S0-BZG-191

PRESENTED TO:

BY:

DATE:

THE

MISSION OF GOD

STUDY BIBLE

THE MISSION OF GOD STUDY BIBLE

ON MISSION. WITH GOD. WHEREVER YOU ARE.

ED STETZER & **PHILIP NATION**

EXECUTIVE EDITOR **GENERAL EDITOR**

NASHVILLE, TENNESSEE

Produced with the assistance of The Livingstone Corporation (www.Livingstonecorp.com). Project staff includes Linda Taylor, David Veerman, Linda Washington, Andy Culbertson, Ashley Taylor, Joel Bartlett. Interior design by Larry Taylor. Typeset by Kathy and Tom Ristow. Proofreading by Peachtree Editorial and Proofreading Service.

Hardcover	**978-1-4336-0156-9**
Paperback	**978-1-4336-0155-2**
Simulated Leather (Brown)	**978-1-4336-0157-6**
Simulated Leather (Brown/Tan)	**978-1-4334-0274-0**
Simulated Leather (Brown/Cream/Taupe)	**978-1-4336-0158-3**

Printed in South Korea
1 2 3 4 5 – 15 14 13 12
SWP

Books of the Bible

Old Testament

New Testament

Purpose of *The Mission of God Study Bible* and How to Use It

Ed Stetzer and Philip Nation

The Mission of God Study Bible exists for the same reason all things exist: to point us to the glory of God. The Scriptures are given by God as a revelation of Himself and to call us to redemption. Throughout the process of His revelatory work, God is honored and we can become the beneficiaries of His grace.

In the preparation of this study Bible, our hope is that you will clearly learn how God, in His great mercy, is active in creation to bring about the work of redeeming people and eventually restoring creation. The Scriptures exist for this purpose, and we have endeavored to create a study edition of the Bible that traces how God reveals Himself through redemption and restoration.

It is the natural inclination of people continually to seek self-fulfillment and self-satisfaction. The study notes in this work will give the practical application of how life is to be lived and how decisions should be made to bring fulfillment to each of us. However, these decisions and actions are a response to the character and work of God. As you read the study helps that follow, we ask that you do so in the framework of seeking to understand how God is revealing Himself as the primary reason for the Bible. As a response to learning more about God's character and work, it will then naturally follow for you to respond in discovering how to be rightly related to God through Christ and join in His mission of redemption.

We want to introduce you to the features you will encounter in *The Mission of God Study Bible*.

Missional Manifesto

The word "missional" has been in the English vocabulary since the early twentieth century. It is a term that has been embraced by various groups in Christianity throughout its short existence. The terminology that undergirds the word "missional" has its origins with the missiologists who were at work in the conciliar missions movement and the International Missionary Council (IMC) meetings of the twentieth century. The meetings were held to debate and better understand the theological concepts of "mission" and "church." In the IMC meetings, the term became more consistently used to describe the way in which all Christians should live—with the mission of God as the center point of life. However, like many technical terms, the word has been redefined in numerous ways once it entered the more common vernacular of church leaders in the English-speaking world. Both editors of this study Bible and many of the essay contributors have been identified with various missional movements within the church.

In 2010, a group of framers led by Ed Stetzer and Alan Hirsch sought to produce a document that would help bring clarity to the ideas housed in the term *missional*. The framers' intent was simply to state what they meant when using the term. From their work, the "Missional Manifesto" was crafted and published. It is included in this project in order to give readers a sense of what we mean by the term *missional* and to paint a picture of what life centered on God and His mission might look like.

Book Introductions

The Book Introductions will highlight the overarching story that is occurring in each book. The books of the Bible were written under the inspiration of the Holy Spirit by more than 40 authors. These authors lived over the course of 2,000 years and across three continents (Europe, Asia, and Africa). However, the entire content of the Scriptures has one main character and one central story: God and His mission. As the Bible is primarily about God and His work, the introductions will highlight how He is at work in the storyline and people recorded in each book of the Bible.

God's Heart for the World

It is God's intention to glorify Himself through creation and through its restoration. In fact, God's glory is a central theme of the Bible. The notes entitled "God's Heart for the World" explore the idea of God's concern and call to glorify His name. It is a work that is not reserved only for the Old Testament people residing in Jerusalem and greater Israel. Rather, it is seen throughout the entire history of the Bible—from the creation story in Genesis and into eternity as shown in Revelation—that God will cause His name to be glorified and His character to be known throughout the temporal and eternal realms.

Feature Essays

The feature essays in this project are unique in both their content and their authors. In the process of crafting the vision for this project, the decision was made to ask a wide array of leaders to contribute to the study Bible. The authors of the feature essays are those who lead the church through full-time vocational ministry and those who serve the church by training leaders in academic settings. Each author was assigned a topic or passage relating to their passion and contribution to the body of work dealing with the mission of God. The feature essays are intended to focus the reader on the central person and content of the Bible—God and His mission. Though every part of the Scripture is profitable for knowing how we should live, these essays help to guide us toward a well-rounded understanding of how God is at work and how He involves us with the mission of His kingdom.

QR Codes

QR codes (quick response codes) are small squares that are composed of odd formations of black dots and lines. You will find QR codes attached to many of the feature essays. By using a QR code scanner app with a smart phone, you will be taken to a Web page that has additional digital information about the subject covered in the essay. In many instances, the information will include a teaching video from Ed Stetzer or Philip Nation about the subject. Also, the Web page will include additional background information about the subject or text.

***God Who Sends* Notes**

Francis Dubose was a minister, author, and professor who focused his life's attention on understanding the mission of God. In 1983, he published the book *God Who Sends* as a biblical theology focused on how God reveals Himself as the One who can affect redemption and the One who sends out His people in the ministry of reconciliation.

In the preface to the book, Dubose wrote,

"This work is a comprehensive and systematic study of the biblical concept of the sending aimed at a better understanding of biblical mission. The title 'God Who Sends' was chosen because God as Sender is the basis

of all the Bible has to say on the subject. The subtitle, 'A Fresh Quest for Biblical Mission,' reflects both my desire for a more satisfying theological understanding and my realization that this can only be a quest, not a final word on the subject." (7)

Dubose's book was one of the earliest in our era to focus on the understanding of God's mission as revealed in the Bible. Throughout this project, you will find quotes from *God Who Sends* connected with various biblical passages that highlight the significance of God's mission for every believer.

Text Messages

As the Bible is God's revelation of Himself and His work, we can find the expression of His good news throughout the entire canon of the Bible. In Text Messages, brief notes are given that show how the gospel can be expressed from multiple places throughout the Bible. Recognizing these different ways of speaking about the gospel helps to develop a robustly biblical view of the gospel.

On the Frontlines

Though the mission of God is occurring in every place and in every time throughout history, the church is called to the specific task of carrying the gospel into those places and among those people that are potentially hostile to the message and the messengers. The Old Testament prophets often ministered in places where they were rejected; many were hunted down for the message they delivered. The majority of the early apostles became martyrs for the Christ they loved so dearly because they refused to give up preaching the gospel. Though we do not call believers to actively seek out persecution for their faith, it is a reality that we should expect when we live out our faith.

In the feature called "On the Frontlines" we share the stories of how some Christian believers have endured persecution or even martyrdom. The stories told are both ancient and recent in their historical context. All of them, however, should inspire us to live for more than the temporary pleasures this world has to offer. The mission of God is the greatest and highest good for which we should be willing to pay any price.

Worldview

The gospel is a message that transcends historical ages and cultural circumstances. In the Worldview feature, we will introduce you to some of the unique details in differing worldviews from around the world.

One issue all humans have in common is the need for reconciliation to God. The gospel is God's message that is applicable to every person in every culture. But, to effectively communicate the gospel, Christians must understand the culture in which they are sharing it. The intent of the Worldview essays is to help believers be better equipped for sharing the gospel in different cultural environments.

Praying for the World

The Praying for the World features will give you guidance about how to better pray for the work of God in the world. The short study notes focus on specific work that will help press believers and the church forward in God's mission. Each note will include information to help inform your prayers for the nations and a prayer that can be used to inspire your own intercession for God's work among the nations as He builds His church.

Cross-Reference Notes
Scripture is best interpreted by Scripture. The Cross-Reference Notes in this project will help you understand how various passages of Scripture relate to one another. By accessing these notes, you can better understand the biblical context for the passage you are currently studying.

Church Unleashed
Throughout the world, Christians serve in the role of cross-cultural mission work. It is a work that should happen naturally within our own cultural context. But God calls some people to move into a new culture in order to share the gospel where it is not known and where the people have little access to the Scriptures. In Church Unleashed, missionary personnel from around the world will share their own stories of how God's mission is pressing forward in the new cultures where they live. In some of these stories, pseudonyms are used as the authors are in areas where it is illegal to serve as a foreign missionary or even to share the gospel of Jesus Christ. Reading these stories will remind readers of how critical the work of God's mission is to all people. You will be inspired to ask Christ to involve you more deeply in His work wherever you might be called to live.

Letters to the Church
One of the great privileges of the Christian life is to learn from those who have served Christ longer and have experienced more of His mission. The essays that make up Letters to the Church are from some of our "older leaders" in the faith. The names will be familiar to many readers as they are some of the trusted leaders of the church in our time. We are all blessed to gain a deeper appreciation about remaining true to the mission of God from their letters to us as believers.

We are deeply indebted to God for His magnanimous work of grace on our behalf. As we study His Word, we do so to gain a greater understanding of who God the Father is, the work accomplished through God the Son, and how God the Holy Spirit is now at work in the church and the world. Our prayer is that God will continually draw you to Himself and teach you how to fully participate in His great mission.

Introduction to the Holman Christian Standard Bible®

The Bible is God's written revelation to man. It is the only book that gives us entirely accurate and authenticated information about God, man's need, and God's provision for that need. It provides us with guidance for life and tells us how to receive eternal life. The Bible can do these things because it is God's inspired Word, inerrant in the original manuscripts.

The Bible describes God's dealings with the ancient Jewish people and the early Christian church. It tells us about the great gift of God's Son, Jesus Christ, who fulfilled Jewish prophecies of the Messiah. It tells us about the salvation He accomplished through His death on the cross, His triumph over death in the resurrection, and His promised return to earth. It is the only book that gives us completely reliable information about the future, about what will happen to us when we die, and about where history is headed.

Bible translation is both a science and an art. It is a bridge that brings God's Word from the ancient world to the world today. In dependence on God to accomplish this sacred task, Holman Bible Publishers presents the Holman Christian Standard Bible, an English translation of God's Word.

Textual base of the HCSB

The textual base for the New Testament [NT] is the Nestle-Aland *Novum Testamentum Graece*, 27th edition, and the United Bible Societies' *Greek New Testament*, 4th corrected edition. The text for the Old Testament [OT] is the *Biblia Hebraica Stuttgartensia*, 5th edition.

Where there are significant differences among Hebrew [Hb] and Aramaic [Aram] manuscripts of the OT or among Greek [Gk] manuscripts of the NT, the translators have followed what they believe is the original reading and have indicated the main alternative(s) in footnotes. The HCSB uses the traditional verse divisions found in most Protestant Bibles.

Goals of this translation

- to provide English-speaking people across the world with an accurate, readable Bible in contemporary English
- to equip serious Bible students with an accurate translation for personal study, private devotions, and memorization
- to give those who love God's Word a text that has numerous reader helps, is visually attractive on the page, and is appealing when heard
- to affirm the authority of Scripture as God's Word and to champion its absolute truth against social or cultural agendas that would compromise its accuracy
- to continue making improvements to the translation in each printing

The name, Holman Christian Standard Bible, captures these goals: *Holman* Bible Publishers presents a *Bible* translation, for *Christian* and English-speaking communities, which will be a *standard* in Bible translations for years to come.

Why is there a need for another English translation of the Bible?

There are several good reasons why Holman Bible Publishers invested its resources in a modern language translation of the Bible:

Each generation needs a fresh translation of the Bible in its own language. The Bible is the world's most important book, confronting each individual and each culture with issues that affect life, both now and forever. Since each new generation must be introduced to God's Word in its own language, there will always be a need for new translations such as the HCSB. The majority of Bible translations on the market today are revisions of translations from previous generations. The HCSB is a new translation for today's generation.

English, one of the world's greatest languages, is rapidly changing, and Bible translations must keep in step with those changes. English is the first truly global language in history. It is the language of education, business, medicine, travel, research, and the Internet. More than 1.3 billion people around the world speak or read English as a primary or secondary language. The HCSB seeks to serve many of those people with a translation they can easily use and understand. English is also the world's most rapidly changing language. The HCSB seeks to reflect recent changes in English by using modern punctuation, formatting, and vocabulary, while avoiding slang, regionalisms, or changes made specifically for the sake of political or social agendas. Modern linguistic and semantic advances have been incorporated into the HCSB, including modern grammar.

Rapid advances in biblical research provide new data for Bible translators. This has been called the "information age," a term that accurately describes the field of biblical research. Never before in history has there been as much information about the Bible as there is today—from archaeological discoveries to analysis of ancient manuscripts to years of study and statistical research on individual Bible books. Translations made as recently as the late 20th century do not reflect many of these advances in biblical research. The HCSB translators have taken into consideration as much of this new data as possible.

Advances in computer technology have opened a new door for Bible translation. The HCSB has used computer technology and telecommunications in its creation perhaps more than any Bible translation in history. Electronic mail was used daily and sometimes hourly for communication and transmission of manuscripts. An advanced Bible software program, Accordance®, was used to create and revise the translation at each step in its production. A developmental copy of the translation itself was used within Accordance to facilitate cross-checking during the translation process—something never done before with a Bible translation.

Translation philosophy of the HCSB

Most discussions of Bible translations speak of two opposite approaches: formal equivalence and dynamic equivalence. Although this terminology is meaningful, Bible translations cannot be neatly sorted into these two categories any more than people can be neatly sorted into two categories according to height or weight. Holman Bible Publishers is convinced there is room for another category of translation philosophy that capitalizes on the strengths of the other two.

Formal Equivalence: Often called "word-for-word" (or "literal") translation, the principle of formal equivalence seeks as nearly as possible to preserve the structure of the original language. It seeks to represent each word of the original text with an exact equivalent word in the translation so that the reader can see word for word what the original human author wrote. The merits of this approach include its consistency with the conviction that the Holy Spirit did inspire the very words of Scripture in the original manuscripts. It also provides the English Bible student some access to the structure of the text in the original language. Formal equivalence can achieve accuracy to the degree that English has an exact equivalent for each word and that the grammatical patterns of the original language can be reproduced in understandable English. However, it can sometimes result in awkward, if not incomprehensible, English or in a misunderstanding of the author's intent. The literal rendering of ancient idioms is especially difficult.

Dynamic or Functional Equivalence: Often called "thought-for-thought" translation, the principle of dynamic equivalence rejects as misguided the desire to preserve the structure of the original language. It proceeds by extracting the meaning of a text from its form and then translating that meaning so that it makes the same impact on modern readers that the ancient text made on its original readers. Strengths of this approach include a high degree of clarity and readability, especially in places where the original is difficult to render word for word. It also acknowledges that accurate and effective translation requires interpretation. However, the meaning of a text cannot always be neatly separated from its form, nor can it always be precisely determined. A biblical author may have intended multiple meanings but these may be lost with the elimination of normal structures. In striving for readability, dynamic equivalence also sometimes overlooks and loses some of the less prominent elements of meaning. Furthermore, lack of formal correspondence to the original makes it difficult to verify accuracy and thus can affect the usefulness of the translation for in-depth Bible study.

Optimal Equivalence: In practice, translations are seldom if ever purely formal or dynamic but favor one theory of Bible translation or the other to varying degrees. Optimal equivalence as a translation philosophy recognizes that form cannot always be neatly separated from meaning and should not be changed (for example, nouns to verbs or third person "they" to second person "you") unless comprehension demands it. The primary goal of translation is to convey the sense of the original with as much clarity as the original text and the translation language permit. Optimal equivalence appreciates the goals of formal equivalence but also recognizes its limitations.

Optimal equivalence starts with an exhaustive analysis of the text at every level (word, phrase, clause, sentence, discourse) in the original language to determine its original meaning and intention (or purpose). Then relying on the latest and best language tools and experts, the nearest corresponding semantic and linguistic equivalents are used to convey as much of the information and intention of the original text with as much clarity and readability as possible. This process assures the maximum transfer of both the words and thoughts contained in the original.

The HCSB uses optimal equivalence as its translation philosophy. When a literal translation meets these criteria, it is used. When clarity and readability demand an idiomatic translation, the reader can still access the form of the original text by means of a footnote with the abbreviation "Lit."

The gender language policy in Bible translation

Some people today are uncomfortable with the Bible's teachings on distinctive roles for men and women in family and church settings and desire to gloss over those distinctions. They seek to correct a perceived male bias in the biblical culture and the English language, including English translations of the Bible. For example, they seek to move away from the traditional linguistic practices such as the generic use of "man" or "men," as well as "he," "him," and "his."

A group of Bible scholars, translators, and other evangelical leaders met in 1997 to respond to this

Lutzer, Erwin –
Senior Pastor of the Moody Church, Chicago, IL

Mason, Eric M. –
Co-founder and Lead Pastor of Epiphany Fellowship, Philadelphia

McCrary, Larry E. –
Director of The Upstream Collective and missionary in Germany

Miller, Calvin –
Research Professor and Distinguished Writer in Residence, Beeson Divinity School

Mullins, Andrea –
Publisher, New Hope Publishers

Nation, Philip –
Director of Ministry Development, LifeWay Research

Ott, Craig –
Associate Professor of Mission and Intercultural Studies at Trinity Evangelical Divinity School

Pocock, Michael –
Senior Professor of World Missions and Intercultural Studies at Dallas Theological Seminary

Roberts, Mark D. –
Senior Director and scholar-in-residence for Laity Lodge

Sanchez, Juan –
Preaching Pastor of High Pointe Baptist Church, Austin, TX

Sproul, R. C. –
President of Ligonier Academy of Biblical and Theological Studies
Founder and president of Ligonier Ministries

Stetzer, Ed –
President of LifeWay Research

Tchividjian, Tullian –
Senior Pastor of Coral Ridge Presbyterian Church in Ft. Lauderdale, FL

Thorn, Joe –
Lead Pastor of Redeemer Fellowship, Chicago, IL

Wan, Enoch –
Professor of Intercultural Studies and Program Director of Doctor of Missiology at Western Seminary

Warnock, Adrian –
Top missional blogger, www.adrianwarnock.com

Wax, Trevin –
Managing Editor, The Gospel Project, LifeWay Christian Resources

Whitfield, Keith –
Pastor of The Oaks Church, Nashville, TN

Wright, Christopher –
International Director of the Langham Partnership International

Ziafat, Afshin –
Lead Pastor of Providence Church, Frisco, TX

The Mission of God in the Scriptures

Ed Stetzer and Philip Nation

The mission of God is one of the great themes throughout the Scriptures. As God reveals Himself in the earliest portions of the history of the human race, it is He who reaches out to us. In fact, at the creation of the first man, God establishes an abiding relationship with Adam. Even with the sinful decisions made by the first man and woman, God continues in His mission by working to reestablish His relationship with humanity.

God's mission among us is to glorify Himself through the work of redeeming people and restoring creation. In Isaiah 42:8, God stated that He would not surrender His glory to another. In all that He does, whether extending mercy or judgment, God has every right to call all of creation to worship Him because He alone is God. He has no equals. There are not even any rivals to His nature and character. God alone deserves all honor, praise, and worship.

In His mercy, God has chosen to reveal Himself in such ways that humanity can know about Him and people can come into a relationship with Him. Again, the biblical record shows this to be the case. When Adam and Eve believe the false statements of a jealous usurper to God's kingdom, it is God who seeks reconciliation with them. Later, it is God who establishes Israel as a nation to bless all the peoples of the world. It is by Israel's covenantal relationship with Yahweh that this blessing to the rest of the world can occur. God goes on to provide priests, judges, kings, and prophets to communicate His law, will, judgment upon sin, and love for people. The Scriptures recount how God worked through those who were faithful to His covenant and regardless of those who rebelled against it. Throughout all of the Old Testament, in fact, we learn how God is on a consistent mission to reestablish the relationship with humanity that has been cast into ruins by our sinful nature and sinful choices.

Moving into the New Testament, obviously the focus shifts immediately to Jesus the Messiah. With the Incarnation, God the Son personally takes on human flesh and arrives here on mission. He brings with Him the kingdom of God and inaugurates His reign upon the earth declaring in Mark 1:15, "The time is fulfilled, and the kingdom of God has come near. Repent and believe in the good news!" The mission of God in the ministry of Jesus is the announcement of God's rule and reign renewed among us. But the announcement is a precursor to Jesus' greatest act: His death as an atonement for sin and His resurrection as victory over death. God's mission finds its pinnacle in the hinge point of human history as Jesus defeats sin, death, and hell in the act of divine mercy that only God can accomplish. By God's mission and God's mission alone can we come back into fellowship with Him.

At the Son's ascension back to heaven, the Holy Spirit then comes on mission to inhabit all Christians. From Pentecost forward, the presence of God the Spirit in the life of every believer enlivens the missionary nature of the church. Throughout the book of Acts, the mission of God begins to move through the church and presses against the boundaries of culture. In the narrative of this historical NT book, we read the descriptions of how the Holy Spirit works through people to make disciples of both Israelites and Gentiles, how the church extends mercy to the marginalized and oppressed in society, and how God's name will be lifted up through the work of believers on mission.

Throughout the balance of the New Testament we learn about the doctrines behind our salvation, how the church can live in unity, proclaim the gospel to people in every culture in a contextually appropriate way, and participate in God's mission. The epistles following Acts were originally a series of letters from church leaders that were to encourage, teach, and sometimes rebuke the early church in how to live on mission with God and for His kingdom. Inspired by God as all of Scripture is, the epistles of the NT give us yet one more lens through which to view God's activity among humanity. It is not enough for us to read this portion of the Bible and picture the Apostles Paul and Peter along with the church simply doing their best to be nice people. These letters reveal the subversive nature of God's kingdom at work among the empires of humanity. God set in motion a rebellion against the rebellions of men. Our new rebellion is to serve as God's coworkers as He reestablishes His reign among all the peoples of the earth. We are given a glimpse into this eternal reality as the Scriptures come to a close with the Revelation given to John in the last book of the Bible. Though wrapped in mysterious language, its theme nevertheless shines through: God is glorified in all things, victorious over all powers, and has extended mercy to draw men and women into a covenant relationship with Him.

The Scripture, from beginning to end, is the great recounting of God's love for fallen humanity. He reaches out to His creation with a redemption plan that He could accomplish alone and without assistance from any created thing, including humanity. However, He has chosen to involve us in the work of His mission. He calls believers to be "ambassadors for Christ," with the result that "God is appealing through us." For this reason "we plead on Christ's behalf, 'Be reconciled to God'" (2Co 5:20).

Our desire is that you will be a part of God's great plan so that men, women, and children from every tongue, tribe, and nation will believe the message of the gospel as it comes to them through the proclamation and life of the church. As you read the Scriptures and consider the study tools included with this study Bible, do so with the mission of God as your lens and framework. Before looking to see what God can do for you, consider what He has done for His own glory and how you are invited to participate in His great mission. We encourage you to closely heed the words of Jesus when He said in John 20:21, "As the Father has sent Me, I also send you."

Missional Manifesto

In 2010-2011, a group of church leaders led by Ed Stetzer and Alan Hirsch collaborated on a statement to define what they meant when using the term "missional." The result was the Missional Manifesto, reproduced here in full.

Preamble

God is a sending God, a missionary God, who has called His people, the church, to be missionary agents of His love and glory. The concept *missional* epitomizes this idea. This manifesto seeks to serve the church by clarifying its calling and helping it theologically understand and practically live out God's mission in the world today. Although it is frequently stated "God's church has a mission," according to missional theology, a more accurate expression is "God's mission has a church" (Ephesians 3:7-13).

One of the goals of theology is to safeguard the meaning of words in order to uphold truth and articulate a biblical worldview within the community of faith. Redeeming the integrity of the word *missional* is especially critical. It is not our intent (or within our ability) to define words for others, but we thought it helpful to describe and define how we are using the term—and to invite others to do the same. A biblically faithful, missional understanding of God and the church is essential to the advancement of our role in His mission, and thus to the dynamism of Christianity in the world.

It is first necessary to be clear about what missional does not mean. Missional is not synonymous with movements attempting to culturally contextualize Christianity, implement church growth, or engage in social action. The word *missional* can encompass all of the above, but it is not limited to any one of these.

Properly understanding the meaning of missional begins with recognizing God's missionary nature. The Father is the source of mission, the Son is the embodiment of that mission, and mission is done in the power of the Spirit. By nature, God is the "sending one" who initiates the redemption of His whole creation. Jesus consistently spoke of Himself as being "sent" in John's gospel and subsequently commissioned His disciples for this same purpose (John 17:3, 8, 18, 21, 23, 25). As the "sent" people of God, the church is the instrument of His mission (John 20:21).

A strong foundation in the gospel, obedience to Christ, and posture to the world are critical components to both individuals and churches living missionally. A missional community is one that regards mission as both its originating impulse and organizing principle (Acts 1:8). It makes decisions accordingly, believing that Christ sends His followers into the world, just as the Father sent Him into the world.

The Church, therefore, properly encourages all believers to live out their primary calling as Christ's ambassadors (2 Corinthians 5:20) to those who do not know Jesus. The ministry of reconciliation is applicable to both its native culture and in cross-cultural ministry throughout the world. In this sense, every believer is a missionary sent by the Spirit into a non-Christian culture activating the whole of his or her life in seeking to participate more fully in God's mission.

Missional represents a significant shift in the way we understand the church. As the people of a missionary God, we are entrusted to participate in the world the same way He does—by committing to be His ambassadors. *Missional* is the perspective to see people as God does and to engage in the activity of reaching them. The church on mission is the church as God intended.

Affirmations

With this in mind, we affirm the following:

1. Authority: As a revelation about the nature of God, we can only truly understand the mission of God by what is revealed through the Scriptures. Therefore, our understanding of the *missio Dei* and the missional church must always be directed and shaped by, and cannot be contrary to, God's revealed Word in scripture.

2. Gospel: We affirm that God, who is more holy than we can imagine, looked with compassion upon humanity made up of people who are more sinful than we will admit and sent Jesus into history to establish His Kingdom and reconcile people and the world to Himself. Jesus, whose love is more extravagant than we can measure, gave His life as a substitutionary death on the cross and was physically resurrected thereby propitiating the wrath of God. Through the grace of God, when a person repents of their sin, confesses the Messiah as Lord, and believes in His resurrection, they gain what the Bible defines as new and eternal life. All believers are then joined together into the church, a covenant community working as "agents of reconciliation" to proclaim and live out the gospel.

3. Kingdom: We affirm that the gospel is the good news of God's Kingdom. The Kingdom is the active and comprehensive rule of God over His whole creation. The sovereign reign of God brings righteousness (right relationships with God, others, and creation), restores justice, and brings healing to a broken world. The Kingdom of God has been inaugurated but is still "not yet." It will not be fully revealed until Jesus returns. The church, birthed in the wake of the Kingdom, serves as an agent of the King in the "already and not yet" of the Kingdom by proclaiming and spreading the gospel and living out its implications.

4. Mission: We affirm that the *missio Dei* is the mission of the triune God to glorify Himself. God does so in this world by redeeming sinful humans and, in the future, restoring corrupted creation. The Father sent the Son to accomplish this redemption and sends the Spirit to apply this redemption to the hearts of men and women. Included in God's mission is the *missio ecclesia* whereby He empowers the church for witness and service that leads to witness. Believers are called to share the gospel with people so they can come to know Christ. Moving from God, through the church, to the world, God's redemptive work results in people of every tribe, tongue, and nation responding in lifelong worship of God. Ultimately the *missio Dei* will encompass all of creation when God creates a new heaven and new earth.

5. Church: The church is a sign and instrument of the Kingdom of God, birthed by the gospel of the Kingdom and tasked with the mission of the Kingdom. The church is a covenant community of imperfect but redeemed believers living in our world. Followers of Christ do not live out their mission in isolation, but rather the Spirit of God enfolds believers into local Christian communities, i.e. churches. It is in and through such community their mission in the world is enhanced.

6. Christocentric: We believe that Jesus is the center of God's plan. By extension, the church as the body of Christ is the primary medium of God's mission to His world. We affirm that while God's work and presence is not limited to the church, nonetheless the proclamation of the gospel of Christ comes through the church and believers everywhere. Members of the church, living by the power of the Spirit, are being conformed into the likeness of Christ in their attitudes and actions.

7. Disciple-making: We believe that discipling of the nations is the essential aspect of the mission of God (Matthew 28:18-20). The gospel calls people to respond in faith and repentance to the good news of the Kingdom in and by the gospel's power. The maturing of believers is inherent to the work of the church ushering those who place faith in Jesus from spiritual infancy to spiritual maturity (Colossians 1:28). This means the church trains its members to be leaders in deeds of justice and ministry to the poor, as well as to live out the implications of their faith in business, the arts, in politics, the academy, the home, and in all of life. As the church makes disciples, it equips them to bring their faith to bear on every area of their lives, private and public.

8. Duality: We believe the mission and responsibility of the church includes both the proclamation of the Gospel and its demonstration. From Jesus, we learn the truth is to be proclaimed with authority and lived with grace. The church must constantly evangelize, respond lovingly to human needs, as well as "seek the welfare of the city" (Jeremiah 29:7). By living out the implications of the gospel, the missional church offers a verbal defense and a living example of its power.

9. Universality: We believe God's mission, and thus the mission of His people, extends to every people, nation, tribe, and tongue; to persons of every gender, age, education, social standing, and religious persuasion (or lack thereof). Thus a missional church will intentionally embrace diversity locally and will cross social, cultural, and geographic barriers as agents of the *missio Dei*. God's mission furthermore universally encompasses every aspect of life: personal, familial, social, cultural, and economic. This is grounded upon the universal authority and lordship of Jesus Christ.

10. Application: We believe the mission of the church continues in multiplying and maturing the followers of Christ (discipleship), increasing the number of congregations (church planting) dedicated to God's Kingdom (living under His lordship), extending God's fame throughout the earth (worship), and doing good in the name of Christ (works of mercy).

Because we believe these things, we are compelled to action. We urge God's people to align around the lordship of Jesus, the missional nature of His church, and the reality of His Kingdom. We invite the body of Christ everywhere to see people and the world through the lens of God's Kingdom, to live holy lives as Jesus' disciples, and to intentionally represent Him together as the church. We affirm that Jesus was sent to fulfill God's purposes in the world through His perfect life, substitutionary death, and physical resurrection so that redemption could be made available to us. With Christ as our focal point, His Kingdom as our destiny, and His Spirit as our empowerment, we accept the privilege and joy of His mission.

Missional Manifesto Framers

Ed Stetzer
President of LifeWay Research

Alan Hirsch
Founding Director of Forge Mission Training Network

Tim Keller
Pastor of Redeemer Presbyterian Church, NYC

Dan Kimball
Teaching Pastor of Vintage Faith Church

Eric Mason
Lead Pastor of Epiphany Fellowship

J. D. Greear
Lead Pastor of The Summit Church

Craig Ott
Associate Professor of Mission and Intercultural Studies at Trinity Evangelical Divinity School

Linda Bergquist
Church Starting Strategist, California Southern Baptist Convention

Philip Nation
Ministry Development Director with LifeWay Research

Brad Andrews
Lead Pastor of Mercyview Church

OLD TESTAMENT

■ **AUTHOR:** Moses

■■ **DATE:** Most likely written during Israel's wandering in the wilderness (around 1445–1406 B.C.)

The biggest question about the creation of the world—why did God do it? The book of Genesis begins the answer.

Did God get orders to invent a universe? No, there's nobody calling the shots behind God's back. To ask why God did it is to probe God alone, no one else.

Did God need to create this planet? Its amazing beauty is a wonder to behold. But why did God do it? Was He obligated? Everywhere the Bible relieves God of a "need to act." God is under no compulsion, no obligations. Creation was not a need-based decision for God.

Nor was it for sheer enjoyment that God brought the world into existence. You can't read two chapters into Genesis before God is disappointed and grieved. In much of the Bible, there's more grief for God than pleasure.

GENESIS

God's mission in creating the world, from the Genesis account, was to glorify Himself by sharing life. God lives, the Scriptures affirm. All the rest of creation lives because God wanted to share this rare gift. Another word for this sharing is love. God's nature and character is love. Love wants to share.

From the first, God is reported to walk the earth conversing with Adam and Eve. Throughout Genesis, God is urging people to come alongside, share the journey, redeem the relationship that will eventually bring His spoiled creation back to what it should be.

Spoiled? Yes, spoiled rotten. The sharing God initiated had this one condition, also a core value of God's character: holiness. God and sin are like fire and water, light and dark. God and sin don't keep company. When the first humans follow the serpent's alluring suggestion to eat from the infamous Tree in defiance of God's command, creation breaks. This crisis could have been the end of it, but God's resolve to share life, to be with us, overcomes the wreckage of Adam and Eve's disobedience. The mission of God is to redeem, to save, to repair the break, to get back to love. God promises to redeem and restore in chapter 3. From that moment on, the Bible's trajectory aims at reconciling men and women to their Creator, the God of love and holiness.

Many notable persons show up in Genesis. Noah and his ark, Abraham and his son, Joseph and his colorful coat. These and other names are widely known, their stories largely romanticized and made into fables of popular entertainment. But Genesis itself is rock-solid serious. Humanity is in desperate trouble. Our link to life is broken by sin. We need God's voice and presence, yet angels guard the gate to the paths where once God and humankind walked in peace and unity.

Our trouble reconnecting with God requires a divine plan. Abraham is called to move from his homeland, searching and trusting, as God shows the way back to fellowship and wholeness. Isaac is spared, and his son, the trickster Jacob, saves his clan with Joseph's help and sets the stage for the creation of a nation, which God will uniquely lead to a land of promise.

The Creation

1 In the beginning[a] God created the heavens and the earth.[A,b]

2 Now the earth was[B] formless and empty,[c] darkness covered the surface of the watery depths, and the Spirit of God was hovering over the surface of the waters.[d] 3 Then God said, "Let there be light,"[e] and there was light. 4 God saw that the light was good, and God separated the light from the darkness. 5 God called the light "day," and He called the darkness "night." Evening came and then morning: the first day.

6 Then God said, "Let there be an expanse[C] between the waters, separating water from water."[f] 7 So God made the expanse and separated the water under the expanse from the water above the expanse.[g] And it was so. 8 God called the expanse "sky."[D] Evening came and then morning: the second day.

9 Then God said, "Let the water under the sky be gathered into one place,[h] and let the dry land appear." And it was so. 10 God called the dry land "earth," and He called the gathering of the water "seas." And God saw that it was good. 11 Then God said, "Let the earth produce vegetation: seed-bearing plants and fruit trees on the earth bearing fruit with seed in it according to their kinds."[i] And it was so. 12 The earth produced vegetation: seed-bearing plants according to their kinds and trees bearing fruit with seed in it according to their kinds. And God saw that it was good. 13 Evening came and then morning: the third day.

14 Then God said, "Let there be lights in the expanse of the sky to separate the day from the night. They will serve as signs[j] for festivals[E] and for days and years.[k] 15 They will be lights in the expanse of the sky to provide light on the earth." And it was so. 16 God made the two great lights — the greater light to have dominion over the day and the lesser light to have dominion over the night — as well as the stars.[l] 17 God placed them in the expanse of the sky to provide light on the earth, 18 to dominate the day and the night, and to separate light from darkness.[m] And God saw that it was good. 19 Evening came and then morning: the fourth day.

20 Then God said, "Let the water swarm with[F] living creatures, and let birds fly above the earth across the expanse of the sky." 21 So God created the large sea-creatures[G] and every living creature that moves and swarms in the water,[n] according to their kinds. He also created every winged bird according to its kind. And God saw that it was good. 22 So God blessed them, "Be fruitful, multiply, and fill the waters of the seas, and let the birds multiply on the earth."[o] 23 Evening came and then morning: the fifth day.

24 Then God said, "Let the earth produce living creatures according to their kinds: livestock, creatures that crawl, and the wildlife of the earth according to their kinds." And it was so. 25 So God made the wildlife of the earth according to their kinds, the livestock according to their kinds, and creatures that crawl on the ground according to their kinds. And God saw that it was good.

26 Then God said, "Let Us[p] make man in Our image, according to Our likeness.[q] They will rule the fish of the sea, the birds of the sky, the livestock, all the earth,[H] and the creatures that crawl[I] on the earth."[r]

27 So God created man in His own image;
He created him in the image of God;
He created them male and female.[s]

28 God blessed them, and God said to them, "Be fruitful, multiply, fill the earth,[t] and subdue it. Rule the fish of the sea, the birds of the sky, and every creature that crawls[J] on the earth." 29 God also said, "Look, I have given you every seed-bearing plant on the surface of the entire earth and every tree whose fruit contains seed. This food will be for you,[u] 30 for all the wildlife of the earth, for every bird of the sky, and for every creature that crawls on the earth — everything having the breath of life in it. I have given every green plant for food."[v] And it was so. 31 God saw all that He had made, and it was very good.[w] Evening came and then morning: the sixth day.

[a] **1:1** Ps 90:2; 102:12; Is 40:21; Jn 1:1-3; Eph 3:21 [b] Neh 9:6; Is 40:12-14; 43:7; Jr 10:12-16; Am 4:13; Rm 1:25; 1Co 11:9; Col 1:16; Rv 4:11 [c] **1:2** Jr 4:23 [d] Jb 26:13; 33:4; Ps 33:6; 104:30 [e] **1:3** 2Co 4:6 [f] **1:6** Is 44:24; Jr 10:12 [g] **1:7** Ps 148:4 [h] **1:9** Jb 38:8-11; Ps 33:7; 136:6; Jr 5:22; 2Pt 3:5 [i] **1:11** Ps 65:9-13; 104:14 [j] **1:14** Jr 10:2 [k] Ps 104:19 [l] **1:16** Dt 4:19; Ps 136:7-9; Is 40:26 [m] **1:18** Jr 31:35 [n] **1:21** Ps 104:25-28 [o] **1:22** Gn 8:17; 9:1 [p] **1:26** Gn 3:22; 11:7 [q] Gn 5:1,3; 9:6; Rm 8:29; 1Co 11:7; 15:49; 2Co 3:18; 4:4; Eph 4:24; Col 1:15; Jms 3:9 [r] Gn 9:2; Ps 8:6-8; Jms 3:7 [s] **1:27** Gn 5:2; Mt 19:4; Mk 10:6 [t] **1:28** Gn 9:1,7 [u] **1:29** Gn 9:3; Ps 104:14-15; 136:25; 145:15-16 [v] **1:30** Ps 147:9 [w] **1:31** 1Tm 4:4

[A] **1:1** Or *created the universe* [B] **1:1-2** Or *When God began to create the sky and the earth, [2] the earth was* [C] **1:6** The Hb word for *expanse* is from a root meaning "to spread out, stamp, beat firmly," which suggests something like a dome; Jb 37:16-18; Is 40:22. [D] **1:8** Or *"heavens"* [E] **1:14** Or *for the appointed times* [F] **1:20** Lit *with swarms of* [G] **1:21** Or *created sea monsters* [H] **1:26** Syr reads *sky, and over every animal of the land* [I] **1:26** Lit *scurry* [J] **1:28** Lit *and all scurrying animals that scurry*

2
So the heavens and the earth and everything in them[A] were completed.[a] ²By the
seventh[B] day God completed His work that
He had done, and He rested[C] on the seventh
day from all His work that He had done.[b]
³God blessed the seventh day and declared
it holy, for on it He rested[c] from His work of
creation.[D,d]

Man and Woman in the Garden

⁴These are the records[e] of the heavens and
the earth, concerning their creation at the
time[E] that the LORD God made the earth and
the heavens. ⁵No shrub of the field[f] had yet
grown on the land,[F] and no plant of the field
had yet sprouted, for the LORD God had not
made it rain on the land, and there was no
man to work the ground. ⁶But water would
come out of the ground and water the entire surface of the land. ⁷Then the LORD God
formed the man out of the dust from the
ground[g] and breathed the breath of life into
his nostrils,[h] and the man became a living being.[i]

⁸The LORD God planted a garden in Eden,
in the east,[j] and there He placed the man He
had formed. ⁹The LORD God caused to grow
out of the ground every tree pleasing in appearance and good for food, including the
tree of life in the middle of the garden,[k] as
well as the tree of the knowledge of good and
evil.[l]

¹⁰A river went[G] out from Eden to water the
garden. From there it divided and became the
source of four rivers.[H] ¹¹The name of the first
is Pishon, which flows through the entire
land of Havilah,[I,m] where there is gold. ¹²Gold
from that land is pure;[J] bdellium[K] and onyx[L]
are also there. ¹³The name of the second river
is Gihon, which flows through the entire land
of •Cush. ¹⁴The name of the third river is the
Tigris,[n] which runs east of Assyria. And the
fourth river is the Euphrates.[o]

¹⁵The LORD God took the man and placed
him in the garden of Eden to work it and
watch over it. ¹⁶And the LORD God commanded the man, "You are free to eat from
any tree of the garden,[p] ¹⁷but you must not
eat[M] from the tree of the knowledge of good
and evil, for on the day you eat from it, you
will certainly die."[q] ¹⁸Then the LORD God
said, "It is not good for the man to be alone. I
will make a helper as his complement."[r] ¹⁹So
the LORD God formed out of the ground every wild animal and every bird of the sky,
and brought each to the man to see what he
would call it.[s] And whatever the man called a
living creature, that was its name. ²⁰The man
gave names to all the livestock, to the birds
of the sky, and to every wild animal; but for
the man[N] no helper was found as his complement. ²¹So the LORD God caused a deep sleep
to come over the man,[t] and he slept. God took
one of his ribs and closed the flesh at that
place. ²²Then the LORD God made the rib He
had taken from the man into a woman and
brought her to the man.[u] ²³And the man said:

> This one, at last, is bone of my bone
> and flesh of my flesh;
> this one will be called "woman,"
> for she was taken from man.[v]

²⁴This is why a man leaves his father and
mother and bonds with his wife, and they become one flesh.[w] ²⁵Both the man and his wife
were naked, yet felt no shame.

The Temptation and the Fall

3
Now the serpent was the most cunning
of all the wild animals that the LORD God
had made. He said to the woman, "Did God
really say, 'You can't eat from any tree in the
garden'?"[x]

²The woman said to the serpent, "We may
eat the fruit from the trees in the garden.
³But about the fruit of the tree in the middle
of the garden, God said, 'You must not eat it
or touch it, or you will die.'"[y]

⁴"No! You will not die," the serpent said to
the woman.[z] ⁵"In fact, God knows that when[O]
you eat it your eyes will be opened and you
will be like God,[P] knowing good and evil."
⁶Then the woman saw that the tree was good
for food and delightful to look at, and that it
was desirable for obtaining wisdom. So she
took some of its fruit and ate it; she also gave
some to her husband, who was with her, and

[a]**2:1** Neh 9:6; Ps 33:6; Is 34:4; 45:12 [b]**2:2** Ex 20:8-11; 31:17; Dt 5:12-14; Heb 4:4 [c]**2:3** Ex 31:17 [d]Ex 20:11; 31:17; Ps 121:2 [e]**2:4** Gn 5:1; 6:9; 10:1; 11:10,27; 25:12,19; 36:1,9; 37:2 [f]**2:5** Gn 1:11-12 [g]**2:7** Gn 3:19,23; 18:27; Ps 103:14; Ec 12:7; 1Co 15:47 [h]Gn 7:22; Jb 33:4; Is 2:22 [i]1Co 15:45 [j]**2:8** Gn 13:10; Is 51:3; Ezk 28:13; 31:8; Jl 2:3 [k]**2:9** Gn 3:22; Rv 2:7; 22:2,14 [l]Pr 3:18 [m]**2:11** Gn 10:7,29; 25:18; 1Sm 15:7 [n]**2:14** Dn 10:4 [o]Gn 15:18 [p]**2:16** Gn 3:1-2 [q]**2:17** Gn 3:5; Dt 30:15,19-20; Rm 6:23; 1Tm 5:6; Jms 1:15 [r]**2:18** Pr 31:11-12; 1Co 11:9; 1Tm 2:13 [s]**2:19** Ps 8:6 [t]**2:21** Gn 15:12 [u]**2:22** 1Co 11:8,12 [v]**2:23** Eph 5:28-30 [w]**2:24** Mal 2:15; Mt 19:5; Mk 10:7-8; 1Co 6:16; Eph 5:31 [x]**3:1** Mt 10:16; 2Co 11:3; Rv 12:9; 20:2 [y]**3:3** Gn 2:17 [z]**3:4** Jn 8:44

[A]**2:1** Lit *and all their host* [B]**2:2** Sam, LXX, Syr read *sixth* [C]**2:2** Or *ceased* [D]**2:3** Lit *work that God created to make* [E]**2:4** Lit *creation on the day* [F]**2:5** Or *earth* [G]**2:10** Or *goes* [H]**2:10** Lit *became four heads* [I]**2:11** Or *of the Havilah* [J]**2:12** Lit *good* [K]**2:12** A yellowish, transparent gum resin [L]**2:12** Identity of this precious stone uncertain [M]**2:17** Lit *eat from it* [N]**2:20** Or *for Adam* [O]**3:5** Lit *on the day* [P]**3:5** Or *gods*, or *divine beings*

he ate it.[a] 7 Then the eyes of both of them were
opened, and they knew they were naked; so
they sewed fig leaves together and made loin-
cloths for themselves.

Sin's Consequences

8 Then the man and his wife heard the
sound of the LORD God walking in the garden
at the time of the evening breeze,[A] and they
hid themselves from the LORD God among
the trees of the garden.[b] 9 So the LORD God
called out to the man and said to him, "Where
are you?"

10 And he said, "I heard You[B] in the garden
and I was afraid because I was naked, so I hid."

11 Then He asked, "Who told you that you
were naked? Did you eat from the tree that I
commanded you not to eat from?"

[a] **3:6** 1Tm 2:14; Jms 1:14-15; 1Jn 2:16 [b] **3:8** Jb 34:22-23

The Messiah Foretold

Philip Nation

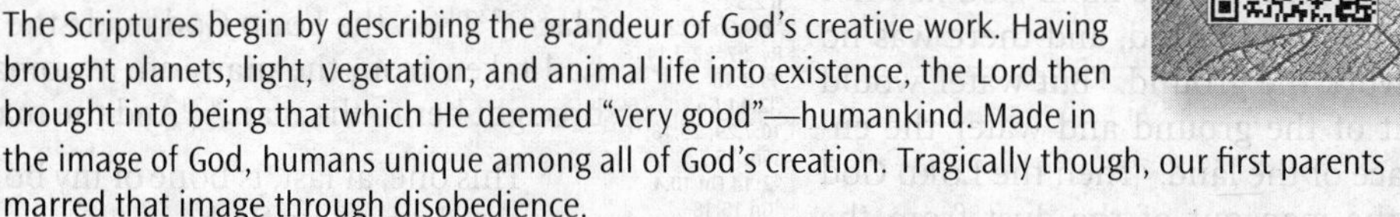

The Scriptures begin by describing the grandeur of God's creative work. Having brought planets, light, vegetation, and animal life into existence, the Lord then brought into being that which He deemed "very good"—humankind. Made in the image of God, humans unique among all of God's creation. Tragically though, our first parents marred that image through disobedience.

When Adam and Eve faced temptation, they chose to believe a lie rather than God's truth. They trusted in their own potential and did not hold God as trustworthy for their future. Because of their choice, sin entered the world and humanity's pure relationship with the Heavenly Father became broken. Goaded along by the cunning of our enemy—the fallen angel Lucifer in the form of a serpent—humanity seemed to have met its end right at its beginning. Ashamed of their unclothed state, Adam and Eve hid from God and covered themselves from one another's sight.

It is, however, for His glory and our benefit that God is by nature on mission. This is seen first in the fact that God sought out the shamed and sinful pair. He sought reconciliation with Adam and Eve even though it would be at great cost to Him. He confronted their sinful state and the deceitful serpent who had coaxed them into ruin. Adam and Eve had excuses and accusations on their lips, but God was undaunted. He was committed to the mission to reconcile humanity to Himself by being the One who does the seeking. Though Adam and Eve hid because of their shame, God sought them out for their benefit. He is committed to more than just scolding them for their sin. In Genesis 3:14-15, the Lord pronounces judgment on the enemy and promises to send a Messiah. He said to the serpent, "I will put hostility between you and the woman, and between your seed and her seed. He will strike your head and you will strike his heel" (v. 15). God said life would be difficult due to the curse, but He also said that the "seed" of the woman would strike the head of our enemy and prevail against Satan.

This statement about the One to come is the first prophecy of the Christ. As inheritors of a sin nature that opposes God, it should amaze us that God so quickly moved from His role as Creator to that of Redeemer. We expect wrath and judgment, not grace and a promise of a coming Savior. But God shatters our expectations. His love for humanity drove Him to provide the Savior who can make all things new.

From the beginning, God has done every work necessary so that we might know Him and abide with Him. He sought us when we did not want to be found. And at just the right time, God sent the Christ to die as a ransom for sin and rise in victory over hell itself. Our God is a God who sends, redeems, and restores.

[A] **3:8** Lit *at the wind of the day* [B] **3:10** Lit *the sound of You*

12 Then the man replied,[a] "The woman You
gave to be with me — she gave me some fruit
from the tree, and I ate."
13 So the LORD God asked the woman, "What
is this you have done?"

And the woman said, "It was the serpent.
He deceived me, and I ate."[b]
14 Then the LORD God said to the serpent:

Because you have done this,
you are cursed more than any livestock
and more than any wild animal.
You will move on your belly
and eat dust all the days of your life.[c]
15 I will put hostility between you
and the woman,
and between your •seed and her seed.
He will strike your head,
and you will strike his heel.[d]

16 He said to the woman:

I will intensify your labor pains;
you will bear children in anguish.[e]
Your desire[f] will be for your husband,
yet he will rule over you.

17 And He said to Adam, "Because you listened to your wife's voice and ate from the
tree about which I commanded you, 'Do not
eat from it':

The ground is cursed because of you.[g]
You will eat from it by means of
painful labor[A]
all the days of your life.
18 It will produce thorns and thistles
for you,
and you will eat the plants of the field.[h]
19 You will eat bread[B] by the sweat
of your brow
until you return to the ground,[i]
since you were taken from it.
For you are dust,
and you will return to dust."

20 Adam named his wife Eve[C] because she
was the mother of all the living. 21 The LORD
God made clothing out of skins for Adam and
his wife, and He clothed them.
22 The LORD God said, "Since man has become like one of Us, knowing good and evil, he
must not reach out, take from the tree of life,
eat, and live forever."[j] 23 So the LORD God sent
him away from the garden of Eden to work the
ground from which he was taken. 24 He drove
man out and stationed the •cherubim and the
flaming, whirling sword east of the garden of
Eden to guard the way to the tree of life.[k]

Cain Murders Abel

4 Adam was intimate with his wife Eve,
and she conceived and gave birth to
Cain. She said, "I have had a male child with
the LORD's help."[D] 2 Then she also gave birth
to his brother Abel. Now Abel became a shepherd of flocks, but Cain worked the ground.
3 In the course of time Cain presented some of
the land's produce as an offering to the LORD.[l]
4 And Abel also presented an offering — some
of the firstborn of his flock and their fat portions.[m] The LORD had regard for Abel and his
offering,[n] 5 but He did not have regard for
Cain and his offering. Cain was furious, and
he looked despondent.[E]
6 Then the LORD said to Cain, "Why are
you furious?[o] And why do you look despondent?[F] 7 If you do what is right, won't you be
accepted? But if you do not do what is right,
sin is crouching at the door. Its desire is for
you, but you must rule over it."[p]

Genesis and "Proto-Mission"

GOD WHO SENDS

The Genesis mission which paves the way for all subsequent missions is the "incipient sending." God is the "source" and "medium" (agent), and his first redemptive promise to man is the "purpose." The proto-missio (the "original mission") precedes the proto evangelium (the "original gospel") of Genesis 3:15. What flowers ultimately in all Scripture has its roots in this primal mission and the purpose behind it.

(DUBOSE, 57)

[a] 3:12 Jb 31:33; Pr 28:13 [b] 3:13 Rm 7:11; 2Co 11:3; 1Tm 2:14 [c] 3:14 Is 65:25; Mc 7:17 [d] 3:15 Heb 2:14; 1Jn 3:8 [e] 3:16 Jn 16:21; 1Tm 2:15 [f] Gn 4:7 [g] 3:17 Gn 5:29; Rm 8:20-22; Heb 6:8 [h] 3:18 Gn 2:5 [i] 3:19 Ps 90:3; 104:29; Ec 12:7 [j] 3:22 Gn 2:9; Rv 2:7 [k] 3:24 Ex 25:18-22; Ps 104:4; Ezk 10:1-20; Heb 1:7 [l] 4:3 Ex 23:19; 34:26; Neh 10:35 [m] 4:4 Ex 13:12; Nm 18:17; Pr 3:9 [n] Heb 11:4 [o] 4:6 Jnh 4:4 [p] 4:7 Gn 3:16

[A] 3:17 Lit *it through pain* [B] 3:19 Or *food* [C] 3:20 Lit *Living*, or *Life* [D] 4:1 Lit *the LORD* [E] 4:5 Lit *and his face fell* [F] 4:6 Lit *why has your face fallen*

8Cain said to his brother Abel, "Let's go out
to the field."[A] And while they were in the field,
Cain attacked his brother Abel and killed
him.[a]
9Then the LORD said to Cain, "Where is
your brother Abel?"
"I don't know," he replied. "Am I my brother's guardian?"
10Then He said, "What have you done? Your
brother's blood cries out to Me from the
ground![b] 11So now you are cursed, alienated,
from the ground that opened its mouth to receive your brother's blood you have shed.[B] 12If
you work the ground, it will never again give
you its yield. You will be a restless wanderer
on the earth."[c]
13But Cain answered the LORD, "My punishment[C] is too great to bear! 14Since You are
banishing me today from the soil, and I must
hide myself from Your presence and become
a restless wanderer on the earth, whoever
finds me will kill me."[d]
15Then the LORD replied to him, "In that
case,[D] whoever kills Cain will suffer vengeance seven times over."[E] And He placed a
mark[e] on Cain so that whoever found him
would not kill him. 16Then Cain went out
from the LORD's presence and lived in the
land of Nod, east of Eden.

The Line of Cain

17Cain was intimate with his wife, and she
conceived and gave birth to Enoch. Then Cain
became the builder of a city, and he named
the city Enoch after his son. 18Irad was born to
Enoch, Irad fathered Mehujael, Mehujael fathered Methushael, and Methushael fathered
Lamech. 19Lamech took two wives for himself,
one named Adah and the other named Zillah.
20Adah bore Jabal; he was the father of the nomadic herdsmen.[F] 21His brother was named
Jubal; he was the father of all who play the
lyre and the flute. 22Zillah bore Tubal-cain,
who made all kinds of bronze and iron tools.
Tubal-cain's sister was Naamah.
23Lamech said to his wives:

Adah and Zillah, hear my voice;
wives of Lamech, pay attention
to my words.
For I killed a man for wounding me,
a young man for striking me.
24 If Cain is to be avenged
seven times over,
then for Lamech it will be
seventy-seven times!

25Adam was intimate with his wife again,
and she gave birth to a son and named him
Seth, for she said, "God has given[G] me another
child in place of Abel, since Cain killed him."
26A son was born to Seth[f] also, and he named
him Enosh. At that time people began to call
on the name of ·Yahweh.[g]

The Line of Seth

5 These are the family[H] records[h] of the descendants of Adam. On the day that God
created man,[I] He made him in the likeness
of God; 2He created them male and female.
When they were created, He blessed them
and called them man.[I]
3Adam was 130 years old when he fathered
a son in his likeness, according to his image,
and named him Seth. 4Adam lived 800 years
after the birth of Seth, and he fathered other
sons and daughters. 5So Adam's life lasted 930
years; then he died.
6Seth was 105 years old when he fathered
Enosh. 7Seth lived 807 years after the birth
of Enosh, and he fathered other sons and
daughters. 8So Seth's life lasted 912 years;
then he died.
9Enosh was 90 years old when he fathered
Kenan. 10Enosh lived 815 years after the birth
of Kenan, and he fathered other sons and
daughters. 11So Enosh's life lasted 905 years;
then he died.
12Kenan was 70 years old when he fathered
Mahalalel. 13Kenan lived 840 years after the
birth of Mahalalel, and he fathered other
sons and daughters. 14So Kenan's life lasted
910 years; then he died.
15Mahalalel was 65 years old when he fathered Jared. 16Mahalalel lived 830 years after
the birth of Jared, and he fathered other sons
and daughters. 17So Mahalalel's life lasted 895
years; then he died.
18Jared was 162 years old when he fathered
Enoch. 19Jared lived 800 years after the birth

[a]**4:8** Mt 23:35; Lk 11:51; 1Jn 3:12-15; Jd 11
[b]**4:10** Nm 35:33; Dt 21:1-9; Heb 12:24; Rv 6:9-10
[c]**4:12** Dt 28:16-18; Is 26:21
[d]**4:14** Nm 35:26-27
[e]**4:15** Ex 9:4; Ezk 9:4,6; Rv 13:16-17
[f]**4:26** Lk 3:38
[g]Gn 12:8; 26:25; 1Kg 18:24; Ps 116:17; Jl 2:32; Zph 3:9; 1Co 1:2
[h]**5:1** Gn 2:4

[A]**4:8** Sam, LXX, Syr, Vg; MT omits *Let's go out to the field* [B]**4:11** Lit *blood from your hand* [C]**4:13** Or *sin* [D]**4:15** LXX, Syr, Vg read *Not so!* [E]**4:15** Or *suffer severely* [F]**4:20** Lit *the dweller of tent and livestock* [G]**4:25** The Hb word for given sounds like the name "Seth." [H]**5:1** Lit *written family* [I]**5:1,2** Or *Adam* of Enoch, and he fathered other sons and daughters. 20 So Jared's life lasted 962 years; then he died.

21 Enoch was 65 years old when he fathered Methuselah. 22 And after the birth of Methuselah, Enoch walked with God[a] 300 years and fathered other sons and daughters. 23 So Enoch's life lasted 365 years. 24 Enoch walked with God; then he was not there because God took him.[b]

25 Methuselah was 187 years old when he fathered Lamech. 26 Methuselah lived 782 years after the birth of Lamech, and he fathered other sons and daughters. 27 So Methuselah's life lasted 969 years; then he died.

28 Lamech was 182 years old when he fathered a son. 29 And he named him Noah,[A] saying, "This one will bring us relief from the agonizing labor of our hands, caused by the ground the LORD has cursed."[c] 30 Lamech lived 595 years after Noah's birth, and he fathered other sons and daughters. 31 So Lamech's life lasted 777 years; then he died.

32 Noah was 500 years old, and he fathered Shem, Ham, and Japheth.

Sons of God and Daughters of Men

6 When mankind began to multiply on the earth and daughters were born to them, 2 the sons of God[d] saw that the daughters of mankind were beautiful, and they took any they chose as wives[B] for themselves.[e] 3 And the LORD said, "My Spirit will not remain[C] with[D] mankind forever,[f] because they are corrupt.[E,g] Their days will be 120 years." 4 The Nephilim[F] were on the earth both in those days and afterward, when the sons of God came to the daughters of mankind, who bore children to them. They were the powerful men of old, the famous men.

Judgment Decreed

5 When the LORD saw that man's wickedness was widespread on the earth and that every scheme his mind thought of was nothing but evil all the time,[h] 6 the LORD regretted that He had made man on the earth,[i] and He was grieved in His heart. 7 Then the LORD said, "I will wipe off from the face of the earth mankind, whom I created, together with the animals, creatures that crawl, and birds of the sky — for I regret that I made them." 8 Noah, however, found favor in the sight of the LORD.[j]

God Warns Noah

9 These are the family records[k] of Noah. Noah was a righteous man,[l] blameless among his contemporaries;[m] Noah walked with God.[n] 10 And Noah fathered three sons: Shem, Ham, and Japheth.

11 Now the earth was corrupt in God's sight, and the earth was filled with wickedness.[G] 12 God saw how corrupt the earth was, for every creature had corrupted its way on the earth.[o] 13 Then God said to Noah, "I have decided to put an end to every creature, for the earth is filled with wickedness[G] because of them; therefore I am going to destroy them along with the earth.

14 "Make yourself an ark of gopher[H] wood. Make rooms in the ark, and cover it with pitch inside and outside. 15 This is how you are to make it: The ark will be 450 feet long, 75 feet wide, and 45 feet high.[I] 16 You are to make a roof,[J] finishing the sides of the ark to within 18 inches[K] of the roof. You are to put a door in the side of the ark. Make it with lower, middle, and upper decks.

17 "Understand that I am bringing a flood — floodwaters on the earth[p] to destroy every creature under heaven with the breath of life in it. Everything on earth will die. 18 But I will establish My covenant with you,[q] and you will enter the ark with your sons, your wife, and your sons' wives. 19 You are also to bring into the ark two of all the living creatures, male and female, to keep them alive with you. 20 Two of everything — from the birds according to their kinds, from the livestock according to their kinds, and from the animals that crawl on the ground according to their kinds — will come to you so that you can keep them alive. 21 Take with you every kind of food that is eaten; gather it as food for you and for them." 22 And Noah did this.

[a] **5:22** Gn 6:9; 17:1; 24:40; 48:15; Mc 6:8; Mal 2:6; 1Th 2:12
[b] **5:24** 2Kg 2:11; Heb 11:5
[c] **5:29** Gn 3:17-19; 4:11
[d] **6:2** Jb 1:6; 2:1; 38:7
[e] 1Pt 3:19-20; Jd 6
[f] **6:3** Gl 5:16-17; 1Pt 3:20
[g] Ps 78:39
[h] **6:5** Gn 8:21; Ps 14:1-3; Pr 6:18; Mt 15:19; Rm 1:28-32
[i] **6:6** Nm 23:19; 1Sm 15:11,29; 2Sm 24:16; Jl 2:13
[j] **6:8** Gn 19:19; Ex 33:17; Lk 1:30
[k] **6:9** Gn 2:4
[l] Ps 37:39; 2Pt 2:5
[m] Gn 17:1; Dt 18:13; Jb 1:1
[n] Gn 5:22
[o] **6:12** Jb 22:15-17; Ps 14:2-3; 53:2-3
[p] **6:17** Gn 7:4; 2Pt 2:5
[q] **6:18** Gn 9:9-16; 17:7

[A] **5:29** In Hb, the name Noah sounds like the phrase "bring us relief." [B] **6:2** Or *women* [C] **6:3** Or *strive* [D] **6:3** Or *in* [E] **6:3** Lit *flesh* [F] **6:4** Possibly means "fallen ones"; traditionally, "giants"; Nm 13:31-33 [G] **6:11,13** Or *injustice* [H] **6:14** Unknown species of tree; perhaps pine or cypress [I] **6:15** Or *300 cubits long, 50 cubits wide, and 30 cubits high* [J] **6:16** Or *window*, or *hatch*; Hb uncertain [K] **6:16** Lit *to a cubit*

He did everything that God had commanded
him.[a]

Entering the Ark

7 Then the LORD said to Noah, "Enter the
ark, you and all your household, for I have
seen that you alone are righteous before Me
in this generation.[b] 2You are to take with you
seven pairs, a male and its female, of all the
•clean animals,[c] and two of the animals that
are not clean, a male and its female, 3and
seven pairs, male and female, of the birds of
the sky — in order to keep •offspring alive on
the face of the whole earth. 4Seven days from
now I will make it rain on the earth 40 days
and 40 nights, and I will wipe off from the
face of the earth every living thing I have
made." 5And Noah did everything that the
LORD commanded him.[d]

6Noah was 600 years old when the flood
came and water covered the earth. 7So Noah,
his sons, his wife, and his sons' wives entered
the ark because of the waters of the flood.
8From the clean animals, •unclean animals,
birds, and every creature that crawls on the
ground, 9two of each, male and female, entered the ark with Noah, just as God had commanded him. 10Seven days later the waters of
the flood came on the earth.

The Flood

11In the six hundredth year of Noah's life,
in the second month, on the seventeenth day
of the month, on that day all the sources of
the watery depths burst open,[e] the floodgates
of the sky were opened,[f] 12and the rain fell on
the earth 40 days and 40 nights. 13On that
same day Noah along with his sons Shem,
Ham, and Japheth, Noah's wife, and his three
sons' wives entered the ark with him. 14They
entered it with all the wildlife according to
their kinds, all livestock according to their
kinds, the creatures that crawl on the earth
according to their kinds, all birds, every fowl,
and everything with wings according to their
kinds. 15Two of all flesh that has the breath of
life in it entered the ark with Noah. 16Those
that entered, male and female of all flesh, entered just as God had commanded him. Then
the LORD shut him in.

17The flood continued for 40 days on the
earth; the waters increased and lifted up
the ark so that it rose above the earth. 18The
waters surged and increased greatly on the
earth, and the ark floated on the surface of
the water. 19Then the waters surged even
higher on the earth, and all the high mountains under the whole sky were covered.
20The mountains were covered as the waters
surged above them more than 20 feet.[A] 21Ev-
ery creature perished — those that crawl on
the earth, birds, livestock, wildlife, and those
that swarm[B] on the earth, as well as all mankind. 22Everything with the breath of the
spirit of life in its nostrils[g] — everything on
dry land died. 23He wiped out every living
thing that was on the surface of the ground,
from mankind to livestock, to creatures that
crawl, to the birds of the sky, and they were
wiped off the earth. Only Noah was left, and
those that were with him in the ark.[h] 24And
the waters surged on the earth 150 days.

The Flood Recedes

8 God remembered Noah,[i] as well as all the
wildlife and all the livestock that were
with him in the ark. God caused a wind[C] to
pass over the earth,[j] and the water began to
subside. 2The sources of the watery depths
and the floodgates of the sky were closed,
and the rain from the sky stopped.[k] 3The water steadily receded from the earth, and by
the end of 150 days the waters had decreased
significantly.[l] 4The ark came to rest in the seventh month, on the seventeenth day of the
month, on the mountains of Ararat.[D,m]

5The waters continued to recede until the
tenth month; in the tenth month, on the first
day of the month, the tops of the mountains
were visible. 6After 40 days Noah opened the
window of the ark that he had made, 7and he
sent out a raven. It went back and forth until the waters had dried up from the earth.
8Then he sent out a dove to see whether the
water on the earth's surface had gone down,
9but the dove found no resting place for her
foot. She returned to him in the ark because
water covered the surface of the whole earth.
He reached out and brought her into the ark
to himself. 10So Noah waited seven more days

[a]6:22 Gn 7:5 [b]7:1 Mt 24:38-39; Lk 17:26-27; Heb 11:7 [c]7:2 Gn 8:20; Lv 11:1-31; Dt 14:3-20 [d]7:5 Gn 6:22 [e]7:11 Gn 8:2; Pr 8:28; Am 9:6 [f]2Kg 7:19; Ps 78:23; Is 24:18; Mal 3:10 [g]7:22 Gn 2:7 [h]7:23 1Pt 3:20; 2Pt 2:5 [i]8:1 Gn 19:29; Ex 2:24; 1Sm 1:19; Ps 105:42 [j]Ex 14:21; 15:10; Jb 12:15; Ps 29:10; Is 44:27; Nah 1:4 [k]8:2 Gn 7:11 [l]8:3 Gn 7:24 [m]8:4 2Kg 19:37; Is 37:38; Jr 51:27

A7:20 Lit *surged 15 cubits* B7:21 Lit *all the swarming swarms* C8:1 Or *spirit*; Gn 1:2 D8:4 Turkey or Armenia

and sent out the dove from the ark again.
11 When the dove came to him at evening,
there was a plucked olive leaf in her beak. So
Noah knew that the water on the earth's surface had gone down. 12 After he had waited
another seven days, he sent out the dove, but
she did not return to him again. 13 In the six
hundred and first year,[A] in the first month,
on the first day of the month, the water that
had covered the earth was dried up. Then
Noah removed the ark's cover and saw that
the surface of the ground was drying. 14 By the
twenty-seventh day of the second month, the
earth was dry.

The Lord's Promise

15 Then God spoke to Noah, 16 "Come out of
the ark, you, your wife, your sons, and your
sons' wives with you. 17 Bring out all the living creatures[B] that are with you — birds, livestock, those that crawl on the ground — and
they will spread over the earth and be fruitful
and multiply on the earth."[a] 18 So Noah, along
with his sons, his wife, and his sons' wives,
came out. 19 All wildlife, all livestock, every
bird, and every creature that crawls on the
earth came out of the ark by their groups.

20 Then Noah built an altar to the Lord. He
took some of every kind of ·clean animal and
every kind of clean bird and offered ·burnt
offerings on the altar. 21 When the Lord
smelled the pleasing aroma,[b] He said to Himself, "I will never again curse the ground[c] because of man, even though man's inclination
is evil from his youth.[d] And I will never again
strike down every living thing as I have done.[e]

22 As long as the earth endures,
seedtime and harvest, cold and heat,
summer and winter, and day and night
will not cease."[f]

God's Covenant with Noah

9 God blessed Noah and his sons and said
to them, "Be fruitful and multiply and fill
the earth.[g] 2 The fear and terror of you will be
in every living creature on the earth, every
bird of the sky, every creature that crawls on
the ground, and all the fish of the sea. They
are placed under your authority.[C] 3 Every liv-

[a]8:17 Gn 1:22,28; 9:1
[b]8:21 Ex 29:18; Lv 1:9; Ezk 16:19; 20:41; 2Co 2:15; Eph 5:2; Php 4:18
[c]Gn 3:17; 5:29; 6:7; Is 54:9
[d]Gn 6:5; Ps 51:5; Jr 17:9; Rm 1:21; 3:23; Eph 2:1-3
[e]Gn 9:11,15
[f]8:22 Jr 33:20,25
[g]9:1 Gn 1:28; 8:17; 9:7; 35:11
[h]9:3 Dt 12:15; 1Tm 4:3-4
[i]9:1-3 Gn 1:28-30
[j]9:4 Lv 3:17; 7:20; 17:10-16; 19:26; Dt 12:16,23; 15:23; 1Sm 14:34; Ac 15:20,29
[k]9:5 Ex 21:28
[l]Gn 4:2,8
[m]9:6 Ex 21:12-14; Lv 24:17; Nm 35:33; Mt 26:52
[n]Gn 1:26-27
[o]9:7 Gn 1:28
[p]9:9 Gn 6:18; 8:22; 17:2; Ex 6:4; 19:5; Lv 26:9
[q]9:11 Is 54:9-10
[r]9:12 Gn 17:11
[s]9:13 Ezk 1:28; Rv 4:3; 10:1
[t]9:15 Lv 26:42,45; Dt 7:9; 1Kg 8:23; Ezk 16:60
[u]9:16 Gn 17:13; 2Sm 23:5; 1Ch 16:17; Is 24:5
[v]9:19 Gn 9:1,7; 10:32; 1Ch 1:4

ing creature will be food for you;[h] as I gave
the green plants, I have given you everything.[i]
4 However, you must not eat meat with its lifeblood in it.[j] 5 I will require the life of every animal[k] and every man for your life and your
blood. I will require the life of each man's
brother for a man's life.[l]

6 Whoever sheds man's blood,
his blood will be shed by man,[m]
for God made man in His image.[n]

7 But you, be fruitful and multiply; spread out
over the earth and multiply on it."[o]

8 Then God said to Noah and his sons with
him, 9 "Understand that I am confirming My
covenant[p] with you and your descendants after you, 10 and with every living creature that
is with you — birds, livestock, and all wildlife
of the earth that are with you — all the animals of the earth that came out of the ark.
11 I confirm My covenant with you that never
again will every creature be wiped out by the
waters of a flood; there will never again be a
flood to destroy the earth."[q]

12 And God said, "This is the sign of the covenant[r] I am making between Me and you and
every living creature with you, a covenant
for all future generations: 13 I have placed My
bow in the clouds,[s] and it will be a sign of the
covenant between Me and the earth. 14 Whenever I form clouds over the earth and the bow
appears in the clouds, 15 I will remember My
covenant[t] between Me and you and all the
living creatures:[D] water will never again become a flood to destroy every creature. 16 The
bow will be in the clouds, and I will look at
it and remember the everlasting covenant[u]
between God and all the living creatures[E] on
earth." 17 God said to Noah, "This is the sign of
the covenant that I have confirmed between
Me and every creature on earth."

Prophecies about Noah's Family

18 Noah's sons who came out of the ark were
Shem, Ham, and Japheth. Ham was the father
of Canaan. 19 These three were Noah's sons, and
from them the whole earth was populated.[v]

20 Noah, a man of the soil, was the first to
plant[F] a vineyard. 21 He drank some of the

A8:13 = of Noah's life B8:17 Lit *creatures of all flesh* C9:2 Lit *are given in your hand* D9:15 Lit *and creatures of all flesh* E9:16 Lit *creatures of all flesh*

F9:20 Or *Noah began to be a farmer and planted*

wine, became drunk, and uncovered himself inside his tent. 22 Ham, the father of Canaan, saw his father naked and told his two brothers outside.[a] 23 Then Shem and Japheth took a cloak and placed it over both their shoulders, and walking backward, they covered their father's nakedness. Their faces were turned away, and they did not see their father naked.

24 When Noah awoke from his drinking and learned what his youngest son had done to him, 25 he said:

Canaan will be cursed.[b]
He will be the lowest of slaves
to his brothers.[c]

26 He also said:

Praise the LORD, the God of Shem;
Canaan will be[A] his slave.
27 God will extend[B] Japheth;
he will dwell in the tents of Shem;
Canaan will be his slave.

28 Now Noah lived 350 years after the flood. 29 So Noah's life lasted 950 years; then he died.

The Table of Nations

10 These are the family records[d] of Noah's sons, Shem, Ham, and Japheth. They also had sons after the flood.

2 Japheth's sons:[e] Gomer, Magog, Madai, Javan, Tubal, Meshech, and Tiras. 3 Gomer's sons: Ashkenaz, Riphath, and Togarmah. 4 And Javan's sons: Elishah, Tarshish,[f] Kittim, and Dodanim.[C] 5 The coastland peoples spread out into their lands. These are Japheth's sons by their clans, in their nations. Each group had its own language.

6 Ham's sons:[g] Cush, Egypt, Put, and Canaan. 7 Cush's sons: Seba, Havilah, Sabtah, Raamah, and Sabteca. And Raamah's sons: Sheba and Dedan.

8 Cush fathered Nimrod, who was the first powerful man on earth. 9 He was a powerful hunter in the sight of the LORD. That is why it is said, "Like Nimrod, a powerful hunter in the sight of the LORD." 10 His kingdom started with Babylon,[h] Erech,[D] Accad,[E] and Calneh,[F] in the land of ˙Shinar.[G,i] 11 From that land he went to Assyria[j] and built Nineveh, Rehoboth-ir, Calah, 12 and Resen, between Nineveh and the great city Calah.

13 Mizraim[H,k] fathered Ludim, Anamim, Lehabim, Naphtuhim, 14 Pathrusim, Casluhim (the Philistines came from them), and Caphtorim.[l]

15 Canaan fathered Sidon his firstborn, then Heth, 16 the Jebusites, the Amorites, the Girgashites,[m] 17 the Hivites, the Arkites, the Sinites, 18 the Arvadites, the Zemarites, and the Hamathites. Afterward the Canaanite clans scattered. 19 The Canaanite border went from Sidon going toward Gerar as far as Gaza, and going toward Sodom, Gomorrah, Admah, and Zeboiim as far as Lasha.

20 These are Ham's sons, by their clans, according to their languages, in their own lands and their nations.

21 And Shem, Japheth's older brother, also had sons. Shem was the father of all the sons of Eber.[n] 22 Shem's sons[o] were Elam, Asshur,[I] Arpachshad, Lud, and Aram.

23 Aram's sons: Uz, Hul, Gether, and Mash.

24 Arpachshad fathered[J] Shelah,[p] and Shelah fathered Eber. 25 Eber had two sons. One was named Peleg, for during his days the earth was divided;[q] his brother was named Joktan. 26 And Joktan fathered Almodad, Sheleph, Hazarmaveth, Jerah, 27 Hadoram, Uzal, Diklah, 28 Obal, Abimael, Sheba, 29 Ophir, Havilah, and Jobab. All these were Joktan's sons. 30 Their settlements extended from Mesha to Sephar, the eastern hill country.

31 These are Shem's sons by their clans, according to their languages, in their lands and their nations.

32 These are the clans of Noah's sons, according to their family records, in their nations. The nations on earth spread out from these after the flood.[r]

The Tower of Babylon

11 At one time the whole earth had the same language and vocabulary.[K] 2 As people[L] migrated from the east,[M] they found a valley in the land of ˙Shinar and settled there.[s] 3 They said to each other, "Come, let

[a] **9:22** Lm 4:21; Hab 2:15
[b] **9:25** Dt 27:16
[c] Jos 9:23; Jdg 1:28; 1Kg 9:20-21
[d] **10:1** Gn 2:4
[e] **10:2-5** 1Ch 1:5-7; Ezk 38:1-6
[f] **10:4** 1Kg 10:22; Is 2:16
[g] **10:6-7** 1Ch 1:8-10
[h] **10:10** Gn 11:9
[i] Gn 11:2; 14:1
[j] **10:11** Mc 5:6
[k] **10:13-18** 1Ch 1:11-16
[l] **10:14** Jr 47:4; Am 9:7
[m] **10:16** Gn 15:19-21
[n] **10:21** Gn 11:13-14
[o] **10:22-29** 1Ch 1:17-23
[p] **10:24** Gn 11:12; Lk 3:35
[q] **10:25** Gn 11:8; Ps 55:9
[r] **10:32** Gn 9:19
[s] **11:2** Gn 10:10; 14:1; Dn 1:2

[A] **9:26** As a prophecy; others interpret the verbs in vv. 26-27 as a wish or prayer: *let Canaan be . . .* [B] **9:27** In Hb, the name Japheth sounds like the word "extend." [C] **10:4** Some Hb mss, Sam, LXX read *Rodanim*; 1Ch 1:7 [D] **10:10** Or *Uruk* [E] **10:10** Or *Akkad* [F] **10:10** Or *and all of them* [G] **10:10** Or *in Babylonia* [H] **10:13** = Egypt [I] **10:22** Or *Assyria* [J] **10:24** LXX reads *fathered Cainan, and Cainan fathered*; Gn 11:12-13; Lk 3:35-36 [K] **11:1** Lit *one lip and the same words* [L] **11:2** Lit *they* [M] **11:2** Or *migrated eastward*

us make oven-fired bricks." They used brick
for stone and asphalt for mortar.[a] 4 And they
said, "Come, let us build ourselves a city and
a tower with its top in the sky.[b] Let us make
a name for ourselves; otherwise, we will be
scattered over the face of the whole earth."
5 Then the LORD came down[c] to look over
the city and the tower that the •men were
building. 6 The LORD said, "If they have begun to do this as one people all having the
same language, then nothing they plan to do
will be impossible for them. 7 Come, let Us go
down there and confuse[A] their language[B] so
that they will not understand one another's
speech."[C] 8 So from there the LORD scattered
them over the face of the whole earth,[d] and
they stopped building the city. 9 Therefore its
name is called Babylon,[D,e] for there the LORD
confused the language of the whole earth,
and from there the LORD scattered them over
the face of the whole earth.

From Shem to Abram

10 These are the family records[f] of Shem.
Shem lived 100 years and fathered Arpachshad two years after the flood. 11 After he fathered Arpachshad, Shem lived 500 years
and fathered other sons and daughters. 12 Arpachshad lived 35 years[E] and fathered Shelah. 13 After he fathered Shelah, Arpachshad
lived 403 years and fathered other sons and
daughters. 14 Shelah lived 30 years and fathered Eber. 15 After he fathered Eber, Shelah lived 403 years and fathered other sons
and daughters. 16 Eber lived 34 years and fathered Peleg. 17 After he fathered Peleg, Eber
lived 430 years and fathered other sons and
daughters. 18 Peleg lived 30 years and fathered
Reu. 19 After he fathered Reu, Peleg lived 209
years and fathered other sons and daughters. 20 Reu lived 32 years and fathered Serug.
21 After he fathered Serug, Reu lived 207 years
and fathered other sons and daughters. 22 Serug lived 30 years and fathered Nahor. 23 After he fathered Nahor, Serug lived 200 years
and fathered other sons and daughters. 24 Nahor lived 29 years and fathered Terah.[g] 25 After
he fathered Terah, Nahor lived 119 years and
fathered other sons and daughters. 26 Terah
lived 70 years and fathered Abram, Nahor,
and Haran.
27 These are the family records of Terah. Terah fathered Abram, Nahor, and Haran, and
Haran fathered Lot. 28 Haran died in his native land, in Ur of the Chaldeans, during his
father Terah's lifetime. 29 Abram and Nahor
took wives: Abram's wife was named Sarai,[h]
and Nahor's wife was named Milcah.[i] She
was the daughter of Haran, the father of both
Milcah and Iscah. 30 Sarai was unable to conceive;[j] she did not have a child.
31 Terah took his son Abram, his grandson
Lot (Haran's son), and his daughter-in-law
Sarai, his son Abram's wife, and they set out
together from Ur of the Chaldeans[k] to go to
the land of Canaan. But when they came to
Haran, they settled there. 32 Terah lived 205
years and died in Haran.

The Call of Abram

12 The LORD said to Abram:

Go out from your land,
your relatives,
and your father's house
to the land that I will show you.[l]
2 I will make you into a great nation,[m]
I will bless you,[n]
I will make your name great,
and you will be a blessing.[F,o]
3 I will bless those who bless you,
I will curse those who treat you
with contempt,[p]
and all the peoples[G] on earth
will be blessed[H] through you.[I,q]

4 So Abram went, as the LORD had told him,
and Lot went with him. Abram was 75 years
old when he left Haran.[r] 5 He took his wife Sarai, his nephew Lot, all the possessions they
had accumulated, and the people he had acquired in Haran, and they set out for the land
of Canaan. When they came to the land of Canaan, 6 Abram passed through the land to the
site of Shechem,[s] at the oak of Moreh. At that
time the Canaanites were in the land. 7 Then
the LORD appeared to Abram and said, "I will

[a] **11:3** Gn 14:10; Ex 2:3 [b] **11:4** Dt 1:28; 9:1; Ps 107:26 [c] **11:5** Gn 18:21; Ex 3:8; 19:11,18,20 [d] **11:8** Gn 11:4; Ps 92:9; Lk 1:51 [e] **11:9** Gn 10:10 [f] **11:10** Gn 2:4; 11:27 [g] **11:24** Jos 24:2 [h] **11:29** Gn 17:15; 20:12 [i] Gn 22:20,23; 24:15 [j] **11:30** Gn 25:21; 29:31; Ex 23:26; Jdg 13:2-3; 1Sm 2:5; Jb 24:21; Is 54:1; Lk 1:36; 23:29; Gl 4:27; Heb 11:11 [k] **11:31** Gn 15:7; Neh 9:7; Ac 7:4 [l] **12:1** Gn 15:7; Ac 7:3; Heb 11:8 [m] **12:2** Gn 17:4-6; 18:18; 46:3; Dt 26:5 [n] Gn 22:17 [o] Zch 8:13 [p] **12:3** Gn 27:29; Nm 24:9 [q] Gn 18:18; 26:4; 28:14; Ac 3:25; Gl 3:8 [r] **12:4** Gn 11:27,31 [s] **12:6** Gn 35:4; Dt 11:30; Heb 11:9

[A] **11:7** Or *confound* [B] **11:7** Lit *lip* [C] **11:7** Lit *understand each man the lip of his companion* [D] **11:9** In Hb, the name Babylon sounds like the word "confuse." [E] **11:12-13** LXX reads *years and fathered Cainan. 13 After he fathered Cainan, Arphachshad lived 430 years and fathered other sons and daughters, and he died. Cainan lived 130 years and fathered Shelah. After he fathered Shelah, Cainan lived 330 years and fathered other sons and daughters, and he died*; Gn 10:24; Lk 3:35-36 [F] **12:2** Or *great. Be a blessing!* [G] **12:3** Lit *clans* [H] **12:3** Or *will find blessing* [I] **12:3** Or *will bless themselves by you*

give this land to your •offspring."[a] So he built
an altar there to the LORD who had appeared
to him. [8]From there he moved on to the hill
country east of Bethel and pitched his tent,
with Bethel on the west and Ai on the east. He
built an altar to •Yahweh there, and he called
on the name of Yahweh.[b] [9]Then Abram journeyed by stages to the •Negev.

Abram in Egypt

[10]There was a famine in the land,[c] so Abram
went down to Egypt to live there for a while
because the famine in the land was severe.
[11]When he was about to enter Egypt, he said
to his wife Sarai, "Look, I know what a beautiful woman you are. [12]When the Egyptians see
you, they will say, 'This is his wife.' They will
kill me but let you live.[d] [13]Please say you're my
sister so it will go well for me because of you,
and my life will be spared on your account."
[14]When Abram entered Egypt, the Egyptians
saw that the woman was very beautiful.
[15]Pharaoh's officials saw her and praised her
to Pharaoh, so the woman was taken to Pharaoh's household. [16]He treated Abram well
because of her, and Abram acquired flocks
and herds, male and female donkeys, male
and female slaves, and camels.

[17]But the LORD struck Pharaoh and his
household with severe plagues because of
Abram's wife Sarai.[e] [18]So Pharaoh sent for
Abram and said, "What have you done to me?
Why didn't you tell me she was your wife?
[19]Why did you say, 'She's my sister,' so that I
took her as my wife? Now, here is your wife.
Take her and go!" [20]Then Pharaoh gave his
men orders about him, and they sent him
away with his wife and all he had.

Abram and Lot Separate

13 Then Abram went up from Egypt to the
•Negev[f]—he, his wife, and all he had,
and Lot with him. [2]Abram was very rich[A] in
livestock, silver, and gold. [3]He went by stages
from the Negev to Bethel, to the place between Bethel and Ai where his tent had for-

[a]12:7 Gn 13:15; Ex 33:1; Ps 105:9-12; Ac 7:5; Gl 3:16
[b]12:8 Gn 4:26; 21:33
[c]12:10 Gn 26:1; 43:1
[d]12:12 Gn 20:1-18; 26:6-11
[e]12:17 Gn 20:18; 1Ch 16:21; Ps 105:14
[f]13:1 Gn 12:9

God's Initiative

I will make you into a great nation, I will bless you . . . and all the peoples on earth will be blessed through you. (Genesis 12:2-3)

From the very beginning of His interactions with Abraham, God had sought to bless not just Abraham's direct descendents, but "all the peoples on earth." Through Israel, Abraham's descendants, God would allow the nations to see what it looked like to be Yahweh's people. Through Christ, a descendant of Israel, God would extend Israel's blessing to the whole world. Through the church, brought together and held together by Christ, God would continue to bless all people as the church would share Christ's message of salvation everywhere.

God has chosen to use people to make His glory known throughout the world, but He has never been dependent on us. It has always been God's plan and God's work. When Abraham tried to take becoming "a great nation" into His own hands, he gave birth to Ishmael, who was not the son of the promise. By the time Abraham died, he had only Isaac, a far cry from a nation. Yet God's promise to Abraham was eventually fulfilled. Key to it all was God's faithfulness even when Abraham tried by his own might or cleverness to fulfill God's promise.

In the same way, we may not understand how God is working, but we can know He is at work. We look at current nations and leaders and sometimes wonder where God is in all of this. Rest assured, He is there and He is not idle. Our task is to continue to declare His glory to the world, remembering that it is not our initiative or our hard work that will bring blessing to the world, it is the work of God in us, His people—just as it has always been.

GOD'S HEART FOR THE WORLD

[A]13:2 Lit *heavy*

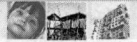

merly been, 4to the site where he had built the altar. And Abram called on the name of •Yahweh there.[a]

5Now Lot, who was traveling with Abram, also had flocks, herds, and tents. 6But the land was unable to support them as long as they stayed together, for they had so many possessions that they could not stay together,[b] 7and there was quarreling between the herdsmen of Abram's livestock and the herdsmen of Lot's livestock.[c] At that time the Canaanites and the Perizzites were living in the land.[d]

8Then Abram said to Lot, "Please, let's not have quarreling between you and me, or between your herdsmen and my herdsmen, since we are relatives.[A] 9Isn't the whole land before you? Separate from me: if you go to the left, I will go to the right; if you go to the right, I will go to the left."

10Lot looked out and saw that the entire Jordan Valley[e] as far as[B] Zoar[f] was well watered everywhere like the LORD's garden[g] and the land of Egypt. This was before the LORD destroyed Sodom and Gomorrah.[h] 11So Lot chose the entire Jordan Valley for himself. Then Lot journeyed eastward, and they separated from each other. 12Abram lived in the land of Canaan, but Lot lived in the cities of the valley and set up his tent near Sodom. 13Now the men of Sodom were evil, sinning greatly[C] against the LORD.[i]

14After Lot had separated from him, the LORD said to Abram, "Look from the place where you are. Look north and south, east and west,[j] 15for I will give you and your •offspring forever all the land that you see.[k] 16I will make your offspring like the dust of the earth,[l] so that if anyone could count the dust of the earth, then your offspring could be counted. 17Get up and walk around the land, through its length and width, for I will give it to you."

18So Abram moved his tent and went to live near the oaks of Mamre at Hebron,[m] where he built an altar to the LORD.

Abram Rescues Lot

14 In those days Amraphel king of •Shinar,[n] Arioch king of Ellasar, Chedorlaomer king of Elam,[D,o] and Tidal[E] king of Goiim[F] 2waged war against Bera king of Sodom, Birsha king of Gomorrah, Shinab king of Admah, and Shemeber king of Zeboiim,[p] as well as the king of Bela (that is, Zoar[q]). 3All of these came as allies to the Valley of Siddim (that is, the Dead Sea[r]). 4They were subject to Chedorlaomer for 12 years, but in the thirteenth year they rebelled. 5In the fourteenth year Chedorlaomer and the kings who were with him came and defeated the Rephaim[s] in Ashteroth-karnaim, the Zuzim in Ham,[t] the Emim in Shaveh-kiriathaim, 6and the Horites[u] in the mountains of Seir, as far as El-paran[v] by the wilderness. 7Then they came back to invade En-mishpat (that is, Kadesh[w]), and they defeated all the territory of the Amalekites, as well as the Amorites who lived in Hazazon-tamar.[x]

8Then the king of Sodom, the king of Gomorrah, the king of Admah, the king of Zeboiim, and the king of Bela (that is, Zoar) went out and lined up for battle in the Valley of Siddim 9against Chedorlaomer king of Elam, Tidal king of Goiim, Amraphel king of Shinar, and Arioch king of Ellasar—four kings against five. 10Now the Valley of Siddim contained many asphalt pits, and as the kings of Sodom and Gomorrah fled, some fell into them,[G] but the rest fled to the mountains.[y] 11The four kings took all the goods of Sodom and Gomorrah and all their food and went on. 12They also took Abram's nephew Lot and his possessions, for he was living in Sodom,[z] and they went on.

13One of the survivors came and told Abram the Hebrew,[aa] who lived near the oaks belonging to Mamre the Amorite, the brother of Eshcol and the brother of Aner. They were bound by a treaty with[H] Abram. 14When Abram heard that his relative had been taken prisoner, he assembled[I] his 318 trained men, born in his household,[ab] and they went in pursuit as far as Dan.[ac] 15And he and his servants deployed against them by night, attacked them, and pursued them as far as Hobah to the north of Damascus. 16He brought back all the goods and also his relative Lot and his goods, as well as the women and the other people.

[a] **13:4** Gn 12:7,8
[b] **13:6** Gn 36:7
[c] **13:7** Gn 26:20
[d] Gn 12:6; 15:20-21
[e] **13:10** Gn 19:17-29
[f] Gn 14:2,8; Dt 34:3
[g] Gn 2:8-10
[h] Gn 19:24-25
[i] **13:13** Gn 18:20; Ezk 16:49; 2Pt 2:7-8
[j] **13:14** Gn 28:14
[k] **13:15** Gn 12:7; 15:18; 17:8; 24:7; 26:4; 28:13; 35:12; Dt 34:4; 2Ch 20:7; Ac 7:5
[l] **13:16** Gn 16:10; 28:14; Nm 23:10
[m] **13:18** Gn 14:13; 18:1; 23:17-19
[n] **14:1** Gn 10:10; 11:2
[o] Gn 10:22; Is 11:11; Dn 8:2
[p] **14:2** Hs 11:8
[q] Gn 19:22-23
[r] **14:3** Nm 34:12; Dt 3:17; Jos 3:16
[s] **14:5** Gn 15:20; Dt 2:11,20-21; 3:11,13; Jos 12:4
[t] Dt 1:4; Jos 9:10
[u] **14:6** Gn 36:20; Dt 2:12,22
[v] Gn 21:21; Nm 10:12
[w] **14:7** Nm 13:26
[x] 2Ch 20:2
[y] **14:10** Gn 19:17
[z] **14:12** Gn 13:12
[aa] **14:13** Gn 39:14; 40:15
[ab] **14:14** Gn 12:5; 15:3; 17:27; Ec 2:7
[ac] Dt 34:1; Jdg 18:29; 1Kg 15:20

[A] **13:8** Lit *brothers* [B] **13:10** Lit *Valley as you go to* [C] **13:13** Lit *evil and sinful* [D] **14:1** A region in southwest Iran [E] **14:1** The name Tidal may be related to the Hittite royal name *Tudhaliya.* [F] **14:1** Or *nations* [G] **14:10** Sam, LXX; MT reads *fell there* [H] **14:13** Lit *were possessors of a covenant of* [I] **14:14** Sam; MT reads *poured out*

Melchizedek's Blessing

17 After Abram returned from defeating
Chedorlaomer and the kings who were with
him, the king of Sodom went out to meet him
in the Valley of Shaveh (that is, the King's Valley[a]). 18 Then Melchizedek, king of Salem,[A,b]
brought out bread and wine; he was a priest to
God ·Most High.[c] 19 He blessed him and said:

> Abram is blessed by God Most High,
> Creator[B] of heaven and earth,
> 20 and I give praise to[C] God Most High
> who has handed over your enemies
> to you.

And Abram gave him a tenth of everything.[d]
21 Then the king of Sodom said to Abram,
"Give me the people, but take the possessions
for yourself."
22 But Abram said to the king of Sodom, "I
have raised my hand in an oath to ·Yahweh,
God Most High, Creator of heaven and earth,
23 that I will not take a thread or sandal strap
or anything that belongs to you, so you can
never say, 'I made Abram rich.' 24 I will take
nothing[D] except what the servants have eaten.
But as for the share of the men who came
with me — Aner, Eshcol, and Mamre — they
can take their share."

The Abrahamic Covenant

15 After these events, the word of the
LORD came[e] to Abram in a vision:

> Do not be afraid,[f] Abram.
> I am your shield;[g]
> your reward will be very great.

2 But Abram said, "Lord GOD, what can You
give me, since I am childless and the heir of
my house is Eliezer of Damascus?"[E] 3 Abram
continued, "Look, You have given me no ·off-
spring, so a slave born in[F] my house will be
my heir."
4 Now the word of the LORD came to him:
"This one will not be your heir; instead, one
who comes from your own body[G] will be your
heir." 5 He took him outside and said, "Look at
the sky and count the stars, if you are able to
count them." Then He said to him, "Your offspring will be that numerous."[h]
6 Abram believed the LORD, and He credited
it to him as righteousness.[i]
7 He also said to him, "I am ·Yahweh who
brought you from Ur of the Chaldeans to give
you this land to possess."[j]
8 But he said, "Lord GOD, how can I know[k]
that I will possess it?"
9 He said to him, "Bring Me a three-year-old
cow, a three-year-old female goat, a three-
year-old ram, a turtledove, and a young pigeon."
10 So he brought all these to Him, split them
down the middle, and laid the pieces opposite each other, but he did not cut up the
birds.[l] 11 Birds of prey came down on the carcasses, but Abram drove them away. 12 As the
sun was setting, a deep sleep[m] fell on Abram,
and suddenly great terror and darkness descended on him.
13 Then the LORD said to Abram,[n] "Know this
for certain: Your offspring will be foreigners[o]
in a land that does not belong to them; they
will be enslaved and oppressed[H] 400 years.[p]
14 However, I will judge the nation they serve,[q]
and afterward they will go out with many
possessions.[r] 15 But you will go to your fathers
in peace and be buried at a ripe old age.[s] 16 In
the fourth generation they will return here,
for the iniquity of the Amorites has not yet
reached its full measure."[I,t]
17 When the sun had set and it was dark,
a smoking fire pot and a flaming torch appeared and passed between the divided animals. 18 On that day the LORD made a covenant
with Abram, saying, "I give this land to your
offspring,[u] from the brook of Egypt[v] to the
Euphrates River:[J] 19 the land of the Kenites,
Kenizzites, Kadmonites, 20 Hittites, Perizzites, Rephaim, 21 Amorites, Canaanites, Girgashites, and Jebusites."

Hagar and Ishmael

16 Abram's wife Sarai had not borne
any children for him, but she owned
an Egyptian slave named Hagar. 2 Sarai said
to Abram, "Since the LORD has prevented
me from bearing children, go to my slave;
perhaps through her I can build a family."
And Abram agreed to what Sarai said.[K] 3 So

[a] **14:17** 2Sm 18:18 [b] **14:18** Ps 110:4; Heb 5:6; 7:1 [c] Ps 57:2 [d] **14:20** Heb 7:4 [e] **15:1** 1Sm 15:10; 2Sm 7:4; 1Kg 6:11; Is 38:4; Jr 1:2 [f] Gn 26:24; Is 41:10; Jr 30:10; Lk 1:13,30 [g] Dt 33:29; 2Sm 22:3,31; Ps 3:3; 7:10 [h] **15:5** Gn 22:17; 26:4; Ex 32:13; Dt 1:10; 10:22; 1Ch 27:23; Rm 4:18; Heb 11:12 [i] **15:6** Rm 4:3,9,22; Gl 3:6; Jms 2:23 [j] **15:7** Gn 11:31; 12:1; Neh 9:7-8; Ac 7:2-4 [k] **15:8** Jdg 6:17; 2Kg 20:8; Ps 86:17; Is 7:11-13; Lk 1:18 [l] **15:10** Lv 1:17 [m] **15:12** Gn 2:21 [n] **15:13-14** Ac 7:6-7 [o] **15:13** Ex 22:21; 23:9 [p] Ex 12:40; Gl 3:17 [q] **15:14** Ex 6:6; 7:4; 12:12 [r] Ex 3:22 [s] **15:15** Gn 25:8; 47:30 [t] **15:16** Lv 18:24-28; Dn 8:23; Mt 23:32; 1Th 2:16 [u] **15:18** Gn 12:7; 13:15; 17:8; 24:7; 26:4; Nm 34:2; Dt 34:4; Jos 21:43; Neh 9:8; Ac 7:5 [v] Ex 23:31; Nm 34:1-15; Dt 1:7-8; 2Kg 24:7

[A] **14:18** = Jerusalem [B] **14:19** Or *Possessor* [C] **14:20** Or *and blessed be* [D] **14:24** Lit *Nothing to me* [E] **15:2** Hb obscure [F] **15:3** Lit *a son of* [G] **15:4** Lit *loins* [H] **15:13** Lit *will serve them and they will oppress them* [I] **15:16** Lit *Amorites is not yet complete* [J] **15:18** Lit *the great river, the river Euphrates* [K] **16:2** Lit *Abram listened to the voice of Sarai*

Abram's wife Sarai took Hagar, her Egyptian
slave, and gave her to her husband Abram as
a wife for him. This happened after Abram
had lived in the land of Canaan 10 years. 4 He
slept with[A] Hagar, and she became pregnant.
When she realized that she was pregnant, she
treated her mistress with contempt. 5 Then
Sarai said to Abram, "You are responsible for
my suffering![B] I put my slave in your arms,[C]
and ever since she saw that she was pregnant,
she has treated me with contempt. May the
LORD judge between me and you."[a]

6 Abram replied to Sarai, "Here, your slave
is in your hands; do whatever you want with
her." Then Sarai mistreated her so much that
she ran away from her.

7 The Angel of the LORD[b] found her by a
spring of water in the wilderness, the spring
on the way to Shur. 8 He said, "Hagar, slave of
Sarai, where have you come from and where
are you going?"

She replied, "I'm running away from my
mistress Sarai."

9 Then the Angel of the LORD said to her,
"You must go back to your mistress and submit to her mistreatment."[D] 10 The Angel of the
LORD also said to her, "I will greatly multiply
your •offspring,[c] and they will be too many to
count."

11 Then the Angel of the LORD said to her:

You have conceived and will have a son.
You will name him Ishmael,[E]
for the LORD has heard
your cry of affliction.
12 This man will be like a wild donkey.
His hand will be against everyone,
and everyone's hand will be
against him;
he will live at odds with[F] all
his brothers.[d]

13 So she called the LORD who spoke to her:
The God Who Sees,[G] for she said, "In this
place, have I actually seen[e] the One who sees
me?"[H] 14 That is why she named the spring, "A
Well of the Living One Who Sees Me."[I] It is located between Kadesh and Bered.

15 So Hagar gave birth to Abram's son, and
Abram gave the name Ishmael to the son
Hagar had. 16 Abram was 86 years old when
Hagar bore Ishmael to him.

Covenant Circumcision

17 When Abram was 99 years old, the LORD
appeared to him, saying, "I am •God Almighty.[f] Live in My presence and be blameless.[g] 2 I will establish My covenant between
Me and you, and I will multiply you greatly."

3 Then Abram fell facedown and God spoke
with him: 4 "As for Me, My covenant is with
you: you will become the father of many nations.[J] 5 Your name will no longer be Abram,[K]
but your name will be Abraham,[L] for I will
make you the father of many nations.[h] 6 I will
make you extremely fruitful and will make
nations and kings come from you. 7 I will keep
My covenant between Me and you, and your
future •offspring throughout their generations, as an everlasting covenant[i] to be your
God and the God of your offspring after you.[j]
8 And to you and your future offspring[k] I will
give the land where you are residing—all the
land of Canaan—as an eternal possession,[l]
and I will be their God."

9 God also said to Abraham, "As for you,
you and your offspring after you throughout
their generations are to keep My covenant.
10 This is My covenant, which you are to keep,
between Me and you and your offspring after
you: Every one of your males must be circumcised. 11 You must circumcise the flesh of your
foreskin to serve as a sign of the covenant
between Me and you.[M,m] 12 Throughout your
generations, every male among you at eight
days old is to be circumcised.[n] This includes a
slave born in your house and one purchased
with money from any foreigner. The one who
is not your offspring, 13 a slave born in your
house, as well as one purchased with money,
must be circumcised. My covenant will be
marked in your flesh as an everlasting covenant. 14 If any male is not circumcised in the
flesh of his foreskin, that man will be cut off
from his people; he has broken My covenant."

15 God said to Abraham, "As for your wife
Sarai, do not call her Sarai, for Sarah[N] will be

[a] 16:5 Gn 31:49; Jos 22:25; 1Sm 24:12 [b] 16:7 Gn 22:11; Ex 3:2; Nm 22:22; Jdg 2:1; 2Sm 24:16; 1Kg 19:7; 2Kg 19:35; Ps 34:7 [c] 16:10 Gn 15:5; 17:2; 26:24; Lv 26:9; Dt 7:13; 30:5; Ps 107:38 [d] 16:12 Gn 25:18 [e] 16:13 Gn 32:30; Ex 33:23; Ps 139:1-12 [f] 17:1 Gn 28:3; 35:11; Ex 6:3 [g] Gn 6:9; Ps 15:2; Lk 1:6 [h] 17:5 Gn 35:11; 48:19; Rm 4:11-12,16-18 [i] 17:7 Gn 9:16 [j] Ex 6:7; Lv 11:45; 26:12,45; Dt 29:13; Heb 11:16; Rv 21:7 [k] 17:8 Gl 3:16 [l] Gn 48:4; Ac 7:5 [m] 17:11 Ex 12:48; Dt 10:16; Ac 7:8; Rm 4:11 [n] 17:12 Lv 12:3; Lk 1:59; 2:21; Php 3:5

[A] 16:4 Lit *He came to* [B] 16:5 Or *May my suffering be on you* [C] 16:5 Lit *bosom* [D] 16:9 Lit *to mistreatment under her hand* [E] 16:11 = God Hears [F] 16:12 Or *live away from* [G] 16:13 Lit *her: You God Who Sees* [H] 16:13 Hb obscure [I] 16:14 Or *Beer-lahai-roi* [J] 17:4 Abraham was the father of the Israelites, Ishmaelites, Edomites, and Midianites. Spiritually, he is the father of all believers; Gl 3:7,29. [K] 17:5 = The Father Is Exalted [L] 17:5 = Father of a Multitude [M] 17:11 *You* in v. 11 is pl. [N] 17:15 = Princess

her name. 16 I will bless her; indeed, I will give
you a son by her.[a] I will bless her, and she will
produce nations; kings of peoples will come
from her."

17 Abraham fell facedown. Then he laughed[b]
and said to himself, "Can a child be born to a
hundred-year-old man? Can Sarah, a ninety-
year-old woman, give birth?" 18 So Abraham
said to God, "If only Ishmael were acceptable
to You!"[A]

19 But God said, "No. Your wife Sarah will
bear you a son, and you will name him Isaac.[B]
I will confirm My covenant with him as an
everlasting covenant for his future offspring.
20 As for Ishmael, I have heard you. I will certainly bless him; I will make him fruitful and
will multiply him greatly. He will father 12
tribal leaders,[c] and I will make him into a
great nation. 21 But I will confirm My covenant with Isaac, whom Sarah will bear to you
at this time next year."[d] 22 When He finished
talking with him, God withdrew[C] from Abraham.[e]

23 Then Abraham took his son Ishmael
and all the slaves born in his house or purchased with his money—every male among
the members of Abraham's household—and
he circumcised the flesh of their foreskin
on that very day, just as God had said to
him. 24 Abraham was 99 years old when the
flesh of his foreskin was circumcised, 25 and
his son Ishmael was 13 years old when the
flesh of his foreskin was circumcised. 26 On
that same day Abraham and his son Ishmael
were circumcised. 27 And all the men of his
household—both slaves born in his house
and those purchased with money from a foreigner—were circumcised with him.

Abraham's Three Visitors

18 Then the LORD appeared to Abraham
at the oaks of Mamre[f] while he was sitting in the entrance of his tent during the
heat of the day. 2 He looked up, and he saw
three men standing near him.[g] When he saw
them, he ran from the entrance of the tent to
meet them and bowed to the ground. 3 Then
he said, "My lord,[D] if I have found favor in
your sight, please do not go on past your servant. 4 Let a little water be brought, that you
may wash your feet and rest yourselves under
the tree. 5 I will bring a bit of bread so that you
may strengthen yourselves.[E] This is why you
have passed your servant's way. Later, you can
continue on."

"Yes," they replied, "do as you have said."

6 So Abraham hurried into the tent and
said to Sarah, "Quick! Knead three measures[F]
of fine flour and make bread."[G] 7 Meanwhile,
Abraham ran to the herd and got a tender,
choice calf. He gave it to a young man, who
hurried to prepare it. 8 Then Abraham took
curds[H] and milk, and the calf that he had
prepared, and set them before the men. He
served[I] them as they ate under the tree.

Sarah Laughs

9 "Where is your wife Sarah?" they asked
him.

"There, in the tent," he answered.

10 The LORD said, "I will certainly come back
to you in about a year's time, and your wife
Sarah will have a son!"[h] Now Sarah was listening at the entrance of the tent behind him.
11 Abraham and Sarah were old and getting
on in years.[J] Sarah had passed the age of childbearing.[K,i] 12 So she laughed to herself: "After I
have become shriveled up and my lord is old,
will I have delight?"[j]

13 But the LORD asked Abraham, "Why did
Sarah laugh, saying, 'Can I really have a baby
when I'm old?' 14 Is anything impossible for the
LORD?[k] At the appointed time I will come back
to you, and in about a year she will have a son."

15 Sarah denied it. "I did not laugh," she said,
because she was afraid.

But He replied, "No, you did laugh."

Abraham's Plea for Sodom

16 The men got up from there and looked out
over Sodom, and Abraham was walking with
them to see them off. 17 Then the LORD said,
"Should I hide what I am about to do from
Abraham?[l] 18 Abraham is to become a great
and powerful nation, and all the nations of
the earth will be blessed through him.[m] 19 For
I have chosen[L] him so that he will command
his children and his house after him to keep

[a] **17:16** Gn 18:10
[b] **17:17** Gn 21:6-7; Rm 4:19
[c] **17:20** Gn 25:13-16
[d] **17:21** Gn 18:10,14; 21:1
[e] **17:22** Gn 35:13
[f] **18:1** Gn 13:18; 14:13; 23:17-19
[g] **18:2** Gn 18:16,22; 19:1; 32:24; Jos 5:13; Jdg 13:6-11; Heb 13:2
[h] **18:10** Gn 17:10; 21:1; Rm 9:9
[i] **18:11** Gn 17:17; Rm 4:19; Heb 11:11-12
[j] **18:12** Gn 17:17; Lk 1:18; 1Pt 3:6
[k] **18:14** Jb 34:10; Jr 32:17,27; Mt 19:26; Mk 10:27; Lk 1:37; 18:27; Heb 6:18
[l] **18:17** Am 3:7
[m] **18:18** Gn 12:3; 26:4; Gl 3:8

[A] **17:18** Lit *Ishmael would live in Your sight* [B] **17:19** = He Laughs [C] **17:22** Lit *went up*, or *ascended* [D] **18:3** Or *My Lord*, or *The Lord* [E] **18:5** Lit *may sustain your heart* [F] **18:6** Lit *three seahs*; about 21 quarts [G] **18:6** A round, thin, unleavened bread [H] **18:8** Or *butter* [I] **18:8** Lit *was standing by* [J] **18:11** Lit *days* [K] **18:11** Lit *The way of women had ceased for Sarah* [L] **18:19** Lit *known* the way of the LORD by doing what is right and just. This is how the LORD will fulfill to Abraham what He promised him." 20Then the LORD said, "The outcry against Sodom and Gomorrah is immense, and their sin is extremely serious. 21I will go down[a] to see if what they have done justifies the cry that has come up to Me. If not, I will find out."

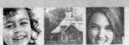

[a]18:21 Gn 11:5; Ex 3:8; Ps 14:2
[b]18:22 Gn 19:1
[c]18:23 Ex 23:7; Nm 16:22; 2Sm 24:17; Ps 11:4-7

22The men turned from there and went toward Sodom[b] while Abraham remained standing before the LORD.[A] 23Abraham stepped forward and said, "Will You really sweep away the righteous with the wicked?[c] 24What if there are 50 righteous people in the city? Will You really sweep it away instead of sparing the place for the sake of the 50 righteous

Abraham Intercedes

Andrea Mullins

When the Lord appeared to Abraham at the oaks of Mamre, He came with serious news. He was on His way to bring judgment on Sodom and Gomorrah (Gn 18:20-21). The Lord knew He would find moral degradation when He arrived in these cities, but His foremost desire was for their redemption. The people there had urgent need for someone to intercede. The Lord had covenanted with Abraham that Abraham would keep to the Lord's way by doing what was right and just (vv. 18-19), and now He came looking to Abraham to share His burden for the sinful condition of Sodom and Gomorrah. Only as Abraham and his descendents fulfilled their roles as intercessors would the nations of the world be blessed. The Lord's visit posed an unspoken question for Abraham: Will you intercede?

The condition of Sodom and Gomorrah and the Lord's plan must have been hard for Abraham to absorb, but the Lord waited while "Abraham remained standing" before Him (v. 22). Abraham surely remembered his nephew Lot as He listened to God's plans, and recalled the times he had been reminded of God's covenant to make him a blessing to the nations. The Lord gave him time to decide his answer to the unspoken question: Will you intercede?

Abraham, the father of many nations, stepped forward, setting the example for generations to come. He asked for something that might have seemed impossible to anyone but Abraham. He asked God to extend to Lot and other righteous citizens in the cities the same grace that had been shown to him. The next morning Abraham looked toward Sodom and Gomorrah (19:27). No doubt he grieved to see smoke rising from the plain! Had the Lord chosen not to answer his prayers? In fact the Lord had remembered Abraham and rescued Lot (v. 29). The Lord is always ready to forgive and may choose to intervene without our intercession, but He is amazed and dismayed when His people fail to intercede (Is 59:15-16). The Lord's unspoken question had been answered. Abraham had chosen to intercede on behalf of others.

Intercession demonstrates God's compassion, righteousness, and justice. When we pray, He listens. When we give, He multiplies. When we serve Him as missions volunteers, business leaders, homemakers, teachers, or students, He empowers us to transform lives. Intercession is making Christ known. The covenant between the Lord and Abraham was an everlasting covenant that reaches to us through Jesus Christ, and because of Him we are blessed with every spiritual blessing (Eph 1:3).

We do not always know the people for whom we have been called to intercede. Even so, the Lord expects us to care about each person's redemption. He is making His plans known and waits for us to be His intercessors. Will you intercede by praying, or giving, or teaching, or telling, or going? Every day God invites you to hear from Him and respond. Will you intercede?

[A]18:22 Ancient Jewish tradition reads *while the LORD remained standing before Abraham*

people who are in it? 25You could not possibly
do such a thing: to kill the righteous with the
wicked, treating the righteous and the wicked
alike. You could not possibly do that! Won't
the Judge of all the earth do what is just?"[a]
26The LORD said, "If I find 50 righteous people in the city of Sodom, I will spare the whole
place for their sake."[b]
27Then Abraham answered, "Since I have
ventured to speak to the Lord — even though
I am dust and ashes — 28suppose the 50 righteous lack five. Will you destroy the whole
city for lack of five?"

He replied, "I will not destroy it if I find 45
there."
29Then he spoke to Him again, "Suppose 40
are found there?"

He answered, "I will not do it on account
of 40."
30Then he said, "Let the Lord not be angry, and I will speak further. Suppose 30 are
found there?"

He answered, "I will not do it if I find 30
there."
31Then he said, "Since I have ventured to
speak to the Lord, suppose 20 are found
there?"

He replied, "I will not destroy it on account
of 20."
32Then he said, "Let the Lord not be angry,
and I will speak one more time.[c] Suppose 10
are found there?"

He answered, "I will not destroy it on account of 10." 33When the LORD had finished
speaking with Abraham, He departed, and
Abraham returned to his place.

The Destruction of Sodom and Gomorrah

19 The two angels entered Sodom[d] in the
evening as Lot was sitting at Sodom's
gate. When Lot saw them, he got up to meet
them. He bowed with his face to the ground
2and said, "My lords, turn aside to your servant's
house, wash your feet, and spend the night.
Then you can get up early and go on your way."

"No," they said. "We would rather spend
the night in the square." 3But he urged them
so strongly that they followed him and went
into his house. He prepared a feast and baked
unleavened bread for them, and they ate.

[a]**18:25** Dt 1:16-17; 32:4; Jb 8:3,20; Ps 58:11; 94:2; Is 3:10-11; Rm 3:5-6
[b]**18:26** Jr 5:1
[c]**18:32** Jdg 6:39
[d]**19:1** Gn 18:2,22
[e]**19:5** Lv 18:22; Jdg 19:22
[f]**19:8** Jdg 19:24
[g]**19:9** Ex 2:14
[h]**19:11** Dt 28:28-29; 2Kg 6:18; Ac 13:11
[i]**19:13** Gn 18:20-21; Ex 3:7; 22:23; 1Sm 9:16; Jb 27:9
[j]**19:14** Nm 16:21,26,45; Jr 51:6; Rv 18:4

4Before they went to bed, the men of the
city of Sodom, both young and old, the whole
population, surrounded the house. 5They
called out to Lot and said, "Where are the
men who came to you tonight? Send them
out to us so we can have sex with them!"[e]
6Lot went out to them at the entrance and
shut the door behind him. 7He said, "Don't
do this evil, my brothers. 8Look, I've got two
daughters who haven't had sexual relations
with a man.[f] I'll bring them out to you, and
you can do whatever you want[A] to them.
However, don't do anything to these men, because they have come under the protection of
my roof."
9"Get out of the way!" they said, adding,
"This one came here as a foreigner, but he's
acting like a judge![g] Now we'll do more harm
to you than to them." They put pressure on
Lot and came up to break down the door.
10But the angels[B] reached out, brought Lot
into the house with them, and shut the door.
11They struck the men who were at the entrance of the house, both young and old, with
a blinding light so that they were unable to
find the entrance.[h]
12Then the angels[B] said to Lot, "Do you have
anyone else here: a son-in-law, your sons and
daughters, or anyone else in the city who belongs to you? Get them out of this place, 13for
we are about to destroy this place because the
outcry against its people is so great before the
LORD, that the LORD has sent us to destroy it."[i]
14So Lot went out and spoke to his sons-in-
law, who were going to marry[C] his daughters.
"Get up," he said. "Get out of this place, for the
LORD is about to destroy the city!"[j] But his
sons-in-law thought he was joking.
15At daybreak the angels urged Lot on: "Get
up! Take your wife and your two daughters
who are here, or you will be swept away in
the punishment[D] of the city." 16But he hesitated. Because of the LORD's compassion for
him, the men grabbed his hand, his wife's
hand, and the hands of his two daughters.
Then they brought him out and left him outside the city.
17As soon as the angels got them outside,
one of them[E] said, "Run for your lives! Don't
look back and don't stop anywhere on the

[A]**19:8** Lit *do what is good in your eyes* [B]**19:10,12** Lit *men* [C]**19:14** Lit *take* [D]**19:15** Or *iniquity*, or *guilt* [E]**19:17** LXX, Syr, Vg read *outside, they*

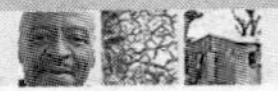

plain! Run to the mountains, or you will be
swept away!"
18 But Lot said to them, "No, my lords[A] —
please. 19 Your servant has indeed found favor
in your sight, and you have shown me great
kindness by saving my life. But I can't run
to the mountains; the disaster will overtake
me, and I will die. 20 Look, this town is close
enough for me to run to. It is a small place.
Please let me go there — it's only a small
place, isn't it? — so that I can survive."
21 And he said to him, "All right,[B] I'll grant
your request[C] about this matter too and
will not demolish the town you mentioned.
22 Hurry up! Run there, for I cannot do anything until you get there." Therefore the
name of the city is Zoar.[D,a]
23 The sun had risen over the land when Lot
reached Zoar. 24 Then out of the sky the LORD
rained burning sulfur on Sodom and Gomorrah from the LORD.[b] 25 He demolished these
cities, the entire plain, all the inhabitants of
the cities, and whatever grew on the ground.
26 But his wife looked back and became a pillar of salt.[c]
27 Early in the morning Abraham went
to the place where he had stood before the
LORD.[d] 28 He looked down toward Sodom and
Gomorrah and all the land of the plain, and
he saw that smoke was going up from the
land like the smoke of a furnace. 29 So it was,
when God destroyed the cities of the plain,
He remembered Abraham and brought Lot
out of the middle of the upheaval when He
demolished the cities where Lot had lived.

The Origin of Moab and Ammon

30 Lot departed from Zoar and lived in the
mountains along with his two daughters, because he was afraid to live in Zoar. Instead, he
and his two daughters lived in a cave. 31 Then
the firstborn said to the younger, "Our father is old, and there is no man in the land to
sleep with us as is the custom of all the land.
32 Come, let's get our father to drink wine
so that we can sleep with him and preserve
our father's line." 33 So they got their father
to drink wine that night, and the firstborn
came and slept with her father; he did not
know when she lay down or when she got up.
34 The next day the firstborn said to the
younger, "Look, I slept with my father last
night. Let's get him to drink wine again tonight so you can go sleep with him and we can
preserve our father's line." 35 That night they
again got their father to drink wine, and the
younger went and slept with him; he did not
know when she lay down or when she got up.
36 So both of Lot's daughters became pregnant by their father. 37 The firstborn gave birth
to a son and named him Moab.[E] He is the father of the Moabites of today.[e] 38 The younger
also gave birth to a son, and she named him
Ben-ammi.[F] He is the father of the Ammonites of today.[f]

Sarah Rescued from Abimelech

20 From there Abraham traveled to the
region of the •Negev and settled between Kadesh and Shur. While he lived in Gerar,[g] 2 Abraham said about his wife Sarah, "She
is my sister."[h] So Abimelech king of Gerar had
Sarah brought to him.
3 But God came to Abimelech in a dream by
night and said to him, "You are about to die
because of the woman you have taken, for she
is a married woman."[G]
4 Now Abimelech had not approached her,
so he said, "Lord, would You destroy a nation
even though it is innocent? 5 Didn't he himself say to me, 'She is my sister'? And she herself said, 'He is my brother.' I did this with a
clear conscience[H] and •clean[I] hands."
6 Then God said to him in the dream, "Yes,
I know that you did this with a clear conscience.[J] I have also kept you from sinning
against Me. Therefore I have not let you
touch her. 7 Now return the man's wife, for he
is a prophet,[i] and he will pray for you and you
will live. But if you do not return her, know
that you will certainly die, you and all who
are yours."
8 Early in the morning Abimelech got up,
called all his servants together, and personally[K] told them all these things, and the men
were terrified.

a19:22 Gn 14:2 b19:24 Dt 29:23; Ps 11:6; Is 13:19; Jr 20:16; Ezk 16:49-50; Lk 17:28-29; 2Pt 2:6-8; Jd 7 c19:26 Lk 17:32 d19:27 Gn 18:22 e19:37 Dt 2:9 f19:38 Dt 2:19 g20:1 Gn 26:1,6 h20:2 Gn 12:13; 26:7 i20:7 1Sm 7:5; 2Kg 5:11; Jb 42:8

A19:18 Or *My Lord*, or *My lords* B19:21 Or *Look!* C19:21 Lit *I will lift up your face* D19:22 In Hb, the name Zoar is related to the phrase "small place" in v. 20; its original name was Bela; Gn 14:2. E19:37 = From My Father F19:38 = Son of My People G20:3 Lit *is possessed by a husband* H20:5 Lit *with integrity of my heart* I20:5 Lit *cleanness of my* J20:6 Lit *with integrity of your heart* K20:8 Lit *in their ears*

9Then Abimelech called Abraham in and
said to him, "What have you done to us? How
did I sin against you that you have brought
such enormous ·guilt on me and on my kingdom? You have done things to me that should
never be done."[a] 10Abimelech also said to
Abraham, "What did you intend when you
did this thing?"
11Abraham replied, "I thought, 'There is absolutely no ·fear of God in this place.[b] They
will kill me because of my wife.' 12Besides, she
really is my sister, the daughter of my father
though not the daughter of my mother, and
she became my wife. 13So when God had me
wander from my father's house,[c] I said to her:
Show your loyalty to me wherever we go and
say about me: 'He's my brother.' "[d]
14Then Abimelech took sheep and cattle and male and female slaves, gave them
to Abraham, and returned his wife Sarah to
him. 15Abimelech said, "Look, my land is before you.[e] Settle wherever you want."[A] 16And
he said to Sarah, "Look, I am giving your
brother 1,000 pieces of silver. It is a verifica-
tion of your honor[B] to all who are with you.
You are fully vindicated."
17Then Abraham prayed to God,[f] and
God healed Abimelech, his wife, and his female slaves so that they could bear children,
18for the LORD had completely closed all the
wombs in Abimelech's household on account
of Sarah, Abraham's wife.

The Birth of Isaac

21 The LORD came to Sarah as He had
said, and the LORD did for Sarah what
He had promised.[g] 2Sarah became pregnant
and bore a son to Abraham in his old age,
at the appointed time God had told him.[h]
3Abraham named his son who was born to
him—the one Sarah bore to him—Isaac.[i]
4When his son Isaac was eight days old,
Abraham circumcised him, as God had commanded him.[j] 5Abraham was 100 years old
when his son Isaac was born to him.[k]
6Sarah said, "God has made me laugh, and
everyone who hears will laugh with me."[C,l]
7She also said, "Who would have told Abraham that Sarah would nurse children? Yet I
have borne a son for him[D] in his old age."

Hagar and Ishmael Sent Away

8The child grew and was weaned, and
Abraham held a great feast on the day Isaac
was weaned. 9But Sarah saw the son mocking[E]—the one Hagar the Egyptian had borne
to Abraham.[m] 10So she said to Abraham,
"Drive out this slave with her son, for the son
of this slave will not be a coheir with my son
Isaac!"[n]
11Now this was a very difficult thing for[F]
Abraham because of his son. 12But God said
to Abraham, "Do not be concerned[G] about
the boy and your slave. Whatever Sarah says
to you, listen to her, because your ·offspring
will be traced through Isaac.[o] 13But I will also
make a nation of the slave's son[p] because he is
your offspring."
14Early in the morning Abraham got up,
took bread and a waterskin, put them on
Hagar's shoulders, and sent her and the boy
away.[H] She left and wandered in the Wilderness of Beer-sheba. 15When the water in the
skin was gone, she left the boy under one of
the bushes. 16Then she went and sat down
nearby, about a bowshot away, for she said, "I
can't bear to watch the boy die!" So as she sat
nearby, she[I] wept loudly.[q]
17God heard the voice of the boy, and the[J]
angel of God called to Hagar from heaven and
said to her, "What's wrong, Hagar? Don't be
afraid, for God has heard the voice of the boy
from the place where he is. 18Get up, help the
boy up, and support him, for I will make him
a great nation." 19Then God opened her eyes,[r]
and she saw a well of water. So she went and
filled the waterskin and gave the boy a drink.
20God was with the boy, and he grew; he settled in the wilderness and became an archer.
21He settled in the Wilderness of Paran, and
his mother got a wife for him from the land
of Egypt.

Abraham's Covenant with Abimelech

22At that time Abimelech, accompanied by
Phicol the commander of his army,[s] said to

[a]**20:9** Gn 12:19; 26:9 [b]**20:11** Neh 5:15; Pr 16:6 [c]**20:13** Gn 12:1 [d]Gn 12:13; 20:5 [e]**20:15** Gn 13:9; 34:10; 47:6 [f]**20:17** Nm 12:13; 21:7; Jms 5:16 [g]**21:1** Gn 17:16; 18:10; Gl 4:23 [h]**21:2** Gn 17:21; 18:10,14; Heb 11:11 [i]**21:3** Gn 17:19 [j]**21:4** Gn 17:10,12; Ac 7:8 [k]**21:5** Gn 17:1,17; Rm 4:19 [l]**21:6** Gn 18:12-15 [m]**21:9** Gn 16:1,15; Gl 4:29 [n]**21:10** Gl 4:30 [o]**21:12** Rm 9:7; Heb 11:18 [p]**21:13** Gn 16:10; 21:18; 25:12-18 [q]**21:16** Jr 6:26; Am 8:10 [r]**21:19** Nm 22:31; 2Kg 6:17-18,20; Lk 24:16,31 [s]**21:22** Gn 20:2; 26:1,26

[A]**20:15** Lit *Settle in the good in your eyes* [B]**20:16** Lit *a covering of the eyes* [C]**21:6** Isaac = He laughs; Gn 17:19 [D]**21:7** Sam, Tg Jonathan; MT omits *him* [E]**21:9** LXX, Vg add *Isaac her son* [F]**21:11** Lit *was very bad in the eyes of* [G]**21:12** Lit *Let it not be bad in your eyes* [H]**21:14** To "send away" a woman = divorce her; Dt 24:1. To "send away" a slave = free her; Dt 15:13. [I]**21:16** LXX reads *the boy* [J]**21:17** Or *an*

Abraham, "God is with you in everything you
do.[a] 23 Swear to me by God here and now, that
you will not break an agreement with me or
with my children and descendants. As I have
been loyal to you, so you will be loyal to me
and to the country where you are a foreign
resident."
24 And Abraham said, "I swear it." 25 But
Abraham complained to Abimelech because
of the water well that Abimelech's servants
had seized.[b]
26 Abimelech replied, "I don't know who did
this thing. You didn't report anything to me,
so I hadn't heard about it until today."
27 Abraham took sheep and cattle[A] and gave
them to Abimelech, and the two of them
made a covenant.[c] 28 Abraham separated
seven ewe lambs from the flock. 29 And Abimelech said to Abraham, "Why have you separated these seven ewe lambs?"
30 He replied, "You are to accept the seven
ewe lambs from my hand so that this act[B]
will serve as my witness that I dug this
well." 31 Therefore that place was called Beer-
sheba[C,d] because it was there that the two of
them swore an oath. 32 After they had made a
covenant at Beer-sheba, Abimelech and Phicol, the commander of his army, left and returned to the land of the Philistines.
33 Abraham planted a tamarisk tree in Beer-
sheba, and there he called on the name of
•Yahweh, the Everlasting God.[e] 34 And Abraham lived as a foreigner in the land of the
Philistines for many days.

The Sacrifice of Isaac

22 After these things God tested Abraham[f] and said to him, "Abraham!"
"Here I am," he answered.
2 "Take your son," He said, "your only son
Isaac, whom you love,[g] go to the land of Moriah,[h] and offer him there as a •burnt offering
on one of the mountains I will tell you about."
3 So Abraham got up early in the morning,[i]
saddled his donkey, and took with him two
of his young men and his son Isaac. He split
wood for a burnt offering and set out to go
to the place God had told him about. 4 On the
third day[j] Abraham looked up and saw the
place in the distance. 5 Then Abraham said to
his young men, "Stay here with the donkey.
The boy and I will go over there to worship;
then we'll come back to you." 6 Abraham took
the wood for the burnt offering and laid it
on his son Isaac.[k] In his hand he took the fire
and the sacrificial knife,[D] and the two of them
walked on together.
7 Then Isaac spoke to his father Abraham
and said, "My father."
And he replied, "Here I am, my son."
Isaac said, "The fire and the wood are here,
but where is the lamb for the burnt offering?"
8 Abraham answered, "God Himself will
provide[E,l] the lamb for the burnt offering,
my son." Then the two of them walked on together.
9 When they arrived at the place that God
had told him about, Abraham built the altar there and arranged the wood. He bound
his son Isaac[F] and placed him on the altar[m]
on top of the wood. 10 Then Abraham reached
out and took the knife to slaughter his son.
11 But the Angel of the LORD called to him
from heaven and said, "Abraham, Abraham!"
He replied, "Here I am."
12 Then He said, "Do not lay a hand on the
boy or do anything to him. For now I know
that you •fear God, since you have not withheld your only son from Me."[n] 13 Abraham
looked up and saw a ram[G] caught in the
thicket by its horns. So Abraham went and
took the ram and offered it as a burnt offering in place of his son. 14 And Abraham named
that place The LORD Will Provide,[H] so today
it is said: "It will be provided[I] on the LORD's
mountain."
15 Then the Angel of the LORD called to Abraham a second time from heaven 16 and said,
"By Myself I have sworn,"[o] this is the LORD's
declaration: "Because you have done this
thing and have not withheld your only son,[J]
17 I will indeed bless you[p] and make your •off-
spring as numerous as the stars of the sky[q]
and the sand on the seashore.[r] Your offspring
will possess the gates of their enemies.[s] 18 And
all the nations of the earth will be blessed[K] by

[a] **21:22** Gn 26:28
[b] **21:25** Gn 26:15,18,20-22
[c] **21:27** Gn 26:31
[d] **21:31** Gn 26:33
[e] **21:33** Ps 45:6; 48:14; 90:2; 93:2; Is 40:28; Jr 10:10; Rm 16:26; Heb 13:8
[f] **22:1** Dt 8:2,16; 1Co 10:13; Heb 11:17; Jms 1:12-14; 1Pt 1:6-7
[g] **22:2** Gn 22:12,16; Jr 6:26; Am 8:10; Mk 12:6; Lk 7:12; Jn 3:16; 1Jn 4:9
[h] 2Ch 3:1
[i] **22:3** Jos 3:1
[j] **22:4** Ex 19:11,16; Jos 9:17; Jdg 20:30; 2Sm 1:2; 1Kg 12:12; 2Kg 20:5; Est 5:1; Hs 6:2; Mt 17:23
[k] **22:6** Jn 19:17
[l] **22:8** Gn 22:14
[m] **22:9** Heb 11:17; Jms 2:21
[n] **22:12** Rm 8:32
[o] **22:16** Ps 105:9; Lk 1:73; Heb 6:13
[p] **22:17** Heb 6:14
[q] Gn 15:5; 26:4; Jr 33:22; Heb 11:12
[r] Gn 13:16; 32:12
[s] Gn 24:60

[A] **21:27** A covenant or treaty was regularly ratified by animal sacrifice (Gn 8:20–9:9; 15:9-17; Ex 24:8) and often involved an exchange of gifts (1Kg 15:19; Hs 12:1). The animals here could serve both purposes. [B] **21:30** Lit *that it* [C] **21:31** = Well of the Oath, or Seven Wells [D] **22:6** The same word is used in Jdg 19:29 and Pr 30:14. [E] **22:8** Lit *see* [F] **22:9** Or *Isaac hand and foot* [G] **22:13** Some Hb mss, Sam, LXX, Syr, Tg; other Hb mss read *saw behind him a ram* [H] **22:14** Or *Yahweh-yireh* [I] **22:14** Or *He will be seen* [J] **22:16** Sam, LXX, Syr, Vg add *from Me* [K] **22:18** Or *will bless themselves*, or *will find blessing*

your offspring[a] because you have obeyed My
command."
19 Abraham went back to his young men,
and they got up and went together to Beer-
sheba. And Abraham settled in Beer-sheba.

Rebekah's Family

20 Now after these things Abraham was told,
"Milcah also has borne sons to your brother
Nahor:[b] 21 Uz his firstborn, his brother Buz,
Kemuel the father of Aram, 22 Chesed, Hazo,
Pildash, Jidlaph, and Bethuel." 23 And Bethuel
fathered Rebekah.[c] Milcah bore these eight to
Nahor, Abraham's brother. 24 His concubine,
whose name was Reumah, also bore Tebah,
Gaham, Tahash, and Maacah.

Sarah's Burial

23 Now Sarah lived 127 years; these were
all the years of her life. 2 Sarah died in
Kiriath-arba (that is, Hebron[d]) in the land
of Canaan, and Abraham went to mourn for
Sarah and to weep for her.
3 Then Abraham got up from beside his
dead wife and spoke to the Hittites:[A] 4 "I am a
foreign resident among you.[e] Give me a burial
site among you so that I can bury my dead."[B,f]
5 The Hittites replied to Abraham,[C] 6 "Listen
to us, lord.[D] You are God's chosen one[E] among
us. Bury your dead in our finest burial place.[F]
None of us will withhold from you his burial
place for burying your dead."
7 Then Abraham rose and bowed down to
the Hittites, the people of the land. 8 He said
to them, "If you are willing for me to bury
my dead, listen to me and ask Ephron son of
Zohar on my behalf 9 to give me the cave of
Machpelah that belongs to him; it is at the
end of his field. Let him give it to me in your
presence, for the full price, as a burial place."
10 Ephron was sitting among the Hittites. So
in the presence[G] of all the Hittites who came
to the ·gate of his city,[g] Ephron the Hittite answered Abraham: 11 "No, my lord. Listen to
me. I give you the field, and I give you the cave
that is in it. I give it to you in the presence[H] of
my people. Bury your dead."
12 Abraham bowed down to the people of
the land 13 and said to Ephron in the presence[G] of the people of the land, "Please listen
to me. Let me pay the price of the field. Accept
it from me, and let me bury my dead there."
14 Ephron answered Abraham and said to
him, 15 "My lord, listen to me. Land worth 400
·shekels of silver[h] — what is that between you
and me? Bury your dead." 16 Abraham agreed
with Ephron, and Abraham weighed out to
Ephron the silver that he had agreed to in the
presence[G] of the Hittites: 400 shekels of silver at the current commercial rate.[i] 17 So Ephron's field[j] at Machpelah near Mamre — the
field with its cave and all the trees anywhere
within the boundaries of the field — became
18 Abraham's possession in the presence of all
the Hittites who came to the gate of his city.
19 After this, Abraham buried his wife Sarah
in the cave of the field at Machpelah near
Mamre (that is, Hebron) in the land of Canaan. 20 The field with its cave passed from
the Hittites to Abraham[k] as a burial place.

A Wife for Isaac

24 Abraham was now old, getting on in
years,[I,l] and the LORD had blessed him
in everything. 2 Abraham said to his servant,
the elder of his household who managed all
he owned, "Place your hand under my thigh,[m]
3 and I will have you swear by the LORD, God
of heaven and God of earth, that you will not
take a wife for my son from the daughters of
the Canaanites among whom I live,[n] 4 but will
go to my land and my family to take a wife for
my son Isaac."
5 The servant said to him, "Suppose the
woman is unwilling to follow me to this land?
Should I have your son go back to the land
you came from?"
6 Abraham answered him, "Make sure that
you don't take my son back there. 7 The LORD,
the God of heaven,[o] who took me from my father's house and from my native land,[p] who
spoke to me and swore to me, 'I will give this
land to your ·offspring'[q] — He will send His
angel before you,[r] and you can take a wife
for my son from there. 8 If the woman is unwilling to follow you, then you are free from
this oath to me,[s] but don't let my son go back
there." 9 So the servant placed his hand un-

[a] **22:18** Gn 12:3; 26:4; Ac 3:25; Gl 3:8
[b] **22:20** Gn 11:29
[c] **22:23** Gn 24:15
[d] **23:2** Gn 35:27; Jos 14:15; 15:13; 21:11; Jdg 1:10
[e] **23:4** Gn 17:8; Lv 25:23; 1Ch 29:15; Ps 39:12; 105:12; Heb 11:9,13
[f] Gn 49:30; Ac 7:16
[g] **23:10** Gn 34:20,24; Ru 4:1
[h] **23:15** Ex 30:13; Ezk 45:12
[i] **23:16** Jr 32:9; Zch 11:12
[j] **23:17** Gn 25:9; 49:29-32; 50:13
[k] **23:20** Jr 32:10-14
[l] **24:1** Gn 18:11; Jos 13:1; 23:1-2; 1Kg 1:1
[m] **24:2** Gn 47:29; Ex 1:5
[n] **24:3** Gn 26:34,35; 27:46; Dt 7:3; 2Co 6:14
[o] **24:7** 2Ch 36:23; Ezr 1:2
[p] Gn 12:1
[q] Gn 12:7; 13:15; 15:18; Ex 32:13
[r] Gn 16:7; 21:17; 22:11; Ex 23:20,23
[s] **24:8** Jos 2:17-20

[A] **23:3** Or *sons of Heth*; also in vv. 5,7,10,16,18,20 [B] **23:4** Lit *dead from before me* [C] **23:5** Lit *Abraham, saying to him* [D] **23:6** Lit *my lord* [E] **23:6** Or *prince of God*, or *mighty prince* [F] **23:6** Or *finest graves* [G] **23:10,13,16** Lit *ears* [H] **23:11** Lit *in the eyes of the sons* [I] **24:1** Lit *days*

der his master Abraham's thigh and swore an
oath to him concerning this matter.
10The servant took 10 of his master's camels and departed with all kinds of his master's
goods in hand. Then he set out for Nahor's
town Aram-naharaim. 11He made the camels kneel beside a well of water outside the
town at evening. This was the time when the
women went out to draw water.
12"LORD, God of my master Abraham," he
prayed, "give me success today,[a] and show
kindness to my master Abraham. 13I am
standing here[b] at the spring where the daughters of the men of the town are coming out
to draw water. 14Let the girl to whom I say,
'Please lower your water jug so that I may
drink,' and who responds, 'Drink, and I'll water your camels also'—let her be the one You
have appointed for Your servant Isaac. By this
I will know that You have shown kindness to
my master."
15Before he had finished speaking, there
was Rebekah—daughter of Bethuel son of
Milcah,[c] the wife of Abraham's brother Nahor—coming with a jug on her shoulder.
16Now the girl was very beautiful,[d] a young
woman who had not known a man intimately. She went down to the spring, filled
her jug, and came up. 17Then the servant ran
to meet her and said, "Please let me have a little water from your jug."
18She replied, "Drink, my lord." She quickly
lowered her jug to her hand and gave him a
drink. 19When she had finished giving him
a drink, she said, "I'll also draw water for
your camels until they have had enough to
drink."[A] 20She quickly emptied her jug into
the trough and hurried to the well again to
draw water. She drew water for all his camels
21while the man silently watched her to see
whether or not the LORD had made his journey a success.
22After the camels had finished drinking, the
man took a gold ring weighing half a •shekel,
and for her wrists two bracelets weighing 10
shekels of gold. 23"Whose daughter are you?"
he asked. "Please tell me, is there room in your
father's house for us to spend the night?"
24She answered him, "I am the daughter of
Bethuel son of Milcah, whom she bore to Nahor." 25She also said to him, "We have plenty
of straw and feed and a place to spend the
night."
26Then the man bowed down, worshiped
the LORD,[e] 27and said, "Praise the LORD, the
God of my master Abraham, who has not
withheld His kindness and faithfulness from
my master.[f] As for me, the LORD has led me
on the journey to the house of my master's
relatives."
28The girl ran and told her mother's household about these things. 29Now Rebekah had
a brother named Laban,[g] and Laban ran out
to the man at the spring. 30As soon as he had
seen the ring and the bracelets on his sister's wrists, and when he had heard his sister Rebekah's words—"The man said this to
me!"—he went to the man. He was standing
there by the camels at the spring.
31Laban said, "Come, you who are blessed
by the LORD.[h] Why are you standing out here?
I have prepared the house and a place for the
camels." 32So the man came to the house,
and the camels were unloaded.[i] Straw and
feed were given to the camels, and water was
brought to wash his feet and the feet of the
men with him.
33A meal was set before him, but he said, "I
will not eat until I have said what I have to
say."
So Laban said, "Please speak."
34"I am Abraham's servant," he said. 35"The
LORD has greatly blessed my master, and he
has become rich. He has given him sheep
and cattle, silver and gold, male and female
slaves, and camels and donkeys. 36Sarah, my
master's wife, bore a son to my master in her[B]
old age,[j] and he has given him everything he
owns.[k] 37My master put me under this oath:
'You will not take a wife for my son from the
daughters of the Canaanites in whose land I
live 38but will go to my father's household and
to my family to take a wife for my son.' 39But
I said to my master, 'Suppose the woman will
not come back with me?' 40He said to me,
'The LORD before whom I have walked[l] will
send His angel with you and make your journey a success, and you will take a wife for my
son from my family and from my father's
household. 41Then you will be free from my

[a] **24:12** Gn 27:20
[b] **24:13-14** Gn 24:43-44
[c] **24:15** Gn 11:29; 22:23
[d] **24:16** Gn 12:11; 26:7; 29:17
[e] **24:26** Ex 4:31
[f] **24:27** Ru 2:20; Ezr 9:9; Neh 9:17
[g] **24:29** Gn 25:20; 28:2; 29:5
[h] **24:31** Gn 26:29; Jdg 17:2; Ru 3:10
[i] **24:32** Gn 43:24; Jdg 19:21
[j] **24:36** Gn 21:2
[k] Gn 25:5
[l] **24:40** Gn 17:1; 1Sm 2:30; 1Kg 2:4; 8:23; 2Kg 20:3; Ps 116:9

[A] **24:19** Lit *they are finished drinking* [B] **24:36** Sam, LXX read *his* oath if you go to my family and they do not give her to you—you will be free from my oath.'

42 "Today when I came to the spring, I prayed: LORD, God of my master Abraham, if only You will make my journey successful! 43 I am standing here at a spring. Let the virgin who comes out to draw water, and I say to her: Please let me drink a little water from your jug, 44 and who responds to me, 'Drink, and I'll draw water for your camels also'—let her be the woman the LORD has appointed for my master's son.

45 "Before I had finished praying silently,[a] there was Rebekah coming with her jug on her shoulder, and she went down to the spring and drew water. So I said to her: Please let me have a drink. 46 She quickly lowered her jug from her shoulder and said, 'Drink, and I'll water your camels also.' So I drank, and she also watered the camels. 47 Then I asked her: Whose daughter are you? She responded, 'The daughter of Bethuel son of Nahor, whom Milcah bore to him.' So I put the ring on her nose[b] and the bracelets on her wrists. 48 Then I bowed down, worshiped the LORD, and praised the LORD, the God of my master Abraham, who guided me on the right way to take the granddaughter of my master's brother for his son. 49 Now, if you are going to show kindness and faithfulness to my master,[c] tell me; if not, tell me, and I will go elsewhere."[A]

50 Laban and Bethuel answered, "This is from the LORD; we have no choice in the matter.[B,d] 51 Rebekah is here in front of you. Take her and go, and let her be a wife for your master's son, just as the LORD has spoken."

52 When Abraham's servant heard their words, he bowed to the ground before the LORD. 53 Then he brought out objects of silver and gold, and garments, and gave them to Rebekah. He also gave precious gifts to her brother and her mother. 54 Then he and the men with him ate and drank and spent the night.

When they got up in the morning, he said, "Send me to my master."

55 But her brother and mother said, "Let the girl stay with us for about 10 days.[C] Then she[D] can go."

56 But he responded to them, "Do not delay me, since the LORD has made my journey a success. Send me away so that I may go to my master."

57 So they said, "Let's call the girl and ask her opinion."[E]

58 They called Rebekah and said to her, "Will you go with this man?"

She replied, "I will go." 59 So they sent away their sister Rebekah with the one who had nursed and raised her,[F,e] and Abraham's servant and his men.

60 They blessed Rebekah, saying to her:

> Our sister, may you become
> thousands upon ten thousands.[f]
> May your offspring possess
> the gates of their[G] enemies.[g]

61 Then Rebekah and her female servants got up, mounted the camels, and followed the man. So the servant took Rebekah and left.

62 Now Isaac was returning from Beer-lahai-roi,[H,h] for he was living in the ·Negev region. 63 In the early evening Isaac went out to walk[I] in the field, and looking up he saw camels coming. 64 Rebekah looked up, and when she saw Isaac, she got down from her camel 65 and asked the servant, "Who is that man in the field coming to meet us?"

The servant answered, "It is my master." So she took her veil and covered herself. 66 Then the servant told Isaac everything he had done. 67 And Isaac brought her into the tent of his mother Sarah and took Rebekah to be his wife. Isaac loved her, and he was comforted after his mother's death.[i]

Abraham's Other Wife and Sons

25 Now Abraham had taken another wife, whose name was Keturah,[j] 2 and she bore him Zimran, Jokshan, Medan, Midian, Ishbak, and Shuah. 3 Jokshan fathered Sheba and Dedan. Dedan's sons were the Asshurim, Letushim, and Leummim. 4 And Midian's sons were Ephah, Epher, Hanoch, Abida, and Eldaah. All these were sons of Keturah. 5 Abraham gave everything he owned to Isaac.[k] 6 And

[a] **24:45** 1Sm 1:13
[b] **24:47** Ezk 16:11-12
[c] **24:49** Gn 47:29; Jos 2:14
[d] **24:50** Gn 31:24,29; 2Sm 13:22
[e] **24:59** Gn 35:8
[f] **24:60** Gn 17:16
[g] Gn 22:17
[h] **24:62** Gn 16:14; 25:11
[i] **24:67** Gn 23:1-2
[j] **25:1-4** 1Ch 1:32-33
[k] **25:5** Gn 24:35-36

[A] **24:49** Lit *go to the right or to the left* [B] **24:50** Lit *we cannot say to you anything bad or good* [C] **24:55** Lit *us a few days or 10* [D] **24:55** Or *you* [E] **24:57** Lit *mouth* [F] **24:59** Lit *with her wet nurse*; Gn 35:8 [G] **24:60** Lit *his* [H] **24:62** = A Well of the Living One Who Sees Me [I] **24:63** Or *pray*, or *meditate*; Hb obscure

Abraham gave gifts to the sons of his concubines, but while he was still alive he sent them eastward, away from his son Isaac, to the land of the East.[a]

Abraham's Death

7 This is the length of Abraham's life:[A] 175 years. 8 He took his last breath and died at a ripe old age,[b] old and contented,[B] and he was gathered to his people.[c] 9 His sons Isaac and Ishmael buried him in the cave of Machpelah[d] near Mamre, in the field of Ephron son of Zohar the Hittite. 10 This was the field that Abraham bought from the Hittites.[e] Abraham was buried there with his wife Sarah. 11 After Abraham's death, God blessed his son Isaac, who lived near Beer-lahai-roi.[f]

Ishmael's Family Records

12 These are the family records[g] of Abraham's son Ishmael,[h] whom Hagar the Egyptian, Sarah's slave, bore to Abraham. 13 These are the names of Ishmael's sons; their names according to the family records are: Nebaioth, Ishmael's firstborn, then Kedar, Adbeel, Mibsam, 14 Mishma, Dumah, Massa, 15 Hadad, Tema, Jetur, Naphish, and Kedemah. 16 These are Ishmael's sons, and these are their names by their villages and encampments: 12 leaders[C,i] of their clans.[D] 17 This is the length[E] of Ishmael's life: 137 years. He took his last breath and died, and was gathered to his people. 18 And they[F] settled from Havilah to Shur, which is opposite Egypt as you go toward Asshur. He[G] lived in opposition to[H] all his brothers.[j]

The Birth of Jacob and Esau

19 These are the family records of Isaac son of Abraham. Abraham fathered Isaac.[k] 20 Isaac was 40 years old when he took as his wife Rebekah[l] daughter of Bethuel the Aramean from Paddan-aram[m] and sister of Laban the Aramean.[n] 21 Isaac prayed to the LORD on behalf of his wife because she was childless.[o] The LORD heard his prayer, and his wife Rebekah conceived.[p] 22 But the children inside her struggled with each other, and she said, "Why is this happening to me?"[I] So she went to inquire of the LORD.[q] 23 And the LORD said to her:

> Two nations are in your womb;
> two people will come from you
> and be separated.
> One people will be stronger
> than the other,[r]
> and the older will serve the younger.[s]

24 When her time came to give birth, there were indeed twins in her womb. 25 The first one came out red-looking,[J] covered with hair[K] like a fur coat, and they named him Esau.[t] 26 After this, his brother came out grasping Esau's heel with his hand.[u] So he was named Jacob.[L,v] Isaac was 60 years old when they were born.

Esau Sells His Birthright

27 When the boys grew up, Esau became an expert hunter, an outdoorsman,[M] but Jacob was a quiet man who stayed at home.[N] 28 Isaac loved Esau because he had a taste for wild game, but Rebekah loved Jacob.[w]

29 Once when Jacob was cooking a stew, Esau came in from the field exhausted. 30 He said to Jacob, "Let me eat some of that red stuff, because I'm exhausted." That is why he was also named Edom.[O]

31 Jacob replied, "First sell me your birthright."

32 "Look," said Esau, "I'm about to die, so what good is a birthright to me?"

33 Jacob said, "Swear to me first." So he swore to Jacob and sold his birthright to him. 34 Then Jacob gave bread and lentil stew to Esau; he ate, drank, got up, and went away. So Esau despised his birthright.[x]

The Promise Reaffirmed to Isaac

26 There was another famine in the land in addition to the one that had occurred in Abraham's time.[y] And Isaac went to Abimelech, king of the Philistines, at Gerar.[z] 2 The LORD appeared to him and said, "Do not go down to Egypt. Live in the land that I tell you about; 3 stay in this land as a

[a] **25:6** Gn 21:14 [b] **25:8** Gn 15:15; 47:8-9 [c] Gn 25:17; 35:29; 49:29,33 [d] **25:9** Gn 23:17-18; 49:29-30; 50:13 [e] **25:10** Gn 23:16; 50:13 [f] **25:11** Gn 16:14; 24:62 [g] **25:12** Gn 2:4; 25:19 [h] **25:12-16** 1Ch 1:29-31 [i] **25:16** Gn 17:20 [j] **25:18** Gn 16:12 [k] **25:19** Mt 1:2 [l] **25:20** Gn 24:15,29,67 [m] Gn 22:23 [n] Gn 24:29 [o] **25:21** Gn 11:30; 29:31; Ex 23:26; Jdg 13:2-3; 1Sm 2:5; Jb 24:21; Is 54:1; Lk 1:36; 23:29; Gl 4:27; Heb 11:11 [p] 1Sm 1:17; 1Ch 5:20; 2Ch 33:13; Ezr 8:23; Ps 127:3; Rm 9:10 [q] **25:22** 1Sm 9:9; 10:22 [r] **25:23** 2Sm 8:14; Ob 18-21 [s] Gn 27:29; Mal 1:2-3; Rm 9:12 [t] **25:25** Gn 27:11,16,23 [u] **25:26** Hs 12:3 [v] Gn 27:36 [w] **25:28** Gn 27:4-9 [x] **25:34** Heb 12:16-17 [y] **26:1** Gn 12:10 [z] Gn 20:2

[A] **25:7** Lit *And these are the days of the years of the lives of Abraham that he lived* [B] **25:8** Sam, LXX, Syr read *full of days* [C] **25:16** Or *chieftains* [D] **25:16** Or *peoples* [E] **25:17** Lit *And these are the years* [F] **25:18** LXX, Vg read *he* [G] **25:18** = Ishmael and his descendants [H] **25:18** Or *He settled down alongside of* [I] **25:22** Lit *If thus, why this I* [J] **25:25** In Hb, the word red-looking sounds like "Edom"; Gn 32:3. [K] **25:25** In Hb, the word hair sounds like "Seir"; Gn 32:3. [L] **25:26** = He Grasps the Heel [M] **25:27** Lit *a man of the field* [N] **25:27** Lit *man living in tents* [O] **25:30** = Red

foreigner, and I will be with you and bless
you.[a] For I will give all these lands to you and
your ·offspring,[b] and I will confirm the oath
that I swore to your father Abraham.[c] 4 I will
make your offspring as numerous as the stars
of the sky, I will give your offspring all these
lands, and all the nations of the earth will be
blessed[A] by your offspring,[d] 5 because Abraham listened to My voice and kept My mandate, My commands, My statutes, and My
instructions."[e] 6 So Isaac settled in Gerar.

Isaac's Deception

7 When the men of the place asked about
his wife, he said, "She is my sister,"[f] for he was
afraid to say "my wife," thinking,[g] "The men
of the place will kill me on account of Rebekah, for she is a beautiful woman."[h] 8 When
Isaac had been there for some time, Abimelech king of the Philistines looked down from
the window and was surprised to see[B] Isaac
caressing his wife Rebekah.

9 Abimelech sent for Isaac and said, "So she
is really your wife! How could you say, 'She is
my sister'?"

Isaac answered him, "Because I thought I
might die on account of her."

10 Then Abimelech said, "What is this you've
done to us? One of the people could easily
have slept with your wife, and you would have
brought ·guilt on us."[i] 11 So Abimelech warned
all the people with these words: "Whoever
harms this man or his wife will certainly die."

Conflicts over Wells

12 Isaac sowed seed in that land, and in that
year he reaped[C] a hundred times what was
sown. The LORD blessed him,[j] 13 and the man
became rich and kept getting richer until he
was very wealthy. 14 He had flocks of sheep,
herds of cattle, and many slaves, and the Philistines were envious of him. 15 The Philistines
stopped up all the wells that his father's slaves
had dug in the days of his father Abraham,[k]
filling them with dirt. 16 And Abimelech said
to Isaac, "Leave us, for you are much too powerful for us."[D]

17 So Isaac left there, camped in the Valley
of Gerar, and lived there. 18 Isaac reopened the
water wells that had been dug in the days of
his father Abraham and that the Philistines
had stopped up after Abraham died. He gave
them the same names his father had given
them. 19 Then Isaac's slaves dug in the valley
and found a well of spring[E] water there. 20 But
the herdsmen of Gerar quarreled with Isaac's
herdsmen and said, "The water is ours!" So he
named the well Quarrel[F] because they quarreled with him.[l] 21 Then they dug another well
and quarreled over that one also, so he named
it Hostility.[G] 22 He moved from there and dug
another, and they did not quarrel over it. He
named it Open Spaces[H] and said, "For now the
LORD has made room for us, and we will be
fruitful in the land."

The LORD Appears to Isaac

23 From there he went up to Beer-sheba,
24 and the LORD appeared to him that night
and said, "I am the God of your father Abraham.[m] Do not be afraid, for I am with you.[n]
I will bless you and multiply your offspring
because of My servant Abraham."

25 So he built an altar there,[o] called on the
name of ·Yahweh, and pitched his tent there.
Isaac's slaves also dug a well there.[p]

Covenant with Abimelech

26 Now Abimelech came to him from Gerar with Ahuzzath his adviser and Phicol the
commander of his army.[q] 27 Isaac said to them,
"Why have you come to me? You hated me
and sent me away from you."

28 They replied, "We have clearly seen how
the LORD has been with you. We think there
should be an oath between two parties — between us and you. Let us make a covenant
with you: 29 You will not harm us, just as we
have not harmed you but have only done
what was good to you, sending you away in
peace. You are now blessed by the LORD."[r]

30 So he prepared a banquet for them, and
they ate and drank. 31 They got up early in the
morning and swore an oath to each other.[I,s]
Then Isaac sent them on their way, and they
left him in peace. 32 On that same day Isaac's
slaves came to tell him about the well they
had dug, saying to him, "We have found

[a]**26:3** Gn 12:2; 26:24; 28:15; 31:3 [b]Gn 12:7; 13:15; 15:18 [c]Gn 22:16-18; Ps 105:9 [d]**26:4** Gn 12:3; 18:18; Ac 3:25; Gl 3:8 [e]**26:5** Lv 18:30; Dt 11:1 [f]**26:7** Gn 12:13; 20:5 [g]Pr 29:25 [h]Gn 24:16 [i]**26:10** Gn 20:8-10 [j]**26:12** Gn 24:1,35 [k]**26:15** Gn 21:30 [l]**26:20** Gn 21:25 [m]**26:24** Gn 17:7-8; 24:12; Ex 3:6; Ac 7:32 [n]Gn 21:17; Ex 20:20; 2Kg 6:16; Is 41:10; 43:1,5 [o]**26:25** Gn 8:20; 12:7; 13:18; 35:7; Ex 17:15; Jos 8:30 [p]Gn 26:32 [q]**26:26** Gn 21:22 [r]**26:29** Gn 24:31; Ps 115:15 [s]**26:31** Gn 21:31

[A]**26:4** Or *will bless themselves* [B]**26:8** Or *and he looked and behold—* [C]**26:12** Lit *found* [D]**26:16** Or *are more numerous than we are* [E]**26:19** Lit *living* [F]**26:20** Or *Esek* [G]**26:21** Or *Sitnah* [H]**26:22** Or *Rehoboth* [I]**26:31** Lit *swore, each man to his brother*

water!"[a] 33He called it Sheba.[A] Therefore the
name of the city is Beer-sheba[B,b] to this day.

Esau's Wives

34When Esau was 40 years old, he took as
his wives Judith daughter of Beeri the Hittite, and Basemath daughter of Elon the Hittite.[c] 35They made life bitter[C] for Isaac and
Rebekah.[d]

The Stolen Blessing

27 When Isaac was old and his eyes were
so weak that he could not see,[e] he called
his older son Esau and said to him, "My son."
And he answered, "Here I am."
2He said, "Look, I am old and do not know
the day of my death. 3Take your hunting gear,
your quiver and bow, and go out in the field
to hunt some game for me.[f] 4Then make me a
delicious meal that I love and bring it to me to
eat, so that I can bless you before I die."[g]
5Now Rebekah was listening to what Isaac
said to his son Esau. So while Esau went to
the field to hunt some game to bring in, 6Re-
bekah said to her son Jacob, "Listen! I heard
your father talking with your brother Esau.
He said, 7'Bring me the game and make a delicious meal for me to eat so that I can bless
you in the LORD's presence before I die.' 8Now
obey every order I give you, my son. 9Go to the
flock and bring me two choice young goats,
and I will make them into a delicious meal for
your father — the kind he loves. 10Then take it
to your father to eat so that he may bless you
before he dies."
11Jacob answered Rebekah his mother,
"Look, my brother Esau is a hairy man, but
I am a man with smooth skin.[h] 12Suppose my
father touches me. Then I will be revealed to
him as a deceiver and bring a curse rather
than a blessing on myself."
13His mother said to him, "Your curse be on
me, my son. Just obey me and go get them for
me."
14So he went and got the goats and brought
them to his mother, and his mother made
the delicious food his father loved. 15Then Rebekah took the best clothes of her older son
Esau, which were in the house, and had her
younger son Jacob wear them. 16She put the
skins of the young goats on his hands and the
smooth part of his neck. 17Then she handed
the delicious food and the bread she had
made to her son Jacob.
18When he came to his father, he said, "My
father."
And he answered, "Here I am. Who are you,
my son?"
19Jacob replied to his father, "I am Esau,
your firstborn. I have done as you told me.
Please sit up and eat some of my game so that
you may bless me."
20But Isaac said to his son, "How did you
ever find it so quickly, my son?"
He replied, "Because the LORD your God
worked it out for me."
21Then Isaac said to Jacob, "Please come
closer so I can touch you, my son. Are you
really my son Esau or not?"
22So Jacob came closer to his father Isaac.
When he touched him, he said, "The voice
is the voice of Jacob, but the hands are the
hands of Esau." 23He did not recognize him,
because his hands were hairy like those of his
brother Esau; so he blessed him. 24Again he
asked, "Are you really my son Esau?"
And he replied, "I am."
25Then he said, "Serve me, and let me eat
some of my son's game so that I can bless
you." Jacob brought it to him, and he ate; he
brought him wine, and he drank.
26Then his father Isaac said to him, "Please
come closer and kiss me, my son." 27So he came
closer and kissed him. When Isaac smelled[D]
his clothes, he blessed him and said:

Ah, the smell of my son
is like the smell of a field
that the LORD has blessed.
28 May God give to you —
from the dew of the sky[i]
and from the richness of the land[j] —
an abundance of grain and new wine.[k]
29 May peoples serve you[l]
and nations bow down to you.
Be master over your brothers;
may your mother's sons bow down
to you.
Those who curse you will be cursed,
and those who bless you
will be blessed.[m]

[a]26:32 Gn 26:19
[b]26:33 Gn 21:30-31
[c]26:34 Gn 28:9; 36:2-3
[d]26:35 Gn 27:46
[e]27:1 Gn 48:10; 1Sm 3:2
[f]27:3 Gn 25:27-28
[g]27:4 Gn 27:19,25,31; 48:9,15-16; Dt 33:1; Heb 11:20
[h]27:11 Gn 25:25
[i]27:28 Gn 27:39; Dt 32:2; 33:13,28; 2Sm 1:21; Pr 3:20; Is 18:4; Hs 14:5; Hg 1:10; Zch 8:12
[j]Nm 18:12
[k]Dt 7:13; Jl 2:19
[l]27:29 Gn 25:23; Is 45:14; 49:7,23; 60:12-14
[m]Gn 12:3; Nm 24:9

[A]26:33 Or *Shibah* [B]26:33 = Well of the Oath [C]26:35 Lit *And they became bitterness of spirit* [D]27:27 Lit *smelled the smell of*

30 As soon as Isaac had finished blessing Jacob and Jacob had left the presence of his father Isaac, his brother Esau arrived from the
hunt. 31 He had also made some delicious food
and brought it to his father. Then he said to
his father, "Let my father get up and eat some
of his son's game, so that you may bless me."
32 But his father Isaac said to him, "Who are
you?"

He answered, "I am Esau your firstborn
son."

33 Isaac began to tremble uncontrollably.
"Who was it then," he said, "who hunted
game and brought it to me? I ate it all before
you came in, and I blessed him. Indeed, he
will be blessed!"

34 When Esau heard his father's words, he
cried out with a loud and bitter cry and said
to his father, "Bless me too, my father!"[a]

35 But he replied, "Your brother came deceitfully and took your blessing."

36 So he said, "Isn't he rightly named Jacob?[A,b] For he has cheated me twice now. He
took my birthright, and look, now he has
taken my blessing." Then he asked, "Haven't
you saved a blessing for me?"

37 But Isaac answered Esau: "Look, I have
made him a master over you, have given him
all of his relatives as his servants, and have
sustained him with grain and new wine.
What then can I do for you, my son?"

38 Esau said to his father, "Do you only have
one blessing, my father? Bless me too, my father!" And Esau wept loudly.[B]

39 Then his father Isaac answered him:

> Look, your dwelling place will be
> away from the richness of the land,
> away from the dew of the sky above.
> 40 You will live by your sword,
> and you will serve your brother.
> But when you rebel,[C]
> you will break his yoke from your neck.

Esau's Anger

41 Esau held a grudge against Jacob because
of the blessing his father had given him. And
Esau determined in his heart: "The days of
mourning for my father are approaching;
then I will kill my brother Jacob."

42 When the words of her older son Esau
were reported to Rebekah, she summoned
her younger son Jacob and said to him, "Listen, your brother Esau is consoling himself
by planning to kill you. 43 So now, my son, listen to me. Flee at once to my brother Laban
in Haran, 44 and stay with him for a few days
until your brother's anger subsides— 45 until your brother's rage turns away from you
and he forgets what you have done to him.
Then I will send for you and bring you back
from there. Why should I lose you both in one
day?"

46 So Rebekah said to Isaac, "I'm sick of my
life because of these Hittite women.[c] If Jacob
marries a Hittite woman like one of them,[D]
what good is my life?"[d]

Jacob's Departure

28 Isaac summoned Jacob, blessed him,
and commanded him: "Don't take a
wife from the Canaanite women. 2 Go at once
to Paddan-aram, to the house of Bethuel, your
mother's father. Marry one of the daughters
of Laban, your mother's brother. 3 May ˙God
Almighty bless you and make you fruitful and
multiply you[e] so that you become an assembly of peoples.[f] 4 May God give you and your
˙offspring the blessing of Abraham[g] so that
you may possess the land where you live as
a foreigner, the land God gave to Abraham."[h]
5 So Isaac sent Jacob to Paddan-aram, to Laban son of Bethuel the Aramean, the brother
of Rebekah, the mother of Jacob and Esau.

6 Esau noticed that Isaac blessed Jacob and
sent him to Paddan-aram to get a wife there.
When he blessed him, Isaac commanded Jacob, "Do not marry a Canaanite woman."
7 And Jacob listened to his father and mother
and went to Paddan-aram. 8 Esau realized that
his father Isaac disapproved of the Canaanite
women,[i] 9 so Esau went to Ishmael and married, in addition to his other wives, Mahalath
daughter of Ishmael, Abraham's son. She was
the sister of Nebaioth.

Jacob at Bethel

10 Jacob left Beer-sheba and went toward
Haran. 11 He reached a certain place and spent
the night there because the sun had set. He

[a] **27:34** Heb 12:17
[b] **27:36** Gn 25:26,32-34
[c] **27:46** Gn 26:34-35; 28:8
[d] Gn 24:3
[e] **28:3** Gn 1:28
[f] Gn 48:4
[g] **28:4** Gn 12:1-3
[h] Gn 12:7; 15:18
[i] **28:8** Gn 24:3; 26:34-35; 27:46

[A] **27:36** = He Grasps the Heel [B] **27:38** Lit *Esau lifted up his voice and wept* [C] **27:40** Hb obscure [D] **27:46** Lit *of these daughters of the land*

took one of the stones from the place, put it
there at his head, and lay down in that place.
12 And he dreamed:[a] A stairway was set on the
ground with its top reaching heaven, and
God's angels were going up and down on it.[b]
13 Yahweh was standing there beside him,[A]
saying, "I am Yahweh,[c] the God of your father
Abraham and the God of Isaac. I will give you
and your offspring the land that you are now
sleeping on. 14 Your offspring will be like the
dust of the earth,[d] and you will spread out
toward the west, the east, the north, and the
south. All the peoples on earth will be blessed
through you and your offspring.[e] 15 Look, I am
with you and will watch over you wherever
you go. I will bring you back to this land,[f] for
I will not leave you until I have done what I
have promised you."

16 When Jacob awoke from his sleep, he said,
"Surely the LORD is in this place, and I did not
know it."[g] 17 He was afraid and said, "What an
awesome place this is! This is none other than
the house of God. This is the gate of heaven."

18 Early in the morning Jacob took the
stone that was near his head and set it up
as a marker. He poured oil on top of it 19 and
named the place Bethel,[B] though previously
the city was named Luz.[h] 20 Then Jacob made
a vow:[i] "If God will be with me and watch
over me on this journey, if He provides me
with food to eat and clothing to wear, 21 and
if I return safely to my father's house,[j] then
the LORD will be my God.[k] 22 This stone that I
have set up as a marker will be God's house,
and I will give to You a tenth of all that You
give me."[l]

Jacob Meets Rachel

29 Jacob resumed his journey[C] and went
to the eastern country.[D,m] 2 He looked
and saw a well in a field. Three flocks of sheep
were lying there beside it because the sheep
were watered from this well. A large stone
covered the opening of the well. 3 When all
the flocks[E] were gathered there, the shepherds would roll the stone from the opening
of the well and water the sheep. The stone was
then placed back on the well's opening.

4 Jacob asked the men at the well, "My
brothers! Where are you from?"

"We're from Haran," they answered.

5 "Do you know Laban grandson of Nahor?"
Jacob asked them.

They answered, "We know him."

6 "Is he well?" Jacob asked.

"Yes," they said, "and here is his daughter
Rachel, coming with his sheep."

7 Then Jacob said, "Look, it is still broad
daylight. It's not time for the animals to be
gathered. Water the flock, then go out and let
them graze."

8 But they replied, "We can't until all the
flocks have been gathered and the stone is
rolled from the well's opening. Then we will
water the sheep."

9 While he was still speaking with them, Rachel came with her father's sheep, for she was
a shepherdess. 10 As soon as Jacob saw his uncle Laban's daughter Rachel with his sheep,[F]
he went up and rolled the stone from the
opening and watered his uncle Laban's sheep.
11 Then Jacob kissed Rachel and wept loudly.[G]
12 He told Rachel that he was her father's relative, Rebekah's son. She ran and told her father.

Jacob Deceived

13 When Laban heard the news about his sister's son Jacob, he ran to meet him, hugged
him, and kissed him. Then he took him to his
house, and Jacob told him all that had happened.

14 Laban said to him, "Yes, you are my own
flesh and blood."[H,n]

After Jacob had stayed with him a month,
15 Laban said to him, "Just because you're my
relative, should you work for me for nothing?
Tell me what your wages should be."

16 Now Laban had two daughters: the older
was named Leah, and the younger was named
Rachel. 17 Leah had ordinary[I] eyes, but Rachel
was shapely and beautiful. 18 Jacob loved Rachel, so he answered Laban, "I'll work for you
seven years for your younger daughter Rachel."[o]

19 Laban replied, "Better that I give her to

[a] **28:12** Gn 41:1; Nm 12:6; Jb 33:15-16
[b] Jn 1:51
[c] **28:13** Gn 15:7; Ex 6:8
[d] **28:14** Gn 13:16
[e] Gn 12:3
[f] **28:15** Gn 48:21; Dt 30:3; 1Kg 8:34; Zph 3:20
[g] **28:16** Ex 3:4-6; Jos 5:13-15; Ps 139:7-12
[h] **28:19** Gn 35:6; 48:3; Jdg 1:23,26
[i] **28:20** Gn 31:13
[j] **28:21** Gn 33:18; Jdg 11:31; 2Sm 15:7-9
[k] Dt 26:17
[l] **28:22** Gn 14:20; Lv 27:30; Dt 14:22
[m] **29:1** Nm 23:7; Jdg 6:3
[n] **29:14** Gn 2:23; 37:27; Jdg 9:2; 2Sm 5:1; 19:12-13; 1Ch 11:1
[o] **29:18** Gn 30:26; 31:41; Hs 12:12

[A] **28:13** Or *there above it* [B] **28:19** = House of God [C] **29:1** Lit *Jacob picked up his feet* [D] **29:1** Lit *the land of the children of the east* [E] **29:3** Sam, some LXX mss read *flocks and the shepherds* [F] **29:10** Lit *with the sheep of Laban his mother's brother* [G] **29:11** Lit *and he lifted his voice and wept* [H] **29:14** Lit *my bone and my flesh* [I] **29:17** Lit *tender*

you than to some other man. Stay with me."
20So Jacob worked seven years for Rachel, and
they seemed like only a few days to him because of his love for her.
21Then Jacob said to Laban, "Give me my
wife, for my time is completed. I want to sleep
with[A] her." 22So Laban invited all the men of
the place to a feast. 23That evening, Laban
took his daughter Leah and gave her to Jacob,
and he slept with her. 24And Laban gave his
slave Zilpah to his daughter Leah as her slave.
25When morning came, there was Leah! So
he said to Laban, "What is this you have done
to me? Wasn't it for Rachel that I worked for
you? Why have you deceived me?"
26Laban answered, "It is not the custom
in this place to give the younger daughter in
marriage before the firstborn. 27Complete
this week of wedding celebration, and we will
also give you this younger one in return for
working yet another seven years for me."
28And Jacob did just that. He finished the
week of celebration, and Laban gave him his
daughter Rachel as his wife. 29And Laban gave
his slave Bilhah to his daughter Rachel as her
slave. 30Jacob slept with Rachel also, and indeed, he loved Rachel more than Leah. And
he worked for Laban another seven years.[a]

Jacob's Sons

31When the LORD saw that Leah was unloved,[b] He opened her womb;[c] but Rachel was
unable to conceive.[d] 32Leah conceived, gave
birth to a son, and named him Reuben,[B] for
she said, "The LORD has seen my affliction;[e]
surely my husband will love me now."
33She conceived again, gave birth to a son,
and said, "The LORD heard that I am unloved
and has given me this son also." So she named
him Simeon.[C]
34She conceived again, gave birth to a son,
and said, "At last, my husband will become attached to me because I have borne three sons
for him." Therefore he was named Levi.[D]
35And she conceived again, gave birth to
a son, and said, "This time I will praise the
LORD." Therefore she named him Judah.[E,f]
Then Leah stopped having children.

[a]**29:30** Gn 31:41 [b]**29:31** Gn 25:28; Dt 21:15-16; 22:13; 24:3; Lk 14:26; 16:13 [c]Gn 30:22 [d]Gn 11:30; 25:21; Jdg 13:2-3; 1Sm 2:5; Lk 1:36 [e]**29:32** Gn 31:42; Ex 3:7; 4:31; Dt 26:7 [f]**29:35** Gn 49:8; Mt 1:2 [g]**30:1** 1Sm 1:5-6 [h]**30:3** Gn 50:23 [i]**30:13** Lk 1:48 [j]**30:14** Sg 7:13

30

When Rachel saw that she was not
bearing Jacob any children, she en-
vied her sister. "Give me sons, or I will die!"[g]
she said to Jacob.
2Jacob became angry with Rachel and said,
"Am I in God's place, who has withheld children[F] from you?"
3Then she said, "Here is my slave Bilhah.
Go sleep with her, and she'll bear children
for me[G,h] so that through her I too can build
a family." 4So Rachel gave her slave Bilhah to
Jacob as a wife, and he slept with her. 5Bilhah
conceived and bore Jacob a son. 6Rachel said,
"God has vindicated me; yes, He has heard
me and given me a son," and she named him
Dan.[H]
7Rachel's slave Bilhah conceived again and
bore Jacob a second son. 8Rachel said, "In my
wrestlings with God,[I] I have wrestled with my
sister and won," and she named him Naphtali.[J]
9When Leah saw that she had stopped having children, she took her slave Zilpah and
gave her to Jacob as a wife. 10Leah's slave Zilpah bore Jacob a son. 11Then Leah said, "What
good fortune!"[K] and she named him Gad.[L]
12When Leah's slave Zilpah bore Jacob a
second son, 13Leah said, "I am happy that the
women call me happy,"[i] so she named him
Asher.[M]
14Reuben went out during the wheat harvest and found some mandrakes in the field.[j]
When he brought them to his mother Leah,
Rachel asked, "Please give me some of your
son's mandrakes."
15But Leah replied to her, "Isn't it enough
that you have taken my husband? Now you
also want to take my son's mandrakes?"
"Well," Rachel said, "you can sleep with
him tonight in exchange for your son's mandrakes."
16When Jacob came in from the field that
evening, Leah went out to meet him and said,
"You must come with me, for I have hired
you with my son's mandrakes." So Jacob slept
with her that night.
17God listened to Leah, and she conceived
and bore Jacob a fifth son. 18Leah said, "God

[A]**29:21** Lit *to go to* [B]**29:32** = See, a Son; in Hb, the name Reuben sounds like "has seen my affliction." [C]**29:33** In Hb, the name Simeon sounds like "has heard." [D]**29:34** In Hb, the name Levi sounds like "attached to." [E]**29:35** In Hb, the name Judah sounds like "praise." [F]**30:2** Lit *the fruit of the womb* [G]**30:3** Lit *bear on my knees* [H]**30:6** In Hb, the name Dan sounds like "has vindicated," or "has judged." [I]**30:8** Or *With mighty wrestlings* [J]**30:8** In Hb, the name Naphtali sounds like "my wrestling." [K]**30:11** Alt Hb tradition, LXX, Vg read *Good fortune has come* [L]**30:11** = Good Fortune [M]**30:13** = Happy

has rewarded me for giving my slave to my
husband," and she named him Issachar.[A]
19 Then Leah conceived again and bore Jacob a sixth son. 20 "God has given me a good
gift," Leah said. "This time my husband will
honor me because I have borne six sons for
him," and she named him Zebulun.[B] 21 Later,
Leah bore a daughter and named her Dinah.
22 Then God remembered Rachel. He listened to her and opened her womb.[a] 23 She
conceived and bore a son, and said, "God has
taken away my shame."[b] 24 She named him
Joseph:[C] "May the LORD add another son to
me."[c]

Jacob's Flocks Multiply

25 After Rachel gave birth to Joseph, Jacob
said to Laban, "Send me on my way so that
I can return to my homeland. 26 Give me my
wives and my children that I have worked
for, and let me go.[d] You know how hard I have
worked for you."
27 But Laban said to him, "If I have found
favor in your sight, stay. I have learned by
•divination that the LORD has blessed me because of you." 28 Then Laban said, "Name your
wages, and I will pay them."[e]
29 So Jacob said to him, "You know what I
have done for you and your herds.[f] 30 For you
had very little before I came, but now your
wealth has increased. The LORD has blessed
you because of me. And now, when will I also
do something for my own family?"
31 Laban asked, "What should I give you?"
And Jacob said, "You don't need to give me
anything. If you do this one thing for me, I
will continue to shepherd and keep your
flock. 32 Let me go through all your sheep today and remove every sheep that is speckled
or spotted, every dark-colored sheep among
the lambs, and the spotted and speckled
among the female goats. Such will be my
wages. 33 In the future when you come to
check on my wages, my honesty will testify
for me. If I have any female goats that are not
speckled or spotted, or any lambs that are not
black, they will be considered stolen."
34 "Good," said Laban. "Let it be as you have
said."

[a]30:22 Gn 29:31 [b]30:23 Is 4:1; Lk 1:25 [c]30:24 Gn 35:17 [d]30:26 Gn 29:18,20,27; Hs 12:12 [e]30:28 Gn 29:15; 31:7,41 [f]30:29 Gn 31:6,38-40 [g]30:39 Gn 31:10-12 [h]30:43 Gn 12:16; 13:2; 24:35; 26:13-14; 30:30 [i]31:3 Gn 28:15; 32:10

35 That day Laban removed the streaked and
spotted male goats and all the speckled and
spotted female goats — every one that had
any white on it — and every dark-colored one
among the lambs, and he placed his sons in
charge of them. 36 He put a three-day journey between himself and Jacob. Jacob, meanwhile, was shepherding the rest of Laban's
flock.
37 Jacob then took branches of fresh poplar, almond, and plane wood, and peeled the
bark, exposing white stripes on the branches.
38 He set the peeled branches in the troughs
in front of the sheep — in the water channels where the sheep came to drink. And the
sheep bred when they came to drink. 39 The
flocks bred in front of the branches and bore
streaked, speckled, and spotted young.[g] 40 Jacob separated the lambs and made the flocks
face the streaked and the completely dark
sheep in Laban's flocks. Then he set his own
stock apart and didn't put them with Laban's
sheep.
41 Whenever the stronger of the flock were
breeding, Jacob placed the branches in the
troughs, in full view of the flocks, and they
would breed in front of the branches. 42 As
for the weaklings of the flocks, he did not put
out the branches. So it turned out that the
weak sheep belonged to Laban and the stronger ones to Jacob. 43 And the man became very
rich.[D] He had many flocks, male and female
slaves, and camels and donkeys.[h]

Jacob Separates from Laban

31 Now Jacob heard what Laban's sons
were saying: "Jacob has taken all that
was our father's and has built this wealth
from what belonged to our father." 2 And Jacob saw from Laban's face that his attitude
toward him was not the same.
3 Then the LORD said to him, "Go back to the
land of your fathers and to your family, and I
will be with you."[i]
4 Jacob had Rachel and Leah called to the
field where his flocks were. 5 He said to them,
"I can see from your father's face that his attitude toward me is not the same, but the
God of my father has been with me. 6 You

[A]30:18 In Hb, the name Issachar sounds like "reward." [B]30:20 In Hb, the name Zebulun sounds like "honored." [C]30:24 = He Adds

[D]30:43 Lit *The man spread out very much, very much*

know that I've worked hard[A] for your father[a]
7and that he has cheated me and changed
my wages 10 times. But God has not let him
harm me. 8If he said, 'The spotted sheep will
be your wages,' then all the sheep were born
spotted. If he said, 'The streaked sheep will
be your wages,' then all the sheep were born
streaked.[b] 9God has taken away your father's
herds and given them to me.

10"When the flocks were breeding, I saw
in a dream that the streaked, spotted, and
speckled males were mating with the females.
11In that dream the Angel of God said to me,
'Jacob!' and I said, 'Here I am.' 12And He said,
'Look up and see: all the males that are mating with the flocks are streaked, spotted, and
speckled, for I have seen all that Laban has
been doing to you.[c] 13I am the God of Bethel,
where you poured oil on the stone marker
and made a solemn vow to Me.[d] Get up, leave
this land, and return to your native land.'"

14Then Rachel and Leah answered him, "Do
we have any portion or inheritance in our father's household? 15Are we not regarded by
him as outsiders? For he has sold us[e] and has
certainly spent our money. 16In fact, all the
wealth that God has taken away from our father belongs to us and to our children. So do
whatever God has said to you."

17Then Jacob got up and put his children
and wives on the camels. 18He took all the
livestock and possessions he had acquired in
Paddan-aram, and he drove his herds to go to
the land of his father Isaac in Canaan. 19When
Laban had gone to shear his sheep, Rachel
stole her father's household idols.[f] 20And Jacob deceived[B] Laban the Aramean, not telling him that he was fleeing. 21He fled with all
his possessions, crossed the Euphrates, and
headed for[C] the hill country of Gilead.

Laban Overtakes Jacob

22On the third day Laban was told that Jacob had fled. 23So he took his relatives with
him, pursued Jacob for seven days, and overtook him at Mount Gilead. 24But God came
to Laban the Aramean in a dream at night.
"Watch yourself!" God warned him. "Don't
say anything to Jacob, either good or bad."[g]
25When Laban overtook Jacob, Jacob had
pitched his tent in the hill country, and Laban and his brothers also pitched their tents
in the hill country of Gilead. 26Then Laban
said to Jacob, "What have you done? You have
deceived me and taken my daughters away
like prisoners of war! 27Why did you secretly
flee from me, deceive me, and not tell me? I
would have sent you away with joy and singing, with tambourines and lyres, 28but you
didn't even let me kiss my grandchildren and
my daughters. You have acted foolishly. 29I
could do you great harm, but last night the
God of your father said to me: 'Watch yourself. Don't say anything to Jacob, either good
or bad.' 30Now you have gone off because you
long for your father — but why have you stolen my gods?"[h]

31Jacob answered, "I was afraid, for I
thought you would take your daughters from
me by force. 32If you find your gods with anyone here, he will not live![i] Before our relatives, point out anything that is yours and
take it." Jacob did not know that Rachel had
stolen the idols.

33So Laban went into Jacob's tent, then Leah's tent, and then the tents of the two female
slaves, but he found nothing. Then he left
Leah's tent and entered Rachel's. 34Now Rachel had taken Laban's household idols, put
them in the saddlebag of the camel, and sat
on them. Laban searched the whole tent but
found nothing.

35She said to her father, "Sir, don't be angry
that I cannot stand up in your presence;[j] I am
having my period." So Laban searched, but
could not find the household idols.

Jacob's Covenant with Laban

36Then Jacob became incensed and
brought charges against Laban. "What is my
crime?" he said to Laban. "What is my sin,
that you have pursued me? 37You've searched
all my possessions! Have you found anything
of yours? Put it here before my relatives and
yours, and let them decide between the two
of us. 38I've been with you these 20 years.
Your ewes and female goats have not miscarried, and I have not eaten the rams from your
flock. 39I did not bring you any of the flock
torn by wild beasts; I myself bore the loss. You

[a]**31:6** Gn 30:29
[b]**31:8** Gn 30:32
[c]**31:12** Gn 30:37-40; Ex 3:7
[d]**31:13** Gn 28:18-19
[e]**31:15** Gn 29:19-30
[f]**31:19** Jdg 17:5; 1Sm 15:23; 19:13; Ezk 21:21; Hs 3:4; Zch 10:2
[g]**31:24** Gn 24:50; 31:29; 2Sm 13:22
[h]**31:30** Gn 31:19; Jos 24:2; Jdg 18:24
[i]**31:32** Gn 44:9
[j]**31:35** Lv 19:32

[A]**31:6** Lit *worked with all my strength* [B]**31:20** Lit *And he stole the heart of* [C]**31:21** Lit *and set his face to*

demanded payment from me for what was
stolen by day or by night. 40 There I was — the
heat consumed me by day and the frost by
night, and sleep fled from my eyes. 41 For 20
years I have worked in your household — 14
years for your two daughters and six years
for your flocks[a] — and you have changed my
wages 10 times! 42 If the God of my father, the
God of Abraham, the Fear of Isaac, had not
been with me, certainly now you would have
sent me off empty-handed. But God has seen
my affliction and my hard work,[A] and He issued His verdict last night."

43 Then Laban answered Jacob, "The daughters are my daughters; the sons, my sons;
and the flocks, my flocks! Everything you see
is mine! But what can I do today for these
daughters of mine or for the children they
have borne? 44 Come now, let's make a covenant, you and I.[b] Let it be a witness between
the two of us."

45 So Jacob picked out a stone and set it up
as a marker.[c] 46 Then Jacob said to his relatives,
"Gather stones." And they took stones and
made a mound, then ate there by the mound.
47 Laban named the mound Jegar-sahadutha,
but Jacob named it Galeed.[B]

48 Then Laban said, "This mound is a witness between you and me today." Therefore
the place was called Galeed 49 and also Mizpah,[C,d] for he said, "May the LORD watch between you and me when we are out of each
other's sight. 50 If you mistreat my daughters
or take other wives, though no one is with
us, understand that God will be a witness
between you and me."[e] 51 Laban also said to
Jacob, "Look at this mound and the marker
I have set up between you and me. 52 This
mound is a witness and the marker is a witness that I will not pass beyond this mound to
you, and you will not pass beyond this mound
and this marker to do me harm. 53 The God of
Abraham, and the gods[f] of Nahor — the gods
of their father[D] — will judge between us." And
Jacob swore by the Fear of his father Isaac.
54 Then Jacob offered a sacrifice on the mountain and invited his relatives to eat a meal. So
they ate a meal and spent the night on the
mountain. 55 [E] Laban got up early in the morning, kissed his grandchildren and daughters,
and blessed them. Then Laban left to return
home.

Preparing to Meet Esau

32 Jacob went on his way, and God's angels met him.[g] 2 When he saw them,
Jacob said, "This is God's camp." So he called
that place Mahanaim.[F,h]

3 Jacob sent messengers ahead of him to his
brother Esau in the land of Seir, the country
of Edom. 4 He commanded them, "You are to
say to my lord Esau, 'This is what your servant Jacob says. I have been staying with Laban and have been delayed until now. 5 I have
oxen, donkeys, flocks, male and female slaves.
I have sent this message to inform my lord, in
order to seek your favor.'"[i]

6 When the messengers returned to Jacob,
they said, "We went to your brother Esau; he
is coming to meet you — and he has 400 men
with him."[j] 7 Jacob was greatly afraid and distressed; he divided the people with him into
two camps, along with the flocks, cattle, and
camels. 8 He thought, "If Esau comes to one
camp and attacks it, the remaining one can
escape."[k]

9 Then Jacob said, "God of my father Abraham and God of my father Isaac,[l] the LORD
who said to me, 'Go back to your land and to
your family, and I will cause you to prosper,'[m]
10 I am unworthy of all the kindness and faithfulness You have shown Your servant. Indeed,
I crossed over this Jordan with my staff, and
now I have become two camps. 11 Please rescue me from the hand of my brother Esau, for
I am afraid of him; otherwise, he may come
and attack me, the mothers, and their children. 12 You have said, 'I will cause you to prosper, and I will make your ·offspring like the
sand of the sea, which cannot be counted.'"[n]

13 He spent the night there and took part of
what he had brought with him as a gift for
his brother Esau:[o] 14 200 female goats, 20 male
goats, 200 ewes, 20 rams, 15 30 milk camels
with their young, 40 cows, 10 bulls, 20 female
donkeys, and 10 male donkeys. 16 He entrusted
them to his slaves as separate herds and said

[a] 31:41 Gn 29:27,30
[b] 31:44 Gn 21:27,32; 26:28
[c] 31:45 Jos 24:26-27
[d] 31:49 Jdg 11:29; 1Sm 7:5-6
[e] 31:50 Jdg 11:10; 1Sm 12:5; Jb 16:19; Jr 42:5; Mc 1:2
[f] 31:53 Jos 24:2
[g] 32:1 Ps 91:9-11
[h] 32:2 Jos 21:38; 2Sm 2:8; 17:24,27; 1Kg 2:8
[i] 32:5 Gn 33:8,15
[j] 32:6 Gn 33:1
[k] 32:8 Gn 27:41
[l] 32:9 Gn 28:13; 31:42,53
[m] Gn 31:3,13
[n] 32:12 Gn 28:13-15
[o] 32:13 Gn 43:11

[A] 31:42 Lit *and the work of my hands* [B] 31:47 *Jegar-sahadutha* is Aram, and *Galeed* is Hb; both names = Mound of Witness [C] 31:49 = Watchtower [D] 31:53 Two Hb mss, LXX omit *the gods of their father* [E] 31:55 Gn 32:1 in Hb [F] 32:2 = Two Camps

to them, "Go on ahead of me, and leave some
distance between the herds."
17 And he told the first one: "When my
brother Esau meets you and asks, 'Who do you
belong to? Where are you going? And whose
animals are these ahead of you?' 18 then tell
him, 'They belong to your servant Jacob. They
are a gift sent to my lord Esau. And look, he is
behind us.'"
19 He also told the second one, the third,
and everyone who was walking behind the
animals, "Say the same thing to Esau when
you find him. 20 You are also to say, 'Look,
your servant Jacob is right behind us.'" For
he thought, "I want to appease Esau with the
gift that is going ahead of me. After that, I can
face him, and perhaps he will forgive me."
21 So the gift was sent on ahead of him while
he remained in the camp that night. 22 During the night Jacob got up and took his two
wives, his two female slaves, and his 11 sons,
and crossed the ford of Jabbok.[a] 23 He took
them and sent them across the stream, along
with all his possessions.

Jacob Wrestles with God

24 Jacob was left alone, and a man wrestled
with him until daybreak.[b] 25 When the man
saw that He could not defeat him, He struck
Jacob's hip socket as they wrestled and dislocated his hip. 26 Then He said to Jacob, "Let Me
go, for it is daybreak."
But Jacob said, "I will not let You go unless
You bless me."
27 "What is your name?" the man asked.
"Jacob," he replied.
28 "Your name will no longer be Jacob,"[c] He
said. "It will be Israel[A] because you have struggled with God[d] and with men and have prevailed."
29 Then Jacob asked Him, "Please tell me
Your name."
But He answered, "Why do you ask My
name?"[e] And He blessed him there.
30 Jacob then named the place Peniel,[B] "For
I have seen God face to face," he said, "and I
have been delivered."[f] 31 The sun shone on
him as he passed by Penuel[C,g] — limping because of his hip. 32 That is why, to this day, the
Israelites don't eat the thigh muscle that is at
the hip socket: because He struck Jacob's hip
socket at the thigh muscle.[D]

Jacob Meets Esau

33 Now Jacob looked up and saw Esau
coming toward him with 400 men. So
he divided the children among Leah, Rachel,
and the two female slaves. 2 He put the female
slaves and their children first, Leah and her
children next, and Rachel and Joseph last.
3 He himself went on ahead and bowed to the
ground[h] seven times until he approached his
brother.
4 But Esau ran to meet him, hugged him,
threw his arms around him, and kissed him.
Then they wept.[i] 5 When Esau looked up and
saw the women and children, he asked, "Who
are these with you?"
He answered, "The children God has graciously given your servant."[j] 6 Then the female
slaves and their children approached him
and bowed down. 7 Leah and her children
also approached and bowed down, and then
Joseph and Rachel approached and bowed
down.
8 So Esau said, "What do you mean by this
whole procession[E] I met?"[k]
"To find favor with you, my lord,"[l] he answered.
9 "I have enough, my brother," Esau replied.
"Keep what you have."
10 But Jacob said, "No, please! If I have found
favor with you, take this gift from my hand.
For indeed, I have seen your face, and it is like
seeing God's face, since you have accepted
me. 11 Please take my present that was brought
to you, because God has been gracious to me
and I have everything I need." So Jacob urged
him until he accepted.
12 Then Esau said, "Let's move on, and I'll go
ahead of you."
13 Jacob replied, "My lord knows that the
children are weak, and I have nursing sheep
and cattle. If they are driven hard for one
day, the whole herd will die. 14 Let my lord
go ahead of his servant. I will continue on
slowly, at a pace suited to the livestock and
the children, until I come to my lord at Seir."
15 Esau said, "Let me leave some of my people with you."

[a] 32:22 Dt 2:37; 3:16; Jos 12:2
[b] 32:24 Hs 12:3-4
[c] 32:28 Gn 35:10; 2Kg 17:34
[d] Hs 12:3-4
[e] 32:29 Jdg 13:18
[f] 32:30 Gn 16:13; Ex 24:10-11; 33:20; Nm 12:8; Jdg 6:22; 13:22
[g] 32:31 Jdg 8:8
[h] 33:3 Gn 18:2; 42:6; 43:26
[i] 33:4 Gn 45:14
[j] 33:5 Gn 48:9; Ps 127:3; Is 8:18
[k] 33:8 Gn 32:13-16
[l] Gn 32:5

[A] 32:28 In Hb, the name Israel sounds like "he struggled (with) God." [B] 32:30 = Face of God [C] 32:31 Variant of *Peniel* [D] 32:32 Or *tendon* [E] 33:8 Lit *camp*

But he replied, "Why do that? Please indulge me,[A] my lord."[a]
16 That day Esau started on his way back to
Seir, 17 but Jacob went on to Succoth. He built a
house for himself and stalls for his livestock;
that is why the place was called Succoth.[B,b]
18 After Jacob came from Paddan-aram, he
arrived safely[c] at Shechem[d] in the land of Canaan and camped in front of the city. 19 He
purchased a section of the field where he had
pitched his tent from the sons of Hamor, Shechem's father, for 100 *qesitahs*.[C,e] 20 And he set
up an altar there and called it "God, the God
of Israel."[D]

Dinah Defiled

34 Dinah, Leah's daughter[f] whom she
bore to Jacob, went out to see some
of the young women of the area. 2 When Shechem son of Hamor the Hivite, a prince of the
region, saw her, he took her and raped her.
3 He became infatuated with Dinah, daughter
of Jacob. He loved the young girl and spoke
tenderly to her.[E] 4 "Get me this girl as a wife,"[g]
he told his father Hamor.
5 Jacob heard that Shechem had defiled his
daughter Dinah, but since his sons were with
his livestock in the field, he remained silent
until they returned. 6 Meanwhile, Shechem's
father Hamor came to speak with Jacob. 7 Jacob's sons returned from the field when they
heard about the incident and were deeply
grieved and angry. For Shechem had committed an outrage against Israel by raping Jacob's daughter,[h] and such a thing should not
be done.
8 Hamor said to Jacob's sons, "My son Shechem is strongly attracted to your[F] daughter.
Please give her to him as a wife. 9 Intermarry
with us; give your daughters to us, and take
our daughters for yourselves. 10 Live with
us. The land is before you. Settle here, move
about, and acquire property in it."
11 Then Shechem said to Dinah's father and
brothers, "Grant me this favor,[G] and I'll give
you whatever you say. 12 Demand of me a high
compensation[H] and gift; I'll give you whatever
you ask me. Just give the girl to be my wife!"

13 But Jacob's sons answered Shechem and
his father Hamor deceitfully because he had
defiled their sister Dinah. 14 "We cannot do
this thing," they said to them. "Giving our sister to an uncircumcised man is a disgrace to
us. 15 We will agree with you only on this condition: if all your males are circumcised as we
are.[i] 16 Then we will give you our daughters,
take your daughters for ourselves, live with
you, and become one people. 17 But if you will
not listen to us and be circumcised, then we
will take our daughter and go."
18 Their words seemed good to Hamor and
his son Shechem. 19 The young man did not
delay doing this, because he was delighted
with Jacob's daughter. Now he was the most
important in all his father's house. 20 So Hamor and his son Shechem went to the ·gate of
their city[j] and spoke to the men there.
21 "These men are peaceful toward us," they
said. "Let them live in our land and move
about in it, for indeed, the region is large
enough for them. Let us take their daughters
as our wives and give our daughters to them.
22 But the men will agree to live with us and
be one people only on this condition: if all
our men are circumcised as they are. 23 Won't
their livestock, their possessions, and all their
animals become ours? Only let us agree with
them, and they will live with us."
24 All the able-bodied men[I,k] listened to Hamor and his son Shechem, and all the able-
bodied men[J] were circumcised. 25 On the
third day, when they were still in pain, two of
Jacob's sons, Simeon and Levi,[l] Dinah's brothers, took their swords, went into the unsuspecting city, and killed every male. 26 They
killed Hamor and his son Shechem with their
swords, took Dinah from Shechem's house,
and went away. 27 Jacob's other sons came to
the slaughter and plundered the city because
their sister had been defiled. 28 They took their
sheep, cattle, donkeys, and whatever was in
the city and in the field. 29 They captured all
their possessions, children, and wives and
plundered everything in the houses.
30 Then Jacob said to Simeon and Levi, "You
have brought trouble on me,[m] making me

[a] **33:15** Gn 34:11; 47:25; Ru 2:13
[b] **33:17** Jos 13:27; Jdg 8:5; Ps 60:6
[c] **33:18** Gn 28:21
[d] Jos 24:1; Jdg 9:1; Ps 60:6; Ac 7:16
[e] **33:19** Jos 24:32; Jn 4:5
[f] **34:1** Gn 30:21
[g] **34:4** Jdg 14:2
[h] **34:7** Dt 22:20-30; Jdg 20:6; 2Sm 13:12
[i] **34:15** Gn 17:23-27
[j] **34:20** Ru 4:1; 2Sm 15:2
[k] **34:24** Gn 23:10
[l] **34:25** Gn 49:5-7
[m] **34:30** Jos 7:25

[A] **33:15** Lit *May I find favor in your eyes* [B] **33:17** = Stalls or Huts [C] **33:19** The value of this currency is unknown. [D] **33:20** Or *El-Elohe-Israel* [E] **34:3** Lit *spoke to her heart* [F] **34:8** The Hb word for "your" is pl, showing that Hamor is speaking to Jacob and his sons. [G] **34:11** Lit *May I find favor in your eyes* [H] **34:12** Or *bride-price*, or *betrothal present* [I] **34:24** Lit *All who went out of the city gate* [J] **34:24** Lit *all the males who went out of the city gate*

odious to the inhabitants of the land,[a] the
Canaanites and the Perizzites.[b] We are few in
number; if they unite against me and attack
me, I and my household will be destroyed."[c]
31 But they answered, "Should he have
treated our sister like a prostitute?"

Return to Bethel

35 God said to Jacob, "Get up! Go to
Bethel and settle there.[d] Build an altar
there to the God who appeared to you when
you fled from your brother Esau."[e]
2 So Jacob said to his family and all who
were with him, "Get rid of the foreign gods
that are among you.[f] Purify yourselves and
change your clothes.[g] 3 We must get up and go
to Bethel. I will build an altar there to the God
who answered me in my day of distress.[h] He
has been with me everywhere I have gone."[i]
4 Then they gave Jacob all their foreign gods
and their earrings, and Jacob hid them under
the oak near Shechem. 5 When they set out, a
terror from God came over the cities around
them, and they did not pursue Jacob's sons.[j]
6 So Jacob and all who were with him came to
Luz (that is, Bethel[k]) in the land of Canaan.
7 Jacob built an altar there and called the place
God of Bethel[A] because it was there that God
had revealed Himself to him when he was
fleeing from his brother.
8 Deborah, the one who had nursed and
raised Rebekah,[B,l] died and was buried under
the oak south of Bethel. So Jacob named it
Oak of Weeping.[C]
9 God appeared to Jacob again after he returned from Paddan-aram, and He blessed
him. 10 God said to him:

> Your name is Jacob;
> you will no longer be named Jacob,
> but your name will be Israel.[m]

So He named him Israel. 11 God also said to
him:

> I am ˙God Almighty.[n]
> Be fruitful and multiply.[o]
> A nation, indeed an assembly
> of nations,
> will come from you,[p]
> and kings will descend from you.[D,q]
> 12 I will give to you the land
> that I gave to Abraham and Isaac.[r]
> And I will give the land
> to your future descendants.

13 Then God withdrew[E,s] from him at the place
where He had spoken to him.
14 Jacob set up a marker at the place where
He had spoken to him—a stone marker. He
poured a drink offering on it and anointed it
with oil.[t] 15 Jacob named the place where God
had spoken with him Bethel.

Rachel's Death

16 They set out from Bethel. When they were
still some distance from Ephrath, Rachel began to give birth, and her labor was difficult.
17 During her difficult labor, the midwife said
to her, "Don't be afraid, for you have another
son."[u] 18 With her last breath—for she was dying—she named him Ben-oni,[F] but his father
called him Benjamin.[G] 19 So Rachel died and was
buried on the way to Ephrath (that is, Bethlehem[v]). 20 Jacob set up a marker on her grave; it
is the marker at Rachel's grave to this day.

Israel's Sons

21 Israel set out again and pitched his tent
beyond the Tower of Eder.[H] 22 While Israel
was living in that region, Reuben went in and
slept with his father's concubine Bilhah, and
Israel heard about it.[w]
Jacob had 12 sons:[x]

> 23 Leah's sons were Reuben
> (Jacob's firstborn),
> Simeon, Levi, Judah,
> Issachar, and Zebulun.
> 24 Rachel's sons were
> Joseph and Benjamin.
> 25 The sons of Rachel's slave Bilhah
> were Dan and Naphtali.
> 26 The sons of Leah's slave Zilpah
> were Gad and Asher.

These are the sons of Jacob, who were born to
him in Paddan-aram.

Isaac's Death

27 Jacob came to his father Isaac at Mamre[y]
in Kiriath-arba (that is, Hebron[z]), where Abra-

[a] **34:30** Ex 5:21; 1Sm 13:4; 2Sm 10:6
[b] Gn 13:7; 34:2
[c] Gn 46:26-27; Dt 4:27; 1Ch 16:19; Ps 105:12
[d] **35:1** Gn 28:19
[e] Gn 27:43
[f] **35:2** Gn 31:19; Jos 24:23; 1Sm 7:3
[g] Ex 19:10
[h] **35:3** 1Sm 7:9; 2Sm 24:25; Jb 12:4; Ps 20:1; 34:4
[i] Gn 28:10-22
[j] **35:5** Ex 23:27
[k] **35:6** Gn 28:19; 48:3
[l] **35:8** Gn 24:59
[m] **35:10** Gn 17:5; 32:28
[n] **35:11** Gn 17:1; 28:3; Ex 6:3
[o] Gn 9:1,7
[p] Gn 48:4
[q] Gn 17:6,16; 36:31
[r] **35:12** Gn 12:7; 13:15; 26:3-4; 28:13; Ex 32:13
[s] **35:13** Gn 17:22; 18:33
[t] **35:14** Gn 28:18-19; 31:45
[u] **35:17** Gn 30:24
[v] **35:19** Mc 5:2; Mt 2:18
[w] **35:22** Gn 49:3-4
[x] **35:22-26** 1Ch 2:1-2
[y] **35:27** Gn 13:18; 18:1; 23:19
[z] Jos 14:15

[A] **35:7** Or *El-bethel* [B] **35:8** Lit *Deborah, Rebekah's wet nurse*; Gn 24:59 [C] **35:8** Or *Allon-bacuth* [D] **35:11** Lit *will come from your loins* [E] **35:13** Lit *went up* [F] **35:18** = Son of My Sorrow [G] **35:18** = Son of the Right Hand [H] **35:21** Or *beyond Migdal-eder*

ham and Isaac had stayed. 28 Isaac lived 180
years. 29 He took his last breath and died, and
was gathered to his people,[a] old and full of
days. His sons Esau and Jacob buried him.

Esau's Family

36 These are the family records[b] of Esau
(that is, Edom[c]). 2 Esau took his wives
from the Canaanite women: Adah daughter
of Elon the Hittite,[d] Oholibamah daughter
of Anah and granddaughter[A] of Zibeon the
Hivite, 3 and Basemath daughter of Ishmael
and sister of Nebaioth.[e] 4 Adah bore Eliphaz
to Esau, Basemath bore Reuel, 5 and Oholibamah bore Jeush, Jalam, and Korah. These
were Esau's sons, who were born to him in
the land of Canaan.
6 Esau took his wives, sons, daughters, and
all the people of his household, as well as his
herds, all his livestock, and all the property
he had acquired in Canaan; he went to a land
away from his brother Jacob. 7 For their possessions were too many for them to live together,[f] and because of their herds, the land
where they stayed could not support them.[g]
8 So Esau (that is, Edom) lived in the mountains of Seir.[h]
9 These are the family records of Esau, father of the Edomites in the mountains of Seir.

10 These are the names of Esau's sons:[i]
Eliphaz son of Esau's wife Adah,
and Reuel son of Esau's wife Basemath.
11 The sons of Eliphaz were
Teman, Omar, Zepho, Gatam,
and Kenaz.
12 Timna, a concubine of Esau's son
Eliphaz,
bore Amalek to Eliphaz.
These were the sons of Esau's wife Adah.
13 These are Reuel's sons:
Nahath, Zerah, Shammah, and Mizzah.
These were the sons of Esau's wife
Basemath.
14 These are the sons of Esau's wife
Oholibamah
daughter of Anah and granddaughter[A]
of Zibeon:
She bore Jeush, Jalam, and Korah
to Edom.

[a] 35:29 Gn 25:8,17; 49:33; Nm 20:24,26; Dt 32:50
[b] 36:1 Gn 2:4; 36:9
[c] Gn 25:30
[d] 36:2 Gn 26:34
[e] 36:3 Gn 28:9
[f] 36:7 Gn 13:6
[g] Gn 17:8; Heb 11:9
[h] 36:8 Dt 2:5
[i] 36:10-14 1Ch 1:35-37
[j] 36:20-28 Gn 14:6; Dt 2:12,22; 1Ch 1:38-42

15 These are the chiefs of Esau's sons:
the sons of Eliphaz, Esau's firstborn:
Chiefs Teman, Omar, Zepho, Kenaz,
16 Korah,[B] Gatam, and Amalek.
These are the chiefs of Eliphaz
in the land of Edom.
These are the sons of Adah.

17 These are the sons of Reuel, Esau's son:
Chiefs Nahath, Zerah, Shammah,
and Mizzah.
These are the chiefs of Reuel
in the land of Edom.
These are the sons of Esau's wife
Basemath.

18 These are the sons of Esau's wife
Oholibamah:
Chiefs Jeush, Jalam, and Korah.
These are the chiefs of Esau's wife
Oholibamah
daughter of Anah.
19 These are the sons of Esau
(that is, Edom),
and these are their chiefs.

Seir's Family

20 These are the sons of Seir the Horite,[j]
the inhabitants of the land:
Lotan, Shobal, Zibeon, Anah,
21 Dishon, Ezer, and Dishan.
These are the chiefs of the Horites,
the sons of Seir, in the land of Edom.
22 The sons of Lotan were Hori
and Heman.
Timna was Lotan's sister.
23 These are Shobal's sons:
Alvan, Manahath, Ebal, Shepho,
and Onam.
24 These are Zibeon's sons: Aiah and Anah.
This was the Anah who found
the hot springs[C] in the wilderness
while he was pasturing the donkeys
of his father Zibeon.
25 These are the children of Anah:
Dishon and Oholibamah
daughter of Anah.
26 These are Dishon's sons:
Hemdan, Eshban, Ithran, and Cheran.
27 These are Ezer's sons:
Bilhan, Zaavan, and Akan.

[A] 36:2,14 Sam, LXX read *Anah son* [B] 36:16 Sam omits *Korah* [C] 36:24 Syr, Vg; Tg reads *the mules*; Hb obscure

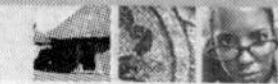

28 These are Dishan's sons: Uz and Aran.
29 These are the chiefs of the Horites:
Chiefs Lotan, Shobal, Zibeon, Anah,
30 Dishon, Ezer, and Dishan.
These are the chiefs of the Horites,
according to their divisions, in the land
of Seir.

Rulers of Edom

31 These are the kings who ruled
in the land of Edom[a]
before any king ruled
over the Israelites:
32 Bela son of Beor ruled in Edom;
the name of his city was Dinhabah.
33 When Bela died, Jobab son of Zerah
from Bozrah became king
in his place.
34 When Jobab died, Husham
from the land of the Temanites
became king in his place.
35 When Husham died, Hadad
son of Bedad became king
in his place.
He defeated Midian in the field
of Moab;
the name of his city was Avith.
36 When Hadad died, Samlah
from Masrekah became king
in his place.
37 When Samlah died, Shaul
from Rehoboth on the
Euphrates River became king
in his place.
38 When Shaul died, Baal-hanan
son of Achbor became king
in his place.
39 When Baal-hanan son of Achbor died,
Hadar[A] became king in his place.
His city was Pau, and his wife's name
was Mehetabel
daughter of Matred daughter
of Me-zahab.
40 These are the names of Esau's chiefs,
according to their families
and their localities,
by their names:
Chiefs Timna, Alvah, Jetheth,
41 Oholibamah, Elah, Pinon,

[a]36:31-43 Gn 17:6,16; 35:11; 1Ch 1:43-54
[b]37:1 Gn 26:3
[c]37:2 Gn 30:1-13
[d]1Sm 2:22-24
[e]37:3 Gn 44:20
[f]37:7 Gn 42:6,9; 43:26; 44:14
[g]37:11 Ac 7:9
[h]Dn 7:28; Lk 2:19,51

42 Kenaz, Teman, Mibzar,
43 Magdiel, and Iram.
These are Edom's chiefs,
according to their settlements
in the land they possessed.
Esau[B] was father of the Edomites.

Joseph's Dreams

37 Jacob lived in the land where his father
had stayed, the land of Canaan.[b] 2These
are the family records of Jacob.
At 17 years of age, Joseph tended sheep
with his brothers. The young man was working with the sons of Bilhah and Zilpah, his
father's wives,[c] and he brought a bad report
about them to their father.[d]
3Now Israel loved Joseph more than his
other sons because Joseph was a son born
to him in his old age,[e] and he made a robe of
many colors[C] for him. 4When his brothers
saw that their father loved him more than all
his brothers, they hated him and could not
bring themselves to speak peaceably to him.
5Then Joseph had a dream. When he told
it to his brothers, they hated him even more.
6He said to them, "Listen to this dream I had:
7There we were, binding sheaves of grain in
the field. Suddenly my sheaf stood up, and
your sheaves gathered around it and bowed
down to my sheaf."[f]
8"Are you really going to reign over us?" his
brothers asked him. "Are you really going to
rule us?" So they hated him even more because of his dream and what he had said.
9Then he had another dream and told it to
his brothers. "Look," he said, "I had another
dream, and this time the sun, moon, and 11
stars were bowing down to me."
10He told his father and brothers, but his
father rebuked him. "What kind of dream
is this that you have had?" he said. "Are your
mother and brothers and I going to come and
bow down to the ground before you?" 11His
brothers were jealous of him,[g] but his father
kept the matter in mind.[h]

Joseph Sold into Slavery

12His brothers had gone to pasture their
father's flocks at Shechem. 13Israel said to
Joseph, "Your brothers, you know, are pas-

[A]36:39 Many Hb mss, Sam, Syr read *Hadad* [B]36:43 Lit *He Esau* [C]37:3 Or *robe with long sleeves*

turing the flocks at Shechem. Get ready. I'm
sending you to them."
"I'm ready," Joseph replied.
14 Then Israel said to him, "Go and see how
your brothers and the flocks are doing, and
bring word back to me." So he sent him from
the Valley of Hebron,[a] and he went to Shechem.
15 A man found him there, wandering in the
field, and asked him, "What are you looking
for?"
16 "I'm looking for my brothers," Joseph
said. "Can you tell me where they are pasturing their flocks?"
17 "They've moved on from here," the man
said. "I heard them say, 'Let's go to Dothan.'"[b]
So Joseph set out after his brothers and found
them at Dothan.
18 They saw him in the distance, and before he had reached them, they plotted to kill
him.[c] 19 They said to one another, "Here comes
that dreamer![A] 20 Come on, let's kill him and
throw him into one of the pits. We can say
that a vicious animal ate him. Then we'll see
what becomes of his dreams!"
21 When Reuben heard this, he tried to save
him from them.[B] He said, "Let's not take his
life."[d] 22 Reuben also said to them, "Don't shed
blood. Throw him into this pit in the wilderness, but don't lay a hand on him" — intending to rescue him from their hands and
return him to his father.
23 When Joseph came to his brothers, they
stripped off his robe, the robe of many colors that he had on. 24 Then they took him and
threw him into the pit. The pit was empty;
there was no water in it.
25 Then they sat down to eat a meal.[e] They
looked up, and there was a caravan of Ishmaelites coming from Gilead.[f] Their camels were
carrying aromatic gum, balsam, and resin,
going down to Egypt.[g]
26 Then Judah said to his brothers, "What
do we gain if we kill our brother and cover
up his blood? 27 Come, let's sell him to the Ishmaelites and not lay a hand on him, for he is
our brother, our own flesh," and they agreed.
28 When Midianite[h] traders passed by, his
brothers pulled Joseph out of the pit and sold
him for 20 pieces of silver to the Ishmaelites,
who took Joseph to Egypt.[i]
29 When Reuben returned to the pit and saw
that Joseph was not there, he tore his clothes.[j]
30 He went back to his brothers and said, "The
boy is gone! What am I going to do?"[C] 31 So
they took Joseph's robe, slaughtered a young
goat, and dipped the robe in its blood. 32 They
sent the robe of many colors to their father
and said, "We found this. Examine it. Is it
your son's robe or not?"
33 His father recognized it. "It is my son's
robe," he said. "A vicious animal has devoured
him. Joseph has been torn to pieces!"[k] 34 Then
Jacob tore his clothes, put *sackcloth around
his waist, and mourned for his son many
days. 35 All his sons and daughters tried to
comfort him, but he refused to be comforted.
"No," he said. "I will go down to *Sheol to my
son, mourning." And his father wept for him.
36 Meanwhile, the Midianites sold Joseph in
Egypt to Potiphar, an officer of Pharaoh and
the captain of the guard.

Judah and Tamar

38 At that time Judah left his brothers and settled near an Adullamite[l]
named Hirah. 2 There Judah saw the daughter
of a Canaanite named Shua; he took her as a
wife and slept with her. 3 She conceived and
gave birth to a son, and he named him Er.[m]
4 She conceived again, gave birth to a son, and
named him Onan. 5 She gave birth to another
son and named him Shelah. It was at Chezib
that[D,E] she gave birth to him.
6 Judah got a wife for Er, his firstborn, and
her name was Tamar. 7 Now Er, Judah's firstborn, was evil in the LORD's sight, and the
LORD put him to death.[n] 8 Then Judah said to
Onan, "Sleep with your brother's wife. Perform your duty as her brother-in-law[o] and
produce *offspring for your brother."[p] 9 But
Onan knew that the offspring would not be
his, so whenever he slept with his brother's
wife, he released his semen on the ground so
that he would not produce offspring for his
brother. 10 What he did was evil in the LORD's
sight, so He put him to death also.
11 Then Judah said to his daughter-in-law

[a]**37:14** Gn 13:18; 35:27
[b]**37:17** 2Kg 6:13
[c]**37:18** Ps 31:13; 37:12,32; Mk 14:1; Jn 11:53; Ac 23:12
[d]**37:21** Gn 42:22
[e]**37:25** Gn 42:21
[f]Gn 39:1
[g]Gn 43:11; Jr 8:22; 46:11
[h]**37:28** Dt 25:5,7; Jdg 8:22-24; Mt 22:24; Mk 12:19; Lk 20:28
[i]Gn 45:4-5; Ps 105:17; Ac 7:9
[j]**37:29** Gn 44:13; Nm 14:6; 2Sm 1:11; 3:31; Jb 1:20
[k]**37:33** Gn 44:28
[l]**38:1** Jos 15:35; 1Sm 22:1
[m]**38:3** Gn 46:12; Nm 26:19
[n]**38:7** 1Ch 2:3
[o]**38:8** Dt 25:5-10
[p]Mt 22:24

[A]**37:19** Lit *comes the lord of the dreams* [B]**37:21** Lit *their hands* [C]**37:30** Lit *And I, where am I going* [D]**38:5** LXX reads *She was at Chezib when* [E]**38:5** Or *He was at Chezib when*

Tamar, "Remain a widow in your father's
house until my son Shelah grows up."[a] For he
thought, "He might die too, like his brothers."
So Tamar went to live in her father's house.
12 After a long time[A] Judah's wife, the
daughter of Shua, died. When Judah had
finished mourning, he and his friend Hirah
the Adullamite went up to Timnah[b] to the
sheepshearers. 13 Tamar was told, "Your father-in-law is going up to Timnah to shear his
sheep." 14 So she took off her widow's clothes,
veiled her face,[c] covered herself, and sat at the
entrance to Enaim,[B] which is on the way to
Timnah. For she saw that, though Shelah had
grown up, she had not been given to him as a
wife. 15 When Judah saw her, he thought she
was a prostitute, for she had covered her face.
16 He went over to her and said, "Come, let
me sleep with you," for he did not know that
she was his daughter-in-law.[d]

She said, "What will you give me for sleeping with me?"
17 "I will send you a young goat from my
flock," he replied.

But she said, "Only if you leave something
with me until you send it."
18 "What should I give you?" he asked.

She answered, "Your signet ring, your cord,
and the staff in your hand." So he gave them
to her and slept with her, and she got pregnant by him. 19 She got up and left, then removed her veil and put her widow's clothes
back on.
20 When Judah sent the young goat by his
friend the Adullamite in order to get back the
items he had left with the woman, he could
not find her. 21 He asked the men of the place,
"Where is the cult prostitute who was beside
the road at Enaim?"

"There has been no cult prostitute here,"
they answered.
22 So the Adullamite returned to Judah, saying, "I couldn't find her, and furthermore, the
men of the place said, 'There has been no cult
prostitute here.'"
23 Judah replied, "Let her keep the items for
herself; otherwise we will become a laughingstock. After all, I did send this young goat, but
you couldn't find her."
24 About three months later Judah was told,
"Your daughter-in-law, Tamar, has been acting like a prostitute, and now she is pregnant."

"Bring her out!" Judah said. "Let her be
burned to death!"[e]
25 As she was being brought out, she sent her
father-in-law this message: "I am pregnant by
the man to whom these items belong." And
she added, "Examine them. Whose signet
ring, cord, and staff are these?"
26 Judah recognized them and said, "She is
more in the right[C] than I,[f] since I did not give
her to my son Shelah." And he did not know
her intimately again.
27 When the time came for her to give birth,
there were twins in her womb. 28 As she was
giving birth, one of them put out his hand,
and the midwife took it and tied a scarlet
thread around it, announcing, "This one
came out first." 29 But then he pulled his hand
back, and his brother came out. Then she
said, "You have broken out first!" So he was
named Perez.[D,g] 30 Then his brother, who had
the scarlet thread tied to his hand, came out,
and was named Zerah.[E]

Joseph in Potiphar's House

39 Now Joseph had been taken to Egypt.
An Egyptian named Potiphar, an officer of Pharaoh and the captain of the guard,
bought him from the Ishmaelites[h] who had
brought him there. 2 The LORD was with Joseph,[i] and he became a successful man, serving[F] in the household of his Egyptian master.
3 When his master saw that the LORD was with
him and that the LORD made everything he
did successful,[j] 4 Joseph found favor in his
master's sight[k] and became his personal attendant. Potiphar also put him in charge of
his household and placed all that he owned
under his authority.[G] 5 From the time that he
put him in charge of his household and of all
that he owned, the LORD blessed the Egyptian's house because of Joseph.[l] The LORD's
blessing was on all that he owned, in his
house and in his fields. 6 He left all that he
owned under Joseph's authority;[H] he did not
concern himself with anything except the
food he ate.

[a] **38:11** Ru 1:12-13
[b] **38:12** Jos 15:10,57
[c] **38:14** Gn 24:65
[d] **38:16** Lv 18:15
[e] **38:24** Lv 20:14
[f] **38:26** 1Sm 24:17
[g] **38:29** Gn 46:12; Nm 26:20; 1Ch 2:4; Mt 1:3
[h] **39:1** Gn 37:25,28,36; Ps 105:17
[i] **39:2** Gn 39:3,21,23; Ac 7:9
[j] **39:3** Ps 1:3
[k] **39:4** Gn 18:3; 19:19; 33:10
[l] **39:5** Gn 30:27

[A] **38:12** Lit *And there were many days* [B] **38:14** Or *sat by the mouth of the springs* [C] **38:26** Or *more righteous* [D] **38:29** = Breaking Out [E] **38:30** = Brightness of Sunrise; perhaps related to the scarlet thread [F] **39:2** Lit *and he was* [G] **39:4** Lit *owned in his hand* [H] **39:6** Lit *owned in Joseph's hand*

Now Joseph was well-built and handsome.[a]
7 After some time[A] his master's wife looked
longingly at Joseph and said, "Sleep with me."
8 But he refused. "Look," he said to his master's wife, "with me here my master does not
concern himself with anything in his house,
and he has put all that he owns under my authority.[B] 9 No one in this house is greater than
I am. He has withheld nothing from me except you, because you are his wife. So how
could I do such a great evil and sin against
God?"[b]
10 Although she spoke to Joseph day after day, he refused[C] to go to bed with her.[D]
11 Now one day he went into the house to do
his work, and none of the household servants were there.[E] 12 She grabbed him by his
garment and said, "Sleep with me!" But leaving his garment in her hand, he escaped and
ran outside. 13 When she saw that he had left
his garment with her and had run outside,
14 she called the household servants. "Look,"
she said to them, "my husband brought a Hebrew man to make fools of us. He came to me
so he could sleep with me, and I screamed as
loud as I could. 15 When he heard me scream-
ing for help,[F] he left his garment with me and
ran outside."
16 She put Joseph's garment beside her until his master came home. 17 Then she told
him the same story: "The Hebrew slave you
brought to us came to make a fool of me,
18 but when I screamed for help,[G] he left his
garment with me and ran outside."
19 When his master heard the story his wife
told him—"These are the things your slave
did to me"—he was furious 20 and had him
thrown into prison,[c] where the king's prisoners were confined. So Joseph was there in
prison.

Joseph in Prison

21 But the LORD was with Joseph and extended kindness to him.[d] He granted him favor in the eyes of the prison warden.[e] 22 The
warden put all the prisoners who were in
the prison under Joseph's authority,[H] and he
was responsible for everything that was done
there. 23 The warden did not bother with anything under Joseph's authority,[I] because the
LORD was with him, and the LORD made everything that he did successful.[f]

Joseph Interprets Two Prisoners' Dreams

40 After this, the Egyptian king's cupbearer[g] and baker offended their
master, the king of Egypt. 2 Pharaoh was angry with his two officers, the chief cupbearer
and the chief baker, 3 and put them in custody
in the house of the captain of the guard[h] in
the prison where Joseph was confined. 4 The
captain of the guard assigned Joseph to them,
and he became their personal attendant. And
they were in custody for some time.[J]
5 The Egyptian king's cupbearer and baker,
who were confined in the prison, each had a
dream. Both had a dream on the same night,
and each dream had its own meaning. 6 When
Joseph came to them in the morning, he saw
that they looked distraught. 7 So he asked
Pharaoh's officers who were in custody with
him in his master's house, "Why do you look
so sad today?"[i]
8 "We had dreams," they said to him, "but
there is no one to interpret them."
Then Joseph said to them, "Don't interpretations belong to God? Tell me your dreams."[j]
9 So the chief cupbearer told his dream to
Joseph: "In my dream there was a vine in front
of me. 10 On the vine were three branches. As
soon as it budded, its blossoms came out and
its clusters ripened into grapes. 11 Pharaoh's
cup was in my hand, and I took the grapes,
squeezed them into Pharaoh's cup, and
placed the cup in Pharaoh's hand."
12 "This is its interpretation,"[k] Joseph said to
him. "The three branches are three days. 13 In
just three days Pharaoh will lift up your head[l]
and restore you to your position. You will put
Pharaoh's cup in his hand the way you used to
when you were his cupbearer. 14 But when all
goes well for you, remember that I was with
you. Please show kindness to me by mentioning me to Pharaoh, and get me out of this
prison. 15 For I was kidnapped from the land
of the Hebrews,[m] and even here I have done
nothing that they should put me in the dungeon."[n]

[a] **39:6** Gn 29:17; 1Sm 16:12 [b] **39:9** Gn 20:6; 42:18; 2Sm 12:13; Ps 51:4; Pr 6:29 [c] **39:20** Gn 40:3; Ps 105:18 [d] **39:21** Gn 39:2; Ps 105:19; Ac 7:9 [e] Ex 3:21; 11:3; 12:36 [f] **39:23** Gn 39:2-3 [g] **40:1** Neh 1:11 [h] **40:3** Gn 39:20 [i] **40:7** Neh 2:2 [j] **40:8** Dn 2:11,20-24 [k] **40:12** Gn 41:12; Dn 2:36 [l] **40:13** Gn 40:19-22 [m] **40:15** Gn 37:28 [n] Gn 39:20

[A] **39:7** Lit *And after these things* [B] **39:8** Lit *owns in my hand* [C] **39:10** Lit *did not listen to her* [D] **39:10** Lit *refused to lie beside her, to be with her* [E] **39:11** Lit *there in the house* [F] **39:15** Lit *me raise my voice and scream* [G] **39:18** Lit *I raised my voice and screamed* [H] **39:22** Lit *prison in the hand of Joseph* [I] **39:23** Lit *anything in his hand* [J] **40:4** Lit *custody days*

16 When the chief baker saw that the interpretation was positive, he said to Joseph,
"I also had a dream. Three baskets of white
bread were on my head. 17 In the top basket
were all sorts of baked goods for Pharaoh, but
the birds were eating them out of the basket
on my head."
18 "This is its interpretation," Joseph replied. "The three baskets are three days. 19 In
just three days Pharaoh will lift up your
head—from off you—and hang you on a
tree.[A] Then the birds will eat the flesh from
your body."[B]
20 On the third day, which was Pharaoh's
birthday, he gave a feast for all his servants.
He lifted up the heads of the chief cupbearer
and the chief baker.[a] 21 Pharaoh restored the
chief cupbearer to his position as cupbearer,
and he placed the cup in Pharaoh's hand.
22 But Pharaoh hanged[C] the chief baker, just as
Joseph had explained to them. 23 Yet the chief
cupbearer did not remember Joseph; he forgot him.[b]

Joseph Interprets Pharaoh's Dreams

41 Two years later Pharaoh had a dream:
He was standing beside the Nile,[c] 2 when
seven healthy-looking, well-fed cows came up
from the Nile and began to graze among the
reeds. 3 After them, seven other cows, sickly
and thin, came up from the Nile and stood
beside those cows along the bank of the Nile.
4 The sickly, thin cows ate the healthy, well-fed
cows. Then Pharaoh woke up. 5 He fell asleep
and dreamed a second time: Seven heads of
grain, plump and ripe, came up on one stalk.
6 After them, seven heads of grain, thin and
scorched by the east wind, sprouted up. 7 The
thin heads of grain swallowed up the seven
plump, ripe ones. Then Pharaoh woke up,
and it was only a dream.
8 When morning came, he was troubled,[d]
so he summoned all the magicians of Egypt
and all its wise men.[e] Pharaoh told them his
dreams, but no one could interpret them for
him.
9 Then the chief cupbearer said to Pharaoh,
"Today I remember my faults. 10 Pharaoh had
been angry with his servants, and he put me
and the chief baker in the custody of the
captain of the guard. 11 He and I had dreams
on the same night; each dream had its own
meaning. 12 Now a young Hebrew, a slave of
the captain of the guards, was with us there.
We told him our dreams, he interpreted our
dreams for us, and each had its own interpretation. 13 It turned out just the way he interpreted them to us: I was restored to my
position, and the other man was hanged."[f]
14 Then Pharaoh sent for Joseph, and they
quickly brought him from the dungeon.[g]
He shaved, changed his clothes, and went to
Pharaoh.[h]
15 Pharaoh said to Joseph, "I have had a
dream, and no one can interpret it. But I have
heard it said about you that you can hear a
dream and interpret it."[i]
16 "I am not able to,"[j] Joseph answered Pharaoh. "It is God who will give Pharaoh a favorable answer."[D,k]
17 So Pharaoh said to Joseph: "In my dream I
was standing on the bank of the Nile, 18 when
seven well-fed, healthy-looking cows came up
from the Nile and began to graze among the
reeds. 19 After them, seven other cows—ugly,
very sickly, and thin—came up. I've never
seen such ugly ones as these in all the land
of Egypt. 20 Then the thin, ugly cows ate the
first seven well-fed cows. 21 When they had
devoured them, you could not tell that they
had devoured them; their appearance was
as bad as it had been before. Then I woke
up. 22 In my dream I had also seen seven
heads of grain, plump and ripe, coming up
on one stalk. 23 After them, seven heads of
grain—withered, thin, and scorched by the
east wind—sprouted up. 24 The thin heads of
grain swallowed the seven plump ones. I told
this to the magicians, but no one can tell me
what it means."[l]
25 Then Joseph said to Pharaoh, "Pharaoh's
dreams mean the same thing. God has revealed to Pharaoh what He is about to do.[m]
26 The seven good cows are seven years, and the
seven ripe heads are seven years. The dreams
mean the same thing. 27 The seven thin, ugly
cows that came up after them are seven years,
and the seven worthless, scorched heads of
grain are seven years of famine.[n]
28 "It is just as I told Pharaoh: God has shown

[a] 40:20 2Kg 25:27; Jr 52:31; Mt 14:6
[b] 40:23 Ec 9:15-16
[c] 41:1-7 Gn 41:17-23
[d] 41:8 Dn 2:1,3
[e] Ex 7:11,22; Dn 1:20; 2:2
[f] 41:13 Gn 40:1-22
[g] 41:14 Ps 105:20
[h] Dn 2:25
[i] 41:15 Dn 5:16
[j] 41:16 Dn 2:30
[k] Gn 40:8; Dn 2:22,28,47
[l] 41:24 Is 8:19; Dn 4:7
[m] 41:25 Dn 2:28-29,45; Rv 4:1
[n] 41:27 2Kg 8:1

A 40:19 Or *and impale you on a pole* B 40:19 Lit *eat your flesh from upon you* C 40:22 Or *impaled* D 41:16 Or *"God will answer Pharaoh with peace of mind."*

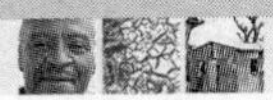

Pharaoh what He is about to do. 29 Seven[A] years
of great abundance are coming throughout
the land of Egypt. 30 After them, seven years of
famine will take place, and all the abundance
in the land of Egypt will be forgotten. The
famine will devastate the land.[a] 31 The abundance in the land will not be remembered
because of the famine that follows it, for the
famine will be very severe. 32 Since the dream
was given twice to Pharaoh, it means that the
matter has been determined by God, and He
will carry it out soon.
33 "So now, let Pharaoh look for a discerning
and wise man and set him over the land of
Egypt. 34 Let Pharaoh do this: Let him appoint
overseers over the land and take a fifth of the
harvest of the land of Egypt during the seven
years of abundance. 35 Let them gather all the
excess food during these good years that are
coming. Under Pharaoh's authority, store
the grain in the cities, so they may preserve
it as food. 36 The food will be a reserve for the
land during the seven years of famine that
will take place in the land of Egypt. Then the
country will not be wiped out by the famine."

Joseph Exalted

37 The proposal pleased Pharaoh and all his
servants. 38 Then Pharaoh said to his servants,
"Can we find anyone like this, a man who has
God's spirit[B] in him?"[b] 39 So Pharaoh said to
Joseph, "Since God has made all this known to
you, there is no one as intelligent and wise as
you are. 40 You will be over my house, and all
my people will obey your commands.[C,c] Only
with regard to the throne will I be greater
than you." 41 Pharaoh also said to Joseph, "See,
I am placing you over all the land of Egypt."
42 Pharaoh removed his signet ring from his
hand and put it on Joseph's hand, clothed
him with fine linen garments, and placed
a gold chain around his neck.[d] 43 He had Joseph ride in his second chariot, and servants
called out before him, *"Abrek!"*[D] So he placed
him over all the land of Egypt. 44 Pharaoh said
to Joseph, "I am Pharaoh, but no one will be
able to raise his hand or foot in all the land of
Egypt without your permission." 45 Pharaoh
gave Joseph the name Zaphenath-paneah and
gave him a wife, Asenath daughter of Potiphera, priest at On.[E] And Joseph went throughout[F] the land of Egypt.

Joseph's Administration

46 Joseph was 30 years old when he entered
the service of Pharaoh king of Egypt. Joseph
left Pharaoh's presence and traveled throughout the land of Egypt.
47 During the seven years of abundance the
land produced outstanding harvests. 48 Joseph gathered all the excess food in the land
of Egypt during the seven years and put it in
the cities. He put the food in every city from
the fields around it. 49 So Joseph stored up
grain in such abundance—like the sand of
the sea—that he stopped measuring it because it was beyond measure.
50 Two sons were born to Joseph before
the years of famine arrived.[e] Asenath daughter of Potiphera, priest at On,[E] bore them to
him. 51 Joseph named the firstborn Manasseh, meaning, "God has made me forget all
my hardship in my father's house." 52 And the
second son he named Ephraim, meaning,
"God has made me fruitful in the land of my
affliction."
53 Then the seven years of abundance in
the land of Egypt came to an end, 54 and the
seven years of famine began, just as Joseph
had said. There was famine in every country,
but throughout the land of Egypt there was
food. 55 Extreme hunger came to all the land
of Egypt, and the people cried out to Pharaoh
for food. Pharaoh told all Egypt, "Go to Joseph and do whatever he tells you." 56 Because
the famine had spread across the whole country, Joseph opened up all the storehouses and
sold grain to the Egyptians, for the famine
was severe in the land of Egypt. 57 Every nation
came to Joseph in Egypt to buy grain, for the
famine was severe in every land.[f]

Joseph's Brothers in Egypt

42 When Jacob learned that there was
grain in Egypt,[g] he said to his sons,
"Why do you keep looking at each other?
2 Listen," he went on, "I have heard there is
grain in Egypt. Go down there and buy some

[a] **41:30** Gn 41:54,56; 47:13; Ps 105:16
[b] **41:38** Jb 32:8; Dn 4:8,9,18; 5:11,14
[c] **41:40** Ps 105:21; Ac 7:10
[d] **41:42** Est 3:10; 8:2; Dn 5:7,16,29
[e] **41:50** Gn 46:20; 48:5
[f] **41:57** Gn 12:10
[g] **42:1** Ac 7:12

[A] **41:29** Lit *Look! Seven* [B] **41:38** Or *the spirit of the gods*, or *a god's spirit* [C] **41:40** Lit *will kiss your mouth* [D] **41:43** Perhaps an Egyptian word meaning "Attention" or a Hb word meaning "Kneel." [E] **41:45,50** Or *Heliopolis* [F] **41:45** Or *Joseph gained authority over* for us so that we will live and not die."[a] 3So 10 of Joseph's brothers went down to buy grain from Egypt. 4But Jacob did not send Joseph's brother Benjamin with his brothers, for he thought, "Something might happen to him."

5The sons of Israel were among those who came to buy grain, for the famine was in the land of Canaan. 6Joseph was in charge of the country; he sold grain to all its people. His brothers came and bowed down before him with their faces to the ground.[b] 7When Joseph saw his brothers, he recognized them, but he treated them like strangers and spoke harshly to them.

"Where do you come from?" he asked.

"From the land of Canaan to buy food," they replied.

8Although Joseph recognized his brothers, they did not recognize him. 9Joseph remembered his dreams about them[c] and said to them, "You are spies. You have come to see the weakness[A] of the land."

10"No, my lord. Your servants have come to buy food," they said. 11"We are all sons of one man. We are honest; your servants are not spies."

12"No," he said to them. "You have come to see the weakness of the land."

13But they replied, "We, your servants, were 12 brothers, the sons of one man in the land of Canaan. The youngest is now[B] with our father, and one is no longer living."

14Then Joseph said to them, "I have spoken:[C] 'You are spies!' 15This is how you will be tested: As surely as Pharaoh lives, you will not leave this place unless your youngest brother comes here. 16Send one from among you to get your brother. The rest of you will be imprisoned so that your words can be tested to see if they are true. If they are not, then as surely as Pharaoh lives, you are spies!" 17So Joseph imprisoned them together for three days.

18On the third day Joseph said to them, "I *fear God[d]—do this and you will live. 19If you are honest, let one of you[D] be confined to the guardhouse, while the rest of you go and take grain to relieve the hunger of your households. 20Bring your youngest brother to me so that your words can be confirmed; then you won't die." And they consented to this.

21Then they said to each other, "Obviously, we are being punished for what we did to our brother. We saw his deep distress when he pleaded with us, but we would not listen. That is why this trouble has come to us."[e]

22But Reuben replied: "Didn't I tell you not to harm the boy?[f] But you wouldn't listen. Now we must account for his blood!"[E]

23They did not realize that Joseph understood them, since there was an interpreter between them. 24He turned away from them and wept. Then he turned back and spoke to them. He took Simeon from them and had him bound before their eyes. 25Joseph then gave orders to fill their containers with grain, return each man's money to his sack, and give them provisions for their journey. This order was carried out. 26They loaded the grain on their donkeys and left there.

The Brothers Return Home

27At the place where they lodged for the night, one of them opened his sack to get feed for his donkey, and he saw his money there at the top of the bag. 28He said to his brothers, "My money has been returned! It's here in my bag." Their hearts sank. Trembling, they turned to one another and said, "What is this that God has done to us?"

29When they reached their father Jacob in the land of Canaan, they told him all that had happened to them: 30"The man who is the lord of the country spoke harshly to us and accused us of spying on the country. 31But we told him: We are honest and not spies. 32We were 12 brothers, sons of the same[F] father. One is no longer living, and the youngest is now[B] with our father in the land of Canaan. 33The man who is the lord of the country said to us, 'This is how I will know if you are honest: Leave one brother with me, take food to relieve the hunger of your households, and go. 34Bring back your youngest brother to me, and I will know that you are not spies but honest men. I will then give your brother back to you, and you can trade in the country.'"

[a] **42:2** Gn 43:8
[b] **42:6** Gn 37:7-10; 41:43; Is 60:14
[c] **42:9** Gn 37:5-11
[d] **42:18** Gn 39:9; Lv 25:43; Neh 5:15
[e] **42:21** Gn 37:26-28
[f] **42:22** Gn 37:22

[A] **42:9** Lit *nakedness* [B] **42:13,32** Or *today* [C] **42:14** Lit *"That which I spoke to you saying* [D] **42:19** Lit *your brothers* [E] **42:22** Lit *Even his blood is being sought* [F] **42:32** Lit *of our*

35As they began emptying their sacks, there
in each man's sack was his bag of money!
When they and their father saw their bags of
money, they were afraid.
36Their father Jacob said to them, "You have
deprived me of my sons. Joseph is gone and
Simeon is gone. Now you want to take Benjamin. Everything happens to me!"
37Then Reuben said to his father, "You can
kill my two sons if I don't bring him back to
you. Put him in my care,[A] and I will return
him to you."
38But Jacob answered, "My son will not go
down with you, for his brother is dead and
he alone is left.[a] If anything happens to him
on your journey, you will bring my gray hairs
down to ·Sheol in sorrow."[b]

Decision to Return to Egypt

43 Now the famine in the land was severe.[c] 2When they had used up the
grain they had brought back from Egypt,
their father said to them, "Go back and buy
us some food."
3But Judah said to him, "The man specifically warned us: 'You will not see me again
unless your brother is with you.' 4If you will
send our brother with us, we will go down
and buy food for you. 5But if you will not
send him, we will not go, for the man said
to us, 'You will not see me again unless your
brother is with you.'"[d]
6"Why did you cause me so much trouble?"
Israel asked. "Why did you tell the man that
you had another brother?"
7They answered, "The man kept asking
about us and our family: 'Is your father still
alive? Do you have another brother?' And
we answered him accordingly. How could we
know that he would say, 'Bring your brother
here'?"
8Then Judah said to his father Israel, "Send
the boy with me. We will be on our way so
that we may live and not die—neither we,
nor you, nor our children. 9I will be responsible for him. You can hold me personally accountable![B] If I do not bring him back to you
and set him before you, I will be ·guilty before
you forever.[e] 10If we had not wasted time, we
could have come back twice by now."

[a]**42:38** Gn 37:33-34; 42:13; 44:27-28 [b]Gn 44:29 [c]**43:1** Gn 12:10; 41:56-57; 47:20 [d]**43:5** Gn 42:18-20; 44:23 [e]**43:9** Gn 42:37; 44:32 [f]**43:11** Gn 37:25; Jr 8:22; Ezk 27:17 [g]**43:14** Gn 42:36 [h]**43:21** Gn 42:27,35 [i]**43:24** Gn 18:4; 19:2; 24:32

11Then their father Israel said to them, "If it
must be so, then do this: Put some of the best
products of the land in your packs and take
them down to the man as a gift—some balsam and some honey, aromatic gum and resin,
pistachios and almonds.[f] 12Take twice as much
money with you. Return the money that was
returned to you in the top of your bags. Perhaps it was a mistake. 13Take your brother also,
and go back at once to the man. 14May ·God Almighty cause the man to be merciful to you
so that he will release your other brother and
Benjamin to you. As for me, if I am deprived of
my sons, then I am deprived."[g]

The Return to Egypt

15The men took this gift, double the amount
of money, and Benjamin. They made their
way down to Egypt and stood before Joseph.
16When Joseph saw Benjamin with them,
he said to his steward,[C] "Take the men to my
house. Slaughter an animal and prepare it,
for they will eat with me at noon." 17The man
did as Joseph had said and brought them to
Joseph's house.
18But the men were afraid because they
were taken to Joseph's house. They said, "We
have been brought here because of the money
that was returned in our bags the first time.
They intend to overpower us, seize us, make
us slaves, and take our donkeys." 19So they approached Joseph's steward[D] and spoke to him
at the doorway of the house.
20They said, "Sir, we really did come down
here the first time only to buy food. 21When
we came to the place where we lodged for
the night and opened our bags of grain, each
one's money was at the top of his bag![h] It was
the full amount of our money, and we have
brought it back with us. 22We have brought
additional money with us to buy food. We
don't know who put our money in the bags."
23Then the steward said, "May you be well.
Don't be afraid. Your God and the God of your
father must have put treasure in your bags.
I received your money." Then he brought
Simeon out to them. 24The steward brought
the men into Joseph's house, gave them water to wash their feet,[i] and got feed for their
donkeys. 25Since the men had heard that they

[A]**42:37** Lit *hand* [B]**43:9** Lit *can seek him from my hand* [C]**43:16** Lit *to the one who was over his house* [D]**43:19** Lit *approached the one who was over the house* were going to eat a meal there, they prepared their gift for Joseph's arrival at noon. 26When Joseph came home, they brought him the gift they had carried into the house, and they bowed to the ground before him.

27He asked if they were well, and he said, "How is your elderly father that you told me about? Is he still alive?"

28They answered, "Your servant our father is well. He is still alive." And they bowed down to honor him.

29When he looked up and saw his brother Benjamin, his mother's son, he asked, "Is this your youngest brother that you told me about?" Then he said, "May God be gracious to you, my son." 30Joseph hurried out because he was overcome with emotion for his brother, and he was about to weep. He went into an inner room to weep. 31Then he washed his face and came out. Regaining his composure,[a] he said, "Serve the meal."

32They served him by himself, his brothers by themselves, and the Egyptians who were eating with him by themselves, because Egyptians could not eat with Hebrews, since that is abhorrent to them.[b] 33They were seated before him in order by age, from the firstborn to the youngest. The men looked at each other in astonishment. 34Portions were served to them from Joseph's table, and Benjamin's portion was five times larger than any of theirs.[c] They drank, and they got intoxicated with Joseph.

Joseph's Final Test

44 Then Joseph commanded his steward: "Fill the men's bags with as much food as they can carry, and put each one's money at the top of his bag.[d] 2Put my cup, the silver one, at the top of the youngest one's bag, along with his grain money." So he did as Joseph told him.

3At morning light, the men were sent off with their donkeys. 4They had not gone very far from the city when Joseph said to his steward, "Get up. Pursue the men, and when you overtake them, say to them, 'Why have you repaid evil for good?[A] 5Isn't this the cup that my master drinks from and uses for *divination?[e] What you have done is wrong!'"

6When he overtook them, he said these words to them. 7They said to him, "Why does my lord say these things? Your servants could not possibly do such a thing. 8We even brought back to you from the land of Canaan the money we found at the top of our bags. How could we steal gold and silver from your master's house? 9If any of us is[B] found to have it, he must die, and we also will become my lord's slaves."[f]

10The steward replied, "What you have said is right, but only the one who is found to have it will be my slave, and the rest of you will be blameless."

11So each one quickly lowered his sack to the ground and opened it. 12The steward searched, beginning with the oldest and ending with the youngest, and the cup was found in Benjamin's sack. 13Then they tore their clothes,[g] and each one loaded his donkey and returned to the city.

14When Judah and his brothers reached Joseph's house, he was still there. They fell to the ground before him.[h] 15"What is this you have done?" Joseph said to them. "Didn't you know that a man like me could uncover the truth by divination?"

16"What can we say to my lord?" Judah replied. "How can we plead? How can we justify ourselves? God has exposed your servants' iniquity. We are now my lord's slaves — both we and the one in whose possession the cup was found."

17Then Joseph said, "I swear that I will not do this. The man in whose possession the cup was found will be my slave. The rest of you can go in peace to your father."

Judah's Plea for Benjamin

18But Judah approached him and said, "Sir, please let your servant speak personally to my lord.[C] Do not be angry with your servant, for you are like Pharaoh.[i] 19My lord asked his servants, 'Do you have a father or a brother?' 20and we answered my lord, 'We have an elderly father and a younger brother, the child of his old age.[j] The boy's brother is dead. He is the only one of his mother's sons left, and his father loves him.' 21Then you said to your servants, 'Bring him to me so that I can see

[a]**43:31** Gn 45:1
[b]**43:32** Gn 46:34; Ex 8:26
[c]**43:34** Gn 35:24; 45:22
[d]**44:1** Gn 42:25
[e]**44:5** Gn 30:27; 44:15; Lv 19:26; Dt 18:10-14
[f]**44:9** Gn 31:32
[g]**44:13** Gn 37:29
[h]**44:14** Gn 37:7-10; 42:6; 43:26-28
[i]**44:18** Gn 37:7-8; 41:40-44
[j]**44:20** Gn 37:3; 43:8; 44:30

[A]**44:4** LXX adds *Why have you stolen my silver cup?* [B]**44:9** Lit *If your servants are* [C]**44:18** Lit *speak a word in my lord's ears* him.'[a] 22 But we said to my lord, 'The boy cannot leave his father. If he were to leave, his father would die.' 23 Then you said to your servants, 'If your younger brother does not come down with you, you will not see me again.'[b]

24 "This is what happened when we went back to your servant my father: We reported your words to him. 25 But our father said, 'Go again, and buy us some food.'[c] 26 We told him, 'We cannot go down unless our younger brother goes with us. So if our younger brother isn't with us, we cannot see the man.' 27 Your servant my father said to us, 'You know that my wife bore me two sons. 28 One left — I said that he must have been torn to pieces — and I have never seen him again.[d] 29 If you also take this one from me and anything happens to him, you will bring my gray hairs down to ˚Sheol in sorrow.'[e]

30 "So if I come to your servant my father and the boy is not with us — his life is wrapped up with the boy's life — 31 when he sees that the boy is not with us, he will die. Then your servants will have brought the gray hairs of your servant our father down to Sheol in sorrow. 32 Your servant became accountable to my father for the boy, saying, 'If I do not return him to you, I will always bear the ˚guilt for sinning against you, my father.'[f] 33 Now please let your servant remain here as my lord's slave, in place of the boy. Let him go back with his brothers. 34 For how can I go back to my father without the boy? I could not bear to see the grief that would overwhelm my father."

Joseph Reveals His Identity

45 Joseph could no longer keep his composure in front of all his attendants,[A] so he called out, "Send everyone away from me!" No one was with him when he revealed his identity to his brothers.[g] 2 But he wept so loudly that the Egyptians heard it, and also Pharaoh's household heard it. 3 Joseph said to his brothers, "I am Joseph! Is my father still living?" But they could not answer him because they were terrified in his presence.

4 Then Joseph said to his brothers, "Please, come near me," and they came near. "I am Joseph, your brother," he said, "the one you sold into Egypt.[h] 5 And now don't be worried or angry with yourselves for selling me here, because God sent me ahead of you to preserve life.[i] 6 For the famine has been in the land these two years, and there will be five more years without plowing or harvesting. 7 God sent me ahead of you to establish you as a remnant within the land and to keep you alive by a great deliverance.[B] 8 Therefore it was not you who sent me here, but God. He has made me a father to Pharaoh, lord of his

[a] **44:21** Gn 42:15,20 [b] **44:23** Gn 43:3,5 [c] **44:25** Gn 43:2 [d] **44:28** Gn 37:31-35 [e] **44:29** Gn 42:38 [f] **44:32** Gn 43:9 [g] **45:1** Ac 7:13 [h] **45:4** Gn 37:18-36 [i] **45:5** Gn 45:7-8; 50:20; Ps 105:17

GOD WHO SENDS

"God sent me ahead of you"

The climactic use of the sending in Genesis is seen in Joseph's words to his brothers, "God *sent* me before you" (45:5, author's italics). That Joseph should discern the hand of God in his getting to Egypt was remarkable in light of the ungodly deeds which were the human side of the story. Three times Joseph is explicit in his use of the sending (vv. 5, 7-8). "God sent me before you to preserve life. . . . to preserve for you a remnant on earth," he emphasizes. This passage is profound in its covenantal and salvific implications. There is more than providence here. Joseph's words reach both back to the Abrahamic covenant and forward to the Exodus deliverance. The Hebrew people later corroborated Joseph's conviction that God had sent him to Egypt, and it is not surprising that Hebrew hymnody repeated the sending language in the celebration of God's redemptive leadership in Joseph's life. The sending of Joseph was seen as a prelude to the sending of Moses and Aaron (Ps 105:17,26) and, therefore, of the Exodus. *(DUBOSE, 41–42)*

[A] **45:1** Lit *all those standing about him* [B] **45:7** Or *keep alive for you many survivors*

entire household, and ruler over all the land
of Egypt.
9“Return quickly to my father and say to
him, ‘This is what your son Joseph says: “God
has made me lord of all Egypt. Come down to
me without delay. 10You can settle in the land
of Goshen[a] and be near me — you, your children, and grandchildren, your sheep, cattle,
and all you have. 11There I will sustain you, for
there will be five more years of famine. Otherwise, you, your household, and everything
you have will become destitute.” ’[b] 12Look!
Your eyes and my brother Benjamin’s eyes
can see that it is I, Joseph, who am[A] speaking
to you. 13Tell my father about all my glory in
Egypt and about all you have seen. And bring
my father here quickly.”[c]
14Then Joseph threw his arms around Benjamin and wept, and Benjamin wept on his
shoulder. 15Joseph kissed each of his brothers as he wept,[B] and afterward his brothers
talked with him.

The Return for Jacob

16When the news reached Pharaoh’s palace, “Joseph’s brothers have come,” Pharaoh
and his servants were pleased. 17Pharaoh said
to Joseph, “Tell your brothers, ‘Do this: Load
your animals and go on back to the land of
Canaan. 18Get your father and your families,
and come back to me. I will give you the best
of the land of Egypt, and you can eat from
the richness of the land.’ 19You are also commanded, ‘Do this: Take wagons from the land
of Egypt for your young children and your
wives and bring your father here.[d] 20Do not
be concerned about your belongings, for the
best of all the land of Egypt is yours.’ ”[e]
21The sons of Israel did this. Joseph gave
them wagons as Pharaoh had commanded,
and he gave them provisions for the journey.
22He gave each of the brothers changes of
clothes,[f] but he gave Benjamin 300 pieces of
silver and five changes of clothes.[g] 23He sent
his father the following: 10 donkeys carrying
the best products of Egypt and 10 female donkeys carrying grain, food, and provisions for
his father on the journey. 24So Joseph sent his
brothers on their way, and as they were leaving, he said to them, “Don’t argue on the way.”

[a]**45:10** Gn 46:34; 47:1,4,6,11,27; 50:8; Ex 8:22; Jos 10:41
[b]**45:11** Gn 47:12; 50:21
[c]**45:13** Ac 7:14
[d]**45:19** Gn 46:5
[e]**45:20** Dt 32:9-14
[f]**45:22** 2Kg 5:5
[g]Gn 43:34
[h]**46:1** Gn 21:14; 28:10; Jos 15:28; Jdg 20:1; 2Sm 24:7; 1Kg 19:3
[i]**46:2** Gn 15:1; Jb 33:14-15
[j]**46:3** Gn 12:2; 15:13-14; 35:11; Ex 1:7,9; Dt 26:5
[k]**46:4** Gn 15:16; 28:15; 48:21; 50:24; Ex 3:8
[l]Gn 50:1
[m]**46:5** Gn 45:19,21
[n]**46:6** Dt 26:5; Jos 24:4; Ps 105:23; Is 52:4; Ac 7:15
[o]**46:8-27** Ex 1:1-5; Nm 26:4-5
[p]**46:9** Ex 6:14
[q]**46:10** Ex 6:15
[r]**46:11** Ex 6:16; 1Ch 6:16

25So they went up from Egypt and came
to their father Jacob in the land of Canaan.
26They said, “Joseph is still alive, and he is
ruler over all the land of Egypt!” Jacob was
stunned,[C] for he did not believe them. 27But
when they told Jacob all that Joseph had said
to them, and when he saw the wagons that Joseph had sent to transport him, the spirit of
their father Jacob revived.
28Then Israel said, “Enough! My son Joseph
is still alive. I will go to see him before I die.”

Jacob Leaves for Egypt

46 Israel set out with all that he had and
came to Beer-sheba,[h] and he offered
sacrifices to the God of his father Isaac. 2That
night God spoke to Israel in a vision:[i] “Jacob,
Jacob!” He said.
And Jacob replied, “Here I am.”
3God said, “I am God, the God of your father. Do not be afraid to go down to Egypt, for
I will make you into a great nation there.[j] 4I
will go down with you to Egypt, and I will also
bring you back.[k] Joseph will put his hands on
your eyes.”[D,l]
5Jacob left Beer-sheba. The sons of Israel
took their father Jacob in the wagons Pharaoh
had sent to carry him,[m] along with their children and their wives. 6They also took their cattle and possessions they had acquired in the
land of Canaan. Then Jacob and all his children went with him to Egypt.[n] 7His sons and
grandsons, his daughters and granddaugh-
ters, indeed all his ˙offspring, he brought with
him to Egypt.

Jacob’s Family

8These are the names of the Israelites, Jacob
and his sons, who went to Egypt:[o]

Jacob’s firstborn: Reuben.
9 Reuben’s sons:[p] Hanoch, Pallu, Hezron,
and Carmi.
10 Simeon’s sons:[q] Jemuel, Jamin, Ohad,
Jachin, Zohar, and Shaul, the son
of a Canaanite woman.
11 Levi’s sons:[r] Gershon, Kohath,
and Merari.
12 Judah’s sons: Er, Onan, Shelah, Perez,
and Zerah; but Er and Onan died
in the land of Canaan.

[A]**45:12** Lit *that my mouth is* [B]**45:15** Lit *brothers, and he wept over them* [C]**45:26** Lit *Jacob’s heart was numb* [D]**46:4** = Joseph will close your eyes after you die

Perez's sons:[a] Hezron and Hamul.
13 Issachar's sons:[b] Tola, Puvah,[A] Jashub,[B]
and Shimron.
14 Zebulun's sons: Sered, Elon, and Jahleel.
15 These were Leah's sons born
to Jacob in Paddan-aram,
as well as his daughter Dinah.
The total number of persons:[C] 33.
16 Gad's sons: Ziphion, Haggi, Shuni,
Ezbon, Eri, Arodi, and Areli.
17 Asher's sons:[c] Imnah, Ishvah, Ishvi,
Beriah, and their sister Serah.
Beriah's sons were Heber and Malchiel.
18 These were the sons
of Zilpah — whom Laban gave
to his daughter Leah — that she bore
to Jacob: 16 persons.
19 The sons of Jacob's wife Rachel:
Joseph and Benjamin.
20 Manasseh and Ephraim were born
to Joseph in the land of Egypt.
They were born to him by Asenath
daughter of Potiphera, a priest at On.[D]
21 Benjamin's sons:[d] Bela, Becher, Ashbel,
Gera, Naaman, Ehi, Rosh, Muppim,
Huppim, and Ard.
22 These were Rachel's sons
who were born to Jacob: 14 persons.
23 Dan's son:[E] Hushim.
24 Naphtali's sons:[e] Jahzeel, Guni, Jezer,
and Shillem.
25 These were the sons of Bilhah,
whom Laban gave to his daughter
Rachel.[f] She bore to Jacob:
seven persons.
26 The total number of persons
belonging to Jacob —
his direct descendants,[F] not including
the wives of Jacob's sons —
who came to Egypt: 66.
27 And Joseph's sons who were born
to him in Egypt: two persons.
All those of Jacob's household
who had come to Egypt: 70[G] persons.[g]

Jacob Arrives in Egypt

28 Now Jacob had sent Judah ahead of him
to Joseph to prepare for his arrival[H] at Goshen.[h] When they came to the land of Goshen,
29 Joseph hitched the horses to his chariot and
went up to Goshen to meet his father Israel.
Joseph presented himself to him, threw his
arms around him, and wept for a long time.[i]
30 Then Israel said to Joseph, "At last I can
die, now that I have seen your face and know
you are still alive!"
31 Joseph said to his brothers and to his father's household, "I will go up and inform
Pharaoh, telling him: My brothers and my
father's household, who were in the land of
Canaan, have come to me.[j] 32 The men are
shepherds; they also raise livestock. They
have brought their sheep and cattle and all
that they have. 33 When Pharaoh addresses
you and asks, 'What is your occupation?'
34 you are to say, 'Your servants, both we and
our fathers, have raised livestock[I] from our
youth until now.' Then you will be allowed
to settle in the land of Goshen, since all shepherds are abhorrent to Egyptians."[k]

Pharaoh Welcomes Jacob

47 So Joseph went and informed Pharaoh:
"My father and my brothers, with their
sheep and cattle and all that they own, have
come from the land of Canaan and are now
in the land of Goshen."[l]
2 He took five of his brothers and presented
them before Pharaoh.[m] 3 Then Pharaoh asked
his brothers, "What is your occupation?"
And they said to Pharaoh, "Your servants,
both we and our fathers, are shepherds."[n]
4 Then they said to Pharaoh, "We have come
to live in the land for a while because there
is no grazing land for your servants' sheep,
since the famine in the land of Canaan has
been severe.[o] So now, please let your servants
settle in the land of Goshen."
5 Then Pharaoh said to Joseph, "Now that
your father and brothers have come to you,
6 the land of Egypt is open before you; settle
your father and brothers in the best part of
the land.[p] They can live in the land of Goshen.
If you know of any capable men among them,
put them in charge of my livestock."[q]
7 Joseph then brought his father Jacob and
presented him before Pharaoh, and Jacob

[a] **46:12** Gn 38:29; 1Ch 2:5
[b] **46:13** 1Ch 7:1
[c] **46:17** 1Ch 7:30-31
[d] **46:21** Nm 26:38-40; 1Ch 7:6-12; 8:1
[e] **46:24** 1Ch 7:13
[f] **46:25** Gn 29:29; 30:5-8
[g] **46:27** Ex 1:5; Dt 10:22; Ac 7:14
[h] **46:28** Gn 45:10
[i] **46:29** Gn 45:14
[j] **46:31** Gn 47:1
[k] **46:34** Gn 43:32; Ex 8:26
[l] **47:1** Gn 45:10; 46:28
[m] **47:2** Ac 7:13
[n] **47:3** Gn 46:32-34
[o] **47:4** Gn 15:13; Dt 26:5
[p] **47:6** Gn 45:10,18; 47:11
[q] Ex 18:21,25; 1Kg 11:28; Pr 22:29

[A] **46:13** Sam, Syr read *Puah*; 1Ch 7:1 [B] **46:13** Sam, LXX; MT reads *Iob* [C] **46:15** Lit *All persons his sons and his daughters* [D] **46:20** Or *Heliopolis* [E] **46:23** Alt Hb tradition reads *sons* [F] **46:26** Lit *Jacob who came out from his loins* [G] **46:27** LXX reads *75*; Ac 7:14 [H] **46:28** Lit *to give directions before him* [I] **46:34** Lit *fathers, are men of livestock* blessed Pharaoh. 8 Then Pharaoh said to Jacob, "How many years have you lived?"[A]

9 Jacob said to Pharaoh, "My pilgrimage[a] has lasted 130 years. My years have been few and hard,[b] and they have not surpassed the years of my fathers during their pilgrimages."[c] 10 So Jacob blessed Pharaoh and departed from Pharaoh's presence.

11 Then Joseph settled his father and brothers in the land of Egypt and gave them property in the best part of the land, the land of Rameses,[d] as Pharaoh had commanded. 12 And Joseph provided his father, his brothers, and all his father's household with food for their dependents.[e]

The Land Becomes Pharaoh's

13 But there was no food in that entire region, for the famine was very severe. The land of Egypt and the land of Canaan were exhausted by the famine. 14 Joseph collected all the money to be found in the land of Egypt and the land of Canaan in exchange for the grain they were purchasing, and he brought the money to Pharaoh's palace.[f] 15 When the money from the land of Egypt and the land of Canaan was gone, all the Egyptians came to Joseph and said, "Give us food. Why should we die here in front of you? The money is gone!"

16 But Joseph said, "Give me your livestock. Since the money is gone, I will give you food in exchange for your livestock." 17 So they brought their livestock to Joseph, and he gave them food in exchange for the horses, the herds of sheep, the herds of cattle, and the donkeys. That year he provided them with food in exchange for all their livestock.

18 When that year was over, they came the next year and said to him, "We cannot hide from our lord that the money is gone and that all our livestock belongs to our lord. There is nothing left for our lord except our bodies and our land. 19 Why should we die here in front of you — both us and our land? Buy us and our land in exchange for food. Then we with our land will become Pharaoh's slaves. Give us seed so that we can live and not die, and so that the land won't become desolate."

[a]**47:9** 1Ch 29:15; Ps 39:12; 119:19,54; Heb 11:9,13
[b]Jb 14:1; Ps 39:4-5; Jms 4:14
[c]Gn 11:32; 25:7; 35:28
[d]**47:11** Gn 45:10; Ex 1:11; 12:37
[e]**47:12** Gn 45:11; 50:21
[f]**47:14** Gn 41:56
[g]**47:24** Gn 41:34
[h]**47:27** Gn 17:6; 26:4; 35:11; Ex 1:7; Dt 26:5; Ac 7:17
[i]**47:29** Dt 31:14; 1Kg 2:1
[j]Gn 24:2
[k]Gn 24:49
[l]**47:30** Gn 23:17-20; 25:9-10; 35:29; 49:29-32; 50:5,13; Ac 7:15-16
[m]**47:31** Gn 48:2; 1Kg 1:47; Heb 11:21

20 In this way, Joseph acquired all the land in Egypt for Pharaoh, because every Egyptian sold his field since the famine was so severe for them. The land became Pharaoh's, 21 and Joseph moved the people to the cities[B] from one end of Egypt to the other. 22 The only land he didn't acquire was the priests' portion, for it was given to them by Pharaoh. They lived off[C] the rations Pharaoh had given them; therefore they did not sell their land.

23 Then Joseph said to the people, "Understand today that I have acquired you and your land for Pharaoh. Here is seed for you. Sow it in the land. 24 At harvest, you are to give a fifth of it to Pharaoh,[g] and four-fifths will be yours as seed for the field and as food for yourselves, your households, and your dependents."

25 And they said, "You have saved our lives. We have found favor in our lord's eyes and will be Pharaoh's slaves." 26 So Joseph made it a law, still in effect today in the land of Egypt, that a fifth of the produce belongs to Pharaoh. Only the priests' land does not belong to Pharaoh.

Israel Settles in Goshen

27 Israel settled in the land of Egypt, in the region of Goshen. They acquired property in it and became fruitful and very numerous.[h] 28 Now Jacob lived in the land of Egypt 17 years, and his life span was 147 years. 29 When the time drew near for him to die,[i] he called his son Joseph and said to him, "If I have found favor in your eyes, put your hand under my thigh[j] and promise me that you will deal with me in kindness and faithfulness.[k] Do not bury me in Egypt. 30 When I rest with my fathers, carry me away from Egypt and bury me in their burial place."[l]

Joseph answered, "I will do what you have asked."

31 And Jacob said, "Swear to me." So Joseph swore to him. Then Israel bowed in thanks at the head of his bed.[D,m]

Jacob Blesses Ephraim and Manasseh

48 Some time after this, Joseph was told, "Your father is weaker." So he set out with his two sons, Manasseh and Ephraim.

[A]**47:8** Lit *many are the days of the years* [B]**47:21** Sam, LXX, Vg read *and he made the people servants* [C]**47:22** Lit *They ate* [D]**47:31** Or *Israel worshiped while leaning on the top of his staff*

2When Jacob was told, "Your son Joseph has
come to you," Israel summoned his strength
and sat up in bed.
3Jacob said to Joseph, "God Almighty[a] appeared to me at Luz[b] in the land of Canaan
and blessed me. 4He said to me, 'I will make
you fruitful and numerous; I will make many
nations come from you, and I will give this
land as an eternal possession[c] to your future
descendants.'[d] 5Your two sons[e] born to you
in the land of Egypt before I came to you in
Egypt are now mine.[f] Ephraim and Manasseh belong to me just as Reuben and Simeon
do. 6Children born to you after them will be
yours and will be recorded under the names
of their brothers with regard to their inheritance. 7When I was returning from Paddan,
to my sorrow Rachel died along the way,[g]
some distance from Ephrath in the land of
Canaan. I buried her there along the way to
Ephrath," (that is, Bethlehem).
8When Israel saw Joseph's sons, he said,
"Who are these?"
9And Joseph said to his father, "They are my
sons God has given me here."
So Jacob said, "Bring them to me and I will
bless them."[h] 10Now his eyesight was poor because of old age; he could hardly[A] see.[i] Joseph
brought them to him, and he kissed and embraced them.[j] 11Israel said to Joseph, "I never
expected to see your face again, but now God
has even let me see your offspring." 12Then
Joseph took them from his father's knees and
bowed with his face to the ground.[k]

Ephraim's Greater Blessing

13Then Joseph took them both — with his
right hand Ephraim toward Israel's left, and
with his left hand Manasseh toward Israel's
right — and brought them to Israel. 14But Israel stretched out his right hand and put it
on the head of Ephraim, the younger, and
crossing his hands, put his left on Manasseh's
head, although Manasseh was the firstborn.[l]
15Then he blessed Joseph and said:

The God before whom my fathers
  Abraham and Isaac walked,[m]
the God who has been my shepherd[n]
  all my life to this day,
16 the Angel who has redeemed me
  from all harm[o] —
may He bless these boys.
And may they be called by my name
and the names of my fathers Abraham
  and Isaac,[p]
and may they grow to be numerous
  within the land.

17When Joseph saw that his father had
placed his right hand on Ephraim's head,
he thought it was a mistake[B] and took his father's hand to move it from Ephraim's head
to Manasseh's. 18Joseph said to his father, "Not
that way, my father! This one is the firstborn.
Put your right hand on his head."
19But his father refused and said, "I know,
my son, I know! He too will become a tribe,[C]
and he too will be great; nevertheless, his
younger brother will be greater than he, and
his offspring will become a populous nation."[D] 20So he blessed them that day with
these words:

The nation Israel will invoke blessings
  by you, saying,
"May God make you like Ephraim
  and Manasseh,"
putting Ephraim before Manasseh.

21Then Israel said to Joseph, "Look, I am
about to die, but God will be with you and
will bring you back to the land of your fathers.[q] 22Over and above what I am giving
your brothers, I am giving you the one mountain slope[E] that I took from the hand of the
Amorites with my sword and bow."[r]

Jacob's Last Words

49 Then Jacob called his sons and said,
"Gather around, and I will tell you
what will happen to you in the days to come.[F,s]

2 Come together and listen,
  sons of Jacob;
listen to your father Israel:

3 Reuben, you are my firstborn,[t]
my strength and the firstfruits
  of my virility,[u]
excelling in prominence,
  excelling in power.

[a]**48:3** Gn 17:1 [b]Gn 28:13,19; 35:6,9 [c]**48:4** Gn 17:8 [d]Gn 35:9-12 [e]**48:5** Gn 41:50-52; 46:20 [f]Jos 13:7; 14:4; 17:17 [g]**48:7** Gn 35:9-19 [h]**48:9** Gn 27:4; 49:25-26; Heb 11:21 [i]**48:10** Gn 27:1 [j]Gn 27:27 [k]**48:12** Gn 18:2; 24:52; 33:3; 42:6; 43:26; Ex 34:8 [l]**48:14** Gn 25:23; 27:18-30 [m]**48:15** Gn 17:1; 24:40 [n]Gn 49:24; Ps 23:1; Jr 31:10 [o]**48:16** Gn 28:13-15; 31:11; Is 63:9; Ac 7:35 [p]Dt 28:10; 2Ch 7:14; Is 4:1; 43:1; 48:1 [q]**48:21** Gn 46:4; 50:24 [r]**48:22** Gn 34:25-29; Jos 24:32; Jn 4:5 [s]**49:1** Nm 24:14; Dt 4:30; 31:29; Is 2:2; Jr 23:20; Dn 2:28; 10:14; Hs 3:5 [t]**49:3** Gn 29:32 [u]Dt 21:17

[A]**48:10** Lit *he was not able to in his eyes* [B]**48:17** Or *he was displeased*; lit *head, it was bad* [C]**48:19** Lit *people* [D]**48:19** Or *a multitude of nations*; lit *a fullness of nations* [E]**48:22** Or *Shechem*, Joseph's burial place; lit *one shoulder* [F]**49:1** Or *in the last days*

4 Turbulent as water, you will
no longer excel,
because you got into your father's bed[a]
and you defiled it — he[A] got
into my bed.
5 Simeon and Levi are brothers;
their knives are vicious weapons.[b]
6 May I never enter their council;
may I never join their assembly.
For in their anger they kill men,
and on a whim they hamstring oxen.
7 Their anger is cursed, for it is strong,
and their fury, for it is cruel!
I will disperse them throughout Jacob
and scatter them throughout Israel.[c]
8 Judah, your brothers will praise you.[d]
Your hand will be on the necks
of your enemies;
your father's sons will bow down
to you.[e]
9 Judah is a young lion[f] —
my son, you return from the kill.
He crouches; he lies down like a lion
or a lioness — who dares to rouse him?
10 The scepter will not depart from Judah
or the staff from between his feet
until He whose right it is comes[B,g]
and the obedience of the peoples
belongs to Him.[h]
11 He ties his donkey to a vine,
and the colt of his donkey
to the choice vine.
He washes his clothes in wine
and his robes in the blood of grapes.
12 His eyes are darker than wine,
and his teeth are whiter than milk.
13 Zebulun will live by the seashore
and will be a harbor for ships,
and his territory will be next to Sidon.[i]
14 Issachar is a strong donkey
lying down between the saddlebags.[C]
15 He saw that his resting place was good
and that the land was pleasant,
so he leaned his shoulder to bear a load
and became a forced laborer.[j]
16 Dan will judge his people[k]
as one of the tribes of Israel.

[a]**49:4** Gn 35:22 [b]**49:5** Gn 34:25,30 [c]**49:7** Ex 32:28; Nm 3:5-13; Dt 33:10; Jos 19:1-9; 1Ch 4:24-39; 2Ch 34:6; Neh 11:25-28 [d]**49:8** Gn 29:35 [e]Gn 27:29; 1Ch 5:2 [f]**49:9** Nm 24:9; Ezk 19:5-7; Mc 5:8; Rv 5:5 [g]**49:10** Nm 2:9; 10:14; 24:17; Jdg 1:1-2; Ps 60:7; 108:8; Ezk 21:27 [h]Ps 2:6-9; 72:8-11; Is 42:1,4; 49:6 [i]**49:13** Dt 33:19; Jos 19:10-16 [j]**49:15** Jdg 5:15-16 [k]**49:16** Dt 33:22; Jdg 13:2,25; 18:25-27 [l]**49:19** Dt 33:20; 1Ch 5:18-22; Jr 49:1 [m]**49:20** Dt 33:24-25; Jos 19:24-31; Jdg 5:17; 1Kg 4:7 [n]**49:21** Jos 19:32-39 [o]**49:24** Gn 31:42; Ps 132:2,5; Is 1:24; 49:26 [p]Gn 48:15; Ps 23:1; Jr 31:10 [q]Ps 118:22; Is 28:16; 1Pt 2:6-8 [r]**49:26** Dt 33:15-16 [s]**49:27** Jdg 5:14; 20:21; 1Sm 14:47-48 [t]**49:29** Gn 25:8

17 He will be a snake by the road,
a viper beside the path,
that bites the horses' heels
so that its rider falls backward.
18 I wait for Your salvation, LORD.
19 Gad will be attacked by raiders,
but he will attack their heels.[l]
20 Asher's[D] food will be rich,
and he will produce royal delicacies.[m]
21 Naphtali is a doe set free
that bears beautiful fawns.[n]
22 Joseph is a fruitful vine,
a fruitful vine beside a spring;
its branches[E] climb over the wall.[F]
23 The archers attacked him,
shot at him, and were hostile
toward him.
24 Yet his bow remained steady,
and his strong[G] arms were made agile
by the hands of the Mighty One of Jacob,[o]
by the name of[H] the Shepherd,[p]
the Rock of Israel,[q]
25 by the God of your father
who helps you,
and by the ·Almighty who blesses you
with blessings of the heavens above,
blessings of the deep that lies below,
and blessings of the breasts
and the womb.
26 The blessings of your father excel
the blessings of my ancestors[I]
and[J] the bounty of the eternal hills.[F,r]
May they rest on the head of Joseph,
on the crown of the prince
of his brothers.
27 Benjamin is a wolf; he tears his prey.
In the morning he devours the prey,
and in the evening he divides
the plunder."[s]

28 These are the tribes of Israel, 12 in all, and
this was what their father said to them. He
blessed them, and he blessed each one with a
suitable blessing.

Jacob's Burial Instructions

29 Then he commanded them: "I am about
to be gathered to my people.[t] Bury me with

[A]**49:4** LXX, Syr, Tg read *you* [B]**49:10** Or *until tribute comes to him*, or *until Shiloh comes*, or *until He comes to Shiloh* [C]**49:14** Or *sheepfolds* [D]**49:19-20** LXX, Syr, Vg; MT reads *their heel.* [20]*From Asher* [E]**49:22** Lit *daughters* [F]**49:22,26** Hb obscure [G]**49:24** Lit *and the hands of his* [H]**49:24** Syr, Tg; MT reads *Jacob, from there* [I]**49:26** Or *of the mountains* [J]**49:26** Lit *to*

my fathers[a] in the cave in the field of Ephron
the Hittite.[b] 30 The cave is in the field of Machpelah near Mamre, in the land of Canaan.
This is the field Abraham purchased from
Ephron the Hittite as a burial site.[c] 31 Abraham
and his wife Sarah are buried there,[d] Isaac
and his wife Rebekah are buried there,[e] and I
buried Leah there.[f] 32 The field and the cave in
it were purchased from the Hittites." 33 When
Jacob had finished instructing his sons, he
drew his feet into the bed and died. He was
gathered to his people.

Jacob's Burial

50 Then Joseph, leaning over his father's
face, wept and kissed him. 2 He commanded his servants who were physicians to
embalm his father. So they embalmed Israel.
3 They took 40 days to complete this, for em-
balming takes that long, and the Egyptians
mourned for him 70 days.[g]
4 When the days of mourning were over, Joseph said to Pharaoh's household, "If I have
found favor with you, please tell[A] Pharaoh
that 5 my father made me take an oath,[h] saying, 'I am about to die. You must bury me
there in the tomb that I made for myself in
the land of Canaan.'[i] Now let me go and bury
my father. Then I will return."
6 So Pharaoh said, "Go and bury your father
in keeping with your oath."
7 Then Joseph went to bury his father, and
all Pharaoh's servants, the elders of his household, and all the elders of the land of Egypt
went with him, 8 along with all Joseph's household, his brothers, and his father's household.
Only their children, their sheep, and their
cattle were left in the land of Goshen. 9 Horses
and chariots went up with him; it was a very
impressive procession. 10 When they reached
the threshing floor of Atad, which is across
the Jordan, they lamented and wept loudly,
and Joseph mourned seven days for his father. 11 When the Canaanite inhabitants of the
land saw the mourning at the threshing floor
of Atad, they said, "This is a solemn mourning on the part of the Egyptians." Therefore
the place is named Abel-mizraim.[B] It is across
the Jordan.
12 So Jacob's sons did for him what he had
commanded them. 13 They carried him to the
land of Canaan and buried him in the cave
at Machpelah in the field near Mamre, which
Abraham had purchased as a burial site from
Ephron the Hittite.[j] 14 After Joseph buried his
father, he returned to Egypt with his brothers and all who had gone with him to bury
his father.

Joseph's Kindness

15 When Joseph's brothers saw that their
father was dead, they said to one another,
"If Joseph is holding a grudge against us, he
will certainly repay us for all the suffering we
caused him."[k]
16 So they sent this message to Joseph, "Before he died your father gave a command:
17 'Say this to Joseph: Please forgive your
brothers' transgression and their sin — the
suffering they caused you.' Therefore, please
forgive the transgression of the servants of
the God of your father." Joseph wept[l] when
their message came to him. 18 Then his brothers also came to him, bowed down before
him, and said, "We are your slaves!"
19 But Joseph said to them, "Don't be afraid.
Am I in the place of God?[m] 20 You planned evil
against me; God planned it for good to bring
about the present result — the survival of
many people.[n] 21 Therefore don't be afraid. I
will take care of you and your little ones."[o] And
he comforted them and spoke kindly to them.[C]

Joseph's Death

22 Joseph and his father's household remained in Egypt. Joseph lived 110 years. 23 He
saw Ephraim's sons to the third generation;[p]
the sons of Manasseh's son Machir were recognized by[D,E] Joseph.[q]
24 Joseph said to his brothers, "I am about to
die,[r] but God will certainly come to your aid
and bring you up from this land to the land
He promised Abraham,[s] Isaac,[t] and Jacob."[u]
25 So Joseph made the sons of Israel take an
oath: "When God comes to your aid, you are
to carry my bones up from here."[v]
26 Joseph died at the age of 110. They embalmed him and placed him in a coffin in
Egypt.

[a] **49:29** Gn 47:30 [b] Gn 23:16-20; 50:13 [c] **49:30** Gn 23:3-20 [d] **49:31** Gn 23:19; 25:9 [e] Gn 35:29 [f] Gn 48:7 [g] **50:3** Gn 50:10; Nm 20:29; Dt 34:8 [h] **50:5** Gn 47:29-31 [i] 2Ch 16:14; Is 22:16; Mt 27:60 [j] **50:13** Gn 23:16-20 [k] **50:15** Gn 37:28; 42:21-22 [l] **50:17** Gn 43:30; 46:29; 50:1 [m] **50:19** Gn 3:5 [n] **50:20** Gn 45:7; Rm 8:28 [o] **50:21** Gn 45:11; 47:12 [p] **50:23** Jb 42:16; Ps 128:6 [q] Gn 30:3 [r] **50:24** Gn 48:21; Ex 3:16-17; Heb 11:22 [s] Gn 13:15-17; 15:7-8 [t] Gn 26:3 [u] Gn 28:13; 35:12 [v] **50:25** Ex 13:19

[A] **50:4** Lit *please speak in the ears of* [B] **50:11** = Mourning of Egypt [C] **50:21** Lit *spoke to their hearts* [D] **50:23** Lit *were born on the knees of* [E] **50:23** Referring to a ritual of adoption or of legitimation; Gn 30:3

AUTHOR: Moses

DATE: Most likely written during Israel's wandering in the wilderness (around 1445–1406 B.C.)

Good intentions have gone bad. Joseph, Jacob's next-to-the-last son, saved his family from starvation by relocating them in Egypt. But years later, the many families who trace their origin to Jacob are trapped in slavery. As tortures grow in Egypt, tension builds. The Hebrews cry out to God.

In this mess, God has a plan. It starts in civil disobedience: a mom hides her forbidden baby boy in a reed basket. Found by royalty, that baby (Moses) grows into a leader of Egypt, serving as pharaoh's chief of staff. His destiny, however, is not power and prestige, but wandering and freedom. Exodus narrates the breakout of the nation chosen to be the people of God, the nation which hears God speak. They alone among the nations will be used to fulfill the divine promise to redeem and save, and step toward it.

EXODUS

Those steps falter, to be sure. The Hebrews' flight from Egypt is anything but quick and easy. Once free of pharaoh's grip, the peoples' doubt, fatigue, and disobedience combine to prolong the journey by an entire generation. Moses dies before reaching the destination.

Yet vital new elements of God's promise show up during this journey. The most revered set of rules in world history are given to these people on a remote mountainside called Sinai. The tablets of ten commands guide the peoples' worship, government, business, and personal relations from then on. No other law document in history has had such widespread and profound influence on human behavior. God spoke with clarity about what obedience and faithfulness require: devote yourself to none other but God, never take His name lightly, only worship Him, and live in humility and respect for each other. These commands tame the wild heart and point the God-adored human toward a future when the promise will show up more real than anyone imagined it could.

In Exodus, the mission of God creates a nation, grants them a homeland, reveals a way to live peaceably, and patiently guides them past each pothole of doubt and terror. Pharaoh's slave masters essentially told the Hebrews, "Make more bricks and with less straw, faster, faster, or else." God, on the contrary, tells the Hebrews to make a land prosper, raise your children in reverent love and trust, and worship the true God, whom they knew by the name, I AM. Do this, and by your life show all people that God is alive, powerful, and—most surprising—God is love. The mission of God is not complete yet, but the message is strong and the Hebrews now know God as guide and protector.

Can they do it? As the great leader Moses bids them farewell, will Hebrew hearts turn again, weighted with fear, confused by setbacks? Will they give up on God or God on them? By the end of Exodus, there's no road except the one that points forward. Move ahead, or lose everything. It is quite like decisions we all face: With God, a future bristling with hope. Without God, not too clear, not too good, not much love out there. Which will it be?

Israel Oppressed in Egypt

1 These are the names of the sons of Israel who came to Egypt with Jacob; each came with his family:[a]

2 Reuben, Simeon, Levi, and Judah;
3 Issachar, Zebulun, and Benjamin;
4 Dan and Naphtali; Gad and Asher.

5 The total number of Jacob's descendants[A] was 70;[B,b] Joseph was already in Egypt.

6 Then Joseph and all his brothers and all that generation died.[c] 7 But the Israelites were fruitful, increased rapidly, multiplied, and became extremely numerous[d] so that the land was filled with them.

8 A new king, who had not known Joseph, came to power in Egypt. 9 He said to his people, "Look, the Israelite people are more numerous and powerful than we are.[e] 10 Let us deal shrewdly with them; otherwise they will multiply further, and if war breaks out, they may join our enemies, fight against us, and leave the country."[f] 11 So the Egyptians assigned taskmasters over the Israelites to oppress them with forced labor.[g] They built Pithom and Rameses as supply cities[h] for Pharaoh. 12 But the more they oppressed them, the more they multiplied and spread so that the Egyptians came to dread[C] the Israelites. 13 They worked the Israelites ruthlessly[i] 14 and made their lives bitter with difficult labor in brick and mortar and in all kinds of fieldwork. They ruthlessly imposed all this work on them.[j]

15 Then the king of Egypt said to the Hebrew midwives, one of whom was named Shiphrah and the other Puah, 16 "When you help the Hebrew women give birth, observe them as they deliver.[D] If the child is a son, kill him, but if it's a daughter, she may live." 17 The Hebrew midwives, however, ·feared God[k] and did not do as the king of Egypt had told them;[l] they let the boys live. 18 So the king of Egypt summoned the midwives and asked them, "Why have you done this and let the boys live?"

19 The midwives said to Pharaoh, "The Hebrew women are not like the Egyptian women, for they are vigorous and give birth before a midwife can get to them."[m]

20 So God was good to the midwives,[n] and the people multiplied and became very numerous. 21 Since the midwives feared God, He gave them families.[o] 22 Pharaoh then commanded all his people: "You must throw every son born to the Hebrews[E] into the Nile, but let every daughter live."[p]

Moses' Birth and Adoption

2 Now a man from the family of Levi married a Levite woman.[q] 2 The woman became pregnant and gave birth to a son; when she saw that he was beautiful,[F] she hid him for three months.[r] 3 But when she could no longer hide him, she got a papyrus basket for him and coated it with asphalt and pitch. She placed the child in it and set it among the reeds by the bank of the Nile. 4 Then his sister[s] stood at a distance in order to see what would happen to him.

5 Pharaoh's daughter went down to bathe at the Nile while her servant girls walked along the riverbank. Seeing the basket among the reeds, she sent her slave girl to get it. 6 When she opened it, she saw the child — a little boy, crying. She felt sorry for him and said, "This is one of the Hebrew boys."

7 Then his sister said to Pharaoh's daughter, "Should I go and call a woman from the Hebrews to nurse the boy for you?"

8 "Go," Pharaoh's daughter told her. So the girl went and called the boy's mother. 9 Then Pharaoh's daughter said to her, "Take this child and nurse him for me, and I will pay your wages." So the woman took the boy and nursed him. 10 When the child grew older, she brought him to Pharaoh's daughter, and he became her son. She named him Moses, "Because," she said, "I drew him out of the water."[G]

Moses in Midian

11 Years later,[H] after Moses had grown up, he went out to his own people[I] and observed their forced labor.[t] He saw an Egyptian beating a Hebrew, one of his people. 12 Looking all around and seeing no one, he struck the Egyptian dead and hid him in the sand. 13 The

[a]**1:1** Gn 46:8
[b]**1:5** Gn 46:26-27; Dt 10:22
[c]**1:6** Gn 50:26
[d]**1:7** Gn 12:2; 46:3; Dt 26:5; Ac 7:17
[e]**1:9** Ps 105:24
[f]**1:10** Ps 83:3-4; Ac 7:19
[g]**1:11** Gn 15:13; Ex 2:11; 3:7; 5:4-5; 6:6; Dt 26:6
[h]Gn 47:11; 1Kg 9:19; 2Ch 8:4
[i]**1:13** Dt 4:20
[j]**1:14** Ex 2:23; Nm 20:15; Ac 7:19
[k]**1:17** Ex 1:21; Pr 16:6
[l]Dn 3:16-18; Ac 4:18-20; 5:29
[m]**1:19** Jos 2:4; 2Sm 17:20
[n]**1:20** Pr 11:18; Is 3:10
[o]**1:21** 1Sm 2:35; 2Sm 7:11,27; 1Kg 11:38; Ps 127:1
[p]**1:22** Gn 41:1; Ac 7:19
[q]**2:1** Ex 6:20; Nm 26:59; 1Ch 23:14
[r]**2:2** Ac 7:20; Heb 11:23
[s]**2:4** Ex 15:20; Nm 26:59
[t]**2:11** Ex 1:11; Ac 7:23; Heb 11:24-26

[A]**1:5** Lit *of people issuing from Jacob's loins* [B]**1:5** LXX, DSS read *75*; Gn 46:27; Ac 7:14 [C]**1:12** Or *Egyptians loathed* [D]**1:16** Lit *birth, look at the stones* [E]**1:22** Sam, LXX, Tg; MT omits *to the Hebrews* [F]**2:2** Or *healthy* [G]**2:10** The name Moses sounds like "drawing out" in Hb and "born" in Egyptian. [H]**2:11** Lit *And it was in those days* [I]**2:11** Lit *his brothers*

next day he went out and saw two Hebrews
fighting. He asked the one in the wrong,
"Why are you attacking your neighbor?"[A]
14 "Who made you a leader and judge over
us?" the man replied. "Are you planning to
kill me as you killed the Egyptian?"
Then Moses became afraid and thought:
What I did is certainly known. 15 When Pharaoh heard about this, he tried to kill Moses.
But Moses fled from Pharaoh and went to
live in the land of Midian,[a] and sat down by
a well.[b]
16 Now the priest of Midian[c] had seven
daughters. They came to draw water and
filled the troughs to water their father's flock.
17 Then some shepherds arrived and drove
them away, but Moses came to their rescue
and watered their flock. 18 When they returned to their father Reuel[B,d] he asked, "Why
have you come back so quickly today?"
19 They answered, "An Egyptian rescued us
from the shepherds. He even drew water for
us and watered the flock."
20 "So where is he?" he asked his daughters.
"Why then did you leave the man behind? Invite him to eat dinner."
21 Moses agreed to stay with the man, and
he gave his daughter Zipporah[e] to Moses in
marriage. 22 She gave birth to a son whom he
named Gershom, for he said, "I have been a
foreigner[f] in a foreign land."[C]
23 After a long time, the king of Egypt died.
The Israelites groaned because of their difficult labor, and they cried out;[g] and their
cry for help ascended to God because of the
difficult labor. 24 So God heard their groaning, and He remembered[h] His covenant with
Abraham, Isaac, and Jacob.[i] 25 God saw the Israelites, and He took notice.[j]

Moses and the Burning Bush

3 Meanwhile, Moses was shepherding the
flock of his father-in-law Jethro,[D] the
priest of Midian. He led the flock to the far
side of the wilderness and came to Horeb,[E]
the mountain of God.[k] 2 Then the Angel of
the LORD appeared to him in a flame of fire
within a bush.[l] As Moses looked, he saw that
the bush was on fire but was not consumed.
3 So Moses thought: I must go over and look
at this remarkable sight. Why isn't the bush
burning up?
4 When the LORD saw that he had gone over
to look, God called out to him from the bush,
"Moses, Moses!"
"Here I am," he answered.
5 "Do not come closer," He said. "Remove the
sandals from your feet, for the place where
you are standing is holy ground."[m] 6 Then He
continued, "I am the God of your father,[F] the
God of Abraham, the God of Isaac, and the
God of Jacob."[n] Moses hid his face because he
was afraid to look at God.
7 Then the LORD said, "I have observed the
misery of My people in Egypt, and have heard
them crying out[o] because of their oppressors,
and I know about their sufferings. 8 I have
come down to rescue them from the power
of the Egyptians and to bring them from that
land to a good and spacious land, a land flowing with milk and honey[p]—the territory of
the Canaanites, Hittites, Amorites, Perizzites,
Hivites, and Jebusites.[q] 9 The Israelites' cry
for help has come to Me, and I have also seen
the way the Egyptians are oppressing[r] them.
10 Therefore, go. I am sending you to Pharaoh
so that you may lead My people, the Israelites,
out of Egypt."
11 But Moses asked God, "Who am I[s] that I
should go to Pharaoh and that I should bring
the Israelites out of Egypt?"
12 He answered, "I will certainly be with
you,[t] and this will be the sign to you that I
have sent you: when you bring the people
out of Egypt, you will all worship[G] God at this
mountain."
13 Then Moses asked God, "If I go to the Israelites and say to them: The God of your fathers
has sent me to you, and they ask me, 'What is
His name?' what should I tell them?"
14 God replied to Moses, "I AM WHO I AM.[H,u]
This is what you are to say to the Israelites:
I AM has sent me to you." 15 God also said to
Moses, "Say this to the Israelites: Yahweh, the
God of your fathers, the God of Abraham, the
God of Isaac, and the God of Jacob, has sent

[a] **2:15** Ac 7:29; Heb 11:27
[b] Gn 24:11; 29:2
[c] **2:16** Ex 3:1; 1Sm 9:11
[d] **2:18** Ex 3:1; 4:18; Nm 10:29
[e] **2:21** Ex 4:25; 18:2
[f] **2:22** Ex 18:3-4; Ac 7:29; Heb 11:13
[g] **2:23** Ex 3:7,9; Dt 26:7; Jms 5:4
[h] **2:24** Gn 9:15; Ex 6:5; 1Ch 16:15; Ps 105:8; 106:45; 111:4
[i] Ps 22:23; Lk 1:33,55
[j] **2:25** Ex 3:7; 4:31; Lk 1:25
[k] **3:1** Ex 2:18; 18:5; 1Kg 19:8
[l] **3:2** Dt 33:16; Ac 7:30
[m] **3:5** Jos 5:15; Ac 7:33
[n] **3:6** Gn 28:13; Mt 22:32; Mk 12:26; Lk 20:37; Ac 7:32
[o] **3:7** Ex 2:23-25; Neh 9:9; Ps 106:44
[p] **3:8** Gn 50:24; Ex 6:6
[q] Gn 15:18-21; Ex 3:17; 13:5; Dt 1:25; Jr 11:5; Ezk 20:6
[r] **3:9** Ex 1:14; 2:23
[s] **3:11** Ex 6:12; 1Sm 18:18
[t] **3:12** Gn 31:3; Jos 1:5; Rm 8:31
[u] **3:14** Ex 6:3; Ps 68:4; Jn 8:58; Heb 13:8; Rv 1:4; 4:8

[A] **2:13** Or *fellow Hebrew* [B] **2:18** Jethro's clan or last name was Reuel; Ex 3:1. [C] **2:22** In Hb the name Gershom sounds like the phrase "a stranger there." [D] **3:1** Moses' father-in-law's first name was Jethro; Ex 2:18. [E] **3:1** = Desolation; another name for Mount Sinai; Dt 4:10,15; 18:16; Mal 4:4 [F] **3:6** Sam, some LXX mss read *fathers*; Ac 7:32 [G] **3:12** Or *serve* [H] **3:14** Or *I AM BECAUSE I AM*, or *I WILL BE WHO I WILL BE* me to you. This is My name forever;[a] this is how I am to be remembered in every generation.

[16]"Go and assemble the elders of Israel and say to them: Yahweh, the God of your fathers, the God of Abraham, Isaac, and Jacob, has appeared to me and said: I have paid close attention to you and to what has been done to you in Egypt.[b] [17]And I have promised you that I will bring you up from the misery of Egypt[c] to the land of the Canaanites, Hittites, Amorites, Perizzites, Hivites, and Jebusites—a land flowing with milk and honey. [18]They will listen to what you say. Then you, along with the elders of Israel, must go to the king of Egypt and say to him: Yahweh, the God of the Hebrews, has met with us. Now please let us go on a three-day trip into the wilderness so that we may sacrifice to Yahweh our God.[d]

[19]"However, I know that the king of Egypt will not allow you to go, unless he is forced by a strong hand.[e] [20]I will stretch out My hand and strike Egypt with all My miracles that I will perform in it. After that, he will let you go.[f] [21]And I will give these people such favor in the sight of the Egyptians that when you go, you will not go empty-handed.[g] [22]Each woman will ask her neighbor and any woman staying in her house for silver and gold jewelry, and clothing, and you will put them on your sons and daughters. So you will plunder the Egyptians."[h]

Miraculous Signs for Moses

4 Then Moses answered, "What if they won't believe me and will not obey me but say, 'The LORD did not appear[i] to you'?"

[2]The LORD asked him, "What is that in your hand?"

"A staff," he replied.

[3]Then He said, "Throw it on the ground." He threw it on the ground, and it became a snake. Moses ran from it, [4]but the LORD told him, "Stretch out your hand and grab it by the tail." So he stretched out his hand and caught it, and it became a staff in his hand. [5]"This will take place," He continued, "so they will believe that ˙Yahweh, the God of their fathers, the God of Abraham, the God of Isaac, and the God of Jacob, has appeared to you."[j]

[6]In addition the LORD said to him, "Put your hand inside your cloak." So he put his hand inside his cloak, and when he took it out, his hand was diseased, white as snow.[A,k] [7]Then He said, "Put your hand back inside your cloak." He put his hand back inside his cloak, and when he took it out,[B] it had again become like the rest of his skin.[l] [8]"If they will not believe you and will not respond to the evidence of the first sign, they may believe the evidence of the second sign. [9]And if they

[a]3:15 Ps 102:12; 135:13; Hs 12:5
[b]3:16 Ex 4:29; Lk 1:68
[c]3:17 Gn 15:16; Jos 24:11
[d]3:18 Ex 4:31; 5:1; Nm 23:3-4,15-16
[e]3:19 Ex 5:2; 6:1
[f]3:20 Ex 6:6; 9:15; 12:31; Dt 6:22; Neh 9:10
[g]3:21 Ex 11:3; 12:36
[h]3:22 Gn 15:14; Ex 11:2; Ezk 39:10
[i]4:1 Ex 3:18; 6:30
[j]4:1-5 Ex 3:6,15; 4:17,20; 19:9
[k]4:6 Nm 12:10; 2Kg 5:27
[l]4:7 Nm 12:13-14; Dt 32:39; 2Kg 5:14

Exodus and the Theme of Sending

In the Book of Exodus, there are some seventeen references to the sending, all of them related in some way to the mighty salvation event of the Exodus. In 3:10-15, there are five references to the sending. God said to Moses, "I will send you" (v. 10) and "I have sent you" (v. 12). In addition, he said to Moses that he was to tell the people "the God of your fathers has sent me to you" (v. 13); "I AM has sent me to you" (v. 14). "The God of Abraham, the God of Isaac, and the God of Jacob, has sent me to you" (v. 15). (All italics by author.) Thus the great salvation event of the Old Testament was to be accomplished by God's mission through Moses. Moreover, the fact that in this sending context God revealed himself, not simply as the covenant God of the patriarchs, but for the first time as Yahweh, adds a sublime dimension to it. As the story of God's sending of Moses unfolds, the language of the sending attends the descriptions of the succeeding events (4:13,28; 5:22; 7:16). *(DuBose, 42)*

GOD WHO SENDS

A4:6 A reference to whiteness or flakiness of the skin B4:7 Lit *out of his cloak*

don't believe even these two signs or listen to
what you say, take some water from the Nile
and pour it on the dry ground. The water you
take from the Nile will become blood on the
ground."[a]
10But Moses replied to the LORD, "Please,
Lord, I have never been eloquent — either in
the past or recently or since You have been
speaking to Your servant[A] — because I am
slow and hesitant in speech."[B,b]
11Yahweh said to him, "Who made the human mouth? Who makes him mute or deaf,
seeing or blind? Is it not I, Yahweh?[c] 12Now
go! I will help[C] you speak and I will teach you
what to say."[d]
13Moses said, "Please, Lord, send someone
else."[D]
14Then the LORD's anger burned against
Moses, and He said, "Isn't Aaron the Levite
your brother? I know that he can speak well.
And also, he is on his way now to meet you. He
will rejoice when he sees you. 15You will speak
with him and tell him what to say.[e] I will help[E]
both you and him to speak and will teach you
both what to do. 16He will speak to the people
for you. He will be your spokesman, and you
will serve as God to him. 17And take this staff
in your hand that you will perform the signs
with."[f]

Moses' Return to Egypt

18Then Moses went back to his father-in-
law Jethro and said to him, "Please let me return to my relatives in Egypt and see if they
are still living."
Jethro said to Moses, "Go in peace."
19Now in Midian the LORD told Moses, "Return to Egypt, for all the men who wanted
to kill you are dead."[g] 20So Moses took his
wife and sons, put them on a donkey, and returned to the land of Egypt. And Moses took
God's staff[h] in his hand.
21The LORD instructed Moses, "When you go
back to Egypt, make sure you do all the wonders before Pharaoh that I have put within
your power. But I will harden his heart[F,i] so
that he won't let the people go. 22Then you
will say to Pharaoh: This is what Yahweh says:
Israel is My firstborn son.[j] 23I told you: Let My
son go so that he may worship Me, but you refused to let him go. Now I will kill your firstborn son!"[k]
24On the trip, at an overnight campsite, it
happened that the LORD confronted him and
sought to put him to death. 25So Zipporah
took a flint, cut off her son's foreskin, and
threw it at Moses' feet.[G] Then she said, "You
are a bridegroom of blood to me!"[l] 26So He
let him alone. At that time she said, "You are
a bridegroom of blood," referring to the circumcision.[H]

Reunion of Moses and Aaron

27Now the LORD had said to Aaron, "Go and
meet Moses in the wilderness." So he went
and met him at the mountain of God and
kissed him.[m] 28Moses told Aaron everything
the LORD had sent him to say, and about all
the signs He had commanded him to do.
29Then Moses and Aaron went and assembled all the elders of the Israelites. 30Aaron
repeated everything the LORD had said to
Moses and performed the signs before the
people. 31The people believed, and when they
heard that the LORD had paid attention[n] to
them and that He had seen their misery,[o] they
bowed down and worshiped.

Moses Confronts Pharaoh

5 Later, Moses and Aaron went in and said
to Pharaoh, "This is what ·Yahweh, the
God of Israel, says: Let My people go, so that
they may hold a festival for Me in the wilderness."[p]
2But Pharaoh responded, "Who is Yahweh
that I should obey Him by letting Israel go?
I do not know anything about Yahweh, and
besides, I will not let Israel go."[q]
3Then they answered, "The God of the Hebrews has met with us. Please let us go on a
three-day trip into the wilderness so that we
may sacrifice to Yahweh our God, or else He
may strike us with plague or sword."
4The king of Egypt said to them, "Moses
and Aaron, why are you causing the people to
neglect their work? Get to your work!" 5Pha-

[a]4:9 Ex 7:19
[b]4:10 Ex 6:12; Jr 1:6
[c]4:11 Ps 94:9
[d]4:12 Is 50:4; Jr 1:9; Mt 10:19-20; Mk 13:11; Lk 12:11-12; 21:14-15
[e]4:15 Ex 7:1-2; Nm 23:5,12,16
[f]4:17 Ex 4:2; 7:15
[g]4:19 Ex 2:15,23; Mt 2:20
[h]4:20 Ex 17:9; Nm 20:8-9
[i]4:21 Ex 7:13; 9:12,35; 14:8; Dt 2:30; Jos 11:20; Is 63:17; Jn 12:40; Rm 9:18
[j]4:22 Is 63:16; 64:8; Jr 31:9; Hs 11:1; Rm 9:4
[k]4:23 Ex 11:5; 12:29
[l]4:25 Gn 17:14; Jos 5:2-3
[m]4:27 Ex 3:1; 4:14
[n]4:31 Ex 2:25; 3:7,18; 4:8-9
[o]Gn 24:26; 1Ch 29:20
[p]5:1 Ex 3:18; 10:9
[q]5:2 Ex 3:19; 2Kg 18:35; Jb 21:15

A4:10 = Moses B4:10 Lit *heavy of mouth and heavy of tongue* C4:12 Lit *will be with you* D4:13 Lit *send by the hand of whom You will send* E4:15 Lit *be with* F4:21 Or *will make him stubborn* G4:25 Some interpret "feet" as a euphemism for genitals. H4:25-26 Zipporah appeased God on Moses' behalf by circumcising Gershom.

raoh also said, "Look, the people of the land
are so numerous, and you would stop them
from working."[a]

Further Oppression of Israel

6 That day Pharaoh commanded the overseers[b] of the people as well as their foremen:
7 "Don't continue to supply the people with
straw for making bricks, as before. They must
go and gather straw for themselves. 8 But require the same quota of bricks from them as
they were making before; do not reduce it.
For they are slackers—that is why they are
crying out,[c] 'Let us go and sacrifice to our
God.' 9 Impose heavier work on the men. Then
they will be occupied with it and not pay attention to deceptive words."

10 So the overseers and foremen of the people went out and said to them, "This is what
Pharaoh says:[d] 'I am not giving you straw.
11 Go get straw yourselves wherever you can
find it, but there will be no reduction at all
in your workload.'" 12 So the people scattered
throughout the land of Egypt to gather stubble for straw. 13 The overseers insisted, "Finish
your assigned work each day, just as you did
when straw was provided." 14 Then the Israelite foremen, whom Pharaoh's slave drivers
had set over the people, were beaten[e] and
asked, "Why haven't you finished making
your prescribed number of bricks yesterday
or today, as you did before?"

15 So the Israelite foremen went in and cried
for help to Pharaoh: "Why are you treating
your servants this way? 16 No straw has been
given to your servants, yet they say to us,
'Make bricks!' Look, your servants are being
beaten, but it is your own people who are at
fault."

17 But he said, "You are slackers. Slackers!
That is why you are saying, 'Let us go sacrifice
to the LORD.' 18 Now get to work. No straw will
be given to you, but you must produce the
same quantity of bricks."

19 The Israelite foremen saw that they were
in trouble when they were told, "You cannot
reduce your daily quota of bricks." 20 When
they left Pharaoh, they confronted Moses and
Aaron, who stood waiting to meet them.
21 "May the LORD take note of you and
judge," they said to them, "because you have
made us reek in front of Pharaoh and his officials—putting a sword in their hand to kill
us!"[f]

22 So Moses went back to the LORD and
asked, "Lord, why have You caused trouble for
this people? And why did You ever send me?[g]
23 Ever since I went in to Pharaoh to speak in
Your name he has caused trouble for this people, and You haven't delivered Your people at
6 all." 1 But the LORD replied to Moses, "Now
you are going to see what I will do to Pharaoh: he will let them go because of My strong
hand; he will drive them out of his land because of My strong hand."[h]

God Promises Freedom

2 Then God spoke to Moses, telling him, "I
am ·Yahweh. 3 I appeared to Abraham, Isaac,
and Jacob as ·God Almighty, but I did not reveal My name Yahweh to them.[i] 4 I also established My covenant with them to give them
the land of Canaan, the land they lived in as
foreigners.[j] 5 Furthermore, I have heard the
groaning of the Israelites, whom the Egyptians are forcing to work as slaves, and I have
remembered[k] My covenant.

6 "Therefore tell the Israelites: I am Yahweh,
and I will deliver you from the forced labor
of the Egyptians and free you from slavery to
them. I will redeem you with an outstretched
arm[l] and great acts of judgment. 7 I will take
you as My people,[m] and I will be your God.
You will know[n] that I am Yahweh your God,
who delivered you from the forced labor of
the Egyptians. 8 I will bring you to the land
that I swore[A,o] to give to Abraham, Isaac, and
Jacob, and I will give it to you as a possession.
I am Yahweh." 9 Moses told this to the Israelites, but they did not listen[p] to him because of
their broken spirit and hard labor.

10 Then the LORD spoke to Moses, 11 "Go and
tell Pharaoh king of Egypt to let the Israelites
go from his land."

12 But Moses said in the LORD's presence: "If
the Israelites will not listen to me, then how
will Pharaoh listen to me, since I am such a
poor speaker?"[B,q] 13 Then the LORD spoke to
Moses and Aaron and gave them commands
concerning both the Israelites and Pharaoh

[a] **5:3-5** Ex 1:7,9,11; 3:18
[b] **5:6** Ex 1:1; 3:7
[c] **5:8** Ex 2:23; 3:7; 5:15
[d] **5:10** Ex 4:22; 5:1
[e] **5:14** Is 10:24
[f] **5:21** Gn 34:30; Ex 6:9; 14:11
[g] **5:22** Nm 11:11; Jr 4:10
[h] **6:1** Ex 3:19; 12:31,33,39
[i] **6:3** Gn 17:1; Ex 3:14; Ps 68:4; 83:18; Jn 8:58
[j] **6:4** Gn 15:18; 28:4
[k] **6:5** Gn 9:15; Ex 2:24; 1Ch 16:15; Ps 105:8; 106:45; 111:4
[l] **6:6** Ex 3:17; Dt 7:8; 26:8; 1Ch 17:21
[m] **6:7** Dt 4:20; 2Sm 7:24
[n] Ex 16:12; 29:45; Is 41:20; Rv 21:7
[o] **6:8** Gn 14:22; 15:18; 26:3
[p] **6:9** Ex 5:21; Ac 7:25
[q] **6:12** Ex 4:10; 6:30; Jr 1:6

[A] **6:8** Lit *raised My hand* [B] **6:12** Lit *I have uncircumcised lips*

king of Egypt to bring the Israelites out of the
land of Egypt.

Genealogy of Moses and Aaron

[14]These are the heads of their fathers' families:

The sons of Reuben,[a] the firstborn
of Israel:
Hanoch and Pallu, Hezron and Carmi.
These are the clans of Reuben.
15 The sons of Simeon:[b]
Jemuel, Jamin, Ohad, Jachin,
Zohar, and Shaul, the son
of a Canaanite woman.
These are the clans of Simeon.

16 These are the names of the sons of Levi
according to their genealogy:
Gershon, Kohath, and Merari.[c]
Levi lived 137 years.
17 The sons of Gershon:
Libni and Shimei, by their clans.
18 The sons of Kohath:
Amram, Izhar, Hebron, and Uzziel.
Kohath lived 133 years.
19 The sons of Merari:
Mahli and Mushi.
These are the clans of the Levites[d]
according to their genealogy.
20 Amram married his father's sister
Jochebed,
and she bore him Aaron and Moses.[e]
Amram lived 137 years.
21 The sons of Izhar:[f]
Korah, Nepheg, and Zichri.
22 The sons of Uzziel:
Mishael, Elzaphan,[g] and Sithri.
23 Aaron married Elisheba,
daughter of Amminadab[h] and sister
of Nahshon.
She bore him Nadab and Abihu, Eleazar
and Ithamar.[i]
24 The sons of Korah:[j]
Assir, Elkanah, and Abiasaph.
These are the clans of the Korahites.
25 Aaron's son Eleazar married
one of the daughters of Putiel
and she bore him Phinehas.[k]
These are the heads of the Levite
families by their clans.

[26]It was this Aaron and Moses whom the
LORD told, "Bring the Israelites out of the
land of Egypt according to their divisions."[l]
[27]Moses and Aaron were the ones who spoke
to Pharaoh king of Egypt in order to bring the
Israelites out of Egypt.

Moses and Aaron before Pharaoh

[28]On the day the LORD spoke to Moses in
the land of Egypt, [29]He said to him, "I am Yahweh;[m] tell Pharaoh king of Egypt everything I
am telling you."
[30]But Moses replied in the LORD's presence,
"Since I am such a poor speaker,[A,n] how will
Pharaoh listen to me?"
7 The LORD answered Moses, "See, I have
made you like God to Pharaoh, and Aaron
your brother will be your prophet. [2]You must
say whatever I command you; then Aaron
your brother must declare it to Pharaoh so
that he will let the Israelites go from his land.
[3]But I will harden Pharaoh's heart[o] and multiply My signs and wonders in the land of
Egypt. [4]Pharaoh will not listen to you, but I
will put My hand on Egypt and bring the divisions of My people the Israelites out of the
land of Egypt by great acts of judgment. [5]The
Egyptians will know that I am 'Yahweh[p] when
I stretch out My hand[q] against Egypt, and
bring out the Israelites from among them."
[6]So Moses and Aaron did this; they did just
as the LORD commanded them. [7]Moses was
80 years old[r] and Aaron 83 when they spoke
to Pharaoh.
[8]The LORD said to Moses and Aaron,
[9]"When Pharaoh tells you, 'Perform a miracle,' tell Aaron, 'Take your staff and throw
it down before Pharaoh. It will become a
serpent.'"[s] [10]So Moses and Aaron went in to
Pharaoh and did just as the LORD had commanded. Aaron threw down his staff before
Pharaoh and his officials, and it became a serpent. [11]But then Pharaoh called the wise men
and sorcerers — the magicians[t] of Egypt, and
they also did the same thing by their occult
practices.[u] [12]Each one threw down his staff,
and it became a serpent. But Aaron's staff
swallowed their staffs. [13]However, Pharaoh's
heart hardened,[v] and he did not listen to
them, as the LORD had said.

[a]**6:14** Gn 46:9; 1Ch 5:3
[b]**6:15** Gn 46:10; 1Ch 4:24
[c]**6:16** Gn 46:11; Nm 3:17
[d]**6:17-19** Nm 3:18-20; 1Ch 6:17-19; 23:21
[e]**6:20** Ex 2:1-2; Nm 26:59
[f]**6:21** Nm 16:1; 1Ch 6:37-38
[g]**6:22** Lv 10:4; Nm 3:30
[h]**6:23** Ru 4:19-20; 1Ch 2:10; Mt 1:4
[i]Lv 10:1; Nm 3:2; 26:60
[j]**6:24** Nm 26:11; 1Ch 6:22-23,37
[k]**6:25** Nm 25:7,11; Jos 24:33; Ps 106:30
[l]**6:26** Ex 7:4; 12:17,51; Nm 33:1
[m]**6:29** Ex 6:11; 7:2
[n]**6:30** Ex 4:10; 6:12
[o]**7:3** Ex 4:21
[p]**7:5** Ex 7:17; 8:19,22; 14:4,18
[q]Ex 3:20; 6:6
[r]**7:7** Dt 29:5; 31:2; 34:7; Ac 7:23,30
[s]**7:9** Ex 4:2; Is 7:11; Jn 2:18; 6:30
[t]**7:11** Gn 41:8; 2Tm 3:8
[u]Ex 7:22; 8:7,18
[v]**7:13** Ex 4:21; 7:22; 8:15,19,32; 9:7,12,34; 10:1,20,27; 11:10; 14:8

[A]**6:30** Lit *I have uncircumcised lips*

The First Plague: Water Turned to Blood

14 Then the LORD said to Moses, "Pharaoh's
heart is hard: he refuses to let the people go.
15 Go to Pharaoh in the morning. When you
see him walking out to the water, stand ready
to meet him by the bank of the Nile. Take in
your hand the staff that turned into a snake.[a]
16 Tell him: Yahweh, the God of the Hebrews,
has sent me to tell you: Let My people go, so
that they may worship[A] Me in the wilderness,
but so far you have not listened. 17 This is what
Yahweh says: Here is how you will know that
I am Yahweh. Watch. I will strike the water in
the Nile with the staff in my hand, and it will
turn to blood. 18 The fish in the Nile will die,
the river will stink, and the Egyptians will be
unable to drink water from it."
19 So the LORD said to Moses, "Tell Aaron:
Take your staff and stretch out your hand[b]
over the waters of Egypt—over their rivers, canals,[B] ponds, and all their water reservoirs—and they will become blood. There
will be blood throughout the land of Egypt,
even in wooden and stone containers."
20 Moses and Aaron did just as the LORD had
commanded; in the sight of Pharaoh and his
officials, he raised the staff and struck the water in the Nile, and all the water in the Nile
was turned to blood.[c] 21 The fish in the Nile
died, and the river smelled so bad the Egyptians could not drink water from it. There
was blood throughout the land of Egypt.
22 But the magicians of Egypt did the same
thing by their occult practices. So Pharaoh's
heart hardened, and he would not listen to
them, as the LORD had said. 23 Pharaoh turned
around, went into his palace, and didn't even
take this to heart. 24 All the Egyptians dug
around the Nile for water to drink because
they could not drink the water from the river.
25 Seven days passed after the LORD struck the
Nile.

The Second Plague: Frogs

8 [C] Then the LORD said to Moses, "Go in to
Pharaoh and tell him: This is what ·Yah-
weh says: Let My people go, so that they may
worship Me.[d] 2 But if you refuse to let them go,
then I will plague all your territory with frogs.[e]
3 The Nile will swarm with frogs; they will come
up and go into your palace, into your bedroom
and on your bed, into the houses of your officials and your people, and into your ovens and
kneading bowls. 4 The frogs will come up on
you, your people, and all your officials."
5 [D] The LORD then said to Moses, "Tell Aaron:
Stretch out your hand with your staff over
the rivers, canals, and ponds, and cause the
frogs to come up onto the land of Egypt."[f]
6 When Aaron stretched out his hand over the
waters of Egypt, the frogs[g] came up and covered the land of Egypt. 7 But the magicians did
the same thing by their occult practices and
brought frogs up onto the land of Egypt.
8 Pharaoh summoned Moses and Aaron
and said, "Ask[h] Yahweh to remove the frogs
from me and my people. Then I will let the
people go and they can sacrifice to Yahweh."
9 Moses said to Pharaoh, "You make the
choice rather than me. When should I ask on
behalf of you, your officials, and your people,
that the frogs be taken away from you and
your houses, and remain only in the Nile?"
10 "Tomorrow," he answered.
Moses replied, "As you have said, so you
may know there is no one like Yahweh our
God,[i] 11 the frogs will go away from you, your
houses, your officials, and your people. The
frogs will remain only in the Nile." 12 After Moses and Aaron went out from Pharaoh, Moses
cried out to the LORD for help concerning the
frogs that He had brought against[E] Pharaoh.
13 The LORD did as Moses had said: the frogs in
the houses, courtyards, and fields died. 14 They
piled them in countless heaps, and there was
a terrible odor in the land. 15 But when Pharaoh saw there was relief, he hardened his
heart[j] and would not listen to them, as the
LORD had said.

The Third Plague: Gnats

16 Then the LORD said to Moses, "Tell Aaron:
Stretch out your staff and strike the dust of the
earth, and it will become gnats[F] throughout
the land of Egypt." 17 And they did this. Aaron
stretched out his hand with his staff, and
when he struck the dust of the earth, gnats
were on man and beast. All the dust of the

[a] **7:14-15** Ex 4:2-3; 8:15; 10:1,20,27
[b] **7:19** Ex 8:5-6,16-17; 9:22; 10:12,21; 14:21,26
[c] **7:20** Ex 17:5; Ps 78:44; 105:29
[d] **8:1** Ex 3:12,18; 4:23
[e] **8:2** Ex 7:14; 9:2; Rv 16:13
[f] **8:3-5** Ex 7:19; 10:6
[g] **8:6** Ps 78:45; 105:30
[h] **8:8** Ex 8:28; 9:28; 10:17
[i] **8:10** Ex 9:14; Dt 33:26; 2Sm 7:22; 1Ch 17:20; Is 46:9; Jr 10:6-7
[j] **8:15** Ex 7:4; Ec 8:11

[A] **7:16** Or *serve*; Ex 4:23 [B] **7:19** The Hb word refers specifically to the various branches and canals of the Nile River; Ex 8:5. [C] **8:1** Ex 7:26 in Hb [D] **8:5** Ex 8:1 in Hb [E] **8:12** Or *frogs, as he had agreed with* [F] **8:16** Perhaps sand fleas or mosquitoes

earth became gnats throughout the land of Egypt. 18The magicians tried to produce gnats using their occult practices, but they could not. The gnats remained on man and beast.[a]

19"This is the finger of God,"[b] the magicians said to Pharaoh. But Pharaoh's heart hardened, and he would not listen to them, as the LORD had said.

The Fourth Plague: Swarms of Flies

20The LORD said to Moses, "Get up early in the morning and present yourself to Pharaoh when you see him going out to the water. Tell him: This is what Yahweh says: Let My people go, so that they may worship[A] Me.[c] 21But if you will not let My people go, then I will send swarms of flies[B] against you, your officials, your people, and your houses. The Egyptians' houses will swarm with flies, and so will the land where they live.[C] 22But on that day I will give special treatment to the land of Goshen, where My people are living;[d] no flies will be there. This way you will know that I, Yahweh, am in the land. 23I will make a distinction[D] between My people and your people. This sign will take place tomorrow."

24And the LORD did this. Thick swarms of flies went into Pharaoh's palace and his officials' houses. Throughout Egypt the land was ruined because of the swarms of flies.[e] 25Then Pharaoh summoned Moses and Aaron and said, "Go sacrifice to your God within the country."

26But Moses said, "It would not be right[E] to do that, because what we will sacrifice to the LORD our God is detestable to the Egyptians.[f] If we sacrifice what the Egyptians detest in front of them, won't they stone us? 27We must go a distance of three days into the wilderness and sacrifice to the LORD our God as He instructs us."

28Pharaoh responded, "I will let you go and sacrifice to the LORD your God in the wilderness, but don't go very far. Make an appeal[g] for me."

29"As soon as I leave you," Moses said, "I will appeal to the LORD, and tomorrow the swarms of flies will depart from Pharaoh, his officials, and his people. But Pharaoh must not act deceptively again by refusing to let the people go and sacrifice to the LORD." 30Then Moses left Pharaoh's presence and appealed to the LORD. 31The LORD did as Moses had said: He removed the swarms of flies from Pharaoh, his officials, and his people; not one was left. 32But Pharaoh hardened his heart this time also and did not let the people go.

The Fifth Plague: Death of Livestock

9 Then the LORD said to Moses, "Go in to Pharaoh and say to him: This is what •Yahweh, the God of the Hebrews, says: Let My people go, so that they may worship Me. 2But if you refuse to let them go and keep holding them, 3then the LORD's hand will bring a severe plague against your livestock in the field—the horses, donkeys, camels, herds, and flocks. 4But the LORD will make a distinction between the livestock of Israel and the livestock of Egypt, so that nothing of all that the Israelites own will die." 5And the LORD set a time, saying, "Tomorrow the LORD will do this thing in the land."[h] 6The LORD did this the next day. All the Egyptian livestock died,[i] but none among the Israelite livestock died. 7Pharaoh sent messengers who saw that not a single one of the Israelite livestock was dead. But Pharaoh's heart was hardened,[j] and he did not let the people go.

The Sixth Plague: Boils

8Then the LORD said to Moses and Aaron, "Take handfuls of furnace soot, and Moses is to throw it toward heaven in the sight of Pharaoh. 9It will become fine dust over the entire land of Egypt. It will become festering boils[k] on man and beast throughout the land of Egypt." 10So they took furnace soot and stood before Pharaoh. Moses threw it toward heaven, and it became festering boils on man and beast. 11The magicians could not stand before Moses because of the boils, for the boils were on the magicians as well as on all the Egyptians.[l] 12But the LORD hardened Pharaoh's heart[m] and he did not listen to them, as the LORD had told Moses.

The Seventh Plague: Hail

13Then the LORD said to Moses, "Get up early in the morning and present yourself to

[a]**8:18** Ex 7:11; 9:11; Dn 5:8
[b]**8:19** Ps 8:3; Lk 11:20
[c]**8:20** Ex 2:5; 7:15; 8:1; 9:13
[d]**8:22** Ex 9:4,6; 10:23; 11:7
[e]**8:24** Ps 78:45; 105:31
[f]**8:26** Gn 43:32; 46:34
[g]**8:28** Ex 8:8; 9:28; 1Kg 13:6
[h]**9:1-5** Ex 7:4,16; 8:1-2,22; 11:7
[i]**9:6** Ex 9:19; Ps 78:50
[j]**9:7** Ex 7:14; 8:32
[k]**9:9** Dt 28:27; Rv 16:2
[l]**9:11** Ex 8:18; 2Tm 3:9
[m]**9:12** Ex 4:21; 7:22

[A]**8:20** Or *serve* [B]**8:21** Or *insects* [C]**8:21** Lit *are* [D]**8:23** LXX, Syr, Vg; MT reads *will place deliverance* [E]**8:26** Or *allowable*

Pharaoh. Tell him: This is what Yahweh, the
God of the Hebrews says: Let My people go,
so that they may worship Me. 14Otherwise, I
am going to send all My plagues against you,[A]
your officials, and your people. Then you
will know there is no one like Me in all the
earth. 15By now I could have stretched out My
hand and struck you and your people with a
plague, and you would have been obliterated
from the earth.[a] 16However, I have let you live
for this purpose: to show you My power[b] and
to make My name known in all the earth.
17You are still acting arrogantly against[B] My
people by not letting them go. 18Tomorrow
at this time I will rain down the worst hail[c]
that has ever occurred in Egypt from the day
it was founded until now. 19Therefore give
orders to bring your livestock and all that
you have in the field into shelters. Every person and animal that is in the field and not
brought inside will die when the hail falls
on them." 20Those among Pharaoh's officials
who ·feared the word of the LORD made their
servants and livestock flee to shelters, 21but
those who didn't take the LORD's word seriously left their servants and livestock in the
field.

22Then the LORD said to Moses, "Stretch
out your hand toward heaven and let there
be hail throughout the land of Egypt — on
man and beast and every plant of the field
in the land of Egypt." 23So Moses stretched
out his staff toward heaven, and the LORD
sent thunder and hail.[d] Lightning struck the
earth, and the LORD rained hail on the land
of Egypt. 24The hail, with lightning flashing
through it, was so severe that nothing like
it had occurred in the land of Egypt since it
had become a nation. 25Throughout the land
of Egypt, the hail struck down everything in
the field, both man and beast. The hail beat
down every plant of the field and shattered
every tree in the field. 26The only place it
didn't hail was in the land of Goshen where
the Israelites were.[e]

27Pharaoh sent for Moses and Aaron. "I have
sinned this time," he said to them. "Yahweh is
the Righteous[f] One, and I and my people are
the ·guilty ones. 28Make an appeal to Yahweh.
There has been enough of God's thunder and
hail. I will let you go;[g] you don't need to stay
any longer."

29Moses said to him, "When I have left the
city, I will extend my hands[h] to Yahweh. The
thunder will cease, and there will be no more
hail, so that you may know the earth[i] belongs
to Yahweh. 30But as for you and your officials,
I know that you still do not fear Yahweh our
God."

31The flax and the barley were destroyed
because the barley was ripe[C] and the flax was
budding,[j] 32but the wheat and the spelt were
not destroyed since they are later crops.[D]

33Moses went out from Pharaoh and the
city, and extended his hands to the LORD.
Then the thunder and hail ceased, and rain
no longer poured down on the land. 34When
Pharaoh saw that the rain, hail, and thunder
had ceased, he sinned again and hardened
his heart, he and his officials. 35So Pharaoh's
heart hardened, and he did not let the Israelites go, as the LORD had said through Moses.

The Eighth Plague: Locusts

10 Then the LORD said to Moses, "Go to
Pharaoh, for I have hardened his heart
and the hearts of his officials so that I may
do these miraculous signs of Mine among
them,[E,k] 2and so that you may tell[F] your son
and grandson[l] how severely I dealt with the
Egyptians and performed miraculous signs
among them, and you will know that I am
·Yahweh."

3So Moses and Aaron went in to Pharaoh
and told him, "This is what Yahweh, the God
of the Hebrews, says: How long will you refuse
to humble yourself before Me? Let My people
go, that they may worship Me.[m] 4But if you
refuse to let My people go, then tomorrow I
will bring locusts[n] into your territory. 5They
will cover the surface of the land so that no
one will be able to see the land. They will eat
the remainder left[o] to you that escaped the
hail; they will eat every tree you have growing in the fields. 6They will fill your houses,
all your officials' houses, and the houses of all
the Egyptians — something your fathers and
ancestors never saw since the time they occupied the land until today." Then he turned
and left Pharaoh's presence.

[a] **9:15** Ex 3:20; 8:10,20
[b] **9:16** Ex 14:17; Pr 16:4; Rm 9:17
[c] **9:18** Jos 10:11; Jb 38:22; Ps 18:12; Is 28:2; 30:30; Ezk 13:11; 38:22
[d] **9:23** Ps 78:47-48; 105:32; 148:8; Rv 8:7; 11:19; 16:21
[e] **9:26** Ex 8:22; 9:4,6; 11:7; 12:13; Is 32:18
[f] **9:27** Ex 10:16; 2Ch 12:6; Ps 129:4; 145:17; Lm 1:18
[g] **9:28** Ex 8:8; 10:17
[h] **9:29** 1Kg 8:22,38; Ps 143:6; Is 1:15
[i] Ps 24:1; 1Co 10:26
[j] **9:31** Ru 1:22; 2:23
[k] **10:1** Ex 4:21; 7:4,13
[l] **10:2** Ex 13:8,14; Dt 4:9; 6:20-22; Ps 44:1; 78:5-7; Jl 1:3
[m] **10:3** 1Kg 21:29; Jms 4:10; 1Pt 5:6
[n] **10:4** Pr 30:27; Rv 9:3
[o] **10:5** Ex 9:32; Jl 1:4

[A] **9:14** Lit *your heart* [B] **9:17** Or *still obstructing* [C] **9:31** Lit *was ears of grain* [D] **9:32** Lit *are late* [E] **10:1** Lit *Mine in his midst* [F] **10:2** Lit *tell in the ears of*

7Pharaoh's officials asked him, "How long
must this man be a snare[a] to us? Let the men
go, so that they may worship Yahweh their
God. Don't you realize yet that Egypt is devastated?"
8So Moses and Aaron were brought back
to Pharaoh. "Go, worship Yahweh your God,"
Pharaoh said. "But exactly who will be going?"
9Moses replied, "We will go with our young
and our old; we will go with our sons and
daughters and with our flocks and herds because we must hold Yahweh's festival."[b]
10He said to them, "May Yahweh be with
you if I ever let you and your families go![A]
Look out—you are planning evil. 11No, only
the men may go and worship Yahweh, for
that is what you have been asking for." And
they were driven from Pharaoh's presence.
12The LORD then said to Moses, "Stretch out
your hand over the land of Egypt and the locusts will come up over it and eat every plant
in the land, everything that the hail left." 13So
Moses stretched out his staff over the land of
Egypt, and the LORD sent an east wind over
the land all that day and through the night.
By morning the east wind had brought in the
locusts. 14The locusts went up over the entire
land of Egypt and settled on the whole territory of Egypt. Never before had there been
such a large number of locusts, and there
never will be again.[c] 15They covered the surface of the whole land so that the land was
black, and they consumed all the plants on
the ground and all the fruit on the trees that
the hail had left. Nothing green was left on the
trees or the plants in the field throughout the
land of Egypt.[d]
16Pharaoh urgently sent for Moses and
Aaron and said, "I have sinned against Yahweh your God and against you. 17Please forgive my sin once more and make an appeal
to Yahweh your God, so that He will take this
death away from me." 18Moses left Pharaoh's
presence and appealed to the LORD.[e] 19Then
the LORD changed the wind to a strong west[B]
wind, and it carried off the locusts and blew
them into the ·Red Sea.[f] Not a single locust
was left in all the territory of Egypt. 20But the
LORD hardened Pharaoh's heart,[g] and he did
not let the Israelites go.

The Ninth Plague: Darkness

21Then the LORD said to Moses, "Stretch out
your hand toward heaven, and there will be
darkness over the land of Egypt, a darkness
that can be felt." 22So Moses stretched out
his hand toward heaven, and there was thick
darkness throughout the land of Egypt for
three days. 23One person could not see another, and for three days they did not move
from where they were. Yet all the Israelites
had light where they lived.[h]
24Pharaoh summoned Moses and said, "Go,
worship Yahweh. Even your families may go
with you; only your flocks and herds must
stay behind."
25Moses responded, "You must also let us
have[C] sacrifices and ·burnt offerings to prepare for Yahweh our God. 26Even our livestock must go with us; not a hoof will be left
behind because we will take some of them to
worship Yahweh our God. We will not know
what we will use to worship Yahweh until we
get there."
27But the LORD hardened Pharaoh's heart,[i]
and he was unwilling to let them go. 28Pha-
raoh said to him, "Leave me! Make sure you
never see my face again, for on the day you see
my face, you will die."
29"As you have said," Moses replied, "I will
never see your face again."[j]

The Tenth Plague: Death of the Firstborn

11 The LORD said[D] to Moses, "I will bring
one more plague on Pharaoh and on
Egypt. After that, he will let you go from here.
When he lets you go,[E] he will drive you out of
here. 2Now announce to the people that both
men and women should ask their neighbors
for silver and gold jewelry." 3The LORD gave[F]
the people favor in the sight of the Egyptians.
And the man Moses was highly regarded[G] in
the land of Egypt by[H] Pharaoh's officials and
the people.[k]
4So Moses said, "This is what ·Yahweh says:
'About midnight I will go throughout Egypt,
5and every firstborn male in the land of Egypt

[a]**10:7** Ex 23:33; Jos 23:13; 1Sm 18:21; Ec 7:26
[b]**10:8-9** Ex 5:1; 8:8
[c]**10:14** Ps 78:46; 105:34; Jl 2:2
[d]**10:15** Ex 10:5; Ps 105:35
[e]**10:16-18** Ex 8:8,30; 9:27
[f]**10:19** Ex 13:18; 15:4,22; 23:31; Nm 14:25; 21:4; 33:10-11
[g]**10:20** Ex 4:21; 11:10
[h]**10:22-23** Ex 8:22; Ps 105:28
[i]**10:27** Ex 4:21; 10:20
[j]**10:29** Heb 11:27
[k]**11:1-3** Ex 3:21-22; 12:35-36

[A]**10:10** Pharaoh's reply is sarcastic. [B]**10:19** Lit *sea* [C]**10:25** Lit *also give in our hand* [D]**11:1** Or *had said* [E]**11:1** Or *go, it will be finished—* [F]**11:3** Or *had given* [G]**11:3** Lit *was very great* [H]**11:3** Or *in the eyes of*

will die, from the firstborn of Pharaoh who
sits on his throne to the firstborn of the servant girl who is behind the millstones, as
well as every firstborn of the livestock. 6Then
there will be a great cry of anguish through
all the land of Egypt such as never was before,
or ever will be again. 7But against all the Israelites, whether man or beast, not even a dog
will snarl,[A] so that you may know that Yahweh
makes a distinction between Egypt and Israel.
8All these officials of yours will come down to
me and bow before me, saying: Leave, you and
all the people who follow you.[B] After that, I
will leave.'" And he left Pharaoh's presence in
fierce anger.[a]
9The LORD said to Moses, "Pharaoh will not
listen[b] to you, so that My wonders may be
multiplied in the land of Egypt." 10Moses and
Aaron did all these wonders before Pharaoh,
but the LORD hardened Pharaoh's heart,[c] and
he would not let the Israelites go out of his
land.

Instructions for the Passover

12 1The LORD said to Moses and Aaron
in the land of Egypt: 2"This month is
to be the beginning of months for you; it is
the first month of your year.[d] 3Tell the whole
community of Israel that on the tenth day
of this month they must each select an animal of the flock according to their fathers'
households, one animal per household. 4If
the household is too small for a whole animal, that person and the neighbor nearest his house are to select one based on the
combined number of people; you should apportion the animal according to what each
person[C] will eat. 5You must have an unblemished[e] animal, a year-old male; you may take
it from either the sheep or the goats. 6You
are to keep it until the fourteenth day of
this month; then the whole assembly of the
community of Israel will slaughter the animals at twilight.[f] 7They must take some of
the blood and put it on the two doorposts
and the lintel of the houses where they eat
them. 8They are to eat the meat that night;
they should eat it, roasted over the fire along
with unleavened bread and bitter herbs.[g]
9Do not eat any of it raw or cooked in boiling[D] water, but only roasted[h] over fire—its
head as well as its legs and inner organs.
10Do not let any of it remain until morning;[i]
you must burn up any part of it that does
remain before morning. 11Here is how you
must eat it: you must be dressed for travel,[E]
your sandals on your feet, and your staff in
your hand. You are to eat it in a hurry; it is
the LORD's •Passover.[j]
12"I will pass through[k] the land of Egypt on
that night and strike every firstborn male in
the land of Egypt, both man and beast. I am
•Yahweh; I will execute judgments against all
the gods of Egypt.[l] 13The blood on the houses
where you are staying will be a distinguishing mark for you; when I see the blood, I will
pass over you. No plague will be among you to
destroy you when I strike the land of Egypt.
14"This day is to be a memorial for you, and
you must celebrate it as a festival to the LORD.
You are to celebrate it throughout your generations as a permanent statute.[m] 15You must
eat unleavened bread for seven days. On the
first day you must remove yeast[n] from your
houses. Whoever eats what is leavened from
the first day through the seventh day must
be cut off[o] from Israel. 16You are to hold a sacred assembly[p] on the first day and another
sacred assembly on the seventh day. No work
may be done on those days except for preparing what people need to eat—you may
do only that.
17"You are to observe the Festival of •Unleav-
ened Bread because on this very day I brought
your divisions out of the land of Egypt.[q] You
must observe this day throughout your generations as a permanent statute. 18You are to
eat unleavened bread in the first month,[r] from
the evening of the fourteenth day of the month
until the evening of the twenty-first day. 19Yeast
must not be found in your houses for seven
days. If anyone eats something leavened, that
person, whether a foreign resident or native of
the land, must be cut off from the community
of Israel. 20Do not eat anything leavened; eat
unleavened bread in all your homes."[F]
21Then Moses summoned all the elders of
Israel and said to them, "Go, select an animal
from the flock according to your families,
and slaughter the Passover animal.[s] 22Take

[a] **11:8** Ex 12:3; Am 5:17
[b] **11:9** Ex 3:19; 7:4; 10:1
[c] **11:10** Ex 4:21; 10:20,27
[d] **12:2** Ex 13:4; 23:15; 34:18; Dt 16:1
[e] **12:5** Lv 22:19-21; Mal 1:8,14
[f] **12:6** Lv 23:5; Nm 9:3; Dt 16:6
[g] **12:8** Ex 34:25; Nm 9:11; Dt 16:3; 1Co 5:8
[h] **12:9** Dt 16:7; 2Ch 35:13
[i] **12:10** Ex 23:18; 34:25
[j] **12:11** Ex 12:27; Dt 16:5
[k] **12:12** Ex 11:4-5; Am 5:17
[l] Ex 6:2; Nm 33:4
[m] **12:14** Ex 12:17,43; 13:9-10; 2Kg 23:21
[n] **12:15** Ex 13:6-7; 23:15; 34:18; Lv 23:6; Dt 16:3,8
[o] Gn 17:14; Nm 9:13
[p] **12:16** Lv 23:7-8; Nm 28:18,25
[q] **12:17** Ex 12:41,51; 13:3
[r] **12:18** Lv 23:5-8; Nm 28:16-25
[s] **12:21** Ex 12:3; Mk 14:12-16

[A] **11:7** Lit *point its tongue* [B] **11:8** Lit *people at your feet* [C] **12:4** Or *household* [D] **12:9** Or *or boiled at all in* [E] **12:11** Lit *it: with your loins girded* [F] **12:20** Or *settlements*

a cluster of hyssop, dip it in the blood[a] that
is in the basin, and brush the lintel and the
two doorposts with some of the blood in the
basin. None of you may go out the door of
his house until morning. 23 When the LORD
passes through to strike Egypt and sees the
blood on the lintel and the two doorposts,
He will pass over the door and not let the destroyer enter your houses to strike you.[b]
24 "Keep this command permanently as a
statute for you and your descendants. 25 When
you enter the land that the LORD will give you
as He promised, you are to observe this ritual.
26 When your children[c] ask you, 'What does
this ritual mean to you?' 27 you are to reply,
'It is the Passover sacrifice[d] to the LORD, for
He passed over the houses of the Israelites
in Egypt when He struck the Egyptians and
spared our homes.'" So the people bowed
down and worshiped. 28 Then the Israelites
went and did this; they did just as the LORD
had commanded Moses and Aaron.

The Exodus

29 Now at midnight the LORD struck every
firstborn male in the land of Egypt, from the
firstborn of Pharaoh who sat on his throne
to the firstborn of the prisoner who was in
the dungeon, and every firstborn of the livestock.[e] 30 During the night Pharaoh got up, he
along with all his officials and all the Egyptians, and there was a loud wailing[f] throughout Egypt because there wasn't a house
without someone dead. 31 He summoned Moses and Aaron during the night and said, "Get
up, leave my people, both you and the Israelites, and go, worship Yahweh as you have
asked. 32 Take even your flocks and your herds
as you asked and leave, and also bless me."
33 Now the Egyptians pressured the people in order to send them quickly out of the
country, for they said, "We're all going to
die!"[g] 34 So the people took their dough before it was leavened, with their kneading
bowls wrapped up in their clothes on their
shoulders.
35 The Israelites acted on Moses' word and
asked the Egyptians for silver and gold jewelry and for clothing.[h] 36 And the LORD gave
the people such favor in the Egyptians' sight
that they gave them what they requested. In
this way they plundered the Egyptians.
37 The Israelites traveled from Rameses to
Succoth,[i] about 600,000[j] soldiers on foot,
besides their families. 38 An ethnically diverse
crowd also went up with them, along with a
huge number of livestock, both flocks and
herds. 39 The people baked the dough they had
brought out of Egypt into unleavened loaves,
since it had no yeast; for when they had been
driven[k] out of Egypt they could not delay and
had not prepared any provisions for themselves.
40 The time that the Israelites lived in Egypt[A]
was 430 years.[l] 41 At the end of 430 years, on
that same day, all the LORD's divisions went out
from the land of Egypt. 42 It was a night of vigil
in honor of the LORD, because He would bring
them out of the land of Egypt. This same night
is in honor of the LORD, a night vigil for all the
Israelites throughout their generations.[m]

Passover Instruction

43 The LORD said to Moses and Aaron, "This
is the statute of the Passover: no foreigner
may eat it. 44 But any slave a man has purchased may eat it, after you have circumcised
him. 45 A temporary resident or hired hand
may not eat the Passover.[n] 46 It is to be eaten in
one house. You may not take any of the meat
outside the house, and you may not break any
of its bones.[o] 47 The whole community of Israel must celebrate[B] it. 48 If a foreigner resides
with you and wants to celebrate the LORD's
Passover, every male in his household must
be circumcised, and then he may participate;[C]
he will become like a native of the land. But
no uncircumcised person may eat it. 49 The
same law will apply to both the native and the
foreigner[p] who resides among you."
50 Then all the Israelites did this; they did
just as the LORD had commanded Moses and
Aaron. 51 On that same day the LORD brought
the Israelites out of the land of Egypt according to their divisions.[q]

13 The LORD spoke to Moses: 2 "Consecrate every firstborn male[r] to Me, the
firstborn from every womb among the Israelites, both man and domestic animal; it is
Mine."

[a] **12:22** Ex 12:7; Heb 11:28
[b] **12:23** Ezk 9:6; 1Co 10:10; Rv 7:3
[c] **12:26** Ex 10:2; 13:8,14; Dt 6:20; 32:7; Jos 4:6,21; Ps 78:3-6
[d] **12:27** Ex 4:31; 12:11
[e] **12:29** Ex 4:23; 11:4; Nm 8:17; 33:4; Ps 78:51; 135:8
[f] **12:30** Ex 11:6; Am 5:17
[g] **12:33** Ex 11:8; Ps 105:38
[h] **12:35** Gn 15:14; Ex 3:21; Ps 105:37
[i] **12:37** Gn 47:11; Nm 33:3,5
[j] Ex 38:26; Nm 1:46; 11:21
[k] **12:39** Ex 6:1; 12:33
[l] **12:40** Gn 15:13-16; Ac 7:6; Gl 3:17
[m] **12:42** Ex 13:10; Dt 16:1,6
[n] **12:43-45** Gn 17:11-13; Lv 22:10; Nm 9:14
[o] **12:46** Nm 9:12; Ps 34:20; Jn 19:33,36
[p] **12:49** Nm 9:14; 15:15-16,19; Gl 3:28
[q] **12:51** Ex 6:26; 12:41
[r] **13:2** Ex 13:12-13,15; 22:29-30; Nm 3:13; Dt 15:9; Lk 2:23

[A] **12:40** LXX, Sam add *and in Canaan* [B] **12:47** Lit *do* [C] **12:48** Lit *may come near to do it*

3 Then Moses said to the people, "Remember this day when you came out of Egypt, out of the place of slavery, for the LORD brought you out of here by the strength of His hand. Nothing leavened may be eaten.[a] 4 Today, in the month of Abib,[A,b] you are leaving. 5 When the LORD brings you into the land of the Canaanites, Hittites, Amorites, Hivites, and Jebusites,[B] which He swore to your fathers that He would give you, a land flowing with milk and honey,[c] you must carry out this ritual in this month.[d] 6 For seven days you must eat unleavened bread, and on the seventh day there is to be a festival to the LORD. 7 Unleavened bread is to be eaten for those seven days. Nothing leavened may be found among you, and no yeast may be found among you in all your territory. 8 On that day explain to your son, 'This is because of what the LORD did for me when I came out of Egypt.'[e] 9 Let it serve as a sign for you on your hand and as a reminder on your forehead,[C,f] so that the LORD's instruction may be in your mouth; for the LORD brought you out of Egypt with a strong hand. 10 Keep this statute at its appointed time from year to year.

11 "When the LORD brings you into the land of the Canaanites, as He swore to you and your fathers, and gives it to you, 12 you are to present to the LORD every firstborn male of the womb. All firstborn offspring of the livestock you own that are males will be the LORD's. 13 You must redeem every firstborn of a donkey with a flock animal, but if you do not redeem it, break its neck. However, you must redeem every firstborn among your sons.[g]

14 "In the future, when your son[h] asks you, 'What does this mean?' say to him, 'By the strength of His hand the LORD brought us out of Egypt, out of the place of slavery. 15 When Pharaoh stubbornly refused to let us go, the LORD killed every firstborn male in the land of Egypt, from the firstborn of man to the firstborn of livestock. That is why I sacrifice to the LORD all the firstborn of the womb that are males, but I redeem all the firstborn of my sons.' 16 So let it be a sign on your hand and a symbol[D] on your forehead, for the LORD brought us out of Egypt by the strength of His hand."[i]

The Route of the Exodus

17 When Pharaoh let the people go, God did not lead them along the road to the land of the Philistines, even though it was nearby; for God said, "The people will change their minds and return to Egypt if they face war."[j] 18 So He led the people around toward the ˙Red Sea along the road of the wilderness. And the Israelites left the land of Egypt in battle formation.[k]

19 Moses took the bones of Joseph[l] with him, because Joseph had made the Israelites swear a solemn oath, saying, "God will certainly come to your aid; then you must take my bones with you from this place."

20 They set out from Succoth and camped at Etham on the edge of the wilderness. 21 The LORD went ahead of them in a pillar of cloud[m] to lead them on their way during the day and in a pillar of fire to give them light at night, so that they could travel day or night. 22 The pillar of cloud by day and the pillar of fire by night never left its place in front of the people.

14 Then the LORD spoke to Moses: 2 "Tell the Israelites to turn back and camp in front of Pi-hahiroth, between Migdol and the sea; you must camp in front of Baal-zephon, facing it by the sea.[n] 3 Pharaoh will say of the Israelites: They are wandering around the land in confusion; the wilderness has boxed them in. 4 I will harden Pharaoh's heart so that he will pursue them. Then I will receive glory by means of Pharaoh and all his army, and the Egyptians will know that I am ˙Yahweh." So the Israelites did this.[o]

The Egyptian Pursuit

5 When the king of Egypt was told that the people had fled, Pharaoh and his officials changed their minds about the people and said: "What have we done? We have released Israel from serving us." 6 So he got his chariot ready and took his troops[E] with him; 7 he took 600 of the best chariots and all the rest of the chariots of Egypt, with officers in each one.

[a] **13:3** Ex 6:1; 12:8,42; Dt 16:3
[b] **13:4** Ex 12:2; 23:15; 34:18; Dt 16:1
[c] **13:5** Ex 3:8; 33:3; Nm 16:14; Jos 5:6; Jr 32:22
[d] Ex 6:8; 12:25
[e] **13:8** Ex 12:26-27; 3:14
[f] **13:9** Ex 13:16; Dt 6:8; 11:18
[g] **13:13** Ex 34:20; Nm 3:46-47; 18:15
[h] **13:14** Ex 12:26-27; Dt 6:20
[i] **13:15-16** Ex 12:29; 13:9
[j] **13:17** Ex 14:11; Nm 14:1-4; Dt 17:16
[k] **13:18** Ex 14:2; Nm 33:6; Jos 1:14
[l] **13:19** Gn 50:25; Jos 24:32; Ac 7:16; Heb 11:22
[m] **13:21** Ex 14:19; Nm 9:15-16; Dt 1:33; Neh 9:12; Ps 78:14; 99:7; Is 4:5; 1Co 10:1
[n] **14:2** Ex 13:18; Nm 33:7; Jr 44:1
[o] **14:4** Ex 4:21; 7:5; Rm 9:17,22-23

[A] **13:4** March–April; called Nisan in the post-exilic period; Neh 2:1; Est 3:7
[B] **13:5** DSS, Sam, LXX, Syr add *Girgashites* and *Perizzites*; Jos 3:10
[C] **13:9** Lit *reminder between your eyes*
[D] **13:16** Or *phylactery*
[E] **14:6** Lit *people*

8 The LORD hardened the heart of Pharaoh king of Egypt, and he pursued the Israelites, who were going out triumphantly.[A,a] 9 The Egyptians—all Pharaoh's horses and chariots, his horsemen,[B] and his army—chased[b] after them and caught up with them as they camped by the sea beside Pi-hahiroth, in front of Baal-zephon.

10 As Pharaoh approached, the Israelites looked up and saw the Egyptians coming after them. Then the Israelites were terrified and cried out[c] to the LORD for help. 11 They said to Moses: "Is it because there are no graves in Egypt that you took us to die in the wilderness? What have you done to us by bringing us out of Egypt? 12 Isn't this what we told you in Egypt: Leave us alone so that we may serve the Egyptians? It would have been better for us to serve the Egyptians than to die in the wilderness."[d]

13 But Moses said to the people, "Don't be afraid. Stand firm and see[e] the LORD's salvation He will provide for you today; for the Egyptians you see today, you will never see again. 14 The LORD will fight for you; you must be quiet."[f]

Escape through the Red Sea

15 The LORD said to Moses, "Why are you crying out to Me? Tell the Israelites to break camp. 16 As for you, lift up your staff, stretch out your hand over the sea, and divide it so that the Israelites can go through the sea on dry ground.[g] 17 I am going to harden the hearts of the Egyptians so that they will go in after them, and I will receive glory by means of Pharaoh, all his army, and his chariots and horsemen. 18 The Egyptians will know that I am Yahweh when I receive glory through Pharaoh, his chariots, and his horsemen."

19 Then the Angel of God,[h] who was going in front of the Israelite forces, moved and went behind them. The pillar of cloud moved from in front of them and stood behind them.[i] 20 It came between the Egyptian and Israelite forces. The cloud was there in the darkness, yet it lit up the night.[C] So neither group came near the other all night long.

21 Then Moses stretched out his hand over the sea. The LORD drove the sea back with a powerful east wind all that night and turned the sea into dry land. So the waters were divided,[j] 22 and the Israelites went through the sea on dry ground, with the waters like a wall to them on their right and their left.[k]

23 The Egyptians set out in pursuit—all Pharaoh's horses, his chariots, and his horsemen—and went into the sea after them. 24 Then during the morning watch, the LORD looked down on the Egyptian forces from the pillar of fire[l] and cloud, and threw them into confusion. 25 He caused their chariot wheels to swerve[D,E] and made them drive[F] with difficulty. "Let's get away from Israel," the Egyptians said, "because Yahweh is fighting for them against Egypt!"

26 Then the LORD said to Moses, "Stretch out your hand over the sea so that the waters may come back on the Egyptians, on their chariots and horsemen." 27 So Moses stretched out his hand over the sea, and at daybreak the sea returned to its normal depth. While the Egyptians were trying to escape from it, the LORD threw them into the sea.[m] 28 The waters came back and covered the chariots[n] and horsemen, the entire army of Pharaoh, that had gone after them into the sea. None of them survived.

29 But the Israelites had walked through the sea on dry ground, with the waters like a wall to them on their right and their left. 30 That day the LORD saved Israel from the power of the Egyptians, and Israel saw the Egyptians dead on the seashore. 31 When Israel saw the great power that the LORD used against the Egyptians, the people •feared the LORD and believed[o] in Him and in His servant Moses.

Israel's Song

15 Then Moses and the Israelites sang this song to the LORD. They said:

I will sing to the LORD,
for He is highly exalted;
He has thrown the horse
and its rider into the sea.
2 The LORD is my strength and my song;[G]
He has become my salvation.[p]
This is my God, and I will praise Him,

[a] 14:8 Ex 6:1; 13:9; Nm 33:3; Ac 13:17 [b] 14:9 Ex 15:9; Jos 24:6 [c] 14:10 Jos 24:7; Neh 9:9; Ps 34:17 [d] 14:12 Ex 5:21; Ps 106:7-8 [e] 14:13 Gn 15:1; 46:3; Ex 20:20; 2Ch 20:15,17; Is 41:10 [f] 14:14 Ex 14:25; Dt 1:30; 3:22; Jos 10:14; 2Ch 20:29; Is 30:15 [g] 14:16 Ex 4:17; Nm 20:8-9; Is 10:26 [h] 14:19 Ex 23:20,23; 32:34; 33:2 [i] Ex 13:21; Is 63:9 [j] 14:21 Ex 15:8; Jos 3:16; Neh 9:11; Ps 74:13; 114:3,5; Is 63:12-13 [k] 14:22 Ex 15:19; Ps 66:6; Is 63:13; Hab 3:10; 1Co 10:1; Heb 11:29 [l] 14:24 Ex 13:21; Nm 14:14; Neh 9:12 [m] 14:27 Ex 5:1,7; Jos 4:18; Ps 78:53; Heb 11:29 [n] 14:28 Ps 106:11; Heb 3:8,13 [o] 14:31 Ps 106:12; Jn 2:11 [p] 15:2 Ps 18:2; 59:17; Is 12:2; Hab 3:18

[A] 14:8 Lit *with a raised hand* [B] 14:9 Or *chariot drivers* [C] 14:20 Perhaps the cloud brought darkness to the Egyptians but light to the Israelites; Ex 10:22-23; Ps 105:39. [D] 14:25 Sam, LXX, Syr read *He bound their chariot wheels* [E] 14:25 Or *fall off* [F] 14:25 Or *and they drove them* [G] 15:2 Or *might*

my father's God, and I will exalt Him.[a]
3 The LORD is a warrior;[b]
·Yahweh is His name.[c]

4 He threw Pharaoh's chariots
and his army into the sea;
the elite of his officers
were drowned in the ·Red Sea.[d]
5 The floods covered them;
they sank to the depths like a stone.[e]
6 LORD, Your right hand is glorious
in power.
LORD, Your right hand shattered
the enemy.[f]
7 You overthrew Your adversaries
by Your great majesty.
You unleashed Your burning wrath;
it consumed them like stubble.[g]
8 The waters heaped up[h] at the blast
of Your nostrils;
the currents stood firm like a dam.
The watery depths congealed
in the heart of the sea.
9 The enemy said:
"I will pursue, I will overtake,
I will divide the spoil.[i]
My desire will be gratified
at their expense.
I will draw my sword;
my hand will destroy[A] them."
10 But You blew with Your breath,
and the sea covered them.
They sank like lead
in the mighty waters.

11 LORD, who is like You among the gods?
Who is like You, glorious in holiness,[j]
revered with praises,
performing wonders?[k]
12 You stretched out Your right hand,
and the earth swallowed them.
13 You will lead the people
You have redeemed
with Your faithful love;
You will guide them
to Your holy dwelling
with Your strength.[l]

14 When the peoples hear,
they will shudder;
anguish will seize the inhabitants
of Philistia.
15 Then the chiefs of Edom will be
terrified;[m]
trembling will seize the leaders
of Moab;
the inhabitants of Canaan will panic;
16 and terror[n] and dread will fall on them.
They will be as still[B] as a stone
because of Your powerful arm
until Your people pass by, LORD,
until the people whom You purchased[C]
pass by.[o]
17 You will bring them in and plant them
on the mountain of Your possession;[p]
LORD, You have prepared the place
for Your dwelling;
Lord,[D] Your hands have established
the sanctuary.
18 The LORD will reign[q] forever and ever!

19 When Pharaoh's horses with his chariots
and horsemen went into the sea, the LORD
brought the waters of the sea back over them.
But the Israelites walked through the sea on
dry ground. 20 Then Miriam the prophetess,[r]
Aaron's sister, took a tambourine in her hand,
and all the women followed her with their
tambourines and danced.[s] 21 Miriam sang to
them:

Sing to the LORD,
for He is highly exalted;
He has thrown the horse
and its rider into the sea.

Water Provided

22 Then Moses led Israel on from the Red
Sea, and they went out to the Wilderness of
Shur. They journeyed for three days in the
wilderness without finding water. 23 They
came to Marah, but they could not drink the
water at Marah because it was bitter — that
is why it was named Marah.[E] 24 The people
grumbled to Moses, "What are we going to
drink?"[t] 25 So he cried out to the LORD, and
the LORD showed him a tree. When he threw
it into the water, the water became drinkable.

He made a statute and ordinance for them
at Marah and He tested them there.[u] 26 He said,
"If you will carefully obey the LORD your God,
do what is right in His eyes, pay attention

[a] **15:2** Gn 28:21; Ex 3:6,15,18; Is 25:1
[b] **15:3** Ps 24:8; Rv 19:11
[c] Ex 6:3; Ps 83:18
[d] **15:4** Ex 13:18; 15:22; 23:31
[e] **15:5** Ex 14:28; 15:10; Neh 9:11
[f] **15:6** Ps 118:15-16
[g] **15:7** Dt 33:26; Is 5:24
[h] **15:8** Ex 14:21; Ps 78:13
[i] **15:9** Ex 14:9; Jdg 5:30; Is 53:12
[j] **15:11** Dt 3:24; 1Kg 8:23
[k] Ps 77:14; Is 6:3; Rv 4:8
[l] **15:13** Ps 77:15,20; 78:54
[m] **15:15** Gn 36:15,40; Nm 22:3; Dt 2:4; Jos 5:1
[n] **15:16** Ex 23:27; Jos 2:9
[o] 1Sm 25:37; Ps 74:2; 1Pt 2:9
[p] **15:17** Ps 44:2; 78:54
[q] **15:18** Ps 10:16; 29:10; Is 57:15
[r] **15:20** Nm 26:59; Jdg 4:4
[s] Jdg 11:34; 1Sm 18:6; Ps 150:4
[t] **15:23-24** Ex 16:2; Nm 33:8
[u] **15:25** Ex 14:10; Dt 8:2,16; Jdg 2:22; 3:1,4; 2Kg 2:21; Ps 66:10

A **15:9** Or *conquer* B **15:16** Or *silent* C **15:16** Or *created* D **15:17** Some Hb mss, DSS, Sam, Tg read *LORD* E **15:23** = bitter or bitterness to His commands, and keep all His statutes, I will not inflict any illnesses on you that I inflicted on the Egyptians. For I am Yahweh who heals you."[a]

27 Then they came to Elim, where there were 12 springs of water and 70 date palms, and they camped there by the waters.

Manna and Quail Provided

16 The entire Israelite community departed from Elim and came to the Wilderness of Sin, which is between Elim and Sinai, on the fifteenth day of the second month after they had left the land of Egypt.[b] 2 The entire Israelite community grumbled[c] against Moses and Aaron in the wilderness. 3 The Israelites said to them, "If only we had died by the LORD's hand in the land of Egypt, when we sat by pots of meat and ate all the bread we wanted. Instead, you brought us into this wilderness to make this whole assembly die of hunger!"[d]

4 Then the LORD said to Moses, "I am going to rain bread from heaven for you. The people are to go out each day and gather enough for that day. This way I will test them to see whether or not they will follow My instructions.[e] 5 On the sixth day, when they prepare what they bring in, it will be twice as much as they gather on other days."[A]

6 So Moses and Aaron said to all the Israelites: "This evening you will know that it was the LORD who brought you out of the land of Egypt;[f] 7 in the morning you will see the LORD's glory because He has heard your complaints about Him. For who are we that you complain about us?"[g] 8 Moses continued, "The LORD will give you meat to eat this evening and more than enough bread in the morning, for He has heard the complaints that you are raising against Him. Who are we? Your complaints are not against us but against the LORD."[h]

9 Then Moses told Aaron, "Say to the entire Israelite community, 'Come before the LORD, for He has heard your complaints.'" 10 As Aaron was speaking to the entire Israelite community, they turned toward the wilderness, and there in a cloud the LORD's glory appeared.[i]

11 The LORD spoke to Moses, 12 "I have heard the complaints of the Israelites. Tell them: At twilight you will eat meat, and in the morning you will eat bread until you are full. Then you will know that I am Yahweh your God."

13 So at evening quail[j] came and covered the camp. In the morning there was a layer of dew all around the camp. 14 When the layer of dew evaporated, there were fine flakes on the desert surface, as fine as frost on the ground. 15 When the Israelites saw it, they asked one another, "What is it?" because they didn't know what it was.

Moses told them, "It is the bread the LORD has given you to eat.[k] 16 This is what the LORD has commanded: 'Gather as much of it as each person needs to eat. You may take two quarts[B] per individual, according to the number of people each of you has in his tent.'"

17 So the Israelites did this. Some gathered a lot, some a little. 18 When they measured it by quarts,[C] the person who gathered a lot had no surplus, and the person who gathered a little had no shortage. Each gathered as much as he needed to eat.[l] 19 Moses said to them, "No one is to let any of it remain until morning." 20 But they didn't listen to Moses; some people left part of it until morning, and it bred worms and smelled. Therefore Moses was angry with them.

21 They gathered it every morning. Each gathered as much as he needed to eat, but when the sun grew hot, it melted. 22 On the sixth day they gathered twice as much food, four quarts[D] apiece, and all the leaders of the community came and reported this to Moses. 23 He told them, "This is what the LORD has said: 'Tomorrow is a day of complete rest, a holy Sabbath[m] to the LORD. Bake what you want to bake, and boil what you want to boil, and set aside everything left over to be kept until morning.'"

24 So they set it aside until morning as Moses commanded, and it didn't smell or have any maggots in it. 25 "Eat it today," Moses said, "because today is a Sabbath to the LORD. Today you won't find any in the field. 26 For six days you may gather it, but on the seventh day, the Sabbath, there will be none."

27 Yet on the seventh day some of the people

[a] **15:26** Ex 23:25; Dt 7:12,15; 28:27,60; Ps 103:3
[b] **16:1** Nm 33:10-11
[c] **16:2** Ex 15:24; 1Co 10:10
[d] **16:3** Nm 11:4-5; Lm 4:9
[e] **16:4** Dt 8:2; Jn 6:31
[f] **16:6** Ex 6:7; Nm 16:28-30
[g] **16:7** Nm 14:27; 16:11; Is 35:2; 40:5
[h] **16:8** 1Sm 8:7; Lk 10:16; Rm 13:2
[i] **16:10** Ex 13:21-22; Nm 16:19; 1Kg 8:10
[j] **16:13** Nm 11:9,31; Ps 78:27-28; 105:40
[k] **16:15** Ex 16:4; Jn 6:31
[l] **16:18** 2Co 8:15
[m] **16:23** Gn 2:3; Ex 20:8; 31:15; 35:3; Lv 23:3

[A] **16:5** Lit *as gathering day to day* [B] **16:16** Lit *an omer* [C] **16:18** Lit *by an omer* [D] **16:22** Lit *two omers* went out to gather, but they did not find any. 28 Then the LORD said to Moses, "How long will you[A] refuse to keep My commands[a] and instructions? 29 Understand that the LORD has given you the Sabbath; therefore on the sixth day He will give you two days' worth of bread. Each of you stay where you are; no one is to leave his place on the seventh day." 30 So the people rested on the seventh day.

31 The house of Israel named the substance manna.[B,b] It resembled coriander seed, was white, and tasted like wafers made with honey. 32 Moses said, "This is what the LORD has commanded: 'Two quarts[C] of it are to be preserved throughout your generations, so that they may see the bread I fed you in the wilderness when I brought you out of the land of Egypt.'"

33 Moses told Aaron, "Take a container and put two quarts[C] of manna in it. Then place it before the LORD to be preserved throughout your generations." 34 As the LORD commanded Moses, Aaron placed it before the •testimony[c] to be preserved.

35 The Israelites ate manna for 40 years, until they came to an inhabited land. They ate manna until they reached the border of the land of Canaan.[d] 36 (Two quarts are[D] a tenth of an ephah.)

Water from the Rock

17 The entire Israelite community left the Wilderness of Sin, moving from one place to the next according to the LORD's command. They camped at Rephidim, but there was no water for the people to drink.[e] 2 So the people complained to Moses, "Give us water to drink."

"Why are you complaining to me?" Moses replied to them. "Why are you testing[f] the LORD?"

3 But the people thirsted there for water, and grumbled against Moses. They said, "Why did you ever bring us out of Egypt to kill us and our children and our livestock with thirst?"[g]

4 Then Moses cried out to the LORD, "What should I do with these people? In a little while they will stone me!"[h]

[a] **16:28** 2Kg 17:14; Ps 78:10
[b] **16:31** Ex 16:14; Nm 11:7; Dt 8:3
[c] **16:34** Ex 25:16,21; 27:21; 40:20; Nm 17:10
[d] **16:35** Jos 5:12; Neh 9:20-21; Jn 6:31,49
[e] **17:1** Ex 16:1; Nm 33:12,14
[f] **17:2** Nm 20:3; Dt 6:16; Ps 78:18,41; 1Co 10:9
[g] **17:3** Ex 15:24; 16:2,7-8; Nm 14:2,27,29,36; 16:11
[h] **17:4** Nm 14:10; 1Sm 30:6; Jn 8:59; 10:31
[i] **17:6** Ex 20:10-11; Ps 114:8; 1Co 10:9
[j] **17:7** Nm 20:13,24; Ps 81:7; 95:8
[k] **17:8** Gn 36:12; Nm 13:29; 24:20; Dt 25:17; Jdg 3:13; 6:3; 10:12; 1Sm 14:48
[l] **17:9** Ex 24:13; 32:17; 33:11; Ac 7:45
[m] **17:11** Ex 24:14; Jms 5:16
[n] **17:14** Ex 34:27; Dt 25:17-19; 1Sm 15:3
[o] **17:15** Ex 20:24-26; 24:4; Jdg 6:24
[p] **18:1** Ex 2:16,18; 3:1

5 The LORD answered Moses, "Go on ahead of the people and take some of the elders of Israel with you. Take the staff you struck the Nile with in your hand and go. 6 I am going to stand there in front of you on the rock at Horeb; when you hit the rock, water[i] will come out of it and the people will drink." Moses did this in the sight of the elders of Israel. 7 He named the place Massah[E] and Meribah[F,j] because the Israelites complained, and because they tested the LORD, saying, "Is the LORD among us or not?"

The Amalekites Attack

8 At Rephidim, Amalek[G,k] came and fought against Israel. 9 Moses said to Joshua,[l] "Select some men for us and go fight against Amalek. Tomorrow I will stand on the hilltop with God's staff in my hand."

10 Joshua did as Moses had told him, and fought against Amalek, while Moses, Aaron, and Hur went up to the top of the hill. 11 While Moses held up his hand,[H] Israel prevailed, but whenever he put his hand[H] down, Amalek prevailed.[m] 12 When Moses' hands grew heavy, they took a stone and put it under him, and he sat down on it. Then Aaron and Hur supported his hands, one on one side and one on the other so that his hands remained steady until the sun went down. 13 So Joshua defeated Amalek and his army[I] with the sword.

14 The LORD then said to Moses, "Write this down on a scroll as a reminder and recite it to Joshua: I will completely blot out the memory of Amalek under heaven."[n]

15 And Moses built an altar[o] and named it, "The LORD Is My Banner."[J] 16 He said, "Indeed, my hand is lifted up toward[K] the LORD's throne. The LORD will be at war with Amalek from generation to generation."

Jethro's Visit

18 Moses' father-in-law Jethro, the priest of Midian,[p] heard about everything that God had done for Moses and His people Israel, and how the LORD had brought Israel out of Egypt.

2 Now Jethro, Moses' father-in-law, had

[A] **16:28** The Hb word for you is pl, referring to the whole nation. [B] **16:31** = what?; Ex 16:15 [C] **16:32,33** Lit *A full omer* [D] **16:36** Lit *The omer is* [E] **17:7** = testing [F] **17:7** = arguing [G] **17:8** A semi-nomadic people descended from Amalek, a grandson of Esau; Gn 36:12 [H] **17:11** Sam, LXX, Syr, Tg, Vg read *hands* [I] **17:13** Or *people* [J] **17:15** Or *Yahweh-nissi* [K] **17:16** Or *hand was on*, or *hand was against*; Hb obscure

taken in Zipporah,[a] Moses' wife, after he
had sent her back, 3along with her two sons,
one of whom was named Gershom (because
Moses had said, "I have been a foreigner in a
foreign land")[A,b] 4and the other Eliezer (because he had said, "The God of my father was
my helper and delivered me from Pharaoh's
sword").[B]

5Moses' father-in-law Jethro, along with
Moses' wife and sons, came to him in the wilderness where he was camped at the mountain of God.[c] 6He sent word to Moses, "I, your
father-in-law Jethro, am coming to you with
your wife and her two sons."

7So Moses went out to meet his father-in-
law, bowed down,[d] and then kissed him. They
asked each other how they had been[C] and
went into the tent. 8Moses recounted to his
father-in-law all that the LORD had done to
Pharaoh and the Egyptians for Israel's sake,
all the hardships that confronted them on
the way, and how the LORD delivered them.[e]

9Jethro rejoiced over all the good things
the LORD had done for Israel when He rescued them from the power of the Egyptians.
10"Praise the LORD,"[f] Jethro exclaimed, "who
rescued you from Pharaoh and the power of
the Egyptians and snatched the people from
the power of the Egyptians. 11Now I know
that ·Yahweh is greater than all gods, because
He did wonders when the Egyptians acted arrogantly against Israel."[D,g]

12Then Jethro, Moses' father-in-law,
brought a ·burnt offering and sacrifices to
God, and Aaron came with all the elders of
Israel to eat a meal with Moses' father-in-law
in God's presence.

13The next day Moses sat down to judge the
people, and they stood around Moses from
morning until evening. 14When Moses' father-in-law saw everything he was doing for
them he asked, "What is this thing you're doing for the people? Why are you alone sitting
as judge, while all the people stand around
you from morning until evening?"

15Moses replied to his father-in-law, "Because the people come to me to inquire
of God. 16Whenever they have a dispute, it
comes to me, and I make a decision between
one man and another. I teach them God's
statutes and laws."[h]

17"What you're doing is not good," Moses'
father-in-law said to him. 18"You will certainly
wear out both yourself and these people who
are with you, because the task is too heavy for
you. You can't do it alone.[i] 19Now listen to me;
I will give you some advice, and God be with
you. You be the one to represent the people
before God and bring their cases to Him.
20Instruct them about the statutes and laws,
and teach them the way to live and what they
must do.[j] 21But you should select from all the
people able men, God-fearing, trustworthy,
and hating bribes.[k] Place them over the people as commanders of thousands, hundreds,
fifties, and tens.[l] 22They should judge the people at all times. Then they can bring you every
important case but judge every minor case
themselves. In this way you will lighten your
load,[E] and they will bear it with you.[m] 23If you
do this, and God so directs you, you will be
able to endure, and also all these people will
be able to go home satisfied."[F]

24Moses listened to his father-in-law and
did everything he said. 25So Moses chose able

[a]**18:2** Ex 2:21; 4:25 [b]**18:3** Ex 2:22; 4:20; Ac 7:29 [c]**18:4-5** Ex 3:1; 1Ch 23:15 [d]**18:7** Gn 29:13; Ex 18:2 [e]**18:8** Ex 15:6,16; Ps 81:7 [f]**18:10** Gn 14:20; 2Sm 18:28 [g]**18:11** 2Ch 2:5; Lk 1:51 [h]**18:15-16** Ex 24:14; Lv 24:12; Nm 15:34; Dt 17:8 [i]**18:18** Ex 3:12; 4:16; Nm 27:5 [j]**18:20** Dt 1:18; 5:1; Ps 143:8 [k]**18:21** Ex 18:8; Dt 16:19; Ac 6:3 [l]Dt 1:15; 2Ch 19:5-10 [m]**18:22** Lv 24:11; Nm 11:17; Dt 1:17

TEXT MESSAGES

Text Message

Moses testifies to God's work in his life, much like anyone would tell a personal story. Moses' life had seen many hard days by that time, yet God's love and care had never left him. A chapter later (Ex 19:5), Moses records God Himself elaborating on that care with a metaphor: "I carried you on eagles' wings." Whether Moses used this same figure of speech in his testimony to Jethro is unknown. But Moses did this well: He seized the opportunity to tell of God's faithfulness, giving God all the credit.

[A]**18:3** In Hb the name Gershom sounds like the phrase "a stranger there." [B]**18:4** = My God Is Help [C]**18:7** Lit *other about well-being* [D]**18:11** Hb obscure [E]**18:22** Lit *lighten from on you* [F]**18:23** Lit *go to their place in peace*

men from all Israel and made them leaders over the people as commanders of thousands, hundreds, fifties, and tens. 26 They judged the people at all times; they would bring the hard cases to Moses, but they would judge every minor case themselves.

27 Then Moses said good-bye to his father-in-law, and he journeyed to his own land.[a]

Israel at Sinai

19 In the third month, on the same day of the month that the Israelites had left the land of Egypt, they entered the Wilderness of Sinai. 2 After they departed from Rephidim, they entered the Wilderness of Sinai and camped in the wilderness, and Israel camped there in front of the mountain.[b]

3 Moses went up the mountain to God, and the LORD called[c] to him from the mountain: "This is what you must say to the house of Jacob, and explain to the Israelites: 4 'You have seen what I did to the Egyptians and how I carried you on eagles' wings and brought you to Me.[d] 5 Now if you will listen to Me and carefully keep My covenant,[e] you will be My own possession[f] out of all the peoples, although all the earth is Mine, 6 and you will be My kingdom of priests and My holy nation.'[g] These are the words that you are to say to the Israelites."

7 After Moses came back, he summoned the elders of the people and set before them all these words that the LORD had commanded him. 8 Then all the people responded together, "We will do all that the LORD has spoken."[h] So Moses brought the people's words back to the LORD.

9 The LORD said to Moses, "I am going to come to you in a dense cloud,[i] so that the people will hear when I speak[j] with you and will always believe you." Then Moses reported the people's words to the LORD. 10 And the LORD told Moses, "Go to the people and consecrate them today and tomorrow. They must wash their clothes[k] 11 and be prepared by the third day, for on the third day the LORD will come down on Mount Sinai in the sight of all the people.[l] 12 Put boundaries for the people all around the mountain and say: Be careful that you don't go up on the mountain or touch its base. Anyone who touches the mountain will be put to death.[m] 13 No hand may touch him; instead he will be stoned or shot with arrows. No animal or man will live. When the ram's horn sounds a long blast, they may go up the mountain."

14 Then Moses came down from the mountain to the people and consecrated them, and they washed their clothes. 15 He said to the people, "Be prepared by the third day. Do not have sexual relations with women."

16 On the third day, when morning came, there was thunder and lightning, a thick cloud on the mountain, and a loud trumpet sound, so that all the people in the camp shuddered. 17 Then Moses brought the people out of the camp to meet God, and they stood at the foot of the mountain. 18 Mount Sinai was completely enveloped in smoke because the LORD came down on it in fire.[n] Its smoke went up like the smoke of a furnace,[o] and the whole mountain shook violently.[p] 19 As the sound of the trumpet grew louder and louder, Moses spoke and God answered him in the thunder.[q]

20 The LORD came down on Mount Sinai at the top of the mountain. Then the LORD summoned Moses to the top of the mountain, and he went up. 21 The LORD directed Moses, "Go down and warn the people not to break through to see the LORD; otherwise many of them will die.[r] 22 Even the priests who come near the LORD must purify themselves or the LORD will break out in anger against them."[s]

23 But Moses responded to the LORD, "The people cannot come up Mount Sinai, since You warned us: Put a boundary around the mountain and consider it holy." 24 And the LORD replied to him, "Go down and come back with Aaron. But the priests and the people must not break through to come up to the LORD, or He will break out in anger against them." 25 So Moses went down to the people and told them.

The Ten Commandments

20 Then God spoke all these words:

2 I am the LORD your God, who brought
you out of the land of Egypt, out of the
place of slavery.[t]

3 Do not have other gods besides Me.[u]

---

[a] 18:25-27 Ex 18:22; Nm 10:29-30; Dt 1:15
[b] 19:2 Ex 3:1; 17:1,8
[c] 19:3 Ex 3:4; Ac 7:38
[d] 19:4 Dt 29:2; Is 63:9
[e] 19:5 Ex 15:26; Dt 5:2
[f] Dt 7:6; 14:2; 26:18; Ps 135:4; Ti 2:14
[g] 19:6 Dt 26:19; Is 62:12; 1Pt 2:5,9
[h] 19:8 Ex 24:3,7; Dt 5:27
[i] 19:9 Ex 24:15-16; Mt 17:5
[j] Dt 4:12,36; Jn 12:29
[k] 19:10 Gn 35:2; Lv 11:44-45; Heb 10:22
[l] 19:11 Ex 19:16; 34:5
[m] 19:12 Heb 12:20
[n] 19:18 Ex 3:2; 24:17; Dt 4:11; 2Ch 7:1
[o] Ps 144:5; Rv 15:8
[p] Jdg 5:5; Ps 68:7; Jr 4:24; Heb 12:26
[q] 19:19 Neh 9:13; Ps 81:7
[r] 19:21 Ex 3:5; 1Sm 6:19
[s] 19:22 Lv 10:3; 2Sm 6:7-8
[t] 20:2 Ex 13:3; Hs 13:4
[u] 20:3 Dt 6:14; Jr 35:15

4 Do not make an idol[a] for yourself,
whether in the shape of anything in
the heavens above or on the earth
below or in the waters under the earth.
5 You must not bow down to them or
worship them; for I, the LORD your
God, am a jealous God,[b] punishing
the children for the fathers' sin, to the
third and fourth generations[c] of those
who hate Me, 6 but showing faithful
love to a thousand generations of those
who love Me and keep My commands.[d]
7 Do not misuse the name of the LORD
your God, because the LORD will not
leave anyone unpunished who misuses
His name.[e]
8 Remember the Sabbath day, to keep it
holy:[f] 9 You are to labor six days and do
all your work,[g] 10 but the seventh day is
a Sabbath to the LORD your God. You
must not do any work — you, your son
or daughter, your male or female slave,
your livestock, or the foreigner who is
within your gates.[h] 11 For the LORD made
the heavens and the earth, the sea, and
everything in them in six days; then He
rested on the seventh day. Therefore
the LORD blessed the Sabbath day and
declared it holy.
12 Honor your father and your mother[i] so
that you may have a long life in the land
that the LORD your God is giving you.
13 Do not murder.[j]
14 Do not commit adultery.[k]
15 Do not steal.[l]
16 Do not give false testimony against
your neighbor.[m]
17 Do not covet your neighbor's house.
Do not covet your neighbor's wife, his
male or female slave, his ox or donkey,
or anything that belongs to your
neighbor.[n]

The People's Reaction

18 All the people witnessed[A] the thunder and
lightning, the sound of the trumpet, and the
mountain surrounded by smoke. When the
people saw it[B] they trembled and stood at a
distance.[o] 19 "You speak to us, and we will listen," they said to Moses, "but don't let God
speak to us, or we will die."[p]
20 Moses responded to the people, "Don't be
afraid, for God has come to test you, so that
you will ·fear Him and will not[C] sin."[q] 21 And
the people remained standing at a distance as
Moses approached the thick darkness where
God was.[r]

Moses Receives Additional Laws

22 Then the LORD told Moses, "This is what
you are to say to the Israelites: You have seen
that I have spoken to you from heaven.[s] 23 You
must not make gods of silver to rival Me; you
must not make gods of gold for yourselves.[D,t]
24 "You must make an earthen altar for Me
and sacrifice on it your ·burnt offerings and
·fellowship offerings, your sheep and goats,
as well as your cattle. I will come to you and
bless you in every place where I cause My
name to be remembered.[u] 25 If you make a
stone altar for Me, you must not build it out
of cut stones. If you use your chisel on it, you
will defile it.[v] 26 You must not go up to My altar on steps, so that your nakedness is not exposed on it.

21 "These are the ordinances that you
must set before them:

Laws about Slaves

2 "When you buy a Hebrew slave, he is to
serve for six years; then in the seventh he is
to leave as a free man[E] without paying anything.[w] 3 If he arrives alone, he is to leave
alone; if he arrives with[F] a wife, his wife is to
leave with him. 4 If his master gives him a wife
and she bears him sons or daughters, the wife
and her children belong to her master, and
the man must leave alone.
5 "But if the slave declares: 'I love my master,
my wife, and my children; I do not want to
leave as a free man,'[x] 6 his master is to bring
him to the judges[G] and then bring him to the
door or doorpost. His master must pierce his
ear with an awl, and he will serve his master
for life.
7 "When a man sells his daughter as a slave,[H]
she is not to leave as the male slaves do.[y] 8 If
she is displeasing to her master, who chose

[a] **20:4** Lv 26:1; Dt 27:15 [b] **20:5** Ex 34:14; Dt 4:24; Is 44:15,19 [c] Nm 14:18; Ps 79:8; Jr 32:18 [d] **20:6** Dt 7:9 [e] **20:7** Lv 19:12; Mt 5:33 [f] **20:8** Ex 31:13-16; Lv 26:2 [g] **20:9** Ex 34:21; Lk 13:14 [h] **20:10** Gn 2:2-3; Neh 13:16-19 [i] **20:12** Lv 19:3; Mt 15:4; Mk 7:10; Lk 18:20; Eph 6:2 [j] **20:13** Mt 5:21; Rm 13:9 [k] **20:14** Dt 5:18; Mt 5:27 [l] **20:15** Lv 19:11; Mt 19:18 [m] **20:16** Ex 23:1 [n] **20:17** Dt 5:21; Mt 5:28; Lk 12:15; Rm 7:7; 13:9; Eph 5:3,5; Heb 13:5 [o] **20:18** Ex 19:18; Heb 12:18 [p] **20:19** Dt 5:25,27; Gl 3:19 [q] **20:20** Dt 13:3; Pr 16:6; Is 8:13 [r] **20:21** Ex 19:16; Dt 5:22 [s] **20:22** Dt 4:36; Neh 9:13 [t] **20:23** Ex 20:3; 32:4 [u] **20:24** Gn 12:2; Dt 12:5; 16:6,11; 1Kg 9:3; 2Ch 6:6 [v] **20:25** Dt 27:5-6; Jos 8:31 [w] **21:2** Dt 4:14; Jr 34:14 [x] **21:5** Dt 15:16-17 [y] **21:7** Neh 5:5

[A] **20:18** Lit *saw* [B] **20:18** Sam, LXX, Syr, Tg, Vg read *smoking; the people* (or *they*) *were afraid* [C] **20:20** Lit *that the fear of Him may be in you, and you do not* [D] **20:23** Hb obscure [E] **21:2** Lit *to go forth* [F] **21:3** Lit *he is the husband of* [G] **21:6** Or *to God*; that is, to His sanctuary or court [H] **21:7** Or *concubine*

her for himself, then he must let her be redeemed. He has no right to sell her to foreigners because he has acted treacherously
toward her. 9 Or if he chooses her for his son,
he must deal with her according to the customary treatment of daughters. 10 If he takes
an additional wife, he must not reduce the
food, clothing, or marital rights of the first
wife.[a] 11 And if he does not do these three
things for her, she may leave free of charge,
without any exchange of money.[A]

Laws about Personal Injury

12 "Whoever strikes a person so that he dies
must be put to death.[b] 13 But if he didn't intend any harm,[B] and yet God caused it to happen by his hand, I will appoint a place for you
where he may flee.[c] 14 If a person schemes and
willfully[C] acts against his neighbor to murder
him, you must take him from My altar to be
put to death.[d]

15 "Whoever strikes his father or his mother
must be put to death.

16 "Whoever kidnaps a person must be put
to death, whether he sells him or the person
is found in his possession.[e]

17 "Whoever curses his father or his mother
must be put to death.[f]

18 "When men quarrel and one strikes the
other with a stone or his fist, and the injured
man does not die but is confined to bed, 19 if
he can later get up and walk around outside
leaning on his staff, then the one who struck
him will be exempt from punishment. Nevertheless, he must pay for his lost work time[D]
and provide for his complete recovery.

20 "When a man strikes his male or female
slave with a rod, and the slave dies under his
abuse,[E] the owner must be punished.[F] 21 However, if the slave can stand up after a day or
two, the owner should not be punished[G] because he is his owner's property.[H,g]

22 "When men get in a fight and hit a pregnant woman so that her children are born
prematurely[I] but there is no injury, the one
who hit her must be fined as the woman's
husband demands[h] from him, and he must
pay according to judicial assessment. 23 If
there is an injury, then you must give life for
life, 24 eye for eye, tooth for tooth,[i] hand for
hand, foot for foot, 25 burn for burn, bruise
for bruise, wound for wound.

26 "When a man strikes the eye of his male
or female slave and destroys it, he must let the
slave go free in compensation for his eye. 27 If
he knocks out the tooth of his male or female
slave, he must let the slave go free in compensation for his tooth.

28 "When an ox[J] gores a man or a woman to
death, the ox must be stoned,[j] and its meat
may not be eaten, but the ox's owner is innocent. 29 However, if the ox was in the habit
of goring, and its owner has been warned yet
does not restrain it, and it kills a man or a
woman, the ox must be stoned, and its owner
must also be put to death. 30 If instead a ransom[k] is demanded of him, he can pay a redemption price for his life in the full amount
demanded from him. 31 If it gores a son or a
daughter, he is to be dealt with according
to this same law. 32 If the ox gores a male or
female slave, he must give 30 ·shekels[l] of silver[K] to the slave's master, and the ox must be
stoned.

33 "When a man uncovers a pit or digs a pit,
and does not cover it, and an ox or a donkey
falls into it, 34 the owner of the pit must give
compensation; he must pay money to its
owner, but the dead animal will become his.

35 "When a man's ox injures his neighbor's
ox and it dies, they must sell the live ox and
divide its proceeds; they must also divide
the dead animal. 36 If, however, it is known
that the ox was in the habit of goring, yet its
owner has not restrained it, he must compensate fully, ox for ox; the dead animal will become his.

Laws about Theft

22 [L] "When a man steals an ox or a sheep
and butchers it or sells it, he must repay[m] five cattle for the ox or four sheep for
the sheep. 2 [M]If a thief is caught in the act of
breaking in, and he is beaten to death, no one
is ·guilty of bloodshed.[n] 3 But if this happens
after sunrise,[N] there is guilt of bloodshed. A

[a] **21:10** 1Co 7:5
[b] **21:12** Gn 9:6; Mt 26:52
[c] **21:13** Nm 35:11,22-25; Dt 19:2-5; Jos 20:2-9; 1Sm 24:4,10,18
[d] **21:14** Dt 19:11-12; 1Kg 2:28-34
[e] **21:16** Gn 37:28; Ex 22:4; Dt 24:7
[f] **21:17** Lv 20:9; Mt 15:4; Mk 7:10
[g] **21:21** Lv 25:44-46
[h] **21:22** Ex 21:30; Dt 22:18-19
[i] **21:24** Lv 24:20; Dt 19:21; Mt 5:38
[j] **21:28** Gn 9:5
[k] **21:30** Nm 35:31
[l] **21:32** Zch 11:12; Mt 26:15; 27:3,9
[m] **22:1** 2Sm 12:6; Pr 6:31; Lk 19:8
[n] **22:2** Nm 35:27; Mt 24:43

[A] **21:11** She doesn't have to pay any redemption price. [B] **21:13** Lit *he was not lying in wait* [C] **21:14** Or *maliciously* [D] **21:19** Lit *his inactivity* [E] **21:20** Lit *hand* [F] **21:20** Or *must suffer vengeance* [G] **21:21** Or *not suffer vengeance* [H] **21:21** Lit *money* [I] **21:22** Either a live birth or a miscarriage [J] **21:28** Or *a bull*, or *a steer* [K] **21:32** About 1 pound of silver [L] **22:1** Ex 21:37 in Hb [M] **22:2** Ex 22:1 in Hb [N] **22:3** Lit *if the sun has risen over him*

thief must make full restitution. If he is unable, he is to be sold because of his theft.[a] 4If
what was stolen — whether ox, donkey, or
sheep — is actually found alive in his possession, he must repay double.

Laws about Crop Protection

5"When a man lets a field or vineyard be
grazed in, and then allows his animals to go
and graze in someone else's field, he must
repay[A] with the best of his own field or vineyard.

6"When a fire gets out of control, spreads
to thornbushes, and consumes stacks of cut
grain, standing grain, or a field, the one who
started the fire must make full restitution for
what was burned.

Laws about Personal Property

7"When a man gives his neighbor money
or goods to keep, but they are stolen from
that person's house, the thief, if caught, must
repay double. 8If the thief is not caught, the
owner of the house must present himself to
the judges[B] to determine[C] whether or not he
has taken his neighbor's property.[b] 9In any
case of wrongdoing involving an ox, a donkey, a sheep, a garment, or anything else lost,
and someone claims, 'That's mine,'[D] the case
between the two parties is to come before the
judges.[E] The one the judges condemn[F] must
repay double to his neighbor.

10"When a man gives his neighbor a donkey, an ox, a sheep, or any other animal to
care for, but it dies, is injured, or is stolen,
while no one is watching, 11there must be
an oath before the LORD between the two
of them to determine whether or not he has
taken his neighbor's property. Its owner must
accept the oath, and the other man does not
have to make restitution. 12But if, in fact, the
animal was stolen from his custody, he must
make restitution to its owner.[c] 13If it was actually torn apart by a wild animal, he is to bring
it as evidence; he does not have to make restitution for the torn carcass.

14"When a man borrows an animal from
his neighbor, and it is injured or dies while
its owner is not there with it, the man must
make full restitution. 15If its owner is there
with it, the man does not have to make restitution. If it was rented, the loss is covered by[G]
its rental price.

Laws about Seduction

16"If a man seduces a virgin who is not engaged, and he has sexual relations with her,
he must certainly pay the bridal price for
her to be his wife. 17If her father absolutely
refuses to give her to him, he must pay an
amount in silver equal to the bridal price for
virgins.[d]

Capital Offenses

18"You must not allow a sorceress[e] to live.

19"Whoever has sexual intercourse with an
animal[f] must be put to death.

20"Whoever sacrifices to any gods, except
the LORD alone, is to be •set apart for destruction.[g]

Laws Protecting the Vulnerable

21"You must not exploit a foreign resident[h]
or oppress him, since you were foreigners in
the land of Egypt.

22"You must not mistreat any widow or
fatherless child.[i] 23If you do mistreat them,
they will no doubt cry to Me, and I will certainly hear their cry.[j] 24My anger will burn,
and I will kill you with the sword; then your
wives will be widows and your children fatherless.[k]

25"If you lend money to My people, to the
poor person among you, you must not be like
a moneylender to him; you must not charge
him interest.[l]

26"If you ever take your neighbor's cloak
as collateral, return it to him before sunset.
27For it is his only covering; it is the clothing
for his body.[H] What will he sleep in? And if
he cries out to Me, I will listen because I am
compassionate.[m]

Respect for God

28"You must not blaspheme God[I] or curse a
leader among your people.[n]

[a]**22:3** Ex 21:2,16
[b]**22:8** Dt 17:8-9
[c]**22:11-12** Gn 31:39; Heb 6:16
[d]**22:16-17** Gn 34:12; Dt 22:28-29
[e]**22:18** Lv 20:27; Dt 18:11; 1Sm 28:3
[f]**22:19** Lv 18:23; 20:15; Dt 27:21
[g]**22:20** Dt 17:2-5
[h]**22:21** Lv 19:33; Dt 10:19
[i]**22:22** Dt 24:17; Jms 1:27
[j]**22:23** Ps 18:6; Lk 18:7
[k]**22:24** Ps 69:4; 109:9
[l]**22:25** Lv 25:36-37; Dt 23:20; Ps 15:5
[m]**22:26-27** Ex 34:6; Dt 24:6
[n]**22:28** Ec 10:20; Ac 23:5

[A]**22:5** LXX adds *from his field according to its produce. But if someone lets his animals graze an entire field, he must repay*; DSS, Sam also support this reading. [B]**22:8** Or *to God* [C]**22:8** LXX, Tg, Vg read *swear* [D]**22:9** Lit *That is it* [E]**22:9** Or *before God* [F]**22:9** Or *one whom God condemns* [G]**22:15** Lit *rented, it comes with* [H]**22:27** Lit *skin* [I]**22:28** Or *judges*

29"You must not hold back offerings[a] from
your harvest or your vats. Give Me the firstborn of your sons. 30Do the same with your
cattle and your flock. Let them stay with their
mothers for seven days, but on the eighth day
you are to give them to Me.[b]
31"Be My holy people. You must not eat the
meat of a mauled animal[c] found in the field;
throw it to the dogs.

Laws about Honesty and Justice

23 "You must not spread a false report.
Do not join[A] the wicked to be a malicious witness.[d]
2"You must not follow a crowd in wrongdoing. Do not testify in a lawsuit and go along
with a crowd to pervert justice.[e] 3Do not show
favoritism to a poor person in his lawsuit.
4"If you come across your enemy's stray ox
or donkey, you must return it to him.
5"If you see the donkey of someone who
hates you lying helpless under its load, and
you want to refrain from helping it, you must
help with it.[B,f]
6"You must not deny justice to a poor person among you in his lawsuit. 7Stay far away
from a false accusation. Do not kill the innocent and the just, because I will not justify
the •guilty.[g] 8You must not take a bribe,[h] for
a bribe blinds the clear-sighted and corrupts
the words[C] of the righteous. 9You must not
oppress a foreign resident;[i] you yourselves
know how it feels to be a foreigner because
you were foreigners in the land of Egypt.

Sabbaths and Festivals

10"Sow your land for six years and gather
its produce.[j] 11But during the seventh year
you are to let it rest and leave it uncultivated,
so that the poor among your people may eat
from it and the wild animals may consume
what they leave. Do the same with your vineyard and your olive grove.
12"Do your work[k] for six days but rest on the
seventh day so that your ox and your donkey
may rest, and the son of your female slave as
well as the foreign resident may be refreshed.
13"Pay strict attention to everything I have
said to you. You must not invoke the names of
other gods; they must not be heard on your
lips.[D,l]
14"Celebrate a festival in My honor three
times a year.[m] 15Observe the Festival of •Un-
leavened Bread. As I commanded you,
you are to eat unleavened bread for seven
days at the appointed time in the month
of Abib,[E] because you came out of Egypt in
that month. No one is to appear before Me
empty-handed.[n] 16Also observe the Festival of
Harvest[F] with the •firstfruits of your produce
from what you sow in the field, and observe
the Festival of Ingathering[G,o] at the end of the
year, when you gather your produce[H] from
the field. 17Three times a year all your males
are to appear before the Lord GOD.
18"You must not offer the blood of My sacrifices with anything leavened. The fat of My
festival offering must not remain until morning.[p]
19"Bring the best of the firstfruits of your
land to the house of the LORD your God.
"You must not boil a young goat in its
mother's milk.[q]

Promises and Warnings

20"I am going to send an angel[r] before you
to protect you on the way and bring you to
the place I have prepared. 21Be attentive to
him and listen to his voice. Do not defy[I] him,
because he will not forgive your acts of rebellion, for My name is in him.[s] 22But if you
will carefully obey him and do everything I
say, then I will be an enemy[t] to your enemies
and a foe to your foes. 23For My angel will go
before you and bring you to the land of the
Amorites, Hittites, Perizzites, Canaanites,
Hivites, and Jebusites, and I will wipe them
out.[u] 24You must not bow down to their gods
or worship them. Do not imitate their practices. Instead, demolish them[J] and smash
their sacred pillars to pieces.[v] 25Worship the
LORD your God, and He[K] will bless your bread
and your water. I will remove illnesses from
you.[w] 26No woman will miscarry or be childless in your land. I will give you the full number of your days.[x]

[a]22:29 Ex 13:2; 23:16 [b]22:30 Lv 22:27; Dt 15:19 [c]22:31 Ex 19:2; Ezk 4:14 [d]23:1 Ps 35:11; 101:5; Ac 6:11 [e]23:2 Dt 16:19; 24:17; 27:19 [f]23:5 Dt 22:1,4; Rm 12:20 [g]23:6-7 Ec 5:8; Eph 4:25 [h]23:8 Dt 10:17; 16:19; Pr 15:27 [i]23:9 Ex 22:21 [j]23:10 Lv 25:3-4 [k]23:12 Ex 20:9 [l]23:13 Dt 4:9; Jos 23:7; Hs 2:17; 1Tm 4:16 [m]23:14 Ex 34:23; Dt 16:16 [n]23:15 Ex 12:15; 34:20 [o]23:16 Ex 34:22; Lv 23:39; Dt 16:13 [p]23:18 Ex 34:25; Dt 16:4 [q]23:19 Ex 22:29; 26:2,10; Dt 14:21 [r]23:20 Ex 14:19; 15:16-17; 23:23; 32:34; 33:2 [s]23:21 Nm 14:11; Dt 18:19; Ps 78:40,56 [t]23:22 Gn 12:3; Dt 30:7; Jr 30:20 [u]23:23 Ex 23:20; Jos 24:8 [v]23:24 Ex 20:5; 34:13; Nm 33:52; Dt 12:30 [w]23:25 Ex 15:26; Dt 6:13; 7:15; 28:5,8; Mt 4:10 [x]23:26 Dt 7:14; Jb 5:26; Mal 3:11

A23:1 Lit *join hands with* B23:5 Or *load, you must refrain from leaving it to him; you must set it free with him* C23:8 Or *and subverts the cause* D23:13 Lit *mouth* E23:15 March–April; called Nisan in the post-exilic period; Neh 2:1; Est 3:7 F23:16 The Festival of Harvest is called Festival of Weeks elsewhere; Ex 34:22. In the NT it is called Pentecost; Ac 2:1. G23:16 The Festival of Ingathering is called Festival of Booths elsewhere; Lv 23:34-36. H23:16 Lit *labors* I23:21 Or *embitter* J23:24 Probably the idols K23:25 LXX, Vg read *I*

27 "I will cause the people ahead of you to feel terror[A] and throw into confusion[a] all the nations you come to. I will make all your enemies turn their backs to you in retreat. 28 I will send the hornet[B,b] in front of you, and it will drive the Hivites, Canaanites, and Hittites away from you. 29 I will not drive them out ahead of you in a single year; otherwise, the land would become desolate, and wild animals would multiply against you. 30 I will drive them out little by little ahead of you until you have become numerous[C] and take possession of the land. 31 I will set your borders from the ·Red Sea to the Mediterranean Sea,[D] and from the wilderness to the Euphrates River.[E] For I will place the inhabitants of the land under your control, and you will drive them out ahead of you.[c] 32 You must not make a covenant[d] with them or their gods. 33 They must not remain in your land, or else they will make you sin against Me. If you worship their gods, it will be a snare for you."[e]

The Covenant Ceremony

24 Then He said to Moses, "Go up to the LORD, you and Aaron, Nadab, and Abihu, and 70 of Israel's elders,[f] and bow in worship at a distance. 2 Moses alone is to approach the LORD, but the others are not to approach, and the people are not to go up with him."

3 Moses came and told the people all the commands of the LORD and all the ordinances. Then all the people responded with a single voice, "We will do everything that the LORD has commanded."[g] 4 And Moses wrote[h] down all the words of the LORD. He rose early the next morning and set up an altar and 12 pillars for the 12 tribes of Israel at the base of the mountain. 5 Then he sent out young Israelite men, and they offered ·burnt offerings and sacrificed bulls as ·fellowship offerings to the LORD. 6 Moses took half the blood and set it in basins; the other half of the blood he sprinkled on the altar. 7 He then took the covenant scroll and read it aloud to the people. They responded, "We will do and obey everything that the LORD has commanded."

[a]**23:27** Dt 2:25; 7:23 [b]**23:28** Dt 7:20; Jos 24:12 [c]**23:31** Gn 15:18; Dt 11:24; Jos 21:44; 1Kg 4:21 [d]**23:32** Ex 34:12,15; Dt 7:2 [e]**23:33** Dt 7:16; Ps 106:36 [f]**24:1** Ex 6:23; Lv 10:1-2; Nm 11:16 [g]**24:3** Ex 19:8; Dt 5:27 [h]**24:4** Gn 28:18; Dt 31:9 [i]**24:6-8** Heb 9:18-20; 1Pt 1:2 [j]**24:10** Jn 1:18; 1Jn 4:12 [k]Ezk 1:26; Mt 17:2; Rv 4:3 [l]**24:11** Gn 32:30; Ex 19:21 [m]**24:12** Ex 32:15; Dt 5:22 [n]**24:13** Ex 3:1; 17:9 [o]**24:15** Ex 19:9; Mt 17:5 [p]**24:16** Ex 16:10 [q]**24:17** Ex 3:2; Dt 4:36; Heb 12:18,29 [r]**24:18** Ex 34:28; Dt 9:9 [s]**25:2** Ex 35:5,21; 1Ch 29:5; Ezr 2:68; Neh 11:2; 2Co 8:12; 9:7 [t]**25:5** Ex 26:14; 35:7,23; 36:19; 39:34 [u]**25:6** Ex 27:20; 30:23-24 [v]**25:7** Ex 28:4,6-15 [w]**25:8** Ex 36:1–5: Heb 9:12 [x]Ex 29:45; 1Kg 6:13; 2Co 6:16; Rv 21:3

8 Moses took the blood, sprinkled it on the people, and said, "This is the blood of the covenant that the LORD has made with you concerning all these words."[i]

9 Then Moses went up with Aaron, Nadab, and Abihu, and 70 of Israel's elders, 10 and they saw[j] the God of Israel. Beneath His feet was something like a pavement made of sapphire[F] stone, as clear as the sky itself.[k] 11 God did not harm[G] the Israelite nobles; they saw[l] Him, and they ate and drank.

12 The LORD said to Moses, "Come up to Me on the mountain and stay there so that I may give you the stone tablets[m] with the law and commandments I have written for their instruction."

13 So Moses arose with his assistant Joshua and went up the mountain of God.[n] 14 He told the elders, "Wait here for us until we return to you. Aaron and Hur are here with you. Whoever has a dispute should go to them." 15 When Moses went up the mountain, the cloud[o] covered it. 16 The glory of the LORD settled on Mount Sinai, and the cloud covered it for six days. On the seventh day He called to Moses from the cloud.[p] 17 The appearance of the LORD's glory to the Israelites was like a consuming fire[q] on the mountaintop. 18 Moses entered the cloud as he went up the mountain, and he remained on the mountain 40 days and 40 nights.[r]

Offerings to Build the Tabernacle

25 The LORD spoke to Moses: 2 "Tell the Israelites to take an offering for Me. You are to take My offering from everyone who is willing to give.[s] 3 This is the offering you are to receive from them: gold, silver, and bronze; 4 blue, purple, and scarlet yarn; fine linen and goat hair; 5 ram skins dyed red[t] and manatee skins;[H] acacia wood; 6 oil[u] for the light; spices for the anointing oil and for the fragrant incense; 7 and onyx[I] along with other gemstones for mounting on the ·ephod and breastpiece.[J,v]

8 "They are to make a sanctuary[w] for Me so that I may dwell[x] among them. 9 You must make it according to all that I show you — the

[A]**23:27** Lit *will send terror of Me ahead of you* [B]**23:28** Or *send panic* [C]**23:30** Lit *fruitful* [D]**23:31** Lit *the Sea of the Philistines* [E]**23:31** Lit *the River* [F]**24:10** Or *lapis lazuli* [G]**24:11** Lit *not stretch out His hand against* [H]**25:5** Or *and dolphin skins*, or *and fine leather*; Hb obscure [I]**25:7** Or *carnelian* [J]**25:7** Traditionally, *breastplate*

pattern[a] of the tabernacle as well as the pattern of all its furnishings.

The Ark

10“They are to make an ark[b] of acacia wood,
45 inches long, 27 inches wide, and 27 inches
high.[A] 11Overlay it with pure gold; overlay it
both inside and out. Also make a gold molding
all around it. 12Cast four gold rings for it and
place them on its four feet, two rings on one
side and two rings on the other side. 13Make
poles of acacia wood and overlay them with
gold. 14Insert the poles into the rings on the
sides of the ark in order to carry the ark with
them. 15The poles are to remain in the rings
of the ark; they must not be removed from it.
16Put the tablets of the ˙testimony that I will
give you into the ark.[c] 17Make a ˙mercy seat[d] of
pure gold, 45 inches long and 27 inches wide.[B]
18Make two ˙cherubim of gold; make them of
hammered work at the two ends of the mercy
seat. 19Make one cherub at one end and one
cherub at the other end. At its two ends, make
the cherubim of one piece with the mercy
seat. 20The cherubim are to have wings spread
out above, covering[e] the mercy seat with their
wings, and are to face one another. The faces
of the cherubim should be toward the mercy
seat. 21Set the mercy seat on top of the ark and
put the testimony that I will give you into the
ark.[f] 22I will meet with you there above the
mercy seat, between the two cherubim[g] that
are over the ark of the testimony; I will speak
with you from there about all that I command you regarding the Israelites.

The Table

23“You are to construct a table[h] of acacia
wood, 36 inches long, 18 inches wide, and 27
inches high.[C] 24Overlay it with pure gold and
make a gold molding all around it. 25Make
a three-inch[D] frame all around it and make
a gold molding for it all around its frame.
26Make four gold rings for it, and attach the
rings to the four corners at its four legs. 27The
rings should be next to the frame as holders
for the poles to carry the table. 28Make the
poles of acacia wood and overlay them with
gold, and the table can be carried by them.
29You are also to make its plates[i] and cups,
as well as its pitchers and bowls for pouring
˙drink offerings. Make them out of pure gold.
30Put the ˙bread of the Presence[j] on the table
before Me at all times.

The Lampstand

31“You[k] are to make a lampstand[l] out of
pure, hammered gold. It is to be made of one
piece: its base and shaft, its ornamental cups,
and its calyxes[E] and petals. 32Six branches are
to extend from its sides, three branches of the
lampstand from one side and three branches
of the lampstand from the other side. 33There
are to be three cups shaped like almond blossoms, each with a calyx and petals, on the
first branch, and three cups shaped like almond blossoms, each with a calyx and petals, on the next branch. It is to be this way for
the six branches that extend from the lampstand. 34There are to be four cups shaped like
almond blossoms on the lampstand shaft
along with its calyxes and petals. 35For the six
branches that extend from the lampstand, a
calyx must be under the first pair of branches
from it, a calyx under the second pair of
branches from it, and a calyx under the third
pair of branches from it. 36Their calyxes and
branches are to be of one piece.[F] All of it is to
be a single hammered piece of pure gold.
37“Make seven lamps[m] on it. Its lamps are to
be set up so they illuminate the area in front
of it. 38Its snuffers and firepans must be of
pure gold. 39The lampstand[G] with all these
utensils is to be made from 75 pounds[H] of
pure gold. 40Be careful to make them according to the pattern[n] you have been shown on
the mountain.

The Tabernacle

26 “You[o] are to construct the tabernacle
itself with 10 curtains. You must make
them of finely spun linen, and blue, purple,
and scarlet yarn, with a design of ˙cherubim
worked into them. 2The length of each curtain should be 42 feet,[I] and the width of each
curtain six feet;[J] all the curtains are to have

[a]**25:9** Ex 25:40; 26:30; Ac 7:44; Heb 8:2,5
[b]**25:10** Ex 37:1,3-4; Dt 10:3; Heb 9:4
[c]**25:16** Ex 16:34; Dt 31:26; 1Kg 8:9
[d]**25:17** Ex 37:6; Rm 3:25; Heb 9:5
[e]**25:20** 1Kg 8:7; 1Ch 28:18; Heb 9:5
[f]**25:21** Ex 25:16; 26:34
[g]**25:22** Nm 7:89; 1Sm 4:4; 2Sm 6:2; 2Kg 19:15; Ps 80:1; Is 37:16
[h]**25:23** Ex 37:10; 1Kg 7:48; 2Ch 4:8; Heb 9:2
[i]**25:29** Ex 37:16; Nm 4:7
[j]**25:30** Ex 35:13; 39:36; 40:23; Lv 24:5-9; Nm 4:7
[k]**25:31-39** Ex 37:17-24
[l]**25:31** 1Kg 7:49; Zch 4:2; Heb 9:2; Rv 1:12
[m]**25:37** Ex 27:21; 37:23; Lv 24:3-4; Nm 8:2; 2Ch 13:11
[n]**25:40** Ex 26:30; Nm 8:4; 1Ch 28:11,19; Ac 7:44; Heb 8:5
[o]**26:1-37** Ex 36:8-38

[A]**25:10** Lit *two and a half cubits its length, one and a half cubits its width, and one and a half cubits its height* [B]**25:17** Lit *two and a half cubits its length, one and a half cubits its width* [C]**25:23** Lit *two cubits its length, one cubit its width, and one and a half cubits its height* [D]**25:25** Lit *Make it a handbreadth* [E]**25:31** = the outer covering of a flower [F]**25:36** Lit *piece with it* [G]**25:39** Lit *It* [H]**25:39** Lit *a talent* [I]**26:2** Lit *28 cubits* [J]**26:2** Lit *four cubits*

the same measurements. 3 Five of the curtains
should be joined together, and the other five
curtains joined together. 4 Make loops of blue
yarn on the edge of the last curtain[A] in the
first set, and do the same on the edge of the
outermost curtain in the second set. 5 Make
50 loops on the one curtain and make 50
loops on the edge of the curtain in the second
set, so that the loops line up together. 6 Also
make 50 gold clasps and join the curtains together with the clasps, so that the tabernacle
may be a single unit.
7 "You are to make curtains of goat hair for
a tent over the tabernacle; make 11 of these
curtains. 8 The length of each curtain should
be 45 feet[B] and the width of each curtain
six feet.[C] All 11 curtains are to have the same
measurements. 9 Join five of the curtains by
themselves, and the other six curtains by
themselves. Then fold the sixth curtain double at the front of the tent. 10 Make 50 loops
on the edge of the one curtain, the outermost
in the first set, and make 50 loops on the edge
of the corresponding curtain of the second
set. 11 Make 50 bronze clasps; put the clasps
through the loops and join the tent together
so that it is a single unit. 12 As for the flap that
is left over from the tent curtains, the leftover
half curtain is to hang down over the back of
the tabernacle. 13 The half yard[D] on one side
and the half yard[E] on the other of what is left
over along the length of the tent curtains
should be hanging down over the sides of the
tabernacle on either side to cover it. 14 Make
a covering for the tent from ram skins dyed
red[a] and a covering of manatee skins[F] on top
of that.
15 "You are to make upright planks[G] of acacia wood[b] for the tabernacle. 16 The length
of each plank is to be 15 feet,[H] and the width
of each plank 27 inches.[I] 17 Each plank must
be connected together with two tenons. Do
the same for all the planks of the tabernacle.
18 Make the planks for the tabernacle as follows: 20 planks for the south side, 19 and make
40 silver bases under the 20 planks, two bases
under the first plank for its two tenons, and
two bases under the next plank for its two
tenons; 20 20 planks for the second side of the
tabernacle, the north side, 21 along with their
40 silver bases, two bases under the first
plank and two bases under each plank; 22 and
make six planks for the west side of the tabernacle. 23 Make two additional planks for the
two back corners of the tabernacle. 24 They
are to be paired at the bottom, and joined together[J] at the top in a single ring. So it should
be for both of them; they will serve as the two
corners. 25 There are to be eight planks with
their silver bases: 16 bases; two bases under
the first plank and two bases under each
plank.
26 "You are to make five crossbars of acacia
wood for the planks on one side of the tabernacle, 27 five crossbars for the planks on the
other side of the tabernacle, and five crossbars for the planks of the back side of the tabernacle on the west. 28 The central crossbar
is to run through the middle of the planks
from one end to the other. 29 Then overlay the
planks with gold, and make their rings of gold
as the holders for the crossbars. Also overlay
the crossbars with gold. 30 You are to set up
the tabernacle according to the plan for it
that you have been shown on the mountain.[c]
31 "You are to make a veil of blue, purple,
and scarlet yarn, and finely spun linen with a
design of cherubim worked into it.[d] 32 Hang it
on four gold-plated posts of acacia wood that
have gold hooks and that stand on four silver
bases. 33 Hang the veil under the clasps[K] and
bring the ark of the •testimony there behind
the veil, so the veil will make a separation for
you between the holy place[e] and the most
holy place. 34 Put the •mercy seat on the ark of
the testimony in the most holy place.[f] 35 Place
the table outside the veil and the lampstand
on the south side of the tabernacle, opposite
the table; put the table on the north side.[g]
36 "For the entrance to the tent you are to
make a screen embroidered with blue, purple, and scarlet yarn, and finely spun linen.
37 Make five posts of acacia wood for the
screen and overlay them with gold; their
hooks are to be gold, and you are to cast five
bronze bases for them.

[a] **26:14** Ex 25:5; 35:7; 36:19; 39:34; Nm 4:25
[b] **26:15** Ex 25:28; 26:37; 27:1,6; 30:1,5; 35:33; 36:20; 37:15; 38:6
[c] **26:30** Ex 25:9,40; Ac 7:44; Heb 8:5
[d] **26:31** Ex 36:35; 2Ch 3:14; Mt 27:51; Heb 9:3
[e] **26:33** Ex 25:16; 40:21; Lv 16:2; Heb 9:2
[f] **26:34** Ex 25:21; 40:20; Heb 9:5
[g] **26:35** Ex 40:22,24; Heb 9:2

[A] **26:4** Lit *the one curtain on the end* [B] **26:8** Lit *30 cubits* [C] **26:8** Lit *four cubits* [D] **26:13** Lit *The cubit* [E] **26:13** Lit *the cubit* [F] **26:14** Or *of dolphin skins*, or *of fine leather*; Hb obscure [G] **26:15** Or *frames*, or *beams* [H] **26:16** Lit *10 cubits* [I] **26:16** Lit *a cubit and a half* [J] **26:24** Lit *and together they are to be complete* [K] **26:33** The clasps that join the 10 curtains of the tabernacle; Ex 26:6

The Altar of Burnt Offering

27 "You[a] are to construct the altar of acacia wood. The altar must be square, 7½ feet long, and 7½ feet wide;[A] it must be 4½ feet high.[B] 2 Make horns for it on its four corners; the horns are to be of one piece.[C] Overlay it with bronze.[b] 3 Make its pots for removing ashes, and its shovels, basins, meat forks, and firepans; make all its utensils of bronze. 4 Construct a grate for it of bronze mesh, and make four bronze rings on the mesh at its four corners. 5 Set it below, under the altar's ledge,[D] so that the mesh comes halfway up[E] the altar. 6 Then make poles for the altar, poles of acacia wood, and overlay them with bronze. 7 The poles are to be inserted into the rings so that the poles are on two sides of the altar when it is carried. 8 Construct the altar with boards so that it is hollow. They are to make it just as it was shown to you on the mountain.[c]

The Courtyard

9 "You[d] are to make the courtyard for the tabernacle. Make the hangings on the south of the courtyard out of finely spun linen, 150 feet[F] long on that side. 10 There are to be 20 posts and 20 bronze bases. The hooks and bands[G] of the posts must be silver. 11 Then make the hangings on the north side 150 feet[F] long. There are to be 20 posts and 20 bronze bases. The hooks and bands[G] of the posts must be silver. 12 Make the hangings of the courtyard on the west side 75 feet[H] long, including their 10 posts and 10 bases. 13 Make the hangings of the courtyard on the east side toward the sunrise 75 feet.[H] 14 Make the hangings on one side of the gate 22½ feet,[I] including their three posts and their three bases. 15 And make the hangings on the other side 22½ feet,[I] including their three posts and their three bases. 16 The gate of the courtyard is to have a thirty-foot[J] screen[e] embroidered with blue, purple, and scarlet yarn, and finely spun linen. It is to have four posts including their four bases.

17 "All the posts around the courtyard are to be banded with silver and have silver hooks and bronze bases. 18 The length of the courtyard is to be 150 feet, the width 75 feet at each end, and the height 7½ feet,[K] all of it made of finely spun linen. The bases of the posts must be bronze. 19 All the tools of the tabernacle for every use and all its tent pegs as well as all the tent pegs of the courtyard are to be made of bronze.

The Lampstand Oil

20 "You are to command the Israelites to bring you pure oil from crushed olives for the light, in order to keep the lamp burning continually. 21 In the tent of meeting outside the veil that is in front of the *testimony,[f] Aaron and his sons are to tend the lamp[g] from evening until morning before the LORD. This is to be a permanent statute[h] for the Israelites throughout their generations.

The Priestly Garments

28 "Have your brother Aaron, with his sons, come to you from the Israelites to serve Me as priest — Aaron, his sons Nadab and Abihu, Eleazar and Ithamar.[i] 2 Make holy garments[j] for your brother Aaron, for glory and beauty. 3 You are to instruct all the skilled craftsmen,[L,k] whom I have filled with a spirit of wisdom, to make Aaron's garments for consecrating him to serve Me as priest. 4 These are the garments that they must make: a breastpiece, an *ephod, a robe, a specially woven tunic,[M] a turban, and a sash. They are to make holy garments for your brother Aaron and his sons so that they may serve Me as priests. 5 They should use[N] gold; blue, purple, and scarlet yarn; and fine linen.

The Ephod

6 "They[l] are to make the ephod of finely spun linen embroidered with gold, and with blue, purple, and scarlet yarn. 7 It must have two shoulder pieces attached to its two edges so that it can be joined together. 8 The artistically woven waistband that is on the ephod[O] must be of one piece,[P] according to the same workmanship of gold, of blue, purple, and scarlet yarn, and of finely spun linen.

[a] **27:1-8** Ex 38:1-7; Ezk 43:13
[b] **27:2** Nm 16:38; Ps 118:27
[c] **27:8** Ex 25:40; 26:30
[d] **27:9-19** Ex 38:9-20
[e] **27:16** Ex 35:17; 38:18; 39:40; 40:8,33; Nm 3:26; 4:26
[f] **27:21** Ex 30:8; 1Sm 3:3; 2Ch 13:11
[g] Ex 26:31,33; 28:43
[h] Ex 29:9; Lv 3:17; 16:34; Nm 18:23; 19:21
[i] **28:1** Nm 18:7; Ps 99:6; Heb 5:1
[j] **28:2** Ex 29:5,9; 31:10; 39:1-2; Lv 8:7,30; Nm 20:26,28
[k] **28:3** Ex 31:6; 35:25; 36:1
[l] **28:6-12** Ex 39:2-7; Lv 8:7

[A] **27:1** Lit *five cubits in length and five cubits in width* [B] **27:1** Lit *wide; and its height three cubits* [C] **27:2** Lit *piece with it* [D] **27:5** Perhaps a ledge around the altar on which the priests could stand; Lv 9:22 [E] **27:5** Or *altar's rim, so that the grid comes halfway down* [F] **27:9,11** Lit *100 cubits* [G] **27:10,11** Or *connecting rods* [H] **27:12,13** Lit *50 cubits* [I] **27:14,15** Lit *15 cubits* [J] **27:16** Lit *twenty-cubit* [K] **27:18** Lit *be 100 by the cubit, and the width 50 by 50, and the height five cubits* [L] **28:3** Lit *all wise of heart* [M] **28:4** Hb obscure [N] **28:5** Lit *receive* [O] **28:8** Lit *waistband of its ephod, which is on it* [P] **28:8** Lit *piece with the ephod*

9 "Take two onyx stones and engrave on
them the names of Israel's sons: 10 six of their
names on the first stone and the remaining
six names on the second stone, in the order
of their birth. 11 Engrave the two stones with
the names of Israel's sons as a gem cutter engraves a seal. Mount them, surrounded with
gold filigree settings. 12 Fasten both stones on
the shoulder pieces of the ephod as memorial stones for the Israelites. Aaron will carry
their names on his two shoulders before the
LORD as a reminder.[a] 13 Fashion gold filigree
settings 14 and two chains of pure gold; you
will make them of braided cord work, and attach the cord chains to the settings.

The Breastpiece

15 "You[b] are to make an embroidered breastpiece for making decisions.[A] Make it with the
same workmanship as the ephod; make it of
gold, of blue, purple, and scarlet yarn, and
of finely spun linen. 16 It must be square and
folded double, nine inches long and nine
inches wide.[B] 17 Place a setting of gemstones[C]
on it, four rows of stones:

The first row should be
a row of carnelian, topaz, and emerald;[D]
18 the second row,
a turquoise,[E] a sapphire,[F]
and a diamond;[G]
19 the third row,
a jacinth,[H] an agate, and an amethyst;
20 and the fourth row,
a beryl, an onyx, and a jasper.

They should be adorned with gold filigree
in their settings. 21 The 12 stones are to correspond to the names of Israel's sons. Each
stone must be engraved like a seal, with one
of the names of the 12 tribes.

22 "You are to make braided chains[I] of pure
gold cord work for the breastpiece. 23 Fashion
two gold rings for the breastpiece and attach
them to its two corners. 24 Then attach the two
gold cords to the two gold rings at the corners
of the breastpiece. 25 Attach the other ends of
the two cords to the two filigree settings, and
in this way attach them to the ephod's shoulder pieces in the front. 26 Make two other gold
rings and put them at the two other corners
of the breastpiece on the edge that is next to
the inner border of the ephod. 27 Make two
more gold rings and attach them to the bottom of the ephod's two shoulder pieces on
its front, close to its seam,[J] and above the
ephod's woven waistband. 28 The craftsmen
are to tie the breastpiece from its rings to the
rings of the ephod with a cord of blue yarn,
so that the breastpiece is above the ephod's
waistband and does not come loose from the
ephod.

29 "Whenever he enters the sanctuary, Aaron
is to carry the names of Israel's sons over his
heart on the breastpiece for decisions, as a
continual reminder before the LORD. 30 Place
the *Urim and Thummim[c] in the breastpiece
for decisions, so that they will also be over
Aaron's heart whenever he comes before the
LORD. Aaron will continually carry the means
of decisions for the Israelites over his heart
before the LORD.

The Robe

31 "You[d] are to make the robe of the ephod
entirely of blue yarn. 32 There should be an
opening at its top in the center of it. Around
the opening, there should be a woven collar
with an opening like that of body armor[K] so
that it does not tear. 33 Make pomegranates of
blue, purple, and scarlet yarn[L] on its lower
hem and all around it. Put gold bells between
them all the way around, 34 so that gold bells
and pomegranates alternate around the
lower hem of the robe. 35 The robe must be
worn by Aaron whenever he ministers, and
its sound will be heard when he enters the
sanctuary before the LORD and when he exits, so that he does not die.

The Turban

36 "You are to make a pure gold medallion
and engrave it, like the engraving of a seal:[e]

HOLY TO THE LORD.

37 Fasten it to a cord of blue yarn so it can be
placed on the turban; the medallion is to be

[a] **28:12** Ex 28:29; Jos 4:7; Zch 6:14
[b] **28:15-28** Ex 39:8-21
[c] **28:30** Lv 8:8; Nm 27:21; Dt 33:8; Ezr 2:63; Neh 7:65
[d] **28:31-40** Ex 39:22-31
[e] **28:36** Lv 8:9; Zch 14:20

[A] **28:15** Used for determining God's will; Nm 27:21 [B] **28:16** Lit *a span its length and a span its width* [C] **28:17** Many of these stones cannot be identified with certainty. [D] **28:17** Or *beryl* [E] **28:18** Or *malachite, or garnet* [F] **28:18** Or *lapis lazuli* [G] **28:18** Hb obscure; LXX, Vg read *jasper* [H] **28:19** Hb obscure [I] **28:22** The same chains mentioned in v. 14 [J] **28:27** The place where the shoulder pieces join the front of the ephod [K] **28:32** Hb obscure [L] **28:33** Sam, LXX add *of finely spun linen* on the front of the turban. 38 It will be on Aaron's forehead so that Aaron may bear the ·guilt[a] connected with the holy offerings that the Israelites consecrate as all their holy gifts. It is always to be on his forehead, so that they may find acceptance with the LORD.

Other Priestly Garments

39 "You are to weave the tunic from fine linen, make a turban of fine linen, and make an embroidered sash. 40 Make tunics, sashes, and headbands for Aaron's sons to give them glory and beauty.[b] 41 Put these on your brother Aaron and his sons; then anoint,[c] ordain,[A] and consecrate[d] them, so that they may serve Me as priests. 42 Make them linen undergarments[e] to cover their naked bodies; they must extend from the waist[B] to the thighs. 43 These must be worn by Aaron and his sons whenever they enter the tent of meeting or approach the altar to minister in the sanctuary area, so that they do not incur guilt[f] and die. This is to be a permanent statute[g] for Aaron and for his future descendants.

Instructions about Consecration

29 "This is what you are to do for them to consecrate them to serve Me as priests. Take a young bull and two unblemished rams, 2 with unleavened bread, unleavened cakes mixed with oil, and unleavened wafers coated with oil. Make them out of fine wheat flour,[h] 3 put them in a basket, and bring them in the basket, along with the bull and two rams. 4 Bring Aaron and his sons to the entrance to the tent of meeting and wash them with water.[i] 5 Then take the garments and clothe Aaron with the tunic, the robe for the ·ephod, the ephod itself, and the breastpiece; fasten the ephod on him with its woven waistband.[j] 6 Put the turban on his head and place the holy diadem[k] on the turban. 7 Take the anointing oil, pour it on his head, and anoint[l] him. 8 You must also bring his sons and clothe them with tunics. 9 Tie the sashes on Aaron and his sons and fasten headbands on them. The priesthood is to be theirs by a permanent statute. This is the way you will ordain Aaron and[C] his sons.[m]

10 "You are to bring the bull to the front of the tent of meeting, and Aaron and his sons must lay their hands on the bull's head.[n] 11 Slaughter the bull before the LORD at the entrance to the tent of meeting. 12 Take some of the bull's blood and apply it to the horns[o] of the altar with your finger; then pour out all the rest of the blood at the base of the altar. 13 Take all the fat[p] that covers the entrails, the fatty lobe of the liver, and the two kidneys with the fat on them, and burn them on the altar. 14 But burn up the bull's flesh, its hide, and its dung outside the camp;[q] it is a ·sin offering.

15 "Take one ram, and Aaron and his sons are to lay their hands on the ram's head.[r] 16 You are to slaughter the ram, take its blood, and sprinkle it on all sides of the altar. 17 Cut the ram into pieces. Wash its entrails and shanks, and place them with its head and its pieces on the altar. 18 Then burn the whole ram on the altar; it is a ·burnt offering to the LORD. It is a pleasing aroma,[s] a fire offering to the LORD.

19 "You are to take the second ram, and Aaron and his sons must lay their hands on the ram's head.[t] 20 Slaughter the ram, take some of its blood, and put it on Aaron's right earlobe, on his sons' right earlobes, on the thumbs of their right hands, and on the big toes of their right feet. Sprinkle the remaining blood on all sides of the altar. 21 Take some of the blood that is on the altar and some of the anointing oil,[u] and sprinkle them on Aaron and his garments, as well as on his sons and their garments. In this way, he and his garments will become holy, as well as his sons and their garments.

22 "Take the fat from the ram, the fat tail, the fat covering the entrails, the fatty lobe of the liver, the two kidneys and the fat on them, and the right thigh (since this is a ram for ordination[D]); 23 take one loaf of bread, one cake of bread made with oil, and one wafer from the basket of unleavened bread that is before the LORD; 24 and put all of them in the hands of Aaron and his[E] sons and wave them as a presentation offering before the LORD.[v] 25 Take them from their hands and burn them on the altar on top of the burnt offering, as

[a] 28:38 Lv 10:17; 22:16; Nm 18:1; Is 53:11; Ezk 4:4-6; Jn 1:29; Heb 9:28; 1Pt 2:24
[b] 28:40 Ex 39:41; Ezk 44:17-18
[c] 28:41 Ex 29:7; 30:30; 40:15; Lv 10:7
[d] Ex 29:9; Heb 7:28
[e] 28:42 Lv 6:10; 16:4; Ezk 44:18
[f] 28:43 Ex 20:26; Lv 5:1,17; 20:19
[g] Ex 27:21; Lv 17:7
[h] 29:2 Lv 2:4; 6:19-23
[i] 29:4 Ex 40:12; Lv 8:6; Heb 10:22
[j] 29:5 Ex 28:2,8; Lv 8:7
[k] 29:6 Ex 28:36-37; Lv 8:9
[l] 29:7 Ex 30:25; Lv 8:12; 10:7; 21:10; Nm 35:25
[m] 29:9 Ex 28:41; Nm 18:7
[n] 29:10 Lv 1:4; 8:14
[o] 29:12 Ex 27:2; Lv 8:15
[p] 29:13 Lv 3:3-4
[q] 29:14 Lv 4:11-12,21; Heb 13:11
[r] 29:15 Lv 1:4; 8:18
[s] 29:18 Gn 8:21; Ex 29:25
[t] 29:19 Ex 29:3; Lv 8:22
[u] 29:21 Ex 30:25,31; Heb 9:22
[v] 29:23-24 Lv 7:30; 8:22

[A] 28:41 Lit *anoint them, fill their hand* [B] 28:42 Lit *loins* [C] 29:9 Lit *you will fill the hand of Aaron and the hand of*; Ex 29:23-24 [D] 29:22 The priest would normally receive the right thigh to be eaten, but here it is burned; Lv 7:32-34. [E] 29:24 Lit *in the hands of his* a pleasing aroma before the LORD; it is a fire offering to the LORD.

26 “Take the breast from the ram of Aaron’s ordination and wave it as a presentation offering before the LORD; it is to be your portion.[a] 27 Consecrate for Aaron and his sons[b] the breast of the presentation offering that is waved and the thigh of the contribution that is lifted up from the ram of ordination. 28 This will belong to Aaron and his sons as a regular portion from the Israelites, for it is a contribution. It will be the Israelites’ contribution from their ·fellowship sacrifices, their contribution to the LORD.

29 “The holy garments that belong to Aaron are to belong to his sons after him, so that they can be anointed and ordained[A] in them.[c] 30 Any priest who is one of his sons and who succeeds him and enters the tent of meeting to minister in the sanctuary must wear them for seven days.[d]

31 “You are to take the ram of ordination and boil its flesh in a holy place. 32 Aaron and his sons are to eat the meat of the ram and the bread that is in the basket at the entrance to the tent of meeting.[e] 33 They must eat those things by which ·atonement was made at the time of their ordination[B] and consecration. An unauthorized person must not eat[f] them, for these things are holy. 34 If any of the meat of ordination or any of the bread is left until morning, burn up what is left over. It must not be eaten because it is holy.

35 “This is what you are to do for Aaron and his sons based on all I have commanded you. Take seven days to ordain them. 36 Sacrifice a bull as a sin offering each day for atonement. Purify[C] the altar when you make atonement for it, and anoint it in order to consecrate it.[g] 37 For seven days you must make atonement for the altar and consecrate it. The altar will become especially holy; whatever touches the altar will become holy.[h]

38 “This is what you are to offer regularly on the altar every day: two year-old lambs.[i] 39 In the morning offer one lamb, and at twilight offer the other lamb.[j] 40 With the first lamb offer two quarts[D] of fine flour mixed with one quart[E] of oil from crushed olives, and a ·drink offering of one quart[E] of wine. 41 You are to offer the second lamb at twilight. Offer a ·grain offering and a drink offering with it, like the one in the morning, as a pleasing aroma, a fire offering to the LORD. 42 This will be a regular burnt offering throughout your generations at the entrance to the tent of meeting before the LORD, where I will meet you[F] to speak with you.[k] 43 I will also meet with the Israelites there, and that place will be consecrated by My glory.[l] 44 I will consecrate the tent of meeting and the altar; I will also consecrate Aaron and his sons to serve Me as priests. 45 I will dwell[m] among the Israelites and be their God.[n] 46 And they will know that I am ·Yahweh their God, who brought them out of the land of Egypt, so that I might dwell among them. I am Yahweh their God.[o]

The Incense Altar

30 “You are to make an altar for the burning of incense; make it of acacia wood.[p] 2 It must be square, 18 inches long and 18 inches wide;[G] it must be 36 inches high.[H] Its horns must be of one piece.[I] 3 Overlay its top, all around its sides, and its horns with pure gold; make a gold molding all around it. 4 Make two gold rings for it under the molding on two of its sides; put these on opposite sides of it to be holders for the poles to carry it with. 5 Make the poles of acacia wood and overlay them with gold.

6 “You are to place the altar in front of the veil by the ark of the ·testimony—in front of the ·mercy seat that is over the testimony—where I will meet with you. 7 Aaron must burn fragrant incense on it; he must burn it every morning when he tends the lamps.[q] 8 When Aaron sets up the lamps at twilight, he must burn incense. There is to be an incense offering before the LORD throughout your generations. 9 You must not offer unauthorized incense on it,[r] or a ·burnt or ·grain offering; you are not to pour a ·drink offering on it.

10 “Once a year Aaron is to perform the purification rite[J] on the horns of the altar.

[a] 29:26 Lv 7:3; 8:29
[b] 29:27 Lv 7:31,34; Nm 18:11,18; Dt 18:3
[c] 29:29 Nm 18:8; 20:26,28
[d] 29:30 Lv 8:35; Nm 20:28
[e] 29:31-32 Lv 8:31; Mt 12:4
[f] 29:33 Lv 10:14-15,17; 22:10
[g] 29:36 Ex 40:10; Heb 10:11
[h] 29:37 Ex 30:29; Mt 23:19
[i] 29:38 Nm 28:3; 1Ch 16:40; Ezr 3:3; Dn 12:11
[j] 29:39 1Kg 18:29,36; 2Kg 16:15; Ezr 9:4-5; Ps 141:2; Ezk 46:13-15
[k] 29:42 Ex 25:22; 30:8
[l] 29:43 1Kg 8:11; 2Ch 5:14; Ezk 43:5; Hg 2:7,9
[m] 29:45 Zch 2:10; Jn 14:17
[n] Ex 25:8; Lv 26:12
[o] 29:46 Ex 20:2
[p] 30:1 Ex 37:25; Rv 8:3
[q] 30:7 Ex 27:21; 1Sm 2:28; 1Ch 23:13; Lk 1:9
[r] 30:9 Lv 10:1

[A] 29:29 Lit *him for anointing in them and for filling their hand* [B] 29:33 Lit *made to fill their hand* [C] 29:36 Or *Make a sin offering on* [D] 29:40 Lit *offer a tenth* [E] 29:40 Lit *a fourth of a hin* [F] 29:42 = Moses [G] 30:2 Lit *one cubit its length and one cubit its width* [H] 30:2 Lit *wide; and two cubits its height* [I] 30:2 Lit *piece with it* [J] 30:10 Or *to make atonement*

Throughout your generations he is to perform the purification rite[A] for[B] it once a
year, with the blood of the ·sin offering for
·atonement.[a] The altar is especially holy to
the LORD."

The Atonement Money

11 The LORD spoke to Moses: 12 "When you
take a census[b] of the Israelites to register
them, each of the men must pay a ransom[c]
for himself to the LORD as they are registered.
Then no plague[d] will come on them as they
are registered. 13 Everyone who is registered
must pay half a ·shekel[C] according to the sanctuary shekel (20 *gerahs* to the shekel). This
half shekel is a contribution to the LORD.[e]
14 Each man who is registered, 20 years old
or more, must give this contribution to the
LORD. 15 The wealthy may not give more and
the poor may not give less[f] than half a shekel
when giving the contribution to the LORD to
atone for[D] your lives. 16 Take the atonement
money[E] from the Israelites and use it for the
service of the tent of meeting. It will serve as
a reminder for the Israelites before the LORD
to atone for[D] your lives."[g]

The Bronze Basin

17 The LORD spoke to Moses: 18 "Make a
bronze basin[h] for washing and a bronze
stand for it. Set it between the tent of meeting and the altar, and put water in it. 19 Aaron
and his sons must wash their hands and feet
from the basin. 20 Whenever they enter the
tent of meeting or approach the altar to minister by burning up an offering to the LORD,
they must wash with water so that they will
not die. 21 They must wash their hands and
feet so that they will not die; this is to be a permanent statute[i] for them, for Aaron and his
descendants throughout their generations."

The Anointing Oil

22 The LORD spoke to Moses: 23 "Take for
yourself the finest spices:[j] 12 1/2 pounds[F] of
liquid myrrh, half as much (6 1/4 pounds[G]) of
fragrant cinnamon, 6 1/4 pounds[G] of fragrant
cane, 24 12 1/2 pounds[F] of cassia (by the sanctuary shekel), and one gallon[H] of olive oil.[k]
25 Prepare from these a holy anointing oil, a
scented blend, the work of a perfumer; it will
be holy anointing oil.[l]
26 "With it you are to anoint[m] the tent of
meeting, the ark of the testimony, 27 the table
with all its utensils, the lampstand with its
utensils, the altar of incense, 28 the altar of
burnt offering with all its utensils, and the
basin with its stand. 29 Consecrate them and
they will be especially holy. Whatever touches
them will be consecrated. 30 Anoint Aaron
and his sons and consecrate[n] them to serve
Me as priests.
31 "Tell the Israelites: This will be My holy
anointing oil throughout your generations.
32 It must not be used for ordinary anointing
on a person's body, and you must not make
anything like it using its formula. It is holy,
and it must be holy to you. 33 Anyone who
blends something like it or puts some of it
on an unauthorized person must be cut off[o]
from his people."

The Sacred Incense

34 The LORD said to Moses: "Take fragrant
spices: stacte, onycha, and galbanum; the
spices and pure frankincense are to be in
equal measures. 35 Prepare expertly blended
incense from these; it is to be seasoned with
salt, pure and holy. 36 Grind some of it into a
fine powder and put some in front of the testimony in the tent of meeting, where I will
meet with you. It must be especially holy[p] to
you. 37 As for the incense you are making, you
must not make any for yourselves using its
formula. It is to be regarded by you as sacred
to the LORD. 38 Anyone who makes something
like it to smell its fragrance must be cut off
from his people."

God's Provision of the Skilled Workers

31 The LORD also spoke to Moses: 2 "Look, I
have appointed by name Bezalel[q] son of
Uri, son of Hur, of the tribe of Judah. 3 I have
filled him with God's Spirit, with wisdom,
understanding, and ability in every craft[r]
4 to design artistic works in gold, silver, and
bronze, 5 to cut gemstones for mounting, and
to carve wood for work in every craft. 6 I have

[a] **30:10** Lv 16:18
[b] **30:12** Nm 1:2; 2Sm 24:2
[c] Nm 31:50; Mt 20:28
[d] Ex 12:13; 2Sm 24:13,21,25
[e] **30:13** Ex 38:26; Nm 3:47; Mt 17:24
[f] **30:15** Pr 22:2; Eph 6:9
[g] **30:16** Ex 38:25-28; Nm 16:40
[h] **30:18** Ex 38:8; 40:7,30; 1Kg 7:38
[i] **30:21** Ex 27:21; 28:43
[j] **30:23** Sg 4:14; Ezk 27:22
[k] **30:24** Ex 29:40; Ps 45:8
[l] **30:25** Ex 37:29; Nm 35:25
[m] **30:26** Ex 40:9; Lv 8:10; Nm 7:1
[n] **30:30** Ex 29:7; Lv 8:12,30
[o] **30:33** Gn 17:14; Ex 30:38
[p] **30:36** Ex 29:37; Lv 2:3
[q] **31:2** Ex 35:30; 36:1; 1Ch 2:20
[r] **31:3** Ex 35:31; 1Kg 7:14

A **30:10** Or *to make atonement* B **30:10** Or *on* C **30:13** About 2/5 of an ounce of silver D **30:15,16** Or *to ransom* E **30:16** Lit *the silver of the atonement* F **30:23,24** Lit *500* (shekels) G **30:23** Lit *250* (shekels) H **30:24** Lit *a hin*

also selected Oholiab[A] son of Ahisamach, of the tribe of Dan, to be with him. I have placed wisdom within every skilled craftsman[B] in order to make all that I have commanded you: 7 the tent of meeting, the ark of the ·testimony, the ·mercy seat that is on top of it, and all the other furnishings of the tent[a]— 8 the table with its utensils, the pure gold lampstand with all its utensils, the altar of incense, 9 the altar of ·burnt offering with all its utensils, the basin with its stand— 10 the specially woven[C] garments, both the holy garments for Aaron the priest and the garments for his sons to serve as priests, 11 the anointing oil, and the fragrant incense for the sanctuary. They must make them according to all that I have commanded you."[b]

Observing the Sabbath

12 The LORD said to Moses: 13 "Tell the Israelites: You must observe My Sabbaths, for it is a sign between Me and you throughout your generations, so that you will know that I am ·Yahweh who sets you apart.[c] 14 Observe the Sabbath, for it is holy to you. Whoever profanes it must be put to death. If anyone does work on it, that person must be cut off from his people.[d] 15 Work may be done for six days, but on the seventh day there must be a Sabbath of complete rest,[e] dedicated to the LORD. Anyone who does work on the Sabbath day must be put to death. 16 The Israelites must observe the Sabbath, celebrating it throughout their generations as a perpetual covenant. 17 It is a sign forever between Me and the Israelites, for in six days the LORD made the heavens and the earth, but on the seventh day He rested and was refreshed."

The Two Stone Tablets

18 When He finished speaking with Moses on Mount Sinai, He gave him the two tablets of the testimony, stone tablets inscribed by the finger of God.[f]

The Gold Calf

32 When the people saw that Moses delayed in coming down from the mountain, they gathered around Aaron and said to him, "Come, make us a god[D] who will go before us because this Moses, the man who brought us up from the land of Egypt—we don't know what has happened to him!"[g]

2 Then Aaron replied to them, "Take off the gold rings[h] that are on the ears of your wives, your sons, and your daughters and bring them to me." 3 So all the people took off the gold rings that were on their ears and brought them to Aaron. 4 He took the gold from their hands, fashioned it with an engraving tool, and made it into an image of a calf.

Then they said, "Israel, this is your God,[E] who brought you up from the land of Egypt!"[i]

5 When Aaron saw this, he built an altar before it; then he made an announcement: "There will be a festival[j] to the LORD tomorrow." 6 Early the next morning they arose, offered ·burnt offerings, and presented ·fellowship offerings. The people sat down to eat and drink, then got up to play.[k]

7 The LORD spoke to Moses: "Go down at once! For your people you brought up from the land of Egypt have acted corruptly.[l] 8 They have quickly turned from the way I commanded them; they have made for themselves an image of a calf. They have bowed down to it, sacrificed to it, and said, 'Israel, this is your God,[E] who brought you up from the land of Egypt.'"[m] 9 The LORD also said to Moses: "I have seen this people, and they are indeed a stiff-necked[n] people. 10 Now leave Me alone, so that My anger can burn against them and I can destroy them. Then I will make you into a great nation."[o]

11 But Moses interceded with the LORD his God: "LORD, why does Your anger burn against Your people You brought out of the land of Egypt with great power and a strong hand? 12 Why should the Egyptians say, 'He brought them out with an evil intent to kill them in the mountains and wipe them off the face of the earth'? Turn from Your great anger and relent concerning this disaster planned for Your people.[p] 13 Remember Your servants Abraham, Isaac, and Israel—You swore to them by Your very self[q] and declared, 'I will make your ·offspring as numerous as the stars of the sky and will give your offspring all this land that I have promised, and they will inherit it forever.'"[r] 14 So the LORD relented[s]

[a] **31:7** Ex 36:8-38; 37:1-6
[b] **31:8-11** Ex 30:25,31,34; 37:10-29; 38:1,8; 39:1,41
[c] **31:13** Lv 19:3,30; Ezk 20:12,20
[d] **31:14** Nm 15:35
[e] **31:15** Gn 2:2; Ex 16:23; 20:9
[f] **31:18** Ex 24:12; 32:15-16; Dt 4:13; 5:22; 2Co 3:3
[g] **32:1** Ex 13:21; 24:18; Dt 9:9; Ac 7:40
[h] **32:2** Ex 35:22; Jdg 8:24-27
[i] **32:4** Dt 9:16; Jdg 17:3-4; 1Kg 12:28; Neh 9:18; Ps 106:19; Ac 7:41
[j] **32:5** Lv 23:2,37; 2Kg 10:20
[k] **32:6** Nm 25:2; 1Co 10:7
[l] **32:7** Gn 6:11-12; Dt 9:12
[m] **32:8** Ex 20:3-4,23; 34:15; Dt 32:17; 1Kg 12:28
[n] **32:9** Ex 33:3,5; 34:9; 2Ch 30:8; Is 48:4; Ac 7:51
[o] **32:10** Ex 22:24; Nm 14:12; Dt 9:14
[p] **32:11-12** Nm 14:13-16; Dt 9:18,26-29
[q] **32:13** Gn 22:16-18; Heb 6:13
[r] Gn 12:7; 13:15; 15:7,18; 26:4; 35:11-12
[s] **32:14** 2Sm 24:16; Ps 106:45

[A] **31:6** LXX, Syr read *Eliab* [B] **31:6** Lit *every person skilled of heart* [C] **31:10** Hb obscure [D] **32:1** Or *us gods* [E] **32:4,8** Or *Israel, this is your god*, or *Israel, these are your gods*

concerning the disaster He said He would
bring on His people.

15 Then Moses turned and went down the
mountain with the two tablets of the ·testi-
mony in his hands. They were inscribed on
both sides — inscribed front and back. 16 The
tablets were the work of God, and the writing
was God's writing, engraved on the tablets.[a]

17 When Joshua heard the sound of the people as they shouted, he said to Moses, "There
is a sound of war in the camp."

18 But Moses replied:

> It's not the sound of a victory cry
> and not the sound of a cry of defeat;
> I hear the sound of singing!

19 As he approached the camp and saw the calf
and the dancing, Moses became enraged and
threw the tablets out of his hands, smashing
them at the base of the mountain. 20 Then he
took the calf they had made, burned it up, and
ground it to powder. He scattered the powder
over the surface of the water and forced the
Israelites to drink the water.

21 Then Moses asked Aaron, "What did these
people do to you that you have led them into
such a grave sin?"

22 "Don't be enraged, my lord," Aaron replied. "You yourself know that the people
are intent on evil.[b] 23 They said to me, 'Make
us a god[A] who will go before us because this
Moses, the man who brought us up from the
land of Egypt — we don't know what has happened to him!' 24 So I said to them, 'Whoever
has gold, take it off,' and they gave it to me.
When I threw it into the fire, out came this
calf!"

25 Moses saw that the people were out of
control, for Aaron had let them get out of
control, resulting in weakness before their
enemies.[B] 26 And Moses stood at the camp's
entrance and said, "Whoever is for the LORD,
come to me." And all the Levites gathered
around him. 27 He told them, "This is what
the LORD, the God of Israel, says, 'Every man
fasten his sword to his side; go back and forth
through the camp from entrance to entrance,
and each of you kill his brother, his friend,
and his neighbor.'"[c] 28 The Levites did as Moses commanded, and about 3,000 men fell
dead that day among the people. 29 Afterward
Moses said, "Today you have been dedicated[C]
to the LORD, since each man went against
his son and his brother. Therefore you have
brought a blessing on yourselves today."[d]

30 The following day Moses said to the people, "You have committed a grave sin. Now I
will go up to the LORD; perhaps I will be able
to atone for your sin."[e]

31 So Moses returned to the LORD and said,
"Oh, these people have committed a grave sin;
they have made a god of gold for themselves.[f]
32 Now if You would only forgive their sin.
But if not, please erase me from the book You
have written."[g]

33 The LORD replied to Moses: "I will erase
whoever has sinned against Me from My
book.[h] 34 Now go, lead the people to the place
I told you about; see, My angel will go before
you. But on the day I settle accounts, I will
hold them accountable for their sin."[i] 35 And
the LORD inflicted a plague on the people for
what they did with the calf Aaron had made.

The Tent Outside the Camp

33 The LORD spoke to Moses: "Go, leave
here, you and the people you brought
up from the land of Egypt, to the land I promised to Abraham, Isaac, and Jacob, saying: I
will give it to your ·offspring.[j] 2 I will send an
angel ahead of you and will drive out the Canaanites, Amorites, Hittites, Perizzites,[D] Hivites, and Jebusites.[k] 3 Go up to a land flowing
with milk and honey. But I will not go with
you because you are a stiff-necked people;
otherwise, I might destroy you on the way."[l]
4 When the people heard this bad news, they
mourned and didn't put on their jewelry.[m]

5 For the LORD said to Moses: "Tell the Israelites: You are a stiff-necked people. If I
went with you for a single moment, I would
destroy you. Now take off your jewelry, and I
will decide what to do with you." 6 So the Israelites remained stripped of their jewelry
from Mount Horeb onward.

7 Now Moses took a tent and set it up outside the camp, far away from the camp; he
called it the tent of meeting. Anyone who

[a] **32:15-16** Ex 31:18; Dt 9:15
[b] **32:19-22** Gn 20:9; 26:10; Ex 14:11; Dt 9:16-17,21
[c] **32:27** Nm 25:5; Dt 33:9
[d] **32:29** Nm 25:11-13; Zch 13:3
[e] **32:30** 1Sm 12:20; 2Sm 16:12
[f] **32:31** Ex 20:23; Dt 9:18
[g] **32:32** Ps 69:28; Dn 12:1; Rm 9:3; Php 4:3; Rv 3:5; 21:27
[h] **32:33** Dt 29:20; Ps 9:5
[i] **32:34** Dt 32:35; Rm 2:5-6
[j] **33:1** Gn 12:7; Ex 32:7
[k] **33:2** Ex 32:34; Jos 24:11
[l] **33:3** Ex 3:8; 32:9; Nm 16:21,45
[m] **33:4** Nm 14:39; Ezk 24:17,23

[A] **32:23** Or *us gods* [B] **32:25** Hb obscure; or *resulting in derision* [C] **32:29** Text emended; MT reads *Today dedicate yourselves*; LXX, Vg read *Today you have dedicated yourselves* [D] **33:2** Sam, LXX add *Girgashites*

wanted to consult the LORD would go to the
tent of meeting that was outside the camp.[a]
8Whenever Moses went out to the tent, all the
people would stand up, each one at the door
of his tent, and they would watch Moses until he entered the tent. 9When Moses entered
the tent, the pillar of cloud would come down
and remain at the entrance to the tent, and
the LORD would speak with Moses.[b] 10As all
the people saw the pillar of cloud remaining
at the entrance to the tent, they would stand
up, then bow in worship, each one at the door
of his tent. 11The LORD spoke with Moses face
to face, just as a man speaks with his friend.
Then Moses would return to the camp, but
his assistant, the young man Joshua son of
Nun, would not leave the inside of the tent.[c]

The LORD's Glory

12Moses said to the LORD, "Look, You have
told me, 'Lead this people up,' but You have
not let me know whom You will send with
me. You said, 'I know you by name,[d] and you
have also found favor in My sight.' 13Now if I
have indeed found favor in Your sight, please
teach me Your ways,[e] and I will know You and

[a]33:7 Ex 29:42-43; Dt 4:29
[b]33:9 Ex 13:21; 31:18; Ps 99:7
[c]33:11 Ex 24:13; Nm 12:8; Dt 34:10
[d]33:12 Ex 32:34; Jn 10:14-15; 2Tm 2:19
[e]33:13 Ps 25:4; 86:11; 119:33

The Glory of God

Philip Nation

The glory of God is often placed before believers as the motivation for our participation in the mission of God. To fully appreciate this, we must explore the theological idea behind God's glory.

In Exodus 33 we read that Moses took up residence outside the Israelites' camp in the "tent of meeting." Here he spoke with God "face to face, just as a man speaks with his friend" (v. 11). In his conversations with the Lord, Moses made a bold request: "Please, let me see Your glory" (v.18). In the following passages we are given several glimpses into the nature of God's glory.

First, God's glory is the overpowering beauty of His presence. It says in 34:5, "The LORD came down" to where Moses was hidden in a crevice. God hid Moses from the full measure of His presence because it is too powerful for any person to witness and survive (33:20).

Second, the glory of God is found in the excellent reputation of His name. When God passed by Moses, He proclaimed His name: Yahweh (34:6). In fact, it is the first thing God did upon His arrival to display His glory. Yahweh is God's revealed name; it is derived from the verb "to be." Essentially, Yahweh means "I AM." God's glory is seen in that He is self-reliant, self-sustaining, and has no limitations. Philosophers refer to God as the "Prime Mover" as He is the force that moves everything else into existence, not needing any force to bring Himself into existence.

Third, the glory of God is seen in His character. As God passed by Moses, He spoke of His character through how He acts. In 34:6-7, God comments on how He loves, keeps the covenant, and punishes sin. The glory of God is not just an ethereal notion but is made tangible by how God acts.

When we embark on the mission of God, it is first of all for God. We are tempted to miss this point and say we preach the gospel primarily for the sake of the lost. But for God the greatest priority is God. In Isaiah 48:9-11, the work of restraining His judgment and refining His people is for His own praise. Earlier in Isaiah, God said, "I am Yahweh, that is My name; I will not give My glory to another or My praise to idols" (42:8). The greatness of God's character, presence, and reputation are unequalled and the place of priority must not be shared with any other created being.

The people of God are given the honor of reflecting the glory of God to our generation. In 2 Corinthians 3:12-17, the Apostle Paul writes of the time when Moses came off the mountain and hid the glow that was the residual effect of having encountered the glory of God. We, as God's messengers and missionaries, are to be those who have "unveiled faces" to reflect the glory of God and be continually transformed by it.

find favor in Your sight. Now consider that
this nation is Your people."[a]
14 Then He replied, "My presence will go
with you, and I will give you rest."[b]
15 "If Your presence does not go," Moses responded to Him, "don't make us go up from
here. 16 How will it be known that I and Your
people have found favor in Your sight unless
You go with us? I and Your people will be distinguished by this from all the other people
on the face of the earth."[c]
17 The LORD answered Moses, "I will do this
very thing you have asked, for you have found
favor in My sight, and I know you by name."
18 Then Moses said, "Please, let me see Your
glory."[d]
19 He said, "I will cause all My goodness to
pass in front of you, and I will proclaim the
name •Yahweh before you. I will be gracious to
whom I will be gracious, and I will have compassion on whom I will have compassion."[e]
20 But He answered, "You cannot see My face,
for no one can see[f] Me and live." 21 The LORD
said, "Here is a place near Me. You are to stand
on the rock, 22 and when My glory passes by,
I will put you in the crevice of the rock and
cover you with My hand until I have passed
by.[g] 23 Then I will take My hand away, and you
will see My back, but My face will not be seen."

New Stone Tablets

34 The LORD said to Moses, "Cut two
stone tablets like the first ones, and
I will write on them the words that were on
the first tablets, which you broke.[h] 2 Be prepared by morning. Come up Mount Sinai
in the morning and stand before Me on the
mountaintop. 3 No one may go up with you;
in fact, no one must be seen anywhere on the
mountain. Even the flocks and herds are not
to graze in front of that mountain."[i]
4 Moses cut two stone tablets like the first
ones. He got up early in the morning, and
taking the two stone tablets in his hand, he
climbed Mount Sinai, just as the LORD had
commanded him.
5 The LORD came down in a cloud, stood
with him there, and proclaimed His name
•Yahweh. 6 Then the LORD passed in front of
him and proclaimed:

Yahweh — Yahweh is a compassionate
and gracious God, slow to anger and rich
in faithful love and truth,[j] 7 maintaining
faithful love to a thousand generations,
forgiving wrongdoing, rebellion, and
sin.[k] But He will not leave the •guilty[l] unpunished, bringing the consequences
of the fathers' wrongdoing on the children and grandchildren to the third and
fourth generation.

8 Moses immediately bowed down to the
ground and worshiped. 9 Then he said, "My
Lord, if I have indeed found favor in Your
sight, my Lord, please go with us. Even
though this is a stiff-necked people, forgive
our wrongdoing and sin, and accept us as
Your own possession."[m]

Covenant Obligations

10 And the LORD responded: "Look, I am
making a covenant. I will perform wonders
in the presence of all your people[A] that have
never been done[B] in all the earth or in any
nation. All the people you live among will see
the LORD's work, for what I am doing with
you is awe-inspiring."[n] 11 Observe what I command you today. I am going to drive out before you the Amorites, Canaanites, Hittites,
Perizzites, Hivites,[C] and Jebusites. 12 Be careful not to make a treaty with the inhabitants
of the land that you are going to enter; otherwise, they will become a snare among you.[o]
13 Instead, you must tear down their altars,
smash their sacred pillars, and chop down
their •Asherah poles.[p] 14 You are never to bow
down to another god because Yahweh, being
jealous[q] by nature,[D] is a jealous God.
15 "Do not make a treaty with the inhabitants of the land, or else when they prostitute
themselves with their gods and sacrifice to
their gods, they will invite you, and you will
eat their sacrifices.[r] 16 Then you will take some
of their daughters as brides for your sons.
Their daughters will prostitute themselves
with their gods and cause your sons to prostitute themselves with their gods.[s]
17 "Do not make cast images[t] of gods for
yourselves.
18 "Observe the Festival of •Unleavened

[a] **33:13** Ex 34:9; Dt 9:26,29
[b] **33:14** Jos 21:44; 22:4; Is 63:9
[c] **33:16** Ex 34:10; Nm 14:14
[d] **33:18** Ex 33:20; 1Tm 6:16
[e] **33:19** Rm 9:15
[f] **33:20** Gn 32:30; Is 6:5
[g] **33:22** Ps 91:1,4; Is 2:21
[h] **34:1** Ex 32:19; 34:28; Dt 10:2,4
[i] **34:2-3** Ex 19:12-13,20-21
[j] **34:6** Nm 14:18; Neh 9:17; Ps 86:15; 103:8; 108:4; Jl 2:13; Rm 2:4
[k] **34:7** Ex 20:6; Ps 103:3; 130:4; Dn 9:9; 1Jn 1:9
[l] Jos 24:19; Jb 10:14; Nah 1:3
[m] **34:9** Ex 33:15-16; Ps 33:12; 94:14
[n] **34:10** Dt 4:32; 5:2; Ps 77:14; 145:6
[o] **34:11-12** Ex 23:32-33; 33:2
[p] **34:13** Ex 23:24; Dt 12:3; 2Kg 18:4; 2Ch 34:3-4
[q] **34:14** Ex 20:3,5; Dt 4:24
[r] **34:15** Nm 25:2; Jdg 2:17; 1Co 8:4,7,10
[s] **34:16** Dt 7:3; 1Kg 11:2,4; Ezr 9:2; Neh 13:25
[t] **34:17** Ex 32:8; Lv 19:14

[A] **34:10** Lit *in all nations* [B] **34:10** Lit *created* [C] **34:11** DSS, Sam, LXX add *Girgashites* [D] **34:14** Lit *Yahweh — His name is Jealous*, or *Yahweh is jealous for His name, He*

Bread. You are to eat unleavened bread for seven days at the appointed time in the month of Abib[A] as I commanded you. For you came out of Egypt in the month of Abib.[a]

19 "The firstborn[b] male from every womb belongs to Me, including all your male[B,C] livestock, the firstborn of cattle or sheep. 20 You must redeem the firstborn of a donkey with a sheep, but if you do not redeem it, break its neck.[c] You must redeem all the firstborn of your sons. No one is to appear before Me empty-handed.

21 "You are to labor six days but you must rest[d] on the seventh day; you must even rest during plowing and harvesting times.

22 "Observe the Festival of Weeks with the ·firstfruits of the wheat harvest, and the Festival of Ingathering[D] at the turn of the agricultural year. 23 Three times a year[e] all your males are to appear before the Lord God, the God of Israel. 24 For I will drive out nations[f] before you and enlarge your territory.[g] No one will covet your land when you go up three times a year to appear before the LORD your God.

25 "Do not present[E] the blood for My sacrifice with anything leavened. The sacrifice of the ·Passover Festival must not remain until morning.[h]

26 "Bring the best firstfruits[i] of your land to the house of the LORD your God.

"You must not boil a young goat in its mother's milk."

27 The LORD also said to Moses, "Write[j] down these words, for I have made a covenant with you and with Israel based on these words."

28 Moses was there with the LORD 40 days and 40 nights; he did not eat bread or drink water. He wrote the Ten Commandments,[k] the words of the covenant, on the tablets.

Moses' Radiant Face

29 As Moses descended from Mount Sinai — with the two tablets of the ·testimony in his hands as he descended the mountain — he did not realize that the skin of his face shone as a result of his speaking with the LORD.[F,l] 30 When Aaron and all the Israelites saw Moses, the skin of his face shone![m] They were afraid to come near him. 31 But Moses called out to them, so Aaron and all the leaders of the community returned to him, and Moses spoke to them. 32 Afterward all the Israelites came near, and he commanded them to do everything the LORD had told him on Mount Sinai. 33 When Moses had finished speaking with them, he put a veil over his face. 34 But whenever Moses went before the LORD to speak with Him, he would remove the veil until he came out. After he came out, he would tell the Israelites what he had been commanded,[n] 35 and the Israelites would see that Moses' face[G] was radiant. Then Moses would put the veil over his face again until he went to speak with the LORD.

The Sabbath Command

35 Moses assembled the entire Israelite community and said to them, "These are the things that the LORD has commanded you to do:[o] 2 For six days work is to be done, but on the seventh day you are to have a holy day, a Sabbath[p] of complete rest to the LORD. Anyone who does work on it must be executed. 3 Do not light a fire in any of your homes on the Sabbath day."[q]

Building the Tabernacle

4 Then Moses said to the entire Israelite community, "This is what the LORD has commanded: 5 Take[r] up an offering among you for the LORD. Let everyone whose heart is willing bring this as the LORD's offering: gold, silver, and bronze; 6 blue, purple, and scarlet yarn; fine linen and goat hair; 7 ram skins dyed red and manatee skins;[H] acacia wood; 8 oil for the light; spices for the anointing oil and for the fragrant incense; 9 and onyx with gemstones to mount on the ·ephod and breastpiece.

10 "Let all the skilled craftsmen[I] among you come and make everything that the LORD has commanded:[s] 11 the tabernacle — its tent and covering, its clasps and planks, its crossbars, its posts and bases; 12 the ark with its poles, the ·mercy seat, and the veil for the screen; 13 the table with its poles, all its utensils, and

[a] **34:18** Ex 12:15; 13:4
[b] **34:19** Ex 13:2; 22:29
[c] **34:20** Ex 13:13,15; 23:15; Dt 16:16
[d] **34:21** Ex 20:9; Lk 13:14
[e] **34:23** Ex 23:14
[f] **34:24** Ex 33:2; Ps 78:55
[g] Dt 12:20; 19:8
[h] **34:25** Ex 12:10; 23:18
[i] **34:26** Ex 23:19; Dt 26:2
[j] **34:27** Ex 17:14; 24:4
[k] **34:28** Ex 24:18; 31:18; Dt 4:13; 10:2,4
[l] **34:29** Ex 32:15
[m] **34:30** Ps 34:5; Mt 17:2; 2Co 3:7,13
[n] **34:34** Ex 24:3; 2Co 3:13-16
[o] **35:1** Ex 34:32
[p] **35:2** Ex 20:9; Lv 23:3
[q] **35:3** Ex 16:23
[r] **35:5-9** Ex 25:2-7
[s] **35:10** Ex 31:6

[A] **34:18** March–April; called Nisan in the post-exilic period; Neh 2:1; Est 3:7 [B] **34:19** LXX, Theod, Vg, Tg read *males* [C] **34:19** Hb obscure [D] **34:22** The Festival of Ingathering is called Festival of Booths elsewhere; Lv 23:34-36. [E] **34:25** Lit *slaughter* [F] **34:29** Lit *with Him* [G] **34:35** Lit *see Moses' face, that the skin of his face* [H] **35:7** Or *and dolphin skins*, or *and fine leather*; Hb obscure [I] **35:10** Lit *the skilled of heart*

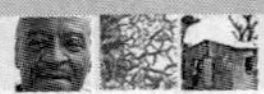

the ·bread of the Presence; [14]the lampstand
for light with its utensils and lamps as well as
the oil for the light; [15]the altar of incense with
its poles; the anointing oil and the fragrant
incense; the entryway screen for the entrance
to the tabernacle; [16]the altar of ·burnt offering with its bronze grate, its poles, and all its
utensils; the basin with its stand; [17]the hangings of the courtyard, its posts and bases, and
the screen for the gate of the courtyard; [18]the
tent pegs for the tabernacle and the tent pegs
for the courtyard, along with their ropes;
[19]and the specially woven[A] garments for ministering in the sanctuary — the holy garments
for Aaron the priest and the garments for his
sons to serve as priests."[a]

[20]Then the entire Israelite community left
Moses' presence. [21]Everyone whose heart was
moved and whose spirit prompted him came
and brought an offering to the LORD for the
work on the tent of meeting, for all its services, and for the holy garments.[b] [22]Both men
and women came; all who had willing hearts
brought brooches, earrings, rings, necklaces,
and all kinds of gold jewelry — everyone who
waved a presentation offering of gold to the
LORD. [23]Everyone who had in his possession
blue, purple, or scarlet yarn,[c] fine linen or goat
hair, ram skins dyed red or manatee skins,[B]
brought them. [24]Everyone making an offering of silver or bronze brought it as a contribution to the LORD. Everyone who possessed
acacia wood useful for any task in the work
brought it. [25]Every skilled[C] woman[d] spun yarn
with her hands and brought it: blue, purple,
and scarlet yarn, and fine linen. [26]And all the
women whose hearts were moved spun the
goat hair by virtue of their skill. [27]The leaders[e] brought onyx and gemstones to mount
on the ephod and breastpiece, [28]as well as
the spice[f] and oil for the light, for the anointing oil, and for the fragrant incense. [29]So the
Israelites brought a freewill offering to the
LORD, all the men and women whose hearts
prompted them to bring something for all
the work that the LORD, through Moses, had
commanded to be done.[g]

[a]**35:11-19** Ex 24:5-6; 25:10,23,30-31; 26:1-2; 27:1,9; 30:1,25,34; 31:10; 39:1,41; Lv 24:5-6; Nm 4:5
[b]**35:21** Ex 36:2
[c]**35:23** 1Ch 29:8
[d]**35:25** Ex 28:3
[e]**35:27** 1Ch 29:6; Ezr 2:68
[f]**35:28** Ex 30:23
[g]**35:29** Ex 35:21; 36:3; 1Ch 29:9
[h]**35:30-34** Ex 31:1-6; 2Ch 2:14
[i]**35:35** Ex 31:3,6; 1Kg 7:14
[j]**36:1** Ex 25:8; 28:3; 31:6; 35:10,35
[k]**36:2** Ex 25:2; 35:21,26; 1Ch 29:5
[l]**36:5** 2Ch 31:10; 2Co 8:2-3
[m]**36:8-19** Ex 26:1-14

Bezalel and Oholiab

[30]Moses[h] then said to the Israelites: "Look,
the LORD has appointed by name Bezalel son
of Uri, son of Hur, of the tribe of Judah. [31]He
has filled him with God's Spirit, with wisdom,
understanding, and ability in every kind of
craft [32]to design artistic works in gold, silver,
and bronze, [33]to cut gemstones for mounting,
and to carve wood for work in every kind of
artistic craft. [34]He has also given both him
and Oholiab son of Ahisamach, of the tribe
of Dan, the ability to teach others. [35]He has
filled them with skill[D] to do all the work[i] of
a gem cutter; a designer; an embroiderer in
blue, purple, and scarlet yarn and fine linen;
and a weaver. They can do every kind of craft
36 and design artistic designs. [1]Bezalel,
Oholiab, and all the skilled[C] people
are to work based on everything the LORD has
commanded. The LORD has given them wisdom and understanding to know how to do
all the work of constructing the sanctuary."[j]

[2]So Moses summoned Bezalel, Oholiab,
and every skilled[C] person in whose heart the
LORD had placed wisdom, everyone whose
heart moved him,[k] to come to the work and
do it. [3]They took from Moses' presence all the
contributions that the Israelites had brought
for the task of making the sanctuary. Meanwhile, the people continued to bring freewill
offerings morning after morning.

[4]Then all the craftsmen who were doing all
the work for the sanctuary came one by one
from the work they were doing [5]and said to
Moses, "The people are bringing more than is
needed[l] for the construction of the work the
LORD commanded to be done."

[6]After Moses gave an order, they sent a proclamation throughout the camp: "Let no man
or woman make anything else as an offering
for the sanctuary." So the people stopped.
[7]The materials were sufficient for them to do
all the work. There was more than enough.

Building the Tabernacle

[8]All[m] the skilled craftsmen[E] among those
doing the work made the tabernacle with 10
curtains. Bezalel made them of finely spun
linen, as well as blue, purple, and scarlet

A**35:19** Hb obscure B**35:23** Or *or dolphin skins*, or *or fine leather*; Hb obscure
C**35:25; 36:1,2** Lit *wise of heart* D**35:35** Lit *with wisdom of heart*
E**36:8** Lit *the wise of heart*

yarn, with a design of ·cherubim worked into them. 9The length of each curtain was 42 feet,[A] and the width of each curtain six feet;[B] all the curtains had the same measurements. 10He joined five of the curtains to each other, and the other five curtains he joined to each other. 11He made loops of blue yarn on the edge of the last curtain in the first set and did the same on the edge of the outermost curtain in the second set. 12He made 50 loops on the one curtain and 50 loops on the edge of the curtain in the second set, so that the loops lined up with each other. 13He also made 50 gold clasps and joined the curtains to each other, so that the tabernacle became a single unit.

14He made curtains of goat hair for a tent over the tabernacle; he made 11 of them. 15The length of each curtain was 45 feet,[C] and the width of each curtain six feet.[B] All 11 curtains had the same measurements. 16He joined five of the curtains together, and the other six together. 17He made 50 loops on the edge of the outermost curtain in the first set and 50 loops on the edge of the corresponding curtain in the second set. 18He made 50 bronze clasps to join the tent together as a single unit. 19He also made a covering for the tent from ram skins dyed red and a covering of manatee skins[D] on top of it.

20He[a] made upright planks[E] of acacia wood for the tabernacle. 21The length of each plank was 15 feet,[F] and the width of each was 27 inches.[G] 22There were two tenons connected to each other for each plank. He did the same for all the planks of the tabernacle. 23He made planks for the tabernacle as follows: 20 for the south side, 24and he made 40 silver bases to put under the 20 planks, two bases under the first plank for its two tenons, and two bases under each of the following planks for their two tenons; 25for the second side of the tabernacle, the north side, he made 20 planks, 26with their 40 silver bases, two bases under the first plank and two bases under each of the following ones; 27and for the west side of the tabernacle he made six planks. 28He also made two additional planks for the two back corners of the tabernacle. 29They were paired at the bottom and joined together[H] at the[I] top in a single ring. This is what he did with both of them for the two corners. 30So there were eight planks with their 16 silver bases, two bases under each one.

31He made five crossbars of acacia wood for the planks on one side of the tabernacle, 32five crossbars for the planks on the other side of the tabernacle, and five crossbars for those at the back of the tabernacle on the west. 33He made the central crossbar run through the middle of the planks from one end to the other. 34He overlaid them with gold and made their rings out of gold as holders for the crossbars. He also overlaid the crossbars with gold.

35Then[b] he made the veil with blue, purple, and scarlet yarn, and finely spun linen. He made it with a design of cherubim worked into it. 36He made four posts of acacia wood for it and overlaid them with gold; their hooks were of gold. And he cast four silver bases for the posts.

37He made a screen embroidered with blue, purple, and scarlet yarn, and finely spun linen for the entrance to the tent, 38together with its five posts and their hooks. He overlaid the tops of the posts and their bands with gold, but their five bases were bronze.

[a]36:20-34 Ex 25:5; 26:15-29 [b]36:35-38 Ex 26:31-37 [c]37:1-9 Ex 25:10-20

Making the Ark

37 Bezalel[c] made the ark of acacia wood, 45 inches long, 27 inches wide, and 27 inches high.[J] 2He overlaid it with pure gold inside and out and made a gold molding all around it. 3He cast four gold rings for it, for its four feet, two rings on one side and two rings on the other side. 4He made poles of acacia wood and overlaid them with gold. 5He inserted the poles into the rings on the sides of the ark for carrying the ark.

6He made a ·mercy seat of pure gold, 45 inches long and 27 inches wide.[K] 7He made two ·cherubim of gold; he made them of hammered work at the two ends of the mercy seat, 8one cherub at one end and one cherub at the other end. At each end, he made a cherub

A36:9 Lit *28 cubits* B36:9,15 Lit *four cubits* C36:15 Lit *30 cubits* D36:19 Or *of dolphin skins*, or *of fine leather*; Hb obscure E36:20 Or *made frames* F36:21 Lit *10 cubits* G36:21 Lit *a cubit and a half* H36:29 Lit *and together they are to be complete* I36:29 Lit *its* J37:1 Lit *two and a half cubits its length, one and a half cubits its width, and one and a half cubits its height* K37:6 Lit *two and a half cubits its length and one and a half cubits its width*

of one piece with the mercy seat. 9 They had wings spread out. They faced each other and covered the mercy seat with their wings. The faces of the cherubim were looking toward the mercy seat.

Making the Table

10 He[a] constructed the table of acacia wood, 36 inches long, 18 inches wide, and 27 inches high.[A] 11 He overlaid it with pure gold and made a gold molding all around it. 12 He made a three-inch[B] frame all around it and made a gold molding all around its frame. 13 He cast four gold rings for it and attached the rings to the four corners at its four legs. 14 The rings were next to the frame as holders for the poles to carry the table. 15 He made the poles for carrying the table from acacia wood and overlaid them with gold. 16 He also made the utensils that would be on the table out of pure gold: its plates and cups, as well as its bowls and pitchers for pouring •drink offerings.

Making the Lampstand

17 Then[b] he made the lampstand out of pure hammered gold. He made it all of one piece: its base and shaft, its ornamental cups, and its calyxes[C] and petals. 18 Six branches extended from its sides, three branches of the lampstand from one side and three branches of the lampstand from the other side. 19 There were three cups shaped like almond blossoms, each with a calyx and petals, on the first branch, and three cups shaped like almond blossoms, each with a calyx and petals, on the next branch. It was this way for the six branches that extended from the lampstand. 20 On the lampstand shaft there were four cups shaped like almond blossoms with its calyxes and petals. 21 For the six branches that extended from it, a calyx was under the first pair of branches from it, a calyx under the second pair of branches from it, and a calyx under the third pair of branches from it. 22 Their calyxes and branches were of one piece.[D] All of it was a single hammered piece of pure gold. 23 He also made its seven lamps, snuffers, and firepans of pure gold. 24 He made it and all its utensils of 75 pounds[E] of pure gold.

Making the Altar of Incense

25 He[c] made the altar of incense out of acacia wood. It was square, 18 inches long and 18 inches wide; it was 36 inches high.[F] Its horns were of one piece.[D] 26 He overlaid it, its top, all around its sides, and its horns with pure gold. Then he made a gold molding all around it. 27 He made two gold rings for it under the molding on two of its sides; he put these on opposite sides of it to be holders for the poles to carry it with. 28 He made the poles of acacia wood and overlaid them with gold.

29 He also made the holy anointing oil and the pure, fragrant, and expertly blended incense.[d]

Making the Altar of Burnt Offering

38 Bezalel[e] constructed the altar of •burnt offering from acacia wood. It was square, $7\frac{1}{2}$ feet long and $7\frac{1}{2}$ feet wide,[G] and was $4\frac{1}{2}$ feet[H] high. 2 He made horns for it on its four corners; the horns were of one piece.[D] Then he overlaid it with bronze.

3 He made all the altar's utensils: the pots, shovels, basins, meat forks, and firepans; he made all its utensils of bronze. 4 He constructed for the altar a grate of bronze mesh under its ledge,[I] halfway up from the bottom. 5 At the four corners of the bronze grate he cast four rings as holders for the poles. 6 Also, he made the poles of acacia wood and overlaid them with bronze. 7 Then he inserted the poles into the rings on the sides of the altar in order to carry it with them. He constructed the altar with boards so that it was hollow.

Making the Bronze Basin

8 He made the bronze basin and its stand from the bronze mirrors of the women who served at the entrance to the tent of meeting.[f]

Making the Courtyard

9 Then[g] he made the courtyard. The hangings on the south side of the courtyard were

[a] 37:10-16 Ex 25:23-29 [b] 37:17-24 Ex 25:31-39 [c] 37:25-28 Ex 30:1-5 [d] 37:29 Ex 30:23-24,34-35 [e] 38:1-7 Ex 27:1-8 [f] 38:8 Ex 30:18; 1Sm 2:22 [g] 38:9-20 Ex 27:9-19

A 37:10 Lit *two cubits its length, one cubit its width, and one and a half cubits its height* B 37:12 Lit *a handbreadth* C 37:17 = the outer covering of a flower D 37:22,25; 38:2 Lit *piece with it* E 37:24 Lit *a talent* F 37:25 Lit *a cubit its length, a cubit its width, and two cubits its height* G 38:1 Lit *five cubits its length and five cubits its width* H 38:1 Lit *three cubits* I 38:4 Or *rim*

of finely spun linen, 150 feet in length,[A] 10 including their 20 posts and 20 bronze bases.
The hooks and bands[B] of the posts were silver. 11 The hangings on the north side were
also 150 feet in length,[A] including their 20
posts and 20 bronze bases. The hooks and
bands[B] of the posts were silver. 12 The hangings on the west side were 75 feet in length,[C]
including their 10 posts and 10 bases. The
hooks and bands of the posts were silver.
13 The hangings on the east toward the sunrise were also 75 feet in length.[C] 14 The hangings on one side of the gate were 22½ feet,[D]
including their three posts and three bases.
15 It was the same for the other side. The
hangings were 22½ feet,[D] including their
three posts and three bases on both sides
of the courtyard gate. 16 All the hangings
around the courtyard were of finely spun
linen. 17 The bases for the posts were bronze;
the hooks and bands[B] of the posts were silver; and the plating for the tops of the posts
was silver. All the posts of the courtyard were
banded with silver.

18 The screen for the gate of the courtyard
was embroidered with blue, purple, and scarlet yarn, and finely spun linen. It was 30 feet[E]
long, and like the hangings of the courtyard,
7½ feet[F] high.[G] 19 It had four posts, including
their four bronze bases. Their hooks were
silver, and the bands[B] as well as the plating
of their tops were silver. 20 All the tent pegs
for the tabernacle and for the surrounding
courtyard were bronze.

Inventory of Materials

21 This is the inventory for the tabernacle,
the tabernacle of the ·testimony,[a] that was recorded at Moses' command. It was the work
of the Levites under the direction of[H] Ithamar
son of Aaron the priest.[b] 22 Bezalel son of Uri,
son of Hur, of the tribe of Judah, made everything that the LORD commanded Moses.
23 With him was Oholiab son of Ahisamach, of
the tribe of Dan, a gem cutter, a designer, and
an embroiderer with blue, purple, and scarlet
yarn, and fine linen.

24 All the gold of the presentation offering
that was used for the project in all the work
on the sanctuary, was 2,193 pounds,[I] according to the sanctuary ·shekel.[c] 25 The silver from
those of the community who were registered
was 7,544 pounds,[J] according to the sanctuary shekel — 26 ⅖ of an ounce[K] per man, that
is, half a shekel according to the sanctuary
shekel, from everyone 20 years old or more
who had crossed over to the registered group,
603,550 men. 27 There were 7,500 pounds[L] of
silver used to cast the bases of the sanctuary
and the bases of the veil — 100 bases from
7,500 pounds,[L] 75 pounds[M] for each base.[d]
28 With the remaining 44 pounds[N] he made
the hooks for the posts, overlaid their tops,
and supplied bands[B] for them.

29 The bronze of the presentation offering
totaled 5,310 pounds.[O] 30 He made with it the
bases for the entrance to the tent of meeting,
the bronze altar and its bronze grate, all the
utensils for the altar, 31 the bases for the surrounding courtyard, the bases for the gate of
the courtyard, all the tent pegs for the tabernacle, and all the tent pegs for the surrounding courtyard.

Making the Priestly Garments

39 They made specially woven[P] garments
for ministry in the sanctuary, and
the holy garments for Aaron from the blue,
purple, and scarlet yarn, just as the LORD had
commanded Moses.[e]

Making the Ephod

2 Bezalel[f] made the ·ephod of gold, of blue,
purple, and scarlet yarn, and of finely spun
linen. 3 They hammered out thin sheets of
gold, and he[Q] cut threads from them to inter-
weave with the blue, purple, and scarlet yarn,
and the fine linen in a skillful design. 4 They
made shoulder pieces for attaching it; it was
joined together at its two edges. 5 The artistically woven waistband that was on the ephod
was of one piece with the ephod, according to
the same workmanship of gold, of blue, purple, and scarlet yarn, and of finely spun linen,
just as the LORD had commanded Moses.

6 Then they mounted the onyx stones sur-

[a] **38:21** Nm 1:50,53; 9:15; 10:11; 17:7-8; 2Ch 24:6; Ac 7:44
[b] Nm 4:28,33
[c] **38:24** Ex 30:13; Lv 27:25; Nm 3:47; 18:16
[d] **38:26-27** Ex 26:19,21,25,32; 30:13; Nm 1:46
[e] **39:1** Ex 28:2,4; 31:10; 35:19,23; 39:41
[f] **39:2-7** Ex 28:6-12

[A] **38:9,11** Lit *100 cubits* [B] **38:10,11,17,28** Or *connecting rods* [C] **38:12,13** Lit *50 cubits* [D] **38:14,15** Lit *15 cubits* [E] **38:18** Lit *20 cubits* [F] **38:18** Lit *five cubits* [G] **38:18** Lit *high in width* [H] **38:21** Lit *Levites by the hand of* [I] **38:24** Lit *29 talents and 730 shekels* [J] **38:25** Lit *100 talents and 1,775 shekels* [K] **38:26** Lit *a beka* [L] **38:27** Lit *100 talents* [M] **38:27** Lit *one talent* [N] **38:28** Lit *1,775* (shekels) [O] **38:29** Lit *70 talents and 2,400 shekels* [P] **39:1** Hb obscure [Q] **39:3** Sam, Syr, Tg read *they*

rounded with gold filigree settings, engraved
with the names of Israel's sons as a gem cutter engraves a seal. 7 He fastened them on the
shoulder pieces of the ephod as memorial
stones for the Israelites, just as the LORD had
commanded Moses.

Making the Breastpiece

8 He[a] also made the embroidered breastpiece with the same workmanship as the
ephod of gold, of blue, purple, and scarlet
yarn, and of finely spun linen. 9 They made
the breastpiece square and folded double,
nine inches long and nine inches wide.[A]
10 They mounted four rows of gemstones[B] on
it. The first row was a row of carnelian, topaz,
and emerald;[C] 11 the second row, a turquoise,[D]
a sapphire,[E] and a diamond;[F] 12 the third row,
a jacinth,[G] an agate, and an amethyst; 13 and
the fourth row, a beryl, an onyx, and a jasper.
They were surrounded with gold filigree in
their settings.
14 The 12 stones corresponded to the names
of Israel's sons. Each stone was engraved like
a seal with one of the names of the 12 tribes.
15 They made braided chains of pure gold
cord for the breastpiece. 16 They also fashioned two gold filigree settings and two gold
rings and attached the two rings to its two
corners. 17 Then they attached the two gold
cords to the two gold rings on the corners
of the breastpiece. 18 They attached the other
ends of the two cords to the two filigree settings and, in this way, attached them to the
ephod's shoulder pieces in front. 19 They made
two other gold rings and put them at the two
other corners of the breastpiece on the edge
that is next to the inner border of the ephod.
20 They made two more gold rings and attached them to the bottom of the ephod's two
shoulder pieces on its front, close to its seam,[H]
above the ephod's woven waistband. 21 Then
they tied the breastpiece from its rings to the
rings of the ephod with a cord of blue yarn,
so that the breastpiece was above the ephod's
waistband and did not come loose from the
ephod. They did just as the LORD had commanded Moses.

[a]39:8-21 Ex 28:15-28
[b]39:22-26 Ex 28:31-34
[c]39:28 Ex 28:39,42; Ezk 44:18
[d]39:30 Ex 28:36-37; 29:6
[e]39:32 Ex 25:40; 39:42-43

Making the Robe

22 They[b] made the woven robe of the ephod
entirely of blue yarn. 23 There was an opening in the center of the robe like that of body
armor[G] with a collar around the opening so
that it would not tear. 24 They made pomegranates of finely spun blue, purple, and scarlet yarn[I] on the lower hem of the robe. 25 They
made bells of pure gold and attached the
bells between the pomegranates, all around
the hem of the robe between the pomegranates, 26 a bell and a pomegranate alternating
all around the lower hem of the robe[J] to be
worn for ministry. They made it just as the
LORD had commanded Moses.

The Other Priestly Garments

27 They made the tunics of fine woven linen
for Aaron and his sons. 28 They also made the
turban and the ornate headbands[K] of fine
linen, the undergarments,[c] 29 and the sash
of finely spun linen of embroidered blue,
purple, and scarlet yarn. They did just as the
LORD had commanded Moses.

Making the Holy Diadem

30 They also made a medallion, the holy diadem, out of pure gold and wrote on it an inscription like the engraving on a seal:[d]

HOLY TO THE LORD.

31 Then they attached a cord of blue yarn to it
in order to mount it on the turban, just as the
LORD had commanded Moses.

Moses' Inspection of the Tabernacle

32 So all the work for the tabernacle, the tent
of meeting, was finished. The Israelites did
everything just as the LORD had commanded
Moses.[e] 33 Then they brought the tabernacle
to Moses: the tent with all its furnishings, its
clasps, its planks, its crossbars, and its posts
and bases; 34 the covering of ram skins dyed
red and the covering of manatee skins;[L] the
veil for the screen; 35 the ark of the •testimony
with its poles and the •mercy seat; 36 the table,
all its utensils, and the •bread of the Presence;
37 the pure gold lampstand, with its lamps

[A]39:9 Lit *a span its length and a span its width* [B]39:10 Many of these stones cannot be identified with certainty. [C]39:10 Or *beryl* [D]39:11 Or *malachite, or garnet* [E]39:11 Or *lapis lazuli* [F]39:11 Hb uncertain; LXX, Vg read *jasper* [G]39:12,23 Hb obscure [H]39:20 The place where the shoulder pieces join the front of the ephod [I]39:24 Sam, LXX, Vg add *and linen* [J]39:26 Lit *bell and pomegranate, bell and pomegranate, on the hem of the robe around* [K]39:28 Lit *and the headdresses of headbands* [L]39:34 Or *of dolphin skins*, or *of fine leather*; Hb obscure

arranged and all its utensils, as well as the oil
for the light; 38the gold altar; the anointing
oil; the fragrant incense; the screen for the
entrance to the tent; 39the bronze altar with
its bronze grate, its poles, and all its utensils;
the basin with its stand; 40the hangings of the
courtyard, its posts and bases, the screen for
the gate of the courtyard, its ropes and tent
pegs, and all the equipment for the service of
the tabernacle, the tent of meeting; 41and the
specially woven[A] garments for ministering in
the sanctuary, the holy garments for Aaron
the priest and the garments for his sons to
serve as priests. 42The Israelites had done all
the work according to everything the LORD
had commanded Moses.[a] 43Moses inspected
all the work they had accomplished. They had
done just as the LORD commanded. Then Moses blessed them.[b]

Setting up the Tabernacle

40 The LORD spoke to Moses: 2"You are
to set up the tabernacle, the tent of
meeting, on the first day of the first month.[B,c]
3Put the ark[d] of the ·testimony there and
screen off the ark with the veil. 4Then bring
in the table and lay out its arrangement; also
bring in the lampstand and set up its lamps.
5Place the gold altar for incense in front of
the ark of the testimony. Put up the screen
for the entrance to the tabernacle. 6Position
the altar of ·burnt offering in front of the entrance to the tabernacle, the tent of meeting.
7Place the basin[e] between the tent of meeting
and the altar, and put water in it. 8Assemble
the surrounding courtyard and hang the
screen for the gate of the courtyard.

9"Take the anointing oil and anoint[f] the
tabernacle and everything in it; consecrate it
along with all its furnishings so that it will be
holy. 10Anoint the altar of burnt offering and
all its utensils; consecrate the altar so that it
will be especially holy. 11Anoint the basin and
its stand and consecrate it.

12"Then bring Aaron and his sons to the entrance to the tent of meeting and wash them
with water.[g] 13Clothe Aaron with the holy
garments,[h] anoint him, and consecrate him,
so that he can serve Me as a priest. 14Have
his sons come forward and clothe them in
tunics. 15Anoint them just as you anointed
their father, so that they may also serve Me
as priests. Their anointing will serve to inaugurate a permanent priesthood for them
throughout their generations."[i]

16Moses did everything just as the LORD
had commanded him. 17The tabernacle was
set up in the first month of the second year,
on the first day of the month.[C,j] 18Moses set up
the tabernacle: he laid its bases, positioned
its planks, inserted its crossbars, and set up
its posts. 19Then he spread the tent over the
tabernacle and put the covering of the tent
on top of it, just as the LORD had commanded
Moses.

20Moses took the testimony[k] and placed it
in the ark, and attached the poles to the ark.
He set the ·mercy seat on top of the ark. 21He
brought the ark into the tabernacle, put up
the veil for the screen, and screened off the
ark of the testimony, just as the LORD had
commanded him.

22Moses placed the table in the tent of
meeting on the north side of the tabernacle,
outside the veil. 23He arranged the bread on
it before the LORD, just as the LORD had commanded him. 24He also put the lampstand in
the tent of meeting opposite the table on the
south side of the tabernacle 25and set up the
lamps before the LORD, just as the LORD had
commanded him.

26Moses also installed the gold altar in the
tent of meeting, in front of the veil, 27and
burned fragrant incense on it, just as the
LORD had commanded him. 28He put up
the screen at the entrance to the tabernacle.
29Then he placed the altar of burnt offering
at the entrance to the tabernacle, the tent of
meeting, and offered the burnt offering and
the ·grain offering on it, just as the LORD had
commanded him.

30He set the basin between the tent of meeting and the altar and put water in it for washing. 31Moses, Aaron, and his sons washed
their hands and feet from it. 32They washed
whenever they came to the tent of meeting
and approached the altar, just as the LORD
had commanded Moses.

33Next Moses set up the surrounding courtyard for the tabernacle and the altar and

[a] 39:33-42 Ex 25:31; 27:9-15; 30:3; 35:10
[b] 39:43 Lv 9:22-23; Nm 6:23-27; Jos 22:6; 2Sm 6:18; 1Kg 8:14; 2Ch 30:27
[c] 40:2 Ex 12:12; 13:4; 26:30
[d] 40:3 Ex 26:33; 40:21; Nm 4:5
[e] 40:7 Ex 30:18; 40:30
[f] 40:9 Ex 30:26; Lv 8:10
[g] 40:12 Lv 8:1-3
[h] 40:13 Ex 28:41
[i] 40:15 Ex 29:9; Nm 25:13
[j] 40:17 Ex 40:2; Nm 7:1
[k] 40:20 Ex 16:34; 25:16

[A] 39:41 Hb obscure [B] 40:2 Lit *on the day of the first month, on the first of the month* [C] 40:17 DSS, Sam, LXX add *of their coming out of Egypt*

hung a screen for the gate of the courtyard.
So Moses finished the work.[a]

The LORD's Glory

34 The cloud covered the tent of meeting,
and the glory of the LORD filled the tabernacle.[b] 35 Moses was unable to enter the tent of
meeting because the cloud rested on it, and
the glory of the LORD filled the tabernacle.

36 The Israelites set out whenever the cloud
was taken up from the tabernacle throughout all the stages of their journey.[c] 37 If the
cloud was not taken up, they did not set out
until the day it was taken up.[d] 38 For the cloud
of the LORD was over the tabernacle by day,
and there was a fire inside the cloud by night,
visible to the entire house of Israel throughout all the stages of their journey.

[a] **40:21-33** Ex 25:37; 26:33,35-36; 27:9,16; 29:38; 30:5-7,19-20; 40:1-7
[b] **40:34** Lv 16:2; Nm 9:15; 1Kg 8:10-11; 2Ch 5:13-14; 7:2; Is 6:4; Hg 2:7,9; Rv 15:8
[c] **40:36** Nm 9:17; Neh 9:19
[d] **40:37** Nm 9:19-22

GOD'S HEART FOR THE WORLD

Down from the Mountain

For the cloud of the LORD was over the tabernacle by day, and there was a fire inside the cloud by night, visible to the entire house of Israel throughout all the stages of their journey. (Exodus 40:38)

If you have been a Christian for a long time the language of "God with us" might have become stale. Maybe you read over this last bit of Exodus quickly because you were excited that you had *finally* finished such a long book. But let's stop and ponder what we have just seen.

In the Ancient Near East belief system it was typical for gods to dwell on mountaintops (think, Mount Olympus). They were seen as far off, distant, and not necessarily working for the people. They were, in fact, interested mostly in themselves. They were powerful and strong, but fickle.

In the book of Exodus, Yahweh, too, is on the top of a mountain, but that's not where He stays. Israel's One God, the creator of all, comes down from the mountain and makes His home right in their front yard. He makes Himself "visible to the entire house of Israel throughout all the stages of their journey." He does not simply stand far off and give rules and instructions. He comes close, He pursues intimacy. He is *with* His people.

In the same way that God set Himself right in the middle of Israel's everyday, in Jesus God came to be with His people in an even more personal way, becoming "Immanuel, which is translated 'God is with us'" (Mt 1:23). He walked, talked, sat, sailed, ate, and wept with them. Then He died for them. And when God's Kingdom comes in full, we will be given even more of the nearness of God, even more intimacy, even more love. Then we will know, even as we are fully known.

■ **AUTHOR:** Moses

■■ **DATE:** Most likely written during Israel's wandering in the wilderness (around 1445–1406 B.C.)

This third book of the Pentateuch begins with instructions on burnt offerings. The animal to be sacrificed must be qualified, taken to the right place, and handled the right way. Instructions on offerings of grain follow, then fellowship offerings, and then sin offering—all with precise instructions that Aaron's sons, the priests of Israel, must follow.

The book continues with minute details about every area of the people's lives. There's medical advice, mostly when to quarantine the sick; cooking advice; health advice. Few of these instructions are likely to be used today. So what is the point of this book? Why read Leviticus today? There are at least three crucial insights every generation of readers can draw from Leviticus.

LEVITICUS

First, the instructions on religious ritual and everyday life created a nation from a group of distantly related tribes and clans. The wilderness tabernacle, made at the foot of Mount Sinai following the giving of the Ten Commandments, became the center of life and worship for a new people who would represent God and witness to God's truth. These instructions formed the basis of the Hebrew national identity, and differentiated them from the nations around them.

Second, the Hebrews learned one major lesson about God. Of all the adjectives attached to God, this one is most important: holiness. The Leviticus code stresses, above all, God's character, and by direct implication, the people's corporate responsibility. God is holy; be holy yourselves. Do not give in to sin.

Third, the codes of Leviticus point beyond themselves to a plan of God for salvation. Yes, the people camped at Mount Sinai were told to worship God by the blood of animals and the offering of grains, but this ritual sacrifice was only provisional. Another sacrifice was coming who would fulfill (not nullify) these laws of sacrifice. That future sacrifice would be one with God Himself, of God's own person—called in the Gospel of John "the Word," Jesus Christ. In the mission plan of God, Jesus would be the great and final sacrifice, forever overcoming sin and appropriating God's holiness to all who put faith in Him.

Today when we read Leviticus, we do not comply with the details of worship ordered here. Rather, we praise God that these sacrifices, essential in their era, have been superseded by the cross of Christ. The renewal these sacrifices intended to bring has been ratified and fulfilled in Jesus' resurrection. The promised new spiritual life is now the work of the Holy Spirit, given to all God's children as a resource and comfort. Leviticus points to but cannot supply these unsurpassable gifts of love. God Himself supplied our needs once for all in Jesus Christ.

The mission of God takes different forms, all the while leading people to trust and obey God's holy will—making an eternal Kingdom of love, peace, and joy.

The Burnt Offering

1 Then the LORD summoned Moses[a] and
spoke to him from the tent of meeting:[b]
2“Speak to the Israelites and tell them: When
any of you brings an offering to the LORD
from the livestock, you[A] may bring your offering from the herd or the flock.
3“If his gift is a •burnt offering[c] from the
herd, he is to bring an unblemished male.[d]
He must bring it to the entrance to the tent
of meeting so that he[B] may be accepted by the
LORD.[e] 4He is to lay his hand on[f] the head of
the burnt offering so it can be accepted[g] on
his behalf to make •atonement for him.[h] 5He
is to slaughter the bull before the LORD; Aaron’s sons the priests[i] are to present the blood[j]
and sprinkle it[k] on all sides of the altar that is
at the entrance to the tent of meeting. 6Then
he must skin the burnt offering[l] and cut it
into pieces.[C] 7The sons of Aaron the priest will
prepare a fire on the altar and arrange wood
on the fire. 8Aaron’s sons the priests are to arrange the pieces, the head, and the suet[m] on
top of the burning wood on the altar. 9The offerer must wash its entrails[n] and shanks[o] with
water. Then the priest will burn all of it on the
altar as a burnt offering, a fire offering[p] of a
pleasing aroma[q] to the LORD.
10“But if his gift for a burnt offering is from
the flock, from sheep or goats,[r] he is to present an unblemished male. 11He will slaughter it on the north side of the altar before the
LORD. Aaron’s sons the priests will sprinkle its
blood against the altar on all sides. 12He will
cut the animal into pieces[C] with its head and
its suet, and the priest will arrange them on
top of the burning wood on the altar. 13But he
is to wash the entrails and shanks with water.
The priest will then present all of it and burn
it on the altar; it is a burnt offering, a fire offering of a pleasing aroma to the LORD.
14“If his gift to the LORD is a burnt offering
of birds,[s] he is to present his offering from
the turtledoves[t] or young pigeons.[D,u] 15Then
the priest must bring it to the altar, and must
twist off its head and burn it on the altar; its
blood should be drained at the side of the altar. 16He will remove its digestive tract,[E] cutting off the tail feathers, and throw it on the
east side of the altar at the place for ashes.[v]
17He will tear it open by its wings without dividing the bird.[w] Then the priest is to burn it
on the altar on top of the burning wood. It is
a burnt offering, a fire offering of a pleasing
aroma to the LORD.

The Grain Offering

2 “When anyone presents a •grain offering[x]
as a gift to the LORD, his gift must consist
of fine flour.[F,y] He is to pour olive oil[z] on it,
put frankincense on it,[G,aa] 2and bring it to
Aaron’s sons the priests. The priest will take
a handful of fine flour and oil from it, along
with all its frankincense, and will burn this
memorial portion[ab] of it on the altar, a fire offering of a pleasing aroma to the LORD. 3But
the rest of the grain offering will belong to
Aaron and his sons; it is the holiest part[ac] of
the fire offerings to the LORD.
4“When you present a grain offering baked
in an oven, it must be made of fine flour, either unleavened cakes[ad] mixed with oil or unleavened wafers[ae] coated with oil. 5If your gift
is a grain offering prepared on a griddle,[af] it
must be unleavened bread[ag] made of fine flour
mixed with oil. 6Break it into pieces and pour
oil on it; it is a grain offering. 7If your gift is a
grain offering prepared in a pan,[ah] it must be
made of fine flour with oil. 8When you bring[H]
to the LORD the grain offering made in any of
these ways, it is to be presented to the priest,
and he will take it to the altar. 9The priest will
remove the memorial portion[I] from the grain
offering and burn it on the altar, a fire offering of a pleasing aroma to the LORD. 10But the
rest of the grain offering will belong to Aaron
and his sons;[ai] it is the holiest part of the fire
offerings to the LORD.
11“No grain offering that you present to the
LORD is to be made with yeast, for you are not
to burn[J] any yeast[aj] or honey[ak] as a fire offering
to the LORD. 12You may present them to the
LORD as an offering of •firstfruits,[al] but they
are not to be offered on the altar as a pleasing
aroma. 13You are to season each of your grain
offerings with salt; you must not omit from
your grain offering the salt of the covenant[am]

[a]**1:1** Ps 77:20; Mt 8:4; Heb 3:2
[b]Ex 27:21
[c]**1:3** Gn 22:2; Lv 3:5
[d]Ex 29:1
[e]Lv 19:5; Heb 9:14; 1Pt 1:19
[f]**1:4** Ex 29:10; Lv 3:2; 8:14,18,22; 16:21; Nm 8:10,12
[g]Gn 33:10; Lv 7:18; 19:7; 22:23,25,27
[h]Ex 30:15
[i]**1:5** Lv 4:16
[j]Heb 9:12
[k]Ex 24:6; 29:16,20
[l]**1:6** Lv 7:8; 9:11; 2Ch 29:34
[m]**1:8** Lv 1:12; 8:20
[n]**1:9** Ex 12:9; 29:13,22; Lv 1:13; 3:3
[o]Ex 12:9; 29:17; Lv 1:13; 4:11; 8:21; 9:14; Am 3:12
[p]Dt 18:1
[q]Lv 2:2; 23:13
[r]**1:10** Lv 4:23
[s]**1:14** Gn 40:17; Lv 17:13
[t]Gn 15:9; Lv 1:14; 5:7,11; 12:6,8; 14:22,30; 15:14,29; Nm 6:10; Ps 74:19; Sg 2:12; Jr 8:7
[u]Gn 8:8-12; Lv 5:7,11
[v]**1:16** Lv 4:12; 6:10-11; 1Kg 13:3,5; Jr 31:40
[w]**1:17** Gn 15:9-10
[x]**2:1** Ex 40:29
[y]Gn 18:6; Ex 29:2,40; Lv 2:1-7
[z]Gn 28:18; 35:14
[aa]Ex 30:34
[ab]**2:2** Lv 2:9,16; 5:12; 6:8; 24:7; Nm 5:26; Ac 10:4
[ac]**2:3** Lv 14:13
[ad]**2:4** Ex 29:2
[ae]Ex 29:2,23; Lv 7:12; 8:26; Nm 6:15,19; 1Ch 23:29
[af]**2:5** Lv 6:14; 7:9; 1Ch 23:29; Ezk 4:3
[ag]Ex 12:8; Mt 16:6,11-12; 1Co 5:6-8
[ah]**2:7** Lv 7:9
[ai]**2:10** Lv 7:9-10
[aj]**2:11** Ex 12:14
[ak]Jdg 14:8
[al]**2:12** Gn 49:3; Ex 23:16,19
[am]**2:13** Ex 19:5; Nm 18:19; 2Ch 13:5

[A]**1:2** Or *LORD, from the livestock you* [B]**1:3** Or *it* [C]**1:6,12** Lit *its pieces* [D]**1:14** Or *or pigeons* [E]**1:16** Or *its crop*, or *its crissum* [F]**2:1** = wheat flour; Ex 29:2 [G]**2:1** DSS, Sam, LXX add *it is a grain offering* [H]**2:8** DSS, LXX read *When he brings* [I]**2:9** Lit *portion of it* [J]**2:11** Some Hb mss, Sam, LXX, Tg read *present*

with your God. You are to present salt[A] with
each of your offerings.
14 "If you present a grain offering of firstfruits to the LORD, you must present fresh
heads of grain, crushed kernels, roasted on
the fire, for your grain offering of firstfruits.
15 You are to put oil and frankincense on it; it
is a grain offering. 16 The priest will then burn
some of its crushed kernels and oil with all
its frankincense as a fire offering to the LORD.

The Fellowship Offering

3 "If his offering is a •fellowship sacrifice,[a]
and he is presenting an animal from the
herd, whether male or female, he must present one without blemish[b] before the LORD.
2 He is to lay his hand on the head of his offering and slaughter it at the entrance to the tent
of meeting. Then Aaron's sons the priests will
sprinkle the blood on all sides of the altar.[c]
3 He will present part of the fellowship sacrifice as a fire offering to the LORD: the fat[d]
surrounding the entrails,[e] all the fat that is on
the entrails, 4 and the two kidneys[f] with the
fat on them at the loins; he will also remove
the fatty lobe of the liver[g] with the kidneys.
5 Aaron's sons will burn it on the altar along
with the •burnt offering[h] that is on the burning wood, a fire offering of a pleasing aroma
to the LORD.
6 "If his offering as a fellowship sacrifice to
the LORD is from the flock, he must present a
male or female without blemish. 7 If he is presenting a lamb for his offering, he is to present it before the LORD. 8 He must lay his hand
on the head of his offering, then slaughter it
before the tent of meeting. Aaron's sons will
sprinkle its blood on all sides of the altar. 9 He
will then present part of the fellowship sacrifice as a fire offering to the LORD consisting
of its fat and the entire fat tail,[i] which he is to
remove close to the backbone. He will also remove the fat surrounding the entrails,[j] all the
fat on the entrails, 10 the two kidneys with the
fat on them at the loins, and the fatty lobe of
the liver above the kidneys. 11 Then the priest
will burn the food on the altar,[k] as a fire offering to the LORD.
12 "If his offering is a goat,[l] he is to present
it before the LORD. 13 He must lay his hand on
its head and slaughter it before the tent of
meeting. Aaron's sons will sprinkle[B] its blood
on all sides of the altar. 14 He will present part
of his offering as a fire offering to the LORD:
the fat surrounding the entrails, all the fat
that is on the entrails, 15 and the two kidneys
with the fat on them at the loins; he will also
remove the fatty lobe of the liver with the
kidneys. 16 Then the priest will burn the food
on the altar, as a fire offering for a pleasing
aroma.[C]
"All fat belongs to the LORD. 17 This is a permanent statute[m] throughout your generations, wherever you live: you must not eat any
fat or any blood."[n]

The Sin Offering

4 Then the LORD spoke to Moses: 2 "Tell the
Israelites: When someone sins unintentionally[o] against any of the LORD's commands
and does anything prohibited by them —
3 "If the anointed priest[D,p] sins, bringing
•guilt[q] on the people, he is to present to the
LORD a young, unblemished[r] bull as a •sin[E]
offering[s] for the sin he has committed. 4 He
must bring the bull to the entrance to the
tent of meeting before the LORD, lay his hand
on the bull's head, and slaughter it before the
LORD. 5 The anointed priest must then take
some of the bull's blood and bring it into
the tent of meeting. 6 The priest is to dip his
finger in the blood and sprinkle some of it
seven times[t] before the LORD in front of the
veil[u] of the sanctuary.[v] 7 The priest must apply
some of the blood to the horns of the altar
of fragrant incense[w] that is before the LORD
in the tent of meeting. He must pour out the
rest of the bull's blood at the base of the altar of burnt offering[x] that is at the entrance
to the tent of meeting. 8 He is to remove all
the fat from the bull of the sin offering: the
fat surrounding the entrails, all the fat that
is on the entrails, 9 and the two kidneys with
the fat on them at the loins. He will also remove the fatty lobe of the liver with the kidneys, 10 just as the fat is removed from the ox
of the •fellowship sacrifice.[y] The priest is to
burn them on the altar of burnt offering.

[a] **3:1** Lv 7:11
[b] Ex 29:1
[c] **3:2** Lv 1:5
[d] **3:3** Ex 23:18; 29:13,22
[e] Ex 12:9
[f] **3:4** Lv 7:4
[g] Lv 9:10
[h] **3:5** Lv 1:3-4
[i] **3:9** Ex 29:22; Lv 7:3; 8:25; 9:19
[j] Lv 1:9
[k] **3:11** Lv 3:16; 21:6,8,17,21-22; 22:25; 26:5; Nm 28:24
[l] **3:12** Lv 4:23
[m] **3:17** Ex 28:43; Lv 11:46
[n] Lv 7:26; 17:10,14; 19:26; Dt 12:16,23; 15:23
[o] **4:2** Nm 15:22,24
[p] **4:3** Lv 4:16; 6:15
[q] Lv 6:5,7; 22:16
[r] Ex 29:1
[s] Ex 29:14
[t] **4:6** Lv 16:14
[u] Mk 15:38; Lk 23:45
[v] Ex 15:17; Lv 10:4
[w] **4:7** Ex 30:27
[x] Ex 3:5; 35:16
[y] **4:8-10** Lv 7:11

[A] **2:13** Salt, used as a preservative, is a symbol of the permanence of the covenant. [B] **3:13** Or *dash* [C] **3:16** Sam, LXX add *to the LORD* [D] **4:3** Probably the high priest; Lv 6:22 [E] **4:3** Or *purification*

[11]But the hide[a] of the bull and all its flesh, with its head and shanks, and its entrails and dung — [12]all the rest of the bull — he must bring to a ceremonially •clean place[b] outside the camp[c] to the ash heap, and must burn it on a wood fire. It is to be burned at the ash heap.

[13]"Now if the whole community of Israel[d] errs,[e] and the matter escapes the notice of the assembly,[f] so that they violate any of the LORD's commands and incur guilt[g] by doing what is prohibited, [14]then the assembly must present a young bull as a sin offering. When the sin they have committed in regard to the command becomes known, they are to bring it before the tent of meeting. [15]The elders[h] of the community are to lay their hands on the bull's head before the LORD and it is to be slaughtered before the LORD. [16]The anointed priest will bring some of the bull's blood into the tent of meeting. [17]The priest is to dip his finger in the blood and sprinkle it seven times before the LORD in front of the veil. [18]He is to apply some of the blood to the horns of the altar that is before the LORD in the tent of meeting. He must pour out the rest of the blood at the base of the altar of burnt offering that is at the entrance to the tent of meeting. [19]He is to remove all the fat from it and burn it on the altar. [20]He is to offer this bull just as he did with the bull in the sin offering; he will offer it the same way. So the priest will make •atonement[i] on their behalf, and they will be forgiven.[j] [21]Then he will bring the bull outside the camp[k] and burn it just as he burned the first bull. It is the sin offering for the assembly.

[22]"When a leader[A,l] sins and unintentionally violates any of the commands of the LORD his God by doing what is prohibited, and incurs guilt, [23]or someone informs him about the sin he has committed, he is to bring an unblemished male goat[m] as his offering. [24]He is to lay his hand on the head of the goat and slaughter it at the place where the •burnt offering[n] is slaughtered before the LORD. It is a sin offering.[o] [25]Then the priest must take some of the blood from the sin offering with his finger and apply it to the horns of the altar of burnt offering.[p] The rest of its blood he must pour out at the base of the altar of burnt offering. [26]He must burn all its fat on the altar, like the fat of the fellowship sacrifice. In this way the priest will make atonement on his behalf for that person's sin, and he will be forgiven.

[27]"Now if any of the common people[B] sins unintentionally by violating one of the LORD's commands, does what is prohibited, and incurs guilt, [28]or if someone informs him about the sin he has committed, then he is to bring an unblemished female goat as his offering for the sin that he has committed. [29]He is to lay his hand on the head of the sin offering and slaughter it at the place of the burnt offering. [30]Then the priest must take some of its blood with his finger and apply it to the horns of the altar of burnt offering. He must pour out the rest of its blood at the base of the altar. [31]He is to remove all its fat just as the fat is removed from the fellowship sacrifice. The priest is to burn it on the altar as a pleasing aroma to the LORD. In this way the priest will make atonement on his behalf, and he will be forgiven.

[32]"Or if the offering that he brings as a sin offering is a lamb,[q] he is to bring an unblemished female. [33]He is to lay his hand on the head of the sin offering and slaughter it as a sin offering at the place where the burnt offering is slaughtered. [34]Then the priest must take some of the blood of the sin offering with his finger and apply it to the horns of the altar of burnt offering. He must pour out the rest of its blood at the base of the altar. [35]He is to remove all its fat just as the fat of the lamb is removed from the fellowship sacrifice. The priest will burn it on the altar along with the fire offerings to the LORD. In this way the priest will make atonement on his behalf for the sin he has committed, and he will be forgiven.

Cases Requiring Sin Offerings

5 "When someone sins in any of these ways:

If he has seen, heard, or known about something he has witnessed, and did not respond to a public call to testify, he is responsible for his sin.[r]

[a]**4:11** Lv 7:8 [b]**4:12** Lv 6:4; 10:14; Nm 19:9 [c]Lv 8:17; Heb 13:11-13 [d]**4:13** Ex 12:47 [e]Nm 15:22 [f]Ex 16:3; Lv 4:21; Nm 10:7; 15:15; 20:6,10 [g]Nm 5:6; Ps 68:21 [h]**4:15** Ex 18:12 [i]**4:20** Ex 30:15 [j]Lv 5:16; 6:7 [k]**4:21** Lv 8:17 [l]**4:22** Ex 34:31 [m]**4:23** Lv 9:3; 16:5; 23:19; Nm 7:16-82 [n]**4:24** Gn 22:2; Ex 20:24; Lv 3:5 [o]Ex 29:14 [p]**4:25** Lv 5:9 [q]**4:32** Lv 9:3 [r]**5:1** Gn 4:13; Ex 20:5; Lv 16:21-22; Nm 5:15,31; Dt 19:15

[A]**4:22** Or *ruler* [B]**4:27** Lit *the people of the land*

2 Or if someone touches anything ·unclean[a] — a carcass of an unclean wild animal,[b] or unclean livestock, or an unclean swarming creature[A,c] — without being aware of it, he is unclean and ·guilty.[d]

3 Or if he touches human uncleanness[e] — any uncleanness by which one can become defiled[f] — without being aware of it, but later recognizes it, he is guilty.

4 Or if someone swears rashly[g] to do what is good or evil — concerning anything a person may speak rashly in an oath — without being aware of it, but later recognizes it, he incurs guilt in such an instance.[B]

5 If someone incurs guilt in one of these cases, he is to confess[h] he has committed that sin. 6 He must bring his restitution[i] for the sin he has committed to the LORD: a female lamb or goat from the flock as a ·sin offering. In this way the priest will make ·atonement[j] on his behalf for his sin.

7 "But if he cannot afford an animal from the flock, then he may bring to the LORD two turtledoves or two young pigeons[k] as restitution for his sin — one as a sin offering and the other as a ·burnt offering. 8 He is to bring them to the priest, who will first present the one for the sin offering. He must twist its head at the back of the neck without severing it.[l] 9 Then he will sprinkle some of the blood of the sin offering on the side of the altar, while the rest of the blood is to be drained out at the base of the altar;[m] it is a sin offering. 10 He must prepare the second bird as a burnt offering according to the regulation.[n] In this way the priest will make atonement on his behalf for the sin he has committed, and he will be forgiven.

11 "But if he cannot afford[C] two turtledoves or two young pigeons,[o] he may bring two quarts[D] of fine[E] flour[F,p] as an offering for his sin. He must not put olive oil or frankincense on it, for it is a sin offering. 12 He is to bring it to the priest, who will take a handful from it as its memorial portion[q] and burn it on the altar along with the fire offerings to the LORD; it is a sin offering. 13 In this way the priest will make atonement on his behalf concerning the sin he has committed in any of these cases, and he will be forgiven. The rest will belong to the priest, like the ·grain offering."[r]

The Restitution Offering

14 Then the LORD spoke to Moses: 15 "If someone offends[s] by sinning unintentionally[t] in regard to any of the LORD's holy things,[G] he must bring his ·restitution offering to the LORD: an unblemished ram from the flock (based on your assessment of its value in silver ·shekels, according to the sanctuary shekel[u]) as a restitution offering. 16 He must make restitution[v] for his sin regarding any holy[w] thing, adding a fifth of its value to it,[x] and give it to the priest. Then the priest will make atonement on his behalf with the ram of the restitution offering, and he will be forgiven.[y]

17 "If someone sins and without knowing it violates any of the LORD's commands concerning anything prohibited, he bears the consequences of his guilt. 18 He must bring an unblemished ram from the flock according to your assessment of its value as a restitution offering to the priest. Then the priest will make atonement on his behalf for the error he has committed unintentionally, and he will be forgiven. 19 It is a restitution offering; he is indeed guilty before the LORD."

6 [H] The LORD spoke to Moses: 2 "When someone sins and offends the LORD by deceiving[z] his neighbor in regard to a deposit,[a] a security,[I] or a robbery;[b] or defrauds[c] his neighbor; 3 or finds something lost and lies about it;[d] or swears falsely[e] about any of the sinful things a person may do — 4 once he has sinned[f] and acknowledged his ·guilt[g] — he must return what he stole or defrauded, or the deposit entrusted to him, or the lost item he found, 5 or anything else about which he swore falsely. He must make full restitution for it and add a fifth of its value to it.[h] He is to pay it to its owner on the day he acknowledges his guilt.[i] 6 Then he must bring his ·restitution offering[j] to the LORD: an unblem-

[a] **5:2** Lv 11:4; Nm 19:13
[b] Lv 26:6
[c] Lv 11:24-40; Dt 14:8
[d] Nm 5:6; Ps 68:21
[e] **5:3** Lv 14:19
[f] Lv 11:24
[g] **5:4** Ps 106:33; Pr 12:18
[h] **5:5** Lv 16:21
[i] **5:6** Lv 14:12
[j] Ex 30:15
[k] **5:7** Lv 1:14
[l] **5:8** Gn 15:10; Lv 1:15,17
[m] **5:9** Lv 4:25,30
[n] **5:10** Lv 1:14-17
[o] **5:11** Lk 2:24
[p] Lv 2:1
[q] **5:12** Lv 2:2
[r] **5:13** Lv 2:3,10
[s] **5:15** Dt 32:51
[t] Nm 15:24
[u] Lv 27:3; Nm 3:47
[v] **5:16** Lv 14:12; 24:18
[w] Lv 25:12
[x] Lv 27:13
[y] Lv 4:20,26,31,35; 6:7
[z] **6:2** Lv 19:11
[a] Ex 22:7-13
[b] Is 61:8; Ezk 22:29
[c] Dt 24:14
[d] **6:3** Ex 23:4; Dt 22:1-3
[e] Ex 22:11; Lv 19:12
[f] **6:4** Gn 44:32; Jdg 10:10; Neh 1:6; Ps 39:1; Is 1:4
[g] Lv 4:3
[h] **6:5** Lv 27:13
[i] **6:4-5** Ex 22:9-12; 23:4-5; Dt 22:13; Mt 5:23-24; Lk 19:8-9
[j] **6:6** Lv 14:12

[A] **5:2** Perhaps a fish, insect, rodent, or reptile; Gn 1:20; Lv 11:20-23,29-31 [B] **5:4** Lit *in one of such things* [C] **5:11** Lit *if his hand is not sufficient for* [D] **5:11** Lit *one-tenth of an ephah* [E] **5:11** Or *wheat*; Ex 29:2 [F] **5:11** Lit *flour as a sin offering* [G] **5:15** Things dedicated to the LORD such as tabernacle furnishings, priestly portions of the sacrifices, tenths, firstfruits, and firstborn livestock [H] **6:1** Lv 5:20 in Hb [I] **6:2** Or *an investment*

ished[a] ram from the flock according to your assessment of its value as a restitution offering to the priest. 7 In this way the priest will make ·atonement on his behalf before the LORD, and he will be forgiven for anything he may have done to incur guilt."[b]

The Burnt Offering

8[A] The LORD spoke to Moses: 9 "Command Aaron and his sons: This is the law of the ·burnt offering; the burnt offering itself must remain on the altar's hearth all night until morning, while the fire of the altar is kept burning on it. 10 The priest is to put on his linen robe and linen undergarments.[B,c] He is to remove the ashes of the burnt offering the fire has consumed on the altar, and place them beside the altar. 11 Then he must take off his garments, put on other clothes,[d] and bring the ashes outside the camp to a ceremonially ·clean place. 12 The fire on the altar is to be kept burning; it must not go out. Every morning the priest will burn wood on the fire. He is to arrange the burnt offering on the fire and burn the fat portions from the ·fellowship offerings[e] on it. 13 Fire must be kept burning on the altar continually; it must not go out.

The Grain Offering

14 "Now this is the law of the ·grain offering:[f] Aaron's sons will present it before the LORD in front of the altar. 15 The priest is to remove a handful of fine flour and olive oil from the grain offering, with all the frankincense that is on the offering, and burn its memorial portion on the altar as a pleasing aroma to the LORD. 16 Aaron and his sons may eat the rest of it.[g] It is to be eaten in the form of unleavened bread[h] in a holy place;[i] they are to eat it in the courtyard[j] of the tent of meeting. 17 It must not be baked with yeast; I have assigned it as their portion[k] from My fire offerings.[l] It is especially holy, like the ·sin offering[m] and the restitution offering. 18 Any male among Aaron's descendants[n] may eat it. It is a permanent portion[C,o] throughout your generations from the fire offerings to the LORD. Anything that touches the offerings will become holy."[p]

[a]**6:6** Ex 29:1
[b]**6:7** Lv 5:10,13,18
[c]**6:10** Ex 28:42-43; Lv 16:4; Ezk 44:17-19
[d]**6:11** Lv 16:23; Ezk 42:14; 44:19
[e]**6:12** Lv 1:2; 7:11
[f]**6:14-18** Lv 2:1-16
[g]**6:16** 1Co 9:13
[h]Ex 12:8; 1Co 5:8
[i]Lv 16:24
[j]Ex 27:9
[k]**6:17** Lv 6:10; Nm 18:20; 31:36; Dt 10:9; 12:12
[l]Dt 18:1
[m]Ex 29:14
[n]**6:18** Lv 21:18-23
[o]Lv 7:34; Heb 13:10
[p]Ex 29:37; Lk 11:2
[q]**6:23** Dt 13:17; 33:10; 1Sm 7:9; Ps 51:19
[r]**6:25** Ex 29:14
[s]**6:26** Lv 16:24; 1Co 9:13
[t]**7:1** Lv 14:12-13
[u]**7:2** Gn 22:2; Lv 3:5; Nm 6:11; Jos 8:31; 1Ch 16:1; Ps 20:3; Mc 6:6
[v]**7:3** Lv 3:9
[w]**7:4** Lv 9:10

19 The LORD spoke to Moses: 20 "This is the offering that Aaron and his sons must present to the LORD on the day that he is anointed: two quarts[D] of fine flour as a regular[E] grain offering, half of it in the morning and half in the evening. 21 It is to be prepared with oil on a griddle; you are to bring it well-kneaded. You must present it as a grain offering of baked pieces,[F] a pleasing aroma to the LORD. 22 The priest, who is one of Aaron's sons and will be anointed to take his place, is to prepare it. It must be completely burned as a permanent portion for the LORD. 23 Every grain offering for a priest will be a whole burnt offering;[q] it is not to be eaten."

The Sin Offering

24 The LORD spoke to Moses: 25 "Tell Aaron and his sons: This is the law of the sin offering.[r] The sin offering is most holy and must be slaughtered before the LORD at the place where the burnt offering is slaughtered. 26 The priest who offers it as a sin offering is to eat it. It must be eaten in a holy place,[s] in the courtyard of the tent of meeting. 27 Anything that touches its flesh will become holy, and if any of its blood spatters on a garment, then you must wash that garment[G] in a holy place. 28 A clay pot in which the sin offering is boiled must be broken; if it is boiled in a bronze vessel, it must be scoured and rinsed with water. 29 Any male among the priests may eat it; it is especially holy. 30 But no sin offering may be eaten if its blood has been brought into the tent of meeting to make atonement in the holy place; it must be burned up.

The Restitution Offering

7 "Now this is the law of the ·restitution offering;[t] it is especially holy. 2 The restitution offering must be slaughtered at the place where the ·burnt offering[u] is slaughtered, and the priest is to sprinkle its blood on all sides of the altar. 3 The offerer must present all the fat from it: the fat tail,[v] the fat surrounding the entrails,[H] 4 and the two kidneys with the fat on them at the loins; he will also remove the fatty lobe of the liver[w] with the kidneys. 5 The priest will burn them on the altar as a

[A]**6:8** Lv 6:1 in Hb [B]**6:10** Lit *undergarments on his flesh* [C]**6:18** Or *statute* [D]**6:20** Lit *a tenth of an ephah* [E]**6:20** Daily [F]**6:21** Hb obscure [G]**6:27** Lit *wash what it spattered on* [H]**7:3** LXX, Sam add *and all the fat that is on the entrails;* Lv 3:3,9,14; 4:8

fire offering[a] to the LORD; it is a restitution offering. 6 Any male among the priests may eat it.[b] It is to be eaten in a holy place;[c] it is especially holy.[d]

7 "The restitution offering is like the ·sin offering;[e] the law is the same for both. It belongs to the priest[f] who makes ·atonement[g] with it. 8 As for the priest who presents someone's burnt offering, the hide of the burnt offering he has presented belongs to him; it is the priest's. 9 Any ·grain offering[h] that is baked in an oven or prepared in a pan or on a griddle belongs to the priest who presents it; it is his. 10 But any grain offering, whether dry or mixed with oil, belongs equally[A] to all of Aaron's sons.

The Fellowship Sacrifice

11 "Now this is the law of the ·fellowship sacrifice[i] that someone may present to the LORD: 12 If he presents it for thanksgiving, in addition to the thanksgiving sacrifice,[B,j] he is to present unleavened cakes[k] mixed with olive oil, unleavened wafers[l] coated with oil, and well-kneaded cakes of fine flour mixed with oil. 13 He is to present as his offering cakes of leavened bread[C] with his thanksgiving sacrifice of fellowship. 14 From the cakes he must present one portion of each offering as a contribution[m] to the LORD. It will belong to the priest who sprinkles the blood of the fellowship offering; it is his. 15 The meat of his thanksgiving sacrifice of fellowship must be eaten on the day he offers it;[n] he may not leave any of it until morning.[o]

16 "If the sacrifice he offers is a vow[D,p] or a freewill offering,[E,q] it is to be eaten on the day he presents his sacrifice, and what is left over may be eaten on the next day. 17 But what remains of the sacrificial meat by the third day must be burned up.[r] 18 If any of the meat of his fellowship sacrifice is eaten on the third day, it will not be accepted.[s] It will not be credited to the one who presents it; it is repulsive.[t] The person who eats any of it will be responsible for his sin.[F]

19 "Meat that touches anything ·unclean must not be eaten; it is to be burned up. Everyone who is ·clean may eat any other meat. 20 But the one who eats meat from the LORD's fellowship sacrifice while he is unclean,[G] that person must be cut off from his people.[u] 21 If someone touches anything unclean, whether human uncleanness, an unclean animal, or any unclean, detestable[H,v] creature, and eats meat from the LORD's fellowship sacrifice, that person must be cut off from his people."

Fat and Blood Prohibited

22 The LORD spoke to Moses: 23 "Tell the Israelites: You are not to eat any fat[w] of an ox, a sheep, or a goat. 24 The fat of an animal that dies naturally or is mauled by wild beasts[I,x] may be used for any purpose, but you must not eat it.[y] 25 If anyone eats animal fat from a fire offering presented to the LORD, the person who eats it must be cut off from his people. 26 Wherever you live, you must not eat the blood[z] of any bird or animal. 27 Whoever eats any blood, that person must be cut off from his people."

The Portion for the Priests

28 The LORD spoke to Moses: 29 "Tell the Israelites: The one who presents a fellowship sacrifice to the LORD must bring an offering to the LORD from his sacrifice. 30 His own hands will bring the fire offerings to the LORD. He will bring the fat together with the breast. The breast is to be waved as a presentation offering[a] before the LORD. 31 The priest is to burn the fat on the altar, but the breast belongs to Aaron and his sons. 32 You are to give the right thigh[b] to the priest as a contribution from your fellowship sacrifices. 33 The son of Aaron who presents the blood of the fellowship offering and the fat will have the right thigh as a portion. 34 I have taken from the Israelites the breast of the presentation offering and the thigh of the contribution from their fellowship sacrifices, and have assigned

[a] **7:5** Dt 18:1 [b] **7:6** 1Co 9:13 [c] Lv 16:24 [d] Lv 14:13 [e] **7:7** Ex 29:14 [f] Lv 14:13 [g] Ex 30:15 [h] **7:9** Ex 40:29 [i] **7:11** Lv 3:1,3,6,9 [j] **7:12** Lv 22:29 [k] Ex 12:8 [l] Lv 2:4 [m] **7:14** Ex 36:3 [n] **7:15** Lv 22:30 [o] Ex 12:10; 34:25; Lv 19:5-8; Dt 16:4 [p] **7:16** Lv 27:8 [q] Ex 35:29 [r] **7:17** Lv 19:6 [s] **7:18** Lv 1:4 [t] Lv 19:7; Is 65:4; Ezk 4:14 [u] **7:20** Gn 17:14; Lv 7:27; 19:8; Nm 9:13 [v] **7:21** Lv 11:10-13,20,23,41-42; Is 66:17; Ezk 8:10 [w] **7:23** Lv 3:16-17 [x] **7:24** Lv 17:15; 22:8 [y] Ex 22:31; Lv 3:17; 17:15; 22:8; Dt 14:21; Ezk 4:14; 44:31 [z] **7:26** Gn 9:3-4; Lv 17:10-12; Dt 12:16,23 [a] **7:30** Ex 29:24 [b] **7:32** Ex 29:22; Lv 8:25-26; 9:21; Nm 18:18

[A] **7:10** Lit *oil, will be a man like his brother* [B] **7:12** The thanksgiving sacrifice is the first of three kinds of fellowship sacrifices. It was given to express gratitude to God (Jr 33:11) in circumstances such as answered prayer (Ps 50:14-15) or safe travel (Ps 107:22-25). [C] **7:13** Although yeast was prohibited from being burned on the altar (Lv 2:11), leavened bread could still be an offering (Lv 23:17-20) to be eaten by the priests and their families. [D] **7:16** The vow offering, the second category of fellowship sacrifice, was brought as an expression of gratitude to fulfill a vow; Gn 28:20; 2Sm 15:7-8; Pr 7:14. [E] **7:16** The freewill offering, the third category of fellowship sacrifice, was a voluntary expression of gratitude toward God for any reason; Dt 16:10; Ps 54:6. [F] **7:18** Or *will bear his guilt* [G] **7:20** Lit *while his uncleanness is upon him* [H] **7:21** Some Hb mss, Sam, Syr, Tg read *swarming* [I] **7:24** Lit *fat of a carcass or the fat of a mauled beast*

them to Aaron the priest and his sons as a permanent portion[A,a] from the Israelites."

35 This is the portion from the fire offerings to the LORD for Aaron and his sons[b] since the day they were presented to serve the LORD as priests. 36 The LORD commanded this to be given to them by the Israelites on the day He anointed them.[c] It is a permanent portion[A] throughout their generations.

37 This is the law for the burnt offering, the grain offering, the sin offering, the restitution offering, the ordination offering,[d] and the fellowship sacrifice, 38 which the LORD commanded Moses on Mount Sinai[e] on the day He[B] commanded the Israelites to present their offerings to the LORD in the Wilderness of Sinai.[f]

Ordination of Aaron and His Sons

8 The LORD spoke to Moses: 2 "Take Aaron, his sons with him, the garments, the anointing oil,[g] the bull of the ·sin[C] offering, the two rams, and the basket[h] of unleavened bread, 3 and assemble the whole community[i] at the entrance to the tent of meeting." 4 So Moses did as the LORD commanded him, and the community assembled at the entrance to the tent of meeting. 5 Moses said to them, "This is what the LORD has commanded to be done."

6 Then Moses presented Aaron and his sons and washed them with water. 7 He put the tunic on Aaron, wrapped the sash around him, clothed him with the robe, and put the ·ephod[j] on him. He put the woven band of the ephod around him and fastened it to him. 8 Then he put the breastpiece on him and placed the ·Urim and Thummim[k] into the breastpiece. 9 He also put the turban[l] on his head and placed the gold medallion, the holy diadem, on the front of the turban, as the LORD had commanded Moses.[m]

10 Then Moses took the anointing oil and anointed the tabernacle and everything in it to consecrate[n] them. 11 He sprinkled some of the oil on the altar seven times, anointing the altar with all its utensils, and the basin with its stand, to consecrate them.[o] 12 He poured some of the anointing oil on Aaron's head and anointed and consecrated him.[p] 13 Then Moses presented Aaron's sons, clothed them with tunics, wrapped sashes around them, and fastened headbands on them, as the LORD had commanded Moses.

14 Then he brought the bull near for the sin offering, and Aaron and his sons laid their hands on the head of the bull for the sin offering. 15 Then Moses slaughtered it,[D] took the blood, and applied it with his finger to the horns of the altar on all sides, purifying[q] the altar. He poured out the blood at the base of the altar and consecrated it so that ·atonement can be made on it.[E,r] 16 Moses took all the fat that was on the entrails, the fatty lobe of the liver, and the two kidneys[s] with their fat, and he burned them on the altar.[t] 17 He burned up the bull with its hide, flesh, and dung outside the camp,[u] as the LORD had commanded Moses.

18 Then he presented the ram for the ·burnt offering, and Aaron and his sons laid their hands on the head of the ram. 19 Moses slaughtered it and[F] sprinkled the blood on all sides of the altar. 20 Moses cut the ram into pieces and burned the head, the pieces, and the suet,[v] 21 but he washed the entrails and shanks with water. He then burned the entire ram on the altar. It was a burnt offering for a pleasing aroma, a fire offering to the LORD as He had commanded Moses.

22 Next he presented the second ram, the ram of ordination,[w] and Aaron and his sons laid their hands on the head of the ram. 23 Moses slaughtered it,[G] took some of its blood, and put it on Aaron's right earlobe, on the thumb of his right hand, and on the big toe of his right foot.[x] 24 Moses also presented Aaron's sons and put some of the blood on their right earlobes, on the thumbs of their right hands, and on the big toes of their right feet. Then Moses sprinkled the blood on all sides of the altar. 25 He took the fat — the fat tail,[y] all the fat that was on the entrails, the fatty lobe of the liver, and the two kidneys with their fat — as well as the right thigh. 26 From the basket of unleavened bread that was before the LORD he took one cake of unleavened bread, one cake of bread made with oil, and

[a] **7:34** Ex 29:28; 30:21; Lv 6:11,15; 10:15; 24:9; Nm 18:8,11,19; Jr 5:22
[b] **7:35** Mt 10:10; 1Co 9:13-14; 1Tm 5:17-18
[c] **7:36** Ex 40:13-15; Lv 8:12,30
[d] **7:37** Lv 8:22
[e] **7:38** Ex 34:2
[f] Ex 31:18; 34:32; Lv 26:46; Neh 9:13
[g] **8:2** Ex 29:7
[h] Gn 40:16
[i] **8:3** Ex 12:47
[j] **8:7** Ex 28:4
[k] **8:8** Ex 28:30; Nm 27:21; Dt 33:8; 1Sm 28:6; Ezr 2:63; Neh 7:65
[l] **8:9** Lv 16:4
[m] **8:1-9** Ex 28:1-43; 29:1-8; 39:1-31
[n] **8:10** Ex 19:10,14,23; 20:11
[o] **8:10-11** Ex 30:18-28; 38:8; 40:7-11
[p] **8:12** Ex 29:7; 30:30; Lv 21:10-12
[q] **8:15** Ex 29:36; Lv 14:49,52; Nm 19:19; Ps 51:7; Ezk 43:22-23; 45:18
[r] **8:14-15** Ex 29:10-12,36-37; Lv 4:7
[s] **8:16** Lv 7:4
[t] Ex 29:13; Lv 4:7-10
[u] **8:17** Ex 29:14; 33:7; Lv 4:12,21; 6:4; 9:11; 10:4-5; 13:46; 14:3; 16:27; 17:3; 24:14,23
[v] **8:20** Lv 1:8
[w] **8:22** Ex 29:22,26-34; Lv 7:37; 8:28-33
[x] **8:23** Ex 29:20; Lv 14:14,17,25,28
[y] **8:25** Lv 3:9

[A] **7:34,36** Or *statute* [B] **7:38** Or *he* [C] **8:2** Or *purification* [D] **8:14-15** Or *offering, and he slaughtered it.* [15] *Then Moses* [E] **8:15** Or *it by making ·atonement for it* [F] **8:18-19** Or *ram,* [19] *and he slaughtered it. Moses* [G] **8:22-23** Or *ram,* [23] *and he slaughtered it. Moses* one wafer, and placed them on the fat portions and the right thigh.[a] 27 He put all these in the hands of Aaron and his sons and waved them before the LORD as a presentation offering. 28 Then Moses took them from their hands and burned them on the altar with the burnt offering. This was an ordination offering for a pleasing aroma, a fire offering to the LORD. 29 He also took the breast and waved it before the LORD as a presentation offering; it was Moses' portion of the ordination ram as the LORD had commanded him.

30 Then Moses took some of the anointing oil and some of the blood that was on the altar and sprinkled them on Aaron and his garments, as well as on his sons and their garments. In this way he consecrated Aaron and his garments, as well as his sons and their garments.[b]

31 Moses said to Aaron and his sons, "Boil the meat at the entrance to the tent of meeting and eat it there with the bread that is in the basket for the ordination offering as I commanded:[A] Aaron and his sons are to eat it.[c] 32 You must burn up what remains of the meat and bread.[d] 33 You must not go outside the entrance to the tent of meeting for seven days, until the time your days of ordination are completed, because it will take seven days to ordain you.[B] 34 The LORD commanded what has been done today in order to make atonement for you.[e] 35 You must remain at the entrance to the tent of meeting day and night for seven days and keep the LORD's charge[f] so that you will not die,[g] for this is what I was commanded." 36 So Aaron and his sons did everything the LORD had commanded through Moses.

The Priestly Ministry Inaugurated

9 On the eighth day Moses summoned Aaron, his sons, and the elders of Israel.[h] 2 He said to Aaron, "Take a young bull for a *sin[C] offering and a ram for a *burnt offering, both without blemish,[i] and present them before the LORD. 3 And tell the Israelites:[D] Take a male goat for a sin offering; a calf and a lamb, male yearlings without blemish, for a burnt offering; 4 an ox and a ram for a *fellowship offering to sacrifice before the LORD; and a *grain offering mixed with oil. For today the LORD is going to appear[j] to you."

5 They brought what Moses had commanded to the front of the tent of meeting, and the whole community came forward and stood before the LORD. 6 Moses said, "This is what the LORD commanded you to do, that the glory of the LORD[k] may appear to you." 7 Then Moses said to Aaron, "Approach the altar and sacrifice your sin offering and your burnt offering; make *atonement for yourself and the people.[E,l] Sacrifice the people's offering and make atonement for them, as the LORD commanded."

8 So Aaron approached the altar and slaughtered the calf as a sin offering for himself. 9 Aaron's sons brought the blood to him, and he dipped his finger in the blood and applied it to the horns of the altar. He poured out the blood at the base of the altar. 10 He burned the fat, the kidneys, and the fatty lobe of the liver from the sin offering on the altar, as the LORD had commanded Moses. 11 He burned up the flesh and the hide[m] outside the camp.[n]

12 Then he slaughtered the burnt offering. Aaron's sons brought him the blood, and he sprinkled it on all sides of the altar. 13 They brought him the burnt offering piece by piece, along with the head, and he burned them on the altar. 14 He washed the entrails and the shanks and burned them with the burnt offering on the altar.

15 Aaron presented the people's offering. He took the male goat for the people's sin offering, slaughtered it, and made a sin offering with it as he did before. 16 He presented the burnt offering and sacrificed it according to the regulation.[o] 17 Next he presented the grain offering, took a handful of it, and burned it on the altar in addition to the morning burnt offering.[p]

18 Finally, he slaughtered the ox and the ram as the people's fellowship sacrifice. Aaron's sons brought him the blood, and he sprinkled it on all sides of the altar. 19 They also brought the fat portions from the ox and the ram — the fat tail, the fat surrounding the

[a]**8:26** Ex 29:3,23; Lv 7:32; Nm 6:15-19
[b]**8:30** Ex 29:21; Is 6:6-7; Heb 10:22
[c]**8:31** Lv 6:16,18; 10:12; 1Co 9:13-14
[d]**8:32** Ex 29:34
[e]**8:33-34** Ex 29:35-37; Heb 7:28
[f]**8:35** Gn 26:5
[g]Lv 10:1-2
[h]**9:1** Ex 18:12
[i]**9:2** Ex 29:1
[j]**9:4** Gn 35:9
[k]**9:6** Ex 40:34; Lk 9:32
[l]**9:7** Heb 5:1-3; 7:26-27
[m]**9:11** Lv 7:8
[n]Ex 29:14; Lv 4:8-10,12,21; 8:17; 16:27
[o]**9:16** Lv 18:26
[p]**9:17** Ex 29:38-42; Lv 2:2

[A]**8:31** LXX, Syr, Tg read *was commanded*; Ex 29:31-32 [B]**8:33** Lit *because he will fill your hands for seven days* [C]**9:2** Or *purification* [D]**9:3** Sam, LXX read *elders of Israel* [E]**9:7** LXX reads *and your household*

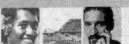

entrails, the kidneys, and the fatty lobe of the liver — 20 and placed these on the breasts. Aaron burned the fat portions on the altar, 21 but he waved the breasts[a] and the right thigh as a presentation offering[b] before the LORD, as Moses had commanded.[A]

22 Aaron lifted up his hands toward the people and blessed[c] them. He came down after sacrificing the sin offering, the burnt offering, and the fellowship offering. 23 Moses and Aaron then entered the tent of meeting. When they came out, they blessed the people, and the glory of the LORD appeared to all the people. 24 Fire came from the LORD and consumed[d] the burnt offering and the fat portions on the altar. And when all the people saw it, they shouted[e] and fell facedown on the ground.[f]

Nadab and Abihu

10 Aaron's sons Nadab[g] and Abihu[h] each took his own firepan,[i] put fire in it, placed incense on it,[j] and presented unauthorized[k] fire before the LORD, which He had not commanded them to do. 2 Then fire came from the LORD[l] and burned them to death before the LORD.[m] 3 So Moses said to Aaron, "This is what the LORD meant when He said:

I will show My holiness[B,n]
to those who are near Me,[o]
and I will reveal My glory[C,p]
before all the people."

But Aaron remained silent.

4 Moses summoned Mishael and Elzaphan,[q] sons of Aaron's uncle Uzziel,[r] and said to them, "Come here and carry your relatives away from the front of the sanctuary to a place outside the camp."[s] 5 So they came forward and carried them in their tunics outside the camp, as Moses had said.

6 Then Moses said to Aaron and his sons Eleazar and Ithamar,[t] "Do not let your hair hang loose[u] and do not tear your garments,[v] or else you will die, and the LORD will become angry[w] with the whole community. However, your brothers, the whole house of Israel, may mourn[x] over that tragedy when the LORD sent the fire. 7 You must not go outside the entrance to the tent of meeting or you will die, for the LORD's anointing oil[y] is on you." So they did as Moses said.

Regulations for Priests

8 The LORD spoke to Aaron: 9 "You and your sons are not to drink wine[z] or beer[aa] when you enter the tent of meeting, or else you will die; this is a permanent statute[ab] throughout your generations. 10 You must distinguish[ac] between the holy and the common,[ad] and the •clean and the •unclean,[ae] 11 and teach the Israelites all the statutes[af] that the LORD has given to them through Moses."

12 Moses spoke to Aaron and his remaining sons, Eleazar and Ithamar: "Take the •grain offering that is left over from the fire offerings[ag] to the LORD, and eat it prepared without yeast beside the altar, because it is especially holy. 13 You must eat it in a holy place because it is your portion[D] and your sons' from the fire offerings to the LORD, for this is what I was commanded. 14 But you and your sons and your daughters may eat the breast of the presentation offering and the thigh of the contribution in any ceremonially clean place, because these portions have been assigned to you and your children from the Israelites' •fellowship sacrifices. 15 They are to bring the thigh of the contribution and the breast of the presentation offering, together with the offerings of fat portions made by fire, to wave as a presentation offering before the LORD. It will belong permanently[ah] to you and your children, as the LORD commanded."

16 Later, Moses inquired about the male goat of the •sin offering, but it had already been burned up. He was angry with Eleazar and Ithamar, Aaron's surviving sons, and asked, 17 "Why didn't you eat the sin offering in the sanctuary area?[ai] For it is especially holy, and He has assigned it to you to take away the •guilt[aj] of the community[ak] and make •atonement for them before the LORD. 18 Since its blood was not brought inside the sanctuary, you should have eaten it in the sanctuary area, as I commanded."[al]

19 But Aaron replied to Moses, "See, today they presented their sin offering and their

[a] **9:21** Ex 29:26-27; Lv 7:30-34; 8:26; 10:14-15; Nm 6:20; 18:18 [b] Ex 29:24 [c] **9:22** Gn 14:19; Nm 6:24-26 [d] **9:24** 1Kg 18:38-39; 2Ch 7:1 [e] Ps 35:27; Is 12:6; 24:14 [f] Nm 16:4 [g] **10:1** Ex 6:23; 28:1; Nm 3:2,4; 26:60-61; 1Ch 6:3 [h] Ex 24:1 [i] Ex 27:3; 38:3; 1Kg 7:50; 2Kg 25:15; Jr 52:19 [j] Ex 30:7-9; Lv 16:12; Nm 16:17,46 [k] Ex 30:9; Nm 3:4; 26:61; Jr 2:25; 3:13; Hs 5:7 [l] **10:2** Gn 4:14 [m] Nm 26:61; Dt 4:24; 2Sm 6:7 [n] **10:3** Nm 20:13; Ezk 20:41; 28:22,25; 36:23; 38:16; 39:27 [o] Dt 30:14; Heb 7:19 [p] Ex 14:4,17-18; Is 26:15; Ezk 28:22; 39:13; Hg 1:8 [q] **10:4** Ex 6:22 [r] Nm 3:19 [s] Lv 8:17; Heb 13:11-13 [t] **10:6** Ex 6:23 [u] Lv 13:45; 21:10; Nm 5:18; Jdg 5:2 [v] Lv 21:10; Mk 14:63 [w] Ex 16:20 [x] Gn 37:34 [y] **10:7** Ex 29:7; Lv 21:12 [z] **10:9** Gn 9:21 [aa] Nm 6:3-4; Dt 7:13; 11:14; Jdg 13:4; Pr 20:1; Ezk 44:21; Dn 1:3-16; 10:3; Am 2:12; Mk 4:23-25; Lk 1:15; Jn 2:1-11; Rm 14:21; 1Tm 3:3,8 [ab] Ex 28:43; Lv 11:46 [ac] **10:10** Lv 20:25 [ad] Ezk 22:26; 42:20; 44:23; 48:15; Ac 10:28 [ae] Lv 11:4; Nm 19:13 [af] **10:11** Gn 47:26 [ag] **10:12** Dt 18:1 [ah] **10:15** Ex 29:28; 30:21; Lv 6:11,15; 24:9; Nm 18:8,11,19; Jr 5:22 [ai] **10:17** Lv 6:26,29 [aj] Nm 5:31 [ak] Ex 28:38; Hs 14:2; Jn 1:29 [al] **10:18** Lv 6:26,29-30

[A] **9:21** Some Hb mss, LXX, Sam read *as the LORD commanded Moses* [B] **10:3** Or *will be treated as holy* [C] **10:3** Or *will be glorified* [D] **10:13** Or *statute* *burnt offering before the LORD. Since these things have happened to me, if I had eaten the sin offering today, would it have been acceptable in the LORD's sight?" 20 When Moses heard this, it was acceptable to him.[A]

Clean and Unclean Land Animals

11 The LORD spoke to Moses and Aaron: 2 "Tell the Israelites: You may eat[a] all these kinds of land animals.[b] 3 You may eat any animal with divided hooves and that chews the cud. 4 But among the ones that chew the cud or have divided hooves you are not to eat these:

the camel,[c] though it chews the cud,
does not have divided hooves — it is
*unclean for you;
5 the hyrax,[B,d] though it chews the cud,
does not have hooves — it is unclean
for you;
6 the hare, though it chews the cud,
does not have hooves — it is unclean
for you;
7 the pig, though it has divided hooves,
does not chew the cud — it is unclean
for you.

8 Do not eat any of their meat or touch their carcasses — they are unclean for you.[e]

Clean and Unclean Aquatic Animals

9 "This is what you may eat from all that is in the water: You may eat everything in the water that has fins and scales, whether in the seas or streams. 10 But these are to be detestable to you: everything in the seas or streams that does not have fins and scales among all the swarming things and other living creatures[f] in the water. 11 They are to remain detestable to you; you must not eat any of their meat, and you must detest their carcasses. 12 Everything in the water that does not have fins and scales will be detestable to you.

Unclean Birds

13 "You are to detest these birds. They must not be eaten because they are detestable:

the eagle,[C,g] the bearded[D] vulture,
the black vulture,[E] 14 the kite,[F]
any kind of falcon,[G,h]
15 every kind of raven, 16 the ostrich,[H]
the short-eared owl,[I] the gull,[J]
any kind of hawk,[i]
17 the little[K] owl, the cormorant,[L]
the long-eared owl,[M,j]
18 the white[N] owl, the desert owl,[O,k]
the osprey,[P] 19 the stork,[Q]
any kind of heron,[R]
the hoopoe, and the bat.

Clean and Unclean Flying Insects

20 "All winged insects that walk on all fours are to be detestable to you. 21 But you may eat these kinds of all the winged insects that walk on all fours: those that have jointed legs above their feet for hopping on the ground. 22 You may eat these:

any kind of locust,[l] katydid, cricket,
and grasshopper.

23 All other winged insects that have four feet are to be detestable to you.

Purification after Touching Dead Animals

24 "These will make you unclean. Whoever touches their carcasses will be unclean[m] until evening, 25 and whoever carries any of their carcasses must wash his clothes and will be unclean until evening.[n] 26 All animals that have hooves but do not have a divided hoof and do not chew the cud are unclean for you. Whoever touches them becomes unclean. 27 All the four-footed animals[o] that walk on their paws are unclean for you. Whoever touches their carcasses will be unclean until evening, 28 and anyone who carries their carcasses must wash his clothes and will be unclean until evening. They are unclean for you.

29 "These creatures that swarm[p] on the ground are unclean for you:

the weasel,[S] the mouse,[q]
any kind of large lizard,[T]
30 the gecko, the monitor lizard,[U]
the common lizard,[V] the skink,[W]
and the chameleon.[X]

[a] 11:2 Lv 11:1-23; Dt 14:3-21; Dn 1:3-16; Ac 10:9-16; 11:3; Rm 14:2; Gl 2:11-14
[b] Dt 14:4-21; Ac 10:9-16; Rm 14:14
[c] 11:4 Gn 24:64; 31:34; Dt 14:7; Jr 2:23; Mt 19:24; 23:24; Mk 10:25; Lk 18:25
[d] 11:5 Dt 14:7; Ps 104:18; Pr 30:26
[e] 11:8 Lv 7:21; 11:24-27; Is 52:11; 2Co 6:17
[f] 11:10 Gn 1:20; 2:19; Lv 11:46
[g] 11:13 Dt 14:12; 28:49; 32:11; Pr 23:5; Is 40:31
[h] 11:14 Dt 14:13; Jb 28:7
[i] 11:16 Dt 14:15; Jb 39:26
[j] 11:17 Dt 14:16
[k] 11:18 Dt 14:17; Ps 102:6; Is 34:11; Zph 2:14
[l] 11:22 Dt 28:38
[m] 11:24 Ezk 22:3-4; 23:17; 44:25; Mc 2:10; Hg 2:13
[n] 11:25 Lv 16:28; 17:15-16; 22:6; Nm 19:7-10
[o] 11:27 Rv 18:2
[p] 11:29 Ex 8:3
[q] 1Sm 6:4-5,11,18; Is 66:17

[A] 10:20 Lit *acceptable in his sight* [B] 11:5 A rabbit-like animal [C] 11:13 Or *griffon-vulture* [D] 11:13 Or *black* [E] 11:13 Or *the osprey, or the bearded vulture* [F] 11:14 Or *hawk* [G] 11:14 Or *buzzards, or hawks* [H] 11:16 Or *eagle owl* [I] 11:16 Or *the night hawk, or the screech owl* [J] 11:16 Or *long-eared owl* [K] 11:17 Or *tawny* [L] 11:17 Or *fisher owl, or pelican* [M] 11:17 Or *the ibis* [N] 11:18 Or *little* [O] 11:18 Or *the pelican, or the horned owl* [P] 11:18 Or *Egyptian vulture* [Q] 11:19 Or *heron* [R] 11:19 Or *cormorant, or hawk* [S] 11:29 Or *mole rat, or rat* [T] 11:29 Or *of thorn-tailed or dabb lizard, or of crocodile* [U] 11:30 Or *the spotted lizard, or the chameleon* [V] 11:30 Or *the gecko, or the newt, or the salamander* [W] 11:30 Or *sand lizard, or newt, or snail* [X] 11:30 Or *salamander, or mole*

31These are unclean for you among all the
swarming creatures. Whoever touches them
when they are dead will be unclean until evening. 32When any one of them dies and falls
on anything it becomes unclean — any item
of wood, clothing, leather, •sackcloth,[a] or any
implement used for work. It is to be rinsed
with water and will remain unclean until evening; then it will be •clean. 33If any of them
falls into any clay pot, everything in it will become unclean; you must break it. 34Any edible
food[b] coming into contact with that unclean
water will become unclean, and any drinkable liquid in any container will become unclean. 35Anything one of their carcasses falls
on will become unclean. If it is an oven or
stove, it must be smashed; it is unclean and
will remain unclean for you. 36A spring or cistern containing water will remain clean, but
someone who touches a carcass in it will become unclean. 37If one of their carcasses falls
on any seed that is to be sown, it is clean; 38but
if water has been put on the seed and one of
their carcasses falls on it, it is unclean for you.
39"If one of the animals that you use for
food dies,[A] anyone who touches its carcass
will be unclean until evening. 40Anyone who
eats some of its carcass must wash his clothes
and will be unclean until evening. Anyone
who carries its carcass must wash his clothes
and will be unclean until evening.

Unclean Swarming Creatures

41"All the creatures that swarm on the earth
are detestable; they must not be eaten. 42Do
not eat any of the creatures that swarm on
the earth, anything that moves on its belly or
walks on all fours or on many feet,[B] for they
are detestable. 43Do not become contaminated by any creature that swarms; do not become unclean or defiled by them. 44For I am
•Yahweh your God,[c] so you must consecrate
yourselves[d] and be holy because I am holy.[e]
You must not defile yourselves by any swarming creature that crawls on the ground. 45For
I am Yahweh, who brought you up from the
land of Egypt to be your God,[f] so you must be
holy because I am holy.[g]
46"This is the law concerning animals,
birds, all living creatures that move in the
water, and all creatures that swarm on the
ground, 47in order to distinguish between
the unclean and the clean, between the animals[h] that may be eaten and those that may
not be eaten."

Purification after Childbirth

12 The LORD spoke to Moses: 2"Tell the
Israelites: When a woman becomes
pregnant and gives birth to a male child,[i] she
will be •unclean seven days, as she is during
the days of her menstrual impurity.[j] 3The
flesh of his foreskin[k] must be circumcised[l] on
the eighth day.[m] 4She will continue in purification[n] from her bleeding[o] for 33 days. She
must not touch any holy thing or go into the
sanctuary until completing her days of purification. 5But if she gives birth to a female
child, she will be unclean for two weeks as she
is during her menstrual impurity. She will
continue in purification from her bleeding
for 66 days.
6"When her days of purification are complete, whether for a son or daughter, she is to
bring to the priest at the entrance to the tent
of meeting a year-old male lamb for a •burnt
offering, and a young pigeon or a turtledove
for a •sin[C] offering. 7He will present them before the LORD and make •atonement on her
behalf; she will be •clean from her discharge
of blood. This is the law for a woman giving
birth, whether to a male or female. 8But if she
doesn't have sufficient means[D,p] for a sheep,
she may take two turtledoves or two young
pigeons,[q] one for a burnt offering and the
other for a sin[C] offering. Then the priest will
make atonement on her behalf, and she will
be clean."

Skin Diseases

13 The LORD spoke to Moses and Aaron:
2"When a person has a swelling,[E] scab,[F]
or spot on the skin of his body, and it becomes a disease on the skin[r] of his body, he
is to be brought to Aaron the priest or to one
of his sons, the priests. 3The priest will examine the infection[s] on the skin of his body. If
the hair in the infection has turned white

[a] **11:32** Gn 37:34
[b] **11:34** Lv 26:5
[c] **11:44** Nm 15:41
[d] Ex 19:22; Lv 20:7; Nm 11:18; Ezk 38:23
[e] Lv 19:2; 20:7,26; 1Pt 1:16
[f] **11:45** Ex 20:2; 6:7; Lv 25:38,42; 26:13,45
[g] Lv 21:8
[h] **11:47** Lv 26:6
[i] **12:2** Lv 10:14
[j] Lv 15:19
[k] **12:3** Ex 4:25
[l] Gn 34:14
[m] Gn 17:12-13; 21:4; Lk 2:21; Gl 3:5; 5:6; 6:15
[n] **12:4** Lv 14:2
[o] Lk 8:43
[p] **12:8** Lv 14:21
[q] Lk 2:24
[r] **13:2** Lv 14:3, 7,32,44,54-57; Dt 24:8; 2Kg 5:3,6-7,27; 2Ch 26:19
[s] **13:3** Ex 11:1; Dt 17:8; 21:5; Is 53:8

[A] **11:39** Dies of itself or by predators; this does not apply to animals slaughtered for food. [B] **11:42** Lit *fours, to anything multiplying pairs of feet* [C] **12:6,8** Or *purification* [D] **12:8** Lit *if her hand cannot obtain what is sufficient* [E] **13:2** Or *discoloration* [F] **13:2** Or *rash*, or *eruption*

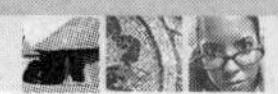

and the infection appears to be deeper than
the skin of his body, it is a skin disease. After
the priest examines him, he must pronounce
him ˙unclean. 4But if the spot on the skin
of his body is white and does not appear to
be deeper than the skin, and the hair in it
has not turned white, the priest must quarantine the infected person for seven days.[a]
5The priest will then reexamine him on the
seventh day. If he sees that the infection remains unchanged and has not spread on the
skin, the priest must quarantine him for another seven days. 6The priest will examine
him again on the seventh day. If the infection
has faded and has not spread on the skin, the
priest is to pronounce him ˙clean;[b] it is a scab.
The person is to wash his clothes and will become clean. 7But if the scab spreads further
on his skin after he has presented himself to
the priest for his cleansing,[c] he must present
himself again to the priest. 8The priest will
examine him, and if the scab has spread on
the skin, then the priest must pronounce him
unclean; he has a skin disease.

9"When a skin disease develops on a person, he is to be brought to the priest. 10The
priest will examine him. If there is a white
swelling on the skin that has turned the hair
white, and there is a patch of raw flesh in the
swelling, 11it is a chronic disease on the skin of
his body, and the priest must pronounce him
unclean.[d] He need not quarantine him, for he
is unclean. 12But if the skin disease breaks out
all over the skin so that it covers all the skin of
the infected person from his head to his feet
so far as the priest can see, 13the priest will
look, and if the skin disease has covered his
entire body, he is to pronounce the infected
person clean.[e] Since he has turned totally
white, he is clean. 14But whenever raw flesh
appears on him, he will be unclean. 15When
the priest examines the raw flesh, he must
pronounce him unclean. Raw flesh is unclean; it is a skin disease. 16But if the raw flesh
changes[A] and[B] turns white, he must go to the
priest. 17The priest will examine him, and if
the infection has turned white, the priest
must pronounce the infected person clean;
he is clean.

18"When a boil appears on the skin[f] of one's
body[g] and it heals, 19and a white swelling or
a reddish-white spot develops where the boil
was, the person must present himself to the
priest. 20The priest will make an examination,
and if the spot seems to be beneath the skin
and the hair in it has turned white, the priest
must pronounce him unclean; it is a skin
disease that has broken out in the boil. 21But
when the priest examines it, if there is no
white hair in it, and it is not beneath the skin
but is faded, the priest must quarantine him
seven days. 22If it spreads further on the skin,
the priest must pronounce him unclean; it is
an infection. 23But if the spot remains where
it is and does not spread, it is only the scar
from the boil. The priest is to pronounce him
clean.

24"When there is a burn on the skin of one's
body produced by fire, and the patch made
raw by the burn becomes reddish-white or
white, 25the priest is to examine it. If the hair
in the spot has turned white and the spot appears to be deeper than the skin, it is a skin
disease that has broken out in the burn. The
priest must pronounce him unclean; it is a
skin disease. 26But when the priest examines
it, if there is no white hair in the spot and it
is not beneath the skin but is faded, the priest
must quarantine him seven days. 27The priest
will reexamine him on the seventh day. If
it has spread further on the skin, the priest
must pronounce him unclean; it is a skin disease. 28But if the spot has remained where
it was and has not spread on the skin but is
faded, it is the swelling from the burn. The
priest is to pronounce him clean, for it is only
the scar from the burn.

29"When a man or woman has an infection
on the head or chin, 30the priest must examine the infection. If it appears to be deeper
than the skin,[h] and the hair in it is yellow and
sparse, the priest must pronounce the person
unclean. It is a scaly outbreak,[C] a skin disease
of the head or chin. 31When the priest examines the scaly infection, if it does not appear
to be deeper than the skin, and there is no
black hair in it, the priest must quarantine
the person with the scaly infection for seven
days. 32The priest will reexamine the infection on the seventh day. If the scaly outbreak

[a] **13:4** Nm 12:14-15; 2Kg 15:5
[b] **13:6** Nm 8:6-7; Ps 51:2; Ezk 24:13
[c] **13:7** Lv 14:2
[d] **13:11** Lv 11:4
[e] **13:13** Lv 10:10
[f] **13:18** Lv 13:2
[g] Ex 9:9-11; Dt 28:27,35; Jb 2:7
[h] **13:30** Lv 13:2

[A] **13:16** Or *recedes* [B] **13:16** Or *flesh again* [C] **13:30** Or *is scall*; Hb obscure

has not spread and there is no yellow hair in
it and it does not appear to be deeper than
the skin, 33 the person must shave himself[a] but
not shave the scaly area. Then the priest must
quarantine the person who has the scaly outbreak for another seven days. 34 The priest will
examine the scaly outbreak on the seventh
day, and if it has not spread on the skin and
does not appear to be deeper than the skin,
the priest is to pronounce the person clean.
He is to wash his clothes, and he will be clean.
35 But if the scaly outbreak spreads further on
the skin after his cleansing, 36 the priest is to
examine the person. If the scaly outbreak has
spread on the skin, the priest does not need
to look for yellow hair; the person is unclean.
37 But if as far as he can see, the scaly outbreak
remains unchanged and black hair has grown
in it, then it has healed; he is clean. The priest
is to pronounce the person clean.
38 "When a man or a woman has white
spots on the skin of the body, 39 the priest is
to make an examination. If the spots on the
skin of the body are dull white, it is only a
rash[A] that has broken out on the skin; the
person is clean.
40 "If a man loses the hair of his head, he is
bald,[b] but he is clean. 41 Or if he loses the hair
at his hairline, he is bald on his forehead, but
he is clean. 42 But if there is a reddish-white
infection on the bald head or forehead, it is a
skin disease breaking out on his head or forehead.[c] 43 The priest is to examine him, and if
the swelling of the infection on his bald head
or forehead is reddish-white, like the appearance of a skin disease on his body, 44 the man
is afflicted with a skin disease;[d] he is unclean.
The priest must pronounce him unclean; the
infection is on his head.
45 "The person afflicted with an infectious
skin disease is to have his clothes torn[e] and
his hair hanging loose, and he must cover his
mouth[f] and cry out, 'Unclean, unclean!' 46 He
will remain unclean as long as he has the infection; he is unclean. He must live alone in a
place outside the camp.[g]

Contaminated Fabrics

47 "If a fabric is contaminated with mildew — in wool or linen fabric, 48 in the warp
or woof of linen or wool, or in leather or
anything made of leather — 49 and if the contamination is green or red in the fabric, the
leather, the warp, the woof, or any leather article, it is a mildew contamination and is to be
shown to the priest. 50 The priest is to examine
the contamination and quarantine the contaminated fabric for seven days. 51 The priest
is to reexamine the contamination on the
seventh day. If it has spread in the fabric, the
warp, the woof, or the leather, regardless of
how it is used, the contamination is harmful
mildew; it is unclean.[h] 52 He is to burn the fabric, the warp or woof in wool or linen, or any
leather article, which is contaminated. Since
it is harmful mildew it must be burned up.
53 "When the priest examines it, if the contamination has not spread in the fabric, the
warp or woof, or any leather article, 54 the
priest is to order whatever is contaminated
to be washed and quarantined for another
seven days. 55 After it has been washed, the
priest is to reexamine the contamination. If
the appearance of the contaminated article
has not changed, it is unclean. Even though
the contamination has not spread, you must
burn up the fabric. It is a fungus[A] on the front
or back of the fabric.
56 "If the priest examines it, and the contamination has faded after it has been washed, he
must cut the contaminated section out of the
fabric, the leather, or the warp or woof. 57 But
if it reappears in the fabric, the warp or woof,
or any leather article, it has broken out again.
You must burn up whatever is contaminated.
58 But if the contamination disappears from
the fabric, the warp or woof, or any leather
article, which have been washed, it is to be
washed again, and it will be clean.
59 "This is the law concerning a mildew contamination in wool or linen fabric, warp or
woof, or any leather article, in order to pronounce it clean or unclean."[i]

Cleansing of Skin Diseases

14 The LORD spoke to Moses: 2 "This is the
law[j] concerning the person afflicted
with a skin disease on the day of his cleansing.[k] He is to be brought to the priest,[l] 3 who
will go outside the camp[m] and examine him."[n]

[a] **13:33** Gn 41:14; Lv 14:8-9; 21:5; Nm 6:9,18-19; Dt 21:12; Jdg 16:17,19,22
[b] **13:40** 2Kg 2:23
[c] **13:42** 2Ch 26:19-20
[d] **13:44** Ex 4:6; Lv 14:2-3; 22:4; Nm 5:2; 12:10
[e] **13:45** Lv 10:6; 21:10
[f] Ezk 24:17,22; Mc 3:7
[g] **13:46** Nm 5:1-4; 8:17; 12:14-15
[h] **13:51** Lv 11:24; 15:10-12,21-27; Hg 2:12-13
[i] **13:59** Lv 10:10-11
[j] **14:2** Lv 11:46
[k] Lv 12:4-5; Nm 6:9; Ezk 44:26
[l] Lv 4:16
[m] **14:3** Lv 8:17
[n] Lv 13:2-3

[A] **13:39,55** Hb obscure

If the skin disease has disappeared from the afflicted person,[A] 4the priest will order that two live ·clean birds,[a] cedar wood,[b] scarlet[c] yarn, and hyssop[d] be brought for the one who is to be cleansed. 5Then the priest will order that one of the birds be slaughtered over fresh water in a clay pot. 6He is to take the live bird together with the cedar wood, scarlet yarn, and hyssop, and dip them all into the blood of the bird that was slaughtered over the fresh water. 7He will then sprinkle the blood seven times on the one who is to be cleansed from the skin disease. He is to pronounce him clean and release the live bird over the open countryside.[e] 8The one who is to be cleansed must wash his clothes, shave off all his hair, and bathe with water; he is clean. Afterward he may enter the camp, but he must remain outside his tent for seven days. 9He is to shave off all his hair again on the seventh day: his head, his beard, his eyebrows, and the rest of his hair. He is to wash his clothes and bathe himself with water; he is clean.

10"On the eighth day he must take two unblemished[f] male lambs, an unblemished year-old ewe lamb, a ·grain offering of three quarts[B] of fine flour mixed with olive oil, and one-third of a quart[C] of olive oil. 11The priest who performs the cleansing will place the person who is to be cleansed, together with these offerings, before the LORD at the entrance to the tent of meeting. 12The priest is to take one male lamb and present it as a ·restitution offering,[g] along with the one-third quart[C] of olive oil, and he must wave them as a presentation offering[h] before the LORD. 13He is to slaughter the male lamb at the place in the sanctuary area where the ·sin offering[i] and ·burnt offering[j] are slaughtered,[k] for like the sin offering, the restitution offering belongs to the priest;[l] it is especially holy.[m] 14The priest is to take some of the blood from the restitution offering and put it on the lobe of the right ear of the one to be cleansed, on the thumb of his right hand, and on the big toe of his right foot.[n] 15Then the priest will take some of the one-third quart[C] of olive oil and pour it into his left palm. 16The priest will dip his right finger into the oil in his left palm and sprinkle some of the oil with his finger seven times before the LORD. 17From the oil remaining in his palm the priest will put some on the lobe of the right ear of the one to be cleansed, on the thumb of his right hand, and on the big toe of his right foot, on top of the blood of the restitution offering.[o] 18What is left of the oil in the priest's palm he is to put on the head of the one to be cleansed. In this way the priest will make ·atonement for him before the LORD. 19The priest must sacrifice the sin offering and make atonement for the one to be cleansed from his uncleanness.[p] Afterward he will slaughter the burnt offering. 20The priest is to offer the burnt offering and the grain offering on the altar. The priest will make atonement for him, and he will be clean.[q]

21"But if he is poor[r] and cannot afford these,[D,s] he is to take one male lamb for a restitution offering to be waved in order to make atonement for him, along with two quarts[E] of fine flour mixed with olive oil for a grain offering, one-third of a quart[C] of olive oil, 22and two turtledoves or two young pigeons, whatever he can afford,[F] one to be a sin offering and the other a burnt offering. 23On the eighth day he is to bring these things for his cleansing to the priest at the entrance to the tent of meeting before the LORD. 24The priest will take the male lamb for the restitution offering and the one-third quart[C] of olive oil, and wave them as a presentation offering before the LORD. 25After he slaughters the male lamb for the restitution offering, the priest is to take some of the blood of the restitution offering and put it on the right earlobe of the one to be cleansed, on the thumb of his right hand, and on the big toe of his right foot. 26Then the priest will pour some of the oil into his left palm. 27With his right finger the priest will sprinkle some of the oil in his left palm seven times before the LORD. 28The priest will also put some of the oil in his palm on the right earlobe of the one to be cleansed, on the thumb of his right hand, and on the big toe of his right foot, on the same place as the blood of the restitution offering. 29What is left of the oil in the priest's palm he is to put on the head of the one to be cleansed to

[a] **14:4** Gn 40:17 [b] Jdg 9:15; 2Sm 5:11; 7:2,7; 1Kg 5:13; 6:9-10; Ps 29:5; Sg 1:17; 8:9; Am 2:9; Zch 11:1-2 [c] Ex 25:4; Nm 4:8; 19:6 [d] Ex 12:22 [e] **14:7** Lv 14:53; 16:21-22 [f] **14:10** Ex 29:1 [g] **14:12** Lv 5:6-19 [h] Ex 29:24 [i] **14:13** Ex 29:14 [j] Gn 22:2; Lv 3:5; Nm 6:11; Jos 8:31; 1Ch 16:1; Ps 20:3; Mc 6:6 [k] Lv 1:11; 6:25; 7:2 [l] Lv 7:7 [m] Lv 2:3; 6:10; 7:1,6; 10:12; 24:9; 27:28 [n] **14:14** Ex 29:20; Lv 8:23-24; 14:25,28 [o] **14:17** Lv 14:14 [p] **14:19** Lv 5:3 [q] **14:20** Mt 8:1-4; Mk 1:21-44; Lk 5:12-14 [r] **14:21** Am 5:11 [s] Lv 5:7-13; 12:8

[A] **14:3** Lit *the person afflicted with skin disease* [B] **14:10** Lit *three-tenths*; probably $^3/_{10}$ of an ephah [C] **14:10,12,15,21,24** Lit *one log* [D] **14:21** Lit *and his hand is not* [E] **14:21** Lit *him, and one-tenth*; probably $^1/_{10}$ of an ephah [F] **14:22** Lit *pigeons, for which his hand is sufficient*

make atonement for him before the LORD.[a]
30 He must then sacrifice one type of what he
can afford,[A] either the turtledoves or young
pigeons, 31 one as a sin offering and the other
as a burnt offering, sacrificing what he can afford[B,C] together with the grain offering. In this
way the priest will make atonement before
the LORD for the one to be cleansed. 32 This is
the law for someone who has[D] a skin disease
and cannot afford[E] the cost of his cleansing."

Cleansing of Contaminated Objects

33 The LORD spoke to Moses and Aaron:
34 "When you enter the land of Canaan[b] that
I am giving you as a possession,[c] and I place
a mildew contamination in a house in the
land you possess,[F] 35 the owner of the house
is to come and tell the priest: Something like
mildew contamination has appeared[G] in my
house. 36 The priest must order them to clear
the house before he enters to examine the
contamination, so that nothing in the house
becomes •unclean. Afterward the priest will
come to examine the house. 37 He will examine
it, and if the contamination in the walls of the
house consists of green or red indentations[H]
that appear to be beneath the surface of the
wall, 38 the priest is to go outside the house
to its doorway and quarantine the house for
seven days. 39 The priest is to return on the
seventh day and examine it. If the contamination has spread on the walls of the house,
40 the priest must order that the stones with
the contamination be pulled out and thrown
into an unclean place outside the city. 41 He
is to have the inside of the house completely
scraped, and the plaster[I] that is scraped off
must be dumped in an unclean place outside the city. 42 Then they must take different
stones to replace the former ones and take additional plaster[I] to replaster the house.

43 "If the contamination reappears in the
house after the stones have been pulled out,
and after the house has been scraped and replastered, 44 the priest must come and examine it. If the contamination has spread in the
house, it is harmful mildew; the house is unclean. 45 It must be torn down with its stones,

[a] 14:29 Lv 14:18
[b] 14:34 Gn 37:1
[c] Gn 17:8; 23:4; 36:43; 47:11; 48:4; 49:30; 50:13; Dt 32:49; Jos 21:12,41
[d] 14:53 Lv 14:7
[e] 15:2 Lv 15:33; 22:4; Nm 5:2; 2Sm 3:29

its beams, and all its plaster, and taken outside the city to an unclean place. 46 Whoever
enters the house during any of the days the
priest quarantines it will be unclean until
evening. 47 Whoever lies down in the house is
to wash his clothes, and whoever eats in it is
to wash his clothes.

48 "But when the priest comes and examines it, if the contamination has not spread
in the house after it was replastered, he is to
pronounce the house clean because the contamination has disappeared.[J] 49 He is to take
two birds, cedar wood, scarlet yarn, and hyssop to purify the house, 50 and he is to slaughter one of the birds over a clay pot containing
fresh water. 51 He will take the cedar wood,
the hyssop, the scarlet yarn, and the live bird,
dip them in the blood of the slaughtered bird
and the fresh water, and sprinkle the house
seven times. 52 He will purify the house with
the blood of the bird, the fresh water, the
live bird, the cedar wood, the hyssop, and the
scarlet yarn. 53 Then he is to release the live
bird into the open countryside[d] outside the
city. In this way he will make atonement for
the house, and it will be clean.

54 "This is the law for any skin disease or
mildew, for a scaly outbreak,[K] 55 for mildew in
clothing or on a house, 56 and for a swelling,
scab, or spot, 57 to determine when something
is unclean or clean. This is the law regarding
skin disease and mildew."

Bodily Discharges

15 The LORD spoke to Moses and Aaron:
2 "Speak to the Israelites and tell them:
When any man has a discharge[e] from his
body, he is •unclean. 3 This is uncleanness
of his discharge: Whether his body secretes
the discharge or retains it, he is unclean. All
the days that his body secretes or retains
anything because of his discharge,[L] he is unclean.[M] 4 Any bed the man with the discharge
lies on will be unclean, and any furniture he
sits on will be unclean. 5 Anyone who touches
his bed is to wash his clothes and bathe with
water, and he will remain unclean until evening. 6 Whoever sits on furniture that the

A 14:30 Lit *of that for which his hand is sufficient* B 14:31 LXX, Syr, Vg omit *what he can afford* C 14:31 Lit *sacrificing that for which his hand is sufficient* D 14:32 Lit *someone on whom there is* E 14:32 Lit *disease whose hand is not sufficient for* F 14:34 Lit *land of your possession* G 14:35 Lit *appeared to me*

H 14:37 Or *eruptions*; Hb obscure I 14:41,42 Lit *dust* J 14:48 Lit *healed* K 14:54 Or *for a scall* L 15:3 DSS, Sam, LXX; MT omits *he is unclean. All the days that his body secretes or retains anything because of his discharge* M 15:3 A urinary tract infection man with the discharge was sitting on is to wash his clothes and bathe with water, and he will remain unclean until evening. 7Whoever touches the body of the man with a discharge is to wash his clothes and bathe with water, and he will remain unclean until evening. 8If the man with the discharge spits on anyone who is •clean, he is to wash his clothes and bathe with water, and he will remain unclean until evening. 9Any saddle the man with the discharge rides on will be unclean.[a] 10Whoever touches anything that was under him will be unclean until evening, and whoever carries such things is to wash his clothes and bathe with water, and he will remain unclean until evening. 11If the man with the discharge touches anyone without first rinsing his hands in water,[b] the person who was touched is to wash his clothes and bathe with water, and he will remain unclean until evening. 12Any clay pot that the man with the discharge touches must be broken, while any wooden utensil must be rinsed with water.[c]

13"When the man with the discharge has been cured of it, he is to count seven days for his cleansing, wash his clothes, and bathe his body in fresh water; he will be clean. 14He must take two turtledoves or two young pigeons on the eighth day, come before the LORD at the entrance to the tent of meeting, and give them to the priest. 15The priest is to sacrifice them, one as a •sin offering and the other as a •burnt offering.[d] In this way the priest will make •atonement for him before the LORD because of his discharge.

16"When a man has an emission of semen,[e] he is to bathe himself completely with water, and he will remain unclean until evening. 17Any clothing or leather on which there is an emission of semen must be washed with water, and it will remain unclean until evening. 18If a man sleeps with a woman and has an emission of semen, both of them are to bathe with water, and they will remain unclean until evening.[f]

19"When a woman has a discharge, and it consists of blood from her body, she will be unclean because of her menstruation[g] for seven days. Everyone who touches her will be unclean until evening. 20Anything she lies on during her menstruation will become unclean, and anything she sits on will become unclean. 21Everyone who touches her bed is to wash his clothes and bathe with water, and he will remain unclean until evening. 22Everyone who touches any furniture she was sitting on is to wash his clothes and bathe with water, and he will remain unclean until evening. 23If discharge is on the bed or the furniture she was sitting on, when he touches it he will be unclean until evening. 24If a man sleeps with her, and blood from her menstruation gets on him, he will be unclean for seven days, and every bed he lies on will become unclean.[h]

25"When a woman has a discharge of her blood for many days, though it is not the time of her menstruation, or if she has a discharge beyond her period, she will be unclean all the days of her unclean discharge, as she is during the days of her menstruation. 26Any bed she lies on during the days of her discharge will be like her bed during menstrual impurity; any furniture she sits on will be unclean as in her menstrual period. 27Everyone who touches them will be unclean; he must wash his clothes and bathe with water, and he will remain unclean until evening. 28When she is cured of her discharge, she is to count seven days, and after that she will be clean.[i] 29On the eighth day she must take two turtledoves or two young pigeons and bring them to the priest at the entrance to the tent of meeting. 30The priest is to sacrifice one as a sin offering and the other as a burnt offering. In this way the priest will make atonement for her before the LORD because of her unclean discharge.

31"You must keep the Israelites from their uncleanness, so that they do not die by defiling My tabernacle[j] that is among them. 32This is the law for someone with a discharge: a man who has an emission of semen, becoming unclean by it; 33a woman who is in her menstrual period; anyone who has a discharge, whether male or female; and a man who sleeps with an unclean woman."

The Day of Atonement

16 The LORD spoke to Moses after the death of two of Aaron's sons when they approached the presence[k] of[A] the LORD

[a] **15:9** Gn 31:34-35
[b] **15:11** Ex 30:19; Mt 15:2; Mk 7:3
[c] **15:12** Lv 6:28; 11:33
[d] **15:15** Gn 22:2; Lv 3:5; Nm 6:11; Jos 8:31; 1Ch 16:1; Ps 20:3; Mc 6:6
[e] **15:16** Lv 15:32; 19:20; 22:4; Nm 5:13
[f] **15:18** 2Sm 11:2-4
[g] **15:19** Lv 12:2,5; 18:19; Ezk 22:10; 36:17
[h] **15:24** Lv 18:19; 20:18; Ezk 18:6
[i] **15:28** Lv 15:13; Mt 9:20-22
[j] **15:31** Ex 25:9; Nm 5:2-3
[k] **16:1** Gn 4:14

[A] **16:1** LXX, Tg, Syr, Vg read *they brought strange fire before*; Nm 3:4

and died.[a] 2 The LORD said to Moses: "Tell your
brother Aaron that he may not come whenever he wants into the holy place[b] behind the
veil[c] in front of the •mercy seat[d] on the ark or
else he will die, because I appear in the cloud[e]
above the mercy seat.[f]

3 "Aaron is to enter the most holy place[g] in
this way: with a young bull for a •sin offering and a ram for a •burnt offering.[h] 4 He is
to wear a holy linen tunic, and linen undergarments are to be on his body. He must tie
a linen sash around him and wrap his head
with a linen turban.[i] These are holy garments;
he must bathe his body with water before he
wears them. 5 He is to take from the Israelite
community two male goats for a sin offering
and one ram for a burnt offering.[j]

6 "Aaron will present the bull for his sin offering and make •atonement for himself and
his household. 7 Next he will take the two
goats and place them before the LORD at the
entrance to the tent of meeting. 8 After Aaron
casts lots[k] for the two goats, one lot for the
LORD and the other for azazel,[A,l] 9 he is to present the goat chosen by lot for the LORD and
sacrifice it as a sin offering.[m] 10 But the goat
chosen by lot for azazel[A] is to be presented
alive before the LORD to make purification
with it by sending it into the wilderness[n] for
azazel.

11 "When Aaron presents the bull for his sin
offering and makes atonement for himself
and his household, he will slaughter the bull
for his sin offering. 12 Then he must take a firepan full of fiery coals from the altar before
the LORD and two handfuls of finely ground
fragrant incense,[o] and bring them inside the
veil.[p] 13 He is to put the incense on the fire before the LORD, so that the cloud[q] of incense
covers the mercy seat that is over the •testi-
mony,[r] or else he will die.[s] 14 He is to take some
of the bull's blood[t] and sprinkle it with his
finger against the east side of the mercy seat;
then he will sprinkle some of the blood with
his finger before the mercy seat seven times.[u]

15 "When he slaughters the male goat for
the people's sin offering and brings its blood
inside the veil, he must do the same with its
blood as he did with the bull's blood: he is to
sprinkle it against the mercy seat and in front
of it. 16 He will purify the most holy place in
this way for all their sins because of the Israelites' impurities and rebellious acts.[v] He will
do the same for the tent of meeting that remains among them, because it is surrounded
by their impurities. 17 No one may be in the
tent of meeting from the time he enters to
make atonement in the most holy place until he leaves after he has made atonement
for himself, his household, and the whole assembly of Israel.[w] 18 Then he will go out to the
altar that is before the LORD and make atonement for it. He is to take some of the bull's
blood and some of the goat's blood and put
it on the horns on all sides of the altar. 19 He
is to sprinkle some of the blood on it with his
finger seven times to cleanse and set it apart[x]
from the Israelites' impurities.[y]

20 "When he has finished purifying the
most holy place, the tent of meeting, and
the altar, he is to present the live male goat.
21 Aaron will lay both his hands on the head of
the live goat and confess[z] over it all the Israelites' wrongdoings[a] and rebellious acts — all
their sins.[b] He is to put them on the goat's
head and send it away into the wilderness[c] by
the man appointed for the task.[B] 22 The goat
will carry on it all their wrongdoings into a
desolate land,[d] and he will release it there.

23 "Then Aaron is to enter the tent of meeting, take off the linen garments[e] he wore
when he entered the most holy place, and
leave them there. 24 He will bathe his body
with water in a holy place[f] and put on his
clothes.[g] Then he must go out and sacrifice
his burnt offering and the people's burnt offering; he will make atonement for himself
and for the people. 25 He is to burn the fat of
the sin offering on the altar. 26 The man who
released the goat for azazel[A] is to wash his
clothes and bathe his body with water; afterward he may reenter the camp. 27 The bull
for the sin offering and the goat for the sin
offering, whose blood was brought into the
most holy place to make atonement, must be
brought outside the camp[h] and their hide,[i]
flesh, and dung burned up.[j] 28 The one who
burns them is to wash his clothes and bathe

[a] **16:1** Lv 10:1-2
[b] **16:2** Heb 6:19
[c] Mk 15:38
[d] Ex 31:7
[e] Ex 16:10
[f] Nm 7:89; 16:42; 1Kg 8:10-12; Heb 9:5
[g] **16:3** Lv 4:1-12; Heb 9:7,24-25
[h] Gn 22:2; Lv 3:5; Nm 6:11; Jos 8:31; 1Ch 16:1; Ps 20:3; Mc 6:6
[i] **16:4** Ex 28:42-43; Lv 6:10; 8:7-8; Ezk 44:17-19
[j] **16:5** Lv 4:23-24; 8:18-21; 9:15
[k] **16:8** Nm 26:55
[l] Lv 16:26
[m] **16:9** Nm 29:11
[n] **16:10** Gn 14:6
[o] **16:12** Nm 7:14
[p] Mk 15:38
[q] **16:13** Ex 16:10
[r] Ex 31:18
[s] Lv 10:1; Nm 16:46-48; Ps 141:2; Rv 8:3-5
[t] **16:14** Heb 9:22
[u] Lv 4:6; Heb 9:4-5
[v] **16:16** Ex 22:9
[w] **16:17** 1Tm 2:5; Heb 9:7
[x] **16:19** Lv 8:10
[y] **16:17-19** Heb 9:11-14
[z] **16:21** Lv 5:5; 26:40; Nm 5:7; 2Ch 30:22; Neh 1:6; 9:2; Dn 9:4,20
[a] Lv 5:1
[b] Ezr 10:1; Neh 9:2-3; Dn 9:20; 2Co 5:21; Jms 5:16; 1Jn 1:9
[c] Lv 14:7
[d] **16:22** Ps 103:12; Is 53:4,6,11-12; Jn 1:29; Heb 9:28; 1Pt 2:24; 1Jn 3:5
[e] **16:23** Lv 6:11
[f] **16:24** Ex 29:31; Lv 6:16,26-27; 7:6; 10:13; 24:9; Ec 8:10; Ezk 42:13
[g] Lv 8:6-9
[h] **16:27** Lv 8:17
[i] Lv 7:8
[j] Lv 4:11-12; Heb 13:11-12

A **16:8,10,26** Perhaps a term that means "for the goat that departs," or "for removal," or "for a rough, difficult place," or "for a goat demon"; Hb obscure

B **16:21** Lit *wilderness in the hand of a ready man*

Martin Burnham (1959—2002)

Martin Burnham was an MK, a missionary kid. When he was ten years old, he accompanied his parents to Manila Bay, Philippines, where they went to serve with New Tribes Mission. Attending boarding school and flying back and forth from school to home gave him his lifelong fascination with airplanes. He knew at a young age that he wanted to be a missionary pilot.

Martin returned to the United States to attend Calvary Bible College and the Wichita Aviation Education Center. In 1982, Martin met Gracia Jones and they were married a year later. After graduating from the New Tribes Mission Training Institute, located in Mississippi, Martin and Gracia left the States in March 1986 for a mission aviation assignment with New Tribes Mission in Northern Luzon, Philippines. They worked as New Tribes missionaries in the Philippines from 1986 to May 2001.

Martin served missionaries in remote areas by flying supplies, mail, and medicines to them, and occasionally transporting the sick or injured back to hospitals. Martin had a huge heart for the tribal peoples of the Philippines and for the missionaries who served them so selflessly. He and Gracia worked hard to go the extra mile whenever help was needed.

On May 27, 2001, Martin and his wife were kidnapped by the Abu Sayyaf, an Islamist separatist group fighting for an independent Islamist province in the Philippines. Martin and Gracia were held hostage for over a year in the jungles of the Philippines. On June 7, 2002, Martin was shot in the chest during military action between the Abu Sayyaf and Philippine forces, a rescue attempt that resulted in Martin's death and Gracia's release.

Martin's uncle summed up Martin's life, referring to a talk Martin gave to his home congregation in Wichita, Kansas, less than a week before his abduction: "Martin not only spoke of following [Jesus], but he took on that responsibility. Of course, at that time neither he nor any of us expected how far he was going to be required to go to. But he was willing to go."[1]

[1] Ralph Burnham, quoted at http://www.christianitytoday.com/ct/2002/juneweb-only/6-17-13.0.html (accessed May 23, 2011).

himself with water; afterward he may reenter the camp.

29 "This is to be a permanent statute[a] for you: In the seventh month, on the tenth day of the month you are to practice self-denial[A,b] and do no work,[c] both the native and the foreigner[d] who resides among you. 30 Atonement will be made for you on this day to cleanse you,[e] and you will be •clean from all your sins before the LORD. 31 It is a Sabbath[f] of complete rest for you,[g] and you must practice self-denial; it is a permanent statute. 32 The priest who is anointed and ordained[B,h] to serve as high priest[i] in place of his father will make atonement. He will put on the linen garments, the holy garments, 33 and purify the most holy place. He will purify the tent of meeting and the altar and will make atonement for the priests and all the people of the assembly. 34 This is to be a permanent statute for you, to make atonement for the Israelites once a year[j] because of all their sins." And all this was done as the LORD commanded Moses.

Forbidden Sacrifices

17 The LORD spoke to Moses: 2 "Speak to Aaron, his sons, and all the Israelites and tell them: This is what the LORD has commanded: 3 Anyone from the house of Israel who slaughters[k] an ox, sheep, or goat in the camp, or slaughters it outside the camp, 4 instead of bringing it to the entrance to the tent of meeting to present it as an offering to the LORD before His tabernacle—that person will be considered •guilty.[C,l] He has shed blood[m] and must be cut off from his people.[n] 5 This is so the Israelites will bring to the LORD the sacrifices[o] they have been offering in the open country. They are to bring them to the priest at the entrance to the tent of meeting and offer them as •fellowship sacrifices[p] to the LORD. 6 The priest will then sprinkle the blood on the LORD's altar at the entrance to the tent of meeting and burn the fat as a pleasing aroma to the LORD. 7 They must no longer offer their sacrifices to the goat-demons[q] that they have prostituted[r] themselves with. This will be a permanent statute[s] for them throughout their generations.

8 "Say to them: Anyone from the house of Israel or from the foreigners[t] who live among them who offers a •burnt offering or a sacrifice 9 but does not bring it to the entrance to the tent of meeting to sacrifice it to the LORD, that person must be cut off from his people.

Eating Blood and Carcasses Prohibited

10 "Anyone from the house of Israel or from the foreigners who live among them who eats any blood,[u] I will turn[D] against that person who eats blood and cut him off from his people. 11 For the life of a creature is in the blood, and I have appointed it to you to make •atonement on the altar for[E] your lives, since it is the lifeblood that makes atonement.[v] 12 Therefore I say to the Israelites: None of you and no foreigner who lives among you may eat blood.

13 "Any Israelite or foreigner living among them, who hunts[w] down a wild animal or bird that may be eaten must drain its blood[x] and cover it with dirt. 14 Since the life of every creature is its blood, I have told the Israelites: You must not eat the blood of any creature,[y] because the life of every creature is its blood; whoever eats it must be cut off.

15 "Every person, whether the native or the foreigner,[z] who eats an animal that died a natural death or was mauled by wild beasts[a] is to wash his clothes and bathe with water, and he will remain •unclean until evening; then he will be •clean. 16 But if he does not wash his clothes and bathe himself, he will bear his punishment."

Prohibited Pagan Practices

18 •Yahweh spoke to Moses: 2 "Speak to the Israelites and tell them: I am Yahweh your God.[b] 3 Do not follow the practices of the land of Egypt,[c] where you used to live, or follow the practices of the land of Canaan,[d] where I am bringing you. You must not follow their customs.[e] 4 You are to practice My ordinances[f] and you are to keep My statutes[g] by following them; I am Yahweh your God. 5 Keep My statutes and ordinances; a person will live[h] if he does them.[i] I am Yahweh.

[a] **16:29** Ex 28:43; Lv 11:46 [b] Lv 23:27-32; Nm 29:7; Ps 35:13; Is 58:3,5; Dn 10:12 [c] Ex 12:16; Lv 23:3,28,31; Nm 29:7; Jr 17:22 [d] Ex 12:49; Lv 17:15; 18:26 [e] **16:30** Lv 13:6 [f] **16:31** Gn 2:2 [g] Ex 16:23; 31:15; 35:2; Lv 23:3,24,32,39; 25:4-5 [h] **16:32** Ex 29:33 [i] Lv 8:12,33 [j] **16:34** Heb 9:7 [k] **17:3** Dt 12:5-21 [l] **17:4** Ex 22:1; Lv 20:9; Nm 35:27; Dt 19:10; Ps 55:23; Is 33:15 [m] Gn 9:6 [n] Nm 9:13 [o] **17:5** Gn 46:1; Ex 34:25 [p] Lv 7:11 [q] **17:7** 2Ch 11:15; Is 13:21; 34:14 [r] Dt 22:21 [s] Gn 26:5; Ex 12:14; Lv 3:17; Nm 9:3; Dt 6:2; 8:11 [t] **17:8** Gn 19:9; Ex 2:22 [u] **17:10** Gn 9:4; Lv 3:17 [v] **17:11** Mt 26:28; Mk 14:24; Rm 3:25; 5:9; Eph 1:7; Col 1:14,20; Heb 13:12; 1Jn 1:7; Rv 1:5 [w] **17:13** Gn 25:27 [x] Ex 29:12; Lv 17:4; Dt 12:16,24; 15:23; Ezk 24:7 [y] **17:14** Lv 3:17 [z] **17:15** Lv 16:29 [a] Ex 22:31; Lv 7:24; 22:8; Dt 14:21 [b] **18:2** Nm 15:41 [c] **18:3** Lv 11:45; 19:34,36 [d] Dt 18:9-12 [e] Ex 23:24; Lv 18:24-30; 2Kg 17:7-8 [f] **18:4** Lv 18:26; Nm 29:18; Jos 6:15; Ezr 3:4; Jb 9:19; Ps 119:13; Is 1:17; Ezk 18:5 [g] Lv 7:7 [h] **18:5** Dt 4:1; Neh 9:29; Ezk 20:13,21,25; 33:12; Rm 7:10; Php 1:21 [i] Dt 6:24; Pr 6:23; Lk 10:26-28; Rm 7:10; 10:5; Gl 3:12

[A] **16:29** Traditionally, fasting, abstinence from sex, and refraining from personal grooming [B] **16:32** Lit *and will fill his hand* [C] **17:4** Lit *tabernacle—blood will be charged against that person* [D] **17:10** Lit *will set My face* [E] **17:11** Or *to ransom*

6“You are not to come near[a] any close relative[A] for sexual intercourse;[b] I am Yahweh.
7You are not to shame your father[c] by having
sex with your mother. She is your mother; you
must not have sexual intercourse with her.
8You are not to have sex with your father’s
wife;[d] it will shame your father.[e] 9You are not
to have sexual intercourse with your sister,
either your father’s daughter or your mother’s,[f] whether born at home or born elsewhere. You are not to have sex with her. 10You
are not to have sexual intercourse with your
son’s daughter or your daughter’s daughter,
because it will shame your family.[B] 11You are
not to have sexual intercourse with your father’s wife’s daughter,[C] who is adopted by[D]
your father; she is your sister. 12You are not
to have sexual intercourse with your father’s
sister;[g] she is your father’s close relative. 13You
are not to have sexual intercourse with your
mother’s sister,[h] for she is your mother’s close
relative. 14You are not to shame your father’s
brother by coming near his wife to have
sexual intercourse; she is your aunt.[i] 15You
are not to have sexual intercourse with your
daughter-in-law.[j] She is your son’s wife; you
are not to have sex with her. 16You are not to
have sexual intercourse with your brother’s
wife; it will shame your brother.[k] 17You are not
to have sexual intercourse with a woman and
her daughter.[l] You are not to marry her son’s
daughter or her daughter’s daughter and
have sex with her. They are close relatives; it
is depraved.[m] 18You are not to marry a woman
as a rival to her sister and have sexual intercourse with her during her sister’s lifetime.[n]

19“You are not to come near[o] a woman during her menstrual impurity to have sexual
intercourse with her.[p] 20You are not to have
sexual intercourse with[E] your neighbor’s
wife, defiling yourself with her.[q]

21“You are not to make any of your children
pass through the fire to ˙Molech.[r] Do not profane the name[s] of your God; I am Yahweh.
22You are not to sleep with a man as with a
woman;[t] it is detestable.[u] 23You are not to have
sexual intercourse with[F] any animal, defiling
yourself with it; a woman is not to present
herself to an animal to mate with it;[v] it is a
perversion.

24“Do not defile yourselves by any of these
practices, for the nations I am driving out
before you have defiled themselves by all
these things. 25The land has become defiled,
so I am punishing it for its sin, and the land
will vomit out its inhabitants.[w] 26But you
are to keep My statutes and ordinances. You
must not commit any of these detestable
things — not the native or the foreigner who
lives among you. 27For the men who were
in the land prior to you have committed all
these detestable things, and the land has become defiled. 28If you defile the land, it will
vomit[x] you out as it has vomited out the nations that were before you. 29Any person who
does any of these detestable practices must
be cut off from his people. 30You must keep
My instruction to not do any of the detestable
customs[y] that were practiced before you, so
that you do not defile yourselves by them; I
am Yahweh your God.”

Laws of Holiness

19 The Lord spoke to Moses: 2“Speak to
the entire Israelite community and tell
them: Be holy[z] because I, ˙Yahweh your God,
am holy.[a]

3“Each of you is to respect his mother and
father.[b] You are to keep My Sabbaths; I am
Yahweh your God. 4Do not turn to idols[c] or
make cast images[d] of gods for yourselves;[e] I
am Yahweh your God.

5“When you offer a ˙fellowship sacrifice to
the Lord, sacrifice it so that you may be accepted. 6It is to be eaten on the day you sacrifice it or on the next day, but what remains
on the third day must be burned up.[f] 7If any is
eaten on the third day, it is a repulsive thing;
it will not be accepted.[g] 8Anyone who eats
it will bear his punishment, for he has profaned what is holy to the Lord. That person
must be cut off from his people.[h]

9“When you reap the harvest of your land,
you are not to reap to the very edge of your
field or gather the gleanings[i] of your harvest.
10You must not strip your vineyard bare or
gather its fallen grapes. Leave them for the

[a]**18:6** Gn 20:4
[b]1Tm 4:3
[c]**18:7** Ezk 22:10
[d]**18:8** Gn 35:22; 49:4; Lv 20:11; 2Sm 16:21-22; Am 2:7; 1Co 5:1
[e]Lv 20:11
[f]**18:9** Lv 20:17; Dt 27:22; 2Sm 13:11-14; Ezk 22:11
[g]**18:12** Ex 6:20
[h]**18:13** Lv 20:19
[i]**18:14** Lv 20:20
[j]**18:15** Gn 38:16; Lv 20:12; Ezk 22:11
[k]**18:16** Lv 20:21; Dt 25:5-10; Mt 14:3-4; Mk 6:18
[l]**18:17** Lv 20:14; Dt 27:23; Am 2:7
[m]Lv 19:29
[n]**18:18** Gn 29:21-28
[o]**18:19** Gn 20:4
[p]Lv 15:19-24; 20:18; Ezk 18:6
[q]**18:20** Ex 20:14; Lv 20:10; Nm 5:11-31; Dt 22:22; 1Co 6:9; Heb 13:4
[r]**18:21** Lv 20:2-5; Dt 18:10; 1Kg 11:7; 2Kg 23:10; Jr 32:35; Ac 7:43
[s]Ex 20:7; Lv 20:3; Jn 10:25
[t]**18:22** Gn 19:5; Lv 20:13; Dt 23:18; Rm 1:26-27; 1Co 6:9-11; Gl 5:21; 1Tm 1:10; Rv 21:8
[u]Gn 46:34
[v]**18:23** Ex 22:19
[w]**18:25** Nm 35:33-34; Dt 9:4; Ezr 9:11; Is 24:5-6; Jr 2:7; Ezk 36:1
[x]**18:28** Lv 20:22; Dt 8:20
[y]**18:30** Lv 7:7
[z]**19:2** Ex 19:5-6
[a]Lv 11:44; 21:8
[b]**19:3** Ex 20:12; 21:15
[c]**19:4** Lv 26:1
[d]Nm 33:52
[e]Ex 20:3,23; 32:31; Dt 4:15-16
[f]**19:6** Lv 7:17
[g]**19:7** Lv 1:4
[h]**19:7-8** Lv 7:18,20
[i]**19:9** Lv 23:22; Dt 24:19-22; Ru 2:2-7,15-19,23; Is 17:5

[A]**18:6** Lit *any flesh of his flesh* [B]**18:10** Lit *because they are your nakedness* [C]**18:11** This must refer to a daughter from a previous marriage. [D]**18:11** Lit *daughter, a relative of* [E]**18:20** Lit *to give your emission of semen to* [F]**18:23** Lit *to give your emission to* poor[a] and the foreign resident;[b] I am Yahweh your God.

11 "You must not steal.[c] You must not act deceptively[d] or lie[e] to one another. 12 You must not swear falsely by My name, profaning the name of your God;[f] I am Yahweh.

13 "You must not oppress[g] your neighbor or rob[h] him. The wages due a hired hand[i] must not remain with you until morning. 14 You must not curse the deaf or put a stumbling block in front of the blind,[j] but you are to •fear your God;[k] I am Yahweh.[l]

15 "You must not act unjustly[m] when deciding a case. Do not be partial[n] to the poor or give preference to the rich;[o] judge your neighbor fairly. 16 You must not go about spreading slander[p] among your people; you must not jeopardize[A] your neighbor's life; I am Yahweh.

17 "You must not harbor hatred against your brother.[B,q] Rebuke your neighbor directly, and you will not incur •guilt because of him.[r] 18 Do not take revenge[s] or bear a grudge against members of your community, but love your neighbor as yourself;[t] I am Yahweh.

19 "You are to keep My statutes. You must not crossbreed two different kinds of your livestock, sow your fields with two kinds of seed, or put on a garment made of two kinds of material.[u]

20 "If a man has sexual intercourse with a woman who is a slave designated for another man, but she has not been redeemed[v] or given her freedom, there must be punishment.[C] They are not to be put to death, because she had not been freed. 21 However, he must bring a ram as his •restitution offering to the LORD at the entrance to the tent of meeting.[w] 22 The priest will make •atonement on his behalf before the LORD with the ram of the restitution offering for the sin he has committed, and he will be forgiven for the sin he committed.

23 "When you come into the land and plant any kind of tree for food, you are to consider the fruit forbidden.[D] It will be forbidden to you for three years; it is not to be eaten. 24 In the fourth year all its fruit must be consecrated as a praise offering[x] to the LORD. 25 But in the fifth year you may eat its fruit. In this way its yield will increase for you;[y] I am Yahweh your God.

26 "You are not to eat anything with blood in it.[E,z] You are not to practice •divination[aa] or sorcery.[ab] 27 You are not to cut off the hair at the sides of your head or mar the edge of your beard.[ac] 28 You are not to make gashes on your bodies for the dead[ad] or put tattoo marks on yourselves; I am Yahweh.

29 "Do not debase[F,ae] your daughter by making her a prostitute,[af] or the land will be prostituted and filled with depravity. 30 You must keep My Sabbaths and revere My sanctuary;[ag] I am Yahweh.

31 "Do not turn to mediums[G,ah] or consult spiritists,[H,ai] or you will be defiled by them; I am Yahweh your God.

32 "You are to rise in the presence of the elderly and honor the old.[aj] Fear your God; I am Yahweh.

33 "When a foreigner lives with you in your land, you must not oppress[ak] him. 34 You must regard the foreigner who lives with you as the native-born among you. You are to love him as yourself,[al] for you were foreigners in the land of Egypt;[am] I am Yahweh your God.

35 "You must not be unfair[an] in measurements of length, weight, or volume. 36 You are to have honest balances,[ao] honest weights, an honest dry measure,[I] and an honest liquid measure;[J,ap] I am Yahweh your God, who brought you out of the land of Egypt. 37 You must keep all My statutes and all My ordinances and do them; I am Yahweh."

Molech Worship and Spiritism

20 The LORD spoke to Moses: 2 "Say to the Israelites: Any Israelite or foreigner living in Israel who gives any of his children to •Molech[aq] must be put to death; the people of the country are to stone him.[ar] 3 I will

[a] 19:10 Dt 15:11 [b] Ex 2:22; Dt 24:20-21; Is 17:5-6; 24:13 [c] 19:11 Ex 20:15; 22:1; Rm 13:9; Eph 4:28 [d] Pr 30:9; Is 30:9; 59:13; Jr 5:12; Hs 4:2; 7:3; 9:2; 10:13; Nah 3:1; Hab 3:17; Zch 13:4 [e] Gn 21:23; Ex 20:16; 1Sm 15:29; Ps 44:18; 89:34; Is 63:8; Eph 4:25 [f] 19:12 Ex 20:7; Lv 18:21; 20:3; Mal 3:5; Jms 5:12 [g] 19:13 Dt 24:14 [h] Dt 28:29 [i] Ex 12:45; 22:14; Lv 22:10; 25:6,40,50,53; Is 7:20; Jr 46:21; Ezk 18:7; Mal 3:5; Jms 5:4 [j] 19:14 Ex 4:11; Dt 27:18 [k] Ps 147:11; Pr 1:7; Ac 10:2; Rv 14:7 [l] Ex 31:13 [m] 19:15 Dt 25:16 [n] Ex 23:2-3; Dt 1:17; Jms 2:9 [o] Gn 24:35; Jb 34:19 [p] 19:16 Ps 15:3; Jr 6:28; 9:4; Lk 6:22; 2Co 6:8; 12:20; Eph 4:31; Col 3:8; Ti 3:2; 1Pt 2:1; 4:4; Rv 2:9 [q] 19:17 2Th 3:15; 1Jn 2:9,11; 3:15; 4:20 [r] Pr 9:8; 27:5; Ezk 3:18; Mt 18:15; Gl 6:1 [s] 19:18 Dt 32:35; Pr 20:22; Rm 12:17,19; Heb 10:30; Rv 19:2 [t] Pr 17:17; Mt 5:43; 22:39; Mk 12:31; Lk 10:27; Rm 13:9; Gl 5:14; Jms 2:8 [u] 19:19 Dt 22:9-11 [v] 19:20 Ex 6:6; 21:7-11; Lv 27:29; Dt 22:23-27 [w] 19:21 Ex 27:21 [x] 19:24 Jdg 9:27 [y] 19:25 Lv 25:18-22 [z] 19:26 Gn 9:4; Lv 3:17; 17:10-12; 1Sm 14:32-35; Ezk 33:25 [aa] 1Kg 20:33 [ab] Dt 18:10,14; Jdg 9:37; 2Kg 21:6; 2Ch 33:6; Is 2:6; 57:3; Jr 27:9 [ac] 19:27 Lv 21:5; Dt 14:1; 2Sm 10:4-5; Jr 41:5; 48:37; Ezk 5:1-5; 44:20 [ad] 19:28 1Kg 18:28; Jr 16:6; 41:5; 47:5; 48:37 [ae] 19:29 Lv 21:12 [af] Ex 34:31; Lv 21:9; Dt 23:17-18 [ag] 19:30 Ex 15:17; Lv 20:3; 26:2; Nm 19:20 [ah] 19:31 Lv 20:6 [ai] Dt 18:11; Ac 16:16 [aj] 19:32 Jb 12:12; 32:4; Pr 23:22; Lm 5:12; 1Tm 5:1 [ak] 19:33 Dt 23:16 [al] 19:34 Lv 19:18 [am] Ex 23:9; Lv 18:3; Dt 10:19; 23:7 [an] 19:35 Dt 25:16 [ao] 19:36 Hs 12:8; Am 8:5; Mc 6:11 [ap] Dt 25:13-16; Pr 16:11; Ezk 45:10 [aq] 20:2 Lv 18:21; Dt 18:10; 2Kg 23:10; Ac 7:43 [ar] Lv 24:14; Nm 15:35-36; Dt 17:2-7; 21:21; Jos 7:25

A 19:16 Lit *not stand against* B 19:17 Or *your fellow Israelite* C 19:20 Or *compensation* D 19:23 Lit *uncircumcised* E 19:26 Or *anything over its blood* F 19:29 Lit *profane* G 19:31 Or *spirits of the dead* H 19:31 Or *familiar spirits* I 19:36 Lit *honest ephah*; an *ephah* is a dry measure of grain equivalent to about 23 quarts. J 19:36 Lit *honest hin*; a *hin* is a liquid measure of about 1 gallon.

turn[A] against that man and cut him off from
his people, because he gave his •offspring to
Molech, defiling My sanctuary[a] and profaning My holy name.[b] 4But if the people of the
country look the other way when that man[B]
gives any of his children to Molech, and
do not put him to death, 5then I will turn[A]
against that man and his family, and cut off
from their people both him and all who follow[C] him in prostituting[c] themselves with
Molech.

6"Whoever turns to mediums[D,d] or spiritists[E] and prostitutes himself with them, I will
turn[A] against that person and cut him off
from his people. 7Consecrate yourselves and
be holy, for I am •Yahweh your God. 8Keep My
statutes and do them; I am Yahweh who sets
you apart.

Family and Sexual Offenses

9"If anyone curses his father or mother,
he must be put to death.[e] He has cursed his
father or mother; his blood is on his own
hands.[F]

10If a man commits adultery[f] with a married woman—if he commits adultery with
his neighbor's wife—both the adulterer
and the adulteress must be put to death. 11If
a man sleeps with his father's wife, he has
shamed his father.[g] Both of them must be put
to death; their blood is on their own hands.[G]
12If a man sleeps with his daughter-in-law,[h]
both of them must be put to death. They have
acted perversely; their blood is on their own
hands.[G] 13If a man sleeps with a man as with a
woman,[i] they have both committed a detestable thing.[j] They must be put to death; their
blood is on their own hands.[G] 14If a man marries a woman and her mother,[k] it is depraved.
Both he and they must be burned with fire,[l]
so that there will be no depravity among you.
15If a man has sexual intercourse with[H] an animal, he must be put to death; you are also to
kill the animal. 16If a woman comes near any
animal and mates with it, you are to kill the
woman and the animal.[m] They must be put
to death; their own blood is on them. 17If a
man marries his sister,[n] whether his father's
daughter or his mother's daughter, and they
have sexual relations,[I,o] it is a disgrace.[p] They
must be cut off publicly from their people.
He has had sexual intercourse with his sister; he will bear his punishment. 18If a man
sleeps with a menstruating woman and has
sexual intercourse with her, he has exposed
the source of her flow, and she has uncovered
the source of her blood.[q] Both of them must
be cut off from their people. 19You must not
have sexual intercourse with your mother's
sister or your father's sister,[r] for it is exposing one's own blood relative; both people will
bear their punishment. 20If a man sleeps with
his aunt, he has shamed his uncle;[s] they will
bear their •guilt and die childless. 21If a man
marries his brother's wife, it is impurity.[t] He
has shamed his brother;[u] they will be childless.

Holiness in the Land

22"You are to keep all My statutes and all
My ordinances, and do them, so that the land
where I am bringing you to live will not vomit
you out.[v] 23You must not follow the statutes
of the nations I am driving out before you,
for they did all these things, and I abhorred
them.[w] 24And I promised you: You will inherit
their land, since I will give it to you to possess, a land flowing with milk and honey.[x] I
am Yahweh your God who set you apart from
the peoples. 25Therefore you must distinguish
the •clean animal from the •unclean one,
and the unclean bird from the clean one. Do
not become contaminated[y] by any land animal, bird, or whatever crawls on the ground; I
have set these apart as unclean for you.[z] 26You
are to be holy to Me because I, Yahweh, am
holy, and I have set you apart from the nations to be Mine.[aa]

27A man or a woman who is[J] a medium or a
spiritist must be put to death. They are to be
stoned; their blood is on their own hands."[K]

The Holiness of the Priests

21 The LORD said to Moses: "Speak to Aaron's sons, the priests, and tell them: A
priest is not to make himself ceremonially

[a]**20:3** Ex 15:17 [b]Lv 18:21; 19:12; 22:2,32; Jr 34:16; Ezk 36:20; 39:7; Am 2:7 [c]**20:5** Dt 22:21 [d]**20:6** Lv 19:31; 20:27; Dt 18:11; 1Sm 28:3,7-9; 2Kg 21:6; 23:24; 1Ch 10:13; 2Ch 33:6; Is 8:19; 19:3; 29:4 [e]**20:9** Ex 21:17; Dt 21:18-21; 27:16; Pr 20:20; 30:11; Mt 15:4; Mk 7:10 [f]**20:10** Ex 20:14; Dt 5:18; 22:22; 31:16; Pr 6:32; Mal 3:5; Mt 5:27-28,32; 19:9,18 [g]**20:11** Lv 18:8; Dt 22:30; 27:20; 1Co 5:1 [h]**20:12** Gn 38:16; Lv 18:15; Ezk 22:11 [i]**20:13** Gn 19:5 [j]Gn 46:34 [k]**20:14** Lv 18:17 [l]Gn 38:24; Lv 18:22; 21:9; Jdg 14:15; Rv 17:16 [m]**20:15-16** Ex 22:19 [n]**20:17** Lv 18:13 [o]Lv 18:9 [p]Lv 19:29 [q]**20:18** Lv 18:19 [r]**20:19** Ex 6:20; Lv 18:12-13 [s]**20:20** Lv 18:14 [t]**20:21** Mk 6:18 [u]Lv 18:16 [v]**20:22** Lv 18:25 [w]**20:23** Ex 23:24; Lv 18:3 [x]**20:24** Ex 3:8; 13:5; Nm 14:8; 16:13-14 [y]**20:25** Dt 7:26 [z]Lv 11:1-47 [aa]**20:26** Ex 19:5-6; Lv 11:44-45; Is 1:4; 6:3

[A]**20:3,5,6** Lit *will set My face* [B]**20:4** Lit *country ever close their eyes from that man when he* [C]**20:5** Lit *prostitute themselves with* [D]**20:6** Or *spirits of the dead* [E]**20:6** Or *familiar spirits* [F]**20:9** Lit *on him* [G]**20:11,12,13** Lit *on them* [H]**20:15** Lit *man gives his emission to* [I]**20:17** Lit *and he sees her nakedness and she sees his nakedness* [J]**20:27** Lit *is in them* [K]**20:27** Lit *on them*

•unclean for a dead person among his relatives,[a] 2 except for his immediate family: his mother, father, son, daughter, or brother. 3 He may make himself unclean for his young unmarried sister in his immediate family. 4 He is not to make himself unclean for those related to him by marriage[A] and so defile himself.

5 "Priests may not make bald spots on their heads, shave the edge of their beards, or make gashes on their bodies.[b] 6 They are to be holy to their God and not profane the name of their God.[c] For they present the fire offerings to •Yahweh, the food of their God, and they must be holy. 7 They are not to marry a woman defiled by prostitution.[B,d] They are not to marry one divorced[e] by her husband, for the priest is holy to his God. 8 You are to consider him holy since he presents the food of your God. He will be holy to you because I, Yahweh who sets you apart, am holy. 9 If a priest's daughter defiles herself by promiscuity,[C,f] she defiles her father; she must be burned up.[g]

10 "The priest who is highest among his brothers, who has had the anointing oil poured on his head and has been ordained[D] to wear the garments, must not dishevel his hair[E] or tear his garments.[h] 11 He must not go near any dead person or make himself unclean even for his father or mother.[i] 12 He must not leave the sanctuary or he will desecrate the sanctuary of his God, for the consecration of the anointing oil of his God is on him;[j] I am Yahweh.

13 "He is to marry a woman who is a virgin. 14 He is not to marry a widow,[k] a divorced woman,[l] or one defiled by prostitution. He is to marry a virgin from his own people, 15 so that he does not corrupt his bloodline[F] among his people, for I am Yahweh who sets him apart."

Physical Defects and Priests

16 The LORD spoke to Moses: 17 "Tell Aaron: None of your descendants throughout your generations who has a physical defect[m] is to come near to present the food[n] of his God. 18 No man who has any defect is to come near: no man who is blind, lame, facially disfigured, or deformed; 19 no man who has a broken foot or hand, 20 or who is a hunchback or a dwarf,[G,o] or who has an eye defect, a festering rash, scabs,[p] or a crushed testicle.[q] 21 No descendant of Aaron the priest who has a defect is to come near to present the fire offerings to the LORD. He has a defect and is not to come near to present the food of his God. 22 He may eat the food of his God from what is especially holy as well as from what is holy. 23 But because he has a defect, he must not go near the curtain[r] or approach the altar. He is not to desecrate My sanctuaries, for I am Yahweh who sets them apart."[s] 24 Moses said this to Aaron and his sons and to all the Israelites.

Priests and Their Food

22 The LORD spoke to Moses: 2 "Tell Aaron and his sons to deal respectfully with the holy offerings of the Israelites that they have consecrated to Me, so they do not profane My holy name;[t] I am •Yahweh. 3 Say to them: If any man from any of your descendants throughout your generations is in a state of uncleanness yet approaches the holy offerings that the Israelites consecrate to the LORD, that person will be cut off from My presence; I am Yahweh. 4 No man of Aaron's descendants who has a skin disease[H] or a discharge is to eat from the holy offerings until he is •clean. Whoever touches anything made •unclean by a dead person or by a man who has an emission of semen, 5 or whoever touches any swarming creature that makes him unclean or any person who makes him unclean—whatever his uncleanness— 6 the man who touches any of these will remain unclean until evening[u] and is not to eat from the holy offerings unless he has bathed his body with water. 7 When the sun has set, he will become clean, and then he may eat from the holy offerings, for that is his food.[v] 8 He must not eat an animal that died naturally or was mauled by wild beasts,[I,w] making himself unclean by it; I am Yahweh. 9 They must keep My instruction,[x] or they will be •guilty and die because they profane it; I am Yahweh who sets them apart.

[a] **21:1** Nm 5:2-3; 6:6; 19:11-13; 31:19; Ezk 44:25
[b] **21:5** Lv 19:27-28
[c] **21:6** Ex 20:7; Lv 20:3; Jn 10:25
[d] **21:7** Gn 34:31
[e] Dt 22:19,29; 24:1,3; Mal 2:16; Mt 1:19; 5:31-32; 19:3-9
[f] **21:9** Dt 22:21
[g] Gn 38:24; Lv 20:14; Jdg 15:6; Rv 17:16
[h] **21:10** Lv 10:6; Ezk 44:20; Mk 14:63
[i] **21:11** Ezk 44:25
[j] **21:12** Lv 10:7
[k] **21:14** Ex 22:22
[l] Lv 21:7; 22:13; Nm 30:10; Ezk 44:22
[m] **21:17** Nm 19:2
[n] Lv 3:11
[o] **21:20** Gn 41:3-4,6-7,23-24; Ex 16:14; Lv 13:30; 16:12; 1Kg 19:12; Is 29:5; 40:15,22
[p] Lv 22:22
[q] **21:18-20** Lv 22:24; Dt 23:1
[r] **21:23** Mk 15:38; Heb 6:19
[s] Ex 31:13; Lv 20:8; 21:8,15; 22:9,16,32; Ezk 20:12
[t] **22:2** Ex 20:7; Jn 10:25
[u] **22:6** Lv 11:24-28,31-32,39-40
[v] **22:7** Lv 6:16-18,29; 7:7-10,32-36; 26:5
[w] **22:8** Ex 22:31; Lv 7:24; 17:15; Ezk 44:31
[x] **22:9** Gn 26:5; Lv 18:30

[A] **21:4** Lit *unclean a husband among his people* [B] **21:7** Or *a prostitute* or *a defiled woman* [C] **21:9** Or *prostitution* [D] **21:10** Lit *and one has filled his hand* [E] **21:10** Or *not uncover his head* [F] **21:15** Lit *not profane his seed* [G] **21:20** Or *or emaciated* [H] **22:4** Or *has leprosy or scale disease* [I] **22:8** Lit *eat a carcass or a mauled beast*

10“No one outside a priest’s family[A,a] is to
eat the holy offering. A foreigner staying with
a priest or a hired hand is not to eat the holy
offering. 11But if a priest purchases someone
with his money, that person may eat it, and
those born in his house may eat his food. 12If
the priest’s daughter is married to a man outside a priest’s family,[B] she is not to eat from
the holy contributions.[C] 13But if the priest’s
daughter becomes widowed or divorced, has
no children, and returns to her father’s house
as in her youth, she may share her father’s
food. But no outsider may share it. 14If anyone eats a holy offering in error,[b] he must add
a fifth to its value and give the holy offering to
the priest.[c] 15The priests must not profane the
holy offerings the Israelites give to the LORD
16by letting the people eat their holy offerings
and having them bear the penalty of restitution.[d] For I am Yahweh who sets them apart.”

Acceptable Sacrifices

17The LORD spoke to Moses: 18“Speak to
Aaron, his sons, and all the Israelites and tell
them: Any man of the house of Israel or of
the foreign residents[e] in Israel who presents
his offering[f]—whether they present freewill gifts or payment of vows to the LORD as
•burnt offerings— 19must offer an unblemished male[g] from the cattle, sheep, or goats in
order for you to be accepted. 20You are not to
present anything that has a defect, because it
will not be accepted on your behalf.

21“When a man presents a •fellowship sacrifice to the LORD to fulfill a vow or as a freewill offering from the herd or flock, it has
to be unblemished to be acceptable; there
must be no defect in it. 22You are not to present any animal to the LORD that is blind,
injured, maimed, or has a running sore, festering rash,[h] or scabs; you may not put any
of them on the altar as a fire offering to the
LORD.[i] 23You may sacrifice as a freewill offering any animal from the herd or flock that
has an elongated or stunted limb, but it is
not acceptable as a vow offering. 24You are
not to present to the LORD anything that has
bruised, crushed, torn, or severed testicles;[j]
you must not sacrifice them in your land.

[a]**22:10** Ex 29:33; Nm 3:10; 18:4,7
[b]**22:14** Nm 15:22,24
[c]Lv 5:14-16
[d]**22:16** Lv 14:12
[e]**22:18** Ex 2:22
[f]Lv 1:2
[g]**22:19** Ex 29:1
[h]**22:22** Dt 28:27; 2Sm 23:38; 1Ch 11:40; Jr 31:39
[i]Lv 21:18-20; Is 28:20
[j]**22:24** Lv 21:20
[k]**22:25** Mal 1:14
[l]**22:27** Ex 22:30
[m]**22:28** Ex 23:19; Dt 22:6-7
[n]**22:29** Lv 7:12-15; 2Ch 29:31; 33:16; Ps 56:13; Jr 17:26; 33:11; Am 4:5
[o]**22:30** Ex 34:25; Lv 7:15; 19:6-7
[p]**22:32** Lv 19:12; 21:6-8,23; 22:2; Lk 11:2
[q]**23:2** Lv 23:37,44; Nm 10:10; 2Ch 2:3; Ezr 3:5
[r]Ex 12:16; Lv 23:21,24,27,35-37; Nm 28:18,25-26; 29:1,7,12
[s]**23:3** Ex 31:15; 35:2; Lv 16:31; 23:32; 25:4
[t]Gn 2:2-3
[u]**23:5** Ex 12:11
[v]**23:6** Ex 12:17

25Neither you nor[D] a foreigner are to present
food to your God from any of these animals.
They will not be accepted for you because
they are deformed and have a defect.”[k]

26The LORD spoke to Moses: 27“When an ox,
sheep, or goat is born, it must remain with[E]
its mother for seven days; from the eighth
day[l] on, it will be acceptable as a gift, a fire
offering to the LORD. 28But you are not to
slaughter an animal from the herd or flock
on the same day as its young.[m] 29When you
sacrifice a thank offering[n] to the LORD, sacrifice it so that you may be accepted. 30It is to
be eaten on the same day.[o] Do not let any of it
remain until morning; I am Yahweh.

31“You are to keep My commands and do
them; I am Yahweh. 32You must not profane
My holy name; I must be treated as holy[p]
among the Israelites. I am Yahweh who sets
you apart, 33the One who brought you out of
the land of Egypt to be your God; I am Yahweh.”

Holy Days

23 The LORD spoke to Moses: 2“Speak to
the Israelites and tell them: These are
My appointed times,[q] the times of the LORD
that you will proclaim as sacred assemblies.[r]

3“Work may be done for six days, but on
the seventh day there must be a Sabbath of
complete rest,[s] a sacred assembly. You are not
to do any work; it is a Sabbath[t] to the LORD
wherever you live.

4“These are the LORD’s appointed times, the
sacred assemblies you are to proclaim at their
appointed times. 5The •Passover[u] to the LORD
comes in the first month, at twilight on the
fourteenth day of the month. 6The Festival of
•Unleavened Bread[v] to the LORD is on the fifteenth day of the same month. For seven days
you must eat unleavened bread. 7On the first
day you are to hold a sacred assembly; you are
not to do any daily work. 8You are to present
a fire offering to the LORD for seven days. On
the seventh day there will be a sacred assembly; you must not do any daily work.”

9The LORD spoke to Moses: 10“Speak to the
Israelites and tell them: When you enter the
land I am giving you and reap its harvest,[F] you

[A]**22:10** Lit *No stranger* [B]**22:12** Lit *man, a stranger* [C]**22:12** Lit *the contribution of holy offerings* [D]**22:25** Lit *nor from the hand of* [E]**22:27** Lit *under*

[F]**23:10** = the barley harvest

are to bring the first sheaf of your harvest to the priest. 11 He will wave the sheaf before the LORD so that you may be accepted; the priest is to wave it on the day after the Sabbath. 12 On the day you wave the sheaf, you are to offer a year-old male lamb[A] without blemish[a] as a •burnt offering to the LORD. 13 Its •grain offering is to be four quarts[B] of fine flour mixed with oil as a fire offering to the LORD, a pleasing aroma, and its •drink offering will be one quart[C] of wine. 14 You must not eat bread, roasted grain, or any new grain[D] until this very day, and until you have brought the offering to your God. This is to be a permanent statute throughout your generations wherever you live.

15 "You are to count seven[E] complete weeks[F,b] starting from the day after the Sabbath, the day you brought the sheaf of the presentation offering.[c] 16 You are to count 50 days until the day after the seventh Sabbath and then present an offering of new grain[G] to the LORD. 17 Bring two loaves of bread from your settlements as a presentation offering, each of them made from four quarts[B] of fine flour, baked with yeast, as •firstfruits[d] to the LORD. 18 You are to present with the bread seven unblemished male lambs a year old, one young bull, and two rams. They will be a burnt offering to the LORD, with their grain offerings and drink offerings, a fire offering of a pleasing aroma to the LORD. 19 You are also to prepare one male goat as a •sin offering, and two male lambs a year old as a •fellowship sacrifice. 20 The priest will wave the lambs with the bread of firstfruits as a presentation offering before the LORD; the bread and the two lambs will be holy to the LORD for the priest. 21 On that same day you are to make a proclamation and hold a sacred assembly. You are not to do any daily work. This is to be a permanent statute wherever you live throughout your generations. 22 When you reap the harvest of your land, you are not to reap all the way to the edge of your field or gather the gleanings of your harvest. Leave them for the poor and the foreign resident;[e] I am •Yahweh your God."

23 The LORD spoke to Moses: 24 "Tell the Israelites: In the seventh month, on the first day of the month, you are to have a day of complete rest, commemoration, and joyful shouting[H,f] — a sacred assembly.[g] 25 You must not do any daily work, but you must present a fire offering to the LORD."

26 The LORD again spoke to Moses: 27 "The tenth day of this seventh month is the Day of •Atonement.[h] You are to hold a sacred assembly and practice self-denial;[I,i] you are to present a fire offering to the LORD. 28 On this particular day you are not to do any work, for it is a Day of Atonement to make atonement for yourselves before the LORD your God. 29 If any person does not practice self-denial on this particular day, he must be cut off from his people. 30 I will destroy among his people anyone who does any work on this same day. 31 You are not to do any work. This is a permanent statute throughout your generations wherever you live. 32 It will be a Sabbath of complete rest for you, and you must practice self-denial. You are to observe your Sabbath from the evening of the ninth day of the month until the following evening."

33 The LORD spoke to Moses: 34 "Tell the Israelites: The Festival of Booths[J,j] to the LORD begins on the fifteenth day of this seventh month and continues for seven days. 35 There is to be a sacred assembly on the first day; you are not to do any daily work. 36 You are to present a fire offering to the LORD for seven days. On the eighth day you are to hold a sacred assembly and present a fire offering to the LORD. It is a solemn gathering;[k] you are not to do any daily work.

37 "These are the LORD's appointed times that you are to proclaim as sacred assemblies for presenting fire offerings to the LORD, burnt offerings and grain offerings, sacrifices and drink offerings, each on its designated day. 38 These are in addition to the offerings for the LORD's Sabbaths, your gifts, all your vow offerings, and all your freewill offerings that you give to the LORD.

39 "You are to celebrate the LORD's festival on the fifteenth day of the seventh month

[a] **23:12** Ex 29:1
[b] **23:15** Ex 34:22; Nm 28:26; Dt 16:10; Ac 2:1
[c] Ex 29:24
[d] **23:17** Lv 2:12; 1Co 15:20; Rv 14:4
[e] **23:22** Ex 2:22; Lv 19:9-10; Ac 6:1; 11:29
[f] **23:24** Lv 25:9; Nm 5:15
[g] Nm 29:1; Ps 81:3
[h] **23:27** Ex 30:10; Lv 16:29-30; 25:9; Nm 29:7-11
[i] Ac 27:9
[j] **23:34** Ex 23:16; Jn 7:37
[k] **23:36** Nm 29:35

[A] **23:12** Or *a male lamb in its first year* [B] **23:13,17** Lit *two-tenths of an ephah* [C] **23:13** Lit *one-fourth of a hin* [D] **23:14** Grain or bread from the new harvest [E] **23:15** Lit *count; they will be seven* [F] **23:15** Or *Sabbaths* [G] **23:16** = the wheat harvest; Ex 34:22 [H] **23:24** Or *blast*; traditionally trumpet blasts [I] **23:27** Traditionally, fasting, abstinence from sex, and refraining from personal grooming [J] **23:34** Or *Feast of Tabernacles* for seven days after you have gathered the produce of the land. There will be complete rest on the first day and complete rest on the eighth day. 40On the first day you are to take the product[a] of majestic trees — palm fronds,[b] boughs of leafy trees,[c] and willows of the brook[d] — and rejoice before the LORD your God for seven days. 41You are to celebrate it as a festival to the LORD seven days each year. This is a permanent statute for you throughout your generations; you must celebrate it in the seventh month. 42You are to live in booths[e] for seven days. All the native-born of Israel must live in booths, 43so that your generations may know that I made the Israelites live in booths when I brought them out of the land of Egypt; I am Yahweh your God." 44So Moses declared the LORD's appointed times to the Israelites.

Tabernacle Oil and Bread

24 The LORD spoke to Moses: 2"Command the Israelites to bring you pure oil from crushed olives for the light, in order to keep the lamp burning continually.[f] 3Aaron is to tend it continually from evening until morning before the LORD outside the veil[g] of the •testimony[h] in the tent of meeting. This is a permanent statute throughout your generations. 4He must continually tend the lamps on the pure gold lampstand in the LORD's presence.[i]

5"Take fine flour and bake it into 12 loaves;[j] each loaf is to be made with four quarts.[A] 6Arrange them in two rows, six to a row, on the pure gold table[k] before the LORD. 7Place pure frankincense[l] near each row, so that it may serve as a memorial portion[m] for the bread and a fire offering[n] to the LORD. 8The bread is to be set out before the LORD every Sabbath day as a perpetual covenant[o] obligation on the part of the Israelites. 9It belongs to Aaron and his sons, who are to eat it in a holy place, for it is the holiest portion for him from the fire offerings to the LORD; this is a permanent rule."

A Case of Blasphemy

10Now the son of an Israelite mother and an Egyptian father was[B] among the Israelites. A fight broke out in the camp between the Israelite woman's son and an Israelite man. 11Her son cursed and blasphemed the Name,[p] and they brought him to Moses. (His mother's name was Shelomith, a daughter of Dibri of the tribe of Dan.[q]) 12They put him in custody[r] until the LORD's decision[s] could be made clear to them.

13Then the LORD spoke to Moses: 14"Bring the one who has cursed to the outside of the camp and have all who heard him lay their hands on his head; then have the whole community stone him.[t] 15And tell the Israelites: If anyone curses his God, he will bear the consequences of his sin. 16Whoever blasphemes the name of •Yahweh is to be put to death;[u] the whole community must stone him. If he blasphemes the Name, he is to be put to death, whether the foreign resident or the native.

17"If a man kills anyone, he must be put to death.[v] 18Whoever kills an animal is to make restitution for it, life for life. 19If any man inflicts a permanent injury on his neighbor, whatever he has done is to be done to him: 20fracture for fracture, eye for eye, tooth for tooth. Whatever injury he inflicted on the person, the same is to be inflicted on him.[w] 21Whoever kills an animal is to make restitution for it, but whoever kills a person is to be put to death.[x] 22You are to have the same law for the foreign resident and the native, because I am Yahweh your God."

23After Moses spoke to the Israelites, they brought the one who had cursed to the outside of the camp and stoned him. So the Israelites did as the LORD had commanded Moses.

Sabbath Years and Jubilee

25 The LORD spoke to Moses on Mount Sinai: 2"Speak to the Israelites and tell them: When you enter the land I am giving you, the land will observe a Sabbath to the LORD. 3You may sow your field for six years, and you may prune your vineyard and gather its produce for six years. 4But there will be a Sabbath of complete rest[y] for the land in the seventh year, a Sabbath to the LORD: you are not to sow your field or prune your vineyard. 5You are not to reap what grows by itself from

[a]**23:40** Gn 1:11 [b]Ex 15:27; Nm 33:9; Jdg 4:5; Neh 8:15; Ps 92:12; Sg 7:8-9; Jl 1:12; Rv 7:9 [c]Neh 8:15; Ezk 6:13; 20:28 [d]Jb 40:22; Is 44:4 [e]**23:42** Gn 33:17; Dt 16:13,16; 31:10; Neh 8:14-17; Am 9:11; Jnh 4:5 [f]**24:2** Ex 25:37 [g]**24:3** Mk 15:38; Heb 6:19 [h]Ex 31:18 [i]**24:4** Gn 4:14; Ex 25:31; 37:17; Zch 4:2 [j]**24:5** Ex 25:30 [k]**24:6** Ex 25:23; Heb 9:2 [l]**24:7** Ex 30:34 [m]Lv 2:2 [n]Dt 18:1 [o]**24:8** Ex 19:5 [p]**24:11** Ex 20:7; Lv 24:16; Nm 15:30; 1Sm 3:13; Neh 9:18 [q]Gn 49:16 [r]**24:12** Gn 40:3-7; 41:10; 42:17 [s]Nm 3:39; 15:32-36 [t]**24:14** Lv 20:2,27; 24:16,23; Nm 14:10; 15:35-36; Dt 21:21; Jos 7:25; 1Kg 12:18; Ezk 16:40; 23:47; Jn 10:33 [u]**24:16** Ex 20:7; 22:28; 1Kg 21:10,13; Jn 8:59; 19:7; 2Tm 2:19 [v]**24:17** Gn 9:5-6; Ex 20:13; 21:12-14; Nm 35:30-31 [w]**24:19-20** Ex 21:24; Dt 19:21; Mt 5:38-39; 7:12 [x]**24:21** Nm 35:30-33 [y]**25:4** Lv 16:31

[A]**24:5** Lit *two-tenths of an ephah* [B]**24:10** Lit *went out* your crop, or harvest the grapes of your untended vines. It must be a year of complete rest for the land. 6Whatever the land produces during the Sabbath year can be food for you — for yourself, your male or female slave, and the hired hand or foreigner who stays with you. 7All of its growth may serve as food for your livestock and the wild animals in your land.

8"You are to count seven sabbatical years, seven times seven years, so that the time period of the seven sabbatical years amounts to 49. 9Then you are to sound a trumpet loudly in the seventh month, on the tenth day of the month; you will sound it throughout your land on the Day of •Atonement.[a] 10You are to consecrate the fiftieth year and proclaim freedom in the land for all its inhabitants. It will be your Jubilee,[b] when each of you is to return to his property and each of you to his clan. 11The fiftieth year will be your Jubilee; you are not to sow, reap what grows by itself, or harvest its untended vines. 12It is to be holy to you because it is the Jubilee; you may only eat its produce directly from the field.

13"In this Year of Jubilee, each of you will return to his property. 14If you make a sale to your neighbor or a purchase from him, do not cheat[c] one another. 15You are to make the purchase from your neighbor based on the number of years since the last Jubilee. He is to sell to you based on the number of remaining harvest years. 16You are to increase its price in proportion to a greater amount of years, and decrease its price in proportion to a lesser amount of years, because what he is selling to you is a number of harvests. 17You are not to cheat one another, but •fear your God, for I am •Yahweh your God.

18"You are to keep My statutes and ordinances and carefully observe them, so that you may live securely in the land.[d] 19Then the land will yield its fruit, so that you can eat, be satisfied, and live securely in the land. 20If you wonder: 'What will we eat in the seventh year if we don't sow or gather our produce?' 21I will appoint My blessing for you in the sixth year, so that it will produce a crop sufficient for three years. 22When you sow in the eighth year, you will be eating from the previous harvest. You will be eating this until the ninth year when its harvest comes in.

23"The land is not to be permanently sold because it is Mine, and you are only foreigners and temporary residents on My land.[A,e] 24You are to allow the redemption of any land you occupy. 25If your brother becomes destitute and sells part of his property, his nearest relative may come and redeem what his brother has sold. 26If a man has no •family redeemer, but he prospers[B] and obtains enough to redeem his land, 27he may calculate the years since its sale, repay the balance to the man he sold it to, and return to his property. 28But if he cannot obtain enough to repay him, what he sold will remain in the possession of its purchaser until the Year of Jubilee. It is to be released at the Jubilee, so that he may return to his property.

29"If a man sells a residence in a walled city, his right of redemption will last until a year has passed after its sale; his right of redemption will last a year. 30If it is not redeemed by the end of a full year, then the house in the walled city is permanently transferred to its purchaser throughout his generations. It is not to be released on the Jubilee. 31But houses in villages that have no walls around them are to be classified as open fields. The right to redeem such houses stays in effect, and they are to be released at the Jubilee.

32"Concerning the Levitical cities,[f] the Levites always have the right to redeem houses in the cities they possess. 33Whatever property one of the Levites can redeem[C] — a house sold in a city they possess — must be released at the Jubilee, because the houses in the Levitical cities are their possession among the Israelites. 34The open pastureland around their cities may not be sold, for it is their permanent possession.

35"If your brother becomes destitute and cannot sustain himself among[D] you, you are to support him as a foreigner or temporary resident, so that he can continue to live among you. 36Do not profit or take interest from him,[g] but fear your God and let your brother live among you. 37You are not to lend him your silver with interest or sell him your food for profit. 38I am Yahweh your God, who

[a] **25:9** Lv 23:27 [b] **25:10** Lv 27:17-24; Nm 36:4; Dt 15:1 [c] **25:14** Dt 23:16 [d] **25:18** Lv 18:4-5,26; 19:37; 20:8,22; 26:3-5 [e] **25:23** 1Ch 29:15; Heb 11:13 [f] **25:32** Nm 35:1-8; Dt 18:1-2; 19:2-9; Jos 21; 1Ch 6:54-81 [g] **25:36** Ex 22:25; Dt 23:19-20; Ezk 22:12

A**25:23** Lit *residents with Me* B**25:26** Lit *but his hand reaches* C**25:33** Hb obscure D**25:35** Lit *and his hand falters with*

brought you out of the land of Egypt to give
you the land of Canaan and to be your God.
39"If your brother among you becomes
destitute and sells himself to you,[a] you must
not force him to do slave labor. 40Let him stay
with you as a hired hand or temporary resident; he may work for you until the Year of
Jubilee. 41Then he and his children are to be
released from you, and he may return to his
clan and his ancestral property.[b] 42They are
not to be sold as slaves,[A] because they are My
slaves that I brought out of the land of Egypt.
43You are not to rule over them harshly[c] but
fear your God. 44Your male and female slaves
are to be from the nations around you; you
may purchase male and female slaves. 45You
may also purchase them from the foreigners
staying with you, or from their families living among you — those born in your land.
These may become your property. 46You may
leave them to your sons after you to inherit as
property; you can make them slaves for life.
But concerning your brothers, the Israelites,
you must not rule over one another harshly.
47"If a foreigner or temporary resident living among you prospers, but your brother
living near him becomes destitute and sells
himself to the foreigner living among you,
or to a member of the foreigner's clan, 48he
has the right of redemption after he has been
sold. One of his brothers may redeem him.
49His uncle or cousin may redeem him, or
any of his close relatives from his clan may
redeem him. If he prospers, he may redeem
himself. 50The one who purchased him is to
calculate the time from the year he sold himself to him until the Year of Jubilee. The price
of his sale will be determined by the number
of years. It will be set for him like the daily
wages of a hired hand. 51If many years are still
left, he must pay his redemption price in proportion to them based on his purchase price.
52If only a few years remain until the Year of
Jubilee, he will calculate and pay the price of
his redemption in proportion to his remaining years. 53He will stay with him like a man
hired year by year. A foreign owner is not to
rule over him harshly in your sight. 54If he is
not redeemed in any of these ways, he and his
children are to be released at the Year of Jubilee. 55For the Israelites are My slaves.[d] They
are My slaves that I brought out of the land of
Egypt; I am Yahweh your God.

Covenant Blessings and Discipline

26 "Do not make idols for yourselves,[e] set
up a carved image or sacred pillar for
yourselves, or place a sculpted stone in your
land to bow down to it, for I am •Yahweh your
God. 2You must keep My Sabbaths and revere
My sanctuary;[f] I am Yahweh.
3"If you follow My statutes and faithfully
observe My commands, 4I will give you rain
at the right time, and the land will yield its
produce, and the trees of the field will bear
their fruit. 5Your threshing will continue until grape harvest, and the grape harvest will
continue until sowing time; you will have
plenty of food to eat and live securely in your
land.[g] 6I will give peace to the land, and you
will lie down with nothing to frighten you.
I will remove dangerous animals from the
land, and no sword will pass through your
land.[h] 7You will pursue your enemies, and
they will fall before you by the sword. 8Five
of you will pursue 100, and 100 of you will
pursue 10,000; your enemies will fall before
you by the sword.[i]
9"I will turn to you, make you fruitful and
multiply you, and confirm My covenant with
you. 10You will eat the old grain of the previous year and will clear out the old to make
room for the new. 11I will place My residence[B]
among you, and I will not reject you.[j] 12I will
walk among you and be your God, and you
will be My people.[k] 13I am Yahweh your God,
who brought you out of the land of Egypt, so
that you would no longer be their slaves. I
broke the bars of your yoke[l] and enabled you
to live in freedom.[C]
14"But if you do not obey Me and observe all
these commands — 15if you reject My statutes
and despise My ordinances, and do not observe all My commands — and break My covenant, 16then I will do this to you: I will bring
terror[m] on you — wasting disease and fever
that will cause your eyes to fail and your life
to ebb away. You will sow your seed in vain
because your enemies will eat it. 17I will turn[D]
against you, so that you will be defeated by

[a]**25:39** 2Kg 4:1; Neh 5:5; Is 50:1; Mt 18:25 [b]**25:41** Ex 21:3-6 [c]**25:43** Ex 1:13-14 [d]**25:55** Ex 4:10 [e]**26:1** Ex 20:3-4; Ps 81:9 [f]**26:2** Ex 15:17; Lv 19:30; Ezk 20:13,16,21; 23:38 [g]**26:3-5** Lv 25:18-19; Dt 28:1-2,12; Is 30:21-23; Am 9:13 [h]**26:6** Jr 30:10; Ezk 34:25,28; Mc 4:4 [i]**26:7-8** Dt 3:22; 32:30; Jos 10:19; 23:3,10 [j]**26:11** Ex 25:8; 29:45-46; Lv 26:44; 1Kg 6:13 [k]**26:12** Jr 7:23; Lk 1:68; 2Co 6:16; Rv 21:3 [l]**26:13** Ex 6:6-7; Is 9:4; Jr 5:5; 28:10-11 [m]**26:16** Ps 78:33; Is 65:23; Jr 15:8

[A]**25:42** Lit *sold with a sale of a slave* [B]**26:11** Or *tabernacle* [C]**26:13** Lit *to walk uprightly* [D]**26:17** Lit *will set My face*

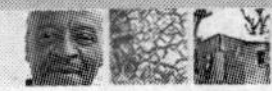

your enemies. Those who hate you will rule over you, and you will flee even though no one is pursuing you.[a]

18 "But if after these things you will not obey Me, I will proceed to discipline you seven times for your sins.[b] 19 I will break down your strong pride. I will make your sky like iron and your land like bronze, 20 and your strength will be used up for nothing.[c] Your land will not yield its produce, and the trees of the land will not bear their fruit.

21 "If you act with hostility toward Me and are unwilling to obey Me, I will multiply your plagues seven times for your sins.[d] 22 I will send wild animals against you that will deprive you of your children, ravage your livestock, and reduce your numbers until your roads are deserted.[e]

23 "If in spite of these things you do not accept My discipline, but act with hostility toward Me, 24 then I will act with hostility toward you; I also will strike you seven times for your sins. 25 I will bring a sword against you[f] to execute the vengeance of the covenant. Though you withdraw into your cities, I will send a pestilence among you, and you will be delivered into enemy hands. 26 When I cut off your supply of bread, 10 women will bake your bread in a single oven and ration out your bread by weight, so that you will eat but not be satisfied.[g]

27 "And if in spite of this you do not obey Me but act with hostility toward Me, 28 I will act with furious hostility toward you; I will also discipline you seven times for your sins. 29 You will eat the flesh of your sons; you will eat the flesh of your daughters.[h] 30 I will destroy your *high places, cut down your incense altars, and heap your dead bodies on the lifeless bodies of your idols;[i] I will reject you. 31 I will reduce your cities to ruins and devastate your sanctuaries. I will not smell the pleasing aroma of your sacrifices.[j] 32 I also will devastate the land, so that your enemies who come to live there will be appalled by it. 33 But I will scatter you among the nations, and I will draw a sword to chase after you. So your land will become desolate, and your cities will become ruins.

34 "Then the land will make up for its Sabbath years during the time it lies desolate, while you are in the land of your enemies. At that time the land will rest and make up for its Sabbaths. 35 As long as it lies desolate, it will have the rest it did not have during your Sabbaths when you lived there.

36 "I will put anxiety in the hearts of those of you who survive in the lands of their enemies. The sound of a wind-driven leaf will put them to flight, and they will flee as one flees from a sword, and fall though no one is pursuing them. 37 They will stumble over one another as if fleeing from a sword though no one is pursuing them. You will not be able to stand against your enemies. 38 You will perish among the nations; the land of your enemies will devour you. 39 Those[A] who survive in the lands of your enemies will waste away because of their sin; they will also waste away because of their fathers' sins along with theirs.

40 "But if they will confess their sin and the sin of their fathers—their unfaithfulness that they practiced against Me, and how they acted with hostility toward Me, 41 and I acted with hostility toward them and brought them into the land of their enemies—and if their uncircumcised hearts will be humbled,[k] and if they will pay the penalty for their sin, 42 then I will remember My covenant with Jacob. I will also remember My covenant with Isaac and My covenant with Abraham, and I will remember the land. 43 For the land abandoned by them will make up for its Sabbaths by lying desolate without the people, while they pay the penalty for their sin, because they rejected My ordinances and abhorred My statutes. 44 Yet in spite of this, while they are in the land of their enemies, I will not reject or abhor them so as to destroy them and break My covenant with them, since I am Yahweh their God.[l] 45 For their sake I will remember the covenant with their fathers, whom I brought out of the land of Egypt in the sight of the nations to be their God; I am Yahweh."

46 These are the statutes, ordinances, and laws the LORD established between Himself and the Israelites through Moses on Mount Sinai.

[a] **26:17** Ex 12:23; Dt 28:25
[b] **26:18** Gn 4:15,24; Heb 12:4-11
[c] **26:20** Dt 28:23; Am 4:7-8
[d] **26:21** Gn 4:15,24
[e] **26:22** Dt 32:24; Jdg 5:6; Is 33:8; Lm 1:1-4; Ezk 14:15; Zch 7:14
[f] **26:25** Ezk 14:21
[g] **26:26** Is 3:1; Ezk 4:16; 14:13; Am 4:6; Mc 6:14
[h] **26:29** Dt 28:53-57; 2Kg 6:28-29; Jr 19:9; Lm 4:10; Mc 3:2-3
[i] **26:30** Gn 31:19; Ezk 6:3-6
[j] **26:31** Gn 8:21; 1Sm 26:19; Am 5:21-22
[k] **26:41** Dt 30:6; Jr 4:4; 9:25; Ezk 44:7,9
[l] **26:44** Gn 17:8; Ezk 36:22; Hs 11:8-9; Zch 10:9

[A] **26:39** Lit *Those of you*

Funding the Sanctuary

27 The LORD spoke to Moses: 2"Speak to
the Israelites and tell them: When
someone makes a special vow[a] to the LORD
that involves the assessment of people, 3if the
assessment concerns a male from 20 to 60
years old, your assessment is 50 silver •shek-
els[b] measured by the standard sanctuary
shekel.[c] 4If the person is a female, your assessment is 30 shekels.[d] 5If the person is from five
to 20 years old, your assessment for a male is
20 shekels[e] and for a female 10 shekels. 6If the
person is from one month to five years old,
your assessment for a male is five silver shekels,[f] and for a female your assessment is three
shekels of silver. 7If the person is 60 years or
more, your assessment is 15 shekels for a male
and 10 shekels for a female. 8But if one is too
poor to pay the assessment, he must present
the person before the priest and the priest
will set a value for him. The priest will set a
value for him according to what the one making the vow can afford.

9"If the vow involves one of the animals
that may be brought as an offering to the
LORD, any of these he gives to the LORD will
be holy. 10He may not replace it or make a substitution for it, either good for bad, or bad for
good.[g] But if he does substitute one animal
for another, both that animal and its substitute will be holy.

11"If the vow involves any of the •unclean
animals that may not be brought as an offering to the LORD, the animal must be presented before the priest. 12The priest will set
its value, whether high or low; the price will
be set as the priest makes the assessment for
you. 13If the one who brought it decides to redeem it, he must add a fifth to the[A] assessed
value.[h]

14"When a man consecrates his house as
holy to the LORD, the priest will assess its
value, whether high or low. The price will
stand just as the priest assesses it. 15But if the
one who consecrated his house redeems it, he
must add a fifth to the[A] assessed value, and it
will be his.[i]

16"If a man consecrates to the LORD any
part of a field that he possesses, your assessment of value will be proportional to the seed
needed to sow it, at the rate of 50 silver shekels for every five bushels[B] of barley seed.[C] 17If
he consecrates his field during the Year of Jubilee,[j] the price will stand according to your
assessment. 18But if he consecrates his field
after the Jubilee, the priest will calculate the
price for him in proportion to the years left
until the next Year of Jubilee, so that your assessment will be reduced. 19If the one who
consecrated the field decides to redeem it, he
must add a fifth to the[A] assessed value, and
the field will transfer back to him. 20But if he
does not redeem the field or if he has sold it
to another man, it is no longer redeemable.
21When the field is released in the Jubilee, it
will be holy to the LORD like a field permanently set apart; it becomes the priest's property.

22"If a person consecrates to the LORD a
field he has purchased that is not part of his
inherited landholding, 23then the priest will
calculate for him the amount of the[A] assessment up to the Year of Jubilee, and the person will pay the assessed value on that day
as a holy offering to the LORD. 24In the Year
of Jubilee the field will return to the one he
bought it from,[k] the original owner. 25All
your assessed values will be measured by the
standard sanctuary shekel, 20 *gerahs* to the
shekel.[l]

26"But no one can consecrate a firstborn
of the livestock, whether an animal from
the herd or flock, to the LORD, because a
firstborn already belongs to the LORD.[m] 27If
it is one of the unclean livestock, it must be
ransomed according to your assessment by
adding a fifth of its value to it. If it is not redeemed, it can be sold according to your assessment.[n]

28"Nothing that a man permanently sets
apart to the LORD from all he owns, whether a
person, an animal, or his inherited landholding, can be sold or redeemed; everything set
apart is especially holy to the LORD. 29No person who has been set apart for destruction is
to be ransomed; he must be put to death.[o]

30"Every tenth of the land's produce, grain
from the soil or fruit from the trees, belongs
to the LORD;[p] it is holy to the LORD. 31If a man
decides to redeem any part of this tenth, he

[a]**27:2** Lv 27:8 [b]**27:3** 2Kg 15:20 [c]Ex 30:13; Lv 5:15; 27:25; Nm 3:47 [d]**27:4** Ex 21:32 [e]**27:5** Gn 37:28 [f]**27:6** Nm 3:46-47; 18:15-16 [g]**27:10** Mal 1:8 [h]**27:13** Gn 47:24; Lv 5:16; 6:5 [i]**27:14-15** Lv 25:29-31 [j]**27:17** Lv 25:10 [k]**27:24** Lv 25:28 [l]**27:25** Ex 30:13; Nm 18:16; Ezk 45:12 [m]**27:26** Ex 13:2,15; 34:19; Nm 18:15 [n]**27:27** Ex 13:13; 34:20 [o]**27:29** Nm 21:1-3; 31:7,13-17; Jos 6:17; 1Sm 15:17-33 [p]**27:30** Nm 18:21-32; Dt 14:22-29; Neh 10:37-39

[A]**27:13,15,19,23** Lit *your* [B]**27:16** Lit *for a homer* [C]**27:16** Or *grain*

must add a fifth to its value. 32 Every tenth
animal from the herd or flock, which passes
under the shepherd's rod,[a] will be holy to the
LORD. 33 He is not to inspect whether it is good
or bad, and he is not to make a substitution
for it. But if he does make a substitution, both
the animal and its substitute will be holy;[b]
they cannot be redeemed."[c]

34 These are the commands the LORD gave
Moses for the Israelites on Mount Sinai.[d]

[a] 27:32 Gn 28:22; 2Ch 31:6; Jr 33:13
[b] 27:33 Lv 12:4; 25:12
[c] Lv 27:10
[d] 27:34 Nm 36:13

AUTHOR: Moses

DATE: Most likely written during Israel's wandering in the wilderness (around 1445–1406 B.C.)

God has made His plan clear. He will create a special people, a nation to whom He will reveal His will and grace. To this people, the true God will be known through a long series of failures and successes.

The book of Numbers describes the wilderness wanderings of the Hebrews. They had been rescued from Egypt and directed by God to Canaan, the promised land. Once there, they would thrive and grow as a nation, becoming a witness to the world about the One and only true God.

You might think that a mission this important would inspire the Israelites to eager obedience. You might think that after all they saw God do for them, they would know that He would not fail them against the people (some very large people) who currently occupy Canaan. But just the opposite happens: The people refuse to trust God. And the result is forty years of wandering in circles and zigzags with a strange diet and the sad certainty that all the generation who escaped from Pharaoh will die before entering Canaan. This is God's way of insisting that His mission is serious; it requires faith and perseverance. Disobedience carries consequences. That lesson is as important in the twenty-first century as it was three millennia ago. Disobedience is a costly mistake. It breaks faith with God. It disregards God's heart.

NUMBERS

One of the most shocking episodes in the Bible occurs during these wilderness wanderings. King Balak of Moab hires a prophet, Balaam, whose profession is to curse or bless—depending on who's paying. In this odd assignment, Balaam's boss wants him to curse the Israelites because he's afraid of their growing army and seeks whatever divine power he can muster against them. Little does Balaam suspect that the real God is about to speak to him. Balaam's own donkey opens her mouth and speaks after he beats her for trying to save both of their lives. When God wants to teach a lesson, He will use whatever resources are at His disposal.

Yet the most obvious part of God's mission revealed in Numbers is not punitive but powerful and restorative. God will punish disobedience, but He will not break faith with people who have heard His promise.

Christians can learn from the Israelites' experience. God is faithful, loyal, trustworthy, powerful; He will save. Through the rebellions, battles, deaths, and uncertainties, God is moving toward His goal. The kingdom of God will be established on the earth. His desire to see people from every corner of the globe come to salvation will be accomplished. God is patient and determined. God is a loving, forgiving Father to these people, but He does not lightly dismiss their disloyalty. God will teach the Hebrews first to love and obey, and then, all will see and follow.

As Numbers ends, we stand on the riverbank and look across the Jordan into the promised land. God has proven Himself trustworthy. Will they trust Him this time?

The Census of Israel

1 The LORD spoke to Moses in the tent of
meeting in the Wilderness of Sinai, on the
first day of the second month of the second
year[a] after Israel's departure from the land of
Egypt: 2"Take a census[b] of the entire Israelite
community by their clans and their ancestral
houses, counting the names of every male
one by one. 3You and Aaron are to register
those who are 20 years old or more by their
military divisions—everyone who can serve
in Israel's army.[A] 4A man from each tribe is to
be with you, each one the head of his ancestral house.[c] 5These are the names of the men
who are to assist you:

Elizur son of Shedeur from Reuben;
6 Shelumiel son of Zurishaddai
from Simeon;
7 Nahshon son of Amminadab
from Judah;
8 Nethanel son of Zuar from Issachar;
9 Eliab son of Helon from Zebulun;
10 from the sons of Joseph:
Elishama son of Ammihud
from Ephraim,
Gamaliel son of Pedahzur
from Manasseh;
11 Abidan son of Gideoni
from Benjamin;
12 Ahiezer son of Ammishaddai
from Dan;
13 Pagiel son of Ochran from Asher;
14 Eliasaph son of Deuel[B] from Gad;
15 Ahira son of Enan from Naphtali.

16These are the men called from the community; they are leaders of their ancestral tribes,
the heads of Israel's clans."

17So Moses and Aaron took these men who
had been designated by name, 18and they assembled the whole community on the first
day of the second month. They recorded
their ancestry by their clans and their ancestral houses, counting one by one the names of
those 20 years old or more, 19just as the LORD
commanded Moses. He registered them in
the Wilderness of Sinai:

20The descendants of Reuben,[d] the firstborn of Israel: according to their family
records by their clans and their ancestral
houses, counting one by one the names
of every male 20 years old or more, everyone who could serve in the army, 21those
registered for the tribe of Reuben numbered 46,500.

22The descendants of Simeon:[e] according
to their family records by their clans and
their ancestral houses, those registered
counting one by one the names of every
male 20 years old or more, everyone who
could serve in the army, 23those registered for the tribe of Simeon numbered
59,300.

24The descendants of Gad:[f] according to
their family records by their clans and
their ancestral houses, counting the
names of those 20 years old or more,
everyone who could serve in the army,
25those registered for the tribe of Gad
numbered 45,650.

26The descendants of Judah:[g] according
to their family records by their clans
and their ancestral houses, counting the
names of those 20 years old or more,
everyone who could serve in the army,
27those registered for the tribe of Judah
numbered 74,600.

28The descendants of Issachar:[h] according to their family records by their clans
and their ancestral houses, counting the
names of those 20 years old or more,
everyone who could serve in the army,
29those registered for the tribe of Issachar numbered 54,400.

30The descendants of Zebulun:[i] according to their family records by their clans
and their ancestral houses, counting the
names of those 20 years old or more,
everyone who could serve in the army,
31those registered for the tribe of Zebulun numbered 57,400.

32The descendants of Joseph:[j]

The descendants of Ephraim:[k] according to their family records by their
clans and their ancestral houses, counting the names of those 20 years old or

[a]1:1 Ex 12:40-41; 19:1; 40:17
[b]1:2 Ex 30:11-16; Nm 26:2
[c]1:4 Nm 1:16; Jos 22:14
[d]1:20 Gn 29:32; 49:3-4; 1Ch 5:1
[e]1:22 Gn 29:33; 42:14-24; 49:5-7
[f]1:24 Gn 30:11; 49:19
[g]1:26 Gn 29:35; 49:8-12; Mt 1:2-3; Rv 5:5
[h]1:28 Gn 30:18; 49:14-15
[i]1:30 Gn 30:20; 49:13
[j]1:32 Gn 30:22-24; 49:22-26
[k]Gn 46:20; 48:13-20

[A]1:3 Lit *everyone going out to war in Israel* [B]1:14 LXX, Syr read *Reuel* more, everyone who could serve in the army, 33 those registered for the tribe of Ephraim numbered 40,500.

34 The descendants of Manasseh:[a] according to their family records by their clans and their ancestral houses, counting the names of those 20 years old or more, everyone who could serve in the army, 35 those registered for the tribe of Manasseh numbered 32,200.

36 The descendants of Benjamin:[b] according to their family records by their clans and their ancestral houses, counting the names of those 20 years old or more, everyone who could serve in the army, 37 those registered for the tribe of Benjamin numbered 35,400.

38 The descendants of Dan:[c] according to their family records by their clans and their ancestral houses, counting the names of those 20 years old or more, everyone who could serve in the army, 39 those registered for the tribe of Dan numbered 62,700.

40 The descendants of Asher:[d] according to their family records by their clans and their ancestral houses, counting the names of those 20 years old or more, everyone who could serve in the army, 41 those registered for the tribe of Asher numbered 41,500.

42 The descendants of Naphtali:[e] according to their family records by their clans and their ancestral houses, counting the names of those 20 years old or more, everyone who could serve in the army, 43 those registered for the tribe of Naphtali numbered 53,400.

44 These are the men Moses and Aaron registered, with the assistance of the 12 leaders of Israel; each represented his ancestral house. 45 So all the Israelites 20 years old or more, everyone who could serve in Israel's army, were registered by their ancestral houses. 46 All those registered numbered 603,550.[f]

Duties of the Levites

47 But the Levites were not registered with them by their ancestral tribe. 48 For the LORD had told Moses: 49 "Do not register or take a census of the tribe of Levi with the other Israelites. 50 Appoint the Levites over the tabernacle of the ·testimony, all its furnishings, and everything in it. They are to transport the tabernacle and all its articles, take care of it, and camp around it. 51 Whenever the tabernacle is to move, the Levites are to take it down, and whenever it is to stop at a campsite, the Levites are to set it up. Any unauthorized person who comes near it must be put to death.[g]

52 "The Israelites are to camp by their military divisions, each man with his encampment and under his banner. 53 The Levites are to camp around the tabernacle of the testimony and watch over it, so that no wrath will fall on the Israelite community."[h] 54 The Israelites did everything just as the LORD had commanded Moses.

Organization of the Camps

2 The LORD spoke to Moses and Aaron: 2 "The Israelites are to camp under their respective banners beside the flags of their ancestral houses. They are to camp around the tent of meeting at a distance from it:

3 Judah's military divisions will camp on the east side toward the sunrise under their banner. The leader of the descendants of Judah is Nahshon son of Amminadab. 4 His military division numbers 74,600. 5 The tribe of Issachar will camp next to it. The leader of the Issacharites is Nethanel son of Zuar. 6 His military division numbers 54,400. 7 The tribe of Zebulun will be next. The leader of the Zebulunites is Eliab son of Helon. 8 His military division numbers 57,400. 9 The total number in their military divisions who belong to Judah's encampment is 186,400; they will move out first.

10 Reuben's military divisions will camp on the south side under their banner. The leader of the Reubenites is Elizur son of Shedeur. 11 His military division numbers 46,500. 12 The tribe of Simeon will camp next to it. The leader of the Simeonites is Shelumiel son of Zurishaddai. 13 His military division numbers 59,300. 14 The tribe of Gad will be next. The leader of the

[a] **1:34** Gn 46:20; 48:13-20
[b] **1:36** Gn 35:18; 49:27
[c] **1:38** Gn 30:6; 49:16-17
[d] **1:40** Gn 30:13; 49:20
[e] **1:42** Gn 30:8; 49:21
[f] **1:46** Ex 12:37; Nm 26:51
[g] **1:51** Nm 3:10,38; 8:19; 18:7
[h] **1:53** Nm 3:7; 18:4-5; 1Ch 23:32; Ezk 44:15-16

Gadites is Eliasaph son of Deuel.[A] 15His
military division numbers 45,650. 16The
total number in their military divisions
who belong to Reuben's encampment is
151,450; they will move out second.

17The tent of meeting is to move out with
the Levites' camp, which is in the middle
of the camps. They are to move out just as
they camp, each in his place,[B] with their
banners.

18Ephraim's military divisions will camp
on the west side under their banner.
The leader of the Ephraimites is Elishama son of Ammihud. 19His military division numbers 40,500. 20The tribe of
Manasseh will be next to it. The leader
of the Manassites is Gamaliel son of Pedahzur. 21His military division numbers
32,200. 22The tribe of Benjamin will be
next. The leader of the Benjaminites is
Abidan son of Gideoni. 23His military
division numbers 35,400. 24The total
in their military divisions who belong
to Ephraim's encampment number
108,100; they will move out third.

25Dan's military divisions will camp on
the north side under their banner. The
leader of the Danites is Ahiezer son of
Ammishaddai. 26His military division
numbers 62,700. 27The tribe of Asher
will camp next to it. The leader of the
Asherites is Pagiel son of Ochran. 28His
military division numbers 41,500. 29The
tribe of Naphtali will be next. The leader
of the Naphtalites is Ahira son of Enan.
30His military division numbers 53,400.
31The total number who belong to Dan's
encampment is 157,600; they are to move
out last, with their banners."

32These are the Israelites registered by
their ancestral houses. The total number
in the camps by their military divisions
is 603,550. 33But the Levites were not registered among the Israelites, just as the
LORD had commanded Moses.[a]

34The Israelites did everything the LORD commanded Moses; they camped by their banners in this way and moved out the same way,
each man by his clan and by his ancestral
house.[b]

Aaron's Sons and the Levites

3 These are the family records of Aaron and
Moses at the time the LORD spoke with
Moses on Mount Sinai.[c] 2These are the names
of Aaron's sons: Nadab, the firstborn, and
Abihu, Eleazar, and Ithamar. 3These are the
names of Aaron's sons, the anointed priests,
who were ordained to serve as priests. 4But
Nadab and Abihu died in the LORD's presence when they presented unauthorized fire[d]
before the LORD in the Wilderness of Sinai,
and they had no sons. So Eleazar and Ithamar
served as priests under the direction of Aaron
their father.[e]

5The LORD spoke to Moses: 6"Bring the tribe
of Levi near and present them to Aaron the
priest to assist him. 7They are to perform duties for[C] him and the entire community before the tent of meeting by attending to the
service of the tabernacle. 8They are to take
care of[D] all the furnishings of the tent of
meeting[f] and perform duties for[C] the Israelites by attending to the service of the tabernacle. 9Assign the Levites to Aaron and his
sons; they have been assigned exclusively to
him[E] from the Israelites.[g] 10You are to appoint
Aaron and his sons to carry out their priestly
responsibilities, but any unauthorized person who comes near the sanctuary must be
put to death."[h]

11The LORD spoke to Moses: 12"See, I have
taken the Levites from the Israelites in place
of every firstborn Israelite from the womb.[i]
The Levites belong to Me, 13because every
firstborn belongs to Me. At the time I struck
down every firstborn in the land of Egypt,[j] I
consecrated every firstborn in Israel to Myself, both man and animal. They are Mine; I
am ·Yahweh."[k]

The Levitical Census

14The LORD spoke to Moses in the Wilderness of Sinai: 15"Register the Levites by their
ancestral houses and their clans. You are to
register every male one month old or more."

[a]**2:33** Nm 1:49
[b]**2:34** Nm 10:10-28
[c]**3:1** Ex 19:3
[d]**3:4** Lv 10:1-2
[e]Lv 10:6; Nm 4:16,28,33
[f]**3:8** Nm 1:50,53
[g]**3:9** Nm 8:16,19,22; 18:6
[h]**3:10** Nm 1:51; 3:38; 8:19; 18:7
[i]**3:12** Ex 13:1-2; Nm 8:16-18
[j]**3:13** Ex 13:15-16
[k]Ex 3:14-16; 6:6-7; Nm 3:41,45

[A]**2:14** Some Hb mss, Sam, Vg; other Hb mss read *Reuel* [B]**2:17** Lit *each on his hand* [C]**3:7,8** Or *to guard* [D]**3:8** Or *and guard* [E]**3:9** Some Hb mss, LXX, Sam read *Me*; Nm 8:16

16 So Moses registered them in obedience to the LORD as he had been commanded:

17 These were Levi's sons by name: Gershon, Kohath, and Merari. 18 These were the names of Gershon's sons by their clans: Libni and Shimei. 19 Kohath's sons by their clans were Amram, Izhar, Hebron, and Uzziel. 20 Merari's sons by their clans were Mahli and Mushi. These were the Levite clans by their ancestral houses.[a]

21 The Libnite clan and the Shimeite clan came from Gershon; these were the Gershonite clans. 22 Those registered, counting every male one month old or more, numbered 7,500. 23 The Gershonite clans camped behind the tabernacle on the west side,[b] 24 and the leader of the Gershonite family was Eliasaph son of Lael. 25 The Gershonites' duties[c] at the tent of meeting involved the tabernacle, the tent, its covering, the screen for the entrance to the tent of meeting,[d] 26 the hangings of the courtyard, the screen for the entrance[e] to the courtyard that surrounds the tabernacle and the altar, and the tent ropes — all the work relating to these.

27 The Amramite clan, the Izharite clan, the Hebronite clan, and the Uzzielite clan came from Kohath; these were the Kohathites. 28 Counting every male one month old or more, there were 8,600[A] responsible for the duties of[B] the sanctuary. 29 The clans of the Kohathites camped on the south side of the tabernacle,[f] 30 and the leader of the family of the Kohathite clans was Elizaphan son of Uzziel. 31 Their duties involved the ark, the table, the lampstand, the altars, the sanctuary utensils that were used with these, and the screen[C,g] — and all the work relating to them.[h] 32 The chief of the Levite leaders was Eleazar[i] son of Aaron the priest; he had oversight of those responsible for the duties of[D] the sanctuary.

33 The Mahlite clan and the Mushite clan came from Merari; these were the Merarite clans. 34 Those registered, counting every male one month old or more, numbered 6,200. 35 The leader of the family of the Merarite clans was Zuriel son of Abihail; they camped on the north side of the tabernacle.[j] 36 The assigned duties of Merari's descendants involved the tabernacle's supports, crossbars, posts, bases, all its equipment, and all the work related to these,[k] 37 in addition to the posts of the surrounding courtyard with their bases, tent pegs, and ropes.

38 Moses, Aaron, and his sons, who performed the duties of[E] the sanctuary as a service on behalf of the Israelites, camped in front of the tabernacle on the east,[l] in front of the tent of meeting toward the sunrise. Any unauthorized person who came near it was to be put to death.[m]

39 The total number of all the Levite males one month old or more that Moses and Aaron[F] registered by their clans at the LORD's command was 22,000.

Redemption of the Firstborn

40 The LORD told Moses: "Register every firstborn male of the Israelites[n] one month old or more, and list their names. 41 You are to take the Levites for Me — I am Yahweh — in place of every firstborn among the Israelites, and the Levites' cattle in place of every firstborn among the Israelites' cattle." 42 So Moses registered every firstborn among the Israelites, as the LORD commanded him. 43 The total number of the firstborn males one month old or more listed by name was 22,273.

44 The LORD spoke to Moses again: 45 "Take the Levites in place of every firstborn among the Israelites, and the Levites' cattle in place of their cattle. The Levites belong to Me; I am Yahweh.[o] 46 As the redemption price for the 273 firstborn Israelites who outnumber the Levites, 47 collect five *shekels for each person, according to the standard sanctuary shekel — 20 *gerahs* to the shekel.[p] 48 Give the money to Aaron and his sons as the redemp-

[a] **3:17-20** Ex 6:17-19; 1Ch 6:1,16,20-29 [b] **3:23** Nm 2:18-24 [c] **3:25-26** Nm 4:24-26 [d] **3:25** Ex 26:7,14,36-37; 35:11,15 [e] **3:26** Ex 27:9-19; 35:17-18; 38:9-31 [f] **3:29** Nm 2:10-16 [g] **3:31** Ex 35:12 [h] Ex 25:10–27:21 [i] **3:32** Ex 6:23-25; 28:1; Lv 10:6,12,16; Nm 3:2,4 [j] **3:35** Nm 2:25-31 [k] **3:36-37** Ex 35:1-13; Nm 4:31-32 [l] **3:38** Nm 2:3-9 [m] Nm 1:51; 3:10; 8:19; 18:7 [n] **3:40** Ex 13:1-2; Nm 8:16-18 [o] **3:45** Nm 3:13,41; 10:10; 15:40-41 [p] **3:47** Nm 18:16

[A] **3:28** LXX reads *8,300* [B] **3:28** Or *for guarding* [C] **3:31** The screen between the most holy place and the holy place; Ex 35:12 [D] **3:32** Or *for guarding* [E] **3:38** Or *who guarded* [F] **3:39** Some Hb mss, Sam, Syr omit *and Aaron*

tion price for those who are in excess among
the Israelites."
49 So Moses collected the redemption
money from those in excess of the ones redeemed by the Levites. 50 He collected the
money from the firstborn Israelites: 1,365
shekels[A] measured by the standard sanctuary
shekel. 51 He gave the redemption money to
Aaron and his sons in obedience to the LORD,
just as the LORD commanded Moses.

Duties of the Kohathites

4 The LORD spoke to Moses and Aaron:
2 "Among the Levites, take a census of the
Kohathites[a] by their clans and their ancestral
houses, 3 men from 30 years old to 50 years
old — everyone who is qualified[B] to do work
at the tent of meeting.
4 "The service of the Kohathites at the tent
of meeting concerns the most holy objects.[b]
5 Whenever the camp is about to move on,
Aaron and his sons are to go in, take down the
screening veil, and cover the ark of the •tes-
timony with it.[c] 6 They are to place over this
a covering made of manatee skin,[C] spread a
solid blue cloth on top, and insert its poles.[d]
7 "They are to spread a blue cloth over the
table of the Presence and place the plates and
cups on it, as well as the bowls and pitchers
for the •drink offering. The regular bread
offering is to be on it.[e] 8 They are to spread a
scarlet cloth over them, cover them with a
covering made of manatee skin,[C] and insert
the poles in the table.[f]
9 "They are to take a blue cloth and cover
the lampstand[g] used for light, with its lamps,
snuffers, and firepans,[h] as well as its jars of
oil by which they service it. 10 Then they must
place it with all its utensils inside a covering
made of manatee skin[C] and put them on the
carrying frame.
11 "They are to spread a blue cloth over the
gold altar,[i] cover it with a covering made of
manatee skin,[C] and insert its poles.[j] 12 They are
to take all the serving utensils they use in the
sanctuary, place them in a blue cloth, cover
them with a covering made of manatee skin,[C]
and put them on a carrying frame.

[a] **4:2** Ex 6:16,18; Nm 3:27-31; 1Ch 6:22-28
[b] **4:4** Nm 3:30-31; 4:15-19
[c] **4:5** Ex 25:10-22; 26:31-33
[d] **4:6** Ex 25:13-15
[e] **4:7** Ex 25:30; Lv 24:5-9
[f] **4:8** Ex 25:26-28
[g] **4:9** Ex 25:31-35; 26:35; 37:17-20
[h] Ex 25:38; 37:23; Nm 4:14
[i] **4:11** Ex 30:1-3; 31:8; 39:38; 40:5,26
[j] Ex 30:4; 35:15
[k] **4:14** Ex 27:3; 38:3; Nm 7:13–8:4
[l] Ex 27:7
[m] **4:15** Nm 1:51; 4:20; 8:19; 18:7
[n] **4:16** Ex 25:6; 27:20; Lv 4:2
[o] Ex 25:6; 30:7; Lv 4:7
[p] Lv 6:20-22
[q] Ex 25:6; 29:7,21; Lv 8:2,10,12,30
[r] **4:19** Nm 3:31; 4:4
[s] **4:22** Nm 3:17,21-26
[t] **4:25** Ex 26:1-13; 36:8-17

13 "They are to remove the ashes from the
bronze altar, spread a purple cloth over it,
14 and place all the equipment on it that they
use in serving: the firepans, meat forks, shovels, and basins — all the equipment of the
altar.[k] They are to spread a covering made of
manatee skin[C] over it and insert its poles.[D,l]
15 "Aaron and his sons are to finish covering the holy objects and all their equipment whenever the camp is to move on. The
Kohathites will come and carry them, but they
are not to touch the holy objects or they will
die.[m] These are the transportation duties of
the Kohathites regarding the tent of meeting.
16 "Eleazar, son of Aaron the priest, has oversight of the lamp oil,[n] the fragrant incense,[o]
the daily •grain offering,[p] and the anointing
oil.[q] He has oversight of the entire tabernacle and everything in it, the holy objects and
their utensils."[E]
17 Then the LORD spoke to Moses and Aaron:
18 "Do not allow the Kohathite tribal clans
to be wiped out from the Levites. 19 Do this
for them so that they may live and not die
when they come near the most holy objects:[r]
Aaron and his sons are to go in and assign
each man his task and transportation duty.
20 The Kohathites are not to go in and look at
the holy objects, even for a moment,[F] or they
will die."

Duties of the Gershonites

21 The LORD spoke to Moses: 22 "Take a census of the Gershonites[s] also, by their ancestral
houses and their clans. 23 Register men from
30 years old to 50 years old, everyone who is
qualified to perform service, to do work at
the tent of meeting. 24 This is the service of the
Gershonite clans regarding work and transportation duties: 25 They are to transport the
tabernacle curtains,[t] the tent of meeting with
its covering and the covering made of manatee skin[C] on top of it, the screen for the entrance to the tent of meeting, 26 the hangings
of the courtyard, the screen for the entrance
at the gate of the courtyard that surrounds
the tabernacle and the altar, along with their
ropes and all the equipment for their service.

[A] **3:50** Over 34 pounds of silver [B] **4:3** Lit *everyone entering the service* [C] **4:6,8,10,11,12,14,25** Or *of dolphin skin*, or *of fine leather*; Hb obscure [D] **4:14** Sam, LXX add *They are to take a purple cloth and cover the wash basin and its base. They are to place them in a covering made of manatee skin and put them on the carrying frame.* [E] **4:16** Or *the sanctuary and its furnishings* [F] **4:20** Or *at the covering of the holy objects*

They will carry out everything that needs to be done with these items.

27"All the service of the Gershonites, all their transportation duties and all their other work, is to be done at the command of Aaron and his sons; you are to assign to them all that they are responsible to carry. 28This is the service of the Gershonite clans at the tent of meeting, and their duties will be under the direction of Ithamar son of Aaron the priest.

Duties of the Merarites

29"As for the Merarites, you are to register them by their clans[a] and their ancestral houses. 30Register men from 30 years old to 50 years old, everyone who is qualified to do the work of the tent of meeting. 31This is what they are responsible to carry as the whole of their service at the tent of meeting: the supports of the tabernacle, with its crossbars, posts, and bases, 32the posts of the surrounding courtyard with their bases, tent pegs, and ropes, including all their equipment and all the work related to them. You are to assign by name the items that they are responsible to carry. 33This is the service of the Merarite clans regarding all their work at the tent of meeting, under the direction of Ithamar son of Aaron the priest."

Census of the Levites

34So Moses, Aaron, and the leaders of the community registered the Kohathites by their clans and their ancestral houses, 35men from 30 years old to 50 years old, everyone who was qualified for work at the tent of meeting. 36The men registered by their clans numbered 2,750. 37These were the registered men of the Kohathite clans, everyone who could serve at the tent of meeting. Moses and Aaron registered them at the LORD's command through Moses.

38The Gershonites were registered by their clans and their ancestral houses, 39men from 30 years old to 50 years old, everyone who was qualified for work at the tent of meeting. 40The men registered by their clans and their ancestral houses numbered 2,630. 41These were the registered men of the Gershonite clans. At the LORD's command Moses and Aaron registered everyone who could serve at the tent of meeting.

42The men of the Merarite clans were registered by their clans and their ancestral houses, 43those from 30 years old to 50 years old, everyone who was qualified for work at the tent of meeting. 44The men registered by their clans numbered 3,200. 45These were the registered men of the Merarite clans; Moses and Aaron registered them at the LORD's command through Moses.

46Moses, Aaron, and the leaders of Israel registered all the Levites by their clans and their ancestral houses, 47from 30 years old to 50 years old, everyone who was qualified to do the work of serving at the tent of meeting and transporting it. 48Their registered men numbered 8,580. 49At the LORD's command they were registered under the direction of Moses, each one according to his work and transportation duty, and his assignment was as the LORD commanded Moses.

Isolation of the Unclean

5 The LORD instructed Moses: 2"Command the Israelites to send away anyone from the camp who is afflicted with a skin disease, anyone who has a bodily discharge, or anyone who is defiled because of a corpse.[b] 3You must send away both male or female; send them outside the camp, so that they will not defile their camps where I dwell among them." 4The Israelites did this, sending them outside the camp. The Israelites did as the LORD instructed Moses.

Compensation for Wrongdoing

5The LORD spoke to Moses: 6"Tell the Israelites: When a man or woman commits any sin against another, that person acts unfaithfully toward the LORD and is *guilty. 7The person is to confess the sin he has committed. He is to pay full compensation, add a fifth of its value to it, and give it to the individual he has wronged.[c] 8But if that individual has no relative[d] to receive compensation,[A] the compensation goes to the LORD for the priest, along with the *atonement ram by which the priest will make atonement for the guilty person.[e] 9Every holy contribution the Israelites pre-

[a] **4:29** Ex 6:16,19; Nm 3:17,33-37
[b] **5:2** Lv 14:2-3; 15:2; 22:4; Nm 9:6-7
[c] **5:7** Lv 6:1-5
[d] **5:8** Lv 25:25,48-49; Jr 32:7
[e] Lv 6:6-7

[A] **5:8** If the individual has died

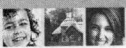

sent to the priest will be his.[a] 10 Each one's
holy contribution is his to give; what each
one gives to the priest will be his."

The Jealousy Ritual

11 The LORD spoke to Moses: 12 "Speak to the
Israelites and tell them: If any man's wife goes
astray, is unfaithful to him, 13 and sleeps with
another,[A] but it is concealed from her husband, and she is undetected, even though she
has defiled herself, since there is no witness
against her, and she wasn't caught in the act;
14 and if a feeling of jealousy comes over the
husband and he becomes jealous because
of his wife who has defiled herself — or if a
feeling of jealousy comes over him and he becomes jealous of her though she has not defiled herself — 15 then the man is to bring his
wife to the priest. He is also to bring an offering for her of two quarts[B] of barley flour. He
is not to pour oil over it or put frankincense
on it because it is a *grain offering of jealousy,
a grain offering for remembrance that brings
sin to mind.

16 "The priest is to bring her forward and
have her stand before the LORD. 17 Then the
priest is to take holy water in a clay bowl, and
take some of the dust from the tabernacle
floor and put it in the water. 18 After the priest
has the woman stand before the LORD, he is
to let down her hair[C] and place in her hands
the grain offering for remembrance, which
is the grain offering of jealousy. The priest is
to hold the bitter water that brings a curse.
19 The priest will require the woman to take an
oath and will say to her, 'If no man has slept
with you, if you have not gone astray and become defiled while under your husband's authority, be unaffected by this bitter water that
brings a curse. 20 But if you have gone astray
while under your husband's authority, if you
have defiled yourself and a man other than
your husband has slept with you' — 21 at this
point the priest must make the woman take
the oath with the sworn curse, and he is to
say to her — 'May the LORD make you into an
object of your people's cursing and swearing
when He makes your thigh[D] shrivel and your

[a] **5:9** Ex 25:2-3; 29:27-28; Lv 7:14,32,34
[b] **6:2** Jdg 13:5,7; 16:17; Am 2:11-12
[c] **6:3** Jdg 13:4,7,14

belly swell.[E] 22 May this water that brings a
curse enter your stomach, causing your belly
to swell and your thigh to shrivel.'

"And the woman must reply, "Amen, Amen.'
23 "Then the priest is to write these curses
on a scroll and wash them off into the bitter
water. 24 He will require the woman to drink
the bitter water that brings a curse, and it will
enter her and cause bitter suffering. 25 The
priest is to take the grain offering of jealousy
from the woman's hand, wave the offering before the LORD, and bring it to the altar. 26 The
priest is to take a handful of the grain offering as a memorial portion and burn it on
the altar. Then he will require the woman to
drink the water.

27 "When he makes her drink the water, if
she has defiled herself and been unfaithful
to her husband, the water that brings a curse
will enter her and cause bitter suffering; her
belly will swell, and her thigh will shrivel. She
will become a curse among her people. 28 But
if the woman has not defiled herself and is
pure, she will be unaffected and will be able
to conceive children.

29 "This is the law regarding jealousy when a
wife goes astray and defiles herself while under her husband's authority, 30 or when a feeling of jealousy comes over a husband and he
becomes jealous of his wife. He is to have the
woman stand before the LORD, and the priest
will apply this entire ritual to her. 31 The husband will be free of guilt, but that woman will
bear the consequences of her guilt."

The Nazirite Vow

6 The LORD instructed Moses: 2 "Speak to
the Israelites and tell them: When a man
or woman makes a special vow, a Nazirite
vow,[b] to consecrate himself to[F] the LORD, 3 he
is to abstain[G] from wine and beer.[c] He must
not drink vinegar made from wine or from
beer. He must not drink any grape juice or eat
fresh grapes or raisins. 4 He is not to eat anything produced by the grapevine, from seeds
to skin,[H] during his vow.

5 "You must not cut his hair[I] throughout
the time of his vow of consecration. He must

[A] **5:13** Lit *and man lies with her and has an emission of semen* [B] **5:15** Lit *a tenth of an ephah* [C] **5:18** Or *to uncover her head* [D] **5:21-22** Possibly a euphemism for the reproductive organs [E] **5:21** Or *flood* [F] **6:2** Or *vow, to live as a Nazirite for* [G] **6:3** In Hb, the words Nazirite, consecrate, and abstain are related and involve the idea of separation. [H] **6:4** Or *from unripe grapes to hulls* [I] **6:5** Lit *A razor is not to pass over his head* be holy until the time is completed during which he consecrates himself to the LORD; he is to let the hair of his head grow long. 6 He must not go near a dead body during the time he consecrates himself to the LORD.[a] 7 He is not to defile himself for his father or mother, or his brother or sister, when they die, because the hair consecrated to his God is on his head. 8 He is holy to the LORD[b] during the time of consecration.

9 "If someone suddenly dies near him, defiling his consecrated head of hair, he must shave his head on the day of his purification; he is to shave it on the seventh day.[c] 10 On the eighth day he is to bring two turtledoves or two young pigeons to the priest at the entrance to the tent of meeting.[d] 11 The priest is to offer one as a ·sin offering and the other as a ·burnt offering[e] to make ·atonement on behalf of the Nazirite, since he sinned because of the corpse. On that day he must consecrate[A] his head again.[f] 12 He is to rededicate his time of consecration to the LORD and to bring a year-old male lamb as a ·restitution offering.[g] But do not count the previous period, because his consecrated hair became defiled.

13 "This is the law of the Nazirite: On the day his time of consecration is completed, he must be brought to the entrance to the tent of meeting.[h] 14 He is to present an offering to the LORD[i] of one unblemished year-old male lamb as a burnt offering, one unblemished year-old female lamb as a sin offering, one unblemished ram as a ·fellowship offering,[j] 15 along with their ·grain offerings and ·drink offerings,[k] and a basket of unleavened cakes made from fine flour mixed with oil, and unleavened wafers coated with oil.[l]

16 "The priest is to present these before the LORD and sacrifice the Nazirite's sin offering and burnt offering. 17 He will also offer the ram as a fellowship sacrifice to the LORD, together with the basket of unleavened bread. Then the priest will offer the accompanying grain offering and drink offering.

18 "The Nazirite is to shave his consecrated head at the entrance to the tent of meeting, take the hair from his head, and put it on the fire under the fellowship sacrifice. 19 The priest is to take the boiled shoulder from the ram, one unleavened cake from the basket, and one unleavened wafer, and put them into the hands[m] of the Nazirite after he has shaved his consecrated head. 20 The priest is to wave them as a presentation offering before the LORD.[n] It is a holy portion for the priest, in addition to the breast of the presentation offering and the thigh of the contribution.[o] After that, the Nazirite may drink wine.

21 "This is the ritual of the Nazirite who vows his offering to the LORD for his consecration,[p] in addition to whatever else he can afford; he must fulfill whatever vow he makes in keeping with the ritual for his consecration."

The Priestly Blessing

22 The LORD spoke to Moses: 23 "Tell Aaron and his sons how you are to bless the Israelites. Say to them:

24 May ·Yahweh bless you
and protect you;[q]
25 may Yahweh make His face shine
on you
and be gracious to you;[r]
26 may Yahweh look with favor on you[B]
and give you peace.[C,s]

27 In this way they will pronounce My name over[D] the Israelites, and I will bless them."

Offerings from the Leaders

7 On the day Moses finished setting up the tabernacle,[t] he anointed and consecrated it and all its furnishings, along with the altar and all its utensils. After he anointed and consecrated these things, 2 the leaders of Israel, the heads of their ancestral houses, presented an offering. They were the tribal leaders who supervised the registration.[u] 3 They brought as their offering before the LORD six covered carts and 12 oxen, a cart from every two leaders and an ox from each one, and presented them in front of the tabernacle.

4 The LORD said to Moses, 5 "Accept these from them to be used in the work of the tent of meeting, and give this offering to the Levites, to each division according to their service."

6 So Moses took the carts and oxen and gave

[a] **6:6** Nm 19:11-16 [b] **6:8** Nm 6:5; Dt 7:6; 14:2,21; 26:19; 2Ch 35:3 [c] **6:9** Nm 19:11 [d] **6:10** Ex 29:42-43; Lv 5:7; Nm 6:18 [e] **6:11** Lv 1:14-17; 5:7-10 [f] Lv 15:13-15 [g] **6:12** Lv 5:14-19; 7:1-6 [h] **6:13** Lv 14:11; Nm 8:9 [i] **6:14** Ac 21:24 [j] Lv 1:10-13; 3:1-5; 4:32-35 [k] **6:15** Ex 29:40-41; Lv 23:12-13,18; Nm 15:1-12 [l] Ex 29:2; Lv 2:4-11; 7:12 [m] **6:19** Ex 29:24; Lv 2:4-11 [n] **6:20** Ex 29:25-27 [o] Ex 25:2-3; 29:27-28; Lv 7:14,32,34 [p] **6:21** Ac 21:24 [q] **6:24** Ps 121:4,7; 128:5; 134:3 [r] **6:25** Ps 67:1; 80:3; 89:15; 119:135 [s] **6:26** Ps 4:6; 147:14 [t] **7:1** Ex 39:32; 40:17; Nm 9:15 [u] **7:2** Nm 1:4-16

[A] **6:11** Lit *set apart* [B] **6:26** Lit *LORD lift His face to you* [C] **6:26** Or *prosperity* [D] **6:27** Or *put My name on*

them to the Levites. 7He gave the Gershonites two carts and four oxen corresponding
to their service,[a] 8and gave the Merarites four
carts and eight oxen corresponding to their
service,[b] under the direction of Ithamar son
of Aaron the priest. 9But he did not give any
to the Kohathites, since their responsibility
was service related to the holy objects[c] carried on their shoulders.[d]

10The leaders also presented the dedication
gift for the altar when it was anointed.[e] The
leaders presented their offerings in front of
the altar. 11The LORD told Moses, "Each day
have one leader present his offering for the
dedication of the altar."[f]

12The one who presented his offering on
the first day was Nahshon son of Amminadab[g] from the tribe of Judah. 13His offering was one silver dish weighing 3¼
pounds[A] and one silver basin weighing
1¾ pounds,[B] measured by the standard
sanctuary ·shekel, both of them full of
fine flour mixed with oil for a ·grain offering;[h] 14one gold bowl weighing four
ounces,[C] full of incense; 15one young bull,
one ram, and one male lamb a year old,
for a ·burnt offering;[i] 16one male goat for
a ·sin offering;[j] 17and two bulls, five rams,
five male breeding goats, and five male
lambs a year old, for the ·fellowship sacrifice.[k] This was the offering of Nahshon
son of Amminadab.

18On the second day Nethanel son of
Zuar,[l] leader of Issachar, presented an offering. 19As his offering, he presented one
silver dish weighing 3¼ pounds[A] and
one silver basin weighing 1¾ pounds,[B]
measured by the standard sanctuary
shekel, both of them full of fine flour
mixed with oil for a grain offering; 20one
gold bowl weighing four ounces,[C] full of
incense; 21one young bull, one ram, and
one male lamb a year old, for a burnt
offering; 22one male goat for a sin offering; 23and two bulls, five rams, five male
breeding goats, and five male lambs a
year old, for the fellowship sacrifice. This
was the offering of Nethanel son of Zuar.

24On the third day Eliab son of Helon,[m]
leader of the Zebulunites, presented an
offering. 25His offering was one silver
dish weighing 3¼ pounds[A] and one silver basin weighing 1¾ pounds,[B] measured by the standard sanctuary shekel,
both of them full of fine flour mixed with
oil for a grain offering; 26one gold bowl
weighing four ounces,[C] full of incense;
27one young bull, one ram, and one male
lamb a year old, for a burnt offering;
28one male goat for a sin offering; 29and
two bulls, five rams, five male breeding
goats, and five male lambs a year old, for
the fellowship sacrifice. This was the offering of Eliab son of Helon.

30On the fourth day Elizur son of Shedeur,[n] leader of the Reubenites, presented
an offering. 31His offering was one silver
dish weighing 3¼ pounds[A] and one silver basin weighing 1¾ pounds,[B] measured by the standard sanctuary shekel,
both of them full of fine flour mixed with
oil for a grain offering; 32one gold bowl
weighing four ounces,[C] full of incense;
33one young bull, one ram, and one male
lamb a year old, for a burnt offering;
34one male goat for a sin offering; 35and
two bulls, five rams, five male breeding
goats, and five male lambs a year old, for
the fellowship sacrifice. This was the offering of Elizur son of Shedeur.

36On the fifth day Shelumiel son of Zurishaddai,[o] leader of the Simeonites, presented an offering. 37His offering was one
silver dish weighing 3¼ pounds[A] and one
silver basin weighing 1¾ pounds,[B] measured by the standard sanctuary shekel,
both of them full of fine flour mixed with
oil for a grain offering; 38one gold bowl
weighing four ounces,[C] full of incense;
39one young bull, one ram, and one male
lamb a year old, for a burnt offering;
40one male goat for a sin offering; 41and
two bulls, five rams, five male breeding
goats, and five male lambs a year old, for
the fellowship sacrifice. This was the offering of Shelumiel son of Zurishaddai.

[a]**7:7** Nm 4:23-28,32
[b]**7:8** Nm 3:36-37; 4:30-33
[c]**7:9** Nm 4:4-16
[d]Nm 3:28-31; 4:4-20
[e]**7:10** Nm 7:11,84,88; 1Kg 8:62-64; 2Ch 7:4-9; Neh 12:27
[f]**7:11** Ex 40:10
[g]**7:12** Nm 1:7; 2:3; 10:14
[h]**7:13** Lv 2:1-2; 6:14-18
[i]**7:15** Lv 1:1-13; 6:8-13
[j]**7:16** Lv 4:1–5:13; 6:24-30; Nm 28:11-15
[k]**7:17** Lv 3:1-17; 7:11-21
[l]**7:18** Nm 1:8; 2:5; 10:15
[m]**7:24** Nm 1:9; 2:7; 10:16
[n]**7:30** Nm 1:5; 2:10; 10:18
[o]**7:36** Nm 1:6; 2:12; 10:19

[A]**7:13,19,25,31,37** Lit *dish, 130 its shekel-weight* [B]**7:13,19,25,31,37** Lit *70 shekels* [C]**7:14,20,26,32,38** Lit *10* (shekels)

42 On the sixth day Eliasaph son of
Deuel,[A,a] leader of the Gadites, presented
an offering. 43 His offering was one silver
dish weighing 3 1/4 pounds[B] and one silver
basin weighing 1 3/4 pounds,[C] measured
by the standard sanctuary shekel, both
of them full of fine flour mixed with
oil for a grain offering; 44 one gold bowl
weighing four ounces,[D] full of incense;
45 one young bull, one ram, and one male
lamb a year old, for a burnt offering;
46 one male goat for a sin offering; 47 and
two bulls, five rams, five male breeding
goats, and five male lambs a year old, for
the fellowship sacrifice. This was the offering of Eliasaph son of Deuel.[A]

48 On the seventh day Elishama son of
Ammihud,[b] leader of the Ephraimites,
presented an offering. 49 His offering was
one silver dish weighing 3 1/4 pounds[B] and
one silver basin weighing 1 3/4 pounds,[C]
measured by the standard sanctuary
shekel, both of them full of fine flour
mixed with oil for a grain offering; 50 one
gold bowl weighing four ounces,[D] full of
incense; 51 one young bull, one ram, and
one male lamb a year old, for a burnt
offering; 52 one male goat for a sin offering; 53 and two bulls, five rams, five male
breeding goats, and five male lambs a
year old, for the fellowship sacrifice. This
was the offering of Elishama son of Ammihud.

54 On the eighth day Gamaliel son of Pedahzur,[c] leader of the Manassites, presented an offering. 55 His offering was one
silver dish weighing 3 1/4 pounds[B] and one
silver basin weighing 1 3/4 pounds,[C] measured by the standard sanctuary shekel,
both of them full of fine flour mixed with
oil for a grain offering; 56 one gold bowl
weighing four ounces,[D] full of incense;
57 one young bull, one ram, and one male
lamb a year old, for a burnt offering;
58 one male goat for a sin offering; 59 and
two bulls, five rams, five male breeding
goats, and five male lambs a year old, for
the fellowship sacrifice. This was the offering of Gamaliel son of Pedahzur.

[a] **7:42** Nm 1:14; 2:14; 10:20
[b] **7:48** Nm 1:10; 2:18; 10:22
[c] **7:54** Nm 1:10; 2:20; 10:23
[d] **7:60** Nm 1:11; 2:22; 10:24
[e] **7:66** Nm 1:12; 2:25; 10:25
[f] **7:72** Nm 1:13; 2:27; 10:26

60 On the ninth day Abidan son of Gideoni,[d] leader of the Benjaminites, presented an offering. 61 His offering was one
silver dish weighing 3 1/4 pounds[B] and one
silver basin weighing 1 3/4 pounds,[C] measured by the standard sanctuary shekel,
both of them full of fine flour mixed with
oil for a grain offering; 62 one gold bowl
weighing four ounces,[D] full of incense;
63 one young bull, one ram, and one male
lamb a year old, for a burnt offering;
64 one male goat for a sin offering; 65 and
two bulls, five rams, five male breeding
goats, and five male lambs a year old, for
the fellowship sacrifice. This was the offering of Abidan son of Gideoni.

66 On the tenth day Ahiezer son of Ammishaddai,[e] leader of the Danites, presented
an offering. 67 His offering was one silver
dish weighing 3 1/4 pounds[B] and one silver
basin weighing 1 3/4 pounds,[C] measured
by the standard sanctuary shekel, both of
them full of fine flour mixed with oil for
a grain offering; 68 one gold bowl weighing four ounces,[D] full of incense; 69 one
young bull, one ram, and one male lamb
a year old, for a burnt offering; 70 one
male goat for a sin offering; 71 and two
bulls, five rams, five male breeding goats,
and five male lambs a year old, for the fellowship sacrifice. This was the offering of
Ahiezer son of Ammishaddai.

72 On the eleventh day Pagiel son of
Ochran,[f] leader of the Asherites, presented an offering. 73 His offering was one
silver dish weighing 3 1/4 pounds[B] and one
silver basin weighing 1 3/4 pounds,[C] measured by the standard sanctuary shekel,
both of them full of fine flour mixed with
oil for a grain offering; 74 one gold bowl
weighing four ounces,[D] full of incense;
75 one young bull, one ram, and one male
lamb a year old, for a burnt offering;
76 one male goat for a sin offering; 77 and
two bulls, five rams, five male breeding
goats, and five male lambs a year old, for
the fellowship sacrifice. This was the offering of Pagiel son of Ochran.

[A] **7:42,47** LXX, Syr read *Reuel* [B] **7:43,49,55,61,67,73** Lit *dish, 130 its shekel-weight* [C] **7:43,49,55,61,67,73** Lit *70 shekels* [D] **7:44,50,56,62,68,74** Lit *10* (shekels)

[78]On the twelfth day Ahira son of Enan,[a] leader of the Naphtalites, presented an offering. [79]His offering was one silver dish weighing 3 1/4 pounds[A] and one silver basin weighing 1 3/4 pounds,[B] measured by the standard sanctuary shekel, both of them full of fine flour mixed with oil for a grain offering; [80]one gold bowl weighing four ounces,[C] full of incense; [81]one young bull, one ram, and one male lamb a year old, for a burnt offering; [82]one male goat for a sin offering; [83]and two bulls, five rams, five male breeding goats, and five male lambs a year old, for the fellowship sacrifice. This was the offering of Ahira son of Enan.

[84]This was the dedication gift from the leaders of Israel for the altar when it was anointed:[b] 12 silver dishes, 12 silver basins, and 12 gold bowls. [85]Each silver dish weighed 3 1/4 pounds,[D] and each basin 1 3/4 pounds.[B] The total weight of the silver articles was 60 pounds[E] measured by the standard sanctuary shekel. [86]The 12 gold bowls full of incense each weighed four ounces[C] measured by the standard sanctuary shekel. The total weight of the gold bowls was three pounds.[F] [87]All the livestock for the burnt offering[c] totaled 12 bulls, 12 rams, and 12 male lambs a year old, with their grain offerings, and 12 male goats for the sin offering.[d] [88]All the livestock for the fellowship sacrifice[e] totaled 24 bulls, 60 rams, 60 male breeding goats, and 60 male lambs a year old. This was the dedication gift for the altar after it was anointed.

[89]When Moses entered the tent of meeting to speak with the LORD, he heard the voice speaking to him[f] from above the ·mercy seat that was on the ark of the ·testimony, from between the two ·cherubim.[g] He spoke to him that way.

The Lighting in the Tabernacle

8 The LORD spoke to Moses: [2]"Speak to Aaron and tell him: When you set up the lamps, the seven lamps are to give light in front of the lampstand." [3]So Aaron did this; he set up its lamps to give light in front of the lampstand just as the LORD had commanded Moses. [4]This is the way the lampstand was made: it was a hammered work of gold, hammered from its base to its flower petals. The lampstand was made according to the pattern the LORD had shown Moses.[h]

Consecration of the Levites

[5]The LORD spoke to Moses: [6]"Take the Levites from among the Israelites and ceremonially cleanse them. [7]This is what you must do to them for their purification: Sprinkle them with the purification water.[i] Have them shave their entire bodies and wash their clothes, and so purify themselves.[j]

[8]"They are to take a young bull and its ·grain offering of fine flour mixed with oil, and you are to take a second young bull for a ·sin offering. [9]Bring the Levites before the tent of meeting and assemble the entire Israelite community.[k] [10]Then present the Levites before the LORD, and have the Israelites lay their hands on them. [11]Aaron is to present the Levites before the LORD as a presentation offering from the Israelites, so that they may perform the LORD's work.[l] [12]Next the Levites are to lay their hands on the heads of the bulls. Sacrifice one as a sin offering and the other as a ·burnt offering to the LORD, to make ·atonement for the Levites.[m]

[13]"You are to have the Levites stand before Aaron and his sons, and you are to present them before the LORD as a presentation offering. [14]In this way you are to separate the Levites from the rest of the Israelites so that the Levites will belong to Me.[n] [15]After that the Levites may come to serve at the tent of meeting, once you have ceremonially cleansed them and presented them as a presentation offering.[o] [16]For they have been exclusively assigned to Me from the Israelites.[p] I have taken them for Myself in place of all who come first from the womb, every Israelite firstborn.[q] [17]For every firstborn among the Israelites is Mine, both man and animal. I consecrated them to Myself[r] on the day I struck down every firstborn in the land of Egypt. [18]But I have taken the Levites in place of every firstborn among the Israelites. [19]From the Israelites, I have given the Levites exclusively to Aaron and his sons to perform the work for the

[a]**7:78** Nm 1:15; 2:29; 10:27 [b]**7:84** Nm 7:1,10 [c]**7:87** Lv 1:1-13; 6:8-13 [d]Lv 4:22-26; 6:24-30; Nm 28:11-15 [e]**7:88** Lv 3:1-17; 7:11-21 [f]**7:89** Nm 12:8 [g]Ex 25:10-22; 37:1-9; 1Kg 6:25 [h]**8:2-4** Ex 25:31-40 [i]**8:7** Lv 14:51; Nm 19:7,13,17,20; Heb 9:13,23 [j]Lv 8:1-6; 14:8-9; Nm 6:19 [k]**8:9** Ex 29:4; Lv 8:1-6 [l]**8:11** Nm 1:50,53; 3:6-7 [m]**8:12** Lv 1:3-5; 4:3-4 [n]**8:14** Nm 3:12,45; 16:8-9 [o]**8:15** Ex 29:26-27; Lv 8:26-29; Nm 6:20 [p]**8:16** Nm 3:9; 18:6 [q]Ex 13:2,12,15; Nm 3:12,41-45 [r]**8:17** Ex 13:1-2,11-12,15-16

[A]**7:79** Lit *dish, 130 its shekel-weight* [B]**7:79,85** Lit *70 shekels* [C]**7:80,86** Lit *10* (shekels) [D]**7:85** Lit *130* (shekels) [E]**7:85** Lit *2,400* (shekels) [F]**7:86** Lit *120* (shekels)

Israelites at the tent of meeting and to make
atonement on their behalf, so that no plague
will come against the Israelites when they approach the sanctuary."[a]
20 Moses, Aaron, and the entire Israelite
community did this to the Levites. The Israelites did everything to them the LORD commanded Moses regarding the Levites. 21 The
Levites purified themselves and washed their
clothes; then Aaron presented[A] them before
the LORD as a presentation offering. Aaron
also made atonement for them to ceremonially cleanse them. 22 After that, the Levites
came to do their work at the tent of meeting
in the presence of Aaron and his sons. So they
did to them as the LORD had commanded Moses concerning the Levites.
23 The LORD spoke to Moses: 24 "In regard to
the Levites: From 25 years old or more, a man
enters the service in the work at the tent of
meeting.[b] 25 But at 50 years old he is to retire
from his service in the work and no longer
serve. 26 He may assist his brothers to fulfill
responsibilities[B] at the tent of meeting,[c] but
he must not do the work. This is how you are
to deal with the Levites regarding their duties."

The Second Passover

9 In the first month of the second year
after their departure from the land of
Egypt, the LORD told Moses in the Wilderness
of Sinai:[d] 2 "The Israelites are to observe the
·Passover at its appointed time.[e] 3 You must
observe it at its appointed time on the fourteenth day of this month at twilight; you are
to observe it according to all its statutes and
ordinances."[f] 4 So Moses told the Israelites to
observe the Passover, 5 and they observed it in
the first month on the fourteenth day at twilight in the Wilderness of Sinai. The Israelites
did everything as the LORD had commanded
Moses.
6 But there were some men who were ·un-
clean because of a human corpse, so they
could not observe the Passover on that day.[g]
These men came before Moses and Aaron the
same day 7 and said to him, "We are unclean
because of a human corpse. Why should we
be excluded from presenting the LORD's offering at its appointed time with the other
Israelites?"
8 Moses replied to them, "Wait here until I
hear what the LORD commands for you."
9 Then the LORD spoke to Moses: 10 "Tell the
Israelites: When any one of you or your descendants is unclean because of a corpse[h] or
is on a distant journey, he may still observe
the Passover to the LORD. 11 Such people are
to observe it in the second month, on the
fourteenth day at twilight. They are to eat
the animal with unleavened bread and bitter herbs;[i] 12 they may not leave any of it until morning or break any of its bones.[j] They
must observe the Passover according to all
its statutes.
13 "But the man who is ceremonially ·clean,
is not on a journey, and yet fails to observe the
Passover is to be cut off from his people, because he did not present the LORD's offering
at its appointed time. That man will bear the
consequences of his sin.
14 "If a foreigner resides with you and wants
to observe the Passover to the LORD,[k] he is to
do so according to the Passover statute and its
ordinances. You are to apply the same statute
to both the foreign resident and the native of
the land."[l]

Guidance by the Cloud

15 On the day the tabernacle was set up, the
cloud covered the tabernacle, the tent of the
·testimony,[m] and it appeared like fire above
the tabernacle from evening until morning.
16 It remained that way continuously: the
cloud would cover it,[C] appearing like fire at
night.[n] 17 Whenever the cloud was lifted up
above the tent, the Israelites would set out;
at the place where the cloud stopped, there
the Israelites camped.[o] 18 At the LORD's command the Israelites set out, and at the LORD's
command they camped. As long as the cloud
stayed over the tabernacle, they camped.
19 Even when the cloud stayed over the tabernacle many days, the Israelites carried out
the LORD's requirement and did not set out.
20 Sometimes the cloud remained over the
tabernacle for only a few days. They would
camp at the LORD's command and set out at
the LORD's command. 21 Sometimes the cloud

[a] **8:19** Nm 1:51,53; 16:1-3,32-50; 18:1-7
[b] **8:24** Nm 4:3,23,30
[c] **8:26** Nm 3:7-8
[d] **9:1** Ex 19:1-2; Nm 1:1; 3:4,14
[e] **9:2** Ex 13:10; 23:15
[f] **9:3** Ex 12:2-27; Lv 23:4-8; Nm 28:16-25; Dt 16:1-8
[g] **9:6** 2Ch 30:3
[h] **9:10** Lv 21:1-3; Nm 5:2; 6:6-12
[i] **9:11** Ex 12:8,15; Dt 16:3-4,8
[j] **9:12** Ex 12:10,46; Ps 34:20; Jn 19:36
[k] **9:14** Ex 12:48
[l] Ex 12:49; Lv 24:22; Nm 15:14-16
[m] **9:15** Ex 40:17,34; Nm 7:1
[n] **9:16** Ex 13:21-22; 40:38
[o] **9:17** Ex 40:36-38; Nm 10:11,33-34

[A] **8:21** Lit *waved* [B] **8:26** Or *to keep guard* [C] **9:16** LXX, Vg, Syr, Tg read *it by day*

remained only from evening until morning;
when the cloud lifted in the morning, they set
out. Or if it remained a day and a night, they
moved out when the cloud lifted. 22 Whether
it was two days, a month, or longer,[A] the Israelites camped and did not set out as long
as the cloud stayed over the tabernacle.
But when it was lifted, they set out. 23 They
camped at the LORD's command, and they
set out at the LORD's command. They carried
out the LORD's requirement according to His
command through Moses.

Two Silver Trumpets

10 The LORD spoke to Moses: 2 "Make two
trumpets of hammered silver to summon the community[a] and have the camps set
out. 3 When both are sounded in long blasts,
the entire community is to gather before you
at the entrance to the tent of meeting. 4 However, if one is sounded, only the leaders, the
heads of Israel's clans,[b] are to gather before
you.

5 "When you sound short blasts, the camps
pitched on the east[c] are to set out. 6 When you
sound short blasts a second time, the camps
pitched on the south[d] are to set out. Short
blasts are to be sounded for them to set out.
7 When calling the assembly together, you are
to sound long blasts, not short ones. 8 The
sons of Aaron, the priests, are to sound the
trumpets. Your use of these is a permanent
statute throughout your generations.

9 "When you enter into battle in your land
against an adversary who is attacking you,
sound short blasts on the trumpets, and you
will be remembered before the LORD your
God and be delivered from your enemies.[e]
10 You are to sound the trumpets over your
•burnt offerings and your •fellowship sacrifices and on your joyous occasions, your appointed festivals, and the beginning of each
of your months. They will serve as a reminder
for you before your God: I am •Yahweh your
God."[f]

From Sinai to Paran

11 During the second year, in the second
month on the twentieth day of the month,
the cloud was lifted up above the tabernacle
of the •testimony. 12 The Israelites traveled on
from the Wilderness of Sinai, moving from
one place to the next[g] until the cloud stopped
in the Wilderness of Paran.[h] 13 They set out for
the first time according to the LORD's command through Moses.[i]

14 The military divisions of the camp of Judah with their banner set out first, and Nahshon son of Amminadab[j] was over Judah's
divisions. 15 Nethanel son of Zuar[k] was over
the division of the Issachar tribe, 16 and Eliab
son of Helon was over the division of the Zebulun tribe. 17 The tabernacle was then taken
down, and the Gershonites and the Merarites
set out, transporting the tabernacle.

18 The military divisions of the camp of Reuben with their banner set out, and Elizur son
of Shedeur was over Reuben's division. 19 Shelumiel son of Zurishaddai[l] was over the division of Simeon's tribe, 20 and Eliasaph son
of Deuel was over the division of the tribe of
Gad. 21 The Kohathites then set out, transporting the holy objects;[m] the tabernacle was to be
set up before their arrival.

22 Next the military divisions of the camp of
Ephraim with their banner set out, and Elishama son of Ammihud[n] was over Ephraim's division. 23 Gamaliel son of Pedahzur was over
the division of the tribe of Manasseh, 24 and
Abidan son of Gideoni was over the division
of the tribe of Benjamin.

25 The military divisions of the camp of Dan
with their banner set out, serving as rear
guard for all the camps, and Ahiezer son of
Ammishaddai[o] was over Dan's division. 26 Pagiel son of Ochran was over the division of
the tribe of Asher, 27 and Ahira son of Enan
was over the division of the tribe of Naphtali.
28 This was the order of march for the Israelites by their military divisions as they set out.

29 Moses said to Hobab, son of Moses' father-in-law[B] Reuel[C,p] the Midianite: "We're
setting out for the place the LORD promised:
'I will give it to you.'[q] Come with us, and we
will treat you well, for the LORD has promised
good things to Israel."[r]

30 But he replied to him, "I don't want to go.
Instead, I will go to my own land and my relatives."

31 "Please don't leave us," Moses said, "since

[a] **10:2** Jl 2:15-16
[b] **10:4** Nm 1:5-16
[c] **10:5** Nm 2:3-9; 10:14-16
[d] **10:6** Nm 2:10-16; 10:18-20
[e] **10:9** Dt 20:4; 2Ch 13:12; Ps 18:3
[f] **10:10** Ex 6:7; Lv 18:2,4,30; 19:2-4
[g] **10:12** Ex 17:1; 19:1; Nm 1:1
[h] Gn 21:21; Nm 12:16; 13:3,26; 1Sm 25:1
[i] **10:13** Nm 9:18-23
[j] **10:14** Nm 1:7; 2:3; 7:12; 1Ch 2:10
[k] **10:15** Nm 1:8; 2:5; 7:18
[l] **10:19** Nm 1:6; 2:12; 7:36
[m] **10:21** Nm 3:27-31; 4:2-4,15,18-20
[n] **10:22** Nm 1:10; 2:18; 7:48
[o] **10:25** Nm 1:12; 2:25; 7:66
[p] **10:29** Ex 2:16-18; 3:1; 4:18; Jdg 4:11
[q] Gn 12:7; 13:14-17; 15:7; Ac 7:5
[r] Ex 18:9

[A] **9:22** Or *a year* [B] **10:29** Or *said to Hobab's brother-in-law* [C] **10:29** = Jethro; Ex 2:16-18; 3:1; 4:18

you know where we should camp in the wilderness, and you can serve as our eyes. 32 If
you come with us, whatever good the LORD
does for us we will do for you."[a]
33 They set out from the mountain of the
LORD on a three-day journey with the ark of
the LORD's covenant traveling ahead of them
for those three days to seek a resting place for
them.[b] 34 Meanwhile, the cloud of the LORD
was over them by day when they set out from
the camp.
35 Whenever the ark set out, Moses would
say:

> Arise, LORD!
> Let Your enemies be scattered,
> and those who hate You flee
> from Your presence.[c]

36 When it came to rest, he would say:

> Return, LORD,
> to the countless thousands of Israel.[d]

Complaints about Hardship

11 Now the people began complaining openly before[A] the LORD about
hardship. When the LORD heard, His anger burned,[e] and fire[f] from the LORD blazed
among them and consumed the outskirts
of the camp. 2 Then the people cried out to
Moses, and he prayed to the LORD, and the
fire died down. 3 So that place was named
Taberah,[B,g] because the LORD's fire had blazed
among them.

Complaints about Food

4 Contemptible people[C] among them[h] had
a strong craving[i] for other food. The Israelites cried again and said, "Who will feed us
meat? 5 We remember the free fish we ate in
Egypt,[j] along with the cucumbers, melons,
leeks, onions, and garlic. 6 But now our appetite is gone;[D] there's nothing to look at but
this manna!"
7 The manna[k] resembled coriander seed,
and its appearance was like that of bdellium.[E]
8 The people walked around and gathered it.
They ground it on a pair of grinding stones
or crushed it in a mortar, then boiled it in a
cooking pot and shaped it into cakes. It tasted
like a pastry cooked with the finest oil. 9 When
the dew fell on the camp at night, the manna
would fall with it.[l]
10 Moses heard the people, family after
family, crying at the entrance of their tents.
The LORD was very angry;[m] Moses was also
provoked.[F] 11 So Moses asked the LORD, "Why
have You brought such trouble on Your servant? Why are You angry with me, and why
do You burden me with all these people?[n]
12 Did I conceive all these people? Did I give
them birth so You should tell me, 'Carry them
at your breast, as a nursing woman carries
a baby,'[o] to the land that You[G] swore to give
their fathers?[p] 13 Where can I get meat to give
all these people? For they are crying to me:
'Give us meat to eat!' 14 I can't carry all these
people by myself. They are too much for me.
15 If You are going to treat me like this, please
kill me right now.[q] If You are pleased with
me,[r] don't let me see my misery[H] anymore."

Seventy Elders Anointed

16 The LORD answered Moses, "Bring Me 70
men from Israel known to you as elders and
officers of the people. Take them to the tent
of meeting and have them stand there with
you. 17 Then I will come down and speak with
you there. I will take some of the Spirit who
is on you and put the Spirit on them.[s] They
will help you bear the burden of the people,
so that you do not have to bear it by yourself.[t]
18 "Tell the people: Purify yourselves in
readiness for tomorrow, and you will eat
meat because you cried before the LORD:
'Who will feed us meat? We really had it good
in Egypt.' The LORD will give you meat and
you will eat. 19 You will eat, not for one day, or
two days, or five days, or 10 days, or 20 days,
20 but for a whole month — until it comes out
of your nostrils and becomes nauseating to
you — because you have rejected the LORD
who is among you, and cried to Him: 'Why
did we ever leave Egypt?'"[u]
21 But Moses replied, "I'm in the middle of
a people with 600,000 foot soldiers,[v] yet You
say, 'I will give them meat, and they will eat for

[a]10:32 Jdg 1:16; 4:11 [b]10:33 Dt 1:33 [c]10:35 Ps 68:1 [d]10:36 Gn 15:5; Dt 1:8,10 [e]11:1 Ex 22:24; 32:10-11; Nm 11:1,33; 32:13; Dt 6:15 [f]1Kg 18:38; 19:12; Is 66:16 [g]11:3 Dt 9:22 [h]11:4 Ex 12:38 [i]Nm 11:34; Ps 78:29-31; 106:14-15; 1Co 10:5-6 [j]11:5 Ex 16:3 [k]11:7 Ex 16:4-35; Dt 8:3,16; Jos 5:12; Neh 9:20; Ps 78:24; Jn 6:48-51; Rv 2:17 [l]11:9 Ex 16:13-14 [m]11:10 Ex 22:24; 32:10-11; Nm 11:1,33; 32:13; Dt 6:15 [n]11:11 Ex 5:22; Dt 1:9-13 [o]11:12 Is 40:11; 66:11-12 [p]Gn 12:7; 26:3-4; Nm 14:16,23; Dt 6:10,23 [q]11:15 Ex 32:32; Jb 6:9; 7:15-16 [r]Gn 6:8; Ex 33:12-17; Ru 2:2,10,13 [s]11:17 2Kg 2:9,15 [t]Ex 18:18; Dt 1:9-13; Ac 6:1-6 [u]11:20 Ex 17:3 [v]11:21 Ex 12:37; Nm 1:45-46; 2:32; 26:51

[A]11:1 Lit *in the ears of* [B]11:3 = blaze [C]11:4 Or *The mixed multitude*; Hb obscure [D]11:6 Or *our lives are wasting away*, or *our throat is dry* [E]11:7 A yellowish, transparent gum resin [F]11:10 Lit *and it was evil in the eyes of Moses* [G]11:12 One Hb ms, Sam, LXX, Syr, Tg read *I* [H]11:15 Ancient Jewish tradition reads *Your misery*

a month.' 22 If flocks and herds were slaughtered for them, would they have enough? Or
if all the fish in the sea were caught for them,
would they have enough?"[a]
23 The LORD answered Moses, "Is the LORD's
power limited?[A,b] You will see whether or not
what I have promised will happen to you."
24 Moses went out and told the people the
words of the LORD. He brought 70 men from
the elders of the people and had them stand
around the tent. 25 Then the LORD descended
in the cloud and spoke to him.[c] He took some
of the Spirit that was on Moses and placed the
Spirit on the 70 elders. As the Spirit rested on
them, they prophesied,[d] but they never did
it again. 26 Two men had remained in the
camp, one named Eldad and the other Medad; the Spirit rested on them — they were
among those listed, but had not gone out to
the tent — and they prophesied in the camp.
27 A young man ran and reported to Moses,
"Eldad and Medad are prophesying in the
camp."
28 Joshua son of Nun, assistant to Moses
since his youth,[B] responded, "Moses, my lord,
stop them!"
29 But Moses asked him, "Are you jealous
on my account?[e] If only all the LORD's people
were prophets and the LORD would place His
Spirit on them!" 30 Then Moses returned to
the camp along with the elders of Israel.

Quail in the Camp

31 A wind sent by the LORD[f] came up and
blew quail in from the sea; it dropped them
at the camp all around, three feet[C] off[D] the
ground, about a day's journey in every direction.[g] 32 The people were up all that day
and night and all the next day gathering the
quail — the one who took the least gathered
50 bushels[E] — and they spread them out all
around the camp.[F,h]
33 While the meat was still between their
teeth, before it was chewed, the LORD's anger burned[i] against the people, and the LORD
struck them with a very severe plague.[j] 34 So
they named that place Kibroth-hattaavah,[G]
because there they buried the people who
had craved the meat.
35 From Kibroth-hattaavah the people moved
on to Hazeroth[H,k] and remained there.

Miriam and Aaron Rebel

12 Miriam[l] and Aaron criticized Moses because of the ·Cushite[I,J] woman
he married (for he had married a Cushite
woman). 2 They said, "Does the LORD speak
only through Moses? Does He not also speak
through us?" And the LORD heard it. 3 Moses
was a very humble man, more so than any
man on the face of the earth.
4 Suddenly the LORD said to Moses, Aaron,
and Miriam, "You three come out to the
tent of meeting." So the three of them went
out. 5 Then the LORD descended in a pillar of
cloud,[m] stood at the entrance to the tent, and
summoned Aaron and Miriam. When the
two of them came forward, 6 He said:

"Listen to what I say:
If there is a prophet among you
from the LORD,
I make Myself known to him
in a vision;[n]
I speak with him in a dream.
7 Not so with My servant Moses;
he is faithful in[K] all My household.[o]
8 I speak with him[p] directly,[L]
openly, and not in riddles;
he sees the form of the LORD.[q]

So why were you not afraid to speak against
My servant Moses?" 9 The LORD's anger
burned against them,[r] and He left.
10 As the cloud moved away from the tent,
Miriam's skin suddenly became diseased, as
white as snow. When Aaron turned toward
her, he saw that she was diseased 11 and said
to Moses, "My lord, please don't hold against
us this sin we have so foolishly committed.
12 Please don't let her be like a dead baby[M]
whose flesh is half eaten away when he comes
out of his mother's womb."
13 Then Moses cried out to the LORD, "God,
please heal her!"[s]
14 The LORD answered Moses, "If her father

[a] 11:22 Mt 15:33; Mk 6:37; 8:4
[b] 11:23 Jb 38:1–42:6; Is 50:2; 59:1
[c] 11:25 Ex 19:9; 33:9-10; Nm 12:5-8
[d] 1Sm 10:6-10; 19:20-24; Is 63:11; Jl 2:28
[e] 11:29 Nm 12:2; 16:3
[f] 11:31 Ex 14:21
[g] Ex 16:12-13; Ps 78:26-28
[h] 11:32 2Sm 17:19; Ezk 26:5,14
[i] 11:33 Ex 22:24; 32:10-11; Nm 11:1,10; 32:13; Dt 6:15
[j] Ps 78:29-31; 106:14-15
[k] 11:35 Nm 12:16; 33:16-17
[l] 12:1 Ex 15:20-21; Nm 20:1; 26:59; Dt 24:9
[m] 12:5 Dt 31:15
[n] 12:6 1Sm 3:15; Ezk 1:1; Dn 10:7-8,16; Rv 1:10-12
[o] 12:7 Heb 3:2,5
[p] 12:8 Ex 33:11; Nm 7:89; Jdg 6:22
[q] 1Co 13:12
[r] 12:9 Ex 22:24; 32:10-11; Nm 11:1,10,33; 32:13; Dt 6:15
[s] 12:13 Gn 20:17; Ex 15:26; Lv 14:3; Dt 32:39

[A] 11:23 Lit *LORD's arm too short* [B] 11:28 LXX, some Sam mss read *Moses, from his chosen ones* [C] 11:31 Lit *two cubits* [D] 11:31 Or *on*, or *above* [E] 11:32 Lit *10 homers* [F] 11:32 To dry or cure the meat; 2Sm 17:19; Ezk 26:5,14 [G] 11:34 = Graves of Craving [H] 11:35 = settlements; Nm 12:16; 33:16-17 [I] 12:1 LXX reads *Ethiopian* [J] 12:1 = Sudan and Ethiopia [K] 12:7 Or *is entrusted with* [L] 12:8 Lit *mouth to mouth* [M] 12:12 Ancient Jewish tradition reads *baby who comes out of our mother's womb and our flesh is half eaten away.*

had merely spit in her face, wouldn't she remain in disgrace for seven days? Let her be
confined outside the camp[a] for seven days;[b]
after that she may be brought back in." 15 So
Miriam was confined outside the camp for
seven days, and the people did not move on
until Miriam was brought back in.[c] 16 After
that, the people set out from Hazeroth and
camped in the Wilderness of Paran.

Scouting Out Canaan

13 The LORD spoke to Moses: 2 "Send men
to scout out the land of Canaan[d] I am
giving to the Israelites. Send one man who is a
leader among them from each of their ancestral tribes." 3 Moses sent them from the Wilderness of Paran at the LORD's command. All
the men were leaders in Israel.[e] 4 These were
their names:

Shammua son of Zaccur from the tribe
of Reuben;
5 Shaphat son of Hori from the tribe
of Simeon;
6 Caleb[f] son of Jephunneh from the tribe
of Judah;
7 Igal son of Joseph from the tribe
of Issachar;
8 Hoshea son of Nun[g] from the tribe
of Ephraim;
9 Palti son of Raphu from the tribe
of Benjamin;
10 Gaddiel son of Sodi from the tribe
of Zebulun;
11 Gaddi son of Susi from the tribe
of Manasseh (from the tribe
of Joseph);
12 Ammiel son of Gemalli from the tribe
of Dan;
13 Sethur son of Michael from the tribe
of Asher;
14 Nahbi son of Vophsi from the tribe
of Naphtali;
15 Geuel son of Machi from the tribe
of Gad.

16 These were the names of the men Moses
sent to scout out the land, and Moses renamed Hoshea son of Nun, Joshua.
17 When Moses sent them to scout out the
land of Canaan, he told them, "Go up this way
to the •Negev, then go up into the hill country. 18 See what the land is like, and whether
the people who live there are strong or weak,
few or many. 19 Is the land they live in good[h]
or bad? Are the cities they live in encampments or fortifications?[i] 20 Is the land fertile
or unproductive?[j] Are there trees in it or not?
Be courageous. Bring back some fruit from
the land." It was the season for the first ripe
grapes.[k]
21 So they went up and scouted out the land
from the Wilderness of Zin[A] as far as Rehob[B]
near the entrance to Hamath.[C] 22 They went
up through the Negev and came to Hebron,
where Ahiman, Sheshai, and Talmai, the descendants of Anak,[l] were living. Hebron was
built seven years before Zoan[m] in Egypt.
23 When they came to the Valley of Eshcol,[n]
they cut down a branch with a single cluster
of grapes, which was carried on a pole by two
men. They also took some pomegranates and
figs.[o] 24 That place was called the Valley of Eshcol[D] because of the cluster of grapes the Israelites cut there. 25 At the end of 40 days[p] they
returned from scouting out the land.

Report about Canaan

26 The men went back to Moses, Aaron, and
the entire Israelite community in the Wilderness of Paran at Kadesh. They brought back a
report for them and the whole community,
and they showed them the fruit of the land.[q]
27 They reported to Moses: "We went into the
land where you sent us. Indeed it is flowing
with milk and honey,[r] and here is some of its
fruit. 28 However, the people living in the land
are strong, and the cities are large and fortified.[s] We also saw the descendants of Anak[t]
there. 29 The Amalekites[u] are living in the
land of the Negev; the Hittites, Jebusites, and
Amorites live in the hill country; and the Canaanites live by the sea and along the Jordan."
30 Then Caleb[v] quieted the people in the
presence of Moses and said, "We must go up
and take possession of the land because we
can certainly conquer it!"
31 But the men who had gone up with him
responded, "We can't go up against the people because they are stronger than we are!"

[a] **12:14** Lv 13:46; Nm 5:1-4; 2Kg 15:5 [b] Lv 13:4 [c] **12:15** Lv 14:2,8 [d] **13:2** Dt 1:22-26 [e] **13:3** Ex 18:25-26; Dt 1:13-18 [f] **13:6** Nm 14:6,24,30,38; 26:65 [g] **13:8** Ex 33:11; Nm 14:30,38; 27:18-23 [h] **13:19** Nm 14:7; Dt 1:25 [i] Dt 1:28; 3:5; 9:1; Jos 14:12 [j] **13:20** Neh 9:25,35; Is 30:23; Ezk 34:14,20 [k] Nm 13:23 [l] **13:22** Nm 13:28,33; Dt 1:28; 2:10-11,21 [m] Ps 78:12; Is 19:11; 30:4; Ezk 30:14 [n] **13:23** Nm 32:9; Dt 1:24 [o] Nm 20:5; Dt 8:8 [p] **13:25** Nm 14:33-34; 32:13; Ps 95:10 [q] **13:26** Nm 32:9; Dt 1:24-25 [r] **13:27** Ex 3:8; Lv 20:24; Nm 14:8; 16:13-14 [s] **13:28** Dt 1:28; 3:5; 9:1; Jos 14:12 [t] Nm 13:22,33; Dt 1:28; 2:10-11,21 [u] **13:29** Ex 17:8-16; Nm 14:25,43,45; Dt 25:17-19 [v] **13:30** Nm 14:6,24,30,38; 26:65

[A] **13:21** Southern border of the promised land [B] **13:21** Northern border of the promised land [C] **13:21** Or *near Lebo-hamath* [D] **13:24** = cluster

32So they gave a negative report to the Israelites about the land they had scouted: "The
land we passed through to explore is one that
devours its inhabitants, and all the people we
saw in it are men of great size. 33We even saw
the Nephilim[A,a] there—the descendants of
Anak come from the Nephilim![b] To ourselves
we seemed like grasshoppers, and we must
have seemed the same to them."

Israel's Refusal to Enter Canaan

14 Then the whole community broke into
loud cries, and the people wept that
night. 2All the Israelites complained about
Moses and Aaron,[c] and the whole community
told them, "If only we had died in the land of
Egypt, or if only we had died in this wilderness! 3Why is the LORD bringing us into this
land to die by the sword? Our wives and little
children will become plunder.[d] Wouldn't it be
better for us to go back to Egypt?"[e] 4So they
said to one another, "Let's appoint a leader
and go back to Egypt."

5Then Moses and Aaron fell down with
their faces to the ground in front of the whole
assembly of the Israelite community. 6Joshua
son of Nun and Caleb son of Jephunneh, who
were among those who scouted out the land,
tore their clothes 7and said to the entire Israelite community: "The land we passed
through and explored is an extremely good
land.[f] 8If the LORD is pleased with us, He will
bring us into this land, a land flowing with
milk and honey,[g] and give it to us. 9Only don't
rebel against the LORD, and don't be afraid
of the people of the land, for we will devour
them.[h] Their protection[i] has been removed
from them, and the LORD is with us. Don't be
afraid of them!"

10While the whole community threatened to stone them,[j] the glory of the LORD
appeared to all the Israelites at the tent of
meeting.

God's Judgment of Israel's Rebellion

11The LORD said to Moses, "How long will
these people despise Me? How long will they
not trust in Me despite all the signs I have
performed among them?[k] 12I will strike them
with a plague and destroy them. Then I will
make you into a greater and mightier nation
than they are."[l]

13But Moses replied to the LORD, "The Egyptians will hear about it, for by Your strength
You brought up this people from them. 14They
will tell it to the inhabitants of this land.[m]
They have heard that You, LORD, are among
these people, how You, LORD, are seen face to
face, how Your cloud stands over them, and
how You go before them in a pillar of cloud by
day and in a pillar of fire by night.[n] 15If You kill
this people with a single blow,[B,o] the nations
that have heard of Your fame[p] will declare,
16'Since the LORD wasn't able to bring this
people into the land He swore to give them,[q]
He has slaughtered them in the wilderness.'[r]

17"So now, may my Lord's power be magnified just as You have spoken: 18The LORD is
slow to anger and rich in faithful love,[s] forgiving wrongdoing and rebellion.[t] But He will
not leave the •guilty unpunished,[u] bringing
the consequences of the fathers' wrongdoing
on the children to the third and fourth generation.[v] 19Please pardon the wrongdoing of
this people, in keeping with the greatness of
Your faithful love,[w] just as You have forgiven
them from Egypt until now."

20The LORD responded, "I have pardoned
them as you requested. 21Yet as surely as I live
and as the whole earth is filled with the LORD's
glory,[x] 22none of the men who have seen My
glory and the signs I performed in Egypt and
in the wilderness, and have tested Me these
10 times and did not obey Me, 23will ever see
the land I swore to give their fathers.[y] None of
those who have despised Me[z] will see it. 24But
since My servant Caleb has a different spirit
and has followed Me completely, I will bring
him into the land where he has gone, and his
descendants will inherit it.[aa] 25Since the Amalekites and Canaanites are living in the low-
lands,[C] turn back tomorrow and head for the
wilderness in the direction of the •Red Sea."[ab]

26Then the LORD spoke to Moses and Aaron:
27"How long must I endure this evil community that keeps complaining about Me? I have
heard the Israelites' complaints that they
make against Me.[ac] 28Tell them: As surely as
I live," this is the LORD's declaration, "I will
do to you exactly as I heard you say. 29Your

[a]**13:33** Gn 6:4 [b]Dt 2:10-11,20-21 [c]**14:2** Ex 16:2,7-8; 17:3; Nm 14:27; 16:11,41; Ps 59:15 [d]**14:3** Gn 34:29; Nm 14:31 [e]Nm 11:5; Dt 17:16; Neh 9:17; Ac 7:39 [f]**14:7** Ex 3:8; Nm 13:27; Dt 1:25; 3:25 [g]**14:8** Ex 3:8; Lv 20:24; Nm 13:17; 16:13-14 [h]**14:9** Nm 14:3 [i]Ps 17:8; 36:7; 57:1; 63:7; 91:1; Is 49:2; 51:16 [j]**14:10** Ex 17:4; Mt 23:37 [k]**14:11** Ex 4:1–12:31; 14:11,21-22; Nm 14:22 [l]**14:12** Gn 12:2; Ex 32:10 [m]**14:14** Ex 15:13-15; Dt 2:25 [n]Ex 13:21-22; Nm 9:16-17; Dt 1:33 [o]**14:15** Ex 32:9-12 [p]Dt 2:25; Jos 2:10; 9:9; Is 66:19; Hab 3:2 [q]**14:16** Gn 12:7; 13:14-17; 15:7; Ac 7:5 [r]Dt 9:28 [s]**14:18** Neh 9:17; Ps 86:5,15; 103:8; 145:8; Jl 2:13; Jnh 4:2 [t]Ezr 9:13; Ps 78:38; 85:2; Is 43:25; 44:22 [u]Pr 11:21; Jr 25:29; Nah 1:3 [v]Ex 20:5; 34:6-7; Dt 5:9; Jr 32:18 [w]**14:19** Ex 34:9; Ps 25:11; 86:5; Jl 2:13 [x]**14:21** Ps 72:19; Hab 2:14 [y]**14:23** Gn 12:7; 13:14-17; 15:7; Ac 7:5 [z]Nm 14:11; Dt 31:20; Ps 74:18 [aa]**14:24** Jos 14:6-15; Jdg 1:10-12,20 [ab]**14:25** Nm 21:4; Dt 1:40; 2:1 [ac]**14:27** Ex 16:2,7-8; 17:3; Nm 14:29,36; 16:11,41; Dt 1:27

[A]**13:33** Possibly means fallen ones; traditionally, "giants"; Gn 6:4 [B]**14:15** Lit *people as one man* [C]**14:25** Lit *valley*

corpses will fall in this wilderness — all of you
who were registered in the census, the entire
number of you 20 years old or more[a] — because you have complained about Me. 30 I
swear that none of you will enter the land I
promised[A] to settle you in, except Caleb son
of Jephunneh and Joshua son of Nun. 31 I will
bring your children whom you said would
become plunder[b] into the land you rejected,
and they will enjoy it.[c] 32 But as for you, your
corpses will fall in this wilderness. 33 Your
children will be shepherds in the wilderness
for 40 years and bear the penalty for your
acts of unfaithfulness until all your corpses
lie scattered in the wilderness. 34 You will
bear the consequences of your sins 40 years
based on the number of the 40 days that you
scouted the land, a year for each day.[B,d] You
will know My displeasure.[C] 35 I, •Yahweh, have
spoken. I swear that I will do this to the entire
evil community that has conspired against
Me.[e] They will come to an end in the wilderness, and there they will die."[f]

36 So the men Moses sent to scout out the
land, and who returned and incited the entire community to complain about him
by spreading a negative report about the
land — 37 those men who spread the negative
report about the land were struck down by
the LORD. 38 Only Joshua son of Nun and Caleb son of Jephunneh remained alive of those
men who went to scout out the land.

Israel Routed

39 When Moses reported these words to all
the Israelites, the people were overcome with
grief. 40 They got up early the next morning
and went up the ridge of the hill country, saying, "Let's go to the place the LORD promised,
for we were wrong."[g]

41 But Moses responded, "Why are you going against the LORD's command? It won't
succeed. 42 Don't go, because the LORD is not
among you and you will be defeated by your
enemies. 43 The Amalekites and Canaanites
are right in front of you, and you will fall by
the sword. The LORD won't be with you, since
you have turned from following Him."

44 But they dared to go up the ridge of
the hill country, even though the ark of the
LORD's covenant and Moses did not leave the
camp. 45 Then the Amalekites and Canaanites who lived in that part of the hill country
came down, attacked them, and routed them
as far as Hormah.[h]

Laws about Offerings

15 The LORD instructed Moses: 2 "Speak
to the Israelites and tell them: When
you enter the land I am giving you to settle
in, 3 and you make a fire offering to the LORD
from the herd or flock — either a •burnt offering or a sacrifice, to fulfill a vow,[i] or as a
freewill offering, or at your appointed festivals — to produce a pleasing aroma for the
LORD, 4 the one presenting his offering to the
LORD must also present a •grain offering of
two quarts[D] of fine flour mixed with a quart[E]
of oil. 5 Prepare a quart[E] of wine as a •drink offering with the burnt offering or sacrifice of
each lamb.

6 "If you prepare a grain offering with a
ram, it must be four quarts[F] of fine flour
mixed with a third of a gallon[G] of oil. 7 Also
present a third of a gallon[G] of wine for a drink
offering as a pleasing aroma to the LORD.

8 "If you prepare a young bull as a burnt offering or as a sacrifice, to fulfill a vow, or as a
•fellowship offering to the LORD, 9 a grain offering of six quarts[H] of fine flour mixed with
two quarts[I] of oil must be presented with the
bull. 10 Also present two quarts[I] of wine as a
drink offering. It is a fire offering of pleasing
aroma to the LORD. 11 This is to be done for
each ox, ram, lamb, or goat. 12 This is how you
must prepare each of them, no matter how
many.

13 "Every Israelite is to prepare these things
in this way when he presents a fire offering
as a pleasing aroma to the LORD. 14 When a
foreigner resides with you or someone else
is among you and wants to prepare a fire offering as a pleasing aroma to the LORD, he is
to do exactly as you do throughout your generations. 15 The assembly is to have the same
statute for[J] both you and the foreign resident

[a] **14:29** Nm 1:3
[b] **14:31** Nm 14:3
[c] Dt 1:39
[d] **14:34** Nm 13:25; 32:13; Dt 2:14; Ps 95:10; Ezk 4:6
[e] **14:35** Nm 16:11; 27:3; Ps 2:1-3
[f] Nm 14:30; 26:64-65; 1Co 10:5
[g] **14:40** Dt 1:41-44
[h] **14:45** Nm 21:3; Jdg 1:17
[i] **15:3** Lv 22:21; 27:2; Nm 15:8

[A] **14:30** Lit *I raised My hand* [B] **14:34** Lit *a day for the year, a day for the year* [C] **14:34** Or *My opposition* [D] **15:4** Lit *a tenth* (of an ephah) [E] **15:4,5** Lit *a fourth hin* [F] **15:6** Lit *two-tenths* (of an ephah) [G] **15:6,7** Lit *a third hin* [H] **15:9** Lit *three-tenths* (of an ephah) [I] **15:9,10** Lit *a half hin* [J] **15:14-15** Sam, LXX read [14] *. . . the LORD, the assembly must do exactly as you do.* [15] *The same statute will apply to . . .*

as a permanent statute throughout your generations. You and the foreigner will be alike
before the LORD. 16 The same law and the same
ordinance will apply to both you and the foreigner who resides with you."[a]
17 The LORD instructed Moses: 18 "Speak to
the Israelites and tell them: After you enter
the land where I am bringing you, 19 you are
to offer a contribution to the LORD when you
eat from the food of the land. 20 You are to offer a loaf from your first batch of dough[b] as a
contribution; offer it just like a contribution
from the threshing floor.[c] 21 Throughout your
generations, you are to give the LORD a contribution from the first batch of your dough.
22 "When you sin unintentionally and do
not obey all these commands that the LORD
spoke to Moses[d] — 23 all that the LORD has
commanded you through Moses, from the
day the LORD issued the commands and onward throughout your generations — 24 and if
it was done unintentionally without the community's awareness, the entire community is
to prepare one young bull for a burnt offering as a pleasing aroma to the LORD, with its
grain offering and drink offering according
to the regulation, and one male goat as a ·sin
offering. 25 The priest must then make ·atone-
ment for the entire Israelite community so
that they may be forgiven, for the sin was unintentional. They are to bring their offering,
one made by fire to the LORD, and their sin
offering before the LORD for their unintentional sin. 26 The entire Israelite community
and the foreigner who resides among them
will be forgiven, since it happened to all the
people unintentionally.
27 "If one person sins unintentionally,[e] he is
to present a year-old female goat as a sin offering. 28 The priest must then make atonement
before the LORD on behalf of the person who
acts in error sinning unintentionally, and
when he makes atonement for him, he will be
forgiven. 29 You are to have the same law for
the person who acts in error, whether he is an
Israelite or a foreigner who lives among you.
30 "But the person who acts defiantly,[A]
whether native or foreign resident, blasphemes the LORD.[f] That person is to be cut
off from his people. 31 He will certainly be cut
off, because he has despised the LORD's word
and broken His command; his ·guilt remains
on him."

Sabbath Violation

32 While the Israelites were in the wilderness, they found a man gathering wood on the
Sabbath day.[g] 33 Those who found him gathering wood brought him to Moses, Aaron, and
the entire community. 34 They placed him
in custody because it had not been decided
what should be done to him. 35 Then the LORD
told Moses, "The man is to be put to death.
The entire community is to stone him outside the camp." 36 So the entire community
brought him outside the camp and stoned
him to death, as the LORD had commanded
Moses.

Tassels for Remembrance

37 The LORD said to Moses, 38 "Speak to the
Israelites and tell them that throughout their
generations they are to make tassels[h] for the
corners of their garments, and put a blue
cord on the tassel at each corner. 39 These will
serve as tassels for you to look at, so that you
may remember all the LORD's commands and
obey them and not become unfaithful by following your own heart and your own eyes.
40 This way you will remember and obey all
My commands and be holy to your God. 41 I
am ·Yahweh your God who brought you out
of the land of Egypt to be your God; I am Yahweh your God."[i]

Korah Incites Rebellion

16 Now Korah son of Izhar, son of Kohath, son of Levi,[j] with Dathan and
Abiram,[k] sons of Eliab, and On son of Peleth,
sons of Reuben, took 2 250 prominent Israelite men who were leaders of the community
and representatives in the assembly, and they
rebelled against Moses. 3 They came together
against Moses and Aaron and told them, "You
have gone too far![B] Everyone in the entire
community is holy, and the LORD is among
them.[l] Why then do you exalt yourselves
above the LORD's assembly?"
4 When Moses heard this, he fell facedown.
5 Then he said to Korah and all his followers,

[a] **15:16** Ex 12:19,49; Lv 16:29-31; 17:8-16
[b] **15:20** Neh 10:37; Ezk 44:30
[c] Lv 2:14
[d] **15:22** Lv 4:2
[e] **15:27** Lv 4:27
[f] **15:30** 2Kg 19:6,22; Is 37:6,23; Ezk 20:27
[g] **15:32** Ex 35:2-3
[h] **15:38** Dt 22:12; Mt 23:5
[i] **15:41** Ex 29:46; Lv 19:36; 25:38; 26:13
[j] **16:1** Ex 6:16-21
[k] Nm 26:9; Dt 11:6; Ps 106:16-18
[l] **16:3** Nm 14:14; Ezk 37:26-28

[A] **15:30** Lit *with a high hand* [B] **16:3** Lit *Enough of you*

"Tomorrow morning the LORD will reveal
who belongs to Him, who is set apart, and the
one He will let come near[a] Him. He will let
the one He chooses come near Him. 6 Korah,
you and all your followers are to do this: take
firepans, and tomorrow 7 place fire in them
and put incense on them before the LORD.[b]
Then the man the LORD chooses will be the
one who is set apart.[c] It is you Levites who
have gone too far!"[A]
8 Moses also told Korah, "Now listen, Levites! 9 Isn't it enough for you that the God
of Israel has separated you from the Israelite
community to bring you near to Himself, to
perform the work at the LORD's tabernacle,
and to stand before the community to minister to them? 10 He has brought you near,
and all your fellow Levites who are with you,
but you are seeking the priesthood as well.
11 Therefore, it is you and all your followers
who have conspired against the LORD![d] As for
Aaron, who is he[B] that you should complain
about him?"
12 Moses sent for Dathan and Abiram, the
sons of Eliab, but they said, "We will not
come! 13 Is it not enough that you brought
us up from a land flowing with milk and
honey to kill us in the wilderness? Do you
also have to appoint yourself as ruler over
us? 14 Furthermore, you didn't bring us to a
land flowing with milk and honey or give us
an inheritance of fields and vineyards. Will
you gouge out the eyes of these men? We will
not come!"
15 Then Moses became angry and said to the
LORD, "Don't respect their offering. I have not
taken one donkey from them or mistreated
a single one of them." 16 So Moses told Korah,
"You and all your followers are to appear before the LORD tomorrow—you, they, and
Aaron. 17 Each of you is to take his firepan,
place incense on it, and present his firepan
before the LORD—250 firepans. You and
Aaron are each to present your firepan also."
18 Each man took his firepan, placed fire in
it, put incense on it, and stood at the entrance
to the tent of meeting along with Moses and
Aaron. 19 After Korah assembled the whole
community against them at the entrance to
the tent of meeting, the glory of the LORD ap-

[a]**16:5** Ex 40:12-15
[b]**16:7** Lv 10:1-2; 16:12
[c]Nm 17:5
[d]**16:11** Nm 14:35; 27:3; Ps 2:1-3
[e]**16:21** Nm 16:45
[f]**16:22** Nm 27:16
[g]Gn 18:24-26
[h]**16:28** Ex 3:10-12
[i]**16:32** Ex 15:12; Nm 26:10
[j]**16:35** Gn 19:24; Lv 10:1-2; Nm 11:1; 2Kg 1:10

peared to the whole community. 20 The LORD
spoke to Moses and Aaron, 21 "Separate yourselves from this community so I may consume them instantly."[e]
22 But Moses and Aaron fell facedown and
said, "God, God of the spirits[C,f] of all flesh,
when one man sins, will You vent Your wrath
on the whole community?"[g]
23 The LORD replied to Moses, 24 "Tell the
community: Get away from the dwellings of
Korah, Dathan, and Abiram."
25 Moses got up and went to Dathan and
Abiram, and the elders of Israel followed
him. 26 He warned the community, "Get away
now from the tents of these wicked men.
Don't touch anything that belongs to them,
or you will be swept away because of all their
sins." 27 So they got away from the dwellings
of Korah, Dathan, and Abiram. Meanwhile,
Dathan and Abiram came out and stood at
the entrance of their tents with their wives,
children, and infants.
28 Then Moses said, "This is how you will
know that the LORD sent me[h] to do all these
things and that it was not of my own will: 29 If
these men die naturally as all people would,
and suffer the fate of all, then the LORD has
not sent me. 30 But if the LORD brings about
something unprecedented, and the ground
opens its mouth and swallows them along
with all that belongs to them so that they go
down alive into *Sheol, then you will know
that these men have despised the LORD."
31 Just as he finished speaking all these
words, the ground beneath them split open.
32 The earth opened its mouth and swallowed
them and their households, all Korah's people,[i] and all their possessions. 33 They went
down alive into Sheol with all that belonged
to them. The earth closed over them, and they
vanished from the assembly. 34 At their cries,
all the people of Israel who were around
them fled because they thought, "The earth
may swallow us too!" 35 Fire also came out
from the LORD and consumed the 250 men
who were presenting the incense.[j]
36 [D]Then the LORD spoke to Moses: 37 "Tell Eleazar son of Aaron the priest to remove the
firepans from the burning debris, because
they are holy, and scatter the fire far away.

[A]**16:7** Lit *Enough of you, sons of Levi* [B]**16:11** Or *Aaron, what has he done* [C]**16:22** Or *breath*; Nm 27:16 [D]**16:36** Nm 17:1 in Hb

38 As for the firepans of those who sinned at
the cost of their own lives, make them into
hammered sheets as plating for the altar, for
they presented them before the LORD, and
the firepans are holy. They will be a sign to
the Israelites."
39 So Eleazar the priest took the bronze firepans that those who were burned had presented, and they were hammered into plating
for the altar, 40 just as the LORD commanded
him through Moses. It was to be a reminder
for the Israelites that no unauthorized person outside the lineage of Aaron should approach to offer incense before the LORD[a] and
become like Korah and his followers.
41 The next day the entire Israelite community complained about Moses and Aaron,[b]
saying, "You have killed the LORD's people!"
42 When the community assembled against
them, Moses and Aaron turned toward the
tent of meeting, and suddenly the cloud covered it, and the LORD's glory appeared.
43 Moses and Aaron went to the front of the
tent of meeting, 44 and the LORD said to Moses, 45 "Get away from this community so that
I may consume them instantly."[c] But they fell
facedown.
46 Then Moses told Aaron, "Take your firepan, place fire from the altar in it, and add
incense. Go quickly to the community and
make •atonement for them, because wrath
has come from the LORD; the plague has begun." 47 So Aaron took his firepan as Moses
had ordered, ran into the middle of the assembly, and saw that the plague had begun
among the people. After he added incense,
he made atonement for the people. 48 He
stood between the dead and the living, and
the plague was halted. 49 But those who died
from the plague numbered 14,700, in addition to those who died because of the Korah
incident. 50 Aaron then returned to Moses at
the entrance to the tent of meeting, since the
plague had been halted.[d]

Aaron's Staff Chosen

17[A] The LORD instructed Moses: 2 "Speak
to the Israelites and take one staff
from them for each ancestral house, 12 staffs
from all the leaders of their ancestral houses.
Write each man's name on his staff. 3 Write
Aaron's name on Levi's staff, because there
must be one staff for the head of each ancestral house. 4 Then place them in the tent of
meeting in front of the •testimony where I
meet with you. 5 The staff of the man I choose
will sprout, and I will rid Myself of the Israelites' complaints that they have been making
about you."
6 So Moses spoke to the Israelites, and each
of their leaders gave him a staff, one for each
of the leaders of their ancestral houses, 12
staffs in all. Aaron's staff was among them.
7 Moses placed the staffs before the LORD in
the tent of the testimony.
8 The next day Moses entered the tent of
the testimony and saw that Aaron's staff, representing the house of Levi, had sprouted,
formed buds, blossomed, and produced almonds! 9 Moses then brought out all the staffs
from the LORD's presence to all the Israelites.
They saw them, and each man took his own
staff. 10 The LORD told Moses, "Put Aaron's
staff back in front of the testimony to be
kept as a sign[e] for the rebels, so that you may
put an end to their complaints before Me, or
else they will die." 11 So Moses did as the LORD
commanded him.
12 Then the Israelites declared to Moses,
"Look, we're perishing! We're lost; we're all
lost! 13 Anyone who comes near the LORD's
tabernacle will die.[f] Will we all perish?"

Provision for the Priesthood

18 The LORD said to Aaron, "You, your
sons, and your ancestral house[g] will be
responsible for sin against the sanctuary. You
and your sons will be responsible for sin involving your priesthood. 2 But also bring your
relatives with you from the tribe of Levi, your
ancestral tribe, so they may join you and assist you and your sons in front of the tent of
the •testimony.[h] 3 They are to perform duties
for you and for the whole tent. They must not
come near the sanctuary equipment or the
altar; otherwise, both they and you will die.
4 They are to join you and guard the tent of
meeting, doing all the work at the tent, but
no unauthorized person may come near you.
5 "You are to guard the sanctuary and the

[a] **16:40** Ex 28:1; Nm 3:10,38; 18:4,7
[b] **16:41** Ex 16:2,7-8; 17:3; Nm 14:27; 17:6; 1Co 10:10
[c] **16:45** Nm 16:21
[d] **16:47-50** Nm 25:1-9; 2Sm 24:15-25
[e] **17:10** Heb 9:4
[f] **17:13** Nm 3:10,38; 8:19; 18:7
[g] **18:1** Nm 10:21
[h] **18:2** Nm 8:5-26

[A] **17:1** Nm 17:16 in Hb

 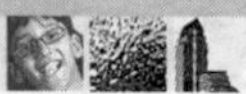

altar so that wrath may not fall on the Israelites again.[a] 6Look, I have selected your fellow
Levites from the Israelites as a gift for you,[A]
assigned by the LORD to work at the tent of
meeting. 7But you and your sons will carry
out your priestly responsibilities for everything concerning the altar and for what is
inside the veil, and you will do that work. I
am giving you the work of the priesthood as a
gift,[B] but an unauthorized person who comes
near the sanctuary will be put to death."

Support for the Priests and Levites

8Then the LORD spoke to Aaron, "Look, I
have put you in charge of the contributions
brought to Me. As for all the holy offerings
of the Israelites, I have given them to you
and your sons as a portion and a permanent
statute.[b] 9A portion of the holiest offerings
kept from the fire will be yours; every one of
their offerings that they give Me, whether the
·grain offering, ·sin offering, or ·restitution
offering will be most holy for you and your
sons. 10You are to eat it as a most holy offering.[C] Every male may eat it; it is to be holy to
you.

11"The contribution of their gifts also belongs to you. I have given all the Israelites'
presentation offerings to you and to your
sons and daughters as a permanent statute.[c]
Every ceremonially ·clean person in your
house may eat it. 12I am giving you all the best
of the fresh olive oil, new wine, and grain,
which the Israelites give to the LORD as their
·firstfruits. 13The firstfruits of all that is in
their land, which they bring to the LORD, belong to you. Every clean person in your house
may eat them.

14"Everything in Israel that is permanently
dedicated to the LORD[d] belongs to you. 15The
firstborn of every living thing, man or animal, presented to the LORD belongs to you.
But you must certainly redeem the firstborn
of man,[e] and redeem the firstborn of an ·un-
clean animal. 16You will pay the redemption
price for a month-old male according to your
assessment: five ·shekels of silver by the standard sanctuary shekel, which is 20 *gerahs*.[f]

17"However, you must not redeem the firstborn of an ox, a sheep, or a goat; they are
holy. You are to sprinkle their blood on the
altar and burn their fat as a fire offering for a
pleasing aroma to the LORD. 18But their meat
belongs to you. It belongs to you like the
breast of the presentation offering and the
right thigh.

19"I give to you and to your sons and daughters all the holy contributions that the Israelites present to the LORD as a permanent
statute. It is a permanent covenant of salt[g]
before the LORD for you as well as your ·off-
spring."

20The LORD told Aaron, "You will not have
an inheritance in their land; there will be no
portion among them for you. I am your portion and your inheritance among the Israelites.[h]

21"Look, I have given the Levites every tenth
in Israel as an inheritance in return for the
work they do, the work of the tent of meeting. 22The Israelites must never again come
near the tent of meeting, or they will incur
·guilt and die. 23The Levites will do the work
of the tent of meeting, and they will bear the
consequences of their sin. The Levites will
not receive an inheritance among the Israelites;[i] this is a permanent statute throughout
your generations. 24For I have given them the
tenth that the Israelites present to the LORD
as a contribution for their inheritance. That
is why I told them that they would not receive
an inheritance among the Israelites."

25The LORD instructed Moses, 26"Speak to
the Levites and tell them: When you receive
from the Israelites the tenth that I have given
you as your inheritance, you must present
part of it as an offering to the LORD — a tenth
of the tenth. 27Your offering will be credited to you as if it were your grain from the
threshing floor or the full harvest from the
winepress. 28You are to present an offering to
the LORD from every tenth you receive from
the Israelites. Give some of it to Aaron the
priest as an offering to the LORD. 29You must
present the entire offering due the LORD
from all your gifts. The best part of the tenth[j]
is to be consecrated.

30"Tell them further: Once you have presented the best part of the tenth, and it is
credited to you Levites as the produce of the

[a]**18:5** Nm 1:53; 16; 17:12-13
[b]**18:8** Lv 10:12-15; Nm 5:9
[c]**18:11** Lv 7:34-36
[d]**18:14** Lv 27:28
[e]**18:15** Ex 13:11-16
[f]**18:16** Lv 27:6; Nm 3:46-47
[g]**18:19** Lv 2:13; 2Ch 13:5
[h]**18:20** Dt 10:9; Jos 18:7; Ezk 44:28-30
[i]**18:23** Dt 10:8-9; 18:1-2; Jos 13:14,33
[j]**18:29** Nm 18:12

[A]**18:6** LXX, Syr, Vg omit *for you* [B]**18:7** Or *veil. So you are to perform the service; a gift of your priesthood I grant* [C]**18:10** Or *it in a most holy place* threshing floor or the winepress, 31then you and your household may eat it anywhere. It is your wage in return for your work at the tent of meeting. 32You will not incur guilt because of it once you have presented the best part of it, but you must not defile the Israelites' holy offerings, so that you will not die."

Purification Ritual

19 The LORD spoke to Moses and Aaron,
2"This is the legal statute that the LORD
has commanded: Instruct the Israelites to
bring you an unblemished red cow that has
no defect and has never been yoked.[a] 3Give
it to Eleazar the priest, and he will have it
brought outside the camp and slaughtered
in his presence. 4Eleazar the priest is to take
some of its blood with his finger and sprinkle it seven times toward the front of the
tent of meeting. 5The cow must be burned in
his sight. Its hide, flesh, and blood, are to be
burned along with its dung. 6The priest is to
take cedar wood, hyssop, and crimson yarn,[b]
and throw them onto the fire where the cow
is burning. 7Then the priest must wash his
clothes and bathe his body in water; after
that he may enter the camp, but he will remain ceremonially •unclean until evening.
8The one who burned the cow must also wash
his clothes and bathe his body in water, and
he will remain unclean until evening.
9"A man who is •clean is to gather up the
cow's ashes and deposit them outside the
camp in a ceremonially clean place. The ashes
must be kept by the Israelite community for
preparing the water to remove impurity; it is
a •sin offering.[c] 10Then the one who gathers
up the cow's ashes must wash his clothes, and
he will remain unclean until evening. This is
a permanent statute for the Israelites and for
the foreigner who resides among them.
11"The person who touches any human
corpse will be unclean for seven days. 12He
is to purify himself with the water[A] on the
third day and the seventh day; then he will
be clean.[d] But if he does not purify himself
on the third and seventh days, he will not be
clean. 13Anyone who touches a body of a person who has died, and does not purify himself, defiles the tabernacle of the LORD. That
person will be cut off from Israel. He remains
unclean because the water for impurity has
not been sprinkled on him, and his uncleanness is still on him.
14"This is the law when a person dies in a
tent: everyone who enters the tent and everyone who is already in the tent will be unclean
for seven days, 15and any open container
without a lid tied on it is unclean. 16Anyone
in the open field who touches a person who
has been killed by the sword or has died, or
who even touches a human bone, or a grave,
will be unclean for seven days. 17For the purification of the unclean person, they are to
take some of the ashes of the burnt sin offering, put them in a jar, and add fresh water to them. 18A person who is clean is to take
hyssop, dip it in the water, and sprinkle the
tent, all the furnishings, and the people who
were there. He is also to sprinkle the one who
touched a bone, a grave, a corpse, or a person
who had been killed.
19"The one who is clean is to sprinkle the
unclean person on the third day and the seventh day. After he purifies the unclean person
on the seventh day, the one being purified
must wash his clothes and bathe in water, and
he will be clean by evening. 20But a person
who is unclean and does not purify himself,
that person will be cut off from the assembly
because he has defiled the sanctuary of the
LORD.[e] The water for impurity has not been
sprinkled on him; he is unclean. 21This is a
permanent statute for them. The person who
sprinkles the water for impurity is to wash
his clothes, and whoever touches the water
for impurity will be unclean until evening.
22Anything the unclean person touches will
become unclean, and anyone who touches it
will be unclean until evening."

Water from the Rock

20 The entire Israelite community entered the Wilderness of Zin in the
first month, and they[B] settled in Kadesh. Miriam[f] died and was buried there.
2There was no water for the community,
so they assembled against Moses and Aaron.
3The people quarreled with Moses and said,
"If only we had perished when our brothers

[a]19:2 Dt 21:3; 1Sm 6:7; Heb 9:13
[b]19:6 Lv 14:4-7,49-52; Heb 9:19
[c]19:9 Lv 4
[d]19:12 Nm 31:19
[e]19:20 1Co 6:19-20
[f]20:1 Ex 15:20-21; Nm 12:1; 26:59; Dt 24:9

A19:12 Or *ashes*; lit *with it* B20:1 Lit *the people*

Haralan Popov (1907–1988)

Some believers can strongly identify with the life of Joseph (son of Jacob) and the apostle Paul. Haralan Popov is one of them. Born on March 7, 1907, in Krasno Gradishte, Haralan Popov was a professed atheist early in life but became a Christian as a teen. After graduating from a Bible school in London, he later became the pastor of the Bulgarian Pentecostal Church, the nation's largest Protestant church, in 1929. He also married Ruth, a citizen of Sweden.

Popov pastored during a time of turmoil—the Communists' occupation of Bulgaria. His faithfulness to the mission of Christ made him enemies. On July 23, 1948, Popov and fourteen other ministers were arrested in Sofia, Bulgaria's capital city, and charged with treason and being spies for the United States and Britain—completely false charges. After being tortured by the KGB for eight months, Popov pled guilty to the charges and received a fifteen-year prison sentence. He served thirteen years in various prisons and labor camps, suffering abuse, before being released on September 25, 1961. Another year passed before he was reunited with his family in Sweden.

Popov and his family moved to the United States in 1970. There he founded Evangelism to Communist Lands, Inc., in 1972, which later became Door of Hope International. This organization was established to offer relief to persecuted Christians and alert others to their plight.

Popov wrote his autobiography, *Tortured for His Faith: An Epic of Christian Courage and Heroism in Our Day* (Zondervan, 1980), which details the story of his life in prison. It has been published in more than twenty languages all over the world.

In 1988 Popov was allowed to return to Bulgaria to visit the church he once pastored. A month later, November 14, 1988, he died of cancer in Glendale, California.

perished before the LORD.[a] 4Why have you brought the LORD's assembly into this wilderness for us and our livestock to die here? 5Why have you led us up from Egypt to bring us to this evil place? It's not a place of grain, figs, vines, and pomegranates,[b] and there is no water to drink!"

6Then Moses and Aaron went from the presence of the assembly to the doorway of the tent of meeting. They fell down with their faces to the ground, and the glory of the LORD appeared to them. 7The LORD spoke to Moses, 8"Take the staff[c] and assemble the community. You and your brother Aaron are to speak to the rock while they watch, and it will yield its water. You will bring out water for them from the rock and provide drink for the community and their livestock."

9So Moses took the staff from the LORD's presence[d] just as He had commanded him. 10Moses and Aaron summoned the assembly in front of the rock, and Moses said to them, "Listen, you rebels! Must we bring water out of this rock for you?" 11Then Moses raised his hand and struck the rock twice with his staff, so that a great amount of water gushed out, and the community and their livestock drank.[e]

12But the LORD said to Moses and Aaron, "Because you did not trust Me to show My holiness in the sight of the Israelites, you will not bring this assembly into the land I have given them."[f] 13These are the waters of Meribah,[A,g] where the Israelites quarreled with the LORD, and He showed His holiness to them.

Edom Denies Passage

14Moses sent messengers from Kadesh to the king of Edom, "This is what your brother Israel[h] says, 'You know all the hardships that have overtaken us. 15Our fathers went down to Egypt, and we lived in Egypt many years, but the Egyptians treated us and our fathers badly. 16When we cried out to the LORD, He heard our voice, sent an angel,[B,i] and brought us out of Egypt. Now look, we are in Kadesh, a city on the border of your territory. 17Please let us travel through your land. We won't travel through any field or vineyard, or drink any well water. We will travel the King's Highway; we won't turn to the right or the left until we have traveled through your territory.'"[j]

18But Edom answered him, "You must not travel through our land, or we will come out and confront you with the sword."

19"We will go on the main road," the Israelites replied to them, "and if we or our herds drink your water, we will pay its price.[k] There will be no problem; only let us travel through on foot."

20Yet Edom insisted, "You must not travel through." And they came out to confront them with a large force of heavily-armed people.[C] 21Edom refused to allow Israel to travel through their territory, and Israel turned away from them.

Aaron's Death

22After they set out from Kadesh, the entire Israelite community came to Mount Hor.[l] 23The LORD said to Moses and Aaron at Mount Hor on the border of the land of Edom, 24"Aaron will be gathered to his people; he will not enter the land I have given the Israelites, because you both rebelled against My command at the waters of Meribah. 25Take Aaron and his son Eleazar and bring them up Mount Hor. 26Remove Aaron's garments and put them on his son Eleazar. Aaron will be gathered to his people and die there."

27So Moses did as the LORD commanded, and they climbed Mount Hor in the sight of the whole community. 28After Moses removed Aaron's garments and put them on his son Eleazar, Aaron died there on top of the mountain. Then Moses and Eleazar came down from the mountain. 29When the whole community saw that Aaron had passed away, the entire house of Israel mourned for him 30 days.

Canaanite King Defeated

21 When the Canaanite king of Arad,[m] who lived in the ·Negev, heard that Israel was coming on the Atharim road, he fought against Israel and captured some prisoners. 2Then Israel made a vow to the LORD, "If You will deliver this people into our hands, we will ·completely destroy their cities."[n] 3The LORD listened to Israel's request, the Canaanites

[a] **20:3** Nm 16:31-35,41-50
[b] **20:5** Ex 13:5; Nm 13:23-27; Dt 8:8
[c] **20:8** Ex 4:2-5; 17:4-9; Nm 17:8
[d] **20:9** Nm 17:10
[e] **20:11** Ex 17:6; Ps 78:15; 1Co 10:4
[f] **20:12** Nm 27:12-14
[g] **20:13** Ex 17:7; Nm 27:14; Dt 32:51; Ps 95:8; 106:32
[h] **20:14** Gn 25:23-26,30; 36:8
[i] **20:16** Ex 3:7-10; 14:19; 23:20
[j] **20:17** Nm 21:22; Dt 2:27
[k] **20:19** Dt 2:1-7
[l] **20:22** Nm 21:4; 33:37-41; Dt 32:50
[m] **21:1** Nm 33:40; Jos 12:14; Jdg 1:16
[n] **21:2** Dt 2:34; 13:16-17; Jos 6:18,21

A**20:13** = quarreling B**20:16** Or *a messenger* C**20:20** Lit *with numerous people and a strong hand* were defeated, and Israel completely destroyed them and their cities. So they named the place Hormah.[A,a]

The Bronze Snake

4 Then they set out from Mount Hor by way of the •Red Sea to bypass the land of Edom, but the people[B] became impatient because of the journey. 5 The people spoke against God and Moses: "Why have you led us up from Egypt to die in the wilderness? There is no bread or water, and we detest this wretched food!" 6 Then the LORD sent poisonous[C,D] snakes among the people, and they bit them so that many Israelites died.[b]

7 The people then came to Moses and said, "We have sinned by speaking against the LORD and against you. Intercede with the LORD so that He will take the snakes away from us." And Moses interceded for the people.

8 Then the LORD said to Moses, "Make a snake image and mount it on a pole. When anyone who is bitten looks at it, he will recover."[c] 9 So Moses made a bronze snake and mounted it on a pole. Whenever someone was bitten, and he looked at the bronze snake, he recovered.

Journey around Moab

10 The Israelites set out and camped at Oboth.[d] 11 They set out from Oboth and camped at Iye-abarim in the wilderness that borders Moab on the east. 12 From there they went and camped at Zered Valley. 13 They set out from there and camped on the other side of the Arnon River, in the wilderness that extends from the Amorite border, because the Arnon was the Moabite border between Moab and the Amorites. 14 Therefore it is stated in the Book of the LORD's Wars:

> Waheb[E] in Suphah
> and the ravines of the Arnon,
> 15 even the slopes of the ravines
> that extend to the site of Ar[F,e]
> and lie along the border of Moab.

16 From there they went to Beer,[G] the well the LORD told Moses about, "Gather the people so I may give them water." 17 Then Israel sang this song:

> Spring up, well — sing to it!
> 18 The princes dug the well;
> the nobles of the people hollowed it out
> with a scepter and with their staffs.

They went from the wilderness to Mattanah, 19 from Mattanah to Nahaliel, from Nahaliel to Bamoth, 20 from Bamoth to the valley in the territory of Moab near the Pisgah highlands[H,f] that overlook the wasteland.[I,g]

Amorite Kings Defeated

21 Israel sent messengers to say to Sihon[h] king of the Amorites: 22 "Let us travel through your land. We won't go into the fields or vineyards. We won't drink any well water. We will travel the King's Highway until we have traveled through your territory."[i] 23 But Sihon would not let Israel travel through his territory. Instead, he gathered his whole army and went out to confront Israel in the wilderness. When he came to Jahaz,[j] he fought against Israel. 24 Israel struck him with the sword and took possession of his land from the Arnon to the Jabbok,[k] but only up to the Ammonite border, because it was fortified.[J,K]

25 Israel took all the cities and lived in all these Amorite cities, including Heshbon and all its villages. 26 Heshbon was the city of Sihon king of the Amorites, who had fought against the former king of Moab and had taken control of all his land as far as the Arnon. 27 Therefore the poets[L] say:

> Come to Heshbon, let it be rebuilt;
> let the city of Sihon be restored.[M]
> 28 For fire came out of Heshbon,
> a flame from the city of Sihon.
> It consumed Ar of Moab,
> the lords of[N] Arnon's heights.
> 29 Woe to you, Moab!
> You have been destroyed,
> people of Chemosh![l]
> He gave up his sons as refugees,
> and his daughters into captivity
> to Sihon the Amorite king.

[a] **21:3** Nm 14:45; Dt 1:44; Jdg 1:17
[b] **21:6** 1Co 10:9
[c] **21:8** 2Kg 18:4; Jn 3:14-15
[d] **21:10-11** Nm 33:43-44
[e] **21:15** Nm 21:28; Dt 2:9,18,29; Is 15:1
[f] **21:20** Nm 23:14; Dt 3:17,27; 4:49; 34:1; Jos 12:3; 13:20
[g] Nm 23:28
[h] **21:21** Nm 32:33; Dt 1:4; 2:24–4:46
[i] **21:22** Nm 20:17; Dt 2:26-33
[j] **21:23** Dt 2:32; Jdg 11:20; 1Ch 6:78
[k] **21:21-24** Jdg 11:19-22
[l] **21:27-29** Jdg 11:24; 1Kg 11:7,33; Jr 48:45-47

[A] **21:3** = destruction [B] **21:4** Lit *soul of the people* [C] **21:6** LXX reads *deadly*; Syr reads *cruel*; Vg reads *fiery* [D] **21:6** Lit *burning* [E] **21:14** = the source of the Arnon River [F] **21:15** A city in Moab; Nm 21:28; Dt 2:9,18,29; Is 15:1 [G] **21:16** = well [H] **21:20** = Moabite mountain plateau; Nm 23:14; Dt 3:17,27; 4:49; 34:1; Jos 12:3; 13:20 [I] **21:20** Or *overlook Jeshimon* [J] **21:24** LXX reads *was Jazer* [K] **21:24** Or *was at Az* [L] **21:27** Lit *ones who speak proverbs* [M] **21:27** Or *firmly founded* [N] **21:28** LXX reads *Moab, and swallowed*

30 We threw them down;
Heshbon has been destroyed
as far as Dibon.[A,a]
We caused desolation as far as Nophah,
which reaches as far as Medeba.[B,b]

31 So Israel lived in the Amorites' land. 32 After
Moses sent spies to Jazer, Israel captured its
villages and drove out the Amorites who were
there.
33 Then they turned and went up the road
to Bashan, and Og king of Bashan[c] came out
against them with his whole army to do battle
at Edrei.[d] 34 But the LORD said to Moses, "Do
not fear him, for I have handed him over to
you along with his whole army and his land.
Do to him as you did to Sihon king of the
Amorites, who lived in Heshbon."[e] 35 So they
struck him, his sons, and his whole army until no one was left,[C] and they took possession
of his land.[f]

Balak Hires Balaam

22 The Israelites traveled on and camped
in the plains of Moab near the Jordan across from Jericho. 2 Now Balak[g] son
of Zippor saw all that Israel had done to the
Amorites. 3 Moab was terrified of the people
because they were numerous, and Moab
dreaded the Israelites. 4 So the Moabites said
to the elders of Midian, "This horde will devour everything around us like an ox eats up
the green plants in the field."
Since Balak son of Zippor was Moab's king
at that time, 5 he sent messengers to Balaam[h]
son of Beor at Pethor, which is by the Euphrates in the land of his people.[D,E] Balak said to
him: "Look, a people has come out of Egypt;
they cover the surface of the land and are living right across from me. 6 Please come and
put a curse on these people for me because
they are more powerful than I am. I may be
able to defeat them and drive them out of
the land, for I know that those you bless are
blessed and those you curse are cursed."
7 The elders of Moab and Midian departed
with fees for •divination in hand.[i] They
came to Balaam and reported Balak's words
to him. 8 He said to them, "Spend the night
here, and I will give you the answer the LORD
tells me." So the officials of Moab stayed with
Balaam.
9 Then God came to Balaam and asked,
"Who are these men with you?"
10 Balaam replied to God, "Balak son of Zippor, king of Moab, sent this message to me:
11 'Look, a people has come out of Egypt, and
they cover the surface of the land. Now come
and put a curse on them for me. I may be able
to fight against them and drive them away.'"
12 Then God said to Balaam, "You are not to
go with them. You are not to curse this people, for they are blessed."
13 So Balaam got up the next morning and
said to Balak's officials, "Go back to your land,
because the LORD has refused to let me go
with you."
14 The officials of Moab arose, returned to
Balak, and reported, "Balaam refused to come
with us."
15 Balak sent officials again who were more
numerous and higher in rank than the others. 16 They came to Balaam and said to him,
"This is what Balak son of Zippor says: 'Let
nothing keep you from coming to me, 17 for I
will greatly honor you and do whatever you
ask me. So please come and put a curse on
these people for me!'"
18 But Balaam responded to the servants
of Balak, "If Balak were to give me his house
full of silver and gold, I could not go against
the command of the LORD my God to do anything small or great. 19 Please stay here overnight as the others did, so that I may find out
what else the LORD has to tell me."
20 God came to Balaam at night and said to
him, "Since these men have come to summon
you, get up and go with them, but you must
only do what I tell you." 21 When he got up in
the morning, Balaam saddled his donkey and
went with the officials of Moab.

Balaam's Donkey and the Angel

22 But God was incensed that Balaam was
going, and the Angel of the LORD took His
stand on the path to oppose him. Balaam
was riding his donkey, and his two servants
were with him. 23 When the donkey saw the
Angel of the LORD standing on the path with

[a] 21:30 Nm 32:34; Neh 11:25; Jr 48:18,22
[b] Jos 13:9,16; 1Ch 19:7; Is 15:2
[c] 21:33 Nm 32:33; Dt 3:1-13; 4:47
[d] Dt 3:1,10; Jos 12:4; 13:12,31
[e] 21:34 Dt 3:2
[f] 21:35 Ps 135:10-11
[g] 22:2 Jos 24:9-10; Mc 6:5; Rv 2:14
[h] 22:5 Dt 23:3-5; Jos 24:9-10; Mc 6:5; 2Pt 2:15-16; Jd 11; Rv 2:14
[i] 22:7 2Pt 2:15; Jd 11

[A] 21:30 LXX reads *Their seed will perish from Heshbon*; Vg reads *Their yoke has perished from Heshbon* [B] 21:30 LXX reads *Dibon. And their women have further kindled a fire against Moab*; Hb uncertain [C] 21:35 Lit *left to him* [D] 22:5 Sam, Vg, Syr read *of the Ammonites* [E] 22:5 Or *of the Amawites* a drawn sword in His hand, she turned off the path and went into the field. So Balaam hit her to return her to the path. 24 Then the Angel of the LORD stood in a narrow passage between the vineyards, with a stone wall on either side. 25 The donkey saw the Angel of the LORD and pressed herself against the wall, squeezing Balaam's foot against it. So he hit her once again. 26 The Angel of the LORD went ahead and stood in a narrow place where there was no room to turn to the right or the left. 27 When the donkey saw the Angel of the LORD, she crouched down under Balaam. So he became furious and beat the donkey with his stick.

28 Then the LORD opened the donkey's mouth, and she asked Balaam, "What have I done to you that you have beaten me these three times?"[a]

29 Balaam answered the donkey, "You made me look like a fool. If I had a sword in my hand, I'd kill you now!"

30 But the donkey said, "Am I not the donkey you've ridden all your life until today? Have I ever treated you this way before?"

"No," he replied.

31 Then the LORD opened Balaam's eyes, and he saw the Angel of the LORD standing in the path with a drawn sword in His hand. Balaam knelt and bowed with his face to the ground. 32 The Angel of the LORD asked him, "Why have you beaten your donkey these three times? Look, I came out to oppose you, because what you are doing is evil in My sight. 33 The donkey saw Me and turned away from Me these three times. If she had not turned away from Me, I would have killed you by now and let her live."

34 Balaam said to the Angel of the LORD, "I have sinned, for I did not know that You were standing in the path to confront me. And now, if it is evil in Your sight, I will go back."

35 Then the Angel of the LORD said to Balaam, "Go with the men, but you are to say only what I tell you." So Balaam went with Balak's officials.

36 When Balak heard that Balaam was coming, he went out to meet him at the Moabite city[A] on the Arnon border at the edge of his territory. 37 Balak asked Balaam, "Did I not send you an urgent summons? Why didn't you come to me? Am I really not able to reward you?"

38 Balaam said to him, "Look, I have come to you, but can I say anything I want? I must speak only the message God puts in my mouth." 39 So Balaam went with Balak, and they came to Kiriath-huzoth.[B] 40 Balak sacrificed cattle and sheep, and sent for Balaam and the officials who were with him.

41 In the morning, Balak took Balaam and brought him to Bamoth-baal.[C] From there he saw the outskirts of the people's camp.

Balaam's Oracles

23 Then Balaam said to Balak, "Build me seven altars here and prepare seven bulls and seven rams for me." 2 So Balak did as Balaam directed, and they offered a bull and a ram on each altar. 3 Balaam said to Balak, "Stay here by your •burnt offering while I am gone. Maybe the LORD[D] will meet with me. I will tell you whatever He reveals to me." So he went to a barren hill.

4 God[E] met with him and Balaam said to Him, "I have arranged seven altars and offered a bull and a ram on each altar." 5 Then the LORD put a message in Balaam's mouth and said, "Return to Balak and say what I tell you."

6 So he returned to Balak, who was standing there by his burnt offering with all the officials of Moab.

Balaam's First Oracle

7 Balaam proclaimed his poem:

Balak brought me from Aram;[b]
the king of Moab,
from the eastern mountains:
"Come, put a curse on Jacob for me;
come, denounce Israel!"[c]
8 How can I curse someone
God has not cursed?
How can I denounce someone the LORD
has not denounced?
9 I see them from the top of rocky cliffs,
and I watch them from the hills.
There is a people living alone;[d]

[a] 22:28 2Pt 2:15-16
[b] 23:7 Dt 23:4
[c] Nm 22:6,17
[d] 23:9 Dt 33:28

[A] 22:36 Or *at Ir-moab*, or *at Ar of Moab* [B] 22:39 = The City of Streets
[C] 22:41 = The High Places of Baal [D] 23:3 DSS, LXX, Sam read *Maybe God*
[E] 23:4 DSS, Sam read *The Angel of God*

it does not consider itself
among the nations.
10 Who has counted the dust of Jacob
or numbered the dust clouds[A] of Israel?
Let me die the death of the upright;
let the end of my life be like theirs.

11 "What have you done to me?" Balak asked
Balaam. "I brought you to curse my enemies,
but look, you have only blessed them!"
12 He answered, "Shouldn't I say exactly
what the LORD puts in my mouth?"[a]

Balaam's Second Oracle

13 Then Balak said to him, "Please come with
me to another place where you can see them.
You will only see the outskirts of their camp;
you won't see all of them. From there, put a
curse on them for me." 14 So Balak took him to
Lookout Field[B] on top of Pisgah, built seven
altars, and offered a bull and a ram on each
altar.
15 Balaam said to Balak, "Stay here by your
burnt offering while I seek the LORD over
there."
16 The LORD met with Balaam and put a message in his mouth. Then He said, "Return to
Balak and say what I tell you."
17 So he returned to Balak, who was standing there by his burnt offering with the officials of Moab. Balak asked him, "What did
the LORD say?"
18 Balaam proclaimed his poem:

Balak, get up and listen;
son of Zippor, pay attention to what
I say!
19 God is not a man who lies,
or a son of man who changes His mind.
Does He speak and not act,
or promise and not fulfill?[b]
20 I have indeed received a command
to bless;
since He has blessed,[C]
I cannot change it.
21 He considers no disaster for Jacob;
He sees no trouble for Israel.[D]
The LORD their God is with them,[c]
and there is rejoicing over the King
among them.

[a]23:12 Nm 22:38 [b]23:19 1Sm 15:29; Rm 11:29; 2Tm 2:13; Heb 6:17-18 [c]23:21 Dt 2:7; 20:1; Jos 1:17; Zph 3:17; Rv 21:3 [d]23:22 Nm 24:8 [e]23:24 Nm 24:9 [f]23:26 Nm 22:38 [g]23:28 Nm 21:20 [h]23:29 Nm 23:1-2 [i]24:2 Ex 35:31; Nm 11:17,25-26,29; 1Sm 10:10 [j]24:4 Is 13:6,9; Ezk 30:2-3; Jl 2:1-2,11,31

22 God brought them out of Egypt;
He is like the horns of a wild ox
for them.[E,d]
23 There is no magic curse against Jacob
and no ·divination against Israel.
It will now be said about Jacob
and Israel,
"What great things God has done!"
24 A people rise up like a lioness;
They rouse themselves like a lion.[e]
They will not lie down
until they devour the prey
and drink the blood of the slain.

25 Then Balak told Balaam, "Don't curse
them and don't bless them!"
26 But Balaam answered him, "Didn't I tell
you: Whatever the LORD says, I must do?"[f]

Balaam's Third Oracle

27 Again Balak said to Balaam, "Please come.
I will take you to another place. Maybe it
will be agreeable to God that you can put a
curse on them for me there." 28 So Balak took
Balaam to the top of Peor, which overlooks
the wasteland.[F,g]
29 Balaam told Balak, "Build me seven altars
here and prepare seven bulls and seven rams
for me."[h] 30 So Balak did as Balaam said and offered a bull and a ram on each altar.

24 Since Balaam saw that it pleased the
LORD to bless Israel, he did not go
to seek omens as on previous occasions,
but turned[G] toward the wilderness. 2 When
Balaam looked up and saw Israel encamped
tribe by tribe, the Spirit of God[i] came on him,
3 and he proclaimed his poem:

The ·oracle of Balaam son of Beor,
the oracle of the man whose eyes
are opened,[H]
4 the oracle of one who hears the sayings
of God,
who sees a vision from the ·Almighty,[j]
who falls into a trance with his eyes
uncovered:
5 How beautiful are your tents, Jacob,
your dwellings, Israel.
6 They stretch out like river valleys,[I]
like gardens beside a stream,

A23:10 Or *numbered a fourth* B23:14 Or *to the field of Zophim* C23:20 Sam, LXX read *since I will bless* D23:21 Or *not observe sin in Jacob; not see wrongdoing* E23:22 Or *Egypt; they have the horns of a wild ox* F23:28 Or *overlooks Jeshimon* G24:1 Lit *set his face* H24:3 LXX reads *true*; Vg reads *closed* I24:6 Or *like date palms*

like aloes the LORD has planted,
like cedars beside the water.
7 Water will flow from his buckets,
and his seed will be
by abundant water.
His king will be greater than Agag,[A,a]
and his kingdom will be exalted.
8 God brought him out of Egypt;
He is like[B] the horns of a wild ox
for them.[b]
He will feed on enemy nations
and gnaw their bones;
he will strike them with his arrows.
9 He crouches, he lies down like a lion
or a lioness — who dares to rouse him?[c]
Those who bless you will be blessed,
and those who curse you
will be cursed.[d]

10 Then Balak became furious with Balaam,
struck his hands together, and said to him, "I
summoned you to put a curse on my enemies,
but instead, you have blessed them these
three times. 11 Now go to your home! I said I
would reward you richly,[e] but look, the LORD
has denied you a reward."
12 Balaam answered Balak, "Didn't I previously tell the messengers you sent me: 13 If
Balak were to give me his house full of silver
and gold, I could not go against the LORD's
command, to do anything good or bad of my
own will? I will say whatever the LORD says.[f]
14 Now I am going back to my people, but first,
let me warn you what these people will do to
your people in the future."

Balaam's Fourth Oracle

15 Then he proclaimed his poem:

The oracle of Balaam son of Beor,
the oracle of the man whose eyes
are opened;[C]
16 the oracle of one who hears the sayings
of God
and has knowledge
from the •Most High,
who sees a vision from the Almighty,
who falls into a trance with his
eyes uncovered:[g]
17 I see him,[D] but not now;
I perceive him,[D] but not near.
A star will come from Jacob,
and a scepter will arise from Israel.[h]
He will smash the forehead[E] of Moab
and strike down[F] all the Shethites.[G]
18 Edom will become a possession;
Seir[i] will become a possession
of its enemies,
but Israel will be triumphant.
19 One who comes from Jacob will rule;
he will destroy the city's survivors.

20 Then Balaam saw Amalek and proclaimed
his poem:

Amalek was first among the nations,[j]
but his future is destruction.

21 Next he saw the Kenites and proclaimed
his poem:

Your dwelling place is enduring;
your nest is set in the cliffs.
22 Kain will be destroyed
when Asshur takes you captive.

23 Once more he proclaimed his poem:

Ah, who can live when God does this?
24 Ships will come from the coast
of Kittim;[k]
they will afflict Asshur and Eber,[l]
but they too will come to destruction.

25 Balaam then arose and went back to his
homeland, and Balak also went his way.

Israel Worships Baal

25 While Israel was staying in the Acacia Grove,[H,m] the people began to have
sexual relations with the women of Moab.
2 The women invited them to the sacrifices
for their gods, and the people ate and bowed
in worship to their gods.[n] 3 So Israel aligned
itself with •Baal of Peor,[o] and the LORD's anger burned against Israel.[p] 4 The LORD said
to Moses, "Take all the leaders of the people
and execute[I] them in broad daylight before
the LORD so that His burning anger may turn
away from Israel."
5 So Moses told Israel's judges, "Kill each of
the men who aligned themselves with Baal of
Peor."

[a] 24:7 Ex 17:14-16; 1Sm 15:8-33 [b] 24:8 Nm 23:22 [c] 24:9 Gn 49:9; Nm 23:24 [d] Gn 12:3; 27:29 [e] 24:11 Nm 22:17 [f] 24:13 Nm 22:18,38 [g] 24:15-16 Nm 24:3-4 [h] 24:17 Gn 49:10; Mt 2:2; Rv 22:16 [i] 24:18 Gn 32:3 [j] 24:20 Ex 17:8-16; 1Sm 15 [k] 24:24 Gn 10:4; Is 23:1,12; Jr 2:10; Dn 11:30 [l] Gn 10:21,24-25; 11:14-27 [m] 25:1 Nm 33:49; Jos 2:1; 3:1; Mc 6:5 [n] 25:2 Ex 34:15-16; 1Co 10:8; Rv 2:14 [o] 25:3 Nm 23:28 [p] Dt 4:3; Ps 106:28-29; Hs 9:10

[A] 24:7 Sam, LXX, Sym, Theod read *Gog* [B] 24:8 Or *He has* [C] 24:15 LXX reads *true*; Vg reads *closed* [D] 24:17 Or *Him* [E] 24:17 Or *frontiers* [F] 24:17 Sam reads *and the skulls of*; Jr 48:45 [G] 24:17 Or *Sethites* [H] 25:1 Or *in Shittim* [I] 25:4 Or *impale*, or *hang*, or *expose*; Hb obscure

Phinehas Intervenes

6 An Israelite man came bringing a Midianite woman to his relatives in the sight of Moses and the whole Israelite community while
they were weeping at the entrance to the tent
of meeting. 7 When Phinehas son of Eleazar,
son of Aaron the priest, saw this, he got up
from the assembly, took a spear in his hand,
8 followed the Israelite man into the tent,[A] and
drove it through both the Israelite man and the
woman — through her belly. Then the plague
on the Israelites was stopped, 9 but those who
died in the plague numbered 24,000.[a]

10 The LORD spoke to Moses, 11 "Phinehas son
of Eleazar, son of Aaron the priest, has turned
back My wrath from the Israelites because he
was zealous among them with My zeal,[B,b] so
that I did not destroy the Israelites in My zeal.
12 Therefore declare: I grant him My covenant
of peace.[c] 13 It will be a covenant of perpetual
priesthood for him and his future descendants,[d] because he was zealous for his God
and made ·atonement for the Israelites."

14 The name of the slain Israelite man, who
was struck dead with the Midianite woman,
was Zimri son of Salu, the leader of a Simeonite ancestral house. 15 The name of the slain
Midianite woman was Cozbi, the daughter
of Zur, a tribal head of an ancestral house in
Midian.

Vengeance against the Midianites

16 The LORD told Moses: 17 "Attack the Midianites and strike them dead. 18 For they attacked you with the treachery that they used
against you in the Peor incident. They did the
same in the case involving their sister Cozbi,
daughter of the Midianite leader who was
killed the day the plague came at Peor."

The Second Census

26 After the plague, the LORD said to
Moses and Eleazar son of Aaron the
priest, 2 "Take a census of the entire Israelite community by their ancestral houses of
those 20 years old or more who can serve in
Israel's army."[e]

3 So Moses and Eleazar the priest said to
them in the plains of Moab by the Jordan
across from Jericho, 4 "Take a census of those
20 years old or more, as the LORD had commanded Moses and the Israelites who came
out of the land of Egypt."[f]

5 Reuben[g] was the firstborn of Israel.
Reuben's descendants:
the Hanochite clan from Hanoch;
the Palluite clan from Pallu;
6 the Hezronite clan from Hezron;
the Carmite clan from Carmi.
7 These were the Reubenite clans,
and their registered men
numbered 43,730.
8 The son of Pallu was Eliab.
9 The sons of Eliab were Nemuel, Dathan,
and Abiram.
(It was Dathan and Abiram, chosen by
the community, who fought against
Moses and Aaron; they and Korah's
followers fought against the LORD.[h]
10 The earth opened its mouth and
swallowed them with Korah, when his
followers died and the fire consumed
250 men.[i] They serve as a warning sign.
11 The sons of Korah, however, did not
die.)

12 Simeon's descendants by their clans:
the Nemuelite clan from Nemuel;[C,j]
the Jaminite clan from Jamin;
the Jachinite clan from Jachin;
13 the Zerahite clan from Zerah;
the Shaulite clan from Shaul.
14 These were the Simeonite clans,
numbering 22,200 men.

15 Gad's descendants by their clans:
the Zephonite clan from Zephon;
the Haggite clan from Haggi;
the Shunite clan from Shuni;
16 the Oznite clan from Ozni;
the Erite clan from Eri;
17 the Arodite clan from Arod;
the Arelite clan from Areli.
18 These were the Gadite clans numbered
by their registered men: 40,500.

19 Judah's sons included Er and Onan,
but they died in the land of Canaan.[k]
20 Judah's descendants by their clans:
the Shelanite clan from Shelah;
the Perezite clan from Perez;

[a] **25:9** 1Co 10:8
[b] **25:11** Ex 34:14; Zch 8:2
[c] **25:12** Is 54:10; Ezk 34:25; 37:26; Mal 2:5
[d] **25:13** Ex 40:15; Ps 106:30-31
[e] **26:2** Nm 1:2-3
[f] **26:4** Nm 1
[g] **26:5** Gn 46:8-27; Ex 6:14-25
[h] **26:9** Nm 16:1-3
[i] **26:10** Nm 16:31-35
[j] **26:12** Gn 46:10; Ex 6:15; 1Ch 4:24
[k] **26:19** Gn 38:3-4,6-11

[A] **25:8** Perhaps a tent shrine or bridal tent [B] **25:11** Or *jealousy* [C] **26:12** Syr reads *Jemuel* (Gn 46:10; Ex 6:15); 1Ch 4:24 reads *Nemuel*

the Zerahite clan from Zerah.
21 The descendants of Perez:
the Hezronite clan from Hezron;
the Hamulite clan from Hamul.
22 These were Judah's clans numbered
by their registered men: 76,500.

23 Issachar's descendants by their clans:
the Tolaite clan from Tola;
the Punite clan from Puvah;[A,a]
24 the Jashubite clan from Jashub;
the Shimronite clan from Shimron.
25 These were Issachar's clans numbered
by their registered men: 64,300.

26 Zebulun's descendants by their clans:
the Seredite clan from Sered;
the Elonite clan from Elon;
the Jahleelite clan from Jahleel.
27 These were the Zebulunite
clans numbered by their
registered men: 60,500.

28 Joseph's descendants by their clans
from Manasseh and Ephraim:
29 Manasseh's descendants:
the Machirite clan from Machir.
Machir fathered Gilead;
the Gileadite clan from Gilead.
30 These were Gilead's descendants:
the Iezerite clan from Iezer;
the Helekite clan from Helek;
31 the Asrielite clan from Asriel;
the Shechemite clan from Shechem;
32 the Shemidaite clan from Shemida;
the Hepherite clan from Hepher;
33 Zelophehad son of Hepher had no
sons — only daughters. The names
of Zelophehad's daughters were
Mahlah, Noah, Hoglah, Milcah, and
Tirzah.[b]
34 These were Manasseh's
clans, numbered by their
registered men: 52,700.
35 These were Ephraim's descendants
by their clans:
the Shuthelahite clan from Shuthelah;
the Becherite clan from Becher;
the Tahanite clan from Tahan.
36 These were Shuthelah's descendants:
the Eranite clan from Eran.
37 These were the Ephraimite

[a]26:23 1Ch 7:1
[b]26:33 Nm 27:1-11; Jos 17:3

clans numbered by their
registered men: 32,500.
These were Joseph's descendants
by their clans.

38 Benjamin's descendants by their clans:
the Belaite clan from Bela;
the Ashbelite clan from Ashbel;
the Ahiramite clan from Ahiram;
39 the Shuphamite clan from Shupham;[B]
the Huphamite clan from Hupham.
40 Bela's descendants from Ard
and Naaman:
the Ardite clan from Ard;
the Naamite clan from Naaman.
41 These were the Benjaminite
clans numbered by their
registered men: 45,600.

42 These were Dan's descendants
by their clans:
the Shuhamite clan from Shuham.
These were the clans of Dan
by their clans.
43 All the Shuhamite clans numbered
by their registered men: 64,400.

44 Asher's descendants by their clans:
the Imnite clan from Imnah;
the Ishvite clan from Ishvi;
the Beriite clan from Beriah.
45 From Beriah's descendants:
the Heberite clan from Heber;
the Malchielite clan from Malchiel.
46 And the name of Asher's daughter
was Serah.
47 These were the Asherite
clans numbered by their
registered men: 53,400.

48 Naphtali's descendants by their clans:
the Jahzeelite clan from Jahzeel;
the Gunite clan from Guni;
49 the Jezerite clan from Jezer;
the Shillemite clan from Shillem.
50 These were the Naphtali
clans numbered by their
registered men: 45,400.

51 These registered Israelite men
numbered 601,730.

52 The LORD spoke to Moses, 53 "The land is
to be divided among them as an inheritance

[A]26:23 Sam, LXX, Vg, Syr read *Puite clan from Puah*; 1Ch 7:1 [B]26:39 Some Hb mss, Sam, LXX, Syr, Tg, Vg; other Hb mss read *Shephupham*

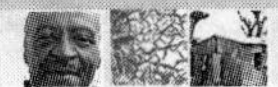

based on the number of names. 54Increase
the inheritance for a large tribe and decrease
it for a small one. Each is to be given its inheritance according to those who were registered in it. 55The land must be divided by lot;
they will receive an inheritance according to
the names of their ancestral tribes. 56Each
inheritance will be divided by lot among the
larger and smaller tribes."[a]

57 These were the Levites registered
by their clans:
the Gershonite clan from Gershon;
the Kohathite clan from Kohath;
the Merarite clan from Merari.
58 These were the Levite family groups:
the Libnite clan,
the Hebronite clan,
the Mahlite clan,
the Mushite clan,
and the Korahite clan.[b]

Kohath was the ancestor of Amram. 59The
name of Amram's wife was Jochebed, a descendant of Levi, born to Levi in Egypt. She
bore to Amram: Aaron, Moses, and their
sister Miriam. 60Nadab, Abihu, Eleazar, and
Ithamar were born to Aaron, 61but Nadab
and Abihu died when they presented unauthorized fire before the LORD.[c] 62Those registered were 23,000, every male one month old
or more; they were not registered among the
other Israelites, because no inheritance was
given to them among the Israelites.

63These were the ones registered by Moses and Eleazar the priest when they registered the Israelites on the plains of Moab by
the Jordan across from Jericho. 64But among
them there was not one of those who had
been registered by Moses and Aaron the
priest when they registered the Israelites in
the Wilderness of Sinai.[d] 65For the LORD had
said to them that they would all die in the wilderness. None of them was left except Caleb
son of Jephunneh and Joshua son of Nun.

A Case of Daughters' Inheritance

27 The daughters of Zelophehad approached; Zelophehad was the son of
Hepher, son of Gilead, son of Machir, son of
Manasseh from the clans of Manasseh, the
son of Joseph. These were the names of his
daughters: Mahlah, Noah, Hoglah, Milcah,
and Tirzah. 2They stood before Moses, Eleazar the priest, the leaders, and the entire community at the entrance to the tent of meeting
and said, 3"Our father died in the wilderness,
but he was not among Korah's followers, who
gathered together against the LORD.[e] Instead,
he died because of his own sin, and he had no
sons. 4Why should the name of our father be
taken away from his clan? Since he had no son,
give us property among our father's brothers."

5Moses brought their case before the LORD,
6and the LORD answered him, 7"What Zelophehad's daughters say is correct. You are
to give them hereditary property among
their father's brothers and transfer their father's inheritance to them.[f] 8Tell the Israelites: When a man dies without having a son,
transfer his inheritance to his daughter. 9If
he has no daughter, give his inheritance to
his brothers. 10If he has no brothers, give his
inheritance to his father's brothers. 11If his
father has no brothers, give his inheritance
to the nearest relative of his clan, and he will
take possession of it. This is to be a statutory
ordinance for the Israelites as the LORD commanded Moses."

Joshua Commissioned to Succeed Moses

12Then the LORD said to Moses,[g] "Go up this
mountain of the Abarim range[A] and see the
land that I have given the Israelites. 13After
you have seen it, you will also be gathered
to your people, as Aaron your brother was.[h]
14When the community quarreled in the Wilderness of Zin, both of you rebelled against
My command to show My holiness in their
sight at the waters." Those were the waters of
Meribah[B] of Kadesh in the Wilderness of Zin.[i]

15So Moses appealed to the LORD, 16"May
the LORD, the God of the spirits of all flesh,[j]
appoint a man over the community 17who
will go out before them and come back in before them,[k] and who will bring them out and
bring them in, so that the LORD's community
won't be like sheep without a shepherd."[l]

18The LORD replied to Moses, "Take Joshua
son of Nun, a man who has the Spirit in him,
and lay your hands on him.[m] 19Have him stand

[a]**26:56** Nm 33:53-54; 36:2; Jos 18:6-11
[b]**26:58** Ex 6:21,24; Nm 3:17-20
[c]**26:61** Lv 10:1-2
[d]**26:64** Nm 1:17-46; 3:39
[e]**27:3** Nm 16:1-3
[f]**27:7** Jos 17:4
[g]**27:12-14** Dt 32:48-51
[h]**27:13** Nm 20:22-29
[i]**27:14** Nm 20:2-13
[j]**27:16** Nm 16:22
[k]**27:17** Jos 14:11; 1Sm 18:13-16; 2Sm 5:2; 11:1; 1Kg 3:7; 2Kg 11:9
[l]1Kg 22:17; 2Ch 18:16; Ezk 34:5; Mt 9:36; Mk 6:34
[m]**27:18** Dt 34:9

[A]**27:12** = Mount Nebo; Nm 33:47-48; Dt 32:49; Jr 22:20 [B]**27:14** = quarreling before Eleazar the priest and the whole community, and commission[a] him in their sight. 20 Confer some of your authority on him so that the entire Israelite community will obey him. 21 He will stand before Eleazar who will consult the LORD for him with the decision of the ·Urim.[b] He and all the Israelites with him, even the entire community, will go out and come back in at his command."

22 Moses did as the LORD commanded him. He took Joshua, had him stand before Eleazar the priest and the entire community, 23 laid his hands on him, and commissioned him, as the LORD had spoken through Moses.

Prescribed Offerings

28 The LORD spoke to Moses, 2 "Command the Israelites and say to them: Be sure to present to Me at its appointed time My offering and My food[c] as My fire offering, a pleasing aroma to Me. 3 And say to them: This is the fire offering you are to present to the LORD:[d]

Daily Offerings

"Each day present two unblemished year-old male lambs as a regular ·burnt offering. 4 Offer one lamb in the morning and the other lamb at twilight, 5 along with two quarts[A] of fine flour for a ·grain offering mixed with a quart[B] of olive oil from crushed olives.[e] 6 It is a regular burnt offering established at Mount Sinai for a pleasing aroma, a fire offering to the LORD. 7 The ·drink offering is to be a quart[B] with each lamb. Pour out the offering of beer to the LORD in the sanctuary area. 8 Offer the second lamb at twilight, along with the same kind of grain offering and drink offering as in the morning. It is a fire offering, a pleasing aroma to the LORD.

Sabbath Offerings

9 "On the Sabbath day present two unblemished year-old male lambs, four quarts[C] of fine flour mixed with oil as a grain offering, and its drink offering. 10 It is the burnt offering for every Sabbath, in addition to the regular burnt offering and its drink offering.

Monthly Offerings

11 "At the beginning of each of your months present a burnt offering to the LORD: two young bulls, one ram, seven male lambs a year old — all unblemished — 12 with six quarts[D] of fine flour mixed with oil as a grain offering for each bull, four quarts[C] of fine flour mixed with oil as a grain offering for the ram, 13 and two quarts[E] of fine flour mixed with oil as a grain offering for each lamb. It is a burnt offering, a pleasing aroma, a fire offering to the LORD. 14 Their drink offerings are to be two quarts[F] of wine with each bull, one and a third quarts[G] with the ram, and one quart[H] with each male lamb. This is the monthly burnt offering for all the months of the year. 15 And one male goat is to be offered as a ·sin offering to the LORD, in addition to the regular burnt offering with its drink offering.

Offerings for Passover

16 "The ·Passover[f] to the LORD comes in the first month, on the fourteenth day of the month. 17 On the fifteenth day of this month there will be a festival; unleavened bread is to be eaten for seven days. 18 On the first day there is to be a sacred assembly; you are not to do any daily work.[g] 19 Present a fire offering, a burnt offering to the LORD: two young bulls, one ram, and seven male lambs a year old. Your animals are to be unblemished. 20 The grain offering with them is to be of fine flour mixed with oil; offer six quarts[D] with each bull and four quarts[C] with the ram. 21 Offer two quarts[E] with each of the seven lambs 22 and one male goat for a sin offering to make ·atonement for yourselves. 23 Offer these with the morning burnt offering that is part of the regular burnt offering. 24 You are to offer the same food each day for seven days as a fire offering,[h] a pleasing aroma to the LORD. It is to be offered with its drink offering and the regular burnt offering. 25 On the seventh day you are to hold a sacred assembly; you are not to do any daily work.

Offerings for the Festival of Weeks

26 "On the day of ·firstfruits, you are to hold a sacred assembly when you present an of-

[a] **27:19** Dt 31:14,23; Ps 91:11; Is 10:6
[b] **27:21** Ex 28:30
[c] **28:2** Lv 3:11,16; 22:25; Nm 28:24
[d] **28:3-8** Ex 29:38-41
[e] **28:5** Ex 27:20; Lv 24:2
[f] **28:16-17** Ex 12:18; Lv 23:5-6; Ezk 45:21
[g] **28:18** Ex 12:16; Lv 23:3,7,28; Nm 29:7
[h] **28:24-25** Lv 23:8

[A] **28:5** Lit *one-tenth of an ephah* [B] **28:5,7** Lit *a fourth of a hin* [C] **28:9,12,20** Lit *two-tenths* (of an ephah) [D] **28:12,20** Lit *three-tenths* (of an ephah) [E] **28:13,21** Lit *one-tenth* (of an ephah) [F] **28:14** Lit *a half hin* [G] **28:14** Lit *bull, a third hin* [H] **28:14** Lit *a fourth hin*

fering of new grain to the LORD at your Festival of Weeks;[a] you are not to do any daily
work. 27 Present a burnt offering for a pleasing aroma to the LORD: two young bulls, one
ram, and seven male lambs a year old, 28 with
their grain offering of fine flour mixed with
oil, six quarts[A] with each bull, four quarts[B]
with the ram, 29 and two quarts[C] with each of
the seven lambs, 30 and one male goat to make
atonement for yourselves. 31 Offer them with
their drink offerings in addition to the regular burnt offering and its grain offering. Your
animals are to be unblemished.

Festival of Trumpets Offerings

29 "You are to hold a sacred assembly in
the seventh month, on the first day of
the month, and you are not to do any daily
work.[b] This will be a day of joyful shouting[D]
for you.[c] 2 Offer a ·burnt offering as a pleasing aroma to the LORD: one young bull, one
ram, seven male lambs a year old—all unblemished— 3 with their ·grain offering of
fine flour mixed with oil, six quarts[A] with
the bull, four quarts[B] with the ram, 4 and two
quarts[C] with each of the seven male lambs.
5 Also offer one male goat as a ·sin offering to
make ·atonement for yourselves. 6 These are
in addition to the monthly and regular burnt
offerings with their prescribed grain offerings and ·drink offerings. They are a pleasing
aroma, a fire offering to the LORD.

Offerings for the Day of Atonement

7 "You are to hold a sacred assembly on
the tenth day of this seventh month and
practice self-denial;[E,d] you must not do any
work. 8 Present a burnt offering to the LORD,
a pleasing aroma: one young bull, one ram,
and seven male lambs a year old. All your animals are to be unblemished. 9 Their grain offering is to be of fine flour mixed with oil, six
quarts[A] with the bull, four quarts[B] with the
ram, 10 and two quarts[C] with each of the seven
lambs. 11 Offer one male goat for a sin offering. The regular burnt offering with its grain
offering and drink offerings are in addition
to the sin offering of atonement.

[a]28:26 Ex 34:22; Dt 16:9-10
[b]29:1 Ex 12:16
[c]Lv 23:23-25
[d]29:7 Lv 23:27-28
[e]29:12 Lv 23:34-35
[f]29:18 Nm 15:1-12

Offerings for the Festival of Booths

12 "You are to hold a sacred assembly on the
fifteenth day of the seventh month;[e] you must
not do any daily work. You are to celebrate a
seven-day festival for the LORD. 13 Present a
burnt offering, a fire offering as a pleasing
aroma to the LORD: 13 young bulls, two rams,
and 14 male lambs a year old. They are to be
unblemished. 14 Their grain offering is to be
of fine flour mixed with oil, six quarts[A] with
each of the 13 bulls, four quarts[B] with each of
the two rams, 15 and two quarts[C] with each of
the 14 lambs. 16 Also offer one male goat as a
sin offering. These are in addition to the regular burnt offering with its grain and drink
offerings.

17 "On the second day present 12 young
bulls, two rams, and 14 male lambs a year
old—all unblemished— 18 with their grain
and drink offerings[f] for the bulls, rams, and
lambs, in proportion to their number. 19 Also
offer one male goat as a sin offering. These
are in addition to the regular burnt offering
with its grain and drink[F] offerings.

20 "On the third day present 11 bulls, two
rams, 14 male lambs a year old—all unblemished— 21 with their grain and drink
offerings for the bulls, rams, and lambs, in
proportion to their number. 22 Also offer one
male goat as a sin offering. These are in addition to the regular burnt offering with its
grain and drink offerings.

23 "On the fourth day present 10 bulls, two
rams, 14 male lambs a year old—all unblemished— 24 with their grain and drink
offerings for the bulls, rams, and lambs, in
proportion to their number. 25 Also offer one
male goat as a sin offering. These are in addition to the regular burnt offering with its
grain and drink offerings.

26 "On the fifth day present nine bulls, two
rams, 14 male lambs a year old—all unblemished— 27 with their grain and drink
offerings for the bulls, rams, and lambs, in
proportion to their number. 28 Also offer one
male goat as a sin offering. These are in addition to the regular burnt offering with its
grain and drink offerings.

[A]28:28; 29:3,9,14 Lit *three-tenths* (of an ephah) [B]28:28; 29:3,9,14 Lit *two-tenths* (of an ephah) [C]28:29; 29:4,10,15 Lit *one-tenth* (of an ephah) [D]29:1 Or *blast*; traditionally, *trumpet blasts* [E]29:7 Traditionally, fasting, abstinence from sex, and refraining from personal grooming [F]29:19 Some Hb mss, Syr, Vg, Sam; other Hb mss, LXX read *and their drink*

29“On the sixth day present eight bulls, two rams, 14 male lambs a year old—all unblemished— 30with their grain and drink offerings for the bulls, rams, and lambs, in proportion to their number. 31Also offer one male goat as a sin offering. These are in addition to the regular burnt offering with its grain and drink[A] offerings.

32“On the seventh day present seven bulls, two rams, and 14 male lambs a year old—all unblemished— 33with their grain and drink offerings for the bulls, rams, and lambs, in proportion to their number. 34Also offer one male goat as a sin offering. These are in addition to the regular burnt offering with its grain and drink offerings.

35“On the eighth day you are to hold a solemn assembly; you are not to do any daily work.[a] 36Present a burnt offering, a fire offering as a pleasing aroma to the LORD: one bull, one ram, seven male lambs a year old—all unblemished— 37with their grain and drink offerings for the bulls, rams, and lambs, in proportion to their number. 38Also offer one male goat as a sin offering. These are in addition to the regular burnt offering with its grain and drink offerings.

39“You must offer these to the LORD at your appointed times in addition to your vow and freewill offerings, whether burnt, grain, drink, or ˙fellowship offerings.” 40[B]So Moses told the Israelites everything the LORD had commanded him.

Regulations about Vows

30 Moses told the leaders of the Israelite tribes, “This is what the LORD has commanded: 2When a man makes a vow to the LORD or swears an oath to put himself under an obligation, he must not break his word; he must do whatever he has promised.[b]

3“When a woman in her father's house during her youth makes a vow to the LORD or puts herself under an obligation, 4and her father hears about her vow or the obligation she put herself under, and he says nothing to her, all her vows and every obligation she put herself under are binding. 5But if her father prohibits her on the day he hears about it, none of her vows and none of the obligations she put herself under are binding. The LORD will absolve her because her father has prohibited her.

6“If a woman marries while her vows or the rash commitment she herself made are binding, 7and her husband hears about it and says nothing to her when he finds out, her vows are binding, and the obligations she put herself under are binding. 8But if her husband prohibits her when he hears about it, he will cancel her vow that is binding or the rash commitment she herself made, and the LORD will forgive her.

9“Every vow a widow or divorced woman puts herself under is binding on her.

10“If a woman in her husband's house has made a vow or put herself under an obligation with an oath, 11and her husband hears about it, says nothing to her, and does not prohibit her, all her vows are binding, and every obligation she put herself under is binding. 12But if her husband cancels them on the day he hears about it, nothing that came from her lips, whether her vows or her obligation, is binding. Her husband has canceled them, and the LORD will absolve her. 13Her husband may confirm or cancel any vow or any sworn obligation to deny herself. 14If her husband says nothing at all to her from day to day, he confirms all her vows and obligations, which are binding. He has confirmed them because he said nothing to her when he heard about them. 15But if he cancels them after he hears about them, he will be responsible for her[C] commitment.”[D]

16These are the statutes that the LORD commanded Moses concerning the relationship between a man and his wife, or between a father and his daughter in his house during her youth.

War with Midian

31 The LORD spoke to Moses, 2“Execute vengeance for the Israelites against the Midianites. After that, you will be gathered to your people.”

3So Moses spoke to the people, “Equip some of your men for war. They will go against Mid-

[a]**29:35** Ex 12:16; Lv 23:36
[b]**30:2** Mt 5:33

[A]**29:31** Some Hb mss, Syr, Tg, Vg; other Hb mss, Sam read *and their drink*
[B]**29:40** Nm 30:1 in Hb [C]**30:15** Sam, LXX, some Syr mss read *his*
[D]**30:15** Or *will bear her guilt*

ian to inflict the LORD's vengeance[a] on them.
4 Send 1,000 men to war from each Israelite
tribe." 5 So 1,000 were recruited from each
Israelite tribe out of the thousands[A] in Israel — 12,000 equipped for war. 6 Moses sent
1,000 from each tribe to war. They went with
Phinehas son of Eleazar the priest, in whose
care were the holy objects and signal trumpets.
7 They waged war against Midian, as the
LORD had commanded Moses, and killed
every male. 8 Along with the others slain by
them, they killed the Midianite kings — Evi,
Rekem, Zur, Hur, and Reba, the five kings of
Midian.[b] They also killed Balaam son of Beor[c]
with the sword. 9 The Israelites took the Midianite women and their children captive, and
they plundered all their cattle, flocks, and
property.[d] 10 Then they burned all the cities where the Midianites lived, as well as all
their encampments, 11 and took away all the
spoils of war and the captives, both man and
beast. 12 They brought the prisoners, animals,
and spoils of war to Moses, Eleazar the priest,
and the Israelite community at the camp on
the plains of Moab by the Jordan across from
Jericho.
13 Moses, Eleazar the priest, and all the leaders of the community went to meet them
outside the camp. 14 But Moses became furious with the officers, the commanders of
thousands and commanders of hundreds,
who were returning from the military campaign. 15 "Have[B] you let every female live?" he
asked them. 16 "Yet they are the ones who, at
Balaam's advice, incited the Israelites to unfaithfulness against the LORD in the Peor incident, so that the plague came against the
LORD's community.[e] 17 So now, kill all the male
children and kill every woman who has had
sexual relations with a man, 18 but keep alive
for yourselves all the young females who have
not had sexual relations.
19 "You are to remain outside the camp for
seven days. All of you and your prisoners who
have killed a person or touched the dead are
to purify yourselves on the third day and the
seventh day. 20 Also purify everything: garments, leather goods, things made of goat
hair, and every article of wood."[f]

[a] 31:3 Ps 18:47; 79:10; 94:1; Jr 11:20
[b] 31:8 Jos 13:21-22
[c] Nm 22:5–24:25
[d] 31:9 Gn 34:28-29; Dt 20:13-14
[e] 31:16 Nm 25; Dt 20:18
[f] 31:19-20 Lv 11:32; Nm 19:11-20
[g] 31:23 Nm 19:1-9,17-20

21 Then Eleazar the priest said to the soldiers who had gone to battle, "This is the legal
statute the LORD commanded Moses: 22 Only
the gold, silver, bronze, iron, tin, and lead —
23 everything that can withstand fire — you
are to pass through fire, and it will be •clean.
It must still be purified with the purification
water.[g] Anything that cannot withstand fire,
pass through the water. 24 On the seventh day
wash your clothes, and you will be clean. After that you may enter the camp."
25 The LORD told Moses, 26 "You, Eleazar the
priest, and the family leaders of the community are to take a count of what was captured,
man and beast. 27 Then divide the captives between the troops who went out to war and
the entire community. 28 Set aside a tribute
for the LORD from what belongs to the fighting men who went out to war: one out of every 500 humans, cattle, donkeys, sheep, and
goats. 29 Take the tribute from their half and
give it to Eleazar the priest as a contribution
to the LORD. 30 From the Israelites' half, take
one out of every 50 from the people, cattle,
donkeys, sheep, and goats, all the livestock,
and give them to the Levites who perform the
duties of[C] the LORD's tabernacle."
31 So Moses and Eleazar the priest did as
the LORD commanded Moses. 32 The captives
remaining from the plunder the army had
taken totaled:

675,000 sheep and goats,
33 72,000 cattle,
34 61,000 donkeys,
35 and 32,000 people, all the females
who had not had sexual relations
with a man.

36 The half portion for those who went out
to war numbered:

337,500 sheep and goats,
37 and the tribute to the LORD was 675
from the sheep and goats;
38 from the 36,000 cattle,
the tribute to the LORD was 72;
39 from the 30,500 donkeys,
the tribute to the LORD was 61;
40 and from the 16,000 people,
the tribute to the LORD was 32 people.

[A] 31:5 Or *clans* [B] 31:15 Sam, LXX, Syr, Vg read *Why have* [C] 31:30 Or *who protect*

41 Moses gave the tribute to Eleazar the priest as a contribution for the LORD, as the LORD had commanded Moses.

42 From the Israelites' half, which Moses separated from the men who fought, 43 the community's half was:

337,500 sheep and goats,
44 36,000 cattle,
45 30,500 donkeys,
46 and 16,000 people.

47 Moses took one out of every 50, selected from the people and the livestock of the Israelites' half. He gave them to the Levites who perform the duties of the LORD's tabernacle, as the LORD had commanded him.

48 The officers who were over the thousands of the army, the commanders of thousands and of hundreds, approached Moses 49 and told him, "Your servants have taken a census of the fighting men under our command, and not one of us is missing. 50 So we have presented to the LORD an offering of the gold articles each man found—armlets, bracelets, rings, earrings, and necklaces—to make •atonement for ourselves before the LORD."[a]

51 Moses and Eleazar the priest received from them all the articles made out of gold. 52 All the gold of the contribution they offered to the LORD, from the commanders of thousands and of hundreds, was 420 pounds.[A] 53 Each of the soldiers had taken plunder for himself. 54 Moses and Eleazar the priest received the gold from the commanders of thousands and of hundreds and brought it into the tent of meeting as a memorial for the Israelites before the LORD.

Transjordan Settlements

32 The Reubenites and Gadites had a very large number of livestock. When they surveyed the lands of Jazer and Gilead, they saw that the region was a good one for livestock. 2 So the Gadites and Reubenites came to Moses, Eleazar the priest, and the leaders of the community and said: 3 "The territory of Ataroth, Dibon, Jazer, Nimrah, Heshbon, Elealeh, Sebam,[B] Nebo, and Beon, 4 which the LORD struck down[b] before the community of Israel, is good land for livestock, and your servants own livestock." 5 They said, "If we have found favor in your sight, let this land be given to your servants as a possession. Don't make us cross the Jordan."

6 But Moses asked the Gadites and Reubenites, "Should your brothers go to war while you stay here? 7 Why are you discouraging[C] the Israelites from crossing into the land the LORD has given them? 8 That's what your fathers did when I sent them from Kadesh-barnea to see the land.[c] 9 After they went up as far as Eshcol Valley and saw the land, they discouraged the Israelites from entering the land the LORD had given them. 10 So the LORD's anger burned that day, and He swore an oath: 11 'Because they did not follow Me completely,[d] none of the men 20 years old or more who came up from Egypt will see the land I swore to give Abraham, Isaac, and Jacob— 12 none except Caleb[e] son of Jephunneh the Kenizzite and Joshua[f] son of Nun, because they did follow the LORD completely.' 13 The LORD's anger burned against Israel, and He made them wander in the wilderness 40 years until the whole generation that had done what was evil in the LORD's sight was gone. 14 And here you, a brood of sinners, stand in your fathers' place adding even more to the LORD's burning anger against Israel. 15 If you turn back from following Him, He will once again leave this people in the wilderness, and you will destroy all of them."

16 Then they approached him and said, "We want to build sheepfolds here for our livestock and cities for our dependents. 17 But we will arm ourselves and be ready to go ahead of the Israelites until we have brought them into their place. Meanwhile, our dependents will remain in the fortified cities because of the inhabitants of the land. 18 We will not return to our homes until each of the Israelites has taken possession of his inheritance. 19 Yet we will not have an inheritance with them across the Jordan and beyond, because our inheritance will be across the Jordan to the east."

20 Moses replied to them, "If you do this—if you arm yourselves for battle before the LORD, 21 and every one of your armed men crosses the Jordan before the LORD until He has

[a] **31:50** Ex 30:12-16
[b] **32:4** Nm 21:24
[c] **32:8** Nm 13:1-3,32-33
[d] **32:11-12** Nm 14:22-24,29-30
[e] **32:12** Nm 14:6,24,30,38; 26:65
[f] Ex 33:11; Nm 27:18-23

[A] **31:52** Lit *16,750 shekels* [B] **32:3** Sam, LXX read *Sibmah* (v. 38); Syr reads *Sebah* [C] **32:7** Lit *discouraging the hearts of*

driven His enemies from His presence, 22 and
the land is subdued before the LORD — afterward you may return and be free from obligation to the LORD and to Israel. And this land
will belong to you as a possession before the
LORD. 23 But if you don't do this, you will certainly sin against the LORD; be sure your sin
will catch up with you. 24 Build cities for your
dependents and folds for your flocks, but do
what you have promised."[a]
25 The Gadites and Reubenites answered
Moses, "Your servants will do just as my lord
commands. 26 Our little children, wives, livestock, and all our animals will remain here
in the cities of Gilead, 27 but your servants are
equipped for war before the LORD and will go
across to the battle as my lord orders."
28 So Moses gave orders about them to Eleazar the priest, Joshua son of Nun, and the
family leaders of the Israelite tribes. 29 Moses told them, "If the Gadites and Reubenites
cross the Jordan with you, every man in battle
formation before the LORD, and the land is
subdued before you, you are to give them the
land of Gilead as a possession.[b] 30 But if they
don't go across with you in battle formation,
they must accept land in Canaan with you."
31 The Gadites and Reubenites replied,
"What the LORD has spoken to your servants
is what we will do. 32 We will cross over in battle formation before the LORD into the land
of Canaan, but we will keep our hereditary
possession across the Jordan."
33 So Moses gave them — the Gadites, Reubenites, and half the tribe of Manasseh son
of Joseph — the kingdom of Sihon king of
the Amorites and the kingdom of Og king
of Bashan, the land including its cities with
the territories surrounding them. 34 The Gadites rebuilt Dibon, Ataroth, Aroer, 35 Atroth-
shophan, Jazer, Jogbehah, 36 Beth-nimrah,
and Beth-haran[c] as fortified cities, and built
sheepfolds. 37 The Reubenites rebuilt Heshbon, Elealeh, Kiriathaim, 38 as well as Nebo
and Baal-meon (whose names were changed),
and Sibmah. They gave names to the cities
they rebuilt.
39 The descendants of Machir[d] son of
Manasseh went to Gilead, captured it, and
drove out the Amorites who were there. 40 So
Moses gave Gilead to the clan of Machir son
of Manasseh, and they settled in it. 41 Jair, a
descendant of Manasseh, went and captured
their villages, which he renamed Jair's Villages.[A,e] 42 Nobah went and captured Kenath
with its villages and called it Nobah after his
own name.

Wilderness Travels Reviewed

33 These were the stages of the Israelites'
journey when they went out of the
land of Egypt by their military divisions under the leadership of Moses and Aaron. 2 At
the LORD's command, Moses wrote down the
starting points for the stages of their journey; these are the stages listed by their starting points:

3 They departed from Rameses[f] in the
first month, on the fifteenth day of the
month. On the day after the ·Passover[g]
the Israelites went out triumphantly[B,h]
in the sight of all the Egyptians.
4 Meanwhile, the Egyptians were
burying every firstborn male the LORD
had struck down among them, for the
LORD had executed judgment against
their gods.[i] 5 The Israelites departed
from Rameses and camped at Succoth.[j]
6 They departed from Succoth and
camped at Etham,[k] which is on the edge
of the wilderness.
7 They departed from Etham and turned
back to Pi-hahiroth, which faces
Baal-zephon, and they camped before
Migdol.[l]
8 They departed from Pi-hahiroth[C] and
crossed through the middle of the sea[m]
into the wilderness. They took a
three-day journey into the Wilderness
of Etham and camped at Marah.[n]
9 They departed from Marah and came
to Elim.[o] There were 12 springs of water
and 70 date palms at Elim, so they
camped there.
10 They departed from Elim and camped
by the ·Red Sea.
11 They departed from the Red Sea and
camped in the Wilderness of Sin.[p]

[a] 32:24 Nm 30:2; Jos 1:12-18; 4:12
[b] 32:29 Jos 22:9
[c] 32:36 Jos 13:27
[d] 32:39 Gn 50:23; Nm 26:29; Jos 17:1,3
[e] 32:41 Dt 3:14; Jos 13:30; 1Kg 4:13; 1Ch 2:23
[f] 33:3 Gn 47:11; Ex 1:11; 12:37
[g] Ex 12:11-48; Lv 23:5; Nm 9:2-14
[h] Ex 14:8
[i] 33:4 Ex 12:12
[j] 33:5 Ex 12:37
[k] 33:6 Ex 13:20
[l] 33:7 Ex 14:2,9; Jr 46:14; Ezk 30:6
[m] 33:8 Ex 14:22-26
[n] Ex 15:23
[o] 33:9 Ex 15:27; 16:1
[p] 33:11 Ex 16:1; 17:1

A 32:41 Or *renamed Havvoth-jair* B 33:3 Lit *with a raised hand*; Ex 14:8 C 33:8 Some Hb mss, Sam, Syr, Vg; other Hb mss read *from before Hahiroth*

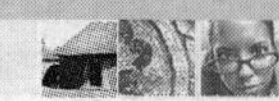

12 They departed from the Wilderness of Sin and camped in Dophkah.
13 They departed from Dophkah and camped at Alush.
14 They departed from Alush and camped at Rephidim,[a] where there was no water for the people to drink.[b]
15 They departed from Rephidim and camped in the Wilderness of Sinai.[c]
16 They departed from the Wilderness of Sinai and camped at Kibroth-hattaavah.[d]
17 They departed from Kibroth-hattaavah and camped at Hazeroth.[e]
18 They departed from Hazeroth and camped at Rithmah.
19 They departed from Rithmah and camped at Rimmon-perez.
20 They departed from Rimmon-perez and camped at Libnah.
21 They departed from Libnah and camped at Rissah.
22 They departed from Rissah and camped at Kehelathah.
23 They departed from Kehelathah and camped at Mount Shepher.
24 They departed from Mount Shepher and camped at Haradah.
25 They departed from Haradah and camped at Makheloth.
26 They departed from Makheloth and camped at Tahath.
27 They departed from Tahath and camped at Terah.
28 They departed from Terah and camped at Mithkah.
29 They departed from Mithkah and camped at Hashmonah.
30 They departed from Hashmonah and camped at Moseroth.
31 They departed from Moseroth and camped at Bene-jaakan.[f]
32 They departed from Bene-jaakan and camped at Hor-haggidgad.
33 They departed from Hor-haggidgad and camped at Jotbathah.
34 They departed from Jotbathah and camped at Abronah.
35 They departed from Abronah and camped at Ezion-geber.[g]

[a]**33:14** Ex 17:1,8; 19:2 [b]Ex 17:1-7 [c]**33:15** Ex 19:1-2 [d]**33:16** Nm 11:34-35; Dt 9:22 [e]**33:17** Nm 11:35; 12:16; Dt 1:1 [f]**33:31-33** Dt 10:6-7 [g]**33:35** Dt 2:8; 1Kg 9:26 [h]**33:36** Nm 10:12 [i]**33:37** Nm 21:4; 33:37-41; Dt 32:50 [j]**33:38** Nm 20:23-29 [k]**33:40** Nm 21:1-3 [l]**33:43** Nm 21:10-11 [m]**33:44** Nm 21:11 [n]**33:45** Nm 32:34; Neh 11:25; Jr 48:18,22 [o]**33:46** Jr 48:22 [p]**33:47** Nm 27:12; Dt 32:49; Jr 22:20 [q]Dt 32:49; 34:1 [r]**33:48** Nm 22:1 [s]**33:49** Jos 12:3; 13:20; Ezk 25:9 [t]Nm 25:1; Jos 2:1; 3:1; Jl 3:18; Mc 6:5 [u]**33:52** Lv 26:1; Ezk 8:12 [v]Ex 32:4,8; 34:17; Lv 19:4; Dt 27:15 [w]**33:53** Gn 12:7; 15:18; 24:7; 35:12

36 They departed from Ezion-geber and camped in the Wilderness of Zin[h] (that is, Kadesh).
37 They departed from Kadesh and camped at Mount Hor[i] on the edge
of the land of Edom. 38 At the LORD's
command, Aaron the priest climbed Mount Hor and died there on the first day of the fifth month in the fortieth year after the Israelites went out of the
land of Egypt.[j] 39 Aaron was 123 years
old when he died on Mount Hor. 40 At
that time the Canaanite king of Arad, who lived in the ·Negev in the land of Canaan,[k] heard the Israelites were coming.
41 They departed from Mount Hor and camped at Zalmonah.
42 They departed from Zalmonah and camped at Punon.
43 They departed from Punon and camped at Oboth.[l]
44 They departed from Oboth and camped at Iye-abarim on the border of Moab.[m]
45 They departed from Iyim[A] and camped at Dibon-gad.[n]
46 They departed from Dibon-gad and camped at Almon-diblathaim.[o]
47 They departed from Almon-diblathaim and camped in the Abarim[p] range facing Nebo.[q]
48 They departed from the Abarim range and camped on the plains of Moab by
the Jordan across from Jericho.[r] 49 They
camped by the Jordan from Beth-jeshimoth[s] to the Acacia Meadow[B,t] on the plains of Moab.

Instructions for Occupying Canaan

50 The LORD spoke to Moses in the plains of Moab by the Jordan across from Jericho,
51 "Tell the Israelites: When you cross the Jor-
dan into the land of Canaan, 52 you must drive
out all the inhabitants of the land before you, destroy all their stone images[u] and cast images,[v] and demolish all their ·high places.
53 You are to take possession of the land and settle in it because I have given you the land[w]
to possess. 54 You are to receive the land as an

[A]**33:45** A shortened form of Iye-abarim [B]**33:49** Or *Abel-shittim*

inheritance by lot according to your clans. Increase the inheritance for a large clan and decrease it for a small one. Whatever place the
lot indicates for someone will be his. You will
receive an inheritance according to your ancestral tribes. 55 But if you don't drive out the
inhabitants of the land before you, those you
allow to remain will become thorns in your
eyes and in your sides; they will harass you in
the land where you will live. 56 And what I had
planned to do to them, I will do to you."[a]

Boundaries of the Promised Land

34 The LORD spoke to Moses, 2 "Command the Israelites and say to them:
When you enter the land of Canaan, it will be
allotted to you as an inheritance[A] with these
borders:

3 Your southern side will be from the
Wilderness of Zin along the boundary of
Edom. Your southern border on the east
will begin at the east end of the Dead Sea.
4 Your border will turn south of the Ascent of Akrabbim,[B] proceed to Zin, and
end south of Kadesh-barnea. It will go
to Hazar-addar and proceed to Azmon.[b]
5 The border will turn from Azmon[c] to the
Brook of Egypt,[d] where it will end at the
Mediterranean Sea.

6 Your western border will be the coastline of the Mediterranean Sea; this will
be your western border.

7 This will be your northern border: From
the Mediterranean Sea draw a line to
Mount Hor;[C,e] 8 from Mount Hor draw a
line to the entrance of Hamath,[D,f] and the
border will reach Zedad.[g] 9 Then the border will go to Ziphron and end at Hazar-
enan.[h] This will be your northern border.

10 For your eastern border, draw a line
from Hazar-enan to Shepham. 11 The border will go down from Shepham to Riblah east of Ain.[i] It will continue down
and reach the eastern slope of the Sea of
Chinnereth.[E,j] 12 Then the border will go
down to the Jordan and end at the Dead
Sea. This will be your land defined by its
borders on all sides."

[a] 33:56 Dt 28:15
[b] 34:4 Jos 15:3; Jdg 1:36
[c] 34:4-5 Jos 15:4
[d] 34:5 Jos 15:47; Is 27:12; Ezk 47:19
[e] 34:7 Nm 20:22-28; 33:37-56
[f] 34:8 Nm 13:21; 2Kg 14:25; 2Ch 7:8; Ezk 48:1
[g] Ezk 47:15
[h] 34:9 Ezk 47:17; 48:1
[i] 34:11 Jos 15:32
[j] Jos 12:3; 13:27; Lk 5:1
[k] 34:15 Nm 32:33
[l] 34:19 Nm 14:6,24,30,38; 26:65

13 So Moses commanded the Israelites, "This
is the land you are to receive by lot as an inheritance, which the LORD commanded to be
given to the nine and a half tribes. 14 For the
tribe of the Reubenites and the tribe of the
Gadites have received their inheritance according to their ancestral houses, and half
the tribe of Manasseh has received its inheritance. 15 The two and a half tribes have
received their inheritance[k] across the Jordan
from Jericho, eastward toward the sunrise."

Leaders for Distributing the Land

16 The LORD spoke to Moses, 17 "These are the
names of the men who are to distribute
the land as an inheritance for you: Eleazar the
priest and Joshua son of Nun. 18 Take one
leader from each tribe to distribute the land.
19 These are the names of the men:

Caleb[l] son of Jephunneh from the tribe
of Judah;
20 Shemuel son of Ammihud from the
tribe of Simeon;
21 Elidad son of Chislon from the tribe
of Benjamin;
22 Bukki son of Jogli, a leader from the
tribe of Dan;
23 from the sons of Joseph:
Hanniel son of Ephod, a leader from
the tribe of Manasseh,
24 Kemuel son of Shiphtan, a leader
from the tribe of Ephraim;
25 Eli-zaphan son of Parnach, a leader
from the tribe of Zebulun;
26 Paltiel son of Azzan, a leader from the
tribe of Issachar;
27 Ahihud son of Shelomi, a leader from
the tribe of Asher;
28 Pedahel son of Ammihud, a leader
from the tribe of Naphtali."

29 These are the ones the LORD commanded to
distribute the inheritance to the Israelites in
the land of Canaan.

Cities for the Levites

35 The LORD again spoke to Moses in the
plains of Moab by the Jordan across
from Jericho: 2 "Command the Israelites to

[A] 34:2 Lit *inheritance — the land of Canaan* [B] 34:4 Lit *of Scorpions*; Jos 15:3; Jdg 1:36 [C] 34:7 In Lebanon; Nm 20:22-28; 33:37-56 [D] 34:8 Or *to Lebo-hamath*
[E] 34:11 = the Sea of Galilee; Jos 12:3; 13:27; Lk 5:1

give cities out of their hereditary property for
the Levites to live in and pastureland around
the cities.[a] 3The cities will be for them to live
in, and their pasturelands will be for their
herds, flocks, and all their other animals.
4The pasturelands of the cities you are to give
the Levites will extend from the city wall 500
yards[A] on every side. 5Measure 1,000 yards[B]
outside the city for the east side, 1,000 yards[B]
for the south side, 1,000 yards[B] for the west
side, and 1,000 yards[B] for the north side, with
the city in the center. This will belong to them
as pasturelands for the cities.

6"The cities you give the Levites will include
six cities of refuge,[b] which you must provide
so that the one who kills someone may flee
there; in addition to these, give 42 other cities.[c] 7The total number of cities you give the
Levites will be 48, along with their pasturelands. 8Of the cities that you give from the
Israelites' territory, you should take more
from a larger tribe and less from a smaller
one. Each tribe is to give some of its cities to
the Levites in proportion to the inheritance
it receives."

Cities of Refuge

9The LORD said to Moses, 10"Speak to the
Israelites and tell them: When you cross the
Jordan into the land of Canaan, 11designate
cities to serve as cities of refuge for you, so
that a person who kills someone unintentionally may flee there.[d] 12You will have the cities
as a refuge from the avenger, so that the one
who kills someone will not die until he stands
trial before the assembly. 13The cities you select will be your six cities of refuge. 14Select
three cities across the Jordan and three cities
in the land of Canaan to be cities of refuge.
15These six cities will serve as a refuge for the
Israelites and for the foreigner or temporary
resident among them, so that anyone who
kills a person unintentionally may flee there.

16"If anyone strikes a person with an iron
object and death results, he is a murderer; the
murderer must be put to death. 17If a man has
in his hand a stone capable of causing death
and strikes another person and he dies, the
murderer must be put to death. 18If a man
has in his hand a wooden object capable of
causing death and strikes another person and
he dies, the murderer must be put to death.
19The avenger of blood himself is to kill the
murderer; when he finds him, he is to kill
him. 20Likewise, if anyone in hatred pushes a
person or throws an object at him with malicious intent and he dies, 21or if in hostility he
strikes him with his hand and he dies, the one
who struck him must be put to death; he is a
murderer. The avenger of blood is to kill the
murderer when he finds him.

22"But if anyone suddenly pushes a person
without hostility or throws any object at him
without malicious intent 23or without looking drops a stone that could kill a person and
he dies, but he was not his enemy and wasn't
trying to harm him, 24the assembly is to judge
between the slayer and the avenger of blood
according to these ordinances. 25The assembly is to protect the one who kills someone
from the hand of the avenger of blood. Then
the assembly will return him to the city of refuge he fled to, and he must live there until the
death of the high priest who was anointed
with the holy oil.[e]

26"If the one who kills someone ever goes
outside the border of the city of refuge he fled
to, 27and the avenger of blood finds him outside the border of his city of refuge and kills
him, the avenger will not be •guilty of bloodshed, 28for the one who killed a person was
supposed to live in his city of refuge until the
death of the high priest. Only after the death
of the high priest may the one who has killed
a person return to the land he possesses.
29These instructions will be a statutory ordinance for you throughout your generations
wherever you live.

30"If anyone kills a person, the murderer is
to be put to death based on the word of witnesses. But no one is to be put to death based
on the testimony of one witness.[f] 31You are
not to accept a ransom for the life of a murderer who is guilty of killing someone; he
must be put to death. 32Neither should you
accept a ransom for the person who flees to
his city of refuge, allowing him to return and
live in the land before the death of the high
priest.[C]

33"Do not defile the land where you are,[D]

[a]**35:2** Jos 21:2-3 [b]**35:6** Dt 19:1-13; Jos 20:7-9 [c]Jos 21:13 [d]**35:11** Dt 4:42; 19:3-4,6; Jos 20:3-6 [e]**35:22-25** Ex 21:13 [f]**35:30** Dt 17:6; 19:15; Mt 18:16

[A]**35:4** Lit *1,000 cubits* [B]**35:5** Lit *2,000 cubits* [C]**35:32** Sam, LXX, Syr read *high priest* [D]**35:33** Sam, LXX, Syr, Vg, Tg read *live*

for bloodshed defiles the land,[a] and there can
be no ·atonement for the land because of the
blood that is shed on it, except by the blood
of the person who shed it. 34Do not make the
land ·unclean where you live and where I reside; for I, ·Yahweh, reside among the Israelites."

The Inheritance of Zelophehad's Daughters

36 The family leaders from the clan of the
descendants of Gilead—the son of
Machir, son of Manasseh—who were from
the clans of the sons of Joseph, approached
and addressed Moses and the leaders who
were over the Israelite families. 2They said,
"·Yahweh commanded my lord to give the
land as an inheritance by lot to the Israelites.
My lord was further commanded by Yahweh
to give our brother Zelophehad's inheritance
to his daughters.[b] 3If they marry any of the
men from the other Israelite tribes, their
inheritance will be taken away from our fathers' inheritance and added to that of the
tribe into which they marry. Therefore, part
of our allotted inheritance would be taken
away. 4When the Jubilee[c] comes for the Israelites, their inheritance will be added to that
of the tribe into which they marry, and their
inheritance will be taken away from the inheritance of our ancestral tribe."

[a]**35:33** Ps 106:38; Is 24:5; Jr 3:9
[b]**36:2** Nm 27:1-11
[c]**36:4** Lv 25:8-55; 27:7-24

5So Moses commanded the Israelites at
the word of the LORD, "What the tribe of Joseph's descendants says is right. 6This is what
the LORD has commanded concerning Zelophehad's daughters: They may marry anyone
they like provided they marry within a clan of
their ancestral tribe. 7An inheritance belonging to the Israelites must not transfer from
tribe to tribe, because each of the Israelites
is to retain the inheritance of his ancestral
tribe. 8Any daughter who possesses an inheritance from an Israelite tribe must marry
someone from the clan of her ancestral tribe,
so that each of the Israelites will possess the
inheritance of his fathers. 9No inheritance is
to transfer from one tribe to another, because
each of the Israelite tribes is to retain its inheritance."

10The daughters of Zelophehad did as the
LORD commanded Moses. 11Mahlah, Tirzah,
Hoglah, Milcah, and Noah, the daughters
of Zelophehad, married cousins on their father's side. 12They married men from the
clans of the descendants of Manasseh son
of Joseph, and their inheritance remained
within the tribe of their father's clan.

13These are the commands and ordinances
the LORD commanded the Israelites through
Moses in the plains of Moab by the Jordan
across from Jericho.

■ **AUTHOR:** Moses, although Joshua probably wrote the last chapter.

■■ **DATE:** Deuteronomy was completed around 1406 B.C.

The book of Deuteronomy is a collection of sermons delivered by Moses just before the people enter the promised land. The old generation had died in the wilderness, just as God had promised. This new generation needs to hear of God's great deeds and learn what it means to be God's chosen people. God delivers this blueprint for life to the people destined to become the Israelite nation. This is the end of Moses' long life. He will not cross the Jordan and must turn over leadership to one who will lead the people into the land. The transfer ceremony will be Moses' greatest gift to the people in a lifetime of great gifts: the law of God spoken and the blessing of God invoked.

God's mission in this last book of Moses is to remind the people of His covenant of love and loyalty, sharing and wholeness. God says through Moses: I have rescued you.

DEUTERONOMY

I will never leave you. Go forward in total trust that I AM (God's name) is with you. On your part, stay with Me. Worship in truth and confidence. Follow My ways.

God's assurance to the people comes at a crucial moment. They are camped on the Plains of Moab, facing Canaan, on the east side of the Jordan River. Difficult challenges face them on the other side of the Jordan. There will be no red carpet welcome. Every step forward will be a test of faith. So the great moment of decision—the choice to obey and discover, or not—awaits them as Moses speaks God's message.

God's mission for the people takes shape in these laws: how to deal with property, including inheritance; what form marriage should take; care for animals; Sabbath rest and worship; disputes and fair trade; personal dignity; right treatment of servants and foreigners.

Again, the details of these laws may not apply today, but the principles behind the laws—integrity, honesty, kindness, restitution—certainly do. These laws are best used as guides and pointers to the mission of God, His plan and purpose for the Hebrew nation. The people are to tell the world about God the loving Redeemer, the sovereign Lord. God's mission is to be their mission.

Christians are likewise called to witness to God's careful, sacrificial plan to save and restore. Callings vary, but all Christians share with Moses the privilege of speaking God's truth, urging all people to return to God in humble trust and gratitude. Assignments and giftedness vary, but all Christians are responsible to live in service to God, following God's way, contributing to church and society. Deuteronomy, the "second-time law," reveals how God is concerned for every part of life.

The enduring lesson is to become a friend of God, living today in the power of the living Christ, guided by the Holy Spirit, carrying out God's mission.

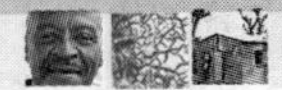

Introduction

1 These are the words Moses spoke to all Israel across the Jordan in the wilderness,[a] in the ·Arabah opposite Suph,[A] between Paran[b] and Tophel, Laban, Hazeroth,[c] and Di-zahab. 2 It is an eleven-day journey from Horeb to Kadesh-barnea by way of Mount Seir. 3 In the fortieth year, in the eleventh month, on the first of the month, Moses told the Israelites everything the LORD had commanded him to say to them. 4 This was after he had defeated Sihon king of the Amorites, who lived in Heshbon, and Og king of Bashan, who lived in Ashtaroth, at Edrei.[d] 5 Across the Jordan in the land of Moab, Moses began to explain this law, saying:

Departure from Horeb

6 "The LORD our God spoke to us at Horeb: 'You have stayed at this mountain long enough. 7 Resume your journey and go to the hill country of the Amorites and their neighbors in the Arabah, the hill country, the Judean foothills,[B] the ·Negev and the sea coast — to the land of the Canaanites and to Lebanon as far as the Euphrates River.[C] 8 See, I have set the land before you. Enter and take possession of the land the LORD swore to give to your fathers[e] Abraham, Isaac, and Jacob and their future descendants.'[f]

Leaders for the Tribes

9 "I said to you at that time: I can't bear the responsibility for you on my own. 10 The LORD your God has so multiplied you that today you are as numerous as the stars of the sky.[g] 11 May ·Yahweh, the God of your fathers, increase you a thousand times more, and bless you as He promised you. 12 But how can I bear your troubles, burdens, and disputes by myself? 13 Appoint for yourselves wise, understanding, and respected men from each of your tribes, and I will make them your leaders.

14 "You replied to me, 'What you propose to do is good.'

15 "So I took the leaders of your tribes, wise and respected men, and set them over you as leaders: officials for thousands, hundreds, fifties, and tens, and officers for your tribes. 16 I commanded your judges at that time: Hear the cases between your brothers, and judge rightly between a man and his brother or a foreign resident. 17 Do not show partiality when deciding a case;[h] listen to small and great alike. Do not be intimidated by anyone, for judgment belongs to God.[i] Bring me any case too difficult for you, and I will hear it. 18 At that time I commanded you about all the things you were to do.[j]

Israel's Disobedience at Kadesh-barnea

19 "We then set out from Horeb and went across all the great and terrible wilderness you saw on the way to the hill country of the Amorites, just as the LORD our God had commanded us. When we reached Kadesh-barnea, 20 I said to you: You have reached the hill country of the Amorites, which the LORD our God is giving us. 21 See, the LORD your God has set the land before you. Go up and take possession of it as Yahweh, the God of your fathers, has told you. Do not be afraid or discouraged.

22 "Then[k] all of you approached me and said, 'Let's send men ahead of us, so that they may explore the land for us and bring us back a report about the route we should go up and the cities we will come to.' 23 The plan seemed good to me, so I selected 12 men from among you, one man for each tribe. 24 They left and went up into the hill country and came to the Valley of Eshcol, scouting the land. 25 They took some of the fruit from the land in their hands, carried it down to us, and brought us back a report: 'The land the LORD our God is giving us is good.'[l]

26 "But you were not willing to go up, rebelling against the command of the LORD your God. 27 You grumbled in your tents[m] and said, 'The LORD brought us out of the land of Egypt to deliver us into the hands of the Amorites so they would destroy us, because He hated us. 28 Where can we go? Our brothers have discouraged us,[n] saying: The people are larger and taller than we are; the cities are large, fortified to the heavens.[o] We also saw the descendants of the Anakim[p] there.'

29 "So I said to you: Don't be terrified or afraid of them![q] 30 The LORD your God who

[a] **1:1** Gn 50:10-11; Dt 4:41,46-47; 11:30; Jos 1:14-15
[b] Nm 12:16; Dt 33:2
[c] Nm 11:35
[d] **1:4** Nm 21:21-35
[e] **1:8** Dt 1:35
[f] Gn 15:18-21; 26:3; 35:12
[g] **1:10** Gn 22:17; 26:4; Ex 32:13
[h] **1:17** Lv 19:15; Dt 16:19; Pr 24:23
[i] 2Ch 19:6
[j] **1:9-18** Ex 18:13-26
[k] **1:22-46** Nm 13–14
[l] **1:25** Dt 8:7
[m] **1:27** Ps 106:25
[n] **1:28** Jos 14:8
[o] Dt 9:1-2
[p] Dt 2:10; 9:2; Jos 11:21; 14:12
[q] **1:29** Dt 31:6

[A] **1:1** LXX, Tg, Vg read *the Red Sea* [B] **1:7** Or *the Shephelah* [C] **1:7** Lit *the great river, the river Euphrates*

goes before you[a] will fight for you,[b] just as you saw Him do for you in Egypt. 31 And you saw in the wilderness how the LORD your God carried you as a man carries his son all along the way you traveled until you reached this place. 32 But in spite of this you did not trust the LORD your God, 33 who went before you on the journey to seek out a place for you to camp. He went in the fire by night and in the cloud by day to guide you on the road you were to travel.

34 "When the LORD heard your[A] words, He grew angry and swore an oath: 35 'None of these men in this evil generation will see the good land I swore to give your fathers,[c] 36 except Caleb the son of Jephunneh. He will see it, and I will give him and his descendants the land on which he has set foot, because he followed the LORD completely.'

37 "The LORD was angry with me also because of you and said: 'You will not enter there either.[d] 38 Joshua son of Nun, who attends you, will enter it. Encourage him, for he will enable Israel to inherit it.[e] 39 Your little children, whom you said would be plunder, your sons who[B] don't know good from evil, will enter there. I will give them the land, and they will take possession of it. 40 But you are to turn back and head for the wilderness by way of the •Red Sea.'[f]

41 "You answered me, 'We have sinned against the LORD. We will go up and fight just as the LORD our God commanded us.' Then each of you put on his weapons of war and thought it would be easy to go up into the hill country.

42 "But the LORD said to me, 'Tell them: Don't go up and fight, for I am not with you to keep you from being defeated by your enemies.'[g] 43 So I spoke to you, but you didn't listen. You rebelled against the LORD's command and defiantly went up into the hill country. 44 Then the Amorites who lived there came out against you and chased you like a swarm of bees. They routed you from Seir as far as Hormah.[h] 45 When you returned, you wept before the LORD, but He didn't listen to your requests or pay attention to you. 46 For this reason you stayed in Kadesh as long as you did.[C]

Journey past Seir

2 "Then we turned back and headed for the wilderness by way of the •Red Sea, as the LORD had told me, and we traveled around the hill country of Seir for many days. 2 The LORD then said to me, 3 'You've been traveling around this hill country long enough; turn north. 4 Command the people: You are about to travel through the territory of your brothers, the descendants of Esau, who live in Seir. They will be afraid of you, so you must be very careful. 5 Don't fight with them, for I will not give you any of their land, not even an inch of it,[D] because I have given Esau the hill country of Seir as his possession. 6 You may purchase food from them with silver, so that you may eat, and buy water from them to drink.[i] 7 For the LORD your God has blessed you in all the work of your hands.[j] He has watched over your journey through this immense wilderness. The LORD your God has been with you this past 40 years, and you have lacked nothing.'

Journey past Moab

8 "So we bypassed our brothers, the descendants of Esau, who live in Seir. We turned away from the •Arabah road and from Elath and Ezion-geber. We traveled along the road to the Wilderness of Moab. 9 The LORD said to me, 'Show no hostility toward Moab, and do not provoke them to battle, for I will not give you any of their land as a possession, since I have given Ar as a possession to the descendants of Lot.'"[k]

10 The Emim, a great and numerous people as tall as the Anakim, had previously lived there. 11 They were also regarded as Rephaim,[l] like the Anakim, though the Moabites called them Emim.[m] 12 The Horites had previously lived in Seir, but the descendants of Esau drove them out, destroying them completely[E] and settling in their place, just as Israel did in the land of its possession the LORD gave them.

13 "The LORD said, 'Now get up and cross the Zered Valley.' So we crossed the Zered Valley.[n] 14 The time we spent traveling from Kadesh-barnea until we crossed the Zered Valley was 38 years until the entire generation of fight-

[a] **1:30** Ex 23:23; 32:34; Dt 31:8; Jdg 4:14; Is 52:12
[b] Ex 14:14; Dt 20:4; Jdg 9:17
[c] **1:35** Dt 1:8; 6:18; 10:11; 11:21; 30:20; 31:7,20; Ezk 20:42
[d] **1:37** Nm 20:12
[e] **1:38** Nm 27:12-21
[f] **1:40** Nm 14:25
[g] **1:42** Nm 14:42
[h] **1:44** Nm 14:45
[i] **2:1-6** Nm 20:14-21
[j] **2:7** Dt 30:9
[k] **2:9** Gn 19:36-37
[l] **2:11** Gn 14:5; 15:20; Jos 13:13; 2Sm 21:15-22
[m] Gn 14:5
[n] **2:8-13** Nm 21:10-20

[A] **1:34** Lit *the sound of your* [B] **1:39** Lit *who today* [C] **1:46** Lit *Kadesh for many days, according to the days you stayed* [D] **2:5** Lit *land as far as the width of a sole of a foot* [E] **2:12** Lit *them before them* ing men had perished from the camp, as the LORD had sworn to them. 15 Indeed, the LORD's hand was against them, to eliminate them from the camp until they had all perished.

Journey past Ammon

16 "When all the fighting men had died among the people, 17 the LORD spoke to me, 18 'Today you are going to cross the border of Moab at Ar. 19 When you get close to the Ammonites, don't show any hostility to them or fight with them, for I will not give you any of the Ammonites' land as a possession; I have given it as a possession to the descendants of Lot.' "[a]

20 This too used to be regarded as the land of the Rephaim. The Rephaim lived there previously, though the Ammonites called them Zamzummim, 21 a great and numerous people, tall as the Anakim. The LORD destroyed the Rephaim at the advance of the Ammonites, so that they drove them out and settled in their place. 22 This was just as He had done for the descendants of Esau who lived in Seir, when He destroyed the Horites before them; they drove them out and have lived in their place until now. 23 The Caphtorim, who came from Caphtor,[A] destroyed the Avvim, who lived in villages as far as Gaza, and settled in their place.

Defeat of Sihon the Amorite

24 "The LORD also said, 'Get up, move out, and cross the Arnon Valley. See, I have handed Sihon the Amorite, king of Heshbon, and his land over to you. Begin to take possession of it; engage him in battle. 25 Today I will begin to put the fear and dread of you on the peoples everywhere under heaven. They will hear the report about you, tremble, and be in anguish because of you.'

26 "So I sent messengers with an offer of peace to Sihon king of Heshbon from the Wilderness of Kedemoth, saying, 27 'Let us travel through your land; we will keep strictly to the highway. We will not turn to the right or the left.[b] 28 You can sell us food in exchange for silver so we may eat, and give us water for silver so we may drink. Only let us travel through on foot, 29 just as the descendants of Esau who live in Seir did for us, and the Moabites who live in Ar, until we cross the Jordan into the land the LORD our God is giving us.' 30 But Sihon king of Heshbon would not let us travel through his land, for the LORD your God had made his spirit stubborn and his heart obstinate in order to hand him over to you, as has now taken place.

31 "Then the LORD said to me, 'See, I have begun to give Sihon and his land to you. Begin to take possession of it.' 32 So Sihon and his whole army came out against us for battle at Jahaz. 33 The LORD our God handed him over to us, and we defeated him, his sons, and his whole army. 34 At that time we captured all his cities and ·completely destroyed the people of every city, including the women and children. We left no survivors. 35 We took only the livestock and the spoil from the cities we captured as plunder for ourselves. 36 There was no city that was inaccessible to[B] us, from Aroer on the rim of the Arnon Valley, along with the city in the valley, even as far as Gilead.[c] The LORD our God gave everything to us. 37 But you did not go near the Ammonites' land, all along the bank of the Jabbok River,[d] the cities of the hill country, or any place that the LORD our God had forbidden.[e]

Defeat of Og of Bashan

3 "Then we turned and went up the road to Bashan, and Og king of Bashan[f] came out against us with his whole army to do battle at Edrei.[g] 2 But the LORD said to me, 'Do not fear him, for I have handed him over to you along with his whole army and his land. Do to him as you did to Sihon king of the Amorites,[h] who lived in Heshbon.' 3 So the LORD our God also handed over Og king of Bashan and his whole army to us. We struck him until there was no survivor left. 4 We captured all his cities at that time. There wasn't a city that we didn't take from them: 60 cities, the entire region of Argob, the kingdom of Og in Bashan. 5 All these were fortified with high walls, gates, and bars, besides a large number of rural villages. 6 We ·completely destroyed them, as we had done to Sihon king of Heshbon, destroying the men, women, and children of every city. 7 But we took all the livestock and

[a] **2:19** Gn 19:36,38
[b] **2:27** Nm 20:17
[c] **2:36** Jos 13:9,16
[d] **2:37** Nm 21:24; Jos 12:2
[e] **2:24-37** Nm 21:21-31
[f] **3:1** Nm 32:33
[g] Nm 21:33,35; Dt 1:4; 3:10; 29:6-7; Jos 12:4; 13:12,31
[h] **3:2** Nm 21:23-26,34

A **2:23** Probably Crete B **2:36** Or *was too high for*

the spoil from the cities as plunder for ourselves.[a]

The Land of the Transjordan Tribes

8 "At that time we took the land from the two Amorite kings across the Jordan, from the Arnon Valley as far as Mount Hermon, 9 which the Sidonians call Sirion, but the Amorites call Senir, 10 all the cities of the plateau, Gilead, and Bashan as far as Salecah and Edrei, cities of Og's kingdom in Bashan.[b] 11 (Only Og king of Bashan was left of the remnant of the Rephaim. His bed was made of iron.[A] Isn't it in Rabbah of the Ammonites? It is 13 feet six inches long and six feet wide by a standard measure.[B])

12 "At that time we took possession of this land.[c] I gave to the Reubenites and Gadites the area extending from Aroer by the Arnon Valley, and half the hill country of Gilead along with its cities. 13 I gave to half the tribe of Manasseh the rest of Gilead and all Bashan, the kingdom of Og. The entire region of Argob, the whole territory of Bashan, used to be called the land of the Rephaim. 14 Jair, a descendant of Manasseh, took over the entire region of Argob as far as the border of the Geshurites and Maacathites. He called Bashan by his own name, Jair's Villages,[C] as it is today. 15 I gave Gilead to Machir, 16 and I gave to the Reubenites and Gadites the area extending from Gilead to the Arnon Valley (the middle of the valley was the border) and up to the Jabbok River, the border of the Ammonites. 17 The *Arabah and Jordan are also borders from Chinnereth[D] as far as the Sea of the Arabah, the Dead Sea, under the slopes of Pisgah on the east.[d]

18 "I commanded you at that time: The LORD your God has given you this land to possess. All your fighting men will cross over in battle formation ahead of your brothers the Israelites. 19 But your wives, young children, and livestock—I know that you have a lot of livestock—will remain in the cities I have given you 20 until the LORD gives rest to your brothers as He has to you, and they also take possession of the land the LORD your God is giving them across the Jordan. Then each of you may return to his possession that I have given you.[e]

[a]3:1-7 Nm 21:32-35 **[b]3:10** Jos 13:11 **[c]3:12** Gn 28:4; Lv 20:24; Dt 4:5; 6:1; 7:1; 8:1; 12:29; 30:5 **[d]3:8-17** Nm 32:1-19,33-42; Jos 12:2-3 **[e]3:18-20** Nm 32:20-32; Jos 1:14-15 **[f]3:25** Dt 8:7 **[g]3:26-27** Nm 20:1-13 **[h]3:27-28** Nm 27:12-23 **[i]4:2** Dt 12:32; Rv 22:18-19 **[j]4:3** Nm 25:1-9

The Transfer of Israel's Leadership

21 "I commanded Joshua at that time: Your own eyes have seen everything the LORD your God has done to these two kings. The LORD will do the same to all the kingdoms you are about to enter. 22 Don't be afraid of them, for the LORD your God fights for you.

23 "At that time I begged the LORD: 24 Lord GOD, You have begun to show Your greatness and power to Your servant, for what god is there in heaven or on earth who can perform deeds and mighty acts like Yours? 25 Please let me cross over and see the beautiful land[f] on the other side of the Jordan, that good hill country and Lebanon.

26 "But the LORD was angry with me on account of you and would not listen to me. The LORD said to me, 'That's enough! Do not speak to Me again about this matter. 27 Go to the top of Pisgah and look to the west, north, south, and east, and see it with your own eyes, for you will not cross this Jordan.[g] 28 But commission Joshua and encourage and strengthen him, for he will cross over ahead of the people and enable them to inherit this land that you will see.'[h] 29 So we stayed in the valley facing Beth-peor.

Call to Obedience

4 "Now, Israel, listen to the statutes and ordinances I am teaching you to follow, so that you may live, enter, and take possession of the land *Yahweh, the God of your fathers, is giving you. 2 You must not add anything to what I command you or take anything away from it,[i] so that you may keep the commands of the LORD your God I am giving you. 3 Your eyes have seen what the LORD did at Baal-peor, for the LORD your God destroyed every one of you who followed *Baal of Peor.[j] 4 But you who have remained faithful[E] to the LORD your God are all alive today. 5 Look, I have taught you statutes and ordinances as the LORD my God has commanded me, so that you may follow them in the land you are entering to possess. 6 Carefully follow them, for this will

[A]**3:11** Or *His sarcophagus was made of basalt* [B]**3:11** Lit *Nine cubits its length and four cubits its width, by a man's cubit* [C]**3:14** Or *Havvoth-jair* [D]**3:17** = the Sea of Galilee; Jos 12:3; 13:27; Lk 5:1 [E]**4:4** Lit *have held on*

show your wisdom and understanding in the
eyes of the peoples. When they hear about all
these statutes, they will say, 'This great nation
is indeed a wise and understanding people.'
7 For what great nation is there that has a god
near to it as the LORD our God is to us whenever we call to Him? 8 And what great nation
has righteous statutes and ordinances like
this entire law I set before you today?

9 "Only be on your guard and diligently
watch yourselves, so that you don't forget the
things your eyes have seen and so that they
don't slip from your mind as long as you live.
Teach them to your children and your grandchildren.[a] 10 The day you stood before the
LORD your God at Horeb, the LORD said to me,
'Assemble the people before Me, and I will let
them hear My words, so that they may learn
to fear Me all the days they live on the earth
and may instruct their children.' 11 You came
near and stood at the base of the mountain, a
mountain blazing with fire into the heavens
and enveloped in a dense, black cloud. 12 Then
the LORD spoke to you from the fire. You kept
hearing the sound of the words, but didn't see
a form; there was only a voice.[b] 13 He declared
His covenant[c] to you. He commanded you to
follow the Ten Commandments, which He
wrote on two stone tablets. 14 At that time the
LORD commanded me to teach you statutes
and ordinances for you to follow in the land
you are about to cross into and possess.

Worshiping the True God

15 "For your own good, be extremely careful—because you did not see any form on
the day the LORD spoke to you out of the fire
at Horeb— 16 not to act corruptly and make
an idol for yourselves in the shape of any figure: a male or female form, 17 or the form of
any beast on the earth, any winged creature
that flies in the sky, 18 any creature that crawls
on the ground, or any fish in the waters under the earth. 19 When you look to the heavens
and see the sun, moon, and stars—all the array of heaven—do not be led astray to bow
down and worship them. The LORD your God
has provided them for all people everywhere
under heaven. 20 But the LORD selected you
and brought you out of Egypt's iron furnace
to be a people for His inheritance, as you are
today.

21 "The LORD was angry with me on your account. He swore that I would not cross the
Jordan and enter the good land[d] the LORD
your God is giving you as an inheritance.[e] 22 I
won't be crossing the Jordan because I am going to die in this land. But you are about to
cross over and take possession of this good
land. 23 Be careful not to forget the covenant
of the LORD your God that He made with you,
and make an idol for yourselves in the shape
of anything He has forbidden you. 24 For the
LORD your God is a consuming fire,[f] a jealous
God.[g]

25 "When you have children and grandchildren and have been in the land a long time,
and if you act corruptly, make an idol in the
form of anything, and do what is evil in the
sight of the LORD your God, provoking Him
to anger, 26 I call heaven and earth as witnesses
against you today that you will quickly perish[h] from the land you are about to cross the
Jordan to possess. You will not live long there,
but you will certainly be destroyed. 27 The
LORD will scatter you among the peoples,
and you will be reduced to a few survivors[A]
among the nations where the LORD your God
will drive you. 28 There you will worship man-
made gods of wood and stone, which cannot
see, hear, eat, or smell. 29 But from there, you
will search for the LORD your God, and you
will find Him when you seek Him with all
your heart and all your soul.[i] 30 When you are
in distress and all these things have happened
to you, you will return to the LORD your God
in later days and obey Him. 31 He will not leave
you, destroy you, or forget the covenant[j] with
your fathers that He swore to them by oath,
because the LORD your God is a compassionate God.[k]

32 "Indeed, ask about the earlier days that
preceded you, from the day God created man
on the earth and from one end of the heavens to the other: Has anything like this great
event ever happened, or has anything like it
been heard of? 33 Has a people heard God's
voice speaking from the fire as you have, and
lived? 34 Or has a god attempted to go and
take a nation as his own out of another na-

[a] **4:9-10** Ex 12:26; Dt 6:7,20-25; 11:2-7,18-21; 31:12-13,19-22; 32:46; Jos 4:6,21-22; 8:35
[b] **4:9-12** Ex 19:10-19; Heb 12:18-19
[c] **4:13** Dt 31:16
[d] **4:21** Dt 8:7
[e] Dt 15:4
[f] **4:24** Ex 24:17; Dt 9:3; 2Sm 22:9; Is 29:6; 30:27,30; 34:14
[g] **4:23-24** Ex 20:5; 34:14; Dt 5:9; 6:15; Jos 24:19; Heb 12:29
[h] **4:26** Dt 8:19
[i] **4:29** Jr 29:13
[j] **4:31** Lv 26:45; Dt 5:3; 7:12; 8:18; 31:20
[k] Ex 34:6

[A] **4:27** Lit *be left few in number*

tion, by trials, signs, wonders, and war, by
a strong hand and an outstretched arm, by
great terrors, as the LORD your God did for
you in Egypt before your eyes? 35 You were
shown these things so that you would know
that the LORD is God; there is no other besides Him.[a] 36 He let you hear His voice from
heaven to instruct you.[b] He showed you His
great fire on earth, and you heard His words
from the fire.[c] 37 Because He loved[d] your fathers, He chose their descendants after them
and brought you out of Egypt by His presence and great power, 38 to drive out before
you nations greater and stronger than you
and to bring you in and give you their land
as an inheritance,[e] as is now taking place.
39 Today, recognize and keep in mind that the
LORD is God in heaven above and on earth
below; there is no other. 40 Keep His statutes
and commands, which I am giving you today,
so that you and your children after you may
prosper and so that you may live long in the
land the LORD your God is giving you for all
time."

Cities of Refuge

41 Then Moses set apart three cities across
the Jordan to the east. 42 Someone could flee
there who committed manslaughter, killing
his neighbor accidentally without previously
hating him. He could flee to one of these cities and stay alive: 43 Bezer in the wilderness
on the plateau land, belonging to the Reubenites; Ramoth in Gilead, belonging to the
Gadites; or Golan in Bashan, belonging to the
Manassites.[f]

Introduction to the Law

44 This is the law Moses gave the Israelites.
45 These are the decrees, statutes, and ordinances Moses proclaimed to them after they
came out of Egypt, 46 across the Jordan in the
valley facing Beth-peor in the land of Sihon
king of the Amorites. He lived in Heshbon,
and Moses and the Israelites defeated him after they came out of Egypt. 47 They took possession of his land and the land of Og king
of Bashan, the two Amorite kings who were
across the Jordan to the east, 48 from Aroer on
the rim of the Arnon Valley as far as Mount
Sion (that is, Hermon) 49 and all the ˙Arabah
on the east side of the Jordan as far as the
Dead Sea below the slopes of Pisgah.

The Ten Commandments

5 Moses summoned all Israel and said to
them, "Israel, listen to the statutes and ordinances I am proclaiming as you hear them
today. Learn and follow them carefully. 2 The
LORD our God made a covenant[g] with us at
Horeb. 3 He did not make this covenant with
our fathers,[h] but with all of us who are alive
here today. 4 The LORD spoke to you face to
face from the fire on the mountain. 5 At that
time I was standing between the LORD and
you to report the word[A] of the LORD to you,
because you were afraid of the fire and did
not go up the mountain. And He said:

6 I am the LORD your God,[i] who brought
you out of the land of Egypt, out of the
place of slavery.[j]
7 Do not have other gods besides Me.
8 Do not make an idol for yourself in the
shape of anything in the heavens above
or on the earth below or in the waters
under the earth. 9 You must not bow
down to them or worship them, because
I, the LORD your God, am a jealous God,
punishing the children for the fathers'
sin to the third and fourth generations
of those who hate Me,[k] 10 but showing
faithful love to a thousand generations
of those who love Me and keep My commands.
11 Do not misuse the name[l] of the LORD
your God, because the LORD will not
leave anyone unpunished who misuses
His name.
12 Be careful to remember the Sabbath day,
to keep it holy as the LORD your God has
commanded you. 13 You are to labor six
days and do all your work, 14 but the seventh day is a Sabbath to the LORD your
God. You must not do any work — you,
your son or daughter, your male or female slave, your ox or donkey, any of
your livestock, or the foreigner who
lives within your gates, so that your
male and female slaves may rest as you

[a] **4:35** 1Kg 8:60; Is 43:11; 44:8; 45:5-6,18-22; 46:9; Dn 3:29; Jl 2:27; Mk 12:32
[b] **4:36** Ex 20:22
[c] Ex 19:18
[d] **4:37** Dt 7:6-8; 10:15; 23:5; 33:3; Jr 31:3; Hs 11:1; Mal 1:2
[e] **4:38** Lv 20:24
[f] **4:41-43** Nm 35:6-15; Dt 19:2-13; Jos 20:7-9
[g] **5:2** Dt 31:16
[h] **5:3** Dt 4:31
[i] **5:6-21** Ex 20:2-17; Dt 8:14
[j] **5:6** Lv 26:13; Dt 6:12; 8:14; 13:5,10; Jos 24:17; Jr 34:13
[k] **5:9** Ex 34:7; Nm 14:18; Dt 7:10; Ezk 18
[l] **5:11** Ex 3:13; 6:3; 33:19

[A] **5:5** One Hb ms, DSS, Sam, LXX, Syr, Vg read *words*

do. 15 Remember that you were a slave in the land of Egypt, and the LORD your God brought you out of there with a strong hand and an outstretched arm. That is why the LORD your God has commanded you to keep the Sabbath day.

16 Honor your father and your mother,[a] as the LORD your God has commanded you, so that you may live long and so that you may prosper in the land the LORD your God is giving you.[b]

17 Do not murder.[c]

18 Do not commit adultery.[d]

19 Do not steal.

20 Do not give dishonest testimony against your neighbor.[e]

21 Do not covet your neighbor's wife or desire your neighbor's house, his field, his male or female slave, his ox or donkey, or anything that belongs to your neighbor.[f]

The People's Response

22 "The LORD spoke these commands in a loud voice to your entire assembly from the fire, cloud, and thick darkness on the mountain; He added nothing more. He wrote them on two stone tablets and gave them to me. 23 All of you approached me with your tribal leaders and elders when you heard the voice from the darkness and while the mountain was blazing with fire. 24 You said, 'Look, the LORD our God has shown us His glory and greatness, and we have heard His voice from the fire. Today we have seen that God speaks with a person, yet he still lives. 25 But now, why should we die? This great fire will consume us and we will die if we hear the voice of the LORD our God any longer. 26 For who out of all mankind has heard the voice of the living God speaking from the fire, as we have, and lived? 27 Go near and listen to everything the LORD our God says. Then you can tell us everything the LORD our God tells you; we will listen and obey.'[g]

28 "The LORD heard your[A] words when you spoke to me. He said to me, 'I have heard the words that these people have spoken to you. Everything they have said is right. 29 If only they had such a heart to •fear Me and keep all My commands always, so that they and their children will prosper forever. 30 Go and tell them: Return to your tents. 31 But you stand here with Me, and I will tell you every command—the statutes and ordinances—you are to teach them, so that they may follow them in the land I am giving them to possess.'

32 "Be careful to do as the LORD your God has commanded you; you are not to turn aside to the right or the left. 33 Follow the whole instruction the LORD your God has commanded you, so that you may live, prosper, and have a long life in the land you will possess.

The Greatest Command

6 "This is the command—the statutes and ordinances—the LORD your God has instructed me to teach you, so that you may follow them in the land you are about to enter and possess.[h] 2 Do this so that you may •fear[i] the LORD your God all the days of your life by keeping all His statutes and commands I am giving you, your son, and your grandson, and so that you may have a long life. 3 Listen, Israel, and be careful to follow them, so that you may prosper and multiply greatly, because •Yahweh, the God of your fathers, has promised you a land flowing with milk and honey.[j]

4 "Listen, Israel: The LORD our God, the LORD is One.[B,k] 5 Love the LORD your God with all your heart, with all your soul, and with all your strength.[l] 6 These words that I am giving you today are to be in your heart.[m] 7 Repeat them to your children.[n] Talk about them when you sit in your house and when you walk along the road, when you lie down and when you get up. 8 Bind them as a sign on your hand and let them be a symbol[C] on your forehead.[D,o] 9 Write them on the doorposts of your house and on your gates.

Remembering God through Obedience

10 "When the LORD your God brings you into the land He swore to your fathers Abraham, Isaac, and Jacob that He would give you—a land with large and beautiful cities

[a] **5:16-20** Mt 19:18-19; Mk 10:19; Lk 18:20; Rm 13:9 [b] **5:16** Mt 15:4; Mk 7:10; Eph 6:2-3 [c] **5:17** Mt 5:21; Jms 2:11 [d] **5:18** Mt 5:27 [e] **5:20** Pr 25:18 [f] **5:16-21** Mt 19:18-19; Mk 10:19; Lk 18:20; Rm 13:9 [g] **5:22-27** Ex 20:18-21 [h] **6:1** Dt 3:12 [i] **6:2** Dt 14:23 [j] **6:3** Dt 11:9 [k] **6:4** Mk 12:29,32; Jms 2:19 [l] **6:5** Mt 22:37; Mk 12:30; Lk 10:27 [m] **6:6-9** Dt 11:18-20 [n] **6:7** Dt 4:9-10 [o] **6:8** Ex 13:16; Dt 11:18

[A] **5:28** Lit *the sound of your* [B] **6:4** Or *Yahweh is our God; Yahweh is One*, or *The LORD is our God, the LORD alone*, or *The LORD our God is one LORD* [C] **6:8** Or *phylactery*; Mt 23:5 [D] **6:8** Lit *symbol between your eyes*

that you did not build, 11 houses full of every
good thing that you did not fill them with,
wells dug that you did not dig, and vineyards
and olive groves that you did not plant[a] — and
when you eat and are satisfied,[b] 12 be careful
not to forget the LORD who brought you out
of the land of Egypt, out of the place of slavery.[c] 13 Fear Yahweh your God, worship Him,
and take your oaths in His name.[d] 14 Do not
follow other gods, the gods of the peoples
around you, 15 for the LORD your God, who is
among you, is a jealous God.[e] Otherwise, the
LORD your God will become angry with you
and wipe you off the face of the earth. 16 Do
not test[f] the LORD your God as you tested
Him at Massah.[g] 17 Carefully observe the commands of the LORD your God, the decrees and
statutes He has commanded you. 18 Do what
is right and good in the LORD's sight, so that
you may prosper and so that you may enter
and possess the good land[h] the LORD your
God swore to give your fathers,[i] 19 by driving
out all your enemies before you, as the LORD
has said.[j]

[a] **6:10-11** Jos 24:13 [b] **6:11** Dt 8:10; Neh 9:25 [c] **6:12** Lv 26:13; Dt 5:6; 8:14; 13:5,10; Jos 24:17; Jr 34:13 [d] **6:13** Dt 10:12,20; 13:4; Jos 24:14; 1Sm 12:24; Mt 4:10; Lk 4:8; Rv 14:7 [e] **6:15** Dt 5:9 [f] **6:16** Ex 15:25; 16:4; Nm 14:22; Ps 78:18,41,56; 106:14; Mal 3:15; Mt 4:7; Lk 4:12 [g] Ex 17:1-7; Dt 9:22; 33:8; Ps 95:8-9 [h] **6:18** Dt 8:7 [i] Dt 1:35 [j] **6:19** Ex 34:11

Family and God's Mission

Juan Sanchez

After God created Adam and Eve in His image, He gave them a mission—"Be fruitful, multiply, fill the earth, and subdue it" (Gn 1:28). Adam and Eve's mission was to rule over creation, which included extending the borders of the garden until human domain covered the entire earth, and filling the earth with children who reflected God's image. In this way the whole earth would be filled with God's glory as Adam and Eve fulfilled their God-given roles as parents who raised their children to know God and live to fulfill His will. The Bible confirms this goal when it declares in Malachi 2:15 that the reason God created man and woman was because He was seeking godly children.

Unfortunately, Adam and Eve rebelled against God (Gn 3) and compromised God's mission. As a result of their sin, all humans are born into a fallen spiritual condition (Ps 51:5; Rm 3:23). Rather than an earth filled with the godly children God seeks, we have a world marred by sin and rebellion against God. Rather than declare His mission at an end, God promised that someday a child would come who would defeat the tempter (Gn 3:15). The New Testament reveals that the long-awaited child is Jesus Christ. By His obedient life and sacrificial death, Jesus defeated the devil and set free from slavery to sin and death all those who call on His name in faith (Hb 2:14-18).

God's mission has not changed today. He is still seeking godly children. By turning away from sin and turning to Christ in faith, we are transferred from the kingdom of darkness to the kingdom of the Son God loves, becoming children of God (Col 1:13). Jesus is the new Adam who is ruling over God's creation and filling the earth with the glory of God—children who reflect God's image (Rm 8:29; 2Co 3:18).

As Christian parents, our family is our first mission field. We join God's mission as we bring up our children in the training and instruction of the Lord (Eph 6:4; Col 3:21). How? First, the truths of the gospel must be hidden in our own hearts (Dt 6:5-6). If this is true of us, our children will see in us the fruits of the gospel life. Second, as parents we must read and know God's Word because only then can we pass on to our children what we know to be true about God, His Word and His works (Ps 78:5). Finally, we are to teach these truths to our children diligently (Dt 6:7-9), getting them into the Word regularly, so they may know truth from error and set their hope in God (Ps 78:7).

The goal of biblical parenting is not merely to raise well-behaved children, but to raise generations of children who are fulfilling God's design—to fill the earth with His renown through image bearers who live on mission.

20 "When your son asks you in the future, 'What is the meaning of the decrees, statutes, and ordinances, which the LORD our God has commanded you?' 21 tell him, 'We were slaves of Pharaoh in Egypt, but the LORD brought us out of Egypt with a strong hand. 22 Before our eyes the LORD inflicted great and devastating signs and wonders on Egypt, on Pharaoh, and on all his household, 23 but He brought us from there in order to lead us in and give us the land that He swore to our fathers. 24 The LORD commanded us to follow all these statutes and to fear the LORD our God for our prosperity always and for our preservation, as it is today. 25 Righteousness will be ours if we are careful to follow every one of these commands before the LORD our God, as He has commanded us.'

Israel to Destroy Idolatrous Nations

7 "When the LORD your God brings you into the land[a] you are entering to possess,[b] and He drives out many nations before you — the Hittites, Girgashites, Amorites, Canaanites, Perizzites, Hivites and Jebusites, seven nations more numerous and powerful than you — 2 and when the LORD your God delivers them over to you and you defeat them, you must ˚completely destroy them. Make no treaty with them and show them no mercy. 3 Do not intermarry with them. Do not give your daughters to their sons or take their daughters for your sons,[c] 4 because they will turn your sons away from Me to worship other gods. Then the LORD's anger will burn against you, and He will swiftly destroy you. 5 Instead, this is what you are to do to them: tear down their altars, smash their sacred pillars, cut down their ˚Asherah poles,[d] and burn up their carved images. 6 For you are a holy people[e] belonging to the LORD your God. The LORD your God has chosen you to be His own possession[f] out of all the peoples on the face of the earth.

7 "The LORD was devoted to you and chose you, not because you were more numerous than all peoples, for you were the fewest of all peoples. 8 But because the LORD loved[g] you and kept the oath He swore to your fathers, He brought you out with a strong hand and redeemed[h] you from the place of slavery, from the power of Pharaoh king of Egypt. 9 Know that ˚Yahweh your God is God, the faithful God who keeps His gracious covenant loyalty for a thousand generations with those who love Him and keep His commands.[i] 10 But He directly pays back[A] and destroys those who hate Him.[j] He will not hesitate to directly pay back[A] the one who hates Him. 11 So keep the command — the statutes and ordinances — that I am giving you to follow today.

12 "If you listen to and are careful to keep these ordinances, the LORD your God will keep His covenant loyalty with you, as He swore to your fathers.[k] 13 He will love you, bless you, and multiply you. He will bless your descendants,[B,l] and the produce of your land — your grain, new wine, and oil — the young of your herds, and the newborn of your flocks, in the land He swore to your fathers that He would give you. 14 You will be blessed above all peoples; there will be no infertile male or female among you or your livestock. 15 The LORD will remove all sickness from you; He will not put on you[m] all the terrible diseases of Egypt that you know about, but He will inflict them on all who hate you. 16 You must destroy all the peoples the LORD your God is delivering over to you and not look on them with pity. Do not worship their gods, for that will be a snare to you.

17 "If you say to yourself, 'These nations are greater than I; how can I drive them out?' 18 do not be afraid of them. Be sure to remember what the LORD your God did to Pharaoh and all Egypt: 19 the great trials that you saw, the signs and wonders, the strong hand and outstretched arm, by which the LORD your God brought you out. The LORD your God will do the same to all the peoples you fear. 20 The LORD your God will also send the hornet against them until all the survivors and those hiding from you perish.[n] 21 Don't be terrified of them, for the LORD your God, a great and awesome God, is among you. 22 The LORD your God will drive out these nations before you little by little. You will not be able to destroy them all at once; otherwise, the wild animals will become too numerous for you.[o] 23 The LORD your God will give them over to

[a] 7:1-5 Ex 23:23-26
[b] 7:1 Dt 3:12
[c] 7:3 Jos 23:12-13; 1Kg 11:12; Ezr 9:12,14
[d] 7:5 Ex 34:13; Dt 12:2-3
[e] 7:6 Dt 14:2,21; 26:19; 28:9
[f] Ex 19:5; Dt 14:2; 26:18-19
[g] 7:8 Dt 4:37
[h] Dt 9:26; 15:15; 24:18
[i] 7:9 Neh 1:5; Dn 9:4
[j] 7:10 Ex 34:6-7
[k] 7:12 Dt 4:31
[l] 7:13 Dt 28:4
[m] 7:15 Ex 15:26; 23:25; Dt 28:27,60
[n] 7:20 Ex 23:28; Jos 24:12
[o] 7:22 Ex 23:29-30

[A] 7:10 Lit *He pays back to their faces* [B] 7:13 Lit *bless the fruit of your womb* you and throw them into great confusion until they are destroyed. 24 He will hand their kings over to you, and you will wipe out their names under heaven. No one will be able to stand against you; you will annihilate them. 25 You must burn up the carved images of their gods. Don't covet the silver and gold on the images and take it for yourself, or else you will be ensnared by it, for it is abhorrent to the LORD your God. 26 You must not bring any abhorrent thing into your house, or you will be •set apart for destruction like it. You are to utterly detest and abhor it, because it is set apart for destruction.

Remember the LORD

8 "You must carefully follow every command I am giving you today, so that you may live and increase, and may enter and take possession of the land[a] the LORD swore to your fathers. 2 Remember that the LORD your God led you on the entire journey these 40 years in the wilderness, so that He might humble you and test you to know what was in your heart, whether or not you would keep His commands. 3 He humbled you by letting you go hungry; then He gave you manna to eat, which you and your fathers had not known, so that you might learn that man does not live on bread alone but on every word that comes from the mouth of the LORD.[b] 4 Your clothing did not wear out, and your feet did not swell these 40 years.[c] 5 Keep in mind that the LORD your God has been disciplining you just as a man disciplines his son. 6 So keep the commands of the LORD your God by walking in His ways and •fearing Him. 7 For the LORD your God is bringing you into a good land,[d] a land with streams of water, springs, and deep water sources, flowing in both valleys and hills; 8 a land of wheat, barley, vines, figs, and pomegranates; a land of olive oil and honey; 9 a land where you will eat food without shortage, where you will lack nothing; a land whose rocks are iron and from whose hills you will mine copper. 10 When you eat and are full,[e] you will praise the LORD your God for the good land[f] He has given you.

11 "Be careful that you don't forget the LORD your God by failing to keep His command—the ordinances and statutes—I am giving you today. 12 When you eat and are full, and build beautiful houses to live in, 13 and your herds and flocks grow large, and your silver and gold multiply, and everything else you have increases, 14 be careful that your heart doesn't become proud and you forget the LORD your God who brought you out of the land of Egypt, out of the place of slavery.[g] 15 He led you through the great and terrible wilderness with its poisonous[A] snakes and scorpions, a thirsty land where there was no water. He brought water out of the flint-like rock for you. 16 He fed you in the wilderness with manna[h] that your fathers had not known, in order to humble and test you, so that in the end He might cause you to prosper. 17 You may say to yourself, 'My power and my own ability have gained this wealth for me,' 18 but remember that the LORD your God gives you the power to gain wealth, in order to confirm His covenant He swore to your fathers,[i] as it is today. 19 If you ever forget the LORD your God and go after other gods to worship and bow down to them, I testify against you today that you will perish.[j] 20 Like the nations the LORD is about to destroy before you, you will perish if you do not obey the LORD your God.

Warning against Self-Righteousness

9 "Listen, Israel: Today you are about to cross the Jordan to go and drive out nations greater and stronger than you, with large cities fortified to the heavens.[k] 2 The people are strong and tall, the descendants of the Anakim.[l] You know about them and you have heard it said about them, 'Who can stand up to the sons of Anak?'[m] 3 But understand that today the LORD your God will cross over ahead of you[n] as a consuming fire; He will devastate and subdue them before you. You will drive them out and destroy them swiftly, as the LORD has told you. 4 When the LORD your God drives them out before you, do not say to yourself, 'The LORD brought me in to take possession of this land because of my righteousness.' Instead, the LORD will drive out these nations before you because of their wickedness. 5 You are not going to take possession of their land because of your righ-

[a] **8:1** Dt 3:12
[b] **8:3** Mt 4:4; Lk 4:4
[c] **8:4** Dt 29:5; Neh 9:21
[d] **8:7** Ex 3:8; Nm 14:7; Dt 1:25,35; 3:25; 4:21-22; 6:18; 8:10; 9:6; 11:17; Jos 23:16
[e] **8:10** Dt 11:15
[f] Dt 8:7
[g] **8:14** Lv 26:13; Dt 5:6; 6:12; 13:5,10; Jos 24:17; Jr 34:13
[h] **8:16** Ex 16:4
[i] **8:18** Dt 4:31
[j] **8:19** Dt 4:26
[k] **9:1** Dt 1:28
[l] **9:2** Dt 2:10; Jos 11:21; 14:12
[m] Nm 13:22; Jos 15:13-14; 21:11; Jdg 1:20
[n] **9:3** Dt 31:3

[A] **8:15** Lit *burning*

teousness or your integrity. Instead, the LORD
your God will drive out these nations before
you because of their wickedness, in order to
keep the promise He swore to your fathers,
Abraham, Isaac, and Jacob. 6Understand that
the LORD your God is not giving you this good
land[a] to possess because of your righteousness, for you are a stiff-necked people.

Israel's Rebellion and Moses' Intercession

7"Remember[b] and do not forget how you
provoked the LORD your God in the wilderness. You have been rebelling against the
LORD from the day you left the land of Egypt
until you reached this place. 8You provoked
the LORD at Horeb, and He was angry enough
with you to destroy you. 9When I went up the
mountain to receive the stone tablets, the
tablets of the covenant the LORD made with
you, I stayed on the mountain 40 days and
40 nights. I did not eat bread or drink water.
10On the day of the assembly the LORD gave
me the two stone tablets, inscribed by God's
finger. The exact words were on them, which
the LORD spoke to you from the fire on the
mountain. 11The LORD gave me the two stone
tablets, the tablets of the covenant, at the end
of the 40 days and 40 nights.

12"The LORD said to me, 'Get up and go
down immediately from here. For your people whom you brought out of Egypt have
acted corruptly. They have quickly turned
from the way that I commanded them; they
have made a cast image for themselves.' 13The
LORD also said to me, 'I have seen this people,
and indeed, they are a stiff-necked people.
14Leave Me alone, and I will destroy them and
blot out their name under heaven. Then I will
make you into a nation stronger and more
numerous than they.'

15"So I went back down the mountain,
while it was blazing with fire, and the two
tablets of the covenant were in my hands. 16I
saw how you had sinned against the LORD
your God; you had made a calf image for
yourselves. You had quickly turned from
the way the LORD had commanded for you.
17So I took hold of the two tablets and threw
them from my hands, shattering them before your eyes. 18Then I fell down like the first
time in the presence of the LORD for 40 days
and 40 nights; I did not eat bread or drink
water because of all the sin you committed,
doing what was evil in the LORD's sight and
provoking Him to anger. 19I was afraid of the
fierce anger the LORD had directed against
you,[c] because He was about to destroy you.
But again the LORD listened to me on that occasion.[d] 20The LORD was angry enough with
Aaron to destroy him. But I prayed for Aaron
at that time also. 21I took the sinful calf you
had made, burned it up, and crushed it, thoroughly grinding it to powder as fine as dust.
Then I threw it into the stream that came
down from the mountain.[e]

22"You continued to provoke the LORD at
Taberah, Massah, and Kibroth-hattaavah.[f]
23When the LORD sent you from Kadesh-barnea, He said, 'Go up and possess the land I
have given you'; you rebelled against the command of the LORD your God. You did not believe or obey Him.[g] 24You have been rebelling
against the LORD ever since I have[A] known
you.[h]

25"I fell down in the presence of the LORD
40 days and 40 nights because the LORD had
threatened to destroy you. 26I prayed to the
LORD:

> Lord GOD, do not annihilate Your people,
> Your inheritance, whom You redeemed[i]
> through Your greatness and brought out
> of Egypt with a strong hand. 27Remember
> Your servants Abraham, Isaac, and Jacob.
> Disregard this people's stubbornness,
> and their wickedness and sin. 28Other-
> wise, those in the land you brought us
> from will say, 'Because the LORD wasn't
> able to bring them into the land He had
> promised them, and because He hated
> them, He brought them out to kill them
> in the wilderness.'[j] 29But they are Your
> people, Your inheritance, whom You
> brought out by Your great power and
> outstretched arm.[k]

The Covenant Renewed

10 "The LORD said to me at that time, 'Cut
two stone tablets like the first ones
and come to Me on the mountain and make

[a]**9:6** Dt 8:7
[b]**9:7–10:11** Ex 32–34
[c]**9:19** Heb 12:21
[d]Dt 10:10
[e]**9:21** Ex 32:20
[f]**9:22** Nm 11:1-35; Ex 17:1-7
[g]**9:23** Nm 13–14
[h]**9:24** Ps 95; 106
[i]**9:26** Dt 7:8; 15:15; 24:18
[j]**9:28** Nm 14:16
[k]**9:29** 2Kg 17:36; Neh 1:10; Jr 27:5; 32:17

A**9:24** Sam, LXX read *since He has*

a wooden ark. 2I will write on the tablets the
words that were on the first tablets you broke,
and you are to place them in the ark.’ 3So I
made an ark of acacia wood, cut two stone
tablets like the first ones, and climbed the
mountain with the two tablets in my hand.
4Then on the day of the assembly, the LORD
wrote on the tablets what had been written
previously, the Ten Commandments that He
had spoken to you on the mountain from the
fire. The LORD gave them to me, 5and I went
back down the mountain and placed the tablets in the ark I had made. And they have remained there, as the LORD commanded me.”

6The Israelites traveled from Beeroth Bene-
jaakan[A] to Moserah. Aaron died and was buried there, and Eleazar his son became priest
in his place.[a] 7They traveled from there to
Gudgodah, and from Gudgodah to Jotbathah,
a land with streams of water.[b]

8“At that time the LORD set apart the tribe
of Levi[c] to carry the ark of the LORD’s covenant, to stand before •Yahweh to serve Him,
and to pronounce blessings in His name, as it
is today. 9For this reason, Levi does not have a
portion or inheritance like his brothers; the
LORD is his inheritance, as the LORD your God
told him.[d]

10“I stayed on the mountain 40 days and 40
nights like the first time. The LORD also listened to me on this occasion;[e] He agreed not
to annihilate you. 11Then the LORD said to me,
‘Get up. Continue your journey ahead of the
people, so that they may enter and possess the
land I swore to give their fathers.’[f]

What God Requires

12“And now, Israel, what does the LORD
your God ask of you except to •fear[g] the LORD
your God by walking in all His ways, to love
Him, and to worship the LORD your God with
all your heart and all your soul? 13Keep the
LORD’s commands and statutes I am giving
you today, for your own good. 14The heavens, indeed the highest heavens, belong to
the LORD your God, as does the earth and
everything in it. 15Yet the LORD was devoted
to your fathers and loved them.[h] He chose
their descendants after them — He chose you
out of all the peoples, as it is today. 16There-
fore, circumcise your hearts[i] and don’t be
stiff-necked any longer. 17For the LORD your
God is the God of gods and Lord of lords,
the great, mighty, and awesome God, showing no partiality and taking no bribe. 18He
executes justice for the fatherless and the
widow, and loves the foreigner, giving him
food and clothing. 19You also must love the
foreigner, since you were foreigners in the
land of Egypt.[j] 20You are to fear Yahweh your
God and worship Him. Remain faithful[B] to
Him and take oaths in His name.[k] 21He is your
praise and He is your God, who has done for
you these great and awesome works your
eyes have seen. 22Your fathers went down to
Egypt, 70 people in all,[l] and now the LORD
your God has made you as numerous as the
stars of the sky.[m]

Remember and Obey

11 “Therefore, love the LORD your God and
always keep His mandate and His statutes, ordinances, and commands. 2You must
understand today that it is not your children
who experienced or saw the discipline of the
LORD your God:

> His greatness, strong hand, and out-
> stretched arm; 3His signs and the works
> He did in Egypt to Pharaoh king of Egypt
> and all his land;[n] 4what He did to Egypt’s
> army, its horses and chariots, when He
> made the waters of the •Red Sea flow
> over them as they pursued you, and He
> destroyed them[o] completely;[C] 5what He
> did to you in the wilderness until you
> reached this place; 6and what He did to
> Dathan and Abiram, the sons of Eliab
> the Reubenite, when in the middle of the
> whole Israelite camp the earth opened
> its mouth and swallowed them, their
> households, their tents, and every living
> thing with them.[p]

7Your own eyes have seen every great work
the LORD has done.

8“Keep every command I am giving you today, so that you may have the strength to cross
into and possess the land you are to inherit,
9and so that you may live long in the land the
LORD swore to your fathers to give them and

[a]10:6 Nm 20:22-29 [b]10:6-7 Nm 33:31-33 [c]10:8 Ex 32:26-29 [d]10:9 Lv 25:32-34; Nm 18:20; 26:62; Dt 18:1-2; Jos 13:14,33; Ezk 44:28-30 [e]10:10 Dt 9:19 [f]10:11 Dt 1:35 [g]10:12 Dt 14:23 [h]10:15 Dt 4:37 [i]10:16 Jr 4:4; Rm 2:29 [j]10:19 Lv 19:34 [k]10:20 Dt 6:13; 13:4 [l]10:22 Gn 46:27; Ex 1:5 [m]Gn 15:5; 22:17; 26:4 [n]11:3 Ex 7–12 [o]11:4 Ex 14 [p]11:6 Nm 16

[A]10:6 Or *from the wells of Bene-jaakan*, or *from the wells of the Jaakanites* [B]10:20 Lit *Hold on* [C]11:4 Lit *to this day*

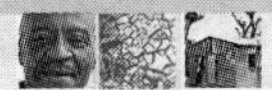

their descendants, a land flowing with milk
and honey.[a] 10For the land you are entering
to possess is not like the land of Egypt, from
which you have come, where you sowed your
seed and irrigated by hand[A] as in a vegetable
garden. 11But the land you are entering to possess is a land of mountains and valleys, watered by rain from the sky. 12It is a land the
LORD your God cares for. He is always watching over it from the beginning to the end of
the year.

13"If you carefully obey my commands I am
giving you today, to love the LORD your God
and worship Him with all your heart and all
your soul, 14I[B] will provide rain for your land
in the proper time, the autumn and spring
rains,[C] and you will harvest your grain, new
wine, and oil.[b] 15I[B] will provide grass in your
fields for your livestock. You will eat and be
satisfied.[c] 16Be careful that you are not enticed to turn aside, worship, and bow down
to other gods. 17Then the LORD's anger will
burn against you. He will close the sky, and
there will be no rain; the land will not yield
its produce, and you will perish quickly from
the good land[d] the LORD is giving you.

18"Imprint these words of mine on your
hearts and minds, bind them as a sign on
your hands, and let them be a symbol[D] on
your foreheads.[E] 19Teach them to your children,[e] talking about them when you sit in
your house and when you walk along the
road, when you lie down and when you get
up. 20Write them on the doorposts of your
house and on your gates,[f] 21so that as long as
the heavens are above the earth, your days
and those of your children may be many in
the land the LORD swore to give your fathers.[g]
22For if you carefully observe every one of
these commands I am giving you to follow—to love the LORD your God, walk in all
His ways, and remain faithful[F] to Him—23the
LORD will drive out all these nations before
you, and you will drive out nations greater
and stronger than you are. 24Every place the
sole of your foot treads will be yours.[h] Your
territory will extend from the wilderness
to Lebanon and from the Euphrates River[G]
to the Mediterranean Sea.[i] 25No one will be
able to stand against you; the LORD your God
will put fear and dread of you in all the land
where you set foot, as He has promised you.[j]

A Blessing and a Curse

26"Look, today I set before you a blessing
and a curse:[k] 27there will be a blessing, if you
obey the commands of the LORD your God I
am giving you today, 28and a curse, if you do
not obey the commands of the LORD your
God and you turn aside from the path I command you today by following other gods you
have not known. 29When the LORD your God
brings you into the land you are entering to
possess, you are to proclaim the blessing at
Mount Gerizim and the curse at Mount Ebal.
30Aren't these mountains across the Jordan,
beyond the western road in the land of the
Canaanites, who live in the *Arabah, opposite
Gilgal, near the oaks[H] of Moreh? 31For you are
about to cross the Jordan to enter and take
possession of the land the LORD your God is
giving you. When you possess it and settle in
it, 32be careful to follow all the statutes and
ordinances I set before you today.

The Chosen Place of Worship

12 "Be careful to follow these statutes
and ordinances in the land that *Yahweh, the God of your fathers, has given you
to possess all the days you live on the earth.
2Destroy completely all the places where the
nations that you are driving out worship
their gods[l]—on the high mountains, on the
hills, and under every green tree. 3Tear down
their altars, smash their sacred pillars, burn
up their *Asherah poles, cut down the carved
images of their gods, and wipe out their
names from every[I] place. 4Don't worship the
LORD your God this way. 5Instead, you must
turn to the place Yahweh your God chooses
from all your tribes to put His name for His
dwelling and go there. 6You are to bring there
your *burnt offerings and sacrifices, your
tenths and personal contributions,[J] your
vow offerings and freewill offerings, and the
firstborn of your herds and flocks. 7You will

[a]**11:9** Ex 3:17; Lv 20:24; Nm 13:27; Dt 6:3; 26:9,15; 27:3; 31:20; Jos 5:6; Jr 11:5; Ezk 20:6
[b]**11:14** Hs 2:22; Jl 2:19,24
[c]**11:15** Lv 25:19; Dt 6:11; 8:10; 31:20
[d]**11:17** Dt 8:7
[e]**11:19** Dt 4:9-10
[f]**11:18-20** Dt 6:6-9
[g]**11:21** Dt 1:35
[h]**11:24-25** Jos 1:3-5
[i]**11:24** Gn 15:18-20; Ex 23:31
[j]**11:25** Dt 2:25
[k]**11:26** Dt 30:15; Jr 21:8
[l]**12:2** Ex 23:23-26; 34:13; Dt 7:1-5

[A]**11:10** Lit *foot* [B]**11:14,15** DSS, Sam, LXX read *He* [C]**11:14** Following the Hb calendar, the early rain came in September/October and the late rain in March/April. [D]**11:18** Or *phylactery*; Mt 23:5 [E]**11:18** Lit *symbol between your eyes*; Ex 13:16; Dt 6:8 [F]**11:22** Lit *and hold on* [G]**11:24** Some Hb mss, LXX, Tg, Vg read *the great river, the river Euphrates* [H]**11:30** Sam, LXX, Syr, Aq, Sym read *oak*; Gn 12:6 [I]**12:3** Lit *that* [J]**12:6** Lit *and the contributions from your hands*

eat there in the presence of the LORD your
God and rejoice with your household in everything you do,[A] because the LORD your God
has blessed you.
8 "You are not to do as we are doing here
today; everyone is doing whatever seems
right in his own eyes. 9 Indeed, you have not
yet come into the resting place[a] and the inheritance[b] the LORD your God is giving you.
10 When you cross the Jordan and live in the
land the LORD your God is giving you to inherit,[c] and He gives you rest from all the enemies around you and you live in security,
11 then Yahweh your God will choose the place
to have His name dwell.[d] Bring there everything I command you: your burnt offerings,
sacrifices, offerings of the tenth, personal
contributions,[B] and all your choice offerings you vow to the LORD. 12 You will rejoice[e]
before the LORD your God—you, your sons
and daughters, your male and female slaves,
and the Levite who is within your gates, since
he has no portion or inheritance among you.[f]
13 Be careful not to offer your burnt offerings
in all the sacred places you see. 14 You must offer your burnt offerings only in the place the
LORD chooses in one of your tribes, and there
you must do everything I command you.

Slaughtering Animals to Eat

15 "But whenever you want, you may slaughter and eat meat within any of your gates,[g]
according to the blessing the LORD your God
has given you. Those who are ·clean or ·un-
clean may eat it, as they would a gazelle or
deer, 16 but you must not eat the blood; pour
it on the ground like water.[h] 17 Within your
gates you may not eat: the tenth of your grain,
new wine, or oil; the firstborn of your herd
or flock; any of your vow offerings that you
pledge; your freewill offerings; or your personal contributions.[C] 18 You must eat them
in the presence of the LORD your God at the
place the LORD your God chooses—you,
your son and daughter, your male and female
slave, and the Levite who is within your gates.
Rejoice before the LORD your God in everything you do,[A] 19 and be careful not to neglect
the Levite, as long as you live in your land.
20 "When the LORD your God enlarges your
territory as He has promised you,[i] and you
say, 'I want to eat meat' because you have
a strong desire to eat meat, you may eat it
whenever you want. 21 If the place where
Yahweh your God chooses to put His name
is too far from you, you may slaughter any of
your herd or flock He has given you, as I have
commanded you, and you may eat it within
your gates whenever you want. 22 Indeed, you
may eat it as the gazelle and deer are eaten;
both the clean and the unclean may eat it.
23 But don't eat the blood, since the blood is
the life, and you must not eat the life with
the meat. 24 Do not eat blood; pour it on the
ground like water. 25 Do not eat it, so that you
and your children after you will prosper, because you will be doing what is right in the
LORD's sight.
26 "But you are to take the holy offerings you
have and your vow offerings and go to the
place the LORD chooses. 27 Present the meat
and blood of your burnt offerings on the altar of the LORD your God. The blood of your
other sacrifices is to be poured out beside the
altar of the LORD your God, but you may eat
the meat. 28 Be careful to obey all these things
I command you, so that you and your children after you may prosper forever, because
you will be doing what is good and right in
the sight of the LORD your God.
29 "When the LORD your God annihilates the
nations before you,[j] which you are entering
to take possession of,[k] and you drive them out
and live in their land, 30 be careful not to be
ensnared by their ways after they have been
destroyed before you. Do not inquire about
their gods, asking, 'How did these nations
worship their gods? I'll also do the same.'
31 You must not do the same to the LORD your
God, because they practice every detestable
thing, which the LORD hates, for their gods.
They even burn their sons and daughters in
the fire to their gods. 32[D] You must be careful
to do everything I command you; do not add
anything to it or take anything away from it.[l]

The False Prophet

13 "If a prophet or someone who has
dreams arises among you and proclaims a sign or wonder to you, 2 and that

[a] **12:9** Dt 3:20; 5:14; 25:19; 28:65
[b] Dt 15:4
[c] **12:10** Dt 15:4
[d] **12:11** Dt 14:23; 16:2,6,11; 26:2
[e] **12:12** Lv 23:40; Dt 14:26; 16:11-15; 26:11; 27:7
[f] Nm 18:20
[g] **12:15-16** Dt 15:22-23
[h] **12:16** Lv 17:10-14
[i] **12:20** Ex 34:24
[j] **12:29** Dt 19:1
[k] Dt 3:12
[l] **12:32** Dt 4:2; Rv 22:18-19

[A] **12:7,18** Lit *you put your hand to* [B] **12:11** Lit *tenth, the contributions from your hands* [C] **12:17** Lit *or the contributions from your hands* [D] **12:32** Dt 13:1 in Hb

sign or wonder he has promised you comes
about, but he says, 'Let us follow other gods,'
which you have not known, 'and let us worship them,' 3do not listen to that prophet's
words or to that dreamer. For the LORD your
God is testing you to know whether you love
the LORD your God with all your heart and
all your soul. 4You must follow the LORD
your God and ˚fear Him. You must keep
His commands and listen to His voice; you
must worship Him and remain faithful[A] to
Him.[a] 5That prophet or dreamer must be
put to death, because he has urged rebellion
against the LORD your God who brought you
out of the land of Egypt and redeemed you
from the place of slavery,[b] to turn you from
the way the LORD your God has commanded
you to walk. You must purge the evil from
you.

Don't Tolerate Idolatry

6"If your brother, the son of your mother,[B]
or your son or daughter, or the wife you embrace, or your closest friend secretly entices
you, saying, 'Let us go and worship other
gods'—which neither you nor your fathers
have known, 7any of the gods of the peoples
around you, near you or far from you, from
one end of the earth to the other— 8you
must not yield to him or listen to him. Show
him no pity,[C] and do not spare him or shield
him. 9Instead, you must kill him. Your hand
is to be the first against him to put him to
death, and then the hands of all the people.[c]
10Stone him to death for trying to turn you
away from the LORD your God who brought
you out of the land of Egypt, out of the place
of slavery. 11All Israel will hear and be afraid,
and they will no longer do anything evil like
this among you.[d]

12"If[e] you hear it said about one of your
cities the LORD your God is giving you to
live in, 13that ˚wicked men have sprung up
among you, led the inhabitants of their city
astray, and said, 'Let us go and worship other
gods,' which you have not known, 14you are
to inquire, investigate, and interrogate thoroughly. If the report turns out to be true that
this detestable thing has happened among
you, 15you must strike down the inhabitants

[a]13:4 Dt 10:20 [b]13:5 Lv 26:13; Dt 5:6; 6:12; 8:14; 13:10; Jos 24:17; Jr 34:13 [c]13:9 Dt 17:7 [d]13:11 Dt 19:20 [e]13:12-15 Dt 17:2-5 [f]14:1 Ex 4:22-23; Dt 32:6 [g]Lv 19:28 [h]14:2 Ex 19:5; Dt 7:6 [i]14:4-8 Lv 11:1-8

of that city with the sword. ˚Completely destroy everyone in it as well as its livestock
with the sword. 16You are to gather all its
spoil in the middle of the city square and
completely burn up the city and all its spoil
for the LORD your God. The city must remain
a mound of ruins forever; it is not to be rebuilt. 17Nothing ˚set apart for destruction is
to remain in your hand, so that the LORD will
turn from His burning anger and grant you
mercy, show you compassion, and multiply
you as He swore to your fathers. 18This will
occur if you obey the LORD your God, keeping all His commands I am giving you today,
doing what is right in the sight of the LORD
your God.

Forbidden Practices

14 "You are sons of the LORD your God;[f]
do not cut yourselves or make a bald
spot on your head[D] on behalf of the dead,[g]
2for you are a holy people belonging to the
LORD your God. The LORD has chosen you to
be His own possession[h] out of all the peoples
on the face of the earth.

Clean and Unclean Foods

3"You must not eat any detestable thing.
4These are the animals you may eat:

the ox, the sheep, the goat,
5 the deer, the gazelle, the roe deer,
the wild goat, the ibex, the antelope,
and the mountain sheep.

6You may eat any animal that has hooves divided in two and chews the cud. 7But among
the ones that chew the cud or have divided
hooves, you are not to eat these:

the camel, the hare, and the hyrax,
though they chew the cud, they do not
have hooves—
they are ˚unclean for you;
8 and the pig, though it has hooves,
it does not chew the cud—
it is unclean for you.

You must not eat their meat or touch their
carcasses.[i]

9"You may eat everything from the water that has fins and scales, 10but you may

[A]13:4 Lit *and hold on* [B]13:6 DSS, Sam, LXX read *If the son of your father or the son of your mother* [C]13:8 Lit *Your eye must not pity him* [D]14:1 Or *forehead*

not eat anything that does not have fins and
scales — it is unclean for you.[a]
[11]"You may eat every ·clean bird, [12]but these
are the ones you may not eat:

the eagle, the bearded vulture,
the black vulture, [13]the kite,
any kind of falcon,[A]
[14] every kind of raven, [15]the ostrich,
the short-eared owl, the gull,
any kind of hawk,
[16] the little owl, the long-eared owl,
the white owl, [17]the desert owl,
the osprey, the cormorant, [18]the stork,
any kind of heron,
the hoopoe, and the bat.[B,b]

[19]All winged insects are unclean for you; they
may not be eaten. [20]But you may eat every
clean flying creature.[c]
[21]"You are not to eat any carcass; you may
give it to a temporary resident living within
your gates, and he may eat it, or you may sell
it to a foreigner. For you are a holy people belonging to the LORD your God. You must not
boil a young goat in its mother's milk.

A Tenth for the LORD

[22]"Each year you are to set aside a tenth of
all the produce grown in your fields. [23]You
are to eat a tenth of your grain, new wine,
and oil, and the firstborn of your herd and
flock, in the presence of ·Yahweh your God at
the place where He chooses to have His name
dwell,[d] so that you will always learn to ·fear[e]
the LORD your God. [24]But if the distance is
too great for you to carry it, since the place
where Yahweh your God chooses to put His
name is too far away from you and since the
LORD your God has blessed you, [25]then exchange it for money, take the money in your
hand, and go to the place the LORD your God
chooses. [26]You may spend the money on anything you want: cattle, sheep, wine, beer, or
anything you desire. You are to feast there in
the presence of the LORD your God and rejoice with your family. [27]Do not neglect the
Levite within your gates, since he has no portion or inheritance among you.[f]
[28]"At the end of every three years, bring a
tenth of all your produce for that year and
store it within your gates. [29]Then the Levite,
who has no portion or inheritance among
you, the foreigner, the fatherless, and the
widow within your gates may come, eat, and
be satisfied.[g] And the LORD your God will
bless you in all the work of your hands that
you do.[h]

Debts Canceled

15 "At the end of every seven years you
must cancel debts.[i] [2]This is how to cancel debt: Every creditor[C] is to cancel what he
has lent his neighbor. He is not to collect anything from his neighbor or brother, because
the LORD's release of debts has been proclaimed. [3]You may collect something from
a foreigner, but you must forgive whatever
your brother owes you.
[4]"There will be no poor among you, however, because the LORD is certain to bless you
in the land the LORD your God is giving you to
possess as an inheritance[j] — [5]if only you obey
the LORD your God and are careful to follow
every one of these commands I am giving
you today. [6]When the LORD your God blesses
you as He has promised you, you will lend to
many nations but not borrow; you will rule
over many nations, but they will not rule over
you.

Lending to the Poor

[7]"If there is a poor person among you, one
of your brothers within any of your gates in
the land the LORD your God is giving you, you
must not be hardhearted or tightfisted toward your poor brother. [8]Instead, you are to
open your hand to him and freely loan him
enough for whatever need he has. [9]Be careful
that there isn't this wicked thought in your
heart, 'The seventh year, the year of cancel-
ing debts, is near,' and you are stingy toward
your poor brother and give him nothing. He
will cry out to the LORD against you, and you
will be ·guilty. [10]Give to him, and don't have a
stingy heart[D] when you give, and because of
this the LORD your God will bless you in all
your work and in everything you do.[E] [11]For
there will never cease to be poor people in

[a]**14:9-10** Lv 11:9-12 [b]**14:11-18** Lv 11:13-19 [c]**14:19-20** Lv 11:20-23 [d]**14:23** Dt 12:11 [e]Dt 4:10; 6:2; 10:12; 17:19; 31:12-13; Jos 4:24; 24:14; 1Sm 12:14; 2Kg 17:25; Ps 15:4 [f]**14:26-27** Dt 12:12,18-19 [g]**14:28-29** Dt 26:12 [h]**14:29** Dt 30:9 [i]**15:1** Ex 22:25-27; Lv 25 [j]**15:4** Ex 32:13; Lv 20:24; Dt 4:21; 12:10; 16:20; 19:10; 21:23; 24:4; 25:19; 26:1; 29:8; Jos 1:6

[A]**14:13** Some Hb mss, Sam, LXX; other Hb mss, Vg read *the falcon, the various kinds of kite* [B]**14:5-18** The identification of some of these animals is uncertain. [C]**15:2** Lit *owner of a loan of his hand* [D]**15:10** Lit *and let not your heart be grudging* [E]**15:10** Lit *you put your hand to*

the land;[a] that is why I am commanding you,
‘You must willingly open your hand to your
afflicted and poor brother in your land.’

Release of Slaves

12“If your fellow Hebrew, a man or woman,
is sold to you and serves you six years, you
must set him free in the seventh year.[b]
13When you set him free, do not send him
away empty-handed. 14Give generously to
him from your flock, your threshing floor,
and your winepress. You are to give him
whatever the LORD your God has blessed
you with. 15Remember that you were a slave
in the land of Egypt and the LORD your God
redeemed[c] you; that is why I am giving you
this command today.[d] 16But if your slave says
to you, ‘I don’t want to leave you,’ because he
loves you and your family, and is well off with
you, 17take an awl and pierce through his ear
into the door, and he will become your slave
for life. Also treat your female slave the same
way. 18Do not regard it as a hardship[A] when
you set him free, because he worked for you
six years — worth twice the wages of a hired
hand. Then the LORD your God will bless you
in everything you do.[e]

Consecration of Firstborn Animals

19“You must consecrate to the LORD your
God every firstborn male produced by your
herd and flock.[f] You are not to put the firstborn of your oxen to work or shear the firstborn of your flock. 20Each year you and your
family are to eat it before the LORD your God
in the place the LORD chooses. 21But if there
is a defect in the animal, if it is lame or blind
or has any serious defect, you must not sacrifice it to the LORD your God. 22Eat it within
your gates; both the ·unclean person and the
·clean may eat it, as though it were a gazelle
or deer. 23But you must not eat its blood; pour
it on the ground like water.[g]

The Festival of Passover

16 “Observe the month of Abib[B,h] and celebrate the ·Passover to the LORD your
God, because the LORD your God brought
you out of Egypt by night in the month of
Abib. 2Sacrifice to ·Yahweh your God a Passover animal from the herd or flock in the
place where the LORD chooses to have His
name dwell.[i] 3You must not eat leavened
bread with it. For seven days you are to eat
unleavened bread with it, the bread of hardship — because you left the land of Egypt in
a hurry — so that you may remember for the
rest of your life the day you left the land of
Egypt. 4No yeast is to be found anywhere in
your territory for seven days, and none of the
meat you sacrifice in the evening of the first
day is to remain until morning. 5You are not
to sacrifice the Passover animal in any of the
towns the LORD your God is giving you. 6You
must only sacrifice the Passover animal at
the place where Yahweh your God chooses to
have His name dwell. Do this in the evening
as the sun sets at the same time of day you departed from Egypt. 7You are to cook and eat it
in the place the LORD your God chooses, and
you are to return to your tents in the morning. 8You must eat unleavened bread for six
days. On the seventh day there is to be a solemn assembly to the LORD your God, and you
must not do any work.

The Festival of Weeks

9“You are to count seven weeks, counting
the weeks from the time the sickle is first
put to the standing grain.[j] 10You are to celebrate the Festival of Weeks to the LORD your
God with a freewill offering that you give in
proportion to how the LORD your God has
blessed you. 11Rejoice[k] before Yahweh your
God in the place where He chooses to have
His name dwell — you, your son and daughter, your male and female slave, the Levite
within your gates, as well as the foreigner,
the fatherless, and the widow among you.
12Remember that you were slaves in Egypt;
carefully follow these statutes.

The Festival of Booths

13“You are to celebrate the Festival of Booths
for seven days when you have gathered in everything from your threshing floor and winepress.[l] 14Rejoice during your festival — you,
your son and daughter, your male and female
slave, as well as the Levite, the foreigner, the
fatherless, and the widow within your gates.

[a] **15:11** Mt 26:11
[b] **15:12** Jr 34:14
[c] **15:15** Ex 15:13; Dt 7:8; 9:26; 24:18
[d] Dt 24:18,22
[e] **15:12-18** Ex 21:2-11
[f] **15:19** Lv 23:9-14
[g] **15:22-23** Dt 12:15-16,22-24
[h] **16:1-8** Ex 12
[i] **16:2** Dt 12:11
[j] **16:9-12** Lv 23:15-21
[k] **16:11** Lv 23:40; Dt 12:12; 14:26; 26:11; 27:7
[l] **16:13-15** Lv 23:33-43

[A] **15:18** Lit *Let it not be hard in your sight* [B] **16:1** March–April; called Nisan in the post-exilic period; Neh 2:1; Est 3:7

15You are to hold a seven-day festival for the LORD your God in the place He chooses, because the LORD your God will bless you in all your produce and in all the work of your hands,[a] and you will have abundant joy.

16"All your males are to appear three times a year[b] before the LORD your God in the place He chooses: at the Festival of ·Unleavened Bread, the Festival of Weeks, and the Festival of Booths. No one is to appear before the LORD empty-handed. 17Everyone must appear with a gift suited to his means, according to the blessing the LORD your God has given you.

Appointing Judges and Officials

18"Appoint judges and officials for your tribes in all your towns the LORD your God is giving you. They are to judge the people with righteous judgment. 19Do not deny justice or show partiality to anyone. Do not accept a bribe, for it blinds the eyes of the wise and twists the words of the righteous. 20Pursue justice and justice alone, so that you will live and possess the land the LORD your God is giving you.[c]

Forbidden Worship

21"Do not set up an ·Asherah of any kind of wood next to the altar you will build for the LORD your God, 22and do not set up a sacred pillar; the LORD your God hates them.[d]

17 "You must not sacrifice to the LORD your God an ox or sheep with a defect or any serious flaw, for that is detestable to the LORD your God.[e]

The Judicial Procedure for Idolatry

2"If[f] a man or woman among you in one of your towns that the LORD your God will give you is discovered doing evil in the sight of the LORD your God and violating His covenant[g] 3and has gone to worship other gods by bowing down to the sun, moon, or all the stars in the sky—which I have forbidden— 4and if you are told or hear about it, you must investigate it thoroughly. If the report turns out to be true that this detestable thing has happened in Israel, 5you must bring out to your ·gates that man or woman who has done this evil thing and stone them to death. 6The one condemned to die is to be executed on the testimony of two or three witnesses. No one is to be executed on the testimony of a single witness. 7The witnesses' hands are to be the first in putting him to death, and after that, the hands of all the people.[h] You must purge the evil from you.[i]

Difficult Cases

8"If a case is too difficult for you—concerning bloodshed,[j] lawsuits,[k] or assaults[l]—cases disputed at your gates,[m] you must go up to the place the LORD your God chooses. 9You are to go to the Levitical priests and to the judge who presides at that time. Ask, and they will give you a verdict in the case. 10You must abide by the verdict they give you at the place the LORD chooses. Be careful to do exactly as they instruct you. 11You must abide by the instruction they give you and the verdict they announce to you. Do not turn to the right or the left from the decision they declare to you. 12The person who acts arrogantly, refusing to listen either to the priest who stands there serving the LORD your God or to the judge, must die. You must purge the evil from Israel. 13Then all the people will hear about it, be afraid, and no longer behave arrogantly.

Appointing a King

14"When you enter the land the LORD your God is giving you,[n] take possession of it, live in it, and say, 'I will set a king over me like all the nations around me,' 15you are to appoint over you the king the LORD your God chooses.[o] Appoint a king from your brothers. You are not to set a foreigner over you, or one who is not of your people.[p] 16However, he must not acquire many horses for himself or send the people back to Egypt to acquire many horses, for the LORD has told you, 'You are never to go back that way again.'[q] 17He must not acquire many wives for himself so that his heart won't go astray. He must not acquire very large amounts of silver and gold for himself. 18When he is seated on his royal throne, he is to write a copy of this instruction for himself on a scroll in the presence of the Levitical priests. 19It is to remain with him, and he is to read from it all the days of his life, so that he may learn to ·fear[r] the LORD his God, to observe all the words of this in-

[a] **16:15** Dt 30:9
[b] **16:16** Ex 23:14,17; 34:23-24; 1Kg 9:25; Lk 2:42
[c] **16:19-20** Ex 23:2-9
[d] **16:21-22** Dt 7:1-5; 12:2-3
[e] **17:1** Lv 22:17-25
[f] **17:2-5** Dt 13:12-15
[g] **17:2** Dt 31:16
[h] **17:7** Dt 13:9
[i] 1Co 5:13
[j] **17:8** Ex 21:12-14,18-25; Nm 35:9-34; Dt 19:1-13; 25:7
[k] Ex 22:6-14
[l] Ex 21:22-26; Lv 24:19-20
[m] Dt 21:19; 22:15
[n] **17:14** Dt 26:1
[o] **17:14-15** 1Sm 8:4-22
[p] **17:15** Gn 17:6,16; 35:11; Nm 24:17-19
[q] **17:16** 1Kg 10:28-29
[r] **17:19** Dt 14:23

struction, and to do these statutes. 20Then his
heart will not be exalted above his countrymen, he will not turn from this command to
the right or the left, and he and his sons will
continue ruling many years[A] over Israel.

Provisions for the Levites

18 "The Levitical priests, the whole tribe
of Levi, will have no portion or inheritance with Israel. They will eat the LORD's
fire offerings; that is their[B,C] inheritance. 2Al-
though Levi has no inheritance among his
brothers, the LORD is his inheritance, as He
promised him.[a] 3This is the priests' share from
the people who offer a sacrifice, whether it is
an ox, a sheep, or a goat; the priests are to be
given the shoulder, jaws, and stomach. 4You
are to give him the ·firstfruits of your grain,
new wine, and oil, and the first sheared wool
of your flock. 5For ·Yahweh your God has chosen him and his sons from all your tribes to
stand and minister in His name from now
on.[D] 6When a Levite leaves one of your towns
where he lives in Israel and wants to go to the
place the LORD chooses, 7he may serve in the
name of Yahweh his God like all his fellow
Levites who minister there in the presence
of the LORD. 8They will eat equal portions besides what he has received from the sale of
the family estate.[E,b]

Occult Practices versus Prophetic Revelation

9"When you enter the land the LORD your
God is giving you, do not imitate the detestable customs of those nations. 10No one
among you is to make his son or daughter
pass through the fire,[F,c] practice ·divina-
tion, tell fortunes, interpret omens, practice
sorcery, 11cast spells, consult a medium or a
familiar spirit, or inquire of the dead.[d] 12Ev-
eryone who does these things is detestable to
the LORD, and the LORD your God is driving
out the nations before you because of these
detestable things. 13You must be blameless
before the LORD your God. 14Though these
nations you are about to drive out listen to
fortune-tellers and diviners, the LORD your
God has not permitted you to do this.
15"The LORD your God will raise up for you a
prophet like me from among your own brothers.[e] You must listen to him. 16This is what you
requested from the LORD your God at Horeb
on the day of the assembly when you said, 'Let
us not continue to hear the voice of the LORD
our God or see this great fire any longer, so
that we will not die!'[f] 17Then the LORD said to
me, 'They have spoken well. 18I will raise up
for them a prophet like you from among their
brothers. I will put My words in his mouth,
and he will tell them everything I command
him. 19I will hold accountable whoever does
not listen to My words that he speaks in My
name.[g] 20But the prophet who dares to speak
a message in My name that I have not commanded him to speak, or who speaks in the
name of other gods — that prophet must die.'
21You may say to yourself, 'How can we recognize a message the LORD has not spoken?'
22When a prophet speaks in the LORD's name,
and the message does not come true or is not
fulfilled, that is a message the LORD has not
spoken. The prophet has spoken it presump-
tuously. Do not be afraid of him.

Cities of Refuge

19 "When the LORD your God annihilates
the nations whose land He is giving
you,[h] so that you drive them out and live in
their cities and houses, 2you are to set apart
three cities for yourselves within the land the
LORD your God is giving you to possess.[i] 3You
are to determine the distances[G] and divide
the land the LORD your God is granting you
as an inheritance into three regions, so that
anyone who commits manslaughter can flee
to these cities.[H]
4"Here is the law concerning a case of
someone who kills a person and flees there
to save his life, having killed his neighbor accidentally without previously hating him:
5If he goes into the forest with his neighbor
to cut timber, and his hand swings the ax to
chop down a tree, but the blade flies off the
handle and strikes his neighbor so that he
dies, that person may flee to one of these cities and live. 6Otherwise, the avenger of blood
in the heat of his anger[I] might pursue the one
who committed manslaughter, overtake him

[a] **18:2** Nm 18:20
[b] **18:8** Nm 18:8-32
[c] **18:10** Lv 18:21
[d] **18:11** Lv 20:27; Is 8:19
[e] **18:15** Mt 21:11; Lk 2:25-34; 7:16; 24:19; Jn 1:21,25; 4:19; Ac 3:22; 7:37
[f] **18:16** Ex 20:19; Dt 5:23-27
[g] **18:19** Ac 3:23
[h] **19:1** Dt 12:29
[i] **19:2-13** Nm 35:6-34; Jos 20

[A] **17:20** Lit *will lengthen days on his kingdom* [B] **18:1** LXX; MT reads *his* [C] **18:1** Or *His* [D] **18:5** Lit *name all the days* [E] **18:8** Hb obscure [F] **18:10** Either a Canaanite cult practice or child sacrifice [G] **19:3** Or *to prepare the roads* [H] **19:3** Lit *flee there* [I] **19:6** Lit *heart*

because the distance is great, and strike him
dead. Yet he did not deserve to die,[A] since he
did not previously hate his neighbor. 7This is
why I am commanding you to set apart three
cities for yourselves. 8If the LORD your God
enlarges your territory as He swore to your
fathers, and gives you all the land He promised to give them — 9provided you keep every
one of these commands I am giving you today
and follow them, loving the LORD your God
and walking in His ways at all times — you
are to add three more cities to these three.
10In this way, innocent blood will not be shed,
and you will not become •guilty of bloodshed
in the land the LORD your God is giving you
as an inheritance.[a] 11But if someone hates
his neighbor, lies in ambush for him, attacks
him, and strikes him fatally, and flees to one
of these cities, 12the elders of his city must
send for him, take him from there, and hand
him over to the avenger of blood and he will
die. 13You must not look on him with pity but
purge from Israel the guilt of shedding innocent blood, and you will prosper.

Boundary Markers

14"You must not move your neighbor's
boundary marker,[b] established at the start in
the inheritance you will receive in the land
the LORD your God is giving you to possess.

Witnesses in Court

15"One witness cannot establish any wrongdoing or sin against a person, whatever that
person has done.[c] A fact must be established
by the testimony of two or three witnesses.[d]

16"If a malicious witness[e] testifies against
someone accusing him of a crime, 17the two
people in the dispute must stand in the presence of the LORD before the priests and judges
in authority at that time. 18The judges are to
make a careful investigation, and if the witness turns out to be a liar who has falsely accused his brother, 19you must do to him as he
intended to do to his brother. You must purge
the evil from you. 20Then everyone else will
hear and be afraid, and they will never again do
anything evil like this among you.[f] 21You must
not show pity: life for life, eye for eye, tooth for
tooth, hand for hand, and foot for foot.[g]

[a]**19:10** Dt 15:4
[b]**19:14** Dt 27:17; Pr 22:28; Hs 5:10
[c]**19:15** Nm 35:30
[d]Mt 18:16; Jn 8:17; 2Co 13:1
[e]**19:16** Ex 23:1
[f]**19:20** Dt 13:11
[g]**19:21** Ex 21:23-25; Lv 24:19-20; Mt 5:38
[h]**20:1** Dt 1:26-40
[i]**20:4** Ex 14:14; Dt 1:30; Jdg 9:17

Rules for War

20 "When you go out to war against
your enemies and see horses, chariots, and an army larger than yours, do not be
afraid of them, for the LORD your God, who
brought you out of the land of Egypt,[h] is with
you. 2When you are about to engage in battle, the priest is to come forward and address
the army. 3He is to say to them: 'Listen, Israel:
Today you are about to engage in battle with
your enemies. Do not be cowardly. Do not be
afraid, alarmed, or terrified because of them.
4For the LORD your God is the One who goes
with you to fight for you[i] against your enemies to give you victory.'

5"The officers are to address the army, 'Has
any man built a new house and not dedicated
it? Let him leave and return home. Otherwise,
he may die in battle and another man dedicate it. 6Has any man planted a vineyard and
not begun to enjoy its fruit?[B] Let him leave
and return home. Otherwise he may die in
battle and another man enjoy its fruit.[C] 7Has
any man become •engaged to a woman and
not married her? Let him leave and return
home. Otherwise he may die in battle and another man marry her.' 8The officers will continue to address the army and say, 'Is there
any man who is afraid or cowardly? Let him
leave and return home, so that his brothers'
hearts won't melt like his own.' 9When the officers have finished addressing the army, they
will appoint military commanders to lead it.

10"When you approach a city to fight
against it, you must make an offer of peace.
11If it accepts your offer of peace and opens its
gates to you, all the people found in it will become forced laborers for you and serve you.
12However, if it does not make peace with
you but wages war against you, lay siege to it.
13When the LORD your God hands it over to
you, you must strike down all its males with
the sword. 14But you may take the women,
children, animals, and whatever else is in the
city — all its spoil — as plunder. You may enjoy the spoil of your enemies that the LORD
your God has given you. 15This is how you are
to treat all the cities that are far away from
you and are not among the cities of these
nations. 16However, you must not let any liv-

[A]**19:6** Lit *did not have a judgment of death* [B]**20:6** Lit *not put it to use* [C]**20:6** Lit *man put it to use*

ing thing survive among the cities of these
people the LORD your God is giving you as
an inheritance. 17 You must ·completely destroy them — the Hittite, Amorite, Canaanite,
Perizzite, Hivite, and Jebusite — as the LORD
your God has commanded you, 18 so that they
won't teach you to do all the detestable things
they do for their gods, and you sin against the
LORD your God.[a]
19 "When you lay siege to a city for a long
time, fighting against it in order to capture
it, you must not destroy its trees by putting
an ax to them, because you can get food from
them. You must not cut them down. Are trees
of the field human, to come under siege by
you? 20 But you may destroy the trees that you
know do not produce food. You may cut them
down to build siege works against the city
that is waging war against you, until it falls.

Unsolved Murders

21 "If a murder victim is found lying in
a field in the land the LORD your God
is giving you to possess, and it is not known
who killed him, 2 your elders and judges must
come out and measure the distance from the
victim to the nearby cities. 3 The elders of the
city nearest to the victim are to get a young
cow that has not been yoked or used for
work. 4 The elders of that city will bring the
cow down to a continually flowing stream, to
a place not tilled or sown, and they will break
its neck there by the stream. 5 Then the priests,
the sons of Levi, will come forward, for ·Yah-
weh your God has chosen them to serve Him
and pronounce blessings in His name, and
they are to give a ruling in[A] every dispute and
case of assault. 6 All the elders of the city nearest to the victim will wash their hands by the
stream over the young cow whose neck has
been broken. 7 They will declare, 'Our hands
did not shed this blood; our eyes did not see
it. 8 LORD, forgive Your people Israel You redeemed, and do not hold the shedding of innocent blood against them.' Then they will
be absolved of responsibility for bloodshed.
9 You must purge from yourselves the ·guilt of
shedding innocent blood, for you will be doing what is right in the LORD's sight.

[a]**20:17-18** Dt 7:1-5 [b]**21:15-17** Gn 29:30-33; 49:3 [c]**21:19** Dt 17:8; 22:15; 25:7 [d]**21:21** Ex 21:17; Lv 20:9

Fair Treatment of Captured Women

10 "When you go to war against your enemies and the LORD your God hands them
over to you and you take some of them prisoner, and 11 if you see a beautiful woman
among the captives, desire her, and want to
take her as your wife, 12 you are to bring her
into your house. She must shave her head,
trim her nails, 13 remove the clothes she was
wearing when she was taken prisoner, live
in your house, and mourn for her father and
mother a full month. After that, you may have
sexual relations with her and be her husband,
and she will be your wife. 14 Then if you are
not satisfied with her, you are to let her go
where she wants, but you must not sell her
for money or treat her as merchandise,[B] because you have humiliated her.

The Right of the Firstborn

15 "If a man has two wives, one loved and the
other unloved, and both the loved and the unloved bear him sons, and if the unloved wife
has the firstborn son, 16 when that man gives
what he has to his sons as an inheritance, he is
not to show favoritism to the son of the loved
wife as his firstborn over the firstborn of the
unloved wife. 17 He must acknowledge the firstborn, the son of the unloved wife, by giving him
two shares[C,D] of his estate, for he is the firstfruits
of his virility; he has the rights of the firstborn.[b]

A Rebellious Son

18 "If a man has a stubborn and rebellious
son who does not obey his father or mother
and doesn't listen to them even after they discipline him, 19 his father and mother must
take hold of him and bring him to the elders
of his city, to the ·gate[c] of his hometown.
20 They will say to the elders of his city, 'This
son of ours is stubborn and rebellious; he
doesn't obey us. He's a glutton and a drunkard.' 21 Then all the men of his city will stone
him to death.[d] You must purge the evil from
you, and all Israel will hear and be afraid.

Display of Executed People

22 "If anyone is found guilty of an offense
deserving the death penalty and is executed,

[A]**21:5** Lit *and according to their mouth will be* [B]**21:14** Hb obscure [C]**21:17** Lit *mouth of two*, or *two mouthfuls* [D]**21:17** Or *two-thirds*; the two-thirds interpretation holds that the firstborn son receives two-thirds of the total estate no matter how many sons are in the family.

and you hang his body on a tree, 23you are not
to leave his corpse on the tree overnight but
are to bury him that day, for anyone hung on
a tree is under God's curse.[a] You must not defile the land the LORD your God is giving you
as an inheritance.[b]

Caring for Your Brother's Property

22 "If you see your brother's ox or sheep
straying, you must not ignore it;
make sure you return it to your brother. 2If
your brother does not live near you or you
don't know him, you are to bring the animal
to your home to remain with you until your
brother comes looking for it; then you can return it to him. 3Do the same for his donkey,
his garment, or anything your brother has
lost and you have found. You must not ignore
it.[c] 4If you see your brother's donkey or ox
fallen down on the road, you must not ignore
it; you must help him lift it up.

Preserving Natural Distinctions

5"A woman is not to wear male clothing,
and a man is not to put on a woman's garment, for everyone who does these things is
detestable to the LORD your God.
6"If you come across a bird's nest with
chicks or eggs, either in a tree or on the
ground along the road, and the mother is sitting on the chicks or eggs, you must not take
the mother along with the young. 7You may
take the young for yourself, but be sure to let
the mother go free, so that you may prosper
and live long. 8If you build a new house, make
a railing around your roof, so that you don't
bring bloodguilt on your house if someone
falls from it. 9Do not plant your vineyard
with two types of seed; otherwise, the entire harvest, both the crop you plant and the
produce of the vineyard, will be defiled. 10Do
not plow with an ox and a donkey together.
11Do not wear clothes made of both wool and
linen.[d] 12Make tassels on the four corners of
the outer garment you wear.[e]

Violations of Proper Sexual Conduct

13"If a man marries a woman, has sexual relations with her, and comes to hate her, 14and
accuses her of shameful conduct, and gives
her a bad name, saying, 'I married this woman
and was intimate with her, but I didn't find
any evidence of her virginity,' 15the young
woman's father and mother will take the evidence of her virginity and bring it to the city
elders at the •gate.[f] 16The young woman's father will say to the elders, 'I gave my daughter
to this man as a wife, but he hates her. 17He
has accused her of shameful conduct, saying:
"I didn't find any evidence of your daughter's virginity," but here is the evidence of
my daughter's virginity.' They will spread out
the cloth before the city elders. 18Then the elders of that city will take the man and punish him.[g] 19They will also fine him 100 silver
shekels and give them to the young woman's
father, because that man gave an Israelite virgin a bad name. She will remain his wife; he
cannot divorce her as long as he lives. 20But if
this accusation is true and no evidence of the
young woman's virginity is found, 21they will
bring the woman to the door of her father's
house, and the men of her city will stone her
to death. For she has committed an outrage
in Israel by being promiscuous in her father's
house. You must purge the evil from you.
22"If a man is discovered having sexual relations with another man's wife, both the man
who had sex with the woman and the woman
must die. You must purge the evil from Israel.
23If there is a young woman who is a virgin
•engaged to a man, and another man encounters her in the city and has sex with her, 24you
must take the two of them out to the gate
of that city and stone them to death — the
young woman because she did not cry out
in the city and the man because he has violated his neighbor's fiancée. You must purge
the evil from you. 25But if the man encounters an engaged woman in the open country,
and he seizes and rapes her, only the man
who raped her must die. 26Do nothing to the
young woman, because she is not •guilty of
an offense deserving death. This case is just
like one in which a man attacks his neighbor
and murders him. 27When he found her in
the field, the engaged woman cried out, but
there was no one to rescue her. 28If a man encounters a young woman, a virgin who is not
engaged, takes hold of her and rapes her, and
they are discovered, 29the man who raped
her must give the young woman's father 50
silver shekels, and she must become his wife

[a] **21:23** Gl 3:13
[b] Dt 15:4
[c] **22:1-3** Ex 23:4
[d] **22:11** Lv 19:19
[e] **22:12** Nm 15:38-39
[f] **22:15** Dt 17:8; 21:19; 25:7
[g] **22:18** Dt 25:1-3

because he violated her.[a] He cannot divorce
her as long as he lives.
30 "A man is not to marry his father's wife; he
must not violate his father's marriage bed.[A,B,b]

Exclusion and Inclusion

23 "No man whose testicles have been
crushed[C] or whose penis has been cut
off may enter the LORD's assembly. 2 No one of
illegitimate birth may enter the LORD's assembly; none of his descendants, even to the tenth
generation, may enter the LORD's assembly.
3 No Ammonite or Moabite may enter the
LORD's assembly;[c] none of their descendants,
even to the tenth generation, may ever enter
the LORD's assembly. 4 This is because they did
not meet you with food and water on the journey after you came out of Egypt, and because
Balaam son of Beor from Pethor in Aram-naharaim was hired to curse you.[d] 5 Yet the LORD
your God would not listen to Balaam, but He
turned the curse into a blessing for you because the LORD your God loves[e] you.[f] 6 Never
seek their peace or prosperity as long as you
live. 7 Do not despise an Edomite, because he is
your brother. Do not despise an Egyptian, because you were a foreign resident in his land.
8 The children born to them in the third generation may enter the LORD's assembly.

Cleanliness of the Camp

9 "When you are encamped against your
enemies, be careful to avoid anything offensive. 10 If there is a man among you who is •un-
clean because of a bodily emission during the
night, he must go outside the camp; he may
not come anywhere inside the camp. 11 When
evening approaches, he must wash with water, and when the sun sets he may come inside
the camp.[g] 12 You must have a place outside the
camp and go there to relieve yourself. 13 You
must have a digging tool in your equipment;
when you relieve yourself, dig a hole with it
and cover up your excrement. 14 For the LORD
your God walks throughout your camp to
protect you and deliver your enemies to you;
so your encampments must be holy. He must
not see anything improper among you or He
will turn away from you.

[a] **22:28-29** Ex 22:16-17
[b] **22:30** Lv 18:8; 20:10-11
[c] **23:3-4** Neh 13:1-2
[d] **23:4** Nm 22:5-6
[e] **23:5** Dt 4:37
[f] Nm 23:11; 24:10
[g] **23:11** Lv 15:16-17
[h] **23:19-20** Ex 22:25
[i] **23:21-23** Nm 30:2-15; Jb 22:27; Ps 50:14; 56:12; 61:8; Pr 20:25; Ec 5:4-7; Mal 1:14
[j] **24:1** Mt 5:31; 19:7; Mk 10:4

Fugitive Slaves

15 "Do not return a slave to his master when
he has escaped from his master to you. 16 Let
him live among you wherever he wants
within your gates. Do not mistreat him.

Cult Prostitution Forbidden

17 "No Israelite woman is to be a cult prostitute, and no Israelite man is to be a cult prostitute. 18 Do not bring a female prostitute's
wages or a male prostitute's[D] earnings into
the house of the LORD your God to fulfill any
vow, because both are detestable to the LORD
your God.

Interest on Loans

19 "Do not charge your brother interest on
money, food, or anything that can earn interest. 20 You may charge a foreigner interest, but
you must not charge your brother interest, so
that the LORD your God may bless you in everything you do[E] in the land you are entering
to possess.[h]

Keeping Vows

21 "If you make a vow to the LORD your God,
do not be slow to keep it, because He will require it of you, and it will be counted against
you as sin. 22 But if you refrain from making a
vow, it will not be counted against you as sin.
23 Be careful to do whatever comes from your
lips, because you have freely vowed what you
promised[F] to the LORD your God.[i]

Neighbor's Crops

24 "When you enter your neighbor's vineyard, you may eat as many grapes as you want
until you are full, but you must not put any in
your container. 25 When you enter your neighbor's standing grain, you may pluck heads of
grain with your hand, but you must not put a
sickle to your neighbor's grain.

Marriage and Divorce Laws

24 "If a man marries a woman, but she
becomes displeasing to him because
he finds something improper about her, he
may write her a divorce certificate, hand it
to her, and send her away from his house.[j] 2 If

[A] **22:30** Dt 23:1 in Hb [B] **22:30** Lit *not uncover the edge of his father's garment*; Ru 3:9; Ezk 16:8 [C] **23:1** Lit *man bruised by crushing* [D] **23:18** Lit *a dog's* [E] **23:20** Lit *you put your hand to* [F] **23:23** Lit *promised with your mouth*

after leaving his house she goes and becomes
another man's wife, 3 and the second man
hates her, writes her a divorce certificate,
hands it to her, and sends her away from his
house or if he[A] dies, 4 the first husband who
sent her away may not marry her again after
she has been defiled, because that would be
detestable to the LORD. You must not bring
·guilt on the land the LORD your God is giving you as an inheritance.[a]
5 "When a man takes a bride, he must not
go out with the army or be liable for any duty.
He is free to stay at home for one year, so that
he can bring joy to the wife he has married.

Safeguarding Life

6 "Do not take a pair of millstones or an upper millstone as security for a debt, because
that is like taking a life as security.
7 "If a man is discovered kidnapping[b] one of
his Israelite brothers, whether he treats him
as a slave or sells him, the kidnapper must die.
You must purge the evil from you.
8 "Be careful in a case of infectious skin disease, following carefully everything the Levitical priests instruct you to do. Be careful to
do as I have commanded them. 9 Remember
what the LORD your God did to Miriam on
the journey after you left Egypt.[c]

Consideration for People in Need

10 "When you make a loan of any kind to
your neighbor, do not enter his house to collect what he offers as security. 11 You must
stand outside while the man you are making
the loan to brings the security out to you. 12 If
he is a poor man, you must not sleep in the
garment he has given as security. 13 Be sure to
return it[B] to him at sunset. Then he will sleep
in it and bless you, and this will be counted
as righteousness to you before the LORD your
God.[d]
14 "Do not oppress a hired hand who is poor
and needy, whether one of your brothers or
one of the foreigners residing within a town[C]
in your land. 15 You are to pay him his wages
each day before the sun sets, because he is
poor and depends on them.[e] Otherwise he
will cry out to the LORD against you, and you
will be held guilty.

[a]24:4 Dt 15:4
[b]24:7 Gn 40:15; Ex 21:16; 22:1; 1Sm 30:2-3,5; 1Tm 1:10
[c]24:9 Nm 12:1-15; Dt 25:17
[d]24:12-13 Ex 22:26-27
[e]24:14-15 Lv 19:13
[f]24:16 2Kg 14:6; 2Ch 25:4; Ezk 18:20; 33:10-20
[g]24:18 Dt 7:8; 9:26; 15:15
[h]Dt 15:15; 24:22
[i]24:18-19 Ex 23:2-3,6-9; Dt 30:9
[j]24:19-22 Ex 22:26-27; Lv 19:9-10,13,15
[k]25:4 1Co 9:9; 1Tm 5:18
[l]25:5-6 Gn 38:8; Mt 22:24; Mk 12:19; Lk 20:28

16 "Fathers are not to be put to death for
their children or children for their fathers;
each person will be put to death for his own
sin.[f] 17 Do not deny justice to a foreigner or fatherless child, and do not take a widow's garment as security. 18 Remember that you were
a slave in Egypt, and the LORD your God redeemed[g] you from there. Therefore I am commanding you to do this.[h]
19 "When you reap the harvest in your field,
and you forget a sheaf in the field, do not go
back to get it. It is to be left for the foreigner,
the fatherless, and the widow, so that the
LORD your God may bless you in all the work
of your hands.[i] 20 When you knock down the
fruit from your olive tree, you must not go
over the branches again. What remains will
be for the foreigner, the fatherless, and the
widow. 21 When you gather the grapes of your
vineyard, you must not glean what is left.
What remains will be for the foreigner, the
fatherless, and the widow. 22 Remember that
you were a slave in the land of Egypt. Therefore I am commanding you to do this.[j]

Fairness and Mercy

25 "If there is a dispute between men,
they are to go to court, and the judges
will hear their case. They will clear the innocent and condemn the ·guilty. 2 If the guilty
party deserves to be flogged, the judge will
make him lie down and be flogged in his
presence with the number of lashes appropriate for his crime. 3 He may be flogged with
40 lashes, but no more. Otherwise, if he is
flogged with more lashes than these, your
brother will be degraded in your sight.
4 "Do not muzzle an ox while it treads out
grain.[k]

Preserving the Family Line

5 "When brothers live on the same property[D]
and one of them dies without a son, the wife
of the dead man may not marry a stranger
outside the family. Her brother-in-law is to
take her as his wife, have sexual relations with
her, and perform the duty of a brother-in-law
for her. 6 The first son she bears will carry on
the name of the dead brother, so his name
will not be blotted out from Israel.[l] 7 But if the

A24:3 Lit *if the second man who has taken her as his wife* B24:13 Lit *return what he has given as security* C24:14 Lit *within the gates* D25:5 Lit *live together*

man doesn't want to marry his sister-in-law,
she must go to the elders at the city ·gate[a] and
say, 'My brother-in-law refuses to preserve
his brother's name in Israel. He isn't willing
to perform the duty of a brother-in-law for
me.' 8The elders of his city will summon him
and speak with him. If he persists and says,
'I don't want to marry her,' 9then his sister-
in-law will go up to him in the sight of the
elders, remove his sandal from his foot, and
spit in his face. Then she will declare, 'This is
what is done to a man who will not build up
his brother's house.' 10And his family name
in Israel will be called 'The house of the man
whose sandal was removed.'[b]
11"If two men are fighting with each other,
and the wife of one steps in to rescue her husband from the one striking him, and she puts
out her hand and grabs his genitals, 12you are
to cut off her hand. You must not show pity.

Honest Weights and Measures

13"You must not have two different weights[A]
in your bag, one heavy and one light.[c] 14You
must not have two differing dry measures in
your house, a larger and a smaller. 15You must
have a full and honest weight, a full and honest dry measure, so that you may live long in
the land the LORD your God is giving you.
16For everyone who does such things and acts
unfairly is detestable to the LORD your God.[d]

Revenge on the Amalekites

17"Remember what the Amalekites did
to you on the journey after you left Egypt.[e]
18They met you along the way and attacked
all your stragglers from behind when you
were tired and weary. They did not ·fear God.
19When the LORD your God gives you rest[f]
from all the enemies around you in the land
the LORD your God is giving you to possess as
an inheritance,[g] blot out the memory of Amalek under heaven. Do not forget.[h]

Giving the Firstfruits

26 "When you enter the land the LORD
your God is giving you as an inheritance,[i] and you take possession of it and live
in it, 2you must take some of the first of all
the land's produce that you harvest from the

[a]**25:7** Dt 17:8; 21:19; 22:15
[b]**25:10** Gn 38; Ru 4:1-12
[c]**25:13** Pr 20:10
[d]**25:16** Lv 19:35-36
[e]**25:17** Dt 24:9
[f]**25:19** Dt 3:20; 5:14; 12:9-11; 28:65
[g]Dt 15:4
[h]Ex 17:8-16; 1Sm 15; 30
[i]**26:1** Dt 15:4; 17:14
[j]**26:2** Dt 12:11
[k]**26:5** Gn 28:5
[l]Ex 1:1-3
[m]**26:7** Ex 3:7
[n]**26:9** Dt 11:9; Jr 32:22
[o]**26:11** Lv 23:40; Dt 12:12; 14:26; 16:11; 27:7
[p]**26:12** Dt 14:28-29

land ·Yahweh your God is giving you and put
it in a container. Then go to the place where
the LORD your God chooses to have His name
dwell.[j] 3When you come before the priest
who is serving at that time, you must say to
him, 'Today I acknowledge to the LORD your[B]
God that I have entered the land the LORD
swore to our fathers to give us.'
4"Then the priest will take the container
from your hand and place it before the altar
of the LORD your God. 5You are to respond by
saying in the presence of the LORD your God:

> My father was a wandering Aramean.[k]
> He went down to Egypt with a few peo-
> ple and lived there.[l] There he became a
> great, powerful, and populous nation.
> 6But the Egyptians mistreated and af-
> flicted us, and forced us to do hard labor.
> 7So we called out to Yahweh, the God of
> our fathers, and the LORD heard our cry
> and saw our misery, hardship, and op-
> pression.[m] 8Then the LORD brought us
> out of Egypt with a strong hand and an
> outstretched arm, with terrifying power,
> and with signs and wonders. 9He led us
> to this place and gave us this land, a land
> flowing with milk and honey.[n] 10I have
> now brought the first of the land's pro-
> duce that You, LORD, have given me.

You will then place the container before
the LORD your God and bow down to Him.
11You, the Levite, and the foreign resident
among you will rejoice[o] in all the good things
the LORD your God has given you and your
household.

The Tenth in the Third Year

12"When you have finished paying all the
tenth of your produce in the third year,[p] the
year of the tenth, you are to give it to
the Levite, the foreigner, the fatherless, and
the widow, so that they may eat in your towns
and be satisfied. 13Then you will say in the
presence of the LORD your God:

> I have taken the consecrated portion out
> of my house; I have also given it to the Le-
> vite, the foreigner, the fatherless, and the
> widow, according to all the commands

[A]**25:13** Lit *have a stone and a stone* [B]**26:3** LXX reads *my*

You gave me. I have not violated or forgotten Your commands. 14 I have not eaten
any of it while in mourning, or removed
any of it while ·unclean, or offered any of
it for the dead.[a] I have obeyed the LORD
my God; I have done all You commanded
me. 15 Look down from Your holy dwelling, from heaven, and bless Your people
Israel and the land You have given us as
You swore to our fathers, a land flowing
with milk and honey.

Covenant Summary

16 "The LORD your God is commanding you
this day to follow these statutes and ordinances. You must be careful to follow them
with all your heart and all your soul. 17 Today
you have affirmed that the LORD is your God
and that you will walk in His ways, keep His
statutes, commands, and ordinances, and
obey Him. 18 And today the LORD has affirmed
that you are His special people as He promised you, that you are to keep all His commands, 19 that He will elevate you to praise,
fame, and glory above all the nations He has
made, and that you will be a holy people[b] to
the LORD your God as He promised."

The Law Written on Stones

27 Moses and the elders of Israel commanded the people, "Keep every command I am giving you today. 2 At the time
you cross the Jordan into the land the LORD
your God is giving you, you must set up large
stones and cover them with plaster.[c] 3 Write
all the words of this law on the stones after
you cross to enter the land the LORD your God
is giving you, a land flowing with milk and
honey,[d] as ·Yahweh, the God of your fathers,
has promised you. 4 When you have crossed
the Jordan, you are to set up these stones on
Mount Ebal, as I am commanding you today, and you are to cover them with plaster.
5 Build an altar of stones there to the LORD
your God — you must not use any iron tool
on them.[e] 6 Use uncut stones to build the altar
of the LORD your God and offer ·burnt offerings to the LORD your God on it. 7 There you
are to sacrifice ·fellowship offerings, eat, and
rejoice in the presence of the LORD your God.

[a] 26:14 Jr 16:7; Ezk 24:17; Hs 9:4
[b] 26:19 Dt 7:6
[c] 27:2-8 Jos 8:30-32
[d] 27:3 Dt 11:9
[e] 27:5-7 Ex 20:25
[f] 27:12-13 Dt 11:29-30; Jos 8:33-35

8 Write clearly all the words of this law on the
plastered stones."

The Covenant Curses

9 Moses and the Levitical priests spoke to
all Israel, "Be silent, Israel, and listen! This
day you have become the people of the LORD
your God. 10 Obey the LORD your God and follow His commands and statutes I am giving
you today."

11 On that day Moses commanded the people, 12 "When you have crossed the Jordan,
these tribes will stand on Mount Gerizim
to bless the people: Simeon, Levi, Judah, Issachar, Joseph, and Benjamin. 13 And these
tribes will stand on Mount Ebal to deliver
the curse: Reuben, Gad, Asher, Zebulun, Dan,
and Naphtali.[f] 14 The Levites will proclaim in a
loud voice to every Israelite:

15 'The person who makes a carved idol
or cast image, which is detestable to the
LORD, the work of a craftsman, and sets
it up in secret is cursed.'
And all the people will reply, 'Amen!'
16 'The one who dishonors his father or
mother is cursed.'
And all the people will say, 'Amen!'
17 'The one who moves his neighbor's
boundary marker is cursed.'
And all the people will say, 'Amen!'
18 'The one who leads a blind person
astray on the road is cursed.'
And all the people will say, 'Amen!'
19 'The one who denies justice to a
foreigner, a fatherless child, or a widow
is cursed.'
And all the people will say, 'Amen!'
20 'The one who sleeps with his father's
wife is cursed, for he has violated his
father's marriage bed.'[A]
And all the people will say, 'Amen!'
21 'The one who has sexual intercourse
with any animal is cursed.'
And all the people will say, 'Amen!'
22 'The one who sleeps with his sister,
whether his father's daughter or his
mother's daughter is cursed.'
And all the people will say, 'Amen!'
23 'The one who sleeps with his
mother-in-law is cursed.'

[A] 27:20 Lit *has uncovered the edge of his father's garment*; Ru 3:9; Ezk 16:8

And all the people will say, 'Amen!'
24 'The one who secretly kills his
neighbor is cursed.'
And all the people will say, 'Amen!'
25 'The one who accepts a bribe to kill an
innocent person is cursed.'
And all the people will say, 'Amen!'
26 'Anyone who does not put the words
of this law into practice is cursed.'
And all the people will say, 'Amen!'

Blessings for Obedience

28 "Now if you faithfully obey the LORD
your God and are careful to follow
all His commands I am giving you today, the
LORD your God will put you far above all the
nations of the earth.[a] 2 All these blessings will
come and overtake you, because you obey the
LORD your God:

3 You will be blessed in the city
and blessed in the country.
4 Your descendants[A] will be blessed,
and your land's produce,
and the offspring of your livestock,
including the young of your herds
and the newborn of your flocks.[b]
5 Your basket and kneading bowl
will be blessed.
6 You will be blessed
when you come in
and blessed when you go out.

7 "The LORD will cause the enemies who
rise up against you to be defeated before you.
They will march out against you from one direction but flee from you in seven directions.
8 The LORD will grant you a blessing on your
storehouses and on everything you do;[B] He
will bless you in the land the LORD your God
is giving you. 9 The LORD will establish you as
His holy people,[c] as He swore to you, if you
obey the commands of the LORD your God
and walk in His ways. 10 Then all the peoples
of the earth will see that you are called by
·Yahweh's name, and they will stand in awe of
you. 11 The LORD will make you prosper abundantly with children,[C] the offspring of your
livestock, and your land's produce in the land
the LORD swore to your fathers to give you.
12 The LORD will open for you His abundant
storehouse, the sky, to give your land rain in
its season and to bless all the work of your
hands.[d] You will lend to many nations, but
you will not borrow. 13 The LORD will make
you the head and not the tail; you will only
move upward and never downward if you listen to the LORD your God's commands I am
giving you today and are careful to follow
them. 14 Do not turn aside to the right or the
left from all the things I am commanding you
today, and do not go after other gods to worship them.

Curses for Disobedience

15 "But if you do not obey the LORD your God
by carefully following all His commands and
statutes I am giving you today, all these curses
will come and overtake you:[e]

16 You will be cursed in the city
and cursed in the country.
17 Your basket and kneading bowl
will be cursed.
18 Your descendants[A] will be cursed,
and your land's produce,
the young of your herds,
and the newborn of your flocks.
19 You will be cursed
when you come in
and cursed when you go out.

20 The LORD will send against you curses, confusion, and rebuke in everything you do[B]
until you are destroyed and quickly perish,
because of the wickedness of your actions in
abandoning Me. 21 The LORD will make pestilence cling to you until He has exterminated
you from the land you are entering to possess. 22 The LORD will afflict you with wasting
disease, fever, inflammation, burning heat,
drought,[D] blight, and mildew; these will pursue you until you perish. 23 The sky above you
will be bronze, and the earth beneath you
iron. 24 The LORD will turn the rain of your
land into falling[E] dust; it will descend on you
from the sky until you are destroyed. 25 The
LORD will cause you to be defeated before
your enemies. You will march out against
them from one direction but flee from them
in seven directions. You will be an object
of horror to all the kingdoms of the earth.

[a] **28:1-14** Lv 26:3-13
[b] **28:4** Dt 7:13
[c] **28:9** Dt 7:6
[d] **28:12** Dt 30:9
[e] **28:15-68** Lv 26:14-46

[A] 28:4,18 Lit *The fruit of your womb* [B] 28:8,20 Lit *you put your hand to* [C] 28:11 Lit *abundantly in the fruit of your womb* [D] 28:22 Or *sword* [E] 28:24 Lit *powder and*

26 Your corpses will be food for all the birds of the sky and the wild animals of the land, with no one to scare them away.[a]

27 "The LORD will afflict you with the boils of Egypt, tumors, a festering rash, and scabies, from which you cannot be cured. 28 The LORD will afflict you with madness, blindness, and mental confusion, 29 so that at noon you will grope as a blind man gropes in the dark.[b] You will not be successful in anything you do. You will only be oppressed and robbed continually, and no one will help you. 30 You will become •engaged to a woman, but another man will rape her. You will build a house but not live in it. You will plant a vineyard but not enjoy its fruit. 31 Your ox will be slaughtered before your eyes, but you will not eat any of it. Your donkey will be taken away from you and not returned to you. Your flock will be given to your enemies, and no one will help you. 32 Your sons and daughters will be given to another people, while your eyes grow weary looking for them every day. But you will be powerless to do anything.[A] 33 A people you don't know will eat your land's produce and everything you have labored for. You will only be oppressed and crushed continually. 34 You will be driven mad by what you see. 35 The LORD will afflict you with painful and incurable boils on your knees and thighs — from the sole of your foot to the top of your head.[c]

36 "The LORD will bring you and your king that you have appointed to a nation neither you nor your fathers have known, and there you will worship other gods, of wood and stone. 37 You will become an object of horror, scorn, and ridicule among all the peoples where the LORD will drive you.[d]

38 "You will sow much seed in the field but harvest little, because locusts will devour it. 39 You will plant and cultivate vineyards but not drink the wine or gather the grapes, because worms will eat them. 40 You will have olive trees throughout your territory but not anoint yourself with oil, because your olives will drop off. 41 You will father sons and daughters, but they will not remain yours, because they will be taken prisoner. 42 Whirring insects will take possession of all your trees and your land's produce. 43 The foreign resident among you will rise higher and higher above you, while you sink lower and lower. 44 He will lend to you, but you won't lend to him. He will be the head, and you will be the tail.

45 "All these curses will come, pursue, and overtake you until you are destroyed, since you did not obey the LORD your God and keep the commands and statutes He gave you. 46 These curses will be a sign and a wonder against you and your descendants forever. 47 Because you didn't serve the LORD your God with joy and a cheerful heart, even though you had an abundance of everything, 48 you will serve your enemies the LORD will send against you, in famine, thirst, nakedness, and a lack of everything. He will place an iron yoke[e] on your neck until He has destroyed you. 49 The LORD will bring a nation from far away, from the ends of the earth, to swoop down on you like an eagle, a nation whose language you don't understand, 50 a ruthless nation,[B] showing no respect for the old and not sparing the young. 51 They will eat the offspring of your livestock and your land's produce until you are destroyed. They will leave you no grain, new wine, oil, young of your herds, or newborn of your flocks until they cause you to perish. 52 They will besiege you within all your gates until your high and fortified walls, that you trust in, come down throughout your land. They will besiege you within all your gates throughout the land the LORD your God has given you.

53 "You will eat your children,[C] the flesh of your sons and daughters the LORD your God has given you[f] during the siege and hardship your enemy imposes on you. 54 The most sensitive and refined man among you will look grudgingly[D] at his brother, the wife he embraces,[E] and the rest of his children, 55 refusing to share with any of them his children's flesh that he will eat because he has nothing left during the siege and hardship your enemy imposes on you in all your towns. 56 The most sensitive and refined woman among you, who would not venture to set the sole of her foot on the ground because of her refinement and sensitivity, will begrudge the husband

[a] **28:26** Jr 7:33; 16:4
[b] **28:28-29** Is 59:9-10
[c] **28:35** Is 1:6
[d] **28:37** 1Kg 9:7; 2Ch 7:20; Jr 24:9
[e] **28:48** Jr 28:13-14
[f] **28:53** 2Kg 6:25-29; Jr 19:9; Lm 2:20; 4:10

[A] **28:32** Lit *day, and not for power your hand* [B] **28:50** Lit *a nation strong of face* [C] **28:53** Lit *eat the fruit of your womb* [D] **28:54** Lit *you his eye will be evil* [E] **28:54** Lit *wife of his bosom*

she embraces, her son, and her daughter,
[57]the afterbirth that comes out from between her legs and the children she bears, because she will secretly eat them for lack of anything else during the siege and hardship your enemy imposes on you within your gates.
[58]“If you are not careful to obey all the words of this law, which are written in this scroll, by ·fearing this glorious and awesome
name — Yahweh, your God — [59]He will bring
extraordinary plagues on you and your descendants, severe and lasting plagues, and terrible and chronic sicknesses. [60]He will afflict
you again with all the diseases of Egypt, which
you dreaded, and they will cling to you. [61]The
LORD will also afflict you with every sickness and plague not recorded in the book of this
law, until you are destroyed. [62]Though you
were as numerous as the stars of the sky, you will be left with only a few people, because
you did not obey the LORD your God. [63]Just
as the LORD was glad to cause you to prosper and to multiply you, so He will also be glad to cause you to perish and to destroy you. You will be deported from the land you are entering to possess. [64]Then the LORD will scatter
you among all peoples from one end of the earth to the other, and there you will worship other gods, of wood and stone, which neither
you nor your fathers have known. [65]You will
find no peace among those nations, and there will be no resting place[a] for the sole of your foot. There the LORD will give you a trembling heart, failing eyes, and a despondent spirit.
[66]Your life will hang in doubt before you. You will be in dread night and day, never certain
of survival. [67]In the morning you will say, ‘If
only it were evening!’ and in the evening you will say, ‘If only it were morning!’ — because of the dread you will have in your heart and
because of what you will see. [68]The LORD will
take you back in ships to Egypt by a route that I said you would never see again.[b] There you will sell yourselves to your enemies as male and female slaves, but no one will buy you.”

Renewing the Covenant

29 [A] These are the words of the covenant[c] the LORD commanded Moses to make with the Israelites in the land of Moab, in addition to the covenant He had made with
them at Horeb. [2][B]Moses summoned all Israel
and said to them, “You have seen with your own eyes everything the LORD did in Egypt to Pharaoh, to all his officials, and to his entire
land. [3]You saw with your own eyes the great
trials and those great signs and wonders.[d]
[4]Yet to this day the LORD has not given you a mind to understand, eyes to see, or ears
to hear.[e] [5]I led you 40 years in the wilderness; your clothes and the sandals on your
feet did not wear out; [6]you did not eat bread
or drink wine or beer — so that you might
know that I am ·Yahweh your God. [7]When
you reached this place, Sihon king of Heshbon and Og king of Bashan came out against
us in battle, but we defeated them. [8]We took
their land and gave it as an inheritance to the Reubenites, the Gadites, and half the tribe of
Manasseh.[f] [9]Therefore, observe the words of
this covenant[g] and follow them, so that you will succeed in everything you do.
[10]“All of you are standing today before the LORD your God — your leaders, tribes, elders,
officials, all the men of Israel, [11]your children,
your wives, and the foreigners in your camps who cut your wood and draw your water —
[12]so that you may enter into the covenant of the LORD your God, which He is making with you today, so that you may enter into His oath
[13]and so that He may establish you today as His people and He may be your God as He promised you and as He swore to your fathers
Abraham, Isaac, and Jacob. [14]I am making this
covenant and this oath not only with you,
[15]but also with those who are standing here with us today in the presence of the LORD our God and with those who are not here today.

Abandoning the Covenant

[16]“Indeed, you know how we lived in the land of Egypt and passed through the nations
where you traveled. [17]You saw their detestable
images and idols made of wood, stone, silver,
and gold, which were among them. [18]Be sure
there is no man, woman, clan, or tribe among you today whose heart turns away from the LORD our God to go and worship the gods of those nations. Be sure there is no root among you bearing poisonous and bitter

[a]**28:65** Dt 12:9 [b]**28:68** Dt 17:16 [c]**29:1** Dt 31:16 [d]**29:3** Ex 7:3; Dt 6:22; 7:19; 26:8; 34:11; Neh 9:10; Ps 135:9; Jr 32:20-21 [e]**29:4** Is 6:9-10; Ezk 12:2; Mt 13:14; Ac 28:26-27; Rm 11:8 [f]**29:7-8** Nm 21:21-35; 32 [g]**29:9** Dt 31:16

[A]**29:1** Dt 28:69 in Hb [B]**29:2** Dt 29:1 in Hb

fruit.[a] 19 When someone hears the words of this oath, he may consider himself exempt,[A] thinking, 'I will have peace even though I follow my own stubborn heart.' This will lead to the destruction of the well-watered land as well as the dry land. 20 The LORD will not be willing to forgive him. Instead, His anger and jealousy will burn against that person, and every curse written in this scroll will descend on him. The LORD will blot out his name under heaven, 21 and single him out for harm from all the tribes of Israel, according to all the curses of the covenant written in this book of the law.

22 "Future generations of your children who follow you and the foreigner who comes from a distant country will see the plagues of the land and the sicknesses the LORD has inflicted on it. 23 All its soil will be a burning waste of sulfur and salt, unsown, producing nothing, with no plant growing on it, just like the fall of Sodom and Gomorrah, Admah and Zeboiim, which the LORD demolished in His fierce anger.[b] 24 All the nations will ask, 'Why has the LORD done this to this land? Why this great outburst of anger?' 25 Then people will answer, 'It is because they abandoned the covenant of Yahweh, the God of their fathers, which He had made with them when He brought them out of the land of Egypt. 26 They began to worship other gods, bowing down to gods they had not known — gods that the LORD had not permitted them to worship.[c] 27 Therefore the LORD's anger burned against this land, and He brought every curse written in this book on it. 28 The LORD uprooted them from their land in His anger, rage, and great wrath, and threw them into another land where they are today.' 29 The hidden things belong to the LORD our God, but the revealed things belong to us and our children forever, so that we may follow all the words of this law.

Returning to the LORD

30 "When all these things happen to you — the blessings and curses I have set before you — and you come to your senses while you are in all the nations where the LORD your God has driven you, 2 and you and your children return to the LORD your God and obey Him with all your heart and all your soul by doing[B] everything I am giving you today, 3 then He will restore your fortunes,[C] have compassion on you, and gather you again from all the peoples where the LORD your God has scattered you.[d] 4 Even if your exiles are at the ends of the earth,[D] He will gather you and bring you back from there.[e] 5 The LORD your God will bring you into the land your fathers possessed, and you will take possession of it.[f] He will cause you to prosper and multiply you more than He did your fathers. 6 The LORD your God will circumcise your heart[g] and the hearts of your descendants, and you will love Him with all your heart and all your soul so that you will live. 7 The LORD your God will put all these curses on your enemies who hate and persecute you. 8 Then you will again obey Him and follow all His commands I am giving you today. 9 The LORD your God will make you prosper abundantly in all the work of your hands[h] with children,[E] the offspring of your livestock, and your land's produce. Indeed, the LORD will again delight in your prosperity, as He delighted in that of your fathers, 10 when you obey the LORD your God by keeping His commands and statutes that are written in this book of the law and return to Him with all your heart and all your soul.

Choose Life

11 "This command that I give you today is certainly not too difficult or beyond your reach. 12 It is not in heaven so that you have to ask, 'Who will go up to heaven, get it for us, and proclaim it to us so that we may follow it?' 13 And it is not across the sea so that you have to ask, 'Who will cross the sea, get it for us, and proclaim it to us so that we may follow it?' 14 But the message is very near you, in your mouth and in your heart, so that you may follow it.[i] 15 See, today I have set before you life and prosperity, death and adversity.[j] 16 For[F] I am commanding you today to love the LORD your God, to walk in His ways, and to keep His commands, statutes, and ordinances, so that you may live[G] and multiply, and the LORD

[a] **29:18** Heb 12:15
[b] **29:23** Gn 14:2,8; 19:23-29
[c] **29:26** Dt 4:19; 1Kg 9:8-9; Jr 22:8-9
[d] **30:3** Lv 26:40-45; 1Kg 8:46-50; Jr 29:14
[e] **30:4** Neh 1:9
[f] **30:5** Dt 3:12
[g] **30:6** Dt 10:16; Jr 4:4
[h] **30:9** Dt 2:7; 14:29; 16:15; 24:19; 28:12; Ec 5:6; Hg 2:17
[i] **30:12-14** Rm 10:6-8
[j] **30:15** Dt 11:26; Jr 21:8

[A] 29:19 Lit *may bless himself in his heart* [B] 30:2 Lit *soul according to* [C] 30:3 Or *will end your captivity* [D] 30:4 Lit *skies* [E] 30:9 Lit *hands in the fruit of your womb* [F] 30:16 LXX reads *If you obey the commands of the LORD your God that* [G] 30:16 LXX reads *ordinances, then you will live*

your God may bless you in the land you are
entering to possess. 17 But if your heart turns
away and you do not listen and you are led
astray to bow down to other gods and worship them, 18 I tell you today that you will certainly perish and will not live long in the land
you are entering to possess across the Jordan.
19 I call heaven and earth as witnesses against
you today that I have set before you life and
death, blessing and curse. Choose life[a] so that
you and your descendants may live, 20 love the
LORD your God, obey Him, and remain faithful[A] to Him. For He is your life, and He will
prolong your life in the land the LORD swore
to give to your fathers[b] Abraham, Isaac, and
Jacob."

Joshua Takes Moses' Place

31 Then Moses continued to speak these[B]
words to all Israel, 2 saying, "I am now
120 years old; I can no longer act as your
leader.[C] The LORD has told me, 'You will not
cross this Jordan.'[c] 3 The LORD your God is the
One who will cross ahead of you.[d] He will destroy these nations before you, and you will
drive them out. Joshua is the one who will
cross ahead of you, as the LORD has said.[e] 4 The
LORD will deal with them as He did Sihon and
Og, the kings of the Amorites, and their land
when He destroyed them.[f] 5 The LORD will deliver them over to you, and you must do to
them exactly as I have commanded you. 6 Be
strong and courageous;[g] don't be terrified or
afraid of them. For it is the LORD your God
who goes with you;[h] He will not leave you or
forsake you."[i]
7 Moses then summoned Joshua and said to
him in the sight of all Israel, "Be strong and
courageous, for you will go with[D] this people
into the land the LORD swore to give to their
fathers.[j] You will enable them to take possession of it. 8 The LORD is the One who will go

[a] **30:19** Dt 4:1; 5:33; 6:24; 8:1,3; 16:20; 32:46-47 [b] **30:20** Dt 1:35 [c] **31:2** Dt 3:27 [d] **31:3** Dt 9:3 [e] Dt 3:28 [f] **31:4** Nm 21:21-35; Dt 29:6 [g] **31:6** Dt 31:23; Jos 1:6-7,9,18; 10:25 [h] Dt 1:29; 7:21; 20:3 [i] Heb 13:5 [j] **31:7** Dt 1:35; 31:20; Ezk 20:42

Covenant Community

GOD WHO SENDS

There is a powerful progression in the manifestation of God and in the experience of his reality by the people of the Exodus. First, he appeared to Moses in a specialized manifestation of a natural object. Then he spoke, identifying himself. Then he revealed his nature reflected in his loving concern for his people. Then he revealed his purpose to send Moses on his mission to deliver his people. In that missional context, he named himself in terms of being. Then language gives way to action. He first declared his intent to send—then he sent. He first said "I AM who I AM"—then he demonstrated who he is by his mighty act of deliverance.

The progression is also demonstrated in the movement from God's relation to Moses, to God's relation to Moses and Aaron and their relation to Pharaoh and his aides, and finally to God's relation to all the people of Israel and all the land of Egypt. God's reality was evident to all through the Exodus deliverance. God's existence was established by his actions, and the people's relationship to and involvement in that action was the witness to God's being.

However, there was more than a manifestation of God first on an individual and then on a communitarian and societal basis. And there was more than the witness of persons and people to God's existence through the reality of his redemptive deed. The very existence of this covenant community which emerged from a slave people of Egypt was the result of the mission of God through Moses. Of course, there were biological, cultural, and even religious antecedents to this people. However, their very missional identity—the fact that they emerged as a community of faith out of the sending of God—forged them into the channel of God's redemptive purpose in the world. *(DUBOSE, 80-81)*

[A] **30:20** Lit *and hold on* [B] **31:1** Some Hb mss, DSS, LXX, Syr, Vg read *all these* [C] **31:2** Lit *no longer go out or come in* [D] **31:7** Some Hb mss, Sam, Syr, Vg read *you will bring*

before you.[a] He will be with you; He will not
leave you or forsake you.[b] Do not be afraid or
discouraged."
9 Moses wrote down this law and gave it to
the priests, the sons of Levi, who carried the
ark of the LORD's covenant, and to all the elders of Israel. 10 Moses commanded them, "At
the end of every seven years, at the appointed
time in the year of debt cancellation,[c] during the Festival of Booths,[d] 11 when all Israel
assembles[A] in the presence of the LORD your
God at the place He chooses, you are to read
this law aloud before all Israel.[e] 12 Gather the
people — men, women, children, and foreigners living within your gates — so that they
may listen and learn to ·fear[f] the LORD your
God and be careful to follow all the words of
this law. 13 Then their children[g] who do not
know the law will listen and learn to fear the
LORD your God as long as you live in the land
you are crossing the Jordan to possess."
14 The LORD said to Moses, "The time of
your death is now approaching. Call Joshua
and present yourselves at the tent of meeting
so that I may commission him." When Moses
and Joshua went and presented themselves
at the tent of meeting, 15 the LORD appeared
at the tent in a pillar of cloud, and the cloud
stood at the entrance to the tent.[h]
16 The LORD said to Moses, "You are about to
rest with your fathers, and these people will
soon commit adultery with the foreign gods
of the land they are entering. They will abandon Me and break the covenant[i] I have made
with them. 17 My anger will burn against them
on that day; I will abandon them and hide My
face from them so that they will become easy
prey.[B] Many troubles and afflictions will come
to them. On that day they will say, 'Haven't
these troubles come to us because our God
is no longer with us?' 18 I will certainly hide
My face on that day because of all the evil they
have done by turning to other gods. 19 Therefore write down this song[j] for yourselves and
teach it to the Israelites; have them recite
it,[C] so that this song may be a witness for Me
against the Israelites. 20 When I bring them
into the land I swore to give their fathers, a
land flowing with milk and honey,[k] they will
eat their fill[l] and prosper.[D] They will turn to
other gods and worship them, despising Me
and breaking My covenant.[m] 21 And when
many troubles and afflictions come to them,
this song will testify against them, because[E]
their descendants will not have forgotten it.
For I know what they are prone to do,[F] even
before I bring them into the land I swore to
give them." 22 So Moses wrote down this song
on that day and taught it to the Israelites.
23 The LORD commissioned Joshua son of
Nun, "Be strong and courageous, for you will
bring the Israelites into the land I swore to
them, and I will be with you."[n]

Moses Warns the People

24 When Moses had finished writing down
on a scroll every single word[G] of this law, 25 he
commanded the Levites who carried the ark
of the LORD's covenant, 26 "Take this book of
the law and place it beside the ark of the covenant of the LORD your God so that it may
remain there as a witness against you. 27 For
I know how rebellious and stiff-necked you
are. If you are rebelling against the LORD
now, while I am still alive, how much more
will you rebel after I am dead! 28 Assemble
all your tribal elders and officers before me
so that I may speak these words directly to
them and call heaven and earth as witnesses
against them.[o] 29 For I know that after my
death you will become completely corrupt
and turn from the path I have commanded
you. Disaster will come to you in the future,
because you will do what is evil in the LORD's
sight, infuriating Him with what your hands
have made."[p] 30 Then Moses recited aloud every single word[H] of this song to the entire assembly of Israel:

Song of Moses

32 Pay attention, heavens, and I
will speak;
listen, earth, to the words
of my mouth.[q]
2 Let my teaching fall like rain
and my word settle like dew,
like gentle rain on new grass
and showers on tender plants.

[a] **31:8** Ex 23:23; 32:34; Dt 1:30; Jdg 4:14; Is 52:12
[b] Jos 1:5; 1Ch 28:20; Heb 13:5
[c] **31:10** Dt 15:1-2
[d] Lv 23:34; Dt 16:3
[e] **31:10-11** Jr 2:8; Mal 2:1-9
[f] **31:12** Dt 14:23
[g] **31:13** Dt 4:9-10
[h] **31:15** Nm 12:5
[i] **31:16** Dt 4:13,23; 5:2-3; 17:2; 29:1,9-14,21,25
[j] **31:19** Dt 32:1-43
[k] **31:20** Dt 11:9
[l] Dt 11:15
[m] Dt 4:31
[n] **31:23** Jos 1:1-9
[o] **31:28** Dt 4:26; 30:19
[p] **31:27-29** Dt 4:25; Jdg 2:6-13
[q] **32:1** Is 1:2

[A] **31:11** Lit *comes to appear* [B] **31:17** Lit *will be for devouring* [C] **31:19** Lit *Israelites; put it in their mouths* [D] **31:20** Lit *be fat* [E] **31:21** Lit *because the mouths of* [F] **31:21** Or *know the plans they are devising* [G] **31:24** Lit *scroll the words to their completion* [H] **31:30** Lit *recited the words to their completion*

3 For I will proclaim ˙Yahweh's name.
Declare the greatness of our God!
4 The Rock — His work is perfect;
all His ways are entirely just.
A faithful God, without prejudice,
He is righteous and true.

5 His people have acted corruptly
toward Him;
this is their defect[A] — they are not
His children
but a devious and crooked generation.
6 Is this how you repay the LORD,
you foolish and senseless people?
Isn't He your Father and Creator?
Didn't He make you and sustain you?
7 Remember the days of old;
consider the years long past.
Ask your father, and he will tell you,
your elders, and they will teach you.
8 When the ˙Most High gave the nations
their inheritance[B]
and divided the ˙human race,[a]
He set the boundaries of the peoples
according to the number of the people
of Israel.[C]
9 But the LORD's portion is His people,
Jacob, His own inheritance.

10 He found him in a desolate land,
in a barren, howling wilderness;
He surrounded him, cared for him,
and protected him as the pupil
of His eye.[b]
11 He watches over[D] His nest like an eagle
and hovers over His young;
He spreads His wings, catches him,
and lifts him up on His pinions.[c]
12 The LORD alone led him,
with no help from a foreign god.[E]
13 He made him ride on the heights
of the land[d]
and eat the produce of the field.
He nourished him with honey
from the rock
and oil from flint-like rock,
14 cream from the herd and milk
from the flock,
with the fat of lambs,
rams from Bashan, and goats,

[a]32:8 Gn 11:1-9
[b]32:10 Pr 7:2
[c]32:11 Ex 19:4; Ps 91:4
[d]32:13 Is 58:14
[e]32:15 Is 44:2
[f]32:16 Ps 78:58
[g]32:17 1Co 10:19-20
[h]32:21 Rm 10:19; 11:14

with the choicest grains of wheat;
you drank wine from the finest grapes.[F]

15 Then[G] Jeshurun[H,e] became fat
and rebelled —
you became fat, bloated, and gorged.
He abandoned the God who made him
and scorned the Rock of his salvation.
16 They provoked His jealousy
with foreign gods;
they enraged Him
with detestable practices.[f]
17 They sacrificed to demons, not God,
to gods they had not known,
new gods that had just arrived,
which your fathers did not fear.[g]
18 You ignored the Rock
who gave you birth;
you forgot the God who gave birth
to you.

19 When the LORD saw this,
He despised them,
provoked to anger by His sons
and daughters.
20 He said: "I will hide My face from them;
I will see what will become of them,
for they are a perverse generation —
unfaithful children.
21 They have provoked My jealousy
with their so-called gods;[I]
they have enraged Me
with their worthless idols.
So I will provoke their jealousy
with an inferior people;[J]
I will enrage them
with a foolish nation.[h]
22 For fire has been kindled because of
My anger
and burns to the depths of ˙Sheol;
it devours the land and its produce,
and scorches the foundations
of the mountains.

23 "I will pile disasters on them;
I will use up My arrows against them.
24 They will be weak from hunger,
ravaged by pestilence and bitter plague;
I will unleash on them wild beasts
with fangs,

A32:5 Or *Him; through their fault*; Hb obscure B32:8 Or *Most High divided the nations* C32:8 One DSS reads *number of the sons of God*; LXX reads *number of the angels of God* D32:11 Or *He stirs up* E32:12 Lit *him, and no foreign god with Him* F32:14 Lit *the blood of grapes* G32:15 DSS, Sam, LXX add *Jacob ate his fill;* H32:15 = Upright One, referring to Israel I32:21 Lit *with no gods* J32:21 Lit *with no people*

as well as venomous snakes that slither
in the dust.
25 Outside, the sword will take
their children,
and inside, there will be terror;
the young man and the young woman
will be killed,
the infant and the gray-haired man.[a]

26 "I would have said: I will cut them
to pieces[A]
and blot out the memory of them
from mankind,
27 if I had not feared insult
from the enemy,
or feared that these foes
might misunderstand
and say: 'Our own hand has prevailed;
it wasn't the LORD who did all this.'"

28 Israel is a nation lacking sense
with no understanding at all.[B]
29 If only they were wise,
they would figure it out;
they would understand their fate.
30 How could one man pursue a thousand,
or two put ten thousand to flight,
unless their Rock had sold them,
unless the LORD had given them up?
31 But their "rock" is not like our Rock;
even our enemies concede.
32 For their vine is from the vine of Sodom
and from the fields of Gomorrah.
Their grapes are poisonous;
their clusters are bitter.
33 Their wine is serpents' venom,
the deadly poison of cobras.

34 "Is it not stored up with Me,
sealed up in My vaults?
35 Vengeance[C] belongs to Me; I will repay.[D,b]
In time their foot will slip,
for their day of disaster is near,
and their doom is coming quickly."
36 The LORD will indeed vindicate
His people
and have compassion on His servants[c]
when He sees that their strength is gone
and no one is left — slave or free.

[a]**32:22-25** Is 5:8-30; Jr 9:17-21
[b]**32:35** Rm 12:19; Heb 10:30
[c]**32:36** Ps 135:14
[d]**32:39** Is 40:25; 43:11-13; 46:9; Ezk 36:23
[e]1Sm 2:6-8
[f]**32:43** Rm 15:10
[g]Ps 79:10
[h]**32:48-51** Nm 27:12-14

37 He will say: "Where are their gods,
the 'rock' they found refuge in?
38 Who ate the fat of their sacrifices
and drank the wine
of their •drink offerings?
Let them rise up and help you;
let it[E] be a shelter for you.
39 See now that I alone am He;
there is no God but Me.[d]
I bring death and I give life;
I wound and I heal.
No one can rescue anyone
from My hand.[e]
40 I raise My hand to heaven and declare:
As surely as I live forever,
41 when I sharpen My flashing sword,
and My hand takes hold of judgment,
I will take vengeance on My adversaries
and repay those who hate Me.
42 I will make My arrows drunk
with blood
while My sword devours flesh —
the blood of the slain and the captives,
the heads of the enemy leaders."[F]

43 Rejoice, you nations,
concerning His people,[G,f]
for He will avenge the blood
of His servants.[H]
He will take vengeance
on His adversaries;[I,g]
He will purify His land and His people.[J]

44 Moses came with Joshua[K] son of Nun and
recited all the words of this song in the presence of the people. 45 After Moses finished re-
citing all these words to all Israel, 46 he said to
them, "Take to heart all these words I am giving as a warning to you today, so that you may
command your children to carefully follow
all the words of this law. 47 For they are not
meaningless words to you but they are your
life, and by them you will live long in the land
you are crossing the Jordan to possess."

Moses' Impending Death

48 On that same day the LORD spoke to Moses,[h] 49 "Go up Mount Nebo in the Abarim

[A]**32:26** LXX reads *will scatter them* [B]**32:28** Lit *understanding in them* [C]**32:35** Sam, LXX read *On a day of vengeance* [D]**32:35** LXX, Tg, Vg read *Me; and recompense I will recompense* [E]**32:38** Sam, LXX, Tg, Vg read *them* [F]**32:42** Or *the long-haired heads of the enemy* [G]**32:43** LXX reads *Rejoice, you heavens, along with Him, and let all the sons of God worship Him; rejoice, you nations, with His people, and let all the angels of God strengthen themselves in Him*; DSS read *Rejoice, you heavens, along with Him, and let all the angels worship Him*; Heb 1:6 [H]**32:43** DSS, LXX read *sons* [I]**32:43** DSS, LXX add *and He will recompense those who hate Him*; v. 41 [J]**32:43** Syr, Tg; DSS, Sam, LXX, Vg read *His people's land* [K]**32:44** LXX, Syr, Vg; MT reads *Hoshea*; Nm 13:8,16

range in the land of Moab, across from Jericho, and view the land of Canaan I am giving
the Israelites as a possession. 50 Then you will
die on the mountain that you go up, and you
will be gathered to your people, just as your
brother Aaron died on Mount Hor and was
gathered to his people.[a] 51 For both of you
broke faith with Me among the Israelites at
the waters of Meribath-kadesh in the Wilderness of Zin by failing to treat Me as holy in
their presence. 52 Although from a distance
you will view the land that I am giving the Israelites, you will not go there."[b]

Moses' Blessings

33 This is the blessing that Moses, the man of God, gave the Israelites before his death.[c] 2 He said:

The LORD came from Sinai
and appeared to them from Seir;
He shone on them from Mount Paran
and came with ten thousand holy ones,[A]
with lightning[B] from His right hand[C]
for them.[d]
3 Indeed He loves the people.[D,e]
All Your[E] holy ones[F] are in Your hand,
and they assemble[G] at Your feet.
Each receives Your words.
4 Moses gave us instruction,
a possession for the assembly of Jacob.
5 So He became King in Jeshurun[H]
when the leaders of the people gathered
with the tribes of Israel.
6 Let Reuben live and not die
though his people become few.[f]

7 He said this about Judah:

LORD, hear Judah's cry and bring him
to his people.
He fights for his cause[I]
with his own hands,
but may You be a help against his foes.

8 He said about Levi:

Your Thummim and ·Urim belong to
Your faithful one;[J]
You tested him at Massah
and contended with him at the waters
of Meribah.[g]
9 He said about his father and mother,
"I do not regard them."
He disregarded his brothers
and didn't acknowledge his sons,
for they kept Your word
and maintained Your covenant.[h]
10 They will teach Your ordinances
to Jacob
and Your instruction to Israel;[i]
they will set incense before You
and whole ·burnt offerings
on Your altar.
11 LORD, bless his possessions,[K]
and accept the work of his hands.
Smash the loins of his adversaries
and enemies,
so that they cannot rise again.

12 He said about Benjamin:

The LORD's beloved rests[L] securely
on Him.
He[M] shields him all day long,
and he rests on His shoulders.[N]

13 He said about Joseph:

May his land be blessed by the LORD
with the dew of heaven's bounty
and the watery depths that lie beneath;[j]
14 with the bountiful harvest from the sun
and the abundant yield of the seasons;
15 with the best products
of the ancient mountains
and the bounty of the eternal hills;
16 with the choice gifts of the land
and everything in it;
and with the favor of Him
who appeared[O] in the burning bush.[k]
May these rest on the head of Joseph,
on the crown of the prince
of his brothers.[l]
17 His firstborn bull has[P] splendor,
and horns like[Q] those of a wild ox;
he gores all the peoples with them
to the ends of the earth.
Such are the ten thousands of Ephraim,

[a] **32:50** Nm 20:22-29
[b] **32:51-52** Nm 20:2-13
[c] **33:1-29** Gn 49:1-33
[d] **33:2** Jdg 5:4-5; Ps 68:7-8; Hab 3:3
[e] **33:3** Dt 4:37
[f] **33:6** Gn 49:3-4; Jdg 5:15-16
[g] **33:8** Ex 17:1-7; Nm 20:2-13
[h] **33:9** Ex 32:25-29
[i] **33:10** Dt 31:9-13
[j] **33:13** Pr 3:20
[k] **33:16** Ex 3:2-4
[l] Gn 49:26

[A] **33:2** LXX reads *Mount Paran with ten thousands from Kadesh* [B] **33:2** Or *fiery law*; Hb obscure [C] **33:2** Or *ones, from His southland to the mountain slopes* [D] **33:3** Or *peoples* [E] **33:3** Lit *His*, or *its* [F] **33:3** Either the saints of Israel or angels [G] **33:3** Hb obscure [H] **33:5** = Upright One, referring to Israel [I] **33:7** Or *He contends for them* [J] **33:8** DSS, LXX read *Give to Levi Your Thummim, Your Urim to Your favored one* [K] **33:11** Or *abilities* [L] **33:12** Or *Let the LORD's beloved rest* [M] **33:12** LXX reads *The Most High* [N] **33:12** Or *and He dwells among his mountain slopes* [O] **33:16** Lit *dwelt* [P] **33:17** Some DSS, Sam, LXX, Syr, Vg read *A firstborn bull — he has* [Q] **33:17** Lit *and his horns are*

and such are the thousands
of Manasseh.

18 He said about Zebulun:

Rejoice, Zebulun, in your journeys,
and Issachar, in your tents.
19 They summon the peoples
to a mountain;
there they offer acceptable sacrifices.
For they draw from the wealth of the seas
and the hidden treasures of the sand.[a]

20 He said about Gad:

The one who enlarges Gad's territory
will be blessed.
He lies down like a lion
and tears off an arm or even a head.[b]
21 He chose the best part for himself,
because a ruler's portion was assigned
there for him.
He came with the leaders of the people;
he carried out the LORD's justice
and His ordinances for Israel.[c]

22 He said about Dan:

Dan is a young lion,
leaping out of Bashan.[d]

23 He said about Naphtali:

Naphtali, enjoying approval,
full of the LORD's blessing,
take[A] possession to the west
and the south.

24 He said about Asher:

May Asher[B] be the most blessed
of the sons;
may he be the most favored
among his brothers
and dip his foot in olive oil.[C,e]
25 May the bolts of your gate be iron
and bronze,
and your strength last as long as you live.
26 There is none like the God of Jeshurun,[D]
who rides the heavens to your aid,
the clouds in His majesty.[f]
27 The God of old is your dwelling place,[g]
and underneath are the everlasting arms.
He drives out the enemy before you
and commands, "Destroy!"
28 So Israel dwells securely;
Jacob lives untroubled[E,h]
in a land of grain and new wine;
even his skies drip with dew.[i]
29 How happy you are, Israel!
Who is like you,
a people saved by the LORD?
He is the shield that protects you,
the sword you boast in.
Your enemies will cringe before you,[j]
and you will tread on their backs.[F,k]

Moses' Death

34 Then Moses went up from the plains
of Moab to Mount Nebo, to the top of
Pisgah,[l] which faces Jericho, and the LORD
showed him all the land: Gilead as far as Dan,
2 all of Naphtali, the land of Ephraim and
Manasseh, all the land of Judah as far as the
Mediterranean[G] Sea, 3 the ·Negev, and the region from the Valley of Jericho, the City of
Palms, as far as Zoar. 4 The LORD then said to
him, "This is the land I promised Abraham,
Isaac, and Jacob, 'I will give it to your descendants.'[m] I have let you see it with your own
eyes, but you will not cross into it."
5 So Moses the servant of the LORD died
there in the land of Moab, as the LORD had
said. 6 He buried him[H] in the valley[n] in the
land of Moab facing Beth-peor, and no one
to this day knows where his grave is.[o] 7 Moses
was 120 years old when he died; his eyes were
not weak, and his vitality had not left him.
8 The Israelites wept for Moses in the plains
of Moab 30 days. Then the days of weeping
and mourning for Moses came to an end.
9 Joshua son of Nun was filled with the spirit
of wisdom because Moses had laid his hands
on him. So the Israelites obeyed him and did
as the LORD had commanded Moses. 10 No
prophet has arisen again in Israel like Moses,
whom the LORD knew face to face.[p] 11 He was
unparalleled for all the signs and wonders
the LORD sent him to do against the land of
Egypt — to Pharaoh, to all his officials, and
to all his land, 12 and for all the mighty acts of
power and terrifying deeds that Moses performed in the sight of all Israel.

[a] **33:18-19** Gn 49:13; Jdg 5:15,18 [b] **33:20** 1Ch 12:8 [c] **33:20-21** Nm 32:1-38 [d] **33:22** Jdg 5:17 [e] **33:24** Gn 49:20 [f] **33:26** 2Sm 22:8-20; Ps 18:7-19 [g] **33:27** Ps 91:9 [h] **33:28** Nm 23:9 [i] Dt 8:7-9 [j] **33:29** 2Sm 22:44-46; Ps 18:43-45 [k] Dt 32:13; Hab 3:19 [l] **34:1-4** Dt 3:27 [m] **34:4** Gn 12:7; 15:18-20; 26:3; 35:12; Ex 33:1 [n] **34:6** Nm 21:20 [o] Jd 9 [p] **34:10** Ex 33:11

[A] **33:23** Sam, LXX, Syr, Vg, Tg read *he will take* [B] **33:24** = Happy or Blessed; Gn 30:13 [C] **33:24** A symbol for prosperity [D] **33:26** = Upright One, referring to Israel [E] **33:28** Text emended; MT reads *Jacob's fountain is alone* [F] **33:29** Or *high places* [G] **34:2** Lit *Western* [H] **34:6** Or *He was buried*

■ **AUTHOR:** Joshua (but Phinehas might have written the last chapter)

■■ **DATE:** After the conquest of Canaan (around 1406–1380 B.C.)

JOSHUA

God wants the twelve tribes of Israel safely inside Canaan, east of the Jordan. Getting there will not be easy.

The land is occupied already by people unwilling to move. They have cities, walls, fields, families, and armies. They must be conquered. By force of arms and the power of God, walls fall, kings are dethroned, armies beaten. People on both sides will die, but the conquest will present subsequent believers with courageous models of faith and stamina. The battle accounts reveal the seriousness of God's desire for His will to be accomplished. In this era of Joshua's leadership, God's worldwide mission takes a very specific focus on Israel. The people of Canaan long ago gave themselves to pagan worship, and nothing in that fits with God's plan for His people. They are eradicated in order for God to protect His people and grow His nation—the nation that worships Him alone.

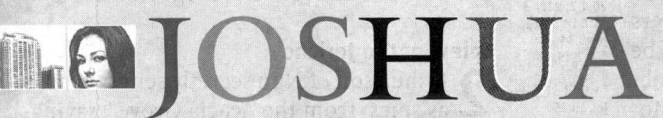

In the book of Joshua, the mission of God is forceful, and uncompromising. Even in relation to the Israelites, disobedience is punished to the full extent of the law. Achan learns this the hard way. The harsh punishment of Achan and his family instills a deep, fearful respect for God's law, but that terrible episode also inspires faith. With sin purged and the sinner judged, God once again leads Joshua's army. Only with God in front will well-equipped Canaanites back away.

The last part of the book documents Joshua's land grants to tribes and clans. At the end, much of Canaan remains to be conquered, but the people are building their nation, still a loose confederation of tribes with two central worship sites. After a string of victories (and some tragic defeats), Israel rests. God's mission is done for now. The people reaffirm their loyalty to God. Joshua's last speech is not a renewed call to war, but a warning on how to worship—with sincere fidelity to God. The covenant between God and the people must hold. All else is second-tier business.

Today Christians are not called to arms against non-Christians, but to prayer and battle against spiritual imposters. Christians conquer not by weaponry, but by power granted by God through the Spirit, enabling witness and service which take God's message to all people and demonstrates its validity. The battle is joined whenever the truth of Jesus Christ is spoken, in word or deed. The conquest is partial, as in Joshua's day, but still the promise is the victory of God, good over evil, and the restoration of all God has made. The mission continues with tactics adjusted, and now, the resurrected Christ is at the lead. Joshua's glimpse into God's mission was rough and bloody; ours is through the eyes and heart of Jesus, who did not draw a sword but gave Himself for the salvation of all who believe.

Every Christian faces Jordan Rivers, Jerichos, and valleys of Achor. But the only faithful way is forward. Fear meets with faith at every turn. Adversaries threaten. Yet faith points us forward into God's mission, then and now.

Encouragement of Joshua

1 After the death of Moses[a] the LORD's servant, the LORD spoke to Joshua[A] son of
Nun,[b] who had served Moses: 2"Moses My
servant is dead.[c] Now you and all the people
prepare to cross over the Jordan[d] to the land I
am giving the Israelites. 3I have given you every place where the sole of your foot treads,[e]
just as I promised Moses. 4Your territory will
be from the wilderness and Lebanon[f] to the
great Euphrates River—all the land of the
Hittites[g]—and west to the Mediterranean
Sea.[B,h] 5No one will be able to stand against
you as long as you live.[i] I will be with you, just
as I was with Moses. I will not leave you or
forsake you.[j]
6"Be strong and courageous,[k] for you will
distribute the land I swore to their fathers
to give them as an inheritance.[l] 7Above all, be
strong and very courageous to carefully observe the whole instruction My servant Moses commanded you.[m] Do not turn from it to
the right or the left, so that you will have success wherever you go. 8This book of instruction must not depart from your mouth;[n] you
are to recite[C] it day and night so that you may
carefully observe everything written in it. For
then you will prosper and succeed in whatever you do.[o] 9Haven't I commanded you: be
strong and courageous?[p] Do not be afraid or
discouraged, for the LORD your God is with
you wherever you go."

Joshua Prepares the People

10Then Joshua commanded the officers of
the people: 11"Go through the camp and tell
the people, 'Get provisions ready for yourselves, for within three days you will be crossing the Jordan to go in and take possession
of the land the LORD your God is giving you
to inherit.'"[q]
12Joshua said to the Reubenites, the Gadites,
and half the tribe of Manasseh:[r] 13"Remember
what Moses the LORD's servant commanded
you when he said, 'The LORD your God will
give you rest, and He will give you this land.'[s]
14Your wives, young children, and livestock
may remain in the land Moses gave you on
this side of the Jordan.[D] But your fighting
men must cross over in battle formation[E]
ahead of your brothers[F] and help them 15until
the LORD gives your brothers rest, as He has
given you, and they too possess the land the
LORD your God is giving them. You may then
return to the land of your inheritance[t] and
take possession of what Moses the LORD's servant[u] gave you on the east side of the Jordan."
16They answered Joshua, "Everything you
have commanded us we will do, and everywhere you send us we will go. 17We will obey
you, just as we obeyed Moses in everything.
And may the LORD your God be with you, as He
was with Moses.[v] 18Anyone who rebels against
your order and does not obey your words in all
that you command him, will be put to death.
Above all, be strong and courageous!"[w]

Spies Sent to Jericho

2 Joshua son of Nun secretly sent two men
as spies[x] from the Acacia Grove,[G] saying,
"Go and scout the land, especially Jericho."
So they left, and they came to the house of
a woman, a prostitute named Rahab,[y] and
stayed there.
2The king of Jericho was told, "Look, some
of the Israelite men have come here tonight
to investigate the land." 3Then the king of Jericho sent word to Rahab and said, "Bring out
the men who came to you and entered your
house, for they came to investigate the entire
land."
4But the woman had taken the two men
and hidden them.[z] So she said, "Yes, the men
did come to me, but I didn't know where
they were from. 5At nightfall, when the gate
was about to close, the men went out, and I
don't know where they were going. Chase after them quickly, and you can catch up with
them!" 6But she had taken them up to the
roof and hidden them[aa] among the stalks of
flax that she had arranged on the roof. 7The
men pursued them along the road to the
fords of the Jordan, and as soon as they left to
pursue them, the gate was shut.

The Promise to Rahab

8Before the men fell asleep, she went up on
the roof 9and said to them, "I know that the

[a]**1:1** Dt 34:5 [b]Ex 17:8-13; 33:11; Nm 13:8,16; 14:6-9; 27:18-23; Dt 31:2-8; 1Ch 7:20,27 [c]**1:2** Dt 34:5-8 [d]Jos 1:11 [e]**1:3-5** Dt 11:24-25 [f]**1:4** Gn 15:18; Nm 34:3 [g]Gn 10:15; 15:19-21 [h]Dt 11:24; 1Kg 4:21,24-25; 8:65 [i]**1:5** Dt 7:24 [j]Dt 31:6-8; Heb 13:5 [k]**1:6** Jos 1:18; 10:25; 1Kg 2:2-3; 1Ch 22:13; 28:20; Ps 27:14; 31:24 [l]Gn 15:18; Ex 32:13; Dt 15:4 [m]**1:7** Dt 5:32; 20:1-2; 21:1-3 [n]**1:8** Dt 31:24; Jos 8:34 [o]Dt 29:9; Ps 1:1-3 [p]**1:9** Dt 31:7-8; Jos 10:25 [q]**1:11** Jos 3:2 [r]**1:12** Nm 32:20-22 [s]**1:13-15** Dt 3:18-20 [t]**1:15** Jos 22:4 [u]Jos 1:1 [v]**1:17** Jos 1:5,9 [w]**1:18** Dt 31:7; Jos 1:6-7,9; 10:25 [x]**2:1** Gn 42:9; Nm 13:2,16-17; Jos 7:2; Jdg 18:2 [y]Heb 11:31; Jms 2:25 [z]**2:4** 2Sm 17:19 [aa]**2:6** Jms 2:25

[A]**1:1** = The LORD Will Save, or The LORD Is Salvation; Joshua is related to the name Jesus. [B]**1:4** Lit *and to the Great Sea, the going down of the sun* [C]**1:8** Or *meditate on* [D]**1:14** = east of the Jordan River [E]**1:14** Or *over armed* [F]**1:14** = fellow Israelites [G]**2:1** Or *from Shittim*

LORD has given you this land[a] and that the
terror of you has fallen on us, and everyone
who lives in the land is panicking because
of you.[A] 10 For we have heard how the LORD
dried up the waters of the •Red Sea before you
when you came out of Egypt,[b] and what you
did to Sihon and Og, the two Amorite kings
you •completely destroyed[c] across the Jordan.
11 When we heard this, we lost heart, and everyone's courage failed[B] because of you,[d] for
the LORD your God is God in heaven above
and on earth below. 12 Now please swear to
me by the LORD that you will also show kindness to my family, because I showed kindness
to you.[C] Give me a sure sign[D] 13 that you will
spare the lives of my father, mother, brothers,
sisters, and all who belong to them, and save
us from death."

14 The men answered her, "We will give our
lives for yours. If you don't report our mission, we will show kindness and faithfulness
to you when the LORD gives us the land."

15 Then she let them down by a rope through
the window, since she lived in a house that
was built into the wall of the city. 16 "Go to the
hill country so that the men pursuing you
won't find you," she said to them. "Hide yourselves there for three days until they return;
afterward, go on your way."

17 The men said to her, "We will be free from
this oath you made us swear, 18 unless, when
we enter the land, you tie this scarlet cord to
the window through which you let us down.
Bring your father, mother, brothers, and
all your father's family into your house. 19 If
anyone goes out the doors of your house, his
blood will be on his own head,[e] and we will be
innocent. But if anyone with you in the house
should be harmed,[E] his blood will be on our
heads. 20 And if you report our mission, we are
free from the oath you made us swear."

21 "Let it be as you say," she replied, and she
sent them away. After they had gone, she tied
the scarlet cord to the window.

22 So the two men went into the hill country
and stayed there three days until the pursuers had returned. They searched all along the
way, but did not find them. 23 Then the men
returned, came down from the hill country,
and crossed the Jordan. They went to Joshua
son of Nun and reported everything that had
happened to them. 24 They told Joshua, "The
LORD has handed over the entire land to us.
Everyone who lives in the land is also panicking because of us."[F]

Crossing the Jordan

3 Joshua started early the next morning and
left the Acacia Grove[G] with all the Israelites. They went as far as the Jordan and stayed
there before crossing. 2 After three days the
officers went through the camp[f] 3 and commanded the people: "When you see the ark of
the covenant of the LORD your God carried
by the Levitical priests,[g] you must break camp
and follow it. 4 But keep a distance of about
1,000 yards[H] between yourselves and the ark.
Don't go near it, so that you can see the way to
go, for you haven't traveled this way before."[I]

5 Joshua told the people, "Consecrate yourselves,[h] because the LORD will do wonders
among you tomorrow." 6 Then he said to the
priests, "Take the ark of the covenant and go
on ahead of the people." So they carried the
ark of the covenant and went ahead of them.

7 The LORD spoke to Joshua: "Today I will
begin to exalt you in the sight of all Israel,[i] so
they will know that I will be with you just as I
was with Moses. 8 Command the priests carrying the ark of the covenant: When you reach
the edge of the waters,[J] stand in the Jordan."

9 Then Joshua told the Israelites, "Come
closer and listen to the words of the LORD
your God." 10 He said: "You will know that the
living God is among you[j] and that He will
certainly dispossess before you the Canaanites, Hittites, Hivites, Perizzites, Girgashites,
Amorites, and Jebusites[k] 11 when the ark of
the covenant of the Lord of all the earth[l] goes
ahead of you into the Jordan. 12 Now choose
12 men from the tribes of Israel, one man for
each tribe.[m] 13 When the feet[K] of the priests
who carry the ark of the LORD, the Lord of all
the earth, come to rest in the Jordan's waters,
its waters will be cut off. The water flowing
downstream will stand up in a mass."[n]

[a] **2:9** Nm 20:24; Jos 9:24
[b] **2:10** Ex 14:21-30
[c] Nm 21:23-30,33-35; Dt 2:32-34; 3:1-3; Jos 6:21
[d] **2:11** Jos 5:1; 7:5; Ps 22:14; Is 13:7; 19:1
[e] **2:19** Mt 27:25
[f] **3:2** Jos 1:11
[g] **3:3** Dt 31:9
[h] **3:5** Ex 19:10; Jos 7:13
[i] **3:7** Jos 4:14
[j] **3:10** Dt 5:26
[k] Ex 33:2; Dt 7:1
[l] **3:11** Zch 6:5
[m] **3:12** Jos 4:2
[n] **3:13** Ex 15:8

[A] **2:9** Or *land panics at your approach* [B] **2:11** Lit *and spirit no longer remained in anyone* [C] **2:12** Lit *to your father's house* [D] **2:12** Or *a sign of truth* [E] **2:19** Lit *if a hand should be on him* [F] **2:24** Or *also panics at our approach* [G] **3:1** Or *left Shittim* [H] **3:4** Lit *2,000 cubits* [I] **3:4** Lit *yesterday and the day before* [J] **3:8** Lit *waters of the Jordan* [K] **3:13** Lit *soles of the feet*

14 When the people broke camp to cross the Jordan, the priests carried the ark of the covenant[a] ahead of the people. 15 Now the Jordan overflows its banks throughout the harvest season.[b] But as soon as the priests carrying the ark reached the Jordan, their feet touched the water at its edge 16 and the water flowing downstream stood still, rising up in a mass that extended as far as[A] Adam, a city next to Zarethan. The water flowing downstream into the Sea of the •Arabah[c] (the Dead Sea) was completely cut off, and the people crossed opposite Jericho. 17 The priests carrying the ark of the LORD's covenant stood firmly on dry ground in the middle of the Jordan,[d] while all Israel crossed on dry ground until the entire nation had finished crossing the Jordan.

The Memorial Stones

4 After the entire nation had finished crossing the Jordan,[e] the LORD spoke to Joshua: 2 "Choose 12 men from the people, one man for each tribe,[f] 3 and command them: Take 12 stones from this place in the middle of the Jordan where the priests[B] are standing, carry them with you, and set them down at the place where you spend the night."

4 So Joshua summoned the 12 men he had selected from the Israelites, one man for each tribe, 5 and said to them, "Go across to the ark of the LORD your God in the middle of the Jordan. Each of you lift a stone onto his shoulder, one for each[C] of the Israelite tribes, 6 so that this will be a sign among you. In the future, when your children ask you, 'What do these stones mean to you?'[g] 7 you should tell them, 'The waters of the Jordan were cut off in front of the ark of the LORD's covenant. When it crossed the Jordan, the Jordan's waters were cut off.' Therefore these stones will always be a memorial for the Israelites."[h]

8 The Israelites did just as Joshua had commanded them. The 12 men took stones from the middle of the Jordan, one for each[D] of the Israelite tribes, just as the LORD had told Joshua. They carried them to the camp and set them down there. 9 Joshua also set up 12 stones in the middle[E] of the Jordan where the priests[B] who carried the ark of the covenant were standing. The stones are there to this day.[i]

10 The priests carrying the ark continued standing in the middle of the Jordan until everything was completed that the LORD had commanded Joshua to tell the people, in keeping with all that Moses had commanded Joshua. The people hurried across, 11 and after everyone had finished crossing, the priests with the ark of the LORD crossed in the sight of the people. 12 The Reubenites, Gadites, and half the tribe of Manasseh went in battle formation in front of the Israelites,[j] as Moses had instructed them. 13 About 40,000 equipped for war crossed to the plains of Jericho in the LORD's presence.

14 On that day the LORD exalted Joshua in the sight of all Israel, and they revered him throughout his life, as they had revered Moses.[k] 15 The LORD told Joshua, 16 "Command the priests who carry the ark of the •testimony[F,l] to come up from the Jordan."

17 So Joshua commanded the priests, "Come up from the Jordan." 18 When the priests carrying the ark of the LORD's covenant came up from the middle of the Jordan, and their feet[G] stepped out on solid ground, the waters of the Jordan resumed their course, flowing over all the banks as before.

19 The people came up from the Jordan on the tenth day of the first month,[H] and camped at Gilgal on the eastern limits of Jericho. 20 Then Joshua set up in Gilgal the 12 stones they had taken from the Jordan, 21 and he said to the Israelites, "In the future, when your children ask their fathers, 'What is the meaning of these stones?' 22 you should tell your children, 'Israel crossed the Jordan on dry ground.'[m] 23 For the LORD your God dried up the waters of the Jordan before you until you had crossed over,[n] just as the LORD your God did to the •Red Sea, which He dried up before us until we had crossed over. 24 This is so that all the people of the earth may know[o] that the LORD's hand is mighty,[p] and so that you may always •fear the LORD your God."[q]

[a] **3:14** Ac 7:44-45
[b] **3:15** 1Ch 12:15; Jr 12:5; 49:19
[c] **3:16** Dt 1:1
[d] **3:17** Ex 14:29
[e] **4:1** Jos 3:17
[f] **4:2** Jos 3:12
[g] **4:6** Ex 12:26-27; 13:8-9,14; Dt 6:20-24; Jos 4:21-22
[h] **4:7** Ex 12:14; Nm 16:40
[i] **4:9** Jos 6:25
[j] **4:12** Nm 32:17
[k] **4:14** Jos 3:7
[l] **4:16** Ex 25:16
[m] **4:22** Jos 3:17
[n] **4:23** Ex 14:21
[o] **4:24** Ex 9:14-16; 14:31; 1Kg 8:42
[p] Ps 89:13
[q] Ex 14:31

[A] **3:16** Alt Hb tradition reads *mass at* [B] **4:3,9** Lit *feet of the priests* [C] **4:5** Lit *shoulder according to the number* [D] **4:8** Lit *Jordan according to the number* [E] **4:9** Or *Now Joshua set up the 12 stones that had been in the middle* [F] **4:16** = the ark of the covenant [G] **4:18** Lit *and the soles of the feet of the priests* [H] **4:19** = Nisan (March–April)

Circumcision of the Israelites

5 When all the Amorite kings across the Jordan to the west and all the Canaanite kings near the sea[a] heard how the LORD had dried up the waters of the Jordan before the Israelites until they had crossed over,[b] they lost heart and their courage failed[A] because of the Israelites.

2 At that time the LORD said to Joshua, "Make flint knives and circumcise the Israelite men again."[c] 3 So Joshua made flint knives and circumcised the Israelite men at Gibeath-haaraloth.[B] 4 This is the reason Joshua circumcised them: All the people who came out of Egypt who were males — all the men of war — had died in the wilderness along the way after they had come out of Egypt. 5 Though all the people who came out were circumcised, none of the people born in the wilderness along the way were circumcised after they had come out of Egypt. 6 For the Israelites wandered in the wilderness 40 years until all the nation's men of war who came out of Egypt had died off because they did not obey the LORD.[d] So the LORD vowed never to let them see the land He had sworn to their fathers to give us, a land flowing with milk and honey.[e] 7 Joshua raised up their sons in their place; it was these he circumcised. They were still uncircumcised, since they had not been circumcised along the way. 8 After the entire nation had been circumcised, they stayed where they were in the camp until they recovered.[f] 9 The LORD then said to Joshua, "Today I have rolled away the disgrace of Egypt from you." Therefore, that place is called Gilgal[C] to this day.[g]

Food from the Land

10 While the Israelites camped at Gilgal on the plains of Jericho, they kept the ·Passover on the evening of the fourteenth day of the month.[D] 11 The day after Passover they ate unleavened bread and roasted grain from the produce of the land. 12 And the day after they ate from the produce of the land, the manna ceased.[h] Since there was no more manna for the Israelites, they ate from the crops of the land of Canaan that year.

[a] **5:1** Nm 13:29
[b] Jos 2:11
[c] **5:2** Gn 17:10-14; Ex 4:24-26; 12:44,48; Lv 12:3
[d] **5:6** Dt 2:7,14
[e] Nm 14:23-24; Dt 11:9
[f] **5:8** Dt 30:6; Hs 6:1-2
[g] **5:9** Jos 6:25
[h] **5:12** Ex 16:35; Ps 78:25; Jn 6:48-51
[i] **5:13** Gn 18:2; 32:24; Nm 22:31
[j] **5:14** Gn 17:3
[k] **5:15** Ex 3:5
[l] **6:2** Dt 7:24
[m] **6:4** Ex 19:13; Ps 24:7; Is 18:3; 1Co 15:52; 1Th 4:16; Rv 11:15
[n] **6:9** Is 52:12

Commander of the LORD's Army

13 When Joshua was near Jericho, he looked up and saw a man standing in front of him with a drawn sword in His hand.[i] Joshua approached Him and asked, "Are You for us or for our enemies?"

14 "Neither," He replied. "I have now come as commander of the LORD's army."

Then Joshua bowed with his face to the ground in worship[j] and asked Him, "What does my Lord want to say to His servant?"

15 The commander of the LORD's army said to Joshua, "Remove the sandals from your feet, for the place where you are standing is holy."[k] And Joshua did so.

The Conquest of Jericho

6 Now Jericho was strongly fortified because of the Israelites — no one leaving or entering. 2 The LORD said to Joshua, "Look, I have handed Jericho, its king, and its fighting men over to you.[l] 3 March around the city with all the men of war, circling the city one time. Do this for six days. 4 Have seven priests carry seven ram's-horn trumpets in front of the ark. But on the seventh day, march around the city seven times, while the priests blow the trumpets.[m] 5 When there is a prolonged blast of the horn and you hear its sound, have all the people give a mighty shout. Then the city wall will collapse, and the people will advance, each man straight ahead."

6 So Joshua son of Nun summoned the priests and said to them, "Take up the ark of the covenant and have seven priests carry seven trumpets in front of the ark of the LORD." 7 He said to the people, "Move forward, march around the city, and have the armed troops go ahead of the ark of the LORD."

8 After Joshua had spoken to the people, seven priests carrying seven trumpets before the LORD moved forward and blew the trumpets; the ark of the LORD's covenant followed them. 9 While the trumpets were blowing, the armed troops went in front of the priests who blew the trumpets, and the rear guard went behind the ark.[n] 10 But Joshua had commanded the people: "Do not shout or let your voice be heard. Don't let one word come out of your mouth until the time I say, 'Shout!'

[A] **5:1** Lit *and they did not have spirit in them any more* [B] **5:3** Or *The Hill of Foreskins* [C] **5:9** = to roll [D] **5:10** = Nisan (March–April)

Then you are to shout." 11So the ark of the
LORD was carried around the city, circling it
once. They returned to the camp and spent
the night there.[A]
12Joshua got up early the next morning.
The priests took the ark of the LORD, 13and
the seven priests carrying seven trumpets
marched in front of the ark of the LORD.
While the trumpets were blowing, the armed
troops went in front of them, and the rear
guard went behind the ark of the LORD. 14On
the second day they marched around the city
once and returned to the camp. They did this
for six days.
15Early on the seventh day, they started at
dawn and marched around the city seven
times in the same way. That was the only day
they marched around the city seven times.
16After the seventh time, the priests blew
the trumpets, and Joshua said to the people,
"Shout! For the LORD has given you the city.
17But the city and everything in it are ·set
apart to the LORD for destruction. Only Rahab the prostitute and everyone with her in
the house will live,[a] because she hid the men[B]
we sent. 18But keep yourselves from the things
set apart, or you will be set apart for destruction. If you[C] take any of those things, you will
set apart the camp of Israel for destruction
and bring disaster on it. 19For all the silver
and gold, and the articles of bronze and iron,
are dedicated to the LORD and must go into
the LORD's treasury."
20So the people shouted, and the trumpets
sounded. When they heard the blast of the
trumpet, the people gave a great shout, and
the wall collapsed.[b] The people advanced
into the city, each man straight ahead, and
they captured the city. 21They ·completely
destroyed[c] everything in the city with the
sword — every man and woman, both young
and old, and every ox, sheep, and donkey.

Rahab and Her Family Spared

22Joshua said to the two men who had
scouted the land, "Go to the prostitute's
house and bring the woman out of there, and
all who are with her, just as you promised
her."[d] 23So the young men who had scouted
went in and brought out Rahab and her father, mother, brothers, and all who belonged
to her. They brought out her whole family
and settled them outside the camp of Israel.
24They burned up the city and everything in
it, but they put the silver and gold and the articles of bronze and iron into the treasury of
the LORD's house. 25However, Joshua spared
Rahab the prostitute, her father's household,
and all who belonged to her, because she hid
the men Joshua had sent to spy on Jericho,
and she lives in Israel[e] to this day.[f]
26At that time Joshua imposed this curse:

> The man who undertakes
> the rebuilding of this city, Jericho,
> is cursed before the LORD.
> He will lay its foundation
> at the cost of his firstborn;
> he will set up its gates
> at the cost of his youngest.[g]

27And the LORD was with Joshua, and his
fame spread throughout the land.

Defeat at Ai

7 The Israelites, however, were unfaithful[h]
regarding the things ·set apart for destruction. Achan son of Carmi, son of Zabdi,
son of Zerah, of the tribe of Judah, took some
of what was set apart, and the LORD's anger
burned against the Israelites.
2Joshua sent men from Jericho to Ai, which
is near Beth-aven,[i] east of Bethel, and told
them, "Go up and scout the land." So the men
went up and scouted Ai.
3After returning to Joshua they reported
to him, "Don't send all the people, but send
about 2,000 or 3,000[D] men to attack Ai. Since
the people of Ai are so few, don't wear out all
our people there." 4So about 3,000 men[E] went
up there, but they fled from the men of Ai.[j]
5The men of Ai struck down about 36 of them
and chased them from outside the gate to the
quarries,[F] striking them down on the descent.
As a result, the people's hearts melted and became like water.[k]
6Then Joshua tore his clothes and fell before the ark of the LORD with his face to the
ground until evening, as did the elders of Is-

[a] 6:17 Dt 7:2 [b] 6:20 Heb 11:30 [c] 6:21 Jos 2:10; 8:26 [d] 6:22 Jos 2:14 [e] 6:25 Ex 6:23; Ru 4:21-22; 1Ch 2:10-12; Mt 1:4-5 [f] Jos 4:9; 5:9; 7:26; 14:14; 15:63 [g] 6:26 1Kg 16:34 [h] 7:1 Lv 6:2; Nm 5:27; 31:16; Dt 32:51; Jos 22:16; Ezr 9:2-4 [i] 7:2 Jos 18:12; 1Sm 13:5; 14:23 [j] 7:4 Lv 26:17; Dt 28:25 [k] 7:5 Jos 2:11

A 6:11 Lit *at the camp* B 6:17 Lit *messengers* C 6:18 LXX reads *you covet and*; Jos 7:21 D 7:3 Or *send two or three military units of* E 7:4 Lit *men from the people* F 7:5 Or *to Shebarim*

rael; they all put dust on their heads. 7"Oh,
Lord GOD," Joshua said, "why did You ever
bring these people across the Jordan to hand
us over to the Amorites for our destruction?
If only we had been content to remain on
the other side of the Jordan! 8What can I say,
Lord, now that Israel has turned its back and
run from its enemies? 9When the Canaanites
and all who live in the land hear about this,
they will surround us and wipe out our name
from the earth. Then what will You do about
Your great name?"
10The LORD then said to Joshua, "Stand up!
Why are you on the ground?[A] 11Israel has

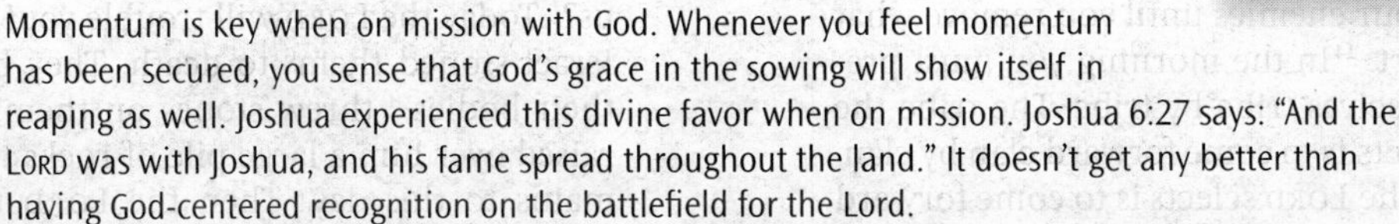

The Impact of Sin on the Mission of God

Eric M. Mason

Momentum is key when on mission with God. Whenever you feel momentum has been secured, you sense that God's grace in the sowing will show itself in reaping as well. Joshua experienced this divine favor when on mission. Joshua 6:27 says: "And the LORD was with Joshua, and his fame spread throughout the land." It doesn't get any better than having God-centered recognition on the battlefield for the Lord.

But as good as things can go on mission, they can go just as badly as well. The Lord God commanded the Hebrews in Joshua 6:17-18 to destroy everything and let the silver and gold be added to the treasury of the Lord. "The Israelites, however, were unfaithful regarding the things set apart for destruction. Achan son of Carmi, son of Zabdi, son of Zerah, of the tribe of Judah, took some of what was set apart, and the LORD's anger burned against the Israelites" (Jos 7:1).

"Unfaithful" points to the fact that this sin flows out of unbelief. In Chapter 6:22-25 an entire family was spared because of faithfulness, but in this chapter an entire family was punished because of unfaithfulness. Sin impacts the life of the missionary community no matter how large or small. As large in number as Israel was at this point, you might assume that such a sin would not impact the entire community. But sin is no trivial matter. It was a distraction from the mission God called His people to and it impacted their effectiveness in moving forward (7:2-5).

God's fame is eternal (Is 63:12) and will not be diminished by human sin, and yet He will call the community that bears His name to face the issues of sin in its midst, in order to restore the community to Himself and call them to further faithfulness.

On the mission field, the question is not whether there will be sin, but whether sin will be dealt with in a way that honors God and His gospel. Unrepentance delays resolution. Time spent working on the unrepentant is time that could have been dedicated to mission. Achan was given opportunity to repent seven times (Jos 7:12-18). His expeditious repentance would have saved the community time and energy and kept them on task.

As costly as confrontation and restoration are, the community must engage these tasks just as fully as all other aspects of mission (7:25-26). Even under the New Covenant the people of God are called to discipline the unrepentant in a Christ-centered way (1Co 5). By letting the sin fester, God's people would have experienced a further setback in the mission of God. Refusing to deal with sin is the same as joining the unrepentant in their sin.

When sin is dealt with properly, mission is not hindered but strengthened as with Ananias and Sapphira in Acts 5:1-11. Mission increased in Acts 5:14 because the sin was dealt with fully. The same is true in any context. Sin is a mission killer, but repentance invites blessing.

[A]7:10 Lit *Why have you fallen on your face?*

sinned. They have violated My covenant that
I appointed for them. They have taken some
of what was set apart. They have stolen, deceived, and put the things with their own belongings.[a] 12 This is why the Israelites cannot
stand against their enemies. They will turn
their backs and run from their enemies, because they have been set apart for destruction.[b] I will no longer be with you unless you
remove from you what is set apart.
13 "Go and consecrate the people. Tell them
to consecrate themselves for tomorrow,[c] for
this is what the LORD, the God of Israel, says:
There are things that are set apart among
you, Israel. You will not be able to stand
against your enemies until you remove what
is set apart. 14 In the morning you must present yourselves tribe by tribe. The tribe the
LORD selects is to come forward clan by clan.
The clan the LORD selects is to come forward
family by family. The family the LORD selects
is to come forward man by man. 15 The one
who is caught with the things set apart must
be burned,[A] along with everything he has,
because he has violated the LORD's covenant
and committed an outrage in Israel."[d]

Achan Judged

16 Joshua got up early the next morning. He
had Israel come forward tribe by tribe, and
the tribe of Judah was selected. 17 He had the
clans of Judah come forward, and the Zerahite clan was selected. He had the Zerahite
clan come forward by heads of families,[B] and
Zabdi was selected. 18 He then had Zabdi's
family come forward man by man, and Achan
son of Carmi, son of Zabdi, son of Zerah, of
the tribe of Judah, was selected.
19 So Joshua said to Achan, "My son, give
glory to the LORD, the God of Israel,[e] and
make a confession to Him.[C] I urge you, tell
me what you have done. Don't hide anything
from me."
20 Achan replied to Joshua, "It is true. I have
sinned against the LORD, the God of Israel.
This is what I did: 21 When I saw among the
spoils a beautiful cloak from Babylon,[D] 200
silver ˙shekels,[E] and a bar of gold weighing
50 shekels,[F] I coveted them and took them.[f]
You can see for yourself. They are concealed
in the ground inside my tent, with the money
under the cloak." 22 So Joshua sent messengers
who ran to the tent, and there was the cloak,
concealed in his tent, with the money underneath. 23 They took the things from inside the
tent, brought them to Joshua and all the Israelites, and spread them out in the LORD's
presence.
24 Then Joshua and all Israel with him took
Achan son of Zerah, the silver, the cloak, and
the bar of gold, his sons and daughters, his
ox, donkey, and sheep, his tent, and all that
he had, and brought them up to the Valley of
Achor.[g] 25 Joshua said, "Why have you troubled
us?[h] Today the LORD will trouble you!" So all
Israel stoned them[G] to death. They burned
their bodies,[H] threw stones on them, 26 and
raised over him a large pile of rocks that remains to this day.[i] Then the LORD turned
from His burning anger. Therefore that place
is called the Valley of Achor[I] to this day.

Conquest of Ai

8 The LORD said to Joshua, "Do not be afraid
or discouraged.[j] Take the whole military
force with you and go attack Ai. Look, I have
handed over to you the king of Ai, his people,
city, and land.[k] 2 Treat Ai and its king as you
did Jericho and its king;[l] you may plunder its
spoil and livestock for yourselves. Set an ambush behind the city."
3 So Joshua and the whole military force
set out to attack Ai. Joshua selected 30,000
fighting men and sent them out at night. 4 He
commanded them: "Pay attention. Lie in ambush behind the city, not too far from it, and
all of you be ready.[m] 5 Then I and all the people who are with me will approach the city.
When they come out against us as they did
the first time, we will flee from them. 6 They
will come after us until we have drawn them
away from the city, for they will say, 'They are
fleeing from us as before.' While we are fleeing from them, 7 you are to come out of your
ambush and seize the city, for the LORD your
God has handed it over to you. 8 After taking
the city, set it on fire. Follow the LORD's command — see that you do as I have ordered

[a] **7:11** Jos 6:18
[b] **7:12** Nm 14:45; Jdg 2:14
[c] **7:13** Jos 3:5
[d] **7:15** Gn 34:7; Dt 22:21; Jdg 19:23-24; 20:6
[e] **7:19** 1Sm 6:5; 2Ch 30:22; Jr 13:16; Jn 9:24
[f] **7:21** Gn 3:6; 2Sm 12:2-4; 1Jn 2:16
[g] **7:24** Jos 15:7
[h] **7:25** Jos 6:18
[i] **7:26** Jos 6:25; 8:28-29; 10:27; 13:13
[j] **8:1** Jos 1:9
[k] Jos 6:2
[l] **8:2** Jos 6:17
[m] **8:4** Jdg 20:29

[A] **7:15** Lit *burned with fire* [B] **7:17** Lit *forward man by man* [C] **7:19** Or *and praise Him* [D] **7:21** Lit *Shinar* [E] **7:21** About 5 pounds of silver [F] **7:21** About 1 pound of gold [G] **7:25** Lit *him* [H] **7:25** Lit *burned them with fire* [I] **7:26** Or *of Trouble*

you." 9 So Joshua sent them out, and they went to the ambush site and waited between Bethel and Ai, to the west of Ai. But he spent that night with the troops.

10 Joshua started early the next morning and mobilized them. Then he and the elders of Israel led the troops up to Ai. 11 All those[A] who were with him went up and approached the city, arriving opposite Ai, and camped to the north of it, with a valley between them and the city. 12 Now Joshua had taken about 5,000 men and set them in ambush between Bethel and Ai, to the west of the city. 13 The military force was stationed in this way: the main[B] camp to the north of the city and its rear guard to the west of the city. And that night Joshua went into the valley.

14 When the king of Ai saw the Israelites, the men of the city hurried and went out early in the morning so that he and all his people could engage Israel in battle at a suitable place facing the •Arabah. But he did not know there was an ambush waiting for him behind the city. 15 Joshua and all Israel pretended to be beaten back by them and fled toward the wilderness. 16 Then all the troops of Ai were summoned to pursue them, and they pursued Joshua and were drawn away from the city. 17 Not a man was left in Ai or Bethel who did not go out after Israel, leaving the city exposed while they pursued Israel.

18 Then the LORD said to Joshua, "Hold out the sword in your hand toward Ai, for I will hand the city over to you." So Joshua held out his sword toward it. 19 When he held out his hand, the men in ambush rose quickly from their position. They ran, entered the city, captured it, and immediately set it on fire.

20 The men of Ai turned and looked back, and smoke from the city was rising to the sky! They could not escape in any direction, and the troops who had fled to the wilderness now became the pursuers. 21 When Joshua and all Israel saw that the men in ambush had captured the city and that smoke was rising from it, they turned back and struck down the men of Ai. 22 Then men in ambush came out of the city against them, and the men of Ai were trapped between the Israelite forces, some on one side and some on the other. They struck them down until no survivor or fugitive remained, 23 but they captured the king of Ai alive and brought him to Joshua.

24 When Israel had finished killing everyone living in Ai who had pursued them into the open country, and when every last one of them had fallen by the sword, all Israel returned to Ai and struck it down with the sword. 25 The total of those who fell that day, both men and women, was 12,000—all the people of Ai. 26 Joshua did not draw back his hand that was holding the sword until all the inhabitants of Ai were •completely destroyed.[a] 27 Israel plundered only the cattle and spoil of that city for themselves, according to the LORD's command that He had given Joshua.

28 Joshua burned Ai and left it a permanent ruin, desolate to this day.[b] 29 He hung[C] the body of the king of Ai on a tree[D] until evening, and at sunset Joshua commanded that they take his body down from the tree.[c] They threw it down at the entrance of the city gate and put a large pile of rocks over it, which remains to this day.

Renewed Commitment to the Law

30 At that time Joshua built an altar on Mount Ebal[d] to the LORD, the God of Israel, 31 just as Moses the LORD's servant had commanded the Israelites. He built it according to what is written in the book of the law of Moses: an altar of uncut stones on which no iron tool has been used.[e] Then they offered •burnt offerings to the LORD and sacrificed •fellowship offerings on it. 32 There on the stones, Joshua copied the law of Moses, which he had written in the presence of the Israelites.[f] 33 All Israel, foreigner and citizen alike, with their elders, officers, and judges, stood on either side of the ark of the LORD's covenant facing the Levitical priests who carried it. As Moses the LORD's servant had commanded earlier, half of them were in front of Mount Gerizim and half in front of Mount Ebal,[g] to bless the people of Israel.[h] 34 Afterward, Joshua read aloud all the words of the law—the blessings as well as the curses—according to all that is written in the book of the law. 35 There was not a word of all that Moses had commanded

[a] 8:26 Nm 21:2-3; Dt 2:34; Jos 2:10; 6:21; 10:1,28,35-40; 11:11-12,20-21; 24:20
[b] 8:28 Dt 13:16; Jos 6:25
[c] 8:29 Dt 21:21-23
[d] 8:30 Dt 27:4-6
[e] 8:31 Dt 27:5-7
[f] 8:32 Dt 27:2-3
[g] 8:33 Dt 11:29
[h] Dt 27:12-13

A 8:11 Lit *the people of war* B 8:13 Lit *way: all the* C 8:29 Or *impaled* D 8:29 Or *wooden stake* that Joshua did not read before the entire assembly of Israel, including the women, the little children, and the foreigners who were with them.[a]

Deception by Gibeon

9 When all the kings heard about Jericho and Ai, those who were west of the Jordan in the hill country,[b] in the Judean foothills,[A] and all along the coast of the Mediterranean Sea[c] toward Lebanon — the Hittites, Amorites, Canaanites, Perizzites, Hivites, and Jebusites — 2 they formed a unified alliance to fight against Joshua and Israel.

3 When the inhabitants of Gibeon heard what Joshua had done to Jericho and Ai,[d] 4 they acted deceptively. They gathered provisions[B] and took worn-out sacks on their donkeys and old wineskins, cracked and mended. 5 They wore old, patched sandals on their feet and threadbare clothing on their bodies. Their entire provision of bread was dry and crumbly. 6 They went to Joshua in the camp at Gilgal and said to him and the men of Israel, "We have come from a distant land. Please make a treaty with us."[e]

7 The men of Israel replied to the Hivites,[C] "Perhaps you live among us. How can we make a treaty with you?"[f]

8 They said to Joshua, "We are your servants."

Then Joshua asked them, "Who are you and where do you come from?"

9 They replied to him, "Your servants have come from a far away land because of the reputation of the LORD your God. For we have heard of His fame, and all that He did in Egypt, 10 and all that He did to the two Amorite kings beyond the Jordan — Sihon king of Heshbon and Og king of Bashan, who was in Ashtaroth. 11 So our elders and all the inhabitants of our land told us, 'Take provisions with you for the journey; go and meet them and say, "We are your servants. Please make a treaty with us."' 12 This bread of ours was warm when we took it from our houses as food on the day we left to come to you. But take a look, it is now dry and crumbly. 13 These wineskins were new when we filled them, but look, they are cracked. And these clothes and sandals of ours are worn out from the extremely long journey." 14 Then the men of Israel took some of their provisions, but did not seek the LORD's counsel.[g] 15 So Joshua established peace with them and made a treaty to let them live, and the leaders of the community swore an oath to them.[h]

Gibeon's Deception Discovered

16 Three days after making the treaty with them, they heard that the Gibeonites were their neighbors, living among them. 17 So the Israelites set out and reached the Gibeonite cities on the third day. Now their cities were Gibeon, Chephirah, Beeroth, and Kiriath-jearim.[i] 18 But the Israelites did not attack them, because the leaders of the community had sworn an oath[j] to them by the LORD, the God of Israel. Then the whole community grumbled against the leaders.

19 All the leaders answered them, "We have sworn an oath to them by the LORD, the God of Israel, and now we cannot touch them. 20 This is how we will treat them: we will let them live, so that no wrath will fall on us because of the oath we swore to them." 21 They also said, "Let them live." So the Gibeonites became woodcutters and water carriers[k] for the whole community, as the leaders had promised them.

22 Joshua summoned the Gibeonites and said to them, "Why did you deceive us by telling us you live far away from us, when in fact you live among us? 23 Therefore you are cursed and will always be slaves — woodcutters and water carriers for the house of my God."

24 The Gibeonites answered him, "It was clearly communicated to your servants that the LORD your God had commanded His servant Moses to give you all the land and to destroy all the inhabitants of the land before you. We greatly feared for our lives because of you, and that is why we did this. 25 Now we are in your hands. Do to us whatever you think is right."[D] 26 This is what Joshua did to them: he delivered them from the hands of the Israelites, and they did not kill them. 27 On that day

[a]8:35 Dt 31:12
[b]9:1 Jos 3:10
[c]Nm 34:6
[d]9:3 Jos 10:2
[e]9:6 Jos 5:10
[f]9:7 Ex 23:32; Dt 7:2-5; 20:10-18
[g]9:14 Nm 27:21
[h]9:15 2Sm 21:1-2
[i]9:17 Jos 18:25
[j]9:18 Ps 15:1-4; Ezk 17:16-20
[k]9:21 Dt 29:11

A9:1 Or *the Shephelah* B9:4 Some Hb mss, LXX, Syr, Vg; other Hb mss read *They went disguised as ambassadors* C9:7 = the men of Gibeon

D9:25 Lit *us as is good and as is right in your eyes do*

he made them woodcutters and water carriers — as they are today — for the community and for the LORD's altar at the place He would choose.[a]

The Day the Sun Stood Still

10 Now Adoni-zedek king of Jerusalem heard that Joshua had captured Ai and ·completely destroyed[b] it, treating Ai and its king as he had Jericho and its king, and that the inhabitants of Gibeon[c] had made peace with Israel and were living among them.[d] 2 So Adoni-zedek and his people were[A] greatly alarmed because Gibeon was a large city like one of the royal cities; it was larger than Ai, and all its men were warriors. 3 Therefore Adoni-zedek king of Jerusalem sent word to Hoham king of Hebron, Piram king of Jarmuth, Japhia king of Lachish, and Debir king of Eglon, saying, 4 "Come up and help me. We will attack Gibeon, because they have made peace with Joshua and the Israelites." 5 So the five Amorite kings — the kings of Jerusalem, Hebron, Jarmuth, Lachish, and Eglon — joined forces, advanced with all their armies, besieged Gibeon, and fought against it.

6 Then the men of Gibeon sent word to Joshua in the camp at Gilgal: "Don't abandon[B] your servants. Come quickly and save us! Help us, for all the Amorite kings living in the hill country have joined forces against us." 7 So Joshua and his whole military force, including all the fighting men, came from Gilgal.[e]

8 The LORD said to Joshua, "Do not be afraid of them,[f] for I have handed them over to you. Not one of them will be able to stand against you."

9 So Joshua caught them by surprise, after marching all night from Gilgal. 10 The LORD threw them into confusion[g] before Israel. He defeated them in a great slaughter at Gibeon, chased them through the ascent of Beth-horon, and struck them down as far as Azekah and Makkedah. 11 As they fled before Israel, the LORD threw large hailstones on them[h] from the sky along the descent of Beth-horon all the way to Azekah, and they died. More of

[a] **9:27** Dt 12:5
[b] **10:1** Jos 8:26; 10:28,35-40; 11:11-12,20-21; 24:20; Jdg 1:17; 21:11
[c] Jos 8:22
[d] Jos 9:15
[e] **10:7** Jos 8:1
[f] **10:8** Jos 1:5
[g] **10:10** Ex 14:24; 23:27; 1Sm 7:10
[h] **10:11** Ps 18:12-14
[i] **10:12** Hab 3:11
[j] **10:14** Ex 14:14,25; Dt 1:30; 3:22; 20:4; Jos 10:42; 23:3,10; 2Ch 20:29; 32:8; Ps 35:1; Zch 14:3

them died from the hail than the Israelites killed with the sword.

12 On the day the LORD gave the Amorites over to the Israelites, Joshua spoke to the LORD in the presence of Israel:

"Sun,[i] stand still over Gibeon,
and moon, over the Valley of Aijalon."
13 And the sun stood still
and the moon stopped
until the nation took vengeance
on its enemies.

Isn't this written in the Book of Jashar?[C]

So the sun stopped
in the middle of the sky
and delayed its setting
almost a full day.

14 There has been no day like it before or since, when the LORD listened to the voice of a man, because the LORD fought for Israel.[j] 15 Then Joshua and all Israel with him returned to the camp at Gilgal.

Execution of the Five Kings

16 Now the five defeated kings had fled and hidden themselves in the cave at Makkedah. 17 It was reported to Joshua: "The five kings have been found; they are hiding in the cave at Makkedah."

18 Joshua said, "Roll large stones against the mouth of the cave, and station men by it to guard the kings. 19 But as for the rest of you, don't stay there. Pursue your enemies and attack them from behind. Don't let them enter their cities, for the LORD your God has handed them over to you." 20 So Joshua and the Israelites finished inflicting a terrible slaughter on them until they were destroyed, although a few survivors ran away to the fortified cities. 21 The people returned safely to Joshua in the camp at Makkedah. And no one dared to threaten[D] the Israelites.

22 Then Joshua said, "Open the mouth of the cave, and bring those five kings to me out of there." 23 That is what they did. They brought the five kings of Jerusalem, Hebron, Jarmuth, Lachish, and Eglon to Joshua out of the cave. 24 When they had brought the kings to him, Joshua summoned all the men of Israel and

[A] **10:2** One Hb ms, Syr, Vg read *So he was* [B] **10:6** Lit *Don't let your hand go from* [C] **10:13** Or *of the Upright* [D] **10:21** Lit *No one sharpened his tongue against* said to the military commanders who had accompanied him, "Come here and put your feet on the necks of these kings." So the commanders came forward and put their feet on their necks. 25 Joshua said to them, "Do not be afraid or discouraged. Be strong and courageous,[a] for the LORD will do this to all the enemies you fight."

26 After this, Joshua struck them down and executed them. He hung[A] their bodies on five trees[B] and they were there until evening.[b] 27 At sunset Joshua commanded that they be taken down from the trees[B,c] and thrown into the cave where they had hidden. Then large stones were placed against the mouth of the cave, and the stones are there to this day.[d]

Conquest of Southern Cities

28 On that day Joshua captured Makkedah and struck it down with the sword, including its king. He completely destroyed it[C] and everyone in it, leaving no survivors. So he treated the king of Makkedah as he had the king of Jericho.[e]

29 Joshua and all Israel with him crossed from Makkedah to Libnah and fought against Libnah.[f] 30 The LORD also handed it and its king over to Israel. He struck it down, putting everyone in it to the sword, and left no survivors in it. He treated Libnah's king as he had the king of Jericho.

31 From Libnah, Joshua and all Israel with him crossed to Lachish. They laid siege to it and attacked it. 32 The LORD handed Lachish over to Israel, and Joshua captured it on the second day. He struck it down, putting everyone in it to the sword, just as he had done to Libnah. 33 At that time Horam king of Gezer went to help Lachish,[g] but Joshua struck him down along with his people, leaving no survivors in it.

34 Then Joshua crossed from Lachish to Eglon and all Israel with him. They laid siege to it and attacked it. 35 On that day they captured it and struck it down, putting everyone in it to the sword. He completely destroyed it that day, just as he had done to Lachish.

36 Next, Joshua and all Israel with him went up from Eglon to Hebron[h] and attacked it. 37 They captured it and struck down its king, all its villages, and everyone in it with the sword. He left no survivors, just as he had done at Eglon. He completely destroyed Hebron and everyone in it.

38 Finally, Joshua turned toward Debir[i] and attacked it. And all Israel was with him. 39 He captured it — its king and all its villages. They struck them down with the sword and completely destroyed everyone in it, leaving no survivors. He treated Debir and its king as he had treated Hebron and as he had treated Libnah and its king.

40 So Joshua conquered the whole region — the hill country, the ˚Negev, the Judean foothills,[D] and the slopes — with all their kings, leaving no survivors. He completely destroyed every living being, as the LORD, the God of Israel, had commanded.[j] 41 Joshua conquered everyone from Kadesh-barnea to Gaza, and all the land of Goshen[k] as far as Gibeon. 42 Joshua captured all these kings and their land in one campaign,[E] because the LORD, the God of Israel, fought for Israel. 43 Then Joshua returned with all Israel to the camp at Gilgal.

Conquest of Northern Cities

11 When Jabin king of Hazor heard this news, he sent a message to:

Jobab king of Madon,
the kings of Shimron and Achshaph,
2 and the kings of the north
in the hill country,
the ˚Arabah south of Chinnereth,[l]
the Judean foothills,[D]
and the Slopes of Dor[F] to the west,
3 the Canaanites in the east and west,
the Amorites, Hittites, Perizzites,
and Jebusites in the hill country,
and the Hivites at the foot of Hermon
in the land of Mizpah.[m]

4 They went out with all their armies — a multitude as numerous as the sand on the seashore — along with a vast number of horses and chariots. 5 All these kings joined forces; they came together and camped at the waters of Merom to attack Israel.[n]

[a] **10:25** Dt 31:7; Jos 1:6-7,9,18
[b] **10:26** Jos 8:29
[c] **10:27** Dt 21:22-23
[d] Jos 6:25
[e] **10:28** Jos 6:21
[f] **10:29** Jos 21:13
[g] **10:33** Jos 16:10; Jdg 1:29; 1Kg 9:16-17
[h] **10:36** Jdg 1:10
[i] **10:38** Jos 15:15; Jdg 1:11
[j] **10:40** Dt 20:16
[k] **10:41** Jos 15:50
[l] **11:2** Dt 3:17; Jos 12:3; 13:27; 19:35; 1Kg 15:20; Mt 14:34; Lk 5:1
[m] **11:3** Jdg 3:3
[n] **11:5** Jdg 7:12

[A] **10:26** Or *impaled* [B] **10:26,27** Or *wooden stakes* [C] **10:28** Some Hb mss read *them* [D] **10:40,11:2** Or *the Shephelah* [E] **10:42** Lit *land at one time* [F] **11:2** Or *and in Naphoth-dor*

6 The LORD said to Joshua, "Do not be afraid
of them, for at this time tomorrow I will cause
all of them to be killed before Israel.[a] You are
to hamstring their horses and burn up their
chariots."[b] 7 So Joshua and his whole military
force surprised them at the waters of Merom
and attacked them. 8 The LORD handed them
over to Israel, and they struck them down,
pursuing them as far as Great Sidon and Misrephoth-maim, and to the east as far as the
Valley of Mizpeh.[A,c] They struck them down,
leaving no survivors. 9 Joshua treated them as
the LORD had told him; he hamstrung their
horses and burned up their chariots.

10 At that time Joshua turned back, captured Hazor, and struck down its king with
the sword, because Hazor had formerly
been the leader of all these kingdoms. 11 They
struck down everyone in it with the sword,
•completely destroying[d] them; he left no one
alive. Then he burned down Hazor.

12 Joshua captured all these kings and their
cities and struck them down with the sword.
He completely destroyed them, as Moses the
LORD's servant[e] had commanded. 13 However, Israel did not burn any of the cities that
stood on their mounds except Hazor, which
Joshua burned. 14 The Israelites plundered all
the spoils and cattle of these cities for themselves. But they struck down every person
with the sword until they had annihilated
them, leaving no one alive. 15 Just as the LORD
had commanded His servant Moses, Moses
commanded Joshua. That is what Joshua did,
leaving nothing undone of all that the LORD
had commanded Moses.

Summary of Conquests

16 So Joshua took all this land—the hill
country, all the •Negev, all the land of Goshen,[f]
the foothills,[B] the Arabah, and the hill country of Israel with its foothills[C]— 17 from
Mount Halak,[g] which ascends to Seir, as far
as Baal-gad in the Valley of Lebanon at the
foot of Mount Hermon. He captured all their
kings and struck them down, putting them
to death.[h] 18 Joshua waged war with all these
kings for a long time. 19 No city made peace
with the Israelites except the Hivites who
inhabited Gibeon;[i] all of them were taken in
battle. 20 For it was the LORD's intention to
harden their hearts, so that they would engage Israel in battle, be completely destroyed
without mercy, and be annihilated, just as the
LORD had commanded Moses.

21 At that time Joshua proceeded to exterminate the Anakim[j] from the hill country—Hebron, Debir, Anab—all the hill country of
Judah and of Israel. Joshua completely destroyed them with their cities. 22 No Anakim
were left in the land of the Israelites, except
for some remaining in Gaza, Gath,[k] and Ashdod.

23 So Joshua took the entire land, in keeping
with all that the LORD had told Moses. Joshua
then gave it as an inheritance to Israel according to their tribal allotments. After this,
the land had rest from war.[l]

Territory East of the Jordan

12 The Israelites struck down the following kings of the land and took possession of their land beyond the Jordan to the
east and from the Arnon Valley to Mount Hermon, including all the •Arabah eastward:[m]

2 Sihon king of the Amorites lived in
Heshbon. He ruled over the territory
from Aroer[n] on the rim of the Arnon Valley, along the middle of the valley, and
half of Gilead up to the Jabbok River (the
border of the Ammonites[o]), 3 the Arabah
east of the Sea of Chinnereth[D] to the Sea
of the Arabah (that is, the Dead Sea),
eastward through Beth-jeshimoth[p] and
southward[E] below the slopes of Pisgah.[q]

4 Og[F] king of Bashan, of the remnant of
the Rephaim, lived in Ashtaroth and
Edrei.[r] 5 He ruled over Mount Hermon,
Salecah, all Bashan up to the Geshurite
and Maacathite border, and half of Gilead to the border of Sihon, king of Heshbon.[s]

6 Moses the LORD's servant[t] and the Israelites
struck them[u] down. And Moses the LORD's
servant gave their land as an inheritance to
the Reubenites, Gadites, and half the tribe of
Manasseh.[v]

[a] **11:6** Jos 10:8
[b] 2Sm 8:4; Ps 20:7
[c] **11:8** Jos 13:6
[d] **11:11** Jos 10:1; 24:20; Jdg 1:17; 21:11; 1Sm 15:3; 2Ch 8:8; Jr 25:9
[e] **11:12** Dt 20:16-17
[f] **11:16** Jos 15:51
[g] **11:17** Jos 12:7
[h] Dt 7:24
[i] **11:19** Jos 9:3,7
[j] **11:21** Nm 13:22,28,33
[k] **11:22** 1Sm 17:4
[l] **11:23** Jos 14:15; 21:44; 2Ch 14:6; Hs 2:18; Heb 4:8
[m] **12:1** Dt 3:8-9
[n] **12:2** Dt 2:36
[o] Dt 3:16
[p] **12:3** Jos 13:20
[q] Jos 11:2
[r] **12:4** Dt 1:4
[s] **12:5** Dt 3:10,14
[t] **12:6** Nm 32:33; Dt 3:12
[u] Nm 21:21-35; Dt 2:26–3:11; 29:7; 31:4; Ps 135:11; 136:19-20; Neh 9:22-25
[v] Dt 3:12-17; 29:8

[A] **11:8** = Mizpah; Jos 11:3; 18:26 [B] **11:16** Or *the Shephelah* [C] **11:16** Or *its Shephelah* [D] **12:3** = the Sea of Galilee [E] **12:3** Or *and from Teman* [F] **12:4** LXX; MT reads *The territory of Og*

Territory West of the Jordan

[7]Joshua and the Israelites struck down the
following kings of the land beyond the Jordan to the west, from Baal-gad in the Valley
of Lebanon to Mount Halak,[a] which ascends
toward Seir (Joshua gave their land as an inheritance to the tribes of Israel according to
their allotments: [8]the hill country, the Judean
foothills,[A] the Arabah, the slopes, the desert,
and the ˙Negev of the Hittites, Amorites, Canaanites, Perizzites, Hivites, and Jebusites):

9 the king of Jericho[b] one
the king of Ai,[c] which is next to Bethel one
10 the king of Jerusalem[d] one
the king of Hebron one
11 the king of Jarmuth one
the king of Lachish one
12 the king of Eglon one
the king of Gezer one
13 the king of Debir one
the king of Geder one
14 the king of Hormah one
the king of Arad one
15 the king of Libnah one
the king of Adullam one
16 the king of Makkedah one
the king of Bethel one
17 the king of Tappuah one
the king of Hepher one
18 the king of Aphek one
the king of Lasharon one
19 the king of Madon one
the king of Hazor one
20 the king of Shimron-meron one
the king of Achshaph one
21 the king of Taanach one
the king of Megiddo one
22 the king of Kedesh one
the king of Jokneam in Carmel one
23 the king of Dor in Naphath-dor[B] one
the king of Goiim in Gilgal[C] one
24 the king of Tirzah one
the total number of all kings: 31.

Unconquered Lands

13 Joshua was now old, getting on in
years,[e] and the LORD said to him, "You
have become old, getting on in years, but
a great deal of the land remains to be possessed.[f] [2]This is the land that remains:

All the districts of the Philistines and
the Geshurites: [3]from the Shihor east
of Egypt to the border of Ekron on the
north (considered to be Canaanite territory) — the five Philistine rulers of Gaza,
Ashdod, Ashkelon, Gath, and Ekron, as
well as the Avvites [4]in the south; all the
land of the Canaanites: from Arah of
the Sidonians to Aphek and as far as the
border of the Amorites; [5]the land of the
Gebalites;[g] and all Lebanon east from
Baal-gad below Mount Hermon to the
entrance of Hamath[D,h] — [6]all the inhabitants of the hill country from Lebanon
to Misrephoth-maim,[i] all the Sidonians.

I will drive them out before the Israelites,
only distribute the land as an inheritance for
Israel, as I have commanded you. [7]Therefore,
divide this land as an inheritance to the nine
tribes and half the tribe of Manasseh."

The Inheritance East of the Jordan

[8]With the other half of the tribe, the Reubenites and Gadites had received the inheritance Moses gave them beyond the Jordan to
the east, just as Moses the LORD's servant had
given them:[j]

[9]From Aroer on the rim of the Arnon
Valley, along with the city in the middle
of the valley,[k] all the Medeba plateau as
far as Dibon, [10]and all the cities of Sihon king of the Amorites, who reigned
in Heshbon, to the border of the Ammonites; [11]also Gilead[l] and the territory of the Geshurites and Maacathites,
all Mount Hermon, and all Bashan to
Salecah — [12]the whole kingdom of Og
in Bashan, who reigned in Ashtaroth
and Edrei; he was one of the remaining
Rephaim.

Moses struck them down and drove them
out,[m] [13]but the Israelites did not drive out the
Geshurites and Maacathites.[n] So Geshur and
Maacath live in Israel to this day.[o]

[14]He did not give any inheritance to the
tribe of Levi. This was its inheritance, just as

[a]**12:7** Jos 11:16-17 [b]**12:9** Jos 6:2 [c]Jos 8:29 [d]**12:10** Jos 10:23 [e]**13:1** Jos 14:10 [f]Ex 23:27-33 [g]**13:5** 1Kg 5:18 [h]Jos 12:7 [i]**13:6** Jos 11:8 [j]**13:8** Jos 12:6 [k]**13:9** Dt 2:36; Jos 13:16 [l]**13:11** Dt 3:10 [m]**13:12** Nm 21:24 [n]**13:13** Jos 16:10; 17:12-13; Jdg 1:1–2:5 [o]Jos 6:25

[A]**12:8** Or *the Shephelah* [B]**12:23** Or *in the Slopes of Dor* [C]**12:23** LXX reads *Galilee* [D]**13:5** Or *to Lebo-hamath*

He had promised: the offerings made by fire
to the LORD, the God of Israel.[a]

Reuben's Inheritance

15To the tribe of the Reubenites by their
clans, Moses gave 16this as their territory:

From Aroer on the rim of the Arnon Valley, along with the city in the middle of
the valley, to the whole plateau as far
as[A] Medeba, 17with Heshbon and all its
cities on the plateau — Dibon, Bamoth-
baal, Beth-baal-meon, 18Jahaz, Kedemoth, Mephaath,[b] 19Kiriathaim, Sibmah,
Zereth-shahar on the hill in the valley,[c]
20Beth-peor, the slopes of Pisgah, and
Beth-jeshimoth — 21all the cities of the
plateau, and all the kingdom of Sihon
king of the Amorites, who reigned in
Heshbon. Moses had killed him and the
chiefs of Midian — Evi, Rekem, Zur, Hur,
and Reba — the princes of Sihon who
lived in the land.[d] 22Along with those the
Israelites put to death, they also killed
the diviner, Balaam son of Beor, with the
sword.

23The border of the Reubenites was the Jordan and its plain. This was the inheritance of
the Reubenites by their clans, with the cities
and their villages.

Gad's Inheritance

24To the tribe of the Gadites by their clans,
Moses gave 25this as their territory:

Jazer and all the cities of Gilead, and half
the land of the Ammonites to Aroer, near
Rabbah; 26from Heshbon to Ramath-miz-
peh and Betonim, and from Mahanaim
to the border of Debir;[B] 27in the valley:[C]
Beth-haram, Beth-nimrah, Succoth, and
Zaphon — the rest of the kingdom of Sihon king of Heshbon. Their land also included the Jordan and its territory as far
as the edge of the Sea of Chinnereth[D] on
the east side of the Jordan.[E]

28This was the inheritance of the Gadites
by their clans, with the cities and their villages.

[a]13:14 Nm 18:20; Dt 10:9; 18:1-2; Jos 13:33; 14:3-4; 18:7; 21:1-42
[b]13:18 Nm 21:23
[c]13:19 Nm 32:37
[d]13:21 Nm 31:8
[e]13:30 Nm 32:41
[f]13:33 Dt 18:1-2; Jos 13:14
[g]14:1 Nm 34:17-18
[h]Jos 19:51
[i]14:2 Nm 33:54; 34:13
[j]14:5 Nm 35:1-2; Jos 21:2
[k]14:6 Nm 14:24,30
[l]14:7 Nm 13:1-29

East Manasseh's Inheritance

29And to half the tribe of Manasseh, that is,
to half the tribe of Manasseh's descendants
by their clans, Moses gave 30this as their territory:

From Mahanaim through all Bashan
— all the kingdom of Og king of Bashan, including all of Jair's Villages[F,e]
that are in Bashan — 60 cities. 31But half
of Gilead, and Og's royal cities in Bashan — Ashtaroth and Edrei — are for
the descendants of Machir son of Manasseh, that is, half the descendants of
Machir by their clans.

32These were the portions Moses gave them
on the plains of Moab beyond the Jordan east
of Jericho. 33But Moses did not give a portion
to the tribe of Levi. The LORD, the God of Israel, was their inheritance, just as He had
promised them.[f]

Israel's Inheritance in Canaan

14 The Israelites received these portions
that Eleazar the priest,[g] Joshua son of
Nun, and the heads of the families of the Israelite tribes gave them in the land of Canaan.[h]
2Their inheritance was by lot[i] as the LORD
commanded through Moses for the nine and
a half tribes, 3because Moses had given the
inheritance to the two and a half tribes beyond the Jordan.[G] But he gave no inheritance
among them to the Levites. 4The descendants
of Joseph became two tribes, Manasseh and
Ephraim. No portion of the land was given to
the Levites except cities to live in, along with
pasturelands for their cattle and livestock.
5So the Israelites did as the LORD commanded
Moses,[j] and they divided the land.

Caleb's Inheritance

6The descendants of Judah approached
Joshua at Gilgal, and Caleb son of Jephunneh
the Kenizzite said to him, "You know what
the LORD promised Moses the man of God at
Kadesh-barnea about you and me.[k] 7I was 40
years old when Moses the LORD's servant sent
me from Kadesh-barnea to scout the land,
and I brought back an honest report.[l] 8My

[A]13:16 Some Hb mss read *plateau near* [B]13:26 Or *Lidbir*, or *Lo-debar* [C]13:27 = the Jordan River Valley [D]13:27 = the Sea of Galilee [E]13:27 Lit *Chinnereth beyond the Jordan to the east* [F]13:30 Or *all of Havvoth-jair* [G]14:3 = east of the Jordan River brothers who went with me caused the people's hearts to melt with fear, but I remained loyal to the LORD my God.[a] 9 On that day Moses promised me: 'The land where you have set foot will be an inheritance for you and your descendants forever, because you have remained loyal to the LORD my God.'[b]

10 "As you see, the LORD has kept me alive these 45 years as He promised,[c] since the LORD spoke this word to Moses while Israel was journeying in the wilderness. Here I am today, 85 years old. 11 I am still as strong today as I was the day Moses sent me out. My strength for battle and for daily tasks[A] is now as it was then.[d] 12 Now give me this hill country the LORD promised me on that day, because you heard then that the Anakim are there, as well as large fortified cities.[e] Perhaps the LORD will be with me and I will drive them out as the LORD promised."

13 Then Joshua blessed Caleb son of Jephunneh and gave him Hebron as an inheritance.[f] 14 Therefore, Hebron belongs to Caleb son of Jephunneh the Kenizzite as an inheritance to this day,[g] because he remained loyal to the LORD, the God of Israel. 15 Hebron's name used to be Kiriath-arba; Arba was the greatest man among the Anakim.[h] After this, the land had rest from war.

Judah's Inheritance

15 Now the allotment for the tribe of the descendants of Judah by their clans[i] was in the southernmost region, south to the Wilderness of Zin and over to the border of Edom.

2 Their southern border began at the tip
of the Dead Sea on the south bay[B] 3 and
went south of the Ascent of Akrabbim,[C]
proceeded to Zin, ascended to the south
of Kadesh-barnea, passed Hezron, ascended to Addar, and turned to Karka.
4 It proceeded to Azmon and to the Brook
of Egypt and so the border ended at the
Mediterranean Sea. This is your[D] southern border.

5 Now the eastern border was along the
Dead Sea to the mouth of the Jordan.[E]

The border on the north side was from the bay of the sea at the mouth of the Jordan. 6 It ascended to Beth-hoglah, proceeded north of Beth-arabah, and ascended to the Stone of Bohan son of Reuben. 7 Then the border ascended to Debir from the Valley of Achor, turning north to the Gilgal that is opposite the Ascent of Adummim, which is south of the ravine. The border proceeded to the waters of En-shemesh and ended at En-rogel. 8 From there the border ascended the Valley of Hinnom to the southern Jebusite slope (that is, Jerusalem) and ascended to the top of the hill that faces the Valley of Hinnom on the west, at the northern end of the Valley of Rephaim. 9 From the top of the hill the border curved to the spring of the Waters of Nephtoah, went to the cities of Mount Ephron, and then curved to Baalah (that is, Kiriath-jearim[j]). 10 The border turned westward from Baalah to Mount Seir, went to the northern slope of Mount Jearim (that is, Chesalon), descended to Beth-shemesh, and proceeded to Timnah.[k] 11 Then the border reached to the slope north of Ekron, curved to Shikkeron, proceeded to Mount Baalah, went to Jabneel, and ended at the Mediterranean Sea.

12 Now the western border was the coastline of the Mediterranean Sea.

This was the boundary of the descendants of Judah around their clans.

Caleb and Othniel

13 He gave Caleb son of Jephunneh the following portion among the descendants of Judah based on the LORD's instruction to Joshua: Kiriath-arba (that is, Hebron; Arba was the father of Anak). 14 Caleb drove out from there the three sons of Anak: Sheshai, Ahiman, and Talmai, descendants of Anak. 15 From there he marched against the inhabitants of Debir whose name used to be Kiriath-sepher,[l] 16 and Caleb said, "I will give my daughter Achsah as a wife to the one who strikes down and captures Kiriath-sepher."

[a] **14:8** Nm 13:30–14:3
[b] **14:9** Dt 1:36
[c] **14:10** Nm 14:30; 26:65; 32:12
[d] **14:11** Dt 34:7
[e] **14:12** Nm 13:28
[f] **14:13-15** Jos 15:13; Jdg 1:10,20
[g] **14:14** Jos 6:25
[h] **14:15** Nm 13:33
[i] **15:1** Nm 34:3
[j] **15:9** 1Ch 13:6
[k] **15:10** Gn 38:13; Jdg 14:1
[l] **15:15-19** Jdg 1:11-15

[A] **14:11** Lit *for going out and coming in* [B] **15:2** Lit *Sea at the tongue that turns southward* [C] **15:3** Lit *of scorpions* [D] **15:4** LXX reads *their* [E] **15:5** = the southern end of the Jordan River at the Dead Sea

17 So Othniel[a] son of Caleb's brother, Kenaz,
captured it, and Caleb gave his daughter Achsah to him as a wife.[b] 18 When she arrived,
she persuaded Othniel to ask her father for
a field. As she got off her donkey, Caleb asked
her, "What do you want?" 19 She replied, "Give
me a blessing. Since you have given me land in
the ·Negev, give me the springs of water also."
So he gave her the upper and lower springs.

Judah's Cities

20 This was the inheritance of the tribe of
the descendants of Judah by their clans.

21 These were the outermost cities of the
tribe of the descendants of Judah toward the border of Edom in the Negev:
Kabzeel, Eder, Jagur,[c] 22 Kinah, Dimonah,
Adadah, 23 Kedesh, Hazor, Ithnan, 24 Ziph,
Telem, Bealoth, 25 Hazor-hadattah, Ke-
rioth-hezron (that is, Hazor), 26 Amam,
Shema, Moladah, 27 Hazar-gaddah, Hesh-
mon, Beth-pelet, 28 Hazar-shual, Beer-
sheba, Biziothiah,[d] 29 Baalah, Iim, Ezem,
30 Eltolad, Chesil, Hormah, 31 Ziklag, Madmannah, Sansannah,[e] 32 Lebaoth, Shil-
him, Ain, and Rimmon — 29 cities in all,
with their villages.

33 In the Judean foothills:[A] Eshtaol, Zo-
rah, Ashnah, 34 Zanoah, En-gannim,
Tappuah,[B] Enam, 35 Jarmuth, Adullam,[f]
Socoh,[C] Azekah, 36 Shaaraim, Adithaim,
Gederah, and Gederothaim — 14 cities,
with their villages; 37 Zenan, Hadashah,
Migdal-gad, 38 Dilan, Mizpeh, Jokthe-el,
39 Lachish, Bozkath, Eglon, 40 Cabbon,
Lahmam, Chitlish, 41 Gederoth, Beth-
dagon, Naamah, and Makkedah — 16 cities, with their villages; 42 Libnah, Ether,
Ashan, 43 Iphtah, Ashnah, Nezib, 44 Keilah,
Achzib, and Mareshah — nine cities,
with their villages; 45 Ekron, with its
towns and villages; 46 from Ekron to the
sea, all the cities near Ashdod, with their
villages; 47 Ashdod, with its towns and villages; Gaza, with its towns and villages,
to the Brook of Egypt and the coastline
of the Mediterranean Sea.

48 In the hill country: Shamir, Jattir, Socoh, 49 Dannah, Kiriath-sannah (that is,
Debir), 50 Anab, Eshtemoh, Anim, 51 Goshen, Holon, and Giloh — 11 cities, with
their villages; 52 Arab, Dumah,[D] Eshan,
53 Janim, Beth-tappuah, Aphekah, 54 Hum-
tah, Kiriath-arba (that is, Hebron), and
Zior — nine cities, with their villages;
55 Maon, Carmel, Ziph, Juttah, 56 Jezreel,
Jokdeam, Zanoah, 57 Kain, Gibeah, and
Timnah — 10 cities, with their villages;
58 Halhul, Beth-zur, Gedor, 59 Maarath,
Beth-anoth, and Eltekon — six cities,
with their villages;[E] 60 Kiriath-baal (that
is, Kiriath-jearim), and Rabbah — two
cities, with their villages.

61 In the wilderness: Beth-arabah, Mid-
din, Secacah, 62 Nibshan, the City of Salt,[F]
and En-gedi — six cities, with their villages.

63 But the descendants of Judah could not
drive out the Jebusites who lived in Jerusalem.[g] So the Jebusites live in Jerusalem among
the descendants of Judah to this day.[h]

Joseph's Inheritance

16 The allotment for the descendants
of Joseph[G] went from the Jordan at
Jericho to the waters of Jericho on the
east, through the wilderness[i] ascending from Jericho into the hill country of
Bethel. 2 From Bethel it went to Luz and
proceeded to the border of the Archites
by Ataroth.[j] 3 It then descended westward
to the border of the Japhletites as far as
the border of lower Beth-horon, then to
Gezer,[k] and ended at the Mediterranean
Sea. 4 So Ephraim and Manasseh, the sons
of Joseph,[l] received their inheritance.[m]

Ephraim's Inheritance

5 This was the territory of the descendants
of Ephraim by their clans:
The border of their inheritance went
from Ataroth-addar[n] on the east of Upper Beth-horon. 6 In the north the border went westward from Michmethath;[o]

[a] 15:17 Jdg 3:8-11 [b] 1Sm 17:25 [c] 15:21 Gn 35:21 [d] 15:28 Gn 21:31 [e] 15:31 1Sm 27:6; 30:1 [f] 15:35 1Sm 22:1 [g] 15:63 Jdg 1:21; 2Sm 5:5-9 [h] Jos 6:25; 16:10; 22:17; 23:8-9 [i] 16:1 Jos 8:15; 18:12 [j] 16:2 Jos 18:13 [k] 16:3 Jos 10:33 [l] 16:4 Jos 17:14 [m] Gn 48:5-20 [n] 16:5 Jos 18:13 [o] 16:6 Jos 17:7

A 15:33 Or *the Shephelah* B 15:34 Or *En-gannim-tappuah* C 15:35 Or *Adullam-socoh* D 15:52 Some Hb mss read *Rumah* E 15:59 LXX adds *Tekoa, Ephrathah (that is, Bethlehem), Peor, Etam, Culom, Tatam, Sores, Carem, Gallim, Baither, and Manach — 11 cities, with their villages* F 15:62 Or *Ir-hamelach* G 16:1 = the tribes of Ephraim and Manasseh

it turned eastward from Taanath-shiloh and passed it east of Janoah. 7From Janoah it descended to Ataroth and Naarah,[a] and then reached Jericho and went to the Jordan. 8From Tappuah the border[A] went westward along the Brook of Kanah and ended at the Mediterranean Sea.[b]

This was the inheritance of the tribe of the descendants of Ephraim by their clans, together with 9the cities set apart for the descendants of Ephraim within the inheritance of the descendants of Manasseh—all these cities with their villages. 10But, they did not drive out the Canaanites who lived in Gezer.[c] So the Canaanites live in Ephraim to this day,[d] but they are forced laborers.

West Manasseh's Inheritance

17 This was the allotment for the tribe of Manasseh[e] as Joseph's firstborn. Gilead and Bashan came to Machir, the firstborn of Manasseh and the father of Gilead, who was a man of war.[f] 2So the allotment was for the rest of Manasseh's descendants by their clans, for the sons of Abiezer, Helek, Asriel, Shechem, Hepher, and Shemida. These are the male descendants of Manasseh son of Joseph, by their clans.

3Now Zelophehad son of Hepher, son of Gilead, son of Machir, son of Manasseh, had no sons, only daughters. These are the names of his daughters: Mahlah, Noah, Hoglah, Milcah, and Tirzah.[g] 4They came before Eleazar the priest, Joshua son of Nun, and the leaders, saying, "The LORD commanded Moses to give us an inheritance among our male relatives."[B] So they gave them an inheritance among their father's brothers, in keeping with the LORD's instruction.[h] 5As a result, 10 tracts fell to Manasseh, besides the land of Gilead and Bashan, which are beyond the Jordan,[C] 6because Manasseh's daughters received an inheritance among his sons. The land of Gilead belonged to the rest of Manasseh's sons.

7The border of Manasseh went from Asher to Michmethath near Shechem. It then went southward toward the inhabitants of En-tappuah. 8The region of Tappuah belonged to Manasseh, but Tappuah itself on Manasseh's border[i] belonged to the descendants of Ephraim. 9From there the border descended to the Brook of Kanah; south of the brook, cities belonged to Ephraim among Manasseh's cities. Manasseh's border was on the north side of the brook and ended at the Mediterranean Sea. 10Ephraim's territory was to the south and Manasseh's to the north, with the Sea as its border. They[D] reached Asher on the north and Issachar on the east. 11Within Issachar and Asher, Manasseh had Beth-shean with its towns, Ibleam with its towns, and the inhabitants of Dor with its towns;[j] the inhabitants of En-dor with its towns, the inhabitants of Taanach with its towns, and the inhabitants of Megiddo with its towns—the three cities of[E] Naphath.[k]

12The descendants of Manasseh could not possess these cities, because the Canaanites were determined to stay in this land. 13However, when the Israelites grew stronger, they imposed forced labor on the Canaanites but did not drive them out completely.[l]

Joseph's Additional Inheritance

14Joseph's descendants said to Joshua, "Why did you give us only one tribal allotment[F] as an inheritance? We have many people, because the LORD has been blessing us greatly."

15"If you have so many people," Joshua replied to them, "go to the forest and clear an area for yourselves there in the land of the Perizzites and the Rephaim, because Ephraim's hill country is too small for you."

16But the descendants of Joseph said, "The hill country is not enough for us, and all the Canaanites who inhabit the valley area have iron chariots, both at Beth-shean with its towns and in the Jezreel Valley."

17So Joshua replied to Joseph's family (that is, Ephraim and Manasseh), "You have many people and great strength. You will not have just one allotment, 18because the hill country will be yours also. It is a forest; clear it and

[a]16:7 1Ch 7:28 [b]16:8 Jos 17:8 [c]16:10 Jdg 1:29; 1Kg 9:16 [d]Jos 6:25 [e]17:1 Gn 41:51; 46:20; 48:18 [f]1Ch 28:3 [g]17:3 Nm 26:33 [h]17:4 Nm 27:1-11 [i]17:8 Jos 16:8-9 [j]17:11 1Ch 7:29 [k]Jos 11:2; 12:23 [l]17:13 Jdg 1:27-28

[A]16:8 Ephraim's northern border [B]17:4 Lit *our brothers* [C]17:5 = east of the Jordan River [D]17:10 The people of Manasseh, or Manasseh's borders [E]17:11 LXX, Vg read *the third is* [F]17:14-17 Lit *one lot and one territory*

its outlying areas will be yours. You can also drive out the Canaanites, even though they have iron chariots and are strong."

Land Distribution at Shiloh

18 The entire Israelite community assembled at Shiloh[a] where it set up the tent of meeting there; the land had been subdued by them. 2 Seven tribes among the Israelites were left who had not divided up their inheritance. 3 So Joshua said to the Israelites, "How long will you delay going out to take possession of the land that the LORD, the God of your fathers, gave you?[b] 4 Appoint for yourselves three men from each tribe, and I will send them out. They are to go and survey the land, write a description of it for the purpose of their inheritance, and return to me. 5 Then they are to divide it into seven portions. Judah is to remain in its territory in the south and Joseph's family in their[A] territory in the north.[c] 6 When you have written a description of the seven portions of land and brought it to me, I will cast lots for you here in the presence of the LORD our God.[d] 7 But the Levites among you do not get a portion, because their inheritance is the priesthood of the LORD.[e] Gad, Reuben, and half the tribe of Manasseh have taken their inheritance beyond the Jordan to the east, which Moses the LORD's servant gave them."

8 As the men prepared to go, Joshua commanded them[B] to write down a description of the land, saying, "Go and survey the land, write a description of it, and return to me. I will then cast lots for you here in Shiloh in the presence of the LORD." 9 So the men left, went through the land, and described it by towns in a document of seven sections. They returned to Joshua at the camp in Shiloh. 10 Joshua cast lots for them at Shiloh in the presence of the LORD where he distributed the land to the Israelites according to their divisions.

Benjamin's Inheritance

11 The lot came up for the tribe of Benjamin's descendants by their clans, and their allotted territory lay between Judah's descendants and Joseph's descendants.

[a] **18:1** Jos 19:51; Jdg 18:31; 1Sm 1:9; 3:3
[b] **18:3** Jdg 18:9
[c] **18:5** Jos 15:1
[d] **18:6** Jos 14:2
[e] **18:7** Jos 13:33
[f] **18:12** Jos 16:1
[g] **18:13** Jos 16:3
[h] **18:17** Jos 15:6

12 Their border on the north side began at the Jordan, ascended to the slope of Jericho on the north, through the hill country westward, and ended at the wilderness of Beth-aven.[f] 13 From there the border went toward Luz, to the southern slope of Luz (that is, Bethel); it then went down by Ataroth-addar, over the hill south of Lower Beth-horon.[g]

14 On the west side, from the hill facing Beth-horon on the south, the border curved, turning southward, and ended at Kiriath-baal (that is, Kiriath-jearim), a city of the descendants of Judah. This was the west side of their border.

15 The south side began at the edge of Kiriath-jearim, and the border extended westward; it went to the spring at the Waters of Nephtoah. 16 The border descended to the foot of the hill that faces the Valley of Hinnom at the northern end of the Valley of Rephaim. It ran down the Valley of Hinnom toward the south Jebusite slope and downward to En-rogel. 17 It curved northward and went to En-shemesh and on to Geliloth, which is opposite the Ascent of Adummim, and continued down to the Stone of Bohan[h] son of Reuben. 18 Then it went north to the slope opposite the Jordan Valley[C,D] and proceeded into the valley.[D] 19 The border continued to the north slope of Beth-hoglah and ended at the northern bay of the Dead Sea, at the southern end of the Jordan. This was the southern border.

20 The Jordan formed the border on the east side.

This was the inheritance of Benjamin's descendants, by their clans, according to its surrounding borders.

Benjamin's Cities

21 These were the cities of the tribe of Benjamin's descendants by their clans:

Jericho, Beth-hoglah, Emek-keziz, 22 Beth-arabah, Zemaraim, Bethel, 23 Avvim,

[A] **18:5** = the tribes of Ephraim and Manasseh [B] **18:8** Lit *the ones going around* [C] **18:18** LXX reads *went northward to Beth-arabah* [D] **18:18** Or *the Arabah*

Parah, Ophrah, 24 Chephar-ammoni, Ophni, and Geba — 12 cities, with their villages; 25 Gibeon, Ramah, Beeroth, 26 Mizpeh,[A] Chephirah, Mozah, 27 Rekem, Irpeel, Taralah, 28 Zela, Haeleph, Jebus[B] (that is, Jerusalem), Gibeah, and Kiriath[C] — 14 cities, with their villages.

This was the inheritance for Benjamin's descendants by their clans.

Simeon's Inheritance

19 The second lot came out for Simeon, for the tribe of his descendants by their clans, but their inheritance was within the portion of Judah's descendants. 2 Their inheritance included:

Beer-sheba (or Sheba[a]), Moladah, 3 Hazar-shual, Balah, Ezem, 4 Eltolad, Bethul, Hormah, 5 Ziklag, Beth-marcaboth, Hazar-susah, 6 Beth-lebaoth, and Sharuhen — 13 cities, with their villages; 7 Ain, Rimmon, Ether, and Ashan — four cities, with their villages; 8 and all the villages surrounding these cities as far as Baalath-beer (Ramah of the south[D]).

This was the inheritance of the tribe of Simeon's descendants by their clans. 9 The inheritance of Simeon's descendants was within the territory of Judah's descendants, because the share for Judah's descendants was too large for them. So Simeon's descendants received an inheritance within Judah's portion.

Zebulun's Inheritance

10 The third lot came up for Zebulun's descendants by their clans.

The territory of their inheritance stretched as far as Sarid; 11 their border went up westward to Maralah, reached Dabbesheth, and met the brook east of Jokneam. 12 From Sarid, it turned east toward the sunrise along the border of Chisloth-tabor, went to Daberath, and went up to Japhia. 13 From there, it went east toward the sunrise to Gath-hepher and to Eth-kazin; it extended to Rimmon, curving around to Neah. 14 The border then circled around Neah on the north to Hannathon and ended at the Valley of Iphtah-el, 15 along with Kattath, Nahalal, Shimron, Idalah, and Bethlehem — 12 cities, with their villages.

16 This was the inheritance of Zebulun's descendants by their clans, these cities, with their villages.

Issachar's Inheritance

17 The fourth lot came out for the tribe of Issachar's descendants by their clans.

18 Their territory went to Jezreel, and included Chesulloth, Shunem,[b] 19 Hapharaim, Shion, Anaharath, 20 Rabbith, Kishion, Ebez, 21 Remeth, En-gannim, En-haddah, Beth-pazzez. 22 The border reached Tabor, Shahazumah, and Beth-shemesh, and ended at the Jordan — 16 cities, with their villages.

23 This was the inheritance of the tribe of Issachar's descendants by their clans, the cities, with their villages.

Asher's Inheritance

24 The fifth lot came out for the tribe of Asher's descendants by their clans.

25 Their boundary included Helkath, Hali, Beten, Achshaph, 26 Allammelech, Amad, and Mishal and reached westward to Carmel and Shihor-libnath. 27 It turned eastward to Beth-dagon, passed Zebulun and the Valley of Iphtah-el, north toward Beth-emek and Neiel, and went north to Cabul,[c] 28 Ebron, Rehob, Hammon, and Kanah, as far as Great Sidon. 29 The boundary then turned to Ramah as far as the fortified city of Tyre; it turned back to Hosah and ended at the sea, including Mahalab, Achzib,[E] 30 Ummah, Aphek, and Rehob — 22 cities, with their villages.

31 This was the inheritance of the tribe of Asher's descendants by their clans, these cities with their villages.

Naphtali's Inheritance

32 The sixth lot came out for Naphtali's descendants by their clans.

[a] **19:2** 1Ch 4:28
[b] **19:18** 1Sm 28:4
[c] **19:27** 1Kg 9:13

[A] **18:26** = Mizpah; Jos 11:3,8 [B] **18:28** Lit *Jebusite* [C] **18:28** LXX, Syr read *Kiriath-jearim* [D] **19:8** Or *the Negev* [E] **19:29** Or *sea, in the region of Achzib*

33 Their boundary went from Heleph and
from the oak in Zaanannim, including
Adami-nekeb and Jabneel, as far as Lak-
kum, and ended at the Jordan. 34 To the
west, the boundary turned to Aznoth-
tabor and went from there to Hukkok,
reaching Zebulun on the south, Asher on
the west, and Judah[A] at the Jordan on the
east. 35 The fortified cities were Ziddim,
Zer, Hammath, Rakkath, Chinnereth,[B]
36 Adamah, Ramah, Hazor, 37 Kedesh,
Edrei, En-hazor, 38 Iron, Migdal-el, Ho-
rem, Beth-anath, and Beth-shemesh
— 19 cities, with their villages.

39 This was the inheritance of the tribe of
Naphtali's descendants by their clans, the cities with their villages.

Dan's Inheritance

40 The seventh lot came out for the Danite
tribe by its clans.

41 The territory of their inheritance included Zorah, Eshtaol, Ir-shemesh,
42 Shaalabbin, Aijalon, Ithlah, 43 Elon,
Timnah, Ekron, 44 Eltekeh, Gibbethon,
Baalath, 45 Jehud, Bene-berak, Gath-rimmon, 46 Me-jarkon, and Rakkon, with the
territory facing Joppa.

47 When the territory of the Danites slipped
out of their control,[C] they went up and fought
against Leshem, captured it, and struck it
down with the sword. So they took possession
of it, lived there, and renamed Leshem after[D]
their ancestor Dan. 48 This was the inheritance of the Danite tribe by its clans, these
cities with their villages.

Joshua's Inheritance

49 When they had finished distributing the
land into its territories, the Israelites gave
Joshua son of Nun an inheritance among
them. 50 By the LORD's command, they gave
him the city Timnath-serah in the hill country of Ephraim,[a] which he requested. He rebuilt the city and lived in it.

51 These were the portions that Eleazar the
priest, Joshua son of Nun, and the heads of
the families distributed to the Israelite tribes
by lot at Shiloh in the LORD's presence at the
entrance to the tent of meeting.[b] So they finished dividing up the land.

Cities of Refuge

20 Then the LORD spoke to Joshua, 2 "Tell
the Israelites: Select your cities of
refuge, as I instructed you through Moses,[c]
3 so that a person who kills someone unintentionally or accidentally may flee there.
These will be your refuge from the avenger
of blood.[d] 4 When someone flees to one of
these cities, stands at the entrance of the city
·gate, and states his case before[E] the elders of
that city, they are to bring him into the city
and give him a place to live among them.[e]
5 And if the avenger of blood pursues him,
they must not hand the one who committed
manslaughter over to him, for he killed his
neighbor accidentally and did not hate him
beforehand. 6 He is to stay in that city until he
stands trial before the assembly and until the
death of the high priest serving at that time.[f]
Then the one who committed manslaughter
may return home to his own city from which
he fled."

7 So they designated Kedesh in the hill
country of Naphtali in Galilee,[g] Shechem in
the hill country of Ephraim, and Kiriath-arba
(that is, Hebron) in the hill country of Judah.[h]
8 Across the Jordan east of Jericho, they selected Bezer on the wilderness plateau from
Reuben's tribe, Ramoth in Gilead from Gad's
tribe, and Golan in Bashan from Manasseh's
tribe.

9 These are the cities appointed for all the
Israelites and foreigners among them,[i] so
that anyone who kills a person unintentionally may flee there and not die at the hand of
the avenger of blood until he stands before
the assembly.

Cities of the Levites

21 The heads of the Levite families approached Eleazar the priest, Joshua
son of Nun, and the heads of the families of
the Israelite tribes. 2 At Shiloh, in the land
of Canaan, they told them, "The LORD commanded through Moses that we be given

[a] **19:50** Jos 24:30
[b] **19:51** Jos 14:1
[c] **20:2** Nm 35:6-34; Dt 4:41-43; 19:1-13
[d] **20:3** Nm 5:5-8; Dt 19:6
[e] **20:4** Ru 4:1
[f] **20:6** Nm 35:12; Dt 21:1-9
[g] **20:7** 1Ch 6:76
[h] Jos 21:11; Lk 1:39
[i] **20:9** Nm 35:15

[A] **19:34** LXX omits *Judah* [B] **19:35** A town near the Sea of Galilee [C] **19:47** Lit *territory of the sons of Dan went out from them* [D] **19:47** Lit *and called Leshem, Dan, after the name of* [E] **20:4** Lit *in the ears of*

cities to live in, with their pasturelands for our livestock."[a] 3So the Israelites, by the LORD's command, gave the Levites these cities with their pasturelands from their inheritance.

4The lot came out for the Kohathite clans: The Levites who were the descendants of Aaron the priest received 13 cities by lot from the tribes of Judah, Simeon, and Benjamin. 5The remaining descendants of Kohath[A] received 10 cities by lot from the clans of the tribes of Ephraim, Dan, and half the tribe of Manasseh.

6Gershon's descendants received 13 cities by lot from the clans of the tribes of Issachar, Asher, Naphtali, and half the tribe of Manasseh in Bashan.

7Merari's descendants received 12 cities for their clans from the tribes of Reuben, Gad, and Zebulun.

8The Israelites gave these cities with their pasturelands around them to the Levites by lot, as the LORD had commanded through Moses.

Cities of Aaron's Descendants

9The Israelites gave these cities by name from the tribes of the descendants of Judah and Simeon 10to the descendants of Aaron from the Kohathite clans of the Levites, because they received the first lot. 11They gave them Kiriath-arba[b] (that is, Hebron) with its surrounding pasturelands in the hill country of Judah. Arba was the father of Anak. 12But they gave the fields and villages of the city to Caleb son of Jephunneh as his possession.

13They gave to the descendants of Aaron the priest:

Hebron, the city of refuge for the one who commits manslaughter, with its pasturelands, Libnah with its pasturelands, 14Jattir with its pasturelands, Eshtemoa with its pasturelands, 15Holon with its pasturelands, Debir with its pasturelands, 16Ain with its pasturelands, Juttah with its pasturelands, and Beth-shemesh with its pasturelands — nine cities from these two tribes.

[a]21:2 Nm 35:4-5
[b]21:11 1Ch 6:55
[c]21:21 Jos 20:7
[d]21:27 1Ch 6:71

17From the tribe of Benjamin they gave:

Gibeon with its pasturelands, Geba with its pasturelands, 18Anathoth with its pasturelands, and Almon with its pasturelands — four cities. 19All 13 cities with their pasturelands were for the priests, the descendants of Aaron.

Cities of Kohath's Other Descendants

20The allotted cities to the remaining clans of Kohath's descendants, who were Levites, came from the tribe of Ephraim. 21The Israelites gave them:

Shechem,[c] the city of refuge for the one who commits manslaughter, with its pasturelands in the hill country of Ephraim, Gezer with its pasturelands, 22Kibzaim with its pasturelands, and Beth-horon with its pasturelands — four cities.

23From the tribe of Dan they gave:

Elteke with its pasturelands, Gibbethon with its pasturelands, 24Aijalon with its pasturelands, and Gath-rimmon with its pasturelands — four cities.

25From half the tribe of Manasseh they gave:

Taanach with its pasturelands and Gath-rimmon[B] with its pasturelands — two cities.

26All 10 cities with their pasturelands were for the clans of Kohath's other descendants.

Cities of Gershon's Descendants

27From half the tribe of Manasseh, they gave to the descendants of Gershon,[d] who were one of the Levite clans:

Golan, the city of refuge for the one who commits manslaughter, with its pasturelands in Bashan, and Beeshterah with its pasturelands — two cities.

28From the tribe of Issachar they gave:

Kishion with its pasturelands, Daberath with its pasturelands, 29Jarmuth with its pasturelands, and En-gannim with its pasturelands — four cities.

[A]21:5 Descendants not in Aaron's priestly line [B]21:25 Or *Ibleam*

30 From the tribe of Asher they gave:

Mishal with its pasturelands, Abdon
with its pasturelands, 31 Helkath with its
pasturelands, and Rehob with its pasturelands — four cities.

32 From the tribe of Naphtali they gave:

Kedesh in Galilee, the city of refuge for
the one who commits manslaughter,
with its pasturelands, Hammoth-dor
with its pasturelands, and Kartan with
its pasturelands — three cities.

33 All 13 cities with their pasturelands were for
the Gershonites by their clans.

Cities of Merari's Descendants

34 From the tribe of Zebulun, they gave to
the clans of the descendants of Merari,[a] who
were the remaining Levites:

Jokneam with its pasturelands, Kartah
with its pasturelands, 35 Dimnah with its
pasturelands, and Nahalal with its pasturelands — four cities.

36 From the tribe of Reuben they gave:

Bezer[b] with its pasturelands, Jahzah[A]
with its pasturelands, 37 Kedemoth with
its pasturelands, and Mephaath with its
pasturelands — four cities.[B]

38 From the tribe of Gad they gave:

Ramoth in Gilead, the city of refuge
for the one who commits manslaughter, with its pasturelands, Mahanaim
with its pasturelands, 39 Heshbon with
its pasturelands, and Jazer with its pasturelands — four cities in all. 40 All 12 cities were allotted to the clans of Merari's
descendants, the remaining Levite clans.

41 Within the Israelite possession there
were 48 cities in all with their pasturelands
for the Levites.[c] 42 Each of these cities had its
own surrounding pasturelands; this was true
for all the cities.

The LORD's Promises Fulfilled

43 So the LORD gave Israel all the land He
had sworn to give their fathers, and they took
possession of it and settled there. 44 The LORD
gave them rest on every side according to all
He had sworn to their fathers. None of their
enemies were able to stand against them, for
the LORD handed over all their enemies to
them. 45 None of the good promises the LORD
had made to the house of Israel failed. Everything was fulfilled.[d]

Eastern Tribes Return Home

22 Joshua summoned the Reubenites,
Gadites, and half the tribe of Manasseh 2 and told them, "You have done everything Moses the LORD's servant commanded
you[e] and have obeyed me in everything I commanded you. 3 You have not deserted your
brothers even once this whole time but have
carried out the requirement of the command
of the LORD your God. 4 Now that He has given
your brothers rest, just as He promised them,
return to your homes in your own land that
Moses the LORD's servant gave you across the
Jordan. 5 Only carefully obey the command
and instruction that Moses the LORD's servant gave you: to love the LORD your God,
walk in all His ways, keep His commands, remain faithful[C] to Him, and serve Him with all
your heart and all your soul."[f]
6 Joshua blessed them and sent them on
their way,[g] and they went to their homes.
7 Moses had given territory to half the tribe
of Manasseh in Bashan, but Joshua had given
territory to the other half,[D] with their brothers, on the west side of the Jordan.[h] When
Joshua sent them to their homes and blessed
them, 8 he said, "Return to your homes with
great wealth: a huge number of cattle, and
silver, gold, bronze, iron, and a large quantity
of clothing. Share the spoil of your enemies
with your brothers."[i]

Eastern Tribes Build an Altar

9 The Reubenites, Gadites, and half the tribe
of Manasseh left the Israelites at Shiloh in the
land of Canaan to return to their own land
of Gilead,[j] which they took possession of according to the LORD's command through Moses. 10 When they came to the region of[E] the
Jordan in the land of Canaan, the Reubenites,
Gadites, and half the tribe of Manasseh built
a large, impressive altar there by the Jordan.

[a] **21:34** 1Ch 6:77
[b] **21:36-38** Jos 20:8
[c] **21:41** Nm 35:7
[d] **21:45** Jos 23:14
[e] **22:2** Dt 3:18-20
[f] **22:5** Dt 6:5; 10:12-13; 11:13-17
[g] **22:6** Jos 14:13
[h] **22:7** Nm 32:33; Jos 17:5
[i] **22:8** Nm 31:27; 1Sm 30:24
[j] **22:9** Nm 32:1,26,29

[A] **21:36** Or *Jahaz* [B] **21:36-37** Some Hb mss omit these vv. [C] **22:5** Lit *commands, hold on* [D] **22:7** Lit *to his half* [E] **22:10** Or *to Geliloth by*

11 Then the Israelites heard it said, "Look,
the Reubenites, Gadites, and half the tribe of
Manasseh have built an altar on the frontier
of the land of Canaan at the region of[A] the
Jordan, on the Israelite side." 12 When the Israelites heard this, the entire Israelite community assembled at Shiloh to go to war against
them.[a]

Explanation of the Altar

13 The Israelites sent Phinehas son of Eleazar the priest to the Reubenites, Gadites, and
half the tribe of Manasseh, in the land of Gilead.[b] 14 They sent 10 leaders with him — one
family leader for each tribe of Israel. All of
them were heads of their families among the
clans of Israel.[c] 15 They went to the Reubenites,
Gadites, and half the tribe of Manasseh, in the
land of Gilead, and told them, 16 "This is what
the LORD's entire community says: 'What is
this treachery you have committed today
against the God of Israel by turning away
from the LORD and building an altar for yourselves, so that you are in rebellion against the
LORD today? 17 Wasn't the sin of Peor, which
brought a plague on the LORD's community,
enough for us, so that we have not cleansed
ourselves from it even to this day,[d] 18 and now,
you would turn away from the LORD? If you
rebel against the LORD today, tomorrow He
will be angry with the entire community of
Israel.[e] 19 But if the land you possess is defiled, cross over to the land the LORD possesses where the LORD's tabernacle stands,
and take possession of it among us. But don't
rebel against the LORD or against us by building for yourselves an altar other than the altar of the LORD our God. 20 Wasn't Achan son
of Zerah unfaithful regarding what was •set
apart for destruction, bringing wrath on the
entire community of Israel? He was not the
only one who perished because of his sin.'"[f]

21 The Reubenites, Gadites, and half the
tribe of Manasseh answered the leaders of
the Israelite clans, 22 "•Yahweh is the God of
gods! Yahweh is the God of gods![B] He knows,[g]
and may Israel also know. Do not spare us today, if it was in rebellion or treachery against
the LORD 23 that we have built for ourselves an
altar to turn away from Him. May the LORD
Himself hold us accountable if we intended
to offer •burnt offerings and •grain offerings
on it, or to sacrifice •fellowship offerings on
it. 24 We actually did this from a specific concern that in the future your descendants
might say to our descendants, 'What relationship do you have with the LORD, the God of
Israel? 25 For the LORD has made the Jordan
a border between us and you descendants of
Reuben and Gad. You have no share in the
LORD!' So your descendants may cause our
descendants to stop fearing the LORD.

26 "Therefore we said: Let us take action and
build an altar for ourselves, but not for burnt
offering or sacrifice. 27 Instead, it is to be a witness between us and you,[h] and between the
generations after us, so that we may carry
out the worship of the LORD in His presence
with our burnt offerings, sacrifices, and fellowship offerings.[i] Then in the future, your
descendants will not be able to say to our descendants, 'You have no share in the LORD!'
28 We thought that if they said this to us or
to our generations in the future, we would
reply: Look at the replica of the LORD's altar
that our fathers made, not for burnt offering or sacrifice, but as a witness between us
and you. 29 We would never rebel against the
LORD or turn away from Him today by building an altar for burnt offering, grain offering,
or sacrifice, other than the altar of the LORD
our God, which is in front of His tabernacle."

Conflict Resolved

30 When Phinehas the priest and the community leaders, the heads of Israel's clans
who were with him, heard what the descendants of Reuben, Gad, and Manasseh had to
say, they were pleased. 31 Phinehas son of Eleazar the priest said to the descendants of
Reuben, Gad, and Manasseh, "Today we know
that the LORD is among us, because you have
not committed this treachery against Him.[j]
As a result, you have delivered the Israelites
from the LORD's power."

32 Then Phinehas son of Eleazar the priest
and the leaders returned from the Reubenites
and Gadites in the land of Gilead to the Israelites in the land of Canaan and brought back a
report to them. 33 The Israelites were pleased

[a] **22:12** Lv 17:8-9; Dt 13:12-15
[b] **22:13** Nm 25:7
[c] **22:14** Nm 1:4,16
[d] **22:17** Jos 6:25
[e] **22:18** Nm 16:22
[f] **22:20** Jos 7:1-26
[g] **22:22** 1Kg 8:39
[h] **22:27** Gn 31:48; Jos 24:27
[i] Dt 12:6
[j] **22:31** Lv 26:11-12

[A] **22:11** Or *at Geliloth by* [B] **22:22** Or *The Mighty One, God, the LORD! The Mighty One, God, the LORD!*, or *God, the LORD God! God, the LORD God!*

with the report, and they praised God.[a] They
spoke no more about going to war against
them to ravage the land where the Reubenites
and Gadites lived. 34 So the Reubenites and
Gadites named the altar: It[A] is a witness between us that the LORD is God.

Joshua's Farewell Address

23 A long time after the LORD had given
Israel rest from all the enemies around
them, Joshua was old, getting on in years. 2 So
Joshua summoned all Israel, including its elders, leaders, judges, and officers,[b] and said
to them, "I am old, getting on in years, 3 and
you have seen for yourselves everything the
LORD your God did to all these nations on
your account, because it was the LORD your
God who was fighting for you.[c] 4 See, I have allotted these remaining nations to you as an
inheritance for your tribes, including all the
nations I have destroyed, from the Jordan
westward to the Mediterranean Sea. 5 The
LORD your God will force them back on your
account and drive them out before you so
that you can take possession of their land,[d] as
the LORD your God promised you.
6 "Be very strong[e] and continue obeying
all that is written in the book of the law of
Moses, so that you do not turn from it to the
right or left 7 and so that you do not associate
with these nations remaining among you. Do
not call on the names of their gods or make
an oath to them;[f] do not worship them or
bow down to them. 8 Instead, remain faithful to the LORD your God, as you have done
to this day.[g]
9 "The LORD has driven out great and powerful nations before you,[h] and no one is able
to stand against you to this day.[i] 10 One of you
routed a thousand[j] because the LORD your
God was fighting for you, as He promised.[B,k]
11 So be very diligent to love the LORD your
God for your own well-being. 12 For if you
turn away and cling to the rest of these nations remaining among you,[l] and if you intermarry or associate with them[m] and they with
you, 13 know for certain that the LORD your
God will not continue to drive these nations
out before you. They will become a snare and
a trap for you,[n] a scourge for your sides and
thorns in your eyes, until you disappear from
this good land the LORD your God has given
you.
14 "I am now going the way of all the earth,[C,o]
and you know with all your heart and all your
soul that none of the good promises the LORD
your God made to you has failed. Everything
was fulfilled for you; not one promise has
failed.[p] 15 Since every good thing the LORD
your God promised you has come about, so
He will bring on you every bad thing until
He has annihilated you from this good land
the LORD your God has given you.[q] 16 If you
break the covenant of the LORD your God,
which He commanded you, and go and worship other gods, and bow down to them, the
LORD's anger will burn against you, and you
will quickly disappear from this good land
He has given you."

Review of Israel's History

24 Joshua assembled all the tribes of Israel at Shechem[r] and summoned Israel's elders, leaders, judges, and officers,
and they presented themselves before God.[s]
2 Joshua said to all the people, "This is what
the LORD, the God of Israel, says: 'Long ago
your ancestors, including Terah,[t] the father
of Abraham and Nahor, lived beyond the
Euphrates River and worshiped other gods.
3 But I took your father Abraham from the
region beyond the Euphrates River, led him
throughout the land of Canaan, and multiplied his descendants.[u] I gave him Isaac,[v] 4 and
to Isaac I gave Jacob and Esau.[w] I gave the hill
country of Seir to Esau as a possession,[x] but
Jacob and his sons went down to Egypt.[y]
5 "'Then I sent Moses and Aaron;[z] I plagued
Egypt by what I did there and afterward I
brought you out. 6 When I brought your fathers out of Egypt and you reached the •Red
Sea,[aa] the Egyptians pursued your fathers
with chariots and horsemen as far as the sea.
7 Your fathers cried out to the LORD, so He put
darkness between you and the Egyptians, and
brought the sea over them, engulfing them.
Your own eyes saw what I did to Egypt. After
that, you lived in the wilderness a long time.
8 "'Later, I brought you to the land of the
Amorites who lived beyond the Jordan.[ab] They

[a] **22:33** 1Ch 29:20; Dn 2:19; Lk 2:28
[b] **23:2** Jos 24:1
[c] **23:3** Jos 10:14
[d] **23:5** Nm 33:53
[e] **23:6** Dt 5:32; Jos 1:7
[f] **23:7** Ex 23:13; Ps 16:4
[g] **23:8** Jos 6:25
[h] **23:9** Ex 23:30
[i] Jos 1:5
[j] **23:10** Jdg 15:15-16
[k] Lv 26:8
[l] **23:12** Ex 34:16
[m] Dt 7:3
[n] **23:13** Ex 23:33; Dt 7:16; Jdg 2:3
[o] **23:14** 1Kg 2:2
[p] Jos 21:45
[q] **23:15** Lv 26:14-33; Dt 28:15
[r] **24:1** Gn 12:1-7
[s] Jos 23:2
[t] **24:2** Gn 11:27-32
[u] **24:3** Gn 12:1
[v] Gn 21:3
[w] **24:4** Gn 25:25-26
[x] Gn 36:8; Dt 2:5
[y] Gn 46:6
[z] **24:5** Ex 4:14
[aa] **24:6** Ex 14:2
[ab] **24:8** Nm 21:21-32

[A] **22:34** Some Hb mss, Syr, Tg read *altar Witness because it* [B] **23:10** Lit *promised you* [C] **23:14** = I am going to die

fought against you, but I handed them over to
you. You possessed their land, and I annihilated them before you. 9 Balak son of Zippor,
king of Moab,[a] set out to fight against Israel.
He sent for Balaam son of Beor to curse you,
10 but I would not listen to Balaam. Instead, he
repeatedly blessed you, and I delivered you
from his hand.
11 "'You then crossed the Jordan and came
to Jericho.[b] The people of Jericho—as well as
the Amorites, Perizzites, Canaanites, Hittites,
Girgashites, Hivites, and Jebusites—fought
against you, but I handed them over to you.
12 I sent the hornet[A,c] ahead of you, and it
drove out the two Amorite kings[d] before you.
It was not by your sword or bow. 13 I gave you
a land you did not labor for, and cities you did
not build,[e] though you live in them; you are
eating from vineyards and olive groves you
did not plant.'

The Covenant Renewal

14 "Therefore, ˚fear the LORD and worship
Him in sincerity and truth.[f] Get rid of the
gods your fathers worshiped[g] beyond the
Euphrates River and in Egypt, and worship
˚Yahweh. 15 But if it doesn't please you to worship Yahweh, choose for yourselves today the
one you will worship: the gods your fathers
worshiped beyond the Euphrates River or the
gods of the Amorites in whose land you are
living.[h] As for me and my family, we will worship Yahweh."
16 The people replied, "We will certainly not
abandon the LORD to worship other gods!
17 For the LORD our God brought us and our
fathers out of the land of Egypt, out of the
place of slavery,[i] and performed these great
signs before our eyes. He also protected us all
along the way we went and among all the peoples whose lands we traveled through. 18 The
LORD drove out before us all the peoples, including the Amorites who lived in the land.
We too will worship the LORD, because He is
our God."
19 But Joshua told the people, "You will not
be able to worship Yahweh, because He is a
holy God. He is a jealous God;[j] He will not remove your transgressions and sins.[k] 20 If you
abandon the LORD and worship foreign gods,
He will turn against you, harm you, and completely destroy[l] you, after He has been good
to you."
21 "No!" the people answered Joshua. "We
will worship the LORD."
22 Joshua then told the people, "You are witnesses against yourselves that you yourselves
have chosen to worship Yahweh."
"We are witnesses," they said.
23 "Then get rid of the foreign gods that are
among you and offer your hearts to the LORD,
the God of Israel."
24 So the people said to Joshua, "We will
worship the LORD our God and obey Him."
25 On that day Joshua made a covenant for
the people at Shechem and established a
statute and ordinance for them. 26 Joshua recorded these things in the book of the law
of God;[m] he also took a large stone and set it
up there under the oak next to the sanctuary of the LORD. 27 And Joshua said to all the
people, "You see this stone—it will be a witness against us,[n] for it has heard all the words
the LORD said to us, and it will be a witness
against you, so that you will not deny your
God." 28 Then Joshua sent the people away,
each to his own inheritance.

Burial of Three Leaders

29 After these things, the LORD's servant,
Joshua son of Nun, died at the age of 110.
30 They buried him in his allotted territory
at Timnath-serah, in the hill country of
Ephraim[o] north of Mount Gaash. 31 Israel worshiped Yahweh throughout Joshua's lifetime
and during the lifetimes of the elders who
outlived Joshua[p] and who had experienced
all the works Yahweh had done for Israel.
32 Joseph's bones, which the Israelites had
brought up from Egypt,[q] were buried at
Shechem in the parcel of land Jacob had purchased from the sons of Hamor, Shechem's
father, for 100 *qesitahs*.[B,r] It was an inheritance for Joseph's descendants.
33 And Eleazar son of Aaron died, and they
buried him at Gibeah,[C] which had been given
to his son Phinehas[s] in the hill country of
Ephraim.

[a] **24:9** Nm 22:5
[b] **24:11** Jos 3:14,17
[c] **24:12** Ex 23:27-28; Dt 7:20
[d] Nm 21:21-35; Dt 2:26–3:11; 29:7
[e] **24:13** Dt 6:10-11
[f] **24:14** Dt 10:12; 1Sm 12:24
[g] Gn 35:4
[h] **24:15** Jdg 6:10
[i] **24:17** Lv 26:13; Dt 5:6; 6:12; 8:14; 13:5,10; Jr 34:13
[j] **24:19** Lv 19:2
[k] Ex 23:21
[l] **24:20** Jos 10:1; 11:11; Jdg 1:17
[m] **24:26** Dt 31:24
[n] **24:27** Jos 22:27,34
[o] **24:30** Jos 19:49-50
[p] **24:31** Jdg 2:7
[q] **24:32** Gn 50:25; Ex 13:19
[r] Gn 33:19; Jb 42:11
[s] **24:33** Jos 22:13

[A] **24:12** Or *sent terror* [B] **24:32** The value of this currency is unknown. [C] **24:33** = the Hill

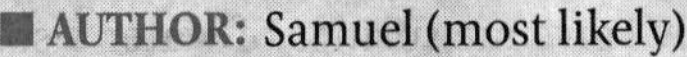

■ **AUTHOR:** Samuel (most likely)

■■ **DATE:** After the conquest of Canaan (around 1380–1060 B.C.)

God's mission is moved forward by the most surprising people: Gideon, the reluctant warrior who uses "the fleece" to insure himself of God's guidance; Jephthah, the all-too-eager warrior, who makes a rash vow and loses what's dearest to him; Samson, legendary strong man (except with his Delilah), who singlehandedly pulls down Philistine strongholds; Deborah, the judge who whips an army into action, then sings about it. Yes, there are ordinary actors in these stories, too, people called by God who did their work over many years and got only a brief mention. Then there's Ruth (not a judge of Israel, but she lived during their time), who became the grandmother of David and ancestor of Jesus. Yet she is a Moabite, not a daughter of Israel. How odd of God to select such a group as this to advance His mission.

JUDGES

The stories are heart-rending. Israel remembers God, forgets God, cries to God, receives deliverance from oppression, lives in peace, and then the cycle begins again. Will they ever learn? Will God run out of patience? Is there no end to the trouble people find when they ignore God? In all this, God's purpose is clear. God wants a people who know Him, follow His ways, and witness to His truth.

In the book of Judges, the mission of God faces all the bumps and potholes of human fickleness—we quickly fall in love with what gives us short-term pleasure. But that longer-term, higher-order mission is directed by a sovereign God who always finds a way, sometimes not at all as we might expect. Throughout this period (from the death of Joshua to the beginning of the monarchy), God sends trouble to Israel when due to forgetfulness or indifference they will wake to the truth by no other means. Then hearing their repentant cries, God raises a leader who beats back the enemy. Or better, a leader who watches God give victory. After all, Gideon had only 300 men against an alliance led by Midian's thousands. And Samson had only himself.

Ruth, the foreigner newly arrived in Israel, is famous for her pledge to stay with her mother-in-law Naomi. She survives her grief by the grace of a wealthy farmer, who is her kinsman-redeemer. He receives her as a blessing that God alone could plan. Neither Boaz nor Ruth—not even the old woman Naomi caressing that baby in the last scene of the story—can know how important their relationships are to the mission of God. They are merely faithful; God does the rest.

Sometimes in public view and sometimes quietly, history unfolds and God works. In the books of Judges and Ruth, God pulls a people from the valleys of failure, doubt, hesitation, excuses, and exasperation, to a new horizon of hope, restoration, and assurance. God is able, and His plan for this world is good.

Judah's Leadership against the Canaanites

1 After the death of Joshua,[a] the Israelites
inquired of the LORD,[b] "Who will be the
first to fight for us against the Canaanites?"
2The LORD answered, "Judah[c] is to go.[d] I
have handed the land over to him."[e]
3Judah said to his brother Simeon, "Come
with me to my territory, and let us fight
against the Canaanites. I will also go with you
to your territory." So Simeon went with him.
4When Judah attacked, the LORD handed
the Canaanites and Perizzites[f] over to them.
They struck down 10,000 men in Bezek.[g]
5They found Adoni-bezek in Bezek, fought
against him, and struck down the Canaanites
and Perizzites.
6When Adoni-bezek fled, they pursued
him, seized him, and cut off his thumbs and
big toes.[h] 7Adoni-bezek said, "Seventy kings
with their thumbs and big toes cut off used
to pick up scraps[A] under my table. God has repaid me for what I have done." They brought
him to Jerusalem, and he died there.
8The men of Judah fought against Jerusalem and captured it. They put the city to the
sword and set it on fire. 9Afterward, the men
of Judah marched down to fight against the
Canaanites who were living in the hill country, the •Negev, and the Judean foothills.[B]
10Judah also marched against the Canaanites who were living in Hebron[i] (Hebron was
formerly named Kiriath-arba[j]). They struck
down Sheshai, Ahiman, and Talmai.[k] 11From
there they marched against the residents of
Debir[l] (Debir was formerly named Kiriath-
sepher).
12Caleb[m] said, "Whoever strikes down and
captures Kiriath-sepher, I will give my daughter Achsah[n] to him as a wife." 13So Othniel[o]
son of Kenaz, Caleb's youngest brother, captured it, and Caleb gave his daughter Achsah
to him as his wife.
14When she arrived, she persuaded Othniel[C]
to ask her father for a field. As she got off
her donkey, Caleb asked her,[D] "What do you
want?" 15She answered him, "Give me a blessing. Since you have given me land in the Negev,[p] give me springs of water also." So Caleb
gave her both the upper and lower springs.[E,q]
16The descendants of the Kenite, Moses'
father-in-law,[r] had gone up with the men of
Judah from the City of Palms[F,s] to the Wilderness of Judah, which was in the Negev of
Arad.[t] They went to live among the people.
17Judah went with his brother Simeon,
struck the Canaanites who were living in
Zephath, and •completely destroyed the
town. So they named the town Hormah.[u] 18Ju-
dah captured Gaza and its territory, Ashkelon
and its territory, and Ekron and its territory.[G]
19The LORD was with[v] Judah and enabled
them to take possession of the hill country,
but they could not drive out[w] the people who
were living in the valley because those people
had iron chariots.[H,x]
20Judah gave Hebron to Caleb, just as Moses had promised.[y] Then Caleb drove out the
three sons of Anak[z] who lived there.[I]

Benjamin's Failure

21At the same time the Benjaminites did not
drive out the Jebusites who were living in Jerusalem. The Jebusites have lived among the
Benjaminites in Jerusalem to this day.[aa]

Success of the House of Joseph

22The house of Joseph also attacked Bethel,
and the LORD was with[ab] them. 23They sent
spies to Bethel (the town was formerly named
Luz[ac]). 24The spies saw a man coming out of
the town and said to him, "Please show us
how to get into town, and we will treat you
well."[ad] 25When he showed them the way into
the town, they put the town to the sword
but released the man and his entire family.
26Then the man went to the land of the Hittites, built a town, and named it Luz. That is
its name to this day.

Failure of the Other Tribes

27At that time Manasseh failed to take possession of Beth-shean[J,ae] and its villages,[K] or

a1:1 Jos 1:1; 24:29-31
bJdg 20:23,27; 1Sm 10:22; 23:2,4; 28:6
c1:2 Gn 29:35; 49:8-12
d1:1-2 Jdg 20:18
e1:2 Gn 35:12; Ex 6:8
f1:4 Gn 13:7; Dt 7:1; Jos 3:10; Ezr 9:1
g1Sm 11:8
h1:6 2Sm 4:12
i1:10 Gn 13:18; 23:2
jGn 23:2; 35:27; Jos 14:15
kNm 13:22; Jos 15:13-14
l1:11 Jos 10:38-39; 11:21; 15:7; 21:15; 1Ch 6:58
m1:12 Nm 13:6,13; 14:6,24,30,38; 26:65; 32:12
n1Ch 2:49
o1:13 Jdg 3:9,11; 1Ch 4:13
p1:15 Gn 12:9; 13:1,3; Nm 13:17,22,29; 2Sm 24:7; Ps 126:4
q1:11-15 Jos 15:15-19
r1:16 Ex 2:18; 3:1; 4:18; 18:1-12; Nm 10:29
sDt 34:3; Jdg 3:13; 2Ch 28:15
tNm 21:1; 33:40; Jos 12:14
u1:17 Nm 21:3; Dt 1:44
v1:19 Gn 39:2,21; Jos 6:27; Jdg 2:18; 1Sm 18:12
wJos 15:63
xJos 17:16,18; Jdg 4:3,13
y1:20 Dt 1:36; Jos 14:9
zNm 13:22
aa1:21 Jos 15:63
ab1:22 Gn 39:2,21; Jos 6:27; Jdg 2:18; 1Sm 18:12
ac1:23 Gn 28:19; 35:6; 48:3
ad1:24 Jos 2:12,14; 2Sm 9:1,3,7
ae1:27 Jos 17:11,16; 1Sm 31:10,12; 2Sm 21:12

A1:7 Lit *toes are gathering* B1:9 Or *the Shephelah* C1:14 LXX reads *arrived, he pressured her* D1:14 LXX reads *. . . field. She grumbled while on the donkey, and she cried out from the donkey, "Into the southland you sent me out," and Caleb said* E1:15 LXX reads *give me redemption of water, and Caleb gave her according to her heart the redemption of the upper and the redemption of the lower* F1:16 = Jericho; Dt 34:3; Jdg 3:13; 2Ch 28:15 G1:18 LXX reads *Judah did not inherit Gaza and its borders nor Ashkelon and its borders nor Ekron and its borders nor Azotus and its surrounding lands* H1:19 LXX reads *hill country, for they were not able to drive out the residents of the valley because Rechab separated it* I1:20 LXX reads *And he inherited from there the three cities of the sons of Anak.* J1:27 LXX reads *Beth-shean, which is a Scythian city* K1:27 LXX reads *its villages or the fields around it*

Taanach[a] and its villages, or the residents
of Dor[b] and its villages, or the residents of
Ibleam[A,c] and its villages, or the residents of
Megiddo[d] and its villages; the Canaanites
refused to leave[B] this land.[e] 28When Israel
became stronger, they made the Canaanites
serve as forced labor but never drove them
out completely.[f]

29At that time Ephraim failed to drive out
the Canaanites who were living in Gezer, so
the Canaanites have lived among them in
Gezer.[C,g]

30Zebulun failed to drive out the residents
of Kitron or the residents of Nahalol,[h] so the
Canaanites lived among them and served as
forced labor.

31Asher failed to drive out the residents of
Acco[D] or of Sidon, or Ahlab, Achzib, Helbah,
Aphik, or Rehob. 32The Asherites lived among
the Canaanites who were living in the land,
because they failed to drive them out.

33Naphtali did not drive out the residents
of Beth-shemesh or the residents of Beth-
anath. They lived among the Canaanites who
were living in the land, but the residents of
Beth-shemesh and Beth-anath served as their
forced labor.

34The Amorites[i] forced the Danites into
the hill country and did not allow them to
go down into the valley. 35The Amorites refused to leave[E] Har-heres, Aijalon,[j] and Shaalbim. When the house of Joseph got the upper
hand,[F] the Amorites[G] were made to serve as
forced labor. 36The territory of the Amorites
extended from the Ascent of Akrabbim,[k] that
is from Sela[l] upward.

Pattern of Sin and Judgment

2 The Angel of the LORD[m] went up from
Gilgal to Bochim[H] and said, "I brought
you out of Egypt and led you into the land[n]
I had promised to your fathers.[o] I also said: I
will never break My covenant with you. 2You
are not to make a covenant[p] with the people
who are living in this land, and you are to tear
down their altars.[I,q] But you have not obeyed
Me. What is this you have done? 3Therefore, I
now say: I will not drive out these people before you.[r] They will be thorns[J,K] in your sides,[s]
and their gods will be a trap for you."[t] 4When
the Angel of the LORD had spoken these
words to all the Israelites, the people wept
loudly. 5So they named that place Bochim[L]
and offered sacrifices there to the LORD.

Joshua's Death

6Joshua sent the people away, and the Israelites went to take possession of the land,
each to his own inheritance.[u] 7The people
worshiped the LORD throughout Joshua's
lifetime and during the lifetimes of the elders
who outlived[M] Joshua. They had seen all the
LORD's great works[v] He had done for Israel.

8Joshua son of Nun, the servant of the
LORD, died at the age of 110. 9They buried him
in the territory of his inheritance, in Tim-
nath-heres, in the hill country of Ephraim,[w]
north of Mount Gaash. 10That whole generation was also gathered to their ancestors.
After them another generation rose up who
did not know the LORD[x] or the works He had
done for Israel.

11The Israelites did what was evil in the
LORD's sight.[y] They worshiped the ·Baals[z]
12and abandoned the LORD, the God of
their fathers, who had brought them out of
Egypt. They went after other gods from the
surrounding peoples[aa] and bowed down to
them. They infuriated the LORD,[ab] 13for they
abandoned Him and worshiped Baal and the
·Ashtoreths.[ac]

14The LORD's anger burned against Israel,
and He handed them over to marauders who
raided them. He sold[ad] them to[N] the enemies
around them, and they could no longer resist
their enemies. 15Whenever the Israelites went
out, the LORD[O] was against them[ae] and brought
disaster on them, just as He had promised and
sworn to them.[af] So they suffered greatly.

16The LORD raised up[ag] judges, who saved

[a]**1:27** Jos 21:25; Jdg 5:19 [b]Jos 11:2; 12:23; 17:11; 1Kg 4:11 [c]Jos 17:11; 2Kg 9:27 [d]Jdg 5:19; 1Kg 9:15; 2Kg 23:29-30 [e]Jdg 1:35; Hs 5:11 [f]**1:27-28** Jos 17:12-13 [g]**1:29** Jos 16:10 [h]**1:30** Jos 19:15; 21:35 [i]**1:34** Ex 3:8; Nm 13:29; 21:31; Jos 2:10 [j]**1:35** Jos 10:12; 1Sm 14:31; 1Ch 8:13; 2Ch 28:18 [k]**1:36** Nm 34:4; Jos 15:3 [l]2Kg 14:7; Is 16:1 [m]**2:1** Gn 22:11; Ex 3:2; Ps 34:7; 35:5-6 [n]Ex 6:8; Nm 14:3,8; Ezk 20:15 [o]Nm 14:23; Dt 6:10,23; 10:11; Jos 1:6 [p]**2:2** Ex 23:32; Dt 7:2 [q]Ex 34:13; Dt 7:5; 12:3; Jdg 6:30-32; 2Ch 34:7 [r]**2:3** Ex 23:29 [s]Nm 33:55 [t]Ex 23:33; 34:12; Dt 7:16; Jos 23:13 [u]**2:6** Dt 9:4; 11:31; Jos 1:11; 18:3; Jdg 18:9; Neh 9:15 [v]**2:7** Dt 11:7 [w]**2:9** Jos 19:50; 1Sm 1:1; 14:22; 1Ch 6:67 [x]**2:10** Ex 5:2; 1Sm 2:12 [y]**2:11** Nm 32:12; Dt 4:25; 31:29; 1Kg 11:6 [z]Jdg 3:7; 8:33; 1Sm 12:10; 2Kg 17:16; Jr 2:23; 9:14 [aa]**2:12** Dt 6:14; 13:7 [ab]1Kg 14:15; 15:30; 2Kg 17:11; 2Ch 28:25 [ac]**2:13** Jdg 10:6; 1Sm 7:3-4; 12:10; 1Kg 11:5,33; 2Kg 23:13 [ad]**2:14** Jdg 3:8; 4:2,9; 10:7; Ps 44:12; Is 50:1; Ezk 30:12; Jl 3:8 [ae]**2:15** Dt 2:15 [af]Lv 26:14-46; Dt 28:15-68 [ag]**2:16** Jdg 3:9,15; 1Kg 11:14; 14:14

[A]**1:27** LXX reads *Balaam* [B]**1:27** LXX reads *Canaanites began to live in* [C]**1:29** LXX reads *Gezer, and became forced labor* [D]**1:31** LXX reads *Acco, and they became for him forced labor and the residents of Dor* [E]**1:35** Or *Amorites determined to live in* [F]**1:35** Lit *When the hand of the house of Joseph was heavy* [G]**1:35** LXX reads *Joseph became strong on the Amorites, they* [H]**2:1** LXX reads *to the weeping place and to Bethel and to the house of Israel* [I]**2:2** LXX reads *with those lying in wait in this land; neither are you to fall down in worship to their gods, but their carved images you must break to pieces and their altars you must destroy* [J]**2:3** LXX reads *affliction* [K]**2:3** Lit *traps* [L]**2:5** Or *Weeping* [M]**2:7** Lit *extended their days after* [N]**2:14** Lit *into the hand of* [O]**2:15** Lit *the hand of the LORD*

On the Frontlines

Clement Shahbaz Bhatti (1968–2011)

Bhatti was born to Christian parents in Pakistan, where few liberties are given to religious minorities. He saw the need to defend not only his own brothers and sisters in Christ, but the right of all people to believe without coercion and to express their faith without fear. His father a teacher, Bhatti became a politician.

Bhatti knew his campaign for liberty—for the privilege of converting without penalty and for free exercise of prayer, worship, and evangelism—could not be achieved without wide networks of support within Pakistan and beyond. He formed the All Pakistan Minorities Alliance in 1985, and the Christian Liberation Front in 1998. Like the celebrated Dietrich Bonhoeffer earlier, Bhatti knew his public work was dangerous, but unlike Bonhoeffer, he did not go underground but consistently stayed in the eye of the storm, disregarding threats and supporting other persecuted Christians. Death threats increased when Bhatti fiercely contested a capital sentence handed down to a Pakistani Christian in 2009 for blasphemy—a crime that covers a multitude of offenses, including conversion. Bhatti also worked on legislation opposing hate speech and supporting educational reforms which would have taught at least the history of other faiths to Pakistani youth.

Bhatti was elected to Pakistan's National Assembly in 2008. He became the first Federal Minister for Minorities and the only Christian member of the Cabinet. For the sake of the oppressed, down-trodden, and marginalized, Bhatti worked with broad coalitions, including international bodies, to free Pakistani Christians and others from official intimidation. He could do little about the unofficial terrors, the Taliban, the secret police.

In December 2010, with threats against his life increasing, Bhatti made a video, kept by a Finnish group for release in the event of his death. He requested security services and an armored car for travel, and was denied. On March 2, 2011 as his car pulled away from his mother's house in Islamabad, three gunmen who later claimed to represent a Taliban branch, opened fire. Dragging Bhatti from the vehicle, they fired again. Bhatti had been eliminated.

Across the world, governments called for his killers to be brought to justice, but in Pakistan, even those who respected his courage and quietly supported his work were careful to avoid too public a show of outrage or grief. Bhatti himself spoke soon after his death, however, as the Finns released the video message he had prepared. It was a message of faith, hope, and perseverance under increasing stress. He was following the way of the Master, undeterred by the way of fear or vengefulness.

them from the power of their marauders, 17 but they did not listen to their judges. Instead, they prostituted[a] themselves with other gods, bowing down to them. They quickly turned from the way[b] of their fathers, who had walked in obedience to the LORD's commands. They did not do as their fathers did. 18 Whenever the LORD raised up a judge for the Israelites, the LORD was with[c] him and saved the people from the power of their enemies while the judge was still alive.[A] The LORD was moved to pity whenever they groaned because of those who were oppressing and afflicting them. 19 Whenever the judge died, the Israelites would act even more corruptly[d] than their fathers, going after other gods to worship and bow down to them. They did not turn from their evil practices or their obstinate[e] ways.

20 The LORD's anger burned against Israel, and He declared, "Because this nation has violated My covenant[f] that I made with their fathers[g] and disobeyed Me, 21 I will no longer drive out before them any of the nations Joshua left[h] when he died.[i] 22 I did this to test Israel and to see whether they would keep the LORD's way[j] by walking in it, as their fathers had."[k] 23 The LORD left these nations and did not drive them out immediately. He did not hand them over to Joshua.

The LORD Tests Israel

3 These are the nations the LORD left in order to test Israel, since the Israelites had fought none of these in[B] any of the wars with Canaan.[l] 2 This was to teach the future generations of the Israelites how to fight in battle, especially those who had not fought before.[C] 3 These nations included: the five rulers[m] of the Philistines[n] and all of the Canaanites, the Sidonians,[o] and the Hivites[p] who lived in the Lebanese mountains[D] from Mount Baal-hermon as far as the entrance to Hamath.[E] 4 The LORD left them to test Israel, to determine if they would keep the LORD's commands He had given their fathers through[F] Moses.[q] 5 But they settled among the Canaanites, Hittites, Amorites, Perizzites, Hivites, and Jebusites. 6 The Israelites took their daughters as wives for themselves, gave their own daughters to their sons, and worshiped their gods.[r]

Othniel, the First Judge

7 The Israelites did what was evil in the LORD's sight; they forgot the LORD their God[s] and worshiped the ˙Baals and the ˙Asherahs. 8 The LORD's anger burned against Israel, and He sold them to[G] Cushan-rishathaim[H] king of Aram-naharaim,[I,t] and the Israelites served him eight years.

9 The Israelites cried out to the LORD.[u] So the LORD raised up Othniel son of Kenaz, Caleb's youngest brother,[v] as a deliverer[w] to save the Israelites. 10 The Spirit of the LORD came on him, and he judged Israel. Othniel went out to battle, and the LORD handed over Cushan-rishathaim king of Aram to him, so that Othniel overpowered him. 11 Then the land was peaceful[x] 40 years, and Othniel son of Kenaz died.

Ehud

12 The Israelites again did what was evil in the LORD's sight. He gave Eglon king of Moab[y] power over Israel, because they had done what was evil in the LORD's sight. 13 After Eglon convinced the Ammonites and the Amalekites to join forces with him, he attacked and defeated Israel and took possession of the City of Palms.[J,z] 14 The Israelites served Eglon king of Moab 18 years.

15 Then the Israelites cried out to the LORD, and He raised up Ehud son of Gera, a left-handed[aa] Benjaminite,[K] as a deliverer for them. The Israelites sent him to Eglon king of Moab with tribute[ab] money.

16 Ehud made himself a double-edged sword 18 inches long.[L] He strapped it to his right thigh under his clothes 17 and brought the tribute to Eglon king of Moab, who was an extremely fat man. 18 When Ehud had finished presenting the tribute, he dismissed the people who had carried it. 19 At the carved images near Gilgal he returned and said, "King Eglon, I have a secret message for you." The king called for silence, and all his

[a] **2:17** Dt 4:30; 1Sm 13:6; 30:6; 2Sm 22:7; Jb 20:22; Ps 59:16; Hs 5:15 [b] Ex 32:8; Dt 9:12,16 [c] **2:18** Gn 39:2,21; Jos 6:27; 1Sm 18:12 [d] **2:19** Gn 6:12; Dt 31:29; Is 1:4 [e] Ex 32:9; Dt 9:6,13; Ezk 2:4 [f] **2:20** Jos 7:11,15; 23:16; Jr 34:18; Hs 6:7 [g] Jdg 3:4; 1Kg 8:58; 2Kg 17:13; Ps 78:5; Jr 11:4 [h] **2:21** Jos 13:1-7; 23:1-16 [i] Jos 24:29-30 [j] **2:22** Gn 18:19; 2Sm 22:22; Ps 138:5 [k] Jos 24:31 [l] **3:1** Jos 1–12 [m] **3:3** Jos 13:3; 1Sm 5:8,11 [n] Gn 10:14; Ex 13:17 [o] Jos 13:4; 1Kg 5:6; Ezk 32:30 [p] Ex 38:17; Dt 20:17; Jos 9:1,7 [q] **3:4** 1Kg 8:58; 2Kg 17:13; Ps 78:5; Jr 11:4 [r] **3:6** Ex 23:33; Dt 7:16 [s] **3:7** Dt 8:11,14,19; 1Sm 12:9; Jr 3:21 [t] **3:8** Gn 24:10; Dt 23:3-4; 1Ch 19:6; Ps 60 title [u] **3:9** Jdg 3:15; 6:6-7; 10:10 [v] Jdg 1:13 [w] Dt 28:29,31; Jdg 6:36; 1Sm 14:39; Is 19:20; 43:11; Hs 13:4 [x] **3:11** Jdg 3:30; 5:31; 8:28; 2Ch 14:1,5-6 [y] **3:12** Nm 22:3; Dt 2:8-9; 32:49 [z] **3:13** Dt 34:3; Jdg 1:16; 2Ch 28:15 [aa] **3:15** Jdg 20:16 [ab] 2Sm 8:2,6; 2Ch 9:24; 17:11

[A] **2:18** Lit *enemies all the days of the judge* [B] **3:1** Lit *had known* [C] **3:2** Lit *not known it* [D] **3:3** LXX reads *in Lebanon* [E] **3:3** Or *as Lebo-hamath* [F] **3:4** Lit *by the hand of* [G] **3:8** Lit *into the hand of* [H] **3:8** Lit *Doubly-Evil* [I] **3:8** = Mesopotamia [J] **3:13** = Jericho; Dt 34:3; Jdg 1:16; 2Ch 28:15 [K] **3:15** = son of the right hand [L] **3:16** Lit *sword a gomed in length*

attendants left him. 20 Then Ehud approached
him while he was sitting alone in his room
upstairs where it was cool. Ehud said, "I
have a word from God for you," and the king
stood up from his throne.[A] 21 Ehud[B] reached
with his left hand, took the sword from his
right thigh, and plunged it into Eglon's belly.
22 Even the handle went in after the blade, and
Eglon's fat closed in over it, so that Ehud did
not withdraw the sword from his belly. And
Eglon's insides came out. 23 Ehud escaped by
way of the porch, closing and locking the
doors of the upstairs room behind him.

24 Ehud was gone when Eglon's servants
came in. They looked and found the doors of
the upstairs room locked and thought he was
relieving himself[C] in the cool room. 25 The servants waited until they became worried and
saw that he had still not opened the doors of
the upstairs room. So they took the key and
opened the doors — and there was their lord
lying dead on the floor!

26 Ehud escaped while the servants waited.
He crossed over the Jordan near the carved
images and reached Seirah. 27 After he arrived,
he sounded the ram's horn throughout the
hill country of Ephraim. The Israelites came
down with him from the hill country, and
he became their leader. 28 He told them, "Follow me, because the LORD has handed over
your enemies, the Moabites, to you." So they
followed him, captured the fords of the Jordan leading to Moab, and did not allow anyone to cross over.[a] 29 At that time they struck
down about 10,000 Moabites, all strong and
able-bodied men. Not one of them escaped.
30 Moab became subject to Israel that day, and
the land was peaceful 80 years.

Shamgar

31 After Ehud, Shamgar son of Anath became judge. He delivered Israel by striking
down 600 Philistines with an oxgoad.

Deborah and Barak

4 The Israelites again did what was evil
in the sight of the LORD after Ehud had
died. 2 So the LORD sold them into the hand of
Jabin[b] king of Canaan, who reigned in Hazor.[c]
The commander of his forces was Sisera[d] who
lived in Harosheth of the Nations.[D] 3 Then
the Israelites cried out[e] to the LORD, because
Jabin had 900 iron chariots, and he harshly
oppressed them 20 years.

4 Deborah, a woman who was a prophetess[f]
and the wife of Lappidoth, was judging Israel
at that time. 5 It was her custom to sit under
the palm tree of Deborah between Ramah
and Bethel in the hill country of Ephraim,
and the Israelites went up to her for judgment.[g]

6 She summoned Barak son of Abinoam
from Kedesh in Naphtali and said to him,
"Hasn't the LORD, the God of Israel,[h] commanded you: 'Go, deploy the troops on
Mount Tabor,[i] and take with you 10,000
men from the Naphtalites[j] and Zebulunites?[k]
7 Then I will lure Sisera commander of Jabin's
forces, his chariots, and his army at the ·Wadi
Kishon[l] to fight against you, and I will hand
him over to you.'"[m]

8 Barak said to her, "If you will go with me,
I will go. But if you will not go with me, I will
not go."

9 "I will go with you," she said, "but you will
receive no honor on the road you are about to
take, because the LORD will sell Sisera into a
woman's hand." So Deborah got up and went
with Barak to Kedesh. 10 Barak summoned
Zebulun and Naphtali to Kedesh; 10,000
men followed him, and Deborah also went
with him.

11 Now Heber the Kenite had moved away
from the Kenites, the sons of Hobab,[n] Moses'
father-in-law,[o] and pitched his tent beside
the oak tree of Zaanannim,[p] which was near
Kedesh.

12 It was reported to Sisera that Barak son of
Abinoam had gone up Mount Tabor. 13 Sisera
summoned all his 900 iron chariots and all
the people who were with him from Harosheth of the Nations[D] to the Wadi Kishon.
14 Then Deborah said to Barak, "Move on, for
this is the day the LORD has handed Sisera
over to you. Hasn't the LORD gone before
you?" So Barak came down from Mount Tabor with 10,000 men following him.

15 The LORD threw Sisera, all his chariot-

[a] **3:28** Jdg 12:5-6
[b] **4:2** Jos 11:1; Ps 83:9
[c] 1Sm 12:9
[d] Jdg 5:20-30; 1Sm 12:9; Ps 83:9
[e] **4:3** Ex 14:10; Nm 12:13; Dt 26:7; Ps 34:17
[f] **4:4** Ex 15:20; 2Kg 22:14; Neh 6:14; Is 8:3
[g] **4:5** Nm 35:12; 2Ch 19:8; Ps 9:4; 76:8-9; Is 3:13-14; Ezk 44:24
[h] **4:6** Ex 5:1; Dt 6:4; Ps 41:13
[i] Jos 19:12,22,34; Ps 89:12
[j] Gn 30:8; 49:21
[k] Gn 30:20; 49:13
[l] **4:7** Jdg 5:21; 1Kg 18:40; Ps 83:9
[m] Dt 2:30; Jdg 7:9; 2Sm 5:19; 1Ch 14:10; Is 47:6
[n] **4:11** Nm 10:29
[o] Ex 3:1; 4:18; 18:1-27
[p] Jos 19:33

A 3:20 LXX reads *"A word of my God for you, O king," and Eglon rose up from the throne near him.* B 3:21 LXX reads *It happened that when he rose up, Ehud immediately* C 3:24 Lit *was covering his feet* D 4:2,13 Or *Harosheth-ha-goiim*

eers, and all his army into confusion[a] with
the sword before Barak. Sisera left his chariot
and fled on foot. 16 Barak pursued the chariots and the army as far as Harosheth of the
Nations,[A] and the whole army of Sisera fell by
the sword; not a single man was left.
17 Meanwhile, Sisera had fled on foot to the
tent of Jael, the wife of Heber the Kenite, because there was peace between Jabin king of
Hazor and the family of Heber the Kenite.
18 Jael went out to greet Sisera and said to him,
"Come in, my lord. Come in with me. Don't
be afraid." So he went into her tent, and she
covered him with a rug. 19 He said to her,
"Please give me a little water to drink for I am
thirsty." She opened a container of milk, gave
him a drink, and covered him again. 20 Then
he said to her, "Stand at the entrance to the
tent. If a man comes and asks you, 'Is there a
man here?' say, 'No.'" 21 While he was sleeping
from exhaustion, Heber's wife Jael took a tent
peg, grabbed a hammer, and went silently to
Sisera. She hammered the peg into his temple
and drove it into the ground, and he died.
22 When Barak arrived in pursuit of Sisera,
Jael went out to greet him and said to him,
"Come and I will show you the man you are
looking for." So he went in with her, and there
was Sisera lying dead with a tent peg through
his temple!
23 That day God subdued Jabin king of Canaan before the Israelites. 24 The power of the
Israelites continued to increase against Jabin
king of Canaan until they destroyed him.

Deborah's Song

5 On that day Deborah and Barak son of
Abinoam sang:

2 When the leaders lead[B] in Israel,
when the people volunteer,
praise the LORD.
3 Listen, kings! Pay attention, princes!
I will sing to the LORD;
I will sing praise to the LORD God
of Israel.
4 LORD, when You came from Seir,[b]
when You marched from the fields
of Edom,
the earth trembled,[c]
the heavens poured[d] rain,
and the clouds poured water.
5 The mountains melted before the LORD,
even Sinai[C] before the LORD, the God
of Israel.[e]
6 In the days of Shamgar[f] son of Anath,
in the days of Jael,[g]
the main ways were deserted
because travelers kept to the side roads.
7 Villages were deserted,[D]
they were deserted in Israel,
until I, Deborah,[E] arose,
a mother in Israel.
8 Israel chose new gods,
then war was in the gates.
Not a shield or spear was seen
among 40,000 in Israel.
9 My heart is with the leaders of Israel,
with the volunteers of the people.
Praise the LORD!
10 You who ride on white[D] donkeys,
who sit on saddle blankets,
and who travel on the road, give
praise!
11 Let them tell the righteous acts[h]
of the LORD,
the righteous deeds of His warriors
in Israel,
with the voices of the singers
at the watering places.[D]

Then the LORD's people went down
to the gates.
12 "Awake! Awake, Deborah!
Awake! Awake, sing a song!
Arise, Barak,
and take hold of your captives,
son of Abinoam!"
13 The survivors[i] came down
to the nobles;[j]
the LORD's people came down to me[F]
with the warriors.
14 Those with their roots in Amalek[G] came
from Ephraim;
Benjamin came with your people
after you.
The leaders came down from Machir,[k]
and those who carry a marshal's staff
came from Zebulun.

[a] **4:15** Ex 14:24; 23:27; Jos 10:10; Ps 18:14; 144:6
[b] **5:4** Gn 14:6; 36:8-9; Dt 2:1
[c] 2Sm 22:8; Ps 18:7; Is 13:13; Ezk 38:20
[d] Jb 29:22; Ps 68:8; Pr 5:3; Jl 3:18
[e] **5:5** Ex 5:1; Dt 6:4; Ps 41:13
[f] **5:6** Jdg 3:31
[g] Jdg 4:17-22
[h] **5:11** 1Sm 12:7; Ps 103:6; Is 45:24; Mc 6:5
[i] **5:13** Nm 21:35; Dt 2:34; Is 1:9
[j] Jdg 5:25; 2Ch 23:20; Neh 3:5; 10:29; Ps 16:3; Jr 14:3; Nah 2:5; 3:18
[k] **5:14** Gn 50:23; Nm 26:29; 32:39-40; Jos 17:1; 2Sm 9:4-5

[A] **4:16** Or *Harosheth-ha-goiim* [B] **5:2** Or *the locks of hair are loose* [C] **5:5** Or *LORD, this One of Sinai* [D] **5:7,10,11** Hb obscure [E] **5:7** Or *you* [F] **5:13** LXX reads *down for him* [G] **5:14** LXX reads *in the valley*

15 The princes of Issachar were
with Deborah;
Issachar was with Barak.
They set out at his heels[a] in the valley.
There was great searching[A] of heart
among the clans of Reuben.
16 Why did you sit among the sheepfolds
listening to the playing of pipes
for the flocks?
There was great searching of heart
among the clans of Reuben.
17 Gilead[b] remained beyond the Jordan.
Dan, why did you linger at the ships?
Asher remained at the seashore
and stayed in his harbors.
18 Zebulun was a people risking
their lives,
Naphtali also, on the heights
of the battlefield.

19 Kings came and fought.
Then the kings of Canaan fought
at Taanach by the waters of Megiddo,
but they took no spoil of silver.
20 The stars fought from the heavens;
the stars fought with Sisera
from their courses.
21 The river Kishon swept them away,[c]
the ancient river, the river Kishon.
March on, my soul, in strength!
22 The horses' hooves then hammered —
the galloping, galloping
of his[B] stallions.
23 "Curse Meroz," says the Angel
of the LORD,
"Bitterly curse her inhabitants,
for they did not come to help the LORD,
to help the LORD against
the mighty warriors."

24 Jael is most blessed of women,
the wife of Heber the Kenite;
she is most blessed among tent-
dwelling women.
25 He asked for water; she gave him milk.
She brought him curdled milk[d]
in a majestic bowl.
26 She reached for a tent peg,
her right hand, for a workman's mallet.
Then she hammered Sisera —
she crushed his head;
she shattered and pierced his temple.
27 He collapsed, he fell, he lay down
at[C] her feet;
he collapsed, he fell at her feet;
where he collapsed,
there he fell — dead.

28 Sisera's mother looked
through the window;
she peered through the lattice,
crying out:
"Why is his chariot so long in coming?
Why don't I hear the hoofbeats
of his horses?"[D]
29 Her wisest princesses answer her;
she even answers herself:[E]
30 "Are they not finding and dividing
the spoil —
a girl or two for each warrior,
the spoil of colored garments for Sisera,
the spoil of an embroidered garment
or two for my neck?"[F]

31 LORD, may all your enemies perish
as Sisera did.[G]
But may those who love Him
be like the rising of the sun
in its strength.

And the land was peaceful 40 years.

Midian Oppresses Israel

6 The Israelites did what was evil in the
sight of the LORD. So the LORD handed[e]
them over to Midian seven years, 2 and they
oppressed Israel.[f] Because of Midian, the Israelites made hiding places[g] for themselves
in the mountains, caves, and strongholds.
3 Whenever the Israelites planted crops, the
Midianites, Amalekites, and the Qedemites[h]
came and attacked them. 4 They encamped
against them and destroyed the produce of
the land, even as far as Gaza. They left nothing for Israel to eat, as well as no sheep, ox or
donkey. 5 For the Midianites came with their
cattle and their tents like a great swarm of
locusts. They and their camels were without
number, and they entered the land to waste
it. 6 So Israel became poverty-stricken be-

[a] **5:15** Jdg 4:10 [b] **5:17** Gn 31:25; Nm 32:40; Jdg 10:17–11:11 [c] **5:20-21** Jdg 4:15 [d] **5:25** Gn 18:8; Dt 32:14; 2Sm 17:29; Jb 20:17; 29:6; Pr 30:3; Is 7:15,22 [e] **6:1** Jos 11:8; Jdg 11:32; 12:3; 13:1; 1Sm 14:10,12 [f] **6:2** Jdg 3:10 [g] 1Sm 23:14,19; 1Ch 11:7; Is 33:16; Jr 48:41 [h] **6:3** Gn 29:1; 1Kg 4:30; Is 11:14

[A] 5:15 Some Hb mss, Syr read *There were great resolves* [B] 5:22 = Sisera's [C] 5:27 Lit *between* [D] 5:28 Lit *Why have the hoofbeats of his chariots delayed* [E] 5:29 Lit *answers her words* [F] 5:30 Hb obscure [G] 5:31 Lit *perish in this way* cause of Midian, and the Israelites cried out to the LORD.

7 When the Israelites cried out to Him because of Midian, 8 the LORD sent a prophet[a] to them. He said to them, "This is what the LORD[b] God of Israel says: 'I brought you out of Egypt and out of the place of slavery.[c] 9 I delivered you from the power of Egypt and the power of all who oppressed[d] you. I drove them out before you and gave you their land. 10 I said to you: I am ·Yahweh your God. Do not fear the gods of the Amorites whose land you live in. But you did not obey Me.' "

The LORD Calls Gideon

11 The Angel[A] of the LORD[e] came, and He[B] sat under the oak that was in Ophrah, which belonged to Joash, the Abiezrite. His son Gideon was threshing wheat in the wine vat in order to hide it from the Midianites. 12 Then the Angel of the LORD appeared to him and said: "The LORD is with you, mighty warrior."

13 Gideon said to Him, "Please Sir,[C] if the LORD is with us, why has all this happened?[D] And where are all His wonders that our fathers told us about? They said, 'Hasn't the LORD brought us out of Egypt?' But now the LORD has abandoned us and handed us over to Midian."

14 The LORD[E] turned to him and said, "Go in the strength you have and deliver Israel from the power of Midian. Am I not sending you?"

15 He said to Him, "Please, Lord, how can I deliver Israel? Look, my family is the weakest in Manasseh, and I am the youngest in my father's house."

16 "But I will be with you,"[f] the LORD said to him. "You will strike Midian down as if it were one man."

17 Then he said to Him, "If I have found favor in Your sight,[g] give me a sign[h] that You are speaking with me. 18 Please do not leave this place until I return to You. Let me bring my gift and set it before You."

And He said, "I will stay until you return."

19 So Gideon went and prepared a young goat and unleavened bread from a half bushel[F] of flour. He placed the meat in a basket and the broth in a pot. He brought them out and offered them to Him under the oak.

20 The Angel of God[i] said to him, "Take the meat with the unleavened bread, put it on this stone, and pour the broth on it." And he did so.

21 The Angel of the LORD extended the tip of the staff that was in His hand and touched the meat and the unleavened bread. Fire came up from the rock and consumed the meat and the unleavened bread. Then the Angel of the LORD vanished from his sight.

22 When Gideon realized that He was the Angel of the LORD, he said, "Oh no, Lord GOD![j] I have seen the Angel of the LORD face to face!"[k]

23 But the LORD said to him, "Peace to you. Don't be afraid, for you will not die." 24 So Gideon built an altar to the LORD there and called it Yahweh Shalom.[G] It is in Ophrah of the Abiezrites until today.

Gideon Tears Down a Baal Altar

25 On that very night the LORD said to him, "Take your father's young bull and a second bull seven years old. Then tear down the altar of ·Baal[l] that belongs to your father and cut down the ·Asherah pole beside it. 26 Build a well-constructed altar to the LORD your God on the top of this rock.[m] Take the second bull and offer it as a ·burnt offering with the wood of the Asherah pole you cut down." 27 So Gideon took 10 of his male servants and did as the LORD had told him. But because he was too afraid of his father's household and the men of the city to do it in the daytime, he did it at night.

28 When the men of the city got up in the morning, they found Baal's altar torn down, the Asherah pole beside it cut down, and the second bull offered up on the altar that had been built. 29 They said to each other, "Who did this?" After they made a thorough investigation, they said, "Gideon son of Joash did it."

30 Then the men of the city said to Joash, "Bring out your son. He must die, because he tore down Baal's altar and cut down the Asherah pole beside it."

31 But Joash said to all who stood against

[a] **6:8** Gn 20:7; Ex 7:1; Nm 11:29; 12:6; Dt 18:15,18,20,22; 34:10
[b] Ex 4:22; 5:1; Dt 6:4; Jos 7:13
[c] Ex 13:3,14; 20:2; Dt 5:6; 7:8; Jr 34:13; Mc 6:4
[d] **6:9** Ex 3:9; 1Sm 10:18; Ps 106:42
[e] **6:11** Ex 3:2
[f] **6:16** Gn 26:3; Ex 3:12
[g] **6:17** Gn 6:8; 18:3; Ex 33:12-13; Ru 2:2,10,13; Est 5:8; 7:3
[h] Ex 3:12; 1Sm 10:7,9; Is 7:11,14
[i] **6:20** Gn 31:11; Ex 14:19; Jdg 13:6,9; 2Sm 14:17,20; 2Ch 36:16
[j] **6:22** Jos 7:7; Jr 1:6; Ezk 4:14
[k] Gn 32:20; Ex 24:10-11; 33:19-23; Jdg 13:21-23; Is 6:5
[l] **6:25** Jdg 2:11,13; 10:6; 1Kg 18:21; 2Ch 33:3; Jr 2:23; Zph 1:4
[m] **6:26** Neh 8:10; Ps 27:1; 37:39; Pr 10:29; Is 17:9-10

[A] **6:11** Or *angel* [B] **6:11** Or *he* [C] **6:13** Lit *Please, my Lord,* or *Please, my lord* [D] **6:13** Lit *this found us out* [E] **6:14** LXX reads *The Angel of the LORD* [F] **6:19** Lit *an ephah* [G] **6:24** = The LORD Is Peace him, "Would you plead Baal's case for him? Would you save him? Whoever pleads his case will be put to death by morning! If he is a god, let him plead his own case because someone tore down his altar." [32]That day, Gideon's father called him Jerubbaal, saying, "Let Baal plead his case with him," because he tore down his altar.

The Sign of the Fleece

[33]All the Midianites, Amalekites, and Qedemites gathered together, crossed over the Jordan, and camped in the Valley of Jezreel.[a]

[34]The Spirit of the LORD took control of[A] Gideon, and he blew the ram's horn and the Abiezrites rallied behind him. [35]He sent messengers throughout all of Manasseh, who rallied behind him. He also sent messengers throughout Asher, Zebulun, and Naphtali, who also came to meet him.

[36]Then Gideon said to God, "If You will deliver Israel by my hand, as You said, [37]I will put a fleece of wool here on the threshing floor. If dew is only on the fleece, and all the ground is dry, I will know that You will deliver Israel by my strength, as You said." [38]And that is what happened. When he got up early in the morning, he squeezed the fleece and wrung dew out of it, filling a bowl with water.

[39]Gideon then said to God, "Don't be angry with me; let me speak one more time. Please allow me to make one more test with the fleece. Let it remain dry, and the dew be all over the ground." [40]That night God did as Gideon requested: only the fleece was dry, and dew was all over the ground.

God Selects Gideon's Army

7 Jerubbaal (that is, Gideon) and everyone who was with him, got up early and camped beside the spring of Harod. The camp of Midian was north of them, below the hill of Moreh, in the valley. [2]The LORD said to Gideon, "You have too many people for Me to hand the Midianites over to you,[B] or else Israel might brag:[C] 'I did it myself.' [3]Now announce in the presence of the people: 'Whoever is fearful and trembling may turn back and leave Mount Gilead.'"[b] So 22,000 of the people turned back, but 10,000 remained.

[a]**6:33** Jos 17:16; 1Sm 29:1,11; 1Kg 21:1
[b]**7:3** Gn 31:21,23,25; Dt 3:12
[c]**7:13** Gn 37:5-6,8-10; 40:5,8-9,16; 41; 42:9; Nm 12:6; Dn 1:17

[4]Then the LORD said to Gideon, "There are still too many people. Take them down to the water, and I will test them for you there. If I say to you, 'This one can go with you,' he can go. But if I say about anyone, 'This one cannot go with you,' he cannot go." [5]So he brought the people down to the water, and the LORD said to Gideon, "Separate everyone who laps water with his tongue like a dog. Do the same with everyone who kneels to drink." [6]The number of those who lapped with their hands to their mouths was 300 men, and all the rest of the people knelt to drink water. [7]The LORD said to Gideon, "I will deliver you with the 300 men who lapped and hand the Midianites over to you. But everyone else is to go home." [8]So Gideon sent all the Israelites to their tents but kept the 300, who took[D] the people's provisions and their trumpets. The camp of Midian was below him in the valley.

Gideon Spies on the Midianite Camp

[9]That night the LORD said to him, "Get up and go into the camp, for I have given it into your hand. [10]But if you are afraid to go to the camp, go with Purah your servant. [11]Listen to what they say, and then you will be strengthened to go to the camp." So he went with Purah his servant to the outpost of the troops[E] who were in the camp.

[12]Now the Midianites, Amalekites, and all the Qedemites had settled down in the valley like a swarm of locusts, and their camels were as innumerable as the sand on the seashore. [13]When Gideon arrived, there was a man telling his friend about a dream. He said, "Listen, I had a dream:[c] a loaf of barley bread came tumbling into the Midianite camp, struck a tent, and it fell. The loaf turned the tent upside down so that it collapsed."

[14]His friend answered: "This is nothing less than the sword of Gideon son of Joash, the Israelite. God has handed the entire Midianite camp over to him."

Gideon Attacks the Midianites

[15]When Gideon heard the account of the dream and its interpretation, he bowed in

[A]**6:34** Lit *LORD clothed Himself with*; 1Ch 12:18; 2Ch 24:20 [B]**7:2** Lit *them* [C]**7:2** Lit *brag against Me* [D]**7:8** Lit *took in their hands* [E]**7:11** Lit *of those who were arranged in companies of 50*

worship. He returned to Israel's camp and said, "Get up, for the LORD has handed the Midianite camp over to you." 16 Then he divided the 300 men into three companies and gave each of the men a trumpet in one hand and an empty pitcher with a torch inside it in the other.

17 "Watch me," he said,[A] "and do the same. When I come to the outpost of the camp, do as I do. 18 When I and everyone with me blow our trumpets, you are also to blow your trumpets all around the camp. Then you will say, 'For ·Yahweh and for Gideon!' "

19 Gideon and the 100 men who were with him went to the outpost of the camp at the beginning of the middle watch after the sentries had been stationed. They blew their trumpets and broke the pitchers that were in their hands. 20 The three companies blew their trumpets and shattered their pitchers. They held their torches in their left hands, their trumpets[B] in their right hands, and shouted, "A sword for Yahweh and for Gideon!" 21 Each Israelite took his position around the camp, and the entire Midianite army fled, and cried out as they ran. 22 When Gideon's men blew their 300 trumpets, the LORD set the swords of each man in the army against each other. They fled to Beth-shittah in the direction of Zererah as far as the border of Abel-meholah[a] near Tabbath. 23 Then the men of Israel were called from Naphtali, Asher, and Manasseh, and they pursued the Midianites.

The Men of Ephraim Join the Battle

24 Gideon sent messengers throughout the hill country of Ephraim with this message: "Come down to intercept the Midianites and take control of the watercourses ahead of them as far as Beth-barah and the Jordan." So all the men of Ephraim[b] were called out, and they took control of the watercourses as far as Beth-barah and the Jordan. 25 They captured Oreb and Zeeb, the two princes of Midian; they killed Oreb at the rock of Oreb and Zeeb at the winepress of Zeeb, while they were pursuing the Midianites. They brought the heads of Oreb and Zeeb to Gideon across the Jordan.

8 The men of Ephraim said to him, "Why have you done this to us, not calling us when you went to fight against the Midianites?" And they argued with him violently.

2 So he said to them, "What have I done now compared to you? Is not the gleaning[c] of Ephraim better than the vintage[d] of Abiezer? 3 God handed over to you Oreb and Zeeb, the two princes of Midian. What was I able to do compared to you?" When he said this, their anger against him subsided.

Gideon Pursues the Kings of Midian

4 Gideon and the 300 men came to the Jordan and crossed it. They were exhausted but still in pursuit. 5 He said to the men of Succoth,[e] "Please give some loaves of bread to the people who are following me,[C] because they are exhausted, for I am pursuing Zebah and Zalmunna, the kings of Midian."

6 But the princes of Succoth asked, "Are[D] Zebah and Zalmunna now in your hands that we should give bread to your army?"

7 Gideon replied, "Very well, when the LORD has handed Zebah and Zalmunna over to me, I will trample[E] your flesh on thorns and briers from the wilderness!" 8 He went from there to Penuel and asked the same thing from them. The men of Penuel[f] answered just as the men of Succoth had answered. 9 He also told the men of Penuel, "When I return in peace, I will tear down this tower!"

10 Now Zebah and Zalmunna were in Karkor, and with them was their army of about 15,000 men, who were all those left of the entire army of the Qedemites. Those who had been killed were 120,000 warriors.[F] 11 Gideon traveled on the caravan route[G] east of Nobah[g] and Jogbehah and attacked their army while the army was unsuspecting. 12 Zebah and Zalmunna fled, and he pursued them. He captured these two kings of Midian and routed the entire army.

13 Gideon son of Joash returned from the battle by the Ascent of Heres. 14 He captured a youth from the men of Succoth and interrogated him. The youth wrote down for him the names of the 77 princes and elders of Succoth. 15 Then he went to the men of Succoth

[a]**7:22** 1Kg 4:12; 19:16 [b]**7:24** Jdg 8:3; Ps 83:11; Is 10:26 [c]**8:2** Lv 19:9-10; 23:22; Dt 24:19-20; Ru 2 [d]Lv 26:5; Is 24:13; 32:10; Mc 7:1 [e]**8:5** Gn 33:17; Jos 13:27; 1Kg 7:46; 2Ch 4:17; Ps 60:6 [f]**8:8** Gn 32:31-32; 1Kg 12:25 [g]**8:11** Nm 32:42

[A]**7:17** Lit *said to them* [B]**7:20** Lit *trumpets to blow* [C]**8:5** Lit *are at my feet* [D]**8:6** Lit *Are the hands of* [E]**8:7** Or *tear* [F]**8:10** Lit *men who drew the sword* [G]**8:11** Lit *on the route of those who live in tents*

and said, "Here are Zebah and Zalmunna. You
taunted me about them, saying, 'Are[A] Zebah
and Zalmunna now in your power that we
should give bread to your exhausted men?'"
16 So he took the elders of the city, and he took
some thorns and briers from the wilderness,
and he disciplined the men of Succoth with
them. 17 He also tore down the tower of Penuel
and killed the men of the city.
18 He asked Zebah and Zalmunna, "What
kind of men did you kill at Tabor?"

"They were like you," they said. "Each resembled the son of a king."

19 So he said, "They were my brothers, the
sons of my mother! As the LORD lives, if
you had let them live, I would not kill you."
20 Then he said to Jether, his firstborn, "Get up
and kill them." The youth did not draw his
sword, for he was afraid because he was still
a youth.

21 Zebah and Zalmunna said, "Get up and
kill us yourself, for a man is judged by his
strength." So Gideon got up, killed Zebah and
Zalmunna, and took the crescent ornaments
that were on the necks of their camels.

Gideon's Legacy

22 Then the Israelites said to Gideon, "Rule
over us, you as well as your sons and your
grandsons, for you delivered us from the
power of Midian."

23 But Gideon said to them, "I will not rule
over you, and my son will not rule over you;
the LORD will rule over you." 24 Then he said
to them, "Let me make a request of you: Everyone give me an earring from his plunder."
Now the enemy had gold earrings because
they were Ishmaelites.
25 They said, "We agree to give them." So
they spread out a mantle, and everyone
threw an earring from his plunder on it.
26 The weight of the gold earrings he requested was about 43 pounds[B] of gold, in
addition to the crescent ornaments and ear
pendants, the purple garments on the kings
of Midian, and the chains on the necks of
their camels. 27 Gideon made an ephod[a] from
all this and put it in Ophrah, his hometown.
Then all Israel prostituted themselves with it
there, and it became a snare to Gideon and
his household.
28 So Midian was subdued before the Israelites, and they were no longer a threat.[C] The
land was peaceful 40 years during the days of
Gideon. 29 Jerubbaal (that is, Gideon) son of
Joash went back to live at his house.
30 Gideon had 70 sons, his own offspring,
since he had many wives. 31 His concubine
who was in Shechem[b] also bore him a son, and
he named him Abimelech. 32 Then Gideon son
of Joash died at a ripe old age and was buried
in the tomb of his father Joash in Ophrah of
the Abiezrites.
33 When Gideon died, the Israelites turned
and prostituted themselves with the *Baals
and made Baal-berith[D] their god. 34 The Israelites did not remember the LORD their God who
had delivered them from the power of the enemies around them. 35 They did not show kindness[c] to the house of Jerubbaal (that is, Gideon)
for all the good he had done for Israel.

Abimelech Becomes King

9 Abimelech son of Jerubbaal went to his
mother's brothers at Shechem and spoke
to them and to all his maternal grandfather's
clan, saying, 2 "Please speak in the presence
of all the lords of Shechem, 'Is it better for
you that 70 men, all the sons of Jerubbaal,[d]
rule over you or that one man rule over you?'
Remember that I am your own flesh and
blood."[E]
3 His mother's relatives spoke all these
words about him in the presence of all the
lords of Shechem, and they were favorable to Abimelech, for they said, "He is our
brother." 4 So they gave him 70 pieces of silver
from the temple of Baal-berith.[D] Abimelech
hired worthless and reckless men with this
money, and they followed him. 5 He went to
his father's house in Ophrah and killed his
70 brothers, the sons of Jerubbaal, on top of
a large stone. But Jotham, the youngest son of
Jerubbaal, survived, because he hid himself.
6 Then all the lords of Shechem and of Beth-millo gathered together and proceeded to
make Abimelech king at the oak of the pillar
in Shechem.

[a] **8:27** Ex 25:7; 28:12; 39:12; Jdg 18:14,17-20; 2Sm 6:14; Hs 3:4
[b] **8:31** Gn 12:6; 37:12-14; Jos 21:22; Ps 60:6; 108:7
[c] **8:35** Gn 24:12,49; Ex 20:6; 2Sm 22:51; Ps 18:50
[d] **9:2** Jdg 6:32

[A] **8:15** Lit *Are the hands of* [B] **8:26** Lit *1,700 shekels* [C] **8:28** Lit *they no longer raised their head* [D] **8:33; 9:4** Lit *Baal of the Covenant*, or *Lord of the Covenant*
[E] **9:2** Lit *your bone and your flesh*

Jotham's Parable

7When they told Jotham, he climbed to the top of Mount Gerizim,[a] raised his voice, and called to them:

Listen to me, lords of Shechem,
and may God listen to you:
8 The trees set out
to anoint a king over themselves.
They said to the olive tree,
"Reign over us."
9 But the olive tree said to them,
"Should I stop giving my oil
that honors both God and man,
and rule[A] over the trees?"
10 Then the trees said to the fig tree,
"Come and reign over us."
11 But the fig tree said to them,
"Should I stop giving
my sweetness and my good fruit,
and rule[A] over trees?"
12 Later, the trees said to the grapevine,
"Come and reign over us."
13 But the grapevine said to them,
"Should I stop giving my wine
that cheers both God and man,
and rule[A] over trees?"
14 Finally, all the trees said to the bramble,
"Come and reign over us."
15 The bramble said to the trees,
"If you really are anointing me
as king over you,
come and find refuge in my shade.
But if not,
may fire come out from the bramble
and consume the cedars of Lebanon."

16"Now if you have acted faithfully[b] and
honestly[c] in making Abimelech king, if you
have done well by Jerubbaal and his family,
and if you have rewarded him appropriately
for what he did — 17for my father fought for
you, risked his life, and delivered you from
the hand of Midian, 18and now you have attacked my father's house today, killed his 70
sons on top of a large stone, and made Abimelech, the son of his slave, king over the lords
of Shechem 'because he is your brother' —
19if then you have acted faithfully and honestly with Jerubbaal and his house this day,
rejoice in Abimelech and may he also rejoice
in you. 20But if not, may fire come from Abimelech and consume the lords of Shechem and
Beth-millo, and may fire come from the lords
of Shechem and Beth-millo and consume
Abimelech." 21Then Jotham fled, escaping to
Beer, and lived there because of his brother
Abimelech.

Abimelech's Punishment

22When Abimelech had ruled over Israel
three years, 23God sent an evil spirit[d] between Abimelech and the lords of Shechem.
They treated Abimelech deceitfully, 24so that
the crime against the 70 sons of Jerubbaal
might come to justice and their blood would
be avenged on their brother Abimelech, who
killed them, and on the lords of Shechem,
who had helped him kill his brothers. 25The
lords of Shechem rebelled against him by
putting people on the tops of the mountains
to ambush[e] and rob everyone who passed by
them on the road. So this was reported to
Abimelech.
26Gaal son of Ebed came with his brothers
and crossed into Shechem, and the lords of
Shechem trusted him. 27So they went out to
the countryside and harvested grapes from
their vineyards. They trampled the grapes
and held a celebration.[f] Then they went to
the house of their god, and as they ate and
drank, they cursed Abimelech. 28Gaal son
of Ebed said, "Who is Abimelech and who
is Shechem that we should serve him? Isn't
he the son of Jerubbaal, and isn't Zebul his
officer? You are to serve the men of Hamor,
the father of Shechem.[g] Why should we serve
Abimelech? 29If only these people were in
my power, I would remove Abimelech." So he
said[B] to Abimelech, "Gather your army and
come out."
30When Zebul, the ruler of the city, heard
the words of Gaal son of Ebed, he was angry.
31So he sent messengers secretly to Abimelech, saying, "Look, Gaal son of Ebed, with
his brothers, have come to Shechem and are
turning the city against you.[C] 32Now tonight,
you and the people with you are to come wait
in ambush in the countryside. 33Then get up

[a]9:7 Dt 11:29; 27:12; Jos 8:33 [b]9:16 1Sm 12:24; 1Kg 2:4; Ps 111:8; Pr 29:14; Jr 32:41 [c]Jos 24:14; Ps 84:11 [d]9:23 1Sm 16:14-23; 18:10-12; 19:9; 2Kg 19:7 [e]9:25 Jos 8:2; 1Sm 15:5; 2Ch 20:22; Ezr 8:31; Ps 10:9; Pr 1:11; Jr 9:8 [f]9:27 Lv 19:24; Jdg 21:20-21 [g]9:28 Gn 33:19; 34:2-26; Jos 24:32

[A]9:9,11,13 Lit *and go to sway* [B]9:29 DSS read *They said*; LXX reads *I would say* [C]9:31 Hb obscure early, and at sunrise charge the city. When he and the people who are with him come out against you, do to him whatever you can."[A] 34 So Abimelech and all the people with him got up at night and waited in ambush for Shechem in four units.

35 Gaal son of Ebed went out and stood at the entrance of the city gate. Then Abimelech and the people who were with him got up from their ambush. 36 When Gaal saw the people, he said to Zebul, "Look, people are coming down from the mountaintops!" But Zebul said to him, "The shadows of the mountains look like men to you."

37 Then Gaal spoke again, "Look, people are coming down from the central part of the land,[a] and one unit is coming from the direction of the Diviners' Oak." 38 Zebul replied,[B] "Where is your mouthing off now? You said, 'Who is Abimelech that we should serve him?' Aren't these the people you despised? Now go and fight them!"

39 So Gaal went out leading the lords of Shechem and fought against Abimelech, 40 but Abimelech pursued him, and Gaal fled before him. Many wounded died[b] as far as the entrance of the gate. 41 Abimelech stayed in Arumah, and Zebul drove Gaal and his brothers from Shechem.

42 The next day when the people went into the countryside, this was reported to Abimelech. 43 He took the people, divided them into three companies, and waited in ambush in the countryside. He looked, and the people were coming out of the city, so he arose against them and struck them down. 44 Then Abimelech and the units that were with him rushed forward and took their stand at the entrance of the city gate. The other two units rushed against all who were in the countryside and struck them down. 45 So Abimelech fought against the city that entire day, captured it, and killed the people who were in it. Then he tore down the city and sowed it with salt.

46 When all the lords of the Tower of Shechem heard, they entered the inner chamber[C] of the temple of El-berith.[D] 47 Then it was reported to Abimelech that all the lords of the Tower of Shechem had gathered together. 48 So Abimelech and all the people who were with him went up to Mount Zalmon. Abimelech took his ax in his hand and cut a branch from the trees. He picked up the branch, put it on his shoulder, and said to the people who were with him, "Hurry and do what you have seen me do." 49 Each person also cut his own branch and followed Abimelech. They put the branches against the inner chamber and set it on fire around the people, and all the people in the Tower of Shechem died — about 1,000 men and women.

50 Abimelech went to Thebez,[c] camped against it, and captured it. 51 There was a strong tower inside the city, and all the men, women, and lords of the city fled there. They locked themselves in and went up to the roof of the tower. 52 When Abimelech came to attack the tower, he approached its entrance to set it on fire. 53 But a woman threw the upper portion of a millstone on Abimelech's head and fractured his skull. 54 He quickly called his armor-bearer and said to him, "Draw your sword and kill me, or they'll say about me, 'A woman killed him.'" So his armor-bearer thrust him through, and he died. 55 When the Israelites saw that Abimelech was dead, they all went home.

56 In this way, God turned back on Abimelech the evil that he had done against his father, by killing his 70 brothers. 57 And God also returned all the evil of the men of Shechem on their heads. So the curse of Jotham son of Jerubbaal came on them.[d]

Tola and Jair

10 After Abimelech, Tola son of Puah, son of Dodo became judge and began to deliver Israel. He was from Issachar and lived in Shamir in the hill country of Ephraim. 2 Tola judged Israel 23 years and when he died, was buried in Shamir.

3 After him came Jair the Gileadite,[e] who judged Israel 22 years. 4 He had 30 sons who rode on 30 donkeys. They had 30 towns[E] in Gilead, which are called Jair's Villages[F] to this day. 5 When Jair died, he was buried in Kamon.

[a] **9:37** Ezk 38:12
[b] **9:40** 1Sm 17:52; 2Ch 13:17; Ezk 6:4,7; Dn 11:26
[c] **9:50** 2Sm 11:21
[d] **9:57** Jdg 9:20
[e] **10:3** Nm 26:29-10; Jos 17:1,3; Jdg 11:1-2; 1Ch 2:12-24; 7:14-17

[A] **9:33** Lit *him as your hand will find* [B] **9:38** Lit *replied to him* [C] **9:46** Or *the crypt*, or *the vault* [D] **9:46** = God of the Covenant [E] **10:4** LXX; MT reads *donkeys* [F] **10:4** Or *called Havvoth-jair*

Israel's Rebellion and Repentance

6Then the Israelites again did what was evil
in the sight of the LORD.[a] They worshiped
the ·Baals and the ·Ashtoreths, the gods of
Aram, Sidon, and Moab, and the gods of the
Ammonites and the Philistines.[b] They abandoned ·Yahweh and did not worship Him.[c]
7So the LORD's anger burned against Israel,
and He sold them to[A] the Philistines and the
Ammonites. 8They shattered and crushed
the Israelites that year, and for 18 years they
did the same to all the Israelites who were
on the other side of the Jordan[d] in the land
of the Amorites[e] in Gilead. 9The Ammonites
also crossed the Jordan to fight against Judah,
Benjamin, and the house of Ephraim. Israel
was greatly oppressed, 10so they cried out to
the LORD, saying, "We have sinned against
You.[f] We have abandoned our God and worshiped the Baals."
11The LORD said to the Israelites, "When
the Egyptians,[g] Amorites, Ammonites, Philistines, 12Sidonians, Amalekites, and Ma-
onites[B,h] oppressed you, and you cried out to
Me, did I not deliver you from their power?
13But you have abandoned Me and worshiped
other gods. Therefore, I will not deliver you
again. 14Go and cry out to the gods you have
chosen.[i] Let them deliver you in the time of
your oppression."
15But the Israelites said, "We have sinned.
Deal with us as You see fit;[C] only deliver us[j]
today!" 16So they got rid of the foreign gods[k]
among them and worshiped the LORD,[l] and
He became weary[m] of Israel's misery.
17The Ammonites were called together, and
they camped in Gilead. So the Israelites assembled and camped at Mizpah.[n] 18The rulers[D] of Gilead said to one another, "Which
man will lead the fight against the Ammonites? He will be the leader of all the inhabitants of Gilead."

Jephthah Becomes Israel's Leader

11 Jephthah[o] the Gileadite was a great
warrior,[p] but he was the son of a prostitute, and Gilead was his father. 2Gilead's
wife bore him sons, and when they grew up,
they drove Jephthah out and said to him,
"You will have no inheritance in our father's
house, because you are the son of another
woman." 3So Jephthah fled from his brothers and lived in the land of Tob.[q] Then some
lawless men joined Jephthah and traveled
with him.
4Some time later, the Ammonites fought
against Israel. 5When the Ammonites made
war with Israel, the elders of Gilead went to
get Jephthah from the land of Tob. 6They said
to him, "Come, be our commander, and let's
fight against the Ammonites."
7Jephthah replied to the elders of Gilead,
"Didn't you hate me and drive me from my
father's house? Why then have you come to
me now when you're in trouble?"
8They answered Jephthah, "Since that's
true, we now turn to you. Come with us, fight
the Ammonites, and you will become leader
of all the inhabitants of Gilead."
9So Jephthah said to them, "If you are bringing me back to fight the Ammonites and the
LORD gives them to me, I will be your leader."
10The elders of Gilead said to Jephthah,
"The LORD is our witness if we don't do as you
say." 11So Jephthah went with the elders of
Gilead. The people put him over themselves
as leader and commander, and Jephthah repeated all his terms in the presence of the
LORD at Mizpah.

Jephthah Rejects Ammonite Claims

12Jephthah sent messengers to the king
of the Ammonites, saying, "What do you
have against me that you have come to fight
against me in my land?"
13The king of the Ammonites said to Jephthah's messengers, "When Israel came from
Egypt, they seized my land from the Arnon
to the Jabbok[r] and the Jordan. Now restore it
peaceably."
14Jephthah again sent messengers to the
king of the Ammonites 15to tell him, "This is
what Jephthah says: Israel did not take away
the land of Moab or the land of the Ammonites. 16But when they came from Egypt, Israel
traveled through the wilderness to the ·Red
Sea and came to Kadesh. 17Israel sent messengers to the king of Edom, saying, 'Please
let us travel through your land,' but the king
of Edom would not listen. They also sent

[a] **10:6** Jdg 3:12; 4:1
[b] 1Kg 11:33
[c] Ex 20:5; 23:24; Dt 5:9; Jos 23:7; 2Kg 17:35; Neh 9:35; Is 60:12; Mal 3:18
[d] **10:8** Gn 50:10-11; Dt 1:1,5; 3:8,20,25; Jos 12:17; Jdg 5:17
[e] Nm 21:31; Jos 24:8; Jdg 11:21; Am 2:10
[f] **10:10** Neh 1:6; Jr 14:20; Dn 9:8
[g] **10:11** Ex 1–15
[h] **10:12** Jos 15:5; 1Sm 23:24-25
[i] **10:14** Dt 32:37-38; Jr 2:28; 11:12
[j] **10:15** 1Sm 12:10; 1Ch 16:35; Ps 79:9
[k] **10:16** Gn 35:2; Jos 24:33; 1Sm 7:3; 2Ch 33:15
[l] Ex 10:7-8; 12:31; Dt 10:12; Jos 24:14-15; 2Ch 30:8
[m] Nm 21:4; Jdg 16:16; Mc 2:7; Zch 11:8
[n] **10:17** Gn 31:49; Jdg 11:11,34; Hs 5:1
[o] **11:1** 1Sm 12:11; Heb 11:32
[p] Jdg 6:12; Ru 2:1; 1Sm 9:1; 16:18; 1Kg 11:28; 2Kg 5:1
[q] **11:3** 2Sm 10:6,8
[r] **11:13** Nm 21:24; Dt 2:37; 3:16

[A] **10:7** Lit *into the hand of* [B] **10:12** LXX reads *Midianites* [C] **10:15** Lit *Do to us what is good in Your eyes* [D] **10:18** Lit *The people, rulers*

messengers to the king of Moab, but he refused. So Israel stayed in Kadesh.
18“Then they traveled through the wilderness and around the lands of Edom and
Moab. They came to the east side of the land
of Moab and camped on the other side of the
Arnon but did not enter into the territory of
Moab, for the Arnon was the boundary of
Moab.
19“Then Israel sent messengers to Sihon
king of the Amorites, king of Heshbon.[a] Israel
said to him, ‘Please let us travel through your
land to our country,’ 20but Sihon would not
trust Israel to pass through his territory. Instead, Sihon gathered all his people, camped
at Jahaz, and fought with Israel. 21Then the
LORD God of Israel handed over Sihon and all
his people to Israel, and they defeated them.
So Israel took possession[b] of the entire land
of the Amorites who lived in that country.
22They took possession of all the territory of
the Amorites from the Arnon to the Jabbok
and from the wilderness to the Jordan.
23“The LORD God of Israel has now driven
out the Amorites before His people Israel,
and will you now force us out? 24Isn’t it true
that you may possess whatever your god Chemosh drives out for you, and we may possess
everything the LORD our God drives out before us? 25Now are you any better than Balak
son of Zippor, king of Moab? Did he ever
contend with Israel or fight against them?
26While Israel lived 300 years in Heshbon
and its villages, in Aroer and its villages, and
in all the cities that are on the banks of the
Arnon, why didn’t you take them back at that
time? 27I have not sinned against you, but
you have wronged me by fighting against me.
Let the LORD who is the Judge[c] decide today
between the Israelites and the Ammonites.”
28But the king of the Ammonites would not
listen to Jephthah’s message that he sent him.

Jephthah’s Vow and Sacrifice

29The Spirit of the LORD came on Jephthah,
who traveled through Gilead and Manasseh,
and then through Mizpah of Gilead. He
crossed over to the Ammonites from Mizpah
of Gilead. 30Jephthah made this vow[d] to the
LORD: “If You will hand over the Ammonites
to me, 31whatever comes out of the doors of
my house to greet me when I return in peace
from the Ammonites will belong to the LORD,
and I will offer it as a ˙burnt offering.”[e]
32Jephthah crossed over to the Ammonites
to fight against them, and the LORD handed
them over[f] to him. 33He defeated 20 of their
cities with a great slaughter from Aroer all
the way to the entrance of Minnith and to
Abel-keramim. So the Ammonites were subdued[g] before the Israelites.
34When Jephthah went to his home in Mizpah, there was his daughter, coming out to
meet him with tambourines and dancing![h]
She was his only child; he had no other son
or daughter besides her. 35When he saw her,
he tore his clothes and said, “No! Not my
daughter! You have devastated me! You have
brought great misery on me.[A] I have given my
word to the LORD and cannot take it back.”
36Then she said to him, “My father, you have
given your word to the LORD. Do to me as you
have said, for the LORD brought vengeance
on your enemies, the Ammonites.” 37She also
said to her father, “Let me do this one thing:
Let me wander two months through the
mountains with my friends and mourn my
virginity.”
38“Go,” he said. And he sent her away two
months. So she left with her friends and
mourned her virginity as she wandered
through the mountains. 39At the end of two
months, she returned to her father, and he
kept the vow he had made about her. And she
had never been intimate with a man. Now it
became a custom in Israel 40that four days
each year the young women of Israel would
commemorate the daughter of Jephthah the
Gileadite.

Conflict with Ephraim

12 The men of Ephraim were called together and crossed the Jordan to Zaphon.[i] They said to Jephthah, “Why have you
crossed over to fight against the Ammonites
but didn’t call us to go with you? We will burn
your house down with you in it!”
2Then Jephthah said to them, “My people
and I had a serious conflict with the Ammonites. So I called for you, but you didn’t deliver

[a]**11:19** Nm 21:25,28,30,34; Dt 3:2,6; Neh 9:22; Is 15:4
[b]**11:21** Nm 21:24; Dt 4:47; Jos 12:1; Jdg 1:19
[c]**11:27** Gn 18:25; Jb 9:15; 23:7; Ps 7:11; 50:6; 75:7; Is 33:22
[d]**11:30** Gn 28:20; Nm 30:2; 1Sm 1:11
[e]**11:31** Ps 66:13
[f]**11:32** Jdg 12:3; 1Sm 14:10
[g]**11:33** Lv 26:41; Jdg 3:30; 8:28; 1Sm 7:13; 1Ch 20:4; 2Ch 13:18; Ps 106:42
[h]**11:34** Ex 15:20; 32:19; Jdg 21:21; Sg 6:13
[i]**12:1** Jos 13:27

[A]**11:35** Lit *have been among those who trouble me*

me from their power. 3When I saw that you weren't going to deliver me, I took my life in my own hands and crossed over to the Ammonites, and the LORD handed them over to me. Why then have you come[A] today to fight against me?"

4Then Jephthah gathered all of the men of Gilead. They fought and defeated Ephraim, because Ephraim had said, "You Gileadites are Ephraimite fugitives in the territories of Ephraim and Manasseh." 5The Gileadites captured the fords of the Jordan leading to Ephraim. Whenever a fugitive from Ephraim said, "Let me cross over," the Gileadites asked him, "Are you an Ephraimite?" If he answered, "No," 6they told him, "Please say Shibboleth." If he said, "Sibboleth," because he could not pronounce it correctly, they seized him and killed him at the fords of the Jordan. At that time 42,000 from Ephraim died.

7Jephthah judged Israel six years, and when he died, he was buried in one of the cities of Gilead.[B]

Ibzan, Elon, and Abdon

8Ibzan, who was from Bethlehem,[a] judged Israel after Jephthah 9and had 30 sons. He gave his 30 daughters in marriage to men outside the tribe and brought back 30 wives for his sons from outside the tribe. Ibzan judged Israel seven years, 10and when he died, he was buried in Bethlehem.

11Elon, who was from Zebulun, judged Israel after Ibzan. He judged Israel 10 years, 12and when he died, he was buried in Aijalon in the land of Zebulun.

13After Elon, Abdon son of Hillel, who was from Pirathon,[b] judged Israel. 14He had 40 sons and 30 grandsons, who rode on 70 donkeys. Abdon judged Israel eight years, 15and when he died, he was buried in Pirathon in the land of Ephraim, in the hill country of the Amalekites.[c]

Birth of Samson, the Last Judge

13 The Israelites again did what was evil in the LORD's sight,[d] so the LORD handed them over to the Philistines 40 years. 2There was a certain man from Zorah,[e] from the family of Dan, whose name was Manoah; his wife was unable to conceive and had no children. 3The Angel of the LORD appeared to the woman and said to her, "It is true that you are unable to conceive and have no children, but you will conceive and give birth to a son. 4Now please be careful not to drink wine or beer,[f] or to eat anything •unclean;[g] 5for indeed, you will conceive and give birth to a son. You must never cut his hair,[C] because the boy will be a Nazirite[h] to God from birth, and he will begin to save Israel from the power of the Philistines."

6Then the woman went and told her husband, "A man of God came to me. He looked like the awe-inspiring Angel of God. I didn't ask Him where He came from, and He didn't tell me His name. 7He said to me, 'You will conceive and give birth to a son. Therefore, do not drink wine or beer, and do not eat anything unclean, because the boy will be a Nazirite to God from birth until the day of his death.'"

8Manoah prayed[i] to the LORD and said, "Please Lord, let the man of God you sent come again to us and teach us what we should do for the boy who will be born."

9God listened[j] to[D] Manoah, and the Angel of God came again to the woman. She was sitting in the field, and her husband Manoah was not with her. 10The woman ran quickly to her husband and told him, "The man who came to me today has just come back!"

11So Manoah got up and followed his wife. When he came to the man, he asked, "Are You the man who spoke to my wife?"

"I am," He said.

12Then Manoah asked, "When Your words come true, what will the boy's responsibilities and mission[E] be?"

13The Angel of the LORD answered Manoah, "Your wife needs to do everything I told her. 14She must not eat anything that comes from the grapevine or drink wine or beer. And she must not eat anything unclean. Your wife must do everything I have commanded her."

15"Please stay here," Manoah told Him, "and we will prepare a young goat[k] for You."

16The Angel of the LORD said to him, "If I stay, I won't eat your food. But if you want to prepare a •burnt offering, offer it to the

[a]**12:8** Gn 35:19; Ru 1:1-2; Mc 5:2
[b]**12:13** 2Sm 23:30; 1Ch 11:31; 27:14
[c]**12:15** Gn 14:7; Nm 14:45; 2Sm 1:8,13
[d]**13:1** Jdg 3:12; 4:1; 10:6
[e]**13:2** Jos 19:42; Jdg 13:25; 16:31; 18:2,8,11
[f]**13:4** Nm 6:3
[g]Lv 7:19,21; 22:8; Dt 12:22; 14:10; 15:22; Hs 9:3-4
[h]**13:5** Nm 6:2
[i]**13:8** Gn 25:21; Ex 10:18; Jb 33:26
[j]**13:9** Gn 16:11; Ex 16:8; Dt 1:45; 33:7; Jos 10:14; Ps 27:7
[k]**13:15** Gn 18:5

[A]**12:3** Lit *come to me* [B]**12:7** LXX reads *in his city in Gilead* [C]**13:5** Lit *And a razor is not to go up on his head* [D]**13:9** Lit *to the voice of* [E]**13:12** Lit *work*

LORD." For Manoah did not know He was the Angel of the LORD.

17 Then Manoah said to Him, "What is Your name, so that we may honor You when Your words come true?"

18 "Why do you ask My name," the Angel of the LORD asked him, "since it is wonderful."[a]

19 Manoah took a young goat and a •grain offering and offered them on a rock to the LORD, and He did a wonderful thing[A] while Manoah and his wife were watching. 20 When the flame went up from the altar to the sky, the Angel of the LORD went up in its flame. When Manoah and his wife saw this, they fell facedown on the ground. 21 The Angel of the LORD did not appear again to Manoah and his wife. Then Manoah realized that it was the Angel of the LORD.

22 "We're going to die," he said to his wife, "because we have seen God!"[b]

23 But his wife said to him, "If the LORD had intended to kill us, He wouldn't have accepted the burnt offering and the grain offering from us, and He would not have shown us all these things or spoken to us now like this."

24 So the woman gave birth to a son and named him Samson.[c] The boy grew,[d] and the LORD blessed him. 25 Then the Spirit of the LORD began to direct him in the Camp of Dan,[B] between Zorah and Eshtaol.[e]

Samson's Riddle

14 Samson went down to Timnah[f] and saw a young Philistine woman there. 2 He went back and told his father and his mother: "I have seen a young Philistine woman in Timnah. Now get her for me as a wife."

3 But his father and mother said to him, "Can't you find[C] a young woman among your relatives or among any of our people? Must you go to the uncircumcised Philistines for a wife?"

But Samson told his father, "Get her for me, because I want her."[D] 4 Now his father and mother did not know this was from the LORD,[g] who was seeking an occasion against the Philistines. At that time, the Philistines were ruling over Israel.

5 Samson went down to Timnah with his father and mother and came to the vineyards of Timnah. Suddenly a young lion came roaring at him, 6 the Spirit of the LORD took control of[E,h] him, and he tore the lion apart with his bare hands as he might have torn a young goat. But he did not tell his father or mother what he had done. 7 Then he went and spoke to the woman, because Samson wanted her.[F]

8 After some time, when he returned to get her, he left the road to see the lion's carcass, and there was a swarm of bees with honey in the carcass. 9 He scooped some honey into his hands and ate it as he went along. When he returned to his father and mother, he gave some to them and they ate it. But he did not tell them that he had scooped the honey from the lion's carcass.[i]

10 His father went to visit the woman, and Samson prepared a feast there, as young men were accustomed to do. 11 When the Philistines saw him, they brought 30 men to accompany him.

12 "Let me tell you a riddle,"[j] Samson said to them. "If you can explain it to me during the seven days of the feast and figure it out, I will give you 30 linen garments and 30 changes of clothes. 13 But if you can't explain it to me, you must give me 30 linen garments and 30 changes of clothes."

"Tell us your riddle," they replied.[G] "Let's hear it."

14 So he said to them:

Out of the eater came something to eat,
and out of the strong came something
sweet.

After three days, they were unable to explain the riddle. 15 On the fourth[H] day they said to Samson's wife, "Persuade your husband to explain the riddle to us, or we will burn you and your father's household to death. Did you invite us here to rob us?"

16 So Samson's wife came to him, weeping, and said, "You hate me and don't love me![k] You told my people the riddle, but haven't explained it to me."

"Look," he said,[I] "I haven't even explained

[a] **13:18** Gn 32:29
[b] **13:22** Gn 33:10; Ex 24:10; 33:20; Jdg 6:22; Is 6:5
[c] **13:24** Heb 11:32
[d] 1Sm 3:19; Lk 1:80
[e] **13:25** Jos 15:33; Jdg 16:31; 18:2,8,11; 1Ch 2:53
[f] **14:1** Jos 15:10; 19:43; 2Ch 28:18
[g] **14:4** Jos 11:20; 1Kg 12:15; 2Kg 6:33
[h] **14:6** Jdg 14:19; 15:14; 1Sm 10:6,10; 11:6; 16:13; 18:10
[i] **14:9** Lv 11:27
[j] **14:12** Nm 12:8; Ps 49:4; Pr 1:6; Ezk 17:2; Dn 8:23
[k] **14:16** Jdg 16:15

[A] **13:19** LXX reads *to the LORD, to the One who works wonders* [B] **13:25** Or *in Mahaneh-dan* [C] **14:3** Lit *Is there not* [D] **14:3** Lit *because she is right in my eyes* [E] **14:6** Lit *LORD rushed on* [F] **14:7** Lit *because she was right in the eyes of Samson* [G] **14:13** Lit *replied to him* [H] **14:15** LXX, Syr; MT reads *seventh* [I] **14:16** Lit *said to her*

it to my father or mother, so why should I explain it to you?"
17She wept the whole seven days of the feast,
and at last, on the seventh day, he explained it
to her, because she had nagged him so much.
Then she explained it to her people. 18On the
seventh day, before sunset, the men of the city
said to him:

What is sweeter than honey?
What is stronger than a lion?

So he said to them:

If you hadn't plowed with
my young cow,
you wouldn't know my riddle now!

19The Spirit of the LORD took control of
him, and he went down to Ashkelon and
killed 30 of their men. He stripped them and
gave their clothes to those who had explained
the riddle. In a rage, Samson returned to his
father's house, 20and his wife was given to one
of the men who had accompanied him.

Samson's Revenge

15 Later on, during the wheat harvest,[a]
Samson took a young goat as a gift and
visited his wife. "I want to go to my wife in
her room," he said. But her father would not
let him enter.
2"I was sure you hated her," her father said,
"so I gave her to one of the men who accompanied you. Isn't her younger sister more
beautiful than she is? Why not take her instead?"
3Samson said to them, "This time I won't
be responsible[b] when I harm the Philistines."
4So he went out and caught 300 foxes.[c] He
took torches, turned the foxes tail-to-tail, and
put a torch between each pair of tails. 5Then
he ignited the torches and released the foxes
into the standing grain of the Philistines. He
burned up the piles of grain and the standing grain as well as the vineyards and olive
groves.[d]
6Then the Philistines asked, "Who did
this?"
They were told, "It was Samson, the Tim-
nite's son-in-law, because he has taken Samson's wife and given her to another man." So
the Philistines went to her and her father and
burned them to death.
7Then Samson told them, "Because you
did this, I swear that I won't rest until I have
taken vengeance on you." 8He tore them limb
from limb[A] with a great slaughter, and he
went down and stayed in the cave at the rock
of Etam.
9The Philistines went up, camped in Judah,
and raided Lehi. 10So the men of Judah said,
"Why have you attacked us?"
They replied, "We have come to arrest Samson and pay him back for what he did to us."
11Then 3,000 men of Judah went to the cave
at the rock of Etam, and they asked Samson,
"Don't you realize that the Philistines rule
over us?[e] What have you done to us?"
"I have done to them what they did to me,"
he answered.[B]
12They said to him, "We've come to arrest
you and hand you over to the Philistines."
Then Samson told them, "Swear to me that
you yourselves won't kill me."
13"No," they said,[C] "we won't kill you, but
we will tie you up securely and hand you over
to them." So they tied him up with two new
ropes[f] and led him away from the rock.
14When he came to Lehi, the Philistines
came to meet him shouting. The Spirit of the
LORD took control of[D] him, and the ropes that
were on his arms became like burnt flax and
his bonds fell off his wrists. 15He found a fresh
jawbone of a donkey, reached out his hand,
took it, and killed 1,000 men with it. 16Then
Samson said:

With the jawbone of a donkey
I have piled them in a heap.
With the jawbone of a donkey
I have killed 1,000 men.

17When he finished speaking, he threw away
the jawbone and named that place Ramath-
lehi.[E] 18He became very thirsty and called out
to the LORD: "You have accomplished this
great victory through[F] Your servant. Must I
now die of thirst and fall into the hands of
the uncircumcised?" 19So God split a hollow
place in the ground at Lehi, and water came

[a]**15:1** Gn 30:14; Ex 34:22; 1Sm 6:13; 12:17
[b]**15:3** Nm 5:19,28,31; 1Sm 26:9; Jr 2:35
[c]**15:4** Neh 4:3; Ps 63:10; Sg 2:15; Lm 5:18; Ezk 13:4
[d]**15:5** Ex 22:6
[e]**15:11** Lv 26:25; Dt 28:43; Jdg 13:1; 14:4; Ps 106:40-42
[f]**15:13** Jdg 16:11-12

[A]**15:8** Lit *He struck them hip on thigh* [B]**15:11** Lit *answered them* [C]**15:13** Lit *said to him* [D]**15:14** Lit *LORD rushed on* [E]**15:17** = High Place of the Jawbone [F]**15:18** Lit *through the hand of*

out of it. After Samson drank, his strength
returned, and he revived.[a] That is why he
named it En-hakkore,[A] which is in Lehi to
this day. 20And he judged Israel 20 years in
the days of the Philistines.

Samson and Delilah

16 Samson went to Gaza,[b] where he saw
a prostitute and went to bed with
her. 2When the Gazites heard that Samson
was there, they surrounded the place and
waited in ambush for him all that night at
the city gate. While they were waiting quietly,[B] they said, "Let us wait until dawn; then
we will kill him." 3But Samson stayed in bed
until midnight when he got up, took hold
of the doors of the city gate along with the
two gateposts, and pulled them out, bar and
all. He put them on his shoulders and took
them to the top of the mountain overlooking Hebron.

4Some time later, he fell in love with a
woman named Delilah, who lived in the
Sorek Valley. 5The Philistine leaders[c] went to
her and said, "Persuade him to tell you[C] where
his great strength comes from, so we can
overpower him, tie him up, and make him
helpless. Each of us will then give you 1,100
pieces of silver."

6So Delilah said to Samson, "Please tell me,
where does your great strength come from?
How could someone tie you up and make you
helpless?"

7Samson told her, "If they tie me up with
seven fresh bowstrings that have not been
dried, I will become weak and be like any
other man."

8The Philistine leaders brought her seven
fresh bowstrings that had not been dried, and
she tied him up with them. 9While the men
in ambush were waiting in her room, she
called out to him, "Samson, the Philistines are
here!"[D] But he snapped the bowstrings as a
strand of yarn snaps when it touches fire. The
secret of his strength remained unknown.

10Then Delilah said to Samson, "You have
mocked me and told me lies! Won't you
please tell me how you can be tied up?"

11He told her, "If they tie me up with new
ropes that have never been used,[d] I will become weak and be like any other man."

12Delilah took new ropes, tied him up with
them, and shouted, "Samson, the Philistines
are here!"[D] But while the men in ambush
were waiting in her room, he snapped the
ropes off his arms like a thread.

13Then Delilah said to Samson, "You have
mocked me all along and told me lies! Tell me
how you can be tied up."

He told her, "If you weave the seven braids
on my head with the web of a loom —"[E]

14She fastened the braids with a pin and
called to him, "Samson, the Philistines are
here!"[D] He awoke from his sleep and pulled
out the pin, with the loom and the web.

15"How can you say, 'I love you,'"[e] she told
him, "when your heart is not with me? This is
the third time you have mocked me and not
told me what makes your strength so great!"

16Because she nagged him day after day and
pleaded with him until she wore him out,[F]
17he told her the whole truth and said to her,
"My hair has never been cut,[G] because I am a
Nazirite[f] to God from birth. If I am shaved,
my strength will leave me, and I will become
weak and be like any other man."

18When Delilah realized that he had told
her the whole truth, she sent this message to
the Philistine leaders: "Come one more time,
for he has told me the whole truth." The Philistine leaders came to her and brought the
money with them.

19Then she let him fall asleep on her lap and
called a man to shave off the seven braids on
his head. In this way, she made him helpless,[H]
and his strength left him. 20Then she cried,
"Samson, the Philistines are here!"[D] When he
awoke from his sleep, he said, "I will escape as
I did before and shake myself free." But he did
not know that the LORD had left him.[g]

Samson's Defeat and Death

21The Philistines seized him and gouged
out his eyes. They brought him down to Gaza
and bound him with bronze shackles, and he
was forced to grind grain in the prison. 22But

[a]**15:19** Gn 45:27; 1Kg 17:22; 2Kg 13:21; Is 38:16,21; Ezk 37:3,14
[b]**16:1** Jos 15:47
[c]**16:5** Jos 13:3
[d]**16:11** Jdg 15:13
[e]**16:15** Jdg 14:6
[f]**16:17** Nm 6:5; Jdg 13:5
[g]**16:20** Nm 14:9,42-43; Jos 7:12; 1Sm 16:14; 18:12; 28:15-16; 2Ch 15:2

[A]**15:19** = Spring of the One Who Cried Out [B]**16:2** Lit *quietly all night* [C]**16:5** Lit *him and see* [D]**16:9,12,14,20** Lit *are on you* [E]**16:13-14** LXX reads *loom and fasten them with a pin into the wall and I will become weak and be like any other man." 14And while he was sleeping, Delilah wove the seven braids on his head into the loom.* [F]**16:16** Lit *him and he became short to death* [G]**16:17** Lit *A razor has not gone up on my head* [H]**16:19** LXX reads *way he began to weaken*

his hair began to grow back after it had been
shaved.
23 Now the Philistine leaders gathered together to offer a great sacrifice to their god
Dagon.[a] They rejoiced and said:

Our god has handed over
our enemy Samson to us.

24 When the people saw him, they praised
their god[b] and said:

Our god has handed over to us
our enemy who destroyed our land
and who multiplied our dead.

25 When they were drunk,[A] they said, "Bring
Samson here to entertain us." So they brought
Samson from prison, and he entertained
them. They had him stand between the pillars.
26 Samson said to the young man who was
leading him by the hand, "Lead me where I
can feel the pillars supporting the temple, so I
can lean against them." 27 The temple was full
of men and women; all the leaders of the Philistines were there, and about 3,000 men and
women were on the roof watching Samson
entertain them. 28 He called out to the LORD:
"Lord GOD, please remember me.[c] Strengthen
me, God, just once more. With one act of vengeance, let me pay back the Philistines for my
two eyes." 29 Samson took hold of the two middle pillars supporting the temple and leaned
against them, one on his right hand and the
other on his left. 30 Samson said, "Let me die
with the Philistines." He pushed with all his
might, and the temple fell on the leaders and
all the people in it. And the dead he killed at
his death were more than those he had killed
in his life.
31 Then his brothers and his father's family came down, carried him back, and buried
him between Zorah and Eshtaol in the tomb
of his father Manoah. So he judged Israel 20
years.

Micah's Priest

17 There was a man from the hill country
of Ephraim named Micah. 2 He said to
his mother, "The 1,100 pieces of silver taken
from you, and that I heard you utter a curse
about — here, I have the silver with me. I took
it. So now I return it to you."[B]
Then his mother said, "My son, you are
blessed by the LORD!"[d]
3 He returned the 1,100 pieces of silver to
his mother, and his mother said, "I personally consecrate[e] the silver to the LORD for my
son's benefit to make a carved image overlaid
with silver."[C] 4 So he returned the silver to his
mother, and she took five pounds of silver
and gave it to a silversmith. He made it into a
carved image overlaid with silver,[C] and it was
in Micah's house.
5 This man Micah had a shrine, and he made
an ·ephod and household idols,[f] and installed
one of his sons to be his priest. 6 In those days
there was no king in Israel;[g] everyone did
whatever he wanted.[D]
7 There was a young man, a Levite from
Bethlehem in Judah, who resided within
the clan of Judah.[h] 8 The man left the town
of Bethlehem in Judah to settle wherever he
could find a place. On his way he came to Micah's home in the hill country of Ephraim.
9 "Where do you come from?" Micah asked
him.
He answered him, "I am a Levite from Bethlehem in Judah, and I'm going to settle wherever I can find a place."
10 Micah replied,[E] "Stay with me and be my
father[i] and priest, and I will give you four
ounces of silver a year, along with your clothing and provisions." So the Levite went in
11 and agreed to stay with the man, and the
young man became like one of his sons. 12 Micah consecrated the Levite, and the young
man became his priest[j] and lived in Micah's
house. 13 Then Micah said, "Now I know that
the LORD will be good to me, because a Levite
has become my priest."

Dan's Invasion and Idolatry

18 In those days, there was no king in Israel,[k] and the Danite tribe was looking
for territory to occupy. Up to that time no territory had been captured by them among the
tribes of Israel. 2 So the Danites sent out five
brave men[l] from all their clans, from Zorah

[a] 16:23 Jos 15:41; 19:27; 1Sm 5:2-5,7; 1Ch 10:10
[b] 16:24 Dn 5:4
[c] 16:28 Jr 15:15
[d] 17:2 Ru 2:20; 1Sm 15:13
[e] 17:3 Lv 22:2-3; 27:14-19; 1Ch 18:11; 26:26-28; 2Ch 30:17
[f] 17:5 Gn 31:19,34-35; Jdg 18:14; 1Sm 19:13; 2Kg 23:24; Hs 3:4
[g] 17:6 Jdg 18:1; 19:1; 21:25
[h] 17:7 Dt 18:6-7
[i] 17:10 Gn 45:8; Jdg 18:19; Jr 3:19
[j] 17:12 Jdg 18:30
[k] 18:1 Jdg 17:6; 19:1; 21:25
[l] 18:2 Dt 3:18; 1Sm 14:52; 18:17; 2Sm 2:7; 13:28; 17:10; 1Kg 1:52; 2Kg 2:16

A16:25 Or *When they were feeling good* B17:2 MT places this sentence at the end of v. 3. C17:3,4 Or *image and a cast image* D17:6 Lit *did what was right in his eyes* E17:10 Lit *replied to him*

and Eshtaol,[a] to scout[b] out the land and explore it. They told them, "Go and explore the
land."

They came to the hill country of Ephraim as
far as the home of Micah and spent the night
there. 3While they were near Micah's home,
they recognized the speech of the young Levite. So they went over to him and asked,
"Who brought you here? What are you doing
in this place? What is keeping you here?" 4He
told them what Micah had done for him and
that he had hired him as his priest.

5Then they said to him, "Please inquire of
God so we will know if we will have a successful journey."

6The priest told them, "Go in peace. The
LORD is watching over the journey you are
going on."

7The five men left and came to Laish. They
saw that the people who were there were living securely, in the same way as the Sidonians,
quiet and unsuspecting. There was nothing
lacking[A] in the land and no oppressive ruler.
They were far from the Sidonians, having no
alliance with anyone.[B]

8When the men went back to their clans at
Zorah and Eshtaol, their people asked them,
"What did you find out?"

9They answered, "Come on, let's go up
against them, for we have seen the land, and
it is very good. Why wait? Don't hesitate to go
and invade and take possession of the land!
10When you get there, you will come to an
unsuspecting people and a spacious land, for
God has handed it over to you. It is a place
where nothing on earth is lacking."[c] 11Six
hundred Danites departed from Zorah and
Eshtaol armed with weapons of war. 12They
went up and camped at Kiriath-jearim[d] in Judah. This is why the place is called the Camp
of Dan[C] to this day; it is west of Kiriath-jearim.
13From there they traveled to the hill country
of Ephraim and arrived at Micah's house.

14The five men who had gone to scout out
the land of Laish told their brothers, "Did you
know that there are an •ephod, household
gods, and a carved image overlaid with silver[D] in these houses? Now think about what
you should do." 15So they detoured there and
went to the house of the young Levite at the
home of Micah and greeted him. 16The 600
Danite men were standing by the entrance of
the gate, armed with their weapons of war.
17Then the five men who had gone to scout
out the land went in and took the carved image overlaid with silver,[D] the ephod, and the
household idols, while the priest was standing by the entrance of the gate with the 600
men armed with weapons of war.

18When they entered Micah's house and
took the carved image overlaid with silver,[D]
the ephod, and the household idols, the priest
said to them, "What are you doing?"

19They told him, "Be quiet. Keep your
mouth shut.[E,e] Come with us and be a father
and a priest to us. Is it better for you to be
a priest for the house of one person or for
you to be a priest for a tribe and family in Israel?" 20So the priest was pleased and took his
ephod, household idols, and carved image,
and went with the people. 21They prepared to
leave, putting their small children, livestock,
and possessions in front of them.

22After they were some distance from Micah's house, the men who were in the houses
near it mobilized and caught up with the
Danites. 23They called to the Danites, who
turned to face them, and said to Micah,
"What's the matter with you that you mobilized the men?"

24He said, "You took the gods I had made
and the priest, and went away. What do I have
left? How can you say to me, 'What's the matter with you?'"

25The Danites said to him, "Don't raise your
voice against us, or angry men will attack you,
and you and your family will lose your lives."
26The Danites went on their way, and Micah
turned to go back home, because he saw that
they were stronger than he was.

27After they had taken the gods Micah had
made and the priest that belonged to him,
they went to Laish, to a quiet and unsuspecting people. They killed them with their
swords and burned down the city.[f] 28There
was no one to rescue them because it was far
from Sidon and they had no alliance with
anyone. It was in a valley that belonged to

[a] **18:2** Jos 19:40-41; Jdg 13:2,25
[b] Nm 13:17; Jos 2:1
[c] **18:10** Dt 8:9
[d] **18:12** Jos 9:17; 1Ch 13:5-6; 2Ch 1:4; Jr 26:20
[e] **18:19** Jb 21:5; 29:9; 40:4; Mc 7:16
[f] **18:27** Jdg 1:8,25; 4:15-16

[A] **18:7** Hb obscure [B] **18:7** MT; some LXX mss, Sym, Old Lat, Syr read *Aram*
[C] **18:12** Or *called Mahaneh-dan* [D] **18:14,17,18** Or *image, the cast image*
[E] **18:19** Lit *Put your hand on your mouth*

Beth-rehob. They rebuilt the city and lived in
it. 29 They named the city Dan, after the name
of their ancestor Dan, who was born to Israel.
The city was formerly named Laish.

30 The Danites set up the carved image for
themselves. Jonathan son of Gershom, son
of Moses,[A] and his sons were priests for the
Danite tribe until the time of the exile from
the land.[a] 31 So they set up for themselves Micah's carved image that he had made, and it
was there as long as the house of God was in
Shiloh.

Outrage in Benjamin

19 In those days, when there was no king
in Israel,[b] a Levite living in a remote
part of the hill country of Ephraim acquired
a woman from Bethlehem in Judah as his
concubine. 2 But she was unfaithful to[B] him
and left him for her father's house in Bethlehem in Judah. She was there for a period of
four months. 3 Then her husband got up and
went after her to speak kindly to her[C,c] and
bring her back. He had his servant with him
and a pair of donkeys. So she brought him
to her father's house, and when the girl's father saw him, he gladly welcomed him. 4 His
father-in-law, the girl's father, detained him,
and he stayed with him for three days. They
ate, drank, and spent the nights there.

5 On the fourth day, they got up early in the
morning and prepared to go, but the girl's father said to his son-in-law, "Have something
to eat to keep up your strength[d] and then you
can go." 6 So they sat down and the two of
them ate and drank together. Then the girl's
father said to the man, "Please agree to stay
overnight and enjoy yourself."[e] 7 The man got
up to go, but his father-in-law persuaded him,
so he stayed and spent the night there again.
8 He got up early in the morning of the fifth
day to leave, but the girl's father said to him,
"Please keep up your strength." So they waited
until late afternoon and the two of them ate.
9 The man got up to go with his concubine and
his servant, when his father-in-law, the girl's
father, said to him, "Look, night is coming.
Please spend the night. See, the day is almost
over. Spend the night here, enjoy yourself,

[a]18:30 2Kg 15:29
[b]19:1 Jdg 17:6; 18:1; 21:25
[c]19:3 Gn 34:3; 50:21
[d]19:5 Gn 18:5
[e]19:6 Jdg 16:25; 19:22; Ru 3:7; 1Kg 21:7; Est 1:10
[f]19:10 Jos 18:28; 1Ch 11:4-5
[g]19:11 Jdg 19:19
[h]19:12 Jos 18:28; 1Sm 10:26; 22:6; Hs 5:8; 9:9; 10:9
[i]19:16 Jdg 19:1
[j]19:21 Gn 24:32-33
[k]19:22 Gn 19:4-5; Dt 13:13; 1Sm 2:12; 1Kg 21:10; Ezk 16:46-48

then you can get up early tomorrow for your
journey and go home."

10 But the man was unwilling to spend the
night. He got up, departed, and arrived opposite Jebus (that is, Jerusalem[f]). The man had
his two saddled donkeys and his concubine
with him. 11 When they were near Jebus and
the day was almost gone, the servant[g] said to
his master, "Please, why not[D] let us stop at this
Jebusite city and spend the night here?"

12 But his master replied to him, "We will
not stop at a foreign city where there are no
Israelites. Let's move on to Gibeah."[h] 13 "Come
on," he said,[E] "let's try to reach one of these
places and spend the night in Gibeah or Ramah." 14 So they continued on their journey,
and the sun set as they neared Gibeah in Benjamin. 15 They stopped[F] to go in and spend
the night in Gibeah. The Levite went in and
sat down in the city square, but no one took
them into their home to spend the night.

16 In the evening, an old man came in from
his work in the field. He was from the hill
country of Ephraim[i] but was residing in
Gibeah, and the men of that place were Benjaminites. 17 When he looked up and saw the
traveler in the city square, the old man asked,
"Where are you going, and where do you
come from?"

18 He answered him, "We're traveling from
Bethlehem in Judah to the remote hill country of Ephraim, where I am from. I went to
Bethlehem in Judah, and now I'm going to the
house of the LORD.[G] No one has taken me into
his home, 19 although we have both straw and
feed for our donkeys, and bread and wine for
me, your female servant, and the young man
with your servant.[H] There is nothing we lack."

20 "Peace to you," said the old man. "I'll take
care of everything you need. Only don't spend
the night in the square." 21 So he brought him
to his house and fed the donkeys. Then they
washed their feet and ate and drank.[j] 22 While
they were enjoying themselves, all of a sudden, •perverted men of the city[k] surrounded
the house and beat on the door. They said to
the old man who was the owner of the house,
"Bring out the man who came to your house
so we can have sex with him!"

[A]18:30 Some Hb mss, LXX, Vg; other Hb mss read *Manasseh* [B]19:2 LXX, Vg read *was angry with* [C]19:3 Lit *speak to her heart* [D]19:11 Lit *Come, please* [E]19:13 Lit *said to his servant* [F]19:15 Lit *stopped there* [G]19:18 LXX reads *to my house* [H]19:19 Some Hb mss, Syr, Tg, Vg; other Hb mss read *servants*

23 The owner of the house went out and said
to them, "No, don't do this evil, my brothers.
After all, this man has come into my house.
Don't do this horrible thing.[a] 24 Here, let me
bring out my virgin daughter[b] and the man's
concubine now. Use them[c] and do whatever
you want[A] to them. But don't do this horrible
thing to this man."

25 But the men would not listen to him, so
the man seized his concubine and took her
outside to them. They raped[B] her and abused
her all night until morning. At daybreak they
let her go. 26 Early that morning, the woman
made her way back, and as it was getting
light, she collapsed at the doorway of the
man's house where her master was.

27 When her master got up in the morning,
opened the doors of the house, and went out
to leave on his journey, there was the woman,
his concubine, collapsed near the doorway of
the house with her hands on the threshold.
28 "Get up," he told her. "Let's go." But there
was no response.[d] So the man put her on his
donkey and set out for home.

29 When he entered his house, he picked up
a knife, took hold of his concubine, cut her
into 12 pieces, limb by limb, and then sent
her throughout the territory of Israel. 30 Everyone who saw it said, "Nothing like this has
ever happened or has been seen since the day
the Israelites came out of the land of Egypt to
this day.[C] Think it over, discuss it, and speak
up!"

War against Benjamin

20 All the Israelites from Dan to Beer-
sheba[e] and from the land of Gilead
came out, and the community assembled as
one body before the LORD at Mizpah.[f] 2 The
leaders[g] of all the people and of all the tribes
of Israel presented themselves in the assembly of God's people: 400,000 armed foot
soldiers. 3 The Benjaminites heard that the Israelites had gone up to Mizpah.

The Israelites asked, "Tell us, how did this
outrage occur?"

4 The Levite, the husband of the murdered
woman, answered: "I went to Gibeah in Benjamin with my concubine to spend the night.
5 Citizens of Gibeah ganged up on me and surrounded the house at night. They intended to
kill me, but they raped my concubine, and
she died. 6 Then I took my concubine and cut
her in pieces, and sent her throughout Israel's territory, because they committed a horrible shame[h] in Israel. 7 Look, all of you are
Israelites. Give your judgment and verdict
here and now."

8 Then all the people stood united and said,
"None of us will go to his tent or return to his
house. 9 Now this is what we will do to Gibeah:
we will go against it by lot. 10 We will take 10
men out of every 100 from all the tribes of
Israel, and 100 out of every 1,000, and 1,000
out of every 10,000 to get provisions for the
people when they go to Gibeah in Benjamin
to punish them for all the horror they did in
Israel."

11 So all the men of Israel gathered united
against the city. 12 Then the tribes of Israel
sent men throughout the tribe of Benjamin, saying, "What is this outrage that has
occurred among you? 13 Hand over the *perverted men in Gibeah so we can put them to
death and eradicate evil from Israel." But the
Benjaminites would not obey their fellow Israelites. 14 Instead, the Benjaminites gathered
together from their cities to Gibeah to go out
and fight against the Israelites. 15 On that day
the Benjaminites rallied 26,000 armed men[i]
from their cities, besides 700 choice men rallied by the inhabitants of Gibeah. 16 There
were 700 choice men who were left-handed
among all these people; all could sling a stone
at a hair and not miss.

17 The Israelites, apart from Benjamin, rallied 400,000 armed men, every one an experienced warrior. 18 They set out, went to
Bethel, and inquired of God.[j] The Israelites asked, "Who is to go first to fight for us
against the Benjaminites?"

And the LORD answered, "Judah will be
first."

19 In the morning, the Israelites set out and
camped near Gibeah. 20 The men of Israel
went out to fight against Benjamin and took
their battle positions against Gibeah. 21 The
Benjaminites came out of Gibeah and slaugh-

[a] **19:23** Gn 34:7; Dt 22:21; Jdg 20:6; 2Sm 13:12; Jb 42:8
[b] **19:24** Gn 19:8
[c] Jdg 20:5; 2Sm 13:12,14; Lm 5:11
[d] **19:28** Jdg 20:5
[e] **20:1** Gn 21:14; 22:19; 1Sm 3:20; 1Kg 4:25
[f] 1Sm 7:5
[g] **20:2** 1Sm 14:38; Is 19:13
[h] **20:6** Lv 18:17; 19:29; Ezk 16:27,43; Jr 13:27
[i] **20:15** Nm 1:36-37; 2:23; 26:41
[j] **20:18** Nm 27:21; Jdg 18:5; 1Sm 14:37; 1Ch 14:10

[A] **19:24** Lit *do what is good in your eyes* [B] **19:25** Lit *knew* [C] **19:30** LXX reads *day." He commanded the men he sent out, saying, "You will say this to all the men of Israel: Has anything like this happened since the day the Israelites came out of Egypt until this day?*

tered 22,000 men of Israel on the field that
day. 22But the Israelite army rallied and again
took their battle positions in the same place
where they positioned themselves on the first
day. 23They went up, wept[a] before the LORD
until evening, and inquired of Him: "Should
we again fight against our brothers the Benjaminites?"

And the LORD answered: "Fight against
them."

24On the second day the Israelites advanced
against the Benjaminites. 25That same day the
Benjaminites came out from Gibeah to meet
them and slaughtered an additional 18,000
Israelites on the field; all were armed men.

26The whole Israelite army went to Bethel
where they wept and sat before the LORD.[b]
They fasted that day until evening and offered
•burnt offerings and •fellowship offerings to
the LORD. 27Then the Israelites inquired of
the LORD. In those days, the ark of the covenant[c] of God was there, 28and Phinehas son
of Eleazar, son of Aaron, was serving before
it. The Israelites asked: "Should we again
fight against our brothers the Benjaminites
or should we stop?"

The LORD answered: "Fight, because I will
hand them over to you tomorrow."[d] 29So Israel set up an ambush[e] around Gibeah. 30On
the third day the Israelites fought against the
Benjaminites and took their battle positions
against Gibeah as before. 31Then the Benjaminites came out against the people and were
drawn away from the city.[f] They began to attack the people as before, killing about 30
men of Israel on the highways, one of which
goes up to Bethel and the other to Gibeah
through the open country. 32The Benjaminites said, "We are defeating them as before."

But the Israelites said, "Let's flee and draw
them away from the city to the highways."
33So all the men of Israel got up from their
places and took their battle positions at
Baal-tamar, while the Israelites in ambush
charged out of their places west of[A] Geba.[g]
34Then 10,000 choice men from all Israel
made a frontal assault against Gibeah, and
the battle was fierce, but the Benjaminites
did not know that disaster was about to strike
them. 35The LORD defeated Benjamin in the
presence of Israel, and on that day the Israelites slaughtered 25,100 men of Benjamin;
all were armed men. 36Then the Benjaminites
realized they had been defeated.

The men of Israel had retreated before Benjamin, because they were confident in the
ambush they had set against Gibeah. 37The
men in ambush had rushed quickly against
Gibeah; they advanced and put the whole city
to the sword. 38The men of Israel had a prear-
ranged signal with the men in ambush: when
they sent up a great cloud of smoke from the
city, 39the men of Israel would return to the
battle. When Benjamin had begun to strike
them down, killing about 30 men of Israel,
they said, "They're defeated before us, just as
they were in the first battle."[h] 40But when the
column of smoke began to go up from the
city, Benjamin looked behind them, and
the whole city was going up in smoke.[B] 41Then
the men of Israel returned, and the men of
Benjamin were terrified when they realized
that disaster had struck them. 42They retreated
before the men of Israel toward the wilderness,[i] but the battle overtook them, and those
who came out of the cities[C] slaughtered those
between them. 43They surrounded the Benjaminites, pursued them, and easily overtook
them near Gibeah toward the east. 44There
were 18,000 men who died from Benjamin; all
were warriors. 45Then Benjamin turned and
fled toward the wilderness to the rock of Rimmon,[j] and Israel killed 5,000 men on the highways. They overtook them at Gidom and struck
2,000 more dead.

46All the Benjaminites who died that day
were 25,000 armed men; all were warriors.
47But 600 men escaped into the wilderness
to the rock of Rimmon and stayed there four
months. 48The men of Israel turned back
against the other Benjaminites and killed
them with their swords—the entire city,
the animals, and everything that remained.
They also burned down all the cities that remained.

Brides for Benjamin

21 The men of Israel had sworn an oath
at Mizpah: "None of us will give his
daughter to a Benjaminite in marriage."[k] 2So

[a] **20:23** Jos 7:6-7
[b] **20:26** Jdg 21:2
[c] **20:27** 1Sm 4:4; 2Sm 15:24; 1Ch 16:6
[d] **20:28** Jdg 7:9
[e] **20:29** Jos 8:4
[f] **20:31** Jos 8:31
[g] **20:33** Jos 8:19
[h] **20:39** Jdg 20:32
[i] **20:42** Jos 8:15,24
[j] **20:45** Jdg 21:13
[k] **21:1** Jdg 21:7,18

[A] **20:33** LXX, Syr, Vg; MT reads *places in the plain of*, or *places in the cave of* [B] **20:40** Lit *up to the sky* [C] **20:42** LXX, Vg read *city*

the people went to Bethel and sat there before God[a] until evening. They wept loudly
and bitterly, 3and cried out, "Why, LORD God
of Israel, has it occurred[A] that one tribe is
missing in Israel today?" 4The next day the
people got up early, built an altar there,[b] and
offered ·burnt offerings and ·fellowship offerings. 5The Israelites asked, "Who of all the
tribes of Israel didn't come to the LORD with
the assembly?" For a great oath had been
taken that anyone who had not come to the
LORD at Mizpah would certainly be put to
death.

6But the Israelites had compassion on their
brothers, the Benjaminites, and said, "Today
a tribe has been cut off from Israel. 7What
should we do about wives for the survivors?
We've sworn to the LORD not to give them
any of our daughters as wives." 8They asked,
"Which city among the tribes of Israel didn't
come to the LORD at Mizpah?" It turned out
that no one from Jabesh-gilead had come to
the camp and the assembly. 9For when the
people were counted, no one was there from
the inhabitants of Jabesh-gilead.

10The congregation sent 12,000 brave warriors[B] there and commanded them: "Go and
kill the inhabitants of Jabesh-gilead with
the sword,[c] including women and children.
11This is what you should do: ·Completely destroy every male, as well as every female who
has slept with a man." 12They found among
the inhabitants of Jabesh-gilead 400 young
women, who had not had sexual relations
with a man, and they brought them to the
camp at Shiloh in the land of Canaan.

13The whole congregation sent a message of
peace[d] to the Benjaminites who were at the
rock of Rimmon. 14Benjamin returned at that
time, and Israel gave them the women they
had kept alive from Jabesh-gilead. But there
were not enough for them.

15The people had compassion on Benjamin,
because the LORD had made this gap in the
tribes of Israel. 16The elders of the congregation said, "What should we do about wives
for those who are left, since the women of
Benjamin have been destroyed?" 17They said,
"There must be heirs for the survivors of
Benjamin, so that a tribe of Israel will not be
wiped out. 18But we can't give them our daughters as wives." For the Israelites had sworn,
"Anyone who gives a wife to a Benjaminite is cursed." 19They also said, "Look, there's
an annual festival to the LORD in Shiloh,[e]
which is north of Bethel, east of the highway
that goes up from Bethel to Shechem, and
south of Lebonah."

20Then they commanded the Benjaminites:
"Go and hide in the vineyards. 21Watch, and
when you see the young women of Shiloh
come out to perform the dances,[f] each of you
leave the vineyards and catch a wife for yourself from the young women of Shiloh, and go
to the land of Benjamin. 22When their fathers
or brothers come to us and protest, we will tell
them, 'Show favor to them, since we did not get
enough wives for each of them in the battle.
You didn't actually give the women to them,
so[C] you are not ·guilty of breaking your oath.'"

23The Benjaminites did this and took the
number of women they needed from the
dancers they caught. They went back to their
own inheritance, rebuilt their cities,[g] and
lived in them. 24At that time, each of the Israelites returned from there to his own tribe
and family. Each returned from there to his
own inheritance.

25In those days there was no king in Israel;[h]
everyone did whatever he wanted.[D]

[a]21:2 Jdg 20:26 [b]21:4 2Sm 24:25 [c]21:10 Nm 31:17 [d]21:13 Dt 20:10 [e]21:19 Jos 18:1; Jdg 18:31; 1Sm 1:3 [f]21:21 Ex 15:20; Jdg 11:34 [g]21:23 Jdg 20:48 [h]21:25 Jdg 17:6; 18:1; 19:1

[A]21:3 Lit *has this occurred in Israel* [B]21:10 Lit *12,000 of their sons of valor* [C]21:22 Lit *at this time* [D]21:25 Lit *did what was right in his eyes*

RUTH

For the introduction to the book of Ruth, see the introduction to the book of
Judges, page 237.

Naomi's Family in Moab

1 During the time[A] of the judges,[a] there was
a famine in the land.[b] A man left Bethlehem[B,c] in Judah with his wife and two sons
to live in the land of Moab for a while. 2 The
man's name was Elimelech,[C] and his wife's
name was Naomi.[D] The names of his two
sons were Mahlon[E] and Chilion.[F] They were
Ephrathites[d] from Bethlehem in Judah. They
entered the land of Moab and settled there.
3 Naomi's husband Elimelech died, and she
was left with her two sons. 4 Her sons took
Moabite women as their wives: one was
named Orpah and the second was named
Ruth. After they lived in Moab about 10 years,
5 both Mahlon and Chilion also died, and
Naomi was left without her two children and
without her husband.

Ruth's Loyalty to Naomi

6 She and her daughters-in-law prepared
to leave the land of Moab, because she had
heard in Moab that the LORD had paid attention to His people's need by providing them
food.[e] 7 She left the place where she had been
living, accompanied by her two daughters-in-
law, and traveled along the road leading back
to the land of Judah.

8 She said to them, "Each of you go back to
your mother's home.[f] May the LORD show
faithful love to you as you have shown to the
dead and to me. 9 May the LORD enable each
of you to find security[g] in the house of your
new husband." She kissed them, and they
wept loudly.

10 "No," they said to her. "We will go with
you to your people."

11 But Naomi replied, "Return home, my
daughters. Why do you want to go with me?
Am I able to have any more sons[G] who could
become your husbands?[h] 12 Return home, my
daughters. Go on, for I am too old to have another husband. Even if I thought there was
still hope for me to have a husband tonight
and to bear sons, 13 would you be willing to
wait for them to grow up? Would you restrain yourselves from remarrying?[H] No, my
daughters, my life is much too bitter for you
to share,[I] because the LORD's hand has turned
against me."[i] 14 Again they wept loudly, and
Orpah kissed her mother-in-law, but Ruth
clung to her. 15 Naomi said, "Look, your sister-
in-law has gone back to her people and to her
god.[J,j] Follow your sister-in-law."

16 But Ruth replied:

> Do not persuade me to leave you
> or go back and not follow you.
> For wherever you go, I will go,
> and wherever you live, I will live;
> your people will be my people,
> and your God will be my God.
> 17 Where you die, I will die,
> and there I will be buried.
> May ·Yahweh punish me,[K,k]
> and do so severely,
> if anything but death separates you
> and me.

18 When Naomi saw that Ruth was determined to go with her, she stopped trying to
persuade her.

19 The two of them traveled until they came
to Bethlehem. When they entered Bethlehem,
the whole town was excited about their arrival[L,l] and the local women exclaimed, "Can
this be Naomi?"

20 "Don't call me Naomi. Call me Mara,"[M]
she answered,[N] "for the ·Almighty[m] has made
me very bitter.[n] 21 I went away full, but the
LORD has brought me back empty.[o] Why do

[a]**1:1** Jdg 2:16-18
[b]Gn 12:10; 26:1; 43:1; 2Kg 8:1
[c]Jdg 17:7; 19:1
[d]**1:2** Gn 35:19; 1Sm 17:12; 1Ch 4:4; Mc 5:2
[e]**1:6** Ex 4:31; 1Sm 2:21
[f]**1:8** Gn 24:28
[g]**1:9** Ru 3:1
[h]**1:11** Gn 38:11; Dt 25:5
[i]**1:13** Jdg 2:15; Jb 19:21; Ps 32:4; 38:2; 39:10
[j]**1:15** Jdg 11:24; 1Kg 11:7; Jr 48:7,13,46
[k]**1:17** 1Sm 3:17; 2Sm 3:9,35; 1Kg 2:23; 2Kg 6:31
[l]**1:19** Mt 21:10
[m]**1:20** Gn 49:25; Ex 6:3; Nm 24:4; Jb 6:4
[n]Ex 15:23
[o]**1:21** Ru 3:17

A**1:1** Lit *In the days of the judging* B**1:1** = House of Bread C**1:2** = My God Is King D**1:2** = Pleasant E**1:2** = Sickly F**1:2** = Weak or failing G**1:11** Lit *More to me sons in my womb* H**1:13** Lit *marrying a man* I**1:13** Lit *daughters, for more bitter to me than you* J**1:15** Or *gods* K**1:17** A solemn oath formula; 1Sm 3:17; 2Sm 3:9,35; 1Kg 2:23; 2Kg 6:31 L**1:19** Lit *excited because of them* M**1:20** = Bitter N**1:20** Lit *answered them* you call me Naomi, since the LORD has pronounced judgment on[A] me, and the Almighty has afflicted me?"

22 So Naomi came back from the land of Moab with her daughter-in-law Ruth the Moabitess. They arrived in Bethlehem at the beginning of the barley harvest.[a]

Ruth and Boaz Meet

2 Now Naomi had a relative on her husband's side named Boaz. He was a prominent man of noble character[b] from Elimelech's family.

2 Ruth the Moabitess asked Naomi, "Will you let me go into the fields and gather fallen grain[c] behind someone who allows me to?"

Naomi answered her, "Go ahead, my daughter." 3 So Ruth left and entered the field to gather grain behind the harvesters. She happened[d] to be in the portion of land belonging to Boaz, who was from Elimelech's family.

4 Later, when Boaz arrived from Bethlehem, he said to the harvesters, "The LORD be with you."[e]

"The LORD bless you,"[f] they replied.

5 Boaz asked his servant who was in charge of the harvesters, "Whose young woman is this?"

6 The servant answered, "She is the young Moabite woman who returned with Naomi from the land of Moab. 7 She asked, 'Will you let me gather fallen grain among the bundles behind the harvesters?' She came and has remained from early morning until now, except that she rested a little in the shelter."[B]

8 Then Boaz said to Ruth, "Listen, my daughter.[C] Don't go and gather grain in another field, and don't leave this one, but stay here close to my female servants. 9 See which field they are harvesting, and follow them. Haven't I ordered the young men not to touch you?[D] When you are thirsty, go and drink from the jars the young men have filled."

10 She bowed with her face to the ground[g] and said to him, "Why are you so kind to notice me, although I am a foreigner?"

11 Boaz answered her, "Everything you have done for your mother-in-law since your husband's death has been fully reported to me: how you left your father and mother and the land of your birth, and how you came to a people you didn't previously know. 12 May the LORD reward you for what you have done,[h] and may you receive a full reward from the LORD God of Israel, under whose wings you have come for refuge."[i]

13 "My lord," she said, "you have been so kind to me, for you have comforted and encouraged[E] your slave, although I am not like one of your female servants."

14 At mealtime Boaz told her, "Come over here and have some bread and dip it in the vinegar sauce." So she sat beside the harvesters, and he offered her roasted grain. She ate and was satisfied and had some left over.

15 When she got up to gather grain, Boaz ordered his young men, "Let her even gather grain among the bundles, and don't humiliate her. 16 Pull out some stalks from the bundles for her and leave them for her to gather. Don't rebuke her." 17 So Ruth gathered grain in the field until evening. She beat out what she had gathered, and it was about 26 quarts[F] of barley. 18 She picked up the grain and went into the town, where her mother-in-law saw what she had gleaned. Then she brought out what she had left over from her meal and gave it to her.

19 Then her mother-in-law said to her, "Where did you gather barley today, and where did you work? May the LORD bless the man who noticed you."[j]

Ruth told her mother-in-law about the men she had worked with and said, "The name of the man I worked with today is Boaz."

20 Then Naomi said to her daughter-in-law, "May he be blessed by the LORD,[k] who has not forsaken his[G] kindness to the living or the dead."[l] Naomi continued, "The man is a close relative. He is one of our ˙family redeemers."[m]

21 Ruth the Moabitess said, "He also told me, 'Stay with my young men until they have finished all of my harvest.'"

22 So Naomi said to her daughter-in-law Ruth, "My daughter, it is good for you to work[H] with his female servants, so that nothing

[a] **1:22** Ex 9:31; Lv 23:10-11
[b] **2:1** Ru 1:2
[c] **2:2** Lv 19:9-10; 23:22
[d] **2:3** Pr 16:33; 20:24
[e] **2:4** 1Sm 20:13
[f] Nm 6:24
[g] **2:10** 1Sm 25:23,41
[h] **2:12** 1Sm 24:19
[i] Ru 1:16; Ps 17:8; 36:7; 57:1; 63:7
[j] **2:19** Ps 41:1
[k] **2:20** 2Sm 2:5
[l] Ru 1:8
[m] Lv 25:25-26; Ru 3:9,12; 4:1-8,14; Ps 19:14; Is 41:14

[A] **1:21** LXX, Syr, Vg read *has humiliated* [B] **2:7** LXX reads *until evening she has not stopped in the field*; Vg reads *now and she did not return to the house*; Hb uncertain [C] **2:8** Lit *Haven't you heard, my daughter?* [D] **2:9** Either sexual or physical harassment [E] **2:13** Lit *and spoken to the heart of* [F] **2:17** Lit *about an ephah* [G] **2:20** Or *His* [H] **2:22** Lit *go out*

Janani Luwum (1922—1977)

He was archbishop of the Church of Uganda, the CEO and priest-in-charge of thousands of Anglican churches there. But his high office was no barrier to the madman who had taken control of his nation and laid waste to its resources and people. Janani Luwum was one of tens of thousands who perished during the purges of Uganda's most well known and evil president.

Luwum was an educated pastor. He had taken degrees in London and shown leadership in the church. He was an active member of the East Africa Revival Fellowship, a movement which has revitalized Christian discipleship since the 1930s. He urged his congregations toward a living relationship with Jesus. Jesus was never absent from us, he taught, no matter how difficult life might become.

In 1974, Luwun became archbishop of the Anglican church in Uganda, Rwanda, Burundi, and parts of Zaire (now the Democratic Republic of the Congo). Already Idi Amin had ruled Uganda for three years since deposing its president in 1971. Public executions, disappearances, expulsions—acts of intimidation and an army gone corrupt—these violations of human rights begged for courageous opposition. Luwum stepped forward, speaking for the church and the gospel on behalf of a suffering nation. Very few people dared to stand against Amin. There were no trials or courts. Amin was his own judge, jury, and sometimes executioner.

Called to the president's office, Luwum knew what the meeting was about. Whether Amin pulled the trigger or one of his goons, no one knows. Where Luwun's body was taken remains a mystery. Many of Amin's victims were simply dumped in the Nile, food for crocodiles.

Two more years of chaos rocked Uganda before Amin himself was deposed and beaten by guerillas who forced him to find sanctuary in Saudi Arabia. Every February 17, Luwum is remembered as a modern martyr. A statue in his memory was placed in Westminster Abbey in London.

The mission of God is righteousness and peace through Jesus Christ. Janani Luwum knew this battle was against powers and principalities that often control the guns but never the truth. He did what Christian leaders throughout history are called to do: trust and obey, live by faith, speak the truth.

will happen to you in another field." 23 Ruth stayed close to Boaz's female servants and gathered grain until the barley and the wheat harvests were finished.[a] And she lived with[A] her mother-in-law.

Ruth's Appeal to Boaz

3 Ruth's mother-in-law Naomi said to her, "My daughter, shouldn't I find security for you, so that you will be taken care of? 2 Now isn't Boaz our relative?[b] Haven't you been working with his female servants? This evening he will be winnowing barley on the threshing floor. 3 Wash, put on perfumed oil, and wear your best clothes. Go down to the threshing floor, but don't let the man know you are there until he has finished eating and drinking. 4 When he lies down, notice the place where he's lying, go in and uncover his feet, and lie down. Then he will explain to you what you should do."

5 So Ruth said to her, "I will do everything you say."[B] 6 She went down to the threshing floor and did everything her mother-in-law had instructed her. 7 After Boaz ate, drank, and was in good spirits,[C] he went to lie down at the end of the pile of barley. Then she went in secretly, uncovered his feet, and lay down.

8 At midnight, Boaz was startled, turned over, and there lying at his feet was a woman! 9 So he asked, "Who are you?"

"I am Ruth, your slave," she replied. "Spread your cloak[D] over me,[c] for you are a ·family redeemer."[d]

10 Then he said, "May the LORD bless you,[e] my daughter. You have shown more kindness now than before,[E] because you have not pursued younger men, whether rich or poor. 11 Now don't be afraid, my daughter. I will do for you whatever you say,[F] since all the people in my town[G] know that you are a woman of noble character.[f] 12 Yes, it is true that I am a family redeemer, but there is a redeemer closer than I am. 13 Stay here tonight, and in the morning, if he wants to redeem you, that's good.[g] Let him redeem you. But if he doesn't want to redeem you, as the LORD lives,[h] I will. Now lie down until morning."

14 So she lay down at his feet until morning but got up while it was still dark.[H] Then Boaz said, "Don't let it be known that a[I] woman came to the threshing floor." 15 And he told Ruth, "Bring the shawl you're wearing and hold it out." When she held it out, he shoveled six measures of barley into her shawl, and she[J] went into the town.

16 She went to her mother-in-law, Naomi, who asked her, "How did it go,[K] my daughter?"

Then Ruth told her everything the man had done for her. 17 She said, "He gave me these six measures of barley, because he said,[L] 'Don't go back to your mother-in-law empty-handed.'"

18 Naomi said, "My daughter, wait until you find out how things go, for he won't rest unless he resolves this today."

Ruth and Boaz Marry

4 Boaz went to the ·gate of the town[i] and sat down there. Soon the ·family redeemer Boaz had spoken about came by. Boaz called him by name and said, "Come[M] over here and sit down." So he went over and sat down. 2 Then Boaz took 10 men of the town's elders[j] and said, "Sit here." And they sat down. 3 He said to the redeemer, "Naomi, who has returned from the land of Moab, is selling a piece of land that belonged to our brother Elimelech.[k] 4 I thought I should inform you:[N] Buy it back in the presence of those seated here and in the presence of the elders of my people. If you want to redeem it, do so. But if you do[O] not want to redeem it, tell me so that I will know, because there isn't anyone other than you to redeem it, and I am next after you."

"I want to redeem it," he answered.

5 Then Boaz said, "On the day you buy the land from Naomi, you will also acquire[P] Ruth the Moabitess, the wife of the deceased man, to perpetuate the man's name on his property."[l]

6 The redeemer replied, "I can't redeem it

[a] **2:23** Dt 16:9
[b] **3:2** Dt 25:5-10
[c] **3:9** Ezk 16:8
[d] Ru 2:12
[e] **3:10** Ru 2:20
[f] **3:11** Ru 2:1; Pr 12:4; 31:10
[g] **3:13** Dt 25:5; Ru 4:5
[h] Jdg 8:19; 1Sm 14:39,45; 19:6; 2Sm 4:9; 12:5; 2Kg 2:2,6
[i] **4:1** Ru 3:11-12; 2Sm 15:2; 18:4,24,33; 19:8; Ps 127:5
[j] **4:2** Dt 19:12; 21:3-6; 1Kg 21:8; Pr 31:23
[k] **4:3** Lv 25:25
[l] **4:5** Gn 38:6-11; Lv 25:23-34; Dt 25:5-10

[A] **2:23** Some Hb mss, Vg read *she returned to* [B] **3:5** Alt Hb tradition reads *say to me* [C] **3:7** Lit *and his heart was glad* [D] **3:9** Or *Spread the edge of your garment*; lit *Spread the wing of your garment*; Ru 2:12 [E] **3:10** Lit *kindness at the last than at the first* [F] **3:11** Some Hb mss, Orig, Syr, Tg, Vg read *say to me* [G] **3:11** Lit *all the gate of my people* [H] **3:14** Lit *up before a man could recognize his companion* [I] **3:14** LXX; MT reads *the* [J] **3:15** Some Hb mss, Aram, Syr, Vg; other Hb mss read *he* [K] **3:16** Lit *Who are you* [L] **3:17** Alt Hb tradition, LXX, Syr, Tg read *said to me* [M] **4:1** Lit *Boaz said so-and-so come* [N] **4:4** Lit *should uncover your ear, saying* [O] **4:4** Some Hb mss, LXX, Syr, Vg; other Hb mss read *if he does* [P] **4:5** Vg; MT reads *Naomi and from*

myself, or I will ruin my own inheritance.
Take my right of redemption, because I can't
redeem it."
7 At an earlier period in Israel, a man removed his sandal[a] and gave it to the other
party in order to make any matter legally
binding concerning the right of redemption or the exchange of property. This was
the method of legally binding a transaction
in Israel.
8 So the redeemer removed his sandal and
said to Boaz, "Buy back the property yourself."
9 Boaz said to the elders and all the people,
"You are witnesses today that I am buying
from Naomi everything that belonged to
Elimelech, Chilion, and Mahlon. 10 I will also
acquire Ruth the Moabitess, Mahlon's widow,
as my wife, to perpetuate the deceased man's
name on his property, so that his name will
not disappear among his relatives or from
the gate of his home. You are witnesses today."
11 The elders and all the people who were
at the gate said, "We are witnesses. May the
LORD make the woman who is entering your
house like Rachel and Leah,[b] who together
built the house of Israel. May you be powerful in Ephrathah and famous in Bethlehem.
12 May your house become like the house of
Perez, the son Tamar bore to Judah,[c] because

[a] **4:7** Dt 25:8-10
[b] **4:11** Gn 29:25-30; 35:16-18
[c] **4:12** Gn 38; 46:12; Ru 4:18
[d] **4:15** Ru 1:16-17; 2:11-12
[e] **4:18-22** Mt 1:3-6

of the offspring the LORD will give you by this
young woman."
13 Boaz took Ruth and she became his wife.
When he was intimate with her, the LORD enabled her to conceive, and she gave birth to a
son. 14 Then the women said to Naomi, "Praise
the LORD, who has not left you without a family redeemer today. May his name become
well known in Israel. 15 He will renew your life
and sustain you in your old age. Indeed, your
daughter-in-law, who loves you and is better
to you than seven sons,[d] has given birth to
him." 16 Naomi took the child, placed him on
her lap, and took care of him. 17 The neighbor
women said, "A son has been born to Naomi,"
and they named him Obed.[A] He was the father of Jesse, the father of David.

David's Genealogy from Judah's Son

18 Now this is the genealogy of Perez:

Perez fathered Hezron.
19 Hezron fathered Ram,[B]
who fathered Amminadab.
20 Amminadab fathered Nahshon,
who fathered Salmon.
21 Salmon fathered Boaz,
who fathered Obed.
22 And Obed fathered Jesse,
who fathered David.[e]

[A] **4:17** = Servant [B] **4:19** LXX reads *Aram*; Mt 1:3-4

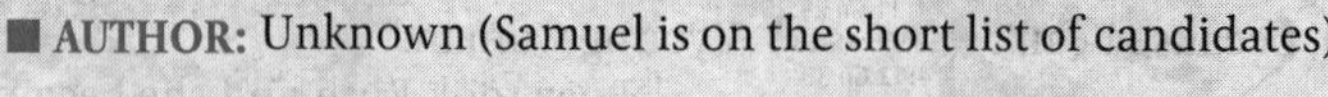

■ **AUTHOR:** Unknown (Samuel is on the short list of candidates)

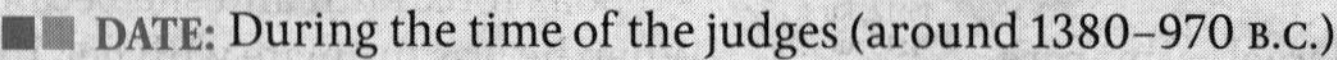

■■ **DATE:** During the time of the judges (around 1380–970 B.C.)

In the books of 1 and 2 Samuel, God's mission changes gears. God already knew this day would come—in fact, He had made provision for the future monarchy in Israel in Moses' famous speech (Dt 17:14-19). Sure enough, the people no longer want to be a theocracy under the direct rule of God; they want a king to rule over them "the same as all the other nations have" (1Sm 8:5).

The book begins with the birth of the last judge, who is also a prophet, Samuel. From Samuel we learn that God's direct rule should always prevail. But the Hebrews want leaders they can see and hear, and as a concession, it seems, God is willing to grant Israel a human king. Surely, however, the real power and driving force behind the king is God Himself. No enemy is defeated, no rule enforced, no project undertaken apart from God's will and approval. The people will have their titled ruler, but the Ruler of All is never far away—even if at times He is left by a faithless people.

1 SAMUEL

Saul appears to be a good candidate for king, but appearances give way to personal weaknesses and outright distortions of reality. Saul wastes precious administration muscle scrambling to find the outlaw David, whom Saul has made a refugee. At critical points, Saul operates independent of God. Finally and tragically, God must replace this failed king with a shepherd lad who composes songs and whose aim with a stone and sling is eagle-eyed.

David becomes the revered leader of the Old Testament. His passion for God is breathtaking; his intuitive sense of mission is true to God's will. David brings the nation together, establishes Jerusalem as the capital, and sets plans for a majestic temple fit for the great God who never fails His people. Yet David also fails. God leads David to repent through Nathan's ministry. Fortunately for Israel, David's heart is open to God. Despite David's famous sin, God moves ahead with a plan to stabilize true worship by making a special place on earth where peace and justice reign. The temple will be built by the son, not the father. So another generation of leader takes over.

First and 2 Samuel were originally one book, separated only by later Bible translators. No one knows for sure who wrote it. Likely several sources were brought together. And that editorial history reflects directly the real history told here. God brings odd pieces of humanity together, shaping His mission through them, pointing forward through the fog of human greed and lust, urging all to see the lamplights shining on something—Someone—yet to come. He will be David's son, born in the lineage of the great king, but greater yet. God's mission through Samuel, Saul, David, and Solomon points to a King whose reign will never end.

Hannah's Vow

1 There was a man from Ramathaim-zophim[a] in[A] the hill country of Ephraim.[b] His name was Elkanah[c] son of Jeroham, son of Elihu, son of Tohu, son of Zuph, an Ephraimite. 2 He had two wives,[d] the first named Hannah[e] and the second Peninnah. Peninnah had children, but Hannah was childless. 3 This man would go up from his town every year[f] to worship and to sacrifice[g] to the LORD of ·Hosts at Shiloh,[h] where Eli's two sons, Hophni and Phinehas, were the LORD's priests.

4 Whenever Elkanah offered a sacrifice, he always gave portions of the meat[i] to his wife Peninnah and to each of her sons and daughters. 5 But he gave a double[B] portion[j] to Hannah, for he loved her even though the LORD had kept her from conceiving. 6 Her rival would taunt her severely just to provoke her, because the LORD had kept Hannah from conceiving. 7 Whenever she went up to the LORD's house,[k] her rival taunted her in this way every year. Hannah wept and would not eat. 8 "Hannah, why are you crying?" her husband Elkanah asked. "Why won't you eat? Why are you troubled? Am I not better to you than 10 sons?"[l]

9 Hannah got up after they ate and drank at Shiloh.[C] Eli the priest was sitting on a chair by the doorpost of the LORD's tabernacle.[m] 10 Deeply hurt, Hannah prayed to the LORD and wept with many tears.[n] 11 Making a vow,[o] she pleaded, "LORD of Hosts, if You will take notice of Your servant's affliction,[p] remember and not forget me, and give Your servant a son,[D] I will give him to the LORD all the days of his life, and his hair will never be cut."[E,q]

12 While she continued praying in the LORD's presence, Eli watched her lips. 13 Hannah was praying silently,[F,r] and though her lips were moving, her voice could not be heard. Eli thought she was drunk 14 and scolded her, "How long are you going to be drunk?[s] Get rid of your wine!"

15 "No, my lord," Hannah replied. "I am a woman with a broken heart. I haven't had any wine or beer; I've been pouring out my heart before the LORD.[t] 16 Don't think of me as a wicked woman;[u] I've been praying from the depth of my anguish and resentment."[v]

17 Eli responded, "Go in peace,"[w] and may the God of Israel grant the petition you've requested from Him."[x]

18 "May your servant find favor with you,"[y] she replied. Then Hannah went on her way; she ate and no longer looked despondent.[G,z]

Samuel's Birth and Dedication

19 The next morning Elkanah and Hannah got up early to bow in worship before the LORD. Afterward, they returned home to Ramah.[aa] Then Elkanah was intimate with his wife Hannah, and the LORD remembered her.[ab] 20 After some time,[H] Hannah conceived and gave birth to a son. She named him Samuel,[I] because she said, "I requested him from the LORD."

21 When Elkanah and all his household went up to make the annual sacrifice[ac] and his vow offering to the LORD, 22 Hannah did not go and explained to her husband, "After the child is weaned, I'll take him to appear in the LORD's presence[ad] and to stay there permanently."[ae]

23 Her husband Elkanah replied, "Do what you think is best,[J,af] and stay here until you've weaned him. May the LORD confirm your[K] word."[ag] So Hannah stayed there and nursed her son until she weaned him. 24 When she had weaned him, she took him with her to Shiloh, as well as a three-year-old bull,[L] half a bushel[M] of flour, and a jar of wine.[ah] Though the boy was still young,[N] she took him to the LORD's house at Shiloh.[ai] 25 Then they slaughtered the bull and brought the boy to Eli.

26 "Please, my lord," she said, "as sure as you live,[aj] my lord, I am the woman who stood here beside you praying to the LORD. 27 I prayed for this boy,[ak] and since the LORD gave me what I asked Him for,[al] 28 I now give the boy to the LORD. For as long as he lives, he is given to the LORD."[am] Then he[O] bowed in worship to the LORD there.[P]

[a] **1:1** 1Sm 1:19
[b] Jos 17:14-18; Jdg 17:1
[c] 1Ch 6:22-28,33-38
[d] **1:2** Dt 21:15-17
[e] Lk 2:36
[f] **1:3** Ex 34:23; Dt 16:16; Lk 2:41
[g] Ex 23:14-17
[h] Jos 18:1
[i] **1:4** Dt 12:17-18
[j] **1:5** Gn 43:34; 48:22
[k] **1:7** Jos 18:1
[l] **1:8** Ru 4:15
[m] **1:9** 1Sm 3:3
[n] **1:10** 1Sm 30:6; 2Kg 4:27
[o] **1:11** Nm 30:6-11
[p] Gn 29:32
[q] Nm 6:5; Jdg 13:5; 16:7
[r] **1:13** Gn 24:42-45
[s] **1:14** Ac 2:4,13
[t] **1:15** Ps 62:8
[u] **1:16** 1Sm 2:12
[v] Lk 6:45
[w] **1:17** 1Sm 25:35; 2Kg 5:19; Mk 5:34
[x] Ru 2:13
[y] **1:18** Ru 2:13
[z] Rm 15:13
[aa] **1:19** 1Sm 1:1; 2:11
[ab] Gn 8:1; 30:22; 1Sm 1:11
[ac] **1:21** Dt 12:11; 1Sm 1:3
[ad] **1:22** Lk 2:22
[ae] 1Sm 1:11,28
[af] **1:23** Nm 30:10-11
[ag] Nm 30:13
[ah] **1:24** Nm 15:9-10
[ai] Jos 18:1; 1Sm 4:3-4
[aj] **1:26** 2Kg 2:2,4,6
[ak] **1:27** 1Sm 1:11-13
[al] 1Sm 1:17,20
[am] **1:28** 1Sm 1:11

[A] **1:1** Or *from Ramathaim, a Zuphite from* [B] **1:5** Or *gave only one*; Hb obscure [C] **1:9** LXX adds *and presented herself before the LORD* [D] **1:11** Lit *a seed of men* [E] **1:11** Lit *and no razor will go up on his head* [F] **1:13** Lit *praying to her heart* [G] **1:18** Lit *and her face was not to her again* [H] **1:20** Lit *In the turning of the days* [I] **1:20** In Hb, the name Samuel sounds like the phrase "requested from God." [J] **1:23** Lit *what is good in your eyes* [K] **1:23** DSS, LXX, Syr; MT reads *His* [L] **1:24** DSS, LXX, Syr; MT reads *Shiloh with three bulls* [M] **1:24** Lit *bull and an ephah* [N] **1:24** Lit *And the youth was a youth* [O] **1:28** DSS read *she*; some Hb mss, Syr, Vg read *they* [P] **1:28** LXX reads *Then she left him there before the LORD*

Hannah's Triumphant Prayer

2 Hannah prayed:[a]

My heart rejoices in the LORD;[b]
my ·horn is lifted up by the LORD.
My mouth boasts over my enemies,
because I rejoice in Your salvation.[c]
2 There is no one holy like the LORD.[d]
There is no one besides You![e]
And there is no rock like our God.[f]
3 Do not boast so proudly,
or let arrogant words come out of
your mouth,
for the LORD is a God of knowledge,
and actions are weighed by Him.[g]
4 The bows of the warriors are broken,[h]
but the feeble are clothed
with strength.[i]
5 Those who are full hire themselves out
for food,
but those who are starving hunger
no more.
The woman who is childless gives birth
to seven,[j]
but the woman with many sons
pines away.[k]
6 The LORD brings death and gives life;[l]
He sends some to ·Sheol, and He raises
others up.[m]
7 The LORD brings poverty and gives
wealth;[n]
He humbles and He exalts.[o]
8 He raises the poor from the dust[p]
and lifts the needy
from the garbage pile.[q]
He seats them with noblemen[r]
and gives them a throne of honor.[A]
For the foundations of the earth
are the LORD's;[s]
He has set the world on them.[t]
9 He guards the steps[B]
of His faithful ones,[u]
but the wicked perish in darkness,[v]
for a man does not prevail by his own
strength.[w]
10 Those who oppose the LORD
will be shattered;[C,x]
He will thunder in the heavens
against them.[y]
The LORD will judge the ends
of the earth.[z]
He will give power to His king;
He will lift up the horn
of His anointed.[aa]

11 Elkanah went home to Ramah,[ab] but the
boy served the LORD in the presence of Eli the
priest.[ac]

Eli's Family Judged

12 Eli's sons were ·wicked men;[ad] they had
no regard for the LORD[ae] 13 or for the priests'
share of the sacrifices from the people. When
any man offered a sacrifice, the priest's servant would come with a three-pronged meat
fork while the meat was boiling 14 and plunge
it into the container or kettle or cauldron
or cooking pot.[af] The priest would claim for
himself whatever the meat fork brought up.
This is the way they treated all the Israelites
who came there to Shiloh. 15 Even before the
fat was burned,[ag] the priest's servant would
come and say to the man who was sacrificing,
"Give the priest some meat to roast, because
he won't accept boiled meat from you — only
raw." 16 If that man said to him, "The fat must
be burned first; then you can take whatever
you want for yourself,"[ah] the servant would
reply, "No, I insist that you hand it over right
now. If you don't, I'll take it by force!" 17 So the
servants' sin was very severe in the presence
of the LORD, because they treated the LORD's
offering with contempt.[ai]
18 The boy Samuel served in the LORD's presence[aj] and wore a linen ephod.[ak] 19 Each year
his mother made him a little robe[al] and took
it to him when she went with her husband to
offer the annual sacrifice.[am] 20 Eli would bless
Elkanah and his wife:[an] "May the LORD give
you children by this woman in place of the
one she[D] has given to the LORD."[ao] Then they
would go home.
21 The LORD paid attention to Hannah's
need,[ap] and she conceived and gave birth to
three sons and two daughters. Meanwhile,
the boy Samuel grew up in the presence of
the LORD.[aq]
22 Now Eli was very old. He heard about
everything his sons were doing to all Israel[ar]

[a] **2:1** Ps 72:20; Hab 3:1; Lk 1:46-55
[b] Ps 75:4-5,10; 92:10
[c] Is 12:2-3
[d] **2:2** Ex 15:11
[e] 2Sm 22:32
[f] 2Sm 7:22; Ps 18:31
[g] **2:3** Pr 16:2; 24:12
[h] **2:4** Ps 37:15; 46:9
[i] Ps 18:39: Heb 11:32-34
[j] **2:5** Ru 4:15; Ps 113:9
[k] Jr 15:9
[l] **2:6** Dt 32:39
[m] Is 26:19
[n] **2:7** Dt 8:17-18
[o] Jb 15:11; Jms 4:10
[p] **2:8** Jb 42:10-12; Ps 75:7
[q] 2Sm 7:8; Dn 2:48; Jms 2:5
[r] Jb 36:7
[s] Jb 38:4-6; Ps 75:3
[t] Ps 113:7-8
[u] **2:9** Ps 91:11-12; 1Pt 1:5
[v] Mt 8:12
[w] Ps 33:16-17
[x] **2:10** Ps 2:9
[y] 1Sm 7:10; Ps 18:13-14
[z] Ps 96:13; 98:9
[aa] 1Sm 2:35; 12:3; 16:6; Ps 89:24
[ab] **2:11** 1Sm 1:1,19
[ac] 1Sm 1:28; 2:18; 3:1
[ad] **2:12** 1Sm 1:15
[ae] Jr 2:8; 9:3,6
[af] **2:14** Lv 7:29-34
[ag] **2:15** Lv 3:3-5,16
[ah] **2:16** Lv 7:25
[ai] **2:17** Mal 2:7-9
[aj] **2:18** 1Sm 2:11; 3:1
[ak] 1Sm 2:28
[al] **2:19** Ex 28:31
[am] 1Sm 1:3,21
[an] **2:20** Lk 2:34
[ao] 1Sm 1:11,22,28
[ap] **2:21** Gn 21:1
[aq] 1Sm 2:26; 3:19-21; Lk 2:40
[ar] **2:22** 1Sm 2:13-17

[A] **2:8** DSS, LXX add *He gives the vow of the one who makes a vow and He blesses the years of the just* [B] **2:9** Lit *feet* [C] **2:10** DSS, LXX read *The LORD shatters those who dispute with Him* [D] **2:20** DSS; MT reads *he*

and how they were sleeping with the women who served at the entrance to the tent of meeting.[a] 23 He said to them, "Why are you doing these things? I have heard about your evil actions from all these people. 24 No, my sons, the report I hear from the LORD's people is not good. 25 If a man sins against another man, God can intercede for him, but if a man sins against the LORD, who can intercede for him?"[b] But they would not listen to their father, since the LORD intended to kill them.[c] 26 By contrast, the boy Samuel grew in stature and in favor with the LORD and with men.[d]

27 A man of God came to Eli and said to him,[e] "This is what the LORD says: 'Didn't I reveal Myself to your ancestral house when it was in Egypt and belonged to Pharaoh's palace?[f] 28 Out of all the tribes of Israel, I selected your house[A] to be priests, to offer sacrifices on My altar, to burn incense, and to wear an ·ephod in My presence.[g] I also gave your house all the Israelite fire offerings. 29 Why, then, do all of you despise My sacrifices and offerings that I require at the place of worship?[h] You have honored your sons more than Me,[i] by making yourselves fat with the best part of all of the offerings of My people Israel.'

30 "Therefore, this is the declaration of the LORD, the God of Israel:

'Although I said
your family and your ancestral house
would walk before Me forever,[j]
the LORD now says, "No longer!"
I will honor those who honor Me,[k]
but those who despise Me
will be disgraced.[l]

31 "'Look, the days are coming when I will cut off your strength and the strength of your ancestral family, so that none in your family will reach old age.[m] 32 You will see distress in the place of worship,[n] in spite of all that is good in Israel, and no one in your family will ever again reach old age.[o] 33 Any man from your family I do not cut off from My altar will bring grief[B] and sadness to you. All your descendants will die violently.[C,D] 34 This will be the sign that will come to you concerning your two sons Hophni and Phinehas:[p] both of them will die on the same day.[q]

35 "'Then I will raise up a faithful priest[r] for Myself. He will do whatever is in My heart and mind. I will establish a lasting dynasty for him,[s] and he will walk before My anointed one for all time.[t] 36 Anyone who is left in your family will come and bow down to him for a piece of silver or a loaf of bread. He will say: Please appoint me to some priestly office so I can have a piece of bread to eat.'"

Samuel's Call

3 The boy Samuel served the LORD in Eli's presence.[u] In those days the word of the LORD was rare and prophetic visions were not widespread.[v]

2 One day Eli, whose eyesight was failing,[w] was lying in his room. 3 Before the lamp of God had gone out,[x] Samuel was lying down in the tabernacle of the LORD, where the ark of God was located.

4 Then the LORD called Samuel,[E] and he answered, "Here I am." 5 He ran to Eli and said, "Here I am; you called me."

"I didn't call," Eli replied. "Go back and lie down." So he went and lay down.

6 Once again the LORD called, "Samuel!"

Samuel got up, went to Eli, and said, "Here I am; you called me."

"I didn't call, my son," he replied. "Go back and lie down."

7 Now Samuel had not yet experienced the LORD, because the word of the LORD had not yet been revealed to him. 8 Once again, for the third time, the LORD called Samuel. He got up, went to Eli, and said, "Here I am; you called me."

Then Eli understood that the LORD was calling the boy. 9 He told Samuel, "Go and lie down. If He calls you, say, 'Speak, LORD, for Your servant is listening.'" So Samuel went and lay down in his place.

10 The LORD came, stood there, and called as before, "Samuel, Samuel!"

Samuel responded, "Speak, for Your servant is listening."

11 The LORD said to Samuel, "I am about to do something in Israel that everyone who hears about it will shudder.[y] 12 On that day I will carry out against Eli everything I said about his family, from beginning to end.[z] 13 I

[a] **2:22** Ex 38:8
[b] **2:25** Nm 15:30-31; Heb 10:26-27
[c] Ex 5:2; 14:17-18; Jos 11:18-20
[d] **2:26** Lk 2:52
[e] **2:27** Dt 33:1; Jdg 13:6
[f] Ex 4:14-16; 12:1,43
[g] **2:28** Ex 28:1-4
[h] **2:29** Dt 12:5-7
[i] Mt 10:37
[j] **2:30** Ex 29:9; 40:12-15; Nm 25:10-13
[k] Ps 50:23
[l] 1Kg 2:26-27
[m] **2:31** 1Sm 4:11-18; 22:17-20
[n] **2:32** 1Kg 2:26-27
[o] Zch 8:4
[p] **2:34** 1Sm 10:7-9; 1Kg 13:3
[q] 1Sm 4:11
[r] **2:35** 1Sm 3:20
[s] 1Sm 8:3-5; 1Kg 11:38
[t] 1Sm 10:9-10; 12:3; 16:13
[u] **3:1** 1Sm 2:11,18
[v] Ps 74:9; Ezk 7:26; Am 8:11-12
[w] **3:2** 1Sm 4:15
[x] **3:3** Ex 27:20-21
[y] **3:11** 2Kg 21:12; Jr 19:3
[z] **3:12** 1Sm 2:27-36

A 2:28 Lit *selected him* B 2:33 Lit *grief to your eyes* C 2:33 DSS, LXX read *die by the sword of men* D 2:33 Lit *die men* E 3:4 DSS, LXX read *called, "Samuel! Samuel!"*

told him that I am going to judge his family forever because of the iniquity he knows
about: his sons are defiling the sanctuary,[A]
and he has not stopped them.[a] 14 Therefore, I
have sworn to Eli's family: The iniquity of Eli's
family will never be wiped out by either sacrifice or offering."[b]
15 Samuel lay down until the morning; then
he opened the doors of the LORD's house. He
was afraid to tell Eli the vision, 16 but Eli called
him and said, "Samuel, my son."
"Here I am," answered Samuel.
17 "What was the message He gave you?"
Eli asked. "Don't hide it from me. May God
punish you and do so severely if you hide
anything from me that He told you."[c] 18 So
Samuel told him everything and did not hide
anything from him. Eli responded, "He is the
LORD. He will do what He thinks is good."[B,d]
19 Samuel grew,[e] and the LORD was with
him,[f] and He fulfilled everything Samuel
prophesied.[C,g] 20 All Israel from Dan to Beer-
sheba knew that Samuel was a confirmed
prophet of the LORD.[h] 21 The LORD continued to appear in Shiloh, because there He
revealed Himself to Samuel by His word.[i]
4 1 And Samuel's words came to all Israel.

The Ark Captured by the Philistines

Israel went out to meet the Philistines in
battle and[D] camped at Ebenezer[j] while the
Philistines camped at Aphek.[k] 2 The Philistines lined up in battle formation against Israel, and as the battle intensified, Israel was
defeated by the Philistines, who struck down
about 4,000 men on the battlefield.
3 When the troops returned to the camp,
the elders of Israel asked, "Why did the LORD
let us be defeated today by the Philistines?[l]
Let's bring the ark of the LORD's covenant
from Shiloh. Then it[E] will go with us and save
us from the hand of our enemies."[m] 4 So the
people sent men to Shiloh to bring back the
ark of the covenant of the LORD of ·Hosts,
who dwells between the ·cherubim.[n] Eli's
two sons, Hophni and Phinehas, were there
with the ark of the covenant of God. 5 When
the ark of the covenant of the LORD entered
the camp, all the Israelites raised such a loud
shout that the ground shook.[o]
6 The Philistines heard the sound of the war
cry and asked, "What's this loud shout in the
Hebrews' camp?" When the Philistines discovered that the ark of the LORD had entered
the camp, 7 they panicked. "The gods have
entered their camp!" they said. "Woe to us,
nothing like this has happened before.[F] 8 Woe
to us, who will rescue us from the hand of
these magnificent gods? These are the gods
that slaughtered the Egyptians with all kinds
of plagues in the wilderness. 9 Show some
courage and be men, Philistines![p] Otherwise,
you'll serve the Hebrews just as they served
you.[q] Now be men and fight!"
10 So the Philistines fought, and Israel was
defeated,[r] and each man fled to his tent.[s] The
slaughter was severe — 30,000 of the Israelite foot soldiers fell. 11 The ark of God was
captured, and Eli's two sons, Hophni and
Phinehas, died.[t]

Eli's Death and Ichabod's Birth

12 That same day, a Benjaminite man ran[u]
from the battle and came to Shiloh. His
clothes were torn,[v] and there was dirt on his
head. 13 When he arrived, there was Eli sitting
on his chair beside the road watching,[w] because he was anxious about the ark of God.
When the man entered the city to give a report, the entire city cried out.
14 Eli heard the outcry and asked, "Why
this commotion?" The man quickly came
and reported to Eli. 15 At that time Eli was 98
years old, and his gaze was fixed[G] because he
couldn't see.[x]
16 The man said to Eli, "I'm the one who
came from the battle.[H] I fled from there today."
"What happened, my son?"[y] Eli asked.
17 The messenger answered, "Israel has
fled from the Philistines, and also there was
a great slaughter among the people. Your
two sons, Hophni and Phinehas, are both
dead, and the ark of God has been captured."
18 When he mentioned the ark of God, Eli fell
backward off the chair by the city gate,[z] and

[a]**3:13** Dt 17:12; 21:18 [b]**3:14** Lv 15:31; Is 22:14 [c]**3:17** 2Sm 3:35 [d]**3:18** Ex 34:5-7; Lv 10:3; Jb 2:10; Is 39:8 [e]**3:19** 1Sm 2:21 [f]Gn 21:22; 28:15 [g]1Sm 9:6 [h]**3:20** 1Sm 2:35 [i]**3:21** 1Sm 3:10 [j]**4:1** 1Sm 7:12 [k]Jos 12:18; 1Sm 29:1 [l]**4:3** Jos 7:7-8 [m]Nm 10:35; Jos 6:6 [n]**4:4** Ex 25:22; Nm 7:89 [o]**4:5** Jos 6:5,20 [p]**4:9** 1Co 16:13 [q]Jdg 13:1; 1Sm 14:21 [r]**4:10** Dt 28:15,25; 1Sm 4:2 [s]2Sm 18:17; 2Kg 14:12 [t]**4:11** 1Sm 2:34; Ps 78:56-64 [u]**4:12** 1Sm 8:11; Jos 7:22 [v]Jos 7:6; 2Sm 1:2; 15:32; Neh 9:1 [w]**4:13** 1Sm 1:9; 4:18 [x]**4:15** 1Kg 14:4 [y]**4:16** 2Sm 1:4 [z]**4:18** 1Sm 4:13

[A]**3:13** Ancient Jewish tradition, LXX, Old Lat read *are cursing God* [B]**3:18** Lit *what is good in His eyes* [C]**3:19** Lit *He let no words fall to the ground* [D]**4:1** LXX reads *In those days the Philistines gathered together to fight against Israel, and Israel went out to engage them in battle. They* [E]**4:3** Or *He* [F]**4:7** Lit *yesterday or the day before* [G]**4:15** Lit *his eyes stood*; 1Kg 14:4 [H]**4:16** LXX reads *camp*

since he was old and heavy, his neck broke
and he died. Eli had judged Israel 40 years.
19 Eli's daughter-in-law, the wife of Phinehas,
was pregnant and about to give birth. When
she heard the news about the capture of God's
ark and the deaths of her father-in-law and
her husband, she collapsed and gave birth
because her labor pains came on her. 20 As she
was dying,[A] the women taking care of her said,
"Don't be afraid. You've given birth to a son!"[a]
But she did not respond or pay attention. 21 She
named the boy Ichabod,[B] saying, "The glory
has departed from Israel,"[b] referring to the
capture of the ark of God[c] and to the deaths
of her father-in-law and her husband. 22 "The
glory has departed from Israel," she said, "because the ark of God has been captured."

The Ark in Philistine Hands

5 After the Philistines had captured the
ark of God, they took it from Ebenezer[d]
to Ashdod,[e] 2 brought it into the temple of
Dagon[C,f] and placed it next to his statue.[D]
3 When the people of Ashdod got up early the
next morning, there was Dagon, fallen with
his face to the ground before the ark of the
LORD.[g] So they took Dagon and returned him
to his place. 4 But when they got up early the
next morning, there was Dagon, fallen with
his face to the ground before the ark of the
LORD. This time, both Dagon's head and the
palms of his hands were broken off and lying on the threshold. Only Dagon's torso remained.[E] 5 That is why, to this day, the priests
of Dagon and everyone who enters the temple
of Dagon in Ashdod do not step on Dagon's
threshold.
6 The LORD's hand was heavy on the people
of Ashdod,[h] terrorizing[i] and afflicting the
people of Ashdod and its territory with tumors.[F,G,j] 7 When the men of Ashdod saw what
was happening, they said, "The ark of Israel's God must not stay here with us, because
His hand is strongly against us and our god
Dagon." 8 So they called all the Philistine rulers together[k] and asked, "What should we do
with the ark of Israel's God?"
"The ark of Israel's God should be moved
to Gath," they replied. So the men of Ashdod
moved the ark. 9 After they had moved it, the
LORD's hand was against the city of Gath,[l]
causing a great panic. He afflicted the men of
the city, from the youngest to the oldest, with
an outbreak of tumors.[m]
10 The Gittites then sent the ark of God to
Ekron, but when it got there, the Ekronites
cried out, "They've moved the ark of Israel's
God to us to kill us and our people!"[H]
11 The Ekronites called all the Philistine rulers together.[n] They said, "Send the ark of Israel's God away. It must return to its place so
it won't kill us and our people!"[I] For the fear
of death pervaded the city; God's hand was
oppressing them.[o] 12 The men who did not die
were afflicted with tumors, and the outcry of
the city went up to heaven.[p]

The Return of the Ark

6 When the ark of the LORD had been in the
land of the Philistines for seven months,
2 the Philistines summoned the priests and
the diviners[q] and pleaded, "What should we
do with the ark of the LORD? Tell us how we
can send it back to its place."
3 They replied, "If you send the ark of Israel's God away, you must not send it without
an offering.[r] You must send back a restitution
offering to Him,[s] and you will be healed. Then
the reason His hand hasn't been removed
from you will be revealed."[J]
4 They asked, "What restitution offering
should we send back to Him?"
And they answered, "Five gold tumors and
five gold mice[t] corresponding to the number of Philistine rulers,[u] since there was one
plague for both you[K] and your rulers. 5 Make
images of your tumors and of your mice that
are destroying the land. Give glory to Israel's God,[v] and perhaps He will stop oppressing you,[L,w] your gods, and your land.[x] 6 Why
harden your hearts as the Egyptians and Pharaoh hardened theirs?[y] When He afflicted
them, didn't they send Israel away, and Israel
left?[z]

[a] **4:20** Gn 35:16-19
[b] **4:21** Ps 26:8; Jr 2:11
[c] 1Sm 4:11
[d] **5:1** 1Sm 4:1; 7:12
[e] Jos 13:3
[f] **5:2** Jdg 16:23-24; 1Ch 10:8-10
[g] **5:3** Is 46:1-9
[h] **5:6** Ex 9:3; 1Sm 5:7,11
[i] 1Sm 6:5
[j] Dt 28:27; Ps 78:66
[k] **5:8** 1Sm 5:11; 29:6-11
[l] **5:9** 1Sm 5:11; 7:13
[m] 1Sm 5:6
[n] **5:11** 1Sm 5:8
[o] 1Sm 5:6,9
[p] **5:12** Ex 12:30
[q] **6:2** Gn 41:8; Ex 7:11; Is 2:6
[r] **6:3** Dt 16:16
[s] Lv 5:15-16
[t] **6:4** 1Sm 5:6,9,12; 6:17
[u] Jos 13:3; Jdg 3:3; 1Sm 6:17-18
[v] **6:5** Jos 7:19; Is 42:2
[w] 1Sm 5:6,11
[x] 1Sm 5:3-4,7
[y] **6:6** Ex 8:15,32; 9:34
[z] Ex 4:21; 12:31

A **4:20** LXX reads *And in her time of delivery, she was about to die* B **4:21** = Where is Glory? C **5:2** A Philistine god of the sea, grain, or storm D **5:2** Lit *to Dagon* E **5:4** LXX; Hb reads *Only Dagon remained on it* F **5:6** LXX adds *He brought up mice against them, and they swarmed in their ships. Then mice went up into the land and there was a mortal panic in the city.* G **5:6** Perhaps bubonic plague H **5:10** DSS, LXX read *Why have you moved . . . people?* I **5:11** DSS, LXX read *Why don't you return it to . . . people?* J **6:3** DSS, LXX read *healed, and an atonement shall be made for you. Shouldn't His hand be removed from you?* K **6:4** Some Hb mss, LXX; other Hb mss read *them* L **6:5** Lit *will lighten the heaviness of His hand from you*

7 "Now then, prepare one new cart and two
milk cows that have never been yoked.[a] Hitch
the cows to the cart, but take their calves away
and pen them up. 8 Take the ark of the LORD,
place it on the cart, and put the gold objects
that you're sending Him as a restitution offering in a box[b] beside the ark.[c] Send it off and
let it go its way. 9 Then watch: If it goes up the
road to its homeland toward Beth-shemesh,[d]
it is the LORD who has made this terrible
trouble for us. However, if it doesn't, we will
know that it was not His hand that punished[e]
us — it was just something that happened to
us by chance."

10 The men did this: They took two milk
cows, hitched them to the cart, and confined
their calves in the pen. 11 Then they put the ark
of the LORD on the cart, along with the box
containing the gold mice and the images of
their tumors. 12 The cows went straight up the
road to Beth-shemesh.[f] They stayed on that
one highway,[g] lowing as they went; they never
strayed to the right or to the left. The Philistine rulers were walking behind them to the
territory of Beth-shemesh.

13 The people of Beth-shemesh were harvesting wheat in the valley, and when they looked
up and saw the ark, they were overjoyed to see
it. 14 The cart came to the field of Joshua of Beth-
shemesh and stopped there near a large rock.
The people of the city chopped up the cart and
offered the cows as a ˙burnt offering to the
LORD.[h] 15 The Levites[i] removed the ark of the
LORD, along with the box containing the gold
objects, and placed them on the large rock. That
day the men of Beth-shemesh offered burnt
offerings and made sacrifices to the LORD.
16 When the five Philistine rulers[j] observed this,
they returned to Ekron that same day.

17 As a restitution offering to the LORD, the
Philistines had sent back one gold tumor for
each city:[k] Ashdod, Gaza, Ashkelon, Gath, and
Ekron. 18 The number of gold mice also corresponded to the number of Philistine cities
of the five rulers, the fortified cities and the
outlying villages.[l] The large rock[A,m] on which
the ark of the LORD was placed is in the field
of Joshua of Beth-shemesh to this day.

[a]**6:7** Nm 19:2
[b]**6:8** 1Sm 6:4-5
[c]1Sm 6:3
[d]**6:9** Jos 15:10
[e]1Sm 6:3
[f]**6:12** 1Sm 6:9
[g]Nm 20:19
[h]**6:14** 1Kg 19:21
[i]**6:15** Nm 4:1-33
[j]**6:16** Jos 13:3
[k]**6:17** 1Sm 6:4
[l]**6:18** Dt 3:5
[m]1Sm 6:14-15
[n]**6:19** Nm 4:15-20; 2Sm 6:7
[o]**6:20** Nm 17:13; Ps 76:7; Ezk 44:9-16
[p]**6:21** Jos 9:17; 15:9,60
[q]**7:1** 2Sm 6:3-4
[r]**7:3** Ex 20:3
[s]Dt 13:4; 1Ch 19:3
[t]Dt 6:5; 30:10; Jl 2:12-14
[u]Jos 24:14,23; Jdg 10:16
[v]Dt 6:13; Mt 4:10
[w]**7:4** Jdg 2:13
[x]**7:5** Jdg 20:1
[y]1Sm 8:6; 12:17,19,23
[z]**7:6** 1Sm 1:15; Ps 62:8; Lm 2:19
[aa]Lv 16:29; Neh 9:1
[ab]Jdg 10:10
[ac]**7:9** Lv 22:27

19 God struck down the men of Beth-shemesh because they looked inside the ark of the
LORD.[B,n] He struck down 70 men out of 50,000
men.[C] The people mourned because the LORD
struck them with a great slaughter. 20 The men
of Beth-shemesh asked, "Who is able to stand
in the presence of this holy LORD God?[o] Who
should the ark go to from here?"

21 They sent messengers to the residents of
Kiriath-jearim,[p] saying, "The Philistines have
returned the ark of the LORD. Come down
and get it."[D]

7 So the men of Kiriath-jearim came for the
ark of the LORD and took it to Abinadab's
house on the hill.[q] They consecrated his son
Eleazar to take care of it.

Victory at Mizpah

2 Time went by until 20 years had passed
since the ark had been taken to Kiriath-
jearim. Then the whole house of Israel began to seek the LORD. 3 Samuel told them,
"If you[r] are returning to the LORD[s] with all
your heart,[t] get rid of the foreign gods[u] and
the ˙Ashtoreths that are among you, dedicate
yourselves to[E] the LORD, and worship only
Him.[v] Then He will rescue you from the hand
of the Philistines." 4 So the Israelites removed
the ˙Baals and the Ashtoreths[w] and only worshiped the LORD.

5 Samuel said, "Gather all Israel at Mizpah,[x] and I will pray to the LORD on your behalf."[y] 6 When they gathered at Mizpah, they
drew water and poured it out in the LORD's
presence.[z] They fasted that day,[aa] and there
they confessed, "We have sinned against the
LORD."[ab] And Samuel judged the Israelites at
Mizpah.

7 When the Philistines heard that the Israelites had gathered at Mizpah, their rulers
marched up toward Israel. When the Israelites heard about it, they were afraid because
of the Philistines. 8 The Israelites said to Samuel, "Don't stop crying out to the LORD our
God for us, so that He will save us from the
hand of the Philistines."

9 Then Samuel took a young lamb[ac] and offered it as a whole ˙burnt offering to the LORD.

[A]**6:18** Some Hb mss, DSS, LXX, Tg; other Hb mss read *meadow* [B]**6:19** LXX reads *But the sons of Jeconiah did not rejoice with the men of Beth-shemesh when they saw the ark of the LORD.* [C]**6:19** Some Hb mss, Josephus read *70 men*; other Hb mss read *50,070 men* [D]**6:21** Lit *and bring it up to you* [E]**7:3** Lit *you and set your hearts on*

He cried out to the LORD on behalf of Israel, and the LORD answered him.[a] 10 Samuel was offering the burnt offering as the Philistines drew near to fight against Israel. The LORD thundered loudly[b] against the Philistines that day and threw them into such confusion that they fled before Israel.[c] 11 Then the men of Israel charged out of Mizpah and pursued the Philistines striking them down all the way to a place below Beth-car.

12 Afterward, Samuel took a stone and set it upright[d] between Mizpah and Shen. He named it Ebenezer,[A] explaining, "The LORD has helped us to this point." 13 So the Philistines were subdued[e] and[B] did not invade Israel's territory again.[f] The LORD's hand was against the Philistines all of Samuel's life. 14 The cities from Ekron to Gath, which they had taken from Israel, were restored; Israel even rescued their surrounding territories from Philistine control. There was also peace between Israel and the Amorites.

15 Samuel judged Israel throughout his life.[g] 16 Every year he would go on a circuit to Bethel, Gilgal, and Mizpah and would judge Israel at all these locations. 17 Then he would return to Ramah[h] because his home was there, he judged Israel there, and he built an altar to the LORD there.

Israel's Demand for a King

8 When Samuel grew old, he appointed his sons as judges over Israel.[i] 2 His firstborn son's name was Joel and his second was Abijah. They were judges in Beer-sheba.[j] 3 However, his sons did not walk in his ways — they turned toward dishonest gain, took bribes, and perverted justice.[k]

4 So all the elders of Israel gathered together and went to Samuel at Ramah.[l] 5 They said to him, "Look, you are old, and your sons do not follow your example. Therefore, appoint a king to judge us the same as all the other nations have."[m]

6 When they said, "Give us a king to judge us," Samuel considered their demand sinful, so he prayed to the LORD. 7 But the LORD told him, "Listen to the people and everything they say to you. They have not rejected you; they have rejected Me as their king.[n] 8 They are doing the same thing to you that they have done to Me,[C] since the day I brought them out of Egypt until this day, abandoning Me and worshiping other gods. 9 Listen to them, but you must solemnly warn them[o] and tell them about the rights of the king who will rule over them."

10 Samuel told all the LORD's words to the people who were asking him for a king. 11 He said, "These are the rights of the king who will rule over you: He will take your sons and put them to his use in his chariots, on his horses, or running in front of his chariots. 12 He can appoint them for his use as commanders of thousands or commanders of fifties,[p] to plow his ground or reap his harvest, or to make his weapons of war or the equipment for his chariots. 13 He can take your daughters to become perfumers, cooks, and bakers. 14 He can take your best fields, vineyards, and olive orchards and give them to his servants.[q] 15 He can take a tenth of your grain and your vineyards and give them to his officials and servants. 16 He can take your male servants, your female servants, your best young men,[D] and your donkeys and use them for his work. 17 He can take a tenth of your flocks, and you yourselves can become his servants. 18 When that day comes, you will cry out because of the king you've chosen for yourselves,[r] but the LORD won't answer you on that day."[s]

19 The people refused to listen to Samuel. "No!" they said. "We must have a king over us. 20 Then we'll be like all the other nations: our king will judge us, go out before us,[t] and fight our battles."

21 Samuel listened to all the people's words and then repeated them to the LORD.[E] 22 "Listen to them," the LORD told Samuel. "Appoint a king for them."[u]

Then Samuel told the men of Israel, "Each of you, go back to your city."

Saul Anointed King

9 There was an influential man of Benjamin named Kish[v] son of Abiel, son of Zeror, son of Becorath, son of Aphiah, son of a Benjaminite. 2 He had a son named Saul,

[a] 7:9 Ps 99:6; Jr 15:1
[b] 7:10 1Sm 2:10; 2Sm 22:14
[c] Ex 23:27; Jos 10:10; Jdg 4:15
[d] 7:12 Jos 4:9
[e] 7:13 Jdg 13:1-15
[f] 1Sm 13:5
[g] 7:15 1Sm 7:6; 12:11
[h] 7:17 1Sm 1:1,19; 2:11
[i] 8:1 Dt 16:18-19
[j] 8:2 Gn 22:19; 1Kg 19:3; Am 5:5
[k] 8:3 Ex 23:1-9
[l] 8:4 1Sm 7:17
[m] 8:5 Dt 17:14-15
[n] 8:7 Ex 16:8; 1Sm 10:19
[o] 8:9 Ezk 3:18
[p] 8:12 Nm 31:14; 1Sm 22:7
[q] 8:14 1Kg 21:7; Ezk 46:18
[r] 8:18 Is 8:21
[s] Pr 1:25-28; Mc 3:4
[t] 8:20 Nm 27:17; 1Sm 18:13; 2Ch 1:10
[u] 8:22 1Sm 8:7
[v] 9:1 1Sm 14:51; 1Ch 9:36-39

A7:12 = Stone of Help B7:13 LXX reads *The LORD humbled the Philistines and they* C8:8 LXX; MT omits *to Me* D8:16 LXX reads *best cattle* E8:21 Lit *them in the LORD's ears*

an impressive young man.[a] There was no
one more impressive among the Israelites
than he. He stood a head taller than anyone
else.[A,b]
3One day the donkeys of Saul's father Kish
wandered off. Kish said to his son Saul, "Take
one of the attendants with you and go look
for the donkeys." **4**Saul and his attendant
went through the hill country of Ephraim[c]
and then through the region of Shalishah,[d]
but they didn't find them. They went through
the region of Shaalim[e]—nothing. Then they
went through the Benjaminite region but still
didn't find them.
5When they came to the land of Zuph,[f]
Saul said to the attendant who was with him,
"Come on, let's go back, or my father will stop
worrying about the donkeys and start worrying about us."[g]
6"Look," the attendant said, "there's a man
of God[h] in this city who is highly respected;
everything he says is sure to come true.[i] Let's
go there now. Maybe he'll tell us which way
we should go."[j]
7"Suppose we do go," Saul said to his attendant, "what do we take the man? The food
from our packs is gone, and there's no gift to
take to the man of God.[k] What do we have?"
8The attendant answered Saul: "Here, I have
a piece[B] of silver. I'll give it to the man of God,
and he will tell us our way."
9Formerly in Israel, a man who was going
to inquire of God would say, "Come, let's go
to the seer," for the prophet of today was formerly called the seer.[l]
10"Good," Saul replied to his attendant.
"Come on, let's go." So they went to the city
where the man of God was. **11**As they were
climbing the hill to the city, they found some
young women coming out to draw water[m]
and asked, "Is the seer here?"
12The women answered, "Yes, he is ahead
of you. Hurry, he just now came to the city,
because there's a sacrifice[n] for the people at
the •high place[o] today. **13**If you go quickly, you
can catch up with him before he goes to the
high place to eat. The people won't eat until
he comes because he must bless the sacrifice;
after that, the guests can eat. Go up immedi-

[a]**9:2** 1Sm 10:24
[b]1Sm 10:23
[c]**9:4** Jos 24:33
[d]2Kg 4:42
[e]Jos 19:42
[f]**9:5** 1Sm 1:1
[g]1Sm 10:2
[h]**9:6** Dt 33:1; 2Kg 5:8
[i]1Sm 3:19
[j]Gn 24:42
[k]**9:7** 1Kg 14:3; 2Kg 5:15; 8:8-9; Ezk 13:19
[l]**9:9** 2Sm 24:11; 1Ch 9:22; 26:28; Is 30:10
[m]**9:11** Gn 24:15; 29:9; Ex 2:16
[n]**9:12** Nm 28:11-15
[o]1Sm 7:17; 10:5
[p]**9:15** 1Sm 15:1; Ac 13:21
[q]**9:16** 1Sm 10:1
[r]Ex 3:7,9
[s]**9:17** 1Sm 16:12
[t]**9:20** 1Sm 9:3
[u]1Sm 8:5; 12:13
[v]**9:21** 1Sm 15:17
[w]Jdg 20:46-48
[x]**9:24** Ex 29:22,27; Lv 7:32-33; Nm 18:18
[y]**9:25** Dt 22:8; Ac 10:9

ately—you can find him now." **14**So they went
up toward the city.
Saul and his attendant were entering the
city when they saw Samuel coming toward
them on his way to the high place. **15**Now the
day before Saul's arrival, the LORD had informed Samuel,[C,p] **16**"At this time tomorrow
I will send you a man from the land of Benjamin. Anoint him ruler over My people Israel.[q] He will save them from the hand of the
Philistines because I have seen the affliction
of My people,[r] for their cry has come to Me."
17When Samuel saw Saul, the LORD told him,
"Here is the man I told you about;[s] he will rule
over My people."
18Saul approached Samuel in the gate area
and asked, "Would you please tell me where
the seer's house is?"
19"I am the seer," Samuel answered.[D] "Go up
ahead of me to the high place and eat with me
today. When I send you off in the morning,
I'll tell you everything that's in your heart.
20As for the donkeys that wandered away
from you three days ago,[t] don't worry about
them because they've been found. And who
does all Israel desire[u] but you and all your father's family?"
21Saul responded, "Am I not a Benjaminite[v]
from the smallest of Israel's tribes and isn't
my clan the least important of all the clans of
the Benjaminite tribe?[w] So why have you said
something like this to me?"
22Samuel took Saul and his attendant,
brought them to the banquet hall, and gave
them a place at the head of the 30[E] or so men
who had been invited. **23**Then Samuel said to
the cook, "Get the portion of meat that I gave
you and told you to set aside."
24The cook picked up the thigh[x] and what
was attached to it and set it before Saul. Then
Samuel said, "Notice that the reserved piece is
set before you. Eat it because it was saved for
you for this solemn event at the time I said,
'I've invited the people.'" So Saul ate with
Samuel that day. **25**Afterward, they went down
from the high place to the city, and Samuel
spoke with Saul on the roof.[F,y]
26They got up early, and just before dawn,
Samuel called to Saul on the roof, "Get up,

[A]**9:2** Lit *From his shoulder and up higher than any of the people* [B]**9:8** Lit *a quarter of a shekel* [C]**9:15** Lit *had uncovered Samuel's ear, saying* [D]**9:19** Lit *answered Saul* [E]**9:22** LXX reads *70* [F]**9:25** LXX reads *city. They prepared a bed for Saul on the roof, and he slept.*

and I'll send you on your way!" Saul got up, and both he and Samuel went outside. 27 As they were going down to the edge of the city, Samuel said to Saul, "Tell the attendant to go on ahead of us, but you stay for a while, and I'll reveal the word of God to you." So the attendant went on.

10 Samuel took the flask of oil,[a] poured it out on Saul's head,[b] kissed him, and said, "Hasn't the LORD anointed you[c] ruler over His inheritance?[A,d] 2 Today when you leave me, you'll find two men at Rachel's Grave[e] at Zelzah in the land of Benjamin. They will say to you, 'The donkeys you went looking for have been found,[f] and now your father has stopped being concerned about the donkeys and is worried about you, asking: What should I do about my son?'

3 "You will proceed from there until you come to the oak of Tabor.[g] Three men going up to God at Bethel[h] will meet you there, one bringing three goats, one bringing three loaves of bread, and one bringing a skin of wine. 4 They will ask how you are and give you two loaves[B] of bread, which you will accept from them.

5 "After that you will come to the Hill of God[C,i] where there are Philistine garrisons.[D] When you arrive at the city, you will meet a group of prophets[j] coming down from the ·high place prophesying.[k] They will be preceded by harps, tambourines, flutes, and lyres. 6 The Spirit of the LORD will control you,[l] you will prophesy with them,[m] and you will be transformed into a different person.[n] 7 When these signs have happened to you, do whatever your circumstances require[E,o] because God is with you. 8 Afterward, go ahead of me to Gilgal. I will come to you to offer ·burnt offerings and to sacrifice ·fellowship offerings. Wait seven days until I come to you and show you what to do."

9 When Saul turned around[F] to leave Samuel, God changed his heart,[G] and all the signs came about that day. 10 When Saul and his attendant arrived at Gibeah, a group of prophets met him. Then the Spirit of God took control of him, and he prophesied along with them.

11 Everyone who knew him previously and saw him prophesy with the prophets asked each other, "What has happened to the son of Kish? Is Saul also among the prophets?"[p]

12 Then a man who was from there asked, "And who is their father?"[q]

As a result, "Is Saul also among the prophets?" became a popular saying. 13 Then Saul finished prophesying and went to the high place.

14 Saul's uncle[r] asked him and his attendant, "Where did you go?"

"To look for the donkeys," Saul answered. "When we saw they weren't there, we went to Samuel."[s]

15 "Tell me," Saul's uncle asked, "what did Samuel say to you?"

16 Saul told him, "He assured us the donkeys had been found." However, Saul did not tell him what Samuel had said about the matter of kingship.

Saul Received as King

17 Samuel summoned the people to the LORD at Mizpah[t] 18 and said to the Israelites, "This is what the LORD, the God of Israel, says:[u] 'I brought Israel out of Egypt, and I rescued you from the power of the Egyptians and all the kingdoms that were oppressing you.' 19 But today you have rejected your God,[v] who saves you from all your troubles and afflictions. You said to Him, 'You[H] must set a king over us.'[w] Now therefore present yourselves before the LORD by your tribes and clans."[x]

20 Samuel had all the tribes of Israel come forward, and the tribe of Benjamin was selected. 21 Then he had the tribe of Benjamin come forward by its clans, and the Matrite clan was selected.[I] Finally, Saul son of Kish was selected.[y] But when they searched for him, they could not find him. 22 They again inquired of the LORD,[z] "Has the man come here yet?"

The LORD replied, "There he is, hidden among the supplies."

23 They ran and got him from there. When

[a] **10:1** Ex 30:23-33; 1Sm 16:13; 2Kg 9:3,6 [b] 2Kg 9:1-3 [c] 1Sm 16:13; 26:9; 2Sm 1:14 [d] Dt 32:9; Ps 78:71 [e] **10:2** Gn 35:19-20 [f] 1Sm 9:3-5 [g] **10:3** Gn 35:8 [h] Gn 28:19; 35:1,3,7 [i] **10:5** 1Sm 13:2-3 [j] 1Sm 19:20; 2Kg 2:3,5,15 [k] 2Kg 3:15; 1Ch 25:1-6 [l] **10:6** Nm 11:25,29; Jdg 14:6 [m] Ec 9:10 [n] 1Sm 19:23-24 [o] **10:7** Jos 1:5 [p] **10:11** 1Sm 19:24; Am 7:14-15; Mt 13:54-57 [q] **10:12** Gn 45:8; Jdg 17:10 [r] **10:14** 1Sm 14:50 [s] 1Sm 9:4-6 [t] **10:17** 1Sm 7:5 [u] **10:18** Jdg 6:8-9 [v] **10:19** 1Sm 8:6-7 [w] 1Sm 8:19 [x] Jos 7:14-18; 24:1; Pr 16:33 [y] **10:20-21** Jos 7:16-18 [z] **10:22** Ex 28:30; Nm 27:21; 1Sm 23:2,4,9-11

[A] **10:1** LXX adds *And you will reign over the LORD's people, and you will save them from the hand of their enemies all around. And this is the sign to you that the LORD has anointed you ruler over his inheritance.* [B] **10:4** DSS, LXX read *wave offerings* [C] **10:5** Or *to Gibeath-elohim* [D] **10:5** Or *governors* [E] **10:7** Lit *do for yourself whatever your hand finds* [F] **10:9** Lit *turned his shoulder* [G] **10:9** Lit *God turned to him another heart* [H] **10:19** Some Hb mss, LXX, Syr, Vg read *You said, 'No, you . . .* [I] **10:21** LXX adds *And he had the Matrite clan come forward, man by man.*

he stood among the people, he stood a head taller than anyone else.[A,a] 24 Samuel said to all the people, "Do you see the one the LORD has chosen?[b] There is no one like him among the entire population."

And all the people shouted,[B] "Long live the king!"[c]

25 Samuel proclaimed to the people the rights of kingship.[d] He wrote them on a scroll, which he placed in the presence of the LORD.[e] Then Samuel sent all the people away, each to his home.

26 Saul also went to his home in Gibeah,[f] and brave men whose hearts God had touched went with him. 27 But some ·wicked men said, "How can this guy save us?" They despised him and did not bring him a gift,[g] but Saul said nothing.[C,D]

Saul's Deliverance of Jabesh-gilead

11 Nahash[E,h] the Ammonite came up and laid siege to Jabesh-gilead.[i] All the men of Jabesh said to him, "Make a treaty[j] with us, and we will serve you."

2 Nahash the Ammonite replied, "I'll make one with you on this condition: that I gouge out everyone's right eye[k] and humiliate all Israel."[l]

3 "Don't do anything to us for seven days," the elders of Jabesh said to him, "and let us send messengers throughout the territory of Israel. If no one saves us, we will surrender to you."

4 When the messengers came to Gibeah,[m] Saul's hometown, and told the terms to[F] the people, all wept aloud.[n] 5 Just then Saul was coming in from the field behind his oxen. "What's the matter with the people? Why are they weeping?" Saul inquired, and they repeated to him the words of the men from Jabesh.

6 When Saul heard these words, the Spirit of God suddenly took control of him,[o] and his anger burned furiously. 7 He took a team of oxen, cut them in pieces,[p] and sent them throughout the land of Israel by messengers who said, "This is what will be done to the ox of anyone who doesn't march behind Saul and Samuel."[q] As a result, the terror of the LORD fell on the people, and they went out united.[r]

8 Saul counted them at Bezek.[s] There were 300,000[G,t] Israelites and 30,000[H] men from Judah. 9 He told the messengers who had come, "Tell this to the men of Jabesh-gilead: 'Deliverance will be yours tomorrow by the time the sun is hot.'" So the messengers told the men of Jabesh, and they rejoiced.

10 Then the men of Jabesh said to Nahash, "Tomorrow we will come out, and you can do whatever you want[I] to us."

11 The next day Saul organized the troops into three divisions.[u] During the morning watch, they invaded the Ammonite camp and slaughtered them until the heat of the day. There were survivors, but they were so scattered that no two of them were left together.

Saul's Confirmation as King

12 Afterward, the people said to Samuel, "Who said that Saul should not[J] reign over us?[v] Give us those men so we can kill them!"[w]

13 But Saul ordered, "No one will be executed this day, for today the LORD has provided deliverance in Israel."[x]

14 Then Samuel said to the people, "Come, let's go to Gilgal, so we can renew the kingship there." 15 So all the people went to Gilgal, and there in the LORD's presence[y] they made Saul king. There they sacrificed ·fellowship offerings[z] in the LORD's presence, and Saul and all the men of Israel greatly rejoiced.

Samuel's Final Public Speech

12 Then Samuel said to all Israel, "I have carefully listened to everything you said to me and placed a king over you.[aa] 2 Now you can see that the king is leading you. As for me, I'm old and gray, and my sons are here with you. I have led you from my youth until today. 3 Here I am. Bring charges against me before the LORD and His anointed:

[a] **10:23** 1Sm 9:2 [b] **10:24** Dt 17:15; 2Sm 21:6 [c] 1Kg 1:25,34,39 [d] **10:25** 1Sm 8:11-17 [e] Dt 17:18-20 [f] **10:26** 1Sm 11:4; 15:34 [g] **10:27** 1Kg 10:25; 2Ch 17:5 [h] **11:1** 1Sm 12:12 [i] 1Sm 12:12; 31:11 [j] 1Kg 20:34; Ezk 17:13 [k] **11:2** Nm 16:14 [l] 1Sm 17:26; Ps 44:13 [m] **11:4** 1Sm 10:26; 15:34 [n] Gn 27:38; Jdg 2:4 [o] **11:6** Jdg 14:6; 1Sm 10:10 [p] **11:7** Jdg 19:29 [q] Jdg 21:5,8,10 [r] Jdg 20:1 [s] **11:8** Jdg 1:5 [t] Jdg 20:2 [u] **11:11** Jdg 7:16 [v] **11:12** 1Sm 10:27 [w] Lk 19:27 [x] **11:13** Ex 14:13; 1Sm 19:5 [y] **11:15** 1Sm 10:17 [z] 1Sm 10:8 [aa] **12:1** 1Sm 8:5-22

[A] **10:23** Lit *people, and he was higher than any of the people from his shoulder and up* [B] **10:24** LXX reads *acknowledged and said* [C] **10:27** DSS add *Nahash king of the Ammonites had been severely oppressing the Gadites and Reubenites. He gouged out the right eye of each of them and brought fear and trembling on Israel. Of the Israelites beyond the Jordan none remained whose right eye Nahash, king of the Ammonites, had not gouged out. But there were 7,000 men who had escaped from the Ammonites and entered Jabesh-gilead.* [D] **10:27** Lit *gift, and he was like a mute person* [E] **11:1** DSS, LXX read *About a month later, Nahash* [F] **11:4** Lit *in the ears of* [G] **11:8** LXX reads *600,000* [H] **11:8** DSS, LXX read *70,000* [I] **11:10** Lit *do what is good in your eyes* [J] **11:12** Some Hb mss, LXX; other Hb mss omit *not*

Whose ox or donkey have I taken?[a] Whom
have I wronged or mistreated? From whose
hand have I taken a bribe to overlook something?[A,B,b] I will return it to you."
4 "You haven't wronged us, you haven't mistreated us, and you haven't taken anything
from anyone's hand," they responded.
5 He said to them, "The LORD is a witness
against you, and His anointed is a witness today that you haven't found anything[c] in my
hand."[d]
"He is a witness," they said.
6 Then Samuel said to the people, "The
LORD, who appointed Moses and Aaron[e] and
who brought your ancestors up from the land
of Egypt, is a witness.[C] 7 Now present yourselves, so I may confront you before the LORD
about all the righteous acts He has done for
you and your ancestors.
8 "When Jacob went to Egypt,[D] your ancestors cried out to the LORD,[f] and He sent them
Moses and Aaron, who led your ancestors out
of Egypt and settled them in this place.[g] 9 But
they forgot the LORD their God, so He handed
them over to Sisera[h] commander of the army
of Hazor, to the Philistines, and to the king
of Moab.[i] These enemies fought against them.
10 Then they cried out to the LORD and said,
'We have sinned, for we abandoned the LORD
and worshiped the ·Baals and the ·Ashtoreths.
Now deliver us from the power of our enemies,[j] and we will serve You.' 11 So the LORD
sent Jerubbaal,[k] Barak,[E,l] Jephthah,[m] and Samuel.[n] He rescued you from the power of the
enemies around you, and you lived securely.
12 But when you saw that Nahash king of the
Ammonites was coming against you, you
said to me, 'No, we must have a king rule over
us'—even though the LORD your God is your
king.
13 "Now here is the king you've chosen,[o] the
one you requested.[p] Look, this is the king
the LORD has placed over you. 14 If you ·fear
the LORD,[q] worship and obey Him, and if you
don't rebel against the LORD's command, then
both you and the king who rules over you will
follow the LORD your God. 15 However, if you
disobey the LORD[r] and rebel against His command, the LORD's hand will be against you[s]
and against your ancestors.[F,t]
16 "Now, therefore, present yourselves and
see this great thing that the LORD will do before your eyes.[u] 17 Isn't the wheat harvest today?[v] I will call on the LORD and He will send
thunder and rain, so that you will know and
see what a great evil you committed in the
LORD's sight by requesting a king for yourselves."[w] 18 Samuel called on the LORD, and on
that day the LORD sent thunder and rain. As a
result, all the people greatly feared the LORD
and Samuel.[x]
19 They pleaded with Samuel, "Pray to the
LORD your God for your servants,[y] so we
won't die! For we have added to all our sins
the evil of requesting a king for ourselves."[z]
20 Samuel replied, "Don't be afraid. Even
though you have committed all this evil,
don't turn away from following the LORD.[aa]
Instead, worship the LORD with all your
heart. 21 Don't turn away to follow worthless[G]
things that can't profit or deliver you; they
are worthless.[ab] 22 The LORD will not abandon
His people,[ac] because of His great name and
because He has determined to make you His
own people.[ad]
23 "As for me, I vow that I will not sin against
the LORD by ceasing to pray for you.[ae] I will
teach you the good and right way. 24 Above
all, fear the LORD and worship Him faithfully
with all your heart; consider the great things
He has done for you.[af] 25 However, if you continue to do what is evil, both you and your
king will be swept away."[ag]

Saul's Failure

13 Saul was 30 years[H] old when he became
king, and he reigned 42 years[I] over Israel.[J] 2 He chose 3,000 men from Israel for
himself: 2,000 were with Saul at Michmash[ah]
and in Bethel's hill country, and 1,000 were
with Jonathan in Gibeah[ai] of Benjamin. He
sent the rest of the troops away, each to his
own tent.
3 Jonathan attacked the Philistine garrison[K,aj] that was in Geba,[ak] and the Philistines
heard about it. So Saul blew the ram's horn

[a] **12:3** Ex 20:17; Nm 16:15
[b] Dt 16:19
[c] **12:5** Ac 23:9; 24:20
[d] Ex 22:4
[e] **12:6** Ex 6:26
[f] **12:8** Ex 2:23-25
[g] Ex 3:1-10
[h] **12:9** Jdg 4:1-2
[i] Jdg 2:11-15
[j] **12:10** Jdg 2:18
[k] **12:11** Jdg 6:11-12,32
[l] Jdg 4:6; 11:1
[m] Jdg 11:1
[n] 1Sm 7:10-14
[o] **12:13** 1Sm 10:24
[p] 1Sm 8:5; Hs 13:11
[q] **12:14** Jos 24:14
[r] **12:15** Jos 24:20; Is 1:20
[s] 1Sm 5:9
[t] Lv 26:14-33; Jos 24:14-27
[u] **12:16** Ex 14:13
[v] **12:17** Pr 26:1
[w] 1Sm 8:7
[x] **12:18** Ex 9:23-25,31; 1Kg 18:37-39; Pr 26:1
[y] **12:19** Ex 9:28; Jr 15:1
[z] 1Sm 17:20
[aa] **12:20** Dt 11:16
[ab] **12:21** Is 44:9-20; Jr 2:8,11; Hab 2:18
[ac] **12:22** Jos 7:9; Ezk 36:22-28
[ad] Dt 7:6-9; 1Pt 2:9
[ae] **12:23** Nm 21:7; 1Sm 7:5-9; Rm 1:9-10
[af] **12:24** Dt 10:21; Ps 103:2-14
[ag] **12:25** 2Kg 17:6-7
[ah] **13:2** 1Sm 14:31
[ai] 1Sm 10:26
[aj] **13:3** 1Sm 10:5
[ak] 1Sm 13:16; 14:5

[A] **12:3** LXX reads *bribe or a pair of shoes? Testify against me.* [B] **12:3** Lit *bribe and will hide my eyes with it?* [C] **12:6** LXX; MT omits *is a witness* [D] **12:8** LXX reads *When Jacob and his sons went to Egypt and Egypt humbled them* [E] **12:11** LXX, Syr; MT reads *Bedan*; Jdg 4:6; Heb 11:32 [F] **12:15** LXX reads *your king* [G] **12:21** LXX reads *away after empty* [H] **13:1** Some LXX mss; MT reads *was one year* [I] **13:1** Text emended; MT reads *two years* [J] **13:1** Some LXX mss omit v. 1 [K] **13:3** Or *governor*

throughout the land[a] saying, "Let the Hebrews hear!"[A,b] 4 And all Israel heard the news, "Saul has attacked the Philistine garrison,[B] and Israel is now repulsive to the Philistines." Then the troops were summoned to join Saul at Gilgal.

5 The Philistines also gathered to fight against Israel: 3,000[C] chariots, 6,000 horsemen, and troops as numerous as the sand on the seashore.[c] They went up and camped at Michmash, east of Beth-aven.[D,d]

6 The men of Israel saw that they were in trouble because the troops were in a difficult situation. They hid in caves, thickets, among rocks, and in holes and cisterns.[e] 7 Some Hebrews even crossed the Jordan to the land of Gad and Gilead.

Saul, however, was still at Gilgal, and all his troops were gripped with fear. 8 He waited seven days for the appointed time that Samuel had set,[f] but Samuel didn't come to Gilgal, and the troops were deserting him. 9 So Saul said, "Bring me the •burnt offering and the •fellowship offerings." Then he offered the burnt offering.

10 Just as he finished offering the burnt offering, Samuel arrived. So Saul went out to greet him, 11 and Samuel asked, "What have you done?"

Saul answered, "When I saw that the troops were deserting me and you didn't come within the appointed days and the Philistines were gathering at Michmash, 12 I thought: The Philistines will now descend on me at Gilgal, and I haven't sought the LORD's favor. So I forced myself to offer the burnt offering."

13 Samuel said to Saul, "You have been foolish.[g] You have not kept the command which the LORD your God gave you.[h] It was at this time that the LORD would have permanently established your reign over Israel,[i] 14 but now your reign will not endure.[j] The LORD has found a man loyal to Him,[E,k] and the LORD has appointed him as ruler over His people, because you have not done what the LORD commanded." 15 Then Samuel went[F] from Gilgal to Gibeah in Benjamin. Saul registered the troops who were with him, about 600 men.

[a]**13:3** Jdg 3:27; 6:34
[b]Nm 10:9; Jdg 3:27; 6:34
[c]**13:5** Jos 11:4
[d]1Sm 14:23
[e]**13:6** Jdg 6:2
[f]**13:8** 1Sm 10:8
[g]**13:13** 2Ch 16:9
[h]1Sm 15:22,28
[i]1Sm 1:22
[j]**13:14** 1Sm 15:28
[k]1Sm 16:7; Ac 13:22
[l]**13:16** 1Sm 13:2-3
[m]**13:17** 1Sm 14:15
[n]Jos 18:23
[o]**13:18** Jos 18:13-14
[p]Neh 11:34
[q]**13:19** Jdg 5:8; 2Kg 24:14
[r]**13:22** Jdg 5:8
[s]**13:23** 1Sm 14:1; 2Sm 23:14
[t]**14:2** Is 10:28
[u]1Sm 13:15-16
[v]1Sm 13:15
[w]**14:3** 1Sm 22:9-12,20
[x]1Sm 2:28
[y]1Sm 4:21
[z]1Sm 1:3
[aa]**14:4** 1Sm 13:23

16 Saul, his son Jonathan, and the troops who were with them were staying in Geba[l] of Benjamin, and the Philistines were camped at Michmash. 17 Raiding parties[m] went out from the Philistine camp in three divisions. One division headed toward the Ophrah[n] road leading to the land of Shual. 18 The next division headed toward the Beth-horon[o] road, and the last division headed down the border road that looks out over the Valley of Zeboim[p] toward the wilderness.

19 No blacksmith could be found in all the land of Israel,[q] because the Philistines had said, "Otherwise, the Hebrews will make swords or spears." 20 So all the Israelites went to the Philistines to sharpen their plows, mattocks, axes, and sickles.[G] 21 The price was two-thirds of a •shekel[H] for plows and mattocks, and one-third of a shekel for pitchforks and axes, and for putting a point on an oxgoad. 22 So on the day of battle not a sword or spear could be found in the hand of any of the troops who were with Saul[r] and Jonathan; only Saul and his son Jonathan had weapons.

Jonathan's Victory over the Philistines

14 23 Now a Philistine garrison[s] took control of the pass at Michmash. 1 That same day Saul's son Jonathan said to the attendant who carried his weapons, "Come on, let's cross over to the Philistine garrison on the other side." However, he did not tell his father.

2 Saul was staying under the pomegranate tree in Migron[t] on the outskirts of Gibeah.[I,u] The troops with him numbered about 600.[v] 3 Ahijah,[w] who was wearing an •ephod,[x] was also there. He was the son of Ahitub, the brother of Ichabod[y] son of Phinehas, son of Eli the LORD's priest at Shiloh.[z] But the troops did not know that Jonathan had left.

4 There were sharp columns[J] of rock on both sides of the pass[aa] that Jonathan intended to cross to reach the Philistine garrison. One was named Bozez and the other Seneh; 5 one stood to the north in front of Michmash and the other to the south in front of Geba. 6 Jonathan said to the attendant who

[A]**13:3** LXX reads *The slaves have revolted* [B]**13:4** Or *governor* [C]**13:5** One LXX ms, Syr; MT reads *30,000* [D]**13:5** LXX reads *Michmash, opposite Beth-horon to the south* [E]**13:14** Lit *man according to His heart* [F]**13:15** LXX reads *Samuel left Gilgal and went on his way, and the rest of the people followed Saul to join the people in his army. They went* [G]**13:20** LXX; MT reads *plowshares* [H]**13:21** Lit *of a pim*; about 1/4 ounce of silver [I]**14:2** LXX reads *on top of the hill* [J]**14:4** Lit *There was a tooth* carried his weapons, "Come on, let's cross over to the garrison of these uncircumcised men.[a] Perhaps the LORD will help us. Nothing can keep the LORD from saving, whether by many or by few."[b]

7His armor-bearer responded, "Do what is in your heart. You choose. I'm right here with you whatever you decide."

8"All right," Jonathan replied, "we'll cross over to the men and then let them see us. 9If they say, 'Wait until we reach you,' then we will stay where we are and not go up to them. 10But if they say, 'Come on up,' then we'll go up, because the LORD has handed them over to us — that will be our sign."

11They let themselves be seen by the Philistine garrison, and the Philistines said, "Look, the Hebrews are coming out of the holes where they've been hiding!" 12The men of the garrison called to Jonathan and his armor-bearer. "Come on up, and we'll teach you a lesson!" they said.

[a]14:6 1Sm 17:26,36; Jr 9:25-26
[b]Jdg 7:4-7

WORLDVIEW

The Mission of God in the Deaf Culture

Deaf culture (with a capital "D") is often contrasted with deafness (with a small "d"). Deaf culture refers to the beliefs, language, and history of people who often do not even think of their deafness as a disability. Small "d" deafness refers simply to the biological impairment of not being able to hear. Members of Deaf culture claim that deafness is primarily a difference that deserves social and political accommodation rather than a disability that needs to be fixed. Many Deaf individuals remember that as children they were forced to try to lip read and prevented from learning or using any kind of sign language, despite the fact that signing was clearly the most natural language for them. Many Deaf individuals report memories of bad experiences with doctors and religious leaders who believed that the answer to their "problem" of deafness was a cure of either science or prayer, and their well-meaning parents imagined the only possibility for their deaf child's future was the hope of a New Testament miracle, "The deaf hear" (Mt 11:5). Even churches that have a Deaf ministry often create a special section of the church where deaf people sit together in front of an interpreter and rarely interact with the rest of the congregation.

Although Deaf people may not regard their deafness as a disability, they do recognize that they are viewed as members of the disabled community. Yet any Christian who approaches members of the Deaf culture hoping to draw them to Christ by promises of healing, on earth or in heaven, risks being regarded as yet another in a long line of blunderers. Well-intentioned Christians who have been subtly influenced by a culture that is fixated on a desire for perfect bodies need to recognize that the message of the gospel is much more comfortable in situations of brokenness and difference. Christ's scars remained even after His resurrection; His resurrection body was not in that sense "perfect."

Churches need to learn how to be faith communities for all people with disabilities, and to accomplish this purpose, they need to fight against the veneration of individualism and self-reliance with a model of mutual communion and interdependence. Individuals with disabilities must be a part of these communities; in fact, they should encourage able-bodied Christians to celebrate difference and recognize their necessary interdependence.

Members of the Deaf culture have often experienced exclusion. Yet because of their confidence in their own culture and value, they can teach the church how to minister *with* rather than *to* people with disabilities. They will respond to a gospel that demonstrates the counter-cultural values of denying the cult of the beautiful body and embracing the mutual needs of all members of the community.

"Follow me," Jonathan told his armor-bearer, "for the LORD has handed them over to Israel."[a] 13 Jonathan climbed up using his hands and feet, with his armor-bearer behind him. Jonathan cut them down, and his armor-bearer followed and finished them off. 14 In that first assault Jonathan and his armor-bearer struck down about 20 men in a half-acre field.

A Defeat for the Philistines

15 Terror spread through the Philistine camp and the open fields to all the troops. Even the garrison and the raiding parties[b] were terrified. The earth shook,[c] and terror spread from God.[A,d] 16 When Saul's watchmen in Gibeah of Benjamin looked, they saw the panicking troops scattering in every direction. 17 So Saul said to the troops with him, "Call the roll and determine who has left us." They called the roll and saw that Jonathan and his armor-bearer were gone.

18 Saul told Ahijah, "Bring the ark of God," for it was with the Israelites[B] at that time. 19 While Saul spoke to the priest,[e] the panic in the Philistine camp increased in intensity. So Saul said to the priest, "Stop what you're doing."[C]

20 Saul and all the troops with him assembled and marched to the battle, and there, the Philistines were fighting against each other in great confusion![f] 21 There were Hebrews from the area who had gone earlier into the camp to join the Philistines, but even they joined the Israelites[g] who were with Saul and Jonathan. 22 When all the Israelite men who had been hiding in the hill country of Ephraim[h] heard that the Philistines were fleeing, they also joined Saul and Jonathan in the battle. 23 So the LORD saved Israel that day.[i]

Saul's Rash Oath

The battle extended beyond Beth-aven, 24 and the men of Israel were worn out that day, for Saul had[D] placed the troops under an oath:[j] "The man who eats food before evening, before I have taken vengeance on my enemies is cursed." So none of the troops tasted any food.

25 Everyone[E] went into the forest, and there was honey on the ground. 26 When the troops entered the forest, they saw the flow of honey, but none of them ate any of it[F] because they feared the oath. 27 However, Jonathan had not heard his father make the troops swear the oath. He reached out with the end of the staff he was carrying and dipped it into the honeycomb.[k] When he ate the honey,[G] he had renewed energy.[l] 28 Then, one of the troops said, "Your father made the troops solemnly swear, 'The man who eats food today is cursed,' and the troops are exhausted."

29 Jonathan replied, "My father has brought trouble to the land.[m] Just look at how I have renewed energy because I tasted a little honey. 30 How much better if the troops had eaten freely today from the plunder they took from their enemies! Then the slaughter of the Philistines would have been much greater."

31 The Israelites struck down the Philistines that day from Michmash[n] all the way to Aijalon.[o] Since the Israelites were completely exhausted, 32 they rushed to the plunder,[p] took sheep, cattle, and calves, slaughtered them on the ground, and ate meat with the blood still in it. 33 Some reported to Saul: "Look, the troops are sinning against the LORD by eating meat with the blood still in it."[q]

Saul said, "You have been unfaithful. Roll a large stone over here at once." 34 He then said, "Go among the troops and say to them, 'Each man must bring me his ox or his sheep. Do the slaughtering here and then you can eat. Don't sin against the LORD by eating meat with the blood in it.'" So every one of the troops brought his ox that night and slaughtered it there. 35 Then Saul built an altar to the LORD; it was the first time he had built an altar to the LORD.[r]

36 Saul said, "Let's go down after the Philistines tonight and plunder them until morning. Don't let even one remain!"

"Do whatever you want,"[H] the troops replied.

But the priest[s] said, "We must consult God here."[t]

37 So Saul inquired of God,[u] "Should I go af-

[a] 14:12 2Sm 5:24
[b] 14:15 1Sm 13:17-18
[c] 1Sm 7:10
[d] 2Kg 7:6
[e] 14:19 Nm 27:21
[f] 14:20 Jdg 7:22; 2Ch 20:23
[g] 14:21 1Sm 29:4
[h] 14:22 1Sm 13:6
[i] 14:23 Ex 14:30
[j] 14:24 Jos 6:26
[k] 14:27 1Sm 14:43
[l] 1Sm 30:12
[m] 14:29 1Kg 18:17-18
[n] 14:31 1Sm 14:5
[o] Jos 10:12
[p] 14:32 1Sm 15:19
[q] 14:33 Gn 9:4; Lv 17:10-12
[r] 14:35 1Sm 7:12,17
[s] 14:36 1Sm 14:3,18-19
[t] Jdg 18:5-6
[u] 14:37 1Sm 10:22

[A] 14:15 Or *and a great terror spread* [B] 14:18 LXX reads *"Bring the ephod." For he wore the ephod before Israel* [C] 14:19 Lit *Withdraw your hand* [D] 14:24 LXX adds *committed a great act of ignorance and* [E] 14:25 Lit *All the land* [F] 14:26 Lit *but there was none who raised his hand to his mouth* [G] 14:27 Lit *he returned his hand to his mouth* [H] 14:36 Lit *Do what is good in your eyes*

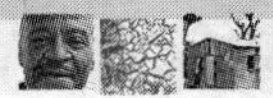

ter the Philistines? Will You hand them over to Israel?" But God did not answer him that day.[a]

38 Saul said, "All you leaders of the troops, come here. Let us investigate how this sin has occurred today. 39 As surely as the LORD lives who saves Israel, even if it is because of my son Jonathan, he must die!" Not one of the troops answered him.

40 So he said to all Israel, "You will be on one side, and I and my son Jonathan will be on the other side."

And the troops replied, "Do whatever you want."[A]

41 So Saul said to the LORD, "God of Israel, give us the right decision."[B,b] Jonathan and Saul were selected, and the troops were cleared of the charge.

42 Then Saul said, "Cast the lot between me and my son Jonathan," and Jonathan was selected. 43 Saul commanded him, "Tell me what you did."[c]

Jonathan told him, "I tasted a little honey[d] with the end of the staff I was carrying. I am ready to die!"

44 Saul declared to him, "May God punish me and do so severely[e] if you do not die, Jonathan!"

45 But the people said to Saul, "Must Jonathan die, who accomplished such a great deliverance for Israel? No, as the LORD lives, not a hair of his head will fall to the ground,[f] for he worked with God's help today."[g] So the people redeemed Jonathan, and he did not die. 46 Then Saul gave up the pursuit of the Philistines, and the Philistines returned to their own territory.

Summary of Saul's Kingship

47 When Saul assumed the kingship over Israel, he fought against all his enemies in every direction: against Moab, the Ammonites,[h] Edom, the kings of Zobah,[i] and the Philistines. Wherever he turned, he caused havoc.[C] 48 He fought bravely, defeated the Amalekites,[j] and delivered Israel from the hand of those who plundered them.

49 Saul's sons[k] were Jonathan, Ishvi, and Malchishua. The names of his two daughters were: Merab,[l] his firstborn, and Michal,[m] the younger. 50 The name of Saul's wife was Ahinoam daughter of Ahimaaz. The name of the commander of his army was Abner son of Saul's uncle Ner.[n] 51 Saul's father was Kish.[o] Abner's father was Ner son of Abiel.

52 The conflict with the Philistines was fierce all of Saul's days, so whenever Saul noticed any strong or brave man, he enlisted him.[p]

Saul Rejected as King

15 Samuel told Saul, "The LORD sent me to anoint you as king over His people Israel.[q] Now, listen to the words of the LORD. 2 This is what the LORD of ·Hosts says: 'I witnessed[D] what the Amalekites did to the Israelites when they opposed them along the way as they were coming out of Egypt.[r] 3 Now go and attack the Amalekites and ·completely destroy everything they have.[s] Do not spare them. Kill men and women, children and infants, oxen and sheep, camels and donkeys.'"[t]

4 Then Saul summoned the troops and counted them at Telaim: 200,000 foot soldiers and 10,000 men from Judah. 5 Saul came to the city of Amalek and set up an ambush in the ·wadi. 6 He warned the Kenites,[u] "Since you showed kindness to all the Israelites when they came out of Egypt,[v] go on and leave! Get away from the Amalekites, or I'll sweep you away with them." So the Kenites withdrew from the Amalekites.

7 Then Saul struck down the Amalekites[w] from Havilah[x] all the way to Shur,[y] which is next to Egypt. 8 He captured Agag[z] king of Amalek alive, but he completely destroyed all the rest of the people with the sword.[aa] 9 Saul and the troops spared Agag, and the best of the sheep, cattle, and choice animals,[E] as well as the young rams and the best of everything else. They were not willing to destroy them, but they did destroy all the worthless and unwanted things.

10 Then the word of the LORD came to Samuel, 11 "I regret that I made Saul king,[ab] for he has turned away from following Me and has

[a] **14:37** 1Sm 28:6
[b] **14:41** Ac 1:24
[c] **14:43** Jos 7:19
[d] 1Sm 14:27
[e] **14:44** 1Sm 25:22
[f] **14:45** 2Sm 14:11; 1Kg 1:52; Ac 27:34
[g] Jn 3:21
[h] **14:47** 1Sm 11:1-13
[i] 2Sm 8:3-10
[j] **14:48** 1Sm 15:3,7
[k] **14:49** 1Sm 31:2; 1Ch 10:2
[l] 1Sm 18:17-19
[m] 1Sm 18:20,27; 19:12; 2Sm 6:20-23
[n] **14:50** 2Sm 2:8
[o] **14:51** 1Sm 9:1,21
[p] **14:52** 1Sm 8:11
[q] **15:1** 1Sm 9:16
[r] **15:2** Ex 17:8-16; Nm 24:20; Dt 25:17-19
[s] **15:3** Nm 24:20; Dt 20:16-18
[t] Jos 6:17-21; 1Sm 22:19
[u] **15:6** Jdg 1:16; 4:11
[v] Ex 18:9-10; Nm 10:29-32
[w] **15:7** 1Sm 14:48
[x] Gn 16:7; 25:17-18
[y] Ex 15:22; 1Sm 27:8
[z] **15:8** Nm 24:7; Est 3:1
[aa] 1Sm 27:8; 30:1; 2Sm 8:12
[ab] **15:11** Gn 6:6-7; Ex 32:14; 2Sm 24:16

[A] **14:40** Lit *Do what is good in your eyes* [B] **14:41** LXX reads *Israel, why have You not answered Your servant today? If the unrighteousness is in me or in my son Jonathan, LORD God of Israel, give Urim; but if the guilt is in Your people Israel, give Thummim."* [C] **14:47** LXX reads *he was victorious* [D] **15:2** LXX reads *I will avenge* [E] **15:9** Lit *and the second*

not carried out My instructions."[a] So Samuel
became angry and cried out to the LORD all
night.[b]
12 Early in the morning Samuel got up to
confront Saul, but it was reported to Samuel,
"Saul went to Carmel[c] where he set up a monument for himself. Then he turned around and
went down to Gilgal."[d] 13 When Samuel came
to him, Saul said, "May the LORD bless you.[e] I
have carried out the LORD's instructions."
14 Samuel replied, "Then what is this sound
of sheep[A] and cattle I hear?"
15 Saul answered, "The troops brought
them from the Amalekites and spared the
best sheep and cattle in order to offer a sacrifice to the LORD your God,[f] but the rest we
destroyed."[g]
16 "Stop!" exclaimed Samuel. "Let me tell
you what the LORD said to me last night."
"Tell me," he replied.
17 Samuel continued, "Although you once
considered yourself unimportant,[h] have you
not become the leader of the tribes of Israel?
The LORD anointed you king over Israel 18 and
then sent you on a mission and said: 'Go and
completely destroy the sinful Amalekites.
Fight against them until you have annihilated
them.' 19 So why didn't you obey the LORD?
Why did you rush on the plunder[i] and do
what was evil in the LORD's sight?"
20 "But I did obey the LORD!" Saul answered.[B] "I went on the mission the LORD
gave me: I brought back Agag, king of Amalek,
and I completely destroyed the Amalekites.
21 The troops took sheep and cattle from the
plunder—the best of what was •set apart for
destruction—to sacrifice to the LORD your
God at Gilgal."[j]
22 Then Samuel said:

Does the LORD[k] take pleasure
in •burnt offerings and sacrifices
as much as in obeying the LORD?
Look: to obey is better than sacrifice,
to pay attention is better than the fat
of rams.[l]
23 For rebellion is like the sin
of •divination,[m]
and defiance is like wickedness[n]
and idolatry.
Because you have rejected the word
of the LORD,
He has rejected you as king.[o]

24 Saul answered Samuel, "I have sinned.[p] I
have transgressed the LORD's command[q] and
your words. Because I was afraid of the people, I obeyed them. 25 Now therefore, please
forgive my sin[r] and return with me so I can
worship the LORD."
26 Samuel replied to Saul, "I will not return
with you. Because you rejected the word of
the LORD,[s] the LORD has rejected you from being king over Israel." 27 When Samuel turned
to go, Saul grabbed the hem of his robe, and
it tore. 28 Samuel said to him, "The LORD has
torn the kingship of Israel away from you today[t] and has given it to your neighbor who is
better than you.[u] 29 Furthermore, the Eternal
One of Israel[v] does not lie or change His mind,
for He is not man who changes his mind."[w]
30 Saul said, "I have sinned. Please honor
me[x] now before the elders of my people and
before Israel. Come back with me so I can
bow in worship to the LORD your God."[y]
31 Then Samuel went back, following Saul, and
Saul bowed down to the LORD.
32 Samuel said, "Bring me Agag king of Amalek."
Agag came to him trembling,[C] for he
thought, "Certainly the bitterness of death
has come."[D,E]
33 Samuel declared:

As your sword has made women
childless,
so your mother will be childless
among women.[z]

Then he hacked Agag to pieces before the
LORD at Gilgal.
34 Samuel went to Ramah,[aa] and Saul went
up to his home in Gibeah[ab] of Saul. 35 Even to
the day of his death, Samuel never again visited Saul.[ac] Samuel mourned for Saul,[ad] and
the LORD regretted He had made Saul king
over Israel.

Samuel Anoints David

16 The LORD said to Samuel, "How long
are you going to mourn for Saul,[ae] since
I have rejected him as king over Israel?[af] Fill

[a] 15:11 1Kg 9:6-7
[b] Ex 32:11-13; Lk 6:12
[c] 15:12 Jos 15:55; 1Sm 25:2
[d] 1Sm 13:13-14
[e] 15:13 Gn 14:19; 2Sm 2:5
[f] 15:15 Gn 3:12-13
[g] 15:14-15 Ex 32:21-24
[h] 15:17 1Sm 9:21
[i] 15:19 1Sm 14:32
[j] 15:21 Ex 32:22-23
[k] 15:22 Ps 40:6-8; 51:16-17; Is 1:11-15; Mc 6:6-8
[l] Heb 10:5-7
[m] 15:23 Dt 18:10
[n] Gn 31:19,34
[o] 1Sm 8:7
[p] 15:24 Nm 22:34; 2Sm 12:13; Ps 51:3-4
[q] Pr 29:25; Is 51:12-13
[r] 15:25 Ex 10:17
[s] 15:26 1Sm 13:14; 16:1
[t] 15:28 1Sm 28:17-18
[u] 15:27-28 1Kg 11:30-36
[v] 15:29 1Ch 29:11; Ps 18:1-2
[w] Nm 23:19; Ezk 24:14
[x] 15:30 Jn 12:43
[y] Is 29:13
[z] 15:33 Gn 9:6; Jdg 1:7; Mt 7:2
[aa] 15:34 1Sm 7:17
[ab] 1Sm 11:4
[ac] 15:35 1Sm 19:24
[ad] 1Sm 16:1
[ae] 16:1 1Sm 15:35
[af] 1Sm 13:13-14; 15:23

[A] 15:14 Lit *sheep in my ears* [B] 15:20 Lit *answered Samuel* [C] 15:32 Hb obscure [D] 15:32 LXX reads *Is death bitter in this way?* [E] 15:32 Lit *turned*

your horn with oil[a] and go. I am sending you
to Jesse of Bethlehem[b] because I have selected
a king from his sons."
2Samuel asked, "How can I go? Saul will
hear about it and kill me!"
The LORD answered, "Take a young cow
with you and say, 'I have come to sacrifice to
the LORD.'[c] 3Then invite Jesse to the sacrifice,
and I will let you know what you are to do.[d]
You are to anoint for Me the one I indicate
to you."[e]
4Samuel did what the LORD directed and
went to Bethlehem.[f] When the elders of the
town met him, they trembled[A] and asked,
"Do[B] you come in peace?"[g]
5"In peace," he replied. "I've come to sacrifice to the LORD. Consecrate yourselves[h]
and come with me to the sacrifice."[C] Then he
consecrated Jesse and his sons and invited
them to the sacrifice. 6When they arrived,
Samuel saw Eliab[i] and said, "Certainly the
LORD's anointed one is here before Him."
7But the LORD said to Samuel, "Do not look
at his appearance or his stature, because I
have rejected him. Man does not see what the
LORD sees,[D] for man sees what is visible,[E] but
the LORD sees the heart."[j]
8Jesse called Abinadab[k] and presented him
to Samuel. "The LORD hasn't chosen this one
either," Samuel said. 9Then Jesse presented
Shammah,[l] but Samuel said, "The LORD hasn't
chosen this one either." 10After Jesse presented seven of his sons to him, Samuel told
Jesse, "The LORD hasn't chosen any of these."
11Samuel asked him, "Are these all the sons
you have?"
"There is still the youngest,"[m] he answered,
"but right now he's tending the sheep." Samuel told Jesse, "Send for him. We won't sit
down to eat until he gets here." 12So Jesse sent
for him. He had beautiful eyes and a healthy,[F]
handsome appearance.[n]
Then the LORD said, "Anoint him, for he is
the one."[o] 13So Samuel took the horn of oil,
anointed him[p] in the presence of his brothers, and the Spirit of the LORD took control of
David from that day forward.[q] Then Samuel
set out and went to Ramah.

[a]**16:1** 1Sm 9:16; 10:1; 2Kg 9:1
[b]Ru 4:17-22
[c]**16:2** 1Sm 20:29
[d]**16:3** Ex 4:15; Ac 9:6
[e]Dt 17:14-15; 1Sm 9:16
[f]**16:4** Gn 48:7; Lk 2:4
[g]1Kg 2:13; 2Kg 9:22; 1Ch 12:17-18
[h]**16:5** Gn 35:2; Ex 19:10
[i]**16:6** 1Sm 17:13
[j]**16:7** 1Kg 8:39; Jr 17:10; Lk 16:15; Jn 2:24-25
[k]**16:8** 1Sm 17:13
[l]**16:9** 1Sm 17:13
[m]**16:11** 1Sm 17:12; 2Sm 13:3
[n]**16:12** 1Sm 17:42
[o]1Sm 9:17
[p]**16:13** 1Sm 10:1
[q]Ps 51:10-12; Ezk 36:27; Ac 2:1-17
[r]**16:14** 1Sm 11:6; 18:12; 28:15
[s]**16:16** 1Sm 18:10; 19:9; 2Kg 3:15
[t]**16:18** 1Sm 17:32-36
[u]1Sm 3:19; 18:12-14
[v]**16:20** 1Sm 10:4,27; Pr 18:16
[w]**16:21** Gn 41:46; Pr 22:29
[x]**16:23** 1Sm 16:14-16
[y]**17:1** 1Sm 13:5
[z]2Ch 28:18
[aa]Jos 10:10
[ab]1Ch 11:13
[ac]**17:2** 1Sm 21:9
[ad]**17:4** 2Sm 21:18-22; 1Ch 20:4-8

David in Saul's Court

14Now the Spirit of the LORD had left Saul,[r]
and an evil spirit sent from the LORD began
to torment him, 15so Saul's servants said to
him, "You see that an evil spirit from God
is tormenting you. 16Let our lord command
your servants here in your presence to look
for someone who knows how to play the lyre.
Whenever the evil spirit from God troubles
you, that person can play the lyre, and you
will feel better."[s]
17Then Saul commanded his servants, "Find
me someone who plays well and bring him to
me."
18One of the young men answered, "I have
seen a son of Jesse of Bethlehem who knows
how to play the lyre. He is also a valiant man,[t]
a warrior, eloquent, handsome, and the LORD
is with him."[u]
19Then Saul dispatched messengers to Jesse
and said, "Send me your son David, who is
with the sheep." 20So Jesse took a donkey
loaded with bread, a skin of wine, and one
young goat and sent them by his son David
to Saul.[v] 21When David came to Saul[w] and entered his service, Saul admired him greatly,
and David became his armor-bearer. 22Then
Saul sent word to Jesse: "Let David remain
in my service, for I am pleased with him."
23Whenever the spirit from God troubled
Saul,[x] David would pick up his lyre and play,
and Saul would then be relieved, feel better,
and the evil spirit would leave him.

David versus Goliath

17 The Philistines[y] gathered their forces
for war at Socoh in Judah and camped
between Socoh[z] and Azekah[aa] in Ephes-dam-
mim.[ab] 2Saul and the men of Israel gathered
and camped in the Valley of Elah;[ac] then they
lined up in battle formation to face the Philistines.
3The Philistines were standing on one hill,
and the Israelites were standing on another
hill with a ravine between them. 4Then a
champion named Goliath, from Gath,[ad] came
out from the Philistine camp. He was nine
feet, nine inches tall[G,H] 5and wore a bronze
helmet[I] and bronze scale armor that weighed

[A]16:4 LXX reads *were astonished* [B]16:4 DSS, LXX read *Seer, do* [C]16:5 LXX reads *and rejoice with me today* [D]16:7 LXX reads *God does not see as a man sees* [E]16:7 Lit *what is of the eyes* [F]16:12 Or *ruddy* [G]17:4 DSS, LXX read *four cubits and a span* [H]17:4 Lit *was six cubits and a span* [I]17:5 Lit *helmet on his head*

125 pounds.[A] 6There was bronze armor on
his shins, and a bronze sword[a] was slung between his shoulders. 7His spear shaft[b] was
like a weaver's beam, and the iron point of
his spear weighed 15 pounds.[B] In addition, a
shield-bearer[c] was walking in front of him.
8He stood and shouted to the Israelite battle formations: "Why do you come out to line
up in battle formation?" He asked them, "Am
I not a Philistine and are you not servants of
Saul?[d] Choose one of your men and have him
come down against me. 9If he wins in a fight
against me and kills me, we will be your servants. But if I win against him and kill him,
then you will be our servants and serve us."[e]
10Then the Philistine said, "I defy the ranks of
Israel today.[f] Send me a man so we can fight
each other!" 11When Saul and all Israel heard
these words from the Philistine, they lost
their courage and were terrified.
12Now David was the son of the Ephrathite[g]
from Bethlehem of Judah named Jesse. Jesse
had eight sons[h] and during Saul's reign was
already an old man. 13Jesse's three oldest sons
had followed Saul to the war, and their names[i]
were Eliab, the firstborn, Abinadab, the next,
and Shammah, the third, 14and David was the
youngest.[j] The three oldest had followed Saul,
15but David kept going back and forth from
Saul[k] to tend his father's flock in Bethlehem.
16Every morning and evening for 40 days
the Philistine came forward and took his
stand. 17One day Jesse had told his son David: "Take this half-bushel[C] of roasted grain
along with these 10 loaves of bread[l] for your
brothers and hurry to their camp. 18Also take
these 10 portions of cheese to the field commander.[D] Check on the welfare of your brothers[m] and bring a confirmation from them.
19They are with Saul and all the men of Israel
in the Valley of Elah fighting with the Philistines."
20So David got up early in the morning, left
the flock with someone to keep it, loaded up,
and set out as Jesse had instructed him.
He arrived at the perimeter of the camp[n] as
the army was marching out to its battle formation shouting their battle cry. 21Israel and
the Philistines lined up in battle formation
facing each other. 22David left his supplies
in the care of the quartermaster[o] and ran to
the battle line. When he arrived, he asked
his brothers how they were. 23While he was
speaking with them, suddenly the champion
named Goliath, the Philistine from Gath,
came forward from the Philistine battle line
and shouted his usual words,[p] which David
heard. 24When all the Israelite men saw Goliath, they retreated from him terrified.
25Previously, an Israelite man had declared:
"Do you see this man who keeps coming out?
He comes to defy Israel. The king will make
the man who kills him very rich and will give
him his daughter.[q] The king will also make
the household of that man's father exempt
from paying taxes in Israel."[r]
26David spoke to the men who were standing with him: "What will be done for the man
who kills that Philistine and removes this
disgrace from Israel?[s] Just who is this uncircumcised Philistine[t] that he should defy the
armies[u] of the living God?"[v]
27The people told him about the offer, concluding, "That is what will be done for the
man who kills him."[w]
28David's oldest brother Eliab listened as
he spoke to the men, and became angry with
him.[x] "Why did you come down here?" he
asked. "Who did you leave those few sheep
with in the wilderness? I know your arrogance and your evil heart — you came down
to see the battle!"
29"What have I done now?" protested David. "It was just a question." 30Then he turned
from those beside him to others in front of
him and asked about the offer. The people
gave him the same answer as before.[y]
31What David said was overheard and reported to Saul, so he had David brought to
him. 32David said to Saul, "Don't let anyone be
discouraged by[E] him;[z] your servant will go[aa]
and fight this Philistine!"
33But Saul replied, "You can't go fight this
Philistine. You're just a youth, and he's been a
warrior since he was young."
34David answered Saul: "Your servant
has been tending his father's sheep. Whenever a lion or a bear came and carried off a
lamb from the flock, 35I went after it, struck
it down, and rescued the lamb from its

[a] **17:6** 1Sm 17:45
[b] **17:7** 2Sm 21:19; 1Ch 11:23
[c] 1Sm 17:41
[d] **17:8** 1Sm 8:17
[e] **17:8-9** 2Sm 2:12-16
[f] **17:10** 1Sm 17:26,36,45
[g] **17:12** Gn 35:19
[h] 1Sm 16:10-11; 1Ch 2:13-15
[i] **17:13** 1Sm 16:6,8-9
[j] **17:14** 1Sm 16:11
[k] **17:15** 1Sm 16:21-23
[l] **17:17** 1Sm 25:18
[m] **17:18** Gn 37:13-14
[n] **17:20** 1Sm 26:5,7
[o] **17:22** Jdg 18:21; Is 10:28
[p] **17:23** 1Sm 17:8-10
[q] **17:25** Jos 15:16
[r] 1Sm 8:11
[s] **17:26** 1Sm 11:2
[t] 1Sm 14:6; 17:36; Jr 9:25-26
[u] 1Sm 17:10
[v] Dt 5:26; 2Kg 19:4
[w] **17:27** 1Sm 17:25
[x] **17:28** Gn 37:4,8-36
[y] **17:30** 1Sm 17:26-27
[z] **17:32** Dt 20:1-4
[aa] 1Sm 16:18

[A] **17:5** Lit *5,000 shekels* [B] **17:7** Lit *600 shekels* [C] **17:17** Lit *this ephah* [D] **17:18** Lit *the leader of 1,000* [E] **17:32** Lit *let a man's heart fall over* mouth.[a] If it reared up against me, I would grab it by its fur,[A] strike it down, and kill it. 36Your servant has killed lions and bears; this uncircumcised Philistine will be like one of them, for he has defied the armies of the living God." 37Then David said, "The LORD who rescued me from the paw of the lion and the paw of the bear will rescue me from the hand of this Philistine."[b]

Saul said to David, "Go, and may the LORD be with you."[c]

38Then Saul had his own military clothes put on David. He put a bronze helmet on David's head and had him put on armor. 39David strapped his sword on over the military clothes and tried to walk, but he was not used to them. "I can't walk in these," David said to Saul, "I'm not used to them." So David took them off. 40Instead, he took his staff in his hand[d] and chose five smooth stones from the •wadi and put them in the pouch, in his shepherd's bag. Then, with his sling in his hand, he approached the Philistine.

41The Philistine came closer and closer to David, with the shield-bearer in front of him. 42When the Philistine looked and saw David, he despised him[e] because he was just a youth, healthy[B,f] and handsome. 43He said to David, "Am I a dog[g] that you come against me with sticks?"[C] Then he cursed David by his gods.[h] 44"Come here," the Philistine called to David, "and I'll give your flesh to the birds of the sky and the wild beasts!"[i]

45David said to the Philistine: "You come against me with a dagger, spear, and sword, but I come against you in the name of •Yahweh of •Hosts, the God of Israel's armies—you have defied Him.[j] 46Today, the LORD will hand you over to me. Today, I'll strike you down, cut your head off, and give the corpses[D] of the Philistine camp to the birds of the sky and the creatures of the earth. Then all the world will know that Israel has a God,[k] 47and this whole assembly will know that it is not by sword or by spear that the LORD saves,[l] for the battle is the LORD's.[m] He will hand you over to us."

48When the Philistine started forward to attack him, David ran quickly to the battle line to meet the Philistine.[n] 49David put his hand in the bag, took out a stone, slung it, and hit the Philistine on his forehead. The stone sank into his forehead, and he fell on his face to the ground. 50David defeated the Philistine with a sling and a stone. Even though David had no sword, he struck down the Philistine and killed him. 51David ran and stood over him. He grabbed the Philistine's sword,[o] pulled it from its sheath, and used it to kill him. Then he cut off his head. When the Philistines saw that their hero was dead, they ran.[p] 52The men of Israel and Judah rallied, shouting their battle cry, and chased the Philistines to the entrance of the valley and to the gates of Ekron.[E,q] Philistine bodies were strewn all along the Shaaraim road[r] to Gath and Ekron.

53When the Israelites returned from the pursuit of the Philistines, they plundered their camps. 54David took Goliath's[F] head and brought it to Jerusalem, but he put Goliath's weapons in his own tent.

55[G] When Saul had seen David going out to confront the Philistine, he asked Abner the commander of the army, "Whose son is this youth, Abner?"[s]

"My king, as surely as you live, I don't know," Abner replied.

56The king said, "Find out whose son the young man is!"

57When David returned from killing the Philistine, Abner took him and brought him before Saul with the Philistine's head still in his hand.[t] 58Saul said to him, "Whose son are you, young man?"

"The son of your servant Jesse of Bethlehem,"[u] David answered.

David's Success

18 When David had finished speaking with Saul, Jonathan committed himself to David, and loved him as much as he loved himself.[v] 2Saul kept David with him from that day on and did not let him return to his father's house.

3Jonathan made a covenant with David[w] because he loved him as much as himself. 4Then Jonathan removed the robe he was wearing

[a]17:35 Am 3:12 [b]17:37 2Tm 4:17-18 [c]1Sm 20:13 [d]17:40 Jdg 20:16 [e]17:42 Pr 16:18 [f]1Sm 16:12 [g]17:43 1Sm 24:14 [h]1Kg 20:10 [i]17:44 1Sm 17:46 [j]17:45 2Ch 32:7-8; Ps 124:8; Heb 11:34 [k]17:46 1Kg 18:36; 2Kg 19:19; Is 37:20 [l]17:47 Hs 1:7 [m]Ex 14:13-14; Ps 33:16-22; 44:4-8 [n]17:48 Ps 27:3 [o]17:51 1Sm 21:9 [p]Heb 11:34 [q]17:52 Jos 15:11 [r]Jos 15:36 [s]17:55 1Sm 16:17-22; 17:25 [t]17:57 1Sm 17:54 [u]17:58 1Sm 17:12 [v]18:1 1Sm 20:17; 2Sm 1:26 [w]18:3 1Sm 20:8,16; 23:18

[A]17:35 LXX reads *throat*; lit *beard* [B]17:42 Or *ruddy* [C]17:43 Some LXX mss add *and stones?" And David said, "No! Worse than a dog!"* [D]17:46 LXX reads *give your limbs and the limbs* [E]17:52 LXX reads *Ashkelon* [F]17:54 Lit *the Philistine's* [G]17:55 LXX omits 1Sm 17:55–18:5

and gave it to David,[a] along with his military tunic, his sword, his bow, and his belt.

5 David marched out with the army and was successful in everything Saul sent him to do. Saul put him in command of the soldiers, which pleased all the people and Saul's servants as well.

6 As the troops were coming back, when David was returning from killing the Philistine, the women came out from all the cities of Israel to meet King Saul,[b] singing and dancing with tambourines, with shouts of joy, and with three-stringed instruments. 7 As they celebrated, the women sang:

> Saul has killed his thousands,
> but David his tens of thousands.[c]

8 Saul was furious and resented this song.[A] "They credited tens of thousands to David," he complained, "but they only credited me with thousands. What more can he have but the kingdom?"[d] 9 So Saul watched David jealously from that day forward.

Saul Attempts to Kill David

10 The next day an evil spirit sent from God took control of Saul,[e] and he began to rave[B] inside the palace. David was playing the lyre as usual,[f] but Saul was holding a spear,[g] 11 and he threw it, thinking, "I'll pin David to the wall."[h] But David got away from him twice.

12 Saul was afraid of David,[i] because the LORD was with David[j] but had left Saul.[k] 13 Therefore, Saul reassigned David and made him commander over 1,000 men. David led the troops[l] 14 and continued to be successful in all his activities because the LORD was with him.[m] 15 When Saul observed that David was very successful, he dreaded him. 16 But all Israel and Judah loved David[n] because he was leading their troops. 17 Saul told David, "Here is my oldest daughter Merab. I'll give her to you as a wife,[o] if you will be a warrior for me and fight the LORD's battles."[p] But Saul was thinking, "My hand doesn't need to be against him; let the hand of the Philistines be against him."[q]

18 Then David responded, "Who am I,[r] and what is my family or my father's clan in Israel that I should become the king's son-in-law?" 19 When it was time to give Saul's daughter Merab to David, she was given to Adriel the Meholathite as a wife.[s]

David's Marriage to Michal

20 Now Saul's daughter Michal[t] loved David, and when it was reported to Saul, it pleased him.[C] 21 "I'll give her to him," Saul thought. "She'll be a trap for him, and the hand of the Philistines will be against him."[u] So Saul said to David a second time, "You can now be my son-in-law."[v]

22 Saul then ordered his servants, "Speak to David in private and tell him, 'Look, the king is pleased with you, and all his servants love you. Therefore, you should become the king's son-in-law.'"

23 Saul's servants reported these words directly to David,[D] but he replied, "Is it trivial in your sight to become the king's son-in-law? I am a poor man who is common."[w]

24 The servants reported back to Saul, "These are the words David spoke."

25 Then Saul replied, "Say this to David: 'The king desires no other bride-price[x] except 100 Philistine foreskins, to take revenge on his enemies.'"[y] Actually, Saul intended to cause David's death at the hands of the Philistines.[z]

26 When the servants reported these terms to David, he was pleased[E] to become the king's son-in-law. Before the wedding day arrived,[F] 27 David and his men went out and killed 200[G] Philistines. He brought their foreskins and presented them as full payment to the king to become his son-in-law. Then Saul gave his daughter Michal to David as his wife.[aa] 28 Saul realized that the LORD was with David and that his daughter Michal loved him, 29 and he became even more afraid of David. As a result, Saul was David's enemy from then on.

30 Every time the Philistine commanders came out to fight,[ab] David was more successful than all of Saul's officers.[ac] So his name became well known.

David Delivered from Saul

19 Saul ordered his son Jonathan and all his servants to kill David.[ad] But Saul's son Jonathan liked David very much,[ae] 2 so he

[a] **18:4** Gn 41:42 [b] **18:6** Ex 15:20-21; Jdg 11:34 [c] **18:7** 1Sm 21:11; 29:5 [d] **18:8** 1Sm 15:28; 24:20 [e] **18:10** 1Sm 16:14; 19:9 [f] 1Sm 16:23 [g] 1Sm 19:9 [h] **18:11** 1Sm 19:10; 20:33 [i] **18:12** 1Sm 18:15,29 [j] 1Sm 16:13,18 [k] 1Sm 16:14; 17:36,47; 2Sm 5:2 [l] **18:13** 2Sm 5:2 [m] **18:14** 1Sm 3:19; 16:18 [n] **18:16** 1Sm 18:5 [o] **18:17** 1Sm 17:25 [p] Nm 21:14; 1Sm 17:36-37; 25:28 [q] 1Sm 18:21; 18:25 [r] **18:18** 1Sm 9:21; 18:23; 2Sm 7:18 [s] **18:19** Jdg 7:22; 2Sm 21:8; 1Kg 19:16 [t] **18:20** 1Sm 18:28 [u] **18:21** 1Sm 18:17 [v] 1Sm 18:20 [w] **18:23** Gn 29:20; 34:12 [x] **18:25** Gn 34:12; Ex 22:17 [y] 1Sm 14:24 [z] 1Sm 18:17 [aa] **18:27** 2Sm 3:14 [ab] **18:30** 2Sm 11:1 [ac] 1Sm 18:5 [ad] **19:1** 1Sm 18:8-9 [ae] 1Sm 18:1-3

[A] **18:8** Lit *furious; this saying was evil in his eyes* [B] **18:10** Or *prophesy* [C] **18:20** Lit *Saul, the thing was right in his eyes* [D] **18:23** Lit *words in David's ears* [E] **18:26** Lit *David, it was right in David's eyes* [F] **18:26** Lit *And the days were not full* [G] **18:27** LXX reads *100*

told him: "My father Saul intends to kill you.
Be on your guard in the morning and hide in
a secret place and stay there. 3 I'll go out and
stand beside my father in the field where you
are and talk to him about you. When I see
what he says, I'll tell you."[a]

4 Jonathan spoke well of David to his father
Saul. He said to him: "The king should not sin
against his servant David.[b] He hasn't sinned
against you; in fact, his actions have been a
great advantage to you. 5 He took his life in his
hands when he struck down the Philistine,[c]
and the LORD brought about a great victory
for all Israel.[d] You saw it and rejoiced, so why
would you sin against innocent blood by killing David for no reason?"[e]

6 Saul listened to Jonathan's advice and
swore an oath: "As surely as the LORD lives,
David will not be killed." 7 So Jonathan summoned David and told him all these words.
Then Jonathan brought David to Saul, and he
served him as he did before.[f]

8 When war broke out again, David went
out and fought against the Philistines. He defeated them with such a great force that they
fled from him.

9 Now an evil spirit sent from the LORD[g]
came on Saul as he was sitting in his palace
holding a spear.[h] David was playing the lyre,[i]
10 and Saul tried to pin David to the wall with
the spear.[j] As the spear struck the wall, David eluded Saul, ran away, and escaped that
night. 11 Saul sent agents to David's house to
watch for him and kill him in the morning.[k]
But his wife Michal[l] warned David, "If you
don't escape tonight, you will be dead tomorrow!" 12 So she lowered David from the
window, and he fled and escaped.[m] 13 Then
Michal took the household idol and put it on
the bed, placed some goat hair on its head,
and covered it with a garment. 14 When Saul
sent agents to seize David, Michal said, "He's
sick."[n]

15 Saul sent the agents back to see David and
said, "Bring him on his bed so I can kill him."
16 When the messengers arrived, to their surprise, the household idol was on the bed with
some goat hair on its head.

17 Saul asked Michal, "Why did you deceive
me like this? You sent my enemy away, and he
has escaped!"

She answered him, "He said to me, 'Let me
go! Why should I kill you?'"

18 So David fled and escaped and went to
Samuel at Ramah[o] and told him everything
Saul had done to him. Then he and Samuel
left and stayed at Naioth.[p]

19 When it was reported to Saul that David
was at Naioth in Ramah, 20 he sent agents to
seize David.[q] However, when they saw the
group of prophets prophesying[r] with Samuel leading them, the Spirit of God came on
Saul's agents, and they also started prophesying. 21 When they reported to Saul, he sent
other agents, and they also began prophesying.[s] So Saul tried again and sent a third
group of agents, and even they began prophesying. 22 Then Saul himself went to Ramah.
He came to the large cistern at Secu, looked
around, and asked, "Where are Samuel and
David?"

"At Naioth in Ramah," someone said.

23 So he went to Naioth in Ramah. The Spirit
of God also came on him,[t] and as he walked
along, he prophesied until he entered Naioth
in Ramah. 24 Saul then removed his clothes
and also prophesied before Samuel; he collapsed and lay naked[u] all that day and all
that night. That is why they say, "Is Saul also
among the prophets?"[v]

Jonathan Protects David

20 David fled from Naioth in Ramah and
came to Jonathan and asked, "What
have I done?[w] What did I do wrong? How
have I sinned against your father so that he
wants to take my life?"

2 Jonathan said to him, "No, you won't die.
Listen, my father doesn't do anything, great
or small, without telling me.[A] So why would
he hide this matter from me? This can't be
true."

3 But David said, "Your father certainly
knows that you have come to look favorably
on me. He has said, 'Jonathan must not know
of this, or else he will be grieved.'" David also
swore, "As surely as the LORD lives and as you
yourself live, there is but a step between me
and death."[x]

[a] 19:3 1Sm 20:32-33
[b] 19:4 Gn 44:22; Pr 17:13; Jr 18:20
[c] 19:5 1Sm 17:42-51
[d] 1Sm 11:13
[e] Dt 19:10-13; 1Sm 20:32
[f] 19:7 1Sm 16:21; 18:2,10,13
[g] 19:9 1Sm 16:14; 18:10-11
[h] 1Sm 18:10
[i] 1Sm 16:14-16; 18:10
[j] 19:10 1Sm 18:11; 20:33
[k] 19:11 Ps 59 title
[l] 1Sm 18:20
[m] 19:12 Jos 2:15; Ac 9:23-25
[n] 19:14 Jos 2:5
[o] 19:18 1Sm 7:17
[p] 2Kg 6:1-2
[q] 19:20 1Sm 19:11; Jn 7:32
[r] 1Sm 10:5-6,10
[s] 19:21 Nm 11:25
[t] 19:23 1Sm 10:10
[u] 19:24 Is 20:2; Mc 1:8
[v] 19:20-24 1Sm 10:5-13
[w] 20:1 1Sm 24:9
[x] 20:3 1Sm 25:26; 2Kg 2:6

[A] 20:2 Lit *without uncovering my ear*

4 Jonathan said to David, "Whatever you say,
I will do for you."
5 So David told him, "Look, tomorrow is the
New Moon,[a] and I'm supposed to sit down
and eat with the king.[b] Instead, let me go, and
I'll hide in the field until the third night.[c] 6 If
your father misses me at all, say, 'David urgently requested my permission to quickly
go to his town Bethlehem[d] for an annual sacrifice[e] there involving the whole clan.' 7 If he
says, 'Good,' then your servant is safe, but if
he becomes angry, you will know he has evil
intentions. 8 Deal faithfully with your servant,
for you have brought me into a covenant with
you before the LORD.[f] If I have done anything
wrong,[g] then kill me yourself; why take me to
your father?"
9 "No!" Jonathan responded. "If I ever find
out my father has evil intentions against you,
wouldn't I tell you about it?"
10 So David asked Jonathan, "Who will tell
me if your father answers you harshly?"
11 He answered David, "Come on, let's go
out to the field." So both of them went out to
the field. 12 "By the LORD, the God of Israel, I
will sound out my father by this time tomorrow or the next day. If I find out that he is
favorable toward you, will I not send for you
and tell you?[A] 13 If my father intends to bring
evil on you, may God punish Jonathan and
do so severely[h] if I do not tell you[B] and send
you away so you may go in peace. May the
LORD be with you,[i] just as He was with my father. 14 If I continue to live, treat me with the
LORD's faithful love, but if I die, 15 don't ever
withdraw your faithful love from my household — not even when the LORD cuts off every one of David's enemies from the face of
the earth."[j] 16 Then Jonathan made a covenant
with the house of David,[k] saying, "May the
LORD hold David's enemies accountable."[C,l]
17 Jonathan once again swore to David[D] in
his love for him, because he loved him as he
loved himself.[m]
18 Then Jonathan said to him, "Tomorrow
is the New Moon;[n] you'll be missed because
your seat will be empty. 19 The following day
hurry down and go to the place where you hid
on the day this incident began and stay beside the rock Ezel. 20 I will shoot three arrows
beside it as if I'm aiming at a target. 21 Then
I will send the young man and say, 'Go and
find the arrows!' Now, if I expressly say to the
young man, 'Look, the arrows are on this side
of you — get them,' then come, because as the
LORD lives, it is safe for you and there is no
problem. 22 But if I say this to the youth: 'Look,
the arrows are beyond you!'[o] then go, for the
LORD is sending you away. 23 As for the matter
you and I have spoken about,[p] the LORD will
be a witness[E] between you and me forever."[q]
24 So David hid in the field.
At the New Moon, the king sat down to eat
the meal. 25 He sat at his usual place on the
seat by the wall. Jonathan sat facing him[F] and
Abner took his place beside Saul, but David's
place was empty.[r] 26 Saul did not say anything
that day because he thought, "Something
unexpected has happened; he must be ceremonially •unclean — yes, that's it, he is unclean."[s]
27 However, the day after the New Moon,
the second day, David's place was still empty,
and Saul asked his son Jonathan, "Why didn't
Jesse's son come to the meal either yesterday
or today?"
28 Jonathan answered, "David asked for my
permission to go to Bethlehem.[t] 29 He said,
'Please let me go because our clan is holding
a sacrifice in the town, and my brother has
told me to be there. So now, if you are pleased
with me, let me go so I can see my brothers.'
That's why he didn't come to the king's table."
30 Then Saul became angry with Jonathan
and shouted, "You son of a perverse and rebellious woman! Don't I know that you are
siding with Jesse's son to your own shame and
to the disgrace of your mother?[G] 31 Every day
Jesse's son lives on earth you and your kingship are not secure. Now send for him and
bring him to me — he deserves to die."[u]
32 Jonathan answered his father back: "Why
is he to be killed? What has he done?"[v]
33 Then Saul threw his spear at Jonathan to
kill him,[w] so he knew that his father was determined to kill David.[x] 34 He got up from the

[a] **20:5** Nm 10:10; 28:11-15; Am 8:5
[b] 1Sm 20:24,27
[c] 1Sm 19:2
[d] **20:6** 1Sm 17:58
[e] Dt 12:5
[f] **20:8** 1Sm 18:3; 20:16; 23:18
[g] 2Sm 14:32
[h] **20:13** Ru 1:17; 1Sm 3:17
[i] 1Sm 18:12
[j] **20:15** 2Sm 9:1
[k] **20:16** 1Sm 18:3; 23:18
[l] Dt 23:21
[m] **20:17** 1Sm 18:1
[n] **20:18** Nm 10:10
[o] **20:22** 1Sm 20:37
[p] **20:23** 1Sm 20:14-15
[q] Gn 31:49,53
[r] **20:25** 1Sm 20:18
[s] **20:26** Lv 7:20-21; Nm 10:10
[t] **20:28** 1Sm 20:6
[u] **20:31** 2Sm 12:5
[v] **20:32** 1Sm 19:5
[w] **20:33** 1Sm 18:11; 19:10
[x] 1Sm 20:7

[A] **20:12** Lit *and uncover your ear* [B] **20:13** Lit *will uncover your ears* [C] **20:16** Lit *LORD require it from the hand of David's enemies* [D] **20:17** LXX; MT reads *Jonathan once again made David swear* [E] **20:23** LXX; MT omits *a witness* [F] **20:25** Text emended; MT reads *Jonathan got up* [G] **20:30** Lit *your mother's genitals*

table in fierce anger and did not eat any food
that second day of the New Moon, for he was
grieved because of his father's shameful behavior toward David.
35 In the morning Jonathan went out to the
field for the appointed meeting with David.
A small young man was with him. 36 He said
to the young man, "Run and find the arrows
I'm shooting."[a] As the young man ran, Jonathan shot an arrow beyond him. 37 He came to
the location of the arrow that Jonathan had
shot, but Jonathan called to him and said,
"The arrow is beyond you, isn't it?"[b] 38 Then
Jonathan called to him, "Hurry up and don't
stop!" Jonathan's young man picked up the
arrow and returned to his master. 39 He did
not know anything; only Jonathan and David knew the arrangement. 40 Then Jonathan
gave his equipment to the young man who
was with him and said, "Go, take it back to
the city."
41 When the young man had gone, David got
up from the south side of the stone Ezel, fell
with his face to the ground, and bowed three
times.[c] Then he and Jonathan kissed each
other and wept with each other, though David wept more.[d]
42 Jonathan then said to David, "Go in the
assurance the two of us pledged in the name
of the LORD when we said: The LORD will be a
witness between you and me and between my
offspring and your offspring forever."[A,e] Then
David left, and Jonathan went into the city.

David Flees to Nob

21 David went to Ahimelech[f] the priest
at Nob.[g] Ahimelech was afraid to meet
David, so he said to him, "Why are you alone
and no one is with you?"
2 David answered Ahimelech the priest,
"The king gave me a mission, but he told me,
'Don't let anyone know anything about the
mission I'm sending you on or what I have
ordered you to do.' I have stationed my young
men at a certain place. 3 Now what do you
have on hand? Give me five loaves of bread or
whatever can be found."
4 The priest told him, "There is no ordinary
bread on hand. However, there is consecrated
bread,[h] but the young men may eat it[B] only
if they have kept themselves from women."[i]
5 David answered him, "I swear that women
are being kept from us, as always when I go
out to battle.[j] The young men's bodies[C] are
consecrated[k] even on an ordinary mission,
so of course their bodies are consecrated today." 6 So the priest gave him the consecrated
bread,[l] for there was no bread there except
the ·bread of the Presence[m] that had been removed from the presence of the LORD. When
the bread was removed, it had been replaced
with warm bread.
7 One of Saul's servants, detained before the
LORD, was there that day. His name was Doeg
the Edomite,[n] chief of Saul's shepherds.
8 David said to Ahimelech, "Do you have a
spear or sword on hand? I didn't even bring
my sword or my weapons since the king's
mission was urgent."
9 The priest replied, "The sword of Goliath
the Philistine,[o] whom you killed in the Valley
of Elah, is here, wrapped in a cloth behind
the ·ephod. If you want to take it for yourself,
then take it, for there isn't another one here."
"There's none like it!" David said. "Give it
to me."

David Flees to Gath

10 David fled that day from Saul's presence and went to King Achish of Gath.[p] 11 But
Achish's servants said to him, "Isn't this David, the king of the land? Don't they sing
about him during their dances:

> Saul has killed his thousands,
> but David his tens of thousands?"[q]

12 David took this to heart[D] and became
very afraid of King Achish of Gath, 13 so he
pretended to be insane in their presence.[r] He
acted like a madman around them,[E] scrib-
bling[F] on the doors of the gate and letting saliva run down his beard.
14 "Look! You can see the man is crazy,"
Achish said to his servants. "Why did you
bring him to me? 15 Do I have such a shortage of crazy people that you brought this one
to act crazy around me? Is this one going to
come into my house?"[s]

[a] **20:36** 1Sm 20:20-21 [b] **20:37** 1Sm 20:22 [c] **20:41** Gn 42:6 [d] 1Sm 18:3 [e] **20:42** 1Sm 20:15-23 [f] **21:1** 1Sm 14:3; Mk 2:26 [g] 1Sm 22:19 [h] **21:4** Ex 25:30; Lv 24:5-9; Mt 12:3-4 [i] Ex 19:15 [j] **21:5** 2Sm 11:11 [k] 1Th 4:4 [l] **21:6** Mt 12:3-4; Mk 2:25 [m] Lv 24:5-9 [n] **21:7** 1Sm 22:9; Ps 52 title [o] **21:9** 1Sm 17:51 [p] **21:10** Ps 56 title [q] **21:11** 1Sm 18:7; 29:5 [r] **21:13** Ps 34 title [s] **21:13-15** Ps 34 title

[A] **20:42** The last sentence of v. 42 is 1Sm 21:1 in Hb. [B] **21:4** DSS; MT omits *may eat it* [C] **21:5** Lit *vessels* [D] **21:12** Lit *David placed these words in his heart* [E] **21:13** Lit *madman in their hand* [F] **21:13** LXX reads *drumming*

Saul's Increasing Paranoia

22 So David left Gath and took refuge in the cave of Adullam.[a] When David's brothers and his father's whole family heard, they went down and joined him there. 2In addition, every man who was desperate, in debt, or discontented rallied around him, and he became their leader. About 400 men were with him.[b]

3From there David went to Mizpeh of Moab where he said to the king of Moab, "Please let my father and mother stay with you until I know what God will do for me." 4So he left them in the care of the king of Moab, and they stayed with him the whole time David was in the stronghold.

5Then the prophet Gad[c] said to David, "Don't stay in the stronghold. Leave and return to the land of Judah." So David left and went to the forest of Hereth.

6Saul heard that David and his men had been discovered. At that time Saul was in Gibeah, sitting under the tamarisk tree[d] at the •high place. His spear was in his hand, and all his servants were standing around him. 7Saul said to his servants, "Listen, men of Benjamin: Is Jesse's son going to give all of you fields and vineyards? Do you think he'll make all of you commanders of thousands and commanders of hundreds?[e] 8That's why all of you have conspired against me! Nobody tells me[A] when my own son makes a covenant with Jesse's son.[f] None of you cares about me[g] or tells me[B] that my son has stirred up my own servant to wait in ambush for me, as is the case today."

9Then Doeg the Edomite,[h] who was in charge of Saul's servants, answered: "I saw Jesse's son come to Ahimelech son of Ahitub at Nob.[i] 10Ahimelech inquired of the LORD for him[j] and gave him provisions.[k] He also gave him the sword of Goliath the Philistine."[l]

Slaughter of the Priests

11The king sent messengers to summon Ahimelech the priest, son of Ahitub, and his father's whole family, who were priests in Nob. All of them came to the king. 12Then Saul said, "Listen, son of Ahitub!"

"I'm at your service,[m] my lord," he said.

13Saul asked him, "Why did you and Jesse's son conspire against me? You gave him bread and a sword and inquired of God for him, so he could rise up against me and wait in ambush, as is the case today."[n]

14Ahimelech replied to the king: "Who among all your servants is as faithful as David?[o] He is the king's son-in-law, captain of your bodyguard, and honored in your house. 15Was today the first time I inquired of God for him?[p] Of course not! Please don't let the king make an accusation against your servant or any of my father's household, for your servant didn't have any idea[C] about all this."

16But the king said, "You will die, Ahimelech — you and your father's whole family!"

17Then the king ordered the guards standing by him, "Turn and kill the priests of the LORD[q] because they sided with David. For they knew he was fleeing, but they didn't tell me."[D] But the king's servants would not lift a hand to execute the priests of the LORD.

18So the king said to Doeg, "Go and execute the priests!" So Doeg the Edomite went and executed the priests himself. On that day, he killed 85 men[r] who wore linen •ephods.[s] 19He also struck down Nob, the city of the priests, with the sword — both men and women, children and infants, oxen, donkeys, and sheep.[t]

20However, one of the sons of Ahimelech son of Ahitub escaped. His name was Abiathar,[u] and he fled to David.[v] 21Abiathar told David that Saul had killed the priests of the LORD. 22Then David said to Abiathar, "I knew that Doeg the Edomite[w] was there that day and that he was sure to report to Saul. I myself am responsible for[E] the lives of everyone in your father's family. 23Stay with me. Don't be afraid, for the one who wants to take my life wants to take your life.[x] You will be safe with me."

Deliverance at Keilah

23 It was reported to David: "Look, the Philistines are fighting against Keilah[y] and raiding the threshing floors."

2So David inquired of the LORD:[z] "Should I launch an attack against these Philistines?"

The LORD answered David, "Launch an

[a]**22:1** Pss 57, 142 titles
[b]**22:2** 1Sm 23:13; 25:13
[c]**22:5** 1Ch 21:9; 29:29; 2Ch 29:25
[d]**22:6** Jdg 4:5; 1Sm 14:2
[e]**22:7** 1Sm 8:12
[f]**22:8** 1Sm 18:3; 20:16
[g]1Sm 23:21
[h]**22:9** Ps 52 title
[i]1Sm 21:1; Ps 52 title
[j]**22:10** 1Sm 10:22
[k]1Sm 21:6,9
[l]1Sm 21:2-9
[m]**22:12** 1Sm 3:4-6; 2Sm 1:7
[n]**22:13** 1Sm 22:8
[o]**22:14** 1Sm 19:4-5
[p]**22:15** 2Sm 5:19,23
[q]**22:17** 2Kg 10:25; 2Ch 12:10
[r]**22:18** 1Sm 2:31
[s]Ex 28:4; 1Sm 2:28
[t]**22:19** 1Sm 2:18
[u]**22:20** 1Sm 23:9; 30:7; 2Sm 2:1; 1Kg 2:26-27
[v]1Sm 2:33
[w]**22:22** 1Sm 21:7
[x]**22:23** 1Kg 2:26
[y]**23:1** Jos 15:44; Neh 3:17-18
[z]**23:2** 1Sm 23:4,6,9-12; 2Sm 5:19,23

[A]**22:8** Lit *No one uncovers my ear* [B]**22:8** Lit *or uncovers my ear* [C]**22:15** Lit *didn't know a thing, small or large* [D]**22:17** Lit *didn't uncover my ear*

[E]**22:22** LXX, Syr, Vg; MT reads *I myself turn in*

attack against the Philistines and rescue Keilah."

3 But David's men said to him, "Look, we're afraid here in Judah; how much more if we go to Keilah against the Philistine forces!"

4 Once again, David inquired of the LORD, and the LORD answered him: "Go at once to Keilah, for I will hand the Philistines over to you."[a] 5 Then David and his men went to Keilah, fought against the Philistines, drove their livestock away, and inflicted heavy losses on them. So David rescued the inhabitants of Keilah. 6 Abiathar son of Ahimelech fled to David at Keilah, and he brought an ·ephod with him.

7 When it was reported to Saul that David had gone to Keilah, he said, "God has handed him over to me, for he has trapped himself by entering a town with barred gates." 8 Then Saul summoned all the troops to go to war at Keilah and besiege David and his men.

9 When David learned that Saul was plotting evil against him, he said to Abiathar the priest,[b] "Bring the ephod."[c]

10 Then David said, "LORD God of Israel, Your servant has heard that Saul intends to come to Keilah and destroy the town because of me. 11 Will the citizens of Keilah hand me over to him? Will Saul come down as Your servant has heard? LORD God of Israel, please tell Your servant."

The LORD answered, "He will come down."

12 Then David asked, "Will the citizens of Keilah hand me and my men over to Saul?"

"They will,"[d] the LORD responded.

13 So David and his men, numbering about 600,[e] left Keilah at once and moved from place to place.[f] When it was reported to Saul that David had escaped from Keilah, he called off the expedition. 14 David then stayed in the wilderness strongholds and in the hill country of the Wilderness of Ziph.[g] Saul searched for him every day, but God did not hand David over to him.[h]

A Renewed Covenant

15 David was in the Wilderness of Ziph in Horesh when he saw that Saul had come out to take his life. 16 Then Saul's son Jonathan came to David in Horesh and encouraged him in his faith in God,[i] 17 saying, "Don't be afraid, for my father Saul will never lay a hand on you. You yourself will be king over Israel,[j] and I'll be your second-in-command. Even my father Saul knows it is true."[k] 18 Then the two of them made a covenant in the LORD's presence.[l] Afterward, David remained in Horesh, while Jonathan went home.

David's Narrow Escape

19 Some Ziphites[m] came up to Saul at Gibeah and said, "David is[A] hiding among us in the strongholds in Horesh on the hill of Hachilah south of Jeshimon. 20 Now, whenever the king wants to come down, let him come down. Our part will be to hand him over to the king."[n]

21 "May you be blessed by the LORD," replied Saul, "for you have taken pity on me.[o] 22 Go and check again. Investigate and watch carefully where he goes[B] and who has seen him there; they tell me he is extremely cunning. 23 Look and find out all the places where he hides. Then come back to me with accurate information, and I'll go with you. If it turns out he really is in the region, I'll search for him among all the clans[C] of Judah." 24 So they went to Ziph ahead of Saul.

Now David and his men were in the wilderness near Maon[p] in the ·Arabah south of Jeshimon, 25 and Saul and his men went to look for him. When David was told about it, he went down to the rock and stayed in the Wilderness of Maon. Saul heard of this and pursued David there.

26 Saul went along one side of the mountain and David and his men went along the other side. Even though David was hurrying to get away from Saul, Saul and his men were closing in on David and his men to capture them.[q] 27 Then a messenger came to Saul saying, "Come quickly, because the Philistines have raided the land!" 28 So Saul broke off his pursuit of David and went to engage the Philistines. Therefore, that place was named the Rock of Separation. 29[D] From there David went up and stayed in the strongholds of En-gedi.[r]

David Spares Saul

24 When Saul returned from pursuing the Philistines,[s] he was told, "David is in the wilderness near En-gedi."[t] 2 So Saul

[a] 23:4 Jos 8:7; Jdg 7:7 [b] 23:9 1Sm 22:20 [c] 1Sm 23:6; 30:7 [d] 23:12 Jdg 15:10-13; 1Sm 23:20 [e] 23:13 1Sm 22:2; 25:13 [f] 2Sm 15:20 [g] 23:14 Jos 15:55; 2Ch 11:8 [h] Ps 32:7 [i] 23:16 1Sm 30:6 [j] 23:17 1Sm 16:1-13; 24:20-22 [k] 1Sm 20:31 [l] 23:18 1Sm 18:3; 20:12-17; 20:42 [m] 23:19 1Sm 26:1; Ps 54 title [n] 23:20 1Sm 23:12 [o] 23:21 1Sm 22:8 [p] 23:24 Jos 15:55; 1Sm 25:2 [q] 23:26 Ps 17:9 [r] 23:29 Jos 15:62; 2Ch 20:2 [s] 24:1 1Sm 23:28-29 [t] 1Sm 23:19

[A] 23:19 Lit *Is David not . . . Jeshimon?* [B] 23:22 Lit *watch his place where his foot will be* [C] 23:23 Or *thousands* [D] 23:29 1Sm 24:1 in Hb took 3,000 of Israel's choice men[a] and went to look for David and his men in front of the Rocks of the Wild Goats. 3 When Saul came to the sheep pens along the road, a cave was there, and he went in to relieve himself.[A,b] David and his men were staying in the back of the cave,[c] 4 so they said to him, "Look, this is the day the LORD told you about: 'I will hand your enemy over to you so you can do to him whatever you desire.'" Then David got up and secretly cut off the corner of Saul's robe.

5 Afterward, David's conscience bothered[B,d] him because he had cut off the corner of Saul's robe.[C] 6 He said to his men, "I swear before the LORD: I would never do such a thing to my lord, the LORD's anointed.[e] I will never lift my hand against him, since he is the LORD's anointed."[f] 7 With these words David persuaded[D] his men, and he did not let them rise up against Saul.

Then Saul left the cave and went on his way. 8 After that, David got up, went out of the cave, and called to Saul, "My lord the king!" When Saul looked behind him, David bowed to the ground in homage.[g] 9 David said to Saul, "Why do you listen to the words of people who say, 'Look, David intends to harm you'? 10 You can see with your own eyes that the LORD handed you over to me today in the cave.[h] Someone advised me to kill you,[i] but I[E,F] took pity on you and said: I won't lift my hand against my lord, since he is the LORD's anointed. 11 See, my father![j] Look at the corner of your robe in my hand, for I cut it off, but I didn't kill you. Look and recognize that there is no evil or rebellion in me. I haven't sinned against you even though you are hunting me down to take my life.[k]

12 "May the LORD judge between you and me, and may the LORD take vengeance on you for me, but my hand will never be against you.[l] 13 As the old proverb says, 'Wickedness comes from wicked people.'[m] My hand will never be against you. 14 Who has the king of Israel come after? What are you chasing after? A dead dog? A flea?[n] 15 May the LORD be judge and decide between you and me. May He take notice and plead my case and deliver[G] me from you."[o]

[a]24:2 1Sm 13:2; 26:2 [b]24:3 Jdg 3:24 [c]Pss 57, 142 titles [d]24:5 2Sm 24:10 [e]24:6 1Sm 26:9-11 [f]1Sm 10:1 [g]24:8 1Sm 25:23-24; 1Kg 1:31 [h]24:10 Ps 7:3-4 [i]1Sm 24:4 [j]24:11 2Kg 5:13 [k]1Sm 23:14,23; 26:20 [l]24:12 1Sm 26:10-11,23 [m]24:13 Mt 7:16-20; Lk 6:43-45 [n]24:14 1Sm 26:20; 2Sm 9:8 [o]24:15 Ps 35:1 [p]24:16 1Sm 26:17 [q]24:17 1Sm 26:21 [r]24:18 1Sm 26:23 [s]24:19 1Sm 23:17; Pr 16:29 [t]24:20 1Sm 13:14; 16:1-13 [u]24:21 Gn 21:23; 1Sm 20:14-17; 2Sm 21:6-8 [v]24:22 1Sm 23:29 [w]25:1 1Sm 28:3 [x]Dt 34:8 [y]2Kg 21:18; 2Ch 33:20 [z]Gn 21:21; Nm 10:12; 13:3 [aa]25:2 1Sm 23:24 [ab]Jos 15:55 [ac]25:3 Jos 15:13; 1Sm 30:14 [ad]25:6 1Ch 12:18 [ae]25:7 1Sm 23:24-25; 25:15-16 [af]25:8 Neh 8:10-12

16 When David finished saying these things to him, Saul replied, "Is that your voice, David my son?"[p] Then Saul wept aloud 17 and said to David, "You are more righteous than I, for you have done what is good to me though I have done what is evil to you.[q] 18 You yourself have told me today what good you did for me: when the LORD handed me over to you, you didn't kill me.[r] 19 When a man finds his enemy, does he let him go unharmed?[H,s] May the LORD repay you with good for what you've done for me today.

20 "Now I know for certain you will be king, and the kingdom of Israel will be established[I] in your hand.[t] 21 Therefore swear to me by the LORD that you will not cut off my descendants or wipe out my name from my father's family."[u] 22 So David swore to Saul. Then Saul went back home, and David and his men went up to the stronghold.[v]

David, Nabal, and Abigail

25 Samuel died,[w] and all Israel assembled to mourn for him,[x] and they buried him by his home in Ramah.[y] David then went down to the Wilderness of Paran.[J,z]

2 A man in Maon[aa] had a business in Carmel;[ab] he was a very rich man with 3,000 sheep and 1,000 goats and was shearing his sheep in Carmel. 3 The man's name was Nabal, and his wife's name, Abigail. The woman was intelligent and beautiful, but the man, a Calebite,[ac] was harsh and evil in his dealings.

4 While David was in the wilderness, he heard that Nabal was shearing sheep, 5 so David sent 10 young men instructing them, "Go up to Carmel, and when you come to Nabal, greet him in my name.[K] 6 Then say this: 'Long life to you,[L] and peace to you, to your family, and to all that is yours.[ad] 7 I hear that you are shearing.[M] When your shepherds were with us, we did not harass them, and nothing of theirs was missing the whole time they were in Carmel.[ae] 8 Ask your young men, and they will tell you. So let my young men find favor with you, for we have come on a feast[N] day.[af] Please give whatever you can afford to your servants and to your son David.'"

[A]24:3 Lit *to cover his feet* [B]24:5 Lit *David's heart struck* [C]24:5 Some Hb mss, LXX, Syr, Vg; other Hb mss omit *robe* [D]24:7 Or *restrained* [E]24:10 LXX, Syr, Tg; MT reads *she* or *it* [F]24:10 Or *my eye* [G]24:15 Lit *render a verdict for* [H]24:19 Lit *go on a good way* [I]24:20 Or *will flourish* [J]25:1 LXX reads *to Maon* [K]25:5 Or *Nabal, and ask him for peace* [L]25:6 Lit *To life* [M]25:7 Lit *you have shearers* [N]25:8 Lit *good*

9David's young men went and said all these
things to Nabal on David's behalf,[A] and they
waited.[B] 10Nabal asked them, "Who is David?[a]
Who is Jesse's son? Many slaves these days
are running away from their masters. 11Am
I supposed to take my bread, my water, and
my meat that I butchered for my shearers and
give them to these men? I don't know where
they are from."
12David's men retraced their steps. When
they returned to him, they reported all these
words. 13He said to his men, "All of you, put on
your swords!" So David and all his men put
on their swords. About 400 men followed David while 200 stayed with the supplies.[b]
14One of Nabal's young men informed Abigail, Nabal's wife: "Look, David sent messengers from the wilderness to greet our master,[c]
but he yelled at them. 15The men treated us
well. When we were in the field, we weren't
harassed[d] and nothing of ours was missing
the whole time we were living among them.
16They were a wall around us, both day and
night,[e] the entire time we were herding the
sheep. 17Now consider carefully what you
must do, because there is certain to be trouble for our master and his entire family. He
is such a worthless fool nobody can talk to
him!"
18Abigail hurried, taking 200 loaves of
bread, two skins of wine, five butchered
sheep, a bushel[C] of roasted grain, 100 clusters
of raisins, and 200 cakes of pressed figs, and
loaded them on donkeys.[f] 19Then she said to
her male servants, "Go ahead of me. I will be
right behind you."[g] But she did not tell her
husband Nabal.
20As she rode the donkey down a mountain
pass hidden from view, she saw David and his
men coming toward her and met them. 21Da-
vid had just said, "I guarded everything that
belonged to this man in the wilderness for
nothing. He was not missing anything, yet he
paid me back evil for good. 22May God punish
me[D] and do so severely[h] if I let any of his men[E]
survive until morning."[i]
23When Abigail saw David, she quickly got
off the donkey and fell with her face to the
ground in front of David.[j] 24She fell at his feet
and said, "The *guilt is mine, my lord, but
please let your servant speak to you directly.
Listen to the words of your servant. 25My lord
should pay no attention to this worthless
man Nabal, for he lives up to his name:[F] His
name is Nabal,[G] and stupidity is all he knows.[H]
I, your servant, didn't see my lord's young
men whom you sent. 26Now my lord, as surely
as the LORD lives and as you yourself live, it
is the LORD who kept you from participating
in bloodshed and avenging yourself[k] by your
own hand. May your enemies and those who
want trouble for my lord be like Nabal.[l] 27Ac-
cept this gift[m] your servant has brought to my
lord, and let it be given to the young men who
follow my lord. 28Please forgive your servant's
offense,[n] for the LORD is certain to make a
lasting dynasty for my lord[o] because he fights
the LORD's battles.[p] Throughout your life,
may evil[I] not be found in you.[q]
29"When someone pursues you and attempts to take your life, my lord's life will be
tucked safely in the place[J] where the LORD
your God protects the living. However, He
will fling away your enemies' lives like stones
from a sling.[r] 30When the LORD does for my
lord all the good He promised and appoints
you ruler over Israel,[s] 31there will not be remorse or a troubled conscience for my lord
because of needless bloodshed or my lord's
revenge. And when the LORD does good
things for my lord, may you remember me
your servant."[t]
32Then David said to Abigail, "Praise to the
LORD God of Israel,[u] who sent you to meet
me today! 33Your discernment is blessed, and
you are blessed. Today you kept me from participating in bloodshed and avenging myself
by my own hand.[v] 34Otherwise, as surely as
the LORD God of Israel lives, who prevented
me from harming you, if you had not come
quickly to meet me, Nabal wouldn't have had
any men[K] left by morning light." 35Then David
accepted what she had brought him and said,
"Go home in peace.[w] See, I have heard what
you said and have granted your request."[x]
36Then Abigail went to Nabal, and there

[a]**25:10** Jdg 9:28 [b]**25:13** 1Sm 23:13; 30:9-10 [c]**25:14** 1Sm 13:10; 15:13 [d]**25:15** 1Sm 25:7,21 [e]**25:16** Ex 14:22 [f]**25:18** 2Sm 16:1; 1Ch 12:40 [g]**25:19** Gn 32:16,20 [h]**25:22** 1Sm 3:17; 20:13 [i]1Kg 14:10 [j]**25:23** 1Sm 20:41 [k]**25:26** Heb 10:30 [l]2Sm 18:32 [m]**25:27** Gn 33:11; 1Sm 30:26 [n]**25:28** 1Sm 25:24 [o]1Sm 2:35; 22:14; 2Sm 7:11,16 [p]1Sm 18:17 [q]1Sm 24:11; Ps 7:3 [r]**25:29** Jr 10:18 [s]**25:30** 1Sm 13:14 [t]**25:31** Gn 40:14; 1Sm 25:30 [u]**25:32** Ex 18:10 [v]**25:33** 1Sm 25:26 [w]**25:35** 1Sm 20:42; 2Kg 5:19 [x]Gn 19:21

[A]**25:9** Lit *name* [B]**25:9** LXX reads *and he became arrogant* [C]**25:18** Lit *sheep, five seahs* [D]**25:22** LXX; MT reads *David's enemies* [E]**25:22** Lit *of those of his who are urinating against the wall* [F]**25:25** Lit *for as is his name is, so he is* [G]**25:25** = Fool [H]**25:25** Lit *and foolishness is with him* [I]**25:28** Or *trouble* [J]**25:29** Lit *bundle* [K]**25:34** Lit *had anyone urinating against a wall*

he was in his house, holding a feast fit for a king.[a] Nabal was in a good mood[A] and very drunk, so she didn't say anything[B] to him[b] until morning light.

37 In the morning when Nabal sobered up,[C] his wife told him about these events. Then he had a seizure[D] and became paralyzed.[E] 38 About 10 days later, the LORD struck Nabal dead.[c]

39 When David heard that Nabal was dead, he said, "Praise the LORD who championed my cause against Nabal's insults[d] and restrained His servant from doing evil.[e] The LORD brought Nabal's evil deeds back on his own head."[f]

Then David sent messengers to speak to Abigail about marrying him. 40 When David's servants came to Abigail at Carmel, they said to her, "David sent us to bring you to him as a wife."

41 She stood up, then bowed her face to the ground[g] and said, "Here I am, your servant, to wash the feet of my lord's servants."[h] 42 Then Abigail got up quickly, and with her five female servants accompanying her, rode on the donkey following David's messengers.[i] And so she became his wife.

43 David also married Ahinoam of Jezreel,[j] and the two of them became his wives. 44 But Saul gave his daughter Michal, David's wife, to Palti[k] son of Laish, who was from Gallim.[l]

David Again Spares Saul

26 Then the Ziphites came to Saul at Gibeah saying, "David is hiding on the hill of Hachilah opposite Jeshimon."[m] 2 So Saul, accompanied by 3,000 of the choice men of Israel,[n] went to the Wilderness of Ziph to search for David there. 3 Saul camped beside the road at the hill of Hachilah[o] opposite Jeshimon. David was living in the wilderness and discovered Saul had come there after him.[p] 4 So David sent out spies and knew for certain that Saul had come. 5 Immediately, David went to the place where Saul had camped. He saw the place where Saul and Abner son of Ner,[q] the general of his army, were lying down. Saul was lying inside the inner circle of the camp with the troops camped around him. 6 Then David asked Ahimelech the Hittite[r] and Joab's brother Abishai[s] son of Zeruiah, "Who will go with me into the camp[t] to Saul?"

"I'll go with you," answered Abishai.

7 That night, David and Abishai came to the troops, and Saul was lying there asleep in the inner circle of the camp with his spear stuck in the ground by his head. Abner and the troops were lying around him. 8 Then Abishai said to David, "Today God has handed your enemy over to you. Let me thrust the spear through him into the ground just once. I won't have to strike him twice!"

9 But David said to Abishai, "Don't destroy him, for who can lift a hand against the LORD's anointed and be blameless?"[u] 10 David added, "As the LORD lives, the LORD will certainly strike him down:[v] either his day will come and he will die, or he will go into battle and perish. 11 However, because of the LORD, I will never lift my hand against the LORD's anointed.[w] Instead, take the spear and the water jug by his head, and let's go."

12 So David took the spear and the water jug by Saul's head, and they went their way. No one saw them, no one knew, and no one woke up; they all remained asleep because a deep sleep from the LORD[x] came over them. 13 David crossed to the other side and stood on top of the mountain at a distance; there was a considerable space between them. 14 Then David shouted to the troops and to Abner son of Ner: "Aren't you going to answer, Abner?"

"Who are you who calls to the king?" Abner asked.

15 David called to Abner, "You're a man, aren't you? Who in Israel is your equal? So why didn't you protect your lord the king when one of the people came to destroy him? 16 What you have done is not good. As the LORD lives, all of you deserve to die since you didn't protect your lord, the LORD's anointed.[y] Now look around; where are the king's spear and water jug that were by his head?"

17 Saul recognized David's voice and asked, "Is that your voice, my son David?"[z]

"It is my voice, my lord and king," David said. 18 Then he continued, "Why is my lord

[a] **25:36** 2Sm 13:23
[b] 1Sm 25:19
[c] **25:38** 1Sm 26:10
[d] **25:39** 1Sm 24:15
[e] 1Sm 25:26,34
[f] 2Sm 3:28-29
[g] **25:41** 1Sm 25:23
[h] Mk 1:7
[i] **25:42** Gn 24:61-67
[j] **25:43** Jos 15:56
[k] **25:44** 1Sm 18:27; 2Sm 3:14-15
[l] Is 10:30
[m] **26:1** 1Sm 23:19; Ps 54 title
[n] **26:2** 1Sm 13:2; 24:2
[o] **26:3** 1Sm 24:3
[p] 1Sm 23:15
[q] **26:5** 1Sm 14:50-51; 17:55
[r] **26:6** Gn 26:34; Jos 3:10; 1Kg 10:29; 2Kg 7:6
[s] 1Ch 2:15-16
[t] Jdg 7:10-11
[u] **26:9** 1Sm 10:1; 24:6-7; 2Sm 1:14,16
[v] **26:10** 1Sm 25:26,38
[w] **26:11** Dt 32:35; 1Sm 24:6; 25:39; Rm 12:19
[x] **26:12** Gn 2:21; 15:12
[y] **26:16** 1Sm 20:31
[z] **26:17** 1Sm 24:16; 26:21,25

[A] **25:36** Lit *Nabal's heart was good on him* [B] **25:36** Lit *anything small or great* [C] **25:37** Lit *when the wine had gone out of Nabal* [D] **25:37** Lit *Then his heart died within him* [E] **25:37** Lit *became a stone*

pursuing his servant? What have I done? What evil is in my hand?[a] 19 Now, may my lord the king please hear the words of his servant: If it is the LORD who has incited you against me,[b] then may He accept an offering.[c] But if it is people,[d] may they be cursed in the presence of the LORD, for today they have driven me away from sharing in the inheritance of the LORD saying,[e] 'Go and worship other gods.' 20 So don't let my blood fall to the ground far from the LORD's presence, for the king of Israel has come out to search for a flea,[f] like one who pursues a partridge in the mountains."

21 Saul responded, "I have sinned.[g] Come back, my son David, I will never harm you again because today you considered my life precious. I have been a fool! I've committed a grave error."

22 David answered, "Here is the king's spear; have one of the young men come over and get it. 23 May the LORD repay every man for his righteousness[h] and his loyalty. I wasn't willing to lift my hand against the LORD's anointed, even though the LORD handed you over to me today.[i] 24 Just as I considered your life valuable today, so may the LORD consider my life valuable[j] and rescue me from all trouble."[k]

25 Saul said to him, "You are blessed, my son David. You will certainly do great things and will also prevail."[l] Then David went on his way, and Saul returned home.[m]

David Flees to Ziklag

27 David said to himself, "One of these days I'll be swept away by Saul. There is nothing better for me than to escape immediately to the land of the Philistines.[n] Then Saul will stop searching for me everywhere in Israel, and I'll escape from him." 2 So David set out with his 600 men[o] and went to Achish son of Maoch,[p] the king of Gath. 3 David and his men stayed with Achish in Gath. Each man had his family with him,[q] and David had his two wives: Ahinoam of Jezreel and Abigail of Carmel,[r] Nabal's widow. 4 When it was reported to Saul that David had fled to Gath, he no longer searched for him.

5 Now David said to Achish, "If I have found favor with you, let me be given a place in one of the outlying towns, so I can live there. Why should your servant live in the royal city with you?" 6 That day Achish gave Ziklag[s] to him, and it still belongs to the kings of Judah today. 7 The time that David stayed in the Philistine territory amounted to a year and four months.[t]

8 David and his men went up and raided the Geshurites,[u] the Girzites,[A] and the Amalekites.[v] From ancient times they had been the inhabitants of the region through Shur[w] as far as the land of Egypt. 9 Whenever David attacked the land, he did not leave a single person alive, either man or woman, but he took flocks, herds, donkeys, camels, and clothing.[x] Then he came back to Achish, 10 who inquired, "Where did you raid today?"[B,y]

David replied, "The south country of Judah," "The south country of the Jerahmeelites,"[z] or "Against the south country of the Kenites."[aa]

11 David did not let a man or woman live to be brought to Gath, for he said, "Or they will inform on us and say, 'This is what David did.'" This was David's custom during the whole time he stayed in the Philistine territory. 12 So Achish trusted David, thinking, "Since he has made himself detestable to his people Israel, he will be my servant forever."

Saul and the Medium

28 At that time, the Philistines[ab] brought their military units together into one army to fight against Israel. So Achish said to David, "You know, of course, that you and your men must march out in the army[C] with me."

2 David replied to Achish, "Good, you will find out what your servant can do."

So Achish said to David, "Very well, I will appoint you as my permanent bodyguard."[ac]

3 By this time Samuel had died,[ad] and all Israel had mourned for him and buried him in Ramah, his city,[ae] and Saul had removed the mediums and spiritists from the land.[af] 4 The Philistines came together and camped at Shunem. So Saul gathered all Israel, and they camped at Gilboa. 5 When Saul saw the Philistine camp, he was afraid and trembled violently. 6 He inquired of the LORD, but the LORD did not answer him in dreams or by the

[a] **26:18** 1Sm 24:11
[b] **26:19** 2Sm 16:11
[c] Gn 8:21
[d] 1Sm 24:9
[e] Jos 22:25-27
[f] **26:20** 1Sm 24:14
[g] **26:21** 1Sm 15:24,30; 24:17
[h] **26:23** 1Sm 24:19
[i] 1Sm 24:10-12; 26:10-11
[j] **26:24** 1Sm 18:30
[k] Ps 54:7
[l] **26:25** 1Sm 24:19
[m] 1Sm 24:22
[n] **27:1** 1Sm 26:19
[o] **27:2** 1Sm 25:13
[p] 1Sm 2:10; 1Kg 2:39
[q] **27:3** 1Sm 30:3; 2Sm 2:3
[r] 1Sm 25:42-44
[s] **27:6** Jos 15:31; 19:5; Neh 11:28
[t] **27:7** 1Sm 29:1-11
[u] **27:8** Jos 13:2,13
[v] Ex 17:8; 1Sm 15:7-8
[w] Ex 15:22
[x] **27:9** 1Sm 15:3; Jb 1:3
[y] **27:10** 1Sm 23:27
[z] 1Sm 30:29; 1Ch 2:9,25
[aa] Jdg 1:16; 4:11
[ab] **28:1** 1Sm 29:1
[ac] **28:2** 1Sm 1:22,28
[ad] **28:3** 1Sm 25:1
[ae] 1Sm 7:17
[af] Lv 19:31; 20:27; Dt 18:10-11

[A] **27:8** Alt Hb tradition reads *Gezerites* [B] **27:10** Some Hb mss, Syr, Tg; LXX, Vg, DSS read *Against whom did you raid today?* [C] **28:1** DSS, LXX read *battle*

Urim or by the prophets.[a] 7 Saul then said to his servants, "Find me a woman who is a medium, so I can go and consult her."

His servants replied, "There is a woman at En-dor[b] who is a medium."[c]

8 Saul disguised himself[d] by putting on different clothes and set out with two of his men. They came to the woman at night, and Saul said, "Consult a spirit for me.[e] Bring up for me the one I tell you."[f]

9 But the woman said to him, "You surely know what Saul has done,[g] how he has killed the mediums and spiritists in the land. Why are you setting a trap for me to get me killed?"

10 Then Saul swore to her by the LORD: "As surely as the LORD lives, nothing bad will happen to you because of this."

11 "Who is it that you want me to bring up for you?" the woman asked.

"Bring up Samuel for me," he answered.

12 When the woman saw Samuel, she screamed, and then she asked Saul, "Why did you deceive me? You are Saul!"

13 But the king said to her, "Don't be afraid. What do you see?"

"I see a spirit form[A] coming up out of the earth," the woman answered.

14 Then Saul asked her, "What does he look like?"

"An old man is coming up," she replied. "He's wearing a robe."[h] Then Saul knew that it was Samuel, and he bowed his face to the ground and paid homage.[i]

15 "Why have you disturbed me by bringing me up?" Samuel asked Saul.

"I'm in serious trouble," replied Saul. "The Philistines are fighting against me and God has turned away from me.[j] He doesn't answer me anymore,[k] either through the prophets or in dreams. So I've called on you to tell me what I should do."

16 Samuel answered, "Since the LORD has turned away from you and has become your enemy, why are you asking me? 17 The LORD has done[B] exactly what He said through me: The LORD has torn the kingship out of your hand and given it to your neighbor David.[l] 18 You did not obey the LORD and did not carry out His burning anger against Amalek;[m] therefore the LORD has done this to you today. 19 The LORD will also hand Israel over to the Philistines along with you. Tomorrow you and your sons will be with me,[C,n] and the LORD will hand Israel's army over to the Philistines."

20 Immediately, Saul fell flat on the ground. He was terrified by Samuel's words and was also weak because he hadn't had any food all day and all night. 21 The woman came over to Saul, and she saw that he was terrified and said to him, "Look, your servant has obeyed you. I took my life in my hands[o] and did what you told me to do. 22 Now please listen to your servant. Let me set some food in front of you. Eat and it will give you strength so you can go on your way."

23 He refused, saying, "I won't eat," but when his servants and the woman urged him, he listened to them.[p] He got up off the ground and sat on the bed.[q]

24 The woman had a fattened calf at her house, and she quickly slaughtered it.[r] She also took flour, kneaded it, and baked unleavened bread. 25 She served it to Saul and his servants, and they ate. Afterward, they got up and left that night.

Philistines Reject David

29 The Philistines[s] brought all their military units together at Aphek[t] while Israel was camped by the spring in Jezreel.[u] 2 As the Philistine leaders were passing in review with their units of hundreds and thousands, David and his men[v] were passing in review behind them with Achish. 3 Then the Philistine commanders asked, "What are these Hebrews doing here?"

Achish answered the Philistine commanders, "That is David, servant of King Saul of Israel. He has been with me a considerable period of time.[D] From the day he defected until today, I've found no fault with him."[w]

4 The Philistine commanders, however, were enraged with Achish and told him, "Send that man back and let him return to the place you assigned him.[x] He must not go down with us into battle only to become our adversary during the battle.[y] What better way could he regain his master's favor than with

[a] 28:6 Ex 28:30; Nm 27:21; 1Kg 3:5
[b] 28:7 Jos 17:1; Ps 83:10
[c] Ac 16:16
[d] 28:8 2Ch 18:29; 35:21-22
[e] Is 8:19
[f] Dt 18:10-11
[g] 28:9 1Sm 28:3
[h] 28:14 1Sm 15:27
[i] 1Sm 24:8
[j] 28:15 1Sm 16:13-14; 18:12
[k] 1Sm 28:6
[l] 28:17 1Sm 15:28
[m] 28:18 1Sm 15:1-9
[n] 28:19 1Sm 31:2; Jb 3:17-19
[o] 28:21 1Sm 19:5
[p] 28:23 2Kg 5:13
[q] Est 1:6; Ezk 23:41
[r] 28:24 Gn 18:6-7
[s] 29:1 1Sm 28:1-2
[t] Jos 12:18; 1Sm 4:1
[u] 1Kg 18:19; 21:1; 2Kg 9:30
[v] 29:2 1Sm 28:1-2
[w] 29:3 1Sm 27:4-12
[x] 29:4 1Sm 27:6
[y] 1Sm 14:21

[A] 28:13 Or *a god*, or *a divine being* [B] 28:17 Some Hb, some LXX mss, Vg read *done to you* [C] 28:19 LXX reads *sons will fall* [D] 29:3 Hb obscure

the heads of our men? 5Isn't this the David
they sing about during their dances:

> Saul has killed his thousands,
> but David his tens of thousands?"[a]

6So Achish summoned David and told him,
"As the LORD lives, you are an honorable man. I
think it is good[A] to have you working[B] with me
in the camp, because I have found no fault in
you from the day you came to me until today.[b]
But the leaders don't think you are reliable.
7Now go back quietly and you won't be doing
anything the Philistine leaders think is wrong."
8"But what have I done?"[c] David replied to
Achish. "From the first day I was with you until today, what have you found against your
servant to keep me from going along to fight
against the enemies of my lord the king?"
9Achish answered David, "I'm convinced
that you are as reliable as the Angel of God.[d]
But the Philistine commanders have said, 'He
must not go into battle with us.'[e] 10So get up
early in the morning, you and your masters'
servants who came with you.[C][f] When you've
all gotten up early, go as soon as it's light." 11So
David and his men got up early in the morning to return to the land of the Philistines.
And the Philistines went up to Jezreel.

David's Defeat of the Amalekites

30 David and his men[g] arrived in Ziklag[h]
on the third day. The Amalekites[i] had
raided the ·Negev and attacked and burned
down Ziklag. 2They also had kidnapped the
women and everyone[D] in it from the youngest
to the oldest. They had killed no one but had
carried them off[j] as they went on their way.
3When David and his men arrived at the
town, they found it burned down. Their wives,
sons, and daughters had been kidnapped. 4Da-
vid and the troops with him wept loudly until
they had no strength left to weep. 5David's two
wives,[k] Ahinoam the Jezreelite and Abigail the
widow of Nabal the Carmelite, had also been
kidnapped. 6David was in a difficult position
because the troops talked about stoning him,[l]
for they were all very bitter over the loss of
their sons and daughters. But David found
strength in the LORD his God.[m]

7David said to Abiathar the priest, son of
Ahimelech, "Bring me the ·ephod."[n] So Abiathar brought it to him, 8and David asked the
LORD:[o] "Should I pursue these raiders? Will I
overtake them?"[p]
The LORD replied to him, "Pursue them, for
you will certainly overtake them and rescue
the people."[q]
9David and the 600 men with him[r] went as
far as the ·Wadi Besor, where 200 men who
were to remain behind would stop.[s] 10They
stopped because they were too exhausted to
cross the Wadi Besor. David and 400 of the
men continued in pursuit.
11They found an Egyptian in the open country and brought him to David. They gave him
some bread to eat and water to drink. 12Then
they gave him some pressed figs and two clusters of raisins. After he ate he revived,[t] for he
hadn't eaten food or drunk water for three
days and three nights.
13Then David said to him, "Who do you belong to? Where are you from?"
"I'm an Egyptian, the slave of an Amalekite
man," he said. "My master abandoned me
when I got sick three days ago. 14We raided
the south country of the Cherethites,[u] the
territory of Judah, and the south country of
Caleb,[v] and we burned down Ziklag."[w]
15David then asked him, "Will you lead me
to these raiders?"
He said, "Swear to me by God that you
won't kill me or turn me over to my master,
and I will lead you to them."
16So he led him, and there were the Amalekites, spread out over the entire area, eating, drinking, and celebrating because of
the great amount of plunder[x] they had taken
from the land of the Philistines and the land
of Judah. 17David slaughtered them from twilight until the evening of the next day.[y] None
of them escaped, except 400 young men who
got on camels and fled.[z]
18David recovered everything the Amalekites had taken; he also rescued his two
wives. 19Nothing of theirs was missing from
the youngest to the oldest, including the sons
and daughters, of all the plunder the Amalekites had taken. David got everything back.[aa]

[a]**29:5** 1Sm 18:7; 21:11
[b]**29:6** 1Sm 27:8-12; 29:3
[c]**29:8** 1Sm 27:10-12
[d]**29:9** 2Sm 14:17,20; 19:27
[e]1Sm 29:4
[f]**29:10** 1Ch 12:19,22
[g]**30:1-18** Gn 14:1-16
[h]**30:1** 1Sm 27:6,8
[i]1Sm 15:7; 27:8-10
[j]**30:2** 1Sm 27:11
[k]**30:5** 1Sm 25:42-43
[l]**30:6** Ex 17:4
[m]1Sm 23:16; Ps 18:2; 27:14
[n]**30:7** 1Sm 23:6-9
[o]**30:8** 1Sm 23:2,4
[p]Ex 15:9
[q]1Sm 30:18
[r]**30:9** 1Sm 27:2
[s]1Sm 30:21
[t]**30:12** Jdg 15:19
[u]**30:14** 1Sm 30:16; 2Sm 8:18; Ezk 25:16
[v]Jos 14:13; 21:11-12
[w]1Sm 30:1
[x]**30:16** 1Sm 30:14
[y]**30:17** 1Sm 11:11
[z]Jdg 7:12; 1Sm 15:3
[aa]**30:19** 1Sm 30:8

[A]**29:6** Lit *It was good in my eyes* [B]**29:6** Lit *you going out and coming in* [C]**29:10** LXX adds *and go to the place I appointed you to. Don't take this evil matter to heart, for you are good before me.* [D]**30:2** LXX; MT omits *and everyone*

20 He took all the sheep and cattle, which were driven ahead of the other livestock, and the people shouted, "This is David's plunder!"[a]

21 When David came to the 200 men who had been too exhausted to go with him and had been left at the Wadi Besor,[b] they came out to meet him and to meet the troops with him. When David approached the men, he greeted them, 22 but all the corrupt and •worthless men among those who had gone with David argued, "Because they didn't go with us, we will not give any of the plunder we recovered to them except for each man's wife and children. They may take them and go."

23 But David said, "My brothers, you must not do this with what the LORD has given us. He protected us and handed over to us the raiders who came against us. 24 Who can agree to your proposal? The share of the one who goes into battle is to be the same as the share of the one who remains with the supplies. They will share equally."[c] 25 And it has been so from that day forward. David established this policy as a law and an ordinance for Israel and it continues to this very day.

26 When David came to Ziklag, he sent some of the plunder to his friends, the elders of Judah, saying, "Here is a gift for you[d] from the plunder of the LORD's enemies."[e] 27 He sent gifts to those in Bethel,[f] in Ramoth of the Negev,[g] and in Jattir;[h] 28 to those in Aroer,[i] in Siphmoth,[j] and in Eshtemoa;[k] 29 to those in Racal, in the towns of the Jerahmeelites,[l] and in the towns of the Kenites;[m] 30 to those in Hormah,[n] in Bor-ashan,[o] and in Athach; 31 to those in Hebron,[p] and to those in all the places where David and his men had roamed.[q]

The Death of Saul and His Sons

31 The Philistines fought against Israel,[r] and Israel's men fled from them. Many were killed on Mount Gilboa.[s] 2 The Philistines overtook Saul and his sons and killed his sons, Jonathan, Abinadab, and Malchishua. 3 When the battle intensified against Saul,[t] the archers caught up with him and severely wounded him.[A] 4 Then Saul said to his armor-bearer,[u] "Draw your sword and run me through with it, or these uncircumcised men[v] will come and run me through and torture me." But his armor-bearer would not do it because he was terrified. Then Saul took his sword and fell on it.[w] 5 When his armor-bearer saw that Saul was dead, he also fell on his own sword and died with him. 6 So on that day, Saul died together with his three sons, his armor-bearer, and all his men.

7 When the men of Israel on the other side of the valley and on the other side of the Jordan saw that Israel's men had run away and that Saul and his sons were dead, they abandoned the cities and fled. So the Philistines came and settled in them.

8 The next day when the Philistines came to strip the dead, they found Saul and his three sons dead on Mount Gilboa. 9 They cut off Saul's head, stripped off his armor, and sent messengers throughout the land of the Philistines to spread the good news[x] in the temples of their idols[y] and among the people. 10 Then they put his armor in the temple of the •Ashtoreths[z] and hung his body[aa] on the wall of Beth-shan.[ab]

11 When the residents of Jabesh-gilead[ac] heard what the Philistines had done to Saul, 12 all their brave men[ad] set out, journeyed all night, and retrieved the body of Saul and the bodies of his sons from the wall of Beth-shan. When they arrived at Jabesh, they burned the bodies there.[ae] 13 Afterward, they took their bones and buried them under the tamarisk tree[af] in Jabesh[ag] and fasted seven days.

[a] **30:20** 1Sm 30:26-31
[b] **30:21** 1Sm 30:9-10
[c] **30:24** Nm 31:25-27; Jos 22:8
[d] **30:26** 1Sm 25:27
[e] 1Sm 18:17; 25:28
[f] **30:27** Jos 15:30; 19:4
[g] Jos 19:8
[h] Jos 15:48; 21:14
[i] **30:28** 1Ch 11:44
[j] 1Ch 27:27
[k] Jos 15:50
[l] **30:29** 1Sm 27:10
[m] 1Sm 15:6
[n] **30:30** Jos 12:14; 15:30; 19:4
[o] Jos 15:42; 19:7
[p] **30:31** Nm 13:22; Jos 14:13-15; 21:11-13
[q] 1Sm 23:22
[r] **31:1-13** 2Sm 1:12; 1Ch 10:1-12
[s] **31:1** 1Sm 28:4
[t] **31:3** 2Sm 1:6
[u] **31:4** Jdg 9:54
[v] Jdg 14:3
[w] 2Sm 1:6,10
[x] **31:9** 2Sm 1:20
[y] Jdg 16:23-24
[z] **31:10** Jdg 2:13; 1Sm 7:3
[aa] 1Sm 31:12; 2Sm 21:14
[ab] Jos 17:11
[ac] **31:11** 1Sm 11:1-13
[ad] **31:12** 2Sm 2:4-7
[ae] 2Ch 16:14
[af] **31:13** 1Sm 22:6
[ag] 2Sm 2:4-7; 21:12-14

[A] **31:3** LXX reads *and he was wounded under the ribs*

2 SAMUEL

For the introduction to the book of 2 Samuel, see the introduction to the book of
1 Samuel, page 268.

Responses to Saul's Death

1 After the death of Saul,[a] David returned
from defeating the Amalekites[b] and stayed
at Ziklag two days. 2 On the third day a man
with torn clothes and dust on his head[c] came
from Saul's camp. When he came to David, he
fell to the ground and paid homage. 3 David
asked him, "Where have you come from?"

He replied to him, "I've escaped from the
Israelite camp."

4 "What was the outcome? Tell me," David
asked him.

"The troops fled from the battle," he answered. "Many of the troops have fallen and
are dead. Also, Saul and his son Jonathan are
dead."[d]

5 David asked the young man who had
brought him the report, "How do you know
Saul and his son Jonathan are dead?"

6 "I happened to be on Mount Gilboa,"[e] he
replied, "and there was Saul, leaning on his
spear. At that very moment the chariots and
the cavalry were closing in on him. 7 When he
turned around and saw me, he called out to
me, so I answered: I'm at your service. 8 He
asked me, 'Who are you?' I told him: I'm an
Amalekite.[f] 9 Then he begged me, 'Stand over
me and kill me, for I'm mortally wounded,[A]
but my life still lingers.'[g] 10 So I stood over
him and killed him because I knew that after
he had fallen he couldn't survive. I took the
crown that was on his head and the armband
that was on his arm, and I've brought them
here to my lord."

11 Then David took hold of his clothes and
tore them,[h] and all the men with him did
the same. 12 They mourned, wept, and fasted
until the evening[i] for those who died by
the sword — for Saul, his son Jonathan, the
LORD's people, and the house of Israel.

13 David inquired of the young man who
had brought him the report, "Where are you
from?"

"I'm the son of a foreigner," he said. "I'm an
Amalekite."

14 David questioned him, "How is it that you
were not afraid to lift your hand to destroy
the LORD's anointed?"[j] 15 Then David summoned one of his servants and said, "Come
here and kill him!" The servant struck him,
and he died.[k] 16 For David had said to the Amalekite, "Your blood is on your own head[l] because your own mouth testified against you
by saying, 'I killed the LORD's anointed.'"

17 David sang the following lament[m] for Saul
and his son Jonathan, 18 and he ordered that
the Judahites be taught The Song of the Bow.
It is written in the Book of Jashar:[B,n]

19 The splendor of Israel lies slain
on your heights.
How the mighty have fallen!
20 Do not tell it in Gath,
don't announce it in the marketplaces
of Ashkelon,
or the daughters of the Philistines
will rejoice,[o]
and the daughters
of the uncircumcised will gloat.
21 Mountains of Gilboa,
let no dew or rain be on you,
or fields of offerings,[C]
for there the shield of the mighty
was defiled[p] —
the shield of Saul, no longer anointed
with oil.[q]
22 Jonathan's bow never retreated,
Saul's sword never returned unstained,[D]
from the blood of the slain,
from the bodies of the mighty.
23 Saul and Jonathan,
loved and delightful,

[a] 1:1 1Sm 31:1-5
[b] 1Sm 30:1-20
[c] 1:2 Jos 7:6; 1Sm 4:12
[d] 1:4 1Sm 31:6
[e] 1:6-10 1Sm 31:1-5; 1Ch 10:1-6
[f] 1:8 Gn 36:12,16; Ex 17:8-16; Nm 24:20; Dt 25:19; 1Sm 15:1-34; 30:1-20; 1Ch 1:36
[g] 1:9 Jdg 9:54
[h] 1:11 Jos 7:6; 2Sm 3:31; 13:31
[i] 1:12 2Sm 3:35
[j] 1:14 1Sm 24:6; 26:6-12; 31:4
[k] 1:15 2Sm 4:10
[l] 1:16 Jos 2:19; Mt 27:24-25; Ac 18:5-6
[m] 1:17 2Sm 3:33; 2Ch 35:24-25
[n] 1:18 Jos 10:12-13
[o] 1:20 1Sm 31:8-9
[p] 1:21 1Sm 31:4
[q] 1Sm 10:1

[A] 1:9 LXX reads *for terrible darkness has taken hold of me* [B] 1:18 Or *of the Upright* [C] 1:21 LXX reads *firstfruits* [D] 1:22 Lit *empty*

they were not parted in life or in death.
They were swifter than eagles,
stronger than lions.
24 Daughters of Israel, weep for Saul,
who clothed you in scarlet,
with luxurious things,
who decked your garments
with gold ornaments.[a]
25 How the mighty have fallen in the thick
of battle!
Jonathan lies slain on your heights.
26 I grieve for you, Jonathan, my brother.
You were such a friend to me.
Your love for me was more wonderful
than the love of women.[b]
27 How the mighty have fallen
and the weapons of war have perished!

David, King of Judah

2 Some time later, David inquired of the
LORD:[c] "Should I go to one of the towns
of Judah?"
The LORD answered him, "Go."
Then David asked, "Where should I go?"
"To Hebron,"[d] the LORD replied.
2 So David went there with his two wives,
Ahinoam the Jezreelite and Abigail, the
widow of Nabal the Carmelite.[e] 3 In addition,
David brought the men who were with him,
each one with his household, and they settled
in the towns near Hebron.[f] 4 Then the men of
Judah came, and there they anointed David
king over the house of Judah.[g] They told David:
"It was the men of Jabesh-gilead who buried
Saul."[h]
5 David sent messengers to the men of Jabesh-gilead
and said to them, "The LORD bless
you, because you have shown this kindness to
Saul your lord when you buried him. 6 Now,
may the LORD show kindness and faithfulness
to you, and I will also show the same
goodness to you because you have done this
deed. 7 Therefore, be strong and courageous,
for though Saul your lord is dead, the house
of Judah has anointed me king over them."
8 Abner son of Ner, commander of Saul's
army,[i] took Saul's son Ish-bosheth[A,B] and
moved him to Mahanaim. 9 He made him
king over Gilead, Asher, Jezreel, Ephraim,
Benjamin — over all Israel. 10 Saul's son Ish-bosheth
was 40 years old when he began his
reign over Israel; he ruled for two years. The
house of Judah, however, followed David.
11 The length of time that David was king in
Hebron over the house of Judah was seven
years and six months.[j]
12 Abner son of Ner and soldiers of Ish-bosheth
son of Saul marched out from Mahanaim
to Gibeon. 13 So Joab son of Zeruiah and
David's soldiers marched out and met them
by the pool of Gibeon.[k] The two groups took
up positions on opposite sides of the pool.
14 Then Abner said to Joab, "Let's have the
young men get up and compete in front of
us."
"Let them get up," Joab replied.
15 So they got up and were counted off — 12
for Benjamin and Ish-bosheth son of Saul,
and 12 from David's soldiers. 16 Then each
man grabbed his opponent by the head and
thrust his sword into his opponent's side
so that they all died together. So this place,
which is in Gibeon, is named Field of Blades.[C]
17 The battle that day was extremely fierce,
and Abner and the men of Israel were defeated
by David's soldiers. 18 The three sons of
Zeruiah were there: Joab, Abishai, and Asahel.[l]
Asahel was a fast runner, like one of the
wild gazelles.[m] 19 He chased Abner and did not
turn to the right or the left in his pursuit of
him. 20 Abner glanced back and said, "Is that
you, Asahel?"
"Yes it is," Asahel replied.
21 Abner said to him, "Turn to your right or
left, seize one of the young soldiers, and take
whatever you can get from him." But Asahel
would not stop chasing him. 22 Once again,
Abner warned Asahel, "Stop chasing me. Why
should I strike you to the ground? How could
I ever look your brother Joab in the face?"[n]
23 But Asahel refused to turn away, so Abner
hit him in the stomach with the end of
his spear. The spear went through his body,
and he fell and died right there. When all who
came to the place where Asahel had fallen and
died, they stopped, 24 but Joab and Abishai
pursued Abner. By sunset, they had gone as
far as the hill of Ammah, which is opposite
Giah on the way to the wilderness of Gibeon.
25 The Benjaminites rallied to Abner; they

[a] **1:24** Ezk 16:1-11
[b] **1:26** 1Sm 18:1-3
[c] **2:1** 1Sm 23:1-12
[d] 1Sm 30:26-31; 2Sm 2:11; 5:5; 1Kg 2:11; 1Ch 3:4; 29:27
[e] **2:2** 1Sm 25:42-43
[f] **2:3** 1Sm 27:2-3; 30:9; 1Ch 12:1,23-37
[g] **2:4** 1Sm 16:13; 2Sm 5:3-5
[h] 1Sm 31:11-13
[i] **2:8** 1Sm 14:50
[j] **2:11** 2Sm 5:5; 1Kg 2:11
[k] **2:13** Jr 41:11-12
[l] **2:18** 1Ch 2:16
[m] 1Ch 12:8; Sg 8:14
[n] **2:22** 2Sm 3:27

A **2:8** Some LXX mss read *Ishbaal*; 1Ch 8:33; 9:39 B **2:8** = Man of Shame C **2:16** Or *Helkath-hazzurim*

formed a single unit and took their stand on
top of a hill. 26 Then Abner called out to Joab:
"Must the sword devour forever? Don't you
realize this will only end in bitterness? How
long before you tell the troops to stop pursuing their brothers?"
27 "As God lives," Joab replied, "if you had
not spoken up, the troops wouldn't have
stopped pursuing their brothers until morning."[a] 28 Then Joab blew the ram's horn, and all
the troops stopped; they no longer pursued
Israel or continued to fight. 29 So Abner and
his men marched through the ·Arabah all
that night. They crossed the Jordan, marched
all morning,[A] and arrived at Mahanaim.[b]
30 When Joab had turned back from pursuing Abner, he gathered all the troops. In addition to Asahel, 19 of David's soldiers were
missing, 31 but they had killed 360 of the Benjaminites and Abner's men. 32 Afterward, they
carried Asahel to his father's tomb in Bethlehem and buried him. Then Joab and his men
marched all night and reached Hebron at
dawn.

Civil War

3 The war between the house of Saul and
the house of David was long and drawn
out, with David growing stronger and the
house of Saul becoming weaker.
2 Sons were born to David in Hebron:

his firstborn was Amnon,
by Ahinoam[c] the Jezreelite;
3 his second was Chileab,
by Abigail, the widow of Nabal
the Carmelite;
the third was Absalom,
son of Maacah the daughter
of King Talmai of Geshur;[d]
4 the fourth was Adonijah,[e]
son of Haggith;
the fifth was Shephatiah,
son of Abital;
5 the sixth was Ithream,
by David's wife Eglah.

These were born to David in Hebron.[f]
6 During the war between the house of Saul
and the house of David, Abner kept acquiring more power in the house of Saul.[g] 7 Now
Saul had a concubine whose name was Rizpah[h] daughter of Aiah, and Ish-bosheth questioned Abner, "Why did you sleep with my
father's concubine?"
8 Abner was very angry about Ish-bosheth's
accusation. "Am I a dog's head[B,i] who belongs
to Judah?" he asked. "All this time I've been
loyal to the house of your father Saul, to
his brothers, and to his friends and haven't
handed you over to David, but now you accuse me of wrongdoing with this woman!
9 May God punish Abner and do so severely
if I don't do for David what the LORD swore
to him: 10 to transfer the kingdom from the
house of Saul and establish the throne of David over Israel and Judah[j] from Dan to Beer-
sheba." 11 Ish-bosheth could not answer Abner
because he was afraid of him.
12 Abner sent messengers as his representatives to say to David, "Whose land is it? Make
your covenant with me, and you can be certain I am on your side to hand all Israel over
to you."
13 David replied, "Good, I will make a covenant with you. However, there's one thing I
require of you: Do not appear before me unless you bring Saul's daughter Michal[k] here
when you come to see me."
14 Then David sent messengers to say to Ish-
bosheth son of Saul, "Give me back my wife,
Michal. I was ·engaged to her for the price of
100 Philistine foreskins."[l]
15 So Ish-bosheth sent someone to take her
away from her husband, Paltiel son of Laish.[m]
16 Her husband followed her, weeping all
the way to Bahurim. Abner said to him, "Go
back." So he went back.

The Assassination of Abner

17 Abner conferred with the elders of Israel:
"In the past you wanted David to be king over
you. 18 Now take action, because the LORD has
spoken concerning David: 'Through My servant David I will save My people Israel from
the power of the Philistines and the power of
all Israel's enemies.'"
19 Abner also informed the Benjaminites
and went to Hebron to inform David about
all that was agreed on by Israel and the whole
house of Benjamin.[n] 20 When Abner and 20

[a] 2:27 2Sm 2:14
[b] 2:29 2Sm 2:8
[c] 3:2 1Sm 25:42-43
[d] 3:3 1Sm 27:8; 2Sm 13:37-38; 14:32; 15:8
[e] 3:4 1Kg 1:5
[f] 3:5 1Ch 3:1-5
[g] 3:6 2Sm 2:8-9
[h] 3:7 2Sm 21:8-10
[i] 3:8 Ex 22:31; 1Sm 17:43; 24:14; 2Sm 9:8; 16:9
[j] 3:10 1Sm 15:28; 16:1-13; 28:17; 1Ch 12:23
[k] 3:13 1Sm 14:49
[l] 3:14 1Sm 18:20-27
[m] 3:15 1Sm 25:44
[n] 3:19 1Ch 12:29

[A] 2:29 Or *marched through the Bithron* [B] 3:8 = a despised person men came to David at Hebron, David held a banquet for him and his men.

21 Abner said to David, "Let me now go and I will gather all Israel to my lord the king. They will make a covenant with you,[a] and you will rule over all you desire." So David dismissed Abner, and he went in peace.

22 Just then David's soldiers and Joab returned from a raid and brought a large amount of plundered goods with them. Abner was not with David in Hebron because David had dismissed him, and he had gone in peace. 23 When Joab and all his army arrived, Joab was informed, "Abner son of Ner came to see the king, the king dismissed him, and he went in peace."

24 Joab went to the king and said, "What have you done? Look here, Abner came to you. Why did you dismiss him? Now he's getting away. 25 You know that Abner son of Ner came to deceive you and to find out about your activities and everything you're doing." 26 Then Joab left David and sent messengers after Abner. They brought him back from the well[A] of Sirah, but David was unaware of it. 27 When Abner returned to Hebron, Joab pulled him aside to the middle of the gateway, as if to speak to him privately, and there Joab stabbed him in the stomach. So Abner died in revenge for the death of Asahel,[B] Joab's brother.[b]

28 David heard about it later and said: "I and my kingdom are forever innocent before the LORD concerning the blood of Abner son of Ner. 29 May it hang over Joab's head and his father's whole house, and may the house of Joab never be without someone who has a discharge or a skin disease,[c] or a man who can only work a spindle,[C] or someone who falls by the sword or starves." 30 Joab and his brother Abishai killed Abner because he had put their brother Asahel to death in the battle at Gibeon.[d]

31 David then ordered Joab and all the people who were with him, "Tear your clothes, put on •sackcloth,[e] and mourn over Abner." And King David walked behind the funeral procession.[D]

32 When they buried Abner in Hebron, the king wept aloud at Abner's tomb. All the people wept, 33 and the king sang a lament for Abner:[f]

> Should Abner die as a fool dies?
> 34 Your hands were not bound,
> your feet not placed in bronze shackles.
> You fell like one who falls victim
> to criminals.

And all the people wept over him even more.

35 Then they came to urge David to eat bread while it was still day, but David took an oath: "May God punish me and do so severely if I taste bread or anything else before sunset!"[g] 36 All the people took note of this, and it pleased them. In fact, everything the king did pleased them. 37 On that day all the troops and all Israel were convinced that the king had no part in the killing of Abner son of Ner.

38 Then the king said to his soldiers, "You must know that a great leader has fallen in Israel today. 39 As for me, even though I am the anointed king, I have little power today. These men, the sons of Zeruiah, are too fierce for me.[h] May the LORD repay the evildoer according to his evil!"[i]

The Assassination of Ish-bosheth

4 When Saul's son Ish-bosheth heard that Abner had died in Hebron, his courage failed, and all Israel was dismayed. 2 Saul's son had two men who were leaders of raiding parties: one named Baanah and the other Rechab, sons of Rimmon the Beerothite of the Benjaminites. Beeroth is also considered part of Benjamin, 3 and the Beerothites fled to Gittaim and still live there as foreigners to this very day.

4 Saul's son Jonathan had a son whose feet were crippled. He was five years old when the report about Saul and Jonathan came from Jezreel. The one who had nursed him[E] picked him up and fled, but as she was hurrying to flee, he fell and became lame. His name was Mephibosheth.[j]

5 Rechab and Baanah, the sons of Rimmon the Beerothite, set out and arrived at Ish-bosheth's house during the heat of the day while the king was taking his midday nap. 6 They entered the interior of the house as if to get wheat and stabbed him in the stom-

[a] **3:21** 2Sm 3:12
[b] **3:27** 2Sm 2:23; 1Kg 2:5,32
[c] **3:29** Lv 14:2-8
[d] **3:30** 2Sm 2:23
[e] **3:31** Gn 37:34; Jos 7:6
[f] **3:33** 2Sm 1:17; 2Ch 35:25
[g] **3:35** 2Sm 12:17
[h] **3:39** 2Sm 16:10; 19:22
[i] Ps 28:4; 2Tm 4:14
[j] **4:4** 2Sm 9:3-7

[A] **3:26** Or *cistern* [B] **3:27** Lit *And he died for the blood of Asahel* [C] **3:29** LXX reads *who uses a crutch* [D] **3:31** Or *the bier*; lit *the bed* [E] **4:4** Lit *His nurse*

ach. Then Rechab and his brother Baanah
escaped. 7They had entered the house while
Ish-bosheth was lying on his bed in his bedroom and stabbed and killed him. Then
they beheaded him, took his head, and traveled by way of the ·Arabah[a] all night. 8They
brought Ish-bosheth's head to David at Hebron and said to the king, "Here's the head
of Ish-bosheth son of Saul, your enemy who
intended to take your life. Today the LORD
has granted vengeance to my lord the king
against Saul and his offspring."

9But David answered Rechab and his
brother Baanah, sons of Rimmon the
Beerothite, "As the LORD lives, the One who
has redeemed my life from every distress,[b]
10when the person told me, 'Look, Saul is
dead,' he thought he was a bearer of good
news, but I seized him and put him to death
at Ziklag.[c] That was my reward to him for his
news! 11How much more when wicked men
kill a righteous man in his own house on his
own bed! So now, should I not require his
blood from your hands and wipe you off the
earth?"[d]

12So David gave orders to the young men,
and they killed Rechab and Baanah. They cut
off their hands and feet and hung their bodies by the pool in Hebron, but they took Ish-
bosheth's head and buried it in Abner's tomb
in Hebron.[e]

David, King of Israel

5 All the tribes of Israel came to David at
Hebron[f] and said, "Here we are, your own
flesh and blood.[A,g] 2Even while Saul was king
over us, you were the one who led us out to
battle and brought us back.[h] The LORD also
said to you, 'You will shepherd My people Israel and be ruler over Israel.'"

3So all the elders of Israel came to the king
at Hebron. King David made a covenant with
them[i] at Hebron in the LORD's presence, and
they anointed David king over Israel.

4David was 30 years old when he began
his reign;[j] he reigned 40 years. 5In Hebron
he reigned over Judah seven years and six
months, and in Jerusalem he reigned 33 years
over all Israel and Judah.

6The king and his men marched to Jerusalem against the Jebusites[k] who inhabited the
land. The Jebusites had said to David: "You
will never get in here. Even the blind and
lame can repel you"; thinking, "David can't
get in here."

7Yet David did capture the stronghold of
·Zion, that is, the city of David.[l] 8He said that
day, "Whoever attacks the Jebusites must go
through the water shaft to reach the lame
and the blind who are despised by David."[B]
For this reason it is said, "The blind and the
lame will never enter the house."[C]

9David took up residence in the stronghold, which he named the city of David. He
built it up all the way around from the supporting terraces inward. 10David became
more and more powerful,[m] and the LORD God
of ·Hosts was with him.[n] 11King Hiram of Tyre
sent envoys to David; he also sent cedar logs,
carpenters, and stonemasons,[o] and they built
a palace for David. 12Then David knew that
the LORD had established him as king over Israel and had exalted his kingdom for the sake
of His people Israel.

13After he arrived from Hebron, David took
more concubines and wives from Jerusalem,
and more sons and daughters were born to
him. 14These are the names of those born to
him in Jerusalem: Shammua, Shobab, Nathan,[p] Solomon, 15Ibhar, Elishua, Nepheg,
Japhia, 16Elishama, Eliada, and Eliphelet.[q]

17When the Philistines heard that David
had been anointed king over Israel,[r] they all
went in search of David, but he heard about
it and went down to the stronghold.[s] 18So the
Philistines came and spread out in the Valley
of Rephaim.

19Then David inquired of the LORD:[t]
"Should I go to war against the Philistines?
Will you hand them over to me?"

The LORD replied to David, "Go, for I will
certainly hand the Philistines over to you."

20So David went to Baal-perazim and defeated them there and said, "Like a bursting
flood, the LORD has burst out against my enemies before me."[u] Therefore, he named that
place the Lord Bursts Out.[D] 21The Philistines
abandoned their idols there, and David and
his men carried them off.

22The Philistines came up again and spread

[a]**4:7** Dt 1:1
[b]**4:9** 1Kg 1:29
[c]**4:10** 2Sm 1:2-15
[d]**4:11** Gn 9:5-6
[e]**4:12** 2Sm 3:32
[f]**5:1-3** 1Ch 11:1-3
[g]**5:1** Gn 29:14
[h]**5:2** 1Sm 18:5,12-16
[i]**5:3** 2Sm 3:12-13,21
[j]**5:4-5** 1Kg 2:11; 1Ch 29:26-27
[k]**5:6** Jos 15:63; Jdg 1:21
[l]**5:7** Lk 2:4
[m]**5:10** 2Sm 3:1
[n]1Ch 11:9
[o]**5:11** 1Kg 5:1,10,18
[p]**5:14** Lk 3:31
[q]**5:11-16** 1Ch 3:5-8; 14:1-7
[r]**5:17-25** 1Ch 14:8-17
[s]**5:17** 1Sm 22:4-5; 2Sm 23:14
[t]**5:19** 2Sm 2:1
[u]**5:20** Is 28:21

[A]**5:1** Lit *your bone and flesh* [B]**5:8** Alt Hb tradition, LXX, Tg, Syr read *who despise David* [C]**5:8** Or *temple*, or *palace* [D]**5:20** Or *Baal-perazim*; 2Sm 6:8; 1Ch 13:11

out in the Valley of Rephaim. 23 So David inquired of the LORD, and He answered, "Do not
make a frontal assault. Circle around behind
them and attack them opposite the balsam
trees. 24 When you hear the sound of marching in the tops of the balsam trees, act deci-
sively, for then the LORD will have marched
out ahead of you to attack the camp of the
Philistines."[a] 25 So David did exactly as the
LORD commanded him, and he struck down
the Philistines all the way from Geba to Gezer.

David Moves the Ark

6 David again assembled all the choice
men in Israel,[b] 30,000. 2 He and all his
troops set out[c] to bring the ark of God from
Baale-judah.[A] The ark is called by the Name,
the name of ·Yahweh of ·Hosts who dwells
between the ·cherubim.[d] 3 They set the ark of
God on a new cart and transported it from
Abinadab's house, which was on the hill. Uzzah and Ahio,[B] sons of Abinadab, were guiding the cart[e] 4 and brought it with the ark of
God from Abinadab's house on the hill. Ahio
walked in front of the ark. 5 David and the
whole house of Israel were celebrating before
the LORD with all kinds of fir wood instruments,[C] lyres, harps, tambourines, sistrums,[D]
and cymbals.[f]
6 When they came to Nacon's threshing
floor, Uzzah reached out to the ark of God and
took hold of it because the oxen had stumbled. 7 Then the LORD's anger burned against
Uzzah,[g] and God struck him dead on the spot
for his irreverence,[h] and he died there next
to the ark of God. 8 David was angry because
of the LORD's outburst against Uzzah, so he
named that place an Outburst Against Uzzah,[E] as it is today. 9 David feared the LORD that
day and said, "How can the ark of the LORD
ever come to me?" 10 So he was not willing to
move the ark of the LORD to the city of David;[i]
instead, he took it to the house of Obed-edom
the Gittite. 11 The ark of the LORD remained in
his house three months, and the LORD blessed
Obed-edom[j] and his whole family.
12 It was reported to King David: "The LORD
has blessed Obed-edom's family and all that
belongs to him because of the ark of God." So
David went and had the ark of God brought
up from Obed-edom's house to the city of David with rejoicing.[k] 13 When those carrying the
ark of the LORD advanced six steps, he sacrificed an ox and a fattened calf.[l] 14 David was
dancing[F] with all his might before the LORD
wearing a linen ·ephod.[m] 15 He and the whole
house of Israel were bringing up the ark of
the LORD with shouts and the sound of the
ram's horn. 16 As the ark of the LORD was entering the city of David,[n] Saul's daughter Michal looked down from the window and saw
King David leaping and dancing before the
LORD, and she despised him in her heart.
17 They brought the ark of the LORD and set
it in its place inside the tent David had set up
for it.[o] Then David offered ·burnt offerings
and ·fellowship offerings in the LORD's presence. 18 When David had finished offering the
burnt offering and the fellowship offerings,
he blessed the people in the name of Yahweh of Hosts. 19 Then he distributed a loaf of
bread, a date cake, and a raisin cake to each
one in the entire Israelite community, both
men and women.[p] Then all the people left,
each to his own home.
20 When David returned home to bless his
household,[q] Saul's daughter Michal came out
to meet him. "How the king of Israel honored
himself today!" she said. "He exposed himself
today in the sight of the slave girls of his subjects like a vulgar person would expose himself."
21 David replied to Michal, "I was dancing[G]
before the LORD who chose me over your father and his whole family to appoint me ruler
over the LORD's people Israel.[r] I will celebrate
before the LORD, 22 and I will humble myself
even more and humiliate myself.[H,I] I will be
honored by the slave girls you spoke about."
23 And Saul's daughter Michal had no child to
the day of her death.

The LORD's Covenant with David

7 When the king had settled into his palace[s]
and the LORD had given him rest on every
side from all his enemies, 2 the king said to

[a] 5:24 2Kg 7:6 [b] 6:1 2Sm 10:9; 1Ch 19:10 [c] 6:2-11 1Ch 13:6-14 [d] 6:2 Ex 25:22; 1Sm 4:4 [e] 6:3 1Ch 15:2,12-15 [f] 6:5 Ps 150:3-5 [g] 6:7 Ex 25:14; Nm 4:5,15,20 [h] 1Sm 6:19-20 [i] 6:10 Lk 2:4 [j] 6:11 1Ch 26:4-8 [k] 6:12 1Ch 15:25 [l] 6:13 1Kg 8:1-5 [m] 6:14 Ex 28:4-28; 1Sm 2:18 [n] 6:16 Lk 2:4 [o] 6:17 1Ch 15:1; 2Ch 1:4 [p] 6:12-19 1Ch 15:25–16:3 [q] 6:20 1Ch 16:43 [r] 6:21 1Sm 13:14; 15:28 [s] 7:1 2Sm 5:11

[A] **6:2** = Kiriath-jearim in 1Sm 7:1; 1Ch 13:6; 2Ch 1:4 [B] **6:3** Or *and his brothers* [C] **6:5** DSS, LXX read *with tuned instruments with strength, with songs*; 1Ch 13:8 [D] **6:5** = an Egyptian percussion instrument [E] **6:8** Or *Perez-uzzah*; 2Sm 5:20 [F] **6:14** Or *whirling* [G] **6:21** LXX; MT omits *I was dancing* [H] **6:22** LXX reads *more and I will be humble in your eyes* [I] **6:22** Lit *more and I will be humble in my own eyes*

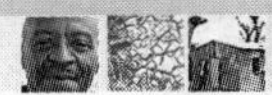

Nathan the prophet, "Look, I am living in a cedar house while the ark of God sits inside tent curtains."[a]

3So Nathan told the king, "Go and do all that is on your heart, for the LORD is with you."

4But that night the word of the LORD came to Nathan: 5"Go to My servant David and say, 'This is what the LORD says: Are you to build a house for Me to live in?[b] 6From the time I brought the Israelites out of Egypt until today I have not lived in a house; instead, I have been moving around with a tent as My dwelling.[c] 7In all My journeys with all the Israelites, have I ever asked anyone among the tribes of Israel, whom I commanded to shepherd My people Israel: Why haven't you built Me a house of cedar?'

8"Now this is what you are to say to My servant David: 'This is what the LORD of •Hosts says: I took you from the pasture and from following the sheep to be ruler over My people Israel.[d] 9I have been with you wherever you have gone, and I have destroyed all your enemies before you. I will make a name for you like that of the greatest in the land.[e] 10I will establish a place for My people Israel and plant them,[f] so that they may live there and not be disturbed again. Evildoers will not afflict them as they have done 11ever since the day I ordered judges to be over My people Israel.[g] I will give you rest from all your enemies.

"'The LORD declares to you: The LORD Himself will make a house for you. 12When your time comes and you rest with your fathers, I will raise up after you your descendant, who will come from your body, and I will establish his kingdom.[h] 13He will build a house for My name,[i] and I will establish the throne of his kingdom forever.[j] 14I will be a father to him, and he will be a son to Me.[k] When he does wrong, I will discipline him with a human rod and with blows from others. 15But My faithful love will never leave him[l] as I removed it from Saul; I removed him from your way.[m] 16Your house and kingdom will endure before Me[A] forever,[n] and your throne will be established forever.'"[o]

17Nathan spoke all these words and this entire vision to David.

David's Prayer of Thanksgiving

18Then King David went in,[p] sat in the LORD's presence, and said,

Who am I, Lord GOD, and what is my house that You have brought me this far? 19What You have done so far[B] was a little thing to You, Lord GOD, for You have also spoken about Your servant's house in the distant future. And this is a revelation[C] for mankind, Lord GOD. 20What more can David say to You? You know Your servant,[q] Lord GOD. 21Because of Your word and according to Your will, You have revealed all these great things to Your servant.

22This is why You are great,[r] Lord GOD. There is no one like You, and there is no God besides You,[s] as all we have heard confirms. 23And who is like Your people Israel? God came to one nation on earth in order to redeem a people for Himself, to make a name for Himself, and to perform for them[D] great and awesome acts, driving out nations and their gods before Your people You redeemed for Yourself from Egypt.[t] 24You established Your people Israel to be Your own people forever, and You, LORD, have become their God.[u]

25Now, LORD God, fulfill the promise forever that You have made to Your servant and his house. Do as You have promised, 26so that Your name will be exalted forever, when it is said, "The LORD of Hosts is God over Israel." The house of Your servant David[v] will be established before You 27since You, LORD of Hosts, God of Israel, have revealed this to Your servant when You said, "I will build a house for you." Therefore, Your servant has found the courage to pray this prayer to You. 28Lord GOD, You are God; Your words are true, and You have promised this grace to Your servant. 29Now, please bless Your servant's house so that it will continue

[a]**7:2** Ex 26:1; 1Ch 17:1
[b]**7:5** 1Kg 5:3; 8:19; 1Ch 22:8; 28:3
[c]**7:6** Ex 25:8-9; 26:1
[d]**7:8** 1Sm 16:11-13
[e]**7:9** 1Sm 18:14; 2Sm 5:10; 8:6
[f]**7:10** Ex 15:17
[g]**7:11** Jdg 2:14-16; 1Sm 12:9-11
[h]**7:12** Ac 13:23
[i]**7:13** 1Kg 5:2-5; 6:12; 8:18-19; Ac 7:47
[j]Lk 1:32-33
[k]**7:14** Ps 2:7; Heb 1:5; Rv 21:7
[l]**7:15** Ps 89:21,28,33
[m]1Sm 15:24-28
[n]**7:16** Lk 1:32-33
[o]Ps 89:3-4,26-37; Ezk 34:23-24; Rv 11:15
[p]**7:18-29** 1Ch 17:16-27
[q]**7:20** Ps 139:1-4
[r]**7:22** 1Ch 16:25; 2Ch 2:5
[s]Mk 12:32
[t]**7:23** Dt 4:32-38
[u]**7:24** Ex 6:7; Dt 26:18
[v]**7:26** Lk 1:69

[A]**7:16** Some Hb mss, LXX, Syr; other Hb mss read *you* [B]**7:19** Lit *Yet this* [C]**7:19** Or *custom*, or *instruction* [D]**7:23** Some Hb mss, Tg, Vg, Syr; other Hb mss read *you*

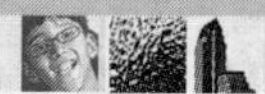

before You forever. For You, Lord God, have spoken, and with Your blessing Your servant's house will be blessed forever.[a]

David's Victories

8 After this, David defeated the Philistines,[b] subdued them, and took Metheg-ammah[A] from Philistine control.[B,c] 2 He also defeated the Moabites, and after making them lie down on the ground, he measured them off with a cord. He measured every two cord lengths of those to be put to death and one length of those to be kept alive. So the Moabites became David's subjects and brought tribute.[d]

3 David also defeated Hadadezer[e] son of Rehob, king of Zobah, who went to restore his control at the Euphrates River. 4 David captured 1,700 horsemen[C] and 20,000 foot soldiers from him, and he hamstrung all the horses[f] and kept 100 chariots.[D]

5 When the Arameans of Damascus[g] came to assist King Hadadezer of Zobah, David struck down 22,000 Aramean men. 6 Then he placed garrisons in Aram of Damascus, and the Arameans became David's subjects and brought tribute. The Lord made David victorious wherever he went.[h]

7 David took the gold shields of Hadadezer's officers and brought them to Jerusalem.[i] 8 King David also took huge quantities of bronze from Betah[E] and Berothai, Hadadezer's cities.

9 When King Toi of Hamath[j] heard that David had defeated the entire army of Hadadezer, 10 he sent his son Joram to King David to greet him and to congratulate him because David had fought against Hadadezer and defeated him, for Toi and Hadadezer had fought many wars. Joram had items of silver, gold, and bronze with him. 11 King David also dedicated these to the Lord, along with the silver and gold he had dedicated from all the nations he had subdued[k]— 12 from Edom,[F] Moab, the Ammonites, the Philistines, the Amalekites, and the spoil of Hadadezer son of Rehob, king of Zobah.

13 David made a reputation for himself when he returned from striking down 18,000 Edomites[G] in the Valley of Salt.[H,l] 14 He placed garrisons throughout Edom, and all the Edomites were subject to David.[m] The Lord made David victorious wherever he went.

15 So David reigned over all Israel, administering justice and righteousness for all his people.

16 Joab son of Zeruiah was over the army;
Jehoshaphat son of Ahilud was
court historian;
17 Zadok son of Ahitub
and Ahimelech son of Abiathar
were priests;
Seraiah was court secretary;
18 Benaiah son of Jehoiada was over
the Cherethites and the Pelethites;[n]
and David's sons were chief officials.[I]

David's Kindness to Mephibosheth

9 David asked, "Is there anyone remaining from Saul's family I can show kindness to because of Jonathan?"[o] 2 There was a servant of Saul's family named Ziba. They summoned him to David, and the king said to him, "Are you Ziba?"

"I am your servant," he replied.

3 So the king asked, "Is there anyone left of Saul's family that I can show the kindness of God to?"

Ziba said to the king, "There is still Jonathan's son who was injured in both feet."[p]

4 The king asked him, "Where is he?"

Ziba answered the king, "You'll find him in Lo-debar at the house of Machir son of Ammiel." 5 So King David had him brought from the house of Machir son of Ammiel in Lo-debar.

6 Mephibosheth son of Jonathan son of Saul came to David, bowed down to the ground and paid homage. David said, "Mephibosheth!"

"I am your servant," he replied.

7 "Don't be afraid," David said to him, "since I intend to show you kindness because of your father Jonathan. I will restore to you all your grandfather Saul's fields, and you will always eat meals at my table."

[a]**7:29** 2Sm 22:51; Ps 89:28-29
[b]**8:1-18** 1Ch 18:1-17
[c]**8:1** 2Sm 3:18
[d]**8:2** Nm 24:17
[e]**8:3** 2Sm 10:16-19
[f]**8:4** Jos 11:6
[g]**8:5** Gn 14:15; Ac 9:2-27
[h]**8:6** 2Sm 8:14
[i]**8:7** 2Kg 11:10; 2Ch 23:9
[j]**8:9** Gn 10:15-18; Ezk 47:16-17
[k]**8:11** 1Kg 7:51; 1Ch 26:26
[l]**8:13** 2Kg 14:7
[m]**8:14** Gn 25:23; 27:29-40; Nm 24:18
[n]**8:18** 2Sm 23:20-23
[o]**9:1** 1Sm 18:3; 20:14-17,42
[p]**9:3** 2Sm 4:4

[A]**8:1** Or *took control of the mother city*; Hb obscure [B]**8:1** LXX reads *them, and David took tribute out of the hand of the Philistines* [C]**8:4** LXX, DSS read *1,000 chariots and 7,000 horsemen* [D]**8:4** Or *chariot horses* [E]**8:8** Some LXX mss, Syr read *Tebah* [F]**8:12** Some Hb mss, LXX, Syr; other Hb mss read *Aram*; 1Ch 18:11 [G]**8:13** Some Hb mss, LXX, Syr; other Hb mss read *Arameans*; 1Ch 18:12 [H]**8:13** = the Dead Sea region [I]**8:18** LXX; MT reads *were priests*; 1Ch 18:17

8 Mephibosheth bowed down and said, "What is your servant that you take an interest in a dead dog like me?"

9 Then the king summoned Saul's attendant Ziba and said to him, "I have given to your master's grandson all that belonged to Saul and his family. 10 You, your sons, and your servants are to work the ground for him, and you are to bring in the crops so your master's grandson will have food to eat. But Mephibosheth, your master's grandson, is always to eat at my table." Now Ziba had 15 sons and 20 servants.

11 Ziba said to the king, "Your servant will do all my lord the king commands."

So Mephibosheth ate at David's[A] table just like one of the king's sons. 12 Mephibosheth had a young son whose name was Mica.[a] All those living in Ziba's house were Mephibosheth's servants. 13 However, Mephibosheth lived in Jerusalem because he always ate at the king's table. His feet had been injured.

War with the Ammonites

10 Some time later the king of the Ammonites died, and his son Hanun became king in his place.[b] 2 Then David said, "I'll show kindness to Hanun son of Nahash, just as his father showed kindness to me."

So David sent his emissaries to console Hanun concerning his father. However, when they arrived in the land of the Ammonites, 3 the Ammonite leaders said to Hanun their lord, "Just because David has sent men with condolences for you, do you really believe he's showing respect for your father? Instead, hasn't David sent his emissaries in order to scout out the city, spy on it, and demolish it?"[c] 4 So Hanun took David's emissaries, shaved off half their beards, cut their clothes in half at the hips, and sent them away.[d]

5 When this was reported to David, he sent someone to meet them, since they were deeply humiliated. The king said, "Stay in Jericho until your beards grow back; then return."

6 When the Ammonites realized they had become repulsive to David, they hired 20,000 foot soldiers from the Arameans of Beth-rehob and Zobah, 1,000 men from the king of Maacah, and 12,000 men from Tob.

7 David heard about it and sent Joab and all the fighting men. 8 The Ammonites marched out and lined up in battle formation at the entrance to the city gate while the Arameans of Zobah and Rehob and the men of Tob and Maacah were in the field by themselves. 9 When Joab saw that there was a battle line in front of him and another behind him, he chose some men out of all the elite troops of Israel and lined up in battle formation to engage the Arameans. 10 He placed the rest of the forces under the command of his brother Abishai who lined up in battle formation to engage the Ammonites.

11 "If the Arameans are too strong for me," Joab said, "then you will be my help. However, if the Ammonites are too strong for you, I'll come to help you. 12 Be strong! We must prove ourselves strong for our people and for the cities of our God.[e] May the LORD's will be done."[B]

13 Joab and his troops advanced to fight against the Arameans, and they fled before him. 14 When the Ammonites saw that the Arameans had fled, they too fled before Abishai and entered the city. So Joab withdrew from the attack against the Ammonites and went to Jerusalem.

15 When the Arameans saw that they had been defeated by Israel, they regrouped. 16 Hadadezer sent messengers to bring the Arameans who were across the Euphrates River, and they came to Helam with Shobach, commander of Hadadezer's army, leading them.

17 When this was reported to David, he gathered all Israel, crossed the Jordan, and went to Helam. Then the Arameans lined up in formation to engage David in battle and fought against him. 18 But the Arameans fled before Israel, and David killed 700 of their charioteers and 40,000 foot soldiers.[C] He also struck down Shobach commander of their army, who died there. 19 When all the kings who were Hadadezer's subjects saw that they had been defeated by Israel, they made peace with Israel and became their subjects. After this, the Arameans were afraid to ever help the Ammonites again.

[a] **9:12** 1Ch 8:34 [b] **10:1-19** 1Ch 19:1-19 [c] **10:3** 1Sm 11:1-10 [d] **10:4** Is 7:20; 20:4 [e] **10:12** Dt 31:6; Jos 1:6

[A] **9:11** LXX; Syr reads *the king's*; Vg reads *your*; MT reads *my* [B] **10:12** Lit *the LORD do what is good in His eyes* [C] **10:18** Some LXX mss; MT reads *horsemen*; 1Ch 19:18

David's Adultery with Bathsheba

11 In the spring when kings march out to war, David sent Joab with his officers and all Israel. They destroyed the Ammonites and besieged Rabbah, but David remained in Jerusalem.[a]

2 One evening David got up from his bed and strolled around on the roof of the palace. From the roof he saw a woman bathing — a very beautiful woman. 3 So David sent someone to inquire about her, and he reported, "This is Bathsheba,[b] daughter of Eliam and wife of Uriah[c] the Hittite."[A]

4 David sent messengers to get her, and when she came to him, he slept with her. Now she had just been purifying herself from her uncleanness.[d] Afterward, she returned home. 5 The woman conceived and sent word to inform David: "I am pregnant."

6 David sent orders to Joab: "Send me Uriah the Hittite." So Joab sent Uriah to David. 7 When Uriah came to him, David asked how Joab and the troops were doing and how the war was going. 8 Then he said to Uriah, "Go down to your house and wash your feet." So Uriah left the palace, and a gift from the king followed him. 9 But Uriah slept at the door of the palace with all his master's servants; he did not go down to his house.

10 When it was reported to David, "Uriah didn't go home," David questioned Uriah, "Haven't you just come from a journey? Why didn't you go home?"

11 Uriah answered David, "The ark, Israel, and Judah are dwelling in tents, and my master Joab and his soldiers[B] are camping in the open field. How can I enter my house to eat and drink and sleep with my wife? As surely as you live and by your life, I will not do this!"[e]

12 "Stay here today also," David said to Uriah, "and tomorrow I will send you back." So Uriah stayed in Jerusalem that day and the next. 13 Then David invited Uriah to eat and drink with him, and David got him drunk. He went out in the evening to lie down on his cot with his master's servants, but he did not go home.

Uriah's Death Arranged

14 The next morning David wrote a letter to Joab and sent it with Uriah. 15 In the letter he wrote:

> Put Uriah[f] at the front of the fiercest fighting, then withdraw from him so that he is struck down and dies.

16 When Joab was besieging the city, he put Uriah in the place where he knew the best enemy soldiers were. 17 Then the men of the city came out and attacked Joab, and some of the men from David's soldiers fell in battle; Uriah the Hittite also died.

18 Joab sent someone to report to David all the details of the battle. 19 He commanded the messenger, "When you've finished telling the king all the details of the battle — 20 if the king's anger gets stirred up and he asks you, 'Why did you get so close to the city to fight? Didn't you realize they would shoot from the top of the wall? 21 At Thebez, who struck Abimelech son of Jerubbesheth?[C,D] Didn't a woman drop an upper millstone on him from the top of the wall so that he died?[g] Why did you get so close to the wall?' — then say, 'Your servant Uriah the Hittite is dead also.'"

22 Then the messenger left.

When he arrived, he reported to David all that Joab had sent him to tell. 23 The messenger reported to David, "The men gained the advantage over us and came out against us in the field, but we counterattacked right up to the entrance of the gate. 24 However, the archers shot down on your soldiers from the top of the wall, and some of the king's soldiers died. Your servant Uriah the Hittite is also dead."

25 David told the messenger, "Say this to Joab: 'Don't let this matter upset you because the sword devours all alike. Intensify your fight against the city and demolish it.' Encourage him."

26 When Uriah's[h] wife heard that her husband Uriah had died, she mourned for him.[E] 27 When the time of mourning ended, David had her brought to his house. She became his wife and bore him a son. However, the LORD considered what David had done to be evil.[i]

Nathan's Parable and David's Repentance

12 So the LORD sent Nathan to David.[j] When he arrived, he said to him:

> There were two men in a certain city, one rich and the other poor. 2 The rich man

[a] **11:1** 2Sm 12:26-29; 1Ch 20:1
[b] **11:3** 2Sm 12:24; Ps 51
[c] Mt 1:6
[d] **11:4** Lv 15:18-30; 18:19
[e] **11:11** 1Sm 21:5
[f] **11:15** Mt 1:6
[g] **11:21** Jdg 9:50-54
[h] **11:26** Mt 1:6
[i] **11:27** 2Sm 12:9; 15:19
[j] **12:1** Ps 51 title

[A] **11:3** DSS add *Joab's armor-bearer* [B] **11:11** Lit *servants* [C] **11:21** LXX reads *Jerubbaal* [D] **11:21** = Gideon [E] **11:26** Lit *her husband*

had a large number of sheep and cattle,
3 but the poor man had nothing except
one small ewe lamb that he had bought.
He raised it, and it grew up, living with
him and his children. It shared his meager food and drank from his cup; it slept
in his arms, and it was like a daughter
to him. 4 Now a traveler came to the rich
man, but the rich man could not bring
himself to take one of his own sheep or
cattle to prepare for the traveler who
had come to him. Instead, he took the
poor man's lamb and prepared it for his
guest.[A]

5 David was infuriated with the man and
said to Nathan: "As the LORD lives, the man
who did this deserves to die! 6 Because he has
done this thing and shown no pity, he must
pay four lambs for that lamb."[a]

7 Nathan replied to David, "You are the
man! This is what the LORD God of Israel
says: 'I anointed you king over Israel,[b] and I
delivered you from the hand of Saul. 8 I gave
your master's house to you and your master's wives into your arms,[B] and I gave you the
house of Israel and Judah, and if that was not
enough, I would have given you even more.
9 Why then have you despised the command
of the LORD by doing what I consider[C] evil?[c]
You struck down Uriah[d] the Hittite with
the sword and took his wife as your own
wife — you murdered him with the Ammonite's sword.[e] 10 Now therefore, the sword will
never leave your house[f] because you despised
Me and took the wife of Uriah the Hittite to
be your own wife.'

11 "This is what the LORD says,[g] 'I am going
to bring disaster on you from your own family: I will take your wives and give them to another[D] before your very eyes, and he will sleep
with them publicly.[E] 12 You acted in secret, but
I will do this before all Israel and in broad
daylight.'"[F]

13 David responded to Nathan, "I have
sinned against the LORD."[h]

Then Nathan replied to David, "The LORD
has taken away your sin; you will not die.[i]
14 However, because you treated[G] the LORD

[a]12:6 Ex 22:1; Lk 19:8
[b]12:7 1Sm 16:13
[c]12:9 Nm 15:30-31; 1Sm 15:19
[d]Mt 1:6
[e]2Sm 11:14-17
[f]12:10 2Sm 12:18; 13:28-29; 18:14-18; 1Kg 2:22-25; 2Kg 11:1
[g]12:11-12 2Sm 16:21-22
[h]12:13 2Sm 24:10; Ps 32:5; 51:4
[i]Lv 20:10; 24:17; Ps 32:1-5; Pr 28:13
[j]12:14 2Sm 12:18
[k]12:15 Mt 1:6
[l]12:16 2Sm 13:31; Jb 1:20
[m]12:23 Jb 7:8-10
[n]12:24 Gn 37:35; Ps 23:4; 119:76,82
[o]1Ch 22:9

with such contempt in this matter, the son
born to you will die."[j] 15 Then Nathan went
home.

The Death of Bathsheba's Son

The LORD struck the baby that Uriah's[k] wife
had borne to David, and he became ill. 16 David pleaded with God for the boy. He fasted,
went home, and spent the night lying on the
ground.[l] 17 The elders of his house stood beside him to get him up from the ground, but
he was unwilling and would not eat anything
with them.

18 On the seventh day the baby died. But David's servants were afraid to tell him the baby
was dead. They said, "Look, while the baby
was alive, we spoke to him, and he wouldn't
listen to us. So how can we tell him the baby is
dead? He may do something desperate."

19 When David saw that his servants were
whispering to each other, he guessed that the
baby was dead. So he asked his servants, "Is
the baby dead?"

"He is dead," they replied.

20 Then David got up from the ground.
He washed, anointed himself, changed his
clothes, went to the LORD's house, and worshiped. Then he went home and requested
something to eat. So they served him food,
and he ate.

21 His servants asked him, "What did you
just do? While the baby was alive, you fasted
and wept, but when he died, you got up and
ate food."

22 He answered, "While the baby was alive,
I fasted and wept because I thought, 'Who
knows? The LORD may be gracious to me and
let him live.' 23 But now that he is dead, why
should I fast? Can I bring him back again? I'll
go to him, but he will never return to me."[m]

The Birth of Solomon

24 Then David comforted[n] his wife Bathsheba; he went and slept with her. She gave
birth to a son and named[H] him Solomon.[I,o]
The LORD loved him, 25 and He sent a message
through Nathan the prophet, who named[J]
him Jedidiah,[K] because of the LORD.

[A]12:4 Lit *for the man who had come to him* [B]12:8 Lit *bosom* [C]12:9 Alt Hb tradition reads *what He considers* [D]12:11 Or *to your neighbor* [E]12:11 Lit *in the eyes of this sun* [F]12:12 Lit *and before the sun* [G]12:14 Ancient Jewish tradition, one LXX ms; MT reads *treated the enemies of*; DSS read *treated the word of* [H]12:24 Alt Hb tradition reads *he named* [I]12:24 In Hb, the name Solomon sounds like "peace." [J]12:25 Or *prophet to name* [K]12:25 = Beloved of the LORD

Capture of the City of Rabbah

26 Joab fought against Rabbah of the Ammonites[a] and captured the royal fortress.
27 Then Joab sent messengers to David to say,
"I have fought against Rabbah and have also
captured the water supply. 28 Now therefore,
assemble the rest of the troops, lay siege
to the city, and capture it. Otherwise I will
be the one to capture the city, and it will be
named after me." 29 So David assembled all the
troops and went to Rabbah; he fought against
it and captured it. 30 He took the crown from
the head of their king,[A] and it was placed on
David's head. The crown weighed 75 pounds[B]
of gold, and it had a precious stone in it. In
addition, David took away a large quantity
of plunder from the city. 31 He removed the
people who were in the city and put them to
work with saws, iron picks, and iron axes, and
to labor at brickmaking.[b] He did the same to
all the Ammonite cities. Then he and all his
troops returned to Jerusalem.

Amnon Rapes Tamar

13 Some time passed. David's son Absalom[c] had a beautiful sister named
Tamar,[d] and David's son Amnon[e] was infatuated with her. 2 Amnon was frustrated to the
point of making himself sick over his sister
Tamar because she was a virgin, but it seemed
impossible to do anything to her. 3 Amnon
had a friend named Jonadab, a son of David's
brother Shimeah.[f] Jonadab was a very shrewd
man, 4 and he asked Amnon, "Why are you,
the king's son, so miserable every morning?
Won't you tell me?"

Amnon replied, "I'm in love with Tamar,
my brother Absalom's sister."

5 Jonadab said to him, "Lie down on your
bed and pretend you're sick. When your father comes to see you, say to him, 'Please let
my sister Tamar come and give me something
to eat. Let her prepare food in my presence so
I can watch and eat from her hand.'"

6 So Amnon lay down and pretended to be
sick. When the king came to see him, Amnon
said to him, "Please let my sister Tamar come
and make a couple of cakes in my presence so
I can eat from her hand."

[a] **12:26-31** 1Ch 20:1-3
[b] **12:31** Ex 1:13-14
[c] **13:1** 2Sm 3:3
[d] 1Ch 3:9
[e] 2Sm 3:2
[f] **13:3** 1Sm 16:9; 17:13; 1Ch 2:13
[g] **13:12** Lv 18:9; 20:17
[h] **13:19** Jr 2:37
[i] **13:20** Is 54:1; 62:4

7 David sent word to Tamar at the palace:
"Please go to your brother Amnon's house
and prepare a meal for him."

8 Then Tamar went to his house while
Amnon was lying down. She took dough,
kneaded it, made cakes in his presence, and
baked them. 9 She brought the pan and set
it down in front of him, but he refused to
eat. Amnon said, "Everyone leave me!" And
everyone left him. 10 "Bring the meal to the
bedroom," Amnon told Tamar, "so I can eat
from your hand." Tamar took the cakes she
had made and went to her brother Amnon's
bedroom. 11 When she brought them to him
to eat, he grabbed her and said,[C] "Come sleep
with me, my sister!"

12 "Don't, my brother!" she cried. "Don't
humiliate me, for such a thing should never
be done in Israel.[g] Don't do this horrible
thing! 13 Where could I ever go with my disgrace? And you — you would be like one of
the immoral men in Israel! Please, speak to
the king, for he won't keep me from you."
14 But he refused to listen to her, and because
he was stronger than she was, he raped
her.

15 After this, Amnon hated Tamar with such
intensity that the hatred he hated her with
was greater than the love he had loved her
with. "Get out of here!" he said.

16 "No," she cried,[D] "sending me away is
much worse than the great wrong you've already done to me!" But he refused to listen
to her. 17 Instead, he called to the servant who
waited on him: "Throw this woman out and
bolt the door behind her!" 18 Amnon's servant
threw her out and bolted the door behind
her. Now Tamar was wearing a long-sleeved[E]
garment, because this is what the king's virgin daughters wore. 19 Tamar put ashes on her
head and tore the long-sleeved garment she
was wearing. She put her hand on her head[h]
and went away crying out.

20 Her brother Absalom said to her: "Has
your brother Amnon been with you? Be quiet
for now, my sister. He is your brother. Don't
take this thing to heart." So Tamar lived as a
desolate woman[i] in the house of her brother
Absalom.

[A] **12:30** LXX reads *of Milcom*; some emend to *Molech*; 1Kg 11:5,33
[B] **12:30** Lit *a talent* [C] **13:11** Lit *said to her* [D] **13:16** Lit *she said to him*
[E] **13:18** Or *an ornamented*; Gn 37:3

Absalom Murders Amnon

21When King David heard about all these
things, he was furious.[A] 22Absalom didn't say
anything to Amnon, either good or bad, because he hated Amnon since he disgraced his
sister Tamar.

23Two years later, Absalom's sheepshearers
were at Baal-hazor near Ephraim, and Absalom invited all the king's sons. 24Then he
went to the king and said, "Your servant has
just hired sheepshearers. Will the king and
his servants please come with your servant?"

25The king replied to Absalom, "No, my son,
we should not all go, or we would be a burden to you." Although Absalom urged him, he
wasn't willing to go, though he did bless him.

26"If not," Absalom said, "please let my
brother Amnon go with us."

The king asked him, "Why should he go
with you?" 27But Absalom urged him, so he
sent Amnon and all the king's sons.[B]

28Now Absalom commanded his young
men, "Watch Amnon until he is in a good
mood from the wine. When I order you to
strike Amnon, then kill him. Don't be afraid.
Am I not the one who has commanded you?
Be strong and courageous!"[a] 29So Absalom's
young men did to Amnon just as Absalom had
commanded. Then all the rest of the king's
sons got up, and each fled on his mule.

30While they were on the way, a report
reached David: "Absalom struck down all the
king's sons; not even one of them survived!"
31In response the king stood up, tore his
clothes, and lay down on the ground, and all
his servants stood by with their clothes torn.[b]

32But Jonadab, son of David's brother
Shimeah,[c] spoke up: "My lord must not think
they have killed all the young men, the king's
sons, because only Amnon is dead. In fact,
Absalom has planned this[C] ever since the day
Amnon disgraced his sister Tamar. 33So now,
my lord the king, don't take seriously the
report that says all the king's sons are dead.
Only Amnon is dead."

34Meanwhile, Absalom had fled. When the
young man who was standing watch looked
up, there were many people coming from the
road west of him from the side of the mountain.[D] 35Jonadab said to the king, "Look, the
king's sons have come! It's exactly like your
servant said." 36Just as he finished speaking,
the king's sons entered and wept loudly. Then
the king and all his servants also wept bitterly.

37Now Absalom fled and went to Talmai
son of Ammihud, king of Geshur.[d] And David
mourned for his son[E] every day. 38Absalom
had fled and gone to Geshur where he stayed
three years. 39Then King David[F] longed to go
to Absalom, for David had finished grieving
over Amnon's death.

Absalom Restored to David

14 Joab son of Zeruiah observed that the
king's mind was on Absalom. 2So Joab
sent someone to Tekoa[e] to bring a clever[f]
woman from there. He told her, "Pretend to
be in mourning: dress in mourning clothes
and don't put on any oil.[g] Act like a woman
who has been mourning for the dead for a
long time. 3Go to the king and speak these
words to him." Then Joab told her exactly
what to say.

4When the woman from Tekoa came[G] to the
king, she fell with her face to the ground in
homage and said, "Help me, my king!"

5"What's the matter?" the king asked her.

"To tell the truth, I am a widow; my husband died," she said.[h] 6"Your servant had two
sons. They were fighting in the field with
no one to separate them, and one struck the
other and killed him. 7Now the whole clan
has risen up against your servant and said,
'Hand over the one who killed his brother so
we may put him to death for the life of the
brother he murdered. We will destroy the
heir!' They would extinguish my one remaining ember by not preserving my husband's
name or posterity on earth."

8The king told the woman, "Go home. I will
issue a command on your behalf."

9Then the woman of Tekoa said to the king,
"My lord the king, may any blame be on me[i]
and my father's house, and may the king and
his throne be innocent."

10"Whoever speaks to you," the king said,

[a]**13:28** Jos 1:9 [b]**13:31** 2Sm 1:11 [c]**13:32** 2Sm 13:3-5 [d]**13:37** 2Sm 3:3; 1Ch 3:2 [e]**14:2** 2Ch 20:20; Am 1:1 [f]2Sm 13:3; 14:20; 20:16; Jb 5:13 [g]Dn 10:2-3 [h]**14:5** 2Sm 12:1 [i]**14:9** 1Sm 25:24

[A]**13:21** LXX, DSS add *but he did not grieve the spirit of Amnon his son, for he loved him because he was his firstborn*; 1Kg 1:6 [B]**13:27** LXX adds *And Absalom prepared a feast like a royal feast.* [C]**13:32** Lit *In fact, it was established on the mouth of Absalom* [D]**13:34** LXX adds *And the watchman came and reported to the king saying, "I see men on the Horonaim road on the side of the mountain."* [E]**13:37** Probably Amnon [F]**13:39** DSS, LXX, Tg read *David's spirit* [G]**14:4** Some Hb mss, LXX, Syr, Tg, Vg; other Hb mss read *spoke*

"bring him to me. He will not trouble you
again!"
11 She replied, "Please, may the king invoke
the LORD your God, so that the avenger of
blood will not increase the loss, and they will
not eliminate my son!"[a]
"As the LORD lives," he vowed, "not a hair of
your son will fall to the ground."[b]
12 Then the woman said, "Please, may your
servant speak a word to my lord the king?"
"Speak," he replied.
13 The woman asked, "Why have you devised
something similar against the people of God?
When the king spoke as he did about this
matter, he has pronounced his own ˚guilt.
The king has not brought back his own banished one. 14 We will certainly die[c] and be like
water poured out on the ground, which can't
be recovered. But God would not take away
a life; He would devise plans so that the one
banished from Him does not remain banished.
15 "Now therefore, I've come to present this
matter to my lord the king because the people
have made me afraid. Your servant thought: I
must speak to the king. Perhaps the king will
grant his servant's request. 16 The king will
surely listen in order to rescue his servant
from the hand of this man who would eliminate both me and my son from God's inheritance. 17 Your servant thought: May the word
of my lord the king bring relief, for my lord
the king is able to discern the good and the
bad like the Angel of God. May the LORD your
God be with you."
18 Then the king answered the woman, "I'm
going to ask you something; don't conceal it
from me!"
"Let my lord the king speak," the woman
replied.
19 The king asked, "Did Joab put you up to[A]
all this?"
The woman answered. "As you live, my lord
the king, no one can turn to the right or left
from all my lord the king says. Yes, your servant Joab is the one who gave orders to me; he
told your servant exactly what to say. 20 Joab
your servant has done this to address the issue indirectly,[B] but my lord has wisdom like
the wisdom of the Angel of God, knowing everything on earth."
21 Then the king said to Joab, "I hereby grant
this request. Go, bring back the young man
Absalom."
22 Joab fell with his face to the ground in
homage and praised the king. "Today," Joab
said, "your servant knows I have found favor
with you, my lord the king, because the king
has granted the request of your servant."
23 So Joab got up, went to Geshur, and
brought Absalom[d] to Jerusalem. 24 However,
the king added, "He may return to his house,
but he may not see my face." So Absalom returned to his house, but he did not see the
king.[C]
25 No man in all Israel was as handsome and
highly praised as Absalom. From the sole of
his foot to the top of his head, he did not have
a single flaw. 26 When he shaved his head — he
shaved it every year because his hair got so
heavy for him that he had to shave it off — he
would weigh the hair from his head and it
would be five pounds[D] according to the royal
standard.
27 Three sons were born to Absalom, and a
daughter named Tamar, who was a beautiful
woman. 28 Absalom resided in Jerusalem two
years but never saw the king. 29 Then Absalom
sent for Joab in order to send him to the king,
but Joab was unwilling to come. So he sent
again, a second time, but he still wouldn't
come. 30 Then Absalom said to his servants,
"See, Joab has a field right next to mine, and
he has barley there. Go and set fire to it!" So
Absalom's servants set the field on fire.[E]
31 Then Joab came to Absalom's house and
demanded, "Why did your servants set my
field on fire?"
32 "Look," Absalom explained to Joab, "I sent
for you and said, 'Come here. I want to send
you to the king to ask: Why have I come back
from Geshur? I'd be better off if I were still
there.' So now, let me see the king. If I am
guilty, let him kill me."
33 Joab went to the king and told him. So David summoned Absalom, who came to the king
and bowed down with his face to the ground
before him. Then the king kissed Absalom.

[a]**14:11** Nm 35:19-21; Dt 19:12
[b]Ac 27:34
[c]**14:14** Jn 8:51
[d]**14:23** 2Sm 13:38

[A]**14:19** Lit *Is the hand of Joab in* [B]**14:20** Lit *to go around the face of the matter* [C]**14:24** Lit *king's face* [D]**14:26** Lit *200 shekels* [E]**14:30** DSS, LXX add *So Joab's servants came to him with their clothes torn and said, "Absalom's servants have set the field on fire!"*

Absalom's Revolt

15 After this, Absalom got himself a chariot, horses, and 50 men to run before
him.[a] 2 He would get up early and stand beside the road leading to the city ·gate.[b] Whenever anyone had a grievance to bring before
the king for settlement, Absalom called out to
him and asked, "What city are you from?" If
he replied, "Your servant is from one of the
tribes of Israel," 3 Absalom said to him, "Look,
your claims are good and right, but the king
does not have anyone to listen to you." 4 He
added, "If only someone would appoint me
judge in the land. Then anyone who had a
grievance or dispute could come to me, and I
would make sure he received justice." 5 When
a person approached to bow down to him,
Absalom reached out his hand, took hold of
him, and kissed him. 6 Absalom did this to
all the Israelites who came to the king for a
settlement. So Absalom stole the hearts of the
men of Israel.

7 When four[A] years had passed, Absalom
said to the king, "Please let me go to Hebron
to fulfill a vow I made to the LORD. 8 For your
servant made a vow when I lived in Geshur
of Aram,[c] saying: If the LORD really brings me
back to Jerusalem, I will worship the LORD in
Hebron."[B,d]

9 "Go in peace," the king said to him.[e] So he
went to Hebron.

10 Then Absalom sent messengers throughout the tribes of Israel with this message:
"When you hear the sound of the ram's horn,
you are to say, 'Absalom has become king in
Hebron!'"[f]

11 Two hundred men from Jerusalem went
with Absalom. They had been invited and
were going innocently, for they knew nothing
about the whole matter. 12 While he was offering the sacrifices, Absalom sent for David's
adviser Ahithophel the Gilonite,[g] from his
city of Giloh. So the conspiracy grew strong,
and the people supporting Absalom continued to increase.

13 Then an informer came to David and reported, "The hearts of the men of Israel are
with Absalom."

14 David said to all the servants with him in
Jerusalem, "Get up. We have to flee, or we will
not escape from Absalom![h] Leave quickly, or
he will soon overtake us, heap disaster on us,
and strike the city with the edge of the sword."

15 The king's servants said to him, "Whatever my lord the king decides, we are your
servants." 16 Then the king set out, and his
entire household followed him. But he left
behind 10 concubines to take care of the palace. 17 So the king set out, and all the people
followed him. They stopped at the last house
18 while all his servants marched past him.
Then all the Cherethites, the Pelethites, and
the Gittites — 600 men who came with him
from Gath[i] — marched past the king.

19 The king said to Ittai the Gittite,[j] "Why are
you also going with us? Go back and stay with
the new king since you're both a foreigner
and an exile from your homeland. 20 Besides,
you only arrived yesterday; should I make
you wander around with us today while I go
wherever I can? Go back and take your brothers with you. May the LORD show you kindness and faithfulness."

21 But in response, Ittai vowed to the king,
"As the LORD lives and as my lord the king
lives, wherever my lord the king is, whether
it means life or death, your servant will be
there!"

22 "March on," David replied to Ittai. So Ittai
the Gittite marched past with all his men and
the children who were with him. 23 Everyone
in the countryside was weeping loudly while
all the people were marching past. As the
king was crossing the Kidron Valley, all the
people were marching past on the road that
leads to the desert.

24 Zadok was also there, and all the Levites
with him were carrying the ark of the covenant of God. They set the ark of God down,
and Abiathar offered sacrifices[C] until the
people had finished marching past.[k] 25 Then
the king instructed Zadok, "Return the ark of
God to the city.[l] If I find favor in the LORD's
eyes, He will bring me back and allow me to
see both it and its dwelling place.[m] 26 However,
if He should say, 'I do not delight in you,' then
here I am — He can do with me whatever
pleases Him."[D,n]

[a] **15:1** 1Sm 8:11; 1Kg 1:5
[b] **15:2** Ru 4:1-11; 2Sm 19:8; Jb 29:7
[c] **15:8** 2Sm 13:37-38
[d] Gn 28:20-21; 1Sm 1:11
[e] **15:9** 1Sm 1:17
[f] **15:10** 1Kg 1:33-34; 2Kg 9:13
[g] **15:12** 1Ch 27:33; Ps 41:9; 55:12-14
[h] **15:14** Ps 3 title
[i] **15:18** 1Sm 27:2-7
[j] **15:19** 2Sm 18:2
[k] **15:24** 2Sm 8:17; 20:25
[l] **15:25** 1Sm 4:3
[m] Ps 43:3
[n] **15:26** 1Sm 3:18

[A] **15:7** Some LXX mss, Syr, Vg; other LXX mss, MT read *40* [B] **15:8** Some LXX mss; MT omits *in Hebron* [C] **15:24** Or *Abiathar went up* [D] **15:26** Lit *me what is good in His eyes*

27 The king also said to Zadok the priest,[a] "Look,[A] return to the city in peace and your two sons with you: your son Ahimaaz and Abiathar's son Jonathan. 28 Remember, I'll wait at the fords of the wilderness until word comes from you to inform me." 29 So Zadok and Abiathar returned the ark of God to Jerusalem and stayed there.

30 David was climbing the slope of the Mount of Olives, weeping as he ascended. His head was covered, and he was walking barefoot.[b] Each of the people with him covered their heads and went up, weeping as they ascended.

31 Then someone reported to David: "Ahithophel is among the conspirators with Absalom."

"LORD," David pleaded, "please turn the counsel of Ahithophel into foolishness!"[c]

32 When David came to the summit where he used to worship God, Hushai the Archite[d] was there to meet him with his robe torn and dust on his head. 33 David said to him, "If you go away with me, you'll be a burden to me, 34 but if you return to the city and tell Absalom, 'I will be your servant, my king! Previously, I was your father's servant, but now I will be your servant,' then you can counteract Ahithophel's counsel for me. 35 Won't Zadok and Abiathar the priests be there with you? Report everything you hear from the king's palace to Zadok and Abiathar the priests. 36 Take note: their two sons, Zadok's son Ahimaaz and Abiathar's son Jonathan, are there with them. Send me everything you hear through them." 37 So Hushai,[e] David's personal adviser, entered Jerusalem just as Absalom was entering the city.

Ziba Helps David

16 When David had gone a little beyond the summit,[B] Ziba, Mephibosheth's servant,[f] was right there to meet him. He had a pair of saddled donkeys loaded with 200 loaves of bread, 100 clusters of raisins, 100 bunches of summer fruit, and a skin of wine. 2 The king said to Ziba, "Why do you have these?"

Ziba answered, "The donkeys are for the king's household to ride, the bread and summer fruit are for the young men to eat, and the wine is for those to drink who become exhausted in the desert."

3 "Where is your master's grandson?" the king asked.

"Why, he's staying in Jerusalem," Ziba replied to the king, "for he said, 'Today, the house of Israel will restore my grandfather's kingdom to me.'"

4 The king said to Ziba, "All that belongs to Mephibosheth is now yours!"[g]

"I bow before you," Ziba said. "May you look favorably on me, my lord the king!"

Shimei Curses David

5 When King David got to Bahurim, a man belonging to the family of the house of Saul was just coming out. His name was Shimei son of Gera,[h] and he was yelling curses as he approached. 6 He threw stones at David and at all the royal[C] servants, the people and the warriors on David's right and left. 7 Shimei said as he cursed: "Get out, get out, you worthless murderer! 8 The LORD has paid you back for all the blood of the house of Saul in whose place you became king, and the LORD has handed the kingdom over to your son Absalom. Look, you are in trouble because you're a murderer!"

9 Then Abishai son of Zeruiah said to the king, "Why should this dead dog[i] curse my lord the king?[j] Let me go over and cut his head off!"

10 The king replied, "Sons of Zeruiah, do we agree on anything?[k] He curses[l] me this way because the LORD[D] told him, 'Curse David!' Therefore, who can say, 'Why did you do that?'" 11 Then David said to Abishai and all his servants, "Look, my own son, my own flesh and blood,[E] intends to take my life[m]—how much more now this Benjaminite! Leave him alone and let him curse me; the LORD has told him to. 12 Perhaps the LORD will see my affliction[F] and restore goodness to me instead of Shimei's curses today." 13 So David and his men proceeded along the road as Shimei was

[a] **15:27** 2Sm 8:17; 20:25-26; 1Kg 1:7-8
[b] **15:30** Is 20:2-4; Mc 1:8
[c] **15:31** 2Sm 16:21; 17:14,23
[d] **15:32** Jos 16:2
[e] **15:37** 1Ch 27:33
[f] **16:1** 2Sm 9:12
[g] **16:4** 2Sm 9:3-11
[h] **16:5** 1Kg 2:8-9,36-46
[i] **16:9** 1Sm 24:14; 2Sm 9:8
[j] Ex 22:28
[k] **16:10** 2Sm 3:39; 19:22
[l] 1Sm 17:43; 2Sm 16:5; Ec 7:21-22
[m] **16:11** 2Sm 12:10-11

[A] **15:27** LXX; MT reads *Are you a seer?* [B] **16:1** = Mount of Olives [C] **16:6** Lit *all King David's* [D] **16:10** Alt Hb tradition reads *If he curses, and if the LORD* [E] **16:11** Lit *son who came from my belly* [F] **16:12** Some Hb mss, LXX, Syr, Vg; one Hb tradition reads *iniquity*; alt Hb tradition reads *eyes*; ancient Jewish tradition reads *will look with His eye*

going along the ridge of the hill opposite him.
As Shimei went, he cursed David, and threw
stones and dirt at him. 14 Finally, the king and
all the people with him arrived[A] exhausted, so
they rested there.

Absalom's Advisers

15 Now Absalom and all the Israelites came
to Jerusalem. Ahithophel was also with him.
16 When David's friend Hushai the Archite
came to Absalom, Hushai said to Absalom,
"Long live the king! Long live the king!"[a]
17 "Is this your loyalty to your friend?" Absalom asked Hushai. "Why didn't you go with
your friend?"
18 "Not at all," Hushai answered Absalom. "I
am on the side of the one that the LORD, the
people, and all the men of Israel have chosen.
I will stay with him. 19 Furthermore, whom
will I serve if not his son? As I served in your
father's presence, I will also serve in yours."[b]
20 Then Absalom said to Ahithophel, "Give
me your advice. What should we do?"
21 Ahithophel replied to Absalom, "Sleep
with your father's concubines he left to take
care of the palace.[c] When all Israel hears that
you have become repulsive to your father,
everyone with you will be encouraged." 22 So
they pitched a tent for Absalom on the roof,
and he slept with his father's concubines in
the sight of all Israel.[d]
23 Now the advice Ahithophel gave in those
days was like someone asking about a word
from God[e] — such was the regard that both
David and Absalom had for Ahithophel's
17 advice. 1 Ahithophel said to Absalom,
"Let me choose 12,000 men, and I will
set out in pursuit of David tonight. 2 I will attack him while he is weak and weary, throw
him into a panic, and all the people with him
will scatter. I will strike down only the king
3 and bring all the people back to you. When
everyone returns except the man you're seeking, all[B] the people will be at peace." 4 This
proposal seemed good to Absalom and all the
elders of Israel.
5 Then Absalom said, "Summon Hushai the
Archite also. Let's hear what he has to say as
well."
6 So Hushai came to Absalom, and Absalom
told him: "Ahithophel offered this proposal.
Should we carry out his proposal? If not,
what do you say?"
7 Hushai replied to Absalom, "The advice
Ahithophel has given this time is not good."
8 Hushai continued, "You know your father
and his men. They are warriors and are desperate like a wild bear robbed of her cubs.
Your father is an experienced soldier who
won't spend the night with the people. 9 He's
probably already hiding in one of the caves[C] or
some other place. If some of our troops fall[D]
first, someone is sure to hear and say, 'There's
been a slaughter among the people who follow Absalom.' 10 Then, even a brave man with
the heart of a lion[f] will melt because all Israel
knows that your father and the valiant men
with him are warriors. 11 Instead, I advise that
all Israel from Dan to Beer-sheba — as numerous as the sand by the sea — be gathered
to you and that you personally go into battle.
12 Then we will attack David wherever we find
him, and we will descend on him like dew on
the ground. Not even one will be left of all the
men with him. 13 If he retreats to some city, all
Israel will bring ropes to that city, and we will
drag its stones into the valley until not even a
pebble can be found there." 14 Since the LORD
had decreed[g] that Ahithophel's good advice
be undermined[h] in order to bring about Absalom's ruin, Absalom and all the men of Israel said, "The advice of Hushai the Archite is
better than Ahithophel's advice."

David Informed of Absalom's Plans

15 Hushai then told the priests Zadok and
Abiathar, "This is what[E] Ahithophel advised
Absalom and the elders of Israel, and this is
what[F] I advised. 16 Now send someone quickly
and tell David, 'Don't spend the night at the
wilderness ford of the Jordan,[i] but be sure to
cross over, or the king and all the people with
him will be destroyed.'"
17 Jonathan and Ahimaaz were staying at
En-rogel, where a servant girl would come
and pass along information to them. They
in turn would go and inform King David, because they dared not be seen entering the city.

[a] 16:16 1Sm 10:24; 1Kg 1:25; 2Kg 11:12
[b] 16:19 2Sm 15:34
[c] 16:21 2Sm 15:16; 20:3
[d] 16:22 2Sm 12:11-12
[e] 16:23 2Sm 15:12
[f] 17:10 Am 3:8
[g] 17:14 Pr 21:30; 1Co 1:19
[h] 2Sm 15:31-34
[i] 17:16 2Sm 15:28

[A] 16:14 LXX adds *at the Jordan* [B] 17:3 LXX reads *to you as a bride returns to her husband. You seek the life of only one man, and all* [C] 17:9 Or *pits*, or *ravines* [D] 17:9 Lit *And it will be when a falling on them at* [E] 17:15 Lit *Like this and like this* [F] 17:15 Lit *and like this and like this*

18 However, a young man did see them and informed Absalom. So the two left quickly and came to the house of a man in Bahurim. He had a well in his courtyard, and they climbed down into it. 19 Then his wife took the cover, placed it over the mouth of the well, and scattered grain on it so nobody would know anything.

20 Absalom's servants came to the woman at the house and asked, "Where are Ahimaaz and Jonathan?"

"They passed by toward the water,"[A] the woman replied to them. The men searched but did not find them, so they returned to Jerusalem.

21 After they had gone, Ahimaaz and Jonathan climbed out of the well and went and informed King David. They told him, "Get up and immediately ford the river, for Ahithophel has given this advice against you." 22 So David and all the people with him got up and crossed the Jordan. By daybreak, there was no one who had not crossed the Jordan. 23 When Ahithophel realized that his advice had not been followed, he saddled his donkey and set out for his house in his hometown. He set his affairs in order[B] and hanged himself. So he died and was buried in his father's tomb.

24 David had arrived at Mahanaim by the time Absalom crossed the Jordan with all the men of Israel. 25 Now Absalom had appointed Amasa[a] over the army in Joab's place. Amasa was the son of a man named Ithra[C] the Israelite;[D,b] Ithra had married Abigail daughter of Nahash.[E] Abigail was a sister to Zeruiah, Joab's mother. 26 And Israel and Absalom camped in the land of Gilead. 27 When David came to Mahanaim, Shobi son of Nahash[c] from Rabbah[d] of the Ammonites, Machir son of Ammiel from Lo-debar,[e] and Barzillai the Gileadite from Rogelim[f] 28 brought beds, basins,[F] and pottery items. They also brought wheat, barley, flour, roasted grain, beans, lentils,[G] 29 honey, curds, sheep, and cheese[H] from the herd for David and the people with him to eat. They had reasoned, "The people must be hungry, exhausted, and thirsty in the desert."

Absalom's Defeat

18 David reviewed his troops and appointed commanders of hundreds and of thousands over them. 2 He then sent out the troops, a third under Joab, a third under Joab's brother Abishai son of Zeruiah, and a third under Ittai the Gittite. The king said to the troops, "I will also march out with you."

3 "You must not go!"[g] the people pleaded. "If we have to flee, they will not pay any attention to us. Even if half of us die, they will not pay any attention to us because you are worth[I] 10,000 of us. Therefore, it is better if you support us from the city."

4 "I will do whatever you think is best," the king replied to them. So he stood beside the gate while all the troops marched out by hundreds and thousands. 5 The king commanded Joab, Abishai, and Ittai, "Treat the young man Absalom gently for my sake." All the people heard the king's orders to all the commanders about Absalom.

6 Then David's forces marched into the field to engage Israel in battle, which took place in the forest of Ephraim. 7 The people of Israel were defeated by David's soldiers, and the slaughter there was vast that day — 20,000 casualties. 8 The battle spread over the entire region, and that day the forest claimed more people than the sword.

Absalom's Death

9 Absalom was riding on his mule when he happened to meet David's soldiers. When the mule went under the tangled branches of a large oak tree, Absalom's head was caught fast in the tree. The mule under him kept going, so he was suspended in midair.[J] 10 One of the men saw him and informed Joab. He said, "I just saw Absalom hanging in an oak tree!"

11 "You just saw him!" Joab exclaimed.[K] "Why didn't you strike him to the ground right there? I would have given you 10 silver pieces[L] and a belt!"

12 The man replied to Joab, "Even if I had the weight of 1,000 pieces of silver[M] in my hand, I would not raise my hand against the king's son. For we heard the king command you,

[a] **17:25** 2Sm 19:13; 20:9-12; 1Kg 2:5,32
[b] 1Ch 2:13-17
[c] **17:27** 2Sm 10:1-2
[d] 2Sm 12:26-29
[e] 2Sm 9:4
[f] 2Sm 19:31-32; 1Kg 2:7; Ezr 2:61
[g] **18:3** 2Sm 21:17

[A] 17:20 Or *brook*; Hb obscure [B] 17:23 Lit *He commanded his house* [C] 17:25 Or *Jether* [D] 17:25 Some LXX mss read *Ishmaelite* [E] 17:25 Some LXX mss read *Jesse* [F] 17:28 LXX reads *brought 10 embroidered beds with double coverings, 10 vessels* [G] 17:28 LXX, Syr; MT adds *roasted grain* [H] 17:29 Hb obscure [I] 18:3 Some Hb mss, LXX, Vg; other Hb mss read *because there would now be about* [J] 18:9 Lit *was between heaven and earth* [K] 18:11 Lit *Joab said to the man who told him* [L] 18:11 About 4 ounces of silver [M] 18:12 About 25 pounds of silver

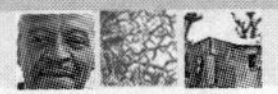

Abishai, and Ittai, 'Protect the young man
Absalom for me.'[A,a] 13 If I had jeopardized my
own[B] life — and nothing is hidden from the
king — you would have abandoned me."
14 Joab said, "I'm not going to waste time
with you!" He then took three spears in his
hand and thrust them into Absalom's heart
while he was still alive in the oak tree, 15 and
10 young men who were Joab's armor-bearers
surrounded Absalom, struck him, and killed
him.
16 Afterward, Joab blew the ram's horn, and
the troops broke off their pursuit of Israel because Joab restrained them. 17 They took Absalom, threw him into a large pit in the forest,
and piled a huge mound of stones over him.[b]
And all Israel fled, each to his tent.[c]
18 When he was alive, Absalom had set up
a pillar[d] for himself in the King's Valley,[e] for
he had said, "I have no son[f] to preserve the
memory of my name." So he gave the pillar
his name. It is still called Absalom's Monument today.
19 Ahimaaz son of Zadok[g] said, "Please let me
run and tell the king the good news that the
LORD has delivered him from his enemies."
20 Joab replied to him, "You are not the man
to take good news today. You may do it another day, but today you aren't taking good
news, because the king's son is dead." 21 Joab
then said to the *Cushite, "Go tell the king
what you have seen." The Cushite bowed to
Joab and took off running.
22 However, Ahimaaz son of Zadok persisted
and said to Joab, "No matter what, please let
me also run behind the Cushite!"
Joab replied, "My son, why do you want to
run since you won't get a reward?"
23 "No matter what, I want to run!"
"Then run!" Joab said to him. So Ahimaaz
ran by way of the plain and outran the Cushite.
24 David was sitting between the two gates[h]
when the watchman went up to the roof of
the gate and over to the wall.[i] The watchman
looked out and saw a man running alone.
25 He called out and told the king.
The king said, "If he's alone, he bears good
news."

[a]18:12 2Sm 18:5
[b]18:17 Jos 7:24-26; 8:29
[c]1Sm 4:10; 2Sm 19:8; 20:1,22; 2Kg 8:21
[d]18:18 Gn 28:18; Dt 16:22; 1Sm 15:12; 2Kg 18:4
[e]Gn 14:17
[f]2Sm 14:27
[g]18:19 2Sm 15:36
[h]18:24 2Sm 19:8
[i]2Sm 13:34; 2Kg 9:17
[j]18:27 2Kg 9:20
[k]1Kg 1:42
[l]18:32 1Sm 25:26
[m]18:33 2Sm 19:4

As the first runner came closer, 26 the watchman saw another man running. He called out
to the gatekeeper, "Look! Another man is running alone!"
"This one is also bringing good news," said
the king.
27 The watchman said, "The way the first
man runs looks to me like the way Ahimaaz
son of Zadok runs."[j]
"This is a good man; he comes with good
news,"[k] the king commented.
28 Ahimaaz called out to the king, "All is
well," and then bowed down to the king with
his face to the ground. He continued, "May
the LORD your God be praised! He delivered
up the men who rebelled against my lord the
king."
29 The king asked, "Is the young man Absalom all right?"
Ahimaaz replied, "When Joab sent the
king's servant and your servant, I saw a big
disturbance, but I don't know what it was."
30 The king said, "Move aside and stand
here." So he stood to one side.
31 Just then the Cushite came and said, "May
my lord the king hear the good news: today
the LORD has delivered you from all those rising up against you!"
32 The king asked the Cushite, "Is the young
man Absalom all right?"
The Cushite replied, "May what has become of the young man happen to the enemies of my lord the king and to all who rise
up against you with evil intent."[l]
33[C] The king was deeply moved and went up
to the gate chamber and wept. As he walked,
he cried, "My son Absalom! My son, my son
Absalom! If only I had died instead of you,
Absalom, my son, my son!"[m]

David's Kingdom Restored

19 It was reported to Joab, "The king is
weeping. He's mourning over Absalom." 2 That day's victory was turned into
mourning for all the troops because on that
day the troops heard, "The king is grieving
over his son." 3 So they returned to the city
quietly that day like people come in when
they are humiliated after fleeing in battle.

[A]18:12 Some Hb mss, LXX, Tg, Vg; other Hb mss read *Protect, whoever, the young man Absalom*; Hb obscure [B]18:13 Alt Hb tradition reads *jeopardized his*
[C]18:33 2Sm 19:1 in Hb

4 But the king hid his face[a] and cried out at the
top of his voice, "My son Absalom! Absalom,
my son, my son!"
5 Then Joab went into the house to the king
and said, "Today you have shamed all your
soldiers — those who rescued your life and
the lives of your sons and daughters, your
wives, and your concubines. 6 You love your
enemies and hate those who love you! Today
you have made it clear that the commanders
and soldiers mean nothing to you. In fact, today I know that if Absalom were alive and all
of us were dead, it would be fine with you![A]
7 "Now get up! Go out and encourage[B] your
soldiers, for I swear by the LORD that if you
don't go out, not a man will remain with you
tonight.[b] This will be worse for you than all
the trouble that has come to you from your
youth until now!"
8 So the king got up and sat in the ·gate,[c] and
all the people were told: "Look, the king is sitting in the gate." Then they all came into the
king's presence.
Meanwhile, each Israelite had fled to his
tent.[d] 9 All the people among all the tribes of
Israel were arguing: "The king delivered us
from the grasp of our enemies,[e] and he rescued us from the grasp of the Philistines,[f] but
now he has fled from the land because of Absalom.[g] 10 But Absalom, the man we anointed
over us, has died in battle. So why do you say
nothing about restoring the king?"
11 King David sent word to the priests, Zadok
and Abiathar:[h] "Say to the elders of Judah,
'Why should you be the last to restore the
king to his palace? The talk of all Israel has
reached the king at his house. 12 You are my
brothers, my flesh and blood.[i] So why should
you be the last to restore the king?' 13 And tell
Amasa,[j] 'Aren't you my flesh and blood? May
God punish me and do so severely if you don't
become commander of the army from now
on instead of Joab!'"
14 So he won over[C] all the men of Judah, and
they sent word to the king: "Come back, you
and all your servants." 15 Then the king returned. When he arrived at the Jordan, Judah
came to Gilgal to meet the king and escort
him across the Jordan.

[a] 19:4 2Sm 15:30
[b] 19:7 Pr 14:28
[c] 19:8 2Sm 18:4,24,33
[d] 2Sm 18:17
[e] 19:9 2Sm 8:1-14
[f] 2Sm 5:20; 8:1
[g] 2Sm 15:14
[h] 19:11 2Sm 15:29
[i] 19:12 Gn 29:14; 2Sm 5:1
[j] 19:13 2Sm 17:25
[k] 19:16 2Sm 16:5; 1Kg 2:8
[l] 19:17 2Sm 16:1-4
[m] 19:19 2Sm 16:5-13
[n] 19:21 Ex 22:28
[o] 19:22 2Sm 3:39; 16:10
[p] 19:23 1Kg 2:8-9,37,46
[q] 19:24 2Sm 9:6
[r] 19:26 2Sm 4:4; 9:3
[s] 19:27 2Sm 16:1-4
[t] 2Sm 14:17,20
[u] 19:28 2Sm 9:1-13

16 Shimei son of Gera,[k] a Benjaminite from
Bahurim, hurried down with the men of Judah to meet King David. 17 There were 1,000
men from Benjamin with him. Ziba, an attendant from the house of Saul,[l] with his 15
sons and 20 servants also rushed down to the
Jordan ahead of the king. 18 They forded the
Jordan to bring the king's household across
and do whatever the king desired.[D]
When Shimei son of Gera crossed the Jordan, he fell down before the king 19 and said
to him, "My lord, don't hold me ·guilty, and
don't remember your servant's wrongdoing
on the day my lord the king left Jerusalem.[m]
May the king not take it to heart. 20 For your
servant knows that I have sinned. But look!
Today I am the first one of the entire house
of Joseph to come down to meet my lord the
king."
21 Abishai son of Zeruiah asked, "Shouldn't
Shimei be put to death for this, because he
cursed the LORD's anointed?"[n]
22 David answered, "Sons of Zeruiah, do we
agree on anything?[o] Have you become my
adversary today? Should any man be killed
in Israel today? Am I not aware that today
I'm king over Israel?" 23 So the king said to
Shimei, "You will not die." Then the king gave
him his oath.[p]
24 Mephibosheth,[q] Saul's grandson, also
went down to meet the king. He had not
taken care of his feet, trimmed his mustache,
or washed his clothes from the day the king
left until the day he returned safely. 25 When
he came from Jerusalem to meet the king, the
king asked him, "Mephibosheth, why didn't
you come with me?"
26 "My lord the king," he replied, "my servant Ziba betrayed me. Actually your servant
said: 'I'll saddle the donkey for myself[E] so
that I may ride it and go with the king' — for
your servant is lame.[r] 27 Ziba slandered your
servant to my lord the king.[s] But my lord the
king is like the Angel of God,[t] so do whatever
you think best.[F] 28 For my grandfather's entire
family deserves death from my lord the king,
but you set your servant among those who eat
at your table.[u] So what further right do I have
to keep on making appeals to the king?"

[A] 19:6 Lit *be right in your eyes* [B] 19:7 Lit *speak to the heart of* [C] 19:14 Lit *he turned the heart of* [D] 19:18 Lit *do what is good in his eyes* [E] 19:26 LXX, Syr, Vg read *said to him, 'Saddle the donkey for me* [F] 19:27 Lit *do what is good in your eyes*

29The king said to him, "Why keep on speaking about these matters of yours? I hereby declare: you and Ziba are to divide the land."[a]
30Mephibosheth said to the king, "Instead,
since my lord the king has come to his palace
safely, let Ziba take it all!"
31Barzillai the Gileadite[b] had come down
from Rogelim and accompanied the king to
the Jordan River to see him off at the Jordan.
32Barzillai was a very old man — 80 years
old — and since he was a very wealthy man,
he had provided for the needs of the king
while he stayed in Mahanaim.[c]
33The king said to Barzillai, "Cross over
with me, and I'll provide for you[A] at my side
in Jerusalem."
34Barzillai replied to the king, "How many
years of my life are left that I should go up to
Jerusalem with the king? 35I'm now 80 years
old.[d] Can I discern what is pleasant and what
is not? Can your servant taste what he eats or
drinks? Can I still hear the voice of male and
female singers? Why should your servant be
an added burden to my lord the king?[e] 36Since
your servant is only going with the king a
little way across the Jordan, why should the
king repay me with such a reward? 37Please
let your servant return so that I may die in
my own city near the tomb of my father and
mother. But here is your servant Chimham:[f]
let him cross over with my lord the king. Do
for him what seems good to you."[B]
38The king replied, "Chimham will cross
over with me, and I will do for him what
seems good to you,[B] and whatever you desire from me I will do for you." 39So all the
people crossed the Jordan, and then the king
crossed. The king kissed Barzillai and blessed
him, and Barzillai returned to his home.
40The king went on to Gilgal, and Chimham
went with him. All the troops of Judah and
half of Israel's escorted the king. 41Suddenly,
all the men of Israel came to the king. They
asked him, "Why did our brothers, the men
of Judah, take you away secretly and transport the king and his household across the
Jordan, along with all of David's men?"
42All the men of Judah responded to the
men of Israel, "Because the king is our relative. Why does this make you angry? Have we
ever eaten anything of the king's or been honored at all?"[C]
43The men of Israel answered the men of
Judah: "We have 10 shares in the king,[g] so we
have a greater claim to David than you. Why
then do you despise us? Weren't we the first
to speak of restoring our king?"[h] But the
words of the men of Judah were harsher than
those of the men of Israel.

Sheba's Revolt

20 Now a •wicked man, a Benjaminite
named Sheba son of Bichri, happened to be there. He blew the ram's horn
and shouted:

> We have no portion in David,
> no inheritance in Jesse's son.
> Each man to his tent, Israel!

2So all the men of Israel deserted David and
followed Sheba son of Bichri, but the men of
Judah from the Jordan all the way to Jerusalem remained loyal to their king.[i]
3When David came to his palace in Jerusalem, he took the 10 concubines he had left to
take care of the palace and placed them under guard.[j] He provided for them, but he was
not intimate with them. They were confined
until the day of their death, living as widows.
4The king said to Amasa, "Summon the
men of Judah to me within three days and be
here yourself." 5Amasa went to summon Judah, but he took longer than the time allotted
him. 6So David said to Abishai, "Sheba son of
Bichri will do more harm to us than Absalom.
Take your lord's soldiers and pursue him, or
he will find fortified cities and elude us."[D]
7So Joab's men, the Cherethites, the Pelethites, and all the warriors marched out under Abishai's command;[E] they left Jerusalem
to pursue Sheba son of Bichri. 8They were at
the great stone in Gibeon when Amasa joined
them. Joab was wearing his uniform and over
it was a belt around his waist with a sword
in its sheath. As he approached, the sword
fell out. 9Joab asked Amasa, "Are you well,
my brother?" Then with his right hand Joab
grabbed Amasa by the beard to kiss him.[k]

[a]**19:29** 2Sm 9:9; 16:4
[b]**19:31** 1Kg 2:7
[c]**19:32** 2Sm 17:27-29
[d]**19:35** Ps 90:10
[e]2Sm 15:33
[f]**19:37** 1Kg 2:7; Jr 41:17
[g]**19:43** 1Kg 11:31
[h]2Sm 19:9-10
[i]**20:1-2** 1Kg 12:16-17
[j]**20:3** 2Sm 15:16; 16:21-22
[k]**20:9** Mt 26:49; Mk 14:45; Lk 22:47

[A]**19:33** LXX reads *for your old age*; Ru 4:15 [B]**19:37,38** Lit *what is good in your eyes* [C]**19:42** LXX reads *king's or has he given us a gift or granted us a portion* [D]**20:6** Lit *and snatch away our eyes* [E]**20:7** Lit *out following him*

10 Amasa was not on guard against the sword
in Joab's hand, and Joab stabbed him in the
stomach with it and spilled his intestines out
on the ground. Joab did not stab him again
for Amasa was dead.[a] Joab and his brother
Abishai pursued Sheba son of Bichri.
11 One of Joab's young men had stood over
Amasa saying, "Whoever favors Joab and
whoever is for David, follow Joab!" 12 Now
Amasa was writhing in his blood in the middle of the highway, and the man had seen that
all the people stopped. So he moved Amasa
from the highway to the field and threw a
garment over him because he realized that
all those who encountered Amasa were stopping. 13 When he was removed from the highway, all the men passed by and followed Joab
to pursue Sheba son of Bichri.
14 Sheba passed through all the tribes of Israel to Abel of Beth-maacah. All the Berites[A]
came together and followed him. 15 Joab's
troops came and besieged Sheba in Abel of
Beth-maacah. They built an assault ramp
against the outer wall of the city. While all
the troops with Joab were battering the wall
to make it collapse, 16 a wise woman called out
from the city, "Listen! Listen! Please tell Joab
to come here and let me speak with him."
17 When he had come near her, the woman
asked, "Are you Joab?"

"I am," he replied.

"Listen to the words of your servant," she
said to him.

He answered, "I'm listening."
18 She said, "In the past they used to say,
'Seek counsel in Abel,' and that's how they settled disputes. 19 I am a peaceful person, one of
the faithful in Israel, but you're trying to destroy a city that is like a mother in Israel. Why
would you devour the LORD's inheritance?"
20 Joab protested: "Never! I do not want to
destroy! 21 That is not my intention. There is
a man named Sheba son of Bichri, from the
hill country of Ephraim, who has rebelled
against King David. Deliver this one man, and
I will withdraw from the city."

The woman replied to Joab, "All right. His
head will be thrown over the wall to you."
22 The woman went to all the people with her
wise counsel,[b] and they cut off the head of
Sheba son of Bichri and threw it to Joab. So he
blew the ram's horn, and they dispersed from
the city, each to his own tent. Joab returned to
the king in Jerusalem.
23 Joab commanded the whole army of Israel;[c] Benaiah son of Jehoiada was over the
Cherethites and Pelethites; 24 Adoram[B] was
in charge of forced labor; Jehoshaphat son of
Ahilud was court historian; 25 Sheva was court
secretary; Zadok and Abiathar were priests;
26 and in addition, Ira the Jairite was David's
priest.

Justice for the Gibeonites

21 During David's reign there was a famine for three successive years, so David
inquired of the LORD. The LORD answered, "It
is because of the blood shed by Saul and his
family when he killed the Gibeonites."
2 The Gibeonites were not Israelites but
rather a remnant of the Amorites. The Israelites had taken an oath concerning them,[d] but
Saul had tried to kill them in his zeal for the
Israelites and Judah. So David summoned
the Gibeonites and spoke to them. 3 He asked
the Gibeonites, "What should I do for you?
How can I make atonement so that you will
bring a blessing on[C] the LORD's inheritance?"
4 The Gibeonites said to him, "We are not
asking for money from[D] Saul or his family,[e]
and we cannot put anyone to death in Israel."[f]

"Whatever you say, I will do for you," he
said.
5 They replied to the king, "As for the man
who annihilated us and plotted to destroy us
so we would not exist within the whole territory of Israel, 6 let seven of his male descendants be handed over to us so we may hang[E]
them in the presence of the LORD[g] at Gibeah
of Saul,[h] the LORD's chosen."[i]

The king answered, "I will hand them over."
7 David spared Mephibosheth, the son of
Saul's son Jonathan, because of the oath of
the LORD that was between David and Jonathan, Saul's son.[j] 8 But the king took Armoni
and Mephibosheth, who were the two sons
whom Rizpah[k] daughter of Aiah had borne to
Saul, and the five sons whom Merab[F,l] daugh-

[a]**20:10** 1Kg 2:5 [b]**20:22** Ec 9:14-15 [c]**20:23-26** 2Sm 8:16-18; 1Kg 4:3-6 [d]**21:2** Jos 9:3-17 [e]**21:4** Nm 35:31-32 [f]Lv 24:21-22 [g]**21:6** Nm 25:4 [h]1Sm 15:34 [i]1Sm 10:24 [j]**21:7** 1Sm 18:3; 20:12-17; 23:18 [k]**21:8** 2Sm 3:7 [l]1Sm 18:19

[A]**20:14** LXX, Vg read *Bichrites* [B]**20:24** Some Hb mss, LXX, Syr read *Adoniram*; 1Kg 4:6; 5:14 [C]**21:3** Lit *will bless* [D]**21:4** Lit *"Not for us silver and gold with* [E]**21:6** Or *impale,* or *expose* [F]**21:8** Some Hb mss, LXX, Syr, Tg; other Hb mss read *Michal* ter of Saul had borne to Adriel son of Barzillai the Meholathite 9 and handed them over to the Gibeonites. They hanged[A] them on the hill in the presence of the LORD; the seven of them died together. They were executed in the first days of the harvest at the beginning of the barley harvest.[B]

The Burial of Saul's Family

10 Rizpah, Aiah's daughter, took ˙sackcloth and spread it out for herself on the rock from the beginning of the harvest[C] until the rain poured down from heaven on the bodies. She kept the birds of the sky from them by day and the wild animals by night.

11 When it was reported to David what Saul's concubine Rizpah, daughter of Aiah, had done, 12 he went and got the bones of Saul and his son Jonathan from the leaders of Jabesh-gilead. They had stolen them from the public square of Beth-shan where the Philistines had hung the bodies the day the Philistines killed Saul at Gilboa.[a] 13 David had the bones brought from there. They gathered up the bones of Saul's family who had been hung[A] 14 and buried the bones of Saul and his son Jonathan at Zela in the land of Benjamin in the tomb of Saul's father Kish. They did everything the king commanded. After this, God answered prayer for the land.[b]

The Philistine Giants

15 The Philistines again waged war against Israel. David went down with his soldiers, and they fought the Philistines, but David became exhausted. 16 Then Ishbi-benob, one of the descendants of the giant,[D] whose bronze spear weighed about eight pounds[E] and who wore new armor, intended to kill David. 17 But Abishai son of Zeruiah came to his aid, struck the Philistine, and killed him. Then David's men swore to him: "You must never again go out with us to battle. You must not extinguish the lamp of Israel."[c]

18 After this,[d] there was another battle with the Philistines at Gob. At that time Sibbecai the Hushathite killed Saph, who was one of the descendants of the giant.[D]

[a] **21:12** 1Sm 31:11-13
[b] **21:14** 2Sm 24:25
[c] **21:17** 2Sm 18:3; 1Kg 11:36; 15:4; 2Ch 21:7; Ps 132:17
[d] **21:18-22** 1Ch 20:4-8
[e] **21:19** 1Sm 17:7
[f] **22:2-51** Ps 18:2-50
[g] **22:2** Ps 31:3; 71:3
[h] **22:3** Lk 1:69
[i] Ps 9:9; 59:9,16-17; 62:2,6
[j] Ps 14:6; 71:7; Jr 16:19
[k] **22:4** 1Ch 16:25; Ps 48:1; 96:4
[l] **22:5** Ps 42:7; Jnh 2:3
[m] **22:6** Ps 116:3
[n] **22:7** Ps 116:4; 120:1; Jnh 2:2
[o] **22:8** Jdg 5:4; Ps 77:18; 97:4
[p] Jb 26:11

19 Once again there was a battle with the Philistines at Gob, and Elhanan son of Jaare-oregim the Bethlehemite killed[F] Goliath the Gittite. The shaft of his spear was like a weaver's beam.[e]

20 At Gath there was still another battle. A huge man was there with six fingers on each hand and six toes on each foot — 24 in all. He, too, was descended from the giant.[D] 21 When he taunted Israel, Jonathan, son of David's brother Shimei, killed him.

22 These four were descended from the giant[D] in Gath and were killed by David and his soldiers.

David's Song of Thanksgiving

22 David spoke the words of this song to the LORD on the day the LORD rescued him from the hand of all his enemies and from the hand of Saul. 2 He said:[f]

The LORD is my rock, my fortress,[g]
and my deliverer,
3 my God, my mountain[G] where I seek
refuge.
My shield, the ˙horn of my salvation,[h]
my stronghold,[i] my refuge,[j]
and my Savior, You save me
from violence.
4 I called to the LORD, who is worthy
of praise,[k]
and I was saved from my enemies.
5 For the waves of death engulfed me;[l]
the torrents of destruction terrified me.
6 The ropes of ˙Sheol entangled me;
the snares of death confronted me.[m]
7 I called to the LORD in my distress;
I called to my God.[n]
From His temple He heard my voice,
and my cry for help reached His ears.
8 Then the earth shook and quaked;
the foundations of the heavens[H]
trembled;[o]
they shook because He burned
with anger.[p]
9 Smoke rose from His nostrils,
and consuming fire came
from His mouth;
coals were set ablaze by it.[I]

[A] 21:9,13 Or *impaled*, or *exposed* [B] 21:9 = March–April [C] 21:10 = April to October [D] 21:16,18,20,22 Or *Raphah* [E] 21:16 Lit *300* (shekels) [F] 21:19 1Ch 20:5 adds *the brother of* [G] 22:3 LXX; MT reads *God of my mountain*; Ps 18:2 [H] 22:8 Some Hb mss, Syr, Vg read *mountains*; Ps 18:7 [I] 22:9 Or *ablaze from Him*

10 He parted the heavens and came down,[a]
a dark cloud beneath His feet.
11 He rode on a cherub and flew,
soaring[A] on the wings of the wind.
12 He made darkness a canopy
around Him,
a gathering[B] of water and thick clouds.[b]
13 From the radiance of His presence,
flaming coals were ignited.
14 The LORD thundered from heaven;
the •Most High projected His voice.[c]
15 He shot arrows and scattered them;[d]
He hurled lightning bolts
and routed them.[e]
16 The depths of the sea became visible,
the foundations of the world
were exposed
at the rebuke of the LORD,
at the blast of the breath[f]
of His nostrils.[g]

17 He reached down from heaven
and took hold of me;
He pulled me out of deep waters.[h]
18 He rescued me
from my powerful enemy
and from those who hated me,
for they were too strong for me.
19 They confronted me in the day
of my distress,
but the LORD was my support.
20 He brought me out to a spacious place;[i]
He rescued me because He delighted
in me.
21 The LORD rewarded me
according to my righteousness;[j]
He repaid me
according to the cleanness
of my hands.[k]
22 For I have kept the ways of the LORD[l]
and have not turned from my God
to wickedness.
23 Indeed, I have kept all His ordinances[m]
in mind[C]
and have not disregarded His statutes.
24 I was blameless before Him
and kept myself from sinning.
25 So the LORD repaid me
according to my righteousness,
according to my cleanness[D]
in His sight.
26 With the faithful
You prove Yourself faithful;
with the blameless man
You prove Yourself blameless;
27 with the pure
You prove Yourself pure,
but with the crooked
You prove Yourself shrewd.
28 You rescue an afflicted people,[n]
but Your eyes are set
against the proud—
You humble them.[o]
29 LORD, You are my lamp;
the LORD illuminates my darkness.[p]
30 With You I can attack a barrier,[E]
and with my God I can leap over a wall.[q]
31 God—His way is perfect;[r]
the word of the LORD is pure.[s]
He is a shield to all who take refuge
in Him.

32 For who is God besides the LORD?
And who is a rock? Only our God.
33 God is my strong refuge;[F]
He makes my way perfect.[G]
34 He makes my feet like the feet of a deer
and sets me securely on the[H] heights.[I]
35 He trains my hands for war;[t]
my arms can bend a bow of bronze.
36 You have given me the shield
of Your salvation;[u]
Your help[J] exalts me.
37 You widen a place beneath me
for my steps,
and my ankles do not give way.
38 I pursue my enemies and destroy them;
I do not turn back until they are
wiped out.
39 I wipe them out and crush them,
and they do not rise;
they fall beneath my feet.
40 You have clothed me with strength
for battle;
You subdue my adversaries
beneath me.[v]

[a]**22:10** Ps 144:5; Is 64:1 [b]**22:12** Ps 97:2 [c]**22:14** Jb 37:4 [d]**22:15** Dt 32:23; Ps 7:13; 77:17; Hab 3:11 [e]Ps 144:6 [f]**22:16** Jb 4:9; Is 30:33 [g]Ex 15:8 [h]**22:17** Ps 144:7 [i]**22:20** Ps 31:8; 118:5 [j]**22:21** 1Sm 26:23; 1Kg 8:32; Ps 7:8 [k]Ps 24:3-4 [l]**22:22** Pr 8:32 [m]**22:23** Ps 119:30,102 [n]**22:28** Ps 72:12-13 [o]Is 2:11-12,17; Lk 1:51 [p]**22:29** Jb 29:3; Ps 27:1 [q]**22:30** 2Sm 5:6-9 [r]**22:31** Dt 32:4 [s]Ps 119:140 [t]**22:35** Ps 144:1 [u]**22:36** Eph 6:16-17 [v]**22:40** Ps 44:5

[A]**22:11** Some Hb mss; other Hb mss, Syr, Tg read *He was seen* [B]**22:12** Or *sieve,* or *mass*; Hb obscure [C]**22:23** Lit *Indeed, all His ordinances have been in front of me* [D]**22:25** LXX, Syr, Vg read *to the cleanness of my hands*; Ps 18:24 [E]**22:30** Or *ridge* [F]**22:33** DSS, some LXX mss, Syr, Vg read *God clothes me with strength*; Ps 18:32 [G]**22:33** Some LXX mss, Syr; MT reads *He sets free the blameless His way*; Hb obscure [H]**22:34** LXX; some Hb mss read *my*; other Hb mss read *His* [I]**22:34** Or *on my high places* [J]**22:36** LXX reads *humility*; Ps 18:35

41 You have made my enemies retreat
before me;[A]
I annihilate those who hate me.
42 They look, but there is no one
to save them —
they look to the LORD, but He does not
answer them.[a]
43 I pulverize them like dust of the earth;
I crush them and trample them
like mud in the streets.[b]

44 You have freed me from the feuds
among my people;[c]
You have appointed me the head
of nations;
a people I had not known serve me.[d]
45 Foreigners submit to me grudgingly;
as soon as they hear, they obey me.
46 Foreigners lose heart
and come trembling
from their fortifications.[e]

47 The LORD lives — may my rock
be praised!
God, the rock of my salvation,[f]
is exalted.
48 God — He gives me vengeance
and casts down peoples under me.[g]
49 He frees me from my enemies.
You exalt me above my adversaries;
You rescue me from violent men.[h]
50 Therefore I will praise You, LORD,
among the nations;
I will sing about Your name.[i]
51 He is a tower of salvation for[B] His king;
He shows loyalty to His anointed,
to David and his descendants forever.[j]

David's Last Words

23 These are the last words of David:

The declaration of David son of Jesse,[k]
the declaration of the man
raised on high,[C]
the one anointed by the God of Jacob,[l]
the favorite singer of Israel:
2 The Spirit of the LORD spoke
through me,
His word was on my tongue.[m]
3 The God of Israel spoke;
the Rock of Israel said to me,
"The one who rules the people
with justice,
who rules in the •fear of God,[n]
4 is like the morning light when the sun
rises
on a cloudless morning,
the glisten of rain on sprouting grass."

5 Is it not true my house is with God?
For He has established
an everlasting covenant[o] with me,
ordered and secured in every detail.[p]
Will He not bring about
my whole salvation
and my every desire?
6 But all the wicked are like thorns
raked aside;
they can never be picked up by hand.
7 The man who touches them
must be armed with iron and the shaft
of a spear.
They will be completely burned up
on the spot.

Exploits of David's Warriors

8 These are the names of David's warriors:[q]
Josheb-basshebeth the Tahchemonite was
chief of the officers.[D] He wielded his spear[E]
against 800 men that he killed at one time.
9 After him, Eleazar son of Dodo son of an
Ahohite was among the three warriors with
David when they defied the Philistines. The
men of Israel retreated in the place they had
gathered for battle, 10 but Eleazar stood his
ground and attacked the Philistines until his
hand was tired and stuck to his sword. The
LORD brought about a great victory that day.
Then the troops came back to him, but only
to plunder the dead.
11 After him was Shammah son of Agee the
Hararite. The Philistines had assembled in
formation where there was a field full of lentils.
The troops fled from the Philistines, 12 but
Shammah took his stand in the middle of the
field, defended it, and struck down the Philistines.
So the LORD brought about a great
victory.
13 Three of the 30 leading warriors went
down at harvest time and came to David at the

[a]22:42 1Sm 28:6; Pr 1:28 [b]22:43 Is 10:6; Mc 7:10; Zch 10:5 [c]22:44 2Sm 2:8-10; 15:1-6; 20:1-2 [d]2Sm 8:1-14; Is 55:5 [e]22:46 Mc 7:17 [f]22:47 Ps 89:26; 95:1 [g]22:48 Ps 144:2 [h]22:49 Ps 140:1 [i]22:50 Rm 15:9 [j]22:51 2Sm 7:12-16; Lk 1:55 [k]23:1 Lk 3:32 [l]1Sm 16:12-13; Ps 89:20 [m]23:2 Mt 22:43; 2Pt 1:21 [n]23:3 Ps 72:1-3; Is 11:1-5 [o]23:5 Gn 9:16; 17:7,19; 1Ch 16:17; Ps 105:10 [p]2Sm 7:12-16; Ps 89:29; Is 55:3 [q]23:8-39 1Ch 11:11-47

A22:41 Lit *You gave me the neck of my enemies* B22:51 DSS read *He gives great victory to* C23:1 Or *raised up by the high God* D23:8 Some Hb mss, LXX read *Three* E23:8 Some Hb mss; other Hb mss, LXX read *He was Adino the Eznite*

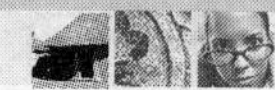

cave of Adullam,[a] while a company of Philistines was camping in the Valley of Rephaim.
14 At that time David was in the stronghold,[b]
and a Philistine garrison was at Bethlehem.
15 David was extremely thirsty[A] and said, "If
only someone would bring me water to drink
from the well at the city gate of Bethlehem!"
16 So three of the warriors broke through the
Philistine camp and drew water from the
well at the gate of Bethlehem. They brought
it back to David, but he refused to drink it.
Instead, he poured it out to the LORD. 17 David
said, "LORD, I would never do such a thing!
Is this not the blood of men who risked their
lives?" So he refused to drink it. Such were
the exploits of the three warriors.

18 Abishai, Joab's brother and son of Zeruiah,[c] was leader of the Three.[B] He raised his
spear against 300 men and killed them, gaining a reputation among the Three. 19 Was he
not more honored than the Three? He became their commander even though he did
not become one of the Three.[d]

20 Benaiah son of Jehoiada[e] was the son of
a brave man from Kabzeel, a man of many
exploits. Benaiah killed two sons[C] of Ariel[D]
of Moab, and he went down into a pit on a
snowy day and killed a lion. 21 He also killed
an Egyptian, a huge man. Even though the
Egyptian had a spear in his hand, Benaiah
went down to him with a club, snatched the
spear out of the Egyptian's hand, and then
killed him with his own spear. 22 These were
the exploits of Benaiah son of Jehoiada, who
had a reputation among the three warriors.
23 He was the most honored of the Thirty, but
he did not become one of the Three. David
put him in charge of his bodyguard.

24 Among the Thirty were:

Joab's brother Asahel,[f]
Elhanan son of Dodo of Bethlehem,
25 Shammah the Harodite,
Elika the Harodite,
26 Helez the Paltite,
Ira son of Ikkesh the Tekoite,
27 Abiezer the Anathothite,
Mebunnai the Hushathite,
28 Zalmon the Ahohite,
Maharai the Netophathite,
29 Heleb son of Baanah the Netophahite,
Ittai son of Ribai from Gibeah
of the Benjaminites,
30 Benaiah the Pirathonite,
Hiddai from the 'wadis of Gaash,[E]
31 Abi-albon the Arbathite,
Azmaveth the Barhumite,
32 Eliahba the Shaalbonite,
the sons of Jashen,
Jonathan son of[F] 33 Shammah
the Hararite,
Ahiam son of Sharar the Hararite,
34 Eliphelet son of Ahasbai
son of the Maacathite,
Eliam son of Ahithophel the Gilonite,[g]
35 Hezro the Carmelite,
Paarai the Arbite,
36 Igal son of Nathan from Zobah,
Bani the Gadite,
37 Zelek the Ammonite,
Naharai the Beerothite, the
armor-bearer for Joab son of Zeruiah,
38 Ira the Ithrite,
Gareb the Ithrite,
39 and Uriah[h] the Hittite.[i]

There were 37 in all.

David's Military Census

24 The LORD's anger burned against Israel again, and He stirred up David
against them to say: "Go, count the people of
Israel and Judah."[j]
2 So the king said to Joab, the commander
of his army, "Go through all the tribes of Israel from Dan to Beer-sheba and register the
troops so I can know their number."[k]
3 Joab replied to the king, "May the LORD
your God multiply the troops 100 times more
than they are[l] — while my lord the king looks
on! But why does my lord the king want to
do this?"
4 Yet the king's order prevailed over Joab
and the commanders of the army. So Joab and
the commanders of the army left the king's
presence to register the troops of Israel.
5 They crossed the Jordan and camped in
Aroer,[m] south of the town in the middle of the
valley, and then proceeded toward Gad and
Jazer. 6 They went to Gilead and to the land of

[a] **23:13** 1Sm 22:1
[b] **23:14** 1Sm 22:4-5
[c] **23:18** 1Sm 26:3-6
[d] **23:19** 1Ch 11:21
[e] **23:20** 2Sm 8:18; 20:23
[f] **23:24** 2Sm 2:18-23; 1Ch 27:7
[g] **23:34** 2Sm 15:12
[h] **23:39** Mt 1:6
[i] 2Sm 11:3-26
[j] **24:1-25** 1Ch 21:1-28
[k] **24:2** Nm 1:2-3; 1Sm 13:15
[l] **24:3** Dt 1:11
[m] **24:5** Dt 2:36; Jos 13:19,16

[A] **23:15** Lit *And David craved* [B] **23:18** Some Hb mss, Syr read *the Thirty* [C] **23:20** LXX; MT omits *sons* [D] **23:20** Or *two warriors* [E] **23:30** Or *from Nahale-gaash* [F] **23:32** Some LXX mss; MT omits *son of*; 1Ch 11:34

the Hittites[A] and continued on to Dan-jaan
and around to Sidon. 7They went to the fortress of Tyre and all the cities of the Hivites
and Canaanites. Afterward, they went to the
•Negev of Judah at Beer-sheba.
8When they had gone through the whole
land, they returned to Jerusalem at the end of
nine months and 20 days. 9Joab gave the king
the total of the registration of the troops.
There were 800,000 fighting men from Israel
and 500,000 men from Judah.[a]
10David's conscience troubled him[b] after he
had taken a census of the troops. He said to
the LORD, "I have sinned greatly in what I've
done. Now, LORD, because I've been very foolish,[c] please take away Your servant's •guilt."

David's Punishment

11When David got up in the morning, a
revelation from the LORD had come to the
prophet Gad,[d] David's seer:[e] 12"Go and say to
David, 'This is what the LORD says: I am offering you three choices. Choose one of them,
and I will do it to you.'"
13So Gad went to David, told him the
choices, and asked him, "Do you want three[B]
years of famine to come on your land, to flee
from your foes three months while they pursue you, or to have a plague in your land three
days? Now, think it over and decide what
answer I should take back to the One who
sent me."
14David answered Gad, "I have great anxiety. Please, let us fall into the LORD's hands because His mercies are great,[f] but don't let me
fall into human hands."
15So the LORD sent a plague on Israel from
that morning until the appointed time, and
from Dan to Beer-sheba 70,000 men died.
16Then the angel extended his hand toward
Jerusalem to destroy it,[g] but the LORD relented concerning the destruction[h] and said
to the angel who was destroying[i] the people,

[a]**24:9** Nm 1:45-46
[b]**24:10** 1Sm 24:5
[c]Nm 12:9-12; 1Sm 13:13
[d]**24:11** 1Sm 22:5
[e]1Sm 9:9
[f]**24:14** Ps 103:8-18; 119:156
[g]**24:16** 2Kg 19:35
[h]Ex 32:14; Am 7:3-6
[i]1Co 10:10
[j]2Ch 3:1
[k]**24:21** Nm 16:44-50
[l]**24:22** 1Sm 6:14; 1Kg 19:21
[m]**24:25** 2Sm 21:14

"Enough, withdraw your hand now!" The
angel of the LORD was then at the threshing
floor of Araunah[C] the Jebusite.[j]
17When David saw the angel striking the
people, he said to the LORD, "Look, I am the
one who has sinned; I am the one[D] who has
done wrong. But these sheep, what have they
done? Please, let Your hand be against me
and my father's family."

David's Altar

18Gad came to David that day and said to
him, "Go up and set up an altar to the LORD
on the threshing floor of Araunah the Jebusite." 19David went up in obedience to Gad's
command, just as the LORD had commanded.
20Araunah looked down and saw the king and
his servants coming toward him, so he went
out and bowed to the king with his face to the
ground.
21Araunah said, "Why has my lord the king
come to his servant?"
David replied, "To buy the threshing floor
from you in order to build an altar to the
LORD, so the plague on the people may be
halted."[k]
22Araunah said to David, "My lord the king
may take whatever he wants[E] and offer it.
Here are the oxen for a •burnt offering and
the threshing sledges and ox yokes for the
wood.[l] 23My king, Araunah gives everything
here to the king." Then he said to the king,
"May the LORD your God accept you."
24The king answered Araunah, "No, I insist
on buying it from you for a price, for I will
not offer to the LORD my God burnt offerings that cost me nothing." David bought the
threshing floor and the oxen for 20 ounces[F]
of silver. 25He built an altar to the LORD there
and offered burnt offerings and •fellowship
offerings. Then the LORD answered prayer on
behalf of the land,[m] and the plague on Israel
ended.

[A]**24:6** LXX; MT reads *of Tahtim-hodshi*; Hb obscure [B]**24:13** LXX; MT reads *seven*; 1Ch 21:12 [C]**24:16** = Ornan in 1Ch 21:15-28; 2Ch 3:1 [D]**24:17** LXX reads *shepherd* [E]**24:22** Lit *take what is good in his eyes* [F]**24:24** Lit *50 shekels*

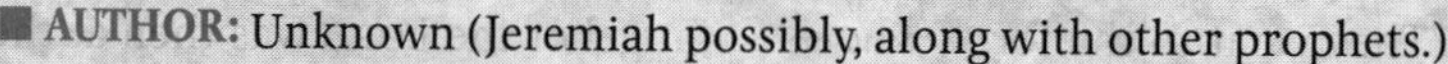

AUTHOR: Unknown (Jeremiah possibly, along with other prophets.)

DATE: 560 B.C.

Although the events depicted in these books took place from the time of the kings through the fall of Jerusalem (a period extending from roughly 970 to 586 B.C.), 1 and 2 Kings may have been written in Babylon during the exile (after the fall of Jerusalem).

Read any modern history and you'll learn politics, economics, warfare, and maybe something about how the common person lived. You'll get the lives of leaders, celebrities, and sports heroes. The books of 1 and 2 Kings, originally one book, are history of a special kind. Read the books of Kings and you'll learn about the covenant—God's plan for relationships of happiness and prosperity—gone amok. Kings is written, in fact, long after the kings it describes have lost everything. The dream is gone. Assyria beat up on the northern kingdom of Israel. Later Babylon captured and destroyed the southern kingdom of Judah. Moses' promised land, Joshua's great conquest, the unity under David's reign, the temple—all gone. The first readers of the books of Kings, captives in Babylon, want explanations.

1 KINGS

Kings makes it clear why the nation now sits in bondage—Israel disregarded God's laws and ignored God's prophets. God's law, expressed in the books of Exodus through Deuteronomy, spelled out clearly how the people were to live. The Ten Commandments put it all in a brief list, easy to remember. But the people broke one command after the other.

The writer of Kings stays close to the facts, narrating the sad stories of mostly rotten leaders who care nothing about their privileged place in God's mission to the world. One by one they come and go. The northern kingdom of Israel has a series of kings, not one of them follows after God. The first king of that part of the newly divided nation, Jeroboam, sets up an idol and begins the cycle of idolatry that defiles the nation. The sad refrain is repeated over and over; succeeding kings did not turn away from the sins of Jeroboam. Ahab and his queen Jezebel set new low standards for leadership. Finally, Israel falls and is taken into captivity in Assyria.

Meanwhile, in the southern kingdom of Judah, the same downward spiral evident in Judges shows up. A few good kings arise to clean up previous mistakes, only to have their sons be sinful and idolatrous leaders. Israel's captor, Assyria, has fallen to the Babylonian empire, and Babylon invades and destroys Judah.

From the smallest miracle of Elisha removing the poison from a pot of stew to the powers that overrun the world and conquer nations, God is completely and always in control. Nothing gets in the way of His mission. Nothing happens that surprises Him. The promises still stand. Yahweh will not break from His covenant.

How will it play out in the impossible world of exile? Dim and distant, the mission of God is still at work, waiting for the right time.

David's Last Days

1 Now King David was old and getting on
in years.[a] Although they covered him with
bedclothes, he could not get warm.[b] 2 So his
servants said to him: "Let us[A] search for a
young virgin for my lord the king.[c] She is to
attend the king and be his caregiver. She is to
lie by your side so that my lord the king will
get warm." 3 They searched for a beautiful girl
throughout the territory of Israel; they found
Abishag[d] the Shunammite[B,e] and brought her
to the king. 4 The girl was of unsurpassed
beauty,[f] and she became the king's caregiver.
She served him, but he was not intimate
with[C] her.

Adonijah's Bid for Power

5 Adonijah son of Haggith[g] kept exalting
himself, saying, "I will be king!" He prepared
chariots, cavalry, and 50 men to run ahead
of him.[D,h] 6 But his father had never once rep-
rimanded[E,i] him by saying, "Why do you act
this way?"[j] In addition, he was quite handsome[k] and was born after Absalom.[l] 7 He conspired[F] with Joab son of Zeruiah[m] and with
Abiathar the priest.[n] They supported[o] Adonijah, 8 but Zadok the priest,[p] Benaiah son of
Jehoiada,[q] Nathan the prophet,[r] Shimei,[s]
Rei, and David's warriors[t] did not side with
Adonijah.

9 Adonijah sacrificed sheep, oxen, and fattened cattle near the stone of Zoheleth,
which is next to En-rogel.[u] He invited all his
royal brothers and all the men of Judah, the
servants of the king,[v] 10 but he did not invite
Nathan the prophet, Benaiah, the warriors,
or his brother Solomon.[w]

Nathan's and Bathsheba's Appeals

11 Then Nathan[x] said to Bathsheba, Solomon's mother,[y] "Have you not heard that
Adonijah son of Haggith has become king[z]
and our lord David does not know it?[aa] 12 Now
please come and let me advise[ab] you. Save your
life and the life of your son Solomon.[ac] 13 Go,
approach King David and say to him, 'My lord
the king, did you not swear to your servant:
Your son Solomon is to become king after me,
and he is the one who is to sit on my throne?[ad]
So why has Adonijah become king?' 14 At that
moment, while you are still there speaking
with the king, I'll come in after you and confirm your words."[ae]

15 So Bathsheba went to the king in his bedroom. Since the king was very old, Abishag
the Shunammite was serving him.[af] 16 Bathsheba bowed down and paid homage to the
king, and he asked, "What do you want?"

17 She replied, "My lord, you swore to your
servant by the LORD your God, 'Your son Solomon is to become king after me, and he is the
one who is to sit on my throne.' 18 Now look,
Adonijah has become king. And,[G] my lord the
king, you didn't know it. 19 He has lavishly
sacrificed oxen, fattened cattle, and sheep.
He invited all the king's sons, Abiathar the
priest, and Joab the commander of the army,
but he did not invite your servant Solomon.
20 Now, my lord the king, the eyes of all Israel
are on you to tell them who will sit on the
throne of my lord the king after him. 21 Otherwise, when my lord the king rests with his
fathers,[ag] I and my son Solomon will be regarded as criminals."[ah]

22 At that moment, while she was still speaking with the king, Nathan the prophet arrived,[ai] 23 and it was announced to the king,
"Nathan the prophet is here." He came into
the king's presence and bowed to him with
his face to the ground.

24 "My lord the king," Nathan said, "did you
say, 'Adonijah is to become king after me, and
he is the one who is to sit on my throne'? 25 For
today he went down and lavishly sacrificed
oxen, fattened cattle, and sheep. He invited
all the sons of the king, the commanders of
the army, and Abiathar the priest. And look!
They're eating and drinking in his presence,
and they're saying, 'Long live King Adonijah!'
26 But he did not invite me — me, your servant — or Zadok the priest or Benaiah son of
Jehoiada or your servant Solomon. 27 I'm certain my lord the king would not have let this
happen without letting your servant[H] know
who will sit on my lord the king's throne after him."

[a] **1:1** 2Sm 5:4; 1Kg 2:10-11; 1Ch 23:1
[b] Ec 4:11
[c] **1:2** Est 2:2
[d] **1:3** 1Kg 1:15; 2:17
[e] Jos 19:18; 1Sm 28:4
[f] **1:4** Est 2:7
[g] **1:5** 2Sm 3:4
[h] 2Sm 15:1
[i] **1:6** 1Sm 3:13
[j] 2Sm 13:21
[k] 2Sm 14:25
[l] 2Sm 3:3-4
[m] **1:7** 1Ch 11:6
[n] 1Sm 22:20-23; 2Sm 20:25
[o] 1Kg 2:22
[p] **1:8** 2Sm 20:25; 1Ch 16:39-40
[q] 2Sm 8:18
[r] 2Sm 7:2; 2:1-25
[s] 1Kg 4:18
[t] 2Sm 23:8-39
[u] **1:9** Jos 15:7; 18:16; 2Sm 17:17
[v] 2Sm 15:11-12
[w] **1:10** 1Kg 1:8,26
[x] **1:11** 2Sm 12:1,25; 1Kg 1:8,10
[y] 2Sm 12:24
[z] 2Sm 15:10; 1Kg 1:25; 2:15
[aa] 2Sm 3:26; 1Kg 1:18; 2:32
[ab] **1:12** Pr 15:22
[ac] 1Kg 15:29; 2Kg 10:11
[ad] **1:13** 1Kg 1:17,30; 1Ch 22:9-13
[ae] **1:14** 1Kg 1:22-27
[af] **1:15** 1Kg 1:1-4
[ag] **1:21** Dt 31:16; 2Sm 7:12; 1Kg 2:10
[ah] 1Kg 1:12
[ai] **1:22** 1Kg 1:14

[A] **1:2** Lit *them* [B] **1:3** Shunem was a town in the hill country of Issachar at the foot of Mt. Moreh; Jos 19:17-18. [C] **1:4** Lit *he did not know* [D] **1:5** Heralds announcing his procession [E] **1:6** Or *grieved* [F] **1:7** Lit *His words were* [G] **1:18** Some Hb mss, LXX, Vg, Syr; other Hb mss read *And now* [H] **1:27** Some Hb mss, LXX; alt Hb tradition reads *servants*

Solomon Confirmed King

28 King David responded by saying, "Call in Bathsheba for me." So she came into the king's presence and stood before him. 29 The king swore an oath and said, "As the LORD lives, who has redeemed my life from every difficulty,[a] 30 just as I swore to you by the LORD God of Israel: Your son Solomon is to become king after me, and he is the one who is to sit on my throne in my place,[b] that is exactly what I will do this very day."[c]

31 Bathsheba bowed with her face to the ground, paying homage to the king,[d] and said, "May my lord King David live forever!"[e]

32 King David then said, "Call in Zadok the priest, Nathan the prophet, and Benaiah son of Jehoiada for me."[f] So they came into the king's presence. 33 The king said to them, "Take my servants[g] with you, have my son Solomon ride on my own mule,[h] and take him down to Gihon.[i] 34 There, Zadok the priest and Nathan the prophet are to anoint him as king over Israel.[j] You are to blow the ram's horn[k] and say, 'Long live King Solomon!'[l] 35 You are to come up after him, and he is to come in and sit on my throne. He is the one who is to become king in my place; he is the one I have commanded to be ruler[m] over Israel and Judah."[n]

36 "Amen," Benaiah son of Jehoiada replied to the king. "May the LORD, the God of my lord the king, so affirm it.[o] 37 Just as the LORD was with my lord the king,[p] so may He[A] be with Solomon and make his throne greater than the throne of my lord King David."[q]

38 Then Zadok the priest, Nathan the prophet, Benaiah son of Jehoiada, the Cherethites, and the Pelethites[r] went down, had Solomon ride on King David's mule, and took him to Gihon. 39 Zadok the priest took the horn of oil from the tabernacle and anointed Solomon.[s] Then they blew the ram's horn,[t] and all the people proclaimed, "Long live King Solomon!"[u] 40 All the people followed him, playing flutes and rejoicing with such a great joy[v] that the earth split open from the sound.[B]

Adonijah Hears of Solomon's Coronation

41 Adonijah and all the invited guests who were with him[w] heard the noise as they finished eating. Joab heard the sound of the ram's horn and said, "Why is the town in such an uproar?"[x] 42 He was still speaking when Jonathan son of Abiathar the priest,[y] suddenly arrived. Adonijah said, "Come in, for you are an excellent man, and you must be bringing good news."[z]

43 "Unfortunately not," Jonathan answered him. "Our lord King David has made Solomon king. 44 And with Solomon, the king has sent Zadok the priest, Nathan the prophet, Benaiah son of Jehoiada, the Cherethites, and the Pelethites, and they have had him ride on the king's mule. 45 Zadok the priest and Nathan the prophet have anointed him king in Gihon.[aa] They have gone from there rejoicing. The town has been in an uproar; that's the noise you heard. 46 Solomon has even taken his seat on the royal throne.[ab]

47 "The king's servants have also gone to congratulate our lord King David, saying, 'May your God make the name of Solomon more well known than your name, and may He make his throne greater than your throne.'[ac] Then the king bowed in worship on his bed.[ad] 48 And the king went on to say this: 'May the LORD God of Israel be praised! Today He has provided one to sit on my throne,[ae] and I am a witness.'"[C]

49 Then all of Adonijah's guests got up trembling and went their separate ways. 50 Adonijah was afraid of Solomon, so he got up and went to take hold of the horns of the altar.[af]

51 It was reported to Solomon: "Look, Adonijah fears King Solomon, and he has taken hold of the horns of the altar, saying, 'Let King Solomon first[D] swear to me that he will not kill his servant with the sword.'"

52 Then Solomon said, "If he is a man of character, not a single hair of his will fall to the ground,[ag] but if evil is found in him, he dies."[ah] 53 So King Solomon sent for him, and they took him down from the altar. He came and paid homage to King Solomon, and Solomon said to him, "Go to your home."

David's Dying Instructions to Solomon

2 As the time approached for David to die,[ai] he instructed his son Solomon, 2 "As for me, I am going the way of all of the earth.[aj] Be

[a] **1:29** 2Sm 4:9
[b] **1:30** 1Kg 1:13
[c] 1Kg 1:33-35
[d] **1:31** 1Kg 1:16
[e] Neh 2:3; Dn 2:4; 3:9
[f] **1:32** 1Kg 1:8,10,26
[g] **1:33** 2Sm 20:6
[h] 2Sm 18:9; Est 6:8; Zch 9:9; Jn 12:14-15
[i] 2Ch 32:30; 33:14
[j] **1:34** 1Sm 10:1; 16:3,13
[k] 2Sm 15:10
[l] 1Sm 10:24; 1Kg 1:25
[m] **1:35** 1Sm 13:14
[n] 2Sm 2:4; 5:3
[o] **1:36** Jr 28:6
[p] **1:37** 1Sm 20:13
[q] 1Kg 1:47
[r] **1:38** 2Sm 8:18
[s] **1:39** 1Ch 29:22
[t] 2Kg 11:14
[u] 1Sm 10:24
[v] **1:40** Ezr 6:16
[w] **1:41** 1Kg 1:5,7-10
[x] 2Kg 11:12-13
[y] **1:42** 2Sm 15:27,36
[z] 2Sm 18:26-27
[aa] **1:43-45** 1Kg 1:33-35
[ab] **1:46** 1Ch 29:23
[ac] **1:47** 1Kg 1:37
[ad] Gn 47:31
[ae] **1:48** 2Sm 7:12; 1Kg 3:6
[af] **1:50** Ex 21:12-14; 1Kg 2:28
[ag] **1:52** 1Sm 14:45; 2Sm 14:11; Ac 27:34
[ah] 1Kg 2:23-25
[ai] **2:1** Gn 47:29; Nm 27:13
[aj] **2:2** Jos 23:14

[A] **1:37** Alt Hb tradition reads *so He will* [B] **1:40** LXX reads *the land resounded with their noise* [C] **1:48** Lit *and my eyes are seeing* [D] **1:51** Some Hb mss, LXX, Syr, Vg read *today*

strong and be courageous like a man,[a] 3 and
keep your obligation to the LORD your God
to walk in His ways and to keep His statutes,
commands, ordinances, and decrees. This
is written in the law of Moses, so that you
will have success in everything you do[b] and
wherever you turn, 4 and so that the LORD will
carry out His promise that He made to me: 'If
your sons are careful to walk faithfully before
Me with their whole mind and heart,[c] you
will never fail to have a man on the throne of
Israel.'[d]
5 "You also know what Joab son of Zeruiah
did to me[e] and what he did to the two commanders of Israel's army, Abner son of Ner[f]
and Amasa son of Jether.[g] He murdered them
in a time of peace to avenge blood shed in
war. He spilled that blood on his own waistband and on the sandals of his feet.[A] 6 Act according to your wisdom, and do not let his
gray head descend to ·Sheol in peace.
7 "Show loyalty to the sons of Barzillai the
Gileadite and let them be among those who
eat at your table[h] because they supported me
when I fled from your brother Absalom.[i]
8 "Keep an eye on Shimei son of Gera, the
Benjaminite from Bahurim who is with you.
He uttered malicious curses against me the
day I went to Mahanaim.[j] But he came down
to meet me at the Jordan River, and I swore
to him by the LORD: 'I will never kill you with
the sword.'[k] 9 So don't let him go unpunished,
for you are a wise man. You know how to
deal with him to bring his gray head down to
Sheol with blood."
10 Then David rested with his fathers[l] and
was buried in the city of David.[m] 11 The length
of time David reigned over Israel was 40
years: he reigned seven years in Hebron and
33 years in Jerusalem.[n] 12 Solomon sat on the
throne of his father David, and his kingship
was firmly established.[o]

Adonijah's Foolish Request

13 Now Adonijah son of Haggith[p] came to
Bathsheba, Solomon's mother. She asked, "Do
you come peacefully?"
"Peacefully," he replied,[q] 14 and then asked,
"May I talk with you?"[B]
"Go ahead," she answered.
15 "You know the kingship was mine,"[r] he
said. "All Israel expected me to be king, but
then the kingship was turned over to my
brother,[s] for the LORD gave it to him.[t] 16 So
now I have just one request of you; don't turn
me down."[C]
She said to him, "Go on."
17 He replied, "Please speak to King Solomon
since he won't turn you down. Let him give
me Abishag the Shunammite[u] as a wife."
18 "Very well," Bathsheba replied. "I will
speak to the king for you."
19 So Bathsheba went to King Solomon to
speak to him about Adonijah. The king stood
up to greet her, bowed to her, sat down on his
throne, and had a throne placed for the king's
mother.[v] So she sat down at his right hand.[w]
20 Then she said, "I have just one small request of you. Don't turn me down."
"Go ahead and ask, mother," the king replied, "for I won't turn you down."
21 So she said, "Let Abishag the Shunammite
be given to your brother Adonijah as a wife."
22 King Solomon answered his mother,
"Why are you requesting Abishag the Shunammite for Adonijah? Since he is my elder
brother,[x] you might as well ask the kingship
for him,[y] for Abiathar the priest, and for Joab
son of Zeruiah."[D,z] 23 Then Solomon took an
oath by the LORD: "May God punish me and
do so severely[aa] if Adonijah has not made this
request at the cost of his life. 24 And now, as
the LORD lives, the One who established me,
seated me on the throne of my father David,
and made me a dynasty as He promised[ab]—I
swear Adonijah will be put to death today!"
25 Then King Solomon gave the order to Benaiah son of Jehoiada,[ac] who struck down Adonijah, and he died.

Abiathar's Banishment

26 The king said to Abiathar the priest,[ad]
"Go to your fields in Anathoth.[ae] Even though
you deserve to die, I will not put you to death
today, since you carried the ark of the Lord
GOD in the presence of my father David[af] and
you suffered through all that my father suffered."[ag] 27 So Solomon banished Abiathar

[a] 2:2 Jos 1:6-7,9 [b] 2:3 Dt 29:9; 1Ch 22:12-13 [c] 2:4 Dt 6:5; Mt 22:37 [d] 2Sm 7:12-13; 1Kg 8:25; 9:5 [e] 2:5 2Sm 18:5,12,14 [f] 2Sm 3:27 [g] 2Sm 20:10 [h] 2:7 2Sm 9:7; 19:28 [i] 2Sm 19:31-39 [j] 2:8 2Sm 16:5-13 [k] 2Sm 19:16-23 [l] 2:10 Ac 2:29; 13:36 [m] 2Sm 5:7 [n] 2:11 2Sm 5:4-5; 1Ch 29:27 [o] 2:12 1Kg 2:46; 1Ch 17:14 [p] 2:13 1Kg 1:5,51-53 [q] 1Sm 16:4-5 [r] 2:15 1Kg 1:11 [s] 1Kg 1:38-46 [t] 1Ch 23:9-10; 28:5,7; Dn 2:21; 4:17; Jn 19:11; Rm 13:1 [u] 2:17 1Kg 1:3-4,15 [v] 2:19 2Sm 15:16; 1Kg 15:13 [w] Ps 110:1; Mt 20:21 [x] 2:22 1Kg 1:6; 1Ch 3:2,5 [y] 2Sm 16:20-22 [z] 1Kg 1:7 [aa] 2:23 Ru 1:17; 1Sm 3:17 [ab] 2:24 2Sm 7:11-13 [ac] 2:25 1Kg 1:8,26,38 [ad] 2:26 1Kg 1:7,19 [ae] Jos 21:18; Jr 1:1 [af] 2Sm 15:24-25,29 [ag] 1Sm 22:20-23; 2Sm 19:11

[A] 2:5 LXX, Old Lat read *on my waistband and . . . my feet*; v. 31 [B] 2:14 Lit *then said, "I have a word for you."* [C] 2:16 Lit *don't make me turn my face* [D] 2:22 LXX, Vg, Syr read *kingship for him, and on his side are Abiathar the priest and Joab son of Zeruiah*

from being the LORD's priest, and it fulfilled
the LORD's prophecy He had spoken at Shiloh
against Eli's family.[a]

Joab's Execution

28The news reached Joab. Since he had supported Adonijah[b] but not Absalom,[c] Joab fled
to the LORD's tabernacle and took hold of the
horns of the altar.[d]
29It was reported to King Solomon: "Joab
has fled to the LORD's tabernacle and is now
beside the altar." Then Solomon sent[A] Benaiah son of Jehoiada[e] and told him, "Go and
strike him down!"[f]
30So Benaiah went to the tabernacle and
said to Joab, "This is what the king says:
'Come out!'"[g]

But Joab said, "No, for I will die here."

So Benaiah took a message back to the king,
"This is what Joab said, and this is how he answered me."
31The king said to him, "Do just as he says.
Strike him down and bury him in order to
remove from me and from my father's house
the blood that Joab shed without just cause.[h]
32The LORD will bring back his own blood on
his head because he struck down two men
more righteous and better than he, without my father David's knowledge. With his
sword, Joab murdered Abner[i] son of Ner,
commander of Israel's army, and Amasa[j] son
of Jether, commander of Judah's army. 33Their
blood will come back on Joab's head and on
the head of his descendants forever, but for
David, his descendants, his dynasty, and his
throne, there will be peace from the LORD
forever."[k]
34Benaiah son of Jehoiada[l] went up, struck
down Joab, and put him to death. He was buried at his house in the wilderness.[m] 35Then the
king appointed Benaiah son of Jehoiada in
Joab's place over the army,[n] and he appointed
Zadok the priest in Abiathar's place.

Shimei's Banishment and Execution

36Then the king summoned Shimei[o] and
said to him, "Build a house for yourself in Jerusalem and live there, but don't leave there
and go anywhere else. 37On the day you do
leave and cross the Kidron Valley,[p] know for
sure that you will certainly die. Your blood
will be on your own head."[q]
38Shimei said to the king, "The sentence is
fair; your servant will do as my lord the king
has spoken." And Shimei lived in Jerusalem
for a long time.
39But then, at the end of three years, two
of Shimei's slaves ran away to Achish[r] son of
Maacah, king of Gath.[s] Shimei was informed,
"Look, your slaves are in Gath." 40So Shimei
saddled his donkey and set out to Achish at
Gath to search for his slaves. He went and
brought them back from Gath.
41It was reported to Solomon that Shimei
had gone from Jerusalem to Gath and had returned. 42So the king summoned Shimei and
said to him, "Didn't I make you swear by the
LORD and warn you, saying, 'On the day you
leave and go anywhere else, know for sure
that you will certainly die'? And you said to
me, 'The sentence is fair; I will obey.' 43So why
have you not kept the LORD's oath and the
command that I gave you?" 44The king also
said, "You yourself know all the evil that you
did to my father David.[t] Therefore, the LORD
has brought back your evil on your head,
45but King Solomon will be blessed, and David's throne will remain established before
the LORD forever."[u]
46Then the king commanded Benaiah son
of Jehoiada, and he went out and struck
Shimei down, and he died. So the kingdom
was established in Solomon's hand.[v]

The LORD Appears to Solomon

3 Solomon made an alliance[B] with Pharaoh
king of Egypt by marrying Pharaoh's
daughter.[w] Solomon brought her to live in
the city of David[x] until he finished building
his palace,[y] the LORD's temple,[z] and the wall
surrounding Jerusalem.[aa] 2However, the people were sacrificing on the *high places,[ab] because until that time a temple for the LORD's
name[ac] had not been built. 3Solomon loved
the LORD[ad] by walking in the statutes of his
father David,[ae] but he also sacrificed and
burned incense on the high places.
4The king went to Gibeon[af] to sacrifice

[a]2:27 1Sm 2:31-35 [b]2:28 1Kg 1:7 [c]2Sm 18:1-5 [d]Ex 21:12-14; 1Kg 1:50 [e]2:29 1Kg 1:8 [f]Ex 12:12,14; 2Sm 3:27; 18:14; 20:10 [g]2:30 Ex 21:14 [h]2:31 Nm 35:33; Dt 21:8-9 [i]2:32 2Sm 3:26-27 [j]2Sm 20:8-10 [k]2:33 2Sm 3:28-29 [l]2:34 2Kg 2:25 [m]2Sm 2:32 [n]2:35 1Kg 4:4 [o]2:36 2Sm 16:5-13; 1Kg 2:8-9 [p]2:37 Jn 18:1 [q]Gn 2:17; 2Sm 1:16 [r]2:39 1Sm 27:2 [s]Jos 13:3; 1Sm 6:16-17; 21:10 [t]2:44 1Kg 2:8-9 [u]2:45 2Sm 7:13 [v]2:46 1Kg 2:12; 2Ch 1:1 [w]3:1 Dt 7:3; 1Kg 7:8; 9:24; Ezr 9:14 [x]2Sm 5:7; 7:8; 9:10 [y]2Sm 7:1-2 [z]2Sm 6:1,14; 1Kg 6:37; 7:51 [aa]1Kg 9:15 [ab]3:2 Dt 12:13-14 [ac]Dt 14:23 [ad]3:3 Dt 6:5 [ae]1Kg 3:14 [af]3:4 Jos 9:3-27; 21:17

A2:29 LXX adds *Joab a message: "What is the matter with you, that you have fled to the altar?" And Joab replied, "Because I feared you, I have fled to the Lord."* And Solomon the king sent B3:1 Lit *Solomon made himself a son-in-law*

there because it was the most famous high
place. He offered 1,000 •burnt offerings on
that altar.[a] 5At Gibeon the LORD appeared
to Solomon[b] in a dream at night.[c] God said,
"Ask.[d] What should I give you?"

6And Solomon replied, "You have shown
great and faithful love to Your servant, my
father David, because he walked before You
in faithfulness, righteousness, and[A] integrity.
You have continued this great and faithful
love for him by giving him a son to sit on his
throne,[e] as it is today.[f]

7"LORD my God, You have now made Your
servant king in my father David's place.[g] Yet
I am just a youth with no experience in leadership.[B,h] 8Your servant is among Your people
You have chosen,[i] a[C] people too numerous to
be numbered or counted.[j] 9So give Your servant an obedient heart to judge[k] Your people
and to discern between good and evil. For who
is able to judge this great people of Yours?"[l]

10Now it pleased the Lord that Solomon had
requested this. 11So God said to him, "Because
you have requested this and did not ask for
long life[D] or riches for yourself,[m] or the death[E]
of your enemies, but you asked discernment
for yourself to understand justice,[n] 12I will
therefore do what you have asked.[o] I will give
you a wise and understanding heart, so that
there has never been anyone like you before
and never will be again.[p] 13In addition, I will
give you what you did not ask for: both riches
and honor,[q] so that no man in any kingdom
will be your equal during your entire life.[r] 14If
you walk in My ways and keep My statutes
and commands just as your father David did,
I will give you a long life."[s]

15Then Solomon woke up[t] and realized it had
been a dream.[u] He went to Jerusalem, stood
before the ark of the Lord's covenant,[v] and
offered burnt offerings and •fellowship offerings.[w] Then he held a feast[x] for all his servants.

Solomon's Wisdom

16Then two women who were prostitutes
came to the king and stood before him.[y] 17One
woman said, "Please my lord, this woman
and I live in the same house, and I had a baby
while she was in the house. 18On the third day
after I gave birth, she also had a baby and we
were alone. No one else[F] was with us in the
house; just the two of us were there. 19During
the night this woman's son died because she
lay on him. 20She got up in the middle of the
night and took my son from my side while
your servant was asleep. She laid him at her
breast, and she put her dead son in my arms.
21When I got up in the morning to nurse my
son, I discovered he was dead. That morning,
when I looked closely at him I realized that
he was not the son I gave birth to."

22"No," the other woman said. "My son is
the living one; your son is the dead one."

The first woman said, "No, your son is the
dead one; my son is the living one." So they
argued before the king.

23The king replied, "This woman says, 'This
is my son who is alive, and your son is dead,'
but that woman says, 'No, your son is dead,
and my son is alive.'" 24The king continued,
"Bring me a sword." So they brought the
sword to the king. 25Solomon said, "Cut the
living boy in two and give half to one and half
to the other."

26The woman whose son was alive spoke to
the king because she felt great compassion[G,z]
for her son. "My lord, give her the living baby,"
she said, "but please don't have him killed!"

But the other one said, "He will not be mine
or yours. Cut him in two!"

27The king responded, "Give the living baby
to the first woman, and don't kill him. She is
his mother." 28All Israel heard about the judgment the king had given, and they stood in
awe of the king because they saw that God's
wisdom[aa] was in him to carry out justice.

Solomon's Officials

4 King Solomon ruled over Israel,[ab] 2and
these were his officials:[ac]

Azariah son of Zadok, priest;
3Elihoreph and Ahijah the sons of
Shisha, secretaries;
Jehoshaphat son of Ahilud, court
historian;
4Benaiah son of Jehoiada, in charge of
the army;
Zadok and Abiathar, priests;

[a]**3:4** 2Ch 1:3,6
[b]**3:5-15** 2Ch 1:7-13
[c]**3:5** Nm 12:6; 1Kg 9:2; 11:9
[d]Mt 7:7; Jn 15:7
[e]**3:6** 1Kg 1:48
[f]1Kg 2:4; 9:4; 2Ch 1:8
[g]**3:7** 2Ch 1:8
[h]1Ch 29:1; Jr 1:6-7
[i]**3:8** Ex 19:5-6; Dt 7:6
[j]Gn 15:5; 22:17
[k]**3:9** Dt 1:16-17
[l]2Ch 1:10
[m]**3:11** Jms 4:3
[n]1Ch 22:12
[o]**3:12** 1Jn 5:14-15
[p]1Kg 4:29-31; 10:23-24
[q]**3:13** Mt 6:33; Lk 12:31
[r]1Kg 10:23
[s]**3:14** 1Kg 3:6; Pr 3:1-2
[t]**3:15** Gn 41:7
[u]Dn 2:3; 4:5
[v]2Sm 6:12
[w]1Sm 11:15
[x]1Kg 8:65
[y]**3:16** Dt 16:18-19; 2Sm 15:2-4
[z]**3:26** Gn 43:30; Jr 31:20; Hs 11:8
[aa]**3:28** 2Sm 14:20; 1Kg 3:9,11-12
[ab]**4:1** 2Sm 5:5; 8:15
[ac]**4:2** 1Kg 12:6

[A]**3:6** Lit *and with You* [B]**3:7** Lit *am a little youth and do not know to go out or come in* [C]**3:8** Lit *chosen many* [D]**3:11** Lit *for many days* [E]**3:11** Lit *life* [F]**3:18** Lit *No stranger* [G]**3:26** Lit *because her compassion grew hot*

5 Azariah son of Nathan, in charge of
the deputies;
Zabud son of Nathan, a priest and
adviser to the king;
6 Ahishar, in charge of the palace;
and Adoniram son of Abda, in charge
of forced labor.

7 Solomon had 12 deputies for all Israel.
They provided food for the king and his
household; each one made provision for one
month out of the year.[a] 8 These were their
names:

Ben-hur, in the hill country of
Ephraim;
9 Ben-deker, in Makaz, Shaalbim,
Beth-shemesh, and Elon-beth-hanan;
10 Ben-hesed, in Arubboth (he had
Socoh and the whole land of Hepher);
11 Ben-abinadab, in all Naphath-dor
(Taphath daughter of Solomon was his
wife);
12 Baana son of Ahilud, in Taanach,
Megiddo, and all Beth-shean which is
beside Zarethan below Jezreel, from
Beth-shean to Abel-meholah, as far as
the other side of Jokmeam;
13 Ben-geber, in Ramoth-gilead (he had
the villages of Jair son of Manasseh,
which are in Gilead, and he had the
region of Argob, which is in Bashan, 60
great cities with walls and bronze bars);
14 Ahinadab son of Iddo, in Mahanaim;
15 Ahimaaz, in Naphtali (he
also had married a daughter of
Solomon — Basemath);
16 Baana son of Hushai, in Asher and
Bealoth;
17 Jehoshaphat son of Paruah, in
Issachar;
18 Shimei son of Ela, in Benjamin;
19 Geber son of Uri, in the land of
Gilead, the country of Sihon king of the
Amorites and of Og king of Bashan.

There was one deputy in the land of Judah.[A]

Solomon's Provisions

20 Judah and Israel were as numerous as the
sand by the sea;[b] they were eating, drinking,
and rejoicing. 21 [B]Solomon ruled over all the
kingdoms from the Euphrates River to the
land of the Philistines and as far as the border of Egypt.[c] They offered tribute and served
Solomon all the days of his life.[d]

22 Solomon's provisions for one day were 150
bushels[C] of fine flour and 300 bushels[D] of meal,
23 10 fattened oxen, 20 range oxen, and 100
sheep, besides deer, gazelles, roebucks, and
pen-fed poultry,[E,e] 24 for he had dominion over
everything west of the Euphrates from Tiphsah to Gaza and over all the kings west of the
Euphrates. He had peace on all his surrounding borders. 25 Throughout Solomon's reign,
Judah and Israel lived in safety from Dan to
Beer-sheba,[f] each man under his own vine and
his own fig tree.[g] 26 Solomon had 40,000[F] stalls
of horses for his chariots, and 12,000 horsemen.[h] 27 Each of those deputies for a month in
turn provided food for King Solomon and for
everyone who came to King Solomon's table.
They neglected nothing. 28 Each man brought
the barley and the straw for the chariot teams
and the other horses[i] to the required place according to his assignment.[G]

Solomon's Wisdom and Literary Gifts

29 God gave Solomon wisdom, very great insight, and understanding[j] as vast as the sand
on the seashore. 30 Solomon's wisdom was
greater than the wisdom of all the people
of the East,[k] greater than all the wisdom of
Egypt.[l] 31 He was wiser than anyone[m] — wiser
than Ethan the Ezrahite,[n] and Heman, Calcol,
and Darda, sons of Mahol.[o] His reputation extended to all the surrounding nations.[p]

32 Solomon composed 3,000 proverbs,[q] and
his songs numbered 1,005.[r] 33 He described
trees, from the cedar in Lebanon to the hyssop growing out of the wall. He also taught
about animals, birds, reptiles, and fish. 34 People came from everywhere, sent by every king
on earth who had heard of his wisdom, to listen to Solomon's wisdom.[s]

Hiram's Building Materials

5 [H]Hiram king of Tyre[t] sent his servants
to Solomon when he heard that he had
been anointed king in his father's place,[u]

[a] **4:7** 1Kg 4:27 [b] **4:20** Gn 22:17; 1Kg 3:8 [c] **4:21** Gn 15:18; 2Ch 9:26 [d] 2Sm 8:2,6 [e] **4:22-23** 1Kg 10:5; Neh 5:18 [f] **4:25** Jdg 20:1; 1Sm 3:20 [g] Mc 4:3-4; Zch 3:10 [h] **4:26** Dt 17:16; 1Kg 10:26; 2Ch 1:14 [i] **4:28** Est 8:10,14 [j] **4:29** 1Kg 3:12 [k] **4:30** Gn 29:1 [l] Is 19:11; Ac 7:22 [m] **4:31** 1Kg 3:12 [n] 1Ch 15:19; Pss 88, 89 titles [o] 1Ch 2:6 [p] 1Kg 10:1,6 [q] **4:32** Pr 1:1; Ec 9:12 [r] Sg 1:1 [s] **4:34** 1Kg 10:1,6 [t] **5:1** 2Ch 2:3 [u] 1Kg 1:34,39

[A] **4:19** LXX; MT omits *of Judah* [B] **4:21** 1Kg 5:1 in Hb [C] **4:22** Lit *30 cors* [D] **4:22** Lit *60 cors* [E] **4:23** Hb obscure [F] **4:26** 2Ch 9:25 reads *4,000 stalls* [G] **4:28** Lit *judgment* [H] **5:1** 1Kg 5:15 in Hb

for Hiram had always been friends with David.[a]
2Solomon sent this message to Hiram:
3"You know my father David was not able
to build a temple for the name of •Yahweh
his God. This was because of the warfare all
around him until the LORD put his enemies
under his feet.[b] 4The LORD my God has now
given me rest all around; there is no enemy
or crisis.[c] 5So I plan to build a temple for the
name of Yahweh my God,[d] according to what
the LORD promised my father David: 'I will
put your son on your throne in your place,
and he will build the temple for My name.'[e]
6"Therefore, command that cedars from
Lebanon be cut down for me. My servants
will be with your servants, and I will pay your
servants' wages according to whatever you
say, for you know that not a man among us
knows how to cut timber like the Sidonians."[f]
7When Hiram heard Solomon's words, he
greatly rejoiced and said, "May the LORD be
praised today![g] He has given David a wise
son to be over this great people!" 8Then Hiram sent a reply to Solomon, saying, "I have
heard your message; I will do everything you
want regarding the cedar and cypress timber.
9My servants will bring the logs down from
Lebanon to the sea, and I will make them into
rafts to go by sea to the place you indicate. I
will break them apart there, and you can take
them away. You then can meet my needs by
providing my household with food."[h]
10So Hiram provided Solomon with all the
cedar and cypress timber he wanted, 11and
Solomon provided Hiram with 100,000
bushels[A] of wheat as food for his household
and 110,000 gallons[B] of oil from crushed olives.[i] Solomon did this for Hiram year after
year.
12The LORD gave Solomon wisdom, as He
had promised him.[j] There was peace between
Hiram and Solomon, and the two of them
made a treaty.[k]

Solomon's Work Force

13Then King Solomon drafted forced laborers from all Israel;[l] the labor force numbered
30,000 men. 14He sent 10,000 to Lebanon
each month in shifts; one month they were
in Lebanon, two months they were at home.
Adoniram was in charge of the forced labor.
15Solomon had 70,000 porters and 80,000
stonecutters in the mountains,[m] 16not including his 3,300[C] deputies[n] in charge of the
work. They ruled over the people doing the
work. 17The king commanded them to quarry
large, costly stones to lay the foundation of
the temple with dressed stones.[o] 18So Solomon's builders and Hiram's builders,[p] along
with the Gebalites,[q] quarried the stone and
prepared the timber and stone for the temple's construction.

Building the Temple

6 Solomon began to build the temple for
the LORD in the four hundred eightieth
year[r] after the Israelites came out of the land
of Egypt, in the fourth year of his reign over
Israel, in the second month, in the month of
Ziv.[D,s] 2The temple that King Solomon built
for the LORD[t] was 90 feet[E] long, 30 feet[F] wide,
and 45 feet[G] high.[u] 3The portico in front of the
temple sanctuary was 30 feet[F] long extending
across the temple's width, and 15 feet deep[H] in
front of the temple.[v] 4He also made windows
with beveled frames[I] for the temple.[w]
5He then built a chambered structure[J]
along the temple wall, encircling the walls
of the temple, that is, the sanctuary and the
inner sanctuary.[x] And he made side chambers[K] all around.[y] 6The lowest chamber was
$7^1/_2$ feet[L] wide, the middle was nine feet[M]
wide, and the third was $10^1/_2$ feet[N] wide. He
also provided offset ledges for the temple all
around the outside so that nothing would be
inserted into the temple walls. 7The temple's
construction used finished stones cut at the
quarry so that no hammer, chisel, or any iron
tool was heard in the temple while it was being built.[z]
8The door for the lowest[O] side chamber
was on the right side of the temple. They[P]
went up a stairway[I] to the middle chamber,
and from the middle to the third. 9When he
finished building the temple,[aa] he paneled it

[a]**5:1** 2Sm 5:11; 1Ch 14:1
[b]**5:3** 1Ch 28:2-3
[c]**5:4** 1Kg 4:24-25
[d]**5:5** 2Ch 2:4
[e]2Sm 7:12-13
[f]**5:6** 2Ch 2:8
[g]**5:7** 1Kg 10:9
[h]**5:9** 2Ch 2:16; Ezr 3:7
[i]**5:11** 2Ch 2:10
[j]**5:12** 1Kg 3:12
[k]1Kg 15:19
[l]**5:13** 1Kg 4:6; 9:15
[m]**5:15** 2Ch 2:17-18
[n]**5:16** 1Kg 9:23
[o]**5:17** 1Kg 6:7; 1Ch 22:2
[p]**5:18** 1Kg 5:6,9
[q]Jos 13:5
[r]**6:1** Ac 13:20
[s]1Kg 6:37; 2Ch 3:1-2; Ezr 3:8
[t]**6:2** Ezr 5:11
[u]2Ch 3:3; Ezk 41:1
[v]**6:3** 2Ch 3:4; Ezk 40:49
[w]**6:4** Ezk 41:16
[x]**6:5** 1Kg 6:16,19-21
[y]Jr 35:2; Ezk 41:5-6
[z]**6:7** 1Kg 5:17
[aa]**6:9** 1Kg 6:1,14,38

[A]**5:11** Lit *20,000 cors* [B]**5:11** LXX reads *20,000 baths*; MT reads *20 cors* [C]**5:16** Some LXX mss read *3,600*; 2Ch 2:2,18 [D]**6:1** April–May [E]**6:2** Lit *60 cubits* [F]**6:2,3** Lit *20 cubits* [G]**6:2** Lit *30 cubits* [H]**6:3** Lit *10 cubits wide* [I]**6:4,8** Hb obscure [J]**6:5** Lit *built the house of chamber* [K]**6:5** Lit *made ribs* or *sides* [L]**6:6** Lit *five cubits* [M]**6:6** Lit *six cubits* [N]**6:6** Lit *seven cubits* [O]**6:8** LXX, Tg; MT reads *middle* [P]**6:8** = people with boards and planks of cedar. 10 He built the chambers along the entire temple, joined to the temple with cedar beams;[a] each story was 7½ feet[A] high.

11 The word of the LORD came to Solomon:[b] 12 "As for this temple you are building—if you walk in My statutes, observe My ordinances, and keep all My commands by walking in them,[c] I will fulfill My promise to you, which I made to your father David.[d] 13 I will live among the Israelites and not abandon My people Israel."[e]

14 When Solomon finished building the temple,[B,f] 15 he paneled the interior temple walls with cedar boards; from the temple floor to the surface of the ceiling he overlaid the interior with wood. He also overlaid the floor with cypress boards.[g] 16 Then he lined 30 feet[C] of the rear of the temple with cedar boards from the floor to the surface of the ceiling,[D] and he built the interior as an inner sanctuary, the most holy place.[h] 17 The temple, that is, the sanctuary in front of the most holy place,[E] was 60 feet[F] long. 18 The cedar paneling inside the temple was carved with ornamental gourds[i] and flower blossoms. Everything was cedar;[j] not a stone could be seen.

19 He prepared the inner sanctuary[k] inside the temple to put the ark of the LORD's covenant[l] there. 20 The interior of the sanctuary was 30 feet[C] long, 30 feet[C] wide, and 30 feet[C] high; he overlaid it with pure gold.[m] He also overlaid the cedar altar. 21 Next, Solomon overlaid the interior of the temple with pure gold, and he hung[G] gold chains[n] across the front of the inner sanctuary[o] and overlaid it with gold. 22 So he added the gold overlay to the entire temple until everything was completely finished, including the entire altar[p] that belongs to the inner sanctuary.

23 In the inner sanctuary he made two ·cherubim[q] 15 feet[H] high out of olive wood. 24 One wing of the first cherub was 7½ feet long,[A] and the other wing was 7½ feet long. The wingspan was 15 feet[H] from tip to tip. 25 The second cherub also was 15 feet;[H] both cherubim had the same size and shape. 26 The first cherub's height was 15 feet[H] and so was the second cherub's. 27 Then he put the cherubim inside the inner temple. Since their wings were spread out, the first one's wing touched one wall while the second cherub's wing touched the other[I] wall, and in the middle of the temple their wings were touching wing to wing.[r] 28 He also overlaid the cherubim with gold.

29 He carved all the surrounding temple walls with carved engravings—cherubim,[s] palm trees and flower blossoms—in both the inner and outer sanctuaries. 30 He overlaid the temple floor with gold in both the inner and outer sanctuaries.

31 For the entrance of the inner sanctuary, he made olive wood doors.[t] The pillars of the doorposts were five-sided.[J] 32 The two doors were made of olive wood. He carved cherubim, palm trees, and flower blossoms on them and overlaid them with gold, hammering gold over the cherubim and palm trees. 33 In the same way, he made four-sided[J] olive wood doorposts for the sanctuary entrance. 34 The two doors[u] were made of cypress wood; the first door had two folding sides, and the second door had two folding panels. 35 He carved cherubim, palm trees, and flower blossoms on them and overlaid them with gold applied evenly over the carving. 36 He built the inner courtyard[v] with three rows of dressed stone[w] and a row of trimmed cedar beams.

37 The foundation of the LORD's temple was laid in Solomon's fourth year in the month of Ziv. 38 In his eleventh year in the eighth month, in the month of Bul,[K] the temple was completed in every detail and according to every specification.[x] So he built it in seven years.[y]

Solomon's Palace Complex

7 Solomon completed his entire palace complex after 13 years of construction.[z] 2 He built the House of the Forest of Lebanon.[aa] It was 150 feet[L] long, 75 feet[M] wide, and 45 feet[N] high on four rows of cedar pillars, with cedar beams on top of the pillars. 3 It was paneled above with cedar at the top

[a] **6:9-10** 1Kg 5:6,8,10 [b] **6:11** 1Kg 3:5,11-15; 9:2 [c] **6:12** 1Kg 11:10 [d] 2Sm 7:12-16; 1Kg 9:5 [e] **6:13** Lv 26:11; Jos 1:5-6; Heb 13:5 [f] **6:14** 1Kg 6:1,38 [g] **6:15** 1Kg 5:8,10; 7:7; Ezk 41:16 [h] **6:16** Ex 26:33-34; 1Kg 8:6; Heb 9:3 [i] **6:18** 1Kg 7:24 [j] 1Kg 5:8,10 [k] **6:19** Ezk 41:3-4 [l] Dt 10:16; Jos 3:11 [m] **6:20** 2Ch 3:8-9 [n] **6:21** 2Ch 3:14; Mt 27:51 [o] 2Ch 3:16 [p] **6:22** 1Kg 7:48; Heb 9:3-4 [q] **6:23-27** Ex 25:18-22; 2Ch 3:10-13 [r] **6:27** 2Ch 5:8 [s] **6:29** Ezk 41:18,25 [t] **6:31-32** Ezk 41:23 [u] **6:34-35** Ezk 41:23-25 [v] **6:36** 2Ch 4:9; Jr 36:10 [w] 1Kg 7:12; Ezr 6:4 [x] **6:38** 1Kg 6:1,14 [y] 1Kg 7:1 [z] **7:1** 1Kg 9:10; 2Ch 8:1 [aa] **7:2** 1Kg 10:21; 2Ch 9:16

[A] **6:10,24** Lit *five cubits* [B] **6:11-14** LXX omits these vv. [C] **6:16,20** Lit *20 cubits* [D] **6:16** LXX; MT omits *of the ceiling*; 1Kg 6:15 [E] **6:17** Lit *front of me*; Hb obscure [F] **6:17** Lit *40 cubits* [G] **6:21** Lit *he caused to pass across* [H] **6:23,24,25,26** Lit *10 cubits* [I] **6:27** Lit *the second* [J] **6:31,33** Hb obscure [K] **6:38** = October–November [L] **7:2** Lit *100 cubits* [M] **7:2** Lit *50 cubits* [N] **7:2** Lit *30 cubits*

of the chambers that rested on 45 pillars, 15 per row. [4]There were three rows of window frames, facing each other[A] in three tiers.[B,a] [5]All the doors and doorposts had rectangular frames, the openings facing each other[C] in three tiers.[B] [6]He made the hall of pillars 75 feet[D] long and 45 feet[E] wide. A portico was in front of the pillars, and a canopy with pillars[F] was in front of them. [7]He made the Hall of the Throne where he would judge[b]—the Hall of Judgment. It was paneled with cedar from the floor to the rafters.[G] [8]Solomon's own palace where he would live, in the other courtyard behind the hall, was of similar construction. And he made a house like this hall for Pharaoh's daughter, his wife.[H,c]

[9]All of these buildings were of costly stones, cut to size and sawed with saws on the inner and outer surfaces, from foundation to coping and from the outside to the great courtyard. [10]The foundation was made of large, costly stones 12 and 15 feet[I] long. [11]Above were also costly stones, cut to size, as well as cedar wood. [12]Around the great courtyard, as well as the inner courtyard of the LORD's temple and the portico of the temple, were three rows of dressed stone and a row of trimmed cedar beams.[d]

[13]King Solomon had Hiram[J,e] brought from Tyre. [14]He was a widow's son from the tribe of Naphtali, and his father was a man of Tyre, a bronze craftsman. Hiram had great skill,[f] understanding, and knowledge to do every kind of bronze work. So he came to King Solomon and carried out all his work.[g]

The Bronze Pillars

[15]He cast two hollow bronze pillars:[h] each 27 feet[K] high and 18 feet[L] in circumference.[M,i] [16]He also made two capitals[j] of cast bronze to set on top of the pillars; 7½ feet[N] was the height of the first capital, and 7½ feet[N] was also the height of the second capital. [17]The capitals on top of the pillars had gratings of latticework, wreaths[O] made of chainwork—seven for the first capital and seven for the second.

[18]He made the pillars with two encircling rows of pomegranates on the one grating to cover the capital on top; he did the same for the second capital. [19]And the capitals on top of the pillars in the portico were shaped like lilies, six feet[P] high. [20]The capitals on the two pillars were also immediately above the rounded surface next to the grating, and 200 pomegranates[k] were in rows encircling each[Q] capital. [21]He set up the pillars at the portico[l] of the sanctuary: he set up the right pillar and named it Jachin;[R] then he set up the left pillar and named it Boaz.[S,m] [22]The tops of the pillars were shaped like lilies. Then the work of the pillars was completed.[n]

The Reservoir

[23]He made the cast metal reservoir,[T,o] 15 feet[U] from brim to brim, perfectly round. It was 7½ feet[N] high and 45 feet[E] in circumference. [24]Ornamental gourds[p] encircled it below the brim, 10 every half yard,[V] completely encircling the reservoir.[q] The gourds were cast in two rows when the reservoir was cast. [25]It stood on 12 oxen,[r] three facing north, three facing west, three facing south, and three facing east. The reservoir was on top of them and all their hindquarters were toward the center. [26]The reservoir was three inches[W] thick, and its rim was fashioned like the brim of a cup or of a lily blossom. It held 11,000 gallons.[X]

The Bronze Water Carts

[27]Then he made 10 bronze water carts.[Y,s] Each water cart was six feet[P] long, six feet[P] wide, and 4½ feet[Z] high. [28]This was the design of the carts: They had frames; the frames were between the cross-pieces, [29]and on the frames between the cross-pieces were lions, oxen, and •cherubim.[t] On the cross-pieces there was a pedestal above, and below the lions and oxen were wreaths of hanging[AA] work. [30]Each cart[u] had four bronze wheels with bronze axles. Underneath the four corners of the basin were cast supports, each next to a wreath.

[a]**7:3-4** 1Kg 10:16-17 [b]**7:7** 1Kg 3:16-28 [c]**7:8** 1Kg 3:1; 9:24; 2Ch 8:11 [d]**7:12** 1Kg 6:36 [e]**7:13** 1Kg 5:1-11; 2Ch 2:13-14 [f]**7:14** Ex 31:2-5 [g]2Ch 4:11 [h]**7:15** 2Kg 25:16-17; 2Ch 3:15 [i]1Kg 7:41 [j]**7:16** 1Kg 7:42; 2Kg 25:17 [k]**7:20** 2Ch 3:16; 4:13 [l]**7:21** 1Kg 6:3 [m]2Ch 3:17 [n]**7:22** 2Kg 25:17 [o]**7:23** 2Kg 25:13; 1Ch 18:8; 2Ch 4:6 [p]**7:24** 1Kg 6:18 [q]2Ch 4:3 [r]**7:25** 2Kg 16:17; 2Ch 4:4-5; Jr 52:20 [s]**7:27** 2Kg 25:13; 2Ch 4:14 [t]**7:29** 1Kg 6:29,32 [u]**7:30** 2Kg 16:17

[A]**7:4** Lit *frames, window to window* [B]**7:4,5** Lit *three times*; = at 3 different places [C]**7:5** Lit *frames, opposing window to window* [D]**7:6** Lit *50 cubits* [E]**7:6,23** Lit *30 cubits* [F]**7:6** Hb obscure [G]**7:7** Syr, Vg; MT reads *floor* [H]**7:8** Lit *daughter he had taken* [I]**7:10** Lit *ten cubits and eight cubits* [J]**7:13** = Huram in 2Ch 4:11 [K]**7:15** Lit *18 cubits* [L]**7:15** Lit *12 cubits* [M]**7:15** LXX adds *and the thickness of the pillar was four fingers hollowed and similarly the second pillar* [N]**7:16,23** Lit *five cubits* [O]**7:17** Lit *tassels* [P]**7:19,27** Lit *four cubits* [Q]**7:20** Lit *encircling the second* [R]**7:21** = He Will Establish [S]**7:21** = In Him Is Strength [T]**7:23** Lit *sea* [U]**7:23** Lit *10 cubits* [V]**7:24** Lit *10 per cubit* [W]**7:26** Lit *a handbreadth* [X]**7:26** Lit *2,000 baths* [Y]**7:27** Lit *bronze stands* [Z]**7:27** Lit *three cubits* [AA]**7:29** Or *hammered-down*

31 And the water cart's opening inside the crown on top was 18 inches[A] wide. The opening was round, made as a pedestal 27 inches[B] wide. On it were carvings, but their frames were square, not round. 32 There were four wheels under the frames, and the wheel axles were part of the water cart; each wheel was 27 inches[C] tall. 33 The wheels' design was similar to that of chariot wheels: their axles, rims, spokes, and hubs were all of cast metal. 34 Four supports were at the four corners of each water cart; each support was one piece with the water cart. 35 At the top of the cart was a band nine inches[D] high encircling it; also, at the top of the cart, its braces and its frames were one piece with it. 36 He engraved cherubim, lions, and palm trees[a] on the plates of its braces and on its frames, wherever each had space, with encircling wreaths. 37 In this way he made the 10 water carts using the same casting, dimensions, and shape for all of them.

Bronze Basins and Other Utensils

38 Then he made 10 bronze basins[b] — each basin holding 220 gallons[E] and each was six feet[F] wide — one basin for each of the 10 water carts. 39 He set five water carts on the right side of the temple and five on the left side. He put the reservoir near the right side of the temple toward the southeast.[c] 40 Then Hiram made[d] the basins, the shovels, and the sprinkling basins.

Completion of the Bronze Works

So Hiram finished all the work that he was doing for King Solomon on the LORD's temple: 41 two pillars;[e] bowls for the capitals that were on top of the two pillars; the two gratings for covering both bowls of the capitals that were on top of the pillars;[f] 42 the 400 pomegranates for the two gratings (two rows of pomegranates for each grating covering both capitals' bowls on top of the pillars[g]); 43 the 10 water carts;[h] the 10 basins on the water carts;[i] 44 the reservoir;[j] the 12 oxen underneath the reservoir;[k] 45 and the pots, shovels, and sprinkling basins.[l] All the utensils that Hiram made for King Solomon at the LORD's temple were made of burnished bronze. 46 The king had them cast in clay molds in the Jordan Valley between Succoth[m] and Zarethan.[n] 47 Solomon left all the utensils unweighed because there were so many; the weight of the bronze was not determined.[o]

Completion of the Gold Furnishings

48 Solomon also made all the equipment in the LORD's temple: the gold altar; the gold table that the *bread of the Presence was placed on;[p] 49 the pure gold lampstands in front of the inner sanctuary, five on the right and five on the left;[q] the gold flowers, lamps, and tongs; 50 the pure gold ceremonial bowls, wick trimmers, sprinkling basins, ladles,[G] and firepans;[r] and the gold hinges for the doors of the inner temple (that is, the most holy place) and for the doors of the temple sanctuary.

51 So all the work King Solomon did in the LORD's temple was completed.[s] Then Solomon brought in the consecrated things of his father David[t] — the silver, the gold, and the utensils — and put them in the treasuries of the LORD's temple.[u]

Solomon's Dedication of the Temple

8 At that time Solomon assembled the elders[v] of Israel,[w] all the tribal heads[x] and the ancestral leaders of the Israelites before him at Jerusalem in order to bring the ark of the LORD's covenant from the city of David,[y] that is *Zion.[z] 2 So all the men of Israel were assembled in the presence of King Solomon in the seventh month, the month of Ethanim,[H] at the festival.[aa]

3 All the elders[ab] of Israel came, and the priests[ac] picked up the ark.[ad] 4 The priests and the Levites brought the ark of the LORD, the tent of meeting,[ae] and the holy utensils that were in the tent.[af] 5 King Solomon and the entire congregation of Israel, who had gathered around him and were with him in front of the ark, were sacrificing sheep and cattle that could not be counted or numbered, because there were so many.[ag] 6 The priests brought the ark of the LORD's covenant to its place, into the inner sanctuary of the temple, to the most holy place[ah] beneath the wings of the *cherubim. 7 For the cherubim were spread-

[a] **7:36** 1Kg 6:29
[b] **7:38** Ex 30:18; 2Ch 4:6
[c] **7:39** 2Ch 4:10
[d] **7:40-51** 2Ch 4:11–5:1
[e] **7:41** 1Kg 7:15
[f] 1Kg 7:17
[g] **7:42** 1Kg 7:20
[h] **7:43** 1Kg 7:27
[i] 1Kg 7:38
[j] **7:44** 1Kg 7:23
[k] 1Kg 7:25
[l] **7:45** Ex 27:3
[m] **7:46** Gn 33:17
[n] Jos 3:16; 1Kg 4:12
[o] **7:47** 1Ch 22:3,14
[p] **7:48** Ex 25:30; 30:1-3; 2Ch 29:18
[q] **7:49** Ex 25:31-36
[r] **7:50** 2Kg 25:15
[s] **7:51** 1Kg 6:37-38
[t] 2Sm 8:9-12; 2Ch 5:1
[u] 2Ch 36:18
[v] **8:1** Ex 3:16; Nm 11:16
[w] **8:1-11** 2Ch 5:2-14
[x] **8:1** Nm 1:5-16; 7:2
[y] 2Sm 5:7
[z] 2Sm 6:12-15,17
[aa] **8:2** Lv 23:34; Dt 16:13-15; 1Kg 8:65
[ab] **8:3** Nm 11:16
[ac] Dt 31:9; Jos 3:3,6
[ad] 2Sm 6:12,17
[ae] **8:4** 2Ch 1:3
[af] 2Ch 5:4-5
[ag] **8:5** 2Ch 1:6; 30:24
[ah] **8:6** 1Kg 6:19

[A] 7:31 Lit *a cubit* [B] 7:31 Lit *one and a half cubits* [C] 7:32 Lit *was one and a half cubits* [D] 7:35 Lit *half a cubit* [E] 7:38 Lit *40 baths* [F] 7:38 Lit *four cubits* [G] 7:50 Or *dishes*, or *spoons*; lit *palms* [H] 8:2 = September–October

ing their wings over[A] the place of the ark, so
that the cherubim covered the ark and its
poles from above.[a] 8 The poles were so long
that their ends were seen from the holy place
in front of the inner sanctuary, but they were
not seen from outside the sanctuary; they are
there to this day.[b] 9 Nothing was in the ark except the two stone tablets that Moses had put
there at Horeb,[B,c] where the LORD made a covenant with the Israelites when they came out
of the land of Egypt.[d]

10 When the priests came out of the holy
place, the cloud filled the LORD's temple,[e]
11 and because of the cloud, the priests were
not able to continue ministering, for the
glory[f] of the LORD filled the temple.

12 Then Solomon said:

The LORD said that He would dwell
in thick darkness.[g]
13 I have indeed built an exalted temple[h]
for You,
a place for Your dwelling forever.[i]

14 The king turned around and blessed[j] the
entire congregation of Israel while they were
standing. 15 He said:

May the LORD God of Israel be praised!
He spoke directly to my father David,
and He has fulfilled the promise[k]
by His power.
He said,
16 "Since the day I brought
My people Israel out of Egypt,[l]
I have not chosen a city to build
a temple in
among any of the tribes of Israel,
so that My name[m] would be there.
But I have chosen David to rule
My people Israel."[n]
17 It was in the desire of my father David
to build a temple for the name
of ·Yahweh, the God of Israel.[o]
18 But the LORD said to my father David,
"Since it was your desire to build
a temple for My name,
you have done well to have this desire.[p]
19 Yet you are not the one to build it;
instead, your son, your own offspring,
will build it for My name."[q]
20 The LORD has fulfilled
what He promised.
I have taken the place
of my father David,[r]
and I sit on the throne of Israel,
as the LORD promised.[s]
I have built the temple for the name
of Yahweh, the God of Israel.
21 I have provided a place there
for the ark,
where the LORD's covenant is
that He made with our ancestors
when He brought them out of the land
of Egypt.[t]

Solomon's Prayer

22 Then Solomon stood[u] before the altar of
the LORD in front of the entire congregation
of Israel and spread out his hands toward
heaven.[v] 23 He said:

LORD God of Israel,
there is no God like You
in heaven above or on earth below,[w]
keeping the gracious covenant
with Your servants who walk
before You
with their whole heart.[x]
24 You have kept what You promised
to Your servant, my father David.
You spoke directly to him
and You fulfilled Your promise
by Your power
as it is today.[y]
25 Therefore, LORD God of Israel,
keep what You promised
to Your servant, my father David:
You will never fail to have a man
to sit before Me on the throne of Israel,[z]
if only your sons guard their walk
before Me
as you have walked before Me.[aa]
26 Now LORD[C] God of Israel,
please confirm what You promised
to Your servant, my father David.[ab]
27 But will God indeed live on earth?
Even heaven, the highest heaven,
cannot contain You,
much less this temple I have built.[ac]

[a] 8:6-7 1Kg 6:23-28
[b] 8:8 Ex 25:13-15; 37:4-5
[c] 8:9 Ex 25:21; Dt 10:5
[d] Ex 24:7-8; Dt 4:13
[e] 8:10 Ex 40:34-35; 2Ch 7:1
[f] 8:11 2Ch 7:2; Ezk 10:4,18-19; 43:4-5
[g] 8:12 Ex 20:21; Lv 16:2; Dt 5:22
[h] 8:13 2Sm 7:13
[i] Ps 132:14
[j] 8:14 Ex 39:43; 2Sm 6:18; 1Kg 8:55
[k] 8:15 2Sm 7:15-16,25
[l] 8:16 2Sm 7:6; 1Ch 17:5
[m] Dt 12:5,11
[n] 1Sm 16:1; 2Sm 7:8
[o] 8:17 2Sm 7:2-3; 1Ch 22:7
[p] 8:18 2Ch 6:8
[q] 8:19 2Sm 7:12-13; 1Kg 5:5; Ac 7:47
[r] 8:20 2Sm 7:12
[s] 1Ch 28:5-6
[t] 8:21 Dt 31:26; 1Kg 8:9
[u] 8:22-53 2Ch 6:12-42
[v] 8:22 1Kg 8:54; 2Ch 6:12
[w] 8:23 1Sm 2:2; 2Sm 7:22
[x] Dt 7:16; Neh 1:5; Dn 9:4
[y] 8:24 2Sm 7:15-16
[z] 8:25 1Kg 2:4; 9:5
[aa] 1Kg 9:4-9; 2Ch 7:17-22
[ab] 8:26 2Sm 7:25
[ac] 8:27 2Ch 2:6; Ac 7:47; 17:24

[A] 8:7 LXX; MT reads *toward* [B] 8:9 = Sinai [C] 8:26 Some Hb mss, LXX, Syr, Tg, Vg, 2Ch 6:16; other Hb mss omit *LORD*

28 Listen[A] to Your servant's prayer
and his petition,[a]
LORD my God,
so that You may hear the cry
and the prayer
that Your servant prays
before You today,
29 so that Your eyes may watch over
this temple night and day,[b]
toward the place where You said:
My name will be there,[c]
and so that You may hear the prayer
that Your servant prays
toward this place.
30 Hear the petition of Your servant[d]
and Your people Israel,
which they pray toward this place.[e]
May You hear in Your dwelling place
in heaven.
May You hear and forgive.

31 When a man sins against his neighbor
and is forced to take an oath,[B,f]
and he comes to take an oath
before Your altar in this temple,
32 may You hear in heaven and act.
May You judge Your servants,
condemning the wicked man
by bringing
what he has done on his own head
and providing justice for the righteous
by rewarding him according to
his righteousness.[g]

33 When Your people Israel are defeated
before an enemy,
because they have sinned against You,[h]
and they return to You and praise
Your name,
and they pray and plead with You
for mercy in this temple,
34 may You hear in heaven
and forgive the sin
of Your people Israel.
May You restore them to the land
You gave their ancestors.[i]

35 When the skies are shut and there is
no rain,
because they have sinned against You,[j]
and they pray toward this place
and praise Your name,
and they turn from their sins
because You are afflicting them,[k]
36 may You hear in heaven
and forgive the sin of Your servants
and Your people Israel,
so that You may teach them
the good way
they should walk in.[l]
May You send rain on Your land
that You gave Your people
for an inheritance.[m]

37 When there is famine on the earth,
when there is pestilence,
when there is blight, mildew, locust,
or grasshopper,[n]
when their enemy besieges them
in the region of their fortified cities,[C]
when there is any plague or illness,
38 whatever prayer or petition
anyone from Your people Israel
might have —
each man knowing
his own afflictions[D,o]
and spreading out his hands
toward this temple[p] —
39 may You hear in heaven,
Your dwelling place,
and may You forgive, act, and repay
the man,
according to all his ways,
since You know his heart,
for You alone know
every human heart,[q]
40 so that they may •fear[r] You
all the days they live on the land[s]
You gave our ancestors.

41 Even for the foreigner who is not
of Your people Israel
but has come from a distant land[t]
because of Your name —
42 for they will hear of Your great name,
mighty hand,[u] and outstretched arm,
and will come[v] and pray
toward this temple —
43 may You hear in heaven,
Your dwelling place,
and do according to all the foreigner
asks You for.

[a]**8:28** Php 4:6
[b]**8:29** 2Ch 7:15; Neh 1:6
[c]Dt 12:11
[d]**8:30** Neh 1:6; Dn 9:4
[e]Dn 6:10
[f]**8:31** Ex 22:11; Jos 7:19; Jn 9:24
[g]**8:32** Dt 25:1
[h]**8:33** Lv 26:17,25,39
[i]**8:33-34** Lv 26:40-42
[j]**8:35** Dt 28:23-24
[k]Dt 30:1-3; Am 4:7-8
[l]**8:36** 1Sm 12:23
[m]Dt 11:14; Jl 2:23
[n]**8:37** Lv 26:16,25-26
[o]**8:38** 2Ch 6:29
[p]Ex 9:29; 2Ch 6:29
[q]**8:39** 1Sm 16:7; 1Ch 28:9
[r]**8:40** Dt 6:13
[s]Dt 12:1
[t]**8:41** Lv 24:22; Dt 10:18-19
[u]**8:42** Dt 3:24
[v]1Kg 10:1

[A]**8:28** Lit *Turn* [B]**8:31** Lit *and he lifts a curse against him to curse him* [C]**8:37** Lit *besieges him in the land of his gates* [D]**8:38** Lit *knowing in his heart of a plague*

Then all the people on earth will know[a]
Your name,
to fear You as Your people Israel do
and know that this temple I have built
is called by Your name.

44 When Your people go out to fight
against their enemies,[A]
wherever You send them,
and they pray to Yahweh
in the direction of the city
You have chosen[b]
and the temple I have built
for Your name,
45 may You hear their prayer and petition
in heaven
and uphold their cause.[c]
46 When they sin against You—
for there is no one who does not sin[d]—
and You are angry with them
and hand them over to the enemy,
and their captors deport them
to the enemy's country[e]—
whether distant or nearby—
47 and when they come to their senses[B]
in the land where they were deported
and repent and petition You
in their captors' land:
"We have sinned and done wrong;
we have been wicked,"[f]
48 and when they return to You
with their whole mind and heart
in the land of their enemies
who took them captive,[g]
and when they pray to You
in the direction of their land
that You gave their ancestors,
the city You have chosen,[h]
and the temple I have built
for Your name,
49 may You hear in heaven,
Your dwelling place,
their prayer and petition and uphold
their cause.
50 May You forgive Your people
who sinned against You
and all their rebellions[C] against You,
and may You give them compassion
in the eyes of their captors,
so that they may be compassionate
to them.[i]
51 For they are Your people
and Your inheritance;[j]
You brought them out of Egypt,
out of the middle of an iron furnace.[k]
52 May Your eyes be open
to Your servant's petition
and to the petition
of Your people Israel,
listening to them whenever they call
to You.
53 For You, Lord GOD, have set them apart
as Your inheritance
from all the people on earth,
as You spoke
through Your servant Moses
when You brought their ancestors
out of Egypt.[l]

Solomon's Blessing

54 When Solomon finished praying this entire prayer and petition to the LORD, he got up
from kneeling before the altar of the LORD,
with his hands spread out toward heaven,[m]
55 and he stood and blessed the whole congregation of Israel[n] with a loud voice: 56 "May
the LORD be praised! He has given rest[o] to His
people Israel according to all He has said.
Not one of all the good promises He made
through His servant Moses has failed.[p] 57 May
the LORD our God be with us as He was with
our ancestors. May He not abandon us or
leave us[q] 58 so that He causes us to be devoted[D]
to Him,[r] to walk in all His ways, and to keep
His commands, statutes, and ordinances,
which He commanded our ancestors. 59 May
my words I have made my petition with before the LORD be near the LORD our God
day and night, so that He may uphold His
servant's cause and the cause of His people
Israel, as each day requires,[s] 60 and so that
all the peoples of the earth may know that
Yahweh is God. There is no other![t] 61 Let your
heart be completely devoted to the LORD our
God[u] to walk in His statutes and to keep His
commands, as it is today."

62 The king and all Israel with him were
offering sacrifices in the LORD's presence.

[a] 8:43 Jos 4:24; 1Sm 17:46 [b] 8:44 Dt 12:11; 1Ch 5:20; 2Ch 14:11 [c] 8:45 Ps 9:4; 140:12 [d] 8:46 Rm 3:10,23 [e] Lv 26:33-34 [f] 8:47 Lv 26:40-42; Neh 1:6; Dn 9:5 [g] 8:48 Jr 29:10-14 [h] Dn 6:10 [i] 8:50 2Kg 25:28; 2Ch 30:9 [j] 8:51 Ex 32:11; Dt 9:26,29 [k] Dt 4:20 [l] 8:53 Ex 19:5-6; Dt 9:26-29 [m] 8:54 2Ch 6:12-13 [n] 8:55 Nm 6:23-26; 2Sm 6:18 [o] 8:56 Dt 12:10; 1Ch 22:18; Heb 3:18-19 [p] Jos 21:45; 23:15 [q] 8:57 Dt 31:6; Jos 1:5; Heb 13:5 [r] 8:58 Jos 24:23; Jr 31:33; Php 2:13 [s] 8:59 Pr 30:8; Mt 6:11 [t] 8:60 Dt 6:4; Jos 4:24; Mk 12:32 [u] 8:61 Dt 6:5; 1Kg 9:4; 11:4

A 8:44 Some Hb mss, some ancient versions, 2Ch 6:34; other Hb mss read *enemy*
B 8:47 Lit *they return to their heart* C 8:50 Lit *rebellions that they have rebelled*
D 8:58 Lit *causes our hearts to be inclined*

63 Solomon offered a sacrifice of ·fellowship offerings to the LORD: 22,000 cattle and 120,000 sheep.[a] In this manner the king and all the Israelites dedicated[b] the LORD's temple.[c]

64 On the same day, the king consecrated the middle of the courtyard that was in front of the LORD's temple because that was where he offered the ·burnt offering, the ·grain offering, and the fat of the fellowship offerings[d] since the bronze altar before the LORD was too small to accommodate the burnt offerings, the grain offerings, and the fat of the fellowship offerings.[e]

65 Solomon and all Israel with him — a great assembly, from the entrance of Hamath[A,f] to the Brook of Egypt[g] — observed the festival at that time[h] in the presence of the LORD our God, seven days, and seven more days — 14 days.[B,i] 66 On the fifteenth day[C] he sent the people away. So they blessed the king and went home to their tents rejoicing and with joyful hearts for all the goodness that the LORD had done for His servant David and for His people Israel.[j]

The LORD's Response

9 When Solomon finished building the temple of the LORD,[k] the royal palace, and all that Solomon desired to do,[l] 2 the LORD appeared to Solomon a second time just as He had appeared to him at Gibeon.[m] 3 The LORD said to him:

> I have heard your prayer and petition you have made before Me. I have consecrated this temple you have built, to put My name there forever;[n] My eyes and My heart will be there at all times.[o]
>
> 4 As for you, if you walk before Me as your father David walked, with a heart of integrity and in what is right, doing everything I have commanded you, and if you keep My statutes and ordinances,[p] 5 I will establish your royal throne over Israel forever, as I promised your father David: You will never fail to have a man on the throne of Israel.[q]
>
> 6 If you or your sons turn away from following Me and do not keep My commands — My statutes that I have set before you — and if you go and serve other gods and worship them,[r] 7 I will cut off Israel from the land I gave them,[s] and I will reject[D] the temple I have sanctified for My name.[t] Israel will become an object of scorn and ridicule among all the peoples.[u] 8 Though this temple is now exalted,[E] everyone who passes by will be appalled and will mock.[F] They will say: Why did the LORD do this to this land and this temple?[v] 9 Then they will say: Because they abandoned the LORD their God who brought their ancestors out of the land of Egypt. They clung to other gods and worshiped and served them. Because of this, the LORD brought all this ruin on them.[w]

King Hiram's 20 Towns

10 At the end of 20 years during which Solomon had built the two houses, the LORD's temple and the royal palace[x] — 11 Hiram king of Tyre[y] having supplied him with cedar and cypress logs and gold[z] for his every wish[aa] — King Solomon gave Hiram 20 towns in the land of Galilee. 12 So Hiram went out from Tyre to look over the towns that Solomon had given him, but he was not pleased with them. 13 So he said, "What are these towns you've given me, my brother?" So he called them the Land of Cabul,[G] as they are still called today.[ab] 14 Now Hiram had sent the king 9,000 pounds[H] of gold.[ac]

Solomon's Forced Labor

15 This is the account of the forced labor[ad] that King Solomon had imposed to build the LORD's temple, his own palace, the supporting terraces,[ae] the wall of Jerusalem,[af] and Hazor,[ag] Megiddo,[ah] and Gezer.[ai] 16 Pharaoh king of Egypt had attacked and captured Gezer. He then burned it down, killed the Canaanites who lived in the city, and gave it as a dowry to his daughter, Solomon's wife.[aj] 17 Then Solomon rebuilt Gezer, Lower Beth-horon,[ak] 18 Baalath,[al] Tamar[I,J] in the Wilder-

[a] **8:62-63** 1Ch 29:21; 2Ch 7:4-5; Ezr 6:16-17 [b] **8:63** Dt 20:5; Ezr 6:16; Neh 12:27 [c] 2Ch 7:5 [d] **8:64** Lv 6–7 [e] 2Ch 7:7 [f] **8:65** Nm 13:21; 34:8 [g] Gn 15:18 [h] Lv 23:36; 1Kg 8:2 [i] 2Ch 7:9 [j] **8:66** 2Ch 7:10 [k] **9:1-9** 2Ch 7:11-22 [l] **9:1** 1Kg 7:1-2; 2Ch 7:11 [m] **9:2** 1Kg 3:5; 11:9 [n] **9:3** 1Kg 8:29 [o] 2Ch 6:40 [p] **9:4** 1Kg 3:6,14; 11:4,6; 1Ch 28:9 [q] **9:5** 2Sm 7:12,15-16; 1Kg 2:4 [r] **9:6** Dt 28:15; 1Kg 11:10; 1Ch 28:9 [s] **9:7** Lv 26:33; Dt 28:63 [t] Dt 12:5; 1Kg 8:20 [u] Dt 28:37 [v] **9:8** Lv 26:32; Dt 29:24; Mt 23:38 [w] **9:9** Dt 29:25; 31:29 [x] **9:10** 1Kg 6:38; 7:1; 2Ch 8:1 [y] **9:11** 1Kg 5:1 [z] Dt 17:17 [aa] 1Kg 5:10 [ab] **9:11-13** 2Ch 8:2 [ac] **9:14** Dt 17:17 [ad] **9:15** 1Kg 5:13-16 [ae] 2Sm 5:9 [af] 1Kg 3:1 [ag] Jos 11:1 [ah] Jos 17:11 [ai] Jdg 1:29 [aj] **9:16** 1Kg 3:1; 7:8 [ak] **9:17** Jos 16:3; 2Ch 8:5 [al] **9:18** Jos 19:44

[A] **8:65** Or *from Lebo-hamath* [B] **8:65** Temple dedication lasted seven days, and the Festival of Tabernacles lasted seven days. [C] **8:66** Lit *the eighth day* [D] **9:7** Lit *send from My presence* [E] **9:8** Some ancient versions read *temple will become a ruin* [F] **9:8** Lit *hiss* [G] **9:13** = Like Nothing [H] **9:14** Lit *120 talents* [I] **9:18** Alt Hb traditions, LXX, Syr, Tg, Vg read *Tadmor*; 2Ch 8:4 [J] **9:18** Tamar was a city in southern Judah; Ezk 47:19; 48:28.

ness of Judah, 19all the storage cities that
belonged to Solomon, the chariot cities,[a] the
cavalry cities,[b] and whatever Solomon desired to build[c] in Jerusalem, Lebanon, or anywhere else in the land of his dominion.
20As for all the peoples who remained of
the Amorites, Hittites, Perizzites, Hivites, and
Jebusites, who were not Israelites — 21their
descendants who remained in the land after
them, those whom the Israelites were unable
to ·completely destroy[d] — Solomon imposed
forced labor on them; it is this way until today.[e] 22But Solomon did not consign the Israelites to slavery;[f] they were soldiers, his
servants, his commanders, his captains, and
commanders of his chariots and his cavalry.
23These were the deputies[g] who were over Solomon's work: 550 who ruled over the people
doing the work.[h]

Solomon's Other Activities

24Pharaoh's daughter moved from the city
of David[i] to the house that Solomon had built
for her;[j] he then built the terraces.[k]
25Three times a year Solomon offered
·burnt offerings and ·fellowship offerings
on the altar he had built for the LORD, and he
burned incense with them in the LORD's presence.[l] So he completed the temple.[m]
26King Solomon put together a fleet of ships at
Ezion-geber,[n] which is near Eloth on the shore
of the ·Red Sea in the land of Edom. 27With the
fleet, Hiram sent his servants, experienced sea-
men, along with Solomon's servants. 28They
went to Ophir[o] and acquired gold there — 16
tons[A] — and delivered it to Solomon.[p]

The Queen of Sheba

10 The queen of Sheba[q] heard about Solomon's fame[r] connected with the name
of ·Yahweh and came to test him with difficult
questions.[s] 2She came to Jerusalem with a very
large entourage, with camels bearing[t] spices,
gold in great abundance, and precious stones.[u]
She came to Solomon and spoke to him about
everything that was on her mind. 3So Solomon
answered all her questions; nothing was too
difficult for the king to explain to her. 4When
the queen of Sheba observed all of Solomon's

[a]9:19 1Kg 10:26 [b]1Kg 4:26 [c]1Kg 9:1 [d]9:20-21 Jdg 1:21-36; 3:1; 2Ch 8:7-8 [e]9:21 Jdg 1:28,35; Ezr 2:55,58 [f]9:22 Lv 25:39 [g]9:23 1Kg 5:16 [h]9:22-23 2Ch 8:9-10 [i]9:24 2Sm 5:7 [j]1Kg 7:8; 2Ch 8:11 [k]1Kg 9:15; 11:27; 2Ch 32:5 [l]9:25 Dt 16:16 [m]2Ch 8:16 [n]9:26 Nm 33:48; 1Kg 22:48 [o]9:27-28 1Kg 10:11; 22:48-49 [p]9:28 1Kg 9:11,14 [q]10:1 2Ch 9:1; Mt 12:42 [r]10:1-10 2Ch 9:1-12 [s]10:1 Jdg 14:12-14 [t]10:2 Gn 24:10 [u]1Kg 10:10 [v]10:4 1Kg 7:1 [w]10:5 1Kg 4:22-23 [x]10:7 1Ch 29:25 [y]10:8 Pr 8:34 [z]10:9 2Sm 22:20; 1Kg 5:7 [aa]1Ch 17:22; 2Ch 2:11 [ab]2Sm 8:15 [ac]10:10 1Kg 9:28 [ad]10:11 1Kg 9:27-28 [ae]10:12-13 2Ch 9:11-12 [af]10:14-25 2Ch 9:13-24 [ag]10:15 2Ch 1:16 [ah]10:14-15 1Kg 9:28; 10:2

wisdom, the palace he had built,[v] 5the food at
his table,[w] his servants' residence, his attendants' service and their attire, his cupbearers, and the ·burnt offerings he offered at the
LORD's temple, it took her breath away.
6She said to the king, "The report I heard in
my own country about your words and about
your wisdom is true. 7But I didn't believe the
reports until I came and saw with my own
eyes. Indeed, I was not even told half. Your
wisdom and prosperity far exceed the report
I heard.[x] 8How happy are your men.[B] How
happy are these servants of yours, who always
stand in your presence hearing your wisdom.[y] 9May Yahweh your God be praised! He
delighted in you and put you on the throne
of Israel,[z] because of the LORD's eternal love
for Israel.[aa] He has made you king to carry out
justice and righteousness."[ab]
10Then she gave the king four and a half
tons[C] of gold,[ac] a great quantity of spices,
and precious stones. Never again did such a
quantity of spices arrive as those the queen
of Sheba gave to King Solomon.
11In addition, Hiram's fleet that carried
gold from Ophir brought from Ophir a
large quantity of almug[D] wood and precious
stones.[ad] 12The king made the almug wood
into steps for the LORD's temple and the
king's palace and into lyres and harps for the
singers. Never before had such almug wood
come, and the like has not been seen again
even to this very day.
13King Solomon gave the queen of Sheba
her every desire — whatever she asked — besides what he had given her out of his royal
bounty. Then she, along with her servants, returned to her own country.[ae]

Solomon's Wealth

14The weight[af] of gold that came to Solomon
annually was 25 tons,[E] 15besides what came
from merchants,[ag] traders' merchandise, and
all the Arabian kings and governors of the
land.[ah]
16King Solomon made 200 large shields of
hammered gold; 15 pounds[F] of gold went into
each shield. 17He made 300 small shields of
hammered gold; about four pounds[G] of gold

[A]9:28 Lit *420 talents* [B]10:8 LXX, Syr read *your wives* [C]10:10 Lit *120 talents* [D]10:11 = algum in 2Ch 2:8; 9:10-11 [E]10:14 Lit *666 talents* [F]10:16 Lit *600* (shekels) [G]10:17 Lit *three minas* went into each shield. The king put them in the House of the Forest of Lebanon.[a]

18 The king also made a large ivory throne and overlaid it with fine gold. 19 The throne had six steps; there was a rounded top at the back of the throne, armrests on either side of the seat, and two lions standing beside the armrests. 20 Twelve lions were standing there on the six steps, one at each end. Nothing like it had ever been made in any other kingdom. 21 All of King Solomon's drinking cups were gold, and all the utensils of the House of the Forest of Lebanon[b] were pure gold.[c] There was no silver, since it was considered as nothing in Solomon's time, 22 for the king had ships of Tarshish[d] at sea with Hiram's fleet, and once every three years the ships of Tarshish would arrive bearing gold, silver, ivory, apes, and peacocks.[A,e]

23 King Solomon surpassed all the kings of the world in riches and in wisdom.[f] 24 The whole world wanted an audience with Solomon to hear the wisdom that God had put in his heart.[g] 25 Every man would bring his annual tribute: items[B] of silver and gold, clothing, weapons,[C] spices, and horses and mules.[h]

26 Solomon accumulated 1,400 chariots and 12,000 horsemen[i] and stationed them in the chariot cities and with the king in Jerusalem.[j] 27 The king made silver as common in Jerusalem as stones,[k] and he made cedar[l] as abundant as sycamore in the Judean foothills. 28 Solomon's horses were imported from Egypt and Kue.[D] The king's traders bought them from Kue at the going price.[m] 29 A chariot was imported from Egypt for 15 pounds[E] of silver, and a horse for about four pounds.[F] In the same way, they exported them to all the kings of the Hittites and to the kings of Aram through their agents.[n]

Solomon's Unfaithfulness to God

11 King Solomon loved many foreign women in addition to Pharaoh's daughter:[o] Moabite, Ammonite, Edomite, Sidonian, and Hittite women[p] 2 from the nations that the LORD had told the Israelites about, "Do not intermarry with them, and they must not intermarry with you, because they will turn you away from Me to their gods."[q] Solomon was deeply attached to these women and loved them. 3 He had 700 wives who were princesses and 300 concubines,[r] and they turned his heart away from the LORD.[s]

4 When Solomon was old, his wives seduced him to follow other gods. He was not completely devoted to ·Yahweh his God, as his father David had been.[t] 5 Solomon followed ·Ashtoreth,[u] the goddess of the Sidonians, and ·Milcom,[v] the detestable idol of the Ammonites.[w] 6 Solomon did what was evil in the LORD's sight, and unlike his father David, he did not completely follow Yahweh.

7 At that time, Solomon built a ·high place[x] for Chemosh,[y] the detestable idol of Moab, and for Milcom,[G,z] the detestable idol of the Ammonites, on the hill across from Jerusalem.[aa] 8 He did the same for all his foreign wives, who were burning incense and offering sacrifices to their gods.

9 The LORD was angry with Solomon, because his heart had turned away from Yahweh, the God of Israel, who had appeared to him twice.[ab] 10 He had commanded him about this, so that he would not follow other gods, but Solomon did not do what the LORD had commanded.[ac]

11 Then the LORD said to Solomon, "Since you have done this[H] and did not keep My covenant and My statutes, which I commanded you, I will tear the kingdom away from you and give it to your servant.[ad] 12 However, I will not do it during your lifetime because of your father David;[ae] I will tear it out of your son's hand. 13 Yet I will not tear the entire kingdom away from him. I will give one tribe to your son[af] because of my servant David and because of Jerusalem that I chose."

Solomon's Enemies

14 So the LORD raised up[ag] Hadad the Edomite as an enemy against Solomon. He was of the royal family in Edom. 15 Earlier, when David was in Edom, Joab, the commander of the army, had gone to bury the dead and had struck down every male in Edom. 16 For Joab and all Israel had remained there six months, until he had killed every male in Edom.[ah] 17 Ha-

[a] **10:17** 1Kg 7:2-5
[b] **10:21** 1Kg 7:2-5
[c] 1Kg 9:28
[d] **10:22** Jnh 1:3
[e] 1Kg 9:26-28; 22:48
[f] **10:23** 1Kg 3:13
[g] **10:24** 1Kg 3:28; 10:1
[h] **10:23-25** 2Ch 9:22-24
[i] **10:26** 1Kg 4:26
[j] 1Kg 9:19
[k] **10:27** Dt 17:17
[l] 1Kg 5:10; 2Ch 1:15
[m] **10:28** Dt 17:16; 2Ch 9:28
[n] **10:29** 2Ch 1:17
[o] **11:1** 1Kg 3:1; 7:8
[p] Neh 13:23-27
[q] **11:2** Dt 7:3-4
[r] **11:3** 2Sm 5:13; Est 2:14-15; Sg 6:8
[s] Dt 17:17
[t] **11:4** 1Kg 8:61; 9:4; 15:3,14; 1Ch 29:19
[u] **11:5** Jdg 2:13; 10:6; 1Kg 11:33
[v] Lv 18:21
[w] Jdg 2:13; 1Sm 7:3-4
[x] **11:7** Nm 33:52; 1Kg 3:2-3
[y] Nm 21:29
[z] 1Kg 11:33
[aa] 2Kg 23:13
[ab] **11:9** 1Kg 3:5; 9:2
[ac] **11:10** 1Kg 6:12; 9:6-7
[ad] **11:11** 1Kg 11:29-31
[ae] **11:12** 2Sm 7:12-16; 2Kg 19:34; 20:6
[af] **11:12-13** 1Kg 11:31-32
[ag] **11:14** 1Kg 5:4; 1Ch 5:26
[ah] **11:15-16** 2Sm 8:13-14; 1Ch 18:12-13

[A] **10:22** Or *baboons* [B] **10:25** Or *vessels*, or *weapons* [C] **10:25** Or *fragrant balsam* [D] **10:28** = Cilicia [E] **10:29** Lit *600 shekels* [F] **10:29** Lit *150 shekels* [G] **11:7** Lit *Molech* [H] **11:11** Lit *Since this was with you*

dad fled to Egypt, along with some Edomites from his father's servants. At the time Hadad was a small boy. 18 Hadad and his men set out from Midian and went to Paran.[a] They took men with them from Paran and went to Egypt, to Pharaoh king of Egypt,[b] who gave Hadad a house, ordered that he be given food, and gave him land. 19 Pharaoh liked Hadad so much that he gave him a wife, the sister of his own wife, Queen Tahpenes. 20 Tahpenes' sister gave birth to Hadad's son Genubath. Tahpenes herself weaned him in Pharaoh's palace, and Genubath lived there along with Pharaoh's sons.

21 When Hadad heard in Egypt that David rested with his fathers and that Joab, the commander of the army, was dead, Hadad said to Pharaoh, "Let me leave, so I can go to my own country."

22 But Pharaoh asked him, "What do you lack here with me for you to want to go back to your own country?"

"Nothing," he replied, "but please let me leave."

23 God raised up Rezon son of Eliada as an enemy[c] against Solomon. Rezon had fled from his master Hadadezer king of Zobah[d] 24 and gathered men to himself. He became captain of a raiding party when David killed the Zobaites. He[A] went to Damascus,[e] lived there, and became king in Damascus. 25 Rezon was Israel's enemy throughout Solomon's reign, adding to the trouble Hadad had caused. He ruled over Aram,[B,f] but he loathed Israel.

26 Now Solomon's servant,[g] Jeroboam son of Nebat, was an Ephraimite from Zeredah. His widowed mother's name was Zeruah. Jeroboam rebelled[h] against Solomon, 27 and this is the reason he rebelled against the king: Solomon had built the supporting terraces[i] and repaired the opening in the wall of the city of his father David. 28 Now the man Jeroboam was capable, and Solomon noticed the young man because he was getting things done. So he appointed him over the entire labor force of the house of Joseph.[j]

29 During that time, the prophet Ahijah the Shilonite[k] met Jeroboam on the road as Jeroboam came out of Jerusalem. Now Ahijah had wrapped himself with a new cloak, and the two of them were alone in the open field. 30 Then Ahijah took hold of the new cloak he had on, tore it into 12 pieces,[l] 31 and said to Jeroboam, "Take 10 pieces for yourself, for this is what the LORD God of Israel says: 'I am about to tear the kingdom out of Solomon's hand. I will give you 10 tribes, 32 but one tribe will remain his because of my servant David[m] and because of Jerusalem, the city I chose out of all the tribes of Israel.[n] 33 For they have abandoned Me; they have bowed the knee to Ashtoreth, the goddess of the Sidonians, to Chemosh, the god of Moab, and to Milcom, the god of the Ammonites.[o] They have not walked in My ways to do what is right in My eyes and to carry out My statutes and My judgments as his father David did.[p]

34 "'However, I will not take the whole kingdom from his hand but will let him be ruler all the days of his life because of My servant David, whom I chose and who kept My commands and My statutes. 35 I will take 10 tribes of the kingdom from his son's hand and give them to you. 36 I will give one tribe[q] to his son,[r] so that My servant David will always have a lamp before Me[s] in Jerusalem, the city I chose for Myself to put My name there.[t] 37 I will appoint you,[u] and you will reign as king[v] over all you want,[w] and you will be king over Israel.

38 "'After that, if you obey all I command you, walk in My ways, and do what is right in My sight in order to keep My statutes and My commands as My servant David did, I will be with you.[x] I will build you a lasting dynasty just as I built for David,[y] and I will give you Israel. 39 I will humble David's descendants, because of their unfaithfulness, but not forever.'"[C,z]

40 Therefore, Solomon tried to kill Jeroboam,[aa] but he fled to Egypt,[ab] to Shishak king of Egypt,[ac] where he remained until Solomon's death.

Solomon's Death

41 The rest of the events of Solomon's reign, along with all his accomplishments and his wisdom, are written in the Book of Solomon's Events.[ad] 42 The length of Solomon's reign in Jerusalem over all Israel totaled 40 years.[ae]

[a] **11:18** Nm 10:12; Dt 1:1
[b] 1Kg 3:1
[c] **11:23** 1Kg 5:4
[d] 2Sm 8:3
[e] **11:24** 2Sm 8:5
[f] **11:25** Gn 10:22; 2Sm 10:19
[g] **11:26** 1Kg 11:11
[h] 1Kg 11:40; 2Ch 13:6
[i] **11:27** 1Kg 9:15,24
[j] **11:28** 1Kg 5:13-16; 12:4
[k] **11:29** 1Kg 12:15; 14:2
[l] **11:30** 1Sm 15:27-28; 1Kg 11:11-13
[m] **11:32** 2Sm 7:15-16
[n] **11:30-32** 1Kg 11:11-13
[o] **11:33** 1Kg 11:5,7
[p] 1Kg 3:14; 11:9-11
[q] **11:36** 1Kg 12:16-17
[r] **11:34-36** 1Kg 3:14; 11:12-13
[s] **11:36** 2Sm 21:17; 1Kg 15:4; 2Kg 8:19
[t] 1Kg 8:29; 11:13
[u] **11:37** 1Kg 11:11
[v] 1Kg 14:7
[w] 2Sm 3:21
[x] **11:38** Jos 1:5; 1Kg 3:14; 11:11
[y] 2Sm 7:11,27
[z] **11:39** Ezk 37:15-28; Am 9:11-12
[aa] **11:40** 1Kg 11:26-28
[ab] 1Kg 12:2
[ac] 1Kg 14:25-26; 2Ch 12:2-9
[ad] **11:41** 1Kg 15:7,23; 2Ch 9:29
[ae] **11:42** 2Sm 5:5

[A] **11:24** LXX; Hb reads *They* [B] **11:25** Some Hb mss, LXX, Syr read *Edom* [C] **11:38-39** LXX omits *and I will give . . . but not forever*

43 Solomon rested with his fathers and was
buried in the city of his father David. His son
Rehoboam[a] became king in his place.[b]

The Kingdom Divided

12 Then Rehoboam[c] went to Shechem,[d]
for all Israel[e] had gone to Shechem to
make him king.[f] 2 When Jeroboam son of Nebat heard about it, for he was still in Egypt
where he had fled from King Solomon's presence,[g] Jeroboam stayed in Egypt.[A] 3 They summoned him, and Jeroboam and the whole
assembly of Israel came and spoke to Rehoboam: 4 "Your father made our yoke difficult.[h] You, therefore, lighten your father's
harsh service and the heavy yoke he put on
us,[i] and we will serve you."
5 Rehoboam replied, "Go home for three
days and then return to me." So the people
left. 6 Then King Rehoboam consulted with
the elders[j] who had served his father Solomon when he was alive, asking, "How do you
advise me to respond to these people?"
7 They replied, "Today if you will be a servant to these people and serve them, and if
you respond to them by speaking kind words
to them, they will be your servants forever."[k]
8 But he rejected the advice of the elders
who had advised him[l] and consulted with
the young men who had grown up with him
and served him. 9 He asked them, "What message do you advise that we send back to these
people who said to me, 'Lighten the yoke your
father put on us'?"
10 Then the young men who had grown up
with him told him, "This is what you should
say to these people who said to you, 'Your father made our yoke heavy, but you, make it
lighter on us!' This is what you should tell
them: 'My little finger is thicker than my
father's loins! 11 Although my father burdened you with a heavy yoke, I will add to
your yoke; my father disciplined you with
whips, but I will discipline you with barbed
whips.'"[B,m]
12 So Jeroboam and all the people came to
Rehoboam on the third day, as the king had
ordered: "Return to me on the third day."
13 Then the king answered the people harshly.
He rejected the advice the elders had given
him 14 and spoke to them according to the
young men's advice: "My father made your
yoke heavy, but I will add to your yoke; my
father disciplined you with whips, but I will
discipline you with barbed whips."[B]
15 The king did not listen to the people,
because this turn of events came from the
LORD[n] to carry out His word, which the LORD
had spoken through Ahijah the Shilonite to
Jeroboam son of Nebat.[o] 16 When all Israel
saw that the king had not listened to them,
the people answered him:

> What portion do we have in David?
> We have no inheritance in the son
> of Jesse.[p]
> Israel, return to your tents;
> David, now look after your own house![q]

So Israel went to their tents, 17 but Rehoboam
reigned over the Israelites living in the cities
of Judah.[r]
18 Then King Rehoboam sent Adoram,[C,s]
who was in charge of forced labor, but all
Israel stoned him to death. King Rehoboam
managed to get into the chariot and flee to
Jerusalem. 19 Israel is in rebellion against the
house of David until today.[t]

Rehoboam in Jerusalem

20 When all Israel heard that Jeroboam had
come back,[u] they summoned him to the assembly and made him king over all Israel.[v]
No one followed the house of David except
the tribe of Judah alone.[w] 21 When Rehoboam
arrived in Jerusalem,[x] he mobilized 180,000
choice warriors from the entire house of Judah and the tribe of Benjamin[y] to fight against
the house of Israel to restore the kingdom to
Rehoboam son of Solomon. 22 But a revelation from God came to Shemaiah,[z] the man
of God: 23 "Say to Rehoboam son of Solomon,
king of Judah, to the whole house of Judah
and Benjamin, and to the rest of the people,
24 'This is what the LORD says: You are not to
march up and fight against your brothers, the
Israelites. Each of you must return home, for
I have done this.'"[aa]
So they listened to what the LORD said and
went back as He had told them.

[a] **11:43** 1Kg 12:1
[b] **11:42-43** 2Ch 9:30-31
[c] **12:1-19** 2Ch 10:1-19
[d] **12:1** Jos 12:1; 1Kg 12:25
[e] 2Sm 20:1-2; 1Kg 12:16-17
[f] Jdg 9:6
[g] **12:2** 1Kg 11:40
[h] **12:4** 1Sm 8:11-18
[i] 1Kg 4:20
[j] **12:6** 1Kg 4:2-19
[k] **12:7** 2Ch 10:7; Pr 15:1
[l] **12:8** Lv 19:32
[m] **12:10-11** Ex 1:13-14; 5:6-9; 2Ch 10:10-11
[n] **12:15** Dt 2:30; 1Kg 12:24
[o] 1Kg 11:29-39
[p] **12:16** 2Sm 5:3,5
[q] 2Sm 20:1
[r] **12:17** 1Kg 11:13,36
[s] **12:18** 2Sm 20:24; 1Kg 4:6; 5:14
[t] **12:19** 2Kg 21:17
[u] **12:20** 1Kg 12:3
[v] 1Kg 11:11
[w] 1Kg 11:13,36
[x] **12:21-24** 2Ch 11:1-4
[y] **12:21** 2Sm 19:17
[z] **12:22** 2Ch 12:5,7
[aa] **12:24** 1Kg 12:15

[A] **12:2** LXX, Vg read *Jeroboam returned from Egypt*; 2Ch 10:2 [B] **12:11,14** Lit *with scorpions* [C] **12:18** LXX reads *Adoniram*; 1Kg 4:6; 5:14

Jeroboam's Idolatry

25 Jeroboam built Shechem[a] in the hill country of Ephraim and lived there. From there he
went out and built Penuel.[b] 26 Jeroboam said
to himself, "The way things are going now, the
kingdom might return to the house of David.[c]
27 If these people regularly go to offer sacrifices in the LORD's temple in Jerusalem,[d] the
heart of these people will return to their lord,
Rehoboam king of Judah. They will murder
me and go back to the king of Judah." 28 So the
king sought advice.

Then he made two golden calves, and he
said to the people, "Going to Jerusalem is
too difficult for you. Israel, here is your God[A]
who brought you out of the land of Egypt."[e]
29 He set up one in Bethel,[f] and put the other
in Dan.[g] 30 This led to sin;[h] the people walked
in procession before one of the calves all the
way to Dan.[B,i]

31 Jeroboam also built shrines on the ·high
places[j] and set up priests from every class of
people who were not Levites.[k] 32 Jeroboam
made a festival in the eighth month on the
fifteenth day of the month, like the festival
in Judah.[l] He offered sacrifices on the altar;
he made this offering in Bethel to sacrifice to
the calves he had set up. He also stationed the
priests in Bethel for the high places he had
set up.[m] 33 He offered sacrifices on[C] the altar
he had set up in Bethel on the fifteenth day
of the eighth month. He chose this month on
his own.[n] He made a festival for the Israelites,
offered sacrifices on the altar, and burned incense.[o]

Judgment on Jeroboam

13 A man of God[p] came from Judah to
Bethel by a revelation from the LORD
while Jeroboam was standing beside the altar to burn incense.[q] 2 The man of God cried
out against the altar by a revelation from the
LORD: "Altar, altar, this is what the LORD says,
'A son will be born to the house of David,
named Josiah, and he will sacrifice on you the
priests of the ·high places who are burning
incense on you. Human bones will be burned
on you.'"[r] 3 He gave a sign[s] that day. He said,
"This is the sign that the LORD has spoken:
'The altar will now be ripped apart, and the
ashes that are on it will be poured out.'"[t]
4 When the king heard the word that the
man of God had cried out against the altar
at Bethel, Jeroboam stretched out his hand
from the altar and said, "Arrest him!" But the
hand he stretched out against him withered,
and he could not pull it back to himself. 5 The
altar was ripped apart, and the ashes poured
from the altar, according to the sign that the
man of God had given by the word of the
LORD.

6 Then the king responded to the man of
God, "Plead for the favor of the LORD your
God and pray for me[u] so that my hand may be
restored to me." So the man of God pleaded
for the favor of the LORD, and the king's hand
was restored to him and became as it had
been at first.

7 Then the king declared to the man of God,
"Come home with me, refresh yourself, and
I'll give you a reward."[v]

8 But the man of God replied, "If you were
to give me half your house,[w] I still wouldn't go
with you, and I wouldn't eat bread or drink
water in this place, 9 for this is what I was commanded by the word of the LORD:[x] 'You must
not eat bread or drink water or go back the way
you came.'" 10 So he went another way; he did
not go back by the way he had come to Bethel.

The Old Prophet and the Man of God

11 Now a certain old prophet was living in
Bethel.[y] His son[D] came and told him all the
deeds that the man of God had done that day
in Bethel. His sons also told their father the
words that he had spoken to the king.[z] 12 Then
their father said to them, "Which way did
he go?" His sons had seen[E] the way taken by
the man of God who had come from Judah.
13 Then he said to his sons, "Saddle the donkey for me." So they saddled the donkey for
him, and he got on it. 14 He followed the man
of God and found him sitting under an oak
tree. He asked him, "Are you the man of God
who came from Judah?"

"I am," he said.

15 Then he said to him, "Come home with
me and eat bread."

[a] **12:25** Gn 12:6; Jdg 9:6; 1Kg 12:1
[b] Jdg 8:8-9,17
[c] **12:26** 1Kg 11:38
[d] **12:27** Dt 12:5-7,14
[e] **12:28** Ex 32:4,8
[f] **12:29** Gn 12:8; 28:19
[g] Jdg 18:29
[h] **12:30** 1Kg 13:34; 2Kg 17:21
[i] Ex 20:4-6; Dt 5:8-10
[j] **12:31** 1Kg 3:3; 11:7
[k] 2Kg 17:32
[l] **12:32** Lv 23:33-34; Nm 29:12
[m] 2Ch 11:15
[n] **12:33** Nm 15:39
[o] 2Kg 23:15
[p] **13:1** 1Kg 12:22; 2Kg 23:17
[q] 1Kg 12:32-33
[r] **13:2** 2Kg 23:15-16
[s] **13:3** Is 7:14
[t] Jn 2:11,18
[u] **13:6** Jms 5:16
[v] **13:7** 1Sm 9:7; 2Kg 5:15
[w] **13:8** Nm 22:18; Est 5:3; Mk 6:23
[x] **13:9** 1Kg 13:1
[y] **13:11** 1Kg 12:32; 13:1
[z] 1Kg 13:2-6

[A] **12:28** Or *here are your gods* [B] **12:30** Some LXX mss read *calves to Bethel and the other to Dan* [C] **12:33** Or *He went up to* [D] **13:11** Some Hb mss, LXX, Syr, Vg read *sons* [E] **13:12** LXX, Syr, Tg, Vg read *sons showed him*

16 But he answered, "I cannot go back with
you, eat bread, or drink water with you in
this place, 17 for a message came to me by the
word of the LORD: 'You must not eat bread or
drink water there[a] or go back by the way you
came.'"
18 He said to him, "I am also a prophet[b] like
you. An angel spoke to me by the word of the
LORD: 'Bring him back with you to your house
so that he may eat bread and drink water.'"
The old prophet deceived him,[c] 19 and the man
of God went back with him, ate bread in his
house, and drank water.
20 While they were sitting at the table, the
word of the LORD came to the prophet who
had brought him back, 21 and the prophet
cried out to the man of God who had come
from Judah, "This is what the LORD says: 'Because you rebelled against the command of
the LORD and did not keep the command that
the LORD your God commanded you — 22 but
you went back and ate bread and drank water in the place that He said to you, "Do not
eat bread and do not drink water"—[d] your
corpse will never reach the grave of your fathers.'"[e]
23 So after he had eaten bread and after he
had drunk, the old prophet saddled the donkey for the prophet he had brought back.
24 When he left,[A] a lion attacked[B] him along
the way and killed him.[f] His corpse was
thrown on the road, and the donkey was
standing beside it; the lion was standing beside the corpse too.
25 There were men passing by who saw
the corpse thrown on the road and the lion
standing beside it, and they went and spoke
about it in the city where the old prophet
lived. 26 When the prophet who had brought
him back from his way heard about it, he
said, "He is the man of God who disobeyed
the command of the LORD. The LORD has
given him to the lion, and it has mauled and
killed him, according to the word of the LORD
that He spoke to him."
27 Then the old prophet instructed his sons,
"Saddle the donkey for me." They saddled it,[g]
28 and he went and found the corpse of the
man of God thrown on the road with the donkey and the lion standing beside the corpse.
The lion had not eaten the corpse or mauled
the donkey. 29 So the prophet lifted the corpse
of the man of God and laid it on the donkey
and brought it back. The old prophet came
into the city to mourn and bury him. 30 Then
he laid the corpse in his own grave,[h] and they
mourned over him: "Oh, my brother!"[i]
31 After he had buried him, he said to his
sons, "When I die, you must bury me in the
grave where the man of God is buried; lay my
bones beside his bones, 32 for the word that
he cried out by a revelation from the LORD
against the altar in Bethel[j] and against all the
shrines of the high places[k] in the cities of Samaria[l] is certain to happen."[m]
33 After all this[n] Jeroboam did not repent[o] of
his evil way but again set up priests for the
high places from every class of people.[p] He
ordained whoever so desired it, and they became priests of the high places.[q] 34 This was
the sin that caused the house of Jeroboam to
be wiped out and annihilated from the face
of the earth.[r]

Disaster on the House of Jeroboam

14 At that time Abijah son of Jeroboam
became sick.[s] 2 Jeroboam said to his
wife, "Go disguise yourself,[t] so they won't
know that you're Jeroboam's wife, and go to
Shiloh.[u] Ahijah the prophet is there; it was he
who told about me becoming king over this
people.[v] 3 Take with you 10 loaves of bread,
some cakes, and a jar of honey,[w] and go to
him. He will tell you what will happen to the
boy."
4 Jeroboam's wife did that: she went to
Shiloh and arrived at Ahijah's house. Ahijah could not see; his gaze was fixed[C] due to
his age.[x] 5 But the LORD had said to Ahijah,
"Jeroboam's wife is coming soon to ask you
about her son, for he is sick. You are to say
such and such to her. When she arrives, she
will be disguised."[y]
6 When Ahijah heard the sound of her feet
entering the door, he said, "Come in, wife of
Jeroboam! Why are you disguised?[z] I have
bad news for you. 7 Go tell Jeroboam, 'This is
what the LORD God of Israel says: I raised you
up from among the people, appointed you
ruler over My people Israel, 8 tore the king-

[a] **13:16-17** 1Kg 13:8-9
[b] **13:18** 1Jn 4:1
[c] Dt 13:1-3
[d] **13:21-22** 1Kg 13:8-9
[e] **13:22** 1Kg 13:30
[f] **13:24** 1Kg 20:36
[g] **13:27** 1Kg 13:13
[h] **13:30** 1Kg 13:22,24
[i] Jr 22:18
[j] **13:32** 1Kg 13:1-3
[k] 1Kg 12:31-32; 2Kg 17:29
[l] 1Kg 16:28-29,32
[m] 2Kg 23:16
[n] **13:33** 1Kg 13:1-6,24
[o] 1Kg 12:28-33; 13:1; Ac 26:20
[p] 1Kg 12:31
[q] Jdg 17:5; 2Ch 13:9
[r] **13:34** 1Kg 12:28-33; 2Kg 17:21-23
[s] **14:1** 1Kg 14:12,17-18
[t] **14:2** 1Sm 28:8; 2Sm 14:2-3
[u] Jos 18:1
[v] 1Kg 11:29-39
[w] **14:3** 1Sm 9:7-8
[x] **14:4** 1Sm 3:2; 4:15
[y] **14:5** 2Sm 14:1-2
[z] **14:6** 1Sm 28:12

[A] **13:23-24** LXX reads *donkey, and he turned* [24] *and left, and* [B] **13:24** Lit *met* [C] **14:4** Lit *see, for his eyes stood*; 1Sm 4:15

dom away from the house of David, and gave
it to you.[a] But you were not like My servant
David, who kept My commands and followed
Me with all of his heart, doing only what is
right in My eyes. 9 You behaved more wickedly than all who were before you.[b] In order
to provoke Me, you have proceeded to make
for yourself other gods and cast images,[c] but
you have flung Me behind your back.[d] 10 Because of all this, I am about to bring disaster
on the house of Jeroboam:

I will eliminate all of Jeroboam's males,[A]
both slave and free,[B] in Israel;
I will sweep away the house
of Jeroboam
as one sweeps away dung until it is
all gone![e]
11 Anyone who belongs to Jeroboam
and dies in the city,
the dogs will eat,
and anyone who dies in the field,
the birds of the sky will eat,[f]
for the LORD has said it!'

12 "As for you, get up and go to your house.
When your feet enter the city, the boy will
die.[g] 13 All Israel will mourn for him and bury
him. He alone out of Jeroboam's house will
be put in the family tomb, because out of
the house of Jeroboam the LORD God of Israel found something good only in him.[h]
14 The LORD will raise up for Himself a king
over Israel, who will eliminate the house of
Jeroboam.[i] This is the day, yes,[B] even today!
15 For the LORD will strike Israel and the people will shake as a reed shakes in water. He
will uproot Israel from this good soil that He
gave to their ancestors.[j] He will scatter them
beyond the Euphrates[k] because they made
their ·Asherah poles, provoking the LORD.[l]
16 He will give up Israel because of Jeroboam's
sins that he committed and caused Israel to
commit."[m]

17 Then Jeroboam's wife got up and left
and went to Tirzah.[n] As she was crossing the
threshold of the house, the boy died. 18 He was
buried, and all Israel mourned for him, according to the word of the LORD He had spoken through His servant Ahijah the prophet.[o]
19 As for the rest of the events of Jeroboam's
reign, how he waged war[p] and how he
reigned, note that they are written in the Historical Record of Israel's Kings. 20 The length
of Jeroboam's reign was 22 years. He rested
with his fathers, and his son Nadab became
king in his place.[q]

Judah's King Rehoboam

21 Now Rehoboam, Solomon's son, reigned
in Judah.[r] Rehoboam was 41 years old when
he became king; he reigned 17 years in Jerusalem, the city where ·Yahweh had chosen
from all the tribes of Israel to put His name.[s]
Rehoboam's mother's name was Naamah the
Ammonite.[t]
22 Judah did what was evil in the LORD's
eyes.[u] They provoked Him to jealous anger[v]
more than all that their ancestors had done
with the sins they committed. 23 They also
built for themselves ·high places,[w] sacred pillars,[x] and Asherah poles on every high hill
and under every green tree; 24 there were
even male cult prostitutes in the land.[y] They
imitated all the detestable practices of the nations the LORD had dispossessed before the
Israelites.[z]
25 In the fifth year of King Rehoboam,
Shishak king of Egypt[aa] went to war against
Jerusalem.[ab] 26 He seized the treasuries of the
LORD's temple and the treasuries of the royal
palace. He took everything. He took all the
gold shields that Solomon had made.[ac] 27 King
Rehoboam made bronze shields in their place
and committed them into the care of the captains of the royal escorts[C,ad] who guarded the
entrance to the king's palace. 28 Whenever
the king entered the LORD's temple, the royal
escorts would carry the shields, then they
would take them back to the royal escorts'
armory.[ae]
29 The rest of the events of Rehoboam's
reign,[af] along with all his accomplishments,
are written about in the Historical Record
of Judah's Kings. 30 There was war between
Rehoboam and Jeroboam throughout their
reigns.[ag] 31 Rehoboam rested with his fathers
and was buried with his fathers in the city of
David. His mother's name was Naamah the
Ammonite.[ah] His son Abijam[D,ai] became king
in his place.

[a] **14:7-8** 1Kg 11:28-31; 16:2
[b] **14:9** 1Kg 16:25,30
[c] 1Kg 11:33; 12:28-33
[d] Neh 9:26; Ps 50:17
[e] **14:10** 1Kg 15:29; 21:21-22
[f] **14:11** 1Kg 16:4; 21:24
[g] **14:12** 1Kg 14:17
[h] **14:13** 2Ch 12:12; 19:3
[i] **14:14** 1Kg 15:27-29
[j] **14:15** Dt 29:28
[k] 2Kg 15:29; 17:6
[l] Ex 34:14-15; Dt 12:3-4
[m] **14:16** 1Kg 12:28-33; 13:34; 15:30
[n] **14:17** 1Kg 15:33; Sg 6:4
[o] **14:18** 1Kg 14:12-13
[p] **14:19** 1Kg 14:30; 2Ch 13:2-20
[q] **14:20** 1Kg 15:25-26
[r] **14:21** 1Kg 12:1-24
[s] Dt 12:5; 1Kg 9:3; 11:32,36
[t] 2Ch 12:13
[u] **14:22** 2Kg 17:19; 2Ch 12:1,14
[v] Dt 32:21
[w] **14:23** 1Kg 3:2; 12:31
[x] Ex 23:24; Dt 16:21-22
[y] **14:24** Dt 23:17
[z] Ex 23:24; Dt 18:9; 2Kg 16:3; 17:15; 21:2; 3Jn 11
[aa] **14:25** 1Kg 11:40
[ab] **14:25-28** 2Ch 12:2-11
[ac] **14:26** 1Kg 10:16-17
[ad] **14:27** 1Sm 22:17; 2Sm 15:1
[ae] **14:28** 1Kg 10:17
[af] **14:29-31** 2Ch 12:15-16
[ag] **14:30** 1Kg 12:21-24; 15:6
[ah] **14:31** 1Kg 14:21
[ai] 1Kg 15:1-8; 2Ch 11:20; 13:1–14:1

[A] **14:10** Lit *eliminate Jeroboam's one who urinates against the wall* [B] **14:10,14** Hb obscure [C] **14:27** Lit *the runners* [D] **14:31** = Abijah in 2Ch 13

Judah's King Abijam

15 In the eighteenth year of Israel's King Jeroboam son of Nebat, Abijam became king over Judah 2 and reigned three years in Jerusalem.[a] His mother's name was Maacah[b] daughter[A] of Abishalom.

3 Abijam walked in all the sins his father before him had committed,[c] and he was not completely devoted to the LORD his God as his ancestor David had been.[d] 4 But because of David, the LORD his God gave him a lamp in Jerusalem to raise up his son after him and to establish Jerusalem.[e] 5 For David did what was right in the LORD's eyes, and he did not turn aside from anything He had commanded him all the days of his life,[f] except in the matter of Uriah[g] the Hittite.

6 There had been war between Rehoboam and Jeroboam all the days of Rehoboam's life.[h] 7 The rest of the events of Abijam's reign, along with all his accomplishments, are written in the Historical Record of Judah's Kings.[i] There was also war between Abijam and Jeroboam.[j] 8 Abijam rested with his fathers and was buried in the city of David.[k] His son Asa became king in his place.[l]

Judah's King Asa

9 In the twentieth year of Israel's King Jeroboam,[m] Asa became king of Judah 10 and reigned 41 years in Jerusalem. His grandmother's[B] name was Maacah[n] daughter[C] of Abishalom.

11 Asa did what was right in the LORD's eyes, as his ancestor David had done.[o] 12 He banished the male cult prostitutes[p] from the land and removed all of the idols that his fathers had made.[q] 13 He also[r] removed his grandmother[D] Maacah from being queen mother because she had made an obscene image of •Asherah. Asa chopped down her obscene image and burned it[s] in the Kidron Valley.[t] 14 The •high places were not taken away;[u] but Asa's heart was completely devoted to the LORD his entire life.[v] 15 He brought his father's consecrated gifts and his own consecrated gifts into the LORD's temple: silver, gold, and utensils.[w]

16 There was war between Asa and Baasha king of Israel throughout their reigns.[x] 17 Israel's King Baasha went to war against Judah.[y] He built Ramah[z] in order to deny anyone access to Judah's King Asa. 18 So Asa withdrew all the silver and gold that remained in the treasuries of the LORD's temple[aa] and the treasuries of the royal palace and put it into the hands of his servants. Then King Asa sent them to Ben-hadad[ab] son of Tabrimmon son of Hezion king of Aram who lived in Damascus,[ac] saying, 19 "There is a treaty between me and you, between my father and your father.[ad] Look, I have sent you a gift of silver and gold. Go and break your treaty with Baasha king of Israel[ae] so that he will withdraw from me."

20 Ben-hadad listened to King Asa and sent the commanders of his armies against the cities of Israel. He attacked Ijon,[af] Dan,[ag] Abel-beth-maacah,[ah] all Chinnereth,[ai] and the whole land of Naphtali.[aj] 21 When Baasha heard about it, he quit building Ramah and stayed in Tirzah.[ak] 22 Then King Asa gave a command to everyone without exception in Judah, and they carried away the stones of Ramah and the timbers Baasha had built it with. Then King Asa built Geba[al] of Benjamin and Mizpah[am] with them.

23 The rest of all the events of Asa's reign,[an] along with all his might, all his accomplishments, and the cities he built, are written in the Historical Record of Judah's Kings.[ao] But in his old age he developed a disease in his feet.[ap] 24 Then Asa rested with his fathers and was buried in the city of his ancestor David.[aq] His son Jehoshaphat[ar] became king in his place.

Israel's King Nadab

25 Nadab son of Jeroboam[as] became king over Israel in the second year of Judah's King Asa; he reigned over Israel two years. 26 Nadab did what was evil in the LORD's sight and followed the example of his father and the sin he had caused Israel to commit.[at]

27 Then Baasha[au] son of Ahijah of the house of Issachar conspired against Nadab, and Baasha struck him down at Gibbethon[av] of the Philistines while Nadab and all Israel were besieging Gibbethon. 28 In the third year of Judah's King Asa,[aw] Baasha killed Nadab[ax] and reigned in his place.

[a] **15:1-2** 2Ch 13:1-2 [b] **15:2** 1Kg 15:10,13; 2Ch 13:2 [c] **15:3** 1Kg 14:21-22 [d] 1Kg 9:4; 11:4 [e] **15:4** 2Sm 21:17; 1Kg 11:36; 2Ch 21:7 [f] **15:5** 1Kg 9:4; 14:8 [g] 2Sm 11:3,15-17; 12:9-10 [h] **15:6** 1Kg 14:30; 2Ch 12:15 [i] **15:7** 1Kg 14:29 [j] 2Ch 13:4-20 [k] **15:8** 1Kg 14:31; 2Ch 14:1 [l] 1Kg 14:31; 2Ch 14–16 [m] **15:9** 1Kg 15:1 [n] **15:10** 1Kg 15:2 [o] **15:11** 1Kg 9:4-5; 2Ch 14:2 [p] **15:12** Dt 23:17; 1Kg 14:24 [q] **15:11-12** 1Kg 11:7; 14:23; 2Ch 14:3,5 [r] **15:13-15** 2Ch 15:16-18 [s] **15:13** Ex 32:20 [t] 2Kg 23:6 [u] **15:14** 1Kg 22:43 [v] 1Kg 8:61; 15:3 [w] **15:15** 1Kg 7:51 [x] **15:16** 1Kg 15:32 [y] **15:17-22** 2Ch 16:1-6 [z] **15:17** Jos 18:25 [aa] **15:18** 1Kg 14:26 [ab] 1Kg 20:1 [ac] 1Kg 11:23-24 [ad] **15:19** 1Kg 5:12; 2Ch 16:7 [ae] 1Kg 15:27-28 [af] **15:20** 2Kg 15:29 [ag] Jdg 18:29; 1Kg 12:29 [ah] 2Sm 20:15; 2Kg 15:29 [ai] Jos 11:2; 12:3 [aj] Jos 19:32-39; 1Kg 20:34 [ak] **15:21** 1Kg 14:17; 15:33; 16:8,15-18 [al] **15:22** Jos 18:24; 21:17 [am] Jos 11:3; 2Ch 16:6 [an] **15:23-24** 2Ch 16:11-14 [ao] **15:23** 1Kg 14:29; 15:7 [ap] 2Ch 16:12 [aq] **15:24** 1Kg 14:31; 15:8 [ar] 1Kg 22:41-50 [as] **15:25** 1Kg 14:20 [at] **15:26** 1Kg 14:16; 15:30,34 [au] **15:27** 1Kg 14:14; 15:16 [av] Jos 19:44; 1Kg 16:15 [aw] **15:28** 1Kg 15:8-24; 2Ch 14–16 [ax] 1Kg 16:8-10

[A] **15:2** Possibly granddaughter; 2Ch 13:2 [B] **15:10** Lit *mother's* [C] **15:10** Possibly granddaughter; 2Ch 13:2 [D] **15:13** Lit *mother*

29 When Baasha became king, he struck
down the entire house of Jeroboam.[a] He did
not leave Jeroboam any survivors but[A] destroyed his family according to the word of
the LORD He had spoken through His servant
Ahijah the Shilonite.[b] 30 This was because Jeroboam had provoked[B] the LORD God of Israel
by the sins he had committed and had caused
Israel to commit.[c]

31 The rest of the events of Nadab's reign,
along with all his accomplishments, are written in the Historical Record of Israel's Kings.[d]
32 There was war between Asa and Baasha king
of Israel throughout their reigns.[e]

Israel's King Baasha

33 In the third year of Judah's King Asa, Baasha son of Ahijah became king over all Israel
and reigned in Tirzah[f] 24 years. 34 He did what
was evil in the LORD's sight and followed the
example of Jeroboam and the sin he had
caused Israel to commit.[g]

16 Now the word of the LORD came to
Jehu[h] son of Hanani[i] against Baasha:
2 "Because I raised you up from the dust[j] and
made you ruler over My people Israel,[k] but
you have walked in the way of Jeroboam and
have caused My people Israel to sin,[l] provoking Me with their sins, 3 take note: I will sweep
away Baasha and his house, and I will make
your house like the house of Jeroboam son of
Nebat:[m]

4 Anyone who belongs to Baasha and dies
 in the city,
the dogs will eat,
and anyone who is his and dies
 in the field,
the birds of the sky will eat."[n]

5 The rest of the events of Baasha's reign,
along with all his accomplishments and
might, are written in the Historical Record
of Israel's Kings.[o] 6 Baasha rested with his
fathers and was buried in Tirzah. His son
Elah became king in his place. 7 Through the
prophet Jehu[p] son of Hanani the word of the
LORD also came against Baasha and against
his house because of all the evil he had done
in the LORD's sight, provoking Him with the
work of his hands and being like the house
of Jeroboam, and because Baasha had struck
down the house of Jeroboam.[q]

Israel's King Elah

8 In the twenty-sixth year of Judah's King
Asa, Elah son of Baasha became king over Israel and reigned in Tirzah[r] two years.
9 His servant Zimri,[s] commander of half his
chariots, conspired against him while Elah
was in Tirzah getting drunk[t] in the house of
Arza, who was in charge of the household[u]
at Tirzah. 10 In the twenty-seventh year of
Judah's King Asa, Zimri went in, struck Elah
down, killing him. Then Zimri became king
in his place.[v]
11 When he became king, as soon as he was
seated on his throne, Zimri struck down the
entire house of Baasha. He did not leave a
single male,[C,w] including his kinsmen and his
friends. 12 So Zimri destroyed the entire house
of Baasha, according to the word of the LORD
He had spoken against Baasha through Jehu
the prophet.[x] 13 This happened because of all
the sins of Baasha and those of his son Elah,
which they committed and caused Israel to
commit, provoking the LORD God of Israel[y]
with their worthless idols.[z]
14 The rest of the events of Elah's reign, along
with all his accomplishments, are written in
the Historical Record of Israel's Kings.[aa]

Israel's King Zimri

15 In the twenty-seventh year of Judah's
King Asa, Zimri became king for seven days
in Tirzah.[ab] Now the troops were encamped
against Gibbethon of the Philistines.[ac]
16 When these troops heard that Zimri had
not only conspired but had also struck down
the king, then all Israel made Omri, the army
commander, king over Israel that very day
in the camp. 17 Omri along with all Israel
marched up from Gibbethon and besieged
Tirzah.[ad] 18 When Zimri saw that the city was
captured, he entered the citadel of the royal
palace and burned it down over himself. He
died 19 because of the sin he committed by doing what was evil in the LORD's sight and by
following the example of Jeroboam and the
sin he caused Israel to commit.[ae]
20 The rest of the events of Zimri's reign,

[a] 15:29 1Kg 13:34
[b] 1Kg 14:10
[c] 15:30 1Kg 14:7-9
[d] 15:31 1Kg 14:19; 16:5
[e] 15:32 1Kg 15:16
[f] 15:33 1Kg 15:21
[g] 15:34 1Kg 14:16
[h] 16:1 1Kg 16:7; 2Ch 19:2
[i] 2Ch 16:7-10
[j] 16:2 1Sm 2:8
[k] 1Kg 14:7
[l] 1Kg 15:26,34
[m] 16:3 1Kg 14:10; 15:29
[n] 16:4 1Kg 14:11; 21:24
[o] 16:5 1Kg 14:19; 15:31
[p] 16:7 1Kg 16:1; 2Ch 19:2
[q] 1Kg 15:27,29
[r] 16:8 1Kg 15:21
[s] 16:9 2Kg 9:30-33
[t] 1Sm 25:36; 1Kg 20:12,16; Pr 31:4-5; Eph 5:18
[u] 1Kg 18:3
[v] 16:10 1Kg 15:28
[w] 16:11 1Sm 25:22; 1Kg 15:29
[x] 16:12 1Kg 16:1-4
[y] 16:13 1Kg 15:26,30
[z] Dt 32:21; 1Kg 12:28-33
[aa] 16:14 1Kg 15:31
[ab] 16:15 1Kg 15:21
[ac] 1Kg 15:27
[ad] 16:17 1Kg 14:17
[ae] 16:19 1Kg 12:28-33

[A] 15:29 Lit *Jeroboam anyone breathing until* [B] 15:30 Lit *provoked in the provocation of* [C] 16:11 Lit *leave him one who urinates against the wall* along with the conspiracy that he instigated, are written in the Historical Record of Israel's Kings. 21 At that time the people of Israel were divided: half the people followed Tibni son of Ginath, to make him king, and half followed Omri. 22 However, the people who followed Omri proved stronger than those who followed Tibni son of Ginath. So Tibni died and Omri became king.

Israel's King Omri

23 In the thirty-first year of Judah's King Asa, Omri became king over Israel and reigned 12 years. He reigned six years in Tirzah,[a] 24 then he bought the hill of Samaria[b] from Shemer for 150 pounds[A] of silver, and he built up the hill. He named the city he built Samaria[B] based on the name Shemer, the owner of the hill.

25 Omri did what was evil in the LORD's sight; he did more evil than all who were before him.[c] 26 He followed the example of Jeroboam son of Nebat and in his sins that he caused Israel to commit, provoking the LORD God of Israel with their worthless idols.[d] 27 The rest of the events of Omri's reign, along with his accomplishments and the might he exercised, are written in the Historical Record of Israel's Kings. 28 Omri rested with his fathers and was buried in Samaria. His son Ahab became king in his place.

Israel's King Ahab

29 Ahab son of Omri became king over Israel in the thirty-eighth year of Judah's King Asa; Ahab son of Omri reigned over Israel in Samaria 22 years. 30 But Ahab son of Omri did what was evil in the LORD's sight more than all who were before him.[e] 31 Then, as if following the sin of Jeroboam son of Nebat were a trivial matter, he married Jezebel,[f] the daughter of Ethbaal king of the Sidonians,[g] and then proceeded to serve •Baal and worship him.[h] 32 He set up an altar for Baal in the temple of Baal[i] that he had built in Samaria. 33 Ahab also made an •Asherah pole.[j] Ahab did more to provoke the LORD God of Israel than all the kings of Israel who were before him.[k]

34 During his reign, Hiel the Bethelite built Jericho. At the cost of Abiram his firstborn, he laid its foundation, and at the cost of Segub his youngest, he set up its gates, according to the word of the LORD He had spoken through Joshua son of Nun.[l]

Elijah Announces Famine

17 Now Elijah[m] the Tishbite, from the Gilead settlers,[C,n] said to Ahab, "As the LORD God of Israel lives,[o] I stand before Him, and there will be no dew or rain during these years except by my command!"[p]

2 Then a revelation from the LORD came to him: 3 "Leave here, turn eastward, and hide[q] yourself at the •Wadi Cherith where it enters the Jordan. 4 You are to drink from the wadi. I have commanded the ravens[r] to provide for you there."

5 So he did what the LORD commanded. Elijah left and lived by the Wadi Cherith where it enters the Jordan. 6 The ravens kept bringing him bread and meat in the morning and in the evening,[s] and he drank from the wadi. 7 After a while, the wadi dried up because there had been no rain in the land.

Elijah and the Widow

8 Then the word of the LORD came to him: 9 "Get up, go to Zarephath[t] that belongs to Sidon and stay there. Look, I have commanded a woman who is a widow to provide for you there." 10 So Elijah got up and went to Zarephath. When he arrived at the city gate, there was a widow woman gathering wood. Elijah called to her and said, "Please bring me a little water in a cup and let me drink."[u] 11 As she went to get it, he called to her and said, "Please bring me a piece of bread in your hand."

12 But she said, "As the LORD your God lives,[v] I don't have anything baked—only a handful of flour in the jar and a bit of oil[w] in the jug. Just now, I am gathering a couple of sticks in order to go prepare it for myself and my son so we can eat it and die."[x]

13 Then Elijah said to her, "Don't be afraid; go and do as you have said. But first make me a small loaf from it and bring it out to me. Afterward, you may make some for yourself and your son, 14 for this is what the LORD God of Israel says, 'The flour jar will not become

[a] **16:23** 1Kg 15:21
[b] **16:24** 1Kg 13:32
[c] **16:25** 1Kg 14:9; 16:30
[d] **16:25-26** 1Kg 16:13,19
[e] **16:30** 1Kg 14:9; 16:25
[f] **16:31** Dt 7:3-4; 1Kg 18:4,13; Rv 2:20
[g] 1Kg 11:5
[h] Jdg 2:11
[i] **16:32** 2Kg 10:21,26-27
[j] **16:33** 2Kg 13:6
[k] 1Kg 16:30
[l] **16:34** Jos 6:26
[m] **17:1** 1Kg 17–19; 2Kg 1–2; Mal 4:5; Mt 11:14
[n] Jdg 12:4
[o] 1Kg 18:10; 22:14
[p] Dt 11:16-17; Jms 5:17; Rv 11:6
[q] **17:3** 1Kg 18:4
[r] **17:4** 1Kg 17:9; Jb 38:41; Lk 12:24
[s] **17:6** Ex 16:8
[t] **17:9** Ob 20; Lk 4:26
[u] **17:10** Gn 24:17; Jn 4:7
[v] **17:12** 1Kg 17:1
[w] 2Kg 4:2-7
[x] Gn 21:14,16

[A] **16:24** Lit *for two talents* [B] **16:24** = Belonging to Shemer's Clan [C] **17:1** LXX reads *from Tishbe of Gilead*

empty and the oil jug will not run dry until
the day the LORD sends rain on the surface of
the land."[a]
15 So she proceeded to do according to the
word of Elijah. Then the woman, Elijah, and
her household ate for many days.[b] 16 The flour
jar did not become empty, and the oil jug did
not run dry, according to the word of the
LORD He had spoken through[A] Elijah.

The Widow's Son Raised

17 After this, the son of the woman who
owned the house became ill. His illness became very severe until no breath remained in
him.[c] 18 She said to Elijah, "Man of God,[d] what
do we have in common?[e] Have you come to
remind me of my ·guilt[f] and to kill my son?"
19 But Elijah said to her, "Give me your son."
So he took him from her arms, brought him
up to the upper room[g] where he was staying,
and laid him on his own bed. 20 Then he cried
out to the LORD[h] and said, "My LORD God,
have You also brought tragedy on the widow
I am staying with by killing her son?" 21 Then
he stretched himself out over the boy three
times.[i] He cried out to the LORD and said, "My
LORD God, please let this boy's life return to
him!"
22 So the LORD listened to Elijah's voice, and
the boy's life returned to him, and he lived.[j]
23 Then Elijah took the boy, brought him
down from the upper room into the house,
and gave him to his mother.[k] Elijah said,
"Look, your son is alive."
24 Then the woman said to Elijah, "Now I
know you are a man of God[l] and the LORD's
word from your mouth is true."[m]

Elijah's Message to Ahab

18 After a long time, the word of the
LORD[n] came to Elijah in the third year:[o]
"Go and present yourself to Ahab.[p] I will send
rain on the surface of the land." 2 So Elijah
went to present himself to Ahab.
The famine was severe in Samaria.[q] 3 Ahab
called for Obadiah, who was in charge of
the palace.[r] Obadiah was a man who greatly
·feared the LORD[s] 4 and took 100 prophets
and hid them, 50 men to a cave, and provided
them with food and water when Jezebel[t]
slaughtered the LORD's prophets.[u] 5 Ahab said
to Obadiah, "Go throughout the land to every
spring of water and to every ·wadi. Perhaps
we'll find grass so we can keep the horses and
mules alive and not have to destroy any cattle."[v] 6 They divided the land between them
in order to cover it. Ahab went one way by
himself, and Obadiah went the other way by
himself.
7 While Obadiah was walking along the
road, Elijah suddenly met him.[w] When Obadiah recognized him, he fell with his face to
the ground and said, "Is it you, my lord Elijah?"
8 "It is I," he replied. "Go tell your lord, 'Elijah is here!'"
9 But Obadiah said, "What sin have I committed,[x] that you are handing your servant
over to Ahab to put me to death? 10 As the
LORD your God lives, there is no nation or
kingdom where my lord has not sent someone to search for you. When they said, 'He is
not here,' he made that kingdom or nation
swear they had not found you.
11 "Now you say, 'Go tell your lord, "Elijah is
here!"' 12 But when I leave you, the Spirit of
the LORD may carry you off[y] to some place I
don't know. Then when I go report to Ahab
and he doesn't find you, he will kill me. But I,
your servant, have feared the LORD from my
youth. 13 Wasn't it reported to my lord what
I did when Jezebel slaughtered the LORD's
prophets? I hid 100 of the prophets of the
LORD, 50 men to a cave, and I provided them
with food and water. 14 Now you say, 'Go tell
your lord, "Elijah is here!"' He will kill me!"
15 Then Elijah said, "As the LORD of ·Hosts
lives,[z] before whom I stand, today I will present myself to Ahab."
16 Obadiah went to meet Ahab and told him.
Then Ahab went to meet Elijah. 17 When Ahab
saw Elijah, Ahab said to him, "Is that you, you
destroyer of Israel?"[aa]
18 He replied, "I have not destroyed Israel, but
you and your father's house have, because you
have abandoned the LORD's commands[ab] and
followed the ·Baals.[ac] 19 Now summon all Israel
to meet me at Mount Carmel,[ad] along with the
450 prophets of Baal and the 400 prophets of
·Asherah[ae] who eat at Jezebel's table."

[a] **17:14** 1Kg 17:1; Php 4:19
[b] **17:15** Mt 6:11
[c] **17:17** Ac 9:37
[d] **17:18** 1Kg 12:22
[e] 2Sm 16:10; 2Kg 3:13
[f] Lk 5:8
[g] **17:19** Ac 9:37,39
[h] **17:20** 2Kg 4:33
[i] **17:21** 2Kg 4:34; Ac 20:10
[j] **17:22** Lk 7:14
[k] **17:23** Lk 7:15; Heb 11:35
[l] **17:24** Jn 3:2
[m] 1Kg 22:16; Jn 17:17
[n] **18:1** 1Kg 17:8
[o] 1Kg 17:1; Jms 5:17
[p] 1Kg 16:29-33
[q] **18:2** 1Kg 16:24,29
[r] **18:3** 1Kg 16:9
[s] Neh 7:2; Pr 3:5-6
[t] **18:4** 1Kg 16:31; Rv 2:20
[u] 1Kg 18:13
[v] **18:5** Gn 47:4
[w] **18:7** 2Kg 1:6-8
[x] **18:9** 1Kg 17:18
[y] **18:12** 2Kg 2:16; Ac 8:39
[z] **18:15** 1Kg 17:1
[aa] **18:17** Jos 7:25; 1Kg 21:20
[ab] **18:18** 1Kg 9:9; 16:25-26
[ac] 1Kg 16:31-32
[ad] **18:19** Jos 19:26; 2Kg 2:25
[ae] 1Kg 16:33; 22:6

[A] **17:16** Lit *by the hand of*

Elijah at Mount Carmel

20 So Ahab summoned all the Israelites and gathered the prophets at Mount Carmel. 21 Then Elijah approached all the people and said, "How long will you hesitate between two opinions?[a] If •Yahweh is God, follow Him. But if Baal, follow him."[b] But the people didn't answer him a word.

22 Then Elijah said to the people, "I am the only remaining prophet of the LORD,[c] but Baal's prophets are 450 men. 23 Let two bulls be given to us. They are to choose one bull for themselves, cut it in pieces, and place it on the wood but not light the fire. I will prepare the other bull and place it on the wood but not light the fire. 24 Then you call on the name of your god, and I will call on the name of Yahweh.[d] The God who answers with fire, He is God."

All the people answered, "That sounds good."

25 Then Elijah said to the prophets of Baal, "Since you are so numerous, choose for yourselves one bull and prepare it first. Then call on the name of your god but don't light the fire." 26 So they took the bull that he gave them, prepared it, and called on the name of Baal from morning until noon, saying, "Baal, answer us!" But there was no sound;[e] no one answered. Then they danced, hobbling around the altar they had made.

27 At noon Elijah mocked them. He said, "Shout loudly, for he's a god! Maybe he's thinking it over; maybe he has wandered away;[A] or maybe he's on the road. Perhaps he's sleeping and will wake up!"[f] 28 They shouted loudly, and cut themselves[g] with knives and spears, according to their custom, until blood gushed over them. 29 All afternoon they kept on raving until the offering of the evening sacrifice,[h] but there was no sound; no one answered, no one paid attention.[i]

30 Then Elijah said to all the people, "Come near me." So all the people approached him. Then he repaired the LORD's altar that had been torn down:[j] 31 Elijah took 12 stones—according to the number of the tribes of the sons of Jacob, to whom the word of the LORD had come, saying, "Israel will be your name"[k]— 32 and he built an altar[l] with the stones in the name of Yahweh. Then he made a trench around the altar large enough to hold about four gallons.[B,C] 33 Next, he arranged the wood, cut up the bull, and placed it on the wood. He said, "Fill four water pots with water and pour it on the offering to be burned and on the wood." 34 Then he said, "A second time!" and they did it a second time. And then he said, "A third time!" and they did it a third time. 35 So the water ran all around the altar; he even filled the trench with water.

36 At the time for offering the evening sacrifice,[m] Elijah the prophet approached the altar and said, "Yahweh, God of Abraham, Isaac, and Israel,[n] today let it be known[o] that You are God in Israel and I am Your servant, and that at Your word I have done all these things. 37 Answer me, LORD! Answer me so that this people will know that You, Yahweh, are God[p] and that You have turned their hearts back."

38 Then Yahweh's fire fell and consumed the •burnt offering, the wood, the stones, and the dust, and it licked up the water that was in the trench. 39 When all the people saw it, they fell facedown[q] and said, "Yahweh, He is God! Yahweh, He is God!"[r]

40 Then Elijah ordered them, "Seize the prophets of Baal![s] Do not let even one of them escape." So they seized them, and Elijah brought them down to the Wadi Kishon[t] and slaughtered them there.[u] 41 Elijah said to Ahab, "Go up, eat and drink, for there is the sound of a rainstorm."[v]

42 So Ahab went to eat and drink, but Elijah went up to the summit of Carmel.[w] He bowed down on the ground and put his face between his knees.[x] 43 Then he said to his servant, "Go up and look toward the sea."

So he went up, looked, and said, "There's nothing."

Seven times Elijah said, "Go back."

44 On the seventh[y] time, he reported, "There's a cloud as small as a man's hand coming from the sea."

Then Elijah said, "Go and tell Ahab, 'Get your chariot ready and go down so the rain doesn't stop you.'"

45 In a little while, the sky grew dark with clouds and wind, and there was a downpour.

[a] 18:21 2Kg 17:41
[b] Jos 24:15; Mt 6:24
[c] 18:22 1Kg 19:10,14
[d] 18:24 Gn 4:26; Rm 10:13
[e] 18:26 Jr 10:5; 1Co 8:4
[f] 18:27 Hab 2:19
[g] 18:28 Lv 19:28; Dt 14:1
[h] 18:29 Ex 29:39,41
[i] 2Kg 19:12; Is 16:12
[j] 18:30 1Kg 19:10
[k] 18:31 Gn 32:28; 35:10; 2Kg 17:34
[l] 18:32 Gn 12:7,8; 22:9
[m] 18:36 1Kg 18:29
[n] Ex 3:6; 4:5
[o] Nm 16:28
[p] 18:37 Jos 4:24; Jn 11:42
[q] 18:39 Lv 9:24; Mt 17:6
[r] 1Kg 18:21,24
[s] 18:40 1Kg 18:19,22
[t] Jdg 4:7; 5:21
[u] Dt 13:5; 2Kg 10:24-25
[v] 18:41 1Kg 17:1; 18:1
[w] 18:42 1Kg 18:19
[x] 1Sm 12:17; Jms 5:18
[y] 18:44 Jos 6:15; Lk 12:54

A 18:27 Or *has turned aside*; possibly to relieve himself B 18:32 LXX reads *trench containing two measures of seed* C 18:32 Lit *altar corresponding to a house of two seahs of seed*

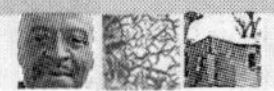

So Ahab got in his chariot and went to Jezreel.[a] 46The power of the LORD[b] was on Elijah,
and he tucked his mantle under his belt[c] and
ran ahead of Ahab to the entrance of Jezreel.

Elijah's Journey to Horeb

19 Ahab told Jezebel[d] everything that Elijah had done[e] and how he had killed all
the prophets with the sword.[f] 2So Jezebel sent
a messenger to Elijah, saying, "May the gods
punish me and do so severely[g] if I don't make
your life like the life of one of them by this
time tomorrow!"
3Then Elijah became afraid[A,h] and immediately ran for his life.[i] When he came to
Beer-sheba[j] that belonged to Judah, he left

[a]18:45 Jos 17:16; Jdg 6:33 [b]18:46 2Kg 3:15 [c]Ex 12:11; 2Kg 4:29; 9:1; Jr 1:17; 1Pt 1:13 [d]19:1 1Kg 16:31; 18:4,14 [e]1Kg 18:30-38 [f]1Kg 18:40 [g]19:2 1Sm 3:17; 1Kg 20:10; 2Kg 6:31

[h]19:3 Pr 29:25 [i]Gn 31:21 [j]Gn 21:31; Jdg 20:1

Mentoring in the Mission

Chris Conrad

"I believe in you." Perhaps some of the most powerful words we can say to someone. These four simple words evoke confidence and anticipation in all that a person can and will become by God's grace and power. If you have ever had the privilege of someone uttering those words to you, you know the emotion it evokes. They inspire you to become all God wants you to become.

In a very real way, this is exactly what Elijah did with Elisha. The cloak (often referred to as a mantle) was one of the most important possessions a person had in Elijah's day. It served as an outer garment, a blanket, a cushion to sit on, and when tied up correctly, even a type of luggage device to carry things home from the market.

So when Elijah took one of his most important possessions, his cloak, and placed it on Elisha, it was a way of saying: "I believe in you. God's Spirit is on you. Your future, Elisha, is bright."

Although we do not know all of Elisha's history, what unfolds in this story gives us a hint that what Elijah did for him that day was one of the most powerful events of Elisha's life. A person who Elisha deeply respected had walked up to him and, through one simple interchange, radically changed how Elisha looked at life, his future, and what he wanted to give his life to.

Missional leaders understand that for the work of God to be accomplished in ever-increasing ways, potential leaders must continually be identified, developed, and deployed. That is why missional leaders are continually praying that God will give them discernment because all believers have incredible potential for Kingdom work. Often however individuals have simply not been challenged to join in missional work or have never been encouraged to believe they have God-given talent and strengths to offer.

Missional leaders take personal responsibility to mentor these future leaders. What began that day between Elijah and Elisha was a mentoring process that would eventually lead to Elisha taking over where Elijah left off (see 2Kg 2). But Elijah was the one who initiated the relationship. He took responsibility for it. He did not wait for Elisha to come to him. After this period of mentoring, Elisha was deployed by the Holy Spirit into the specific work God had for him to do.

What Elijah did the day he put his cloak on Elisha did not cost him any money. Nor did it decrease the influence he had with the people of Israel. But he did put into motion leadership multiplication through his life that would serve the Kingdom well going into the future.

As missional leaders we have an incredible opportunity to follow in the footsteps of Elijah and look for the Elishas in our own life. As we initiate the mentoring process with them, only heaven knows the full impact of all God will eventually do through their lives.

[A]19:3 Some Hb mss, LXX, Syr, Vg; other Hb mss read *he saw* his servant there,[a] 4 but he went on a day's journey into the wilderness. He sat down under a broom tree[b] and prayed that he might die. He said, "I have had enough! LORD, take my life,[c] for I'm no better than my fathers." 5 Then he lay down and slept under the broom tree.

Suddenly, an angel touched him.[d] The angel told him, "Get up and eat." 6 Then he looked, and there at his head was a loaf of bread baked over hot stones, and a jug of water.[e] So he ate and drank and lay down again. 7 Then the angel of the LORD[f] returned for a second time and touched him. He said, "Get up and eat, or the journey will be too much for you." 8 So he got up, ate, and drank. Then on the strength from that food, he walked 40 days and 40 nights[g] to Horeb, the mountain of God.[h] 9 He entered a cave[i] there and spent the night.

Elijah's Encounter with the LORD

Then the word of the LORD came to him, and He said to him, "What are you doing here, Elijah?"[j]

10 He replied, "I have been very zealous[k] for the LORD God of ˙Hosts, but the Israelites have abandoned Your covenant,[l] torn down Your altars,[m] and killed Your prophets[n] with the sword. I alone am left,[o] and they are looking for me to take my life."[p]

11 Then He said, "Go out and stand on the mountain in the LORD's presence."[q]

At that moment, the LORD passed by.[r] A great and mighty wind[s] was tearing at the mountains and was shattering cliffs before the LORD, but the LORD was not in the wind. After the wind there was an earthquake,[t] but the LORD was not in the earthquake. 12 After the earthquake there was a fire,[u] but the LORD was not in the fire. And after the fire there was a voice, a soft whisper.[v] 13 When Elijah heard it, he wrapped his face in his mantle[w] and went out and stood at the entrance of the cave.

Suddenly, a voice came to him and said, "What are you doing here, Elijah?"

14 "I have been very zealous for the LORD God of Hosts," he replied, "but the Israelites have abandoned Your covenant, torn down Your altars, and killed Your prophets with the sword. I alone am left, and they're looking for me to take my life."[x]

15 Then the LORD said to him, "Go and return by the way you came to the Wilderness of Damascus. When you arrive, you are to anoint Hazael[y] as king over Aram. 16 You are to anoint Jehu[z] son of Nimshi as king over Israel and Elisha[aa] son of Shaphat from Abel-meholah as prophet in your place. 17 Then Jehu will put to death whoever escapes the sword of Hazael,[ab] and Elisha will put to death whoever escapes the sword of Jehu.[ac] 18 But I will leave 7,000 in Israel[ad]—every knee that has not bowed to ˙Baal[ae] and every mouth that has not kissed him."[af]

Elisha's Appointment as Elijah's Successor

19 Elijah left there and found Elisha[ag] son of Shaphat as he was plowing. Twelve teams of oxen were in front of him, and he was with the twelfth team. Elijah walked by him and threw his mantle over him.[ah] 20 Elisha left the oxen, ran to follow Elijah, and said, "Please let me kiss my father and mother, and then I will follow you."[ai]

"Go on back," he replied, "for what have I done to you?"

21 So he turned back from following him, took the team of oxen, and slaughtered them. With the oxen's wooden yoke and plow,[aj] he cooked the meat and gave it to the people, and they ate. Then he left, followed Elijah, and served him.[ak]

Victory over Ben-hadad

20 Now Ben-hadad[al] king of Aram assembled his entire army. Thirty-two kings,[am] along with horses and chariots, were with him. He marched up, besieged Samaria,[an] and fought against it. 2 He sent messengers into the city to Ahab king of Israel and said to him, "This is what Ben-hadad says: 3 'Your silver and your gold are mine! And your best wives and children are mine as well!'"[ao]

4 Then the king of Israel answered, "Just as you say, my lord the king: I am yours, along with all that I have."

5 The messengers then returned and said, "This is what Ben-hadad says: 'I have sent messengers to you, saying: You are to give me your silver, your gold, your wives, and your children. 6 But at this time tomorrow I will send my servants to you, and they will search your palace and your servants' houses. They

[a] **19:3** Gn 22:5; Mt 14:23; 26:36
[b] **19:4** Jb 30:4
[c] Nm 11:15; Jnh 4:3,8
[d] **19:5** Gn 28:11-16
[e] **19:6** 1Kg 17:10-11
[f] **19:7** Gn 16:7,9,11
[g] **19:8** Ex 24:18; Mt 4:2
[h] Ex 3:1; 4:27
[i] **19:9** Ex 33:22
[j] Gn 3:9
[k] **19:10** Nm 25:13; Ac 22:3
[l] Dt 31:16
[m] 1Kg 18:30
[n] 1Kg 18:4,13; Ac 7:52
[o] 1Kg 18:22
[p] 1Kg 19:2,14; Rm 11:3
[q] **19:11** Ex 19:20
[r] Ex 33:21-22
[s] Ezk 1:4; Ac 2:2
[t] Am 1:1; Rv 6:12; 16:18
[u] **19:12** Ex 3:2
[v] Zch 4:6,10
[w] **19:13** Ex 3:6
[x] **19:14** 1Kg 19:10; Rm 11:3
[y] **19:15** 2Kg 8:8-15
[z] **19:16** 2Kg 19:1-10
[aa] 1Kg 19:19
[ab] **19:17** 2Kg 9:14–10:25
[ac] 2Kg 2:24; 8:1
[ad] **19:18** Rm 11:4
[ae] 1Kg 16:31
[af] Hs 13:2
[ag] **19:19** 1Kg 19:16-17
[ah] 2Kg 2:8,13-14
[ai] **19:20** Mt 8:21-22
[aj] **19:21** 1Sm 6:14; 2Sm 24:22
[ak] Lk 14:26,33
[al] **20:1** 1Kg 15:18,20
[am] 1Kg 22:31
[an] 1Kg 16:24,29
[ao] **20:3** 2Kg 24:14-16; Dn 1:3-4

will lay their hands on and take away whatever is precious to you.'"
7Then the king of Israel called for all the elders of the land and said, "Think it over and
you will see that this one is only looking for
trouble,[a] for he demanded my wives, my children, my silver, and my gold, and I didn't turn
him down."
8All the elders and all the people said to
him, "Don't listen or agree."
9So he said to Ben-hadad's messengers,
"Say to my lord the king, 'Everything you demanded of your servant the first time, I will
do, but this thing I cannot do.'" So the messengers left and took word back to him.
10Then Ben-hadad sent messengers to him
and said, "May the gods punish me and do so
severely[b] if Samaria's dust[c] amounts to a handful for each of the people who follow me."
11The king of Israel answered, "Say this:
'Don't let the one who puts on his armor
boast[d] like the one who takes it off.'"
12When Ben-hadad heard this response,
while he and the kings were drinking[e] in the
tents, he said to his servants, "Take your positions." So they took their positions against
the city.
13A prophet came to Ahab king of Israel and
said, "This is what the LORD says: 'Do you see
this entire great army? Watch, I am handing
it over to you today so that you may know that
I am ⸢Yahweh.'"[f]
14Ahab asked, "By whom?"
And the prophet said, "This is what the
LORD says: 'By the young men of the provincial leaders.'"
Then he asked, "Who is to start the battle?"[g]
He said, "You."
15So Ahab counted the young men of the
provincial leaders, and there were 232. After them he counted all the Israelite troops:
7,000.[h] 16They marched out at noon while
Ben-hadad and the 32 kings[i] who were helping him were getting drunk in the tents. 17The
young men of the provincial leaders marched
out first. Then Ben-hadad sent out scouts,
and they reported to him, saying, "Men are
marching out of Samaria."[j]
18So he said, "If they have marched out
in peace,[k] take them alive, and if they have
marched out for battle, take them alive."
19The young men of the provincial leaders and the army behind them marched out
from the city, 20and each one struck down his
opponent.[l] So the Arameans fled and Israel
pursued them,[m] but Ben-hadad king of Aram
escaped on a horse with the cavalry. 21Then
the king of Israel marched out and attacked
the cavalry and the chariots. He inflicted a
great slaughter on Aram.
22The prophet approached the king of Israel and said to him, "Go and strengthen
yourself, then consider what you should do,
for in the spring[n] the king of Aram will march
against you."
23Now the king of Aram's servants said to
him, "Their gods are gods of the hill country.[o] That's why they were stronger than we
were. Instead, we should fight with them on
the plain; then we will certainly be stronger
than they will be. 24Also do this: remove each
king from his position and appoint captains
in their place. 25Raise another army for yourself like the army you lost — horse for horse,
chariot for chariot — and let's fight with
them on the plain; and we will certainly be
stronger than they will be." The king listened
to them and did so.
26In the spring, Ben-hadad mobilized the
Arameans and went up to Aphek[p] to battle Israel. 27The Israelites mobilized, gathered supplies, and went to fight them. The Israelites
camped in front of them like two little flocks
of goats, while the Arameans filled the landscape.[q]
28Then the man of God[r] approached and
said to the king of Israel, "This is what the
LORD says: 'Because the Arameans have said:
Yahweh is a god of the mountains and not
a god of the valleys,[s] I will hand over all this
great army to you. Then you will know that I
am the LORD.'"[t]
29They camped opposite each other for
seven days. On the seventh day,[u] the battle
took place, and the Israelites struck down
the Arameans — 100,000 foot soldiers in
one day. 30The ones who remained fled into
the city of Aphek, and the wall fell on those
27,000 remaining men.
Ben-hadad also fled and went into an inner
room[v] in the city. 31His servants said to him,
"Consider this: we have heard that the kings

[a]20:7 2Kg 5:7
[b]20:10 1Kg 19:2; 2Kg 6:31
[c]2Sm 22:43
[d]20:11 Pr 27:1
[e]20:12 1Kg 16:9
[f]20:13 1Kg 20:28
[g]20:14 Jdg 1:1; 20:18
[h]20:15 Jdg 7:2
[i]20:16 1Kg 20:1
[j]20:17 1Kg 16:24
[k]20:18 2Kg 14:8
[l]20:20 2Sm 2:15-16
[m]1Sm 14:13-14,22
[n]20:22 2Sm 11:1
[o]20:23 1Kg 14:23; Ps 139:7-12
[p]20:26 2Kg 13:17
[q]20:27 Jdg 6:5; 1Sm 13:5
[r]20:28 1Kg 17:18
[s]1Kg 20:23
[t]1Kg 20:13
[u]20:29 Jos 6:15
[v]20:30 1Kg 22:25

of the house of Israel are merciful kings. So
let's put •sackcloth around our waists[a] and
ropes around our heads, and let's go out to
the king of Israel. Perhaps he will spare your
life."
32 So they dressed with sackcloth around
their waists and ropes around their heads,
went to the king of Israel, and said, "Your servant
Ben-hadad says, 'Please spare my life.'"

So he said, "Is he still alive? He is my
brother."
33 Now the men were looking for a sign of
hope, so they quickly picked up on this[A] and
responded, "Yes, it is your brother Ben-hadad."

Then he said, "Go and bring him."

So Ben-hadad came out to him, and Ahab
had him come up into the chariot. 34 Then
Ben-hadad said to him, "I restore to you the
cities that my father took from your father,[b]
and you may set up marketplaces for yourself
in Damascus, like my father set up in Samaria."[c]

Ahab responded, "On the basis of this
treaty, I release you." So he made a treaty with
him and released him.

Ahab Rebuked by the LORD

35 One of the sons of the prophets[d] said to
his fellow prophet by the word of the LORD,
"Strike me!" But the man refused to strike
him.
36 He told him, "Because you did not listen to
the voice of the LORD, mark my words: When
you leave me, a lion will kill you."[e] When he
left him, a lion attacked and killed him.
37 The prophet found another man and said
to him, "Strike me!" So the man struck him,
inflicting a wound. 38 Then the prophet went
and waited for the king on the road. He disguised[f]
himself with a bandage over his eyes.
39 As the king was passing by, he cried out to
the king and said, "Your servant marched out
into the middle of the battle. Suddenly, a man
turned aside and brought someone to me and
said, 'Guard this man! If he is ever missing,
it will be your life in place of his life,[g] or you
will weigh out 75 pounds[B] of silver.' 40 But
while your servant was busy here and there,
he disappeared."

[a] 20:31 Gn 37:34
[b] 20:34 1Kg 15:20
[c] 2Sm 8:6
[d] 20:35 2Kg 2:3,5,7
[e] 20:36 1Kg 13:24
[f] 20:38 1Kg 14:2
[g] 20:39 Jos 2:14; 2Kg 10:24
[h] 20:40 2Sm 12:5
[i] 20:42 1Kg 19:16
[j] 20:43 1Kg 21:4
[k] 21:1 Jdg 6:33; 1Kg 18:45
[l] 1Kg 20:1
[m] 21:2 1Sm 8:14
[n] 21:3 Lv 25:23; Nm 36:7
[o] 21:4 1Kg 20:43
[p] 2Kg 20:2
[q] 1Sm 28:23
[r] 21:7 1Sm 8:14
[s] 21:8 2Sm 11:14
[t] Est 3:12; 8:8,10
[u] 1Kg 20:7
[v] 21:9 1Sm 7:5-6; 2Ch 20:2-4
[w] 21:10 Dt 13:13

The king of Israel said to him, "That will be
your sentence; you yourself have decided it."[h]
41 He quickly removed the bandage from
his eyes. The king of Israel recognized that he
was one of the prophets. 42 The prophet said
to him, "This is what the LORD says: 'Because
you released from your hand the man I had
•set apart for destruction,[i] it will be your life
in place of his life and your people in place of
his people.'" 43 The king of Israel left for home
resentful and angry,[j] and he entered Samaria.

Ahab and Naboth's Vineyard

21 Some time passed after these events.
Naboth the Jezreelite had a vineyard;
it was in Jezreel[k] next to the palace of Ahab
king of Samaria.[l] 2 So Ahab spoke to Naboth,
saying, "Give me your vineyard[m] so I can have
it for a vegetable garden, since it's right next
to my palace. I will give you a better vineyard
in its place, or if you prefer, I will give you its
value in silver."
3 But Naboth said to Ahab, "I will never give
my fathers' inheritance[n] to you."
4 So Ahab went to his palace resentful and
angry[o] because of what Naboth the Jezreelite
had told him. He had said, "I will not give you
my fathers' inheritance." He lay down on his
bed, turned his face away,[p] and didn't eat any
food.[q]
5 Then his wife Jezebel came to him and said
to him, "Why are you so upset that you refuse
to eat?"
6 "Because I spoke to Naboth the Jezreelite,"
he replied. "I told him: Give me your vineyard
for silver, or if you wish, I will give you a vineyard
in its place. But he said, 'I won't give you
my vineyard!'"
7 Then his wife Jezebel said to him, "Now,
exercise your royal power over Israel. Get up,
eat some food, and be happy. For I will give
you the vineyard of Naboth the Jezreelite."[r]
8 So she wrote letters[s] in Ahab's name and
sealed them with his seal.[t] She sent the letters
to the elders[u] and nobles who lived with Naboth
in his city. 9 In the letters, she wrote:

> Proclaim a fast[v] and seat Naboth at the
> head of the people. 10 Then seat two
> •wicked men[w] opposite him and have

[A] 20:33 Some Hb mss, alt Hb tradition, LXX; other Hb mss read *they hastened and caught hold; "Is this it?"* [B] 20:39 Lit *a talent*

them testify against him, saying, "You
have cursed God and the king!"[a] Then
take him out and stone him to death.[b]

[11]The men of his city, the elders and nobles who lived in his city, did as Jezebel had
commanded them, as was written in the letters she had sent them. [12]They proclaimed
a fast and seated Naboth at the head of the
people. [13]The two wicked men came in and
sat opposite him. Then the wicked men testified against Naboth in the presence of the
people, saying, "Naboth has cursed God and
the king!" So they took him outside the city
and stoned him to death with stones. [14]Then
they sent word to Jezebel, "Naboth has been
stoned to death."[c]

[15]When Jezebel heard that Naboth had
been stoned to death, she said to Ahab, "Get
up and take possession of the vineyard of Naboth the Jezreelite who refused to give it to
you for silver,[d] since Naboth isn't alive, but
dead." [16]When Ahab heard that Naboth was
dead, he got up to go down to the vineyard of
Naboth the Jezreelite to take possession of it.

The LORD's Judgment on Ahab

[17]Then the word of the LORD came to Elijah
the Tishbite:[e] [18]"Get up and go to meet Ahab
king of Israel,[f] who is in Samaria.[g] You'll find
him in Naboth's vineyard, where he has gone
to take possession of it. [19]Tell him, 'This is
what the LORD says: Have you murdered[h] and
also taken possession?'[i] Then tell him, 'This
is what the LORD says: In the place where the
dogs licked Naboth's blood, the dogs will also
lick your blood!'"[j]

[20]Ahab said to Elijah, "So, you have caught
me, my enemy."[k]

He replied, "I have caught you because you
devoted[l] yourself to do what is evil in the
LORD's sight. [21]This is what the LORD says:[A] 'I
am about to bring disaster on you and will
sweep away your descendants:

> I will eliminate all of Ahab's males,[B]
> both slave and free, in Israel;[m]

[22]I will make your house like the house of
Jeroboam[n] son of Nebat and like the house
of Baasha[o] son of Ahijah, because you have

[a]**21:10** Ex 20:16; 23:1; Dt 5:20; Ac 6:11
[b]Lv 24:15-16
[c]**21:14** Lv 24:16
[d]**21:15** 1Kg 21:2-3
[e]**21:17** 1Kg 17:2,8
[f]**21:18** 1Kg 18:1
[g]1Kg 16:29; 2Ch 22:9
[h]**21:19** Ex 20:13; Dt 5:17
[i]Lv 25:23
[j]1Kg 22:38
[k]**21:20** 1Kg 18:17
[l]2Kg 17:17; Rm 7:14
[m]**21:21** 2Kg 9:8
[n]**21:22** 1Kg 14:10-11
[o]1Kg 16:3-4
[p]1Kg 12:30
[q]**21:23** 2Kg 9:10,30-37
[r]**21:24** 1Kg 14:11; 16:4
[s]**21:25** 1Kg 16:30-33
[t]**21:26** 2Kg 17:12
[u]Gn 15:16; 2Kg 21:11
[v]**21:27** Gn 37:34; 2Sm 3:31; 2Kg 6:30
[w]**21:29** 2Kg 20:19; 2Ch 32:26
[x]2Kg 9:25-37; 10:6-11
[y]**22:1-9** 2Ch 18:1-8
[z]**22:1** 1Kg 20:1,26
[aa]**22:2** 1Kg 15:24
[ab]2Ch 18:2
[ac]**22:3** Dt 4:43; Jos 20:8; 1Kg 4:13
[ad]**22:4-6** 2Kg 3:7-8
[ae]**22:4** 2Kg 8:18,27
[af]2Kg 3:7
[ag]**22:5** 1Sm 23:1-5; Jms 4:15
[ah]**22:6** 1Kg 18:19
[ai]1Kg 13:18

provoked My anger and caused Israel to sin.[p]
[23]The LORD also speaks of Jezebel: The dogs
will eat Jezebel in the plot of land[C] at Jezreel:[q]

> [24] He who belongs to Ahab and dies
> in the city, the dogs will eat,
> and he who dies in the field, the birds
> of the sky will eat.'"[r]

[25]Still, there was no one like Ahab, who
devoted himself to do what was evil in the
LORD's sight, because his wife Jezebel incited
him.[s] [26]He committed the most detestable
acts by going after idols[t] as the Amorites[u] had,
whom the LORD had dispossessed before the
Israelites.

[27]When Ahab heard these words, he tore
his clothes, put 'sackcloth over his body, and
fasted. He lay down in sackcloth[v] and walked
around subdued. [28]Then the word of the
LORD came to Elijah the Tishbite: [29]"Have you
seen how Ahab has humbled himself before
Me? I will not bring the disaster during his
lifetime,[w] because he has humbled himself
before Me. I will bring the disaster on his
house during his son's lifetime."[x]

Jehoshaphat's Alliance with Ahab

22 There was[y] a lull of three years[z] without war between Aram and Israel.
[2]However, in the third year, Jehoshaphat[aa]
king of Judah went to visit the king of Israel.[ab] [3]The king of Israel had said to his servants, "Don't you know that Ramoth-gilead[ac]
is ours, but we have failed to take it from the
hand of the king of Aram?" [4]So[ad] he asked Jehoshaphat, "Will you go with me to fight Ramoth-gilead?"[ae]

Jehoshaphat replied to the king of Israel,
"I am as you are, my people as your people,
my horses as your horses."[af] [5]But Jehoshaphat
said to the king of Israel, "First, please ask
what the LORD's will is."[ag]

[6]So the king of Israel gathered the prophets,
about 400 men,[ah] and asked them, "Should I
go against Ramoth-gilead for war or should
I refrain?"

They replied, "March up, and the Lord will
hand it over to the king."[ai]

[7]But Jehoshaphat asked, "Isn't there a

[A]**21:21** LXX; MT omits *This is what the LORD says* [B]**21:21** Lit *eliminate Ahab's one who urinates against the wall* [C]**21:23** Some Hb mss, Syr, Tg, Vg, 2Kg 9:36; other Hb mss, LXX read *the rampart* prophet of •Yahweh here anymore?[a] Let's ask him."

8 The king of Israel said to Jehoshaphat, "There is still one man who can ask Yahweh, but I hate him[b] because he never prophesies good about me,[c] but only disaster. He is Micaiah son of Imlah."

"The king shouldn't say that!" Jehoshaphat replied.

9 So the king of Israel called an officer and said, "Hurry and get Micaiah son of Imlah!"

10 Now the king of Israel and Jehoshaphat king of Judah,[d] clothed in royal attire, were each sitting on his own throne. They were on the threshing floor[e] at the entrance to Samaria's •gate, and all the prophets were prophesying in front of them. 11 Then Zedekiah[f] son of Chenaanah made iron horns[g] and said, "This is what the LORD says: 'You will gore the Arameans with these until they are finished off.'" 12 And all the prophets were prophesying the same: "March up to Ramoth-gilead[h] and succeed, for the LORD will hand it over to the king."

Micaiah's Message of Defeat

13 The messenger[i] who went to call Micaiah instructed him, "Look, the words of the prophets are unanimously favorable for the king. So let your words be like theirs, and speak favorably."

14 But Micaiah said, "As the LORD lives,[j] I will say whatever the LORD says to me."[k]

15 So he went to the king, and the king asked him, "Micaiah, should we go to Ramoth-gilead for war, or should we refrain?"

Micaiah told him, "March up and succeed. Yahweh will hand it over to the king."

16 But the king said to him, "How many times must I make you swear not to tell me anything but the truth in the name of Yahweh?"

17 So Micaiah said:

> I saw all Israel scattered on the hills
> like sheep without a shepherd.[l]
> And the LORD said,
> "They have no master;
> let everyone return home in peace."[m]

18 So the king of Israel said to Jehoshaphat, "Didn't I tell you he never prophesies good about me, but only disaster?"

19 Then Micaiah said, "Therefore, hear the word of the LORD: I saw the LORD sitting on His throne,[n] and the whole heavenly •host[o] was standing by Him at His right hand and at His left hand. 20 And the LORD said, 'Who will entice Ahab to march up and fall at Ramoth-gilead?'[p] So one was saying this and another was saying that.

21 "Then a spirit came forward, stood before the LORD, and said, 'I will entice him.'

22 "The LORD asked him, 'How?'

"He said, 'I will go and become a lying spirit[q] in the mouth of all his prophets.'

"Then He said, 'You will certainly entice him and prevail.[r] Go and do that.'

23 "You see, the LORD has put a lying spirit into the mouth of all these prophets of yours, and the LORD has pronounced disaster against you."

24 Then Zedekiah[s] son of Chenaanah came up, hit Micaiah in the face, and demanded, "Did[A] the Spirit of the LORD leave me to speak to you?"[t]

25 Micaiah replied, "You will soon see when you go to hide yourself in an inner chamber on that day."[u]

26 Then the king of Israel ordered, "Take Micaiah and return him to Amon, the governor of the city, and to Joash, the king's son,[v] 27 and say, 'This is what the king says: Put this guy in prison[w] and feed him only bread and water[B] until I come back safely.'"

28 But Micaiah said, "If you ever return safely, the LORD has not spoken through me."[x] Then he said, "Listen, all you people!"[C,y]

Ahab's Death

29 Then[z] the king of Israel and Judah's King Jehoshaphat went up to Ramoth-gilead.[aa] 30 But the king of Israel said to Jehoshaphat, "I will disguise[ab] myself and go into battle, but you wear your royal attire." So the king of Israel disguised himself and went into battle.[ac]

31 Now the king of Aram had ordered his 32 chariot commanders,[ad] "Do not fight with anyone at all except the king of Israel."[ae]

32 When the chariot commanders saw Jehoshaphat, they shouted, "He must be the

[a] **22:7** 2Kg 1:3; 3:11; 5:8
[b] **22:8** 1Kg 18:17; 21:20
[c] Am 5:10
[d] **22:10-12** 2Ch 18:9-11
[e] **22:10** Jdg 6:37
[f] **22:11** 1Kg 22:24
[g] Dt 33:17; Zch 1:18-21
[h] **22:12** 1Kg 4:13
[i] **22:13-28** 2Ch 18:12-27
[j] **22:14** 1Kg 18:10,15
[k] Nm 22:28; 24:13
[l] **22:17** Nm 27:16-17; Mt 9:36; Mk 6:34
[m] 1Kg 22:35-36
[n] **22:19** Is 6:1; Dn 7:9
[o] Jb 1:6; Dn 7:10; Heb 1:7
[p] **22:20** 1Kg 22:4
[q] **22:22** Jdg 9:23; 1Sm 16:14; Jr 20:7; Ezk 14:9
[r] 2Th 2:11
[s] **22:24** 1Kg 22:11
[t] 2Ch 18:23
[u] **22:25** 1Kg 20:30
[v] **22:26** 1Kg 22:40
[w] **22:27** 2Ch 16:10; Heb 11:36
[x] **22:28** Dt 18:22
[y] Mc 1:2
[z] **22:29-33** 2Ch 18:28-32
[aa] **22:29** 1Kg 22:4
[ab] **22:30** 1Sm 28:8
[ac] 2Ch 35:22
[ad] **22:31** 1Kg 20:1,16
[ae] 2Ch 18:30

[A] **22:24** Lit *Which way did* [B] **22:27** Lit *him on bread of oppression and water of oppression* [C] **22:28** LXX omits *Then he said, "Listen, all you people!"*

king of Israel!" So they turned to fight against
him, but Jehoshaphat cried out. 33 When the
chariot commanders saw that he was not the
king of Israel, they turned back from pursuing him.
34 But a man drew his bow[a] without taking special aim and struck the king of Israel
through the joints of his armor. So he said
to his charioteer, "Turn around and take me
out of the battle,[A] for I am badly wounded!"[b]
35 The battle raged throughout that day, and
the king was propped up in his chariot facing the Arameans. He died that evening,[c] and
blood from his wound flowed into the bottom of the chariot. 36 Then the cry rang out in
the army as the sun set, declaring:

> Each man to his own city,
> and each man to his own land![d]

37 So the king died and was brought to Samaria. They buried the king in Samaria.[e]
38 Then someone washed the chariot at the
pool of Samaria. The dogs licked up his blood,
and the prostitutes bathed in it, according to
the word of the LORD that He had spoken.[f]
39 The rest of the events of Ahab's reign,
along with all his accomplishments, including the ivory palace[g] he built, and all the cities
he built, are written in the Historical Record
of Israel's Kings.[h] 40 Ahab rested with his fathers,[i] and his son Ahaziah[j] became king in
his place.

Judah's King Jehoshaphat

41 Jehoshaphat[k] son of Asa became king over
Judah in the fourth year of Israel's King Ahab.
42 Jehoshaphat was 35 years old when he became king; he reigned 25 years in Jerusalem.
His mother's name was Azubah daughter of
Shilhi. 43 He walked in all the ways of his father Asa;[l] he did not turn away from them but
did what was right in the LORD's sight. However, the ·high places were not taken away;[B]
the people still sacrificed and burned incense
on the high places.[m] 44 Jehoshaphat also made
peace with the king of Israel.[n]
45 The rest of the events of Jehoshaphat's
reign, along with the might he exercised and
how he waged war, are written in the Historical Record of Judah's Kings.[o] 46 He removed
from the land the rest of the male cult prostitutes who were left from the days of his father
Asa.[p] 47 There was no king in Edom;[q] a deputy
served as king. 48 Jehoshaphat made ships of
Tarshish[r] to go to Ophir[s] for gold, but they
did not go because the ships were wrecked at
Ezion-geber.[t] 49 At that time, Ahaziah[u] son of
Ahab said to Jehoshaphat, "Let my servants
go with your servants in the ships," but Jehoshaphat was not willing. 50 Jehoshaphat
rested with his fathers and was buried with
them in the city of his ancestor David.[v] His
son Jehoram[w] became king in his place.

Israel's King Ahaziah

51 Ahaziah[x] son of Ahab became king over
Israel in Samaria[y] in the seventeenth year of
Judah's King Jehoshaphat[z] and reigned over
Israel two years. 52 He did what was evil in
the LORD's sight.[aa] He walked in the way of
his father,[ab] in the way of his mother,[ac] and in
the way of Jeroboam son of Nebat, who had
caused Israel to sin.[ad] 53 He served ·Baal and
worshiped him.[ae] He provoked the LORD God
of Israel just as his father had done.[af]

[a] **22:34** 2Kg 9:24
[b] 2Ch 35:23
[c] **22:34-35** 1Kg 22:17,28; 2Ch 18:33-34
[d] **22:36** 2Sm 20:1; 1Kg 12:16; 22:17; 2Kg 14:12
[e] **22:37** 1Kg 16:28
[f] **22:38** 1Kg 21:19
[g] **22:39** Am 3:15
[h] 1Kg 16:27
[i] **22:40** 1Kg 16:28
[j] 2Kg 1:2
[k] **22:41** 2Ch 20:31
[l] **22:43** 1Kg 15:11
[m] 1Kg 15:14
[n] **22:44** 1Kg 22:2,4
[o] **22:45** 1Kg 15:23; 2Ch 20:34
[p] **22:46** 1Kg 15:12
[q] **22:47** 2Sm 8:14; 2Kg 3:9
[r] **22:48** 1Kg 10:22
[s] 1Kg 9:28
[t] 1Kg 9:26
[u] **22:49** 1Kg 22:40,51
[v] **22:50** 1Kg 15:24; 2Ch 21:1
[w] 2Kg 1:17
[x] **22:51** 1Kg 22:40
[y] 1Kg 16:24
[z] 1Kg 22:41-50
[aa] **22:52** 1Kg 15:26
[ab] 1Kg 21:25-26
[ac] 1Kg 16:31; 18:4; 21:25
[ad] 1Kg 12:28-33
[ae] **22:53** Jdg 2:11; 1Kg 16:32
[af] 1Kg 16:33; 21:25

[A] **22:34** LXX; MT reads *camp* [B] **22:43** LXX, Syr, Vg read *he did not remove the high places*

2 KINGS

For the introduction to the book of 2 Kings, see the introduction to the book of 1 Kings, page 328.

Ahaziah's Sickness and Death

1 After the death of Ahab, Moab[a] rebelled
against Israel.[b] 2 Ahaziah[c] had fallen
through the latticed window of his upper
room in Samaria[d] and was injured. So he sent
messengers instructing them: "Go inquire of
Baal-zebub,[A,e] the god of Ekron,[f] if I will recover from this injury."[g]
3 But the angel of the LORD said to Elijah the
Tishbite,[h] "Go and meet the messengers of the
king of Samaria[i] and ask them, 'Is it because
there is no God in Israel that you are going
to inquire of Baal-zebub, the god of Ekron?'
4 Therefore, this is what the LORD says: 'You
will not get up from your sickbed—you will
certainly die.'" Then Elijah left.
5 The messengers returned to the king, who
asked them, "Why have you come back?"
6 They replied, "A man came to meet us and
said, 'Go back to the king who sent you and
declare to him: This is what the LORD says: Is
it because there is no God in Israel that you're
sending these men to inquire of Baal-zebub,
the god of Ekron? Therefore, you will not get
up from your sickbed—you will certainly
die.'"
7 The king asked them, "What sort of man
came up to meet you and spoke those words
to you?"
8 They replied, "A hairy man with a leather
belt around his waist."[j]
He said, "It's Elijah the Tishbite."[k]
9 So King Ahaziah sent a captain of 50 with
his 50 men[l] to Elijah. When the captain went
up to him, he was sitting on top of the hill. He
announced, "Man of God,[m] the king declares,
'Come down!'"
10 Elijah responded to the captain of the 50,
"If I am a man of God, may fire come down
from heaven and consume you and your 50
men." Then fire came down from heaven and
consumed him and his 50 men.[n]
11 So the king sent another captain of 50
with his 50 men to Elijah. He took in the situation[B] and announced, "Man of God, this is
what the king says: 'Come down immediately!'"
12 Elijah responded, "If I am a man of God,
may fire come down from heaven and consume you and your 50 men." So a divine fire[C]
came down from heaven and consumed him
and his 50 men.
13 Then the king sent a third captain of 50
with his 50 men. The third captain of 50 went
up and fell on his knees in front of Elijah and
begged him, "Man of God,[o] please let my life
and the lives of these 50 servants of yours
be precious in your sight.[p] 14 Already fire has
come down from heaven and consumed the
first two captains of 50 with their fifties, but
this time let my life be precious in your sight."
15 The angel of the LORD[q] said to Elijah, "Go
down with him. Don't be afraid of him."[r] So
he got up and went down with him to the
king.
16 Then Elijah said to King Ahaziah, "This is
what the LORD says: 'Because you have sent
messengers to inquire of Baal-zebub, the god
of Ekron—is it because there is no God in Israel for you to inquire of His will?—you will
not get up from your sickbed; you will certainly die.'"
17 Ahaziah died according to the word of the
LORD that Elijah had spoken. Since he had no
son, Joram[D,s] became king in his place. This
happened in the second year of Judah's King
Jehoram[t] son of Jehoshaphat.[E] 18 The rest of
the events of Ahaziah's reign, along with his
accomplishments, are written in the Historical Record of Israel's Kings.[F,u]

a 1:1 Gn 19:37; 2Sm 8:2
b 2Kg 3:5
c 1:2 1Kg 22:40,51-53
d 1Kg 16:24; 22:51
e Jdg 10:6
f Jos 13:3; 2Kg 1:16
g 2Kg 8:8-9
h 1:3 1Kg 19:7
i 1Sm 28:7-8
j 1:8 Zch 13:4; Mt 3:4
k 1Kg 17:1
l 1:9 2Kg 6:13-14
m 1Kg 13:1
n 1:10 1Kg 18:36-38
o 1:13 1Kg 13:1
p 1Sm 26:21; Ps 72:14
q 1:15 1Kg 19:7; 2Kg 1:3
r Jr 1:17; Ezk 2:6
s 1:17 2Kg 3:1-3
t 1Kg 22:50
u 1:18 1Kg 22:39

A 1:2 = Lord of the Flies B 1:11 Lit *He answered* C 1:12 Lit *a fire of God* D 1:17 Lit *Jehoram*; 2Kg 8:16 E 1:17 LXX omits *in the second year . . . Jehoshaphat* F 1:18 LXX adds 4 more vv. here similar to 2Kg 3:1-3.

Elijah in the Whirlwind

2 The time had come for the LORD to take
Elijah up to heaven[a] in a whirlwind.[b] Elijah and Elisha[c] were traveling from Gilgal,[d]
2and Elijah said to Elisha,[e] "Stay here;[f] the
LORD is sending me on to Bethel."[g]
But Elisha replied, "As the LORD lives and as
you yourself live, I will not leave you."[h] So they
went down to Bethel.
3Then the sons of the prophets[i] who were
at Bethel came out to Elisha and said, "Do
you know that the LORD will take your master away from you today?"[j]
He said, "Yes, I know. Be quiet."
4Elijah said to him, "Elisha, stay here; the
LORD is sending me to Jericho."[k]
But Elisha said, "As the LORD lives and as
you yourself live, I will not leave you." So they
went to Jericho.
5Then the sons of the prophets who were in
Jericho came up to Elisha and said, "Do you
know that the LORD will take your master
away from you today?"
He said, "Yes, I know. Be quiet."
6Elijah said to him, "Stay here; the LORD is
sending me to the Jordan."[l]
But Elisha said, "As the LORD lives and as
you yourself live, I will not leave you." So the
two of them went on.
7Fifty men from the sons of the prophets
came and stood facing them from a distance
while the two of them stood by the Jordan.
8Elijah took his mantle,[m] rolled it up, and
struck the waters, which parted to the right
and left. Then the two of them crossed over
on dry ground.[n] 9After they had crossed over,
Elijah said to Elisha, "Tell me what I can do
for you before I am taken from you."
So Elisha answered, "Please, let me inherit
two shares[A] of your spirit."[o]
10Elijah replied, "You have asked for something difficult. If you see me being taken
from you,[p] you will have it. If not, you won't."
11As they continued walking and talking, a
chariot of fire with horses of fire[q] suddenly
appeared and separated the two of them.
Then Elijah went up into heaven in the whirlwind.[r] 12As Elisha watched, he kept crying
out, "My father, my father, the chariots and
horsemen of Israel!"[s] Then he never saw Elijah again. He took hold of his own clothes
and tore them into two pieces.[t]

Elisha Succeeds Elijah

13Elisha picked up the mantle[u] that had
fallen off Elijah and went back and stood on
the bank of the Jordan. 14Then he took the
mantle Elijah had dropped and struck the
waters. "Where is the LORD God of Elijah?"
he asked. He struck the waters himself, and
they parted to the right and the left, and Elisha crossed over.
15When the sons of the prophets from Jericho who were facing him saw him, they said,
"The spirit of Elijah rests on Elisha." They
came to meet him and bowed down to the
ground in front of him.
16Then the sons of the prophets said to Elisha, "Since there are 50 strong men here with
your servants, please let them go and search
for your master. Maybe the Spirit of the LORD
has carried him away and put him on one of
the mountains or into one of the valleys."[v]
He answered, "Don't send them."
17However, they urged him to the point of
embarrassment,[w] so he said, "Send them."
They sent 50 men, who looked for three days
but did not find him. 18When they returned
to him in Jericho[x] where he was staying, he
said to them, "Didn't I tell you not to go?"
19Then the men of the city said to Elisha,
"Even though our lord can see that the city's
location is good, the water is bad and the land
unfruitful."[y]
20He replied, "Bring me a new bowl and put
salt in it."[z]
After they had brought him one, 21Elisha
went out to the spring of water, threw salt in
it,[aa] and said, "This is what the LORD says: 'I
have healed this water. No longer will death
or unfruitfulness result from it.'" 22There-
fore, the water remains healthy to this very
day according to the word that Elisha spoke.
23From there Elisha went up to Bethel.[ab] As
he was walking up the path, some small boys
came out of the city and harassed him,[ac] chanting, "Go up, baldy! Go up, baldy!" 24He turned
around, looked at them, and cursed them in
the name of the LORD.[ad] Then two female bears
came out of the woods and mauled 42 of the

[a] **2:1** Gn 5:24; Heb 11:5
[b] 2Kg 2:11
[c] 1Kg 19:16-21
[d] Jos 4:19; 2Kg 4:38
[e] **2:2** 1Kg 19:16,19-21
[f] Ru 1:15
[g] 1Kg 12:28-29
[h] 1Sm 1:26; 2Kg 4:30
[i] **2:3** 1Sm 10:5; 1Kg 20:35; 2Kg 4:1,38
[j] Gn 5:24
[k] **2:4** Jos 6:16; 1Kg 16:34
[l] **2:6** Jos 3:8; Mt 3:5-6,13
[m] **2:8** 1Kg 19:13,19
[n] Ex 14:21-22; Jos 3:14-17
[o] **2:9** Nm 11:16-25; Dt 21:15-17
[p] **2:10** Ac 1:9-11
[q] **2:11** 2Kg 6:17
[r] 2Kg 2:1
[s] **2:12** 2Kg 13:14
[t] Gn 37:29,34
[u] **2:13** 1Kg 19:19
[v] **2:16** 1Kg 18:12; Ac 8:39
[w] **2:17** Jdg 3:25; 2Kg 8:11
[x] **2:18** 2Kg 2:4
[y] **2:19** Dt 28:15-18; Jos 6:26; 1Kg 16:34
[z] **2:20** Lv 2:13; Nm 18:19
[aa] **2:21-22** Ex 15:25-26; 2Kg 4:41; 6:6
[ab] **2:23** 2Kg 2:2-3
[ac] 2Ch 36:16; Ps 31:17-18
[ad] **2:24** Lv 26:21-22; Neh 13:25

[A] **2:9** Two shares is the inheritance of blessing for the firstborn son; Dt 21:17. Here Elisha is asking for the leadership role among the prophets.

children. 25 From there Elisha went to Mount Carmel,[a] and then he returned to Samaria.[b]

Israel's King Joram

3 Joram son of Ahab became king over Israel in Samaria during the eighteenth year of Judah's King Jehoshaphat and reigned 12 years.[c] 2 He did what was evil in the LORD's sight, but not like his father and mother,[d] for he removed the sacred pillar of ·Baal his father had made. 3 Nevertheless, Joram clung to the sins that Jeroboam son of Nebat had caused Israel to commit.[e] He did not turn away from them.

Moab's Rebellion against Israel

4 King Mesha of Moab[f] was a sheep breeder. He used to pay[g] the king of Israel 100,000 lambs and the wool of 100,000 rams,[h] 5 but when Ahab died, the king of Moab rebelled against the king of Israel.[i] 6 So King Joram marched out from Samaria at that time and mobilized all Israel. 7 Then he sent a message to King Jehoshaphat[j] of Judah: "The king of Moab has rebelled against me.[k] Will you go with me to fight against Moab?"

Jehoshaphat said, "I will go. I am as you are, my people as your people, my horses as your horses."[l] 8 Then he asked, "Which route should we take?"

Joram replied, "The route of the Wilderness of Edom."

9 So the king of Israel, the king of Judah, and the king of Edom[m] set out. After they had traveled their indirect route for seven days, they had no water for the army or their animals.

10 Then the king of Israel said, "Oh no, the LORD has summoned three kings, only to hand them over to Moab."

11 But Jehoshaphat said, "Isn't there a prophet of the LORD here? Let's inquire of ·Yahweh through him."[n]

One of the servants of the king of Israel answered, "Elisha son of Shaphat,[o] who used to pour water on Elijah's hands, is here."

12 Jehoshaphat affirmed, "The LORD's words are with him." So the king of Israel and Jehoshaphat and the king of Edom went to him.[p]

13 However, Elisha said to King Joram of Israel, "We have nothing in common. Go to the prophets of your father and your mother!"[q]

But the king of Israel replied, "No, because it is the LORD who has summoned these three kings to hand them over to Moab."

14 Elisha responded, "As the LORD of ·Hosts lives,[r] I stand before Him. If I did not have respect for King Jehoshaphat of Judah,[s] I would not look at you; I wouldn't take notice of you. 15 Now, bring me a musician."[t]

While the musician played,[u] the LORD's hand[v] came on Elisha. 16 Then he said, "This is what the LORD says: 'Dig ditch after ditch in this ·wadi.' 17 For the LORD says, 'You will not see wind or rain, but the wadi will be filled with water,[w] and you will drink—you and your cattle and your animals.' 18 This is easy in the LORD's sight.[x] He will also hand Moab over to you.[y] 19 Then you must attack every fortified city and every choice city. You must cut down every good tree and stop up every spring of water. You must ruin every good piece of land with stones."

20 About the time for the ·grain offering[z] the next morning, water suddenly came from the direction of Edom and filled the land.

21 All Moab had heard that the kings[aa] had come up to fight against them. So all who could bear arms, from the youngest to the oldest, were summoned and took their stand at the border. 22 When they got up early in the morning, the sun was shining on the water, and the Moabites saw that the water across from them was red like blood.[ab] 23 "This is blood!" they exclaimed. "The kings[ac] have clashed swords and killed each other. So, to the spoil, Moab!"

24 However, when the Moabites came to Israel's camp, the Israelites attacked them, and they fled from them. So Israel went into the land and struck down the Moabites. 25 They destroyed the cities, and each of them threw stones to cover every good piece of land. They stopped up every spring of water and cut down every good tree. In the end, only the buildings of Kir-hareseth[ad] were left. Then men with slings surrounded the city and attacked it.

26 When the king of Moab saw that the battle was too fierce for him, he took 700 swordsmen with him to try to break through to the king of Edom,[ae] but they could not do it. 27 So he took his firstborn son,[af] who was to

[a] **2:25** 1Kg 18:19-20
[b] 1Kg 16:24; 2Kg 1:2
[c] **3:1** 2Kg 1:17
[d] **3:2** 1Kg 21:25-26
[e] **3:3** 1Kg 16:31-32
[f] **3:4** Gn 19:37; 2Kg 1:1
[g] 2Sm 8:2
[h] Is 16:1-2
[i] **3:5** 2Kg 1:1
[j] **3:7** 1Kg 22:41-50
[k] 2Kg 1:1
[l] 1Kg 22:4
[m] **3:9** 1Kg 22:47; 2Kg 8:20
[n] **3:11** 1Kg 22:7
[o] 1Kg 19:16,19-21; 2Kg 2:9
[p] **3:12** 2Kg 2:25
[q] **3:13** 1Kg 18:19,22; 22:6
[r] **3:14** 1Kg 17:1; 2Kg 5:16
[s] 1Kg 22:41-50
[t] **3:15** 1Sm 10:5
[u] 1Sm 16:23
[v] Ezk 3:14
[w] **3:17** Ps 107:35; Is 32:2
[x] **3:18** Gn 18:14
[y] 2Kg 3:7
[z] **3:20** Ex 29:39-40
[aa] **3:21** 2Kg 3:9
[ab] **3:22** Ex 7:17,20
[ac] **3:23** 2Kg 3:9
[ad] **3:25** Jr 48:31,36
[ae] **3:26** 2Kg 3:9
[af] **3:27** Dt 12:31; 2Kg 16:3

become king in his place, and offered him as a ·burnt offering on the city wall. Great wrath was on the Israelites, and they withdrew from him and returned to their land.

The Widow's Oil Multiplied

4 One of the wives of the sons of the prophets[a] cried out to Elisha, "Your servant, my husband, has died. You know that your servant ·feared the LORD.[b] Now the creditor is coming to take my two children as his slaves."[c]

2 Elisha asked her, "What can I do for you? Tell me, what do you have in the house?"

She said, "Your servant has nothing in the house except a jar of oil."[d]

3 Then he said, "Go and borrow empty containers from everyone — from all your neighbors. Do not get just a few.[e] 4 Then go in and shut the door behind you and your sons, and pour oil into all these containers. Set the full ones to one side." 5 So she left.

After she had shut the door behind her and her sons, they kept bringing her containers, and she kept pouring.[f] 6 When they were full, she said to her son, "Bring me another container."

But he replied, "There aren't any more." Then the oil stopped.

7 She went and told the man of God,[g] and he said, "Go sell the oil and pay your debt; you and your sons can live on the rest."[h]

The Shunammite Woman's Hospitality

8 One day Elisha went to Shunem.[i] A prominent woman who lived there persuaded him to eat some food. So whenever he passed by, he stopped there to eat.[j] 9 Then she said to her husband, "I know that the one who often passes by here is a holy man of God, 10 so let's make a small room upstairs and put a bed, a table, a chair, and a lamp there for him. Whenever he comes, he can stay there."[k]

The Shunammite Woman's Son

11 One day he came there and stopped and went to the room upstairs to lie down. 12 He ordered his attendant Gehazi,[l] "Call this Shunammite woman." So he called her and she stood before him.

13 Then he said to Gehazi, "Say to her, 'Look, you've gone to all this trouble for us. What can we do for you?[m] Can we speak on your behalf to the king or to the commander of the army?'"

She answered, "I am living among my own people."

14 So he asked, "Then what should be done for her?"

Gehazi answered, "Well, she has no son, and her husband is old."

15 "Call her," Elisha said. So Gehazi called her, and she stood in the doorway. 16 Elisha said, "At this time next year you will have a son in your arms."[n]

Then she said, "No, my lord. Man of God, do not deceive your servant."[o]

17 The woman conceived and gave birth to a son at the same time the following year, as Elisha had promised her.

The Shunammite's Son Raised

18 The child grew and one day went out to his father and the harvesters.[p] 19 Suddenly he complained to his father, "My head! My head!"

His father told his servant, "Carry him to his mother." 20 So he picked him up and took him to his mother. The child sat on her lap until noon and then died. 21 Then she went up and laid him on the bed of the man of God, shut him in, and left.

22 She summoned her husband and said, "Please send me one of the servants and one of the donkeys, so I can hurry to the man of God and then come back."

23 But he said, "Why go to him today? It's not a New Moon or a Sabbath."[q]

She replied, "Everything is all right."[r]

24 Then she saddled the donkey and said to her servant, "Hurry, don't slow the pace for me unless I tell you." 25 So she set out and went to the man of God at Mount Carmel.[s]

When the man of God saw her at a distance, he said to his attendant Gehazi,[t] "Look, there's the Shunammite woman.[u] 26 Run out to meet her and ask, 'Are you all right? Is your husband all right? Is your son all right?'"

And she answered, "Everything's all right."

27 When she came up to the man of God at the mountain, she clung to his feet.[v] Gehazi came to push her away, but the man of God

[a] **4:1** 2Kg 2:3,15
[b] Pr 1:7; 9:10
[c] Lv 25:39-41
[d] **4:2** 1Kg 17:12
[e] **4:3** 2Kg 3:16
[f] **4:5** Mt 14:17-21
[g] **4:7** 1Kg 12:22
[h] 1Kg 17:16
[i] **4:8** Jos 19:18
[j] Mt 10:40-42; 3Jn 5-8
[k] **4:10** 1Kg 17:19
[l] **4:12** 2Kg 4:29-31; 5:20-27
[m] **4:13** 2Kg 4:2
[n] **4:16** Gn 18:9-14; Lk 1:7-13
[o] 2Kg 4:28
[p] **4:18** Ru 2:3
[q] **4:23** Nm 10:10; 28:11
[r] 2Sm 18:28; 2Kg 4:26
[s] **4:25** 1Kg 18:19-20
[t] 2Kg 4:12
[u] 2Kg 4:8,12
[v] **4:27** Mt 28:9

said, "Leave her alone — she is in severe anguish,[a] and the LORD has hidden it from me. He hasn't told me."

28 Then she said, "Did I ask my lord for a son? Didn't I say, 'Do not deceive me?'"[b]

29 So Elisha said to Gehazi, "Tuck your mantle[c] under your belt, take my staff with you, and go. If you meet anyone, don't stop to greet him, and if a man greets you, don't answer him.[d] Then place my staff on the boy's face."

30 The boy's mother said to Elisha, "As the LORD lives and as you yourself live, I will not leave you."[e] So he got up and followed her.

31 Gehazi went ahead of them and placed the staff on the boy's face, but there was no sound or sign of life, so he went back to meet Elisha and told him, "The boy didn't wake up."[f]

32 When Elisha got to the house, he discovered the boy lying dead on his bed.[g] 33 So he went in, closed the door behind the two of them, and prayed to the LORD.[h] 34 Then he went up and lay on the boy:[i] he put mouth to mouth, eye to eye, hand to hand. While he bent down over him, the boy's flesh became warm.[j] 35 Elisha got up, went into the house, and paced back and forth. Then he went up and bent down over him again. The boy sneezed seven times and opened his eyes.[k]

36 Elisha called Gehazi and said, "Call the Shunammite woman." He called her and she came. Then Elisha said, "Pick up your son." 37 She came, fell at his feet, and bowed to the ground; she picked up her son and left.[l]

The Deadly Stew

38 When Elisha returned to Gilgal,[m] there was a famine[n] in the land. The sons of the prophets[o] were sitting at his feet.[A,p] He said to his attendant, "Put on the large pot and make stew for the sons of the prophets."

39 One went out to the field to gather herbs and found a wild vine from which he gathered as many wild gourds as his garment would hold. Then he came back and cut them up into the pot of stew, but they were unaware of what they were.

40 They served some for the men to eat, but when they ate the stew they cried out, "There's death in the pot,[q] man of God!" And they were unable to eat it.

41 Then Elisha said, "Get some meal." He threw it into the pot and said, "Serve it for the people to eat." And there was nothing bad in the pot.[r]

The Multiplied Bread

42 A man from Baal-shalishah[s] came to the man of God with his sack full of 20 loaves of barley bread from the first bread of the harvest. Elisha said, "Give it to the people to eat."[t]

43 But Elisha's attendant asked, "What? Am I to set 20 loaves before 100 men?"[u]

"Give it to the people to eat," Elisha said, "for this is what the LORD says: 'They will eat, and they will have some left over.'" 44 So he gave it to them, and as the LORD had promised, they ate and had some left over.[v]

Naaman's Disease Healed

5 Naaman,[w] commander of the army for the king of Aram, was a great man in his master's sight[B] and highly regarded[x] because through him, the LORD had given victory to Aram. The man was a brave warrior, but he had a skin disease.[y]

2 Aram had gone on raids[z] and brought back from the land of Israel a young girl who served Naaman's wife. 3 She said to her mistress, "If only my master would go to[C] the prophet who is in Samaria, he would cure him of his skin disease."

4 So Naaman went and told his master what the girl from the land of Israel had said. 5 Therefore, the king of Aram said, "Go and I will send a letter with you to the king of Israel."

So he went and took with him 750 pounds[D] of silver, 150 pounds[E] of gold, and 10 changes of clothes.[aa] 6 He brought the letter to the king of Israel, and it read:

> When this letter comes to you, note that I have sent you my servant Naaman for you to cure him of his skin disease.

7 When the king of Israel read the letter, he tore his clothes[ab] and asked, "Am I God,[ac] kill-

[a] **4:27** Ru 1:19-21; 1Sm 1:15; Zch 12:10
[b] **4:28** 2Kg 4:16
[c] **4:29** 1Kg 18:46; 2Kg 9:1
[d] Lk 10:4
[e] **4:30** 2Kg 2:2,4,6
[f] **4:31** Jn 11:11
[g] **4:32** 2Kg 4:21
[h] **4:33** Mt 6:6
[i] **4:34** 1Kg 17:21-23
[j] Ac 20:10
[k] **4:35** 2Kg 8:5
[l] **4:37** Heb 11:35
[m] **4:38** 2Kg 2:1
[n] Lv 26:26; 2Kg 8:1
[o] 2Kg 2:3,5,7
[p] Lk 10:39; Ac 22:3
[q] **4:40** Ex 10:17
[r] **4:41** Ex 15:25; 2Kg 2:21
[s] **4:42** 1Sm 9:4
[t] Mt 14:17
[u] **4:43** Lk 9:13; Jn 6:9
[v] **4:43-44** Mt 14:20
[w] **5:1** Lk 4:27
[x] Ex 11:3
[y] 2Kg 7:3,8
[z] **5:2** 2Kg 6:23; 13:20
[aa] **5:5** Jdg 14:12; 2Kg 5:22
[ab] **5:7** Gn 37:29; 2Kg 11:14
[ac] Gn 30:2

[A] **4:38** Lit *sitting before him* [B] **5:1** Lit *man before his master* [C] **5:3** Lit *master was before* [D] **5:5** Lit *10 talents* [E] **5:5** Lit *6,000 shekels*

ing and giving life that this man expects me
to cure a man of his skin disease? Think it
over and you will see that he is only picking
a fight with[A] me."[a]
8When Elisha the man of God heard that
the king of Israel tore his clothes, he sent a
message to the king, "Why have you torn your
clothes? Have him come to me, and he will
know there is a prophet in Israel."[b] 9So Naaman came with his horses and chariots and
stood at the door of Elisha's house.
10Then Elisha sent him a messenger,[c] who
said, "Go wash[d] seven times[e] in the Jordan
and your flesh will be restored and you will
be •clean."
11But Naaman got angry and left, saying, "I
was telling myself: He will surely come out,
stand and call on the name of •Yahweh his
God, and will wave his hand[f] over the spot
and cure the skin disease. 12Aren't Abana and
Pharpar, the rivers of Damascus, better than
all the waters of Israel?[g] Could I not wash in
them and be clean?" So he turned and left in
a rage.[h]

[a]5:7 1Kg 20:7 [b]5:8 1Kg 22:7 [c]5:10 Nm 5:1-4 [d]Jn 9:7 [e]Lv 14:7 [f]5:11 Ex 7:19 [g]5:12 Is 8:6 [h]Pr 14:17; 19:11 [i]5:13 2Kg 2:12; 6:21; 13:14 [j]5:14 Lk 4:27 [k]5:15 Jos 2:11; 1Sm 17:46-47 [l]Gn 33:11 [m]5:16 1Kg 17:1; 2Kg 3:14 [n]Gn 14:22-23 [o]5:17 Ex 20:24 [p]Dt 6:4

13But his servants approached and said to
him, "My father,[i] if the prophet had told you
to do some great thing, would you not have
done it? How much more should you do it
when he tells you, 'Wash and be clean'?" 14So
Naaman went down and dipped himself in
the Jordan seven times, according to the command of the man of God. Then his skin was
restored and became like the skin of a small
boy, and he was clean.[j]
15Then Naaman and his whole company
went back to the man of God, stood before
him, and declared, "I know there's no God in
the whole world except in Israel.[k] Therefore,
please accept a gift[l] from your servant."
16But Elisha said, "As the LORD lives,[m] I
stand before Him. I will not accept it."[n] Naaman urged him to accept it, but he refused.
17Naaman responded, "If not, please let
your servant be given as much soil as a pair
of mules can carry,[o] for your servant will no
longer offer a •burnt offering or a sacrifice to
any other god but Yahweh.[p] 18However, in a
particular matter may the LORD pardon your

GOD'S HEART FOR THE WORLD

Divine Multi-tasking

Naaman and his whole company went back to the man of God, stood before him, and declared, "I know there's no God in the whole world except in Israel." (2 Kings 5:15)

God has a purpose for everything, even the odd, painful, or difficult events that occur. Because we can often see behind the scenes in the lives of Bible people, we are privileged to watch how God works. He weaves together a complex set of choices and events to bring about His will. And His work is never limited. He reaches out to all people and meets them right at their point of need.

Second Kings chapters 4–6 record a series of miracles performed by Elisha, "the man of God." While these might seem like an odd laundry list of unbelievable events piled one on top of another, the point is that we see God's supreme care—from the mundane (the need for enough bread in 4:42-44; the recovery of a borrowed tool in 6:1-7) to the life-altering (raising a dead boy in 4:18-37; removing the poison from a pot of stew in 4:38-41; the saving of a Gentile soldier from the death-sentence of leprosy here in chapter 5).

God is the supreme multi-tasker. His heart for the world can be seen in the way He reaches out to people in their various circumstances with their various needs—whether that need seems minor or major. He reveals Himself in order that those who see and experience His miraculous touch might realize, along with Naaman, that there is no other God.

[A]5:7 Lit *only seeking an occasion against*

servant: When my master, the king of Aram,
goes into the temple of Rimmon to worship
and I, as his right-hand man,[A,a] bow in the
temple of Rimmon — when I bow[B] in the
temple of Rimmon, may the LORD pardon
your servant in this matter."
19 So he said to him, "Go in peace."[b]

Gehazi's Greed Punished

After Naaman had traveled a short distance
from Elisha, 20 Gehazi,[c] the attendant of Elisha the man of God, thought: My master has
let this Aramean Naaman off lightly by not
accepting from him what he brought. As the
LORD lives,[d] I will run after him and get something from him.
21 So Gehazi pursued Naaman. When Naaman saw someone running after him, he
got down from the chariot to meet him and
asked, "Is everything all right?"
22 Gehazi said, "It's all right.[e] My master has
sent me to say, 'I have just now discovered
that two young men from the sons of the
prophets have come to me from the hill country of Ephraim. Please give them 75 pounds[C]
of silver and two changes of clothes.'"[f]
23 But Naaman insisted, "Please, accept 150
pounds."[D] He urged Gehazi and then packed
150 pounds[D] of silver in two bags with two
changes of clothes. Naaman gave them to two
of his young men who carried them ahead of
Gehazi. 24 When Gehazi came to the hill,[E,g] he
took the gifts from them and stored them in
the house. Then he dismissed the men, and
they left.
25 Gehazi came and stood by his master.
"Where did you go, Gehazi?" Elisha asked
him.
"Your servant didn't go anywhere," he replied.
26 But Elisha questioned him, "Wasn't my
spirit[h] there[F] when the man got down from
his chariot to meet you? Is it a time to accept
money and clothes, olive orchards and vineyards, sheep and oxen, and male and female
slaves? 27 Therefore, Naaman's skin disease
will cling to you and your descendants forever." So Gehazi went out from his presence
diseased — white as snow.[i]

[a] **5:18** 2Kg 7:2
[b] **5:19** 1Sm 1:17
[c] **5:20** 2Kg 4:12,31
[d] Ex 20:7
[e] **5:21-22** 2Kg 4:26
[f] **5:22** 2Kg 5:5
[g] **5:24** 2Kg 1:9
[h] **5:26** 2Kg 2:9,15
[i] **5:27** Ex 4:6; Nm 12:10
[j] **6:1** 1Sm 10:5; 2Kg 2:3,5,7; 4:38
[k] **6:5** Ex 22:14
[l] **6:6** 2Kg 4:8-9
[m] Ex 15:25; 2Kg 2:21; 4:41
[n] **6:8** 2Kg 8:28-29
[o] **6:9** 2Kg 4:8-9
[p] **6:13** Gn 37:17

The Floating Ax Head

6 The sons of the prophets[j] said to Elisha,
"Please notice that the place where we
live under your supervision[G] is too small for
us. 2 Please let us go to the Jordan where we
can each get a log and can build ourselves a
place to live there."
"Go," he said.
3 Then one said, "Please come with your servants."
"I'll come," he answered.
4 So he went with them, and when they
came to the Jordan, they cut down trees. 5 As
one of them was cutting down a tree, the iron
ax head fell into the water, and he cried out,
"Oh, my master, it was borrowed!"[k]
6 Then the man of God[l] asked, "Where did
it fall?"
When he showed him the place, the man of
God cut a stick, threw it there, and made the
iron float.[m] 7 Then he said, "Pick it up." So he
reached out and took it.

The Aramean War

8 When the king of Aram[n] was waging war
against Israel, he conferred with his servants,
"My camp will be at such and such a place."
9 But the man of God[o] sent word to the king
of Israel: "Be careful passing by this place, for
the Arameans are going down there." 10 Consequently, the king of Israel sent word to the
place the man of God had told him about. The
man of God repeatedly[H] warned the king, so
the king would be on his guard.
11 The king of Aram was enraged because of
this matter, and he called his servants and demanded of them, "Tell me, which one of us is
for the king of Israel?"
12 One of his servants said, "No one, my lord
the king. Elisha, the prophet in Israel, tells
the king of Israel even the words you speak in
your bedroom."
13 So the king said, "Go and see where he is,
so I can send men to capture him."
When he was told, "Elisha is in Dothan,"[p]
14 he sent horses, chariots, and a massive army
there. They went by night and surrounded
the city.
15 When the servant of the man of God got

[A] **5:18** Lit *worship, and he leans on my hand, and I* [B] **5:18** LXX, Vg read *when he bows himself* [C] **5:22** Lit *a talent* [D] **5:23** Lit *two talents* [E] **5:24** Or *citadel* [F] **5:26** Lit *"Did not my heart go* [G] **6:1** Lit *we are living before you* [H] **6:10** Lit *not once and not twice*

up early and went out, he discovered an army
with horses and chariots surrounding the
city. So he asked Elisha, "Oh, my master, what
are we to do?"
16 Elisha said, "Don't be afraid,[a] for those
who are with us outnumber those who are
with them."[b]
17 Then Elisha prayed, "LORD, please open
his eyes and let him see." So the LORD opened
the servant's eyes. He looked and saw that the
mountain was covered with horses and chariots of fire[c] all around Elisha.
18 When the Arameans came against him,
Elisha prayed to the LORD, "Please strike this
nation with blindness." So He struck them
with blindness,[d] according to Elisha's word.
19 Then Elisha said to them, "This is not the
way, and this is not the city. Follow me, and
I will take you to the man you're looking for."
And he led them to Samaria.[e] 20 When they entered Samaria, Elisha said, "LORD, open these
men's eyes and let them see." So the LORD
opened their eyes. They looked and discovered they were in Samaria.
21 When the king of Israel saw them, he said
to Elisha, "My father,[f] should I kill them? I
will kill them."
22 Elisha replied, "Don't kill them. Do you
kill those you have captured with your sword
or your bow? Set food and water in front of
them so they can eat and drink and go to their
master."[g]
23 So he prepared a great feast for them.
When they had eaten and drunk, he sent
them away, and they went to their master. The
Aramean raiders[h] did not come into Israel's
land again.
24 Some time later, King Ben-hadad[i] of Aram
brought all his military units together and
marched up to besiege Samaria. 25 So there
was a great famine[j] in Samaria, and they continued the siege against it until a donkey's
head sold for 80 silver •shekels,[A] and a cup[B]
of dove's dung[C] sold for five silver shekels.[D,k]
26 As the king of Israel was passing by on the
wall, a woman cried out to him, "My lord the
king, help!"
27 He answered, "If the LORD doesn't help
you, where can I get help for you? From the

[a]6:16 Ex 14:13 [b]2Ch 32:7 [c]6:17 2Kg 2:11; Ps 34:7 [d]6:18 Gn 19:11 [e]6:19 1Kg 16:24; 2Kg 3:6 [f]6:21 2Kg 2:12; 5:13 [g]6:22 2Ch 28:8-15; Rm 12:20 [h]6:23 2Kg 5:2; 24:2 [i]6:24 1Kg 20:1 [j]6:25 2Kg 4:38; 8:1 [k]Lv 26:26 [l]6:27 Hs 9:2 [m]6:26-28 2Sm 14:4-5 [n]6:28-29 Lv 26:29; Dt 28:53,57 [o]6:30 1Kg 21:27 [p]Gn 37:34 [q]6:31 1Kg 19:2 [r]6:32 Ezk 8:1; 14:1 [s]Lk 12:31-32 [t]6:33 Jb 2:9; Is 8:21 [u]7:1 2Kg 7:18 [v]7:2 2Kg 5:18; 7:17 [w]2Kg 4:8-9 [x]Mal 3:10 [y]2Kg 7:17 [z]7:3 Nm 5:2-4; 2Kg 5:1 [aa]7:4 2Kg 6:24

threshing floor or the winepress?"[l] 28 Then
the king asked her, "What's the matter?"[m]
She said, "This woman said to me, 'Give up
your son, and we will eat him today. Then we
will eat my son tomorrow.' 29 So we boiled my
son and ate him, and I said to her the next
day, 'Give up your son, and we will eat him,'[n]
but she has hidden her son."
30 When the king heard the woman's words,
he tore his clothes.[o] Then, as he was passing
by on the wall, the people saw that there was
•sackcloth[p] under his clothes next to his skin.
31 He announced, "May God punish me and
do so severely[q] if the head of Elisha son of
Shaphat remains on his shoulders today."
32 Elisha was sitting in his house, and the elders[r] were sitting with him. The king sent a
man ahead of him, but before the messenger
got to him, Elisha said to the elders, "Do you
see how this murderer[s] has sent someone to
cut off my head? Look, when the messenger
comes, shut the door to keep him out. Isn't
the sound of his master's feet behind him?"
33 While Elisha was still speaking with
them, the messenger[E] came down to him.
Then he said, "This disaster is from the LORD.
Why should I wait for the LORD any longer?"[t]

Aram Defeated

7 Elisha replied, "Hear the word of the
LORD! This is what the LORD says: 'About
this time tomorrow at the gate of Samaria, six
quarts[F] of fine meal will sell for a •shekel[G] and
12 quarts[H] of barley will sell for a shekel.'"[G,u]
2 Then the captain, the king's right-hand
man,[v] responded to the man of God,[w] "Look,
even if the LORD were to make windows in
heaven, could this really happen?"[x]
Elisha announced, "You will in fact see it
with your own eyes, but you won't eat any of
it."[y]
3 Four men with a skin disease[z] were at the
entrance to the gate. They said to each other,
"Why just sit here until we die? 4 If we say,
'Let's go into the city,' we will die there because the famine is in the city, but if we sit
here, we will also die. So now, come on. Let's
go to the Arameans' camp.[aa] If they let us live,
we will live; if they kill us, we will die."

[A]6:25 About 2 pounds of silver [B]6:25 Lit *a fourth of a kab* [C]6:25 Or *seedpods*, or *wild onions* [D]6:25 About 2 ounces of silver [E]6:33 Some emend to *king*

[F]7:1 Lit *a seah* [G]7:1 About $^1/_2$ ounce of silver [H]7:1 Lit *two seahs*

5 So the diseased men got up at twilight to go to the Arameans' camp. When they came to the camp's edge, they discovered that there was not a single man there, 6 for the Lord[A] had caused the Aramean camp to hear the sound of chariots, horses, and a great army.[a] The Arameans had said to each other, "The king of Israel must have hired the kings of the Hittites[b] and the kings of Egypt[c] to attack us." 7 So they had gotten up and fled[d] at twilight, abandoning their tents, horses, and donkeys. The camp was intact, and they had fled for their lives.

8 When these men came to the edge of the camp, they went into a tent to eat and drink. Then they picked up the silver, gold, and clothing and went off and hid them. They came back and entered another tent, picked things up, and hid them.[e] 9 Then they said to each other, "We're not doing what is right. Today is a day of good news.[f] If we are silent and wait until morning light, our sin will catch up with us. Let's go tell the king's household."

10 The diseased men went and called to the city's gatekeepers and told them, "We went to the Aramean camp and no one was there — no human sounds. There was nothing but tethered horses and donkeys, and the tents were intact." 11 The gatekeepers called out, and the news was reported to the king's household.

12 So the king got up in the night and said to his servants, "Let me tell you what the Arameans have done to us. They know we are starving,[g] so they have left the camp to hide in the open country, thinking, 'When they come out of the city, we will take them alive and go into the city.'"[h]

13 But one of his servants responded, "Please, let messengers take five of the horses that are left in the city. Their fate is like the entire Israelite community who will die,[B] so let's send them and see."

14 The messengers took two chariots with horses, and the king sent them after the Aramean army, saying, "Go and see." 15 So they followed them as far as the Jordan. They saw that the whole way was littered with clothes and equipment the Arameans had thrown off in their haste. The messengers returned and told the king. 16 Then the people went out and plundered the Aramean camp.[i]

It was then that six quarts[C] of fine meal sold for a shekel[D] and 12 quarts[E] of barley sold for a shekel,[D] according to the word of the LORD.[j] 17 The king had appointed the captain, his right-hand man,[k] to be in charge of the gate, but the people trampled him in the gateway. He died, just as the man of God had predicted when the king came to him. 18 When the man of God had said to the king, "About this time tomorrow 12 quarts[E] of barley will sell for a shekel[D] and six quarts[C] of fine meal will sell for a shekel[D] at the gate of Samaria," 19 this captain had answered the man of God, "Look, even if the LORD were to make windows in heaven, could this really happen?" Elisha had said, "You will in fact see it with your own eyes, but you won't eat any of it."[l] 20 This is what happened to him: the people trampled him in the gateway, and he died.

[a]**7:6** 2Sm 5:24; 2Kg 5:16-17
[b]1Kg 10:29
[c]2Ch 12:2-3
[d]**7:7** Jdg 7:21
[e]**7:8** Jos 7:21
[f]**7:9** Pr 15:27; 21:17-18
[g]**7:12** 2Kg 6:25
[h]Jos 8:4-12
[i]**7:16** 2Kg 7:8
[j]2Kg 7:1-2
[k]**7:17** 2Kg 7:2
[l]**7:18-19** 2Kg 7:1-2
[m]**8:1** 2Kg 4:8-37
[n]Gn 41:27,54
[o]**8:3** 2Kg 7:1-2
[p]Dt 15:1-6
[q]**8:4** 2Kg 4:12; 5:20-27
[r]**8:5** 2Kg 4:35

The Shunammite's Land Restored

8 Elisha said to the woman whose son he had restored to life,[m] "Get ready, you and your household, and go and live as a foreigner wherever you can. For the LORD has announced a seven-year famine,[n] and it has already come to the land."

2 So the woman got ready and did what the man of God said. She and her household lived as foreigners in the land of the Philistines for seven years. 3 When the woman returned from the land of the Philistines at the end of seven years,[o] she went to appeal to the king for her house and field.[p]

4 The king had been speaking to Gehazi,[q] the attendant of the man of God, saying, "Tell me all the great things Elisha has done."

5 While he was telling the king how Elisha restored the dead son to life, the woman whose son he had restored to life came to appeal to the king for her house and field. So Gehazi said, "My lord the king, this is the woman and this is the son Elisha restored to life."[r]

6 When the king asked the woman, she told him the story. So the king appointed a court

[A]**7:6** Some Hb mss read *LORD* [B]**7:13** Some Hb mss, LXX, Syr, Vg; other Hb mss read *left in it. Indeed, they are like the whole multitude of Israel that are left in it; indeed, they are like the whole multitude of Israel who will die.* [C]**7:16,18** Lit *a seah* [D]**7:16,18** About 1/2 ounce of silver [E]**7:16,18** Lit *two seahs* official for her, saying, "Restore all that was hers, along with all the income from the field from the day she left the country until now."

Aram's King Hazael

7 Elisha came to Damascus[a] while Ben-hadad[b] king of Aram was sick, and the king was told, "The man of God[c] has come here." 8 So the king said to Hazael,[d] "Take a gift[e] with you and go meet the man of God. Inquire of the LORD through him, 'Will I recover from this sickness?' "[f]

9 Hazael went to meet Elisha, taking with him a gift: 40 camel-loads of all kinds of goods from Damascus. When he came and stood before him, he said, "Your son,[g] Ben-hadad king of Aram, has sent me to ask you, 'Will I recover from this sickness?' "

10 Elisha told him, "Go say to him, 'You are sure to[A] recover.' But the LORD has shown me that he is sure to die." 11 Then Elisha stared steadily at him until Hazael was ashamed.[h]

The man of God wept,[i] 12 and Hazael asked, "Why is my lord weeping?"

He replied, "Because I know the evil you will do to the people of Israel. You will set their fortresses on fire. You will kill their young men with the sword. You will dash their little ones to pieces. You will rip open their pregnant women."[j]

13 Hazael said, "How could your servant, a mere dog,[k] do this monstrous thing?"

Elisha answered, "The LORD has shown me that you will be king over Aram."[l]

14 Hazael left Elisha and went to his master, who asked him, "What did Elisha say to you?"

He responded, "He told me you are sure to recover." 15 The next day Hazael took a heavy cloth, dipped it in water, and spread it over the king's face. Ben-hadad died, and Hazael reigned instead of him.

Judah's King Jehoram

16 In the fifth year[m] of Israel's King Joram[n] son of Ahab, Jehoram[B,o] son of Jehoshaphat became king of Judah, replacing his father.[C,p] 17 He was 32 years old when he became king and reigned eight years in Jerusalem.[q] 18 He walked in the way of the kings of Israel, as the house of Ahab had done, for Ahab's daughter was his wife. He did what was evil in the LORD's sight.[r] 19 The LORD was unwilling to destroy Judah because of His servant David, since He had promised to give a lamp[s] to David and his sons forever.[t]

20 During Jehoram's reign, Edom rebelled against Judah's control and appointed their own king.[u] 21 So Jehoram crossed over to Zair with all his chariots. Then at night he set out to attack the Edomites who had surrounded him and the chariot commanders, but his troops fled to their tents.[v] 22 So Edom is still in rebellion against Judah's control today. Libnah[w] also rebelled at that time.

23 The rest of the events of Jehoram's reign, along with all his accomplishments, are written in the Historical Record of Judah's Kings.[x] 24 Jehoram rested with his fathers and was buried with his fathers in the city of David, and his son Ahaziah became king in his place.[y]

Judah's King Ahaziah

25 In the twelfth year of Israel's King Joram son of Ahab,[z] Ahaziah son of Jehoram became king of Judah.[aa] 26 Ahaziah was 22 years old when he became king and reigned one year in Jerusalem. His mother's name was Athaliah, granddaughter of Israel's King Omri.[ab] 27 He walked in the way of the house of Ahab and did what was evil in the LORD's sight like the house of Ahab,[ac] for he was a son-in-law to Ahab's family.

28 Ahaziah went with Joram son of Ahab to fight against Hazael[ad] king of Aram in Ramoth-gilead,[ae] and the Arameans wounded Joram. 29 So King Joram returned to Jezreel[af] to recover from the wounds that the Arameans had inflicted on him in Ramoth-gilead[D] when he fought against Aram's King Hazael.[ag] Then Judah's King Ahaziah son of Jehoram went down to Jezreel to visit Joram son of Ahab since Joram was ill.

Jehu Anointed as Israel's King

9 The prophet Elisha called one of the sons of the prophets[ah] and said, "Tuck your mantle[ai] under your belt, take this flask of oil[aj] with you, and go to Ramoth-gilead.[ak] 2 When you get there, look for Jehu[al] son of

[a] **8:7** 1Kg 11:24
[b] 2Kg 6:24
[c] 2Kg 5:20
[d] **8:8** 1Kg 19:15,17
[e] 1Kg 14:3
[f] 2Kg 1:2
[g] **8:9** 2Kg 5:13
[h] **8:11** Jdg 3:25; 2Kg 2:17
[i] Lk 19:41
[j] **8:12** 1Kg 19:17; 2Kg 10:32-33; 13:3
[k] **8:13** 2Sm 9:8
[l] **8:13-15** 1Kg 19:15
[m] **8:16-24** 2Ch 21:5-20
[n] **8:16** 2Kg 1:17; 3:1
[o] 2Ch 21:1
[p] 1Kg 22:50
[q] **8:17** 2Ch 21:5
[r] **8:18** 2Ch 21:6
[s] **8:19** 1Kg 11:36; 15:4
[t] 2Ch 21:7
[u] **8:20** 1Kg 22:47; 2Kg 3:9
[v] **8:21** 2Sm 18:17; 19:8
[w] **8:22** Jos 21:13; 2Kg 19:8
[x] **8:23** 1Kg 22:39; 2Kg 1:18
[y] **8:24** 1Kg 22:40; 2Kg 1:17
[z] **8:25-29** 2Ch 22:1-6
[aa] **8:25** 2Kg 9:29
[ab] **8:26** 1Kg 16:23; 2Ch 22:2
[ac] **8:27** 2Ch 22:3
[ad] **8:28** 1Kg 19:15
[ae] 1Kg 22:3,29
[af] **8:29** 1Kg 21:1
[ag] 2Kg 9:15
[ah] **9:1** 2Kg 2:3,5,7
[ai] 2Kg 4:29
[aj] 1Sm 10:1; 16:1; 1Kg 1:39
[ak] 1Kg 22:3,29; 2Kg 8:28-29
[al] **9:2** 1Kg 19:16-17; 2Kg 9:14

[A] **8:10** Alt Hb tradition reads *You will not* [B] **8:16** = The LORD is Exalted [C] **8:16** Lit *Judah; Jehoshaphat had been king of Judah* [D] **8:29** Lit *Ramah*

Jehoshaphat, son of Nimshi. Go in, get him away from his colleagues, and take him to an inner room. 3Then, take the flask of oil, pour it on his head, and say, 'This is what the LORD says: "I anoint you king over Israel."'[a] Open the door and escape. Don't wait." 4So the young prophet went to Ramoth-gilead.

5When he arrived, the army commanders were sitting there, so he said, "I have a message for you, commander."

Jehu asked, "For which one of us?"

He answered, "For you, commander."

6So Jehu got up and went into the house. The young prophet poured the oil on his head and said, "This is what the LORD God of Israel says: 'I anoint you king over the LORD's people, Israel. 7You are to strike down the house of your master Ahab so that I may avenge the blood shed by the hand of Jezebel — the blood of My servants the prophets and of all the servants of the LORD.[b] 8The whole house of Ahab will perish, and I will eliminate all of Ahab's males,[A] both slave and free, in Israel.[c] 9I will make the house of Ahab like the house of Jeroboam son of Nebat and like the house of Baasha son of Ahijah.[d] 10The dogs will eat Jezebel in the plot of land at Jezreel — no one will bury her.'"[e] Then the young prophet opened the door and escaped.

11When Jehu came out to his master's servants, they asked, "Is everything all right? Why did this crazy person[f] come to you?"

Then he said to them, "You know the sort and their ranting."

12But they replied, "That's a lie! Tell us!"

So Jehu said, "He talked to me about this and that and said, 'This is what the LORD says: I anoint you king over Israel.'"

13Each man quickly took his garment and put it under Jehu on the bare steps.[B,g] They blew the ram's horn[h] and proclaimed, "Jehu is king!"[i]

14Then Jehu son of Jehoshaphat, son of Nimshi, conspired against Joram.[j] Joram and all Israel had been at Ramoth-gilead on guard against Hazael king of Aram. 15But King Joram had returned to Jezreel to recover from the wounds that the Arameans had inflicted on him when he fought against Aram's King Hazael. Jehu said, "If you commanders wish to make me king, then don't let anyone escape from the city to go tell about it in Jezreel."

Jehu Kills Joram and Ahaziah

16Jehu got into his chariot and went to Jezreel since Joram was laid up there and Ahaziah king of Judah had gone down to visit Joram. 17Now the watchman[k] was standing on the tower in Jezreel. He saw Jehu's troops approaching and shouted, "I see troops!"

Joram responded, "Choose a rider and send him to meet them and have him ask, 'Do you come in peace?'"[l]

18So a horseman went to meet Jehu and said, "This is what the king asks: 'Do you come in peace?'"

Jehu replied, "What do you have to do with peace?[C] Fall in behind me."

The watchman reported, "The messenger reached them but hasn't started back."

19So he sent out a second horseman, who went to them and said, "This is what the king asks: 'Do you come in peace?'"

Jehu answered, "What do you have to do with peace?[C] Fall in behind me."

20Again the watchman reported, "He reached them but hasn't started back. Also, the driving is like that of Jehu son of Nimshi[m] — he drives like a madman."

21"Harness!" Joram shouted, and they harnessed his chariot. Then Joram king of Israel and Ahaziah king of Judah set out, each in his own chariot, and met Jehu at the plot of land of Naboth the Jezreelite.[n] 22When Joram saw Jehu he asked, "Do you come in peace, Jehu?"

He answered, "What peace can there be as long as there is so much prostitution and witchcraft from your mother Jezebel?"[o]

23Joram turned around and fled, shouting to Ahaziah, "It's treachery,[p] Ahaziah!"

24Then Jehu drew his bow and shot Joram between the shoulders. The arrow went through his heart, and he slumped down in his chariot.[q] 25Jehu said to Bidkar his aide, "Pick him up and throw him on the plot of ground belonging to Naboth the Jezreelite.[r] For remember when you and I were riding

[a]**9:3** 2Ch 22:7
[b]**9:7** 1Kg 18:4; 21:15
[c]**9:8** 1Kg 21:21; 2Kg 10:17
[d]**9:9** 1Kg 16:3-5,11-12
[e]**9:10** 1Kg 21:23; 2Kg 9:30-37
[f]**9:11** 1Sm 10:11; Mk 3:21
[g]**9:13** Mt 21:8
[h]2Sm 15:10
[i]1Kg 1:39
[j]**9:14-16** 2Kg 8:28-29; 2Ch 22:6
[k]**9:17** 1Sm 14:16
[l]1Sm 16:4
[m]**9:20** 1Kg 19:17; 2Kg 9:2
[n]**9:21** 1Kg 21:1-7
[o]**9:22** 1Kg 16:30-33; 2Ch 21:13
[p]**9:23** 2Kg 11:14
[q]**9:24** 1Kg 22:34-35
[r]**9:25** 1Kg 21:1

[A]**9:8** Lit *eliminate Ahab's one who urinates against a wall* [B]**9:13** Lit *on the bones of the steps* [C]**9:18,19** Lit *What to you and to peace*

side by side behind his father Ahab, and the
LORD uttered this ˚oracle against him: [26]'As
surely as I saw the blood of Naboth and the
blood of his sons yesterday'—this is the
LORD's declaration—'so will I repay you on
this plot of land'—this is the LORD's declaration. So now, according to the word of the
LORD, pick him up and throw him on the plot
of land."[a]
[27]When King Ahaziah of Judah saw what
was happening, he fled up the road toward
Beth-haggan. Jehu pursued him, shouting,
"Shoot him too!" So they shot him in his
chariot[A] at Gur Pass near Ibleam,[b] but he fled
to Megiddo[c] and died there.[d] [28]Then his servants carried him to Jerusalem in a chariot
and buried him in his fathers' tomb in the
city of David.[e] [29]It was in the eleventh year of
Joram son of Ahab that Ahaziah had become
king over Judah.[f]

Jehu Kills Jezebel

[30]When Jehu came to Jezreel, Jezebel heard
about it, so she painted her eyes,[g] adorned
her head, and looked down from the window.
[31]As Jehu entered the gate, she said, "Do you
come in peace, Zimri,[B,h] killer of your master?"
[32]He looked up toward the window and
said, "Who is on my side? Who?" Two or
three eunuchs[i] looked down at him, [33]and
he said, "Throw her down!" So they threw
her down, and some of her blood splattered
on the wall and on the horses, and Jehu rode
over her.[j]
[34]Then he went in, ate and drank, and
said, "Take care of this cursed[k] woman and
bury her, since she's a king's daughter."[l] [35]But
when they went out to bury her, they did not
find anything but her skull, her feet, and the
palms of her hands. [36]So they went back
and told him, and he said, "This fulfills the
LORD's word that He spoke through His servant Elijah the Tishbite: 'In the plot of land
at Jezreel, the dogs will eat Jezebel's flesh.[m]
[37]Jezebel's corpse will be like manure[n] on the
surface of the field in the plot of land at Jezreel so that no one will be able to say: This is
Jezebel.'"

Jehu Kills the House of Ahab

10 Since Ahab had 70 sons in Samaria,[o]
Jehu wrote letters and sent them to Samaria to the rulers of Jezreel,[p] to the elders,
and to the guardians of Ahab's sons,[C] saying:

> [2]When this letter[q] arrives, since your
> master's sons are with you and you have
> chariots, horses, a fortified city, and
> weaponry, [3]select the most qualified[D]
> of your master's sons, set him on his fa-
> ther's throne, and fight for your master's
> house.

[4]However, they were terrified and reasoned, "Look, two kings[r] couldn't stand
against him; how can we?"
[5]So the overseer of the palace, the overseer
of the city, the elders, and the guardians sent
a message to Jehu: "We are your servants, and
we will do whatever you tell us. We will not
make anyone king. Do whatever you think is
right."[E,s]
[6]Then Jehu wrote them a second letter, saying:

> If you are on my side, and if you will obey
> me, bring me the heads of your master's
> sons at this time tomorrow at Jezreel.

All 70 of the king's sons were being cared
for by the city's prominent men. [7]When the
letter came to them, they took the king's sons
and slaughtered all 70, put their heads in baskets, and sent them to Jehu at Jezreel. [8]When
the messenger came and told him, "They have
brought the heads of the king's sons," the king
said, "Pile them in two heaps at the entrance
of the gate until morning."
[9]The next morning when he went out and
stood at the gate, he said to all the people,
"You are innocent. It was I who conspired
against my master and killed him.[t] But who
struck down all these? [10]Know, then, that not
a word the LORD spoke against the house of
Ahab will fail,[u] for the LORD has done what
He promised through His servant Elijah."[v]
[11]So Jehu killed all who remained of the house
of Ahab in Jezreel—all his great men, close
friends, and priests—leaving him no survivors.

[a]**9:25-26** 1Kg 21:13,19,24 [b]**9:27** Jos 17:11; Jdg 1:27 [c]2Kg 23:29 [d]2Ch 22:7,9 [e]**9:27-28** 2Kg 23:30; 2Ch 22:9 [f]**9:29** 2Kg 8:25 [g]**9:30** Jr 4:30; Ezk 23:40 [h]**9:31** 1Kg 16:9-20 [i]**9:32** Est 1:10; 2:14 [j]**9:33** Ps 7:5 [k]**9:34** 1Kg 21:21-24 [l]1Kg 16:31 [m]**9:36** 1Kg 21:23; 2Kg 9:10 [n]**9:37** Jr 8:1-2; Zph 1:17 [o]**10:1** 1Kg 16:24,29 [p]1Kg 21:1; 2Kg 9:30 [q]**10:2** 2Kg 5:6 [r]**10:4** 2Kg 9:24,27 [s]**10:5** Jos 9:8,11; 1Kg 20:4,32; 2Kg 18:14 [t]**10:9** 2Kg 9:14-24 [u]**10:10** 2Kg 9:7-10 [v]1Kg 21:19-29

[A]**9:27** LXX, Syr, Vg; MT omits *So they shot him* [B]**9:31** A sarcastic reference to Zimri who usurped the throne; 1Kg 16:8-20 [C]**10:1** LXX; MT reads *of Ahab* [D]**10:3** Lit *the good and the upright* [E]**10:5** Lit *Do what is good in your eyes*

12 Then he set out and went on his way to Samaria. On the way, while he was at Beth-eked
of the Shepherds, 13 Jehu met the relatives of
Ahaziah king of Judah and asked, "Who are
you?"

They answered, "We're Ahaziah's[a] relatives.
We've come down to greet the king's sons and
the queen mother's[b] sons."

14 Then Jehu ordered, "Take them alive." So
they took them alive and then slaughtered
them at the pit of Beth-eked — 42 men. He
didn't spare any of them.[c]

15 When he left there, he found Jehonadab
son of Rechab[d] coming to meet him. He
greeted him and then asked, "Is your heart
one with mine?"[A]

"It is," Jehonadab replied.

Jehu said, "If it is,[B] give me your hand."[e]
So he gave him his hand, and Jehu pulled
him up into the chariot with him. 16 Then
he said, "Come with me and see my zeal[f] for
the LORD!" So he let him ride with him in
his chariot. 17 When Jehu came to Samaria,
he struck down all who remained from the
house of Ahab in Samaria until he had annihilated his house, according to the word of
the LORD spoken to Elijah.[g]

Jehu Kills the Baal Worshipers

18 Then Jehu brought all the people together and said to them, "Ahab served •Baal[h]
a little, but Jehu will serve him a lot. 19 Now,
therefore, summon to me all the prophets
of Baal, all his servants, and all his priests.[i]
None must be missing, for I have a great sacrifice for Baal. Whoever is missing will not
live." However, Jehu was acting deceptively in
order to destroy the servants of Baal. 20 Jehu
commanded, "Consecrate a solemn assembly[j]
for Baal." So they called one.

21 Then Jehu sent messengers throughout
all Israel, and all the servants of Baal[C] came;
there was not a man left who did not come.[k]
They entered the temple of Baal,[l] and it was
filled from one end to the other. 22 Then he
said to the custodian of the wardrobe, "Bring
out the garments for all the servants of Baal."
So he brought out their garments.

23 Then Jehu and Jehonadab son of Rechab
entered the temple of Baal, and Jehu said to
the servants of Baal, "Look carefully to see that
there are no servants of the LORD here among
you — only servants of Baal." 24 Then they went
in to offer sacrifices and •burnt offerings.

Now Jehu had stationed 80 men outside,
and he warned them, "Whoever allows any of
the men I am delivering into your hands to
escape will forfeit his life for theirs."[m] 25 When
he finished offering the burnt offering, Jehu
said to the guards and officers, "Go in and kill
them. Don't let anyone out."[n] So they struck
them down with the sword. Then the guards
and officers threw the bodies out and went
into the inner room of the temple of Baal.
26 They brought out the pillars of the temple
of Baal and burned them 27 and tore down the
pillar[o] of Baal. Then they tore down the temple of Baal and made it a latrine[p] — which it
is to this day.

Evaluation of Jehu's Reign

28 Jehu eliminated Baal worship from Israel,
29 but he did not turn away from the sins that
Jeroboam son of Nebat had caused Israel to
commit — worshiping the gold calves that
were in Bethel and Dan.[q] 30 Nevertheless, the
LORD said to Jehu, "Because you have done
well in carrying out what is right in My sight
and have done to the house of Ahab all that
was in My heart, four generations of your
sons will sit on the throne of Israel."[r]

31 Yet Jehu was not careful to follow the instruction of the LORD God of Israel with all
his heart. He did not turn from the sins that
Jeroboam had caused Israel to commit.

32 In those days the LORD began to reduce
the size of Israel.[s] Hazael[t] defeated the Israelites throughout their territory: 33 from the
Jordan eastward, all the land of Gilead — the
Gadites, the Reubenites, and the Manassites — from Aroer[u] which is by the Arnon
Valley[v] through Gilead to Bashan.[D]

34 Now the rest of the events of Jehu's reign,
along with all his accomplishments and all
his might, are written in the Historical Record of Israel's Kings.[w] 35 Jehu rested with his
fathers and was buried in Samaria. His son
Jehoahaz[x] became king in his place. 36 The

[a] 10:13 2Kg 9:27-29
[b] 1Kg 2:19
[c] 10:14 2Ch 22:8
[d] 10:15 Jr 35:6-19
[e] Ezr 10:19
[f] 10:16 1Kg 19:10
[g] 10:17 1Kg 21:19-21; 2Kg 9:8
[h] 10:18 1Kg 16:31-32
[i] 10:19 1Kg 18:19; 22:6
[j] 10:20 Jl 1:14
[k] 10:21 1Kg 22:6
[l] 1Kg 16:32
[m] 10:24 1Kg 20:39
[n] 10:25 1Kg 18:40
[o] 10:27 1Kg 14:23; 2Kg 3:2
[p] Ezr 6:11
[q] 10:29 1Kg 12:28-29
[r] 10:30 2Kg 15:12
[s] 10:32 2Kg 13:25
[t] 1Kg 19:17; 2Kg 8:12
[u] 10:33 Dt 2:36; Jdg 11:26
[v] Nm 21:13
[w] 10:34 2Kg 1:18
[x] 10:35 2Kg 13:1

A 10:15 Lit *heart upright like my heart is with your heart* B 10:15 LXX, Syr, Vg; MT reads *mine?" Jehonadab said, "It is and it is* C 10:21 LXX adds *—all his priests and all his prophets—* D 10:33 Lit *Arnon Valley and Gilead and Bashan*

length of Jehu's reign over Israel in Samaria was 28 years.[a]

Athaliah Usurps the Throne

11 When Athaliah,[b] Ahaziah's mother,[c] saw that her son was dead,[d] she proceeded to annihilate all the royal heirs. [2]Jehosheba,[e] who was King Jehoram's daughter and Ahaziah's[f] sister, secretly rescued Joash son of Ahaziah from the king's sons who were being killed and put him and the one who nursed him in a bedroom. So he was hidden from Athaliah and was not killed. [3]Joash was in hiding with Jehosheba in the LORD's temple six years while Athaliah ruled over the land.

Athaliah Overthrown

[4]Then[g] in the seventh year, Jehoiada[h] sent messengers and brought in the commanders of hundreds, the Carites, and the guards.[i] He had them come to him in the LORD's temple, where he made a covenant with them and put them under oath. He showed them the king's son [5]and commanded them, "This is what you are to do: a third of you who come on duty on the Sabbath[j] are to provide protection for the king's palace. [6]A third are to be at the Sur gate and a third at the gate behind the guards. You are to take turns providing protection for the palace.[A,k]

[7]"Your two divisions that go off duty on the Sabbath are to provide protection for the LORD's temple. [8]You must completely surround the king with weapons in hand. Anyone who approaches the ranks is to be put to death. You must be with the king in all his daily tasks."[B,l]

[9]So the commanders of hundreds did everything Jehoiada the priest commanded. They each brought their men—those coming on duty on the Sabbath and those going off duty—and went to Jehoiada the priest.[m] [10]The priest gave to the commanders of hundreds King David's spears and shields[n] that were in the LORD's temple. [11]Then the guards stood with their weapons in hand surrounding the king—from the right side of the temple to the left side, by the altar and by the temple.

[12]He brought out the king's son, put the crown[o] on him, gave him the ·testimony,[C,p] and made him king. They anointed[q] him and clapped their hands and cried, "Long live the king!"[r]

[13]When Athaliah[s] heard the noise from the guard and the crowd, she went out to the people at the LORD's temple.[t] [14]As she looked, there was the king standing by the pillar[u] according to the custom. The commanders and the trumpeters were by the king, and all the people of the land were rejoicing and blowing trumpets.[v] Athaliah tore her clothes and screamed "Treason! Treason!"[w]

[15]Then Jehoiada[x] the priest ordered the commanders of hundreds[y] in charge of the army, "Take her out between the ranks, and put to death by the sword anyone who follows her," for the priest had said, "She is not to be put to death in the LORD's temple."[z] [16]So they arrested her, and she went through the horse entrance[aa] to the king's palace, where she was put to death.[ab]

Jehoiada's Reforms

[17]Then[ac] Jehoiada made a covenant between the LORD, the king, and the people that they would be the LORD's people[ad] and another covenant between the king and the people.[D,ae] [18]So all the people of the land went to the temple of ·Baal and tore it down. They broke its altars and images into pieces,[af] and they killed Mattan, the priest of Baal, at the altars.[ag]

Then Jehoiada the priest appointed guards for the LORD's temple.[ah] [19]He took the commanders of hundreds, the Carites, the guards,[ai] and all the people of the land, and they brought the king from the LORD's temple. They entered the king's palace by way of the guards' gate. Then Joash[aj] sat on the throne of the kings. [20]All the people of the land rejoiced, and the city was quiet, for they had put Athaliah to death by the sword in the king's palace.

Judah's King Joash

12 [21E]Joash[F,ak] was seven years old when he became king.[al] [1]In the seventh year of Jehu, Joash became king and reigned 40 years

[a]10:36 2Kg 1:17 [b]11:1 2Ch 22:10 [c]2Kg 8:26 [d]2Kg 9:27 [e]11:2 2Kg 11:21; 12:1 [f]2Kg 8:25 [g]11:4-16 2Ch 23:1-15 [h]11:4 2Kg 11:15,17 [i]2Kg 11:19 [j]11:5 1Ch 9:25 [k]11:4-6 2Ch 23:1-2 [l]11:8 Nm 27:16-17 [m]11:9 2Ch 23:8 [n]11:10 2Sm 8:7; 1Ch 18:7 [o]11:12 2Sm 1:10 [p]Ex 31:18; 2Kg 23:3 [q]1Kg 1:39 [r]1Sm 10:24 [s]11:13 2Kg 11:1 [t]2Ch 23:12 [u]11:14 2Kg 23:3; 2Ch 34:31 [v]Nm 10:7-10; 1Kg 1:39-40 [w]2Kg 9:23 [x]11:15 2Kg 11:4 [y]1Kg 11:4; 2Ch 23:1 [z]1Kg 2:30 [aa]11:16 Neh 3:28 [ab]Gn 9:6; Lv 24:17; 2Kg 11:1 [ac]11:17-20 2Ch 23:16-21 [ad]11:17 Jos 24:25; 2Ch 34:31 [ae]1Sm 10:25; 2Sm 5:3 [af]11:18 Dt 12:2-3; 2Kg 10:26-27 [ag]1Kg 18:40 [ah]2Ch 23:18 [ai]11:19 2Kg 11:4,6 [aj]2Kg 11:2-3,12 [ak]11:21–12:3 2Ch 24:1-4 [al]11:21 2Kg 11:2

[A]11:6 Hb obscure [B]11:8 Lit *king when he goes out and when he comes in* [C]11:12 Or *him the copy of the covenant*, or *him a diadem*, or *him jewels* [D]11:17 Some Gk versions, 2Ch 23:16 omit *and another covenant between the king and the people* [E]11:21 2Kg 12:1 in Hb [F]11:21 = The LORD Has Bestowed

in Jerusalem. His mother's name was Zibiah,
who was from Beer-sheba.[a] 2Throughout the
time Jehoiada[b] the priest instructed[c] him,
Joash did what was right in the LORD's sight.[d]
3Yet the ·high places were not taken away; the
people continued sacrificing and burning incense on the high places.[e]

Repairing the Temple

4Then[f] Joash said to the priests, "All the dedicated money brought to the LORD's temple,[g]
census money,[h] money from vows,[i] and all
money voluntarily given[j] for the LORD's temple, 5each priest is to take from his assessor[A]
and repair whatever damage to the temple is
found."[B,k]
6But by the twenty-third year[l] of the reign
of King Joash, the priests had not repaired
the damage[C] to the temple.[m] 7So King Joash
called Jehoiada[n] the priest and the other
priests and said, "Why haven't you repaired
the temple's damage? Since you haven't, don't
take any money from your assessors; instead,
hand it over for the repair of the temple." 8So
the priests agreed they would not take money
from the people and they would not repair
the temple's damage.
9Then Jehoiada the priest took a chest,[o]
bored a hole in its lid, and set it beside the altar on the right side as one enters the LORD's
temple; in it the priests who guarded the
threshold put all the money brought into the
LORD's temple.[p] 10Whenever they saw there
was a large amount of money in the chest, the
king's secretary[q] and the high priest would
go to the LORD's temple and count the money
found there and tie it up in bags.[r] 11Then they
would put the counted money into the hands
of those doing the work—those who oversaw the LORD's temple. They in turn would
pay it out to those working on the LORD's
temple—the carpenters, the builders, 12the
masons, and the stonecutters—and would
use it to buy timber and quarried stone to repair the damage to the LORD's temple[s] and for
all spending for temple repairs.
13However, no silver bowls, wick trimmers,
sprinkling basins, trumpets, or any articles of
gold or silver[t] were made for the LORD's temple from the money brought into the temple.
14Instead, it was given to those doing the work,
and they repaired the LORD's temple with it.
15No accounting was required from the men
who received the money to pay those doing
the work, since they worked with integrity.[u]
16The money from the ·restitution offering
and the ·sin offering was not brought to the
LORD's temple since it belonged to the priests.[v]

Aramean Invasion of Judah

17At that time Hazael[w] king of Aram
marched up and fought against Gath and
captured it. Then he planned to attack Jerusalem.[x] 18So King Joash of Judah took all the
consecrated items that his ancestors—Judah's kings Jehoshaphat, Jehoram, and Ahaziah—had consecrated, along with his own
consecrated items and all the gold found in
the treasuries of the LORD's temple and in the
king's palace, and he sent them to Hazael king
of Aram.[y] Then Hazael withdrew from Jerusalem.

Joash Assassinated

19The rest of the events of Joash's reign,
along with all his accomplishments, are written in the Historical Record of Judah's Kings.[z]
20Joash's servants conspired against him
and killed him[aa] at Beth-millo[ab] on the road
that goes down to Silla. 21His servants Jozabad[D] son of Shimeath and Jehozabad son of
Shomer struck him down, and he died.[ac] Then
they buried him with his fathers in the city
of David, and his son Amaziah became king
in his place.[ad]

Israel's King Jehoahaz

13 In the twenty-third year of Judah's
King Joash[ae] son of Ahaziah, Jehoahaz[af] son of Jehu became king over Israel in
Samaria and reigned 17 years. 2He did what
was evil in the LORD's sight and followed the
sins that Jeroboam son of Nebat had caused
Israel to commit; he did not turn away from
them.[ag] 3So the LORD's anger burned against
Israel,[ah] and He surrendered them to the
power of Hazael[ai] king of Aram and his son
Ben-hadad[aj] during their reigns.

[a]**12:1** 2Kg 11:2,21; 2Ch 24:1
[b]**12:2** 2Kg 11:4,17
[c]Mal 2:6-7
[d]Dt 12:25; 2Sm 8:15
[e]**12:3** 1Kg 3:3; 2Kg 14:4; 15:35
[f]**12:4-12** 2Ch 24:5-12
[g]**12:4** 2Kg 22:4
[h]Ex 30:13-16
[i]Lv 27:2-28
[j]Ex 35:5
[k]**12:5** 2Kg 22:5
[l]**12:6** 2Kg 11:21
[m]2Ch 24:5
[n]**12:7-8** 2Kg 11:4-6
[o]**12:9** 2Ch 23:1; 24:8
[p]Mk 12:41; Lk 21:1
[q]**12:10** 2Sm 8:17; 2Kg 19:2
[r]2Ch 24:11
[s]**12:11-12** 2Kg 22:5-6; 2Ch 24:11-12
[t]**12:13** 1Kg 7:48,50-51; 2Ch 24:14
[u]**12:15** 2Kg 22:7; 2Ch 34:12
[v]**12:16** Lv 4:24,29; 5:15-18; 7:7
[w]**12:17** 1Kg 19:17; 2Kg 8:12; 10:32
[x]**12:17-21** 2Ch 24:23-27
[y]**12:18** 2Kg 16:8; 18:15-16
[z]**12:19** 1Kg 22:45
[aa]**12:20** 2Kg 14:5
[ab]Jdg 9:6
[ac]**12:21** 2Ch 24:26
[ad]2Kg 14:1; 2Ch 24:27
[ae]**13:1** 2Kg 12:1
[af]2Kg 10:35
[ag]**13:2** 1Kg 12:26-33
[ah]**13:3** Dt 31:17; Jdg 2:14
[ai]2Kg 8:12; 12:17
[aj]2Kg 13:24-25

[A]**12:5** Hb obscure [B]**12:5** Lit *repair the breach of the house wherever there is found a breach* [C]**12:6** Lit *breach* in 2Kg 12:5-12 [D]**12:21** Some Hb mss, LXX read *Jozacar*; 2Ch 24:26 reads *Zabad*

4 Then Jehoahaz sought the LORD's favor,
and the LORD heard him, for He saw the oppression the king of Aram inflicted on Israel.[a]
5 Therefore, the LORD gave Israel a deliverer,[b]
and they escaped from the power of the Arameans. Then the people of Israel dwelt in
their tents as before, 6 but they didn't turn
away from the sins that the house of Jeroboam had caused Israel to commit. Jehoahaz walked in them,[c] and the ·Asherah
pole also remained standing in Samaria.
7 Jehoahaz did not have an army left, except
for 50 horsemen, 10 chariots, and 10,000
foot soldiers, because the king of Aram had
destroyed them,[d] making them like dust at
threshing.[e]

8 The rest of the events of Jehoahaz's reign,
along with all his accomplishments and his
might, are written in the Historical Record
of Israel's Kings.[f] 9 Jehoahaz rested with his fathers, and he was buried in Samaria. His son
Jehoash[A] became king in his place.

Israel's King Jehoash

10 In the thirty-seventh year of Judah's King
Joash, Jehoash son of Jehoahaz became king
over Israel in Samaria and reigned 16 years.
11 He did what was evil in the LORD's sight.
He did not turn away from all the sins that
Jeroboam son of Nebat had caused Israel to
commit, but he walked in them.[g]

12 The rest of the events of Jehoash's reign,
along with all his accomplishments and the
power he had to wage war against Judah's
King Amaziah,[h] are written in the Historical
Record of Israel's Kings. 13 Jehoash rested with
his fathers, and Jeroboam[i] sat on his throne.
Jehoash was buried in Samaria with the kings
of Israel.

Elisha's Death

14 When Elisha became sick with the illness
that he died from, Jehoash king of Israel went
down and wept over him and said, "My father,
my father, the chariots and horsemen of Israel!"[j]

15 Elisha responded, "Take a bow and arrows." So he got a bow and arrows.[k] 16 Then Elisha said to the king of Israel, "Put your hand
on the bow." So the king put his hand on it,
and Elisha put his hands on the king's hands.
17 Elisha said, "Open the east window." So he
opened it. Elisha said, "Shoot!" So he shot.[l]
Then Elisha said, "The LORD's arrow of victory, yes, the arrow of victory over Aram. You
are to strike down the Arameans in Aphek[m]
until you have put an end to them."

18 Then Elisha said, "Take the arrows!" So
he took them. Then Elisha said to the king
of Israel, "Strike the ground!" So he struck
the ground three times and stopped. 19 The
man of God[n] was angry with him and said,
"You should have struck the ground five or
six times. Then you would have struck down
Aram until you had put an end to them, but
now you will only strike down Aram three
times." 20 Then Elisha died and was buried.[o]

Now Moabite raiders[p] used to come into
the land in the spring of the year. 21 Once, as
the Israelites were burying a man, suddenly
they saw a raiding party, so they threw the
man into Elisha's tomb. When he touched Elisha's bones, the man revived and stood up![q]

God's Mercy on Israel

22 Hazael[r] king of Aram oppressed Israel
throughout the reign of Jehoahaz, 23 but the
LORD was gracious to them, had compassion
on them,[s] and turned toward them because
of His covenant with Abraham, Isaac, and
Jacob.[t] He was not willing to destroy them.
Even now He has not banished them from
His presence.[u]

24 King Hazael of Aram died, and his son
Ben-hadad[v] became king in his place. 25 Then
Jehoash son of Jehoahaz took back from Ben-
hadad son of Hazael the cities that Hazael had
taken in war from Jehoash's father Jehoahaz.
Jehoash defeated Ben-hadad three times and
recovered the cities of Israel.[w]

Judah's King Amaziah

14 In[x] the second year of Israel's King Jehoash[A,y] son of Jehoahaz,[B] Amaziah[z]
son of Joash became king of Judah. 2 He was 25
years old when he became king and reigned
29 years in Jerusalem. His mother's name was
Jehoaddan[C] and was from Jerusalem. 3 He did
what was right in the LORD's sight, but not
like his ancestor David. He did everything his

[a]13:4 Ex 3:7-9; Nm 21:7-9; 2Kg 14:26
[b]13:5 Jdg 2:18; 2Kg 13:25; 14:25,27
[c]13:6 2Kg 13:2
[d]13:7 2Kg 10:32-33
[e]Am 1:3
[f]13:8-9 2Kg 1:17-18; 10:34-36
[g]13:11 1Kg 12:28-33
[h]13:12-13 2Kg 14:15-16
[i]13:13 2Kg 14:23
[j]13:14 2Kg 2:12
[k]13:15 1Sm 20:20
[l]13:17 Jos 8:18
[m]1Kg 20:26
[n]13:19 2Kg 5:20
[o]13:20 2Kg 2:1,11
[p]2Kg 3:7; 24:2
[q]13:21 Mt 27:52
[r]13:22 1Kg 19:17; 2Kg 8:12-13
[s]13:23 1Kg 8:28
[t]Ex 2:24
[u]2Kg 14:27
[v]13:24 2Kg 13:3
[w]13:25 2Kg 10:32
[x]14:1-14 2Ch 25:1-24
[y]14:1 2Ch 25:1
[z]2Kg 13:10

[A]13:9; 14:1 Lit *Joash* [B]14:1 Lit *Joahaz* [C]14:2 Alt Hb tradition, some Hb mss, Syr, Tg, Vg, 2Ch 25:1; other Hb mss, LXX read *Jehoaddin*

father Joash had done.[a] 4Yet the ·high places were not taken away, and the people continued sacrificing and burning incense on the high places.[b]

5As soon as the kingdom was firmly in his grasp, Amaziah killed his servants who had murdered his father the king.[c] 6However, he did not put the children of the murderers to death, as it is written in the book of the law of Moses where the LORD commanded, "Fathers must not be put to death because of children, and children must not be put to death because of fathers; instead, each one will be put to death for his own sin."[d]

7Amaziah killed 10,000 Edomites in the Valley of Salt.[e] He took Sela[f] in battle and called it Joktheel,[g] which is its name to this very day. 8Amaziah then sent messengers to Jehoash son of Jehoahaz, son of Jehu, king of Israel, saying, "Come, let us meet face to face."[h]

9King Jehoash of Israel sent word to Amaziah king of Judah, saying, "The thistle that was in Lebanon once sent a message to the cedar[i] that was in Lebanon,[j] saying, 'Give your daughter to my son as a wife.' Then a wild animal that was in Lebanon passed by and trampled the thistle. 10You have indeed defeated Edom, and you have become overconfident.[k] Enjoy your glory and stay at home. Why should you stir up such trouble that you fall—you and Judah with you?"

11But Amaziah would not listen, so King Jehoash of Israel advanced. He and King Amaziah of Judah faced off at Beth-shemesh[l] that belongs to Judah. 12Judah was routed before Israel, and everyone fled to his own tent.[m] 13King Jehoash of Israel captured Judah's King Amaziah son of Joash,[A] son of Ahaziah, at Beth-shemesh. Then Jehoash went to Jerusalem and broke down 200 yards[B] of Jerusalem's wall from the Ephraim Gate[n] to the Corner Gate.[o] 14He took all the gold and silver, all the articles found in the LORD's temple and in the treasuries of the king's palace, and some hostages.[p] Then he returned to Samaria.

Jehoash's Death

15The rest of the events of Jehoash's reign, along with his accomplishments, his might, and how he waged war against Amaziah king of Judah, are written in the Historical Record of Israel's Kings.[q] 16Jehoash rested with his fathers, and he was buried in Samaria with the kings of Israel. His son Jeroboam became king in his place.

Amaziah's Death

17Judah's King Amaziah son of Joash lived 15 years after the death of Israel's King Jehoash son of Jehoahaz.[r] 18The rest of the events of Amaziah's reign are written in the Historical Record of Judah's Kings.[s] 19A conspiracy was formed against him in Jerusalem,[t] and he fled to Lachish.[u] However, men were sent after him to Lachish, and they put him to death there. 20They carried him back[v] on horses, and he was buried in Jerusalem with his fathers in the city of David.[w]

21Then all the people of Judah took Azariah,[C,x] who was 16 years old, and made him king in place of his father Amaziah. 22He rebuilt Elath[D,y] and restored it to Judah after Amaziah the king rested with his fathers.

Israel's King Jeroboam

23In the fifteenth year of Judah's King Amaziah son of Joash, Jeroboam[z] son of Jehoash[E] became king of Israel in Samaria and reigned 41 years. 24He did what was evil in the LORD's sight. He did not turn away from all the sins Jeroboam son of Nebat had caused Israel to commit.[aa]

25He restored Israel's border[ab] from Lebo-hamath[ac] as far as the Sea of the ·Arabah,[ad] according to the word the LORD, the God of Israel, had spoken through His servant, the prophet Jonah[ae] son of Amittai from Gath-hepher.[af] 26For the LORD saw that the affliction of Israel was very bitter.[ag] There was no one to help Israel, neither bond nor free. 27However, the LORD had not said He would blot out the name of Israel under heaven,[ah] so He delivered[ai] them by the hand of Jeroboam son of Jehoash.[E]

28The rest of the events of Jeroboam's reign—along with all his accomplishments, the power he had to wage war, and how he recovered for Israel Damascus[aj] and Hamath,[ak] which had belonged to Judah[F]—are written

[a]14:3 2Kg 12:2 [b]14:4 1Kg 3:3; 2Kg 12:3; 16:4 [c]14:5 2Kg 12:20 [d]14:6 Dt 24:16; Jr 31:30; Ezk 18:4,20 [e]14:7 2Sm 8:13 [f]Jdg 1:36 [g]Jos 15:38 [h]14:8 2Sm 2:14-17 [i]14:9 1Kg 4:33 [j]Jdg 9:8-15 [k]14:10 Dt 8:14; 2Ch 26:16; 34:25 [l]14:11 Jos 19:38; 21:16 [m]14:12 2Sm 18:17; 1Kg 22:36 [n]14:13 Neh 8:16; 12:39 [o]2Ch 25:23; Zch 14:10 [p]14:14 1Kg 7:51; 14:26; 2Kg 12:18 [q]14:15-16 2Kg 13:12-13 [r]14:17 2Ch 25:25-28 [s]14:18 2Kg 12:19 [t]14:19 2Ch 25:27 [u]Jos 10:31; 2Kg 18:14 [v]14:20 2Kg 9:28 [w]2Kg 12:21 [x]14:21 2Kg 15:13; 2Ch 26:1-2 [y]14:22 1Kg 9:26; 2Kg 16:6 [z]14:23 2Kg 13:13 [aa]14:24 1Kg 12:30; 15:30 [ab]14:25 2Kg 13:25 [ac]1Kg 8:65 [ad]Nm 34:3-9 [ae]Jnh 1:1; Mt 12:39 [af]Jos 19:13 [ag]14:26 Ex 3:7-9; Dt 32:36; 2Kg 13:4 [ah]14:27 Dt 29:20; 2Kg 13:3 [ai]Jdg 6:14 [aj]14:28 2Sm 8:5; 1Kg 11:24 [ak]2Sm 8:9; 2Ch 8:3

[A]14:13 Lit *Jehoash* [B]14:13 Lit *400 cubits* [C]14:21 = Uzziah in 2Ch 26:1 [D]14:22 = Eloth in 2Ch 26:2 [E]14:23,27 Lit *Joash* [F]14:28 Lit *recovered Damascus and for Judah in Israel*; Hb obscure

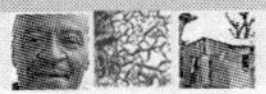

in the Historical Record of Israel's Kings.[a]
29 Jeroboam rested with his fathers, the kings
of Israel. His son Zechariah became king in
his place.[b]

Judah's King Azariah

15 In the twenty-seventh year of Israel's
King Jeroboam, Azariah[A,c] son of Amaziah became king of Judah.[d] 2 He was 16 years
old when he became king and reigned 52
years in Jerusalem. His mother's name was
Jecoliah, who was from Jerusalem. 3 Azariah
did what was right in the LORD's sight[e] just as
his father Amaziah had done. 4 Yet the ˙high
places were not taken away; the people continued sacrificing and burning incense on
the high places.[f]

5 The LORD afflicted the king, and he had
a serious skin disease until the day of his
death.[g] He lived in a separate house,[B,h] while
Jotham,[i] the king's son, was over the household governing the people of the land.[j]

6 The rest of the events of Azariah's reign,
along with all his accomplishments, are written in the Historical Record of Judah's Kings.[k]
7 Azariah rested with his fathers and was buried with his fathers in the city of David. His
son Jotham became king in his place.[l]

Israel's King Zechariah

8 In the thirty-eighth year of Judah's King
Azariah, Zechariah[m] son of Jeroboam became
king over Israel in Samaria for six months.
9 He did what was evil in the LORD's sight as
his fathers had done.[n] He did not turn away
from the sins Jeroboam son of Nebat had
caused Israel to commit.[o]

10 Shallum son of Jabesh conspired against
Zechariah. He struck him down publicly,[C] killed
him, and became king in his place.[p] 11 As for the
rest of the events of Zechariah's reign, they
are written in the Historical Record of Israel's
Kings.[q] 12 The word of the LORD that He spoke to
Jehu was, "Four generations of your sons will sit
on the throne of Israel,"[r] and it was so.

Israel's King Shallum

13 In the thirty-ninth year of Judah's King
Uzziah, Shallum son of Jabesh became king;

[a] 14:28 2Kg 13:8
[b] 14:29 2Kg 13:12-13; 15:8
[c] 15:1 2Kg 14:21
[d] 15:1-3 2Ch 26:3-5
[e] 15:3 1Kg 14:8
[f] 15:4 2Kg 14:3-4
[g] 15:5 2Ch 26:16-21
[h] Lv 13:46
[i] 2Kg 15:32; 2Ch 27:1; Mc 1:1
[j] 2Ch 26:16-21
[k] 15:6 2Kg 14:18
[l] 15:6-7 2Ch 26:22-23
[m] 15:8 2Kg 14:29
[n] 15:9 2Kg 14:24
[o] 1Kg 12:28-33; 13:33-34
[p] 15:10 2Kg 12:20
[q] 15:11 2Kg 13:8
[r] 15:12 2Kg 10:30
[s] 15:13 1Kg 16:24
[t] 15:14 1Kg 14:17
[u] 15:16 1Kg 4:24
[v] Dt 20:11
[w] 2Kg 8:12; Hs 13:16; Am 1:13
[x] 15:18 1Kg 12:28-33; 15:26
[y] 15:19 1Ch 5:25-26
[z] 2Kg 14:5
[aa] 15:20 2Kg 12:18
[ab] 15:22 2Kg 14:29
[ac] 15:24 1Kg 12:28-33
[ad] 15:25 2Ch 28:6
[ae] 2Kg 12:20
[af] 1Kg 16:8

he reigned in Samaria[s] a full month. 14 Then
Menahem son of Gadi came up from Tirzah[t]
to Samaria and struck down Shallum son of
Jabesh there. He killed him and became king
in his place. 15 As for the rest of the events of
Shallum's reign, along with the conspiracy
that he formed, they are written in the Historical Record of Israel's Kings.

Israel's King Menahem

16 At that time, starting from Tirzah, Menahem attacked Tiphsah,[u] all who were in it,
and its territory. Because they wouldn't surrender,[v] he attacked it and ripped open all the
pregnant women.[w]

17 In the thirty-ninth year of Judah's King
Azariah, Menahem son of Gadi became king
over Israel and reigned 10 years in Samaria.
18 He did what was evil in the LORD's sight.
Throughout his reign, he did not turn away
from the sins Jeroboam son of Nebat had
caused Israel to commit.[x]

19 Pul[D,y] king of Assyria invaded the land, so
Menahem gave Pul 75,000 pounds[E] of silver
so that Pul would support him to strengthen
his grip on the kingdom.[z] 20 Then Menahem
exacted 20 ounces[F] of silver from each of the
wealthy men of Israel to give to the king of Assyria. So the king of Assyria withdrew and did
not stay there in the land.[aa]

21 The rest of the events of Menahem's reign,
along with all his accomplishments, are written in the Historical Record of Israel's Kings.
22 Menahem rested with his fathers, and his
son Pekahiah became king in his place.[ab]

Israel's King Pekahiah

23 In the fiftieth year of Judah's King Azariah, Pekahiah son of Menahem became king
over Israel in Samaria and reigned two years.
24 He did what was evil in the LORD's sight and
did not turn away from the sins Jeroboam
son of Nebat had caused Israel to commit.[ac]

25 Then his officer, Pekah[ad] son of Remaliah, conspired against him[ae] and struck him
down in Samaria at the citadel of the king's
palace[af] — as well as Argob and Arieh.[G] There
were 50 Gileadite men with Pekah. He killed
Pekahiah and became king in his place.

A 15:1 = Uzziah in 2Ch 26:3 B 15:5 Lit *house of freedom*, or *house of exemption*
C 15:10 Some LXX mss read *at Ibleam*; Hb uncertain D 15:19 = Tiglath-pileser
E 15:19 Lit *1,000 talents* F 15:20 Lit *50 shekels* G 15:25 Hb obscure

[26]As for the rest of the events of Pekahiah's reign, along with all his accomplishments, they are written in the Historical Record of Israel's Kings.

Israel's King Pekah

[27]In the fifty-second year of Judah's King Azariah, Pekah son of Remaliah became king over Israel in Samaria and reigned 20 years. [28]He did what was evil in the LORD's sight. He did not turn away from the sins Jeroboam son of Nebat had caused Israel to commit.

[29]In the days of Pekah king of Israel, Tiglath-pileser[a] king of Assyria came and captured Ijon,[b] Abel-beth-maacah, Janoah, Kedesh, Hazor, Gilead, and Galilee—all the land of Naphtali[c]—and deported the people to Assyria.[d]

[30]Then Hoshea[e] son of Elah organized a conspiracy against Pekah son of Remaliah. He attacked him, killed him,[f] and became king in his place in the twentieth year of Jotham son of Uzziah.

[31]As for the rest of the events of Pekah's reign, along with all his accomplishments, they are written in the Historical Record of Israel's Kings.

Judah's King Jotham

[32]In the second year of Israel's King Pekah son of Remaliah, Jotham[g] son of Uzziah became king of Judah. [33]He was 25 years old when he became king[h] and reigned 16 years in Jerusalem. His mother's name was Jerusha daughter of Zadok. [34]He did what was right in the LORD's sight just as his father Uzziah had done.[i] [35]Yet the high places were not taken away; the people continued sacrificing and burning incense on the high places.

Jotham built the Upper Gate of the LORD's temple.[j] [36]The rest[k] of the events of Jotham's reign, along with all his accomplishments, they are written in the Historical Record of Judah's Kings.[l] [37]In those days the LORD began sending Rezin king of Aram and Pekah son of Remaliah against Judah.[m] [38]Jotham rested with his fathers and was buried with his fathers in the city of his ancestor David.[n] His son Ahaz became king in his place.

[a]**15:29** 1Ch 5:6,26
[b]1Kg 15:29
[c]Jos 19:32-39
[d]2Kg 17:6
[e]**15:30** 2Kg 17:1
[f]2Kg 12:20
[g]**15:32** 2Kg 15:5,7
[h]**15:33-35** 2Ch 27:1-3
[i]**15:34-35** 2Kg 15:3-4
[j]**15:35** 2Ch 27:3
[k]**15:36-38** 2Ch 27:7-9
[l]**15:36** 2Kg 14:18
[m]**15:37** 2Kg 16:5; Is 7:1
[n]**15:38** 2Kg 15:7
[o]**16:1-4** 2Ch 28:1-4
[p]**16:1** Is 1:1; 7:1
[q]**16:2** 1Kg 14:8
[r]**16:3** 2Kg 17:9-10
[s]Dt 18:10; 2Kg 21:6; 2Ch 33:6
[t]**16:4** 1Kg 22:17
[u]Dt 12:2
[v]**16:5-6** 2Ch 28:5-6; Is 7:1-9
[w]**16:5** 2Kg 15:37; Is 7:1
[x]**16:6** 1Kg 9:26
[y]2Ch 26:2
[z]**16:7** 2Ch 28:16
[aa]2Kg 15:29; 1Ch 5:26
[ab]**16:8** 1Kg 15:19; 2Kg 12:17-18; 18:15
[ac]**16:9** 2Ch 28:21
[ad]Am 1:3-5
[ae]Is 22:6; Am 9:7
[af]**16:10** 2Kg 15:29
[ag]Is 8:2
[ah]**16:12** 2Ch 26:16
[ai]**16:13** Ex 29:40

Judah's King Ahaz

16 In the seventeenth year of Pekah son of Remaliah,[o] Ahaz[p] son of Jotham became king of Judah. [2]Ahaz was 20 years old when he became king and reigned 16 years in Jerusalem. He did not do what was right in the sight of the LORD his God like his ancestor David[q] [3]but walked in the way of the kings of Israel.[r] He even made his son pass through the fire,[A] imitating the detestable practices of the nations the LORD had dispossessed before the Israelites.[s] [4]He sacrificed and burned incense[t] on the •high places, on the hills, and under every green tree.[u]

[5]Then[v] Aram's King Rezin and Israel's King Pekah son of Remaliah came to wage war against Jerusalem. They besieged Ahaz but were not able to conquer him.[w] [6]At that time Rezin king of Aram recovered Elath for Aram and expelled the Judahites from Elath.[x] Then the Arameans came to Elath, and they live there until today.[y]

[7]So Ahaz sent messengers[z] to Tiglath-pileser[aa] king of Assyria, saying, "I am your servant and your son. March up and save me from the power of the king of Aram and of the king of Israel, who are rising up against me." [8]Ahaz also took the silver and gold found in the LORD's temple and in the treasuries of the king's palace and sent them to the king of Assyria as a gift.[ab] [9]So the king of Assyria listened to him[ac] and marched up to Damascus and captured it.[ad] He deported its people to Kir[ae] but put Rezin to death.

Ahaz's Idolatry

[10]King Ahaz went to Damascus to meet Tiglath-pileser[af] king of Assyria. When he saw the altar that was in Damascus, King Ahaz sent a model of the altar and complete plans for its construction to Uriah the priest.[ag] [11]Uriah built the altar according to all the instructions King Ahaz sent from Damascus. Therefore, by the time King Ahaz came back from Damascus, Uriah the priest had completed it. [12]When the king came back from Damascus, he saw the altar. Then he approached the altar[ah] and ascended it. [13]He offered his •burnt offering[ai] and his •grain offering, poured out his drink offering, and sprinkled the blood

[A]**16:3** Either a Canaanite cult practice or child sacrifice

of his ·fellowship offerings[a] on the altar. 14He
took the bronze altar[b] that was before the
LORD in front of the temple between his altar and the LORD's temple, and put it on the
north side of his altar.
15Then King Ahaz commanded Uriah the
priest, "Offer on the great altar the morning
burnt offering, the evening grain offering,
and the king's burnt offering and his grain offering. Also offer the burnt offering of all the
people of the land, their grain offering, and
their drink offerings. Sprinkle on the altar
all the blood of the burnt offering and all the
blood of sacrifice. The bronze altar will be for
me to seek guidance."[A] 16Uriah the priest did
everything King Ahaz commanded.
17Then King Ahaz cut off the frames of the
water carts[B,c] and removed the bronze basin
from each of them. He took the reservoir[C,d]
from the bronze oxen that were under it and
put it on a stone pavement. 18To satisfy the
king of Assyria, he removed from the LORD's
temple the Sabbath canopy they had built in
the palace, and he closed the outer entrance
for the king.

Ahaz's Death

19The rest[e] of the events of Ahaz's reign,
along with his accomplishments, are written in the Historical Record of Judah's Kings.[f]
20Ahaz rested with his fathers[g] and was buried with his fathers in the city of David, and
his son Hezekiah became king in his place.

Israel's King Hoshea

17 In the twelfth year of Judah's King Ahaz,
Hoshea[h] son of Elah became king over
Israel in Samaria and reigned nine years. 2He
did what was evil in the LORD's sight, but not
like the kings of Israel who preceded him.[i]
3Shalmaneser[j] king of Assyria attacked
him,[k] and Hoshea became his vassal and paid
him tribute money. 4But the king of Assyria
discovered Hoshea's conspiracy. He had sent
envoys to So king of Egypt[l] and had not paid
tribute money to the king of Assyria as in
previous years.[D] Therefore the king of Assyria
arrested him and put him in prison. 5Then
the king of Assyria invaded the whole land,
marched up to Samaria, and besieged it for
three years.[m]

The Fall of Samaria

6In the ninth year of Hoshea,[n] the king
of Assyria captured Samaria. He deported[o]
the Israelites to Assyria and settled them in
Halah and by the Habor, Gozan's river, and in
the cities of the Medes.[p]

Why Israel Fell

7This disaster happened because the people
of Israel had sinned against the LORD their
God who had brought them out of the land
of Egypt from the power of Pharaoh king
of Egypt[q] and because they had worshiped[E]
other gods.[r] 8They had lived according to the
customs of the nations that the LORD had dispossessed before the Israelites[s] and the customs the kings of Israel had introduced.[t] 9The
Israelites secretly did what was not right[F]
against the LORD their God. They built ·high
places in all their towns from watchtower[u]
to fortified city. 10They set up for themselves
sacred pillars[v] and ·Asherah poles[w] on every
high hill and under every green tree.[x] 11They
burned incense on all the high places just like
those nations that the LORD had driven out
before them. They did evil things, provoking
the LORD. 12They served idols, although the
LORD had told them, "You must not do this."[y]
13Still, the LORD warned[z] Israel and Judah
through every prophet and every seer, saying,
"Turn from your evil ways and keep My commands and statutes according to all the law I
commanded your ancestors and sent to you
through My servants the prophets."[aa]
14But they would not listen. Instead they became obstinate like[G] their ancestors who did
not believe the LORD their God.[ab] 15They rejected His statutes and His covenant He had
made with their ancestors[ac] and the decrees
He had given them. They pursued worthless
idols and became worthless themselves,[ad] following the surrounding nations the LORD
had commanded them not to imitate.[ae]
16They abandoned all the commands of the
LORD their God. They made cast images[af] for
themselves, two calves, and an Asherah pole.[ag]

[a]16:13 Lv 7:11-21 [b]16:14 Ex 40:24 [c]16:17 1Kg 7:27-28 [d]1Kg 7:23-25 [e]16:19-20 2Ch 28:26-27 [f]16:19 2Kg 15:36 [g]16:20 Is 14:28 [h]17:1 2Kg 15:30 [i]17:2 2Kg 15:24,28 [j]17:3 Hs 10:14 [k]2Kg 18:9-12 [l]17:4 Is 31:1 [m]17:5 2Kg 18:9-10; Hs 13:16 [n]17:6 Hs 1:4; 13:16 [o]Dt 28:64; 29:27-28 [p]1Ch 5:26 [q]17:7 Jos 24:5-7 [r]Jdg 6:10 [s]17:8 Lv 18:3; Dt 18:9 [t]2Kg 16:3; 17:19 [u]17:9 2Kg 18:8 [v]17:10 Ex 23:24 [w]1Kg 14:15,23; 15:13; 2Kg 18:4 [x]Dt 12:2 [y]17:12 Ex 20:4-5 [z]17:13 Neh 9:29-30 [aa]1Kg 9:6-9; 18:18-21 [ab]17:14 Ex 32:9; 33:3; Nm 14:11 [ac]17:15 Ex 24:6-8 [ad]Jr 2:5; Rm 1:21-23 [ae]Dt 12:30-31 [af]17:16 1Kg 12:28 [ag]1Kg 14:15,23

[A]16:15 Hb obscure [B]16:17 Lit *the stands* [C]16:17 Lit *sea* [D]17:4 Lit *as year by year* [E]17:7 Lit *feared* [F]17:9 Or *Israelites spoke untrue words* [G]17:14 Lit *they stiffened their neck like the neck of*

They worshiped the whole heavenly ·host[a]
and served ·Baal.[b] 17They made their sons and
daughters pass through the fire[c] and practiced ·divination and interpreted omens.[d]
They devoted themselves to do what was evil
in the LORD's sight and provoked Him.[e]
18Therefore, the LORD was very angry with
Israel, and He removed them from His presence.[f] Only the tribe of Judah remained.[g]
19Even Judah did not keep the commands
of the LORD their God[h] but lived according
to the customs Israel had introduced.[i] 20So
the LORD rejected all the descendants of Israel, afflicted them, and handed them over to
plunderers until He had banished them from
His presence.[j]

Summary of Israel's History

21When the LORD tore[k] Israel from the
house of David, Israel made Jeroboam son of
Nebat king.[l] Then Jeroboam led Israel away
from following the LORD and caused them to
commit great sin. 22The Israelites persisted
in all the sins that Jeroboam committed and
did not turn away from them.[m] 23Finally, the
LORD removed Israel from His presence just
as He had declared through all His servants
the prophets. So Israel has been exiled to Assyria from their homeland until today.[n]

Foreign Refugees in Israel

24Then the king of Assyria brought people
from Babylon, Cuthah, Avva, Hamath, and
Sepharvaim and settled them in place of the
Israelites in the cities of Samaria. The settlers
took possession of Samaria and lived in its cities.[o] 25When they first lived there, they did not
·fear ·Yahweh. So the LORD sent lions among
them, which killed some of them.[p] 26The settlers spoke to the king of Assyria, saying, "The
nations that you have deported and placed
in the cities of Samaria do not know the requirements of the God of the land. Therefore
He has sent lions among them that are killing
them because the people don't know the requirements of the God of the land."
27Then the king of Assyria issued a command: "Send back one of the priests you deported.[q] Have him go and live there so he can
teach them the requirements of the God of
the land." 28So one of the priests they had
deported came and lived in Bethel,[r] and he
began to teach them how they should fear
Yahweh.
29But the people of each nation were still
making their own gods in the cities where
they lived and putting them in the shrines
of the high places that the people of Samaria
had made.[s] 30The men of Babylon made Suc-
coth-benoth, the men of Cuth made Nergal,
the men of Hamath made Ashima, 31the Avvites made Nibhaz and Tartak, and the Se-
pharvites burned their children in the fire[t]
to Adrammelech and Anammelech, the gods
of the Sepharvaim. 32They feared the LORD,
but they also appointed from their number
priests to serve them in the shrines of the
high places.[u] 33They feared the LORD, but they
also worshiped their own gods[v] according
to the custom of the nations where they had
been deported from.
34They are still practicing the former customs to this day. None of them fear the LORD
or observe their statutes and ordinances,
the law and commandments the LORD commanded the descendants of Jacob. He had
renamed him Israel.[w] 35The LORD made a
covenant with them and commanded them,
"Do not fear other gods; do not bow down to
them;[x] do not serve them; do not sacrifice to
them.[y] 36Instead fear the LORD, who brought
you from the land of Egypt with great power[z]
and an outstretched arm.[aa] You are to bow
down to Him, and you are to sacrifice to Him.
37You are to be careful always[ab] to observe the
statutes, the ordinances, the law, and the
commandments He wrote for you; do not
fear other gods. 38Do not forget the covenant
that I have made with you.[ac] Do not fear other
gods, 39but fear the LORD your God, and He
will deliver you from the hand of all your enemies."[ad]
40However, they would not listen but continued practicing their former customs.
41These nations feared the LORD but also
served their idols. Their children and grandchildren continue doing as their fathers did
until today.[ae]

Judah's King Hezekiah

18 In the third year of Israel's King
Hoshea[af] son of Elah, Hezekiah[ag] son
of Ahaz became king of Judah. 2He was 25
years old when he became king and reigned

---

[a] 17:16 2Kg 21:3
[b] 1Kg 16:31-33; Am 5:26; Zph 1:5
[c] 17:17 2Kg 16:3
[d] Lv 19:26; Dt 18:10-12; 2Kg 16:3
[e] 1Kg 21:20
[f] 17:18 2Kg 17:6
[g] 1Kg 11:13,32,36
[h] 17:19 1Kg 14:22-23
[i] 2Kg 16:3
[j] 17:20 2Kg 15:29; 17:6
[k] 17:21 1Kg 11:11,31
[l] 1Kg 12:20
[m] 17:21-22 1Kg 12:28-33
[n] 17:23 2Kg 17:6,13
[o] 17:24 Ezr 4:10
[p] 17:25 1Kg 13:24
[q] 17:27 2Kg 17:6
[r] 17:28 1Kg 12:29,32-33
[s] 17:29 1Kg 12:31; 13:32
[t] 17:31 2Kg 17:17
[u] 17:32 Jdg 17:5-13; 1Kg 12:31; 13:33
[v] 17:33 Zph 1:5
[w] 17:34 Gn 32:28; 35:10
[x] 17:35 Ex 20:5; Dt 5:9; Jdg 6:10
[y] Dt 5:9
[z] 17:36 Ex 14:15-30
[aa] Ex 6:6; 9:15
[ab] 17:37 Dt 5:32
[ac] 17:38 Dt 4:23; 6:12
[ad] 17:39 Ex 23:22; Dt 20:1-4; 23:14
[ae] 17:41 1Kg 18:21; Ezr 4:2; Mt 6:24
[af] 18:1 2Kg 17:1
[ag] 2Ch 28:27

29 years in Jerusalem. His mother's name
was Abi[A] daughter of Zechariah. 3 He did
what was right in the LORD's sight just as his
ancestor David had done.[a] 4 He removed the
·high places, shattered the sacred pillars, and
cut down the ·Asherah poles.[b] He broke into
pieces the bronze snake that Moses made,[c] for
the Israelites burned incense to it up to that
time. He called it Nehushtan.[B]
5 Hezekiah trusted in the LORD God of Israel;[d] not one of the kings of Judah was like
him, either before him or after him.[e] 6 He remained faithful to ·Yahweh[f] and did not turn
from following Him but kept the commands
the LORD had commanded Moses.
7 The LORD was with him, and wherever he
went he prospered.[g] He rebelled against the
king of Assyria and did not serve him.[h] 8 He
defeated the Philistines as far as Gaza and its
borders,[i] from watchtower[j] to fortified city.

Review of Israel's Fall

9 In the fourth year of King Hezekiah, which
was the seventh year of Israel's King Hoshea
son of Elah, Shalmaneser king of Assyria
marched against Samaria and besieged it.[k]
10 The Assyrians captured it at the end of three
years. In the sixth year of Hezekiah, which
was the ninth year of Israel's King Hoshea, Samaria was captured. 11 The king of Assyria deported the Israelites to Assyria and put them
in Halah and by the Habor, Gozan's river, and
in the cities of the Medes,[l] 12 because they did
not listen to the voice of the LORD their God
but violated His covenant — all He had commanded Moses the servant of the LORD. They
did not listen, and they did not obey.[m]

Sennacherib's Invasion

13 In the fourteenth year of King Hezekiah,
Sennacherib king of Assyria attacked all the
fortified cities of Judah and captured them.[n]
14 So Hezekiah king of Judah sent word to the
king of Assyria at Lachish,[o] saying, "I have
done wrong;[p] withdraw from me. Whatever
you demand from me, I will pay." The king of
Assyria demanded 11 tons[C] of silver and one
ton[D] of gold from King Hezekiah of Judah.
15 So Hezekiah gave him all the silver found in
the LORD's temple and in the treasuries of the
king's palace.
16 At that time Hezekiah stripped the gold
from the doors of the LORD's sanctuary and
from the doorposts he had overlaid and gave
it to the king of Assyria.[q]
17 Then the king of Assyria sent the Tartan,[r]
the Rab-saris, and the ·Rabshakeh, along with
a massive army, from Lachish to King Hezekiah at Jerusalem.[s] They advanced and came
to Jerusalem, and[E] they took their position
by the aqueduct of the upper pool, which is
by the highway to the Fuller's Field.[t] 18 Then
they called for the king, but Eliakim[u] son of
Hilkiah, who was in charge of the palace,
Shebnah[v] the court secretary, and Joah son
of Asaph, the court historian, came out to
them.[w]

The Rabshakeh's Speech

19 Then[x] the Rabshakeh said to them, "Tell
Hezekiah this is what the great king, the king
of Assyria, says: 'What are you relying on?[F,y]
20 You think mere words are strategy and
strength for war. What are you now relying on
so that you have rebelled against me?[z] 21 Look,
you are now trusting in Egypt, that splintered
reed of a staff[aa] that will enter and pierce the
hand of anyone who leans on it.[ab] This is how
Pharaoh king of Egypt is to all who trust in
him. 22 Suppose you say to me: We trust in the
LORD our God. Isn't He the One whose high
places and altars Hezekiah has removed,[ac]
saying to Judah and to Jerusalem: You must
worship at this altar in Jerusalem?'
23 "So now make a bargain with my master
the king of Assyria. I'll give you 2,000 horses
if you're able to supply riders for them!
24 How then can you drive back a single officer[ad] among the least of my master's servants
and trust in Egypt for chariots and for horsemen? 25 Have I attacked this place to destroy it
without the LORD's approval?[ae] The LORD said
to me, 'Attack this land and destroy it.'"
26 Then Eliakim son of Hilkiah, Shebnah,
and Joah said to the Rabshakeh, "Please speak
to your servants in Aramaic,[af] since we understand it. Don't speak with us in Hebrew[G]
within earshot of the people on the wall."

[a] **18:2-3** 2Ch 29:1-2 [b] **18:4** 2Kg 17:10; 18:22; 2Ch 31:1 [c] Nm 21:5-9 [d] **18:5** 2Kg 19:10 [e] 1Kg 3:12; 2Kg 23:25 [f] **18:6** Dt 10:20; Jos 23:8 [g] **18:7** Gn 39:2-3; 1Sm 18:14 [h] 2Kg 16:7 [i] **18:8** 2Ch 28:18; Is 14:29 [j] 2Kg 17:9 [k] **18:9** 2Kg 17:3-7 [l] **18:10-11** 2Kg 17:6; 1Ch 5:26 [m] **18:12** 1Kg 9:6; 2Kg 17:7-18; Dn 9:6,10 [n] **18:13** 2Ch 32:1; Is 36:1 [o] **18:14** 2Kg 19:8 [p] Is 24:5; 33:8 [q] **18:15-16** 2Kg 12:18; 16:8; 2Ch 16:2 [r] **18:17** Is 20:1 [s] 2Ch 32:9 [t] 2Kg 20:20; Is 7:3 [u] **18:18** 2Kg 19:2; Is 22:20 [v] Is 22:15 [w] **18:17-18** Is 36:2-3 [x] **18:19-37** Is 36:4-22 [y] **18:19** 2Kg 18:5; 2Ch 32:10 [z] **18:20** 2Kg 18:7 [aa] **18:21** Is 30:2-3,7 [ab] Ezk 29:6-7 [ac] **18:22** 2Kg 18:4; 2Ch 31:1; 32:11-12 [ad] **18:24** Is 10:8 [ae] **18:25** 2Kg 19:6,22; 24:3; 2Ch 35:21 [af] **18:26** Ezr 4:7; Dn 2:4

[A] **18:2** = Abijah in 2Ch 29:1 [B] **18:4** = A bronze thing [C] **18:14** Lit *300 talents* [D] **18:14** Lit *30 talents* [E] **18:17** LXX, Syr, Vg; MT reads *and came and* [F] **18:19** Lit *What is this trust which you trust* [G] **18:26** Lit *Judahite*

27 But the Rabshakeh said to them, "Has my
master sent me only to your master and to
you to speak these words? Hasn't he also sent
me to the men who sit on the wall, destined
with you to eat their own excrement and
drink their own urine?"[a]

28 The Rabshakeh stood and called out
loudly in Hebrew.[A] Then he spoke: "Hear the
word of the great king, the king of Assyria.
29 This is what the king says: 'Don't let Hezekiah deceive[b] you; he can't deliver you from
my hand.[c] 30 Don't let Hezekiah persuade you
to trust in the LORD by saying: Certainly the
LORD will deliver us! This city will not be
handed over to the king of Assyria.'[d]

31 "Don't listen to Hezekiah, for this is what
the king of Assyria says: 'Make peace[B] with me
and surrender to me. Then every one of you
may eat from his own vine and his own fig
tree,[e] and every one may drink water from his
own cistern 32 until I come and take you away
to a land like your own land — a land of grain
and new wine, a land of bread and vineyards,
a land of olive trees and honey[f] — so that you
may live[g] and not die. But don't listen to Hezekiah when he misleads you, saying: The LORD
will deliver us. 33 Has any of the gods of the nations ever delivered[h] his land from the power
of the king of Assyria? 34 Where are the gods
of Hamath and Arpad? Where are the gods of
Sepharvaim, Hena, and Ivvah?[C] Have they delivered Samaria from my hand?[i] 35 Who
among all the gods of the lands has delivered
his land from my power? So will the LORD deliver Jerusalem?'"[j]

36 But the people kept silent; they didn't say
anything, for the king's command was, "Don't
answer him." 37 Then Eliakim son of Hilkiah,
who was in charge of the palace, Shebna the
court secretary, and Joah son of Asaph, the
court historian,[k] came to Hezekiah with their
clothes torn[l] and reported to him the words
of the Rabshakeh.

Hezekiah Seeks Isaiah's Counsel

19 When King Hezekiah heard their
report, he tore his clothes, covered
himself with ·sackcloth,[m] and went into the
LORD's temple.[n] 2 Then he sent Eliakim, who
was in charge of the palace, Shebna the court
secretary,[o] and the leading priests, who were
wearing sackcloth,[p] to the prophet Isaiah[q]
son of Amoz. 3 They said to him, "This is what
Hezekiah says: 'Today is a day of distress, rebuke, and disgrace, for children have come to
the point of birth,[r] but there is no strength
to deliver them. 4 Perhaps ·Yahweh your God[s]
will hear[t] all the words of the ·Rabshakeh,
whom his master the king of Assyria sent to
mock the living God, and will rebuke[u] him for
the words that Yahweh your God has heard.
Therefore, offer a prayer for the surviving
remnant.'"[v]

5 So the servants of King Hezekiah went to
Isaiah, 6 who said to them, "Tell your master
this, 'The LORD says: Don't be afraid[w] because
of the words you have heard, that the king of
Assyria's attendants[x] have blasphemed[y] Me
with. 7 I am about to put a spirit in him, and
he will hear a rumor and return to his own
land[z] where I will cause him to fall by the
sword.'"[aa]

Sennacherib's Departing Threat

8 When[ab] the Rabshakeh heard that the king
of Assyria had left Lachish,[ac] he returned and
found him fighting against Libnah.[ad] 9 The
king had heard this about Tirhakah king of
·Cush: "Look, he has set out to fight against
you." So he again sent messengers to Hezekiah, saying, 10 "Say this to Hezekiah king of
Judah: 'Don't let your God, whom you trust,[ae]
deceive you by promising that Jerusalem will
not be handed over to the king of Assyria.[af]
11 Look, you have heard what the kings of
Assyria have done to all the countries: they
·completely destroyed them. Will you be rescued? 12 Did the gods of the nations[ag] that my
predecessors destroyed rescue them — nations such as Gozan,[ah] Haran,[ai] Rezeph, and
the Edenites[aj] in Telassar? 13 Where is the king
of Hamath, the king of Arpad, the king of the
city of Sepharvaim, Hena, or Ivvah?'"[ak]

Hezekiah's Prayer

14 Hezekiah took[al] the letter[am] from the
hand of the messengers, read it, then went
up to the LORD's temple, and spread it out before the LORD.[an] 15 Then Hezekiah prayed before the LORD:

[a] **18:26-27** Is 36:11-12
[b] **18:29** 2Kg 19:10
[c] 2Ch 32:15
[d] **18:30** 2Ch 32:18
[e] **18:31** 1Kg 4:25
[f] **18:32** Dt 8:7-9; 11:12
[g] Dt 30:19
[h] **18:33** 2Kg 19:12; Is 10:10-11
[i] **18:34** 2Kg 17:24; 19:13
[j] **18:35** 2Ch 32:14; Ps 2:1-4; Dn 3:15
[k] **18:37** 2Kg 18:26; 19:2
[l] 2Kg 6:30; Is 33:7
[m] **19:1** 1Kg 21:27; 2Kg 18:37; Ps 69:11
[n] 2Ch 32:20; Is 37:1
[o] **19:2** 2Kg 18:26,37
[p] 2Sm 3:31
[q] Is 1:1; 2:1
[r] **19:3** Hs 13:13
[s] **19:4** 1Sm 17:26; 2Kg 18:35
[t] Jos 14:12; 2Sm 16:12
[u] Ps 50:21
[v] 2Kg 19:30; Is 1:9
[w] **19:6** Is 37:6
[x] 2Kg 18:17
[y] 2Kg 18:22-25,30,35
[z] **19:7** 2Kg 7:6
[aa] 2Kg 19:35-37
[ab] **19:8-13** Is 37:8-13
[ac] **19:8** 2Kg 18:14
[ad] Jos 10:29
[ae] **19:10** 2Kg 18:5
[af] 2Kg 18:29-30
[ag] **19:12** 2Kg 18:33,35
[ah] 2Kg 17:6
[ai] Gn 11:31
[aj] Is 37:12
[ak] **19:13** 2Kg 18:34
[al] **19:14-19** Is 37:14-20
[am] **19:14** 2Kg 5:7
[an] Is 37:14

[A] **18:28** Lit *Judahite* [B] **18:31** Lit *a blessing* [C] **18:34** Some LXX mss, Old Lat read *Sepharvaim? Where are the gods of the land of Samaria?*

LORD God of Israel who is enthroned
above the ·cherubim,[a] You are God — You
alone — of all the kingdoms of the earth.
You made the heavens and the earth.[b]
16 Listen closely, LORD, and hear; open
Your eyes, LORD, and see.[c] Hear the words
that Sennacherib has sent to mock the living God.[d] 17 LORD, it is true that the kings
of Assyria have devastated the nations
and their lands.[e] 18 They have thrown
their gods into the fire, for they were not
gods but made by human hands — wood
and stone.[f] So they have destroyed them.
19 Now, LORD our God, please save us from
his hand so that all the kingdoms of the
earth may know that You are the LORD
God — You alone.[g]

God's Answer through Isaiah

20 Then[h] Isaiah son of Amoz sent a message
to Hezekiah: "The LORD, the God of Israel
says: 'I have heard your prayer[i] to Me about
Sennacherib king of Assyria.'[j] 21 This is the
word the LORD has spoken against him:

Virgin Daughter ·Zion[k]
despises you and scorns you:
Daughter Jerusalem
shakes her head behind your back.[A,l]
22 Who is it you mocked
and blasphemed?[m]
Against whom have you raised your voice
and lifted your eyes in pride?
Against the Holy One of Israel![n]
23 You have mocked the Lord[B] through[C]
your messengers.[o]
You have said:
With my many chariots[p]
I have gone up to the heights
of the mountains,
to the far recesses of Lebanon.
I cut down its tallest cedars,
its choice cypress trees.
I came to its farthest outpost,
its densest forest.
24 I dug wells,
and I drank foreign waters.
I dried up all the streams of Egypt[q]
with the soles of my feet.

[a]19:15 Ex 35:22
[b]Gn 1:1; 2Kg 5:15; Is 44:6
[c]19:16 Dn 9:18
[d]2Kg 19:4; Ps 31:2; Is 37:17
[e]19:17 2Kg 18:34
[f]19:18 Is 44:9-20; Jr 10:3-5; Ac 17:29
[g]19:19 1Kg 8:42-43; Is 43:10-11
[h]19:20-34 Is 37:21-35
[i]19:20 2Kg 20:5
[j]Is 37:21
[k]19:21 Jr 14:17; Lm 2:13
[l]Ps 22:7-8; 109:25; Mt 27:39
[m]19:22 2Kg 19:4,6
[n]Is 5:24; 30:11-15; Jr 51:5
[o]19:23 2Kg 18:17; 19:4
[p]Ps 20:7; Jr 50:37
[q]19:24 Is 19:6
[r]19:25 Is 40:21; 45:7
[s]Is 10:5
[t]19:26 Ps 129:6
[u]19:27 Ps 139:1-2
[v]19:28 Ezk 19:9; 29:4; 38:4
[w]19:29 Ex 3:14; 2Kg 20:8-9; Is 7:14
[x]19:30 2Kg 19:4; 2Ch 32:22-23
[y]19:31 Is 10:20
[z]Is 9:7
[aa]19:32 Is 8:7-10
[ab]19:34 1Kg 11:12-13; 2Kg 20:6; Is 31:5

25 Have you not heard?[r]
I designed it long ago;
I planned it in days gone by.
I have now brought it to pass,[s]
and you have crushed fortified cities
into piles of rubble.
26 Their inhabitants have
become powerless,
dismayed, and ashamed.
They are plants of the field,
tender grass,
grass on the rooftops,[t]
blasted by the east wind.[D]

27 But I know your sitting down,[E,u]
your going out and your coming in,
and your raging against Me.
28 Because your raging against Me
and your arrogance have reached
My ears,
I will put My hook in your nose[v]
and My bit in your mouth;
I will make you go back
the way you came.

29 "This will be the sign[w] for you: This year
you will eat what grows on its own, and in the
second year what grows from that. But in the
third year sow and reap, plant vineyards and
eat their fruit. 30 The surviving remnant[x] of
the house of Israel will again take root downward and bear fruit upward. 31 For a remnant
will go out from Jerusalem and survivors,
from Mount Zion.[y] The zeal of the LORD of
·Hosts will accomplish this.[z]

32 Therefore, this is what the LORD says
about the king of Assyria:
He will not enter this city
or shoot an arrow there
or come before it with a shield
or build up an assault ramp
against it.[aa]
33 He will go back
on the road that he came
and he will not enter this city.
This is the LORD's declaration.
34 I will defend this city and rescue it
for My sake and for the sake of My
servant David."[ab]

A19:21 Lit *behind you* B19:23 Many mss read *LORD* C19:23 Lit *by the hand of* D19:26 DSS; MT reads *blasted before standing grain*; Is 37:27 E19:27 LXX, DSS read *your rising up and your sitting down*; Is 37:28

Defeat and Death of Sennacherib

35 That night the angel of the LORD went
out and struck down 185,000 in the camp
of the Assyrians. When the people got up the
next morning — there were all the dead bodies![a] 36 So Sennacherib king of Assyria broke
camp and left. He returned home and lived
in Nineveh.[b]

37 One day, while he was worshiping in the
temple of his god Nisroch, his sons Adrammelech[c] and Sharezer struck him down with
the sword and escaped to the land of Ararat.[d]
Then his son Esar-haddon[e] became king in
his place.

Hezekiah's Illness and Recovery

20 In those days[f] Hezekiah became terminally ill.[g] The prophet Isaiah[h] son
of Amoz came and said to him, "This is what
the LORD says: 'Put your affairs in order,[A] for
you are about to die; you will not recover.'"[i]

2 Then Hezekiah turned his face to the wall[j]
and prayed to the LORD, 3 "Please LORD, remember[k] how I have walked before You faithfully and wholeheartedly and have done what
pleases You."[B,l] And Hezekiah wept bitterly.[m]

4 Isaiah had not yet gone out of the inner
courtyard when the word of the LORD came
to him: 5 "Go back and tell Hezekiah, the
leader[n] of My people, 'This is what the LORD
God of your ancestor David says: I have heard
your prayer;[o] I have seen your tears. Look, I
will heal you. On the third day from now you
will go up to the LORD's temple. 6 I will add 15
years to your life. I will deliver you and this
city from the hand of the king of Assyria. I
will defend this city for My sake and for the
sake of My servant David.'"[p]

7 Then Isaiah said, "Bring a lump of pressed
figs." So they brought it and applied it to his
infected skin, and he recovered.[q]

8 Hezekiah had asked Isaiah, "What is the
sign[r] that the LORD will heal me and that I will
go up to the LORD's temple on the third day?"

9 Isaiah said, "This is the sign[s] to you from
the LORD that He will do what He has promised: Should the shadow go ahead 10 steps or
go back 10 steps?"

10 Then Hezekiah answered, "It's easy

[a] **19:35** 2Ch 32:21; Is 37:36
[b] **19:36** Jnh 1:2
[c] **19:37** 2Kg 17:31
[d] Gn 8:4; Jr 51:27
[e] Gn 10:11; Ezr 4:2
[f] **20:1-11** Is 38:1-8
[g] **20:1** 2Ch 32:24
[h] Is 1:1; 2:1
[i] 2Sm 17:23
[j] **20:2** 1Kg 21:4
[k] **20:3** Neh 5:19; 13:14,22,31
[l] 2Kg 18:3-6
[m] 2Sm 12:21-22
[n] **20:5** 1Sm 9:16; 10:1
[o] Ps 39:12
[p] **20:6** 2Kg 19:34
[q] **20:7** Is 38:21
[r] **20:8** Jdg 6:17,37,39
[s] **20:9** Is 38:7
[t] **20:11** Jos 10:12-14; Is 38:8
[u] **20:12-19** Is 39:1-8
[v] **20:13** 2Ch 32:27
[w] **20:17** 2Kg 24:13; 2Ch 36:10
[x] **20:18** 2Kg 24:12; 2Ch 33:11
[y] Dn 1:3-7,11
[z] **20:19** 1Sm 3:18; 2Kg 22:20
[aa] **20:20** Neh 3:16; Is 7:3
[ab] 2Ch 32:30
[ac] 2Kg 16:19
[ad] **20:20-21** 2Ch 32:32-33

for the shadow to lengthen 10 steps. No,
let the shadow go back 10 steps." 11 So Isaiah
the prophet called out to the LORD, and He
brought the shadow[C] back the 10 steps it had
descended on Ahaz's stairway.[D,t]

Hezekiah's Folly

12 At that time[u] Merodach-baladan[E] son of
Baladan, king of Babylon, sent letters and a
gift to Hezekiah since he heard that he had
been sick. 13 Hezekiah gave them a hearing and showed them his whole treasure
house — the silver, the gold, the spices, and
the precious oil — and his armory, and everything that was found in his treasuries. There
was nothing in his palace and in all his realm
that Hezekiah did not show them.[v]

14 Then the prophet Isaiah came to King Hezekiah and asked him, "Where did these men
come from and what did they say to you?"

Hezekiah replied, "They came from a distant country, from Babylon."

15 Isaiah asked, "What have they seen in
your palace?"

Hezekiah answered, "They have seen everything in my palace. There isn't anything in my
treasuries that I didn't show them."

16 Then Isaiah said to Hezekiah, "Hear the
word of the LORD: 17 'The time will certainly
come when everything in your palace and all
that your fathers have stored up until this day
will be carried off to Babylon; nothing will be
left,'[w] says the LORD. 18 'Some of your descendants who come from you will be taken away,[x]
and they will become eunuchs[F] in the palace
of the king of Babylon.'"[y]

19 Then Hezekiah said to Isaiah, "The word
of the LORD that you have spoken is good,"[z]
for he thought: Why not, if there will be peace
and security during my lifetime?

Hezekiah's Death

20 The rest of the events of Hezekiah's reign,
along with all his might and how he made the
pool[aa] and the tunnel and brought water into
the city,[ab] are written in the Historical Record
of Judah's Kings.[ac] 21 Hezekiah rested with his
fathers, and his son Manasseh became king
in his place.[ad]

[A] **20:1** Lit *Command your house* [B] **20:3** Lit *what is good in Your eyes* [C] **20:11** Lit *shadow on the steps* [D] **20:11** Tg, Vg; DSS read *on the steps of Ahaz's roof chamber*; Is 38:8 [E] **20:12** Some Hb mss, LXX, Syr, Tg, some Vg mss, Is 39:1; other Hb mss read *Berodach-baladan* [F] **20:18** Or *court officials*

Judah's King Manasseh

21 Manasseh[a] was 12 years old when he became king and reigned 55 years in Jerusalem. His mother's name was Hephzibah.[b] 2 He did what was evil in the LORD's sight,[c] imitating the detestable practices of the nations that the LORD had dispossessed before the Israelites.[d] 3 He rebuilt the ·high places that his father Hezekiah had destroyed[e] and reestablished the altars for ·Baal. He made an ·Asherah,[f] as King Ahab of Israel had done;[g] he also worshiped the whole heavenly ·host[h] and served them. 4 He built altars in the LORD's temple,[i] where the LORD had said, "Jerusalem is where I will put My name."[j] 5 He built altars to the whole heavenly host[k] in both courtyards of the LORD's temple.[l] 6 He made his son pass through the fire,[m] practiced witchcraft and ·divination, and consulted mediums and spiritists.[n] He did a great amount of evil in the LORD's sight, provoking Him.[o]

7 Manasseh set up the carved image of Asherah, which he made, in the temple that the LORD had spoken about to David and his son Solomon, "I will establish My name forever in this temple and in Jerusalem, which I have chosen out of all the tribes of Israel.[p] 8 I will never again cause the feet of the Israelites to wander from the land I gave to their ancestors if only they will be careful to do all I have commanded them—the whole law that My servant Moses commanded them."[q] 9 But they did not listen; Manasseh caused them to stray so that they did greater evil than the nations the LORD had destroyed before the Israelites.[r]

10 The LORD spoke through His servants the prophets, saying, 11 "Since Manasseh king of Judah has committed all these detestable things[s]—greater evil than the Amorites[t] who preceded him had done—and by means of his idols has also caused Judah to sin, 12 this is what the LORD God of Israel says: 'I am about to bring such disaster on Jerusalem and Judah that everyone who hears about it will shudder.[u] 13 I will stretch over Jerusalem the measuring line used on Samaria and the mason's level used on the house of Ahab,[v] and I will wipe[w] Jerusalem ·clean as one wipes a bowl—wiping it and turning it upside down. 14 I will abandon the remnant[x] of My inheritance and hand them over to their enemies. They will become plunder and spoil to all their enemies, 15 because they have done what is evil in My sight and have provoked Me from the day their ancestors came out of Egypt until today.'"[y]

16 Manasseh also shed so much innocent blood that he filled Jerusalem with it from one end to another.[z] This was in addition to his sin that he caused Judah to commit. Consequently, they did what was evil in the LORD's sight.

Manasseh's Death

17 The rest[aa] of the events of Manasseh's reign, along with all his accomplishments and the sin that he committed, are written in the Historical Record of Judah's Kings.[ab] 18 Manasseh rested with his fathers and was buried in the garden of his own house, the garden of Uzza. His son Amon became king in his place.

Judah's King Amon

19 Amon was 22 years old when he became king[ac] and reigned two years in Jerusalem. His mother's name was Meshullemeth daughter of Haruz; she was from Jotbah. 20 He did what was evil in the LORD's sight as his father Manasseh had done.[ad] 21 He walked in all the ways his father had walked; he served the idols his father had served, and he worshiped them.[ae] 22 He abandoned the LORD God of his ancestors[af] and did not walk in the way of the LORD.[ag]

23 Amon's servants conspired against the king and killed him in his own house.[ah] 24 Then the common people[A] executed[ai] all those who had conspired against King Amon and made his son Josiah[aj] king in his place.

25 The rest of the events of Amon's reign, along with his accomplishments, are written in the Historical Record of Judah's Kings. 26 He was buried in his tomb in the garden of Uzza, and his son Josiah became king in his place.

Judah's King Josiah

22 Josiah[ak] was eight years old when he became king and reigned 31 years in Jerusalem. His mother's name was Jedidah

[a] **21:1-9** 2Ch 33:1-9
[b] **21:1** Is 62:4
[c] **21:2** 2Kg 20:16; Jr 15:4
[d] 2Kg 16:3
[e] **21:3** 2Kg 18:4; 2Ch 31:1
[f] 2Kg 23:26
[g] 1Kg 16:32-33
[h] 2Kg 17:16; 23:5
[i] **21:4** 2Kg 16:10-16
[j] Dt 12:11,14; 1Kg 11:13
[k] **21:5** 2Kg 23:4-5
[l] 1Kg 7:12; 2Kg 23:12
[m] **21:6** Lv 18:21; 2Kg 16:3; 2Ch 28:3
[n] Lv 19:26,31; Dt 18:10-12; 2Kg 23:24
[o] 2Kg 23:26
[p] **21:7** Dt 12:5; 1Kg 11:32
[q] **21:8** 2Sm 7:10; 1Kg 9:1-9
[r] **21:9** 1Kg 14:9
[s] **21:11** 2Kg 21:2; 24:3-4
[t] Gn 15:16; 1Kg 21:16
[u] **21:12** 1Sm 3:11; Jr 19:3
[v] **21:13** Is 34:11; Am 7:7-8
[w] 2Kg 23:27
[x] **21:14** 2Kg 19:4; Jr 6:9
[y] **21:15** Ex 32:22; Jr 25:7
[z] **21:16** 2Kg 24:4
[aa] **21:17-18** 2Ch 33:18-20
[ab] **21:17** 2Kg 20:20
[ac] **21:19-24** 2Ch 33:21-25
[ad] **21:20** 2Kg 21:2-7,11,16
[ae] **21:21** 2Kg 16:2
[af] **21:22** 1Kg 11:33
[ag] 2Kg 22:17
[ah] **21:23** 2Kg 12:20; 14:19
[ai] **21:24** 2Kg 14:5
[aj] 2Kg 22:1
[ak] **22:1-2** 2Ch 34:1-2

[A] **21:24** Lit *the people of the land*

the daughter of Adaiah; she was from Bozkath.[a] 2He did what was right in the LORD's
sight and walked in all the ways of his ancestor
David;[b] he did not turn to the right or the left.[c]

Josiah Repairs the Temple

3In the eighteenth year of King Josiah, the
king sent the court secretary Shaphan son
of Azaliah, son of Meshullam, to the LORD's
temple,[d] saying, 4"Go up to Hilkiah the high
priest so that he may total up the money
brought into the LORD's temple — the money
the doorkeepers have collected from the people.[e] 5It is to be put into the hands of those
doing the work — those who oversee the
LORD's temple. They in turn are to give it to
the workmen in the LORD's temple to repair
the damage.[f] 6They are to give it to the carpenters, builders, and masons to buy timber and
quarried stone to repair the temple.[g] 7But no
accounting is to be required from them for
the money put into their hands since they
work with integrity."[h]

The Book of the Law Found

8Hilkiah the high priest told Shaphan the
court secretary, "I have found the book of
the law[i] in the LORD's temple," and he gave
the book to Shaphan, who read it.
9Then Shaphan the court secretary went to
the king and reported,[A] "Your servants have
emptied out the money that was found in
the temple and have put it into the hand of
those doing the work — those who oversee
the LORD's temple." 10Then Shaphan the court
secretary told the king, "Hilkiah the priest
has given me a book," and Shaphan read it in
the presence of the king.[j]
11When the king heard the words of the
book of the law, he tore his clothes.[k] 12Then
he commanded Hilkiah the priest, Ahikam[l]
son of Shaphan, Achbor[m] son of Micaiah,
Shaphan the court secretary, and the king's
servant Asaiah: 13"Go and inquire of the LORD
for me, the people, and all Judah about the
instruction in this book that has been found.
For great is the LORD's wrath that is kindled
against us because our ancestors have not
obeyed the words of this book in order to do
everything written about us."[n]

Huldah's Prophecy of Judgment

14So[o] Hilkiah the priest, Ahikam, Achbor,
Shaphan, and Asaiah went to the prophetess[p]
Huldah, wife of Shallum son of Tikvah,[q] son
of Harhas,[B] keeper of the wardrobe. She lived
in Jerusalem in the Second District.[r] They
spoke with her.
15She said to them, "This is what the LORD
God of Israel says, 'Say to the man who sent
you to Me: 16This is what the LORD says: I am
about to bring disaster on this place and on
its inhabitants, fulfilling all the words of the
book that the king of Judah has read,[s] 17be-
cause they have abandoned Me and burned
incense to other gods in order to provoke Me
with all the work of their hands. My wrath
will be kindled against this place, and it will
not be quenched.[t] 18Say this to the king of
Judah who sent you to inquire of the LORD:
This is what the LORD God of Israel says: As
for the words that you heard,[u] 19because your
heart was tender and you humbled yourself before the LORD[v] when you heard what
I spoke against this place and against its inhabitants, that they would become a desolation and a curse,[w] and because you have torn
your clothes and wept before Me, I Myself
have heard you — this is the LORD's declaration — 20therefore, I will indeed gather you
to your fathers, and you will be gathered to
your grave in peace.[x] Your eyes will not see all
the disaster that I am bringing on this place.'"
Then they reported[C] to the king.

Covenant Renewal

23 So the king sent messengers,[y] and they
gathered all the elders[z] of Jerusalem
and Judah to him. 2Then the king went to the
LORD's temple with all the men of Judah and
all the inhabitants of Jerusalem, as well as
the priests and the prophets — all the people
from the youngest to the oldest. As they listened, he read all the words of the book of the
covenant[aa] that had been found in the LORD's
temple.[ab] 3Next, the king stood by the pillar[D,ac]
and made a covenant[ad] in the presence of the
LORD to follow the LORD and to keep His commands, His decrees, and His statutes with all
his mind and with all his heart,[ae] and to carry
out the words of this covenant that were writ-

[a] **22:1** Jos 15:39 [b] **22:2** 1Kg 14:8 [c] Dt 5:32; Jos 1:7 [d] **22:3** 2Ch 34:8 [e] **22:4** 2Kg 12:4,9-10 [f] **22:5** 2Kg 12:5 [g] **22:6** 2Kg 12:11-12 [h] **22:7** 2Kg 12:15; 1Co 4:2 [i] **22:8** Dt 31:24-26; 2Ch 34:14-15 [j] **22:10** Dt 17:18-20 [k] **22:11** Gn 37:34; Jos 7:6 [l] **22:12** 2Kg 25:22; Jr 26:24 [m] 2Ch 34:20 [n] **22:13** Dt 29:24-28; 31:17-18 [o] **22:14-20** 2Ch 34:22-28 [p] **22:14** Ex 15:20 [q] 2Ch 34:22 [r] Zph 1:10 [s] **22:16** Dt 29:27; Dn 9:11-14 [t] **22:17** Dt 29:25-26; 1Kg 9:9 [u] **22:18** 2Ch 34:26 [v] **22:19** 1Sm 24:5; 1Kg 21:29 [w] Dt 28:15; Jr 26:6 [x] **22:20** 2Kg 20:19; 23:30 [y] **23:1** 2Ch 34:29-32 [z] 2Kg 10:1 [aa] **23:2** Dt 31:10-13 [ab] 2Kg 22:8 [ac] **23:3** 1Kg 7:15; 2Kg 11:14 [ad] 2Kg 11:17 [ae] Dt 6:4-6; 13:4

[A] **22:9** Lit *and returned a word to the king and said* [B] **22:14** = Hasrah in 2Ch 34:22 [C] **22:20** Lit *returned a word* [D] **23:3** 2Ch 34:31 reads *platform*

ten in this book; all the people agreed to[A] the
covenant.[a]

Josiah's Reforms

4Then the king commanded Hilkiah[b] the
high priest and the priests of the second
rank[c] and the doorkeepers to bring out of
the LORD's temple all the articles made for
·Baal, ·Asherah, and the whole heavenly
·host.[d] He burned them outside Jerusalem
in the fields of the Kidron and carried their
ashes to Bethel.[e] 5Then he did away with the
idolatrous priests the kings of Judah had appointed to burn incense at the ·high places[f] in
the cities of Judah and in the areas surrounding Jerusalem. They had burned incense to
Baal, and to the sun, moon, constellations,
and the whole heavenly host.[g] 6He brought
out the Asherah pole[h] from the LORD's temple to the Kidron Valley outside Jerusalem. He
burned it at the Kidron Valley,[i] beat it to dust,[j]
and threw its dust on the graves of the common people.[B,k] 7He also tore down the houses
of the male cult prostitutes[l] that were in the
LORD's temple, in which the women were
weaving tapestries[C] for Asherah.[m]
8Then Josiah brought all the priests from
the cities of Judah, and he defiled the high
places[n] from Geba[o] to Beer-sheba,[p] where the
priests had burned incense. He tore down
the high places of the gates at the entrance
of the ·gate of Joshua the governor of the city
(on the left at the city gate). 9The priests of
the high places, however, did not come up to
the altar of the LORD in Jerusalem; instead,
they ate unleavened bread with their fellow
priests.[q]
10He defiled ·Topheth,[r] which is in the Valley of Hinnom,[s] so that no one could make
his son or daughter pass through the fire[t] to
·Molech.[u] 11He did away with the horses that
the kings of Judah had dedicated to the sun.
They had been at the entrance of the LORD's
temple in the precincts by the chamber of
Nathan-melech the court official, and he
burned up the chariots of the sun.[v]
12The king tore down the altars that were
on the roof[w]—Ahaz's upper chamber[x] that
the kings of Judah had made—and the altars

[a]**23:3** Ex 24:3-8; Jos 24:14-28
[b]**23:4** 2Kg 22:8,14
[c]2Kg 25:18; Jr 35:4; 52:24
[d]2Kg 21:3,7; 2Ch 33:3
[e]2Kg 23:15
[f]**23:5** 2Kg 16:4
[g]2Kg 21:3
[h]**23:6** 1Kg 14:15,23; 2Kg 18:4; 21:7
[i]1Kg 15:13
[j]2Kg 23:15
[k]2Ch 34:4; Jr 26:23
[l]**23:7** Dt 23:17; 1Kg 14:24; 15:12
[m]Ex 38:8; Ezk 16:16
[n]**23:8** 2Kg 18:4
[o]Jos 21:17; 1Kg 15:22
[p]1Sm 3:20
[q]**23:9** Ezk 44:10-14
[r]**23:10** Is 30:33; Jr 7:31-32
[s]Jos 15:8
[t]Lv 18:21; 20:2-5
[u]1Kg 11:7; Jr 32:35
[v]**23:11** Dt 4:19; Ezk 8:16
[w]**23:12** Jr 19:13; Zph 1:4-5
[x]2Kg 20:11
[y]2Kg 21:5; 2Ch 33:5
[z]**23:13** 1Kg 11:5-8
[aa]**23:14** Ex 23:24
[ab]2Kg 18:4
[ac]**23:15** 1Kg 13:1-3
[ad]1Kg 12:28-33
[ae]2Kg 23:6
[af]**23:16** 2Ch 34:5
[ag]1Kg 13:2
[ah]**23:17** 1Kg 13:1,31-32
[ai]**23:18** 1Kg 13:29-31
[aj]**23:19** 2Ch 34:6-7
[ak]**23:20** 1Kg 12:31; 13:2
[al]2Kg 10:25; 11:18; 2Ch 34:5
[am]**23:21** Nm 9:1-14; Dt 16:1-8; 2Ch 35:1-6

that Manasseh had made[y] in the two courtyards of the LORD's temple. Then he smashed
them[D] there and threw their dust into the
Kidron Valley. 13The king also defiled the high
places that were across from Jerusalem, to the
south of the Mount of Destruction, which
King Solomon of Israel had built for ·Ashto-
reth, the detestable idol of the Sidonians; for
Chemosh, the detestable idol of Moab; and
for ·Milcom, the abomination of the Ammonites.[z] 14He broke the sacred pillars into
pieces,[aa] cut down the Asherah poles,[ab] then
filled their places with human bones.
15He even tore down the altar at Bethel[ac]
and the high place[ad] that Jeroboam son of Nebat, who caused Israel to sin, had made. Then
he burned the high place, crushed it to dust,
and burned the Asherah.[ae] 16As Josiah turned,
he saw the tombs there on the mountain. He
sent someone to take the bones out of the
tombs, and he burned them on the altar.[af] He
defiled it according to the word of the LORD
proclaimed by the man of God[E] who proclaimed these things.[ag] 17Then he said, "What
is this monument I see?"
The men of the city told him, "It is the tomb
of the man of God who came from Judah and
proclaimed these things that you have done
to the altar at Bethel."[ah]
18So he said, "Let him rest. Don't let anyone
disturb his bones." So they left his bones un-
disturbed with the bones of the prophet who
came from Samaria.[ai]
19Josiah also removed all the shrines of the
high places that were in the cities of Samaria,
which the kings of Israel had made to provoke the LORD.[aj] Josiah did the same things to
them that he had done at Bethel. 20He slaughtered on the altars all the priests of the high
places[ak] who were there, and he burned human bones on the altars.[al] Then he returned
to Jerusalem.

Passover Observed

21The king commanded all the people,
"Keep the ·Passover of the LORD your God as
written in the book of the covenant."[am] 22No
such Passover had ever been kept from the
time of the judges who judged Israel through

[A]23:3 Lit *people took a stand in* [B]23:6 Lit *the sons of the people* [C]23:7 Or *clothing* [D]23:12 Text emended; MT reads *he ran from* [E]23:16 LXX adds *when Jeroboam stood by the altar of the feast. And he turned and raised his eyes to the tomb of the man of God*

the entire time of the kings of Israel and Judah. 23 But in the eighteenth year of King Josiah, this Passover was observed to the LORD
in Jerusalem.[a]

Further Zeal for the LORD

24 In addition, Josiah removed the mediums, the spiritists,[b] household idols,[c] images,
and all the detestable things[d] that were seen
in the land of Judah and in Jerusalem. He did
this in order to carry out the words of the law
that were written in the book that Hilkiah the
priest found in the LORD's temple.[e] 25 Before
him there was no king like him who turned
to the LORD with all his mind and with all
his heart and with all his strength[f] according
to all the law of Moses, and no one like him
arose after him.[g]
26 In spite of all that, the LORD did not
turn from the fury of His great burning anger, which burned against Judah because of
all that Manasseh had provoked Him with.[h]
27 For the LORD had said, "I will also remove
Judah from My sight just as I have removed
Israel.[i] I will reject this city Jerusalem, that I
have chosen, and the temple about which I
said, 'My name will be there.'"[j]

Josiah's Death

28 The rest of the events of Josiah's reign,[k]
along with all his accomplishments, are written in the Historical Record of Judah's Kings.
29 During his reign, Pharaoh Neco king of
Egypt[l] marched up to help the king of Assyria
at the Euphrates River. King Josiah went to
confront him, and at Megiddo[m] when Neco
saw him he killed him. 30 From Megiddo his
servants carried his dead body in a chariot,
brought him into Jerusalem, and buried him
in his own tomb.[n] Then the common people[A]
took Jehoahaz son of Josiah, anointed him,
and made him king in place of his father.[o]

Judah's King Jehoahaz

31 Jehoahaz[p] was[q] 23 years old when he became king and reigned three months in Jerusalem. His mother's name was Hamutal[r]
daughter of Jeremiah, from Libnah. 32 He did
what was evil in the LORD's sight just as his
ancestors had done.[s] 33 Pharaoh Neco imprisoned him at Riblah[t] in the land of Hamath[u] to
keep him from reigning in Jerusalem, and he
imposed on the land a fine of 7,500 pounds[B]
of silver and 75 pounds[C] of gold.

Judah's King Jehoiakim

34 Then[v] Pharaoh Neco made Eliakim[w] son
of Josiah king in place of his father Josiah and
changed Eliakim's name to Jehoiakim.[x] But
Neco took Jehoahaz and went to Egypt, and he
died there.[y] 35 So Jehoiakim gave the silver and
the gold to Pharaoh, but at Pharaoh's command he taxed the land to give the money. He
exacted the silver and the gold from the common people,[A] each man according to his assessment,[z] to give it to Pharaoh Neco.
36 Jehoiakim was 25 years old when he became king and reigned 11 years in Jerusalem.
His mother's name was Zebidah daughter
of Pedaiah, from Rumah. 37 He did what was
evil[aa] in the LORD's sight just as his ancestors
had done.

Jehoiakim's Rebellion and Death

24 During[ab] Jehoiakim's reign,[ac] Nebuchadnezzar[ad] king of Babylon[ae] attacked.[af] Jehoiakim became his vassal for
three years, and then he turned and rebelled
against him. 2 The LORD sent Chaldean, Aramean,[ag] Moabite,[ah] and Ammonite raiders
against Jehoiakim. He sent them against Judah to destroy it, according to the word of the
LORD He had spoken through His servants
the prophets.[ai] 3 Indeed, this happened to Judah at the LORD's command to remove them
from His sight.[aj] It was because of the sins
of Manasseh, according to all he had done,[ak]
4 and also because of all the innocent blood he
had shed. He had filled Jerusalem with innocent blood,[al] and the LORD would not forgive.
5 The rest of the events of Jehoiakim's reign,
along with all his accomplishments, are written in the Historical Record of Judah's Kings.[am]
6 Jehoiakim rested with his fathers, and his
son Jehoiachin became king in his place.[an]
7 Now the king of Egypt did not march out
of his land again,[ao] for the king of Babylon
took everything that belonged to the king of
Egypt,[ap] from the Brook of Egypt to the Euphrates River.[aq]

[a]23:22-23 2Ch 35:18-19 [b]23:24 Lv 19:31; 2Kg 21:6 [c]Gn 31:19 [d]Dt 7:26; 2Kg 16:3 [e]2Kg 22:8; 23:2-3 [f]23:25 Dt 6:4-9; 2Kg 23:3 [g]1Kg 3:12; 2Kg 18:5 [h]23:26 2Kg 21:11-13; Jr 15:4 [i]23:27 2Kg 18:11-12 [j]Dt 12:11; 1Kg 9:3; 2Kg 21:4 [k]23:28-30 2Ch 35:20-27 [l]23:29 Jr 46:2 [m]Jdg 5:19 [n]23:30 2Kg 9:28 [o]2Ch 36:1 [p]23:31 1Ch 3:15; Jr 22:11 [q]23:31-33 2Ch 36:2-3 [r]23:31 2Kg 24:18 [s]23:32 2Kg 21:2-7 [t]23:33 2Kg 25:6 [u]1Kg 8:65 [v]23:34-37 2Ch 36:4-5 [w]23:34 1Ch 3:15 [x]2Kg 24:17; 2Ch 36:4 [y]Jr 22:11-12; Ezk 19:3-4 [z]23:35 Ex 30:12-16; Lv 27:2-8 [aa]23:37 Jr 22:13-19; 36:1-26 [ab]24:1-6 2Ch 36:6-8 [ac]24:1 2Kg 23:26-27 [ad]2Kg 24:10-11; Dn 1:1 [ae]2Kg 20:14 [af]Jr 35:11 [ag]24:2 2Kg 6:23 [ah]2Kg 13:20 [ai]2Kg 23:27 [aj]24:3 2Kg 18:25 [ak]2Kg 23:26 [al]24:4 2Kg 21:16 [am]24:5 2Kg 23:28 [an]24:5-6 Jr 22:18-19 [ao]24:7 Jr 37:5-7 [ap]Jr 46:2 [aq]Gn 15:18; 1Kg 4:21; Is 27:12

[A]23:30,35 Lit *the people of the land* [B]23:33 Lit *100 talents* [C]23:33 Lit *one talent*

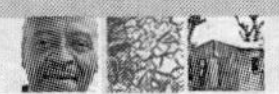

Judah's King Jehoiachin

8Jehoiachin was 18 years old when he became king and reigned three months in Jerusalem. His mother's name was Nehushta
daughter of Elnathan, from Jerusalem.[a] 9He
did what was evil in the LORD's sight as his father had done.

Deportations to Babylon

10At that time[b] the servants of Nebuchadnezzar[c] king of Babylon marched up to Jerusalem, and the city came under siege. 11Then
King Nebuchadnezzar of Babylon came to
the city while his servants were besieging it.
12Jehoiachin king of Judah, along with his
mother, his servants, his commanders, and
his officials, surrendered to the king of Babylon.[d]

So the king of Babylon took him captive
in the eighth year of his reign. 13He also carried off from there all the treasures of the
LORD's temple and the treasures of the king's
palace, and he cut into pieces all the gold articles that Solomon king of Israel had made[e]
for the LORD's sanctuary, just as God had predicted.[f] 14Then he deported all Jerusalem and
all the commanders and all the fighting men,[g]
10,000 captives,[h] and all the craftsmen and
metalsmiths.[i] Except for the poorest people
of the land,[j] no one remained.

15Nebuchadnezzar deported Jehoiachin
to Babylon. Also, he took the king's mother,
the king's wives, his officials, and the leading
men of the land into exile from Jerusalem to
Babylon.[k] 16The king of Babylon also brought
captive into Babylon all 7,000 fighting men
and 1,000 craftsmen and metalsmiths — all
strong and fit for war. 17Then the king of Babylon made Mattaniah, Jehoiachin's[A] uncle,[B]
king in his place and changed his name to
Zedekiah.[l]

Judah's King Zedekiah

18Zedekiah[m] was 21 years old when he became king[n] and reigned 11 years in Jerusalem.
His mother's name was Hamutal[o] daughter of
Jeremiah, from Libnah. 19Zedekiah did what
was evil in the LORD's sight just as Jehoiakim
had done.[p] 20Because of the LORD's anger,[q]
it came to the point in Jerusalem and Judah
that He finally banished them from His presence.[r] Then, Zedekiah rebelled against the
king of Babylon.[s]

Nebuchadnezzar's Siege of Jerusalem

25 In the ninth year[t] of Zedekiah's reign,[u]
on the tenth day of the tenth month,
King Nebuchadnezzar of Babylon advanced
against Jerusalem with his entire army.[v] They
laid siege to the city and built a siege wall
against it all around.[w] 2The city was under
siege until King Zedekiah's eleventh year.

3By the ninth day of the fourth month the
famine was so severe in the city that the people of the land had no food.[x] 4Then the city
was broken into,[y] and all the warriors fled[z]
by night by way of the gate between the two
walls near the king's garden,[aa] even though
the Chaldeans surrounded the city. As the
king made his way along the route to the
•Arabah,[ab] 5the Chaldean army pursued him
and overtook him in the plains of Jericho.
Zedekiah's entire army was scattered from
him.[ac] 6The Chaldeans seized the king[ad] and
brought him up to the king of Babylon[ae] at
Riblah,[af] and they passed sentence on him.
7They slaughtered Zedekiah's sons before
his eyes. Finally, the king of Babylon blinded
Zedekiah, bound him in bronze chains, and
took him to Babylon.[ag]

Jerusalem Destroyed

8On[ah] the seventh day of the fifth month,
which was the nineteenth year of Nebuchadnezzar king of Babylon, Nebuzaradan, the
commander of the guards, a servant of the
king of Babylon, entered Jerusalem.[ai] 9He
burned the LORD's temple,[aj] the king's palace,[ak]
and all the houses of Jerusalem; he burned
down[al] all the great houses. 10The whole Chaldean army with the commander of the guards
tore down the walls[am] surrounding Jerusalem. 11Nebuzaradan, the commander of the
guards, deported the rest of the people who
were left in the city, the deserters who had defected to the king of Babylon, and the rest of
the population.[an] 12But the commander of the
guards left some of the poorest of the land to
be vinedressers and farmers.[ao]

13Now[ap] the Chaldeans broke into pieces

[a] **24:8-9** 2Ch 36:9; Jr 22:24-30
[b] **24:10-17** 2Ch 36:10
[c] **24:10** 2Kg 24:1; Dn 1:1
[d] **24:12** 2Kg 25:27; Jr 22:24-30
[e] **24:13** 1Kg 7:48-50
[f] 2Kg 20:16-18; Is 39:5-7
[g] **24:14** Jr 24:1
[h] Jr 52:28
[i] Jr 24:1; 29:2
[j] 2Kg 25:12
[k] **24:15** 2Ch 36:10; Jr 22:24-28
[l] **24:17** 1Ch 3:15; 2Ch 36:11; Jr 1:3
[m] **24:18** Jr 27:1; 28:1
[n] **24:18-20** 2Ch 36:11-12; Jr 52:1-3
[o] **24:18** 2Kg 23:31
[p] **24:19** 2Kg 23:37
[q] **24:20** Dt 4:26; 29:27; 2Kg 23:26
[r] 2Kg 13:23
[s] 2Ch 36:13; Ezk 17:15
[t] **25:1** Jr 32:1
[u] **25:1-7** Jr 39:1-7; 52:4-11
[v] **25:1** Jr 21:2; 34:1-2; Ezk 24:2
[w] Ezk 21:22
[x] **25:3** 2Kg 6:24-25; Lm 4:9-10
[y] **25:4** Jr 39:2
[z] Ezk 33:21
[aa] Neh 3:15
[ab] Dt 2:8
[ac] **25:5** Lv 26:36; Ezk 12:14; 17:21
[ad] **25:6** Jr 34:21-22
[ae] Jr 32:4
[af] Nm 34:11; 2Kg 23:33; Jr 52:9
[ag] **25:7** Jr 39:6-7; Ezk 12:13
[ah] **25:8-12** Jr 39:8-10; 52:12-16
[ai] **25:8** 2Kg 24:12; Jr 39:9; 52:12
[aj] **25:9** 1Kg 9:8; 2Ch 36:19
[ak] Jr 39:8; Am 2:5
[al] Jr 17:27
[am] **25:10** 2Kg 24:13; Neh 1:3; Jr 50:15
[an] **25:11** 2Ch 36:20; Jr 5:19; 39:1-9
[ao] **25:12** 2Kg 24:14; Jr 39:10; 40:7
[ap] **25:13-21** Jr 52:17-27

[A] **24:17** Lit *his* [B] **24:17** = brother in 2Ch 36:10; Jr 37:1

the bronze pillars[a] of the LORD's temple, the water carts, and the bronze reservoir,[b] which were in the LORD's temple, and carried the bronze to Babylon.[c] 14 They also took the pots, the shovels, the wick trimmers, the dishes, and all the bronze articles used in temple service.[d] 15 The commander of the guards took away the firepans and the sprinkling basins—whatever was gold or silver.[e]

16 As for the two pillars, the one reservoir, and the water carts that Solomon had made for the LORD's temple, the weight of the bronze of all these articles was beyond measure.[f] 17 One pillar was 27 feet[A] tall and had a bronze capital on top of it. The capital, encircled by a grating and pomegranates of bronze, stood five feet[B] high. The second pillar was the same, with its own grating.[g]

18 The commander of the guards[h] also took away Seraiah[i] the chief priest, Zephaniah[j] the priest of the second rank, and the three doorkeepers. 19 He took a court official who had been appointed over the warriors from the city; five trusted royal aides[C,k] found in the city; the secretary of the commander of the army, who enlisted the people of the land for military duty; and 60 men from the common people[D] who were found within the city. 20 Nebuzaradan, the commander of the guards, took them and brought them to the king of Babylon at Riblah.[l] 21 The king of Babylon put them to death at Riblah in the land of Hamath. So Judah went into exile from its land.[m]

Gedaliah Made Governor

22 Nebuchadnezzar king of Babylon appointed Gedaliah[n] son of Ahikam, son of Shaphan, over the rest of the people he left in the land of Judah.[o] 23 When all the commanders of the armies—they and their men—heard that the king of Babylon had appointed Gedaliah, they came to Gedaliah at Mizpah.[p] The commanders included Ishmael son of Nethaniah, Johanan son of Kareah, Seraiah son of Tanhumeth the Netophathite, and Jaazaniah son of the Maacathite—they and their men.[q] 24 Gedaliah swore an oath to them and their men, assuring them, "Don't be afraid of the servants of the Chaldeans. Live in the land and serve the king of Babylon, and it will go well for you."[r]

25 In the seventh month, however, Ishmael son of Nethaniah, son of Elishama, of the royal family, came with 10 men and struck down Gedaliah, and he died. Also, they killed the Judeans and the Chaldeans who were with him at Mizpah.[s] 26 Then all the people, from the youngest to the oldest, and the commanders of the army, left and went to Egypt, for they were afraid of the Chaldeans.[t]

Jehoiachin Pardoned

27 On[u] the twenty-seventh day of the twelfth month of the thirty-seventh year of the exile of Judah's King Jehoiachin, in the year Evil-merodach became king of Babylon, he pardoned King Jehoiachin[v] of Judah and released him from prison.[w] 28 He spoke kindly[x] to him and set his throne over the thrones of the kings who were with him in Babylon.[y] 29 So Jehoiachin changed his prison clothes, and he dined regularly in the presence of the king of Babylon for the rest of his life.[z] 30 As for his allowance, a regular allowance[aa] was given to him by the king, a portion for each day, for the rest of his life.

[a] **25:13** 2Kg 20:17; 2Ch 36:18; Jr 52:17
[b] 1Kg 7:23; 2Ch 4:2-4
[c] Jr 27:19-22
[d] **25:14** Ex 27:3; 1Kg 7:47-50; 2Ch 4:16
[e] **25:15** 2Kg 24:13; Jr 15:13; 20:5
[f] **25:16** 1Kg 7:47
[g] **25:17** 1Kg 7:15-22
[h] **25:18** Jr 39:9-13; 52:12-16,24
[i] 1Ch 6:14; Ezr 7:1
[j] Jr 21:1; 29:25,29
[k] **25:19** Jr 52:25
[l] **25:20** 2Kg 23:33
[m] **25:21** Dt 28:63-64; 2Kg 23:27
[n] **25:22** Jr 39:14; 40:7-9
[o] Is 1:9; Jr 40:5
[p] **25:23** Jos 18:26
[q] Jr 40:7-8
[r] **25:24** Jr 40:9
[s] **25:25** Jr 41:1-2
[t] **25:26** Is 30:2; Jr 43:4-7
[u] **25:27-30** Jr 52:31-34
[v] **25:27** 2Kg 24:12
[w] Gn 40:13,20
[x] **25:28** 1Kg 8:50
[y] Ezr 5:5; 7:6,28
[z] **25:29** 2Sm 9:7
[aa] **25:30** Gn 43:34; Neh 12:47

[A] **25:17** Lit *18 cubits* [B] **25:17** Lit *three cubits* [C] **25:19** Lit *five men who look on the king's face* [D] **25:19** Lit *the people of the land*

■ **AUTHOR:** Ezra (more than likely)

■■ **DATE:** The events narrated in Chronicles occurred during the time of the kings, specifically David and Solomon, through the fall of Jerusalem (around 1010–585 B.C.). First and 2 Chronicles could have been written around 400 B.C.

In audience for the first two histories (1 and 2 Samuel and 1 and 2 Kings) is the nation of Judah struggling with the meaning of God's mission in exile. The record of their nation up to this point is one of high highs but also very low lows. Southern Judah was finally overrun by Babylon in 585 B.C. Where is God now, while His people sit under the thumb of pagan power? In the books of 1 and 2 Chronicles, the situation has changed. Persia has conquered Babylon. Cyrus, the king, permits a group of Jews to return to Jerusalem with some of their former temple treasures (another event already foreseen by God's prophet, proving once again that God is never surprised, see Is 44:28). We may wonder what God is doing now, we are surprised—but God is always in control. Nothing can thwart His plans.

1 CHRONICLES

The books of 1 and 2 Chronicles were almost certainly written and compiled during the time of Ezra (who might have been the author and compiler). The books are God's message for the "restored community." To all who arrive in Jerusalem with high hopes of recovering former grandeur, the stark reality must have shaken their tenuous faith. Is God still interested in us? Do God's promises still hold any hope?

The people need a revival of mission and a resurgence of confidence that God still cares. The books of Chronicles meet that need in special ways. In the genealogies, God's mission is underscored through the record of His word and work done through ancient leaders of the nation. Never forget what God has done, Chronicles urges. The past can guide the present. Learn your history.

Chronicles focuses on the southern kingdom of Judah (skipping most anything that occurred in the northern kingdom of Israel), gives emphasis to the careers of David and Solomon, and underscores the importance of the temple and of the people's worship. Through these stories, God's mission is recalled in a "golden age" history that bypasses much of that era's trouble but highlights the special character and calling of this father-son leadership team. God calls the humble shepherd David to great service. God provides Solomon—the king's son and wisest of all—with resources and peace more than sufficient to build the great temple.

The description of the temple with its architectural detail and sacrificial rites helps people see God's power and scope. The temple symbolizes God's mission. It is not a national monument; the temple is for the nations. In Old Testament terms, the hope of all peoples everywhere is centered on the worship of the one true God, who made the world, ordered it for the benefit of all life, and now "lives" within the temple. "Come and worship" is the open invitation.

One more important focus in the Chronicles gives Christians today every reason to study this book. The promise of a Messiah still rings throughout Israel. Despite the loss of Solomon's temple, despite the trouble Israel has seen, the promise of One who is coming means God is not finished yet. Watch for the deliverance and salvation of all God's people in the One who comes. He will be David's son, the "lamp" (2Ch 21:7) who lights the way.

God's mission looks forward, remembering the past, to a day when the nation, temple, and people of God take new shape, reach a new level of intimacy with God, and place their allegiance in God more fully revealed than ever before. This is the great promise for people who wonder: Does God still care?

From Adam to Abraham

1 Adam,[a] Seth, Enosh,
2 Kenan, Mahalalel, Jared,
3 Enoch, Methuselah, Lamech,
4 Noah, Noah's sons:[A]
Shem, Ham, and Japheth.

5 Japheth's[b] sons: Gomer, Magog, Madai,
Javan, Tubal, Meshech, and Tiras.
6 Gomer's sons: Ashkenaz, Riphath,[B] and
Togarmah.
7 Javan's sons: Elishah, Tarshish, Kittim,
and Rodanim.[C]

8 Ham's sons: Cush, Mizraim,[D] Put, and
Canaan.
9 Cush's sons: Seba, Havilah, Sabta,
Raama, and Sabteca.
Raama's sons: Sheba and Dedan.
10 Cush fathered Nimrod, who was
the first to become a great warrior on
earth.
11 Mizraim[c] fathered Ludim, Anamim,
Lehabim, Naphtuhim, 12 Pathrusim,
Casluhim (the Philistines came from
them), and Caphtorim.[d]
13 Canaan fathered Sidon as his
firstborn, then Heth, 14 the Jebusites,
Amorites, Girgashites, 15 Hivites, Arkites,
Sinites, 16 Arvadites, Zemarites, and
Hamathites.

17 Shem's[e] sons: Elam, Asshur,
Arpachshad, Lud, Aram, Uz, Hul,
Gether, and Meshech.
18 Arpachshad fathered Shelah, and
Shelah fathered Eber. 19 Two sons
were born to Eber. One of them was
named Peleg[E] because the earth was
divided during his lifetime, and the
name of his brother was Joktan.
20 Joktan fathered Almodad, Sheleph,
Hazarmaveth, Jerah, 21 Hadoram, Uzal,
Diklah, 22 Ebal, Abimael, Sheba, 23 Ophir,
Havilah, and Jobab. All of these were
Joktan's sons.
24 Shem,[f] Arpachshad, Shelah,
25 Eber, Peleg, Reu,
26 Serug, Nahor, Terah,
27 and Abram (that is, Abraham).

[a]1:1-4 Gn 4:25–5:32 [b]1:5-7 Gn 10:2-4 [c]1:11-16 Gn 10:13-18 [d]1:12 Dt 2:23; Am 9:7 [e]1:17-23 Gn 10:21-29 [f]1:24-27 Gn 11:10-26; Lk 3:34-36 [g]1:29-31 Gn 25:12-16 [h]1:32-33 Gn 25:1-4 [i]1:34 1Ch 1:28 [j]Gn 25:24-26; 32:28 [k]1:35-37 Gn 36:4-5,9-14 [l]1:38-42 Gn 36:20-30 [m]1:43-50 Gn 36:31-39 [n]1:44 Is 34:6 [o]1:45 Jb 2:11

Abraham's Descendants

28 Abraham's sons: Isaac and Ishmael.

29 These[g] are their family records:
Nebaioth, Ishmael's firstborn, Kedar,
Adbeel, Mibsam, 30 Mishma, Dumah,
Massa, Hadad, Tema, 31 Jetur, Naphish,
and Kedemah.
These were Ishmael's sons.
32 The sons[h] born to Keturah, Abraham's
concubine: Zimran, Jokshan, Medan,
Midian, Ishbak, and Shuah.
Jokshan's sons: Sheba and Dedan.
33 Midian's sons: Ephah, Epher, Hanoch,
Abida, and Eldaah.
All of these were Keturah's sons.

34 Abraham[i] fathered Isaac.
Isaac's sons: Esau and Israel.[j]
35 Esau's[k] sons: Eliphaz, Reuel, Jeush,
Jalam, and Korah.
36 Eliphaz's sons: Teman, Omar, Zephi,
Gatam, and Kenaz; and by Timna,
Amalek.[F]
37 Reuel's sons: Nahath, Zerah,
Shammah, and Mizzah.

The Edomites

38 Seir's[l] sons: Lotan, Shobal, Zibeon,
Anah, Dishon, Ezer, and Dishan.
39 Lotan's sons: Hori and Homam.
Timna was Lotan's sister.
40 Shobal's sons: Alian, Manahath, Ebal,
Shephi, and Onam.
Zibeon's sons: Aiah and Anah.
41 Anah's son: Dishon.
Dishon's sons: Hamran, Eshban, Ithran,
and Cheran.
42 Ezer's sons: Bilhan, Zaavan, and
Jaakan.
Dishan's sons: Uz and Aran.

43 These[m] were the kings who ruled in the
land of Edom before any king ruled over the
Israelites: Bela son of Beor. Bela's town was
named Dinhabah. 44 When Bela died, Jobab
son of Zerah from Bozrah[n] ruled in his place.
45 When Jobab died, Husham from the land
of the Temanites[o] ruled in his place. 46 When
Husham died, Hadad son of Bedad, who de-

[A]1:4 LXX; MT omits *Noah's sons* [B]1:6 Some Hb mss, LXX, Vg; other Hb mss read *Diphath*; Gn 10:3 [C]1:7 Some Hb mss, Syr read *Dodanim*; Gn 10:4 [D]1:8 = Egypt [E]1:19 = Division [F]1:36 LXX; MT reads *and Timna and Amalek*; Gn 36:12

feated Midian in the country of Moab, ruled
in his place. Hadad's town was named Avith.
47 When Hadad died, Samlah from Masrekah
ruled in his place. 48 When Samlah died, Shaul
from Rehoboth on the Euphrates River ruled
in his place. 49 When Shaul died, Baal-hanan
son of Achbor ruled in his place. 50 When Baal-
hanan died, Hadad ruled in his place. Hadad's
city was named Pai, and his wife's name was
Mehetabel daughter of Matred, daughter of
Me-zahab. 51 Then Hadad died.

Edom's[a] chiefs: Timna, Alvah,[A] Jetheth,
52 Oholibamah, Elah, Pinon, 53 Kenaz,
Teman, Mibzar, 54 Magdiel, and Iram.
These were Edom's chiefs.

Israel's Sons

2 These[b] were Israel's sons:
Reuben, Simeon, Levi,
Judah, Issachar, Zebulun,
2 Dan, Joseph, Benjamin,
Naphtali, Gad, and Asher.

Judah's Descendants

3 Judah's[c] sons: Er, Onan, and Shelah.[d]
These three were born to him by Bath-
shua the Canaanite woman. Er, Judah's
firstborn, was evil in the LORD's sight, so
He put him to death. 4 Judah's daughter-
in-law Tamar bore Perez and Zerah to
him. Judah had five sons in all.

5 Perez's sons: Hezron and Hamul.
6 Zerah's sons: Zimri, Ethan, Heman,
Calcol, and Dara[B,e] — five in all.
7 Carmi's son: Achar,[C,f] who brought
trouble on Israel when he was
unfaithful by taking the things •set
apart for destruction.
8 Ethan's son: Azariah.
9 Hezron's sons, who were born to him:
Jerahmeel, Ram, and Chelubai.[D]

10 Ram fathered Amminadab, and
Amminadab fathered Nahshon, a
leader of Judah's descendants.
11 Nahshon fathered Salma, and Salma
fathered Boaz.
12 Boaz fathered Obed, and Obed
fathered Jesse.

[a] **1:51-54** Gn 36:40-43
[b] **2:1-2** Gn 35:22-26; 46:8-25
[c] **2:3-4** Gn 38:6-30
[d] **2:3** Gn 38:2-5; 46:12; Nm 26:19-22
[e] **2:6** 1Kg 4:31
[f] **2:7** Jos 7:1,16-26
[g] **2:21** Nm 26:29

13 Jesse fathered Eliab, his firstborn;
Abinadab was born second, Shimea
third, 14 Nethanel fourth, Raddai fifth,
15 Ozem sixth, and David seventh.
16 Their sisters were Zeruiah and
Abigail. Zeruiah's three sons: Abishai,
Joab, and Asahel. 17 Amasa's mother was
Abigail, and his father was Jether the
Ishmaelite.

18 Caleb son of Hezron had children by
his wife Azubah and by Jerioth. These
were Azubah's sons: Jesher, Shobab, and
Ardon. 19 When Azubah died, Caleb married Ephrath, and she bore Hur to him.
20 Hur fathered Uri, and Uri fathered
Bezalel. 21 After this, Hezron slept with
the daughter of Machir the father of
Gilead.[g] Hezron had married her when
he was 60 years old, and she bore Segub
to him. 22 Segub fathered Jair, who possessed 23 towns in the land of Gilead.
23 But Geshur and Aram captured[E] Jair's
Villages[F] along with Kenath and its villages — 60 towns. All these were the sons
of Machir father of Gilead. 24 After Hezron's death in Caleb-ephrathah, his wife
Abijah bore Ashhur to him. He was the
father of Tekoa.

25 The sons of Jerahmeel, Hezron's
firstborn: Ram, his firstborn, Bunah,
Oren, Ozem, and Ahijah. 26 Jerahmeel
had another wife named Atarah, who
was the mother of Onam.
27 The sons of Ram, Jerahmeel's
firstborn: Maaz, Jamin, and Eker.
28 Onam's sons: Shammai and Jada.
Shammai's sons: Nadab and Abishur.
29 Abishur's wife was named Abihail,
who bore Ahban and Molid to him.
30 Nadab's sons: Seled and Appaim. Seled
died without children.
31 Appaim's son: Ishi.
Ishi's son: Sheshan.
Sheshan's descendant: Ahlai.
32 The sons of Jada, brother of Shammai:
Jether and Jonathan. Jether died
without children.
33 Jonathan's sons: Peleth and Zaza.

[A] **1:51** Alt Hb tradition reads *Aliah* [B] **2:6** Some Hb mss, LXX, Syr, Tg, Vg read *Darda*; 1Kg 4:31 [C] **2:7** = Trouble; Achan in Jos 7:1,16-26 [D] **2:9** = Caleb [E] **2:23** Lit *took from them* [F] **2:23** Or *captured Havvoth-jair*

These were the descendants of
Jerahmeel.
34 Sheshan had no sons, only daughters,
but he did have an Egyptian servant
whose name was Jarha. 35 Sheshan gave
his daughter in marriage to his servant
Jarha, and she bore Attai to him.

36 Attai fathered Nathan, and Nathan
fathered Zabad.
37 Zabad fathered Ephlal, and Ephlal
fathered Obed.
38 Obed fathered Jehu, and Jehu
fathered Azariah.
39 Azariah fathered Helez, and Helez
fathered Elasah.
40 Elasah fathered Sismai, and Sismai
fathered Shallum.
41 Shallum fathered Jekamiah, and
Jekamiah fathered Elishama.

42 The sons of Caleb brother of
Jerahmeel: Mesha, his firstborn,
fathered Ziph, and Mareshah, his
second son,[A] fathered Hebron.
43 Hebron's sons: Korah, Tappuah,
Rekem, and Shema.
44 Shema fathered Raham, who
fathered Jorkeam, and Rekem fathered
Shammai.
45 Shammai's son was Maon, and Maon
fathered Beth-zur.
46 Caleb's concubine Ephah was the
mother of Haran, Moza, and Gazez.
Haran fathered Gazez.
47 Jahdai's sons: Regem, Jotham, Geshan,
Pelet, Ephah, and Shaaph.
48 Caleb's concubine Maacah was
the mother of Sheber and Tirhanah.
49 She was also the mother of Shaaph,
Madmannah's father, and of Sheva, the
father of Machbenah and Gibea. Caleb's
daughter was Achsah.
50 These were Caleb's descendants.

The sons of Hur, Ephrathah's firstborn:
Shobal fathered Kiriath-jearim;
51 Salma fathered Bethlehem,
and Hareph fathered Beth-gader.

52 These were the descendants of Shobal
the father of Kiriath-jearim: Haroeh, half
of the Manahathites,[B] 53 and the families of Kiriath-jearim — the Ithrites, Pu-
thites, Shumathites, and Mishraites. The
Zorathites and Eshtaolites descended
from these.

54 Salma's sons: Bethlehem, the Netopha-
thites, Atroth-beth-joab, and half of the
Manahathites, the Zorites, 55 and the fam-
ilies of scribes who lived in Jabez — the
Tirathites, Shimeathites, and Sucathites.
These are the Kenites who came from
Hammath, the father of Rechab's family.

David's Descendants

3 These[a] were David's sons who were
born to him in Hebron:
Amnon was the firstborn, by Ahinoam
of Jezreel;
Daniel was born second, by Abigail of
Carmel;
2 Absalom son of Maacah, daughter of
King Talmai of Geshur, was third;
Adonijah son of Haggith was fourth;
3 Shephatiah, by Abital, was fifth;
and Ithream, by David's wife Eglah, was
sixth.
4 Six sons were born to David in
Hebron, where he ruled seven years
and six months, and he ruled in
Jerusalem 33 years.[b]
5 These[c] sons were born to him in
Jerusalem:
Shimea, Shobab, Nathan, and
Solomon.[d] These four were born to him
by Bath-shua[e] daughter of Ammiel.
6 David's other sons: Ibhar, Elishua,[C,f]
Eliphelet, 7 Nogah, Nepheg, Japhia,
8 Elishama, Eliada, and Eliphelet — nine
sons.
9 These were all David's sons, with their
sister Tamar,[g] in addition to the sons by
his concubines.

Judah's Kings

10 Solomon's son was Rehoboam;
his son was Abijah, his son Asa,
his son Jehoshaphat, 11 his son
Jehoram,[D,E]
his son Ahaziah, his son Joash,

[a] 3:1-4a 2Sm 3:2-5
[b] 3:4 2Sm 2:11; 5:4-5
[c] 3:5-8 2Sm 5:14-16; 1Ch 14:4-7
[d] 3:5 2Sm 12:24-25
[e] 2Sm 11:3
[f] 3:6 2Sm 5:15; 1Ch 14:5
[g] 3:9 2Sm 13:1

A 2:42 Lit *and the sons of Mareshah* B 2:52 Lit *Manuhoth* C 3:6 Lit *Elishama*; 2Sm 5:15; 1Ch 14:5 D 3:11 Lit *Joram* E 3:11 = The LORD is Exalted

12 his son Amaziah, his son Azariah,
his son Jotham, 13 his son Ahaz,
his son Hezekiah, his son Manasseh,
14 his son Amon, and his son Josiah.
15 Josiah's sons:
Johanan was the firstborn, Jehoiakim second,
Zedekiah third, and Shallum fourth.
16 Jehoiakim's sons:
his sons Jeconiah and Zedekiah.

David's Line After the Exile

17 The sons of Jeconiah the captive:
his sons Shealtiel, 18 Malchiram,
Pedaiah, Shenazzar, Jekamiah,
Hoshama, and Nedabiah.
19 Pedaiah's sons: Zerubbabel and Shimei.
Zerubbabel's sons: Meshullam and
Hananiah, with their sister Shelomith;
20 and five others — Hashubah,
Ohel, Berechiah, Hasadiah, and
Jushab-hesed.
21 Hananiah's descendants: Pelatiah,
Jeshaiah, and the sons of Rephaiah,
Arnan, Obadiah, and Shecaniah.[A]
22 The son[B] of Shecaniah: Shemaiah.
Shemaiah's sons: Hattush, Igal, Bariah,
Neariah, and Shaphat — six.
23 Neariah's sons: Elioenai, Hizkiah, and
Azrikam — three.
24 Elioenai's sons: Hodaviah, Eliashib,
Pelaiah, Akkub, Johanan, Delaiah, and
Anani — seven.

Judah's Descendants

4 Judah's sons:[a] Perez, Hezron, Carmi,
Hur, and Shobal.
2 Reaiah son of Shobal fathered Jahath,
and Jahath fathered Ahumai and
Lahad.
These were the families of the
Zorathites.
3 These were Etam's sons:[C] Jezreel,
Ishma, and Idbash, and their sister was
named Hazzelelponi.
4 Penuel fathered Gedor, and Ezer
fathered Hushah.

[a] 4:1 1Ch 2:5,18,50

These were the sons of Hur,
Ephrathah's firstborn and the father of
Bethlehem:
5 Ashhur fathered Tekoa and had two
wives, Helah and Naarah.
6 Naarah bore Ahuzzam, Hepher,
Temeni, and Haahashtari to him. These
were Naarah's sons.
7 Helah's sons: Zereth, Zohar,[D] and
Ethnan. 8 Koz fathered Anub, Zobebah,[E]
and the families of Aharhel son of
Harum.

9 Jabez[F] was more honorable than his brothers. His mother named him Jabez and said, "I
gave birth to him in pain."
10 Jabez called out to the God of Israel: "If
only You would bless me, extend my border,
let Your hand be with me, and keep me from
harm, so that I will not cause any pain."[G,H]
And God granted his request.

11 Chelub brother of Shuhah fathered
Mehir, who was the father of Eshton.
12 Eshton fathered Beth-rapha, Paseah,
and Tehinnah the father of Irnahash.
These were the men of Recah.
13 Kenaz's sons: Othniel and Seraiah.
Othniel's sons: Hathath and
Meonothai.[I]
14 Meonothai fathered Ophrah,
and Seraiah fathered Joab, the ancestor
of those in the Valley of Craftsmen,[J] for
they were craftsmen.
15 The sons of Caleb son of Jephunneh:
Iru, Elah, and Naam.
Elah's son: Kenaz.
16 Jehallelel's sons: Ziph, Ziphah, Tiria,
and Asarel.
17 Ezrah's sons: Jether, Mered, Epher,
and Jalon. Mered's wife Bithiah gave
birth to Miriam, Shammai, and Ishbah
the father of Eshtemoa. 18 These were
the sons of Pharaoh's daughter Bithiah;
Mered had married her. His Judean
wife gave birth to Jered the father
of Gedor, Heber the father of Soco,
and Jekuthiel the father of Zanoah.
19 The sons of Hodiah's wife, the sister
of Naham: the father of Keilah the

A 3:21 LXX reads *Jeshaiah, his son Rephaiah, his son Arnan, his son Obadiah, and his son Shecaniah* B 3:22 LXX; MT reads *sons* C 4:3 LXX; MT reads *father* D 4:7 Alt Hb tradition reads *Izhar* E 4:8 Or *Hazzobebah* F 4:9 In Hb, the name Jabez sounds like "he causes pain." G 4:10 LXX reads *and act in knowledge which doesn't hurt me* H 4:10 Or *so that I will not experience pain* I 4:13 LXX, Vg; MT omits *and Meonothai* J 4:14 Or *the Ge-harashim*

Garmite and the father of Eshtemoa the
Maacathite.
[20]Shimon's sons: Amnon, Rinnah,
Ben-hanan, and Tilon.
Ishi's sons: Zoheth and Ben-zoheth.

[21]The sons of Shelah son of Judah: Er
the father of Lecah, Laadah the father
of Mareshah, the families of the guild[A]
of linen workers at Beth-ashbea, [22]Jo-
kim, the men of Cozeba; and Joash and
Saraph, who married Moabites[B] and returned to Lehem. These names are from
ancient records. [23]They were the potters
and residents of Netaim and Gederah.
They lived there in the service of the king.

Simeon's Descendants

[24]Simeon's sons:[a] Nemuel, Jamin, Jarib,
Zerah, and Shaul;
[25]Shaul's sons: his son Shallum, his son
Mibsam, and his son Mishma.
[26]Mishma's sons: his son Hammuel, his
son Zaccur, and his son Shimei.

[27]Shimei had 16 sons and six daughters,
but his brothers did not have many children, so their whole family did not become as numerous as the Judeans. [28]They
lived in Beer-sheba, Moladah, Hazar-
shual, [29]Bilhah, Ezem, Tolad, [30]Bethuel,
Hormah, Ziklag, [31]Beth-marcaboth,
Hazar-susim, Beth-biri, and Shaaraim.
These were their cities until David became king. [32]Their villages were Etam,
Ain, Rimmon, Tochen, and Ashan — five
cities, [33]and all their surrounding villages as far as Baal. These were their settlements, and they kept a genealogical
record for themselves.

[34]Meshobab, Jamlech, Joshah son of
Amaziah,
[35]Joel, Jehu son of Joshibiah, son of
Seraiah, son of Asiel,
[36]Elioenai, Jaakobah, Jeshohaiah,
Asaiah, Adiel, Jesimiel, Benaiah, [37]and
Ziza son of Shiphi, son of Allon, son
of Jedaiah, son of Shimri, son of
Shemaiah —

[38]these mentioned by name were leaders
in their families. Their ancestral houses
increased greatly. [39]They went to the entrance of Gedor, to the east side of the
valley to seek pasture for their flocks.
[40]They found rich, good pasture, and the
land was broad, peaceful, and quiet,[b] for
some Hamites had lived there previously.

[41]These[c] who were recorded by name came
in the days of King Hezekiah of Judah, attacked the Hamites' tents and the Meunites
who were found there, and •set them apart for
destruction,[d] as they are today. Then they settled in their place because there was pasture
for their flocks. [42]Now 500 men from these
sons of Simeon went with Pelatiah, Neariah,
Rephaiah, and Uzziel, the sons of Ishi, as their
leaders to Mount Seir.[e] [43]They struck down[f]
the remnant of the Amalekites who had escaped, and they still live there today.

Reuben's Descendants

5 These were the sons of Reuben the firstborn of Israel. He was the firstborn,[g] but
his birthright was given to the sons of Joseph[h]
son of Israel, because Reuben defiled his father's bed.[i] He is not listed in the genealogy
according to birthright. [2]Although Judah became strong among his brothers[j] and a ruler
came from him,[k] the birthright was given to
Joseph.

[3] The sons of Reuben, Israel's firstborn:[l]
Hanoch, Pallu, Hezron, and Carmi.
[4] Joel's sons: his son Shemaiah,
his son Gog, his son Shimei,
[5] his son Micah, his son Reaiah,
his son Baal, [6]and his son Beerah.

Beerah was a leader of the Reubenites, and
Tiglath-pileser[C] king of Assyria took him into
exile. [7]His relatives by their families as they
are recorded in their genealogy:[m]

Jeiel the chief, Zechariah,
[8]and Bela son of Azaz,
son of Shema, son of Joel.

They settled in Aroer[n] as far as Nebo and Baal-
meon. [9]They also settled in the east as far as
the edge of the desert that extends to the
Euphrates River, because their herds had increased in the land of Gilead.[o] [10]During Saul's
reign they waged war against the Hagrites,[p]

[a]**4:24** Gn 46:10 [b]**4:40** Jdg 18:7-10 [c]**4:41** 1Ch 4:33-38 [d]Nm 21:3; Dt 2:34; 7:2; 13:15; Jos 6:17-21 [e]**4:42** Gn 36:8-9 [f]**4:43** 1Sm 15:7-8; 30:17 [g]**5:1** Gn 29:32; 1Ch 2:1 [h]Gn 48:15-22 [i]Gn 35:22; 49:4 [j]**5:2** Gn 49:8-10 [k]Mc 5:2; Mt 2:6 [l]**5:3** Gn 46:9; Nm 26:5-9 [m]**5:7** 1Ch 5:17 [n]**5:8** Nm 32:34; Jos 12:2 [o]**5:9** Jos 22:8-9 [p]**5:10** 1Ch 5:19-21; 11:38; 27:31

[A]**4:21** Lit *house* [B]**4:22** Or *who ruled over Moab* [C]**5:6** LXX; MT reads *Tilgath-pilneser*

who were defeated by their power. And they
lived in their tents throughout the region
east of Gilead.

Gad's Descendants

11 The sons[a] of Gad lived next to them in
the land of Bashan as far as Salecah:[b]
12 Joel the chief, Shapham the second
in command, Janai, and Shaphat in
Bashan.
13 Their relatives according to
their ancestral houses: Michael,
Meshullam, Sheba, Jorai, Jacan, Zia, and
Eber — seven.
14 These were the sons of Abihail son of
Huri,
son of Jaroah, son of Gilead,
son of Michael, son of Jeshishai,
son of Jahdo, son of Buz.
15 Ahi son of Abdiel, son of Guni, was
head of their ancestral houses. 16 They
lived in Gilead, in Bashan and its towns,
and throughout the pasturelands of
Sharon.[c] 17 All of them were registered
in the genealogies during the reigns of
Judah's King Jotham[d] and Israel's King
Jeroboam.[e]

18 The sons of Reuben and Gad and half the
tribe of Manasseh had 44,760 warriors who
could serve[f] in the army — men who carried
shield and sword, drew the bow, and were
trained for war. 19 They waged war against the
Hagrites,[g] Jetur,[h] Naphish, and Nodab. 20 They
received help against these enemies because
they cried out to God in battle, and the Hagrites and all their allies were handed over to
them.[i] He granted their request because they
trusted in Him.[j] 21 They captured the Hagrites'
livestock — 50,000 of their camels, 250,000
sheep, and 2,000 donkeys — as well as 100,000
people. 22 Many of the Hagrites were killed because it was God's battle.[k] And they lived there
in the Hagrites' place[l] until the exile.[m]

Half the Tribe of Manasseh

23 The sons of half the tribe of Manasseh
settled in the land from Bashan to Baal-hermon (that is, Senir[n] or Mount Hermon); they
were numerous. 24 These were the heads of
their ancestral houses: Epher, Ishi, Eliel, Azriel, Jeremiah, Hodaviah, and Jahdiel. They
were brave warriors, famous men, and heads
of their ancestral houses. 25 But they were unfaithful to the God of their ancestors. They
prostituted themselves[o] with the gods of the
nations[A] God had destroyed before them.[p]
26 So the God of Israel put it into the mind of
Pul[q] (that is, Tiglath-pileser[B]) king of Assyria
to take the Reubenites, Gadites, and half the
tribe of Manasseh into exile. He took them to
Halah, Habor, Hara, and Gozan's river, where
they are until today.

The Levites

6 [C] Levi's[r] sons: Gershom,[D] Kohath,
and Merari.
2 Kohath's sons: Amram, Izhar, Hebron,
and Uzziel.
3 Amram's children: Aaron, Moses,
and Miriam.
Aaron's sons: Nadab, Abihu, Eleazar,
and Ithamar.
4 Eleazar fathered Phinehas;[s]
Phinehas fathered Abishua;
5 Abishua fathered Bukki;
Bukki fathered Uzzi;
6 Uzzi fathered Zerahiah;
Zerahiah fathered Meraioth;
7 Meraioth fathered Amariah;
Amariah fathered Ahitub;
8 Ahitub fathered Zadok;
Zadok fathered Ahimaaz;
9 Ahimaaz fathered Azariah;
Azariah fathered Johanan;
10 Johanan fathered Azariah, who served
as priest in the temple that Solomon
built in Jerusalem;
11 Azariah fathered Amariah;
Amariah fathered Ahitub;
12 Ahitub fathered Zadok;
Zadok fathered Shallum;
13 Shallum fathered Hilkiah;
Hilkiah fathered Azariah;
14 Azariah fathered Seraiah;
and Seraiah fathered Jehozadak.
15 Jehozadak went into exile when the
LORD sent Judah and Jerusalem
into exile at the hands of
Nebuchadnezzar.[t]

[a] **5:11-12** Gn 46:16; Nm 26:15-18
[b] **5:11** Dt 3:10
[c] **5:16** 1Ch 27:29
[d] **5:17** 2Kg 15:5,32
[e] 2Kg 14:16,28
[f] **5:18** Nm 1:3
[g] **5:19** 1Ch 5:10
[h] 1Ch 1:31
[i] **5:20** 2Ch 14:11-13
[j] Ps 9:10; 20:7-8
[k] **5:22** Jos 23:10; 2Ch 32:8
[l] 1Ch 4:41
[m] 2Kg 15:29; 17:6
[n] **5:23** Dt 3:9
[o] **5:25** Ex 34:15
[p] 2Kg 17:7-8
[q] **5:26** 2Kg 15:19,29
[r] **6:1-3** Gn 46:11; Ex 6:16,18,20,23; Nm 26:57-60
[s] **6:4** Ex 6:25
[t] **6:15** 2Kg 24:1-2,10,14; 25:1,8,11,21; 1Ch 9:1

[A] **5:25** Lit *the peoples of the land* [B] **5:26** LXX; MT reads *Tilgath-pilneser* [C] **6:1** 1Ch 5:27 in Hb [D] **6:1** Levi's son's name is spelled Gershon in Ex.

16 [A] Levi's[a] sons: Gershom, Kohath,
and Merari.
17 These are the names of Gershom's sons:
Libni and Shimei.
18 Kohath's sons: Amram, Izhar, Hebron
and Uzziel.
19 Merari's sons: Mahli and Mushi.
These are the Levites' families
according to their fathers:
20 Of Gershom: his son Libni,
his son Jahath, his son Zimmah,
21 his son Joah, his son Iddo,
his son Zerah, and his son Jeatherai.
22 Kohath's sons: his son Amminadab,
his son Korah, his son Assir,
23 his son Elkanah, his son Ebiasaph,
his son Assir, 24 his son Tahath,
his son Uriel, his son Uzziah,
and his son Shaul.
25 Elkanah's sons: Amasai and Ahimoth,
26 his son Elkanah, his son Zophai,
his son Nahath, 27 his son Eliab,
his son Jeroham, and his son Elkanah.
28 Samuel's sons: his firstborn Joel,[B,b]
and his second son Abijah.
29 Merari's sons: Mahli, his son Libni,
his son Shimei, his son Uzzah,
30 his son Shimea, his son Haggiah,
and his son Asaiah.

The Musicians

31 These are the men David put in charge of
the music in the LORD's temple[c] after the ark
came to rest there.[d] 32 They ministered with
song in front of the tabernacle, the tent of
meeting, until Solomon built the LORD's temple in Jerusalem, and they performed their
task according to the regulations given to
them. 33 These are the men who served with
their sons.

From the Kohathites: Heman the singer,
son of Joel, son of Samuel,
34 son of Elkanah, son of Jeroham,
son of Eliel, son of Toah,
35 son of Zuph, son of Elkanah,
son of Mahath, son of Amasai,
36 son of Elkanah, son of Joel,
son of Azariah, son of Zephaniah,
37 son of Tahath, son of Assir,
son of Ebiasaph, son of Korah,

[a] **6:16-19** Ex 6:16-19
[b] **6:28** 1Sm 8:2
[c] **6:31** 1Ch 15:16-22; 16:4-6
[d] 2Sm 6:17; 1Ch 15:25–16:1
[e] **6:49** Ex 27:1-8
[f] Ex 30:1-7
[g] Ex 30:10-16
[h] **6:50-53** 1Ch 6:4-8
[i] **6:54** Jos 21:4,10
[j] **6:55-56** Jos 14:13; 15:13
[k] **6:57** Jos 21:13,19

38 son of Izhar, son of Kohath,
son of Levi, son of Israel.
39 Heman's relative was ˙Asaph, who stood
at his right hand:
Asaph son of Berechiah, son of Shimea,
40 son of Michael, son of Baaseiah,
son of Malchijah, 41 son of Ethni,
son of Zerah, son of Adaiah,
42 son of Ethan, son of Zimmah,
son of Shimei, 43 son of Jahath,
son of Gershom, son of Levi.
44 On the left, their relatives were
Merari's sons:
Ethan son of Kishi, son of Abdi,
son of Malluch, 45 son of Hashabiah,
son of Amaziah, son of Hilkiah,
46 son of Amzi, son of Bani,
son of Shemer, 47 son of Mahli,
son of Mushi, son of Merari,
son of Levi.

Aaron's Descendants

48 Their relatives, the Levites, were assigned
to all the service of the tabernacle, God's temple. 49 But Aaron and his sons did all the work
of the most holy place. They presented the offerings on the altar of ˙burnt offerings[e] and
on the altar of incense[f] to make atonement
for Israel according to all that Moses the servant of God had commanded.[g]

50 These[h] are Aaron's sons: his son Eleazar,
his son Phinehas, his son Abishua,
51 his son Bukki, his son Uzzi,
his son Zerahiah, 52 his son Meraioth,
his son Amariah, his son Ahitub,
53 his son Zadok, and his son Ahimaaz.

The Settlements of the Levites

54 These were the places assigned to Aaron's
sons from the Kohathite family for their settlements in their territory, because the first
lot was for them.[i] 55 They[j] were given Hebron
in the land of Judah and its surrounding pasturelands, 56 but the fields and villages around
the city were given to Caleb son of Jephunneh. 57 Aaron's sons were given:[k]

Hebron (a city of refuge), Libnah and
its pasturelands, Jattir, Eshtemoa and

[A] **6:16** 1Ch 6:1 in Hb [B] **6:28** Some LXX mss, Syr, Arabic; other Hb mss omit *Joel*; 1Sm 8:2

its pasturelands, 58 Hilen[A] and its pasturelands, Debir and its pasturelands,
59 Ashan and its pasturelands, and Beth-
shemesh and its pasturelands. 60 From
the tribe of Benjamin they were given
Geba and its pasturelands, Alemeth and
its pasturelands, and Anathoth and its
pasturelands. They had 13 towns in all
among their families.

61 To the rest of the Kohathites, 10 towns
from half the tribe of Manasseh were assigned by lot.[a]
62 The Gershomites were assigned 13 towns
from the tribes of Issachar, Asher, Naphtali,
and Manasseh in Bashan according to their
families.
63 The Merarites were assigned by lot 12
towns from the tribes of Reuben, Gad, and
Zebulun according to their families.[b] 64 So the
Israelites gave these towns and their pasturelands to the Levites.[c] 65 They assigned by lot
the towns named above[d] from the tribes of
the Judahites, Simeonites, and Benjaminites.
66 Some[e] of the families of the Kohathites
were given towns from the tribe of Ephraim
for their territory:

67 Shechem (a city of refuge) with its pasturelands in the hill country of Ephraim,
Gezer and its pasturelands, 68 Jokmeam
and its pasturelands, Beth-horon and its
pasturelands, 69 Aijalon and its pasturelands, and Gath-rimmon and its pasturelands. 70 From half the tribe of Manasseh,
Aner and its pasturelands, and Bileam
and its pasturelands were given to the
rest of the families of the Kohathites.

71 The Gershomites received:

Golan in Bashan and its pasturelands,
and Ashtaroth and its pasturelands
from the families of half the tribe of
Manasseh. 72 From the tribe of Issachar
they received Kedesh and its pasturelands, Daberath and its pasturelands,
73 Ramoth and its pasturelands, and
Anem and its pasturelands. 74 From the
tribe of Asher they received Mashal and
its pasturelands, Abdon and its pasturelands, 75 Hukok and its pasturelands, and
Rehob and its pasturelands. 76 From the
tribe of Naphtali they received Kedesh
in Galilee and its pasturelands, Hammon
and its pasturelands, and Kiriathaim and
its pasturelands.

77 The rest of the Merarites received:

From the tribe of Zebulun they received
Rimmono and its pasturelands and Tabor and its pasturelands. 78 From the tribe
of Reuben across the Jordan at Jericho, to
the east of the Jordan, they received Bezer in the desert and its pasturelands,
Jahzah and its pasturelands, 79 Kedemoth
and its pasturelands, and Mephaath and
its pasturelands. 80 From the tribe of Gad
they received Ramoth in Gilead and its
pasturelands, Mahanaim and its pasturelands, 81 Heshbon and its pasturelands,
and Jazer and its pasturelands.

Issachar's Descendants

7 Issachar's sons:[f] Tola, Puah, Jashub, and
Shimron — four.
2 Tola's sons: Uzzi, Rephaiah, Jeriel,
Jahmai, Ibsam, and Shemuel, the heads
of their ancestral houses. During
David's reign, 22,600 descendants of
Tola were recorded as warriors in their
genealogies.[g]
3 Uzzi's son: Izrahiah.
Izrahiah's sons: Michael, Obadiah, Joel,
Isshiah. All five of them were chiefs.
4 Along with them, they had 36,000
troops for battle according to the
genealogical records of their ancestral
houses, for they had many wives and
children. 5 Their tribesmen who were
warriors belonging to all the families
of Issachar totaled 87,000 in their
genealogies.

Benjamin's Descendants

6 Three[h] of Benjamin's sons: Bela,
Becher, and Jediael.
7 Bela's sons: Ezbon, Uzzi, Uzziel,
Jerimoth, and Iri — five. They were
warriors and heads of their ancestral
houses; 22,034 were listed in their
genealogies.

[a] **6:61** Jos 21:5; 1Ch 6:66-70
[b] **6:63** Jos 21:7; 1Ch 6:77-81
[c] **6:64** Jos 21:3,41-42
[d] **6:65** 1Ch 6:57-60
[e] **6:66-81** Jos 21:20-40
[f] **7:1** Gn 46:13
[g] **7:2** 2Sm 24:1-9
[h] **7:6-12** Gn 46:21; Nm 26:38-41; 1Ch 8

A **6:58** Some Hb mss, LXX; other Hb mss read *Hilez*

[8]Becher's sons: Zemirah, Joash, Eliezer,
Elioenai, Omri, Jeremoth, Abijah,
Anathoth, and Alemeth; all these were
Becher's sons. [9]Their genealogies were
recorded according to the heads of their
ancestral houses — 20,200 warriors.
[10]Jediael's son: Bilhan.
Bilhan's sons: Jeush, Benjamin, Ehud,
Chenaanah, Zethan, Tarshish, and
Ahishahar. [11]All these sons of Jediael
listed by heads of families were
warriors; there were 17,200 who
could serve in the army. [12]Shuppim
and Huppim were sons of Ir, and the
Hushim were the sons of Aher.

Naphtali's Descendants

[13]Naphtali's sons:[a] Jahziel, Guni, Jezer,
and Shallum — Bilhah's sons.

Manasseh's Descendants

[14]Manasseh's[b] sons through his
Aramean concubine: Asriel and Machir
the father of Gilead. [15]Machir took
wives from Huppim and Shuppim. The
name of his sister was Maacah. Another
descendant was named Zelophehad,
but he had only daughters.
[16]Machir's wife Maacah gave birth to
a son, and she named him Peresh. His
brother was named Sheresh, and his
sons were Ulam and Rekem.
[17]Ulam's son: Bedan. These were the
sons of Gilead son of Machir, son of
Manasseh. [18]His sister Hammolecheth
gave birth to Ishhod, Abiezer, and
Mahlah.
[19]Shemida's sons: Ahian, Shechem,
Likhi, and Aniam.

Ephraim's Descendants

20 Ephraim's[c] sons: Shuthelah, and
his son Bered,
his son Tahath, his son Eleadah,
his son Tahath, [21]his son Zabad,
his son Shuthelah, also Ezer, and Elead.

The men of Gath, born in the land,
killed them because they went down to
raid their cattle. [22]Their father Ephraim
mourned a long time, and his relatives[A]
came to comfort him. [23]He slept with
his wife, and she conceived and gave
birth to a son. So he named him Beriah,
because there had been misfortune in
his home.[B] [24]His daughter was Sheerah,
who built Lower and Upper Beth-
horon[d] and Uzzen-sheerah,

25 his son Rephah,[C] his son Resheph,
his son Telah, his son Tahan,
26 his son Ladan, his son Ammihud,
his son Elishama, [27]his son Nun,
and his son Joshua.[e]

[28]Their holdings and settlements were
Bethel[f] and its villages; Naaran to the
east, Gezer and its villages to the west,
and Shechem and its villages as far as
Ayyah and its villages, [29]and along the
borders of the sons of Manasseh, Beth-
shean and its villages, Taanach and its villages, Megiddo and its villages, and Dor
and its villages. The sons of Joseph son of
Israel lived in these towns.

Asher's Descendants

[30]Asher's[g] sons: Imnah, Ishvah, Ishvi,
and Beriah, with their sister Serah.
[31]Beriah's sons: Heber, and Malchiel,
who fathered Birzaith.
[32]Heber fathered Japhlet, Shomer, and
Hotham, with their sister Shua.
[33]Japhlet's sons: Pasach, Bimhal, and
Ashvath. These were Japhlet's sons.
[34]Shemer's sons: Ahi, Rohgah, Hubbah,
and Aram.
[35]His brother Helem's sons: Zophah,
Imna, Shelesh, and Amal.
[36]Zophah's sons: Suah, Harnepher,
Shual, Beri, Imrah, [37]Bezer, Hod,
Shamma, Shilshah, Ithran, and Beera.
[38]Jether's sons: Jephunneh, Pispa, and
Ara.
[39]Ulla's sons: Arah, Hanniel, and Rizia.
[40]All these were Asher's sons. They were
the heads of their ancestral houses,
chosen men, warriors, and chiefs
among the leaders. The number of men
listed in their genealogies for military
service was 26,000.

[a]7:13 Gn 46:24-25 [b]7:14-19 Nm 26:29-34 [c]7:20-21a Nm 26:35-36 [d]7:24 Jos 16:3,5 [e]7:27 Ex 17:9-14; 24:13 [f]7:28 Jos 16:2 [g]7:30-31 Gn 46:17; Nm 26:44-46

[A]7:22 Or *his brothers* [B]7:23 In Hb, the name Beriah sounds like "in misfortune." [C]7:25 Probably Ephraim's son

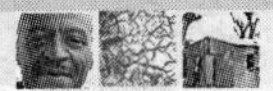

Benjamin's Descendants

8 Benjamin[a] fathered Bela, his firstborn;
Ashbel was born second, Aharah third,
2 Nohah fourth, and Rapha fifth.
3 Bela's sons: Addar, Gera, Abihud,
4 Abishua, Naaman, Ahoah, 5 Gera,
Shephuphan, and Huram.
6 These were Ehud's sons, who were the
heads of the families living in Geba
and who were deported to Manahath:
7 Naaman, Ahijah, and Gera. Gera
deported them and was the father of
Uzza and Ahihud.
8 Shaharaim had sons in the country
of Moab after he had divorced his
wives Hushim and Baara. 9 His sons by
his wife Hodesh: Jobab, Zibia, Mesha,
Malcam, 10 Jeuz, Sachia, and Mirmah.
These were his sons, heads of families.
11 He also had sons by Hushim: Abitub
and Elpaal.
12 Elpaal's sons: Eber, Misham, and
Shemed who built Ono and Lod and
its villages, 13 Beriah and Shema, who
were the heads of families of Aijalon's
residents and who drove out the
residents of Gath, 14 Ahio,[A] Shashak, and
Jeremoth.
15 Zebadiah, Arad, Eder, 16 Michael,
Ishpah, and Joha were Beriah's sons.
17 Zebadiah, Meshullam, Hizki, Heber,
18 Ishmerai, Izliah, and Jobab were
Elpaal's sons.
19 Jakim, Zichri, Zabdi, 20 Elienai,
Zillethai, Eliel, 21 Adaiah, Beraiah, and
Shimrath were Shimei's sons.
22 Ishpan, Eber, Eliel, 23 Abdon, Zichri,
Hanan, 24 Hananiah, Elam, Anthothijah,
25 Iphdeiah, and Penuel were Shashak's
sons.
26 Shamsherai, Shehariah, Athaliah,
27 Jaareshiah, Elijah, and Zichri were
Jeroham's sons.
28 These[b] were heads of families, chiefs
according to their genealogies, and
lived in Jerusalem.

29 Jeiel[B,c] fathered Gibeon and lived in
Gibeon. His wife's name was Maacah.
30 Abdon was his firstborn son, then
Zur, Kish, Baal, Nadab, 31 Gedor, Ahio,
Zecher, 32 and Mikloth who fathered
Shimeah. These also lived opposite
their relatives in Jerusalem, with their
other relatives.
33 Ner fathered Kish, Kish fathered
Saul, and Saul fathered Jonathan,
Malchishua, Abinadab, and
Esh-baal.[C]
34 Jonathan's son was Merib-baal,[D] and
Merib-baal fathered Micah.
35 Micah's sons: Pithon, Melech, Tarea,
and Ahaz.
36 Ahaz fathered Jehoaddah, Jehoaddah
fathered Alemeth, Azmaveth, and
Zimri, and Zimri fathered Moza.
37 Moza fathered Binea. His son was
Raphah, his son Elasah, and his son
Azel.
38 Azel had six sons, and these were their
names: Azrikam, Bocheru, Ishmael,
Sheariah, Obadiah, and Hanan. All
these were Azel's sons.
39 His brother Eshek's sons: Ulam
was his firstborn, Jeush second, and
Eliphelet third.
40 Ulam's sons were warriors and
archers.[E] They had many sons and
grandsons — 150 of them.
All these were among Benjamin's sons.

[a] **8:1-5** Gn 46:21; Nm 26:38-41; 1Ch 7:6-12
[b] **8:28-38** 1Ch 9:34-44
[c] **8:29** 1Ch 9:35
[d] **9:1** 1Ch 6:15
[e] **9:2-9** Neh 11:3-9
[f] **9:2** Ezr 2:43,58; 8:20

After the Exile

9 All Israel was registered in the genealogies that are written in the Book of the
Kings of Israel. But Judah was exiled[d] to Babylon because of their unfaithfulness. 2 The
first[e] to live in their towns on their own property again were Israelites, priests, Levites, and
temple servants.[f]

3 These people from the descendants
of Judah, Benjamin, Ephraim, and
Manasseh settled in Jerusalem:
4 Uthai son of Ammihud, son of Omri,
son of Imri, son of Bani, a descendant[F]
of Perez son of Judah;
5 from the Shilonites:
Asaiah the firstborn and his sons;
6 and from the sons of Zerah:
Jeuel and 690 of their relatives.

[A] **8:13-14** LXX reads *Gath* [14] *and their brother* [B] **8:29** LXX; MT omits *Jeiel*; 1Ch 9:35 [C] **8:33** = Man of Baal [D] **8:34** = Baal Contends [E] **8:40** Lit *valiant ones who string the bow* [F] **9:4** Lit *Bani, from the sons*

[7]The Benjaminites: Sallu son of
Meshullam, son of Hodaviah, son of
Hassenuah;
[8]Ibneiah son of Jeroham;
Elah son of Uzzi, son of Michri;
Meshullam son of Shephatiah, son of
Reuel, son of Ibnijah;
[9]and 956[a] of their relatives according
to their genealogical records. All these
men were heads of their ancestral
houses.

[10]The priests:[b] Jedaiah; Jehoiarib;
Jachin;
[11]Azariah son of Hilkiah, son of
Meshullam, son of Zadok, son of
Meraioth, son of Ahitub, the chief
official[c] of God's temple;
[12]Adaiah son of Jeroham, son of
Pashhur, son of Malchijah;
Maasai son of Adiel, son of Jahzerah,
son of Meshullam, son of Meshillemith,
son of Immer;
[13]and 1,760 of their relatives, the heads
of households. They were capable men
employed in the ministry of God's
temple.

[14]The Levites: Shemaiah son of
Hasshub, son of Azrikam, son of
Hashabiah of the Merarites;
[15]Bakbakkar, Heresh, Galal, and
Mattaniah, son of Mica, son of Zichri,
son of *Asaph;
[16]Obadiah son of Shemaiah, son of
Galal, son of Jeduthun;
and Berechiah son of Asa, son of
Elkanah who lived in the villages of the
Netophathites.

[17]The gatekeepers:[d] Shallum, Akkub,
Talmon, Ahiman, and their relatives.
Shallum was their chief; [18]he was
previously stationed at the King's
Gate on the east side.[e] These were the
gatekeepers from the camp of the
Levites.
[19]Shallum son of Kore, son of Ebiasaph,
son of Korah and his relatives from his
ancestral household, the Korahites,
were assigned to guard the thresholds
of the tent.[A] Their ancestors had
been assigned to the LORD's camp as
guardians of the entrance.[f] [20]In earlier
times Phinehas son of Eleazar had been
their leader, and the LORD was with
him.[g] [21]Zechariah son of Meshelemiah
was the gatekeeper at the entrance to
the tent of meeting.[h]

[22]The total number of those chosen to be
gatekeepers at the thresholds was 212. They
were registered by genealogy in their villages.
David and Samuel the seer had appointed
them[i] to their trusted positions. [23]So they
and their sons were assigned to the gates of
the LORD's temple, which had been the tent-
temple. [24]The gatekeepers were on the four
sides: east, west, north, and south. [25]Their relatives came from their villages[j] at fixed times
to be with them seven days,[k] [26]but the four
chief gatekeepers, who were Levites, were entrusted with the rooms and the treasuries of
God's temple.[l] [27]They spent the night in the
vicinity of God's temple, because they had
guard duty and were in charge of opening it
every morning.[m]

[28]Some of them were in charge of the utensils used in worship. They would count them
when they brought them in and when they
took them out. [29]Others were put in charge
of the furnishings and all the utensils of the
sanctuary,[n] as well as the fine flour,[o] wine,
oil, incense, and spices. [30]Some of the priests'
sons mixed the spices.[p] [31]A Levite called Mattithiah, the firstborn of Shallum the Korahite,
was entrusted with baking the bread.[B] [32]Some
of the Kohathites' relatives were responsible
for preparing the rows of the *bread of the
Presence[q] every Sabbath.

[33]The singers,[r] the heads of the Levite families, stayed in the temple chambers and were
exempt from other tasks because they were
on duty day and night.[s] [34]These[t] were the
heads of the Levite families, chiefs according
to their genealogies, and lived in Jerusalem.

Saul's Family

[35]Jeiel fathered Gibeon and lived in
Gibeon. His wife's name was Maacah.
[36]Abdon was his firstborn son, then

[a]**9:9** Neh 11:8
[b]**9:10-16** Neh 11:10-18
[c]**9:11** Jr 20:1
[d]**9:17-22a** 1Ch 26:1-19; Ezr 2:42; Neh 7:45; 11:19
[e]**9:18** Ezk 46:1-2
[f]**9:19** Nm 4:1-20; 26:11; 1Ch 6:22
[g]**9:20** Nm 25:7-13
[h]**9:21** 1Ch 26:2,14
[i]**9:22** 1Ch 26:1
[j]**9:25** 1Ch 9:16
[k]2Kg 11:5,7; 2Ch 23:8
[l]**9:26** Neh 12:25
[m]**9:27** 1Sm 3:3,15; 1Ch 23:30-32
[n]**9:29** Nm 3:31
[o]1Ch 23:29
[p]**9:30** Ex 30:23-25
[q]**9:32** Lv 24:5-9
[r]**9:33** 1Ch 6:31-47; 25:1
[s]Ps 134:1
[t]**9:34-44** 1Ch 8:28-38

[A]**9:19** = the temple [B]**9:31** Lit *with things prepared in pans*

Zur, Kish, Baal, Ner, Nadab, 37 Gedor,
Ahio, Zechariah, and Mikloth.
38 Mikloth fathered Shimeam. These
also lived opposite their relatives in
Jerusalem with their other relatives.
39 Ner fathered Kish, Kish fathered
Saul, and Saul fathered Jonathan,
Malchishua, Abinadab, and Esh-baal.
40 Jonathan's son was Merib-baal, and
Merib-baal fathered Micah.
41 Micah's sons: Pithon, Melech, Tahrea,
and Ahaz.[A]
42 Ahaz fathered Jarah;
Jarah fathered Alemeth, Azmaveth, and
Zimri;
Zimri fathered Moza.
43 Moza fathered Binea.
His son was Rephaiah, his son Elasah,
and his son Azel.
44 Azel had six sons, and these were their
names: Azrikam, Bocheru, Ishmael,
Sheariah, Obadiah, and Hanan. These
were Azel's sons.

The Deaths of Saul and His Sons

10 The Philistines[a] fought against Israel,
and Israel's men fled from them and
were killed on Mount Gilboa. 2 The Philistines
pursued Saul and his sons and killed Saul's
sons Jonathan, Abinadab, and Malchishua.
3 When the battle intensified against Saul,
the archers found him and severely wounded
him. 4 Then Saul said to his armor-bearer,
"Draw your sword and run me through with
it, or these uncircumcised men will come and
torture me!" But his armor-bearer wouldn't
do it because he was terrified. Then Saul took
his sword and fell on it. 5 When his armor-
bearer saw that Saul was dead, he also fell
on his own sword and died. 6 So Saul and his
three sons died—his whole house died together.

7 When all the men of Israel in the valley
saw that the army had fled and that Saul and
his sons were dead, they abandoned their cities and fled. So the Philistines came and settled in them.

8 The next day when the Philistines came to
strip the slain, they found Saul and his sons
dead on Mount Gilboa. 9 They stripped Saul,
cut off his head, took his armor, and sent
messengers throughout the land of the Philistines to spread the good news to their idols
and their people. 10 Then they put his armor
in the temple of their gods and hung his skull
in the temple of Dagon.[b]

11 When all Jabesh-gilead heard of everything the Philistines had done to Saul, 12 all
their brave men set out and retrieved the
body of Saul and the bodies of his sons and
brought them to Jabesh. They buried their
bones under the oak[B] in Jabesh[c] and fasted
seven days.

13 Saul died for his unfaithfulness to the
LORD because he did not keep the LORD's
word.[d] He even consulted a medium for guidance,[e] 14 but he did not inquire of the LORD.
So the LORD put him to death and turned the
kingdom over to David son of Jesse.[f]

David's Anointing as King

11 All Israel[g] came together to David at Hebron and said, "Here we are, your own
flesh and blood.[C] 2 Even when Saul was king,
you led us out to battle and brought us back.
The LORD your God also said to you, 'You will
shepherd My people Israel and be ruler over
My people Israel.'"

3 So all the elders of Israel came to the king
at Hebron. David made a covenant with them
at Hebron in the LORD's presence, and they
anointed David king over Israel, in keeping
with the LORD's word through Samuel.[h]

David's Capture of Jerusalem

4 David[i] and all Israel marched to Jerusalem
(that is, Jebus[j]); the Jebusites who inhabited
the land were there. 5 The inhabitants of Jebus
said to David, "You will never get in here." Yet
David did capture the stronghold of *Zion,
that is, the city of David.

6 David said, "Whoever is the first to kill
a Jebusite will become chief commander."
Joab[k] son of Zeruiah went up first, so he became the chief.

7 Then David took up residence in the
stronghold; therefore, it was called the city
of David. 8 He built up the city all the way
around, from the supporting terraces to the
surrounding parts, and Joab restored the rest

[a] **10:1-12** 1Sm 31:1-13
[b] **10:10** 1Sm 5:1-4; 17:54
[c] **10:12** 2Sm 21:12-14
[d] **10:13** 1Sm 13:13-14; 15:23
[e] 1Sm 28:7
[f] **10:14** 1Sm 15:28; 1Ch 12:23
[g] **11:1-3** 2Sm 5:1-3
[h] **11:3** 1Sm 16:1-13
[i] **11:4-9** 2Sm 5:6-10
[j] **11:4** Jos 15:8,63; Jdg 1:21
[k] **11:6** 2Sm 8:16; 1Ch 18:15

[A] **9:41** LXX, Syr, Tg, Vg, Arabic; MT omits *and Ahaz*; 1Ch 8:35 [B] **10:12** Or *terebinth*, or *large tree* [C] **11:1** Lit *your bone and flesh*

May Hayman (1906–1942)

"For whoever wants to save his life will lose it, but whoever loses his life because of Me and the gospel will save it" (Mk 8:35).

For many Christians this verse is about giving up our ambition and control or being willing to lose our lives, but some face its ultimate test as their lives are literally demanded of them. Anglican Sister May Hayman, along with Sister Mavis Parkinson, her partner in missions, were two such people, both of whom were martyred at the hands of Japanese soldiers in Papua New Guinea, during World War II.

Hayman began her career as a nurse in Australia before taking her skills to the mission field in 1932, at the age of twenty-six. She served at two mission stations before settling in Gona and taking charge of the hospital and the housekeeping in 1939. There she worked alongside a priest, Father James Benson, and a teacher, Sister Mavis Parkinson. Hayman cared for sick Papuans, sometimes even performing surgery and setting broken bones, which normally would have been the work of a doctor.

When World War II started, it initially had little effect on the people of Papua, but when the Japanese forces entered in 1941, Papua New Guinea became a dangerous place. Many Europeans were evacuated to Australia because of the likelihood of a Japanese invasion, but the bishops of the Anglican church urged their missionaries to stay: "Many already think us fools and mad. What does that matter! If we are fools, we are fools for Christ's sake. . . . I cannot guarantee all will be well. . . . One thing only I can guarantee is that if we do not forsake Christ present here in His Body in Papua, the Church, He will not forsake us."[1] Hayman and the others at her station chose to face danger rather than flee to Australia, staying with the people they loved and served.

When Japanese boats began to appear on the shore near the mission station, Hayman, Parkinson, and Benson tried to avoid the troops. They were helped along by many of the Papuan people who gave them food and shelter and even built them a small cottage in the jungle where they hid safely for a month before moving on again. After nearly running into Japanese soldiers, Hayman and Parkinson found themselves separated from Benson and lost in the jungle. It was not long afterward that they were betrayed by a guide and were taken to their deaths. Hayman and Parkinson were run through with bayonets and buried in unmarked graves.

These two brave women were killed for the sake of Christ and His gospel among the people of Papua New Guinea, and they have received their crowns of glory.

[1] Strong, Rt. Revd. Philip in E. C. Rowland, *Faithful Unto Death: The Story of the New Guinea Martyrs* (Australia: Australian Board of Missions, 1964), http://anglicanhistory.org/aus/png/rowland_faithful1964.html (Accessed on May 18, 2011).

of the city. [9]David steadily grew more powerful,[a] and the LORD of ·Hosts was with him.

Exploits of David's Warriors

[10]The following were the chiefs of David's warriors who, together with all Israel,
strongly supported him in his reign to make
him king according to the LORD's word about
Israel.[b] [11]This[c] is the list of David's warriors:

Jashobeam son of Hachmoni was chief[d] of
the Thirty;[A] he wielded his spear against 300
and killed them at one time.

[12]After him, Eleazar son of Dodo[e] the Ahohite was one of the three warriors. [13]He was
with David at Pas-dammim when the Philistines had gathered there for battle. There
was a portion of a field full of barley, where
the troops had fled from the Philistines.[f]
[14]But Eleazar and David[B] took their stand in
the middle of the field and defended it. They
killed the Philistines, and the LORD gave them
a great victory.

[15]Three of the 30 chief men went down to
David, to the rock at the cave of Adullam,[g]
while the Philistine army was encamped in
the Valley of Rephaim.[h] [16]At that time David
was in the stronghold,[i] and a Philistine garrison[j] was at Bethlehem. [17]David was extremely
thirsty[C] and said, "If only someone would
bring me water to drink from the well at the
city gate of Bethlehem!" [18]So the Three broke
through the Philistine camp and drew water
from the well at the gate of Bethlehem. They
brought it back to David, but he refused to
drink it. Instead, he poured it out to the LORD.
[19]David said, "I would never do such a thing
in the presence of God! How can I drink the
blood of these men who risked their lives?"
For they brought it at the risk of their lives. So
he would not drink it. Such were the exploits
of the three warriors.

[20]Abishai,[k] Joab's brother, was the leader of
the Three.[D] He raised his spear against 300
men and killed them, gaining a reputation
among the Three. [21]He was more honored
than the Three and became their commander
even though he did not become one of the
Three.

[22]Benaiah son of Jehoiada[l] was the son of
a brave man[E] from Kabzeel, a man of many
exploits. Benaiah killed two sons of Ariel
of Moab,[F] and he went down into a pit on a
snowy day and killed a lion. [23]He also killed
an Egyptian who was seven and a half feet
tall.[G] Even though the Egyptian had a spear
in his hand like a weaver's beam,[m] Benaiah
went down to him with a club, snatched the
spear out of the Egyptian's hand, and then
killed him with his own spear. [24]These were
the exploits of Benaiah son of Jehoiada, who
had a reputation among the three warriors.
[25]He was the most honored of the Thirty, but
he did not become one of the Three. David
put him in charge of his bodyguard.

[26]The fighting men[n] were:

Joab's brother Asahel,[o]
Elhanan son of Dodo of Bethlehem,
27 Shammoth the Harorite,
Helez the Pelonite,
28 Ira son of Ikkesh the Tekoite,
Abiezer the Anathothite,
29 Sibbecai the Hushathite,
Ilai the Ahohite,
30 Maharai the Netophathite,
Heled son of Baanah the Netophathite,
31 Ithai son of Ribai from Gibeah
of the Benjaminites,
Benaiah the Pirathonite,
32 Hurai from the ·wadis of Gaash,
Abiel the Arbathite,
33 Azmaveth the Baharumite,
Eliahba the Shaalbonite,
34 the sons of[H,p] Hashem the Gizonite,
Jonathan son of Shagee the Hararite,
35 Ahiam son of Sachar the Hararite,
Eliphal son of Ur,
36 Hepher the Mecherathite,
Ahijah the Pelonite,
37 Hezro the Carmelite,
Naarai son of Ezbai,
38 Joel the brother of Nathan,
Mibhar son of Hagri,
39 Zelek the Ammonite,
Naharai the Beerothite,
the armor-bearer for Joab
son of Zeruiah,
40 Ira the Ithrite,
Gareb the Ithrite,

[a]11:9 2Sm 3:1 [b]11:10 1Ch 11:3 [c]11:11-25 2Sm 23:8-23 [d]11:11 1Ch 12:18 [e]11:12 1Ch 27:4 [f]11:13 2Sm 23:11-12 [g]11:15 1Sm 22:1 [h]1Ch 14:9 [i]11:16 1Sm 22:4-5; 2Sm 5:9 [j]1Sm 10:5 [k]11:20 1Sm 26:6; 2Sm 18:2 [l]11:22 2Sm 8:18; 20:23; 23:20-23; 1Kg 1:8; 1Ch 18:17; 27:5-6,34 [m]11:23 1Sm 17:7; 1Ch 20:5 [n]11:26-47 2Sm 23:24-39 [o]11:26 2Sm 2:18-23 [p]11:34 2Sm 23:32

[A]11:11 Alt Hb tradition reads *Three* [B]11:14 Lit *But they* [C]11:17 Lit *And David craved* [D]11:20 Syr reads *Thirty* [E]11:22 Or *was a valiant man* [F]11:22 Or *He killed two Moabite warriors* [G]11:23 Lit *who measured five cubits* [H]11:34 LXX omits *the sons of*; 2Sm 23:32

41 Uriah the Hittite,
Zabad son of Ahlai,
42 Adina son of Shiza the Reubenite, chief
of the Reubenites, and 30 with him,
43 Hanan son of Maacah,
Joshaphat the Mithnite,
44 Uzzia the Ashterathite,
Shama and Jeiel the sons of Hotham
the Aroerite,
45 Jediael son of Shimri and his brother
Joha the Tizite,
46 Eliel the Mahavite,
Jeribai and Joshaviah, the sons of Elnaam,
Ithmah the Moabite,
47 Eliel, Obed, and Jaasiel the Mezobaite.

David's First Supporters

12 The following were the men who
came to David at Ziklag while he was
still banned from the presence of Saul son
of Kish.[a] They were among the warriors who
helped him in battle. 2 They were archers who
could use either the right or left hand, both
to sling stones and shoot arrows from a bow.[b]
They were Saul's relatives[c] from Benjamin:

3 Their chief was Ahiezer son of
Shemaah the Gibeathite.
Then there was his brother Joash;
Jeziel and Pelet sons of Azmaveth;
Beracah, Jehu the Anathothite;
4 Ishmaiah the Gibeonite, a warrior
among the Thirty and a leader over the
Thirty;
[A]Jeremiah, Jahaziel, Johanan, Jozabad
the Gederathite;
5 Eluzai, Jerimoth, Bealiah, Shemariah,
Shephatiah the Haruphite;
6 Elkanah, Isshiah, Azarel, Joezer, and
Jashobeam, the Korahites;
7 and Joelah and Zebadiah, the sons of
Jeroham from Gedor.

8 Some Gadites defected to David at his
stronghold in the desert. They were fighting
men, trained for battle, expert with shield
and spear. Their faces were like the faces of
lions, and they were as swift as gazelles on the
mountains.[d]

9 Ezer was the chief, Obadiah second,
Eliab third,
10 Mishmannah fourth, Jeremiah fifth,
11 Attai sixth, Eliel seventh,
12 Johanan eighth, Elzabad ninth,
13 Jeremiah tenth, and
Machbannai eleventh.

14 These Gadites were army commanders; the
least of them was a match for a hundred, and
the greatest of them for a thousand.[e] 15 These
are the men who crossed the Jordan in the
first month[B] when it was overflowing all its
banks,[f] and put to flight all those in the valleys to the east and to the west.
16 Other Benjaminites and men from Judah
also went to David at the stronghold.[g] 17 David
went out to meet them and said to them, "If
you have come in peace to help me, my heart
will be united with you, but if you have come
to betray me to my enemies even though my
hands have done no wrong, may the God of
our ancestors look on it and judge."
18 Then the Spirit took control of[C,h] Amasai,[i]
chief of the Thirty, and he said:

We are yours, David,
we are with you, son of Jesse!
Peace, peace to you,
and peace to him who helps you,[j]
for your God helps you.

So David received them and made them leaders of his troops.
19 Some Manassites defected to David when
he went with the Philistines to fight against
Saul. However, they did not help the Philistines because the Philistine rulers sent David
away after a discussion. They said, "It will be
our heads if he defects to his master Saul."[k]
20 When David went to Ziklag, some men
from Manasseh defected to him: Adnah, Jozabad, Jediael, Michael, Jozabad, Elihu, and
Zillethai, chiefs of thousands in Manasseh.
21 They helped David against the raiders,[l] for
they were all brave warriors and commanders in the army. 22 At that time, men came day
after day to help David until there was a great
army, like an army of God.[D,m]

David's Soldiers in Hebron

23 The numbers of the armed troops who
came to David at Hebron to turn Saul's king-

[a] 12:1 1Sm 27:1-7
[b] 12:2 Jdg 3:15; 20:16
[c] 1Ch 12:29
[d] 12:8 2Sm 2:18
[e] 12:14 Lv 26:8; Dt 32:30; Is 30:17
[f] 12:15 Jos 3:15; 4:18
[g] 12:16 1Sm 22:1-2
[h] 12:18 Jdg 6:34; 2Ch 24:20
[i] 1Ch 2:17
[j] 1Sm 25:5-6
[k] 12:19 1Sm 29:1-11
[l] 12:21 1Sm 30:1-20
[m] 12:22 Gn 32:1-2; Jos 5:13-15

[A] 12:4 1Ch 12:5 in Hb [B] 12:15 = Nisan (March–April) [C] 12:18 Lit *Spirit clothed Himself with*; Jdg 6:34; 2Ch 24:20 [D] 12:22 Or *like the ultimate army*

dom over to him,[a] according to the LORD's
word,[b] were as follows:

24 From the Judahites: 6,800 armed troops bearing shields and spears.

25 From the Simeonites: 7,100 brave warriors ready for war.

26 From the Levites: 4,600 27 in addition to Jehoiada, leader of the house of Aaron, with 3,700 men; 28 and Zadok,[c] a young brave warrior, with 22 commanders from his own ancestral house.

29 From the Benjaminites, the relatives of Saul:[d] 3,000 (up to that time the majority of the Benjaminites maintained their allegiance to the house of Saul).

30 From the Ephraimites: 20,800 brave warriors who were famous men in their ancestral houses.

31 From half the tribe of Manasseh: 18,000 designated by name to come and make David king.

32 From the Issacharites, who understood the times[e] and knew what Israel should do: 200 chiefs with all their relatives under their command.

33 From Zebulun: 50,000 who could serve in the army, trained for battle with all kinds of weapons of war, with one purpose[f] to help David.[A]

34 From Naphtali: 1,000 commanders accompanied by 37,000 men with shield and spear.

35 From the Danites: 28,600 trained for battle.

36 From Asher: 40,000 who could serve in the army, trained for battle.

37 From across the Jordan — from the Reubenites, Gadites, and half the tribe of Manasseh: 120,000 men equipped with all the military weapons of war.

38 All these warriors, lined up in battle formation, came to Hebron fully determined to
make David king over all Israel. All the rest
of Israel was also of one mind to make David
king.[g] 39 They spent three days there eating
and drinking with David, for their relatives
had provided for them. 40 In addition, their
neighbors from as far away as Issachar, Zebulun, and Naphtali came and brought food
on donkeys, camels, mules, and oxen — abundant provisions of flour, fig cakes, raisins,
wine and oil, oxen, and sheep.[h] Indeed, there
was joy in Israel.

David and the Ark

13 David consulted with all his leaders,
the commanders of hundreds and of
thousands. 2 Then he said to the whole assembly of Israel, "If it seems good to you, and if
this is from the LORD our God, let us spread
out and send the message to the rest of our
relatives in all the districts of Israel, including the priests and Levites in their cities with
pasturelands,[i] that they should gather together with us. 3 Then let us bring back the ark
of our God, for we did not inquire of Him[j] in
Saul's days." 4 Since the proposal seemed right
to all the people, the whole assembly agreed
to do it.
5 So David assembled all Israel,[k] from the
Shihor of Egypt to the entrance of Hamath,[B,l]
to bring the ark of God from Kiriath-jearim.[m]
6 David[n] and all Israel went to Baalah[o] (that is,
Kiriath-jearim that belongs to Judah) to take
the ark of God from there, which is called
by the name of the LORD who dwells between
the •cherubim.[p] 7 At Abinadab's house[q] they
set the ark of God on a new cart. Uzzah and
Ahio[C] were guiding the cart.
8 David and all Israel were celebrating with
all their might before God with songs and
with lyres, harps, tambourines, cymbals,
and trumpets.[r] 9 When they came to Chi-
don's threshing floor,[s] Uzzah reached out to
hold the ark because the oxen had stumbled.
10 Then the LORD's anger burned against Uzzah, and He struck him dead because he had
reached out to the ark.[t] So he died there in the
presence of God.[u]
11 David was angry because of the LORD's
outburst against Uzzah, so he named that
place Outburst Against Uzzah,[D] as it is still
named today. 12 David feared God that day and
said, "How can I ever bring the ark of God to
me?" 13 So David did not move the ark of God
home[E] to the city of David; instead, he took it

[a] **12:23** 1Sm 15:28; 1Ch 10:14
[b] 1Ch 11:10
[c] **12:28** 2Sm 8:17; 1Ch 6:8,53; 9:11; 15:11; 16:39
[d] **12:29** 1Ch 12:2
[e] **12:32** Est 1:13
[f] **12:33** Ps 12:2
[g] **12:38** 2Sm 5:1-3
[h] **12:40** 1Sm 25:18
[i] **13:2** Nm 35:1-8
[j] **13:3** 1Sm 7:1-2; 1Ch 10:14; 15:13
[k] **13:5** 2Sm 6:1; 1Ch 15:3
[l] 1Kg 8:65
[m] 1Sm 6:21; 7:1
[n] **13:6-14** 2Sm 6:2-11
[o] **13:6** Jos 15:9
[p] 2Kg 19:15
[q] **13:7** 1Sm 7:1
[r] **13:8** 1Ch 15:16
[s] **13:9** 2Sm 6:6
[t] **13:10** 1Ch 15:13,15
[u] Lv 10:2

[A] **12:33** LXX; MT omits *David* [B] **13:5** Or *to Lebo-hamath* [C] **13:7** Or *and his brothers* [D] **13:11** Or *Perez-uzzah* [E] **13:13** Lit *to himself*

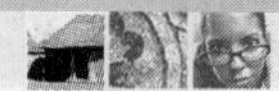

to the house of Obed-edom the Gittite.[a] 14 The ark of God remained with Obed-edom's family in his house for three months, and the LORD blessed his family and all that he had.

God's Blessing on David

14 King Hiram of Tyre sent envoys to David,[b] along with cedar logs, stonemasons, and carpenters to build a palace for him. 2 Then David knew that the LORD had established him as king over Israel and that his kingdom had been exalted for the sake of His people Israel.

3 David took more wives in Jerusalem, and he became the father of more sons and daughters. 4 These[c] are the names of the children born to him in Jerusalem: Shammua, Shobab, Nathan, Solomon, 5 Ibhar, Elishua, Elpelet, 6 Nogah, Nepheg, Japhia, 7 Elishama, Beeliada, and Eliphelet.

8 When the Philistines heard that David had been anointed king over all Israel, they all went in search of David; when David heard of this, he went out to face them. 9 Now the Philistines had come and raided in the Valley of Rephaim,[d] 10 so David inquired of God, "Should I go to war against the Philistines? Will You hand them over to me?"

The LORD replied, "Go, and I will hand them over to you."

11 So the Israelites went up to Baal-perazim, and David defeated the Philistines there. Then David said, "Like a bursting flood, God has used me to burst out against my enemies." Therefore, they named that place the Lord Bursts Out.[A] 12 The Philistines abandoned their idols there, and David ordered that they be burned in the fire.

13 Once again the Philistines raided in the valley. 14 So David again inquired of God, and God answered him, "Do not pursue them directly. Circle around them and attack them opposite the balsam trees. 15 When you hear the sound of marching in the tops of the balsam trees, then march out to battle, for God will have marched out ahead of you to attack the camp of the Philistines." 16 So David did exactly as God commanded him, and they struck down the Philistine army from Gibeon to Gezer. 17 Then David's fame spread throughout the lands, and the LORD caused all the nations to be terrified of him.[e]

The Ark Comes to Jerusalem

15 David built houses for himself in the city of David, and he prepared a place for the ark of God and pitched a tent for it.[f] 2 Then David said, "No one but the Levites may carry the ark of God, because the LORD has chosen them to carry the ark of the LORD and to minister before Him forever."[g]

3 David assembled all Israel at Jerusalem[h] to bring the ark of the LORD to the place he had prepared for it.[i] 4 Then he gathered together the descendants of Aaron and the Levites:

5 From the Kohathites, Uriel the leader and 120 of his relatives; 6 from the Merarites, Asaiah the leader and 220 of his relatives; 7 from the Gershomites,[B] Joel the leader and 130 of his relatives; 8 from the Elizaphanites, Shemaiah the leader and 200 of his relatives; 9 from the Hebronites, Eliel the leader and 80 of his relatives; 10 from the Uzzielites, Amminadab the leader and 112 of his relatives.

11 David summoned the priests Zadok[j] and Abiathar[k] and the Levites Uriel, Asaiah, Joel, Shemaiah, Eliel, and Amminadab. 12 He said to them, "You are the heads of the Levite families. You and your relatives must consecrate yourselves[l] so that you may bring the ark of the LORD God of Israel to the place I have prepared for it.[m] 13 For the LORD our God burst out in anger against us because you Levites were not with us the first time, for we didn't inquire of Him about the proper procedures."[n] 14 So the priests and the Levites consecrated themselves to bring up the ark of the LORD God of Israel. 15 Then the Levites carried the ark of God the way Moses had commanded according to the word of the LORD: on their shoulders with the poles.[o]

16 Then David told the leaders of the Levites to appoint their relatives as singers and to have them raise their voices with joy accompanied by musical instruments — harps, lyres, and cymbals.[p] 17 So the Levites appointed Heman son of Joel; from his relatives, Asaph son of Berechiah; and from their relatives the Merarites, Ethan son of Kushaiah. 18 With them were their relatives second in rank:

[a] **13:13** 1Ch 26:4-5; 2Ch 25:23-24
[b] **14:1-17** 2Sm 5:11-25
[c] **14:4-7** 1Ch 3:5-8
[d] **14:9** 1Ch 11:15; 14:13
[e] **14:17** Ex 15:14-16; Dt 2:25
[f] **15:1** 1Ch 16:1; 17:1-5
[g] **15:2** Nm 4:15; Dt 10:8
[h] **15:3** 1Ch 13:5
[i] 2Sm 6:12,17; 1Ch 15:12
[j] **15:11** 1Ch 12:28; 18:16; 24:3,6,31; 27:17; 29:22
[k] 1Sm 22:20-23; 1Kg 1:7; 2:26-27,35; 1Ch 27:34
[l] **15:12** Ex 19:14; 2Ch 35:6
[m] 1Ch 15:1,3
[n] **15:13** 2Sm 6:3; 1Ch 13:7
[o] **15:15** Ex 25:12-15; Nm 4:6,15
[p] **15:16** 1Ch 13:8; 25:1

[A] **14:11** Or *Baal-perazim* [B] **15:7** = Gershonites

Zechariah, Jaaziel,[A] Shemiramoth, Jehiel,
Unni, Eliab, Benaiah, Maaseiah, Mattithiah,
Eliphelehu, Mikneiah, and the gatekeepers
Obed-edom and Jeiel. 19 The singers Heman,
Asaph, and Ethan were to sound the bronze
cymbals; 20 Zechariah, Aziel, Shemiramoth,
Jehiel, Unni, Eliab, Maaseiah, and Benaiah
were to play harps according to *Alamoth*;[B]
21 and Mattithiah, Eliphelehu, Mikneiah,
Obed-edom, Jeiel, and Azaziah were to lead
the music with lyres according to the •*Sheminith*. 22 Chenaniah, the leader of the Levites
in music, was to direct the music because he
was skillful. 23 Berechiah and Elkanah were
to be gatekeepers for the ark. 24 The priests,
Shebaniah, Joshaphat, Nethanel, Amasai,
Zechariah, Benaiah, and Eliezer, were to blow
trumpets[a] before the ark of God. Obed-edom
and Jehiah were also to be gatekeepers for the
ark.

25 David,[b] the elders of Israel, and the commanders of thousands went with rejoicing
to bring the ark of the covenant of the LORD
from the house of Obed-edom.[c] 26 While the
Levites were carrying the ark of the covenant
of the LORD, with God's help, they sacrificed
seven bulls and seven rams.[d]

27 Now David was dressed in a robe of fine
linen, as were all the Levites who were carrying the ark, as well as the singers and
Chenaniah, the music leader of the singers.
David also wore a linen •ephod. 28 So all Israel brought up the ark of the covenant of
the LORD with shouts, the sound of the ram's
horn, trumpets, and cymbals, and the playing of harps and lyres. 29 As the ark of the covenant of the LORD was entering the city of
David, Saul's daughter Michal looked down
from the window and saw King David dancing[C] and celebrating, and she despised him in
her heart.

16 They[e] brought the ark of God and
placed it inside the tent David had
pitched for it.[f] Then they offered •burnt offerings and •fellowship offerings in God's presence. 2 When David had finished offering the
burnt offerings and the fellowship offerings,
he blessed the people in the name of •Yahweh.
3 Then he distributed to each and every Israelite, both men and women, a loaf of bread, a
date cake, and a raisin cake.

4 David appointed some of the Levites to
be ministers before the ark of the LORD, to
celebrate the LORD God of Israel, and to give
thanks and praise to Him. 5 •Asaph was the
chief and Zechariah was second to him. Jeiel,
Shemiramoth, Jehiel, Mattithiah, Eliab, Benaiah, Obed-edom, and Jeiel played the harps
and lyres, while Asaph sounded the cymbals
6 and the priests Benaiah and Jahaziel blew
the trumpets regularly before the ark of the
covenant of God.

David's Psalm of Thanksgiving

7 On that day David decreed for the first
time that thanks be given to the LORD by
Asaph and his relatives:

8 Give thanks[g] to Yahweh; call on
His name;
proclaim His deeds among
the peoples.[h]
9 Sing to Him; sing praise to Him;
tell about all His wonderful works!
10 Honor His holy name;
let the hearts of those who seek Yahweh
rejoice.
11 Search for the LORD and for
His strength;
seek His face always.[i]
12 Remember the wonderful works
He has done,[j]
His wonders, and the judgments
He has pronounced,[D,k]
13 you offspring of Israel His servant,
Jacob's descendants—His chosen ones.

14 He is the LORD our God;
His judgments govern the whole earth.[l]
15 Remember His covenant forever—
the promise He ordained
for a thousand generations,
16 the covenant He made with Abraham,
swore[E] to Isaac,[m]
17 and confirmed to Jacob as a decree,
and to Israel
as an everlasting covenant:[n]
18 "I will give the land of Canaan to you
as your inherited portion."[o]

[a] 15:24 1Ch 16:6
[b] 15:25-29 2Sm 6:12-16
[c] 15:25 1Ch 13:13
[d] 15:26 Nm 23:1-4,29
[e] 16:1-3 2Sm 6:17-19
[f] 16:1 1Ch 15:1
[g] 16:8-22 Ps 105:1-15
[h] 16:8 1Kg 8:43; 2Kg 19:19
[i] 16:11 Ps 24:6
[j] 16:12 Ps 103:2
[k] Ps 78:43-68
[l] 16:14 Ps 48:10
[m] 16:16 Gn 17:2; 22:16-18; 26:3
[n] 16:17 Gn 35:11-12
[o] 16:18 Gn 13:15

[A] 15:18 Some Hb mss, LXX; other Hb mss read *Zechariah son and Jaaziel*
[B] 15:20 This may refer to a high pitch, perhaps a tune sung by soprano voices; the Hb word means "young women"; Ps 46 title
[C] 15:29 Or *whirling*
[D] 16:12 Lit *judgments of His mouth*
[E] 16:16 Lit *and His oath*

19 When they[A] were few in number,
very few indeed,[a]
and temporary residents in Canaan
20 wandering from nation to nation
and from one kingdom to another,
21 He allowed no one to oppress them;
He rebuked kings on their behalf:[b]
22 "Do not touch My anointed ones
or harm My prophets."[c]

23 Sing[d] to the LORD, all the earth.
Proclaim His salvation from day to day.
24 Declare His glory among the nations,
His wonderful works
among all peoples.

25 For the LORD is great
and highly praised;[e]
He is feared above all gods.[f]
26 For all the gods of the peoples
are idols,[g]
but the LORD made the heavens.[h]
27 Splendor and majesty are before Him;
strength and joy are in His place.
28 Ascribe to the LORD, families
of the peoples,
ascribe to the LORD glory and strength.
29 Ascribe to Yahweh the glory
of His name;
bring an offering and come
before Him.
Worship the LORD
in the splendor of His holiness;[i]
30 tremble[j] before Him, all the earth.
The world is firmly established;
it cannot be shaken.
31 Let the heavens be glad and the earth
rejoice,[k]
and let them say among the nations,
"The LORD is King!"
32 Let the sea and everything in it
resound;
let the fields and all that is in them
exult.[l]
33 Then the trees of the forest will shout
for joy before the LORD,
for He is coming to judge the earth.
34 Give thanks to the LORD, for He is good;
His faithful love endures forever.[m]
35 And say:[n] "Save us, God of our salvation;

[a]**16:19** Gn 34:30; Dt 7:7 [b]**16:21** Gn 12:17; 20:3; Ex 7:15-18 [c]**16:22** Gn 20:7 [d]**16:23-33** Ps 96 [e]**16:25** Ps 144:3-6 [f]Ps 89:7 [g]**16:26** Lv 19:4 [h]Ps 102:25 [i]**16:29** Ps 29:2 [j]**16:30-31** Ps 93:1 [k]**16:31** Is 44:23; 49:13 [l]**16:32** Ps 98:7 [m]**16:34** Ps 106:1; 136:1 [n]**16:35-36a** Ps 106:47-48 [o]**16:36** 1Kg 8:15,56; Ps 72:18 [p]**16:37** 1Ch 16:4-5 [q]2Ch 8:14; Ezr 3:4 [r]**16:38** 1Ch 13:13 [s]1Ch 26:10 [t]**16:39** 1Kg 3:4; 1Ch 21:29 [u]**16:40** Ex 29:38-42; Nm 28:3-4 [v]**16:41** 1Ch 6:33 [w]1Ch 25:1-6 [x]2Ch 5:13 [y]**16:42** 1Ch 25:7; 2Ch 7:6; 29:27 [z]**16:43** 2Sm 6:19-20 [aa]**17:1-2** 2Sm 7:1-3 [ab]**17:1** Hg 1:4 [ac]**17:3-15** 2Sm 7:4-17 [ad]**17:4** 1Ch 22:7-8; 28:2-3

gather us and rescue us from
the nations
so that we may give thanks to
Your holy name
and rejoice in Your praise.
36 May Yahweh, the God of Israel,
be praised[o]
from everlasting to everlasting."

Then all the people said, "*Amen" and "Praise
the LORD."
37 So David left Asaph and his relatives there
before the ark of the LORD's covenant to minister regularly[p] before the ark according to
the daily requirements.[q] 38 He assigned Obed-
edom[r] and his[B] 68 relatives. Obed-edom son
of Jeduthun and Hosah[s] were to be gatekeepers. 39 David left Zadok the priest and his fellow priests before the tabernacle of the LORD
at the *high place in Gibeon[t] 40 to offer burnt
offerings regularly, morning and evening, to
the LORD on the altar of burnt offerings and
to do everything that was written in the law of
the LORD, which He had commanded Israel to
keep.[u] 41 With them were Heman,[v] Jeduthun,
and the rest who were chosen and designated
by name[w] to give thanks to the LORD — for His
faithful love endures forever.[x] 42 Heman and
Jeduthun had with them trumpets and cymbals to play and musical instruments of God.[y]
Jeduthun's sons were at the gate.
43 Then all the people left for their homes,
and David returned home to bless his household.[z]

The LORD's Covenant with David

17 When David[aa] had settled into his palace, he said to Nathan the prophet,
"Look! I am living in a cedar house while the
ark of the LORD's covenant is under tent curtains."[ab]
2 So Nathan told David, "Do all that is on
your heart, for God is with you."
3 But that night[ac] the word of God came to
Nathan: 4 "Go to David My servant and say,
'This is what the LORD says: You are not the
one to build Me a house to dwell in.[ad] 5 From
the time I brought Israel out of Egypt until today I have not lived in a house; instead, I have
moved from tent to tent and from tabernacle

[A]**16:19** One Hb ms, LXX, Vg; other Hb mss read *you* [B]**16:38** LXX, Syr, Vg; Hb reads *their*

to tabernacle.[a] 6In all My travels throughout
Israel, have I ever spoken a word to even one
of the judges of Israel, whom I commanded
to shepherd My people, asking: Why haven't
you built Me a house of cedar?'[b]
7"Now this is what you will say to My servant David: 'This is what the LORD of ·Hosts
says: I took you from the pasture and from
following the sheep to be ruler over My
people Israel.[c] 8I have been with you wherever you have gone, and I have destroyed all
your enemies before you. I will make a name
for you like that of the greatest in the land.
9I will establish a place for My people Israel
and plant them,[d] so that they may live there
and not be disturbed again. Evildoers will not
continue to oppress them as they formerly
have 10ever since the day I ordered judges to
be over My people Israel. I will also subdue all
your enemies.
"'Furthermore, I declare to you that the
LORD Himself will build a house for you.
11When your time comes to be with your fathers, I will raise up after you your descendant, who is one of your own sons, and I will
establish his kingdom. 12He will build a house
for Me,[e] and I will establish his throne forever. 13I will be a father to him, and he will be
a son to Me.[f] I will not take away My faithful
love from him as I took it from the one who
was before you.[g] 14I will appoint him over
My house and My kingdom forever, and his
throne will be established forever.'"[h]
15Nathan reported all these words and this
entire vision to David.

David's Prayer of Thanksgiving

16Then[i] King David went in, sat in the
LORD's presence, and said,

> Who am I, LORD God, and what is my
> house that You have brought me this
> far? 17This was a little thing to You,[A] God,
> for You have spoken about Your servant's
> house in the distant future. You regard
> me as a man of distinction,[B] LORD God.
> 18What more can David say to You for
> honoring Your servant? You know Your
> servant. 19LORD, You have done all this
> greatness, making known all these great
> promises because of Your servant and ac-
> cording to Your will.[j] 20LORD, there is no
> one like You, and there is no God besides
> You, as all we have heard confirms. 21And
> who is like Your people Israel? God, You
> came to one nation on earth to redeem
> a people for Yourself, to make a name
> for Yourself through great and awesome
> works by driving out nations before Your
> people You redeemed from Egypt.[k] 22You
> made Your people Israel Your own peo-
> ple forever, and You, LORD, have become
> their God.[l]
>
> 23Now, LORD, let the word that You have
> spoken concerning Your servant and his
> house be confirmed forever, and do as
> You have promised. 24Let Your name be
> confirmed and magnified forever in the
> saying, "·Yahweh of Hosts, the God of Is-
> rael, is God over Israel." May the house of
> Your servant David be established before
> You. 25Since You, my God, have revealed
> to[C,m] Your servant that You will build him
> a house, Your servant has found courage
> to pray in Your presence. 26Yahweh, You
> indeed are God, and You have promised
> this good thing to Your servant. 27So now,
> You have been pleased to bless Your ser-
> vant's house that it may continue before
> You forever. For You, LORD, have blessed
> it, and it is blessed forever.

David's Military Campaigns

18 After this,[n] David defeated the Philistines, subdued them, and took Gath
and its villages from Philistine control. 2He
also defeated the Moabites, and they became
David's subjects and brought tribute.
3David also defeated King Hadadezer of Zobah at Hamath when he went to establish his
control at the Euphrates River. 4David captured 1,000 chariots, 7,000 horsemen, and
20,000 foot soldiers from him, hamstrung
all the horses, and kept 100 chariots.[D]
5When the Arameans of Damascus came
to assist King Hadadezer of Zobah,[o] David
struck down 22,000 Aramean men. 6Then he
placed garrisons[E,p] in Aram of Damascus, and
the Arameans became David's subjects and

[a]17:5 Ex 40:2-3; 2Sm 7:6
[b]17:6 2Sm 7:7
[c]17:7 1Sm 16:11-13
[d]17:9 Ex 15:17
[e]17:12 1Kg 5:2-5; 6:14,38; 8:17-20; 2Ch 6:2
[f]17:13 Heb 1:5
[g]1Sm 15:23-28; 1Ch 10:14
[h]17:14 Ps 89:29,36
[i]17:16-27 2Sm 7:18-29
[j]17:19 Is 37:35
[k]17:21 Dt 4:32-38
[l]17:22 Ex 6:7; 19:5-6
[m]17:25 Ex 6:7; 19:5-6
[n]18:1-13 2Sm 8:1-14
[o]18:5 1Ch 18:9; 19:6
[p]18:6 2Sm 8:6

[A]17:17 Lit *thing in Your eyes* [B]17:17 Hb obscure [C]17:25 Lit *have uncovered the ear of* [D]18:4 Or *chariot horses* [E]18:6 Some Hb mss, LXX, Vg; other Hb mss omit *garrisons*; 2Sm 8:6

brought tribute. The LORD made David victorious wherever he went.

7 David took the gold shields carried by Hadadezer's officers and brought them to Jerusalem. 8 From Tibhath and Cun, Hadadezer's cities, David also took huge quantities of bronze, from which Solomon made the bronze reservoir, the pillars, and the bronze articles.[a]

9 When King Tou of Hamath heard that David had defeated the entire army of King Hadadezer of Zobah, 10 he sent his son Hadoram to King David to greet him and to congratulate him because David had fought against Hadadezer and defeated him, for Tou and Hadadezer had fought many wars. Hadoram brought all kinds of gold, silver, and bronze items. 11 King David also dedicated these to the LORD, along with the silver and gold he had carried off from all the nations — from Edom, Moab, the Ammonites, the Philistines, and the Amalekites.

12 Abishai son of Zeruiah struck down 18,000 Edomites in the Valley of Salt. 13 He put garrisons in Edom, and all the Edomites were subject to David. The LORD made David victorious wherever he went.

14 So David reigned over all Israel,[b] administering justice and righteousness for all his people.

15 Joab[c] son of Zeruiah was over the army;
Jehoshaphat son of Ahilud was
court historian;
16 Zadok son of Ahitub
and Ahimelech[A,d] son of Abiathar
were priests;
Shavsha was court secretary;
17 Benaiah son of Jehoiada[e] was over
the Cherethites and the Pelethites;
and David's sons were the chief officials
at the king's side.

War with the Ammonites

19 Some time later,[f] King Nahash of the Ammonites died, and his son became king in his place. 2 Then David said, "I'll show kindness to Hanun son of Nahash, because his father showed kindness to me."

So David sent messengers to console him concerning his father. However, when David's emissaries arrived in the land of the Ammonites to console him, 3 the Ammonite leaders said to Hanun, "Just because David has sent men with condolences for you, do you really believe he's showing respect for your father? Instead, hasn't David sent his emissaries in order to scout out, overthrow, and spy on the land?" 4 So Hanun took David's emissaries, shaved them, cut their clothes in half at the hips, and sent them away.[g]

5 It was reported to David about his men, so he sent messengers to meet them, since the men were deeply humiliated. The king said, "Stay in Jericho until your beards grow back; then return."

6 When the Ammonites realized[h] they had made themselves repulsive to David, Hanun and the Ammonites sent 38 tons[B] of silver to hire chariots and horsemen from Aram-naharaim, Aram-maacah, and Zobah.[i] 7 They hired 32,000 chariots and the king of Maacah with his army, who came and camped near Medeba.[j] The Ammonites also came together from their cities for the battle.

8 David heard about this and sent Joab and the entire army of warriors. 9 The Ammonites marched out and lined up in battle formation at the entrance of the city while the kings who had come were in the field by themselves. 10 When Joab saw that there was a battle line in front of him and another behind him, he chose some men out of all the elite troops[C,k] of Israel and lined up in battle formation to engage the Arameans. 11 He placed the rest of the forces under the command of his brother Abishai, and they lined up in battle formation to engage the Ammonites.

12 "If the Arameans are too strong for me," Joab said, "then you'll be my help. However, if the Ammonites are too strong for you, I'll help you. 13 Be strong! We must prove ourselves strong for our people and for the cities of our God.[l] May the LORD's will be done."[D]

14 Joab and the people with him approached the Arameans for battle, and they fled before him. 15 When the Ammonites saw that the Arameans had fled, they likewise fled before Joab's brother Abishai and entered the city. Then Joab went to Jerusalem.

[a] 18:8 1Kg 7:15-47; 2Ch 3:15–4:18
[b] 18:14-17 2Sm 8:15-18
[c] 18:15 1Ch 11:6
[d] 18:16 2Sm 8:17; 1Ch 24:6,31
[e] 18:17 2Sm 23:20-23
[f] 19:1-5 2Sm 10:1-5
[g] 19:4 Is 7:20; 20:4
[h] 19:6-19 2Sm 10:6-19
[i] 19:6 1Ch 18:5,9
[j] 19:7 Nm 21:30; Jos 13:9,16; Is 15:2
[k] 19:10 2Sm 6:1
[l] 19:13 Jos 1:6

[A] 18:16 Some Hb mss, LXX, Syr, Vg; other Hb mss read *Abimelech*; 2Sm 8:17
[B] 19:6 Lit *1,000 talents*
[C] 19:10 Lit *the choice ones*; 2Sm 6:1
[D] 19:13 Lit *the LORD do what is good in His eyes*

16When the Arameans realized that they
had been defeated by Israel, they sent messengers to summon the Arameans who were
across the Euphrates. They were led by Shophach, the commander of Hadadezer's army.
17When this was reported to David, he
gathered all Israel and crossed the Jordan.
He came up to the Arameans and lined up in
battle formation against them. When David
lined up to engage them in battle, they fought
against him. 18But the Arameans fled before
Israel, and David killed 7,000 of their charioteers and 40,000 foot soldiers. He also killed
Shophach, commander of the army. 19When
Hadadezer's subjects saw that they had been
defeated by Israel, they made peace with David and became his subjects. After this, the
Arameans were never willing to help the Ammonites again.

Capture of the City of Rabbah

20 In the spring[A] when kings march
out to war,[a] Joab led the army and
destroyed the Ammonites' land. He came to
Rabbah and besieged it, but David remained
in Jerusalem.[b] Joab attacked Rabbah and demolished it. 2Then David took the crown
from the head of their king,[B,C,c] and it was
placed on David's head. He found that the
crown weighed 75 pounds[D] of gold, and there
was a precious stone in it. In addition, David
took away a large quantity of plunder from
the city. 3He brought out the people who were
in it and put them to work with saws,[E] iron
picks, and axes.[F,d] David did the same to all the
Ammonite cities. Then he and all his troops
returned to Jerusalem.

The Philistine Giants

4After this,[e] a war broke out with the Philistines at Gezer. At that time Sibbecai the
Hushathite killed Sippai, a descendant of the
giants,[G] and the Philistines were subdued.
5Once again there was a battle with the Philistines, and Elhanan son of Jair killed Lahmi
the brother of Goliath the Gittite. The shaft of
his spear was like a weaver's beam.[f]
6There was still another battle at Gath
where there was a man of extraordinary stature with six fingers on each hand and six
toes on each foot — 24 in all. He, too, was descended from the giant.[H] 7When he taunted
Israel, Jonathan son of David's brother
Shimei killed him.
8These were the descendants of the giant[H]
in Gath killed by David and his soldiers.

David's Military Census

21 Satan[I,g] stood up against Israel and
incited David[h] to count the people of
Israel. 2So David said to Joab and the commanders of the troops, "Go and count Israel
from Beer-sheba to Dan and bring a report to
me so I can know their number."[i]
3Joab replied, "May the LORD multiply the
number of His people a hundred times over![j]
My lord the king, aren't they all my lord's servants? Why does my lord want to do this?
Why should he bring ˙guilt on Israel?"
4Yet the king's order prevailed over Joab. So
Joab left and traveled throughout Israel and
then returned to Jerusalem. 5Joab gave the
total troop registration to David. In all Israel
there were 1,100,000 swordsmen and in Judah itself 470,000 swordsmen. 6But he did
not include Levi and Benjamin in the count
because the king's command was detestable
to him. 7This command was also evil in God's
sight, so He afflicted Israel.
8David said to God, "I have sinned greatly
because I have done this thing. Now, please
take away Your servant's guilt, for I've been
very foolish."[k]

David's Punishment

9Then[l] the LORD instructed Gad,[m] David's
seer,[n] 10"Go and say to David, 'This is what the
LORD says: I am offering you three choices.
Choose one of them for yourself, and I will
do it to you.'"
11So Gad went to David and said to him,
"This is what the LORD says: 'Take your choice:
12three years of famine, or three months of
devastation by your foes with the sword of
your enemy overtaking you, or three days
of the sword of the LORD — a plague on the
land, the angel of the LORD bringing destruction to the whole territory of Israel.' Now

[a] **20:1-3** 2Sm 12:26-31
[b] **20:1** 2Sm 11:1
[c] **20:2** 1Kg 11:5,7
[d] **20:3** 2Sm 12:31
[e] **20:4-8** 2Sm 21:18-22
[f] **20:5** 1Sm 17:7; 1Ch 11:23
[g] **21:1** Jb 1:6; Zch 3:1-2
[h] **21:1-8** 2Sm 24:1-10
[i] **21:2** 1Ch 27:23-24
[j] **21:3** Dt 1:11
[k] **21:8** 2Sm 12:13
[l] **21:9-17** 2Sm 24:11-17
[m] **21:9** 1Ch 29:29
[n] 1Sm 9:9; 2Sm 24:11; 1Ch 25:5

[A] **20:1** Lit *At the time of the return of the year* [B] **20:2** LXX, Vg read *of Milcom* [C] **20:2** = Molech; 1Kg 11:5,7 [D] **20:2** Lit *a talent* [E] **20:3** Text emended; MT reads *and sawed them with the saw*; 2Sm 12:31 [F] **20:3** Text emended; MT reads *saws*; 2Sm 12:31 [G] **20:4** Or *the Rephaites* [H] **20:6,8** Or *Raphah* [I] **21:1** Or *An adversary*; Jb 1:6; Zch 3:1-2

decide what answer I should take back to the
One who sent me."
13 David answered Gad, "I'm in anguish.
Please, let me fall into the LORD's hands because His mercies are very great,[a] but don't
let me fall into human hands."
14 So the LORD sent a plague on Israel, and
70,000 Israelite men died. 15 Then God sent
an angel to Jerusalem to destroy it, but when
the angel was about to destroy the city,[A] the
LORD looked, relented concerning the destruction,[b] and said to the angel who was destroying the people, "Enough, withdraw your
hand now!" The angel of the LORD was then
standing at the threshing floor of Ornan[B] the
Jebusite.
16 When David looked up and saw the angel of the LORD standing between earth and
heaven, with his drawn sword in his hand
stretched out over Jerusalem, David and the
elders, clothed in ˙sackcloth,[c] fell down with
their faces to the ground. 17 David said to God,
"Wasn't I the one who gave the order to count
the people? I am the one who has sinned and
acted very wickedly. But these sheep, what
have they done? My LORD God, please let Your
hand be against me and against my father's
family, but don't let the plague be against
Your people."

David's Altar

18 So the angel of the LORD ordered Gad[d] to
tell David to go and set up an altar to the LORD
on the threshing floor of Ornan the Jebusite.[e]
19 David went up at Gad's command spoken in
the name of the LORD.
20 Ornan was threshing wheat when he
turned and saw the angel. His four sons, who
were with him, hid themselves. 21 David came
to Ornan, and when Ornan looked and saw
David, he left the threshing floor and bowed
to David with his face to the ground.
22 Then David said to Ornan, "Give me this
threshing-floor plot so that I may build an
altar to the LORD on it. Give it to me for the
full price, so the plague on the people may be
stopped."
23 Ornan said to David, "Take it! My lord the
king may do whatever he wants.[C] See, I give
the oxen for the ˙burnt offerings, the thresh-

[a]**21:13** Ps 51:1; 130:4,7
[b]**21:15** Ex 32:14; 1Sm 15:11; 2Sm 24:16; Am 7:3,6; Jnh 3:9-10
[c]**21:16** 1Kg 21:27
[d]**21:18-27** 2Sm 24:18-25
[e]**21:18** 2Ch 3:1
[f]**21:26** Lv 9:24; Jdg 6:21
[g]**21:29** 1Kg 3:4; 1Ch 16:39
[h]**22:1** 1Ch 21:18-28; 2Ch 3:1
[i]**22:2** 1Kg 9:20-21; 2Ch 2:17
[j]1Kg 5:17-18
[k]**22:3** 1Ch 29:2,7
[l]**22:4** 1Kg 5:6-10
[m]**22:5** 1Ch 29:1
[n]**22:7** 2Sm 7:2-3; 1Ch 17:1-2; 28:2

ing sledges for the wood, and the wheat for
the ˙grain offering—I give it all."
24 King David answered Ornan, "No, I insist
on paying the full price, for I will not take for
the LORD what belongs to you or offer burnt
offerings that cost me nothing."
25 So David gave Ornan 15 pounds of gold[D]
for the plot. 26 He built an altar to the LORD
there and offered burnt offerings and ˙fel-
lowship offerings. He called on the LORD, and
He answered him with fire from heaven on
the altar of burnt offering.[f]
27 Then the LORD spoke to the angel, and he
put his sword back into its sheath. 28 At that
time, David offered sacrifices there when
he saw that the LORD answered him at the
threshing floor of Ornan the Jebusite. 29 The
tabernacle of the LORD, which Moses made
in the desert, and the altar of burnt offering
were at the ˙high place in Gibeon,[g] 30 but David could not go before it to inquire of God,
because he was terrified of the sword of the
22 LORD's angel. 1 Then David said, "This
is the house of the LORD God, and this
is the altar of ˙burnt offering for Israel."[h]

David's Preparations for the Temple

2 So David gave orders to gather the foreigners that were in the land of Israel,[i] and he appointed stonecutters to cut finished stones
for building God's house.[j] 3 David supplied a
great deal of iron to make the nails for the
doors of the gateways and for the fittings,
together with an immeasurable quantity of
bronze,[k] 4 and innumerable cedar logs because the Sidonians and Tyrians had brought
a large quantity of cedar logs to David.[l] 5 David
said, "My son Solomon is young and inexperienced, and the house that is to be built for the
LORD must be exceedingly great and famous
and glorious in all the lands.[m] Therefore, I
must make provision for it." So David made
lavish preparations for it before his death.
6 Then he summoned his son Solomon and
instructed him to build a house for the LORD
God of Israel. 7 "My son," David said to Solomon, "It was in my heart to build a house for
the name of ˙Yahweh my God,[n] 8 but the word
of the LORD came to me: 'You have shed much
blood and waged great wars. You are not to

[A]**21:15** Lit *but as he was destroying* [B]**21:15-28** = Araunah in 2Sm 24:16-24 [C]**21:23** Lit *do what is good in his eyes* [D]**21:25** Lit *600 shekels of gold by weight*

build a house for My name because you have shed so much blood on the ground before Me.[a] 9 But a son will be born to you; he will be a man of rest. I will give him rest from all his surrounding enemies,[b] for his name will be Solomon,[A,c] and I will give peace and quiet to Israel during his reign.[d] 10 He is the one who will build a house for My name. He will be My son, and I will be his father. I will establish the throne of his kingdom over Israel forever.'[e]

11 "Now, my son, may the LORD be with you,[f] and may you succeed in building the house of the LORD your God, as He said about you. 12 Above all, may the LORD give you insight and understanding when He puts you in charge of Israel so that you may keep the law of the LORD your God.[g] 13 Then you will succeed if you carefully follow the statutes and ordinances the LORD commanded Moses for Israel.[h] Be strong and courageous. Don't be afraid or discouraged.[i]

14 "Notice I have taken great pains to provide for the house of the LORD — 3,775 tons of gold, 37,750 tons of silver,[B,j] and bronze and iron that can't be weighed because there is so much of it. I have also provided timber and stone, but you will need to add more to them. 15 You also have many workers: stonecutters, masons, carpenters, and people skilled in every kind of work 16 in gold, silver, bronze, and iron — beyond number. Now begin the work, and may the LORD be with you."[k]

17 Then David ordered all the leaders of Israel to help his son Solomon: 18 "The LORD your God is with you, isn't He? And hasn't He given you rest on every side?[l] For He has handed the land's inhabitants over to me, and the land has been subdued before the LORD and His people. 19 Now determine in your mind and heart to seek the LORD your God.[m] Get started building the LORD God's sanctuary so that you may bring the ark of the LORD's covenant and the holy articles of God to the temple that is to be built[n] for the name of Yahweh."[o]

The Divisions of the Levites

23 When David was old and full of days,[p] he installed his son Solomon as king over Israel.[q] 2 Then he gathered all the leaders of Israel, the priests, and the Levites. 3 The Levites 30 years old or more were counted;[r] the total number of men was 38,000 by headcount.[s] 4 "Of these," David said, "24,000 are to be in charge of the work on the LORD's temple,[t] 6,000 are to be officers and judges,[u] 5 4,000 are to be gatekeepers, and 4,000 are to praise the LORD with the instruments that I have made for worship."[v]

6 Then David divided them into divisions according to Levi's sons:[w] Gershom,[C] Kohath, and Merari.

7 The Gershonites: Ladan and Shimei.
8 Ladan's sons: Jehiel was the first, then Zetham, and Joel — three.
9 Shimei's sons: Shelomoth, Haziel, and Haran — three. Those were the heads of the families of Ladan.
10 Shimei's sons: Jahath, Zizah,[D] Jeush, and Beriah. Those were Shimei's sons — four. 11 Jahath was the first and Zizah was the second; however, Jeush and Beriah did not have many sons, so they became an ancestral house and received a single assignment.
12 Kohath's sons: Amram, Izhar, Hebron, and Uzziel — four.
13 Amram's sons:[x] Aaron and Moses.

Aaron, along with his descendants,[y] was set apart forever to consecrate the most holy things, to burn incense in the presence of ·Yahweh,[z] to minister to Him, and to pronounce blessings in His name forever. 14 As for Moses the man of God,[aa] his sons were named among the tribe of Levi.

15 Moses' sons: Gershom and Eliezer.
16 Gershom's sons: Shebuel was first.
17 Eliezer's sons were Rehabiah, first; Eliezer did not have any other sons, but Rehabiah's sons were very numerous.
18 Izhar's sons: Shelomith was first.
19 Hebron's sons: Jeriah was first, Amariah second, Jahaziel third, and Jekameam fourth.
20 Uzziel's sons: Micah was first, and Isshiah second.
21 Merari's sons: Mahli and Mushi. Mahli's sons: Eleazar and Kish.

[a] **22:8** 1Ch 28:3
[b] **22:9** 1Kg 4:20,25
[c] 2Sm 12:24-25
[d] 1Ch 28:5
[e] **22:10** 2Sm 7:13-14; 1Ch 17:12-13; 28:6-7
[f] **22:11** 1Ch 22:16
[g] **22:12** 1Kg 3:9-12; 2Ch 1:10-12
[h] **22:13** 1Ch 28:7
[i] Jos 1:6-9
[j] **22:14** 1Ch 29:4
[k] **22:16** 1Ch 22:11
[l] **22:18** 1Ch 22:9; 23:25
[m] **22:19** 1Ch 28:9
[n] 1Kg 8:6,21; 2Ch 5:7
[o] 1Ch 22:7
[p] **23:1** 1Ch 29:28
[q] 1Ch 28:5; 29:22
[r] **23:3** Nm 4:3-49
[s] 1Ch 23:24
[t] **23:4** Ezr 3:8-9
[u] 1Ch 26:29
[v] **23:5** 1Ch 15:16
[w] **23:6** 1Ch 6:1
[x] **23:13** Ex 6:20
[y] Ex 28:1
[z] Ex 30:6-10
[aa] **23:14** Dt 33:1; Ps 90 title

[A] **22:9** In Hb, the name Solomon sounds like "peace." [B] **22:14** Lit *100,000 talents of gold and 1,000,000 talents of silver* [C] **23:6** Lit *Gershon*

[D] **23:10** LXX, Vg; MT reads *Zina*

22 Eleazar died having no sons, only
daughters. Their cousins, the sons of
Kish, married them.
23 Mushi's sons: Mahli, Eder, and
Jeremoth — three.

24 These were the sons of Levi by their ancestral houses — the heads of families, according to their registration by name in
the headcount — 20 years old or more, who
worked in the service of the LORD's temple.[a]
25 For David said, "The LORD God of Israel has
given rest to His people,[b] and He has come to
stay in Jerusalem forever. 26 Also, the Levites
no longer need to carry the tabernacle or any
of the equipment for its service"[c] — 27 for according to the last words of David, the Levites
20 years old or more were to be counted —
28 "but their duty will be to assist the sons of
Aaron with the service of the LORD's temple,
being responsible for the courts and the
chambers, the purification of all the holy
things, and the work of the service of God's
temple — 29 as well as the rows of the •bread
of the Presence,[d] the fine flour for the •grain
offering,[e] the wafers of unleavened bread,
the baking,[A,f] the mixing,[g] and all measurements of volume and length.[h] 30 They are also
to stand every morning to give thanks and
praise to the LORD, and likewise in the evening. 31 Whenever •burnt offerings are offered
to the LORD on the Sabbaths, New Moons,[i]
and appointed festivals, they are to do so
regularly in the LORD's presence according to
the number prescribed for them.[j] 32 They are
to carry out their responsibilities for the tent
of meeting, for the holy place,[k] and for their
relatives, the sons of Aaron,[l] in the service of
the LORD's temple."

The Divisions of the Priests

24 The divisions of the descendants of
Aaron were as follows: Aaron's sons
were Nadab, Abihu, Eleazar, and Ithamar.[m]
2 But Nadab and Abihu died before their father, and they had no sons, so Eleazar and
Ithamar served as priests.[n] 3 Together with
Zadok[o] from the sons of Eleazar and Ahimelech from the sons of Ithamar, David divided
them according to the assigned duties of
their service. 4 Since more leaders were found
among Eleazar's descendants than Ithamar's,
they were divided accordingly: 16 heads of
ancestral houses were from Eleazar's descendants, and eight heads of ancestral houses
were from Ithamar's. 5 They[p] were assigned
by lot, for there were officers of the sanctuary and officers of God among both Eleazar's
and Ithamar's descendants.
6 The secretary, Shemaiah son of Nethanel,
a Levite, recorded them in the presence of
the king and the officers, Zadok the priest,
Ahimelech[q] son of Abiathar, and the heads
of families of the priests and the Levites. One
ancestral house was taken for Eleazar, and
then one for Ithamar.

7 The first lot fell to Jehoiarib, the second
to Jedaiah,
8 the third to Harim, the fourth
to Seorim,
9 the fifth to Malchijah, the sixth
to Mijamin,
10 the seventh to Hakkoz, the eighth
to Abijah,[r]
11 the ninth to Jeshua, the tenth
to Shecaniah,
12 the eleventh to Eliashib, the twelfth
to Jakim,
13 the thirteenth to Huppah,
the fourteenth to Jeshebeab,
14 the fifteenth to Bilgah, the sixteenth
to Immer,
15 the seventeenth to Hezir,
the eighteenth to Happizzez,
16 the nineteenth to Pethahiah,
the twentieth to Jehezkel,
17 the twenty-first to Jachin,
the twenty-second to Gamul,
18 the twenty-third to Delaiah,
and the twenty-fourth to Maaziah.

19 These had their assigned duties for service when they entered the LORD's temple,
according to their regulations, which they
received from their ancestor Aaron, as the
LORD God of Israel had commanded him.

The Rest of the Levites

20 As for the rest of Levi's sons:
from Amram's sons: Shubael;

[a] 23:24 Nm 10:17,21 [b] 23:25 1Ch 22:9,18 [c] 23:26 Nm 4:5,15; 7:9 [d] 23:29 Lv 24:5-9 [e] Lv 6:20 [f] 1Ch 9:31 [g] Lv 6:14-15; 7:12 [h] Ex 29:40; 30:13; Lv 19:35-36 [i] 23:31 Is 1:13-14 [j] Lv 23:2-4 [k] 23:32 Nm 1:53; 1Ch 9:27 [l] Nm 3:6-9,38 [m] 24:1 Ex 6:23 [n] 24:2 Lv 10:1-2 [o] 24:3 1Ch 15:11; 24:6,31 [p] 24:5-6 1Ch 24:31 [q] 24:6 2Sm 8:17; 1Ch 18:16; 24:31 [r] 24:10 Neh 12:4; Lk 1:5

A 23:29 Lit *the griddle*

from Shubael's sons: Jehdeiah.
21 From Rehabiah:
from Rehabiah's sons: Isshiah was the first.
22 From the Izharites: Shelomoth;
from Shelomoth's sons: Jahath.
23 Hebron's[A,a] sons:
Jeriah the first, Amariah the second, Jahaziel the third, and Jekameam the fourth.
24 From Uzziel's sons: Micah;
from Micah's sons: Shamir.
25 Micah's brother: Isshiah;
from Isshiah's sons: Zechariah.
26 Merari's sons: Mahli and Mushi,
and from his sons, Jaaziah his son.[B]
27 Merari's sons, by his son Jaaziah:[C]
Shoham, Zaccur, and Ibri.
28 From Mahli: Eleazar, who had no sons.
29 From Kish, from Kish's sons:
Jerahmeel.
30 Mushi's sons: Mahli, Eder, and
Jerimoth.

Those were the sons of the Levites according to their ancestral houses.
31 They also cast
lots the same way as their relatives the sons of Aaron did in the presence of King David, Zadok, Ahimelech, and the heads of the families of the priests and Levites — the family heads and their younger brothers alike.[b]

The Levitical Musicians

25 David and the officers of the army also set apart some of the sons of ˙Asaph, Heman,[c] and Jeduthun, who were to prophesy[d] accompanied by lyres, harps, and cymbals.[e] This is the list of the men who performed their service:

2 From Asaph's sons:
Zaccur, Joseph, Nethaniah, and Asarelah, sons of Asaph, under Asaph's authority, who prophesied under the authority of the king.
3 From Jeduthun:[f] Jeduthun's sons:
Gedaliah, Zeri, Jeshaiah, Shimei,[D] Hashabiah, and Mattithiah — six — under the authority of their father Jeduthun, prophesying to the accompaniment of lyres, giving thanks and praise to the LORD.
4 From Heman: Heman's sons:
Bukkiah, Mattaniah, Uzziel, Shebuel, Jerimoth, Hananiah, Hanani, Eliathah, Giddalti, Romamti-ezer, Joshbekashah, Mallothi, Hothir, and Mahazioth.
5 All
these sons of Heman, the king's seer,[g] were given by the promises of God to exalt him,[E] for God had given Heman fourteen sons and three daughters.

6 All these men were under their own fathers' authority for the music in the LORD's temple, with cymbals, harps, and lyres for the service of God's temple. Asaph, Jeduthun, and Heman were under the king's authority.
7 They numbered 288 together with their
relatives who were all trained and skillful in music for the LORD.
8 They cast lots for their
duties, young and old alike, teacher as well as pupil.[h]

9 The first lot for Asaph fell to Joseph, his sons, and his brothers — 12
to Gedaliah the second: him, his brothers, and his sons — 12
10 the third to Zaccur, his sons, and his brothers — 12
11 the fourth to Izri,[F] his sons, and his brothers — 12
12 the fifth to Nethaniah, his sons, and his brothers — 12
13 the sixth to Bukkiah, his sons, and his brothers — 12
14 the seventh to Jesarelah, his sons, and his brothers — 12
15 the eighth to Jeshaiah, his sons, and his brothers — 12
16 the ninth to Mattaniah, his sons, and his brothers — 12
17 the tenth to Shimei, his sons, and his brothers — 12
18 the eleventh to Azarel,[G] his sons, and his brothers — 12
19 the twelfth to Hashabiah, his sons, and his brothers — 12
20 the thirteenth to Shubael, his sons, and his brothers — 12

[a]24:23 1Ch 23:19 [b]24:31 1Ch 24:5-6 [c]25:1 1Ch 6:33,39 [d]2Kg 3:15 [e]1Ch 15:16; 25:6 [f]25:3 1Ch 16:41-42 [g]25:5 1Sm 9:9; 2Sm 24:11; 1Ch 21:9 [h]25:8 1Ch 26:13

[A]24:23 Some Hb mss, some LXX mss; other Hb mss omit *Hebron's*; 1Ch 23:19 [B]24:26 Or *Mushi; Jaaziah's sons: Beno.* [C]24:27 Or *sons, Jaaziah: Beno,* [D]25:3 One Hb ms, LXX; other Hb mss omit *Shimei* [E]25:5 Or *Him*; lit *by the words of God to lift a horn* [F]25:11 Variant of Zeri [G]25:18 Variant of Uzziel

21 the fourteenth to Mattithiah, his sons,
and his brothers — 12
22 the fifteenth to Jeremoth, his sons,
and his brothers — 12
23 the sixteenth to Hananiah, his sons,
and his brothers — 12
24 the seventeenth to Joshbekashah,
his sons, and his brothers — 12
25 the eighteenth to Hanani, his sons,
and his brothers — 12
26 the nineteenth to Mallothi, his sons,
and his brothers — 12
27 the twentieth to Eliathah, his sons,
and his brothers — 12
28 the twenty-first to Hothir, his sons,
and his brothers — 12
29 the twenty-second to Giddalti,
his sons, and his brothers — 12
30 the twenty-third to Mahazioth,
his sons, and his brothers — 12
31 and the twenty-fourth
to Romamti-ezer, his sons,
and his brothers — 12.

The Levitical Gatekeepers

26 The following were the divisions of the gatekeepers:

From the Korahites: Meshelemiah son
of Kore, one of the sons of ·Asaph.
2 Meshelemiah had sons:
Zechariah the firstborn, Jediael the
second,
Zebadiah the third, Jathniel the fourth,
3 Elam the fifth, Jehohanan the sixth,
and Eliehoenai the seventh.
4 Obed-edom also had sons:
Shemaiah the firstborn, Jehozabad the
second,
Joah the third, Sachar the fourth,
Nethanel the fifth, 5 Ammiel the sixth,
Issachar the seventh, and Peullethai the
eighth,
for God blessed him.
6 Also, to his son Shemaiah were born
sons who ruled over their ancestral
houses because they were strong,
capable men.
7 Shemaiah's sons: Othni, Rephael, Obed,
and Elzabad; his brothers Elihu and
Semachiah were also capable men. 8 All
of these were among the sons of Obed-
edom with their sons and brothers; they
were capable men with strength for the
work — 62 from Obed-edom.
9 Meshelemiah also had sons and
brothers who were capable men — 18.
10 Hosah,[a] from the Merarites, also had
sons: Shimri the first (although he
was not the firstborn, his father had
appointed him as the first), 11 Hilkiah
the second, Tebaliah the third, and
Zechariah the fourth. The sons and
brothers of Hosah were 13 in all.

12 These divisions of the gatekeepers, under
their leading men, had duties for ministering
in the LORD's temple, just as their brothers
did. 13 They cast lots for each gate according to
their ancestral houses, young and old alike.[b]
14 The lot for the east gate fell to Shelemiah.[A]
They also cast lots for his son Zechariah, an
insightful counselor, and his lot came out for
the north gate. 15 Obed-edom's was the south
gate, and his sons' lot was for the storehouses;
16 it was the west gate and the gate of Shallech-
eth on the ascending highway for Shuppim
and Hosah.
There were guards stationed at every watch.
17 There were six Levites each day[B] on the east,
four each day on the north, four each day on
the south, and two pair at the storehouses.
18 As for the court on the west, there were four
at the highway and two at the court. 19 Those
were the divisions of the gatekeepers from
the sons of the Korahites and Merarites.

The Levitical Treasurers and Other Officials

20 From the Levites, Ahijah was in charge of
the treasuries of God's temple and the treasuries of what had been dedicated.[c] 21 From
the sons of Ladan, who were the sons of the
Gershonites through Ladan and were the
heads of families belonging to Ladan the Gershonite: Jehieli. 22 The sons of Jehieli, Zetham
and his brother Joel, were in charge of the
treasuries of the LORD's temple.
23 From the Amramites, the Izharites, the
Hebronites, and the Uzzielites: 24 Shebuel, a
descendant of Moses' son Gershom, was the

[a]26:10 1Ch 16:38 [b]26:13 1Ch 24:5,31; 25:8 [c]26:20 1Ch 26:24,26; 28:12; Ezr 2:69

[A]26:14 Variant of Meshelemiah [B]26:17 LXX; MT omits *each day*

officer in charge of the treasuries. 25His relative through Eliezer: his son Rehabiah, his son
Jeshaiah, his son Joram, his son Zichri, and
his son Shelomith.[A] 26This Shelomith[A] and his
brothers were in charge of all the treasuries of
what had been dedicated by King David,[a] by
the heads of families who were the commanders of thousands and of hundreds, and by the
army commanders. 27They dedicated part of
the plunder from their battles for the repair
of the LORD's temple. 28All that Samuel the
seer, Saul son of Kish, Abner son of Ner, and
Joab son of Zeruiah had dedicated, along with
everything else that had been dedicated, were
in the care of Shelomith[A] and his brothers.

29From the Izrahites: Chenaniah and his
sons had the outside duties[b] as officers and
judges[c] over Israel. 30From the Hebronites:
Hashabiah[d] and his relatives, 1,700 capable
men, had assigned duties in Israel west of the
Jordan for all the work of the LORD and for
the service of the king. 31From the Hebronites: Jerijah[e] was the head of the Hebronites, according to the genealogical records
of his ancestors. A search was made in the
fortieth year of David's reign and strong, capable men were found among them at Jazer[f]
in Gilead. 32There were among Jerijah's relatives, 2,700 capable men who were heads of
families. King David appointed them over the
Reubenites, the Gadites, and half the tribe of
Manasseh as overseers in every matter relating to God and the king.[g]

David's Secular Officials

27 This is the list of the Israelites, the
heads of families, the commanders
of thousands and the commanders of hundreds, and their officers who served the king
in every matter to do with the divisions that
were on rotated military duty each month
throughout[B] the year. There were 24,000 in
each division:

2Jashobeam son of Zabdiel was in
charge of the first division,[h] for the first
month; 24,000 were in his division. 3He
was a descendant of Perez and chief of
all the army commanders for the first
month.

[a]26:26 2Sm 8:11; 1Ch 18:7-11
[b]26:29 Neh 11:16
[c]1Ch 23:4
[d]26:30 1Ch 27:17
[e]26:31 1Ch 23:19
[f]1Ch 6:81
[g]26:32 2Ch 19:11
[h]27:2-15 2Sm 23:8-30; 1Ch 11:11-31

4Dodai the Ahohite was in charge of
the division for the second month, and
Mikloth was the leader; 24,000 were in
his division.
5The third army commander, as chief
for the third month, was Benaiah son
of Jehoiada the priest; 24,000 were
in his division. 6This Benaiah was a
mighty man among the Thirty and over
the Thirty, and his son Ammizabad was
in charge[C] of his division.
7The fourth commander, for the fourth
month, was Joab's brother Asahel, and
his son Zebadiah was commander after
him; 24,000 were in his division.
8The fifth, for the fifth month, was the
commander Shamhuth the Izrahite;
24,000 were in his division.
9The sixth, for the sixth month, was Ira
son of Ikkesh the Tekoite; 24,000 were
in his division.
10The seventh, for the seventh month,
was Helez the Pelonite from the sons of
Ephraim; 24,000 were in his division.
11The eighth, for the eighth month, was
Sibbecai the Hushathite, a Zerahite;
24,000 were in his division.
12The ninth, for the ninth month, was
Abiezer the Anathothite, a Benjaminite;
24,000 were in his division.
13The tenth, for the tenth month, was
Maharai the Netophathite, a Zerahite;
24,000 were in his division.
14The eleventh, for the eleventh month,
was Benaiah the Pirathonite from the
sons of Ephraim; 24,000 were in his
division.
15The twelfth, for the twelfth month,
was Heldai the Netophathite, of
Othniel's family;[D] 24,000 were in his
division.

16The following were in charge of the
tribes of Israel:
For the Reubenites, Eliezer son of
Zichri was the chief official;
for the Simeonites, Shephatiah son of
Maacah;
17for the Levites, Hashabiah son of
Kemuel; for Aaron, Zadok;

[A]26:25,26,28 Or *Shelomoth* [B]27:1 Lit *that came in and went out month by month for all months of* [C]27:6 LXX; MT omits *in charge* [D]27:15 Lit *belonging to Othniel*

18 for Judah, Elihu, one of David's
brothers; for Issachar, Omri son of
Michael;
19 for Zebulun, Ishmaiah son of
Obadiah;
for Naphtali, Jerimoth son of Azriel;
20 for the Ephraimites, Hoshea son of
Azaziah;
for half the tribe of Manasseh, Joel son
of Pedaiah;
21 for half the tribe of Manasseh in
Gilead, Iddo son of Zechariah;
for Benjamin, Jaasiel son of Abner;
22 for Dan, Azarel son of Jeroham.
Those were the leaders of the tribes of
Israel.[a]

23 David didn't count the men aged 20 or
under, for the LORD had said He would make
Israel as numerous as the stars of heaven.[b]
24 Joab son of Zeruiah began to count them,
but he didn't complete it. There was wrath
against Israel because of this census,[c] and the
number was not entered in the Historical
Record[A] of King David.

25 Azmaveth son of Adiel was in charge
of the king's storehouses.
Jonathan son of Uzziah was in charge
of the storehouses in the country, in
the cities, in the villages, and in the
fortresses.
26 Ezri son of Chelub was in charge of
those who worked in the fields tilling
the soil.
27 Shimei the Ramathite was in charge
of the vineyards.
Zabdi the Shiphmite was in charge of
the produce of the vineyards for the
wine cellars.
28 Baal-hanan the Gederite was in
charge of the olive and sycamore trees[d]
in the Judean foothills.[B]
Joash was in charge of the stores of
olive oil.
29 Shitrai the Sharonite was in charge of
the herds that grazed in Sharon,[e] while
Shaphat son of Adlai was in charge of
the herds in the valleys.
30 Obil the Ishmaelite was in charge of
the camels.
Jehdeiah the Meronothite was in
charge of the donkeys.
31 Jaziz the Hagrite[f] was in charge of the
flocks.
All these were officials in charge of
King David's property.

32 David's uncle Jonathan was a counselor;
he was a man of understanding and a scribe.
Jehiel son of Hachmoni attended[C] the king's
sons. 33 Ahithophel[g] was the king's counselor.
Hushai[h] the Archite was the king's friend.
34 After Ahithophel came Jehoiada son of
Benaiah,[i] then Abiathar.[j] Joab was the commander of the king's army.[k]

David Commissions Solomon to Build the Temple

28 David assembled all the leaders of Israel in Jerusalem:[l] the leaders of the
tribes, the leaders of the divisions in the
king's service, the commanders of thousands
and the commanders of hundreds, and the
officials in charge of all the property and
cattle of the king and his sons, along with the
court officials, the fighting men,[m] and all the
brave warriors. 2 Then King David rose to his
feet and said, "Listen to me, my brothers and
my people. It was in my heart to build a house
as a resting place for the ark of the LORD's covenant[n] and as a footstool[o] for our God. I had
made preparations to build, 3 but God said to
me, 'You are not to build a house for My name
because you are a man of war and have shed
blood.'[p]

4 "Yet the LORD God of Israel chose me out
of all my father's household[q] to be king over
Israel forever.[r] For He chose Judah as leader,[s]
and from the house of Judah, my father's
household, and from my father's sons,[t] He
was pleased to make me king over all Israel.
5 And out of all my sons[u] — for the LORD has
given me many sons — He has chosen my son
Solomon to sit on the throne of the LORD's
kingdom over Israel.[v] 6 He said to me,[w] 'Your
son Solomon is the one who is to build My
house and My courts, for I have chosen him
to be My son, and I will be his father. 7 I will establish his kingdom forever if he perseveres
in keeping My commands and My ordinances
as he is today.'[x]

[a] **27:22** 1Ch 28:1
[b] **27:23** Gn 15:5
[c] **27:24** 2Sm 24:1-15; 1Ch 21:1-7
[d] **27:28** 1Kg 10:27; 2Ch 1:15
[e] **27:29** 1Ch 5:16
[f] **27:31** 1Ch 5:10,18-21; 11:38
[g] **27:33** 2Sm 15:12
[h] 2Sm 15:32,37
[i] **27:34** 2Sm 8:18; 1Kg 1:8; 1Ch 11:22-24; 18:17; 27:5-6
[j] 1Sm 22:20-23; 1Kg 1:7; 2:26-27,35; 1Ch 15:11; 18:16; 24:6
[k] 1Ch 11:6
[l] **28:1** 1Ch 23:2; 27:1-31
[m] 1Ch 11:10-47
[n] **28:2** 2Sm 7:1-3; 1Ch 17:1-2; 22:7
[o] Ps 132:7; Is 66:1
[p] **28:3** 1Ch 22:8
[q] **28:4** 1Sm 16:6-13
[r] 1Ch 17:23,27
[s] Gn 49:8-10; 1Ch 5:2
[t] 1Sm 16:1
[u] **28:5** 1Ch 3:1-9; 14:3-7
[v] 1Ch 22:9
[w] **28:6-7** 2Sm 7:13-14; 1Ch 22:10
[x] **28:7** 1Ch 22:13

[A] **27:24** LXX; MT reads *Number* [B] **27:28** Or *the Shephelah* [C] **27:32** Lit *was with*

8“So now in the sight of all Israel, the assembly of the LORD, and in the hearing of our
God, observe and follow all the commands of
the LORD your God so that you may possess
this good land and leave it as an inheritance
to your descendants forever.
9“As for you, Solomon my son, know the
God of your father, and serve Him with a
whole heart and a willing mind,[a] for the LORD
searches every heart and understands the intention of every thought.[b] If you seek Him, He
will be found by you, but if you forsake Him,
He will reject you forever.[c] 10Realize now that
the LORD has chosen you to build a house for
the sanctuary. Be strong, and do it.”[d]
11Then David gave his son Solomon the
plans[e] for the portico[f] of the temple and
its buildings, treasuries, upper rooms, inner rooms, and a room for the •mercy seat.[g]
12The plans contained everything he had in
mind[A,h] for the courts of the LORD’s house,
all the surrounding chambers, the treasuries[i]
of God’s house, and the treasuries for what
is dedicated. 13Also included were plans for
the divisions of the priests and the Levites;
all the work of service in the LORD’s house; all
the articles of service of the LORD’s house;
14the weight of gold for all the articles for every kind of service; the weight of all the silver
articles for every kind of service; 15the weight
of the gold lampstands[j] and their gold lamps,
including the weight of each lampstand and
its lamps; the weight of each silver lampstand
and its lamps, according to the service of each
lampstand; 16the weight of gold for each table
for the rows of the •bread of the Presence and
the silver for the silver tables; 17the pure gold
for the forks, sprinkling basins, and pitchers; the weight of each gold dish; the weight
of each silver bowl; 18the weight of refined
gold for the altar of incense;[k] and the plans
for the chariot of[B,l] the gold •cherubim that
spread out their wings and cover the ark of
the LORD’s covenant.[m]
19David concluded, “By the LORD’s hand on
me, He enabled me to understand everything
in writing, all the details of the plan.”[C]
20Then David said to his son Solomon, “Be
strong and courageous,[n] and do the work.
Don’t be afraid or discouraged, for the LORD
God, my God, is with you. He won’t leave you
or forsake you[o] until all the work for the service of the LORD’s house is finished. 21Here are
the divisions of the priests and the Levites for
all the service of God’s house.[p] Every willing
man of any skill[q] will be at your disposal for
the work, and the leaders and all the people
are at your every command.”

Contributions for Building the Temple

29 Then King David said to all the assembly, “My son Solomon — God has
chosen him alone — is young and inexperienced. The task is great[r] because the temple
will not be for man but for the LORD God.[s] 2So
to the best of my ability I’ve made provision
for the house of my God:[t] gold for the gold
articles, silver for the silver, bronze for the
bronze, iron for the iron, and wood for the
wood, as well as onyx, stones for mounting,[D]
antimony,[E,u] stones of various colors, all kinds
of precious stones, and a great quantity of
marble. 3Moreover, because of my delight in
the house of my God, I now give my personal
treasures of gold and silver for the house
of my God over and above all that I’ve provided for the holy house: 4100 tons[F,v] of gold
(gold of Ophir[w]) and 250 tons[G] of refined silver for overlaying the walls of the buildings,
5the gold for the gold work and the silver for
the silver, for all the work to be done by the
craftsmen. Now who will volunteer to consecrate himself to the LORD today?”
6Then the leaders of the households, the
leaders of the tribes of Israel, the commanders of thousands and of hundreds,[x] and the
officials in charge of the king’s work[y] gave
willingly. 7For the service of God’s house they
gave 185 tons[H] of gold and 10,000 gold coins,[I,z]
375 tons[J] of silver, 675 tons[K] of bronze, and
4,000 tons[L] of iron. 8Whoever had precious
stones gave them to the treasury of the LORD’s
house under the care of Jehiel[aa] the Gershonite. 9Then the people rejoiced because of their
leaders’ willingness to give, for they had given
to the LORD with a whole heart.[ab] King David
also rejoiced greatly.

[a]28:9 1Kg 8:61; 1Ch 29:17-19 [b]Gn 6:5; 1Sm 16:7; Ps 139 [c]2Ch 15:2; Jr 29:13 [d]28:10 1Ch 22:13 [e]28:11 Ex 25:9,40; 1Ch 28:19 [f]1Kg 6:3 [g]Ex 25:17-22 [h]28:12 1Ch 28:19 [i]1Ch 26:20,22,24,26; Ezr 2:69 [j]28:15 Ex 25:31-39 [k]28:18 Ex 30:1-10 [l]Ps 18:10 [m]Ex 25:18-22; 1Kg 8:6-7; 2Ch 5:7-8 [n]28:20 Jos 1:6-7; 1Ch 22:13; 2Ch 32:7 [o]Dt 31:6; Jos 1:5,9; Heb 13:5 [p]28:21 1Ch 28:13 [q]Ex 35:25-35; 36:1-2 [r]29:1 1Ch 22:5 [s]1Ch 29:19 [t]29:2 1Ch 22:3-5 [u]Ex 28:18 [v]29:4 1Ch 22:14 [w]1Kg 9:28 [x]29:6 1Ch 27:1; 28:1 [y]1Ch 27:25-31 [z]29:7 Ezr 2:69; Neh 7:70 [aa]29:8 1Ch 23:8 [ab]29:9 1Kg 8:61; 1Ch 28:9; 2Co 9:7

A28:12 Or *he received from the Spirit* B28:18 Or *chariot, that is*; Ps 18:10; Ezk 1:5,15 C28:19 Hb obscure D29:2 Or *mosaic* E29:2 In Hb, the word antimony is similar to “turquoise”; Ex 28:18. F29:4 Lit *3,000 talents* G29:4 Lit *7,000 talents* H29:7 Lit *5,000 talents* I29:7 Or *drachmas*, or *darics* J29:7 Lit *10,000 talents* K29:7 Lit *18,000 talents* L29:7 Lit *100,000 talents*

David's Prayer

10 Then David praised the LORD in the sight of all the assembly. David said,

May You be praised, LORD God of our father Israel, from eternity to eternity. 11 Yours, LORD, is the greatness and the power and the glory and the splendor and the majesty, for everything in the heavens and on earth belongs to You. Yours, LORD, is the kingdom, and You are exalted as head over all.[a] 12 Riches and honor come from You, and You are the ruler of everything.[b] Power and might are in Your hand, and it is in Your hand to make great and to give strength to all.[c] 13 Now therefore, our God, we give You thanks and praise Your glorious name.

14 But who am I, and who are my people, that we should be able to give as generously as this? For everything comes from You, and we have given You only what comes from Your own hand.[A] 15 For we live before You as foreigners and temporary residents in Your presence as were all our ancestors.[d] Our days on earth are like a shadow, without hope.[e] 16 •Yahweh our God, all this wealth that we've provided for building You a house for Your holy name comes from Your hand; everything belongs to You. 17 I know, my God, that You test the heart[f] and that You are pleased with what is right.[g] I have willingly given all these things with an upright heart, and now I have seen Your people who are present[B] here giving joyfully and[C] willingly to You. 18 LORD God of Abraham, Isaac, and Israel, our ancestors, keep this desire forever in the thoughts of the hearts of Your people, and confirm their hearts toward You. 19 Give my son Solomon a whole heart to keep and to carry out all Your commands, Your decrees, and Your statutes,[h] and to build the temple for which I have made provision.[i]

20 Then David said to the whole assembly, "Praise the LORD your God." So the whole assembly praised the LORD God of their ancestors.[j] They bowed down and paid homage to the LORD and the king.[k]

21 The following day they offered sacrifices to the LORD and •burnt offerings to the LORD: 1,000 bulls, 1,000 rams, and 1,000 lambs, along with their •drink offerings, and sacrifices in abundance for all Israel.[l] 22 They ate and drank with great joy in the LORD's presence that day.

The Enthronement of Solomon

Then, for a second time,[m] they made David's son Solomon king; they anointed him[D] as the LORD's ruler,[n] and Zadok as the priest. 23 Solomon sat on the LORD's throne as king in place of his father David. He prospered, and all Israel obeyed him.[o] 24 All the leaders and the mighty men, and all of King David's sons as well, pledged their allegiance to King Solomon. 25 The LORD highly exalted Solomon in the sight of all Israel[p] and bestowed on him such royal majesty as had not been bestowed on any king over Israel before him.[q]

A Summary of David's Life

26 David son of Jesse was king over all Israel.[r] 27 The length of his reign over Israel was 40 years; he reigned in Hebron for seven years and in Jerusalem for 33.[s] 28 He died at a ripe old age,[t] full of days,[u] riches, and honor, and his son Solomon became king in his place. 29 As for the events of King David's reign, from beginning to end, note that they are written in the Events of Samuel the Seer,[v] the Events of Nathan the Prophet,[w] and the Events of Gad the Seer,[x] 30 along with all his reign, his might, and the incidents that affected him and Israel and all the kingdoms of the surrounding lands.

[a] **29:11** Mt 6:13; Rv 5:13
[b] **29:12** 2Ch 1:12
[c] 2Ch 20:6
[d] **29:15** Lv 25:23; Heb 11:13
[e] Jb 14:2,10-12
[f] **29:17** 1Ch 28:9
[g] Ps 15:2
[h] **29:19** Ps 72:1
[i] 1Ch 29:2
[j] **29:20** Jos 22:33
[k] Ex 4:31
[l] **29:21** 1Kg 8:62-63
[m] **29:22** 1Ch 23:1
[n] 1Kg 1:33-39
[o] **29:23** 1Kg 2:12
[p] **29:25** 2Ch 1:1
[q] 1Kg 3:13; 2Ch 1:12
[r] **29:26** 1Ch 18:14
[s] **29:27** 2Sm 5:4-5; 1Kg 2:11
[t] **29:28** Gn 15:15; Ac 13:36
[u] 1Ch 23:1
[v] **29:29** 1Sm 9:9
[w] 2Sm 7:2-4; 12:1-7
[x] 1Sm 22:5

[A] **29:14** Lit *and from Your hand we have given to You* [B] **29:17** Lit *found*
[C] **29:17** Or *now with joy I've seen Your people who are present here giving*
[D] **29:22** LXX, Tg, Vg; MT omits *him*

2 CHRONICLES

For the introduction to the book of 2 Chronicles, see the introduction to the book of 1 Chronicles, page 393.

Solomon's Request for Wisdom

1 Solomon son of David strengthened his hold on his kingdom.[a] The LORD his God was with him and highly exalted him.[b] 2 Then Solomon spoke to all Israel, to the commanders of thousands and of hundreds, to the judges, and to every leader in all Israel—the heads of the families.[c] 3 Solomon and the whole assembly with him went to the •high place that was in Gibeon[d] because God's tent of meeting, which the LORD's servant Moses had made[e] in the wilderness, was there. 4 Now David had brought the ark of God from Kiriath-jearim to the place[A] he had set up for it, because he had pitched a tent for it in Jerusalem,[f] 5 but he put[B] the bronze altar, which Bezalel son of Uri, son of Hur, had made,[g] in front of the LORD's tabernacle. Solomon and the assembly inquired of Him[C] there. 6 Solomon offered sacrifices there in the LORD's presence on the bronze altar at the tent of meeting; he offered 1,000 •burnt offerings on it.[h]

7 That night[i] God appeared to Solomon and said to him: "Ask. What should I give you?"

8 And Solomon said to God: "You have shown great and faithful love to my father David, and You have made me king in his place.[j] 9 LORD God, let Your promise to my father David now come true.[k] For You have made me king over a people as numerous as the dust of the earth.[l] 10 Now grant me wisdom and knowledge so that I may lead these people,[m] for who can judge this great people of Yours?"

11 God said to Solomon, "Since this was in your heart, and you have not requested riches, wealth, or glory, or for the life of those who hate you, and you have not even requested long life, but you have requested for yourself wisdom and knowledge that you may judge My people over whom I have made you king, 12 wisdom and knowledge are given to you. I will also give you riches, wealth, and glory, unlike what was given to the kings who were before you, or will be given to those after you."[n] 13 So Solomon went to Jerusalem from[D] the high place that was in Gibeon in front of the tent of meeting, and he reigned over Israel.

[a] 1:1 1Kg 2:12,46 [b] 1Ch 29:25 [c] 1:2 1Ch 28:1 [d] 1:3 1Kg 3:4 [e] Ex 36:8-38 [f] 1:4 1Ch 13:1-14; 15:25–16:1 [g] 1:5 Ex 31:2-11; 38:1-7 [h] 1:6 1Kg 3:4 [i] 1:7-13 1Kg 3:5-15 [j] 1:8 1Ch 28:5 [k] 1:9 2Sm 7:12-16 [l] Gn 13:16; 22:17 [m] 1:10 1Sm 18:16; 2Sm 5:2 [n] 1:12 1Ch 29:25; 2Ch 9:22 [o] 1:14-17 1Kg 10:26-29; 2Ch 9:25-28 [p] 1:14 1Kg 4:26 [q] 1Kg 9:19 [r] 2:1 1Kg 5:5; 2Ch 2:12 [s] 2:2 1Kg 5:15-16; 9:23; 2Ch 2:18; 8:10 [t] 2:3 2Sm 5:11; 1Kg 5:1-2 [u] 2:3-10 1Kg 5:2-6,10-11 [v] 2:3 1Ch 14:1

Solomon's Horses and Wealth

14 Solomon[o] accumulated 1,400 chariots and 12,000 horsemen,[p] which he stationed in the chariot cities[q] and with the king in Jerusalem. 15 The king made silver and gold as common in Jerusalem as stones, and he made cedar as abundant as sycamore in the Judean foothills. 16 Solomon's horses came from Egypt and Kue.[E] The king's traders would get them from Kue at the going price. 17 A chariot could be imported from Egypt for 15 pounds[F] of silver and a horse for about four pounds.[G] In the same way, they exported them to all the kings of the Hittites and to the kings of Aram through their agents.

Solomon's Letter to Hiram

2 [H] Solomon decided to build a temple for the name of •Yahweh and a royal palace for himself,[r] 2[I] so he assigned 70,000 men as porters, 80,000 men as stonecutters in the mountains, and 3,600 as supervisors over them.[s]

3 Then Solomon sent word to King Hiram[J,t] of Tyre:[u]

> Do for me what you did for my father David. You sent him cedars to build him a house to live in.[v] 4 Now I am building a

[A] 1:4 Vg; MT omits *the place* [B] 1:5 Some Hb mss, Tg, Syr; other Hb mss, LXX, Vg read *but there was* [C] 1:5 Or *it* [D] 1:13 LXX, Vg; MT reads *to* [E] 1:16 = Cilicia [F] 1:17 Lit *600 shekels* [G] 1:17 Lit *150 shekels* [H] 2:1 2Ch 1:18 in Hb [I] 2:2 2Ch 2:1 in Hb [J] 2:3 Some Hb mss, LXX, Syr, Vg; other Hb mss read *Huram*; 2Sm 5:11; 1Kg 5:1-2

temple for the name of Yahweh my God
in order to dedicate it to Him for burning fragrant incense before Him,[a] for
displaying the rows of the •bread of the
Presence continuously,[b] and for sacrificing •burnt offerings for the morning and
the evening,[c] the Sabbaths[d] and the New
Moons, and the appointed festivals of the
LORD our God. This is ordained for Israel
forever. 5 The temple that I am building
will be great, for our God is greater than
any of the gods.[e] 6 But who is able to build
a temple for Him, since even heaven and
the highest heaven cannot contain Him?[f]
Who am I then that I should build a temple for Him except as a place to burn incense before Him? 7 Therefore, send me a
craftsman who is skilled in engraving to
work with gold, silver, bronze, and iron,
and with purple, crimson, and blue yarn.
He will work with the craftsmen who
are with me in Judah and Jerusalem,[g]
appointed by my father David.[h] 8 Also,
send me cedar, cypress, and algum[A,i] logs
from Lebanon, for I know that your servants know how to cut the trees of Lebanon. Note that my servants will be with
your servants[j] 9 to prepare logs for me
in abundance because the temple I am
building will be great and wonderful. 10 I
will give your servants, the woodcutters
who cut the trees, 100,000 bushels[B] of
wheat flour, 100,000 bushels[B] of barley,
110,000 gallons[C] of wine, and 110,000
gallons[C] of oil.

Hiram's Reply

11 Then King Hiram of Tyre wrote a letter[D]
and sent it to Solomon:

Because the LORD loves His people, He
set you over them as king.[k]

12 Hiram also said:

May the LORD God of Israel, who made
the heavens and the earth,[l] be praised!
He gave King David a wise son with insight and understanding,[m] who will
build a temple for the LORD and a royal
palace for himself.[n] 13 I have now sent
Huram-abi,[E] a skillful man who has understanding.[o] 14 He is the son of a woman
from the daughters of Dan. His father is
a man of Tyre. He knows how to work
with gold, silver, bronze, iron, stone, and
wood, with purple, blue, crimson yarn,
and fine linen. He knows how to do all
kinds of engraving and to execute any design that may be given him. I have sent
him to be with your craftsmen and the
craftsmen of my lord, your father David.
15 Now, let my lord send the wheat, barley, oil, and wine to his servants as promised.[p] 16 We will cut logs from Lebanon, as
many as you need, and bring them to you
as rafts by sea to Joppa. You can then take
them up to Jerusalem.[q]

Solomon's Work Force

17 Solomon took a census of all the foreign
men in the land of Israel, after the census
that his father David had conducted,[r] and the
total was 153,600. 18 Solomon made 70,000
of them porters, 80,000 stonecutters in the
mountains, and 3,600 supervisors to make
the people work.[s]

Building the Temple

3 Then Solomon began[t] to build the LORD's
temple in Jerusalem on Mount Moriah[u]
where the LORD[F] had appeared to his father
David, at the site David had prepared on the
threshing floor of Ornan[G] the Jebusite. 2 He
began to build on the second day of the second month in the fourth year of his reign.
3 These are Solomon's foundations[H] for building God's temple: the length[I] was 90 feet,[J] and
the width 30 feet.[K] 4 The portico, which was
across the front extending across the width
of the temple, was 30 feet[K] wide; its height
was 30 feet;[K,L] he overlaid its inner surface
with pure gold. 5 The larger room[M] he paneled
with cypress wood, overlaid with fine gold,
and decorated with palm trees and chains.
6 He adorned the temple with precious stones
for beauty, and the gold was the gold of Par-
vaim. 7 He overlaid the temple — the beams,

[a] **2:4** Ex 30:7
[b] Ex 25:30
[c] Ex 29:38-42
[d] Nm 28:9-10
[e] **2:5** Ex 15:11; 1Ch 16:25
[f] **2:6** 1Kg 8:27; 2Ch 6:18
[g] **2:7** Ex 31:3-5; 2Ch 2:13-14
[h] 1Ch 22:14-16; 28:21
[i] **2:8** 1Kg 10:11-12
[j] **2:8-9** 2Ch 9:10-11
[k] **2:11** 1Kg 10:9; 2Ch 9:8
[l] **2:12** Ps 33:6; 102:25
[m] 1Kg 5:7
[n] 2Ch 2:1
[o] **2:13-14** 1Kg 7:14
[p] **2:15** 2Ch 2:10
[q] **2:16** 1Kg 5:8-9
[r] **2:17** 2Sm 24:1-9; 1Ch 21:1-5
[s] **2:18** 1Kg 5:15-16; 2Ch 2:2
[t] **3:1-4** 1Kg 6:1-3
[u] **3:1** Gn 22:2

[A] **2:8** = almug in 1Kg 10:11-12 [B] **2:10** Lit *20,000 cors* [C] **2:10** Lit *20,000 baths* [D] **2:11** Lit *Tyre said in writing* [E] **2:13** Lit *Huram my father* [F] **3:1** LXX; Tg reads *the Angel of the LORD*; MT reads *He* [G] **3:1** = Araunah in 2Sm 24:16-24 [H] **3:3** Tg reads *The measurements which Solomon decreed* [I] **3:3** Lit *length — cubits in the former measure—* [J] **3:3** Lit *60 cubits* [K] **3:3,4** Lit *20 cubits* [L] **3:4** LXX, Syr; MT reads *120 cubits* [M] **3:5** Lit *The house*

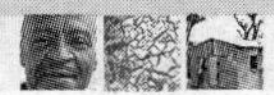

the thresholds, its walls and doors — with
gold,[a] and he carved ·cherubim on the walls.[b]

The Most Holy Place

8 Then he made the most holy place; its
length corresponded to the width of the temple, 30 feet,[A] and its width was 30 feet.[A,c] He
overlaid it with 45,000 pounds[B] of fine gold.
9 The weight of the nails was 20 ounces[C] of
gold, and he overlaid the ceiling with gold.
10 He made[d] two cherubim of sculptured
work, for the most holy place, and he overlaid
them with gold. 11 The overall length of the
wings of the cherubim was 30 feet:[A] the wing
of one was 7 1/2 feet,[D] touching the wall of the
room; its other wing was 7 1/2 feet,[D] touching
the wing of the other cherub. 12 The wing of
the other[E] cherub was 7 1/2 feet,[D] touching the
wall of the room; its other wing was 7 1/2 feet,[D]
reaching the wing of the other cherub. 13 The
wingspan of these cherubim was 30 feet.[A]
They stood on their feet and faced the larger
room.[F]
14 He made the veil of blue, purple, and
crimson yarn and fine linen, and he wove
cherubim into it.[e]

The Bronze Pillars

15 In front of the temple[f] he made two pillars, each 27 feet[G,H] high. The capital on top of
each was 7 1/2 feet[D] high. 16 He had made chainwork in the inner sanctuary and also put it on
top of the pillars.[g] He made 100 pomegranates and fastened them into the chainwork.
17 Then he set up the pillars in front of the
sanctuary, one on the right and one on the
left. He named the one on the right Jachin[I]
and the one on the left Boaz.[J]

The Altar, Reservoir, and Basins

4 He made a bronze altar[h] 30 feet[A] long, 30
feet[A] wide, and 15 feet[K] high.
2 Then he made the cast metal reservoir,[i]
15 feet[K] from brim to brim, perfectly round.
It was 7 1/2 feet[D] high and 45 feet[L] in circumference. 3 The likeness of oxen[M] was below it,
completely encircling it, 10 every half yard,[N]
completely surrounding the reservoir. The
oxen were cast in two rows when the reservoir was cast. 4 It stood on 12 oxen, three facing north, three facing west, three facing
south, and three facing east. The reservoir
was on top of them and all their hindquarters were toward the center. 5 The reservoir
was three inches[O] thick, and its rim was fashioned like the brim of a cup or a lily blossom.
It could hold 11,000 gallons.[P]
6 He made 10 basins for washing and he put
five on the right and five on the left.[j] The parts
of the ·burnt offering were rinsed in them,[k]
but the reservoir was used by the priests for
washing.

The Lampstands, Tables, and Courts

7 He made the 10 gold lampstands according to their specifications and put them in
the sanctuary, five on the right and five on the
left.[l] 8 He made 10 tables and placed them in
the sanctuary, five on the right and five on the
left.[m] He also made 100 gold bowls.
9 He made the courtyard[n] of the priests and
the large court, and doors for the court. He
overlaid the doors with bronze. 10 He put the
reservoir on the right side, toward the southeast.[o] 11 Then Huram[Q,p] made[q] the pots, the
shovels, and the bowls.

Completion of the Bronze Furnishings

So Huram finished doing the work that he
was doing for King Solomon in God's temple:
12 two pillars; the bowls and the capitals on
top of the two pillars; the two gratings for
covering both bowls of the capitals that were
on top of the pillars; 13 the 400 pomegranates
for the two gratings (two rows of pomegranates for each grating covering both capitals'
bowls on top of the pillars[r]). 14 He also made
the water carts[R,s] and the basins on the water
carts. 15 The one reservoir and the 12 oxen underneath it, 16 the pots, the shovels, the forks,
and all their utensils — Huram-abi[S,t] made
them for King Solomon for the LORD's temple. All these were made of polished bronze.
17 The king had them cast in clay molds in the
Jordan Valley between Succoth and Zeredah. 18 Solomon made all these utensils in

[a] **3:7** 1Kg 6:20-22
[b] 1Kg 6:29-35
[c] **3:8** 1Kg 6:16
[d] **3:10-13** 1Kg 6:23-28
[e] **3:14** Ex 26:31
[f] **3:15-17** 1Kg 7:15-22; 2Kg 25:17; Jr 52:21-23
[g] **3:16** 1Kg 6:21; 7:17
[h] **4:1** Ex 27:1-2; 2Kg 16:14
[i] **4:2-5** 1Kg 7:23-26; Ezk 47:1-12; Rv 22:1
[j] **4:6** 1Kg 7:38-39
[k] Ezk 40:38
[l] **4:7** Ex 37:17-24; 1Kg 7:49
[m] **4:8** 1Kg 7:48
[n] **4:9** 1Kg 6:36
[o] **4:10** 1Kg 7:39
[p] **4:11** 1Kg 7:13,40,45
[q] **4:11–5:1** 1Kg 7:40-51
[r] **4:13** 1Kg 7:20
[s] **4:14** 1Kg 7:27-37
[t] **4:16** 1Kg 7:14; 2Ch 2:13

[A] **3:8,11,13; 4:1** Lit *20 cubits* [B] **3:8** Lit *600 talents* [C] **3:9** Lit *50 shekels* [D] **3:11,12,15; 4:2** Lit *five cubits* [E] **3:12** Syr, Vg; MT reads *the one* [F] **3:13** Lit *the house* [G] **3:15** Hb uncertain [H] **3:15** Lit *35 cubits* [I] **3:17** = He Will Establish [J] **3:17** = Strength Is in Him [K] **4:1,2** Lit *10 cubits* [L] **4:2** Lit *30 cubits* [M] **4:3** = gourds in 1Kg 7:24 [N] **4:3** Lit *10 per cubit* [O] **4:5** Lit *a handbreadth* [P] **4:5** Text emended; MT reads *3,000 baths* in 1Kg 7:26 [Q] **4:11** = Hiram in 1Kg 7:13,40,45 [R] **4:14** Lit *the stands* [S] **4:16** Lit *Huram my father*

such great abundance that the weight of the
bronze was not determined.

Completion of the Gold Furnishings

19Solomon also made all the equipment
in God's temple: the gold altar; the tables
on which to put the ·bread of the Presence;[a]
20the lampstands and their lamps of pure
gold to burn in front of the inner sanctuary
according to specifications;[b] 21the flowers,
lamps, and gold tongs — of purest gold; 22the
wick trimmers, sprinkling basins, ladles,[A]
and firepans — of purest gold; and the entryway to the temple, its inner doors to the most
holy place, and the doors of the temple sanctuary — of gold.

5 So all the work Solomon did for the
LORD's temple was completed. Then Solomon brought the consecrated things of his
father David — the silver, the gold, and all the
utensils — and put them in the treasuries of
God's temple.

Preparations for the Temple Dedication

2At that time[c] Solomon assembled at Jerusalem the elders of Israel — all the tribal heads,
the ancestral chiefs of the Israelites — in order to bring the ark of the covenant of the
LORD up from the city of David,[d] that is, ·Zion.
3So all the men of Israel were assembled in
the king's presence at the festival; this was in
the seventh month.[B]
4All the elders of Israel came, and the Levites picked up the ark. 5They brought up
the ark, the tent of meeting, and the holy
utensils that were in the tent. The priests
and the Levites brought them up. 6King Solomon and the entire congregation of Israel
who had gathered around him were in front
of the ark sacrificing sheep and cattle that
could not be counted or numbered because
there were so many. 7The priests brought
the ark of the LORD's covenant to its place,
into the inner sanctuary of the temple, to the
most holy place, beneath the wings of the
·cherubim.[e] 8And the cherubim spread their
wings over the place of the ark so that the
cherubim formed a cover above the ark and
its poles. 9The poles were so long that their
ends were seen from the holy place[C,f] in front
of the inner sanctuary, but they were not
seen from outside; they are there to this very
day. 10Nothing was in the ark except the two
tablets that Moses had put in it at Horeb,[D,g]
where the LORD had made a covenant with
the Israelites when they came out of Egypt.
11Now all the priests who were present had
consecrated themselves regardless of their
divisions.[h] When the priests came out of the
holy place, 12the Levitical singers dressed in
fine linen and carrying cymbals, harps, and
lyres[i] were standing east of the altar, and
with them were 120 priests blowing trumpets.[j] The Levitical singers were descendants
of ·Asaph, Heman, and Jeduthun and their
sons[k] and relatives. 13The trumpeters and
singers joined together to praise and thank
the LORD with one voice. They raised their
voices, accompanied by trumpets, cymbals,
and musical instruments,[l] in praise to the
LORD:

For He is good;
His faithful love endures forever.[m]

The temple, the LORD's temple, was filled
with a cloud.[n] 14And because of the cloud, the
priests were not able to continue ministering,
for the glory of the LORD filled God's temple.[o]

Solomon's Dedication of the Temple

6 Then Solomon said:[p]

The LORD said He would dwell
in thick darkness,[q]
2 but I have built an exalted temple
for You,
a place for Your residence forever.

3Then the king turned and blessed the entire congregation of Israel while they were
standing. 4He said:

May the LORD God of Israel be praised!
He spoke directly to my father David,
and He has fulfilled the promise
by His power.
He said,
5 "Since the day I brought
My people Israel
out of the land of Egypt,[r]

[a]**4:19** Lv 24:5-9
[b]**4:20** Ex 25:31-40; 2Ch 4:7
[c]**5:2-14** 1Kg 8:1-11
[d]**5:2** 2Ch 1:4
[e]**5:7** 2Ch 3:10
[f]**5:9** 1Kg 8:8
[g]**5:10** Dt 10:2-5; Heb 9:4
[h]**5:11** 1Ch 24:1-5
[i]**5:12** 1Ch 13:8; 15:16,24
[j]2Ch 7:6
[k]1Ch 25:1-4
[l]**5:13** 1Ch 16:42
[m]1Ch 16:34; 2Ch 7:3
[n]Ex 40:34-35; Lv 16:2; Nm 9:15-16
[o]**5:14** Ex 13:21-22; 40:34-38; Dt 4:11; 5:22; 31:14-15; 2Ch 7:1-3
[p]**6:1-42** 1Kg 8:12-53
[q]**6:1** Ex 20:21; Dt 4:11; 5:22
[r]**6:5-9** 2Sm 7:1-13

[A]**4:22** Or *dishes*, or *spoons*; lit *palms* [B]**5:3** = Tishri (September–October) [C]**5:9** Some Hb mss, LXX; other Hb mss read *the ark*; 1Kg 8:8 [D]**5:10** = Sinai

I have not chosen a city to build
a temple in
among any of the tribes of Israel,
so that My name would be there,
and I have not chosen a man
to be ruler over My people Israel.
6 But I have chosen Jerusalem
so that My name will be there,[a]
and I have chosen David
to be over My people Israel."[b]

7 Now it was in the heart
of my father David
to build a temple for the name
of ·Yahweh, the God of Israel.[c]
8 However, Yahweh said
to my father David,
"Since it was your desire to build
a temple for My name,
you have done well to have
this desire.
9 Yet, you are not the one to build
the temple,
but your son, your own offspring,
will build the temple for My name."
10 So Yahweh has fulfilled
what He promised.
I have taken the place
of my father David
and I sit on the throne of Israel,
as Yahweh promised.
I have built the temple for the name
of Yahweh, the God of Israel.
11 I have put the ark there,
where Yahweh's covenant is
that He made with the Israelites.[d]

Solomon's Prayer

12 Then Solomon stood before the altar of
the LORD in front of the entire congregation
of Israel and spread out his hands. 13 For Solomon had made a bronze platform 7 1/2 feet[A]
long, 7 1/2 feet[A] wide, and 4 1/2 feet[B] high and
put it in the court. He stood on it,[e] knelt down
in front of the entire congregation of Israel,
and spread out his hands toward heaven.[f]
14 He said:

LORD God of Israel,
there is no God like You
in heaven or on earth,[g]
keeping His gracious covenant
with Your servants who walk
before You
with their whole heart.[h]
15 You have kept what You promised
to Your servant, my father David.
You spoke directly to him,
and You fulfilled Your promise
by Your power,
as it is today.[i]
16 Therefore, LORD God of Israel,
keep what You promised
to Your servant, my father David:
"You will never fail to have a man
to sit before Me on the throne of Israel,[j]
if only your sons guard their way
to walk in My Law
as you have walked before Me."
17 Now, LORD God of Israel,
please confirm
what You promised
to Your servant David.

18 But will God indeed live on earth
with man?
Even heaven, the highest heaven,
cannot contain You,[k]
much less this temple I have built.
19 Listen[C] to Your servant's prayer
and his petition,
LORD my God,
so that You may hear the cry
and the prayer
that Your servant prays before You,
20 so that Your eyes watch over this temple
day and night,
toward the place where You said
You would put Your name;[l]
and so that You may hear the prayer
Your servant prays toward this place.
21 Hear the petitions of Your servant
and Your people Israel,
which they pray toward this place.
May You hear in Your dwelling place
in heaven.
May You hear and forgive.

22 If a man sins against his neighbor
and is forced to take an oath[D]
and he comes to take an oath
before Your altar in this temple,

[a] 6:6 2Ch 12:13 [b] 1Ch 28:4 [c] 6:7 1Kg 5:3 [d] 6:11 2Ch 5:7,10 [e] 6:13 Ex 9:29,33; Ezr 9:5; Neh 8:4 [f] 1Kg 8:54 [g] 6:14 Ex 15:11; Dt 3:24 [h] Dt 7:9 [i] 6:15 1Ch 22:9-10 [j] 6:16 1Kg 2:4; 2Ch 7:18 [k] 6:18 2Ch 2:6 [l] 6:20 Dt 12:11

[A] 6:13 Lit *five cubits* [B] 6:13 Lit *three cubits* [C] 6:19 Lit *Turn* [D] 6:22 Lit *and he lifts a curse against him to curse him*

23 may You hear in heaven and act.
May You judge Your servants,
condemning the wicked man
by bringing
what he has done on his own head
and providing justice for the righteous
by rewarding him according to
his righteousness.

24 If Your people Israel are defeated
before an enemy,
because they have sinned against You,
and they return to You and praise
Your name,
and they pray and plead for mercy
before You in this temple,
25 may You hear in heaven
and forgive the sin
of Your people Israel.
May You restore them to the land
You gave them and their ancestors.

26 When the skies are shut and there is
no rain
because they have sinned against You,
and they pray toward this place
and praise Your name,
and they turn from their sins
because You are afflicting[A,a] them,
27 may You hear in heaven
and forgive the sin of Your servants
and Your people Israel,
so that You may teach them
the good way
they should walk in.
May You send rain on Your land
that You gave Your people
for an inheritance.

28 When there is famine on the earth,
when there is pestilence,
when there is blight, mildew, locust,
or grasshopper,
when their enemies besiege them
in the region of their fortified cities,[B,b]
when there is any plague or illness,
29 whatever prayer or petition
anyone from your people Israel
might have —
each man knowing his own affliction[C]
and suffering,

[a]6:26 1Kg 8:35 [b]6:28 Jos 2:7; Jdg 16:2-3 [c]6:30 1Sm 16:7; 1Ch 28:9 [d]6:32 Is 56:6-8; Zch 8:20-23; 14:16-21 [e]6:33 2Ch 7:14 [f]6:34 Dt 12:11 [g]6:36 Jb 15:14-16; Jms 3:2; 1Jn 1:8-10

and spreading out his hands
toward this temple —
30 may You hear in heaven,
Your dwelling place,
and may You forgive
and repay the man
according to all his ways,
since You know his heart,
for You alone know the human heart,[c]
31 so that they may •fear You
and walk in Your ways
all the days they live on the land
You gave our ancestors.

32 Even for the foreigner who is not of
Your people Israel
but has come from a distant land
because of Your great name
and Your mighty hand
and outstretched arm:[d]
when he comes and prays
toward this temple,
33 may You hear in heaven in Your
dwelling place,
and do all the foreigner asks You.
Then all the peoples of the earth
will know Your name,
to fear You as Your people Israel do
and know that this temple I have built
is called by Your name.[e]

34 When Your people go out
to fight against their enemies,
wherever You send them,
and they pray to You
in the direction of this city
You have chosen[f]
and the temple that I have built
for Your name,
35 may You hear their prayer and petition
in heaven
and uphold their cause.

36 When they sin against You —
for there is no one who does not sin[g] —
and You are angry with them
and hand them over to the enemy,
and their captors deport them
to a distant or nearby country,
37 and when they come to their senses
in the land where they were deported

A6:26 LXX, Vg; MT reads *answering*; 1Kg 8:35 B6:28 Lit *if his* (Israel's) *enemies besiege him in the land of his gates*; Jos 2:7; Jdg 16:2-3 C6:29 Lit *plague*

and repent and petition You
in their captors' land,
saying: "We have sinned
and done wrong;
we have been wicked,"
38 and when they return to You
with their whole mind and heart
in the land of their captivity
where they were taken captive,
and when they pray in the direction
of their land
that You gave their ancestors,
and the city You have chosen,
and toward the temple I have built
for Your name,
39 may You hear their prayer and petitions
in heaven,
Your dwelling place,
and uphold their cause.[A]
May You forgive Your people
who sinned against You.
40 Now, my God,
please let Your eyes be open
and Your ears attentive
to the prayer of this place.[a]
41 Now therefore:[b]

Arise, LORD God, come
to Your resting place,
You and Your powerful ark.
May Your priests, LORD God, be clothed
with salvation,
and may Your godly people rejoice
in goodness.
42 LORD God, do not reject
Your anointed one;[B]
remember the loyalty
of Your servant David.[c]

The Dedication Ceremonies

7 When Solomon finished praying,[d] fire
descended from heaven and consumed
the ·burnt offering and the sacrifices,[e] and
the glory of the LORD filled the temple. 2The
priests were not able to enter the LORD's temple because the glory of the LORD filled the
temple of the LORD. 3All the Israelites were
watching when the fire descended and the
glory of the LORD came on the temple. They
bowed down on the pavement with their
faces to the ground. They worshiped and
praised the LORD:

For He is good,
for His faithful love endures forever.[f]

4The king and all the people were offering sacrifices in the LORD's presence.[g] 5King
Solomon offered a sacrifice of 22,000 cattle
and 120,000 sheep. In this manner the king
and all the people dedicated God's temple.
6The priests and the Levites were standing
at their stations. The Levites had the musical
instruments of the LORD, which King David
had made to praise the LORD—"for His faithful love endures forever"—when he offered
praise with them.[h] Across from the Levites,
the priests were blowing trumpets, and all
the people were standing. 7Since the bronze
altar that Solomon had made[i] could not accommodate the burnt offering, the ·grain
offering, and the fat of the ·fellowship offerings, Solomon first consecrated the middle of
the courtyard[j] that was in front of the LORD's
temple and then offered the burnt offerings
and the fat of the fellowship offerings there.[k]
8So Solomon and all Israel with him—a
very great assembly, from the entrance to Hamath[C] to the Brook of Egypt—observed the
festival at that time for seven days. 9On the
eighth day[D] they held a sacred assembly,[l] for
the dedication of the altar lasted seven days
and the festival seven days. 10On the twenty-
third day of the seventh month he sent the
people away to their tents, rejoicing and with
happy hearts for the goodness the LORD had
done for David, for Solomon, and for His people Israel.
11So Solomon finished the LORD's temple
and the royal palace. Everything that had entered Solomon's heart to do for the LORD's
temple and for his own palace succeeded.[m]

The LORD's Response

12Then the LORD appeared to Solomon at
night and said to him:

I have heard your prayer and have chosen this place for Myself as a temple of
sacrifice.[n] 13If I close the sky so there is no

[a]6:40 2Ch 7:15; Neh 1:6,11; Ps 17:1 [b]6:41-42 Ps 132:8-10 [c]6:42 1Ch 16:8-22; Ps 105:1-15; Is 55:3 [d]7:1-10 1Kg 8:54 [e]7:1 Gn 15:7-17; Lv 9:24; Jdg 6:21-24; 1Kg 18:24,38 [f]7:3 1Ch 16:41; 2Ch 5:13; 20:21; Ezr 3:11; Ps 106:1; Jr 33:11 [g]7:4-5 1Kg 8:62-63 [h]7:6 1Ch 15:16-21; 16:42; 23:5; 2Ch 29:26-30; Neh 12:36 [i]7:7 2Ch 4:1 [j]7:7-10 1Kg 8:64-66 [k]7:7 Lv 7:30-31 [l]7:9 Lv 23:36 [m]7:11-22 1Kg 9:1-9 [n]7:12 Dt 12:5,11

A6:39 Lit *and do their judgment* or *justice* B6:42 Some Hb mss, LXX; other Hb mss read *ones*; Ps 132:10 C7:8 Or *from Lebo-hamath* D7:9 = the day after the festival, or the 15th day

rain, or if I command the grasshopper to
consume the land, or if I send pestilence
on My people,[a] 14 and My people who are
called by My name humble themselves,
pray and seek My face, and turn from
their evil ways, then I will hear from
heaven, forgive their sin, and heal their
land.[b] 15 My eyes will now be open and My
ears attentive to prayer from this place.[c]
16 And I have now chosen and consecrated this temple so that My name may
be there forever; My eyes and My heart
will be there at all times.[d]

17 As for you, if you walk before Me as
your father David walked, doing everything I have commanded you, and if you
keep My statutes and ordinances, 18 I will
establish your royal throne, as I promised your father David: You will never fail
to have a man ruling in Israel.[e]

19 However, if you turn away and abandon My statutes and My commands that
I have set before you and if you go and
serve other gods and worship them,[f]
20 then I will uproot Israel from the soil
that I gave them, and this temple that I
have sanctified for My name I will banish from My presence;[g] I will make it an
object of scorn and ridicule among all
the peoples.[h] 21 As for this temple, which
was exalted, everyone who passes by will
be appalled and will say:[i] Why did the
LORD do this to this land and this temple? 22 Then they will say: Because they
abandoned the LORD God of their ancestors who brought them out of the land of
Egypt. They clung to other gods and worshiped and served them. Because of this,
He brought all this ruin on them.

Solomon's Later Building Projects

8 At the end of 20 years[j] during which Solomon had built the LORD's temple and
his own palace— 2 Solomon had rebuilt the
cities Hiram[A] gave him and settled Israelites
there— 3 Solomon went to Hamath-zobah
and seized it. 4 He built Tadmor in the wilderness along with all the storage cities that he
built in Hamath. 5 He built Upper Beth-horon and Lower Beth-horon[k]— fortified cities
with walls, gates, and bars[l]— 6 Baalath, all the
storage cities that belonged to Solomon, all
the chariot cities, the cavalry cities, and everything Solomon desired to build in Jerusalem, Lebanon, or anywhere else in the land of
his dominion.

7 As for all the peoples who remained of the
Hittites, Amorites, Perizzites, Hivites, and
Jebusites, who were not from Israel[m]— 8 their
descendants who remained in the land after
them, those the Israelites had not completely
destroyed— Solomon imposed forced labor
on them; it is this way today.[n] 9 But Solomon
did not consign the Israelites to be slaves for
his work; they were soldiers, commanders of
his captains, and commanders of his chariots
and his cavalry. 10 These were King Solomon's
deputies: 250 who ruled over the people.

11 Solomon brought the daughter of Pharaoh from the city of David to the house he
had built for her,[o] for he said, "My wife must
not live in the house[B] of David king of Israel
because the places the ark of the LORD has
come into are holy."

Public Worship Established at the Temple

12 At that time[p] Solomon offered •burnt offerings to the LORD on the LORD's altar he
had made in front of the portico.[q] 13 He followed the daily requirement[r] for offerings according to the commandment of Moses[s] for
Sabbaths, New Moons, and the three annual
appointed festivals: the Festival of Unleavened
Bread, the Festival of Weeks, and the Festival
of Booths.[t] 14 According to the ordinances of
his father David, he appointed the divisions
of the priests over their service,[u] of the Levites
over their responsibilities to offer praise and
to minister before the priests following the
daily requirement,[v] and of the gatekeepers by
their divisions with respect to each gate,[w] for
this had been the command of David, the man
of God.[x] 15 They did not turn aside from the
king's command regarding the priests and the
Levites concerning any matter or concerning
the treasuries.[y] 16 All of Solomon's work was
carried out from the day the foundation was
laid for the LORD's temple until it was finished. So the LORD's temple was completed.

[a] **7:13** 2Ch 6:26-28
[b] **7:14** 2Ch 6:37-39
[c] **7:15** 2Ch 6:20,40
[d] **7:16** 2Ch 7:12
[e] **7:18** 2Ch 6:16
[f] **7:19** Lv 26:14; Dt 28:15
[g] **7:20** Lv 26:33; Dt 29:28; 1Kg 14:15
[h] Dt 28:37
[i] **7:21-22** Dt 29:24-25
[j] **8:1-10** 1Kg 9:10-23
[k] **8:5** 1Ch 7:24
[l] 2Ch 14:7
[m] **8:7** Gn 15:18-21
[n] **8:8** 1Kg 4:6; 9:21
[o] **8:11** 1Kg 3:1; 7:8; 9:24
[p] **8:12-13** 1Kg 9:25
[q] **8:12** 2Ch 4:1
[r] **8:13** Ex 29:38-42
[s] Nm 28:3
[t] Ex 23:14-17
[u] **8:14** 1Ch 24:1-3
[v] 1Ch 25:1
[w] 1Ch 26:1,13
[x] Neh 12:24,36
[y] **8:15** 1Ch 26:20-28

[A] **8:2** = the king of Tyre [B] **8:11** LXX reads *city*

Solomon's Fleet

17 At that time[a] Solomon went to Ezion-geber and to Eloth[b] on the seashore in the land
of Edom. 18 So Hiram[A] sent ships to him by his
servants along with crews of experienced sea-
men. They went with Solomon's servants to
Ophir, took from there 17 tons[B] of gold, and
delivered it to King Solomon.[c]

The Queen of Sheba

9 The queen of Sheba heard of Solomon's
fame,[d] so she came to test Solomon with
difficult questions at Jerusalem with a very
large entourage, with camels bearing spices,
gold in abundance, and precious stones. She
came to Solomon and spoke with him about
everything that was on her mind. 2 So Solomon answered all her questions; nothing
was too difficult for Solomon to explain to
her. 3 When the queen of Sheba observed Solomon's wisdom, the palace he had built, 4 the
food at his table, his servants' residence, his
attendants' service and their attire, his cupbearers and their attire, and the •burnt offerings he offered at the LORD's temple, it took
her breath away.

5 She said to the king, "The report I heard in
my own country about your words and about
your wisdom is true. 6 But I didn't believe
their reports until I came and saw with my
own eyes. Indeed, I was not even told half of
your great wisdom! You far exceed the report
I heard. 7 How happy are your men.[C,e] How
happy are these servants of yours, who always
stand in your presence hearing your wisdom.
8 May the LORD your God be praised! He delighted in you and put you on His throne as
king for the LORD your God.[f] Because Your
God loved Israel enough to establish them
forever, He has set you over them as king to
carry out justice and righteousness."[g]

9 Then she gave the king four and a half
tons[D] of gold, a great quantity of spices, and
precious stones. There never were such spices
as those the queen of Sheba gave to King Solomon. 10 In addition, Hiram's servants and
Solomon's servants who brought gold from
Ophir[h] also brought algum wood and precious stones. 11 The king made the algum wood
into walkways for the LORD's temple and for
the king's palace and into lyres and harps for
the singers. Never before had anything like
them been seen in the land of Judah.

12 King Solomon gave the queen of Sheba
her every desire, whatever she asked—far
more than she had brought the king. Then
she, along with her servants, returned to her
own country.

Solomon's Wealth

13 The weight of gold that came to Solomon[i]
annually was 25 tons,[E] 14 besides what was
brought by the merchants and traders. All the
Arabian kings and governors of the land also
brought gold and silver to Solomon.

15 King Solomon made 200 large shields of
hammered gold; 15 pounds[F] of hammered
gold went into each shield. 16 He made 300
small shields of hammered gold; about eight
pounds[G] of gold went into each shield. The
king put them in the House of the Forest of
Lebanon.[j]

17 The king also made a large ivory throne
and overlaid it with pure gold. 18 The throne
had six steps; there was a footstool covered
in gold for the throne, armrests on either
side of the seat, and two lions standing beside the armrests. 19 Twelve lions were standing there on the six steps, one at each end.
Nothing like it had ever been made in any
other kingdom.

20 All of King Solomon's drinking cups were
gold, and all the utensils of the House of the
Forest of Lebanon were pure gold. There was
no silver, since it was considered as nothing
in Solomon's time, 21 for the king's ships kept
going to Tarshish[k] with Hiram's servants, and
once every three years the ships of Tarshish
would arrive bearing gold, silver, ivory, apes,
and peacocks.[H]

22 King Solomon surpassed all the kings of
the world in riches and wisdom.[l] 23 All the
kings of the world wanted an audience with
Solomon to hear the wisdom God had put
in his heart. 24 Each of them would bring his
own gift—items[I] of silver and gold, clothing,
weapons,[J,K] spices, and horses and mules—as
an annual tribute.

[a] **8:17-18** 1Kg 9:26-28 [b] **8:17** 2Kg 14:22 [c] **8:18** 2Ch 9:10,13 [d] **9:1-12** 1Kg 10:1-13; Mt 12:42; Lk 11:31 [e] **9:7** 1Kg 10:8 [f] **9:8** 1Ch 28:5; 29:23 [g] Dt 7:8; 2Ch 2:11 [h] **9:10** 2Ch 8:18 [i] **9:13-24** 1Kg 10:14-25 [j] **9:16** 1Kg 7:2-5 [k] **9:21** 2Ch 20:36-37 [l] **9:22** 1Kg 3:13; 2Ch 1:12

[A] **8:18** Lit *Huram* [B] **8:18** Lit *450 talents* [C] **9:7** LXX, Old Lat read *wives*; 1Kg 10:8 [D] **9:9** Lit *120 talents* [E] **9:13** Lit *666 talents* [F] **9:15** Lit *600* (shekels) [G] **9:16** Lit *300* (shekels) [H] **9:21** Or *baboons* [I] **9:24** Or *vessels*, or *weapons* [J] **9:24** LXX reads *resin* [K] **9:24** Or *fragrant balsam*

25 Solomon[a] had 4,000 stalls for horses and chariots, and 12,000 horsemen.[b] He stationed them in the chariot cities and with the king in Jerusalem. 26 He ruled over all the kings from the Euphrates River to the land of the Philistines and as far as the border of Egypt.[c] 27 The king made silver as common in Jerusalem as stones, and he made cedar as abundant as sycamore in the Judean foothills. 28 They were bringing horses for Solomon from Egypt and from all the countries.

Solomon's Death

29 The remaining events[d] of Solomon's reign, from beginning to end, are written in the Events of Nathan the Prophet, the Prophecy of Ahijah the Shilonite, and the Visions of Iddo the Seer concerning Jeroboam son of Nebat.[e] 30 Solomon reigned in Jerusalem over all Israel for 40 years. 31 Solomon rested with his fathers and was buried in the city of his father David.[f] His son Rehoboam became king in his place.

The Kingdom Divided

10 Then Rehoboam went to Shechem,[g] for all Israel had gone to Shechem to make him king. 2 When Jeroboam son of Nebat heard about it—for he was in Egypt where he had fled from King Solomon's presence—Jeroboam returned from Egypt.[h] 3 So they summoned him. Then Jeroboam and all Israel came and spoke to Rehoboam: 4 "Your father made our yoke difficult. Therefore, lighten your father's harsh service and the heavy yoke he put on us, and we will serve you."

5 Rehoboam replied, "Return to me in three days." So the people left.

6 Then King Rehoboam consulted with the elders who had served his father Solomon when he was alive, asking, "How do you advise me to respond to these people?"

7 They replied, "If you will be kind to these people and please them by speaking kind words to them, they will be your servants forever."

8 But he rejected the advice of the elders who had advised him, and he consulted with the young men who had grown up with him, the ones serving him. 9 He asked them, "What message do you advise we send back to these people who said to me, 'Lighten the yoke your father put on us'?"

10 Then the young men who had grown up with him told him, "This is what you should say to the people who said to you, 'Your father made our yoke heavy, but you, make it lighter on us!' This is what you should say to them: 'My little finger is thicker than my father's loins.[A] 11 Now therefore, my father burdened you with a heavy yoke, but I will add to your yoke; my father disciplined you with whips, but I, with barbed whips.'"[B]

12 So Jeroboam and all the people came to Rehoboam on the third day, just as the king had ordered, saying, "Return to me on the third day." 13 Then the king answered them harshly. King Rehoboam rejected the elders' advice 14 and spoke to them according to the young men's advice, saying, "My father made your yoke heavy,[C,i] but I will add to it; my father disciplined you with whips, but I, with barbed whips."[B]

15 The king did not listen to the people because the turn of events came from God,[j] in order that the LORD might carry out His word that He had spoken through Ahijah the Shilonite to Jeroboam son of Nebat.[k]

16 When[l] all Israel saw[D,m] that the king had not listened to them, the people answered the king:

> What portion do we have in David?
> We have no inheritance in the son
> of Jesse.
> Israel, each man to your tent;
> David, look after
> your own house now!

So all Israel went to their tents. 17 But as for the Israelites living in the cities of Judah, Rehoboam reigned over them.

18 Then King Rehoboam sent Hadoram,[E,n] who was in charge of the forced labor, but the Israelites stoned him to death. However, King Rehoboam managed to get into his chariot to flee to Jerusalem. 19 Israel is in rebellion against the house of David until today.

[a] **9:25-28** Dt 17:16; 1Kg 10:26-29; 2Ch 1:14-17
[b] **9:25** 1Kg 4:26
[c] **9:26** Gn 15:18; 1Kg 4:21,24
[d] **9:29-31** 1Kg 11:41-43
[e] **9:29** 1Ch 29:29; 2Ch 12:15; 13:22
[f] **9:31** 1Kg 2:10
[g] **10:1-19** 1Kg 12:1-20
[h] **10:2** 1Kg 11:40
[i] **10:14** 1Kg 12:14
[j] **10:15** 2Ch 25:16-20
[k] 1Kg 11:29-39
[l] **10:16-17** 2Sm 20:1-2
[m] **10:16** 1Kg 12:16
[n] **10:18** 1Kg 4:6; 5:14; 12:18

[A] **10:10** Or *waist* [B] **10:11,14** Lit *with scorpions* [C] **10:14** Some Hb mss, LXX; other Hb mss read *I will make your yoke heavy*; 1Kg 12:14 [D] **10:16** Some Hb mss, LXX; other Hb mss omit *saw*; 1Kg 12:16 [E] **10:18** = Adoram in 1Kg 12:18

Rehoboam in Jerusalem

11 When Rehoboam arrived in Jerusalem,[a]
he mobilized the house of Judah and
Benjamin — 180,000 choice warriors — to
fight against Israel to restore the reign to
Rehoboam. 2 But the word of the LORD came
to Shemaiah,[b] the man of God: 3 "Say to Rehoboam son of Solomon, king of Judah, to all
Israel in Judah and Benjamin, and to the rest
of the people: 4 'This is what the LORD says:
You are not to march up and fight against
your brothers.[c] Each of you must return
home, for this incident has come from Me.' "[d]
So they listened to what the LORD said and
turned back from going against Jeroboam.

Judah's King Rehoboam

5 Rehoboam stayed in Jerusalem, and he
fortified cities[A,e] in Judah. 6 He built up Bethlehem, Etam, Tekoa, 7 Beth-zur, Soco, Adullam,
8 Gath, Mareshah, Ziph, 9 Adoraim, Lachish,
Azekah, 10 Zorah, Aijalon, and Hebron, which
are fortified cities in Judah and in Benjamin.
11 He strengthened their fortifications and
put leaders in them with supplies of food,
oil, and wine. 12 He also put large shields and
spears in each and every city to make them
very strong. So Judah and Benjamin were his.
13 The priests and Levites from all their regions throughout Israel took their stand with
Rehoboam, 14 for the Levites left their pasturelands and their possessions[f] and went to
Judah and Jerusalem, because Jeroboam and
his sons refused to let them serve as priests
of •Yahweh.[g] 15 Jeroboam appointed his own
priests for the •high places,[h] the goat-demons,[i] and the golden calves he had made.[j]
16 Those from every tribe of Israel who had determined in their hearts to seek Yahweh their
God followed the Levites to Jerusalem to sacrifice to Yahweh, the God of their ancestors.
17 So they strengthened the kingdom of Judah
and supported Rehoboam son of Solomon
for three years,[k] because they walked in the
way of David and Solomon for three years.
18 Rehoboam married Mahalath, daughter
of David's son Jerimoth and of Abihail daughter of Jesse's son Eliab.[l] 19 She bore sons to him:
Jeush, Shemariah, and Zaham. 20 After her, he
married Maacah daughter[B,m] of Absalom. She
bore Abijah, Attai, Ziza, and Shelomith to
him. 21 Rehoboam loved Maacah daughter[B] of
Absalom more than all his wives and concubines. He acquired 18 wives[n] and 60 concubines and was the father of 28 sons and 60
daughters.
22 Rehoboam appointed Abijah son of Maacah as chief, leader among his brothers, intending to make him king.[o] 23 Rehoboam also
showed discernment by dispersing some of
his sons to all the regions of Judah and Benjamin and to all the fortified cities. He gave
them plenty of provisions and sought many
wives for them.

Shishak's Invasion

12 When Rehoboam had established his
sovereignty and royal power,[p] he abandoned the law of the LORD — he and all Israel
with him. 2 Because they were unfaithful to
the LORD, in the fifth year of King Rehoboam,
Shishak[q] king of Egypt went to war against Jerusalem[r] 3 with 1,200 chariots, 60,000 caval-
rymen, and countless people who came with
him from Egypt — Libyans,[s] Sukkiim, and
Cushites. 4 He captured the fortified cities[t] of
Judah and came as far as Jerusalem.
5 Then Shemaiah[u] the prophet went to Rehoboam and the leaders of Judah who were
gathered at Jerusalem because of Shishak. He
said to them: "This is what the LORD says: 'You
have abandoned Me; therefore, I have abandoned you into the hand of Shishak.' "[v]
6 So the leaders of Israel and the king humbled themselves and said, "•Yahweh is righteous."[w]
7 When the LORD saw that they had humbled themselves, the LORD's message came to
Shemaiah: "They have humbled themselves;
I will not destroy them but will grant them
a little deliverance.[x] My wrath will not be
poured out on Jerusalem through Shishak.[y]
8 However, they will become his servants so
that they may recognize the difference between serving Me and serving the kingdoms
of other lands."[z]
9 So King Shishak of Egypt went to war[aa]
against Jerusalem.[ab] He seized the treasuries
of the LORD's temple and the treasuries of the
royal palace. He took everything. He took the

[a] **11:1-4** 1Kg 12:21-24
[b] **11:2** 2Ch 12:5-7,15
[c] **11:4** 2Ch 28:8-11
[d] 2Ch 10:15
[e] **11:5** 2Ch 8:2-6; 11:23
[f] **11:14** Nm 35:2-5
[g] 2Ch 13:9
[h] **11:15** Ex 34:16-17
[i] Lv 17:7
[j] 1Kg 12:25-33; 13:33
[k] **11:17** 2Ch 12:1
[l] **11:18** 1Sm 16:6
[m] **11:20** 2Ch 13:2
[n] **11:21** Dt 17:17
[o] **11:22** Dt 21:15-17
[p] **12:1** 2Ch 11:17; 12:13
[q] **12:2** 1Kg 11:40
[r] 1Kg 14:25
[s] **12:3** 2Ch 16:8; Nah 3:9
[t] **12:4** 2Ch 11:5-12
[u] **12:5** 2Ch 11:2
[v] Dt 28:15,25; 2Ch 15:2
[w] **12:6** Ex 9:27; Dn 9:14
[x] **12:7** 1Kg 21:29
[y] 2Ch 34:25-27; Ps 78:38
[z] **12:8** Dt 28:47-48
[aa] **12:9-11** 1Kg 14:25-28
[ab] **12:9** 2Ch 12:2

[A] **11:5** Lit *he built cities for a fortress* [B] **11:20,21** Possibly *granddaughter*; 2Ch 13:2

gold shields that Solomon had made.[a] 10King
Rehoboam made bronze shields in their place
and committed them into the care of the captains of the royal escorts[A] who guarded the
entrance to the king's palace. 11Whenever the
king entered the LORD's temple, the royal escorts would carry the shields and take them
back to the royal escorts' armory. 12When Rehoboam humbled himself, the LORD's anger
turned away from him, and He did not destroy him completely.[b] Besides that, conditions were good in Judah.[c]

Rehoboam's Last Days

13King Rehoboam[d] established his royal
power in Jerusalem. Rehoboam was 41 years
old when he became king and reigned 17
years in Jerusalem, the city the LORD had
chosen from all the tribes of Israel to put His
name.[e] Rehoboam's mother's name was Naamah the Ammonite. 14Rehoboam did what
was evil, because he did not determine in his
heart to seek the LORD.[f]

15The events[g] of Rehoboam's reign, from beginning to end, are written in the Events of
Shemaiah[h] the Prophet and of Iddo the Seer
concerning genealogies.[i] There was war between Rehoboam and Jeroboam throughout
their reigns. 16Rehoboam rested with his fathers and was buried in the city of David. His
son Abijah[B,j] became king in his place.

Judah's King Abijah

13 In the eighteenth year[k] of Israel's King
Jeroboam, Abijah[B] became king over
Judah 2and reigned three years in Jerusalem.
His mother's name was Micaiah[C,l] daughter of
Uriel; she was from Gibeah.

There was war between Abijah and Jeroboam. 3Abijah set his army of warriors in
order with 400,000 choice men. Jeroboam
arranged his mighty army of 800,000 choice
men in battle formation against him. 4Then
Abijah stood on Mount Zemaraim,[m] which
is in the hill country of Ephraim, and said,
"Jeroboam and all Israel, hear me. 5Don't you
know that the LORD God of Israel gave the
kingship over Israel to David and his descendants forever[n] by a covenant of salt?[o] 6But
Jeroboam son of Nebat, a servant of Solomon
son of David, rose up and rebelled against
his lord.[p] 7Then worthless and ·wicked men
gathered around him to resist Rehoboam
son of Solomon when Rehoboam was young,
inexperienced, and unable to assert himself
against them.

8"And now you are saying you can assert yourselves against the LORD's kingdom,
which is in the hand of one of David's sons.
You are a vast number and have with you the
golden calves that Jeroboam made for you
as gods.[D,q] 9Didn't you banish the priests of
·Yahweh, the descendants of Aaron and the
Levites, and make your own priests like the
peoples of other lands do?[r] Whoever comes
to ordain himself[s] with a young bull and
seven rams may become a priest[t] of what are
not gods.[u]

10"But as for us, Yahweh is our God. We have
not abandoned Him; the priests ministering
to the LORD are descendants of Aaron, and
the Levites serve at their tasks. 11They offer a
·burnt offering and fragrant incense to the
LORD every morning and every evening,[v] and
they set the rows of the ·bread of the Presence
on the ceremonially ·clean table.[w] They light
the lamps of the gold lampstand every evening. We are carrying out the requirements
of Yahweh our God, while you have abandoned Him.[x] 12Look, God and His priests are
with us at our head. The trumpets are ready
to sound the charge against you. Israelites,
don't fight against the LORD God of your ancestors, for you will not succeed."[y]

13Now Jeroboam had sent an ambush[z]
around to advance from behind them. So
they were in front of Judah, and the ambush
was behind them. 14Judah turned and discovered that the battle was in front of them and
behind them, so they cried out to the LORD.[aa]
Then the priests blew the trumpets, 15and
the men of Judah raised the battle cry. When
the men of Judah raised the battle cry, God
routed Jeroboam and all Israel before Abijah
and Judah.[ab] 16So the Israelites fled before Judah, and God handed them over to them.[ac]
17Then Abijah and his people struck them
with a mighty blow, and 500,000 choice men
of Israel were killed. 18The Israelites were subdued at that time. The Judahites succeeded

[a] 12:9 2Ch 9:15-16
[b] 12:12 2Ch 12:6-7
[c] 2Ch 19:3
[d] 12:13-14 1Kg 14:21-22
[e] 12:13 Dt 12:5; 1Kg 9:3
[f] 12:14 2Ch 19:3
[g] 12:15-16 1Kg 14:29-31
[h] 12:15 2Ch 12:5
[i] 2Ch 9:29; 13:22
[j] 12:16 1Kg 14:31–15:8
[k] 13:1-2 1Kg 15:1-2,7
[l] 13:2 1Kg 15:2; 2Ch 11:20,22
[m] 13:4 Jos 18:22
[n] 13:5 2Sm 7:12-16
[o] Lv 2:13; Nm 18:19
[p] 13:6 1Kg 11:26
[q] 13:8 1Kg 12:28
[r] 13:9 2Ch 11:14
[s] Ex 29:29-33
[t] 1Kg 13:33
[u] Jr 2:11; 5:7
[v] 13:11 Ex 29:38; 2Ch 2:4
[w] Ex 25:30; Lv 24:5-9
[x] Ex 25:31-40
[y] 13:12 Nm 10:8-9
[z] 13:13 Jos 8:4-9
[aa] 13:14 2Ch 14:11
[ab] 13:15 2Ch 14:12
[ac] 13:16 2Ch 16:8

A 12:10 Lit *the runners* B 12:16; 13:1 = Abijam in 1Kg 14:31–15:8 C 13:2 LXX, Syr, Arabic read *Maacah*; 1Kg 15:2; 2Ch 11:22 D 13:8 Or *God*; 1Kg 12:28

because they depended on the LORD, the God
of their ancestors.
19 Abijah pursued Jeroboam and captured
some cities from him: Bethel and its villages,
Jeshanah and its villages, and Ephron[A] and its
villages. 20 Jeroboam no longer retained his
power[B] during Abijah's reign; ultimately, the
LORD struck him[a] and he died.[b]
21 However, Abijah grew strong, acquired
14 wives, and fathered 22 sons and 16 daughters. 22 The rest of the events of Abijah's reign,
along with his ways and his sayings, are
14 written in the Writing[c] of the Prophet
Iddo.[d] 1[C] Abijah rested with his fathers
and was buried in the city of David. His
son Asa became king in his place.[e] During
his reign the land experienced peace for 10
years.

Judah's King Asa

2[D] Asa did what was good and right[f] in the
sight of the LORD his God. 3 He removed the
pagan altars and the •high places. He shattered their sacred pillars and chopped down
their •Asherah poles.[g] 4 He told the people of
Judah to seek the LORD God of their ancestors and to carry out the instruction and the
commands. 5 He also removed the high places
and the incense altars from all the cities of
Judah,[h] and the kingdom experienced peace
under him.
6 Because the land experienced peace, Asa
built fortified cities in Judah.[i] No one made
war with him in those days because the LORD
gave him rest.[j] 7 So he said to the people of
Judah, "Let's build these cities and surround
them with walls and towers, with doors and
bars.[k] The land is still ours because we sought
the LORD our God. We sought Him and He
gave us rest on every side." So they built and
succeeded.

The Cushite Invasion

8 Asa had an army of 300,000 from Judah bearing large shields and spears,[l] and
280,000 from Benjamin bearing regular
shields and drawing the bow. All these were
brave warriors. 9 Then Zerah the •Cushite
came against them with an army of one million men and 300[E] chariots. They came as far
as Mareshah. 10 So Asa marched out against
him and lined up in battle formation in the
Valley of Zephathah at Mareshah.[m]
11 Then Asa cried out to the LORD his God:[n]
"LORD, there is no one besides You to help the
mighty and those without strength. Help us,
LORD our God, for we depend on You,[o] and
in Your name we have come against this large
army. •Yahweh, You are our God. Do not let a
mere mortal hinder You."
12 So the LORD routed the Cushites before
Asa and before Judah,[p] and the Cushites
fled. 13 Then Asa and the people who were
with him pursued them as far as Gerar.[q] The
Cushites fell until they had no survivors, for
they were crushed before Yahweh and His
army. So the people of Judah carried off a
great supply of loot. 14 Then they attacked all
the cities around Gerar because the terror of
the LORD was on them.[r] They also plundered
all the cities, since there was a great deal of
plunder in them. 15 They also attacked the
tents of the herdsmen and captured many
sheep and camels. Then they returned to Jerusalem.

Revival Under Asa

15 The Spirit of God came on Azariah son
of Oded.[s] 2 So he went out to meet Asa
and said to him, "Asa and all Judah and Benjamin, hear me. The LORD is with you[t] when
you are with Him. If you seek Him, He will
be found by you,[u] but if you abandon Him,
He will abandon you.[v] 3 For many years Israel
has been without the true God,[w] without a
teaching priest, and without instruction,[x]
4 but when they turned to the LORD God of Israel in their distress and sought Him, He was
found by them. 5 In those times there was no
peace for those who went about their daily
activities because the residents of the lands
had many conflicts. 6 Nation was crushed
by nation and city by city, for God troubled
them with every possible distress. 7 But as
for you, be strong; don't be discouraged,[F] for
your work has a reward."[y]
8 When Asa heard these words and the
prophecy of Azariah son of Oded the prophet,

[a] **13:20** 1Sm 25:38 [b] 1Kg 14:20 [c] **13:22** 2Ch 24:27 [d] 1Kg 15:7; 2Ch 9:29; 12:15 [e] **14:1** 1Kg 15:8 [f] **14:2-3** 1Kg 15:11-12 [g] **14:3** Ex 34:13; Dt 7:5 [h] **14:5** 2Ch 34:4,7 [i] **14:6** 2Ch 11:5 [j] 2Ch 15:15 [k] **14:7** 2Ch 8:5 [l] **14:8** 2Ch 13:3 [m] **14:10** 2Ch 11:8 [n] **14:11** 2Ch 13:14 [o] 2Ch 13:18 [p] **14:12** 2Ch 13:15 [q] **14:13** Gn 10:19 [r] **14:14** 2Ch 17:10 [s] **15:1** 2Ch 20:14; 24:20 [t] **15:2** 2Ch 20:17 [u] Dt 4:29; 2Ch 15:15; Jr 29:13-14 [v] 1Ch 28:9 [w] **15:3** 1Kg 12:28-33 [x] Lv 10:8-11; 2Ch 17:9 [y] **15:7** Jos 1:7,9

[A] **13:19** Alt Hb tradition reads *Ephrain* [B] **13:20** Lit *He did not restrain the power of Jeroboam* [C] **14:1** 2Ch 13:23 in Hb [D] **14:2** 2Ch 14:1 in Hb [E] **14:9** Syr, Arabic read *30,000* [F] **15:7** Lit *don't let your hands fail*

he took courage and removed the detestable
idols from the whole land of Judah and Benjamin and from the cities he had captured
in the hill country of Ephraim.[a] He reno-
vated the altar of the LORD that was in front
of the portico of the LORD's temple.[b] 9 Then he
gathered all Judah and Benjamin, as well as
those from the tribes of Ephraim, Manasseh,
and Simeon who had settled among them,
for they had defected to him from Israel in
great numbers when they saw that ·Yahweh
his God was with him.[c]
10 They were gathered in Jerusalem in the
third month of the fifteenth year of Asa's
reign. 11 At that time they sacrificed to the
LORD 700 cattle and 7,000 sheep from all the
plunder they had brought.[d] 12 Then they entered into a covenant to seek the LORD God
of their ancestors with all their mind and all
their heart.[e] 13 Whoever would not seek the
LORD God of Israel would be put to death,
young or old,[A] man or woman.[f] 14 They took an
oath to the LORD in a loud voice, with shouting, with trumpets, and with rams' horns.
15 All Judah rejoiced over the oath, for they
had sworn it with all their mind. They had
sought Him with all their heart, and He was
found by them.[g] So the LORD gave them rest
on every side.[h]
16 King Asa[i] also removed Maacah, his
grandmother,[B,j] from being queen mother
because she had made an obscene image of
·Asherah. Asa chopped down her obscene
image, then crushed it and burned it in the
Kidron Valley.[k] 17 The ·high places were not
taken away from Israel; nevertheless, Asa was
wholehearted his entire life.[C] 18 He brought
his father's consecrated gifts and his own
consecrated gifts into God's temple: silver,
gold, and utensils.
19 There was no war until the thirty-fifth
year of Asa's reign.

Asa's Treaty with Aram

16 In the thirty-sixth year of Asa,[l] Israel's
King Baasha went to war against Ju-
dah. He built Ramah in order to deny access
to anyone—going or coming—to Judah's
King Asa. 2 So Asa brought out the silver and
gold from the treasuries of the LORD's temple and the royal palace and sent it to Aram's
King Ben-hadad, who lived in Damascus, saying, 3 "There's a treaty between me and you,
between my father and your father. Look, I
have sent you silver and gold. Go break your
treaty with Israel's King Baasha so that he will
withdraw from me."
4 Ben-hadad listened to King Asa and sent
the commanders of his armies to the cities of
Israel. They attacked Ijon, Dan, Abel-maim,[D]
and all the storage cities[E] of Naphtali. 5 When
Baasha heard about it, he quit building Ramah and stopped his work. 6 Then King Asa
brought all Judah, and they carried away the
stones of Ramah and the timbers Baasha had
built it with. Then he built Geba and Mizpah
with them.

Hanani's Rebuke of Asa

7 At that time, Hanani[m] the seer came to
King Asa of Judah and said to him, "Because
you depended on the king of Aram and have
not depended on the LORD your God,[n] the
army of the king of Aram has escaped from
your hand. 8 Were not the ·Cushites and Libyans a vast army with many chariots and horsemen?[o] When you depended on ·Yahweh, He
handed them over to you.[p] 9 For the eyes of
Yahweh roam throughout the earth[q] to show
Himself strong for those whose hearts are
completely His.[r] You have been foolish in this
matter. Therefore, you will have wars from
now on." 10 Asa was angry with the seer and
put him in prison[F] because of his anger over
this. And Asa mistreated some of the people
at that time.

Asa's Death

11 Note that the events[s] of Asa's reign, from
beginning to end, are written in the Book
of the Kings of Judah and Israel. 12 In the
thirty-ninth year of his reign, Asa developed
a disease in his feet, and his disease became
increasingly severe. Yet even in his disease he
didn't seek the LORD but only the physicians.
13 Asa died in the forty-first year of his reign
and rested with his fathers. 14 He was buried
in his own tomb that he had made for him-

[a] **15:8** 2Ch 13:19
[b] 2Ch 4:1; 8:12
[c] **15:9** 2Ch 11:16
[d] **15:11** 2Ch 14:13-15
[e] **15:12** 2Ch 23:16
[f] **15:13** Ex 22:20; Dt 13:6-9; 17:2-7
[g] **15:15** 2Ch 15:2
[h] 2Ch 14:6-7
[i] **15:16-18** 1Kg 15:13-15
[j] **15:16** 1Kg 15:2; 2Ch 11:22
[k] 2Ch 14:2-5
[l] **16:1-6** 1Kg 15:17-22
[m] **16:7** 1Kg 16:1; 2Ch 19:2
[n] 2Ch 14:11
[o] **16:8** 2Ch 12:3
[p] 2Ch 14:9-13
[q] **16:9** Gn 6:8; Ps 33:18; 34:15; Pr 15:3; Zch 4:10; 1Pt 3:12
[r] 2Ch 15:17
[s] **16:11-14** 1Kg 15:23-24

[A] **15:13** Or *insignificant or great* [B] **15:16** Lit *mother*; 1Kg 15:2; 2Ch 11:22
[C] **15:17** Lit *wholehearted all his days* [D] **16:4** *Abel-beth-maacah* in 1Kg 15:20
[E] **16:4** = all Chinnereth in 1Kg 15:20 [F] **16:10** Lit *the house of stocks*

self in the city of David. They laid him out in a coffin that was full of spices and various mixtures of prepared ointments;[a] then they made a great fire in his honor.[b]

Judah's King Jehoshaphat

17 His son Jehoshaphat became king in his place[c] and strengthened himself against Israel. 2He stationed troops in every fortified city of Judah[d] and set garrisons in the land of Judah and in the cities of Ephraim that his father Asa had captured.[e]

3Now the LORD was with Jehoshaphat because he walked in the former ways of his father David.[A] He did not seek the •Baals 4but sought the God of his father and walked by His commands, not according to the practices of Israel.[f] 5So the LORD established the kingdom in his hand. Then all Judah brought him tribute, and he had riches and honor in abundance.[g] 6His mind rejoiced in the LORD's ways, and he again[h] removed the •high places and •Asherah poles from Judah.[i]

Jehoshaphat's Educational Plan

7In the third year of his reign, Jehoshaphat sent his officials — Ben-hail,[B] Obadiah, Zechariah, Nethanel, and Micaiah — to teach in the cities of Judah.[j] 8The Levites with them were Shemaiah, Nethaniah, Zebadiah,[C] Asahel, Shemiramoth, Jehonathan, Adonijah, Tobijah, and Tob-adonijah; the priests, Elishama and Jehoram, were with these Levites. 9They taught throughout Judah, having the book of the LORD's instruction with them.[k] They went throughout the towns of Judah and taught the people.

10The terror of the LORD was on all the kingdoms of the lands that surrounded Judah,[l] so they didn't fight against Jehoshaphat. 11Some of the Philistines also brought gifts and silver as tribute to Jehoshaphat, and the Arabs brought him flocks: 7,700 rams and 7,700 male goats.[m]

Jehoshaphat's Military Might

12Jehoshaphat grew stronger and stronger. He built fortresses[n] and storage cities in Judah 13and carried out great works in the towns of Judah. He had fighting men, brave warriors, in Jerusalem. 14These are their numbers according to their ancestral families. For Judah, the commanders of thousands:

> Adnah the commander and 300,000
> brave warriors with him;
> 15next to him, Jehohanan the
> commander and 280,000 with him;
> 16next to him, Amasiah son of Zichri,
> the volunteer[o] of the LORD, and
> 200,000 brave warriors with him;
> 17from Benjamin, Eliada, a brave
> warrior, and 200,000 with him armed
> with bow and shield;
> 18next to him, Jehozabad and 180,000
> with him equipped for war.

19These were the ones who served the king, besides those he stationed in the fortified cities throughout all Judah.[p]

Jehoshaphat's Alliance with Ahab

18 Now Jehoshaphat[q] had riches and honor in abundance,[r] and he made an alliance with Ahab through marriage.[D,s] 2Then after some years, he went down to visit Ahab in Samaria. Ahab sacrificed many sheep and cattle for him and for the people who were with him. Then he persuaded him to march up to Ramoth-gilead, 3for Israel's King Ahab asked Judah's King Jehoshaphat, "Will you go with me to Ramoth-gilead?"

He replied to him, "I am as you are, my people as your people; we will be with you in the battle." 4But Jehoshaphat said to the king of Israel, "First, please ask what the LORD's will is."

5So the king of Israel gathered the prophets, 400 men, and asked them, "Should we go to Ramoth-gilead for war or should I refrain?"

They replied, "March up, and God will hand it over to the king."

6But Jehoshaphat asked, "Isn't there a prophet of •Yahweh here anymore? Let's ask him."[t]

7The king of Israel said to Jehoshaphat, "There is still one man who can ask Yahweh, but I hate him because he never prophesies

[a] 16:14 Gn 50:2; Jn 12:7; 19:39-40
[b] 2Ch 21:19
[c] 17:1 1Kg 15:24
[d] 17:2 2Ch 11:5
[e] 2Ch 15:8
[f] 17:4 1Kg 12:28
[g] 17:5 2Ch 18:1
[h] 17:6 2Ch 14:2-3
[i] 2Ch 15:17
[j] 17:7 2Ch 15:3; 35:3
[k] 17:9 Dt 6:4-9; 17:18; 28:58,61; 29:21; 30:10; 31:24,26; Jos 1:8; 8:31,34; 23:6; 24:26
[l] 17:10 2Ch 14:14
[m] 17:11 2Ch 9:14; 26:8
[n] 17:12 2Ch 27:4
[o] 17:16 Jdg 5:2,9; 1Ch 29:9
[p] 17:19 2Ch 17:2
[q] 18:1-34 1Kg 22:1-35
[r] 18:1 2Ch 17:5
[s] 1Kg 3:1; 2Kg 8:18; Ezr 9:14
[t] 18:6 2Kg 3:11

[A] 17:3 Some Hb mss, LXX omit *David* [B] 17:7 = Son of Power [C] 17:8 Some Hb mss, Syr, Tg, Arabic read *Zechariah* [D] 18:1 Lit *made himself a son-in-law to Ahab*; 1Kg 3:1; Ezr 9:14

good about me, but only disaster. He is Micaiah son of Imlah."

"The king shouldn't say that," Jehoshaphat replied.

8 So the king of Israel called an officer and said, "Hurry and get Micaiah son of Imlah!"

9 Now the king of Israel and King Jehoshaphat of Judah, clothed in royal attire, were each sitting on his own throne. They were sitting on the threshing floor at the entrance to Samaria's ˙gate,[a] and all the prophets were prophesying in front of them. 10 Then Zedekiah son of Chenaanah made iron horns and said, "This is what the LORD says: 'You will gore the Arameans with these until they are finished off.'" 11 And all the prophets were prophesying the same, saying, "March up to Ramoth-gilead and succeed, for the LORD will hand it over to the king."

Micaiah's Message of Defeat

12 The messenger who went to call Micaiah instructed him, "Look, the words of the prophets are unanimously favorable for the king. So let your words be like theirs, and speak favorably."

13 But Micaiah said, "As the LORD lives, I will say whatever my God says."[A,b]

14 So he went to the king, and the king asked him, "Micaiah, should we go to Ramoth-gilead for war, or should I[B] refrain?"

Micaiah said, "March up and succeed, for they will be handed over to you."

15 But the king said to him, "How many times must I make you swear not to tell me anything but the truth in the name of Yahweh?"

16 So Micaiah said:

> I saw all Israel scattered on the hills
> like sheep without a shepherd.[c]
> And the LORD said,
> "They have no master;
> let each return home in peace."

17 So the king of Israel said to Jehoshaphat, "Didn't I tell you he never prophesies good about me, but only disaster?"

18 Then Micaiah said, "Therefore, hear the word of the LORD. I saw the LORD sitting on His throne, and the whole heavenly ˙host was standing at His right hand and at His left hand.[d] 19 And the LORD said, 'Who will entice Ahab king of Israel to march up and fall at Ramoth-gilead?' So one was saying this and another was saying that.

20 "Then[e] a spirit came forward, stood before the LORD, and said, 'I will entice him.'

"The LORD asked him, 'How?'

21 "So he said, 'I will go and become a lying spirit in the mouth of all his prophets.'

"Then He said, 'You will entice him and also prevail. Go and do that.'

22 "Now, you see, the LORD has put a lying spirit into the mouth of[C] these prophets of yours, and the LORD has pronounced disaster against you."

23 Then Zedekiah son of Chenaanah came up, hit Micaiah in the face, and demanded, "Which way did the spirit from the LORD leave me to speak to you?"

24 Micaiah replied, "You will soon see when you go to hide yourself in an inner chamber on that day."[f]

25 Then the king of Israel ordered, "Take Micaiah and return him[g] to Amon, the governor of the city,[h] and to Joash, the king's son, 26 and say, 'This is what the king says: Put this guy in prison[i] and feed him only bread and water[D] until I come back safely.'"

27 But Micaiah said, "If you ever return safely, the LORD has not spoken through me." Then he said, "Listen, all you people!"[j]

Ahab's Death

28 Then the king of Israel and Judah's King Jehoshaphat went up to Ramoth-gilead. 29 But the king of Israel said to Jehoshaphat, "I will disguise myself and go into battle, but you wear your royal attire." So the king of Israel disguised himself, and they went into battle.[k]

30 Now the king of Aram had ordered his chariot commanders, "Do not fight with anyone, small or great, except the king of Israel."

31 When the chariot commanders saw Jehoshaphat, they shouted, "He must be the king of Israel!" So they turned to attack him, but Jehoshaphat cried out[l] and the LORD helped him. God drew them away from him.

[a]**18:9** Ru 4:1 [b]**18:13** Nm 22:35,38; 24:13 [c]**18:16** Nm 27:16-17; Ezk 34:5-8; Mt 9:36; Mk 6:34 [d]**18:18** Is 6:1-5; Dn 7:9-10 [e]**18:20-21** Dt 13:1-5; 1Sm 16:14; Jr 27:9-10; Ezk 14:9; 2Th 2:9-12 [f]**18:24** 1Kg 20:30 [g]**18:25** 2Ch 18:8 [h]2Ch 34:8 [i]**18:26** 2Ch 16:10 [j]**18:27** Mc 1:2 [k]**18:29** 2Ch 35:22 [l]**18:31** 2Ch 13:14-15

A**18:13** LXX, Vg add *to me*; 1Kg 22:14 B**18:14** LXX reads *we*; 1Kg 22:15 C**18:22** Some Hb mss, LXX, Syr, Vg add *all*; 1Kg 22:23 D**18:26** Lit *him on bread of oppression and water of oppression*

[32]When the chariot commanders saw that he
was not the king of Israel, they turned back
from pursuing him.
[33]But a man drew his bow without taking special aim and struck the king of Israel
through the joints of his armor. So he said
to the charioteer, "Turn around and take me
out of the battle,[A] for I am badly wounded!"[a]
[34]The battle raged throughout that day, and
the king of Israel propped himself up in his
chariot facing the Arameans until evening.
Then he died at sunset.

Jehu's Rebuke of Jehoshaphat

19 Jehoshaphat king of Judah returned to
his home in Jerusalem in peace. [2]Then
Jehu[b] son of Hanani the seer went out to confront him[B] and said to King Jehoshaphat, "Do
you help the wicked and love those who hate
the LORD?[c] Because of this, the LORD's wrath
is on you.[d] [3]However, some good is found in
you, for you have removed the ·Asherah poles
from the land and have decided to seek God."[e]

Jehoshaphat's Reforms

[4]Jehoshaphat lived in Jerusalem, and once
again he went out among the people from
Beer-sheba to the hill country of Ephraim
and brought them back to ·Yahweh, the God
of their ancestors.[f] [5]He appointed judges in
all the fortified cities of the land of Judah, city
by city.[g] [6]Then he said to the judges, "Consider
what you are doing, for you do not judge for
man, but for the LORD, who is with you in the
matter of judgment.[h] [7]And now, may the terror of the LORD be on you. Watch what you
do, for there is no injustice or partiality or
taking bribes with the LORD our God."[i]
[8]Jehoshaphat also appointed in Jerusalem
some of the Levites and priests and some of
the heads of the Israelite families for deciding the LORD's will and for settling disputes of
the residents of[C] Jerusalem. [9]He commanded
them, saying, "In the ·fear of the LORD, with
integrity, and with a whole heart, you are
to do the following: [10]for every dispute that
comes to you from your brothers who dwell
in their cities—whether it regards differences of bloodguilt, law, commandment,
statutes, or judgments[j]—you are to warn
them, so they will not incur ·guilt before the
LORD and wrath will not come on you and
your brothers.[k] Do this, and you will not incur guilt.
[11]"Note that Amariah, the chief priest, is
over you in all matters related to the LORD,
and Zebadiah son of Ishmael, the ruler of the
house of Judah, in all matters related to the
king, and the Levites are officers in your presence. Be strong; may the LORD be with those
who do what is good."[l]

War against Eastern Enemies

20 After this, the Moabites and Ammonites, together with some of the
Meunites,[D,m] came to fight against Jehoshaphat. [2]People came and told Jehoshaphat, "A
vast number from beyond the Dead Sea and
from Edom[E] has come to fight against you;
they are already in Hazazon-tamar"[n] (that is,
En-gedi). [3]Jehoshaphat was afraid, and he resolved[o] to seek the LORD. Then he proclaimed
a fast[p] for all Judah, [4]who gathered to seek the
LORD. They even came from all the cities of
Judah to seek Him.

Jehoshaphat's Prayer

[5]Then Jehoshaphat stood in the assembly
of Judah and Jerusalem in the LORD's temple
before the new courtyard. [6]He said:

·Yahweh, the God of our ancestors, are
You not the God who is in heaven,[q] and
do You not rule over all the kingdoms
of the nations?[r] Power and might are in
Your hand, and no one can stand against
You. [7]Are You not our God who drove out
the inhabitants of this land before Your
people Israel[s] and who gave it forever
to the descendants of Abraham[t] Your
friend? [8]They have lived in the land and
have built You a sanctuary in it for Your
name and have said, [9]"If disaster comes
on us—sword or judgment, pestilence
or famine[u]—we will stand before this
temple and before You, for Your name is
in this temple.[v] We will cry out to You because of our distress, and You will hear
and deliver."

[a]**18:33** 2Ch 35:23
[b]**19:2** 1Kg 16:1; 2Ch 20:34
[c]2Ch 18:1,3
[d]2Ch 24:18
[e]**19:3** 2Ch 12:14; 17:4,6
[f]**19:4** 2Ch 15:8-13
[g]**19:5** Dt 16:18-20
[h]**19:6** Lv 19:15; Dt 1:17
[i]**19:7** Gn 18:25; Dt 10:17-18; 32:4
[j]**19:10** Dt 17:8
[k]2Ch 19:2
[l]**19:11** 1Ch 28:20
[m]**20:1** 2Ch 26:7
[n]**20:2** Gn 14:7
[o]**20:3** 2Ch 19:3
[p]1Sm 7:6; Ezr 8:21
[q]**20:6** Dt 4:39
[r]1Ch 29:11
[s]**20:7** Ps 135:10-12
[t]Is 41:8
[u]**20:9** 2Ch 6:28-30
[v]2Ch 6:20

[A]**18:33** LXX, Vg; MT reads *camp* [B]**19:2** Lit *to his face* [C]**19:8** LXX, Vg; MT reads *disputes and they returned to* [D]**20:1** LXX; MT reads *Ammonites*; 2Ch 26:7 [E]**20:2** Some Hb mss, Old Lat; other Hb mss read *Aram*

10 Now here are the Ammonites, Moabites,
and the inhabitants of Mount Seir.[a] You
did not let Israel invade them when Israel came out of the land of Egypt, but Israel turned away from them and did not
destroy them.[b] 11 Look how they repay us
by coming to drive us out of Your possession that You gave us as an inheritance.
12 Our God, will You not judge them?[c] For
we are powerless before this vast number
that comes to fight against us. We do not
know what to do, but we look to You.[A,d]

God's Answer

13 All Judah was standing before the LORD
with their infants, their wives, and their children. 14 In the middle of the congregation, the
Spirit of the LORD came on[e] Jahaziel (son of
Zechariah, son of Benaiah, son of Jeiel, son
of Mattaniah, a Levite from •Asaph's descendants), 15 and he said, "Listen carefully, all Judah and you inhabitants of Jerusalem, and
King Jehoshaphat. This is what the LORD says:
'Do not be afraid or discouraged because of
this vast number,[f] for the battle is not yours,
but God's.[g] 16 Tomorrow, go down against
them. You will see them coming up the Ascent of Ziz, and you will find them at the end
of the valley facing the Wilderness of Jeruel.
17 You do not have to fight this battle. Position
yourselves, stand still, and see the salvation of
the LORD.[h] He is with you, Judah and Jerusalem. Do not be afraid or discouraged.[i] Tomorrow, go out to face them, for Yahweh is with
you.' "[j]

18 Then Jehoshaphat bowed with his face
to the ground, and all Judah and the inhabitants of Jerusalem fell down before the LORD
to worship Him.[k] 19 Then the Levites from the
sons of the Kohathites and the Korahites[l]
stood up to praise the LORD God of Israel
shouting with a loud voice.

Victory and Plunder

20 In the morning they got up early and
went out to the wilderness of Tekoa. As they
were about to go out, Jehoshaphat stood and
said, "Hear me, Judah and you inhabitants of
Jerusalem. Believe in Yahweh your God, and
you will be established;[m] believe in His prophets, and you will succeed." 21 Then he consulted
with the people and appointed some to sing
for the LORD and some to praise the splendor
of His holiness.[n] When they went out in front
of the armed forces, they kept singing:[B]

> Give thanks to the LORD,
> for His faithful love endures forever.[o]

22 The moment they began their shouts and
praises, the LORD set an ambush[p] against the
Ammonites, Moabites, and the inhabitants of
Mount Seir who came to fight against Judah,
and they were defeated. 23 The Ammonites
and Moabites turned against the inhabitants
of Mount Seir and •completely annihilated
them.[q] When they had finished with the inhabitants of Seir, they helped destroy each
other.[r]

24 When Judah came to a place overlooking the wilderness, they looked for the large
army, but there were only corpses lying on
the ground; nobody had escaped. 25 Then Jehoshaphat and his people went to gather the
plunder. They found among them[C] an abundance of goods on the bodies[D] and valuable
items. So they stripped them until nobody
could carry any more. They were gathering
the plunder for three days because there was
so much. 26 They assembled in the Valley of
Beracah[E] on the fourth day, for there they
praised the LORD. Therefore, that place is still
called the Valley of Beracah today.

27 Then all the men of Judah and Jerusalem
turned back with Jehoshaphat their leader,
returning joyfully to Jerusalem, for the LORD
enabled them to rejoice over their enemies.
28 So they came into Jerusalem to the LORD's
temple with harps, lyres, and trumpets.

29 The terror of God[s] was on all the kingdoms of the lands when they heard that Yahweh had fought against the enemies of Israel.
30 Then Jehoshaphat's kingdom was quiet, for
his God gave him rest on every side.[t]

Summary of Jehoshaphat's Reign

31 Jehoshaphat became king over Judah.[u] He
was 35 years old when he became king and
reigned 25 years in Jerusalem. His mother's
name was Azubah daughter of Shilhi. 32 He
walked in the way of Asa his father; he did not

[a] **20:10** 2Ch 20:1,22
[b] Nm 20:14-21; Dt 2:4-9
[c] **20:12** Jdg 11:27
[d] Ps 25:15; 121:1-2
[e] **20:14** 2Ch 15:1; 24:20
[f] **20:15** Ex 14:13; 2Ch 32:7-8
[g] 1Sm 17:47; 2Ch 13:15; 14:12
[h] **20:17** Ex 14:13-14
[i] Jos 1:9
[j] 2Ch 15:2
[k] **20:18** 2Ch 7:3
[l] **20:19** Ex 6:18; 1Ch 9:19
[m] **20:20** Is 7:9
[n] **20:21** 1Ch 16:29; Ps 29:2
[o] 1Ch 16:34; 2Ch 5:13; 7:3; Ps 118:1,29; 136:1
[p] **20:22** 2Ch 13:13
[q] **20:23** Ezk 38:21; Hg 2:22; Zch 14:13
[r] Jdg 7:22; 1Sm 14:20
[s] **20:29** 2Ch 14:14; 17:10
[t] **20:30** 2Ch 14:6-7; 15:15
[u] **20:31-34** 1Kg 22:41-45

[A] **20:12** Lit *but on You our eyes* [B] **20:21** Lit *saying* [C] **20:25** LXX reads *found cattle* [D] **20:25** Some Hb mss, Old Lat, Vg read *goods, garments* [E] **20:26** = Blessing

turn away from it but did what was right in the LORD's sight. 33 However, the ·high places were not taken away;[a] the people had not yet set their hearts on the God of their ancestors.[b]

34 The rest of the events of Jehoshaphat's reign from beginning to end are written in the Events of Jehu[c] son of Hanani, which is recorded in the Book of Israel's Kings.[d]

Jehoshaphat's Fleet of Ships

35 After this,[e] Judah's King Jehoshaphat made an alliance with Israel's King Ahaziah, who was ·guilty of wrongdoing. 36 Jehoshaphat formed an alliance with him to make ships to go to Tarshish,[f] and they made the ships in Ezion-geber. 37 Then Eliezer son of Dodavahu of Mareshah prophesied against Jehoshaphat, saying, "Because you formed an alliance with Ahaziah, the LORD has broken up what you have made." So the ships were wrecked and were not able to go to Tarshish.

Jehoram Becomes King Over Judah

21 Jehoshaphat rested with his fathers and was buried with his fathers in the city of David. His son Jehoram[A] became king in his place.[g] 2 He had brothers, sons of Jehoshaphat: Azariah, Jehiel, Zechariah, Azariah, Michael, and Shephatiah; all these were the sons of Jehoshaphat, king of Judah.[B] 3 Their father had given them many gifts of silver, gold, and valuable things, along with fortified cities[h] in Judah, but he gave the kingdom to Jehoram because he was the firstborn. 4 When Jehoram had established himself over his father's kingdom, he strengthened his position by killing with the sword all his brothers as well as some of the princes of Israel.

Judah's King Jehoram

5 Jehoram[i] was 32 years old when he became king and reigned eight years in Jerusalem. 6 He walked in the way of the kings of Israel, as the house of Ahab had done,[j] for Ahab's daughter was his wife.[k] He did what was evil in the LORD's sight, 7 but because of the covenant the LORD had made with David, He was unwilling to destroy the house of David since the LORD had promised[l] to give a lamp[m] to David and to his sons forever.

[a] **20:33** 2Ch 17:6
[b] 2Ch 19:3
[c] **20:34** 2Ch 19:2
[d] 1Kg 16:1,7
[e] **20:35-37** 1Kg 22:48-49
[f] **20:36** 2Ch 9:21
[g] **21:1** 1Kg 22:50
[h] **21:3** 2Ch 11:5
[i] **21:5-10** 2Kg 8:17-22
[j] **21:6** 1Kg 12:28-30
[k] 2Ch 18:1
[l] **21:7** 2Sm 7:12-17; 1Kg 11:13
[m] 1Kg 11:36; 15:4
[n] **21:11** 1Kg 11:7
[o] Lv 20:5
[p] **21:12** 2Ch 17:3-4
[q] 2Ch 14:2-5
[r] **21:13** 2Ch 21:6
[s] 1Kg 16:31-33
[t] 2Ch 21:4
[u] **21:15** 2Ch 21:18-19
[v] **21:16** 2Ch 17:11; 22:1
[w] 2Ch 33:11
[x] **21:17** 2Ch 25:23

8 During Jehoram's reign, Edom rebelled against Judah's domination and appointed their own king. 9 So Jehoram crossed into Edom with his commanders and all his chariots. Then at night he set out to attack the Edomites who had surrounded him and the chariot commanders. 10 And now Edom is still in rebellion against Judah's domination today. Libnah also rebelled at that time against his domination because he had abandoned ·Yahweh, the God of his ancestors. 11 Jehoram also built ·high places[n] in the hills[C] of Judah, and he caused the inhabitants of Jerusalem to prostitute themselves,[o] and he led Judah astray.

Elijah's Letter to Jehoram

12 Then a letter came to Jehoram from Elijah the prophet, saying:

> This is what Yahweh, the God of your ancestor David says: "Because you have not walked in the ways of your father Jehoshaphat[p] or in the ways of Asa king of Judah[q] 13 but have walked in the way of the kings of Israel,[r] have caused Judah and the inhabitants of Jerusalem to prostitute themselves like the house of Ahab[s] prostituted itself, and also have killed your brothers,[t] your father's family, who were better than you, 14 Yahweh is now about to strike your people, your sons, your wives, and all your possessions with a horrible affliction. 15 You yourself will be struck with many illnesses, including a disease of the intestines, until your intestines come out day after day because of the disease."[u]

Jehoram's Last Days

16 The LORD put it into the mind of the Philistines and the Arabs[v] who live near the ·Cushites to attack Jehoram.[w] 17 So they went to war against Judah and invaded it. They carried off all the possessions found in the king's palace and also his sons and wives; not a son was left to him except Jehoahaz,[D,x] his youngest son.

18 After all these things, the LORD afflicted him in his intestines with an incurable

[A] **21:1** = Joram [B] **21:2** Some Hb mss, LXX, Syr, Vg, Arabic; other Hb mss read *Israel* [C] **21:11** Some Hb mss, LXX, Vg read *cities* [D] **21:17** LXX, Syr, Tg read *Ahaziah*

disease. 19This continued day after day until two full years passed. Then his intestines
came out because of his disease, and he died
from severe[A] illnesses. But his people did not
hold a fire in his honor like the fire in honor
of his fathers.[a]
20Jehoram[b] was 32 years old when he became king; he reigned eight years in Jerusalem. He died to no one's regret[B,c] and was
buried in the city of David but not in the
tombs of the kings.[d]

Judah's King Ahaziah

22 Then the inhabitants of Jerusalem
made Ahaziah, his youngest son, king
in his place, because the troops that had come
with the Arabs[e] to the camp had killed all the
older sons.[C] So Ahaziah son of Jehoram became king of Judah. 2Ahaziah[f] was 22[D] years
old when he became king and reigned one
year in Jerusalem. His mother's name was
Athaliah, granddaughter[E] of Omri.
3He walked in the ways of the house of
Ahab, for his mother gave him evil advice. 4So
he did what was evil in the LORD's sight like
the house of Ahab, for they were his advisers
after the death of his father, to his destruction. 5He also followed their advice and went
with Joram[F] son of Israel's King Ahab to fight
against Hazael, king of Aram, in Ramoth-
gilead. The Arameans[G] wounded Joram, 6so
he returned to Jezreel to recover from the
wounds they inflicted on him in Ramoth-
gilead[H] when he fought against Aram's King
Hazael. Then Judah's King Ahaziah[I] son of
Jehoram went down to Jezreel to visit Joram
son of Ahab since Joram was ill.
7Ahaziah's downfall came from God when
he went to Joram.[g] When Ahaziah arrived, he
went out with Joram to meet Jehu son of Nimshi,[h] whom the LORD had anointed to destroy
the house of Ahab.[i] 8So when Jehu executed
judgment on the house of Ahab,[j] he found
the rulers of Judah and the sons of Ahaziah's
brothers who were serving Ahaziah, and he
killed them. 9Then Jehu looked for Ahaziah,[k]
and Jehu's soldiers captured him (he was hiding in Samaria). So they brought Ahaziah to
Jehu, and they killed him. The soldiers buried
him, for they said, "He is the grandson of Jehoshaphat who sought the LORD with all his
heart."[l] So no one from the house of Ahaziah
had the strength to rule the kingdom.

Athaliah Usurps the Throne

10When[m] Athaliah, Ahaziah's mother, saw
that her son was dead, she proceeded to annihilate all the royal heirs[J] of the house of
Judah. 11Jehoshabeath,[K] the king's daughter,
rescued Joash son of Ahaziah from the king's
sons who were being killed and put him and
the one who nursed him in a bedroom. Now
Jehoshabeath was the daughter of King Jehoram and the wife of Jehoiada the priest.
Since she was Ahaziah's sister, she hid Joash
from Athaliah so that she did not kill him.
12While Athaliah ruled over the land, he was
hiding with them in God's temple six years.

Athaliah Overthrown

23 Then, in the seventh year,[n] Jehoiada
summoned his courage and took the
commanders of hundreds into a covenant
with him: Azariah son of Jeroham, Ishmael
son of Jehohanan, Azariah son of Obed, Maaseiah son of Adaiah, and Elishaphat son of
Zichri. 2They made a circuit throughout Judah. They gathered the Levites from all the
cities of Judah and the heads of the families
of Israel, and they came to Jerusalem.
3Then the whole assembly made a covenant
with the king in God's temple. Jehoiada said
to them, "Here is the king's son! He must
reign, just as the LORD promised[o] concerning David's sons. 4This is what you are to do:
a third of you, priests and Levites who are
coming on duty on the Sabbath,[p] are to be
gatekeepers. 5A third are to be at the king's
palace, and a third are to be at the Foundation Gate, and all the troops will be in the
courtyards of the LORD's temple. 6No one is
to enter the LORD's temple but the priests and
those Levites who serve;[q] they may enter because they are holy, but all the people are to
obey the requirement of the LORD. 7You must
completely surround the king with weapons

[a]**21:19** 2Ch 16:14
[b]**21:20** 2Kg 8:17,24
[c]Jr 22:18,28
[d]2Ch 24:25
[e]**22:1** 2Ch 21:16
[f]**22:2-6** 2Kg 8:24-29
[g]**22:7** 2Ch 10:15
[h]2Kg 9:21
[i]2Kg 9:6-7
[j]**22:8** 2Kg 10:11-14
[k]**22:9** 2Kg 9:27-28
[l]2Ch 17:4
[m]**22:10-12** 2Kg 11:1-3
[n]**23:1-21** 2Kg 11:4-20
[o]**23:3** 2Ch 21:7
[p]**23:4** 1Ch 9:25
[q]**23:6** 1Ch 23:28-32

[A]**21:19** Lit *evil* [B]**21:20** Lit *He walked in no desirability* [C]**22:1** Lit *the former ones* [D]**22:2** Some LXX mss, Syr; MT reads *42*; 2Kg 8:26 [E]**22:2** Lit *daughter* [F]**22:5** = Jehoram [G]**22:5** Lit *Rammites* [H]**22:6** Lit *in Ramah* [I]**22:6** Some Hb mss, LXX, Syr, Vg; other Hb mss read *Azariah* [J]**22:10** Lit *seed* [K]**22:11** = Jehosheba; 2Kg 11:2

in hand. Anyone who enters the temple is to
be put to death. You must be with the king in
all his daily tasks."[A]
8 So the commanders of hundreds did everything Jehoiada the priest commanded.
They each brought their men — those coming on duty on the Sabbath and those going off duty on the Sabbath — for Jehoiada
the priest did not release the divisions.[a] 9 Jehoiada the priest gave to the commanders of
hundreds King David's spears, shields, and
quivers[B] that were in God's temple. 10 Then he
stationed all the troops with their weapons in
hand surrounding the king — from the right
side of the temple to the left side, by the altar
and by the temple.
11 They brought out the king's son, put the
crown on him, gave him the ·testimony,[b]
and made him king. Jehoiada and his sons
anointed him and cried, "Long live the king!"[c]
12 When Athaliah heard the noise from the
troops, the guards, and those praising the
king, she went to the troops in the LORD's
temple. 13 As she looked, there was the king
standing by his pillar[C] at the entrance. The
commanders and the trumpeters were by
the king, and all the people of the land were
rejoicing and blowing trumpets[d] while the
singers with musical instruments were leading the praise. Athaliah tore her clothes and
screamed, "Treason, treason!"
14 Then Jehoiada the priest sent out the
commanders of hundreds, those in charge
of the army, saying, "Take her out between
the ranks, and put anyone who follows her to
death by the sword," for the priest had said,
"Don't put her to death in the LORD's temple."
15 So they arrested her, and she went by the entrance of the Horses' Gate[e] to the king's palace, where they put her to death.

Jehoiada's Reforms

16 Then Jehoiada made a covenant between
himself, the king, and the people that they
would be the LORD's people. 17 So all the people went to the temple of ·Baal and tore it
down. They broke its altars and images into
pieces and killed Mattan, the priest of Baal,
at the altars.[f]
18 Then Jehoiada put the oversight of the

[a]23:8 1Ch 24:1
[b]23:11 Ex 25:16,21; 31:18
[c]1Sm 10:24
[d]23:13 Nm 10:7-10
[e]23:15 Neh 3:28; Jr 31:40
[f]23:17 Dt 13:6-9; 1Kg 18:40
[g]23:18 2Ch 5:5
[h]1Ch 23:6,25-31
[i]2Kg 14:6; 2Ch 17:9; Ezr 7:6; Neh 8:1
[j]23:19 1Ch 9:22
[k]24:1-2 2Kg 11:21; 12:1-2
[l]24:2 2Ch 26:4-5
[m]24:4-12 2Kg 12:4-12
[n]24:4 2Ch 24:7
[o]24:5 Ex 30:12-16; 2Ch 34:9-10; Neh 10:32; Mt 17:24
[p]24:6 Nm 1:50
[q]24:9 2Ch 36:22

LORD's temple into the hands of the Levitical
priests,[g] whom David had appointed[h] over
the LORD's temple, to offer ·burnt offerings to
the LORD as it is written in the law of Moses,[i]
with rejoicing and song ordained by[D] David.
19 He stationed gatekeepers[j] at the gates of the
LORD's temple so that nothing ·unclean could
enter for any reason. 20 Then he took with him
the commanders of hundreds, the nobles, the
governors of the people, and all the people of
the land and brought the king down from the
LORD's temple. They entered the king's palace through the Upper Gate and seated the
king on the throne of the kingdom. 21 All the
people of the land rejoiced, and the city was
quiet, for they had put Athaliah to death by
the sword.

Judah's King Joash

24 Joash[k] was seven years old when he became king and reigned 40 years in Jerusalem. His mother's name was Zibiah; she
was from Beer-sheba. 2 Throughout the time
of Jehoiada the priest, Joash did what was
right in the LORD's sight.[l] 3 Jehoiada acquired
two wives for him, and he was the father of
sons and daughters.

Repairing the Temple

4 Afterward,[m] Joash took it to heart to renovate[n] the LORD's temple. 5 So he gathered the
priests and Levites and said, "Go out to the
cities of Judah and collect money from all
Israel to repair the temple of your God as
needed year by year,[o] and do it quickly."
However, the Levites did not hurry. 6 So
the king called Jehoiada the high priest and
said, "Why haven't you required the Levites
to bring from Judah and Jerusalem the tax
imposed by the LORD's servant Moses and the
assembly of Israel for the tent[p] of the testimony? 7 For the sons of that wicked Athaliah
broke into the LORD's temple and even used
the sacred things of the LORD's temple for the
·Baals."
8 At the king's command a chest was made
and placed outside the gate of the LORD's temple. 9 Then a proclamation[q] was issued in Judah and Jerusalem that the tax God's servant
Moses imposed on Israel in the wilderness be

[A]23:7 Lit *king when he comes in and when he goes out* [B]23:9 Or *spears and large and small shields* [C]23:13 LXX reads *post* [D]23:18 Lit *song on the hands of*

brought to the LORD. 10 All the leaders and all the people rejoiced, brought the tax, and put it in the chest until it was full. 11 Whenever the chest was brought by the Levites to the king's overseers, and when they saw that there was a large amount of money, the king's secretary and the high priest's deputy came and emptied the chest, picked it up, and returned it to its place. They did this daily and gathered the money in abundance. 12 Then the king and Jehoiada gave it to those in charge of the labor on the LORD's temple, who were hiring stonecutters and carpenters to renovate the LORD's temple, also blacksmiths and coppersmiths to repair the LORD's temple.[a]

13 The workmen did their work, and through them the repairs progressed. They restored God's temple to its specifications and reinforced it. 14 When they finished, they presented the rest of the money to the king and Jehoiada, who made articles for the LORD's temple with it—articles for ministry and for making ·burnt offerings, and ladles[A] and articles of gold and silver. They regularly offered burnt offerings in the LORD's temple throughout Jehoiada's life.

Joash's Apostasy

15 Jehoiada died when he was old and full of days; he was 130 years old at his death. 16 He was buried in the city of David with the kings[b] because he had done what was good in Israel with respect to God and His temple.

17 However, after Jehoiada died, the rulers of Judah came and paid homage to the king. Then the king listened to them, 18 and they abandoned the temple of ·Yahweh, the God of their ancestors and served the ·Asherah poles and the idols.[c] So there was wrath[d] against Judah and Jerusalem for this ·guilt of theirs. 19 Nevertheless, He sent them prophets[e] to bring them back to the LORD; they admonished them, but the people would not listen.[f]

20 The Spirit of God took control of[B,g] Zechariah son of Jehoiada the priest. He stood above the people and said to them, "This is what God says, 'Why are you transgressing the LORD's commands and you do not prosper?[h] Because you have abandoned the LORD, He has abandoned you.'"[i] 21 But they conspired against him and stoned him at the king's command in the courtyard of the LORD's temple.[j] 22 King Joash didn't remember the kindness that Zechariah's father Jehoiada had extended to him, but killed his son. While he was dying, he said, "May the LORD see and demand[k] an account."

Aramean Invasion of Judah

23 At the turn of the year, an Aramean army went to war against Joash.[l] They entered Judah and Jerusalem and destroyed all the leaders of the people among them and sent all the plunder to the king of Damascus. 24 Although the Aramean army came with only a few men, the LORD handed over[m] a vast army to them because the people of Judah had abandoned[n] Yahweh, the God of their ancestors. So they executed judgment on Joash.

Joash Assassinated

25 When[o] the Arameans saw that Joash had many wounds, they left him. His servants conspired against him, and killed him on his bed, because he had shed the blood of the sons of Jehoiada the priest. So he died, and they buried him in the city of David, but they did not bury him in the tombs of the kings.[p]

26 Those who conspired against him were Zabad, son of the Ammonite woman Shimeath, and Jehozabad, son of the Moabite woman Shimrith.[C,q] 27 Concerning his sons, the many ·oracles about him, and the restoration[r] of the LORD's temple, they are recorded in the Writing[s] of the Book of the Kings. His son Amaziah became king in his place.

Judah's King Amaziah

25 Amaziah[t] became king when he was 25 years old and reigned 29 years in Jerusalem. His mother's name was Jehoaddan; she was from Jerusalem. 2 He did what was right in the LORD's sight but not wholeheartedly.[u]

3 As soon as the kingdom was firmly in his grasp,[D] he executed his servants who had murdered his father the king. 4 However, he did not put their children to death, because—as

[a] **24:12** 2Kg 22:4-6
[b] **24:16** 2Ch 21:20; 24:25
[c] **24:18** Ex 34:12-14
[d] Jos 22:20
[e] **24:19** Jr 7:25
[f] Neh 9:30; Ps 81:8-11; Jr 11:6-8
[g] **24:20** Jdg 6:34; 1Ch 12:18
[h] Nm 14:41
[i] 2Ch 15:2
[j] **24:21** Neh 9:26; Mt 23:35; Lk 11:51
[k] **24:22** Gn 9:5
[l] **24:23** 2Kg 12:17
[m] **24:24** 2Ch 16:7-8
[n] 2Ch 24:20
[o] **24:25-27** 2Kg 12:19-21
[p] **24:25** 2Ch 24:16
[q] **24:26** 2Kg 12:21
[r] **24:27** 2Ch 24:12
[s] 2Ch 13:22
[t] **25:1-4** 2Kg 14:2-6
[u] **25:2** 2Kg 25:14

[A] **24:14** Or *dishes*, or *spoons*; lit *palms* [B] **24:20** Lit *God clothed Himself with*; Jdg 6:34; 1Ch 12:18 [C] **24:26** = Shomer in 2Kg 12:21 [D] **25:3** LXX, Syr; MT reads *was strong on him*; 1Kg 14:4

it is written in the Law, in the book of Moses,[a] where the LORD commanded—"Fathers must not die because of children, and children must not die because of fathers, but each one will die for his own sin."[b]

Amaziah's Campaign against Edom

5Then Amaziah gathered Judah and assembled them according to ancestral house,
according to commanders of thousands, and
according to commanders of hundreds. He
numbered those 20 years old or more[c] for
all Judah and Benjamin. He found there to
be 300,000 choice men who could serve in
the army, bearing spear and shield.[d] 6Then
for 7,500 pounds[A] of silver he hired 100,000
brave warriors from Israel.
7However, a man of God[e] came to him and
said, "King, do not let Israel's army go with
you, for the LORD is not with Israel—all the
Ephraimites. 8But if you go with them, do it!
Be strong for battle! But God will make you
stumble before the enemy,[f] for God has the
power to help[g] or to make one stumble."
9Then Amaziah said to the man of God,
"What should I do about the 7,500 pounds[A]
of silver I gave to Israel's division?"
The man of God replied, "The LORD is able
to give you much more than this."
10So Amaziah released the division that
came to him from Ephraim to go home. But
they got very angry with Judah and returned
home in a fierce rage.
11Amaziah strengthened his position and
led his people to the Valley of Salt. He struck
down 10,000 Seirites,[B] 12and the Judahites
captured 10,000 alive. They took them to the
top of a cliff where they threw them off, and
all of them were dashed to pieces.
13As for the men of the division that Amaziah sent back so they would not go with him
into battle, they raided the cities of Judah from
Samaria to Beth-horon, struck down 3,000 of
their people, and took a great deal of plunder.
14After Amaziah came from the attack on
the Edomites, he brought the gods of the
Seirites[B] and set them up as his gods. He
worshiped before them and burned incense
to them.[h] 15So the LORD's anger was against
Amaziah, and He sent a prophet to him, who
said, "Why have you sought a people's gods
that could not deliver their own people from
your hand?"[i]
16While he was still speaking to him, the king
asked, "Have we made you the king's counselor? Stop, why should you lose your life?"
So the prophet stopped, but he said, "I
know that God intends to destroy you, because you have done this and have not listened to my advice."

Amaziah's War With Israel's King Joash

17King Amaziah of Judah took counsel[j] and
sent word to Jehoash[C] son of Jehoahaz, son of
Jehu, king of Israel, saying, "Come, let us meet
face to face."
18King Jehoash of Israel sent word to King
Amaziah of Judah, saying, "The thistle that
was in Lebanon sent a message to the cedar that was in Lebanon, saying, 'Give your
daughter to my son as a wife.' Then a wild
animal that was in Lebanon passed by and
trampled the thistle.[k] 19You have said, 'Look,
I[D] have defeated Edom,' and you have become
overconfident[l] that you will get glory. Now
stay at home. Why stir up such trouble so that
you fall and Judah with you?"
20But Amaziah would not listen, for this
turn of events was from God in order to hand
them over to their enemies because they went
after the gods of Edom. 21So King Jehoash of
Israel advanced. He and King Amaziah of
Judah faced off at Beth-shemesh in Judah.
22Judah was routed before Israel, and each
fled to his own tent. 23King Jehoash of Israel
captured Judah's King Amaziah son of Joash,
son of Jehoahaz,[E,m] at Beth-shemesh. Then
Jehoash took him to Jerusalem and broke
down 200 yards[F] of Jerusalem's wall from the
Ephraim Gate to the Corner Gate.[G,n] 24He took
all the gold, silver, all the utensils that were
found with Obed-edom[o] in God's temple, the
treasures of the king's palace, and the hostages. Then he returned to Samaria.

Amaziah's Death

25Judah's King Amaziah[p] son of Joash
lived 15 years after the death of Israel's King

[a]**25:4** 2Ch 17:9; 23:18
[b]Dt 24:16; Jr 31:30; Ezk 18:4,20
[c]**25:5** Nm 1:3
[d]2Ch 26:13
[e]**25:7** 2Kg 4:9
[f]**25:8** Ps 64:7-8
[g]2Ch 14:11; 20:6
[h]**25:14** 2Ch 28:23
[i]**25:15** 2Ch 25:11-12
[j]**25:17-24** 2Kg 14:8-14
[k]**25:18** Jdg 9:8-15
[l]**25:19** 2Ch 26:16; 32:25
[m]**25:23** 2Ch 21:17; 22:1
[n]2Kg 14:13
[o]**25:24** 1Ch 26:15
[p]**25:25-28** 2Kg 14:17-20

[A]**25:6,9** Lit *100 talents* [B]**25:11,14** = Edomites [C]**25:17** Lit *Joash* [D]**25:19** Some LXX mss, Old Lat, Tg, Vg; MT reads *you* [E]**25:23** = Ahaziah in 2Kg 14:13 [F]**25:23** Lit *400 cubits* [G]**25:23** Some Hb mss; other Hb mss read *to Happoneh*

Jehoash son of Jehoahaz. 26The rest of the
events of Amaziah's reign, from beginning to
end, are written in the Book of the Kings of
Judah and Israel.
27From the time Amaziah turned from following the LORD, a conspiracy was formed
against him in Jerusalem, and he fled to Lachish. However, men were sent after him to
Lachish, and they put him to death there.
28They carried him back on horses and buried him with his fathers in the city of Judah.[A,a]

Judah's King Uzziah

26 All the people[b] of Judah took Uzziah,[B]
who was 16 years old, and made him
king in place of his father Amaziah. 2He rebuilt Eloth[C,c] and restored it to Judah after
Amaziah the king rested with his fathers.
3Uzziah was 16 years old[d] when he became
king and reigned 52 years in Jerusalem. His
mother's name was Jecoliah from Jerusalem.
4He did what was right in the LORD's sight
as his father Amaziah had done. 5He sought
God[e] throughout the lifetime of Zechariah,
the teacher of the ·fear[D,f] of God. During the
time that he sought the LORD, God gave him
success.[g]

Uzziah's Exploits

6Uzziah went out to wage war against the
Philistines,[h] and he tore down the wall of
Gath, the wall of Jabneh, and the wall of Ashdod. Then he built cities in the vicinity of Ashdod and among the Philistines. 7God helped
him against the Philistines, the Arabs that
live in Gur-baal, and the Meunites. 8The Ammonites[E] gave Uzziah tribute money,[i] and his
fame spread as far as the entrance of Egypt,
for God made him very powerful. 9Uzziah
built towers in Jerusalem at the Corner Gate,[j]
the Valley Gate,[k] and the corner buttress, and
he fortified them. 10Since he had many cattle
both in the Judean foothills[F] and the plain,
he built towers in the desert and dug many
wells.[l] And since he was a lover of the soil, he
had farmers and vinedressers in the hills and
in the fertile lands.[G]
11Uzziah had an army equipped for combat that went out to war by division according to their assignments, as recorded by Jeiel
the court secretary and Maaseiah the officer under the authority of Hananiah, one of
the king's commanders. 12The total number
of heads of families was 2,600 brave warriors. 13Under their authority was an army
of 307,500 equipped for combat, a powerful force to help the king against the enemy.[m]
14Uzziah provided the entire army with
shields, spears, helmets, armor, bows and
slingstones. 15He made skillfully designed devices in Jerusalem to shoot arrows and catapult large stones for use on the towers and on
the corners. So his fame spread even to distant places, for he was marvelously helped
until he became strong.

Uzziah's Disease

16But when he became strong, he grew arrogant[n] and it led to his own destruction.
He acted unfaithfully against the LORD his
God by going into the LORD's sanctuary to
burn incense on the incense altar.[o] 17Aza-
riah[p] the priest, along with 80 brave priests
of the LORD, went in after him. 18They took
their stand[q] against King Uzziah and said,
"Uzziah, you have no right to offer incense
to the LORD[r]—only the consecrated priests,
the descendants of Aaron, have the right to
offer incense.[s] Leave the sanctuary, for you
have acted unfaithfully! You will not receive
honor from the LORD God."
19Uzziah, with a firepan in his hand to offer
incense, was enraged. But when he became
enraged with the priests, in the presence of
the priests in the LORD's temple beside the
altar of incense, a skin disease[t] broke out on
his forehead. 20Then Azariah the chief priest
and all the priests turned to him and saw that
he was diseased on his forehead. They rushed
him out of there. He himself also hurried to
get out because the LORD had afflicted him.
21So King Uzziah was diseased to the time of
his death.[u] He lived in quarantine[H,v] with a
serious skin disease and was excluded from
access to the LORD's temple, while his son Jotham was over the king's household governing the people of the land.
22Now the prophet Isaiah[w] son of Amoz

[a]25:28 2Kg 14:20
[b]26:1-2 2Kg 14:21-22
[c]26:2 1Kg 9:26; 2Kg 14:22; 16:6
[d]26:3-4 2Kg 15:2-3
[e]26:5 2Ch 24:2
[f]Dn 1:17
[g]2Ch 15:2
[h]26:6 Is 14:29
[i]26:8 2Ch 17:11
[j]26:9 2Ch 25:23
[k]Neh 2:13,15; 3:13
[l]26:10 Gn 26:18-21
[m]26:13 2Ch 25:5
[n]26:16 Dt 32:15; 2Ch 25:19
[o]1Kg 13:1-4
[p]26:17 1Ch 6:10
[q]26:18 2Ch 19:2
[r]Nm 16:39-40
[s]Ex 30:7-8
[t]26:19 2Kg 5:25-27
[u]26:21-23 2Kg 15:5-7
[v]26:21 Lv 13:46
[w]26:22 Is 1:1

A25:28 Some Hb mss read *city of David* B26:1 = Azariah in 2Kg 14:21 C26:2 LXX, Syr, Vg read *Elath* D26:5 Some Hb mss, LXX, Syr, Tg, Arabic; other Hb mss, Vg read *visions* E26:8 LXX reads *Meunites* F26:10 Or *the Shephelah* G26:10 Or *in Carmel* H26:21 Lit *a house of freedom*

wrote about the rest of the events of Uzziah's reign, from beginning to end. 23Uzziah
rested with his fathers, and he was buried
with his fathers in the burial ground of the
kings' cemetery,[a] for they said, "He has a skin
disease." His son Jotham became king in his
place.

Judah's King Jotham

27 Jotham was 25 years old[b] when he became king and reigned 16 years in Jerusalem.[c] His mother's name was Jerushah
daughter of Zadok. 2He did what was right
in the LORD's sight as his father Uzziah had
done. In addition, he didn't enter the LORD's
sanctuary,[d] but the people still behaved corruptly.
3Jotham built the Upper Gate of the LORD's
temple, and he built extensively on the wall of
Ophel.[e] 4He also built cities in the hill country of Judah and fortresses and towers in the
forests.[f] 5He waged war against the king of
the Ammonites. He overpowered the Ammonites, and that year they gave him 7,500
pounds[A] of silver, 50,000 bushels[B] of wheat,
and 50,000 bushels[B] of barley. They paid him
the same in the second and third years. 6So
Jotham strengthened himself because he did
not waver in obeying[C] the LORD his God.[g]
7As for the rest of the events[h] of Jotham's
reign, along with all his wars and his ways,
note that they are written in the Book of the
Kings of Israel and Judah. 8He was 25 years
old when he became king and reigned 16
years in Jerusalem. 9Jotham rested with his
fathers and was buried in the city of David.
His son Ahaz became king in his place.

Judah's King Ahaz

28 Ahaz was 20 years old[i] when he became king and reigned 16 years in Jerusalem. He did not do what was right in the
LORD's sight[j] like his ancestor David, 2for he
walked in the ways of the kings of Israel[k] and
made cast images of the ·Baals.[l] 3He burned
incense in the Valley of Hinnom[m] and burned
his children in[D,n] the fire, imitating the detestable practices of the nations the LORD
had dispossessed before the Israelites.[o] 4He
sacrificed and burned incense on the ·high
places,[p] on the hills, and under every green
tree.
5So the LORD his God handed Ahaz over[q] to
the king of Aram. He attacked him and took
many captives to Damascus.
Ahaz was also handed over to the king of Israel, who struck him with great force: 6Pekah
son of Remaliah killed 120,000 in Judah in
one day—all brave men—because they had
abandoned the LORD God of their ancestors.
7An Ephraimite warrior named Zichri killed
the king's son Maaseiah, Azrikam governor
of the palace, and Elkanah who was second
to the king. 8Then the Israelites took 200,000
captives from their brothers—women, sons,
and daughters.[r] They also took a great deal of
plunder from them and brought it to Samaria.
9A prophet of the LORD named Oded was
there. He went out to meet the army that
came to Samaria and said to them, "Look, the
LORD God of your ancestors handed them
over to you because of His wrath against Judah,[s] but you slaughtered them in a rage that
has reached heaven.[t] 10Now you plan to reduce the people of Judah and Jerusalem, male
and female, to slavery. Are you not also ·guilty
before ·Yahweh your God? 11Listen to me and
return the captives you took from your brothers,[u] for the LORD's burning anger is on you."
12So some men who were leaders of the
Ephraimites—Azariah son of Jehohanan,
Berechiah son of Meshillemoth, Jehizkiah
son of Shallum, and Amasa son of Had-
lai—stood in opposition to those coming
from the war. 13They said to them, "You must
not bring the captives here, for you plan to
bring guilt on us from the LORD to add to our
sins and our guilt. For we have much guilt,
and burning anger is on Israel."
14The army left the captives and the plunder in the presence of the officers and the
congregation. 15Then the men who were designated by name[v] took charge of the captives
and provided clothes for their naked ones
from the plunder. They clothed them, gave
them sandals, food and drink,[w] dressed their
wounds, and provided donkeys for all the
feeble. The Israelites brought them to Jericho, the City of Palms,[x] among their brothers.
Then they returned to Samaria.

[a] **26:23** 2Ch 21:20
[b] **27:1-3** 2Kg 15:33-35
[c] **27:1** 2Ch 27:8
[d] **27:2** 2Ch 26:16-18
[e] **27:3** 2Ch 33:14; Neh 3:26-27
[f] **27:4** 2Ch 11:5
[g] **27:6** 2Ch 26:5
[h] **27:7-9** 2Kg 15:36-38
[i] **28:1-6** 2Kg 16:2-4
[j] **28:1** 2Ch 27:2
[k] **28:2** 2Ch 22:3
[l] Ex 34:17
[m] **28:3** Jos 15:8; 18:16; 2Kg 23:10; Jr 7:29-34; 19:2-6
[n] Lv 18:21; 2Kg 16:3; 2Ch 33:6
[o] 2Ch 33:2
[p] **28:4** 2Ch 28:25
[q] **28:5** 2Ch 24:24
[r] **28:8** 2Ch 11:4
[s] **28:9** Is 47:6
[t] Ezr 9:6; Rv 18:5
[u] **28:11** 2Ch 28:8
[v] **28:15** 2Ch 28:12
[w] 2Kg 6:22; Pr 25:21-22
[x] Dt 34:3

[A] **27:5** Lit *100 talents* [B] **27:5** Lit *10,000 cors* [C] **27:6** Lit *he established his ways before* [D] **28:3** LXX, Syr, Tg read *and passed his children through*

16 At that time King Ahaz asked the king of
Assyria for help.[a] 17 The Edomites came again,
attacked Judah, and took captives.[b] 18 The
Philistines also raided the cities of the Judean foothills[A] and the ·Negev of Judah[c] and
captured Beth-shemesh, Aijalon, Gederoth,
Soco and its villages, Timnah and its villages, Gimzo and its villages, and they lived
there. 19 For the LORD humbled Judah because of King Ahaz of Judah,[B] who threw off
restraint in Judah and was unfaithful to the
LORD. 20 Then Tiglath-pileser[C,d] king of Assyria came against Ahaz; he oppressed him
and did not give him support.[e] 21 Although
Ahaz plundered the LORD's temple and the
palace of the king and of the rulers and gave
the plunder to the king of Assyria, it did not
help him.

22 At the time of his distress, King Ahaz
himself became more unfaithful to the LORD.
23 He sacrificed to the gods of Damascus
which had defeated him; he said, "Since the
gods of the kings of Aram are helping them,
I will sacrifice to them so that they will help
me."[f] But they were the downfall of him and
of all Israel.

24 Then Ahaz gathered up the utensils of
God's temple, cut them into pieces,[g] shut the
doors of the LORD's temple,[h] and made himself altars on every street corner in Jerusalem.[i] 25 He made high places in every city of
Judah to offer incense to other gods, and he
provoked the LORD, the God of his ancestors.

Ahaz's Death

26 As for the rest of his deeds[j] and all his
ways, from beginning to end, they are written in the Book of the Kings of Judah and Israel. 27 Ahaz rested with his fathers and was
buried in the city, in Jerusalem, but they did
not bring him into the tombs of the kings of
Israel. His son Hezekiah became king in his
place.

Judah's King Hezekiah

29 Hezekiah was 25 years old[k] when he
became king and reigned 29 years in
Jerusalem. His mother's name was Abijah[D]
daughter of Zechariah. 2 He did what was
right in the LORD's sight[l] just as his ancestor
David had done.

3 In the first year of his reign, in the first
month, he opened the doors of the LORD's
temple and repaired them.[m] 4 Then he
brought in the priests and Levites and gathered them in the eastern public square.[n] 5 He
said to them, "Hear me, Levites. Consecrate
yourselves[o] now and consecrate the temple of
·Yahweh, the God of your ancestors. Remove
everything impure from the holy place. 6 For
our fathers were unfaithful and did what is
evil in the sight of the LORD our God. They
abandoned Him, turned their faces away
from the LORD's tabernacle, and turned their
backs on Him.[E,p] 7 They also closed the doors
of the portico, extinguished the lamps, did
not burn incense, and did not offer ·burnt offerings in the holy place of the God of Israel.
8 Therefore, the wrath of the LORD was on Judah and Jerusalem, and He made them an object of terror, horror, and mockery,[F,q] as you
see with your own eyes. 9 Our fathers fell by
the sword, and our sons, our daughters, and
our wives are in captivity because of this.[r] 10 It
is in my heart now to make a covenant with
Yahweh, the God of Israel[s] so that His burning anger may turn away from us. 11 My sons,
don't be negligent now, for the LORD has chosen you to stand in His presence, to serve
Him, and to be His ministers and burners of
incense."[t]

Cleansing the Temple

12 Then the Levites stood up:

Mahath[u] son of Amasai and Joel son of Azariah from the Kohathites;
Kish son of Abdi and Azariah son of Jehallelel from the Merarites;[v]
Joah son of Zimmah and Eden son of Joah from the Gershonites;
13 Shimri and Jeuel from the Elizaphanites;
Zechariah and Mattaniah from the Asaphites;
14 Jehiel[G] and Shimei from the Hemanites;
Shemaiah and Uzziel from the Jeduthunites.

[a] **28:16** 2Kg 16:7
[b] **28:17** Ob 10-14
[c] **28:18** Ezk 16:57
[d] **28:20** 1Ch 5:26
[e] 2Ch 28:16
[f] **28:23** Jr 44:17-18
[g] **28:24** 2Kg 16:17
[h] 2Ch 29:7
[i] 2Ch 30:14; 33:3-5
[j] **28:26-27** 2Kg 16:19-20
[k] **29:1-2** 2Kg 18:2-3
[l] **29:2** 2Ch 28:1; 34:2
[m] **29:3** 2Ch 28:24; 29:7
[n] **29:4** Ezr 10:9; Neh 8:1
[o] **29:5** 2Ch 29:15,34; 35:6
[p] **29:6** Ezk 8:16
[q] **29:8** Dt 28:25; Jr 25:18
[r] **29:9** 2Ch 28:5-8,17
[s] **29:10** 2Ch 23:16
[t] **29:11** Nm 3:6; 8:6
[u] **29:12** 2Ch 31:13
[v] Nm 3:19-20

[A] **28:18** Or *the Shephelah* [B] **28:19** Some Hb mss; other Hb mss read *Israel* [C] **28:20** Text emended; MT reads *Tilgath-pilneser*; 1Ch 5:6,26 [D] **29:1** = Abi in 2Kg 18:2 [E] **29:6** Lit *and they gave the back of the neck* [F] **29:8** Lit *hissing* [G] **29:14** Alt Hb tradition reads *Jehuel*

15They gathered their brothers together, consecrated themselves,[a] and went according to the king's command by the words of the LORD[b] to cleanse the LORD's temple.[c]

16The priests went to the entrance of the LORD's temple to cleanse it. They took all the unclean things they found in the LORD's sanctuary to the courtyard of the LORD's temple. Then the Levites received them and took them outside to the Kidron Valley.[d] 17They began the consecration on the first day of the first month, and on the eighth day of the month they came to the portico of the LORD's temple. They consecrated the LORD's temple for eight days, and on the sixteenth day of the first month they finished.

18Then they went inside to King Hezekiah and said, "We have cleansed the whole temple of the LORD, the altar of burnt offering and all its utensils, and the table for the rows of the •bread of the Presence and all its utensils. 19We have set up and consecrated all the utensils that King Ahaz rejected during his reign[e] when he became unfaithful. They are in front of the altar of the LORD."

Renewal of Temple Worship

20King Hezekiah got up early, gathered the city officials, and went to the LORD's temple. 21They brought seven bulls, seven rams, seven lambs, and seven male goats as a •sin offering for the kingdom, for the sanctuary, and for Judah. Then he told the descendants of Aaron, the priests, to offer them on the altar of the LORD. 22So they slaughtered the bulls, and the priests received the blood and sprinkled it on the altar.[f] They slaughtered the rams and sprinkled the blood on the altar. They slaughtered the lambs and sprinkled the blood on the altar. 23Then they brought the goats for the sin offering right into the presence of the king and the congregation, who laid their hands on them.[g] 24The priests slaughtered the goats and put their blood on the altar for a sin offering, to make •atonement for all Israel,[h] for the king said that the burnt offering and sin offering were for all Israel.

25Hezekiah stationed the Levites in the LORD's temple with cymbals, harps, and lyres[i] according to the command of David,[j] Gad the king's seer,[k] and Nathan the prophet.[l] For the command was from the LORD through His prophets. 26The Levites stood with the instruments of David,[m] and the priests with the trumpets.[n]

27Then Hezekiah ordered that the burnt offering be offered on the altar. When the burnt offerings began, the song of the LORD and the trumpets began, accompanied by the instruments of David king of Israel. 28The whole assembly was worshiping, singing the song, and blowing the trumpets—all of this continued until the burnt offering was completed. 29When the burnt offerings were completed, the king and all those present with him bowed down and worshiped.[o] 30Then King Hezekiah and the officials told the Levites to sing praise to the LORD in the words of David and of •Asaph the seer. So they sang praises with rejoicing and bowed down and worshiped.

31Hezekiah concluded, "Now you are consecrated[A] to the LORD. Come near and bring sacrifices and thank offerings to the LORD's temple." So the congregation brought sacrifices and thank offerings, and all those with willing hearts[p] brought burnt offerings. 32The number of burnt offerings the congregation brought was 70 bulls, 100 rams, and 200 lambs; all these were for a burnt offering to the LORD. 33Six hundred bulls and 3,000 sheep were consecrated.

34However, since there were not enough priests, they weren't able to skin all the burnt offerings, so their Levite brothers helped them[q] until the work was finished and until the priests consecrated themselves. For the Levites were more conscientious[B,r] to consecrate themselves than the priests were.[s] 35Furthermore, the burnt offerings were abundant, along with the fat of the •fellowship offerings[t] and with the •drink offerings[u] for the burnt offering.

So the service of the LORD's temple was established. 36Then Hezekiah and all the people rejoiced over how God had prepared the people, for it had come about suddenly.

Celebration of the Passover

30 Then Hezekiah sent word throughout all Israel and Judah, and he also wrote letters to Ephraim and Manasseh to come to

a29:15 2Ch 29:5
b2Ch 30:12
c1Ch 23:28
d29:16 2Ch 15:16
e29:19 2Ch 28:24
f29:22 Lv 4:18
g29:23 Lv 4:15
h29:24 Lv 4:26
i29:25 1Ch 15:16; 25:6
j2Ch 8:14
k2Sm 24:11
l2Sm 7:2; 1Ch 29:29
m29:26 1Ch 23:5
n2Ch 5:12
o29:29 2Ch 20:18
p29:31 Ex 35:5,22; Ezr 1:4,6; 3:5
q29:34 2Ch 35:11
rPs 32:11; 64:10
s2Ch 30:3
t29:35 Lv 3:16
uNm 15:5-10

A29:31 Lit *Now you have filled your hands* B29:34 Lit *upright of heart*; Ps 32:11; 64:10

the LORD's temple in Jerusalem to observe the •Passover of •Yahweh, the God of Israel.[a] 2 For the king and his officials and the entire congregation in Jerusalem decided to observe the Passover of the LORD in the second month,[b] 3 because they were not able to observe it at the appropriate time. Not enough of the priests had consecrated themselves[c] and the people hadn't been gathered together in Jerusalem. 4 The proposal pleased the king and the congregation, 5 so they affirmed the proposal and spread the message throughout all Israel, from Beer-sheba to Dan,[d] to come to observe the Passover of Yahweh, the God of Israel in Jerusalem, for they hadn't observed it often,[A] as prescribed.[B]

6 So the couriers[e] went throughout Israel and Judah with letters from the hand of the king and his officials, and according to the king's command, saying, "Israelites, return to Yahweh, the God of Abraham, Isaac, and Israel so that He may return to those of you who remain, who have escaped from the grasp of the kings of Assyria.[f] 7 Don't be like your fathers and your brothers who were unfaithful to Yahweh, the God of their ancestors[g] so that He made them an object of horror[h] as you yourselves see. 8 Don't become obstinate[C,i] now like your fathers did. Give your allegiance[D] to Yahweh, and come to His sanctuary that He has consecrated forever. Serve the LORD your God so that He may turn His burning anger away from you,[j] 9 for when you return to Yahweh, your brothers and your sons will receive mercy in the presence of their captors and will return to this land.[k] For Yahweh your God is gracious and merciful;[l] He will not turn His face away from you if you return to Him."

10 The couriers traveled from city to city in the land of Ephraim and Manasseh as far as Zebulun, but the inhabitants[E] laughed at them and mocked them.[m] 11 But some from Asher, Manasseh, and Zebulun humbled themselves and came to Jerusalem.[n] 12 Also, the power of God was at work in Judah to unite them[F] to carry out the command of the king and his officials by the word of the LORD.

13 A very large assembly of people was gathered in Jerusalem to observe the Festival of Unleavened Bread in the second month. 14 They proceeded to take away the altars that were in Jerusalem,[o] and they took away the incense altars and threw them into the Kidron Valley.[p] 15 They slaughtered the Passover lamb[q] on the fourteenth day of the second month. The priests and Levites were ashamed, and they consecrated themselves and brought •burnt offerings to the LORD's temple. 16 They stood at their prescribed posts,[r] according to the law of Moses, the man of God. The priests sprinkled the blood received from the hand of the Levites, 17 for there were many in the assembly who had not consecrated themselves, and so the Levites were in charge of slaughtering the Passover lambs for every •unclean person to consecrate the lambs to the LORD.[s] 18 A large number of the people—many from Ephraim, Manasseh, Issachar, and Zebulun—were ritually unclean, yet they had eaten the Passover[t] contrary to what was written.[u] But Hezekiah had interceded for them, saying, "May the good LORD provide •atonement on behalf of 19 whoever sets his whole heart on seeking God,[v] Yahweh, the God of his ancestors, even though not according to the purification rules of the sanctuary." 20 So the LORD heard Hezekiah and healed the people.[w] 21 The Israelites who were present in Jerusalem observed the Festival of Unleavened Bread seven days with great joy,[x] and the Levites and the priests praised the LORD day after day with loud instruments. 22 Then Hezekiah encouraged[G,y] all the Levites who performed skillfully before the LORD. They ate at the appointed festival for seven days, sacrificing •fellowship offerings and giving thanks to Yahweh, the God of their ancestors.[z]

23 The whole congregation decided to observe[aa] seven more days, so they observed seven days with joy, 24 for Hezekiah king of Judah contributed 1,000 bulls and 7,000 sheep for the congregation. Also, the officials contributed 1,000 bulls and 10,000 sheep for the congregation,[ab] and many priests consecrated themselves.[ac] 25 Then the whole assembly of Judah with the priests and Levites, the whole assembly that came from Israel, the

[a] **30:1** Ex 12:1-28; 13:1-10
[b] **30:2** Nm 9:6-14; 2Ch 30:13,15
[c] **30:3** 2Ch 29:34
[d] **30:5** Jdg 20:1
[e] **30:6** Est 8:14; Jb 9:25; Jr 51:31
[f] 2Ch 28:20
[g] **30:7** Ezk 20:13
[h] 2Ch 29:8
[i] **30:8** Ex 32:9
[j] 2Ch 29:10
[k] **30:9** Dt 30:2-3
[l] Ex 34:6-7; Mc 7:18
[m] **30:10** 2Ch 36:16
[n] **30:11** 2Ch 30:18,21,25
[o] **30:14** 2Ch 28:24
[p] 2Ch 29:16
[q] **30:15** 2Ch 30:2-3
[r] **30:16** 2Ch 35:10,15
[s] **30:17** 2Ch 29:34
[t] **30:18** Nm 9:10
[u] Ex 12:43-49
[v] **30:19** 2Ch 19:3
[w] **30:20** Ps 41:4; Hs 14:4
[x] **30:21** Ex 12:15; 13:6
[y] **30:22** 2Ch 32:6
[z] Ezr 10:11
[aa] **30:23** 1Kg 8:65
[ab] **30:24** 2Ch 35:7-8
[ac] 2Ch 29:34; 30:3

[A] **30:5** Or *in great numbers* [B] **30:5** Lit *often, according to what is written* [C] **30:8** Lit *Don't stiffen your neck* [D] **30:8** Lit *hand* [E] **30:10** Lit *but they* [F] **30:12** Lit *to give them one heart* [G] **30:22** Lit *spoke to the heart of*

foreigners who came from the land of Israel,
and those who were living in Judah, rejoiced.
26 There was great rejoicing in Jerusalem, for
nothing like this was known since the days of
Solomon son of David, the king of Israel.[a]
27 Then the priests and the Levites[b] stood to
bless the people,[c] and God heard their voice,
and their prayer came into His holy dwelling
place[d] in heaven.

Removal of Idolatry

31 When all this was completed, all Israel
who had attended went out to the cities of Judah and broke up the sacred pillars,
chopped down the ·Asherah poles, and tore
down the ·high places and altars[e] throughout
Judah and Benjamin, as well as in Ephraim
and Manasseh, to the last one.[A] Then all the
Israelites returned to their cities, each to his
own possession.

Offerings for Levites

2 Hezekiah reestablished the divisions[f] of
the priests and Levites for the ·burnt offerings and ·fellowship offerings, for ministry,
for giving thanks, and for praise in the gates
of the camp of the LORD,[g] each division corresponding to his service among the priests
and Levites. 3 The king contributed[B] from his
own possessions[h] for the regular morning
and evening burnt offerings, the burnt offerings of the Sabbaths, of the New Moons, and
of the appointed feasts, as written in the law
of the LORD.[i] 4 He told the people who lived
in Jerusalem to give a contribution[j] for the
priests and Levites so that they could devote
their energy to the law of the LORD. 5 When
the word spread, the Israelites gave liberally
of the best of the grain, new wine, oil, honey,
and of all the produce of the field, and they
brought in an abundance, a tenth[k] of everything. 6 As for the Israelites and Judahites who
lived in the cities of Judah, they also brought
a tenth of the cattle and sheep, and a tenth of
the dedicated things that were consecrated
to the LORD their God.[l] They gathered them
into large piles. 7 In the third month they began building up the piles, and they finished
in the seventh month. 8 When Hezekiah and
his officials came and viewed the piles, they
praised the LORD and His people Israel.
9 Hezekiah asked the priests and Levites
about the piles. 10 Azariah, the chief priest
of the household of Zadok,[m] answered him,
"Since they began bringing the offering to the
LORD's temple, we eat and are satisfied and
there is plenty left over because the LORD has
blessed His people; this abundance is what is
left over."[n]
11 Hezekiah told them to prepare chambers[o]
in the LORD's temple, and they prepared them.
12 The offering, the tenth, and the dedicated
things were brought faithfully. Conaniah the
Levite was the officer in charge of them, and
his brother Shimei was second.[p] 13 Jehiel, Azaziah, Nahath, Asahel, Jerimoth, Jozabad, Eliel,
Ismachiah, Mahath, and Benaiah were deputies under the authority of Conaniah and
his brother Shimei by appointment of King
Hezekiah and of Azariah the chief official of
God's temple.
14 Kore son of Imnah the Levite, the keeper
of the East Gate, was over the freewill offerings to God to distribute the contribution to
the LORD and the consecrated things.[q] 15 Eden,[r]
Miniamin, Jeshua, Shemaiah, Amariah, and
Shecaniah in the cities of the priests[s] were
to faithfully distribute it under his authority
to their brothers by divisions, whether large
or small. 16 In addition, they distributed it to
males registered by genealogy three[C,t] years
old and above; to all who would enter the
LORD's temple for their daily duty,[u] for their
service in their responsibilities according
to their divisions. 17 They distributed also to
those recorded by genealogy of the priests
by their ancestral families and the Levites 20
years old and above,[v] by their responsibilities
in their divisions; 18 to those registered by genealogy — with all their infants, wives, sons,
and daughters — of the whole assembly (for
they had faithfully consecrated themselves as
holy); 19 and to the descendants of Aaron, the
priests, in the common fields of their cities,[w]
in each and every city. There were men who
were registered by name[x] to distribute a portion to every male among the priests and to
every Levite recorded by genealogy.
20 Hezekiah did this throughout all Judah.

[a] **30:26** 2Ch 7:8-10
[b] **30:27** 2Ch 23:18
[c] Nm 6:23-27
[d] Dt 26:15; Ps 68:5
[e] **31:1** 2Kg 18:4
[f] **31:2** 1Ch 23:6-23; 24:1-19
[g] 1Ch 23:28-31
[h] **31:3** 2Ch 35:7
[i] Nm 28
[j] **31:4** Nm 18:8
[k] **31:5** Neh 13:12
[l] **31:6** Lv 27:30; Dt 14:28
[m] **31:10** 1Ch 6:8-9
[n] Mal 3:10
[o] **31:11** 1Kg 6:5
[p] **31:12** 2Ch 35:9
[q] **31:14** 1Ch 26:26-28
[r] **31:15** 2Ch 29:12
[s] Jos 21:9-19
[t] **31:16** 1Ch 23:3
[u] Ezr 3:4
[v] **31:17** 1Ch 23:24
[w] **31:19** Lv 25:34; Nm 35:2-5
[x] 2Ch 31:12-15

[A] **31:1** Lit *Manasseh, until finishing* [B] **31:3** Lit *The king's portion* [C] **31:16** Or *30*; 1Ch 23:3

He did what was good and upright and true
before the LORD his God.[a] 21 He was diligent
in every deed that he began in the service of
God's temple, in the instruction and the commands, in order to seek his God, and he prospered.

Sennacherib's Invasion

32 After these faithful deeds, Sennacherib king of Assyria came and entered
Judah. He laid siege to the fortified cities and
intended[A] to break into them.[b] 2 Hezekiah
saw that Sennacherib had come and that he
planned[B] war on Jerusalem, 3 so he consulted
with his officials and his warriors about stopping up the waters of the springs that were
outside the city, and they helped him. 4 Many
people gathered and stopped up all the
springs[c] and the stream that flowed through
the land;[d] they said, "Why should the kings
of Assyria come and find plenty of water?"
5 Then Hezekiah strengthened his position by
rebuilding the entire broken-down wall[e] and
heightening the towers and the other outside
wall.[f] He repaired the supporting terraces[g] of
the city of David, and made an abundance of
weapons and shields.

6 He set military commanders over the people and gathered the people in the square of
the city gate. Then he encouraged them,[C,h]
saying, 7 "Be strong and courageous![i] Don't
be afraid or discouraged before the king of
Assyria or before the large army that is with
him, for there are more with us than with
him.[j] 8 He has only human strength,[D] but
we have ·Yahweh our God to help us and to
fight our battles."[k] So the people relied on the
words of King Hezekiah of Judah.

Sennacherib's Servant's Speech

9 After this,[l] while Sennacherib king of Assyria with all his armed forces besieged[E]
Lachish, he sent his servants to Jerusalem
against King Hezekiah of Judah and against
all those of Judah who were in Jerusalem,
saying, 10 "This is what King Sennacherib of
Assyria says: 'What are you relying on that
you remain in Jerusalem under siege? 11 Isn't
Hezekiah misleading you to give you over
to death by famine and thirst when he says,
"Yahweh our God will deliver us from the
power of the king of Assyria"? 12 Didn't Hezekiah himself remove His ·high places and His
altars[m] and say to Judah and Jerusalem, "You
must worship before one altar, and you must
burn incense on it"?

13 "'Don't you know[n] what I and my fathers
have done to all the peoples of the lands?
Have any of the national gods of the lands
been able to deliver their land from my
power? 14 Who among all the gods of these
nations that my predecessors ·completely
destroyed was able to deliver his people from
my power, that your God should be able to do
the same for you?[o] 15 So now,[p] don't let Hezekiah deceive you, and don't let him mislead
you like this. Don't believe him, for no god of
any nation or kingdom has been able to deliver his people from my power or the power
of my fathers. How much less will your God
deliver you from my power!'"

16 His servants said more against the LORD
God and against His servant Hezekiah. 17 He
also wrote letters to mock Yahweh, the God
of Israel, saying against Him:

> Just like the national gods of the lands
> that did not deliver their people from my
> power, so Hezekiah's God will not deliver
> His people from my power.[q]

18 Then they called out loudly in Hebrew[F]
to the people of Jerusalem, who were on the
wall, to frighten and discourage them in order that he might capture the city. 19 They
spoke against the God of Jerusalem like they
had spoken against the gods of the peoples of
the earth, which were made by human hands.

Deliverance from Sennacherib

20 King Hezekiah and the prophet Isaiah
son of Amoz prayed about this and cried out
to heaven,[r] 21 and the LORD sent an angel who
annihilated every brave warrior, leader, and
commander in the camp of the king of Assyria. So the king of Assyria returned in disgrace to his land. He went to the temple of
his god, and there some of his own children
struck him down with the sword.[s]

[a] 31:20 2Kg 20:3; 22:2
[b] 32:1 2Kg 18:13; Is 36:1
[c] 32:4 2Kg 20:20
[d] 2Ch 32:30
[e] 32:5 2Ch 25:23
[f] 2Kg 25:4
[g] 2Sm 5:9; 1Kg 9:15
[h] 32:6 2Ch 30:22
[i] 32:7 Dt 31:6; Jos 1:6-9; 10:25; 1Ch 22:13; Ps 31:24
[j] 2Kg 6:16; 1Jn 4:4
[k] 32:8 2Ch 20:17; Is 31:3; Jr 17:5
[l] 32:9-12 2Kg 18:17-22; Is 36:2-7
[m] 32:12 2Ch 31:1
[n] 32:13-14 2Kg 18:33-35; Is 36:18-20
[o] 32:14 Is 10:9-11
[p] 32:15-18 2Kg 18:28-30; Is 36:13-15
[q] 32:17 2Ch 32:14
[r] 32:20 2Kg 19:15; Is 37:15-16
[s] 32:21 2Kg 19:35-37; Is 37:36-38

[A] 32:1 Lit *said to himself* [B] 32:2 Lit *that his face was for* [C] 32:6 Lit *he spoke to their hearts* [D] 32:8 Lit *With him an arm of flesh* [E] 32:9 Lit *with his dominion was against* [F] 32:18 Lit *Judahite*

22So the LORD saved Hezekiah and the inhabitants of Jerusalem from the power of
King Sennacherib of Assyria and from the
power of all others. He gave them rest[A,a] on
every side. 23Many were bringing an offering
to the LORD to Jerusalem and valuable gifts to
King Hezekiah of Judah, and he was exalted
in the eyes of all the nations after that.[b]

Hezekiah's Illness and Pride

24In those days Hezekiah became sick to
the point of death, so he prayed to the LORD,
and He spoke to him and gave him a miraculous sign.[c] 25However, because his heart was
proud,[d] Hezekiah didn't respond according
to the benefit that had come to him. So there
was wrath on him, Judah, and Jerusalem.[e]
26Then Hezekiah humbled himself for the
pride of his heart—he and the inhabitants of
Jerusalem—so the LORD's wrath didn't come[f]
on them during Hezekiah's lifetime.[g]

Hezekiah's Wealth and Works

27Hezekiah had abundant riches and glory,
and he made himself treasuries for silver,
gold, precious stones, spices, shields, and every desirable item. 28He made warehouses
for the harvest of grain, new wine, and oil,
and stalls for all kinds of cattle, and pens for
flocks. 29He made cities for himself, and he
acquired herds of sheep and cattle in abundance, for God gave him abundant possessions.
30This same Hezekiah blocked the outlet
of the water of the Upper Gihon[h] and chan-
neled it smoothly downward and westward
to the city of David.[i] Hezekiah succeeded in
everything he did. 31When the ambassadors
of Babylon's rulers[j] were sent[B] to him to inquire about the miraculous sign[k] that happened in the land, God left him to test him
and discover what was in his heart.[l]

Hezekiah's Death

32As for the rest of the events[m] of Hezekiah's
reign and his deeds of faithful love, note that
they are written in the Visions of the Prophet
Isaiah son of Amoz,[n] and in the Book of the
Kings of Judah and Israel.[o] 33Hezekiah rested
with his fathers and was buried on the ascent to the tombs of David's descendants. All
Judah and the inhabitants of Jerusalem paid
him honor at his death. His son Manasseh became king in his place.

Judah's King Manasseh

33 Manasseh was 12 years old[p] when he
became king and reigned 55 years
in Jerusalem. 2He did what was evil in the
LORD's sight, imitating the detestable practices of the nations that the LORD had dispossessed before the Israelites.[q] 3He rebuilt
the ·high places that his father Hezekiah
had torn down[r] and reestablished the altars
for the ·Baals. He made ·Asherah poles, and
he worshiped the whole heavenly ·host and
served them. 4He built altars[s] in the LORD's
temple, where ·Yahweh had said, "Jerusalem
is where My name will remain forever."[t] 5He
built altars to the whole heavenly host in
both courtyards[u] of the LORD's temple. 6He
passed his sons through the fire in the Valley
of Hinnom.[v] He practiced witchcraft, ·divi-
nation, and sorcery, and consulted mediums
and spiritists.[w] He did a great deal of evil in
the LORD's sight, provoking Him.
7Manasseh[x] set up a carved image of the idol
he had made, in God's temple,[y] about which
God had said to David and his son Solomon,
"I will establish My name forever[C,z] in this temple and in Jerusalem, which I have chosen out
of all the tribes of Israel.[aa] 8I will never again
remove the feet of the Israelites from the land
where I stationed your[D,ab] ancestors,[ac] if only
they will be careful to do all that I have commanded them through Moses—all the law,
statutes, and judgments." 9So Manasseh caused
Judah and the inhabitants of Jerusalem to stray
so that they did worse evil than the nations the
LORD had destroyed before the Israelites.

Manasseh's Repentance

10The LORD spoke to Manasseh and his people, but they didn't listen.[ad] 11So He brought
against them the military commanders of
the king of Assyria. They captured Manasseh
with hooks, bound him with bronze shackles,
and took him to Babylon.[ae] 12When he was in

[a] **32:22** Ps 23:2 [b] **32:23** 2Sm 8:10; 2Ch 9:23-24 [c] **32:24** 2Kg 20:1-3,8-11; Is 38:1-3,7-8 [d] **32:25** 2Ch 26:16; 32:31 [e] 2Ch 24:18 [f] **32:26** Jr 26:18-19 [g] 2Kg 20:18-19; Is 39:7-8 [h] **32:30** 1Kg 1:33 [i] 2Kg 20:20 [j] **32:31** 2Kg 20:12; Is 39:1 [k] 2Ch 32:24 [l] Dt 8:2; 13:3 [m] **32:32-33** 2Kg 20:20-21 [n] **32:32** Is 36:1–39:8 [o] 2Kg 18:9–20:19 [p] **33:1-9** 2Kg 21:1-9 [q] **33:2** 2Ch 28:3 [r] **33:3** 2Kg 18:4; 2Ch 31:1 [s] **33:4** 2Ch 28:24 [t] 2Ch 7:16 [u] **33:5** 2Ch 4:9 [v] **33:6** 2Kg 16:3; 2Ch 28:3 [w] Lv 19:31; 20:27; 2Kg 23:24 [x] **33:7-8** 1Kg 9:1-9 [y] **33:7** Dt 16:21 [z] 2Kg 21:7 [aa] Dt 12:5; 1Kg 11:32 [ab] **33:8** 2Kg 21:8 [ac] 2Sm 7:10 [ad] **33:10** 2Kg 21:10-16 [ae] **33:11** 2Ch 36:6

[A] **32:22** Lit *He led them*; Ps 23:2 [B] **32:31** LXX, Tg, Vg; MT reads *of Babylon sent* [C] **33:7** LXX, Syr, Tg, Vg; 2Kg 21:7; MT reads *name for Elom* [D] **33:8** LXX, Syr, Vg read *land I gave to their*; 2Kg 21:8

distress, he sought the favor of Yahweh his God and earnestly humbled himself[a] before the God of his ancestors. 13 He prayed to Him, so He heard his petition and granted his request,[b] and brought him back to Jerusalem, to his kingdom. So Manasseh came to know that Yahweh is God.[c]

14 After this, he built the outer wall of the city of David from west of Gihon[d] in the valley to the entrance of the Fish Gate;[e] he brought it around the Ophel,[f] and he heightened it considerably. He also placed military commanders in all the fortified cities of Judah.

15 He removed the foreign gods and the idol[g] from the LORD's temple, along with all the altars that he had built on the mountain of the LORD's temple and in Jerusalem, and he threw them outside the city. 16 He built[A] the altar of the LORD and offered ·fellowship and thank offerings on it. Then he told Judah to serve Yahweh, the God of Israel. 17 However, the people still sacrificed at the high places,[h] but only to Yahweh their God.

Manasseh's Death

18 The rest of the events[i] of Manasseh's reign, along with his prayer[j] to his God and the words of the seers who spoke to him in the name of Yahweh, the God of Israel, are written in the Records of Israel's Kings. 19 His prayer and how God granted his request, and all his sin and unfaithfulness and the sites where he built high places and set up Asherah poles and carved images before he humbled himself, they are written in the Records of Hozai. 20 Manasseh rested with his fathers, and he was buried in his own house. His son Amon became king in his place.

Judah's King Amon

21 Amon was 22 years old when he became king and reigned two years in Jerusalem. 22 He did what was evil in the LORD's sight just as his father Manasseh had done.[k] Amon sacrificed to all the carved images that his father Manasseh had made, and he served them. 23 But he did not humble himself before the LORD like his father Manasseh humbled himself;[l] instead, Amon increased his ·guilt.

24 So his servants conspired against him and put him to death[m] in his own house. 25 Then the common people[B] executed all those who conspired against King Amon and made his son Josiah king in his place.

Judah's King Josiah

34 Josiah was eight years old[n] when he became king and reigned 31 years in Jerusalem. 2 He did what was right in the LORD's sight and walked in the ways of his ancestor David;[o] he did not turn aside to the right or the left.

Josiah's Reform

3 In the eighth year of his reign, while he was still a youth, Josiah began to seek the God of his ancestor David,[p] and in the twelfth year he began to cleanse Judah and Jerusalem of the ·high places, the ·Asherah poles, the carved images,[q] and the cast images. 4 Then in his presence the altars of the ·Baals were torn down, and he chopped down the incense altars that were above them. He shattered the Asherah poles, the carved images, and the cast images, crushed them to dust, and scattered[r] them over the graves of those who had sacrificed to them.[s] 5 He burned the bones of the priests on their altars.[t] So he cleansed Judah and Jerusalem. 6 He did the same in the cities[u] of Manasseh, Ephraim, and Simeon, and as far as Naphtali and on their surrounding mountain shrines.[C] 7 He tore down the altars, and he smashed the Asherah poles and the carved images to powder. He chopped down all the incense altars throughout the land of Israel and returned to Jerusalem.[v]

Josiah's Repair of the Temple

8 In the eighteenth year of his reign,[w] in order to cleanse the land and the temple, Josiah sent Shaphan son of Azaliah, along with Maaseiah the governor[x] of the city and the court historian Joah son of Joahaz, to repair the temple of the LORD his God.

9 So they went to Hilkiah[y] the high priest, and gave him the money brought into God's temple. The Levites and the doorkeepers had collected money from Manasseh, Ephraim,[z]

[a] **33:12** 2Ch 32:26
[b] **33:13** Ezr 8:23
[c] Dn 4:32
[d] **33:14** 1Kg 1:33; 2Ch 32:30
[e] Neh 3:3
[f] 2Ch 27:3
[g] **33:15** 2Ch 33:3-7
[h] **33:17** 2Ch 32:12
[i] **33:18-25** 2Kg 21:17-24
[j] **33:18** 2Ch 33:12-13
[k] **33:22** 2Ch 33:2
[l] **33:23** 2Ch 33:12,19
[m] **33:24** 2Ch 25:27
[n] **34:1-2** 2Kg 22:1-2
[o] **34:2** 2Ch 29:2
[p] **34:3** 1Ch 28:9; 2Ch 11:16; 14:4; 15:12
[q] 2Ch 33:22
[r] **34:4** Ex 32:20
[s] 2Kg 23:6
[t] **34:5** 2Kg 23:5,8,16,20
[u] **34:6** 2Kg 23:15,19
[v] **34:7** 2Ch 31:1
[w] **34:8-12** 2Kg 22:3-7
[x] **34:8** 2Ch 18:25
[y] **34:9** 2Ch 34:14; 35:8
[z] 2Ch 30:10,18

[A] **33:16** Some Hb mss, Syr, Tg, Arabic; other Hb mss, LXX, Vg read *restored*
[B] **33:25** Lit *the people of the land*
[C] **34:6** One Hb tradition reads *Naphtali with their swords*; alt Hb tradition, Syr, Vg read *Naphtali, the ruins all around*; Hb obscure

and from the entire remnant of Israel, and
from all Judah, Benjamin, and the inhabitants
of Jerusalem. 10 They put it into the hands of
those doing the work—those who oversaw
the LORD's temple. They gave it to the workmen who were working in the LORD's temple,
to repair and restore the temple; 11 they gave it
to the carpenters and builders and also used
it to buy quarried stone and timbers—for
joining and making beams—for the buildings that Judah's kings had destroyed.

12 The men were doing the work with integrity. Their overseers were Jahath and
Obadiah, Levites from the Merarites, and
Zechariah and Meshullam from the Kohathites as supervisors. The Levites were all skilled
with musical instruments.[a] 13 They were also
over the porters and were supervising all
those doing the work task by task. Some of
the Levites were secretaries, officers, and
gatekeepers.

The Recovery of the Book of the Law

14 When they brought out the money that
had been deposited in the LORD's temple,
Hilkiah the priest found the book of the law
of the LORD written by the hand of Moses.[b]
15 Consequently,[c] Hilkiah told Shaphan the
court secretary, "I have found the book of
the law in the LORD's temple," and he gave the
book to Shaphan.

16 Shaphan took the book to the king, and
also reported, "Your servants are doing all
that was placed in their hands. 17 They have
emptied out the money that was found in the
LORD's temple and have put it into the hand
of the overseers and the hand of those doing
the work." 18 Then Shaphan the court secretary told the king, "Hilkiah the priest gave
me a book," and Shaphan read from it in the
presence of the king.[d]

19 When the king heard the words of the law,
he tore his clothes.[e] 20 Then he commanded
Hilkiah, Ahikam son of Shaphan, Abdon son
of Micah, Shaphan the court secretary, and
the king's servant Asaiah, 21 "Go. Ask ·Yahweh
for me and for those remaining in Israel and
Judah, concerning the words of the book that
was found. For great is the LORD's wrath that
is poured out on us[f] because our fathers have
not kept the word of the LORD in order to do
everything written in this book."

Huldah's Prophecy of Judgment

22 So Hilkiah and those the king had designated[A] went to the prophetess Huldah, the
wife of Shallum son of Tokhath, son of Hasrah, keeper of the wardrobe. She lived in Jerusalem in the Second District. They spoke with
her about this.

23 She said to them, "This is what Yahweh,
the God of Israel says: Say to the man who
sent you to Me, 24 'This is what Yahweh says: I
am about to bring disaster on this place and
on its inhabitants,[g] fulfilling all the curses
written in the book that they read in the
presence of the king of Judah,[h] 25 because they
have abandoned Me[i] and burned incense to
other gods in order to provoke Me with all
the works of their hands. My wrath will be
poured out on this place, and it will not be
quenched.' 26 Say this to the king of Judah who
sent you to ask Yahweh, 'This is what Yahweh,
the God of Israel says: As for the words that
you heard, 27 because[j] your heart was tender and you humbled yourself before God
when you heard His words against this place
and against its inhabitants, and because you
humbled yourself before Me, and you tore
your clothes and wept before Me, I Myself
have heard'—this is the LORD's declaration.
28 'I will indeed gather you to your fathers,
and you will be gathered to your grave in
peace. Your eyes will not see all the disaster
that I am bringing on this place and on its inhabitants.'"[k]

Then they reported to the king.

Affirmation of the Covenant by Josiah and the People

29 So the king sent messengers and gathered
all the elders of Judah and Jerusalem. 30 The
king went up to the LORD's temple with all the
men of Judah and the inhabitants of Jerusalem, as well as the priests and the Levites—all
the people from great to small. He read in
their hearing all the words of the book of the
covenant that had been found in the LORD's
temple.[l] 31 Then the king stood at his post[m]
and made a covenant in the LORD's presence[n]

[a] **34:12** 1Ch 25:1
[b] **34:14** Dt 31:24-26
[c] **34:15-32** 2Kg 22:8–23:3
[d] **34:18** Dt 17:18-20
[e] **34:19** Jos 7:6
[f] **34:21** 2Ch 29:8
[g] **34:24** 2Ch 36:15-21
[h] Dt 28:15-68
[i] **34:25** 2Ch 33:3
[j] **34:27-28** 1Kg 21:29; 2Ch 12:6-7; 32:26
[k] **34:28** Is 57:1-2
[l] **34:30** Neh 8:1-3
[m] **34:31** 2Kg 11:14; 2Ch 30:16
[n] 2Ch 23:16; 29:10

[A] **34:22** LXX; MT omits *designated*

to follow the LORD and to keep His commands, His decrees, and His statutes with
all his heart and with all his soul[a] in order to
carry out the words of the covenant written
in this book.[b]
32 He had all those present in Jerusalem and
Benjamin agree[A] to it. So all the inhabitants
of Jerusalem carried out the covenant of God,
the God of their ancestors.
33 So Josiah removed everything that was
detestable from all the lands belonging to
the Israelites,[c] and he required all who were
present in Israel to serve the LORD their God.
Throughout his reign they did not turn aside
from following Yahweh, the God of their ancestors.

Josiah's Passover Observance

35 Josiah observed the LORD's •Passover[d]
and slaughtered the Passover lambs
on the fourteenth day of the first month.[e]
2 He appointed the priests to their responsibilities and encouraged them to serve in the
LORD's temple.[f] 3 He said to the Levites who
taught all Israel[g] the holy things of the LORD,
"Put the holy ark in the temple built by Solomon son of David king of Israel. Since you
do not have to carry it on your shoulders,[h]
now serve •Yahweh your God and His people
Israel.
4 "Organize your ancestral houses by your
divisions[i] according to the written instruction of David king of Israel and that of his
son Solomon.[j] 5 Serve in the holy place by the
divisions of the ancestral houses for your
brothers, the lay people,[B] and the distribution of the tribal household of the Levites.[k]
6 Slaughter the Passover lambs,[l] consecrate
yourselves,[m] and make preparations for your
brothers to carry out the word of the LORD
through Moses."
7 Then Josiah donated 30,000 sheep, lambs,
and young goats, plus 3,000 bulls from his
own possessions, for the Passover sacrifices
for all the lay people[B] who were present.
8 His officials also donated willingly for the
people, the priests, and the Levites. Hilkiah,
Zechariah, and Jehiel, chief officials of God's
temple, gave 2,600 Passover sacrifices and
300 bulls for the priests. 9 Conaniah[n] and his
brothers Shemaiah and Nethanel, and Hashabiah, Jeiel, and Jozabad, officers of the Levites, donated 5,000 Passover sacrifices for the
Levites, plus 500 bulls.
10 So the service was established; the priests
stood at their posts and the Levites in their
divisions according to the king's command.[o]
11 Then they slaughtered the Passover lambs,
and while the Levites were skinning the animals,[p] the priests sprinkled the blood[C] they
had been given.[D] 12 They removed the •burnt
offerings so that they might be given to the divisions of the ancestral houses of the lay people[B] to offer to the LORD, according to what
is written in the book of Moses; they did the
same with the bulls. 13 They roasted the Passover lambs with fire according to regulation.[q]
They boiled the holy sacrifices in pots, kettles,
and bowls; and they quickly brought them to
the lay people.[B] 14 Afterward, they made preparations for themselves and for the priests,
since the priests, the descendants of Aaron,
were busy offering up burnt offerings and fat
until night. So the Levites made preparations
for themselves and for the priests, the descendants of Aaron.
15 The singers, the descendants of •Asaph,
were at their stations according to the command of David, Asaph, Heman, and Jeduthun
the king's seer.[r] Also, the gatekeepers were at
each gate.[s] None of them left their tasks because their Levite brothers had made preparations for them.
16 So all the service of the LORD was established that day for observing the Passover
and for offering burnt offerings on the altar
of the LORD, according to the command of
King Josiah. 17 The Israelites who were present
in Judah also observed the Passover at that
time and the Festival of Unleavened Bread for
seven days.[t] 18 No Passover had been observed[u]
like it in Israel since the days of Samuel the
prophet. None of the kings of Israel ever observed a Passover like the one that Josiah observed with the priests, the Levites, all Judah,
the Israelites who were present in Judah, and
the inhabitants of Jerusalem. 19 In the eighteenth year of Josiah's reign, this Passover
was observed.

[a] Dt 6:4-6
[b] Ex 24:3-8; Jos 24:14-28
[c] **34:33** 2Ch 34:3-7
[d] **35:1** 2Kg 23:21
[e] Ex 12:6; Nm 9:3
[f] **35:2** 2Ch 29:11
[g] **35:3** 2Ch 17:8-9; Neh 8:7
[h] 1Ch 23:26
[i] **35:4** 1Ch 9:10-13
[j] 2Ch 8:14
[k] **35:5** Ezr 6:18
[l] **35:6** 2Ch 35:1,11
[m] 2Ch 29:5
[n] **35:9** 2Ch 31:12-13
[o] **35:10** 2Ch 35:5
[p] **35:11** 2Ch 29:34
[q] **35:13** Ex 12:8-9
[r] **35:15** 1Ch 25:1
[s] 1Ch 26:12-19
[t] **35:17** 2Ch 30:21
[u] **35:18-19** 2Kg 23:22-23

[A] **34:32** Lit *take a stand.* [B] **35:5,7,12,13** Lit *the sons of the people* [C] **35:11** LXX, Vg, Tg; MT omits *blood* [D] **35:11** Lit *sprinkled from their hand*

Josiah's Last Deeds and Death
20After all this[a] that Josiah had prepared
for the temple, Neco king of Egypt[b] marched
up to fight at Carchemish[c] by the Euphrates,
and Josiah went out to confront him. 21But
Neco sent messengers to him, saying, "What
is the issue between you and me, king of Judah?[d] I have not come against you today[A] but
I am fighting another dynasty.[B] God told me
to hurry. Stop opposing God who is with me;
don't make Him destroy you!"
22But Josiah did not turn away from him;
instead, in order to fight with him he disguised himself.[C,e] He did not listen to Neco's
words from the mouth of God, but went to
the Valley of Megiddo[f] to fight. 23The archers
shot King Josiah, and he said to his servants,
"Take me away, for I am severely wounded!"[g]
24So his servants took him out of the war chariot, carried him in his second chariot, and
brought him to Jerusalem. Then he died, and
they buried him in the tomb of his fathers.
All Judah and Jerusalem mourned[h] for Josiah.
25Jeremiah chanted a dirge[i] over Josiah, and
all the singing men and singing women still
speak of Josiah in their dirges to this very day.
They established them as a statute for Israel,
and indeed they are written in the Dirges.
26The rest of the events[j] of Josiah's reign,
along with his deeds of faithful love according to what is written in the law of the LORD,
27and his words, from beginning to end, are
written in the Book of the Kings of Israel and
Judah.

Judah's King Jehoahaz
36 Then[k] the common people[D] took Jehoahaz son of Josiah and made him king
in Jerusalem in place of his father.
2Jehoahaz[E] was 23 years old when he became king and reigned three months in Jerusalem. 3The king of Egypt deposed him in
Jerusalem and fined the land 7,500 pounds[F]
of silver and 75 pounds[G] of gold.

Judah's King Jehoiakim
4Then Neco king of Egypt made Jehoahaz's
brother Eliakim king over Judah and Jerusalem and changed Eliakim's name to Jehoiakim. But Neco took his brother Jehoahaz[E] and
brought him to Egypt.[l]
5Jehoiakim was 25 years old when he became king and reigned 11 years in Jerusalem. He did what was evil in the sight of the
LORD his God.[m] 6Now Nebuchadnezzar king
of Babylon attacked him[n] and bound him
in bronze[o] shackles to take him to Babylon.[p]
7Also Nebuchadnezzar took some of the utensils of the LORD's temple to Babylon and put
them in his temple in Babylon.[q]
8The rest of the deeds of Jehoiakim,[r] the
detestable things he did, and what was found
against him, are written in the Book of Israel's Kings. His son Jehoiachin became king in
his place.

Judah's King Jehoiachin
9Jehoiachin was 18[H] years old[s] when he became king and reigned three months and 10
days in Jerusalem. He did what was evil in the
LORD's sight. 10In the spring[I,t] Nebuchadnezzar sent for him and brought him to Babylon
along with the valuable utensils of the LORD's
temple. Then he made Jehoiachin's brother
Zedekiah king over Judah and Jerusalem.[u]

Judah's King Zedekiah
11Zedekiah was 21 years old[v] when he became king and reigned 11 years in Jerusalem. 12He did what was evil in the sight of the
LORD his God and did not humble himself[w]
before Jeremiah the prophet at the LORD's
command.[x] 13He also rebelled against[y] King
Nebuchadnezzar who had made him swear
allegiance by God. He became obstinate[J,z]
and hardened his heart against returning to
•Yahweh, the God of Israel. 14All the leaders
of the priests and the people multiplied their
unfaithful deeds, imitating all the detestable
practices of the nations, and they defiled the
LORD's temple that He had consecrated in Jerusalem.

The Destruction of Jerusalem
15But Yahweh, the God of their ancestors
sent word against them by the hand of His

[a]**35:20-25** 2Kg 23:29-30a
[b]**35:20** Jr 46:2
[c]Is 10:9
[d]**35:21** Jdg 11:12; 2Ch 25:19
[e]**35:22** 2Ch 18:29
[f]Jdg 5:19
[g]**35:23** 2Ch 18:33
[h]**35:24** Zch 12:11
[i]**35:25** Jr 22:10; Lm 4:20
[j]**35:26-27** 2Kg 23:28
[k]**36:1-4** 2Kg 23:30b-34
[l]**36:4** Jr 22:10-12
[m]**36:5** 2Kg 23:36-37; Jr 22:13-18
[n]**36:6** 2Kg 24:1
[o]2Ch 33:11
[p]Jr 22:18-19
[q]**36:7** 2Kg 24:1-4; Jr 22:13-19; 25:1-9; Dn 1:1; Hab 1:6
[r]**36:8** 2Kg 24:5-6
[s]**36:9-10** 2Kg 24:8-17
[t]**36:10** 2Sm 11:1
[u]Jr 37:1
[v]**36:11-13** 2Kg 24:18-20; Jr 52:1-3
[w]**36:12** 2Ch 33:23
[x]Jr 21:3-7
[y]**36:13** Ezk 17:15
[z]2Ch 30:8

[A]**35:21** LXX, Syr, Tg, Vg; MT reads *Not against you, you today* [B]**35:21** Lit *house* [C]**35:22** LXX reads *he was determined* [D]**36:1** Lit *the people of the land* [E]**36:2,4** = Joahaz [F]**36:3** Lit *100 talents* [G]**36:3** Lit *one talent* [H]**36:9** Some Hb mss, LXX; 2Kg 24:8; other Hb mss read *eight* [I]**36:10** Lit *At the return of the year* [J]**36:13** Lit *He stiffened his neck*

messengers, sending them time and time
again,[a] for He had compassion on His people
and on His dwelling place. **16**But they kept
ridiculing God's messengers,[b] despising His
words,[c] and scoffing at His prophets, until
the LORD's wrath was so stirred up against
His people that there was no remedy.[d] **17**So
He brought up against them the king of the
Chaldeans,[e] who killed their choice young
men with the sword in the house of their
sanctuary. He had no pity on young men or
young women, elderly or aged; He handed
them all over to him. **18**He took everything
to Babylon — all the articles of God's temple,
large and small, the treasures of the LORD's
temple, and the treasures of the king and his
officials. **19**Then the Chaldeans burned God's
temple.[f] They tore down Jerusalem's wall,
burned down all its palaces, and destroyed
all its valuable articles.

20He deported those who escaped from the
sword to Babylon, and they became servants
to him and his sons until the rise of the Persian[A] kingdom.[g] **21**This fulfilled the word of
the LORD through Jeremiah[h] and the land enjoyed its Sabbath rest all the days of the desolation[i] until 70 years were fulfilled.

The Decree of Cyrus

22In the first year of Cyrus king of Persia,[j]
the word of the LORD spoken through[B] Jeremiah[k] was fulfilled. The LORD put it into the
mind of King Cyrus[l] of Persia to issue a proclamation throughout his entire kingdom and
also to put it in writing:

23This is what King Cyrus of Persia says:
The LORD, the God of heaven, has given
me all the kingdoms of the earth and has
appointed me to build Him a temple at
Jerusalem in Judah. Whoever among you
of His people may go up, and may the
LORD his God be with him.

[a]**36:15** Jr 7:13; 25:3,11-12 [b]**36:16** 2Ch 30:10; Jr 5:12-13 [c]Pr 1:24-32 [d]Ezr 5:12 [e]**36:17** 2Kg 25:1-7; Jr 52:4-11 [f]**36:19-20** 2Kg 25:9-11; Jr 52:13-15 [g]**36:20** Jr 27:7 [h]**36:21** Jr 25:11-12; 29:10 [i]Lv 25:4; 26:33 [j]**36:22-23** Ezr 1:1-3 [k]**36:22** Jr 25:11-14; 27:22; 29:10-14; 33:7-10 [l]Is 44:28; 45:1

[A]**36:20** LXX reads *Median* [B]**36:22** Lit *LORD by the mouth of*

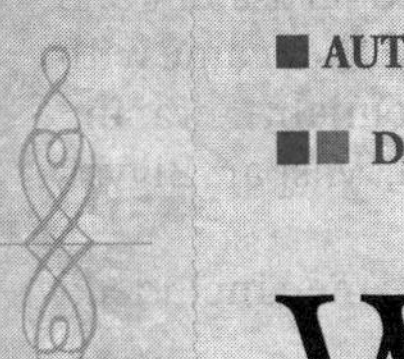

■ **AUTHOR:** Ezra (most likely)

■■ **DATE:** Ezra was written around 400 B.C. Events cover the time of the Babylonian captivity and return of the Jews (around 538–457 B.C.).

With a new era of religious tolerance dawning in the Medo-Persian empire, old antipathies melt away. Persia confidently loosens ties with its long-held captives—many who arrived in the land under Babylonian rule. *What harm could be done by people celebrating their old festivals?* King Cyrus likely thought. *May as well let them go! Their buildings will add to my treasures, their celebrations to the happiness of my kingdom.* But always behind the scenes, the Lord God Almighty works His plan: the salvation of people and worship of the one true God.

The first part of the book of Ezra reads a lot like the last part of 2 Chronicles, leading to the conclusion that the same author wrote and compiled both. Indeed, Ezra contains

EZRA

lists and documents, decrees and messages, much as one might expect in a diplomatic brief, except this brief is God-centered. Nothing happens by farce or folly. No kings or emissaries act apart from the oversight and supervision of God, whose will is made clear through prophets, then enacted by pagan kings who, oddly, appear more reverent than the old, failed kings of Israel and Judah. God works His mission through odd sorts of people. There are no dream teams here, no "special forces" trained in the skill of discerning God's will. But people—some who worship God and some who don't—are caught in the work of God literally, renovating buildings and walls, patiently and in good order. Around a reconstructed temple the people of God began to recover their worship and sense of mission.

That second temple was a pale shadow of the first one, Solomon's majestic edifice. Smaller, modestly ornamented but equipped for animal sacrifice, the people began to relearn their identity. Despite seventy years of exile from their homeland, these people are—no credit due themselves—chosen by God to carry the Word of love and forgiveness that would restore people to the family of God.

Family is important to God. Parents are primary caregivers; children are primary learners and future leaders. You can see a picture of eternity here: There are no orphans in God's kingdom. That's why Ezra speaks emphatically about family as one of the strongest images of God's Kingdom.

Family must be anchored. Family must be focused. Family cannot thrive with divided loyalties or casual indifference to their source of life and love. Ezra directs Israel's families to clean up their mistakes. They have married pagan women. These marriages are state-sanctioned but not God-sanctioned, not God-blessed. Painful corrective measures are in order. Despite the tears these measures will bring, disobedience must be addressed and disloyalty corrected. It must be done.

The challenge for Christian families is to keep the same devotion to God as Ezra insisted, the same clear allegiance to God. Mixed loyalties subvert the very thing God wants in emerging leaders—single-hearted devotion and service. God can help all people endure emotional upset and make painful corrections. Getting back to heartfelt worship and sincere love is what all families must do. Building for the future demands it.

The Decree of Cyrus

1 In[a] the first year of Cyrus king of Persia,[A]
the word of the LORD spoken through Jeremiah was fulfilled.[b] The LORD put it into the
mind[c] of King Cyrus to issue a proclamation
throughout his entire kingdom and to put it
in writing:

> [2]This is what King Cyrus of Persia says:
> "The LORD, the God of heaven, has given
> me all the kingdoms of the earth and has
> appointed me to build Him a house at Je-
> rusalem in Judah.[d] [3]Whoever is among His
> people, may his God be with him, and may
> he go to Jerusalem in Judah and build the
> house of the LORD, the God of Israel,[e] the
> God who is in Jerusalem. [4]Let every survi-
> vor,[f] wherever he lives, be assisted by the
> men of that region with silver, gold, goods,
> and livestock, along with a freewill offer-
> ing for the house of God in Jerusalem."

Return from Exile

[5]So the family leaders of Judah and Benjamin, along with the priests and Levites—everyone God had motivated[B,g]—prepared to
go up and rebuild the LORD's house in Jerusalem. [6]All their neighbors supported them[C,h]
with silver articles, gold, goods, livestock, and
valuables, in addition to all that was given as
a freewill offering. [7]King Cyrus also brought
out the articles of the LORD's house that Nebuchadnezzar had taken from Jerusalem and
had placed in the house of his gods.[i] [8]King
Cyrus of Persia had them brought out under
the supervision of Mithredath the treasurer,
who counted them out to Sheshbazzar the
prince of Judah.[j] [9]This was the inventory:

> 30 gold basins, 1,000 silver basins,
> 29 silver knives, [10]30 gold bowls,
> 410 various[D] silver bowls,
> and 1,000 other articles.

[11]The gold and silver articles totaled 5,400.
Sheshbazzar brought all of them when the
exiles went up from Babylon to Jerusalem.

The Exiles Who Returned

2 These[k] now are the people of the province
who came from those captive exiles King
Nebuchadnezzar of Babylon[E] had deported
to Babylon.[l] They returned to Jerusalem and
Judah, each to his own town. [2]They came with
Zerubbabel,[m] Jeshua,[n] Nehemiah, Seraiah,[o]
Reelaiah, Mordecai, Bilshan, Mispar, Bigvai,
Rehum, and Baanah.

The number of the Israelite men included:[F]

3	Parosh's descendants[p]	2,172
4	Shephatiah's descendants	372
5	Arah's descendants	775
6	Pahath-moab's descendants: Jeshua's and Joab's descendants	2,812
7	Elam's descendants	1,254
8	Zattu's descendants	945
9	Zaccai's descendants	760
10	Bani's descendants	642
11	Bebai's descendants	623
12	Azgad's descendants	1,222
13	Adonikam's descendants[q]	666
14	Bigvai's descendants	2,056
15	Adin's descendants	454
16	Ater's descendants: of Hezekiah	98
17	Bezai's descendants	323
18	Jorah's descendants	112
19	Hashum's descendants	223
20	Gibbar's descendants	95
21	Bethlehem's[r] people	123
22	Netophah's men	56
23	Anathoth's men	128
24	Azmaveth's people	42
25	Kiriatharim's, Chephirah's, and Beeroth's people	743
26	Ramah's[s] and Geba's people	621
27	Michmas's men	122
28	Bethel's and Ai's[t] men	223
29	Nebo's people	52
30	Magbish's people	156
31	the other Elam's people	1,254
32	Harim's people	320
33	Lod's, Hadid's, and Ono's people	725
34	Jericho's[u] people	345
35	Senaah's people	3,630

[36]The priests included:

	Jedaiah's descendants of the house of Jeshua	973
37	Immer's descendants	1,052
38	Pashhur's descendants	1,247
39	and Harim's descendants	1,017

[a]1:1 2Ch 36:22-23 [b]Jr 25:12; 29:10-14 [c]Ezr 7:27 [d]1:2-3 Is 44:28; 45:1,13; Dn 9:17 [e]1:3 Dn 6:26 [f]1:4 Neh 1:2; Is 10:20-22 [g]1:5 Ezr 1:1 [h]1:6 Ezr 6:22 [i]1:7 2Ch 36:7,10,18; Dn 1:2; 5:2-3 [j]1:8 Ezr 5:14,16 [k]2:1-70 Neh 7:6-73 [l]2:1 2Ch 36:17-20 [m]2:2 1Ch 3:19; Ezr 3:2; Hg 1:1; Zch 4:6 [n]Hg 1:1; Zch 3:1-10 [o]Neh 12:1 [p]2:3 Ezr 8:3; 10:25; Neh 3:25 [q]2:13 Ezr 8:13 [r]2:21 Mc 5:2; Mt 2:1,6 [s]2:26 Jr 31:15; Mt 2:18 [t]2:28 Gn 12:8; Jos 7:2; 8:9 [u]2:34 Jos 4:19; 5:13; 6:1-25

A1:1 Cyrus reigned 559–530 B.C. B1:5 Lit *everyone whose spirit God had stirred* C1:6 Lit *supported their hands* D1:10 Or *similar* E2:1 Nebuchadnezzar reigned 605–562 B.C. F2:2 Lit *the men of the people of Israel*

[40]The Levites included:
Jeshua's and Kadmiel's descendants
from Hodaviah's descendants 74
[41]The singers included:
·Asaph's[a] descendants 128
[42]The gatekeepers'[b] descendants included:
Shallum's descendants,
Ater's descendants,
Talmon's descendants,
Akkub's descendants,
Hatita's descendants,
Shobai's descendants, in all 139
[43]The temple servants[c] included:
Ziha's descendants,
Hasupha's descendants,
Tabbaoth's descendants,
[44]Keros's descendants,
Siaha's descendants,
Padon's descendants,
[45] Lebanah's descendants,
Hagabah's descendants,
Akkub's descendants,
[46]Hagab's descendants,
Shalmai's[A] descendants,
Hanan's descendants,
[47] Giddel's descendants,
Gahar's descendants,
Reaiah's descendants,
[48]Rezin's descendants,
Nekoda's descendants,
Gazzam's descendants,
[49] Uzza's descendants,
Paseah's descendants,
Besai's descendants,
[50]Asnah's descendants,
Meunim's[B] descendants,
Nephusim's[C] descendants,
[51] Bakbuk's descendants,
Hakupha's descendants,
Harhur's descendants,
[52]Bazluth's descendants,
Mehida's descendants,
Harsha's descendants,
[53] Barkos's descendants,
Sisera's descendants,
Temah's descendants,
[54]Neziah's descendants,
and Hatipha's descendants.

[a]2:41 1Ch 25:1; 2Ch 5:12; 35:15
[b]2:42 1Ch 9:17-32; Neh 12:25-26
[c]2:43 Ezr 8:20
[d]2:55 Neh 11:3
[e]2:63 Ezr 6:7; Neh 5:14; Hg 1:1
[f]Ex 28:30; Lv 8:8; Nm 27:21; Neh 7:65
[g]2:65 2Ch 35:25
[h]2:68 Nm 15:3; Ezr 1:4

[55]The descendants of Solomon's servants[d] included:
Sotai's descendants,
Hassophereth's descendants,
Peruda's descendants,
[56]Jaalah's descendants,
Darkon's descendants,
Giddel's descendants,
[57] Shephatiah's descendants,
Hattil's descendants,
Pochereth-hazzebaim's descendants,
and Ami's descendants.
[58] All the temple servants
and the descendants
of Solomon's servants 392.

[59]The following are those who came from
Tel-melah, Tel-harsha, Cherub, Addan, and
Immer but were unable to prove that their
families and ancestry were Israelite:
[60] Delaiah's descendants,
Tobiah's descendants,
Nekoda's descendants 652
[61]and from the descendants of the priests: the
descendants of Hobaiah, the descendants of
Hakkoz, the descendants of Barzillai — who
had taken a wife from the daughters of Barzillai the Gileadite and was called by their
name. [62]These searched for their entries in
the genealogical records, but they could not
be found, so they were disqualified from the
priesthood. [63]The governor[e] ordered them
not to eat the most holy things until there
was a priest who could consult the ·Urim and
Thummim.[f]

[64] The whole combined assembly
numbered 42,360
[65] not including their 7,337 male
and female slaves,
and their 200 male and female singers.[g]
[66] They had 736 horses, 245 mules,
[67] 435 camels, and 6,720 donkeys.

Gifts for the Work

[68]After they arrived at the LORD's house in
Jerusalem, some of the family leaders gave
freewill offerings[h] for the house of God in
order to have it rebuilt on its original site.
[69]Based on what they could give, they gave

[A]2:46 Alt Hb tradition reads *Shamlai's* [B]2:50 Alt Hb tradition reads *Meinim's* [C]2:50 Alt Hb tradition reads *Nephisim's*

61,000 gold coins,[A] 6,250 pounds[B] of silver, and 100 priestly garments to the treasury[a] for the project. 70The priests, Levites, singers, gatekeepers, temple servants, and some of the people settled in their towns, and the rest of Israel settled in their towns.[b]

Sacrifice Restored

3 By the seventh month,[c] the Israelites had settled in their towns, and the people gathered together in Jerusalem.[d] 2Jeshua son of Jozadak and his brothers the priests along with Zerubbabel son of Shealtiel[e] and his brothers began to build the altar of Israel's God in order to offer •burnt offerings on it, as it is written in the law of Moses, the man of God.[f] 3They set up the altar on its foundation and offered burnt offerings for the morning and evening on it to the LORD even though they feared the surrounding peoples.[g] 4They celebrated the Festival of Booths as prescribed, and offered burnt offerings each day, based on the number specified by ordinance for each festival day.[h] 5After that, they offered the regular burnt offering and the offerings for the beginning of each month[C,i] and for all the LORD's appointed holy occasions, as well as the freewill offerings brought to[D] the LORD.

6On the first day of the seventh month they began to offer burnt offerings to the LORD,[j] even though the foundation of the LORD's temple had not yet been laid. 7They gave money to the stonecutters and artisans, and gave food, drink, and oil to the people of Sidon and Tyre, so they could bring cedar wood from Lebanon to Joppa by sea,[k] according to the authorization given them by King Cyrus of Persia.[l]

Rebuilding the Temple

8In the second month of the second year after they arrived at God's house in Jerusalem, Zerubbabel son of Shealtiel, Jeshua son of Jozadak,[m] and the rest of their brothers, including the priests, the Levites, and all who had returned to Jerusalem from the captivity, began to build. They appointed the Levites who were 20 years old or more to supervise the work on the LORD's house.[n] 9Jeshua with his sons and brothers, Kadmiel with his sons, and the sons of Judah[E] and of Henadad, with their sons and brothers, the Levites,[o] joined together to supervise those working on the house of God.

Temple Foundation Completed

10When the builders had laid the foundation of the LORD's temple, the priests, dressed in their robes and holding trumpets, and the Levites descended from •Asaph,[p] holding cymbals, took their positions to praise the LORD, as King David of Israel had instructed.[q] 11They sang with praise and thanksgiving to the LORD: "For He is good; His faithful love to Israel endures forever."[r] Then all the people gave a great shout of praise to the LORD because the foundation of the LORD's house had been laid.[s]

12But many of the older priests, Levites, and family leaders, who had seen the first temple, wept loudly when they saw the foundation of this house,[t] but many others shouted joyfully. 13The people could not distinguish the sound of the joyful shouting from that of the[F] weeping,[u] because the people were shouting so loudly. And the sound was heard far away.

Opposition to Rebuilding the Temple

4 When the enemies of Judah and Benjamin[v] heard that the returned exiles[G,w] were building a temple for •Yahweh, the God of Israel, 2they approached Zerubbabel and the leaders of the families and said to them, "Let us build with you, for we also worship your God and have been sacrificing to Him[H] since the time King Esar-haddon of Assyria[I] brought us here."[x]

3But Zerubbabel, Jeshua, and the other leaders of Israel's families answered them, "You may have no part with us in building a house for our God,[y] since we alone must build it for Yahweh, the God of Israel, as King Cyrus, the king of Persia has commanded us."[z] 4Then the people who were already in the land[J] discouraged[K] the people of Judah and made them afraid[aa] to build. 5They also

[a]**2:69** Ezr 8:33-34
[b]**2:70** 1Ch 9:2; Neh 11:3
[c]**3:1** Lv 23:23-43; Nm 29:1-38
[d]Neh 7:73–8:1
[e]**3:2** Ezr 3:8; 5:2; Hg 1:1; 2:21,23
[f]Ex 27:1-8
[g]**3:3** Ezr 4:4
[h]**3:4** Lv 23:33-43; Nm 29:12-38; Neh 8:13-18; Zch 14:16
[i]**3:5** Nm 28:11-14; 1Sm 20:5
[j]**3:6** Lv 23:23-25; Nm 29:1-6
[k]**3:7** 1Kg 5:1-11; 2Ch 2:3-16
[l]Ezr 1:2; 6:3-5
[m]**3:8** Ezr 4:3; 5:2; Hg 1:1
[n]1Ch 23:4,24
[o]**3:9** Ezr 2:40
[p]**3:10** Ezr 2:41
[q]1Ch 6:31; 25:1,6; 2Ch 29:25-26; Neh 12:24,45
[r]**3:11** 1Ch 16:34; 2Ch 5:13; 7:3; Neh 12:31
[s]Hg 2:18; Zch 4:9
[t]**3:12** Hg 2:3
[u]**3:13** Ps 126:5-6
[v]**4:1** Neh 2:19-20
[w]Ezr 1:11; 2:1
[x]**4:2** 2Ki 17:24,27-32; 19:37; Is 37:38
[y]**4:3** Neh 2:20
[z]Ezr 1:1-4
[aa]**4:4** Ezr 3:3

A**2:69** Or *drachmas*, or *darics* B**2:69** Lit *5,000 minas* C**3:5** Lit *for the new moons* D**3:5** Lit *well as those of everyone making a freewill offering to* E**3:9** Or *Hodaviah*; Neh 7:43; 1 Esdras 5:58 F**3:13** Lit *the people* G**4:1** Lit *the sons of the exile* H**4:2** Alt Hb tradition reads *have not been sacrificing* I**4:2** Esar-haddon reigned 681–669 B.C. J**4:4** Lit *people of the land* K**4:4** Lit *relaxed the hands of*

Richard Wurmbrand (1909–2001)

Richard Wurmbrand's life is a testimony that God often uses our suffering for the sake of the world and the sake of His church. Our sufferings are never meaningless when they are in the hands of our redeeming God.

Wurmbrand grew up in Romania as an active communist, but he and his wife were converted to the Christian faith in 1938 through the testimony of a carpenter named Christian Wolfkes. Wurmbrand pursued the ministry and was ordained first in the Anglican church, then the Lutheran.

When the Soviet Union occupied Romania and began to establish communism in the country, Wurmbrand began to speak out against it. He shared the gospel with both the Romanian people and the Russian people. He had Bibles printed in Russian so that the soldiers might also come to know Christ, and his congregants even threw Russian Scriptures into the windows of trains full of Russian soldiers. Eventually the government began to control church activity, so Wurmbrand moved his ministry underground. In 1948, he was kidnapped by the secret police and spent the next eight and a half years in prison. He faced brutal torture and spent three of the years in solitary confinement with no windows, lights, or sounds. Despite the trials of his time in prison, Wurmbrand continued in ministry upon his release in 1956, and was arrested again in 1959. Like Paul, he would not live in fear of those who imprisoned him, but continued to risk himself for the sake of the gospel.

In 1964, Wurmbrand was given amnesty and immigrated to the United States to be free from persecution, but also to be a voice for others whose lives were threatened because of their faith. His suffering in Romania led to the beginning of the Voice of the Martyrs, an organization that helps persecuted Christians all over the world by making their stories heard, equipping them with the Scriptures, food, and other resources as they are needed. Christianity is still illegal in many countries and believers are often persecuted, but even after Wurmbrand's death in 2001, Voice of the Martyrs continues to fight for them, following the words of Hebrews 13:3, "Remember the prisoners, as though you were in prison with them, and the mistreated, as though you yourselves were suffering bodily."

Richard Wurmbrand and his family faced terrible persecution in Romania, but God used and continues to use their lives and their stories to care for and equip Christians all over the world who face similar affliction for their faith in Jesus Christ.

Image of Richard Wurmbrand used with permission by The Voice of the Martyrs/www.persecution.com.

bribed officials to act against them to frus-
trate their plans[a] throughout the reign of
King Cyrus of Persia and until the reign of
King Darius of Persia.[A,b]

Opposition to Rebuilding the City

6 At the beginning of the reign of Ahasuerus,[B,c] the people who were already in the
land[C,d] wrote an accusation against the residents of Judah and Jerusalem. 7 During the
time of King Artaxerxes of Persia,[D,e] Bishlam,
Mithredath, Tabeel and the rest of his colleagues wrote to King Artaxerxes. The letter
was written in Aramaic[f] and translated.[E,F]

8 Rehum the chief deputy and Shimshai the
scribe[g] wrote a letter to King Artaxerxes concerning Jerusalem as follows:

> 9 From Rehum[G] the chief deputy, Shim-
> shai the scribe, and the rest of their col-
> leagues — the judges and magistrates[H]
> from Tripolis, Persia, Erech, Babylon,
> Susa[h] (that is, the people of Elam),[I] 10 and
> the rest of the peoples whom the great
> and illustrious Ashurbanipal[J] deported
> and settled in the cities of Samaria[i] and
> the region west of the Euphrates River.[j]

11 This is the text of the letter they sent to him:

> To King Artaxerxes from your servants,
> the men from the region west of the Eu-
> phrates River:
>
> 12 Let it be known to the king that the Jews
> who came from you have returned to us
> at Jerusalem. They are rebuilding that re-
> bellious and evil city, finishing its walls,
> and repairing its foundations. 13 Let it
> now be known to the king that if that city
> is rebuilt and its walls are finished,[k] they
> will not pay tribute, duty, or land tax,[l]
> and the royal revenue[I] will suffer. 14 Since
> we have taken an oath of loyalty to the
> king,[K] and it is not right for us to witness
> his dishonor, we have sent to inform the
> king 15 that a search should be made in
> your fathers' record books.[m] In these rec-
> ord books you will discover and verify
> that the city is a rebellious city, harmful
> to kings and provinces. There have been
> revolts in it since ancient times. That is
> why this city was destroyed. 16 We advise
> the king that if this city is rebuilt and its
> walls are finished, you will not have any
> possession west of the Euphrates.

Artaxerxes' Reply

17 The king sent a reply to his chief deputy
Rehum, Shimshai the scribe, and the rest of
their colleagues living in Samaria and elsewhere in the region west of the Euphrates
River:

> Greetings.
>
> 18 The letter you sent us has been trans-
> lated and read[L,n] in my presence. 19 I
> issued a decree and a search was con-
> ducted. It was discovered that this city
> has had uprisings against kings since an-
> cient times, and there have been rebel-
> lions and revolts in it. 20 Powerful kings
> have also ruled over Jerusalem and ex-
> ercised authority over the whole region,
> and tribute, duty, and land tax were paid
> to them. 21 Therefore, issue an order for
> these men to stop, so that this city will
> not be rebuilt until a further decree has
> been pronounced by me.[o] 22 See that you
> not neglect this matter. Otherwise, the
> damage will increase and the royal inter-
> ests[M] will suffer.

23 As soon as the text of King Artaxerxes' letter was read to Rehum, Shimshai the scribe,
and their colleagues,[p] they immediately went
to the Jews in Jerusalem and forcibly stopped
them.

Rebuilding of the Temple Resumed

24 Now the construction of God's house in
Jerusalem had stopped and remained at a
standstill until the second year of the reign
of King Darius of Persia.[q] **5** 1 But when the
prophets Haggai and Zechariah son of
Iddo[r] prophesied to the Jews who were in Judah and Jerusalem, in the name of the God
of Israel who was over them, 2 Zerubbabel
son of Shealtiel and Jeshua son of Jozadak[s]
began to rebuild God's house in Jerusalem.

[a] **4:5** Neh 6:12-13; 13:2
[b] Ezr 5:5; 6:1
[c] **4:6** Est 1:1; Dn 9:1
[d] Ezr 3:3
[e] **4:7** Ezr 7:1; Neh 2:1
[f] Dn 1:4; 2:4
[g] **4:8-9** Ezr 4:17,23-24
[h] **4:9** Neh 1:1; Est 1:2; Dn 8:2
[i] **4:10** 2Kg 17:24
[j] **4:10-11** Ezr 4:16-17,20
[k] **4:13** Ezr 4:16,21; Neh 1:3
[l] Ezr 4:20; 7:24
[m] **4:15** Ezr 5:17; 6:1
[n] **4:18** Neh 8:8
[o] **4:21** Neh 2:5,7-8
[p] **4:23** Ezr 4:8-10,17
[q] **4:24** Ezr 4:1-5; Hg 1:1,14
[r] **5:1** Ezr 6:14; Hg 1:1; Zch 1:1
[s] **5:2** Ezr 3:2,8,10

[A] **4:5** Darius reigned 521–486 B.C. [B] **4:6** = Xerxes; he reigned 486–465 B.C. [C] **4:6** Lit *people of the land* [D] **4:7** Artaxerxes reigned 465–425 B.C. [E] **4:7** Lit *translated. Aramaic:* [F] **4:7** Ezr 4:8–6:18 is written in Aram. [G] **4:9** Lit *Then Rehum* [H] **4:9** Or *ambassadors* [I] **4:9,13** Aram obscure [J] **4:10** Lit *Osnappar* [K] **4:14** Lit *have eaten the salt of the palace* [L] **4:18** Or *been read clearly* [M] **4:22** Lit *the kings*

The prophets of God[a] were with them, helping them.
3At that time Tattenai the governor of the
region west of the Euphrates River, Shethar-
bozenai, and their colleagues[b] came to the
Jews and asked, "Who gave you the order
to rebuild this temple and finish this structure?"[A,c] 4They also asked them, "What are the
names of the workers[B] who are constructing
this building?" 5But God was watching[C] over[d]
the Jewish elders. These men wouldn't stop
them until a report was sent to Darius, so that
they could receive written instructions about
this matter.

The Letter to Darius

6This is the text of the letter that Tattenai
the governor of the region west of the Euphrates River, Shethar-bozenai, and their
colleagues, the officials in the region, sent to
King Darius. 7They sent him a report, written
as follows:

To King Darius:

All greetings.

8Let it be known to the king that we went
to the house of the great God in the province of Judah. It is being built with cut[D]
stones, and its beams are being set in the
walls. This work is being done diligently
and succeeding through the people's efforts.[e] 9So we questioned the elders and
asked, "Who gave you the order to rebuild this temple and finish this structure?"[A] 10We also asked them for their
names, so that we could write down the
names of their leaders for your information.

11This is the reply they gave us:

We are the servants of the God of heaven
and earth and are rebuilding the temple
that was built many years ago, which a
great king of Israel built and finished.[f]
12But since our fathers angered the God
of heaven, He handed them over to King
Nebuchadnezzar of Babylon, the Chaldean, who destroyed this temple and
deported the people to Babylon.[g] 13How-
ever, in the first year of Cyrus king of
Babylon, he issued a decree to rebuild
the house of God.[h] 14He also took from
the temple in Babylon the gold and silver
articles of God's house that Nebuchadnezzar had taken from the temple in
Jerusalem and carried them to the temple in Babylon.[i] He released them from
the temple in Babylon to a man named
Sheshbazzar, the governor by the appointment of King Cyrus.[j] 15Cyrus told
him, "Take these articles, put them in the
temple in Jerusalem, and let the house
of God be rebuilt on its original site."[k]
16Then this same Sheshbazzar came and
laid the foundation of God's house in Jerusalem.[l] It has been under construction
from that time until now,[m] yet it has not
been completed.

17So if it pleases the king, let a search of
the royal archives[E] in Babylon be conducted to see if it is true that a decree
was issued by King Cyrus to rebuild the
house of God in Jerusalem.[n] Let the king's
decision regarding this matter be sent
to us.[o]

Darius's Search

6 King Darius gave the order, and they
searched[p] in the library of Babylon in
the archives.[F,q] 2But it was in the fortress
of Ecbatana in the province of Media[r] that
a scroll was found with this record written
on it:

3In the first year of King Cyrus, he issued
a decree[s] concerning the house of God in
Jerusalem:

Let the house be rebuilt as a place for
offering sacrifices, and let its original
foundations be retained.[G] Its height is to
be 90 feet[H] and its width 90 feet,[H,I,t] 4with
three layers of cut[J] stones and one of timber.[u] The cost is to be paid from the royal
treasury.[v] 5The gold and silver articles of
God's house that Nebuchadnezzar took

[a]**5:2** Ezr 6:14
[b]**5:3** Ezr 6:6,13
[c]Ezr 1:1-4; 5:9,13; 6:3
[d]**5:5** Ezr 7:6,9,28; 8:18,22,31
[e]**5:8** Ezr 6:3-4
[f]**5:11** 1Kg 6:1,37-38
[g]**5:12** 2Ch 36:19-20
[h]**5:13** 2Ch 36:22-23; Ezr 1:1-4
[i]**5:14** 2Ch 36:7,10,18; Ezr 1:7; Dn 5:2-3
[j]Ezr 1:8,11
[k]**5:15** Ezr 6:5
[l]**5:16** Ezr 3:10
[m]Ezr 5:1-5
[n]**5:17** 2Ch 36:22-23; Ezr 1:1-4
[o]Ezr 6:1-12
[p]**6:1** Ezr 5:17
[q]Ezr 4:15
[r]**6:2** Dn 9:1; Ac 2:9
[s]**6:3** 2Ch 36:22-23; Ezr 1:1-4
[t]1Kg 6:2
[u]**6:4** 1Kg 6:36; Ezr 5:8
[v]Ezr 3:7

A**5:3,9** Or *finish its furnishings* B**5:4** One Aram ms, LXX, Syr; MT reads *Then we told them exactly what the names of the men were* C**5:5** Lit *But the eye of their God was* D**5:8** Or *huge* E**5:17** Lit *treasure house* F**6:1** Lit *Babylon where the treasures were stored* G**6:3** Lit *be brought forth* H**6:3** Lit *60 cubits*

I**6:3** A copyist seemingly overlooked the term for length and inadvertently read the 60 cubits for height and width. Like Solomon's temple, this temple was probably 90 feet long, 30 feet wide, and 45 feet high. J**6:4** Or *huge*

from the temple in Jerusalem and carried to Babylon must also be returned.
They are to be brought to the temple in
Jerusalem where they belong[A] and put
into the house of God.[a]

Darius's Decree

6Therefore, you must stay away from
that place, Tattenai governor of the region west of the Euphrates River, Shethar-bozenai, and your[B] colleagues, the
officials in the region.[b] 7Leave the construction of the house of God alone. Let
the governor[c] and elders of the Jews rebuild this house of God on its original
site.

8I hereby issue a decree concerning what
you must do, so that the elders of the
Jews can rebuild the house of God:

The cost is to be paid in full to these
men out of the royal revenues[d] from the
taxes of the region west of the Euphrates River, so that the work will not stop.
9Whatever is needed—young bulls,
rams, and lambs for •burnt offerings to
the God of heaven, or wheat, salt, wine,
and oil, as requested by the priests in Jerusalem—let it be given to them every
day without fail,[e] 10so that they can offer
sacrifices of pleasing aroma to the God
of heaven and pray for the life of the king
and his sons.[f]

11I also issue a decree concerning any
man who interferes with this directive:

Let a beam be torn from his house and
raised up; he will be impaled on it, and
his house will be made into a garbage
dump because of this offense.[g] 12May
the God who caused His name to dwell
there[h] overthrow any king or people
who dares[C] to harm or interfere with
this house of God in Jerusalem. I, Darius,
have issued the decree. Let it be carried
out diligently.

13Then Tattenai governor of the region west
of the Euphrates River, Shethar-bozenai, and
their colleagues[i] diligently carried out what
King Darius had decreed. 14So the Jewish elders continued successfully with the building
under the prophesying of Haggai the prophet
and Zechariah son of Iddo.[j] They finished
the building according to the command of
the God of Israel and the decrees of Cyrus,[k]
Darius, and King Artaxerxes[l] of Persia. 15This
house was completed on the third day of the
month of Adar[D,m] in the sixth year of the reign
of King Darius.

Temple Dedication and the Passover

16Then the Israelites, including the priests,
the Levites, and the rest of the exiles, celebrated the dedication of the house of God
with joy. 17For the dedication of God's house
they offered 100 bulls, 200 rams, and 400
lambs, as well as 12 male goats[n] as a •sin offering for all Israel—one for each Israelite
tribe. 18They also appointed the priests by
their divisions and the Levites by their groups
to the service of God in Jerusalem, according
to what is written in the book of Moses.[o]

19The exiles[p] observed the •Passover[q] on the
fourteenth day of the first month. 20All of the
priests and Levites were ceremonially •clean,
because they had purified themselves. They
killed the Passover lamb for themselves, their
priestly brothers, and all the exiles.[r] 21The Israelites who had returned from exile[s] ate it,
together with all who had separated themselves from the uncleanness of the Gentiles
of the land[E,t] in order to worship •Yahweh,
the God of Israel. 22They observed the Festival of •Unleavened Bread for seven days[u] with
joy, because the LORD had made them joyful,
having changed the Assyrian king's attitude
toward them, so that he supported them[F] in
the work on the house of the God of Israel.[v]

Ezra's Arrival

7 After these events, during the reign of
King Artaxerxes[w] of Persia, Ezra—

Seraiah's[x] son, Azariah's son,
Hilkiah's[y] son, 2Shallum's son,
Zadok's[z] son, Ahitub's son,
3 Amariah's son, Azariah's son,
Meraioth's son, 4Zerahiah's son,
Uzzi's son, Bukki's son,
5 Abishua's son, Phinehas's son,

[a]6:5 Ezr 1:7
[b]6:6 Ezr 5:3,6; 6:13
[c]6:7 Neh 5:14; Hg 1:1
[d]6:8 Ezr 7:20
[e]6:9 Ezr 7:17,20-22
[f]6:10 Ezr 7:23; 1Tm 2:1-2
[g]6:11 Est 2:23; 9:14
[h]6:12 Dt 12:5; 2Ch 6:2
[i]6:13 Ezr 5:3,6; 6:6
[j]6:14 Ezr 5:1; Hg 1:1; Zch 1:1
[k]Ezr 1:1-4; 6:3-5
[l]Ezr 7:12-26
[m]6:15 Est 3:7
[n]6:16-17 2Ch 7:4-5
[o]6:18 Ex 29; Nm 18; 1Ch 24
[p]6:19 Ezr 1:11; 2:1
[q]Ex 12:1-11; Nm 28:16
[r]6:20 2Ch 30:15-17
[s]6:21 Ezr 1:11; 2:1
[t]Ezr 9:11; Neh 10:28
[u]6:22 Ex 12:14-20; Dt 16:3-8
[v]Ezr 6:8-12
[w]7:1 Ezr 4:7; 6:14; Neh 2:1
[x]2Kg 25:18-21; Jr 52:24-27
[y]2Kg 22:4; 23:4
[z]7:2 1Sm 8:17; 1Kg 1:7-8; 2:35

[A]6:5 Lit *Jerusalem, to its place,* [B]6:6 Lit *their* [C]6:12 Lit *who stretches out its hand* [D]6:15 = February–March [E]6:21 Lit *land to them* [F]6:22 Lit *their hands*

Eleazar's son, Aaron the chief priest's
son[a]

6 — came up from Babylon. He was a scribe
skilled in the law of Moses,[b] which •Yahweh,
the God of Israel, had given. The king had
granted him everything he requested[c] because the hand of Yahweh his God was on
him.[d] 7 Some of the Israelites, priests, Levites,
singers, gatekeepers, and temple servants[e] accompanied him to Jerusalem in the seventh
year of King Artaxerxes.

8 Ezra[A] came to Jerusalem in the fifth month,
during the seventh year of the king. 9 He began the journey from Babylon on the first day
of the first month[f] and arrived in Jerusalem
on the first day of the fifth month[g] since the
gracious hand of his God was on him.[h] 10 Now
Ezra had determined in his heart to study the
law of the LORD, obey it, and teach[i] its statutes
and ordinances in Israel.

Letter from Artaxerxes

11 This is the text of the letter King Artaxerxes gave to Ezra the priest and scribe, an
expert in matters of the LORD's commands
and statutes for Israel:[B]

> 12 Artaxerxes, king of kings,[j] to Ezra the
> priest, an expert in the law of the God of
> heaven:
>
> Greetings.
>
> 13 I issue a decree that any of the Israelites
> in my kingdom, including their priests
> and Levites, who want to go to Jerusa-
> lem, may go with you.[k] 14 You are sent
> by the king and his seven counselors[l] to
> evaluate Judah and Jerusalem according
> to the law of your God, which is in your
> possession. 15 You are also to bring the sil-
> ver and gold the king and his counselors
> have willingly given to the God of Israel,[m]
> whose dwelling is in Jerusalem,[n] 16 and all
> the silver and gold you receive through-
> out the province of Babylon, together
> with the freewill offerings given by the
> people and the priests to the house of
> their God in Jerusalem.[o] 17 Then you are
> to buy with this money as many bulls,
> rams, and lambs as needed, along with
> their •grain and •drink offerings, and of-
> fer them on the altar at the house of your
> God in Jerusalem.[p] 18 You may do what-
> ever seems best to you and your broth-
> ers with the rest of the silver and gold,
> according to the will of your God. 19 You
> must deliver to the God of Jerusalem all
> the articles given to you for the service
> of the house of your God.[q] 20 You may use
> the royal treasury to pay for anything
> else needed for the house of your God.[r]
>
> 21 I, King Artaxerxes, issue a decree to all
> the treasurers in the region west of the
> Euphrates River:[s]
>
> Whatever Ezra the priest, an expert in
> the law of the God of heaven, asks of
> you must be provided promptly,[t] 22 up to
> 7,500 pounds[C] of silver, 500 bushels[D] of
> wheat, 550 gallons[E] of wine, 550 gallons[E]
> of oil, and salt without limit.[F] 23 What-
> ever is commanded by the God of heaven
> must be done diligently for the house
> of the God of heaven, so that wrath will
> not fall on the realm of the king and his
> sons.[u] 24 Be advised that tribute, duty, and
> land tax must not be imposed on any
> priests, Levites, singers, doorkeepers,
> temple servants, or other servants of this
> house of God.
>
> 25 And you, Ezra, according to[G] God's
> wisdom that you possess, appoint mag-
> istrates and judges to judge all the peo-
> ple in the region west of the Euphrates
> who know the laws of your God and to
> teach anyone who does not know them.[v]
> 26 Anyone who does not keep the law of
> your God and the law of the king, let a
> fair judgment be executed against him,
> whether death, banishment, confisca-
> tion of property, or imprisonment.[w]

27 Praise Yahweh the God of our fathers,
who has put it into the king's mind[x] to glorify
the house of the LORD in Jerusalem,[y] 28 and
who has shown favor to me before the king,[z]
his counselors, and all his powerful officers.
So I took courage because I was strengthened

[a] 7:1-5 1Ch 6:3-15
[b] 7:6 Ezr 7:11-12,21
[c] Neh 2:4-8
[d] Ezr 7:28; 8:22; Neh 2:8,18
[e] 7:7 Ezr 2:1-58; Neh 7:6-60
[f] 7:9 Ezr 8:15,21,31
[g] Ezr 8:32
[h] Ezr 7:28; 8:18,31; Neh 2:8,18
[i] 7:10 Neh 8:1-8
[j] 7:12 Ezk 26:7; Dn 2:37
[k] 7:13 Ezr 1:3
[l] 7:14 Est 1:14
[m] 7:15 Hg 2:8
[n] Dt 12:5-6; 2Ch 6:2
[o] 7:16 Ex 3:22; Ezr 1:6
[p] 7:17 Nm 15:1-14; Ezr 6:9
[q] 7:19 Ezr 8:33
[r] 7:20 Ezr 6:4,8; 7:22-23
[s] 7:21 Ezr 4:10; 7:25
[t] Ezr 6:8
[u] 7:23 Ezr 6:10
[v] 7:25 Ezr 7:10; Neh 8:1-3,8
[w] 7:26 Ezr 6:11
[x] 7:27 Ezr 6:22
[y] Is 60:7,13
[z] 7:28 Ezr 9:9

A 7:8 LXX, Syr, Vg read *They* B 7:11 Ezr 7:12-26 is written in Aram. C 7:22 Lit *100 talents* D 7:22 Lit *100 cors* E 7:22 Lit *100 baths* F 7:22 Lit *without instruction*
G 7:25 Lit *to your*

by Yahweh my God,[A,a] and I gathered Israelite leaders to return with me.[b]

Those Returning with Ezra

8 These are the family leaders and the genealogical records of those who returned with me from Babylon during the reign of King Artaxerxes:[c]

2 Gershom, from Phinehas's descendants;
Daniel, from Ithamar's descendants;
Hattush, from David's descendants,
3 who was of Shecaniah's descendants;[d]
Zechariah, from Parosh's[e] descendants,
and 150 men[B] with him
who were registered by genealogy;
4 Eliehoenai son of Zerahiah
from Pahath-moab's descendants,[f]
and 200 men with him;
5 Shecaniah[C] son of Jahaziel
from Zattu's descendants,
and 300 men with him;
6 Ebed son of Jonathan
from Adin's descendants,[g]
and 50 men with him;
7 Jeshaiah son of Athaliah
from Elam's descendants,
and 70 men with him;
8 Zebadiah son of Michael
from Shephatiah's descendants,
and 80 men with him;
9 Obadiah son of Jehiel
from Joab's descendants,
and 218 men with him;
10 Shelomith[D] son of Josiphiah
from Bani's descendants,
and 160 men with him;
11 Zechariah son of Bebai
from Bebai's descendants,
and 28 men with him;
12 Johanan son of Hakkatan
from Azgad's descendants,
and 110 men with him;
13 these are the last ones,
from Adonikam's descendants,[h]
and their names are:
Eliphelet, Jeuel, and Shemaiah,
and 60 men with them;
14 Uthai and Zaccur[E]
from Bigvai's descendants,
and 70 men with them.

[a]**7:28** Ezr 7:6; 8:18 [b]Ezr 8:1-14,16 [c]**8:1** Ezr 7:7 [d]**8:3** 1Ch 3:22 [e]Ezr 2:3; 10:25 [f]**8:4** Ezr 2:6 [g]**8:6** Ezr 2:15; Neh 7:20 [h]**8:13** Ezr 2:13 [i]**8:15** Ezr 8:21,31 [j]Ezr 2:40; 7:7 [k]**8:16** Ezr 10:15 [l]**8:17** Ezr 2:43; Neh 7:46 [m]**8:18** Ezr 7:6 [n]Ezr 8:24; Neh 8:7 [o]**8:19** Neh 12:24 [p]**8:20** Ezr 2:43; 7:7 [q]**8:21** Is 58:3-8 [r]**8:22** Dt 31:6,17 [s]**8:24** Neh 10:9,11

15 I gathered them at the river[F] that flows to
Ahava,[i] and we camped there for three days.
I searched among the people and priests,
but found no Levites[j] there. 16 Then I summoned the leaders: Eliezer, Ariel, Shemaiah,
Elnathan, Jarib, Elnathan, Nathan, Zechariah, and Meshullam,[k] as well as the teachers
Joiarib and Elnathan. 17 I sent them to Iddo,
the leader at Casiphia, with a message for[G]
him and his brothers, the temple servants[l] at
Casiphia, that they should bring us ministers
for the house of our God. 18 Since the gracious
hand of our God was on us,[m] they brought us
Sherebiah[n] — a man of insight from the descendants of Mahli, a descendant of Levi son
of Israel — along with his sons and brothers,
18 men, 19 plus Hashabiah,[o] along with Jeshaiah, from the descendants of Merari, and
his brothers and their sons, 20 men. 20 There
were also 220 of the temple servants,[p] who
had been appointed by David and the leaders
for the work of the Levites. All were identified
by name.

Preparing to Return

21 I proclaimed a fast[q] by the Ahava River,[H]
so that we might humble ourselves before
our God and ask Him for a safe journey for
us, our children, and all our possessions. 22 I
did this because I was ashamed to ask the
king for infantry and cavalry to protect us
from enemies during the journey, since we
had told him, "The hand of our God is gracious to all who seek Him, but His great anger is against all who abandon Him."[r] 23 So we
fasted and pleaded with our God about this,
and He granted our request.

24 I selected 12 of the leading priests, along
with Sherebiah,[s] Hashabiah, and 10 of their
brothers. 25 I weighed out to them the silver,
the gold, and the articles — the contribution
for the house of our God that the king, his
counselors, his leaders, and all the Israelites
who were present had offered. 26 I weighed
out to them 24 tons[I] of silver, silver articles
weighing 7,500 pounds,[J] 7,500 pounds[J] of

[A]**7:28** Lit *because the hand of the LORD my God was on me* [B]**8:3** Or *males*; also in vv. 4-14 [C]**8:5** LXX, 1 Esdras 8:32; MT reads *the descendants of Shecaniah* [D]**8:10** Some LXX mss, 1 Esdras 8:36; MT reads *the descendants of Shelomith* [E]**8:14** Alt Hb tradition, some LXX mss read *Zabud* [F]**8:15** Or *canal* [G]**8:17** Lit *Casiphia, and I put in their mouth the words to speak to* [H]**8:21** Or *Canal* [I]**8:26** Lit *650 talents* [J]**8:26** Lit *100 talents*

gold, 27 20 gold bowls worth 1,000 gold coins,[A] and two articles of fine gleaming bronze, as valuable as gold.[a] 28 Then I said to them, "You are holy to the LORD, and the articles are holy. The silver and gold are a freewill offering[b] to the LORD God of your fathers. 29 Guard them carefully until you weigh them out in the chambers of the LORD's house before the leading priests, Levites, and heads of the Israelite families in Jerusalem." 30 So the priests and Levites took charge of the silver, the gold, and the articles that had been weighed out, to bring them to the house of our God in Jerusalem.[c]

Arrival in Jerusalem

31 We set out from the Ahava River[B] on the twelfth day of the first month to go to Jerusalem. We were strengthened by our God,[C,d] and He protected us from the power of the enemy and from ambush along the way.[e] 32 So we arrived at Jerusalem and rested there for three days.[f] 33 On the fourth day the silver, the gold, and the articles were weighed out in the house of our God into the care of Meremoth the priest, son of Uriah. Eleazar son of Phinehas was with him. The Levites Jozabad[g] son of Jeshua and Noadiah son of Binnui were also with them. 34 Everything was verified by number and weight, and the total weight was recorded at that time.

35 The exiles who had returned from the captivity[h] offered •burnt offerings to the God of Israel: 12 bulls for all Israel, 96 rams, and 77 lambs, along with 12 male goats as a •sin offering. All this was a burnt offering for the LORD.[i] 36 They also delivered the king's edicts to the royal satraps and governors of the region west of the Euphrates,[j] so that they would support the people and the house of God.[k]

Israel's Intermarriage with Pagans

9 After these things had been done, the leaders approached me and said: "The people of Israel, the priests, and the Levites have not separated themselves[l] from the surrounding peoples whose detestable practices[m] are like those of the Canaanites, Hittites, Perizzites, Jebusites, Ammonites, Moabites, Egyptians, and Amorites.[n] 2 Indeed, the Israelite men[D] have taken some of their daughters as wives for themselves and their sons, so that the holy •seed[o] has become mixed with the surrounding peoples.[p] The leaders[E] and officials have taken the lead in this unfaithfulness!"[q] 3 When I heard this report, I tore my tunic and robe, pulled out some of the hair from my head and beard, and sat down devastated.[r]

Ezra's Confession

4 Everyone who trembled at the words of the God of Israel[s] gathered around me, because of the unfaithfulness of the exiles,[t] while I sat devastated until the evening offering.[u] 5 At the evening offering, I got up from my humiliation, with my tunic and robe torn. Then I fell on my knees and spread out my hands to •Yahweh my God.[v] 6 And I said:[w]

> My God, I am ashamed and embarrassed to lift my face toward You, my God, because our iniquities are higher than our heads and our •guilt is as high as the heavens.[x] 7 Our guilt has been terrible from the days of our fathers until the present. Because of our iniquities we have been handed over, along with our kings and priests, to the surrounding kings, and to the sword, captivity, plundering, and open shame,[y] as it is today. 8 But now, for a brief moment, grace has come from Yahweh our God to preserve a remnant[z] for us and give us a stake[aa] in His holy place. Even in our slavery, God has given us new life and light to our eyes.[ab] 9 Though we are slaves,[ac] our God has not abandoned us in our slavery. He has extended grace to us in the presence of the Persian kings,[ad] giving us new life, so that we can rebuild the house of our God and repair its ruins,[ae] to give us a wall in Judah and Jerusalem.
>
> 10 Now, our God, what can we say in light of[F] this? For we have abandoned the commands 11 You gave through Your servants the prophets, saying: "The land you are entering to possess is an impure land. The surrounding peoples have filled it from end to end with their uncleanness by

[a] **8:25-27** Ezr 7:15-20
[b] **8:28** Ezr 1:4; 2:68-69
[c] **8:29-30** Neh 13:4-5,9
[d] **8:31** Ezr 7:9; Neh 2:18
[e] Ezr 8:21-22
[f] **8:32** Neh 2:11
[g] **8:33** Neh 11:16
[h] **8:35** Ezr 2:1; 6:16
[i] Lv 1:3-15; 2Ch 29:24,27,31-35
[j] **8:36** Ezr 7:21,25
[k] Ezr 7:21-24
[l] **9:1** Ezk 5:10-12
[m] Dt 12:29-31; Ezr 9:11
[n] Gn 15:18; Lv 18:24-30; Dt 7:1
[o] **9:2** Dt 14:2
[p] Dt 7:1-4; Ezr 9:12; Neh 13:1-3,23
[q] Neh 13:28
[r] **9:3** 2Kg 18:37–19:2; Neh 1:4; Dn 9:3
[s] **9:4** Ezr 10:3; Is 66:2,5
[t] Ezr 2:1; 6:16
[u] Ex 29:38-39
[v] **9:5** Ex 9:29; Dn 6:10
[w] **9:6-15** Neh 1:5-11; Dn 9:4-19
[x] **9:6** Jr 51:9; Rv 18:5
[y] **9:7** Neh 9:30,36; Dn 9:7
[z] **9:8** Is 10:20-22
[aa] Is 10:23
[ab] 1Sm 14:29
[ac] **9:9** Neh 9:36
[ad] 2Kg 25:28; Ezr 6:22
[ae] Ezr 1:4; 7:12-20

[A] **8:27** Or *1,000 drachmas*, or *1,000 darics* [B] **8:31** Or *Canal* [C] **8:31** Lit *The hand of our God was on us* [D] **9:2** Lit *they* [E] **9:2** Lit *hand of the leaders* [F] **9:10** Lit *say after* their impurity and detestable practices.[a] 12 So do not give your daughters to their sons in marriage or take their daughters for your sons.[b] Never seek their peace or prosperity,[c] so that you will be strong, eat the good things of the land, and leave it as an inheritance to your sons forever." 13 After all that has happened to us because of our evil deeds and terrible guilt — though You, our God, have punished us less than our sins deserve and have allowed us to survive[A,d] — 14 should we break Your commands again and intermarry with the peoples who commit these detestable practices?[e] Wouldn't You become so angry with us that You would destroy us, leaving no survivors?[f] 15 LORD God of Israel, You are righteous, for we survive as a remnant[g] today. Here we are before You with our guilt, though no one can stand in Your presence because of this.[h]

Sending Away Foreign Wives

10 While Ezra prayed and confessed, weeping and falling facedown[i] before the house of God, an extremely large assembly of Israelite men, women, and children gathered around him. The people also wept bitterly.[j] 2 Then Shecaniah son of Jehiel,[k] an Elamite, responded to Ezra: "We have been unfaithful to our God by marrying foreign women from the surrounding peoples,[l] but there is still hope for Israel in spite of this. 3 Let us therefore make a covenant before our God[m] to send away all the foreign wives and their children, according to the counsel of my lord and of those who tremble at the command of our God.[n] Let it be done according to the law. 4 Get up, for this matter is your responsibility,[o] and we support you. Be strong and take action!"[p]

5 Then Ezra got up and made the leading priests, Levites, and all Israel take an oath to do what had been said; so they took the oath.[q] 6 Ezra then went from the house of God and walked to the chamber of Jehohanan son of Eliashib, where he spent the night.[B] He did not eat food or drink water, because he was mourning over the unfaithfulness of the exiles.[r]

[a] **9:10-11** Dt 12:29-31; Ezr 9:1
[b] **9:12** Dt 7:1-4; Ezr 9:2; Neh 13:23-28
[c] Dt 7:3; 23:6
[d] **9:13** Is 10:20-22
[e] **9:14** Ezr 9:1-2; Neh 13:23-28
[f] Dt 29:26-28
[g] **9:15** Neh 1:3
[h] Ps 130:3
[i] **10:1** Ezr 9:3,5; Neh 1:4; Dn 9:3-4,20
[j] Ezr 3:12-13
[k] **10:2** Ezr 10:26
[l] Ezr 9:1-2; 10:18,44; Neh 13:23-28
[m] **10:3** 2Ch 34:31
[n] Ezr 9:4
[o] **10:4** Ezr 7:25-26
[p] Jos 1:6-9
[q] **10:5** Neh 10:29-30; 13:25
[r] **10:6** Dt 9:18-19
[s] **10:7-8** Ezr 7:26
[t] **10:9** Neh 8:1
[u] **10:10** Ezr 9:1-2; Neh 13:23-27
[v] **10:14** 2Ch 29:10; 30:8
[w] **10:15** Ezr 8:16

7 They circulated a proclamation throughout Judah and Jerusalem that all the exiles should gather at Jerusalem. 8 Whoever did not come within three days would forfeit all his possessions,[C] according to the decision of the leaders and elders, and would be excluded[s] from the assembly of the exiles.

9 So all the men of Judah and Benjamin gathered in Jerusalem within the three days. On the twentieth day of the ninth month, all the people sat in the square at the house of God,[t] trembling because of this matter and because of the heavy rain. 10 Then Ezra the priest stood up and said to them, "You have been unfaithful by marrying foreign women, adding to Israel's •guilt.[u] 11 Therefore, make a confession to •Yahweh the God of your fathers and do His will. Separate yourselves from the surrounding peoples and your foreign wives."

12 Then all the assembly responded with a loud voice: "Yes, we will do as you say! 13 But there are many people, and it is the rainy season. We don't have the stamina to stay out in the open. This isn't something that can be done in a day or two, for we have rebelled terribly in this matter. 14 Let our leaders represent the entire assembly. Then let all those in our towns who have married foreign women come at appointed times, together with the elders and judges of each town, in order to avert the fierce anger of our God[v] concerning[D] this matter." 15 Only Jonathan son of Asahel and Jahzeiah son of Tikvah opposed this, with Meshullam[w] and Shabbethai the Levite supporting them.

16 The exiles did what had been proposed. Ezra the priest selected men[E] who were family leaders, all identified by name, to represent[F] their ancestral houses. They convened on the first day of the tenth month to investigate the matter, 17 and by the first day of the first month they had dealt with all the men who had married foreign women.

Those Married to Foreign Wives

18 The following were found to have married foreign women from the descendants of the priests:

[A] **9:13** Lit *and gave us a remnant like this* [B] **10:6** 1 Esdras 9:2, Syr; MT, Vg read *he went* [C] **10:8** Lit *would •set apart all his possessions for destruction* [D] **10:14** Some Hb mss, LXX, Vg; other Hb mss read *until* [E] **10:16** 1 Esdras 9:16, Syr; MT, Vg read *priest and men were selected* [F] **10:16** Lit *name, for*

from the descendants of Jeshua son of
Jozadak and his brothers: Maaseiah,
Eliezer, Jarib, and Gedaliah. 19 They
pledged[A] to send their wives away, and
being guilty, they offered a ram from
the flock for their guilt;[a]

20 Hanani and Zebadiah from Immer's[b] descendants;
21 Maaseiah, Elijah, Shemaiah, Jehiel, and Uzziah from Harim's[c] descendants;
22 Elioenai, Maaseiah, Ishmael, Nethanel, Jozabad, and Elasah from Pashhur's[d] descendants.

23 The Levites:[e]

Jozabad, Shimei, Kelaiah (that is Kelita), Pethahiah, Judah, and Eliezer.

24 The singers:[f]

Eliashib.

The gatekeepers:[g]

Shallum, Telem, and Uri.

25 The Israelites:[h]

Parosh's descendants:[i] Ramiah, Izziah, Malchijah, Mijamin, Eleazar, Malchijah,[B] and Benaiah;
26 Elam's descendants:[j] Mattaniah, Zechariah, Jehiel, Abdi, Jeremoth, and Elijah;
27 Zattu's descendants:[k] Elioenai, Eliashib, Mattaniah, Jeremoth, Zabad, and Aziza;
28 Bebai's descendants:[l] Jehohanan, Hananiah, Zabbai, and Athlai;
29 Bani's descendants:[m] Meshullam, Malluch, Adaiah, Jashub, Sheal, and Jeremoth;
30 Pahath-moab's descendants:[n] Adna, Chelal, Benaiah, Maaseiah, Mattaniah, Bezalel, Binnui, and Manasseh;
31 Harim's descendants:[o] Eliezer, Isshijah, Malchijah, Shemaiah, Shimeon,
32 Benjamin, Malluch, and Shemariah;
33 Hashum's descendants:[p] Mattenai, Mattattah, Zabad, Eliphelet, Jeremai, Manasseh, and Shimei;

34 Bani's descendants:[q] Maadai, Amram,
Uel, 35 Benaiah, Bedeiah, Cheluhi,
36 Vaniah, Meremoth, Eliashib,
37 Mattaniah, Mattenai, Jaasu, 38 Bani,
Binnui, Shimei, 39 Shelemiah, Nathan,
Adaiah, 40 Machnadebai, Shashai,
Sharai, 41 Azarel, Shelemiah, Shemariah,
42 Shallum, Amariah, and Joseph;

43 Nebo's descendants:[r] Jeiel, Mattithiah, Zabad, Zebina, Jaddai, Joel, and Benaiah.

44 All of these[s] had married foreign women,
and some of the wives had given birth to children.[t]

[a] 10:19 Lv 5:14–6:7
[b] 10:20 1Ch 24:14
[c] 10:21 1Ch 24:8
[d] 10:22 1Ch 9:12
[e] 10:23 Ezr 2:40
[f] 10:24 Ezr 2:41
[g] Ezr 2:42
[h] 10:25-43 Ezr 2:3-35; Neh 7:8-38
[i] 10:25 Ezr 2:3
[j] 10:26 Ezr 2:7; 10:2
[k] 10:27 Ezr 2:8
[l] 10:28 Ezr 2:11
[m] 10:29 Ezr 2:10
[n] 10:30 Ezr 2:6
[o] 10:31 Ezr 2:32
[p] 10:33 Ezr 2:19
[q] 10:34 Ezr 2:10
[r] 10:43 Ezr 2:29
[s] 10:44 Ezr 10:18-43
[t] Neh 13:24

A 10:19 Lit *gave their hand* B 10:25 Some LXX mss, 1 Esdras 9:26 read *Hashabiah*

■ **AUTHOR:** Ezra the scribe (most likely)

■■ **DATE:** During the time of the exile and return of the Jews (around 445–430 B.C.)

To all who imagine that God grants His people an easy, comfortable life, the book of Nehemiah is a powerful corrective. This leader's life and calling are a steady diet of conflict, mistreatment, intimidation, lazy or fearful co-workers, and belligerent bureaucrats. Nevertheless, Jerusalem's walls are rebuilt, new gates are set in place, and the city is made secure. Only then is God's Word taught with the continuity and persuasive power that leads to revival—a solid and steady recovery of the peoples' commitment to God's mission, especially to their personal role in it.

Practical matters appear everywhere in Nehemiah. Building material, areas for settlement of new immigrants, fairness to Levites who technically have no land but serve the people and must be fed and cared for—these problems tie up much of Nehemiah's day. Today we tend to think of blue-collar or white-collar jobs as quite different, even separating social classes. Not so for these pioneers, who deal with all means of practical and priestly challenges just to enable that long-neglected mission to make its first faltering steps of progress after seventy years. Now that freedom has been granted by Persia (God's sovereign order was behind that), the peoples' mission of witness and worship is given new significance. The past must lie behind; the future stretches out before them. Christians are reminded that Paul directs churches not to dwell on faults and failures of years gone by, but to look ahead with joy at the privilege of telling the world that a Savior, crucified, has risen from the dead and holds the power to transform all people. Believe, obey, come and see, is Paul's missionary invitation. God's mission takes new forms as it reaches beyond Israel, beyond the temple and the nation, to all people everywhere.

NEHEMIAH

Nehemiah's work involves making lists, filing documents, recording official correspondence, and conducting affairs in an orderly way. He is surrounded by mismanagement and pettiness, people who slow him down and by their resistance subvert his work. Leaders who know the fatigue of working in God's mission—the seemingly pointless setbacks, the failure of adequate supplies, the half-hearted workers, the reluctant givers—will learn from Nehemiah that faith points toward possibilities that people cannot see. Faith believes that God wants something done; faith takes charge to meet needs and reach mission goals. Nehemiah is a man of hope who refuses to be diverted from God's assignment. He works according to the God who speaks and rewards His people.

God urges His people to follow mentors such as this, to imagine great possibilities and to partner with people of vision. Leaders hear the message for our day: Go and tell, invite and urge, explain and teach, baptize and make disciples. All sorts of tasks—care of people, animals, and landscape—make up God's mission today. All manner of gifts and talents move the message to people who need to know.

1 The words of Nehemiah[a] son of Hacaliah:

News from Jerusalem

During the month of Chislev[A,b] in the
twentieth year,[B,c] when I was in the fortress
city of Susa,[d] 2 Hanani,[e] one of my brothers,
arrived with men from Judah, and I questioned them about Jerusalem and the Jewish
remnant[f] that had survived the exile.[g] 3 They
said to me, "The remnant in the province,[h]
who survived the exile, are in great trouble
and disgrace. Jerusalem's wall has been broken down, and its gates have been burned
down."[i]

Nehemiah's Prayer

4 When I heard these words, I sat down and
wept. I mourned for a number of days, fasting and praying[j] before the God of heaven.[k]
5 I said,[l]

Yahweh, the God of heaven, the great
and awe-inspiring God who keeps His
gracious covenant with those who love
Him[m] and keep His commands,[n] 6 let Your
eyes be open and Your ears be attentive[o]
to hear Your servant's prayer that I now
pray to You day and night[p] for Your servants, the Israelites. I confess the sins[C] we
have committed against You. Both I and
my father's house have sinned.[q] 7 We have
acted corruptly toward You and have not
kept the commands, statutes, and ordinances You gave Your servant Moses.[r]
8 Please remember what You commanded
Your servant Moses: "If you are unfaithful, I will scatter you among the peoples.[s]
9 But if you return to Me and carefully observe My commands, even though your
exiles were banished to the ends of the
earth,[D] I will gather them from there and
bring them to the place where I chose to
have My name dwell."[t] 10 They are Your
servants and Your people. You redeemed
them by Your great power and strong
hand.[u] 11 Please, Lord, let Your ear be attentive[v] to the prayer of Your servant and
to that of Your servants who delight to
revere Your name. Give Your servant success today,[w] and have compassion on him
in the presence of this man.[E,x]

At the time, I was the king's cupbearer.[y]

Nehemiah Sent to Jerusalem

2 During the month of Nisan[F] in the twentieth year of King Artaxerxes,[z] when wine
was set before him, I took the wine and gave it
to the king. I had never been sad in his presence, 2 so the king said to me, "Why are you[G]
sad, when you aren't sick? This is nothing but
depression."[H,aa]

I was overwhelmed with fear 3 and replied
to the king, "May the king live forever! Why
should I[I] not be sad when the city where my
ancestors are buried lies in ruins and its gates
have been destroyed by fire?"[ab]

4 Then the king asked me, "What is your request?"

So I prayed to the God of heaven[ac] 5 and answered the king, "If it pleases the king, and if
your servant has found favor with you, send
me to Judah and to the city where my ancestors are buried,[J,ad] so that I may rebuild it."[ae]

6 The king, with the queen seated beside
him, asked me, "How long will your journey
take, and when will you return?" So I gave
him a definite time,[af] and it pleased the king
to send me.

7 I also said to the king: "If it pleases the
king, let me have letters written to the governors of the region west of the Euphrates
River,[ag] so that they will grant me safe passage
until I reach Judah.[ah] 8 And let me have a letter
written to Asaph, keeper of the king's forest,
so that he will give me timber to rebuild the
gates of the temple's fortress,[ai] the city wall,
and the home where I will live."[K,aj] The king
granted my requests, for I was graciously
strengthened by my God.[L,ak]

9 I went to the governors of the region west
of the Euphrates and gave them the king's letters.[al] The king had also sent officers of the infantry and cavalry with me. 10 When Sanballat
the Horonite[am] and Tobiah the Ammonite official heard that someone had come to seek
the well-being of the Israelites, they were
greatly displeased.[an]

[a] **1:1** Neh 10:1
[b] Zch 7:1
[c] Ezr 7:1,8; Neh 2:1
[d] Est 1:2; Dn 8:2
[e] **1:2** Neh 7:2
[f] Ezr 9:8,15; Is 10:20-22
[g] Ezr 1:11
[h] **1:3** Ezr 2:1; Neh 11:3
[i] Ezr 4:12-13,16; Neh 2:13
[j] **1:4** Ezr 9:3; 10:1; Ps 35:13; Dn 9:3; Lk 2:37; Ac 13:3
[k] Ezr 1:2; Neh 2:4
[l] **1:5-11** Dn 9:4-19
[m] **1:5** Dt 6:5; 7:9-11; Rm 8:28
[n] Dn 9:4
[o] **1:6** 2Ch 6:40
[p] Ps 88:1-2; 2Tm 1:3
[q] Dn 9:5,8,20
[r] **1:7** 2Ch 29:6; Dn 9:5-6,11
[s] **1:8** Dt 4:25-27; 28:64; Dn 9:7
[t] **1:9** Dt 30:1-5
[u] **1:10** Dt 9:29; Dn 9:15
[v] **1:11** 2Ch 6:40
[w] Gn 24:12
[x] Neh 2:1
[y] Gn 40:20
[z] **2:1** Ezr 7:1,8; Neh 1:1
[aa] **2:1-2** Pr 15:13
[ab] **2:3** Ezr 4:12,21; Neh 1:3
[ac] **2:4** Neh 1:4
[ad] **2:5** Neh 1:3
[ae] Ezr 4:21; Dn 9:18
[af] **2:6** Neh 13:6
[ag] **2:7** Ezr 4:8-9; 8:36
[ah] Ezr 8:22
[ai] **2:8** Neh 7:2
[aj] Ezr 3:7
[ak] Ezr 7:6; Neh 2:18
[al] **2:9** Ezr 8:36
[am] **2:10** Jos 16:3,5; 18:13
[an] Neh 4:7

A **1:1** = November–December B **1:1** Artaxerxes reigned 465–425 B.C. C **1:6** Lit *sins of the Israelites* D **1:9** Lit *skies* E **1:11** = the king F **2:1** = March–April; called Abib in the pre-exilic period; Ex 13:4; Dt 16:1 G **2:2** Lit *Why is your face* H **2:2** Lit *sadness of heart* I **2:3** Lit *my face* J **2:5** Lit *city, the house of the graves of my fathers,* K **2:8** Lit *enter* L **2:8** Lit *for the gracious hand of my God was on me*

Preparing to Rebuild the Walls

[11]After I arrived in Jerusalem and had been there three days,[a] [12]I got up at night and took a few men with me. I didn't tell anyone what my God had laid on my heart to do for Jerusalem. The only animal I took[A] was the one I was riding. [13]I went out at night through the Valley Gate toward the Serpent's[B] Well and

[a]2:11 Ezr 8:32

WORLDVIEW

The Mission of God in China and Asia

Every culture reflects a different facet of God's grace. Cultural worldviews influence how we receive the gospel. Chinese culture in particular has traits that help, and perhaps sometimes hurt, the adoption of Christian faith.

Chinese people work extremely hard and pursue learning even when it means sacrificing sleep. They are selfless with their inability to say "No, that's enough!" Anyone with Chinese roots or relatives knows this. An extreme work ethic is driven by a strong sense of loyalty to one's family. It is not uncommon for a Chinese person to have multiple jobs and academic degrees. Hard work has fueled a very active church in China. According to journalist David Aikman, in the next three decades, 20 to 30 percent of China will be Christianized.

Also prominent for the Chinese is the importance of ancestors and authority. This has generated a Christian community that is very respectful of authority, including the authority of an unfriendly state. Persecution seems not to mitigate this respect and submission. The same dynamic applies in family relations. Children respect parents, especially fathers, who have strong influence in major decisions for children, even during their adulthood.

A third social factor is harmony. Deeply embedded in Confucian thought, harmony seeks the welfare of all at the expense of personal interest. Harmony unites under a banner, enforces social norms, and builds Great Walls when national defense is a priority. Notice that the Great Wall has slots for archers only on the side facing outward. Harmony would never require archers shooting at Chinese people, the inward side.

When the gospel announces that God Almighty has sent His Son, Jesus Christ, to redeem the world, Chinese people respect and adhere to the Word of God, knowing that God's Kingdom, whatever else it holds, is perfect harmony. In the Kingdom, now and in the consummation, the aspirations of Chinese people for "togetherness" will be complete and joyous.

Sometimes this stress on authority and submission can generate negative feelings of inferiority and fear. Chinese history, especially in recent decades, has been the story of domination, control, and the violent suppression of dissent. How very Chinese for a student to stand in front of a tank in Tiananmen Square as an expression of his unity with fellow students. Equally Chinese was the respect of the tank crew and artillery commander that day; rather than run the student over, they respected his stance and halted the tank. How these standoffs will play out in the future of China, we will see.

The gospel is spreading like wildfire across China. What parts of the gospel will the Chinese church emphasize? How will China's history and culture affect the mission of God there? The world will watch, while the mission of God in China and throughout Asia wins people eager to find a sure path and the tranquility of knowing that people are at brought to peace with the Almighty through Jesus Christ.

[A]2:12 Lit *animal with me* [B]2:13 Or *Dragon's*

the Dung Gate,[a] and I inspected the walls of Jerusalem that had been broken down and its gates that had been destroyed by fire.[b] 14 I went on to the Fountain Gate[c] and the King's Pool,[d] but farther down it became too narrow for my animal to go through. 15 So I went up at night by way of the valley and inspected the wall. Then heading back, I entered through the Valley Gate[e] and returned. 16 The officials did not know where I had gone or what I was doing, for I had not yet told the Jews, priests, nobles, officials, or the rest of those who would be doing the work. 17 So I said to them, "You see the trouble we are in. Jerusalem lies in ruins and its gates have been burned down.[f] Come, let's rebuild Jerusalem's wall,[g] so that we will no longer be a disgrace." 18 I told them how the gracious hand of my God had been on me,[h] and what the king had said to me.

They said, "Let's start rebuilding," and they were encouraged[A] to do this good work.

19 When Sanballat the Horonite, Tobiah the Ammonite official,[i] and Geshem the Arab[j] heard about this, they mocked and despised us, and said, "What is this you're doing? Are you rebelling against the king?"

20 I gave them this reply, "The God of heaven is the One who will grant us success. We, His servants, will start building, but you have no share, right, or historic claim in Jerusalem."[k]

Rebuilding the Walls

3 Eliashib the high priest[l] and his fellow priests began rebuilding the Sheep Gate.[m] They dedicated it and installed its doors. After building the wall to the Tower of the Hundred and the Tower of Hananel,[n] they dedicated it. 2 The men of Jericho[o] built next to Eliashib,[p] and next to them Zaccur son of Imri built.

Fish Gate

3 The sons of Hassenaah built the Fish Gate.[q] They built it with beams and installed its doors, bolts, and bars.[r] 4 Next to them Meremoth[s] son of Uriah, son of Hakkoz, made repairs. Beside them Meshullam[t] son of Berechiah, son of Meshezabel, made repairs. Next to them Zadok son of Baana made repairs. 5 Beside them the Tekoites[u] made repairs, but their nobles did not lift a finger to help[B] their supervisors.

Old Gate, Broad Wall, and Tower of the Ovens

6 Joiada son of Paseah and Meshullam son of Besodeiah repaired the Old[C] Gate.[v] They built it with beams and installed its doors, bolts, and bars. 7 Next to them the repairs were done by Melatiah the Gibeonite, Jadon the Meronothite, and the men of Gibeon[w] and Mizpah, who were under the authority[D,x] of the governor[y] of the region west of the Euphrates River.[z] 8 After him Uzziel son of Harhaiah, the goldsmith,[aa] made repairs, and next to him Hananiah son of the perfumer made repairs. They restored Jerusalem as far as the Broad Wall.[ab]

9 Next to them Rephaiah son of Hur, ruler over half the district of Jerusalem, made repairs. 10 After them Jedaiah son of Harumaph made repairs across from his house.[ac] Next to him Hattush the son of Hashabneiah made repairs. 11 Malchijah son of Harim and Hasshub son of Pahath-moab made repairs to another section, as well as to the Tower of the Ovens.[ad] 12 Beside him Shallum son of Hallohesh, ruler over half the district of Jerusalem, made repairs—he and his daughters.

Valley Gate, Dung Gate, and Fountain Gate

13 Hanun and the inhabitants of Zanoah repaired the Valley Gate. They rebuilt it and installed its doors, bolts, and bars, and repaired 500 yards[E] of the wall to the Dung Gate.[ae] 14 Malchijah son of Rechab, ruler over the district of Beth-haccherem,[af] repaired the Dung Gate.[ag] He rebuilt it and installed its doors, bolts, and bars.

15 Shallun[F] son of Col-hozeh, ruler over the district of Mizpah, repaired the Fountain Gate.[ah] He rebuilt it and roofed it. Then he installed its doors, bolts, and bars. He also made repairs to the wall of the Pool of Shelah[ai] near the king's garden,[aj] as far as the stairs that descend from the city of David.[ak]

16 After him Nehemiah son of Azbuk, ruler

[a] **2:13** Neh 3:13 [b] Ezr 4:12; Neh 1:3 [c] **2:14** Neh 3:15; 12:37 [d] 2Kg 18:17; 20:20 [e] **2:15** Neh 3:13 [f] **2:17** Ezr 4:12; Neh 1:3; 2:3 [g] Neh 2:5 [h] **2:18** Ezr 7:9; Neh 2:8 [i] **2:19** Neh 4:7 [j] Neh 6:1,6 [k] **2:19-20** Ezr 4:3-4 [l] **3:1** Neh 12:10; 13:4,7,28 [m] Neh 3:32; 12:39; Jn 5:2 [n] Neh 12:39; Zch 14:10 [o] **3:2** Ezr 2:34; Neh 7:36 [p] Neh 12:10 [q] **3:3** Neh 12:39; Zph 1:10 [r] Neh 6:1; 7:1 [s] **3:4** Ezr 8:33 [t] Ezr 10:15; Neh 3:30; 6:17-18 [u] **3:5** Neh 3:27; Am 1:1 [v] **3:6** Neh 12:39 [w] **3:7** Jos 9:3 [x] 2Kg 25:23; Jr 40:5-12 [y] Neh 2:7-8; 5:14 [z] Neh 2:7,9 [aa] **3:8** Neh 3:31,32 [ab] 2Ch 32:5; Neh 12:38 [ac] **3:10** Neh 3:23,28 [ad] **3:11** 2Ch 26:9; Neh 12:38 [ae] **3:13** Neh 2:13 [af] **3:14** Jr 6:1 [ag] Neh 2:13 [ah] **3:15** Neh 2:14; 12:37 [ai] Is 8:6; Jn 9:7 [aj] 2Kg 25:4 [ak] Neh 12:37

A **2:18** Lit *they put their hands* B **3:5** Lit *not bring their neck to the work of* C **3:6** Or *Jeshanah* D **3:7** Or *Mizpah, the seat* E **3:13** Lit *1,000 cubits* F **3:15** Some Hb mss, Syr read *Shallum*

over half the district of Beth-zur,[a] made repairs up to a point opposite the tombs of
David,[b] as far as the artificial pool[c] and the
House of the Warriors.[d] 17 Next to him the
Levites[e] made repairs under Rehum son of
Bani. Beside him Hashabiah, ruler over half
the district of Keilah,[f] made repairs for his
district. 18 After him their fellow Levites made
repairs under Binnui[A] son of Henadad, ruler
over half the district of Keilah. 19 Next to him
Ezer son of Jeshua, ruler over Mizpah, made
repairs to another section opposite the ascent to the armory at the Angle.[g]

The Angle, Water Gate, and Tower on the Ophel

20 After him Baruch son of Zabbai[B] diligently
repaired another section, from the Angle to
the door of the house of Eliashib the high
priest.[h] 21 Beside him Meremoth[i] son of Uriah,
son of Hakkoz, made repairs to another section, from the door of Eliashib's[j] house to the
end of his house. 22 And next to him the priests
from the surrounding area made repairs.
23 After them Benjamin and Hasshub made
repairs opposite their house. Beside them Azariah son of Maaseiah, son of Ananiah, made repairs beside his house. 24 After him Binnui[k] son
of Henadad made repairs to another section,
from the house of Azariah to the Angle and the
corner. 25 Palal son of Uzai made repairs opposite the Angle and tower that juts out from the
upper palace[C] of the king,[l] by the courtyard of
the guard.[m] Beside him Pedaiah son of Parosh,
26 and the temple servants[n] living on Ophel[D,o]
made repairs opposite the Water Gate[p] toward
the east and the tower that juts out. 27 Next to
him the Tekoites[q] made repairs to another section from a point opposite the great tower that
juts out, as far as the wall of Ophel.[r]

Horse Gate, Inspection Gate, and Sheep Gate

28 Each of the priests made repairs above
the Horse Gate,[s] each opposite his own house.
29 After them Zadok son of Immer made repairs opposite his house. And beside him
Shemaiah son of Shecaniah, guard of the East
Gate, made repairs. 30 Next to him Hananiah
son of Shelemiah and Hanun the sixth son of
Zalaph made repairs to another section.
After them Meshullam son of Berechiah
made repairs opposite his room. 31 Next to
him Malchijah, one of the goldsmiths,[t] made
repairs to the house of the temple servants[u]
and the merchants, opposite the Inspection[E]
Gate, and as far as the upper room of the corner. 32 The goldsmiths[v] and merchants made
repairs between the upper room of the corner and the Sheep Gate.[w]

Progress in Spite of Opposition

4 [F] When Sanballat[x] heard that we were rebuilding the wall,[y] he became furious.
He mocked the Jews[z] 2 before his colleagues
and the powerful men[G] of Samaria,[aa] and said,
"What are these pathetic Jews doing? Can they
restore it by themselves? Will they offer sacrifices? Will they ever finish it? Can they bring
these burnt stones[ab] back to life from the
mounds of rubble?"[ac] 3 Then Tobiah the Ammonite,[ad] who was beside him, said, "Indeed,
even if a fox[ae] climbed up what they are building, he would break down their stone wall!"
4 Listen, our God, for we are despised. Make
their insults return on their own heads and
let them be taken as plunder to a land of captivity. 5 Do not cover their ·guilt or let their sin
be erased from Your sight, because they have
provoked[H] the builders.[af]
6 So we rebuilt the wall until the entire wall
was joined together up to half its height, for
the people had the will to keep working.[ag]
7 [I] When Sanballat, Tobiah, and the Arabs,[ah]
Ammonites, and Ashdodites heard that the
repair to the walls of Jerusalem was progress-
ing and that the gaps were being closed,[ai] they
became furious.[aj] 8 They all plotted together to
come and fight against Jerusalem and throw
it into confusion. 9 So we prayed to our God
and stationed a guard because of them day
and night.
10 In Judah, it was said:[J]

The strength of the laborer fails,
since there is so much rubble.
We will never be able
to rebuild the wall.

[a] **3:16** Jos 15:58; 1Ch 2:45
[b] 1Kg 2:10; Ac 2:29
[c] 2Kg 20:20; Is 22:9-11
[d] 2Sm 23:8-39
[e] **3:17** Ezr 2:40; Neh 7:43
[f] 1Sm 23:1-5
[g] **3:19** 2Ch 26:9
[h] **3:20** Neh 3:1; 12:10
[i] **3:21** Ezr 8:33
[j] Neh 3:1
[k] **3:24** Ezr 8:33
[l] **3:25** Neh 12:37
[m] Jr 32:2
[n] **3:26** Ezr 2:43,55-58; 7:7
[o] Ezr 8:20; Neh 11:21
[p] Neh 8:1
[q] **3:27** Neh 3:5; Am 1:1
[r] Neh 11:21
[s] **3:28** 2Ch 23:15
[t] **3:31** Neh 3:8
[u] Neh 7:46-56
[v] **3:32** Neh 3:8,21
[w] Neh 3:1; Jn 5:2
[x] **4:1** Neh 2:10,19; 4:7
[y] Neh 2:17,19
[z] Neh 2:19
[aa] **4:2** Ezr 4:9-10
[ab] 2Ch 26:19
[ac] 2Ch 26:19; Neh 1:3
[ad] **4:3** Neh 2:10,19; 6:1,14
[ae] Lm 5:18
[af] **4:4-5** Neh 6:14; Jr 18:23
[ag] **4:6** Neh 2:20; 6:1,15
[ah] **4:7** Neh 2:19
[ai] Neh 4:2-3
[aj] Neh 2:10

[A] **3:18** Some Hb mss, Syr, LXX; Neh 3:24; other Hb mss, Vg read *Bavvai* [B] **3:20** Alt Hb tradition, Vg read *Zaccai*; Ezr 2:9 [C] **3:25** Or *and the upper tower that juts out from the palace* [D] **3:26** = a hill in Jerusalem [E] **3:31** Or *Muster* [F] **4:1** Neh 3:33 in Hb [G] **4:2** Or *the army* [H] **4:5** Or *provoked You in front of* [I] **4:7** Neh 4:1 in Hb [J] **4:10** Lit *Judah said*

11And our enemies said, "They won't know
or see anything until we're among them and
can kill them and stop the work." 12When the
Jews who lived nearby arrived, they said to us
time and again,[A] "Everywhere you turn, they
attack[B] us." 13So I stationed people behind
the lowest sections of the wall, at the vulnerable areas. I stationed them by families with
their swords, spears, and bows. 14After I made
an inspection, I stood up and said to the nobles, the officials, and the rest of the people,[a]
"Don't be afraid of them.[b] Remember the
great and awe-inspiring Lord, and fight for
your countrymen, your sons and daughters,
your wives and homes."[c]

Sword and Trowel

15When our enemies heard that we knew
their scheme and that God had frustrated it,
every one of us returned to his own work on
the wall. 16From that day on, half of my men
did the work while the other half held spears,
shields, bows, and armor.[d] The officers supported all the people of Judah, 17who were rebuilding the wall. The laborers who carried
the loads worked with one hand and held a
weapon with the other. 18Each of the builders had his sword strapped around his waist
while he was building, and the trumpeter was
beside me. 19Then I said to the nobles, the officials, and the rest of the people:[e] "The work
is enormous and spread out, and we are separated far from one another along the wall.[f]
20Wherever you hear the trumpet sound,
rally to us there. Our God will fight for us!"[g]
21So we continued the work, while half of the
men were holding spears from daybreak until
the stars came out. 22At that time, I also said
to the people, "Let everyone and his servant
spend the night inside Jerusalem, so that they
can stand guard by night and work by day."
23And I, my brothers, my men, and the guards
with me never took off our clothes. Each carried his weapon, even when washing.[C]

Social Injustice

5 There was a widespread outcry from the
people and their wives against their Jewish countrymen. 2Some were saying, "We, our
sons, and our daughters are numerous. Let us
get grain so that we can eat and live." 3Others
were saying, "We are mortgaging our fields,
vineyards, and homes to get grain during the
famine."[h] 4Still others were saying, "We have
borrowed money to pay the king's tax[i] on our
fields and vineyards.[j] 5We and our children are
just like our countrymen and their children,
yet we are subjecting our sons and daughters
to slavery.[k] Some of our daughters are already
enslaved,[l] but we are powerless[D] because our
fields and vineyards belong to others."

6I became extremely angry[m] when I heard
their outcry and these complaints. 7After seriously considering the matter, I accused the
nobles and officials, saying to them, "Each of
you is charging his countrymen interest."[n] So I
called a large assembly against them 8and said,
"We have done our best to buy back our Jewish countrymen who were sold to foreigners,
but now you sell your own countrymen, and
we have to buy them back."[o] They remained
silent and could not say a word.[p] 9Then I said,
"What you are doing isn't right. Shouldn't you
walk in the •fear of our God[q] and not invite
the reproach of our foreign enemies?[r] 10Even
I, as well as my brothers and my servants, have
been lending them money and grain. Please,
let us stop charging this interest.[E] 11Return
their fields, vineyards, olive groves, and houses
to them immediately, along with the percentage[F] of the money, grain, new wine, and olive
oil[s] that you have been assessing them."

12They responded: "We will return these
things and require nothing more from them.[t]
We will do as you say."

So I summoned the priests and made everyone take an oath[u] to do this. 13I also shook the
folds of my robe and said, "May God likewise
shake from his house and property everyone
who doesn't keep this promise. May he be
shaken out[v] and have nothing!"

The whole assembly said, "•Amen," and they
praised the LORD. Then the people did as they
had promised.[w]

Good and Bad Governors

14Furthermore, from the day King Artaxerxes[x] appointed me to be their governor in

[a]**4:14** Neh 2:16 [b]Dt 1:29; Ezr 3:3; 4:4 [c]2Sm 10:12 [d]**4:16** 2Ch 18:33 [e]**4:19** Neh 2:16 [f]Neh 3:1-32 [g]**4:20** Nm 10:1-9; Dt 1:30 [h]**5:3** Hg 1:5-11 [i]**5:4** Ezr 4:13; 7:24 [j]**5:2-4** Dt 15:7-8 [k]**5:5** Lv 25:39-43 [l]Ex 21:7-11 [m]**5:6** Ex 11:8; Eph 4:26-27 [n]**5:7** Ex 22:25; Dt 23:19-20 [o]**5:8** Ex 21:8; Lv 25:39-42 [p]Jr 8:9 [q]**5:9** Lv 25:36 [r]2Sm 12:14; Neh 4:4 [s]**5:11** Neh 10:37 [t]**5:12** Neh 10:31 [u]Ezr 10:5 [v]**5:13** Ac 18:6 [w]Ezr 10:4-5; Neh 13:25 [x]**5:14** Ezr 4:7; 7:1

[A]**4:12** Lit *us 10 times* [B]**4:12** Or *again from every place, "You must return to us"* hand [C]**4:23** Lit *Each his weapon the water* [D]**5:5** Lit *but there is not the power in our hand* [E]**5:10** Or *us forgive these debts* [F]**5:11** Lit *hundredth*

the land of Judah — from the twentieth year
until his thirty-second year, 12 years[a] — I and
my associates never ate from the food allotted to the governor. 15 The governors[b] who
preceded me had heavily burdened the people, taking food and wine from them, as well
as a pound[A] of silver. Their subordinates also
oppressed the people, but I didn't do this, because of the fear of God.[c] 16 Instead, I devoted
myself to the construction of the wall,[d] and
all my subordinates were gathered there for
the work. We didn't buy any land.[e]

17 There were 150 Jews and officials, as well
as guests from the surrounding nations at my
table.[f] 18 Each[B] day, one ox, six choice sheep,
and some fowl were prepared for me. An
abundance of all kinds of wine was provided
every 10 days.[g] But I didn't demand the food
allotted to the governor, because the burden
on the people was so heavy.

19 Remember me favorably, my God, for all
that I have done for this people.[h]

Attempts to Discourage the Builders

6 When Sanballat, Tobiah, Geshem the
Arab, and the rest of our enemies[i] heard
that I had rebuilt the wall and that no gap
was left in it[j] — though at that time I had not
installed the doors in the gates[k] — 2 Sanballat
and Geshem[l] sent me a message: "Come, let's
meet together in the villages of[C] the Ono Valley."[m] But they were planning to harm me.

3 So I sent messengers to them, saying, "I am
doing a great work and cannot come down.
Why should the work cease while I leave it
and go down to you?" 4 Four times they sent
me the same proposal, and I gave them the
same reply.

5 Sanballat[n] sent me this same message a
fifth time by his aide, who had an open letter
in his hand. 6 In it was written:

> It is reported among the nations — and
> Geshem[D,o] agrees — that you and the
> Jews plan to rebel. This is the reason
> you are building the wall. According to
> these reports, you are to become their
> king 7 and have even set up the prophets
> in Jerusalem to proclaim on your behalf:
> "There is a king in Judah."[p] These rumors
> will be heard by the king. So come, let's
> confer together.

8 Then I replied to him, "There is nothing to
these rumors you are spreading; you are in-
venting them in your own mind."[q] 9 For they
were all trying to intimidate[r] us, saying, "They
will become discouraged[E] in the work,[s] and it
will never be finished."

But now, my God, strengthen me.[F,t]

Attempts to Intimidate Nehemiah

10 I went to the house of Shemaiah son
of Delaiah, son of Mehetabel, who was restricted to his house. He said:

> Let us meet at the house of God
> inside the temple.
> Let us shut the temple doors
> because they are coming to kill you.
> They are coming to kill you tonight![G]

11 But I said, "Should a man like me run
away? How can I enter the temple and live?[u]
I will not go." 12 I realized that God had not
sent him, because of the prophecy he spoke
against me. Tobiah and Sanballat[v] had hired
him. 13 He was hired, so that I would be intimidated,[w] do as he suggested, sin, and get a bad
reputation, in order that they could discredit
me.

14 My God, remember[x] Tobiah and Sanballat for what they have done, and also Noadiah
the prophetess[y] and the other prophets who
wanted to intimidate me.

The Wall Completed

15 The wall was completed[z] in 52 days, on the
twenty-fifth day of the month Elul.[aa] 16 When
all our enemies[ab] heard this, all the surrounding nations were intimidated[ac] and lost their
confidence,[H] for they realized that this task
had been accomplished by our God.[ad]

17 During those days, the nobles of Judah
sent many letters to Tobiah,[ae] and Tobiah's
letters came to them. 18 For many in Judah
were bound by oath[af] to him, since he was a
son-in-law of Shecaniah son of Arah, and his
son Jehohanan had married the daughter of
Meshullam[ag] son of Berechiah. 19 These nobles
kept mentioning Tobiah's good deeds to me,

[a] **5:14** Neh 13:6
[b] **5:15** Ezr 5:3,14; Hg 1:1
[c] Lv 25:36
[d] **5:16** Neh 4:1; 6:1; 2Th 3:7-10
[e] Neh 5:3,7,11
[f] **5:17** 1Kg 4:27; 18:19
[g] **5:18** 1Kg 4:22-23
[h] **5:19** Neh 13:14,22,31
[i] **6:1** Neh 2:10,19
[j] Neh 4:6-7
[k] Neh 3:1
[l] **6:2** Neh 2:10
[m] 1Ch 8:12
[n] **6:5** Neh 2:10
[o] **6:6** Neh 2:19
[p] **6:7** Zch 9:9
[q] **6:8** Jb 13:4; Ps 52:2
[r] **6:9** Ezr 3:3
[s] Ezr 4:4
[t] Neh 5:19; 13:22; Ps 138:3
[u] **6:10-11** Nm 18:7
[v] **6:12** Neh 2:10; 6:1
[w] **6:13** Ezr 3:3
[x] **6:14** Neh 13:29
[y] Rv 2:20
[z] **6:15** Neh 4:1,7; 6:1
[aa] Ezr 6:15
[ab] **6:16** Neh 2:10; 6:1
[ac] Ezr 3:3
[ad] Ex 14:25
[ae] **6:17** Neh 6:1; 13:4-5,7-8
[af] **6:18** Ezr 10:5
[ag] Neh 3:4,30

[A] **5:15** Lit *40 shekels* [B] **5:18** Lit *And that which was prepared each* [C] **6:2** Or *together at Kephirim in* [D] **6:6** Lit *Gashmu* [E] **6:9** Lit *saying, "Their hands will fail* [F] **6:9** Lit *my hands* [G] **6:10** Or *by night* [H] **6:16** Lit *and fell greatly in their eyes*

and they reported my words to him. And Tobiah sent letters to intimidate[a] me.

The Exiles Return

7 When the wall had been rebuilt and I had
the doors installed,[b] the gatekeepers,[c]
singers, and Levites were appointed. 2Then I
put my brother Hanani[d] in charge of Jerusalem,[e] along with Hananiah,[f] commander of
the fortress,[g] because he was a faithful man
who ·feared God[h] more than most. 3I said to
them, "Do not open the gates of Jerusalem
until the sun is hot, and let the doors be shut
and securely fastened while the guards are
on duty. Station the citizens of Jerusalem as
guards, some at their posts and some at their
homes."[i]

4The city was large and spacious, but there
were few people in it, and no houses had been
built yet.[j] 5Then my God put it into my mind[k]
to assemble the nobles, the officials, and the
people to be registered by genealogy. I found
the genealogical record of those who came
back first, and I found the following written
in it:[l]

6These are the people of the province who
went up among the captive exiles deported
by King Nebuchadnezzar[m] of Babylon. Each
of them returned to Jerusalem and Judah, to
his own town.[n] 7They came with Zerubbabel,[o]
Jeshua,[p] Nehemiah, Azariah, Raamiah, Naha-
mani, Mordecai, Bilshan, Mispereth, Bigvai,
Nehum, and Baanah.

The number of the Israelite men included:

8 Parosh's descendants[q] 2,172
9 Shephatiah's descendants 372
10 Arah's descendants 652
11 Pahath-moab's descendants:
Jeshua's and Joab's descendants 2,818
12 Elam's descendants 1,254
13 Zattu's descendants 845
14 Zaccai's descendants 760
15 Binnui's descendants 648
16 Bebai's descendants 628
17 Azgad's descendants 2,322
18 Adonikam's descendants[r] 667
19 Bigvai's descendants 2,067
20 Adin's descendants[s] 655
21 Ater's descendants: of Hezekiah 98
22 Hashum's descendants 328
23 Bezai's descendants 324
24 Hariph's descendants 112
25 Gibeon's[A] descendants 95
26 Bethlehem's[t] and Netophah's[u] men 188
27 Anathoth's[v] men 128
28 Beth-azmaveth's men 42
29 Kiriath-jearim's, Chephirah's,
and Beeroth's men 743
30 Ramah's and Geba's men 621
31 Michmas's men 122
32 Bethel's and Ai's men[w] 123
33 the other Nebo's men 52
34 the other Elam's people 1,254
35 Harim's people 320
36 Jericho's people[x] 345
37 Lod's,[y] Hadid's, and Ono's people 721
38 Senaah's people 3,930.

39The priests included:

Jedaiah's[z] descendants
of the house of Jeshua 973
40 Immer's descendants 1,052
41 Pashhur's descendants 1,247
42 Harim's descendants 1,017.

43The Levites[aa] included:

Jeshua's descendants: of Kadmiel
Hodevah's descendants 74.

44The singers[ab] included:

·Asaph's descendants 148.

45The gatekeepers[ac] included:

Shallum's descendants,
Ater's descendants,
Talmon's descendants,
Akkub's descendants,
Hatita's descendants,
Shobai's descendants 138.

46The temple servants[ad] included:

Ziha's descendants,
Hasupha's descendants,
Tabbaoth's descendants,
47Keros's descendants,
Sia's descendants, Padon's descendants,
48 Lebanah's descendants,
Hagabah's descendants,
Shalmai's descendants,
49Hanan's descendants,

[a]**6:19** Neh 6:9,13 [b]**7:1** Neh 6:1 [c]Ezr 2:40-42; Neh 7:43-45 [d]**7:2** Neh 1:2 [e]Neh 3:9,12 [f]Neh 10:23 [g]Neh 2:8 [h]1Kg 18:3; Neh 5:9,15 [i]**7:3** Neh 4:13,16,22-23 [j]**7:4** Neh 11:1 [k]**7:5** Pr 2:6 [l]**7:5-73** Ezr 2:1-70 [m]**7:6** 2Ch 36:20 [n]Ezr 2:1 [o]**7:7** Hg 1:1 [p]Ezr 2:2; 5:2; Zch 3:3,8 [q]**7:8** Ezr 2:3; 8:3; 10:25; Neh 3:25 [r]**7:18** Ezr 2:13; 8:13 [s]**7:20** Ezr 2:15; 8:6 [t]**7:26** Ezr 2:21; Mc 5:2 [u]2Sm 23:28; 2Kg 25:23; Ezr 2:22 [v]**7:27** Ezr 2:23; Neh 11:32; Jr 1:1 [w]**7:32** Gn 12:8; Jos 7:2; Ezr 2:28 [x]**7:36** Jos 6:1; Ezr 2:34; Neh 3:2 [y]**7:37** 1Ch 8:12; Ezr 2:33; Ac 9:32 [z]**7:39** 1Ch 24:7; Ezr 2:36 [aa]**7:43** Ezr 2:40; 7:7; 8:15; Neh 13:30 [ab]**7:44** 1Ch 15:16; Ezr 2:41-43 [ac]**7:45** 1Ch 9:17-27 [ad]**7:46** Neh 11:21

[A]**7:25** = Gibbar's in Ezr 2:20

Giddel's descendants,
Gahar's descendants,
50 Reaiah's descendants,
Rezin's descendants,
Nekoda's descendants,
51Gazzam's descendants,
Uzza's descendants,
Paseah's descendants,
52 Besai's descendants,
Meunim's descendants,
Nephishesim's[A] descendants,
53Bakbuk's descendants,
Hakupha's descendants,
Harhur's descendants,
54 Bazlith's descendants,
Mehida's descendants,
Harsha's descendants,
55Barkos's descendants,
Sisera's descendants,
Temah's descendants,
56 Neziah's descendants,
Hatipha's descendants.

57The descendants of Solomon's servants[a]
included:

Sotai's descendants,
Sophereth's descendants,
Perida's descendants,
58Jaala's descendants,
Darkon's descendants,
Giddel's descendants,
59 Shephatiah's descendants,
Hattil's descendants,
Pochereth-hazzebaim's descendants,
Amon's descendants.

60 All the temple servants
and the descendants of
Solomon's servants[b] 392.

61The following[c] are those who came from
Tel-melah, Tel-harsha, Cherub, Addon, and
Immer, but were unable to prove that their
families and ancestors were Israelite:

62 Delaiah's descendants,
Tobiah's descendants,
and Nekoda's descendants 642

63and from the priests: the descendants of
Hobaiah, the descendants of Hakkoz, and the
descendants of Barzillai — who had taken a

[a]**7:57** 1Kg 9:21; Ezr 2:55
[b]**7:60** Ezr 2:58
[c]**7:61-62** Ezr 2:59-60
[d]**7:65** Ezr 2:63; 5:14
[e]Ex 28:30; Lv 8:8; Ezr 2:63
[f]**7:69-72** Ezr 2:64-70
[g]**7:73** 1Ch 9:2; Ezr 2:70; Neh 7:6
[h]Lv 23:23-43; Ezr 3:1
[i]**8:1** Ezr 3:1
[j]Neh 3:26; 8:16
[k]Ezr 7:6,11,12; Neh 8:9,13
[l]2Ch 34:14; Neh 8:7-9,13-14,18
[m]**8:2** Lv 23:23; Nm 29:1-6; Neh 6:15
[n]Ezr 7:1-5
[o]Neh 8:7,18
[p]**8:3** Neh 3:26
[q]Dt 28:61; 2Ch 17:9; 25:4; 34:14-15
[r]**8:4** 2Ch 6:13

wife from the daughters of Barzillai the Gileadite and was called by their name. 64These
searched for their entries in the genealogical
records, but they could not be found, so they
were disqualified from the priesthood. 65The
governor[d] ordered them not to eat the most
holy things until there was a priest who could
consult the ·Urim and Thummim.[e]

66 The whole combined assembly
numbered 42,360
67 not including their 7,337 male
and female slaves,
as well as their 245 male
and female singers.
68 They had 736 horses, 245 mules,[B]
69 435 camels, and 6,720 donkeys.[f]

70Some of the family leaders gave to the
project. The governor gave 1,000 gold coins,[C]
50 bowls, and 530 priestly garments to the
treasury. 71Some of the family leaders gave
20,000 gold coins and 2,200 silver minas[D]
to the treasury for the project. 72The rest of
the people gave 20,000 gold coins, 2,000 silver minas, and 67 priestly garments. 73So the
priests, Levites, gatekeepers, temple singers,
some of the people, temple servants, and all
Israel settled in their towns.[E,g]

Public Reading of the Law

8 When the seventh month[h] came and the
Israelites had settled in their towns, 1all
the people gathered together[i] at the square in
front of the Water Gate.[j] They asked Ezra the
scribe[k] to bring the book of the law of Moses[l]
that the LORD had given Israel. 2On the first
day of the seventh month,[m] Ezra the priest[n]
brought the law[o] before the assembly of men,
women, and all who could listen with understanding. 3While he was facing the square
in front of the Water Gate,[p] he read out of it
from daybreak until noon before the men,
the women, and those who could understand. All the people listened attentively[F] to
the book of the law.[q] 4Ezra the scribe stood
on a high wooden platform[r] made for this
purpose. Mattithiah, Shema, Anaiah, Uriah,
Hilkiah, and Maaseiah stood beside him on
his right; to his left were Pedaiah, Mishael,

[A]**7:52** Alt Hb tradition reads *Nephushesim's* [B]**7:68** Some Hb mss, LXX; Ezr 2:66; other Hb mss omit v. 68 [C]**7:70** Or *drachmas*, or *darics*; also in vv. 71-72 [D]**7:71** A Babylonian coin worth 50 shekels [E]**7:73** The second half of v. 73 is better understood when placed with 8:1. [F]**8:3** Lit *The ears of all the people listened*

Malchijah, Hashum, Hash-baddanah, Zechariah, and Meshullam. 5 Ezra opened the book
in full view of all the people, since he was elevated above everyone. As he opened it, all the
people stood up. 6 Ezra praised the LORD, the
great God, and with their hands uplifted[a] all
the people said, "•Amen, Amen!"[b] Then they
bowed down and worshiped the LORD with
their faces to the ground.[c]
7 Jeshua, Bani, Sherebiah, Jamin, Akkub,
Shabbethai, Hodiah, Maaseiah, Kelita, Azariah, Jozabad, Hanan, and Pelaiah,[d] who were
Levites,[A,e] explained the law[f] to the people as
they stood in their places. 8 They read out of
the book of the law of God, translating and
giving the meaning so that the people could
understand what was read. 9 Nehemiah the
governor,[g] Ezra the priest and scribe,[h] and
the Levites who were instructing the people
said to all of them, "This day[i] is holy to the
LORD your God. Do not mourn or weep."[j] For
all the people were weeping as they heard
the words of the law. 10 Then he said to them,
"Go and eat what is rich, drink what is sweet,
and send portions to those who have nothing
prepared,[k] since today[l] is holy to our Lord. Do
not grieve, because the joy of the LORD is your
stronghold."[m] 11 And the Levites quieted all the
people, saying, "Be still,[n] since today[o] is holy.
Do not grieve." 12 Then all the people began to
eat and drink, send portions, and have a great
celebration,[p] because they had understood
the words that were explained to them.

Festival of Booths Observed

13 On the second day, the family leaders
of all the people, along with the priests and
Levites,[q] assembled before Ezra the scribe[r]
to study the words of the law. 14 They found
written in the law how the LORD had commanded through Moses that the Israelites
should dwell in booths during the festival
of the seventh month.[s] 15 So they proclaimed
and spread this news throughout their towns
and in Jerusalem, saying, "Go out to the hill
country and bring back branches of olive,
wild olive, myrtle, palm, and other leafy trees
to make booths, just as it is written."[t] 16 The
people went out, brought back branches, and
made booths for themselves on each of their
rooftops,[u] and courtyards, the court of the
house of God, the square by the Water Gate,[v]
and the square by the Gate of Ephraim.[w] 17 The
whole community that had returned from
exile[x] made booths and lived in them. They
had not celebrated like this from the days of
Joshua son of Nun until that day.[y] And there
was tremendous joy.[z] 18 Ezra[B] read out of the
book of the law of God[aa] every day, from the
first day to the last. The Israelites celebrated
the festival for seven days, and on the eighth
day there was an assembly, according to the
ordinance.[ab]

National Confession of Sin

9 On the twenty-fourth day of this month[ac]
the Israelites assembled; they were fasting, wearing •sackcloth, and had put dust
on their heads.[ad] 2 Those of Israelite descent
separated themselves from all foreigners,[ae]
and they stood[af] and confessed their sins and
the •guilt of their fathers.[ag] 3 While they stood
in their places,[ah] they read from the book of
the law of the LORD their God for a fourth
of the day and spent another fourth of the
day[ai] in confession[aj] and worship of the LORD
their God. 4 Jeshua, Bani, Kadmiel, Shebaniah,
Bunni, Sherebiah, Bani, and Chenani stood
on the raised platform built for the Levites[ak]
and cried out loudly to the LORD their God.
5 Then the Levites — Jeshua, Kadmiel, Bani,
Hashabneiah, Sherebiah, Hodiah, Shebaniah,
and Pethahiah[al] — said, "Stand up. Praise
•Yahweh your God from everlasting to everlasting."[am]

Praise Your glorious name,[an]
and may it be exalted above all blessing
and praise.
6 You[C] alone are Yahweh.[ao]
You created the heavens,
the highest heavens with all their host,
the earth and all that is on it,
the seas and all that is in them.
You give life to all of them,[ap]
and the heavenly host worships You.[aq]
7 You are Yahweh,
the God who chose Abram
and brought him out of Ur
of the Chaldeans,[ar]

[a] **8:6** 1Tm 2:8
[b] Neh 5:13
[c] 2Ch 20:18
[d] **8:7** Neh 9:4-5
[e] Ezr 8:15,18-19; Neh 7:43
[f] Lv 10:11; Mal 2:6,8
[g] **8:9** Neh 5:14-15
[h] Ezr 7:1-6
[i] Nm 29:1-6
[j] Ezr 3:12-13; 10:1,6
[k] **8:10** 2Sm 6:19; Est 9:22
[l] Nm 29:1-6
[m] Dt 16:11,14-15
[n] **8:11** Ps 46:10
[o] Nm 29:1-6
[p] **8:12** Est 9:22
[q] **8:13** Neh 10:28-29
[r] Ezr 7:6; Neh 8:1,9
[s] **8:14** Jn 7:2
[t] **8:14-15** Lv 23:4,34-42
[u] **8:16** Dt 22:8
[v] Neh 3:26; 8:1; 12:37
[w] 2Ch 25:23
[x] **8:17** Ezr 1:11; Neh 7:6
[y] 2Ch 7:9; Ezr 3:4
[z] 2Ch 30:21
[aa] **8:18** Neh 8:1,3
[ab] Lv 23:34-36
[ac] **9:1** Neh 7:73; 8:2
[ad] 1Sm 4:12; Neh 1:4; Dn 9:3
[ae] **9:2** Ezr 6:21; 10:11; Neh 13:3
[af] Neh 8:5
[ag] Neh 1:6; Dn 9:4,20
[ah] **9:3** Neh 8:5,7
[ai] Neh 8:3
[aj] Neh 1:6
[ak] **9:4** Neh 8:4
[al] **9:4-5** Neh 8:7
[am] **9:5** 1Ch 16:36; Ps 41:13; 106:48
[an] 1Ch 29:13
[ao] **9:6** Dt 6:4
[ap] 2Kg 19:15
[aq] Ps 89:5-7; Lk 2:13
[ar] **9:7** Gn 11:28,31

[A] **8:7** Vg, 1 Esdras 9:48; MT reads *Pelaiah and the Levites* [B] **8:18** Some Hb mss, Syr read *They* [C] **9:6** LXX reads *And Ezra said: You*

and changed his name to Abraham.[a]
8 You found his heart faithful
in Your sight,[b]
and made a covenant with him
to give the land of the Canaanites,
Hittites, Amorites, Perizzites,
Jebusites, and Girgashites —
to give it to his descendants.[c]
You have kept Your promise,
for You are righteous.

9 You saw the oppression
of our ancestors in Egypt[d]
and heard their cry at the *Red Sea.
10 You performed signs and wonders
against Pharaoh,
all his officials, and all the people
of his land,[e]
for You knew how arrogantly
they treated our ancestors.
You made a name for Yourself
that endures to this day.
11 You divided the sea before them,
and they crossed through it
on dry ground.[f]
You hurled their pursuers
into the depths
like a stone into churning waters.[g]
12 You led them with a pillar of cloud
by day,
and with a pillar of fire by night,
to illuminate the way
they should go.[h]
13 You came down on Mount Sinai,[i]
and spoke to them from heaven.
You gave them impartial ordinances,
reliable instructions,
and good statutes and commands.
14 You revealed Your holy Sabbath
to them,
and gave them commands, statutes,
and instruction
through Your servant Moses.[j]
15 You provided bread from heaven[k]
for their hunger;
You brought them water from the rock[l]
for their thirst.
You told them to go in and possess
the land
You had sworn[A] to give them.[m]

[a]**9:7** Gn 17:5
[b]**9:8** Gn 15:6; 22:15-18
[c]Gn 15:18-21
[d]**9:9** Ex 3:7; 14:10-14,31
[e]**9:10** Ex 3:20; 10:1
[f]**9:11** Ex 14:21-22
[g]Ex 14:26-28
[h]**9:12** Dt 1:32-33
[i]**9:13** Ex 19:20
[j]**9:13-14** Ex 20:1-17
[k]**9:15** Ex 16:4
[l]Ex 17:6
[m]Dt 1:8,21
[n]**9:16-17** Dt 1:26-33
[o]**9:17** Nm 14:4
[p]Ex 34:6; Ps 86:15; 103:8
[q]**9:17-18** Ex 32:4
[r]**9:19** Ex 16:4; 17:6
[s]**9:20** Nm 11:17; Neh 9:30
[t]Ex 16:14-15
[u]Ex 17:6
[v]**9:21** Dt 2:7; 29:5
[w]Dt 8:4
[x]**9:22** Nm 21:21-35
[y]**9:23** Gn 15:5; 22:17

16 But our ancestors acted arrogantly;
they became stiff-necked and did not
listen to Your commands.
17 They refused to listen
and did not remember Your wonders
You performed among them.[n]
They became stiff-necked
and appointed a leader
to return to their slavery in Egypt.[B,o]
But You are a forgiving God,
gracious and compassionate,
slow to anger and rich in faithful love,[p]
and You did not abandon them.
18 Even after they had cast an image
of a calf
for themselves and said,
"This is your God who brought you
out of Egypt,"[q]
and they had committed
terrible blasphemies,
19 You did not abandon them
in the wilderness
because of Your great compassion.
During the day the pillar of cloud
never turned away from them,
guiding them on their journey.
And during the night the pillar of fire
illuminated the way they should go.[r]
20 You sent Your good Spirit[s]
to instruct them.
You did not withhold Your manna[t]
from their mouths,
and You gave them water
for their thirst.[u]
21 You provided for them
in the wilderness 40 years[v]
and they lacked nothing.
Their clothes did not wear out,
and their feet did not swell.[w]
22 You gave them kingdoms and peoples
and assigned them to be a boundary.
They took possession
of the land of Sihon[C] king of Heshbon
and of the land of Og king of Bashan.[x]
23 You multiplied their descendants
like the stars of heaven[y]
and brought them to the land
You told their ancestors to go in
and take possession of it.

[A]**9:15** Lit *lifted Your hand* [B]**9:17** Some Hb mss, LXX; other Hb mss read *in their rebellion* [C]**9:22** One Hb ms, LXX; other Hb mss, Vg read *Sihon, even the land of the*

24 So their descendants went in
and possessed the land:
You subdued the Canaanites
who inhabited the land before them
and handed their kings
and the surrounding peoples over to them,[a]
to do as they pleased with them.
25 They captured fortified cities
and fertile land
and took possession
of well-supplied houses,
cisterns cut out of rock, vineyards,
olive groves, and fruit trees
in abundance.[b]
They ate, were filled,
became prosperous, and delighted
in Your great goodness.
26 But they were disobedient and rebelled
against You.
They flung Your law
behind their backs[c]
and killed Your prophets[d]
who warned them
in order to turn them back to You.
They committed terrible blasphemies.
27 So You handed them over
to their enemies,
who oppressed them.
In their time of distress, they cried out
to You,
and You heard from heaven.
In Your abundant compassion
You gave them deliverers,
who rescued them
from the power of their enemies.
28 But as soon as they had relief,
they again did what was evil
in Your sight.
So You abandoned them to the power
of their enemies,
who dominated them.
When they cried out to You again,
You heard from heaven
and rescued them
many times in Your compassion.[e]
29 You warned them to turn back
to Your law,
but they acted arrogantly
and would not obey Your commands.
They sinned against Your ordinances,
which a person will live by
if he does them.[f]
They stubbornly resisted,[A]
stiffened their necks,
and would not obey.
30 You were patient with them
for many years,
and Your Spirit warned them
through Your prophets,[g]
but they would not listen.
Therefore, You handed them over
to the surrounding peoples.[h]
31 However,
in Your abundant compassion,
You did not destroy them
or abandon them,[i]
for You are a gracious
and compassionate God.[j]
32 So now, our God — the great, mighty,
and awe-inspiring God who keeps
His gracious covenant[k] —
do not view lightly all the hardships
that have afflicted us,
our kings and leaders,
our priests and prophets,
our ancestors and all Your people,
from the days of the Assyrian kings[l]
until today.
33 You are righteous concerning all
that has come on us,
because You have acted faithfully,
while we have acted wickedly.[m]
34 Our kings, leaders, priests,
and ancestors
did not obey Your law
or listen to Your commands
and warnings You gave them.
35 When they were in their kingdom,
with Your abundant goodness that
You gave them,
and in the spacious and fertile land
You set before them,[n]
they would not serve You or turn
from their wicked ways.
36 Here we are today,
slaves in the land You gave
our ancestors

[a]**9:24** Jos 11:23
[b]**9:25** Dt 6:11; 11:11-12
[c]**9:26** 1Kg 14:9
[d]1Kg 18:4; 19:10
[e]**9:26-28** Jdg 2:6–3:6
[f]**9:29** Lv 18:5; Dt 30:16
[g]**9:30** 2Kg 17:13-18; Neh 9:20; Dn 9:6; 1Pt 1:10-12
[h]Jr 16:10-13
[i]**9:31** Jr 4:27
[j]Neh 9:17
[k]**9:32** Neh 1:5; Dn 9:4
[l]2Kg 15:19; 17:3-6
[m]**9:33** Dn 9:7-8,14
[n]**9:35** Neh 9:25

[A]**9:29** Lit *They gave a stubborn shoulder*

so that they could enjoy its fruit
and its goodness.
Here we are — slaves in it![a]
37 Its abundant harvest goes to the kings
You have set over us,
because of our sins.
They rule over our bodies
and our livestock as they please.[b]
We are in great distress.

Israel's Vow of Faithfulness

38[A]In view of all this, we are making a binding agreement[c] in writing on a sealed document containing the names of our leaders,
Levites, and priests.[d]

10 Those whose seals were on the document were:

Nehemiah the governor,[e]
son of Hacaliah, and Zedekiah,
2 Seraiah,[f] Azariah, Jeremiah,
3 Pashhur,[g] Amariah, Malchijah,
4 Hattush, Shebaniah, Malluch,
5 Harim, Meremoth, Obadiah,
6 Daniel, Ginnethon, Baruch,
7 Meshullam, Abijah, Mijamin,
8 Maaziah, Bilgai, and Shemaiah.
These were the priests.
9 The Levites[h] were:
Jeshua son of Azaniah,
Binnui of the sons of Henadad, Kadmiel,
10 and their brothers
Shebaniah, Hodiah, Kelita, Pelaiah,
Hanan,
11 Mica, Rehob, Hashabiah,
12 Zaccur, Sherebiah, Shebaniah,
13 Hodiah, Bani, and Beninu.

14 The leaders of the people[i] were:
Parosh, Pahath-moab, Elam, Zattu, Bani,
15 Bunni, Azgad, Bebai,
16 Adonijah, Bigvai, Adin,[j]
17 Ater, Hezekiah, Azzur,
18 Hodiah, Hashum, Bezai,
19 Hariph, Anathoth, Nebai,
20 Magpiash, Meshullam, Hezir,
21 Meshezabel, Zadok, Jaddua,
22 Pelatiah, Hanan, Anaiah,
23 Hoshea, Hananiah,[k] Hasshub,
24 Hallohesh, Pilha, Shobek,
25 Rehum, Hashabnah, Maaseiah,
26 Ahijah, Hanan, Anan,
27 Malluch, Harim, Baanah.

28The rest of the people — the priests, Levites, gatekeepers, singers, and temple servants, along with their wives, sons, and
daughters, everyone who is able to understand[l] and who has separated themselves
from the surrounding peoples[m] to obey the
law of God — 29join with their noble brothers
and commit themselves with a sworn oath[B,n]
to follow the law of God given through God's
servant Moses[o] and to carefully obey all the
commands, ordinances, and statutes of •Yah-
weh our Lord.

Details of the Vow

30We will not give our daughters in marriage to the surrounding peoples and
will not take their daughters as wives for
our sons.[p]

31When the surrounding peoples bring
merchandise or any kind of grain to sell
on the Sabbath day, we will not buy from
them on the Sabbath or a holy day.[q] We
will also leave the land uncultivated in the
seventh year[r] and will cancel every debt.[s]

32We will impose the following commands on ourselves:

To give an eighth of an ounce of silver[C]
yearly for the service of the house of our
God:[t] 33the bread displayed before the
LORD,[D,u] the daily •grain offering, the
regular •burnt offering, the Sabbath and
New Moon offerings,[v] the appointed festivals, the holy things, the •sin offerings
to •atone for Israel,[w] and for all the work
of the house of our God.

34We have cast lots[x] among the priests,
Levites, and people for the donation
of wood by our ancestral houses at the
appointed times each year. They are to
bring the wood to our God's house to
burn on the altar of the LORD our God,[y]
as it is written in the law.

35We will bring the •firstfruits of our land
and of every fruit tree to the LORD's house

[a]**9:35-36** Dt 28:47-48 [b]**9:37** Dt 28:33,51 [c]**9:38** 2Ch 23:16 [d]Neh 10:1-39 [e]**10:1** Neh 5:14; 8:9; 12:26 [f]**10:2-8** Neh 12:1-7,11-21 [g]**10:3** 1Ch 9:12 [h]**10:9-13** Neh 8:7; 9:4-5; 12:8-9 [i]**10:14-27** Ezr 2:1-61; Neh 7:6-63 [j]**10:16** Ezr 8:6 [k]**10:23** Neh 7:2 [l]**10:28** Neh 8:2-3 [m]Neh 9:2; 13:3 [n]**10:29** Ezr 10:5; Neh 5:12 [o]Neh 8:1 [p]**10:30** Ex 34:16; Neh 13:23 [q]**10:31** Neh 13:16 [r]Ex 23:10-11; Lv 25:1-7 [s]Dt 15:1-3 [t]**10:32** Ex 30:11-16; Mt 17:24 [u]**10:33** Lv 24:5-9 [v]Nm 10:10 [w]Nm 28:2–29:39 [x]**10:34** Lv 16:8; Neh 11:1 [y]Lv 6:12-13; Neh 13:31

[A]**9:38** Neh 10:1 in Hb [B]**10:29** Lit *and enter in a curse and in an oath* [C]**10:32** Lit *give one-third of a shekel* [D]**10:33** Lit *rows of bread*

year by year.[a] 36 We will also bring the
firstborn of our sons and our livestock,
as prescribed by the law, and will bring
the firstborn of our herds and flocks to
the house of our God,[b] to the priests who
serve in our God's house. 37 We will bring a
loaf from our first batch of dough[c] to the
priests at the storerooms of the house of
our God. We will also bring the firstfruits
of our grain offerings, of every fruit tree,
and of the new wine and oil.[d] A tenth of
our land's produce belongs to the Levites,
for the Levites are to collect the one-tenth
offering in all our agricultural towns.[e] 38 A
priest of Aaronic descent must accompany the Levites when they collect the
tenth,[f] and the Levites must take a tenth
of this offering to the storerooms of the
treasury in the house of our God.[g] 39 For
the Israelites and the Levites are to bring
the contributions of grain, new wine,
and oil to the storerooms where the articles of the sanctuary are kept[h] and where
the priests who minister are, along with
the gatekeepers and singers. We will not
neglect the house of our God.[i]

Resettling Jerusalem

11 Now the leaders of the people stayed in
Jerusalem,[j] and the rest of the people
cast lots[k] for one out of ten to come and live
in Jerusalem, the holy city,[l] while the other
nine-tenths remained in their towns.[m] 2 The
people praised all the men who volunteered[n]
to live in Jerusalem.

3 These are the heads of the province who
stayed in Jerusalem[o] (but in the villages of Judah each lived on his own property in their
towns[p]—the Israelites, priests, Levites, temple servants, and descendants of Solomon's
servants[q]— 4 while some of the descendants
of Judah and Benjamin settled in Jerusalem):

Judah's[r] descendants:

Athaiah son of Uzziah, son of Zechariah,
son of Amariah, son of Shephatiah, son
of Mahalalel, of Perez's descendants;
5 and Maaseiah son of Baruch, son of Col-
hozeh, son of Hazaiah, son of Adaiah,
son of Joiarib, son of Zechariah, a descendant of the Shilonite. 6 The total number
of Perez's descendants, who settled in Jerusalem, was 468 capable men.

7 These were Benjamin's descendants:
Sallu son of Meshullam, son of Joed, son
of Pedaiah, son of Kolaiah, son of Maaseiah, son of Ithiel, son of Jeshaiah, 8 and
after him Gabbai and Sallai: 928. 9 Joel
son of Zichri was the officer over them,
and Judah son of Hassenuah was second
in command over the city.

10 The priests:

Jedaiah son of Joiarib, Jachin, and 11 Seraiah son of Hilkiah, son of Meshullam,
son of Zadok, son of Meraioth, son of
Ahitub, the chief official of God's temple,
12 and their relatives who did the work at
the temple: 822. Adaiah son of Jeroham,
son of Pelaliah, son of Amzi, son of Zechariah, son of Pashhur, son of Malchijah
13 and his relatives, the leaders of families: 242. Amashsai son of Azarel, son of
Ahzai, son of Meshillemoth, son of Immer, 14 and their relatives, capable men:
128. Zabdiel son of Haggedolim, was
their chief.

15 The Levites:

Shemaiah son of Hasshub, son of Azrikam, son of Hashabiah, son of Bunni;
16 and Shabbethai and Jozabad, from
the leaders of the Levites, who supervised the work outside the house of God;
17 Mattaniah son of Mica, son of Zabdi,
son of ·Asaph, the leader who began the
thanksgiving in prayer;[s] Bakbukiah, second among his relatives; and Abda son of
Shammua, son of Galal, son of Jeduthun.[t]
18 All the Levites in the holy city:[u] 284.

19 The gatekeepers:

Akkub, Talmon, and their relatives, who
guarded the gates: 172.

20 The rest of Israel, the priests, and the Levites were in all the villages of Judah, each on
his own inherited property.[v] 21 The temple servants lived on Ophel;[A,w] Ziha and Gishpa supervised the temple servants.

[a] **10:35** Lv 26:1-10; Nm 18:12-13
[b] **10:36** Ex 13:2,12-13
[c] **10:37** Lv 23:17; Nm 15:20-21; Ezk 44:30
[d] Nm 18:12-13
[e] Lv 27:30
[f] **10:38** Nm 18:26
[g] Neh 13:12-13
[h] **10:39** Dt 12:6,11
[i] Neh 13:10-11
[j] **11:1** Neh 7:4
[k] Neh 10:34
[l] Neh 11:18; Is 48:2; Rv 11:2; 21:2
[m] Ezr 2:70; Neh 7:73
[n] **11:2** Jdg 5:9
[o] **11:3** 1Ch 9:2-34
[p] Neh 7:73; 11:20
[q] Neh 7:39-43,46-60
[r] **11:4-19** 1Ch 9:3-21
[s] **11:17** 1Ch 6:31,39; 2Ch 5:12
[t] 1Ch 16:42
[u] **11:18** Neh 11:1; Rv 21:2
[v] **11:20** Nm 36:3; Neh 11:3
[w] **11:21** Neh 3:26

[A] **11:21** = a hill in Jerusalem

The Levites and Priests

[22]The leader of the Levites in Jerusalem
was Uzzi son of Bani, son of Hashabiah, son
of Mattaniah, son of Mica, of the descendants
of Asaph, who were singers for the service of
God's house. [23]There was, in fact, a command
of the king regarding them, and an ordinance
regulating[A] the singers'[a] daily tasks. [24]Petha-
hiah son of Meshezabel, of the descendants
of Zerah[b] son of Judah, was the king's[c] agent[B]
in every matter concerning the people.
[25]As for the farming settlements with their
fields:

Some of Judah's descendants lived
in Kiriath-arba[d] and its villages,
Dibon[e] and its villages, and Jekabzeel
and its villages;
26 in Jeshua, Moladah,[f] Beth-pelet,
27 Hazar-shual, and Beer-sheba[g]
and its villages;
28 in Ziklag[h] and Meconah and its villages;
29 in En-rimmon, Zorah,[i] Jarmuth,[j] and
30 Zanoah[k] and Adullam
with their villages;
in Lachish[l] with its fields and Azekah[m]
and its villages.
So they settled from Beer-sheba[n]
to the Valley of Hinnom.[o]

31 Benjamin's descendants:
from Geba,[C,p] Michmash,[q] Aija,
and Bethel[r] — and its villages,
32 Anathoth,[s] Nob,[t] Ananiah,
33 Hazor,[u] Ramah,[v] Gittaim,[w]
34 Hadid, Zeboim,[x] Neballat,
35 Lod, and Ono,[y] the Valley of Craftsmen.
36 Some of the Judean divisions of Levites
were in Benjamin.

12 These[z] are the priests and Levites[aa]
who went up with Zerubbabel[ab] son of
Shealtiel and with Jeshua:

Seraiah, Jeremiah, Ezra,
2 Amariah, Malluch, Hattush,
3 Shecaniah, Rehum, Meremoth,
4 Iddo,[ac] Ginnethoi, Abijah,[ad]
5 Mijamin, Maadiah, Bilgah,
6 Shemaiah, Joiarib, Jedaiah,[ae]
7 Sallu, Amok, Hilkiah, Jedaiah.

[a]11:22-23 1Ch 15:16; Neh 7:44
[b]11:24 Gn 38:30; 1Ch 2:43
[c]Neh 2:1; 5:14
[d]11:25 Jos 14:15
[e]Jos 3:9,17
[f]11:26 Jos 15:26-28
[g]11:27 2Sm 17:11
[h]11:28 1Sm 27:6
[i]11:29 Jos 15:33
[j]Jos 10:5
[k]11:30 Jos 15:34-35
[l]Jos 10:3; 15:39
[m]Jos 10:10
[n]Jos 15:27
[o]2Kg 23:10
[p]11:31 Jos 21:17
[q]1Sm 13:2
[r]Jos 12:9
[s]11:32 Jos 21:18; Jr 1:1
[t]1Sm 21:1; 22:9
[u]11:33 Jos 11:1
[v]Jos 18:25
[w]2Sm 4:3
[x]11:34 1Sm 13:18
[y]11:35 1Ch 8:12; Ac 9:32
[z]12:1-7 Neh 12:12-21
[aa]12:1 Ezr 2:1-2; 7:7
[ab]Ezr 3:2
[ac]12:4 Neh 12:16; Zch 1:1
[ad]1Ch 24:10
[ae]12:6 1Ch 24:7
[af]12:7 Ezr 2:2; 3:2
[ag]12:8 Neh 11:17
[ah]12:10 Neh 3:20
[ai]12:23 1Ch 9:14-22

These were the leaders of the priests and their
relatives in the days of Jeshua.[af]

8 The Levites:
Jeshua, Binnui, Kadmiel,
Sherebiah, Judah, and Mattaniah[ag] —
he and his relatives were in charge
of the praise songs.
9 Bakbukiah, Unni,[D] and their relatives
stood opposite them in the services.
10 Jeshua fathered Joiakim,
Joiakim fathered Eliashib,
Eliashib[ah] fathered Joiada,
11 Joiada fathered Jonathan,
and Jonathan fathered Jaddua.[E]

[12]In the days of Joiakim, the leaders of the
priestly families were:

Meraiah	of Seraiah,
Hananiah	of Jeremiah,
13 Meshullam	of Ezra,
Jehohanan	of Amariah,
14 Jonathan	of Malluchi,
Joseph	of Shebaniah,
15 Adna	of Harim,
Helkai	of Meraioth,
16 Zechariah	of Iddo,
Meshullam	of Ginnethon,
17 Zichri	of Abijah,
Piltai	of Moadiah, of Miniamin,
18 Shammua	of Bilgah,
Jehonathan	of Shemaiah,
19 Mattenai	of Joiarib,
Uzzi	of Jedaiah,
20 Kallai	of Sallai,
Eber	of Amok,
21 Hashabiah	of Hilkiah,
and Nethanel	of Jedaiah.

[22]In the days of Eliashib, Joiada, Johanan,
and Jaddua, the leaders of the families of the
Levites and priests were recorded while Darius the Persian ruled. [23]Levi's descendants,
the leaders of families, were recorded in the
Book of the Historical Records[ai] during the
days of Johanan son of Eliashib. [24]The leaders of the Levites — Hashabiah, Sherebiah,
and Jeshua son of Kadmiel, along with their
relatives opposite them — gave praise and
thanks, division by division, as David the man

[A]11:23 Lit *for* [B]11:24 Lit *was at the king's hand* [C]11:31 Or *descendants from Geba lived in* [D]12:9 Alt Hb tradition reads *Unno*

[E]12:10-11 These men were high priests.

of God had prescribed.[a] 25This included Mattaniah,[b] Bakbukiah, and Obadiah. Meshullam, Talmon, and Akkub were gatekeepers
who guarded the storerooms at the gates.[c]
26These served in the days of Joiakim son of
Jeshua, son of Jozadak, and in the days of Nehemiah the governor[d] and Ezra the priest and
scribe.[e]

Dedication of the Wall

27At the dedication of the wall[f] of Jerusalem,
they sent for the Levites wherever they lived
and brought them to Jerusalem to celebrate
the joyous dedication with thanksgiving and
singing accompanied by cymbals, harps, and
lyres.[g] 28The singers gathered from the region
around Jerusalem, from the villages of the
Netophathites,[h] 29from Beth-gilgal, and from
the fields of Geba and Azmaveth, for they had
built villages for themselves around Jerusalem. 30After the priests and Levites had purified themselves, they purified the people, the
gates, and the wall.[i]

31Then I brought the leaders of Judah up
on top of the wall, and I appointed two large
processions that gave thanks. One went to
the right on the wall, toward the Dung Gate.[j]
32Hoshaiah and half the leaders of Judah followed, 33along with Azariah, Ezra, Meshullam, 34Judah, Benjamin, Shemaiah, Jeremiah,
35and some of the priests' sons with trumpets,
and Zechariah son of Jonathan, son of Shemaiah, son of Mattaniah, son of Micaiah, son
of Zaccur, son of •Asaph followed 36as well
as his relatives—Shemaiah, Azarel, Milalai,
Gilalai, Maai, Nethanel, Judah, and Hanani,
with the musical instruments of David, the
man of God.[k] Ezra the scribe[l] went in front of
them. 37At the Fountain Gate[m] they climbed
the steps of the city of David[n] on the ascent of
the wall and went above the house of David
to the Water Gate[o] on the east.

38The second thanksgiving procession went
to the left, and I followed it with half the people along the top of the wall, past the Tower
of the Ovens[p] to the Broad Wall,[q] 39above
the Gate of Ephraim,[r] and by the Old Gate,[s]
the Fish Gate,[t] the Tower of Hananel, and the
Tower of the Hundred, to the Sheep Gate.[u]
They stopped at the Gate of the Guard.[v] 40The
two thanksgiving processions stood in the
house of God. So did I and half of the officials
accompanying me, 41as well as the priests:

Eliakim, Maaseiah, Miniamin,
Micaiah, Elioenai, Zechariah,
and Hananiah, with trumpets;
42 and Maaseiah, Shemaiah, Eleazar,
Uzzi, Jehohanan, Malchijah, Elam,
and Ezer.

Then the singers sang, with Jezrahiah as the
leader. 43On that day they offered great sacrifices and rejoiced because God had given
them great joy.[w] The women and children
also celebrated, and Jerusalem's rejoicing was
heard far away.[x]

Support of the Levites' Ministry

44On that same day men were placed in
charge of the rooms[y] that housed the supplies, contributions, •firstfruits, and tenths.[z]
The legally required portions for the priests
and Levites[aa] were gathered from the village fields, because Judah was grateful to the
priests and Levites who were serving.[ab] 45They
performed the service of their God and the
service of purification, along with the singers
and gatekeepers,[ac] as David and his son Solomon had prescribed.[ad] 46For long ago, in the
days of David and Asaph,[ae] there were leaders[A]
of the singers and songs of praise and thanksgiving to God.[af] 47So in the days of Zerubbabel[ag] and Nehemiah,[ah] all Israel contributed
the daily portions[ai] for the singers and gatekeepers. They also set aside daily portions for
the Levites, and the Levites set aside daily portions[aj] for the descendants of Aaron.

Nehemiah's Further Reforms

13 At that time[ak] the book of Moses[al]
was read publicly to[B] the people.[am]
The command was found written in it that
no Ammonite or Moabite[an] should ever enter the assembly of God,[ao] 2because they did
not meet the Israelites with food and water.
Instead, they hired Balaam against them to
curse them,[ap] but our God turned the curse
into a blessing.[aq] 3When they heard the law,
they separated all those of mixed descent[ar]
from Israel.

[a] **12:24** 1Ch 16:4; 23:30; 2Ch 29:25
[b] **12:25** Neh 11:17
[c] 1Ch 26:15,17; Ezr 2:42; Neh 11:19
[d] **12:26** Neh 5:14; 10:1
[e] Neh 8:1-2,9
[f] **12:27** Ezr 6:16
[g] 1Ch 15:16
[h] **12:28** 1Ch 2:54; 9:16
[i] **12:30** Neh 13:22,30
[j] **12:31** Neh 2:13
[k] **12:36** 1Ch 15:16,19-21; 2Ch 8:14; Neh 12:24
[l] Neh 8:1,4
[m] **12:37** Neh 2:14
[n] Neh 3:15
[o] Neh 3:26; 8:1
[p] **12:38** Neh 3:11
[q] Neh 3:8
[r] **12:39** 2Kg 14:13; Neh 8:16
[s] Neh 3:6
[t] Neh 3:3
[u] Neh 3:1; Jn 5:2
[v] Neh 3:25
[w] **12:43** Ezr 6:16-17,22
[x] Ezr 3:13
[y] **12:44** Neh 13:4,13
[z] Neh 10:37-39
[aa] Neh 7:39-43
[ab] Dt 18:8
[ac] **12:45** Neh 7:44-45
[ad] 2Ch 8:14
[ae] **12:46** 2Ch 29:30
[af] 1Ch 9:33
[ag] **12:47** Neh 7:7; Hg 1:1
[ah] Neh 1:1; 5:14
[ai] Neh 11:23
[aj] Nm 18:21
[ak] **13:1** Neh 12:27
[al] Dt 28:61; Neh 8:1-3
[am] Neh 9:3
[an] Neh 13:23
[ao] Dt 23:3
[ap] **13:2** Nm 22:2-11; 23:7; 24:10; Dt 23:3-5
[aq] Dt 23:4-5
[ar] **13:3** Dt 23:3,6

A **12:46** Alt Hb tradition reads *there was a leader* B **13:1** Lit *read in the ears of*

4 Now before this, Eliashib the priest[a] had
been put in charge of the storerooms of the
house of our God.[b] He was a relative[A] of Tobiah[c] 5 and had prepared a large room for him
where they had previously stored the ·grain
offerings, the frankincense, the articles, and
the tenths of grain, new wine, and oil[d] prescribed for the Levites, singers, and gatekeepers, along with the contributions for the
priests.[e]
6 While all this was happening, I was not
in Jerusalem, because I had returned to King
Artaxerxes[f] of Babylon[g] in the thirty-second
year of his reign.[h] It was only later that I asked
the king for a leave of absence[i] 7 so I could return to Jerusalem. Then I discovered the evil
that Eliashib had done on behalf of Tobiah
by providing him a room in the courts of
God's house. 8 I was greatly displeased and
threw all of Tobiah's household possessions
out of the room. 9 I ordered that the rooms
be purified,[j] and I had the articles of the
house of God restored there, along with the
grain offering and frankincense.[k] 10 I also
found out that because the portions for the
Levites had not been given,[l] each of the Levites and the singers performing the service
had gone back to his own field.[m] 11 Therefore,
I rebuked the officials, saying, "Why has the
house of God been neglected?"[n] I gathered
the Levites and singers together and stationed them at their posts.[o] 12 Then all Judah
brought a tenth of the grain, new wine, and
oil into the storehouses.[p] 13 I appointed as
treasurers over the storehouses Shelemiah
the priest, Zadok the scribe, and Pedaiah of
the Levites, with Hanan son of Zaccur, son
of Mattaniah to assist them, because they
were considered trustworthy.[q] They were
responsible for the distribution to their
colleagues.[r]
14 Remember me for this, my God, and don't
erase the deeds of faithful love I have done for
the house of my God and for its services.[s]
15 At that time I saw people in Judah treading wine presses on the Sabbath. They were
also bringing in stores of grain and loading
them on donkeys, along with wine, grapes,
and figs. All kinds of goods were being
brought to Jerusalem on the Sabbath day. So
I warned them against selling food on that
day.[t] 16 The Tyrians living there were import-
ing fish and all kinds of merchandise and
selling them on the Sabbath to the people of
Judah in Jerusalem.[u]
17 I rebuked the nobles of Judah and said to
them: "What is this evil you are doing—profaning the Sabbath day?[v] 18 Didn't your ancestors do the same, so that our God brought all
this disaster on us and on this city?[w] And now
you are rekindling His anger against Israel by
profaning the Sabbath!"
19 When shadows began to fall on the gates
of Jerusalem just before the Sabbath, I gave orders that the gates be closed and not opened
until after the Sabbath.[x] I posted some of my
men at the gates, so that no goods could enter during the Sabbath day.[y] 20 Once or twice
the merchants and those who sell all kinds
of goods camped outside Jerusalem, 21 but I
warned them, "Why are you camping in front
of the wall? If you do it again, I'll use force[B]
against you." After that they did not come
again on the Sabbath. 22 Then I instructed the
Levites to purify themselves[z] and guard the
gates in order to keep the Sabbath day holy.[aa]
Remember me for this also, my God,[ab] and
look on me with compassion in keeping with
Your abundant, faithful love.[ac]
23 In those days I also saw Jews who had
married women from Ashdod, Ammon, and
Moab.[ad] 24 Half of their children spoke the
language of Ashdod or the language of one
of the other peoples but could not speak
Hebrew.[C,ae] 25 I rebuked them, cursed them,
beat some of their men, and pulled out their
hair.[af] I forced them to take an oath[ag] before God and said: "You must not give your
daughters in marriage to their sons or take
their daughters as wives for your sons or
yourselves![ah] 26 Didn't King Solomon of Israel sin in matters like this? There was not a
king like him among many nations. He was
loved by his God and God made him king
over all Israel, yet foreign women drew him
into sin.[ai] 27 Why then should we hear about
you doing all this terrible evil and acting unfaithfully against our God by marrying foreign women?"[aj]
28 Even one of the sons of Jehoiada, son of

[a]**13:4** Neh 12:10,22-23 [b]Neh 12:44 [c]Neh 2:10; 6:14 [d]**13:5** Neh 12:44 [e]Nm 13:21-32; Dt 14:28-29; 26:12-15 [f]**13:6** Neh 2:1-8 [g]Ezr 5:13 [h]Neh 2:1; 5:14 [i]Neh 1:11; 2:6 [j]**13:9** 1Ch 23:28; 2Ch 29:5; Neh 13:30 [k]Neh 12:44 [l]**13:10** Dt 12:19; Neh 12:44,47 [m]2Ch 29:5 [n]**13:11** Neh 10:37-39; Mal 3:10 [o]Neh 12:44-45 [p]**13:12** Neh 10:37-38 [q]**13:13** Neh 7:2; Ac 6:1-5; 1Co 4:2 [r]Neh 12:47 [s]**13:14** Neh 5:19; 13:31 [t]**13:15** Ex 20:8-11; Dt 5:12-15 [u]**13:16** Neh 10:31 [v]**13:17** Ex 20:8-11 [w]**13:18** Ezr 9:10-11,13; Jr 17:21-23 [x]**13:19** Lv 23:32 [y]Neh 7:1,3; Jr 17:21-22 [z]**13:22** Neh 12:30; 13:30 [aa]Ex 20:8 [ab]Neh 5:19; 13:14,31 [ac]Neh 1:5; 9:17,27,31 [ad]**13:23** Dt 23:3; Ezr 9:1-2; Neh 13:1-3; Mal 2:11 [ae]**13:24** Est 1:22; 8:9 [af]**13:25** Ezr 9:3; Is 50:6 [ag]Ezr 10:5 [ah]Ezr 9:1-2; Neh 10:30 [ai]**13:26** 1Kg 3:13; 11:1-10 [aj]**13:27** Ezr 9:1-2

[A]**13:4** Or *an associate* [B]**13:21** Lit *again, I will send a hand* [C]**13:24** Lit *Judahite*

Eliashib the high priest,[a] had become a son-
in-law to Sanballat the Horonite.[b] So I drove
him away from me.[c]
29 Remember them, my God, for defiling
the priesthood as well as the covenant of the
priesthood and the Levites.[d]
30 So I purified them from everything foreign[e] and assigned specific duties to each of
the priests and Levites.[f] 31 I also arranged for
the donation of wood at the appointed times
and for the •firstfruits.[g]
Remember me, my God, with favor.[h]

[a] 13:28 Neh 12:10,22-23 [b] Neh 2:10; 4:1; 6:1 [c] Lv 21:10,13-15 [d] 13:29 Neh 6:14; Mal 2:4-8 [e] 13:30 Neh 10:30 [f] Neh 12:44-47 [g] 13:31 Neh 10:34-36 [h] Neh 5:19; 13:14,22

■ **AUTHOR:** Unknown (Mordecai possibly)

■■ **DATE:** During the time of the exile and return of the Jews (around 486–465 B.C.)

She must have been gorgeous in every way, this Hebrew queen of the great Persian king Xerxes. The book named for her claims as much, but in this case, written claims may not do justice to the reality. A search of the entire empire settled finally on this young woman. Though beautiful, she was of no special prominence. Maybe that was part of her mystique and appeal.

Haman, in contrast, must have been arrogant to the core. Recently elevated to high office, perhaps he believed that the esteem that came with his promotion hardly did him justice. So when Mordecai refused to bow and give homage that Haman believed was due him, he decided that genocide of Mordecai's entire race was the due comeuppance.

ESTHER

And what of Mordecai? He is a Jew in a foreign land, yet loyal to the leaders. When he hears of a plot against the king, he does not hesitate to inform those who could protect him. He is not rewarded at the time, but his loyalty is duly recorded in the king's records, which the king reads at just the right time and, at that point, chooses to honor the man Haman is planning to execute.

What of God in all these royal plots and banquets? God is not named in Esther. The entire ten chapters go by without a mention of Him. Is this a secular report? At times, the unfolding story seems to signal an impending collapse of God's plan. Esther's drama is all about the mission of God coming to near failure. But only "near" failure. Never before has the Bible spoken so directly about the extinction of God's people. Only the Flood account in Genesis comes close and there a remnant—survivors of God's judgment—has already been set apart. For the first time now, a military commander with considerable firepower plots to wipe out these chosen ones—all of them, every last one. If Haman succeeds (and with Xerxes' signet ring, how could he fail?), God's mission to redeem the world will be snuffed out in a horrible massacre.

But God has brought Esther here for "such a time as this." We are witnesses as the book of Esther celebrates the sovereign hand of God at every turn by keeping silent about God. The writer never reveals what hearers and readers suspect all along—that God's mission will not fail, that Haman will himself be ruined by his own bloated ego, and that Israel will step back from the precipice and recover their confidence in the God whose promise is worth all their trust.

And so it ends. Israel is saved. Pride is punished. The people have a future after all. The Feast of Purim becomes Israel's way of never forgetting their trustworthy God, and never letting His mission slip too far from their own identity and sense of calling.

Vashti Angers the King

1 These events took place during the days
of Ahasuerus,[A,a] who ruled 127 provinces[b]
from India[B] to ·Cush. 2 In those days King
Ahasuerus reigned from his royal throne[c]
in the fortress at Susa.[d] 3 He held a feast[e] in
the third year of his reign for all his officials
and staff, the army of Persia and Media,[f] the
nobles,[g] and the officials from the provinces.
4 He displayed the glorious wealth of his kingdom and the magnificent splendor of his
greatness[h] for a total of 180 days.
5 At the end of this time, the king held a
week-long banquet[i] in the garden courtyard[j]
of the royal palace[k] for all the people, from
the greatest to the least,[l] who were present in
the fortress of Susa.[m] 6 White and violet linen
hangings were fastened with fine white and
purple linen cords to silver rods on marble[C]
columns. Gold and silver couches[n] were arranged on a mosaic pavement of red feld-
spar,[D] marble,[C] mother-of-pearl, and precious
stones.
7 Beverages were served in an array of gold
goblets,[o] each with a different design. Royal
wine flowed freely, according to the king's
bounty[p] 8 and no restraint was placed on the
drinking. The king had ordered every wine
steward in his household to serve as much as
each person wanted. 9 Queen Vashti also gave
a feast for the women of King Ahasuerus's
palace.
10 On the seventh day, when the king was
feeling good from the wine,[q] Ahasuerus commanded Mehuman, Biztha, Harbona,[r] Big-
tha, Abagtha, Zethar, and Carkas, the seven
eunuchs[s] who personally served him, 11 to
bring Queen Vashti before him with her royal
crown. He wanted to show off her beauty to
the people and the officials, because she was
very beautiful.[t] 12 But Queen Vashti refused to
come at the king's command that was delivered by his eunuchs. The king became furious
and his anger burned within him.[u]

The King's Decree

13 The king consulted the wise men[v] who
understood the times,[E,w] for it was his normal procedure to confer with experts in
law and justice. 14 The most trusted ones[F]
were Carshena, Shethar, Admatha, Tarshish,
Meres, Marsena, and Memucan. They were
the seven officials[x] of Persia and Media[y] who
had personal access to the king[z] and occupied the highest positions in the kingdom.[aa]
15 The king asked, "According to the law, what
should be done with Queen Vashti, since she
refused to obey King Ahasuerus's command
that was delivered by the eunuchs?"
16 Memucan said in the presence of the king
and his officials, "Queen Vashti has wronged
not only the king, but all the officials and the
peoples who are in every one of King Ahasuerus's provinces.[ab] 17 For the queen's action will
become public knowledge to all the women
and cause them to despise their husbands and
say, 'King Ahasuerus ordered Queen Vashti
brought before him, but she did not come.'
18 Before this day is over, the noble women of
Persia and Media who hear about the queen's
act will say the same thing to all the king's officials, resulting in more contempt and fury.
19 "If it meets the king's approval, he should
personally issue a royal decree. Let it be recorded in the laws of Persia and Media, so
that it cannot be revoked:[ac] Vashti is not to enter King Ahasuerus's presence, and her royal
position is to be given to another woman
who is more worthy than she.[ad] 20 The decree
the king issues will be heard throughout his
vast kingdom,[ae] so all women will honor their
husbands,[af] from the least to the greatest."[ag]
21 The king and his counselors approved the
proposal, and he followed Memucan's advice.
22 He sent letters to all the royal provinces, to
each province in its own script and to each
ethnic group in its own language,[ah] that every
man should be master of his own house and
speak in the language of his own people.

Search for a New Queen

2 Some time later,[ai] when King Ahasuerus's
rage[aj] had cooled down, he remembered
Vashti, what she had done, and what was decided against her.[ak] 2 The king's personal attendants[G] suggested, "Let a search be made
for beautiful young women for the king.[al] 3 Let
the king appoint commissioners[am] in each

[a] **1:1** Ezr 4:6; Dn 9:1
[b] Est 8:9; 9:30
[c] **1:2** 1Kg 1:46
[d] Ezr 4:9; Neh 1:1; Dn 8:2
[e] **1:3** Gn 40:20; 1Kg 3:15; Est 2:18
[f] Dn 5:28
[g] Est 6:9; Dn 1:3
[h] **1:4** Dn 4:28-30
[i] **1:5** Est 2:18
[j] 2Kg 21:18; Est 7:7-8
[k] Est 2:8
[l] Est 1:20
[m] Ezr 4:9
[n] **1:6** Est 7:8; Ezk 23:41; Am 6:4
[o] **1:7** Dn 5:1-3
[p] Est 2:18
[q] **1:10** 2Sm 13:28
[r] Est 7:9
[s] 2Kg 20:18; Est 2:21; 6:14; Mt 19:12
[t] **1:11** Est 2:7
[u] **1:12** Est 7:7; Pr 19:12
[v] **1:13** Jr 10:7; Dn 2:2,12; Mt 2:1
[w] 1Ch 12:32
[x] **1:14** Ezr 7:14
[y] Dn 5:28
[z] 2Kg 25:19
[aa] Dn 2:48-49
[ab] **1:16** Est 1:1,3,5; 9:30
[ac] **1:19** Est 8:8; Dn 6:8,15
[ad] Est 2:2,4,17
[ae] **1:20** Est 1:1; 8:9
[af] Est 1:10-12; Eph 5:22,24,33; Col 3:18; 1Tm 2:12; 1Pt 3:1
[ag] Est 1:5
[ah] **1:22** Neh 13:24; Est 3:12; 8:9
[ai] **2:1** Est 1:3,10
[aj] Est 1:12; 7:10
[ak] Est 1:10-12,16-21
[al] **2:2** 1Kg 1:2
[am] **2:3** Gn 41:34

A **1:1** = Xerxes; he reigned 486-465 B.C. B **1:1** = modern Pakistan C **1:6** Or *alabaster* D **1:6** Or *of porphyry* E **1:13** Or *understood propitious times*
F **1:14** Lit *Those near him* G **2:2** Lit *The young men of the king who served him*

province of his kingdom, so that they may assemble all the beautiful young women to the harem at the fortress of Susa.[a] Put them under the care of Hegai, the king's eunuch,[b] who is in charge of the women,[c] and give them the required beauty treatments. 4 Then the young woman who pleases the king[d] will become queen instead of Vashti."[e] This suggestion pleased the king, and he did accordingly.

5 In the fortress of Susa, there was a Jewish man named Mordecai[f] son of Jair, son of Shimei,[g] son of Kish,[h] a Benjaminite. 6 He had been taken into exile from Jerusalem with the other captives when King Nebuchadnezzar of Babylon took King Jeconiah[A] of Judah into exile.[i] 7 Mordecai was the legal guardian of his cousin[B] Hadassah (that is, Esther), because she didn't have a father or mother. The young woman had a beautiful figure and was extremely good-looking. When her father and mother died, Mordecai had adopted her as his own daughter.[j]

8 When the king's command and edict became public knowledge, many young women gathered at the fortress of Susa under Hegai's care. Esther was also taken to the palace and placed under the care of Hegai, who was in charge of the women. 9 The young woman pleased him and gained his favor[C] so that he accelerated the process of the beauty treatments and the special diet that she received. He assigned seven hand-picked female servants to her from the palace and transferred her and her servants to the harem's best quarters.

10 Esther did not reveal her ethnic background or her birthplace, because Mordecai had ordered her not to. 11 Every day Mordecai took a walk in front of the harem's courtyard to learn how Esther was doing and to see what was happening to her.

12 During the year before each young woman's turn to go to King Ahasuerus, the harem regulation required her to receive beauty treatments with oil of myrrh for six months and then with perfumes and cosmetics for another six months. 13 When the young woman would go to the king, she was given whatever she requested to take with her from the harem to the palace. 14 She would go in the evening, and in the morning she would return to a second harem under the supervision of Shaashgaz, the king's eunuch in charge of the concubines.[k] She never went to the king again, unless he desired her and summoned her by name.[l]

[a] 2:3 Neh 1:1; Est 1:1; Dn 8:2
[b] Est 1:10
[c] Est 2:8-9,12-13
[d] 2:4 Est 2:17
[e] Est 1:19
[f] 2:5 Ezr 2:2; Est 2:15; 3:2
[g] 2Sm 6:5-13
[h] 1Sm 9:1
[i] 2:6 2Kg 24:10-15; 2Ch 36:10; Jr 24:1; 29:1-2
[j] 2:7 Est 9:29
[k] 2:14 1Kg 11:3; Dn 5:2
[l] Est 4:11
[m] 2:15 Est 9:29
[n] Est 5:2,8
[o] 2:16 Est 1:2
[p] 2:17 Est 1:10-11; 2:4
[q] 2:18 Est 1:3
[r] Est 1:7
[s] 2:19 Est 2:12-14
[t] Est 5:13
[u] 2:21 Est 1:10,12; 2:3,14
[v] 2:22 Est 6:2-3
[w] 2:23 Gn 40:19,22; Est 5:14; 7:9-10

Esther Becomes Queen

15 Esther was the daughter of Abihail,[m] the uncle of Mordecai who had adopted her as his own daughter. When her turn came to go to the king, she did not ask for anything except what Hegai, the king's trusted official in charge of the harem, suggested. Esther won approval in the sight of everyone who saw her.[n]

16 She was taken to King Ahasuerus in the royal palace in the tenth month, the month Tebeth, in the seventh year of his reign.[o] 17 The king loved Esther more than all the other women. She won more favor and approval from him than did any of the other young women. He placed the royal crown on her head and made her queen in place of Vashti.[p] 18 The king held a great banquet for all his officials and staff.[q] It was Esther's banquet. He freed his provinces from tax payments and gave gifts worthy of the king's bounty.[r]

19 When the young women[s] were assembled together for a second time, Mordecai was sitting at the King's Gate.[t] 20 Esther still had not revealed her birthplace or her ethnic background, as Mordecai had directed. She obeyed Mordecai's orders, as she always had while he raised her.

Mordecai Saves the King

21 During those days while Mordecai was sitting at the King's Gate, Bigthan and Teresh, two eunuchs[u] who guarded the king's entrance, became infuriated and planned to assassinate[D] King Ahasuerus. 22 When Mordecai learned of the plot, he reported it to Queen Esther, and she told the king on Mordecai's behalf.[v] 23 When the report was investigated and verified, both men were hanged on the gallows.[w] This event was recorded in the Historical Record in the king's presence.

[A] **2:6** = Jehoiachin in 2Kg 24; 25:27; 1Ch 3:16-17 [B] **2:7** Lit *uncle's daughter* [C] **2:9** Lit *and carried faithful love before him* [D] **2:21** Lit *and they sought to stretch out a hand against*

Haman's Plan to Kill the Jews

3 After all this took place, King Ahasuerus
honored Haman, son of Hammedatha
the Agagite.[a] He promoted him in rank and
gave him a higher position than all the other
officials.[b] 2The entire royal staff at the King's
Gate[c] bowed down and paid homage to Haman, because the king had commanded this
to be done for him. But Mordecai would not
bow down or pay homage.[d] 3The members of
the royal staff at the King's Gate asked Mordecai, "Why are you disobeying the king's
command?" 4When they had warned him
day after day[e] and he still would not listen to
them, they told Haman to see if Mordecai's
actions would be tolerated, since he had told
them he was a Jew.

5When Haman saw that Mordecai was not
bowing down or paying him homage, he was
filled with rage.[f] 6And when he learned of
Mordecai's ethnic identity, Haman decided
not to do away with[A] Mordecai alone. He
planned to destroy all of Mordecai's people,
the Jews,[g] throughout Ahasuerus's kingdom.[h]

7In the first month, the month of Nisan,[B]
in King Ahasuerus's twelfth year,[C,i] Pur (that
is, the lot) was cast before Haman for each
day in each month, and it fell on the twelfth
month,[j] the month Adar.[D,k] 8Then Haman informed King Ahasuerus, "There is one ethnic
group, scattered throughout the peoples in
every province of your kingdom,[l] yet living
in isolation. Their laws are different from everyone else's and they do not obey the king's
laws.[m] It is not in the king's best interest to
tolerate them.[n] 9If the king approves, let an
order be drawn up authorizing their destruction, and I will pay 375 tons of silver to[E] the ac-
countants for deposit in the royal treasury."[o]

10The king removed his signet ring[p] from
his finger and gave it to Haman son of
Hammedatha the Agagite, the enemy of the
Jewish people.[q] 11Then the king told Haman,
"The money and people are given to you to do
with as you see fit."

12The royal scribes were summoned[r] on
the thirteenth day of the first month, and
the order was written exactly as Haman
commanded. It was intended for the royal
satraps,[s] the governors of each of the provinces, and the officials of each ethnic group
and written for each province in its own
script and to each ethnic group in its own
language.[t] It was written in the name of
King Ahasuerus[u] and sealed with the royal
signet ring.[v] 13Letters were sent by couriers[w]
to each of the royal provinces telling the officials to destroy, kill, and annihilate all the
Jewish people — young and old, women and
children — and plunder their possessions on
a single day,[x] the thirteenth day of Adar, the
twelfth month.[F]

14A copy of the text, issued as law throughout every province, was distributed to all the
peoples so that they might get ready for that
day. 15The couriers left, spurred on by royal
command, and the law was issued in the fortress of Susa.[y] The king and Haman sat down
to drink, while the city of Susa was in confusion.[z]

Mordecai Appeals to Esther

4 When Mordecai learned all that had occurred,[aa] he tore his clothes,[ab] put on •sack-
cloth and ashes,[ac] went into the middle of the
city, and cried loudly and bitterly.[ad] 2He only
went as far as the King's Gate,[ae] since the law
prohibited anyone wearing sackcloth from
entering the King's Gate. 3There was great
mourning among the Jewish people in every province where the king's command and
edict[af] came. They fasted, wept, and lamented,
and many lay on sackcloth and ashes.[ag]

4Esther's female servants and her eunuchs
came and reported the news to her, and the
queen was overcome with fear.[ah] She sent
clothes for Mordecai to wear so he could take
off his sackcloth, but he did not accept them.
5Esther summoned Hathach, one of the king's
eunuchs assigned to her, and dispatched him
to Mordecai to learn what he was doing and
why.[G] 6So Hathach went out to Mordecai in
the city square in front of the King's Gate.
7Mordecai told him everything that had happened as well as the exact amount of money
Haman had promised to pay the royal treasury for the slaughter of the Jews.[ai]

8Mordecai also gave him a copy of the written

[a]3:1 Ex 17:8-16; 1Sm 15:20
[b]Est 1:3,21; 2:18
[c]3:2 Est 2:19,21
[d]Est 5:9
[e]3:4 Gn 39:10
[f]3:5 Est 1:12; 2:21; 7:7; Dn 3:19
[g]3:6 Est 6:10
[h]Est 9:24; Ps 83:2-4
[i]3:7 Est 1:2; 2:16
[j]Est 9:24-28
[k]Ezr 6:15
[l]3:8 Est 1;1; 8:11,17; 9:2
[m]Jr 29:7; Ac 16:20-21
[n]Ezr 4:12-15
[o]3:9 Est 4:7
[p]3:10 Gn 41:42; Est 8:2,8,10; Hg 2:23
[q]Est 7:6; 9:10
[r]3:12 Est 8:9
[s]Ezr 8:36
[t]Est 1:22; 8:9
[u]1Kg 21:8
[v]Est 8:10
[w]3:13 2Ch 30:6; Est 8:14
[x]Est 8:11-13; 9:10
[y]3:14-15 Est 8:13-14
[z]3:15 Est 7:1; 8:15
[aa]4:1 Est 3:7-15
[ab]2Sm 1:11; 3:31; Ezr 9:3
[ac]Is 58:5; Dn 9:3
[ad]Ex 11:6
[ae]4:2 Est 2:19; 3:2
[af]4:3 Est 3:12-15
[ag]Est 8:17; Is 58:5; Dan 9:3; Jnh 3:5-6
[ah]4:4 Est 7:6
[ai]4:7 Est 3:9-15

A3:6 Lit *to stretch out a hand against* B3:7 = March–April; called Abib in the pre-exilic period; Ex 13:4; Dt 16:1 C3:7 474 B.C. D3:7 = February–March E3:9 Lit *will weigh 10,000 silver talents on the hands of* F3:13 LXX adds the text of Ahasuerus's letter here. G4:5 Lit *what is this and why is this*

decree issued in Susa ordering their destruction, so that Hathach might show it to Esther, explain it to her, and command her to
approach the king, implore his favor, and
plead with him personally for her people.[a]
9 Hathach came and repeated Mordecai's response to Esther.
10 Esther spoke to Hathach and commanded him to tell Mordecai, 11 "All the royal officials and the people of the royal provinces
know that one law applies to every man or
woman who approaches the king in the inner courtyard[b] and who has not been summoned — the death penalty.[c] Only if the king
extends the gold scepter will that person live.[d]
I have not been summoned to appear before

[a] 4:8 Est 7:3-4
[b] 4:11 Est 5:1
[c] Dn 2:9,12-13
[d] Est 5:2; 8:4

WORLDVIEW

The Mission of God in Native American Culture

The aboriginal people of North America have had a spirituality so deeply impressive that many religious leaders have advised more aggressive Christian movements to simply leave them alone, as though Native Americans have had enough of the "white man's ways."

That attractive spirituality, however, has become such a regular theme of popular media that reality begs to be understood for what it really was, not for Hollywood's romantic version. Native Americans rested their case for life, family, and tribal survival on a wide and high view of a sovereign deity who may be approached by a supplicant, whose good will may be won, and who finally provides the necessities of life—rain, sun, protection—and who guides the human spirit after death. This great deity sometimes shows himself in visions, but can be obnoxiously indifferent, stoic, or absent when needed most. Under the vast skies of the American plains, seekers of God could well imagine themselves to be shadowed by the presence of the Almighty or conversely, orphans in the universe. Either way, the cycle of life plays out, sometimes all too quickly. Disease, raids, droughts, and the extinction of the great buffalo herds were constant threats and tragic realities, all known to the inscrutable Almighty, all eventually a fit with the inexorable cycle.

The Christian gospel came to Native Americans so tied to the encroachment of European-American culture that its rejection by Native American leaders was nearly an act of cultural justice. But seen for what it is—the revelation that the God of creation has displayed His identity and saving purpose fully in Jesus Christ—the gospel has a claim on Native Americans and has taken hold among them. Churches have been established. Old animosities have softened in bonds of Christian fellowship, and mutual forgiveness for the cruelties perpetrated by both sides extended and received.

The gospel is a big sky story of great and mysterious life forging the contours of rugged lands, filling those lands with life, and protecting creation from evil by the great spiritual warrior, Jesus. It was He who was captured and beaten, then killed, by His oppressors, only to be vindicated by the Almighty and made to rise to new life. That great day of hope and celebration is reminiscent of the feasts and festivals of Native American cultures, as it was of the people of Israel entering and occupying their own land in Old Testament narratives. It is relief to know that God is good, full of lovingkindness, and not the distant deity hard to find and placate.

Reconciliation with white culture was also a gift of the gospel. On the frontier, Indians were often regarded as wild animals and settlers thought nothing of killing them. Indians may have felt much the same about the settlers. Such dehumanization offends God, whose Kingdom is a unity of many colors. The gospel enables people to see the other through eyes of love and kinship. Wounds are healed and mutual goodwill witnesses to the mission of God.

the king[a] for the last[A] 30 days." 12Esther's response was reported to Mordecai.
13Mordecai told the messenger to reply to
Esther, "Don't think that you will escape the
fate of all the Jews because you are in the
king's palace. 14If you keep silent at this time,
liberation and deliverance will come to the
Jewish people from another place,[b] but you
and your father's house will be destroyed.
Who knows, perhaps you have come to your
royal position for such a time as this."[c]
15Esther sent this reply to Mordecai: 16"Go
and assemble all the Jews who can be found
in Susa and fast for me. Don't eat or drink
for three days,[d] day or night. I and my female
servants will also fast[e] in the same way. After
that, I will go to the king even if it is against
the law.[f] If I perish, I perish."[g] 17So Mordecai
went and did everything Esther had ordered
him.

Esther Approaches the King

5 On the third day,[h] Esther dressed up in
her royal clothing and stood in the inner
courtyard[i] of the palace facing it. The king
was sitting on his royal throne in the royal
courtroom, facing its entrance. 2As soon as
the king saw Queen Esther standing in the
courtyard, she won his approval.[B] The king
extended the gold scepter in his hand toward
Esther, and she approached and touched the
tip of the scepter.[j]
3"What is it, Queen Esther?" the king asked
her. "Whatever you want, even to half the
kingdom, will be given to you."[k]
4"If it pleases the king," Esther replied,
"may the king and Haman come today to the
banquet[l] I have prepared for them."
5The king commanded, "Hurry, and get Haman so we can do as Esther has requested."
So the king and Haman went to the banquet
Esther had prepared.
6While drinking the[C] wine,[m] the king asked
Esther, "Whatever you ask will be given to
you. Whatever you want, even to half the
kingdom, will be done."
7Esther answered, "This is my petition and
my request: 8If the king approves of me[D] and
if it pleases the king to grant my petition

[a]**4:11** Est 2:14
[b]**4:14** Gn 50:20
[c]Gn 45:5-7
[d]**4:16** Est 5:1; Jl 1:14
[e]Est 9:31
[f]Est 5:1-2
[g]Gn 43:14
[h]**5:1** Est 4:16
[i]Est 4:11
[j]**5:2** Est 8:4
[k]**5:3** Est 7:2; Mk 6:23
[l]**5:4** Est 1:3,5; 2:18
[m]**5:6** Est 1:7-8,10; 7:1-2
[n]**5:8** Est 7:3; 8:5
[o]Est 6:14
[p]**5:9** 1Kg 8:66; 2Ch 7:10; Pr 15:15
[q]Est 2:19; 3:2,5
[r]**5:10** Est 6:13
[s]**5:11** Est 3:1
[t]**5:14** Est 6:4; 7:9-10
[u]Est 6:13
[v]**6:1** Dn 6:18
[w]**6:1-2** Est 2:21-23
[x]**6:3** Est 10:2-3; Dn 2:48
[y]**6:4** Est 5:14

and perform my request,"[n] may the king and
Haman come to the banquet I will prepare
for them.[o] Tomorrow I will do what the king
has asked."
9That day Haman left full of joy and in good
spirits.[E,p] But when Haman saw Mordecai at
the King's Gate, and Mordecai didn't rise or
tremble in fear at his presence, Haman was
filled with rage toward Mordecai.[q] 10Yet Haman controlled himself and went home. He
sent for his friends and his wife Zeresh[r] to
join him. 11Then Haman described for them
his glorious wealth and his many sons. He
told them all how the king had honored him
and promoted him in rank over the other officials and the royal staff.[s] 12"What's more,"
Haman added, "Queen Esther invited no one
but me to join the king at the banquet she
had prepared. I am invited again tomorrow
to join her with the king. 13Still, none of this
satisfies me since I see Mordecai the Jew sitting at the King's Gate all the time."
14His wife Zeresh and all his friends told
him, "Have them build a gallows 75 feet[F] high.[t]
Ask the king in the morning to hang Mordecai on it. Then go to the banquet with the
king and enjoy yourself." The advice pleased
Haman, so he had the gallows constructed.[u]

Mordecai Honored by the King

6 That night sleep escaped[v] the king, so he
ordered the book recording daily events
to be brought and read to the king. 2They
found the written report of how Mordecai
had informed on Bigthana and Teresh, two
eunuchs who guarded the king's entrance,
when they planned to assassinate King Ahasuerus.[w] 3The king inquired, "What honor and
special recognition have been given to Mordecai for this act?"[x]
The king's personal attendants replied,
"Nothing has been done for him."
4The king asked, "Who is in the court?"
Now Haman was just entering the outer court
of the palace to ask the king to hang Mordecai
on the gallows he had prepared for him.[y]
5The king's attendants answered him, "Haman is there, standing in the court."
"Have him enter," the king ordered.

[A]**4:11** Lit *king these* [B]**5:2** Lit *she obtained favor in his eyes*; Est 2:15,17 [C]**5:6** Lit *During the banquet of* [D]**5:8** Lit *If I have found favor in the eyes of the king*

[E]**5:9** Lit *left rejoicing and good of heart* [F]**5:14** Lit *50 cubits*

6Haman entered, and the king asked him,
"What should be done for the man the king
wants to honor?"[a]
Haman thought to himself, "Who is it the
king would want to honor more than me?"
7Haman told the king, "For the man the king
wants to honor: 8Have them bring a royal garment that the king himself has worn[b] and a
horse the king himself has ridden,[c] which has
a royal diadem on its head. 9Put the garment
and the horse under the charge of one of the
king's most noble officials.[d] Have them clothe
the man the king wants to honor, parade him
on the horse through the city square, and
proclaim before him, 'This is what is done for
the man the king wants to honor.'"
10The king told Haman, "Hurry, and do just
as you proposed. Take a garment and a horse
for Mordecai the Jew,[e] who is sitting at the
King's Gate. Do not leave out anything you
have suggested." 11So Haman took the garment and the horse. He clothed Mordecai
and paraded him through the city square,
crying out before him, "This is what is done
for the man the king wants to honor."
12Then Mordecai returned to the King's
Gate,[f] but Haman, overwhelmed,[A] hurried
off for home with his head covered.[g] 13Haman
told his wife Zeresh and all his friends[h] everything that had happened. His advisers and
his wife Zeresh said to him, "Since Mordecai
is Jewish, and you have begun to fall before
him, you won't overcome him, because your
downfall is certain."[i] 14While they were still
speaking with him, the eunuchs of the king[j]
arrived and rushed Haman to the banquet Esther had prepared.[k]

Haman Is Executed

7 The king and Haman came to feast[B,l] with
Esther the queen. 2Once again, on the second day while drinking wine,[m] the king asked
Esther, "Queen Esther, whatever you ask will
be given to you. Whatever you seek, even to
half the kingdom, will be done."[n]
3Queen Esther answered, "If I have obtained
your approval,[C] my king, and if the king is
pleased,[o] spare my life—this is my request;
and spare my people—this is my desire.[p] 4For
my people and I have been sold out[q] to destruction, death, and extermination.[r] If we had
merely been sold as male and female slaves,[s]
I would have kept silent. Indeed, the trouble
wouldn't be worth burdening the king."
5King Ahasuerus spoke up and asked
Queen Esther, "Who is this, and where is the
one who would devise such a scheme?"[D,t]
6Esther answered, "The adversary and enemy[u] is this evil Haman."
Haman stood terrified[v] before the king and
queen. 7Angered[w] by this, the king arose from
where they were drinking wine and went to
the palace garden.[x] Haman remained to beg
Queen Esther for his life because he realized
the king was planning something terrible for
him.[y] 8Just as the king returned from the palace garden to the house of wine drinking, Haman was falling on the couch[z] where Esther
was reclining. The king exclaimed, "Would
he actually violate the queen while I am in
the palace?" As soon as the statement left the
king's mouth, Haman's face was covered.[aa]
9Harbona, one of the royal eunuchs,[ab] said:
"There is a gallows 75 feet[E] tall at Haman's
house that he made for Mordecai,[ac] who gave
the report that saved[F] the king."[ad]
The king commanded, "Hang him on it."
10They hanged Haman on the gallows he
had prepared for Mordecai.[ae] Then the king's
anger subsided.[af]

Esther Intervenes for the Jews

8 That same day King Ahasuerus awarded
Queen Esther the estate[ag] of Haman, the
enemy of the Jews.[ah] Mordecai entered the
king's presence because Esther had revealed
her relationship to Mordecai.[ai] 2The king removed his signet ring he had recovered from
Haman[aj] and gave it to Mordecai, and Esther
put him in charge of Haman's estate.
3Then Esther addressed the king again.[ak]
She fell at his feet, wept, and begged[al] him to
revoke the evil of Haman the Agagite,[am] and
his plot he had devised against the Jews.[an] 4The
king extended the gold scepter[ao] toward Esther, so she got up and stood before the king.
5She said, "If it pleases the king, and I have
found approval before him, if the matter

[a] **6:6** Est 3:8-9 [b] **6:8-9** Gn 41:42-43 [c] **6:8** 1Kg 1:33 [d] **6:9** Est 5:11 [e] **6:10** Est 3:6 [f] **6:12** Est 5:9,13 [g] 2Sm 15:30 [h] **6:13** Est 5:10,14 [i] Dt 32:10; Zch 2:8 [j] **6:14** Est 1:10-11 [k] Est 5:7-8 [l] **7:1** Gn 40:20 [m] **7:2** Est 5:6 [n] Est 5:3,6 [o] **7:3** Est 2:17; 5:8 [p] Est 4:12-14 [q] **7:4** Est 3:9,13; 4:7 [r] Est 3:13; 8:11; 9:5-10 [s] Dt 28:48,68 [t] **7:5** Est 3:5-6,8-9 [u] **7:6** Est 3:10 [v] Est 4:4 [w] **7:7** Est 1:12; Pr 20:2 [x] Est 1:5-6 [y] Est 6:13 [z] **7:8** Est 1:6 [aa] Est 6:12; Jb 9:24 [ab] **7:9** Est 1:12 [ac] Est 5:14 [ad] Est 2:21-23; 6:1-2 [ae] **7:10** Est 5:14; Ps 7:16; 94:23; Pr 11:5,6; Dn 6:24 [af] Est 1:12; 2:1 [ag] **8:1** Est 3:9; 5:11 [ah] Est 3:10; 7:6 [ai] Est 2:7,10 [aj] **8:2** Est 3:10,12 [ak] **8:3** Est 7:3-4,6 [al] Est 7:7 [am] Ex 17:8-16; Est 3:1 [an] Est 3:5-6,8-15 [ao] **8:4** Est 4:11; 5:2

[A] 6:12 Lit *mourning* [B] 7:1 Lit *drink* [C] 7:3 Lit *If I have found favor in your eyes* [D] 7:5 Lit *who would fill his heart to do this* [E] 7:9 Lit *50 cubits* [F] 7:9 Lit *who spoke good for*

seems right to the king and I am pleasing
in his sight,[a] let a royal edict be written. Let
it revoke the documents the scheming Haman son of Hammedatha the Agagite, wrote
to destroy the Jews who are in all the king's
provinces.[b] 6 For how could I bear to see the
disaster that would come on my people?[c]
How could I bear to see the destruction of
my relatives?"[d]
7 King Ahasuerus said to Esther the Queen
and to Mordecai the Jew, "Look, I have given
Haman's estate to Esther,[e] and he was hanged
on the gallows because he attacked[A] the Jews.[f]
8 You may write in the king's name whatever
pleases you[g] concerning the Jews, and seal it
with the royal signet ring.[h] A document written in the king's name and sealed with the
royal signet ring cannot be revoked."[i]
9 On the twenty-third day of the third
month[j] (that is, the month Sivan),[B] the royal
scribes were summoned. Everything was
written exactly as Mordecai[k] ordered for the
Jews, to the satraps,[l] the governors, and the
officials of the 127 provinces from India[C] to
•Cush.[m] The edict was written for each province in its own script, for each ethnic group
in its own language,[n] and to the Jews in their
own script and language.
10 Mordecai wrote in King Ahasuerus's
name and sealed the edicts with the royal signet ring. He sent the documents by mounted
couriers,[o] who rode fast horses[p] bred from
the royal racing mares.
11 The king's edict gave the Jews in each and
every city the right to assemble and defend
themselves, to destroy, kill, and annihilate
every ethnic and provincial army hostile to
them, including women and children, and to
take their possessions as spoils of war.[q] 12 This
would take place on a single day throughout all the provinces of King Ahasuerus, on
the thirteenth day of the twelfth month, the
month Adar.[D,r]
13 A copy of the text, issued as law throughout every province, was distributed to all the
peoples[s] so the Jews could be ready to avenge
themselves against their enemies on that day.
14 The couriers rode out in haste on their royal
horses at the king's urgent command. The law
was also issued in the fortress of Susa.[t]
15 Mordecai went from the king's presence
clothed in royal purple and white, with a
great gold crown and a purple robe of fine
linen.[u] The city of Susa shouted and rejoiced,[v]
16 and the Jews celebrated[E] with gladness,
joy, and honor.[w] 17 In every province and every city, wherever the king's command and
his law reached, joy and rejoicing took place
among the Jews. There was a celebration and
a holiday.[F,x] And many of the ethnic groups of
the land professed themselves to be Jews because fear of the Jews[y] had overcome them.

Victories of the Jews

9 The king's command and law[z] went into
effect on the thirteenth day of the twelfth
month,[aa] the month Adar.[D] On the day when
the Jews' enemies[ab] had hoped to overpower
them, just the opposite happened. The Jews
overpowered those who hated them.[ac] 2 In
each of King Ahasuerus's provinces[ad] the Jews
assembled in their cities to attack those who
intended to harm them.[G] Not a single person
could withstand them; terror of them[ae] fell
on every nationality.[af]
3 All the officials of the provinces, the satraps, the governors, and the royal civil administrators[H,ag] aided the Jews because they
were afraid of Mordecai.[ah] 4 For Mordecai
exercised great power in the palace,[ai] and his
fame spread throughout the provinces as he
became more and more powerful.[aj]
5 The Jews put all their enemies to the sword,
killing and destroying them.[ak] They did what
they pleased to those who hated them. 6 In
the fortress of Susa[al] the Jews killed and destroyed 500 men, 7 including Parshandatha,
Dalphon, Aspatha, 8 Poratha, Adalia, Arida-
tha, 9 Parmashta, Arisai, Aridai, and Vaizatha.
10 They killed these 10 sons[am] of Haman son of
Hammedatha, the enemy of the Jews.[an] However, they did not seize[I] any plunder.[ao]
11 On that day the number of people killed
in the fortress of Susa was reported to the
king. 12 The king said to Queen Esther, "In
the fortress of Susa the Jews have killed and
destroyed 500 men, including Haman's 10 sons.

[a] **8:5** Est 2:17; 5:8; 7:3
[b] Est 3:13-14
[c] **8:6** Est 4:13-14; 7:3-4
[d] Est 3:13
[e] **8:7** Est 3:9; 5:11; 8:1; Pr 13:22
[f] Est 7:9-10
[g] **8:8** Est 3:11
[h] Est 3:10,12; 8:2; Hg 2:23
[i] Est 1:19; Dn 6:8,12
[j] **8:9** Est 3:7,12
[k] Est 3:12
[l] Ezr 8:36
[m] Est 1:1; 3:13; 9:30
[n] Neh 13:24; Est 1:22; 3:12
[o] **8:10** Est 3:12-13
[p] 1Kg 4:26,28
[q] **8:11** Est 3:13; 9:10
[r] **8:12** Est 3:7
[s] **8:13** Est 3:14
[t] **8:14** Est 3:15
[u] **8:15** Gn 41:42; Est 5:11; Dn 5:29
[v] Est 3:15
[w] **8:16** Ezr 4:1-3; Ps 97:11
[x] **8:17** Est 4:3
[y] Dt 11:25; Est 9:3
[z] **9:1** Est 8:7-8,10
[aa] Est 3:7; 8:12
[ab] Est 3:10; 7:6; 8:1
[ac] 2Sm 22:41; Est 3:5
[ad] **9:2** Est 1:1; 8:9; 9:30
[ae] Est 8:17
[af] Est 3:12,14; 8:13,17
[ag] **9:3** Est 3:12; 8:9
[ah] Est 8:17
[ai] **9:4** Est 10:2-3
[aj] 2Sm 3:1; 1Ch 11:9
[ak] **9:5** Est 3:13
[al] **9:6** Est 1:2; 3:15; 8:14
[am] **9:10** Est 5:11
[an] Est 3:10; 7:6; 8:1
[ao] Est 3:13; 8:11

[A] **8:7** Lit *stretched out his hand against* [B] **8:9** = May–June [C] **8:9** = modern Pakistan [D] **8:12; 9:1** = February–March [E] **8:16** Lit *had light* [F] **8:17** Lit *good day* [G] **9:2** Lit *cities to send out a hand against the seekers of their evil* [H] **9:3** Lit *and those who do the king's work*; Est 3:9 [I] **9:10** Lit *not put their hands on*

What have they done in the rest of the royal provinces? Whatever you ask will be given to you. Whatever you seek will also be done."[a]

13 Esther answered, "If it pleases the king, may the Jews who are in Susa also have tomorrow[b] to carry out today's law,[c] and may the bodies of Haman's 10 sons[d] be hung on the gallows."[e] 14 The king gave the orders for this to be done, so a law was announced in Susa, and they hung the bodies of Haman's 10 sons. 15 The Jews in Susa assembled again on the fourteenth day of the month of Adar[f] and killed 300 men in Susa, but they did not seize[A] any plunder.[g]

16 The rest of the Jews in the royal provinces assembled, defended themselves, and got rid of[B] their enemies. They killed 75,000[C] of those who hated them,[h] but they did not seize[A] any plunder. 17 They fought on the thirteenth day of the month of Adar and rested on the fourteenth, and it became a day of feasting and rejoicing.

18 But the Jews in Susa had assembled on the thirteenth and the fourteenth days of the month. They rested on the fifteenth day of the month, and it became a day of feasting and rejoicing.[i] 19 This explains why the rural Jews who live in villages observe the fourteenth day of the month of Adar as a time of rejoicing and feasting. It is a holiday when they send gifts to one another.[j]

20 Mordecai[k] recorded these events and sent letters to all the Jews in all of King Ahasuerus's provinces, both near and far. 21 He ordered[l] them to celebrate the fourteenth and fifteenth days of the month Adar every year 22 because during those days the Jews got rid of[D,m] their enemies. That was the month when their sorrow was turned into rejoicing and their mourning into a holiday.[n] They were to be days of feasting,[o] rejoicing, and of sending gifts to one another and the poor.

23 So the Jews agreed to continue the practice they had begun, as Mordecai had written them to do. 24 For Haman son of Hammedatha the Agagite, the enemy of all the Jews,[p] had plotted against the Jews to destroy them. He cast the Pur (that is, the lot) to crush and destroy them.[q] 25 But when the matter was brought before the king,[r] he commanded by letter that the evil plan Haman had devised against the Jews return on his own head[s] and that he should be hanged with his sons on the gallows.[t] 26 For this reason these days are called Purim, from the word Pur.[u]

Because of all the instructions in this letter as well as what they had witnessed and what had happened to them, 27 the Jews bound themselves, their descendants, and all who joined[v] with them to a commitment that they would not fail to celebrate these two days each and every year according to the written instructions and according to the time appointed. 28 These days are remembered and celebrated by every generation, family, province, and city, so that these days of Purim will not lose their significance in Jewish life[E] and their memory will not fade from their descendants.[w]

29 Queen Esther daughter of Abihail,[x] along with Mordecai the Jew,[y] wrote this second letter with full authority[z] to confirm the letter about Purim. 30 He sent letters with messages of peace and faithfulness to all the Jews who were in the 127 provinces of the kingdom of Ahasuerus, 31 in order to confirm these days of Purim at their proper time just as Mordecai the Jew and Queen Esther had established them and just as they had committed themselves and their descendants to the practices of fasting[aa] and lamentation.[ab] 32 So Esther's command confirmed these customs of Purim, which were then written into the record.

Mordecai's Fame

10 King Ahasuerus imposed a tax throughout the land[ac] even to the farthest shores.[F,ad] 2 All of his powerful and magnificent accomplishments[ae] and the detailed account of Mordecai's great rank to which the king had honored him,[af] have they not been written in the Historical Records of the Kings of Media and Persia?[ag] 3 Mordecai the Jew was second only to King Ahasuerus,[ah] famous among the Jews, and highly popular with many of his relatives.[ai] He continued to seek good for his people and to speak for the welfare of all his descendants.[aj]

[a] **9:12** Est 5:6; 7:2; 8:8
[b] **9:13** Est 8:12; 9:1
[c] Est 8:11
[d] Est 5:11
[e] Est 7:9-10
[f] **9:15** Est 9:1
[g] Est 8:11
[h] **9:16** Lv 26:7-8; Est 9:5
[i] **9:18** Est 8:16-17
[j] **9:19** Neh 8:10,12; Est 9:22
[k] **9:20** Est 8:15
[l] **9:21** Est 8:15; 9:3-4
[m] **9:22** Est 4:14
[n] Ps 30:11
[o] Est 8:17
[p] **9:24** Est 3:1,10; 7:6
[q] Est 3:6-7
[r] **9:25** Est 7:3-6
[s] Ps 7:16
[t] Est 5:14; 7:9-10; 9:13-14
[u] **9:26** Est 3:7
[v] **9:27** Est 8:17; Is 56:3,6; Zch 2:11
[w] **9:28** Jos 4:6-7; 1Co 11:24-25
[x] **9:29** Est 2:7,15
[y] Est 3:4-6; 5:13
[z] Est 8:8; Dn 6:8
[aa] **9:31** Est 4:16
[ab] Est 4:1-3
[ac] **10:1** Est 1:1; 8:9
[ad] Is 11:11; 24:15
[ae] **10:2** Est 1:4
[af] Est 8:15
[ag] Est 2:23; 6:1-2
[ah] **10:3** Gn 41:40-43; 2Ch 28:7; Est 8:15; Dn 5:7
[ai] Est 8:16-17
[aj] Neh 2:10

[A] **9:15,16** Lit *not put their hands on* [B] **9:16** Lit *and gained relief from* [C] **9:16** Some LXX mss read *10,107*; other LXX mss read *15,000* [D] **9:22** Lit *Jews gained relief from* [E] **9:28** LXX reads *will be celebrated into all times* [F] **10:1** Or *imposed forced labor on the land and the coasts of the sea*

JOB

■ **AUTHOR:** Unknown (Job or possibly Moses or Elihu)

■■ **DATE:** The events possibly occurred during the time of the patriarchs (around 2100–1900 B.C.)

To fully understand God's mission in the book of Job, you must endure a loss so grievous that no platitudes can explain it away, no substitutes can replace the loss—or you must know someone whose life has taken a Job-like turn. You must have walked in the valley and not known your point of exit, not seen how the loss can be salvaged or redeemed. It is not necessary to have shared with Job great riches or a large, successful family—only the terribleness of deep loss.

In our fix-it-fast culture, Job-like losses resist every technology, every psychology, and every calculation of gain versus loss. Job is all loss and sorrow. His friends offer no solace whatsoever; their theologies only satisfy themselves, not Job. His wife even, poor soul—no comfort from her, only reiterations of pointless pain. Job's own conception of God fails him, too. He wants reasons that make sense; none are offered that come close. He wants a God who secures his life's work and legacy. Everyone does. But Job is left with dust and tears.

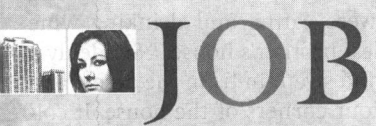

After much distress trying to fit their ideas about God with the realities of Job's life, the friends give up. A dreadful silence sets in. What will come of it? Job wonders whether he is a hapless victim of ideals now quashed by "accidents" no one can explain, an orphan in a cold universe of cause-effect and nothing else—no master plan, no point or purpose. He would be relieved only by his own return to lifeless dust. Then, at least, he would no longer challenge this unpredictable universe which renders no reply to senseless loss. If he were quiet, all would be quiet. Is this how the world is—silence and terror and then nothing?

No, the world is not that way. God speaks. The message is clear, though not particularly comforting, not at first. Job must first hear God; only later is he comforted. When God speaks, Job is compelled only to listen, not to ask for more information or to counter with his own proposals for justice and resolution.

God's message: People suffer because an adversary to whom God allows wide latitude wrecks life and shatters hope for so-called good people as well as obviously bad people. We fret less when bad people suffer; they deserve what they get, we believe. But the moral and the immoral alike share in the pain of this fallen world. God permits people to suffer, stricken by the adversary, hurt beyond repair, it seems. When that happens, Job must not lose sight of God's sovereign goodness.

Job endures a battle between faith and despair that God's entire mission to the world is designed to overcome. Job may surrender hope, handing victory to Satan. Job may persevere in faith—not happy, deeply hurt, but nonetheless confessing that in the valley or at the banquet, bad times and good, God is God: Creator, Redeemer, Savior, Sovereign Lord of life and world. In this confession, Job renders Satan harmless, shown to be a fool for losing the bargain he was so sure he'd win.

God's mission stands when airplanes crash, when viruses destroy a beautiful body, when life goes way past theological explanation and psychological repair. God's mission stands because God is good, and His goodness will shine for all to see. It will, although Job and all who share Job's humanity must wait to see it.

Job and His Family

1 There was a man in the country of Uz[a] named Job.[b] He was a man of perfect integrity,[c] who ˚feared God and turned away from evil.[d] 2 He had seven sons and three daughters. 3 His estate included 7,000 sheep, 3,000 camels, 500 yoke of oxen, 500 female donkeys, and a very large number of servants. Job was the greatest man among all the people of the east.

4 His sons used to take turns having banquets at their homes. They would send an invitation to their three sisters to eat and drink with them. 5 Whenever a round of banqueting was over, Job would send for his children and purify them, rising early in the morning to offer burnt offerings for[A] all of them. For Job thought: Perhaps my children have sinned, having cursed God in their hearts. This was Job's regular practice.

Satan's First Test of Job

6 One day the sons of God[e] came to present themselves before the LORD, and Satan[B] also came with them. 7 The LORD asked Satan, "Where have you come from?"

"From roaming through the earth,"[f] Satan answered Him, "and walking around on it."

8 Then the LORD said to Satan, "Have you considered My servant Job? No one else on earth is like him, a man of perfect integrity, who fears God and turns away from evil."

9 Satan answered the LORD, "Does Job fear God for nothing? 10 Haven't You placed a hedge around[g] him, his household, and everything he owns? You have blessed the work of his hands, and his possessions have increased in the land. 11 But stretch out Your hand and strike[h] everything he owns, and he will surely curse You to Your face."

12 "Very well," the LORD told Satan, "everything he owns is in your power. However, you must not lay a hand on Job himself." So Satan left the LORD's presence.

13 One day when Job's sons and daughters were eating and drinking wine in their oldest brother's house, 14 a messenger came to Job and reported: "While the oxen were plowing and the donkeys grazing nearby, 15 the Sabeans[i] swooped down and took them away. They struck down the servants with the sword, and I alone have escaped to tell you!"

16 He was still speaking when another messenger came and reported: "A lightning storm[C] struck from heaven.[j] It burned up the sheep and the servants and devoured them, and I alone have escaped to tell you!"

17 That messenger was still speaking when yet another came and reported: "The Chaldeans formed three bands, made a raid on the camels, and took them away. They struck down the servants with the sword, and I alone have escaped to tell you!"

18 He was still speaking when another messenger came and reported: "Your sons and daughters were eating and drinking wine in their oldest brother's house. 19 Suddenly a powerful wind swept in from the desert and struck the four corners of the house. It collapsed on the young people so that they died, and I alone have escaped to tell you!"

20 Then Job stood up, tore[k] his robe, and shaved[l] his head.[D] He fell to the ground and worshiped, 21 saying:

Naked I came
 from my mother's womb,[m]
and naked I will leave this life.[E,n]
The LORD gives, and the LORD takes away.
Praise the name of ˚Yahweh.[o]

22 Throughout all this Job did not sin or blame God for anything.[F,p]

Satan's Second Test of Job

2 One day the sons of God[q] came again to present themselves before the LORD, and Satan also came with them to present himself before the LORD. 2 The LORD asked Satan, "Where have you come from?"

"From roaming through the earth," Satan answered Him, "and walking around on it."

3 Then the LORD said to Satan, "Have you considered My servant Job? No one else on earth is like him, a man of perfect integrity,[r] who ˚fears God and turns away from evil.[s] He still retains his integrity, even though you incited Me against him, to destroy him without just cause."

[a] **1:1** Jr 25:20; Lm 4:21
[b] Ezk 14:14,20; Jms 5:11
[c] Jb 2:3; 8:20; 9:20-22
[d] Jb 28:28; Pr 3:7
[e] **1:6** Gn 6:2,4; Jb 2:1; 38:7
[f] **1:7** 1Pt 5:8
[g] **1:10** Ps 34:7
[h] **1:11** Jb 2:5; 4:5; 5:19
[i] **1:15** Gn 10:7; Jb 6:19; Is 45:14
[j] **1:16** Gn 19:24; 1Kg 18:38; 2Kg 1:10-14
[k] **1:20** Gn 37:29,34; Jos 7:6; Jb 2:12
[l] Jr 7:29; Ezk 7:18; Mc 1:16
[m] **1:21** Jb 3:10-11; 10:17-18; Jr 20:17-18
[n] Ps 139:13,15
[o] Jb 38:1; Ps 113:2; 118:26
[p] **1:22** Jb 2:10
[q] **2:1** Gn 6:2,4; Jb 1:6; 38:7
[r] **2:3** Jb 6:29
[s] Jb 1:1,8; 28:28; Pr 3:7

[A] **1:5** Lit *for the number of* [B] **1:6** Or *the adversary* [C] **1:16** Lit *The fire of God*
[D] **1:20** This custom demonstrated mourning. [E] **1:21** Lit *will return there;* Ps 139:13,15 [F] **1:22** Lit *or ascribe blame to God*

4 "Skin for skin!" Satan answered the LORD.
"A man will give up everything he owns in exchange for his life. 5 But stretch out Your hand
and strike[a] his flesh and bones, and he will
surely curse You to Your face."
6 "Very well," the LORD told Satan, "he is in
your power; only spare his life." 7 So Satan left
the LORD's presence and infected Job with
terrible boils from the sole of his foot to the
top of his head.[b] 8 Then Job took a piece of
broken pottery to scrape himself while he sat
among the ashes.[A,c]

a 2:5 Jb 1:11; 4:5; 19:21 b 2:7 Dt 28:27,35 c 2:8 2Sm 13:19; Jb 42:6

WORLDVIEW

The Mission of God in the Middle East

Readers of the Old Testament are dazzled by the hospitality expressed in so many narratives. Abraham entertains strangers. In Judges an old man takes in a Levite for a night and then refuses the crude brutality of brigand neighbors. No guest of his will be victim of a mob. The story ends viciously but the man's sturdy sense of hospitality never falters.

The same sense of awe is real-life experience for visitors to the Middle East, whose people have never forgotten their tradition of opening space and friendship to strangers and pilgrims. Relationships matter in this region. Hospitality is more than casual kindness, timed to fit busy schedules of consumption and self-absorption. It is joy born of ancient dangers of travel and the delight of sharing far-off news. Hospitality is strong commitment to the comfort and safety of guests, at considerable but uncounted cost to hosts.

The gospel is the story of welcoming and incorporation. God's Kingdom is open and God's favor is radiantly attractive to all who follow the way to His table, that way being total trust in the Savior Jesus Christ. As the great host, God imposes no fee and accepts no payment. God's schedule is open. Travelers may knock at any time to seek shelter and be assured of glad welcome. The Scriptures hint that angels sing at the arrival of guests, indeed, that some guests are in fact angels in disguise.

The mission of God is the kind word of welcome and the warm embrace of God's eternal, well-prepared, sumptuous table at life's end. No human hearth matches the promise of God's "welcome home," for heaven is eternal and unspoiled.

Admittedly, there is much concerning heaven that the Bible does not explain, but the assurance of hospitality is guaranteed by the character of the Host and by the point and purpose of the Host's mission in the world of time and space. God has wanted to be known, to be surrounded, to be sought. God has wanted the company of strangers turned friends. God has, in His uniquely divine way, anticipated the buzz of talk and song that warms the house and makes the spirit glad—the company of happy travelers at journey's end, dangers past, struggle over. Now be full, the Host offers. Stay, feast, and rebuild so that your countenance shines like the Son's, and your body turns from "dust" and flesh to the tissue and sinew of the resurrection body of Christ. Be renewed.

Since September 11, 2001 Middle East culture has suffered a metaphoric tsunami. Events since then have devastated any perception of "welcome" once so integral to North African-Red Sea-Fertile Crescent culture. Fighting in Afghanistan, revolutions in other countries, popular uprisings in Libya, Syria, Egypt, news footage of violence and self-inflated leaders merciless to their own people—all speaks to the very opposite of hospitality's virtues. This too shall be redeemed as God's mission of welcome reconciliation takes hold throughout the Middle East. All the world belongs to God. All are invited to God's table.

A 2:8 This custom demonstrated mourning.

9 His wife said to him, "Do you still retain
your integrity? Curse God and die!"
10 "You speak as a foolish woman speaks," he
told her. "Should we accept only good from
God and not adversity?" Throughout all this
Job did not sin in what he said.[A]

Job's Three Friends

11 Now when Job's three friends — Eliphaz
the Temanite,[a] Bildad the Shuhite,[b] and Zophar the Naamathite — heard about all this
adversity that had happened to him, each of
them came from his home. They met together
to go and sympathize with him and comfort[c]
him. 12 When they looked from a distance,
they could barely recognize him. They wept
aloud,[d] and each man tore his robe and threw
dust into the air and on his head.[e] 13 Then they
sat on the ground with him seven days and
nights,[f] but no one spoke a word to him because they saw that his suffering[g] was very
intense.

Job's Opening Speech

3 After this, Job began to speak and cursed
the day he was born. 2 He said:

3 May the day I was born perish,
and the night when they said,
"A boy is conceived."[h]
4 If only that day had turned to darkness!
May God above not care about it,
or light shine on it.
5 May darkness and gloom[i] reclaim it,
and a cloud settle over it.
May an eclipse of the sun[B] terrify it.
6 If only darkness had taken
that night away!
May it not appear[C] among the days
of the year
or be listed in the calendar.[D]
7 Yes, may that night be barren;
may no joyful shout[j] be heard in it.
8 Let those who curse certain days
cast a spell[k] on it,
those who are skilled
in rousing ·Leviathan.[l]
9 May its morning stars grow dark.
May it wait for daylight but have none;
may it not see the breaking[E] of dawn.
10 For that night did not shut
the doors of my mother's womb,
and hide sorrow from my eyes.
11 Why was I not stillborn;
why didn't I die as I came
from the womb?[m]
12 Why did the knees receive me,
and why were there breasts for me
to nurse?[n]
13 Now I would certainly be lying down
in peace;
I would be asleep.[o]
Then I would be at rest[p]
14 with the kings and counselors[q]
of the earth,
who rebuilt ruined cities
for themselves,
15 or with princes who had gold,
who filled their houses[r] with silver.
16 Or why was I not hidden
like a miscarried child,[s]
like infants who never see daylight?
17 There the wicked[t] cease
to make trouble,
and there the weary find rest.
18 The captives are completely at ease;[u]
they do not hear the voice
of their oppressor.[v]
19 Both small and great are there,
and the slave is set free
from his master.[w]
20 Why is light given to one burdened
with grief,
and life to those whose existence
is bitter,[x]
21 who wait for death,[y]
but it does not come,
and search for it more than
for hidden treasure,
22 who are filled with much joy
and are glad when they reach
the grave?[z]
23 Why is life given to a man whose path
is hidden,[aa]
whom God has hedged in?
24 I sigh when food[ab] is put before me,[F]
and my groans pour out like water.[ac]
25 For the thing I feared has overtaken me,

[a] **2:11** Gn 36:34; 1Ch 1:45; Jb 42:9 [b] Gn 25:2; Jb 8:1; 18:1 [c] Jb 42:11; Ps 69:20; Jr 16:5 [d] **2:12** Jdg 21:2; Ru 1:9,14; 2Sm 13:36 [e] Jos 7:6; Lm 2:10; Ezk 27:30 [f] **2:13** Gn 50:10; Ezk 3:15; 45:21 [g] Gn 34:5; Jb 16:6; Ps 39:2 [h] **3:3** Jb 5:7; Pr 23:25; Is 7:14 [i] **3:5** Jb 10:21-22; 12:22; 28:3 [j] **3:7** Jb 20:5; Ps 63:5 [k] **3:8** Nm 22:11,17; Jb 5:3; Pr 11:26 [l] Jb 41; Ps 74:14; 104:26 [m] **3:10-11** Jb 1:21; 10:17-18; Jr 20:17-18 [n] **3:12** Sg 8:1; Is 66:12; Jl 2:16 [o] **3:13** Ps 13:3; Jr 51:39,57; Mt 8:24 [p] Jb 17:16; Dn 12:13; Rv 14:13 [q] **3:14** Is 14:9; Jr 51:57; Ezk 32:29 [r] **3:15** Jb 17:13; 30:23; Ec 12:5 [s] **3:16** Nm 12:12; Ps 58:8; Ec 6:3 [t] **3:17** Jb 9:22; 11:20; 18:5 [u] **3:18** Pr 1:33; Jr 30:10; 46:27 [v] Ex 3:7; 5:10,13-14; Jb 39:7 [w] **3:19** Jb 9:22; Ec 9:2-3; Is 14:9-10 [x] **3:20** Jb 23:2; Ps 71:20; Lm 1:4 [y] **3:21** 1Kg 19:4; Jb 7:15; Jnh 4:3 [z] **3:22** Jb 5:26; 10:19; 17:1 [aa] **3:23** Jb 19:8; Lm 3:9; Hs 2:6 [ab] **3:24** Jb 6:7: 33:20; Ps 102:4 [ac] Ps 6:6; 22:1,14; 32:3

[A] **2:10** Lit *sin with his lips* [B] **3:5** Lit *May a darkening of daylight* [C] **3:6** LXX, Syr, Tg, Vg; MT reads *rejoice* [D] **3:6** Lit *or enter the number of months* [E] **3:9** Lit *the eyelids* [F] **3:24** Or *My sighing serves as my food*

and what I dreaded has happened
to me.[a]
26 I cannot relax or be still;
I have no rest,[b] for trouble comes.

FIRST SERIES OF SPEECHES

Eliphaz Speaks

4 Then Eliphaz the Temanite replied:

2 Should anyone try to speak with you
when you are exhausted?
Yet who can keep from speaking?
3 Indeed, you have instructed many
and have strengthened[c] weak hands.
4 Your words have steadied the one
who was stumbling
and braced the knees
that were buckling.[d]
5 But now that this has happened to you,
you have become exhausted.
It strikes[e] you, and you are dismayed.
6 Isn't your piety your confidence,
and the integrity of your life[A]
your hope?[f]
7 Consider: who has perished when he
was innocent?
Where have the honest
been destroyed?[g]
8 In my experience,
those who plow injustice
and those who sow trouble[h] reap
the same.[i]
9 They perish at a single blast[j] from God
and come to an end by the breath
of His nostrils.[k]
10 The lion may roar and the fierce
lion[l] growl,
but the fangs of young lions
are broken.[m]
11 The strong lion dies if it catches
no prey,
and the cubs of the lioness
are scattered.[n]

12 A word was brought to me in secret;
my ears caught a whisper of it.[o]
13 Among unsettling thoughts
from visions in the night,[p]
when deep sleep[q] descends on men,
14 fear and trembling came over me[r]
and made all my bones shake.
15 A wind[B] passed by me,
and I shuddered with fear.[C]
16 A figure stood there,
but I could not recognize
its appearance;
a form loomed before my eyes.
I heard a quiet voice:
17 "Can a person be more righteous
than God,
or a man more pure than his Maker?"[s]
18 If God puts no trust in His servants
and He charges His angels
with foolishness,[D,t]
19 how much more those who dwell
in clay houses,[u]
whose foundation is in the dust,
who are crushed like a moth!
20 They are smashed to pieces from dawn
to dusk;
they perish forever
while no one notices.[v]
21 Are their tent cords not pulled up?
They die without wisdom.[w]

5 Call out if you please. Will anyone
answer you?
Which of the holy ones[x] will you
turn to?
2 For anger kills a fool,
and jealousy slays the gullible.[y]
3 I have seen a fool taking root,
but I immediately pronounced a curse
on his home.
4 His children are far from safety.
They are crushed at the city ·gate,[z]
with no one to rescue them.
5 The hungry consume his harvest,
even taking it out of the thorns.[E]
The thirsty[F] pant
for his children's wealth.
6 For distress does not grow
out of the soil,
and trouble does not sprout
from the ground.
7 But mankind is born for trouble[aa]
as surely as sparks fly upward.

8 However, if I were you, I would appeal
to God
and would present my case to Him.[ab]

[a]3:25 Jb 9:28; 13:11; 30:15 [b]3:26 Jb 30:17; Pr 25:2; Ec 2:23 [c]4:3 Jb 26:2; Is 35:3; Heb 12:12 [d]4:4 Dt 3:28; Jb 16:15; Is 41:10 [e]4:5 Jb 5:19; 6:7; 19:21 [f]4:6 Jb 11:18; Ps 119:116; Jr 17:7 [g]4:7 Jb 8:20; Ps 37:25; Pr 12:21 [h]4:8 Jb 5:7; 15:35; Is 59:4 [i]Ps 7:15; Pr 22:8; Hs 8:7 [j]4:9 2Sm 22:26; Jb 37:10; Is 30:33 [k]Ex 15:8-10; Ps 18:15; 2Th 2:8 [l]4:10 Ps 10:9; 17:12; 22:13,21 [m]Jb 29:17; Ps 3:7; 58:6 [n]4:11 Ps 59:11; Pr 20:8,20; Is 33:3 [o]4:12 Jb 13:1; 33:16; 36:10,15 [p]4:13 Jb 7:14; 20:8; 33:15 [q]Gn 2:21; 15:12; Jb 33:15 [r]4:14 Jb 21:6; Ps 55:5; 119:120 [s]4:17 Jb 15:14; 25:4; Pr 20:9 [t]4:18 Jb 15:15; 21:22; 25:5 [u]4:19 Jb 10:9; 33:6; Is 64:8 [v]4:20 Jb 14:2; 20:7; Ps 90:5-6 [w]4:21 Jb 36:12; Pr 5:23; 10:21 [x]5:1 Jb 15:15; Ps 89:5-7; Dn 4:17 [y]5:2 Pr 12:16; 14:18; 19:19 [z]5:4 Jb 31:21; Pr 22:22; Is 29:21 [aa]5:7 Jb 4:8; 15:35; Is 59:4 [ab]5:8 Jb 13:18; 23:4; Lm 3:59

[A]4:6 Lit *ways* [B]4:15 Or *A spirit* [C]4:15 Or *and the hair on my body stood up* [D]4:18 Or *error*; Hb obscure [E]5:5 Hb obscure [F]5:5 Aq, Sym, Syr, Vg; MT reads *snares*

9 He does great[a]
and unsearchable things,
wonders without number.[b]
10 He gives rain to the earth
and sends water to the fields.[c]
11 He sets the lowly on high,
and mourners are lifted to safety.[d]
12 He frustrates the schemes of the crafty
so that they[A] achieve no success.
13 He traps the wise in their craftiness
so that the plans of the deceptive
are quickly brought to an end.[e]
14 They encounter darkness by day,
and they grope at noon
as if it were night.[f]
15 He saves the needy
from their sharp words[B,g]
and from the clutches of the powerful.
16 So the poor have hope,
and injustice shuts its mouth.[h]
17 See how happy the man is
God corrects;
so do not reject the discipline
of the ·Almighty.
18 For He crushes but also binds up;
He strikes, but His hands also heal.[i]
19 He will rescue you from six calamities;
no harm will touch you in seven.
20 In famine He will redeem you
from death,
and in battle, from the power
of the sword.[j]
21 You will be safe from slander[C]
and not fear destruction
when it comes.[k]
22 You will laugh at destruction
and hunger
and not fear the animals of the earth.
23 For you will have a covenant
with the stones of the field,
and the wild animals will be at peace
with you.[l]
24 You will know that your tent is secure,[m]
and nothing will be missing
when you inspect your home.
25 You will also know that your offspring
will be many
and your descendants like the grass
of the earth.
26 You will approach the grave[n]
in full vigor,[o]
as a stack of sheaves is gathered
in its season.

27 We have investigated this,
and it is true!
Hear it and understand it
for yourself.

Job's Reply to Eliphaz

6 Then Job answered:

2 If only my grief could be weighed
and my devastation[p] placed with it
in the scales.[q]
3 For then it would outweigh the sand
of the seas!
That is why my words are rash.
4 Surely the arrows of the ·Almighty
have pierced[D] me;
my spirit drinks their poison.
God's terrors are arrayed against me.[r]
5 Does a wild donkey bray
over fresh grass
or an ox low over its fodder?
6 Is bland food eaten without salt?
Is there flavor in an egg white?[E]
7 I refuse to touch them;
they are like contaminated food.[s]
8 If only my request would be granted
and God would provide what
I hope for:
9 that He would decide to crush me,
to unleash His power and cut me off!
10 It would still bring me comfort,
and I would leap for joy
in unrelenting pain
that I have not denied[F] the words
of the Holy One.[t]
11 What strength do I have that I should
continue to hope?
What is my future, that I should
be patient?
12 Is my strength that of stone,
or my flesh made of bronze?
13 Since I cannot help myself,
the hope for success has been banished
from me.

[a]**5:9** Jb 9:10; 37:5; Ps 71:19 [b]Jb 42:5; Ps 40:5; 72:18 [c]**5:10** Jb 36:27-28; 38:26-28; Jr 14:22 [d]**5:11** 1Sm 2:7; Ps 113:6-7; Mt 5:4 [e]**5:13** Ps 9:15-16; Is 29:14; 1Co 3:19 [f]**5:14** Dt 28:29; Jb 12:25; Is 59:10 [g]**5:15** Ps 55:21; 59:7 [h]**5:16** Ps 63:11; 107:42; Rm 3:19 [i]**5:18** Dt 32:39; 1Sm 2:6; Hs 6:1 [j]**5:20** Ps 33:19; 37:19; 144:10 [k]**5:21** Ps 27:5; 31:20; 91:5 [l]**5:23** Ps 91:12; Ezk 34:25; Hs 2:18 [m]**5:24** Jb 8:6; 12:6; 21:9 [n]**5:26** Jb 3:22; 10:19; 17:1 [o]Gn 15:15; 25:8; Jb 21:23 [p]**6:2** Jb 30:13; Ps 57:1; Pr 19:13 [q]Jb 31:6; Dn 5:27; Mc 6:11 [r]**6:4** Jb 30:15; Ps 38:2; 88:16 [s]**6:7** Jb 3:24; 33:20; Ps 107:18 [t]**6:10** Jb 22:22; 23:12; Ps 119:102

A **5:12** Lit *their hands* B **5:15** Lit *from the sword of their mouth*; Ps 55:21; 59:7
C **5:21** Lit *be hidden from the whip of the tongue* D **6:4** Lit *Almighty are in*
E **6:6** Hb obscure F **6:10** Lit *hidden*

14 A despairing man should receive loyalty
from his friends,[A,a]
even if he abandons the ·fear
of the Almighty.
15 My brothers are as treacherous
as a ·wadi,
as seasonal streams that overflow
16 and become darkened[B] because of ice,
and the snow melts into them.
17 The wadis evaporate in warm weather;
they disappear from their channels
in hot weather.
18 Caravans turn away from their routes,
go up into the desert, and perish.
19 The caravans of Tema look
for these streams.
The traveling merchants of Sheba hope
for them.
20 They are ashamed because they
had been confident of finding water.
When they arrive there,
they are frustrated.[b]
21 So this is what you have now become
to me.[C]
When you see something dreadful,
you are afraid.
22 Have I ever said: "Give me something"
or "Pay a bribe for me
from your wealth"
23 or "Deliver me
from the enemy's power"
or "Redeem me from the grasp
of the ruthless"?
24 Teach me, and I will be silent.
Help me understand what I did wrong.
25 How painful honest words can be!
But what does your rebuke prove?
26 Do you think that you can disprove
my words
or that a despairing man's words are
mere wind?[c]
27 No doubt you would cast lots
for a fatherless child
and negotiate a price to sell
your friend.[d]
28 But now, please look at me;
would I lie to your face?[e]
29 Reconsider; don't be unjust.
Reconsider; my righteousness[f] is still
the issue.
30 Is there injustice on my tongue
or can my palate not taste disaster?[g]

7 Isn't mankind consigned
to forced labor[h] on earth?
Are not his days like those
of a hired hand?
2 Like a slave he longs for shade;
like a hired man he waits for his pay.
3 So I have been made to inherit months
of futility,
and troubled nights have been assigned
to me.[i]
4 When I lie down I think:
When will I get up?
But the evening drags on endlessly,
and I toss and turn until dawn.
5 My flesh is clothed with maggots
and encrusted with dirt.[D]
My skin forms scabs[E] and then oozes.[j]
6 My days pass more swiftly
than a weaver's shuttle;
they come to an end without hope.[k]
7 Remember that my life is but a breath.
My eye will never again see
anything good.[l]
8 The eye of anyone who looks on me
will no longer see me.
Your eyes will look for me, but I
will be gone.[m]
9 As a cloud fades away and vanishes,
so the one who goes down to ·Sheol[n]
will never rise again.
10 He will never return to his house;
his hometown will no longer
remember[F] him.[o]
11 Therefore I will not restrain my mouth.
I will speak in the anguish of my spirit;
I will complain in the bitterness
of my soul.
12 Am I the sea[G,p] or a sea monster,[q]
that You keep me under guard?
13 When I say: My bed will comfort me,
and my couch will ease my complaint,
14 then You frighten me with dreams,
and terrify me with visions,[r]
15 so that I prefer strangling[H]—

[a]6:14 Jb 19:21; Ps 38:11; Pr 17:17 [b]6:20 Jr 14:3; Jl 1:11; Am 4:8 [c]6:26 Jb 8:2; 15:2; 16:3 [d]6:27 Jl 3:3; Nah 3:10; 2Pt 2:3 [e]6:28 Jb 24:25; 27:4; 34:6 [f]6:29 Jb 2:3 [g]6:30 Jb 12:11; 27:4 [h]7:1 Jb 14:14; Is 40:2 [i]7:3 Jb 30:17; Ps 6:6; 42:3 [j]7:5 Dt 28:35; Ps 38:5; Is 1:6 [k]7:6 Jb 14:19; 17:15; 19:10 [l]7:7 Jb 9:25; Ps 78:39; Jms 4:14 [m]7:8 Jb 7:21; 20:9; Ps 37:36 [n]7:9 Jb 11:8; 14:13; 17:13,16 [o]7:10 Jb 8:18; 20:9; Ps 103:16 [p]7:12 Jb 26:12; Ps 74:13 [q]Ps 148:7; Is 27:1; Ezk 32:2 [r]7:14 Jb 4:13; 20:8; 33:15

A6:14 Lit *To the despairing his friend loyalty* B6:16 Or *turbid* C6:21 Alt Hb tradition reads *So you have now become nothing* D7:5 Or *and dirty scabs* E7:5 Lit *skin hardens* F7:10 Lit *know* G7:12 Or *the sea god* H7:15 Or *suffocation*

death rather than life in this body.[A,a]
16 I give up! I will not live forever.
Leave me alone,[b] for my days are
a breath.[B]

17 What is man, that You think so highly
of him
and pay so much attention to him?[c]
18 You inspect him every morning,
and put him to the test every moment.[d]
19 Will You ever look away from me,
or leave me alone long enough
to swallow?[C]
20 If I have sinned, what have I done
to You,
Watcher of mankind?
Why have You made me Your target,[e]
so that I have become a burden to You?[D]
21 Why not forgive my sin
and pardon my transgression?[f]
For soon I will lie down in the grave.[g]
You will eagerly seek me, but I
will be gone.[h]

Bildad Speaks

8 Then Bildad the Shuhite replied:

2 How long will you go on saying
these things?
Your words[i] are a blast of wind.[j]
3 Does God pervert justice?[k]
Does the •Almighty pervert
what is right?[l]
4 Since your children sinned against Him,
He gave them over to their rebellion.
5 But if you earnestly seek[m] God
and ask the Almighty for mercy,[n]
6 if you are pure and upright,
then He will move even now
on your behalf
and restore the home where
your righteousness dwells.[o]
7 Then, even if your beginnings
were modest,
your final days will be
full of prosperity.[p]
8 For ask the previous generation,
and pay attention to what
their fathers discovered,[q]

9 since we were born only yesterday
and know nothing.
Our days on earth are but a shadow.[r]
10 Will they not teach you and tell you
and speak from their understanding?
11 Does papyrus grow where there is
no marsh?
Do reeds flourish without water?
12 While still uncut shoots,
they would dry up quicker than
any other plant.
13 Such is the destiny[E] of all
who forget God;
the hope of the godless[s] will perish.
14 His source of confidence is fragile;[F]
what he trusts in is a spider's web.[t]
15 He leans on his web, but it doesn't
stand firm.
He grabs it, but it does not hold up.
16 He is a well-watered plant
in the sunshine;
his shoots spread out over his garden.
17 His roots are intertwined around a pile
of rocks.
He looks for a home
among the stones.
18 If he is uprooted[G] from his place,
it will deny knowing him, saying,
"I never saw you."[u]
19 Surely this is the joy of his way of life;
yet others will sprout from the dust.
20 Look, God does not reject a person
of integrity,
and He will not support evildoers.[v]
21 He will yet fill your mouth
with laughter
and your lips with a shout of joy.[w]
22 Your enemies will be clothed
with shame;[x]
the tent[y] of the wicked will exist
no longer.

Job's Reply to Bildad

9 Then Job answered:

2 Yes, I know what you've said is true,
but how can a person be justified
before God?[z]
3 If one wanted to take[aa] Him to court,

[a]**7:15** 1Kg 19:4; Jb 3:21; Jnh 4:3 [b]**7:16** Jb 7:19; 10:20; Ps 39:13 [c]**7:17** Ps 8:4; 144:3; Heb 2:6 [d]**7:18** Ps 17:3; 73:14; 139:23 [e]**7:20** Jb 16:12; Lm 3:12 [f]**7:21** Jb 11:6; 13:23; 15:5 [g]Jb 17:16; 20:11; Is 26:19 [h]Jb 3:13; 7:8; Ps 37:36 [i]**8:2** Jb 11:2; Pr 10:19; Ec 5:3 [j]Jb 6:26; 15:2; 16:3 [k]**8:3** 2Ch 19:6; Jb 34:12; Ps 9:16 [l]Gn 18:25; Jb 34:17; Rm 3:5 [m]**8:5** Ps 63:1; 78:34; Is 26:9 [n]Jb 9:15; 33:24; Ps 30:8 [o]**8:6** Jb 22:23; 42:10; Pr 3:33 [p]**8:7** Jb 36:11; 42:10,12; Jms 5:11 [q]**8:8** Dt 4:32; 32:7; Jb 15:18 [r]**8:9** Ps 102:11; 144:4; Ec 6:12 [s]**8:13** Jb 13:16; 15:34; 27:8 [t]**8:14-15** Jb 27:18; Is 59:5; Mt 7:26-27 [u]**8:18** Jb 7:10; 20:7; Ps 37:36 [v]**8:20** Gn 18:25; Jb 36:6; 2Pt 2:9 [w]**8:21** Jb 33:26; Ps 27:6; 47:5 [x]**8:22** Ps 35:26; 109:29; 132:18 [y]Jb 18:6,14; Ps 52:5; Pr 14:11 [z]**9:2** Jb 25:4; Ps 143:2; Rm 3:20 [aa]**9:3** Jb 13:19; 33:13; 40:2

[A]**7:15** Lit *than my bones* [B]**7:16** Or *are futile* [C]**7:19** Lit *swallow my saliva?* [D]**7:20** Ancient Jewish tradition, LXX; MT, Vg read *myself* [E]**8:13** Lit *Such are the ways* [F]**8:14** Or *cut off*; Hb obscure [G]**8:18** Lit *swallowed*

he could not answer God[A] once
in a thousand times.[a]
4 God is wise[b] and all-powerful.
Who has opposed Him
and come out unharmed?
5 He removes mountains
without their knowledge,
overturning them in His anger.[c]
6 He shakes the earth from its place
so that its pillars tremble.
7 He commands the sun not to shine
and seals off the stars.[d]
8 He alone stretches out the heavens[e]
and treads on the waves of the sea.[B]
9 He makes the stars: the Bear,[C] Orion,
the Pleiades,[f] and the constellations[D]
of the southern sky.
10 He does great and unsearchable things,
wonders without number.[g]
11 If He passes by me, I wouldn't see Him;[h]
if He goes right by,
I wouldn't recognize Him.
12 If He snatches something,
who can stop[E] Him?
Who can ask Him, "What are
You doing?"[i]
13 God does not hold back His anger;
˙Rahab's[j] assistants cringe in fear
beneath Him!
14 How then can I answer Him
or choose my arguments against Him?
15 Even if I were in the right,
I could not answer.
I could only beg my Judge for mercy.[k]
16 If I summoned Him
and He answered me,
I do not believe He would
pay attention to what I said.
17 He batters me with a whirlwind[l]
and multiplies my wounds
without cause.
18 He doesn't let me catch my breath
but soaks me with bitter experiences.
19 If it is a matter of strength, look, He is
the Mighty One![m]
If it is a matter of justice, who can
summon[n] Him?[F]
20 Even if I were in the right,
my own mouth would condemn me;[o]
if I were blameless, my mouth would
declare me ˙guilty.
21 Though I am blameless,
I no longer care about myself;
I renounce my life.[p]
22 It is all the same. Therefore I say,
"He destroys both the blameless
and the wicked."[q]
23 When disaster brings sudden death,
He mocks the despair of the innocent.
24 The earth[G] is handed over
to the wicked;
He blindfolds[H] its judges.[r]
If it isn't He, then who is it?
25 My days fly by faster than a runner;[I,s]
they flee without seeing any good.[t]
26 They sweep by like boats made
of papyrus,
like an eagle swooping down on its prey.[u]
27 If I said, "I will forget my complaint,
change my expression, and smile,"
28 I would still live in terror of all
my pains.[v]
I know You will not acquit me.[w]
29 Since I will be found guilty,[x]
why should I labor in vain?
30 If I wash myself with snow,
and cleanse my hands with lye,
31 then You dip me in a pit of mud,
and my own clothes despise me!
32 For He is not a man like me, that I can
answer Him,[y]
that we can take each other to court.
33 There is no one to judge between us,
to lay his hand on both of us.
34 Let Him take His rod away from me
so His terror will no longer
frighten me.[z]
35 Then I would speak and not fear Him.
But that is not the case; I am
on my own.

10 I am disgusted with my life.[aa]
I will express my complaint
and speak in the bitterness of my soul.
2 I will say to God:
"Do not declare me ˙guilty!
Let me know why You prosecute me.

[a]9:3 Jb 9:14; 37:19; 40:2 [b]9:4 Jb 11:6; 12:13; 36:5 [c]9:5 Jdg 5:5; Ps 18:7; Mc 1:4 [d]9:7 Is 13:10; Ezk 32:8; Jl 2:10,31 [e]9:8 Ps 104:2-3; Is 40:22; 44:24 [f]9:9 Jb 38:31-32; Is 40:26; Am 5:8 [g]9:10 Jb 5:9; Ps 40:5; 72:18 [h]9:11 Jb 23:8-9; 35:14 [i]9:12 Jb 11:10; Is 45:9; Rm 9:20 [j]9:13 Jb 26:12; Ps 89:10; Is 51:9 [k]9:15 Jb 8:5; 10:15 [l]9:17 Jb 30:22; Ps 83:15; Jnh 1:4 [m]9:19 Jb 9:4; Is 28:2; 40:26 [n]Jr 49:19; 50:44 [o]9:20 Jb 9:28; 40:8; Is 50:9 [p]9:21 Jb 7:16; 10:1 [q]9:22 Jb 3:19; Ec 9:2-3; Is 14:3-11 [r]9:24 Jb 12:6,17; Is 29:14; 44:25 [s]9:25 2Sm 18:19-33; 1Kg 1:5; Est 3:13,15 [t]Jb 7:7; Ps 78:39; Jms 4:14 [u]9:26 Jb 39:29; Is 18:2; Hab 1:8 [v]9:28 Jb 3:25; 13:11; 31:23 [w]Jb 10:14; Jl 3:21; Nah 1:3 [x]9:29 Jb 9:20; 40:8; Is 50:9 [y]9:32 Jb 41:13; Ps 143:2; Ec 6:10 [z]9:34 Jb 6:4; 13:21; Ps 39:10 [aa]10:1 Jb 7:16; 9:21

A9:3 Or *court, God would not answer him* B9:8 Or *and walks on the back of the sea god* C9:9 Or *Aldebaran* D9:9 Or *chambers* E9:12 Or *dissuade* F9:19 LXX; MT reads *me* G9:24 Or *land* H9:24 Lit *covers the faces of* I9:25 = a royal messenger

3 Is it good for You to oppress,
to reject the work of Your hands,
and favor[A] the plans of the wicked?
4 Do You have eyes of flesh,
or do You see as a human sees?
5 Are Your days like those of a human,
or Your years like those of a man,[a]
6 that You look for my wrongdoing[b]
and search for my sin,
7 even though You know that
I am not wicked
and that there is no one
who can deliver from Your hand?

8 "Your hands shaped me
and formed me.
Will You now turn and destroy me?
9 Please remember that You formed me
like clay.
Will You now return me to dust?[c]
10 Did You not pour me out like milk
and curdle me like cheese?
11 You clothed me with skin and flesh,
and wove me together with bones
and tendons.
12 You gave me life and faithful love,
and Your care has guarded my life.

13 "Yet You concealed these thoughts
in Your heart;
I know that this was Your hidden plan:[B]
14 if I sin, You would notice,[C]
and would not acquit me
of my wrongdoing.[d]
15 If I am wicked, woe to me!
And even if I am righteous, I cannot
lift up my head.
I am filled with shame
and aware of my affliction.[e]
16 If I am proud,[D] You hunt me like a lion
and again display
Your miraculous power against me.[f]
17 You produce new witnesses[E] against me
and multiply Your anger toward me.
Hardships assault me, wave after wave.[F]

18 "Why did You bring me out of
the womb?[g]
I should have died and never been seen.
19 I wish[G] I had never existed
but had been carried from the womb
to the grave.[h]
20 Are my days not few? Stop it![H]
Leave me alone, so that I can smile
a little
21 before I go to a land of darkness
and gloom,[i]
never to return.
22 It is a land of blackness
like the deepest darkness,
gloomy and chaotic,
where even the light is
like[I] the darkness."

Zophar Speaks

11 Then Zophar the Naamathite replied:

2 Should this stream of words[j]
go unanswered
and such a talker[J] be acquitted?
3 Should your babbling put others
to silence,
so that you can keep on ridiculing
with no one to humiliate you?
4 You have said, "My teaching[k] is sound,
and I am pure in Your sight."
5 But if only God would speak
and declare His case[K] against you,
6 He would show you the secrets
of wisdom,[l]
for true wisdom has two sides.
Know then that God has chosen
to overlook some of your sin.[m]

7 Can you fathom the depths of God
or discover the limits
of the ·Almighty?[n]
8 They are higher than the heavens—
what can you do?
They are deeper than ·Sheol—what can
you know?[o]
9 Their measure is longer than the earth
and wider than the sea.

10 If He passes by and throws
someone in prison
or convenes a court, who can
stop Him?[p]
11 Surely He knows which people
are worthless.

[a] 10:5 Jb 36:26; Ps 90:4; 2Pt 3:8 [b] 10:6 Jb 13:23,26; 14:17; 22:5 [c] 10:9 Gn 2:7; Jb 4:19; 34:15 [d] 10:14 Ex 34:7; Jb 7:21; Am 3:2 [e] 10:15 Jb 9:15; Ps 25:18; Is 3:11 [f] 10:16 Jb 5:9; Is 38:13; Lm 3:10 [g] 10:18 Jb 1:21; 10:18-19; Jr 20:17-18 [h] 10:19 Jb 3:22; 5:26; 17:1 [i] 10:21 Jb 3:5;12:22; 28:3 [j] 11:2 Jb 8:2; Pr 10:19; Ec 5:3 [k] 11:4 Dt 32:2; Pr 4:2; Is 29:24 [l] 11:6 Jb 28:12; 38:36; Ec 7:23,25 [m] Ezr 9:13; Ps 103:10 [n] 11:7 Ec 3:11; 8:17; Rm 11:33 [o] 11:8 Dt 30:12-13; Ps 139:8-9; Am 9:2-3 [p] 11:10 Jb 9:12; 23:13; Rv 3:7

[A] 10:3 Lit *shine on* [B] 10:13 Lit *was with You* [C] 10:14 Lit *notice me* [D] 10:16 Lit *If he lifts up* [E] 10:17 Or *You bring fresh troops* [F] 10:17 Lit *Changes and a host are with me* [G] 10:19 Lit *As if* [H] 10:20 Alt Hb tradition reads *Will He not leave my few days alone?* [I] 10:22 Lit *chaotic, and shines as* [J] 11:2 Lit *a man of lips* [K] 11:5 Lit *and open His lips*

If He sees iniquity, will He not take note
of it?[a]
12 But a stupid man
will gain understanding
as soon as a wild donkey is born a man!

13 As for you, if you redirect your heart
and lift up your hands to Him
in prayer —
14 if there is iniquity in your hand,
remove it,
and don't allow injustice to dwell
in your tents —
15 then you will hold your head high,
free from fault.
You will be firmly established
and unafraid.[b]
16 For you will forget your suffering,
recalling it only as waters
that have flowed by.
17 Your life will be brighter than noonday;
its darkness[A] will be like the morning.[c]
18 You will be confident, because
there is hope.[d]
You will look carefully about
and lie down in safety.[e]
19 You will lie down without fear,
and many will seek your favor.[f]
20 But the sight of the wicked[g] will fail.
Their way of escape will be cut off,
and their only hope is their last breath.[h]

Job's Reply to Zophar

12 Then Job answered:

2 No doubt you are the people,
and wisdom will die with you!
3 But I also have a mind;
I am not inferior to you.
Who doesn't know the things you are
talking about?[B,i]

4 I am a laughingstock to my[C] friends,
by calling on God, who answers me.[D]
The righteous and upright man is
a laughingstock.[j]
5 The one who is at ease[k] holds calamity
in contempt
and thinks it is prepared for those
whose feet are slipping.

[a]**11:11** Jb 34:25; Ps 10:14
[b]**11:15** Jb 22:26; Ps 119:6; 1Jn 3:21
[c]**11:17** Jb 17:12; Ps 37:6; Is 58:8,10
[d]**11:18** Jb 4:6; Ps 119:116; Jr 17:7
[e]Jb 24:23; Ps 4:8; Pr 3:24
[f]**11:19** Ps 45:12; Pr 19:6; 29:26
[g]**11:20** Jb 3:17; 9:22; 18:5
[h]Jb 8:13; Pr 10:28; 11:7
[i]**12:3** Jb 13:2; 15:9; 16:2
[j]**12:4** Jb 30:1,9; Jr 20:7; Lm 3:14
[k]**12:5** Ps 123:4; Am 6:1
[l]**12:6** Jb 5:24; 8:6; 21:9
[m]Ps 73:11; Jr 12:1; Mt 5:45
[n]**12:7** Jb 35:11; Mt 6:26
[o]**12:9** Ru 1:13; Jb 19:21; Is 41:20
[p]**12:10** Gn 2:7; Jb 27:3; 33:4
[q]**12:12** Jb 12:20; 32:7,9; Ps 119:100
[r]**12:13** Jb 9:4; 36:5; 38:36
[s]**12:14** Jb 11:10; Is 22:22; Rv 3:7
[t]**12:15** Is 41:18; 42:15; 44:3,27
[u]**12:17** Jb 9:24; Is 29:14; 44:25
[v]**12:18** Jb 12:21; Is 45:1
[w]**12:19** Is 40:23; Lk 1:52
[x]**12:22** Ps 90:8; Dn 2:22; 1Co 4:5

6 The tents of robbers are safe,[l]
and those who provoke God are secure;
God's power provides this.[E,m]

7 But ask the animals, and they will
instruct you;
ask the birds of the sky, and they will
tell you.[n]
8 Or speak to the earth, and it will
instruct you;
let the fish of the sea inform you.
9 Which of all these does not know
that the hand of the LORD
has done this?[o]
10 The life of every living thing is
in His hand,
as well as the breath of all mankind.[p]
11 Doesn't the ear test words
as the palate tastes food?
12 Wisdom is found with the elderly,
and understanding comes
with long life.[q]

13 Wisdom and strength belong to God;
counsel and understanding are His.[r]
14 Whatever He tears down cannot
be rebuilt;
whoever He imprisons cannot
be released.[s]
15 When He withholds the waters,
everything dries up,
and when He releases them,
they destroy the land.[t]
16 True wisdom and power belong
to Him.
The deceived and the deceiver are His.
17 He leads counselors away barefoot
and makes judges go mad.[u]
18 He releases the bonds[F] put on by kings[v]
and fastens a belt around their waists.
19 He leads priests away barefoot
and overthrows established leaders.[w]
20 He deprives trusted advisers of speech
and takes away the elders'
good judgment.
21 He pours out contempt on nobles
and disarms[G] the strong.
22 He reveals mysteries from the darkness
and brings the deepest darkness
into the light.[x]

[A]**11:17** Text emended; MT reads *noonday; you are dark, you* [B]**12:3** Lit *With whom are not such things as these* [C]**12:4** Lit *his* [D]**12:4** Lit *him* [E]**12:6** Or *secure; to those who bring their god in their hands* [F]**12:18** Text emended; MT reads *discipline* [G]**12:21** Lit *and loosens the belt of*

23 He makes nations great,
then destroys them;
He enlarges nations,[a]
then leads them away.
24 He deprives the world's leaders
of reason,
and makes them wander
in a trackless wasteland.[b]
25 They grope around in darkness
without light;
He makes them stagger
like drunken men.[c]

13 Look, my eyes have seen all this;
my ears[d] have heard
and understood it.
2 Everything you know, I also know;
I am not inferior to you.[e]
3 Yet I prefer to speak to the ·Almighty
and argue my case before God.[f]
4 But you coat the truth with lies;
you are all worthless doctors.[g]
5 If only you would shut up
and let that be your wisdom!
6 Hear now my argument,
and listen to my defense.[A]
7 Would you testify unjustly
on God's behalf
or speak deceitfully for Him?
8 Would you show partiality[h] to Him
or argue the case in His defense?
9 Would it go well if He examined you?
Could you deceive Him
as you would deceive a man?[i]
10 Surely He would rebuke you
if you secretly showed partiality.
11 Would God's majesty not terrify you?[j]
Would His dread not fall on you?
12 Your memorable sayings are proverbs
of ash;[k]
your defenses are made of clay.

13 Be quiet,[B] and I will speak.
Let whatever comes happen to me.
14 Why do I put myself at risk[C]
and take my life in my own hands?
15 Even if He kills me, I will hope in Him.[D]
I will still defend[l] my ways
before Him.
16 Yes, this will result in my deliverance,
for no godless person[m] can appear
before Him.
17 Pay close attention to my words;
let my declaration ring in your ears.
18 Now then, I have prepared my case;[n]
I know that I am right.
19 Can anyone indict me?
If so, I will be silent and die.

20 Only grant these two things to me, God,
so that I will not have to hide
from Your presence:
21 remove Your hand from me,
and do not let Your terror frighten me.[o]
22 Then call, and I will answer,[p]
or I will speak, and You can respond
to me.
23 How many iniquities[q] and sins
have I committed?[E]
Reveal to me my transgression and sin.
24 Why do You hide Your face
and consider me Your enemy?[r]
25 Will You frighten a wind-driven leaf?
Will You chase after dry straw?
26 For You record bitter accusations
against me
and make me inherit the iniquities
of my youth.
27 You put my feet in the stocks
and stand watch over all my paths,
setting a limit for the soles[F]
of my feet.

28 Man wears out like something rotten,
like a moth-eaten garment.[s]

14 Man born of woman
is short of days and full of trouble.[t]
2 He blossoms like a flower,
then withers;[u]
he flees like a shadow and does not last.
3 Do You really take notice of one
like this?
Will You bring me into judgment
against You?[G,v]
4 Who can produce something pure
from what is impure?
No one!
5 Since man's days are determined
and the number of his months depends
on You,

[a]**12:23** Ex 34:24; Is 9:3; 26:15 [b]**12:24** Ps 107:40; Dn 4:33 [c]**12:25** Dt 28:29; Jb 5:14; Is 59:10 [d]**13:1** Jb 4:12; 33:16; 36:10,15 [e]**13:2** Jb 12:3; 15:9; 16:2 [f]**13:3** Jb 5:8; 23:4; 40:2 [g]**13:4** Jb 16:2; Ps 69:20; Ec 4:1 [h]**13:8** Dt 10:17; Jb 32:21; 34:19 [i]**13:9** Ps 44:21; Pr 18:17; Jr 17:10 [j]**13:11** Ex 15:16; Jb 31:23; Is 2:10 [k]**13:12** 1Sm 24:13; Pr 26:7,9; Is 44:20 [l]**13:15** Jb 13:3; 15:3; 23:7 [m]**13:16** Jb 8:13; 15:34; 27:8 [n]**13:18** Jb 5:8; 23:4; Lm 3:59 [o]**13:21** Jb 6:4; 9:34; Ps 39:10 [p]**13:22** Jb 9:16; 14:15; Jr 33:3 [q]**13:23** Jb 7:21; 10;6,14; Is 43:25 [r]**13:24** Jb 19:11; 33:10; Lm 2:5 [s]**13:28** Ps 102:26; Is 50:9; 51:8 [t]**14:1** Jb 5:7; 15:35; Is 59:4 [u]**14:2** Ps 103:15-16; Is 40:6-7; Jms 1:10-11 [v]**14:3** Jb 22:4; Ps 143:2; 144:3

[A]**13:6** Lit *to the claims of my lips* [B]**13:13** Lit *quiet before me* [C]**13:14** Lit *I take my flesh in my teeth* [D]**13:15** Some Hb mss read *I will be without hope* [E]**13:23** Lit *sins are to me* [F]**13:27** Lit *paths. You mark a line around the roots* [G]**14:3** LXX, Syr, Vg read *him*

and since You have set[A] limits
he cannot pass,[a]
6 look away from him and let him rest
so that he can enjoy his day
like a hired hand.[b]
7 There is hope for a tree:
If it is cut down, it will sprout again,
and its shoots will not die.
8 If its roots grow old in the ground
and its stump starts to die in the soil,
9 the smell of water makes it thrive
and produce twigs like a sapling.[c]
10 But a man dies and fades away;
he breathes his last — where is he?
11 As water disappears from the sea
and a river becomes parched and dry,
12 so man lies down never to rise again.
They will not wake up until the heavens
are no more;[d]
they will not stir from their sleep.
13 If only You would hide me in •Sheol[e]
and conceal me
until Your anger[f] passes.
If only You would appoint a time
for me
and then remember me.
14 When a man dies, will he come back
to life?
If so, I would wait[g] all the days
of my struggle[h]
until my relief comes.
15 You would call, and I would
answer You.
You would long for the work
of Your hands.[i]
16 For then You would count my steps[j]
but would not take note[k] of my sin.
17 My rebellion would be sealed up
in a bag,
and You would cover over
my iniquity.
18 But as a mountain collapses
and crumbles
and a rock is dislodged from its place,
19 as water wears away stones
and torrents wash away the soil
from the land,
so You destroy a man's hope.[l]

[a]**14:5** Jb 21:21; Ps 39:4; 90:12 [b]**14:6** Jb 7:16; 10:20; Ps 39:13 [c]**14:9** Jb 29:19; Ps 1:3; Jr 17:8 [d]**14:12** Is 51:6; Rv 20:11; 21:1 [e]**14:13** Jb 11:8; 17:16; Am 9:2 [f]Jb 16:9; 19:11; Ps 30:5 [g]**14:14** Jb 6:8; 13:13; 35:14 [h]Jb 7:1; Is 40:2 [i]**14:15** Jb 9:16; 10:3; 13:22 [j]**14:16** Jb 10:6; 31:4; 34:21 [k]Jb 10:14; 33:11; Ps 130:3 [l]**14:19** Jb 7:6; 17:15; 19:10 [m]**14:21** Jb 21:21; Ec 9:5; Is 63:16 [n]**15:2** Jb 2:10; 6:26; 27:12 [o]**15:3** Jb 13:3,15; 23:7 [p]**15:5** Jb 13:23,26; 14:17; 22:5 [q]**15:6** 2Sm 1:16; Jb 9:20; Lk 19:22 [r]**15:7** Jb 38:21; Ps 90:2; Pr 8:25 [s]**15:8** Jr 23:18; Rm 11:34; 1Co 2:11

20 You completely overpower him, and he
passes on;
You change his appearance
and send him away.
21 If his sons receive honor, he does not
know it;
if they become insignificant,
he is unaware of it.[m]
22 He feels only the pain of his own body
and mourns only for himself.

SECOND SERIES OF SPEECHES

Eliphaz Speaks

15 Then Eliphaz the Temanite replied:
2 Does a wise man answer
with empty[B] counsel[n]
or fill himself[C] with the hot east wind?
3 Should he argue[o] with useless talk
or with words that serve
no good purpose?
4 But you even undermine the •fear
of God
and hinder meditation before Him.
5 Your iniquity[p] teaches you what to say,
and you choose the language
of the crafty.
6 Your own mouth condemns you, not I;
your own lips testify against you.[q]
7 Were you the first person ever born,
or were you brought forth
before the hills?[r]
8 Do you listen in on the council of God,
or have a monopoly on wisdom?[s]
9 What do you know that we don't?
What do you understand that
is not clear to us?
10 Both the gray-haired and the elderly are
with us,
men older than your father.
11 Are God's consolations not enough
for you,
even the words that deal gently
with you?
12 Why has your heart misled you,
and why do your eyes flash
13 as you turn your anger[D] against God
and allow such words to leave
your mouth?

[A]**14:5** Lit *set his* [B]**15:2** Lit *windy*; Jb 16:3 [C]**15:2** Lit *his belly* [D]**15:13** Or *spirit*

14 What is man, that he should be pure,[a]
or one born of woman, that he
should be righteous?
15 If God puts no trust in His holy ones[b]
and the heavens are not pure
in His sight,[c]
16 how much less one who is revolting
and corrupt,[d]
who drinks injustice[e] like water?
17 Listen to me and I will inform you.
I will describe what I have seen,
18 what was declared by wise men
and was not suppressed
by their ancestors,[f]
19 the land was given to them alone
when no foreigner passed among them.
20 A wicked man writhes in pain
all his days;
only a few[A] years are reserved
for the ruthless.
21 Dreadful sounds fill his ears;
when he is at peace, a robber
attacks him.
22 He doesn't believe he will return
from darkness;
he is destined for the sword.[g]
23 He wanders about for food, saying,
"Where is it?"
He knows the day of darkness is
at hand.
24 Trouble[h] and distress terrify him,
overwhelming him like a king prepared
for battle.
25 For he has stretched out his hand[i]
against God
and has arrogantly opposed
the ·Almighty.
26 He rushes headlong at Him
with his thick, studded shields.
27 Though his face is covered with fat[B]
and his waistline bulges with it,
28 he will dwell in ruined cities,
in abandoned houses destined
to become piles of rubble.[j]
29 He will no longer be rich; his wealth
will not endure.
His possessions[C] will not increase
in the land.
30 He will not escape from the darkness;
flames will wither his shoots,
and by the breath of God's mouth,
he will depart.[k]
31 Let him not put trust
in worthless things, being led astray,
for what he gets in exchange
will prove worthless.
32 It will be accomplished
before his time,
and his branch will not flourish.
33 He will be like a vine that drops
its unripe grapes[l]
and like an olive tree that sheds
its blossoms.
34 For the company of the godless[m]
will have no children,
and fire will consume the tents of those
who offer bribes.
35 They conceive trouble[n] and give birth
to evil;
their womb[o] prepares deception.[p]

Job's Reply to Eliphaz

16 Then Job answered:

2 I have heard many things like these.
You are all miserable comforters.[q]
3 Is there no end to your empty[D,r] words?
What provokes you that you
continue testifying?
4 If you were in my place I could also talk
like you.
I could string words together
against you
and shake my head at you.
5 Instead, I would encourage you
with my mouth,
and the consolation from my lips
would bring relief.[s]
6 Even if I speak, my suffering
is not relieved,
and if I hold back, what have
I lost?
7 Surely He[E] has now exhausted me.
You have devastated my entire family.
8 You have shriveled me up[F] —
it has become a witness;
My frailty rises up against me
and testifies to my face.

[a]**15:14** Jb 4:17; 25:4; Pr 20:9 [b]**15:15** Jb 5:1; Ps 89:5-7; Dn 4:17 [c]Jb 4:18; 21:22; 25:5 [d]**15:16** Ps 14:3; 53:3 [e]Jb 34:7; Ps 14:3 [f]**15:18** Dt 4:32; 32:7; Jb 8:8 [g]**15:22** Dt 32:41-42; Jb 19:29; Is 66:16 [h]**15:24** 1Sm 22:2; Jb 36:19; Ps 107:6,13,19,28 [i]**15:25** Is 5:25; 9:16,20; Jr 21:5 [j]**15:28** Jb 3:14; Ps 109:10; Is 5:9 [k]**15:30** Jb 4:9; 22:20; 2Th 2:8 [l]**15:33** Is 18:5; Jr 31:29-30; Ezk 18:2 [m]**15:34** Jb 8:13; 13:16; 27:8 [n]**15:35** Jb 4:8; 5:7; Is 59:4 [o]Jb 32:19; 37:1; Pr 20:27,30 [p]Ps 7:14; Is 59:4; Hs 10:13 [q]**16:2** Jb 13:4; Ps 69:20; Ec 4:1 [r]**16:3** Jb 15:2 [s]**16:5** Dt 3:28; Jb 4:4; Is 41:10

[A]**15:20** Lit *the number of* [B]**15:27** Lit *with his fat* [C]**15:29** Text emended; MT reads *their gain* [D]**16:3** Lit *windy*; Jb 15:2 [E]**16:7** Or *it* [F]**16:8** Or *have seized me*; Hb obscure

9 His anger tears at me,
and He harasses[a] me.
He gnashes His teeth at me.
My enemy pierces me with His eyes.
10 They open their mouths against me
and strike my cheeks with contempt;[b]
they join themselves together
against me.
11 God hands me over to unjust men;[A]
He throws me into the hands
of the wicked.
12 I was at ease, but He shattered me;
He seized me by the scruff
of the neck
and smashed me to pieces.
He set me up as His target;[c]
13 His archers[B] surround me.
He pierces my kidneys without mercy
and pours my bile on the ground.
14 He breaks through my defenses again
and again;[C]
He charges at me like a warrior.[d]
15 I have sewn ˚sackcloth over my skin;
I have buried my strength[D]
in the dust.[e]
16 My face has grown red with weeping,
and darkness[f] covers my eyes,
17 although my hands are free
from violence[g]
and my prayer is pure.
18 Earth, do not cover my blood;
may my cry for help find
no resting place.[h]
19 Even now my witness is in heaven,
and my advocate is in the heights![i]
20 My friends scoff at me
as I weep before God.
21 I wish that someone might arbitrate
between a man and God[j]
just as a ˚man pleads for his friend.
22 For only a few years will pass
before I go the way of no return.

17 My spirit is broken.
My days are extinguished.
A graveyard[k] awaits me.
2 Surely mockers surround[E] me
and my eyes must gaze
at their rebellion.[l]

[a]**16:9** Gn 49:23; Jb 30:21; Ps 55:3
[b]**16:10** 1Kg 22:24; Lm 3:30; Mc 5:1
[c]**16:12** Jb 7:20; Lm 3:12
[d]**16:14** Jb 30:14; Jl 2:7
[e]**16:15** Jb 30:19; Ps 7:5; 75:10
[f]**16:16** Ps 44:19; 107:10; Jr 13:16
[g]**16:17** Is 53:9; 59:6; Jnh 3:8
[h]**16:18** Gn 4:10; Is 26:21; Ezk 24:7-8
[i]**16:19** Jb 22:12; Rm 1:9; 1Th 2:5
[j]**16:21** Jb 31:35; Ec 6:10; Is 45:9
[k]**17:1** Jb 3:22; 5:26; 10:19
[l]**17:2** Ps 22:7; 119:51; Jr 20:7
[m]**17:3** Gn 43:9; Ps 119:122; Pr 6:1
[n]**17:6** Nm 12:14; Is 50:6; Mt 27:30
[o]**17:8** Jb 18:20; 21:5; Dn 4:19
[p]**17:9** 2Sm 22:21; Jb 22:30; Ps 24:4
[q]**17:12** Jb 11:17; Ps 37:6; Is 58:8,10
[r]**17:14** Jb 3:15; 30:23; Ec 12:5
[s]**17:15** Jb 7:6; 14:19; 19:10
[t]**17:16** Jb 7:9; 11:8; 14:13
[u]**18:1** Jb 2:11; 8:1; 25:1

3 Make arrangements! Put up security
for me.[F,m]
Who else will be my sponsor?[G]
4 You have closed their minds
to understanding,
therefore You will not honor them.
5 If a man informs on his friends
for a price,
the eyes of his children will fail.

6 He has made me an object of scorn
to the people;
I have become a man people spit at.[H,n]
7 My eyes have grown dim from grief,
and my whole body has become
but a shadow.
8 The upright are appalled[o] at this,
and the innocent are roused
against the godless.
9 Yet the righteous person will hold
to his way,
and the one whose hands are ˚clean[p]
will grow stronger.
10 But come back and try again, all of you.[I]
I will not find a wise man among you.
11 My days have slipped by;
my plans have been ruined,
even the things dear to my heart.
12 They turned night into day
and made light seem near in the face
of darkness.[q]
13 If I await ˚Sheol as my home,
spread out my bed in darkness,
14 and say to corruption: You are
my father,
and to the maggot: My mother
or my sister,[r]
15 where then is my hope?[s]
Who can see any hope for me?
16 Will it go down to the gates of Sheol,[t]
or will we descend together to the dust?

Bildad Speaks

18 Then Bildad the Shuhite[u] replied:

2 How long until you stop talking?
Show some sense, and then we can talk.
3 Why are we regarded as cattle,
as stupid in your sight?

[A]16:11 LXX, Vg; MT reads *to a boy* [B]16:13 Or *arrows* [C]16:14 Lit *through me, breach on breach* [D]16:15 Lit *horn* [E]17:2 Lit *are with* [F]17:3 Lit *me with You* [G]17:3 Lit *Who is there that will strike himself into my hand* [H]17:6 Lit *become a spitting to the faces* [I]17:10 Some Hb mss, LXX, Vg; other Hb mss read *them*

4 You who tear yourself in anger[A]—
should the earth be abandoned
on your account,
or a rock be removed from its place?
5 Yes, the light[a] of the wicked[b]
is extinguished;
the flame of his fire does not glow.
6 The light in his tent grows dark,[c]
and the lamp beside him is put out.
7 His powerful stride is shortened,
and his own schemes trip him up.[d]
8 For his own feet lead him into a net,
and he strays into its mesh.
9 A trap catches him by the heel;
a noose seizes him.
10 A rope lies hidden for him
on the ground,
and a snare waits for him
along the path.
11 Terrors frighten him on every side[e]
and harass him at every step.
12 His strength is depleted;
disaster lies ready for him to stumble.[B]
13 Parts of his skin are eaten away;
death's firstborn consumes his limbs.
14 He is ripped from the security
of his tent
and marched away to the king
of terrors.
15 Nothing he owned remains
in his tent.
Burning sulfur[f] is scattered
over his home.
16 His roots below dry up,
and his branches above wither away.[g]
17 All memory[h] of him perishes
from the earth;
he has no name anywhere.[C]
18 He is driven from light to darkness
and chased from the inhabited world.
19 He has no children or descendants
among his people,
no survivor where he used to live.[i]
20 Those in the west are appalled[j]
at his fate,
while those in the east tremble
in horror.
21 Indeed, such is the dwelling of the
unjust man,
and this is the place of the one
who does not know God.[k]

Job's Reply to Bildad

19 Then Job answered:

2 How long will you torment me
and crush me with words?
3 You have humiliated me ten times now,
and you mistreat[D] me without shame.[l]
4 Even if it is true that I have sinned,
my mistake concerns only[E] me.
5 If you really want to appear superior[m]
to me
and would use my disgrace as evidence
against me,
6 then understand that it is God
who has wronged me
and caught me in His net.[n]
7 I cry out: "Violence!"
but get no response;[o]
I call for help, but there is no justice.
8 He has blocked[p] my way so that
I cannot pass through;
He has veiled my paths with darkness.[q]
9 He has stripped me of my honor
and removed the crown from my head.
10 He tears me down on every side so that
I am ruined.[F]
He uproots my hope like a tree.[r]
11 His anger[s] burns against me,
and He regards me as one of
His enemies.[t]
12 His troops advance together;
they construct a ramp[G] against me
and camp[u] around my tent.
13 He has removed my brothers from me;
my acquaintances have abandoned me.[v]
14 My relatives stop coming by,
and my close friends have forgotten me.
15 My house guests[H] and female servants
regard me as a stranger;
I am a foreigner in their sight.[w]
16 I call for my servant, but he
does not answer,
even if I beg him with my own mouth.
17 My breath is offensive to my wife,
and my own family[I] finds me repulsive.

[a]**18:5** Jb 21:17; Pr 13:9; 24:20 [b]Jb 3:17; 9:22; 11:20 [c]**18:6** Jb 8:22; 18:14; Ps 52:5 [d]**18:7** Jb 5:13; Pr 4:12 [e]**18:11** Jb 20:25; 27:20; Jr 6:25 [f]**18:15** Gn 19:24; Ps 11:6; Ezk 38:22 [g]**18:16** Is 5:24; Hs 9:16; Am 2:9 [h]**18:17** Ps 34:16; 109:13,15; Pr 10:7 [i]**18:19** Gn 21:23; Is 14:22; Lm 2:22 [j]**18:20** Jr 2:12; Ezk 27:35; 32:10 [k]**18:21** Jb 21:28; Jr 9:3; 1Th 4:5 [l]**19:3** Gn 31:7; Nm 14:22; Pr 25:8 [m]**19:5** Ps 35:26; 38:16; 55:12 [n]**19:6** Jb 27:2; Lm 3:5; Ezk 12:13 [o]**19:7** Jb 30:20; Lm 3:8; Hab 1:2 [p]**19:8** Jb 3:23; Lm 3:9; Hs 2:6 [q]Jb 29:3; 30:26; Is 59:9 [r]**19:10** Dt 28:63; Jb 24:20; Ps 52:5 [s]**19:11** Jb 16:9; 21:17; 40:11 [t]Jb 13:24; 33:10; Lm 2:5 [u]**19:12** Ps 27:3; Is 29:3; Jr 50:29 [v]**19:13** Ps 31:11; 38:11; 88:8,18 [w]**19:15** Gn 31:15; Ps 69:8; Mt 10:36

[A]18:4 Lit *He who tears himself in his anger* [B]18:12 Or *disaster hungers for him* [C]18:17 Or *name in the streets* [D]19:3 Hb obscure [E]19:4 Lit *mistake lives with* [F]19:10 Lit *gone* [G]19:12 Lit *they raise up their way* [H]19:15 Or *The resident aliens in my household* [I]19:17 Lit *and the sons of my belly*

18 Even young boys scorn me.
When I stand up, they mock me.[a]
19 All of my best friends[A] despise me,[b]
and those I love have turned
against me.[c]
20 My skin and my flesh cling
to my bones;
I have escaped by the skin of my teeth.

21 Have mercy on me, my friends,[d]
have mercy,
for God's hand[e] has struck me.[f]
22 Why do you persecute me as God does?
Will you never get enough of my flesh?

23 I wish that my words
were written down,
that they were recorded on a scroll
24 or were inscribed in stone forever
by an iron stylus and lead!
25 But I know my living Redeemer,[B,g]
and He will stand on the dust[C] at last.[D,h]
26 Even after my skin has been destroyed,[E]
yet I will see God in[F] my flesh.[i]
27 I will see Him myself;
my eyes will look at Him, and not
as a stranger.[G]
My heart longs[H] within me.[j]

28 If you say, "How will we pursue him,
since the root of the problem lies
with him?"[I]
29 then be afraid of the sword,
because wrath brings punishment
by the sword,[k]
so that you may know there is
a judgment.

Zophar Speaks

20 Then Zophar the Naamathite[l] replied:

2 This is why my unsettling thoughts
compel me to answer,
because I am upset![J]
3 I have heard a rebuke that insults me,
and my understanding[K]
makes me reply.[m]

4 Don't you know that
ever since antiquity,
from the time man was placed on earth,
5 the joy of the wicked has been brief
and the happiness of the godless
has lasted only a moment?[n]
6 Though his arrogance reaches heaven,
and his head touches the clouds,[o]
7 he will vanish forever
like his own dung.
Those who know[L] him will ask,
"Where is he?"[p]
8 He will fly away like a dream and never
be found;
he will be chased away like a vision
in the night.[q]
9 The eye that saw him will see him
no more,[r]
and his household will no longer
see him.[s]
10 His children will beg from[M] the poor,
for his own hands must give back
his wealth.
11 His bones may be full of
youthful vigor,
but will lie down with him
in the grave.[t]

12 Though evil tastes sweet in his mouth
and he conceals it under his tongue,
13 though he cherishes it and will not
let it go
but keeps it in his mouth,[u]
14 yet the food in his stomach turns
into cobras' venom inside him.
15 He swallows wealth but must
vomit it up;
God will force it from his stomach.
16 He will suck the poison of cobras;
a viper's fangs[N] will kill him.[v]
17 He will not enjoy the streams,
the rivers flowing with honey
and cream.[w]
18 He must return the fruit of his labor
without consuming it;
he doesn't enjoy the profits
from his trading.
19 For he oppressed and abandoned
the poor;
he seized a house he did not build.[x]

[a]19:18 2Kg 2:23; Jb 29:8
[b]19:19 Jb 30:10; Ps 89:38; Am 5:10
[c]Ps 41:9; 55:11-12; Jn 13:18
[d]19:21 Jb 6:14; Ps 38:11; Pr 17:17
[e]Ru 1:13; Jb 12:9; Is 41:20
[f]Jb 1:11; 2:5; 6:7
[g]19:25 Jb 16:19; Pr 23:11; Jr 50:34
[h]Is 44:6; 48:12; Rv 1:17-18
[i]19:26 Ps 17:15; Is 6:1; 1Co 13:12
[j]19:27 Ps 73:26; 84:2; 119:81
[k]19:29 Jb 15:22; Is 66:16; Ezk 32:10
[l]20:1 Jb 2:11; 11:1; 42:9
[m]20:3 Jb 19:3; 32:18; Ac 2:20
[n]20:5 Jb 8:12-13; Ps 37:35-36; 92:7
[o]20:6 Gn 11:4; Is 14:13-14; Ob 3-4
[p]20:7 Jb 4:20; Ps 90:5-6; Jms 4:14
[q]20:8 Ps 73:20; 90:5; Is 29:7
[r]20:9 Jb 7:8,21; Ps 37:36
[s]Jb 7:10; 8:18; Ps 103:16
[t]20:11 Jb 7:21; 17:16; Ps 7:5
[u]20:12-13 Ps 10:7; Pr 9:17; 20:17
[v]20:16 Dt 32:33; Pr 23:32; Is 59:5
[w]20:17 Dt 32:13; Jb 29:6; Ps 36:8
[x]20:19 Dt 28:30; Is 5:8; Mc 2:2

A19:19 Lit *of the men of my council* B19:25 Or *know that my Redeemer is living* C19:25 Or *earth* D19:25 Or *dust at the last, or dust as the Last One* E19:26 Lit *skin which they destroyed, or skin they destroyed in this way* F19:26 Or *apart from* G19:27 Or *not a stranger* H19:27 Lit *My kidneys grow faint* I19:28 Some Hb mss, LXX, Vg; other Hb mss read *me* J20:2 Lit *because of my feeling within me* K20:3 Lit *and a spirit from my understanding* L20:7 Lit *have seen* M20:10 Or *children must compensate* N20:16 Lit *tongue*

20 Because his appetite is never satisfied,[A]
he does not let anything
he desires escape.
21 Nothing is left for him to consume;[a]
therefore, his prosperity will not last.
22 At the height of his success[B]
distress will come to him;[b]
the full weight of misery[C]
will crush him.
23 When he fills his stomach,
God will send His burning anger
against him,
raining[c] it down on him
while he is eating.[D]
24 If he flees from an iron weapon,
an arrow from a bronze bow
will pierce him.
25 He pulls it out of his back,
the flashing tip out of his liver.[E]
Terrors come over him.[d]
26 Total darkness is reserved
for his treasures.
A fire unfanned by human hands
will consume[e] him;
it will feed on what is left in his tent.
27 The heavens will expose his iniquity,[f]
and the earth will rise up against him.[g]
28 The possessions in his house
will be removed,
flowing away on the day of God's anger.
29 This is the wicked man's lot[h] from God,
the inheritance God ordained for him.

Job's Reply to Zophar

21 Then Job answered:

2 Pay close attention to my words;
let this be the consolation you offer.
3 Bear with me while I speak;
then after I have spoken, you may
continue mocking.
4 As for me, is my complaint[i]
against a man?
Then why shouldn't I be impatient?
5 Look at me and shudder;[j]
put your hand over your mouth.[k]
6 When I think about it, I am terrified
and my body trembles[l] in horror.

[a]20:20-21 Jb 15:29; Pr 17:1; Ec 5:13 [b]20:22 Jdg 2:15; Jb 21:17; Zph 1:17 [c]20:23 Gn 19:24; Ps 11:6; Ezk 38:22 [d]20:25 Jb 18:11; 27:20; Jr 6:25 [e]20:26 Jb 15:34; Ps 21:9; 50:3 [f]20:27 Jb 13:23,26; 15:5; 22:5 [g]Dt 4:26; Jb 16:18-19; Ps 50:4 [h]20:29 Jb 27:13; 31:2; Ps 17:14 [i]21:4 Jb 7:11; 10:1; 27:13 [j]21:5 Jb 17:8; 18:20; Dn 4:19 [k]Jdg 18:19; Jb 29:9; 40:4 [l]21:6 Jb 4:14; Ps 55:5; 119:120 [m]21:9 Jb 5:24; 8:6; 12:6 [n]Jb 9:34; Ps 73:5 [o]21:12 Jb 30:31; Ps 81:2; 150:4 [p]21:13 Jb 36:11; Ps 37:7; 73:12 [q]21:14 Jb 22:17; Ps 95:10; Pr 1:29 [r]21:15 Ex 5:2; Jb 34:9; Mal 3:14 [s]21:16 Jb 22:18; Ps 1:1; Pr 1:10 [t]21:17 Jb 18:5; Pr 13:9; 24:20 [u]21:18 Ps 1:4; 35:5; Is 17:13 [v]21:19 Ex 20:5; Jr 31:29; Lm 5:7 [w]21:20 Ps 75:8; Is 51:17; Jr 25:15 [x]21:21 Jb 14:21; Ec 9:5; Is 63:16 [y]Jb 14:5; Ps 39:4; 90:12 [z]21:22 Is 40:13-14; Rm 11:34; 1Co 2:16

7 Why do the wicked continue to live,
growing old and becoming powerful?
8 Their children are established
while they are still alive,[F]
and their descendants,
before their eyes.
9 Their homes are secure
and free of fear;[m]
no rod from God strikes them.[n]
10 Their bulls breed without fail;
their cows calve and do not miscarry.
11 They let their little ones run
around like lambs;
their children skip about,
12 singing to the tambourine and lyre
and rejoicing at the sound of the flute.[o]
13 They spend[G] their days in prosperity[p]
and go down to •Sheol in peace.
14 Yet they say to God: "Leave us alone!
We don't want to know Your ways.[q]
15 Who is the •Almighty, that we
should serve Him,
and what will we gain by pleading
with Him?"[r]
16 But their prosperity is not
of their own doing.
The counsel of the wicked is far
from me![s]
17 How often is the lamp[t] of the wicked
put out?
Does disaster[H] come on them?
Does He apportion destruction
in His anger?
18 Are they like straw before the wind,
like chaff[u] a storm sweeps away?
19 God reserves a person's punishment
for his children.[v]
Let God repay the person himself,
so that he may know it.
20 Let his own eyes see his demise;
let him drink from
the Almighty's wrath![w]
21 For what does he care about his family
once he is dead,[x]
when the number of his months
has run out?[y]
22 Can anyone teach God knowledge,[z]
since He judges the exalted ones?[I]

[A]20:20 Lit *Because he does not know ease in his stomach* [B]20:22 Lit *In the fullness of his excess* [C]20:22 Some Hb mss, LXX, Vg; other Hb mss read *the hand of everyone in misery* [D]20:23 Text emended; MT reads *him, against his flesh* [E]20:25 Or *gallbladder* [F]21:8 Lit *established before them with them* [G]21:13 Alt Hb tradition reads *fully enjoy* [H]21:17 Lit *their disaster* [I]21:22 Probably angels

23 One person dies in excellent health,[A]
completely secure[B] and at ease.
24 His body is[C] well fed,[D]
and his bones are full of marrow.[E]
25 Yet another person dies
with a bitter[a] soul,
having never tasted prosperity.
26 But they both lie in the dust,
and worms cover them.[b]

27 I know your thoughts very well,
the schemes you would
wrong me with.
28 For you say, "Where now is
the nobleman's house?"
and "Where are the tents[c] the wicked
lived in?"
29 Have you never consulted
those who travel the roads?
Don't you accept their reports?[F]
30 Indeed, the evil man is spared
from the day of disaster,
rescued from the day of wrath.
31 Who would denounce his behavior
to his face?
Who would repay[d] him for what
he has done?
32 He is carried to the grave,
and someone keeps watch over
his tomb.
33 The dirt on his grave is[G] sweet to him.
Everyone follows behind him,
and those who go before him are
without number.

34 So how can you offer me
such futile comfort?
Your answers are deceptive.

THIRD SERIES OF SPEECHES

Eliphaz Speaks

22 Then Eliphaz the Temanite replied:

2 Can a man be of any use to God?
Can even a wise man be of use
to Him?
3 Does it delight the ·Almighty if you
are righteous?
Does He profit if you perfect
your behavior?[e]
4 Does He correct you and take you
to court
because of your piety?[f]
5 Isn't your wickedness abundant
and aren't your iniquities endless?
6 For you took collateral[g]
from your brothers without cause,
stripping off their clothes
and leaving them naked.
7 You gave no water to the thirsty
and withheld food from the famished,[h]
8 while the land belonged
to a powerful man
and an influential man lived on it.
9 You sent widows away empty-handed,
and the strength of the fatherless[i]
was[H] crushed.
10 Therefore snares surround you,
and sudden dread terrifies[j] you,
11 or darkness, so you cannot see,
and a flood of water covers you.[k]

12 Isn't God as high as the heavens?
And look at the highest stars —
how lofty they are!
13 Yet you say: "What does God know?
Can He judge through thick darkness?[l]
14 Clouds[m] veil Him so that
He cannot see,
as He walks on the circle of the sky."
15 Will you continue on the ancient path
that wicked men have walked?
16 They were snatched away
before their time,
and their foundations[n]
were washed away by a river.
17 They were the ones who said to God,
"Leave us alone!"
and "What can the Almighty do
to us?"[I,o]
18 But it was He who filled their houses
with good things.
The counsel of the wicked is
far from me!
19 The righteous see this and rejoice;
the innocent mock them, saying,[p]
20 "Surely our opponents are destroyed,
and fire has consumed
what they left behind."[q]

[a]**21:25** 1Sm 1:10; Jb 7:11; 10:1
[b]**21:26** Jb 20:11; Ec 9:2-3; Is 14:11
[c]**21:28** Jb 8:22,18:21; Ps 55:15
[d]**21:31** Dt 7:10; Jb 34:11; Ps 62:12
[e]**22:2-3** Jb 35:7; Ps 16:2; Lk 17:10
[f]**22:4** Jb 14:3; Ps 143:2
[g]**22:6** Ex 22:26; Dt 24:6,17; Ezk:12,16
[h]**22:7** Jb 31:17; Is 58:7; Mt 25:42
[i]**22:9** Jb 24:3; Is 10:2; Ezk 22:7
[j]**22:10** Jb 3:25; 23:15; 31:23
[k]**22:11** Jb 38:34; Ps 69:1-2; Lm 3:54
[l]**22:13** Ps 73:11; Is 29:15; Ezk 8:12
[m]**22:14** 2Sm 22:12; Jb 26:8; 37:11
[n]**22:16** Jb 4:19; Lm 4:11; Ezk 30:4
[o]**22:17** Jb 21:14; Ps 95:10; 107:42
[p]**22:19** Ps 52:6; 58:10; Pr 1:26-27
[q]**22:20** Jb 1:16; 4:9; 15:30

[A]**21:23** Lit *in bone of his perfection* [B]**21:23** Text emended; MT reads *health, all at ease* [C]**21:24** Or *His sides are*; Hb obscure [D]**21:24** Lit *is full of milk* [E]**21:24** Lit *and the marrow of his bones is watered* [F]**21:29** Lit *signs* [G]**21:33** Lit *The clods of the wadi are* [H]**22:9** LXX, Syr, Vg, Tg read *you have* [I]**22:17** LXX, Syr; MT reads *him*

21 Come to terms with God and be
at peace;[a]
in this way[A] good will come to you.
22 Receive instruction from His mouth,[b]
and place His sayings[c] in your heart.
23 If you return[d] to the Almighty, you will
be renewed.
If you banish injustice from your tent
24 and consign your gold to the dust,
the gold of Ophir[e] to the stones
in the •wadis,
25 the Almighty will be your gold
and your finest silver.
26 Then you will delight[f] in the Almighty
and lift up your face to God.[g]
27 You will pray to Him, and He will
hear you,[h]
and you will fulfill your vows.
28 When you make a decision, it will be
carried out,[B]
and light will shine on your ways.[i]
29 When others are humiliated
and you say, "Lift them up,"
God will save the humble.[C,j]
30 He will even rescue the •guilty one,
who will be rescued by the purity
of your hands.[k]

Job's Reply to Eliphaz

23 Then Job answered:

2 Today also my complaint is bitter.[D,l]
His[E] hand is heavy
despite my groaning.
3 If only I knew how to find Him,
so that I could go to His throne.
4 I would plead my case before Him[m]
and fill my mouth with arguments.
5 I would learn how[F] He would
answer me;
and understand what He would say
to me.
6 Would He prosecute[n] me forcefully?
No, He will certainly pay attention
to me.
7 Then an upright man could reason[o]
with Him,
and I would escape
from my Judge[p] forever.

[a]22:21 Ps 119:165; Pr 3:2; Is 27:5 [b]22:22 Dt 8:3; Pr 2:6; Mal 2:7 [c]Jb 6:10; 23:12; Ps 119:102 [d]22:23 Is 31:6; 55:7; Mal 3:7 [e]22:24 1Kg 9:28; Jb 28:16; Is 13:12 [f]22:26 Jb 27:10; Ps 37:4; Is 55:2 [g]Jb 11:15; 27:10; Is 58:14 [h]22:27 Jb 33:26; Ps 50:14; Is 58:9 [i]22:28 Pr 4:18; Is 60:3; Dn 12:3 [j]22:29 Ps 18:27; Mt 23:12; 1Pt 5:5 [k]22:30 2Sm 22:21; Jb 17:9; Ps 24:4 [l]23:2 Jb 7:11; 10:1; 21:4 [m]23:4 Jb 5:8; 13:18; 35:14 [n]23:6 Jb 13:19; 33:13; Is 45:9 [o]23:7 Jb 13:3,15; 15:3 [p]Gn 18:25; Is 33:22; Jr 11:20 [q]23:8 Jb 9:11; 35:14 [r]23:10 Ps 17:3; 66:10; 1Pt 1:7 [s]23:11 Jb 17:9; Ps 17:5; 44:18 [t]23:12 Jb 6:10; 22:22; Ps 119:102-3,111 [u]23:13 Ps 115:3; Is 14:27; Dn 4:35 [v]23:15 Jb 4:14; 22:10; 23:15 [w]23:16 Dt 20:3; Is 7:4; Jr 51:46 [x]23:17 Jb 19:8; 29:3; 30:26 [y]24:1 Ec 9:12; Is 2:12; Ac 1:7 [z]24:3 Dt 27:19; Jb 22:9; 31:21 [aa]24:4 Jdg 5:6; Pr 28:28; Am 2:7

8 If I go east, He is not there,
and if I go west, I cannot perceive Him.[q]
9 When He is at work to the north,
I cannot see Him;
when He turns south, I cannot
find Him.
10 Yet He knows the way I have taken;[G]
when He has tested me,[r] I will emerge
as pure gold.
11 My feet have followed in His tracks;
I have kept to His way[s] and not
turned aside.
12 I have not departed
from the commands of His lips;
I have treasured[H] the words[t]
of His mouth
more than my daily food.
13 But He is unchangeable; who can
oppose Him?
He does what He desires.[u]
14 He will certainly accomplish
what He has decreed for me,
and He has many more things like these
in mind.[I]
15 Therefore I am terrified[v]
in His presence;
when I consider this, I am afraid
of Him.
16 God has made my heart faint;[w]
the •Almighty has terrified me.
17 Yet I am not destroyed[J]
by the darkness,[x]
by the thick darkness that covers
my face.

24 Why does the •Almighty not reserve
times for judgment?[y]
Why do those who know Him never see
His days?
2 The wicked displace boundary markers.
They steal a flock and provide pasture
for it.
3 They drive away the donkeys owned
by the fatherless[z]
and take the widow's ox as collateral.
4 They push the needy off the road;
the poor of the land are forced
into hiding.[aa]
5 Like wild donkeys in the desert,

[A]22:21 Lit *peace; by them* [B]22:28 Lit *out for you* [C]22:29 Lit *bowed of eyes* [D]23:2 Syr, Tg, Vg; MT reads *rebellion* [E]23:2 LXX, Syr; MT reads *My* [F]23:5 Lit *the words* [G]23:10 Lit *way with me* [H]23:12 LXX, Vg read *treasured in my bosom* [I]23:14 Lit *these with Him* [J]23:17 Or *silenced*

the poor go out to their task of foraging
for food;
the wilderness provides nourishment
for their children.
6 They gather their fodder in the field
and glean the vineyards of the wicked.
7 Without clothing, they spend
the night naked,
having no covering against the cold.[a]
8 Drenched by mountain rains,
they huddle against[A] the rocks,
shelterless.
9 The fatherless infant is snatched
from the breast;
the nursing child of the poor is seized
as collateral.[B]
10 Without clothing,
they wander about naked.
They carry sheaves but go hungry.[b]
11 They crush olives in their presses;[C]
they tread the winepresses,
but go thirsty.
12 From the city, men[D] groan;
the mortally wounded cry for help,
yet God pays no attention
to this crime.[c]

13 The wicked are those who rebel
against the light.
They do not recognize its ways
or stay on its paths.
14 The murderer rises at dawn
to kill the poor and needy,
and by night he becomes a thief.
15 The adulterer's eye watches for twilight,
thinking: No eye will see me;
he covers his face.
16 In the dark they break[E] into houses;
by day they lock themselves in,[F]
never experiencing the light.
17 For the morning is like darkness
to them.
Surely they are familiar with the terrors
of darkness!

18 They float[G] on the surface of the water.
Their section of the land is cursed,
so that they never go to their vineyards.
19 As dry ground and heat snatch away
the melted snow,
so ·Sheol[d] steals those who have sinned.
20 The womb forgets them;
worms feed on them;
they are remembered[e] no more.
So injustice is broken like a tree.
21 They prey on[H] the childless woman
who is unable to conceive,
and do not deal kindly with the widow.
22 Yet God drags away[I] the mighty
by His power;
when He rises up, they have
no assurance of life.
23 He gives them a sense of security,
so they can rely on it,[f]
but His eyes[g] watch over their ways.
24 They are exalted for a moment,
then they are gone;
they are brought low and shrivel up
like everything else.[J]
They wither like heads of grain.[h]

25 If this is not true, then who
can prove me a liar[i]
and show that my speech is worthless?

Bildad Speaks

25 Then Bildad the Shuhite replied:

2 Dominion and dread[j] belong to Him,
the One who establishes harmony
in the heavens.[K]
3 Can His troops be numbered?
Does His light not shine on everyone?
4 How can a person be justified
before God?[k]
How can one born of woman be pure?[l]
5 If even the moon does not shine
and the stars are not pure in His sight,[m]
6 how much less man, who is a maggot,
and the son of man, who is a worm![n]

Job's Reply to Bildad

26 Then Job answered:

2 How you have helped[o] the powerless
and delivered the arm that is weak!
3 How you have counseled the unwise[p]
and thoroughly explained
the path to success!

[a]**24:7** Ex 22:26-27; Dt 24:12-13; Jb 22:6
[b]**24:10** Dt 24:19; 2Tm 2:6; Jms 5:4
[c]**24:12** Jb 1:22; Ps 69:26
[d]**24:19** Jb 7:9; Ps 9:17; Pr 27:20
[e]**24:20** Jb 18:17; Pr 10:7; Jr 11:19
[f]**24:23** Jb 11:18; Ps 4:8; Pr 3:24
[g]Ps 11:4; Pr 15:3; Jr 16:17
[h]**24:24** Jb 14:21; Ps 37:10; 106:43
[i]**24:25** Jb 6:28; 27:4; 34:6
[j]**25:2** 2Ch 20:29; Jb 13:11; Ps 36:1
[k]**25:4** Jb 9:2; Ps 143:2; Rm 3:20
[l]Jb 4:17; 15:14; Pr 20:9
[m]**25:5** Jb 4:18; 15:15; 21:22
[n]**25:6** Ps 8:4; 22:6; Is 41:14
[o]**26:2** Jb 4:3; Is 35:3; Heb 12:12
[p]**26:3** Jb 11:6; Ps 73:24; Jms 1:5

[A]**24:8** Lit *they embrace* [B]**24:9** Text emended; MT reads *breast; they seize collateral against the poor* [C]**24:11** Lit *olives between their rows* [D]**24:12** One Hb ms, Syr read *the dying* [E]**24:16** Lit *dig* [F]**24:16** Lit *they seal for themselves* [G]**24:18** Lit *are insignificant* [H]**24:21** LXX, Tg read *They harm* [I]**24:22** Or *God prolongs the life of* [J]**24:24** LXX reads *like a mallow plant in the heat* [K]**25:2** Lit *in His heights*

4 Who did you speak these words to?
Whose breath came out of your mouth?
5 The departed spirits tremble
beneath the waters and all that
inhabit them.[a]
6 •Sheol[b] is naked before God,
and •Abaddon[c] has no covering.[d]
7 He stretches the northern skies
over empty space;
He hangs the earth on nothing.
8 He wraps up the waters in His clouds,
yet the clouds do not burst
beneath their weight.[e]
9 He obscures the view of His throne,
spreading His cloud over it.
10 He laid out the horizon on the surface
of the waters[f]
at the boundary between light
and darkness.
11 The pillars that hold up the sky tremble,
astounded at His rebuke.[g]
12 By His power He stirred[h] the sea,
and by His understanding
He crushed •Rahab.[i]
13 By His breath the heavens gained
their beauty;
His hand pierced the fleeing serpent.[A,j]
14 These are but the fringes of His ways;
how faint is the word we hear of Him!
Who can understand
His mighty thunder?

27

Job continued his discourse, saying:

2 As God lives, who has deprived me
of justice,[k]
and the •Almighty who has
made me bitter,[l]
3 as long as my breath is still in me
and the breath from God remains
in my nostrils,[m]
4 my lips will not speak unjustly,
and my tongue will not utter deceit.
5 I will never affirm that you are right.
I will maintain my integrity[B,n] until I die.
6 I will cling to my righteousness
and never let it go.
My conscience[o] will not accuse me
as long as I live!

7 May my enemy be like the wicked
and my opponent like the unjust.
8 For what hope does
the godless man[p] have when he is
cut off,
when God takes away his life?[q]
9 Will God hear his cry
when distress comes on him?
10 Will he delight[r] in the Almighty?
Will he call on God at all times?
11 I will teach you about God's power.
I will not conceal what the Almighty
has planned.[C]
12 All of you have seen this for yourselves,
why do you keep up this empty talk?[s]
13 This is a wicked man's lot[t] from God,
the inheritance the ruthless receive
from the Almighty.
14 Even if his children increase,
they are destined for the sword;
his descendants will never
have enough food.
15 Those who survive him will be buried
by the plague,
yet their widows will not weep
for them.[u]
16 Though he piles up silver like dust
and heaps up a wardrobe like clay—
17 he may heap it up, but the righteous
will wear it,
and the innocent will divide up
his silver.[v]
18 The house he built is
like a moth's cocoon
or a booth set up by a watchman.[w]
19 He lies down wealthy, but will do so
no more;
when he opens his eyes, it is gone.
20 Terrors overtake him like a flood;[x]
a storm[y] wind sweeps him away
at night.
21 An east wind picks him up,
and he is gone;
it carries him away from his place.
22 It blasts at him without mercy,
while he flees desperately
from its grasp.
23 It claps[z] its hands at him
and scorns him from its place.

[a]26:5 Ps 88:10; Is 26:14,19; Rv 20:13 [b]26:6 Ps 30:3,9; Pr 1:12; Is 5:14 [c]Jb 28:22; Pr 27:20; Rv 9:11 [d]Ps 139:8; Pr 15:11; Heb 4:13 [e]26:8 Jb 37:11; 38:9; Pr 30:4 [f]26:10 Ps 104:9; Pr 8:27,29; Jr 5:22 [g]26:11 2Sm 22:16; Ps 18:15; 104:7 [h]26:12 Is 51:15; Jr 31:35 [i]Jb 9:13; Ps 89:10; Is 51:9 [j]26:13 Jb 41; Ps 33:6; Is 27:1 [k]27:2 Jb 19:6; 34:5 [l]Ex 1:14; Ru 1:20; Jb 3:20 [m]27:3 Gn 2:7; Jb 12:10; 33:4 [n]27:5 Jb 2:3,9; 31:6; Pr 11:3 [o]27:6 Ac 24:16; 1Co 4:4; Rv 9:11 [p]27:8 Jb 17:8; 20:5; 36:13 [q]Jb 8:13; Mt 16:26; Lk 12:20 [r]27:10 Jb 22:26; Ps 37:4; Is 55:2 [s]27:12 Jb 2:10; 15:2 [t]27:13 Jb 20:29; 31:2; Ps 17:14 [u]27:15 Jb 18:19; Ps 78:64; Jr 22:10 [v]27:17 Pr 13:22; 28:8; Ec 2:26 [w]27:18 Jb 4:19; Is 1:8; Jnh 4:5 [x]27:20 Jb 18:11; 20:25; Jr 6:25 [y]Jb 21:18; Ps 83:15; Is 29:6 [z]27:23 Nm 24:10; Jb 34:37; Lm 2:15

[A]26:13 = Leviathan [B]27:5 Lit *will not remove my integrity from me* [C]27:11 Lit *what is with the Almighty*

Job's Hymn to Wisdom

28 Surely there is a mine for silver
and a place where gold is refined.
2 Iron is taken from the ground,
and copper is smelted from ore.
3 A miner puts an end to the darkness;
he probes[A] the deepest recesses
for ore in the gloomy darkness.
4 He cuts a shaft far
from human habitation,
in places unknown to those who walk
above ground.[B]
Suspended far away from people,
the miners swing back and forth.
5 Food may come from the earth,
but below the surface the earth
is transformed as by fire.
6 Its rocks are a source of sapphire,[C,a]
containing flecks of gold.
7 No bird of prey knows that path;
no falcon's eye has seen it.
8 Proud beasts have never walked on it;
no lion has ever prowled over it.
9 The miner strikes the flint
and transforms the mountains
at their foundations.
10 He cuts out channels in the rocks,
and his eyes spot every treasure.
11 He dams up the streams from flowing[D]
so that he may bring to light
what is hidden.

12 But where can wisdom[b] be found,
and where is understanding located?
13 No man can know its value,[E]
since it cannot be found in the land
of the living.
14 The ocean depths say, "It's not in me,"
while the sea declares, "I don't have it."[c]
15 Gold cannot be exchanged for it,
and silver cannot be weighed out
for its price.
16 Wisdom cannot be valued in the gold
of Ophir,[d]
in precious onyx or sapphire.[C,e]
17 Gold and glass do not compare with it,
and articles of fine gold
cannot be exchanged for it.[f]
18 Coral and quartz are not
worth mentioning.
The price of wisdom is beyond pearls.
19 Topaz from •Cush cannot compare
with it,
and it cannot be valued in pure gold.

20 Where then does wisdom come from,
and where is understanding located?
21 It is hidden from the eyes
of every living thing
and concealed from the birds of the sky.
22 •Abaddon and Death[g] say,
"We have heard news of it
with our ears."
23 But God understands the way
to wisdom,
and He knows its location.
24 For He looks to the ends of the earth
and sees everything under the heavens.
25 When God fixed the weight of the wind
and limited the water by measure,[h]
26 when He established a limit[F]
for the rain[i]
and a path for the lightning,
27 He considered wisdom
and evaluated it;
He established it and examined it.
28 He said to mankind,
"The •fear of the Lord is this: wisdom.
And to turn from evil
is understanding."[j]

Job's Final Claim of Innocence

29 Job continued his discourse, saying:

2 If only I could be as in months
gone by,
in the days when God
watched over me,
3 when His lamp shone above my head,
and I walked through darkness
by His light![k]
4 I would be as I was in the days
of my youth
when God's friendship[l] rested
on my tent,
5 when the •Almighty was still with me
and my children were around me,
6 when my feet were bathed in cream
and the rock[m] poured out streams of oil
for me!

[a]28:6 Ex 24:10; Ezk 1:26; Rv 21:19
[b]28:12 Jb 28:20; Pr 16:16; Ec 7:23,25
[c]28:14 Dt 30:11-13; Ps 92:5; Rm 11:33
[d]28:16 1Kg 9:28; 10:11; Jb 22:24
[e]Pr 3:14-16; 8:10-11; 16:16
[f]28:17 Ps 119:72; Pr 8:19; 20:15
[g]28:22 Jb 25:6; Ps 49:14; Pr 27:20
[h]28:25 Ps 135:7; Pr 30:4; Is 40:12
[i]28:26 Jb 5:10; 37:6; 38:25
[j]28:28 Dt 4:6; Pr 1:7; 9:10
[k]29:3 Jb 11:17; Ps 18:28; 119:105
[l]29:4 Ps 25:14; 55:14; Pr 3:32
[m]29:6 Dt 32:13; Jb 20:17; Ps 81:16

A 28:3 Lit *probes all* B 28:4 Lit *far from with inhabitant, things forgotten by foot* C 28:6,16 Or *lapis lazuli* D 28:11 LXX, Vg read *He explores the sources of the streams* E 28:13 LXX reads *way* F 28:26 Or *decree*

7 When I went out to the city ·gate
and took my seat in the town square,
8 the young men saw me and withdrew,
while older men stood to their feet.
9 City officials stopped talking
and covered their mouths
with their hands.[a]
10 The noblemen's voices were hushed,
and their tongues stuck to the roof
of their mouths.
11 When they heard me, they blessed me,
and when they saw me, they spoke well
of me.[A]
12 For I rescued the poor man
who cried out for help,
and the fatherless child who had
no one to support him.[b]
13 The dying man blessed me,
and I made the widow's heart rejoice.
14 I clothed myself in righteousness,[c]
and it enveloped me;
my just decisions were like a robe
and a turban.
15 I was eyes to the blind
and feet to the lame.[d]
16 I was a father to the needy,
and I examined the case of the stranger.
17 I shattered the fangs of the unjust[e]
and snatched the prey from his teeth.

18 So I thought: I will die in my own nest
and multiply my days as the sand.[B]
19 My roots will have access to water,[f]
and the dew will rest on my branches
all night.
20 My strength will be refreshed
within me,
and my bow will be renewed
in my hand.[g]
21 Men listened to me with expectation,
waiting silently for my advice.
22 After a word from me they did not
speak again;
my speech settled on them like dew.
23 They waited for me as for the rain
and opened their mouths as for
spring showers.
24 If I smiled at them, they couldn't
believe it;
they were thrilled at[C] the light
of my countenance.
25 I directed their course and presided
as chief.
I lived as a king among his troops,
like one who comforts
those who mourn.

30 But now they mock[h] me,
men younger than I am,
whose fathers I would have refused
to put
with my sheep dogs.
2 What use to me was the strength
of their hands?
Their vigor had left them.
3 Emaciated from poverty and hunger,
they gnawed the dry land,
the desolate wasteland by night.
4 They plucked mallow[D,i]
among the shrubs,
and the roots of the broom tree were
their food.
5 They were expelled
from human society;
people shouted at them
as if they were thieves.
6 They are living on the slopes
of the ·wadis,
among the rocks and in holes
in the ground.
7 They bray among the shrubs;
they huddle beneath the thistles.
8 Foolish[j] men, without even a name.
They were forced to leave the land.
9 Now I am mocked by their songs;[k]
I have become an object of scorn
to them.
10 They despise me and keep
their distance from me;[l]
they do not hesitate to spit[m] in my face.
11 Because God has loosened
my[E] bowstring and oppressed me,
they have cast off restraint
in my presence.[n]
12 The rabble[F] rise up at my right;
they trap[G] my feet
and construct their siege ramp[H]
against me.[o]

[a] **29:9** Jdg 18:19; Jb 21:5; 40:4
[b] **29:12** Ps 10:14; 72:12; Pr 21:13
[c] **29:14** Ps 132:9; Is 59:17; Eph 6:14
[d] **29:15** Is 35:6; 42:7,16; Mt 11:5
[e] **29:17** Jb 4:10; Ps 3:7; 58:6
[f] **29:19** Jb 14:9; Ps 1:3; Ezk 31:7
[g] **29:20** Gn 49:24; Is 40:31; 41:1
[h] **30:1** Jb 12:4; Jr 20:7; Lm 3:14
[i] **30:4** Jb 12:4; Jr 20:7; Lm 3:14
[j] **30:8** Pr 26:7,12; Ec 7:5; Is 32:5-6
[k] **30:9** Jb 12:4; 30:1; Lm 3:14
[l] **30:10** Jb 19:19; Ps 89:38; Am 5:10
[m] Nm 12:14; Is 50:6; Mt 26:67
[n] **30:11** Jb 12:18; 29:20; Ps 32:9
[o] **30:12** Jb 16:10; 19:12; Ps 140:4-5

[A] **29:11** Lit *When an ear heard, it called me blessed, and when an eye saw, it testified for me* [B] **29:18** Or *as the phoenix* [C] **29:24** Lit *they did not cast down* [D] **30:4** Or *saltwort* [E] **30:11** Alt Hb tradition, LXX, Vg read *His* [F] **30:12** Hb obscure [G] **30:12** Lit *stretch out* [H] **30:12** Lit *and raise up their destructive paths*

13 They tear up my path;
they contribute to my destruction,[a]
without anyone to help them.
14 They advance as through
a gaping breach;
they keep rolling in through the ruins.[b]
15 Terrors[c] are turned loose against me;
they chase my dignity away
like the wind,
and my prosperity has passed by
like a cloud.

16 Now my life is poured out
before my eyes,
and days of suffering[d] have seized me.
17 Night pierces my bones,
but my gnawing pains never rest.[e]
18 My clothing is distorted
with great force;
He chokes me by the neck
of my garment.[A]
19 He throws me into the mud,
and I have become like dust and ashes.[f]

20 I cry out to You for help, but You do not
answer me;[g]
when I stand up, You merely look at me.
21 You have turned against me
with cruelty;
You harass[h] me with Your strong hand.
22 You lift me up on the wind
and make me ride it;
You scatter me in the storm.[i]
23 Yes, I know that You will lead me
to death —
the place[j] appointed for all who live.

24 Yet no one would stretch out his hand
against a ruined man[B]
when he cries out to him for help
because of his distress.[k]
25 Have I not wept for those
who have fallen on hard times?
Has my soul not grieved for the needy?[l]
26 But when I hoped for good, evil came;
when I looked for light,
darkness[m] came.
27 I am churning within[C] and cannot rest;
days of suffering confront me.
28 I walk about blackened, but not
by the sun.[D]
I stood in the assembly and cried out
for help.
29 I have become a brother to jackals
and a companion of ostriches.
30 My skin blackens and flakes off,[E]
and my bones burn with fever.[n]
31 My lyre is used for mourning
and my flute for the sound
of weeping.[o]

31 I have made a covenant with my eyes.[p]
How then could I look
at a young woman?[F,q]
2 For what portion[r] would I have
from God above,
or what inheritance from the ˙Almighty
on high?
3 Doesn't disaster come to the unjust
and misfortune to evildoers?
4 Does He not see my ways
and number all my steps?[s]

5 If I have walked in falsehood
or my foot has rushed to deceit,
6 let God weigh me in accurate scales,[t]
and He will recognize my integrity.[u]
7 If my step has turned from the way,
my heart has followed my eyes,
or impurity has stained my hands,[v]
8 let someone else eat what I have sown,
and let my crops be uprooted.[w]

9 If my heart has been seduced by
my neighbor's wife
or I have lurked at his door,
10 let my own wife grind grain
for another man,
and let other men sleep with[G] her.
11 For that would be a disgrace;
it would be a crime
deserving punishment.[H,x]
12 For it is a fire that consumes down
to ˙Abaddon;
it would destroy my entire harvest.[y]

13 If I have dismissed the case of my male
or female servants
when they made a complaint
against me,
14 what could I do when God stands up
to judge?

[a]**30:13** Jb 6:2; Ps 57:1; Pr 19:13 [b]**30:14** Jb 16:14; Jl 2:7 [c]**30:15** Jb 18:11; 27:20; Ps 73:19 [d]**30:16** Jb 10:15; 30:27; 36:21 [e]**30:17** Jb 33:19; Ps 6:2; 38:3 [f]**30:19** Jb 16:15; Ps 7:5; 75:10 [g]**30:20** Jb 19:7; Ps 18:41; 88:13-14 [h]**30:21** Gn 49:23; Jb 16:9; Ps 55:3 [i]**30:22** Jb 9:17; Ps 83:15; Jnh 1:4 [j]**30:23** Jb 3:15; 17:13; Ec 12:5 [k]**30:24** Jb 12:5; 31:29; Pr 24:22 [l]**30:25** Jb 5:15; 24:4,14; 31:19 [m]**30:26** Jb 19:8; Is 59:9; Lm 3:2 [n]**30:30** Ps 102:3; Lm 4:8; 5:10 [o]**30:31** Is 24:8; Ezk 26:13; Mt 11:17 [p]**31:1** Pr 4:25; Is 33:15; 2Pt 2:14 [q]Ex 22:6; Pr 17:24; Mt 5:28 [r]**31:2** Jb 20:29; 27:13; Ps 17:14 [s]**31:4** Jb 14:16; 34:21; Pr 5:21 [t]**31:6** Jb 6:2; Dn 5:27; Mc 6:11 [u]Jb 2:3,9; 27:5; Pr 11:3 [v]**31:7** Nm 15:39; Jb 23:11; Ps 7:3 [w]**31:8** Lv 26:16; Dt 28:30; Jb 20:18 [x]**31:11** Gn 38:24; Lv 20:10; Dt 22:22,24 [y]**31:12** Jb 26:6; 28:22; Pr 6:27-29

[A]**30:18** Hb obscure [B]**30:24** Lit *a heap of ruins* [C]**30:27** Lit *My bowels boil* [D]**30:28** Or *walk in sunless gloom* [E]**30:30** Lit *blackens away from me* [F]**31:1** Or *a virgin* [G]**31:10** Lit *men kneel down over* [H]**31:11** Lit *crime judges*

How should I answer Him
when He calls me to account?
15 Did not the One who made me
in the womb also make them?
Did not the same God form us both
in the womb?[a]
16 If I have refused the wishes
of the poor
or let the widow's[b] eyes go blind,
17 if I have eaten my few crumbs alone
without letting the fatherless
eat any of it —
18 for from my youth, I raised him
as his father,
and since the day I was born[A] I guided
the widow —
19 if I have seen anyone dying for lack
of clothing
or a needy person without a cloak,[c]
20 if he[B] did not bless me
while warming himself with the fleece
from my sheep,
21 if I ever cast my vote[C]
against a fatherless child
when I saw that I had support
in the city ·gate,[d]
22 then let my shoulder blade fall
from my back,
and my arm be pulled from its socket.
23 For disaster from God terrifies me,
and because of His majesty
I could not do these things.[e]
24 If I placed my confidence in gold
or called fine gold my trust,[f]
25 if I have rejoiced because my wealth
is great
or because my own hand has acquired
so much,
26 if I have gazed at the sun
when it was shining
or at the moon moving in splendor,[g]
27 so that my heart was secretly enticed
and I threw them a kiss,[D]
28 this would also be a crime
deserving punishment,
for I would have denied God above.
29 Have I rejoiced over
my enemy's distress,

[a]**31:15** Ps 119:73; 139:13; Jr 1:5
[b]**31:16** Jb 22:9; 24:3,21; 29:13
[c]**31:19** Ex 22:26; Jb 22:6
[d]**31:21** Jb 5:4; Pr 22:22; Is 29:21
[e]**31:23** Jb 13:11; 22:10; 23:15
[f]**31:24** Ps 52:7; Mt 6:19; Mk 10:24
[g]**31:26** Dt 4:19; 17:3; Ezk 8:16
[h]**31:33** Jb 7:21; 22:5; 33:9
[i]Ps 32:3-5; Pr 28:13; 1Jn 1:8-10
[j]**31:35** Jb 16:21; Ec 6:10; Is 45:9
[k]**31:36** Pr 4:9; 12:4; 17:6
[l]**31:40** Gn 3:18; Is 34:13; Hs 9:6
[m]Pr 24:31; Is 5:2; Hs 10:4
[n]**32:1** Jb 10:7; 33:9; 34:5-6
[o]**32:2** Gn 22:21; Jr 25:23
[p]Jb 33:32; Jr 3:11; Ezk 16:51-52

or become excited when trouble came
his way?
30 I have not allowed my mouth to sin
by asking for his life with a curse.
31 Haven't the members
of my household said,
"Who is there who has not had enough
to eat at Job's table?"
32 No stranger had to spend the night
on the street,
for I opened my door to the traveler.
33 Have I covered my transgressions[h]
as others do[E]
by hiding my ·guilt in my heart,[i]
34 because I greatly feared the crowds,
and the contempt of the clans
terrified me,
so I grew silent and would not
go outside?
35 If only I had someone to hear my case![j]
Here is my signature; let the Almighty
answer me.
Let my Opponent compose
His indictment.
36 I would surely carry it on my shoulder
and wear it like a crown.[k]
37 I would give Him an account of all
my steps;
I would approach Him like a prince.
38 If my land cries out against me
and its furrows join in weeping,
39 if I have consumed its produce
without payment
or shown contempt for its tenants,[F]
40 then let thorns[l] grow instead of wheat
and stinkweed[m] instead of barley.

The words of Job are concluded.

Elihu's Angry Response

32 So these three men quit answering
Job, because he was righteous in his
own eyes.[n] 2Then Elihu son of Barachel the
Buzite[o] from the family of Ram became angry. He was angry at Job because he had justified[p] himself rather than God. 3He was also
angry at Job's three friends because they had
failed to refute him and yet had condemned
him.[G]

[A]**31:18** Lit *and from my mother's womb* [B]**31:20** Lit *his loins* [C]**31:21** Lit *I raise my hand* [D]**31:27** Lit *and my hand kissed my mouth* [E]**31:33** Or *as Adam* [F]**31:39** Lit *or caused the breath of its tenants to breathe out* [G]**32:3** Ancient Jewish tradition reads *condemned God*

4 Now Elihu had waited to speak to Job because they were all older than he. 5 But when
he saw that the three men could not answer
Job, he became angry.
6 So Elihu son of Barachel the Buzite replied:

I am young in years,
while you are old;
therefore I was timid and afraid
to tell[a] you what I know.
7 I thought that age should speak
and maturity should teach wisdom.
8 But it is a spirit in man[A]
and the breath[b] of the ·Almighty
that give him understanding.
9 It is not only the old who are wise
or the elderly who understand
how to judge.
10 Therefore I say, "Listen to me.
I too will declare what I know."
11 Look, I waited for your conclusions;
I listened to your insights
as you sought for words.
12 I paid close attention to you.
Yet no one proved Job wrong;
not one of you refuted his arguments.
13 So do not claim,
"We have found wisdom;
let God deal with him, not man."
14 But Job has not directed his argument
to me,
and I will not respond to him
with your arguments.

15 Job's friends are dismayed and can
no longer answer;
words have left them.
16 Should I continue to wait now that
they are silent,
now that they stand there
and no longer answer?
17 I too will answer;[B]
yes, I will tell what I know.
18 For I am full of words,
and my spirit[C] compels me to speak.[c]
19 My heart[D] is like unvented wine;
it is about to burst like new wineskins.[d]
20 I must speak so that I can find relief;
I must open my lips and respond.

[a]32:6 Jb 15:17; 36:2
[b]32:8 Gn 2:7; Jb 33:4; Is 42:5
[c]32:18 Jb 19:3; 32:18; Ac 4:20
[d]32:19 Jb 15:35; 37:1; Pr 20:27,30
[e]32:21 Dt 10:17; Jb 13:8; 34:19
[f]33:3 1Kg 9:4; Ps 25:21; 119:7
[g]33:4 Jb 27:2; 32:8; 35:13
[h]Gn 2:7; Jb 27:3; Is 30:33
[i]33:5 Jb 23:4; 32:14; 37:19
[j]1Sm 17:16; Ps 2:2; Jr 46:4,14
[k]33:6 Jb 4:19; 10:9; 13:12
[l]33:7 Jb 20:25; Ps 55:4; 88:15
[m]33:9 Jb 9:21; 11:4; 34:6
[n]33:10 Jb 13:24; 19:11; Lm 2:5
[o]33:11 Jb 10:14; 14:16; Ps 130:3
[p]33:12 Jb 4:17; 9:2; 15:14
[q]33:13 Jb 9:3; 13:19; 40:2
[r]33:15 Jb 4:13; 7:14; 20:8

21 I will be partial to no one,[e]
and I will not give anyone
an undeserved title.
22 For I do not know how to give
such titles;
otherwise, my Maker would remove me
in an instant.

Elihu Confronts Job

33 But now, Job, pay attention
to my speech,
and listen to all my words.
2 I am going to open my mouth;
my tongue will form words
on my palate.
3 My words come from
my upright[f] heart,
and my lips speak with sincerity
what they know.
4 The Spirit of God has made me,
and the breath of the ·Almighty[g]
gives me life.[h]
5 Refute me if you can.
Prepare[i] your case against me;
take your stand.[j]
6 I am just like you before God;
I was also pinched off
from a piece of clay.[k]
7 Fear[l] of me should not terrify you;
the pressure I exert[E] against you
will be light.

8 Surely you have spoken in my hearing,
and I have heard these very[F] words:
9 "I am pure, without transgression;
I am ·clean and have no ·guilt.[m]
10 But He finds reasons to oppose me;
He regards me as His enemy.[n]
11 He puts my feet in the stocks;
He stands watch[o] over all my paths."
12 But I tell you that you are wrong
in this matter,
since God is greater than man.[p]
13 Why do you take[q] Him to court
for not answering anything
a person asks?[G]
14 For God speaks time and again,
but a person may not notice it.
15 In a dream, a vision[r] in the night,

A32:8 Or *is the Spirit in a person* B32:17 Lit *answer my part* C32:18 Lit *and the spirit of my belly* D32:19 Lit *belly* E33:7 Lit *you; my pressure* F33:8 Lit *heard a sound of* G33:13 Lit *court, for He does not answer all his words*

when deep sleep falls on people[a]
as they slumber on their beds,
16 He uncovers their ears[b] at that time
and terrifies them[A] with warnings,
17 in order to turn a person
from his actions
and suppress his pride.[B]
18 God spares his soul from the ·Pit,[c]
his life from crossing the river
of death.[C]
19 A person may be disciplined on his bed[d]
with pain
and constant distress in his bones,[e]
20 so that he detests bread,
and his soul despises his favorite food.[f]
21 His flesh wastes away to nothing,[D]
and his unseen bones stick out.
22 He draws near to the Pit,
and his life to the executioners.
23 If there is an angel[g] on his side,
one mediator out of a thousand,
to tell a person what is right for him[E]
24 and to be gracious to him and say,
"Spare him from going down to the Pit;
I have found a ransom,"[h]
25 then his flesh will be healthier[F] than
in his youth,
and he will return to the days
of his youthful vigor.[i]
26 He will pray to God, and God
will delight in him.
That man will see His face[j] with a shout
of joy,
and God will restore his righteousness
to him.[k]
27 He will look at men and say,
"I have sinned and perverted
what was right;
yet I did not get what I deserved.[G]
28 He redeemed my soul from going down
to the Pit,
and I will continue to see the light."
29 God certainly does all these things
two or three times to a man
30 in order to turn him back
from the Pit,
so he may shine with the light of life.[l]
31 Pay attention, Job, and listen to me.
Be quiet, and I will speak.
32 But if you have something to say,[H]
answer me;
speak, for I would like to justify you.
33 If not, then listen to me;
be quiet, and I will teach you wisdom.

34 Then Elihu continued,[I] saying:

2 Hear my words, you wise men,
and listen to me,
you knowledgeable ones.
3 Doesn't the ear test words
as the palate tastes food?
4 Let us judge for ourselves what is right;
let us decide together what is good.
5 For Job has declared, "I am righteous,
yet God has deprived me of justice.[m]
6 Would I lie about my case?[n]
My wound[J] is incurable,
though I am without transgression."
7 What man is like Job?
He drinks derision[o] like water.
8 He keeps company with evildoers
and walks with wicked men.
9 For he has said, "A man gains nothing
when he becomes God's friend."[p]
10 Therefore listen to me, you men
of understanding.
It is impossible for God to do wrong,
and for the ·Almighty to act unjustly.[q]
11 For He repays[r] a person according to
his deeds,
and He brings his ways on him.
12 Indeed, it is true that God does not
act wickedly
and the Almighty does not
pervert justice.[s]
13 Who gave Him authority
over the earth?
Who put Him in charge of
the entire world?[t]
14 If He put His mind to it
and withdrew the spirit[u] and breath
He gave,
15 every living thing
would perish together
and mankind would return to the dust.[v]
16 If you have understanding, hear this;
listen to what I have to say.

[a]**33:15** Gn 2:21; 15:12; Jb 4:13
[b]**33:16** Jb 4:12; 13:1; 36:10,15
[c]**33:18** Jb 33:28,30; 36:16; Ps 30:9
[d]**33:19** Jb 7:13; Ps 41:3; Hs 7:14
[e]Jb 30:17; Ps 6:2; 38:3
[f]**33:20** Jb 3:24; 6:7; Ps 102:4
[g]**33:23** Ex 23:20,23; Ps 34:7; Is 63:9
[h]**33:24** Ex 30:12; Ps 49:7; Pr 21:18
[i]**33:25** Dt 34:7; 2Kg 5:14; Jb 20:11
[j]**33:26** Gn 33:10; Ps 11:7; 17:15
[k]Ps 23:3; 51:12; 1Jn 1:9
[l]**33:30** Ps 56:13; Jn 1:4,9
[m]**34:5** Jb 10:7; 27:2; 33:9
[n]**34:6** Jb 6:28; 24:25; 27:4
[o]**34:7** Jb 15:16; Pr 19:28
[p]**34:9** Ex 5:2; Jb 21:15; Mal 3:14
[q]**34:10** Dt 32:4; Ps 92:15; Rm 9:14
[r]**34:11** Dt 7:10; Jb 21:31; Is 59:18
[s]**34:12** 2Ch 19:6; Jb 8:3; Ps 9:16
[t]**34:13** Jb 38:4; Ps 50:12; Is 40:12-14
[u]**34:14** Ps 104:29; Ec 3:19; 12:7
[v]**34:15** Gn 2:7; Jb 4:19; 10:9

[A]**33:16** LXX; MT reads *and seals* [B]**33:17** Lit *and cover pride within a man* [C]**33:18** Or *from perishing by the sword* [D]**33:21** Lit *away from sight* [E]**33:23** Or *to vouch for a person's uprightness* [F]**33:25** Hb obscure [G]**33:27** Lit *and the same was not to me* [H]**33:32** Lit *If there are words* [I]**34:1** Lit *answered* [J]**34:6** Lit *arrow*

17 Could one who hates justice
govern the world?
Will you condemn the mighty
Righteous One,[a]
18 who says to a king, "Worthless man!"
and to nobles, "Wicked men!"?[b]
19 God is not partial[c] to princes
and does not favor the rich
over the poor,
for they are all the work of His hands.
20 They die suddenly in the middle
of the night;
people shudder, then pass away.
Even the mighty are removed
without effort.

21 For His eyes watch over a man's ways,
and He observes all his steps.[d]
22 There is no darkness, no deep darkness,
where evildoers can hide themselves.[e]
23 God does not need to examine
a person further,
that one should[A] approach Him
in court.
24 He shatters the mighty
without an investigation
and sets others in their place.[f]
25 Therefore, He recognizes their deeds[g]
and overthrows them by night,
and they are crushed.
26 In full view of the public,[B]
He strikes them for their wickedness,
27 because they turned aside
from following Him
and did not understand any of His ways
28 but caused the poor to cry out to Him,
and He heard the outcry
of the afflicted.[h]
29 But when God is silent, who can declare
Him ·guilty?
When He hides His face, who can
see Him?
Yet He watches over both individuals
and nations,
30 so that godless men should not rule
or ensnare the people.

31 Suppose someone says to God,
"I have endured my punishment;
I will no longer act wickedly.
32 Teach me what I cannot see;
if I have done wrong, I won't
do it again."
33 Should God repay you on your terms
when you have rejected His?
You must choose, not I!
So declare what you know.
34 Reasonable men will say to me,
along with the wise men who hear me,
35 "Job speaks without knowledge;[i]
his words are without insight."
36 If only Job were tested to the limit,
because his answers are like those
of wicked men.
37 For he adds rebellion to his sin;
he scornfully claps[j] in our presence,
while multiplying[k] his words
against God.

35

Then Elihu continued, saying:

2 Do you think it is just when you say,
"I am righteous before God"?
3 For you ask, "What does it profit You,[C]
and what benefit comes to me,
if I do not sin?"[l]
4 I will answer you
and your friends with you.
5 Look at the heavens and see;
gaze at the clouds high above you.
6 If you sin, how does it affect God?
If you multiply your transgressions,
what does it do to Him?
7 If you are righteous, what do you
give Him,
or what does He receive
from your hand?[m]
8 Your wickedness affects a person
like yourself,
and your righteousness another
human being.

9 People cry out because of
severe oppression;
they shout for help because of the arm
of the mighty.[n]
10 But no one asks, "Where is God
my Maker,[o]
who provides us with songs
in the night,[p]
11 who gives us more understanding
than the animals of the earth

[a]34:17 Gn 18:25; 2Sm 23:3; Rm 3:5
[b]34:18 Ex 22:28; Jb 12:21; Ps 107:40
[c]34:19 Dt 10:17; Jb 13:8; 32:21
[d]34:21 Jb 14:16; 31:4; Pr 5:21
[e]34:22 Ps 139:12; Am 9:2-3; Heb 4:13
[f]34:24 Jb 12:19; Ps 2:9; Dn 2:21
[g]34:25 Jb 11:11; Ps 10:14
[h]34:28 Ex 3:7; 22:23; Jms 5:4
[i]34:35 Jb 35:16; 38:2; 42:3
[j]34:37 Nm 24:10; Jb 27:23; Lm 2:15
[k]Jb 16:4; 35:16; Ezk 35:13
[l]35:3 Jb 9:29; 21:15; 34:9
[m]35:7 Jb 22:3; 41:11; Rm 11:35
[n]35:9 Ex 2:23; Jb 24:12; 34:28
[o]35:10 Dt 32:6; Is 51:13; Jr 2:8
[p]Ps 42:8; 77:6; Ac 16:25

A34:23 Some emend to *God has not appointed a time for man to* B34:26 Lit *In a place of spectators* C35:3 Some emend to *me*

and makes us wiser than the birds
of the sky?"[a]
12 There they cry out,
but He does not answer,
because of the pride of evil men.[b]
13 Indeed, God does not listen
to empty cries,
and the ·Almighty does not take note
of it—
14 how much less when[A] you complain[B]
that you do not see Him,
that your case[c] is before Him
and you are waiting[d] for Him.
15 But now, because God's anger
does not punish
and He does not pay attention
to transgression,[C]
16 Job opens his mouth in vain
and multiplies words
without knowledge.[e]

36 Then Elihu continued, saying:
2 Be patient with me a little longer,
and I will inform you,
for there is still more to be said
on God's behalf.
3 I will get my knowledge from a
distant place
and ascribe justice to my Maker.
4 For my arguments are without flaw;[D]
one who has perfect knowledge is
with you.
5 Yes, God is mighty, but He despises
no one;
He understands all things.[E,f]
6 He does not keep the wicked alive,[g]
but He gives justice to the afflicted.
7 He does not remove His gaze
from the righteous,
but He seats them forever
with enthroned kings,
and they are exalted.
8 If people are bound with chains
and trapped by the cords of affliction,
9 God tells them what they have done
and how arrogantly
they have transgressed.
10 He opens their ears[h] to correction
and insists they repent from iniquity.
11 If they serve Him obediently,
they will end their days in prosperity
and their years in happiness.[i]
12 But if they do not obey,
they will cross the river of death[F]
and die without knowledge.[j]
13 Those who have a godless heart
harbor anger;
even when God binds them,
they do not cry for help.
14 They die in their youth;
their life ends among
male cult prostitutes.[k]
15 God rescues the afflicted by
their affliction;
He instructs them by their torment.
16 Indeed, He lured you from the jaws[G]
of distress
to a spacious and unconfined place.
Your table was spread with choice food.
17 Yet now you are obsessed
with the judgment due the wicked;
judgment and justice have seized you.
18 Be careful that no one lures you
with riches;[H]
do not let a large ransom[I]
lead you astray.[l]
19 Can your wealth[J] or all
your physical exertion
keep you from distress?[m]
20 Do not long for the night
when nations will disappear
from their places.
21 Be careful that you do not turn
to iniquity,
for that is why you have been tested
by[K] affliction.
22 Look, God shows Himself exalted
by His power.
Who is a teacher like Him?
23 Who has appointed His way for Him,
and who has declared, "You have
done wrong"?[n]
24 Remember that you should praise
His work,

[a]35:11 Jb 12:7; Mt 6:26 [b]35:12 Pr 1:28; Is 1:15; Zch 7:13 [c]35:14 Jb 13:18; 23:4; 31:13 [d]Jb 6:8; 13:13; 14:14 [e]35:16 Jb 15:2; 21:22; 34:35 [f]36:5 Jb 9:4; 12:13; 38:36 [g]36:6 Gn 18:25; Jb 8:20; 2Pt 2:9 [h]36:10 Jb 4:12; 13:1; 33:16 [i]36:11 Jb 21:13; 22:2; Is 1:19 [j]36:12 Jb 4:21; 33:18; Hs 4:6 [k]36:14 Dt 23:17; 1Kg 14:24; 22:46 [l]36:18 1Sm 12:3; Ps 26:10; Am 5:12 [m]36:19 1Sm 22:2; Jb 15:24; Ps 107:6,13,19,28 [n]36:23 Jb 34:10,13; Is 40:13-14; Rm 11:34

[A]35:14 Or *How then can* [B]35:14 Lit *say* [C]35:15 LXX, Vg; MT reads *folly*, or *arrogance*; Hb obscure [D]36:4 Lit *my words are not false* [E]36:5 Lit *He is mighty in strength of heart* [F]36:12 Or *will perish by the sword* [G]36:16 Lit *from a mouth of narrowness* [H]36:18 Or *you into mockery* [I]36:18 Or *bribe* [J]36:19 Or *cry for help* [K]36:21 Or *for you have preferred this to*

which people have sung about.[a]
25 All mankind has seen it;
people have looked at it
from a distance.[b]
26 Yes, God is exalted
beyond our knowledge;[c]
the number of His years
cannot be counted.[d]
27 For He makes waterdrops evaporate;[A]
they distill the rain into its[B] mist,[e]
28 which the clouds pour out
and shower abundantly on mankind.
29 Can anyone understand how the clouds
spread out
or how the thunder roars
from God's pavilion?[f]
30 See how He spreads His lightning[g]
around Him
and covers the depths of the sea.
31 For He judges the nations with these;
He gives food in abundance.[h]
32 He covers His hands with lightning
and commands it to hit its mark.
33 The[C] thunder declares His presence;[D]
the cattle also, the approaching storm.

37 My heart[i] pounds at this
and leaps from my chest.[E]
2 Just listen to His thunderous voice
and the rumbling that comes
from His mouth.
3 He lets it loose beneath the entire sky;
His lightning to the ends[j] of the earth.
4 Then there comes a roaring sound;
God thunders[k]
with His majestic voice.
He does not restrain the lightning
when His rumbling voice is heard.
5 God thunders marvelously
with His voice;
He does great things that
we cannot comprehend.
6 For He says to the snow,[l]
"Fall to the earth,"
and the torrential rains,
His mighty torrential rains,
7 serve as His sign to all mankind,
so that all men may know His work.
8 The wild animals enter their lairs
and stay in their dens.[m]
9 The windstorm comes
from its chamber,
and the cold
from the driving north winds.
10 Ice is formed by the breath of God,[n]
and watery expanses are frozen.
11 He saturates clouds with moisture;[o]
He scatters His lightning
through them.
12 They swirl about,
turning round and round
at His direction,
accomplishing everything
He commands them
over the surface of the inhabited world.
13 He causes this to happen
for punishment,
for His land, or for His faithful love.
14 Listen to this, Job.
Stop and consider God's wonders.
15 Do you know how God directs
His clouds
or makes their lightning flash?
16 Do you understand
how the clouds float,
those wonderful works of Him who has
perfect knowledge?
17 You whose clothes get hot
when the south wind brings calm
to the land,
18 can you help God spread out the skies
as hard as a cast metal mirror?
19 Teach us what we should say to Him;[p]
we cannot prepare our case because of
our darkness.
20 Should He be told that I want to speak?
Can a man speak when he is confused?
21 Now men cannot even look at the sun
when it is in the skies,
after a wind has swept through
and cleared them away.
22 Yet out of the north He comes,
shrouded in a golden glow;
awesome[q] majesty surrounds Him.
23 The ·Almighty — we cannot
reach Him —
He is exalted in power!
He will not oppress justice and
abundant righteousness,

[a] **36:24** Ps 92:5; 104:33; Rv 15:3
[b] **36:25** Ps 19:3; Rm 1:19-20; Heb 11:13
[c] **36:26** Jb 9:10; 37:5,23; Ec 8:17
[d] Ps 90:2; 102:24,27; Heb 1:12
[e] **36:27** Gn 2:6; Jb 38:28; Ps 147:8
[f] **36:29** Jb 26:14; 37:16; Ps 105:39
[g] **36:30** 2Sm 22:15; Jb 38:28; Ps 18:14
[h] **36:31** Jb 37:13; Ps 136:25; Ac 14:17
[i] **37:1** Jb 15:35; 32:19; Pr 20:27,30
[j] **37:3** Jb 38:13; Is 11:12; Ezk 7:2
[k] **37:4** Jb 40:9; Ps 18:3; 29:3
[l] **37:6** Jb 6:16; 24:19; 38:22
[m] **37:8** Jb 38:40; Ps 104:22; Am 3:4
[n] **37:10** 2Sm 22:21; Jb 4:9; Is 30:33
[o] **37:11** Jb 26:8; 36:29; 38:9
[p] **37:19** Jb 9:3,14; 40:2; Jms 1:5
[q] **37:22** Ex 15:11; Dt 7:21; Hab 3:2

A **36:27** Lit *He draws in waterdrops* B **36:27** Or *His* C **36:33** Lit *His*, or *Its* D **36:33** Lit *thunder announces concerning Him* or *it* E **37:1** Lit *from its place*

24 Therefore, men ·fear Him.
He does not look favorably on any
who are wise[a] in heart.

The Lord Speaks

38 Then the Lord answered Job from the
whirlwind.[b] He said:
2 Who is this who obscures My counsel
with ignorant words?[c]
3 Get ready to answer Me like a man;
when I question[d] you,
you will inform Me.
4 Where were you when I established[e]
the earth?
Tell Me, if you have[A] understanding.
5 Who fixed its dimensions?
Certainly you know!
Who stretched a measuring line
across it?
6 What supports its foundations?
Or who laid its cornerstone
7 while the morning stars sang together
and all the sons of God[f] shouted
for joy?
8 Who enclosed the sea behind doors
when it burst from the womb,
9 when I made the clouds its garment
and thick darkness its blanket,[B,g]
10 when I determined its boundaries[C]
and put its bars and doors in place,
11 when I declared: "You may come
this far, but no farther;
your proud waves stop here"?
12 Have you ever in your life commanded
the morning
or assigned the dawn its place,
13 so it may seize the edges of the earth
and shake the wicked out of it?
14 The earth is changed as clay is by a seal;
its hills stand out like the folds of
a garment.

[a]37:24 Pr 3:7; 26:5,12,16; 28:11
[b]38:1 2Kg 2:11; Jb 40:6; Ezk 13:11,13
[c]38:2 Jb 34:35; 35:16; 42:3
[d]38:3 2Sm 11:7; Jb 40:7; 42:4
[e]38:4 Ps 89:11; 102:25; 104:5
[f]38:7 Gn 6:2,4; Jb 1:6; 2:1
[g]38:9 2Sm 22:10; Jb 22:13; 37:11

GOD'S HEART FOR THE WORLD

Creation's Glory

Where were you when I established the earth? Tell Me, if you have understanding. (Job 38:4)

God's glory is all around us. It declares itself from everything God's hand has touched, the whole of creation.

Chapters 38–41 of Job show us that God rules over the world's greatest forces, enclosing "the sea behind doors" (38:8), and still lovingly beholding the smallest of details, watching "the deer in labor" (39:1). This great power and intimate love are revealed as we watch the sun rise and realize that God has "commanded the morning" (38:12), and when we see the ostrich and know that, though she is foolish with her young, God delights that "when she proudly spreads her wings, she laughs at the horse and its rider" (39:18). David wrote, "the heavens declare the glory of God" (Ps 19:1), catching a glimpse of this creative disclosure, bringing him to praise, to evoke a hymn that has lasted through the ages.

God delights to reveal His glory through what He has made. Job, too, lets this encounter with God impact him—first as he fumbles in speechless awe, and then as he turns and repents. After God's words to Job, it is no wonder that Paul tells us in his letter to the Romans that "from the creation of the world His invisible attributes, that is, His eternal power and divine nature, have been clearly seen, being understood through what He has made. As a result, people are without excuse" (Rm 1:20).

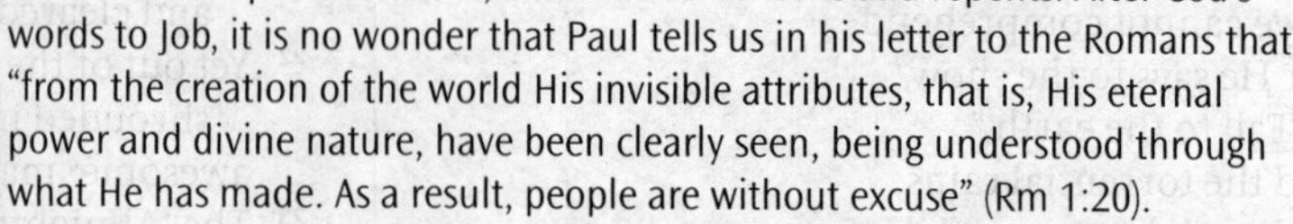

There is no room for being blasé. What we see in God's creation is part of His revelation. This demands a response.

[A]38:4 Lit *know* [B]38:9 Lit *swaddling clothes* [C]38:10 Lit *I broke My statute on it*

15 Light[A] is withheld from the wicked,
and the arm raised in violence
is broken.
16 Have you traveled to the sources
of the sea
or walked in the depths of the oceans?
17 Have the gates[a] of death been revealed
to you?
Have you seen the gates
of deep darkness?
18 Have you comprehended the extent
of the earth?
Tell Me, if you know all this.
19 Where is the road to the home
of light?
Do you know where darkness lives,
20 so you can lead it back to its border?
Are you familiar with the paths
to its home?
21 Don't you know? You were
already born;[b]
you have lived so long![B]
22 Have you entered the place
where the snow is stored?
Or have you seen the storehouses
of hail,[c]
23 which I hold in reserve for times
of trouble,
for the day of warfare and battle?[d]
24 What road leads to the place
where light is dispersed?[C]
Where is the source of the east wind
that spreads across the earth?
25 Who cuts a channel
for the flooding rain
or clears the way for lightning,
26 to bring rain on an uninhabited land,
on a desert with no human life,[D]
27 to satisfy the parched wasteland
and cause the grass to sprout?[e]
28 Does the rain have a father?
Who fathered the drops of dew?[f]
29 Whose womb did the ice come from?
Who gave birth to the frost of heaven
30 when water becomes as hard as stone,[E]
and the surface of the watery depths
is frozen?[g]

[a]**38:17** Ps 9:13; 107:18; Is 38:10
[b]**38:21** Jb 15:7; Ps 90:2; Pr 8:25
[c]**38:22** Ex 9:18; Ps 105:32; Is 28:17
[d]**38:23** Jos 10:11; Is 30:30; Rv 16:21
[e]**38:27** Gn 1:11; 2Sm 23:4; Ps 107:35
[f]**38:28** Jb 5:10; Ps 147:8; Jr 14:22
[g]**38:29-30** Jb 37:10; Ps 147:16-17
[h]**38:31-32** Jb 9:9; Is 40:26; Am 5:8
[i]**38:33** Jr 31:35; 33:25
[j]**38:34** Jb 22:11; Ps 69:1-2; Lm 3:54
[k]**38:35** Ex 19:16; Ps 18:14; 97:4
[l]**38:36** Jb 28:12,18,20; Ps 51:6; Ec 2:26
[m]**38:39** Ps 104:21; 145:15-16
[n]**38:41** 1Kg 17:4,6; Ps 147:9; Lk 12:24
[o]**39:6** Jb 24:5; 38:26; Jr 2:24
[p]Dt 29:23; Ps 107:34; Jr 17:6

31 Can you fasten the chains
of the Pleiades
or loosen the belt of Orion?
32 Can you bring out the constellations[F]
in their season
and lead the Bear[G] and her cubs?[h]
33 Do you know the laws[i] of heaven?
Can you impose its[H] authority
on earth?
34 Can you command[I] the clouds
so that a flood of water covers you?[j]
35 Can you send out lightning[k] bolts,
and they go?
Do they report to you: "Here we are"?
36 Who put wisdom[l] in the heart[J]
or gave the mind understanding?
37 Who has the wisdom to number
the clouds?
Or who can tilt the water jars of heaven
38 when the dust hardens like cast metal
and the clods of dirt stick together?
39 Can you hunt prey for a lioness
or satisfy the appetite of young lions[m]
40 when they crouch in their dens
and lie in wait within their lairs?
41 Who provides the raven's food[n]
when its young cry out to God
and wander about for lack of food?

39 Do you know when mountain goats
give birth?
Have you watched the deer in labor?
2 Can you count the months
they are pregnant[K]
so you can know the time
they give birth?
3 They crouch down to give birth
to their young;
they deliver their newborn.[L]
4 Their offspring are healthy
and grow up in the open field.
They leave and do not return.[M]
5 Who set the wild donkey free?
Who released the swift donkey
from its harness?
6 I made the wilderness[o] its home,
and the salty[p] wasteland its dwelling.
7 It scoffs at the noise of the village

[A]**38:15** Lit *Their light* [B]**38:21** Lit *born; the number of your days is great* [C]**38:24** Or *where lightning is distributed* [D]**38:26** Lit *life in it* [E]**38:30** Lit *water hides itself as the stone* [F]**38:32** Or *Mazzaroth;* Hb obscure [G]**38:32** Or *lead Aldebaran* [H]**38:33** Or *God's* [I]**38:34** Lit *lift up your voice to* [J]**38:36** Or *the inner self;* Ps 51:6 [K]**39:2** Lit *months they fulfill* [L]**39:3** Or *they send away their labor pains* [M]**39:4** Lit *return to them*

and never hears the shouts of a driver.[a]
8 It roams the mountains
for its pastureland,
searching for anything green.
9 Would the wild ox be willing
to serve you?
Would it spend the night
by your feeding trough?
10 Can you hold the wild ox[b] to a furrow
by its harness?
Will it plow the valleys behind you?
11 Can you depend on it because
its strength is great?
Would you leave it to do
your hard work?
12 Can you trust the wild ox to harvest
your grain
and bring it to your threshing floor?

13 The wings of the ostrich flap joyfully,
but are her feathers and plumage
like the stork's?[A,c]
14 She abandons her eggs on the ground
and lets them be warmed in the sand.
15 She forgets that a foot may crush them
or that some wild animal
may trample them.
16 She treats her young harshly, as if
they were not her own,
with no fear that her labor
may have been in vain.
17 For God has deprived her of wisdom;
He has not endowed her
with understanding.[d]
18 When she proudly[A] spreads her wings,
she laughs at the horse and its rider.

19 Do you give strength to the horse?
Do you adorn his neck with a mane?[A]
20 Do you make him leap like a locust?
His proud snorting
fills one with terror.
21 He paws[B] in the valley and rejoices
in his strength;
He charges into battle.[C]
22 He laughs at fear, since he is afraid
of nothing;
he does not run from the sword.
23 A quiver rattles at his side,
along with a flashing spear and a lance.[D]
24 He charges ahead[E] with trembling rage;
he cannot stand still
at the trumpet's sound.
25 When the trumpet blasts,
he snorts defiantly.[F]
He smells the battle from a distance;
he hears the officers' shouts
and the battle cry.

26 Does the hawk take flight
by your understanding
and spread its wings to the south?
27 Does the eagle soar at your command
and make its nest[e] on high?
28 It lives on a cliff where it spends
the night;
its stronghold is on a rocky crag.
29 From there it searches for prey;[f]
its eyes penetrate the distance.
30 Its brood gulps down blood,
and where the slain are, it is there.[g]

40

The LORD answered Job:
2 Will the one who contends
with the ˙Almighty correct Him?
Let him who argues with God
give an answer.[G]

3Then Job answered the LORD:

4 I am so insignificant. How can I
answer You?[h]
I place my hand over my mouth.
5 I have spoken once, and I will not reply;
twice, but now I can add nothing.[i]

6Then the LORD answered Job from the
whirlwind:[j]

7 Get ready to answer Me like a man;
When I question[k] you, you will
inform Me.
8 Would you really challenge My justice?
Would you declare Me ˙guilty[l]
to justify yourself?[m]
9 Do you have an arm like God's?
Can you thunder with a voice like His?
10 Adorn yourself with majesty[n]
and splendor,
and clothe yourself with honor
and glory.

[a]39:7 Ex 3:7; 5:10,13-14; Jb 3:18 [b]39:10 Nm 23:22; 24:8; Dt 33:17 [c]39:13 Ps 104:17; Jr 8:7; Zch 5:9 [d]39:17 Jb 35:11; 38:36 [e]39:27 Jr 49:16; Ob 4; Hab 2:9 [f]39:29 Jb 9:26; Hab 1:8 [g]39:30 Ezk 39:17; Mt 24:28; Lk 17:37 [h]40:4 Ezr 9:6; Jb 29:9; 42:6 [i]40:5 Jb 9:3,15; 33:14; Ps 62:11 [j]40:6 Jb 38:1; Jr 30:23; Ezk 13:11,13 [k]40:7 2Sm 11:7; Jb 38:3; 42:4 [l]40:8 Jb 9:20,28; Ps 37:33; Is 50:9 [m]Jb 32:2; Ps 51:4; Rm 3:4 [n]40:10 Ps 93:1; 96:6; 104:1

[A]39:13,18,19 Hb obscure [B]39:21 LXX, Syr; MT reads *digs* [C]39:21 Lit *He goes out to meet the weapon* [D]39:23 Or *scimitar* [E]39:24 Lit *He swallows the ground* [F]39:25 Lit *he says, "Aha!"* [G]40:2 Lit *God respond to it*

11 Unleash your raging anger;[a]
look on every proud person
and humiliate him.[b]
12 Look on every proud person
and humble him;[c]
trample the wicked where they stand.[A]
13 Hide them together in the dust;
imprison them in the grave.[B]
14 Then I will confess to you
that your own right hand[d]
can deliver you.[e]
15 Look at Behemoth,
which I made along with you.
He eats grass like an ox.
16 Look at the strength of his loins
and the power in the muscles
of his belly.
17 He stiffens his tail like a cedar tree;
the tendons of his thighs are woven
firmly together.
18 His bones are bronze tubes;
his limbs are like iron rods.
19 He is the foremost of God's works;[f]
only his Maker can draw the sword
against him.
20 The hills yield food for him,
while all sorts of wild animals
play there.
21 He lies under the lotus plants,
hiding in the protection[C]
of marshy reeds.
22 Lotus plants cover him
with their shade;
the willows by the brook surround him.
23 Though the river rages,
Behemoth is unafraid;
he remains confident, even if
the Jordan surges up to his mouth.
24 Can anyone capture him
while he looks on,[D]
or pierce his nose with snares?

41 [E] Can you pull in ˙Leviathan[g]
with a hook[h]
or tie his tongue down with a rope?
2 Can you put a cord[F] through his nose
or pierce his jaw with a hook?[i]
3 Will he beg you for mercy
or speak softly to you?

[a]**40:11** Jb 14:13; 19:11; 21:17
[b]Is 2:11; Ezk 21:26; Dn 4:37
[c]**40:12** Ps 18:27; Is 13:11; 63:3
[d]**40:14** Ps 17:7; 20:6; 108:6
[e]Ps 3:8; 49:7; 62:2
[f]**40:19** Jb 26:14; Pr 8:22
[g]**41:1** Jb 3:8; Ps 104:26; Is 27:1
[h]Is 19:8; Hab 1:15
[i]**41:2** 2Kg 19:28; Jb 40:24; Is 37:29
[j]**41:4** Ex 21:6; Dt 15:17; 1Sm 27:12
[k]**41:10** Jb 3:8; Jr 50:44
[l]**41:11** Ps 24:1; Rm 11:35; 1Co 10:26
[m]**41:13** Jr 46:4; 51:3
[n]**41:20** 2Sm 22:9; Jb 39:20; Ps 18:8

4 Will he make a covenant with you
so that you can take him
as a slave forever?[j]
5 Can you play with him like a bird
or put him on a leash[G] for your girls?
6 Will traders bargain for him
or divide him among the merchants?
7 Can you fill his hide with harpoons
or his head with fishing spears?
8 Lay a[H] hand on him.
You will remember the battle
and never repeat it!
9[I] Any hope of capturing him proves false.
Does a person not collapse
at the very sight of him?
10 No one is ferocious enough
to rouse Leviathan;[k]
who then can stand against Me?
11 Who confronted Me, that I
should repay him?
Everything under heaven belongs
to Me.[l]
12 I cannot be silent about his limbs,
his power, and his graceful proportions.
13 Who can strip off his outer covering?
Who can penetrate his double layer
of armor?[J,m]
14 Who can open his jaws,[K]
surrounded by those terrifying teeth?
15 His pride is in his rows of scales,
closely sealed together.
16 One scale is so close to another[L]
that no air can pass between them.
17 They are joined to one another,
so closely connected[M] they cannot
be separated.
18 His snorting[N] flashes with light,
while his eyes are like the rays[O] of dawn.
19 Flaming torches shoot from his mouth;
fiery sparks fly out!
20 Smoke billows from his nostrils[n]
as from a boiling pot or burning reeds.
21 His breath sets coals ablaze,
and flames pour out of his mouth.
22 Strength resides in his neck,
and dismay dances before him.
23 The folds of his flesh
are joined together,

[A]**40:12** Lit *wicked in their place* [B]**40:13** Lit *together; bind their faces in the hidden place* [C]**40:21** Lit *plants, in the hiding place* [D]**40:24** Lit *capture it in its eyes* [E]**41:1** Jb 40:25 in Hb [F]**41:2** Lit *reed* [G]**41:5** Lit *or bind him* [H]**41:8** Lit *your*

[I]**41:9** Jb 41:1 in Hb [J]**41:13** LXX; MT reads *double bridle* [K]**41:14** Lit *open the doors of his face* [L]**41:16** Lit *One by one they approach* [M]**41:17** Lit *another; they cling together and* [N]**41:18** Or *sneezing* [O]**41:18** Lit *eyelids*

solid as metal[A] and immovable.
24 His heart is as hard as a rock,
as hard as a lower millstone!
25 When Leviathan rises, the mighty[B]
are terrified;
they withdraw because of
his thrashing.
26 The sword that reaches him will have
no effect,
nor will a spear, dart, or arrow.
27 He regards iron as straw,
and bronze as rotten wood.
28 No arrow can make him flee;
slingstones become like stubble to him.
29 A club is regarded as stubble,
and he laughs[a] at the sound of a javelin.
30 His undersides are jagged potsherds,
spreading the mud
like a threshing sledge.[b]
31 He makes the depths seethe
like a cauldron;
he makes the sea like an ointment jar.
32 He leaves a shining wake behind him;[C]
one would think the deep had
gray hair!
33 He has no equal on earth —
a creature devoid of fear!
34 He surveys everything that is haughty;
he is king over all the proud beasts.[D]

Job Replies to the LORD

42 Then Job replied to the LORD:
2 I[E] know that You can do anything
and no plan of Yours can be thwarted.[c]
3 You asked, "Who is this who conceals
My counsel with ignorance?"[d]
Surely I spoke about things I did not
understand,
things too wonderful for me to[F] know.[e]
4 You said, "Listen now, and I will speak.
When I question[f] you, you will
inform Me."
5 I had heard rumors about You,
but now my eyes[g] have seen You.
6 Therefore I take back my words
and repent in dust and ashes.[G]

7 After the LORD had finished speaking[H] to
Job, He said to Eliphaz the Temanite: "I am
angry with you and your two friends, for you
have not spoken the truth about Me, as My
servant Job has. 8 Now take seven bulls and
seven rams, go to My servant Job, and offer
a burnt offering for yourselves. Then My servant Job will pray for you.[h] I will surely accept
his prayer and not deal with you as your folly
deserves. For you have not spoken the truth
about Me, as My servant Job has." 9 Then Eliphaz the Temanite, Bildad the Shuhite, and
Zophar the Naamathite went and did as the
LORD had told them, and the LORD accepted
Job's prayer.

God Restores Job

10 After Job had prayed for his friends, the
LORD restored his prosperity and doubled
his previous possessions.[i] 11 All his brothers,
sisters, and former acquaintances[j] came to
his house and dined with him in his house.
They sympathized with him and comforted
him concerning all the adversity the LORD
had brought on him. Each one gave him a
qesitah[I,k] and a gold earring.[l]
12 So the LORD blessed the last part of Job's
life more than the first. He owned 14,000
sheep, 6,000 camels, 1,000 yoke of oxen, and
1,000 female donkeys. 13 He also had seven
sons and three daughters. 14 He named his
first daughter Jemimah, his second Keziah,
and his third Keren-happuch.[m] 15 No women
as beautiful as Job's daughters could be found
in all the land, and their father granted them
an inheritance with their brothers.
16 Job lived 140 years after this and saw his
children and their children to the fourth generation. 17 Then Job died, old and full of days.[n]

[a] **41:29** 2Ch 30:10; Jb 39:7,18; Hab 1:10
[b] **41:30** Is 41:15; Am 1:3
[c] **42:2** Gn 18:14; Jr 23:20; Mt 19:26
[d] **42:3** Jb 34:35; 35:16; 38:2
[e] Ps 40:5; 131:1; 139:6
[f] **42:4** Jb 38:3; 40:7
[g] **42:5** Jb 19:27; Ps 123:1-2; 141:8
[h] **42:8** Gn 20:17; Nm 23:1; 1Jn 5:16
[i] **42:10** Ps 14:7; Is 40:2; Mt 5:44
[j] **42:11** Jb 2:11; 19:13
[k] Gn 33:19; Jos 24:32
[l] Gn 24:22; 35:4; Hs 2:13
[m] **42:14** Ps 45:8; Sg 2:14; Jr 4:30
[n] **42:17** Gn 25:8; 35:29; 1Ch 29:28

[A] **41:23** Lit *together, hard on him* [B] **41:25** Or *the divine beings* [C] **41:32** Lit *a path* [D] **41:34** Lit *the children of pride* [E] **42:2** Alt Hb tradition reads *You* [F] **42:3** Lit *me, and I did not* [G] **42:6** LXX reads *I despise myself and melt; I consider myself dust and ashes* [H] **42:7** Lit *speaking these words* [I] **42:11** The value of the currency is unknown.

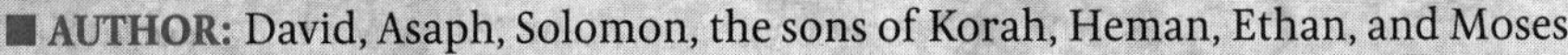

■ **AUTHOR:** David, Asaph, Solomon, the sons of Korah, Heman, Ethan, and Moses

■■ **DATE:** Events cover the time of Moses (1446–1406 B.C.) through the time of the exile (586 B.C.). But David's psalms were written during his kingship (around 1010–970 B.C.)

God likes music, or the psalms would not fill so many pages of God's Word. For centuries these verses have been sung surely as much as they have been read or spoken.

Prophets proclaiming or pastors preaching are not the only ways God's mission is made known to the ears of humankind. Singers tell it too, and artists, composers, sculptors, and poets whose talents are able to send a message straight to the heart and soul. We dance to these psalms. We laugh and weep at God's Word to us. Life is full of weeping and laughing, and we do these human things in God's presence, not away from Him. We give thanks, pray for deliverance, and lament and mourn our troubles because we have learned that both our aspirations and our sorrows have their place in God's mission to the world.

PSALMS

The psalms show us what we have learned about God by living with Him, walking with His people. God is a refuge: No trouble operates independent of God's control. God is holy: We rightly confess the awful frequency of our trespasses. God is fierce in defense of His people: Hs visage turns to the poor and needy. Life is celebration of God's provision. Death is not to be feared. God restores the soul, makes us new.

Without a long education in these truths, we could never sing them. The psalms witness to the foothold God's mission has gained in the human heart. We know better than to imagine a world independent of God, or a God indifferent to the world. God "watches over the way of the righteous" (Ps 1:6)—this we know. Who are the righteous? Those who trust in God.

Like all Bible books before and after, the book of Psalms does not shield human experience from losses and accidents. "With my tears I dampen my pillow and drench my bed every night," says Psalm 6:6, a psalm of David. Even this weeping tells of God's mission, which always carries a cost and is never a dance through daffodils. The psalms honestly portray our pursuit of God and our frequent denial of God's care. "Lord, why do You stand so far away? Why do You hide in times of trouble?" begs Psalm 10, as nearly every person who honestly reflects on life has begged. Struggle, puzzlement, a sense of distance, even divine neglect, the psalms reflect all of these as emotions of the pilgrim called to service in God's plan to save the world.

Above all, the psalms tell of things certain, things true. God is at the center of life and world, and God will deliver His people. God's mission of love, mercy, and redemption will not fail. Though our flesh fails and our emotions falter, God never abandons His creation. All will be set right. The glory of God on display in the redemption of people and restoration of creation is His mission's aim. Our right response is trust and obedience, praise and thanks. With these affirmations the great songs of God's people rise to His ears. Thus is God's mission fulfilled: His people glad to know Him well, glad in the depths of their hearts to know that God is loving-kindness (a favorite term in the psalms), and God's purpose is for us to share in the dwelling where goodness and love never cease. Only then is the glory of God formed in the heart, with a strength and permanence that endures the breakdown of flesh and heart.

"God is the strength of my heart, my portion forever," Psalm 73:26 claims. All who sing that know the mission of God firsthand, personally, and for real.

PSALMS

BOOK I
(Psalms 1–41)

Psalm 1
The Two Ways

1 How happy is the man
who does not follow[A] the advice
of the wicked
or take[B] the path of sinners
or join a group[C] of mockers![a]
2 Instead, his delight is in the LORD's
instruction,
and he meditates on it day and night.[b]
3 He is like a tree planted beside streams
of water[D]
that bears its fruit in season[E,c]
and whose leaf does not wither.[d]
Whatever he does prospers.[e]

4 The wicked are not like this;
instead, they are like chaff
that the wind blows away.[f]
5 Therefore the wicked will not survive[B]
the judgment,[g]
and sinners will not be
in the community of the righteous.
6 For the LORD watches over the way
of the righteous,[h]
but the way of the wicked
leads to ruin.[i]

Psalm 2
Coronation of the Son

1 Why[j] do the nations rebel[F,k]
and the peoples plot in vain?[l]
2 The kings of the earth take their stand,[m]
and the rulers conspire together
against the LORD
and His Anointed One:[G,n]
3 "Let us tear off their chains
and free ourselves
from their restraints."[H,o]

4 The One enthroned[I] in heaven laughs;
the Lord ridicules them.[p]
5 Then He speaks to them in His anger
and terrifies them in His wrath:[q]
6 "I have consecrated My King[J]
on ·Zion, My holy mountain."[r]
7 I will declare the LORD's decree:
He said to Me, "You are My Son;[K]
today I have become Your[L] Father.[s]
8 Ask of Me,
and I will make the nations
Your[L] inheritance
and the ends of the earth
Your[L] possession.[t]
9 You will break[M] them with a rod of iron;
You[N] will shatter them like pottery."[O,u]

10 So now, kings, be wise;
receive instruction, you judges
of the earth.
11 Serve the LORD with reverential awe
and rejoice with trembling.[v]
12 Pay homage to[P] the Son or He[Q]
will be angry
and you will perish in your rebellion,[R,w]
for His[S] anger may ignite
at any moment.[x]
All those who take refuge in Him[T]
are happy.[y]

Psalm 3
Confidence in Troubled Times

A psalm of David when he fled
from his son Absalom.[z]

1 LORD, how my foes increase!
There are many who attack me.[aa]
2 Many say about me,
"There is no help for him
in God."[ab] *·Selah*
3 But You, LORD, are a shield around me,[ac]
my glory,[ad] and the One who lifts up
my head.[ae]
4 I cry aloud to the LORD,
and He answers me
from His holy mountain.[af] *Selah*

5 I lie down and sleep;
I wake again because the LORD
sustains me.[ag]
6 I am not afraid of the thousands
of people
who have taken their stand against me
on every side.[ah]

[a]**1:1** Ps 26:4-5; Pr 4:14-15 [b]**1:2** Jos 1:8; Ps 40:8; 119:14-16 [c]**1:3** Rv 22:2 [d]Ps 92:12-14; Jr 17:8 [e]Dt 5:33 [f]**1:4** Jb 21:18; Ps 35:5; Hs 13:3 [g]**1:5** Ps 5:5; 9:16; 76:7; Jr 25:31 [h]**1:6** Jb 34:21; Ps 37:18; Nah 1:7; Jn 10:14; 2Tm 2:19 [i]Pr 21:12; Jn 3:16 [j]**2:1-2** Ac 4:25-26 [k]**2:1** Is 17:12-13 [l]Ps 83:2-3 [m]**2:2** Jr 49:19; 50:44 [n]1Sm 2:10; 12:3,5; 2Sm 22:51; Ps 18:50; 20:6; 28:8 [o]**2:3** Is 58:6; Jr 5:5; Nah 1:13 [p]**2:4** Ps 37:13; 59:8 [q]**2:5** Ps 90:7 [r]**2:6** Ps 48:2; Is 24:23 [s]**2:7** Mt 3:17; Lk 3:22; Ac 13:33; Heb 1:5; 5:5 [t]**2:8** Jos 23:4; Ps 111:6 [u]**2:8-9** Ps 89:23; Rv 2:26-27; 12:5; 19:15 [v]**2:11** Heb 12:28 [w]**2:12** Jn 3:18 [x]2Th 1:7-8 [y]Ps 5:11; 34:8,22 [z]**3:title** 2Sm 15:13-17 [aa]**3:1** 2Sm 15:12; Ps 69:4 [ab]**3:2** Ps 22:7-8; 71:11 [ac]**3:3** Gn 15:1; Dt 33:29; Ps 5:12; 18:2; 28:7; 119:114 [ad]Ps 62:7 [ae]Ps 110:7 [af]**3:4** Ps 2:6; 43:3; 48:1 [ag]**3:5** Lv 26:6; Ps 4:8; Pr 3:24 [ah]**3:6** Ps 23:4; 27:3; 118:10-13

[A]**1:1** Lit *not walk in* [B]**1:1,5** Lit *stand in* [C]**1:1** Or *or sit in the seat* [D]**1:3** Or *beside irrigation canals* [E]**1:3** Lit *in its season* [F]**2:1** Or *conspire,* or *rage* [G]**2:2** Or *anointed one* [H]**2:3** Lit *and throw their ropes from us* [I]**2:4** Lit *who sits* [J]**2:6** Or *king* [K]**2:7** Or *me, "You are My son* [L]**2:7,8** Or *your* [M]**2:9** LXX, Syr, Tg read *shepherd* [N]**2:9** Or *you* [O]**2:9** Lit *a potter's vessel* [P]**2:12** Lit *Kiss* [Q]**2:12** Or *son, otherwise he* [R]**2:12** Lit *perish way* [S]**2:12** Or *his* [T]**2:12** Or *him*

7 Rise up, LORD![a]
Save me, my God!
You strike all my enemies on the cheek;[b]
You break the teeth of the wicked.[c]
8 Salvation belongs to the LORD;[d]
may Your blessing be on Your people.[e]
Selah

PSALM 4
A Night Prayer

For the choir director: with stringed instruments.[f]
A Davidic psalm.

1 Answer me when I call,
God, who vindicates me.[A,g]
You freed me from affliction;[h]
be gracious to me and hear my prayer.
2 How long, exalted men, will my honor
be insulted?[i]
How long will you love
what is worthless[j]
and pursue a lie? *Selah*
3 Know that the LORD has set apart
the faithful for Himself;
the LORD will hear when I call to Him.
4 Be angry[B] and do not sin;[k]
on your bed, reflect in your heart
and be still.[l] *Selah*
5 Offer sacrifices in righteousness[C,m]
and trust in the LORD.[n]
6 Many are saying, "Who can show us
anything good?"
Look on us with favor, LORD.[o]
7 You have put more joy in my heart
than they have when their grain
and new wine abound.[p]
8 I will both lie down and sleep in peace,[q]
for You alone, LORD, make me live
in safety.[r]

PSALM 5
The Refuge of the Righteous

For the choir director: with the flutes.
A Davidic psalm.

1 Listen to my words, LORD;
consider my sighing.[s]
2 Pay attention to the sound of my cry,[t]
my King and my God,[u]
for I pray to You.
3 At daybreak,[v] LORD, You hear my voice;
at daybreak I plead my case to You[w]
and watch expectantly.
4 For You are not a God who delights
in wickedness;
evil cannot dwell with You.[x]
5 The boastful cannot stand
in Your presence;[y]
You hate all evildoers.[z]
6 You destroy those who tell lies;[aa]
the LORD abhors a man of bloodshed
and treachery.[ab]
7 But I enter Your house
by the abundance
of Your faithful love;[ac]
I bow down toward Your holy temple
in reverential awe of You.[ad]
8 LORD, lead me in Your righteousness[ae]
because of my adversaries;[D]
make Your way straight before me.[af]
9 For there is nothing reliable in what
they say;[E,ag]
destruction is within them;
their throat is an open grave;
they flatter with their tongues.[ah]
10 Punish them, God;
let them fall by their own schemes.[ai]
Drive them out[aj] because of
their many crimes,
for they rebel against You.[ak]
11 But let all who take refuge in You
rejoice;[al]
let them shout for joy forever.
May You shelter them,[am]
and may those who love Your name
boast about You.[an]
12 For You, LORD, bless the righteous one;
You surround him with favor
like a shield.[ao]

PSALM 6
A Prayer for Mercy

For the choir director:
with stringed instruments,
according to *Sheminith.*[ap] A Davidic psalm.

1 LORD, do not rebuke me in Your anger;
do not discipline me in Your wrath.[aq]

[a]**3:7** Ps 7:6 [b]Jb 16:10; Mc 5:1 [c]Ps 58:6 [d]**3:8** Jnh 2:9; Rv 7:10; 19:1 [e]Dt 26:15 [f]**4:title** Ps 6 title; Is 38:20; Hab 3:19 [g]**4:1** Ps 7:8; 26:1; 35:24 [h]Ps 25:17; 107:6,13 [i]**4:2** Ps 69:7-10,19-20 [j]Ps 12:2 [k]**4:4** Eph 4:26 [l]Ps 77:6; 119:55 [m]**4:5** Dt 33:19; Ps 51:19 [n]Ps 37:3,5; 62:8 [o]**4:6** Ps 80:3 [p]**4:7** Is 9:3 [q]**4:8** Ps 3:5 [r]Lv 25:18; Dt 12:10; Jr 32:37; Ezk 34:25 [s]**5:1** Ps 38:9 [t]**5:2** Ps 28:2 [u]Ps 84:3 [v]**5:3** Ps 88:13 [w]Jb 13:18; 23:4; Ps 50:21 [x]**5:4** Ps 92:15 [y]**5:5** Ps 1:5; 73:3; 75:4 [z]Jb 8:20; Ps 11:5; 45:7 [aa]**5:6** Rv 21:8 [ab]Ps 55:23 [ac]**5:7** Ps 69:13; 86:5,15; 106:45; Is 63:7 [ad]Ps 138:2 [ae]**5:8** Ps 27:11 [af]Pr 4:11 [ag]**5:9** Ps 52:2 [ah]Ps 12:3; Pr 26:28; Rm 3:13 [ai]**5:10** Ps 9:16; 35:8; 141:10 [aj]Mt 13:41-42 [ak]Pr 17:11 [al]**5:11** Ps 2:12; 64:10 [am]Ps 31:20; 61:4 [an]Ps 9:2 [ao]**5:12** Gn 15:1; Dt 33:29; Ps 3:3; 18:2; 28:7; 119:114 [ap]**6:title** 1Ch 15:21; Ps 12 title [aq]**6:1** Ps 38:1; Jr 10:24

[A]**4:1** Or *God of my righteousness* [B]**4:4** Or *Tremble* [C]**4:5** Or *Offer right sacrifices*; lit *Sacrifice sacrifices of righteousness* [D]**5:8** Or *of those who lie in wait for me* [E]**5:9** Lit *in his mouth*

2 Be gracious to me, LORD,
for I am weak;[A,a]
heal me,[b] LORD, for my bones
are shaking;[c]
3 my whole being is shaken with terror.[d]
And You, LORD — how long?[e]
4 Turn, LORD! Rescue me;
save me because of Your faithful love.[f]
5 For there is no remembrance of You
in death;
who can thank You in •Sheol?[g]

6 I am weary from my groaning;[h]
with my tears I dampen my pillow[B]
and drench my bed every night.[i]
7 My eyes are swollen from grief;[j]
they[C] grow old because of all
my enemies.

8 Depart from me, all evildoers,
for the LORD has heard the sound
of my weeping.[k]
9 The LORD has heard my plea for help;[l]
the LORD accepts my prayer.[m]
10 All my enemies will be ashamed
and shake with terror;
they will turn back[n] and suddenly
be disgraced.[o]

PSALM 7
Prayer for Justice

A *Shiggaion*[D] of David, which he sang to the LORD concerning the words of •Cush,[E] a Benjaminite.

1 •Yahweh my God, I seek refuge in You;[p]
save me from all my pursuers
and rescue me[q]
2 or they[F] will tear me like a lion,
ripping me apart with no one
to rescue me.[G,r]

3 Yahweh my God, if I have done this,
if there is injustice on my hands,[s]
4 if I have done harm to one at peace
with me[t]
or have plundered[H] my adversary
without cause,[u]
5 may an enemy pursue
and overtake me;
may he trample me to the ground[v]
and leave my honor in the dust.[w] •*Selah*

6 Rise up, LORD, in Your anger;
lift Yourself up against the fury
of my adversaries;[x]
awake for me;[I,y]
You have ordained[J] a judgment.[z]
7 Let the assembly of peoples gather
around You;[aa]
take Your seat[K] on high over it.[ab]
8 The LORD judges the peoples;[ac]
vindicate me, LORD,
according to my righteousness
and my integrity.[L,ad]
9 Let the evil of the wicked come
to an end,[ae]
but establish the righteous.[af]
The One who examines the thoughts
and emotions[M]
is a righteous God.[ag]
10 My shield is with[N] God,[ah]
who saves the upright in heart.[ai]
11 God is a righteous judge
and a God who shows His wrath
every day.[aj]
12 If anyone does not repent,
God[O] will sharpen His sword;[ak]
He has strung[P] His bow
and made it ready.[al]
13 He has prepared
His deadly weapons;
He tips His arrows with fire.[am]

14 See, the wicked one is pregnant
with evil,
conceives trouble, and gives birth
to deceit.[an]
15 He dug a pit and hollowed it out
but fell into the hole he had made.[ao]
16 His trouble comes back
on his own head,
and his violence falls on the top
of his head.[ap]

17 I will thank the LORD
for His righteousness;
I will sing about the name of Yahweh
the •Most High.[aq]

[a]**6:2** Ps 142:6 [b]Ps 41:4; Jr 17:14 [c]Jb 4:14 [d]**6:3** Jb 9:28; Jn 12:27 [e]Nm 14:27; Ps 13:1-2; 35:17; 79:5; 80:4 [f]**6:4** Ps 31:16; 109:26 [g]**6:4-5** Ps 30:9; 88:10-12; 115:17; Ec 9:10; Is 38:18 [h]**6:6** Ps 69:3; 119:28 [i]Ps 42:3; 102:9 [j]**6:7** Jb 17:7; Ps 31:9; 88:9 [k]**6:8** Ps 18:6; 34:6; 40:1 [l]**6:9** Ps 28:6 [m]Ps 3:4; 66:19-20 [n]**6:10** Ex 23:27 [o]Ps 71:13 [p]**7:1** Ps 11:1; 31:1; 71:1 [q]Ps 31:15 [r]**7:2** Ps 57:4; Is 5:29 [s]**7:3** 1Sm 24:11 [t]**7:4** Ps 55:20 [u]1Sm 24:11; 26:18 [v]**7:5** Am 2:7 [w]**7:3-5** Jb 31:5-40 [x]**7:6** Ps 3:7; 17:13 [y]Ps 59:4 [z]Jr 15:3 [aa]**7:7** Ps 22:27 [ab]Ps 68:18 [ac]**7:8** Ps 96:13; 98:9 [ad]Ps 26:1; 35:24; 43:1 [ae]**7:9** Ps 94:23 [af]Is 9:7 [ag]Heb 4:12 [ah]**7:10** 2Sm 22:3; Ps 18:2; 144:2 [ai]Ps 36:10 [aj]**7:11** Ps 9:4; Is 11:4 [ak]**7:12** Nm 22:23; Dt 32:41 [al]Ps 37:14 [am]**7:13** Ps 18:14; 45:5; 64:7; 144:6 [an]**7:14** Jb 15:35; Is 59:4; Jms 1:15 [ao]**7:15** Ps 9:15; 57:6; Pr 26:27; 28:10 [ap]**7:16** 1Sm 25:39; 1Kg 2:33; Est 9:25 [aq]**7:17** Ps 9:2; 71:15-16

[A]**6:2** Or *sick* [B]**6:6** Lit *bed* [C]**6:7** LXX, Aq, Sym, Jer read *I* [D]**7:title** Perhaps a passionate song with rapid changes of rhythm, or a dirge [E]**7:title** LXX, Aq, Sym, Theod, Jer read *of the Cushite* [F]**7:2** Lit *he* [G]**7:2** Lit *ripping, and without a rescuer* [H]**7:4** Or *me and have spared* [I]**7:6** LXX reads *awake, Lord my God* [J]**7:6** Or *me; ordain* [K]**7:7** MT reads *and return* [L]**7:8** Lit *integrity on me* [M]**7:9** Lit *examines hearts and kidneys* [N]**7:10** Lit *on* [O]**7:12** Lit *He* [P]**7:12** Lit *bent*; that is, bent the bow to string it

Psalm 8
God's Glory, Man's Dignity

For the choir director: on the ·*Gittith.*[a] A Davidic psalm.

1 ·Yahweh, our Lord,
how magnificent is Your name
throughout the earth![b]

You have covered the heavens
with Your majesty.[A,c]
2 Because of Your adversaries,
You have established a stronghold[B]
from the mouths of children
and nursing infants[d]
to silence the enemy and the avenger.

3 When I observe Your heavens,
the work of Your fingers,
the moon and the stars,
which You set in place,[e]
4 what is man that You remember him,
the son of man that You look
after him?[f]
5 You made him little less than God[C,D]
and crowned him with glory and honor.
6 You made him lord over the works
of Your hands;
You put everything under his feet:[E,g]
7 all the sheep and oxen,
as well as the animals in the wild,
8 the birds of the sky,
and the fish of the sea
that pass through the currents
of the seas.[h]

9 Yahweh, our Lord,
how magnificent is Your name
throughout the earth!

Psalm 9
Celebration of God's Justice

For the choir director: according to *Muth-labben.*[F] A Davidic psalm.

1 I will thank ·Yahweh with all my heart;
I will declare all Your wonderful works.[i]
2 I will rejoice and boast about You;[j]
I will sing about Your name,
·Most High.[k]

3 When my enemies retreat,
they stumble and perish before You.[l]
4 For You have upheld my just cause;[G,m]
You are seated on Your throne
as a righteous judge.[n]
5 You have rebuked the nations:[o]
You have destroyed the wicked;[p]
You have erased their name forever
and ever.[q]
6 The enemy has come to eternal ruin;
You have uprooted the cities,
and the very memory of them
has perished.[r]

7 But the LORD sits enthroned forever;[s]
He has established His throne
for judgment.[t]
8 He judges the world
with righteousness;
He executes judgment on the nations
with fairness.[u]

9 The LORD is a refuge for the oppressed,
a refuge in times of trouble.[v]
10 Those who know Your name trust in You
because You have not abandoned
those who seek You, Yahweh.[w]

11 Sing to the LORD, who dwells in ·Zion;[x]
proclaim His deeds among the nations.[y]
12 For the One who seeks an accounting
for bloodshed remembers them;[z]
He does not forget the cry
of the afflicted.[aa]

13 Be gracious to me, LORD;
consider my affliction at the hands
of those who hate me.[ab]
Lift me up from the gates of death,[ac]
14 so that I may declare all Your praises.
I will rejoice in Your salvation[ad]
within the gates of Daughter Zion.

15 The nations have fallen into the pit
they made;
their foot is caught in the net
they have concealed.[ae]
16 The LORD has revealed Himself;
He has executed justice,[af]
striking down[H] the wicked[I]
by the work of their hands.[ag]
·Higgaion. ·Selah

[a]**8:title** Ps 81,84 titles [b]**8:1** Is 12:4 [c]Ps 113:4; 148:13 [d]**8:2** Mt 21:16 [e]**8:3** Ps 33:6; 136:9 [f]**8:4** Jb 7:17-18; Ps 144:3 [g]**8:4-6** 1Co 15:27; Eph 1:22; Heb 2:5-8 [h]**8:7-8** Gn 1:26,28 [i]**9:1** 1Ch 16:9,24; Ps 26:7; 96:3; 105:2 [j]**9:2** Ps 5:11 [k]Ps 7:17; 92:1 [l]**9:3** Lv 26:37; Ps 27:2; 92:9 [m]**9:4** 1Kg 8:45,49,59; 2Ch 6:35,39 [n]Ps 7:11 [o]**9:5** Is 17:3 [p]Ps 68:2 [q]Zch 13:2 [r]**9:6** Ps 34:16 [s]**9:7** Ps 29:10; 102:12; Lm 5:19 [t]Ps 89:14 [u]**9:8** Ps 96:13; 98:9; Rv 19:11 [v]**9:9** Ps 14:6; Is 14:32 [w]**9:10** Ps 37:28; 94:14 [x]**9:11** Ps 76:2 [y]1Ch 16:8; Ps 105:1 [z]**9:12** Gn 9:5 [aa]Ps 12:5; Pr 22:22-23 [ab]**9:13** Ps 69:14 [ac]Ps 30:3; 86:13 [ad]**9:14** 1Sm 2:1 [ae]**9:15** Ps 7:15; 57:6; Pr 28:10 [af]**9:16** Is 56:1 [ag]Ps 3:7; Is 11:4

[A]**8:1** Lit *earth, which has set Your splendor upon the heavens* [B]**8:2** LXX reads *established praise* [C]**8:5** LXX reads *angels* [D]**8:5** Or *gods*, or *a god*, or *heavenly beings*; lit *Elohim* [E]**8:6** Or *authority* [F]**9:title** Perhaps a musical term [G]**9:4** Lit *my justice and my cause* [H]**9:16** Or *justice, snaring* [I]**9:16** LXX, Aq, Syr, Tg read *justice, the wicked is trapped*

17 The wicked will return to ˚Sheol[a] —
all the nations that forget God.[b]
18 For the oppressed will not always
be forgotten;
the hope of the afflicted[A] will not perish
forever.[c]
19 Rise up, LORD! Do not let man prevail;
let the nations be judged
in Your presence.[d]
20 Put terror in them, LORD;[e]
let the nations know they are
only men.[f] *Selah*

PSALM 10

1 LORD,[B,C] why do You stand so far away?[g]
Why do You hide in times of trouble?[h]
2 In arrogance the wicked
relentlessly pursue the afflicted;
let them be caught in the schemes
they have devised.[i]
3 For the wicked one boasts about
his own cravings;[j]
the one who is greedy curses[D]
and despises the LORD.[k]
4 In all his scheming,
the wicked arrogantly thinks:[E]
"There is no accountability,
since God does not exist."[l]
5 His ways are always secure;[F]
Your lofty judgments are beyond
his sight;
he scoffs at all his adversaries.[m]
6 He says to himself, "I will never
be moved —
from generation to generation
without calamity."[n]
7 Cursing, deceit, and violence
fill his mouth;
trouble and malice are
under his tongue.[o]
8 He waits in ambush near the villages;[p]
he kills the innocent in secret places.
His eyes are on the lookout
for the helpless;[q]
9 he lurks in secret like a lion in a thicket.
He lurks in order to seize the afflicted;
he seizes the afflicted and drags him
in his net.
10 So he is oppressed and beaten down;
the helpless fall because of
his strength.[r]
11 He says to himself, "God has forgotten;
He hides His face and will never see."[s]
12 Rise up, LORD God! Lift up Your hand.[t]
Do not forget the afflicted.[u]
13 Why has the wicked person
despised God?
He says to himself, "You will not
demand an account."[v]
14 But You Yourself have seen trouble
and grief,
observing it in order to take the matter
into Your hands.[w]
The helpless entrusts himself to You;
You are a helper of the fatherless.[x]
15 Break the arm of the wicked
and evil person;[y]
call his wickedness into account
until nothing remains of it.[G,z]
16 The LORD is King forever and ever;[aa]
the nations will perish from His land.[ab]
17 LORD, You have heard the desire
of the humble;[H]
You will strengthen their hearts.
You will listen carefully,[ac]
18 doing justice for the fatherless
and the oppressed
so that men of the earth
may terrify them no more.[ad]

PSALM 11

Refuge in the LORD

For the choir director. Davidic.

1 I have taken refuge in the LORD.[ae]
How can you say to me,
"Escape to the mountain like a bird![I,af]
2 For look, the wicked string the bow;
they put the[J] arrow on the bowstring
to shoot from the shadows
at the upright in heart.[ag]
3 When the foundations
are destroyed,
what can the righteous do?"[ah]
4 The LORD is in His holy temple;[ai]
the LORD's throne is in heaven.[aj]

[a]**9:17** Ps 31:17; 49:14; 55:15 [b]Jb 8:13; Ps 50:22 [c]**9:18** Ps 12:5; 72:4 [d]**9:19** Ps 82:8; 110:6 [e]**9:20** Ps 14:5 [f]Ps 62:9 [g]**10:1** Ps 22:1; 35:22; 38:21; 71:12 [h]Jb 13:24; Ps 44:24; 88:14 [i]**10:2** Ps 7:15-16 [j]**10:3** Ps 49:6 [k]2Pt 2:3 [l]**10:4** Ps 14:1; 53:1 [m]**10:5** Ps 52:7 [n]**10:6** Ps 49:11; Rv 18:7 [o]**10:7** Ps 73:8; 140:3; Rm 3:13-14 [p]**10:8** Ps 59:3 [q]Ps 64:4; 94:6 [r]**10:8-10** Ps 17:11-12; Pr 28:15 [s]**10:11** Jb 22:13; Ps 59:3 [t]**10:12** Mc 5:9 [u]Ps 9:12 [v]**10:13** Ps 73:11 [w]**10:14** Ps 33:13-15 [x]Ps 68:5; 146:9 [y]**10:15** Ps 37:17 [z]Ps 89:32 [aa]**10:16** Ex 15:18; Ps 29:10; Rv 11:15 [ab]Dt 8:20 [ac]**10:17** 2Ch 7:14; Ps 34:15 [ad]**10:18** Ex 22:22-24; Dt 10:18 [ae]**11:1** Ps 7:1; 31:1; 71:1 [af]Ps 121:1 [ag]**11:2** Ps 37:14; 64:4 [ah]**11:3** Ps 82:5 [ai]**11:4** Ps 27:4; Hab 2:20 [aj]Ps 103:19; Is 66:1; Ac 7:49

[A]**9:18** Alt Hb tradition reads *humble* [B]**10:1** Some Hb mss, LXX connect Pss 9–10. [C]**10:1** Together these 2 psalms form a partial ˚acrostic. [D]**10:3** Or *he blesses the greedy* [E]**10:4** Lit *wicked according to the height of his nose* [F]**10:5** Or *prosperous* [G]**10:15** Lit *account You do not find* [H]**10:17** Some Hb mss, LXX, Syr read *afflicted* [I]**11:1** Lit *to your mountain, bird* [J]**11:2** Lit *their*

His eyes watch;
He examines[A] •everyone.
5 The LORD examines the righteous
and the wicked.
He hates the lover of violence.[a]
6 He will rain burning coals[B] and sulfur
on the wicked;
a scorching wind will be
their portion.[C,b]
7 For the LORD is righteous; He loves
righteous deeds.
The upright will see His face.[c]

PSALM 12

Oppression by the Wicked

For the choir director: according to •*Sheminith*.[d]
A Davidic psalm.

1 Help, LORD, for no
faithful one remains;
the loyal have disappeared
from the •human race.[e]
2 They lie to one another;
they speak with flattering lips
and deceptive hearts.[f]
3 May the LORD cut off all flattering lips
and the tongue that speaks boastfully.[g]
4 They say, "Through our tongues
we have power;[D]
our lips are our own — who can be
our master?"[h]
5 "Because of the oppression
of the afflicted
and the groaning of the poor,
I will now rise up," says the LORD.
"I will put the one who longs for it
in a safe place."[i]
6 The words of the LORD
are pure words,
like silver refined
in an earthen furnace,
purified seven times.[j]
7 You, LORD, will guard us;[E]
You will protect us[F]
from this generation forever.[k]
8 The wicked wander[G] everywhere,
and what is worthless is exalted
by the human race.[l]

[a]**11:4-5** Ps 33:13-15
[b]**11:6** Ezk 38:22
[c]**11:7** Ps 17:15; Rv 22:4
[d]**12:title** 1Ch 15:21; Ps 6 title
[e]**12:1** Ps 14:2-3; 53:2-3; Mc 7:2
[f]**12:2** Ps 41:6; 144:8; Jr 9:8
[g]**12:3** Ps 5:9
[h]**12:4** Ps 73:8-9
[i]**12:5** Ps 9:18; 72:4
[j]**12:6** Ps 18:30; 119:140; Pr 30:5
[k]**12:7** Ps 37:28; 97:10
[l]**12:8** Ps 4:2; 119:37
[m]**13:1** Jb 13:24; Ps 44:24; 89:46
[n]**13:2** Ps 6:3; 38:6; 42:9
[o]**13:3** Ezr 9:8; Ps 19:8; Pr 29:13
[p]**13:4** Ps 89:42
[q]**13:5** Ps 52:8
[r]Ps 9:14
[s]**13:6** Ps 119:17; 142:7
[t]**14:1** Ps 10:4; 53:1
[u]**14:2** Ps 33:13-15
[v]**14:1-3** Ps 12:1; 53:1-3; Mc 7:2; Rm 3:10-12
[w]**14:4** Ps 27:2; Mc 3:3
[x]Is 64:7
[y]**14:5** Ps 53:5

PSALM 13

A Plea for Deliverance

For the choir director. A Davidic psalm.

1 LORD, how long will You forget me?
Forever?
How long will You hide Your face
from me?[m]
2 How long will I store up
anxious concerns[H] within me,
agony in my mind every day?
How long will my enemy dominate me?[n]
3 Consider me and answer, LORD my God.
Restore brightness to my eyes;[o]
otherwise, I will sleep in death.
4 My enemy will say, "I have triumphed
over him,"
and my foes will rejoice
because I am shaken.[p]
5 But I have trusted in Your faithful love;[q]
my heart will rejoice in
Your deliverance.[r]
6 I will sing to the LORD
because He has treated me generously.[s]

PSALM 14

A Portrait of Sinners

For the choir director. Davidic.

1 The fool says in his heart,
"God does not exist."[t]
They are corrupt; they do vile deeds.
There is no one who does good.
2 The LORD looks down from heaven
on the •human race[u]
to see if there is one who is wise,
one who seeks God.
3 All have turned away;
all alike have become corrupt.
There is no one who does good,
not even one.[I,v]
4 Will evildoers never understand?
They consume My people
as they consume bread;[w]
they do not call on the LORD.[x]
5 Then[J] they will be filled with terror,
for God is with those
who are[K] righteous.[y]

[A]**11:4** Lit *His eyelids examine* [B]**11:6** Sym; MT reads *rain snares, fire* [C]**11:6** Lit *be the portion of their cup* [D]**12:4** Lit *That say, "By our tongues we are strengthened* [E]**12:7** Some Hb mss, LXX, Jer; other Hb mss read *them* [F]**12:7** Some Hb mss, LXX; other Hb mss read *him* [G]**12:8** Lit *walk about* [H]**13:2** Or *up counsels* [I]**14:3** Some Hb mss, some LXX mss add the material found in Rm 3:13-18. [J]**14:5** Or *There* [K]**14:5** Lit *with the generation of the*

6 You sinners frustrate the plans
of the afflicted,[a]
but the LORD is his refuge.[b]
7 Oh, that Israel's deliverance
would come from ·Zion!
When the LORD restores the fortunes
of His people,[A]
Jacob will rejoice; Israel will be glad.[B,c]

Psalm 15

A Description of the Godly

A Davidic psalm.

1 LORD, who can dwell in Your tent?
Who can live on Your holy mountain?[e]
2 The one who lives honestly,
practices righteousness,
and acknowledges the truth
in his heart[f] —
3 who does not slander with his tongue,[g]
who does not harm his friend
or discredit his neighbor,[h]
4 who despises the one rejected
by the LORD[C]
but honors those who ·fear the LORD,[i]
who keeps his word whatever the cost,[j]
5 who does not lend his money
at interest[k]
or take a bribe against the innocent[l] —
the one who does these things
will never be moved.[m]

Psalm 16

Confidence in the LORD

A Davidic ·*Miktam*.[n]

1 Protect me, God, for I take refuge
in You.[o]
2 I[D] said to ·Yahweh, "You are my Lord;
I have nothing good besides You."[E,p]
3 As for the holy people who are
in the land,[q]
they are the noble ones.
All my delight is in them.
4 The sorrows of those who take
another god
for themselves will multiply;
I will not pour out
their ·drink offerings of blood,
and I will not speak their names
with my lips.[r]
5 LORD, You are my portion[F]
and my cup of blessing;
You hold my future.[s]
6 The boundary lines have fallen for me
in pleasant places;
indeed, I have a beautiful inheritance.[t]
7 I will praise the LORD
who counsels me[u] —
even at night my conscience
instructs me.[v]
8 I keep the LORD in mind[G] always.
Because He is at my right hand,
I will not be shaken.[w]
9 Therefore my heart is glad
and my spirit rejoices;
my body also rests securely.[x]
10 For You will not abandon me
to ·Sheol;[y]
You will not allow Your Faithful One
to see decay.[z]
11 You reveal the path of life to me;
in Your presence is abundant joy;[aa]
in Your right hand are
eternal pleasures.[ab]

Psalm 17

A Prayer for Protection

A Davidic prayer.

1 LORD, hear a just cause;[ac]
pay attention to my cry;
listen to my prayer —
from lips free of deceit.[ad]
2 Let my vindication come from You,
for You see what is right.[ae]
3 You have tested my heart;[af]
You have examined me at night.
You have tried me and found
nothing evil;[ag]
I have determined that my mouth
will not sin.[H]
4 Concerning what people do:
by the word of Your lips[I]
I have avoided the ways of the violent.[ah]
5 My steps are on Your paths;
my feet have not slipped.[ai]

[a]**14:6** Ezr 4:5
[b]Ps 9:9; 94:22
[c]**14:7** Ps 53:6
[d]**15:1** Ps 61:4
[e]Ps 43:3
[f]**15:1-2** Ps 24:3-5; Is 33:14-16
[g]**15:3** Pr 10:18
[h]Pr 3:29
[i]**15:4** Gn 14:17-24; Ps 119:63
[j]Lv 5:4; Dt 23:21-23
[k]**15:5** Lv 25:35-38; Dt 33:19
[l]Ex 23:18; Dt 16:19
[m]Ps 16:8; 112:6
[n]**16:title** Pss 56–60 titles
[o]**16:1** Ps 94:22
[p]**16:2** Ps 73:25
[q]**16:3** Dt 7:6; 14:2; 26:19
[r]**16:4** Ex 23:13; Jos 23:7
[s]**16:5** Nm 18:20; Ps 119:57; Lm 3:24
[t]**16:6** Jr 3:19
[u]**16:7** Ps 73:24
[v]Ps 77:6
[w]**16:8** Ps 15:5; 112:6
[x]**16:9** Ps 4:7-8; 13:5
[y]**16:10** Ps 49:10; 86:13
[z]Jb 33:18,28; Ps 30:3; 103:4; Ac 13:35
[aa]**16:11** Ps 21:6
[ab]**16:8-11** Ac 2:25-28
[ac]**17:1** Ps 9:4
[ad]Jb 27:4; Ps 34:13; 1Pt 3:10
[ae]**17:2** Ps 26:1; 43:1
[af]**17:3** Ps 66:10; Zch 13:9
[ag]Jb 23:10; Ps 26:2
[ah]**17:4** Pr 4:14-15
[ai]**17:5** Jb 23:11

[A]14:7 Or *restores His captive people* [B]14:7 Or *let Jacob rejoice; let Israel be glad.* [C]15:4 Lit *in his eyes the rejected is despised* [D]16:2 Some Hb mss, LXX, Syr, Jer; other Hb mss read *You* [E]16:2 Or *"Lord, my good; there is none besides You."* [F]16:5 Or *allotted portion* [G]16:8 Lit *front of me* [H]17:3 Or *evil; my mouth will not sin* [I]17:4 God's instruction

6 I call on You, God,
because You will answer me;[a]
listen closely to me; hear what I say.
7 Display the wonders
of Your faithful love,[b]
Savior of all who seek refuge[c]
from those who rebel
against Your right hand.[A]
8 Protect me as the pupil of Your eye;[d]
hide me in the shadow of Your wings[e]
9 from[B] the wicked
who treat me violently,[C]
my deadly enemies who surround me.[f]

10 They have become hardened;[D,g]
their mouths speak arrogantly.[h]
11 They advance against me;[E]
now they surround me.[i]
They are determined[F]
to throw me to the ground.[j]
12 They are[G] like a lion eager to tear,
like a young lion lurking in ambush.[k]

13 Rise up, LORD!
Confront him; bring him down.[l]
With Your sword, save me
from the wicked.[m]
14 With Your hand, LORD, save me
from men,
from men of the world
whose portion is in this life:
You fill their bellies with what You have
in store;
their sons are satisfied,
and they leave their surplus
to their children.[n]

15 But I will see Your face
in righteousness;[o]
when I awake, I will be satisfied
with Your presence.[H,p]

Psalm 18

Praise for Deliverance

For the choir director. Of the servant of the LORD, David, who spoke the words of this song to the LORD on the day the LORD rescued him from the hand of all his enemies and from the hand of Saul.[q] He said:

1 I love You, LORD, my strength.

[a]**17:6** Ps 86:7
[b]**17:7** Ps 85:7
[c]Ps 7:1
[d]**17:8** Pr 7:2
[e]Ps 36:7; 57:1; 63:7; 91:1,4
[f]**17:9** Ps 18:48
[g]**17:10** Ps 119:70
[h]Ps 31:18
[i]**17:11** Ps 88:17
[j]Ps 37:14; 62:4
[k]**17:12** Ps 7:2; 10:9
[l]**17:13** Ps 55:23
[m]Ps 7:12
[n]**17:14** Ps 73:3-7
[o]**17:15** Ps 11:7; Rv 22:4
[p]Ps 16:11; 21:6; 73:28
[q]**18:title** 2Sm 22
[r]**18:2** Ps 62:7; 94:22
[s]Gn 15:1; Dt 33:29; Ps 3:3; 5:12; 28:7; 119:114
[t]1Sm 2:1,10; Lk 1:69
[u]**18:3** Ps 48:1; 96:4; 145:3
[v]Ps 138:7
[w]**18:4** Ps 124:4
[x]**18:5** Ps 116:3
[y]**18:6** Ps 3:4
[z]Ps 34:15
[aa]**18:7** Is 13:13; Hg 2:6
[ab]**18:8** Ps 21:9; 50:3
[ac]**18:9** Ps 144:5; Is 64:1
[ad]**18:10** Ps 104:3
[ae]**18:11** Ps 97:2
[af]**18:12** Ps 50:2; Is 60:3
[ag]**18:13** Ps 29:3; 104:7
[ah]**18:14** Ps 144:6

2 The LORD is my rock,
my fortress, and my deliverer,[r]
my God, my mountain
where I seek refuge,
my shield[s] and the •horn
of my salvation,[t]
my stronghold.
3 I called to the LORD, who is
worthy of praise,[u]
and I was saved from my enemies.[v]

4 The ropes of death were wrapped
around me;
the torrents of destruction
terrified me.[w]
5 The ropes of •Sheol entangled me;
the snares of death confronted me.[x]
6 I called to the LORD in my distress,
and I cried to my God for help.
From His temple He heard my voice,[y]
and my cry to Him reached His ears.[z]

7 Then the earth shook and quaked;
the foundations of the mountains
trembled;[aa]
they shook because He burned
with anger.
8 Smoke rose from His nostrils,
and consuming fire came
from His mouth;
coals were set ablaze by it.[I,ab]
9 He parted the heavens and came down,[ac]
a dark cloud beneath His feet.
10 He rode on a cherub and flew,
soaring on the wings of the wind.[ad]
11 He made darkness His hiding place,
dark storm clouds His canopy
around Him.[e]
12 From the radiance of His presence,[af]
His clouds swept onward with hail
and blazing coals.
13 The LORD thundered from[J] heaven;
the •Most High projected His voice.[K,ag]
14 He shot His arrows and scattered them;
He hurled[L] lightning bolts
and routed them.[ah]
15 The depths of the sea became visible,
the foundations of the world
were exposed,

[A]**17:7** Or *love, You who save with Your right hand those seeking refuge from adversaries* [B]**17:9** Lit *from the presence of* [C]**17:9** Or *who plunder me* [D]**17:10** Lit *have closed up their fat* [E]**17:11** Vg; one Hb ms, LXX read *They cast me out*; MT reads *Our steps* [F]**17:11** Lit *They set their eyes* [G]**17:12** Lit *He is* [H]**17:15** Lit *form*

[I]**18:8** Or *ablaze from Him* [J]**18:13** Some Hb mss, LXX, Tg, Jer; other Hb mss read *in* [K]**18:13** Some Hb mss read *voice, with hail and fiery coals* [L]**18:14** Or *multiplied*

at Your rebuke, LORD,
at the blast of the breath
of Your nostrils.[a]

16 He reached down from heaven
and took hold of me;
He pulled me out of deep waters.[b]
17 He rescued me
from my powerful enemy
and from those who hated me,
for they were too strong for me.[c]
18 They confronted me in the day
of my distress,
but the LORD was my support.[d]
19 He brought me out to a spacious place;[e]
He rescued me because He delighted
in me.[f]

20 The LORD rewarded me
according to my righteousness;[g]
He repaid me
according to the cleanness
of my hands.[h]
21 For I have kept the ways of the LORD
and have not turned from my God
to wickedness.[i]
22 Indeed, I have kept all His ordinances
in mind[A]
and have not disregarded His statutes.[j]
23 I was blameless toward Him[k]
and kept myself from sinning.
24 So the LORD repaid me
according to my righteousness,[l]
according to the cleanness of my hands
in His sight.[m]

25 With the faithful
You prove Yourself faithful;
with the blameless man
You prove Yourself blameless;
26 with the pure
You prove Yourself pure,
but with the crooked
You prove Yourself shrewd.[n]
27 For You rescue an afflicted people,[o]
but You humble those
with haughty eyes.[p]
28 LORD, You light my lamp;
my God illuminates my darkness.[q]
29 With You I can attack a barrier,[B]
and with my God I can leap over a wall.[r]

30 God — His way is perfect;[s]
the word of the LORD is pure.[t]
He is a shield to all who take refuge
in Him.[u]
31 For who is God besides ·Yahweh?[v]
And who is a rock? Only our God.[w]
32 God — He clothes me with strength[x]
and makes my way perfect.
33 He makes my feet like the feet of a deer[y]
and sets me securely on the heights.[C,z]
34 He trains my hands for war;[aa]
my arms can bend a bow of bronze.[ab]
35 You have given me the shield
of Your salvation;
Your right hand upholds me,[ac]
and Your humility exalts me.
36 You widen a place beneath me
for my steps,[ad]
and my ankles do not give way.[ae]

37 I pursue my enemies
and overtake them;
I do not turn back until they are
wiped out.[af]
38 I crush them, and they cannot get up;
they fall beneath my feet.[ag]
39 You have clothed me with strength
for battle;[ah]
You subdue my adversaries
beneath me.[ai]
40 You have made my enemies retreat
before me;[D,aj]
I annihilate those who hate me.[ak]
41 They cry for help, but there is no one
to save them[al] —
they cry to the LORD, but He does not
answer them.[am]
42 I pulverize them like dust
before the wind;[an]
I trample them[E] like mud in the streets.[ao]

43 You have freed me from the feuds
among the people;
You have appointed me the head
of nations;[ap]
a people I had not known serve me.[aq]
44 Foreigners submit to me grudgingly;
as soon as they hear,[F] they obey me.[ar]
45 Foreigners lose heart

[a] **18:15** Ex 15:8; Ps 106:9; Nah 1:4
[b] **18:16** Ps 144:7
[c] **18:17** Ps 35:10; 59:1; 142:6
[d] **18:18** Ps 55:22; 59:16
[e] **18:19** Ps 31:8; 118:5
[f] Ps 41:11
[g] **18:20** Ps 7:8
[h] Ps 24:4
[i] **18:21** Jb 23:11; Ps 119:101
[j] **18:22** Lv 18:4-5
[k] **18:23** Dt 18:13; Ps 37:18; 119:1
[l] **18:24** 2Ch 6:23
[m] Ps 24:4
[n] **18:25-26** Mt 16:27; Rv 22:12
[o] **18:27** Ps 72:12
[p] Ps 138:6
[q] **18:28** Ps 112:4; Is 42:16
[r] **18:29** Mt 19:26; Php 4:13
[s] **18:30** Dt 32:4
[t] Ps 19:7
[u] Ps 91:4; 144:2
[v] **18:31** Dt 32:39; 1Sm 2:2; Ps 86:8
[w] Ps 62:2
[x] **18:32** Is 45:5
[y] **18:33** Hab 3:19
[z] Dt 32:13; Is 58:14
[aa] **18:34** Ps 144:1
[ab] Jb 29:20
[ac] **18:35** Ps 89:21
[ad] **18:36** Ps 31:8; 118:5
[ae] Ps 66:9; Pr 4:12
[af] **18:37** Ps 44:5
[ag] **18:38** Ps 36:12
[ah] **18:39** 1Sm 2:4
[ai] 1Ch 17:10; Ps 81:14
[aj] **18:40** Ex 23:27
[ak] Dt 7:10
[al] **18:41** Ps 50:22
[am] Mc 3:4
[an] **18:42** 2Kg 13:7
[ao] Is 10:6; Mc 7:10
[ap] **18:43** 2Sm 8:1-14
[aq] Is 55:5
[ar] **18:44** Dt 33:29; Ps 66:3

[A] **18:22** Lit *Indeed, all His ordinances have been in front of me* [B] **18:29** Or *ridge*
[C] **18:33** Or *on my high places* [D] **18:40** Or *You gave me the necks of my enemies*
[E] **18:42** Some Hb mss, LXX, Syr, Tg; other Hb mss read *I poured them out*
[F] **18:44** Lit *At the hearing of the ear*

and come trembling
from their fortifications.[a]

46 The LORD lives — may my rock
be praised!
The God of my salvation is exalted.[b]
47 God — He gives me vengeance[c]
and subdues peoples under me.[d]
48 He frees me from my enemies.
You exalt me above my adversaries;
You rescue me from violent men.[e]
49 Therefore I will praise You, Yahweh,
among the nations;
I will sing about Your name.[f]
50 He gives great victories to His king;[g]
He shows loyalty to His anointed,
to David and his descendants forever.[h]

PSALM 19

The Witness of Creation and Scripture

For the choir director. A Davidic psalm.

1 The heavens declare the glory of God,
and the sky[A] proclaims the work
of His hands.[i]
2 Day after day they pour out speech;
night after night
they communicate knowledge.[B]
3 There is no speech; there are no words;
their voice is not heard.
4 Their message[C] has gone out to all
the earth,
and their words to the ends
of the world.[j]

In the heavens[D] He has pitched a tent
for the sun.[k]
5 It is like a groom coming from
the[E] bridal chamber;
it rejoices like an athlete
running a course.
6 It rises from one end of the heavens
and circles[F] to their other end;[l]
nothing is hidden from its heat.

7 The instruction of the LORD is perfect,
renewing one's life;[m]
the ·testimony of the LORD
is trustworthy,
making the inexperienced wise.[n]
8 The precepts of the LORD are right,
making the heart glad;[o]
the command of the LORD is radiant,
making the eyes light up.[p]
9 The ·fear of the LORD is pure,
enduring forever;[q]
the ordinances of the LORD are reliable
and altogether righteous.[r]
10 They are more desirable than gold —
than an abundance of pure gold;[s]
and sweeter than honey,
which comes from the honeycomb.[t]
11 In addition, Your servant is warned
by them;
there is great reward in keeping them.[u]

12 Who perceives his unintentional sins?
Cleanse me from my hidden faults.[v]
13 Moreover, keep Your servant
from willful sins;[w]
do not let them rule over me.[x]
Then I will be innocent
and cleansed from blatant rebellion.[y]
14 May the words of my mouth
and the meditation of my heart
be acceptable to You,[z]
LORD, my rock and my Redeemer.[aa]

PSALM 20

Deliverance in Battle

For the choir director. A Davidic psalm.

1 May ·Yahweh answer you in a day
of trouble;[ab]
may the name of Jacob's God
protect you.[ac]
2 May He send you help
from the sanctuary
and sustain you from ·Zion.[ad]
3 May He remember all your offerings
and accept your ·burnt offering.[ae] ·*Selah*
4 May He give you what
your heart desires[af]
and fulfill your whole purpose.[ag]
5 Let us shout for joy at your victory[ah]
and lift the banner in the name
of our God.[ai]
May Yahweh fulfill all your requests.[aj]
6 Now I know that the LORD gives victory
to His anointed;[ak]

[a]**18:45** Mc 7:17 [b]**18:46** Ps 62:2,6 [c]**18:47** 2Sm 4:8; Ps 94:1 [d]Ps 47:3; 144:2 [e]**18:48** Ps 59:1; 140:1 [f]**18:49** Rm 15:9 [g]**18:50** Ps 144:10 [h]2Sm 7:12-13; Ps 89:4,29 [i]**19:1** Ps 50:6; Rm 1:19-20 [j]**19:4** Rm 10:18 [k]Is 40:22 [l]**19:6** Ec 1:5 [m]**19:7** Ps 111:7 [n]Ps 93:5; 119:130 [o]**19:8** Ps 119:14 [p]Ps 13:3 [q]**19:9** Ps 111:10 [r]Ps 119:30 [s]**19:10** Ps 119:72,127 [t]Ps 119:103 [u]**19:11** Pr 29:18 [v]**19:12** Ps 90:8 [w]**19:13** Nm 15:30 [x]Gn 4:7 [y]Ps 51:7; Ezk 36:25 [z]**19:14** Ps 104:34 [aa]Ps 78:35 [ab]**20:1** Ps 50:15; 77:2; 102:2 [ac]Ps 46:7,11 [ad]**20:2** Ps 3:4; 110:2; 128:5 [ae]**20:3** Ps 119:108 [af]**20:4** Ps 21:2; 145:19 [ag]Ps 138:8 [ah]**20:5** Ps 21:1 [ai]Is 13:2 [aj]Ps 21:2; 1Pt 3:12 [ak]**20:6** Ps 18:50

A**19:1** Or *expanse* B**19:2** Or *Day to day pours out speech, and night to night communicates knowledge* C**19:4** LXX, Sym, Syr, Vg; MT reads *line* D**19:4** Lit *In them* E**19:5** Lit *his* F**19:6** Lit *its circuit is*

He will answer him
from His holy heaven
with mighty victories
from[A] His right hand.[a]
7 Some take pride in chariots, and others
in horses,
but we take pride in the name
of Yahweh our God.[b]
8 They collapse and fall,
but we rise and stand firm.[c]
9 LORD, give victory to the king![d]
May He[B] answer us on the day
that we call.

PSALM 21
The King's Victory

For the choir director. A Davidic psalm.

1 LORD, the king finds joy
in Your strength.
How greatly he rejoices
in Your victory![e]
2 You have given him his heart's desire[f]
and have not denied the request
of his lips.[g] *Selah*
3 For You meet him with rich blessings;
You place a crown of pure gold
on his head.[h]
4 He asked You for life, and You gave it
to him —
length of days forever and ever.[i]
5 His glory is great through Your victory;
You confer majesty and splendor
on him.[j]
6 You give him blessings forever;[k]
You cheer him with joy
in Your presence.[l]
7 For the king relies on the LORD;
through the faithful love
of the *Most High
he is not shaken.[m]
8 Your hand will capture
all your enemies;
your right hand will seize
those who hate you.[n]
9 You will make them burn
like a fiery furnace when you appear;
the LORD will engulf them in His wrath,
and fire will devour them.[o]
10 You will wipe their descendants
from the earth
and their offspring
from the *human race.[p]
11 Though they intend to harm[C] you
and devise a wicked plan,
they will not prevail.[q]
12 Instead, you will put them to flight
when you aim your bow[D]
at their faces.[r]
13 Be exalted, LORD, in Your strength;
we will sing and praise Your might.[s]

PSALM 22
From Suffering to Praise

For the choir director: according to "The Deer of the Dawn."[E] A Davidic psalm.

1 My God, my God, why have You
forsaken me?[t]
Why are You so far
from my deliverance[u]
and from my words of groaning?[F,v]
2 My God, I cry by day, but You
do not answer,
by night, yet I have no rest.[w]
3 But You are holy,
enthroned on the praises of Israel.[x]
4 Our fathers trusted in You;
they trusted, and You rescued them.[y]
5 They cried to You and were set free;
they trusted in You
and were not disgraced.[z]
6 But I am a worm and not a man,[aa]
scorned by men and despised
by people.[ab]
7 Everyone who sees me mocks me;
they sneer[G] and shake their heads:[ac]
8 "He relies on[H] the LORD;
let Him rescue him;
let the LORD[I] deliver him,
since He takes pleasure in him."[ad]
9 You took me from the womb,
making me secure
while at my mother's breast.[ae]
10 I was given over to You at birth;[J]
You have been my God
from my mother's womb.[af]

[a] **20:6** Ps 44:3; 98:1; 118:15
[b] **20:7** Ps 33:17; Is 31:1
[c] **20:8** Is 2:11,17; Mc 7:8
[d] **20:9** Ps 18:50
[e] **21:1** Ps 28:7-8; 59:16-17
[f] **21:2** Ps 20:4; 145:19
[g] Ps 20:5; 1Pt 3:12
[h] **21:3** 2Sm 12:30; 1Ch 20:2
[i] **21:4** Ps 61:6; 91:16
[j] **21:5** Ps 8:5; 96:6
[k] **21:6** 1Ch 17:27
[l] Ps 16:11
[m] **21:7** Ps 10:6; 16:8
[n] **21:8** Ex 15:6; Is 10:10
[o] **21:9** Ps 50:3; 97:3; Mal 4:1
[p] **21:10** 1Kg 13:34; Ps 37:28; Is 14:20
[q] **21:11** Ps 2:1-3; 7:15-16; 10:2
[r] **21:12** Ps 7:12
[s] **21:13** Ps 59:16; 81:1
[t] **22:1** Mt 27:46; Mk 15:34
[u] Ps 10:1
[v] Ps 32:3; 38:8
[w] **22:2** Ps 42:3; 88:1
[x] **22:3** Ps 99:3
[y] **22:4** Ps 107:6
[z] **22:5** Ps 25:2; 31:1; 71:1; Is 49:23
[aa] **22:6** Jb 25:6
[ab] Ps 109:25; Is 53:3
[ac] **22:7** Mt 27:39; Mk 15:29; Lk 23:35
[ad] **22:8** Mt 27:43
[ae] **22:9** Ps 71:6
[af] **22:10** Is 46:3; 49:1; Gl 1:15

[A] **20:6** Some Hb mss, Aq, Sym, Jer, Syr read *with the victorious might of* [B] **20:9** Or *LORD, save. May the king* [C] **21:11** Lit *they stretch out evil against* [D] **21:12** Lit *aim with your bowstrings* [E] **22:title** Perhaps a musical term [F] **22:1** Or *My words of groaning are so far from delivering me* [G] **22:7** Lit *separate with the lip* [H] **22:8** Or *Rely on* [I] **22:8** Lit *let Him* [J] **22:10** Lit *was cast on You from the womb*

11 Do not be far from me, because distress
is near
and there is no one to help.[a]
12 Many bulls surround me;
strong ones of Bashan encircle me.[b]
13 They open their mouths against me —
lions, mauling and roaring.[c]
14 I am poured out like water,[d]
and all my bones are disjointed;[e]
my heart is like wax,
melting within me.[f]
15 My strength is dried up like baked clay;[g]
my tongue sticks to the roof
of my mouth.[h]
You put me into the dust of death.[i]
16 For dogs have surrounded me;[j]
a gang of evildoers has closed in on me;
they pierced[A] my hands and my feet.[k]
17 I can count all my bones;
people[B] look and stare at me.[l]
18 They divided my garments
among themselves,
and they cast lots for my clothing.[m]
19 But You, LORD, don't be far away.[n]
My strength, come quickly to help me.[o]
20 Deliver my life from the sword,[p]
my only life[C] from the power
of these dogs.
21 Save me from the mouth of the lion![q]
You have rescued[D] me
from the horns of the wild oxen.
22 I will proclaim Your name
to my brothers;
I will praise You in the congregation.[r]
23 You who ·fear ·Yahweh, praise Him![s]
All you descendants of Jacob,
honor Him!
All you descendants of Israel,
revere Him![t]
24 For He has not despised or detested
the torment of the afflicted.[u]
He did not hide His face from him[v]
but listened when he cried to Him
for help.[w]
25 I will give praise[E]
in the great congregation
because of You;[x]
I will fulfill my vows
before those who fear You.[F,y]
26 The humble[G] will eat and be satisfied;[z]
those who seek the LORD
will praise Him.
May your hearts live forever![aa]
27 All the ends of the earth will remember
and turn to the LORD.
All the families of the nations
will bow down before You,[ab]
28 for kingship belongs to the LORD;
He rules over the nations.[ac]
29 All who prosper on earth will eat
and bow down;
all those who go down to the dust
will kneel before Him —
even the one who cannot preserve
his life.[ad]
30 Their descendants will serve Him;
the next generation will be told
about the Lord.[ae]
31 They will come and tell a people
yet to be born
about His righteousness —
what He has done.[af]

PSALM 23

The Good Shepherd

A Davidic psalm.

1 The LORD is my shepherd;[ag]
there is nothing I lack.[ah]
2 He lets me lie down
in green pastures;[ai]
He leads me beside quiet waters.[aj]
3 He renews my life;
He leads me along the right paths[H]
for His name's sake.[ak]
4 Even when I go
through the darkest valley,[I]
I fear no danger,
for You are with me;[al]
Your rod
and Your staff[J] — they comfort me.[am]
5 You prepare a table before me
in the presence of my enemies;
You anoint my head with oil;[an]
my cup overflows.[ao]

[a] **22:11** 2Kg 14:26; Ps 71:12; Is 63:5 [b] **22:12** Ps 68:30; Am 4:1 [c] **22:13** Ps 10:9; 17:12 [d] **22:14** Jb 30:16 [e] Jb 4:14; Ps 6:2; 32:3 [f] Nah 2:10 [g] **22:15** Ps 38:10 [h] Lm 4:4 [i] Ps 104:29 [j] **22:16** Ps 59:6,14 [k] Jn 20:25 [l] **22:17** Lk 23:35 [m] **22:18** Mt 27:35; Lk 23:34; Jn 19:24 [n] **22:19** Ps 10:1 [o] Ps 70:5 [p] **22:20** Jr 39:18 [q] **22:21** Ps 35:17; 2Tm 4:17 [r] **22:22** Ps 40:10; Heb 2:12 [s] **22:23** Rv 19:5 [t] Ps 135:20 [u] **22:24** Ps 69:33 [v] Ezk 39:29 [w] Ps 28:2 [x] **22:25** Ps 35:18; 40:9-10 [y] Ps 61:8 [z] **22:26** Ps 107:9 [aa] Ps 40:16; 69:32 [ab] **22:27** Ps 2:8; 86:9 [ac] **22:28** 1Ch 16:31; 2Ch 20:6; Mal 1:14; Rv 15:3 [ad] **22:29** Is 45:23; Rm 14:11; Php 2:10 [ae] **22:30** Ps 102:18,28 [af] **22:31** Ps 71:18; 78:6 [ag] **23:1** Ps 78:52; Jr 31:10; Ezk 34:11-13; Jn 10:11 [ah] Ps 34:9-10; Php 4:19 [ai] **23:2** Ps 65:11-13; Ezk 34:14 [aj] Ps 36:8 [ak] **23:3** Ps 5:8; Pr 4:11 [al] **23:4** Is 43:2 [am] Mc 7:14 [an] **23:5** Ps 92:10 [ao] Ps 16:5

[A] **22:16** Some Hb mss, LXX, Syr; other Hb mss read *me; like a lion* [B] **22:17** Lit *they* [C] **22:20** Lit *my only one* [D] **22:21** Lit *answered* [E] **22:25** Lit *my praise* [F] **22:25** Lit *Him* [G] **22:26** Or *poor*, or *afflicted* [H] **23:3** Or *me in paths of righteousness* [I] **23:4** Or *the valley of the shadow of death* [J] **23:4** A shepherd's equipment

6 Only goodness and faithful love
will pursue me
all the days of my life,[a]
and I will dwell in[A] the house of the LORD
as long as I live.[B,b]

PSALM 24

The King of Glory

A Davidic psalm.

1 The earth and everything in it,
the world and its inhabitants,
belong to the LORD;[c]
2 for He laid its foundation on the seas
and established it on the rivers.[d]

3 Who may ascend the mountain
of the LORD?
Who may stand in His holy place?[e]
4 The one who has •clean hands
and a pure heart,[f]
who has not set his mind[C] on
what is false,[g]
and who has not sworn deceitfully.
5 He will receive blessing from the LORD,[h]
and righteousness from the God
of his salvation.[i]
6 Such is the generation of those
who seek Him,
who seek the face of the God of Jacob.[D,j]
•Selah

7 Lift up your heads, you gates!
Rise up, ancient doors!
Then the King of glory will come in.[k]
8 Who is this King of glory?
The LORD, strong and mighty,
the LORD, mighty in battle.[l]
9 Lift up your heads, you gates!
Rise up, ancient doors!
Then the King of glory will come in.
10 Who is He, this King of glory?
The LORD of •Hosts,
He is the King of glory.[m] *Selah*

PSALM 25

Dependence on the LORD

Davidic.

1 LORD,[E] I turn to You.[F,n]
2 My God, I trust in You.
Do not let me be disgraced;[o]
do not let my enemies gloat over me.[p]
3 No one who waits for You
will be disgraced;[q]
those who act treacherously
without cause
will be disgraced.[r]

4 Make Your ways known to me, LORD;
teach me Your paths.[s]
5 Guide me in Your truth and teach me,[t]
for You are the God of my salvation;[u]
I wait for You all day long.[v]
6 Remember, LORD, Your compassion
and Your faithful love,
for they have existed from antiquity.[G,w]
7 Do not remember the sins of my youth[x]
or my acts of rebellion;[y]
in keeping with Your faithful love,
remember me
because of Your goodness, LORD.[z]

8 The LORD is good and upright;[aa]
therefore He shows sinners the way.[ab]
9 He leads the humble in what is right[ac]
and teaches them His way.[ad]
10 All the LORD's ways show faithful love
and truth
to those who keep His covenant
and decrees.[ae]
11 Because of Your name, •Yahweh,
forgive my sin, for it is great.[af]
12 Who is the man who •fears the LORD?[ag]
He will show him the way
he should choose.[ah]
13 He will live a good life,
and his descendants will inherit
the land.[H,ai]
14 The secret counsel of the LORD
is for those who fear Him,
and He reveals His covenant to them.[aj]
15 My eyes are always on the LORD,
for He will pull my feet out of the net.[ak]

16 Turn to me and be gracious to me,
for I am alone and afflicted.[al]
17 The distresses of my heart increase;[I,am]
bring me out of my sufferings.[an]
18 Consider my affliction and trouble,[ao]
and take away all my sins.[ap]

[a] **23:6** Ps 25:7; 109:21 [b] Ps 27:4-6 [c] **24:1** Dt 10:14; Ps 89:11; 1Co 10:26 [d] **24:2** Ps 104:5; Pr 8:29 [e] **24:3** Ps 15:1 [f] **24:4** Jb 22:30; Ps 73:1; Mt 5:8 [g] Ps 31:6; 119:37 [h] **24:5** Ps 115:13 [i] Ps 65:5 [j] **24:6** Ps 27:8 [k] **24:7** Ps 118:19-20; Is 26:2 [l] **24:8** Ex 15:3; Ps 76:3-6 [m] **24:10** Is 24:23 [n] **25:1** Ps 38:15; 86:4 [o] **25:2** Ps 31:1; 71:1 [p] Ps 13:4; 41:11 [q] **25:3** Is 49:23 [r] Pr 2:22; Is 21:2 [s] **25:4** Ex 33:13; Ps 27:11; 86:11 [t] **25:5** Jn 16:13 [u] Ex 15:2 [v] Ps 40:1 [w] **25:6** Ps 98:3; 103:17 [x] **25:7** Jb 13:26 [y] Ps 51:1 [z] Neh 13:22 [aa] **25:8** Ps 100:5; Nah 1:7 [ab] Ps 32:8 [ac] **25:9** Ps 23:3 [ad] Ex 18:20; Ps 86:11 [ae] **25:10** Ps 40:11; 103:17-18 [af] **25:11** Jb 7:21; Ps 103:3; Jr 31:34 [ag] **25:12** Ps 31:19 [ah] Ps 37:23 [ai] **25:13** Ps 37:11; 69:36 [aj] **25:14** Jn 7:17; 1Co 2:9 [ak] **25:15** Ps 31:4; 124:7 [al] **25:16** Ps 70:5; 73:14 [am] **25:17** Lm 1:20 [an] Jr 10:19 [ao] **25:18** Ps 31:7 [ap] Rm 11:27; 1Jn 3:5

[A] **23:6** LXX, Sym, Syr, Tg, Vg, Jer; MT reads *will return to* [B] **23:6** Lit *LORD for length of days*; traditionally *LORD forever* [C] **24:4** Or *not lifted up his soul* [D] **24:6** LXX; some Hb mss, Syr read *seek Your face, God of Jacob*; other Hb mss read *seek Your face, Jacob* [E] **25:1** The lines of this poem form an •acrostic. [F] **25:1** Or *To You, LORD, I lift up my soul* [G] **25:6** Or *everlasting* [H] **25:13** Or *earth* [I] **25:17** Or *Relieve the distresses of my heart*

19 Consider my enemies;
they are numerous,[a]
and they hate me violently.[b]
20 Guard me and deliver me;[c]
do not let me be put to shame,
for I take refuge in You.[d]
21 May integrity and what is right
watch over me,
for I wait for You.[e]

22 God, redeem Israel, from all
its distresses.[f]

PSALM 26

Prayer for Vindication

Davidic.

1 Vindicate me, LORD,
because I have lived with integrity
and have trusted in the LORD
without wavering.[g]
2 Test me, LORD, and try me;
examine my heart and mind.[h]
3 For Your faithful love is
before my eyes,
and I live by Your truth.[i]
4 I do not sit with the worthless
or associate with hypocrites.
5 I hate a crowd of evildoers,
and I do not sit with the wicked.[j]
6 I wash my hands[A] in innocence[k]
and go around Your altar, LORD,[l]
7 raising my voice in thanksgiving[m]
and telling about
Your wonderful works.[n]
8 LORD, I love the house
where You dwell,
the place where Your glory resides.[o]
9 Do not destroy me along with sinners,
or my life along with men
of bloodshed[p]
10 in whose hands are evil schemes
and whose right hands are filled
with bribes.[q]
11 But I live with integrity;
redeem me and be gracious to me.[r]
12 My foot stands on level ground;[s]
I will praise the LORD in the assemblies.[t]

[a] **25:19** Ps 3:1
[b] Ps 9:13
[c] **25:20** Ps 17:8; 31:15
[d] Ps 86:2
[e] **25:21** Ps 41:12
[f] **25:22** Ps 34:22; 130:8
[g] **26:1** 2Kg 20:3; Ps 7:8
[h] **26:2** Ps 7:9; 17:3; 139:23
[i] **26:3** Ps 40:10; 86:11
[j] **26:4-5** Ps 1:1; Pr 4:14-15
[k] **26:6** Ps 73:13
[l] Ps 43:4
[m] **26:7** Jnh 2:9
[n] Ps 9:1
[o] **26:8** Ps 27:4
[p] **26:9** Ps 28:3
[q] **26:10** Ex 23:8; Dt 16:19; Ps 15:5
[r] **26:11** Jb 31:6; Ps 7:8
[s] **26:12** Ps 27:11
[t] Ps 35:18; 40:9-10
[u] **27:1** Is 60:20; Mc 7:8
[v] Ps 28:8; 118:6
[w] **27:2** Ps 14:4
[x] Ps 9:3
[y] **27:3** Ps 3:6
[z] **27:4** Ps 23:6; 26:8
[aa] Ps 93:5
[ab] Mal 3:1
[ac] **27:5** Ps 31:20; 91:1; Is 25:4
[ad] **27:6** Ps 3:3
[ae] Ps 54:6; 116:17
[af] Eph 5:19
[ag] **27:7** Ps 4:3; 30:10
[ah] **27:8** Ps 24:6; 105:4
[ai] **27:9** Ps 69:17; 102:2; 143:7
[aj] Ps 6:1
[ak] Ps 40:17
[al] **27:9-10** Ps 37:28; 94:14

PSALM 27

My Stronghold

Davidic.

1 The LORD is my light
and my salvation —
whom should I fear?[u]
The LORD is the stronghold of my life —
of whom should I be afraid?[v]
2 When evildoers came against me
to devour my flesh,[w]
my foes and my enemies stumbled
and fell.[x]
3 Though an army deploys against me,
my heart is not afraid;
though a war breaks out against me,
still I am confident.[y]

4 I have asked one thing from the LORD;
it is what I desire:
to dwell in the house of the LORD
all the days of my life,[z]
gazing on the beauty of the LORD[aa]
and seeking Him in His temple.[ab]
5 For He will conceal me in His shelter
in the day of adversity;
He will hide me under the cover
of His tent;
He will set me high on a rock.[ac]
6 Then my head will be high
above my enemies around me;[ad]
I will offer sacrifices in His tent
with shouts of joy.[ae]
I will sing and make music to the LORD.[af]
7 LORD, hear my voice when I call;
be gracious to me and answer me.[ag]
8 My heart says this about You,
"You[B] are to seek My face."
LORD, I will seek Your face.[ah]
9 Do not hide Your face from me;[ai]
do not turn Your servant away
in anger.[aj]
You have been my helper;[ak]
do not leave me or abandon me,
God of my salvation.
10 Even if my father and mother
abandon me,
the LORD cares for me.[al]

11 Because of my adversaries,
show me Your way, LORD,

[A] **26:6** A ritual or ceremonial washing to express innocence [B] **27:8** You is plural in Hb

and lead me on a level path.[a]
12 Do not give me over to the will
of my foes,
for false witnesses rise up against me,
breathing violence.[b]
13 I am certain that I will see
the LORD's goodness
in the land of the living.[c]
14 Wait for the LORD;
be strong[A] and courageous.[d]
Wait for the LORD.[e]

PSALM 28
My Strength

Davidic.

1 LORD, I call to You;
my rock, do not be deaf to me.[f]
If You remain silent to me,
I will be like those going down
to the ˚Pit.[g]
2 Listen to the sound of my pleading
when I cry to You for help,
when I lift up my hands
toward Your holy sanctuary.[h]
3 Do not drag me away with the wicked,
with the evildoers,
who speak in friendly ways
with their neighbors
while malice is in their hearts.[i]
4 Repay them according to what
they have done—
according to the evil of their deeds.
Repay them according to the work
of their hands;
give them back what they deserve.[j]
5 Because they do not consider
what the LORD has done
or the work of His hands,
He will tear them down and not
rebuild them.[k]
6 May the LORD be praised,
for He has heard the sound
of my pleading.[l]
7 The LORD is my strength and my
shield;
my heart trusts in Him,
and I am helped.[m]

[a]27:11 Ps 25:4; 26:12 [b]27:12 Ps 35:11; 41:2; Mt 26:59-60 [c]27:13 Ex 33:19; Ps 116:9; 142:5 [d]27:14 Jos 1:6 [e]Ps 37:34; 130:5 [f]28:1 Ps 83:1 [g]Ps 88:4; 143:7 [h]28:2 Ps 28:2; 134:2; 141:2; 1Tm 2:8 [i]28:3 Ps 26:9-10 [j]28:4 Jr 50:29; Rv 18:6; 22:12 [k]28:5 Jb 34:26-28; Is 5:12 [l]28:6 Ps 31:22 [m]28:7 Gn 15:1; Dt 33:29; Ps 3:3; 5:12; 18:2; 119:114 [n]Ps 59:17; 69:30 [o]28:8 Ps 20:6; 27:1 [p]28:9 Ps 33:12; Is 40:11 [q]29:1-2 1Ch 16:28-29; Ps 96:7-9 [r]29:3 Jb 37:4-5; Ps 18:13; 104:7 [s]29:4 Ps 68:33 [t]29:5 Ps 104:16 [u]29:6 Ps 114:4,6 [v]Dt 3:8-9 [w]29:7 Dt 4:12,33 [x]29:8 Nm 13:26 [y]29:9 Jb 39:1-3 [z]Is 24:1,3 [aa]29:10 Ps 9:7; 10:17 [ab]29:11 Ps 28:8; 68:35 [ac]Php 4:7

Therefore my heart rejoices,
and I praise Him with my song.[n]
8 The LORD is the strength of His people;[B]
He is a stronghold of salvation
for His anointed.[o]
9 Save Your people,
bless Your possession,
shepherd them, and carry
them forever.[p]

PSALM 29
The Voice of the LORD

A Davidic psalm.

1 Ascribe to ˚Yahweh,
you heavenly beings,[C]
ascribe to the LORD glory and strength.
2 Ascribe to Yahweh the glory due
His name;
worship Yahweh
in the splendor of His holiness.[D,q]
3 The voice of the LORD is
above the waters.
The God of glory thunders—
the LORD, above vast waters,[r]
4 the voice of the LORD in power,
the voice of the LORD in splendor.[s]
5 The voice of the LORD
breaks the cedars;
the LORD shatters the cedars
of Lebanon.[t]
6 He makes Lebanon skip like a calf,[u]
and Sirion,[E] like a young wild ox.[v]
7 The voice of the LORD flashes
flames of fire.[w]
8 The voice of the LORD shakes
the wilderness;
the LORD shakes the wilderness
of Kadesh.[x]
9 The voice of the LORD makes the deer
give birth[F,y]
and strips the woodlands bare.[z]
In His temple all cry, "Glory!"
10 The LORD sat enthroned at the flood;
the LORD sits enthroned, King forever.[aa]
11 The LORD gives His people strength;[ab]
the LORD blesses His people
with peace.[ac]

[A]27:14 Lit *LORD; let your heart be strong* [B]28:8 Some Hb mss, LXX, Syr; other Hb mss read *strength for them* [C]29:1 Or *you angels*, or *you sons of the mighty*; lit *LORD sons of the gods* [D]29:2 Or *in holy attire*, or *in holy appearance* [E]29:6 = Mount Hermon [F]29:9 Or *the oaks shake*

Psalm 30

Joy in the Morning

A psalm; a dedication song for the house. Davidic.

1 I will exalt You, LORD,
because You have lifted me up[a]
and have not allowed my enemies
to triumph over me.[b]
2 LORD my God,
I cried to You for help,
and You healed me.[c]
3 LORD, You brought me up from ·Sheol;[d]
You spared me from among those
going down[A] to the ·Pit.[e]

4 Sing to ·Yahweh, you His faithful ones,
and praise His holy name.[f]
5 For His anger lasts only a moment,
but His favor, a lifetime.
Weeping may spend the night,
but there is joy in the morning.[g]

6 When I was secure, I said,
"I will never be shaken."[h]
7 LORD, when You showed Your favor,
You made me stand
like a strong mountain;[i]
when You hid Your face, I was terrified.[j]
8 LORD, I called to You;
I sought favor from my Lord:[k]
9 "What gain is there in my death,
if I go down to the Pit?
Will the dust praise You?
Will it proclaim Your truth?[l]
10 LORD, listen and be gracious to me;
LORD, be my helper."[m]
11 You turned my lament into dancing;
You removed my ·sackcloth
and clothed me with gladness,[n]
12 so that I can sing to You and not
be silent.
LORD my God, I will praise You forever.[o]

Psalm 31

A Plea for Protection

For the choir director. A Davidic psalm.

1 LORD, I seek refuge in You;
let me never be disgraced.[p]
Save me by Your righteousness.
2 Listen closely to me; rescue me quickly.
Be a rock of refuge for me,
a mountain fortress to save me.[q]
3 For You are my rock and my fortress;[r]
You lead and guide me
because of Your name.[s]
4 You will free me from the net
that is secretly set for me,
for You are my refuge.[t]
5 Into Your hand I entrust my spirit;[u]
You redeem[B] me, LORD, God of truth.[v]

6 I[C] hate those who are devoted
to worthless idols,
but I trust in the LORD.[w]
7 I will rejoice and be glad
in Your faithful love
because You have seen my affliction.
You have known the troubles
of my life[x]
8 and have not handed me over
to the enemy.[y]
You have set my feet
in a spacious place.[z]

9 Be gracious to me, LORD,
because I am in distress;[aa]
my eyes are worn out
from angry sorrow—
my whole being[D] as well.[ab]
10 Indeed, my life is consumed with grief
and my years with groaning;[ac]
my strength has failed
because of my sinfulness,[E]
and my bones waste away.[ad]
11 I am ridiculed by all my adversaries
and even by my neighbors.
I am dreaded by my acquaintances;
those who see me in the street
run from me.[ae]
12 I am forgotten: gone from memory
like a dead person—
like broken pottery.[af]
13 I have heard the gossip of many;
terror is on every side.[ag]
When they conspired against me,
they plotted to take my life.[ah]

14 But I trust in You, LORD;
I say, "You are my God."[ai]
15 The course of my life is in Your power;[aj]

[a] **30:1** Ps 3:3
[b] Ps 25:2; 35:19
[c] **30:2** Ps 88:13
[d] **30:3** Ps 86:13
[e] Ps 28:1; 88:4; 143:7
[f] **30:4** Ps 50:5; 149:1
[g] **30:5** Ps 103:9; Is 54:7-8; 2Co 4:17
[h] **30:6** Ps 10:6; 62:2,6
[i] **30:7** Ps 20:8
[j] Ps 104:29
[k] **30:8** Ps 119:58
[l] **30:9** Ps 6:5; 88:10-12
[m] **30:10** Ps 4:1; 27:7
[n] **30:11** Ec 3:4; Is 61:10; Jr 31:13
[o] **30:12** Ps 44:8; 108:1
[p] **31:1** Ps 25:2
[q] **31:2** Ps 71:1-2
[r] **31:3** Ps 18:2; 71:3
[s] Ps 23:3; 25:11
[t] **31:4** Ps 25:15; 46:1
[u] **31:5** Lk 23:46
[v] Ps 25:5
[w] **31:6** Ps 26:5; Jnh 2:8
[x] **31:7** Ps 10:14
[y] **31:8** Dt 32:30
[z] Jb 36:16
[aa] **31:9** Ps 69:17
[ab] Ps 6:7; 63:1
[ac] **31:10** Ps 102:3
[ad] Ps 32:3; 38:3
[ae] **31:11** Jb 19:13; Ps 38:11; 88:8,18
[af] **31:12** Ps 88:5; Ec 9:5
[ag] **31:13** Jr 20:10
[ah] Ps 41:7; Mt 27:1
[ai] **31:14** Ps 140:6
[aj] **31:15** Jb 14:5; 24:1

[A] **30:3** Some Hb mss, LXX, Theod, Orig, Syr; other Hb mss, Aq, Sym, Tg, Jer read *from going down* [B] **31:5** Or *You have redeemed*, or *You will redeem*, or *spirit. Redeem* [C] **31:6** One Hb ms, LXX, Syr, Vg, Jer read *You* [D] **31:9** Lit *my soul and my belly* [E] **31:10** LXX, Syr, Sym read *affliction*

deliver me from the power
of my enemies
and from my persecutors.[a]
16 Show Your favor to Your servant;
save me by Your faithful love.[b]
17 LORD, do not let me be disgraced
when I call on You.[c]
Let the wicked be disgraced;
let them be silent[A,B] in ·Sheol.[d]
18 Let lying lips be quieted;[e]
they speak arrogantly
against the righteous
with pride and contempt.[f]
19 How great is Your goodness
that You have stored up for those
who ·fear You
and accomplished in the sight
of ·everyone
for those who take refuge in You.[g]
20 You hide them in the protection
of Your presence;
You conceal them in a shelter[C]
from the schemes of men,
from quarrelsome tongues.[h]
21 May the LORD be praised,
for He has wonderfully shown
His faithful love to me
in a city under siege.[D,i]
22 In my alarm I had said,
"I am cut off from Your sight."[j]
But You heard the sound
of my pleading
when I cried to You for help.[k]
23 Love the LORD, all His faithful ones.[l]
The LORD protects the loyal,
but fully repays the arrogant.[m]
24 Be strong[E] and courageous,
all you who put your hope in the LORD.[n]

PSALM 32

The Joy of Forgiveness

Davidic. A ·*Maskil.*

1 How joyful is the one
whose transgression is forgiven,
whose sin is covered![o]
2 How joyful is the man
the LORD does not charge with sin[p]
and in whose spirit is no deceit![q]
3 When I kept silent, my bones
became brittle
from my groaning all day long.[r]
4 For day and night Your hand was heavy
on me;[s]
my strength was drained[F]
as in the summer's heat.[t] *·Selah*
5 Then I acknowledged my sin to You
and did not conceal my iniquity.
I said,
"I will confess my transgressions
to the LORD,"
and You took away the ·guilt of my sin.[u]
Selah
6 Therefore let everyone who is faithful
pray to You
at a time that You may be found.[G,v]
When great floodwaters come,
they will not reach him.[w]
7 You are my hiding place;[x]
You protect me from trouble.[y]
You surround me with joyful shouts
of deliverance. *Selah*
8 I will instruct you and show you
the way to go;[z]
with My eye on you, I will give counsel.[aa]
9 Do not be like a horse or mule,
without understanding,
that must be controlled with bit
and bridle
or else it will not come near you.[ab]
10 Many pains come to the wicked,[ac]
but the one who trusts in the LORD
will have faithful love
surrounding him.[ad]
11 Be glad in the LORD and rejoice,
you righteous ones;
shout for joy,
all you upright in heart.[ae]

PSALM 33

Praise to the Creator

1 Rejoice in the LORD, you righteous ones;
praise from the upright is beautiful.[af]
2 Praise the LORD with the lyre;
make music to Him
with a ten-stringed harp.[ag]
3 Sing a new song to Him;[ah]

[a] **31:15** JPs 59:1
[b] **31:16** Ps 6:4; 119:135
[c] **31:17** Ps 25:2-3,20
[d] Ps 94:17; 115:17
[e] **31:18** Ps 120:2
[f] 1Sm 2:3; Ps 94:4
[g] **31:19** Ps 5:11; 23:5
[h] **31:20** Ps 27:5; 32:7
[i] **31:21** Ps 28:6
[j] **31:22** Ps 88:5; Is 38:11-12
[k] Ps 66:19; 145:19
[l] **31:23** Ps 30:4
[m] Ps 94:2
[n] **31:24** Ps 27:14
[o] **32:1** Ps 85:2
[p] **32:1-2** Rm 4:7-8
[q] **32:2** Jn 1:47
[r] **32:3** Ps 31:10; 38:8
[s] **32:4** Jb 23:2; Ps 38:2
[t] Ps 22:15; 39:10
[u] **32:5** Lv 26:40; Ps 38:18; Pr 28:13; 1Jn 1:9
[v] **32:6** Is 55:6
[w] Ps 124:4-5; Is 43:2
[x] **32:7** Ps 31:20; 91:1
[y] Ps 121:7
[z] **32:8** Ps 25:8,12
[aa] Ps 33:18; 73:24
[ab] **32:9** Pr 26:3; Jms 3:3
[ac] **32:10** Pr 13:21; Rm 2:9
[ad] Ps 5:12
[ae] **32:11** Ps 64:10; 68:3; 97:12
[af] **33:1** Ps 32:11; 147:1; Php 4:4
[ag] **33:2** Ps 92:3; 144:9
[ah] **33:3** Ps 40:3; 96:1; Is 42:10

[A] **31:17** LXX reads *brought down* [B] **31:17** Or *them perish*, or *them wail* [C] **31:20** Lit *canopy* [D] **31:21** Or *a fortified city* [E] **31:24** Lit *Let your heart be strong* [F] **32:4** Hb obscure [G] **32:6** Lit *time of finding*

play skillfully on the strings,
with a joyful shout.[a]
4 For the word of the LORD is right,
and all His work is trustworthy.[b]
5 He loves righteousness
and justice;[c]
the earth is full of the LORD's
unfailing love.[d]

[a]33:3 Ps 150:4 [b]33:4 Ps 19:8 [c]33:5 Ps 11:7; 37:28 [d]Ps 119:64 [e]33:6 Heb 11:3; 2Pt 3:5 [f]Jb 26:13; Ps 104:30 [g]33:7 Ex 15:8; Jos 3:13; Ps 78:13

6 The heavens were made by the word
of the LORD,[e]
and all the stars, by the breath
of His mouth.[f]
7 He gathers the waters of the sea
into a heap;[A]
He puts the depths
into storehouses.[g]

Sing a New Song

Mike Harland

Ironic isn't it? The oldest collection of songs known to man includes the admonition to "sing a new song" to the Lord. Six times in the Psalms the exhortation is clear: "Sing a new song to Him" (33:3, 40:3, 96:1, 98:1, 144:9, 149:1).

It makes sense that God would invite us to create new expressions of worship as we praise Him. After all, we are created in His image and of all the titles we give Him, "Creator" is one He gave Himself (Col 1:16). Our inclination to create is one of God's fingerprints on us, one of the ways we reflect His nature. No other part of His creation "creates." We alone share that trait with God.

For clarity's sake it is helpful to see the other references in Scripture that call for "new songs." Isaiah 42:40 reads, "Sing a new song to the Lord; sing His praise from the ends of the earth . . ."

The prophet continues in the next seven verses to describe the vast reach of the praise of our God, across groups of people and mountain ranges of land. No barrier—whether man made or God created—will thwart the new song of praise from God's people.

There are two references to new songs in the New Testament. In Revelation 5:9, the elders fall down before the Lamb and sing a song that fills the halls of heaven. It begins with, "You are worthy to take the scroll . . ." Revelation 14:3 reads, "They sang a new song before the throne . . ." It is noteworthy that just one chapter later the song of God's servant Moses is sung in heaven, proving that old songs will be part of eternity as well (15:3).

So what makes a song "new?" And what is the significance of the Psalmists' exhortation for the worshiper to sing "new songs" to the Lord? It comes with the realization that the qualities of the song itself are not what make it "new."

Think of it this way: your great-grandmother's recipe for bread has been passed on to you and every time you assemble the ingredients to prepare them just the way she used to a hundred years ago, you get the finest bread you have ever tasted. The recipe is old, but the bread you enjoy is fresh and new.

The "new song" does not have new ingredients. The song of faith from today's worshiper has the same truth of the song of faith the Psalmist gave centuries ago. But it must be assembled and prepared in a new heart. The only thing new about the song is the heart of the believer that sings it. And when we sing the new song of praise to the Lord, the world around can smell the freshness of our offering and be drawn in to taste and see the goodness of our God in the person of Jesus Christ, the bread of life.

Sing a new song to the Lord. Let that be our mission.

[A]33:7 LXX, Tg, Syr, Vg, Jer read *sea as in a bottle*

8 Let the whole earth tremble
before the LORD;
let all the inhabitants of the world
stand in awe of Him.[a]
9 For He spoke, and it came into being;
He commanded, and it came
into existence.[b]
10 The LORD frustrates the counsel
of the nations;
He thwarts the plans of the peoples.[c]
11 The counsel of the LORD stands forever,
the plans of His heart from generation
to generation.[d]
12 Happy is the nation whose God
is ˚Yahweh —
the people He has chosen to be
His own possession![e]
13 The LORD looks down from heaven;
He observes everyone.[f]
14 He gazes on all the inhabitants
of the earth
from His dwelling place.[g]
15 He alone shapes their hearts;
He considers all their works.[h]
16 A king is not saved by a large army;
a warrior will not be delivered
by great strength.[i]
17 The horse is a false hope for safety;
it provides no escape by its great power.[j]
18 Now the eye of the LORD is on those
who ˚fear Him —
those who depend on His faithful love[k]
19 to deliver them from death
and to keep them alive in famine.[l]
20 We wait for Yahweh;[m]
He is our help and shield.[n]
21 For our hearts rejoice in Him[o]
because we trust in His holy name.[p]
22 May Your faithful love rest on us, Yahweh,
for we put our hope in You.[q]

PSALM 34

The LORD Delivers the Righteous

Concerning David, when he pretended to be insane in the presence of Abimelech,[A,r] who drove him out, and he departed.

1 I[B] will praise the LORD at all times;
His praise will always be on my lips.[s]
2 I will boast in the LORD;[t]
the humble will hear and be glad.[u]
3 Proclaim ˚Yahweh's greatness with me;[v]
let us exalt His name together.[w]

4 I sought the LORD, and He answered me
and delivered me from all my fears.[x]
5 Those who look to Him are[C] radiant
with joy;[y]
their faces will never be ashamed.[z]
6 This poor man cried, and the LORD
heard him
and saved him from all his troubles.[aa]
7 The Angel of the LORD encamps
around those who ˚fear Him,
and rescues them.[ab]

8 Taste and see that the LORD is good.[ac]
How happy is the man who takes refuge
in Him![ad]
9 You who are His holy ones, fear Yahweh,
for those who fear Him lack nothing.[ae]
10 Young lions[D] lack food and go hungry,[af]
but those who seek the LORD
will not lack any good thing.[ag]

11 Come, children, listen to me;
I will teach you the fear of the LORD.[ah]
12 Who is the man who delights in life,
loving a long life to enjoy what is good?[ai]
13 Keep your tongue from evil
and your lips from deceitful speech.[aj]
14 Turn away from evil and do
what is good;[ak]
seek peace and pursue it.[al]

15 The eyes of the LORD are
on the righteous,
and His ears are open to their cry
for help.[am]
16 The face of the LORD is set
against those who do what is evil,[an]
to erase[E] all memory of them
from the earth.[ao]
17 The righteous[F] cry out,
and the LORD hears,
and delivers them from all
their troubles.[ap]
18 The LORD is near the brokenhearted;
He saves those crushed in spirit.[aq]

[a] 33:8 Ps 67:7; 96:9 [b] 33:9 Gn 1:3; Ps 147:15,18; 148:5 [c] 33:10 Ps 2:1-3; Is 8:10; 19:3 [d] 33:11 Ps 139:17; Pr 19:21; Is 55:8 [e] 33:12 Ex 19:5; Dt 7:6; Ps 144:15 [f] 33:13 Jb 28:24; Ps 11:4; 14:2; 53:2 [g] 33:14 Ps 102:19 [h] 33:15 Jb 34:21 [i] 33:16 Ps 44:6; 60:11 [j] 33:17 Ps 20:7; 147:10; Hs 1:7 [k] 33:18 Jb 36:7; Ps 34:15; 1Pt 3:12 [l] 33:19 Jb 5:20; Ps 37:19; 56:13 [m] 33:20 Ps 130:6; Is 8:17 [n] Gn 15:1; Dt 33:29; Ps 3:3; 5:12; 18:2; 28:7; 115:9-11 [o] 33:21 Ps 13:5; 28:7; Jn 16:22 [p] Zph 3:12 [q] 33:22 Ps 130:7; 147:11 [r] 34:title 1Sm 21:10-15 [s] 34:1 Ps 71:6; Eph 5:20 [t] 34:2 Ps 44:8; Jr 9:24; 1Co 1:31 [u] Ps 69:32 [v] 34:3 Lk 1:46 [w] Ps 69:30 [x] 34:4 Ps 34:6,17,19 [y] 34:5 Is 60:5 [z] Ps 25:3 [aa] 34:6 Ps 34:4 [ab] 34:7 Ps 91:11; Heb 1:14 [ac] 34:8 1Pt 2:3 [ad] Ps 2:12 [ae] 34:9 Ps 23:1 [af] 34:10 Jb 4:10-11 [ag] Ps 84:11 [ah] 34:11 Ps 66:16; 111:10 [ai] 34:12 Ec 3:13; 6:6 [aj] 34:13 Ps 39:1; 141:3; Pr 13:3; Jms 1:26 [ak] 34:14 Ps 37:27; Is 1:16-17 [al] Rm 14:19; Heb 12:14 [am] 34:15 Jb 36:7; Ps 33:18; 1Pt 3:12 [an] 34:12-16 1Pt 3:10-12 [ao] 34:16 Am 9:4 [ap] 34:17 Ps 145:19 [aq] 34:18 Ps 51:17; 147:3; Is 61:1

[A] **34:title** Probably Achish, king of Gath [B] **34:1** The lines of this poem form an ˚acrostic. [C] **34:5** Some Hb mss, LXX, Aq, Syr, Jer read *Look to Him and be* [D] **34:10** LXX, Syr, Vg read *The rich* [E] **34:16** Or *cut off* [F] **34:17** Lit *They*

19 Many adversities come to the one
who is righteous,
but the LORD delivers him
from them all.[a]
20 He protects all his bones;
not one of them is broken.[b]
21 Evil brings death to the wicked,
and those who hate the righteous
will be punished.[c]
22 The LORD redeems the life
of His servants,
and all who take refuge in Him will not
be punished.[d]

PSALM 35
Prayer for Victory

Davidic.

1 Oppose my opponents, LORD;
fight those who fight me.[e]
2 Take Your shields — large and small —
and come to my aid.[f]
3 Draw the spear and javelin
against my pursuers,
and assure me: "I am
your deliverance."[g]

4 Let those who seek to kill me
be disgraced and humiliated;
let those who plan to harm me
be turned back and ashamed.[h]
5 Let them be like chaff in the wind,
with the angel of the LORD
driving them away.[i]
6 Let their way be dark and slippery,
with the angel of the LORD
pursuing them.[j]
7 They hid their net for me
without cause;
they dug a pit for me without cause.[k]
8 Let ruin come on him unexpectedly,
and let the net that he hid
ensnare him;
let him fall into it — to his ruin.[l]

9 Then I will rejoice in the LORD;
I will delight in His deliverance.[m]
10 My very bones will say,
"LORD, who is like You,[n]
rescuing the poor from one too strong
for him,
the poor or the needy from one
who robs him?"[o]

11 Malicious witnesses come forward;
they question me about things
I do not know.[p]
12 They repay me evil for good,
making me desolate.[q]
13 Yet when they were sick,
my clothing was ˙sackcloth;
I humbled myself with fasting,
and my prayer was genuine.[A,r]
14 I went about grieving as if for my friend
or brother;
I was bowed down with grief,
like one mourning a mother.[s]
15 But when I stumbled, they gathered
in glee;
they gathered against me.
Assailants I did not know
tore at me and did not stop.[t]
16 With godless mockery[B]
they gnashed their teeth at me.[u]

17 Lord, how long will You look on?[v]
Rescue my life from their ravages,
my only one from the young lions.[w]
18 I will praise You
in the great congregation;
I will exalt You
among many people.[x]
19 Do not let my deceitful enemies rejoice
over me;
do not let those who hate me
without cause[y]
look at me maliciously.[z]
20 For they do not speak
in friendly ways,
but contrive deceitful schemes[C]
against those who live peacefully
in the land.[aa]
21 They open their mouths wide
against me and say,
"Aha, aha! We saw it!"[D,ab]

22 You saw it, LORD; do not be silent.
Lord, do not be far from me.[ac]
23 Wake up and rise to my defense,
to my cause, my God and my LORD![ad]
24 Vindicate me, LORD my God,
in keeping with Your righteousness,

[a]**34:19** Ps 71:20; 2Tm 3:11-12 [b]**34:20** Jn 19:33,36 [c]**34:21** Ps 94:23; 140:11; Pr 24:16 [d]**34:22** Ps 37:40; Rm 8:33-34 [e]**35:1** Ex 14:25; Is 49:25 [f]**35:2** Ps 5:12; 91:4 [g]**35:3** Ps 13:5; 40:17 [h]**35:4** Ps 40:14; 70:2; 129:5 [i]**35:5** Jb 21:18; Ps 83:13; Is 29:5 [j]**35:6** Ps 73:18; Jr 23:12 [k]**35:7** Ps 140:5 [l]**35:8** Jb 18:8; Ps 7:15 [m]**35:9** Ps 9:14; 13:5 [n]**35:10** Ex 15:11; Ps 86:8; Mc 7:18 [o]Ps 72:12; 82:4 [p]**35:11** Ps 27:12; Pr 19:5,9 [q]**35:12** Ps 38:20; 109:5; Jr 18:20 [r]**35:13** Ps 69:10-11 [s]**35:14** Ps 38:6 [t]**35:15** Jb 30:1,8,12; Ob 12 [u]**35:16** Jb 16:9; Ps 37:12; Lm 2:16 [v]**35:17** Ps 13:1; Hab 1:13 [w]Ps 22:20-21 [x]**35:18** Ps 22:22,25; 40:9-10; Heb 2:12 [y]**35:19** Ps 38:19; Jn 15:25 [z]Ps 13:4; 30:1; 38:16 [aa]**35:20** Ps 55:21; Jr 9:8; Mc 6:12 [ab]**35:21** Jb 16:10; Ps 22:13; 40:15; 70:3 [ac]**35:22** Ps 10:1; 22:11; 28:1 [ad]**35:23** Ps 7:6; 44:23; 59:4

A**35:13** Lit *prayer returned to my chest* B**35:16** Hb obscure C**35:20** Lit *but devise deceitful words* D**35:21** Lit *Our eyes saw!*

and do not let them rejoice over me.[a]
25 Do not let them say in their hearts,
"Aha! Just what we wanted."
Do not let them say,
"We have swallowed him up!"[b]
26 Let those who rejoice
at my misfortune
be disgraced and humiliated;
let those who exalt themselves over me
be clothed with shame and reproach.[c]
27 Let those who want my vindication
shout for joy and be glad;
let them continually say,
"The LORD be exalted.
He takes pleasure in
His servant's well-being."[d]
28 And my tongue will proclaim
Your righteousness,
Your praise all day long.[e]

PSALM 36

Human Wickedness and God's Love

For the choir director. A psalm of David, the LORD's servant.

1 An ˹oracle within my heart
concerning the transgression of the
wicked person:
There is no dread of God
before his eyes,[f]
2 for in his own eyes he flatters himself
too much
to discover and hate his sin.[g]
3 The words of his mouth are malicious
and deceptive;[h]
he has stopped acting wisely
and doing good.[i]
4 Even on his bed he makes
malicious plans.[j]
He sets himself on a path
that is not good
and does not reject evil.[k]
5 LORD, Your faithful love reaches
to heaven,
Your faithfulness to the clouds.[l]
6 Your righteousness is
like the highest mountains;
Your judgments, like the deepest sea.[m]
LORD, You preserve man and beast.[n]
7 God, Your faithful love is so valuable
that ˹people take refuge in the shadow
of Your wings.[o]
8 They are filled from the abundance
of Your house;
You let them drink
from Your refreshing stream,[p]
9 for with You is life's fountain.[q]
In Your light we will see light.[r]
10 Spread Your faithful love over those
who know You,
and Your righteousness
over the upright in heart.[s]
11 Do not let the foot of the arrogant man
come near me
or the hand of the wicked one
drive me away.[t]
12 There the evildoers fall;
they have been thrown down
and cannot rise.[u]

PSALM 37

Instruction in Wisdom

Davidic.

1 Do[A] not be agitated by evildoers;
do not envy those who do wrong.[v]
2 For they wither quickly like grass
and wilt like tender green plants.[w]
3 Trust in the LORD and do
what is good;[x]
dwell in the land and live securely.[B,y]
4 Take delight in the LORD,
and He will give you
your heart's desires.[z]
5 Commit your way to the LORD;
trust in Him, and He will act,[aa]
6 making your righteousness shine
like the dawn,
your justice like the noonday.[ab]
7 Be silent before the LORD and wait
expectantly for Him;[ac]
do not be agitated by one who prospers
in his way,
by the man who carries out evil plans.[ad]
8 Refrain from anger and give up
your rage;
do not be agitated — it can only
bring harm.[ae]

[a]**35:24** Ps 26:1; 43:1 [b]**35:25** Ps 124:3; Lm 2:16 [c]**35:26** Jb 8:22; Ps 40:14; 109:29 [d]**35:27** Ps 40:16; 70:4 [e]**35:28** Ps 71:8,15,24 [f]**36:1** Rm 3:18 [g]**36:2** Dt 29:19; Ps 10:3; 49:18 [h]**36:3** Ps 10:7 [i]Jr 4:22 [j]**36:4** Pr 4:16 [k]Ps 10:7; Is 65:2 [l]**36:5** Ps 57:10; 103:11; 108:4 [m]**36:6** Ps 71:19 [n]Ps 104:14-15 [o]**36:7** Ru 2:12; Ps 17:8; 57:1; 91:4 [p]**36:8** Ps 46:4; 65:4; Jr 31:12-14 [q]**36:9** Jn 4:10,14 [r]Jn 1:9; Ac 26:18 [s]**36:10** Pr 11:6; Jr 22:16 [t]**36:11** Ps 38:16; 119:122 [u]**36:12** Ps 1:5; 140:10; Is 26:14 [v]**37:1** Ps 73:3; Pr 3:31; 23:17; 24:19 [w]**37:2** Ps 92:7; 129:6; Jms 1:11 [x]**37:3** Ps 62:8 [y]Pr 2:21 [z]**37:4** Ps 21:2; 145:19; Is 58:14 [aa]**37:5** Ps 55:22; Pr 16:3; 1Pt 5:7 [ab]**37:6** Ps 97:11; Is 58:8,10 [ac]**37:7** Ps 40:1; Lm 3:26 [ad]Jr 12:1 [ae]**37:8** Eph 4:31; Col 3:8

[A]**37:1** The lines of this poem form an ˹acrostic. [B]**37:3** Or *and cultivate faithfulness*

9 For evildoers will be destroyed,
but those who put their hope
in the LORD
will inherit the land.[A,a]
10 A little while, and the wicked person
will be no more;
though you look for him, he will not
be there.[b]
11 But the humble will inherit the land[A,c]
and will enjoy abundant prosperity.[d]
12 The wicked person schemes
against the righteous
and gnashes his teeth at him.[e]
13 The Lord laughs at him[f]
because He sees that his day is coming.[g]
14 The wicked have drawn the sword
and strung the[B] bow
to bring down the afflicted and needy
and to slaughter those whose way
is upright.[h]
15 Their swords will enter their own hearts,
and their bows will be broken.[i]

[a]37:9 Pr 2:21; Is 57:13; 60:21 [b]37:10 Jb 7:10; 24:24; Ps 37:35-36 [c]37:11 Mt 5:5 [d]Ps 72:7 [e]37:12 Ps 31:13,20; 35:16 [f]37:13 Ps 2:4; 59:8; Hab 1:10 [g]1Sm 26:10 [h]37:14 Ps 11:2; Lm 2:4 [i]37:15 1Sm 2:4; Ps 46:9 [j]37:16 Pr 15:16; 16:8 [k]37:17 Ps 10:15 [l]Ps 145:14 [m]37:18 Ps 1:6 [n]37:19 Jb 5:20; Ps 33:19 [o]37:20 Ps 68:2; Hs 13:3

16 The little that the righteous man has
is better
than the abundance
of many wicked people.[j]
17 For the arms[C] of the wicked
will be broken,[k]
but the LORD supports the righteous.[l]
18 The LORD watches over the blameless
all their days,
and their inheritance will last forever.[m]
19 They will not be disgraced in times
of adversity;
they will be satisfied in days
of hunger.[n]
20 But the wicked will perish;
the LORD's enemies, like the glory
of the pastures,
will fade away —
they will fade away like smoke.[o]
21 The wicked man borrows
and does not repay,

PRAYING FOR THE WORLD

A Call for Justice

Justice fares badly in societies under totalitarian regimes. But in democracies, too, justice can often seem to be in short supply. We thank the Lord for those who seek true justice and plead the cause of the weak and the needy. God's Word is not partial to the powerful; indeed, God cares for the neediest among us.

Democracies that confess to honor Christian values must use their power to press for freedom and justice for all their citizens. God's people, too, must always work for justice even as they spread the gospel message. The mission here takes courage, pushing powers to acknowledge God's will for all people, bringing justice with the message of freedom in Christ.

God of justice, righteousness, and truth, we pray for missionaries who bring the gospel of liberty to nations abroad. They witness the fear and affliction of those living under the yoke of abuse and injustice.

But, Lord, where protest, advocacy, and pleadings have brought relief and restitution, we thank You. Where prayers have dissolved bondage, we thank You. Where the power of Your Word inclined the hearts of rulers to right wrongs, we thank You. Where authorities, because of Your promptings, created better conditions, we thank You. Where our governments were diligent in defending justice, we thank You. Where, in our private dealings, we sought honesty and fairness, even at the cost of personal comfort, we thank You.

May "your righteousness shine like the dawn, your justice like the noonday" (Ps 37:6). Amen.

[A]37:9,11 Or *earth* [B]37:14 Lit *their* [C]37:17 Or *power*

but the righteous one is gracious
and giving.[a]
22 Those who are blessed by Him
will inherit the land,[A]
but those cursed by Him
will be destroyed.[b]

23 A man's steps are established
by the LORD,
and He takes pleasure in his way.[c]
24 Though he falls, he will not
be overwhelmed,
because the LORD holds his hand.[B,d]

25 I have been young and now I am old,
yet I have not seen
the righteous abandoned
or his children begging for bread.[e]
26 He is always generous, always lending,
and his children are a blessing.[f]

27 Turn away from evil and do
what is good,
and dwell there[C] forever.[g]
28 For the LORD loves justice
and will not abandon
His faithful ones.[h]
They are kept safe forever,
but the children of the wicked
will be destroyed.[i]
29 The righteous will inherit the land[A]
and dwell in it permanently.[j]

30 The mouth of the righteous
utters wisdom;
his tongue speaks what is just.[k]
31 The instruction of his God is
in his heart;
his steps do not falter.[l]

32 The wicked one lies in wait
for the righteous
and seeks to kill him;[m]
33 the LORD will not leave him
in the power of the wicked one
or allow him to be condemned
when he is judged.[n]

34 Wait for the LORD and keep His way,
and He will exalt you to inherit
the land.
You will watch when the wicked
are destroyed.[o]

35 I have seen a wicked, violent man
well-rooted[D] like
a flourishing native tree.[p]
36 Then I passed by and[E] noticed
he was gone;
I searched for him, but he could not
be found.[q]

37 Watch the blameless and observe
the upright,
for the man of peace will have
a future.[F,r]
38 But transgressors will all be eliminated;
the future[F] of the wicked
will be destroyed.[s]

39 The salvation of the righteous is
from the LORD,
their refuge in a time of distress.[t]
40 The LORD helps and delivers them;
He will deliver them from the wicked
and will save them
because they take refuge in Him.[u]

PSALM 38

Prayer of a Suffering Sinner

A Davidic psalm for remembrance.[v]

1 LORD, do not punish me in Your anger
or discipline me in Your wrath.[w]
2 For Your arrows have sunk into me,
and Your hand has pressed down
on me.[x]

3 There is no health in my body
because of Your indignation;
there is no strength[G] in my bones
because of my sin.[y]
4 For my sins have flooded
over my head;
they are a burden too heavy for me
to bear.[z]

5 My wounds are foul and festering
because of my foolishness.[aa]
6 I am bent over and brought low;
all day long I go around in mourning.[ab]
7 For my loins are full of burning pain,
and there is no health in my body.[ac]
8 I am faint and severely crushed;
I groan because of the anguish
of my heart.[ad]

[a]**37:21** Ps 112:5,9
[b]**37:22** Pr 3:33
[c]**37:23** 1Sm 2:9; Ps 66:9
[d]**37:24** Ps 145:14; Pr 24:16; Mc 7:8
[e]**37:25** Is 41:17
[f]**37:26** Dt 15:8; Ps 112:5,9; Mt 5:42
[g]**37:27** Ps 34:14; 102:28
[h]**37:28** Dt 31:6; Heb 13:5
[i]Ps 21:10; Pr 2:22
[j]**37:29** Pr 2:21; Is 60:21
[k]**37:30** Ps 49:3; 119:13; Pr 10:13
[l]**37:31** Dt 6:6; Ps 40:8; 119:11
[m]**37:32** Ps 10:8; 17:11
[n]**37:33** Ps 34:22; 109:31; 2Pt 2:9
[o]**37:34** Ps 27:14; 52:5-6; 91:8
[p]**37:35** Jb 5:3; Jr 12:2
[q]**37:36** Jb 20:5
[r]**37:37** Is 57:1-2
[s]**37:38** Ps 1:4-6; Pr 2:22
[t]**37:39** Ps 3:8; 9:9; 62:1
[u]**37:40** Ps 22:4; 34:22; 54:4
[v]**38:title** Ps 70 title
[w]**38:1** Ps 6:1
[x]**38:2** Jb 6:4; Ps 32:4
[y]**38:3** Jb 33:19; Ps 31:10; 102:10
[z]**38:4** Ezr 9:6; Ps 40:12
[aa]**38:5** Is 1:6
[ab]**38:6** Ps 35:14
[ac]**38:7** Ps 38:3; Lm 1:13
[ad]**38:8** Jb 3:24; Ps 6:6; 32:3; Lm 2:11

[A]**37:22,29** Or *earth* [B]**37:24** Or *LORD supports with His hand* [C]**37:27** = dwell in the land [D]**37:35** Hb obscure [E]**37:36** DSS, LXX, Syr, Vg, Jer; MT reads *Then he passed away, and I* [F]**37:37,38** Or *posterity* [G]**38:3** Hb *shalom*

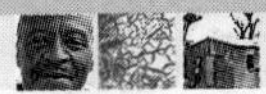

9 Lord, my every desire is known
to[A] You;
my sighing is not hidden from You.[a]
10 My heart races, my strength leaves me,
and even the light of my eyes
has faded.[B,b]
11 My loved ones and friends stand back
from my affliction,
and my relatives stand at a distance.[c]
12 Those who seek my life set traps,
and those who want to harm me
threaten to destroy me;
they plot treachery all day long.[d]
13 I am like a deaf person; I do not hear.
I am like a speechless person
who does not open his mouth.[e]
14 I am like a man who does not hear
and has no arguments in his mouth.[f]
15 I put my hope in You, LORD;
You will answer, Lord my God.[g]
16 For I said, "Don't let them rejoice
over me—
those who are arrogant toward me
when I stumble."[h]
17 For I am about to fall,
and my pain is constantly with me.[i]
18 So I confess my •guilt;
I am anxious because of my sin.[j]
19 But my enemies are vigorous
and powerful;[C]
many hate me for no reason.[k]
20 Those who repay evil for good
attack me for pursuing good.[l]
21 LORD, do not abandon me;
my God, do not be far from me.[m]
22 Hurry to help me,
Lord, my Savior.[n]

PSALM 39

The Fleeting Nature of Life

For the choir director, for Jeduthun.
A Davidic psalm.

1 I said, "I will guard my ways
so that I may not sin with my tongue;
I will guard my mouth with a muzzle
as long as the wicked are
in my presence."[o]
2 I was speechless and quiet;
I kept silent, even from speaking good,
and my pain intensified.[p]
3 My heart grew hot within me;
as I mused, a fire burned.[q]
I spoke with my tongue:
4 "LORD, reveal to me the end of my life
and the number of my days.
Let me know how short-lived I am.[r]
5 You, indeed, have made my days short
in length,
and my life span as nothing
in Your sight.
Yes, every mortal man is only a vapor.[s]
•Selah
6 "Certainly, man walks about
like a mere shadow.
Indeed, they frantically rush around
in vain,
gathering possessions
without knowing who will get them.[t]
7 Now, Lord, what do I wait for?
My hope is in You.[u]
8 Deliver me from all my transgressions;
do not make me the taunt of fools.[v]
9 I am speechless; I do not open my mouth
because of what You have done.[w]
10 Remove Your torment from me;
I fade away because of the force
of Your hand.[x]
11 You discipline a man with punishment
for sin,
consuming like a moth what is precious
to him;[y]
every man is only a vapor.[z] *Selah*
12 "Hear my prayer, LORD,
and listen to my cry for help;
do not be silent at my tears.[aa]
For I am a foreigner residing with You,
a temporary resident like all my fathers.[ab]
13 Turn Your angry gaze from me
so that I may be cheered up
before I die and am gone."[ac]

PSALM 40

Thanksgiving and a Cry for Help

For the choir director. A Davidic psalm.

1 I waited patiently for the LORD,
and He turned to me and heard my cry
for help.[ad]

[a]38:9 Ps 10:17 [b]38:10 Ps 6:7; 69:3; 88:9 [c]38:11 Jb 19:13-20; Ps 31:11; 88:18 [d]38:12 Ps 35:4,20; 54:3; 140:5 [e]38:13 Ps 39:2,9 [f]38:14 Jb 23:4 [g]38:15 Ps 17:6; 39:7 [h]38:16 Ps 13:4; 35:26 [i]38:17 Ps 13:2; 35:15 [j]38:18 Ps 32:5; 2Co 7:9-10 [k]38:19 Ps 18:17; 35:19 [l]38:20 Ps 35:12; 109:5; 3Jn 11 [m]38:21 Ps 22:19; 35:22 [n]38:22 Ps 40:13,17 [o]39:1 Ps 34:13; Jms 3:5-12 [p]39:2 Jb 40:4; Ps 38:13 [q]39:3 Ps 32:4; Jr 20:9; Lk 24:32 [r]39:4 Ps 78:39; 90:12; 103:14 [s]39:5 Ps 62:9; 89:47; 144:4 [t]39:6 Ps 49:10; Ec 2:18-19; Lk 12:20; 1Co 7:31 [u]39:7 Ps 38:15 [v]39:8 Ps 44:13; 79:4; 119:22 [w]39:9 Ps 39:2 [x]39:10 Jb 9:34; 13:21; Ps 32:4 [y]39:11 Is 50:9 [z]Ps 39:5 [aa]39:12 Ps 35:22 [ab]1Ch 29:15; Heb 11:13; 1Pt 2:11 [ac]39:13 Jb 7:19; 10:20-21; Ps 102:24 [ad]40:1 Ps 27:14; 34:15; 37:7

[A]38:9 Lit is *in front of* [B]38:10 Or *and the light of my eyes—even that is not with me* [C]38:19 Or *numerous*

2 He brought me up
from a desolate[A] pit,
out of the muddy clay,[a]
and set my feet on a rock,
making my steps secure.[b]
3 He put a new song in my mouth,
a hymn of praise to our God.[c]
Many will see and fear
and put their trust in the LORD.[d]

4 How happy is the man
who has put his trust in the LORD
and has not turned to the proud
or to those who run after lies![e]
5 LORD my God, You have done
many things—
Your wonderful works and Your plans
for us;
none can compare with You.
If I were to report and speak of them,
they are more than can be told.[f]

6 You do not delight in sacrifice
and offering;
You open my ears to listen.[B]
You do not ask for
a whole ˙burnt offering
or a ˙sin offering.[g]
7 Then I said, "See, I have come;
it is written about me in the volume
of the scroll.[h]
8 I delight to do Your will, my God;[i]
Your instruction lives within me."[C,j]

9 I proclaim righteousness
in the great assembly;
see, I do not keep my mouth closed[D]—
as You know, LORD.[k]
10 I did not hide Your righteousness
in my heart;
I spoke about Your faithfulness
and salvation;
I did not conceal Your constant love
and truth
from the great assembly.[l]

11 LORD, do not withhold
Your compassion from me;
Your constant love and truth
will always guard me.[m]
12 For troubles without number
have surrounded me;
my sins have overtaken me; I am unable
to see.
They are more than the hairs
of my head,
and my courage leaves me.[n]
13 LORD, be pleased to deliver me;
hurry to help me, LORD.[o]

14 Let those who seek to take my life
be disgraced and confounded.
Let those who wish me harm
be driven back and humiliated.[p]
15 Let those who say to me, "Aha, aha!"
be horrified because of their shame.[q]
16 Let all who seek You rejoice and be glad
in You;
let those who love Your salvation
continually say,
"The LORD is great!"[r]
17 I am afflicted and needy;
the Lord thinks of me.
You are my helper and my deliverer;
my God, do not delay.[s]

PSALM 41

Victory in Spite of Betrayal

For the choir director. A Davidic psalm.

1 Happy is one who cares for the poor;
the LORD will save him in a day
of adversity.[t]
2 The LORD will keep him
and preserve him;
he will be blessed in the land.[u]
You will not give him over to the desire
of his enemies.[v]
3 The LORD will sustain him
on his sickbed;
You will heal him on the bed
where he lies.[w]

4 I said, "LORD, be gracious to me;
heal me, for I have sinned
against You."[x]
5 My enemies speak maliciously
about me:
"When will he die and be forgotten?"[y]
6 When one of them comes to visit,
he speaks deceitfully;
he stores up evil in his heart;
he goes out and talks.[z]

[a] **40:2** Ps 69:2,14
[b] Ps 27:5; 37:23
[c] **40:3** Ps 33:3
[d] Dt 13:11
[e] **40:4** Jb 23:11; Ps 84:12
[f] **40:5** Jb 5:9; Ps 71:15; 139:17-18
[g] **40:6** 1Sm 15:22; Ps 51:16; Am 5:22
[h] **40:7** Lk 24:44
[i] **40:8** Ps 119:16,24; Jn 4:34
[j] **40:6-8** Ps 119:11; Heb 10:5-9
[k] **40:9** Ps 22:22,25
[l] **40:10** Ac 20:20
[m] **40:11** Ps 36:5; 57:3; 61:7
[n] **40:12** Ps 38:4; 65:3
[o] **40:13** Ps 70:1
[p] **40:14** Ps 35:4,26; 63:9; 70:2
[q] **40:15** Ps 35:21,25; 70:3
[r] **40:16** Ps 35:27; 70:4
[s] **40:17** Ps 86:1; 109:22
[t] **41:1** Ps 82:3-4; Pr 14:21
[u] **41:2** Ps 37:22,28
[v] Ps 27:12
[w] **41:3** Jr 17:14
[x] **41:4** Ps 6:2; 51:4
[y] **41:5** Ps 38:12
[z] **41:6** Ps 12:2; 62:4; Pr 26:24-26

[A] **40:2** Or *watery* [B] **40:6** Lit *You hollow out ears for me* [C] **40:8** Lit *instruction within my inner being* [D] **40:9** Lit *not restrain my lips*

7 All who hate me whisper together
about me;
they plan to harm me.[a]
8 "Lethal poison has been poured
into him,
and he won't rise again from where
he lies!"[b]
9 Even my friend[A] in whom I trusted,
one who ate my bread,
has raised his heel against me.[c]

10 But You, LORD, be gracious to me
and raise me up;
then I will repay them.[d]
11 By this I know that You delight in me:[e]
my enemy does not shout in triumph
over me.[f]
12 You supported me because of
my integrity[g]
and set me in Your presence forever.[h]

13 May •Yahweh, the God of Israel,
be praised
from everlasting to everlasting.
•Amen and amen.[i]

BOOK II
(Psalms 42–72)

Psalm 42
Longing for God

For the choir director. A •*Maskil*
of the sons of Korah.

1 As a deer longs for streams of water,
so I long for You, God.[j]
2 I thirst for God, the living God.
When can I come and appear
before God?[k]
3 My tears have been my food
day and night,
while all day long people say to me,
"Where is your God?"[l]
4 I remember this as I pour out
my heart:[m]
how I walked with many,
leading the festive procession
to the house of God,
with joyful and thankful shouts.[n]
5 Why am I so depressed?
Why this turmoil within me?
Put your hope in God, for I will
still praise Him,
my Savior and my God.[o]
6 I[B] am deeply depressed;
therefore I remember You
from the land of Jordan
and the peaks of Hermon,
from Mount Mizar.[p]
7 Deep calls to deep in the roar
of Your waterfalls;
all Your breakers and Your billows
have swept over me.[q]
8 The LORD will send His faithful love
by day;[r]
His song will be with me in the night—
a prayer to the God of my life.
9 I will say to God, my rock,[s]
"Why have You forgotten me?
Why must I go about in sorrow
because of the enemy's oppression?"[t]
10 My adversaries taunt me,
as if crushing my bones,
while all day long they say to me,
"Where is your God?"[u]
11 Why am I so depressed?
Why this turmoil within me?
Put your hope in God, for I will
still praise Him,
my Savior and my God.[v]

Psalm 43[C]

1 Vindicate me, God, and defend my cause
against an ungodly nation;
rescue me from the deceitful
and unjust man.[w]
2 For You are the God of my refuge.
Why have You rejected me?
Why must I go about in sorrow
because of the enemy's oppression?[x]

3 Send Your light and Your truth;
let them lead me.[y]
Let them bring me
to Your holy mountain,
to Your dwelling place.[z]
4 Then I will come to the altar of God,
to God, my greatest joy.[aa]
I will praise You with the lyre,
God, my God.[ab]

[a]**41:7** Ps 56:5
[b]**41:8** Ps 71:10-11
[c]**41:9** Jb 19:19; Ps 55:12-13; Jn 13:18
[d]**41:10** Ps 9:13
[e]**41:11** Ps 37:23
[f]Ps 25:2
[g]**41:12** Ps 37:17
[h]Ps 21:6
[i]**41:13** Ps 72:18-19; 89:52
[j]**42:1** Ps 84:2; 119:131
[k]**42:2** Ps 63:1
[l]**42:3** Ps 79:10; 115:2
[m]**42:4** Ps 62:8
[n]Ps 55:14; 100:4
[o]**42:5** Ps 38:6; 43:5; Mt 26:38
[p]**42:6** Ps 61:2; Jnh 2:7
[q]**42:7** Ps 69:1-2; Jnh 2:3
[r]**42:8** Jb 35:10; Ps 77:6
[s]**42:9** Ps 18:2; 31:3
[t]Ps 43:2
[u]**42:10** Jl 2:17
[v]**42:11** Ps 43:5; Mt 26:38
[w]**43:1** Ps 5:6; 26:1; 35:24
[x]**43:2** Ps 42:9; 88:14
[y]**43:3** Ps 36:9
[z]Ps 2:6; 46:4; 84:1
[aa]**43:4** Ps 26:6
[ab]Ps 33:2; 57:8

[A]**41:9** Lit *Even a man of my peace* [B]**42:5-6** Some Hb mss, LXX, Syr; other Hb mss read *Him, the salvation of His presence.* [6]*My God, I* [C]**Ps 43** Many Hb mss connect Pss 42–43

5 Why am I so depressed?
Why this turmoil within me?
Put your hope in God, for I will
still praise Him,
my Savior and my God.[a]

Psalm 44
Israel's Complaint

For the choir director. A *Maskil of the sons of Korah.

1 God, we have heard with our ears —
our ancestors have told us —
the work You accomplished
in their days,
in days long ago:[b]
2 to plant them,
You drove out the nations
with Your hand;
to settle them,
You crushed the peoples.[c]
3 For they did not take the land
by their sword —
their arm did not bring them victory —
but by Your right hand, Your arm,
and the light of Your face,
for You were pleased with them.[d]
4 You are my King, my God,
who ordains[A] victories for Jacob.[e]
5 Through You we drive back our foes;
through Your name we trample
our enemies.[f]
6 For I do not trust in my bow,
and my sword does not
bring me victory.[g]
7 But You give us victory over our foes
and let those who hate us be disgraced.[h]
8 We boast in God all day long;
we will praise Your name forever.[i]
*Selah
9 But You have rejected
and humiliated us;
You do not march out with our armies.[j]
10 You make us retreat from the foe,
and those who hate us
have taken plunder for themselves.[k]
11 You hand us over to be eaten like sheep
and scatter us among the nations.[l]
12 You sell Your people for nothing;
You make no profit from selling them.[m]

[a]43:5 Ps 42:5,11
[b]44:1 Dt 32:7; Ps 78:3
[c]44:2 2Sm 7:10; Ps 78:55; 80:8
[d]44:3 Dt 7:7-8; Ps 77:15; Hs 1:7
[e]44:4 Ps 42:8; 74:12
[f]44:5 Ps 60:12; 108:13; Zch 10:5
[g]44:6 1Sm 17:47; Ps 33:16
[h]44:7 Ps 35:4; 53:5
[i]44:8 Ps 30:12; 34:2
[j]44:9 Ps 60:1,10; 74:1; 108:11
[k]44:10 Lv 26:17; Dt 28:25; Jos 7:8,12
[l]44:11 Lv 26:33; Dt 4:27; 28:64; Ps 106:27
[m]44:12 Dt 32:30; Jdg 2:14; 3:8; Is 52:3-4
[n]44:13 Dt 28:37; Ps 79:4
[o]44:14 Jb 17:6; Ps 109:25; Jr 24:9
[p]44:15 2Ch 32:21; Ps 69:7
[q]44:16 Ps 8:2; 74:10
[r]44:17 Ps 119:61,153
[s]44:18 Jb 23:11; Ps 37:31; 119:51,157
[t]44:19 Jb 30:29; Jr 9:11
[u]44:20 Dt 6:14; Jb 11:13
[v]44:21 Ps 139:1-2; Jr 17:10; Heb 4:13
[w]44:22 Is 53:7; Jr 12:3; Rm 8:36
[x]44:23 Ps 7:6; 35:23; 78:65
[y]44:24 Jb 13:24; Ps 88:14
[z]44:25 Ps 119:25
[aa]44:26 Ps 25:22

13 You make us an object of reproach
to our neighbors,
a source of mockery and ridicule
to those around us.[n]
14 You make us a joke among the nations,
a laughingstock[B] among the peoples.[o]
15 My disgrace is before me all day long,
and shame has covered my face,[p]
16 because of the voice of the scorner
and reviler,
because of the enemy and avenger.[q]
17 All this has happened to us,
but we have not forgotten You
or betrayed Your covenant.[r]
18 Our hearts have not turned back;
our steps have not strayed
from Your path.[s]
19 But You have crushed us in a haunt
of jackals
and have covered us
with deepest darkness.[t]
20 If we had forgotten the name
of our God
and spread out our hands
to a foreign god,[u]
21 wouldn't God have found this out,
since He knows the secrets
of the heart?[v]
22 Because of You we are slain all day long;
we are counted as sheep
to be slaughtered.[w]
23 Wake up, LORD! Why are You sleeping?
Get up! Don't reject us forever![x]
24 Why do You hide Yourself
and forget our affliction
and oppression?[y]
25 For we have sunk down to the dust;
our bodies cling to the ground.[z]
26 Rise up! Help us!
Redeem us because of
Your faithful love.[aa]

Psalm 45
A Royal Wedding Song

For the choir director: according to "The Lilies."[C] A *Maskil of the sons of Korah. A love song.

1 My heart is moved by a noble theme
as I recite my verses to the king;

[A]44:4 LXX, Syr, Aq; MT reads *King, God; ordain* [B]44:14 Lit *shaking of the head* [C]45:title Possibly a tune; Pss 60; 69; 80

my tongue is the pen
of a skillful writer.[a]
2 You are the most handsome of ·men;
grace flows from your lips.[b]
Therefore God has blessed you forever.[c]
3 Mighty warrior, strap your sword
at your side.
In your majesty and splendor[d] —
4 in your splendor ride triumphantly
in the cause of truth, humility,
and justice.
May your right hand show
your awe-inspiring acts.[e]
5 Your arrows pierce the hearts
of the king's enemies;
the peoples fall under you.[f]
6 Your throne,[g] God, is[A] forever
and ever;
the scepter of Your[B] kingdom is
a scepter of justice.[h]
7 You love righteousness
and hate wickedness;[i]
therefore God, your God,
has anointed you with the oil of joy
more than your companions.
8 Myrrh, aloes, and cassia perfume
all your garments;
from ivory palaces harps bring you joy.[j]
9 Kings' daughters are
among your honored women;[k]
the queen, adorned with gold
from Ophir,
stands at your right hand.[l]
10 Listen, daughter, pay attention
and consider:
forget your people
and your father's house,[m]
11 and the king will desire your beauty.
Bow down to him, for he is your lord.[n]
12 The daughter of Tyre,
the wealthy people,
will seek your favor with gifts.[o]
13 In her chamber, the royal daughter
is all glorious,
her clothing embroidered with gold.[p]
14 In colorful garments she is led
to the king;
after her, the virgins, her companions,
are brought to you.[q]
15 They are led in with gladness
and rejoicing;
they enter the king's palace.[r]
16 Your sons will succeed your ancestors;
you will make them princes
throughout the land.[s]
17 I will cause your name
to be remembered
for all generations;
therefore the peoples will praise you
forever and ever.[t]

PSALM 46

God Our Refuge

For the choir director. A song of the sons
of Korah. According to *Alamoth*.[C,u]

1 God is our refuge and strength,
a helper who is always found
in times of trouble.[v]
2 Therefore we will not be afraid,
though the earth trembles
and the mountains topple
into the depths of the seas,[w]
3 though its waters roar and foam
and the mountains quake
with its turmoil.[x] *·Selah*
4 There is a river —
its streams delight the city of God,
the holy dwelling place
of the ·Most High.[y]
5 God is within her;
she will not be toppled.
God will help her
when the morning dawns.[z]
6 Nations rage, kingdoms topple;
the earth melts when He lifts His voice.[aa]
7 The LORD of ·Hosts is with us;
the God of Jacob is our stronghold.[ab]
Selah
8 Come, see the works of the LORD,
who brings devastation on the earth.[ac]
9 He makes wars cease
throughout the earth.
He shatters bows and cuts spears
to pieces;
He burns up the chariots.[D,ad]

[a] **45:1** Ezr 7:6
[b] **45:2** Lk 4:22
[c] Ps 21:6
[d] **45:3** Is 49:2; Rv 1:16; 19:15
[e] **45:4** Ps 65:5; 98:1
[f] **45:5** Dt 23:14; Ps 18:14
[g] **45:6-7** Heb 1:8-9
[h] **45:6** Ps 93:2
[i] **45:7** Ps 33:5
[j] **45:8** Sg 4:14; Jn 19:39
[k] **45:9** Sg 6:8
[l] 1Kg 9:28; 10:11
[m] **45:10** Ru 1:16-17
[n] **45:11** Eph 5:33
[o] **45:12** Ps 68:29; 72:10-11; Is 49:23
[p] **45:13** Ex 39:2-3; Rv 19:7-8
[q] **45:14** Ezk 16:18; 26:16
[r] **45:15** Jr 22:4
[s] **45:16** 1Pt 2:9; Rv 1:6; 5:10
[t] **45:17** Mal 1:11
[u] **46:title** 1Ch 15:20
[v] **46:1** Ps 9:9; 62:7-8
[w] **46:2** Ps 18:7; 82:5
[x] **46:3** Ps 93:3-4; Jr 5:22
[y] **46:4** Ps 43:3; Rv 22:1-2
[z] **46:5** Is 12:6; Zch 2:10-11
[aa] **46:6** Ps 2:1; Jr 25:30
[ab] **46:7** Ps 9:9; Jl 3:16
[ac] **46:8** Ps 66:5
[ad] **46:9** Ps 76:3; Is 2:4; Mc 4:3

A **45:6** Or *Your divine throne is*, or *Your throne is God's* B **45:6** Or *your* C **46:title** This may refer to a high pitch, perhaps a tune sung by soprano voices; the Hb word means "young women." D **46:9** Lit *chariots with fire*

10 "Stop your fighting — and know that
I am God,
exalted among the nations,
exalted on the earth."[a]
11 ·Yahweh of Hosts is with us;
the God of Jacob is our stronghold.[b]
Selah

Psalm 47
God Our King

For the choir director. A psalm
of the sons of Korah.

1 Clap your hands, all you peoples;[c]
shout to God with a jubilant cry.[d]
2 For ·Yahweh, the ·Most High, is awe-
inspiring,
a great King over all the earth.[e]
3 He subdues peoples under us
and nations under our feet.[f]
4 He chooses for us our inheritance —
the pride of Jacob, whom He loves.[g]
·*Selah*
5 God ascends among shouts of joy,
the LORD, among the sound
of trumpets.[h]
6 Sing praise to God, sing praise;
sing praise to our King, sing praise![i]
7 Sing a song of wisdom,[A]
for God is King of all the earth.[j]
8 God reigns over the nations;
God is seated on His holy throne.[k]
9 The nobles of the peoples
have assembled
with the people of the God
of Abraham.[l]
For the leaders[B] of the earth
belong to God;
He is greatly exalted.[m]

Psalm 48
Zion Exalted

A song. A psalm of the sons of Korah.

1 The LORD is great and highly praised
in the city of our God.[n]
His holy mountain, 2 rising splendidly,
is the joy of the whole earth.
Mount ·Zion on the slopes of the north
is the city of the great King.[o]
3 God is known as a stronghold
in its citadels.[p]
4 Look! The kings assembled;
they advanced together.[q]
5 They looked and froze with fear;
they fled in terror.[r]
6 Trembling seized them there,
agony like that of a woman in labor,[s]
7 as You wrecked the ships of Tarshish
with the east wind.[t]
8 Just as we heard, so we have seen
in the city of ·Yahweh of ·Hosts,
in the city of our God;
God will establish it forever.[u] ·*Selah*
9 God, within Your temple,
we contemplate Your faithful love.[v]
10 Your name, God, like Your praise,
reaches to the ends of the earth;[w]
Your right hand is filled with justice.[x]
11 Mount Zion is glad.
The towns[C] of Judah rejoice
because of Your judgments.[y]
12 Go around Zion, encircle it;
count its towers,
13 note its ramparts; tour its citadels
so that you can tell a future generation:[z]
14 "This God, our God forever and ever —
He will always lead us."[D,aa]

Psalm 49
Misplaced Trust in Wealth

For the choir director. A psalm of the sons of Korah.

1 Hear this, all you peoples;
listen, all who inhabit the world,[ab]
2 both low and high,[E]
rich and poor together.[ac]
3 My mouth speaks wisdom;
my heart's meditation
brings understanding.[ad]
4 I turn my ear to a proverb;
I explain my riddle with a lyre.[ae]
5 Why should I fear in times
of trouble?
The iniquity of my foes surrounds me.[af]
6 They trust in their wealth
and boast of their abundant riches.[ag]
7 Yet these cannot redeem a person[F]

[a] **46:10** Ps 100:3; Is 2:11,17
[b] **46:11** Ps 9:9; Jl 3:16
[c] **47:1** Is 55:12
[d] Ps 95:1
[e] **47:2** Dt 7:21; Neh 1:5; Mal 1:14
[f] **47:3** Ps 2:8; 18:47
[g] **47:4** Am 8:7; Nah 2:2
[h] **47:5** 2Sm 6:15; Ps 68:18; 98:6
[i] **47:6** Ps 68:4; 89:18
[j] **47:7** Zch 14:9; 1Co 14:15
[k] **47:8** 1Ch 16:31; Ps 22:28; 97:2
[l] **47:9** Ps 102:22
[m] Ps 72:11; Is 49:7,23
[n] **48:1** Ps 2:6; Mc 4:1; Zch 8:3
[o] **48:2** Mt 5:35
[p] **48:3** Ps 46:7; 50:2
[q] **48:4** 2Sm 10:6-19
[r] **48:5** Ex 15:15
[s] **48:6** Is 13:8; Hs 13:13
[t] **48:7** 1Kg 22:48; Jr 18:17; Ezk 27:26
[u] **48:8** Ps 87:5; Is 2:2; Mc 4:1
[v] **48:9** Ps 26:3; 40:10
[w] **48:10** Ps 113:3; Mal 1:11
[x] Ps 45:4
[y] **48:11** Ps 97:8
[z] **48:12-13** Ps 78:5-7; 122:7
[aa] **48:14** Ps 23:3-4; Is 58:11
[ab] **49:1** Ps 78:1; Mc 1:2
[ac] **49:2** Ps 62:9
[ad] **49:3** Ps 37:30
[ae] **49:4** Nm 12:8; Mt 13:35
[af] **49:5** Ps 23:4; 27:1
[ag] **49:6** Jb 31:24; Ps 52:7; Pr 11:28

[A] **47:7** Hb *a Maskil* [B] **47:9** Lit *shields* [C] **48:11** Lit *daughters* [D] **48:14** Some Hb mss, LXX; other Hb mss read *over death* [E] **49:2** Lit *both sons of Adam and sons of man* [F] **49:7** Or *Certainly he cannot redeem himself,* or *Yet he cannot redeem a brother*

or pay his ransom to God[a] —
8 since the price of redeeming him is
too costly,
one should forever stop trying[A,b] —
9 so that he may live forever
and not see the ·Pit.[c]

10 For one can see that wise men die;
foolish and stupid men also pass away.[d]
Then they leave their wealth to others.[e]
11 Their graves are their eternal homes,[B]
their homes from generation
to generation,
though they have named estates
after themselves.[f]
12 But despite his assets,[C]
man will not last;
he is like the animals that perish.[g]

13 This is the way of those
who are arrogant,
and of their followers,
who approve of their words.[D,h] *·Selah*
14 Like sheep they are headed for ·Sheol;
Death will shepherd them.
The upright will rule over them
in the morning,[i]
and their form will waste away
in Sheol,[E]
far from their lofty abode.[j]
15 But God will redeem my life
from the power of Sheol,
for He will take me.[k] *Selah*

16 Do not be afraid when a man gets rich,
when the wealth[F]
of his house increases.[l]
17 For when he dies, he will take
nothing at all;
his wealth[F] will not follow him down.[m]
18 Though he praises himself
during his lifetime —
and people praise you when you do well
for yourself[n] —
19 he will go to the generation
of his fathers;
they will never see the light.[o]
20 A man with valuable possessions[G]
but without understanding
is like the animals that perish.[p]

Psalm 50

God as Judge

A psalm of ·Asaph.[q]

1 ·Yahweh, the God of gods[H] speaks;
He summons the earth from east
to west.[I,r]
2 From ·Zion, the perfection of beauty,
God appears in radiance.[J,s]
3 Our God is coming; He will not
be silent!
Devouring fire precedes Him,
and a storm rages around Him.[t]
4 On high, He summons heaven
and earth
in order to judge His people.[u]
5 "Gather My faithful ones to Me,
those who made a covenant with Me
by sacrifice."[v]
6 The heavens proclaim
His righteousness,[w]
for God is the Judge.[x] *·Selah*

7 "Listen, My people, and I will speak;
I will testify against you, Israel.
I am God, your God.[y]
8 I do not rebuke you for your sacrifices
or for your ·burnt offerings,
which are continually before Me.[z]
9 I will not accept a bull
from your household
or male goats from your pens,[aa]
10 for every animal of the forest is Mine,
the cattle on a thousand hills.
11 I know every bird of the mountains,[K]
and the creatures of the field are Mine.[ab]
12 If I were hungry, I would not tell you,
for the world and everything in it
is Mine.[ac]
13 Do I eat the flesh of bulls
or drink the blood of goats?[ad]
14 Sacrifice a thank offering to God,[ae]
and pay your vows to the ·Most High.[af]
15 Call on Me in a day of trouble;
I will rescue you,
and you will honor Me."[ag]

16 But God says to the wicked:
"What right do you have to recite
My statutes

[a]**49:7** Jb 36:18-19; Mt 25:8-9
[b]**49:8** Mt 16:26
[c]**49:9** Jb 33:28; Ps 16:10
[d]**49:10** Ec 2:16
[e]Ps 39:6; Ec 2:18-19; Lk 12:20
[f]**49:11** Ps 5:9; 10:6
[g]**49:12** Ec 3:19
[h]**49:13** Ps 31:23; Pr 16:18; 21:24
[i]**49:14** Rv 2:26
[j]Jb 24:19; Ps 9:17
[k]**49:15** Ps 16:10; 56:13; Hs 13:14
[l]**49:16** Ps 37:7
[m]**49:17** Jb 27:19; Ps 17:14; 1Tm 6:7
[n]**49:18** Dt 29:19; Ps 10:3,6
[o]**49:19** Gn 15:15; Jb 33:30; Ps 56:13
[p]**49:20** Ec 3:19
[q]**50:title** 1Ch 16:5,7
[r]**50:1** Jos 22:22; Ps 113:3
[s]**50:2** Dt 33:2; Ps 48:2; Lm 2:15
[t]**50:3** Ps 18:12-13; 97:3
[u]**50:4** Dt 4:26; 31:28; 32:1; Is 1:2
[v]**50:5** Ex 24:4-8; 2Ch 6:11
[w]**50:6** Ps 89:5; 97:6
[x]Ps 75:7; 96:13
[y]**50:7** Dt 31:21; Ps 81:8
[z]**50:8** 1Sm 15:22; Ps 40:6; 51:16
[aa]**50:9** Ps 69:31
[ab]**50:10-11** Ex 19:5; Ps 104:24
[ac]**50:12** Dt 10:14; Ps 24:1; 1Co 10:26
[ad]**50:13** Is 1:11
[ae]**50:14** Lv 7:12; Ps 107:22; 116:17
[af]Dt 23:21; Ps 76:11
[ag]**50:15** Ps 20:1; 59:16; 77:2

[A]**49:8** Or *costly, it will cease forever* [B]**49:11** LXX, Syr, Tg; MT reads *Their inner thought is that their houses are eternal* [C]**49:12** Or *honor* [D]**49:13** Lit *and after them with their mouth they were pleased* [E]**49:14** Hb obscure [F]**49:16,17** Or *glory* [G]**49:20** Or *with honor* [H]**50:1** Or *The Mighty One, God, the LORD*, or *The God of gods, the LORD* [I]**50:1** Lit *from the rising of the sun to its setting* [J]**50:2** Or *God shines forth* [K]**50:11** LXX, Syr, Tg read *heavens*

and to take My covenant on your lips?[a]
17 You hate instruction
and turn your back on My words.[A,b]
18 When you see a thief,
you make friends with him,
and you associate with adulterers.[c]
19 You unleash your mouth for evil
and harness your tongue for deceit.[d]
20 You sit, maligning your brother,
slandering your mother's son.[e]
21 You have done these things,
and I kept silent;
you thought I was just like you.[f]
But I will rebuke you
and lay out the case before you.[B,g]
22 "Understand this,
you who forget God,
or I will tear you apart,
and there will be no one to
rescue you.[h]
23 Whoever sacrifices a thank offering
honors Me,
and whoever orders his conduct,
I will show him the salvation of God."[i]

Psalm 51

A Prayer for Restoration

For the choir director. A Davidic psalm,
when Nathan the prophet came to him
after he had gone to Bathsheba.[j]

1 Be gracious to me, God,
according to Your faithful love;
according to Your abundant
compassion,
blot out my rebellion.[k]
2 Wash away my ·guilt
and cleanse me from my sin.[l]
3 For I am conscious of my rebellion,
and my sin is always before me.[m]
4 Against You — You alone —
I have sinned
and done this evil in Your sight.[n]
So You are right
when You pass sentence;
You are blameless when You judge.[o]
5 Indeed, I was guilty when I was born;
I was sinful when my mother
conceived me.[p]
6 Surely You desire integrity
in the inner self,
and You teach me wisdom
deep within.[q]
7 Purify me with hyssop,
and I will be ·clean;
wash me, and I will be
whiter than snow.[r]
8 Let me hear joy and gladness;
let the bones You have crushed
rejoice.[s]
9 Turn Your face away[C] from my sins
and blot out all my guilt.[t]
10 God, create a clean heart for me
and renew a steadfast[D] spirit
within me.[u]
11 Do not banish me from Your presence
or take Your Holy Spirit from me.[v]
12 Restore the joy of Your salvation
to me,
and give me a willing spirit.[E,w]
13 Then I will teach the rebellious
Your ways,
and sinners will return to You.[x]
14 Save me from the guilt of bloodshed,
God,[y]
the God of my salvation,
and my tongue will sing
of Your righteousness.[z]
15 Lord, open my lips,
and my mouth will declare
Your praise.[aa]
16 You do not want a sacrifice,
or I would give it;
You are not pleased
with a ·burnt offering.[ab]
17 The sacrifice pleasing to God is[F]
a broken spirit.
God, You will not despise a broken
and humbled heart.[ac]
18 In Your good pleasure, cause ·Zion
to prosper;
build[G] the walls of Jerusalem.[ad]
19 Then You will delight
in righteous sacrifices,
whole burnt offerings;
then bulls will be offered
on Your altar.[ae]

[a]**50:16** Is 29:13 [b]**50:17** Pr 5:12; 12:1 [c]**50:18** Rm 1:32; 1Tm 5:22 [d]**50:19** Ps 10:7; 36:3; 52:2 [e]**50:20** Jb 19:18; Mt 10:21 [f]**50:21** Is 42:14; 57:11 [g]Ps 90:8 [h]**50:22** Jb 8:13; Ps 9:17 [i]**50:23** Ps 85:13; 91:16; Gl 6:16 [j]**50:title** 2Sm 12:1 [k]**51:1** Is 43:25; Ac 3:19 [l]**51:2** Is 1:16; Jr 33:8; 1Jn 1:7,9 [m]**51:3** Ps 32:5; Pr 28:13; Is 59:12 [n]**51:4** Ps 41:4 [o]Rm 3:4 [p]**51:5** Jb 15:14; Ps 58:3; Rm 5:12-13 [q]**51:6** Jb 38:36; Pr 2:6; Ec 2:26 [r]**51:7** Lv 14:4,49; Nm 19:18; Is 1:18 [s]**51:8** Ps 35:10; Is 38:13 [t]**51:9** Jr 16:17 [u]**51:10** Ps 24:4; Mt 5:8; Jms 4:8 [v]**51:11** 2Kg 13:23; Is 63:10-11; Jr 7:15 [w]**51:12** Ps 13:5 [x]**51:13** Ex 33:13; Ps 25:4; Jr 2:33 [y]**51:14** Ps 26:9 [z]Ps 35:28; 71:15 [aa]**51:15** Ex 4:15; Ps 9:14 [ab]**51:16** 1Sm 15:22; Ps 40:6 [ac]**51:17** Ps 34:18 [ad]**51:18** Ps 69:35; 102:16; 147:2 [ae]**51:19** Ps 4:5; 66:13,15; Mal 3:3

[A]50:17 Or *and cast My words behind you* [B]50:21 Lit *out before your eyes* [C]51:9 Lit *Hide Your face* [D]51:10 Or *right* [E]51:12 Or *and sustain me with a noble spirit* [F]51:17 Lit *The sacrifices of God are* [G]51:18 Or *rebuild*

Psalm 52
God Judges the Proud

For the choir director. A Davidic ·*Maskil*. When Doeg the Edomite went and reported to Saul, telling him, "David went to Ahimelech's house."[a]

1 Why brag about evil, you hero![b]
God's faithful love is constant.[c]
2 Like a sharpened razor,
your tongue devises destruction,
working treachery.[d]
3 You love evil instead of good,
lying instead of speaking truthfully.[e]
·*Selah*
4 You love any words that destroy,
you treacherous tongue![f]
5 This is why God will bring
you down forever.
He will take you, ripping you out of
your tent;
He will uproot you from the land
of the living.[g] *Selah*
6 The righteous will look on with awe
and will ridicule him:[h]
7 "Here is the man
who would not make God his refuge,
but trusted in the abundance
of his riches,
taking refuge
in his destructive behavior."[A,i]
8 But I am like a flourishing olive tree
in the house of God;[j]
I trust in God's faithful love
forever and ever.[k]
9 I will praise You forever for what
You have done.
In the presence of Your faithful people,
I will put my hope in Your name,
for it is good.[l]

Psalm 53
A Portrait of Sinners

For the choir director: on *Mahalath*.[B,m]
A Davidic ·*Maskil*.

1 The fool says in his heart,
"God does not exist."
They are corrupt, and they do
vile deeds.
There is no one who does good.[n]
2 God looks down from heaven
on the ·human race
to see if there is one who is wise,
one who seeks God.[o]
3 All have turned away;
all alike have become corrupt.
There is no one who does good,
not even one.[p]
4 Will evildoers never understand?
They consume My people
as they consume bread;[q]
they do not call on God.[r]
5 Then they will be filled with terror—
terror like no other[s]—
because God will scatter
the bones of those who besiege you.[t]
You will put them to shame,
for God has rejected them.[u]
6 Oh, that Israel's deliverance
would come from ·Zion!
When God restores the fortunes
of His people,[C]
Jacob will rejoice; Israel will be glad.[v]

Psalm 54
Prayer for Deliverance

For the choir director: with stringed instruments. A Davidic ·*Maskil*. When the Ziphites went and said to Saul, "Is David not hiding among us?"[w]

1 God, save me by Your name,
and vindicate me by Your might![x]
2 God, hear my prayer;
listen to the words of my mouth.[y]
3 For strangers rise up against me,
and violent men seek my life.
They have no regard for God.[D,z] ·*Selah*
4 God is my helper;
the Lord is the sustainer of my life.[E,aa]
5 He will repay my adversaries
for their evil.
Because of Your faithfulness,
annihilate them.[ab]
6 I will sacrifice a freewill offering
to You.[ac]
I will praise Your name, ·Yahweh,
because it is good.[ad]

[a] **52:title** 1Sm 22:9
[b] **52:1** Ps 94:4
[c] Ps 40:10-11; 138:2
[d] **52:2** Ps 5:9; 50:19; 59:7
[e] **52:3** Ps 58:3; Jr 9:4-5
[f] **52:4** Ps 10:7; Pr 17:4
[g] **52:5** Ps 27:13; Pr 2:22
[h] **52:6** Jb 22:19-20; Ps 37:34
[i] **52:7** Ps 10:6; 49:6; Pr 11:28
[j] **52:8** Ps 1:3; 128:3; Jr 11:16
[k] Ps 143:8
[l] **52:9** Ps 30:12; 54:6
[m] **53:title** Ps 88 title
[n] **53:1** Ps 10:4; 14:1
[o] **53:2** Ps 33:13-15
[p] **53:2-3** Rm 3:10-12
[q] **53:4** Ps 27:2; Mc 3:3
[r] Is 64:7
[s] **53:5** Lv 26:36
[t] Jr 8:1-2
[u] Ps 44:7
[v] **53:6** Ps 14:7; Is 52:7-9; Jr 30:18-19
[w] **53:title** 1Sm 23:19; 26:1
[x] **54:1** Ps 6:1; 7:8; 35:24; 43:1
[y] **54:2** Ps 5:1; 17:6; 55:1
[z] **54:3** Ps 86:14; 143:3; Is 25:5
[aa] **54:4** Ps 118:7; Is 41:10
[ab] **54:5** Ps 94:23; 143:12
[ac] **54:6** Nm 15:3; Ps 116:17
[ad] Ps 52:9

[A] **52:7** Or *riches, and grew strong in his evil desire*; lit *his destruction*
[B] **53:title** Perhaps a tune, a musical instrument, or a dance; this may be related to Hb word for "sickness."
[C] **53:6** Or *restores His captive people*
[D] **54:3** Lit *They do not set God before them*
[E] **54:4** Or *is with those who sustain my life*

7 For He has delivered me
from every trouble,
and my eye has looked down on
my enemies.[a]

Psalm 55
Betrayal by a Friend

For the choir director: with stringed instruments. A Davidic ˚*Maskil.*

1 God, listen to my prayer
and do not ignore[A] my plea for help.[b]
2 Pay attention to me and answer me.[c]
I am restless and in turmoil
with my complaint,[d]
3 because of the enemy's voice,
because of the pressure[B] of the wicked.
For they bring down disaster on me[C]
and harass me in anger.[e]

4 My heart shudders within me;[f]
terrors of death sweep over me.
5 Fear and trembling grip me;
horror has overwhelmed me.[g]
6 I said, "If only I had[D] wings like a dove!
I would fly away and find rest.[h]
7 How far away I would flee;
I would stay in the wilderness.[i] ˚*Selah*
8 I would hurry to my shelter
from the raging wind and the storm."[j]

9 Lord, confuse[E] and confound
their speech,[F,k]
for I see violence and strife in the city;
10 day and night they make the rounds
on its walls.
Crime and trouble are within it;[l]
11 destruction is inside it;
oppression and deceit never leave
its marketplace.[m]

12 Now it is not an enemy
who insults me —
otherwise I could bear it;
it is not a foe who rises up against me —
otherwise I could hide from him.
13 But it is you, a man who is my peer,
my companion and good friend![n]
14 We used to have close fellowship;
we walked with the crowd
into the house of God.[o]
15 Let death take them by surprise;[p]
let them go down to ˚Sheol alive,
because evil is in their homes
and within them.[q]
16 But I call to God,
and the LORD will save me.[r]
17 I complain and groan morning, noon,
and night,[s]
and He hears my voice.[t]
18 Though many are against me,
He will redeem me
from my battle unharmed.[u]
19 God, the One enthroned
from long ago,[v]
will hear and will humiliate them *Selah*
because they do not change
and do not ˚fear God.[w]

20 My friend[x] acts violently
against those at peace with him;[y]
he violates his covenant.[z]
21 His buttery words are smooth,[G]
but war is in his heart.
His words are softer than oil,
but they are drawn swords.[aa]

22 Cast your burden on the LORD,
and He will sustain you;[ab]
He will never allow the righteous
to be shaken.[ac]

23 God, You will bring them down
to the ˚Pit of destruction;[ad]
men of bloodshed and treachery
will not live out half their days.[ae]
But I will trust in You.[af]

Psalm 56
A Call for God's Protection

For the choir director: according to "A Silent Dove Far Away."[H] A Davidic ˚*Miktam.* When the Philistines seized him in Gath.[ag]

1 Be gracious to me, God,
for man tramples me;
he fights and oppresses me all day long.
2 My adversaries trample me all day,
for many arrogantly fight against me.[I,ah]

3 When I am afraid,
I will trust in You.[ai]
4 In God, whose word I praise,

[a]**54:7** Ps 59:10; 92:11 [b]**55:1** Lm 3:56 [c]**55:1-2** Ps 4:1; 5:1-2; 54:2 [d]**55:2** Ps 64:1; 142:2 [e]**55:3** 2Sm 16:7-8; Ps 71:11 [f]**55:4** Ps 38:8 [g]**55:4-5** Ps 18:4-5; 116:3 [h]**55:6** Jb 3:13 [i]**55:7** Jr 9:2 [j]**55:8** Is 4:6; 25:4 [k]**55:9** Gn 10:25; 11:7 [l]**55:9-10** Jr 6:7; Hab 1:3 [m]**55:11** Ps 5:9; 10:7 [n]**55:12-13** Jb 19:13,19; Ps 41:9; 88:18 [o]**55:14** Ps 42:4 [p]**55:15** Pr 6:15; Is 47:11; 1Th 5:3 [q]Nm 16:30,33 [r]**55:16** Ps 119:46 [s]**55:17** Ps 92:2 [t]Ps 64:1; 142:2 [u]**55:18** Ps 56:2; 103:4 [v]**55:19** Ps 93:2 [w]Dt 33:27 [x]**55:20** Ps 55:13 [y]Ps 7:4 [z]Ps 89:34 [aa]**55:21** Ps 12:2; 28:3 [ab]**55:22** 1Pt 5:7 [ac]Ps 37:24; 112:6 [ad]**55:23** Is 38:17; Ezk 28:8 [ae]Ps 5:6 [af]Ps 56:3 [ag]**56:title** 1Sm 21:10-11; 22:1 [ah]**56:1-2** Ps 35:1; 57:3 [ai]**56:3** Ps 112:7; Pr 29:25; Is 12:2

[A]55:1 Lit *hide Yourself from* [B]55:3 Or *threat,* or *oppression* [C]55:3 LXX, Syr, Sym; MT reads *they cause me to totter* [D]55:6 Lit *"Who will give to me . . . dove?* [E]55:9 Or *destroy* [F]55:9 Lit *and divide their tongue* [G]55:21 Some Hb mss, Sym, Syr, Tg, Jer read *His speech is smoother than butter* [H]56:title Possibly a tune [I]56:2 Or *many fight against me, O exalted One,* or *many fight against me from the heights*

in God I trust; I will not fear.
What can man do to me?[a]

5 They twist my words all day long;
all their thoughts against me are evil.[b]
6 They stir up strife,[A] they lurk;
they watch my steps
while they wait to take my life.[c]
7 Will they escape in spite of such sin?
God, bring down the nations in wrath.[d]

8 You Yourself have recorded
my wanderings.[B]
Put my tears in Your bottle.
Are they not in Your records?[e]
9 Then my enemies will retreat
on the day when I call.[f]
This I know: God is for me.[g]

10 In God, whose word I praise,
in the LORD, whose word I praise,
11 in God I trust; I will not fear.
What can man do to me?[h]

12 I am obligated by vows[C] to You, God;
I will make my thank offerings to You.[i]
13 For You delivered me from death,
even my feet from stumbling,
to walk before God in the light of life.[j]

PSALM 57

Praise for God's Protection

For the choir director: "Do Not Destroy."[D] A Davidic ·*Miktam*. When he fled before Saul into the cave.[k]

1 Be gracious to me, God, be gracious
to me,
for I take refuge in You.
I will seek refuge in the shadow
of Your wings
until danger passes.[l]
2 I call to God ·Most High,
to God who fulfills His purpose
for me.[E,m]
3 He reaches down from heaven
and saves me,
challenging the one who tramples me.[n]
·*Selah*
God sends His faithful love and truth.[o]
4 I am surrounded by lions;
I lie down with those who devour ·men.
Their teeth are spears and arrows;
their tongues are sharp swords.[p]
5 God, be exalted above the heavens;
let Your glory be over
the whole earth.[q]

6 They prepared a net for my steps;
I was despondent.
They dug a pit ahead of me,
but they fell into it![r] *Selah*

7 My heart is confident, God, my heart
is confident.
I will sing; I will sing praises.[s]
8 Wake up, my soul![F]
Wake up, harp and lyre!
I will wake up the dawn.[t]
9 I will praise You, Lord,
among the peoples;
I will sing praises to You
among the nations.[u]
10 For Your faithful love is as high as
the heavens;
Your faithfulness reaches the clouds.[v]
11 God, be exalted above the heavens;[w]
let Your glory be over the whole earth.[x]

PSALM 58

A Cry against Injustice

For the choir director: "Do Not Destroy."[D] A Davidic ·*Miktam*.

1 Do you really speak righteously,
you mighty ones?[G]
Do you judge ·people fairly?[y]
2 No, you practice injustice
in your hearts;
with your hands you weigh out violence
in the land.[z]

3 The wicked go astray from the womb;
liars err from birth.[aa]
4 They have venom like the venom
of a snake,
like the deaf cobra that stops up
its ears,[ab]
5 that does not listen to the sound
of the charmers
who skillfully weave spells.[ac]

6 God, knock the teeth
out of their mouths;
LORD, tear out the young lions' fangs.[ad]

[a]**56:4** Ps 27:1; 118:6; Heb 13:6
[b]**56:5** Ps 41:7; 2Pt 3:16
[c]**56:6** Ps 10:8-10; 59:3
[d]**56:7** Ezk 17:15; Rm 2:3
[e]**56:8** 2Kg 20:5; Ps 139:3; Mal 3:16
[f]**56:9** Ps 9:3
[g]Ps 118:6; Rm 8:31
[h]**56:10-11** Ps 112:7; Pr 29:25; Is 12:2
[i]**56:12** Ps 50:14
[j]**56:13** Jb 33:30; Ps 116:8-9
[k]**57:title** 1Sm 22:1; 24:1-3
[l]**57:1** Ru 2:12; Ps 17:8; 91:1,4
[m]**57:2** Ps 138:8
[n]**57:3** Ps 56:1-2
[o]Ps 25:10; 40:11
[p]**57:4** Ps 58:6; 64:3; Pr 30:14
[q]**57:5** Ps 108:5; 113:4
[r]**57:6** Ps 9:15; 35:8; Pr 28:10
[s]**57:7** Ps 59:17; 112:7
[t]**57:8** Jdg 5:12; Ps 33:2; 81:2
[u]**57:9** 2Sm 22:50; Ps 9:11; 18:49
[v]**57:10** Ps 36:5; 103:11; Lm 3:22-23
[w]**57:11** Ps 113:4
[x]**57:7-11** Ps 108:1-5
[y]**58:1** Ps 82:2
[z]**58:2** Ps 94:20; Is 10:1; Mal 3:15
[aa]**58:3** Ps 51:5; Is 48:8
[ab]**58:4** Dt 32:33; Ps 140:3
[ac]**58:5** Ec 10:11; Jr 8:17
[ad]**58:6** Jb 4:10; 29:17; Ps 3:7

[A]**56:6** Or *They attack* [B]**56:8** Or *misery* [C]**56:12** Lit *On me the vows*
[D]**57:title; 58:title** Possibly a tune [E]**57:2** Or *who avenges me* [F]**57:8** Lit *glory*
[G]**58:1** Or *Can you really speak righteousness in silence?*

7 They will vanish like water
that flows by;
they will aim their useless arrows.[A,B,a]
8 Like a slug that moves along in slime,
like a woman's miscarried child,
they will not see the sun.[b]
9 Before your pots can feel the heat of
the thorns —
whether green or burning —
He will sweep them away.[C,c]
10 The righteous one will rejoice
when he sees the retribution;[d]
he will wash his feet in the blood
of the wicked.[e]
11 Then people will say,
"Yes, there is a reward for the righteous!
There is a God who judges on earth!"[f]

Psalm 59

God Our Stronghold

For the choir director: "Do Not Destroy."[D]
A Davidic ·*Miktam*. When Saul sent agents
to watch the house and kill him.[g]

1 Deliver me from my enemies, my God;[h]
protect me from those who rise up
against me.[i]
2 Deliver me from those who practice sin,
and save me from men of bloodshed.[j]
3 LORD, look! They set an ambush
for me.[k]
Powerful men attack me,
but not because of any sin or rebellion
of mine.[l]
4 For no fault of mine,
they run and take up a position.
Awake to help me, and take notice.[m]
5 LORD God of ·Hosts, You are the
God of Israel,
rise up to punish all the nations;
do not show grace
to any wicked traitors.[n] ·*Selah*
6 They return at evening,
snarling like dogs
and prowling around the city.[o]
7 Look, they spew from their mouths —
sharp words from[E] their lips.[p]
"For who," they say, "will hear?"[q]
8 But You laugh at them, LORD;
You ridicule all the nations.[r]
9 I will keep watch for You, my[F] strength,
because God is my stronghold.[s]
10 My faithful God[G] will come to meet me;
God will let me look down on
my adversaries.[t]
11 Do not kill them; otherwise, my people
will forget.
By Your power, make them
homeless wanderers[u]
and bring them down,
Lord, our shield.[v]
12 For the sin of their mouths and the
words of their lips,
let them be caught in their pride.
They utter curses and lies.[w]
13 Consume them in rage;
consume them until they are gone.[x]
Then people will know
throughout[H] the earth
that God rules over Jacob.[y] *Selah*
14 And they return at evening,
snarling like dogs
and prowling around the city.[z]
15 They scavenge for food;
they growl if they are not satisfied.[aa]
16 But I will sing of Your strength
and will joyfully proclaim
Your faithful love in the morning.[ab]
For You have been a stronghold for me,
a refuge in my day of trouble.[ac]
17 To You, my strength, I sing praises,
because God is my stronghold —
my faithful God.[ad]

Psalm 60

Prayer in Difficult Times

For the choir director: according to
"The Lily of Testimony."[I] A Davidic ·*Miktam*
for teaching. When he fought with Aram-naharaim
and Aram-zobah, and Joab returned and struck
Edom in the Valley of Salt, killing 12,000.[ae]

1 God, You have rejected us;
You have broken out[J] against us;
You have been angry. Restore us![K,af]

[a]**58:7** Jos 7:5; Ps 112:10; Ezk 21:7
[b]**58:8** Jb 3:16; Ec 6:3
[c]**58:9** Jb 27:21; Pr 10:25; Ec 7:6
[d]**58:10** Jb 22:19
[e]Ps 68:23; Jr 11:20; 20:12
[f]**58:11** Ps 9:8; 67:4; 75:7
[g]**59:title** 1Sm 19:11
[h]**59:1** Ps 143:9
[i]2Sm 22:18; Ps 18:17; 91:14
[j]**59:2** Ps 5:6; 17:7
[k]**59:3** Pr 1:11,18
[l]1Sm 20:1; 24:11
[m]**59:4** Ps 7:3-4; 69:4
[n]**59:5** Jr 18:23
[o]**59:6** Ps 22:16
[p]**59:7** Ps 52:2; 57:4; 64:3
[q]Ps 73:11
[r]**59:8** Ps 2:4; 37:13
[s]**59:9** Ps 28:8; Jr 16:19
[t]**59:10** Ps 54:7
[u]**59:11** Hs 9:17
[v]Gn 15:1; Dt 33:29; 2Sm 22:3,31; Ps 3:3; 5:12; 18:2; 28:7; 119:114
[w]**59:12** Ps 10:7; Pr 12:13
[x]**59:13** Ps 104:35
[y]Ps 83:18
[z]**59:14** Ps 22:16
[aa]**59:15** Jb 15:23; Ps 109:10
[ab]**59:16** Ps 5:3; 88:13; 92:2
[ac]Is 25:4; Nah 1:7
[ad]**59:17** Ps 28:8; Jr 16:19
[ae]**60:title** 1Ch 18:3,12
[af]**60:1** Ps 44:9,23; 79:5

[A]58:7 Or *their arrows as if they were circumcised*; Hb obscure [B]58:7 Or *they wither like trampled grass* [C]58:9 Or *thorns, He will sweep it away, whether raw or cooking*, or *thorns, He will sweep him away alive in fury* [D]59:title Possibly a tune [E]59:7 Lit *swords are on* [F]59:9 Some Hb mss, LXX, Vg, Tg; other Hb mss read *his* [G]59:10 Alt Hb tradition reads *My God in His faithful love* [H]59:13 Lit *know to the ends of* [I]60:title Possibly a tune; Pss 45; 69; 80 [J]60:1 Lit *have burst through* [K]60:1 Or *Turn back to us*

2 You have shaken the land
and split it open.
Heal its fissures, for it shudders.[a]
3 You have made Your people
suffer hardship;
You have given us wine to drink
that made us stagger.[b]
4 You have given a signal flag to those
who ·fear You,
so that they can flee
before the archers.[A,c] ·*Selah*
5 Save with Your right hand,
and answer me,
so that those You love may be rescued.[d]
6 God has spoken in His sanctuary:[B]
"I will triumph!
I will divide up Shechem.[e]
I will apportion the Valley of Succoth.[f]
7 Gilead is Mine, Manasseh is Mine,
and Ephraim is My helmet;[g]
Judah is My scepter.[h]
8 Moab is My washbasin.[i]
I throw My sandal on Edom;[j]
I shout in triumph over Philistia."[k]
9 Who will bring me to the fortified city?
Who will lead me to Edom?[l]
10 God, haven't You rejected us?
God, You do not march out
with our armies.[m]
11 Give us aid against the foe,
for human help is worthless.[n]
12 With God we will perform valiantly;[o]
He will trample our foes.[p]

PSALM 61
Security in God

For the choir director:
on stringed instruments. Davidic.

1 God, hear my cry;
pay attention to my prayer.[q]
2 I call to You from the ends of the earth
when my heart is without strength.[r]
Lead me to a rock that is
high above me,[s]
3 for You have been a refuge for me,
a strong tower[t] in the face of the enemy.
4 I will live in Your tent forever
and take refuge under the shelter
of Your wings.[u] ·*Selah*
5 God, You have heard my vows;[v]
You have given a heritage
to those who ·fear Your name.[w]
6 Add days to the king's life;
may his years span many generations.[x]
7 May he sit enthroned
before God forever;[y]
appoint faithful love and truth
to guard him.[z]
8 Then I will continually sing
of Your name,[aa]
fulfilling my vows day by day.[ab]

PSALM 62
Trust in God Alone

For the choir director: according to Jeduthun.[ac]
A Davidic psalm.

1 I am at rest in God alone;
my salvation comes from Him.[ad]
2 He alone is my rock
and my salvation,[ae]
my stronghold; I will never be shaken.[af]
3 How long will you threaten a man?
Will all of you attack[C]
as if he were a leaning wall
or a tottering stone fence?[ag]
4 They only plan to bring him down
from his high position.
They take pleasure in lying;
they bless with their mouths,
but they curse inwardly.[ah] ·*Selah*
5 Rest in God alone, my soul,
for my hope comes from Him.[ai]
6 He alone is my rock
and my salvation,[aj]
my stronghold; I will not be shaken.[ak]
7 My salvation and glory depend on God,
my strong rock.
My refuge is in God.[al]
8 Trust in Him at all times, you people;
pour out your hearts before Him.
God is our refuge.[am] *Selah*
9 ·Men are only a vapor;
exalted men, an illusion.
Weighed in the scales, they go up;
together they are less than a vapor.[an]
10 Place no trust in oppression,
or false hope in robbery.

[a] **60:2** Ps 18:7
[b] **60:3** Is 51:17-23; Jr 25:15-17
[c] **60:4** Is 5:26; 11:12; 13:2
[d] **60:5** Ps 17:7; 20:6; 138:7
[e] **60:6** Gn 12:6; 33:18
[f] Gn 33:17
[g] **60:7** Dt 33:17; Jos 13:31
[h] Gn 49:10
[i] **60:8** 2Sm 8:2
[j] 2Sm 8:14
[k] 2Sm 8:1
[l] **60:9** Jr 1:18
[m] **60:10** Ps 44:9
[n] **60:11** Ps 146:3
[o] **60:12** Nm 24:18; Ps 44:5; 118:15-16
[p] **60:5-12** Ps 108:6-13
[q] **61:1** Ps 17:1; 88:2; 142:6
[r] **61:2** Ps 88:4
[s] Ps 27:5
[t] **61:3** Pr 18:10
[u] **61:4** Ru 2:12; Ps 17:8; 91:4
[v] **61:5** Jb 22:27; Ps 56:12
[w] Mal 4:2
[x] **61:6** Ps 21:4
[y] **61:7** Ps 41:12
[z] Ps 40:11
[aa] **61:8** Ps 7:17; 9:2; 18:49
[ab] Ps 65:1; 116:14,18
[ac] **62:title** Ps 39 title
[ad] **62:1** Ps 33:20; 37:39
[ae] **62:1-2** Dt 32:15; 2Sm 22:47
[af] **62:2** Ps 37:24; 55:22
[ag] **62:3** Is 30:13
[ah] **62:4** Ps 4:2; 55:21
[ai] **62:5** Ps 71:5
[aj] **62:6** Ps 89:26; 95:1
[ak] Ps 16:8; 21:7
[al] **62:7** Ps 18:2
[am] **62:8** Ps 91:2; 118:8-9
[an] **62:9** Ps 39:5-6,11; Is 40:17

[A] **60:4** Or *can rally before the archers,* or *can rally because of the truth* [B] **60:6** Or *has promised by His holy nature* [C] **62:3** Some Hb mss read *you be struck down*

If wealth increases,
pay no attention to it.[A,a]
11 God has spoken once;
I have heard this twice:
strength belongs to God,[b]
12 and faithful love
belongs to You, LORD.
For You repay each according to
his works.[c]

PSALM 63

Praise God Who Satisfies

A Davidic psalm. When he was in the Wilderness of Judah.[d]

1 God, You are my God; I eagerly
seek You.
I thirst for You;
my body faints for You
in a land that is dry, desolate,
and without water.[e]
2 So I gaze on You in the sanctuary
to see Your strength and Your glory.[f]
3 My lips will glorify You
because Your faithful love is better
than life.[g]
4 So I will praise You as long as I live;
at Your name, I will lift up my hands.[h]
5 You satisfy me as with rich food;[B,i]
my mouth will praise You
with joyful lips.[j]
6 When I think of You as I lie
on my bed,
I meditate on You
during the night watches[k]
7 because You are my helper;[l]
I will rejoice in the shadow
of Your wings.[m]
8 I follow close to You;
Your right hand holds on to me.[n]
9 But those who seek to destroy my life
will go into the depths of the earth.[o]
10 They will be given over to the power
of the sword;[p]
they will become the jackals' prey.
11 But the king will rejoice in God;[q]
all who swear by Him[C] will boast,
for the mouths of liars will be shut.[r]

PSALM 64

Protection from Evildoers

For the choir director. A Davidic psalm.

1 God, hear my voice when I complain.[s]
Protect my life from the terror
of the enemy.[t]
2 Hide me from the scheming
of wicked people,[u]
from the mob of evildoers,[v]
3 who sharpen their tongues like swords
and aim bitter words like arrows,[w]
4 shooting from concealed places
at the innocent.
They shoot at him suddenly
and are not afraid.[x]
5 They encourage each other
in an evil plan;[D,E]
they talk about hiding traps and say,
"Who will see them?"[F,y]
6 They devise crimes and say,
"We have perfected a secret plan."[z]
The inner man and the heart
are mysterious.
7 But God will shoot them with arrows;
suddenly, they will be wounded.[aa]
8 They will be made to stumble;
their own tongues work against them.
All who see them will shake
their heads.[ab]
9 Then everyone will fear
and will tell about God's work,
for they will understand
what He has done.[ac]
10 The righteous one rejoices in the LORD
and takes refuge in Him;
all those who are upright in heart
will offer praise.[ad]

PSALM 65

God's Care for the Earth

For the choir director.
A Davidic psalm. A song.

1 Praise is rightfully Yours,[G]
God, in ˙Zion;
vows to You will be fulfilled.[ae]
2 All humanity will come to You,
the One who hears prayer.[af]

[a]**62:10** Jb 31:24-25; Mk 4:19; 1Tm 6:10,17-19 [b]**62:11** Jb 40:5 [c]**62:12** Mt 16:27; Rm 2:6; Rv 22:12 [d]**63:title** 2Sm 16:14; 17:2,29 [e]**63:1** Ps 42:2; Is 26:9 [f]**63:2** Jb 19:26-27; Ps 17:15; 27:4 [g]**63:3** Ps 69:16 [h]**63:4** Ps 28:2; 143:6; Lm 3:41 [i]**63:5** Ps 36:8 [j]Ps 71:23 [k]**63:6** Ps 77:6; 119:148 [l]**63:7** Ps 27:9; 40:17 [m]Ps 17:8; 36:7; 57:1 [n]**63:8** Ps 18:35 [o]**63:9** Ps 55:15; Ezk 26:20; 31:14-18 [p]**63:10** Jr 18:21; Ezk 35:5 [q]**63:11** Ps 21:1 [r]Ps 107:42; Rm 3:19 [s]**64:1** Ps 55:2 [t]Ps 140:1 [u]**64:2** Ps 35:20; 37:12 [v]Ps 22:16; 26:5 [w]**64:3** Ps 52:2; 57:4; Pr 25:18 [x]**64:4** Ps 10:8; 11:2 [y]**64:5** Ps 35:7; 140:5; 141:9 [z]**64:6** Ps 21:11; 83:3 [aa]**64:7** Ps 7:13; 45:5; 144:6 [ab]**64:8** Jr 18:16; 48:27; Lm 2:15 [ac]**64:9** Ps 40:3 [ad]**64:10** Ps 32:11; 68:3; 97:11-12 [ae]**65:1** Ps 50:14; 116:18 [af]**65:2** Ps 86:9; Is 2:2-4; 66:23

[A]**62:10** Lit *increases, do not set heart* [B]**63:5** Lit *with fat and fatness* [C]**63:11** Or *him* [D]**64:5** Or *thing*; lit *word* [E]**64:5** Or *They hold fast to an evil purpose*, or *They establish for themselves an evil purpose* [F]**64:5** Or *us*, or *it* [G]**65:1** Or *Praise is silence to You*, or *Praise awaits You*

3 Iniquities overwhelm me;
only You can ·atone for[A] our rebellions.[a]
4 How happy is the one You choose
and bring near to live in Your courts!
We will be satisfied with the goodness
of Your house,
the holiness of Your temple.[B,b]
5 You answer us in righteousness,
with awe-inspiring works,
God of our salvation,
the hope of all the ends of the earth
and of the distant seas.[c]
6 You establish the mountains
by Your[C] power,
robed with strength.[d]
7 You silence the roar of the seas,
the roar of their waves,
and the tumult of the nations.[e]
8 Those who live far away are awed
by Your signs;
You make east and west shout for joy.[f]
9 You visit the earth
and water it abundantly,
enriching it greatly.
God's stream is filled with water,
for You prepare the earth[D] in this way,
providing people with grain.[g]
10 You soften it with showers and bless
its growth,
soaking its furrows and leveling
its ridges.[h]
11 You crown the year with Your goodness;
Your ways overflow with plenty.[E,i]
12 The wilderness pastures overflow,
and the hills are robed with joy.[j]
13 The pastures are clothed with flocks
and the valleys covered with grain.[k]
They shout in triumph; indeed,
they sing.[l]

Psalm 66
Praise for God's Mighty Acts

For the choir director. A song. A psalm.

1 Shout joyfully to God, all the earth![m]
2 Sing about the glory of His name;
make His praise glorious.[n]
3 Say to God, "How awe-inspiring
are Your works!
Your enemies will cringe before You
because of Your great strength.[o]
4 All the earth will worship You
and sing praise to You.
They will sing praise to Your name."[p]
·Selah
5 Come and see the wonders of God;[q]
His acts for ·humanity
are awe-inspiring.
6 He turned the sea into dry land,
and they crossed the river on foot.[r]
There we rejoiced in Him.[s]
7 He rules forever by His might;
He keeps His eye on the nations.[t]
The rebellious should not
exalt themselves.[u] *Selah*
8 Praise our God, you peoples;
let the sound of His praise be heard.[v]
9 He keeps us alive[F]
and does not allow our feet to slip.[w]
10 For You, God, tested us;
You refined us as silver is refined.[x]
11 You lured us into a trap;
You placed burdens on our backs.[y]
12 You let men ride over our heads;
we went through fire and water,
but You brought us out to abundance.[G,z]
13 I will enter Your house
with ·burnt offerings;
I will pay You my vows[aa]
14 that my lips promised
and my mouth spoke
during my distress.[ab]
15 I will offer You fattened sheep
as burnt offerings,
with the fragrant smoke of rams;
I will sacrifice oxen with goats.[ac] *Selah*
16 Come and listen, all who ·fear God,
and I will tell what He has done for me.[ad]
17 I cried out to Him with my mouth,
and praise was on my tongue.[ae]
18 If I had been aware of malice
in my heart,
the Lord would not have listened.[af]
19 However, God has listened;
He has paid attention to the sound
of my prayer.[ag]

[a] 65:3 Ps 38:14; 40:12; 79:9
[b] 65:4 Ps 27:4; 84:4
[c] 65:5 Dt 10:21; 2Sm 7:23; Ps 46:8
[d] 65:6 Ps 93:1; Am 4:13
[e] 65:7 Ps 107:29; Is 17:13; Mt 8:26
[f] 65:8 Ps 2:8; 139:9; Is 24:16
[g] 65:9 Ps 104:13; 147:8; Is 45:8
[h] 65:10 Dt 3:22; Ps 72:6; 147:8
[i] 65:11 Ps 104:28; 147:14
[j] 65:12 Jb 38:26-27; Is 55:12; Jl 2:22
[k] 65:13 Ps 72:16; 144:13; Is 30:23
[l] Is 44:23
[m] 66:1 Ps 98:4; 100:1
[n] 66:1-2 1Ch 16:29; Ps 48:10
[o] 66:3 Ps 18:44; 47:2; 145:6
[p] 66:4 Ps 72:11; Is 66:23; Zph 2:11
[q] 66:5 Ps 46:8
[r] 66:6 Ex 14:21; Ps 106:9
[s] Ex 15:1-21
[t] 66:7 Ps 14:2; 33:13-14; Pr 15:3
[u] Ps 140:8
[v] 66:8 Ps 98:4
[w] 66:9 Ps 94:18; 121:3
[x] 66:10 Jb 23:10; Ps 17:3; Is 48:10
[y] 66:11 Lm 1:13; Ezk 12:13; 17:20
[z] 66:12 Ps 18:19; Is 43:2
[aa] 66:13 Ps 22:25; 116:14; Ec 5:4
[ab] 66:14 Ps 18:6
[ac] 66:15 Nm 6:14; Ps 51:19
[ad] 66:16 Ps 9:1; 34:11; 71:15,24
[ae] 66:17 Ps 35:28
[af] 66:18 Jb 36:21; Jn 9:31
[ag] 66:19 Ps 116:1-2

A 65:3 Or *can forgive*, or *can wipe out* B 65:4 Or *house, Your holy temple* C 65:6 Some LXX mss, Vg; MT reads *His* D 65:9 Lit *prepare it* E 65:11 Lit *ways drip with fat* F 66:9 Lit *He sets our soul in life* G 66:12 Or *a place of satisfaction*

20 May God be praised!
He has not turned away my prayer
or turned His faithful love from me.[a]

Psalm 67
All Will Praise God

For the choir director: with stringed instruments.
A psalm. A song.

1 May God be gracious to us and bless us;
look on us with favor[b] ·*Selah*
2 so that Your way may be known
on earth,
Your salvation among all nations.[c]
3 Let the peoples praise You, God;
let all the peoples praise You.[d]
4 Let the nations rejoice and shout
for joy,
for You judge the peoples with fairness
and lead the nations on earth.[e] *Selah*
5 Let the peoples praise You, God,
let all the peoples praise You.[f]
6 The earth has produced its harvest;
God, our God, blesses us.[g]

[a]**66:20** Ps 22:24; 68:35 [b]**67:1** Nm 6:25; Ps 4:6; 80:3,7,19 [c]**67:2** Ps 98:2; Is 52:10; Ti 2:11 [d]**67:3** Ps 45:17; 66:4; 117:1 [e]**67:4** Ps 96:10,13; 100:1-2; Is 11:4 [f]**67:5** Ps 45:17; 66:8; 117:1 [g]**67:6** Lv 26:4; Ps 85:12; Ezk 34:27; Hs 2:22 [h]**67:7** 1Kg 8:43; 2Ch 6:33; Ps 33:8 [i]**68:1** Nm 10:35; Ps 7:6; Ezk 30:26 [j]**68:2** Ps 37:20; Hs 13:3 [k]**68:3** Ps 32:11; 40:16; 64:10 [l]**68:4** Dt 33:26; Ps 7:17; 66:4; Is 19:1

7 God will bless us,
and all the ends of the earth
will ·fear Him.[h]

Psalm 68
God's Majestic Power

For the choir director.
A Davidic psalm. A song.

1 God arises. His enemies scatter,
and those who hate Him flee
from His presence.[i]
2 As smoke is blown away,
so You blow them away.
As wax melts before the fire,
so the wicked are destroyed
before God.[j]
3 But the righteous are glad;
they rejoice before God and celebrate
with joy.[k]

4 Sing to God! Sing praises to His name.
Exalt Him who rides on the clouds[A] —
His name is ·Yahweh[B] — and rejoice
before Him.[l]

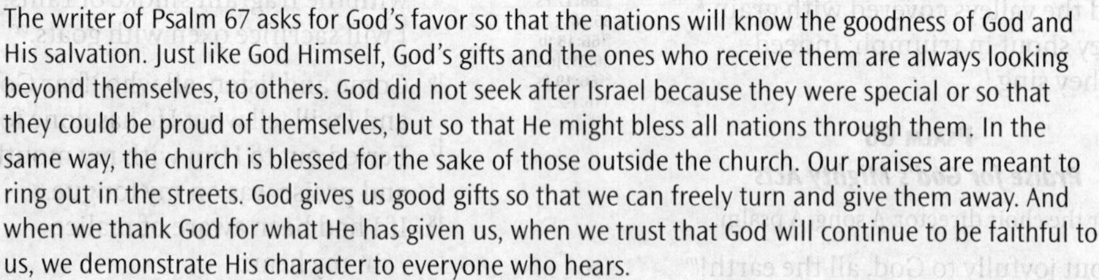

GOD'S HEART FOR THE WORLD

Receiving to Give

May God be gracious to us and bless us; look on us with favor so that Your way may be known on earth, Your salvation among all nations. (Psalm 67:1-2)

God's work in each of our lives is much bigger than our own happiness or well being. God loves us and longs to give us good things, but He does not bless us merely for our own sake. His blessings are always to bring glory to His name and to demonstrate that glory to those who do not know Him. They are meant to bring blessing to "all nations" (v. 2), to "all the ends of the earth" (v. 7), like one seed that, when planted, multiplies to produce hundreds of that same seed.

The writer of Psalm 67 asks for God's favor so that the nations will know the goodness of God and His salvation. Just like God Himself, God's gifts and the ones who receive them are always looking beyond themselves, to others. God did not seek after Israel because they were special or so that they could be proud of themselves, but so that He might bless all nations through them. In the same way, the church is blessed for the sake of those outside the church. Our praises are meant to ring out in the streets. God gives us good gifts so that we can freely turn and give them away. And when we thank God for what He has given us, when we trust that God will continue to be faithful to us, we demonstrate His character to everyone who hears.

Praises multiply like seeds as others come to recognize the truth and goodness of God and join in our song.

[A]**68:4** Or *rides through the desert* [B]**68:4** Lit *Yah*

5 God in His holy dwelling is
a father of the fatherless
and a champion of widows.[a]
6 God provides homes for those
who are deserted.
He leads out the prisoners
to prosperity,[A]
but the rebellious live
in a scorched land.[b]

7 God, when You went out
before Your people,
when You marched through the desert, *Selah
8 the earth trembled and the skies
poured down rain
before God, the God of Sinai,[B]
before God, the God of Israel.[c]
9 You, God, showered abundant rain;
You revived Your inheritance
when it languished.[d]
10 Your people settled in it;
God, You provided for the poor
by Your goodness.[e]
11 The Lord gave the command;
a great company of women brought
the good news:[f]
12 "The kings of the armies flee —
they flee!"
She who stays at home divides
the spoil.[g]
13 While[C] you lie among the sheepfolds,[D]
the wings of a dove are covered
with silver,
and its feathers with glistening gold.[h]
14 When the *Almighty scattered kings
in the land,
it snowed on Zalmon.[E,i]

15 Mount Bashan is
God's towering mountain;
Mount Bashan is a mountain
of many peaks.[j]
16 Why gaze with envy,
you mountain peaks,
at the mountain[F] God desired
for His dwelling?
The LORD will live there forever![k]
17 God's chariots are tens of thousands,
thousands and thousands;[l]
the Lord is among them
in the sanctuary[G]
as He was at Sinai.[m]
18 You ascended to the heights,
taking away captives;
You received gifts from[H] people,
even from the rebellious,
so that the LORD God might live there.[I,n]

19 May the Lord be praised!
Day after day He bears our burdens;
God is our salvation.[o] *Selah*
20 Our God is a God of salvation,
and escape from death belongs
to the Lord GOD.[p]
21 Surely God crushes the heads
of His enemies,
the hairy head of one who goes on
in his *guilty acts.[q]
22 The Lord said, "I will bring them back
from Bashan;
I will bring them back from the depths
of the sea[r]
23 so that your foot may wade[J] in blood
and your dogs' tongues may have
their share
from the enemies."[s]
24 People have seen
Your procession, God,
the procession of my God,
my King, in the sanctuary.[K,t]
25 Singers[L] lead the way,
with musicians following;
among them are young women
playing tambourines.[u]
26 Praise God in the assemblies;
praise the LORD from the fountain
of Israel.[v]
27 There is Benjamin, the youngest,
leading them,
the rulers of Judah in their assembly,[M]
the rulers of Zebulun, the rulers
of Naphtali.[w]

28 Your God has decreed your strength.
Show Your strength, God,
You who have acted on our behalf.[x]
29 Because of Your temple at Jerusalem,
kings will bring tribute to You.[y]

[a]68:5 Dt 24:17,19; Ps 146:9 [b]68:6 Ps 107:14; 113:9; 146:7 [c]68:7-8 Ex 19:16-18; Jdg 5:4-5 [d]68:9 Lv 26:4; Ezk 34:26 [e]68:10 Ps 74:19; 78:20; 107:9 [f]68:11 1Sm 18:6-7 [g]68:12 Jos 10:16; Jdg 5:30 [h]68:13 Gn 49:14; Jdg 5:16 [i]68:14 Jos 10:10; Jdg 9:48 [j]68:15 Ps 36:6 [k]68:16 Ps 48:1-2; 132:13-14; Is 2:2-4 [l]68:17 Hab 3:8 [m]Dt 33:2 [n]68:18 Dt 21:10; Ps 7:7; Eph 4:8 [o]68:19 Ps 55:22; Is 46:3-4 [p]68:20 Dt 32:39; Ps 49:15; 56:13 [q]68:21 Ps 110:6; Hab 3:13 [r]68:22 Nm 21:33; Am 9:1-4 [s]68:23 1Kg 21:19; 22:38; Jr 15:3 [t]68:24 Ps 42:4; Is 60:11 [u]68:25 Ex 15:20; Jdg 11:34; 1Sm 18:6 [v]68:26 Ps 22:25; 26:12 [w]68:27 Jdg 5:14,18; 1Sm 9:21 [x]68:28 Ps 44:4; Is 26:12 [y]68:29 Ps 72:10; Is 18:7; Hg 2:7

[A]68:6 Or *prisoners with joyous music*; Hb uncertain [B]68:8 Lit *God, this Sinai* [C]68:13 Or *If* [D]68:13 Or *campfires*, or *saddlebags*; Hb obscure [E]68:14 Or *Black Mountain* [F]68:16 = Mount Zion [G]68:17 Or *in holiness* [H]68:18 Lit *among* [I]68:18 Or *even those rebelling against the LORD God's living there*, or *even rebels are living with the LORD God*; Hb obscure [J]68:23 LXX, Syr read *dip* [K]68:24 Or *in holiness* [L]68:25 Some Hb mss, LXX, Syr read *Officials* [M]68:27 Hb obscure

30 Rebuke the beast[A] in the reeds,
the herd of bulls with the calves
of the peoples.[a]
Trample underfoot those with bars
of silver.[B]
Scatter the peoples who take pleasure
in war.[b]
31 Ambassadors will come[C] from Egypt;
·Cush will stretch out its hands[D] to God.[c]
32 Sing to God, you kingdoms of the earth;
sing praise to the Lord,[d] *Selah*
33 to Him who rides in the ancient,
highest heavens.[e]
Look, He thunders
with His powerful voice![f]
34 Ascribe power to God.
His majesty is over Israel,
His power among the clouds.[g]
35 God, You are awe-inspiring
in Your sanctuaries.
The God of Israel gives power
and strength to His people.
May God be praised![h]

Psalm 69

A Plea for Rescue

For the choir director: according to "The Lilies."[E] Davidic.

1 Save me, God,
for the water has risen to my neck.[i]
2 I have sunk in deep mud, and there is
no footing;
I have come into deep waters,
and a flood sweeps over me.[j]
3 I am weary from my crying;
my throat is parched.
My eyes fail, looking for my God.[k]
4 Those who hate me without cause
are more numerous than the hairs
of my head;
my deceitful enemies, who would
destroy me,
are powerful.[l]
Though I did not steal, I must repay.[m]
5 God, You know my foolishness,
and my ·guilty acts are not hidden
from You.[n]
6 Do not let those who put their hope
in You
be disgraced because of me,
Lord God of ·Hosts;
do not let those who seek You
be humiliated because of me,
God of Israel.[o]
7 For I have endured insults
because of You,
and shame has covered my face.[p]
8 I have become a stranger
to my brothers
and a foreigner to my mother's sons[q]
9 because zeal for Your house
has consumed me,[r]
and the insults of those who insult You
have fallen on me.[s]
10 I mourned and fasted,
but it brought me insults.[t]
11 I wore ·sackcloth as my clothing,
and I was a joke to them.
12 Those who sit at the city ·gate
talk about me,
and drunkards make up songs
about me.[u]
13 But as for me, Lord,
my prayer to You is for a time of favor.
In Your abundant, faithful love, God,
answer me with Your sure salvation.[v]
14 Rescue me from the miry mud;
don't let me sink.
Let me be rescued from those
who hate me
and from the deep waters.[w]
15 Don't let the floodwaters
sweep over me
or the deep swallow me up;
don't let the ·Pit close its mouth
over me.[x]
16 Answer me, Lord,
for Your faithful love is good;
in keeping with Your great compassion,
turn to me.[y]
17 Don't hide Your face from Your servant,
for I am in distress.
Answer me quickly![z]
18 Draw near to me and redeem me;
ransom me because of my enemies.[aa]

[a] **68:30** Ps 22:12 [b] Ps 18:42; 89:10 [c] **68:31** Is 45:14; Zph 3:10 [d] **68:32** Ps 67:4; 102:22 [e] **68:33** Dt 33:26 [f] Ps 29:3-5; 46:6; Is 30:30 [g] **68:34** Ps 29:1; 150:1 [h] **68:35** Dt 10:21; Ps 29:11; Is 40:29 [i] **69:1** Jb 22:11; Ps 32:6; Jnh 2:5 [j] **69:2** Ps 40:2; 124:4; Jnh 2:3 [k] **69:3** Ps 6:6; 38:10; 119:82,123 [l] **69:4** Ps 38:19 [m] Lv 6:2-5; Ps 35:19; Jn 15:25 [n] **69:5** Ps 38:5; 44:21 [o] **69:6** Ps 25:2-3 [p] **69:7** Ps 44:15; Is 50:6; Jr 51:51 [q] **69:8** Jb 19:13-14; Ps 31:11; 38:11 [r] **69:9** Jn 2:17 [s] Ps 89:50; Rm 15:3 [t] **69:10** Ps 35:13; 109:24-25 [u] **69:11-12** Jb 17:6; 30:9; Ps 44:14; Jr 24:9 [v] **69:13** Ps 109:4; Is 49:8; 2Co 6:2 [w] **69:14** Ps 144:7 [x] **69:15** Nm 16:33; Ps 55:23 [y] **69:16** Ps 25:16; 109:21 [z] **69:17** Ps 27:9; 102:2 [aa] **69:18** Ps 119:134

[A] **68:30** Probably Egypt [B] **68:30** Or *peoples, trampling on those who take pleasure in silver*, or *peoples, trampling on the bars of silver*, or *peoples, who trample each other for bars of silver* [C] **68:31** Or *They bring red cloth*, or *They bring bronze* [D] **68:31** Probably with tribute or in submission [E] **69:title** Possibly a tune; Pss 45; 60; 80

19 You know the insults I endure —
my shame and disgrace.
You are aware of all my adversaries.[a]
20 Insults have broken my heart,
and I am in despair.
I waited for sympathy,
but there was none;
for comforters, but found no one.[b]
21 Instead, they gave me gall[A] for my food,
and for my thirst
they gave me vinegar to drink.[c]

22 Let their table set before them be
a snare,
and let it be a trap for their allies.[d]
23 Let their eyes grow too dim to see,
and let their loins continually shake.[e]
24 Pour out Your rage on them,
and let Your burning anger
overtake them.[f]
25 Make their fortification desolate;
may no one live in their tents.[g]
26 For they persecute the one You struck
and talk about the pain of those
You wounded.[h]
27 Add guilt to their guilt;
do not let them share
in Your righteousness.[i]
28 Let them be erased from the book
of life
and not be recorded
with the righteous.[j]

29 But as for me — poor and in pain —
let Your salvation protect me, God.[k]
30 I will praise God's name with song
and exalt Him with thanksgiving.[l]
31 That will please •Yahweh more than
an ox,
more than a bull with horns
and hooves.[m]
32 The humble will see it and rejoice.
You who seek God, take heart![n]
33 For the LORD listens to the needy
and does not despise
His own who are prisoners.[o]

34 Let heaven and earth praise Him,
the seas and everything that moves
in them,[p]
35 for God will save •Zion
and build up[B] the cities of Judah.
They will live there and possess it.[q]
36 The descendants of His servants
will inherit it,
and those who love His name will live
in it.[r]

PSALM 70
A Call for Deliverance

For the choir director. Davidic.
To bring remembrance.[s]

1 God, deliver me.
Hurry to help me, LORD![t]
2 Let those who seek my life
be disgraced and confounded;
let those who wish me harm
be driven back and humiliated.
3 Let those who say, "Aha, aha!"
retreat because of their shame.[u]
4 Let all who seek You rejoice and be glad
in You;
let those who love Your salvation
continually say, "God is great!"[v]
5 I am afflicted and needy;
hurry to me, God.
You are my help and my deliverer;
LORD, do not delay.[w]

PSALM 71
God's Help in Old Age

1 LORD, I seek refuge in You;
let me never be disgraced.[x]
2 In Your justice, rescue and deliver me;
listen closely to me and save me.[y]
3 Be a rock of refuge for me,
where I can always go.
Give the command to save me,
for You are my rock and fortress.[z]
4 Deliver me, my God, from the power
of the wicked,
from the grasp of the unjust
and oppressive.[aa]
5 For You are my hope, Lord GOD,
my confidence from my youth.[ab]
6 I have leaned on You from birth;
You took me from my mother's womb.[ac]
My praise is always about You.[ad]
7 I have become an ominous sign
to many,

[a] **69:19** Jr 15:15
[b] **69:20** Ps 142:4; Is 63:5
[c] **69:21** Mt 27:34,48; Jn 19:29
[d] **69:22** Ps 35:4-8; Rm 11:9-10; 1Th 5:3
[e] **69:23** Is 6:10; Ezk 29:7; Dn 5:6
[f] **69:24** Ps 79:6; Ezk 21:31; Zph 3:8
[g] **69:25** Mt 23:38; Lk 13:35; Ac 1:20
[h] **69:26** 2Ch 28:9; Is 53:4; Zch 1:15
[i] **69:27** Neh 4:5; Ps 109:14
[j] **69:28** Ex 32:32; Dn 12:1; Rv 3:5
[k] **69:29** Ps 20:1; 70:5
[l] **69:30** Ps 100:4; 107:22
[m] **69:31** Ps 50:13-14; 51:16
[n] **69:32** Ps 22:26; 34:2
[o] **69:33** Ps 12:5; 68:6; 146:7
[p] **69:34** Ps 96:11; Is 44:23; 49:13
[q] **69:35** Ps 147:2; Is 44:26
[r] **69:36** Ps 102:28; Is 65:9
[s] **70:title** Ps 38 title
[t] **70:1** Ps 38:22
[u] **70:2-3** Ps 35:25; 40:14-15
[v] **70:4** Ps 35:27; 77:13
[w] **70:5** Ps 40:17; 141:1
[x] **71:1** Ps 25:20
[y] **71:2** Ps 17:6
[z] **71:1-3** Ps 31:1-3
[aa] **71:4** Ps 140:1,4
[ab] **71:5** Ps 39:7; Jr 17:13
[ac] **71:6** Ps 22:9-10
[ad] Ps 34:1

[A] **69:21** A bitter substance [B] **69:35** Or *and rebuild*

but You are my strong refuge.[a]
8 My mouth is full of praise
and honor to You all day long.[b]
9 Don't discard me in my old age;
as my strength fails,
do not abandon me.[c]
10 For my enemies talk about me,
and those who spy on me plot together,[d]
11 saying, "God has abandoned him;
chase him and catch him,
for there is no one to rescue him."[e]
12 God, do not be far from me;
my God, hurry to help me.[f]
13 May my adversaries be disgraced
and destroyed;
may those who seek my harm
be covered with disgrace
and humiliation.[g]
14 But I will hope continually
and will praise You more and more.[h]
15 My mouth will tell
about Your righteousness
and Your salvation all day long,
though I cannot sum them up.[i]
16 I come because of the mighty acts
of the Lord God;
I will proclaim Your righteousness,
Yours alone.[j]

17 God, You have taught me
from my youth,
and I still proclaim
Your wonderful works.[k]
18 Even when I am old and gray,
God, do not abandon me.[l]
Then I will[A] proclaim Your power
to another generation,
Your strength to all who are to come.[m]
19 Your righteousness
reaches heaven, God,
You who have done great things;
God, who is like You?[n]
20 You caused me to experience
many troubles and misfortunes,[o]
but You will revive me again.[p]
You will bring me up again,
even from the depths of the earth.[q]
21 You will increase my honor
and comfort me once again.[r]
22 Therefore, I will praise You with a harp
for Your faithfulness, my God;
I will sing to You with a lyre,
Holy One of Israel.[s]
23 My lips will shout for joy
when I sing praise to You
because You have redeemed me.[t]
24 Therefore, my tongue will proclaim
Your righteousness all day long,
for those who seek my harm
will be disgraced and confounded.[u]

Psalm 72

A Prayer for the King

Solomonic.[v]

1 God, give Your justice to the king
and Your righteousness
to the king's son.[w]
2 He will judge Your people
with righteousness
and Your afflicted ones with justice.[x]
3 May the mountains bring prosperity[B]
to the people
and the hills, righteousness.[y]
4 May he vindicate the afflicted
among the people,
help the poor,
and crush the oppressor.[z]
5 May he continue[C] while the
sun endures
and as long as the moon,
throughout all generations.[aa]
6 May he be like rain that falls
on the cut grass,
like spring showers that water
the earth.[ab]
7 May the righteous[D] flourish in his days
and prosperity[B] abound
until the moon is no more.[ac]
8 May he rule from sea to sea
and from the Euphrates
to the ends of the earth.[ad]
9 May desert tribes kneel before him
and his enemies lick the dust.[ae]
10 May the kings of Tarshish
and the coasts and islands
bring tribute,
the kings of Sheba and Seba offer gifts.[af]
11 Let all kings bow down to him,
all nations serve him.[ag]

[a] **71:7** Ps 61:3; 62:7; 91:2,9
[b] **71:8** Ps 35:28; 63:5
[c] **71:9** Ps 27:9; 71:18; Is 46:3-4
[d] **71:10** Ps 31:13; 56:6; 83:3
[e] **71:11** Ps 3:2
[f] **71:12** Ps 22:19; 38:21-22; 40:13
[g] **71:13** Ps 71:24
[h] **71:14** Ps 84:4; 130:7; 147:11
[i] **71:15** Ps 35:28; 40:5; 96:2
[j] **71:16** Ps 51:14; 106:2
[k] **71:17** Dt 4:5; 6:7
[l] **71:18** Is 46:4
[m] Ps 22:30-31; 78:4,6
[n] **71:19** Ex 15:11; Dt 3:24; Ps 86:8
[o] **71:20** Ps 60:3
[p] Ps 85:6
[q] Hs 6:1-2
[r] **71:21** Ps 86:17; Is 12:1; 49:13
[s] **71:22** Ps 33:2; 81:2; 92:1-3
[t] **71:23** Ps 34:22; 55:18
[u] **71:24** Ps 35:28; 71:13
[v] **72:title** Ps 127 title
[w] **72:1** 1Kg 3:9; 1Ch 22:12-13; Ps 24:5
[x] **72:2** Is 9:7; 11:2-5; 32:1
[y] **72:3** Is 11:9; 52:7; 55:12
[z] **72:4** Ps 109:31; Is 11:4
[aa] **72:5** Ps 89:36-37
[ab] **72:6** Dt 32:2; 2Sm 23:3-4; Hs 6:3
[ac] **72:7** Ps 37:11; Is 2:4; 60:21
[ad] **72:8** Gn 15:18; Ex 23:31; Zch 9:10
[ae] **72:9** Ps 22:29; Is 49:23; Mc 7:17
[af] **72:10** 1Kg 10:22; 2Ch 9:21; Is 60:6
[ag] **72:11** Ps 86:9; 138:4; Is 49:23

[A] **71:18** Lit *me until I* [B] **72:3,7** Or *peace* [C] **72:5** LXX; MT reads *May they fear you* [D] **72:7** Some Hb mss, LXX, Syr, Jer read *May righteousness*

12 For he will rescue the poor who cry out
and the afflicted who have no helper.[a]
13 He will have pity on the poor
and helpless
and save the lives of the poor.[b]
14 He will redeem them from oppression
and violence,
for their lives are[A] precious[B]
in his sight.[c]

15 May he live long!
May gold from Sheba be given to him.
May prayer be offered
for him continually,
and may he be blessed all day long.[d]
16 May there be plenty of grain
in the land;
may it wave on the tops
of the mountains.
May its crops be like Lebanon.
May people flourish in the cities
like the grass of the field.[e]
17 May his name endure forever;
as long as the sun shines,
may his fame increase.
May all nations be blessed by him
and call him blessed.[f]

18 May the LORD God, the God of Israel,
who alone does wonders, be praised.[g]
19 May His glorious name
be praised forever;
the whole earth is filled with His glory.[h]
·Amen and amen.
20 The prayers of David son of Jesse
are concluded.[i]

BOOK III
(Psalms 73–89)

PSALM 73
God's Ways Vindicated

A psalm of ·Asaph.[j]

1 God is indeed good to Israel,
to the pure in heart.[k]
2 But as for me, my feet almost slipped;
my steps nearly went astray.[l]
3 For I envied the arrogant;
I saw the prosperity of the wicked.[m]
4 They have an easy time until they die,[C]
and their bodies are well fed.[D,n]
5 They are not in trouble like others;
they are not afflicted like most people.[o]
6 Therefore, pride is their necklace,
and violence covers them
like a garment.[p]
7 Their eyes bulge out from fatness;
the imaginations of their hearts
run wild.[q]
8 They mock, and they speak maliciously;
they arrogantly threaten oppression.[r]
9 They set their mouths against heaven,
and their tongues strut
across the earth.[s]
10 Therefore His people turn to them[E]
and drink in their overflowing words.[F,t]
11 The wicked say, "How can God know?
Does the ·Most High
know everything?"[u]
12 Look at them — the wicked!
They are always at ease,
and they increase their wealth.[v]

13 Did I purify my heart
and wash my hands in innocence
for nothing?[w]
14 For I am afflicted all day long
and punished every morning.[x]
15 If I had decided to say
these things aloud,
I would have betrayed Your people.[G,y]
16 When I tried to understand all this,
it seemed hopeless[H,z]
17 until I entered God's sanctuary.
Then I understood their destiny.[aa]
18 Indeed, You put them
in slippery places;
You make them fall into ruin.[ab]
19 How suddenly they become
a desolation!
They come to an end, swept away
by terrors.[ac]
20 Like one waking from a dream,
Lord, when arising, You will despise
their image.[ad]

21 When I became embittered
and my innermost being[I]
was wounded,[ae]

[a]72:12 Jb 29:12-17 [b]72:13 Pr 19:17; 28:8 [c]72:14 Ps 69:18; 116:15 [d]72:15 Is 60:6 [e]72:16 Jb 5:25; Ps 104:16 [f]72:17 Gn 12:2-3; 22:18; Ps 89:36 [g]72:18 Jb 9:10; Ps 86:10; 136:4 [h]72:19 Nm 14:21; Is 6:3 [i]72:20 2Sm 23:1 [j]73:title 1Ch 16:5,7 [k]73:1 Ps 24:4; 51:10; Mt 5:8 [l]73:2 Ps 17:5; 66:9; 94:18 [m]73:3 Ps 37:1; Pr 23:17; 24:1 [n]73:4 Jb 21:23-24 [o]73:5 Jb 21:4 [p]73:6 Ps 37:35; Pr 16:29; 21:24 [q]73:7 Jb 15:27; Jr 5:28 [r]73:8 Ps 17:10; 2Pt 2:18; Jd 16 [s]73:9 Rv 13:6 [t]73:10 Jb 15:16 [u]73:11 Jb 22:13; Ps 10:4,11; Is 29:15 [v]73:12 Ps 49:6; 52:7; Jr 49:31 [w]73:13 Ps 26:6; Mt 27:24 [x]73:14 Jb 33:19; Ps 38:6; 118:18 [y]73:15 Ps 44:17; 89:33 [z]73:16 Ec 8:17 [aa]73:17 Jb 8:13; Ps 37:38 [ab]73:18 Ps 35:6,8 [ac]73:19 Nm 16:21; Jb 18:11; Is 47:11 [ad]73:20 Ps 35:23; 59:5; 78:65 [ae]73:21 Ps 109:22

[A]72:14 Lit *their blood is* [B]72:14 Or *valuable* [C]73:4 Lit *For there are no pangs to their death* [D]73:4 Lit *fat* [E]73:10 Lit *turn here* [F]73:10 Lit *and waters of fullness are drained by them* [G]73:15 Lit *betrayed the generation of Your sons* [H]73:16 Lit *it was trouble in my eyes* [I]73:21 Lit *my kidneys*

22 I was stupid and didn't understand;
I was an unthinking animal
toward You.[a]
23 Yet I am always with You;
You hold my right hand.[b]
24 You guide me with Your counsel,
and afterward You will take me up
in glory.[A,c]
25 Who do I have in heaven but You?
And I desire nothing on earth but You.[d]
26 My flesh and my heart may fail,
but God is the strength[B] of my heart,
my portion forever.[e]
27 Those far from You
will certainly perish;
You destroy all who are
unfaithful to You.[f]
28 But as for me, God's presence is
my good.
I have made the Lord GOD my refuge,
so I can tell about all You do.[g]

PSALM 74
Prayer for Israel

A ·*Maskil* of ·Asaph.[h]

1 Why have You rejected us forever, God?
Why does Your anger burn
against the sheep of Your pasture?[i]
2 Remember Your congregation,
which You purchased long ago
and redeemed as the tribe
for Your own possession.[j]
Remember Mount ·Zion
where You dwell.[k]
3 Make Your way[C] to the everlasting ruins,
to all that the enemy has destroyed
in the sanctuary.[l]
4 Your adversaries roared
in the meeting place
where You met with us.[D]
They set up their emblems as signs.[m]
5 It was like men in a thicket of trees,
wielding axes,[n]
6 then smashing all the carvings
with hatchets and picks.[o]
7 They set Your sanctuary on fire;
they utterly[E] desecrated
the dwelling place of Your name.[p]
8 They said in their hearts,
"Let us oppress them relentlessly."
They burned down every place
throughout the land
where God met with us.[F,q]
9 There are no signs for us to see.
There is no longer a prophet.
And none of us knows how long
this will last.[r]
10 God, how long will the enemy mock?
Will the foe insult Your name forever?[s]
11 Why do You hold back Your hand?
Stretch out[G] Your right hand
and destroy them![t]
12 God my King is from ancient times,
performing saving acts on the earth.[u]
13 You divided the sea with Your strength;
You smashed the heads
of the sea monsters in the waters;[v]
14 You crushed the heads of ·Leviathan;
You fed him to the creatures
of the desert.[w]
15 You opened up springs and streams;[x]
You dried up ever-flowing rivers.[y]
16 The day is Yours, also the night;
You established the moon and the sun.[z]
17 You set all the boundaries of the earth;
You made summer and winter.[aa]
18 Remember this: the enemy
has mocked ·Yahweh,
and a foolish people has insulted
Your name.[ab]
19 Do not give the life of Your dove
to beasts;[H]
do not forget the lives
of Your poor people forever.[ac]
20 Consider the covenant,[ad]
for the dark places of the land
are full of violence.[ae]
21 Do not let the oppressed turn away
in shame;
let the poor and needy
praise Your name.[af]
22 Rise up, God, defend Your cause![ag]
Remember the insults
that fools bring against You
all day long.[ah]
23 Do not forget the clamor
of Your adversaries,

[a]**73:22** Jb 11:12; Ps 92:6
[b]**73:23** Ps 63:8
[c]**73:24** Ps 49:15; Is 58:11
[d]**73:25** Ps 16:2; Php 3:8
[e]**73:26** Ps 16:5; 38:10; 84:2
[f]**73:27** 1Ch 5:25; Ps 37:20
[g]**73:28** Ps 40:5; 118:17
[h]**74:title** 1Ch 16:5,7
[i]**74:1** Ex 32:11; Ps 60:1,10; 108:11
[j]**74:2** Is 63:17; Jr 10:16; 51:19
[k]Is 8:18
[l]**74:3** Ps 79:1; Is 61:4
[m]**74:4** Nm 2:2; Lm 2:6-7
[n]**74:5** Jr 46:22
[o]**74:6** Lm 2:2
[p]**74:7** 2Kg 25:9; Ps 79:1
[q]**74:8** Ps 83:4
[r]**74:9** 1Sm 3:1; Lm 2:9; Ezk 7:26
[s]**74:10** Ps 79:12; 89:51
[t]**74:11** Ps 59:13; Lm 2:3
[u]**74:12** Ps 47:6-8; 95:3; Jr 10:10
[v]**74:13** Ex 14:21; Is 51:9; Ezk 32:2
[w]**74:14** Jb 41:1; Ps 104:26; Is 27:1
[x]**74:15** Ps 104:10-11
[y]Is 42:15; 44:27
[z]**74:16** Gn 1:14-18; Ps 104:19
[aa]**74:17** Gn 8:22; Jb 38:10-11; Pr 8:29; Jr 5:22
[ab]**74:18** Ps 14:1; 53:1; 89:51
[ac]**74:19** Ps 9:18; 68:10
[ad]**74:20** Dt 4:31; Ps 106:45
[ae]Ezk 7:23
[af]**74:21** Ps 9:9; 103:6; Is 41:7
[ag]**74:22** Ps 9:19; 82:8
[ah]Ps 79:12

[A]**73:24** Or *will receive me with honor* [B]**73:26** Lit *rock* [C]**74:3** Lit *Lift up Your steps* [D]**74:4** Lit *in Your meeting place* [E]**74:7** Lit *they to the ground* [F]**74:8** Lit *every meeting place of God in the land* [G]**74:11** Lit *From Your bosom* [H]**74:19** One Hb ms, LXX, Syr read *Do not hand over to beasts a soul that praises You*

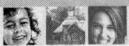

the tumult of Your opponents
that goes up constantly.[a]

Psalm 75

God Judges the Wicked

For the choir director: "Do Not Destroy."[A]
A psalm of ˙Asaph.[b] A song.

1 We give thanks to You, God;
we give thanks to You, for Your name
is near.
People tell about
Your wonderful works.[c]
2 "When I choose a time,
I will judge fairly.[d]
3 When the earth and all
its inhabitants shake,
I am the One who steadies its pillars.[e]
˙*Selah*
4 I say to the boastful, 'Do not boast,'
and to the wicked, 'Do not lift up
your ˙horn.[f]
5 Do not lift up your horn against heaven
or speak arrogantly.'"[g]
6 Exaltation does not come
from the east, the west, or the desert,
7 for God is the Judge:
He brings down one
and exalts another.[h]
8 For there is a cup in the LORD's hand,
full of wine blended with spices,
and He pours from it.
All the wicked of the earth will drink,
draining it to the dregs.[i]
9 As for me, I will tell about Him forever;
I will sing praise to the God of Jacob.[j]
10 "I will cut off all the horns
of the wicked,[k]
but the horns of the righteous will be
lifted up."[l]

Psalm 76

God, the Powerful Judge

For the choir director:
with stringed instruments.
A psalm of ˙Asaph.[m] A song.

1 God is known in Judah;
His name is great in Israel.[n]
2 His tent is in Salem,[B]
His dwelling place in ˙Zion.[o]
3 There He shatters the bow's
flaming arrows,
the shield, the sword, and the weapons
of war.[p] ˙*Selah*
4 You are resplendent and majestic
coming down from the mountains
of prey.[q]
5 The brave-hearted
have been plundered;
they have slipped into their final sleep.
None of the warriors was able to lift
a hand.[r]
6 At Your rebuke, God of Jacob,
both chariot and horse lay still.[s]
7 And You — You are to be ˙feared.[C]
When You are angry,
who can stand before You?[t]
8 From heaven
You pronounced judgment.
The earth feared and grew quiet[u]
9 when God rose up to judge
and to save all the lowly of the earth.[v]
Selah
10 Even human wrath will praise You;
You will clothe Yourself
with their remaining wrath.[D,w]
11 Make and keep your vows
to the LORD your God;[x]
let all who are around Him
bring tribute
to the awe-inspiring One.[E,y]
12 He humbles the spirit of leaders;
He is feared by the kings of the earth.[z]

Psalm 77

Confidence in a Time of Crisis

For the choir director: according to
Jeduthun. Of ˙Asaph.[aa] A psalm.

1 I cry aloud to God,
aloud to God, and He will hear me.[ab]
2 I sought the Lord in my day of trouble.
My hands were continually lifted up
all night long;
I refused to be comforted.[ac]
3 I think of God; I groan;
I meditate; my spirit becomes weak.[ad]
˙*Selah*

[a] **74:23** Ps 65:7 [b] **75:title** 1Ch 16:5,7 [c] **75:1** Dt 4:7; Ps 26:7; 145:18 [d] **75:2** Ps 9:8; 96:10 [e] **75:3** 1Sm 2:8; Ps 46:6; Is 24:19 [f] **75:4** Pr 27:1; Jr 9:23 [g] **75:5** 1Sm 2:3; Ps 94:4 [h] **75:6-7** 1Sm 2:7-8; Ps 50:6; Lk 1:52-53 [i] **75:8** Is 51:17,22; Jr 25:15-17 [j] **75:9** Ps 9:2; 18:49; 81:1 [k] **75:10** Jr 48:25 [l] Ps 89:17; 92:10; 148:14 [m] **76:title** 1Ch 16:5,7 [n] **76:1** Jr 10:6; Mal 1:11 [o] **76:2** Gn 14:18; Ps 9:11 [p] **76:3** Ps 46:9; Is 2:4; Jr 49:35 [q] **76:4** Is 14:25; Nah 2:13 [r] **76:5** Jr 51:39 [s] **76:6** Ex 13:1,21 [t] **76:7** Ps 1:5; 130:3; Nah 1:6 [u] **76:8** 2Ch 20:29-30; Ps 33:8; Hab 2:20 [v] **76:9** Ps 9:7-8; Is 3:13-15 [w] **76:10** Ex 9:16; Rm 9:17 [x] **76:11** Ps 50:14 [y] Ps 68:29; Is 18:7 [z] **76:12** Dn 4:37 [aa] **77:title** 1Ch 16:5,7 [ab] **77:1** Ps 3:4; 142:1 [ac] **77:2** Gn 37:35; Jb 11:13; Jr 31:15 [ad] **77:3** Ps 42:5,11; 43:5; 55:17; 143:4

[A] **75:title** Possibly a tune [B] **76:2** = Jerusalem [C] **76:7** Or *are awe-inspiring* [D] **76:10** Hb obscure [E] **76:11** Or *tribute with awe*

[4] You have kept me from closing
my eyes;
I am troubled and cannot speak.[a]
[5] I consider days of old,
years long past.[b]
[6] At night I remember my music;
I meditate in my heart,
and my spirit ponders.[c]

[7] "Will the Lord reject forever
and never again show favor?[d]
[8] Has His faithful love ceased forever?
Is His promise at an end
for all generations?[e]
[9] Has God forgotten to be gracious?
Has He in anger
withheld His compassion?"[f] *Selah*

[10] So I say, "I am grieved[A]
that the right hand of the •Most High
has changed."[g]
[11] I will remember the LORD's works;
yes, I will remember
Your ancient wonders.[h]
[12] I will reflect on all You have done
and meditate on Your actions.[i]

[13] God, Your way is holy.
What god is great like God?[j]
[14] You are the God who works wonders;
You revealed Your strength
among the peoples.[k]
[15] With power You redeemed Your people,
the descendants of Jacob and Joseph.[l]
Selah

[16] The waters saw You, God.
The waters saw You; they trembled.
Even the depths shook.[m]
[17] The clouds poured down water.
The storm clouds thundered;
Your arrows flashed back and forth.[n]
[18] The sound of Your thunder was
in the whirlwind;
lightning lit up the world.[o]
The earth shook and quaked.[p]
[19] Your way went through the sea
and Your path through
the great waters,
but Your footprints were unseen.[q]
[20] You led Your people like a flock[r]
by the hand of Moses and Aaron.[s]

[a]**77:4** Ps 39:9
[b]**77:5** Dt 32:7; Ps 143:5
[c]**77:6** Ps 4:4; 42:8
[d]**77:7** Ps 44:9,23; 74:1; Lm 2:7; 3:31
[e]**77:8** Ps 33:11; 85:5; 89:49
[f]**77:9** Ps 25:6; 40:11; Is 49:15
[g]**77:10** Ps 31:22; 73:14
[h]**77:11** Ps 105:5; 143:5
[i]**77:12** Ps 9:11; 90:16; 145:5
[j]**77:13** Ex 15:11; Ps 71:19; 86:8
[k]**77:14** Ps 72:18; 106:8
[l]**77:15** Ex 6:6; Dt 9:29; Ps 74:2
[m]**77:16** Ps 114:3; Hab 3:8,10
[n]**77:17** Ps 18:14; Hab 3:11; Zch 9:14
[o]**77:16-18** Ps 29:3,9; 97:4
[p]**77:18** 2Sm 22:8; Ps 18:7; Is 13:13
[q]**77:19** Is 43:16
[r]**77:20** Ps 78:52; 80:1
[s]Ps 105:26; Is 63:11-13
[t]**78:title** 1Ch 16:5,7
[u]**78:1** Pr 5:7; 7:24; Is 55:3
[v]**78:2** Ps 49:4; Pr 1:6; Mt 13:35
[w]**78:3** Ps 44:1
[x]**78:4** Dt 6:7; 11:19; Ps 145:4
[y]**78:5** Ps 19:7; 81:5; 147:19
[z]**78:6** Dt 11:19; Ps 22:31; 102:18
[aa]**78:7** Dt 6:12; Ps 103:2; Pr 3:1
[ab]**78:8** Dt 31:27; 2Kg 17:14; 2Ch 30:7
[ac]**78:9** Ps 44:10
[ad]**78:10** 1Kg 11:11; 2Kg 17:15; Jr 32:23
[ae]**78:11** Ps 106:13
[af]**78:12** Ex 7–12; Ps 78:43
[ag]**78:13** Ex 14:21; 15:8; Ps 136:13

PSALM 78
Lessons from Israel's Past

A •*Maskil* of •Asaph.[t]

[1] My people, hear my instruction;
listen to what I say.[u]
[2] I will declare wise sayings;
I will speak mysteries from the past[v] —
[3] things we have heard and known
and that our fathers have passed down
to us.[w]
[4] We must not hide them
from their children,
but must tell a future generation
the praises of the LORD,
His might, and the wonderful works
He has performed.[x]
[5] He established a •testimony in Jacob
and set up a law in Israel,
which He commanded our fathers
to teach to their children[y]
[6] so that a future generation —
children yet to be born — might know.
They were to rise and tell
their children[z]
[7] so that they might put their confidence
in God
and not forget God's works,
but keep His commands.[aa]
[8] Then they would not be
like their fathers,
a stubborn and rebellious generation,
a generation whose heart was not loyal
and whose spirit was not faithful
to God.[ab]

[9] The Ephraimite archers turned back
on the day of battle.[ac]
[10] They did not keep God's covenant
and refused to live by His law.[ad]
[11] They forgot what He had done,
the wonderful works
He had shown them.[ae]
[12] He worked wonders in the sight of
their fathers
in the land of Egypt, the region
of Zoan.[af]
[13] He split the sea
and brought them across;
the water stood firm like a wall.[ag]

[A]**77:10** Lit *"My piercing*

14 He led them with a cloud by day
and with a fiery light
throughout the night.[a]
15 He split rocks in the wilderness
and gave them drink as abundant
as the depths.[b]
16 He brought streams out of the stone
and made water flow down like rivers.[c]
17 But they continued to sin against Him,
rebelling in the desert
against the ·Most High.[d]
18 They deliberately[A] tested God,
demanding the food they craved.[e]
19 They spoke against God, saying,
"Is God able to provide food
in the wilderness?
20 Look! He struck the rock and water
gushed out;
torrents overflowed.[f]
But can He also provide bread
or furnish meat for His people?"[g]
21 Therefore, the LORD heard
and became furious;
then fire broke out against Jacob,
and anger flared up against Israel[h]
22 because they did not believe God
or rely on His salvation.[i]
23 He gave a command to the clouds above
and opened the doors of heaven.[j]
24 He rained manna for them to eat;
He gave them grain from heaven.[k]
25 People[B] ate the bread of angels.[C]
He sent them an abundant supply
of food.[l]
26 He made the east wind blow in the skies
and drove the south wind
by His might.[m]
27 He rained meat on them like dust,
and winged birds like the sand
of the seas.
28 He made them fall in His camp,
all around His tent.[D,E,n]
29 They ate and were completely satisfied,
for He gave them what they craved.[o]
30 Before they had satisfied their desire,
while the food was still
in their mouths,
31 God's anger flared up against them,
and He killed some of their best men.
He struck down Israel's choice
young men.[p]
32 Despite all this, they kept sinning
and did not believe
His wonderful works.[q]
33 He made their days end in futility,
their years in sudden disaster.[r]
34 When He killed some of them,
the rest began to seek Him;
they repented and searched for God.[s]
35 They remembered that God was
their rock,
the Most High God, their Redeemer.[t]
36 But they deceived Him
with their mouths,
they lied to Him with their tongues,[u]
37 their hearts were insincere
toward Him,
and they were unfaithful
to His covenant.[v]
38 Yet He was compassionate;
He ·atoned for[F] their ·guilt
and did not destroy them.
He often turned His anger aside
and did not unleash[G] all His wrath.[w]
39 He remembered that they were
only flesh,
a wind that passes and does not return.[x]
40 How often they rebelled against Him
in the wilderness
and grieved Him in the desert.
41 They constantly tested God[y]
and provoked the Holy One of Israel.[z]
42 They did not remember
His power shown
on the day He redeemed them
from the foe,[aa]
43 when He performed
His miraculous signs in Egypt
and His wonders in the region
of Zoan.[ab]
44 He turned their rivers into blood,
and they could not drink
from their streams.[ac]
45 He sent among them swarms of flies,[ad]
which fed on them,
and frogs, which devastated them.[ae]
46 He gave their crops to the caterpillar

[a]**78:14** Ex 13:21; Nm 14:14; Ps 105:39
[b]**78:15** Ex 17:6; Nm 20:8-13; Is 48:21
[c]**78:16** Ps 105:41; 114:8
[d]**78:17** Dt 9:22; Is 63:10; Heb 3:16
[e]**78:18** Ex 17:2,7; Ps 106:14; 1Co 10:5-10
[f]**78:20** Nm 20:11
[g]**78:19-20** Ex 16:3; Nm 11:4; 21:5
[h]**78:21** Nm 11:1
[i]**78:22** Dt 1:23; 9:23; Heb 3:18
[j]**78:23** Gn 7:11; Mal 3:10
[k]**78:24** Ex 16:4,31; Jn 6:31
[l]**78:25** Ex 16:3
[m]**78:26** Nm 11:31
[n]**78:27-28** Ex 16:13; Ps 105:40
[o]**78:29** Nm 11:4,34
[p]**78:30-31** Nm 11:33-34; Jb 20:23
[q]**78:32** Nm 14:16-17
[r]**78:33** Nm 14:29,35
[s]**78:34** Nm 21:7; Ps 63:1; Hs 5:15
[t]**78:35** Is 44:6,8
[u]**78:36** Is 29:13; 57:11; Ezk 33:31
[v]**78:37** Ps 51:10; 78:8; Ac 8:21
[w]**78:38** Nm 14:18-20; Dt 4:31; Is 12:1
[x]**78:39** Dt 31:27; Ps 107:11
[y]**78:41** Ps 95:8-9
[z]Dt 9:7-8,22; Ps 106:29; Zch 8:14
[aa]**78:42** Jdg 8:34; Ps 44:3; 106:10
[ab]**78:43** Ex 4:21; 7:3; Ps 105:27
[ac]**78:44** Ex 7:14-25; Ps 105:29
[ad]**78:45** Ex 8:17; Ps 105:31
[ae]Ex 8:3-6; Ps 105:30

[A]**78:18** Lit *in their heart* [B]**78:25** Lit *Man* [C]**78:25** Lit *mighty ones* [D]**78:28** LXX, Syr read *in their camp, all around their tents* [E]**78:28** Or *in its camp, all around its tents* [F]**78:38** Or *He wiped out*, or *He forgave* [G]**78:38** Or *stir up*

and the fruit of their labor
to the locust.[a]
47 He killed their vines with hail
and their sycamore fig trees
with a flood.
48 He handed over their livestock to hail
and their cattle to lightning bolts.[b]
49 He sent His burning anger
against them:
fury, indignation, and calamity—
a band of deadly messengers.[A,c]
50 He cleared a path for His anger.
He did not spare them from death
but delivered their lives to the plague.[d]
51 He struck all the firstborn[e] in Egypt,
the first progeny of the tents of Ham.[B,f]
52 He led His people out like sheep
and guided them like a flock
in the wilderness.[g]
53 He led them safely,
and they were not afraid;
but the sea covered their enemies.[h]
54 He brought them to His holy land,
to the mountain
His right hand acquired.[i]
55 He drove out nations before them.[j]
He apportioned their inheritance by lot
and settled the tribes of Israel
in their tents.[k]

56 But they rebelliously tested
the Most High God,
for they did not keep His decrees.[l]
57 They treacherously turned away
like their fathers;
they became warped like a faulty bow.[m]
58 They enraged Him
with their ·high places
and provoked His jealousy
with their carved images.[n]
59 God heard and became furious;
He completely rejected Israel.[o]
60 He abandoned the tabernacle
at Shiloh,
the tent where He resided
among men.[C,p]
61 He gave up His strength[D] to captivity
and His splendor to the hand of a foe.[q]
62 He surrendered His people
to the sword
because He was enraged
with His heritage.[r]
63 Fire consumed His chosen young men,
and His young women
had no wedding songs.[E,s]
64 His priests fell by the sword,
but the[F] widows could not lament.[G,t]

65 Then the Lord awoke as if from sleep,
like a warrior from the effects of wine.[u]
66 He beat back His foes;
He gave them lasting shame.[v]
67 He rejected the tent of Joseph
and did not choose the tribe
of Ephraim.
68 He chose instead the tribe of Judah,
Mount ·Zion, which He loved.[w]
69 He built His sanctuary like the heights,[H]
like the earth that
He established forever.[x]
70 He chose David His servant
and took him from the sheepfolds;[y]
71 He brought him from tending ewes
to be shepherd over His people Jacob—
over Israel, His inheritance.[z]
72 He shepherded them with a pure heart
and guided them
with his skillful hands.[aa]

Psalm 79

Faith amid Confusion

A psalm of ·Asaph.[ab]

1 God, the nations have invaded
Your inheritance,
desecrated Your holy temple,
and turned Jerusalem into ruins.[ac]
2 They gave the corpses of Your servants
to the birds of the sky for food,
the flesh of Your godly ones
to the beasts of the earth.[ad]
3 They poured out their blood
like water all around Jerusalem,
and there was no one to bury them.[ae]
4 We have become an object of reproach
to our neighbors,
a source of mockery and ridicule
to those around us.[af]

5 How long, ·Yahweh? Will You
be angry forever?

[a]**78:46** Ex 10:14-15; Ps 105:34
[b]**78:47-48** Ex 9:23-24; Ps 105:32
[c]**78:49** Ex 12:13,23; 2Sm 24:16
[d]**78:50** Ex 12:29-30
[e]**78:51** Ex 13:15; Ps 105:36
[f]Ps 105:23,27
[g]**78:52** Ex 15:22; Ps 77:20
[h]**78:53** Ex 14; 15:19; Jos 24:7; Ps 106:11
[i]**78:54** Ex 15:17; Ps 74:2
[j]**78:55** Jos 11:16-23; Ps 44:2
[k]Jos 13:7; 23:4; Ps 135:12
[l]**78:56** Jdg 2:11-13
[m]**78:57** Ezk 20:27-28; Hs 7:16
[n]**78:58** Jdg 2:12; 1Kg 3:2; Ezk 20:28
[o]**78:59** Dt 32:19; Ps 106:40; Am 6:8
[p]**78:60** Jr 7:12,14; 26:6
[q]**78:61** 1Sm 4:17
[r]**78:62** Jdg 20:21; 1Sm 4:10
[s]**78:63** Jr 7:34; 16:9; Lm 2:21
[t]**78:64** Jb 27:15; Ezk 24:23
[u]**78:65** Ps 73:20; 121:4; Is 42:13
[v]**78:66** 1Sm 5:6; Ps 40:14
[w]**78:67-68** Ps 87:2
[x]**78:69** 1Kg 6
[y]**78:70** 1Sm 16:11-13
[z]**78:71** Ps 28:9; Is 40:11
[aa]**78:72** 1Kg 9:4; Ps 101:2
[ab]**79:title** 1Ch 16:5,7
[ac]**79:1** Jr 26:18; Lm 1:10; Mc 3:12
[ad]**79:2** Dt 28:26; Jr 7:33; 16:4
[ae]**79:3** Jr 14:16; 16:4; 22:19
[af]**79:4** Ps 44:13-14; 80:6; Dn 9:16

[A]**78:49** Or *angels* [B]**78:51** Ham's descendants who settled in Egypt [C]**78:60** Hb *adam* [D]**78:61** = the ark of the covenant [E]**78:63** Lit *virgins were not praised* [F]**78:64** Lit *His* [G]**78:64** War probably prevented customary funerals. [H]**78:69** Either the heights of heaven or the mountain heights

Will Your jealousy keep burning
like fire?[a]
6 Pour out Your wrath on the nations
that don't acknowledge You,
on the kingdoms that don't call on
Your name,[b]
7 for they have devoured Jacob
and devastated his homeland.[c]
8 Do not hold past sins[A] against us;
let Your compassion come to us quickly,
for we have become weak.[d]

9 God of our salvation, help us[e] —
for the glory of Your name.
Deliver us and •atone for[B] our sins,
because of Your name.[f]
10 Why should the nations ask,
"Where is their God?"[g]
Before our eyes,
let vengeance for the shed blood
of Your servants
be known among the nations.[h]
11 Let the groans of the prisoners
reach You;
according to Your great power,
preserve those condemned to die.[i]

12 Pay back sevenfold to our neighbors[j]
the reproach they have hurled at You,
Lord.[k]
13 Then we, Your people, the sheep
of Your pasture,[l]
will thank You forever;
we will declare Your praise
to generation after generation.[m]

Psalm 80

A Prayer for Restoration

For the choir director: according to "The Lilies."[C]
A testimony of •Asaph.[n] A psalm.

1 Listen, Shepherd of Israel,
who leads Joseph like a flock;[o]
You who sit enthroned
on the •cherubim,[p]
rise up[q]
2 before Ephraim,
Benjamin, and Manasseh.[D,r]
Rally Your power and come to save us.[s]
3 Restore us, God;
look on us with favor,
and we will be saved.[t]

4 LORD God of •Hosts,
how long will You be angry
with Your people's prayers?[u]
5 You fed them the bread of tears
and gave them a full measure[E]
of tears to drink.[v]
6 You make us quarrel
with our neighbors;
our enemies make fun of us.[w]
7 Restore us, God of Hosts;
look on us with favor, and we will be
saved.[x]

8 You uprooted a vine from Egypt;
You drove out the nations
and planted it.[y]
9 You cleared a place for it;
it took root and filled the land.[z]
10 The mountains were covered
by its shade,
and the mighty cedars[F]
with its branches.[aa]
11 It sent out sprouts toward the Sea[G]
and shoots toward the River.[H,ab]
12 Why have You broken down its walls
so that all who pass by pick its fruit?[ac]
13 The boar from the forest tears it
and creatures of the field feed on it.[ad]
14 Return, God of Hosts.[ae]
Look down from heaven and see;
take care of this vine,
15 the root[I] Your right hand has planted,
the shoot[J] that You made strong
for Yourself.[af]
16 It was cut down and burned up;[K]
they[L] perish at the rebuke
of Your countenance.[ag]
17 Let Your hand be with the man
at Your right hand,
with the son of man
You have made strong for Yourself.[ah]
18 Then we will not turn away from You;
revive us, and we will call on Your name.[ai]
19 Restore us, •Yahweh, the God of Hosts;[aj]
look on us with favor, and we will
be saved.[ak]

[a]79:5 Ps 74:10; 78:58; 80:4
[b]79:6 Ps 14:4; Jr 10:25
[c]79:7 Ps 53:4
[d]79:8 Ps 142:6; Is 64:9
[e]79:9 1Ch 16:35; Ps 85:4
[f]Ps 25:11; 106:8; Jr 14:7
[g]79:10 Ps 42:3,10; 115:2
[h]Dt 32:43; Ps 94:1-2; Jr 46:10
[i]79:11 Ps 102:20
[j]79:12 Lv 26:21,28
[k]Ps 74:10,18,22
[l]79:13 Ps 74:1; 100:3
[m]Ps 89:1; Is 43:21
[n]80:title 1Ch 16:5,7
[o]80:1 Ezk 34:11,16,31
[p]Ps 99:1
[q]Ps 44:26
[r]80:2 Nm 2:17-24
[s]Ps 35:23; 106:47; 118:25
[t]80:3 Ps 60:1; 85:4; Lm 5:21
[u]80:4 Ps 74:10; 79:5; 85:5
[v]80:5 Ps 102:9; Is 30:20; Hs 9:4
[w]80:6 Ps 44:13; 79:4
[x]80:7 Ps 60:1; Lm 5:21
[y]80:8 Jr 2:21; 32:41
[z]80:9 Am 9:15
[aa]80:10 Ezk 17:22-24
[ab]80:11 Ex 23:31; Dt 11:24; Ps 72:8
[ac]80:12 Ps 89:40; Is 5:5
[ad]80:13 Jr 5:6
[ae]80:14 Ps 6:4; 90:13
[af]80:14-15 Is 63:15
[ag]80:16 Ps 39:11; 76:6; Is 33:12
[ah]80:17 Ps 89:21
[ai]80:18 Ps 71:20; 85:6
[aj]80:19 Ps 60:1; 85:4; Lm 5:21
[ak]Mal 1:9

[A]79:8 Or *hold the sins of past generations* [B]79:9 Or *and wipe out*, or *and forgive* [C]80:title Possibly a tune; Pss 45; 60; 69 [D]80:2 This is the marching order for the camp of Israel. [E]80:5 Lit *a one-third measure* [F]80:10 Lit *the cedars of God* [G]80:11 = the Mediterranean [H]80:11 = the Euphrates [I]80:15 Hb obscure [J]80:15 Or *son* [K]80:16 Lit *burned with fire* [L]80:16 Or *may they*

Psalm 81
A Call to Obedience

For the choir director: on the ·*Gittith*. Of ·Asaph.[a]

1 Sing for joy to God our strength;
shout in triumph to the God of Jacob.[b]
2 Lift up a song — play the tambourine,
the melodious lyre, and the harp.[c]
3 Blow the horn on the day of our feasts[A,B]
during the new moon[d]
and during the full moon.
4 For this is a statute for Israel,
a judgment of the God of Jacob.[e]
5 He set it up as an ordinance for Joseph
when He went throughout[C] the land
of Egypt.[f]

I heard an unfamiliar language:
6 "I relieved his shoulder
from the burden;
his hands were freed from carrying
the basket.[g]
7 You called out in distress,
and I rescued you;
I answered you
from the thundercloud.[h]
I tested you at the waters of Meribah.[i]
·Selah
8 Listen, My people, and I will
admonish you.
Israel, if you would only listen to Me![j]
9 There must not be a strange god
among you;
you must not bow down
to a foreign god.[k]
10 I am ·Yahweh your God,
who brought you up from the land
of Egypt.[l]
Open your mouth wide, and I will
fill it.[m]

11 "But My people did not listen to Me;
Israel did not obey Me.[n]
12 So I gave them over
to their stubborn hearts
to follow their own plans.[o]
13 If only My people would listen to Me
and Israel would follow My ways,[p]
14 I would quickly subdue their enemies
and turn My hand against their foes."[q]

15 Those who hate the LORD
would pretend submission to Him;[r]
their doom would last forever.[s]
16 But He would feed Israel[D]
with the best wheat.
"I would satisfy you with honey
from the rock."[t]

Psalm 82
A Plea for Righteous Judgment

A psalm of ·Asaph.[u]

1 God has taken His place
in the divine assembly;
He judges among the gods:[E,v]
2 "How long will you judge unjustly
and show partiality to the wicked?[w]
·Selah
3 Provide justice for the needy
and the fatherless;
uphold the rights of the oppressed
and the destitute.[x]
4 Rescue the poor and needy;
save them from the power of
the wicked."[y]

5 They do not know or understand;
they wander in darkness.[z]
All the foundations of the earth
are shaken.[aa]

6 I said, "You are gods;[ab]
you are all sons of the ·Most High.[ac]
7 However, you will die like men
and fall like any other ruler."[ad]

8 Rise up, God, judge the earth,
for all the nations belong to You.[ae]

Psalm 83
Prayer against Enemies

A song. A psalm of ·Asaph.[af]

1 God, do not keep silent.
Do not be deaf, God; do not be idle.[ag]
2 See how Your enemies make an uproar;
those who hate You
have acted arrogantly.[F,ah]
3 They devise clever schemes
against Your people;
they conspire against
Your treasured ones.[ai]

[a] **81:title** 1Ch 16:5,7; Ps 8,84 titles
[b] **81:1** Ps 59:16; 95:1-2; 98:4
[c] **81:2** Ps 33:2; 71:22; 92:3
[d] **81:3** Lv 23:24; Nm 10:10; 29:1
[e] **81:4** 1Ch 16:17; Ps 105:10
[f] **81:5** Ps 78:5; 122:4
[g] **81:6** Is 9:4; 10:27
[h] **81:7** Ex 14:24; 20:18-20
[i] Ex 17:1-7; Nm 20:2-13
[j] **81:8** Ps 50:7
[k] **81:9** Ex 20:3-5; 22:20; 34:14
[l] **81:10** Ex 20:2; Dt 5:6
[m] Ps 78:25; 107:9
[n] **81:11** Jr 7:24; 13:10
[o] **81:12** Jb 8:4; Jr 11:8
[p] **81:13** Dt 5:29; Is 48:18
[q] **81:14** Ps 18:47; 47:3; Am 1:8
[r] **81:15** Ps 18:44; 66:3
[s] Dt 32:35
[t] **81:16** Nm 18:12; Dt 32:13-14; Ps 147:14
[u] **82:title** 1Ch 16:5,7
[v] **82:1** Jb 21:22; Ps 7:8; 58:11
[w] **82:2** Dt 1:17; Pr 18:5; Mal 2:9
[x] **82:3** Dt 24:17; Is 11:4; Jr 22:16
[y] **82:4** Jb 29:12; Pr 24:11
[z] **82:5** Pr 2:13; Is 44:18
[aa] Ps 11:3
[ab] **82:6** Jn 10:34
[ac] Ps 82:1; Lk 6:35
[ad] **82:7** Ps 49:12
[ae] **82:8** Ps 58:11; 96:13
[af] **83:title** 1Ch 16:5,7
[ag] **83:1** Ps 28:1; 39:12; Is 62:1
[ah] **83:2** Ps 2:1; Is 17:12
[ai] **83:3** Jb 5:12-13; Ps 37:12; 64:2

A 81:3 Lit *feast* B 81:3 Either Passover or Tabernacles C 81:5 LXX, Syr, Jer read *out of* D 81:16 Lit *him* E 82:1 Or *the heavenly beings*, or *the earthly rulers*; lit *elohim* F 83:2 Lit *have lifted their head*

4 They say, "Come, let us wipe them out
as a nation
so that Israel's name will no longer
be remembered."[a]
5 For they have conspired with one mind;
they form an alliance[A] against You[b]—
6 the tents of Edom and the Ishmaelites,[c]
Moab and the Hagrites,[d]
7 Gebal, Ammon, and Amalek,[e]
Philistia with the inhabitants of Tyre.[f]
8 Even Assyria has joined them;
they lend support[B] to the sons of Lot.[C,g]
·Selah

9 Deal with them as You did
with Midian,[h]
as You did with Sisera
and Jabin at the Kishon River.[i]
10 They were destroyed at En-dor;
they became manure for the ground.[j]
11 Make their nobles like Oreb and Zeeb,[k]
and all their tribal leaders like Zebah
and Zalmunna,[l]
12 who said, "Let us seize God's pastures
for ourselves."[m]

13 Make them like tumbleweed, my God,
like straw before the wind.[n]
14 As fire burns a forest,
as a flame blazes through mountains,[o]
15 so pursue them with Your tempest
and terrify them with Your storm.[p]
16 Cover their faces with shame
so that they will seek
Your name ·Yahweh.[q]
17 Let them be put to shame
and terrified forever;
let them perish in disgrace.[r]
18 May they know that You alone—
whose name is Yahweh—
are the ·Most High over all the earth.[s]

Psalm 84

Longing for God's House

For the choir director: on the ·*Gittith*.[t]
A psalm of the sons of Korah.

1 How lovely is Your dwelling place,
LORD of ·Hosts.[u]
2 I long and yearn
for the courts of the LORD;
my heart and flesh cry out
for[D] the living God.[v]

3 Even a sparrow finds a home,
and a swallow, a nest for herself
where she places her young—
near Your altars, LORD of Hosts,
my King and my God.[w]
4 How happy are those who reside
in Your house,
who praise You continually.[x] ·Selah

5 Happy are the people whose strength is
in You,
whose hearts are set on pilgrimage.[y]
6 As they pass through the Valley
of Baca,[E]
they make it a source of springwater;
even the autumn rain will cover it
with blessings.[F,z]
7 They go from strength to strength;
each appears before God in ·Zion.[aa]

8 LORD God of Hosts, hear my prayer;
listen, God of Jacob.[ab] Selah
9 Consider our shield,[G] God;[ac]
look on the face of Your anointed one.[ad]

10 Better a day in Your courts
than a thousand anywhere else.
I would rather be at the door
of the house of my God
than to live in the tents
of wicked people.[ae]
11 For the LORD God is a sun and shield.[af]
The LORD gives grace and glory;
He does not withhold the good
from those who live with integrity.[ag]
12 Happy is the person who trusts in You,
LORD of Hosts![ah]

Psalm 85

Restoration of Favor

For the choir director. A psalm of the sons of Korah.

1 LORD, You showed favor to Your land;[ai]
You restored Jacob's prosperity.[H,aj]
2 You took away Your people's ·guilt;
You covered all their sin.[ak] ·Selah
3 You withdrew all Your fury;
You turned from Your burning anger.[al]

4 Return to us, God of our salvation,

[a]**83:4** Ps 41:5; Jr 11:19 [b]**83:5** Ps 2:2 [c]**83:6** Gn 25:12-16; Ps 137:7 [d]1Ch 5:10; 2Ch 20:10 [e]**83:7** Jos 13:5; 1Sm 15:2 [f]1Sm 4:1; Ezk 27:3 [g]**83:8** 2Kg 15:19 [h]**83:9** Nm 31:7; Jdg 7:1-24 [i]Jdg 4:7; 5:21 [j]**83:10** Jr 9:22; 16:4; 25:33 [k]**83:11** Jdg 7:25; 8:3 [l]Jdg 8:5-21 [m]**83:12** 2Ch 20:11 [n]**83:13** Jb 21:18; Ps 1:4; Is 17:13 [o]**83:14** Is 9:18; 10:16-19 [p]**83:15** Jb 9:17; Ps 58:9 [q]**83:16** Ps 35:26; 109:29; 132:18 [r]**83:17** Ps 35:4; 70:2 [s]**83:18** Ps 97:9 [t]**84:title** Ps 8,81 titles [u]**84:1** Ps 43:3; 132:5 [v]**84:2** Ps 42:1-2; 63:1 [w]**84:3** Ps 5:2; 43:4 [x]**84:4** Ps 65:4 [y]**84:5** Ps 119:2; 122:1 [z]**84:6** Ezk 34:26; Jl 2:23 [aa]**84:7** Pr 4:18; Is 40:31 [ab]**84:8** Ps 39:12; 54:2; 86:6 [ac]**84:9** Ps 3:3; 115:9-11 [ad]1Sm 2:10; 2Ch 6:42; Ps 132:17 [ae]**84:10** Ps 27:4 [af]**84:11** Ps 3:3; 5:12; 18:2; 28:7; 119:114; Is 60:19-20; Rv 21:23 [ag]Pr 2:7 [ah]**84:12** Ps 40:4 [ai]**85:1** Ps 106:4 [aj]Dt 30:3; Ps 14:7; Jr 29:14 [ak]**85:2** 1Kg 8:34; Ps 32:1,5 [al]**85:3** Ps 78:38; 106:23; Jnh 3:9

[A]**83:5** Lit *they cut a covenant* [B]**83:8** Lit *they are an arm* [C]**83:8** = Moab and Edom [D]**84:2** Or *flesh shout for joy to* [E]**84:6** Or *Valley of Tears* [F]**84:6** Or *pools* [G]**84:9** = the king [H]**85:1** Or *restored Jacob from captivity*

and abandon Your displeasure with us.[a]
5 Will You be angry with us forever?
Will You prolong Your anger for all
generations?[b]
6 Will You not revive us again
so that Your people may rejoice in You?[c]
7 Show us Your faithful love, LORD,
and give us Your salvation.[d]

8 I will listen to what God will say;
surely the LORD will declare peace
to His people, His godly ones,
and not let them go back
to foolish ways.[e]
9 His salvation is very near
those who ·fear Him,
so that glory may dwell in our land.[f]
10 Faithful love and truth
will join together;
righteousness and peace will embrace.[g]
11 Truth will spring up from the earth,
and righteousness will look
down from heaven.[h]
12 Also, the LORD will provide
what is good,
and our land will yield its crops.[i]
13 Righteousness will go before Him
to prepare the way for His steps.[j]

PSALM 86

Lament and Petition

A Davidic prayer.

1 Listen, LORD, and answer me,
for I am poor and needy.[k]
2 Protect my life, for I am faithful.[l]
You are my God; save Your servant
who trusts in You.[m]
3 Be gracious to me, Lord,
for I call to You all day long.[n]
4 Bring joy to Your servant's life,
because I turn to You, Lord.[o]
5 For You, Lord, are kind and ready
to forgive,[p]
rich in faithful love to all who call
on You.[q]
6 LORD, hear my prayer;
listen to my plea for mercy.[r]
7 I call on You in the day of my distress,
for You will answer me.[s]

8 Lord, there is no one like You
among the gods,
and there are no works like Yours.[t]
9 All the nations You have made
will come and bow down
before You, Lord,
and will honor Your name.[u]
10 For You are great
and perform wonders;
You alone are God.[v]

11 Teach me Your way, ·Yahweh,
and I will live by Your truth.
Give me an undivided mind to ·fear
Your name.[w]
12 I will praise You with all my heart,
Lord my God,
and will honor Your name forever.[x]
13 For Your faithful love for me is great,
and You deliver my life from the depths
of ·Sheol.[y]

14 God, arrogant people have attacked me;
a gang of ruthless men seeks my life.
They have no regard for You.[z]
15 But You, Lord, are a compassionate
and gracious God,
slow to anger and rich in faithful love
and truth.[aa]
16 Turn to me and be gracious to me.
Give Your strength to Your servant;
save the son of Your female servant.[ab]
17 Show me a sign of Your goodness;
my enemies will see and be put
to shame
because You, LORD, have helped
and comforted me.[ac]

PSALM 87

Zion, the City of God

A psalm of the sons of Korah. A song.

1 His foundation is
on the holy mountains.[ad]
2 The LORD loves the gates of ·Zion
more than all the dwellings of Jacob.[ae]
3 Glorious things are said about you,
city of God.[af] ·*Selah*

4 "I will mention those who know Me:
·Rahab, Babylon, Philistia, Tyre,
and ·Cush —
each one was born there."[ag]
5 And it will be said of Zion,

[a] **85:4** Ps 27:9; 79:9; 80:3,7
[b] **85:5** Ps 74:1; 79:5; 80:4
[c] **85:6** Ps 71:20; 80:18; 149:2
[d] **85:7** Ps 69:13; 119:41
[e] **85:8** Hg 2:9; Zch 9:10
[f] **85:9** Is 46:13; Zch 2:5; Jn 1:14
[g] **85:10** Ps 72:3; 89:14
[h] **85:11** Is 45:8
[i] **85:12** Ps 65:12-13; 67:6; Ezk 34:27
[j] **85:13** Ps 89:14; Is 40:3,10; 58:8
[k] **86:1** Ps 17:6; 31:2; 70:5
[l] **86:2** 1Sm 2:9; Ps 37:28
[m] Ps 109:26
[n] **86:3** Ps 25:5; 88:9
[o] **86:4** Ps 25:1; 43:5
[p] **86:5** Ps 130:4
[q] Ps 103:8; 145:8
[r] **86:6** Ps 55:1-2
[s] **86:7** Gn 35:3; Ps 17:6; 20:1
[t] **86:8** Ex 15:11; Dt 3:24; Ps 89:6
[u] **86:9** Ps 22:7; Is 66:24; Rv 15:4
[v] **86:10** 2Kg 19:15; Ps 72:18; 83:18; Jr 10:6
[w] **86:11** Ps 25:4-5; 26:3
[x] **86:12** Ps 111:1
[y] **86:13** Ps 30:3; Ezk 26:20
[z] **86:14** Ps 54:3
[aa] **86:15** Ex 34:6; Nm 14:18; Neh 9:17
[ab] **86:16** Ps 25:16; 68:35
[ac] **86:17** Ps 112:10; 132:18
[ad] **87:1** Ps 78:69; Is 28:16
[ae] **87:2** Ps 78:67-68
[af] **87:3** Ps 48:8
[ag] **87:4** Is 19:23-25; 56:6-7; Zch 2:10-12

"This one and that one were born
in her."
The ·Most High Himself
will establish her.[a]
6 When He registers the peoples,
the LORD will record,
"This one was born there."[b] *Selah*
7 Singers and dancers alike will say,
"My whole source of joy is[A] in you."[c]

PSALM 88
A Cry of Desperation

A song. A psalm of the sons of Korah. For the choir director: according to *Mahalath Leannoth*. A ·*Maskil* of Heman the Ezrahite.[d]

1 LORD, God of my salvation,
I cry out before You day and night.[e]
2 May my prayer reach Your presence;
listen to my cry.[f]
3 For I have had enough troubles,
and my life is near ·Sheol.[g]
4 I am counted among those going down
to the ·Pit.[h]
I am like a man without strength,[i]
5 abandoned[B] among the dead.
I am like the slain lying
in the grave,[j]
whom You no longer remember,
and who are cut off from Your care.[C,k]

6 You have put me in the lowest part
of the Pit,
in the darkest places, in the depths.[l]
7 Your wrath weighs heavily on me;[m]
You have overwhelmed me with all
Your waves.[n] ·*Selah*
8 You have distanced my friends
from me;
You have made me repulsive to them.[o]
I am shut in and cannot go out.
9 My eyes are worn out from crying.[p]
LORD, I cry out to You all day long;[q]
I spread out my hands to You.[r]

10 Do You work wonders for the dead?
Do departed spirits rise up
to praise You?[s] *Selah*
11 Will Your faithful love be declared
in the grave,
Your faithfulness in ·Abaddon?[t]

[a]**87:5** Ps 48:8; Is 2:2
[b]**87:6** Is 4:3; Ezk 13:9
[c]**87:7** Ps 46:4; 68:25
[d]**88:title** 1Kg 4:31; 1Ch 2:6
[e]**88:1** Ps 22:2; 86:3; Lk 18:7
[f]**88:2** Ps 18:6; 31:2; 86:1
[g]**88:3** Ps 16:10; 116:3
[h]**88:4** Ps 28:1; 143:7
[i]Ps 61:2
[j]**88:5** Ps 31:12
[k]Ps 31:22; Is 53:8
[l]**88:6** Ps 69:15; 86:13; Ezk 26:20
[m]**88:7** Ps 32:4; 39:10
[n]Ps 42:7
[o]**88:8** Jb 19:13-22; Ps 31:11
[p]**88:9** Ps 6:7; 31:9
[q]Ps 86:3
[r]Ps 143:6
[s]**88:10** Ps 6:5; 30:9
[t]**88:11** Jb 26:6; Pr 15:11; 27:20
[u]**88:12** Ec 9:5
[v]**88:13** Ps 5:3; 119:147
[w]**88:14** Ps 43:2
[x]Jb 13:24; Ps 10:1; 13:1
[y]**88:15** Jb 31:23
[z]**88:16** Jb 6:4; 9:34
[aa]**88:17** Ps 22:12,16; 118:10-12
[ab]**88:18** Jb 19:13; Ps 31:11; 38:11
[ac]**89:title** 1Kg 4:31; 1Ch 2:6
[ad]**89:1** Ps 101:1
[ae]Ps 92:2; 119:90
[af]**89:2** Ps 36:5
[ag]**89:3-4** 2Sm 7:8-16; 1Ch 17:7-14; Jr 33:17-21
[ah]**89:5** Ps 19:1; 97:6
[ai]Ps 149:1
[aj]**89:6** Ps 86:8; 113:5

12 Will Your wonders be known in
the darkness
or Your righteousness in the land
of oblivion?[u]

13 But I call to You for help, LORD;
in the morning my prayer meets You.[v]
14 LORD, why do You reject me?[w]
Why do You hide Your face from me?[x]
15 From my youth,
I have been afflicted and near death.
I suffer Your horrors; I am desperate.[y]
16 Your wrath sweeps over me;
Your terrors destroy me.[z]
17 They surround me like water
all day long;
they close in on me from every side.[aa]
18 You have distanced loved one
and neighbor from me;
darkness is my only friend.[D,ab]

PSALM 89
Perplexity about God's Promises

A ·*Maskil* of Ethan the Ezrahite.[ac]

1 I will sing about the LORD's
faithful love forever;[ad]
I will proclaim Your faithfulness to all
generations
with my mouth.[ae]
2 For I will declare,
"Faithful love is built up forever;
You establish Your faithfulness
in the heavens."[af]

3 The LORD said,
"I have made a covenant
with My chosen one;
I have sworn an oath to David
My servant:
4 'I will establish your offspring forever
and build up your throne
for all generations.'"[ag] ·*Selah*

5 LORD, the heavens praise
Your wonders[ah] —
Your faithfulness also —
in the assembly of the holy ones.[ai]
6 For who in the skies can compare
with the LORD?
Who among the heavenly beings[E] is
like the LORD?[aj]

[A]**87:7** Lit *"All my springs, are* [B]**88:5** Or *set free* [C]**88:5** Or *hand* [D]**88:18** Or *from me, my friends. Oh darkness!* [E]**89:6** Or *the angels*, or *the sons of the mighty*

7 God is greatly ·feared in the council
of the holy ones,
more awe-inspiring than[A]
all who surround Him.[a]
8 LORD God of ·Hosts,
who is strong like You, LORD?[b]
Your faithfulness surrounds You.
9 You rule the raging sea;
when its waves surge, You still them.[c]
10 You crushed ·Rahab like one
who is slain;[d]
You scattered Your enemies
with Your powerful arm.[e]
11 The heavens are Yours; the earth also
is Yours.
The world and everything
in it—You founded them.[f]
12 North and south—You created them.[g]
Tabor and Hermon shout for joy
at Your name.[h]
13 You have a mighty arm;
Your hand is powerful;
Your right hand is lifted high.[i]
14 Righteousness and justice are
the foundation
of Your throne;[j]
faithful love and truth go before You.[k]
15 Happy are the people who know
the joyful shout;[l]
·Yahweh, they walk in the light
of Your presence.[m]
16 They rejoice in Your name all day long,
and they are exalted
by Your righteousness.[n]
17 For You are their magnificent strength;[o]
by Your favor our ·horn is exalted.[p]
18 Surely our shield[B] belongs to the LORD,
our king to the Holy One of Israel.[q]
19 You once spoke in a vision
to Your loyal ones
and said: "I have granted help
to a warrior;
I have exalted one chosen[C]
from the people.[r]
20 I have found David My servant;
I have anointed him with My sacred oil.[s]
21 My hand will always be with him,
and My arm will strengthen him.[t]

[a]89:7 Ps 89:5; 96:4
[b]89:8 Ex 15:11; 2Sm 7:22
[c]89:9 Jb 38:11; Ps 104:9; Mt 8:23-27
[d]89:10 Is 30:7; 51:9-10
[e]Ps 68:1; 92:9
[f]89:11 1Ch 29:11; Ps 24:1
[g]89:12 Jb 26:7
[h]Ps 133:3; Jr 46:18
[i]89:13 Ps 98:1; 118:16
[j]89:14 Ps 97:2
[k]Ps 85:13
[l]89:15 Ps 98:6
[m]Ps 56:13; 1Jn 1:7
[n]89:16 Ps 20:5; 105:3
[o]89:17 Ps 28:8
[p]Ps 148:14
[q]89:18 Ps 84:9
[r]89:19 2Sm 17:10; 1Kg 11:34; Ps 78:70
[s]89:20 1Sm 16:13; Ps 47:9; Ac 13:22
[t]89:21 Ps 18:35; 80:17
[u]89:22 2Sm 7:10
[v]89:23 2Sm 7:9; Ps 2:9
[w]89:24 Ps 21:7; 132:17
[x]89:25 Ps 72:8
[y]89:26 2Sm 7:14; 1Ch 22:10
[z]2Sm 22:47; Ps 18:2
[aa]89:27 Ex 4:22; Jr 31:9; Col 1:15
[ab]89:28 2Ch 13:5; Ps 105:8
[ac]89:29 Is 9:7; Jr 33:17
[ad]89:30 2Sm 7:14; 1Kg 2:4
[ae]89:31 1Sm 12:15
[af]89:32 Jb 9:34
[ag]89:33 2Sm 7:15
[ah]89:34 Lv 26:44; Jdg 2:1
[ai]89:35 Am 4:2
[aj]89:36 Ps 72:5,17
[ak]89:37 Jb 16:19; Lk 1:33
[al]89:38 1Ch 28:9; Ps 44:9
[am]89:39 Ps 74:7; Lm 2:7; 5:16
[an]89:40 Ps 80:12; Lm 2:2,5

22 The enemy will not afflict[D] him;
no wicked man will oppress him.[u]
23 I will crush his foes before him
and strike those who hate him.[v]
24 My faithfulness and love will be
with him,
and through My name
his horn will be exalted.[w]
25 I will extend his power to the sea
and his right hand to the rivers.[x]
26 He will call to Me, 'You are my Father,[y]
my God, the rock of my salvation.'[z]
27 I will also make him My firstborn,
greatest of the kings of the earth.[aa]
28 I will always preserve My faithful love
for him,
and My covenant with him
will endure.[ab]
29 I will establish his line forever,
his throne as long as heaven lasts.[E,ac]
30 If his sons forsake My instruction
and do not live by My ordinances,[ad]
31 if they dishonor My statutes
and do not keep My commands,[ae]
32 then I will call their rebellion
to account with the rod,
their sin with blows.[af]
33 But I will not withdraw
My faithful love from him
or betray My faithfulness.[ag]
34 I will not violate My covenant
or change what My lips have said.[ah]
35 Once and for all
I have sworn an oath by My holiness;
I will not lie to David.[ai]
36 His offspring will continue forever,
his throne like the sun before Me,[aj]
37 like the moon, established forever,
a faithful witness in the sky."[ak] *Selah*
38 But You have spurned and rejected him;
You have become enraged
with Your anointed.[al]
39 You have repudiated the covenant
with Your servant;
You have completely dishonored
his crown.[F,am]
40 You have broken down all his walls;
You have reduced his fortified cities
to ruins.[an]

[A]89:7 Or *ones, revered by* [B]89:18 = the king [C]89:19 Or *exalted a young man* [D]89:22 Or *not exact tribute from* [E]89:29 Lit *as days of heaven* [F]89:39 Lit *have dishonored his crown to the ground*

41 All who pass by plunder him;[a]
he has become an object of ridicule
to his neighbors.[b]
42 You have lifted high the right hand
of his foes;
You have made all his enemies rejoice.[c]
43 You have also turned back
his sharp sword
and have not let him stand in battle.[d]
44 You have made his splendor[A] cease
and have overturned his throne.[e]
45 You have shortened the days
of his youth;
You have covered him with shame.[f]
Selah

46 How long, LORD? Will You hide
Yourself forever?
Will Your anger keep burning like fire?[g]
47 Remember how short my life is.
Have You created ·everyone
for nothing?[h]
48 What man can live and never see death?
Who can save himself from the power
of ·Sheol?[i] *Selah*
49 Lord, where are the former acts
of Your faithful love
that You swore to David
in Your faithfulness?[j]
50 Remember, Lord, the ridicule
against Your servants—
in my heart I carry abuse from all
the peoples—
51 how Your enemies
have ridiculed, LORD,
how they have ridiculed every step
of Your anointed.[k]

52 May the LORD be praised forever.
·Amen and amen.[l]

BOOK IV
(Psalms 90–106)

PSALM 90
Eternal God and Mortal Man

A prayer of Moses, the man of God.

1 Lord, You have been our refuge[B]
in every generation.[m]
2 Before the mountains were born,
before You gave birth to the earth
and the world,
from eternity to eternity, You are God.[n]

3 You return mankind to the dust,
saying, "Return, descendants of Adam."[o]
4 For in Your sight a thousand years
are like yesterday that passes by,
like a few hours of the night.[p]
5 You end their lives;[C] they sleep.[q]
They are like grass that grows
in the morning—
6 in the morning it sprouts and grows;
by evening it withers and dries up.[r]

7 For we are consumed by Your anger;
we are terrified by Your wrath.[s]
8 You have set our unjust ways
before You,
our secret sins in the light
of Your presence.[t]
9 For all our days ebb away
under Your wrath;
we end our years like a sigh.[u]
10 Our lives last[D] seventy years
or, if we are strong, eighty years.
Even the best of them are[E] struggle
and sorrow;
indeed, they pass quickly and we
fly away.[v]
11 Who understands the power
of Your anger?
Your wrath matches the fear
that is due You.[w]
12 Teach us to number our days carefully
so that we may develop wisdom
in our hearts.[F,x]

13 LORD—how long?
Turn and have compassion
on Your servants.[y]
14 Satisfy us in the morning
with Your faithful love
so that we may shout with joy
and be glad all our days.[z]
15 Make us rejoice for as many days
as You have humbled us,
for as many years as
we have seen adversity.[aa]
16 Let Your work be seen by Your servants,
and Your splendor by their children.[ab]

[a]**89:41** Jr 30:16 [b]Ps 44:13; 79:4 [c]**89:42** Ps 13:4; 80:6 [d]**89:43** Ps 44:10 [e]**89:44** Ezk 28:7 [f]**89:45** Is 54:4; Ezk 7:18; Ob 10 [g]**89:46** Ps 6:3; 13:1; 35:17; 79:5 [h]**89:47** Ps 39:6-7; 90:5-6,9-10 [i]**89:48** Ps 16:10; 22:29 [j]**89:49** 2Sm 7:15; Jr 30:9; Ezk 34:23 [k]**89:50-51** Ps 69:9; 74:10,18,22 [l]**89:52** Ps 41:13; 72:19-20; 106:48 [m]**90:1** Ps 71:3 [n]**90:2** Jb 36:26; Ps 102:27; Pr 8:25 [o]**90:3** Gn 3:19; Ec 12:7 [p]**90:4** 2Pt 3:8 [q]**90:5** Jb 14:12 [r]**90:5-6** Jb 14:1-2; Ps 37:2; 103:15-16 [s]**90:7** Ps 39:11 [t]**90:8** Ps 19:12; Ec 12:14 [u]**90:9** Ps 78:33 [v]**90:10** Jb 20:8; Ps 78:39 [w]**90:11** Ps 76:7 [x]**90:12** Dt 32:29; Ps 39:4 [y]**90:13** Dt 32:36; Ps 135:14 [z]**90:14** Ps 36:8; 65:4; 103:5 [aa]**90:15** Ps 86:4; 92:4 [ab]**90:16** Ps 96:6; Is 35:2

[A]**89:44** Hb obscure [B]**90:1** Some Hb mss, LXX; other Hb mss read *dwelling place* [C]**90:5** Or *You overwhelm them*; Hb obscure [D]**90:10** Lit *The days of our years in them* [E]**90:10** LXX, Tg, Syr, Vg read *Even their span is*; Hb obscure [F]**90:12** Or *develop a heart of wisdom*

17 Let the favor of the Lord our God be
on us;
establish for us the work
of our hands —
establish the work of our hands![a]

Psalm 91
The Protection of the Most High

1 The one who lives under the protection
of the ·Most High
dwells in the shadow of the ·Almighty.[b]
2 I will say[A] to the Lord, "My refuge
and my fortress,
my God, in whom I trust."[c]
3 He Himself will deliver you
from the hunter's net,[d]
from the destructive plague.
4 He will cover you with His feathers;
you will take refuge under His wings.[e]
His faithfulness will be
a protective shield.[f]
5 You will not fear the terror of the night,
the arrow that flies by day,[g]
6 the plague that stalks in darkness,
or the pestilence that ravages at noon.[h]
7 Though a thousand fall at your side
and ten thousand at your right hand,
the pestilence will not reach you.[i]
8 You will only see it with your eyes
and witness the punishment
of the wicked.[j]

9 Because you have made
the Lord — my refuge,[k]
the Most High — your dwelling place,[l]
10 no harm will come to you;
no plague will come near your tent.[m]
11 For He will give His angels orders
concerning you,
to protect you in all your ways.[n]
12 They will support you with their hands
so that you will not strike your foot
against a stone.[o]
13 You will tread on the lion
and the cobra;
you will trample the young lion
and the serpent.[p]
14 Because he is lovingly devoted to Me,
I will deliver him;
I will protect him because he knows
My name.[q]
15 When he calls out to Me,
I will answer him;
I will be with him in trouble.
I will rescue him and give him honor.[r]
16 I will satisfy him with a long life[s]
and show him My salvation.[t]

Psalm 92
God's Love and Faithfulness

A psalm. A song for the Sabbath day.

1 It is good to praise ·Yahweh,
to sing praise to Your name,
·Most High,[u]
2 to declare Your faithful love
in the morning
and Your faithfulness at night,[v]
3 with a ten-stringed harp
and the music of a lyre.[w]

4 For You have made me rejoice, Lord,
by what You have done;
I will shout for joy
because of the works of Your hands.[x]
5 How magnificent are Your works,
Lord,
how profound Your thoughts![y]
6 A stupid person does not know,
a fool does not understand this:[z]
7 though the wicked sprout like grass
and all evildoers flourish,
they will be eternally destroyed.[aa]
8 But You, Lord, are exalted forever.[ab]
9 For indeed, Lord, Your enemies —
indeed, Your enemies will perish;
all evildoers will be scattered.[ac]
10 You have lifted up my ·horn[ad]
like that of a wild ox;
I have been anointed[B] with oil.[ae]
11 My eyes look down on my enemies;
my ears hear evildoers
when they attack me.[af]

12 The righteous thrive like a palm tree
and grow like a cedar tree in Lebanon.[ag]
13 Planted in the house of the Lord,
they thrive in the courts of our God.[ah]
14 They will still bear fruit in old age,
healthy and green,[ai]

[a] 90:17 Ps 27:4; Is 26:12
[b] 91:1 Ps 27:5; 32:7; 121:5
[c] 91:2 Ps 18:2; 61:4; 62:7-8
[d] 91:3 Ps 124:7; 141:9; Ec 9:12
[e] 91:4 Ps 57:1; 63:7
[f] Ps 5:12
[g] 91:5 Ps 58:7; 76:3
[h] 91:5-6 Jb 5:19-23
[i] 91:7 2Ch 20:9
[j] 91:8 Ps 37:34; 58:10
[k] 91:9 Ps 18:2; 62:7-8
[l] Ps 121:5
[m] 91:10 Pr 12:21
[n] 91:11 Ps 34:7
[o] 91:11-12 Mt 4:6; Lk 4:10-11
[p] 91:13 Lk 10:19
[q] 91:14 Ps 9:10; 37:40; 107:41
[r] 91:15 2Sm 22:20; Ps 18:19; 50:15
[s] 91:16 Dt 4:40; Ps 21:4
[t] Ps 50:23
[u] 92:1 Ps 135:3; 147:1
[v] 92:2 Ps 59:16; 89:1; Lm 3:22-23
[w] 92:3 Ps 33:2
[x] 92:4 Ps 40:5; 143:5
[y] 92:5 Ps 139:17; Is 55:8-9
[z] 92:6 Ps 73:22
[aa] 92:7 Ps 90:5-6
[ab] 92:8 Ps 93:4
[ac] 92:9 Ps 37:20; 68:1
[ad] 92:10 Ps 89:17,24; 112:9
[ae] Ps 45:7
[af] 92:11 Ps 37:34; 54:7
[ag] 92:12 Ps 1:3; Is 61:3; Jr 17:8
[ah] 92:13 Is 60:21
[ai] 92:14 Is 37:31; 46:4

[A] 91:1-2 LXX, Syr, Jer read ²*Almighty, saying,* or ²*Almighty, he will say* [B] 92:10 Syr reads *You have anointed me*

15 to declare: "The LORD is just;
He is my rock,
and there is no unrighteousness
in Him."[a]

PSALM 93
God's Eternal Reign

1 The LORD reigns! He is robed
in majesty;
The LORD is robed,
enveloped in strength.
The world is firmly established;
it cannot be shaken.[b]
2 Your throne has been established
from the beginning;[A]
You are from eternity.[c]
3 The floods have lifted up, LORD,
the floods have lifted up their voice;
the floods lift up
their pounding waves.[d]
4 Greater than the roar
of many waters —
the mighty breakers of the sea —
the LORD on high is majestic.[e]

5 LORD, Your testimonies
are completely reliable;[f]
holiness is the beauty of[B] Your house
for all the days to come.[g]

PSALM 94
The Just Judge

1 LORD, God of vengeance —
God of vengeance, appear.[h]
2 Rise up, Judge of the earth;
repay the proud what they deserve.[i]
3 LORD, how long will the wicked —
how long will the wicked gloat?[j]
4 They pour out arrogant words;
all the evildoers boast.[k]
5 LORD, they crush Your people;
they afflict Your heritage.[l]
6 They kill the widow and the foreigner
and murder the fatherless.[m]
7 They say, "The LORD doesn't see it.
The God of Jacob
doesn't pay attention."[n]

8 Pay attention, you stupid people!
Fools, when will you be wise?[o]

[a]92:15 Dt 32:4; Ps 18:2; 94:22 [b]93:1 1Ch 16:30-31; Ps 96:10; 97:1 [c]93:2 Ps 9:7; 90:2; 103:19 [d]93:3 Ps 96:11; 98:7-8 [e]93:4 Ps 65:7; 89:9; Ezk 43:2 [f]93:5 Ps 19:7 [g]Ps 29:2; 96:9 [h]94:1 2Sm 22:48; Ps 18:47-48; Jr 46:10 [i]94:2 Ps 7:6; 28:4; 98:9 [j]94:3 Ps 74:10; Rv 6:10 [k]94:4 1Sm 2:3; Ps 31:18 [l]94:5 Is 3:15 [m]94:6 Dt 27:19; Is 10:2 [n]94:7 Jb 22:13; Ps 10:11 [o]94:8 Ps 92:6 [p]94:9 Ex 4:11; Pr 20:12 [q]94:10 Jb 35:11; Is 28:26 [r]94:11 Ps 139:2; Is 66:18; 1Co 3:20 [s]94:12 Ps 25:5,9; 71:17; Is 48:17 [t]94:13 Ps 7:15; 9:15; Pr 26:27 [u]94:14 1Sm 12:22; Rm 11:2 [v]94:15 Ps 36:10; 64:10; 97:11 [w]94:16 Ps 59:2 [x]94:17 Ps 124:1-2 [y]94:18 Ps 18:35; 66:9; 121:3 [z]94:19 Is 57:18; 66:13 [aa]94:20 Ps 50:16; 58:2 [ab]94:21 2Kg 21:16; Ps 106:38; Jr 26:15 [ac]94:22 2Sm 22:3; Ps 46:1,7; 62:2,6 [ad]94:23 Ps 73:27; 94:23; 101:5,8 [ae]95:1 Jb 38:7; Ps 81:1; 98:4,6

9 Can the One who shaped the ear
not hear,
the One who formed the eye not see?[p]
10 The One who instructs nations,
the One who teaches man knowledge —
does He not discipline?[q]
11 The LORD knows man's thoughts;
they are meaningless.[r]

12 LORD, happy is the man You discipline
and teach from Your law[s]
13 to give him relief from troubled times
until a pit is dug for the wicked.[t]
14 The LORD will not forsake His people
or abandon His heritage,[u]
15 for justice will again be righteous,
and all the upright in heart
will follow[C] it.[v]

16 Who stands up for me
against the wicked?
Who takes a stand for me
against evildoers?[w]
17 If the LORD had not been my helper,
I would soon rest in the silence
of death.[x]
18 If I say, "My foot is slipping,"
Your faithful love
will support me, LORD.[y]
19 When I am filled with cares,
Your comfort brings me joy.[z]

20 Can a corrupt throne —
one that creates trouble by law —
become Your ally?[aa]
21 They band together against the life
of the righteous
and condemn the innocent to death.[ab]
22 But the LORD is my refuge;
my God is the rock of my protection.[ac]
23 He will pay them back for their sins
and destroy them for their evil.
The LORD our God will destroy them.[ad]

PSALM 95
Worship and Warning

1 Come, let us shout joyfully to the LORD,
shout triumphantly to the rock
of our salvation![ae]
2 Let us enter His presence
with thanksgiving;

[A]93:2 Lit *from then* [B]93:5 Or *holiness characterizes* [C]94:15 Or *heart will support*; lit *heart after*

let us shout triumphantly to Him
in song.[a]
3 For the LORD is a great God,
a great King above all gods.[b]
4 The depths of the earth are in His hand,
and the mountain peaks are His.[c]
5 The sea is His; He made it.
His hands formed the dry land.[d]
6 Come, let us worship and bow down;
let us kneel before the LORD our Maker.[e]
7 For He is our God,
and we are the people of His pasture,
the sheep under His care.[A,f]

Today, if you hear His voice:[g]
8 Do not harden your hearts
as at Meribah,
as on that day at Massah
in the wilderness[h]
9 where your fathers tested Me;
they tried Me, though they had seen
what I did.[i]
10 For 40 years I was disgusted
with that generation;
I said, "They are a people whose hearts
go astray;
they do not know My ways."[j]
11 So I swore in My anger,
"They will not enter My rest."[k]

[a]95:2 Ps 100:4; Jnh 2:9 [b]95:3 Dt 10:17; Ps 47:2; 96:4 [c]95:4 Ps 135:6 [d]95:5 Gn 1:9-10; Ps 146:6; Jnh 1:9 [e]95:6 Ps 96:9; 100:3; Is 17:7 [f]95:7 Ps 79:13 [g]Heb 3:7-11,15; 4:7 [h]95:8 Ex 17:7; Dt 6:16 [i]95:9 Nm 14:22; Ps 78:18 [j]95:10 Dt 9:7; Ac 13:18; Heb 3:10,17 [k]95:11 Nm 14:23,28-30; Dt 12:9 [l]Ps 96 1Ch 16:23-33 [m]96:1 1Ch 16:23; Ps 98:1; Is 42:10 [n]96:2 Is 25:9; 52:7 [o]96:3 1Ch 16:9,24; Ps 145:12

PSALM 96[l]

King of the Earth

1 Sing a new song to the LORD;
sing to the LORD, all the earth.[m]
2 Sing to ·Yahweh, praise His name;
proclaim His salvation from day to day.[n]
3 Declare His glory among the nations,
His wonderful works
among all peoples.[o]
4 For the LORD is great and is
highly praised;

GOD'S HEART FOR THE WORLD

The Lord Reigns

Say among the nations: The Lord reigns." The world is firmly established; it cannot be shaken. (Psalm 96:10)

"The Lord reigns," not the idols. Not money or power. Not the rich or the powerful. Not the beautiful. Not the nicest people, not the worst ones. Not companies or CEOs. Not human kings or presidents. The Lord reigns, and that is our only hope.

Because the Lord is King, the whole world is held together. Because He reigns, people will be judged fairly, with righteousness and faithfulness. We are not subject to the standards of this world, but to a gracious and loving God. In the face of this overwhelming truth, it is not enough for this psalmist that one group of worshipers sing God's glory, or even all of Israel. He seeks worship from the whole of creation, from the vast expanse of the heavens to the field mice and the sea's tiniest bit of plankton. The nations must hear! They must know that their idols are false, and that Israel worships the God who made the skies. Declare to them the amazing things that Yahweh has done so that they too might join in creation's chorus, ascribing glory and strength to the One True God who stands above all the others, promising us life and justice.

When God's people praise His name, the whole world gathers around to listen. "Sing a new song to the Lord; sing to the Lord, all the earth. Sing to the Lord, praise His name; proclaim His salvation from day to day. Declare His glory among the nations, His wonderful works among all peoples" (vv. 1–3).

Let the whole world hear our voices resound!

[A]95:7 Lit *sheep of His hand*

He is feared above all gods.[a]
5 For all the gods of the peoples are idols,
but the LORD made the heavens.[b]
6 Splendor and majesty are before Him;
strength and beauty are
in His sanctuary.[c]

7 Ascribe to the LORD, you families
of the peoples,
ascribe to the LORD glory and strength.[d]
8 Ascribe to Yahweh the glory of His name;[e]
bring an offering and enter His courts.[f]
9 Worship the LORD in the splendor
of His holiness;[g]
tremble before Him, all the earth.[h]

10 Say among the nations:
"The LORD reigns.[i]
The world is firmly established;
it cannot be shaken.[j]
He judges the peoples fairly."[k]
11 Let the heavens be glad
and the earth rejoice;
let the sea and all that fills it resound.[l]
12 Let the fields and everything
in them exult.
Then all the trees of the forest
will shout for joy[m]
13 before the LORD, for He is coming —
for He is coming to judge the earth.
He will judge the world
with righteousness
and the peoples with His faithfulness.[n]

PSALM 97
The Majestic King

1 The LORD reigns! Let the earth rejoice;
let the many coasts and islands be glad.[o]
2 Clouds and thick darkness
surround Him;
righteousness and justice are
the foundation of His throne.[p]
3 Fire goes before Him
and burns up His foes on every side.[q]
4 His lightning lights up the world;
the earth sees and trembles.[r]
5 The mountains melt like wax
at the presence of the LORD —
at the presence of the Lord of all
the earth.[s]

6 The heavens proclaim
His righteousness;[t]
all the peoples see His glory.[u]

7 All who serve carved images,
those who boast in idols, will be
put to shame.[v]
All the gods[A] must worship Him.[w]

8 ·Zion hears and is glad,
and the towns[B] of Judah rejoice
because of Your judgments, LORD.[x]
9 For You, LORD,
are the ·Most High over all the earth;
You are exalted above all the gods.[y]

10 You who love the LORD, hate evil![z]
He protects the lives of His godly ones;[aa]
He rescues them from the power of
the wicked.[ab]
11 Light dawns[C,D] for the righteous,
gladness for the upright in heart.[ac]
12 Be glad in ·Yahweh, you righteous ones,
and praise His holy name.[E,ad]

PSALM 98
Praise the King

A psalm.

1 Sing a new song to the LORD,[ae]
for He has performed wonders;
His right hand and holy arm
have won Him victory.[af]
2 The LORD has made His victory known;
He has revealed His righteousness
in the sight of the nations.[ag]
3 He has remembered His love
and faithfulness to the house of Israel;
all the ends of the earth
have seen our God's victory.[ah]

4 Shout to the LORD, all the earth;
be jubilant, shout for joy, and sing.[ai]
5 Sing to the LORD with the lyre,
with the lyre and melodious song.[aj]
6 With trumpets and the blast
of the ram's horn
shout triumphantly
in the presence of the LORD, our King.[ak]

7 Let the sea and all that fills it,
the world and those who live in it,
resound.[al]

[a] **96:4** 1Ch 16:25; Ps 47:2; 95:3
[b] **96:5** 1Ch 16:27; Jr 10:11
[c] **96:6** Ps 104:1
[d] **96:7** 1Ch 16:28-29; Ps 29:1
[e] **96:8** Ps 79:9
[f] Ps 100:4
[g] **96:8-9** Ps 29:2
[h] **96:9** Ps 33:8; 114:7
[i] **96:10** Ps 93:1; 97:1
[j] 1Ch 16:30
[k] Ps 9:8; 67:4; 98:9
[l] **96:11** 1Ch 16:31-32; Ps 69:34; 98:7
[m] **96:12** Is 35:1; 55:12-13
[n] **96:13** Ps 98:9; Rv 19:11
[o] **97:1** Ps 93:1; 96:10
[p] **97:2** Dt 4:11; 5:20; Ps 18:11
[q] **97:3** Ps 18:8; 50:3
[r] **97:4** Ex 19:16; Ps 77:18
[s] **97:5** Neh 1:5; Mc 1:4
[t] **97:6** Ps 50:6
[u] Is 40:5; 66:18
[v] **97:7** Is 44:9,11; Jr 10:14; 50:2
[w] Heb 1:6
[x] **97:8** Ps 48:11; Zph 3:14
[y] **97:9** 1Ch 16:25; Ps 95:3; 96:4
[z] **97:10** Am 5:15
[aa] Ps 145:20
[ab] Ps 37:40
[ac] **97:11** Ps 112:4; Pr 4:18
[ad] **97:12** Ps 30:4; 32:11
[ae] **98:1** Ps 33:3
[af] Ex 15:6; Is 52:10
[ag] **98:2** Is 56:1; 62:2
[ah] **98:3** Ps 22:27; Is 52:10
[ai] **98:4** Ps 66:1; 100:1; Is 44:23
[aj] **98:5** Ps 51:3; Is 51:3
[ak] **98:6** Nm 10:10; 2Ch 15:14
[al] **98:7** 1Ch 16:31-32; Ps 93:1; 97:1

[A] **97:7** LXX, Syr read *All His angels*; Heb 1:6 [B] **97:8** Lit *daughters* [C] **97:11** One Hb ms, LXX, some ancient versions read *rises to shine*; Ps 112:4 [D] **97:11** Lit *Light is sown* [E] **97:12** Or *memory, of His holiness*; lit *praise the mention*

8 Let the rivers clap their hands;
let the mountains shout together
for joy[a]
9 before the LORD,
for He is coming to judge the earth.
He will judge the world righteously
and the peoples fairly.[b]

PSALM 99
The King Is Holy

1 The LORD reigns! Let
the peoples tremble.
He is enthroned above the ·cherubim.[c]
Let the earth quake.[d]
2 ·Yahweh is great in ·Zion;
He is exalted above all the peoples.[e]
3 Let them praise Your great
and awe-inspiring name.[f]
He is holy.[g]

4 The mighty King loves justice.
You have established fairness;
You have administered justice
and righteousness in Jacob.[h]
5 Exalt the LORD our God;
bow in worship at His footstool.[i]
He is holy.[j]

6 Moses and Aaron were
among His priests;[k]
Samuel also was among those calling on
His name.
They called to Yahweh
and He answered them.[l]
7 He spoke to them in a pillar of cloud;[m]
they kept His decrees and the statutes
He gave them.
8 LORD our God, You answered them.
You were a forgiving God to them,[n]
an avenger of their sinful actions.[o]
9 Exalt the LORD our God;
bow in worship at His holy mountain,
for the LORD our God is holy.[p]

PSALM 100
Be Thankful

A psalm of thanksgiving.

1 Shout triumphantly to the LORD,
all the earth.[q]
2 Serve the LORD with gladness;
come before Him with joyful songs.[r]
3 Acknowledge that ·Yahweh is God.
He made us, and we are His[A,s] —
His people, the sheep of His pasture.[t]
4 Enter His gates with thanksgiving[u]
and His courts with praise.
Give thanks to Him and praise
His name.[v]
5 For Yahweh is good, and His love
is eternal;
His faithfulness endures
through all generations.

PSALM 101
A Vow of Integrity

A Davidic psalm.

1 I will sing of faithful love
and justice;
I will sing praise to You, LORD.[w]
2 I will pay attention to the way
of integrity.
When will You come to me?
I will live with a heart of integrity
in my house.[x]

[a]98:8 Ps 89:12; Is 55:12
[b]98:9 Ps 9:8; 67:4; 96:13
[c]99:1 Ex 25:22; 1Sm 4:4; Ezk 11:22
[d]Ps 33:8
[e]99:2 Ps 48:1; 113:4
[f]99:3 Ps 111:9
[g]Is 6:3
[h]99:4 Ps 33:5; 103:6; Jr 23:5
[i]99:5 Ps 132:7
[j]Is 6:3
[k]99:6 Ex 24:6-8; Lv 8:1-30
[l]1Sm 12:18
[m]99:7 Nm 12:5; 14:14; Dt 31:15-18
[n]99:8 Ps 78:38
[o]Jr 46:28
[p]99:9 Ps 2:6; 48:1; Ezk 20:40
[q]100:1 Ps 66:1; 98:4
[r]100:1-2 Ps 95:1-2; 98:4-6
[s]100:3 Dt 32:6; Ps 95:6
[t]Ps 79:13; 95:7
[u]100:4-5 Ps 119:90; 136:1; Lm 3:22-23
[v]100:4 Ps 75:1; 116:17
[w]101:1 Ps 89:1; 145:7
[x]101:2 1Kg 9:4; Ps 119:1

Text Message

TEXT MESSAGES

The gospel has a core message, and we should stick to it. In Psalm 100, the core is celebrated: God is good, faithful, reliable, loving, enduring. Everything fades away, even life itself, but God's love never fades away. Worship is a wonderful way to rehearse the gospel. We tell it back to God so we will be able to tell it boldly on the street, in a conversation, at a meeting. Let your worship be glad and joyful, for that is the gospel's ultimate emotion. If your worship brings joy, then speaking of God's love to friends will also bring you joy.

A100:3 Alt Hb tradition, some Hb mss, LXX, Syr, Vg read *and not we ourselves*

3 I will not set anything worthless
before my eyes.
I hate the practice of transgression;
it will not cling to me.[a]
4 A devious heart will be far from me;
I will not be involved with[A] evil.[b]
5 I will destroy anyone
who secretly slanders his neighbor;[c]
I cannot tolerate anyone
with haughty eyes
or an arrogant heart.[d]
6 My eyes favor the faithful
of the land
so that they may sit down with me.
The one who follows the way
of integrity
may serve me.[e]
7 No one who acts deceitfully
will live in my palace;
no one who tells lies
will remain in my presence.[B,f]
8 Every morning I will destroy
all the wicked of the land,
eliminating all evildoers
from the LORD's city.[g]

PSALM 102
Affliction in Light of Eternity

A prayer of an afflicted person who is weak and pours out his lament before the LORD.[h]

1 LORD, hear my prayer;
let my cry for help come before You.[i]
2 Do not hide Your face from me
in my day of trouble.
Listen closely to me;
answer me quickly when I call.[j]
3 For my days vanish like smoke,
and my bones burn like a furnace.[k]
4 My heart is afflicted,
withered like grass;[l]
I even forget to eat my food.[m]
5 Because of the sound of my groaning,
my flesh sticks to my bones.[n]
6 I am like a desert owl,[C]
like an owl among the ruins.[o]
7 I stay awake;[p]
I am like a solitary bird on a roof.
8 My enemies taunt me all day long;
they ridicule and curse me.[q]
9 I eat ashes like bread
and mingle my drinks with tears[r]
10 because of Your indignation and wrath;
for You have picked me up
and thrown me aside.[s]
11 My days are like a lengthening shadow,
and I wither away like grass.[t]
12 But You, LORD, are enthroned forever;[u]
Your fame endures to all generations.[v]
13 You will rise up and have compassion
on ·Zion,
for it is time to show favor to her —
the appointed time has come.[w]
14 For Your servants take delight
in its stones
and favor its dust.[x]
15 Then the nations will fear the name
of ·Yahweh,
and all the kings of the earth
Your glory,[y]
16 for the LORD will rebuild Zion;
He will appear in His glory.[z]
17 He will pay attention to the prayer
of the destitute
and will not despise their prayer.[aa]
18 This will be written
for a later generation,
and a newly created people will praise
the LORD:[ab]
19 He looked down from
His holy heights —
the LORD gazed out from heaven
to earth[ac] —
20 to hear a prisoner's groaning,
to set free those condemned to die,[D,ad]
21 so that they might declare
the name of Yahweh in Zion
and His praise in Jerusalem,[ae]
22 when peoples and kingdoms
are assembled
to serve the LORD.[af]
23 He has broken my[E] strength
in midcourse;
He has shortened my days.[ag]
24 I say: "My God, do not take me
in the middle of my life![F]

[a]101:3 Dt 15:9; Ps 40:4 [b]101:4 Pr 3:32; 14:2 [c]101:5 Ps 50:20 [d]Ps 18:27; Is 5:15 [e]101:6 Ps 119:1; Pr 11:20 [f]101:7 Ps 31:18; 52:3; 63:11 [g]101:8 Ps 119:119; Jr 21:12 [h]102:title Ps 142:2 [i]102:1 Ps 18:6; 39:12; 61:1 [j]102:2 Ps 27:9; 31:2; 69:17 [k]102:3 Jb 30:30; Ps 31:10; Lm 1:13 [l]102:4 Ps 37:2 [m]Ezr 10:6; Jb 33:20 [n]102:5 Jb 19:20; Lm 4:8 [o]102:6 Is 34:11; Zph 2:14 [p]102:7 Ps 77:4 [q]102:8 Ps 31:11; 69:19 [r]102:9 Ps 42:3; 80:5 [s]102:10 Jb 30:22 [t]102:11 Jb 8:9; Ps 109:23 [u]102:12 Ps 9:7; Lm 5:19 [v]Ps 135:13 [w]102:13 Is 60:10; Zch 1:12 [x]102:14 Neh 4:2; Lm 4:1 [y]102:15 Ps 138:4; Is 60:3 [z]102:16 Ps 147:2; Is 60:1-2 [aa]102:17 Ps 22:24 [ab]102:18 Dt 31:19; Ps 22:30-31; 78:6 [ac]102:19 Ps 14:2; 33:13; 53:2 [ad]102:20 Ps 79:11 [ae]102:21 Ps 22:22 [af]102:22 Ps 22:27; 86:9; Zch 8:20-23 [ag]102:23 Ps 39:5; 89:45

[A]101:4 Lit *not know* [B]101:7 Lit *in front of my eyes* [C]102:6 Or *a pelican of the desert* [D]102:20 Lit *free sons of death* [E]102:23 Some Hb mss, LXX read *His* [F]102:24 Lit *my days*

Your years continue
through all generations.[a]
25 Long ago You established the earth,
and the heavens are the work
of Your hands.[b]
26 They will perish, but You will endure;
all of them will wear out like clothing.
You will change them like a garment,
and they will pass away.[c]
27 But You are the same,
and Your years will never end.[d]
28 Your servants' children
will dwell securely,
and their offspring will be established
before You."[e]

Psalm 103

The Forgiving God

Davidic.

1 My soul, praise ·Yahweh,
and all that is within me, praise
His holy name.[f]
2 My soul, praise the Lord,
and do not forget all His benefits.[g]
3 He forgives all your sin;[h]
He heals all your diseases.[i]
4 He redeems your life from the ·Pit;[j]
He crowns you with faithful love
and compassion.[k]
5 He satisfies you[A] with goodness;[l]
your youth is renewed like the eagle.[m]
6 The Lord executes acts
of righteousness
and justice for all the oppressed.[n]
7 He revealed His ways to Moses,[o]
His deeds to the people of Israel.[p]
8 The Lord is compassionate
and gracious,
slow to anger and rich in faithful love.[q]
9 He will not always accuse us
or be angry forever.[r]
10 He has not dealt with us as
our sins deserve
or repaid us according to our offenses.[s]
11 For as high as the heavens are above
the earth,
so great is His faithful love
toward those who ·fear Him.[t]
12 As far as the east is from the west,
so far has He removed
our transgressions from us.[u]
13 As a father has compassion
on his children,
so the Lord has compassion on those
who fear Him.[v]
14 For He knows what we are made of,
remembering that we are dust.[w]
15 As for man, his days are like grass —
he blooms like a flower of the field;[x]
16 when the wind passes over it,
it vanishes,
and its place is no longer known.[B,y]
17 But from eternity to eternity
the Lord's faithful love is toward
those who fear Him,
and His righteousness
toward the grandchildren[z]
18 of those who keep His covenant,
who remember to observe His precepts.[aa]
19 The Lord has established His throne
in heaven,
and His kingdom rules over all.[ab]
20 Praise the Lord,
all His angels of great strength,
who do His word,
obedient to His command.[ac]
21 Praise the Lord, all His armies,
His servants who do His will.[ad]
22 Praise the Lord, all His works
in all the places where He rules.[ae]
My soul, praise Yahweh!

Psalm 104

God the Creator

1 My soul, praise ·Yahweh!
Lord my God, You are very great;
You are clothed with majesty
and splendor.[af]
2 He wraps Himself in light as if it were
a robe,
spreading out the sky like a canopy,[ag]
3 laying the beams of His palace
on the waters above,[ah]
making the clouds His chariot,[ai]
walking on the wings of the wind,[aj]
4 and making the winds His messengers,[C]
flames of fire His servants.[ak]

[a]**102:24** Jb 36:26; Ps 90:2 [b]**102:25** Neh 9:6; Ps 96:5; Heb 1:10-12 [c]**102:26** Is 34:4; 51:6; Mt 24:35 [d]**102:27** Mal 3:6; Jms 1:17 [e]**102:28** Ps 69:36; 89:4; 112:2 [f]**103:1** Ps 30:4; 97:12; 104:1 [g]**103:2** Dt 6:12; 8:11 [h]**103:3** Is 43:25 [i]Jr 30:17 [j]**103:4** Ps 49:15 [k]Ps 5:12 [l]**103:5** Ps 107:9 [m]Is 40:31 [n]**103:6** Ps 147:7 [o]**103:7** Ex 33:13 [p]Ps 78:11; 99:7 [q]**103:8** Ex 34:6; Nm 14:18; Neh 9:17 [r]**103:9** Is 57:16; Jr 3:12; Mc 7:19 [s]**103:10** Ezr 9:13; Lm 3:22 [t]**103:11** Ps 36:5; 57:10 [u]**103:12** Is 43:25; Mc 7:19 [v]**103:13** Mal 3:17 [w]**103:14** Gn 3:19; Ps 78:39 [x]**103:15** Jb 14:2; 1Pt 1:24 [y]**103:15-16** Is 40:6-7 [z]**103:17** Ex 20:6; Dt 5:10; Ps 25:6 [aa]**103:18** Dt 7:9; Ps 25:10 [ab]**103:19** Ps 11:4; 47:2 [ac]**103:20** Ps 29:1; 148:2 [ad]**103:21** 1Kg 22:19; Neh 9:6 [ae]**103:22** Ps 145:10 [af]**104:1** Ps 93:1; 103:22 [ag]**104:2** Jb 9:8; Is 40:22 [ah]**104:3** Am 9:6 [ai]Is 19:1 [aj]Ps 18:10 [ak]**104:4** Ps 148:8; Heb 1:7

[A]**103:5** Lit *satisfies your ornament*; Hb obscure [B]**103:16** Lit *place no longer knows it* [C]**104:4** Or *angels*

5 He established the earth
on its foundations;
it will never be shaken.[a]
6 You covered it with the deep
as if it were a garment;
the waters stood above the mountains.[b]
7 At Your rebuke the waters fled;
at the sound of Your thunder
they hurried away[c] —
8 mountains rose and valleys sank[A] —
to the place You established for them.[d]
9 You set a boundary they cannot cross;
they will never cover the earth again.[e]

10 He causes the springs to gush
into the valleys;
they flow between the mountains.[f]
11 They supply water for every wild beast;
the wild donkeys quench their thirst.[g]
12 The birds of the sky live
beside the springs;
they sing among the foliage.[h]
13 He waters the mountains
from His palace;
the earth is satisfied by the fruit
of Your labor.[i]

14 He causes grass to grow
for the livestock
and provides crops for man
to cultivate,
producing food from the earth,[j]
15 wine that makes man's heart glad —
making his face shine with oil —
and bread that sustains man's heart.[k]
16 The trees of the LORD flourish,[B]
the cedars of Lebanon
that He planted.[l]
17 There the birds make their nests;
the stork makes its home
in the pine trees.[m]
18 The high mountains are
for the wild goats;
the cliffs are a refuge for hyraxes.[n]

19 He made the moon to mark
the[C] festivals;[D]
the sun knows when to set.[o]
20 You bring darkness,
and it becomes night,
when all the forest animals stir.[p]
21 The young lions roar for their prey
and seek their food from God.[q]
22 The sun rises; they go back
and lie down in their dens.[r]
23 Man goes out to his work
and to his labor until evening.[s]

24 How countless are Your works, LORD!
In wisdom You have made them all;
the earth is full of Your creatures.[E,t]
25 Here is the sea, vast and wide,
teeming with creatures
beyond number —
living things both large and small.[u]
26 There the ships move about,
and •Leviathan, which You formed
to play there.[v]

27 All of them wait for You
to give them their food
at the right time.[w]
28 When You give it to them,
they gather it;
when You open Your hand,
they are satisfied with good things.[x]
29 When You hide Your face,
they are terrified;
when You take away their breath,
they die and return to the dust.[y]
30 When You send Your breath,[F]
they are created,
and You renew the face of the earth.[z]

31 May the glory of the LORD
endure forever;
may the LORD rejoice in His works.[aa]
32 He looks at the earth,
and it trembles;
He touches the mountains,
and they pour out smoke.[ab]
33 I will sing to the LORD all my life;
I will sing praise to my God while I live.[ac]
34 May my meditation be pleasing
to Him;
I will rejoice in the LORD.[ad]
35 May sinners vanish from the earth
and wicked people be no more.[ae]
My soul, praise Yahweh!
•Hallelujah!

[a]104:5 Jb 38:4; Ps 24:2; 93:1; 96:10
[b]104:6 Gn 7:19
[c]104:7 Ps 18:15; 106:9
[d]104:8 Ps 65:6; Am 4:13
[e]104:9 Jb 26:10; 38:10-11; Jr 5:22
[f]104:10 Ps 107:35; Is 41:18
[g]104:11 Jb 39:5
[h]104:12 Mt 8:20
[i]104:13 Jb 5:10; Ps 65:9
[j]104:14 Jb 28:5; Ps 147:8
[k]104:15 Gn 18:5; Ps 141:5
[l]104:16 Nm 24:6
[m]104:17 Lv 11:19
[n]104:18 Lv 11:5; Pr 30:26
[o]104:19 Gn 1:14; Ps 19:6; 74:16
[p]104:20 Is 45:17
[q]104:21 Jb 38:39
[r]104:22 Jb 37:8
[s]104:23 Gn 3:19
[t]104:24 Pr 3:19; Jr 10:12; 51:15
[u]104:25 Gn 1:21; Ps 69:34
[v]104:26 Jb 41:1; Ps 74:14; Is 27:1
[w]104:27 Ps 136:25; 145:15; 147:9
[x]104:28 Ps 145:16
[y]104:29 Jb 10:9; Ps 90:3
[z]104:30 Jb 33:4
[aa]104:31 Ps 72:17
[ab]104:32 Ex 19:18; Ps 144:5
[ac]104:33 Ps 63:4; 146:2
[ad]104:34 Ps 19:14
[ae]104:35 Ps 37:10; 59:13

A104:7-8 Or *away. They flowed over the mountains and went down valleys*
B104:16 Lit *are satisfied* C104:19 Lit *moon for* D104:19 Or *the appointed times*
E104:24 Lit *possessions* F104:30 Or *Spirit*

Psalm 105

God's Faithfulness to His People

1 Give thanks to •Yahweh, call on
His name;
proclaim His deeds
among the peoples.[a]
2 Sing to Him, sing praise to Him;
tell about all His wonderful works![b]
3 Honor His holy name;
let the hearts of those who seek
Yahweh rejoice.[c]
4 Search for the LORD and for
His strength;
seek His face always.[d]
5 Remember the wonderful works
He has done,
His wonders, and the judgments
He has pronounced,[A,e]
6 you offspring of Abraham His servant,
Jacob's descendants — His chosen ones.[f]
7 He is the LORD our God;
His judgments govern the whole earth.[g]
8 He remembers His covenant forever,
the promise He ordained
for a thousand generations[h] —
9 the covenant He made with Abraham,
swore[B] to Isaac,[i]
10 and confirmed to Jacob as a decree
and to Israel
as an everlasting covenant:[j]
11 "I will give the land of Canaan to you
as your inherited portion."[k]
12 When they were few in number,
very few indeed,
and temporary residents in Canaan,[l]
13 wandering from nation to nation
and from one kingdom to another,[m]
14 He allowed no one to oppress them;
He rebuked kings on their behalf:[n]
15 "Do not touch My anointed ones,[o]
or harm My prophets."[p]
16 He called down famine against the land
and destroyed the entire food supply.[q]
17 He had sent a man ahead of them —
Joseph, who was sold as a slave.[r]
18 They hurt his feet with shackles;
his neck was put in an iron collar.[s]
19 Until the time his prediction came true,
the word of the LORD tested him.[t]
20 The king sent for him and released him;
the ruler of peoples set him free.[u]
21 He made him master of his household,
ruler over all his possessions[v] —
22 binding[C] his officials at will
and instructing his elders.[w]
23 Then Israel went to Egypt;
Jacob lived as a foreigner in the land
of Ham.[D,x]
24 The LORD[E] made His people
very fruitful;
He made them more numerous
than their foes,[y]
25 whose hearts He turned to hate
His people
and to deal deceptively
with His servants.[z]
26 He sent Moses His servant,
and Aaron, whom He had chosen.[aa]
27 They performed His miraculous signs
among them,
and wonders in the land of Ham.[D,ab]
28 He sent darkness, and it became dark —
for did they not defy[F] His commands?[ac]
29 He turned their water into blood
and caused their fish to die.[ad]
30 Their land was overrun with frogs,
even in their royal chambers.[ae]
31 He spoke, and insects came[af] —
gnats throughout their country.[ag]
32 He gave them hail for rain,
and lightning throughout their land.[ah]
33 He struck their vines and fig trees
and shattered the trees
of their territory.[ai]
34 He spoke, and locusts came —
young locusts without number.
35 They devoured all the vegetation
in their land
and consumed the produce
of their land.[aj]
36 He struck all the firstborn in their land,
all their first progeny.[ak]
37 Then He brought Israel out with silver
and gold,

[a]105:1 Ps 9:11; Is 12:4
[b]105:2 Ps 96:3
[c]105:3 Ps 33:21
[d]105:4 Ps 27:8; 63:2
[e]105:5 Ps 77:11; 119:13
[f]105:6 Ps 135:4
[g]105:7 Is 26:9
[h]105:8 Dt 7:9; Ps 106:45; Lk 1:42
[i]105:9 Gn 12:7; 22:16-18
[j]105:10 Gn 28:13-15
[k]105:11 Gn 13:15; 15:18; Ps 78:55
[l]105:12 Gn 34:30; Dt 7:7
[m]105:13 Dt 26:5
[n]105:14 Gn 12:17; 20:3,7
[o]105:15 Gn 20:6-7; 26:11
[p]105:1-15 1Ch 16:8-22
[q]105:16 Gn 41:54; Lv 26:26; Ezk 4:16
[r]105:17 Gn 37:28-36; 45:5; Ac 7:9
[s]105:18 Gn 39:20
[t]105:19 Gn 40:20-21
[u]105:20 Gn 41:14
[v]105:21 Gn 41:40-43
[w]105:22 Gn 41:44
[x]105:23 Gn 46:6; Ac 7:15; 13:17
[y]105:24 Ex 1:7,9; Dt 26:5
[z]105:25 Ex 1:8-14; Ac 7:19
[aa]105:26 Ex 3:10; 4:12,14
[ab]105:27 Ex 7:3; 11:9-10; Ps 78:43-51
[ac]105:28 Ex 10:21-23; Ps 99:7
[ad]105:29 Ex 7:20-21
[ae]105:30 Ex 8:3,6
[af]105:31 Ex 8:21
[ag]Ex 8:16-17
[ah]105:32-33 Ex 9:23-25
[ai]105:33 Ps 78:47
[aj]105:34-35 Ex 10:12-15
[ak]105:36 Ex 12:29; 13:15; Ps 78:51

[A]105:5 Lit *judgments of His mouth* [B]105:9 Lit *and His oath* [C]105:22 LXX, Syr, Vg read *teaching* [D]105:23,27 = Egypt [E]105:24 Lit *He* [F]105:28 LXX, Syr read *for they did defy*

and no one among
His tribes stumbled.[a]
38 Egypt was glad when they left,
for the dread of Israel[A] had fallen
on them.[b]
39 He spread a cloud as a covering
and gave a fire to light up the night.[c]
40 They asked, and He brought quail
and satisfied them with bread
from heaven.[d]
41 He opened a rock, and water
gushed out;
it flowed like a stream in the desert.[e]
42 For He remembered His holy promise
to Abraham His servant.[f]
43 He brought His people out
with rejoicing,
His chosen ones with shouts of joy.[g]
44 He gave them the lands of the nations,
and they inherited
what other peoples had worked for.[h]
45 All this happened
so that they might keep His statutes
and obey His instructions.[i]
•Hallelujah!

Psalm 106

Israel's Unfaithfulness to God

1 •Hallelujah!
Give thanks to the Lord, for He is good;
His faithful love endures forever.[j]
2 Who can declare the Lord's mighty acts
or proclaim all the praise due Him?[k]
3 How happy are those
who uphold justice,
who practice righteousness at all times.[l]
4 Remember me, Lord,
when You show favor to Your people.[m]
Come to me with Your salvation
5 so that I may enjoy the prosperity
of Your chosen ones,
rejoice in the joy of Your nation,
and boast about Your heritage.[n]
6 Both we and our fathers have sinned;
we have done wrong
and have acted wickedly.[o]
7 Our fathers in Egypt did not grasp
the significance of
Your wonderful works
or remember Your many acts
of faithful love;
instead, they rebelled
by the sea — the •Red Sea.[p]
8 Yet He saved them because of His name,
to make His power known.[q]
9 He rebuked the Red Sea, and it dried up;
He led them through the depths
as through a desert.[r]
10 He saved them from the hand
of the adversary;
He redeemed them from the hand
of the enemy.[s]
11 Water covered their foes;
not one of them remained.[t]
12 Then they believed His promises
and sang His praise.[u]
13 They soon forgot His works
and would not wait for His counsel.[v]
14 They were seized with craving
in the wilderness
and tested God in the desert.[w]
15 He gave them what they asked for,
but sent a wasting disease
among them.[x]
16 In the camp they were envious of Moses
and of Aaron, the Lord's holy one.[y]
17 The earth opened up
and swallowed Dathan;
it covered the assembly of Abiram.[z]
18 Fire blazed throughout their assembly;
flames consumed the wicked.[aa]
19 At Horeb they made a calf
and worshiped the cast metal image.[ab]
20 They exchanged their glory[B,C]
for the image of a grass-eating ox.[ac]
21 They forgot God their Savior,
who did great things in Egypt,[ad]
22 wonderful works in the land of Ham,[D]
awe-inspiring acts at the Red Sea.[ae]
23 So He said
He would have destroyed them —
if Moses His chosen one
had not stood before Him in the breach
to turn His wrath away
from destroying them.[af]

[a] 105:37 Ex 12:35-36
[b] 105:38 Ex 12:33; 15:16
[c] 105:39 Ex 13:21; Neh 9:12; Ps 78:14
[d] 105:40 Ex 16:15; Ps 78:24
[e] 105:41 Ex 17:6; Nm 20:11; Ps 78:15
[f] 105:42 Ex 2:24
[g] 105:43 Ex 15:1; Ps 106:12
[h] 105:44 Jos 24:13; Ps 78:55
[i] 105:45 Dt 4:1,40; Ps 78:7
[j] 106:1 1Ch 16:34,41; Ps 100:5
[k] 106:2 Ps 145:4,12; 150:2
[l] 106:3 Ps 15:2
[m] 106:4 Ps 119:132
[n] 106:5 Dt 32:9; Ps 105:6,43
[o] 106:6 Lv 26:40; Jr 3:25; 14:20
[p] 106:7 Ex 14:10-12; Ps 78:17
[q] 106:8 Ex 9:16; Ezk 20:9
[r] 106:9 Ps 18:15; 104:7; Is 63:11-13
[s] 106:10 Ex 14:30; Ps 107:2
[t] 106:11 Ex 14:27-28; 15:5; Ps 78:53
[u] 106:12 Ex 14:31; 15:1-21; Ps 105:43
[v] 106:13 Ex 15:24; Ps 78:11; 107:11
[w] 106:14 Nm 11:4; Ps 78:18
[x] 106:15 Nm 11:31; Ps 78:29
[y] 106:16 Nm 16:1-3
[z] 106:17 Nm 16:31-32; Dt 11:6
[aa] 106:18 Nm 16:35
[ab] 106:19 Ex 32:4; Dt 9:8; Ac 7:41
[ac] 106:20 Jr 2:11; Rm 1:23
[ad] 106:21 Dt 10:21; Ps 78:11
[ae] 106:22 Ps 105:27
[af] 106:23 Ex 32:10; Dt 9:14; Ezk 20:8

A105:38 Lit *them* B106:20 Alt Jewish tradition reads *His* or *My glory* C106:20 = God D106:22 = Egypt

24 They despised the pleasant land
and did not believe His promise.[a]
25 They grumbled in their tents
and did not listen to the LORD's voice.[b]
26 So He raised His hand against them
with an oath
that He would make them fall
in the desert[c]
27 and would disperse their descendants[A]
among the nations,
scattering them throughout the lands.[d]

28 They aligned themselves with •Baal
of Peor
and ate sacrifices offered
to lifeless gods.[B,e]
29 They provoked the LORD
with their deeds,
and a plague broke out against them.[f]
30 But Phinehas stood up and intervened,
and the plague was stopped.[g]
31 It was credited to him as righteousness
throughout all generations to come.[h]

32 They angered the LORD at the waters
of Meribah,
and Moses suffered[C] because of them;[i]
33 for they embittered his spirit,[D]
and he spoke rashly with his lips.[j]

34 They did not destroy the peoples
as the LORD had commanded them[k]
35 but mingled with the nations
and adopted their ways.[l]
36 They served their idols,
which became a snare to them.[m]
37 They sacrificed their sons
and daughters to demons.[n]
38 They shed innocent blood —
the blood of their sons and daughters
whom they sacrificed to the idols
of Canaan;
so the land became polluted
with blood.[o]
39 They defiled themselves by their actions
and prostituted themselves
by their deeds.[p]

40 Therefore the LORD's anger burned
against His people,
and He abhorred His own inheritance.[q]

[a]106:24 Nm 14:31; Dt 9:23; Heb 3:19
[b]106:25 Nm 14:2; Dt 1:27
[c]106:26 Nm 14:28-35; Ezk 20:15; Heb 3:11
[d]106:27 Lv 26:33; Dt 4:27; Ps 44:11
[e]106:28 Nm 25:3; Dt 4:3; Hs 9:10
[f]106:29 Nm 25:4
[g]106:30 Nm 25:7-8
[h]106:31 Gn 15:6; Nm 25:10-13
[i]106:32 Nm 20:2-13; Ps 81:7
[j]106:33 Ps 78:40; Is 63:10
[k]106:34 Dt 7:2,16; Jdg 1:21,27-36
[l]106:35 Jdg 3:5-6
[m]106:36 Dt 7:16; Jdg 2:12
[n]106:37 Lv 17:7; Dt 32:17
[o]106:38 Nm 35:33; Is 24:5
[p]106:39 Lv 18:24; Ezk 20:18,30-31
[q]106:40 Dt 32:19; Ps 78:59
[r]106:41 Jdg 2:14; Neh 9:27
[s]106:42 Jdg 4:3; 10:12
[t]106:43 Jdg 2:16-18; Ps 81:12
[u]106:44 Jdg 3:3; 6:7; 10:10
[v]106:45 Lv 26:42; Ps 105:8
[w]106:46 1Kg 8:50; 2Ch 30:9; Ezr 9:9
[x]106:47 Ps 107:3; 147:2
[y]106:48 Ps 41:13; 72:18; 89:52
[z]106:47-48 1Ch 16:35-36
[aa]107:1 1Ch 16:34; Ps 100:5; 106:1
[ab]107:2 Ps 78:42; 106:10
[ac]107:3 Is 11:12; 43:5; Ezk 20:34
[ad]107:4 Nm 14:33; 32:13
[ae]107:5 Ps 77:3

41 He handed them over to the nations;
those who hated them ruled them.[r]
42 Their enemies oppressed them,
and they were subdued
under their power.[s]
43 He rescued them many times,
but they continued
to rebel deliberately
and were beaten down by their sin.[t]

44 When He heard their cry,
He took note of their distress,[u]
45 remembered His covenant with them,
and relented according to the riches
of His faithful love.[v]
46 He caused them to be pitied
before all their captors.[w]

47 Save us, •Yahweh our God,
and gather us from the nations,
so that we may give thanks
to Your holy name
and rejoice in Your praise.[x]

48 May Yahweh, the God of Israel,
be praised
from everlasting to everlasting.[y]
Let all the people say, "•Amen!"
Hallelujah![z]

BOOK V

(Psalms 107–150)

PSALM 107

Thanksgiving for God's Deliverance

1 Give thanks to the LORD, for He is good;
His faithful love endures forever.[aa]
2 Let the redeemed of the LORD proclaim
that He has redeemed them
from the hand of the foe[ab]
3 and has gathered them
from the lands —
from the east and the west,
from the north and the south.[ac]

4 Some[E] wandered
in the desolate wilderness,
finding no way to a city
where they could live.[ad]
5 They were hungry and thirsty;
their spirits failed[F] within them.[ae]

[A]106:27 Syr; MT reads *would make their descendants fall* [B]106:28 Lit *sacrifices for dead ones* [C]106:32 Lit *and it was evil for Moses* [D]106:33 Some Hb mss, LXX, Syr, Jer; other Hb mss read *they rebelled against His Spirit* [E]107:4 Lit *They* [F]107:5 Lit *their soul fainted*

6 Then they cried out to the LORD
in their trouble;
He rescued them from their distress.[a]
7 He led them by the right path
to go to a city where they could live.[b]
8 Let them give thanks to the LORD
for His faithful love
and His wonderful works for
all ·humanity.[c]
9 For He has satisfied the thirsty
and filled the hungry
with good things.[d]

10 Others[A] sat in darkness and gloom[B] —
prisoners in cruel chains[e] —
11 because they rebelled
against God's commands
and despised the counsel
of the ·Most High.[f]
12 He broke their spirits[C]
with hard labor;
they stumbled, and there was no one
to help.[g]
13 Then they cried out to the LORD
in their trouble;
He saved them from their distress.[h]
14 He brought them out of darkness
and gloom[B]
and broke their chains apart.[i]
15 Let them give thanks to the LORD
for His faithful love
and His wonderful works for
all humanity.[j]
16 For He has broken down
the bronze gates
and cut through the iron bars.[k]

17 Fools suffered affliction
because of their rebellious ways
and their sins.[l]
18 They loathed all food
and came near the gates of death.[m]
19 Then they cried out to the LORD
in their trouble;
He saved them from their distress.[n]
20 He sent His word and healed them;
He rescued them from the ·Pit.[o]
21 Let them give thanks to the LORD
for His faithful love
and His wonderful works for
all humanity.[p]
22 Let them offer sacrifices
of thanksgiving
and announce His works with shouts
of joy.[q]

23 Others[A] went to sea in ships,
conducting trade
on the vast waters.[r]
24 They saw the LORD's works,
His wonderful works in the deep.[s]
25 He spoke and raised a tempest
that stirred up the waves of the sea.[D,t]
26 Rising up to the sky, sinking down
to the depths,
their courage[E] melting away
in anguish,[u]
27 they reeled and staggered
like drunken men,
and all their skill was useless.[v]
28 Then they cried out to the LORD
in their trouble,
and He brought them
out of their distress.[w]
29 He stilled the storm to a murmur,
and the waves of the sea[F]
were hushed.[x]
30 They rejoiced when the waves[G]
grew quiet.
Then He guided them to the harbor
they longed for.[y]
31 Let them give thanks to the LORD
for His faithful love
and His wonderful works for
all humanity.[z]
32 Let them exalt Him in the assembly
of the people
and praise Him in the council
of the elders.[aa]

33 He turns rivers into desert,
springs of water into thirsty ground,[ab]
34 and fruitful land into salty wasteland,
because of the wickedness
of its inhabitants.[ac]
35 He turns a desert into a pool of water,
dry land into springs of water.[ad]
36 He causes the hungry to settle there,
and they establish a city
where they can live.[ae]
37 They sow fields and plant vineyards
that yield a fruitful harvest.[af]

[a] **107:6** Ps 106:44
[b] **107:7** Jr 31:9
[c] **107:8** Ps 75:1
[d] **107:9** Ps 22:26; 34:10; Lk 1:53
[e] **107:10** Ps 102:20; Is 42:7; Lk 1:79
[f] **107:11** 2Ch 36:16; Ps 78:40; 106:7
[g] **107:12** Ex 6:9; Dt 26:6; Is 14:3
[h] **107:13** Ex 2:23-25
[i] **107:14** Jr 2:20
[j] **107:15** Ps 75:1
[k] **107:16** Is 45:1-2
[l] **107:17** Jr 30:14-15
[m] **107:18** Jb 33:20
[n] **107:19** Nm 21:7-9
[o] **107:20** Jb 33:28,30; Ps 30:3
[p] **107:21** Ps 75:1
[q] **107:22** Ps 9:11; 105:43; 116:17
[r] **107:23** Is 42:10
[s] **107:24** Is 33:21
[t] **107:25** Ps 93:3-4; Ezk 26:19
[u] **107:26** Ps 22:14; 119:28
[v] **107:27** Jb 12:25; Is 29:9
[w] **107:28** Jnh 1:14; Mk 4:39
[x] **107:29** Ps 89:9; Mt 8:26; Lk 8:24
[y] **107:30** Ex 15:13; Ps 78:72
[z] **107:31** Ps 75:1
[aa] **107:32** Ps 22:22,25
[ab] **107:33** Is 42:15; 50:2
[ac] **107:34** Gn 19:24-28; Dt 29:23
[ad] **107:35** Is 35:6-7; 41:18
[ae] **107:36** Ps 60:9; 146:7
[af] **107:37** Is 65:21; Am 9:14

[A] **107:10,23** Lit *They* [B] **107:10,14** Or *the shadow of death* [C] **107:12** Lit *hearts* [D] **107:25** Lit *of it* [E] **107:26** Lit *souls* [F] **107:29** Lit *of them* [G] **107:30** Lit *when they*

38 He blesses them,
and they multiply greatly;[a]
He does not let
their livestock decrease.[b]
39 When they are diminished
and are humbled
by cruel oppression and sorrow,[c]
40 He pours contempt on nobles[d]
and makes them wander
in a trackless wasteland.[e]
41 But He lifts the needy out of
their suffering[f]
and makes their families multiply
like flocks.[g]
42 The upright see it and rejoice,[h]
and all injustice shuts its mouth.[i]
43 Let whoever is wise pay attention
to these things
and consider[A] the LORD's acts
of faithful love.[j]

PSALM 108
A Plea for Victory

A song. A Davidic psalm.

1 My heart is confident, God;[B]
I will sing; I will sing praises
with the whole of my being.[C,k]
2 Wake up, harp and lyre!
I will wake up the dawn.[l]
3 I will praise You, LORD,
among the peoples;
I will sing praises to You
among the nations.[m]
4 For Your faithful love is higher
than the heavens,
and Your faithfulness reaches to
the clouds.[n]
5 God, be exalted above the heavens,[o]
and let Your glory be over
the whole earth.[p]
6 Save with Your right hand
and answer me
so that those You love may be rescued.[q]
7 God has spoken in His sanctuary:[D]
"I will triumph!
I will divide up Shechem.[r]
I will apportion the Valley of Succoth.[s]
8 Gilead is Mine, Manasseh is Mine,
and Ephraim is My helmet;[t]
Judah is My scepter.[u]
9 Moab is My washbasin;[v]
I throw My sandal on Edom.[w]
I shout in triumph over Philistia."[x]
10 Who will bring me
to the fortified city?
Who will lead me to Edom?[y]
11 God, haven't You rejected us?
God, You do not march out
with our armies.[z]
12 Give us aid against the foe,
for human help is worthless.[aa]
13 With God we will perform valiantly;[ab]
He will trample our foes.[ac]

PSALM 109
Prayer against an Enemy

For the choir director. A Davidic psalm.

1 God of my praise, do not be silent.[ad]
2 For wicked and deceitful mouths open
against me;
they speak against me
with lying tongues.[ae]
3 They surround me with hateful words
and attack me without cause.[af]
4 In return for my love they accuse me,
but I continue to pray.[E,ag]
5 They repay me evil for good,
and hatred for my love.[ah]
6 Set a wicked person over him;
let an accuser[F] stand at his right hand.[ai]
7 When he is judged, let him
be found ·guilty,
and let his prayer be counted as sin.[aj]
8 Let his days be few;
let another take over his position.[ak]
9 Let his children be fatherless
and his wife a widow.[al]
10 Let his children wander as beggars,
searching for food far[G]
from their demolished homes.[am]
11 Let a creditor seize all he has;
let strangers plunder what he has
worked for.[an]
12 Let no one show him kindness,

[a]107:38 Gn 12:2; Ex 1:7
[b]Dt 7:14
[c]107:39 Ps 44:25
[d]107:40 Jb 12:21
[e]Jb 12:24
[f]107:41 1Sm 2:8; Ps 113:7-8
[g]Jb 21:11
[h]107:42 Jb 22:19; Ps 64:10
[i]Jb 5:16
[j]107:43 Ps 64:9; Hs 14:9
[k]108:1 Ps 59:17; 112:7
[l]108:2 Jdg 5:12; Ps 33:2; 81:2
[m]108:3 2Sm 22:50; Ps 9:11; 18:49
[n]108:4 Ps 36:5; 103:11; Lm 3:22-23
[o]108:5 Ps 113:4
[p]108:1-5 Ps 57:7-11
[q]108:6 Ps 17:7; 20:6; 138:7
[r]108:7 Gn 12:6; 33:18
[s]Gn 33:17
[t]108:8 Dt 33:17; Jos 13:31
[u]Gn 49:10
[v]108:9 2Sm 8:2
[w]2Sm 8:14
[x]2Sm 8:1
[y]108:10 Jr 1:18
[z]108:11 Ps 44:9
[aa]108:12 Ps 146:3
[ab]108:13 Nm 24:18; Ps 44:5; 118:15-16
[ac]108:6-13 Ps 60:5-12
[ad]109:1 Ps 28:1; 83:1
[ae]109:2 Ps 10:7; 52:4; 120:2
[af]109:3 Ps 35:7; 69:4; Jn 15:25
[ag]109:4 Ps 69:13
[ah]109:5 Ps 35:12; 38:20
[ai]109:6 Zch 3:1
[aj]109:7 Ps 1:5; Pr 28:9
[ak]109:8 Ps 55:23; Ac 1:20
[al]109:9 Ex 22:24
[am]109:10 Jb 30:5-8; Ps 59:15
[an]109:11 Dt 28:43-44; Lm 5:2

[A]107:43 Lit *and let them consider* [B]108:1 Some Hb mss, LXX, Syr add *my heart is confident* [C]108:1 Lit *praises, even my glory* [D]108:7 Or *has promised by His holy nature* [E]109:4 Lit *but I, prayer* [F]109:6 Or *adversary* [G]109:10 LXX reads *beggars, driven far*

and let no one be gracious
to his fatherless children.[a]
13 Let the line of his descendants
be cut off;
let their name be blotted out
in the next generation.[b]
14 Let his ancestors' guilt
be remembered before the LORD,[c]
and do not let his mother's sin
be blotted out.[d]
15 Let their sins[A] always remain
before the LORD,
and let Him erase[B] all memory of them
from the earth.[e]

16 For he did not think to show kindness,
but pursued the afflicted, poor, and
brokenhearted
in order to put them to death.[f]
17 He loved cursing — let it fall on him;
he took no delight in blessing —
let it be far from him.[g]
18 He wore cursing like his coat —
let it enter his body like water
and go into his bones like oil.[h]
19 Let it be like a robe he wraps
around himself,
like a belt he always wears.[i]
20 Let this be the LORD's payment
to my accusers,
to those who speak evil against me.[j]
21 But You, ˙Yahweh my Lord,
deal kindly with me
because of Your name;[k]
deliver me because of the goodness
of Your faithful love.[l]
22 For I am afflicted and needy;[m]
my heart is wounded within me.[n]
23 I fade away like a lengthening shadow;[o]
I am shaken off like a locust.
24 My knees are weak from fasting,
and my body is emaciated.[C,p]
25 I have become an object of ridicule
to my accusers;[D]
when they see me, they shake
their heads in scorn.[q]

26 Help me, LORD my God;
save me according to Your faithful love[r]
27 so they may know that this is Your hand
and that You, LORD, have done it.[s]
28 Though they curse, You will bless.
When they rise up, they will be
put to shame,
but Your servant will rejoice.[t]
29 My accusers will be clothed
with disgrace;
they will wear their shame like a cloak.[u]
30 I will fervently thank the LORD
with my mouth;
I will praise Him in the presence
of many.[v]
31 For He stands at the right hand of
the needy
to save him from those who would
condemn him.[w]

PSALM 110

The Priestly King

A Davidic psalm.

1 This is the declaration of the LORD
to my Lord:
"Sit at My right hand
until I make Your enemies
Your footstool."[x]
2 The LORD will extend
Your mighty scepter from ˙Zion.
Rule[E] over Your surrounding[F] enemies.[y]
3 Your people will volunteer
on Your day of battle.[G,z]
In holy splendor, from the womb
of the dawn,
the dew of Your youth
belongs to You.[H,aa]
4 The LORD has sworn an oath
and will not take it back:
"Forever, You are a priest
like Melchizedek."[ab]

5 The Lord is at Your right hand;
He will crush kings on the day
of His anger.[ac]
6 He will judge the nations,
heaping up corpses;[ad]
He will crush leaders
over the entire world.[ae]
7 He will drink from the brook
by the road;[af]
therefore, He will lift up His head.[ag]

[a]**109:12** Jb 5:4
[b]**109:13** Jb 18:17,19; Ps 9:5; Pr 10:7
[c]**109:14** Ex 20:5; Nm 14:18
[d]Neh 4:5; Jr 18:23
[e]**109:15** Ps 34:16; 90:8; Jr 16:17
[f]**109:16** Ps 34:18; 94:6
[g]**109:17** Pr 14:14; Ezk 35:6; Mt 7:2
[h]**109:18** Nm 5:22
[i]**109:19** Ps 73:26
[j]**109:20** Ps 54:5; 94:23; Is 3:11
[k]**109:21** Ps 79:9; 106:8
[l]Ps 69:16
[m]**109:22** Ps 40:17; 86:1
[n]Ps 143:4
[o]**109:23** Ps 102:11
[p]**109:24** Jb 16:8; Ps 35:13
[q]**109:25** Ps 22:6-7; 69:19
[r]**109:26** Ps 119:86
[s]**109:27** Jb 37:7
[t]**109:28** 2Sm 16:11-12; Is 65:14
[u]**109:29** Jb 8:22; Ps 35:26; 132:18
[v]**109:30** Ps 22:22,25; 35:18; 111:1
[w]**109:31** Ps 16:8; 110:5; 121:5
[x]**110:1** Mt 22:44; Mk 12:36; Lk 20:42-43; Ac 2:34-35; 1Co 15:25; Heb 1:13
[y]**110:2** Ps 45:6; Ezk 19:14
[z]**110:3** Jdg 5:2
[aa]1Ch 16:29; Ps 96:9
[ab]**110:4** Gn 14:18; Heb 5:6,10; 7:17,21
[ac]**110:5** Ps 16:8; 68:14
[ad]**110:6** Is 66:24; Rv 19:17-18
[ae]Ps 68:21
[af]**110:7** Jdg 7:5-6
[ag]Ps 27:6

[A]**109:15** Lit *Let them* [B]**109:15** Or *cut off* [C]**109:24** Lit *denied from fat* [D]**109:25** Lit *to them* [E]**110:2** One Hb ms, LXX, Tg read *You will rule* [F]**110:2** Lit *Rule in the midst of Your* [G]**110:3** Lit *power* [H]**110:3** Hb obscure

PSALM 111
Praise for the LORD's Works

1 ·Hallelujah![A]
I will praise the LORD with all my heart
in the assembly of the upright
and in the congregation.[a]

2 The LORD's works are great,
studied by all who delight in them.[b]
3 All that He does is splendid
and majestic;[c]
His righteousness endures forever.[d]
4 He has caused His wonderful works
to be remembered.[e]
The LORD is gracious
and compassionate.[f]
5 He has provided food for those
who fear Him;[g]
He remembers His covenant forever.[h]
6 He has shown His people the power
of His works
by giving them the inheritance
of the nations.[i]
7 The works of His hands are truth
and justice;
all His instructions are trustworthy.[j]
8 They are established forever and ever,
enacted in truth and in what is right.[k]
9 He has sent redemption
to His people.[l]
He has ordained His covenant forever.
His name is holy and awe-inspiring.[m]

10 The ·fear of the LORD is the beginning
of wisdom;[n]
all who follow His instructions[B] have
good insight.[o]
His praise endures forever.[p]

PSALM 112
The Traits of the Righteous

1 ·Hallelujah![A]
Happy is the man who ·fears the LORD,
taking great delight in His commands.[q]

2 His descendants will be powerful
in the land;
the generation of the upright
will be blessed.[r]
3 Wealth and riches are in his house,[s]
and his righteousness endures forever.[t]
4 Light shines in the darkness
for the upright.[u]
He is gracious, compassionate,
and righteous.[v]
5 Good will come to a man
who lends generously
and conducts his business fairly.[w]
6 He will never be shaken.[x]
The righteous man will be
remembered forever.[y]
7 He will not fear bad news;
his heart is confident,
trusting in the LORD.[z]
8 His heart is assured; he will not fear.[aa]
In the end he will look in triumph
on his foes.[ab]
9 He distributes freely to the poor;
his righteousness endures forever.[ac]
His ·horn will be exalted in honor.[ad]

10 The wicked man will see it
and be angry;
he will gnash his teeth in despair.[ae]
The desire of the wicked man will come
to nothing.[af]

PSALM 113
Praise to the Merciful God

1 ·Hallelujah!
Give praise, servants of ·Yahweh;
praise the name of Yahweh.[ag]
2 Let the name of Yahweh be praised
both now and forever.[ah]
3 From the rising of the sun
to its setting,
let the name of Yahweh be praised.[ai]
4 Yahweh is exalted above all the nations,[aj]
His glory above the heavens.[ak]
5 Who is like Yahweh our God—
the One enthroned on high,[al]
6 who stoops down to look
on the heavens and the earth?[am]
7 He raises the poor from the dust
and lifts the needy
from the garbage pile[an]
8 in order to seat them with nobles—
with the nobles of His people.[ao]
9 He gives the childless woman
a household,

[a]**111:1** Ps 35:18; 149:1 [b]**111:2** Ps 92:5; 143:5 [c]**111:3** Ps 145:5 [d]Ps 112:3,9; 119:142 [e]**111:4** Ps 78:4 [f]Ps 103:8; 145:8 [g]**111:5** Mt 6:31-33 [h]Ps 105:8 [i]**111:6** Dt 4:38; 32:8; Ps 78:55 [j]**111:7** Ps 19:7; 93:5 [k]**111:8** Ps 119:160; Is 40:8; Mt 5:18 [l]**111:9** Lk 1:68 [m]Ps 99:3; Lk 1:49 [n]**111:10** Pr 1:7; 9:10 [o]Ps 119:98 [p]Ps 44:8; 145:2 [q]**112:1** Ps 1:2; 119:16; 128:1 [r]**112:2** Ps 102:28 [s]**112:3** Pr 3:16; 8:18 [t]Ps 111:3 [u]**112:4** Ps 97:11 [v]Ex 34:6; Neh 9:17; Ps 116:5 [w]**112:5** Ps 15:5; 37:26 [x]**112:6** Ps 55:22 [y]Pr 10:7 [z]**112:7** Ps 56:4; 57:7; Pr 1:33 [aa]**112:8** Ps 27:1; 56:11 [ab]Ps 54:7; 59:10 [ac]**112:9** 2Co 9:9 [ad]Ps 75:10; 89:17 [ae]**112:10** Jb 16:9; Ps 35:16 [af]Pr 10:28; 11:7 [ag]**113:1** Ps 34:22; 69:36; 135:1 [ah]**113:2** Ps 115:18; 145:21 [ai]**113:3** Mal 1:11 [aj]**113:4** Ps 99:2 [ak]Ps 57:5,11; 148:13 [al]**113:5** Ex 15:11; Ps 89:6 [am]**113:6** Ps 11:4; 138:6 [an]**113:7** 1Sm 2:8; Ps 107:41 [ao]**113:8** Jb 36:7

[A]**111:1; 112:1** The lines of this poem form an ·acrostic. [B]**111:10** Lit *follow them*

making her the joyful mother
of children.[a]
Hallelujah!

Psalm 114
God's Deliverance of Israel

1 When Israel came out of Egypt —
the house of Jacob from a people
who spoke a foreign language[b] —
2 Judah became His sanctuary,
Israel, His dominion.[c]
3 The sea looked and fled;[d]
the Jordan turned back.[e]
4 The mountains skipped like rams,
the hills, like lambs.[f]
5 Why was it, sea, that you fled?
Jordan, that you turned back?[g]
6 Mountains, that you skipped like rams?
Hills, like lambs?[h]

7 Tremble, earth, at the presence
of the Lord,
at the presence of the God of Jacob,[i]
8 who turned the rock into a pool
of water,
the flint into a spring of water.[j]

Psalm 115
Glory to God Alone

1 Not to us, ·Yahweh, not to us,
but to Your name give glory
because of Your faithful love,
because of Your truth.[k]
2 Why should the nations say,
"Where is their God?"[l]
3 Our God is in heaven
and does whatever He pleases.[m]
4 Their idols are silver and gold,
made by human hands.[n]
5 They have mouths but cannot speak,
eyes, but cannot see.
6 They have ears but cannot hear,
noses, but cannot smell.[o]
7 They have hands but cannot feel,
feet, but cannot walk.[p]
They cannot make a sound
with their throats.[q]
8 Those who make them are[A] just like them,
as are all who trust in them.[r]
9 Israel,[B] trust in the LORD![s]
He is their help and shield.[t]
10 House of Aaron, trust in the LORD![u]
He is their help and shield.[v]
11 You who ·fear the LORD,
trust in the LORD![w]
He is their help and shield.
12 The LORD remembers us
and will bless us.
He will bless the house of Israel;
He will bless the house of Aaron;[x]
13 He will bless those who fear
the LORD —
small and great alike.[y]
14 May the LORD add to your numbers,
both yours and your children's.[z]
15 May you be blessed by the LORD,
the Maker of heaven and earth.[aa]
16 The heavens are the LORD's,[C]
but the earth He has given
to the ·human race.[ab]
17 It is not the dead who praise the LORD,
nor any of those descending
into the silence of death.[ac]
18 But we will praise the LORD,
both now and forever.[ad]
·Hallelujah!

Psalm 116
Thanks to God for Deliverance

1 I love the LORD because He has heard
my appeal for mercy.[ae]
2 Because He has turned His ear to me,
I will call out to Him as long as I live.[af]
3 The ropes of death were wrapped
around me,
and the torments of ·Sheol
overcame me;
I encountered trouble and sorrow.[ag]
4 Then I called on the name of ·Yahweh:
"Yahweh, save me!"[ah]
5 The LORD is gracious and righteous;
our God is compassionate.[ai]
6 The LORD guards the inexperienced;
I was helpless, and He saved me.[aj]
7 Return to your rest, my soul,
for the LORD has been good to you.[ak]
8 For You, LORD, rescued me from death,

[a] 113:9 1Sm 2:5; Ps 68:6 [b] 114:1 Ex 13:3; Ps 81:5 [c] 114:2 Ex 15:17; Ps 78:68-69 [d] 114:3 Ex 14:21; Ps 77:16 [e] Jos 3:13-16 [f] 114:4 Ex 19:18; Ps 29:6 [g] 114:5 Hab 3:8 [h] 114:6 Hab 3:10 [i] 114:7 Ps 96:9 [j] 114:8 Ex 17:6; Nm 20:11; Dt 8:15 [k] 115:1 Ezk 36:22; Dn 9:18-19 [l] 115:2 Ps 42:3,10; 79:10 [m] 115:3 Ps 135:6; Dn 4:35 [n] 115:4 2Kg 19:18; Is 37:19 [o] 115:5-6 Is 46:7 [p] 115:7 Jr 10:5 [q] Hab 2:18 [r] 115:4-8 Ps 135:15-18 [s] 115:9 Ps 118:2 [t] Gn 15:1; Dt 33:29; Ps 3:3; 5:12; 18:2; 28:7; 33:20; 119:114 [u] 115:10 Ps 118:3; 135:19 [v] 115:10-11 Ps 33:20 [w] 115:11 Ps 22:23; 118:4 [x] 115:12 Ps 98:3 [y] 115:13 Rv 11:18; 19:5 [z] 115:14 Dt 1:11 [aa] 115:15 Ps 121:2; 124:8; 134:3 [ab] 115:16 Ps 89:11 [ac] 115:17 Ps 6:5; 31:17; 88:10-12 [ad] 115:18 Ps 113:2; Dn 2:20 [ae] 116:1 Ps 18:1; 66:19 [af] 116:2 Ps 17:6; 40:1 [ag] 116:3 Ps 18:4-5 [ah] 116:4 Ps 18:6; 118:5 [ai] 116:5 Ex 34:6; Neh 9:17; Ps 112:4 [aj] 116:6 Ps 19:7; 79:8; 142:6 [ak] 116:7 Ps 13:6; Jr 6:16

[A] 115:8 Or *May those who make them become* [B] 115:9 Some Hb mss, LXX, Syr read *House of Israel* [C] 115:16 Lit *LORD's heavens*

my eyes from tears,
my feet from stumbling.[a]
9 I will walk before the LORD
in the land of the living.[b]
10 I believed, even when I said,
"I am severely afflicted."[c]
11 In my alarm I said,
"Everyone is a liar."[d]

12 How can I repay the LORD
for all the good He has done for me?[e]
13 I will take the cup of salvation
and call on the name of Yahweh.[f]
14 I will fulfill my vows to the LORD
in the presence of all His people.[g]
15 The death of His faithful ones
is valuable in the LORD's sight.[h]
16 LORD, I am indeed Your servant;
I am Your servant, the son
of Your female servant.
You have loosened my bonds.[i]
17 I will offer You a sacrifice
of thanksgiving
and call on the name of Yahweh.[j]
18 I will fulfill my vows to the LORD
in the presence of all His people,[k]
19 in the courts of the LORD's house—
within you, Jerusalem.[l]
·Hallelujah!

PSALM 117

Universal Call to Praise

1 Praise the LORD, all nations!
Glorify Him, all peoples![m]
2 For His faithful love to us is great;
the LORD's faithfulness
endures forever.[n]
·Hallelujah!

PSALM 118

Thanksgiving for Victory

1 Give thanks to the LORD, for He is good;
His faithful love endures forever.[o]
2 Let Israel say,
"His faithful love endures forever."[p]
3 Let the house of Aaron say,
"His faithful love endures forever."[q]
4 Let those who fear the LORD say,
"His faithful love endures forever."[r]

[a]116:8 Ps 49:15; 56:13 [b]116:9 Ps 27:13 [c]116:10 2Co 4:13 [d]116:11 Ps 31:22; 62:9; Rm 3:4 [e]116:12 2Ch 32:25; 1Th 3:9 [f]116:13 Ps 16:5; 105:1 [g]116:14 Ps 22:25; 50:14 [h]116:15 Ps 72:14 [i]116:16 Jb 12:18; Ps 86:16; 107:14 [j]116:17 Lv 7:12; Ps 50:14 [k]116:18 Ps 22:25; 50:14 [l]116:19 Ps 96:8; 102:21 [m]117:1 Rm 15:11 [n]117:2 Ps 100:5; 103:11; 146:6 [o]118:1 2Ch 5:13; Ezr 3:11; Ps 100:5 [p]118:2 Ps 115:9 [q]118:3 Ps 115:10; 135:19 [r]118:4 Ps 22:23; 115:11 [s]118:5 Ps 18:6; 120:1 [t]Ps 18:19 [u]118:6 Ps 56:4,11; Heb 13:6 [v]118:7 Ps 54:4,7; 59:10 [w]118:8 Ps 40:4; 108:12; Jr 17:5 [x]118:9 Ps 146:3 [y]118:10 Ps 3:6; 88:17 [z]118:11 Ps 18:40 [aa]118:12 Dt 1:44 [ab]Ps 58:9; Nah 1:10 [ac]118:13 Ps 140:4 [ad]118:14 Ex 15:2; Ps 27:1; Is 12:2 [ae]118:15 Ex 15:6; Lk 1:51 [af]118:16 Ps 89:13 [ag]118:17 Ps 73:28; Hab 1:12 [ah]118:18 Ps 86:13; Jr 30:11; 2Co 6:9 [ai]118:19 Is 26:2 [aj]118:20 Ps 24:3-6; Rv 22:14 [ak]118:21 Ps 116:1

5 I called to the LORD in distress;[s]
the LORD answered me
and put me in a spacious place.[A,t]
6 The LORD is for me; I will not be afraid.
What can man do to me?[u]
7 The LORD is my helper,
Therefore, I will look in triumph
on those who hate me.[v]

8 It is better to take refuge in the LORD
than to trust in man.[w]
9 It is better to take refuge in the LORD
than to trust in nobles.[x]

10 All the nations surrounded me;
in the name of ·Yahweh
I destroyed them.[y]
11 They surrounded me, yes,
they surrounded me;
in the name of Yahweh
I destroyed them.[z]
12 They surrounded me like bees;[aa]
they were extinguished like a fire
among thorns;
in the name of Yahweh
I destroyed them.[ab]
13 You[B] pushed me[C] hard to make me fall,
but the LORD helped me.[ac]
14 The LORD is my strength and my song;
He has become my salvation.[ad]

15 There are shouts of joy and victory
in the tents of the righteous:
"The LORD's right hand
performs valiantly![ae]
16 The LORD's right hand is raised.
The LORD's right hand
performs valiantly!"[af]
17 I will not die, but I will live
and proclaim what the LORD has done.[ag]
18 The LORD disciplined me severely
but did not give me over to death.[ah]

19 Open the gates of righteousness for me;
I will enter through them
and give thanks to the LORD.[ai]
20 This is the gate of the LORD;
the righteous will enter through it.[aj]
21 I will give thanks to You
because You have answered me
and have become my salvation.[ak]
22 The stone that the builders rejected

[A]118:5 Or *answered me with freedom* [B]118:13 Perhaps the enemy [C]118:13 LXX, Syr, Jer read *I was pushed*

has become the cornerstone.[a]
23 This came from the LORD;
it is wonderful in our eyes.[b]
24 This is the day the LORD has made;
let us rejoice and be glad in it.[c]

25 LORD, save us!
LORD, please grant us success![d]
26 He who comes in the name
of the LORD is blessed.[e]
From the house of the LORD
we bless you.[f]
27 The LORD is God and has given us light.
Bind the festival sacrifice with cords
to the horns of the altar.[g]
28 You are my God, and I will give
You thanks.
You are my God; I will exalt You.[h]
29 Give thanks to the LORD,
for He is good;
His faithful love endures forever.[i]

PSALM 119

Delight in God's Word

א Alef

1 How[A] happy are those whose way
is blameless,[j]
who live according to the LORD's
instruction![k]
2 Happy are those who keep His decrees[l]
and seek Him with all their heart.[m]
3 They do nothing wrong;[n]
they follow His ways.
4 You have commanded
that Your precepts[o]
be diligently kept.
5 If only my ways were committed
to keeping Your statutes![p]
6 Then I would not be ashamed[q]
when I think about all Your commands.
7 I will praise You with a sincere heart[r]
when I learn Your righteous judgments.
8 I will keep Your statutes;
never abandon me.[s]

ב Bet

9 How can a young man keep his way
pure?
By keeping Your[B] word.[t]
10 I have sought You with all my heart;[u]
don't let me wander
from Your commands.[v]
11 I have treasured Your word
in my heart[w]
so that I may not sin against You.
12 LORD, may You be praised;
teach me Your statutes.[x]
13 With my lips I proclaim
all the judgments from Your mouth.[y]
14 I rejoice in the way revealed by
Your decrees[z]
as much as in all riches.
15 I will meditate on Your precepts[aa]
and think about Your ways.[ab]
16 I will delight in Your statutes;[ac]
I will not forget Your word.

ג Gimel

17 Deal generously with Your servant[ad]
so that I might live;
then I will keep Your word.
18 Open my eyes so that
I may contemplate
wonderful things
from Your instruction.
19 I am a stranger on earth;[ae]
do not hide Your commands from me.
20 I am continually overcome
with longing for Your judgments.[af]
21 You rebuke the proud,
the ones under a curse,[ag]
who wander from Your commands.[ah]
22 Take insult and contempt away
from me,[ai]
for I have kept Your decrees.
23 Though princes sit together speaking
against me,[aj]
Your servant will think
about Your statutes;[ak]
24 Your decrees are my delight
and my counselors.[al]

ד Dalet

25 My life is down in the dust;[am]
give me life[an] through Your word.
26 I told You about my life,
and You listened to me;

[a]**118:22** Lk 20:17; Ac 4:11; 1Pt 2:4,7 [b]**118:23** Mt 21:42; Mk 12:11 [c]**118:24** Ps 31:7 [d]**118:25** Neh 2:20; Ps 122:6-7 [e]**118:25-26** Mt 21:9; Mk 11:9-10; Lk 13:35; Jn 12:13 [f]**118:26** Ps 129:8 [g]**118:27** Ex 27:2; Ps 18:28; 1Pt 2:9 [h]**118:28** Is 25:1 [i]**118:29** 2Ch 5:13; Ezr 3:11; Ps 100:5 [j]**119:1** Ps 101:6; Pr 11:20 [k]Ps 128:1; Mc 4:2 [l]**119:2** Ps 25:10; 119:10,22,168 [m]Dt 4:29; 10:12; 11:13; 13:3; 30:2 [n]**119:3** 1Jn 3:9; 5:18 [o]**119:4** Dt 4:13; Neh 9:13; Ps 19:8 [p]**119:5** Dt 12:1; 2Ch 7:17; Pr 4:26 [q]**119:6** Jb 22:26; Ps 119:80 [r]**119:7** Ps 119:62,106 [s]**119:8** Ps 38:21; 71:9,18 [t]**119:9** 2Sm 22:31; Ps 12:6; 19:9-10; 119:140; Pr 20:11; 30:5; Php 4:8 [u]**119:10** Ps 119:2 [v]Ps 119:21,118 [w]**119:11** Ps 37:31; 40:8; Lk 2:19,51 [x]**119:12** Ps 119:26,64,108, 124,135,171 [y]**119:13** Ps 40:9; 119:72 [z]**119:14** Ps 119:111,162; Pr 3:13-15; 8:10,11,18,19 [aa]**119:15** Ps 1:2; 119:23,48,78, 97,148 [ab]Ps 25:4; 27:11; Is 58:2 [ac]**119:16** Ps 1:2; 119:24,47,70, 77,92,143,174 [ad]**119:17** Ps 13:6; 119:144 [ae]**119:19** 1Ch 29:15; Ps 39:12; 119:54; Heb 11:13 [af]**119:20** Ps 42:1,2; 63:1; 84:2; 119:40,131 [ag]**119:21** Dt 27:26 [ah]Ps 119:10,118 [ai]**119:22** Ps 39:8; 119:39 [aj]**119:23** Ps 119:161 [ak]Ps 119:15,27-28 [al]**119:24** Ps 119:16; Rm 7:22 [am]**119:25** Ps 44:25 [an]Ps 119:37,40,88,93,107,149,154,156,159

A**119:1** The stanzas of this poem form an *acrostic. B**119:9** Or *keeping it according to Your*

teach me Your statutes.[a]
27 Help me understand
the meaning of Your precepts
so that I can meditate on
Your wonders.[b]
28 I am weary[A] from grief;
strengthen me through Your word.[c]
29 Keep me from the way of deceit
and graciously give me
Your instruction.
30 I have chosen the way of truth;
I have set Your ordinances before me.[d]
31 I cling to Your decrees;
LORD, do not put me to shame.[e]
32 I pursue the way of Your commands,
for You broaden my understanding.[B,f]

ה He

33 Teach me, LORD, the meaning[C]
of Your statutes,
and I will always keep them.[D,g]
34 Help me understand
Your instruction,[h]
and I will obey it
and follow it with all my heart.[i]
35 Help me stay on the path
of Your commands,[j]
for I take pleasure in it.[k]
36 Turn my heart to Your decrees[l]
and not to material gain.[m]
37 Turn my eyes
from looking at what is worthless;[n]
give me life in Your ways.[E,o]
38 Confirm what You said
to Your servant,[p]
for it produces reverence for You.
39 Turn away the disgrace I dread;[q]
indeed, Your judgments are good.
40 How I long for Your precepts![r]
Give me life through
Your righteousness.

ו Vav

41 Let Your faithful love
come to me, LORD,[s]
Your salvation, as You promised.[t]
42 Then I can answer the one
who taunts me,[u]
for I trust in Your word.
43 Never take the word of truth
from my mouth,
for I hope in Your judgments.[v]
44 I will always obey Your instruction,
forever and ever.[w]
45 I will walk freely in an open place[x]
because I seek Your precepts.[y]
46 I will speak of Your decrees
before kings
and not be ashamed.[z]
47 I delight in Your commands,
which I love.[aa]
48 I will lift up my hands[ab]
to Your commands,
which I love,
and will meditate on Your statutes.[ac]

ז Zayin

49 Remember Your word to Your servant;
You have given me hope through it.
50 This is my comfort in my affliction:[ad]
Your promise has given me life.
51 The arrogant constantly ridicule me,
but I do not turn away
from Your instruction.[ae]
52 LORD, I remember Your judgments
from long ago
and find comfort.
53 Rage seizes me[af] because of the wicked
who reject Your instruction.[ag]
54 Your statutes are the theme of my song
during my earthly life.[F]
55 •Yahweh, I remember Your name[ah]
in the night,[ai]
and I obey Your instruction.
56 This is my practice:
I obey Your precepts.[aj]

ח Khet

57 The LORD is my portion;[G,ak]
I have promised to keep Your words.
58 I have sought Your favor[al] with all
my heart;
be gracious to me[am] according to
Your promise.
59 I thought about my ways[an]
and turned my steps back
to Your decrees.

[a]**119:26** Ps 25:4; 86:11; 119:12,26,64, 68,124,135,171 [b]**119:27** Ps 105:2; 119:15,73,125; 145:5 [c]**119:28** 1Pt 5:10 [d]**119:30** Ps 16:8 [e]**119:31** Ps 119:116 [f]**119:32** 1Kg 4:29; 2Co 6:11,13 [g]**119:33** Ps 119:112; Mt 10:22; Heb 3:6; Rv 2:26 [h]**119:34** Ps 119:125, 144,169 [i]1Ch 22:12; Ps 119:2,69 [j]**119:35** Ps 25:4; Is 40:14 [k]Ps 119:16 [l]**119:36** 1Kg 8:58 [m]Ezk 33:31; Mk 7:21,22; Lk 12:15; Heb 13:5 [n]**119:37** Is 33:15 [o]Ps 119:25 [p]**119:38** 2Sm 7:25 [q]**119:39** Ps 119:22 [r]**119:40** Ps 119:20 [s]**119:41** Ps 119:77 [t]Ps 119:58,76, 116,170 [u]**119:42** Ps 102:8; Pr 27:11 [v]**119:43** Ps 119:49,74,81, 114,147 [w]**119:44** Ps 119:33 [x]**119:45** Pr 4:12 [y]Ps 119:94,155 [z]**119:46** Mt 10:18; Ac 26:1,2 [aa]**119:47** Ps 119:16,97,127, 159 [ab]**119:48** Ps 63:4 [ac]Ps 119:15 [ad]**119:50** Rm 15:4 [ae]**119:51** Jb 23:11; Ps 44:18 [af]**119:53** Ezr 9:3; Neh 13:25; Ps 119:158 [ag]Ps 89:30 [ah]**119:55** Ps 63:6 [ai]Ps 42:8; 92:2; Is 26:9; Ac 16:25 [aj]**119:56** Ps 119:22,69,100 [ak]**119:57** Ps 16:5; Lm 3:24 [al]**119:58** 1Kg 13:6 [am]Ps 41:4; 56:1; 57:1 [an]**119:59** Lk 15:17

[A]**119:28** Or *I weep* [B]**119:32** Lit *You enlarge my heart* [C]**119:33** Lit *way* [D]**119:33** Or *will keep it as my reward* [E]**119:37** Some Hb mss, Tg read *word* [F]**119:54** Lit *song in the house of my sojourning* [G]**119:57** Lit *You are my portion, LORD*

60 I hurried, not hesitating
to keep Your commands.
61 Though the ropes of the wicked[a]
were wrapped around me,
I did not forget Your instruction.[b]
62 I rise at midnight to thank You[c]
for Your righteous judgments.[d]
63 I am a friend to all who ·fear You,[e]
to those who keep Your precepts.
64 LORD, the earth is filled with
Your faithful love;[f]
teach me Your statutes.[g]

ט Tet

65 LORD, You have treated
Your servant well,
just as You promised.
66 Teach me good judgment
and discernment,[h]
for I rely on Your commands.
67 Before I was afflicted I went astray,[i]
but now I keep Your word.
68 You are good,[j] and You do
what is good;[k]
teach me Your statutes.
69 The arrogant have smeared me
with lies,[l]
but I obey Your precepts with all
my heart.[m]
70 Their hearts are hard and insensitive,[n]
but I delight in Your instruction.[o]
71 It was good for me to be afflicted[p]
so that I could learn Your statutes.
72 Instruction from Your lips[q] is better
for me
than thousands of gold
and silver pieces.

י Yod

73 Your hands made me and formed me;[r]
give me understanding
so that I can learn Your commands.[s]
74 Those who fear You will see me
and rejoice,[t]
for I put my hope in Your word.[u]
75 I know, LORD, that Your judgments
are just
and that You have afflicted me fairly.[v]
76 May Your faithful love comfort me
as You promised Your servant.
77 May Your compassion come to me[w]
so that I may live,
for Your instruction is my delight.[x]
78 Let the arrogant be put to shame[y]
for slandering me with lies;
I will meditate on Your precepts.
79 Let those who fear You,
those who know Your decrees,
turn to me.
80 May my heart be blameless
regarding Your statutes[z]
so that I will not be put to shame.

כ Kaf

81 I long for Your salvation;[aa]
I put my hope in Your word.[ab]
82 My eyes grow weary
looking for what You have promised;[ac]
I ask, "When will You comfort me?"
83 Though I have become like a wineskin
dried by smoke,
I do not forget Your statutes.
84 How many days must
Your servant wait?
When will You execute judgment
on my persecutors?[ad]
85 The arrogant have dug pits for me;[ae]
they violate Your instruction.
86 All Your commands are true;
people persecute me with lies—
help me![af]
87 They almost ended my life on earth,
but I did not abandon Your precepts.
88 Give me life in accordance with
Your faithful love,
and I will obey the decree
You have spoken.

ל Lamed

89 LORD, Your word is forever;[ag]
it is firmly fixed in heaven.
90 Your faithfulness is for all generations;[ah]
You established the earth,
and it stands firm.[ai]
91 They stand today in accordance with
Your judgments,[aj]
for all things are Your servants.[ak]
92 If Your instruction had not been
my delight,
I would have died in my affliction.[al]
93 I will never forget Your precepts,
for You have given me life
through them.[am]
94 I am Yours; save me,[an]

[a] 119:61 Jb 36:8; Ps 140:5 [b] Ps 119:83,141,153,176 [c] 119:62 Ps 119:55 [d] Ps 119:7 [e] 119:63 Ps 101:6 [f] 119:64 Ps 33:5 [g] Ps 119:12 [h] 119:66 Php 1:9,10 [i] 119:67 Ps 119:71,75; Jr 31:18,19; Heb 12:5-11 [j] 119:68 Ps 100:5; 106:1; 107:1 [k] Ps 125:4 [l] 119:69 Jb 13:4; Ps 109:2 [m] Ps 119:56 [n] 119:70 Ps 17:10 [o] Ps 119:16 [p] 119:71 Ps 119:67,75 [q] 119:72 Ps 19:10; 119:127; Pr 8:10,11,19 [r] 119:73 Jb 10:8; 31:15; Ps 100:3; 139:15-16 [s] Ps 119:34 [t] 119:74 Ps 34:2; 107:42 [u] Ps 119:43 [v] 119:75 Ps 119:138; Heb 12:10 [w] 119:77 Ps 119:41 [x] Ps 119:16 [y] 119:78 Jr 50:32 [z] 119:80 Ps 119:1 [aa] 119:81 Ps 84:2 [ab] Ps 119:43 [ac] 119:82 Ps 69:3; 119:123; Is 38:14 [ad] 119:84 Rv 6:10 [ae] 119:85 Ps 35:7; 57:6; Jr 18:22 [af] 119:86 Ps 35:19; 109:26; 119:78 [ag] 119:89 Ps 89:2; 119:160; Is 40:8; Mt 24:35; 1Pt 1:25 [ah] 119:90 Ps 89:1,2 [ai] Ps 148:6; Ec 1:4 [aj] 119:91 Jr 31:35 [ak] Ps 104:2-4 [al] 119:92 Ps 119:16,50 [am] 119:93 Ps 119:16,25 [an] 119:94 Ps 119:146

for I have sought Your precepts.[a]
95 The wicked hope to destroy me,[b]
but I contemplate Your decrees.
96 I have seen a limit to all perfection,
but Your command is without limit.

מ *Mem*

97 How I love Your instruction![c]
It is my meditation all day long.[d]
98 Your commands make me wiser
than my enemies,[e]
for they are always with me.
99 I have more insight than
all my teachers
because Your decrees are
my meditation.[f]
100 I understand more than the elders[g]
because I obey Your precepts.[h]
101 I have kept my feet from every evil path[i]
to follow Your word.
102 I have not turned from
Your judgments,[j]
for You Yourself have instructed me.
103 How sweet Your word is[k] to my taste —
sweeter than honey in my mouth.
104 I gain understanding
from Your precepts;[l]
therefore I hate every false way.[m]

נ *Nun*

105 Your word is a lamp for my feet[n]
and a light on my path.
106 I have solemnly sworn[o]
to keep Your righteous judgments.
107 I am severely afflicted;
LORD, give me life through Your word.[p]
108 LORD, please accept
my willing offerings of praise,[q]
and teach me Your judgments.[r]
109 My life is constantly in danger,[A]
yet I do not forget Your instruction.[s]
110 The wicked have set a trap for me,[t]
but I have not wandered
from Your precepts.[u]
111 I have Your decrees
as a heritage forever;
indeed, they are the joy of my heart.[v]
112 I am resolved to obey Your statutes
to the very end.[B,w]

ס *Samek*

113 I hate those who are double-minded,[x]
but I love Your instruction.[y]
114 You are my shelter and my shield;[z]
I put my hope in Your word.[aa]
115 Depart from me,[ab] you evil ones,
so that I may obey
my God's commands.[ac]
116 Sustain me as You promised,[ad]
and I will live;
do not let me be ashamed of my hope.[ae]
117 Sustain me so that I can be safe[af]
and always be concerned about
Your statutes.[ag]
118 You reject all who stray
from Your statutes,[ah]
for their deceit is a lie.
119 You remove all the wicked on earth
as if they were[C] dross;[ai]
therefore, I love Your decrees.[aj]
120 I tremble[D] in awe of You;[ak]
I fear Your judgments.

ע *Ayin*

121 I have done what is just and right;[al]
do not leave me to my oppressors.
122 Guarantee Your servant's well-being;[am]
do not let the arrogant oppress me.
123 My eyes grow weary[an] looking for
Your salvation
and for Your righteous promise.
124 Deal with Your servant based on
Your faithful love;[ao]
teach me Your statutes.
125 I am Your servant;[ap]
give me understanding[aq]
so that I may know Your decrees.
126 It is time for the LORD to act,[ar]
for they have violated Your instruction.
127 Since I love Your commands[as]
more than gold, even the purest gold,
128 I carefully follow[E] all Your precepts[at]
and hate every false way.[au]

פ *Pe*

129 Your decrees are wonderful;[av]
therefore I obey them.[aw]

[a]**119:94** Ps 119:45 [b]**119:95** Ps 40:14 [c]**119:97** Ps 119:47,127,163,165 [d]Ps 1:2; 119:15 [e]**119:98** Dt 4:6; Ps 119:130 [f]**119:99** Ps 119:15 [g]**119:100** Jb 32:7-9 [h]Ps 119:56 [i]**119:101** Pr 1:15 [j]**119:102** Dt 17:20; Jos 23:6; 1Kg 15:5 [k]**119:103** Ps 19:10; Pr 8:11; 24:13,14 [l]**119:104** Ps 119:130 [m]Ps 119:128 [n]**119:105** Pr 6:23 [o]**119:106** Neh 10:29 [p]**119:107** Ps 119:25,50 [q]**119:108** Hs 14:2; Heb 13:15 [r]Ps 119:12 [s]**119:109** Ps 119:16 [t]**119:110** Ps 140:5; 141:9 [u]Ps 119:10 [v]**119:111** Ps 119:14,162 [w]**119:112** Ps 119:33,36 [x]**119:113** 1Kg 18:21; Jms 1:8; 4:8 [y]Ps 119:47 [z]**119:114** Gn 15:1; Dt 33:29; Ps 3:3; 28:7; 115:9-11; 144:2; Pr 2:7 [aa]Ps 119:74 [ab]**119:115** Ps 6:8; 139:19; Mt 4:10 [ac]Ps 119:22 [ad]**119:116** Ps 54:4 [ae]Ps 25:20; 31:1; Rm 9:33; Php 1:20 [af]**119:117** Pr 29:25 [ag]Ps 119:15 [ah]**119:118** Ps 119:10,21 [ai]**119:119** Is 1:25; Ezk 22:18,19 [aj]Ps 119:47 [ak]**119:120** Jb 4:14; Hab 3:16 [al]**119:121** Jb 29:14 [am]**119:122** Ps 119:134 [an]**119:123** Ps 119:82 [ao]**119:124** Ps 51:1; 109:26; 119:88,149,159 [ap]**119:125** Ps 116:16

[aq]Ps 119:27 [ar]**119:126** Jr 18:23 [as]**119:127** Ps 19:10; 119:47 [at]**119:128** Ps 19:8 [au]Ps 119:104 [av]**119:129** Ps 119:18 [aw]Ps 119:22

[A]**119:109** Lit *in my hand* [B]**119:112** Or *statutes; the reward is eternal* [C]**119:119** Some Hb mss, DSS, LXX, Aq, Sym, Jer read *All the wicked of the earth You count as* [D]**119:120** Lit *My flesh shudders* [E]**119:128** Lit *I therefore follow carefully*

130 The revelation of Your words[a]
brings light
and gives understanding
to the inexperienced.[b]
131 I open my mouth and pant[c]
because I long for Your commands.
132 Turn to me and be gracious to me,[d]
as is Your practice toward those
who love Your name.
133 Make my steps steady
through Your promise;[e]
don't let any sin dominate me.[f]
134 Redeem me from human oppression,[g]
and I will keep Your precepts.
135 Show favor to Your servant,[h]
and teach me Your statutes.[i]
136 My eyes pour out streams of tears[j]
because people do not follow
Your instruction.

צ *Tsade*

137 You are righteous, LORD,[k]
and Your judgments are just.
138 The decrees You issue are righteous
and altogether trustworthy.[l]
139 My anger overwhelms me
because my foes forget Your words.[m]
140 Your word is completely pure,[n]
and Your servant loves it.[o]
141 I am insignificant and despised,[p]
but I do not forget Your precepts.[q]
142 Your righteousness is
an everlasting righteousness,
and Your instruction is true.[r]
143 Trouble and distress
have overtaken me,
but Your commands are my delight.[s]
144 Your decrees are righteous forever.[t]
Give me understanding, and I will live.

ק *Qof*

145 I call with all my heart;
answer me, LORD.
I will obey Your statutes.[u]
146 I call to You; save me,
and I will keep Your decrees.[v]
147 I rise before dawn and cry out for help;[w]
I put my hope in Your word.
148 I am awake through each watch
of the night
to meditate on Your promise.[x]
149 In keeping with Your faithful love,
hear my voice.
LORD, give me life in keeping with
Your justice.[y]
150 Those who pursue evil plans[A,z]
come near;
they are far from Your instruction.
151 You are near, LORD,[aa]
and all Your commands are true.[ab]
152 Long ago I learned from Your decrees
that You have established them forever.[ac]

ר *Resh*

153 Consider my affliction and rescue me,[ad]
for I have not forgotten
Your instruction.[ae]
154 Defend my cause and redeem me;[af]
give me life as You promised.
155 Salvation is far from the wicked
because they do not seek Your statutes.[ag]
156 Your compassions are many, LORD;[ah]
give me life according to
Your judgments.
157 My persecutors and foes are many.[ai]
I have not turned from Your decrees.[aj]
158 I have seen the disloyal[ak]
and feel disgust[al]
because they do not keep Your word.
159 Consider how I love Your precepts;
LORD, give me life according to
Your faithful love.[am]
160 The entirety of Your word is truth,
and all Your righteous judgments
endure forever.[an]

ש *Sin* / ש *Shin*

161 Princes have persecuted me
without cause,
but my heart fears only Your word.[ao]
162 I rejoice over Your promise[ap]
like one who finds vast treasure.
163 I hate and abhor falsehood,[aq]
but I love Your instruction.[ar]
164 I praise You seven times a day
for Your righteous judgments.[as]
165 Abundant peace belongs to those[at]
who love Your instruction;

[a] 119:130 Pr 6:23 [b] Ps 19:7 [c] 119:131 Ps 42:1 [d] 119:132 Ps 25:16 [e] 119:133 Ps 17:5 [f] Ps 19:13; Rm 6:12 [g] 119:134 Ps 142:6; Lk 1:74 [h] 119:135 Ps 31:16; 80:3,7,19 [i] Ps 119:12 [j] 119:136 Jr 9:1; 14:17; Lm 3:48 [k] 119:137 Neh 9:33; Ps 129:4; 145:17; Lm 1:18 [l] 119:138 Ps 19:7-9; 119:86,90, 144,172 [m] 119:139 Ps 69:9; Jn 2:17 [n] 119:140 Ps 12:6; 19:9 [o] Ps 119:47 [p] 119:141 Ps 22:6 [q] Ps 119:61 [r] 119:142 Ps 119:151,160 [s] 119:143 Ps 119:24 [t] 119:144 Ps 19:9 [u] 119:145 Ps 119:10,55 [v] 119:146 Ps 3:7 [w] 119:147 Ps 5:3 [x] 119:148 Ps 119:15 [y] 119:149 Ps 119:25,124 [z] 119:150 Pr 6:17,18; 12:20; 14:22; 24:8 [aa] 119:151 Ps 34:18; 145:18; Is 50:8 [ab] Ps 119:142 [ac] 119:152 Ps 119:89; Lk 21:33 [ad] 119:153 Ps 119:50; Lm 5:1 [ae] Ps 119:16; Hs 4:6 [af] 119:154 1Sm 24:15; Ps 35:1; Mc 7:9 [ag] 119:155 Ps 119:45,94 [ah] 119:156 2Sm 24:14 [ai] 119:157 Ps 7:1 [aj] Ps 119:51 [ak] 119:158 Pr 14:14 [al] Ps 139:21 [am] 119:159 Ps 119:25,47 [an] 119:160 Ps 119:89,142,152 [ao] 119:161 Ps 119:23,120 [ap] 119:162 Ps 119:14,111 [aq] 119:163 Ps 119:104,128; Pr 13:5 [ar] Ps 119:47 [as] 119:164 Ps 119:7,160 [at] 119:165 Pr 3:1,2; Is 26:3; 32:17

A 119:150 Some Hb mss, LXX, Sym, Jer read *who maliciously persecute me*

nothing makes them stumble.[a]
166 LORD, I hope for Your salvation[b]
and carry out Your commands.
167 I obey Your decrees
and love them greatly.[c]
168 I obey Your precepts and decrees,
for all my ways are before You.[d]

ת *Tav*

169 Let my cry reach You, LORD;[e]
give me understanding according to
Your word.[f]
170 Let my plea reach You;[g]
rescue me according to Your promise.[h]
171 My lips pour out praise,[i]
for You teach me Your statutes.[j]
172 My tongue sings about Your promise,[k]
for all Your commands are righteous.[l]
173 May Your hand be ready to help me,[m]
for I have chosen Your precepts.[n]
174 I long for Your salvation, LORD,
and Your instruction is my delight.[o]
175 Let me live, and I will praise You;[p]
may Your judgments help me.
176 I wander like a lost sheep;[q]
seek Your servant,[r]
for I do not forget Your commands.[s]

PSALM 120

A Cry for Truth and Peace

A •song of ascents.

1 In my distress I called to the LORD,
and He answered me.[t]
2 "LORD, deliver me from lying lips
and a deceitful tongue."[u]

3 What will He give you,
and what will He do to you,
you deceitful tongue?[v]
4 A warrior's sharp arrows
with burning charcoal![A,w]
5 What misery that I have stayed
in Meshech,[B,x]
that I have lived among the tents
of Kedar![C,y]
6 I have lived too long
with those who hate peace.[z]
7 I am for peace; but when I speak,
they are for war.[aa]

PSALM 121

The LORD Our Protector

A •song of ascents.

1 I lift my eyes toward the mountains.
Where will my help come from?[ab]
2 My help comes from the LORD,
the Maker of heaven and earth.[ac]

3 He will not allow your foot to slip;
your Protector will not slumber.[ad]
4 Indeed, the Protector of Israel
does not slumber or sleep.[ae]
5 The LORD protects you;
the LORD is a shelter right by your side.[D,af]
6 The sun will not strike you by day
or the moon by night.[ag]

7 The LORD will protect you
from all harm;
He will protect your life.[ah]
8 The LORD will protect your coming
and going
both now and forever.[ai]

PSALM 122

A Prayer for Jerusalem

A Davidic •song of ascents.

1 I rejoiced with those who said to me,
"Let us go to the house of the LORD."[aj]
2 Our feet are standing
within your gates, Jerusalem[ak] —
3 Jerusalem, built as a city should be,
solidly joined together,[al]
4 where the tribes, •Yahweh's tribes, go up
to give thanks to the name of Yahweh.[am]
(This is an ordinance for Israel.[an])
5 There, thrones for judgment are placed,
thrones of the house of David.[ao]

6 Pray for the peace of Jerusalem:
"May those who love you prosper;[ap]
7 may there be peace within your walls,
prosperity within your fortresses."[aq]
8 Because of my brothers and friends,
I will say, "Peace be with you."[ar]
9 Because of the house of the LORD
our God,
I will seek your good.[as]

[a]**119:165** Pr 3:23; Is 63:13 [b]**119:166** Gn 49:18; Ps 119:81,174 [c]**119:167** Ps 119:47,129 [d]**119:168** Ps 139:3; Pr 5:21 [e]**119:169** Ps 18:6; 102:1; 140:6 [f]Ps 119:144 [g]**119:170** Ps 28:2; 130:2; 143:1 [h]Ps 22:20; 59:1 [i]**119:171** Ps 51:15; 63:3 [j]Ps 119:12 [k]**119:172** Ps 51:14 [l]Ps 119:138 [m]**119:173** Ps 37:24; 73:23 [n]Jos 24:22 [o]**119:174** Ps 119:16,24,166 [p]**119:175** Ps 119:25 [q]**119:176** Is 53:6; Jr 50:6 [r]Mt 18:12; Lk 15:4 [s]Ps 119:16 [t]**120:1** Ps 18:6; Jnh 2:2 [u]**120:2** Pr 12:22 [v]**120:3** Zph 3:13 [w]**120:4** Pr 25:18,22 [x]**120:5** Ezk 27:13 [y]Sg 1:5; Ezk 27:21 [z]**120:6** Ps 35:20 [aa]**120:7** Ps 109:4 [ab]**121:1** Ps 87:1; 123:1 [ac]**121:2** Ps 115:15; 124:8 [ad]**121:3** Ps 41:2; 66:9; 127:1 [ae]**121:4** Dt 33:29 [af]**121:5** Ps 16:8; 91:1,4 [ag]**121:6** Is 49:10; Rv 7:16 [ah]**121:7** Ps 41:2; 91:10-12 [ai]**121:8** Dt 28:6 [aj]**122:1** Is 2:3; Mc 4:2; Zch 8:21 [ak]**122:2** Ps 9:14; Jr 7:2 [al]**122:3** Neh 4:6; Ps 147:2 [am]**122:4** Is 2:3; Mc 4:2 [an]1Ch 22:13 [ao]**122:5** Dt 17:8; 2Ch 19:8 [ap]**122:6** Ps 51:18; Jr 29:7 [aq]**122:7** Ps 48:3 [ar]**122:8** 1Sm 25:6; Ps 85:8 [as]**122:9** Neh 2:10; Est 10:3

[A]**120:4** Lit *with coals of the broom bush* [B]**120:5** = a people far to the north of Palestine [C]**120:5** = a nomadic people of the desert to the southeast

[D]**121:5** Lit *is your shelter at your right hand*

Psalm 123

Looking for God's Favor

A ·song of ascents.

1 I lift my eyes to You,
the One enthroned in heaven.[a]
2 Like a servant's eyes
on his master's hand,
like a servant girl's eyes
on her mistress's hand,
so our eyes are on the LORD our God
until He shows us favor.[b]
3 Show us favor, LORD, show us favor,
for we've had more than enough
contempt.[c]
4 We've had more than enough
scorn from the arrogant
and contempt from the proud.[d]

Psalm 124

The LORD Is on Our Side

A Davidic ·song of ascents.

1 If the LORD had not been on our side—
let Israel say—
2 If the LORD had not been on our side[e]
when men attacked us,[f]
3 then they would have
swallowed us alive
in their burning anger against us.[g]
4 Then the waters would have
engulfed us;
the torrent would have swept over us;
5 the raging waters would have swept
over us.[h]
6 Praise the LORD,
who has not let us be ripped apart
by their teeth.[i]
7 We have escaped like a bird
from the hunter's net;
the net is torn, and we have escaped.[j]
8 Our help is in the name of ·Yahweh,
the Maker of heaven and earth.[k]

Psalm 125

Israel's Stability

A ·song of ascents.

1 Those who trust in the LORD are
like Mount ·Zion.
It cannot be shaken; it remains forever.[l]
2 Jerusalem—the mountains
surround her.
And the LORD surrounds His people,
both now and forever.[m]
3 The scepter of the wicked
will not remain
over the land allotted to the righteous,
so that the righteous will not apply
their hands to injustice.[n]
4 Do what is good, LORD, to the good,
to those whose hearts are upright.[o]
5 But as for those who turn aside
to crooked ways,
the LORD will banish them
with the evildoers.[p]

Peace be with Israel.[q]

Psalm 126

Zion's Restoration

A ·song of ascents.

1 When the LORD restored the fortunes
of ·Zion,[A]
we were like those who dream.[r]
2 Our mouths were filled
with laughter then,[s]
and our tongues with shouts of joy.[t]
Then they said among the nations,
"The LORD has done great things
for them."[u]
3 The LORD had done great things for us;
we were joyful.[v]
4 Restore our fortunes,[B] LORD,
like watercourses in the ·Negev.[w]
5 Those who sow in tears
will reap with shouts of joy.[x]
6 Though one goes along weeping,
carrying the bag of seed,
he will surely come back with shouts
of joy,
carrying his sheaves.[y]

Psalm 127

The Blessing of the LORD

A Solomonic ·song of ascents.

1 Unless the LORD builds a house,
its builders labor over it in vain;[z]
unless the LORD watches over a city,

[a] 123:1 Ps 2:4; 121:1; 141:8
[b] 123:2 Ps 25:15
[c] 123:3 Neh 4:4; Ps 4:1; 119:22
[d] 123:4 Is 32:9,11; Am 6:1
[e] 124:1-2 Ps 94:17
[f] 124:2 Ps 129:1
[g] 124:3 Ps 35:25; 56:1; Pr 1:12
[h] 124:4-5 Jb 22:11; Ps 32:6; 69:2
[i] 124:6 Ps 27:2; Pr 30:14
[j] 124:7 Ps 91:3
[k] 124:8 Ps 115:15; 121:2
[l] 125:1 Ps 46:5
[m] 125:2 Zch 2:5
[n] 125:3 Ps 89:22; Is 14:5
[o] 125:4 Ps 7:10; 119:68
[p] 125:5 Ps 92:7,9; 94:4
[q] 125:4-5 Ps 128:5-6
[r] 126:1 Ps 85:1; Jr 29:14
[s] 126:2 Jb 8:21
[t] Ps 51:14
[u] Ps 71:19
[v] 126:3 Is 25:9
[w] 126:4 Is 35:6; 43:19
[x] 126:5 Jr 31:9
[y] 126:6 Is 35:10; 51:11
[z] 127:1 Ps 78:69

A126:1 Or *LORD returned those of Zion who had been captives* B126:4 Or *Return our captives*

the watchman stays alert in vain.[a]
2 In vain you get up early
and stay up late,
working hard to have enough food —
yes, He gives sleep to the one He loves.[A,b]

3 Sons are indeed a heritage
from the LORD,
children, a reward.[c]
4 Like arrows in the hand of a warrior
are the sons born in one's youth.[d]
5 Happy is the man who has filled
his quiver with them.[e]
Such men will never be put to shame
when they speak with their enemies
at the city ·gate.[f]

PSALM 128
Blessings for Those Who Fear God

A ·song of ascents.

1 How happy is everyone who ·fears
the LORD,
who walks in His ways![g]
2 You will surely eat
what your hands have worked for.[h]
You will be happy,
and it will go well for you.[i]
3 Your wife will be like a fruitful vine
within your house,
your sons, like young olive trees
around your table.[j]
4 In this very way
the man who fears the LORD
will be blessed.[k]

5 May the LORD bless you from ·Zion,
so that you will see the prosperity
of Jerusalem
all the days of your life[l]
6 and will see your children's children!

Peace be with Israel.[m]

PSALM 129
Protection of the Oppressed

A ·song of ascents.

1 Since my youth they have often
attacked me —
let Israel say —
2 Since my youth they have often
attacked me,
but they have not prevailed against me.[n]
3 Plowmen plowed over my back;
they made their furrows long.[o]
4 The LORD is righteous;
He has cut the ropes of the wicked.[p]

5 Let all who hate ·Zion
be driven back in disgrace.[q]
6 Let them be like grass on the rooftops,
which withers before it grows up[B,r]
7 and can't even fill the hands
of the reaper
or the arms of the one
who binds sheaves.[s]
8 Then none who pass by will say,
"May the LORD's blessing be on you."
We bless you in the name of ·Yahweh.[t]

PSALM 130
Awaiting Redemption

A ·song of ascents.

1 Out of the depths I call
to You, ·Yahweh![u]
2 Lord, listen to my voice;
let Your ears be attentive
to my cry for help.[v]

3 Yahweh, if You considered sins,
Lord, who could stand?[w]
4 But with You there is forgiveness,
so that You may be revered.[x]

5 I wait for Yahweh; I wait
and put my hope in His word.[y]
6 I wait for the Lord
more than watchmen
for the morning —
more than watchmen for the morning.[z]

7 Israel, put your hope in the LORD.[aa]
For there is faithful love with the LORD,
and with Him is redemption
in abundance.[ab]
8 And He will redeem Israel
from all its sins.[ac]

PSALM 131
A Childlike Spirit

A Davidic ·song of ascents.

1 LORD, my heart is not proud;
my eyes are not haughty.[ad]

[a] **127:1** Ps 121:4
[b] **127:2** Ps 3:5; 4:8; Pr 3:24
[c] **127:3** Dt 7:13; Ps 113:9
[d] **127:4** Ps 120:4
[e] **127:5** Ps 128:2-3
[f] Jl 2:26-27
[g] **128:1** Ps 112:1; 119:1,3
[h] **128:2** Is 3:10
[i] Ec 8:12
[j] **128:3** Ps 52:8; Ezk 19:10
[k] **128:4** Ps 115:13
[l] **128:5** Ps 20:2; 134:3; 135:21
[m] **128:6** Ps 125:5; Pr 17:6
[n] **129:1-2** Jr 1:19; 20:11
[o] **129:3** Mc 3:12
[p] **129:4** Ps 2:3
[q] **129:5** Ps 35:4; 70:3; 71:13
[r] **129:6** 2Kg 19:26; Is 37:27
[s] **129:7** Ps 79:12
[t] **129:8** Ru 2:4; Ps 118:26
[u] **130:1** Ps 69:2; Lm 3:55
[v] **130:2** 2Ch 6:40; Ps 28:6; 140:6
[w] **130:3** Ps 76:7; Mal 3:2; Rv 6:17
[x] **130:4** 1Kg 8:39-40; Ps 86:5; Jr 33:8-9
[y] **130:5** Ps 33:20; 119:74,81
[z] **130:6** Ps 63:6; 119:147
[aa] **130:7** Ps 131:3
[ab] Ps 111:9
[ac] **130:8** Lk 1:68; Ti 2:14
[ad] **131:1** Ps 101:5; Rm 12:16

A **127:2** Or *yes, He gives such things to His loved ones while they sleep* B **129:6** Or *it can be pulled out*

I do not get involved with things
too great or too difficult for me.[a]
2 Instead, I have calmed
and quieted myself
like a little weaned child
with its mother;
I am like a little child.[b]

3 Israel, put your hope in the LORD,
both now and forever.[c]

PSALM 132

David and Zion Chosen

A •song of ascents.

1 LORD, remember David
and all the hardships he endured,[d]
2 and how he swore an oath to the LORD,
making a vow to the Mighty One
of Jacob:[e]
3 "I will not enter my house[A]
or get into my bed,[B]
4 I will not allow my eyes to sleep
or my eyelids to slumber[f]
5 until I find a place for the LORD,
a dwelling for the Mighty One of Jacob."[g]

6 We heard of the ark in Ephrathah;[C,h]
we found it in the fields of Jaar.[D,i]
7 Let us go to His dwelling place;
let us worship at His footstool.[j]
8 Rise up, LORD, come to
Your resting place,
You and Your powerful ark.[k]
9 May Your priests be clothed
with righteousness,
and may Your godly people shout
for joy.[l]
10 Because of Your servant David,
do not reject Your anointed one.[E,m]

11 The LORD swore an oath to David,
a promise He will not abandon:
"I will set one of your descendants[F]
on your throne.[n]
12 If your sons keep My covenant
and My decrees that I will teach them,
their sons will also sit on
your throne forever."[o]

13 For the LORD has chosen •Zion;
He has desired it for His home:[p]
14 "This is My resting place forever;
I will make My home here
because I have desired it.[q]
15 I will abundantly bless its food;
I will satisfy its needy with bread.[r]
16 I will clothe its priests with salvation,
and its godly people will shout for joy.[s]
17 There I will make a •horn grow
for David;[t]
I have prepared a lamp for
My anointed one.[u]
18 I will clothe his enemies with shame,[v]
but the crown he wears[G]
will be glorious."[w]

PSALM 133

Living in Harmony

A Davidic •song of ascents.

1 How good and pleasant it is
when brothers live together
in harmony![x]
2 It is like fine oil on the head,
running down on the beard,
running down Aaron's beard
onto his robes.[y]
3 It is like the dew of Hermon[H]
falling on the mountains of •Zion.[z]
For there the LORD has appointed
the blessing —
life forevermore.[aa]

PSALM 134

Call to Evening Worship

A •song of ascents.

1 Now praise the LORD,
all you servants of the LORD
who stand in the LORD's house
at night![ab]
2 Lift up your hands in the holy place
and praise the LORD![ac]

3 May the LORD,
Maker of heaven and earth,
bless you from •Zion.[ad]

PSALM 135

Yahweh Is Great

1 •Hallelujah!
Praise the name of •Yahweh.

a131:1 Jb 42:3; Ps 139:6 **b131:2** Mt 18:3; 1Co 14:20 **c131:3** Ps 130:7 **d132:1** 2Sm 16:12 **e132:2** Gn 49:24; Is 49:26; 60:16 **f132:3-4** Pr 6:4 **g132:5** 1Ch 22:7; Ac 7:46 **h132:6** Gn 35:19; Ru 4:11; 1Sm 17:12; Mc 5:2 **i**1Sm 7:1 **j132:7** 1Ch 28:2; Ps 99:5 **k132:8** 2Ch 6:41; Ps 68:1; 78:61 **l132:9** Jb 29:14; Ps 149:5 **m132:10** 2Ch 6:42 **n132:11** 2Sm 7:12-16; Ps 89:3; Ac 2:30 **o132:12** 1Kg 8:25; Lk 1:32 **p132:13** Ps 68:16; 78:68 **q132:14** Mt 23:21 **r132:15** Ps 107:9; 147:14 **s132:16** 2Ch 6:41 **t132:17** 2Sm 23:5; Lk 1:69 **u**1Kg 11:36 **v132:18** Jb 8:22 **w**Ps 21:3 **x133:1** Gn 13:8; Heb 13:1 **y133:2** Ex 30:25,30; Lv 8:12 **z133:3** Ps 48:1-2; Mc 5:7 **aa**Ps 21:4 **ab134:1** 1Ch 9:23-27; Ps 135:1-2 **ac134:2** Ps 28:2; 63:2; 1Tm 2:8 **ad134:3** Ps 115:15; 128:5

A**132:3** Lit *enter the tent of my house* B**132:3** Lit *into the couch of my bed* C**132:6** = Bethlehem D**132:6** = Kiriath-jearim E**132:10** = the king F**132:11** Lit *set the fruit of your womb* G**132:18** Lit *but on him his crown* H**133:3** The tallest mountain in the region, noted for its abundant precipitation

Give praise, you servants of Yahweh[a]
2 who stand in the house of Yahweh,
in the courts of the house of our God.[b]
3 Praise Yahweh, for Yahweh is good;
sing praise to His name,
for it is delightful.[c]
4 For Yahweh has chosen Jacob
for Himself,
Israel as His treasured possession.[d]

5 For I know that Yahweh is great;
our Lord is greater than all gods.[e]
6 Yahweh does whatever He pleases
in heaven and on earth,
in the seas and all the depths.[f]
7 He causes the clouds to rise
from the ends of the earth.
He makes lightning for the rain
and brings the wind
from His storehouses.[g]

8 He struck down the firstborn of Egypt,
both man and beast.[h]
9 He sent signs and wonders
against you, Egypt,
against Pharaoh and all his officials.[i]
10 He struck down many nations
and slaughtered mighty kings:[j]
11 Sihon king of the Amorites,
Og king of Bashan,
and all the kings of Canaan.[k]
12 He gave their land as an inheritance,
an inheritance to His people Israel.[l]

13 Yahweh, Your name endures forever,
Your reputation, Yahweh,
through all generations.[m]
14 For Yahweh will vindicate His people
and have compassion on His servants.[n]

15 The idols of the nations are of silver
and gold,
made by human hands.[o]
16 They have mouths but cannot speak,[p]
eyes, but cannot see.
17 They have ears but cannot hear;
indeed, there is no breath
in their mouths.[q]
18 Those who make them are just
like them,
as are all who trust in them.[r]

19 House of Israel, praise Yahweh![s]
House of Aaron, praise Yahweh![t]
20 House of Levi, praise Yahweh!
You who revere the LORD,
praise the LORD![u]
21 May the LORD be praised from °Zion;[v]
He dwells in Jerusalem.[w]
Hallelujah!

PSALM 136

God's Love Is Eternal

1 Give thanks to the LORD,
for He is good.[x]
His love is eternal.
2 Give thanks to the God of gods.
His love is eternal.
3 Give thanks to the Lord of lords.[y]
His love is eternal.
4 He alone does great wonders.[z]
His love is eternal.
5 He made the heavens skillfully.[aa]
His love is eternal.
6 He spread the land on the waters.[ab]
His love is eternal.
7 He made the great lights:[ac]
His love is eternal.
8 the sun to rule by day,
His love is eternal.
9 the moon and stars to rule by night.[ad]
His love is eternal.

10 He struck the firstborn
of the Egyptians[ae]
His love is eternal.
11 and brought Israel out
from among them
His love is eternal.
12 with a strong hand
and outstretched arm.[af]
His love is eternal.
13 He divided the °Red Sea[ag]
His love is eternal.
14 and led Israel through,[ah]
His love is eternal.
15 but hurled Pharaoh and his army
into the Red Sea.[ai]
His love is eternal.
16 He led His people in the wilderness.[aj]
His love is eternal.

17 He struck down great kings
His love is eternal.
18 and slaughtered famous kings —
His love is eternal.
19 Sihon king of the Amorites
His love is eternal.

[a] **135:1** Ps 113:1; 134:1
[b] **135:2** Ps 92:13; 116:19
[c] **135:3** Ps 100:5; 147:1
[d] **135:4** Ex 19:5; Dt 7:6-7; 10:15
[e] **135:5** Ps 95:3; 97:9
[f] **135:6** Ps 115:3; Is 45:7; Lm 3:37-38; Dn 4:35
[g] **135:7** Jb 28:25-26; Jr 10:13; 51:16
[h] **135:8** Ex 12:12; Ps 78:51; 105:36
[i] **135:9** Dt 6:22; Ps 78:43
[j] **135:10** Ps 44:2; 136:17-22
[k] **135:11** Nm 21:21-35
[l] **135:12** Dt 29:8; Ps 78:55
[m] **135:13** Ex 3:15; Ps 102:12
[n] **135:14** Dt 32:36; Ps 90:13; 106:46
[o] **135:15** 2Kg 19:18; Is 37:19
[p] **135:16** Hab 2:18
[q] **135:16-17** Is 46:7
[r] **135:15-18** Ps 115:4-11
[s] **135:19** Ps 115:9; 118:2
[t] Ps 115:10; 118:3
[u] **135:20** Ps 22:23; 115:11; 118:4
[v] **135:21** Ps 128:5
[w] Ps 132:13-14
[x] **136:1** Ps 106:1; 107:1; 118:1
[y] **136:2-3** Dt 10:17
[z] **136:4** Jb 9:10; Ps 72:18
[aa] **136:5** Pr 3:19; Jr 10:12; 51:15
[ab] **136:6** Ps 24:2
[ac] **136:7** Ps 74:16
[ad] **136:8-9** Gn 1:16
[ae] **136:10** Ex 12:29; Ps 78:51; 135:8
[af] **136:12** Ex 6:1; Dt 4:34
[ag] **136:13** Ex 14:21; Ps 66:6; 78:13
[ah] **136:14** Ex 14:21-22; Ps 106:9
[ai] **136:15** Ex 14:27; Ps 78:53; 106:11
[aj] **136:16** Dt 8:15; Ps 78:52

20 and Og king of Bashan —
His love is eternal.
21 and gave their land as an inheritance,
His love is eternal.
22 an inheritance to Israel His servant.[a]
His love is eternal.
23 He remembered us
in our humiliation[b]
His love is eternal.
24 and rescued us from our foes.[c]
His love is eternal.
25 He gives food to every creature.[d]
His love is eternal.
26 Give thanks to the God of heaven![e]
His love is eternal.

PSALM 137
Lament of the Exiles

1 By the rivers of Babylon —
there we sat down and wept
when we remembered ˙Zion.[f]
2 There we hung up our lyres
on the poplar trees,[g]
3 for our captors there asked us
for songs,
and our tormentors, for rejoicing:
"Sing us one of the songs of Zion."[h]

4 How can we sing the LORD's song
on foreign soil?[i]
5 If I forget you, Jerusalem,
may my right hand forget its skill.[j]
6 May my tongue stick to the roof
of my mouth
if I do not remember you,
if I do not exalt Jerusalem
as my greatest joy![k]

7 Remember, LORD,
what the Edomites said
that day[A] at Jerusalem:
"Destroy it! Destroy it
down to its foundations!"[l]
8 Daughter Babylon,
doomed to destruction,
happy is the one who pays you back
what you have done to us.[m]
9 Happy is he who takes
your little ones
and dashes them against the rocks.[n]

[a]**136:17-22** Nm 21:21-35; Ps 135:10-12
[b]**136:23** Ps 106:45
[c]**136:24** Ps 107:2
[d]**136:25** Ps 104:27; 145:15
[e]**136:26** Neh 1:5
[f]**137:1** Ezk 1:1,3
[g]**137:2** Jb 30:31; Ezk 26:13
[h]**137:3** Ps 80:6
[i]**137:4** Neh 12:46
[j]**137:5** Is 65:11
[k]**137:6** Jb 29:10; Ps 22:15; Ezk 3:26
[l]**137:7** Is 34:5-6; Ezk 35:2; Ob 10-14
[m]**137:8** Jr 50:1-46; 51:1-64
[n]**137:9** 2Kg 8:12; Is 13:16; Nah 3:10
[o]**138:1** Ps 111:1
[p]Ps 82:1,6-7; 95:3; 96:5
[q]**138:2** 1Kg 8:29; Ps 5:7; 28:2
[r]**138:3** Ps 28:7; 46:1
[s]**138:4** Ps 72:11; 102:15
[t]**138:5** Ps 21:5; 145:7
[u]**138:6** Ps 113:4-7; Pr 3:34; Jms 4:6
[v]**138:7** Ps 23:4
[w]Ps 20:6; 60:5
[x]**138:8** Ps 57:2; Php 1:6
[y]Jb 10:3; Ps 100:3
[z]**139:1** Ps 17:3; 44:21; Jr 12:3
[aa]**139:2** 2Kg 19:27; Is 66:18; Mt 9:4

PSALM 138
A Thankful Heart

Davidic.

1 I will give You thanks
with all my heart;[o]
I will sing Your praise
before the heavenly beings.[B,p]
2 I will bow down
toward Your holy temple
and give thanks to Your name
for Your constant love and truth.
You have exalted Your name
and Your promise above
everything else.[q]
3 On the day I called, You answered me;
You increased strength within me.[C,r]

4 All the kings on earth
will give You thanks, LORD,
when they hear
what You have promised.[D,s]
5 They will sing of the LORD's ways,
for the LORD's glory is great.[t]
6 Though the LORD is exalted,
He takes note of the humble;
but He knows the haughty
from a distance.[u]

7 If I walk into the thick of danger,
You will preserve my life
from the anger of my enemies.[v]
You will extend Your hand;
Your right hand will save me.[w]
8 The LORD will fulfill His purpose
for me.[x]
LORD, Your love is eternal;
do not abandon the work
of Your hands.[y]

PSALM 139
The All-Knowing, Ever-Present God

For the choir director. A Davidic psalm.

1 LORD, You have searched me
and known me.[z]
2 You know when I sit down and when
I stand up;
You understand my thoughts
from far away.[aa]
3 You observe my travels and my rest;

[A]**137:7** The day Jerusalem fell to the Babylonians in 586 B.C. [B]**138:1** Or *before the gods*, or *before judges*, or *before kings*; Hb *elohim* [C]**138:3** Hb obscure [D]**138:4** Lit *hear the words of Your mouth*

You are aware of all my ways.[a]
4 Before a word is on my tongue,
You know all about it, LORD.[b]
5 You have encircled me;
You have placed Your hand on me.[c]
6 This extraordinary knowledge is
beyond me.
It is lofty; I am unable to reach it.[d]

7 Where can I go to escape Your Spirit?
Where can I flee from Your presence?[e]
8 If I go up to heaven, You are there;[f]
if I make my bed in ·Sheol,
You are there.[g]
9 If I live at the eastern horizon
or settle at the western limits,[A]
10 even there Your hand will lead me;
Your right hand will hold on to me.[h]
11 If I say, "Surely the darkness will hide me,
and the light around me
will be night"[i] —
12 even the darkness is not dark to You.
The night shines like the day;
darkness and light are alike to You.[j]

13 For it was You who created
my inward parts;[B]
You knit me together
in my mother's womb.[k]
14 I will praise You
because I have been remarkably
and wonderfully made.[C,D]
Your works are wonderful,
and I know this very well.[l]
15 My bones were not hidden from You
when I was made in secret,
when I was formed in the depths
of the earth.[m]
16 Your eyes saw me when I was formless;
all my days were written in Your book
and planned
before a single one of them began.[n]

17 God, how difficult[E] Your thoughts are
for me to comprehend;
how vast their sum is!
18 If I counted them,
they would outnumber the grains
of sand;[o]
when I wake up,[F] I am still with You.[p]

[a]139:3 Jb 14:16; 31:4
[b]139:4 Heb 4:13
[c]139:5 Jb 9:33; Ps 125:2
[d]139:6 Jb 42:3; Rm 11:33
[e]139:7 Jr 23:24
[f]139:8 Am 9:2-4
[g]Jb 26:6; Is 14:11
[h]139:9-10 Ps 23:2-3
[i]139:11 Jb 22:13-14
[j]139:12 Jb 34:22; Dn 2:22
[k]139:13 Jb 10:11; Ps 119:73
[l]139:14 Ps 40:5
[m]139:15 Jb 10:8-10; Ps 63:9; Ec 11:5
[n]139:16 Jb 14:5
[o]139:17-18 Ps 40:5; 92:5
[p]139:18 Ps 3:5
[q]139:19 Ps 5:6; 6:8; Is 11:4
[r]139:20 Ex 20:7; Jd 15
[s]139:21-22 Ps 26:5; 31:16
[t]139:23 Jb 31:6; Ps 26:2
[u]139:24 Ps 16:11
[v]140:1 Ps 18:48; 71:4
[w]140:2 Ps 36:4; 56:6; Pr 6:14
[x]140:3 Ps 58:4; Rm 3:13; Jms 3:8
[y]140:4 Ps 71:4
[z]Ps 36:11
[aa]140:5 Ps 35:7; 141:9; 142:3
[ab]140:6 Ps 31:14; 130:2
[ac]140:7 Ps 28:8; 118:14
[ad]140:8 Ps 10:2-3
[ae]140:9 Ps 7:16; Pr 18:7

19 God, if only You would kill
the wicked —
you bloodthirsty men, stay away
from me[q] —
20 who invoke You deceitfully.
Your enemies swear by You falsely.[r]
21 LORD, don't I hate those who hate You,
and detest those who rebel against You?
22 I hate them with extreme hatred;
I consider them my enemies.[s]

23 Search me, God, and know my heart;
test me and know my concerns.[t]
24 See if there is any offensive[G] way in me;
lead me in the everlasting way.[u]

PSALM 140

Prayer for Rescue

For the choir director. A Davidic psalm.

1 Rescue me, LORD, from evil men.
Keep me safe from violent men[v]
2 who plan evil in their hearts.
They stir up wars all day long.[w]
3 They make their tongues
as sharp as a snake's bite;
viper's venom is under their lips.[x] *·Selah*

4 Protect me, LORD,
from the clutches of the wicked.[y]
Keep me safe from violent men
who plan to make me stumble.[H,z]
5 The proud hide a trap with ropes
for me;
they spread a net along the path
and set snares for me.[aa] *Selah*

6 I say to the LORD, "You are my God."
Listen, LORD, to my cry for help.[ab]
7 Lord GOD, my strong Savior,
You shield my head on the day
of battle.[ac]
8 LORD, do not grant the desires
of the wicked;
do not let them achieve their goals.
Otherwise, they will become proud.[ad]
Selah

9 When those who surround me rise up,[I]
may the trouble their lips cause
overwhelm them.[ae]

[A]139:9 Lit *I take up the wings of the dawn; I dwell at the end of the sea* [B]139:13 Lit *my kidneys* [C]139:14 DSS, some LXX mss, Syr, Jer read *because You are remarkable and wonderful* [D]139:14 Hb obscure [E]139:17 Or *precious* [F]139:18 Some Hb mss read *I come to an end* [G]139:24 Or *idolatrous* [H]140:4 Lit *to trip up my steps* [I]140:9 Lit *Head of those who surround me*

10 Let hot coals fall on them.
Let them be thrown into the fire,
into the abyss, never again to rise.[a]
11 Do not let a slanderer stay in the land.
Let evil relentlessly[A] hunt down
a violent man.[b]

12 I[B] know that the LORD upholds
the just cause of the poor,
justice for the needy.[c]
13 Surely the righteous will praise
Your name;
the upright will live in Your presence.[d]

PSALM 141
Protection from Sin and Sinners

A Davidic psalm.

1 LORD, I call on You; hurry to help me.
Listen to my voice when I call on You.[e]
2 May my prayer be set before You
as incense,[f]
the raising of my hands
as the evening offering.[g]

3 LORD, set up a guard for my mouth;
keep watch at the door of my lips.[h]
4 Do not let my heart turn
to any evil thing
or perform wicked acts
with men who commit sin.
Do not let me feast on their delicacies.[i]
5 Let the righteous one strike me—
it is an act of faithful love;
let him rebuke me—
it is oil for my head;
let me[C] not refuse it.[j]
Even now my prayer is against
the evil acts of the wicked.[D,k]
6 When their rulers[E] will be thrown off
the sides of a cliff,
the people[F] will listen to my words,
for they are pleasing.[l]

7 As when one plows and breaks up
the soil,
turning up rocks,
so our[G] bones have been scattered
at the mouth of *Sheol.[m]

8 But my eyes look to You, Lord GOD.
I seek refuge in You; do not let me die.[H,n]

[a]140:10 Ps 11:6; 36:12 [b]140:11 Ps 34:21 [c]140:12 1Kg 8:45,49; Ps 9:4; 82:3 [d]140:13 Ps 11:7; 64:10 [e]141:1 Ps 22:19; 38:22; 70:5 [f]141:2 Ex 30:8 [g]Lk 1:10; Rv 5:8; 8:3-4 [h]141:3 Ps 34:13; 39:1; Pr 13:3; Mc 7:5 [i]141:4 Ps 119:36; Pr 23:6; Is 32:6 [j]141:5 Ec 7:5; Gl 6:1 [k]Ps 109:4 [l]141:6 2Ch 25:12 [m]141:7 Ps 53:5; 88:3-5 [n]141:8 Ps 7:1; 57:1; 144:2 [o]141:9 Ps 38:12; 140:5 [p]141:10 Ps 7:15; 35:8; 57:6 [q]142:title 1Sm 22:1; 24:3 [r]142:1 Ps 3:4; 77:1 [s]Ps 30:8 [t]142:2 Ps 77:2; 102 title [u]142:3 Ps 77:3; 143:4 [v]Ps 140:5 [w]142:4 Ps 69:20; Jr 25:35 [x]142:5 Ps 16:5; 27:13 [y]142:6 Ps 79:8; 116:6 [z]Ps 18:17 [aa]142:7 Ps 13:6; 143:11 [ab]143:1 Ps 71:2; 140:6 [ac]143:2 Jb 14:3 [ad]Jb 15:14; Ps 130:3; Rm 3:23

9 Protect me from[I] the trap they have set
for me,
and from the snares of evildoers.[o]
10 Let the wicked fall into their own nets,
while I pass by safely.[p]

PSALM 142
A Cry of Distress

A Davidic *Maskil. When he was
in the cave.[q] A prayer.

1 I cry aloud to the LORD;[r]
I plead aloud to the LORD for mercy.[s]
2 I pour out my complaint before Him;
I reveal my trouble to Him.[t]
3 Although my spirit is weak within me,
You know my way.[u]

Along this path I travel
they have hidden a trap for me.[v]
4 Look to the right and see:[J]
no one stands up for me;
there is no refuge for me;
no one cares about me.[w]

5 I cry to You, LORD;
I say, "You are my shelter,
my portion in the land of the living."[x]
6 Listen to my cry,
for I am very weak.[y]
Rescue me from those who pursue me,
for they are too strong for me.[z]
7 Free me from prison
so that I can praise Your name.
The righteous will gather around me
because You deal generously with me.[aa]

PSALM 143
A Cry for Help

A Davidic psalm.

1 LORD, hear my prayer.
In Your faithfulness listen to my plea,
and in Your righteousness answer me.[ab]
2 Do not bring Your servant
into judgment,[ac]
for no one alive is righteous
in Your sight.[ad]

3 For the enemy has pursued me,
crushing me to the ground,
making me live in darkness

[A]140:11 Hb obscure [B]140:12 Alt Hb tradition reads *You* [C]141:5 Lit *my head* [D]141:5 Lit *of them* [E]141:6 Or *judges* [F]141:6 Lit *cliff, and they* [G]141:7 DSS reads *my*; some LXX mss, Syr read *their* [H]141:8 Or *not pour out my life* [I]141:9 Lit *from the hands of* [J]142:4 DSS, LXX, Syr, Vg, Tg read *I look to the right and I see*

like those long dead.[a]
4 My spirit is weak within me;
my heart is overcome
with dismay.[b]

5 I remember the days of old;
I meditate on all You have done;
I reflect on the work of Your hands.[c]
6 I spread out my hands to You;
I am like parched land before You.[d]
·Selah

7 Answer me quickly, LORD;
my spirit fails.[e]
Don't hide Your face from me,
or I will be like those
going down to the ·Pit.[f]
8 Let me experience
Your faithful love in the morning,
for I trust in You.[g]
Reveal to me the way I should go
because I long for You.[h]
9 Rescue me from my enemies, LORD;
I come to You for protection.[A,i]
10 Teach me to do Your will,
for You are my God.[j]
May Your gracious Spirit
lead me on level ground.[k]

11 Because of Your name, ·Yahweh,
let me live.
In Your righteousness deliver me
from trouble,[l]
12 and in Your faithful love
destroy my enemies.
Wipe out all those who attack me,
for I am Your servant.[m]

PSALM 144
A King's Prayer

Davidic.

1 May the LORD, my rock, be praised,[n]
who trains my hands for battle
and my fingers for warfare.[o]
2 He is my faithful love
and my fortress,
my stronghold and my deliverer.
He is my shield,[p] and I take refuge
in Him;[q]
He subdues my people[B] under me.[r]

3 LORD, what is man,
that You care for him,
the son of man, that
You think of him?[s]
4 Man is like a breath;
his days are like a passing shadow.[t]

5 LORD, part Your heavens
and come down.[u]
Touch the mountains,
and they will smoke.[v]
6 Flash Your lightning and scatter
the foe;[C]
shoot Your arrows and rout them.[w]
7 Reach down[D] from heaven;[x]
rescue me from deep water,
and set me free
from the grasp of foreigners[y]
8 whose mouths speak lies,
whose right hands are deceptive.[z]

9 God, I will sing a new song to You;
I will play on a ten-stringed harp
for You[aa]—
10 the One who gives victory to kings,
who frees His servant David
from the deadly sword.[ab]
11 Set me free and rescue me
from the grasp of foreigners[ac]
whose mouths speak lies,
whose right hands are deceptive.[ad]

12 Then our sons will be like plants
nurtured in their youth,
our daughters, like corner pillars
that are carved in the palace style.[ae]
13 Our storehouses will be full,
supplying all kinds of produce;[af]
our flocks will increase by thousands
and tens of thousands in
our open fields.[ag]
14 Our cattle will be well fed.[E]
There will be no breach
in the walls,
no going into captivity,[F]
and no cry of lament in
our public squares.[ah]
15 Happy are the people with
such blessings.
Happy are the people
whose God is ·Yahweh.[ai]

[a] **143:3** Ps 88:3-6; Lm 3:6
[b] **143:4** Ps 77:3; 142:3
[c] **143:5** Ps 77:5,10-12
[d] **143:6** Jb 11:13; Ps 42:2; 63:1
[e] **143:7** Ps 69:17; 102:2
[f] Ps 28:1; 88:4
[g] **143:8** Ps 90:14
[h] Ps 25:1,4
[i] **143:9** Ps 31:15; 59:1; 142:6
[j] **143:10** Ps 25:4-5; 31:14; 63:1; 86:2; 119:12
[k] Ps 23:3
[l] **143:11** Ps 25:11; 71:20
[m] **143:12** Ps 54:5; 116:16
[n] **144:1** 1Sm 2:2; Ps 18:2; 19:14; 92:15; 95:1; Is 26:4
[o] Ps 18:34
[p] **144:2** Dt 33:29; Ps 3:3; 28:7; 115:9-11; Pr 2:7
[q] 2Sm 22:3; Ps 18:2; 71:1-3; 91:4; 144:2; Pr 30:5
[r] Ps 18:39,47
[s] **144:3** Jb 7:17; Ps 8:4; Heb 2:6
[t] **144:4** Ps 102:11; 109:23
[u] **144:5** 2Sm 22:10; Ps 18:9-10
[v] Ps 104:32
[w] **144:6** Ps 18:14; Hab 3:11; Zch 9:14
[x] **144:7** Ps 18:16
[y] Ps 69:14
[z] **144:8** Ps 12:2; 41:6; 106:26
[aa] **144:9** Ps 33:2-3; 40:3
[ab] **144:10** Ps 18:50
[ac] **144:11** Ps 69:14
[ad] Ps 12:2; 41:6; 106:26
[ae] **144:12** Ps 92:12-14; 128:3
[af] **144:13** Ps 107:37-38
[ag] Pr 3:9-10
[ah] **144:14** Is 24:11; Jr 14:2
[ai] **144:15** Ps 33:12

[A] **143:9** One Hb ms, LXX; some Hb mss read *I cover myself to You* [B] **144:2** Some Hb mss, DSS, Aq, Syr, Tg, Jer read *subdues peoples*; 2Sm 22:48; Ps 18:47 [C] **144:6** Lit *scatter them* [D] **144:7** Lit *down Your hands* [E] **144:14** Or *will bear heavy loads*, or *will be pregnant* [F] **144:14** Or *be no plague, no miscarriage*

Psalm 145

Praising God's Greatness

A Davidic hymn.

1 I[A] exalt You, my God the King,
and praise Your name forever and ever.[a]
2 I will praise You every day;
I will honor Your name
forever and ever.[b]

3 ˚Yahweh is great and is highly praised;[c]
His greatness is unsearchable.[d]
4 One generation will declare Your works
to the next
and will proclaim Your mighty acts.[e]
5 I[B] will speak of Your splendor and
glorious majesty
and[C] Your wonderful works.[f]
6 They will proclaim the power
of Your awe-inspiring acts,
and I will declare Your greatness.[D,g]
7 They will give a testimony
of Your great goodness
and will joyfully sing
of Your righteousness.[h]

8 The LORD is gracious
and compassionate,
slow to anger and great in faithful love.[i]
9 The LORD is good to everyone;[j]
His compassion rests
on all He has made.[k]
10 All You have made
will thank You, LORD;
the[E] godly will praise You.[l]
11 They will speak of the glory
of Your kingdom
and will declare Your might,[m]
12 informing all ˚people
of Your mighty acts
and of the glorious splendor
of Your[F] kingdom.[n]
13 Your kingdom is
an everlasting kingdom;
Your rule is for all generations.[o]
The LORD is faithful in all His words
and gracious in all His actions.[G,p]

14 The LORD helps all who fall;
He raises up all who are oppressed.[H,q]
15 All eyes look to You,
and You give them their food at the
proper time.[r]
16 You open Your hand
and satisfy the desire
of every living thing.[s]

17 The LORD is righteous in all His ways
and gracious in all His acts.[t]
18 The LORD is near all who call out
to Him,
all who call out to Him with integrity.[u]
19 He fulfills the desires of those
who ˚fear Him;
He hears their cry for help
and saves them.[v]
20 The LORD guards all those
who love Him,
but He destroys all the wicked.[w]
21 My mouth will declare Yahweh's praise;
let every living thing
praise His holy name forever and ever.[x]

Psalm 146

The God of Compassion

1 ˚Hallelujah!
My soul, praise the LORD.[y]
2 I will praise the LORD all my life;
I will sing to my God as long as I live.[z]
3 Do not trust in nobles,
in man, who cannot save.[aa]
4 When his breath[I] leaves him,
he returns to the ground;
on that day his plans die.[ab]

5 Happy is the one whose help is the God
of Jacob,
whose hope is in the LORD his God,[ac]
6 the Maker of heaven and earth,
the sea and everything in them.[ad]
He remains faithful forever,[ae]
7 executing justice for the exploited
and giving food to the hungry.[af]
The LORD frees prisoners.[ag]
8 The LORD opens the eyes of the blind.[ah]
The LORD raises up those
who are oppressed.[H,ai]
The LORD loves the righteous.[aj]
9 The LORD protects foreigners

[a]**145:1** Ps 30:1; 34:1; 99:5,9 [b]**145:2** Ps 146:2 [c]**145:3** Ps 48:1; 147:5 [d]Jb 5:9; 9:10; Is 40:28 [e]**145:4** Ps 22:30-31 [f]**145:5** Ps 119:27 [g]**145:6** Dt 10:21; Ps 106:2 [h]**145:7** Is 63:7 [i]**145:8** Ex 34:6; Ps 86:5,15; 103:8 [j]**145:9** Ac 14:17 [k]Ps 100:5 [l]**145:10** Ps 19:1; 103:22 [m]**145:11** Jr 14:21 [n]**145:12** Ps 105:1; 145:5 [o]**145:13** Ps 10:16; 2Pt 1:11 [p]Ps 103:8 [q]**145:14** Ps 37:24; 146:8 [r]**145:15** Ps 104:27; 136:25 [s]**145:16** Ps 104:28 [t]**145:17** Ps 116:5 [u]**145:18** Dt 4:7; Ps 34:18; Jn 4:23-24 [v]**145:19** Ps 10:17; 21:2; 37:4 [w]**145:20** Ps 31:23; 97:10 [x]**145:21** Ps 65:2; 150:6 [y]**146:1** Ps 103:1 [z]**146:2** Ps 63:4; 104:33 [aa]**146:3** Ps 60:11; 108:12; 118:8-9 [ab]**146:4** Gn 2:7; 3:19 [ac]**146:5** Ps 144:15; Jr 17:7 [ad]**146:6** Ps 115:15; Ac 14:15 [ae]Ps 117:2 [af]**146:7** Ps 103:6; 107:9 [ag]Is 61:1 [ah]**146:8** Mt 9:27-30; Jn 9:7 [ai]Ps 145:15 [aj]Ps 11:7

[A]**145:1** The lines of this poem form an ˚acrostic. [B]**145:5** LXX, Syr read *They* [C]**145:5** LXX, Syr read *and they will tell of* [D]**145:6** Alt Hb tradition, Jer read *great deeds* [E]**145:10** Lit *Your* [F]**145:12** LXX, Syr, Jer; MT reads *His* [G]**145:13** One Hb ms, DSS, LXX, Syr; some Hb mss omit *The LORD is faithful in all His words and gracious in all His actions.* [H]**145:14; 146:8** Lit *bowed down* [I]**146:4** Or *spirit*

and helps the fatherless
and the widow,[a]
but He frustrates the ways
of the wicked.[b]

10 The LORD reigns forever;
·Zion, your God reigns
for all generations.[c]
Hallelujah!

PSALM 147

God Restores Jerusalem

1 ·Hallelujah!
How good it is to sing to our God,
for praise is pleasant and lovely.[d]
2 The LORD rebuilds Jerusalem;[e]
He gathers Israel's exiled people.[f]
3 He heals the brokenhearted
and binds up their wounds.[g]
4 He counts the number of the stars;
He gives names to all of them.[h]
5 Our Lord is great, vast in power;
His understanding is infinite.[A,i]
6 The LORD helps the afflicted
but brings the wicked to the ground.[j]

7 Sing to the LORD with thanksgiving;
play the lyre to our God,[k]
8 who covers the sky with clouds,
prepares rain for the earth,
and causes grass to grow on the hills.[l]
9 He provides the animals
with their food,
and the young ravens,
what they cry for.[m]

10 He is not impressed by the strength
of a horse;
He does not value the power[B] of a man.[n]
11 The LORD values those who fear Him,
those who put their hope
in His faithful love.[o]
12 Exalt the LORD, Jerusalem;
praise your God, ·Zion![p]
13 For He strengthens the bars
of your gates
and blesses your children within you.[q]
14 He endows your territory
with prosperity;[C,r]
He satisfies you with the finest wheat.[s]

[a]146:9 Ex 22:22-23; Dt 10:18 [b]Ps 147:6 [c]146:10 Ex 15:18; Ps 10:16 [d]147:1 Ps 33:1; 135:3 [e]147:2 Ps 51:18; 102:16 [f]Dt 30:3; Ezk 39:28 [g]147:3 Ps 34:18; Is 61:1 [h]147:4 Gn 15:5; Is 40:26 [i]147:5 Ps 48:1; Is 40:28 [j]147:6 Ps 146:8-9 [k]147:7 Ps 33:2; 95:1-2 [l]147:8 Jb 5:10; 38:27; Ps 104:14 [m]147:9 Jb 38:41; Ps 104:27-28 [n]147:10 Ps 33:17 [o]147:11 Ps 33:18; 149:4 [p]147:12 Ps 99:5,9 [q]147:13 Neh 7:3 [r]147:14 Is 54:13 [s]Dt 32:14; Ps 81:16 [t]147:15 Ps 104:4 [u]147:16 Jb 37:6; 38:29 [v]147:17 Jb 37:9-10 [w]147:18 Ps 33:9; 107:20 [x]147:19 Dt 33:2-4; Mal 4:4 [y]147:20 Dt 4:7,32-34 [z]148:1 Ps 69:34; Mt 21:9 [aa]148:2 Ps 103:20-21 [ab]148:3 1Co 15:41 [ac]148:4 Gn 1:7; Dt 10:14; 1Kg 8:27 [ad]148:5 Ps 33:6,9 [ae]148:6 Jr 31:35-36; 33:20,25 [af]148:7 Gn 1:2,21; Ps 74:13 [ag]148:8 Ps 18:12; 103:20; 147:16 [ah]148:9 Is 44:23; 49:13; 55:12 [ai]148:10 Is 43:20; Hs 2:18 [aj]148:11 Ps 102:15 [ak]148:11-12 Rv 7:9

15 He sends His command
throughout the earth;
His word runs swiftly.[t]
16 He spreads snow like wool;
He scatters frost like ashes;[u]
17 He throws His hailstones like crumbs.
Who can withstand His cold?[v]
18 He sends His word and melts them;
He unleashes His winds,[D]
and the waters flow.[w]

19 He declares His word to Jacob,
His statutes and judgments to Israel.[x]
20 He has not done this for any nation;
they do not know[E] His judgments.[y]
Hallelujah!

PSALM 148

Creation's Praise of the LORD

1 ·Hallelujah!
Praise the LORD from the heavens;
praise Him in the heights.[z]
2 Praise Him, all His angels;
praise Him, all His ·hosts.[aa]
3 Praise Him, sun and moon;
praise Him, all you shining stars.[ab]
4 Praise Him, highest heavens,
and you waters above the heavens.[ac]
5 Let them praise the name of ·Yahweh,
for He commanded,
and they were created.[ad]
6 He set them in position
forever and ever;
He gave an order that will never
pass away.[ae]

7 Praise the LORD from the earth,
all sea monsters and ocean depths,[af]
8 lightning[F] and hail, snow and cloud,
powerful wind that executes
His command,[ag]
9 mountains and all hills,
fruit trees and all cedars,[ah]
10 wild animals and all cattle,
creatures that crawl and flying birds,[ai]
11 kings of the earth and all peoples,
princes and all judges of the earth,[aj]
12 young men as well as young women,
old and young together.[ak]
13 Let them praise the name of Yahweh,

[A]147:5 Lit *understanding has no number* [B]147:10 Lit *legs* [C]147:14 Or *peace* [D]147:18 Or *breath* [E]147:20 DSS, LXX, Syr, Tg read *He has not made known to them* [F]148:8 Or *fire*

for His name alone is exalted.
His majesty covers heaven and earth.[a]
14 He has raised up a ·horn for His people,
resulting in praise to all His godly ones,
to the Israelites, the people
close to Him.[b]
Hallelujah!

Psalm 149

Praise for God's Triumph

1 ·Hallelujah!
Sing to the Lord a new song,[c]
His praise in the assembly of the godly.[d]
2 Let Israel celebrate its Maker;
let the children of ·Zion rejoice
in their King.[e]
3 Let them praise His name with dancing
and make music to Him
with tambourine and lyre.[f]
4 For ·Yahweh takes pleasure
in His people;[g]
He adorns the humble with salvation.[h]
5 Let the godly celebrate
in triumphal glory;
let them shout for joy on their beds.[i]

6 Let the exaltation of God be
in their mouths[A]
and a double-edged sword
in their hands,[j]
7 inflicting vengeance on the nations
and punishment on the peoples,[k]
8 binding their kings with chains
and their dignitaries
with iron shackles,[l]
9 carrying out the judgment
decreed against them.
This honor is for all His godly people.[m]
Hallelujah!

Psalm 150

Praise the Lord

1 ·Hallelujah!
Praise God in His sanctuary.
Praise Him in His mighty heavens.[n]
2 Praise Him for His powerful acts;[o]
praise Him
for His abundant greatness.[p]

3 Praise Him with trumpet blast;[q]
praise Him with harp and lyre.[r]
4 Praise Him with tambourine
and dance;[s]
praise Him with flute and strings.[t]
5 Praise Him with resounding cymbals;
praise Him with clashing cymbals.[u]

6 Let everything that breathes
praise the Lord.[v]
Hallelujah!

[a] **148:13** Ps 8:1; 113:4; Is 12:4
[b] **148:14** Dt 10:21; Jr 17:14; Eph 2:17
[c] **149:1** Ps 33:3
[d] Ps 35:18; 89:5
[e] **149:2** Ps 95:6; Zch 9:9
[f] **149:3** Ps 30:11; 81:2
[g] **149:4** Ps 147:11; Rm 8:8; 1Co 1:21
[h] Ps 35:27; Is 61:3
[i] **149:5** Jb 35:10; Ps 132:16
[j] **149:6** Ps 66:17; Heb 4:12
[k] **149:7** Ezk 25:16-17; Mc 5:15
[l] **149:8** Jb 36:8
[m] **149:9** Ps 148:14; Ezk 28:26
[n] **150:1** Ps 11:4; 19:1
[o] **150:2** Ps 145:12
[p] Dt 3:24
[q] **150:3** Ps 98:6
[r] Ps 33:2
[s] **150:4** Ps 149:3
[t] Jb 21:12; Ps 45:8
[u] **150:5** 2Sm 6:5; 1Ch 13:8
[v] **150:6** Ps 145:21

[A] **149:6** Lit *throat*

■ **AUTHOR:** Solomon mainly, along with Agur and Lemuel

■■ **DATE:** During the time of Solomon's reign (around 970–931 B.C.)

The aphorisms of the book Proverbs aim to make us wise. This education in wisdom is an important element in the mission of God. In our service to God, we're never to stagnate, but always to mature in wisdom and understanding.

It is fitting that Solomon, the king who asked for wisdom, is closely associated with this book. The sayings of others—Agur and King Lemuel—however, are included. Many of the proverbs include two-word combinations like "wisdom and understanding" to make their point. A couplet may frame a contrast or suggest a comparison. "Good news from a distant land is like cold water to a parched throat" (Pr 25:25).

PROVERBS

Why seek wisdom and understanding? Why all the fuss over living well? It is because decisions have consequences. The Proverbs equip people to grow closer to God through discernment, discipleship, and devotion. Practical choices must be made—good choices leading to the greatest good. Becoming weary from time to time suggests that effort and labor are part of this growth. When our decisions take account of God's laws and purposes, then we are living according to the principles of God's mission. When we do not, we fight God's intentions.

Does God's mission depend on wise decisions by leaders, parents, teachers, or young people? We might wonder if God's mission is so fragile that its success hinges on human wisdom. The answer, throughout the Bible, is both yes and no. Decisions matter. The fruit of this can be seen throughout Israel's history. The book of Numbers shows that for a full generation Israel wandered in the wilderness thanks to a poor decision. The book of Judges records a series of poor decisions followed by repentance and recovery. But the strength and grit of God's mission towers above human decisions. God Himself has decided what the point and purpose of creation will be. God's glory will be manifest. God's family (His Kingdom) will be established. Decisions we make today may advance or hinder God's mission, but nothing we do will stop it. Our calling is to know God as the source of all wisdom, to learn through experience to trust God, and to offer our lives in obedient, joyous service to God.

Training is necessary in just about all professions. No doctor enters surgery without training. We cannot live well, we cannot flourish as human beings bearing God's image, apart from an education in wisdom. Huge gaps in our moral senses must be filled. We must learn who we are and how to master setbacks and disabilities. This education in wisdom is, by any assessment, a large part of God's curriculum for the world, our "lifetime learning" in the master teacher's classroom.

The Purpose of Proverbs

1 The proverbs of Solomon[a] son of David,
king of Israel:
2 For learning what wisdom
and discipline are;
for understanding insightful sayings;
3 for receiving wise instruction
in righteousness, justice, and integrity;[b]
4 for teaching shrewdness
to the inexperienced,[A,c]
knowledge and discretion[d]
to a young man—
5 a wise man will listen and increase
his learning,[e]
and a discerning man
will obtain guidance—
6 for understanding a proverb
or a parable,[B]
the words of the wise,
and their riddles.[f]

7 The ·fear of the LORD
is the beginning of knowledge;[g]
fools despise wisdom and discipline.[h]

Avoid the Path of the Violent

8 Listen, my son,
to your father's instruction,
and don't reject
your mother's teaching,[i]
9 for they will be a garland[j] of grace
on your head
and a gold chain around your neck.[k]
10 My son, if sinners entice you,[l]
don't be persuaded.[m]
11 If they say—"Come with us!
Let's set an ambush[n] and kill someone.[C]
Let's attack some innocent person[o]
just for fun![D]
12 Let's swallow them alive,[p] like ·Sheol,
still healthy as they go down to the ·Pit.[q]
13 We'll find all kinds of valuable property
and fill our houses with plunder.[r]
14 Throw in your lot with us,
and we'll all share our money"[E]—
15 my son, don't travel that road
with them[s]
or set foot on their path,[t]
16 because their feet run toward trouble
and they hurry to commit murder.[F,u]

[a]**1:1** 1Kg 4:32; Pr 10:1; 25:1; Ec 12:9
[b]**1:3** Pr 2:9
[c]**1:4** Pr 8:5
[d]Pr 2:11; 3:21
[e]**1:5** Pr 9:9; 16:21,23
[f]**1:6** Nm 12:8; Jdg 14:12; Ps 49:4; Hab 2:6
[g]**1:7** Jb 28:28; Ps 111:10; Pr 9:10; 15:33
[h]Eph 5:17
[i]**1:8** Pr 6:20; 31:1
[j]**1:9** Pr 4:9
[k]Gn 41:42; Pr 6:21; Dn 5:29
[l]**1:10** Pr 16:29
[m]Ps 141:4
[n]**1:11** Pr 12:6; Jr 5:26
[o]Ps 10:8
[p]**1:12** Ps 124:3
[q]Ps 28:1
[r]**1:13** Pr 24:4
[s]**1:15** Ps 1:1; Pr 4:14
[t]Ps 119:101; Pr 16:19
[u]**1:16** Pr 6:17-18; Is 59:7; Rm 3:15
[v]**1:19** Pr 15:27; Ezk 22:27; Hab 2:6-12
[w]**1:20** Pr 8:1-3; 9:3
[x]**1:22** Ps 1:1
[y]Jb 21:14; Pr 1:29; 5:12
[z]**1:23** Pr 3:11; 15:5,31-32
[aa]Jl 2:28
[ab]**1:24** Is 65:12; 66:4; Jr 7:13; Zch 7:11
[ac]Is 65:2; Rm 10:21
[ad]**1:25** Ps 107:11; Lk 7:30
[ae]**1:26** Ps 2:4
[af]**1:28** 1Sm 8:18
[ag]**1:29** Pr 1:7
[ah]**1:30** Pr 5:12; 15:5
[ai]**1:31** Jr 6:19
[aj]Pr 14:14; 28:19
[ak]**1:32** Jr 2:19

17 It is foolish to spread a net
where any bird can see it,
18 but they set an ambush
to kill themselves;[G]
they attack their own lives.
19 Such are the paths of all who make
profit dishonestly;[v]
it takes the lives of those
who receive it.[H]

Wisdom's Plea

20 Wisdom calls out in the street;
she raises her voice
in the public squares.[w]
21 She cries out above[I] the commotion;
she speaks at the entrance
of the city ·gates:
22 "How long, foolish ones, will you
love ignorance?
How long will you mockers[x]
enjoy mocking
and you fools hate knowledge?[y]
23 If you respond to my warning,[J,z]
then I will pour out my spirit on you[aa]
and teach you my words.
24 Since I called out and you refused,[ab]
extended my hand and no one
paid attention,[ac]
25 since you neglected all my counsel[ad]
and did not accept my correction,
26 I, in turn, will laugh at your calamity.[ae]
I will mock when terror strikes you,
27 when terror strikes you like a storm
and your calamity comes
like a whirlwind,
when trouble and stress overcome you.
28 Then they will call me,
but I won't answer;
they will search for me, but won't
find me.[af]
29 Because they hated knowledge,
didn't choose to fear the LORD,[ag]
30 were not interested in my counsel,
and rejected all my correction,[ah]
31 they will eat the fruit of their way[ai]
and be glutted with their own schemes.[aj]
32 For the turning away
of the inexperienced will kill them,[ak]

[A]**1:4** Or *simple*, or *gullible* [B]**1:6** Or *an enigma* [C]**1:11** Lit *Let's ambush for blood* [D]**1:11** Lit *person for no reason* [E]**1:14** Lit *us; one bag will be for all of us* [F]**1:16** Lit *to shed blood* [G]**1:18** Lit *they ambush for their blood* [H]**1:19** Lit *takes the life of its masters* [I]**1:21** Lit *at the head of* [J]**1:23** Lit *back to my reprimand*

and the complacency of fools
will destroy them.
33 But whoever listens to me
will live securely
and be free from the fear of danger."[a]

Wisdom's Worth

2 My son, if you accept my words[b]
and store up my commands within you,
2 listening closely[A] to wisdom
and directing your heart
to understanding;
3 furthermore, if you call out to insight
and lift your voice to understanding,
4 if you seek it like silver
and search for it like hidden treasure,[c]
5 then you will understand the •fear
of the LORD
and discover the knowledge of God.
6 For the LORD gives wisdom;
from His mouth come knowledge
and understanding.[d]
7 He stores up success[B] for the upright;
He is a shield for those who live
with integrity[e]
8 so that He may guard the paths
of justice
and protect the way
of His loyal followers.[f]
9 Then you will understand
righteousness, justice,
and integrity—every good path.
10 For wisdom will enter your mind,
and knowledge will delight your heart.
11 Discretion will watch over you,
and understanding will guard you,[g]
12 rescuing you from the way of evil—
from the one who says perverse things,
13 from those who abandon
the right paths
to walk in ways of darkness,[h]
14 from those who enjoy doing evil[i]
and celebrate perversion,
15 whose paths are crooked,[j]
and whose ways are devious.[k]
16 It will rescue you
from a forbidden woman,[l]
from a stranger[C]
with her flattering talk,[m]

[a]1:33 Ps 112:7-8; Pr 3:24-26 [b]2:1 Pr 4:10 [c]2:4 Jb 3:21; Mt 13:44 [d]2:6 Jb 32:8 [e]2:7 Ps 84:11; Pr 10:9; 20:7; 28:18; 30:5 [f]2:8 1Sm 2:9; Ps 66:9 [g]2:11 Pr 4:6; 6:22 [h]2:11-13 Ps 82:5; Pr 15:19; 16:17; Jn 3:19,20 [i]2:14 Pr 10:23 [j]2:15 Ps 125:5; Pr 21:8 [k]Pr 3:32; 14:2 [l]2:16 Pr 9:13-18 [m]Pr 5:3,20; 6:24; 7:5,21; 23:27 [n]2:17 Mal 2:14-15 [o]2:18 Pr 7:27; 9:18; 21:16 [p]2:16-19 Ps 16:11; Pr 5:6; 7:5,21-27; 23:27-28; Ec 7:26 [q]2:20 Heb 6:12 [r]2:21 Pr 10:30; Mt 5:5-6 [s]2:22 Ps 37:38 [t]Dt 28:63; Ps 52:5 [u]3:1 Dt 30:16 [v]3:2 Ps 91:16; Pr 3:16; 4:10; 9:11; 10:27 [w]3:1-2 Pr 4:1-4; 6:20-23; 7:1-3 [x]3:3 Pr 1:9; 6:21; 7:3; 2Co 3:3 [y]3:4 Dt 4:6; 1Sm 2:26; Lk 2:52; Rm 14:18 [z]3:5 Ps 37:3,5 [aa]Jr 9:23 [ab]3:6 Pr 11:5 [ac]3:7 Pr 26:5,12; 28:11,26; Rm 12:16 [ad]Jb 1:1; 28:28; Ps 37:27; Pr 16:6 [ae]3:8 Pr 4:22 [af]Jb 21:24 [ag]3:9 Ex 23:19; Lv 23:9-14; Dt 26:2 [ah]3:10 Dt 28:8; Mal 3:10 [ai]3:11 Pr 5:11-13; 15:5,31-33

17 who abandons the companion
of her youth[n]
and forgets the covenant of her God;
18 for her house sinks down to death
and her ways to the land
of the departed spirits.[o]
19 None return who go to her;
none reach the paths of life.[p]
20 So follow the way of good people,[q]
and keep to the paths of the righteous.
21 For the upright will inhabit the land,
and those of integrity will remain in it;[r]
22 but the wicked will be cut off
from the land,[s]
and the treacherous uprooted from it.[t]

Trust the LORD

3 My son, don't forget my teaching,
but let your heart keep my commands;[u]
2 for they will bring you
many days, a full life,[D,v] and well-being.[w]
3 Never let loyalty and faithfulness
leave you.
Tie them around your neck;
write them on the tablet of your heart.[x]
4 Then you will find favor
and high regard
in the sight of God and man.[y]
5 Trust in the LORD with all your heart,[z]
and do not rely on
your own understanding;[aa]
6 think about Him in all your ways,
and He will guide you
on the right paths.[E,ab]
7 Don't consider yourself to be wise;[ac]
•fear the LORD and turn away
from evil.[ad]
8 This will be healing for your body[F,ae]
and strengthening for your bones.[af]
9 Honor the LORD with your possessions
and with the first produce
of your entire harvest;[ag]
10 then your barns will be
completely filled,
and your vats will overflow
with new wine.[ah]
11 Do not despise the LORD's instruction,
my son,
and do not loathe His discipline;[ai]

[A]2:2 Lit *you, stretching out your ear* [B]2:7 Or *resourcefulness* [C]2:16 Or *foreign woman* [D]3:2 Lit *days, years of life* [E]3:6 Lit *will make your paths straight* [F]3:8 Lit *navel*

12 for the LORD disciplines the one
He loves,
just as a father, the son he delights in.[a]

Wisdom Brings Happiness

13 Happy is a man who finds wisdom[b]
and who acquires understanding,
14 for she is more profitable than silver,
and her revenue is better than gold.[c]
15 She is more precious than jewels;[d]
nothing you desire compares
with her.[e]
16 Long life[A] is in her right hand;
in her left, riches and honor.[f]
17 Her ways are pleasant,[g]
and all her paths, peaceful.
18 She is a tree of life[h] to those
who embrace her,
and those who hold on to her
are happy.
19 The LORD founded the earth
by wisdom[i]
and established the heavens
by understanding.
20 By His knowledge the watery depths
broke open,[j]
and the clouds dripped with dew.[k]
21 Maintain your competence
and discretion.
My son, don't lose sight of them.[l]
22 They will be life for you[B,C,m]
and adornment[D] for your neck.
23 Then you will go safely on your way;
your foot will not stumble.[n]
24 When you lie[E] down, you will not
be afraid;[o]
you will lie down, and your sleep
will be pleasant.
25 Don't fear sudden danger
or the ruin of the wicked
when it comes,[p]
26 for the LORD will be your confidence[F]
and will keep your foot from a snare.[q]

Treat Others Fairly

27 When it is in your power,[G]
don't withhold good[r] from the one
it belongs to.
28 Don't say to your neighbor, "Go away!
Come back later.
I'll give it tomorrow"—when it is there
with you.[s]
29 Don't plan any harm
against your neighbor,[t]
for he trusts you and lives near you.
30 Don't accuse anyone without cause,[u]
when he has done you no harm.
31 Don't envy a violent man[v]
or choose any of his ways;
32 for the devious are detestable
to the LORD,
but He is a friend[H] to the upright.[w]
33 The LORD's curse is on the household
of the wicked,[x]
but He blesses the home
of the righteous;
34 He mocks those who mock,
but gives grace to the humble.[y]
35 The wise will inherit honor,
but He holds up fools to dishonor.[I]

A Father's Example

4 Listen, my sons, to a father's discipline,[z]
and pay attention so that
you may gain understanding,
2 for I am giving you good instruction.[aa]
Don't abandon my teaching.
3 When I was a son with my father,
tender and precious to my mother,
4 he taught me and said:
"Your heart must hold on to my words.
Keep my commands and live.[ab]
5 Get wisdom, get understanding;[ac]
don't forget or turn away
from the words of my mouth.
6 Don't abandon wisdom, and she will
watch over you;
love her,[ad] and she will guard you.
7 Wisdom is supreme—so get wisdom.
And whatever else you get,
get understanding.[ae]
8 Cherish her, and she will exalt you;
if you embrace her, she will
honor you.[af]
9 She will place a garland of grace
on your head;
she will give you a crown of beauty."[ag]

[a]**3:12** Dt 8:5; Jb 5:17-18; Pr 13:24; Heb 12:5-7 [b]**3:13** Pr 8:32,34 [c]**3:14** Jb 28:15-19; Pr 8:10,19; 16:16; 22:1 [d]**3:15** Jb 28:18 [e]Pr 8:11; 20:15 [f]**3:16** Pr 8:18; 21:21; 22:4 [g]**3:17** Mt 11:19 [h]**3:18** Gn 2:9; Pr 11:30; 13:12; 15:4; Rv 2:7 [i]**3:19** Ps 104:24; Pr 8:27 [j]**3:20** Gn 7:11 [k]Dt 33:28; Jb 36:28 [l]**3:21** Pr 4:21 [m]**3:22** Pr 4:22 [n]**3:23** Ps 91:12; Pr 4:12 [o]**3:24** Jb 11:19; Ps 3:5; Pr 6:22 [p]**3:25** Jb 5:21; Ps 91:5; 1Pt 3:14 [q]**3:26** 1Sm 2:9 [r]**3:27** Gl 6:10 [s]**3:28** Lv 19:13; Dt 24:15 [t]**3:29** Pr 6:14; 14:22 [u]**3:30** Pr 24:28; Rm 12:18 [v]**3:31** Ps 37:1; Pr 23:17; 24:1,19 [w]**3:32** Ps 25:14; Pr 11:20; 12:22; 15:8-9 [x]**3:33** Zch 5:3-4; Mal 2:2 [y]**3:34** Jms 4:6; 1Pt 5:5 [z]**4:1** Ps 34:11; Pr 1:8 [aa]**4:2** Jb 11:4 [ab]**4:4** Pr 3:1-2; 6:20-23; 7:1-2 [ac]**4:5** Pr 16:16 [ad]**4:6** 2Th 2:10 [ae]**4:7** Pr 16:16 [af]**4:8** 1Sm 2:30 [ag]**4:9** Pr 1:9; 16:31

[A]3:16 Lit *Length of days* [B]3:22 Or *be your throat* [C]3:22 In Hb, *nephesh* can mean throat, soul, or life. [D]3:22 Or *grace* [E]3:24 LXX reads *sit* [F]3:26 Or *be at your side* [G]3:27 Lit *in the power of your hands* [H]3:32 Or *confidential counsel* [I]3:35 Or *but haughty fools dishonor*, or *but fools exalt dishonor*

Two Ways of Life

10 Listen, my son. Accept my words,[a]
and you will live many years.[b]
11 I am teaching you the way of wisdom;
I am guiding you on straight paths.[c]
12 When you walk, your steps will not
be hindered;[d]
when you run, you will not stumble.[e]
13 Hold on to instruction; don't let go.[f]
Guard it, for it is your life.
14 Don't set foot on the path
of the wicked;[g]
don't proceed in the way of evil ones.
15 Avoid it; don't travel on it.
Turn away from it, and pass it by.
16 For they can't sleep
unless they have done what is evil;
they are robbed of sleep
unless they make someone stumble.[h]
17 They eat the bread of wickedness
and drink the wine of violence.
18 The path of the righteous is
like the light of dawn,[i]
shining brighter and brighter
until midday.
19 But the way of the wicked is
like the darkest gloom;[j]
they don't know what makes
them stumble.[k]

The Straight Path

20 My son, pay attention to my words;
listen closely to my sayings.[l]
21 Don't lose sight of them;[m]
keep them within your heart.
22 For they are life to those
who find them,
and health to one's whole body.
23 Guard your heart above all else,[A]
for it is the source of life.[n]
24 Don't let your mouth
speak dishonestly,[o]
and don't let your lips talk deviously.
25 Let your eyes look forward;
fix your gaze[B] straight ahead.[p]
26 Carefully consider the path[C]
for your feet,[q]
and all your ways will be established.
27 Don't turn to the right or to the left;[r]
keep your feet away from evil.

Avoid Seduction

5 My son, pay attention to my wisdom;
listen closely[D] to my understanding[s]
2 so that you may maintain discretion
and your lips safeguard knowledge.[t]
3 Though the lips
of the forbidden woman drip honey
and her words are[E] smoother than oil,
4 in the end she's as bitter
as 'wormwood[u]
and as sharp as a double-edged sword.[v]
5 Her feet go down to death;
her steps head straight for 'Sheol.[w]
6 She doesn't consider the path of life;
she doesn't know that her ways
are unstable.

7 So now, my sons, listen to me,
and don't turn away from the words
of my mouth.[x]
8 Keep your way far from her.
Don't go near the door of her house.[y]
9 Otherwise, you will give up your vitality
to others
and your years to someone cruel;
10 strangers will drain your resources,
and your earnings will end up
in a foreigner's house.
11 At the end of your life, you will lament
when your physical body
has been consumed,
12 and you will say,
"How I hated discipline,
and how my heart despised correction.[z]
13 I didn't obey my teachers
or listen closely[F] to my mentors.
14 I am on the verge of complete ruin
before the entire community."

Enjoy Marriage

15 Drink water from your own cistern,
water flowing from your own well.[aa]
16 Should your springs flow in the streets,
streams of water in the public squares?[ab]
17 They should be for you alone
and not for you to share with strangers.
18 Let your fountain be blessed,
and take pleasure in the wife
of your youth.[ac]
19 A loving doe, a graceful fawn —

[a] **4:10** Pr 2:1 [b] Pr 3:2 [c] **4:11** 1Sm 12:23 [d] **4:12** Jb 18:7; Ps 18:36 [e] Pr 3:23 [f] **4:13** Pr 3:18 [g] **4:14** Ps 1:1; Pr 1:15 [h] **4:16** Ps 36:4; Mc 2:1 [i] **4:18** 2Sm 23:4 [j] **4:19** Is 59:9-10; Jr 23:12; Jn 12:35 [k] Pr 24:16; Jn 11:10 [l] **4:20** Pr 5:1 [m] **4:21** Pr 3:21 [n] **4:23** Mt 15:19; Mk 7:18-23 [o] **4:24** Pr 6:12 [p] **4:25** Heb 12:2 [q] **4:26** Pr 5:6,21; Heb 12:13 [r] **4:27** Dt 5:32-33; 28:13-14; Jos 1:7; 23:6; 1Kg 15:5 [s] **5:1** Pr 4:20; 22:17 [t] **5:2** Mal 2:7 [u] **5:4** Pr 5:8-11; 6:32-33; Ec 7:26 [v] Ps 55:21; 57:4 [w] **5:5** Pr 7:27; 9:18 [x] **5:7** Pr 7:24 [y] **5:8** Pr 2:18; 7:8; 9:14 [z] **5:12** Ps 107:11; Pr 1:7,28-31; 12:1; 13:18 [aa] **5:15** Sg 4:12,15 [ab] **5:16** Pr 7:12 [ac] **5:18** Ec 9:9; Mal 2:14

[A] **4:23** Or *heart with all diligence* [B] **4:25** Lit *eyelids* [C] **4:26** Or *Clear a path* [D] **5:1** Lit *wisdom; stretch out your ear* [E] **5:3** Lit *her palate is* [F] **5:13** Lit *or turn my ear*

let her breasts always satisfy you;[a]
be lost in her love forever.
20 Why, my son, would you be infatuated
with a forbidden woman
or embrace the breast of a stranger?[b]
21 For a man's ways are
before the LORD's eyes,[c]
and He considers all his paths.[d]
22 A wicked man's iniquities entrap him;[e]
he is entangled in the ropes
of his own sin.[f]
23 He will die because there is
no discipline,[g]
and be lost because of
his great stupidity.

Financial Entanglements

6 My son, if you have put up security
for your neighbor[A]
or entered into an agreement
with[B] a stranger,[C,h]
2 you have been trapped by the words
of your lips[D] —
ensnared by the words of your mouth.
3 Do this, then, my son, and free yourself,
for you have put yourself
in your neighbor's power:
Go, humble yourself, and plead
with your neighbor.
4 Don't give sleep to your eyes
or slumber to your eyelids.[i]
5 Escape like a gazelle from a hunter,[E]
like a bird from a fowler's trap.[E,j]

Laziness

6 Go to the ant,[k] you slacker![l]
Observe its ways and become wise.
7 Without leader, administrator,
or ruler,
8 it prepares its provisions in summer;
it gathers its food during harvest.[m]
9 How long will you stay in bed,
you slacker?
When will you get up from your sleep?
10 A little sleep, a little slumber,
a little folding of the arms to rest,[n]
11 and your poverty will come like
a robber,
your need, like a bandit.[o]

The Malicious Man

12 A worthless person,[p] a wicked man
goes around speaking dishonestly,[q]
13 winking[r] his eyes, signaling
with his feet,
and gesturing with his fingers.
14 He always plots evil[s] with perversity
in his heart —
he stirs up trouble.[t]
15 Therefore calamity
will strike him suddenly;
he will be shattered
instantly — beyond recovery.[u]

What the LORD Hates

16 The LORD hates six things;
in fact, seven are detestable to Him:
17 arrogant eyes,[v] a lying tongue,[w]
hands that shed innocent blood,[x]
18 a heart that plots wicked schemes,[y]
feet eager to run to evil,[z]
19 a lying witness who gives
false testimony,[aa]
and one who stirs up trouble
among brothers.[ab]

Warning against Adultery

20 My son, keep your father's command,
and don't reject
your mother's teaching.[ac]
21 Always bind them to your heart;
tie them around your neck.[ad]
22 When you walk here and there,
they will guide you;
when you lie down, they will
watch over you;
when you wake up, they will
talk to you.
23 For a command is a lamp,
teaching is a light,[ae]
and corrective discipline is the way
to life.[af]
24 They will protect you
from an evil woman,[F]
from the flattering[G] tongue
of a stranger.[ag]
25 Don't lust in your heart for her beauty[ah]
or let her captivate you
with her eyelashes.[ai]

[a] **5:19** Sg 4:5
[b] **5:20** Pr 2:16
[c] **5:21** Jb 14:16; Ps 119:168; Hs 7:2; Heb 4:13
[d] Pr 4:25-26
[e] **5:22** Nm 32:23; Ps 7:15-16
[f] Pr 11:6
[g] **5:23** Jb 4:21
[h] **6:1** Pr 11:15; 17:18; 20:16; 22:26; 27:13
[i] **6:4** Ps 132:4
[j] **6:5** Ps 91:3; 124:7
[k] **6:6** Pr 30:24-25
[l] Pr 10:26; 13:4; 20:4; 26:16
[m] **6:8** Pr 10:5; 30:25
[n] **6:10** Pr 26:14; Ec 4:5
[o] **6:10-11** Pr 20:13; 24:33-34; Ec 4:5
[p] **6:12** 1Sm 25:25; Pr 16:27; 19:28
[q] Pr 4:24
[r] **6:13** Ps 35:19; Pr 10:10; 16:30
[s] **6:14** Pr 3:29; Mc 2:1
[t] Pr 6:19; 16:27-28; 28:25
[u] **6:15** 2Ch 36:16; Pr 24:22; 29:1; Is 30:13-14; Jr 19:11
[v] **6:17** Ps 18:27; Pr 21:4; 30:13
[w] Ps 31:18; 120:2; Pr 12:22; 17:7
[x] Dt 19:10; Pr 1:16; Is 1:15; 59:7
[y] **6:18** Gn 6:5
[z] Pr 1:16
[aa] **6:19** Ex 20:16; Ps 27:12; Pr 12:17; 14:5,25
[ab] Pr 6:14; 16:27-28; 28:25
[ac] **6:20** Pr 1:8; 31:1
[ad] **6:21** Pr 1:9; 3:3; 7:3
[ae] **6:23** Ps 119:105
[af] Pr 3:1-2; 4:4; 7:2; 19:16
[ag] **6:24** Pr 7:5
[ah] **6:25** Mt 5:28
[ai] Sg 4:9

[A] **6:1** Or *friend* [B] **6:1** Lit *or shaken hands for* or *with* [C] **6:1** The Hb word for *stranger* can refer to a foreigner, an Israelite outside one's family, or simply to another person. [D] **6:2** Lit *mouth* [E] **6:5** Lit *hand* [F] **6:24** LXX reads *from a married woman* [G] **6:24** Lit *smooth*

26 For a prostitute's fee is only a loaf
of bread,[A]
but an adulteress[B] goes after
a precious life.[a]
27 Can a man embrace fire[C]
and his clothes not be burned?
28 Can a man walk on burning coals
without scorching his feet?
29 So it is with the one who sleeps with
another man's wife;
no one who touches her
will go unpunished.[b]
30 People don't despise the thief
if he steals
to satisfy himself when he is hungry.[c]
31 Still, if caught, he must pay seven times
as much;[d]
he must give up all the wealth
in his house.
32 The one who commits adultery[D]
lacks sense;
whoever does so destroys himself.[e]
33 He will get a beating[E] and dishonor,
and his disgrace will never be removed.
34 For jealousy enrages a husband,[f]
and he will show no mercy
when he takes revenge.
35 He will not be appeased by anything
or be persuaded by lavish gifts.

7 My son, obey my words,
and treasure my commands.[g]
2 Keep my commands and live;[h]
protect my teachings
as the pupil of your eye.[i]
3 Tie them to your fingers;
write them on the tablet of your heart.[j]
4 Say to wisdom, "You are my sister,"[k]
and call understanding your relative.
5 She will keep you
from a forbidden woman,
a stranger with her flattering talk.[l]

A Story of Seduction

6 At the window of my house
I looked through my lattice.[m]
7 I saw among the inexperienced,[F]
I noticed among the youths,
a young man lacking sense.
8 Crossing the street near her corner,
he strolled down the road to her house
9 at twilight, in the evening,
in the dark of the night.[n]
10 A woman came to meet him
dressed like a prostitute,[o]
having a hidden agenda.[G]
11 She is loud and defiant;[p]
her feet do not stay at home.[q]
12 Now in the street, now in the squares,[r]
she lurks at every corner.[s]
13 She grabs him and kisses him;
she brazenly says[H] to him,
14 "I've made ·fellowship offerings;[I]
today I've fulfilled my vows.[t]
15 So I came out to meet you,
to search for you, and I've found you.
16 I've spread coverings on my bed[u] —
richly colored linen from Egypt.[v]
17 I've perfumed my bed
with myrrh, aloes, and cinnamon.[w]
18 Come, let's drink deeply of lovemaking
until morning.[x]
Let's feast on each other's love!
19 My husband isn't home;
he went on a long journey.
20 He took a bag of money with him
and will come home at the time
of the full moon."
21 She seduces him
with her persistent pleading;
she lures with her flattering[J] talk.
22 He follows her impulsively
like an ox going to the slaughter,
like a deer bounding toward a trap[K]
23 until an arrow pierces its[L] liver,[y]
like a bird darting into a snare[z] —
he doesn't know it will cost him his life.
24 Now, my sons, listen to me,
and pay attention to the words
of my mouth.
25 Don't let your heart turn aside
to her ways;
don't stray onto her paths.[aa]
26 For she has brought many
down to death;

[a]**6:26** Pr 2:18-19; 7:21-23,27; 23:27-28; Ezk 13:18
[b]**6:29** Pr 16:5
[c]**6:30** Jr 49:9; Ob 5
[d]**6:31** Ex 22:1-4; Ps 79:12
[e]**6:32** Pr 7:22-23
[f]**6:34** Pr 27:4; Sg 8:6
[g]**7:1** Pr 2:1
[h]**7:2** Pr 3:1-2; 4:4; 6:23; 19:16
[i]Dt 32:10; Ps 17:8; Zch 2:8
[j]**7:3** Dt 11:18; Pr 3:3; 6:21
[k]**7:4** Sg 4:9
[l]**7:5** Pr 5:3,20; 6:24; 7:21
[m]**7:6** Jdg 5:28; Sg 2:9
[n]**7:9** Jb 24:15
[o]**7:10** Gn 38:14-15
[p]**7:11** Pr 9:13
[q]1Tm 5:13
[r]**7:12** Pr 5:16; 9:14
[s]Pr 23:28
[t]**7:14** Lv 7:11-18; Dt 23:18; Ps 56:12
[u]**7:16** Pr 31:22
[v]Ezk 27:7
[w]**7:17** Ex 30:23; Ps 45:8
[x]**7:18** Sg 5:1
[y]**7:21-23** Pr 2:16-19; 5:3-6; 23:27-28
[z]**7:23** Ec 9:12
[aa]**7:25** Pr 5:8

[A]**6:26** Or *On account of a prostitute, one is left with only a loaf of bread* [B]**6:26** Lit *but a wife of a man* [C]**6:27** Lit *man take fire to his bosom* [D]**6:32** Lit *commits adultery with a woman* [E]**6:33** Or *plague* [F]**7:7** Or *simple*, or *gullible*, or *naive* [G]**7:10** Or *prostitute with a guarded heart* [H]**7:13** Lit *she makes her face strong and says* [I]**7:14** Meat from a fellowship offering had to be eaten on the day it was offered; therefore she is inviting him to a feast at her house. [J]**7:21** Lit *smooth* [K]**7:22** Text emended; MT reads *like a shackle to the discipline of a fool*; Hb obscure [L]**7:23** Or *his*

her victims are countless.[A]
27 Her house is the road to ˙Sheol,
descending to the chambers of death.[a]

Wisdom's Appeal

8 Doesn't Wisdom[b] call out?
Doesn't Understanding make her voice
heard?
2 At the heights overlooking the road,
at the crossroads, she takes her stand.
3 Beside the gates[c] at the entry
to[B] the city,
at the main entrance, she cries out:
4 "People, I call out to you;
my cry is to mankind.
5 Learn to be shrewd,
you who are inexperienced;
develop common sense,
you who are foolish.
6 Listen, for I speak of noble things,
and what my lips say is right.
7 For my mouth tells the truth,[d]
and wickedness is detestable to my lips.
8 All the words of my mouth
are righteous;
none of them are deceptive
or perverse.[e]
9 All of them are clear to the perceptive,[f]
and right to those
who discover knowledge.
10 Accept my instruction instead of silver,
and knowledge rather than pure gold.[g]
11 For wisdom is better than jewels,[h]
and nothing desirable can compare
with it.[i]
12 I, Wisdom, share a home
with shrewdness
and have knowledge and discretion.[j]
13 To ˙fear the LORD is to hate evil.[k]
I hate arrogant pride, evil conduct,
and perverse speech.
14 I possess good advice and competence;[C]
I have understanding and strength.[l]
15 It is by me that kings reign[m]
and rulers enact just law;
16 by me, princes lead,
as do nobles and all righteous judges.[D]
17 I love those who love me,[n]
and those who search for me find me.[o]
18 With me are riches and honor,[p]
lasting wealth and righteousness.[q]
19 My fruit is better than solid gold,
and my harvest than pure silver.[r]
20 I walk in the way of righteousness,
along the paths of justice,
21 giving wealth as an inheritance to those
who love me,
and filling their treasuries.

22 "The LORD made[E] me
at the beginning of His creation,[F]
before His works of long ago.[s]
23 I was formed before ancient times,
from the beginning,
before the earth began.[t]
24 I was born
when there were no watery depths[u]
and no springs filled with water.
25 I was delivered
before the mountains and hills
were established,[v]
26 before He made the land, the fields,
or the first soil on earth.
27 I was there when He established
the heavens,[w]
when He laid out the horizon
on the surface of the ocean,[x]
28 when He placed the skies above,
when the fountains of the ocean
gushed out,
29 when He set a limit for the sea
so that the waters would not violate
His command,[y]
when He laid out the foundations
of the earth.[z]
30 I was a skilled craftsman[G] beside Him.[aa]
I was His[H] delight every day,
always rejoicing before Him.
31 I was rejoicing in His inhabited world,[ab]
delighting in the ˙human race.[ac]

32 "And now, my sons, listen to me;
those who keep my ways are happy.[ad]
33 Listen to instruction and be wise;[ae]
don't ignore it.
34 Anyone who listens to me is happy,[af]
watching at my doors every day,
waiting by the posts of my doorway.
35 For the one who finds me finds life[ag]

[a]**7:27** Pr 2:18; 5:5; 9:18; 1Co 6:9; Rv 22:15 [b]**8:1-3** Pr 1:20-21; 9:3,13-15 [c]**8:3** Jb 29:7 [d]**8:7** Ps 37:30 [e]**8:8** Dt 32:5; Pr 2:15; Php 2:15 [f]**8:9** Pr 14:6 [g]**8:10** Pr 3:14-15; 8:19; 16:16 [h]**8:11** Jb 28:12-19 [i]Pr 3:15; 20:15 [j]**8:12** Pr 1:4 [k]**8:13** Pr 16:6 [l]**8:14** Ec 7:19 [m]**8:15** 2Ch 1:10; Dn 2:21; Rm 13:1 [n]**8:17** 1Sm 2:30; Jn 14:21 [o]Pr 1:28; 2:4-5; Jms 1:5 [p]**8:18** Pr 3:16 [q]Ps 112:3; Mt 6:33 [r]**8:19** Jb 28:15; Pr 3:14; 8:10; 16:16 [s]**8:22** Gn 1:1; Jb 28:26-28; Ps 104:24 [t]**8:23** Jn 1:1-3; 17:5 [u]**8:24** Gn 1:2; Pr 3:20 [v]**8:25** Ps 90:2 [w]**8:27** Pr 3:19 [x]Jb 26:10 [y]**8:29** Jb 38:8-11; Ps 104:9 [z]Jb 38:4-5; Ps 104:5 [aa]**8:30** Jb 28:20-27; 38–39; Pr 3:19-20; Jr 10:12; 51:15; Zch 13:7; Jn 1:2-3 [ab]**8:31** Jb 38:4-7 [ac]Heb 2:6-8 [ad]**8:32** Ps 119:1-2; 128:1; Lk 11:28 [ae]**8:33** Pr 4:1 [af]**8:34** Pr 3:13 [ag]**8:35** Pr 4:4,22; 7:2; 9:11; 12:28; Jn 17:3

[A]**7:26** Or *and powerful men are all her victims* [B]**8:3** Lit *the mouth of* [C]**8:14** Or *resourcefulness* [D]**8:16** Some Hb mss, LXX read *nobles who judge the earth* [E]**8:22** Or *possessed*, or *begot* [F]**8:22** Lit *way* [G]**8:30** Or *a confidant*, or *a child*, or *was constantly* [H]**8:30** LXX; MT omits *His*

and obtains favor from the LORD,[a]
36 but the one who misses me[A]
harms himself;[b]
all who hate me love death."[c]

Wisdom versus Foolishness

9 Wisdom has built her house;[d]
she has carved out her seven pillars.
2 She has prepared her meat;[e]
she has mixed her wine;[f]
she has also set her table.[g]
3 She has sent out her female servants;[h]
she calls out from the highest points
of the city:[i]
4 "Whoever is inexperienced,
enter here!"
To the one who lacks sense,[j] she says,
5 "Come, eat my bread,[k]
and drink the wine I have mixed.
6 Leave inexperience behind,
and you will live;
pursue the way of understanding.
7 The one who corrects a mocker
will bring dishonor on himself;
the one who rebukes a wicked man
will get hurt.[B]
8 Don't rebuke a mocker, or he will
hate you;[l]
rebuke a wise man, and he will
love you.[m]
9 Instruct a wise man, and he will be
wiser still;
teach a righteous man, and he will
learn more.[n]
10 "The ·fear of the LORD is the beginning
of wisdom,[o]
and the knowledge of the Holy One[p]
is understanding.
11 For by Wisdom your days will be many,
and years will be added to your life.
12 If you are wise, you are wise
for your own benefit;[q]
if you mock, you alone will bear
the consequences."
13 The woman Folly is rowdy;[r]
she is gullible and knows nothing.[s]
14 She sits by the doorway of her house,
on a seat at the highest point of the city,
15 calling to those who pass by,
who go straight ahead on their paths:[t]
16 "Whoever is inexperienced,
enter here!"
To the one who lacks sense, she says,
17 "Stolen water is sweet,
and bread eaten secretly is tasty!"[u]
18 But he doesn't know
that the departed spirits are there,[v]
that her guests are in the depths
of ·Sheol.[w]

A Collection of Solomon's Proverbs

10 Solomon's proverbs:[x]

A wise son brings joy to his father,
but a foolish son, heartache
to his mother.[y]

2 Ill-gotten gains do not profit anyone,
but righteousness rescues from death.[z]

3 The LORD will not let the righteous
go hungry,[aa]
but He denies the wicked
what they crave.[ab]

4 Idle hands make one poor,
but diligent hands bring riches.[ac]

5 The son who gathers during summer
is prudent;
the son who sleeps during harvest
is disgraceful.[ad]

6 Blessings are on the head
of the righteous,
but the mouth of the wicked
conceals violence.[ae]

7 The remembrance of the righteous is
a blessing,
but the name of the wicked will rot.[af]

8 A wise heart accepts commands,[ag]
but foolish lips will be destroyed.

9 The one who lives with integrity
lives securely,[ah]
but whoever perverts his ways will be
found out.[ai]

10 A sly wink of the eye[aj] causes grief,
and foolish lips will be destroyed.

11 The mouth of the righteous is
a fountain of life,[ak]

[a] **8:35** Pr 3:4; 12:2; 13:13; 18:22 [b] **8:36** Pr 15:32 [c] Pr 11:19; 21:6 [d] **9:1** Pr 14:1; Eph 2:20-22; 1Pt 2:5 [e] **9:2** Mt 22:4 [f] Sg 8:2 [g] Lk 14:17 [h] **9:3** Ps 68:11; Mt 22:3 [i] Pr 8:2-3; 9:14-15; Mt 10:27 [j] **9:4** Pr 6:32 [k] **9:5** Is 55:1; Jn 6:27,51 [l] **9:8** Pr 15:12; Mt 7:6 [m] Ps 141:5 [n] **9:9** Pr 1:5; 16:21,23 [o] **9:10** Jb 28:28; Ps 111:10; Pr 1:7; 15:33 [p] Pr 30:3; Hs 11:12; Rv 16:5 [q] **9:12** Jb 22:2 [r] **9:13** Pr 7:11 [s] Pr 5:6 [t] **9:14-15** Pr 7:11-12; 9:3-4 [u] **9:17** Pr 20:17 [v] **9:18** Pr 2:18; 21:16 [w] Pr 5:5; 7:27 [x] **10:1** Pr 1:1 [y] Pr 15:20; 17:25; 23:24-25; 29:3,15 [z] **10:2** Pr 11:4,18; 12:28; 21:6; Ezk 7:19; Lk 12:19-20 [aa] **10:3** Ps 37:25; Mt 6:33 [ab] Ps 112:10 [ac] **10:4** Pr 12:24,27; 13:4,11; 19:15; 21:5 [ad] **10:5** Pr 6:6-11; 30:25 [ae] **10:6** Pr 10:11 [af] **10:7** Ps 9:5-6; 112:6 [ag] **10:8** Mt 7:24 [ah] **10:9** Ps 23:4; Pr 2:7; 3:23; 19:1; 20:7; 28:6,18; Is 33:15-16 [ai] Pr 26:26; Mt 10:26; 1Tm 5:25 [aj] **10:10** Ps 35:19; Pr 6:13; 16:30 [ak] **10:11** Ps 37:30; Pr 13:14; 14:27; 16:22

[A] **8:36** Or *who sins against me* [B] **9:7** Lit *man his blemish*

but the mouth of the wicked
conceals violence.[a]

12 Hatred stirs up conflicts,
but love covers all offenses.[b]

13 Wisdom is found on the lips
of the discerning,
but a rod is for the back of the one
who lacks sense.[c]

14 The wise store up knowledge,
but the mouth of the fool
hastens destruction.[d]

15 A rich man's wealth is
his fortified city;[e]
the poverty of the poor is
their destruction.

16 The labor of the righteous leads to life;
the activity of the wicked leads to sin.[f]

17 The one who follows instruction is
on the path to life,
but the one who rejects correction
goes astray.[g]

18 The one who conceals hatred has
lying lips,
and whoever spreads slander is a fool.[h]

19 When there are many words,
sin is unavoidable,
but the one who controls his lips
is wise.[i]

20 The tongue of the righteous is
pure silver;
the heart of the wicked is of little value.[j]

21 The lips of the righteous feed many,
but fools die for lack of sense.[k]

22 The LORD's blessing enriches,[l]
and struggle adds nothing to it.[A,m]

23 As shameful conduct is pleasure
for a fool,[n]
so wisdom is for a man
of understanding.

24 What the wicked dreads will come
to him,[o]
but what the righteous desire
will be given to them.[p]

25 When the whirlwind passes,
the wicked are no more,[q]
but the righteous are secure forever.[r]

26 Like vinegar to the teeth and smoke
to the eyes,[s]
so the slacker is to the one
who sends him on an errand.

27 The ·fear of the LORD prolongs life,[B,t]
but the years of the wicked
are cut short.[u]

28 The hope of the righteous is joy,[v]
but the expectation of the wicked
comes to nothing.[w]

29 The way of the LORD is a stronghold
for the honorable,
but destruction awaits the malicious.[x]

30 The righteous will never be shaken,
but the wicked will not remain
on the earth.[y]

31 The mouth of the righteous
produces wisdom,[z]
but a perverse tongue will be cut out.[aa]

32 The lips of the righteous know
what is appropriate,[ab]
but the mouth of the wicked,
only what is perverse.[ac]

11 Dishonest scales are detestable
to the LORD,[ad]
but an accurate weight is His delight.[ae]

2 When pride comes, disgrace follows,
but with humility comes wisdom.[af]

3 The integrity of the upright
guides them,[ag]
but the perversity of the treacherous
destroys them.[ah]

4 Wealth is not profitable on a day
of wrath,
but righteousness rescues from death.[ai]

5 The righteousness of the blameless
clears his path,
but the wicked person will fall
because of his wickedness.

6 The righteousness of the upright
rescues them,

[a]**10:11** Pr 10:6
[b]**10:12** Pr 17:9; Jms 5:20; 1Pt 4:8
[c]**10:13** Pr 19:29; 26:3
[d]**10:14** Pr 10:8; 12:13; 13:3; 18:7
[e]**10:15** Ps 52:7; Pr 18:11
[f]**10:16** Pr 11:19
[g]**10:17** Pr 5:12-13,22-23; 6:23; 13:13-14
[h]**10:18** Pr 11:13
[i]**10:19** Pr 17:27-28; Jms 1:19; 3:2
[j]**10:20** Pr 8:19; 10:32
[k]**10:21** Hs 4:6
[l]**10:22** Gn 24:35; 26:12; Dt 8:18; Jms 1:17
[m]Mt 6:31-32
[n]**10:23** Pr 2:14; 15:21
[o]**10:24** Pr 1:26-27; Is 66:4; Heb 10:27
[p]Ps 37:4; 145:19; Pr 11:23; Mt 5:6; 1Jn 5:14-15
[q]**10:25** Jb 21:18; Is 29:5-7
[r]Ps 15:5; Pr 10:30; 12:3,7; Mt 7:24-27
[s]**10:26** Pr 26:6
[t]**10:27** Pr 3:2
[u]Jb 15:32-33; Pr 14:26-27; 15:16; 19:23
[v]**10:28** Pr 11:23; 23:18; Jr 29:11
[w]Jb 8:13; 14:9; Pr 11:7; Ezk 37:11
[x]**10:29** Pr 13:6; 21:15
[y]**10:30** Ps 21:7; 37:29; 125:1; Pr 2:21-22; 12:3
[z]**10:31** Ps 37:30
[aa]Ps 37:38; 120:2-4
[ab]**10:32** Ec 10:12
[ac]Pr 2:12; 10:20; 15:28
[ad]**11:1** Dt 25:13-16; Pr 20:10,23; Mc 6:10-11
[ae]Lv 19:36; Pr 16:11; Ezk 45:10
[af]**11:2** Pr 15:33; 18:12; 22:4; 29:23
[ag]**11:3** Pr 13:6
[ah]Pr 11:17-19; 19:3
[ai]**11:4** Gn 7:1; Pr 10:2; 11:28; 12:28; Zph 1:18

A**10:22** Or *and He adds no trouble to it* B**10:27** Lit *LORD adds to days*

but the treacherous are trapped
by their own desires.[a]

7 When the wicked man dies,
his expectation comes to nothing,
and hope placed in wealth[A,B]
vanishes.[b]

8 The righteous one is rescued
from trouble;
in his place, the wicked one goes in.[c]

9 With his mouth the ungodly
destroys his neighbor,
but through knowledge the righteous
are rescued.

10 When the righteous thrive,
a city rejoices,[d]
and when the wicked die, there is
joyful shouting.

11 A city is built up by the blessing
of the upright,[e]
but it is torn down by the mouth
of the wicked.[f]

12 Whoever shows contempt
for his neighbor lacks sense,
but a man with understanding
keeps silent.[g]

13 A gossip goes around revealing
a secret,
but a trustworthy person keeps
a confidence.[h]

14 Without guidance, people fall,
but with many counselors
there is deliverance.[i]

15 If someone puts up security
for a stranger,
he will suffer for it,[j]
but the one who hates such agreements
is protected.

16 A gracious woman gains honor,
but violent[C] men gain only riches.

17 A kind man benefits himself,[k]
but a cruel man brings disaster
on himself.[l]

18 The wicked man earns an empty wage,
but the one who sows righteousness,
a true reward.[m]

19 Genuine righteousness leads to life,[n]
but pursuing evil leads to death.[o]

20 Those with twisted minds
are detestable to the LORD,
but those with blameless conduct are
His delight.[p]

21 Be assured[D] that the wicked
will not go unpunished,[q]
but the offspring of the righteous
will escape.

22 A beautiful woman who rejects
good sense
is like a gold ring in a pig's snout.[r]

23 The desire of the righteous
turns out well,[s]
but the hope of the wicked
leads to wrath.[t]

24 One person gives freely,
yet gains more;[u]
another withholds what is right,
only to become poor.[v]

25 A generous person will be enriched,[w]
and the one who gives a drink of water
will receive water.[x]

26 People will curse[y] anyone
who hoards grain,
but a blessing will come to the one
who sells it.[z]

27 The one who searches
for what is good[aa] finds favor,
but if someone looks for trouble,
it will come to him.[ab]

28 Anyone trusting in his riches will fall,[ac]
but the righteous will flourish
like foliage.[ad]

29 The one who brings ruin
on his household[ae]
will inherit the wind,[af]
and a fool will be a slave
to someone whose heart is wise.

30 The fruit of the righteous is a tree
of life,[ag]
but violence[E] takes lives.

31 If the righteous will be repaid on earth,
how much more the wicked and sinful.[ah]

[a]**11:6** Ps 7:15-16; Pr 5:22; Ec 10:8 [b]**11:7** Jb 8:13; Pr 10:28; 24:14 [c]**11:8** Pr 21:18 [d]**11:10** Pr 28:12 [e]**11:11** Pr 14:34 [f]Pr 14:1; 29:4 [g]**11:12** Pr 14:21 [h]**11:13** Lv 19:16; Pr 10:18; 20:19; 1Tm 5:13 [i]**11:14** Pr 15:22; 20:18; 24:6 [j]**11:15** Pr 6:1-2; 17:18; 22:26 [k]**11:17** Mt 5:7; 25:34-36 [l]Pr 11:3 [m]**11:18** Pr 10:2-3; Hs 10:12; Gl 6:8-9; Jms 3:18 [n]**11:19** Pr 10:16-17; 19:23 [o]Rm 6:23; Jms 1:15 [p]**11:20** 1Ch 29:17; Ps 119:1; Pr 3:32; 12:22; 13:6; 15:8-9,26 [q]**11:21** Pr 16:5 [r]**11:22** Gn 24:47 [s]**11:23** Ps 37:4-5; Pr 10:24; Jr 29:11 [t]Pr 10:28; 11:7; Rm 2:8-9 [u]**11:24** Ps 112:9; Pr 11:25; 21:26 [v]Pr 13:7; 22:16; 28:27 [w]**11:25** Pr 3:9-10; 2Co 9:6-11 [x]Mt 5:7; 10:42 [y]**11:26** Pr 24:24 [z]Gn 42:6 [aa]**11:27** Php 4:8 [ab]Est 7:10; Ps 7:15-16 [ac]**11:28** Ps 49:6 [ad]Ps 1:3; 92:12; Pr 11:4; 14:11; Jr 17:8 [ae]**11:29** Pr 15:27 [af]Ec 5:16 [ag]**11:30** Pr 3:18 [ah]**11:31** Dt 32:25; Pr 13:21; 1Pt 4:18

[A]**11:7** LXX reads *hope of the ungodly* [B]**11:7** Or *strength* [C]**11:16** Or *ruthless* [D]**11:21** Lit *Hand to hand* [E]**11:30** LXX, Syr; MT reads *but a wise one*

12

Whoever loves discipline
loves knowledge,
but one who hates correction is stupid.[a]

2 The good person obtains favor
from the LORD,[b]
but He condemns a man who schemes.[c]

3 Man cannot be made secure
by wickedness,
but the root of the righteous
is immovable.[d]

4 A capable wife[A] is her husband's crown,[e]
but a wife who causes shame
is like rottenness in his bones.[f]

5 The thoughts of the righteous are just,
but guidance from the wicked
leads to deceit.

6 The words of the wicked are
a deadly ambush,[g]
but the speech of the upright
rescues them.[h]

7 The wicked are overthrown
and perish,[i]
but the house of the righteous
will stand.[j]

8 A man is praised for his insight,
but a twisted mind is despised.

9 Better to be dishonored, yet have
a servant,
than to act important but have
no food.[k]

10 A righteous man cares about
his animal's health,[l]
but even the merciful acts of the wicked
are cruel.

11 The one who works his land will have
plenty of food,[m]
but whoever chases fantasies
lacks sense.[n]

12 The wicked desire what evil men have,[B]
but the root of the righteous
produces fruit.

13 An evil man is trapped
by his rebellious speech,[o]
but a righteous one escapes
from trouble.[p]

14 A man will be satisfied with good
by the words of his mouth,[q]
and the work of a man's hands
will reward him.[r]

15 A fool's way is right in his own eyes,[s]
but whoever listens to counsel is wise.

16 A fool's displeasure is known at once,
but whoever ignores an insult
is sensible.[t]

17 Whoever speaks the truth declares
what is right,
but a false witness, deceit.[u]

18 There is one who speaks rashly,
like a piercing sword;[v]
but the tongue of the wise
brings healing.[w]

19 Truthful lips endure forever,
but a lying tongue, only a moment.[x]

20 Deceit is in the hearts of those
who plot evil,
but those who promote peace have joy.[y]

21 No disaster overcomes the righteous,[z]
but the wicked are full of misery.

22 Lying lips are detestable to the LORD,[aa]
but faithful people are His delight.[ab]

23 A shrewd person conceals knowledge,
but a foolish heart publicizes stupidity.[ac]

24 The diligent hand will rule,
but laziness will lead to forced labor.[ad]

25 Anxiety in a man's heart weighs it down,
but a good word cheers it up.[ae]

26 A righteous man is careful in dealing
with his neighbor,[C]
but the ways of the wicked
lead them astray.[af]

27 A lazy man doesn't roast his game,[ag]
but to a diligent man, his wealth
is precious.[ah]

28 There is life in the path
of righteousness,
but another path leads to death.[D,ai]

[a] **12:1** Pr 3:11; 5:11-13; 15:5,31-32 [b] **12:2** Pr 8:35 [c] Pr 14:17; 24:8 [d] **12:3** Ps 16:8; 21:7; Pr 10:30 [e] **12:4** Pr 18:22; 19:14; 31:10 [f] Pr 14:30 [g] **12:6** Pr 1:11 [h] Pr 14:2 [i] **12:7** Jb 34:25 [j] Ps 103:17-18; Pr 10:25; Mt 7:24-27 [k] **12:9** Pr 11:24; 13:7; Rm 12:3 [l] **12:10** Dt 25:4; Pr 27:23; Jnh 4:11 [m] **12:11** Pr 24:27 [n] Pr 28:19 [o] **12:13** Pr 10:14; 13:3; 18:7 [p] Pr 21:23; 29:6 [q] **12:14** Pr 13:2; 18:20 [r] Pr 1:31; 28:19; Is 3:10 [s] **12:15** Pr 16:2; 21:2 [t] **12:16** Pr 11:13; 12:23; 17:9; 29:11 [u] **12:17** Pr 6:19; 14:5,25 [v] **12:18** Ps 57:4 [w] Pr 4:22; 15:4 [x] **12:19** Ps 52:4-5; Pr 19:9 [y] **12:20** Pr 14:22 [z] **12:21** Ps 91:10; 1Pt 3:13 [aa] **12:22** Rv 22:15 [ab] Pr 3:32; 11:20; 15:8-9,26 [ac] **12:23** Pr 11:13; 12:16; 13:16; 15:2 [ad] **12:24** Pr 10:4; 13:4; 19:15 [ae] **12:25** Ps 94:19; Pr 15:13; 16:24; Mt 6:25-34 [af] **12:26** Pr 14:22 [ag] **12:27** Pr 19:15,24; 26:15 [ah] Pr 10:4; 13:4 [ai] **12:28** Pr 10:2; 13:14; 14:27

[A] **12:4** Or *A wife of quality*, or *A wife of good character* [B] **12:12** Or *desire a stronghold of evil* [C] **12:26** Or *man guides his neighbor* [D] **12:28** Or *righteousness, and in its path there is no death*

13 A wise son responds to his
father's discipline,
but a mocker doesn't listen to rebuke.

2 From the words of his mouth,
a man will enjoy good things,[a]
but treacherous people have
an appetite for violence.[b]

3 The one who guards his mouth protects
his life;[c]
the one who opens his lips invites
his own ruin.[d]

4 The slacker craves, yet has nothing,
but the diligent is fully satisfied.[e]

5 The righteous hate lying,
but the wicked act disgustingly
and disgracefully.

6 Righteousness guards people
of integrity,[A]
but wickedness undermines the sinner.[f]

7 One man pretends to be rich
but has nothing;[g]
another pretends to be poor but has
great wealth.[h]

8 Riches are a ransom for a man's life,[i]
but a poor man hears no threat.

9 The light of the righteous
shines brightly,[j]
but the lamp of the wicked is put out.[k]

10 Arrogance leads to nothing but strife,[l]
but wisdom is gained by those
who take advice.

11 Wealth obtained by fraud
will dwindle,[m]
but whoever earns it through labor[B]
will multiply it.[n]

12 Delayed hope makes the heart sick,
but fulfilled desire is a tree of life.[o]

13 The one who has contempt
for instruction will pay the penalty,[p]
but the one who respects a command
will be rewarded.[q]

14 A wise man's instruction is a fountain
of life,[r]
turning people away from the snares
of death.[s]

15 Good sense wins favor,[t]
but the way of the treacherous
never changes.[C]

16 Every sensible person
acts knowledgeably,
but a fool displays his stupidity.[u]

17 A wicked messenger falls into trouble,
but a trustworthy courier
brings healing.[v]

18 Poverty and disgrace come to those
who ignore discipline,
but the one who accepts correction
will be honored.[w]

19 Desire fulfilled is sweet to the taste,
but to turn from evil[x]
is an abomination to fools.

20 The one who walks with the wise
will become wise,
but a companion of fools
will suffer harm.

21 Disaster pursues sinners,
but good rewards the righteous.[y]

22 A good man leaves an inheritance
to his[D] grandchildren,
but the sinner's wealth is stored up
for the righteous.[z]

23 The uncultivated field of the poor
yields abundant food,
but without justice, it is swept away.

24 The one who will not use the rod hates
his son,[aa]
but the one who loves him disciplines
him diligently.[ab]

25 A righteous man eats
until he is satisfied,
but the stomach of the wicked
is empty.[ac]

14 Every wise woman builds her house,[ad]
but a foolish one tears it down
with her own hands.[ae]

2 Whoever lives with integrity
*fears the LORD,[af]

[a]**13:2** Pr 12:14 [b]Pr 1:10-12,31; 18:20-21; Is 32:6-8 [c]**13:3** Pr 18:21; 21:23; Jms 3:2 [d]Pr 10:14; 12:13; 18:7 [e]**13:4** Pr 10:4; 12:24,27; 19:15 [f]**13:6** Pr 10:29; 11:3 [g]**13:7** Pr 11:24; Lk 12:20-21; 1Tm 6:17-19; Rv 3:17-18 [h]Lk 12:33; 2Co 6:10; Jms 2:5 [i]**13:8** Jb 2:4; Pr 10:15 [j]**13:9** Pr 4:18 [k]Jb 18:5-6; Pr 20:20; 24:20 [l]**13:10** Pr 17:19 [m]**13:11** Pr 10:2; 20:21; 23:5 [n]Pr 10:4; 21:5-6 [o]**13:12** Pr 11:30; 15:4 [p]**13:13** Nm 15:31; 2Ch 36:16 [q]Pr 3:1-2; 4:4; 6:23 [r]**13:14** Pr 10:11; 14:27 [s]Ps 18:5; 116:3 [t]**13:15** Pr 3:4 [u]**13:16** Pr 12:23; 15:2; Ec 10:3 [v]**13:17** Pr 25:13 [w]**13:18** Pr 5:12-14; 12:1; 15:31-33 [x]**13:19** Pr 16:22; 29:27 [y]**13:21** Ps 32:10; Pr 11:31; 13:13 [z]**13:22** Jb 27:13-17; Pr 28:8; Ec 2:26 [aa]**13:24** Pr 19:18; 22:15; 23:13-14; 29:15,17 [ab]Dt 8:5; Pr 3:12; Heb 12:5-7 [ac]**13:25** Pr 10:3 [ad]**14:1** Ru 4:11; Pr 9:1; 24:3; 31:10-27 [ae]Pr 11:11; 29:4 [af]**14:2** Pr 19:1; 28:6

[A]**13:6** Lit *guards integrity of way* [B]**13:11** Lit *whoever gathers upon his hand* [C]**13:15** LXX, Syr, Tg read *treacherous will perish* [D]**13:22** Or *inheritance: his*

but the one who is devious in his ways
despises Him.[a]

3 The proud speech of a fool brings a rod
of discipline,[A]
but the lips of the wise protect them.[b]

4 Where there are no oxen, the
feeding trough is empty,[B]
but an abundant harvest comes
through the strength of an ox.

5 An honest witness does not deceive,
but a dishonest witness utters lies.[c]

6 A mocker seeks wisdom
and doesn't find it,
but knowledge comes easily
to the perceptive.

7 Stay away from a foolish man;
you will gain no knowledge
from his speech.[d]

8 The sensible man's wisdom is
to consider his way,
but the stupidity of fools deceives them.

9 Fools mock at making restitution,[C]
but there is goodwill
among the upright.

10 The heart knows its own bitterness,
and no outsider shares in its joy.

11 The house of the wicked
will be destroyed,
but the tent of the upright will stand.[D,e]

12 There is a way that seems right
to a man,[f]
but its end is the way to death.[g]

13 Even in laughter a heart may be sad,
and joy may end in grief.[h]

14 The disloyal one will get
what his conduct deserves,
and a good man,
what his deeds deserve.[i]

15 The inexperienced one believes
anything,[j]
but the sensible one watches[E] his steps.

16 A wise man is cautious and turns
from evil,[k]

[a]**14:2** Pr 2:15
[b]**14:3** Pr 12:6
[c]**14:5** Ex 20:16; 23:1; Pr 6:19; 12:17; 14:25
[d]**14:7** Pr 20:15
[e]**14:11** Pr 10:25; 11:28; 12:7; Mt 7:24-27
[f]**14:12** Pr 12:15; 16:25
[g]Pr 5:4; Rm 6:21
[h]**14:13** Ec 2:1-2; Lk 6:25
[i]**14:14** Pr 1:31; 12:14; 18:20; 28:19
[j]**14:15** Eph 4:14; Jms 1:5-8
[k]**14:16** Jb 28:28; Ps 34:14; Pr 3:7; 22:3
[l]**14:17** Pr 12:2; 24:8
[m]**14:20** Pr 19:7
[n]Pr 19:4
[o]**14:21** Pr 11:12
[p]Ps 41:1
[q]**14:22** Pr 6:14-15; 12:26
[r]Pr 12:20
[s]**14:23** Pr 21:5
[t]**14:25** Pr 6:19; 12:17; 14:5
[u]**14:26** Pr 29:25
[v]**14:27** Pr 13:14; 16:22; 19:23
[w]**14:29** Pr 16:32; 19:11; Ec 7:9; Jms 1:19

but a fool is easily angered
and is careless.[F]

17 A quick-tempered man acts foolishly,
and a man who schemes is hated.[l]

18 The inexperienced inherit foolishness,
but the sensible are crowned
with knowledge.

19 The evil bow before those
who are good,
the wicked, at the gates
of the righteous.

20 A poor man is hated even
by his neighbor,[m]
but there are many who love the rich.[n]

21 The one who despises
his neighbor sins,[o]
but whoever shows kindness
to the poor will be happy.[p]

22 Don't those who plan evil go astray?[q]
But those who plan good find loyalty
and faithfulness.[r]

23 There is profit in all hard work,
but endless talk[G] leads only
to poverty.[s]

24 The crown of the wise is their wealth,
but the foolishness of fools
produces foolishness.

25 A truthful witness rescues lives,
but one who utters lies is deceitful.[t]

26 In the fear of the LORD one has
strong confidence
and his children have a refuge.[u]

27 The fear of the LORD is a fountain
of life,
turning people away from the snares
of death.[v]

28 A large population is
a king's splendor,
but a shortage of people is
a ruler's devastation.

29 A patient person shows great
understanding,[w]
but a quick-tempered one
promotes foolishness.

[A]**14:3** Some emend to *In the mouth of a fool is a rod for his back* [B]**14:4** Or *clean* [C]**14:9** Or *at guilt offerings* [D]**14:11** Lit *flourish* [E]**14:15** Lit *the prudent understand* [F]**14:16** Or *and falls* [G]**14:23** Lit *but word of lips*

30 A tranquil heart is life to the body,[a]
but jealousy is rottenness to the bones.[b]

31 The one who oppresses the poor person
insults his Maker,[c]
but one who is kind to the needy
honors Him.[d]

32 The wicked one is thrown down
by his own sin,[e]
but the righteous one has a refuge
in his death.[f]

33 Wisdom resides in the heart
of the discerning;[g]
she is known[A] even among fools.

34 Righteousness exalts a nation,
but sin is a disgrace to any people.[h]

35 A king favors a wise servant,[i]
but his anger falls on a disgraceful one.

15 A gentle answer turns away anger,[j]
but a harsh word stirs up wrath.[k]

2 The tongue of the wise
makes knowledge attractive,
but the mouth of fools
blurts out foolishness.[l]

3 The eyes of the LORD are everywhere,
observing the wicked and the good.[m]

4 The tongue that heals is a tree of life,[n]
but a devious tongue[B] breaks the spirit.

5 A fool despises his father's discipline,
but a person who accepts correction
is sensible.[o]

6 The house of the righteous
has great wealth,
but trouble accompanies the income
of the wicked.

7 The lips of the wise
broadcast knowledge,
but not so the heart of fools.

8 The sacrifice of the wicked is detestable
to the LORD,[p]
but the prayer of the upright is
His delight.[q]

9 The LORD detests the way of the wicked,
but He loves the one
who pursues righteousness.[r]

10 Discipline is harsh for the one
who leaves the path;
the one who hates correction will die.

11 ·Sheol and ·Abaddon lie open
before the LORD[s]—
how much more, human hearts.[t]

12 A mocker doesn't love one
who corrects him;[u]
he will not consult the wise.

13 A joyful heart makes a face cheerful,
but a sad heart produces
a broken spirit.[v]

14 A discerning mind seeks knowledge,[w]
but the mouth of fools feeds
on foolishness.[x]

15 All the days of the oppressed
are miserable,
but a cheerful heart has
a continual feast.

16 Better a little with the ·fear
of the LORD
than great treasure with turmoil.[y]

17 Better a meal of vegetables
where there is love
than a fattened ox[z] with hatred.[aa]

18 A hot-tempered man stirs up conflict,[ab]
but a man slow to anger[ac] calms strife.

19 A slacker's way is like a thorny hedge,
but the path of the upright is
a highway.[ad]

20 A wise son brings joy to his father,
but a foolish man despises his mother.[ae]

21 Foolishness brings joy to one
without sense,
but a man with understanding walks
a straight path.[af]

22 Plans fail when there is no counsel,
but with many advisers they succeed.[ag]

23 A man takes joy in giving an answer;[C]
and a timely word — how good that is![ah]

24 For the discerning the path of life
leads upward,
so that he may avoid going down
to Sheol.

[a]**14:30** Pr 3:8; 4:22; 16:24 [b]Pr 12:4; 27:4; Jms 3:16 [c]**14:31** Pr 17:5; 21:13; Mt 25:40; 1Jn 3:17 [d]Pr 3:9; 14:21; 19:17; 22:2 [e]**14:32** Ps 17:15; 73:24; Pr 24:16; 2Co 1:9; 5:8; 2Tm 4:18 [f]Pr 10:25 [g]**14:33** Pr 15:14; 18:15; Ec 7:9 [h]**14:34** Pr 11:11 [i]**14:35** Pr 22:29; Mt 24:45-47; 25:21 [j]**15:1** Jdg 8:1-3; Pr 25:15; Ec 10:4 [k]1Sm 25:10-13; 1Kg 12:13-16 [l]**15:2** Pr 12:23; 13:16; 15:28 [m]**15:3** 2Ch 16:9; Jb 31:4; Zch 4:10; Heb 4:13 [n]**15:4** Pr 11:30; 13:12 [o]**15:5** Pr 3:11; 12:1; 15:31-33 [p]**15:8** Pr 21:27; 28:9; Ec 5:1; Is 1:11; Jr 6:20; Mc 6:7 [q]Pr 15:29 [r]**15:9** Pr 3:32; 11:20; 12:22; 1Tm 6:11 [s]**15:11** Jb 26:6; Ps 139:8 [t]1Sm 16:7; 2Ch 6:30; Ps 44:21; Ac 1:24 [u]**15:12** Pr 9:8; Am 5:10 [v]**15:13** Pr 12:25; 14:30; 15:30; 17:22; 18:14 [w]**15:14** Pr 14:33; 18:15 [x]Mt 12:34 [y]**15:16** Ps 37:16; Pr 16:8; Ec 4:6; 1Tm 6:6 [z]**15:17** Mt 22:4; Lk 15:23 [aa]Pr 16:19; 17:1 [ab]**15:18** Pr 16:28; 26:21; 29:22 [ac]Pr 14:29 [ad]**15:19** Pr 16:17,31; 22:5-6 [ae]**15:20** Pr 10:1; 23:24-25; 29:3,15 [af]**15:21** Pr 4:11,25; 10:23; Eph 5:15 [ag]**15:22** Pr 8:14-16; 11:14; 24:6 [ah]**15:23** Pr 25:11; Is 50:4

[A]**14:33** LXX reads *unknown* [B]**15:4** Lit *but crookedness in it* [C]**15:23** Lit *in an answer of his mouth*

25 The LORD destroys the house
of the proud,
but He protects the widow's territory.[a]

26 The LORD detests the plans
of an evil man,
but pleasant words are pure.[b]

27 The one who profits dishonestly[c]
troubles his household,
but the one who hates bribes will live.[d]

28 The mind of the righteous person
thinks before answering,[e]
but the mouth of the wicked blurts out
evil things.[f]

29 The LORD is far from the wicked,[g]
but He hears the prayer
of the righteous.[h]

30 Bright eyes cheer the heart;
good news strengthens[A] the bones.[i]

31 One who[B] listens to life-giving rebukes[j]
will be at home among the wise.

32 Anyone who ignores discipline
despises himself,[k]
but whoever listens to correction
acquires good sense.[C,l]

33 The fear of the LORD is what
wisdom teaches,
and humility comes before honor.[m]

16 The reflections of the heart
belong to man,
but the answer of the tongue is
from the LORD.[n]

2 All a man's ways seem right to him,
but the LORD evaluates the motives.[D,o]

3 Commit your activities to the LORD,
and your plans will be achieved.[p]

4 The LORD has prepared everything
for His purpose—
even the wicked for the day of disaster.[q]

5 Everyone with a proud heart is
detestable to the LORD;[r]
be assured,[E] he will not go unpunished.[s]

6 Wickedness is ·atoned for by loyalty
and faithfulness,[t]
and one turns from evil by the ·fear
of the LORD.[u]

7 When a man's ways please the LORD,
He[F] makes even his enemies to be
at peace with him.[v]

8 Better a little with righteousness
than great income with injustice.[w]

9 A man's heart plans his way,
but the LORD determines his steps.[x]

10 God's verdict is on the lips of a king;[G,y]
his mouth should not give
an unfair judgment.[z]

11 Honest balances and scales are
the LORD's;
all the weights in the bag[H] are
His concern.[aa]

12 Wicked behavior[I] is detestable
to kings,[ab]
since a throne is established
through righteousness.[ac]

13 Righteous lips are a king's delight,
and he loves one who speaks honestly.

14 A king's fury is a messenger of death,
but a wise man appeases it.[ad]

15 When a king's face lights up,
there is life;
his favor is like a cloud with spring rain.

16 Get wisdom—
how much better it is than gold!
And get understanding—
it is preferable to silver.[ae]

17 The highway of the upright[af]
avoids evil;
the one who guards his way protects
his life.[ag]

18 Pride comes before destruction,
and an arrogant spirit before a fall.[ah]

19 Better to be lowly of spirit
with the humble[J,ai]
than to divide plunder with the proud.[aj]

20 The one who understands a matter
finds success,[ak]

[a]**15:25** Ps 68:5; 146:9 [b]**15:26** Pr 11:20; 15:8-9; 16:24 [c]**15:27** Pr 1:19; Jr 17:11 [d]Ex 23:8; Dt 16:19; Ps 15:5; Pr 17:23; 28:16 [e]**15:28** Pr 18:13; 1Pt 3:15 [f]Pr 15:2 [g]**15:29** Ps 18:41; Pr 28:9 [h]Ps 145:18-19; Pr 15:8 [i]**15:30** Pr 14:30; 15:13; 17:22 [j]**15:31** Pr 3:11 [k]**15:32** Pr 12:1 [l]Pr 3:11; 5:12-14 [m]**15:33** Pr 18:12; 22:4; 29:23 [n]**16:1** Pr 16:9; 19:21 [o]**16:2** 1Sm 16:7; Pr 17:3; 19:21; 21:2 [p]**16:3** Ps 37:4-5 [q]**16:4** Ex 9:16; Rm 9:21-22 [r]**16:5** 2Ch 32:25; Pr 6:16-17; 8:13 [s]Ps 101:5; Pr 11:21; 16:18 [t]**16:6** Dn 4:27; Lk 11:41 [u]Jb 28:28; Pr 3:7; 14:16 [v]**16:7** 2Ch 17:10 [w]**16:8** Ps 37:16; Pr 15:16-17; 16:19; 28:6 [x]**16:9** Ps 37:23; Pr 16:1; 19:21; 20:24; Jr 10:23 [y]**16:10** 2Sm 14:17,20; 1Kg 3:28 [z]2Sm 23:2-3; Pr 18:14-15 [aa]**16:11** Lv 19:36; Pr 11:1; Ezk 45:10; Mc 6:11 [ab]**16:12** Pr 31:3-5 [ac]Ps 101; Pr 25:5 [ad]**16:14** Ec 10:4 [ae]**16:16** Pr 3:14; 8:10,19; 22:1 [af]**16:17** Is 35:8 [ag]Pr 2:11-13; 15:19 [ah]**16:18** Pr 11:2; 16:5; 18:12; 29:23; Dn 4:37; Ob 3-4 [ai]**16:19** Pr 29:23; Is 57:15 [aj]Ex 15:9; Ps 37:16; Pr 1:13-14; 15:16-17; 16:8 [ak]**16:20** Pr 19:8

[A]**15:30** Lit *makes fat* [B]**15:31** Lit *An ear that* [C]**15:32** Lit *acquires a heart* [D]**16:2** Lit *weighs spirits* [E]**16:5** Lit *hand to hand* [F]**16:7** Or *he* [G]**16:10** Or *A divination is on the lips of a king* [H]**16:11** Merchants kept the stones for their scales in a bag. [I]**16:12** Either the king's or someone else's behavior [J]**16:19** Alt Hb tradition reads *afflicted*

and the one who trusts in the LORD
will be happy.[a]

21 Anyone with a wise heart
is called discerning,
and pleasant speech[A]
increases learning.[b]

22 Insight is a fountain of life[c]
for its possessor,
but the discipline of fools is folly.

23 A wise heart instructs its mouth
and increases learning
with its speech.[B,d]

24 Pleasant words are a honeycomb:[e]
sweet to the taste[C] and health
to the body.[D,f]

25 There is a way that seems right
to a man,
but its end is the way to death.[g]

26 A worker's appetite works for him
because his hunger[E] urges him on.

27 A worthless man digs up evil,
and his speech is like a scorching fire.[h]

28 A contrary man spreads conflict,
and a gossip separates close friends.[i]

29 A violent man lures his neighbor,[j]
leading him in a way that is not good.[k]

30 The one who narrows his eyes
is planning deceptions;
the one who compresses his lips
brings about evil.[l]

31 Gray hair is a glorious crown;[m]
it is found in the way
of righteousness.[n]

32 Patience is better than power,
and controlling one's temper,[F]
than capturing a city.[o]

33 The lot is cast into the lap,
but its every decision is from the LORD.[p]

17 Better a dry crust with peace
than a house full of feasting
with strife.[q]

2 A wise servant will rule over
a disgraceful son

[a]**16:20** Ps 2:12; 34:8; 40:4; 84:12; 146:5; Jr 17:7
[b]**16:21** Pr 1:5; 9:9; 16:23
[c]**16:22** Pr 10:11; 13:14; 14:27
[d]**16:23** Ps 37:30; Pr 1:5; 9:9; Mt 12:34
[e]**16:24** Ps 19:10; Pr 15:26
[f]Pr 4:22; 15:30; 25:13
[g]**16:25** Pr 14:12; 24:20
[h]**16:27** Pr 6:12; 19:28; 26:23; Jms 3:6
[i]**16:28** Pr 6:14,19; 17:9; 26:20-21; 28:25
[j]**16:29** Pr 1:10
[k]1Sm 12:23; Ps 36:4; Pr 28:10
[l]**16:30** Ps 35:19; Pr 6:12-14; 10:10
[m]**16:31** Lv 19:32; Pr 4:9; 20:29
[n]Pr 3:1-2
[o]**16:32** Pr 25:15,28; 29:11
[p]**16:33** Pr 16:1; 19:21; 21:31
[q]**17:1** Pr 15:17; 21:9,19; 25:24
[r]**17:3** Pr 27:21
[s]1Ch 29:17; Ps 26:2; Pr 16:2; 21:2; Is 48:10; Jr 17:10; Mal 3:3
[t]**17:5** Pr 14:31; 21:13
[u]Jb 31:29; Pr 24:17; Lm 1:21-22; Ezk 25:6-7; 35:15; Ob 12
[v]**17:8** Ex 23:8; Is 1:23; Am 5:12
[w]Pr 18:16; 19:6; 21:14
[x]**17:9** Pr 10:12; Jms 5:20; 1Pt 4:8
[y]Lv 19:16; Pr 11:13; 16:28
[z]**17:11** Ps 78:49
[aa]**17:12** 2Sm 17:8; Hs 13:8
[ab]**17:13** Ps 35:12; 109:5
[ac]2Sm 12:10
[ad]**17:14** Pr 20:3; 25:8
[ae]**17:15** Ex 23:7; Pr 17:26; 18:5; 24:23-24; Is 5:23
[af]**17:16** Pr 4:5,7; 18:15; 23:23

and share an inheritance
among brothers.

3 A crucible for silver, and a smelter
for gold,[r]
and the LORD is the tester of hearts.[s]

4 A wicked person listens to
malicious talk;[G]
a liar pays attention to
a destructive tongue.

5 The one who mocks the poor insults
his Maker,[t]
and one who rejoices over calamity
will not go unpunished.[u]

6 Grandchildren are the crown
of the elderly,
and the pride of sons is their fathers.

7 Eloquent words are not appropriate
on a fool's lips;
how much worse are lies for a ruler.

8 A bribe[v] seems like a magic stone
to its owner;
wherever he turns, he succeeds.[w]

9 Whoever conceals an offense
promotes love,[x]
but whoever gossips about it
separates friends.[y]

10 A rebuke cuts into a perceptive person
more than a hundred lashes into a fool.

11 An evil man seeks only rebellion;
a cruel messenger[H,z] will be sent
against him.

12 Better for a man to meet a bear robbed
of her cubs[aa]
than a fool in his foolishness.

13 If anyone returns evil for good,[ab]
evil will never depart from his house.[ac]

14 To start a conflict is to release a flood;
stop the dispute before it breaks out.[ad]

15 Acquitting the ˈguilty and condemning
the just[ae] —
both are detestable to the LORD.

16 Why does a fool have money in his hand
with no intention of buying wisdom?[af]

[A]**16:21** Lit *and sweetness of lips* [B]**16:23** Lit *learning upon his lips* [C]**16:24** Lit *throat* [D]**16:24** Lit *bones* [E]**16:26** Lit *mouth* [F]**16:32** Lit *and ruling over one's spirit* [G]**17:4** Lit *to lips of iniquity* [H]**17:11** Or *a merciless angel*

17 A friend loves at all times,[a]
and a brother is born for
a difficult time.

18 One without sense enters
an agreement[A]
and puts up security for his friend.[b]

19 One who loves to offend loves strife;[c]
one who builds a high threshold
invites injury.

20 One with a twisted mind
will not succeed,
and one with deceitful speech will fall
into ruin.[d]

21 A man fathers a fool
to his own sorrow;
the father of a fool has no joy.[e]

22 A joyful heart is good medicine,
but a broken spirit dries up
the bones.[f]

23 A wicked man secretly takes a bribe[g]
to subvert the course of justice.[h]

24 Wisdom is the focus of the perceptive,
but a fool's eyes[i] roam to the ends
of the earth.

25 A foolish son is grief to his father
and bitterness to the one
who bore him.[j]

26 It is certainly not good to fine
an innocent person
or to beat a noble for his honesty.[B,k]

27 The intelligent person restrains
his words,[l]
and one who keeps a cool head[C]
is a man of understanding.

28 Even a fool is considered wise
when he keeps silent,
discerning when he seals his lips.[m]

18

One who isolates himself pursues
selfish desires;
he rebels against all sound judgment.

2 A fool does not delight
in understanding,
but only wants to show off
his opinions.[D,n]

3 When a wicked man comes,
contempt also does,
and along with dishonor, disgrace.

4 The words of a man's mouth
are deep waters,[o]
a flowing river, a fountain of wisdom.[E]

5 It is not good to show partiality
to the ·guilty[p]
by perverting the justice
due the innocent.[q]

6 A fool's lips lead to strife,
and his mouth provokes a beating.[r]

7 A fool's mouth is his devastation,
and his lips are a trap for his life.[s]

8 A gossip's words are like choice food
that goes down
to one's innermost being.[F,t]

9 The one who is truly lazy in his work
is brother to a vandal.[G,u]

10 The name of ·Yahweh is a strong tower;[v]
the righteous run to it
and are protected.[H,w]

11 A rich man's wealth is his fortified city;
in his imagination it is like a high wall.[x]

12 Before his downfall a man's heart
is proud,[y]
but humility comes before honor.[z]

13 The one who gives an answer
before he listens —
this is foolishness and disgrace
for him.[aa]

14 A man's spirit can endure sickness,
but who can survive a broken spirit?[ab]

15 The mind of the discerning
acquires knowledge,
and the ear of the wise seeks it.[ac]

16 A gift opens doors[I] for a man
and brings him before the great.[ad]

17 The first to state his case seems right
until another comes
and cross-examines him.[ae]

18 Casting the lot[af] ends quarrels
and separates powerful opponents.

[a]**17:17** Ru 1:16; Pr 18:24; 27:10
[b]**17:18** Pr 6:1-5; 11:15; 22:26
[c]**17:19** Pr 29:22
[d]**17:20** Jr 23:36
[e]**17:21** Pr 10:1; 17:25; 19:13; 23:24-25
[f]**17:22** Ps 22:15; Pr 14:30; 15:13; 18:14
[g]**17:23** Pr 17:8
[h]Dt 16:19; Ps 15:5; Pr 18:5; Mc 3:11; 7:3
[i]**17:24** Ec 2:14
[j]**17:25** Pr 10:1; 17:21; 19:13
[k]**17:26** Pr 17:15; 18:5; 24:23-24
[l]**17:27** Pr 10:19; Jms 1:19; 3:2
[m]**17:28** Jb 13:5; Pr 10:19
[n]**18:2** Pr 12:23; 13:16; Ec 10:3
[o]**18:4** Pr 20:5
[p]**18:5** Lv 19:15; Dt 1:17; 24:17; Ps 15:5; 82:2; Pr 24:23-24; 28:21
[q]Pr 17:15
[r]**18:6** Pr 19:29
[s]**18:7** Ps 64:8; 140:9; Pr 10:14; 12:13; 13:3; Ec 10:12
[t]**18:8** Pr 26:22
[u]**18:9** Pr 28:24
[v]**18:10** Ps 18:2; 61:3; 91:2; 144:2
[w]Pr 29:25
[x]**18:11** Pr 10:15
[y]**18:12** Pr 16:18
[z]Pr 11:2; 15:33; 29:23
[aa]**18:13** Pr 15:28
[ab]**18:14** Pr 15:13; 17:22
[ac]**18:15** Pr 14:33; 15:14
[ad]**18:16** Gn 32:20; 1Sm 25:27; Pr 17:8; 19:6; 21:14
[ae]**18:17** 1Kg 3:16-28
[af]**18:18** Pr 16:33

[A]**17:18** Lit *sense shakes hands* [B]**17:26** Or *noble unfairly* [C]**17:27** Lit *spirit* [D]**18:2** Lit *to uncover his heart* [E]**18:4** Or *waters; a fountain of wisdom is a flowing river.* [F]**18:8** Lit *to the chambers of the belly* [G]**18:9** Lit *master of destruction* [H]**18:10** Lit *raised high* [I]**18:16** Lit *gift makes room*

19 An offended brother is harder to reach[A]
than a fortified city,
and quarrels are like the bars
of a fortress.

20 From the fruit of his mouth
a man's stomach is satisfied;
he is filled with the product of his lips.[a]

21 Life and death are in the power
of the tongue,
and those who love it will eat its fruit.[b]

22 A man who finds a wife finds
a good thing[c]
and obtains favor from the LORD.[d]

23 The poor man pleads,[e]
but the rich one answers roughly.[f]

24 A man with many friends
may be harmed,[B]
but there is a friend who stays closer
than a brother.[g]

19 Better a poor man who lives
with integrity[h]
than someone who has deceitful lips
and is a fool.

2 Even zeal is not good
without knowledge,[i]
and the one who acts hastily[C] sins.[j]

3 A man's own foolishness leads
him astray,
yet his heart rages against the LORD.[k]

4 Wealth attracts many friends,[l]
but a poor man is separated
from his friend.

5 A false witness will not
go unpunished,[m]
and one who utters lies
will not escape.[n]

6 Many seek a ruler's favor,[o]
and everyone is a friend of one
who gives gifts.[p]

7 All the brothers of a poor man hate him;[q]
how much more do his friends
keep their distance from him!
He may pursue them with words,[r]
but they are not there.[D]

8 The one who acquires good sense[E]
loves himself;
one who safeguards understanding
finds success.[s]

9 A false witness will not go unpunished,
and one who utters lies perishes.[t]

10 Luxury is not appropriate for a fool[u]—
how much less for a slave to rule
over princes![v]

11 A person's insight gives him patience,[w]
and his virtue is to overlook an offense.[x]

12 A king's rage is like the roaring
of a lion,[y]
but his favor is like dew on the grass.[z]

13 A foolish son is his father's ruin,[aa]
and a wife's nagging is
an endless dripping.[ab]

14 A house and wealth are inherited
from fathers,[ac]
but a sensible wife is from the LORD.

15 Laziness induces deep sleep,
and a lazy person will go hungry.[ad]

16 The one who keeps commands
preserves himself;[ae]
one who disregards[F] his ways will die.[af]

17 Kindness to the poor is a loan
to the LORD,[ag]
and He will give a reward
to the lender.[G,ah]

18 Discipline your son while there is hope;
don't be intent on killing him.[H,ai]

19 A person with great anger bears
the penalty;
if you rescue him, you'll have to do
it again.[aj]

20 Listen to counsel
and receive instruction
so that you may be wise later in life.[I,ak]

21 Many plans are in a man's heart,
but the LORD's decree will prevail.[al]

22 What is desirable in a man is
his fidelity;
better to be a poor man than a liar.[am]

[a] **18:20** Pr 1:31; 12:14; 14:14 [b] **18:21** Pr 13:2; Mt 12:37; 15:11,18-20; Jms 3:8 [c] **18:22** Pr 12:4; 19:14; 31:10-31 [d] Pr 8:35 [e] **18:23** Pr 19:7 [f] Jms 2:6 [g] **18:24** Pr 17:17; 27:10; Jn 15:13 [h] **19:1** Ps 26:11; 37:16; Pr 10:9; 14:2; 20:7; 28:6 [i] **19:2** Rm 10:2 [j] Pr 21:5; 28:20; 29:20 [k] **19:3** Is 8:21 [l] **19:4** Pr 14:20; 19:6 [m] **19:5** Dt 19:16-19; Pr 19:9; 21:28 [n] Pr 6:19 [o] **19:6** Pr 29:26 [p] Pr 14:20; 17:8; 19:4 [q] **19:7** Ps 38:11 [r] Pr 18:23 [s] **19:8** Pr 16:20 [t] **19:9** Pr 19:5; 21:28 [u] **19:10** Pr 17:7; 26:1 [v] Pr 30:22; Ec 10:6-7 [w] **19:11** Pr 14:29 [x] Pr 11:13; 17:9 [y] **19:12** Pr 16:14 [z] Ps 133:3; Pr 20:2; 28:15; Hs 14:5; Mc 5:7 [aa] **19:13** Pr 10:1; 17:25; 28:7 [ab] Pr 21:9,19; 27:15 [ac] **19:14** 2Co 12:14 [ad] **19:15** Pr 6:9-11; 10:4; 13:4; 21:25 [ae] **19:16** Lk 10:28 [af] Pr 3:1-2; 4:4; 13:13 [ag] **19:17** Dt 15:7-10; Pr 14:31; 28:27; Ec 11:1-2; Mt 10:42; 25:40; 2Co 9:6-8; Heb 6:10 [ah] Lk 6:38 [ai] **19:18** Pr 13:24; 23:13-14; 29:17 [aj] **19:19** Pr 22:24-25; 29:22 [ak] **19:20** Pr 12:1; 15:5,31-32 [al] **19:21** Ps 33:10-11; Pr 16:1,9,33; 21:31; Is 14:26-27 [am] **19:22** Pr 19:1; 28:6

[A] **18:19** LXX, Syr, Tg, Vg read *is stronger* [B] **18:24** Some LXX mss, Syr, Tg, Vg read *friends must be friendly* [C] **19:2** Lit *who is hasty with feet* [D] **19:7** Hb uncertain [E] **19:8** Lit *acquires a heart* [F] **19:16** Or *despises*, or *treats lightly* [G] **19:17** Lit *to him* [H] **19:18** Lit *don't lift up your soul to his death* [I] **19:20** Lit *in your end*

23 The ·fear of the LORD leads to life;
one will sleep at night[A] without danger.[a]

24 The slacker buries his hand in the bowl;
he doesn't even bring it back
to his mouth.[b]

25 Strike a mocker, and the inexperienced
learn a lesson;[c]
rebuke the discerning,
and he gains knowledge.[d]

26 The one who assaults his father
and evicts his mother
is a disgraceful and shameful son.

27 If you stop listening to correction,
my son,
you will stray from the words
of knowledge.

28 A worthless witness mocks justice,
and a wicked mouth swallows iniquity.[e]

29 Judgments are prepared for mockers,
and beatings for the backs of fools.[f]

20 Wine is a mocker,[g] beer is a brawler,
and whoever staggers
because of them is not wise.

2 A king's terrible wrath is
like the roaring of a lion;
anyone who provokes him
endangers himself.[h]

3 It is honorable for a man to resolve
a dispute,[i]
but any fool can get himself
into a quarrel.[j]

4 The slacker does not plow
during planting season;[B]
at harvest time he looks,[C] and there is
nothing.[k]

5 Counsel in a man's heart is deep water;[l]
but a man of understanding
draws it out.

6 Many a man proclaims his own loyalty,
but who can find a trustworthy man?[m]

7 The one who lives with integrity
is righteous;[n]
his children[D] who come after him
will be happy.[o]

[a]**19:23** Pr 14:26-27
[b]**19:24** Pr 12:27; 20:4; 26:14-15
[c]**19:25** Pr 21:11
[d]Pr 9:8
[e]**19:28** Jb 15:16; 34:7
[f]**19:29** Pr 10:13; 18:6; 26:3
[g]**20:1** Gn 9:21; Pr 23:29-30; Is 28:7; Hs 4:11
[h]**20:2** Nm 16:38; Est 4:11; Pr 8:36; 19:12; 28:15; Hab 2:10
[i]**20:3** Pr 17:14
[j]Pr 15:18; 18:6; 22:10
[k]**20:4** Pr 24:27,30-34
[l]**20:5** Pr 18:4
[m]**20:6** Ps 53:2-3; Pr 28:20; Ec 7:28; Lk 18:8
[n]**20:7** Pr 2:7,20-21; 10:9; 13:6
[o]Ps 37:26; 112:2
[p]**20:8** Pr 20:26; 25:5; Mt 25:32
[q]**20:9** 1Kg 8:46; Jb 15:15-16; Ps 14:2-3; Ec 7:20; Rm 3:9-12; 1Jn 1:8
[r]**20:10** Dt 25:14-15; Pr 11:1; 20:23; Mc 6:10-11
[s]**20:11** Pr 21:8; Mt 7:16
[t]**20:12** Ex 4:11; Ps 94:9; Pr 22:2; 29:13
[u]**20:13** Pr 6:10-11; 19:15; 24:33-34
[v]**20:15** Pr 3:15; 8:11
[w]**20:16** Dt 24:12-13; Pr 6:1-5; 11:15; 27:13
[x]**20:17** Pr 9:17
[y]**20:18** Pr 11:14; 15:22
[z]Pr 24:6; Lk 14:31
[aa]**20:19** Lv 19:16; Pr 11:13
[ab]Pr 13:3
[ac]**20:20** Ex 21:17; Pr 24:20; 30:11
[ad]Jb 18:5
[ae]**20:21** Pr 21:5; 23:5; 28:22; Lk 15:11-13
[af]**20:22** Pr 24:29; Mt 5:39; Rm 12:17,19; 1Th 5:15; 1Pt 3:9
[ag]Ps 27:14
[ah]Ps 37:7-9

8 A king sitting on a throne to judge
sifts out all evil with his eyes.[p]

9 Who can say, "I have kept
my heart pure;
I am cleansed from my sin"?[q]

10 Differing weights
and varying measures[E] —
both are detestable to the LORD.[r]

11 Even a young man is known
by his actions —
if his behavior is pure and upright.[s]

12 The hearing ear and the seeing eye —
the LORD made them both.[t]

13 Don't love sleep, or you will
become poor;
open your eyes, and you'll have
enough to eat.[u]

14 "It's worthless, it's worthless!"
the buyer says,
but after he is on his way, he gloats.

15 There is gold and a multitude of jewels,
but knowledgeable lips are
a rare treasure.[v]

16 Take his garment,[F]
for he has put up security
for a stranger;
get collateral if it is for foreigners.[w]

17 Food gained by fraud is sweet to a man,[x]
but afterward his mouth is full of gravel.

18 Finalize plans with counsel,[y]
and wage war with sound guidance.[z]

19 The one who reveals secrets is
a constant gossip;[aa]
avoid someone with a big mouth.[ab]

20 Whoever curses his father
or mother[ac] —
his lamp will go out in deep darkness.[ad]

21 An inheritance gained prematurely
will not be blessed ultimately.[ae]

22 Don't say, "I will avenge this evil!"[af]
Wait on the LORD,[ag] and He will
rescue you.[ah]

[A]**19:23** Lit *will spend the night satisfied* [B]**20:4** Lit *plow in winter* [C]**20:4** Lit *inquires* [D]**20:7** Lit *sons* [E]**20:10** Lit *Stone and stone, measure and measure*

[F]**20:16** A debtor's outer garment was held as collateral.

23 Differing weights[A] are detestable
to the LORD,[a]
and dishonest scales[b] are unfair.

24 A man's steps are determined
by the LORD,[c]
so how can anyone understand
his own way?

25 It is a trap for anyone to dedicate
something rashly
and later to reconsider his vows.[d]

26 A wise king separates out the wicked[e]
and drives the threshing wheel[f]
over them.

27 The LORD's lamp sheds light on
a person's life,[B]
searching the innermost parts.[C,g]

28 Loyalty and faithfulness deliver a king;
through loyalty he maintains
his throne.

29 The glory of young men is
their strength,
and the splendor of old men is
gray hair.[h]

30 Lashes and wounds purge away evil,[i]
and beatings cleanse
the innermost parts.[D]

21 A king's heart is like streams of water
in the LORD's hand:
He directs it wherever He chooses.[j]

2 All a man's ways seem right to him,
but the LORD evaluates the motives.[E,k]

3 Doing what is righteous and just
is more acceptable to the LORD
than sacrifice.[l]

4 The lamp[F] that guides the wicked—
haughty eyes
and an arrogant heart[m]—is sin.

5 The plans of the diligent certainly lead
to profit,
but anyone who is reckless
certainly becomes poor.[n]

6 Making a fortune
through a lying tongue
is a vanishing mist,[G] a pursuit
of death.[H,I,o]

7 The violence of the wicked
sweeps them away
because they refuse to act justly.

8 A ·guilty man's conduct is crooked,[p]
but the behavior of the innocent
is upright.[q]

9 Better to live on the corner of a roof
than to share a house
with a nagging wife.[r]

10 A wicked person desires evil;
he has no consideration[J]
for his neighbor.[s]

11 When a mocker is punished,
the inexperienced become wiser;
when one teaches a wise man,
he acquires knowledge.[t]

12 The Righteous One considers the house
of the wicked;
He brings the wicked to ruin.

13 The one who shuts his ears to the cry
of the poor
will himself also call out
and not be answered.[u]

14 A secret gift soothes anger,
and a covert bribe,[K] fierce rage.[v]

15 Justice executed is a joy
to the righteous
but a terror to those
who practice iniquity.[w]

16 The man who strays from the way
of wisdom
will come to rest
in the assembly
of the departed spirits.[x]

17 The one who loves pleasure
will become a poor man;
whoever loves wine and oil will not
get rich.[y]

18 The wicked are a ransom
for the righteous,
and the treacherous, for[L] the upright.[z]

[a]**20:23** Pr 20:10; Mc 6:11 [b]Pr 11:1 [c]**20:24** Pr 16:9,33; 19:21 [d]**20:25** Nm 30:2; Dt 23:21; Ec 5:4-6 [e]**20:26** Pr 20:8 [f]Is 28:27 [g]**20:27** Ps 139:23; Pr 20:30; 1Co 2:11 [h]**20:29** Lv 19:32; Pr 16:31 [i]**20:30** Is 53:5 [j]**21:1** Ezr 6:22 [k]**21:2** Pr 12:15; 16:2; 17:3; 24:12; Lk 16:15 [l]**21:3** 1Sm 15:22; Pr 15:8; Hs 6:6; Mc 6:7-8; Mt 9:13 [m]**21:4** Ps 101:5; Pr 6:16-17; 30:13 [n]**21:5** Pr 10:4; 14:23; 21:20; 28:22 [o]**21:6** Pr 8:36; 13:11; 20:21 [p]**21:8** Pr 2:15 [q]Pr 20:11 [r]**21:9** Pr 15:16-17; 17:1; 21:19; 25:24 [s]**21:10** Pr 14:21 [t]**21:11** Pr 19:25 [u]**21:13** Pr 14:31; 17:5; Mt 18:30-34; Jms 2:13; 1Jn 3:17 [v]**21:14** Pr 17:8; 18:16; 19:6 [w]**21:15** Pr 10:29; Rm 13:13 [x]**21:16** Ps 49:14; Pr 2:18; 9:18 [y]**21:17** Ec 2:1-3,10-11 [z]**21:18** Pr 11:8; Is 43:3

[A]**20:23** Lit *A stone and a stone* [B]**20:27** Lit *breath* [C]**20:27** Lit *the chambers of the belly* [D]**20:30** Lit *beatings the chambers of the belly* [E]**21:2** Lit *LORD weighs the hearts* [F]**21:4** Some Hb mss, ancient versions read *tillage* [G]**21:6** Or *a breath blown away* [H]**21:6** Some Hb mss, LXX, Vg read *a snare of death* [I]**21:6** Lit *is vanity, ones seeking death* [J]**21:10** Or *favor* [K]**21:14** Lit *a bribe in the bosom* [L]**21:18** Or *in place of*

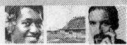

19 Better to live in a wilderness
than with a nagging
and hot-tempered wife.[a]

20 Precious treasure and oil are
in the dwelling of a wise person,
but a foolish man consumes them.[A,b]

21 The one who pursues righteousness
and faithful love
will find life, righteousness, and honor.[c]

22 A wise person went up against a city
of warriors
and brought down its secure fortress.[d]

23 The one who guards his mouth
and tongue
keeps himself out of trouble.[e]

24 The proud and arrogant person,
named "Mocker,"
acts with excessive pride.[f]

25 A slacker's craving will kill him
because his hands refuse to work.[g]

26 He is filled with craving[B] all day long,
but the righteous give and don't
hold back.[h]

27 The sacrifice of a wicked person
is detestable —
how much more so
when he brings it
with ulterior motives![i]

28 A lying witness will perish,[j]
but the one who listens
will speak successfully.

29 A wicked man puts on a bold face,[k]
but the upright man considers his way.

30 No wisdom, no understanding,
and no counsel
will prevail against the LORD.[l]

31 A horse is prepared for the day of battle,[m]
but victory comes from the LORD.[n]

22 A good name is to be chosen
over great wealth;
favor is better than silver and gold.[o]

2 The rich and the poor have this
in common:[C]
the LORD made them both.[D,p]

3 A sensible person sees danger
and takes cover,
but the inexperienced keep going
and are punished.[q]

4 The result of humility is ·fear
of the LORD,
along with wealth, honor, and life.[r]

5 There are thorns and snares
on the path of the crooked;[s]
the one who guards himself stays
far from them.

6 Teach a youth about the way
he should go;[t]
even when he is old he will not depart
from it.

7 The rich rule over the poor,[u]
and the borrower is a slave
to the lender.[v]

8 The one who sows injustice
will reap disaster,[w]
and the rod of his fury
will be destroyed.

9 A generous person[E] will be blessed,[x]
for he shares his food with the poor.[y]

10 Drive out a mocker,[z] and conflict
goes too;
then quarreling and dishonor
will cease.[aa]

11 The one who loves a pure heart
and gracious lips — the king is
his friend.[ab]

12 The LORD's eyes keep watch
over knowledge,
but He overthrows the words
of the treacherous.

13 The slacker says, "There's a lion outside!
I'll be killed in the public square!"[ac]

14 The mouth of the forbidden woman is
a deep pit;
a man cursed by the LORD will fall
into it.[ad]

15 Foolishness is tangled up in the heart
of a youth;
the rod of discipline will drive it away
from him.[ae]

[a] 21:19 Pr 21:9 [b] 21:20 Jb 20:15,18; Ps 112:3; Pr 10:4; 28:20; Mt 25:1-13 [c] 21:21 Pr 3:16; 8:18; 15:9; Mt 5:6; 6:33 [d] 21:22 2Sm 5:6-9; Pr 14:26; 24:5; Ec 7:19; 9:14-18 [e] 21:23 Pr 12:13; 13:3; Jms 3:2 [f] 21:24 Ps 1:1; Pr 1:22; 21:11 [g] 21:25 Pr 10:4; 12:24; 13:4; 19:15,24 [h] 21:26 Ps 37:26; Pr 11:24-25 [i] 21:27 Pr 15:8; 28:9; Is 66:3 [j] 21:28 Pr 19:5,9 [k] 21:29 Pr 7:13 [l] 21:30 Is 8:9-10; 1Co 3:19-20 [m] 21:31 Ps 20:7; 33:17; 108:10-13; Is 31:1 [n] Jr 3:23; 1Co 15:57 [o] 22:1 Pr 10:7; 8:10; Ec 7:1 [p] 22:2 Jb 31:13,15; Pr 29:13 [q] 22:3 Pr 14:16; 27:12; Is 26:20 [r] 22:4 Pr 15:33; 21:21; 29:23 [s] 22:5 Pr 7:23; 15:19 [t] 22:6 Eph 6:4 [u] 22:7 Pr 18:23; Jms 2:6 [v] Dt 28:12-13 [w] 22:8 Jb 4:8; Hs 10:13-14 [x] 22:9 Pr 19:17; 2Co 9:6 [y] Lk 14:13-14 [z] 22:10 Gn 21:9-10 [aa] Pr 26:20 [ab] 22:11 Pr 16:13 [ac] 22:13 Pr 26:13 [ad] 22:14 Pr 2:16-19; 7:5,21,27; 23:27-28; Ec 7:26 [ae] 22:15 Pr 13:24; 23:13-14; 29:15

[A] 21:20 Lit *it* [B] 21:26 Lit *He craves a craving* [C] 22:2 Lit *poor meet* [D] 22:2 Lit *all* [E] 22:9 Lit *Good of eye*

16 Oppressing the poor to enrich oneself,
and giving to the rich — both lead
only to poverty.[a]

Words of the Wise

17 Listen closely,[A] pay attention
to the words of the wise,[b]
and apply your mind to my knowledge.
18 For it is pleasing if you keep them
within you
and if[B] they are constantly on your lips.
19 I have instructed you today —
even you —
so that your confidence may be
in the LORD.
20 Haven't I written for you
thirty sayings[C]
about counsel and knowledge,
21 in order to teach you true
and reliable words,
so that you may give
a dependable report[D,c]
to those who sent you?[d]

22 Don't rob a poor man
because he is poor,
and don't crush the oppressed[e]
at the ·gate,[f]
23 for the LORD will take up their case[g]
and will plunder those
who plunder them.

24 Don't make friends with an angry man,[E]
and don't be a companion
of a hot-tempered man,[h]
25 or you will learn his ways[i]
and entangle yourself in a snare.

26 Don't be one of those
who enter agreements,[F]
who put up security for loans.[j]
27 If you have no money to pay,
even your bed will be taken
from under you.[k]

28 Don't move
an ancient boundary marker
that your fathers set up.[l]

29 Do you see a man skilled in his work?
He will stand in the presence of kings.
He will not stand in the presence
of unknown men.[m]

23 When you sit down to dine
with a ruler,
consider carefully what[G] is before you,
2 and put a knife to your throat
if you have a big[H] appetite;
3 don't desire his choice food,[n]
for that food is deceptive.

4 Don't wear yourself out to get rich;[o]
stop giving your attention to it.
5 As soon as your eyes fly to it,
it disappears,[p]
for it makes wings for itself
and flies like an eagle to the sky.

6 Don't eat a stingy person's bread,[I,q]
and don't desire his choice food,[r]
7 for it's like someone calculating
inwardly.[J,s]
"Eat and drink," he says to you,
but his heart is not with you.[t]
8 You will vomit the little you've eaten
and waste your pleasant words.

9 Don't speak to[K] a fool,
for he will despise the insight
of your words.[u]

10 Don't move
an ancient boundary marker,[v]
and don't encroach on the fields
of the fatherless,
11 for their Redeemer is strong,[w]
and He will take up their case
against you.[x]

12 Apply yourself to discipline
and listen to words of knowledge.

13 Don't withhold discipline
from a youth;
if you beat him with a rod,
he will not die.[y]
14 Strike him with a rod,
and you will rescue his life
from ·Sheol.[z]

15 My son, if your heart is wise,
my heart will indeed rejoice.[aa]

[a]**22:16** Pr 11:24; 22:7; 28:27 [b]**22:17** Pr 5:1 [c]**22:21** Lk 1:3-4 [d]Pr 10:26; 25:13 [e]**22:22** Ex 23:6; Jb 31:16; Zch 7:10; Mal 3:5 [f]Ru 4:11; Pr 24:7; Zch 8:16 [g]**22:23** 1Sm 25:39; Ps 12:5; 35:10; 68:5; 140:12; Pr 23:10-11; Is 3:13-15 [h]**22:24** Pr 15:18; 19:19 [i]**22:25** 1Co 15:33 [j]**22:26** Pr 6:1-5; 11:15; 17:18 [k]**22:27** Ex 22:26; Pr 20:16 [l]**22:28** Dt 19:14; 27:17; Jb 24:2; Pr 23:10; Hs 5:10 [m]**22:29** Gn 41:46; 1Kg 10:8; Pr 14:35 [n]**23:3** Gn 27:4; Pr 23:6; Dn 1:8 [o]**23:4** Pr 15:27; 28:20; Mt 6:19; 1Tm 6:9-10; Heb 13:5 [p]**23:5** Pr 27:24 [q]**23:6** Dt 15:9; Pr 28:22; Mt 6:23 [r]Pr 23:3 [s]**23:7** Mt 6:21; Lk 12:34 [t]Pr 26:24-25 [u]**23:9** Mt 7:6 [v]**23:10** Pr 22:28 [w]**23:11** Jr 50:34 [x]Pr 22:22-23 [y]**23:13** Pr 13:24; 19:18; 22:15 [z]**23:14** 1Co 5:5 [aa]**23:15** Pr 10:1; 15:20; 23:24-25; 29:3

[A]**22:17** Lit *Stretch out your ear* [B]**22:18** Or *you; let them be*, or *you, so that* [C]**22:20** Text emended; one Hb tradition reads *you previously*; alt Hb tradition reads *you excellent things*; LXX, Syr, Vg read *you three times* [D]**22:21** Lit *give dependable words* [E]**22:24** Lit *with a master of anger* [F]**22:26** Lit *who shakes hands* [G]**23:1** Or *who* [H]**23:2** Lit *you are the master of an* [I]**23:6** Lit *eat bread of an evil eye* [J]**23:7** LXX reads *it is like someone swallowing a hair in the throat* [K]**23:9** Lit *in the ears of*

16 My innermost being will cheer
when your lips say what is right.[a]
17 Don't let your heart envy sinners;[b]
instead, always ·fear the LORD.[c]
18 For then you will have a future,
and your hope will never fade.[d]
19 Listen, my son, and be wise;
keep your mind on the right course.
20 Don't associate with those who drink
too much wine[e]
or with those who gorge themselves
on meat.[f]
21 For the drunkard and the glutton
will become poor,
and grogginess will clothe them
in rags.[g]
22 Listen to your father who gave you life,
and don't despise your mother
when[A] she is old.[h]
23 Buy — and do not sell — truth,
wisdom, instruction,
and understanding.[i]
24 The father of a righteous son
will rejoice greatly,
and one who fathers a wise son
will delight in him.[j]
25 Let your father and mother have joy,[k]
and let her who gave birth to you
rejoice.
26 My son, give me your heart,
and let your eyes observe my ways.
27 For a prostitute is a deep pit,[l]
and a stranger is a narrow well;
28 indeed, she sets an ambush
like a robber[m]
and increases those among men
who are unfaithful.
29 Who has woe? Who has sorrow?
Who has conflicts?
Who has complaints?
Who has wounds for no reason?[n]
Who has red eyes?
30 Those who linger over wine,
those who go looking for mixed wine.[o]
31 Don't gaze at wine because it is red,[p]
when it gleams in the cup
and goes down smoothly.[q]
32 In the end it bites like a snake
and stings like a viper.
33 Your eyes will see strange things,
and you will say absurd things.[B,r]
34 You'll be like someone sleeping
out at sea
or lying down on the top
of a ship's mast.
35 "They struck me, but[C] I feel no pain!
They beat me, but I didn't know it![s]
When will I wake up?
I'll look for another drink."[t]

24

Don't envy evil men[u]
or desire to be with them,[v]
2 for their hearts plan violence,
and their words stir up trouble.[w]
3 A house is built by wisdom,[x]
and it is established by understanding;
4 by knowledge the rooms are filled
with every precious
and beautiful treasure.
5 A wise warrior is better
than a strong one,[D]
and a man of knowledge than one
of strength;[E,y]
6 for you should wage war
with sound guidance —
victory comes with many counselors.[z]
7 Wisdom is inaccessible to[F] a fool;[aa]
he does not open his mouth
at the ·gate.[ab]
8 The one who plots evil[ac]
will be called a schemer.
9 A foolish scheme is sin,
and a mocker is detestable to people.
10 If you do nothing in a difficult time,
your strength is limited.
11 Rescue those being taken off to death,
and save those stumbling
toward slaughter.[ad]
12 If you say, "But we didn't know
about this,"
won't He who weighs hearts[ae]
consider it?
Won't He who protects your life[af] know?
Won't He repay a person according to
his work?[ag]

[a] **23:16** Pr 8:6 [b] **23:17** Ps 37:1; Pr 24:1,19 [c] Pr 28:14 [d] **23:18** Ps 9:18; Pr 10:28; 24:14; Jr 29:11 [e] **23:20** Pr 20:1; 23:29-30; Is 5:22; Mt 24:49; Lk 21:34; Rm 13:13; Eph 5:18 [f] Pr 28:7 [g] **23:21** Pr 6:10-11 [h] **23:22** Pr 1:8; 15:20; Eph 6:1 [i] **23:23** Pr 4:5,7; 16:16; 18:15; Mt 13:44 [j] **23:24** Pr 10:1; 23:15; 29:3 [k] **23:25** Pr 27:11 [l] **23:27** Pr 22:14 [m] **23:28** Pr 6:26; 7:12,22-23; Ec 7:26 [n] **23:29** Pr 23:35 [o] **23:30** Is 5:11,22 [p] **23:31** Eph 5:18 [q] Sg 7:9 [r] **23:33** Is 28:7 [s] **23:35** Pr 23:29; Jr 5:3 [t] Is 56:12 [u] **24:1** Ps 37:1; Pr 23:17; 24:19 [v] Ps 1:1; Pr 1:15 [w] **24:2** Ps 10:7 [x] **24:3** Pr 14:1 [y] **24:5** Pr 21:22 [z] **24:6** Pr 11:14; 15:22; 20:18 [aa] **24:7** Pr 14:6; 17:16,24 [ab] Jb 5:4; Ps 127:5 [ac] **24:8** Rm 1:30 [ad] **24:11** Ps 82:4; Is 58:6-7 [ae] **24:12** 1Sm 16:7; Ps 44:21; Pr 21:2 [af] Ps 121:3-8 [ag] Jb 34:11; Ps 62:12

A 23:22 Or *because* B 23:33 Or *will speak perversities* or *inverted things* C 23:35 LXX, Syr, Tg, Vg read *me," you will say, "But* D 24:5 LXX, Syr; MT reads *one is in strength* E 24:5 LXX, Syr, Tg; MT reads *knowledge exerts strength* F 24:7 Lit *is too high for*

13 Eat honey,[a] my son, for it is good,
and the honeycomb is sweet
to your palate;[b]
14 realize that wisdom is the same
for you.[c]
If you find it, you will have a future,
and your hope will never fade.[d]

15 Wicked man, don't set an ambush,
at the camp of the righteous man;[e]
don't destroy his dwelling.
16 Though a righteous man falls
seven times,
he will get up,[f]
but the wicked will stumble into ruin.[g]
17 Don't gloat when your enemy falls,
and don't let your heart rejoice
when he stumbles,[h]
18 or the LORD will see, be displeased,
and turn His wrath away from him.
19 Don't be agitated by evildoers,
and don't envy the wicked.[i]
20 For the evil have no future;[j]
the lamp of the wicked will be put out.[k]
21 My son, ˙fear the LORD, as well as
the king,[l]
and don't associate with rebels,[A]
22 for destruction from them
will come suddenly;
who knows what distress these two
can bring?

23 These sayings also belong to the wise:[m]
It is not good to show partiality
in judgment.[n]
24 Whoever says to the ˙guilty,
"You are innocent"[o] —
people will curse him,[p] and tribes
will denounce him;
25 but it will go well with those
who convict the guilty,
and a generous blessing will come
to them.

26 He who gives an honest answer
gives a kiss on the lips.
27 Complete your outdoor work,
and prepare your field;[q]
afterward, build your house.

28 Don't testify against your neighbor
without cause.[r]
Don't deceive with your lips.
29 Don't say, "I'll do to him what he did
to me;
I'll repay the man for what
he has done."[s]

30 I went by the field of a slacker
and by the vineyard of a man
lacking sense.
31 Thistles had come up everywhere,
weeds covered the ground,[t]
and the stone wall was ruined.
32 I saw, and took it to heart;
I looked, and received instruction:
33 a little sleep, a little slumber,
a little folding of the arms to rest,
34 and your poverty will come
like a robber,
your need, like a bandit.[u]

Hezekiah's Collection

25 These too are proverbs of Solomon,[v]
which the men of Hezekiah,[w]
king of Judah, copied.

2 It is the glory of God to conceal
a matter[x]
and the glory of kings to investigate
a matter.
3 As the heaven is high and the earth
is deep,
so the hearts of kings cannot
be investigated.
4 Remove impurities from silver,[y]
and a vessel will be produced[B]
for a silversmith.[z]
5 Remove the wicked
from the king's presence,[aa]
and his throne will be established
in righteousness.[ab]

6 Don't brag about yourself
before the king,
and don't stand in the place
of the great;
7 for it is better for him to say to you,
"Come up here!"
than to demote you in plain view
of a noble.[C,ac]

[a]**24:13** Pr 25:16 [b]Sg 5:1 [c]**24:14** Ps 19:10; 119:103 [d]Pr 10:28; 23:18; Jr 29:11 [e]**24:15** Pr 10:9-10 [f]**24:16** Jb 5:19; Ps 37:24 [g]Pr 14:32; 29:16 [h]**24:17** Ps 35:15,19; Pr 17:5; Ob 12; Mc 7:8 [i]**24:19** Ps 37:1; Pr 23:17; 24:1 [j]**24:20** Ps 37:38; Pr 14:11; 16:25 [k]Jb 18:5; 21:17; Pr 13:9; 20:20 [l]**24:21** Mt 22:21; Rm 13:1-7; 1Pt 2:13-14,17 [m]**24:23** Pr 1:6; 22:17 [n]Dt 1:17; 16:19; Pr 18:5; 28:21 [o]**24:24** Pr 17:15 [p]Pr 11:26 [q]**24:27** Pr 20:4 [r]**24:28** Ex 20:16; Pr 25:18 [s]**24:29** Dt 32:35; Pr 20:22; Mt 5:39; Rm 12:17,19 [t]**24:31** Gn 3:18; Pr 20:4 [u]**24:34** Pr 6:10-11; 20:13 [v]**25:1** Pr 1:1 [w]2Kg 18–20 [x]**25:2** Dt 29:29; Rm 11:33 [y]**25:4** Ezk 22:18; Mal 3:2-3 [z]2Tm 2:21 [aa]**25:5** Pr 20:8,26 [ab]Pr 16:12 [ac]**25:7** Lk 14:7-11

[A]**24:21** Or *those given to change* [B]**25:4** Lit *will come out*; Ex 32:24 [C]**25:7** Lit *you before a noble whom your eyes see*

8 Don't take a matter to court hastily.[a]
Otherwise, what will you do afterward
if your opponent[A] humiliates you?
9 Make your case with your opponent[A]
without revealing another's secret;[b]
10 otherwise, the one who hears
will disgrace you,
and you'll never live it down.[B]
11 A word spoken at the right time
is like gold apples on a silver tray.[C,c]
12 A wise correction to a receptive ear[d]
is like a gold ring or an ornament
of gold.
13 To those who send him,
a trustworthy messenger
is like the coolness of snow
on a harvest day;
he refreshes the life of his masters.[e]
14 The man who boasts about a gift
that does not exist
is like clouds and wind without rain.[f]
15 A ruler can be persuaded
through patience,
and a gentle tongue can break a bone.[g]
16 If you find honey,[h] eat only
what you need;
otherwise, you'll get sick from it
and vomit.[i]
17 Seldom set foot
in your neighbor's house;
otherwise, he'll get sick of you
and hate you.
18 A man giving false testimony
against his neighbor[j]
is like a club, a sword, or a sharp arrow.[k]
19 Trusting an unreliable person in a
difficult time
is like a rotten tooth
or a faltering foot.[l]
20 Singing songs to a troubled heart
is like taking off clothing on a cold day
or like pouring vinegar on soda.[D,m]
21 If your enemy is hungry, give him food
to eat,
and if he is thirsty, give him water
to drink;[n]

[a]25:8 Pr 17:14; Mt 5:25; 1Co 6:7 [b]25:9 Pr 17:9; Mt 18:15 [c]25:11 Pr 8:10; 15:23; 16:16 [d]25:12 Pr 15:31 [e]25:13 Pr 13:17; 16:24; 25:25 [f]25:14 Jd 12 [g]25:15 Pr 15:1; 16:14,32; Ec 10:4 [h]25:16 Jdg 14:8; 1Sm 14:25 [i]Pr 25:27 [j]25:18 Ex 20:16; Pr 24:28 [k]Ps 57:4; Pr 12:18 [l]25:19 2Kg 18:21 [m]25:20 Rm 12:15 [n]25:21 Ex 23:4-5; 2Kg 6:22; 2Ch 28:15; Mt 5:44; Rm 12:20 [o]25:22 Mt 6:4 [p]25:24 Pr 15:17; 17:1; 21:9,19 [q]25:25 Pr 15:30 [r]25:26 Dt 13:6-8; Gl 2:4-5 [s]Ezk 32:2; 34:18-19 [t]25:27 Pr 25:16 [u]Pr 27:2 [v]25:28 Pr 16:32; 29:11 [w]Neh 1:3 [x]26:1 1Sm 12:17 [y]Pr 17:7; 19:10 [z]26:2 Pr 27:8 [aa]Nm 23:8; Dt 23:5; 2Sm 16:12 [ab]26:3 Ps 32:9 [ac]Pr 10:13; 19:29 [ad]26:4 Pr 23:9; 29:9; Mt 7:6; Lk 23:9 [ae]26:5 Mt 16:1-4; 21:24-27 [af]Pr 26:12; 28:11; Rm 12:16 [ag]26:6 Pr 10:26; 25:13 [ah]Pr 13:2

22 for you will heap burning coals
on his head,
and the LORD will reward you.[o]
23 The north wind produces rain,
and a backbiting tongue, angry looks.
24 Better to live on the corner of a roof
than to share a house
with a nagging wife.[p]
25 Good news from a distant land
is like cold water to a parched throat.[E,q]
26 A righteous person who yields
to the wicked[r]
is like a muddied spring
or a polluted well.[s]
27 It is not good to eat too much honey[t]
or to seek glory after glory.[F,u]
28 A man who does not control
his temper[v]
is like a city whose wall
is broken down.[w]

26 Like snow in summer and rain
at harvest,[x]
honor is inappropriate for a fool.[y]
2 Like a flitting sparrow
or a fluttering swallow,[z]
an undeserved curse goes nowhere.[aa]
3 A whip for the horse, a bridle
for the donkey,[ab]
and a rod for the backs of fools.[ac]
4 Don't answer a fool according to
his foolishness[ad]
or you'll be like him yourself.
5 Answer a fool according to
his foolishness[ae]
or he'll become wise in his own eyes.[af]
6 The one who sends a message
by a fool's hand[ag]
cuts off his own feet
and drinks violence.[ah]
7 A proverb in the mouth of a fool
is like lame legs that hang limp.
8 Giving honor to a fool
is like binding a stone in a sling.[G]
9 A proverb in the mouth of a fool
is like a stick with thorns,
brandished by[H] the hand of a drunkard.
10 The one who hires a fool or who hires
those passing by

[A]25:8,9 Or *neighbor* [B]25:10 Lit *and your evil report will not turn back* [C]25:11 Or *like apples of gold in settings of silver* [D]25:20 Lit *natron, or sodium carbonate* [E]25:25 Or *a weary person* [F]25:27 Lit *seek their glory, glory* [G]26:8 A stone bound in a sling would not release and could harm the person using the sling. A modern equivalent is jamming a cork in a gun barrel. [H]26:9 Lit *thorn that goes up into*

is like an archer who wounds everyone.
11 As a dog returns to its vomit,
so a fool repeats his foolishness.[a]
12 Do you see a man who is wise
in his own eyes?[b]
There is more hope for a fool
than for him.[c]
13 The slacker says, "There's a lion
in the road —
a lion in the public square!"[d]
14 A door turns on its hinges,
and a slacker, on his bed.[e]
15 The slacker buries his hand
in the bowl;
he is too weary to bring it to his mouth.[f]
16 In his own eyes, a slacker is wiser[g]
than seven men
who can answer sensibly.
17 A person who is passing by and
meddles in a quarrel that's not his
is like one who grabs a dog by the ears.
18 Like a madman who throws
flaming darts and deadly arrows,[h]
19 so is the man who deceives
his neighbor
and says, "I was only joking!"
20 Without wood, fire goes out;
without a gossip, conflict dies down.[i]
21 As charcoal for embers and wood
for fire,
so is a quarrelsome man
for kindling strife.[j]
22 A gossip's words are like choice food
that goes down to
one's innermost being.[A,k]
23 Smooth[B] lips with an evil heart
are like glaze on an earthen vessel.[l]
24 A hateful person disguises himself
with his speech
and harbors deceit within.
25 When he speaks graciously,
don't believe him,
for there are seven abominations
in his heart.[m]
26 Though his hatred is concealed
by deception,
his evil will be revealed in the assembly.
27 The one who digs a pit will fall into it,
and whoever rolls a stone —
it will come back on him.[n]
28 A lying tongue hates those it crushes,
and a flattering mouth causes ruin.

27

Don't boast about tomorrow,
for you don't know what a day
might bring.[o]
2 Let another praise you, and not
your own mouth —
a stranger, and not your own lips.[p]
3 A stone is heavy and sand, a burden,
but aggravation from a fool
outweighs them both.
4 Fury is cruel, and anger a flood,
but who can withstand jealousy?[q]
5 Better an open reprimand
than concealed love.[r]
6 The wounds of a friend
are trustworthy,[s]
but the kisses of an enemy
are excessive.[t]
7 A person who is full tramples
on a honeycomb,[u]
but to a hungry person, any bitter thing
is sweet.
8 A man wandering from his home
is like a bird wandering from its nest.[v]
9 Oil[w] and incense bring joy to the heart,
and the sweetness of a friend is better
than self-counsel.[C]
10 Don't abandon your friend
or your father's friend,[x]
and don't go to your brother's house
in your time of calamity;
better a neighbor nearby
than a brother far away.[y]
11 Be wise, my son, and bring
my heart joy,[z]
so that I can answer anyone
who taunts me.[aa]
12 A sensible person sees danger
and takes cover;
the inexperienced keep going
and are punished.[ab]

[a]**26:11** 2Pt 2:22
[b]**26:12** Pr 3:7; 26:5; Rm 12:16
[c]Pr 29:20
[d]**26:13** Pr 22:13
[e]**26:14** Pr 6:9-10; 19:15
[f]**26:15** Pr 12:27; 19:24
[g]**26:16** Pr 26:5,12; 28:11
[h]**26:18** Is 50:11
[i]**26:20** Pr 16:28; 22:10
[j]**26:21** Pr 15:18
[k]**26:22** Pr 18:8
[l]**26:23** Mt 23:27; Lk 11:39
[m]**26:25** Ps 28:3
[n]**26:27** Est 7:10; Jb 4:8; Pr 28:10; Dn 6:24; Mt 26:52
[o]**27:1** Lk 12:19-20; Jms 4:13-14
[p]**27:2** Pr 25:27; 2Co 10:12,18; 12:11
[q]**27:4** Pr 6:34
[r]**27:5** Pr 28:23
[s]**27:6** Ps 141:5
[t]Lk 22:48
[u]**27:7** Pr 25:16
[v]**27:8** Pr 26:2
[w]**27:9** Ps 23:5
[x]**27:10** 2Sm 10:2
[y]Pr 17:17
[z]**27:11** Pr 10:1; 23:24-25; 29:3
[aa]Ps 119:42; 127:5
[ab]**27:12** Pr 22:3

[A]**26:22** Lit *to the chambers of the belly* [B]**26:23** LXX; MT reads *Burning* [C]**27:9** LXX reads *heart, but the soul is torn up by affliction*

13 Take his garment,[A]
for he has put up security
for a stranger;
get collateral if it is for foreigners.[B,a]
14 If one blesses his neighbor
with a loud voice early in the morning,
it will be counted as a curse to him.
15 An endless dripping on a rainy day
and a nagging wife are alike.[b]
16 The one who controls her controls
the wind
and grasps oil with his right hand.
17 Iron sharpens iron,
and one man sharpens another.[C]
18 Whoever tends a fig tree[c] will eat
its fruit,[d]
and whoever looks after his master
will be honored.
19 As water reflects the face,
so the heart reflects the person.
20 ·Sheol and ·Abaddon[e] are
never satisfied,[f]
and people's eyes are never satisfied.[g]
21 A crucible for silver, and a smelter
for gold,
and a man for the words
of his praise.[D,h]
22 Though you grind a fool
in a mortar with a pestle
along with grain,
you will not separate his foolishness
from him.[i]
23 Know well the condition of your flock,[j]
and pay attention to your herds,
24 for wealth is not forever;[k]
not even a crown lasts for all time.
25 When hay is removed
and new growth appears
and the grain from the hills
is gathered in,
26 lambs will provide your clothing,
and goats, the price of a field;
27 there will be enough goat's milk
for your food —
food for your household
and nourishment for your
female servants.[l]

28

The wicked flee when no one
is pursuing them,[m]
but the righteous are as bold
as a lion.[n]
2 When a land is in rebellion, it has
many rulers,[o]
but with a discerning
and knowledgeable person,
it endures.
3 A destitute leader[E] who oppresses
the poor
is like a driving rain that leaves
no food.[p]
4 Those who reject the law
praise the wicked,[q]
but those who keep the law battle
against them.[r]
5 Evil men do not understand justice,[s]
but those who seek the LORD
understand everything.[t]
6 Better a poor man who lives
with integrity[u]
than a rich man who distorts right
and wrong.[F,v]
7 A discerning son keeps the law,
but a companion of gluttons humiliates
his father.[w]
8 Whoever increases his wealth
through excessive interest[x]
collects it for one who is kind
to the poor.[y]
9 Anyone who turns his ear
away from hearing the law —
even his prayer is detestable.[z]
10 The one who leads the upright
into an evil way
will fall into his own pit,[aa]
but the blameless will inherit
what is good.[ab]
11 A rich man is wise in his own eyes,
but a poor man who has discernment
sees through him.

[a]**27:13** Pr 6:1-5; 11:15; 20:16
[b]**27:15** Pr 19:13
[c]**27:18** Am 7:14
[d]Sg 8:12; 1Co 3:8; 9:7; 2Tm 2:6
[e]**27:20** Jb 26:6; Pr 15:11
[f]Pr 30:15-16; Hab 2:5
[g]Ec 1:8; 4:8
[h]**27:21** Pr 16:2; 17:3
[i]**27:22** Pr 23:35; 26:11; Jr 5:3
[j]**27:23** Ezk 34:12; Jn 10:3,14; Ac 20:28
[k]**27:24** Lk 16:9
[l]**27:27** Pr 31:15
[m]**28:1** Lv 26:17; Ps 53:5
[n]Eph 6:19-20
[o]**28:2** 1Kg 16:8-28; 2Kg 15:8-15
[p]**28:3** Ex 9:25
[q]**28:4** Rm 1:32
[r]1Kg 18:18; Neh 13:11,15; Mt 3:7; 14:4; Eph 5:11
[s]**28:5** Ps 92:6
[t]Ps 119:100; Jn 7:17; 1Co 2:15; Jms 1:5; 1Jn 2:20,27
[u]**28:6** Pr 19:1; 20:7
[v]Pr 16:8,19; 19:22; Is 5:20
[w]**28:7** Dt 21:20; Pr 17:25; 23:20; 29:3
[x]**28:8** Ex 22:25; Lv 25:36
[y]Jb 27:17; Pr 13:22; Ec 2:26; Ezk 18:13,17
[z]**28:9** Ps 109:7; Pr 15:8,29; 21:27
[aa]**28:10** Ps 7:15; Pr 16:29; 26:27; Mt 18:6
[ab]Mt 5:6

[A]**27:13** A debtor's outer garment held as collateral; Dt 24:12-13,17; Jb 22:6; Am 2:8 [B]**27:13** Lit *a foreign woman* [C]**27:17** Lit *and a man sharpens his friend's face* [D]**27:21** *Or gold, but a man is tested by his praise* [E]**28:3** LXX reads *A wicked man* [F]**28:6** Lit *who twists two ways*

12 When the righteous triumph,
there is great rejoicing,[A]
but when the wicked come to power,
people hide themselves.[a]

13 The one who conceals his sins
will not prosper,[b]
but whoever confesses
and renounces them
will find mercy.[c]

14 Happy is the one who is always
reverent,[d]
but one who hardens his heart falls
into trouble.[e]

15 A wicked ruler over a helpless people[f]
is like a roaring lion
or a charging bear.[g]

16 A leader who lacks understanding
is very oppressive,
but one who hates dishonest profit
prolongs his life.[h]

17 A man burdened by bloodguilt[B]
will be a fugitive until death.[i]
Let no one help him.[j]

18 The one who lives with integrity
will be helped,
but one who distorts right and wrong[C]
will suddenly fall.[k]

19 The one who works his land
will have plenty of food,[l]
but whoever chases fantasies
will have his fill of poverty.[m]

20 A faithful man will have
many blessings,[n]
but one in a hurry to get rich[o]
will not go unpunished.

21 It is not good to show partiality[p] —
yet a man may sin for a piece
of bread.[q]

22 A greedy man[D] is in a hurry for wealth;
he doesn't know that poverty will come
to him.[r]

23 One who rebukes a person
will later find more favor[s]
than one who flatters[E] with his tongue.[t]

[a]28:12 Pr 11:10; 28:28; 29:2; Ec 10:5-6 [b]28:13 Jb 31:33; Ps 32:3 [c]Ps 32:5; Jms 5:16; 1Jn 1:9 [d]28:14 2Ch 19:7; Pr 23:17 [e]Ps 95:8 [f]28:15 Ex 1:14; Pr 29:2; Mt 2:16 [g]Pr 19:12; 1Pt 5:8 [h]28:16 1Kg 12:1-19; Ps 15:5; Pr 15:27 [i]28:17 Gn 4:14; 9:6; Ex 21:14 [j]Nm 35:31 [k]28:18 Pr 2:7; 10:9; 20:7 [l]28:19 Pr 24:27 [m]Pr 1:31; 12:11,14; 14:14 [n]28:20 Pr 10:6; Mt 25:21 [o]Pr 20:21; 28:22; 1Tm 6:9 [p]28:21 Pr 18:5; 24:23 [q]Ezk 13:19 [r]28:22 Pr 13:11; 20:21; 21:5; 22:16 [s]28:23 Pr 27:5-6 [t]Pr 26:28; 29:5 [u]28:24 Pr 19:6 [v]Pr 30:20; Mk 7:11 [w]Pr 18:9 [x]28:25 Pr 15:18 [y]Ps 37:3-5; Pr 3:5-6; Jr 17:7-8 [z]28:26 Pr 3:5-7 [aa]28:27 Pr 11:24; 19:17; 22:16 [ab]28:28 Pr 28:12; 29:2 [ac]29:1 Pr 1:24-31; 6:14-15 [ad]29:2 Ex 2:23; Est 8:15; Pr 11:10; 28:12,28 [ae]29:3 Pr 10:1; 15:20; 23:24-25; 27:11; 28:7 [af]Pr 5:9-10; 6:26; Lk 15:13,30 [ag]29:4 2Ch 9:8; Pr 29:14 [ah]Pr 17:23 [ai]29:5 Pr 26:28; 27:6; 28:23 [aj]29:6 Pr 12:13; 18:7; Ec 9:12 [ak]Ex 15:1 [al]29:7 Jb 29:16; Ps 41:1

24 The one who robs his father or mother[u]
and says, "That's no sin,"[v]
is a companion to a man who destroys.[w]

25 A greedy person provokes conflict,[x]
but whoever trusts in the LORD
will prosper.[y]

26 The one who trusts in himself[F]
is a fool,
but one who walks in wisdom
will be safe.[z]

27 The one who gives to the poor
will not be in need,
but one who turns his eyes away[G]
will receive many curses.[aa]

28 When the wicked come to power,
people hide,
but when they are destroyed,
the righteous flourish.[ab]

29 One who becomes stiff-necked,
after many reprimands
will be shattered instantly —
beyond recovery.[ac]

2 When the righteous flourish,
the people rejoice,
but when the wicked rule,
people groan.[ad]

3 A man who loves wisdom brings joy
to his father,[ae]
but one who consorts with prostitutes
destroys his wealth.[af]

4 By justice a king brings stability
to a land,[ag]
but a man who demands
"contributions"[H]
demolishes it.[ah]

5 A man who flatters[I] his neighbor
spreads a net for his feet.[ai]

6 An evil man is caught by sin,[aj]
but the righteous one sings
and rejoices.[ak]

7 The righteous person knows the rights[J]
of the poor,[al]
but the wicked one does not
understand these concerns.

[A]28:12 Lit *glory* [B]28:17 Lit *the blood of a person* [C]28:18 Lit *who is twisted regarding two ways* [D]28:22 Lit *A man with an evil eye* [E]28:23 Lit *is smooth* [F]28:26 Lit *his heart* [G]28:27 Lit *who shuts his eyes* [H]29:4 The Hb word for "contributions" usually refers to offerings in worship. [I]29:5 Lit *is smooth on* [J]29:7 Lit *justice*

8 Mockers inflame a city,[a]
but the wise turn away anger.

9 If a wise man goes to court with a fool,
there will be ranting and raving
but no resolution.[A,b]

10 Bloodthirsty men hate
an honest person,[c]
but the upright care about him.[B]

11 A fool gives full vent to his anger,[C,d]
but a wise man holds it in check.[e]

12 If a ruler listens to lies,[f]
all his officials will be wicked.

13 The poor and the oppressor have this
in common:[D]
the LORD gives light to the eyes of both.[g]

14 A king who judges the poor
with fairness —
his throne will be established forever.[h]

15 A rod of correction imparts wisdom,[i]
but a youth left to himself[E]
is a disgrace to his mother.[j]

16 When the wicked increase,
rebellion increases,
but the righteous will see
their downfall.[k]

17 Discipline your son, and it will bring
you peace of mind[l]
and give you delight.

18 Without revelation[F,m] people run wild,[n]
but one who listens to instruction
will be happy.[o]

19 A slave cannot be disciplined
by words;
though he understands,
he doesn't respond.[p]

20 Do you see a man who speaks
too soon?[q]
There is more hope for a fool
than for him.[r]

21 A slave pampered from his youth
will become arrogant[G] later on.

22 An angry man stirs up conflict,
and a hot-tempered man[H]
increases rebellion.[s]

23 A person's pride will humble him,[t]
but a humble spirit will gain honor.[u]

24 To be a thief's partner is to hate oneself;
he hears the curse but will not testify.[I,v]

25 The fear of man is a snare,[w]
but the one who trusts in the LORD
is protected.[J,x]

26 Many seek a ruler's favor,[y]
but a man receives justice
from the LORD.[z]

27 An unjust man is detestable
to the righteous,
and one whose way is upright
is detestable to the wicked.[aa]

The Words of Agur

30 The words of Agur son of Jakeh.
The oracle.[K,ab]

The man's oration to Ithiel, to Ithiel
and Ucal:[L]

2 I am more stupid than
any other man,[M]
and I lack man's ability
to understand.[ac]

3 I have not gained wisdom,
and I have no knowledge
of the Holy One.[ad]

4 Who has gone up to heaven
and come down?[ae]
Who has gathered the wind
in His hands?
Who has bound up the waters
in a cloak?[af]
Who has established all the ends
of the earth?[ag]
What is His name,
and what is the name of His Son —
if you know?[ah]

5 Every word of God is pure;[N,ai]
He is a shield to those who take refuge
in Him.[aj]

[a]**29:8** Pr 11:11; 26:21; 29:22 [b]**29:9** Pr 26:4 [c]**29:10** Gn 4:5-8; 1Jn 3:12 [d]**29:11** Pr 12:16 [e]Pr 16:32; 25:28 [f]**29:12** 1Kg 22:8,21-23 [g]**29:13** Pr 22:2 [h]**29:14** Ps 72:4; Pr 16:12; 25:5; Is 11:4 [i]**29:15** Pr 13:24; 22:15 [j]Pr 10:1; 17:25 [k]**29:16** Ps 37:34,36; 58:10; 91:8; 92:11 [l]**29:17** Pr 13:24 [m]**29:18** 1Sm 3:1; Ps 74:9; Am 8:11-12 [n]Ex 32:25 [o]Ps 119:2; Pr 8:32; Jn 13:17; Jms 1:25 [p]**29:19** Mt 18:17 [q]**29:20** Lv 5:4; Jdg 11:30-31,34; Pr 10:19; 17:27; 19:2; 20:25 [r]Pr 26:12 [s]**29:22** Pr 15:18; 26:21; 28:25 [t]**29:23** 2Sm 22:28; Mt 23:12; Jms 4:6 [u]Pr 11:2; 15:33; 18:12; 22:4 [v]**29:24** Lv 5:1 [w]**29:25** Gn 12:12; 20:2; 1Sm 13:11; Lk 12:4; Jn 12:42-43 [x]Pr 14:27; 18:10 [y]**29:26** Pr 16:15; 19:6 [z]Is 49:4; 1Co 4:4-5 [aa]**29:27** Pr 29:10; Mt 10:22; Jn 15:18; 1Jn 3:13 [ab]**30:1** Nm 24:3; Pr 31:1; Nah 1:1; Hab 1:1; Zch 9:1; Mal 1:1 [ac]**30:2** 1Kg 3:7 [ad]**30:3** Pr 9:10 [ae]**30:4** Jn 3:13; Eph 4:9-10 [af]Jb 26:8; 38:9 [ag]Jb 38:4-5; Ps 93:1; 119:90; Is 45:18 [ah]Mt 11:27; Rv 19:12-13 [ai]**30:5** Ps 12:6; 18:30 [aj]Ps 3:3

[A]**29:9** Lit *rest* [B]**29:10** Or *person, and seek the life of the upright* [C]**29:11** Lit *spirit* [D]**29:13** Lit *oppressor meet* [E]**29:15** Lit *youth sent away* [F]**29:18** Lit *vision* [G]**29:21** Hb obscure [H]**29:22** Lit *a master of rage* [I]**29:24** When a call for witnesses was made public, anyone with information who did not submit his testimony was under a curse. [J]**29:25** Lit *raised high* [K]**30:1** Or *son of Jakeh from Massa*; Pr 31:1 [L]**30:1** Hb uncertain. Sometimes read with different word division as *oration: I am weary, God, I am weary, God, and I am exhausted*, or *oration: I am not God, I am not God, that I should prevail.* LXX reads *My son, fear my words and when you have received them repent. The man says these things to the believers in God, and I pause.* [M]**30:2** Lit *I am more stupid than a man* [N]**30:5** Lit *refined*

6 Don't add to His words,[a]
or He will rebuke you, and you will be
proved a liar.[b]

7 Two things I ask of You;
don't deny them to me before I die:
8 Keep falsehood and deceitful words
far from me.
Give me neither poverty nor wealth;
feed me with the food I need.[c]
9 Otherwise, I might have too much[d]
and deny You,[e] saying,
"Who is the LORD?"[f]
or I might have nothing and steal,[g]
profaning[A] the name of my God.[h]

10 Don't slander a servant to his master
or he will curse you,[i] and you will
become ˚guilty.

11 There is a generation that curses
its father
and does not bless its mother.[j]
12 There is a generation that is pure
in its own eyes,[k]
yet is not washed from its filth.
13 There is a generation — how haughty
its eyes
and pretentious its looks.[B]
14 There is a generation whose teeth
are swords,[l]
whose fangs are knives,[m]
devouring the oppressed from the land[n]
and the needy from among mankind.

15 The leech has two daughters:
"Give, Give!"
Three things[o] are never satisfied;
four never say, "Enough!":
16 ˚Sheol;[p] a childless womb;[q]
earth, which is never satisfied
with water;
and fire, which never says, "Enough!"

17 As for the eye that ridicules a father[r]
and despises obedience to a mother,
may ravens of the valley pluck it out
and young vultures eat it.[s]

18 Three things are beyond me;
four I can't understand:
19 the way of an eagle in the sky,
the way of a snake on a rock,
the way of a ship at sea,
and the way of a man
with a young woman.

20 This is the way of an adulteress:
she eats and wipes her mouth
and says, "I've done nothing wrong."[t]

21 The earth trembles under three things;
it cannot bear up under four:
22 a servant when he becomes king,[u]
a fool when he is stuffed with food,
23 an unloved woman when she marries,[v]
and a servant girl when she ousts
her queen.

24 Four things on earth are small,
yet they are extremely wise:
25 the ants are not a strong people,
yet they store up their food
in the summer;[w]
26 hyraxes are not a mighty people,
yet they make their homes in the cliffs;[x]
27 locusts have no king,
yet all of them march in ranks;[y]
28 a lizard[C] can be caught in your hands,
yet it lives in kings' palaces.

29 Three things are stately in their stride,
even four are stately in their walk:
30 a lion, which is mightiest
among beasts
and doesn't retreat before anything,
31 a strutting rooster,[D] a goat,
and a king at the head of his army.[E]

32 If you have been foolish
by exalting yourself
or if you've been scheming,
put your hand over your mouth.[z]
33 For the churning of milk
produces butter,
and twisting a nose draws blood,
and stirring up anger produces strife.[aa]

The Words of Lemuel

31 The words of King Lemuel,
an oracle[F,ab] that his mother
taught him:

2 What should I say, my son?
What, son of my womb?[ac]
What, son of my vows?

[a]30:6 Dt 4:2; 12:32; Rv 22:18
[b]Dt 18:22
[c]30:8 Jb 23:12; Mt 6:11; Php 4:11-12
[d]30:9 Dt 6:10-12; 8:11-14
[e]Jos 24:27; Jb 31:28
[f]Ex 5:2
[g]Ex 20:5; Eph 4:28
[h]Lv 19:11-12
[i]30:10 Ec 7:21
[j]30:11 Ex 21:17; Pr 20:20
[k]30:12 Pr 16:2; Lk 18:11
[l]30:14 Ps 57:4
[m]Jb 29:17
[n]Ps 14:4
[o]30:15 Pr 6:16; 30:18,21,29
[p]30:16 Pr 27:20; Hab 2:5
[q]Gn 30:1
[r]30:17 Gn 9:22
[s]Dt 28:26
[t]30:20 Pr 28:24; 1Jn 1:8
[u]30:22 Pr 19:10; Ec 10:7
[v]30:23 Gn 29:30-31; Dt 21:15
[w]30:25 Pr 6:6-8
[x]30:26 Lv 11:5; Ps 104:18
[y]30:27 Jl 2:7-8
[z]30:32 Jb 21:5; Mc 7:16
[aa]30:33 Pr 10:12; 29:22
[ab]31:1 Pr 30:1
[ac]31:2 Is 49:15

[A]30:9 Lit *grabbing* [B]30:13 Lit *and its eyelids lifted up* [C]30:28 Or *spider* [D]30:31 Or *a greyhound* [E]30:31 LXX reads *king addressing his people* [F]31:1 Or *of Lemuel, king of Massa*, or *of King Lemuel, a burden*

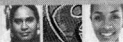

3 Don't spend your energy[a] on women
or your efforts on those
who destroy kings.[b]
4 It is not for kings, Lemuel,
it is not for kings[c] to drink wine[d]
or for rulers to desire beer.
5 Otherwise, they[A] will drink,
forget what is decreed,[e]
and pervert justice for all
the oppressed.[B,f]
6 Give beer to one who is dying
and wine to one whose life
is bitter.[g]
7 Let him drink so that he can forget
his poverty
and remember his trouble no more.[h]

[a]31:3 Pr 5:9 [b]Dt 17:17; 1Kg 11:1; Neh 13:26 [c]31:4 1Kg 16:9; 20:16; Ec 10:17 [d]Pr 20:1 [e]31:5 Hs 4:11 [f]Ps 72:1-2; Is 28:7 [g]31:6 Jb 3:20 [h]31:7 Ps 104:15

The Proverbs 31 Woman

Wendy Alsup

The capable wife of Proverbs 31 reflects back on the first woman created in the image of God in Genesis 2:18 to be a helper to her husband. God is called the helper of His people throughout Scripture (Ex 18:4, Ps 10:14), and the first woman was gifted at creation to reflect particular aspects of His strong advocacy and care for His children. But the helper created in Genesis 2 was marred by the fall. The battle of the sexes began. Supportive relationships between spouses became the exception rather than the norm.

The Proverbs 31 wife also reflects forward to the wife of Ephesians 5 who, redeemed by Christ, is equipped to reclaim the image of God in her relationship with her husband. In Paul's beautiful discourse on the gospel in Ephesians 1 and 2, he writes of God's plan to redeem all that was lost in the fall. We see that, in Christ, we are now equipped to be "imitators of God" (Eph 5:1), once again living as the image bearers He created us to be. In that context, Paul paints a picture of what marriage looks like between husbands and wives who are in Christ and image bearers of God. Proverbs 31 gives us a similar picture of the kind of love and support that a woman who is faithful to the Lord and an image bearer of God can provide in her home. She is a precious gift to her husband, valued far above earthly riches.

Some translations refer to this *woman* as the virtuous or capable woman rather than the virtuous or capable *wife*. The Hebrew word can mean either, but wife seems the better translation in context. To guard against a false notion that the only pathway to virtue for a woman is through a husband and children, Scripture gives us the story of Ruth and others. Ruth is a childless widow, and her virtue and capable nature are clearly evident. Rather than serving as a taunting, unattainable goal to single women who love and serve Christ, the capable wife of Proverbs 31 is a model to those who are in marriages tainted by the fall who long for a practical vision of what is possible in their marriage and home through Christ.

The author of this proverb paints a picture of a woman who is FOR her husband. She does him good all his days. She can be trusted with his heart, the place that holds his innermost fears and desires.

She is also FOR her family. She is aware of their needs and is diligent to support, protect, and encourage them. The great summary statement of the entire section is found in verse 30, "a woman who fears the Lord will be praised." Her horizontal relationship with her husband and family is based on her vertical relationship with God. She remains in close relationship with her God, for without Him, she can do nothing (Jn 15:5). That is what equips her to be *capable*.

[A]31:5 Lit *he* [B]31:5 Lit *sons of affliction*

8 Speak up[A] for those who have
no voice,[B,a]
for the justice of all
who are dispossessed.[C]
9 Speak up,[A] judge righteously,[b]
and defend the cause of[D] the oppressed
and needy.[c]

In Praise of a Capable Wife

10 Who can find a capable wife?[E,d]
She is far more precious than jewels.[F]
11 The heart of her husband trusts in her,
and he will not lack anything good.
12 She rewards him with good, not evil,
all the days of her life.
13 She selects wool and flax
and works with willing hands.
14 She is like the merchant ships,
bringing her food from far away.[e]
15 She rises while it is still night[f]
and provides food for her household
and portions[G] for her female servants.[g]
16 She evaluates a field and buys it;
she plants a vineyard
with her earnings.[H,h]
17 She draws on her strength[I]
and reveals that her arms are strong.[i]
18 She sees that her profits are good,
and her lamp never goes out at night.[j]
19 She extends her hands
to the spinning staff,
and her hands hold the spindle.[k]
20 Her hands reach[J] out to the poor,
and she extends her hands
to the needy.[l]
21 She is not afraid for her household
when it snows,
for all in her household
are doubly clothed.[K]
22 She makes her own bed coverings;[m]
her clothing is fine linen[n] and purple.[o]
23 Her husband is known
at the city ˚gates,
where he sits among the elders
of the land.[p]
24 She makes and sells linen garments;
she delivers belts[L] to the merchants.
25 Strength[q] and honor are her clothing,[r]
and she can laugh at the time to come.[s]
26 She opens her mouth with wisdom
and loving instruction[M] is
on her tongue.
27 She watches over the activities
of her household[t]
and is never idle.[N]
28 Her sons rise up and call her blessed.
Her husband also praises her:
29 "Many women[O] are capable,
but you surpass them all!"[u]
30 Charm is deceptive and beauty
is fleeting,[v]
but a woman who ˚fears the LORD
will be praised.
31 Give her the reward of her labor,[P]
and let her works praise her
at the city gates.

[a] **31:8** Jb 29:12-17 [b] **31:9** Lv 19:15; Dt 1:16 [c] Is 1:17; Jr 22:16 [d] **31:10** Ru 3:11; Pr 12:4; 18:22; 19:14 [e] **31:14** 1Kg 10:22 [f] **31:15** Pr 20:13 [g] Pr 27:27; Lk 12:42 [h] **31:16** Mt 21:33 [i] **31:17** Pr 31:25 [j] **31:18** Mt 25:8 [k] **31:19** Pr 31:13 [l] **31:20** Dt 15:11; Pr 22:9; 31:9; Rm 12:13; Eph 4:28 [m] **31:22** Pr 7:16 [n] Gn 41:42; Rv 19:8,14 [o] Jdg 8:26; Lk 16:19 [p] **31:23** Ru 4:1-2; Pr 24:7; 31:31 [q] **31:25** Pr 31:17 [r] 1Tm 2:9-10 [s] Pr 31:21 [t] **31:27** Pr 31:15 [u] **31:29** Pr 12:4; 31:10; Sg 6:8-9 [v] **31:30** 1Pt 3:3-4

[A] **31:8,9** Lit *Open your mouth* [B] **31:8** Lit *who are mute* [C] **31:8** Lit *all the sons of passing away* [D] **31:9** Lit *and justice for* [E] **31:10** Or *a wife of quality*, or *a wife of noble character* [F] **31:10** Vv. 10-31 form an ˚acrostic. [G] **31:15** Or *tasks* [H] **31:16** Or *vineyard by her own labors* [I] **31:17** Lit *She wraps strength around her like a belt* [J] **31:20** Lit *Her hand reaches* [K] **31:21** LXX, Vg; MT reads *are dressed in scarlet* [L] **31:24** Or *sashes* [M] **31:26** Or *and the teaching of kindness* [N] **31:27** Lit *and does not eat the bread of idleness* [O] **31:29** Lit *daughters* [P] **31:31** Lit *the fruit of her hands*

■ **AUTHOR:** Solomon

■■ **DATE:** During the time of Solomon's reign (around 970–931 B.C.)

The book of Ecclesiastes is a testament to the relevance of Scripture in a postmodern age. While some may resonate with the "Everything is futile" message (Ec 1:2) and see life as an unsolvable puzzle, Ecclesiastes teaches that unlike life centered on worldly pursuits, a life centered on God has purpose, point, and significance.

Some people live a long time and never gain an understanding of this truth. As teens, they missed crucial lessons on the importance of following good mentors and making good friends. As young adults, they imagine the world should bend to their will or admire their beauty. As they grow older, they wonder when their well-deserved fortune will at last catapult them into status and fashion. In old age, they ponder all

ECCLESIASTES

they missed and lost. This all-too-common trajectory seems to be the perspective of the author of Ecclesiastes. Many of us can relate to his exposed sense of misfortune and lost chances.

Ecclesiastes dispels any illusions about a happy, trouble-free, life. In that sense, this is one of the most honest accounts of human emptiness and boredom ever written. The author could be rich or poor; the conclusions would be the same either way. He's tired of what money cannot buy, and weary of what it can. He's sick of trying to spin a web of meaningfulness between the disconnected dots of his life. Happiness is elusive. William Ernest Henley's famous poem "Invictus" says, "I am the master of my fate: I am the captain of my soul." This is just as silly and shallow as the piety of religious fanatics. Both types end up disillusioned.

A careful reading of Ecclesiastes encourages you to sign on to God's mission before your years expire. Develop friendship with God from youth to old age. Don't put it off. Find your needs met and your purpose fulfilled in God's work, His reason for creation and redemption. Be one to delight in God's glory through good times and bad.

If you measure your life with faith in God, the writer confesses, you will find the one vantage-point that stabilizes all others. Professional goals, wealth, esteem, and power all fade. The mission of God remains. God has one point and purpose in the world—to share His glory with humankind, to open the door to His Kingdom, to invite us in. We were made to know God's glory and to share it as citizens of heaven.

Fix your life on knowing and serving God, and the puzzle takes on a new face. We need not have all the answers; we finite creatures cannot explain all the "whys." God is there, calling us to faith and service of many kinds. God's approval at the end is enough. God's purpose, often hidden, gives us reason to go on. God's love guides us toward the great meaning of life.

Everything is Futile

1 The words of the Teacher,[A,a] son of David,
king in Jerusalem.[b]

2 "Absolute futility," says the Teacher.
"Absolute futility. Everything is futile."[c]
3 What does a man gain for all
his efforts
that he labors at under the sun?[d]
4 A generation goes and a generation
comes,
but the earth remains forever.[e]
5 The sun rises and the sun sets;
panting, it returns to its place[f]
where it rises.
6 Gusting to the south,
turning to the north,
turning, turning, goes the wind,[g]
and the wind returns in its cycles.
7 All the streams flow to the sea,
yet the sea is never full.
The streams are flowing to the place,
and they flow there again.
8 All things[B] are wearisome;
man is unable to speak.
The eye is not satisfied by seeing[h]
or the ear filled with hearing.
9 What has been is what will be,
and what has been done is
what will be done;
there is nothing new under the sun.
10 Can one say about anything,
"Look, this is new"?
It has already existed in the ages
before us.
11 There is no remembrance of those
who[C] came before;[i]
and of those who[C] will come after
there will also be no remembrance
by those who follow them.

The Limitations of Wisdom

12 I, the Teacher,[j] have been[D] king over Israel
in Jerusalem. 13 I applied my mind to seek[k] and
explore through wisdom all that is done under heaven.[l] God has given ·people this miserable task to keep them occupied.[m] 14 I have
seen all the things that are done under the
sun and have found everything to be futile, a
pursuit of the wind.[E,n]

15 What is crooked cannot
be straightened;[o]
what is lacking cannot be counted.

16 I said to myself,[F] "Look, I have amassed
wisdom far beyond all those who were over
Jerusalem before me,[p] and my mind has thoroughly grasped[G] wisdom and knowledge."
17 I applied my mind to know wisdom and
knowledge,[q] madness and folly;[r] I learned
that this too is a pursuit of the wind.[E,s]

18 For with much wisdom is
much sorrow;[t]
as knowledge increases, grief increases.

The Emptiness of Pleasure

2 I said to myself, "Go ahead, I will test you
with pleasure;[u] enjoy what is good." But it
turned out to be futile. 2 I said about laughter,[v]
"It is madness," and about pleasure, "What
does this accomplish?" 3 I explored with my
mind how to let my body enjoy life[H] with
wine[w] and how to grasp folly[x] — my mind still
guiding me with wisdom — until I could see
what is good for ·people to do under heaven[I]
during the few days of their lives.[y]

The Emptiness of Possessions

4 I increased my achievements. I built
houses[z] and planted vineyards[aa] for myself.
5 I made gardens[ab] and parks for myself and
planted every kind of fruit tree in them. 6 I
constructed reservoirs of water for myself
from which to irrigate a grove of flourishing
trees.[ac] 7 I acquired male and female servants
and had slaves who were born in my house.[ad]
I also owned many herds of cattle and flocks,
more than all who were before me in Jerusalem.[ae] 8 I also amassed silver and gold for myself, and the treasure of kings and provinces.[af]
I gathered male and female singers for myself,[ag] and many concubines, the delights of
men.[J,K] 9 So I became great and surpassed all
who were before me in Jerusalem;[ah] my wisdom also remained with me. 10 All that my
eyes desired, I did not deny them.[ai] I did not

[a] **1:1** Ec 1:12; 7:27; 12:8-10
[b] 1Kg 2:12; Pr 1:1
[c] **1:2** Ps 39:5-6; 62:9; 144:4; Ec 12:8; Rm 8:20
[d] **1:3** Ec 2:11,22; 3:9; 5:16
[e] **1:4** Ps 104:5; 119:90; 1Jn 2:17
[f] **1:5** Ps 19:6
[g] **1:6** Ec 11:5; Jn 3:8
[h] **1:8** Pr 27:20; Ec 4:8
[i] **1:11** Dt 9:14; Ec 2:16; 9:5
[j] **1:12** Ec 1:1; 7:27; 12:8-10
[k] **1:13** Ec 1:17
[l] 1Kg 4:29-34; Ec 3:10-11; 7:25; 8:17
[m] Gn 3:19; Ec 2:23,26; 3:10; 4:8
[n] **1:14** Pr 27:16; Ec 2:11,17; 4:4; 6:9
[o] **1:15** Ec 7:13
[p] **1:16** 1Kg 3:12; 4:30; 10:23; Ec 2:9
[q] **1:17** Ec 1:13
[r] Ec 2:12; 7:25
[s] Ec 2:11,17; 4:4,6,16; 6:9
[t] **1:18** Ec 2:23; 12:12
[u] **2:1** Ec 7:4; 8:15; Lk 12:19
[v] **2:2** Pr 14:13; Ec 7:3,6
[w] **2:3** Ps 104:15; Ec 10:19
[x] Ec 7:25
[y] Ec 2:24; 3:12,13; 5:18; 8:15
[z] **2:4** 1Kg 7:1-12
[aa] Sg 8:11
[ab] **2:5** Sg 4:16
[ac] **2:6** Neh 2:14; 3:15-16
[ad] **2:7** Gn 14:14; 15:3
[ae] 1Kg 4:23
[af] **2:8** 1Kg 9:28; 10:10,14,21
[ag] 2Sm 19:35
[ah] **2:9** 1Ch 29:25; Ec 1:16
[ai] **2:10** Ec 6:2

[A] **1:1** Or *of Qoheleth*, or *of the Leader of the Assembly* [B] **1:8** Or *words* [C] **1:11** Or *of the things that* [D] **1:12** Or *Teacher, was* [E] **1:14,17** Or *a feeding on wind*, or *an affliction of spirit* [F] **1:16** Lit *said with my heart* [G] **1:16** Or *discerned* [H] **2:3** Lit *to pull my body* [I] **2:3** Two Hb mss, LXX, Syr read *the sun* [J] **2:8** LXX, Theod, Syr read *and male cupbearers and female cupbearers*; Aq, Tg, Vg read *a cup and cups*; Hb obscure [K] **2:8** Or *many treasures that people delight in* refuse myself any pleasure, for I took pleasure in all my struggles. This was my reward for all my struggles.[a] 11When I considered all that I had accomplished[A] and what I had labored to achieve, I found everything to be futile and a pursuit of the wind.[b] There was nothing to be gained under the sun.[c]

[a]**2:10** Ec 3:22; 5:18; 9:9 [b]**2:11** Ec 1:14; 2:22-23 [c]Ec 1:3; 3:9; 5:16 [d]**2:12** Ec 1:17 [e]Ec 1:9-10; 3:15 [f]**2:13** Ec 7:11-12,19; 9:18; 10:10

The Relative Value of Wisdom

12Then I turned to consider wisdom,[d] madness, and folly, for what will the man be like who comes after the king? He[B] will do what has already been done.[e] 13And I realized that there is an advantage to wisdom over folly, like the advantage of light over darkness.[f]

The Mission of God in Pragmatic America

WORLDVIEW

If it isn't broken, don't fix it. If it works, run with it. Rambling theory is less persuasive in America than a plan that produces results. Entrepreneurs have always been America's heroes. America loves winners.

The mission of God strikes many Americans as the right message at the right time. America is a nation of eager church-goers. Many American churches are thriving operations with large ministry staffs and a corps of volunteers. Non-profits and charities extend the work of the church into specialized sectors: urban renewal, youth, the underemployed and homeless. Many American Christians employ the same "can-do" attitude to church work as to business and manufacturing.

At the center of this spiritual dynamo, however, can be profound misunderstandings of the gospel. Salvation is God's gift. It comes by faith, not by works. God's mission centers on Jesus' death on the cross and resurrection to new life, not on pragmatic production or workaholic projects. Americans need to breathe easy, relax, and receive the grace of God given freely without price. That can be hard, when all the rest of life seems to require total effort.

Americans love to be entertained. Motion pictures, television, and popular music are thriving businesses. The passion for stories is an open door for churches to teach the Bible in fresh ways and to hear the testimonies of Christian believers whose lives are transformed by God's power. Narratives speak to the heart. American hearts are open to stories of courage, love, and devotion.

America has suffered. Its story includes a costly civil war. Its best leaders have urged the nation to depend on God who providentially controls history and whose presence is never far from those who make autos, build roads, or send soldiers into harm's way. African American leaders have been among the most notable ministers in American history. Martin Luther King's "I have a dream" is considered one of the greatest speeches ever spoken, full of reference to eschatological hope and assurance that justice will "roll down," as the prophet Amos said. American immigrants arrived with bold hope for religious freedom and business opportunity, and never let either dream die, no matter the obstacles. For all of America's pragmatic common sense, there has been no atheist president—all have practiced or at least claimed some degree of faith in God. Many have been outspoken Christians who publically acknowledged their dependence on God and asked for the nation's prayers.

The mission of God in America has been a builder's mission. From few apparent resources the gospel makes life effective and enduring. It keeps people active. It encourages smart action, learning, and leadership. The challenge for Americans is to share, to delegate, and then to rest. The Bible's many occasions when disciples walk and talk with the Lord remind Americans to slow down, get out of their cars and off their exercise bikes and re-learn the serenity of friendship, loyalty, and worship—off the clock.

By grace, America, the gift of God comes.

[A]**2:11** Lit *all my works that my hands had done* [B]**2:12** Some Hb mss read *They*

14 The wise man has eyes in his head,
but the fool walks in darkness.[a]

Yet I also knew that one fate comes to them
both.[b] 15 So I said to myself, "What happens
to the fool will also happen to me. Why then
have I been overly wise?"[c] And I said to myself that this is also futile. 16 For, just like the
fool, there is no lasting remembrance of the
wise man,[d] since in the days to come both will
be forgotten. How is it that the wise man dies
just like the fool? 17 Therefore, I hated life because the work that was done under the sun
was distressing to me. For everything is futile
and a pursuit of the wind.

The Emptiness of Work

18 I hated all my work that I labored at under the sun[e] because I must leave it to the
man who comes after me.[f] 19 And who knows
whether he will be a wise man or a fool?[g] Yet
he will take over all my work that I labored
at skillfully under the sun. This too is futile.
20 So I began to give myself over[A] to despair
concerning all my work that I had labored at
under the sun. 21 When there is a man whose
work was done with wisdom, knowledge, and
skill,[h] and he must give his portion to a man
who has not worked for it, this too is futile
and a great wrong. 22 For what does a man get
with all his work and all his efforts[i] that he
labors at under the sun? 23 For all his days are
filled with grief, and his occupation is sorrowful;[j] even at night, his mind does not rest.[k]
This too is futile.

24 There is nothing better for man than to
eat, drink, and enjoy[B,C] his work.[l] I have seen
that even this is from God's hand,[m] 25 because
who can eat and who can enjoy life[D] apart
from Him?[E] 26 For to the man who is pleasing
in His sight, He gives wisdom, knowledge,
and joy,[n] but to the sinner He gives the task of
gathering and accumulating in order to give
to the one who is pleasing in God's sight.[o] This
too is futile and a pursuit of the wind.[p]

[a] **2:14** Pr 2:10-13; 1Jn 2:11
[b] Ps 49:10; Ec 3:19; 6:6; 7:2; 9:2-3
[c] **2:15** Ec 6:8,11; 7:16
[d] **2:16** Dt 32:26; 2Sm 18:18; Ec 1:11; 9:5
[e] **2:18** Ec 1:3; 2:11
[f] Ps 39:6; 49:10; Pr 13:22
[g] **2:19** Ezk 18:9-10
[h] **2:21** Ec 4:4
[i] **2:22** Ec 1:3; 2:11
[j] **2:23** Jb 5:7; 14:1
[k] Ps 127:2
[l] **2:24** Ec 2:3; 3:12-13,22; 5:18; 6:12; 8:15; 9:7; Is 56:12; Lk 12:19; 1Co 15:32; 1Tm 6:17
[m] Ec 3:13
[n] **2:26** Jb 32:8; Pr 2:6
[o] Jb 27:16-17; Pr 13:22; 28:8
[p] Ec 1:14

Go and Sow

The daily needs of cities such as New York, Rio De Janeiro, and Tokyo boggle the mind. Trains loaded with foods and other necessities roll in and out, day and night. In villages around the globe, people work hard to maintain daily sustenance.

Human beings are the same everywhere, and everyone has the same daily needs for food and shelter. Even more than that, however, is the same basic spiritual need, a hunger in the heart for some meaning in this life and some hope of a better future. Scripture records that God has "put eternity in [our] hearts" (Ec 3:11). People everywhere need the Savior, and they will be able to meet Him as people called by God plant the seeds, plant the churches, and nurture new believers to spiritual maturity.

We may be the members of such seedling churches. We may be able to give and help such churches to be planted. We may be able to go as sowers into the fields. We pray for good soil, that these churches may grow, flourish, and multiply.

Dear Savior, we acknowledge You as King of kings and Lord of lords. You watch over Your church in every place. Bless all the many church-planting efforts undertaken all across the continents. Bless ministries that seek out people living in poverty and distress. Bless ministries that spread the gospel via the printed page. Touch our hearts, Lord, so that we support with our resources all the various church planting efforts near and far. Amen.

PRAYING FOR THE WORLD

[A] **2:20** Lit *And I turned to cause my heart* [B] **2:24** Syr, Tg; MT reads *There is no good in man who eats and drinks and enjoys* [C] **2:24** Lit *and his soul sees good* [D] **2:25** LXX, Theod, Syr read *can drink* [E] **2:25** Some Hb mss, LXX, Syr read *me*

The Mystery of Time

3 There is an occasion for everything,
and a time for every activity
under heaven:[a]
2 a time to give birth and a time to die;[b]
a time to plant and a time to uproot;[A]
3 a time to kill and a time to heal;
a time to tear down and a time to build;
4 a time to weep and a time to laugh;[c]
a time to mourn and a time to dance;[d]
5 a time to throw stones and a time
to gather stones;[e]
a time to embrace and a time
to avoid embracing;[f]
6 a time to search and a time to count
as lost;
a time to keep and a time
to throw away;
7 a time to tear and a time to sew;
a time to be silent and a time to speak;[g]
8 a time to love and a time to hate;
a time for war and a time for peace.[h]

9 What does the worker gain from his struggles?[i] 10 I have seen the task that God has given •people to keep them occupied.[j] 11 He has made everything appropriate[B] in its time.[k] He has also put eternity in their hearts,[C] but man cannot discover the work God has done from beginning to end.[l] 12 I know that there is nothing better for them than to rejoice and enjoy the[D] good life. 13 It is also the gift of God whenever anyone eats, drinks, and enjoys all his efforts.[m] 14 I know that all God does will last forever; there is no adding to it or taking from it.[n] God works so that people will be in awe of Him.[o] 15 Whatever is, has already been,[p] and whatever will be, already is. God repeats what has passed.[E]

The Mystery of Injustice and Death

16 I also observed under the sun: there is wickedness at the place of judgment and there is wickedness at the place of righteousness.[q] 17 I said to myself, "God will judge the righteous and the wicked,[r] since there is a time for every activity and every work."[s] 18 I said to myself, "This happens concerning people, so that God may test them and they may see for themselves that they are like animals."[t] 19 For the fate of people and the fate of animals is the same.[u] As one dies, so dies the other; they all have the same breath. People have no advantage over animals since everything is futile. 20 All are going to the same place; all come from dust, and all return to dust.[v] 21 Who knows if the spirit of people rises upward and the spirit of animals goes downward to the earth? 22 I have seen that there is nothing better than for a person to enjoy his activities[w] because that is his reward. For who can enable him to see what will happen after he dies?[F,x]

4 Again, I observed all the acts of oppression being done under the sun.[y] Look at the tears of those who are oppressed; they have no one to comfort them. Power is with those who oppress them; they have no one to comfort them. 2 So I admired the dead,[z] who have already died, more than the living, who are still alive. 3 But better than either of them is the one who has not yet existed,[aa] who has not seen the evil activity that is done under the sun.

The Loneliness of Wealth

4 I saw that all labor and all skillful work is due to a man's jealousy of his friend.[ab] This too is futile and a pursuit of the wind.[ac]

5 The fool folds his arms[ad]
and consumes his own flesh.[ae]
6 Better one handful with rest
than two handfuls with effort and a
pursuit of the wind.[af]

7 Again, I saw futility under the sun: 8 There is a person without a companion,[G] without even a son or brother, and though there is no end to all his struggles, his eyes are still not content with riches.[ag] "So who am I struggling for," he asks, "and depriving myself from good?" This too is futile and a miserable task.

9 Two are better than one because they have a good reward for their efforts. 10 For if either falls, his companion can lift him up; but pity the one who falls without another to lift him up. 11 Also, if two lie down together, they can keep warm; but how can one person alone keep warm?[ah] 12 And if someone overpowers

[a] 3:1 Ec 3:17; 8:6
[b] 3:2 Jb 14:5; Heb 9:27
[c] 3:4 Rm 12:15
[d] Ex 15:20
[e] 3:5 2Kg 3:19,25; Is 5:2
[f] 1Co 7:5
[g] 3:7 Am 5:13; 1Co 14:26-32
[h] 3:8 Mt 5:9; 10:34
[i] 3:9 Ec 1:3
[j] 3:10 Ec 1:13; 2:26
[k] 3:11 Gn 1:31
[l] Jb 5:9; Ec 7:23; 8:17; Rm 11:33
[m] 3:13 Ec 2:24; 5:19
[n] 3:14 Rv 22:18-19
[o] Ex 7:5; Ezk 36:23
[p] 3:15 Ec 1:9; 6:10
[q] 3:16 Ec 4:1; 5:8; 8:9
[r] 3:17 Ec 11:9; Mt 16:27; Rm 2:6-10; 2Th 1:6-9
[s] Ec 3:1
[t] 3:18 Ps 49:12,20; 73:22
[u] 3:19 Ec 9:12
[v] 3:20 Gn 3:19; Ec 12:7
[w] 3:22 Ec 2:24
[x] Ec 2:18; 6:12; 8:7; 10:14
[y] 4:1 Jb 35:9; Ec 3:16; 5:8
[z] 4:2 Jb 3:11-26
[aa] 4:3 Ec 6:3; Lk 23:29
[ab] 4:4 1Sm 18:9; Ec 2:21; Ac 13:45; 2Co 12:20
[ac] Ec 1:14
[ad] 4:5 Pr 6:10; 24:33
[ae] Is 9:20
[af] 4:6 Pr 15:16-17
[ag] 4:8 Pr 27:20; Ec 1:8; 5:10
[ah] 4:11 1Kg 1:1-4

A 3:2 Lit *uproot what is planted* B 3:11 Or *beautiful* C 3:11 Or *has put a sense of past and future into their minds*, or *has placed ignorance in their hearts* D 3:12 Lit *his* E 3:15 Or *God calls the past to account*, or *God seeks what is past*, or *God seeks the persecuted*; lit *God seeks the pursued* F 3:22 Lit *after him* G 4:8 Lit *person, but there is not a second,*

one person, two can resist him. A cord of three
strands is not easily broken.
13 Better is a poor but wise youth than an old
but foolish king who no longer pays attention to warnings.[a] 14 For he came from prison
to be king,[b] even though he was born poor in
his kingdom. 15 I saw all the living, who move
about under the sun, follow[A] a second youth
who succeeds him. 16 There is no limit to all
the ·people who were before them, yet those
who come later will not rejoice in him. This
too is futile and a pursuit of the wind.[c]

Caution in God's Presence

5 [B] Guard your steps when you go to the
house of God. Better to draw near in
obedience than to offer the sacrifice as fools
do,[d] for they ignorantly do wrong. 2 [C] Do not
be hasty to speak, and do not be impulsive to
make a speech before God. God is in heaven
and you are on earth, so let your words be
few.[e] 3 For dreams result from much work
and a fool's voice from many words.[f] 4 When
you make a vow to God,[g] don't delay fulfilling it, because He does not delight in fools.
Fulfill what you vow. 5 Better that you do not
vow than that you vow and not fulfill it.[h] 6 Do
not let your mouth bring ·guilt on you,[i] and
do not say in the presence of the messenger
that it was a mistake.[j] Why should God be
angry with your words and destroy the work
of your hands? 7 For many dreams bring
futility, so do many words.[k] Therefore, ·fear
God.

The Realities of Wealth

8 If you see oppression of the poor[l] and perversion of justice and righteousness in the
province, don't be astonished at the situation,[m] because one official protects another
official, and higher officials protect them.
9 The profit from the land is taken by all; the
king is served by the field.[D,n]
10 The one who loves money is never satisfied with money, and whoever loves wealth is
never satisfied with income. This too is futile.
11 When good things increase, the ones who
consume them multiply; what, then, is the
profit to the owner, except to gaze at them

[a] **4:13** Ec 9:15
[b] **4:14** Gn 41:14,41-43
[c] **4:16** Ec 1:14
[d] **5:1** 1Sm 15:22; Mt 5:23-24
[e] **5:2** Pr 10:19; Mt 6:7
[f] **5:3** Jb 11:2
[g] **5:4** Nm 30:2; Dt 6:13; 23:21-22; Pr 20:25
[h] **5:5** Pr 20:25; Mt 5:33-37; Ac 5:4; Jms 5:12
[i] **5:6** Jdg 11:30-31,34
[j] Nm 15:25
[k] **5:7** Ec 6:11
[l] **5:8** Ec 4:1
[m] 1Pt 4:12
[n] **5:9** Pr 27:23-27
[o] **5:13** Ec 6:1-2
[p] **5:15** Jb 1:21
[q] **5:16** Ec 1:3
[r] Pr 11:29
[s] **5:17** Ps 127:2
[t] **5:18** Ec 2:24
[u] Ec 2:10
[v] **5:19** 2Ch 1:12
[w] Ec 6:2
[x] Ec 3:13
[y] **6:1** Ec 5:13
[z] **6:2** 1Kg 3:13
[aa] Ps 17:14; 73:7
[ab] **6:3** Is 14:20; Jr 8:2; 22:19
[ac] Jb 3:16; Ec 4:3
[ad] **6:7** Pr 16:26

with his eyes? 12 The sleep of the worker is
sweet, whether he eats little or much, but the
abundance of the rich permits him no sleep.
13 There is a sickening tragedy I have seen
under the sun: wealth kept by its owner to
his harm.[o] 14 That wealth was lost in a bad
venture, so when he fathered a son, he was
empty-handed. 15 As he came from his mother's womb, so he will go again, naked as he
came;[p] he will take nothing for his efforts that
he can carry in his hands. 16 This too is a sickening tragedy: exactly as he comes, so he will
go. What does the one gain[q] who struggles for
the wind?[r] 17 What is more, he eats in darkness
all his days,[s] with much sorrow, sickness, and
anger.
18 Here is what I have seen to be good:[t] it
is appropriate to eat, drink, and experience
good in all the labor one does under the sun
during the few days of his life God has given
him, because that is his reward.[u] 19 Furthermore, every man to whom God has given
riches and wealth,[v] He has also allowed him
to enjoy them, take his reward, and rejoice in
his labor.[w] This is a gift of God,[x] 20 for he does
not often consider the days of his life because
God keeps him occupied with the joy of his
heart.

6 Here is a tragedy I have observed under
the sun,[y] and it weighs heavily on humanity:[E] 2 God gives a man riches, wealth,
and honor[z] so that he lacks nothing of all he
desires for himself,[aa] but God does not allow
him to enjoy them. Instead, a stranger will
enjoy them. This is futile and a sickening tragedy. 3 A man may father a hundred children
and live many years. No matter how long he
lives,[F] if he is not satisfied by good things and
does not even have a proper burial,[ab] I say that
a stillborn child is better off than he.[ac] 4 For he
comes in futility and he goes in darkness, and
his name is shrouded in darkness. 5 Though a
stillborn child does not see the sun and is not
conscious, it has more rest than he. 6 And if
he lives a thousand years twice, but does not
experience happiness, do not both go to the
same place?

7 All man's labor is for his stomach,[G,ad]
yet the appetite is never satisfied.

[A] **4:15** Lit *with* [B] **5:1** Ec 4:17 in Hb [C] **5:2** Ec 5:1 in Hb [D] **5:9** Or *An advantage for the land in every respect is a king for a cultivated field*; Hb obscure [E] **6:1** Or *it is common among men* [F] **6:3** Lit *how many years* [G] **6:7** Lit *mouth*

8 What advantage then does the wise man
have over the fool?[a] What advantage is there
for the poor person who knows how to conduct himself before others? 9 Better what the
eyes see than wandering desire.[b] This too is
futile and a pursuit of the wind.[c]
10 Whatever exists was given its name long
ago,[A,d] and it is known what man is. But he
is not able to contend with the One stronger
than he.[e] 11 For when there are many words,
they increase futility.[f] What is the advantage
for man? 12 For who knows what is good for
man in life, in the few days of his futile life that
he spends like a shadow?[g] Who can tell man
what will happen after him under the sun?

Wise Sayings

7 A good name is better than
fine perfume,[h]
and the day of one's death than the day
of one's birth.[i]
2 It is better to go to a house of mourning
than to go to a house of feasting,
since that is the end of all mankind,
and the living should take it to heart.[j]
3 Grief is better than laughter,
for when a face is sad, a heart
may be glad.[k]
4 The heart of the wise is in a house
of mourning,
but the heart of fools is in a house
of pleasure.
5 It is better to listen to rebuke
from a wise person
than to listen to the song of fools,[l]
6 for like the crackling of burning thorns
under the pot,[m]
so is the laughter of the fool.
This too is futile.
7 Surely, the practice of extortion turns
a wise person into a fool,[n]
and a bribe destroys the mind.[o]
8 The end of a matter is better
than its beginning;
a patient spirit is better
than a proud spirit.[p]
9 Don't let your spirit rush to be angry,
for anger abides in the heart of fools.[q]
10 Don't say, "Why were the former days
better than these?"[r]
since it is not wise of you to ask this.
11 Wisdom is as good as an inheritance
and an advantage to those who see
the sun,
12 because wisdom is protection as money
is protection,
and the advantage of knowledge
is that wisdom preserves the life
of its owner.[s]
13 Consider the work of God,[t]
for who can straighten out
what He has made crooked?[u]

14 In the day of prosperity be joyful,[v] but in
the day of adversity, consider: God has made
the one as well as the other,[w] so that man cannot discover anything that will come after
him.

Avoiding Extremes

15 In my futile life[B] I have seen everything:[x]
there is a righteous man who perishes in spite
of his righteousness,[y] and there is a wicked
man who lives long in spite of his evil.[z]
16 Don't be excessively righteous, and don't be
overly wise.[aa] Why should you destroy yourself? 17 Don't be excessively wicked, and don't
be foolish. Why should you die before your
time?[ab] 18 It is good that you grasp the one and
do not let the other slip from your hand. For
the one who ˚fears God will end up with both
of them.

19 Wisdom makes the wise man stronger
than ten rulers of a city.[ac]
20 There is certainly no righteous man
on the earth
who does good and never sins.[ad]

21 Don't pay attention[C] to everything ˚peo-
ple say, or you may hear your servant cursing
you,[ae] 22 for you know that many times you
yourself have cursed others.

What the Teacher Found

23 I have tested all this by wisdom. I resolved, "I will be wise," but it was beyond
me. 24 What exists is beyond reach and very
deep.[af] Who can discover it? 25 I turned my
thoughts to know, explore, and seek wisdom[ag]
and an explanation for things, and to know

[a] 6:8 Ec 2:15
[b] 6:9 Ec 11:9
[c] Ec 1:14
[d] 6:10 Gn 2:19; Ec 1:9-10; 3:15
[e] Jb 9:32; Is 45:9
[f] 6:11 Pr 10:19; Mt 6:7
[g] 6:12 Ec 3:22
[h] 7:1 Pr 22:1; Ezk 36:21
[i] Ec 4:2
[j] 7:2 Ps 90:12
[k] 7:3 Pr 14:13
[l] 7:5 Pr 13:1
[m] 7:6 Ps 58:9; 118:12
[n] 7:7 Ec 4:1
[o] Dt 16:19; Pr 17:8
[p] 7:8 Pr 14:29
[q] 7:9 Pr 14:17; Jms 1:19
[r] 7:10 Jdg 6:13
[s] 7:12 Pr 3:18
[t] 7:13 Ec 3:11
[u] Ec 1:15
[v] 7:14 Ec 3:22
[w] Lm 3:38
[x] 7:15 Ec 6:12; 9:9
[y] Ec 8:14
[z] Ec 8:12-13
[aa] 7:16 Ec 2:15; Rm 12:3
[ab] 7:17 Jb 22:16; Ps 55:23; Pr 10:27
[ac] 7:19 Ec 9:13-18
[ad] 7:20 1Kg 8:46; Rm 3:23
[ae] 7:21 Pr 30:10
[af] 7:24 Rm 11:33
[ag] 7:25 Ec 1:15,17

A 6:10 Lit *name already* B 7:15 Lit *days* C 7:21 Lit *Don't give your heart* that wickedness is stupidity and folly is madness. 26 And I find more bitter than death[a] the woman who is a trap,[b] her heart a net, and her hands chains. The one who pleases God will escape her, but the sinner will be captured by her. 27 "Look," says the Teacher, "I have discovered this by adding one thing to another to find out the explanation, 28 which my soul continually searches for but does not find: among a thousand people I have found one true man, but among all these I have not found a true woman.[c] 29 Only see this: I have discovered that God made people upright,[d] but they pursued many schemes."

Wisdom, Authorities, and Inequities

8 Who is like the wise person, and who knows the interpretation of a matter? A man's wisdom brightens his face, and the sternness of his face is changed.[e]

2 Keep[A] the king's command because of your oath made before God.[f] 3 Do not be in a hurry; leave his presence,[g] and don't persist in a bad cause, since he will do whatever he wants. 4 For the king's word is authoritative, and who can say to him, "What are you doing?"[h] 5 The one who keeps a command will not experience anything harmful,[i] and a wise heart knows the right time and procedure. 6 For every activity there is a right time and procedure,[j] even though man's troubles are heavy on him. 7 Yet no one knows what will happen[k] because who can tell him what will happen? 8 No one has authority over the wind[B] to restrain it,[l] and there is no authority over the day of death;[m] there is no furlough in battle, and wickedness will not allow those who practice it to escape. 9 All this I have seen, applying my mind to all the work that is done under the sun, at a time when one man has authority over another to his harm.

10 In such circumstances, I saw the wicked buried. They came and went from the holy place,[n] and they were praised[C] in the city where they did so. This too is futile. 11 Because the sentence against a criminal act is not carried out quickly,[o] the heart of ·people is filled with the desire to commit crime. 12 Although a sinner commits crime a hundred times and prolongs his life,[p] yet I also know that it will go well with God-fearing people,[q] for they are reverent before Him. 13 However, it will not go well with the wicked,[r] and they will not lengthen their days like a shadow,[s] for they are not reverent before God.

14 There is a futility that is done on the earth: there are righteous people who get what the actions of the wicked deserve,[t] and there are wicked people who get what the actions of the righteous deserve.[u] I say that this too is futile. 15 So I commended enjoyment because there is nothing better for man under the sun than to eat, drink, and enjoy himself,[v] for this will accompany him in his labor during the days of his life that God gives him under the sun.

16 When I applied my mind to know wisdom[w] and to observe the activity that is done on the earth (even though one's eyes do not close in sleep day or night), 17 I observed all the work of God and concluded that man is unable to discover the work that is done under the sun. Even though a man labors hard to explore it, he cannot find it;[x] even if the wise man claims to know it, he is unable to discover it.

Enjoy Life Despite Death

9 Indeed, I took all this to heart and explained it all: the righteous, the wise, and their works are in God's hands.[y] People don't know whether to expect love or hate. Everything lies ahead of them. 2 Everything is the same for everyone:[z] there is one fate for the righteous and the wicked,[aa] for the good and the bad,[D] for the ·clean and the ·unclean, for the one who sacrifices and the one who does not sacrifice. As it is for the good, so it is for the sinner; as for the one who takes an oath, so for the one who fears an oath. 3 This is an evil in all that is done under the sun: there is one fate for everyone. In addition, the hearts of people are full of evil, and madness is in their hearts while they live[ab] — after that they go to the dead. 4 But there is hope for whoever is joined[E] with all the living, since a live dog is better than a dead lion. 5 For the living know that they will die, but the dead don't

[a] **7:26** Pr 5:4
[b] Pr 6:25
[c] **7:28** 1Kg 11:3
[d] **7:29** Gn 1:27
[e] **8:1** Dt 28:50
[f] **8:2** Ex 22:11; 2Sm 21:7; Ezk 17:18
[g] **8:3** Ec 10:4
[h] **8:4** Jb 9:12; Dn 4:35
[i] **8:5** Rm 13:3
[j] **8:6** Ec 3:1,17
[k] **8:7** Ec 3:22; 6:12; 9:12; 10:14
[l] **8:8** Ps 148:8; Pr 30:4; Mk 4:39
[m] Jn 10:18; 2Tm 1:10
[n] **8:10** Ec 9:5
[o] **8:11** Rm 2:4; 2Pt 3:9
[p] **8:12** Ec 7:15
[q] Dt 12:25; Ps 37:11; Pr 1:33; Is 3:10
[r] **8:13** Is 3:11
[s] Jb 14:2; Ec 6:12
[t] **8:14** Ec 7:15
[u] Jb 21:7; Ps 73:3; Jr 12:1
[v] **8:15** Ec 2:24
[w] **8:16** Ec 1:13-14
[x] **8:17** Ec 3:11; 7:25-29; 11:5
[y] **9:1** Dt 33:3
[z] **9:2** Jb 9:22
[aa] Ec 2:14
[ab] **9:3** Ec 1:17

[A] **8:2** Some Hb mss, LXX, Vg, Tg, Syr; other Hb mss read *I, keep* [B] **8:8** Or *life-breath* [C] **8:10** Some Hb mss, LXX, Aq, Theod, Sym; other Hb mss read *forgotten*

[D] **9:2** LXX, Aq, Syr, Vg; MT omits *and the bad* [E] **9:4** Alt Hb tradition reads *chosen*

know anything. There is no longer a reward
for them because the memory of them is forgotten.[a] 6 Their love, their hate, and their envy
have already disappeared, and there is no
longer a portion for them in all that is done
under the sun.
7 Go, eat your bread with pleasure, and
drink your wine with a cheerful heart, for
God has already accepted your works.[b] 8 Let
your clothes be white all the time, and never
let oil be lacking on your head.[c] 9 Enjoy life
with the wife you love all the days of your
fleeting[A] life,[d] which has been given to you
under the sun, all your fleeting days. For that
is your portion in life and in your struggle[e]
under the sun. 10 Whatever your hands find to
do, do with all your strength,[f] because there is
no work, planning, knowledge, or wisdom[g] in
•Sheol where you are going.

The Limitations of Wisdom

11 Again I saw under the sun that the race is
not to the swift,[h] or the battle to the strong,[i]
or bread to the wise, or riches to the discerning, or favor to the skillful; rather, time and
chance happen to all of them. 12 For man
certainly does not know his time:[j] like fish
caught in a cruel net or like birds caught in a
trap,[k] so people are trapped in an evil time[l] as
it suddenly falls on them.[m]
13 I have observed that this also is wisdom
under the sun, and it is significant to me:
14 There was a small city with few men in it.
A great king came against it, surrounded it,
and built large siege works against it. 15 Now
a poor wise man was found in the city,[n] and
he delivered the city by his wisdom.[o] Yet no
one remembered that poor man. 16 And I said,
"Wisdom is better than strength,[p] but the
wisdom of the poor man is despised, and his
words are not heeded."

17 The calm words of the wise
are heeded
more than the shouts of a ruler
over fools.
18 Wisdom is better
than weapons of war,
but one sinner can destroy much good.[q]

The Burden of Folly

10 Dead flies make a perfumer's oil
ferment and stink;[r]
so a little folly outweighs wisdom
and honor.
2 A wise man's heart goes to the[B] right,
but a fool's heart to the[B] left.
3 Even when the fool walks
along the road, his heart lacks sense,
and he shows everyone he is a fool.[s]
4 If the ruler's anger rises against you,
don't leave your place,[t]
for calmness puts great offenses
to rest.[u]

5 There is an evil I have seen under the sun,
an error proceeding from the presence of the
ruler:

6 The fool is appointed to great heights,[v]
but the rich remain
in lowly positions.
7 I have seen slaves on horses,[w]
but princes walking on the ground
like slaves.[x]
8 The one who digs a pit may fall into it,[y]
and the one who breaks through a wall
may be bitten by a snake.[z]
9 The one who quarries stones
may be hurt by them;
the one who splits trees
may be endangered by them.
10 If the ax is dull, and one does not
sharpen its edge,
then one must exert more strength;
however, the advantage of wisdom is
that it brings success.
11 If the snake bites before
it is charmed,[aa]
then there is no advantage
for the charmer.[C]
12 The words from the mouth
of a wise man are gracious,[ab]
but the lips of a fool consume him.[ac]
13 The beginning of the words
of his mouth is folly,
but the end of his speaking
is evil madness.
14 Yet the fool multiplies words.
No one knows what will happen,

[a] 9:5 Ec 2:16 [b] 9:7 Ec 2:24; 3:13; 5:18; 8:15 [c] 9:8 Ps 23:5 [d] 9:9 Ec 6:12; 7:15 [e] Ec 2:10 [f] 9:10 Rm 12:11; Col 3:23 [g] Ec 9:5 [h] 9:11 Am 2:14-15 [i] 2Ch 20:15 [j] 9:12 Ec 8:7 [k] Pr 7:23 [l] Pr 29:6 [m] Lk 21:34-35 [n] 9:15 Ec 4:13 [o] 2Sm 20:22 [p] 9:16 Ec 7:19 [q] 9:18 Jos 7:1 [r] 10:1 Ex 30:25 [s] 10:3 Pr 13:16; 18:2 [t] 10:4 Ec 8:3 [u] 1Sm 25:24-33; Pr 25:15 [v] 10:6 Est 3:1; Pr 28:12; 29:2 [w] 10:7 Pr 19:10 [x] Est 6:8-10 [y] 10:8 Ps 7:15 [z] Am 5:19 [aa] 10:11 Jr 8:17 [ab] 10:12 Pr 10:32; 22:11; Lk 4:22 [ac] Pr 18:7

[A] 9:9 Or *futile* [B] 10:2 Lit *his* [C] 10:11 Lit *master of the tongue*

and who can tell anyone
what will happen after him?[a]
15 The struggles of fools weary them,
for they don't know how to go
to the city.
16 Woe to you, land, when your king is
a youth[b]
and your princes feast in the morning.
17 Blessed are you, land, when your king is
a son of nobles
and your princes feast
at the proper time —
for strength and not
for drunkenness.[c]
18 Because of laziness the roof caves in,
and because of negligent hands
the house leaks.
19 A feast is prepared for laughter,
and wine makes life happy,[d]
and money is the answer
for everything.[e]
20 Do not curse the king
even in your thoughts,[f]
and do not curse a rich person
even in your bedroom,[g]
for a bird of the sky may carry
the message,
and a winged creature may report
the matter.

Invest in Life

11 Send your bread on the surface
of the waters,[h]
for after many days you may find it.
2 Give a portion to seven or even
to eight,[i]
for you don't know what disaster
may happen on earth.
3 If the clouds are full, they will pour out
rain on the earth;
whether a tree falls to the south
or the north,
the place where the tree falls,
there it will lie.
4 One who watches the wind
will not sow,
and the one who looks at the clouds
will not reap.
5 Just as you don't know the path
of the wind,
or how bones develop in[A] the womb
of a pregnant woman,
so you don't know the work of God
who makes everything.[j]
6 In the morning sow your seed,
and at evening do not let
your hand rest,
because you don't know
which will succeed,
whether one or the other,
or if both of them will be
equally good.
7 Light is sweet,
and it is pleasing for the eyes to see
the sun.[k]
8 Indeed, if a man lives many years,
let him rejoice in them all,
and let him remember the days
of darkness,[l] since they
will be many.
All that comes is futile.
9 Rejoice, young man,
while you are young,
and let your heart be glad in the days
of your youth.
And walk in the ways of your heart
and in the sight of your eyes;[m]
but know that for all of these things
God will bring you to judgment.
10 Remove sorrow from your heart,
and put away pain from your flesh,[n]
because youth and the prime of life
are fleeting.

The Twilight of Life

12 So remember your Creator in the days
of your youth:
Before the days of adversity come,
and the years approach
when you will say,[o]
"I have no delight in them";
2 before the sun and the light
are darkened,[p]
and the moon and the stars,
and the clouds return after[B] the rain;
3 on the day when the guardians
of the house tremble,
and the strong men stoop,

[a]10:14 Ec 8:7,17 [b]10:16 Pr 30:21-22; Is 3:4,12 [c]10:17 Pr 31:4; Is 5:11 [d]10:19 Ps 104:15 [e]Ec 7:12 [f]10:20 Ex 22:28 [g]2Kg 6:12; Lk 12:3 [h]11:1 Dt 15:10; Pr 19:17; Mt 10:42; Gl 6:9-10; Heb 6:10 [i]11:2 Ps 112:9; Mt 5:42; Lk 6:30; 1Tm 6:18-19 [j]11:5 Jb 10:10-11; Ps 139:14-16; Is 55:9; Jn 3:6-8; Rm 11:33 [k]11:7 Ec 6:5; 7:11 [l]11:8 Ec 12:1 [m]11:9 Ec 2:24; 3:12-13,22; 5:18; 8:15; 9:7-9 [n]11:10 2Co 7:1; 2Tm 2:22 [o]12:1 Ec 11:8 [p]12:2 Is 5:30; Ezk 32:7-8

[A]11:5 Or *know how the life-breath comes to the bones in* [B]12:2 Or *with*

the women who grind cease because
they are few,
and the ones who watch
through the windows see dimly,[a]
4 the doors at the street are shut
while the sound of the mill fades;[b]
when one rises at the sound of a bird,
and all the daughters of song
grow faint.
5 Also, they are afraid of heights
and dangers on the road;
the almond tree blossoms,
the grasshopper loses its spring,[A]
and the caper berry has no effect;
for man is headed to his eternal home,[c]
and mourners will walk around
in the street;[d]
6 before the silver cord is snapped,[B]
and the gold bowl is broken,[e]
and the jar is shattered at the spring,
and the wheel is broken into the well;
7 and the dust returns to the earth
as it once was,
and the spirit returns to God
who gave it.[f]

8 "Absolute futility," says the Teacher. "Everything is futile."[g]

The Teacher's Objectives and Conclusion

9 In addition to the Teacher being a wise
man, he constantly taught the ·people knowledge; he weighed, explored, and arranged
many proverbs.[h] 10 The Teacher sought to find
delightful sayings and write words of truth
accurately. 11 The sayings of the wise are like
goads,[i] and those from masters of collections
are like firmly embedded nails.[j] The sayings
are given by one Shepherd.[C]

12 But beyond these, my son, be warned:
there is no end to the making of many books,[k]
and much study wearies the body.[l] 13 When all
has been heard, the conclusion of the matter
is: ·fear God[m] and keep His commands, because this is for all humanity.[n] 14 For God will
bring every act to judgment,[o] including every
hidden thing, whether good or evil.

[a] **12:3** Gn 27:1; 48:10; 1Sm 3:2 [b] **12:4** Jr 25:10; Rv 18:22 [c] **12:5** Jb 17:13; 30:23 [d] Jr 9:17 [e] **12:6** Zch 4:2-3 [f] **12:7** Gn 2:7; 3:19; Ec 3:21 [g] **12:8** Ec 1:2 [h] **12:9** 1Kg 4:32; Pr 1:1 [i] **12:11** Pr 1:6; 22:17 [j] Ezr 9:8; Is 22:23 [k] **12:12** 1Kg 4:32-33; Jn 21:25 [l] Ec 1:18 [m] **12:13** Pr 1:7; Ec 3:14; 5:7; 7:18; 8:12-13 [n] Ps 97:5; Ac 4:12; Rm 10:12 [o] **12:14** Ec 3:17; 11:9; Rv 20:12

A **12:5** Or *grasshopper is weighed down, or grasshopper drags itself along* B **12:6** Alt Hb tradition reads *removed* C **12:11** Or *by a shepherd*

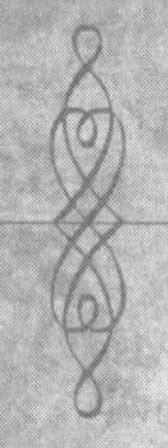

AUTHOR: Solomon

DATE: During the time of Solomon's reign (around 970–931 B.C.)

Song of Songs gets far too little attention in most churches. Perhaps its language is too intense, its images and intimacies too personal for preaching or Bible studies. If only the beauty of the love celebrated here were more the common experience of humankind, we would be far happier, less stressed, more delighted in each day's treasured moments. We would probably avoid lusting after forbidden sexual fruit.

The love expressed by the lovers in this song is almost tangible. God designed us for this level of committed love. Sadly, we don't often seek it with wisdom and earnestness.

The Song is sometimes made into an analogy by interpreters. The two lovers delighting in their passions are said to be a picture of God's love for His people.

SONG OF SONGS

Some adherents to this approach take sexuality completely out of the Song in favor of something spiritual. Yet Song of Songs is clearly a celebration of sexual love in cherished tones and wondrous feelings. God made man and woman for this extraordinary pleasure. A culture may object, or try to write alternatives between the lines, but the magnetism is undeniable.

God's mission to the world is redemptive love, one that embraces suffering (Jesus on the cross) and triumph (Jesus risen from the dead). God's mission in the world generates a love which grows as it touches, brings new life, and nurtures the soul. It acknowledges the worth and beauty of the beloved. The Song's love reflects wonderfully on God's love, without taking a moment away from the lovers.

How many failed substitutes do we try? We have only to look at the latest cultural version of glamour and sexuality to see the unfilled longings of many. "The heart wants what the heart wants," a famous serial adulterer once said to explain his affairs. No, the Song insists, the heart wants this: love so sure, strong, and exciting that to settle for less is to trade gold for copper pennies.

It is God's great gift that marital love is of such great worth and satisfaction. Strive for and remain with God's plan for man and woman. Find it, experience it, treasure it—and say "thank You, Lord" for the supple steel and fire of delirious love, made for completing what you alone can never know.

1 Solomon's Finest Song.[A,a]

W[B] 2 Oh, that he would kiss me
with the kisses of his mouth!
For your[C] love is[D] more delightful
than wine.[b]
3 The fragrance of your perfume
is intoxicating;[c]
your name is perfume poured out.[d]
No wonder young women[E] adore you.
4 Take me with you[e] — let us hurry.
Oh, that the king would bring[F] me
to his chambers.

Y We will rejoice and be glad for you;
we will praise your love
more than wine.

W It is only right that they adore you.
5 Daughters of Jerusalem,[f]
I am dark like the tents of Kedar,[g]
yet lovely[h] like the curtains of Solomon.
6 Do not stare at me because I am dark,
for the sun has gazed on me.
My mother's sons were angry
with me;[i]
they made me a keeper
of the vineyards.[j]
I have not kept my own vineyard.[G]
7 Tell me, you, the one I love:[k]
Where do you pasture your sheep?[l]
Where do you let them rest at noon?[m]
Why should I be like one who veils
herself[H,I]
beside the flocks
of your companions?[n]

M[J] 8 If you do not know,
most beautiful of women,[o]
follow[K] the tracks of the flock,
and pasture your young goats
near the shepherds' tents.
9 I compare you, my darling,[p]
to a[L] mare
among Pharaoh's chariots.[M,q]
10 Your cheeks are beautiful
with jewelry,[r]
your neck with its necklace.
11 We will make gold jewelry for you,
accented with silver.

W 12 While the king is on his couch,[N]
my perfume[O] releases its fragrance.[s]
13 My love is a sachet of myrrh to me,[t]
spending the night
between my breasts.
14 My love is a cluster of henna blossoms
to me,[u]
in the vineyards of En-gedi.[P,v]

M 15 How beautiful you are, my darling.
How very beautiful!
Your eyes are doves.[w]

W 16 How handsome you are, my love.[x]
How delightful!
Our bed is lush with foliage;
17 the beams of our house are cedars,
and our rafters are cypresses.[Q]

2 I am a rose[R,S] of Sharon,
a lily[T] of the valleys.[y]

M 2 Like a lily among thorns,
so is my darling
among the young women.

W 3 Like an apricot[U] tree among the trees
of the forest,
so is my love among the young men.
I delight to sit in his shade,
and his fruit is sweet to my taste.
4 He brought me
to the banquet hall,[V,z]
and he looked on me with love.[W,aa]
5 Sustain me with raisins;
refresh me with apricots,[X]
for I am lovesick.[ab]
6 His left hand is under my head,
and his right arm embraces me.[Y,ac]
7 Young women of Jerusalem,
I charge you
by the gazelles and the wild does
of the field:

[a] 1:1 1Kg 4:32
[b] 1:2 Sg 4:10
[c] 1:3 Jn 12:3
[d] Ec 7:1
[e] 1:4 Hs 11:4
[f] 1:5 Sg 2:7; 3:5,10; 5:8,16; 8:4
[g] Ps 120:5; Is 60:7
[h] Sg 2:14; 4:3; 6:4
[i] 1:6 Ps 69:8
[j] Sg 8:11
[k] 1:7 Sg 3:1-4
[l] Sg 2:16; 6:3
[m] Is 13:20; Jr 33:12
[n] Sg 8:13
[o] 1:8 Sg 5:9; 6:1
[p] 1:9 Sg 1:15
[q] 2Ch 1:16-17
[r] 1:10 Sg 5:13
[s] 1:12 Sg 4:14; Mk 14:3; Jn 12:3
[t] 1:13 Ps 45:8; Jn 19:39
[u] 1:14 Sg 4:13
[v] 1Sm 23:29
[w] 1:15 Sg 4:1
[x] 1:16 Sg 2:3
[y] 2:1 Sg 5:13; 7:2; Hs 14:5
[z] 2:4 Sg 1:4
[aa] Ps 20:5
[ab] 2:5 Sg 5:8
[ac] 2:6 Sg 8:3

[A] 1:1 Or *The Song of Songs, which is Solomon's* [B] 1:2 The **W, M, Y, N,** and **B** indicate the editors' opinions of the changes of speakers: **W** = Woman, **M** = Man, **Y** = Young women of Jerusalem, **N** = Narrator, **B** = Brothers. If a letter is in parenthesis **(W)**, there is a question about the identity of the speaker. [C] 1:2 Unexpected change of grammatical persons, here from *he* and *his* to *your*, is a Hb poetic device. [D] 1:2 Or *your caresses are*, or *your lovemaking is* [E] 1:3 Or *wonder virgins* [F] 1:4 Or *The king has brought* [G] 1:6 Lit *my vineyard, which is mine* [H] 1:7 Or *who wanders* [I] 1:7 To express shame or grief, or to conceal identity as a prostitute would; Gn 38:14-15 [J] 1:8 Some understand the young women to be the speakers in this verse. [K] 1:8 Lit *go out for yourself into* [L] 1:9 Lit *my* [M] 1:9 Pharaoh's chariot horses were stallions. [N] 1:12 Or *is at his table* [O] 1:12 Lit *nard* [P] 1:14 = Wellspring of the Young Goat [Q] 1:17 Or *firs*, or *pines* [R] 2:1 Or *meadow saffron* [S] 2:1 Not the modern flower but a common wildflower in northern Israel [T] 2:1 Or *lotus* [U] 2:3 Or *apple* [V] 2:4 Lit *the house of wine* [W] 2:4 Or *and his banner over me is love* [X] 2:5 Or *apples* [Y] 2:6 Or *Let his left hand be under . . . and his right arm embrace me*

do not stir up or awaken love
until the appropriate time.[A,a]

8 Listen! My love is approaching.
Look! Here he comes,
leaping over the mountains,[b]
bounding over the hills.
9 My love is like a gazelle
or a young stag.[c]
Look, he is standing behind our wall,
gazing through the windows,
peering through the lattice.
10 My love calls to me:

M Arise,[d] my darling.
Come away, my beautiful one.
11 For now the winter is past;
the rain has ended and gone away.
12 The blossoms appear
in the countryside.
The time of singing[B] has come,
and the turtledove's cooing is heard
in our land.[e]
13 The fig tree ripens its figs;[f]
the blossoming vines give off
their fragrance.[g]
Arise, my darling.
Come away, my beautiful one.

14 My dove,[h] in the clefts of the rock,[i]
in the crevices of the cliff,
let me see your face,[C]
let me hear your voice;[j]
for your voice is sweet,
and your face is lovely.[k]

(W)15 Catch the foxes for us[l] —
the little foxes that ruin
the vineyards —
for our vineyards are in bloom.[m]

W 16 My love is mine and I am his;[n]
he feeds among the lilies.
17 Before the day breaks[D]
and the shadows flee,
turn to me, my love, and be
like a gazelle
or a young stag[o]
on the divided mountains.[E,p]

3 In my bed at night[F]
I sought the one I love;[q]
I sought him, but did not find him.[G,r]

2 I will arise now and go about the city,
through the streets and the plazas.[s]
I will seek the one I love.
I sought him, but did not find him.
3 The guards who go about the city
found me.[t]
I asked them, "Have you seen the one
I love?"
4 I had just passed them
when I found the one I love.
I held on to him and would not
let him go
until I brought him
to my mother's house[u] —
to the chamber of the one
who conceived me.
5 Young women of Jerusalem,
I charge you
by the gazelles and the wild does
of the field:
do not stir up or awaken love
until the appropriate time.[A,v]

N 6 What is this[w] coming up
from the wilderness
like columns of smoke,
scented with myrrh and frankincense[x]
from every fragrant powder
of the merchant?
7 It is Solomon's royal litter[H]
surrounded by 60 warriors
from the mighty of Israel.
8 All of them are skilled with swords
and trained in warfare.
Each has his sword at his side[y]
to guard against the terror
of the night.[z]

9 King Solomon made a sedan chair[I]
for himself
with wood from Lebanon.
10 He made its posts of silver,
its back[J] of gold,
and its seat of purple.
Its interior is inlaid with love[K]
by the young women of Jerusalem.[aa]
11 Come out, young women of ·Zion,[ab]
and gaze at King Solomon,
wearing the crown his mother placed
on him

[a]2:7 Sg 3:5; 5:8; 8:4 [b]2:8 Is 52:7 [c]2:9 Sg 2:17; 8:14 [d]2:10 Sg 2:13 [e]2:12 Jr 8:7 [f]2:13 Mt 24:32 [g]Sg 7:12 [h]2:14 Sg 5:2; 6:9 [i]Jr 48:28 [j]Sg 8:13 [k]Sg 1:5 [l]2:15 Ezk 13:4 [m]Sg 2:13 [n]2:16 Sg 6:3; 7:10; 8:6 [o]2:17 Sg 2:9 [p]Sg 4:5-6; 8:14 [q]3:1 Sg 1:7 [r]Sg 5:6 [s]3:2 Jr 5:1 [t]3:3 Sg 5:7 [u]3:4 Sg 8:2 [v]3:5 Sg 2:7; 5:8; 8:4 [w]3:6 Sg 6:10; 8:5 [x]Sg 4:6,14 [y]3:8 Ps 45:3 [z]Ps 91:5 [aa]3:10 Sg 1:5 [ab]3:11 Is 3:16-17; 4:4

A2:7; 3:5 Lit *until it pleases* B2:12 Or *pruning* C2:14 Or *form* D2:17 Lit *breathes* E2:17 Or *the Bether mountains*, or *the mountains of spices*; Hb obscure F3:1 Or *bed night after night* G3:1 LXX adds *I called him, but he did not answer me* H3:7 A conveyance carried on the shoulders of servants I3:9 In Hb, the term sedan chair is possibly a synonym for "litter"; it is also called a palanquin. J3:10 Or *base*, or *canopy* K3:10 Or *leather*

the day of his wedding[a] —
the day of his heart's rejoicing.

4 M How beautiful you are, my darling.
How very beautiful!
Behind your veil,
your eyes are doves.[b]
Your hair is like a flock of goats
streaming down Mount Gilead.[c]
2 Your teeth are like a flock
of newly shorn sheep
coming up from washing,
each one having a twin,
and not one missing.[A,d]
3 Your lips are like a scarlet cord,[e]
and your mouth[B] is lovely.
Behind your veil,
your brow[C] is like a slice
of pomegranate.[f]
4 Your neck is like the tower of David,[g]
constructed in layers.
A thousand bucklers are hung on it —
all of them shields of warriors.[D]
5 Your breasts are like two fawns,
twins of a gazelle,[h] that feed
among the lilies.
6 Before the day breaks[E]
and the shadows flee,[i]
I will make my way to the mountain
of myrrh
and the hill of frankincense.[j]
7 You are absolutely beautiful,[k] my darling,
with no imperfection in you.
8 Come with me from Lebanon,[F,l]
my bride[m] —
with me from Lebanon!
Descend from the peak of Amana,
from the summit of Senir and Hermon,[n]
from the dens of the lions,
from the mountains of the leopards.
9 You have captured my heart,[o]
my sister,[G,p] my bride.
You have captured my heart
with one glance of your eyes,
with one jewel of your necklace.
10 How delightful your love is, my sister,
my bride.
Your love is much better than wine,[q]
and the fragrance of your perfume
than any balsam.
11 Your lips drip sweetness like
the honeycomb, my bride.[r]
Honey and milk[s] are
under your tongue.
The fragrance of your garments is like
the fragrance of Lebanon.
12 My sister, my bride, you are
a locked garden —
a locked garden[H] and a sealed spring.[t]
13 Your branches are a paradise[I]
of pomegranates
with choicest fruits,[u]
henna with nard —
14 nard and saffron, calamus
and cinnamon,[v]
with all the trees of frankincense,[w]
myrrh and aloes,[x]
with all the best spices.
15 You are a garden spring,
a well of flowing water[y]
streaming from Lebanon.

W 16 Awaken,[z] north wind —
come, south wind.
Blow on my garden,
and spread the fragrance of its spices.
Let my love come to his garden
and eat its choicest fruits.[aa]

5 M I have come to my garden — my sister,
my bride.
I gather[J] my myrrh with my spices.
I eat my honeycomb with my honey.
I drink my wine with my milk.

N Eat, friends!
Drink, be intoxicated with love![K,ab]

W 2 I sleep, but my heart is awake.
A sound! My love is knocking![ac]

M Open to me, my sister, my darling,
my dove, my perfect one.
For my head is drenched with dew,
my hair with droplets of the night.

W 3 I have taken off my clothing.[ad]
How can I put it back on?
I have washed my feet.

[a]3:11 Is 62:5 [b]4:1 Sg 1:15; 5:12 [c]Sg 6:5 [d]4:2 Sg 6:6 [e]4:3 Jos 2:18 [f]Sg 6:7 [g]4:4 Sg 7:4 [h]4:5 Sg 7:3 [i]4:6 Sg 2:17 [j]Sg 3:6; 4:14 [k]4:7 Sg 1:15; Eph 5:27 [l]4:8 1Kg 4:33 [m]Is 62:5 [n]Dt 3:9; 1Ch 5:23 [o]4:9 Sg 6:5; 7:5 [p]Sg 5:1-2 [q]4:10 Sg 1:2,4 [r]4:11 Pr 5:3 [s]Ex 3:8,17; Nm 14:8; 16:13-14 [t]4:12 1Kg 21:8; Est 8:10; Jb 9:7 [u]4:13 Sg 7:13 [v]4:14 Ex 30:23 [w]Sg 4:6 [x]Sg 3:6; Jn 19:39 [y]4:15 Gn 26:19; Lv 14:5; Jr 2:13 [z]4:16 Sg 2:7; 3:5; 8:4 [aa]Sg 7:13 [ab]5:1 Pr 5:19 [ac]5:2 Sg 2:8 [ad]5:3 Lk 11:7

A4:2 Lit *and no one bereaved among them* B4:3 Or *speech* C4:3 Or *temple*, or *cheek*, or *lips* D4:4 Perhaps describing the woman's necklace E4:6 Lit *breathes* F4:8 In Hb, the word for Lebanon is similar to "frankincense" in Sg 4:6,14,15. G4:9 A term of endearment H4:12 Some Hb mss read *locked fountain* I4:13 Or *park*, or *orchard* J5:1 Lit *pluck* K5:1 Or *Drink your fill, lovers*

How can I get them dirty?
4 My love thrust his hand
through the opening,
and my feelings were stirred for him.
5 I rose to open for my love.
My hands dripped with myrrh,[a]
my fingers with flowing myrrh
on the handles of the bolt.
6 I opened to my love,
but my love had turned
and gone away.
I was crushed[A] that he had left.[B]
I sought him, but did not find him.[b]
I called him, but he did not answer.
7 The guards who go about the city
found me.[c]
They beat and wounded me;
they took my cloak[C] from me —
the guardians of the walls.[d]
8 Young women of Jerusalem,
I charge you:[e]
if you find my love,
tell him that I am lovesick.[f]

Y 9 What makes the one you love better
than another,
most beautiful of women?[g]
What makes him better than another,
that you would give us this charge?

W 10 My love is fit and strong,[D,h]
notable among ten thousand.[i]
11 His head is purest gold.
His hair is wavy[E,j]
and black as a raven.
12 His eyes are like doves[k]
beside streams of water,
washed in milk
and set like jewels.[F]
13 His cheeks[l] are like beds of spice,
towers of[G] perfume.
His lips are lilies,
dripping with flowing myrrh.[m]
14 His arms[H] are rods of gold
set[I] with topaz.[J,n]
His body[K] is an ivory panel
covered with sapphires.[o]
15 His legs are alabaster pillars
set on pedestals of pure gold.
His presence is like Lebanon,[p]
as majestic as the cedars.[q]
16 His mouth is sweetness.
He is absolutely desirable.[r]
This is my love, and this is my friend,
young women of Jerusalem.

6

Y Where has your love gone,
most beautiful of women?
Which way has he[L] turned?
We will seek him with you.

W 2 My love has gone down to his garden,[s]
to beds of spice,[t]
to feed in the gardens[u]
and gather lilies.[v]
3 I am my love's and my love is mine;[w]
he feeds among the lilies.

M 4 You are as beautiful as Tirzah,[M]
my darling,
lovely as Jerusalem,
awe-inspiring as an army
with banners.[x]
5 Turn your eyes away from me,
for they captivate me.[y]
Your hair is like a flock of goats
streaming down from Gilead.[z]
6 Your teeth are like a flock of ewes
coming up from washing,
each one having a twin,
and not one missing.[N,aa]
7 Behind your veil,[ab]
your brow[O] is like a slice of pomegranate.
8 There are 60 queens
and 80 concubines[ac]
and young women[P] without number.
9 But my dove,[ad] my virtuous one,
is unique;[ae]
she is the favorite of her mother,
perfect to the one who gave her birth.
Women see her and declare
her fortunate;[af]
queens and concubines also,
and they sing her praises:

Y[Q] 10 Who is this[R,ag] who shines
like the dawn —
as beautiful as the moon,

[a]**5:5** Sg 5:13
[b]**5:6** Sg 3:1-2
[c]**5:7** Sg 3:3
[d]Sg 8:9-10
[e]**5:8** Sg 2:7; 3:5; 8:4
[f]Sg 2:5
[g]**5:9** Sg 1:8; 6:1
[h]**5:10** 1Sm 16:12
[i]Ps 45:2
[j]**5:11** Sg 5:2
[k]**5:12** Sg 1:15; 4:1
[l]**5:13** Sg 1:10
[m]Sg 5:5
[n]**5:14** Ex 28:20; 39:13; Ezk 1:16
[o]Ex 24:10
[p]**5:15** Sg 7:4-5
[q]1Kg 4:33
[r]**5:16** Sg 4:7
[s]**6:2** Sg 4:16; 5:1
[t]Sg 5:13
[u]Sg 1:7
[v]Sg 2:1
[w]**6:3** Sg 2:16; 7:10; 8:6
[x]**6:4** Nm 2:2-3; Sg 6:10
[y]**6:5** Sg 4:9
[z]Sg 4:1
[aa]**6:6** Sg 4:2
[ab]**6:7** Sg 4:3
[ac]**6:8** 1Kg 11:3
[ad]**6:9** Sg 2:14; 5:2
[ae]Pr 31:29
[af]Gn 30:13
[ag]**6:10** Sg 3:6; 8:5

[A]**5:6** Lit *My soul went out* [B]**5:6** Or *spoken* [C]**5:7** Or *veil*, or *shawl* [D]**5:10** Or *is radiant and ruddy* [E]**5:11** Or *is like palm leaves*; Hb obscure [F]**5:12** Lit *milk sitting in fullness* [G]**5:13** LXX, Vg read *spice, yielding* [H]**5:14** Lit *hands* [I]**5:14** Lit *filled*; Sg 5:2,12 [J]**5:14** Probably yellow topaz [K]**5:14** Lit *abdomen* [L]**6:1** Lit *your love* [M]**6:4** = a mountain city in Manasseh [N]**6:6** Lit *and no one bereaved among them* [O]**6:7** Or *temple*, or *cheek*, or *lips* [P]**6:8** Or *and virgins*; Sg 1:3 [Q]**6:10** Some see v. 10 as spoken by **M**. [R]**6:10** In Hb, the word for "this" is feminine.

bright as the sun,
awe-inspiring as an army
with banners?[a]

W 11 I came down to the walnut grove
to see the blossoms of the valley,
to see if the vines were budding[b]
and the pomegranates blooming.
12 Before I knew it,
my desire put me
among the chariots of
my noble people.[A]

Y 13B Come back, come back,
Shulammite![C,D]
Come back, come back, that
we may look at you!

M Why are you looking
at the Shulammite,
as you look at the dance[c]
of the two camps?[E,d]

7 How beautiful are your sandaled feet,
princess![F,e]
The curves of your thighs
are like jewelry,
the handiwork of a master.
2 Your navel is a rounded bowl;
it never lacks mixed wine.
Your waist[G] is a mound of wheat
surrounded by lilies.
3 Your breasts are like two fawns,
twins of a gazelle.[f]
4 Your neck is like a tower of ivory,[g]
your eyes like pools in Heshbon
by the gate of Bath-rabbim.
Your nose is like the tower of Lebanon
looking toward Damascus.
5 Your head crowns you[H]
like Mount Carmel,
the hair of your head
like purple cloth —
a king could be held captive[h]
in your tresses.
6 How beautiful you are
and how pleasant,[i]
my love, with such delights!
7 Your stature is like a palm tree;
your breasts are clusters of fruit.

[a]**6:10** Sg 6:4
[b]**6:11** Sg 7:12
[c]**6:13** Jdg 21:21
[d]Gn 32:2; 2Sm 17:24
[e]**7:1** Ps 45:13
[f]**7:3** Sg 4:5
[g]**7:4** Sg 4:4
[h]**7:5** Sg 4:9
[i]**7:6** Sg 1:15-16
[j]**7:8** Pr 5:19
[k]Sg 2:3
[l]**7:9** Sg 5:16
[m]**7:10** Gn 3:16; 4:7
[n]Sg 2:16; 6:3; 8:6
[o]**7:12** Sg 6:11
[p]**7:13** Gn 30:14-16
[q]**8:2** Sg 3:4
[r]**8:3** Sg 2:6
[s]**8:4** Sg 2:7; 3:5
[t]**8:5** Sg 3:6; 6:10

8 I said, "I will climb the palm tree
and take hold of its fruit."[j]
May your breasts be like clusters
of grapes,
and the fragrance of your breath
like apricots.[k]
9 Your mouth[I] is like fine wine[l] —

W flowing smoothly for my love,
gliding past my lips and teeth![J]
10 I belong to my love,
and his desire[m] is for me.[n]
11 Come, my love,
let's go to the field;
let's spend the night
among the henna blossoms.[K]
12 Let's go early to the vineyards;
let's see if the vine has budded,
if the blossom has opened,
if the pomegranates are in bloom.[o]
There I will give you my love.
13 The mandrakes[p] give off a fragrance,
and at our doors is every delicacy —
new as well as old.
I have treasured them up for you,
my love.

8 If only I could treat you
like my brother,[L]
one who nursed
at my mother's breasts,
I would find you in public
and kiss you,
and no one would scorn me.
2 I would lead you, I would take you,
to the house of my mother[q]
who taught me.[M]
I would give you spiced wine to drink
from my pomegranate juice.
3 His left hand is under my head,
and his right arm embraces me.[r]
4 Young women of Jerusalem,
I charge you:
do not stir up or awaken love
until the appropriate time.[s]

Y 5 Who is this[t] coming up
from the wilderness,
leaning on the one she loves?

[A]**6:12** Or *of Amminadib*, or *of my people of a prince*; Hb obscure [B]**6:13** Sg 7:1 in Hb [C]**6:13** Or *the peaceable one* [D]**6:13** Perhaps an inhabitant of the town of Shunem, or a feminine form of Solomon's name [E]**6:13** Or *dance of Mahanaim* [F]**7:1** Lit *daughter of a nobleman* or *prince* [G]**7:2** Or *belly* [H]**7:5** Lit *head upon you is* [I]**7:9** Lit *palate* [J]**7:9** LXX, Syr, Vg; MT reads *past lips of sleepers* [K]**7:11** Or *the villages* [L]**8:1** Lit *Would that you were like a brother to me* [M]**8:2** LXX adds *and into the chamber of the one who bore me*

W I awakened you under
the apricot tree.[a]
There your mother conceived you;
there she conceived and gave
you birth.
6 Set me as a seal on your heart,
as a seal on your arm.[b]
For love is as strong as death;[c]
ardent love is as unrelenting
as *Sheol.
Love's flames are fiery flames[d] —
the fiercest of all.[A]
7 Mighty waters cannot extinguish love;
rivers cannot sweep it away.
If a man were to give all his wealth[B]
for love,[e]
it would be utterly scorned.

B 8 Our sister is young;
she has no breasts.[f]
What will we do for our sister
on the day she is spoken for?
9 If she is a wall,
we will build a silver parapet on it.
If she is a door,
we will enclose it with cedar planks.[C,g]

W 10 I am[D] a wall
and my breasts like towers.
So in his eyes I have become
like one who finds peace.[E]
11 Solomon owned a vineyard
in Baal-hamon.[h]
He leased the vineyard to tenants.[i]
Each was to bring for his fruit
1,000 pieces of silver.[j]
12 I have my own vineyard.[F,k]
The 1,000 are for you, Solomon,
but 200 for those who guard its fruits.

M 13 You[G] who dwell in the gardens —
companions[l] are listening
for your voice —
let me hear you![m]

W 14 Hurry to me, my love,
and be like a gazelle
or a young stag
on the mountains of spices.[n]

[a]8:5 Sg 2:3 [b]8:6 Sg 2:16; 6:3; 7:10 [c]Rm 8:38-39; 1Co 13:8 [d]Dt 32:21-22; Pr 6:34; 27:4 [e]8:7 Pr 6:35 [f]8:8 Ezk 16:7 [g]8:9 1Kg 6:15 [h]8:11 Ec 2:4 [i]Mt 21:33 [j]Is 7:23 [k]8:12 Sg 1:6 [l]8:13 Sg 1:7 [m]Sg 2:14 [n]8:14 Sg 2:17

[A]8:6 Or *the blaze of the LORD* [B]8:7 Lit *all the wealth of his house* [C]8:8-9 Vv. 8-9 may record what the girl's brothers used to say. [D]8:10 Or *was* [E]8:10 In Hb, the word for peace sounds similar to Solomon and Shulammite. [F]8:12 Lit *My vineyard, which is mine, is before me*; Sg 1:6 [G]8:13 In Hb, the word for You is feminine.

■ **AUTHOR:** Isaiah

■■ **DATE:** Isaiah prophesied during the reigns of Uzziah, Jotham, Ahaz, and Hezekiah—around 740–681 B.C.

Isaiah is called the greatest of the writing prophets, a testament to his God-given talent for framing in words the majestic mission of God—the judgment and salvation of humankind.

Every prophet announces bad news: God condemns disobedience. Sometimes God's judgment is a mere about-face, turning away, leaving unrepentant sinners alone in their own distress. Sometimes judgment is active punishment, often enacted by foreign armies.

In Isaiah's day, around 700 B.C., the foreign armies were Assyria, which had conquered the northern kingdom in 722 B.C., and Babylon, threatening the southern kingdom. How could the faithful God of the covenant—Moses' God, Joshua's commander, David's Lord—ever employ Israel's enemies to enact His will? To most Israelite leaders, the answer was "impossible, never." To the prophets, however, the threat of conquest due to the nation's spiritual unfaithfulness was quite real.

ISAIAH

More real, however, especially to Isaiah, was the final victory of God—the recovery of people's deepest hopes and the rehearsal of God's glory by all the nations. Visions of that wondrous day were far-off, cloudy, but certain. To get there, Isaiah announced, would require a most unusual plan.

Swinging swords and battle cries had been the customary way Israel won many battles—God at the lead advancing; God at the rear protecting; God in the ranks encouraging. Challenging superior armies, Israel's best days came after glorious victories followed by appropriate celebration and worship. But God's mission revealed through Isaiah shows a different face.

It seems that the Servant of the Lord, deliverer of His people and Savior of all, will appear disfigured, despised, and crushed. The Servant's wisdom will not save Him from oppression, affliction, and wrongful death. His accusers will have no case, but God Himself will make the case by placing on the Servant's shoulders our penalty for sin. Thus will God's mission be accomplished by suffering, rather than by sabers or spears. This loss (the death of His Servant) would achieve a greater gain: the justification of many.

Many years after Isaiah wrote his quotable lines, other writers—missionaries, pioneer preachers, disciples—explained the mission that the ancient prophets foretold. God would make His victory over sin and evil certain, once for all, through Jesus. The love of God would show like the rising sun in the person of Jesus. By faith, all God's people would be freed, renewed, forgiven, and welcomed to share God's Kingdom.

Such hope is worth an oratorio without end. And that's just what God has in mind—an everlasting Kingdom of justice, peace, and love. The Servant has won your victory. You are forgiven and welcomed.

1 The vision[a] concerning Judah and Jerusalem that Isaiah[b] son of Amoz saw during the reigns[A,B] of Uzziah,[c] Jotham,[d] Ahaz,[e] and Hezekiah,[f] kings of Judah.[g]

Judah on Trial

2 Listen, heavens,
and pay attention, earth,[h]
for the LORD has spoken:
"I have raised children[C]
and brought them up,
but they have rebelled against Me.[i]
3 The ox knows its owner,
and the donkey its master's
feeding trough,
but Israel does not know;
My people do not understand."[j]

4 Oh sinful nation,
people weighed down with iniquity,[k]
brood of evildoers,[l]
depraved children![C]
They have abandoned[m] the LORD;
they have despised[n] the Holy One
of Israel;[o]
they have turned their backs on Him.

5 Why do you want more beatings?
Why do you keep on rebelling?
The whole head is hurt,
and the whole heart is sick.
6 From the sole of the foot
even to the head,[p]
no spot is uninjured[q]—
wounds, welts, and festering sores
not cleansed, bandaged,
or soothed with oil.

7 Your land is desolate,
your cities burned with fire;[r]
foreigners devour your fields
before your very eyes—
a desolation demolished by foreigners.
8 Daughter ·Zion[s] is abandoned
like a shelter in a vineyard,
like a shack in a cucumber field,
like a besieged city.
9 If the LORD of ·Hosts[t]
had not left us a few survivors,[u]
we would be like Sodom,
we would resemble Gomorrah.[v]

10 Hear the word of the LORD,[w]
you rulers of Sodom!
Listen to the instruction of our God,
you people of Gomorrah![x]
11 "What are all your sacrifices to Me?"
asks the LORD.
"I have had enough of ·burnt offerings
and rams
and the fat of well-fed cattle;
I have no desire for the blood of bulls,
lambs, or male goats.[y]
12 When you come to appear before Me,
who requires this from you—
this trampling of My courts?
13 Stop bringing useless offerings.[z]
Your incense is detestable to Me.
New Moons and Sabbaths,[aa]
and the calling
of solemn assemblies[ab]—
I cannot stand iniquity[ac] with a festival.
14 I hate your New Moons
and prescribed festivals.
They have become a burden to Me;
I am tired of putting up with them.
15 When you lift up your hands in prayer,[ad]
I will refuse to look at you;
even if you offer countless prayers,
I will not listen.[ae]
Your hands are covered with blood.[af]

Purification of Jerusalem

16 "Wash yourselves. Cleanse yourselves.[ag]
Remove your evil deeds
from My sight.
Stop doing evil.[ah]
17 Learn to do what is good.
Seek justice.[ai]
Correct the oppressor.[D]
Defend the rights of the fatherless.
Plead the widow's cause.

18 "Come, let us discuss this,"[aj]
says the LORD.
"Though your sins are like scarlet,
they will be as white as snow;[ak]
though they are as red as crimson,
they will be like wool.
19 If you are willing and obedient,
you will eat the good things of the land.[al]
20 But if you refuse and rebel,

[a]**1:1** Pr 29:18; Dn 8:1; Ob 1; Nah 1:1; Hab 2:2-3 [b]Is 2:1; 13:1 [c]2Ch 26:3-5 [d]2Kg 15:32-38 [e]2Kg 16:1-4 [f]2Kg 18:1-8 [g]Hs 1:1; Mc 1:1 [h]**1:2** Dt 4:26; 32:1; Is 30:1; Mc 1:2 [i]Is 30:1 [j]**1:3** Jr 8:7 [k]**1:4** Is 13:11 [l]Is 14:20; Mt 3:7 [m]Dt 4:31 [n]Nm 14:11; Dt 31:20; Pr 5:12; Is 5:24 [o]Is 5:19,24; 10:20; 12:6; 29:19; 30:11-15 [p]**1:6** Jb 2:7 [q]Ps 38:3 [r]**1:7** Lv 26:33; Dt 28:51-52; Is 6:11-12; Jr 44:6 [s]**1:8** Is 10:32; 37:22; Zch 2:10; 9:9 [t]**1:9** 1Sm 17:45 [u]Is 10:21-22 [v]Gn 19:24-25; Is 3:9; 13:19; Rm 9:29 [w]**1:10** Is 28:14 [x]Is 3:9; Ezk 16:46-49,55; Rv 11:8 [y]**1:11** 1Sm 15:22; Jr 6:20; Hs 6:6; Am 5:21-24; Mt 23:23; Mk 12:33 [z]**1:13** Mal 1:10 [aa]Nm 28:11; 1Ch 23:31 [ab]Ex 12:16; Lv 23:36 [ac]Is 13:11 [ad]**1:15** 1Kg 8:22 [ae]Is 59:2; Jr 7:16; Ezk 8:18; Am 5:23; Hab 1:2; Zch 7:13 [af]Pr 1:28; Is 59:1-3; Mc 3:4 [ag]**1:16** Ps 26:6; Is 4:4; 52:11 [ah]Jr 25:5 [ai]**1:17** Dt 16:20; 1Kg 3:11; Ps 89:14; Is 10:2; 11:4; Am 5:15; Zch 7:9 [aj]**1:18** Is 41:1,21; 43:26; Mc 6:2 [ak]Ps 51:7; Is 43:25; 44:22; Rv 7:14 [al]**1:19-20** Dt 30:15-20

[A]**1:1** Lit *saw in the days* [B]**1:1** ca 792–686 B.C. [C]**1:2,4** Or *sons* [D]**1:17** Or *Aid the oppressed*

you will be devoured by the sword."[a]
For the mouth of the LORD has spoken.[b]

21 The faithful city —
what an adulteress[A] she has become!
She was once full of justice.
Righteousness once dwelt in her —
but now, murderers!
22 Your silver has become dross,[B]
your beer[C] is diluted with water.
23 Your rulers are rebels,
friends of thieves.[c]
They all love graft
and chase after bribes.[d]
They do not defend the rights
of the fatherless,
and the widow's case never comes
before them.[e]

24 Therefore the Lord GOD of Hosts,
the Mighty One of Israel, declares:
"Ah, I will gain satisfaction
from My foes;
I will take revenge
against My enemies.[f]
25 I will turn My hand against you[g]
and will burn away
your dross[B] completely;[D]
I will remove all your impurities.[h]
26 I will restore your judges[i] to what
they once were,[E]
and your advisers to their former state.[F]
Afterward you will be called
the Righteous City,[j]
a Faithful City."

27 Zion will be redeemed by justice,
her repentant ones by righteousness.[k]
28 But both rebels and sinners
will be destroyed,
and those who abandon the LORD
will perish.
29 Indeed, they[G] will be ashamed
of the sacred trees
you desired,[l]
and you will be embarrassed because of
the gardens
you have chosen.[m]
30 For you will become like an oak
whose leaves are withered,
and like a garden without water.[n]
31 The strong one will become tinder,
and his work a spark;
both will burn together,[o]
with no one to quench the flames.[p]

The City of Peace

2 The vision that Isaiah[q] son of Amoz saw
concerning Judah and Jerusalem:

2 In[r] the last days[s]
the mountain of the LORD's house[t]
will be established
at the top of the mountains
and will be raised above the hills.
All nations will stream to it,[u]
3 and many peoples will come and say,
"Come, let us go up to the mountain
of the LORD,
to the house of the God of Jacob.[v]
He will teach us about His ways
so that we may walk in His paths."
For instruction will go out of ·Zion
and the word of the LORD
from Jerusalem.
4 He will settle disputes
among the nations
and provide arbitration
for many peoples.
They will turn their swords
into plows
and their spears into pruning knives.[w]
Nations will not take up the sword
against other nations,
and they will never again train for war.[x]

The Day of the LORD

5 House of Jacob,
come and let us walk
in the LORD's light.[y]
6 For You have abandoned[z] Your people,
the house of Jacob,
because they are full of ·divination
from the East
and of fortune-tellers[aa]
like the Philistines.[ab]
They are in league[H] with foreigners.
7 Their[I,J] land is full of silver and gold,
and there is no limit to their treasures;
their land is full of horses,
and there is no limit to their chariots.[ac]

[a]1:20 Jr 12:12 [b]Is 24:3; 40:5; 58:14; Mc 4:4 [c]1:23 Hs 5:10 [d]Ex 23:8; Mc 7:2-6 [e]Ex 22:22; Dt 24:17; Is 10:2; Jr 5:28; Ezk 22:7; Zch 7:10 [f]1:24 Is 35:4; 59:18; Jr 46:10 [g]1:25 Ps 81:14; Is 5:25; Am 1:8 [h]Ezk 22:20; Mal 3:3 [i]1:26 Is 60:17; Mt 19:28 [j]Is 33:5; 60:14; 62:1-2; Zch 8:3 [k]1:27 Rm 3:26 [l]1:29 Is 2:8; 57:5; Hs 4:13 [m]Is 65:3; 66:17 [n]1:30 Ps 1:3; Is 64:6 [o]1:31 Is 5:24; 9:19; 26:11; 33:11-14 [p]Is 66:24; Mt 3:12; Mk 9:43 [q]2:1 2Kg 19:2; 20:1; 2Ch 26:22; 32:20; Is 1:1; 13:1 [r]2:2-4 Mc 4:1-4; Rm 2:20 [s]2:2 Nm 24:14; Dt 4:30; Ezk 38:16; Hs 3:5 [t]2Ch 33:15; Is 27:13; 66:20 [u]Ps 22:27; Is 56:7; Zch 14:10 [v]2:3 Is 29:23; 45:23; 60:13; 66:18 [w]2:4 Is 11:6-9; 32:17-18; Jl 3:10 [x]Ps 72:3,7; Is 9:7; Hs 2:18; Zch 9:10 [y]2:5 Ps 27:1; 43:3 [z]2:6 Dt 31:17; Ps 94:14; Is 1:4 [aa]Lv 19:26; Dt 18:10-14; 2Kg 21:6; 2Ch 33:6; Jr 27:9; Mc 5:12 [ab]Jdg 14:3; 1Sm 6:2; 2Kg 1:2-6 [ac]2:7 Dt 17:17

A1:21 Or *prostitute* B1:22,25 Or *burnished lead* C1:22 Or *wine* D1:25 Lit *dross as with lye* E1:26 Lit *judges as at the first* F1:26 Lit *advisers as at the beginning* G1:29 Some Hb mss; other Hb mss, Tg read *you* H2:6 Or *They teem*, or *They partner*; Hb obscure I2:7 Lit *Its* J2:7 = the house of Jacob

8 Their land is full of idols;[a]
they bow down to the work
of their hands,
to what their fingers have made.[b]
9 So humanity is brought low,
and man is humbled.
Do not forgive them![c]
10 Go into the rocks[d]
and hide in the dust
from the terror of the LORD[e]
and from His majestic splendor.[f]
11 Human pride[A] will be humbled,[g]
and the loftiness of men
will be brought low;
the LORD alone will be exalted
on that day.
12 For a day belonging to the LORD
of ·Hosts is coming
against all that is proud and lofty,[h]
against all that is lifted up — it will
be humbled —
13 against all the cedars of Lebanon,[i]
lofty and lifted up,
against all the oaks of Bashan,[j]
14 against all the high mountains,[k]
against all the lofty hills,
15 against every high tower,[l]
against every fortified wall,
16 against every ship of Tarshish,[m]
and against every splendid sea vessel.
17 So human pride will be brought low,
and the loftiness of men
will be humbled;
the LORD alone will be exalted
on that day.[n]
18 The idols will vanish completely.
19 People will go into caves in the rocks[o]
and holes in the ground,
away from the terror of the LORD
and from His majestic splendor,
when He rises to terrify the earth.[p]
20 On that day people will throw
their silver and gold idols,[q]

[a]**2:8** Is 10:10-11; 19:1-3; 31:7; Jr 2:28 [b]Is 41:21-29; 44:9-17 [c]**2:9** Ex 34:7 [d]**2:10** Rv 6:15 [e]1Sm 11:7; 2Ch 14:14; 17:10; 19:7; Is 2:19,21 [f]2Th 1:9 [g]**2:11** Ps 18:27; Is 2:17; Mc 2:3; 2Co 10:5 [h]**2:12** Mal 4:1 [i]**2:13** Ps 29:5; Is 14:8; Hs 14:5 [j]Ezk 27:6; Zch 11:2 [k]**2:14** Is 40:4 [l]**2:15** Is 25:12; Zph 1:16 [m]**2:16** 1Kg 10:22; Is 23:1,14; 60:9 [n]**2:17** Mt 25:13 [o]**2:19** Is 2:10 [p]Ps 18:7; Is 13:13; 24:1,19-20; Hg 2:6-7; Heb 12:26 [q]**2:20** Is 30:22; 31:7

GOD'S HEART FOR THE WORLD

God's Promise of Peace

He will settle disputes among the nations and provide arbitration for many peoples. They will turn their swords into plows and their spears into pruning knives. Nations will not take up the sword against other nations, and they will never again train for war. (Isaiah 2:4)

The prophets reveal the tension between God's overwhelming love for all He has created and His hatred for the sin that destroys it. Isaiah 2–12 provide a great example. From 2:6 to the end of chapter 11 we read about God's judgment on several nations and His disappointment that, again, His people have failed Him. He has loved and provided for them, but still, "He looked for justice but saw injustice, for righteousness, but heard cries of wretchedness" (5:7). But Isaiah 2:2-5 and chapter 12 form a border of hope around this judgment, not just for Israel, but for all nations. God does not flippantly lose control of His emotions. He brings judgment in order to draw wayward nations back to Himself. Hebrews 12 says it well: "the Lord disciplines the one He loves . . . for our benefit, so that we can share in His holiness."

Discipline and judgment might still seem unfair if we see God's holiness as some abstract rule that He wants us to obey, but it is so much more than that. To follow Him is to live as we were created to live. It is God's holiness that allows us to pound our weapons into tools bringing peace between the nations.

Can you imagine a world where nations need "never again train for war"? This is what God promises in the midst of His judgment. Come, let us walk in the light of the Lord.

[A]**2:11** Lit *Mankind's proud eyes*

which they made to worship,
to the moles and the bats.
21 They will go into the caves of the rocks
and the crevices in the cliffs,
away from the terror of the LORD
and from His majestic splendor,[a]
when He rises to terrify the earth.
22 Put no more trust in man,
who has only the breath in his nostrils.[b]
What is he really worth?

Judah's Leaders Judged

3 Observe this: The Lord GOD of ·Hosts
is about to remove from Jerusalem
and from Judah
every kind of security:
the entire supply of bread and water,
2 the hero and warrior,[c]
the judge and prophet,
the fortune-teller and elder,
3 the commander of 50 and the dignitary,
the counselor, cunning magician,[A]
and necromancer.[B]
4 "I will make youths their leaders,[d]
and the unstable[C] will govern them."
5 The people will oppress one another,[e]
man against man, neighbor
against neighbor;
the youth will act arrogantly
toward the elder,
and the worthless toward the honorable.
6 A man will even seize his brother
in his father's house, saying:
"You have a cloak — you be our leader!
This heap of rubble will be
under your control."
7 On that day he will cry out, saying:
"I'm not a healer.
I don't even have food or clothing
in my house.
Don't make me the leader
of the people!"
8 For Jerusalem has stumbled
and Judah has fallen
because they have spoken and acted
against the LORD,[f]
defying His glorious presence.[g]
9 The look on their faces testifies
against them,
and like Sodom,[h] they flaunt their sin.
They do not conceal it.
Woe to them,
for they have brought evil
on themselves.[i]
10 Tell the righteous that it will go well
for them,
for they will eat the fruit of their labor.
11 Woe to the wicked — it will go badly
for them,
for what they have done will be done
to them.
12 Youths oppress My people,[j]
and women rule over them.
My people, your leaders mislead you;
they confuse the direction
of your paths.[k]
13 The LORD rises to argue the case
and stands to judge the people.[l]
14 The LORD brings this charge
against the elders and leaders
of His people:[m]
"You have devastated the vineyard.
The plunder from the poor is
in your houses.[n]
15 Why do you crush My people
and grind the faces of the poor?"
This is the declaration
of the Lord GOD of Hosts.

Jerusalem's Women Judged

16 The LORD also says:

Because the daughters of ·Zion
are haughty,[o]
walking with heads held high
and seductive eyes,
going along with prancing steps,
jingling their ankle bracelets,
17 the Lord will put scabs on the heads
of the daughters of Zion,
and the LORD will shave
their foreheads bare.

18 On that day[p] the Lord will strip their fin-
ery: ankle bracelets, headbands, crescents,[q]
19 pendants, bracelets, veils, 20 headdresses,
ankle jewelry, sashes, perfume bottles, amulets,[r] 21 signet rings, nose rings,[s] 22 festive
robes, capes, cloaks, purses, 23 garments, linen
clothes, turbans, and veils.

[a] **2:21** Is 2:10
[b] **2:22** Ps 39:11; 144:4; 146:3; Jr 17:5; Jms 4:14
[c] **3:2** 2Kg 24:14; Ezk 17:13-14
[d] **3:4** Ec 10:16
[e] **3:5** Mc 7:3-6
[f] **3:8** Ps 73:9-11
[g] Nm 14:22-23; Is 43:7; 48:11; 59:19
[h] **3:9** Is 1:9-10; 13:19
[i] Rm 6:23
[j] **3:12** Is 3:4
[k] Is 28:14-22
[l] **3:13** Ps 7:6; Hs 4:1
[m] **3:14** Mc 3:1-3
[n] Ezk 18:10-18; 33:15
[o] **3:16** Is 32:9-15; 1Pt 3:3-4
[p] **3:18** Is 27:12
[q] Jdg 8:21,26
[r] **3:20** Ezk 24:17
[s] **3:21** Gn 24:47; Ezk 16:12

[A] **3:3** Or *skilled craftsman* [B] **3:3** Or *medium* [C] **3:4** Or *mischief-makers*

24 Instead of perfume there will be
a stench;
instead of a belt, a rope;
instead of
beautifully styled hair,[a] baldness;[b]
instead of fine clothes, ·sackcloth;[c]
instead of beauty, branding.[A]
25 Your men will fall by the sword,
your warriors in battle.
26 Then her gates[d] will lament and mourn;
deserted, she will sit on the ground.[e]

4 On that day seven women
will seize one man,[f] saying,
"We will eat our own bread
and provide our own clothing.
Just let us be called by your name.
Take away our disgrace."[g]

Zion's Future Glory

2On that day the Branch of[B] the LORD will
be beautiful and glorious,[h] and the fruit of
the land[i] will be the pride and glory[j] of Israel's
survivors.[k] 3Whoever remains in ·Zion and
whoever is left in Jerusalem[l] will be called
holy[m] — all in Jerusalem who are destined to
live[n] — 4when the Lord has washed away the
filth[o] of the daughters of Zion and cleansed
the bloodguilt[p] from the heart of Jerusalem
by a spirit of judgment[q] and a spirit of burning.[r] 5Then the LORD will create[s] a cloud of
smoke by day[t] and a glowing flame of fire by
night over the entire site of Mount Zion and
over its assemblies. For there will be a canopy
over all the glory,[C] 6and there will be a booth
for shade from heat by day, and a refuge and
shelter from storm and rain.[u]

Song of the Vineyard

5 I will sing about the one I love,
a song about my loved one's vineyard:[v]
The one I love had a vineyard
on a very fertile hill.
2 He broke up the soil, cleared it
of stones,
and planted it with the finest vines.[w]
He built a tower in the middle of it
and even dug out a winepress there.
He expected[x] it to yield good grapes,
but it yielded worthless grapes.[y]

[a]3:24 1Pt 3:3 [b]Is 15:2; 22:12; Ezk 27:31; Am 8:10; Mc 1:16 [c]Gn 37:34; Is 15:3; Jr 48:36-38; Lm 2:10 [d]3:26 Jr 14:2; Lm 1:4 [e]Jb 2:13; Is 47:1; Lm 2:10 [f]4:1 Is 3:25 [g]Gn 19:31-32; 30:23; Neh 1:3; Is 54:4; Lk 1:25 [h]4:2 2Sm 23:4-5; Ps 132:17; Jr 23:5; 33:15; Zch 3:8; 6:12 [i]Ps 72:16; Is 27:6 [j]Is 3:18 [k]Gn 45:7; Jdg 21:17; 2Kg 19:30-31; Is 10:20; 37:31-32; Jl 2:32; Ob 17 [l]4:3 Is 28:5; Rm 11:4-5 [m]Is 52:1; 62:12 [n]Ex 32:32; Ps 69:28; 139:16; Is 49:16; Ezk 13:9; Lk 10:20; Ac 13:48 [o]4:4 2Ch 4:6; Ezk 40:38; Zch 13:1 [p]Is 1:15; 3:13-15 [q]Is 28:6 [r]Is 1:31; 9:19; 33:14; Mal 3:2; Mt 3:11; Lk 3:17 [s]4:5 Gn 1:1; Is 40:26,28; 41:20; 43:1,7,15; 45:7-8; 65:17-18 [t]Ex 13:21-22; 14:20; 40:34; Nm 9:15-23 [u]4:6 Ps 27:5; Is 25:4; 32:1-2 [v]5:1 Ps 80:8; Jr12:10; Mt 21:33; Lk 20:9 [w]5:2 Jr 2:21 [x]Is 40:31 [y]Mt 21:19; Mk 11:13; Lk 13:6 [z]5:4 Mc 6:3-4; Mt 23:37 [aa]5:5 Ps 89:40; Jr 5:10 [ab]Ps 80:12 [ac]5:6 2Ch 36:19-21; Is 7:19-25; 24:1,3; 27:2-6; Jr 25:11 [ad]Gn 3:18; Is 7:23-25; 9:18; 10:17; 27:4; 32:13 [ae]5:7 Ps 80:8-11 [af]5:8 Jr 22:13-17; Mc 2:2; Hab 2:9-12 [ag]5:9 Am 3:10,15 [ah]5:11 Lv 10:9; Nm 6:3; Dt 29:6; Jdg 13:4; Is 5:22; 24:9; 28:7; 56:12

3 So now, residents of Jerusalem
and men of Judah,
please judge between Me
and My vineyard.
4 What more could I have done
for My vineyard
than I did?[z]
Why, when I expected a yield
of good grapes,
did it yield worthless grapes?
5 Now I will tell you
what I am about to do to My vineyard:
I will remove its hedge,[aa]
and it will be consumed;
I will tear down its wall,[ab]
and it will be trampled.
6 I will make it a wasteland.[ac]
It will not be pruned or weeded;
thorns and briers will grow up.[ad]
I will also give orders to the clouds
that rain should not fall on it.
7 For the vineyard of the LORD of ·Hosts
is the house of Israel,[ae]
and the men[D] of Judah,
the plant He delighted in.
He looked for justice
but saw injustice,
for righteousness,
but heard cries of wretchedness.

Judah's Sins Denounced

8 Woe to those who add house to house[af]
and join field to field
until there is no more room
and you alone are left in the land.
9I heard the LORD of Hosts say:
Indeed, many houses[ag]
will become desolate,
grand and lovely ones
without inhabitants.
10 For a ten-acre[E] vineyard will yield
only six gallons,[F]
and 10 bushels[G] of seed will yield
only one bushel.[H]
11 Woe to those who rise early
in the morning
in pursuit of beer,[ah]
who linger into the evening,

[A]3:24 DSS read *shame* [B]4:2 Or *plant* [C]4:5 Or *For glory will be a canopy over all* [D]5:7 Lit *man* [E]5:10 Lit *ten-yoke* [F]5:10 Lit *one bath* [G]5:10 Lit *one homer* [H]5:10 Lit *one ephah*

inflamed by wine.
12 At their feasts they have lyre, harp,
tambourine, flute, and wine.
They do not perceive the LORD's actions,[a]
and they do not see the work
of His hands.[b]

13 Therefore My people will go into exile
because they lack knowledge;[c]
her[A] dignitaries are starving,
and her[A] masses are parched
with thirst.
14 Therefore ·Sheol enlarges its throat
and opens wide its enormous jaws,[d]
and down go ·Zion's dignitaries,
her masses,
her crowds, and those who carouse
in her!
15 Humanity is brought low,
man is humbled,
and haughty eyes are humbled.[e]
16 But the LORD of Hosts is exalted
by His justice,[f]
and the holy God[g] is distinguished
by righteousness.[h]
17 Lambs will graze
as if in[B] their own pastures,[i]
and strangers[C] will eat
among the ruins of the rich.

18 Woe to those who drag wickedness
with cords of deceit[j]
and pull sin along with cart ropes,
19 to those who say:
"Let Him hurry up and do
His work quickly
so that we can see it!
Let the plan[k] of the Holy One of Israel[l]
take place
so that we can know it!"
20 Woe to those who call evil good
and good evil,[m]
who substitute darkness for light
and light for darkness,
who substitute bitter for sweet
and sweet for bitter.
21 Woe to those who are wise
in their own opinion
and clever in their own sight.[D,n]
22 Woe to those who are heroes
at drinking wine,
who are fearless at mixing beer,[o]
23 who acquit the ·guilty for a bribe[p]
and deprive the innocent of justice.
24 Therefore, as a tongue of fire
consumes straw
and as dry grass shrivels in the flame,
so their roots will become
like something rotten
and their blossoms will blow away
like dust,
for they have rejected[q]
the instruction of the LORD of Hosts,
and they have despised
the word of the Holy One of Israel.[r]
25 Therefore the LORD's anger burns[s]
against His people.
He raised His hand against them
and struck them;
the mountains quaked,[t]
and their corpses were like garbage
in the streets.
In all this, His anger is not removed,
and His hand is still raised to strike.[u]

26 He raises a signal flag
for the distant nations[v]
and whistles[w] for them from the ends
of the earth.
Look — how quickly and swiftly
they come!
27 None of them grows weary
or stumbles;[x]
no one slumbers or sleeps.
No belt is loose
and no sandal strap broken.
28 Their arrows are sharpened,
and all their bows strung.
Their horses' hooves are like flint;
their chariot wheels are
like a whirlwind.
29 Their roaring is like a lion's;[y]
they roar like young lions;[z]
they growl and seize their prey
and carry it off,
and no one can rescue it.
30 On that day they will roar over it,
like the roaring of the sea.
When one looks at the land,
there will be darkness and distress;
light will be obscured by clouds.[E]

[a]**5:12** Dt 32:4; Jb 34:27; 36:24; Ps 28:5; 44:1; 64:9-10 [b]Ex 32:16; 34:10; Ps 8:3,6; 19:1; 92:4-5; Is 10:12; 29:23 [c]**5:13** Is 1:3; 27:11; Hs 4:6; Lk 11:52; 19:42; 1Tm 1:13 [d]**5:14** Pr 30:16; Hab 2:5 [e]**5:15** Is 2:9,11,17; 10:33 [f]**5:16** Is 33:5,10 [g]Is 6:3 [h]Is 8:13; 29:23; 1Pt 3:15 [i]**5:17** Mc 2:12 [j]**5:18** Pr 5:22; Is 59:4-8; Jr 23:10-14 [k]**5:19** Jb 38:2; 42:3; Ps 33:11; 106:13; 107:11; Pr 19:21; Is 14:26; 19:17; 46:10-11 [l]Is 1:4 [m]**5:20** Pr 17:15; Am 5:7; Mal 2:17 [n]**5:21** Pr 3:7; Rm 12:16; 1Co 3:18 [o]**5:22** Is 5:11 [p]**5:23** Ex 23:8; Pr 17:15; Is 1:23; 33:15 [q]**5:24** Is 8:6; 30:9,12; Am 2:4; Ac 13:41 [r]Is 5:19; Jr 51:5 [s]**5:25** Nm 11:10,33; 32:10-13; Dt 6:15; Jos 7:1; 23:16; 2Kg 13:3; Ps 106:40 [t]Am 1:1; Zch 14:5 [u]Is 9:12,17,21; 10:4; 14:27 [v]**5:26** Is 10:5; 11:10,12; 13:2; 18:3 [w]Is 7:18; Zch 10:8 [x]**5:27** 1Jn 2:10 [y]**5:29** Jdg 14:5; Hs 13:8; Jl 1:6; Nah 2:12-13 [z]Rv 9:17

[A]**5:13** Lit *its* [B]**5:17** Syr reads *graze in* [C]**5:17** LXX reads *sheep* [D]**5:21** Lit *clever before their face* [E]**5:30** Lit *its clouds*

Isaiah's Call and Mission

6 In the year that King Uzziah[a] died, I saw
the Lord[b] seated on a high and lofty[c]
throne,[d] and His robe[A] filled the temple. 2 Seraphim[B] were standing above Him; each one
had six wings:[e] with two he covered his face,
with two he covered his feet, and with two he
flew.[f] 3 And one called to another:

> Holy, holy, holy is the LORD of ·Hosts;
> His glory[g] fills the whole earth.[h]

4 The foundations of the doorways shook[i] at
the sound of their voices, and the temple was
filled with smoke.
5 Then I said:

> Woe is me[j] for I am ruined[C]
> because I am a man of ·unclean lips
> and live among a people
> of unclean lips,[k]
> and because my eyes have seen the King,
> the LORD of Hosts.

6 Then one of the seraphim flew to me, and
in his hand was a glowing coal that he had
taken from the altar[l] with tongs. 7 He touched
my mouth[m] with it and said:

> Now that this has touched your lips,
> your wickedness is removed
> and your sin is atoned for.[n]

8 Then I heard the voice of the Lord saying:

> Who should I send?
> Who will go for Us?

I said:

> Here I am. Send me.

9 And He replied:

> Go! Say to these people:
> Keep listening, but do not understand;[o]
> keep looking, but do not perceive.
> 10 Dull the minds[D] of these people;
> deafen their ears and blind their eyes;
> otherwise they might see
> with their eyes
> and hear with their ears,

[a] **6:1** 2Kg 15:1-7; Is 1:1; 14:28
[b] Gn 32:30; Ex 3:1-6; 24:9-10; Jos 5:13-15; 1Kg 22:19; Is 31:3; Jn 1:18; 4:24; 12:41
[c] Is 52:13; 57:15
[d] Ps 9:7; 11:4; 45:6; Is 66:1; Jr 3:17; Ezk 1:26; 10:1; 43:7
[e] **6:2** Rv 4:8
[f] Ezk 1:14
[g] **6:3** Ex 16:10; 24:16-17; 40:34-35; 1Kg 8:11; Is 35:2; 40:5; 60:1; Ezk 1:28; Lk 9:32
[h] Nm 14:21; Ps 72:19
[i] **6:4** Ex 19:8; Hab 3:3-10; Rv 15:8
[j] **6:5** Ex 33:20; Jdg 13:22; Is 59:3; Jr 9:3-8; Lk 5:8
[k] Ex 6:12,30
[l] **6:6** Lv 6:12-13; 17:11
[m] **6:7** Jr 1:9; Dn 10:16
[n] Ex 21:30; 30:12-16
[o] **6:9-10** Mt 13:14-15; Mk 4:12; Lk 8:10; Jn 12:40; Ac 28:26-27

GOD'S HEART FOR THE WORLD

Meeting the Infinite

Holy, holy, holy is the LORD of Hosts; His glory fills the whole earth. (Isaiah 6:3)

Few passages in Scripture depict God's "otherness," His complete and total differentness from us, with as much clarity as Isaiah 6. God's infinite, eternal, holy presence is so overwhelming that when Isaiah tries to describe it, he gets only as far as the hem of God's robe (and even that filled the whole temple!). The seraphim, who sing with enough intensity to shake the temple, get a much more detailed description, but they are still hard to picture. At once we seem to be brought into this glorious moment, while also finding it difficult to fully grasp. God's glory is awesome and somewhat elusive, yet Isaiah is there. He is right in the middle of it all. The Infinite makes Himself present to the finite. It's like Niagara Falls introducing itself to the leak in your kitchen sink; like Mount Everest making itself known to the stone in your driveway; like the whole of the Sahara Desert visiting the dust under your living room sofa.

Despite the incalculable difference, this is how God relates to all of us when we come to meet with Him in prayer or in worship. It is no coincidence that when we meet Him at worship, we respond in the same way that Isaiah did: praise, confession, assurance of our forgiveness, hearing His Word to us, and in the end, being sent out to serve the world in His name.

When God asks, "Who should I send? Who will go for Us?" may we be as eager as Isaiah: "Here I am. Send me."

[A] **6:1** Lit *seam* [B] **6:2** = heavenly beings [C] **6:5** Or *I must be silent* [D] **6:10** Lit *heart*

understand with their minds,
turn back, and be healed.[a]

11 Then I said, "Until when, Lord?"[b] And He replied:

Until cities lie in ruins
without inhabitants,[c]
houses are without people,

the land is ruined and desolate,
12 and the LORD drives the people far away,
leaving great emptiness in the land.
13 Though a tenth will remain in the land,
it will be burned again.
Like the terebinth or the oak
that leaves a stump when felled,
the holy °seed[d] is the stump.[e]

[a] 6:10 Zch 7:11-12; 1Th 2:16
[b] 6:11 Ps 79:5; 89:46
[c] Is 1:7; 27:10
[d] 6:13 Is 41:8; 43:5; 45:25; 53:10; 59:21; 65:9,23; 66:22
[e] Is 11:1

Facilitating Church Transformation

Glenn Burris, Jr.

Leading change, although an opportunity, is often fraught with opposition and obstacles. Resisting it can cause us to drift into irrelevance and obscurity, while embracing it has its own risks and rewards. It can be an open door to new beginnings, but it may also wrestle away from us things we hold dear. Sometimes it leaves us excited about the future, while at other times it frightens us to our core.

The prophet Isaiah and the nation of Israel found themselves at an intersection of change upon the death of King Uzziah (Is 6), who reigned for 52 years but died in relative isolation due to leprosy. Change oftentimes heightens our senses and ignites an adrenalin rush. In this case, the prophet is confronted with a new revelation of God, and it humbles him. He is suddenly made aware of the greatness of God, and it exposes his own frailty. Change is coming, Isaiah has no idea what it will mean, and he feels vulnerable. In spite of his shortcomings, the Lord extends a compelling invitation for the prophet to help facilitate the possibilities of transforming a nation in crisis.

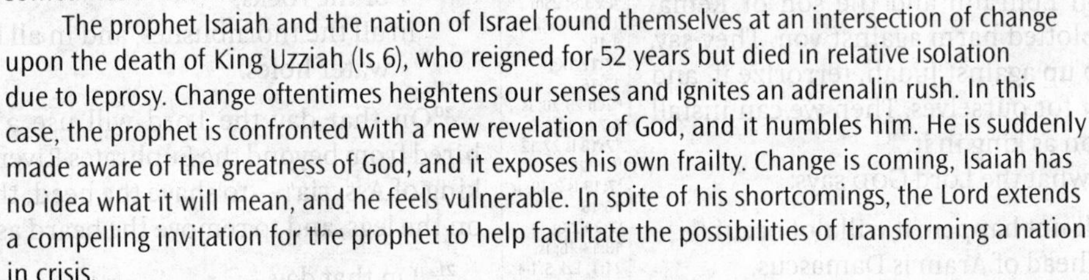

The current reviews and initial prospects were not very encouraging. Israel will experience a season of consequence, and the prophet is informed that it will get worse before it gets better. In these desperate times, the actions or inactions of a leader may determine the length and breadth of the crisis. We could contribute to decline or we may be used by God as an instrument to bring about transformation. The word "transform" means to change in character or condition. Good leaders bring deep change, not surface or temporary change.

Observing this national transformation from a distance offers some significant takeaways. First, if a leader is going to help open the door to a different future than the present, they must have a realistic and uncensored view of current realities. Only when we are willing to have the lights on and the windows open can we get a healthy assessment of the present. Without that accurate data, all of our decisions and plans for the future will be flawed. With it, the leader can be relentless in their pursuit of effective transformation. Isaiah postured himself well by taking an unfiltered view of the entire landscape, including his own limitations.

Second, if a leader doesn't also possess the ability to imagine a future filled with possibilities even though there is impending catastrophe and significant limitations, it will greatly hinder their ability to navigate those present issues and will translate into a culture of managing the minutia of the ministry rather than leading the church into healthy transformation.

Third, if the leader does not regularly acknowledge their absolute dependency on the Lord, and lead accordingly, the ultimate success of their ministry will always be limited to only what they can accomplish through their own means, and their gains will not be sustainable.

Facilitating effective church transformation requires clear vision, unbridled hope and sincere humility.

The Message to Ahaz

7 This took place during the reign of Ahaz,
son of Jotham, son of Uzziah king of Judah:[a] Rezin king of Aram, along with Pekah,
son of Remaliah, king of Israel, waged war
against Jerusalem,[b] but he could not succeed.
2 When it became known to the house of David[c] that Aram had occupied Ephraim,[d] the
heart of Ahaz[A] and the hearts of his people
trembled like trees of a forest shaking in the
wind.

3 Then the LORD said to Isaiah, "Go out with
your son Shear-jashub[e] to meet Ahaz at the
end of the conduit of the upper pool,[f] by the
road to the Fuller's Field. 4 Say to him: Calm
down and be quiet. Don't be afraid or cowardly[g] because of these two smoldering stubs
of firebrands, the fierce anger of Rezin and
Aram, and the son of Remaliah. 5 For Aram,
along with Ephraim and the son of Remaliah, has plotted harm against you. They say,
6 'Let us go up against Judah, terrorize it, and
conquer it for ourselves. Then we can install
Tabeel's son as king in it.'"

7 This is what the Lord GOD says:

It will not happen; it will not occur.[h]
8 The[B] head of Aram is Damascus,
the head of Damascus is Rezin
(within 65 years
Ephraim will be too shattered to be
a people),
9 the head of Ephraim is Samaria,
and the head of Samaria is the son
of Remaliah.
If you do not stand firm in your faith,
then you will not stand at all.

The Immanuel Prophecy

10 Then the LORD spoke again to Ahaz: 11 "Ask
for a sign[i] from the LORD your God — from
the depths of *Sheol to the heights of heaven."

12 But Ahaz replied, "I will not ask. I will not
test the LORD."

13 Isaiah[j] said, "Listen, house of David! Is
it not enough for you to try the patience of
men? Will you also try the patience of my
God?[k] 14 Therefore, the Lord Himself will
give you[C] a sign: The virgin will conceive,[D]
have a son, and name him Immanuel.[E,l] 15 By
the time he learns to reject what is bad and
choose what is good,[m] he will be eating butter[F] and honey.[n] 16 For before the boy knows
to reject what is bad and choose what is good,
the land of the two kings you dread will be
abandoned. 17 The LORD will bring on you,
your people, and the house of your father,
such a time as has never been since Ephraim
separated from Judah[o] — the king of Assyria[p]
is coming."

18 On that day[q]
the LORD will whistle[r] to the fly
that is at the farthest streams
of the Nile
and to the bee that is in the land
of Assyria.
19 All of them will come and settle
in the steep ravines, in the clefts
of the rocks,[s]
in all the thornbushes, and in all the
water holes.

20 On that day the Lord will use a razor[t]
hired from beyond the Euphrates River — the
king of Assyria[u] — to shave the head, the hair
on the legs, and to remove the beard as well.

21 On that day
a man will raise a young cow
and two sheep,
22 and from the abundant milk they give
he will eat butter,
for every survivor in the land
will eat butter and honey.[v]
23 And on that day
every place where there were
1,000 vines,
worth 1,000 pieces of silver,
will become thorns and briers.[w]
24 A man will go there with bow
and arrows
because the whole land will be thorns
and briers.
25 You will not go to all the hills
that were once tilled with a hoe,
for fear of the thorns and briers.
Those hills will be places for oxen
to graze
and for sheep to trample.

[a] **7:1** Is 1:1 [b] 2Kg 15:25,37; 16:5 [c] **7:2** Is 7:13; 9:7; 16:5; 22:9,22; 29:1; 37:35; 38:5; 55:3 [d] Is 8:12; 9:9 [e] **7:3** Is 8:3,18 [f] 2Kg 18:17; Is 36:2 [g] **7:4** Gn 15:1; Ex 14:13; 20:20; Nm 14:9; Dt 20:3; 31:6; Jos 10:8,25; Is 10:24; 35:4; 41:14 [h] **7:7** Is 8:10 [i] **7:11** 2Kg 19:29; Is 37:30; 38:7-8; 55:13 [j] **7:13** Mt 3:3; 12:17 [k] Is 1:14; 43:24; Jr 15:6; 20:9; Mal 2:17 [l] **7:14** Is 8:8,10; Mt 1:23; Lk 1:31 [m] **7:15** Dt 1:39 [n] Ex 3:8; 2Sm 17:29; Is 7:22; 8:15 [o] **7:17** 1Kg 12:16 [p] 2Ch 28:20; Is 8:7-8; 10:5-6 [q] **7:18** Is 27:12 [r] Is 5:25 [s] **7:19** Is 2:19; Jr 16:16 [t] **7:20** 2Kg 18:13-16; Is 24:1; Ezk 5:1-4 [u] Is 8:7; 11:15; Jr 2:18 [v] **7:22** Is 8:15 [w] **7:23** Is 5:6

[A] **7:2** Lit *Aram has rested upon Ephraim, his heart* [B] **7:8** Lit *For the* [C] **7:14** In Hb, the word you is pl [D] **7:14** Or *virgin is pregnant, will* [E] **7:14** = God With Us [F] **7:15** Or *sour milk*

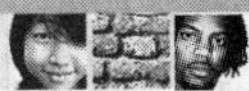

The Coming Assyrian Invasion

8 Then the LORD said to me, "Take a large
piece of parchment[A] and write on it
with an ordinary pen:[B,a] Maher-shalal-hash-
baz.[C] 2I have appointed[D] trustworthy witnesses — Uriah the priest and Zechariah son
of Jeberechiah."[b]
3I was then intimate with the prophetess,
and she conceived and gave birth to a son.
The LORD said to me, "Name him Maher-shal-
al-hash-baz, 4for before the boy knows how
to call out father or mother,[c] the wealth of
Damascus and the spoils of Samaria will be
carried off to the king of Assyria."[d]
5The LORD spoke to me again:

6 Because these people rejected
the slowly flowing waters of Shiloah
and rejoiced with[E] Rezin
and the son of Remaliah,[e]
7 the Lord will certainly bring
against them
the mighty rushing waters
of the Euphrates River —
the king of Assyria and all his glory.
It will overflow its channels
and spill over all its banks.
8 It will pour into Judah,
flood over it, and sweep through,
reaching up to the neck;[f]
and its spreading streams[F]
will fill your entire land, Immanuel![g]

9 Band together, peoples,
and be broken;
pay attention, all you distant lands;
prepare for war, and be broken;
prepare for war, and be broken.
10 Devise a plan; it will fail.[h]
Make a prediction; it will not happen.
For God is with us.[G,i]

The LORD of Hosts, the Only Refuge

11For this is what the LORD said to me with
great power, to keep[H] me from going the way
of this people:[j]

12 Do not call everything an alliance
these people say is an alliance.[k]
Do not fear what they fear;[l]
do not be terrified.
13 You are to regard only the LORD
of •Hosts as holy.[m]
Only He should be •feared;[n]
only He should be held in awe.
14 He will be a sanctuary;[o]
but for the two houses of Israel,
He will be a stone[p] to stumble over
and a rock to trip over,[q]
and a trap and a snare
to the inhabitants of Jerusalem.
15 Many will stumble over these;[r]
they will fall and be broken;
they will be snared and captured.

16 Bind up the •testimony.[s]
Seal up the instruction[t]
among my disciples.
17 I will wait for the LORD,[u]
who is hiding His face from the house
of Jacob.[v]
I will wait for Him.

18Here I am with the children the LORD
has given me[w] to be signs and wonders in Israel from the LORD of Hosts who dwells on
Mount •Zion. 19When they say to you, "Consult the spirits of the dead and the spiritists
who chirp and mutter,"[x] shouldn't a people
consult their God?[I] Should they consult the
dead on behalf of the living?[y] 20To the law
and to the testimony![z] If they do not speak
according to this word, there will be no dawn
for them.
21They will wander through the land, dejected and hungry. When they are famished,
they will become enraged, and, looking upward, will curse their king and their God.
22They will look toward the earth[aa] and see
only distress, darkness, and the gloom of affliction, and they will be driven into thick
darkness.

Birth of the Prince of Peace

9 [J] Nevertheless, the gloom of the distressed
land will not be like that of the former
times when He humbled the land of Zebulun
and the land of Naphtali.[ab] But in the future
He will bring honor to the Way of the Sea, to
the land east of the Jordan, and to Galilee of
the nations.

[a]**8:1** Is 30:8; Hab 2:2
[b]**8:2** 2Kg 16:10-11,15-16
[c]**8:4** Is 7:16
[d]Is 7:8-9
[e]**8:6** Is 7:1
[f]**8:8** Is 30:28
[g]Is 7:14; 8:10
[h]**8:10** Is 14:27
[i]Is 8:8
[j]**8:11** Ezk 2:8
[k]**8:12** Is 7:2; 30:1
[l]1Pt 3:14
[m]**8:13** Nm 20:12
[n]1Pt 3:15
[o]**8:14** Is 4:6; 25:4; Ezk 11:16
[p]Ps 91:12; Is 26:4
[q]Lk 2:34; Rm 9:33; 1Pt 2:8
[r]**8:15** Is 28:13; 59:10; Lk 20:18; Rm 9:32
[s]**8:16** Is 8:1-2; 29:11-12
[t]Dn 12:4
[u]**8:17** Ps 27:14; 33:20; 37:34; 130:5-6; Is 25:9; 30:18; Lm 3:26; Hab 2:3; 1Co 1:7; Php 3:20
[v]Dt 31:17; Is 1:15; 45:15; 54:8
[w]**8:18** Heb 2:13
[x]**8:19** Lv 20:6; 2Kg 21:6; 23:24; Is 19:3; 29:4; 47:12-13
[y]1Sm 28:8-11
[z]**8:20** Is 1:10; Lk 16:29
[aa]**8:22** Is 5:30; 59:9; Jr 13:16; Am 5:18,20; Zph 1:14-15
[ab]**9:1** Mt 4:15

[A]**8:1** Hb obscure [B]**8:1** Lit *with the pen of a man* [C]**8:1** = Speeding to the Plunder, Hurrying to the Spoil [D]**8:2** Vg; MT, one DSS ms read *I will appoint*; one DSS ms, LXX, Syr, Tg read *Appoint* [E]**8:6** Or *and rejoiced over* [F]**8:8** Or *wings* [G]**8:10** Or *For Immanuel* [H]**8:11** DSS; MT reads *instruct* [I]**8:19** Or *gods* [J]**9:1** Is 8:23 in Hb

2[A] The people walking in darkness
have seen a great light;[a]
a light has dawned
on those living in the land
of darkness.[b]
3 You have enlarged the nation
and increased its joy.[B,c]
The people have rejoiced before You
as they rejoice at harvest time
and as they rejoice
when dividing spoils.[d]
4 For You have shattered
their oppressive yoke[e]
and the rod on their shoulders,
the staff of their oppressor,
just as You did on the day of Midian.[f]
5 For the trampling boot of battle
and the bloodied garments of war
will be burned as fuel for the fire.
6 For a child will be born for us,
a son will be given to us,[g]
and the government will be
on His shoulders.[h]
He will be named
Wonderful Counselor,[i] Mighty God,[j]
Eternal Father,[k] Prince of Peace.[l]
7 The dominion will be vast,
and its prosperity will never end.[m]
He will reign on the throne of David
and over his kingdom,
to establish and sustain it
with justice and righteousness
from now on and forever.
The zeal of the LORD of ˙Hosts
will accomplish this.[n]

The Hand Raised against Israel

8 The Lord sent a message against Jacob;
it came against Israel.
9 All the people —
Ephraim and the inhabitants
of Samaria[o] — will know it.
They will say with pride and arrogance:
10 "The bricks have fallen,
but we will rebuild with cut stones;
the sycamores have been cut down,
but we will replace them with cedars."
11 The LORD has raised up
Rezin's adversaries against him
and stirred up his enemies.
12 Aram from the east and Philistia
from the west
have consumed Israel
with open mouths.
In all this, His anger is not removed,
and His hand is still raised to strike.[p]
13 The people did not turn to Him
who struck them;
they did not seek the LORD of Hosts.
14 So the LORD cut off Israel's head
and tail,[q]
palm branch and reed in a single day.
15 The head is the elder, the honored one;[r]
the tail is the prophet,
the lying teacher.[s]
16 The leaders of the people mislead them,
and those they mislead
are swallowed up.[C]
17 Therefore the Lord does not rejoice
over[D] Israel's young men
and has no compassion
on its fatherless and widows,
for everyone is a godless evildoer,[t]
and every mouth speaks folly.
In all this, His anger is not removed,
and His hand is still raised to strike.
18 For wickedness burns like a fire[u]
that consumes thorns and briers
and kindles the forest thickets
so that they go up in a column
of smoke.
19 The land is scorched
by the wrath of the LORD of Hosts,
and the people are like fuel for the fire.[v]
No one has compassion on his brother.[w]
20 They carve meat on the right,
but they are still hungry;[x]
they have eaten on the left,
but they are still not satisfied.
Each one eats the flesh of his own arm.[y]
21 Manasseh is with Ephraim,
and Ephraim with Manasseh;
together, both are against Judah.[z]
In all this, His anger is not removed,
and His hand is still raised to strike.[aa]

10 Woe to those enacting
crooked statutes
and writing oppressive laws

[a]**9:2** Mt 4:16; Eph 5:8 [b]Lk 1:79 [c]**9:3** Is 26:15 [d]1Sm 30:16 [e]**9:4** Is 10:27; 14:25 [f]Jdg 7:25; Is 10:26 [g]**9:6** Is 7:14; 11:1-2; 53:2; Lk 2:11; Jn 3:16 [h]Is 22:22; Mt 28:18; 1Co 15:25 [i]Is 28:29 [j]Dt 10:17; Neh 9:32; Is 10:21 [k]Is 63:16; 64:8 [l]Is 26:3,12; 54:10; 66:12 [m]**9:7** Ps 89:4; Dn 2:44; Lk 1:32-33 [n]Is 37:32; 59:17 [o]**9:9** Ac 1:8 [p]**9:12** Is 5:25 [q]**9:14** Is 19:15 [r]**9:15** Is 3:2-3 [s]Is 28:15; 59:3-4; Jr 23:14,32; Mt 24:24 [t]**9:17** Is 1:4; 10:6; 14:20; 31:2; 32:6 [u]**9:18** Ps 83:14; Is 1:7; Nah 1:10; Mal 4:1 [v]**9:19** Is 1:31; 24:6 [w]Mc 7:2,6 [x]**9:20** Is 8:21-22 [y]Dt 28:53-57; Is 49:26 [z]**9:21** 2Ch 28:6,8; Is 11:13 [aa]Is 5:25

[A]**9:2** Is 9:1 in Hb [B]**9:3** Alt Hb tradition reads *have not increased joy* [C]**9:16** Or *are confused* [D]**9:17** DSS read *not spare*

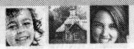

2 to keep the poor from getting
a fair trial
and to deprive the afflicted
among my people of justice,
so that widows can be their spoil
and they can plunder the fatherless.
3 What will you do on the day
of punishment
when devastation comes
from far away?
Who will you run to for help?
Where will you leave your wealth?
4 There will be nothing to do
except crouch among the prisoners
or fall among the slain.
In all this, His anger is not removed,
and His hand is still raised to strike.

Assyria, the Instrument of Wrath

5 Woe to Assyria, the rod of My anger —
the staff in their hands is My wrath.
6 I will send him against a godless nation;
I will command him to go
against a people destined for My rage,
to take spoils, to plunder,
and to trample them down like clay[a]
in the streets.
7 But this is not what he intends;
this is not what he plans.
It is his intent to destroy
and to cut off many nations.
8 For he says,
"Aren't all my commanders kings?
9 Isn't Calno like Carchemish?
Isn't Hamath like Arpad?
Isn't Samaria[b] like Damascus?[A]
10 As my hand seized
the idolatrous kingdoms,
whose idols exceeded
those of Jerusalem and Samaria,
11 and as I did to Samaria and its idols
will I not also do to Jerusalem
and its idols?"

Judgment on Assyria

12 But when the Lord finishes all His work
against Mount *Zion and Jerusalem, He will
say, "I[B] will punish the king of Assyria for his
arrogant acts and the proud look in his eyes."
13 For he said:

[a] 10:6 2Sm 22:43; Ps 18:42; Ezk 26:11; Mc 7:10
[b] 10:9 Ac 1:8
[c] 10:20 Is 1:4

I have done this by my own strength
and wisdom, for I am clever.
I abolished the borders of nations
and plundered their treasures;
like a mighty warrior, I subjugated
the inhabitants.[C]
14 My hand has reached out, as if
into a nest,
to seize the wealth of the nations.
Like one gathering abandoned eggs,
I gathered the whole earth.
No wing fluttered;
no beak opened or chirped.
15 Does an ax exalt itself
above the one who chops with it?
Does a saw magnify itself
above the one who saws with it?
It would be like a staff waving the one
who lifts[D] it!
It would be like a rod lifting a man
who isn't wood!
16 Therefore the Lord GOD of *Hosts
will inflict an emaciating disease
on the well-fed of Assyria,
and He will kindle a burning fire
under its glory.
17 Israel's Light will become a fire,
and its Holy One, a flame.
In one day it will burn up
Assyria's thorns and thistles.
18 He will completely destroy
the glory of its forests and orchards
as a sickness consumes a person.
19 The remaining trees of its forest
will be so few in number
that a child could count them.

The Remnant Will Return

20 On that day the remnant of Israel and the
survivors of the house of Jacob will no longer
depend on the one who struck them, but they
will faithfully depend on the LORD, the Holy
One of Israel.[c]

21 The remnant will return, the remnant
of Jacob,
to the Mighty God.
22 Israel, even if your people were
as numerous
as the sand of the sea,

[A] 10:9 Cities conquered by Assyria [B] 10:12 LXX reads *Jerusalem, He* [C] 10:13 Or *I brought down their kings* [D] 10:15 Some Hb mss, Syr, Vg read *wave he who lifts*

only a remnant of them will return.[a]
Destruction has been decreed;
justice overflows.
23 For throughout the land
the Lord GOD of Hosts
is carrying out a destruction
that was decreed.

24 Therefore, the Lord GOD of Hosts says
this: "My people who dwell in Zion, do not
fear Assyria, though he strikes you with a rod
and raises his staff over you as the Egyptians
did. 25 In just a little while My wrath will be
spent and My anger will turn to their destruction." 26 And the LORD of Hosts will brandish
a whip against him as He did when He struck
Midian at the rock of Oreb;[b] and He will raise
His staff over the sea as He did in Egypt.

God Will Judge Assyria

27 On that day
his burden will fall
from your shoulders,
and his yoke from your neck.
The yoke will be broken
because of fatness.[A]
28 Assyria has come to Aiath
and has gone through Migron,
storing his equipment at Michmash.
29 They crossed over
at the ford, saying,
"We will spend the night at Geba."
The people of Ramah
are trembling;
those at Gibeah of Saul have fled.
30 Cry aloud, daughter of Gallim!
Listen, Laishah!
Anathoth is miserable.
31 Madmenah has fled.
The inhabitants of Gebim
have sought refuge.
32 Today he will stand at Nob,
shaking his fist at the mountain
of Daughter Zion,
the hill of Jerusalem.
33 Look, the Lord GOD of Hosts
will chop off the branches
with terrifying power,
and the tall trees will be cut down,
the high trees felled.

[a] 10:22 Rm 9:27-28
[b] 10:26 Jdg 7:25
[c] 11:1 Is 9:7; 11:10; Ac 13:23
[d] Is 14:19; 60:21; Jr 23:5; 33:15; Dn 11:7; Zch 3:8; 6:12
[e] 11:2 Is 42:1; 48:16; 61:1; Mt 3:16; Jn 1:32
[f] 11:3 Jn 2:25; 7:24
[g] 11:4 Ps 72:2,13-14; Is 3:14
[h] Ps 2:9; Is 49:2; Mal 4:6
[i] Gn 18:25; Ps 139:19; Ezk 3:18-19; 18:20-24; 33:8-15
[j] Jb 4:9; Is 30:28,33; 2Th 2:8
[k] 11:5 Eph 6:14
[l] Eph 6:14
[m] 11:6 Is 65:25; Jr 5:6; Hs 2:18; 13:6-9
[n] 11:9 Ps 98:2-3; Is 45:6; 52:10; 66:18-23; Hab 2:14

34 He is clearing the thickets of the forest
with an ax,
and Lebanon with its majesty will fall.

Reign of the Davidic King

11 Then a shoot will grow
from the stump of Jesse,[c]
and a branch[d] from his roots
will bear fruit.
2 The Spirit of the LORD will rest
on Him[e]—
a Spirit of wisdom and understanding,
a Spirit of counsel and strength,
a Spirit of knowledge and of the ·fear
of the LORD.
3 His delight will be in the fear
of the LORD.
He will not judge
by what He sees with His eyes,[f]
He will not execute justice
by what He hears with His ears,
4 but He will judge the poor righteously[g]
and execute justice for the oppressed
of the land.
He will strike the land
with discipline[B] from His mouth,[h]
and He will kill the wicked[i]
with a command[C] from His lips.[j]
5 Righteousness will be a belt
around His loins;[k]
faithfulness will be a belt
around His waist.[l]
6 The wolf will live with the lamb,[m]
and the leopard will lie down
with the goat.
The calf, the young lion, and the fatling
will be together,
and a child will lead them.
7 The cow and the bear will graze,
their young ones will lie down together,
and the lion will eat straw like the ox.
8 An infant will play
beside the cobra's pit,
and a toddler will put his hand
into a snake's den.
9 None will harm or destroy another
on My entire holy mountain,
for the land will be as full
of the knowledge of the LORD
as the sea is filled with water.[n]

[A] 10:27 Hb obscure [B] 11:4 Lit *the rod* [C] 11:4 Lit *with the breath*

Israel Regathered

10 On that day the root of Jesse[a]
will stand as a banner for the peoples.[b]
The nations will seek Him,[c]
and His resting place will be glorious.[d]

11On that day[e] the Lord will extend His
hand a second time to recover — from Assyria, Egypt, Pathros, ·Cush, Elam, ·Shinar,
Hamath, and the coasts and islands of the
west — the remnant of His people who survive.[f]

12 He will lift up a banner for the nations
and gather the dispersed of Israel;[g]
He will collect the scattered of Judah
from the four corners of the earth.[h]
13 Ephraim's envy will cease;[i]
Judah's harassment will end.
Ephraim will no longer be envious
of Judah,
and Judah will not harass Ephraim.
14 But they will swoop down
on the Philistine flank to the west.
Together they will plunder the people
of the east.[j]
They will extend their power
over Edom and Moab,
and the Ammonites will be
their subjects.[k]
15 The LORD will divide[A,B] the Gulf
of Suez.[C]
He will wave His hand
over the Euphrates
with His mighty wind[l]
and will split it into seven streams,
letting people walk through on foot.
16 There will be a highway
for the remnant of His people
who will survive from Assyria,[m]
as there was for Israel
when they came up from the land
of Egypt.[n]

A Song of Praise

12 On that day you will say:
"I will praise You, LORD,
although You were angry with me.
Your anger has turned away,
and You have had compassion[o] on me.
2 Indeed, God is my salvation;
I will trust Him and not be afraid,
for ·Yah, the LORD,
is my strength and my song.
He has become my salvation."[p]
3 You will joyfully draw water[q]
from the springs of salvation,
4 and on that day you will say:
"Give thanks to Yahweh;
proclaim His name!
Celebrate His works
among the peoples.[r]
Declare that His name is exalted.
5 Sing to Yahweh, for He has done
glorious things.[s]
Let this be known
throughout the earth.
6 Cry out and sing, citizen of ·Zion,
for the Holy One of Israel[t] is
among you
in His greatness."

An Oracle against Babylon

13 An ·oracle[u] against Babylon[v] that Isaiah son of Amoz saw:

2 Lift up a banner
on a barren mountain.[w]
Call out to them.
Wave your hand, and they will go
through the gates of the nobles.
3 I have commanded My chosen ones;
I have also called My warriors,
who exult in My triumph,
to execute My wrath.[x]
4 Listen, a tumult on the mountains,
like that of a mighty people!
Listen, an uproar among the kingdoms,
like nations being gathered together!
The LORD of ·Hosts is mobilizing
an army for war.
5 They are coming from a far land,
from the distant horizon —
the LORD and the weapons
of His wrath —
to destroy the whole country.[D]

6 Wail! For the day of the LORD is near.[y]
It will come like destruction
from the ·Almighty.[z]
7 Therefore everyone's hands
will become weak,

[a]**11:10** Is 11:1 [b]Is 49:22; 62:10; Jn 3:14-15; 12:32 [c]Rm 15:12; Rv 5:5 [d]Is 14:3; 28:12; 32:17-18 [e]**11:11** Is 27:12 [f]Is 10:20-22; 37:4,31-32; 46:3 [g]**11:12** Is 56:8; Zph 3:10; Zch 10:6 [h]Rv 7:1; 20:8 [i]**11:13** Is 9:21; Jr 3:18; Ezk 37:16-17,22; Hs 1:11 [j]**11:14** Jr 49:28 [k]Ps 60:8; 83:6 [l]**11:15** Is 7:20; 8:7; Rv 16:12 [m]**11:16** Is 19:23; 35:8; 40:3; 62:10 [n]Ex 14:26-29 [o]**12:1** Is 40:1 [p]**12:2** Ex 15:2; Ps 118:14 [q]**12:3** Jn 4:10; 7:37-38 [r]**12:4** 1Ch 16:8; Ps 105:1; 145:4 [s]**12:5** Ex 15:1; Ps 98:1; Is 24:14; 42:10-11; 44:23 [t]**12:6** Is 1:4 [u]**13:1** Is 14:28; 15:1; 17:1; 19:1; 21:1,11,13; 22:1; 23:1; 30:6 [v]Is 13:19; 14:4; 47:1-15; Jr 24:1; 50:1–51:64; Mt 1:11; Rv 14:8 [w]**13:2** Is 5:26; Jr 50:2 [x]**13:3** Ps 78:21,50; Ezk 5:15; 20:8 [y]**13:6** Is 2:12; 10:3; 13:9; 34:2,8; 61:2; Ezk 30:3; Am 5:18; Zph 1:7 [z]Is 10:25; 14:23; Jl 1:15

[A]**11:15** Text emended; MT reads *destroy* [B]**11:15** Or *dry up* [C]**11:15** Lit *the Sea of Egypt* [D]**13:5** Or *earth*

and every man's heart will melt.
8 They will be horrified;
pain and agony will seize them;
they will be in anguish like a woman
in labor.[a]
They will look at each other,
their faces flushed with fear.
9 Look, the day[b] of the LORD is coming —
cruel, with rage and burning anger —
to make the earth a desolation
and to destroy the sinners on it.[c]
10 Indeed, the stars of the sky
and its constellations[A]
will not give their light.
The sun will be dark when it rises,
and the moon will not shine.[d]
11 I will bring disaster on the world,
and their own iniquity,[e] on the wicked.
I will put an end to the pride
of the arrogant[f]
and humiliate the insolence of tyrants.
12 I will make man scarcer than gold,
and mankind more rare than the gold
of Ophir.[g]
13 Therefore I will make
the heavens tremble,
and the earth will shake
from its foundations[h]
at the wrath of the LORD of Hosts,
on the day of His burning anger.
14 Like wandering gazelles
and like sheep without a shepherd,[i]
each one will turn to his own people,
each one will flee to his own land.
15 Whoever is found will be stabbed,
and whoever is caught will die
by the sword.
16 Their children will be smashed to death
before their eyes;[j]
their houses will be looted,
and their wives raped.
17 Look! I am stirring up the Medes
against them,[k]
who cannot be bought off with[B] silver
and who have no desire for gold.
18 Their bows will cut young men
to pieces.
They will have no compassion
on little ones;
they will not look with pity on children.

[a]**13:8** Is 26:17; Jr 4:31; Jn 16:21
[b]**13:9** Mt 25:13
[c]Dt 32:43
[d]**13:10** Is 34:4; Mt 24:29; Mk 13:24-25; Lk 21:26; Rv 8:12
[e]**13:11** Jr 23:2; 36:31; 44:29
[f]Is 2:11; 23:9; Dn 5:22-23
[g]**13:12** 1Kg 9:28; Jb 28:16; Ps 45:9
[h]**13:13** Ps 18:7; Is 2:19; 24:1,19-20; Hg 2:6
[i]**13:14** 1Kg 22:17; Mt 9:36; Mk 6:34; 1Pt 2:25
[j]**13:16** Ps 137:8-9; Is 13:18; 14:21; Hs 10:14; Nah 3:10
[k]**13:17** Jr 51:11; Dn 5:28
[l]**13:19** Gn 19:24; Jr 14:18; 50:40; Am 4:11
[m]**13:20** Is 14:23; 34:10-15; Jr 51:37-43
[n]**13:21** Is 34:11-15; Zph 2:14; Rv 18:2
[o]**14:1** 1Kg 3:26
[p]Dt 7:7; Ps 102:13; Zch 1:17
[q]Dt 12:10; 2Sm 7:1
[r]Dt 14:21,29; Zch 8:22, 23; Eph 2:12-14
[s]**14:2** Is 9:7; 45:14-25; 49:22-26; 60:9; 61:5; 66:19-24
[t]**14:3** Gn 3:16; Is 14:3; Jr 44:19
[u]Ex 1:14
[v]**14:4** Mc 2:4; Hab 2:6

19 And Babylon, the jewel
of the kingdoms,
the glory of the pride
of the Chaldeans,
will be like Sodom and Gomorrah
when God overthrew them.[l]
20 It will never be inhabited
or lived in from generation
to generation;[m]
a nomad will not pitch his tent there,
and shepherds will not let their flocks
rest there.
21 But desert creatures
will lie down there,
and owls will fill the houses.
Ostriches will dwell there,
and wild goats will leap about.[n]
22 Hyenas will howl in the fortresses,
and jackals, in the luxurious palaces.
Babylon's time is almost up;
her days are almost over.

Israel's Return

14 For the LORD will have compassion[o]
on Jacob and will choose Israel again.[p]
He will settle them on their own land.[q] The
foreigner will join them and be united with
the house of Jacob.[r] 2 The nations will escort
Israel and bring it to its homeland. Then the
house of Israel will possess them as male and
female slaves in the LORD's land.[s] They will
make captives of their captors and will rule
over their oppressors.

Downfall of the King of Babylon

3 When the LORD gives you rest from your
pain,[t] torment, and the hard labor[u] you were
forced to do, 4 you will sing this song of contempt about the king of Babylon[v] and say:

How the oppressor has quieted down,
and how the raging[C] has become quiet!
5 The LORD has broken the staff
of the wicked,
the scepter of the rulers.
6 It struck the peoples in anger
with unceasing blows.
It subdued the nations in rage
with relentless persecution.
7 All the earth is calm and at rest;

[A]**13:10** Or *Orions* [B]**13:17** Lit *who have no regard for* [C]**14:4** DSS; Hb uncertain

people shout with a ringing cry.
8 Even the cypresses and the cedars
of Lebanon
rejoice over you:[a]
"Since you have been laid low,
no woodcutter has come against us."
9 ·Sheol below is eager to greet
your coming.
He stirs up the spirits of the departed
for you —
all the rulers[A] of the earth.
He makes all the kings of the nations
rise from their thrones.
10 They all respond to you, saying:
"You too have become as weak
as we are;
you have become like us!
11 Your splendor has been brought down
to Sheol,
along with the music of your harps.
Maggots are spread out under you,
and worms cover you."
12 Shining morning star,[B,b]
how you have fallen from the heavens![c]
You destroyer of nations,
you have been cut down to the ground.
13 You said to yourself:
"I will ascend to the heavens;[d]
I will set up my throne
above the stars of God.[e]
I will sit on the mount
of the gods' assembly,
in the remotest parts of the North.[C,f]
14 I will ascend above the highest clouds;
I will make myself
like the ·Most High."
15 But you will be brought down to Sheol
into the deepest regions of the ·Pit.[g]
16 Those who see you will stare at you;
they will look closely at you:
"Is this the man who caused the earth
to tremble,
who shook the kingdoms,
17 who turned the world
into a wilderness,[h]
who destroyed its cities
and would not release the prisoners
to return home?"

[a]**14:8** Ps 104:16; Is 55:12; Ezk 31:16
[b]**14:12** 2Pt 1:19; Rv 2:28; 22:16
[c]Is 34:4; Lk 10:18; Rv 8:10; 9:1
[d]**14:13** Jr 51:53; Ezk 28:2; Am 9:2
[e]Dn 5:22-23; 8:10; 2Th 2:4
[f]Ps 48:2
[g]**14:15** Ps 28:1; Is 38:18; Ezk 28:8; Mt 11:23; Lk 10:15
[h]**14:17** Jl 1:19-20; 2:3,22; 4:19
[i]**14:20** Jb 18:16,19; Ps 21:10; 37:28; Is 1:4; 31:2
[j]**14:21** Is 13:11
[k]**14:24** Pr 16:4; Is 46:11; Jr 23:20; 30:24; 51:29; Zch 1:6; Eph 1:11; Rv 17:17
[l]**14:25** Is 8:7; 10:5-15,27
[m]**14:26** Is 5:19

18 All the kings of the nations
lie in splendor, each in his own tomb.
19 But you are thrown out without a grave,
like a worthless branch,
covered by those slain with the sword
and dumped into a rocky pit
like a trampled corpse.
20 You will not join them in burial,
because you destroyed your land
and slaughtered your own people.
The offspring of evildoers
will never be remembered.[i]
21 Prepare a place of slaughter
for his sons,
because of the iniquity[j] of their fathers.
They will never rise up to possess a land
or fill the surface of the earth
with cities.

22 "I will rise up against them" — this is the
declaration of the LORD of ·Hosts — "and I
will cut off from Babylon her reputation,
remnant, offspring, and posterity" — this is
the LORD's declaration. 23 "I will make her a
swampland and a region for screech owls,[D]
and I will sweep her away with a broom of
destruction."

This is the declaration
of the LORD of Hosts.

Assyria Will Be Destroyed

24 The LORD of Hosts has sworn:

As I have purposed, so it will be;
as I have planned it, so it will happen.[k]
25 I will break Assyria[l] in My land;
I will tread him down
on My mountain.
Then his yoke will be taken
from them,
and his burden will be removed
from their shoulders.
26 This is the plan[m] prepared
for the whole earth,
and this is the hand stretched out
against all the nations.
27 The LORD of Hosts Himself
has planned it;
therefore, who can stand in its way?
It is His hand that is outstretched,
so who can turn it back?

[A]14:9 Lit *rams* [B]14:12 Or *Day Star, son of the dawn* [C]14:13 Or *of Zaphon* [D]14:23 Or *hedgehogs*

An Oracle against Philistia

28 In the year that King Ahaz died,[a] this ·oracle came:[b]

29 Don't rejoice, all of you in Philistia,
because the rod of the one
who struck you[c] is broken.
For a viper will come from the root[A]
of a snake,
and from its egg comes
a flying serpent.[d]
30 Then the firstborn[e] of the poor will be
well fed,
and the impoverished will lie down
in safety,
but I will kill your root with hunger,
and your remnant will be slain.[B]
31 Wail, you gates![f] Cry out, city!
Tremble with fear,[g] all Philistia!
For a cloud of dust is coming
from the north,[h]
and there is no one missing from
the invader's ranks.
32 What answer will be given
to the messengers from that nation?
The LORD has founded ·Zion,[i]
and His afflicted people find refuge
in her.

An Oracle against Moab

15 An ·oracle against Moab:[j]

Ar in Moab is devastated,[k]
destroyed in a night.
Kir in Moab is devastated,
destroyed in a night.
2 Dibon went up to its temple
to weep at its ·high places.
Moab wails on Nebo and at[C] Medeba.
Every head is shaved;
every beard is cut off.
3 In its streets they wear ·sackcloth;
on its rooftops and in its public squares
everyone wails,
falling down and weeping.
4 Heshbon and Elealeh cry out;
their voices are heard as far away
as Jahaz.[l]
Therefore the soldiers of Moab cry out,
and they tremble.[D]
5 My heart cries out over Moab,
whose fugitives flee as far as Zoar,[m]
to Eglath-shelishiyah;
they go up the slope of Luhith weeping;
they raise a cry of destruction
on the road to Horonaim.
6 The waters of Nimrim[n] are desolate;
the grass is withered, the foliage
is gone,
and the vegetation has vanished.
7 So they carry their wealth
and belongings
over the ·Wadi of the Willows.[o]
8 For their cry echoes
throughout the territory of Moab.
Their wailing reaches Eglaim;
their wailing reaches Beer-elim.
9 The waters of Dibon[E] are full of blood,[p]
but I will bring on Dibon[F] even more
than this —
a lion for those who escape
from Moab,
and for the survivors in the land.[q]

16 Send lambs to the ruler of the land,[r]
from Sela in the desert[s]
to the mountain of Daughter ·Zion.
2 Like a bird fleeing,
forced from the nest,
the daughters of Moab
will be at the fords of the Arnon.
3 Give us counsel and make a decision.
Shelter us at noonday
with shade that is as dark as night.
Hide the refugees;[t]
do not betray the one who flees.
4 Let my refugees stay with you;
be a refuge for Moab[G]
from the aggressor.
When the oppressor has gone,
destruction has ended,
and marauders have vanished
from the land.
5 Then in the tent of David
a throne will be established
by faithful love.[u]
A judge who seeks what is right
and is quick to execute justice
will sit on the throne forever.

[a] **14:28** 2Kg 16:20; 2Ch 28:27; Is 6:1 [b] Is 13:1 [c] **14:29** 1Sm 17:50; 18:25-30; 19:8; 23:1-5; 2Sm 5:17-25; 8:1 [d] Ex 4:2-3; 7:10-12; Is 30:6 [e] **14:30** Ex 4:22 [f] **14:31** Is 3:26; 24:12; 45:2 [g] Jos 2:9,24 [h] Is 41:25; Jr 1:13-14; 4:6; 6:1; 47:2; 50:3,9,41 [i] **14:32** Ps 87:1,5; 102:16; Is 28:16; 44:28; 54:11 [j] **15:1-7** Gn 19:31-37; Is 11:14; 25:10; Jr 48:1-38; Ezk 25:8-11; Am 2:1-3; Zph 2:8-9 [k] **15:1** Nm 21:28 [l] **15:4** Nm 21:28; 32:3; Jr 48:34 [m] **15:5** Gn 19:21-22 [n] **15:6** Nm 32:3,36; Jos 13:27 [o] **15:7** Is 30:6; Jr 48:36 [p] **15:9** 2Kg 3:22-23 [q] 2Sm 23:20; 1Ch 11:22 [r] **16:1** 2Kg 3:4 [s] 2Kg 14:7; Is 42:11 [t] **16:3** 1Kg 18:4 [u] **16:5** Is 9:6-7; 32:1; 55:4; Dn 7:14; Mc 4:7; Lk 1:33

[A] **14:29** Or *stock* [B] **14:30** DSS, Syr, Tg; MT reads *and he will kill* [C] **15:2** Or *wails over Nebo and over* [D] **15:4** Lit *out, he trembles within himself* [E] **15:9** DSS, some LXX mss, Vg; MT reads *Dimon* [F] **15:9** DSS, some LXX mss, Vg; MT reads *Dimon* [G] **16:4** Or *you; Moab — be a refuge for him*

6 We have heard of Moab's pride[a] —
how very proud he is —
his haughtiness, his pride,
his arrogance,
and his empty boasting.
7 Therefore let Moab wail;
let every one of them wail for Moab.
Mourn, you who are
completely devastated,
for the raisin cakes[b] of Kir-hareseth.[c]
8 For Heshbon's terraced vineyards
and the grapevines of Sibmah
have withered.
The rulers of the nations
have trampled its choice vines
that reached as far as Jazer[d]
and spread to the desert.
Their shoots spread out
and reached the Dead Sea.[e]
9 So I join with Jazer
to weep for the vines of Sibmah;
I drench Heshbon and Elealeh
with my tears.
Triumphant shouts have fallen silent[A]
over your summer fruit
and your harvest.
10 Joy and rejoicing[f] have been removed
from the orchard;
no one is singing or shouting for joy
in the vineyards.[g]
No one tramples grapes[B]
in the winepresses.
I have put an end to the shouting.
11 Therefore I moan like the sound of
a lyre for Moab,[h]
as does my innermost being
for Kir-heres.
12 When Moab appears
on the ·high place,
when he tires[C] himself out[i]
and comes to his sanctuary to pray,
it will do him no good.[j]

13This is the message that the LORD previously announced about Moab. 14And now the
LORD says, "In three years, as a hired worker
counts years,[k] Moab's splendor will become
an object of contempt, in spite of a very large
population. And those who are left will be
few and weak."

An Oracle against Damascus

17 An ·oracle[l] against Damascus:[m]

Look, Damascus is no longer a city.
It has become a ruined heap.
2 The cities of Aroer are forsaken;
they will be places for flocks.
They will lie down without fear.
3 The fortress disappears from Ephraim,[n]
and a kingdom from Damascus.
The remnant of Aram will be
like the splendor of the Israelites.
This is the declaration
of the LORD of ·Hosts.

Judgment against Israel

4 On that day
the splendor of Jacob will fade,
and his healthy body[D]
will become emaciated.[o]
5 It will be as if a reaper had gathered
standing grain —
his arm harvesting the heads
of grain —
and as if one had gleaned heads
of grain
in the Valley of Rephaim.[p]
6 Only gleanings will be left in Israel,[q]
as if an olive tree had been beaten —
two or three berries at the very top
of the tree,
four or five on its fruitful branches.
This is the declaration
of the LORD,
the God of Israel.

7On that day people will look to their
Maker and will turn their eyes to the Holy
One of Israel.[r] 8They will not look to the al-
tars[s] they made with their hands or to the
·Asherahs and incense altars[t] they made with
their fingers.

9 On that day their strong cities will be
like the abandoned woods
and mountaintops[E]
that were abandoned because of
the Israelites;
there will be desolation.
10 For you have forgotten the God
of your salvation,

[a]16:6 Jr 48:29; Am 2:1; Ob 3-4; Zph 2:8,10 [b]16:7 2Sm 6:19; 1Ch 16:3; Sg 2:5; Hs 3:1 [c]2Kg 3:25; Jr 48:31 [d]16:8 Nm 21:32; Jos 13:25 [e]Jr 48:32 [f]16:10 Is 24:8; Jr 48:33 [g]Jdg 9:27; Is 24:7; Am 5:11,17 [h]16:11 Is 15:5; 63:15; Jr 48:36; Hs 11:8; Php 2:1 [i]16:12 1Kg 18:29 [j]Is 15:2 [k]16:14 Jb 7:1; 14:6; Is 21:16 [l]17:1 Is 13:1 [m]Gn 14:15; 15:2; 2Kg 16:9; Jr 49:23; Am 1:3-5; Zch 9:1; Ac 9:2 [n]17:3 Is 7:8,16; 8:4 [o]17:4 Is 10:16 [p]17:5 2Sm 5:18,22 [q]17:6 Dt 4:27; Is 24:13; 27:12; Ob 5; Rm 11:19 [r]17:7 Is 1:4 [s]17:8 2Ch 34:7; Is 27:9 [t]Ex 34:13; Dt 7:5; Mc 5:14

[A]16:9 Or *Battle cries have fallen* [B]16:10 Lit *wine* [C]16:12 DSS read *place, he will tire* [D]17:4 Lit *and the fat of his flesh* [E]17:9 Some Hb mss read *like the Horesh and the Amir*; LXX reads *like the Amorites and the Hivites*

and you have failed to remember
the rock of your strength;[a]
therefore you will plant
beautiful plants
and set out cuttings from exotic vines.
11 On the day that you plant,
you will help them to grow,
and in the morning
you will help your seed to sprout,
but the harvest will vanish
on the day of disease
and incurable pain.

Judgment against the Nations

12 Ah! The roar of many peoples —
they roar like the roaring of the seas.
The raging of the nations —
they rage like the raging
of mighty waters.[b]
13 The nations rage like the raging
of many waters.[c]
He rebukes them, and they flee
far away,[d]
driven before the wind like chaff
on the hills[e]
and like tumbleweeds before a gale.
14 In the evening — sudden terror!
Before morning — it is gone!
This is the fate of those
who plunder us
and the lot of those who ravage us.

The LORD's Message to Cush

18 Ah! The land of buzzing insect wings[A]
beyond the rivers of ·Cush[f]
2 sends couriers by sea,
in reed vessels on the waters.

Go, swift messengers,
to a nation tall and smooth-skinned,
to a people feared far and near,
a powerful nation
with a strange language,[B]
whose land is divided by rivers.
3 All you inhabitants of the world
and you who live on the earth,
when a banner is raised
on the mountains, look!
When a trumpet sounds, listen!

4 For, the LORD said to me:

I will quietly look out from My place,
like shimmering heat in sunshine,
like a rain cloud in harvest heat.
5 For before the harvest,
when the blossoming is over
and the blossom becomes
a ripening grape,
He will cut off the shoots
with a pruning knife,
and tear away and remove
the branches.
6 They will all be left for the birds of prey
on the hills
and for the wild animals of the land.
The birds will spend the summer
on them,
and all the animals, the winter
on them.

7 At that time a gift will be brought to ·Yah-
weh of ·Hosts from[C] a people tall and smooth-
skinned,[g] a people feared far and near, a
powerful nation with a strange language,
whose land is divided by rivers — to Mount
·Zion, the place of the name of Yahweh of
Hosts.

An Oracle against Egypt

19 An ·oracle[h] against Egypt:[i]

Look, the LORD rides
on a swift cloud[j]
and is coming to Egypt.
Egypt's idols will tremble before Him,[k]
and Egypt's heart will melt within it.[l]
2 I will provoke Egypt against Egypt;
each will fight against his brother[m]
and each against his friend,
city against city,
kingdom against kingdom.[n]
3 Egypt's spirit will be disturbed
within it,
and I will frustrate its plans.
Then they will seek idols, ghosts,
spirits of the dead, and spiritists.[o]
4 I will deliver Egypt into the hands
of harsh masters,[p]
and a strong king will rule it.
This is the declaration
of the Lord GOD of ·Hosts.

[a] **17:10** Is 8:14; 26:4
[b] **17:12** Ps 93:1-5; Is 8:9-10; Lk 21:25
[c] **17:13** Is 33:3
[d] Ps 9:5; Is 41:11
[e] Jb 21:18; Ps 1:4; 83:13; Is 29:5; 41:15-16
[f] **18:1** 2Kg 19:9; Is 20:3-5; Ezk 30:4-5,9; Zph 2:12; 3:10
[g] **18:7** Ps 68:31; Is 45:14; Zph 3:10; Ac 8:27-38
[h] **19:1** Is 13:1
[i] Jr 46:13-26; Ezk 29:1–31:2; 31:18–32:32; Jl 3:19
[j] Ps 18:9-10; 104:3; Mt 26:64; Rv 1:7
[k] Ex 12:12; Jr 43:12; 44:8
[l] Jos 2:11; Is 13:7
[m] **19:2** Mk 13:12
[n] Jdg 7:22; 1Sm 14:20; 2Ch 20:23; Mt 10:21,36; Mk 13:8; Lk 21:10
[o] **19:3** 1Ch 10:13; Is 8:19; Dn 2:2
[p] **19:4** Is 20:4; Jr 46:26; Ezk 29:19

[A] **18:1** Or *of sailing ships* [B] **18:2** Hb obscure [C] **18:7** DSS, LXX, Vg; MT omits *from*

5 The waters of the sea will dry up,
and the river will be parched and dry.
6 The channels will stink;
they will dwindle, and Egypt's canals
will be parched.
Reed and rush will die.[A]
7 The reeds by the Nile, by the mouth
of the river,
and all the cultivated areas of the Nile
will wither, blow away, and vanish.
8 Then the fishermen will mourn.
All those who cast hooks into the Nile
will lament,
and those who spread nets on the water
will shrivel up.
9 Those who work with flax
will be dismayed;[a]
the combers and weavers
will turn pale.[B]
10 Egypt's weavers[C] will be dejected;
all her wage earners
will be demoralized.

11 The princes of Zoan
are complete fools;[b]
Pharaoh's wisest advisers
give stupid advice!
How can you say to Pharaoh,
"I am one[D] of the wise,
a student of eastern[E] kings"?
12 Where then are your wise men?
Let them tell you and reveal
what the LORD of Hosts has planned
against Egypt.
13 The princes of Zoan have been fools;
the princes of Memphis are deceived.[c]
Her tribal chieftains have led
Egypt astray.
14 The LORD has mixed within her a spirit
of confusion.
The leaders have made Egypt stagger
in all she does,
as a drunkard staggers in his vomit.
15 No head or tail, palm or reed,[d]
will be able to do anything for Egypt.

Egypt Will Know the LORD

16 On that day Egypt will be like women. She
will tremble with fear because of the threatening hand of the LORD of Hosts when He
raises it against her. 17 The land of Judah will
terrify Egypt; whenever Judah is mentioned,
Egypt will tremble because of what the LORD
of Hosts has planned[e] against it.

18 On that day five cities in the land of Egypt
will speak the language of Canaan and swear
loyalty to the LORD of Hosts. One of the cities
will be called the City of the Sun.[F,G]

19 On that day there will be an altar to the
LORD in the center of the land of Egypt and a
pillar to the LORD near her border.[f] 20 It will be
a sign and witness to the LORD of Hosts in the
land of Egypt. When they cry out to the LORD
because of their oppressors, He will send
them a savior and leader, and he will rescue
them.[g] 21 The LORD will make Himself known
to Egypt, and Egypt will know the LORD on
that day. They will offer sacrifices and offerings;[h] they will make vows to the LORD and
fulfill them. 22 The LORD will strike Egypt,
striking and healing. Then they will return to
the LORD and He will hear their prayers and
heal them.

23 On that day there will be a highway[i] from
Egypt to Assyria. Assyria will go to Egypt,
Egypt to Assyria, and Egypt will worship with
Assyria.

24 On that day Israel will form a triple alliance with Egypt and Assyria—a blessing
within the land. 25 The LORD of Hosts will
bless them, saying, "Egypt My people, Assyria
My handiwork,[j] and Israel My inheritance
are blessed."[k]

No Help from Cush or Egypt

20 In the year that the chief commander,[l] sent by Sargon king of Assyria, came to Ashdod[m] and attacked and
captured it— 2 during that time the LORD had
spoken through Isaiah[n] son of Amoz, saying,
"Go, take off your *sackcloth[H] and remove the
sandals from your feet," and he did so, going
naked and barefoot[o]— 3 the LORD said, "As
My servant Isaiah has gone naked and barefoot three years as a sign and omen against
Egypt and *Cush,[p] 4 so the king of Assyria will
lead the captives of Egypt[q] and the exiles of

[a] **19:9** Pr 7:16; Ezk 27:7 [b] **19:11** Nm 13:22; Ps 78:12,43; Is 30:4 [c] **19:13** Jr 2:16; 46:14,19; Ezk 30:13 [d] **19:15** Is 9:14-16 [e] **19:17** Is 5:19 [f] **19:19** Gn 28:18; Ex 24:4; Jos 22:10,26-27 [g] **19:20** Jdg 3:9,15; 6:7; 10:10 [h] **19:21** Is 56:7; 60:7; Zch 14:16-18 [i] **19:23** Is 11:16; 35:8; 49:11; 62:10 [j] **19:25** Ps 100:3; Is 29:23; 45:11; 60:21; 64:8; Eph 2:10 [k] Dt 9:26,29; 32:9; Ps 28:9; Is 47:6; 63:17 [l] **20:1** 2Kg 18:17 [m] 1Sm 5:1 [n] **20:2** Mt 3:3; 12:17 [o] 1Sm 19:24; Mc 1:8 [p] **20:3** Is 8:18 [q] **20:4** Is 19:4

[A] **19:6** Or *wilt*, or *become black* [B] **19:9** DSS, Tg; MT reads *weavers of white cloth* [C] **19:10** Or *foundations* [D] **19:11** Lit *a son* [E] **19:11** Lit *a son of ancient* [F] **19:18** Some Hb mss, DSS, Sym, Tg, Vg, Arabic; other Hb mss read *of Destruction*; LXX reads *of Righteousness* [G] **19:18** = the ancient Egyptian city Heliopolis [H] **20:2** Lit *off the sackcloth from your loins*

Cush, young and old alike, naked and barefoot, with bared buttocks — to Egypt's shame.
5 Those who made Cush their hope and Egypt their boast will be dismayed and ashamed.[a]
6 And the inhabitants of this coastland will say on that day, 'Look, this is what has happened to those we relied on and fled to for help to rescue us from the king of Assyria! Now, how will we escape?'"

A Judgment on Babylon

21 An ·oracle[b] against the desert by the sea:[c]

Like storms that pass over the ·Negev,
it comes from the desert, from the land of terror.
2 A troubling vision is declared to me:
"The treacherous one
acts treacherously,[d]
and the destroyer destroys.
Advance, Elam! Lay siege, you Medes!
I will put an end to all her groaning."
3 Therefore I am[A] filled with anguish.
Pain grips me, like the pain of a woman
in labor.[e]
I am too perplexed to hear,
too dismayed to see.
4 My heart staggers;
horror terrifies me.
He has turned my last glimmer of hope[B]
into sheer terror.[f]
5 Prepare a table,[g] and spread out
a carpet!
Eat and drink!
Rise up, you princes,
and oil the shields!
6 For the Lord has said to me,
"Go, post a lookout;
let him report what he sees.
7 When he sees riders —
pairs of horsemen,
riders on donkeys,
riders on camels —
he must pay close attention."
8 Then the lookout[C] reported,
"Lord, I stand on the watchtower
all day,[h]
and I stay at my post all night.
9 Look, riders come —
horsemen in pairs."
And he answered, saying,
"Babylon has fallen,[i] has fallen.
All the images of her gods
have been shattered on the ground."[j]
10 My people who have been crushed
on the threshing floor,[k]
I have declared to you
what I have heard from the LORD
of ·Hosts,
the God of Israel.

An Oracle against Dumah

11 An oracle[l] against Dumah:[D,m]

One calls to me from Seir,[n]
"Watchman, what is left of the night?
Watchman, what is left of the night?"
12 The watchman said,
"Morning has come, and also night.
If you want to ask, ask!
Come back again."

An Oracle against Arabia

13 An oracle against Arabia:[o]

In the desert[E] brush
you will camp for the night,
you caravans of Dedanites.[p]
14 Bring water for the thirsty.
The inhabitants of the land of Tema[q]
meet[F] the refugees with food.
15 For they have fled from swords,
from the drawn sword,
from the bow that is strung,
and from the stress of battle.

16 For the Lord said this to me: "Within one year,[r] as a hired worker counts years, all the glory of Kedar[s] will be gone. 17 The remaining Kedarite archers will be few in number." For the LORD, the God of Israel, has spoken.

An Oracle against Jerusalem

22 An ·oracle[t] against the Valley of Vision:[u]

What's the matter with you?
Why have all of you gone up
to the rooftops?[v]

[a] **20:5** 2Kg 18:21; Is 30:3-5; 31:1; Ezk 29:6-7 [b] **21:1** Is 13:1 [c] Is 13:20-22; 14:23; 21:9; Jr 51:41-44 [d] **21:2** Is 24:16; 33:1 [e] **21:3** Ps 48:6; Is 13:8; 16:11; 26:17-18; Jr 4:31; 6:24; 22:23; 30:6; 50:43; Mc 4:9-10; 1Th 5:3 [f] **21:4** Dt 28:67 [g] **21:5** Jr 51:39,57; Dn 5:1-4 [h] **21:8** Hab 2:1 [i] **21:9** 2Sm 1:19; Is 3:8; 14:12; Jr 51:8; Ezk 32:22; Rv 14:8; 18:2 [j] Is 46:1; Jr 50:2; 51:44 [k] **21:10** Jr 51:33; Mc 4:13 [l] **21:11** Is 21:1 [m] Gn 25:14 [n] Dt 2:8; Ezk 35:2 [o] **21:13** Jr 25:23-24; 49:28 [p] Gn 10:7; Jr 25:23; 49:8; Ezk 27:15 [q] **21:14** Gn 25:15; Jb 6:19 [r] **21:16** Is 16:14 [s] Ps 120:5; Sg 1:5; Is 42:11; 60:7; Jr 2:10; Ezk 27:21 [t] **22:1** Is 13:1 [u] Ps 125:2; Jr 21:13; Jl 3:12,14 [v] Is 15:3

[A] **21:3** Lit *Therefore my loins are* [B] **21:4** Lit *my twilight* [C] **21:8** DSS, Syr; MT reads *Then a lion* [D] **21:11** Some Hb mss, LXX read *Edom* [E] **21:13** LXX, Syr, Tg, Vg read *desert at evening* [F] **21:14** LXX, Syr, Tg, Vg read *meet* as a command

2 The noisy city, the jubilant town,[a]
is filled with revelry.
Your dead did not die by the sword;
they were not killed in battle.
3 All your rulers have fled together,
captured without a bow.
All your fugitives
were captured together;
they had fled far away.
4 Therefore I said,
"Look away from me!
Let me weep bitterly![b]
Do not try to comfort me
about the destruction
of my dear[A] people."
5 For the Lord GOD of ·Hosts
had a day of tumult, trampling,
and confusion[c]
in the Valley of Vision —
people shouting[B] and crying
to the mountains;
6 Elam took up a quiver
with chariots and horsemen,[C]
and Kir[d] uncovered the shield.
7 Your best valleys were full of chariots,
and horsemen were positioned
at the gates.
8 He removed the defenses of Judah.

On that day you looked to the weapons in
the House of the Forest.[e] 9You saw that there
were many breaches in the walls of the city
of David.[f] You collected water from the lower
pool.[g] 10You counted the houses of Jerusalem
so that you could tear them down to fortify
the wall. 11You made a reservoir between the
walls[h] for the waters of the ancient pool,[i] but
you did not look to the One who made it, or
consider the One who created it long ago.

12 On that day the Lord GOD of Hosts
called for weeping,[j] for wailing,
for shaven heads,
and for the wearing of ·sackcloth.
13 But look: joy and gladness,
butchering of cattle,
slaughtering of sheep,
eating of meat, and drinking of wine —
"Let us eat and drink, for tomorrow
we die!"[k]
14 The LORD of Hosts has directly revealed
to me:[l]
"This sin of yours will never[D] be
wiped out."[m]
The Lord GOD of Hosts has spoken.

An Oracle against Shebna

15The Lord GOD of Hosts said: "Go to
Shebna,[n] that steward who is in charge of the
palace, and say to him: 16What are you doing here? Who authorized you to carve out a
tomb for yourself here, carving your tomb on
the height and cutting a crypt for yourself out
of rock?[o] 17Look, you strong man! The LORD
is about to shake you violently. He will take
hold of you, 18wind you up into a ball, and
sling you into a wide land.[E] There you will die,
and there your glorious chariots will be — a
disgrace to the house of your lord. 19I will remove you from your office; you will be ousted
from your position.

20"On that day I will call for my servant,
Eliakim son of Hilkiah.[p] 21I will clothe him
with your robe and tie your sash around him.
I will put your authority into his hand, and
he will be like a father to the inhabitants of
Jerusalem and to the House of Judah.[q] 22I will
place the key[r] of the House of David on his
shoulder; what he opens, no one can close;
what he closes, no one can open.[s] 23I will drive
him, like a peg, into a firm place. He will be a
throne of honor for his father's house. 24They
will hang on him the whole burden of his
father's house: the descendants and the off-
shoots — all the small vessels, from bowls to
every kind of jar. 25On that day" — the declaration of the LORD of Hosts — "the peg that
was driven into a firm place will give way, be
cut off, and fall, and the load on it will be destroyed." Indeed, the LORD has spoken.

An Oracle against Tyre

23 An ·oracle[t] against Tyre:[u]

Wail, ships of Tarshish,[v]
for your haven has been destroyed.
Word has reached them from the land
of Cyprus.[F,w]
2 Mourn, inhabitants of the coastland,

[a]**22:2** Is 23:7; 32:13
[b]**22:4** Is 15:3; 33:7; Jr 9:1; Zch 12:10
[c]**22:5** Is 10:6; 37:3; 63:3
[d]**22:6** 2Kg 16:9; Am 1:5; 9:7
[e]**22:8** 1Kg 7:2; 10:17
[f]**22:9** Lk 2:4
[g]2Kg 20:20; Neh 3:16
[h]**22:11** 2Kg 25:4; Jr 39:4
[i]2Kg 20:20; 2Ch 32:3-4
[j]**22:12** Is 32:11; Jl 1:13; 2:17
[k]**22:13** Is 56:12; 1Co 15:32
[l]**22:14** Is 5:9
[m]1Sm 3:14; Ezk 24:13
[n]**22:15** 2Kg 18:18,26,37; Is 36:3,11,22; 37:2
[o]**22:16** 2Sm 18:18; 2Ch 16:14; Mt 27:60
[p]**22:20** 2Kg 18:18; Is 36:3,22; 37:2
[q]**22:21** Gn 45:8; Jb 29:16
[r]**22:22** Mt 16:19; Rv 3:7
[s]Jb 12:14
[t]**23:1** Is 13:1
[u]Jos 19:29; 1Kg 5:1; Jr 25:22; 47:4; Ezk 26:1–27:36; Jl 3:4-8; Am 1:9; Zch 9:2-4
[v]Gn 10:4; 1Kg 10:22
[w]Jr 2:10; Ezk 27:6; Ac 11:19

[A]**22:4** Lit *of the daughter of my* [B]**22:5** Or *Vision — a tearing down of a wall,* or *Vision — Kir raged;* Hb obscure [C]**22:6** Lit *chariots of man* [D]**22:14** Lit *will not until you die* [E]**22:17-18** Hb obscure [F]**23:1** Hb *Kittim*

you merchants of Sidon;[a]
your agents have crossed the sea[A]
3 on many waters.
Tyre's revenue was the grain
from Shihor—
the harvest of the Nile.
She was the merchant
among the nations.[b]
4 Be ashamed Sidon, the stronghold
of the sea,
for the sea has spoken:
"I have not been in labor or given birth.
I have not raised young men
or brought up young women."
5 When the news reaches Egypt,
they will be in anguish over the news
about Tyre.[c]
6 Cross over to Tarshish;
wail, inhabitants of the coastland!
7 Is this your jubilant city,
whose origin was in ancient times,
whose feet have taken her
to settle far away?
8 Who planned this against Tyre,
the bestower of crowns,
whose traders are princes,
whose merchants are the honored ones
of the earth?
9 The LORD of ˙Hosts planned it,
to desecrate all its glorious beauty,
to disgrace all the honored ones
of the earth.
10 Overflow[B] your land like the Nile,
daughter of Tarshish;
there is no longer anything
to restrain you.[C]
11 He stretched out His hand over the sea;[d]
He made kingdoms tremble.
The LORD has commanded
that the Canaanite fortresses
be destroyed.
12 He said,
"You will not rejoice anymore,
ravished young woman,
daughter of Sidon.
Get up and cross over to Cyprus[e]—
even there you will have no rest!"
13 Look at the land of the Chaldeans—
a people who no longer exist.
Assyria destined it for desert creatures.

[a]**23:2** Gn 10:15; Jos 19:28; Jr 25:22; 27:3; Ezk 27:8; 32:30; Jl 3:4; Zch 9:2
[b]**23:3** Ezk 27:3-23
[c]**23:5** Ac 21:7
[d]**23:11** Ex 14:21; Is 14:26
[e]**23:12** Is 23:1; Jr 2:10; Ezk 27:6; Ac 4:36; 11:19-20; 13:4; 15:39; 21:3,16; 27:4
[f]**23:17** Jr 25:11,22
[g]Ac 21:7
[h]**24:3** Is 1:20; 6:11
[i]**24:5** Gn 3:17; 6:5,11-12; Nm 35:33; Is 9:17; 10:6

They set up their siege towers
and stripped its palaces.
They made it a ruin.
14 Wail, ships of Tarshish,
because your fortress is destroyed!

15 On that day Tyre will be forgotten for 70
years—the life span of one king. At the end
of 70 years, what the song says about the
prostitute will happen to Tyre:

16 Pick up your lyre,
stroll through the city,
prostitute forgotten by men.
Play skillfully,
sing many a song,
and you will be thought of again.

17 And at the end of the 70 years,[f] the LORD
will restore Tyre[g] and she will go back into
business, prostituting herself with all the
kingdoms of the world on the face of the
earth. 18 But her profits and wages will be dedicated to the LORD. They will not be stored or
saved, for her profit will go to those who live
in the LORD's presence, to provide them with
ample food and sacred clothing.

The Earth Judged

24 Look, the LORD is stripping
the earth bare
and making it desolate.
He will twist its surface and scatter
its inhabitants:
2 people and priest alike,
servant and master,
female servant and mistress,
buyer and seller,
lender and borrower,
creditor and debtor.
3 The earth will be stripped
completely bare
and will be totally plundered,
for the LORD has spoken this message.[h]
4 The earth mourns and withers;
the world wastes away and withers;
the exalted people of the earth
waste away.
5 The earth is polluted by its inhabitants,[i]
for they have transgressed teachings,
overstepped decrees,

[A]**23:2** DSS; MT reads *Sidon, whom the seafarers have filled* [B]**23:10** DSS, LXX read *Work* [C]**23:10** Or *longer any harbor*

and broken the everlasting covenant.[a]
6 Therefore a curse has consumed
the earth,[b]
and its inhabitants
have become ·guilty;
the earth's inhabitants
have been burned,
and only a few survive.
7 The new wine mourns;[c]
the vine withers.
All the carousers now groan.
8 The joyful tambourines[d] have ceased.
The noise of the jubilant has stopped.
The joyful lyre has ceased.
9 They no longer sing and drink wine;
beer is bitter to those who drink it.
10 The city of chaos is shattered;[e]
every house is closed to entry.[f]
11 In the streets they cry[A] for wine.
All joy grows dark;
earth's rejoicing goes into exile.
12 Only desolation remains in the city;
its gate has collapsed in ruins.
13 For this is how it will be on earth
among the nations:
like a harvested olive tree,
like a gleaning after a grape harvest.[g]

14 They raise their voices, they sing out;
they proclaim in the west
the majesty of the LORD.
15 Therefore, in the east honor the LORD!
In the islands of the west
honor the name of ·Yahweh,
the God of Israel.
16 From the ends of the earth
we hear songs:
The Splendor of the Righteous One.[h]
But I said, "I waste away! I waste away![B]
Woe is me."
The treacherous act treacherously;
the treacherous deal
very treacherously.[i]

17 Panic, pit, and trap await you[j]
who dwell on the earth.[k]
18 Whoever flees at the sound of panic
will fall into a pit,
and whoever escapes from the pit
will be caught in a trap.
For the windows are opened
from heaven,[l]
and the foundations of the earth
are shaken.[m]
19 The earth is completely devastated;
the earth is split open;
the earth is violently shaken.
20 The earth staggers like a drunkard[n]
and sways like a hut.
Earth's rebellion weighs it down,
and it falls, never to rise again.

21 On that day[o] the LORD will punish
the host of heaven above
and kings of the earth below.
22 They will be gathered together
like prisoners in a pit.[p]
They will be confined to a dungeon;[q]
after many days they will be punished.
23 The moon will be put to shame
and the sun disgraced,
because the LORD of ·Hosts will reign
as king
on Mount ·Zion in Jerusalem,
and He will display His glory
in the presence of His elders.[r]

Salvation and Judgment on That Day

25 ·Yahweh, You are my God;[s]
I will exalt You. I will praise
Your name,
for You have accomplished wonders,
plans formed long ago,
with perfect faithfulness.
2 For You have turned the city into a pile
of rocks,[t]
a fortified city, into ruins;
the fortress of barbarians[u] is no longer
a city;
it will never be rebuilt.
3 Therefore, a strong people
will honor You.
The cities of violent nations
will ·fear You.
4 For You have been a stronghold
for the poor,
a stronghold for the needy[v] person
in his distress,
a refuge from the rain, a shade
from the heat.[w]

[a] **24:5** Gn 9:16; 17:7; Ex 31:16; Lv 24:8; 2Sm 23:5; Ps 105:10; Is 55:3; 61:8; Jr 32:40; Ezk 16:60
[b] **24:6** Jos 23:15; Is 34:5; 43:28; Zch 5:3-4
[c] **24:7** Is 16:10; Jl 1:10,12
[d] **24:8** Ex 15:20; Jdg 11:34; 1Sm 18:6; Is 30:32; Jr 31:4
[e] **24:10** Is 34:11
[f] Is 23:1
[g] **24:13** Is 17:6
[h] **24:16** Ex 9:27; Pr 21:12; Ac 3:14; 7:52; 22:14
[i] Is 21:2; 33:1; Jr 3:20; 5:11
[j] **24:17** Am 5:19
[k] **24:17-18** Jr 48:43-44
[l] **24:18** Gn 7:11
[m] Ps 18:7; 46:2; Is 2:19,21; 13:13
[n] **24:20** Is 19:14
[o] **24:21** Is 27:12
[p] **24:22** Rv 20:1-3
[q] Rv 20:2
[r] **24:23** Is 2:2-4; 1Co 15:54
[s] **25:1** Ex 15:2; Ps 118:28; Is 7:13; 44:17
[t] **25:2** Is 17:1; 26:5
[u] Col 3:11
[v] **25:4** Mt 11:29
[w] Is 4:6; 32:2

[A] **24:11** Lit *streets she cries* [B] **24:16** Hb obscure

When the breath of the violent
is like rain against a wall,
5 like heat in a dry land,
You subdue the uproar of barbarians.
As[A] the shade of a cloud cools the heat
of the day,
so He silences the song of the violent.

6 The LORD of ·Hosts will prepare a feast[a]
for all the peoples
on this mountain[B,b] —
a feast of aged wine, choice meat,[C]
finely aged wine.
7 On this mountain
He will destroy the burial shroud,
the shroud over all the peoples,
the sheet covering all the nations;[c]
8 He will destroy death forever.[d]
The Lord GOD will wipe away the tears
from every face[e]
and remove His people's disgrace[f]
from the whole earth,
for the LORD has spoken.

9 On that day it will be said,
"Look, this is our God;
we have waited for Him, and He has
saved us.
This is the LORD; we have waited for Him.
Let us rejoice and be glad
in His salvation."[g]
10 For the LORD's power will rest
on this mountain.

But Moab[h] will be trampled in his place[D]
as straw is trampled in a dung pile.
11 He will spread out his arms
in the middle of it,
as a swimmer spreads out his arms
to swim.
His pride will be brought low,
along with the trickery of his hands.[i]
12 The high-walled fortress
will be brought down,
thrown to the ground, to the dust.[j]

The Song of Judah

26 On that day this song will be sung in
the land of Judah:

We have a strong city.
Salvation is established as walls
and ramparts.[k]
2 Open the gates
so a righteous nation can come in —
one that remains faithful.
3 You will keep the mind that is
dependent on You
in perfect peace,[l]
for it is trusting in You.
4 Trust in the LORD forever,
because in ·Yah, the LORD, is
an everlasting rock![m]
5 For He has humbled those who live
in lofty places —
an inaccessible city.[n]
He brings it down; He brings it down
to the ground;
He throws it to the dust.
6 Feet trample it,
the feet of the humble,
the steps of the poor.

God's People Vindicated

7 The path of the righteous is level;[o]
You clear a straight path
for the righteous.
8 Yes, Yahweh, we wait for You
in the path of Your judgments.
Our desire is for Your name
and renown.[p]
9 I long for You in the night;[q]
yes, my spirit within me
diligently seeks You,
for when Your judgments are
in the land,
the inhabitants of the world
will learn righteousness.
10 But if the wicked man is shown favor,
he does not learn righteousness.
In a righteous land he acts unjustly
and does not see the majesty
of the LORD.

11 LORD, Your hand is lifted up
to take action,
but they do not see it.
They will see Your zeal
for Your people,
and they will be put to shame.
The fire for Your adversaries
will consume them!
12 LORD, You will establish peace for us,

[a]**25:6** Is 24:23; Rv 19:9
[b]Is 2:2-4
[c]**25:7** 2Co 3:15-16; Eph 4:18
[d]**25:8** Hs 13:14; 1Co 15:54; Rv 21:4
[e]Is 30:19; 35:10; 51:11; 65:19; Rv 7:17; 21:4
[f]Ps 89:50-51; Is 51:7; 54:4; Mt 5:11; 1Pt 4:14
[g]**25:9** Is 35:1-2,10; 66:10
[h]**25:10** Nm 24:17; Is 15:1
[i]**25:11** Is 2:10-12,15-17; 16:6,14
[j]**25:10-12** Is 26:5-6
[k]**26:1** Is 60:18
[l]**26:3** Is 26:12; 27:5; 57:19; 66:12
[m]**26:4** Ps 73:26; Is 17:10; 30:29; 44:8
[n]**26:5-6** Is 25:10-12
[o]**26:7** Ps 27:11
[p]**26:8** Ex 3:15
[q]**26:9** Ps 77:2; 84:2; 119:20,81

[A]**25:5** Lit *In* [B]**25:6** = Mount Zion [C]**25:6** Lit *wine, fat full of marrow* [D]**25:10** Or *trampled under Him*

for You have also done all our work
for us.
13 Yahweh our God, lords other than You
have ruled over us,
but we remember Your name alone.[a]

14 The dead do not live;
departed spirits do not rise up.
Indeed, You have visited
and destroyed them;
You have wiped out all memory of them.[b]
15 You have added to the nation, LORD.[c]
You have added to the nation;
You are honored.
You have expanded all the borders
of the land.[d]
16 LORD, they went to You
in their distress;[e]
they poured out whispered prayers
because Your discipline fell on them.[A]
17 As a pregnant woman
about to give birth
writhes and cries out in her pains,[f]
so we were before You, LORD.
18 We became pregnant, we writhed
in pain;
we gave birth to wind.
We have won no victories on earth,
and the earth's inhabitants
have not fallen.
19 Your dead will live; their bodies[B]
will rise.[g]
Awake and sing, you who dwell
in the dust!
For you will be covered
with the morning dew,[C]
and the earth will bring out
the departed spirits.
20 Go, my people, enter your rooms
and close your doors behind you.
Hide for a little while until the wrath
has passed.[h]
21 For look, the LORD is coming
from His place[i]
to punish the inhabitants of the earth
for their iniquity.[j]
The earth will reveal the blood shed
on it
and will no longer conceal her slain.

Leviathan Slain

27 On that day the LORD with His harsh, great, and strong sword, will bring judgment on ·Leviathan,[k] the fleeing serpent — Leviathan, the twisting serpent. He will slay the monster that is in the sea.[l]

The LORD's Vineyard

2 On that day
sing about a desirable vineyard:[m]
3 I, ·Yahweh, watch over it;
I water it regularly.
I guard it night and day
so that no one disturbs it.
4 I am not angry,
but if it produces thorns and briers[n]
for Me,
I will fight against it, trample it,
and burn it to the ground.
5 Or let it take hold of My strength;
let it make peace with Me —
make peace with Me.
6 In days to come, Jacob will take root.[o]
Israel will blossom and bloom[p]
and fill the whole world with fruit.

7 Did the LORD strike Israel
as He struck the one
who struck Israel?[q]
Was he killed like those killed by Him?
8 You disputed with her
by banishing and driving her away.[A]
He removed her with His severe storm
on the day of the east wind.
9 Therefore Jacob's iniquity[r]
will be purged in this way,
and the result of the removal of his sin
will be this:[s]
when he makes all the altar stones
like crushed bits of chalk,
no ·Asherah poles or incense altars
will remain standing.
10 For the fortified city will be deserted,
pastures abandoned and forsaken
like a wilderness.
Calves will graze there,
and there they will spread out and strip
its branches.
11 When its branches dry out, they will be
broken off.

[a] **26:13** Jn 10:25
[b] **26:14** Jb 18:17; Ps 9:6
[c] **26:15** Is 9:3
[d] Is 33:17; 54:2-3
[e] **26:16** Is 37:3; Hs 5:15
[f] **26:17** Is 13:8
[g] **26:19** Is 25:8; Ezk 37:1-14; Dn 12:2; Hs 13:14; Mt 11:5; Lk 7:22; Jn 8:51
[h] **26:20** Is 10:5,25; 13:5; 34:2; 66:14
[i] **26:21** Mc 1:3
[j] Is 13:11
[k] **27:1** Jb 3:8; 41:1,34; Ps 74:14; 104:26
[l] Is 51:9
[m] **27:2** Ps 80:8; Is 5:7; Jr 2:21
[n] **27:4** 2Sm 23:6; Is 10:17
[o] **27:6** Is 37:31
[p] Is 35:1-2; Hs 14:5-6
[q] **27:7** Is 10:12,17; 30:31-33; 31:8-9; 37:36-38
[r] **27:9** Is 13:11
[s] Rm 11:27

[A] **26:16; 27:8** Hb obscure [B] **26:19** Lit *live; my body they* [C] **26:19** Lit *For your dew is a dew of lights*

Women will come and make fires
with them,
for they are not a people
with understanding.[a]
Therefore their Maker[b] will not
have compassion on them,
and their Creator will not be gracious
to them.

12 On that day[c]
the LORD will thresh grain
from the Euphrates River
as far as the ˙Wadi of Egypt,[d]
and you Israelites will be gathered
one by one.
13 On that day
a great trumpet[e] will be blown,
and those lost in the land of Assyria
will come,
as well as those dispersed in the land
of Egypt;
and they will worship the LORD
at Jerusalem on the holy mountain.

Woe to Samaria

28 Woe to the majestic crown
of Ephraim's drunkards,[f]
and to the fading flower
of its beautiful splendor,
which is on the summit above
the rich valley.
Woe to those overcome with wine.
2 Look, the Lord has a strong
and mighty one[g] —
like a devastating hail storm,
like a storm with strong
flooding waters.
He will bring it across the land
with His hand.
3 The majestic crown
of Ephraim's drunkards
will be trampled underfoot.
4 The fading flower
of his beautiful splendor,
which is on the summit
above the rich valley,
will be like a ripe fig
before the summer harvest.[h]
Whoever sees it will swallow it
while it is still in his hand.

[a]**27:11** Ps 32:9; 49:20; Jr 4:22 [b]Jb 4:17; Ps 95:6; Pr 14:31; Is 17:7; 29:16; 44:2; 45:9,11; 51:13; 54:5; Hs 8:14 [c]**27:12** Is 3:18; 7:18,20; 11:11; 24:21; Zch 12:8 [d]Gn 15:18 [e]**27:13** Lv 25:9; 1Ch 15:24; Mt 24:31; 1Th 4:16; Rv 11:15 [f]**28:1** Is 28:7; Hs 7:5 [g]**28:2** Is 8:7; 40:10 [h]**28:4** Hs 9:10; Mc 7:1; Nah 3:12 [i]**28:5** Is 62:3 [j]**28:6** 1Kg 3:28; Is 11:2; 32:1,15-16; Jn 5:30 [k]**28:7** Is 5:11,22; 9:15; 22:13; 56:12; Hs 4:11 [l]**28:11-12** Is 5:26-29; 33:19; 1Co 14:21 [m]**28:12** Is 11:10; 30:15; 32:17-18; Jr 6:16; Mt 11:28-29 [n]**28:13** Is 8:15; Mt 21:44 [o]**28:14** Is 1:10; 39:5,8; 66:5 [p]Is 29:20

5 On that day
the LORD of ˙Hosts will become a crown
of beauty
and a diadem of splendor[i]
to the remnant of His people,
6 a spirit of justice
to the one who sits in judgment,[j]
and strength
to those who turn back the battle
at the gate.
7 These also stagger because of wine
and stumble under the influence
of beer:
priest and prophet stagger
because of beer,
they are confused by wine.[k]
They stumble because of beer,
they are muddled in their visions,
they stumble in their judgments.
8 Indeed, all their tables are covered
with vomit;
there is no place without a stench.
9 Who is he[A] trying to teach?
Who is he[A] trying to instruct?
Infants[B] just weaned from milk?
Babies[B] removed from the breast?
10 For he says: "Law after law, law after law,
line after line, line after line,
a little here, a little there."[C,D]
11 So He will speak to this people
with stammering speech
and in a foreign language.[l]
12 He had said to them:
"This is the place of rest,
let the weary rest;[m]
this is the place of repose."
But they would not listen.
13 Then the word of the LORD came
to them:
"Law after law, law after law,
line after line, line after line,
a little here, a little there,"[C,E]
so they go stumbling backward,
to be broken, trapped, and captured.[n]

A Deal with Death

14 Therefore hear the word of the LORD,[o]
you mockers[p]

[A]**28:9** Or *He* [B]**28:9** Lit *Those* [C]**28:10,13** Hb obscure [D]**28:10** Perhaps the mockers of v. 9 are mimicking the prophet's words as baby talk. [E]**28:13** The LORD quotes the mockers' words in v. 10 to represent the unintelligible language of the Assyrian invaders.

who rule this people in Jerusalem.
15 For you said, "We have cut a deal
with Death,
and we have made an agreement
with ·Sheol;
when the overwhelming scourge
passes through,[a]
it will not touch us,
because we have made falsehood
our refuge
and have hidden behind treachery."
16 Therefore the Lord GOD said:
"Look, I have laid a stone[b] in ·Zion,
a tested stone,
a precious cornerstone,
a sure foundation;[c]
the one who believes
will be unshakable.[A,d]
17 And I will make justice
the measuring line
and righteousness the mason's level."[e]
Hail will sweep away the false refuge,
and water will flood your hiding place.
18 Your deal with Death
will be dissolved,
and your agreement with Sheol
will not last.
When the overwhelming scourge
passes through,
you will be trampled.
19 Every time it passes through,
it will carry you away;
it will pass through every morning —
every day and every night.
Only terror[f] will cause you
to understand the message.[B]
20 Indeed, the bed is too short
to stretch out on,
and its cover too small to wrap up in.
21 For the LORD will rise up as He did
at Mount Perazim.[g]
He will rise in wrath, as at the Valley
of Gibeon,[h]
to do His work, His strange work,
and to perform His task,
His disturbing task.
22 So now, do not mock,
or your shackles will become stronger.
Indeed, I have heard
from the Lord GOD of Hosts
a decree of destruction
for the whole land.[i]

God's Wonderful Advice

23 Listen and hear my voice.
Pay attention and hear what I say.
24 Does the plowman plow every day
to plant seed?
Does he continuously break up
and cultivate the soil?
25 When he has leveled its surface,
does he not then scatter black cumin
and sow cumin?
He plants wheat in rows and barley
in plots,
with spelt as their border.
26 His God teaches him order;
He instructs him.
27 Certainly black cumin is not threshed
with a threshing board,
and a cart wheel is not rolled
over the cumin.
But black cumin is beaten out
with a stick,
and cumin with a rod.
28 Bread grain is crushed,
but is not threshed endlessly.
Though the wheel
of the farmer's cart rumbles,
his horses do not crush it.
29 This also comes from the LORD
of Hosts.
He gives wonderful advice;
He gives great wisdom.[j]

Woe to Jerusalem

29 Woe to Ariel,[C] Ariel,
the city where David camped![k]
Continue year after year;
let the festivals recur.
2 I will oppress Ariel,
and there will be mourning
and crying,
and she will be to Me like an Ariel.[C]
3 I will camp in a circle around you;
I will besiege you with earth ramps,
and I will set up my siege towers
against you.
4 You will be brought down;
you will speak from the ground,

[a]**28:15** Is 8:7-8 [b]**28:16** Is 8:14; 26:4 [c]Mt 21:42; Mk 12:10; Lk 20:17; Ac 4:11; 1Co 3:11; Eph 2:20 [d]Rm 9:33; 1Pt 2:6 [e]**28:17** 2Kg 21:13; Is 5:16; 30:18; 61:8; Am 7:7-9 [f]**28:19** 2Ch 29:8; Jr 15:4; 24:9; 29:18 [g]**28:21** 2Sm 5:20; 1Ch 14:11 [h]Jos 10:10,12; 2Sm 5:25; 1Ch 14:16 [i]**28:22** Is 10:22-23; Rm 9:27-28 [j]**28:29** Is 9:6; Jr 32:19 [k]**29:1** 2Sm 5:9

[A]**28:16** Lit *will not hurry* [B]**28:19** Or *The understanding of the message will cause sheer terror* [C]**29:1,2** Or *Altar Hearth*, or *Lion of God*; Hb obscure

and your words will come from low
in the dust.
Your voice will be like that of a spirit
from the ground;[a]
your speech will whisper from the dust.
5 Your many foes[A] will be like fine dust,[b]
and many of the ruthless,
like blowing chaff.
Then suddenly, in an instant,[c]
6 you will be visited by the LORD of ·Hosts
with thunder, earthquake,
and loud noise,
storm, tempest, and a flame
of consuming fire.[d]
7 All the many nations[e]
going out to battle against Ariel —
all the attackers, the siege works
against her,
and those who oppress her —
will then be like a dream, a vision
in the night.[f]
8 It will be like a hungry one who dreams
he is eating,
then wakes and is still hungry;
and like a thirsty one who dreams
he is drinking,
then wakes and is still thirsty,
longing for water.
So it will be for all the many nations
who go to battle
against Mount ·Zion.

9 Stop and be astonished;
blind yourselves and be blind!
They are drunk,[B] but not with wine;
they stagger,[C] but not with beer.[g]
10 For the LORD has poured out on you
an overwhelming urge to[D] sleep;[h]
He has shut your eyes — the prophets,
and covered your heads — the seers.[i]

11 For you the entire vision will be like the
words of a sealed document.[j] If it is given
to one who can read and he is asked to read
it,[E] he will say, "I can't read it, because it is
sealed." 12 And if the document is given to one
who cannot read and he is asked to read it,[F]
he will say, "I can't read."
13 The Lord said:

[a]29:4 Is 8:19 [b]29:5 Is 17:13; 41:15-16 [c]Is 17:14; 30:13; 47:11; 1Th 5:3 [d]29:6 Ex 9:23; 19:16,19; 20:18; 1Sm 2:10; 12:18; Jb 40:9; Ps 77:18; Zch 14:5; Rv 4:5; 11:13 [e]29:7 Mc 4:11-12; Zch 12:9 [f]Jb 20:8; Ps 73:20; Is 17:14 [g]29:9 Lk 1:15 [h]29:10 Ps 69:23; Is 6:9-10; Mc 3:6 [i]Rm 11:8 [j]29:11 Is 8:16; Dn 12:4,9; Mt 13:11; Rv 5:1 [k]29:13 Ezk 33:31; Mt 15:8-9; Mk 7:6-7 [l]29:14 Is 6:9-10; 28:21; 65:7; Hab 1:5 [m]Is 44:25; Jr 8:9; 49:7; 1Co 1:19 [n]29:15 Ps 10:11,13; Is 28:15; 30:1 [o]Jb 22:13; Is 57:12; Ezk 8:12 [p]29:16 Rm 9:20 [q]29:17 Ps 84:6; 107:33,35; Is 32:15 [r]29:18 Is 35:5; 42:18-19; 43:8; Mt 11:5; Mk 7:37 [s]29:19 Ps 69:32; Is 49:13 [t]Is 1:4 [u]29:20 Is 28:14

Because these people approach Me
with their mouths[k]
to honor Me with lip-service[G] —
yet their hearts are far from Me,
and their worship consists
of man-made rules
learned by rote —
14 therefore I will again confound
these people
with wonder after wonder.[l]
The wisdom of their wise men
will vanish,[m]
and the understanding
of the perceptive will be hidden.
15 Woe to those who go to great lengths
to hide their plans from the LORD.[n]
They do their works in darkness,
and say, "Who sees us?
Who knows us?"[o]
16 You have turned things around,
as if the potter were the same
as the clay.
How can what is made say
about its maker,
"He didn't make me"?[p]
How can what is formed
say about the one who formed it,
"He doesn't understand
what he's doing"?
17 Isn't it true that in just a little while
Lebanon will become an orchard,
and the orchard will seem
like a forest?[q]
18 On that day the deaf will hear[r]
the words of a document,
and out of a deep darkness
the eyes of the blind will see.
19 The humble will have joy
after joy in the LORD,
and the poor people will rejoice[s]
in the Holy One of Israel.[t]
20 For the ruthless one will vanish,
the scorner will disappear,[u]
and all those who lie in wait
with evil intent
will be killed —
21 those who, with their speech,
accuse a person of wrongdoing,

[A]29:5 Lit *foreigners* [B]29:9 LXX, Tg, Vg read *Be drunk* [C]29:9 Tg, Vg read *wine; stagger* [D]29:10 Lit *you a spirit of* [E]29:11 Lit *If one gives it to one who knows the document, saying, "Read this, please"* [F]29:12 Lit *who does not know the document, saying, "Read this, please"* [G]29:13 Lit *their mouth and honor Me with its lips*

who set a trap at the ·gate
for the mediator,
and without cause deprive
the righteous of justice.[a]

22 Therefore, the LORD who redeemed Abraham[b] says this about the house of Jacob:

Jacob will no longer be ashamed
and his face will no longer be pale.
23 For when he sees his children,
the work of My hands
within his nation,
they will honor My name,
they will honor the Holy One of Jacob[c]
and stand in awe of the God of Israel.[d]
24 Those who are confused
will gain understanding,
and those who grumble
will accept instruction.

Condemnation of the Egyptian Alliance

30 Woe to the rebellious children![e]
This is the LORD's declaration.
They carry out a plan,[f] but not Mine;
they make an alliance,
but against My will,
piling sin on top of sin.
2 They set out to go down to Egypt[g]
without asking My advice,
in order to seek shelter
under Pharaoh's protection
and take refuge in Egypt's shadow.[h]
3 But Pharaoh's protection will become
your shame,
and refuge in Egypt's shadow
your disgrace.[i]
4 For though his[A] princes are at Zoan[j]
and his messengers reach
as far as Hanes,
5 everyone will be ashamed
because of a people who can't help.
They are of no benefit, they are no help;
they are good for nothing but shame
and reproach.[k]

6 An ·oracle[l] about the animals of the
·Negev:[B]

Through a land of trouble and distress,
of lioness and lion,
of viper and flying serpent,[m]
they carry their wealth on the backs
of donkeys
and their treasures on the humps
of camels,
to a people who will not help them.
7 Egypt's help is completely worthless;
therefore, I call her:
·Rahab Who Just Sits.[n]

8 Go now, write it on a tablet
in their presence
and inscribe it on a scroll;
it will be for the future,
forever and ever.
9 They are a rebellious people,
deceptive children,[o]
children who do not want to obey
the LORD's instruction.
10 They say to the seers, "Do not see,"
and to the prophets,
"Do not prophesy the truth to us.
Tell us flattering things.[p]
Prophesy illusions.
11 Get out of the way!
Leave the pathway.
Rid us of the Holy One of Israel."[q]
12 Therefore the Holy One of Israel says:
"Because you have rejected this message
and have trusted in oppression
and deceit,
and have depended on them,
13 this iniquity[r] of yours will be
like a spreading breach,
a bulge in a high wall
whose collapse will come
in an instant—suddenly!
14 Its collapse will be like the shattering
of a potter's jar,[s] crushed to pieces,
so that not even a fragment of pottery
will be found among
its shattered remains—
no fragment large enough to take fire
from a hearth
or scoop water from a cistern."
15 For the Lord GOD, the Holy One
of Israel, has said:
"You will be delivered by returning
and resting;
your strength will lie
in quiet confidence.

[a] **29:21** Is 32:7; Am 5:10,12
[b] **29:22** Is 41:8; 51:2; 63:16
[c] **29:23** 2Sm 23:1; Ps 24:6; 76:6; 114:7; Is 2:3
[d] Is 5:16; 8:13
[e] **30:1** Dt 21:18-21; Is 1:2,23; 30:9; 65:2
[f] Is 29:15
[g] **30:2** Is 31:1; Jr 43:7
[h] Is 36:9
[i] **30:3** Is 20:5-6; 36:6; Jr 42:18,22
[j] **30:4** Is 19:11
[k] **30:5** Jr 2:36
[l] **30:6** Is 13:1
[m] Dt 8:15
[n] **30:7** Ps 87:4; 89:10; Is 51:9; Ezk 29:3,7
[o] **30:9** Is 30:1
[p] **30:10** 1Kg 22:8,13; Jr 6:14; 23:17,26; Ezk 13:8-16; Rm 16:18; 2Tm 4:3-4
[q] **30:11** Is 1:4; 41:14-20; 43:14; 45:11; 48:17; 49:7; 54:5; 55:5; 60:9,14
[r] **30:13** Is 13:11
[s] **30:14** Ps 2:9; Jr 19:10-11

[A] **30:4** Or *Judah's* [B] **30:6** Or *Southland*

But you are not willing."
16 You say, "No!
We will escape on horses" —
therefore you will escape! —
and, "We will ride on fast horses" —
but those who pursue you
will be faster.[a]
17 One thousand will flee at the threat
of one,[b]
at the threat of five you will flee,
until you alone remain
like a solitary pole on a mountaintop
or a banner on a hill.

The LORD's Mercy to Israel

18 Therefore the LORD is waiting
to show you mercy,
and is rising up
to show you compassion,[c]
for the LORD is a just God.
All who wait patiently for Him
are happy.

19 For you people will live on ·Zion in Jerusalem and will never cry again. He will show
favor to you at the sound of your cry; when
He hears, He will answer you. 20 The Lord
will give you meager bread and water during oppression,[d] but your Teacher[A] will not
hide Himself[B] any longer. Your eyes will see
your Teacher,[A] 21 and whenever you turn to
the right or to the left, your ears will hear
this command behind you: "This is the way.
Walk in it."[e] 22 Then you will defile your silver-
plated idols and your gold-plated images. You
will throw them away like menstrual cloths,
and call them filth.

23 Then He will send rain for your seed that
you have sown in the ground, and the food,
the produce of the ground, will be rich and
plentiful. On that day your cattle will graze
in open pastures.[f] 24 The oxen and donkeys
that work the ground will eat salted fodder
scattered with winnowing shovel[g] and fork.
25 Streams flowing with water will be on every high mountain and every raised hill on
the day of great slaughter when the towers
fall. 26 The moonlight will be as bright as the
sunlight, and the sunlight will be seven times
brighter[h] — like the light of seven days — on
the day[i] that the LORD bandages His people's
injuries and heals the wounds He inflicted.[j]

Annihilation of the Assyrians

27 Look, ·Yahweh[C] comes from far away,
His anger burning and heavy
with smoke.[D]
His lips are full of fury,
and His tongue is
like a consuming fire.
28 His breath is like
an overflowing torrent[k]
that rises to the neck.[l]
He comes to sift the nations in a sieve
of destruction
and to put a bridle on the jaws
of the peoples
to lead them astray.[m]
29 Your singing will be like that
on the night of a holy festival,
and your heart will rejoice
like one who walks to the music
of a flute,
going up to the mountain
of the LORD,
to the Rock of Israel.[n]
30 And the LORD will make the splendor
of His voice heard
and reveal His arm[o] striking in
angry wrath
and a flame of consuming fire,
in driving rain, a torrent,
and hailstones.
31 Assyria will be shattered by the voice
of the LORD.
He will strike with a rod.
32 And every stroke
of the appointed[E] staff
that the LORD brings down on him
will be to the sound of tambourines
and lyres;
He will fight against him
with brandished weapons.
33 Indeed! ·Topheth has been ready[p]
for the king for a long time now.
Its funeral pyre is deep and wide,
with plenty of fire and wood.
The breath of the LORD,[q] like a torrent
of brimstone,
kindles it.

[a] **30:16** Is 31:1,3
[b] **30:17** Lv 26:36; Dt 28:25; 32:30; Jos 23:10; Pr 28:1
[c] **30:18** 2Pt 3:9
[d] **30:20** 1Kg 22:27; Ps 80:5
[e] **30:21** Is 35:8-9
[f] **30:23** Ps 144:13; Is 32:20; Hs 4:16
[g] **30:24** Mt 3:12
[h] **30:26** Is 24:23; 60:19-20; Rv 21:23; 22:5
[i] Mt 25:13
[j] Is 33:24; Jr 33:6; Hs 6:1-2
[k] **30:28** Is 11:4; 30:33; 2Th 2:8
[l] Is 8:8
[m] 2Kg 19:28; Is 37:29
[n] **30:29** Is 8:14; 26:4
[o] **30:30** Ex 6:6; Dt 4:34; Jb 40:9; Is 53:1; Jr 32:17; Ezk 20:33
[p] **30:33** 2Kg 23:10; Jr 7:31; 19:6
[q] Is 40:7

[A] **30:20** Or *teachers* [B] **30:20** Or *themselves* [C] **30:27** Lit *the name Yahweh* [D] **30:27** Hb obscure [E] **30:32** Some Hb mss read *punishing*

The LORD, the Only Help

31 Woe to those who go down to Egypt
for help[a]
and who depend on horses!
They trust in the abundance of chariots
and in the large number of horsemen.[b]
They do not look[c] to the Holy One
of Israel
and they do not seek the LORD's help.
2 But He also is wise and brings disaster.[d]
He does not go back on what He says;[e]
He will rise up against the house
of wicked men
and against the allies of evildoers.
3 Egyptians are men, not God;
their horses are flesh, not spirit.
When the LORD raises His hand
to strike,
the helper will stumble
and the one who is helped will fall;
both will perish together.

4 For this is what the LORD said to me:

As a lion or young lion growls
over its prey[f]
when a band of shepherds is called out
against it,
and is not terrified by their shouting
or subdued by their noise,
so the LORD of ·Hosts will come down
to fight on Mount ·Zion
and on its hill.[g]
5 Like hovering birds,
so the LORD of Hosts
will protect Jerusalem[h] —
by protecting it, He will rescue it,
by sparing it, He will deliver it.

6 Return to the One the Israelites have
greatly rebelled against.[i] 7 For on that day,
every one of you will reject the silver and
gold idols that your own hands have sinfully
made.[j]

8 Then Assyria will fall,
but not by human sword;
a sword will devour him,
but not one made by man.[k]
He will flee from the sword;
his young men will be put
to forced labor.[l]
9 His rock[A] will pass away
because of fear,[m]
and his officers will be afraid
because of the signal flag.[n]

This is the LORD's declaration — whose fire is
in Zion and whose furnace is in Jerusalem.[o]

The Righteous Kingdom Announced

32 Indeed, a king will reign righteously,
and rulers will rule justly.[p]
2 Each will be like a shelter
from the wind,
a refuge from the rain,[q]
like streams of water[r] in a dry land
and the shade of a massive rock
in an arid land.
3 Then the eyes of those who see will not
be closed,
and the ears of those who hear
will listen.[s]
4 The reckless mind will gain knowledge,
and the stammering tongue[t]
will speak clearly and fluently.
5 A fool will no longer be called a noble,[u]
nor a scoundrel said to be important.
6 For a fool speaks foolishness
and his mind plots iniquity.
He lives in a godless way
and speaks falsely about the LORD.
He leaves the hungry empty
and deprives the thirsty of drink.[v]
7 The scoundrel's weapons
are destructive;
he hatches plots to destroy the needy
with lies,
even when the poor says what is right.
8 But a noble person plans noble things;
he stands up for noble causes.
9 Stand up, you complacent women;[w]
listen to me.
Pay attention to what I say,
you overconfident daughters.
10 In a little more than a year
you overconfident ones will shudder,
for the vintage will fail
and the harvest will not come.
11 Shudder, you complacent ones;
tremble, you overconfident ones!
Strip yourselves bare[x]

a **31:1** Is 30:2,7; 36:6
b Dt 17:16; Ps 20:7; 33:17; Is 2:7; 30:16; 36:9
c Is 9:13; 17:7-8; Dn 9:13; Am 5:4-8
d **31:2** Is 45:7
e Nm 23:19; Is 22:14; Jr 44:29
f **31:4** Nm 24:9; Hs 11:10; Am 3:8
g Is 42:13; Zch 12:8
h **31:5** Dt 32:11; Ps 91:4
i **31:6** Is 1:5; 59:13
j **31:7** Is 2:20; 30:22
k **31:8** Is 37:7,36-38
l Gn 49:15; Is 14:2
m **31:9** Dt 32:31,37
n Is 5:26; 13:2; Jr 4:6,21; 51:12,27
o Lv 10:2; Is 10:17; 30:33
p **32:1** Ps 72:1-4; Is 9:6-7; 11:4-5; Jr 23:5; Zch 9:9; 14:9
q **32:2** Is 4:6; 25:4
r Is 30:25
s **32:3** Is 29:18
t **32:4** Is 33:19
u **32:5** Ps 107:40; 118:9; 146:3
v **32:6** Is 3:15; 10:2
w **32:9** Is 47:8; Am 6:1; Zph 2:15
x **32:11** Is 47:2-3

A **31:9** Perhaps the Assyrian king

and put ˙sackcloth around your waists.
12 Beat your breasts in mourning[a]
for the delightful fields
and the fruitful vines,[b]
13 for the ground of my people
growing thorns and briers,[c]
indeed, for every joyous house
in the joyful city.
14 For the palace will be forsaken,
the busy city abandoned.
The hill and the watchtower
will become
barren places forever,
the joy of wild donkeys,
and a pasture for flocks,
15 until the Spirit from heaven
is poured out on us.[d]
Then the desert will become
an orchard,
and the orchard will seem like a forest.[e]
16 Then justice will inhabit the wilderness,
and righteousness will dwell
in the orchard.
17 The result of righteousness
will be peace;[f]
the effect of righteousness
will be quiet confidence forever.
18 Then my people will dwell
in a peaceful place,
in safe and secure dwellings.
19 But hail will level the forest,[A,g]
and the city will sink into the depths.[h]
20 Those who sow seed are happy
beside abundant waters;[i]
they let ox and donkey range freely.[j]

The LORD Rises Up

33 Woe, you destroyer never destroyed,
you traitor never betrayed!
When you have finished destroying,
you will be destroyed.
When you have finished betraying,
they will betray you.[k]
2 LORD, be gracious to us! We wait
for You.[l]
Be our strength every morning
and our salvation in time of trouble.[m]
3 The peoples flee
at the thunderous noise;[n]
the nations scatter when You rise
in Your majesty.
4 Your spoil will be gathered as locusts
are gathered;
people will swarm over it
like an infestation of locusts.
5 The LORD is exalted, for He dwells
on high;
He has filled ˙Zion with justice
and righteousness.
6 There will be times of security
for you —
a storehouse of salvation, wisdom,
and knowledge.
The ˙fear of the LORD is Zion's treasure.[o]
7 Listen! Their warriors cry loudly
in the streets;
the messengers of peace weep bitterly.[p]
8 The highways are deserted;
travel has ceased.
An agreement has been broken,[q]
cities[B] despised,
and human life disregarded.
9 The land mourns and withers;[r]
Lebanon is ashamed and decayed.
Sharon is like a desert;
Bashan and Carmel shake off
their leaves.
10 "Now I will rise up,"[s] says the LORD.
"Now I will lift Myself up.
Now I will be exalted.
11 You will conceive chaff;[t]
you will give birth to stubble.
Your breath is fire that will
consume you.
12 The peoples will be burned to ashes,
like thorns cut down and burned
in a fire.
13 You who are far off, hear what
I have done;
you who are near,[u] know My strength."
14 The sinners in Zion are afraid;
trembling seizes the ungodly:
"Who among us can dwell
with a consuming fire?[v]
Who among us can dwell
with ever-burning flames?"
15 The one who lives righteously
and speaks rightly,[w]

[a]32:12 Nah 2:7 [b]Mk 14:25 [c]32:13 Is 5:6; 7:23-25; 9:18; 27:4 [d]32:15 Is 11:2; 44:3; 59:21; Ezk 39:29; Jl 2:28 [e]Is 29:17; 35:1-2 [f]32:17 Ps 72:2-3; 85:8; 119:165; Is 2:4; Rm 14:17; Jms 3:18 [g]32:19 Is 28:2,17; 30:30 [h]Is 24:10,12; 26:5; 27:10; 29:4 [i]32:20 Nm 24:7; Ec 11:1; Is 30:23-24 [j]Is 30:24 [k]33:1 2Kg 18:14-36; Is 17:14; 21:2 [l]33:2 Is 25:9; 26:8 [m]Ex 15:2; Ps 28:8; Is 12:2; 17:10; 51:5 [n]33:3 Is 17:13; 21:15 [o]33:6 Is 11:2-3; Ac 9:31 [p]33:7 2Kg 18:18,37; Is 36:3,22 [q]33:8 2Kg 18:14-17; Is 24:5 [r]33:9 Is 3:26; 24:4; 29:2 [s]33:10 Ps 12:5; Is 2:19,21 [t]33:11 Ps 7:14; Is 26:18; 59:4; Jms 1:15 [u]33:13 Is 18:2; Eph 2:17 [v]33:14 Is 30:27,30; 66:15; Heb 12:29 [w]33:15 Ps 15:2; 24:4; Is 58:6-11

A32:19 Hb obscure B33:8 DSS read *witnesses*

who refuses gain from extortion,
whose hand never takes a bribe,
who stops his ears from listening
to murderous plots[A]
and shuts his eyes to avoid
endorsing evil[B,a] —
16 he will dwell on the heights;
his refuge will be the rocky fortresses,
his food provided, his water assured.
17 Your eyes will see the King
in His beauty;[b]
you will see a vast land.[c]
18 Your mind will meditate
on the past terror:
"Where is the accountant?[C]
Where is the tribute collector?[D]
Where is the one who spied out
our defenses?"[E]
19 You will no longer see the barbarians,
a people whose speech is difficult
to comprehend —
who stammer in a language that is
not understood.[d]
20 Look at Zion, the city
of our festival times.
Your eyes will see Jerusalem,
a peaceful pasture,[e] a tent
that does not wander;
its tent pegs will not be pulled up
nor will any of its cords be loosened.[f]
21 For the majestic One, our LORD,
will be there,[g]
a place of rivers and broad streams
where ships that are rowed
will not go,
and majestic vessels will not pass.[h]
22 For the LORD is our Judge,
the LORD is our lawgiver,[i]
the LORD is our King.
He will save us.[j]
23 Your ropes are slack;
they cannot hold the base
of the mast
or spread out the flag.
Then abundant spoil will be divided,
the lame will plunder it,
24 and none there will say, "I am sick."
The people who dwell there
will be forgiven[k] their iniquity.[l]

The Judgment of the Nations

34 You nations, come here and listen;
you peoples, pay attention![m]
Let the earth hear, and all that fills it,
the world and all that comes from it.[n]
2 The LORD is angry with all
the nations —
furious with all their armies.[o]
He will set them apart for destruction,[p]
giving them over to slaughter.
3 Their slain will be thrown out,
and the stench of their corpses
will rise;[q]
the mountains will flow[F]
with their blood.[r]
4 All[G] the heavenly bodies[s] will dissolve.
The skies will roll up like a scroll,[t]
and their stars will all wither
as leaves wither on the vine,
and foliage on the fig tree.[u]

The Judgment of Edom

5 When My sword has drunk its fill[H,v]
in the heavens,
it will then come down on Edom[w]
and on the people I have *set apart
for destruction.
6 The LORD's sword is covered
with blood.
It drips with fat,
with the blood of lambs and goats,
with the fat of the kidneys of rams.[x]
For the LORD has a sacrifice in Bozrah,[y]
a great slaughter in the land of Edom.
7 The wild oxen will be struck[I] down
with them,
and young bulls with the mighty bulls.
Their land will be soaked with[J] blood,
and their soil will be saturated
with fat.
8 For the LORD has a day of vengeance,[z]
a time of paying back Edom
for its hostility against *Zion.
9 Edom's streams will be turned
into pitch,
her soil into sulfur;[aa]
her land will become burning pitch.
10 It will never go out — day or night.
Its smoke will go up forever.[ab]

[a]**33:15** Ps 119:37
[b]**33:17** Is 6:5; 24:23; 33:21-22; Zch 9:9
[c]Is 54:2-3
[d]**33:19** Dt 28:49-50; Is 28:11; Jr 5:15
[e]**33:20** Ps 46:5; 125:1-2; Is 32:18
[f]Is 54:2
[g]**33:21** Rm 8:31
[h]Is 41:18; 43:19-20; 48:18; 66:12
[i]**33:22** Is 1:10; 51:4,7; Jms 4:12
[j]2Sm 22:3; 23:5; 2Kg 19:19,34; Is 25:9; 35:4; 38:20
[k]**33:24** Is 40:2; 44:22; Jr 50:20; Mc 7:18-19; 1Jn 1:7-9
[l]Is 13:11
[m]**34:1** Ps 49:1; Is 1:2; 41:1; 43:9; 45:20
[n]Ps 24:1; Is 6:3; 42:5
[o]**34:2** Is 13:5; Jr 10:10; 50:13
[p]Jos 6:21; 1Sm 15:3; Is 11:5; 24:1,6; 43:28
[q]**34:3** Is 14:21; 18:6; Ezk 39:17; Jl 2:10; Am 4:10; Rv 19:17-19
[r]Ps 46:2-3
[s]**34:4** 2Kg 17:16; 21:3,5; 23:4-5
[t]Rv 6:12-14
[u]Ps 102:25-27; Is 13:10; 51:6; Ezk 32:7-8; Jl 3:15; Mt 24:29; Mk 13:24-25; 2Pt 3:10,12
[v]**34:5** Dt 32:41-43; Jr 46:10; Ezk 21:3-5
[w]Nm 20:14-21; Is 63:1; Jr 49:7-8,20; Ezk 25:12-14; 35:1-15; Jl 3:19; Am 1:11-12; Ob 1-14; Mal 1:4
[x]**34:6** Is 25:6; 30:32; Jr 46:10; 51:40; Ezk 39:17; Zph 1:7-9
[y]Gn 36:33; Is 63:1; Jr 49:13,22
[z]**34:8** Is 13:6; 35:4; 47:3; 61:2; 63:4
[aa]**34:9** Gn 19:24; Dt 29:23; Ps 11:6; Is 30:33; Ezk 38:22
[ab]**34:10** Is 1:31; 66:24; Rv 14:11; 19:3

[A]**33:15** Lit *to bloods* [B]**33:15** Lit *eyes from seeing evil* [C]**33:18** Lit *counter* [D]**33:18** Lit *weigher* [E]**33:18** Lit *who counts towers* [F]**34:3** Or *melt*, or *dissolve* [G]**34:4** DSS read *And the valleys will be split, and all* [H]**34:5** DSS read *sword will appear* [I]**34:7** Or *will go* [J]**34:7** Or *will drink its fill of*

It will be desolate, from generation
to generation;
no one will pass through it forever
and ever.[a]
11 The desert owl[A] and the screech owl[B]
will possess it,
and the great owl and the raven
will dwell there.[b]
The LORD will stretch out
a measuring line
and a plumb line over her
for her destruction and chaos.[c]
12 No nobles will be left to proclaim
a king,
and all her princes will come
to nothing.
13 Her palaces will be overgrown
with thorns;
her fortified cities, with thistles
and briers.[d]
She will become a dwelling for jackals,
an abode[C] for ostriches.[e]
14 The desert creatures will meet hyenas,
and one wild goat will call to another.
Indeed, the screech owl
will stay there
and will find a resting place
for herself.
15 The sand partridge[D] will make
her nest there;
she will lay and hatch her eggs
and will gather her brood
under her shadow.
Indeed, the birds of prey
will gather there,
each with its mate.[f]
16 Search and read the scroll
of the LORD:[g]
Not one of them will be missing,
none will be lacking its mate,
because He has ordered it
by my[E] mouth,
and He will gather them by His Spirit.
17 He has ordained a lot for them;
His hand allotted their portion
with a measuring line.
They will possess it forever;[h]
they will dwell in it from generation
to generation.

The Ransomed Return to Zion

35 The wilderness and the dry land
will be glad;
the desert will rejoice and blossom
like a rose.[F,G,i]
2 It will blossom abundantly
and will also rejoice with joy
and singing.
The glory of Lebanon will be given to it,
the splendor of Carmel and Sharon.[j]
They will see the glory of the LORD,[k]
the splendor of our God.[l]
3 Strengthen the weak hands,
steady the shaking knees![m]
4 Say to the cowardly:
"Be strong; do not fear!
Here is your God; vengeance is coming.[n]
God's retribution is coming; He will
save you."[o]
5 Then the eyes of the blind
will be opened,
and the ears of the deaf unstopped.[p]
6 Then the lame will leap like a deer,[q]
and the tongue of the mute will sing
for joy,[r]
for water will gush in the wilderness,
and streams in the desert;[s]
7 the parched ground will become a pool
of water,
and the thirsty land springs of water.[t]
In the haunt of jackals,[u] in their lairs,
there will be grass, reeds,
and papyrus.
8 A road will be there and a way;[v]
it will be called the Holy Way.[w]
The *unclean will not travel on it,[x]
but it will be for the one who walks
the path.[y]
Even the fool will not go astray.
9 There will be no lion there,
and no vicious beast will go up on it;
they will not be found there.
But the redeemed will walk on it,
10 and the redeemed of the LORD
will return[z]
and come to *Zion with singing,
crowned with unending joy.
Joy and gladness will overtake them,
and sorrow and sighing will flee.[aa]

[a] **34:10** Is 13:20-22; Ezk 29:11; Mal 1:3-4
[b] **34:11** Is 13:21-22; 14:23; Zph 2:14
[c] 2Kg 21:13; Is 24:10; Lm 2:8
[d] **34:13** Is 32:13
[e] Ps 44:19; Is 13:22; Jr 9:11; 10:22; Mal 1:3
[f] **34:15** Dt 14:13
[g] **34:16** Ps 40:7; 139:16; Is 8:16; 30:8; Dn 7:10; Mal 3:16; Rv 20:12
[h] **34:17** Nm 24:18
[i] **35:1** Ps 65:12; Is 6:11; 7:21-25; 27:10; 32:15; 41:18-19; 51:3; 55:12-13
[j] **35:2** Sg 2:1; 5:15; 7:5; Is 33:9
[k] Ex 16:7,10; Lv 9:6,23; Nm 29:6; Is 40:5; Ezk 1:28; 3:23
[l] Ps 45:3-4; 96:6; 104:1; 145:5,12; Is 2:10,19,21; 53:2; 63:1; Ezk 16:14
[m] **35:3** Heb 12:12
[n] **35:4** Is 1:24; 34:8; 47:3; 59:17; 61:2; 63:4
[o] Is 33:22
[p] **35:5** Is 29:18; 32:3-4; 42:7,16,18; 50:4; Mt 11:5; Lk 7:22; Jn 9:6-7
[q] **35:6** Zph 3:19; Mt 11:5; 15:30-31; 21:14; Ac 3:1-8; 8:7; 14:8-10
[r] Ex 4:11; Mk 7:32; 9:25
[s] Is 41:18; 43:19; Jn 7:38-39
[t] **35:7** Is 49:10
[u] Is 13:22; 34:13
[v] **35:8** Is 40:3; 42:16; 43:16,19; 49:11; 51:10; 57:14; 62:10
[w] Is 4:3; 52:1; Mt 7:13-14; 1Pt 1:15-16
[x] Is 52:1; Rv 21:27
[y] Ps 139:24; Is 2:3; 8:11; 30:21; 42:24; 48:17; 58:13
[z] **35:10** Is 51:11
[aa] Is 65:19; Rm 9:2; Rv 21:4

[A] **34:11** Or *The pelican* [B] **34:11** Or *the hedgehog* [C] **34:13** DSS, LXX, Syr, Tg; MT reads *jackals, grass* [D] **34:15** Or *The arrow snake*, or *The owl* [E] **34:16** Some Hb mss; other Hb mss, DSS, Syr, Tg read *His* [F] **35:1** Or *meadow saffron* [G] **35:1** Not the modern flower but a common wildflower in northern Israel

Sennacherib's Invasion

36 In the fourteenth year of King Hezekiah,[a] Sennacherib king of Assyria attacked all the fortified cities of Judah and captured them. 2 Then the king of Assyria sent the ·Rabshakeh, along with a massive army, from Lachish[b] to King Hezekiah at Jerusalem. The Assyrian stood near the conduit of the upper pool, by the road to the Fuller's Field.[c] 3 Eliakim son of Hilkiah, who was in charge of the palace, Shebna the court secretary,[d] and Joah son of Asaph, the court historian, came out to him.

4 The Rabshakeh said to them, "Tell Hezekiah:

> The great king, the king of Assyria, says this: What are you relying on?[A] 5 I[B] say that your strategy and military preparedness are mere words. What are you now relying on that you have rebelled against me?[e] 6 Look, you are trusting in Egypt, that splintered reed of a staff[f] that will enter and pierce the hand of anyone who leans on it. This is how Pharaoh king of Egypt is to all who trust in him.[g] 7 Suppose you say to me, 'We trust in the LORD our God.' Isn't He the One whose ·high places and altars Hezekiah has removed, saying to Judah and Jerusalem, 'You are to worship at this altar'?[h]
>
> 8 Now make a deal with my master, the king of Assyria. I'll give you 2,000 horses if you're able to supply riders for them! 9 How then can you drive back a single officer among the weakest of my master's officers and trust in Egypt for chariots and horsemen?[i] 10 Have I attacked this land to destroy it without the LORD's approval? The LORD said to me, 'Attack this land and destroy it.'"

11 Then Eliakim, Shebna, and Joah said to the Rabshakeh, "Please speak to your servants in Aramaic,[j] since we understand it. Don't speak to us in Hebrew[C] within earshot of the people who are on the wall."

12 But the Rabshakeh replied, "Has my master sent me to speak these words to your master and to you, and not to the men who are sitting on the wall, who are destined with you to eat their own excrement and drink their own urine?"

13 Then the Rabshakeh stood and called out loudly in Hebrew:[C]

> Listen to the words of the great king, the king of Assyria! 14 This is what the king says: "Don't let Hezekiah deceive you,[k] for he cannot deliver you. 15 Don't let Hezekiah persuade you to trust in the LORD, saying, 'The LORD will certainly deliver us! This city will not be handed over to the king of Assyria.'"
>
> 16 Don't listen to Hezekiah, for this is what the king of Assyria says: "Make peace[D] with me and surrender to me. Then every one of you may eat from his own vine and his own fig tree[l] and drink water from his own cistern 17 until I come and take you away to a land like your own land—a land of grain and new wine, a land of bread and vineyards. 18 Beware that Hezekiah does not mislead you by saying, 'The LORD will deliver us.'[m] Has any one of the gods of the nations[n] delivered his land from the power of the king of Assyria? 19 Where are the gods of Hamath and Arpad?[o] Where are the gods of Sepharvaim? Have they delivered Samaria from my power?[p] 20 Who among all the gods of these lands ever delivered his land from my power? So will the LORD deliver Jerusalem."

21 But they kept silent; they didn't say anything, for the king's command was, "Don't answer him."[q] 22 Then Eliakim son of Hilkiah, who was in charge of the palace, Shebna the court secretary, and Joah son of Asaph, the court historian, came to Hezekiah with their clothes torn and reported to him the words of the Rabshakeh.

Hezekiah Seeks Isaiah's Counsel

37 When King Hezekiah heard their report,[r] he tore his clothes, put on ·sackcloth,[s] and went to the LORD's temple. 2 Then he sent Eliakim, who was in charge of the palace, Shebna the court secretary, and the

[a] **36:1-22** 2Kg 18:13,17-37; 2Ch 32:1-16,18
[b] **36:2** Jos 15:20,39
[c] Is 7:3
[d] **36:3** Is 22:15,20-21
[e] **36:5** 2Kg 18:7
[f] **36:6** Ezk 29:6-7
[g] Is 30:3-7
[h] **36:7** Dt 12:2-5; 2Kg 18:4-5
[i] **36:9** Is 20:5; 30:2-5,7; 31:3
[j] **36:11** Ezr 4:7; Dn 2:4
[k] **36:14** Is 37:10
[l] **36:16** 1Kg 4:25; Mc 4:4; Zch 3:10
[m] **36:18** Is 37:10
[n] 1Ch 5:25; Is 37:12
[o] **36:19** Is 10:9-11; 37:11-13; Jr 49:23
[p] 2Kg 17:6
[q] **36:21** Pr 26:4
[r] **37:1-35** 2Kg 19:1-34
[s] **37:1** Gn 37:34; 2Sm 3:31; 1Kg 21:27; Is 3:24

[A] **36:4** Lit *What is this trust that you trust* [B] **36:5** DSS read *You* [C] **36:11,13** Lit *Judahite* [D] **36:16** Lit *a blessing*

leading priests, who were wearing sackcloth,
to the prophet Isaiah son of Amoz. 3 They said
to him, "This is what Hezekiah says: 'Today is
a day of distress, rebuke, and disgrace,[a] for
children have come to the point of birth, and
there is no strength to deliver them.[b] 4 Perhaps
•Yahweh your God will hear all the words of
the •Rabshakeh, whom his master the king of
Assyria sent to mock the living God,[c] and will
rebuke him for the words that Yahweh your
God has heard. Therefore offer a prayer for
the surviving remnant.' "[d]

5 So the servants of King Hezekiah went to
Isaiah, 6 who said to them, "Tell your master
this, 'The LORD says: Don't be afraid[e] because
of the words you have heard, which the king
of Assyria's attendants have blasphemed Me
with.[f] 7 I am about to put a spirit[g] in him and he
will hear a rumor and return to his own land,
where I will cause him to fall by the sword.' "[h]

Sennacherib's Letter

8 When the Rabshakeh heard that the king
of Assyria had left Lachish,[i] he returned and
found him fighting against Libnah.[j] 9 The
king had heard this about Tirhakah king of
•Cush:[k] "He has set out to fight against you."
So when he heard this, he sent messengers
to Hezekiah, saying, 10 "Say this to Hezekiah
king of Judah: 'Don't let your God, whom you
trust, deceive you[l] by promising that Jerusalem won't be handed over to the king of Assyria. 11 Look, you have heard what the kings
of Assyria have done to all the countries: they
•completely destroyed them. Will you be rescued? 12 Did the gods of the nations[m] that my
predecessors destroyed rescue them — Gozan,[n] Haran,[o] Rezeph, and the Edenites in
Telassar? 13 Where is the king of Hamath, the
king of Arpad, the king of the city of Sepharvaim, Hena, or Ivvah?' "

Hezekiah's Prayer

14 Hezekiah took the letter from the messengers, read it, then went up to the LORD's
temple and spread it out before the LORD.[p]
15 Then Hezekiah prayed[q] to the LORD:
16 LORD of •Hosts, God of Israel, who is
enthroned above the •cherubim,[r] You are

[a]37:3 Is 22:5; 26:16; 33:2; Nah 1:7; Hab 3:16 [b]Is 26:17-18; 66:9; Hs 13:13 [c]37:4 Dt 5:26; 1Sm 17:26,36; Jr 10:10 [d]Is 1:9; 46:3 [e]37:6 Is 7:4; 35:4 [f]Ps 44:7,13-16; Is 52:5; Rm 2:24 [g]37:7 Nm 5:14; Is 19:14; Hs 4:12; Zch 13:2; 2Tm 1:7 [h]Is 37:36-38 [i]37:8 Jos 10:31-32 [j]Nm 33:20; Jos 10:29 [k]37:9 Is 18:1; 20:5 [l]37:10 Is 36:14-15 [m]37:12 Is 36:18 [n]2Kg 17:6; 18:11 [o]Gn 11:31; 12:1-4; Ac 7:2 [p]37:14 Dt 22:17; 1Kg 8:22; Ezk 2:10 [q]37:15 2Ch 32:20 [r]37:16 Ex 25:22; Nm 7:89; 1Sm 4:4; 2Sm 6:2; Ps 80:1; 99:1 [s]Dt 10:17; 2Sm 7:28; Ps 86:10; 90:2; 136:2-3 [t]1Kg 8:39; Neh 9:6; Ps 4:8; 83:18; 86:10; Rv 15:4 [u]2Ch 36:20; Ps 68:32; Rv 11:15 [v]Ex 20:11; Neh 9:6; Ps 146:6; Ac 4:24 [w]37:17 2Ch 6:40; Ps 17:6; Dn 9:18 [x]Is 42:5; 45:12; Jr 10:12 [y]Is 37:4 [z]37:19 Dt 32:17; 2Ch 13:9; Jr 2:11; 5:7; 16:20; Hs 8:6; Ac 19:26; Gl 4:8 [aa]Is 2:8,20; 17:8; 31:7; 41:24,29; 44:9-20; 46:6 [ab]Dt 4:28; 28:36,64; 29:17; Ezk 20:32 [ac]37:20 Jos 4:24; 1Kg 8:60; 20:13; Is 45:3,6 [ad]Is 37:16 [ae]37:22 Is 1:8; 3:16-17; 4:4; 52:2; 62:11; Lm 2:13 [af]Ps 22:7; 109:25; Jb 16:4;

God[s] — You alone[t] — of all the kingdoms
of the earth.[u] You made the heavens and
the earth.[v] 17 Listen closely, LORD, and
hear;[w] open Your eyes, LORD, and see.[x]
Hear all the words that Sennacherib has
sent to mock the living God.[y] 18 LORD, it is
true that the kings of Assyria have devastated all these countries and their lands.
19 They have thrown their gods into the
fire, for they were not gods[z] but made by
human hands[aa] — wood and stone.[ab] So
they have destroyed them. 20 Now, LORD
our God, save us from his power so that
all the kingdoms of the earth may know
that You are the LORD[ac] — You alone.[ad]

God's Answer through Hezekiah

21 Then Isaiah son of Amoz sent a message
to Hezekiah: "The LORD, the God of Israel,
says: 'Because you prayed to Me about Sennacherib king of Assyria, 22 this is the word
the LORD has spoken against him:

Virgin Daughter •Zion[ae]
despises you and scorns you:
Daughter Jerusalem shakes her head[af]
behind your back.[A]
23 Who is it you have mocked[ag]
and blasphemed?
Who have you raised your voice against
and lifted your eyes in pride?[ah]
Against the Holy One of Israel![ai]
24 You have mocked the LORD
through[B] your servants.
You have said, "With my many chariots[aj]
I have gone up to the heights
of the mountains,
to the far recesses of Lebanon.
I cut down its tallest cedars,
its choice cypress trees.
I came to its distant heights,
its densest forest.
25 I dug wells[C] and drank water.
I dried up all the streams of Egypt
with the soles of my feet."[ak]
26 Have you not heard?[al]
I designed it long ago;

Jr 18:16; Lm 2:15 [ag]37:23 Ps 74:10,18; Is 37:4; Gl 6:7 [ah]Is 2:11; 5:15,21 [ai]Gn 12:3; Ex 23:22 [aj]37:24 Ex 14:26-28; 15:4,19; Dt 20:1; Jos 11:4-9; 2Ch 16:8; Ps 68:17 [ak]37:25 Dt 11:10; 1Kg 20:10 [al]37:26 Is 40:21,28

[A]37:22 Lit *behind you* [B]37:24 Lit *by the hand of* [C]37:25 DSS add *in foreign lands*

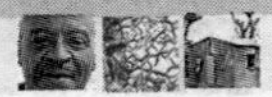

I planned it in days gone by.[a]
I have now brought it to pass,
and you have crushed fortified cities[b]
into piles of rubble.

27 Their inhabitants have become powerless,
dismayed, and ashamed.
They are plants of the field,
tender grass,
grass on the rooftops,
blasted by the east wind.[A]

28 But I know[B] your sitting down,
your going out and your coming in,[c]
and your raging against Me.

29 Because your raging against Me
and your arrogance have reached
My ears,[d]
I will put My hook in your nose[e]
and My bit in your mouth;[f]
I will make you go back
the way you came.

30 "'This will be the sign for you:[g] This year
you will eat what grows on its own, and in the
second year what grows from that. But in the
third year sow and reap, plant vineyards and
eat their fruit. 31 The surviving remnant of the
house of Judah will again take root[h] downward and bear fruit upward. 32 For a remnant[i]
will go out from Jerusalem and survivors,
from Mount Zion. The zeal of the LORD of
Hosts will accomplish this.'[j]

33 "Therefore, this is what the LORD says
about the king of Assyria:

He will not enter this city
or shoot an arrow there
or come before it with a shield
or build up an assault ramp against it.

34 He will go back
the way he came,
and he will not enter this city.
This is the LORD's declaration.

35 I will defend this city and rescue it
because of Me[k]
and because of My servant David."[l]

Defeat and Death of Sennacherib

36 Then[m] the angel of the LORD[n] went out
and struck down 185,000 in the camp of the
Assyrians. When the people got up the next
morning—there were all the dead bodies! 37 So Sennacherib king of Assyria broke
camp and left. He returned home and lived
in Nineveh.[o]

38 One day, while he was worshiping in the
temple of his god Nisroch, his sons Adrammelech and Sharezer struck him down with
the sword and escaped to the land of Ararat.[p]
Then his son Esar-haddon[q] became king in
his place.

Hezekiah's Illness and Recovery

38 In those days Hezekiah became terminally ill.[r] The prophet Isaiah son of
Amoz came and said to him, "This is what the
LORD says: 'Put your affairs in order,[C,s] for you
are about to die; you will not recover.'"[D]

2 Then Hezekiah turned his face to the wall
and prayed to the LORD. 3 He said, "Please,
LORD, remember how I have walked before
You faithfully and wholeheartedly,[t] and have
done what pleases You."[E,u] And Hezekiah wept
bitterly.

4 Then the word of the LORD came to Isaiah:
5 "Go and tell Hezekiah that this is what the
LORD God of your ancestor David says: I have
heard your prayer; I have seen your tears.
Look, I am going to add 15 years to your life.[F,v]
6 And I will deliver you and this city from the
power of the king of Assyria; I will defend this
city.[w] 7 This is the sign to you[x] from the LORD
that He will do what[G] He has promised:[H]
8 I am going to make the sun's shadow that
goes down on Ahaz's stairway go back by 10
steps."[y] So the sun's shadow[I] went back the 10
steps it had descended.

9 A poem by Hezekiah king of Judah after
he had been sick and had recovered from his
illness:

10 I said: In the prime[J] of my life[F,z]
I must go to the gates of ˚Sheol;[aa]
I am deprived of the rest of my years.

11 I said: I will never see the LORD,
the LORD in the land of the living;[ab]
I will not look on humanity any longer
with the inhabitants of what is
passing away.[K]

[a] **37:26** Is 5:19; 10:5-6; 14:24-26; 22:11; 46:11; Jr 18:11; Ac 2:23; 4:27-28; 1Pt 2:8
[b] Is 34:13
[c] **37:28** Ps 139:1
[d] **37:29** Is 10:12
[e] Ezk 19:9; 29:4; 38:4
[f] Is 30:28
[g] **37:30** Ex 3:12; 1Sm 2:34; 1Kg 13:3; Is 7:14; 38:7; Jr 44:29; Lk 2:12
[h] **37:31** Is 27:6
[i] **37:32** Ezr 9:14; Is 10:20-22
[j] 2Kg 19:31; Is 9:7; 59:17; Jl 2:18; Zch 1:14
[k] **37:35** Is 43:25; 48:9,11
[l] 1Kg 11:13,32-38; 2Kg 20:6; Ezk 34:23
[m] **37:36-38** 2Kg 19:35-37; 2Ch 32:21
[n] **37:36** Gn 16:7-11; Ex 3:2; Nm 22:22-35; Jdg 6:11-12; 2Sm 24:16; Ps 34:7
[o] **37:37** Gn 10:11; Jnh 1:2; 3:3; 4:11; Zph 2:13
[p] **37:38** Gn 8:4; Jr 51:27
[q] Ezr 4:2
[r] **38:1-8** 2Kg 20:1-6,9-11; 2Ch 32:24
[s] **38:1** 2Sm 17:23
[t] **38:3** Gn 17:1; 1Kg 2:4; 3:6; 8:23; 2Kg 18:5-6; Ps 26:3
[u] Dt 6:18
[v] **38:5** 2Kg 18:2,13
[w] **38:6** Is 31:5; 37:35
[x] **38:7** Is 37:30
[y] **38:8** Jos 10:12-14
[z] **38:10** Ps 102:24
[aa] Ps 107:18
[ab] **38:11** Ps 27:13; 116:9

[A] **37:27** DSS; MT reads *rooftops, field before standing grain* [B] **37:28** DSS read *know your rising up and* [C] **38:1** Lit *Command your house* [D] **38:1** Lit *live* [E] **38:3** Lit *what is good in Your eyes* [F] **38:5,10** Lit *days* [G] **38:7** Lit *this thing* [H] **38:7** Lit *said* [I] **38:8** Lit *And the sun* [J] **38:10** Lit *quiet* [K] **38:11** Some Hb mss, Tg read *of the world*

12 My dwelling is plucked up and removed
from me
like a shepherd's tent.[a]
I have rolled up my life like a weaver;[b]
He cuts me off from the loom.[A,c]
You make an end of me from day
until night.[d]
13 I thought until the morning:
He will break all my bones like a lion;
You make an end of me day and night.
14 I chirp like a swallow or a crane;
I moan like a dove.[e]
My eyes grow weak looking upward.
Lord, I am oppressed; support me.[f]

15 What can I say?
He has spoken to me,
and He Himself has done it.
I walk along slowly all my years[g]
because of the bitterness of my soul,[h]
16 Lord, because of these promises
people live,[i]
and in all of them is the life of my spirit
as well;
You have restored me to health[j]
and let me live.[k]
17 Indeed, it was for my own welfare
that I had such great bitterness;[l]
but Your love has delivered me
from the ·Pit of destruction,[m]
for You have thrown all my sins
behind Your back.[n]
18 For Sheol cannot thank You;
Death cannot praise You.[o]
Those who go down to the Pit
cannot hope for Your faithfulness.
19 The living, only the living
can thank You,
as I do today;
a father will make Your faithfulness
known to children.[p]
20 The LORD will[B] save me;
we will play stringed instruments
all the days of our lives
at the house of the LORD.[q]

21 Now Isaiah[r] had said, "Let them take a
lump of pressed figs and apply it to his infected skin, so that he may recover." 22 And
Hezekiah had asked, "What is the sign that I
will go up to the LORD's temple?"

[a] 38:12 2Co 5:1,4; 2Pt 1:13-14
[b] Jb 7:6; Heb 1:12
[c] Jb 6:9
[d] Jb 4:20; Ps 73:14
[e] 38:14 Is 59:11; Ezk 7:16; Nah 2:7
[f] Jb 17:3; Ps 119:122
[g] 38:15 1Kg 21:27
[h] 1Sm 1:10; Ezk 27:31; Jb 3:20; 7:11; 10:1
[i] 38:16 Ps 119:71,75
[j] Ps 39:13
[k] Ps 119:25
[l] 38:17 Heb 12:11
[m] Jb 33:18,30; Ps 103:4; 106:23; Ezk 20:17; Jnh 2:6
[n] Is 43:25; Jr 31:34; Mc 7:19
[o] 38:18 Ps 6:5; 30:9; 88:10-12; 115:17
[p] 38:19 Dt 6:7; 11:19; Ps 78:5-7
[q] 38:20 Ps 23:6; 116:17-19
[r] 38:21-22 2Kg 20:7-8
[s] 39:1-8 2Kg 20:12-19; 2Ch 32:31
[t] 39:2 2Kg 18:15-16
[u] 2Ch 32:25
[v] 39:5 Is 28:14; Zch 7:4; 8:1,18
[w] 39:6 2Kg 24:13; 25:13-15; Jr 20:5
[x] 39:8 2Ch 32:26
[y] 40:1 Is 12:1; 49:13; 51:3,12; 52:9; 61:2; 66:13; Jr 31:10-14; Zph 3:14-17; 2Co 1:4
[z] 40:2 Is 13:11
[aa] Lv 26:41,43; Is 27:9
[ab] Ex 22:7-8; Jr 16:18; Zch 9:12; Rv 18:6
[ac] 40:3 Mal 3:1; 4:5-6

Hezekiah's Folly

39 At that time[s] Merodach-baladan son of
Baladan, king of Babylon, sent letters
and a gift to Hezekiah since he heard that he
had been sick and had recovered. 2 Hezekiah
was pleased with them, and showed them
his treasure house—the silver, the gold, the
spices, and the precious oil—and all his armory, and everything that was found in his
treasuries.[t] There was nothing in his palace
and in all his realm that Hezekiah did not
show them.[u]
3 Then the prophet Isaiah came to King Hezekiah and asked him, "Where did these men
come from and what did they say to you?"
Hezekiah replied, "They came to me from a
distant country, from Babylon."
4 Isaiah asked, "What have they seen in your
palace?"
Hezekiah answered, "They have seen everything in my palace. There isn't anything in my
treasuries that I didn't show them."
5 Then Isaiah said to Hezekiah, "Hear the
word of the LORD of ·Hosts:[v] 6 'The time will
certainly come when everything in your palace and all that your fathers have stored up
until this day will be carried off to Babylon;
nothing will be left,' says the LORD.[w] 7 'Some of
your descendants who come from you will be
taken away, and they will become eunuchs in
the palace of the king of Babylon.'"
8 Then Hezekiah said to Isaiah, "The word
of the LORD that you have spoken is good," for
he thought: There will be peace and security
during my lifetime.[x]

God's People Comforted

40 "Comfort, comfort My people,"[y]
says your God.
2 "Speak tenderly to[C] Jerusalem,
and announce to her
that her time of forced labor is over,
her iniquity[z] has been pardoned,[aa]
and she has received
from the LORD's hand
double for all her sins."[ab]

3 A voice of one crying out:

Prepare the way of the LORD
in the wilderness;[ac]

[A] 38:12 Lit *thrum* [B] 38:20 Lit *to* [C] 40:2 Lit *Speak to the heart of*

make a straight highway for our God
in the desert.[a]
4 Every valley will be lifted up,
and every mountain and hill
will be leveled;
the uneven ground will become smooth
and the rough places, a plain.[b]
5 And the glory of the LORD will appear,[c]
and all humanity[A] together will see it,[d]
for the mouth of the LORD has spoken.[e]

6 A voice was saying, "Cry out!"
Another[B] said, "What should I cry out?"
"All humanity is grass,[f]
and all its goodness is like the flower
of the field.[g]
7 The grass withers, the flowers fade
when the breath[C] of the LORD blows
on them;[D]
indeed, the people are grass.
8 The grass withers, the flowers fade,[h]
but the word of our God
remains forever."[i]

9 ·Zion, herald of good news,
go up on a high mountain.[j]
Jerusalem, herald of good news,[k]
raise your voice loudly.
Raise it, do not be afraid!
Say to the cities of Judah,
"Here is your God!"[l]
10 See, the Lord GOD comes with strength,
and His power establishes His rule.[m]
His reward is with Him,[n]
and His gifts accompany Him.
11 He protects His flock like a shepherd;[o]
He gathers the lambs in His arms
and carries them in the fold
of His garment.
He gently leads those that are nursing.

12 Who has measured the waters
in the hollow of his hand
or marked off the heavens
with the span of his hand?[p]
Who has gathered the dust of the earth
in a measure
or weighed the mountains in a balance
and the hills in the scales?
13 Who has directed[E] the Spirit
of the LORD,
or who gave Him His counsel?[q]
14 Who did He consult with?
Who gave Him understanding[r]
and taught Him the paths of justice?
Who taught Him knowledge
and showed Him the way
of understanding?
15 Look, the nations are like a drop
in a bucket;
they are considered as a speck of dust
in the scales;
He lifts up the islands like fine dust.
16 Lebanon is not enough for fuel,
or its animals enough
for a ·burnt offering.[s]
17 All the nations are as nothing
before Him;
they are considered by Him
as nothingness and emptiness.[t]

18 Who will you compare God with?
What likeness will you
compare Him to?[u]
19 To an idol? — something that
a smelter casts,
and a metalworker plates with gold
and makes silver welds for it?[v]
20 To one who shapes a pedestal,
choosing wood that does not rot?[F]
He looks for a skilled craftsman
to set up an idol that
will not fall over.[w]

21 Do you not know?[x]
Have you not heard?
Has it not been declared to you
from the beginning?
Have you not considered
the foundations of the earth?[y]
22 God is enthroned above the circle
of the earth;
its inhabitants are like grasshoppers.[z]
He stretches out the heavens
like thin cloth[aa]
and spreads them out like a tent
to live in.[ab]
23 He reduces princes to nothing[ac]
and makes judges of the earth
irrational.
24 They are barely planted, barely sown,

[a]40:3 Mt 3:3; Mk 1:3; Lk 3:4; Jn 1:23 [b]40:4-5 Lk 3:5-6 [c]40:5 Is 35:2 [d]Is 52:10; Jl 2:28 [e]Is 1:20; 34:16; 58:14 [f]40:6-8 1Pt 1:24-25 [g]40:6 Jb 14:2; Ps 102:11; 103:15 [h]40:8 Jms 1:11 [i]Is 55:11; 59:21; Mk 13:31; Lk 21:33 [j]40:9 Is 52:7 [k]Is 61:1 [l]Is 25:9; 35:2 [m]40:10 Is 59:16-18 [n]Is 62:11; Rv 22:12 [o]40:11 Jr 31:10; Ezk 34:12-14,23,31; Mc 5:4; Jn 10:11,14-16 [p]40:12 Is 48:13; Heb 1:10-12 [q]40:13 Rm 11:34; 1Co 2:16 [r]40:14 Jb 21:22; Col 2:3 [s]40:16 Ps 50:9-11; Mc 6:6-7; Heb 10:5-9 [t]40:17 Is 29:7 [u]40:18 Ex 8:10; 15:11; 1Sm 2:2; Is 40:25; 46:5; Mc 7:18; Ac 17:29 [v]40:19 Is 2:20; 30:22; 41:7; 44:10 [w]40:20 1Sm 5:3; Is 44:9-15; 46:6-7; Jr 10:3-5 [x]40:21 Ps 19:1; 50:6; Is 37:26; Ac 14:17; Rm 1:19-20 [y]Is 48:13; 51:13 [z]40:22 Nm 13:33 [aa]Jb 9:8; Is 37:16; 42:5; 44:24 [ab]Jb 36:29; Ps 18:11; 19:4; 104:2 [ac]40:23 Jb 12:21; Ps 107:40; Is 34:12

A **40:5** Lit *flesh* B **40:6** DSS, LXX, Vg read *I* C **40:7** Or *wind*, or *Spirit* D **40:7** Lit *it* E **40:13** Or *measured*, or *comprehended* F **40:20** Or *who is too poor for such an offering, or who chooses mulberry wood as a votive gift*; Hb obscure

their stem hardly takes root
in the ground
when He blows on them
and they wither,
and a whirlwind carries them away
like stubble.[a]
25 "Who will you compare Me to,[b]
or who is My equal?"
asks the Holy One.
26 Look up[A] and see:
who created[c] these?
He brings out the starry host
by number;
He calls all of them by name.[d]
Because of His great power
and strength,
not one of them is missing.
27 Jacob, why do you say,
and Israel, why do you assert:
"My way is hidden from the LORD,
and my claim is ignored by my God"?[e]
28 Do you not know?
Have you not heard?
·Yahweh is the everlasting God,[f]
the Creator of the whole earth.
He never grows faint or weary;
there is no limit to His understanding.[g]
29 He gives strength to the weary
and strengthens the powerless.
30 Youths may faint and grow weary,
and young men stumble and fall,
31 but those who trust in the LORD
will renew their strength;[h]
they will soar on wings like eagles;[i]
they will run and not grow weary;
they will walk and not faint.

The LORD versus the Nations' Gods

41 "Be silent before Me, islands![j]
And let peoples renew their strength.
Let them approach,
then let them testify;
let us come together for the trial.
2 Who has stirred him up from the east?[k]
He calls righteousness to his feet.[B,l]
The LORD hands nations over to him,[m]
and he subdues kings.
He makes them like dust
with his sword,
like wind-driven stubble with his bow.
3 He pursues them, going on safely,
hardly touching the path with his feet.
4 Who has performed and done this,
calling the generations
from the beginning?
I, ·Yahweh, am the first,
and with the last[n] — I am He."[o]
5 The islands see and are afraid,
the whole earth trembles.[p]
They approach and arrive.
6 Each one helps the other,
and says to another, "Take courage!"
7 The craftsman encourages
the metalworker;[q]
the one who flattens with the hammer
supports the one who strikes the anvil,
saying of the soldering, "It is good."
He fastens it with nails so that
it will not fall over.[r]
8 But you, Israel, My servant,[s]
Jacob, whom I have chosen,[t]
descendant of Abraham, My friend[u] —
9 I brought[C] you from the ends
of the earth
and called you
from its farthest corners.
I said to you: You are My servant;
I have chosen you and not rejected you.[v]
10 Do not fear, for I am with you;[w]
do not be afraid, for I am your God.[x]
I will strengthen you; I will help you;
I will hold on to you with My righteous
right hand.[y]
11 Be sure that all who are enraged
against you
will be ashamed and disgraced;[z]
those who contend with you
will become as nothing and will perish.
12 You will look for those who contend
with you,
but you will not find them.
Those who war against you
will become absolutely nothing.
13 For I, Yahweh your God,[aa]
hold your right hand
and say to you: Do not fear,
I will help you.

[a] **40:24** Ps 1:4; Is 41:2,16; 64:6; Ezk 17:10,24; Nah 1:4
[b] **40:25** Is 46:5; Ac 17:29
[c] **40:26** Is 42:5; 48:12-13
[d] Ps 147:4-5
[e] **40:27** Is 7:13; 49:4,14
[f] **40:28** Gn 21:33; Ps 90:2
[g] Ps 147:5; Rm 11:33
[h] **40:31** Jb 17:9; Ps 103:5; 2Co 4:8-10,16; 12:9
[i] Ex 19:4; Dt 32:11; Lk 18:1; 2Co 4:1,16; Gl 6:9; Heb 12:3
[j] **41:1** Is 11:11; Hab 2:20; Zch 2:13
[k] **41:2** Is 41:25; 45:1-3; 46:11; Rv 16:12
[l] Is 42:6
[m] 2Ch 36:23; Ezr 1:2
[n] **41:4** Is 43:10; 44:6; Rv 1:8,17; 22:13
[o] Is 43:13; 46:4; 48:12
[p] **41:5** Ps 67:7
[q] **41:7** Is 40:19
[r] Is 40:20; 46:7
[s] **41:8** Is 42:19; 43:10; 44:1-2,21; 45:4; 48:20; 49:3; 54:17; Ezk 28:25; 37:25; Lk 1:54
[t] Is 42:1; 43:10,20; 44:1-2; 45:4; 49:7; 65:9,15,22
[u] 2Ch 20:7; Jms 2:23
[v] **41:9** Is 43:5-7
[w] **41:10** Gn 26:24; 28:15; Is 43:5; Jr 1:19; 15:20; 42:11
[x] Ezk 34:31
[y] Ex 15:6,12; Ps 18:35; 48:10; 63:8; 138:7; 139:10
[z] **41:11** Is 45:24
[aa] **41:13** Is 43:3

[A] **40:26** Lit *Lift up your eyes on high* [B] **41:2** Hb obscure [C] **41:9** Or *seized*

14 Do not fear, you worm Jacob,[a]
you men[A] of Israel:
I will help you —
this is the LORD's declaration.
Your Redeemer[b] is the Holy One
of Israel.[c]
15 See, I will make you
into a sharp threshing board,
new, with many teeth.
You will thresh mountains
and pulverize them
and make hills into chaff.[d]
16 You will winnow them[e]
and a wind will carry them away,
a gale will scatter them.
But you will rejoice in the LORD;
you will boast in the Holy One of Israel.

17 The poor and the needy seek water,
but there is none;
their tongues are parched with thirst.
I, Yahweh, will answer them;[f]
I, the God of Israel, will not
forsake them.
18 I will open rivers
on the barren heights,[g]
and springs in the middle of the plains.
I will turn the desert into a pool
of water
and dry land into springs of water.[h]
19 I will plant cedars in the desert,
acacias, myrtles, and olive trees.[i]
I will put juniper trees in the desert,
elms and cypress trees together,
20 so that all may see and know,
consider and understand,
that the hand of the LORD
has done this,[j]
the Holy One of Israel has created[k] it.

21 "Submit your case," says the LORD.
"Present your arguments,"
says Jacob's King.
22 "Let them come and tell us
what will happen.[l]
Tell us the past events,
so that we may reflect on them
and know the outcome,
or tell us the future.
23 Tell us the coming events,[m]
then we will know that you are gods.
Indeed, do something good or bad,
then we will be in awe[B] and perceive.
24 Look, you are nothing[n]
and your work is worthless.
Anyone who chooses you is detestable.

25 "I have raised up one from the north,[o]
and he has come,
one from the east[p] who invokes
My[C] name.[q]
He will march over rulers as if
they were mud,
like a potter who treads the clay.
26 Who told about this
from the beginning,
so that we might know,
and from times past,
so that we might say: He is right?
No one announced it,
no one told it,
no one heard your words.
27 I was the first to say to 'Zion:[D]
Look! Here they are!
And I gave a herald of good news
to Jerusalem.[r]
28 When I look, there is no one;
there is no counselor among them;
when I ask them, they have
nothing to say.[s]
29 Look, all of them are a delusion;[E]
their works are nonexistent;
their images are wind and emptiness.

The Servant's Mission

42 "This[t] is My Servant;[u]
I strengthen Him,
this is My Chosen One;[v] I delight
in Him.[w]
I have put My Spirit on Him;[x]
He will bring justice[F] to the nations.[y]
2 He will not cry out or shout
or make His voice
heard in the streets.
3 He will not break a bruised reed,
and He will not put out
a smoldering wick;
He will faithfully bring justice.
4 He will not grow weak
or be discouraged

[a]**41:14** Jb 25:6; Ps 22:6 [b]Is 43:14; 44:6,24; 47:4; 48:17; 49:7,26; 54:5,8; 59:20; 60:16; 63:16 [c]Is 1:4 [d]**41:15** Mc 4:13; Hab 3:12 [e]**41:16** Jr 51:2 [f]**41:17** Is 43:20; 44:3; 49:10; 55:1 [g]**41:18** Is 30:25 [h]Ps 107:35; Is 35:6-7; 43:19 [i]**41:19** Is 35:1; 55:13; 60:13 [j]**41:20** Jb 12:9; Is 66:14 [k]Is 4:5 [l]**41:22** Is 44:7-8; 45:21; 46:10 [m]**41:23** Is 42:9; 45:3; Jn 13:19 [n]**41:24** Ps 115:8; Is 44:9; 1Co 8:4 [o]**41:25** Jr 50:3 [p]Is 41:2; 46:11 [q]Ezr 1:2-4 [r]**41:27** Is 40:9; 44:28; 52:7; Nah 1:15 [s]**41:28** Is 46:7 [t]**42:1-4** Mt 12:18-21 [u]**42:1** Is 49:3-7; 50:10 [v]Is 41:8-9; Lk 9:35; 23:35; 1Pt 2:4,6 [w]Mt 3:17; 17:5; Mk 1:11; Lk 3:22; 2Pt 1:17 [x]Nm 11:16-17; 1Sm 16:13; Ps 33:6; 139:7; Is 11:2; 40:7; 59:21; Lk 4:18-21 [y]Is 2:4; 51:4-5

[A]**41:14** LXX reads *small number*; DSS read *dead ones* [B]**41:23** DSS read *we may hear* [C]**41:25** DSS read *his* [D]**41:27** Lit *First to Zion* [E]**41:29** DSS, Syr read *are nothing* [F]**42:1** DSS read *His justice*

until He has established justice
on earth.
The islands will wait
for His instruction."[a]

5 This is what God, Yahweh, says —
who created the heavens and stretched
them out,[b]
who spread out the earth
and what comes from it,[c]
who gives breath to the people on it
and life[A] to those who walk on it[d] —
6 "I, Yahweh, have called You
for a righteous purpose,[B,e]
and I will hold You by Your hand.[f]
I will keep You and appoint You
to be a covenant for the people[g]
and a light to the nations,[h]
7 in order to open blind eyes,[i]
to bring out prisoners
from the dungeon,[j]
and those sitting in darkness
from the prison house.
8 I am Yahweh, that is My name;
I will not give My glory to another[k]
or My praise to idols.
9 The past events have indeed happened.
Now I declare new events;[l]
I announce them to you
before they occur."

A Song of Praise

10 Sing a new song to the LORD;[m]
sing His praise from the ends
of the earth,
you who go down to the sea with all
that fills it,[n]
you islands with your[C] inhabitants.
11 Let the desert and its cities shout,
the settlements where Kedar dwells
cry aloud.[o]
Let the inhabitants of Sela sing for joy;[p]
let them cry out
from the mountaintops.
12 Let them give glory to the LORD
and declare His praise in the islands.
13 The LORD advances like a warrior;
He stirs up His zeal like a soldier.[q]
He shouts, He roars aloud,
He prevails over His enemies.

[a]42:4 Is 11:11; 24:15; 42:10,12; 49:1; 51:5; 60:9; 66:19
[b]42:5 Ps 104:2; Is 40:22
[c]Ps 136:6; Is 34:1
[d]Jb 12:10; 33:4; Is 57:16; Dn 5:23; Ac 17:25
[e]42:6 Is 5:7,16; 9:7; 11:4-5; 32:1; 41:2; 45:8,13; 51:5-8; 56:1; 60:21; Jr 23:5-6
[f]Is 41:10,13
[g]Is 49:8
[h]Is 49:6
[i]42:7 Ac 26:17-18
[j]Is 35:5; 49:9; 61:1; Heb 2:14-15
[k]42:8 Ex 20:3-5; Is 48:11
[l]42:9 Is 43:19; 48:3,6; Rv 21:4
[m]42:10 Ps 33:3; 96:1; 98:1; 144:9
[n]Ps 96:11; 98:7
[o]42:11 Is 21:16; 60:7
[p]Is 16:1
[q]42:13 Is 9:7; 26:11; 37:32; 59:17
[r]42:14 Ps 50:21; Is 57:11; 62:1; 64:12; 65:6
[s]Is 13:8
[t]42:15 Is 44:27; 50:2; Nah 1:4-6
[u]42:16 Is 29:18; 30:21; 32:3; Jr 31:8-9; Lk 1:78-79
[v]Eph 5:8
[w]Is 40:4; Lk 3:5
[x]Jos 1:5; Ps 94:14; Is 41:17; Heb 13:5
[y]42:17 Ps 97:7; Is 1:29; 44:9,11; 45:16
[z]42:18 Is 35:5
[aa]42:19 Is 41:8-9; 43:10; 44:1-2,21; 45:4; 48:20; 49:3; 54:17; Ezk 28:25; 37:25; Lk 1:54
[ab]42:20 Rm 2:21-23
[ac]42:22 Dt 1:39; Jr 2:14; Ezk 34:8; 36:4

14 "I have kept silent from ages past;
I have been quiet
and restrained Myself.[r]
But now, I will groan like a woman
in labor,[s]
gasping breathlessly.
15 I will lay waste mountains and hills
and dry up all their vegetation.
I will turn rivers into islands
and dry up marshes.[t]
16 I will lead the blind by a way
they did not know;[u]
I will guide them on paths
they have not known.
I will turn darkness to light in front
of them[v]
and rough places into level ground."[w]
This is what I will do for them,
and I will not forsake them.[x]
17 They will be turned back
and utterly ashamed —
those who trust in idols
and say to metal-plated images:
You are our gods![y]

Israel's Blindness and Deafness

18 "Listen, you deaf!
Look, you blind, so that you may see.[z]
19 Who is blind but My servant,[aa]
or deaf like My messenger
I am sending?
Who is blind like My dedicated one,[D]
or blind like the servant of the LORD?
20 Though seeing many things,[E]
you do not obey.
Though his ears are open,
he does not listen."[ab]
21 The LORD was pleased, because of
His righteousness,
to magnify His instruction
and make it glorious.
22 But this is a people plundered
and looted,
all of them trapped in holes
or imprisoned in dungeons.
They have become plunder[ac]
with no one to rescue them
and loot, with no one saying,
"Give it back!"

[A]42:5 Lit *spirit* [B]42:6 Or *you by My righteousness*; lit *you in righteousness* [C]42:10 Lit *their* [D]42:19 Hb obscure [E]42:20 Alt Hb tradition reads *You see many things;*

23 Who among you will pay attention
to this?
Let him listen and obey in the future.
24 Who gave Jacob to the robber,[A]
and Israel to the plunderers?
Was it not the LORD?
Have we not sinned against Him?
They were not willing to walk
in His ways,
and they would not listen
to His instruction.
25 So He poured out on Jacob
His furious anger
and the power of war.
It surrounded him with fire,
but he did not know it;
it burned him, but he paid
no attention.[B,a]

Restoration of Israel

43 Now this is what the LORD says—
the One who created you, Jacob,
and the One who formed
you, Israel[b]—
"Do not fear, for I have redeemed you;[c]
I have called you by your name;
you are Mine.[d]
2 I will be with you[e]
when you pass through the waters,[f]
and when you pass through the rivers,
they will not overwhelm you.
You will not be scorched
when you walk through the fire,[g]
and the flame will not burn you.
3 For I ·Yahweh your God,[h]
the Holy One of Israel, and your Savior,[i]
give Egypt as a ransom for you,
·Cush and Seba in your place.
4 Because you are precious in My sight[j]
and honored, and I love you,[k]
I will give people in exchange for you
and nations instead of your life.
5 Do not fear, for I am with you;
I will bring your descendants
from the east,[l]
and gather you from the west.[m]
6 I will say to the north: Give them up!
and to the south:
Do not hold them back!
Bring My sons from far away,[n]
and My daughters from the ends
of the earth[o]—
7 everyone called by My name
and created for My glory.
I have formed him;
indeed, I have made him."
8 Bring out a people who are blind,
yet have eyes,[p]
and are deaf, yet have ears.
9 All the nations are gathered together,
and the peoples are assembled.[q]
Who among them can declare this,[r]
and tell us the former things?
Let them present their witnesses
to vindicate themselves,
so that people may hear and say,
"It is true."
10 "You are My witnesses"[s]—
this is the LORD's declaration—
"and My servant whom I have chosen,[t]
so that you may know and believe Me
and understand that I am He.[u]
No god was formed before Me,
and there will be none after Me.[v]
11 I, I am Yahweh,
and there is no other Savior but Me.[w]
12 I alone declared, saved,
and proclaimed—
and not some foreign god[C] among you.
So you are My witnesses"—
this is the LORD's declaration—
"and[D] I am God.[x]
13 Also, from today on I am He alone,
and none can deliver from My hand.[y]
I act, and who can reverse it?"[z]

God's Deliverance of Rebellious Israel

14 This is what the LORD, your Redeemer,[aa]
the Holy One of Israel[ab] says:

Because of you, I will send to Babylon
and bring all of them as fugitives,[E]
even the Chaldeans[ac] in the ships
in which they rejoice.[F]
15 I am Yahweh, your Holy One,
the Creator of Israel, your King.
16 This is what the LORD says—
who makes a way in the sea,
and a path through surging waters,[ad]

[a] 42:25 Is 29:13; 47:7; 57:1; Jr 12:11; Hs 7:9
[b] 43:1 Is 43:7,15,21; 44:2,21,24
[c] Is 44:22-23; 48:20
[d] Gn 32:28; Is 45:3-4
[e] 43:2 Dt 31:6,8,23; Jos 1:5; 3:7; Jr 1:8; 30:11; 46:28
[f] Ps 66:12; Is 8:7-8
[g] Is 29:6; 30:27-29; Dn 3:25,27
[h] 43:3 Ex 20:2; Is 41:13
[i] Is 19:20; 43:11; 45:15,21; 49:26; 60:16; 63:8
[j] 43:4 2Kg 1:13-14; Ps 36:7; 72:14; Pr 3:15; Is 28:16
[k] Is 63:9
[l] 43:5 Is 41:8; 61:9
[m] Is 49:12
[n] 43:6 2Co 6:18
[o] Is 45:22
[p] 43:8 Is 6:9; 42:19; Ezk 12:2
[q] 43:9 Is 34:1; 41:1
[r] Is 41:22-23,26
[s] 43:10 Is 44:8; Ac 1:8
[t] Is 41:8
[u] Is 41:4
[v] Is 44:6,8; 45:5-6
[w] 43:11 Is 43:3; 45:21; Hs 13:4
[x] 43:12 Ps 46:10; 50:7; Is 45:22; 46:9
[y] 43:13 Dt 32:39; Jn 10:28-29
[z] Jb 9:12; Is 14:27
[aa] 43:14 Jb 19:25; Ps 19:14; 78:35; Pr 23:11; Is 41:14; Jr 50:34
[ab] Is 1:4
[ac] Is 23:13
[ad] 43:16 Ex 14:21-22; Ps 77:19; Is 11:15; 44:27; 50:2; 51:10; 63:11-12

[A] 42:24 Lit *to loot* [B] 42:25 Lit *he did not put on heart* [C] 43:12 Lit *not a foreigner* [D] 43:12 Or *that* [E] 43:14 Or *will break down all their bars* [F] 43:14 Hb obscure

17 who brings out the chariot and horse,[a]
the army and the mighty one together
(they lie down, they do not rise again;
they are extinguished,
quenched like a wick[b]) —
18 "Do not remember the past events,
pay no attention to things of old.[c]
19 Look, I am about to do something new;[d]
even now it is coming.
Do you not see it?
Indeed, I will make a way
in the wilderness,[e]
rivers[A] in the desert.
20 The animals of the field will honor Me,
jackals and ostriches,
because I provide water
in the wilderness,
and rivers in the desert,[f]
to give drink to My chosen people.
21 The people I formed for Myself
will declare My praise.[g]
22 "But Jacob, you have not called on Me,
because, Israel, you have become weary
of Me.[h]
23 You have not brought Me your sheep
for ˙burnt offerings
or honored Me with your sacrifices.[i]
I have not burdened you with offerings
or wearied you with incense.[B]
24 You have not bought Me aromatic cane
with silver,
or satisfied Me with the fat
of your sacrifices.
But you have burdened Me
with your sins;
you have wearied Me[j]
with your iniquities.[k]
25 "It is I who sweep away
your transgressions[l]
for My own sake[m]
and remember your sins no more.[n]
26 Take Me to court; let us argue
our case together.[o]
State your case, so that you may
be vindicated.
27 Your first father sinned,[p]
and your mediators have rebelled
against Me.[q]
28 So I defiled the officers
of the sanctuary,
and ˙set Jacob apart for destruction[r]
and Israel for abuse.

Spiritual Blessing

44 "And now listen, Jacob My servant,
Israel whom I have chosen.[s]
2 This is the word of the LORD
your Maker who formed you
from the womb;
He[C] will help you:
Do not fear; Jacob is My servant;
I have chosen Jeshurun.[D,t]
3 For I will pour water on
the thirsty land
and streams on the dry ground;
I will pour out My Spirit[u]
on your descendants
and My blessing on your offspring.
4 They will sprout among[E] the grass
like poplars by flowing streams.
5 This one will say, 'I am the LORD's';
another will call himself by the name
of Jacob;
still another will write on his hand,
'The LORD's,'
and name himself by the name
of Israel."

No God Other Than Yahweh

6 This is what the LORD, the King of Israel
and its Redeemer,[v] the LORD of ˙Hosts, says:
I am the first and I am the last.[w]
There is no God but Me.[x]
7 Who, like Me, can announce
the future?
Let him say so and make a case
before Me,[y]
since I have established
an ancient people.
Let these gods declare[F]
the coming things,
and what will take place.
8 Do not be startled or afraid.
Have I not told you and declared it
long ago?
You are my witnesses![z]
Is there any God but Me?[aa]

[a] **43:17** Ex 15:19
[b] Ps 118:12; Is 1:31
[c] **43:18** Is 65:17; Jr 23:7
[d] **43:19** Is 42:9; 48:6; 2Co 5:17
[e] Ex 17:6; Nm 20:11; Dt 8:15; Ps 78:16; Is 35:1,6; 41:18-19; 49:10; 51:3
[f] **43:20** Is 41:17-18; 48:21
[g] **43:21** Ps 102:18; Is 42:12; Lk 1:74-75; 1Pt 2:9
[h] **43:22** Mc 6:3; Mal 1:13; 3:14
[i] **43:23** Zch 7:5-6; Mal 1:6-8
[j] **43:24** Ps 95:10; Is 1:14; 7:13; Ezk 6:9; Mal 2:17
[k] Is 13:11
[l] **43:25** Is 44:22; 55:7; Jr 50:20; Heb 2:17
[m] Is 37:35; 48:9,11; Ezk 36:22
[n] Is 38:17; Jr 31:34; Mk 2:7
[o] **43:26** Is 1:18; 41:1; 50:8
[p] **43:27** Is 51:2; Ezk 16:3
[q] Is 9:15; 28:7; 29:10; Jr 5:31
[r] **43:28** Is 24:6; 34:5; Jr 24:9; Dn 9:11; Zch 8:13
[s] **44:1** Is 41:8-9; 42:1; 43:10,20; 45:4; 49:7; 65:9,15,22
[t] **44:2** Dt 32:15; 33:5,26
[u] **44:3** Is 32:15; Jl 2:28
[v] **44:6** Is 41:14; 43:14
[w] Is 41:4; 43:10; 48:12; Rv 1:8,17; 22:13
[x] Is 43:11; 44:8; 45:5-6
[y] **44:7** Is 41:22,26
[z] **44:8** Is 43:10
[aa] Dt 4:35,39; 1Sm 2:2; Is 45:5; Jl 2:27

[A] **43:19** DSS read *paths* [B] **43:23** With demands for offerings and incense
[C] **44:2** Lit *from the womb, and He* [D] **44:2** = Upright One, referring to Israel
[E] **44:4** Some Hb mss, DSS, LXX read *as among* [F] **44:7** Lit *declare them—*

There is no other Rock;[a]
I do not know any.
9 All who make idols are nothing,
and what they treasure does not profit.
Their witnesses do not see
or know anything,
so they will be put to shame.[b]
10 Who makes a god or casts
a metal image
for no profit?[c]
11 Look, all its worshipers will be
put to shame,
and the craftsmen are humans.
They all will assemble and stand;
they all will be startled
and put to shame.
12 The ironworker labors over the coals,
shapes the idol with hammers,
and works it with his strong arm.
Also he grows hungry
and his strength fails;
he doesn't drink water and is faint.
13 The woodworker stretches out
a measuring line,
he outlines it with a stylus;
he shapes it with chisels
and outlines it with a compass.
He makes it according to
a human likeness,[d]
like a beautiful person,
to dwell in a temple.
14 He cuts down[A] cedars for his use,
or he takes a cypress or an oak.
He lets it grow strong among the trees
of the forest.
He plants a laurel, and the rain
makes it grow.
15 It serves as fuel for man.
He takes some of it and warms himself;
also he kindles a fire and bakes bread;
he even makes it into a god
and worships it;
he makes an idol from it
and bows down to it.
16 He burns half of it in a fire,
and he roasts meat on that half.
He eats the roast and is satisfied.
He warms himself and says, "Ah!
I am warm, I see the blaze."

17 He makes a god or his idol with the rest
of it.
He bows down to it and worships;
He prays to it,[e] "Save me, for you are
my god."
18 Such people[B] do not comprehend
and cannot understand,
for He has shut their eyes[C]
so they cannot see,
and their minds
so they cannot understand.
19 No one reflects,
no one has the perception or insight
to say,
"I burned half of it in the fire,
I also baked bread on its coals,
I roasted meat and ate.
I will make something detestable[f]
with the rest of it,
and I will bow down to a block
of wood."
20 He feeds on[D] ashes.
His deceived mind has led him astray,
and he cannot deliver himself,
or say, "Isn't there a lie
in my right hand?"[g]
21 Remember these things, Jacob,
and Israel, for you are My servant;
I formed you, you are My servant;
Israel, you will never be forgotten
by Me.[E,h]
22 I have swept away your transgressions
like a cloud,[i]
and your sins like a mist.
Return to Me,[j]
for I have redeemed you.[k]
23 Rejoice, heavens,[l] for the LORD has acted;
shout, depths of the earth.
Break out into singing, mountains,
forest, and every tree in it.
For the LORD has redeemed Jacob,
and glorifies Himself through Israel.[m]

Restoration of Israel through Cyrus

24 This is what the LORD, your Redeemer[n]
who formed you from the womb,[o] says:

I am ˈYahweh, who made everything;
who stretched out the heavens
by Myself;[p]

[a] **44:8** Is 17:10; 26:4; 30:29 [b] **44:9** Ps 97:7; Is 42:17; 44:11; 45:16 [c] **44:10** Is 41:29; Jr 10:5; Hab 2:18; Ac 19:26 [d] **44:13** Ps 115:5-7 [e] **44:17** 1Kg 18:26,28; Is 45:20 [f] **44:19** Dt 27:15; 1Kg 11:5,7; 2Kg 23:13-14 [g] **44:20** Is 57:11; 59:3-4,13; Rm 1:25 [h] **44:21** Is 49:15 [i] **44:22** Ps 51:1,9; Is 43:25; Ac 3:19 [j] Is 31:6; 55:7 [k] Is 43:1; 48:20; 1Co 6:20; 1Pt 1:18-19 [l] **44:23** Ps 69:34; 96:11-12; Is 42:10; 49:13 [m] Is 49:3; 61:3 [n] **44:24** Is 41:14; 43:14 [o] Is 44:2 [p] Is 40:22; 42:5; 45:12,18; 51:13

[A] **44:14** Lit *To cut down for himself* [B] **44:18** Lit *They* [C] **44:18** Or *for their eyes are shut* [D] **44:20** Or *He shepherds* [E] **44:21** DSS, LXX, Tg read *Israel, do not forget Me*

who alone spread out the earth;
25 who destroys the omens
of the false prophets
and makes fools of diviners;
who confounds the wise
and makes
their knowledge foolishness;[a]
26 who confirms the message
of His servant
and fulfills the counsel
of His messengers;
who says to Jerusalem, "She will
be inhabited,"
and to the cities of Judah, "They will
be rebuilt,"
and I will restore her ruins;
27 who says to the depths of the sea,
"Be dry,"
and I will dry up your rivers;
28 who says to Cyrus,[b] "My shepherd,
he will fulfill all My pleasure"[c]
and says to Jerusalem, "She will
be rebuilt,"[d]
and of the temple, "Its foundation
will be laid."

45

The LORD says this to Cyrus,
His anointed,[e]
whose right hand I have grasped[f]
to subdue nations before him,
to disarm[A] kings,[g]
to open the doors before him
and the gates will not be shut:
2 "I will go before you
and level the uneven places;[B,h]
I will shatter the bronze doors
and cut the iron bars in two.[i]
3 I will give you the treasures of darkness
and riches from secret places,[j]
so that you may know that I, ·Yahweh,
the God of Israel call you by your name.[k]
4 I call you by your name,
because of Jacob My servant[l]
and Israel My chosen one.
I give a name to you,
though you do not know Me.
5 I am Yahweh, and there is no other;[m]
there is no God but Me.[n]
I will strengthen[C] you,
though you do not know Me,
6 so that all may know from the rising
of the sun to its setting
that there is no one but Me.[o]
I am Yahweh, and there is no other.
7 I form light and create darkness,[p]
I make success and create disaster;[q]
I, Yahweh, do all these things.

8 "Heavens, sprinkle from above,
and let the skies shower righteousness.[r]
Let the earth open up
so that salvation will sprout
and righteousness will spring up
with it.[s]
I, Yahweh, have created it.

9 "Woe to the one who argues
with his Maker —
one clay pot among many.[D]
Does clay say to the one forming it,
'What are you making?'[t]
Or does your work say,
'He has no hands'?[E]
10 How absurd is the one who says
to his father,
'What are you fathering?'
or to his mother,
'What are you giving birth to?'"
11 This is what the LORD,
the Holy One of Israel[u]
and its Maker, says:
"Ask Me what is to happen to[F] My sons,[v]
and instruct Me about the work
of My hands.[w]
12 I made the earth,
and created man on it.
It was My hands that stretched out
the heavens,[x]
and I commanded all their host.
13 I have raised him up in righteousness,[y]
and will level all roads for him.
He will rebuild My city,[z]
and set My exiles free,[aa]
not for a price or a bribe,"
says the LORD of ·Hosts.

God Alone is the Savior

14 This is what the LORD says:

The products of Egypt
and the merchandise of ·Cush

[a]**44:25** 2Sm 15:31; Jb 5:12-14; Ps 33:10; Is 29:14; Jr 51:57; 1Co 1:20,27
[b]**44:28** Is 45:1
[c]Eph 1:9
[d]2Ch 36:22-23; Ezr 1:1; Is 14:32; 45:13; 54:11
[e]**45:1** Is 44:28
[f]Ps 73:23; Is 41:13; 42:6
[g]Jb 12:21; Is 45:5
[h]**45:2** Is 40:4
[i]Ps 107:16
[j]**45:3** Jr 41:8; 50:37
[k]Ex 33:12,17; Is 43:1; 49:1
[l]**45:4** Is 41:8; 42:19
[m]**45:5** Is 45:6,14,18,21; 46:9
[n]Is 44:6,8
[o]**45:6** Ps 102:15; Is 37:20; Mal 1:11
[p]**45:7** Ps 104:20; 105:28
[q]Gn 50:20; 1Sm 16:14; 1Kg 21:21; 22:8; 2Kg 6:33; Ps 78:49; Jb 2:10; Is 13:11; 31:2; 47:11; Jr 1:14; Lm 3:38; Am 3:6
[r]**45:8** Hs 10:12
[s]Ps 85:11; Is 61:11
[t]**45:9** Is 29:16; 64:8; Jr 18:6; Rm 9:20-21
[u]**45:11** Is 1:4
[v]Jr 31:9
[w]Is 19:25; 29:23; 60:21; 64:8
[x]**45:12** Ps 104:2; Is 42:5; 44:24
[y]**45:13** Is 41:2
[z]2Ch 36:22-23; Is 44:28
[aa]Is 52:3

[A]**45:1** Lit *unloosen the loins* [B]**45:2** DSS, LXX read *the mountains* [C]**45:5** Lit *gird* [D]**45:9** Lit *a clay pot with clay pots of the ground* [E]**45:9** Or *making? Your work has no hands.* [F]**45:11** Or *Me the coming things about*

and the Sabeans, men of stature,[a]
will come over to you[b]
and will be yours;
they will follow you,
they will come over in chains
and bow down to you.
They will confess[A] to you:
God is indeed with you,[c] and there is
no other;
there is no other God.
15 Yes, You are a God who hides Himself,[d]
God of Israel, Savior.[e]
16 All of them are put to shame,
even humiliated;[f]
the makers of idols
go in humiliation together.
17 Israel will be saved by the LORD
with an everlasting salvation;
you will not be put to shame
or humiliated
for all eternity.[g]

18 For this is what the LORD says —
God is the Creator of the heavens.
He formed the earth and made it.
He established it;
He did not create it to be empty,
but formed it to be inhabited[h] —
"I am Yahweh,
and there is no other.
19 I have not spoken in secret,[i]
somewhere in a land of darkness.
I did not say to the descendants
of Jacob:
Seek Me in a wasteland.[j]
I, Yahweh, speak truthfully;[k]
I say what is right.

20 "Come, gather together,
and draw near, you fugitives
of the nations.
Those who carry their wooden idols,
and pray to a god who cannot save,[l]
have no knowledge.[m]
21 Speak up and present your case[B,n] —
yes, let them take counsel together.
Who predicted this long ago?
Who announced it from ancient times?
Was it not I, Yahweh?
There is no other God but Me,
a righteous God and Savior;[o]
there is no one except Me.[p]
22 Turn to Me and be saved,
all the ends of the earth.
For I am God,
and there is no other.
23 By Myself I have sworn;[q]
Truth has gone from My mouth,[r]
a word that will not be revoked:
Every knee will bow[s] to Me,
every tongue will swear allegiance.
24 It will be said to Me: Righteousness
and strength
is only in the LORD."
All who are enraged against Him
will come to Him and be
put to shame.[t]
25 All the descendants of Israel
will be justified and find glory
through the LORD.

There is No One Like God

46 Bel crouches; Nebo cowers.[u]
Their idols are consigned to beasts
and cattle.
The images you carry are loaded,
as a burden for the weary animal.
2 The gods cower; they crouch together;
they are not able to rescue the burden,
but they themselves go into captivity.[v]

3 "Listen to Me, house of Jacob,
all the remnant of the house of Israel,
who have been sustained
from the womb,
carried along since birth.
4 I will be the same until your old age,[w]
and I will bear you up when you
turn gray.
I have made you, and I will carry you;
I will bear and save you.

5 "Who will you compare Me or make Me
equal to?
Who will you measure Me with,
so that we should be like each other?[x]
6 Those who pour out their bags of gold
and weigh out silver on scales —
they hire a goldsmith and he makes it
into a god.
Then they kneel and bow down to it.[y]

[a]45:14 Is 18:1; 43:3 [b]Is 14:1-2; 49:23; 54:3 [c]1Co 14:25 [d]45:15 Ps 44:24; Is 1:15; 8:17; 57:17 [e]Is 43:3 [f]45:16 Is 42:17; 44:9 [g]45:17 Is 49:23; 50:7; 54:4 [h]45:18 Gn 1:26; Ps 115:16 [i]45:19 Is 48:16 [j]2Ch 15:2; Ps 78:34; Jr 29:13-14 [k]Ps 19:8; Is 45:23; 63:1 [l]45:20 Is 44:17; 46:1,7; Jr 10:5 [m]Is 44:18-19; 48:5-7 [n]45:21 Is 41:21-23; 43:9 [o]Is 43:3,11 [p]Dt 4:35; 6:4; Mk 12:32 [q]45:23 Gn 22:16; Is 62:8; Heb 6:13 [r]Is 55:11 [s]Rm 14:11; Php 2:10 [t]45:24 Is 41:11 [u]46:1 Jr 50:2-4; 51:44 [v]46:2 Jdg 18:17-18,24; 2Sm 5:21; Jr 43:12-13; 48:7; Hs 10:5-6 [w]46:4 Ps 71:18 [x]46:5 Is 40:18,25 [y]46:6 Is 40:19; 41:7; 44:12-17; Jr 10:4

A45:14 Lit *pray* B45:21 Lit *and approach*

7 They lift it to their shoulder
and bear it along;[a]
they set it in its place, and there
it stands;
it does not budge from its place.[b]
They cry out to it but it doesn't answer;
it saves no one from his trouble.

8 "Remember this and be brave;[A]
take it to heart, you transgressors!
9 Remember what happened long ago,[c]
for I am God, and there is no other;
I am God, and no one is like Me.
10 I declare the end from the beginning,
and from long ago
what is not yet done,
saying: My plan will take place,
and I will do all My will.[d]
11 I call a bird of prey[B] from the east,[e]
a man for My purpose
from a far country.
Yes, I have spoken; so I will also
bring it about.[f]
I have planned it; I will also do it.
12 Listen to me, you hardhearted,
far removed from justice:
13 I am bringing My justice near;[g]
it is not far away,
and My salvation will not delay.
I will put salvation in ˙Zion,
My splendor in Israel.

The Fall of Babylon

47 "Go down and sit in the dust,[h]
Virgin Daughter Babylon.[i]
Sit on the ground without a throne,
Daughter Chaldea!
For you will no longer be called
pampered and spoiled.
2 Take millstones and grind meal;[j]
remove your veil,
strip off your skirt, bare your thigh,
wade through the streams.
3 Your nakedness will be uncovered,
and your shame will be exposed.[k]
I will take vengeance;
I will spare no one.[A]
4 The Holy One of Israel is
our Redeemer;[l]
˙Yahweh of ˙Hosts is His name.

5 "Daughter Chaldea,
sit in silence[m] and go into darkness.
For you will no longer be called
mistress of kingdoms.
6 I was angry with My people;
I profaned My possession,
and I placed them under your control.
You showed them no mercy;
you made your yoke very heavy
on the elderly.
7 You said, 'I will be the mistress forever.'
You did not take these things to heart
or think about their outcome.

8 "So now hear this, lover of luxury,
who sits securely,[n]
who says to herself,
'I exist, and there is no one else.
I will never be a widow
or know the loss of children.'[o]
9 These two things will happen to you
suddenly, in one day:
loss of children and widowhood.
They will happen to you
in their entirety,
in spite of your many sorceries[p]
and the potency of your spells.
10 You were secure in your wickedness;
you said, 'No one sees me.'[q]
Your wisdom and knowledge
led you astray.
You said to yourself,
'I exist, and there is no one else.'
11 But disaster will happen to you;
you will not know how to avert it.
And it will fall on you,
but you will be unable to ward it off.[C]
Devastation will happen
to you suddenly
and unexpectedly.[r]
12 So take your stand with your spells
and your many sorceries,
which you have wearied yourself with
from your youth.
Perhaps you will be able to succeed;
perhaps you will inspire terror!
13 You are worn out
with your many consultations.
So let them stand and save you —
the astrologers,[D] who observe the stars,[s]

[a]**46:7** Is 45:20; 46:1; Jr 10:5 [b]Is 40:20; 41:7 [c]**46:9** Dt 32:7; Is 42:9; 65:17 [d]**46:10** Ps 33:11; Pr 19:21; Is 5:19; 14:24; 25:1; 40:8; Ac 5:39 [e]**46:11** Is 44:28–45:1 [f]Nm 23:19; Is 14:24; 37:26 [g]**46:13** Is 51:5; 61:11; Rm 3:21 [h]**47:1** Is 3:26; Jr 48:18 [i]Ps 137:8; Jr 50:42; 51:33; Zch 2:7 [j]**47:2** Ex 11:5; Jb 31:10; Mt 24:41 [k]**47:3** Jr 13:26; Lm 1:8; Ezk 16:37; Nah 3:5 [l]**47:4** Is 41:14; 43:14 [m]**47:5** Is 23:2; Jr 8:14; Lm 2:10; 3:2,28 [n]**47:8** Zph 2:15 [o]Rv 18:7 [p]**47:9** Is 47:13; Nah 3:4; Rv 18:23 [q]**47:10** Ps 139:3,11 [r]**47:11** Is 13:6; Jr 51:8,43; Lk 17:27; 1Th 5:3 [s]**47:13** Is 8:19; 44:25; 47:9; Dn 2:2,10

[A]**46:8; 47:3** Hb obscure [B]**46:11** = Cyrus [C]**47:11** Or *to atone for it* [D]**47:13** Lit *dividers of the heavens*

who predict monthly
what will happen to you.
14 Look, they are like stubble;[a]
fire burns them up.[b]
They cannot deliver themselves
from the power[A] of the flame.
This is not a coal
for warming themselves,
or a fire to sit beside!
15 This is what they are to you —
those who have wearied you
and have traded with you
from your youth —
each wanders on his own way;
no one can save you.

Israel Must Leave Babylon

48 "Listen to this, house of Jacob —
those who are called
by the name Israel
and have descended from[B] Judah,[c]
who swear by the name of ·Yahweh[d]
and declare the God of Israel,
but not in truth or righteousness.
2 For they are named after the Holy City,
and lean on the God of Israel;[e]
His name is Yahweh of ·Hosts.
3 I declared the past events long ago;
they came out of My mouth;
I proclaimed them.
Suddenly I acted, and they occurred.
4 Because I know that you are stubborn,
and your neck is iron[C]
and your forehead bronze,[f]
5 therefore I declared to you long ago.
I announced it to you
before it occurred,
so you could not claim, 'My idol
caused them;
my carved image and cast idol
control them.'[g]
6 You have heard it. Observe it all.
Will you not acknowledge it?
From now on I will announce
new things to you,
hidden things that
you have not known.[h]
7 They have been created now, and not
long ago;
you have not heard of them
before today,
so you could not claim, 'I already
knew them!'
8 You have never heard; you have
never known;
For a long time your ears have not
been open.
For I knew that you
were very treacherous,
and were known as a rebel
from birth.[i]
9 I will delay My anger for the honor
of My name,
and I will restrain Myself
for your benefit and for My praise,
so that you will not be destroyed.
10 Look, I have refined you,[j] but not
as silver;
I have tested[D] you in the furnace
of affliction.
11 I will act for My own sake,
indeed, My own,[k]
for how can I[E] be defiled?
I will not give My glory to another.[l]
12 "Listen to Me, Jacob,
and Israel, the one called by Me:
I am He; I am the first,
I am also the last.[m]
13 My own hand founded the earth,
and My right hand spread out
the heavens;[n]
when I summoned them,
they stood up together.
14 All of you, assemble and listen!
Who among the idols[F] has declared
these things?
The LORD loves him;[G]
he will accomplish His will
against Babylon,[o]
and His arm will be against
the Chaldeans.
15 I — I have spoken;
yes, I have called him;[p]
I have brought him,
and he will succeed in his mission.[q]
16 Approach Me and listen to this.
From the beginning I have not spoken
in secret;[r]

[a]47:14 Is 5:24; Nah 1:10; Mal 4:1
[b]Is 10:17; Jr 51:30-32,58
[c]48:1 Nm 24:7; Dt 33:28; Ps 68:26
[d]Dt 6:13; Is 45:23; 65:16
[e]48:2 Is 10:20; Jr 7:4; 21:2; Mc 3:11; Rm 2:17
[f]48:4 Ex 32:9; Dt 31:27; Ezk 2:4; 3:7-9
[g]48:5 Jr 44:15-18
[h]48:6 Is 42:9; 43:19
[i]48:8 Dt 9:7,24; Ps 58:3; Is 46:8
[j]48:10 Dt 4:20; 1Kg 8:51; Jr 11:4; Ezk 22:18-22; 1Pt 1:7
[k]48:11 Is 43:25; Ezk 20:9
[l]Is 42:8
[m]48:12 Is 41:4; 43:10-13; 46:4; Rv 1:17
[n]48:13 Ps 102:25; Is 42:5; 45:12,18; Heb 1:10-12
[o]48:14 Is 13:4-5,17-19; 46:10-11
[p]48:15 Is 41:2; 45:1-2
[q]Is 53:10
[r]48:16 Is 45:19

[A]47:14 Lit *hand* [B]48:1 Lit *have come from the waters of* [C]48:4 Lit *is an iron sinew* [D]48:10 Or *chosen* [E]48:11 DSS, Syr; MT reads *it* [F]48:14 Lit *among them* [G]48:14 = Cyrus

from the time anything existed,
I was there."
And now the Lord GOD
has sent me and His Spirit.[a]

17 This is what the LORD, your Redeemer,[b]
the Holy One of Israel[c] says:
I am Yahweh your God,
who teaches you for your benefit,
who leads you in the way you should go.
18 If only you had paid attention
to My commands.
Then your peace would have been
like a river,[d]
and your righteousness like the waves
of the sea.[e]
19 Your descendants would have been
as countless as the sand,[f]
and the offspring of your body
like its grains;
their name would not be cut off
or eliminated from My presence.

20 Leave Babylon,
flee from the Chaldeans!
Declare with a shout of joy,
proclaim this,
let it go out to the end of the earth;
announce,
"The LORD has redeemed
His servant[g] Jacob!"
21 They did not thirst
when He led them through the deserts;
He made water flow for them
from the rock;[h]
He split the rock, and water
gushed out.
22 "There is no peace for the wicked,"
says the LORD.[i]

The Servant Brings Salvation

49 Coastlands,[A] listen to me;
distant peoples, pay attention.
The LORD called[j] me before I was born.
He named me while I was
in my mother's womb.[k]
2 He made my words like a sharp sword;[l]
He hid me in the shadow of His hand.[m]
He made me like a sharpened arrow;
He hid me in His quiver.

[a] 48:16 Nm 27:18; Ps 51:11; Is 61:1; 63:7,10; Zch 2:9,11
[b] 48:17 Is 41:14; 43:14
[c] Is 1:4
[d] 48:18 Is 32:16-18; 66:12
[e] Dt 5:29; 32:29; Ps 81:13-16; Am 5:24
[f] 48:19 Gn 22:17; Is 10:22; 44:3-4; 54:3; Hs 1:10
[g] 48:20 Is 41:8-9; 42:19; 43:10; 44:1-2,21; 45:4; 49:3; 54:17; Lk 1:54
[h] 48:21 Ex 17:6; Ps 78:15-16
[i] 48:22 Is 57:21
[j] 49:1 Is 44:2,24; 46:3; Jr 1:5
[k] Lk 1:15
[l] 49:2 Is 11:4; Heb 4:12; Rv 1:16; 2:12,16
[m] Is 51:16
[n] 49:3 Is 41:8-9; 42:1; 49:5-7; 50:10; 52:13; 53:11; Ezk 34:23-24; Zch 3:8; Ac 3:13
[o] 49:6 Is 42:6; 51:4; Lk 2:32; Ac 13:47; 26:23
[p] Ac 13:47
[q] 49:7 Is 41:14; 43:14
[r] Ps 22:6-8; 69:7-9; Is 53:3
[s] Is 1:4
[t] Is 41:8-9; 42:1; 43:10,20; 44:1-2; 45:4; 65:9,15,22
[u] 49:8 Ps 69:13; 2Co 6:2
[v] Is 42:6
[w] 49:9 Is 42:7; 61:1; Lk 4:18

3 He said to me, "You are
My Servant, Israel;[n]
I will be glorified in him."
4 But I myself said: I have labored
in vain,
I have spent my strength for nothing
and futility;
yet my vindication is with the LORD,
and my reward is with my God.
5 And now, says the LORD,
who formed me from the womb to be
His Servant,
to bring Jacob back to Him
so that Israel might be gathered
to Him;
for I am honored in the sight
of the LORD,
and my God is my strength—
6 He says,
"It is not enough for you to be
My Servant
raising up the tribes of Jacob
and restoring the protected ones
of Israel.
I will also make you a light
for the nations,[o]
to be My salvation to the ends
of the earth."[p]
7 This is what the LORD,
the Redeemer[q] of Israel,
his Holy One, says
to one who is despised,
to one abhorred by people,[B,r]
to a servant of rulers:
"Kings will see and stand up,
and princes[C] will bow down,
because of the LORD, who is faithful,
the Holy One of Israel[s]—
and He has chosen you."[t]

8 This is what the LORD says:

I will answer you in a time of favor,
and I will help you in the day
of salvation.[u]
I will keep you, and I will appoint you
to be a covenant for the people,[v]
to restore the land,
to make them possess
the desolate inheritances,
9 saying to the prisoners: Come out,[w]

[A] 49:1 Or *Islands* [B] 49:7 Or *by the nation* [C] 49:7 Lit *princes and they*

and to those who are in darkness:
Show yourselves.
They will feed along the pathways,
and their pastures will be on all
the barren heights.[a]
10 They will not hunger or thirst,
the scorching heat or sun will not
strike them;
for their compassionate One
will guide them,
and lead them to springs of water.[b]
11 I will make all My mountains
into a road,
and My highways will be raised up.[c]
12 See, these will come from far away,
from the north and from the west,[A,d]
and from the land of Sinim.[B,C]

13 Shout for joy, you heavens![e]
Earth, rejoice!
Mountains break into joyful shouts!
For the LORD has comforted
His people,[f]
and will have compassion
on His afflicted ones.[g]

Zion Remembered

14 ·Zion says, "The LORD
has abandoned me;
The Lord has forgotten me!"
15 "Can a woman forget her nursing child,
or lack compassion for the child
of her womb?
Even if these forget,
yet I will not forget you.
16 Look, I have inscribed you on the palms
of My hands;[h]
your walls are continually before Me.
17 Your builders[D] hurry;
those who destroy and devastate you
will leave you.
18 Look up, and look around.
They all gather together; they come
to you.[i]
As I live" —
this is the LORD's declaration —
"you will wear all your children[E]
as jewelry,
and put them on as a bride does.
19 For your waste and desolate places
and your land marked by ruins —
will now be indeed too small
for the inhabitants,[j]
and those who swallowed you up
will be far away.
20 Yet as you listen, the children
that you have been deprived of will say,
'This place is too small for me;
make room for me so that I may settle.'[k]
21 Then you will say within yourself,
'Who fathered these for me?
I was deprived of my children
and unable to conceive,
exiled and wandering —
but who brought them up?
See, I was left by myself —
but these, where did they
come from?'"[F]
22 This is what the Lord GOD says:

Look, I will lift up My hand
to the nations,
and raise My banner to the peoples.[l]
They will bring your sons in their arms,
and your daughters will be carried
on their shoulders.[m]
23 Kings will be your foster fathers,
and their queens[G]
your nursing mothers.[n]
They will bow down to you
with their faces to the ground,
and lick the dust at your feet.[o]
Then you will know that I am ·Yahweh;[p]
those who put their hope in Me
will not be put to shame.[q]

24 Can the prey be taken
from the mighty,
or the captives of the righteous[H]
be delivered?
25 For this is what the LORD says:
"Even the captives of a mighty man
will be taken,
and the prey of a tyrant
will be delivered;
I will contend with the one
who contends with you,
and I will save your children.
26 I will make your oppressors eat
their own flesh,[r]

[a] 49:9 Is 41:18
[b] 49:10 Ps 23:2; Is 40:11; Jn 4:10; Rv 7:16-17
[c] 49:11 Is 40:4
[d] 49:12 Is 43:5-6
[e] 49:13 Is 44:23
[f] Is 40:1
[g] Is 54:7-10; Mt 11:29
[h] 49:16 Sg 8:6; Hg 2:23
[i] 49:18 Is 60:4
[j] 49:19 Is 54:1-2; Zch 10:10
[k] 49:20 Is 54:1-3
[l] 49:22 Is 11:10-12; 18:3; 62:10
[m] Is 14:2; 43:6; 60:4
[n] 49:23 Is 60:3,10-11
[o] Is 14:1-2
[p] Is 41:20; 43:10; 60:16
[q] Ps 25:3; Is 45:17; Jl 2:27
[r] 49:26 Is 9:20

[A] 49:12 Lit *sea* [B] 49:12 DSS read *of the Syenites* [C] 49:12 Perhaps modern Aswan in southern Egypt [D] 49:17 DSS, Aq, Theod, Vg; MT, Syr, Sym read *sons* [E] 49:18 Lit *all of them* [F] 49:21 Lit *where are they* [G] 49:23 Lit *princesses* [H] 49:24 DSS, Syr, Vg read *fearsome one*, or *tyrant*

and they will be drunk
with their own blood
as with sweet wine.
Then all flesh will know
that I, Yahweh, am your Savior,[a]
and your Redeemer,[b] the Mighty One
of Jacob."[c]

50 This is what the LORD says:

Where is your mother's
divorce certificate
that I used to send her away?[d]
Or who were My creditors
that I sold you to?[e]
Look, you were sold for your iniquities,[f]
and your mother was put away
because of your transgressions.
2 Why was no one there when I came?
Why was there no one to answer
when I called?
Is My hand too short to redeem?[g]
Or do I have no power to deliver?
Look, I dry up the sea by My rebuke;[h]
I turn the rivers into a wilderness;
their fish rot because of lack of water
and die of thirst.
3 I dress the heavens in black
and make •sackcloth their clothing.[i]

The Obedient Servant

4 The Lord GOD has given Me
the tongue of those who are instructed[j]
to know how to sustain the weary
with a word.
He awakens Me each morning;
He awakens My ear to listen like those
being instructed.[k]
5 The Lord GOD has opened My ear,
and I was not rebellious;
I did not turn back.[l]
6 I gave My back to those who beat Me,
and My cheeks to those who tore out
My beard.
I did not hide My face from scorn
and spitting.[m]
7 The Lord GOD will help Me;
therefore I have not been humiliated;
therefore I have set My face like flint,[n]
and I know I will not be put to shame.
8 The One who vindicates Me is near;[o]
who will contend with Me?
Let us confront each other.[A]
Who has a case against Me?[B]
Let him come near Me!
9 In truth, the Lord GOD will help Me;
who will condemn Me?[p]
Indeed, all of them will wear out
like a garment;
a moth will devour them.[q]
10 Who among you •fears the LORD,
listening to the voice of His Servant?[r]
Who among you walks in darkness,
and has no light?
Let him trust in the name of •Yahweh;
let him lean on his God.
11 Look, all you who kindle a fire,
who encircle yourselves
with[C] firebrands;
walk in the light of your fire
and in the firebrands you have lit!
This is what you'll get from My hand:
you will lie down in a place
of torment.

Salvation for Zion

51 Listen to Me, you
who pursue righteousness,
you who seek the LORD:
Look to the rock from which
you were cut,
and to the quarry from which
you were dug.
2 Look to Abraham your father,
and to Sarah who gave birth to you
in pain.
When I called him, he was only one;
I blessed him and made him many.[s]
3 For the LORD will comfort •Zion;[t]
He will comfort all her waste places,
and He will make her wilderness
like Eden,[u]
and her desert like the garden
of the LORD.[v]
Joy and gladness will be found in her,
thankgiving and melodious song.
4 Pay attention to Me, My people,
and listen to Me, My nation;
for instruction will come from Me,

[a]**49:26** Is 43:3 [b]Is 41:14 [c]Gn 49:24; Ps 132:2,5; Is 60:16 [d]**50:1** Dt 24:1-3; Jr 3:8 [e]Dt 32:30; 2Kg 4:1; Neh 5:5 [f]Is 13:11 [g]**50:2** Gn 18:14; Nm 11:23; Is 59:1 [h]Ex 14:21; Is 43:16; 44:27 [i]**50:3** Rv 6:12 [j]**50:4** Is 8:16; 54:13 [k]Jn 4:34 [l]**50:5** Jn 8:29; 14:31; 15:10; Php 2:8; Heb 5:8 [m]**50:6** Mt 26:67; 27:26; Mk 14:65; 15:19; Lk 22:63; Jn 19:1-5 [n]**50:7** Ezk 3:8-9 [o]**50:8** Is 45:25 [p]**50:9** Rm 8:33-34 [q]Jb 13:28; Is 51:8; Hs 5:12 [r]**50:10** Is 42:1; 49:3-7; 52:13; 53:11; Ezk 34:23-24; Zch 3:8; Ac 3:13 [s]**51:2** Gn 12:1; 15:5; Dt 1:10; Is 29:22; 41:8; 63:16; Ezk 33:24 [t]**51:3** Is 40:1 [u]Gn 2:8; Jl 2:3 [v]Gn 13:10

[A]**50:8** Lit *us stand* [B]**50:8** Lit *Who is lord of My judgment* [C]**50:11** Syr reads *who set ablaze*

and My justice for a light
to the nations.[a]
I will bring it about quickly.
5 My righteousness is near,[b]
My salvation appears,
and My arms will bring justice
to the nations.[c]
The coastlands[A] will put their hope in Me,
and they will look to My strength.[B]
6 Look up to the heavens,
and look at the earth beneath;
for the heavens will vanish like smoke,
the earth will wear out like a garment,
and its inhabitants will die like gnats.[C,d]
But My salvation will last forever,[e]
and My righteousness will never
be shattered.

7 Listen to Me, you who
know righteousness,
the people in whose heart is
My instruction:[f]
do not fear disgrace by men,
and do not be shattered by their taunts.
8 For the moth will devour them
like a garment,[g]
and the worm will eat them like wool.[h]
But My righteousness will last forever,
and My salvation for all generations.

9 Wake up, wake up!
Put on the strength
of the LORD's power.
Wake up as in days past,
as in generations of long ago.
Wasn't it You who hacked •Rahab
to pieces,[i]
who pierced the sea monster?[j]
10 Wasn't it You who dried up the sea,[k]
the waters of the great deep,
who made the sea-bed into a road
for the redeemed to pass over?[l]
11 And the redeemed of the LORD
will return[m]
and come to Zion with singing,
crowned with unending joy.
Joy and gladness will overtake them,
and sorrow and sighing will flee.

12 I—I am the One who comforts you.
Who are you that you should fear man
who dies,[n]
or a son of man who is given up
like grass?[o]
13 But you have forgotten the LORD,
your Maker,
who stretched out the heavens
and laid the foundations of the earth.[p]
You are in constant dread all day long
because of the fury of the oppressor,
who has set himself to destroy.
But where is the fury of the oppressor?[q]
14 The prisoner[D] is soon to be set free;
he will not die and go to the •Pit,
and his food will not be lacking.
15 For I am •Yahweh your God
who stirs up the sea so that
its waves roar[r]—
His name is Yahweh of •Hosts.
16 I have put My words in your mouth,[s]
and covered you in the shadow
of My hand,[t]
in order to plant[E] the heavens,
to found the earth,
and to say to Zion, "You are My people."

17 Wake yourself, wake yourself up!
Stand up, Jerusalem,
you who have drunk the cup
of His fury[u]
from the hand of the LORD;
you who have drunk the goblet
to the dregs—
the cup that causes people to stagger.
18 There is no one to guide her
among all the children she has raised;
there is no one to take hold of her hand
among all the offspring
she has brought up.
19 These two things have happened
to you:[v]
devastation and destruction,
famine and sword.
Who will grieve for you?
How can I[F] comfort you?
20 Your children have fainted;
they lie at the head of every street
like an antelope in a net.
They are full of the LORD's fury,
the rebuke of your God.

21 So listen to this, afflicted
and drunken one—but not with wine.[w]

[a]**51:4** Is 42:6; 49:6 [b]**51:5** Is 46:13; 54:17 [c]Is 40:10 [d]**51:6** Ps 102:25-26; Is 34:4; Mt 24:35; Heb 1:10-12; 2Pt 3:10 [e]Is 45:17; 2Tm 2:10; Heb 5:9 [f]**51:7** Ps 37:31 [g]**51:8** Is 50:9 [h]Is 14:11 [i]**51:9** Jb 26:12; Ps 89:10; Is 30:7 [j]Ps 74:13; Is 27:1 [k]**51:10** Is 11:15-16; 50:2; 63:11-12 [l]Ex 15:13 [m]**51:11** Is 35:10 [n]**51:12** Ps 118:6; Is 2:22 [o]Is 40:6-7; Jms 1:10-11; 1Pt 1:24 [p]**51:13** Is 44:24; 45:12, Am 9:6; Zch 12:1 [q]Is 49:26 [r]**51:15** Ps 107:25; Jr 31:35 [s]**51:16** Is 59:21 [t]Ex 33:22; Is 49:2 [u]**51:17** Jb 21:20; Is 63:6; Jr 25:15; Mt 20:22; 26:39; Jn 18:1; Rv 14:10 [v]**51:19** Is 47:9 [w]**51:21** Is 29:9

[A]**51:5** Or *islands* [B]**51:5** Lit *arm* [C]**51:6** Or *die in like manner* [D]**51:14** Hb obscure [E]**51:16** Syr reads *to stretch out* [F]**51:19** DSS, LXX, Syr, Vg read *you? Who can*

22 This is what your Lord says —
Yahweh, even your God,
who defends His people[a] —
"Look, I have removed
the cup of staggering from your hand;
that goblet, the cup of My fury.
You will never drink it again.
23 I will put it into the hands
of your tormentors,
who said to you:[b]
Lie down, so we can walk over you.
You made your back like the ground,
and like a street for those who walk
on it.

52 "Wake up, wake up;
put on your strength, ˚Zion!
Put on your beautiful garments,[c]
Jerusalem, the Holy City![d]
For the uncircumcised
and the ˚unclean
will no longer enter you.[e]
2 Stand up, shake the dust off yourself!
Take your seat, Jerusalem.
Remove the bonds[A] from your neck,
captive Daughter Zion."
3 For this is what the LORD says:
"You were sold for nothing,
and you will be redeemed
without silver."[f]
4 For this is what the Lord GOD says:
"At first My people went down to Egypt
to live there,[g]
then Assyria oppressed them
without cause.[B]
5 So now what have I here" —
this is the LORD's declaration —
"that My people are taken away
for nothing?
Its rulers wail" —
this is the LORD's declaration —
"and My name is continually
blasphemed all day long.[h]
6 Therefore My people will know
My name;[i]
therefore they will know on that day
that I am He who says:
Here I am."
7 How beautiful on the mountains
are the feet of the herald,
who proclaims peace,
who brings news of good things,[j]
who proclaims salvation,
who says to Zion, "Your God reigns!"[k]
8 The voices of your watchmen[l] —
they lift up their voices,
shouting for joy together;
for every eye will see
when the LORD returns to Zion.
9 Be joyful, rejoice together,
you ruins of Jerusalem![m]
For the LORD has comforted
His people;[n]
He has redeemed Jerusalem.
10 The LORD has displayed His holy arm
in the sight of all the nations;[o]
all the ends of the earth will see
the salvation of our God.[p]

[a]**51:22** Is 3:12-13; 49:25; Jr 50:34
[b]**51:23** Is 49:26; Jr 25:15-17,26,28; Zch 12:2
[c]**52:1** Is 61:3
[d]Neh 11:1; Is 48:2
[e]Is 35:8; Rv 21:27
[f]**52:3** Is 45:13; 1Pt 1:18
[g]**52:4** Gn 46:6
[h]**52:5** Ezk 36:20; Rm 2:24
[i]**52:6** Is 49:23
[j]**52:7** Nah 1:15; Rm 10:15
[k]Ps 93:1; Is 24:23
[l]**52:8** Is 62:6
[m]**52:9** Is 44:26; 51:3; 61:4
[n]Is 40:1
[o]**52:10** Ps 98:1-3; Is 51:9; 66:18-19
[p]Is 40:5; Lk 3:6

GOD WHO SENDS

Beauty of the Missional Task

The missional vision is a call to the missional task. To be involved in this task is to be at the very center of God's purpose in the world. This is conceived by Paul in esthetic terms. In Romans 10:13-15, Paul wrote of the necessity of hearing if one is to believe and call upon the name of the Lord for salvation. Then he emphasized the necessity for a preacher if one is to hear. However, the evangelistic sequence does not stop here. "How can men preach unless they are sent?" Then Paul quoted from Isaiah 52:7: "As it is written, 'How beautiful are the feet of those who preach good news!'" Here the idea of sending and the idea of beauty are clearly linked.

(DUBOSE, 93-94)

[A]**52:2** Alt Hb tradition reads *The bonds are removed* [B]**52:4** Or *them at last*, or *them for nothing*

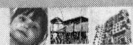

11 Leave, leave, go out from there![a]
Do not touch anything unclean;
go out from her, purify yourselves,[b]
you who carry the vessels of the LORD.
12 For you will not leave in a hurry,[c]
and you will not have to take flight;
because the LORD is going before you,[d]
and the God of Israel is your rear guard.[e]

[a]52:11 Is 48:20; Jr 50:8; Ezk 20:34,41; Zch 2:6,7; 2Co 6:17 [b]2Co 6:17; 2Tm 2:19 [c]52:12 Ex 12:11,33; Dt 16:3 [d]Ex 23:23; Dt 1:30; 31:8; Is 45:2

The Servant's Suffering and Exaltation

13 See, My Servant[A,f] will act wisely;[B]
He will be raised and lifted up
and greatly exalted.[g]
14 Just as many were appalled at You[C]—
His appearance was so disfigured

[e]Jos 6:9,13; Is 58:8 [f]52:13 Is 42:1; 49:3-7; 50:10; 53:11; Ezk 34:23-24; Zch 3:8; Ac 3:13 [g]Php 2:9-11

The Mission of God in the Old Testament

Mark D. Roberts

God created humans so we might have fellowship with Him and serve as faithful stewards of His creation (Gn 1–2). God the King reigns over all, and we were created to be His royal family through whom He would implement His reign.

Yet we sinned against God. We wanted to be kings and queens. Our sin was not some minor peccadillo God could ignore, but outright rebellion against His reign. The result of sin was pervasive brokenness in our relationship with God, with each other, and with creation (Gn 3).

From the moment of the first sin, we have tried to earn our way back into God's favor. But no human effort works. Only God can mend what we have broken. That is His fundamental mission: to reconcile us to Himself and to one another, and to bring reconciliation to all creation. Though we have rebelled, God wants us to have fellowship with Him and to serve as stewards of His renewed creation.

God begins to fulfill His reconciling mission by forming a special people—Israel—with whom He will have covenant relationship and through whom He will bless all nations (Gn 12:1-3; Ex 19:3-6). He reveals His gracious nature to the Israelites and rules over them as king (Ex 34:4-7; Jdg 8:23). But they repeatedly rebel, rejecting God and choosing idols instead (1Sm 10:19; Ezk 20:16).

What seems like an irreparable setback in God's plan actually prepares the way for the crucial step in His mission. God uses the occasion of Israel's rebellion to promise future reconciliation. Through the prophets, the Lord reveals that He will save His chosen people through a unique individual who will extend divine salvation to the ends of the earth (Is 49:6). This Savior will be the suffering Servant of God, who bears the sin of all humanity, offering His life for us so we might be reconciled to God (Is 53). Isaiah speaks words that would one day fill the mouth of God's redeeming Messiah:

The Spirit of the Lord God is on me, because the Lord has anointed me to bring good news to the poor. He has sent me to heal the brokenhearted, to proclaim liberty to the captives, and freedom to the prisoners; to proclaim the year of the Lord's favor . . . (Is 61:1-2a).

In that time of favor, God will remove the rebellion of sin and restore His rightful reign upon earth. That which has been damaged by sin will be mended, as God reconciles people to Himself and to each other. It will be a day of great rejoicing:

How beautiful on the mountains are the feet of the herald who proclaims peace, who brings news of good things, who proclaims salvation, who say to Zion, "Your God reigns!" The voices of your watchmen—they lift up their voices, shouting for joy together. (Is 52:7-8a)

Someday, God's mission will be fulfilled and He will reign. God's people will be reconciled to their Creator and restored to their created purpose.

[A]52:13 Tg adds *the Messiah* [B]52:13 Or *will be successful* [C]52:14 Some Hb mss, Syr, Tg read *Him*

that He did not look
like a man,
and His form did not resemble
a human being —
15 so He will sprinkle[A,B]
many nations.[C,a]
Kings will shut their mouths
because of Him,
For they will see
what had not been told them,
and they will understand
what they had not heard.[b]

[a]52:15 Nm 19:18-21; Ezk 36:25 [b]Rm 15:21; Eph 3:5

The Promises of God in the Mission of God

Andreas J. Köstenberger

While God, being eternal and the fountainhead of all life, was never sent by anyone, His mission, in pursuit of His divine purposes, reaches back all the way to creation. God made Adam and Eve in His image and placed them on this earth so they might accomplish His mandate to multiply and fill the earth. Through their obedience to God's command, and through their offspring, His vice-regents on this earth would take God's presence to the ends of the earth, expanding the scope of His reign and extending His rule (Gn 1:26–31).

When the first man and woman transgressed the boundaries set by their Creator and fell into sin, God's mission took on a new element. No longer did humans enjoy direct communion with God. They now required redemption from sin and reconciliation with their Creator. God's story of salvation is the account of His quest to reclaim a people for Himself who will take His presence to the ends of the earth once again. The Creator immediately instilled hope when He promised that Eve's offspring would overcome the curse (Gn 3:15). The prospect of restoring creation rested on God's faithfulness to His promise.

Yet, again, God's mission was potentially thwarted almost immediately. In keeping with the creation mandate, humanity began to multiply and to fill the earth. But rather than take God's presence to the ends of the earth, humans plunged into evil, sin, and destruction (Gn 6:1–4). God judged their rebellion through a universal flood, but He renewed His promise of a new creation to Noah and His family (Gn 6–9). At the Tower of Babylon, God dispersed humanity in judgment (Gn 11), but then called Abraham in order to bless all the peoples of the earth through him and his descendants (Gn 12, 15, 17, 22).

Faithful to His promise, God made the children of Abraham into a great nation and delivered them from bondage in Egypt through the exodus. As a nation formed by God, Israel would display God's character to all nations, summoning them to participate in the renewal of all things by worshiping Him alone (Ex 19:5–6). In this way, God would bless all nations through Israel, Abraham's offspring. Once Israel was in the land, God further focused the promise of an offspring on a son of King David, declaring that his descendant would establish an eternal kingdom (2Sm 7:14).

Yet Israel disobeyed, and God scattered her across the nations. The exile posed the greatest threat to the promise and mission of God, and the Old Testament ends with the promises of God in doubt yet with the hope of divine restoration still intact. How will God remain faithful to His promises and complete His mission if the people whom He has chosen—the recipients of His promises—are disobedient and in ruins? It is in the offspring of Adam, Abraham, and David, the suffering Servant (Is 52:13–53:12), the true Israel, that God will fulfill His promises and His mission.

[A]52:15 Or *startle* [B]52:15 As the blood of a sacrifice is sprinkled on the altar on behalf of the people [C]52:15 LXX reads *so many nations will marvel at Him*

53 Who has believed
what we have heard?[A]
And who has the arm of the LORD[a]
been revealed to?[b]
2 He grew up before Him
like a young plant[c]
and like a root out of dry ground.
He didn't have an impressive form
or majesty that we should look at Him,
no appearance that we should
desire Him.[d]
3 He was despised and rejected by men,[e]
a man of suffering who knew
what sickness was.[f]
He was like someone
people turned away from;[B]
He was despised, and we didn't
value Him.

4 Yet He Himself bore our sicknesses,
and He carried our pains;[g]
but we in turn regarded Him stricken,
struck down by God,[h] and afflicted.
5 But He was pierced because of
our transgressions,[i]
crushed because of our iniquities;[j]
punishment[k] for our peace was on Him,
and we are healed by His wounds.[l]
6 We all went astray like sheep;[m]
we all have turned to our own way;
and the LORD has punished Him
for[C] the iniquity[n] of us all.[o]

7 He was oppressed and afflicted,
yet He did not open His mouth.
Like a lamb led to the slaughter
and like a sheep silent
before her shearers,
He did not open His mouth.[p]
8 He was taken away because of
oppression and judgment;
and who considered His fate?[D]
For He was cut off from the land
of the living;
He was struck because of
my people's rebellion.
9 They[E] made His grave with the wicked
and with a rich man at His death,[q]
although He had done no violence
and had not spoken deceitfully.[r]

10 Yet the LORD was pleased[s] to crush Him
severely.[F,t]
When[G] You make Him
a ·restitution offering,[u]
He will see His ·seed, He will prolong
His days,
and by His hand, the LORD's pleasure
will be accomplished.[v]
11 He will see it[H] out of His anguish,
and He will be satisfied
with His knowledge.
My righteous[w] Servant[x]
will justify many,[y]
and He will carry their iniquities.
12 Therefore I will give Him[I] the many
as a portion,
and He will receive[J] the mighty as spoil,
because He submitted Himself
to death,[z]
and was counted among the rebels;[aa]
yet He bore the sin of many[ab]
and interceded for the rebels.[ac]

Future Glory for Israel

54 "Rejoice, childless one, who did not
give birth;
burst into song and shout,
you who have not been in labor![ad]
For the children of the forsaken one
will be more
than the children
of the married woman,"[ae]
says the LORD.
2 "Enlarge the site of your tent,
and let your tent curtains
be stretched out;[af]
do not hold back;
lengthen your ropes,
and drive your pegs deep.
3 For you will spread out to the right
and to the left,[ag]
and your descendants
will dispossess nations
and inhabit the desolate cities.

4 "Do not be afraid, for you will not
be put to shame;[ah]
don't be humiliated, for you will not
be disgraced.

[a]**53:1** Is 30:30; 40:10; 48:14; 51:9; 52:10; Lk 1:51; Ac 13:17
[b]Jn 12:38; Rm 10:16
[c]**53:2** Is 11:1
[d]Is 52:14
[e]**53:3** Ps 22:6; Is 49:7; Lk 18:31-33
[f]Mk 8:31; Jn 1:10-11; Heb 4:15
[g]**53:4** Mt 8:17; 1Pt 2:21
[h]Ps 69:26
[i]**53:5** Is 53:8; Rm 4:25; 1Co 15:3; Heb 9:28
[j]Is 1:4
[k]Jr 2:30; Zph 3:2; Heb 5:8
[l]**53:5-6** 1Pt 2:24-25
[m]**53:6** Mt 18:12
[n]Is 13:11
[o]2Co 5:21; Col 2:14
[p]**53:7** Jr 11:19; Mt 26:63; 27:12-14; Lk 23:9; Jn 19:9; Ac 8:32-33; 1Pt 2:23
[q]**53:9** Mt 27:57-60
[r]Heb 4:15; 1Pt 2:22; 1Jn 3:5
[s]**53:10** Is 44:28; 55:11
[t]Dt 29:22; Is 17:11
[u]Lv 5:1-19
[v]Is 46:10
[w]**53:11** 1Jn 2:1
[x]Is 42:1
[y]Ac 13:39; Rm 5:18-19
[z]**53:12** Mt 26:42; Jn 10:14-18; Php 2:6-8
[aa]Lk 22:37
[ab]Heb 9:28
[ac]Lk 23:34; Rm 8:34; Heb 7:25
[ad]**54:1** Gl 4:27
[ae]1Sm 2:5; Is 62:4
[af]**54:2** Is 49:19-20
[ag]**54:3** Gn 28:14; Is 43:5-6; 60:3
[ah]**54:4** Is 45:17

[A]**53:1** Or *believed our report* [B]**53:3** Lit *And like a hiding of faces from Him* [C]**53:6** Or *has placed on Him*; lit *with* [D]**53:8** Or *and as for His generation, who considered Him?* [E]**53:9** DSS; MT reads *He* [F]**53:10** Or *Him; He made Him sick.* [G]**53:10** Or *If* [H]**53:11** DSS, LXX read *see light* [I]**53:12** Or *Him with* [J]**53:12** Or *receive with*

For you will forget the shame
of your youth,
and you will no longer remember
the disgrace of your widowhood.[a]
5 Indeed, your husband is
your Maker[b] —
His name is •Yahweh of •Hosts —
and the Holy One of Israel[c] is
your Redeemer;[d]
He is called the God of all the earth.
6 For the LORD has called you,
like a wife deserted and wounded
in spirit,[e]
a wife of one's youth[f]
when she is rejected,"
says your God.
7 "I deserted you for a brief moment,[g]
but I will take you back
with great compassion.
8 In a surge of anger
I hid My face[h] from you for a moment,
but I will have compassion on you
with everlasting love,"[i]
says the LORD your Redeemer.
9 "For this is like the days[A] of Noah to Me:
when I swore that the waters of Noah
would never flood the earth again,[j]
so I have sworn that I will not be angry
with you
or rebuke you.[k]
10 Though the mountains move
and the hills shake,
My love will not be removed from you
and My covenant of peace[l] will not
be shaken,"
says your compassionate LORD.
11 "Poor Jerusalem, storm-tossed,
and not comforted,
I will set your stones in black mortar,[B]
and lay your foundations
in sapphires.[C,m]
12 I will make your fortifications[D]
out of rubies,
your gates out of sparkling stones,
and all your walls out of
precious stones.
13 Then all your children will be taught
by the LORD,"[n]
their prosperity will be great,

[a]54:4 Is 4:1; 25:8; 51:7
[b]54:5 Jr 3:14; Hs 2:19
[c]Is 1:4
[d]Is 41:14; 43:14
[e]54:6 Is 49:14-21; 50:1-2; 62:4
[f]Mal 2:14
[g]54:7 Is 26:20
[h]54:8 Dt 31:17-18; Is 8:17
[i]Ps 100:5; Jr 31:3; 33:11
[j]54:9 Gn 9:11
[k]Ezk 39:29
[l]54:10 Nm 25:12; Ezk 34:25; Mal 2:5
[m]54:11 Rv 21:19
[n]54:13 Jn 6:45
[o]54:17 Is 41:8-9; Lk 1:54
[p]Is 45:24; 46:13
[q]55:1 Ps 42:1-2; 63:1; 143:6; Is 41:17; 44:3; Jn 4:14; 7:37; Rv 21:6
[r]55:3 Gn 9:16; 17:7; 2Sm 23:5; Is 24:5; 59:21; 61:8
[s]Ac 13:34
[t]55:4 Ps 18:43
[u]Ezk 34:24; 37:24-25; Dn 9:25; Mc 5:2

14 and you will be established
on a foundation of righteousness.
You will be far from oppression,
you will certainly not be afraid;
you will be far from terror,
it will certainly not come near you.
15 If anyone attacks you,
it is not from Me;
whoever attacks you
will fall before you.
16 Look, I have created the craftsman
who blows on the charcoal fire
and produces a weapon suitable
for its task;
and I have created the destroyer
to cause havoc.
17 No weapon formed against you
will succeed,
and you will refute any accusation[E]
raised against you in court.
This is the heritage
of the LORD's servants,[o]
and their righteousness is from Me."[p]
This is the LORD's declaration.

Come to the LORD

55 "Come, everyone who is thirsty,[q]
come to the waters;
and you without money,
come, buy, and eat!
Come, buy wine and milk
without money and without cost!
2 Why do you spend money on what
is not food,
and your wages on what
does not satisfy?
Listen carefully to Me, and eat
what is good,
and you will enjoy the choicest
of foods.[F]
3 Pay attention and come to Me;
listen, so that you will live.
I will make an everlasting covenant
with you,[r]
the promises assured to David.[s]
4 Since I have made him a witness
to the peoples,[t]
a leader and commander
for the peoples,[u]

[A]54:9 DSS, Cairo Geniza; MT, LXX read *waters* [B]54:11 Lit *in antimony* [C]54:11 Or *lapis lazuli* [D]54:12 Lit *suns*; perhaps *shields*; Ps 84:11 [E]54:17 Lit *refute every tongue* [F]55:2 Lit *enjoy fatness*

5 so you will summon a nation
you do not know,[a]
and nations who do not know you
will run to you.[b]
For the LORD your God,
even the Holy One of Israel,[c]
has glorified you."[d]

6 Seek the LORD
while He may be found;
call to Him while He is near.[e]
7 Let the wicked one abandon his way
and the sinful one his thoughts;[f]
let him return to the LORD,
so He may have compassion on him,
and to our God, for He will
freely forgive.[g]

8 "For My thoughts are not
your thoughts,
and your ways are not My ways."
This is the LORD's declaration.
9 "For as heaven is higher than earth,[h]
so My ways are higher
than your ways,
and My thoughts than your thoughts.
10 For just as rain and snow fall
from heaven
and do not return there
without saturating the earth
and making it germinate and sprout,
and providing seed to sow
and food to eat,[i]
11 so My word that comes
from My mouth
will not return to Me empty,
but it will accomplish what I please
and will prosper in what I send it
to do."[j]

12 You will indeed go out with joy
and be peacefully guided;
the mountains and the hills will break
into singing before you,
and all the trees of the field will clap
their hands.[k]
13 Instead of the thornbush, a cypress
will come up,
and instead of the brier, a myrtle
will come up;[l]
it will make a name for ·Yahweh[m]
as an everlasting sign that will not
be destroyed.

[a] **55:5** Is 45:14,22-24; 49:6
[b] Zch 8:22
[c] Is 1:4
[d] Is 60:9
[e] **55:6** Ps 32:6; Am 5:4
[f] **55:7** Ps 33:10; Is 32:7; 59:7; 65:2
[g] Is 1:18; 43:25; 44:22
[h] **55:9** Ps 103:11
[i] **55:10** 2Co 9:10
[j] **55:11** Is 45:23; 46:10; 53:10
[k] **55:12** Ps 98:8; Is 44:23
[l] **55:13** Is 35:1-2; 41:19; 60:13
[m] Is 63:12-14; Jr 33:9
[n] **56:1** Gn 18:19; Ps 106:3; Pr 21:3
[o] Ps 98:2; Is 46:13; 51:5; Rm 1:17; 3:21
[p] **56:2** Is 58:13
[q] **56:3** Is 14:1; 56:6
[r] Dt 23:1
[s] **56:5** Is 55:13; Rv 2:17
[t] **56:7** Is 2:2-3
[u] Mal 1:11
[v] Jr 7:11; Mt 21:13; Mk 11:17; Lk 19:46
[w] **56:8** Is 11:12; 60:3-11; 66:18-21; Jn 10:16

A House of Prayer for All

56 This is what the LORD says:

Preserve justice and do what is right,[n]
for My salvation is coming soon,
and My righteousness will be revealed.[o]
2 Happy is the man who does this,
anyone who maintains this,
who keeps the Sabbath
without desecrating it,
and keeps his hand from doing any evil.[p]

3 No foreigner who has joined himself
to the LORD
should say,
"The LORD will exclude me
from His people";[q]
and the eunuch should not say,
"Look, I am a dried-up tree."[r]
4 For the LORD says this:
"For the eunuchs who keep
My Sabbaths,
and choose what pleases Me,
and hold firmly to My covenant,
5 I will give them, in My house
and within My walls,
a memorial and a name
better than sons and daughters.
I will give each of them
an everlasting name
that will never be cut off.[s]
6 And the foreigners who join themselves
to the LORD
minister to Him,
love the name of ·Yahweh
and become His servants,
all who keep the Sabbath
without desecrating it
and who hold firmly to My covenant —
7 I will bring them to My holy mountain[t]
and let them rejoice in My house
of prayer.
Their ·burnt offerings and sacrifices
will be acceptable on My altar,[u]
for My house will be called a house
of prayer
for all nations."[v]
8 This is the declaration
of the Lord GOD, who gathers
the dispersed of Israel:
"I will gather to them still others
besides those already gathered."[w]

Unrighteous Leaders Condemned

9 All you animals of the field and forest,
come and eat!
10 Israel's[A] watchmen are blind,
all of them,
they know nothing;
all of them are mute dogs,
they cannot bark;
they dream, lie down,
and love to sleep.
11 These dogs have fierce appetites;
they never have enough.
And they are shepherds
who have no discernment;
all of them turn to their own way,
every last one for his own gain.[a]
12 "Come, let me get some wine,
let's guzzle some beer;
and tomorrow will be like today,
only far better!"[b]

57 The righteous one perishes,
and no one takes it to heart;
faithful men are swept away,
with no one realizing
that the righteous one is swept away
from the presence[B] of evil.
2 He will enter into peace —
they will rest on their beds[C] —
everyone who lives uprightly.

Pagan Religion Denounced

3 But come here,
you sons of a sorceress,
offspring of an adulterer
and a prostitute![D]
4 Who is it you are mocking?
Who is it you are opening your mouth
and sticking out your tongue at?
Isn't it you, you rebellious children,[c]
you race of liars,
5 who burn with lust among the oaks,
under every green tree,[d]
who slaughter children in the •wadis
below the clefts of the rocks?[e]
6 Your portion is
among the smooth stones
of the wadi;
indeed, they are your lot.
You have even poured out
a •drink offering to them;
you have offered a •grain offering;
should I be satisfied with these?
7 You have placed your bed
on a high and lofty mountain;[f]
you also went up there to offer sacrifice.
8 You have set up your memorial
behind the door and doorpost.
For away from Me, you stripped,
went up, and made your bed wide,[g]
and you have made a bargain[E]
for yourself with them.
You have loved their bed;
you have gazed on their genitals.[F,G]
9 You went to the king with oil
and multiplied your perfumes;
you sent your couriers far away[h]
and sent them down even to •Sheol.
10 You became weary
on your many journeys,
but you did not say, "I give up!"[i]
You found a renewal of your strength;[H]
therefore you did not grow weak.
11 Who was it you dreaded and feared,
so that you lied and didn't
remember Me
or take it to heart?
Have I not kept silent for such
a long time[I,j]
and you do not •fear Me?
12 I will expose your righteousness,
and your works — they will not
profit you.
13 When you cry out,
let your collection of idols deliver you!
The wind will carry all of them off,
a breath will take them away.
But whoever takes refuge in Me
will inherit the land[k]
and possess My holy mountain.[l]

Healing and Peace

14 He said,
"Build it up, build it up,
prepare the way,
remove every obstacle
from My people's way."[m]
15 For the High and Exalted One

[a]56:11 Jr 10:21; 23:1; 50:6; Ezk 34:2
[b]56:12 Lk 12:19; 1Co 15:32
[c]57:4 Is 30:1,9
[d]57:5 2Kg 16:4; Jr 2:20; 3:13
[e]2Kg 23:10; Ps 106:37-38; Jr 7:31; Ezk 16:20-21
[f]57:7 Jr 3:6; Ezk 16:16
[g]57:8 Ezk 23:17-18
[h]57:9 Ezk 16:26-29
[i]57:10 Jr 2:25; 18:12
[j]57:11 Ps 50:21; Is 42:14
[k]57:13 Ps 37:3,9; Is 25:4
[l]Is 65:9
[m]57:14 Is 62:10; Jr 18:15

[A]56:10 Or *His*, or *Its* [B]57:1 Or *away because* [C]57:2 Either their deathbeds or their graves [D]57:3 Lit *and she acted as a prostitute* [E]57:8 Lit *you cut* [F]57:8 Lit *hand* [G]57:8 In Hb, the word hand is probably a euphemism for "genitals." [H]57:10 Lit *found life of your hand* [I]57:11 LXX reads *And I, when I see you, I pass by*

who lives forever, whose name is Holy[a]
says this:
"I live in a high and holy place,
and with the oppressed and lowly
of spirit,[b]
to revive the spirit of the lowly
and revive the heart of the oppressed.[c]
16 For I will not accuse you forever,
and I will not always be angry;[d]
for then the spirit would grow weak
before Me,
even the breath of man,
which I have made.
17 Because of his sinful greed I was angry,[e]
so I struck him; I was angry and hid;[A]
but he went on turning back
to the desires of his heart.
18 I have seen his ways, but I will heal him;
I will lead him and restore comfort
to him and his mourners,[f]
19 creating words of praise."[B,g]
The LORD says,
"Peace, peace to the one who is far
or near,[h]
and I will heal him.
20 But the wicked are
like the storm-tossed sea,[i]
for it cannot be still,
and its waters churn up mire
and muck.
21 There is no peace for the wicked,"
says my God.[j]

True Fasting

58 "Cry out loudly,[C] don't hold back!
Raise your voice like a trumpet.
Tell My people their transgression
and the house of Jacob their sins.
2 They seek Me day after day
and delight to know My ways,
like a nation that does what is right
and does not abandon the justice
of their God.
They ask Me for righteous judgments;
they delight in the nearness of God."[k]
3 "Why have we fasted,
but You have not seen?[l]
We have denied ourselves,
but You haven't noticed!"[D]

[a]57:15 Lk 1:49 [b]Ps 34:18; 51:17; Is 66:2 [c]Ps 147:3; Is 61:1-3 [d]57:16 Gn 6:3; Ps 103:9; Jr 3:12 [e]57:17 Is 2:7; 56:11; Jr 6:13 [f]57:18 Is 61:1-3 [g]57:19 Is 6:7; 51:16; 59:21; Heb 13:15 [h]Ac 2:39; Eph 2:17 [i]57:20 Ps 107:29 [j]57:21 Is 48:22; 59:8 [k]58:2 Ps 119:151; Is 29:13; 57:3; Jms 4:8 [l]58:3 Mal 3:14; Lk 18:12 [m]Is 22:12-13; Zch 7:5-6 [n]58:5 Est 4:3; Dn 9:3 [o]58:6 Jb 36:8; Ps 107:10; Ec 7:26 [p]Neh 5:10-12; Is 58:9; Jr 34:8 [q]58:7 Jb 31:19-20; Is 58:10; Ezk 18:7,16 [r]Mt 25:35-36; Lk 3:11 [s]Dt 22:1-4; Lk 10:31-32 [t]58:8 Is 30:26; 33:24; Jr 30:17; 33:6 [u]Ps 85:13; Is 62:1 [v]Ex 14:19; Is 52:12 [w]58:9 Ps 50:15; Is 55:6; 65:24 [x]Pr 6:13 [y]58:10 Jb 11:17; Ps 37:6; Is 42:16; 58:8 [z]58:11 Sg 4:15; Is 27:3; Jr 31:12

"Look, you do as you please on the day
of your fast,
and oppress all your workers."[m]
4 You fast with contention and strife
to strike viciously with your fist.
You cannot fast as you do today,
hoping to make your voice heard
on high.
5 Will the fast I choose be like this:
A day for a person to deny himself,
to bow his head like a reed,
and to spread out •sackcloth
and ashes?[n]
Will you call this a fast
and a day acceptable to the LORD?
6 Isn't the fast I choose:
To break the chains of wickedness,[o]
to untie the ropes of the yoke,
to set the oppressed free,
and to tear off every yoke?[p]
7 Is it not to share your bread
with the hungry,[q]
to bring the poor and homeless
into your house,
to clothe the naked when you see him,[r]
and not to ignore[E] your own flesh
and blood?[s]
8 Then your light will appear
like the dawn,
and your recovery will come quickly.[t]
Your righteousness will go before you,[u]
and the LORD's glory will be
your rear guard.[v]
9 At that time, when you call, the LORD
will answer;[w]
when you cry out, He will say,
'Here I am.'
If you get rid of the yoke among you,[F]
the finger-pointing
and malicious speaking,[x]
10 and if you offer yourself[G] to the hungry,
and satisfy the afflicted one,
then your light will shine
in the darkness,[y]
and your night will be like noonday.
11 The LORD will always lead you,
satisfy you in a parched land,
and strengthen your bones.
You will be like a watered garden[z]

[A]57:17 Lit *him; hiding and I am angry* [B]57:19 Lit *creating fruit of the lips* [C]58:1 Lit *with throat* [D]58:3 These are Israel's words to God. [E]58:7 Lit *not hide yourself from* [F]58:9 Lit *yoke from your midst* [G]58:10 Some Hb mss, LXX, Syr read *offer your bread*

and like a spring whose waters
never run dry.[a]
12 Some of you will rebuild
the ancient ruins;[b]
you will restore the foundations laid
long ago;[A,c]
you will be called the repairer
of broken walls,
the restorer of streets
where people live.

13 "If you keep from desecrating[B]
the Sabbath,[d]
from doing whatever you want
on My holy day;
if you call the Sabbath a delight,
and the holy day
of the LORD honorable;
if you honor it, not going
your own ways,[e]
seeking your own pleasure, or talking
too much;[C]
14 then you will delight yourself
in the LORD,[f]
and I will make you ride
over the heights of the land,[g]
and let you enjoy the heritage
of your father Jacob."
For the mouth of the LORD has spoken.[h]

Sin and Redemption

59 Indeed, the LORD's hand is not
too short to save,[i]
and His ear is not too deaf to hear.
2 But your iniquities[j] have built barriers
between you and your God,
and your sins have made Him
hide His face from you[k]
so that He does not listen.[l]
3 For your hands are defiled with blood
and your fingers, with iniquity;
your lips have spoken lies,
and your tongues mutter injustice.
4 No one makes claims justly;
no one pleads honestly.
They trust in empty
and worthless words;
they conceive trouble and give birth
to iniquity.[m]
5 They hatch viper's eggs
and weave spider's webs.
Whoever eats their eggs will die;
crack one open, and a viper is hatched.
6 Their webs cannot become clothing,
and they cannot cover themselves
with their works.
Their works are sinful works,
and violent acts are in their hands.
7 Their feet run after evil,[n]
and they rush to shed innocent blood.[o]
Their thoughts are sinful thoughts;[p]
ruin and wretchedness are
in their paths.
8 They have not known the path
of peace,[q]
and there is no justice in their ways.
They have made their roads crooked;
no one who walks on them
will know peace.[r]

9 Therefore justice is far from us,
and righteousness does not reach us.
We hope for light, but there is darkness;
for brightness, but we live in the night.
10 We grope along a wall like the blind;
we grope like those without eyes.[s]
We stumble at noon as though
it were twilight;
we are like the dead among those
who are healthy.
11 We all growl like bears
and moan like doves.[t]
We hope for justice, but there is none;
for salvation, but it is far from us.
12 For our transgressions have multiplied
before You,[u]
and our sins testify against us.[v]
For our transgressions are with us,
and we know our iniquities:[w]
13 transgression and deception
against the LORD,
turning away from following our God,
speaking oppression and revolt,
conceiving and uttering lying words
from the heart.
14 Justice is turned back,
and righteousness stands far off.
For truth has stumbled
in the public square,
and honesty cannot enter.

[a] **58:11** Jn 4:14; 7:38 [b] **58:12** Ezr 6:14; Neh 4:6; Is 49:8; 61:4; Ezk 36:10 [c] 1Kg 6:37; Ezr 3:10-12 [d] **58:13** Ex 31:16-17; 35:2-3; Is 56:2-6; Jr 17:21-27 [e] Is 55:8 [f] **58:14** Jb 22:26; Ps 37:4 [g] Dt 32:13; 33:29; Is 33:16; Hab 3:19 [h] Is 1:20; 40:5 [i] **59:1** Nm 11:23; Is 50:2; Jr 32:17 [j] **59:2** Is 13:11 [k] Dt 31:17-18; 32:20; Is 50:6; Ezk 39:29; Mc 3:4 [l] Dt 3:26; 23:5; Jb 35:13; Is 1:15 [m] **59:4** Jb 15:35; Ps 7:14; Is 33:11 [n] **59:7-8** Rm 3:15-17 [o] **59:7** Pr 1:16; 6:17 [p] Mk 7:21-22 [q] **59:8** Lk 1:79 [r] Is 57:20-21 [s] **59:10** Dt 28:29; Jb 5:14 [t] **59:11** Is 38:14; Ezk 7:16 [u] **59:12** Ezr 9:6 [v] Is 3:9; Jr 14:7; Hs 5:5 [w] Is 13:11

[A] **58:12** Lit *foundations generation and generation* [B] **58:13** Lit *keep your foot from* [C] **58:13** Lit *or speak a word*

15 Truth is missing,
and whoever turns from evil
is plundered.

The LORD saw that there was no justice,
and He was offended.
16 He saw that there was no man —
He was amazed that there was
no one interceding;[a]
so His own arm brought salvation,
and His own righteousness
supported Him.
17 He put on righteousness
like a breastplate,
and a helmet of salvation on His head;[b]
He put on garments of vengeance
for clothing,
and He wrapped Himself in zeal
as in a cloak.[c]
18 So He will repay according to
their deeds:[d]
fury to His enemies,
retribution to His foes,
and He will repay the coastlands.
19 They will ·fear the name of ·Yahweh
in the west
and His glory in the east;[e]
for He will come like a rushing stream[f]
driven by the wind of the LORD.
20 "The Redeemer[g] will come to ·Zion,
and to those in Jacob who turn
from transgression."[h]
This is the LORD's declaration.

21"As for Me, this is My covenant with
them,"[i] says the LORD: "My Spirit who is on
you, and My words that I have put in your
mouth,[j] will not depart from your mouth, or
from the mouth of your children, or from the
mouth of your children's children, from now
on and forever," says the LORD.

The LORD's Glory in Zion

60 Arise, shine, for your light has come,[k]
and the glory of the LORD shines
over you.[A,l]
2 For look, darkness covers the earth,
and total darkness the peoples;
but the LORD will shine over you,
and His glory will appear over you.
3 Nations will come to your light,
and kings to the brightness
of your radiance.[m]
4 Raise your eyes and look around:
they all gather and come to you;
your sons will come from far away,
and your daughters will be carried
on the hip.[n]
5 Then you will see and be radiant,[o]
and your heart will tremble
and rejoice,[B]
because the riches of the sea
will become yours
and the wealth of the nations will come
to you.[p]
6 Caravans of camels will cover
your land[C] —
young camels of Midian and Ephah —
all of them will come from Sheba.[q]
They will carry gold and frankincense[r]
and proclaim the praises of the LORD.
7 All the flocks of Kedar will be gathered
to you;
the rams of Nebaioth will serve you[s]
and go up on My altar
as an acceptable sacrifice.[t]
I will glorify My beautiful house.[u]

8 Who are these who fly like a cloud,
like doves to their shelters?[v]
9 Yes, the islands will wait for Me[w]
with the ships of Tarshish in the lead,[x]
to bring your children from far away,[y]
their silver and gold with them,
for the honor of the LORD your God,
the Holy One of Israel,[z]
who has glorified you.[aa]
10 Foreigners will build up your walls,[ab]
and their kings will serve you.[ac]
Although I struck you in My wrath,
yet I will show mercy to you
with My favor.[ad]
11 Your gates will always be open;
they will never be shut day or night
so that the wealth of the nations
may be brought into you,[ae]
with their kings being led
in procession.
12 For the nation and the kingdom
that will not serve you will perish;
those nations will be annihilated.[af]

[a]**59:16** Is 41:28; 63:5; Ezk 22:30 [b]**59:17** Eph 6:14,17; 1Th 5:8 [c]Is 9:7; 37:32; Zch 1:14 [d]**59:18** Jr 25:14; Rv 22:12 [e]**59:19** Ps 113:3 [f]Is 30:28; 66:12 [g]**59:20** Is 41:14; 43:14 [h]**59:20-21** Ezk 18:30-31; Rm 11:26-27 [i]**59:21** Jr 31:31-34 [j]Is 51:16 [k]**60:1** Is 9:2; 26:19; 30:26; 51:17; 52:2; Eph 5:14 [l]Is 40:5; 58:8; Mal 4:2 [m]**60:3** Is 42:6; 49:6; Rv 21:24 [n]**60:4** Is 49:18-22 [o]**60:5** Ps 34:5 [p]Is 61:6 [q]**60:6** Gn 25:3; Ps 72:10 [r]Mt 2:11 [s]**60:7** Gn 25:13 [t]Is 19:19; 56:7 [u]Is 60:13; Hg 2:7,9 [v]**60:8** Hs 11:11 [w]**60:9** Is 51:5 [x]Ps 48:7; Is 2:16 [y]Is 14:2; 43:6; 49:22 [z]Is 1:4; 60:14 [aa]Is 55:5 [ab]**60:10** Is 14:1-2; 61:5; Zch 6:15 [ac]Is 49:7,23; Rv 21:24 [ad]Hab 3:2 [ae]**60:11** Rv 21:25-26 [af]**60:12** Zch 14:17-19

A**60:1** = Jerusalem B**60:5** Lit *expand* C**60:6** Lit *cover you*

13 The glory of Lebanon will come
to you[a] —
its pine, fir, and cypress together[b] —
to beautify the place of My sanctuary,
and I will glorify My dwelling place.[A]
14 The sons of your oppressors
will come and bow down to you;[c]
all who reviled you
will fall facedown at your feet.[d]
They will call you the City of the LORD,
•Zion of the Holy One of Israel.[e]
15 Instead of your being deserted
and hated,
with no one passing through,[f]
I will make you an object
of eternal pride,[g]
a joy from age to age.
16 You will nurse on the milk of nations,
and nurse at the breast of kings;[h]
you will know that I, •Yahweh,
am your Savior[i]
and Redeemer,[j] the Mighty One
of Jacob.[k]

17 I will bring gold instead of bronze;
I will bring silver instead of iron,
bronze instead of wood,
and iron instead of stones.
I will appoint peace as your guard
and righteousness as your ruler.
18 Violence will never again be heard of
in your land;[l]
devastation and destruction
will be gone from your borders.
But you will name your walls salvation[m]
and your gates, praise.
19 The sun will no longer be your light
by day,
and the brightness of the moon
will not shine on you;
but the LORD will be
your everlasting light,[n]
and your God will be your splendor.
20 Your sun will no longer set,
and your moon will not fade;
for the LORD will be
your everlasting light,
and the days of your sorrow
will be over.[o]
21 Then all your people will be righteous;[p]
they will possess the land forever;[q]
they are the branch I planted,
the work of My[B] hands,
so that I may be glorified.[r]
22 The least will become a thousand,
the smallest a mighty nation.
I am Yahweh;
I will accomplish it quickly in its time.

Messiah's Jubilee

61 The Spirit of the Lord GOD is on Me,[s]
because the LORD has anointed Me
to bring good news to the poor.[t]
He has sent Me to heal[C]
the brokenhearted,
to proclaim liberty to the captives
and freedom to the prisoners;[u]
2 to proclaim the year
of the LORD's favor,[v]
and the day of our God's vengeance;[w]
to comfort[x] all who mourn,
3 to provide for those who mourn
in •Zion;
to give them a crown of beauty
instead of ashes,
festive oil instead of mourning,[y]

[a]**60:13** Is 35:2
[b]Is 41:19
[c]**60:14** Is 14:1-2; Zch 8:23
[d]Is 49:23; Rv 3:9
[e]Is 1:26
[f]**60:15** Is 34:10
[g]Is 65:18
[h]**60:16** Is 49:23; 66:11-12
[i]Is 43:3; 49:26
[j]Is 41:14; 43:14
[k]Gn 49:24; Ps 132:2,5; Is 49:26
[l]**60:18** Is 11:9
[m]Is 26:1
[n]**60:19** Zch 14:6-7; Rv 21:23; 22:5
[o]**60:20** Is 35:10; 65:19; Rv 21:4
[p]**60:21** Is 52:1
[q]Ps 37:9; Ezk 37:25
[r]Is 61:3
[s]**61:1-2** Is 11:2; 42:1; 48:16; Lk 4:18-19
[t]**61:1** Lk 7:22
[u]Is 42:7; 49:9
[v]**61:2** Is 49:8
[w]Is 2:12; 13:6; 34:2,8
[x]Is 40:1
[y]**61:3** Ps 45:7; Heb 1:9

GOD WHO SENDS

Care for the Oppressed

Our mission is ethical in both purpose and implication. To be sent to bind up the brokenhearted—an Old Testament idea which Jesus incarnated (Is 61; Lk 4)—is to be on mission to bring the loving nature of God to bear upon our relationships in life. There is an apostolate of morality inherent in the apostolate of proclamation in the larger evangelistic purpose of the Christian mission.

(DUBOSE, 86)

[A]**60:13** Lit *glorify the place of My feet* [B]**60:21** LXX, DSS read *His* [C]**61:1** Lit *bind up*

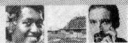

and splendid clothes
instead of despair.[A]
And they will be called righteous trees,
planted by the LORD
to glorify Him.[a]
4 They will rebuild the ancient ruins;[b]
they will restore
the former devastations;
they will renew the ruined cities,
the devastations of many generations.
5 Strangers will stand and feed
your flocks,
and foreigners will be your plowmen
and vinedressers.[c]
6 But you will be called
the LORD's priests;[d]

[a]61:3 Is 60:21; Jr 17:7-8 [b]61:4 Is 49:8; 58:12; Ezk 36:33; Am 9:14 [c]61:5 Is 14:2; 60:10 [d]61:6 Ex 19:6; Is 66:21; 1Pt 2:5,9

Care for the Outcast

Matthew Barnett

The name Isaiah means "salvation of the LORD," and the book of Isaiah stresses that salvation comes from God and not mankind. Considered one of the greatest and most eloquent prophets, Isaiah's writings were a message of salvation for the people of Judah. He urged them to let go of their sin and embrace the saving grace of the Lord.

Believers are to strive for purity and set an example for those who are separated from God. We must live our lives serving God's mission, striving to be representative of His character. We are emissaries for God's love, and the most important way we can show this love is in the way we care for the poor and downtrodden. As it says in Isaiah 61:1, "The Spirit of the Lord GOD is on Me, because the LORD has anointed Me to bring good news to the poor."

If every church took in one homeless person, homelessness would be eradicated. Salvation is the ultimate goal, but few will consider spiritual salvation when they are physically starving. I believe there is a movement where churches are pushing the limits of the way they help the world. They are taking on ambitious projects to feed the homeless, clean up cities, and speak life into people. When I came to Los Angeles I had a dream of a 24/7 church that would be a refuge to hurting people. For over 15 years the Dream Center has served Los Angeles, showing broken people that they can have an amazing future. Thousands have gone through our discipleship program, turning from hopelessness to new beginnings. Weekly we feed thousands in poverty-stricken areas. Families who were living on the street have found a place to stay while they get their lives together.

God is the only path to salvation and all glory goes to Him. Once people have seen the restorative power of God's love, a transformation begins to occur. They find hope. They have peace and joy when they wake up. Poverty and regret once consumed their lives; now they see a future of possibilities.

We are to be an unrelenting source of help to our communities, never giving up on a single person. The church should live every day with the intent of encouraging someone, showing them such joy and love that they would be inspired to turn to the God of salvation and restoration. My father, Pastor Tommy Barnett, always lived with the philosophy of "find a need and fill it, find a hurt and heal it." As Christians we are to be a light to the world. As we live our lives with a message of hope and salvation, this light will only grow brighter. It is our duty as representatives of God to encourage where no one else would, to love someone and give them hope no matter how far they have fallen, to feed the poor and care for the sick, to restore broken lives, and by showing this love, lead them to salvation in Christ.

[A]61:3 Lit *a dim spirit*

they will speak of you as ministers
of our God;
you will eat the wealth of the nations,
and you will boast in their riches.
7 Because your shame was double,[a]
and they cried out,
"Disgrace is their portion,"
therefore, they will possess double
in their land,[b]
and eternal joy will be theirs.
8 For I ·Yahweh love justice;[c]
I hate robbery and injustice;[A]
I will faithfully reward them
and make an everlasting covenant[d]
with them.
9 Their descendants will be known
among the nations,
and their posterity among the peoples.
All who see them will recognize
that they are a people the LORD
has blessed.
10 I greatly rejoice in the LORD,
I exult in my God;
for He has clothed me
with the garments of salvation
and wrapped me in a robe
of righteousness,[e]
as a groom wears a turban
and as a bride adorns herself
with her jewels.[f]
11 For as the earth produces its growth,
and as a garden enables what is sown
to spring up,
so the Lord GOD
will cause righteousness and praise
to spring up before all the nations.[g]

Zion's Restoration

62 I will not keep silent because of ·Zion,
and I will not keep still
because of Jerusalem,[h]
until her righteousness shines
like a bright light[i]
and her salvation, like a flaming torch.
2 Nations will see your righteousness[j]
and all kings, your glory.
You will be called by a new name
that the LORD's mouth will announce.[k]

[a]**61:7** Is 54:4 [b]Is 40:2; Zch 9:12 [c]**61:8** Ps 11:7; Is 59:15 [d]Is 24:5; 55:3 [e]**61:10** Is 49:18; 52:1; 59:17 [f]Rv 21:2 [g]**61:11** Is 45:23-24; 60:18,21 [h]**62:1** Ps 83:1; Is 64:12; 65:6 [i]Is 1:26; 58:8; 61:11 [j]**62:2** Is 60:3 [k]Is 60:14; Rv 2:17; 3:12 [l]**62:3** Is 28:5; Zch 9:16; 1Th 2:19 [m]**62:4** Is 54:6-7; 60:15,18 [n]Hs 2:19-20 [o]**62:5** Is 65:19 [p]**62:6** Is 52:8; Jr 6:17; Ezk 3:17; 33:7 [q]**62:7** Is 60:18; Jr 33:9; Zph 3:19-20 [r]**62:8** Lv 26:16; Dt 28:31,33; Jdg 6:3-6; Is 1:7; Jr 5:17 [s]**62:10** Is 11:16; 19:23; 35:8; 49:11; 57:14 [t]Is 11:10,12; 49:22 [u]**62:11** Mt 21:5; Zch 9:9

3 You will be a glorious crown
in the LORD's hand,
and a royal diadem in the palm
of your God.[l]
4 You will no longer be called Deserted,[m]
and your land will not
be called Desolate;
instead, you will be called My Delight
is in Her,[B]
and your land Married;[C,n]
for the LORD delights in you,
and your land will be married.
5 For as a young man marries
a young woman,
so your sons will marry you;
and as a groom rejoices[D] over his bride,
so your God will rejoice over you.[o]
6 Jerusalem,
I have appointed watchmen
on your walls;[p]
they will never be silent, day or night.
There is no rest for you,
who remind the LORD.
7 Do not give Him rest
until He establishes
and makes Jerusalem
the praise of the earth.[q]
8 The LORD has sworn
with His right hand
and His strong arm:
I will no longer give your grain
to your enemies for food,[r]
and foreigners will not drink
your new wine
you have labored for.
9 For those who gather grain will eat it
and praise the LORD,
and those who harvest the grapes
will drink the wine
in My holy courts.
10 Go out, go out through the gates;
prepare a way for the people!
Build it up, build up the highway;[s]
clear away the stones!
Raise a banner for the peoples.[t]
11 Look, the LORD has proclaimed
to the ends of the earth,
"Say to Daughter Zion:[u]

[A]**61:8** Some Hb mss, DSS, LXX, Syr, Tg, Vg; other Hb mss read *robbery with a burnt offering* [B]**62:4** Or *Hephzibah* [C]**62:4** Or *Beulah* [D]**62:5** Lit *and the rejoicing of the groom*

Look, your salvation is coming,
His reward is with Him,[a]
and His gifts accompany Him."
12 And they will be called[A]
the Holy People,[b]
the LORD's Redeemed;
and you will be called Cared For,
A City Not Deserted.

The LORD's Day of Vengeance

63 Who is this coming from Edom[c]
in crimson-stained garments
from Bozrah —
this One who is splendid in His apparel,
rising up proudly[B] in His great might?

It is I, proclaiming vindication,[C]
powerful to save.

2 Why are Your clothes red,
and Your garments like one who treads
a winepress?[d]

3 I trampled the winepress alone,
and no one from the nations was
with Me.
I trampled them in My anger
and ground them underfoot in My fury;
their blood spattered My garments,
and all My clothes were stained.
4 For I planned the day of vengeance,[D,e]
and the year of My redemption[E] came.
5 I looked, but there was no one to help,[f]
and I was amazed that no one assisted;
so My arm accomplished victory
for Me,
and My wrath assisted Me.
6 I crushed nations in My anger;
I made them drunk with My wrath[g]
and poured out their blood
on the ground.[h]

Remembrance of Grace

7 I will make known
the LORD's faithful love
and the LORD's praiseworthy acts,
because of all the LORD has done
for us —
even the many good things
He has done for the house of Israel
and has done for them based on
His compassion
and the abundance of His faithful love.
8 He said, "They are indeed My people,
children who will not be disloyal,"
and He became their Savior.
9 In all their suffering, He suffered,[F,i]
and the Angel of His Presence
saved them.
He redeemed them
because of His love and compassion;[j]
He lifted them up and carried them
all the days of the past.[k]
10 But they rebelled
and grieved His Holy Spirit.[l]
So He became their enemy
and fought against them.
11 Then He[G] remembered the days
of the past,
the days of Moses and his people.
Where is He who brought them
out of the sea
with the shepherds[H] of His flock?
Where is He who put His Holy Spirit
among the flock?
12 He sent His glorious arm
to be at Moses' right hand,
divided the waters before them[m]
to obtain eternal fame for Himself,
13 and led them through the depths
like a horse in the wilderness,
so that they did not stumble.
14 Like cattle that go down into the valley,
the Spirit of the LORD gave them[I] rest.
You led Your people this way
to make a glorious name for Yourself.

Israel's Prayer

15 Look down from heaven and see[n]
from Your lofty home —
holy and beautiful.
Where is Your zeal and Your might?
Your yearning[J] and Your compassion
are withheld from me.
16 Yet You are our Father,
even though Abraham does not
know us
and Israel doesn't recognize us.

[a]62:11 Is 40:10; Rv 22:12 [b]62:12 Dt 7:6; Is 4:3; 1Pt 2:9 [c]63:1 Ps 137:7; Is 34:5-6; Ezk 25:12-14; 35:1-15; Ob 1-14; Mal 1:2-5 [d]63:2 Rv 19:13-15 [e]63:4 Is 34:8; 61:2; Jr 46:10 [f]63:5 Is 59:16 [g]63:6 Is 29:9; 51:17; Jr 51:39 [h]Rv 14:20 [i]63:9 Jdg 10:16 [j]Dt 7:7-8 [k]Dt 1:31; 32:10-12; Is 46:3 [l]63:10 Ps 51:11; 78:40; 106:33; Is 48:16; Ac 7:51; Eph 4:30 [m]63:12 Ex 14:21; Ps 74:13 [n]63:15 Dt 26:15; Ps 80:14

[A]62:12 Lit *will call them* [B]63:1 Syr, Vg read *apparel, striding forward* [C]63:1 Or *righteousness* [D]63:4 Lit *For day of vengeance in My heart* [E]63:4 Or *blood revenge* [F]63:9 Alt Hb tradition reads *did not suffer* [G]63:11 Or *he*, or *they* [H]63:11 LXX, Tg, Syr read *shepherd* [I]63:14 Lit *him* [J]63:15 Lit *The agitation of Your inward parts*

You, ·Yahweh, are our Father;
from ancient times,
Your name is our Redeemer.[a]
17 Why, Yahweh, do You make us stray
from Your ways?
You harden our hearts so we do not
·fear[A] You.[b]
Return, because of Your servants,
the tribes of Your heritage.
18 Your holy people had a possession[B]
for a little while,
but our enemies have trampled down
Your sanctuary.[c]
19 We have become like those
You never ruled over,
like those not called by Your name.[d]

64 [C] If only You would tear
the heavens open
and come down,[e]
so that mountains would quake
at Your presence[f] —
2[D] as fire kindles the brushwood,
and fire causes water to boil —
to make Your name known
to Your enemies,
so that nations will tremble
at Your presence!
3 When You did awesome works[g]
that we did not expect,
You came down,[h]
and the mountains quaked
at Your presence.
4 From ancient times no one has heard,
no one has listened,
no eye has seen any God except You,
who acts on behalf of the one
who waits for Him.[i]
5 You welcome the one who joyfully does
what is right;
they remember You in Your ways.
But we have sinned, and You
were angry.
How can we be saved if we remain
in our sins?[E]
6 All of us have become
like something ·unclean,
and all our righteous acts are
like a polluted[F] garment;[j]
all of us wither like a leaf,[k]
and our iniquities[l] carry us away
like the wind.
7 No one calls on Your name,
striving to take hold of You.
For You have hidden Your face from us[m]
and made us melt because of[G,H]
our iniquity.
8 Yet LORD, You are our Father;[n]
we are the clay, and You are our potter;
we all are the work of Your hands.[o]
9 LORD, do not be terribly angry
or remember our iniquity forever.[p]
Please look — all of us are Your people!
10 Your holy cities have become
a wilderness;
·Zion has become a wilderness,
Jerusalem a desolation.[q]
11 Our holy and beautiful[I] temple,
where our fathers praised You,
has been burned with fire,
and all that was dear to us lies in ruins.[r]
12 LORD, after all this, will You
restrain Yourself?
Will You keep silent
and afflict severely?[s]

The LORD's Response

65 "I was sought by those
who did not ask;[J]
I was found by those
who did not seek Me.
I said: Here I am, here I am,
to a nation that was not called
by[K] My name.[t]
2 I spread out My hands all day long
to a rebellious people[u]
who walk in the wrong path,
following their own thoughts.
3 These people continually provoke Me
to My face,
sacrificing in gardens,[v]
burning incense on bricks,
4 sitting among the graves,
spending nights in secret places,
eating the meat of pigs,[w]
and putting polluted broth
in their bowls.[L]

[a]**63:16** Is 41:14; 43:14 [b]**63:17** Is 6:10 [c]**63:18** Ps 74:3-7; Is 64:11 [d]**63:19** Dt 28:10; Is 43:7; 65:1 [e]**64:1** Ex 19:18; Ps 18:9; 144:5 [f]Jdg 5:5; Ps 68:8; Nah 1:5 [g]**64:3** Dt 10:21; 2Sm 7:23; Ps 65:5 [h]Mc 1:3-4; Hab 3:13 [i]**64:4** 1Co 2:9 [j]**64:6** Is 61:10; Php 3:7-9 [k]Ps 90:5-6; Is 1:30 [l]Is 13:11 [m]**64:7** Is 54:8 [n]**64:8** Is 63:16 [o]Is 29:16; 45:9; Rm 9:20-21 [p]**64:9** Is 43:25; 57:17; Mc 7:18 [q]**64:10** Is 62:4 [r]**64:11** 2Kg 25:9; Ps 74:5-7; Is 63:18; Mt 23:38 [s]**64:12** Is 42:14 [t]**65:1** Is 63:19; Hs 1:10; Rm 10:20; Jms 2:7 [u]**65:2** Rm 10:21 [v]**65:3** Is 1:29; 66:17 [w]**65:4** Lv 11:7; Is 66:3,17

[A]**63:17** Lit *our heart from fearing* [B]**63:18** Or *Your people possessed Your holy place* [C]**64:1** Is 63:19b in Hb [D]**64:2** Is 64:1 in Hb [E]**64:5** Lit *angry; in them continually and we will be saved*; Hb obscure [F]**64:6** Lit *menstrual* [G]**64:7** LXX, Syr, Vg, Tg read *and delivered us into the hand of* [H]**64:7** Lit *melt by the hand* [I]**64:11** Or *glorious*; Is 60:7 [J]**65:1** LXX, Syr, DSS, Tg read *ask for Me* [K]**65:1** LXX, Syr, DSS, Tg, Vg read *that did not call on* [L]**65:3-4** These vv. describe pagan worship.

5 They say, 'Keep to yourself,
don't come near me, for I am too holy
for you!'
These practices are smoke
in My nostrils,
a fire that burns all day long.
6 It is written before Me:
I will not keep silent,[a] but I will repay;[b]
I will repay them fully[A]
7 for your iniquities and the iniquities[c]
of your[B] fathers together,"
says the LORD.
"Because they burned incense
on the mountains
and reproached Me on the hills,[d]
I will reward them fully[C]
for their former deeds."

8 The LORD says this:

As the new wine is found in a bunch
of grapes,
and one says, 'Don't destroy it,
for there's some good[D] in it,'
so I will act because of My servants
and not destroy them all.
9 I will produce descendants from Jacob,[e]
and heirs to My mountains from Judah;
My chosen[f] ones will possess it,
and My servants will dwell there.[g]
10 Sharon will be a pasture for flocks,[h]
and the Valley of Achor a place
for cattle to lie down,[i]
for My people who have sought Me.[j]
11 But you who abandon the LORD,
who forget My holy mountain,
who prepare a table for Fortune
and fill bowls of mixed wine for Destiny,[E]
12 I will destine you for the sword,
and all of you will kneel down
to be slaughtered,
because I called
and you did not answer,
I spoke and you did not hear;
you did what was evil in My sight
and chose what I did not delight in.[k]

13 Therefore, this is what the Lord GOD says:

My servants will eat,
but you will be hungry;

[a]**65:6** Ps 50:3,21; Is 42:14; 64:12 [b]Jr 16:18 [c]**65:7** Is 13:11 [d]Ezk 20:27-28; Hs 9:10; Zch 8:14; Mal 3:7 [e]**65:9** Jr 31:36-37 [f]Is 41:8 [g]Is 49:8; 60:21; Am 9:11-15 [h]**65:10** Is 33:9; 35:2 [i]Jos 7:26; Hs 2:15 [j]Is 51:1 [k]**65:12** 2Ch 36:15-16; Pr 1:24; Is 41:28; 50:2; 66:4; Jr 7:13 [l]**65:15** Jr 24:9; 25:18; Zch 8:13 [m]Is 62:2 [n]**65:16** Ps 31:5; 2Co 1:20; Rv 3:7,14 [o]**65:17** Is 66:22; 2Pt 3:13; Rv 21:1 [p]**65:19** Is 25:8; 30:19; 35:10; 51:11; Rv 7:17; 21:4 [q]**65:20** Ec 8:12-13; Is 3:11; 22:14 [r]**65:21** Jos 24:13; Is 37:30; Jr 29:5,28; Ezk 28:26; Zph 1:13

My servants will drink,
but you will be thirsty;
My servants will rejoice,
but you will be put to shame.
14 My servants will shout for joy
from a glad heart,
but you will cry out
from an anguished heart,
and you will lament out of
a broken spirit.
15 You will leave your name behind
as a curse for My chosen ones,[l]
and the Lord GOD will kill you;
but He will give His servants
another name.[m]
16 Whoever is blessed in the land
will be blessed by the God of truth,[n]
and whoever swears in the land
will swear by the God of truth.
For the former troubles
will be forgotten
and hidden from My sight.

A New Creation

17 "For I will create a new heaven
and a new earth;[o]
the past events will not be remembered
or come to mind.
18 Then be glad and rejoice forever
in what I am creating;
for I will create Jerusalem to be
a joy
and its people to be a delight.
19 I will rejoice in Jerusalem
and be glad in My people.
The sound of weeping and crying
will no longer be heard in her.[p]
20 In her, a nursing infant
will no longer live
only a few days,[F]
or an old man not live out his days.
Indeed, the youth will die
at a hundred years,
and the one who misses
a hundred years will be cursed.[q]
21 People will build houses and live
in them;
they will plant vineyards and eat
their fruit.[r]

[A]65:6 Lit *repay into their lap* [B]65:7 LXX, Syr read *for their iniquities and the iniquities of their* [C]65:7 Lit *reward into their lap* [D]65:8 Or *there's a blessing* [E]65:11 Pagan gods [F]65:20 Lit *her, no longer infant of days*

22 They will not build and others live
in them;
they will not plant and others eat.
For My people's lives will be
like the lifetime of a tree.[a]
My chosen ones will fully enjoy
the work of their hands.
23 They will not labor without success[b]
or bear children destined for disaster,
for they will be a people blessed
by the LORD
along with their descendants.[c]
24 Even before they call, I will answer;[d]
while they are still speaking, I will hear.
25 The wolf and the lamb
will feed together,[A]
and the lion will eat straw like the ox,[e]
but the serpent's food will be dust![f]
They will not do what is evil or destroy
on My entire holy mountain,"[g]
says the LORD.

Final Judgment and Joyous Restoration

66 This is what the LORD says:

Heaven[h] is My throne,[i]
and earth is My footstool.[j]
What house could you possibly build
for Me?
And what place could be My home?[k]
2 My hand made all these things,
and so they all came into being.
This is the LORD's declaration.
I will look favorably on this kind
of person:
one who is humble,[l]
submissive[B] in spirit,[m]
and trembles at My word.
3 One slaughters an ox, one kills a man;
one sacrifices a lamb, one breaks
a dog's neck;
one offers a ·grain offering, one offers
pig's blood;
one offers incense, one praises an idol —
all these have chosen their ways
and delight
in their detestable practices.[n]
4 So I will choose their punishment,
and I will bring on them
what they dread
because I called and no one answered;
I spoke and they didn't hear;
they did what was evil in My sight
and chose what I didn't delight in.[o]

5 You who tremble at His word,[p]
hear the word of the LORD:[q]
"Your brothers who hate
and exclude you
because of Me have said,[r]
'Let the LORD be glorified
so that we can see your joy!'
But they will be put to shame."[s]
6 A sound of uproar from the city!
A voice from the temple —
the voice of the LORD,
paying back His enemies
what they deserve![t]

7 Before ·Zion was in labor,
she gave birth;
before she was in pain, she delivered
a boy.
8 Who has heard of such a thing?
Who has seen such things?
Can a land be born in one day
or a nation be delivered in an instant?
Yet as soon as Zion was in labor,
she gave birth to her sons.
9 "Will I bring a baby to the point
of birth
and not deliver it?"
says the LORD;
"or will I who deliver, close the womb?"
says your God.
10 Be glad for Jerusalem and rejoice
over her,
all who love her.[u]
Rejoice greatly with her,
all who mourn over her —
11 so that you may nurse and be satisfied
from her comforting breast
and drink deeply and delight yourselves
from her glorious breasts.

12 For this is what the LORD says:

I will make peace flow to her
like a river,[v]
and the wealth[C] of nations like a flood;[w]
you will nurse and be carried
on her hip[x]

[a]**65:22** Ps 92:12-14 [b]**65:23** Dt 28:3-12; Is 55:2 [c]Is 61:9 [d]**65:24** Ps 91:15; Is 55:6; 58:9; Dn 9:20-23; 10:12 [e]**65:25** Is 11:6-9 [f]Gn 3:14; Mc 7:17 [g]Is 11:9; 27:13; 56:7 [h]**66:1-2** Ac 7:49-50 [i]**66:1** Ps 11:4; Mt 5:34-35; 23:22 [j]1Ch 28:2; Ps 99:5 [k]2Sm 7:5; 1Kg 8:27; Jer 23:24 [l]**66:2** Ps 86:1; Pr 16:19; Mt 11:29 [m]Ps 34:18; Mt 5:3; 1Ti 2:11 [n]**66:3** Am 5:21-25 [o]**66:4** 2Kg 21:2,6; Is 59:7; 65:12; Jr 7:30 [p]**66:5** Ezr 9:4; 10:3 [q]Is 28:14 [r]Mt 5:10-12; 10:22; Jn 9:34; 15:18-20 [s]Is 26:11; 44:9; 65:13 [t]**66:6** Is 59:18; 65:6; Jl 3:7 [u]**66:10** Ps 122:6; 137:6; Is 65:18 [v]**66:12** Ps 72:3,7; Is 48:18 [w]Is 61:6 [x]Is 60:4-5

[A]**65:25** Lit *as one* [B]**66:2** Lit *broken* [C]**66:12** Or *glory*

and bounced on her lap.
13 As a mother comforts her son,
so I will comfort you,[a]
and you will be comforted in Jerusalem.

14 You will see, you will rejoice,
and you[A] will flourish like grass;[b]
then the LORD's power will be revealed
to His servants,
but He will show His wrath
against His enemies.
15 Look, the LORD will come with fire[c] —
His chariots are like the whirlwind[d] —
to execute His anger with fury
and His rebuke with flames of fire.
16 For the LORD will execute judgment
on all flesh[e] with His fiery sword,
and many will be slain by the LORD.

17 "Those who dedicate and purify themselves to enter the groves[f] following their
leader,[B] eating meat from pigs, vermin, and
rats, will perish together."
This is the LORD's declaration.
18 "Knowing[C] their works and their
thoughts, I have come to gather all nations
and languages;[g] they will come and see My
glory. 19 I will establish a sign among them,
and I will send survivors from them to the
nations — to Tarshish, Put,[D] Lud (who are
archers), Tubal, Javan,[h] and the islands far
away — who have not heard of My fame or
seen My glory. And they will proclaim My
glory among the nations.[i] 20 They will bring
all your brothers from all the nations as a
gift to the LORD on horses and chariots, in
litters, and on mules and camels, to My holy
mountain Jerusalem,"[j] says the LORD, "just as
the Israelites bring an offering in a •clean vessel to the house of the LORD. 21 I will also take
some of them as priests and Levites,"[k] says the
LORD.

22 "For just as the new heavens
and the new earth,[l]
which I will make,
will endure before Me" —
this is the LORD's declaration —
"so your offspring and your name
will endure.
23 All mankind will come to worship Me
from one New Moon to another
and from one Sabbath to another,"
says the LORD.

24 "As they leave, they will see the dead bodies of the men who have rebelled against Me;[m]
for their worm[n] will never die, their fire will
never go out,[o] and they will be a horror to all
mankind."[p]

[a] **66:13** Ps 86:17; Is 40:1; 49:13; 51:13; 52:9; 2Co 1:3-4 [b] **66:14** Ps 72:16; Pr 11:28; Is 58:11 [c] **66:15** Is 33:14; Mal 3:1-2; 2Th 1:7-8; 2Pt 3:7 [d] Ps 68:17; Is 5:28; Hab 3:8 [e] **66:16** Gn 6:12; Jr 12:12; 25:31; Ezk 20:48; 21:4-5 [f] **66:17** Is 65:3-5 [g] **66:18** Is 45:22-25; Jr 3:17 [h] **66:19** Gn 10:2,5; 1Kg 10:22; Jr 46:9; Ezk 27:10,13 [i] 1Ch 16:24; Ps 96:3 [j] **66:20** Ps 2:6; Is 56:7; Ezk 20:40; Jl 3:17 [k] **66:21** Ex 19:6; Is 61:6; 1Pt 2:5,9; Rv 1:6 [l] **66:22** Is 65:17; Heb 12:26-27; 2Pt 3:13; Rv 21:1 [m] **66:24** Is 1:2; 5:25; 34:3 [n] Jb 7:5; Is 14:11 [o] Mk 9:44-48 [p] Dn 12:2

[A] **66:14** Lit *your bones* [B] **66:17** Hb obscure [C] **66:18** LXX, Syr; MT omits *Knowing* [D] **66:19** LXX; MT reads *Pul*

AUTHOR: Jeremiah

DATE: Jeremiah prophesied during the time of the last five kings of Judah (Josiah, Jehoahaz, Jehoiakim, Jehoiachin, and Zedekiah—around 626–586 B.C.)

The book of Jeremiah teaches the mission of God to a people who see the "old mission"—a Land of Promise as a witness to all nations—withering away. Could God's people ever recover?

The prophet Jeremiah wrote and preached during the final years of Judah. Judah's kings were mostly scoundrels, though well-meaning Josiah reinstituted the celebration of the Passover and other reforms. Finally, the nation was besieged by the juggernaut of Babylon. Jeremiah urged survivors to submit to Babylon, not rebel, because their military position was hopeless. More accurately, because God was no longer fighting for Israel. Sometimes, searching for God's purpose in loss is better than resistance to it. As P. T. Forsyth stated, "It is a better thing to pray for pain's conversion than for its removal."

JEREMIAH

That Jeremiah is called the "weeping prophet" is no surprise. He had much to weep over. As Israel succumbed, Jeremiah was told by God not to marry or raise children because the next generation—those who would bear the judgment for Israel's sin—would be swept away. To his lonely life and ominous prophecies add the opposition of most of Judah's last kings, who deeply resented Jeremiah's unmitigated bad news. Jeremiah was calling kings to repent for crimes against God that those very kings called "the good life." No wonder Jeremiah struggled. His book is one of the most personal and transparent records in the Bible of a man fully conscious of his calling and deeply troubled by the message God had given him to publicize.

God's mission to the world takes two odd turns in Jeremiah. First, God chose not to deliver Judah from defeat. Defeat is God's judgment for Israel's idolatry, an act expressly forbidden in the Decalogue. To compromise with pagan worship is to deny the core of God's mission. As a result, God allowed Jerusalem to fall.

Second, God provided through Jeremiah the promise of recovery through new life. God promises a day when the Word cast on tablets for Moses on Mount Sinai will be written "on their hearts. I will be their God, and they will be My people" (31:33). The determination of God to see past the present trauma to a day of recovery and even rejoicing is underscored by a great promise that God-followers everywhere have prayed and told to their children: "'For I know the plans I have for you'—this is the LORD's declaration—'plans for your welfare, not for disaster, to give you a future and a hope'" (29:11).

Every person facing stress and struggle must hear Jeremiah's robust call to hope: God's mission does not end in defeat and judgment. It will move on. It will be certified and magnified in the life of One to come. A Branch will sprout from David's line, Jeremiah says. In that Branch, Jesus, will be salvation and safety—good news in hard times.

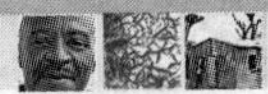

1 The words of Jeremiah,[a] the son of Hilkiah,
one of the priests living in Anathoth[b] in
the territory of Benjamin. 2 The word of the
LORD came to him in the thirteenth year of
the reign of Josiah[c] son of Amon, king of Judah. 3 It also came throughout the days of Jehoiakim[d] son of Josiah, king of Judah, until
the fifth month of the eleventh year of Zedekiah[e] son of Josiah, king of Judah, when the
people of Jerusalem went into exile.

The Call of Jeremiah

4 The word of the LORD came to me:

5 I chose you before I formed you
in the womb;
I set you apart before you were born.[f]
I appointed you a prophet
to the nations.[g]

6 But I protested, "Oh no, Lord GOD! Look,
I don't know how to speak[h] since I am only
a youth."[i]
7 Then the LORD said to me:

Do not say, "I am only a youth,"[j]
for you will go to everyone I send you to
and speak whatever I tell you.[k]
8 Do not be afraid of anyone,[l]
for I will be with you to deliver you.[m]
This is the LORD's declaration.

9 Then the LORD reached out His hand,
touched my mouth,[n] and told me:

I have now filled your mouth
with My words.[o]
10 See, I have appointed you today
over nations and kingdoms
to uproot and tear down,
to destroy and demolish,[p]
to build and plant.[q]

Two Visions

11 Then the word of the LORD came to me,
asking, "What do you see, Jeremiah?"[r]
I replied, "I see a branch of an almond tree."
12 The LORD said to me, "You have seen correctly, for I watch over My word to accomplish it."[s] 13 Again the word of the LORD came
to me inquiring, "What do you see?"
And I replied, "I see a boiling pot,[t] its lip
tilted from the north to the south."

[a] **1:1** 2Ch 35:25; 36:12; Ezr 1:1; Dn 9:2; Mt 2:17; 16:14; 27:9
[b] Jos 21:18; 1Kg 2:26; Jr 32:7
[c] **1:2** 2Kg 21:24; 22:1; Jr 25:3; 36:2; Zph 1:1
[d] **1:3** 2Kg 23:34; 24:2; 1Ch 3:15; Jr 22:18; 25:1; 35:1
[e] 2Kg 24:17-20; 1Ch 3:16; Jr 21:1; 27:1; 39:2
[f] **1:5** 1Sm 1:22; Ps 22:9-10; 139:13-16; Is 44:2; 49:1-6; Lk 1:15; Gl 1:15
[g] Jr 25:15-26
[h] **1:6** Ex 4:10; 1Co 2:1-5
[i] 1Kg 3:7
[j] **1:7** 1Tm 4:12
[k] Dt 18:18; Jr 1:17; Ezk 2:7
[l] **1:8** Ezk 2:6
[m] Gn 26:3; 31:3; Ex 3:12; Is 43:2; Jr 15:20
[n] **1:9** Is 6:7
[o] Is 51:16
[p] **1:10** 2Co 10:4-5
[q] Jr 12:14-17; 18:7,9; 19:7; 24:6; 31:28; Col 2:6-7
[r] **1:11** Jr 24:3; Am 8:2; Zch 4:2
[s] **1:12** Jr 31:28; Php 1:6
[t] **1:13** Ezk 24:3
[u] **1:14** Jr 4:6,20; 6:1; 15:12; 47:2; 50:3,9,41; 51:48
[v] **1:15** Jr 25:9

14 Then the LORD said to me, "Disaster will
be poured out[A] from the north[u] on all who live
in the land. 15 Indeed, I am about to summon
all the clans and kingdoms of the north."[v]
This is the LORD's declaration.

They will come, and each king
will set up his throne
at the entrance to Jerusalem's gates.
They will attack
all her surrounding walls
and all the other cities of Judah.

16 "I will pronounce My judgments against them
for all the evil they did when they abandoned

Prophets Sent

GOD WHO SENDS

The prophets were first and foremost men whom God had sent. The dramatic call and sending of Isaiah is recorded in 6:8: "Whom shall I send, and who will go for us? . . . Here am I! Send me." In God's call to Jeremiah, he said: "all to whom I send you you shall go" (1:7). Haggai 1:12 emphasizes that the people had obeyed the words of the prophet Haggai whom the Lord had sent. Zechariah declared that the Lord had sent him to the nations (2:8), and he repeated this declaration a number of times (2:9; 4:9; 6:15).

The prophets emphasized strongly the fact that God sent his prophets to do his will. Jeremiah spoke a number of times of the fact that God repeatedly and persistently sent his servants the prophets to the people (7:25; 25:4; 26:5; 29:19; 35:15; 44:4). God sent his messengers even though they were not always what they should be (Is 42:19).

(DUBOSE, 46)

[A] **1:14** LXX reads *will boil*

Me to burn incense to other gods and to worship the works of their own hands.[a]
17 "Now, get ready. Stand up and tell them
everything that I command you. Do not be
intimidated by them[b] or I will cause you to
cower before them. 18 Today, I am the One
who has made you a fortified city,[c] an iron
pillar, and bronze walls[d] against the whole
land — against the kings of Judah, its officials, its priests, and the population. 19 They
will fight against you but never prevail over
you,[e] since I am with you to rescue you."[f]

This is the LORD's declaration.

Israel Accused of Apostasy

2 The word of the LORD came to me: 2 "Go
and announce directly to Jerusalem that
this is what the LORD says:

I remember the loyalty of your youth,[g]
your love as a bride —
how you followed Me in the wilderness,
in a land not sown.
3 Israel was holy to the LORD,[h]
the ·firstfruits of His harvest.[i]
All who ate of it found
themselves ·guilty;[j]
disaster came on them."
This is the LORD's declaration.

4 Hear the word of the LORD,
house of Jacob
and all families of the house of Israel.
5 This is what the LORD says:

What fault did your fathers find in Me[k]
that they went so far from Me,
followed worthless idols,[l]
and became worthless themselves?[m]
6 They stopped asking, "Where is
the LORD[n]
who brought us from the land of Egypt,
who led us through the wilderness,[o]
through a land of deserts and ravines,
through a land of drought
and darkness,[A]
a land no one traveled through
and where no one lived?"
7 I brought you to a fertile land[p]
to eat its fruit and bounty,
but after you entered, you defiled
My land;[q]
you made My inheritance[r] detestable.
8 The priests quit asking, "Where is
the LORD?"
The experts in the law no longer
knew Me,[s]
and the rulers[t] rebelled against Me.
The prophets prophesied by[B] ·Baal[u]
and followed useless idols.[v]

9 Therefore, I will bring a case
against you again.
This is the LORD's declaration.
I will bring a case
against your children's children.[w]
10 Cross over to Cyprus[C,x] and take a look.
Send someone to Kedar[y]
and consider carefully;
see if there has ever been
anything like this:
11 Has a nation ever exchanged its gods?[z]
(But they were not gods![aa])
Yet My people have exchanged
their[D] Glory
for useless idols.[ab]
12 Be horrified at this, heavens;[ac]
be shocked and utterly appalled.
This is the LORD's declaration.
13 For My people have committed
a double evil:
They have abandoned Me,[ad]
the fountain of living water,[ae]
and dug cisterns for themselves,
cracked cisterns that cannot
hold water.[af]

Consequences of Apostasy

14 Is Israel a slave?
Was he born into slavery?[E]
Why else has he become a prey?
15 The young lions have roared at him;[ag]
they have roared loudly.
They have laid waste his land.[ah]
His cities are in ruins,
without inhabitants.
16 The men of Memphis and Tahpanhes[ai]
have also broken your skull.
17 Have you not brought this on yourself[aj]
by abandoning the LORD your God
while He was leading you
along the way?

[a] **1:16** Ex 20:3; Is 37:19; 44:15; Ac 7:41 [b] **1:17** Ezk 2:6-7; 1Th 2:2 [c] **1:18-19** Jr 15:20 [d] **1:18** Jr 6:27; Ezk 3:8-9 [e] **1:19** Ps 129:2 [f] Jr 1:6 [g] **2:2** Ezk 16:8,60; Hos 2:15; Rv 2:4 [h] **2:3** Dt 7:6 [i] Jms 1:18 [j] Gn 12:3; Ps 105:14-15; Is 41:11 [k] **2:5** Is 5:4; Mc 6:3 [l] 2Kg 17:15; Jr 2:25; Hs 2:5 [m] Ps 115:8; Hs 9:10; Rm 1:21 [n] **2:6** Jdg 6:13; Jb 35:10 [o] Dt 8:15; 32:10 [p] **2:7** Ex 3:8; Dt 8:7-10; Jr 4:26 [q] Nm 35:33; Ezk 36:17 [r] Jr 16:18 [s] **2:8** Hs 4:6; Mal 2:7; Lk 11:52 [t] Jr 23:1-4; Ezk 34 [u] Jr 2:23; 9:14 [v] Hab 2:8 [w] **2:9** Ex 20:5; Is 3:13; Mc 6:1-8 [x] **2:10** Gn 10:4; Nm 24:24; Is 23:1,12; Am 6:2; Ac 13:4 [y] Ps 120:5 [z] **2:11** Mc 4:5 [aa] Jr 16:20; Gl 4:8 [ab] Ps 106:20; Hs 4:7; Rm 1:23; 1Pt 1:18 [ac] **2:12** Dt 32:1; Is 1:2; Mc 6:1 [ad] **2:13** Jdg 10:13 [ae] Ps 36:9; Jr 17:13; Jn 4:10 [af] Is 55:2; Gl 1:6-7 [ag] **2:15** Is 5:29 [ah] Is 1:7 [ai] **2:16** Jr 44:1; 46:14,19; Ezk 30:13,16,18 [aj] **2:17** Jr 4:18

[A] **2:6** Or *shadow of death* [B] **2:8** = in the name of [C] **2:10** Lit *to the islands of Kittim* [D] **2:11** Ancient Jewish tradition reads *My* [E] **2:14** Lit *born of a house*

18 Now what will you gain
by traveling along the way to Egypt[a]
to drink the waters of the Nile?[A]
What will you gain
by traveling along the way to Assyria[b]
to drink the waters of the Euphrates?[c]
19 Your own evil will discipline you;[d]
your own apostasies
will reprimand you.
Think it over and see how evil
and bitter[e] it is
for you to abandon the LORD your God
and to have no ·fear of Me.
This is the declaration
of the Lord GOD of ·Hosts.

20 For long ago I[B] broke your yoke;[f]
I[B] tore off your chains.
You insisted, "I will not serve!"
On every high hill
and under every green tree[g]
you lie down like a prostitute.[h]

21 I planted you, a choice vine[i]
from the very best seed.
How then could you turn into
a degenerate, foreign vine?[j]

22 Even if you wash with lye
and use a great amount of soap,[k]
the stain of your sin is still
in front of Me.[l]
This is the Lord GOD's declaration.

23 How can you protest, "I am not defiled;
I have not followed the Baals"?[m]
Look at your behavior in the valley;
acknowledge what you have done.[n]
You are a swift young camel
twisting and turning on her way,
24 a wild donkey[o] at home[C]
in the wilderness.
She sniffs the wind in the heat
of her desire.
Who can control her passion?
All who look for her will not
become tired;
they will find her
in her mating season.[D]
25 Keep your feet from going bare
and your throat from thirst.
But you say, "It's hopeless;[p]
I love strangers,[q]
and I will continue to follow them."

26 Like the shame of a thief
when he is caught,
so the house of Israel has been
put to shame.[r]
They, their kings, their officials,
their priests, and their prophets[s]
27 say to a tree, "You are my father,"
and to a stone, "You gave birth to me."
For they have turned their back to Me
and not their face,[t]
yet in their time of disaster[u] they beg,
"Rise up and save us!"
28 But where are your gods you made
for yourself?
Let them rise up and save you[v]
in your time of disaster if they can,
for your gods are as numerous
as your cities, Judah.

Judgment Deserved

29 Why do you bring a case against Me?[w]
All of you have rebelled against Me.
This is the LORD's declaration.

30 I have struck down your children
in vain;
they would not accept discipline.[x]
Your own sword has devoured
your prophets[y]
like a ravaging lion.
31 Evil generation,
pay attention to the word of the LORD!
Have I been a wilderness to Israel
or a land of dense darkness?[z]
Why do My people claim,
"We will go where we want;[E]
we will no longer come to You"?
32 Can a young woman forget her jewelry[aa]
or a bride her wedding sash?
Yet My people have forgotten Me[ab]
for countless days.
33 How skillfully you pursue love;
you also teach evil women your ways.
34 Moreover, your skirts are stained
with the blood of the innocent poor.[ac]
You did not catch them breaking
and entering.[ad]
But in spite of all these things

[a]**2:18** Is 30:1-2; 31:1 [b]Hs 7:11 [c]Is 8:7 [d]**2:19** Is 3:9; Hs 5:5 [e]Jr 4:18 [f]**2:20** Lv 26:13; Is 10:27; Nah 1:13 [g]Dt 12:2; 1Kg 14:23; 2Kg 17:10; Is 57:5; Jr 3:6; Ezk 6:13; Hs 4:13 [h]Ezk 16:28; Hs 2:5 [i]**2:21** Gn 49:11; Ps 80:8; Is 5:2 [j]Is 5:4 [k]**2:22** Ps 51:2,7; Mal 3:2; Eph 5:26 [l]Ps 90:8 [m]**2:23** Jr 2:8; 9:14 [n]Gn 3:13; 1Sm 15:13; Pr 28:13; Jr 3:13; 1Jn 1:8 [o]**2:24** Jb 39:5; Hs 8:9 [p]**2:25** Jr 18:12 [q]Dt 32:16; Jr 3:13 [r]**2:26** Jr 2:36; 6:15; 8:9,12; Rm 6:21 [s]Ezr 9:7 [t]**2:27** 2Ch 29:6; Jr 18:17; 32:33; Ezk 8:16 [u]Jdg 10:9-10; Is 26:16 [v]**2:28** Dt 32:37-38; Jdg 10:14; Is 45:20 [w]**2:29** Jr 2:9 [x]**2:30** Pr 3:11; Is 1:5; 9:13; Jr 5:3; 17:23; 32:33; Am 4:10 [y]Mt 23:34 [z]**2:31** Jr 50:12; Hs 2:3 [aa]**2:32** Is 61:10 [ab]Ps 106:21; Jr 13:25; 18:15; Ezk 22:12; 23:35; Hs 8:14 [ac]**2:34** 2Kg 21:16; 24:4; Ps 106:38; Jr 19:4; 22:3,17 [ad]Ex 22:2

[A]**2:18** Lit *of Shihor* [B]**2:20** LXX reads *you* [C]**2:24** Lit *donkey taught* [D]**2:24** Lit *her month* [E]**2:31** Or *We have taken control*, or *We can roam*

35 you claim, "I am innocent.[a]
His anger is sure to turn away
from me."
But I will certainly judge you
because you have said, "I have
not sinned."[b]
36 How unstable you are,[c]
constantly changing your ways!
You will be put to shame by Egypt[d]
just as you were put to shame
by Assyria.
37 Moreover, you will be led out
from here
with your hands on your head[e]
since the LORD has rejected
those you trust;[f]
you will not succeed even with
their help.[A]

Wages of Apostasy

3 If[B] a man divorces his wife
and she leaves him to marry another,
can he ever return to her?[g]
Wouldn't such a land[C] become
totally defiled?
But you!
You have played the prostitute
with many partners[h] —
can you return to Me?[i]
This is the LORD's declaration.
2 Look to the barren heights[j] and see.
Where have you not been immoral?
You sat waiting for them
beside the highways[k]
like a nomad in the desert.
You have defiled the land
with your prostitution and wickedness.[l]
3 This is why the showers
haven't come[m] —
why there has been no spring rain.
You have the brazen look[n]
of a prostitute[D]
and refuse to be ashamed.[o]
4 Have you not lately called to Me,
"My Father.[p]
You were my friend in my youth.[q]
5 Will He bear a grudge forever?[r]
Will He be endlessly infuriated?"
This is what you have said,
but you have done the evil things
you are capable of.

Unfaithful Israel, Treacherous Judah

6 In the days of King Josiah the LORD asked
me, "Have you seen what unfaithful Israel has
done? She has ascended every high hill and
gone under every green tree to prostitute herself there.[s] 7 I thought: After she has done all
these things, she will return to Me.[t] But she
didn't return, and her treacherous sister Judah[u] saw it. 8 I[E] observed that it was because
unfaithful Israel had committed adultery
that I had sent her away and had given her
a certificate of divorce.[v] Nevertheless, her
treacherous sister Judah was not afraid but
also went and prostituted herself.[w] 9 Indifferent to[F] her prostitution, she defiled the land
and committed adultery with stones[x] and
trees.[y] 10 Yet in spite of all this, her treacherous sister Judah didn't return to Me with all
her heart[z] — only in pretense."
This is the LORD's declaration.
11 The LORD announced to me, "Unfaithful
Israel has shown herself more righteous than
treacherous Judah.[aa] 12 Go, proclaim these
words to the north, and say:

Return, unfaithful Israel.[ab]
This is the LORD's declaration.
I will not look on you with anger,[G]
for I am unfailing in My love.[ac]
This is the LORD's declaration.
I will not be angry forever.[ad]
13 Only acknowledge your ·guilt[ae] —
you have rebelled against the LORD
your God.[af]
You have scattered your favors
to strangers
under every green tree[ag]
and have not obeyed My voice.
This is the LORD's declaration.

14 "Return, you faithless children"[ah] — this
is the LORD's declaration — "for I am your
master,[ai] and I will take you,[aj] one from a
city and two from a family, and I will bring
you to ·Zion. 15 I will give you shepherds who
are loyal to Me,[H,ak] and they will shepherd
you with knowledge and skill. 16 When you

[a] **2:35** Jb 33:9 [b] Pr 28:13; 1Jn 1:8,10 [c] **2:36** Jms 1:8 [d] Is 30:3 [e] **2:37** 2Sm 13:19 [f] 1Sm 15:23,26; 2Kg 17:20; Jr 7:29 [g] **3:1** Dt 24:1-4 [h] Ezk 16:26,28 [i] Hs 2:7 [j] **3:2** Dt 12:2; Ezk 16:52 [k] Gn 38:14; Pr 7:10-12; Ezk 16:25 [l] Nm 14:33 [m] **3:3** Zch 14:7 [n] Ezk 3:7-8 [o] Jr 6:15; 8:12 [p] **3:4** Ex 4:22; Is 1:2; 64:8; Hs 11:1; Gl 4:6 [q] Ps 71:17; Hs 2:15 [r] **3:5** Lv 19:18; Ps 103:9; Is 57:16; Nah 1:2 [s] **3:6** Jr 2:20 [t] **3:7** Hs 14:1 [u] Ezk 16:46 [v] **3:8** Dt 24:1-4; Is 50:1; Hs 2:2 [w] Ezk 23:11 [x] **3:9** Is 57:6 [y] Dt 28:36; Jr 2:27; Ezk 20:32; Hab 2:19; Rv 9:20 [z] **3:10** Hs 7:14 [aa] **3:11** Ezk 16:51-52; 23:11 [ab] **3:12** Pr 28:13 [ac] Ps 86:5; 145:17 [ad] Ps 103:9; Is 57:16; Mc 7:18 [ae] **3:13** Lv 26:40; 1Jn 1:9 [af] 2Kg 18:20; Is 36:5; Jr 2:29 [ag] Dt 12:2; 2Kg 16:4; 2Ch 28:4; Is 57:5; Jr 2:20; 3:6,13; Ezk 20:47 [ah] **3:14** Hs 14:1 [ai] Hs 2:16-17 [aj] Hs 2:19-20 [ak] **3:15** 1Sm 13:14; Jr 23:4; Ezk 34:23; Ac 20:28; Eph 4:11

[A] **2:37** Lit *with them* [B] **3:1** One Hb ms, LXX, Syr; other Hb mss read *Saying: If* [C] **3:1** LXX reads *woman* [D] **3:3** Lit *have a prostitute's forehead* [E] **3:8** One Hb ms, Syr read *She* [F] **3:9** Lit *From the lightness of* [G] **3:12** Lit *not cause My face to fall on you* [H] **3:15** Lit *shepherds according to My heart*

multiply and increase in the land,[a] in those
days" — the LORD's declaration — "no one
will say any longer, 'The ark of the LORD's
covenant.'[b] It will never come to mind, and
no one will remember or miss it. It will never
again be made. 17 At that time Jerusalem will
be called, ·Yahweh's Throne,[c] and all the nations will be gathered to it,[d] to the name of
Yahweh in Jerusalem.[e] They will cease to follow the stubbornness of their evil hearts. 18 In
those days the house of Judah will join with
the house of Israel,[f] and they will come together from the land of the north to the land
I have given your ancestors to inherit."[g]

True Repentance

19 I thought: How I long to make you
My sons
and give you a desirable land,
the most beautiful inheritance[h] of all
the nations.
I thought: You will call Me, my Father,
and never turn away from Me.
20 However, as a woman may betray
her lover,[A]
so you have betrayed[i] Me,
house of Israel.
This is the LORD's declaration.

21 A sound is heard on the barren heights,
the children of Israel weeping
and begging for mercy,
for they have perverted their way;
they have forgotten the LORD
their God.[j]
22 Return, you faithless children.
I will heal your unfaithfulness.[k]
"Here we are, coming to You,
for You are the LORD our God.
23 Surely, falsehood comes from the hills,
commotion from the mountains,[l]
but the salvation of Israel
is only in the LORD our God.[m]
24 From the time of our youth
the shameful one[B] has consumed
what our fathers have worked for —
their flocks and their herds,
their sons and their daughters.
25 Let us lie down in our shame;
let our disgrace cover us.[n]
We have sinned against the LORD
our God,[o]
both we and our fathers,
from the time of our youth
even to this day.[p]
We have not obeyed the voice
of the LORD our God."

Blessing or Curse

4 If you return,[C] Israel —
this is the LORD's declaration —
you will return to Me,[q]
if you remove your detestable idols[r]
from My presence
and do not waver,
2 then you can swear, "As the LORD lives,"[s]
in truth,[t] in justice,
and in righteousness,[u]
then the nations will be blessed[D]
by Him[v]
and will pride themselves in Him.[w]

3 For this is what the LORD says to the men
of Judah and Jerusalem:

Break up the unplowed ground;[x]
do not sow among the thorns.[y]
4 Circumcise yourselves to the LORD;
remove the foreskin of your hearts,[z]
men of Judah and residents
of Jerusalem.
Otherwise, My wrath will break out
like fire
and burn with no one to extinguish it[aa]
because of your evil deeds.

Judgment from the North

5 Declare in Judah, proclaim in Jerusalem,
and say:

Blow the ram's horn
throughout the land.[ab]
Cry out loudly and say:
Assemble yourselves,
and let's flee to the fortified cities.
6 Lift up a signal flag toward ·Zion.[ac]
Run for cover! Don't stand still!
For I am bringing disaster
from the north —
a great destruction.[ad]
7 A lion has gone up from his thicket;[ae]

[a] **3:16** Gn 1:28; Ex 1:12
[b] Ex 37:1-9; Dt 31:24-29; 1Kg 8:6
[c] **3:17** Ezk 43:7; Rv 22:1,3
[d] Is 2:2-4; 43:9; 56:6-7; 66:18; Jr 16:19
[e] Dt 12:5
[f] **3:18** Is 11:12-13; Jr 50:4-5; Ezk 37:15-22; Hs 11:1
[g] Am 9:15
[h] **3:19** Dt 32:8-9; Ps 16:6; Lm 2:15; Ezk 20:6,15
[i] **3:20** Ex 21:8-9; Is 48:8; Hs 1:2; 5:7; 6:7
[j] **3:21** Is 17:10
[k] **3:22** Is 57:18; Hs 5:15–6:3; 14:1-3
[l] **3:23** Ps 121:1-2
[m] Ps 3:8; Jr 17:5-8
[n] **3:25** Jb 8:22; Ezr 9:6
[o] Is 64:5; Jr 8:14; 14:7,20; Lm 3:42; 5:16; Dn 9:5
[p] Ezr 9:7; Ezk 2:3
[q] **4:1** Zch 1:3
[r] Jr 7:30; 16:18; 32:34
[s] **4:2** Dt 6:13; 10:20; Jr 5:2
[t] Is 65:16
[u] Hs 2:19
[v] Gn 26:3-4
[w] Gn 12:1-3; 18:18; 22:18; 1Co 1:31
[x] **4:3** Hs 10:12
[y] Mt 13:7
[z] **4:4** Gn 17:14; Dt 10:16; Jr 9:25; Rm 2:28-29
[aa] Is 1:31; Jr 21:12; Am 5:6; Mal 4:1
[ab] **4:5** Jr 6:1; Hs 5:8; Jl 2:1; 1Th 4:16-17
[ac] **4:6** Is 62:10
[ad] Is 14:31; 41:25; Jr 1:13; 4:20; 6:1; 15:12; 47:2; 50:3,9,41; 51:48; Ezk 26:7
[ae] **4:7** Ps 10:9; 17:12; Is 5:29; Jr 2:15; 5:6; 25:38; 49:19; 50:17,44

[A] **3:20** Lit *friend* [B] **3:24** = Baal [C] **4:1** Or *Repent* [D] **4:2** Or *will bless themselves*

a destroyer of nations has set out.
He has left his lair
to make your land a waste.
Your cities will be reduced
to uninhabited ruins.[a]
8 Because of this, put on *sackcloth;
mourn and wail,[b]
for the LORD's burning anger[c]
has not turned away from us.

9"On that day" — this is the LORD's declaration — "the king and the officials will lose
their courage. The priests will tremble in fear,
and the prophets will be scared speechless."
10I said, "Oh no, Lord GOD, You have certainly deceived[d] this people and Jerusalem,
by announcing, 'You will have peace,'[e] while
a sword is at[A] our throats."
11"At that time it will be said to this people
and to Jerusalem, 'A searing wind[f] blows from
the barren heights in the wilderness on the
way to My dear[B] people. It comes not to winnow or to sift; 12a wind too strong for this
comes at My call.[C] Now I will also pronounce
judgments against them.'"[g]

13 Look, he advances like clouds;[h]
his chariots are like a storm.[i]
His horses are swifter than eagles.[j]
Woe to us, for we are ruined![k]
14 Wash the evil
from your heart,[l] Jerusalem,
so that you will be delivered.
How long will you harbor
malicious thoughts within you?[m]
15 For a voice announces from Dan,
proclaiming malice
from Mount Ephraim.
16 Warn the nations: Look!
Proclaim to Jerusalem:
Those who besiege are coming
from a distant land;[n]
they raise their voices
against the cities of Judah.
17 They have her surrounded[o]
like those who guard a field,
because she has rebelled
against Me.[p]
This is the LORD's declaration.
18 Your way of life and your actions
have brought this on you.[q]
This is your punishment. It is
very bitter,
because it has reached your heart!

Jeremiah's Lament

19 My anguish, my anguish![D] I writhe
in agony!
Oh, the pain in[E] my heart![r]
My heart pounds;
I cannot be silent.
For you, my soul,
have heard the sound
of the ram's horn —
the shout of battle.
20 Disaster after disaster[s] is reported
because the whole land is destroyed.
Suddenly my tents are destroyed,
my tent curtains, in a moment.
21 How long must I see the signal flag
and hear the sound
of the ram's horn?

22 "For My people are fools;
they do not know Me.
They are foolish children,
without understanding.[t]
They are skilled in doing what is evil,
but they do not know how to do
what is good."[u]

23 I looked at the earth,
and it was formless and empty.[v]
I looked to the heavens,
and their light was gone.[w]
24 I looked at the mountains,
and they were quaking;[x]
all the hills shook.
25 I looked, and no man was left;[y]
all the birds of the sky had fled.[z]
26 I looked, and the fertile field[aa]
was a wilderness.[ab]
All its cities were torn down
because of the LORD
and His burning anger.[ac]

27For this is what the LORD says:

The whole land will be a desolation,[ad]
but I will not finish it off.[ae]
28 Because of this, the earth will mourn;[af]
the skies above will grow dark.[ag]
I have spoken; I have planned,

[a]**4:7** Is 1:7; 6:11 [b]**4:8** Jl 1:13 [c]Nm 25:4; Ps 78:49 [d]**4:10** 1Kg 22:22; Ezk 14:9; 2Th 2:11 [e]Jr 6:14; 23:17 [f]**4:11** Ezk 17:10 [g]**4:12** Jr 1:16; Ezk 5:8 [h]**4:13** Rv 1:7 [i]Is 5:28; 66:15 [j]2Sm 1:23; Jb 9:26; Lm 4:19 [k]Lm 5:16 [l]**4:14** Ps 51:2,7; Is 1:16; Jr 2:22; Ti 3:5; Jms 4:8 [m]Ps 119:113 [n]**4:16** Is 39:3 [o]**4:17** 2Kg 25:1-4 [p]Is 1:20 [q]**4:18** Ps 107:17; Pr 1:31; Jr 7:3,5; 17:10; 18:11; 23:22; 25:5; 26:3,13; 32:19; Hs 4:9; 12:2; Zch 1:4,6 [r]**4:19** Is 16:11; Hab 3:16; Rm 9:1-2 [s]**4:20** Ezk 7:26 [t]**4:22** Ps 82:5; Is 1:3 [u]Rm 16:19 [v]**4:23** Gn 1:2; Jb 26:7; Is 45:18 [w]Is 5:30; 13:10 [x]**4:24** Jdg 5:5; Ps 46:1-3 [y]**4:25** Gn 2:5 [z]Zph 1:3 [aa]**4:26** Jr 2:7 [ab]Ps 107:34 [ac]Ps 76:7 [ad]**4:27** Is 6:11 [ae]Neh 9:31; Jr 5:10,18; Rm 11:1-7 [af]**4:28** Jr 8:13; 14:2; Hs 4:3 [ag]Ps 105:28; Is 13:10; 50:3; Ezk 30:18

[A]**4:10** Lit *sword touches* [B]**4:11** Lit *to the daughter of My* [C]**4:12** Lit *comes for Me* [D]**4:19** Lit *My inner parts, my inner parts* [E]**4:19** Lit *the walls of*

and I will not relent or turn back
from it.[a]
29 Every city flees[b]
at the sound of the horseman
and the archer.
They enter the thickets
and climb among the rocks.[c]
Every city is abandoned;
no inhabitant is left.
30 And you, devastated one, what are
you doing[d]
that you dress yourself in scarlet,
that you adorn yourself
with gold jewelry,
that you enlarge your eyes with paint?[e]
You beautify yourself for nothing.
Your lovers reject you;[f]
they want to take your life.[g]
31 I hear a cry like a woman in labor,[h]
a cry of anguish like one bearing
her first child.
The cry of Daughter Zion
gasping for breath,
stretching out her hands:[i]
Woe is me, for my life is weary
because of the murderers!

The Depravity of Jerusalem

5 Roam[j] through the streets of Jerusalem.
Look and take note;
search in her squares.
If you find one person,[k]
any who acts justly,
who seeks to be faithful,
then I will forgive her.[l]
2 When they say, "As the LORD lives,"[m]
they are swearing falsely.[n]
3 LORD, don't Your eyes
look for faithfulness?[o]
You have struck them, but they felt
no pain.[p]
You finished them off,
but they refused to accept discipline.[q]
They made their faces harder than rock,[r]
and they refused to return.[s]

4 Then I thought:

They are just the poor;
they have played the fool.
For they don't understand the way
of the LORD,[t]
the justice of their God.[u]
5 I will go to the powerful
and speak to them.
Surely they know the way of the LORD,
the justice of their God.[v]
However, these also had broken
the yoke
and torn off the chains.[w]
6 Therefore, a lion from the forest
will strike them down.[x]
A wolf from an arid plain
will ravage them.
A leopard[y] keeps watch over their cities.
Anyone who leaves them will be torn
to pieces
because their rebellious acts are many,[z]
their unfaithful deeds numerous.[aa]

7 Why should I forgive you?
Your children have abandoned Me
and sworn by those who are not gods.[ab]
I satisfied their needs, yet they
committed adultery;[ac]
they gashed themselves[ad]
at the[A] prostitute's house.
8 They are well-fed,[B] eager[C] stallions,[ae]
each neighing[af] after
someone else's wife.[ag]
9 Should I not punish them
for these things?[ah]
This is the LORD's declaration.
Should I not avenge Myself[ai]
on such a nation as this?

10 Go up among her vineyard terraces
and destroy them,[aj]
but do not finish them off.[ak]
Prune away her shoots,
for they do not belong to the LORD.[al]
11 They, the house of Israel and the house
of Judah,
have dealt very treacherously with Me.[am]
This is the LORD's declaration.
12 They have contradicted the LORD
and insisted, "It won't happen.[D,an]
Harm won't come to us;
we won't see sword or famine."
13 The prophets become only wind,

[a] **4:28** Nm 23:19; Is 46:11; 48:15; Ezk 37:14
[b] **4:29** 2Kg 25:4
[c] Is 2:19-21
[d] **4:30** Is 10:3
[e] 2Kg 9:30
[f] Jr 30:14; Lm 1:19
[g] Ezk 23:9-10,22
[h] **4:31** Ps 48:6; Is 13:8; 21:3; 42:14; Jr 6:24; 13:21; 22:23; 30:6; 50:43; Mc 4:9-10; 1Th 5:3
[i] Is 1:15
[j] **5:1** 2Ch 16:9
[k] Ps 14:1-3; Ezk 22:30; Rm 3:10
[l] Gn 18:26-32
[m] **5:2** Jr 4:2
[n] Lv 19:12; Is 48:1; Jr 7:9
[o] **5:3** 2Ch 16:9; Ps 51:6
[p] Pr 23:35
[q] Pr 27:22
[r] Ezk 3:7-9
[s] Hs 11:5
[t] **5:4** Gn 18:19; 2Kg 17:26; 21:22; Ps 95:10; Jr 8:7; Hs 4:6
[u] Mc 3:1
[v] **5:5** Ps 103:7
[w] Ps 2:3; Jr 2:20
[x] **5:6** 2Kg 17:26; Jr 4:7; 25:38
[y] Hs 13:7; Rv 13:2
[z] Is 59:12
[aa] Jr 3:6,8,11-12,22; 14:7; 30:15; Am 5:12
[ab] **5:7** Dt 32:21; Jos 23:7; Gl 4:8
[ac] Hs 4:10
[ad] 1Kg 18:24
[ae] **5:8** Ezk 23:20
[af] Jr 13:27
[ag] Ex 20:14; Ezk 22:11
[ah] **5:9** Jr 5:29; 8:10; 9:9
[ai] Dt 32:35; Heb 10:30
[aj] **5:10** 2Kg 24:2
[ak] Jr 4:27
[al] Hs 1:9
[am] **5:11** Is 21:2; 24:16; 48:8; Hs 6:7
[an] **5:12** Is 28:15; Jr 23:17

[A] **5:7** Or *adultery and trooped to the*, or *adultery and lodged at the*; Hb obscure
[B] **5:8** Lit *well-equipped*; Hb obscure [C] **5:8** Lit *early-rising*; Hb obscure
[D] **5:12** Lit *He does not exist*

for the LORD's word is not in them.
This will in fact happen to them.

Coming Judgment

14 Therefore, this is what the Lord GOD of
•Hosts says:

Because you have spoken this word,
I am going to make My words
become fire in your mouth.[a]
These people are the wood,
and the fire will consume them.[b]
15 I am about to bring a nation
from far away against you,[c]
house of Israel.
This is the LORD's declaration.
It is an established nation,
an ancient nation,
a nation whose language
you do not know
and whose speech
you do not understand.[d]
16 Their quiver is like an open grave;[e]
they are all mighty warriors.
17 They will consume your harvest
and your food.[f]
They will consume your sons
and your daughters.
They will consume your flocks
and your herds.
They will consume your vines
and your fig trees.
They will destroy with the sword
your fortified cities[g] in which you trust.

18 "But even in those days"—this is the
LORD's declaration—"I will not finish you
off.[h] 19 When people ask, 'For what offense
has the LORD our God done all these things
to us?' You will respond to them: Just as you
abandoned Me[i] and served foreign gods in
your land, so will you serve strangers in a
land that is not yours.[j]
20 "Declare this in the house of Jacob; proclaim it in Judah, saying:

21 Hear this,
you foolish and senseless[A] people.[k]
They have eyes, but they don't see.
They have ears, but they don't hear.[l]
22 Do you not •fear Me?
This is the LORD's declaration.

[a] **5:14** Hs 6:5; Rv 11:5
[b] Zch 12:6
[c] **5:15** Is 10:3; 13:5; 30:27; Jr 4:16
[d] Dt 28:49; Is 28:11; 33:19; 1Co 14:21
[e] **5:16** Ps 5:9; Rm 3:13
[f] **5:17** Lv 26:16; Dt 28:31,33,51
[g] Hs 8:14
[h] **5:18** 2Ch 12:12; Jr 4:27; 5:10; 30:11; Ezk 11:13; 20:17; Rm 11:1-5
[i] **5:19** Dt 28:20; 29:24-25; 31:16; Jdg 2:12; 1Sm 8:8; 1Kg 9:8-9; Is 1:4,28; Jr 1:16; 2:13,17,19; 16:11; 17:13
[j] Dt 4:27-28; 28:47-48
[k] **5:21** Dt 32:6
[l] Ps 115:5-6; 135:16-17; Is 6:9; 42:20; Ezk 12:2; Mt 13:14; Mk 8:18
[m] **5:22** Jb 26:10; 38:10-11; Ps 104:9; Pr 8:29
[n] **5:23** Dt 21:18,20; Ps 78:8; Is 1:5; Heb 3:12
[o] **5:24** Pr 9:10; Hs 6:1
[p] Mt 5:45
[q] Jl 2:23
[r] Dt 11:14
[s] **5:25** Is 59:2
[t] **5:26** Pr 1:11
[u] Ps 10:9
[v] **5:27** Ps 10:7; 50:19; Is 3:14; 5:18; 30:12; Jr 8:5; Zph 1:9; Ac 13:10; Rm 1:29
[w] **5:28** Dt 32:15
[x] Deut 24:14; Jb 29:16; 30:25; 31:19; Ps 82:3-4; 140:12; Pr 14:31; 31:9; Is 1:23; Zch 7:10; Ac 4:34
[y] **5:29** Jr 5:9; 8:19; Heb 10:30
[z] **5:30** Hs 6:10
[aa] **5:31** Jr 6:13; 8:10; 14:14; 20:6; 23:14,25,26,32; 27:10,14-16; 28:15; 29:9,21,31; Lm 2:14; Zch 13:3
[ab] Dt 32:29; Is 10:3

Do you not tremble before Me,
the One who set the sand
as the boundary of the sea,
an enduring barrier that
it cannot cross?[m]
The waves surge, but they
cannot prevail.
They roar but cannot pass over it.
23 But these people have stubborn
and rebellious hearts.[n]
They have turned aside
and have gone away.
24 They have not said to themselves,
'Let's fear the LORD our God,[o]
who gives the rain,[p] both early
and late,[q] in its season,[r]
who guarantees to us the fixed weeks
of the harvest.'
25 Your •guilty acts have diverted
these things from you.
Your sins have withheld My bounty
from you,[s]
26 for wicked men live among My people.
They watch like fowlers lying in wait.[B,t]
They set a trap;[u]
they catch men.
27 Like a cage full of birds,
so their houses are full of deceit.[v]
Therefore they have grown powerful
and rich.
28 They have become fat[w] and sleek.
They have also excelled in evil matters.
They have not taken up cases,
such as the case of the fatherless,
so they might prosper,
and they have not defended the rights
of the needy.[x]
29 Should I not punish them
for these things?
This is the LORD's declaration.
Should I not avenge Myself[y]
on such a nation as this?
30 A horrible, terrible thing
has taken place in the land.[z]
31 The prophets prophesy falsely,[aa]
and the priests rule
by their own authority.
My people love it like this.
But what will you do at the end of it?[ab]

[A] **5:21** Lit *without heart* [B] **5:26** Hb obscure

Threatened Siege of Jerusalem

6 "Run for cover,[a] Benjaminites,
out of Jerusalem!
Sound the ram's horn[b] in Tekoa;[c]
raise a smoke signal[d]
over Beth-haccherem,[A]
for disaster threatens from the north,[e]
even great destruction.
2 Though she is beautiful and delicate,
I will destroy[B] Daughter ·Zion.
3 Shepherds and their flocks will come
against her;
they will pitch their tents
all around her.[f]
Each will pasture his own portion.
4 Set them apart for war[g] against her;
rise up, let's attack at noon.
Woe to us, for the day is passing;
the evening shadows grow long.
5 Rise up, let's attack by night.
Let us destroy her fortresses."

6 For this is what the LORD of ·Hosts says:

Cut down the trees;[h]
raise a siege ramp against Jerusalem.
This city must be punished.
There is nothing but oppression
within her.[i]
7 As a well gushes out its water,
so she pours out her evil.[C]
Violence and destruction[j] resound
in her.
Sickness and wounds keep coming
to My attention.
8 Be warned, Jerusalem,
or I will turn away from you;[k]
I will make you a desolation,
a land without inhabitants.[l]

Wrath on Israel

9 This is what the LORD of Hosts says:

Glean the remnant of Israel[m]
as thoroughly as a vine.
Pass your hand once more
like a grape gatherer
over the branches.

10 Who can I speak to and give
such a warning[D]
that they will listen?
Look, their ear is uncircumcised,[E,n]
so they cannot pay attention.
See, the word of the LORD
has become contemptible to them —
they find no pleasure in it.[o]
11 But I am full of the LORD's wrath;
I am tired of holding it back.[p]
Pour it out on the children
in the street,[q]
on the gang of young men as well.
For both husband and wife
will be captured,
the old with the very old.[F]
12 Their houses will be turned over
to others,[r]
their fields and wives as well,
for I will stretch out My hand[s]
against the inhabitants of the land.
This is the LORD's declaration.

13 For from the least to the greatest
of them,[t]
everyone is making
profit dishonestly.[u]
From prophet to priest,
everyone deals falsely.[v]
14 They have treated
My people's brokenness superficially,
claiming, "Peace, peace,"[w]
when there is no peace.
15 Were they ashamed when they acted
so abhorrently?
They weren't at all ashamed.
They can no longer feel humiliation.[x]
Therefore, they will fall
among the fallen.
When I punish them,
they will collapse,[y]
says the LORD.

Disaster because of Disobedience

16 This is what the LORD says:

Stand by the roadways and look.
Ask about the ancient paths:[z]
Which is the way to what is good?
Then take it
and find rest for yourselves.[aa]
But they protested, "We won't!"
17 I appointed watchmen over you[ab]

[a]**6:1** Ex 9:19; Is 10:31; Jr 4:6 [b]Jr 4:5; 51:27; Am 3:6 [c]2Sm 14:2; 2Ch 11:6; 20:20 [d]Jdg 20:38,40; Neh 3:14 [e]Jr 1:13; 4:6,20; 6:22; 15:12; 47:2; 50:3,9,41; 51:48 [f]**6:3** Jr 4:17 [g]**6:4** Jr 51:27; Mc 3:5 [h]**6:6** Dt 20:19-20 [i]Is 30:12; 59:9-15; Jr 22:17; Ezk 22:7,12,29; Am 3:9; Hab 1:3 [j]**6:7** Jr 20:8; Am 3:10; Hab 1:3 [k]**6:8** Ezk 23:18; Hs 9:12 [l]Jr 9:11; 25:9; 29:18; 34:22; Ezk 30:12 [m]**6:9** Is 10:20; Jr 31:7; Ezk 9:8; 11:13; Mc 2:12; Zph 3:13 [n]**6:10** Lv 26:41; Jr 9:26; Ezk 44:7,9 [o]1Sm 15:23; Jr 8:9 [p]**6:11** Jr 20:9; Hs 5:10 [q]Jr 9:21 [r]**6:12** Jr 8:10-12 [s]Ex 3:20; Jr 15:6; Ezk 6:14; 14:13; 25:7; Zph 1:4 [t]**6:13** Est 1:20; Jr 8:10; 31:34; 42:1,8; 44:12 [u]Pr 1:19; 15:27; Hab 2:9 [v]Jr 5:31; 8:10; 14:14; 20:6; 23:14,25,26,32; 27:10,14-16; 28:15; 29:9,21,31; Lm 2:14; Zch 13:3 [w]**6:14** 1Ch 12:18; Is 57:19 [x]**6:15** Jr 3:3; 8:12 [y]**6:13-15** Jr 8:10-12 [z]**6:16** Is 59:8; Jr 18:15; Jb 24:13; Pr 8:20; 12:28 [aa]Mt 11:29 [ab]**6:17** Is 21:11; 58:1; Hs 9:8

[A]**6:1** = House of the Vineyard [B]**6:2** Or *silence* [C]**6:7** Or *well keeps its water fresh, so she keeps her evil fresh* [D]**6:10** Or *and bear witness* [E]**6:10** They are unresponsive to God. [F]**6:11** Lit *with fullness of days*

and said: Listen for the sound
of the ram's horn.
But they protested, "We won't listen!"
18 Therefore listen, you nations
and you witnesses,
learn what the charge is against them.
19 Listen, earth!
I am about to bring disaster
on these people,
the fruit of their own plotting,[a]
for they have paid no attention
to My word.
They have rejected My instruction.[b]
20 What use to Me is frankincense
from Sheba[c]
or sweet cane[d] from a distant land?
Your •burnt offerings
are not acceptable;
your sacrifices do not please Me.[e]
21 Therefore, this is what the LORD says:
I am going to place stumbling blocks
before these people;
fathers and sons together will stumble
over them;[f]
friends and neighbors will also perish.

A Cruel Nation from the North

22 This is what the LORD says:

Look, an army is coming
from a northern land;[g]
a great nation will be awakened
from the remote regions of the earth.[h]
23 They grasp bow and javelin.
They are cruel and show no mercy.[i]
Their voice roars like the sea,[j]
and they ride on horses,
lined up like men in battle formation
against you, Daughter Zion.

24 We have heard about it,
and we are discouraged.[A]
Distress has seized us —
pain like a woman in[k] labor.[l]
25 Don't go out to the fields;
don't walk on the road.
For the enemy has a sword;
terror is on every side.[m]
26 My dear[B] people, dress yourselves
in •sackcloth
and roll in the dust.[n]
Mourn as you would for an only son,[o]
a bitter lament,
for suddenly the destroyer[p] will come
on us.[q]

Jeremiah Appointed as an Examiner

27 I have appointed you to be an assayer
among My people —
a refiner[C] —
so you may know and assay their way
of life.[r]
28 All are stubborn rebels
spreading slander.[s]
They are bronze and iron;
all of them are corrupt.[t]
29 The bellows blow,
blasting the lead with fire.
The refining is completely in vain;
the evil ones are not separated out.
30 They are called rejected silver,
for the LORD has rejected them.[u]

False Trust in the Temple

7 This is the word that came to Jeremiah
from the LORD: 2 "Stand in the gate of the
house of the LORD[v] and there call out this
word: Hear the word of the LORD, all you people of Judah who enter through these gates to
worship the LORD.
3 "This is what the LORD of •Hosts, the God
of Israel, says: Correct your ways and your
deeds,[w] and I will allow you to live in this
place. 4 Do not trust deceitful words, chanting: This is the temple of the LORD, the temple
of the LORD, the temple of the LORD. 5 Instead,
if you really change your ways and your actions, if you act justly toward one another,[D,x]
6 if you no longer oppress the foreigner, the
fatherless, and the widow[y] and no longer
shed innocent blood in this place or follow
other gods, bringing harm on yourselves, 7 I
will allow you to live in this place, the land
I gave to your ancestors[z] long ago and forever. 8 But look, you keep trusting in deceitful
words that cannot help.
9 "Do you steal, murder, commit adultery,
swear falsely, burn incense to •Baal, and follow other gods that you have not known?[aa]
10 Then do you come and stand before Me in

[a] **6:19** Pr 1:31 [b] Is 5:24; Jr 23:17 [c] **6:20** 1Kg 10:1; Is 60:6 [d] Ex 30:23; Is 43:24; Ezk 27:19 [e] Ps 40:6; Is 1:11; 43:23; 66:3; Hs 9:4; Am 5:21; Mc 6:6; Mal 1:10 [f] **6:21** Is 8:15; Jr 31:9; Ezk 7:19 [g] **6:22** Is 13:4; Jr 1:13; 6:1; 38:3; Lm 1:15; Ezk 38:15; Jl 2:25 [h] Jr 25:32; 31:8 [i] **6:23** Is 13:18; Jr 50:42; Hab 1:6-17 [j] Is 5:30; 17:12 [k] **6:24** Ps 48:6; Is 13:8; 21:3; 42:14; Jr 4:31; 13:21; 22:23; 30:6; 50:43; Mc 4:9-10; 1Th 5:3 [l] **6:22-24** Jr 50:41-43 [m] **6:25** Ps 31:13; Jr 20:3,10; 49:29 [n] **6:26** Jr 25:34; Ezk 27:30; Mc 1:10 [o] Am 8:10 [p] Ex 12:23; Is 21:2; 54:16; Jr 48:8,15,18,32; 1Co 10:10; Heb 11:28 [q] Is 47:11; Jr 4:20; 15:8 [r] **6:27** 1Ch 29:17; Ps 7:9; Pr 17:3 [s] **6:28** Lv 19:16; Pr 11:13; 20:19; Is 1:23 [t] 2Ch 27:2; Is 1:4 [u] **6:30** 1Sm 15:23,26; Jr 2:37; 7:29 [v] **7:2** Jr 26:2 [w] **7:3** Jr 4:18; 18:11; 26:13 [x] **7:5** Jr 22:3 [y] **7:6** Dt 19:10,13; 21:8-9; 2Kg 21:16; 24:4; Jr 22:3,17; 26:15; Mt 27:4 [z] **7:7** Gn 12:7; Jos 1:2; Jr 30:3 [aa] **7:9** Ex 20:3-17; Lv 19:11-12; Dt 5:7-21; Ezk 18:5-9,14-18; 22:6-12; Hs 4:2

[A] **6:24** Lit *and our hands fail* [B] **6:26** Lit *Daughter of My* [C] **6:27** Text emended; MT reads *fortress* [D] **7:5** Lit *justly between a man and his neighbor*

this house[a] called by My name and say, 'We are delivered, so we can continue doing all these detestable acts'? [11]Has this house, which is called by My name, become a den of robbers[b] in your view? Yes, I too have seen it."[c] This is the LORD's declaration.

Shiloh As a Warning

[12]"But return to My place that was at Shiloh, where I made My name dwell at first.[d] See what I did to it because of the evil of My people Israel. [13]Now, because you have done all these things"—this is the LORD's declaration—"and because I have spoken to you time and time again[A] but you wouldn't listen,[e] and I have called to you, but you wouldn't answer,[f] [14]what I did to Shiloh I will do to the house that is called by My name[g]—the house in which you trust—the place that I gave you and your ancestors. [15]I will drive you from My presence, just as I drove out all of your brothers, all the descendants of Ephraim.[h]

Do Not Pray for Judah

[16]"As for you, do not pray for these people.[i] Do not offer a cry or a prayer on their behalf, and do not beg Me,[j] for I will not listen to you.[k] [17]Don't you see how they behave in the cities of Judah and in the streets of Jerusalem? [18]The sons gather wood, the fathers light the fire, and the women knead dough to make cakes for the queen of heaven,[B,l] and they pour out ·drink offerings to other gods so that they provoke Me to anger. [19]But are they really provoking Me?"[m] This is the LORD's declaration. "Isn't it they themselves being provoked to disgrace?"

[20]Therefore, this is what the Lord GOD says: "Look, My anger—My burning wrath—is about to be poured out on this place,[n] on man and beast, on the tree of the field, and on the produce of the land. My wrath will burn and not be quenched."[o]

Obedience Over Sacrifice

[21]This is what the LORD of Hosts, the God of Israel, says: "Add your ·burnt offerings to your other sacrifices, and eat the meat yourselves,[p] [22]for when I brought your ancestors out of the land of Egypt, I did not speak with them[q] or command them concerning burnt offering and sacrifice. [23]However, I did give them this command: Obey Me, and then I will be your God, and you will be My people. You must follow every way I command you so that it may go well with you.[r] [24]Yet they didn't listen or pay attention[s] but followed their own advice and according to their own stubborn, evil heart. They went backward and not forward.[t] [25]Since the day your ancestors came out of the land of Egypt until this day, I have sent all My servants the prophets[u] to you time and time again.[C,v] [26]However, they wouldn't listen to Me or pay attention but became obstinate;[D,w] they did more evil than their ancestors.[x]

A Lament for Disobedient Judah

[27]"When you speak all these things to them, they will not listen to you. When you call to them, they will not answer you. [28]You must therefore declare to them: This is the nation that would not listen to the voice of the LORD their God and would not accept discipline. Truth[E] has perished—it has disappeared from their mouths. [29]Cut off the hair of your sacred vow[F,y] and throw it away. Raise up a dirge on the barren heights,[z] for the LORD has rejected and abandoned the generation under His wrath.[aa]

[30]"For the Judeans have done what is evil in My sight." This is the LORD's declaration. "They have set up their detestable things[ab] in the house that is called by My name and defiled it.[ac] [31]They have built the ·high places of ·Topheth[G,ad] in the Valley of Hinnom[H,ae] in order to burn their sons and daughters in the fire,[af] a thing I did not command; I never entertained the thought.[I]

[32]"Therefore, take note! Days are coming"[ag]—the LORD's declaration—"when this place will no longer be called Topheth and the Valley of Hinnom, but the Valley of Slaughter.[ah] Topheth will become a cemetery,[J] because there will be no other burial place. [33]The corpses of these people will become

[a]7:10 Jr 32:34 [b]7:11 Is 56:7; Mt 21:13; Mk 11:17; Lk 19:46 [c]Ps 33:13-15; Ezk 8:12; Am 9:1-4 [d]7:12 Dt 12:11; 14:23; 16:6,11 [e]7:13 Jr 7:25; 11:7; 25:3; 26:5; 29:19; ; 32:33; 35:14,15; 44:4 [f]Pr 1:24; Is 65:12 [g]7:14 Dt 12:5; 1Kg 9:7; Mk 13:2 [h]7:15 Dt 29:28; 2Kg 17 [i]7:16 Jr 11:14; 14:11-12; 15:1 [j]Gn 23:8; Ru 1:16; Jr 27:18 [k]Ex 32:11-13,20-34; Jr 14:11; 15:1 [l]7:18 Jr 44:17-19,25 [m]7:19 Jb 35:6 [n]7:20 Jr 42:18; Lm 4:11 [o]Nah 1:6 [p]7:21 Dt 12:4-28; Ps 50:13; Hs 8:13 [q]7:22 Hs 6:6 [r]7:23 Dt 5:33 [s]7:24 Ps 81:11 [t]Jr 15:6 [u]7:25 2Kg 9:7; 17:13; Jr 26:5; 29:19; 35:15; 44:4; Ezk 38:17; Zch 1:6 [v]2Ch 36:15-16; Jr 25:4 [w]7:26 Ex 32:9; Dt 9:6,13; 2Kg 17:14; Jr 17:23; 19:15 [x]1Kg 16:25; 2Kg 21:11 [y]7:29 Nm 6:1-8 [z]Jr 3:2,21 [aa]Is 2:6 [ab]7:30 Jr 4:1; 16:18; 32:34 [ac]2Kg 23:24 [ad]7:31 2Kg 23:10; Jr 19:6,11-14 [ae]Jos 15:8; Jr 19:5; 32:35 [af]Lv 18:21; Dt 12:31; 2Kg 17:17,31; 2Ch 28:3; Jr 19:5; Ezk 16:21; 20:31; 23:25,37,47 [ag]7:32 Jr 16:14; 19:6; 23:5; 48:12; 49:2; 51:47,52 [ah]Jr 19:6

A7:13 Lit *you rising early and speaking* B7:18 = a pagan goddess C7:25 Lit *you, each day rising early and sending* D7:26 Lit *but stiffened their neck* E7:28 Or *Faithfulness* F7:29 Lit *off your consecration* G7:31 Lit *of the fireplace* H7:31 A valley south of Jerusalem I7:31 Lit *command, and it did not arise on My heart* J7:32 Lit *They will bury in Topheth*

food for the birds of the sky and for the wild
animals of the land, with no one to scare them
away.[a] 34 I will remove from the cities of Judah
and the streets of Jerusalem the sound of joy
and gladness and the voices of the groom and
the bride,[b] for the land will become a desolate
waste.[c]

Death over Life

8 "At that time" — this is the LORD's declaration — "the bones of the kings of Judah, the bones of her officials, the bones of
the priests, the bones of the prophets, and
the bones of the residents of Jerusalem will
be brought out of their graves. 2 They will
be exposed[d] to the sun, the moon, and the
whole heavenly ·host,[e] which they have loved,
served, followed, consulted, and worshiped.
Their bones will not be collected and buried
but will become like manure on the surface
of the soil.[f] 3 Death will be chosen over life[g] by
all the survivors of this evil family, those who
remain wherever I have banished them." This
is the declaration of the LORD of Hosts.
4 "You are to say to them: This is what the
LORD says:

Do people fall and not get up again?[h]
If they turn away, do they not return?
5 Why have these people turned away?
Why is Jerusalem always turning away?
They take hold of deceit;[i]
they refuse to return.[j]
6 I have paid careful attention.
They do not speak what is right.
No one regrets his evil,
asking, 'What have I done?'
Everyone has stayed his course
like a horse rushing into battle.[k]
7 Even the stork in the sky
knows her seasons.
The turtledove, swallow, and crane[A]
are aware of their migration,
but My people do not know
the requirements of the LORD.[l]

Punishment for Judah's Leaders

8 "How can you claim, 'We are wise;
the law of the LORD is with us'?
In fact, the lying pen of scribes[m]
has produced falsehood.
9 The wise will be put to shame;
they will be dismayed and snared.
They have rejected the word
of the LORD,
so what wisdom do they really have?
10 Therefore, I will give[n] their wives
to other men,
their fields to new occupants,
for from the least to the greatest,
everyone is making profit dishonestly.
From prophet to priest,
everyone deals falsely.
11 They have treated superficially
the brokenness
of My dear[B] people,
claiming, 'Peace, peace,'
when there is no peace.
12 Were they ashamed when they acted
so abhorrently?
They weren't at all ashamed.
They can no longer feel humiliation.
Therefore, they will fall
among the fallen.
When I punish them, they will collapse,"[o]
says the LORD.

13 I will gather them and bring them
to an end.[C,p]
This is the LORD's declaration.
There will be no grapes on the vine,
no figs on the fig tree,
and even the leaf will wither.
Whatever I have given them will be lost
to them.

God's People Unrepentant

14 Why are we just sitting here?
Gather together; let us enter
the fortified cities
and perish there,[D]
for the LORD our God has destroyed[E] us.
He has given us poisoned water
to drink,[q]
because we have sinned
against the LORD.
15 We hoped for peace, but there was
nothing good;
for a time of healing, but there was
only terror.[r]

[a] 7:33 Dt 28:26; Ps 79:2; Jr 16:4; 19:7; 34:27; Ezk 29:5 [b] 7:34 Jr 16:9; 25:10; 33:11 [c] Lv 26:31,33; Is 64:11; Jr 25:9,11,18; 27:17; 44:2,6,22 [d] 8:2 2Sm 21:12-14; Ps 53:5; Ezk 6:5 [e] Dt 4:19; 2Kg 17:16; 23:4-5 [f] Ps 83:10; Jr 9:22; 16:4 [g] 8:3 Dt 30:11-20 [h] 8:4 Is 24:20; Jr 25:27; Am 5:2 [i] 8:5 Jr 14:14; 23:26; Zph 3:13 [j] Jr 5:3; Hs 11:5 [k] 8:6 Jb 39:19-25 [l] 8:7 Jr 5:4 [m] 8:8 Jb 19:24; Ps 45:1; Jr 17:1 [n] 8:10-12 Jr 6:13-15 [o] 8:12 Jr 10:15; 49:8; 51:18 [p] 8:13 Zph 1:2 [q] 8:14 Jr 9:15 [r] 8:15 Jr 14:19; 33:9

[A] 8:7 Hb obscure [B] 8:11 Lit *of the daughter of My* [C] 8:13 Lit *Gathering I will end them* [D] 8:14 Or *there be silenced* [E] 8:14 Or *silenced*

16 From Dan the snorting
of horses is heard.
At the sound of the neighing
of mighty steeds,[a]
the whole land quakes.
They come to devour the land
and everything in it,
the city and all its residents.
17 Indeed, I am about to send snakes
among you,
poisonous vipers[b] that cannot
be charmed.[c]
They will bite you.
This is the LORD's declaration.

Lament over Judah

18 My joy has flown away;
grief has settled on me.
My heart is sick.[d]
19 Listen — the cry of my dear[A] people
from a far away land,
"Is the LORD no longer in ˙Zion,[e]
her King not within her?"
Why have they provoked me
to anger
with their carved images,
with their worthless foreign idols?[f]
20 Harvest has passed,
summer has ended,
but we have not been saved.
21 I am broken by the brokenness
of my dear[A] people.[g]
I mourn; horror has taken hold of me.
22 Is there no balm in Gilead?[h]
Is there no physician there?
So why has the healing
of my dear[A] people
not come about?

9 [B] If my head were a spring of water,
my eyes a fountain of tears,
I would weep day and night[i]
over the slain of my dear[C] people.
2[D] If only I had a traveler's lodging place
in the wilderness,
I would abandon my people
and depart from them,
for they are all adulterers,[j]
a solemn assembly
of treacherous people.[k]

[a]8:16 Jdg 5:22; Jr 47:3; 50:11 [b]8:17 Nm 21:6-9; Dt 32:24 [c]Ps 58:4-5; Ec 10:11 [d]8:18 Lm 5:17 [e]8:19 Ps 99:2; 102:21; Jl 3:17,21 [f]Jr 2:5 [g]8:21 Jr 6:14; 8:11 [h]8:22 Gn 37:25; Jr 46:11 [i]9:1 Ps 42:3; Jr 13:17; Lm 2:11; Lk 19:41 [j]9:2 Jr 23:10; Hs 7:4; Mal 3:5 [k]Is 24:16; 33:1; Jr 12:1 [l]9:3 Jr 4:22 [m]9:4 Jr 6:28 [n]9:6 Rm 1:17 [o]9:7 Is 1:25; Jr 6:27 [p]9:8 Ps 28:3 [q]9:9 Jr 5:9,29 [r]9:10 Jr 4:25; 12:4

3 They bent their tongues like their bows;
lies and not faithfulness prevail
in the land,
for they proceed from one evil
to another,
and they do not take Me into account.[l]
This is the LORD's declaration.

Imminent Ruin and Exile

4 Everyone has to be on guard
against his friend.
Don't trust any brother,
for every brother will certainly deceive,
and every friend spread slander.[m]
5 Each one betrays his friend;
no one tells the truth.
They have taught their tongues
to speak lies;
they wear themselves out doing wrong.
6 You live in a world of deception.[E]
In their deception they refuse
to know Me.[n]
This is the LORD's declaration.

7Therefore, this is what the LORD of ˙Hosts
says:

I am about to refine them
and test them,[o]
for what else can I do
because of My dear[F] people?[G]
8 Their tongues are deadly arrows —
they speak deception.[p]
With his mouth
a man speaks peaceably with his friend,
but inwardly he sets up an ambush.
9 Should I not punish them
for these things?
This is the LORD's declaration.
Should I not avenge Myself[q]
on such a nation as this?
10 I will raise weeping and a lament
over the mountains,
a dirge over the wilderness
grazing land,
for they have been so scorched
that no one passes through.
The sound of cattle is no longer heard.
From the birds of the sky
to the animals,[r]

[A]8:19,21,22 Lit *of the daughter of my* [B]9:1 Jr 8:23 in Hb [C]9:1 Lit *slain among the daughter of my* [D]9:2 Jr 9:1 in Hb [E]9:6 LXX reads *Oppression on oppression, deceit on deceit* [F]9:7 Lit *of the daughter of My* [G]9:7 LXX, Tg read *because of their evils*

everything has fled — they have
gone away.
11 I will make Jerusalem a heap of rubble,[a]
a jackals' den.[b]
I will make the cities of Judah
a desolation,
an uninhabited place.

12 Who is the man wise enough to understand this?[c] Who has the LORD spoken to, that
he may explain it? Why is the land destroyed
and scorched like a wilderness, so no one can
pass through?
13 The LORD said, "It is because they abandoned My instruction[d] that I set in front of
them and did not obey My voice or walk according to it. 14 Instead, they followed the
stubbornness of their hearts[e] and followed
after the •Baals as their fathers taught them."[f]
15 Therefore, this is what the LORD of Hosts,
the God of Israel, says: "I am about to feed
this people •wormwood[g] and give them poisonous water to drink.[h] 16 I will scatter them
among the nations[i] that they and their fathers have not known. I will send a sword after them until I have finished them off."

Mourning over Judah

17 This is what the LORD of Hosts says:

Consider, and summon the women
who mourn;[j]
send for the skillful women.
18 Let them come quickly to raise a lament
over us
so that our eyes may overflow
with tears,
our eyelids soaked with weeping.
19 For a sound of lamentation is heard
from •Zion:
How devastated we are.
We are greatly ashamed,[k]
for we have abandoned the land;
our dwellings have been torn down.

20 Now hear the word of the LORD,
you women.
Pay attention to[A] the word
of His mouth.
Teach your daughters a lament
and one another a dirge,
21 for Death[l] has climbed
through our windows;
it has entered our fortresses,
cutting off children from the streets,
young men from the squares.

22 Speak as follows:
This is what the LORD says:

Human corpses will fall
like manure on the surface of the field,
like newly cut grain[m] after the reaper
with no one to gather it.

Boast in the LORD

23 This is what the LORD says:

The wise man must not boast
in his wisdom;
the strong man must not boast
in his strength;
the wealthy man must not boast
in his wealth.
24 But the one who boasts should boast
in this,
that he understands
and knows Me[n] —
that I am •Yahweh,
showing faithful love,
justice, and righteousness on the earth,
for I delight in these things.
This is the LORD's declaration.

25 "The days are coming" — the LORD's declaration — "when I will punish all the circumcised yet uncircumcised:[o] 26 Egypt, Judah,
Edom, the Ammonites, Moab, and all the inhabitants of the desert who clip the hair on
their temples.[B] All these nations are uncircumcised, and the whole house of Israel is
uncircumcised in heart."[p]

False Gods Contrasted with the Creator

10 Hear the word that the LORD has spoken to[C] you, house of Israel. 2 This is
what the LORD says:

Do not learn the way of the nations[q]
or be terrified by signs in the heavens,
although the nations are terrified
by them,
3 for the customs of the peoples
are worthless.

[a] 9:11 2Kg 19:25; Is 25:2; Jr 51:37 [b] Jr 10:22; 49:33; 51:37 [c] 9:12 Ps 107:43; Ec 8:1; Hs 14:9 [d] 9:13 2Ch 12:1 [e] 9:14 Dt 29:19; Ps 81:12 [f] Jr 2:8,23 [g] 9:15 Dt 29:18; Jr 23:15; Lm 3:19 [h] Jr 8:14; 23:15 [i] 9:16 Lv 26:33; Dt 4:27; 28:64 [j] 9:17 Ec 12:5; Am 5:16 [k] 9:19 Jr 2:26; 6:15; 8:12 [l] 9:21 Jb 18:13; 28:22; Ps 49:14 [m] 9:22 Am 2:13; Mc 4:12; Zch 12:6 [n] 9:24 Ps 34:2; 64:10; 105:3; 1Co 1:31; 2Co 10:17 [o] 9:25 Jr 4:4; Rm 2:28-29 [p] 9:26 Lv 19:27; Jr 25:23; 49:32; Ezk 44:7,9 [q] 10:2 Jr 2:23,36

[A] 9:20 Lit *Your ears must receive* [B] 9:26 Or *who live in distant places* [C] 10:1 Or *against*

Someone cuts down a tree
from the forest;
it is worked by the hands of a craftsman
with a chisel.
4 He decorates it with silver and gold.[a]
It is fastened with hammer and nails,[b]
so it won't totter.
5 Like scarecrows in a cucumber patch,
their idols cannot speak.[c]
They must be carried[d] because
they cannot walk.
Do not fear them for they can do
no harm[e] —
and they cannot do any good.[f]
6 ·Yahweh, there is no one like You.[g]
You are great;
Your name is great in power.[h]
7 Who should not ·fear You,
King of the nations?[i]
It is what You deserve.
For among all the wise people
of the nations
and among all their kingdoms,
there is no one like You.
8 They are both stupid and foolish,
instructed by worthless idols
made of wood!
9 Beaten silver is brought from Tarshish,[j]
and gold from Uphaz[A,k]
from the hands of a goldsmith,
the work of a craftsman.
Their clothing is blue and purple,
all the work of skilled artisans.
10 But Yahweh is the true God;[l]
He is the living God[m] and eternal King.[n]
The earth quakes at His wrath,[o]
and the nations cannot endure
His rage.

11You are to say this to them, "The gods that
did not make the heavens[p] and the earth will
perish from the earth[q] and from under these
heavens."[B]

12 He made the earth by His power,
established the world[r] by His wisdom,[s]
and spread out the heavens
by His understanding.[t]
13 When He thunders,[C]
the waters in the heavens
are in turmoil,[u]

[a]**10:4** Is 40:19 [b]Is 41:7 [c]**10:5** Ps 115:5; 1Co 12:2 [d]Ps 115:7; Is 46:7 [e]Is 41:23-24 [f]**10:3-5** Is 44:9-20 [g]**10:6** Ex 15:11; 2Sm 7:22; 1Kg 8:23 [h]Ps 76:1; 86:10; Mal 1:11 [i]**10:7** Ps 22:28; 47:7-8; Jr 8:19 [j]**10:9** Ezk 27:12,25; 38:13 [k]Dn 10:5 [l]**10:10** 2Ch 15:3 [m]**10:10** Dt 5:26; 1Sm 17:26,36; 2Kg 19:4,16 [n]Ex 15:18; Ps 10:16; 29:10 [o]2Sm 22:8; Ps 18:7; Is 13:13 [p]**10:11** Ps 96:5 [q]Is 2:18 [r]**10:12** Jb 38:4; Ps 93:1; 96:10 [s]Pr 3:19-20; 8:22-29 [t]Jb 9:8; Ps 104:2; Is 45:12 [u]**10:13** Jr 5:22; 31:35 [v]Jb 38:25-30,34-38; Ps 135:7 [w]**10:14** Is 40:18-31; 46:1-7 [x]Is 41:29 [y]Hab 2:19 [z]**10:15** Jr 8:12; 51:18 [aa]**10:16** Gn 2:7-8,19; Ps 94:9; 95:5 [ab]Dt 4:20; 32:8-9; Ps 74:2 [ac]**10:12-16** Jr 51:15-19 [ad]**10:17** Ezk 12:3 [ae]**10:18** 1Sm 25:29 [af]**10:19** Jr 14:17; 30:12; Nah 3:19 [ag]**10:20** Jr 4:20 [ah]**10:21** 2Ch 16:12; Is 9:13; 31:1

and He causes the clouds to rise
from the ends of the earth.
He makes lightning for the rain
and brings the wind
from His storehouses.[v]
14 Everyone is stupid and ignorant.
Every goldsmith is put to shame
by his carved image,[w]
for his cast images are a lie;[x]
there is no breath in them.[y]
15 They are worthless, a work
to be mocked.
At the time of their punishment
they will be destroyed.[z]
16 Jacob's Portion[D] is not like these
because He is the One who formed
all things.[aa]
Israel is the tribe of His inheritance;[ab]
Yahweh of ·Hosts is His name.[ac]

Exile After the Siege

17 Gather up your belongings[E]
from the ground,[ad]
you who live under siege.
18For this is what the LORD says:

Look, I am slinging out[ae]
the land's residents at this time
and bringing them such distress
that they will feel it.

Jeremiah Grieves

19 Woe to me because of
my brokenness —
I am severely wounded![af]
I exclaimed, "This is
my intense suffering,
but I must bear it."
20 My tent is destroyed;[ag]
all my tent cords are snapped.
My sons have departed from me
and are no more.
I have no one to pitch my tent again
or to hang up my curtains.
21 For the shepherds are stupid:
they don't seek the LORD.[ah]
Therefore they have not prospered,
and their whole flock is scattered.
22 Listen! A noise — it is coming —

[A]**10:9** Or *Ophir* [B]**10:11** This is the only Aram v. in Jr. [C]**10:13** Lit *At His giving of the voice* [D]**10:16** = the LORD [E]**10:17** Lit *bundle*

a great commotion[a] from the land
to the north.
The cities of Judah will be
made desolate,
a jackals' den.[b]

23 I know, LORD,
that a man's way of life is not his own;
no one who walks determines
his own steps.[c]
24 Discipline me, LORD, but with justice—
not in Your anger,[d]
or You will reduce me to nothing.
25 Pour out Your wrath on the nations
that don't recognize You
and on the families
that don't call on Your name,
for they have consumed Jacob;
they have consumed him and finished
him off
and made his homeland desolate.[e]

Reminder of the Covenant

11 This is the word that came to Jeremiah
from the LORD: 2 "Listen to the words of
this covenant[f] and tell them to the men of Judah and the residents of Jerusalem. 3 You must
tell them: This is what the LORD, the God of Israel, says: 'Let a curse be on the man who does
not obey the words of this covenant,[g] 4 which
I commanded your ancestors when I brought
them out of the land of Egypt,[h] out of the iron
furnace.'[i] I declared: 'Obey Me, and do everything that I command you, and you will be
My people, and I will be your God,'[j] 5 in order
to establish the oath I swore to your ancestors,[k] to give them a land flowing with milk
and honey, as it is today."
I answered, "·Amen, LORD."[l]
6 The LORD said to me, "Proclaim all these
words in the cities of Judah and in the streets
of Jerusalem: Obey the words of this covenant
and carry them out. 7 For I strongly warned
your ancestors when I brought them out of
the land of Egypt until today, warning them
time and time again,[A,m] 'Obey My voice.' 8 Yet
they would not obey or pay attention; each
one followed the stubbornness of his evil
heart.[n] So I brought on them all the curses
of this covenant, because they had not done
what I commanded them to do."
9 The LORD said to me, "A conspiracy has
been discovered among the men of Judah[o]
and the residents of Jerusalem. 10 They have
returned to the sins of their ancestors[p] who
refused to obey My words and have followed
other gods to worship them.[q] The house of
Israel and the house of Judah broke My covenant I made with their ancestors.
11 "Therefore, this is what the LORD says: I
am about to bring on them disaster that they
cannot escape.[r] They will cry out to Me, but I
will not hear them. 12 Then the cities of Judah
and the residents of Jerusalem will go and cry
out to the gods they have been burning incense to, but they certainly will not save them
in their time of disaster.[s] 13 Your gods are indeed as numerous as your cities, Judah,[t] and
the altars you have set up to Shame[B,u]—altars to burn incense to ·Baal—as numerous
as the streets of Jerusalem.
14 "As for you, do not pray for these people.
Do not raise up a cry or a prayer on their behalf,[v] for I will not be listening when they call
out to Me at the time of their disaster.

15 What right does My beloved have
to be in My house,[w]
having carried out so many
evil schemes?
Can holy meat[C,x] prevent
your disaster[D]
so you can rejoice?
16 The LORD named you
a flourishing olive tree,[y]
beautiful with well-formed fruit.
He has set fire to it,
and its branches are consumed[E,z]
with a great roaring sound.[aa]

17 "The LORD of ·Hosts who planted you[ab]
has decreed disaster against you, because of
the harm the house of Israel and the house of
Judah brought on themselves, provoking Me
to anger by burning incense to Baal."

18 The LORD informed me, so I knew.
Then You helped me to see their deeds,
19 for I was like a docile[F] lamb led
to slaughter.[ac]
I didn't know that they had
devised plots against me:

[a] **10:22** Jr 4:29; 6:22-23
[b] Jr 9:11
[c] **10:23** Ps 37:23; Pr 3:5-6; 16:9
[d] **10:24** Ps 6:1; 38:1
[e] **10:25** Ps 79:6-7
[f] **11:2** Dt 29:9
[g] **11:3** Dt 27:26; Gl 3:10
[h] **11:4** Dt 29:25; Jr 7:22; 34:13
[i] Dt 4:20; 1Kg 8:51
[j] Dt 29:13; Jr 24:7; 30:22
[k] **11:5** Gn 26:3; Dt 7:8
[l] Dt 27:15-16
[m] **11:7** 2Ch 36:15; Jr 7:25
[n] **11:8** Jr 3:17; 7:24; 16:12
[o] **11:9** Ezk 22:25; Hs 6:9
[p] **11:10** Lv 26:39-40; Neh 9:2; Is 65:7
[q] Dt 28:14; Jr 13:10; 35:15
[r] **11:11** Jr 39:4-7; Am 9:1-4
[s] **11:12** Dt 32:35-37
[t] **11:13** Jr 2:28
[u] Jr 3:24; Hs 9:10
[v] **11:14** Jr 7:16; 14:11
[w] **11:15** Jr 7:1-15
[x] Hg 2:12
[y] **11:16** Ps 52:8; 128:3
[z] Ezk 31:12
[aa] Ezk 1:24
[ab] **11:17** Is 5:2,7; Jr 2:21
[ac] **11:19** Ps 44:11,22; Is 53:7; Jr 12:3

[A] **11:7** Lit *today, rising early and warning* [B] **11:13** = Baal [C] **11:15** = sacrificial meat [D] **11:15** LXX; MT reads *meat pass from you* [E] **11:16** Vg; MT reads *broken* [F] **11:19** Or *pet*

"Let's destroy the tree with its fruit;[A]
let's cut him off from the land
of the living[a]
so that his name will no longer
be remembered."
20 But, LORD of Hosts,
who judges righteously,
who tests[b] heart[B] and mind,[c]
let me see Your vengeance on them,
for I have presented my case to You.[d]

21 Therefore, here is what the LORD says concerning the people of Anathoth[e] who want
to take your life. They warn, "You must not
prophesy in the name of •Yahweh, or you will
certainly die at our hand." 22 Therefore, this
is what the LORD of Hosts says: "I am about
to punish them. The young men will die by
the sword; their sons and daughters will die
by famine.[f] 23 They will have no remnant, for I
will bring disaster on the people of Anathoth[g]
in the year of their punishment."

Jeremiah's Complaint

12 You will be righteous, LORD,[h]
even if I bring a case against You.
Yet, I wish to contend with You:[i]
Why does the way of the wicked
prosper?[j]
Why do all the treacherous live at ease?
2 You planted them,[k] and they
have taken root.
They have grown and produced fruit.
You are ever on their lips,[C]
but far from their conscience.[B,l]
3 As for You, LORD, You know me;
You see me.[m]
You test whether my heart is
with You.[n]
Drag the wicked away like sheep
to slaughter[o]
and set them apart for the day
of killing.
4 How long will the land mourn[p]
and the grass of every field wither?
Because of the evil of its residents,
animals and birds have been
swept away,
for the people have said,
"He cannot see what our end will be."[D,q]

The LORD's Response

5 If you have raced with runners
and they have worn you out,
how can you compete with horses?
If you stumble[E] in a peaceful land,
what will you do in the thickets
of the Jordan?[r]
6 Even your brothers — your own
father's household —
even they were treacherous to you;[s]
even they have cried out loudly
after you.[t]
Do not have confidence in them,
though they speak well of you.

7 I have abandoned My house;[u]
I have deserted My inheritance.
I have given the love of My life
into the hands of her enemies.
8 My inheritance has acted toward Me
like a lion in the forest.
She has roared against Me.
Therefore, I hate her.[v]
9 Is My inheritance like a hyena[F] to Me?
Are birds of prey circling her?
Go, gather all the wild animals;[w]
bring them to devour her.
10 Many shepherds have destroyed
My vineyard;
they have trampled My plot of land.[x]
They have turned My desirable plot
into a desolate wasteland.
11 They have made it a desolation.
It mourns, desolate, before Me.
All the land is desolate,
but no one takes it to heart.[y]
12 Over all the barren heights
in the wilderness
the destroyers have come,
for the LORD has a sword that devours
from one end of the earth to the other.
No one has peace.[z]
13 They have sown wheat
but harvested thorns.[aa]
They have exhausted themselves
but have no profit.[ab]
Be put to shame by your harvests
because of the LORD's burning anger.[ac]

14 This is what the LORD says: "Concerning all My evil neighbors who attack the

[a] 11:19 Ps 27:13; Is 53:8; Ezk 26:20
[b] 11:20 Jr 9:7; 12:3
[c] Ps 7:9; 17:3; 26:2
[d] Jr 20:12
[e] 11:21 Jr 1:1; 32:7-9
[f] 11:21-22 Am 7:16-17
[g] 11:23 Jr 23:12
[h] 12:1 Ezr 9:15; Neh 9:8,33; Ps 119:137
[i] Jb 9:14-15; 13:13-28; 23:2-17
[j] Ps 73
[k] 12:2 Ps 1:3; Jr 17:7-8
[l] Ps 28:3; Is 29:13
[m] 12:3 Ps 139; Jr 1:5
[n] Ps 7:9; Jr 11:20
[o] Jr 11:19
[p] 12:4 Is 24:4-7; Jr 4:28; 23:10
[q] Dt 32:20; Jb 22:13; Jr 29:11
[r] 12:5 Jr 50:44
[s] 12:6 Jn 1:11
[t] Jr 11:19
[u] 12:7 Ezk 8:1–11:25
[v] 12:8 Hs 9:15; Am 6:8
[w] 12:9 Is 56:9; Jr 7:33
[x] 12:10 Is 63:18
[y] 12:11 Is 42:25
[z] 12:12 2Ch 15:5; Is 48:22; Ezk 13:16
[aa] 12:13 Lv 26:16; Dt 28:38; Mc 6:15; Hg 1:6
[ab] Is 55:2
[ac] Jr 4:26; 25:37-38

[A] 11:19 Lit *bread* [B] 11:20; 12:2 Lit *kidneys* [C] 12:2 Lit *are near in their mouth* [D] 12:4 LXX reads *see our ways* [E] 12:5 Or *you are secure* [F] 12:9 Hb obscure

inheritance that I bequeathed to My people,
Israel, I am about to uproot them[a] from their
land, and I will uproot the house of Judah from
them. 15 After I have uprooted them, I will once
again have compassion[b] on them and return
each one to his inheritance and to his land.
16 If they will diligently learn the ways of My
people[c] — to swear by My name, 'As •Yahweh
lives,' just as they taught My people to swear by
•Baal — they will be built up among My people.
17 However, if they will not obey, then I will uproot and destroy that nation."[d]
This is the LORD's declaration.

Linen Underwear

13 This is what the LORD said to me: "Go
and buy yourself a linen undergar-
ment[e] and put it on,[A] but do not put it in
water." 2 So I bought underwear as the LORD
instructed me and put it on.
3 Then the word of the LORD came to me a
second time: 4 "Take the underwear that you
bought and are wearing,[B] and go at once to
the Euphrates[C] and hide it in a rocky crevice."[f]
5 So I went and hid it by the Euphrates, as the
LORD commanded me.
6 A long time later the LORD said to me, "Go
at once to the Euphrates and get the underwear that I commanded you to hide there."
7 So I went to the Euphrates and dug up the underwear and got it from the place where I had
hidden it, but it was ruined — of no use at all.
8 Then the word of the LORD came to me:
9 "This is what the LORD says: Just like this I
will ruin the great pride of both Judah and
Jerusalem.[g] 10 These evil people, who refuse
to listen to Me, who follow the stubbornness
of their own hearts,[h] and who have followed
other gods to serve and worship — they will
be like this underwear, of no use at all. 11 Just
as underwear clings to one's waist, so I fastened the whole house of Israel and of Judah
to Me"[i] — this is the LORD's declaration — "so
that they might be My people for My fame,
praise, and glory,[j] but they would not obey.

The Wine Jars

12 "Say this to them: This is what the LORD,
the God of Israel, says: Every jar should be
filled with wine. Then they will respond to
you, 'Don't we know that every jar should be
filled with wine?' 13 And you will say to them:
This is what the LORD says: I am about to
fill all who live in this land — the kings who
reign for David on his throne, the priests,
the prophets and all the residents of Jerusalem — with drunkenness. 14 I will smash
them against each other, fathers and sons
alike" — this is the LORD's declaration. "I will
allow no mercy, pity, or compassion to keep
Me from destroying them."[k]

The LORD's Warning

15 Listen and pay attention.
Do not be proud,
for the LORD has spoken.
16 Give glory to the LORD your God[l]
before He brings darkness,
before your feet stumble
on the mountains at dusk.
You wait for light,
but He brings darkest gloom[D]
and makes thick darkness.
17 But if you will not listen,
my innermost being will weep in secret
because of your pride.
My eyes will overflow with tears,
for the LORD's flock[m] has been
taken captive.

18 Say to the king and the queen mother:[n]
Take a humble seat,
for your glorious crowns
have fallen from your heads.
19 The cities of the •Negev are under siege;
no one can help them.
All of Judah has been taken into exile,
taken completely into exile.
20 Look up and see
those coming from the north.[o]
Where is the flock entrusted to you,
the sheep that were your pride?

The Destiny of Jerusalem

21 What will you say when He appoints
close friends as leaders over you,
ones you yourself trained?
Won't labor pains seize you,[p]
as they do a woman in labor?

[a] 12:14 Jr 1:10; 18:7-8
[b] 12:15 Jr 48:47; 49:6
[c] 12:16 Is 2:2-4; Mc 4:1-5
[d] 12:17 Is 60:12
[e] 13:1 Ex 39:27-29; Lv 16:4; Ezk 44:17-18
[f] 13:4 Jr 51:63
[g] 13:9 Lv 26:19
[h] 13:10 Jr 16:12
[i] 13:11 Dt 4:3-4; 10:20
[j] Dt 26:19; Ezk 16:8-14
[k] 13:14 Lm 2:2,17,21; 3:43
[l] 13:16 Jos 7:19; 1Sm 6:5; Ps 29:1-2
[m] 13:17 Ps 80:1; 95:7; Jr 23:1-4
[n] 13:18 2Kg 24:12; Jr 22:26
[o] 13:20 Jr 1:13-15; 4:6; 10:22
[p] 13:21 Is 13:8

[A] 13:1 Lit *around your waist* [B] 13:4 Lit *wearing around your waist*
[C] 13:4-7 Perhaps a place near Anathoth with the same spelling as river
[D] 13:16 Or *brings a shadow of death*

22 And when you ask yourself,
"Why have these things happened
to me?"
It is because of your great ·guilt[a]
that your skirts have been stripped off,[b]
your body exposed.[A]
23 Can the ·Cushite change his skin,
or a leopard his spots?
If so, you might be able to do
what is good,[c]
you who are instructed in evil.
24 I will scatter you[B] like drifting chaff[d]
before the desert wind.
25 This is your lot,
what I have decreed for you —
this is the LORD's declaration —
because you have forgotten Me
and trusted in Falsehood.[C,e]
26 I will pull your skirts up over your face
so that your shame might be seen.[f]
27 Your adulteries and
your lustful neighing,[g]
your heinous prostitution
on the hills, in the fields —
I have seen your detestable acts.
Woe to you, Jerusalem!
You are ·unclean —
for how long yet?[h]

The Drought

14 The word of the LORD that came to Jeremiah concerning the drought:[i]

2 Judah mourns;
her gates languish.[j]
Her people are on the ground
in mourning;
Jerusalem's cry rises up.[k]
3 Their nobles send their servants[D]
for water.
They go to the cisterns;
they find no water;
their containers return empty.
They are ashamed and humiliated;
they cover their heads.[l]
4 The ground is cracked
since no rain has fallen on the land.
The farmers are ashamed;[m]
they cover their heads.
5 Even the doe in the field
gives birth and abandons her fawn
since there is no grass.
6 Wild donkeys stand
on the barren heights[n]
panting for air like jackals.
Their eyes fail
because there are no green plants.
7 Though our ·guilt testifies against us,
·Yahweh, act for Your name's sake.
Indeed, our rebellions[o] are many;
we have sinned against You.
8 Hope of Israel,[p]
its Savior in time of distress,
why are You like a foreigner in the land,
like a traveler stopping only
for the night?
9 Why are You like a helpless man,
like a warrior unable to save?[q]
Yet You are among us, Yahweh,[r]
and we are called by Your name.
Don't leave us!

10 This is what the LORD says concerning these people:

Truly they love to wander;[s]
they never rest their feet.
So the LORD does not accept them.
Now He will remember their guilt
and punish their sins.[t]

False Prophets to be Punished

11 Then the LORD said to me, "Do not pray for the well-being of these people.[u] 12 If they fast, I will not hear their cry of despair. If they offer ·burnt offering and ·grain offering, I will not accept them. Rather, I will finish them off by sword, famine, and plague."[v]

13 And I replied, "Oh no, Lord GOD! The prophets are telling them, 'You won't see sword or suffer famine. I will certainly give you true peace in this place.'"[w]

14 But the LORD said to me, "These prophets are prophesying a lie in My name. I did not send them, nor did I command them or speak to them. They are prophesying to you a false vision, worthless ·divination, the deceit[x] of their own minds.

15 "Therefore, this is what the LORD says concerning the prophets who prophesy in My name, though I did not send them, and

[a]13:22 Jr 5:6; 30:15 [b]Ezk 16:37-39; Hs 2:3,10; Nah 3:5 [c]13:23 Ec 5:1; Jr 4:22; Hs 5:4 [d]13:24 Jb 13:25; Ps 83:13; Is 40:24 [e]13:25 Jr 3:23 [f]13:26 Is 47:2-3; Jr 49:10; Nah 3:5 [g]13:27 Jr 2:23-24; 5:8 [h]Hs 8:5 [i]14:1 Jr 17:8 [j]14:2 Is 3:26 [k]1Sm 5:12 [l]14:3 Est 6:12; 7:8 [m]14:4 Jl 1:11 [n]14:6 Jr 2:24 [o]14:7 Jr 2:19; 3:6,22; 5:6 [p]14:8 Jr 17:13; 50:7 [q]14:9 Is 59:1 [r]Ex 29:45 [s]14:10 Jr 5:31; Am 8:12 [t]Hs 8:13 [u]14:11 Jr 7:16; 11:14; 15:1 [v]14:12 Jr 5:12 [w]14:13 Jr 4:10; 6:13-14; 8:10-12 [x]14:14 Ps 119:118; Jr 8:5; 23:26

[A]13:22 Lit *your heels have suffered violence* [B]13:24 Lit *them* [C]13:25 = Baal [D]14:3 Lit *little ones*

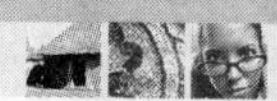

who say, 'There will never be sword or famine in this land.' By sword and famine these
prophets will meet their end. 16The people
they are prophesying to will be thrown into
the streets of Jerusalem because of the famine and the sword. There will be no one to
bury them[a]—they, their wives, their sons,
and their daughters. I will pour out their own
evil on them."

Jeremiah's Request

17 You are to speak this word to them:
Let my eyes overflow with tears;
day and night may they not stop,[b]
for the virgin daughter of my people
has been destroyed by a great disaster,[c]
an extremely severe wound.[d]
18 If I go out to the field,
look—those slain by the sword!
If I enter the city,
look—those ill[e] from famine!
For both prophet and priest
travel to a land they do not know.

19 Have You completely rejected Judah?
Do You detest[f] •Zion?
Why do You strike us
with no hope of healing for us?
We hoped for peace,
but there was nothing good;
for a time of healing,
but there was only terror.[g]
20 We acknowledge our wickedness, LORD,
the guilt of our fathers;[h]
indeed, we have sinned against You.
21 Because of Your name, don't despise us.
Don't disdain Your glorious throne.[i]
Remember Your covenant[j] with us;
do not break it.
22 Can any of the worthless idols
of the nations[k] bring rain?
Or can the skies alone give showers?
Are You not the LORD our God?
We therefore put our hope in You,[l]
for You have done all these things.

The LORD's Negative Response

15 Then the LORD said to me: "Even if[m]
Moses and[n] Samuel should[o] stand before Me,[p] My compassions would not reach
out to these people. Send them from My presence, and let them go. 2If they ask you, 'Where
will we go?' you must tell them: This is what
the LORD says:

Those destined for death,[q] to death;
those destined for the sword,
to the sword.
Those destined for famine, to famine;
those destined for captivity, to captivity.

3"I will ordain four kinds[A] of judgment for
them"—this is the LORD's declaration—"the
sword to kill, the dogs to drag away,[r] and
the birds of the sky and the wild animals of
the land[s] to devour and destroy. 4I will make
them a horror to all the kingdoms of the earth
because of Manasseh[t] son of Hezekiah, the
king of Judah, for what he did in Jerusalem.

5 Who will have pity on you, Jerusalem?[u]
Who will show sympathy toward you?[v]
Who will turn aside
to ask about your welfare?
6 You have left Me.
This is the LORD's declaration.
You have turned your back,
so I have stretched out My hand
against you
and destroyed you.
I am tired of showing compassion.
7 I scattered them
with a winnowing fork
at the gates of the land.
I made them childless; I destroyed
My people.
They would not turn from their ways.[w]
8 I made their widows more numerous
than the sand of the seas.[x]
I brought a destroyer at noon
against the mother of young men.
I suddenly released on her
agitation and terrors.
9 The mother of seven grew faint;[y]
she breathed her last breath.
Her sun set while it was still day;
she was ashamed and humiliated.
The rest of them I will give over
to the sword
in the presence of their enemies."
This is the LORD's declaration.

[a]**14:16** Jr 7:33; 9:22
[b]**14:17** Jr 9:1,10; 13:17
[c]Jr 4:6; 6:1
[d]Jr 10:19; 30:12
[e]**14:18** Dt 29:22
[f]**14:19** Lv 26:11,30,43-44
[g]Jr 8:15; 33:9
[h]**14:20** Jr 3:25; 11:10; 16:12-13
[i]**14:21** Jr 17:12
[j]Lv 26:44; Jdg 2:1; Is 33:8
[k]**14:22** Jr 8:19; 10:8,15; 16:19
[l]Is 8:17; 25:9
[m]**15:1** Ps 99:6; Ezk 14:14
[n]Ex 32:11-14; Ps 106:23
[o]1Sm 7:9; 12:23
[p]Jr 15:19; 35:19
[q]**15:2** Jr 14:12; 43:11; Ezk 5:12; Zch 11:9
[r]**15:3** Jr 22:19; 49:20–50:45
[s]Is 18:6; Jr 7:33; 19:7
[t]**15:4** 2Kg 21:1-18; 2Ch 33:1-20
[u]**15:5** Lm 1:1-2; Am 5:2
[v]Is 51:19; Nah 3:7
[w]**15:7** Jr 18:11; 25:5; 35:15
[x]**15:8** Gn 22:17; 32:12; 41:49
[y]**15:9** Ru 4:15; 1Sm 2:5; Jb 42:13

[A]**15:3** Lit *families*

Jeremiah's Complaint

10 Woe is me, my mother,
that you gave birth to me,[a]
a man who incites dispute
and conflict
in all the land.
I did not lend or borrow,
yet everyone curses me.[b]

The LORD's Response

11 The LORD said:

I will certainly set you free and care
for you.[A]
I will certainly intercede for you
in a time of trouble,
in your time of distress,
with the enemy.
12 Can anyone smash iron,
iron from the north, or bronze?
13 I will give up your wealth
and your treasures as plunder,
without cost,[c] for all your sins
in all your borders.
14 Then I will make you serve
your enemies[B]
in a land you do not know,
for My anger will kindle a fire
that will burn against you.[d]

Jeremiah's Prayer for Vengeance

15 You know,[e] LORD;
remember me and take note of me.
Avenge me against my persecutors.[f]
In Your patience,[C] don't take me away.
Know that I suffer disgrace
for Your honor.[g]
16 Your words were found,
and I ate them.[h]
Your words became a delight to me
and the joy of my heart,
for I am called by Your name,[i]
*Yahweh God of *Hosts.
17 I never sat with the band of revelers,
and I did not celebrate with them.
Because Your hand was on me,
I sat alone,[j]
for You filled me with indignation.
18 Why has my pain become unending,
my wound incurable,[k]
refusing to be healed?
You truly have become like a mirage
to me —
water that is not reliable.

Jeremiah Told to Repent

19 Therefore, this is what the LORD says:

If you return, I will restore you;
you will stand in My presence.
And if you speak noble words,
rather than worthless ones,
you will be My spokesman.[l]
It is they who must return to you;
you must not return to them.
20 Then I will make you a fortified wall
of bronze
to this people.
They will fight against you
but will not overcome you,
for I am with you
to save you and deliver you.[m]
This is the LORD's declaration.
21 I will deliver you from the power
of evil people
and redeem you from the control
of the ruthless.

No Marriage for Jeremiah

16 The word of the LORD came to me:
2 "You must not marry or have sons or
daughters in this place. 3 For this is what the
LORD says concerning sons and daughters
born in this place as well as concerning the
mothers who bear them and the fathers who
father them in this land: 4 They will die from
deadly diseases. They will not be mourned or
buried but will be like manure on the face of
the earth.[n] They will be finished off by sword
and famine. Their corpses will become food
for the birds of the sky and for the wild animals of the land.[o]

5 "For this is what the LORD says: Don't enter a house where a mourning feast is taking place.[D] Don't go to lament or sympathize
with them, for I have removed My peace
from these people" — this is the LORD's declaration — "as well as My faithful love and
compassion.[p] 6 Both great and small will die
in this land without burial. No lament will

[a] 15:10 Jb 3:1-10 [b] Is 53:3 [c] 15:13 Ps 44:12; Is 52:3 [d] 15:13-14 Jr 17:3-4 [e] 15:15 Jr 12:3 [f] Jr 11:20 [g] Ps 69:7-9 [h] 15:16 Ezk 3:3 [i] Jr 14:9 [j] 15:17 Ps 102:7; Lm 3:28 [k] 15:18 Jr 19:8; 30:12,14,17 [l] 15:19 Ex 4:16 [m] 15:20 Jr 1:8,19; 30:11; 42:11 [n] 16:4 Jr 8:2; 9:22; 25:33 [o] Dt 28:26; Is 18:6; Jr 7:33 [p] 16:5 Ps 25:6; 40:11; 69:16

[A] 15:11 Lit *free for good* [B] 15:14 Some Hb mss, LXX, Syr, Tg; other Hb mss read *you pass through* [C] 15:15 Lit *In the slowness of Your anger* [D] 16:5 Lit *house of mourning*

be made for them, nor will anyone cut himself or[a] shave his head for them.[A] 7 Food won't
be provided for the mourner[b] to comfort
him because of the dead. A cup of consolation won't be given him because of the loss
of his father or mother. 8 You must not enter
the house where feasting is taking place to sit
with them to eat and drink. 9 For this is what
the LORD of ·Hosts, the God of Israel, says: I
am about to eliminate from this place, before
your very eyes and in your time, the sound of
joy and gladness, the voice of the groom and
the bride.[c]

Abandoning the LORD and His Law

10 "When you tell these people all these
things, they will say to you, 'Why has the
LORD declared all this great disaster against
us?[d] What is our ·guilt? What is our sin that
we have committed against the LORD our
God?' 11 Then you will answer them: Because
your fathers abandoned Me"[e]—this is the
LORD's declaration—"and followed other
gods, served them, and worshiped them.[f] Indeed, they abandoned Me and did not keep
My instruction. 12 You did more evil than your
fathers.[g] Look, each one of you was following
the stubbornness of his evil heart, not obeying Me. 13 So I will hurl you from this land
into a land that you and your fathers are not
familiar with.[h] There you will worship other
gods[i] both day and night, for I will not grant
you grace.[B]

14 "However, take note! The days are coming"—the LORD's declaration—"when it
will no longer be said, 'As the LORD lives
who brought the Israelites from the land of
Egypt,'[j] 15 but rather, 'As the LORD lives who
brought the Israelites from the land of the
north[k] and from all the other lands where He
had banished them.' For I will return them to
their land that I gave to their ancestors.[l]

Punishment of Exile

16 "I am about to send for many fishermen"[m]—this is the LORD's declaration—"and they will fish for them. Then I
will send for many hunters, and they will
hunt them down on every mountain and hill
and out of the clefts of the rocks, 17 for My
gaze takes in all their ways.[n] They are not concealed from Me, and their guilt is not hidden
from My sight. 18 I will first repay them double for their guilt[o] and sin because they have
polluted My land. They have filled My inheritance with the lifelessness of their detestable
and abhorrent idols."

19 LORD, my strength and my stronghold,
my refuge in a time of distress,[p]
the nations will come to You
from the ends of the earth,
and they will say,
"Our fathers inherited only lies,
worthless idols[q] of no benefit at all."
20 Can one make gods for himself?
But they are not gods.[r]
21 "Therefore, I am about
to inform them,
and this time I will make them know
My power and My might;
then they will know that My name
is ·Yahweh."[s]

The Persistent Sin of Judah

17 The sin of Judah is written
with an iron stylus.[t]
With a diamond point
it is engraved on the tablet
of their hearts[u]
and on the horns of their[C] altars,
2 while their children remember
their altars
and their ·Asherah poles,
by the green trees
on the high hills—
3 My mountains in the countryside.
I will give up your wealth
and all your treasures as plunder
because of the sin of your ·high places[D]
in all your borders.[v]
4 You will, on your own, relinquish
your inheritance
that I gave you.
I will make you serve your enemies
in a land you do not know,[w]
for you have set My anger on fire;[x]
it will burn forever.

[a] **16:6** Dt 14:1
[b] **16:7** Dt 26:14; Ezk 24:17; Hs 9:4
[c] **16:9** Jr 7:34; 25:10; 33:11
[d] **16:10** Jr 5:19
[e] **16:11** Dt 29:25; Jr 22:9
[f] Dt 29:26
[g] **16:12** Jr 7:26
[h] **16:13** Jr 15:14; 17:4; 22:26
[i] Dt 4:28; 28:36,64
[j] **16:14-15** Jr 23:7-8
[k] **16:15** Jr 3:18
[l] Jr 23:8
[m] **16:16** Am 4:2; Hab 1:14-15
[n] **16:17** Jr 32:19; 2Ch 16:9; Jb 34:21; Ps 90:8; Pr 5:21
[o] **16:18** Jr 17:18
[p] **16:19** Ps 37:39; Nah 1:7
[q] Jr 8:19; 10:8,15; 14:22
[r] **16:20** Jr 2:11
[s] **16:21** Jr 33:2
[t] **17:1** Jb 19:24
[u] Pr 3:3; 7:3; Jr 31:33-34
[v] **17:3** Jr 15:13
[w] **17:4** Jr 16:13; 22:28; Ezk 32:9
[x] Dt 32:22; Jr 15:14

[A] **16:6** This custom demonstrated pagan mourning rituals. [B] **16:13** Or *compassion* [C] **17:1** Some Hb mss, Syr, Vg; other Hb mss read *your*

[D] **17:3** Lit *plunder, your high places because of sin*

Curse and Blessing

5 This is what the LORD says:

The man who trusts in mankind,[a]
who makes human flesh his strength[b]
and turns his heart from the LORD
is cursed.
6 He will be like a juniper in the ·Arabah;[c]
he cannot see when good comes
but dwells in the parched places
in the wilderness,
in a salt land where no one lives.[d]
7 The man who trusts in the LORD,
whose confidence indeed is the LORD,
is blessed.[e]
8 He will be like a tree planted by water:[f]
it sends its roots out toward a stream,
it doesn't fear when heat comes,
and its foliage remains green.
It will not worry in a year of drought
or cease producing fruit.

The Deceitful Heart

9 The heart is more deceitful
than anything else,
and incurable—who can understand it?[g]
10 I, ·Yahweh, examine the mind,
I test the heart[A,h]
to give to each according to his way,
according to what his actions deserve.[i]
11 He who makes a fortune unjustly
is like a partridge that hatches eggs
it didn't lay.
In the middle of his days
his riches will abandon him,
so in the end he will be a fool.[j]
12 A throne of glory[k]
on high[l] from the beginning
is the place of our sanctuary.[m]
13 LORD, the hope of Israel,[n]
all who abandon You
will be put to shame.
All who turn away from Me
will be written in the dirt,
for they have abandoned
the LORD, the fountain of living water.[o]

Jeremiah's Plea

14 Heal me, LORD, and I will be healed;
save me, and I will be saved,
for You are my praise.[p]
15 Hear how they keep challenging me,[q]
"Where is the word of the LORD?
Let it come!"
16 But I have not run away from being
Your shepherd,
and I have not longed for the fatal day.
You know my words were spoken
in Your presence.
17 Don't become a terror to me.
You are my refuge[r] in the day
of disaster.
18 Let my persecutors be put to shame,[s]
but don't let me be put to shame.
Let them be terrified, but don't let me
be terrified.
Bring on them the day of disaster;[t]
shatter them with total[B] destruction.

Observing the Sabbath

19 This is what the LORD said to me, "Go and
stand at the People's Gate, through which the
kings of Judah enter and leave, as well as at all
the gates of Jerusalem. 20 Announce to them:
Hear the word of the LORD, kings of Judah, all
Judah, and all the residents of Jerusalem who
enter through these gates. 21 This is what the
LORD says: Watch yourselves; do not pick up
a load and bring it in through the gates of Jerusalem on the Sabbath day.[u] 22 You must not
carry a load out of your houses on the Sabbath day or do any work,[v] but you must consecrate the Sabbath day, just as I commanded
your ancestors.[w] 23 They wouldn't listen or pay
attention but became obstinate,[x] not listening or accepting discipline.
24 "However, if you listen to Me, says the
LORD, and do not bring loads through the
gates of this city on the Sabbath day and consecrate the Sabbath day and do no work on
it, 25 kings and princes will enter through the
gates of this city. They will sit on the throne of
David, riding in chariots and on horses[y] with
their officials, the men of Judah, and the residents of Jerusalem. This city will be inhabited forever. 26 Then people will come from
the cities of Judah and from the area around
Jerusalem, from the land of Benjamin and
from the Judean foothills, from the hill country and from the ·Negev[z] bringing ·burnt

[a]17:5 Ps 146:3 [b]2Ch 32:8 [c]17:6 Jr 48:6 [d]Gn 19:24-26; Ps 107:34 [e]17:7 Ps 40:4 [f]17:8 Ps 1:3; Ezk 17:5-8 [g]17:9 Jr 15:18; Mc 1:9 [h]17:10 Dt 8:2; Ps 17:3; 26:2 [i]Jr 32:19; Rm 2:6 [j]17:11 Lk 12:20 [k]17:12 Is 6:1-3; Jr 14:21; Ezk 1:26-28 [l]Ps 102:19; Jr 25:30 [m]Ps 68:33-35; Is 60:13 [n]17:13 Jr 14:8; 50:7 [o]Jr 2:13 [p]17:14 Ps 22:25; 71:6; 109:1 [q]17:15 Is 5:19; 2Pt 3:4 [r]17:17 Ps 46:1; 61:3; 62:7-8 [s]17:18 Ps 35:4 [t]Ps 35:8 [u]17:21 Neh 13:15-21; Jn 5:9-12 [v]17:22 Ex 20:8-10; Dt 5:12-14; Is 56:2-6 [w]Ezk 20:12 [x]17:23 Jr 7:26 [y]17:25 Jr 22:4 [z]17:26 Jr 32:44; 33:13

[A]17:10 Lit *kidneys* [B]17:18 Lit *double*

offerings and sacrifice, ˚grain offerings and
frankincense, and thank offerings to the
house of the LORD. 27 If you do not listen to Me
to consecrate the Sabbath day by not carrying
a load while entering the gates of Jerusalem
on the Sabbath day, I will set fire to its gates,[a]
and it will consume the citadels[b] of Jerusalem[c] and not be extinguished."[d]

Parable of the Potter

18 This is the word that came to Jeremiah
from the LORD: 2 "Go down at once to
the potter's house;[e] there I will reveal My
words to you." 3 So I went down to the potter's
house, and there he was, working away at the
wheel.[A] 4 But the jar that he was making from
the clay became flawed in the potter's hand,
so he made it into another jar, as it seemed
right for him to do.[f]

5 The word of the LORD came to me: 6 "House
of Israel, can I not treat you as this potter
treats his clay?"—this is the LORD's declaration. "Just like clay in the potter's hand,
so are you in My hand, house of Israel.[g] 7 At
one moment I might announce concerning a
nation or a kingdom that I will uproot, tear
down, and destroy it.[h] 8 However, if that nation I have made an announcement about
turns from its evil, I will relent concerning
the disaster I had planned to do to it.[i] 9 At another time I announce that I will build and
plant a nation or a kingdom.[j] 10 However, if it
does what is evil in My sight by not listening
to My voice, I will relent concerning the good
I had said I would do to it.[k] 11 So now, say to the
men of Judah and to the residents of Jerusalem: This is what the LORD says: I am about
to bring harm to you and make plans against
you. Turn now, each from your evil way, and
correct your ways and your deeds.[l] 12 But they
will say, 'It's hopeless.[m] We will continue to
follow our plans, and each of us will continue to act according to the stubbornness of
his evil heart.'"

Deluded Israel

13 Therefore, this is what the LORD says:

Ask among the nations,
Who has heard things like these?
Virgin Israel has done
a most terrible thing.[n]
14 Does the snow of Lebanon ever leave
the highland crags?
Or does cold water flowing
from a distance ever fail?
15 Yet My people have forgotten Me.[o]
They burn incense to false idols
that make them stumble in their ways
on the ancient roads[p]
and walk on new paths,
not the highway.
16 They have made their land a horror,[q]
a perpetual object of scorn;[B,r]
everyone who passes by it
will be horrified[s]
and shake his head.[t]
17 I will scatter them before the enemy
like the east wind.[u]
I will show them[C] My back and not
My face
on the day of their calamity.

Plot against Jeremiah

18 Then certain ones said, "Come, let's
make plans against Jeremiah,[v] for instruction will never be lost from the priest,[w] or
counsel from the wise, or an ˚oracle from the
prophet.[x] Come, let's denounce him[D] and pay
no attention to all his words."

19 Pay attention to me, LORD.
Hear what my opponents are saying![y]
20 Should good be repaid with evil?
Yet they have dug a pit for me.[z]
Remember how I stood before You
to speak good on their behalf,
to turn Your anger from them.
21 Therefore, hand their children
over to famine,[aa]
and pour the sword's power on them.
Let their wives become childless
and widowed,
their husbands slain by deadly disease,[E]
their young men struck down
by the sword in battle.
22 Let a cry be heard from their houses
when You suddenly bring raiders
against them,
for they have dug a pit to capture me

[a] **17:27** Lm 4:11 [b] Jr 49:27; Am 1:14 [c] 2Kg 25:9 [d] Jr 7:20 [e] **18:2** Jr 19:1-2 [f] **18:4** Rm 9:21 [g] **18:6** Gn 2:7-8; Is 43:1; 64:8 [h] **18:7** Jr 1:10; 24:6; 31:28 [i] **18:8** 2Sm 24:1; Jr 42:10; Jnh 3:10 [j] **18:9** Jr 1:10 [k] **18:10** Ezk 18:25-29; 33:12-13 [l] **18:11** Jr 7:3 [m] **18:12** Jr 2:25 [n] **18:13** Jr 5:30; Hs 6:10 [o] **18:15** Jr 2:32; 3:21; 13:25 [p] Jr 6:16 [q] **18:16** Jr 25:9; 50:13 [r] Lm 2:15 [s] Jr 19:8; 49:17 [t] Ps 22:7 [u] **18:17** Jr 13:24 [v] **18:18** Jr 11:19 [w] Jr 2:8 [x] Jr 5:13 [y] **18:19** Ps 55:2-3; 142:6 [z] **18:20** Ps 35:7; 57:6 [aa] **18:21** Ps 109:9-20

[A] **18:3** Lit *pair of stones* [B] **18:16** Lit *hissing* [C] **18:17** LXX, Lat, Syr, Tg; MT reads *will look at them* [D] **18:18** Lit *let's strike him with the tongue* [E] **18:21** Lit *by death*

and have hidden snares for my feet.[a]
23 But You, LORD, know
all their deadly plots against me.
Do not wipe out their ·guilt;[b]
do not blot out their sin before You.
Let them be forced to stumble
before You;
deal with them in the time of Your anger.

The Clay Jar

19 This is what the LORD says: "Go, buy a
potter's clay[c] jar. Take[A] some of the elders of the people and some of the leading
priests[d] 2 and go out to the Valley of Hinnom[e]
near the entrance of the Potsherd Gate. Proclaim there the words I speak to you. 3 Say:
Hear the word of the LORD, kings of Judah
and residents of Jerusalem.[f] This is what the
LORD of ·Hosts, the God of Israel, says: I am
going to bring such disaster on this place that
everyone who hears about it will shudder[B,g]
4 because they have abandoned Me and made
this a foreign place. They have burned incense
in it to other gods that they, their fathers, and
the kings of Judah have never known. They
have filled this place with the blood of the innocent.[h] 5 They have built ·high places to ·Baal
on which to burn their children in the fire
as burnt offerings to Baal, something I have
never commanded or mentioned; I never entertained the thought.[C,i]
6 "Therefore, take note! The days are coming" — this is the LORD's declaration — "when
this place will no longer be called Topheth
and the Valley of Hinnom, but the Valley of
Slaughter.[j] 7 I will spoil the plans of Judah and
Jerusalem in this place. I will make them fall
by the sword before their enemies, by the
hand of those who want to take their life. I
will provide their corpses as food for the
birds of the sky and for the wild animals of
the land.[k] 8 I will make this city desolate, an
object of scorn. Everyone who passes by it
will be horrified and scoff because of all its
wounds.[l] 9 I will make them eat the flesh of
their sons and their daughters, and they will
eat each other's flesh in the siege and distress
that their enemies, those who want to take
their life, inflict on them.[m]

[a] **18:22** Ps 140:5; 142:3 [b] **18:23** Neh 4:5 [c] **19:1** Jr 18:2 [d] 2Kg 19:2 [e] **19:2** 2Kg 23:10; 2Ch 28:3; Jr 7:31-32 [f] **19:3** Jr 17:20 [g] 1Sm 3:11 [h] **19:4** 2Kg 21:6,16; Jr 2:34 [i] **19:5** Jr 7:31; 32:35 [j] **19:6** Jr 7:32 [k] **19:7** Dt 28:26; Jr 7:33; 15:3 [l] **19:8** Jr 18:16; Mc 1:9; Nah 3:19 [m] **19:9** Dt 28:53-57; Ezk 5:10; Lm 4:10 [n] **19:11** Jr 7:32 [o] **19:13** Dt 4:19; 2Kg 17:16; 23:4-5 [p] **19:14** 2Ch 20:5; Jr 26:2 [q] **19:15** Jr 7:26 [r] **20:1** 1Ch 24:14; Ezr 2:37-38 [s] **20:4** Jr 6:25 [t] **20:5** Dt 28:33; Ezk 23:29

10 "Then you are to shatter the jar in the
presence of the people traveling with you,
11 and you are to proclaim to them: This is
what the LORD of Hosts says: I will shatter
these people and this city, like one shatters a
potter's jar that can never again be mended.
They will bury the dead in Topheth because
there is no other place for burials.[n] 12 I will
do so to this place" — this is the declaration
of the LORD — "and to its residents, making
this city like Topheth. 13 The houses of Jerusalem and the houses of the kings of Judah will
become impure like that place Topheth — all
the houses on whose rooftops they have
burned incense to the whole heavenly host[o]
and poured out ·drink offerings to other
gods."
14 Jeremiah came back from Topheth, where
the LORD had sent him to prophesy, stood
in the courtyard of the LORD's temple,[p] and
proclaimed to all the people, 15 "This is what
the LORD of Hosts, the God of Israel, says: 'I
am about to bring on this city — and on all
its dependent villages — all the disaster that
I spoke against it, for they have become obstinate, not obeying My words.'"[q]

Jeremiah Beaten by Pashhur

20 Pashhur the priest, the son of Immer[r] and chief official in the temple
of the LORD, heard Jeremiah prophesying
these things. 2 So Pashhur had Jeremiah the
prophet beaten and put him in the stocks at
the Upper Benjamin Gate in the LORD's temple. 3 The next day, when Pashhur released
Jeremiah from the stocks, Jeremiah said to
him, "The LORD does not call you Pashhur,
but Magor-missabib,[D] 4 for this is what the
LORD says, 'I am about to make you a terror
to both yourself and those you love.[s] They will
fall by the sword of their enemies before your
very eyes. I will hand Judah over to the king
of Babylon, and he will deport them to Babylon and put them to the sword. 5 I will give
away all the wealth of this city, all its products[t] and valuables. Indeed, I will hand all the
treasures of the kings of Judah over to their
enemies. They will plunder them, seize them,
and carry them off to Babylon. 6 As for you,

[A] **19:1** Syr, Tg; MT omits *Take* [B] **19:3** Lit *shudder their ears*; 1Sm 3:11; 2Kg 21:12 [C] **19:5** Lit *mentioned, and it did not arise on My heart*

[D] **20:3** = Terror Is on Every Side; Jr 6:25; 20:10; 46:5

Pashhur, and all who live in your house, you will go into captivity. You will go to Babylon. There you will die, and there you will be buried, you and all your friends that you prophesied falsely[a] to.'"

Jeremiah Compelled to Preach

7 You deceived me, LORD,
and I was deceived.
You seized me and prevailed.
I am a laughingstock all the time;[b]
everyone ridicules me.
8 For whenever I speak, I cry out,
I proclaim, "Violence
and destruction!"[c]
because the word of the LORD
has become for me
constant disgrace and derision.
9 If I say, "I won't mention Him
or speak any longer in His name,"
His message becomes a fire burning
in my heart,[d]
shut up in my bones.
I become tired of holding it in,
and I cannot prevail.
10 For I have heard the gossip
of many people,
"Terror is on every side![A,e]
Report him; let's report him!"
Everyone I trusted[B] watches
for my fall.[f]
"Perhaps he will be deceived
so that we might prevail against him
and take our vengeance on him."
11 But the LORD is with me
like a violent warrior.[g]
Therefore, my persecutors will stumble
and not prevail.
Since they have not succeeded,
they will be utterly shamed,
an everlasting humiliation that will
never be forgotten.
12 LORD of *Hosts, testing the righteous
and seeing the heart[C] and mind,
let me see Your vengeance on them,
for I have presented my case to You.[h]
13 Sing to the LORD!
Praise the LORD,
for He rescues the life of the needy
from the hand of evil people.

Jeremiah's Lament

14 May the day I was born
be cursed.[i]
May the day my mother bore me
never be blessed.
15 May the man be cursed
who brought the news
to my father, saying,
"A male child is born to you,"
bringing him great joy.
16 Let that man be like the cities
the LORD demolished
without compassion.[j]
Let him hear an outcry in the morning[k]
and a war cry at noontime
17 because he didn't kill me in the womb[l]
so that my mother might have been
my grave,
her womb eternally pregnant.
18 Why did I come out of the womb
to see only struggle and sorrow,[m]
to end my life in shame?

Zedekiah's Request Denied

21 This is the word that came to Jeremiah
from the LORD when King Zedekiah
sent Pashhur[n] son of Malchijah and the priest
Zephaniah[o] son of Maaseiah to Jeremiah, asking, 2"Ask the LORD on our behalf, since Nebuchadnezzar[D,p] king of Babylon is making war
against us. Perhaps the LORD will perform
for us something like all His past wonderful
works so that Nebuchadnezzar will withdraw
from us."
3But Jeremiah answered, "This is what
you are to say to Zedekiah: 4'This is what the
LORD, the God of Israel, says: I will repel the
weapons of war in your hands,[q] those you are
using to fight the king of Babylon and the
Chaldeans[E] who are besieging you outside the
wall, and I will bring them into the center of
this city.[r] 5I will fight against you[s] with an outstretched hand and a mighty arm,[t] with anger,
rage, and great wrath. 6I will strike the residents of this city, both man and beast. They
will die in a great plague. 7Afterward'" — this
is the LORD's declaration — "'King Zedekiah
of Judah, his officers, and the people — those
in this city who survive the plague, the sword,
and the famine — I will hand over to King

[a]**20:6** Jr 14:14 [b]**20:7** Lm 3:14 [c]**20:8** Jr 6:7 [d]**20:9** Jb 32:18-20; Ps 39:3 [e]**20:10** Jr 6:25; 46:5 [f]Ps 35:15; 41:9; 56:6 [g]**20:11** Ex 15:3 [h]**20:12** Jr 11:20 [i]**20:14** Jb 3:3 [j]**20:16** Gn 19:25 [k]Jr 18:22 [l]**20:17** Jb 3:10-11 [m]**20:18** Jb 3:20; Lm 3:1 [n]**21:1** 1Ch 9:12; Neh 11:12; Jr 38:1 [o]Jr 29:24-29; 37:3; 52:24-27 [p]**21:2** 2Kg 24:11; 25:22; 2Ch 36:6-13 [q]**21:4** Jr 32:5; 37:8-10 [r]Is 13:4 [s]**21:5** 1Sm 4:1–5:12; Lm 2:5 [t]Dt 5:15; 26:8; Ps 136:12

[A]**20:10** Hb *Magor-missabib*; Jr 20:3 [B]**20:10** Lit *Every man of my peace* [C]**20:12** Lit *kidneys* [D]**21:2** Lit *Nebuchadrezzar* [E]**21:4** = Babylonians

Nebuchadnezzar of Babylon,[a] to their enemies, yes, to those who want to take their
lives. He will put them to the sword; he won’t
spare them or show pity or compassion.’[b]

A Warning for the People

8“But you must say to this people, ‘This is
what the LORD says: Look, I am presenting
to you the way of life and the way of death.[c]
9Whoever stays in this city will die by the
sword, famine, and plague, but whoever goes
out and surrenders to the Chaldeans who are
besieging you will live and will retain his life
like the spoils of war.[d] 10For I have turned[A]
against this city to bring disaster[e] and not
good’” — this is the LORD’s declaration. “‘It
will be handed over to the king of Babylon,
who will burn it down.’[f]
11“And to the house of the king of Judah say
this: ‘Hear the word of the LORD! 12House of
David, this is what the LORD says:

Administer justice every morning,
and rescue the victim of robbery
from the hand of his oppressor,[g]
or My anger will flare up like fire
and burn unquenchably
because of their evil deeds.
13 Beware! I am against you,[h]
you who sit above the valley,
you atop the rocky plateau —
this is the LORD’s declaration —
you who say, “Who can come down
against us?[i]
Who can enter our hiding places?”
14 I will punish you according to
what you have done[j] —
this is the LORD’s declaration.
I will kindle a fire in its forest[k]
that will consume everything
around it.’”[l]

Judgment against Sinful Kings

22 This is what the LORD says: “Go down
to the palace of the king of Judah and
announce this word there. 2You are to say:
Hear the word of the LORD, king of Judah, you
who sit on the throne of David — you, your officers, and your people who enter these gates.
3This is what the LORD says: Administer justice
and righteousness.[m] Rescue the victim of robbery from the hand of his oppressor.[n] Don’t
exploit or brutalize the foreigner, the fatherless, or the widow. Don’t shed innocent blood
in this place. 4For if you conscientiously carry
out this word, then kings sitting on David’s
throne will enter through the gates of this
palace[o] riding on chariots and horses — they,
their officers, and their people. 5But if you
do not obey these words, then I swear by Myself” — this is the LORD’s declaration — “that
this house will become a ruin.”[p]
6For this is what the LORD says concerning
the house of the king of Judah:

You are like Gilead to Me,
or the summit of Lebanon,
but I will certainly turn you
into a wilderness,
uninhabited cities.
7 I will appoint destroyers against you,
each with his weapons.
They will cut down the choicest
of your cedars
and throw them into the fire.

8“Many nations will pass by this city and
ask one another, ‘Why did the LORD do such
a thing to this great city?’ 9They will answer,
‘Because they abandoned the covenant[q] of
Yahweh their God and worshiped and served
other gods.’”[r]

A Message Concerning Shallum

10 Do not weep for the dead;
do not mourn for him.
Weep bitterly for the one[B]
who has gone away,
for he will never return again
and see his native land.

11For this is what the LORD says concerning
Shallum[s] son of Josiah, king of Judah, who became king in place of his father Josiah: “He
has left this place — he will never return here
again, 12but he will die in the place where they
deported him, never seeing this land again.”

A Message concerning Jehoiakim

13 Woe for the one who builds his palace
through unrighteousness,[t]

[a]**21:7** Jr 37:17; 39:5-9; 52:9
[b]2Ch 36:17
[c]**21:8** Dt 30:15-19; Pr 12:28; Jr 8:3
[d]**21:9** Jr 38:2; 39:18; 45:5
[e]**21:10** Jr 44:11
[f]Jr 34:2,22; 37:8; 38:18
[g]**21:12** Dt 28:29; Ec 4:1; Jr 22:3
[h]**21:13** Ezk 13:8
[i]Jr 49:4
[j]**21:14** Is 3:10
[k]Ezk 20:47
[l]Jr 50:32
[m]**22:3** 2Sm 8:15; 2Ch 9:8; Jr 23:5
[n]Dt 28:29; Ec 4:1; Jr 21:12
[o]**22:4** Jr 17:25
[p]**22:5** Jr 17:27
[q]**22:8-9** Dt 29:24-25
[r]**22:9** Dt 30:17
[s]**22:11** 2Kg 23:32-35; 1Ch 3:15
[t]**22:13** Mc 3:10

[A]**21:10** Lit *set My face* [B]**22:10** = Shallum (Jehoahaz) in v. 11

his upper rooms through injustice,
who makes his fellow man serve
without pay
and will not give him his wages,[a]
14 who says, "I will build myself
a massive palace,
with spacious upper rooms."
He will cut windows[A] in it,
and it will be paneled with cedar
and painted with vermilion.
15 Are you a king because you excel
in cedar?
Didn't your father eat and drink
and administer justice
and righteousness?[b]
Then it went well with him.
16 He took up the case of the poor
and needy,
then it went well.
Is this not what it means to know Me?
This is the LORD's declaration.
17 But you have eyes and a heart
for nothing
except your own dishonest profit,
shedding innocent blood
and committing extortion
and oppression.

18 Therefore, this is what the LORD says
concerning Jehoiakim[c] son of Josiah, king of
Judah:

They will not mourn for him, saying,
"Woe, my brother!" or "Woe,
my sister!"
They will not mourn for him, saying,
"Woe, lord! Woe, his majesty!"
19 He will be buried like a donkey,[d]
dragged off and thrown
outside the gates of Jerusalem.
20 Go up to Lebanon and cry out;
raise your voice in Bashan;
cry out from Abarim,[e]
for all your lovers[B] have been crushed.[f]
21 I spoke to you when you were secure.
You said, "I will not listen."
This has been your way since youth;[g]
indeed, you have never listened
to Me.
22 The wind will take charge of[C] all
your shepherds,
and your lovers[B] will go into captivity.
Then you will be ashamed
and humiliated[h]
because of all your evil.
23 You residents of Lebanon,
nestled among the cedars,
how you will groan[D] when labor pains
come on you,
agony like a woman in labor.[i]

A Message concerning Coniah

24 "As I live," says the LORD, "though you, Coniah[E,j] son of Jehoiakim, the king of Judah,
were a signet ring[k] on My right hand, I would
tear you from it. 25 In fact, I will hand you
over to those you dread,[l] who want to take
your life, to Nebuchadnezzar king of Babylon
and the Chaldeans. 26 I will hurl you and the
mother who gave birth[m] to you into another
land,[n] where neither of you were born, and
there you will both die. 27 They will never return to the land they long to return to."

28 Is this man Coniah
a despised, shattered pot,[o]
a jar no one wants?
Why are he and his descendants
hurled out
and cast into a land
they have not known?
29 Earth, earth, earth,
hear the word of the LORD!

30 This is what the LORD says:

Record this man as childless,[p]
a man who will not be successful
in his lifetime.
None of his descendants will succeed
in sitting on the throne of David[q]
or ruling again in Judah.

The LORD and His Sheep

23 "Woe to the shepherds who destroy
and scatter the sheep of My pasture!"[r]
This is the LORD's declaration. 2 "Therefore,
this is what the LORD, the God of Israel, says
about the shepherds who shepherd My people: You have scattered My flock, banished
them, and have not attended to them.[s] I will
attend to you because of your evil acts"—this

[a] **22:13** Lv 19:13; Jms 5:4
[b] **22:15** Jr 22:3
[c] **22:18** 2Kg 23:34–24:6; 2Ch 36:4-8
[d] **22:19** Jr 36:30
[e] **22:20** Nm 27:12; Dt 32:49
[f] Jr 3:1
[g] **22:21** Jr 3:25
[h] **22:22** Is 41:11
[i] **22:23** Jr 6:24
[j] **22:24** 2Kg 24:6-17; Jr 37:1; 52:31
[k] Gn 38:18; 1Kg 21:8; Hg 2:23
[l] **22:25** Jr 34:20-21
[m] **22:26** 2Kg 24:15
[n] 2Kg 24:8
[o] **22:28** Ps 31:12; Jr 48:38; Hs 8:8
[p] **22:30** 1Ch 3:17; Mt 1:12
[q] Jr 36:30
[r] **23:1** Ps 100:3; Ezk 34:31
[s] **23:2** Ps 8:4; Is 23:16

[A] **22:14** Lit *My windows* [B] **22:20,22** Or *friends*, or *allies* [C] **22:22** Lit *will shepherd* [D] **22:23** LXX, Syr, Vg; MT reads *will be pitied* [E] **22:24** = Jehoiachin

is the LORD's declaration. 3"I will gather the
remnant of My flock from all the lands where
I have banished them, and I will return them
to their grazing land. They will become fruitful and numerous.[a] 4I will raise up shepherds
over them who will shepherd them.[b] They
will no longer be afraid or dismayed, nor will
any be missing." This is the LORD's declaration.

The Righteous Branch of David

5 "The days are coming"[c] — this is
the LORD's declaration—
"when I will raise up a Righteous
Branch of David.[d]
He will reign wisely as king
and administer justice and
righteousness in the land.[e]
6 In His days Judah will be saved,
and Israel will dwell securely.[f]
This is what He will be named:
·Yahweh Our Righteousness.[g]

7"The days are coming" — the LORD's declaration — "when it will no longer be said,
'As the LORD lives who brought the Israelites
from the land of Egypt,'[h] 8but, 'As the LORD
lives, who brought and led the descendants of
the house of Israel from the land of the north
and from all the other countries where I[A] had
banished them.' They will dwell once more in
their own land."[i]

False Prophets Condemned

9Concerning the prophets:

My heart is broken within me,[j]
and all my bones tremble.
I have become like a drunkard,
like a man overcome by wine,
because of the LORD,
because of His holy words.
10 For the land is full of adulterers;[k]
the land mourns because
of the curse,
and the grazing lands in the wilderness
have dried up.
Their way of life[B] has become evil,
and their power is not rightly used
11 because both prophet and priest
are ungodly,[l]

[a]23:3 Gn 1:26-28; 9:1-7; 35:11
[b]23:4 Ezk 34:23; Mc 5:2-6
[c]23:5-6 Jr 33:14-16
[d]23:5 Zch 3:8; 6:12
[e]Is 11:1-9
[f]23:6 Dt 33:12
[g]Ps 4:1
[h]23:7 Jr 16:14
[i]23:8 Jr 16:15
[j]23:9 Hab 3:16
[k]23:10 Jr 9:2; Hs 7:4; Mal 3:5
[l]23:11 Jr 6:13; Zph 3:4
[m]23:12 Ps 35:6; 73:18
[n]23:13 Pr 12:26; Is 3:12; Jr 50:6
[o]23:14 Gn 13:10-13; 18:16–19:28; Is 1:10-17
[p]23:15 Jr 8:14; 9:15
[q]23:17 Jr 4:10
[r]23:18 Jb 15:8; Ps 25:14; 89:7
[s]23:19 Ps 83:15; Is 29:6; Zch 9:14

even in My house I have found
their evil.
This is the LORD's declaration.
12 Therefore, their way will be to them
like slippery paths in the gloom.[m]
They will be driven away
and fall down there,
for I will bring disaster on them,
the year of their punishment.
This is the LORD's declaration.
13 Among the prophets of Samaria
I saw something disgusting:
They prophesied by[C] ·Baal
and led My people Israel astray.[n]
14 Among the prophets of Jerusalem also
I saw a horrible thing:
They commit adultery and walk
in lies.
They strengthen the hands of evildoers,
and none turns his back on evil.
They are all like Sodom[o] to Me;
Jerusalem's residents are
like Gomorrah.

15Therefore, this is what the LORD of ·Hosts
says concerning the prophets:

I am about to feed them ·wormwood
and give them poisoned water
to drink,[p]
for from the prophets of Jerusalem
ungodliness[D] has spread
throughout the land.

16This is what the LORD of Hosts says: "Do
not listen to the words of the prophets who
prophesy to you. They are making you worthless. They speak visions from their own
minds, not from the LORD's mouth. 17They
keep on saying to those who despise Me, 'The
LORD has said: You will have peace.'[q] They
have said to everyone who follows the stubbornness of his heart, 'No harm will come to
you.' "

18 For who has stood in the council[r]
of the LORD
to see and hear His word?
Who has paid attention to His word
and obeyed?
19 Look, a storm from the LORD![s]
Wrath has gone out,

[A]23:8 LXX reads *He* [B]23:10 Lit *Their manner of running* [C]23:13 = in the name of [D]23:15 Or *pollution*

a whirling storm.
It will whirl about the heads
of the wicked.
20 The LORD's anger will not turn back
until He has completely fulfilled
the purposes of His heart.
In time to come you will
understand it clearly.[a]

21 I did not send these prophets,[b]
yet they ran with a message.
I did not speak to them,
yet they prophesied.
22 If they had really stood in My council,
they would have enabled My people
to hear My words
and would have turned them back
from their evil ways
and their evil deeds.

23 "Am I a God who is only near"[c] — this is
the LORD's declaration — "and not a God who
is far away? 24 Can a man hide himself in secret places where I cannot see him?"[d] — the
LORD's declaration. "Do I not fill the heavens
and the earth?"[e] — the LORD's declaration.

25 "I have heard what the prophets who
prophesy a lie in My name have said, 'I had a
dream! I had a dream!' 26 How long will this
continue in the minds of the prophets prophesying lies, prophets of the deceit of their own
minds? 27 Through their dreams that they tell
one another, they plan to cause My people to
forget My name as their fathers forgot My
name through Baal worship.[f] 28 The prophet
who has only a dream should recount the
dream, but the one who has My word should
speak My word truthfully, for what is straw
compared to grain?" — this is the LORD's declaration. 29 "Is not My word like fire" — this is
the LORD's declaration — "and like a hammer
that pulverizes rock? 30 Therefore, take note!
I am against the prophets"[g] — the LORD's declaration — "who steal My words from each
other. 31 I am against the prophets" — the
LORD's declaration — "who use their own
tongues to make a declaration. 32 I am against
those who prophesy false dreams"[h] — the
LORD's declaration — "telling them and leading My people astray with their falsehoods
and their boasting. It was not I who sent or
commanded them, and they are of no benefit at all[i] to these people" — this is the LORD's
declaration.

The Burden of the LORD

33 "Now when these people or a prophet or
a priest asks you, 'What is the burden of the
LORD?' you will respond to them: What is
the burden? I will throw you away" — this is
the LORD's declaration. 34 "As for the prophet,
priest, or people who say, 'The burden of the
LORD,' I will punish that man and his household. 35 This is what each man is to say to his
friend and to his brother, 'What has the LORD
answered?' or 'What has the LORD spoken?'
36 But no longer refer to[A] the burden of the
LORD, for each man's word becomes his burden and you pervert the words of the living
God, the LORD of Hosts, our God. 37 You must
say to the prophet: What has the LORD answered you? and What has the LORD spoken?
38 But if you say, 'The burden of the LORD,' then
this is what the LORD says: Because you have
said, 'The burden of the LORD,' and I specifically told you not to say, 'The burden of the
LORD,' 39 I will surely forget you[B] and throw
away from My presence both you and the city
that I gave you and your fathers. 40 I will bring
on you everlasting shame and humiliation[j]
that will never be forgotten."

The Good and the Bad Figs

24 After Nebuchadnezzar king of Babylon had deported Jeconiah[C] son of Jehoiakim king of Judah, the officials of Judah,
and the craftsmen and metalsmiths[k] from Jerusalem and had brought them to Babylon,
the LORD showed me two baskets of figs[l]
placed before the temple of the LORD. 2 One
basket contained very good figs, like early
figs,[m] but the other basket contained very
bad figs, so bad they were inedible. 3 The LORD
said to me, "What do you see, Jeremiah?" I
said, "Figs! The good figs are very good, but
the bad figs are extremely bad, so bad they are
inedible."

4 The word of the LORD came to me: 5 "This
is what the LORD, the God of Israel, says: Like
these good figs, so I regard as good the exiles
from Judah I sent away from this place to the

[a] **23:19-20** Jr 30:23-24 [b] **23:21** Jr 14:14 [c] **23:23** Ps 139:1-10 [d] **23:24** Gn 3:8; 4:14; Jb 34:22 [e] Ps 139:7-12; Am 9:2-4 [f] **23:27** Jdg 3:7; 8:33-34 [g] **23:30** Dt 18:20; Jr 14:14-15; Ezk 13:8 [h] **23:32** Dt 18:20 [i] Is 30:5-6; Jr 2:8,11 [j] **23:40** Ps 78:66; Jr 20:11 [k] **24:1** 2Kg 24:14,16; Jr 29:2 [l] Am 8:1 [m] **24:2** Is 28:4; Hs 9:10; Mc 7:1

[A] **23:36** Or *longer remember* [B] **23:39** Some Hb mss; other Hb mss, LXX, Syr, Vg read *surely lift you up* [C] **24:1** = Jehoiachin

land of the Chaldeans. 6 I will keep My eyes on
them for their good and will return them to
this land. I will build them up and not demolish them; I will plant them and not uproot
them.[a] 7 I will give them a heart to know Me,[b]
that I am •Yahweh. They will be My people,
and I will be their God because they will return to Me with all their heart.[c]

8 "But as for the bad figs, so bad they are inedible,[d] this is what the LORD says: in this way
I will deal with king Zedekiah of Judah, his officials, and the remnant of Jerusalem — those
remaining in this land and those living in the
land of Egypt.[e] 9 I will make them an object of
horror[f] and disaster to all the kingdoms of the
earth, a disgrace, an object of scorn, ridicule,[g]
and cursing, wherever I have banished them.
10 I will send the sword, famine, and plague[h]
against them until they have perished from
the land I gave to them and their ancestors."

The Seventy-Year Exile

25 This is the word that came to Jeremiah
concerning all the people of Judah
in the fourth year of Jehoiakim[i] son of Josiah, king of Judah (which was the first year
of Nebuchadnezzar king of Babylon). 2 The
prophet Jeremiah spoke concerning all the
people of Judah and all the residents of Jerusalem as follows: 3 "From the thirteenth year
of Josiah son of Amon,[j] king of Judah, until
this very day — 23 years — the word of the
LORD has come to me, and I have spoken to
you time and time again,[A,k] but you have not
obeyed. 4 The LORD sent all His servants the
prophets to you time and time again,[B] but you
have not obeyed or even paid attention.[C,l] 5 He
announced, 'Turn, each of you, from your[D]
evil way of life and from your evil deeds.[m]
Live in the land the LORD gave to you and
your ancestors long ago and forever. 6 Do not
follow other gods to serve them and to worship them,[n] and do not provoke Me to anger
by the work of your hands.[o] Then I will do you
no harm.

7 "'But you would not obey Me' — this is
the LORD's declaration — 'in order that you
might provoke Me to anger by the work of
your hands and bring disaster on yourselves.'
8 "Therefore, this is what the LORD of

[a]**24:6** Jr 1:10 [b]**24:7** Dt 30:6; Jr 31:33; 32:40 [c]2Ch 6:38; Jr 29:13 [d]**24:8** Jr 29:17 [e]Jr 44:1 [f]**24:9** 2Ch 29:8; Jr 15:4; 29:18 [g]Dt 28:37; 1Kg 9:7; 2Ch 7:20 [h]**24:10** Jr 14:12; 21:9; 29:17-18 [i]**25:1** 2Kg 23:34–24:6; 2Ch 36:4-8 [j]**25:3** Jr 1:2 [k]Jr 11:7; 26:5 [l]**25:4** Jr 7:25-26 [m]**25:5** Jr 18:11; 35:15 [n]**25:6** Dt 8:19; Jr 13:10 [o]Dt 31:29; 1Kg 16:7; Jr 44:8 [p]**25:9** Jr 1:13 [q]Is 45:1 [r]Jr 4:7; 18:16; 19:8 [s]**25:10** Jr 7:34; 16:9; 33:11 [t]**25:11** 2Ch 36:21; Jr 29:10; Dn 9:2 [u]**25:12** Is 13:19 [v]**25:14** Jr 50:29 [w]**25:15** Ps 75:8; Is 51:17; Jr 49:12

•Hosts says: 'Because you have not obeyed
My words, 9 I am going to send for all the
families of the north'[p] — this is the LORD's
declaration — 'and send for My servant[q] Nebuchadnezzar king of Babylon, and I will bring
them against this land, against its residents,
and against all these surrounding nations,
and I will •completely destroy them and
make them a desolation,[r] a derision, and ruins forever. 10 I will eliminate the sound of joy
and gladness from them — the voice of the
groom and the bride,[s] the sound of the millstones and the light of the lamp. 11 This whole
land will become a desolate ruin, and these
nations will serve the king of Babylon for 70
years.[t] 12 When the 70 years are completed, I
will punish the king of Babylon and that nation' — this is the LORD's declaration — 'the
land of the Chaldeans, for their •guilt, and I
will make it a ruin forever.[u] 13 I will bring on
that land all My words I have spoken against
it, all that is written in this book that Jeremiah prophesied against all the nations.
14 For many nations and great kings will enslave them, and I will repay them according
to their deeds[v] and the work of their hands.'"

The Cup of God's Wrath

15 This is what the LORD, the God of Israel,
said to me: "Take this cup of the wine of
wrath from My hand and make all the nations I am sending you to, drink from it.[w]
16 They will drink, stagger,[E] and go out of their
minds because of the sword I am sending
among them."

17 So I took the cup from the LORD's hand
and made all the nations drink from it, everyone the LORD sent me to. 18 These included:

Jerusalem and the other cities of Judah,
its kings and its officials, to make them
a desolate ruin, an object of scorn and
cursing — as it is today;
19 Pharaoh king of Egypt, his officers,
his leaders, all his people,
20 and all the mixed peoples;
all the kings of the land of Uz;
all the kings of the land of the
Philistines — Ashkelon, Gaza, Ekron,
and the remnant of Ashdod;

[A]**25:3** Lit *you; rising early and speaking* [B]**25:4** Lit *prophets, rising early and sending* [C]**25:4** Lit *even inclined your ears* [D]**25:5** Lit *his* [E]**25:16** Or *vomit*

21 Edom, Moab, and the Ammonites;
22 all the kings of Tyre,
all the kings of Sidon,
and the kings of the coastlands across
the sea;
23 Dedan, Tema, Buz, and all those who
shave their temples;[A,a]
24 all the kings of Arabia,
and all the kings of the mixed peoples
who have settled in the desert;
25 all the kings of Zimri,
all the kings of Elam,
and all the kings of Media;
26 all the kings of the north, both near
and far from one another;
that is, all the kingdoms of the world
which are on the face of the earth.
Finally, the king of Sheshach[B] will drink
after them.

27 "Then you are to say to them: This is what
the LORD of Hosts, the God of Israel, says:
Drink,[b] get drunk, and vomit. Fall down and
never get up again, as a result of the sword I
am sending among you. 28 If[C] they refuse to
take the cup from you and drink, you are to
say to them: This is what the LORD of Hosts
says: You must drink! 29 For I am already
bringing disaster on the city that bears My
name,[c] so how could you possibly go unpunished? You will not go unpunished, for I am
summoning a sword against all the inhabitants of the earth"—this is the declaration
of the LORD of Hosts.[d]

Judgment on the Whole World

30 "As for you, you are to prophesy all these
things to them, and say to them:

The LORD roars from heaven;
He raises His voice
from His holy dwelling.[e]
He roars loudly over His grazing land;
He calls out with a shout, like those
who tread grapes,
against all the inhabitants of the earth.
31 The tumult reaches to the ends
of the earth
because the LORD brings a case
against[f] the nations.
He enters into judgment with all flesh.
As for the wicked, He hands them over
to the sword—
this is the LORD's declaration.

32 "This is what the LORD of Hosts says:

Pay attention! Disaster spreads
from nation to nation.
A great storm is stirred up
from the ends of the earth."[g]

33 Those slain by the LORD[h] on that day will
be spread from one end of the earth to the
other. They will not be mourned,[i] gathered,
or buried. They will be like manure on the
surface of the ground.

34 Wail, you shepherds, and cry out.
Roll in the dust,[D,j] you leaders
of the flock.
Because the days of your slaughter
have come,
you will fall and become shattered
like a precious vase.
35 Flight will be impossible
for the shepherds,
and escape, for the leaders
of the flock.
36 Hear the sound of the shepherds' cry,
the wail of the leaders of the flock,
for the LORD is destroying
their pasture.
37 Peaceful grazing land
will become lifeless
because of the LORD's burning anger.[k]
38 He has left His den like a lion,
for their land has become a desolation
because of the sword[E] of the oppressor,[l]
because of His burning anger.

Jeremiah's Speech in the Temple

26 At the beginning of the reign of Jehoiakim[m] son of Josiah, king of Judah,
this word came from the LORD: 2 "This is what
the LORD says: Stand in the courtyard of the
LORD's temple and speak all the words I have
commanded you to speak to all Judah's cities
that are coming to worship there. Do not hold
back a word.[n] 3 Perhaps they will listen and return—each from his evil way of life—so that

[a]**25:23** Lv 19:27; Jr 9:26; 49:32
[b]**25:27** Jr 25:16; Hab 2:16
[c]**25:29** Dn 9:18
[d]**25:28-29** Jr 49:12-13
[e]**25:30** Dt 26:15; 2Ch 30:27; Ps 76:2; Am 1:2; Jl 3:16
[f]**25:31** Hs 4:1; 12:3; Mc 6:2
[g]**25:32** Jr 23:19; 30:23
[h]**25:33** Is 66:16
[i]Jr 16:4
[j]**25:34** Jb 2:8,12; Jr 6:26; Ezk 27:30
[k]**25:37** Nm 32:14; 2Ch 28:11; Zph 2:2
[l]**25:38** Jr 46:16
[m]**26:1** 2Kg 23:34–24:6; 2Ch 36:4-8
[n]**26:2** Dt 4:2; Ec 3:14

A**25:23** Or *who live in distant places* B**25:26** Probably a name for Babylon
C**25:28** Or *When* D**25:34** This custom demonstrated mourning.
E**25:38** Some Hb mss, LXX, Tg; other Hb mss read *burning*

I might relent[a] concerning the disaster that I
plan to do to them because of the evil of their
deeds. 4You are to say to them: This is what
the LORD says: If you do not listen to Me by
living according to My instruction that I set
before you[b] 5and by listening to the words of
My servants the prophets[c] I have been sending you time and time again,[A] though you did
not listen, 6I will make this temple like Shiloh.[d] I will make this city an object of cursing
for all the nations of the earth."

Jeremiah Seized

7The priests, the prophets, and all the people heard Jeremiah speaking these words in
the temple of the LORD. 8He finished the address the LORD had commanded him to deliver to all the people. Then the priests, the
prophets, and all the people took hold of
him, yelling, "You must surely die! 9How dare
you prophesy in the name of ·Yahweh, 'This
temple will become like Shiloh and this city
will become an uninhabited ruin'!" Then all
the people assembled against Jeremiah at the
LORD's temple.

10When the officials of Judah heard these
things, they went from the king's palace to the
LORD's temple and sat at the entrance of the
New Gate.[B,e] 11Then the priests and prophets
said to the officials and all the people, "This
man deserves the death sentence because he
has prophesied against this city, as you have
heard with your own ears."[f]

Jeremiah's Defense

12Then Jeremiah said to all the officials and
the people, "The LORD sent me to prophesy
all the words that you have heard against this
temple and city. 13So now, correct your ways
and deeds[g] and obey the voice of the LORD
your God so that He might relent concerning
the disaster that He warned about. 14As for
me, here I am in your hands; do to me what
you think is good and right. 15But know for
certain that if you put me to death, you will
bring innocent blood[h] on yourselves, on this
city, and on its residents, for it is certain the
LORD has sent me to speak all these things directly to you."

[a]**26:3** Ex 32:12,14; Am 7:3,6; Jnh 3:9-10
[b]**26:4** Lv 26:14
[c]**26:5** Jr 25:3-4
[d]**26:6** Jos 18:1,8-10; 21:2; 1Sm 1:3
[e]**26:10** Jr 36:10; Ezk 46:1,3
[f]**26:11** Jr 38:4
[g]**26:13** Jr 7:3-5; 18:11
[h]**26:15** Dt 19:10; 2Kg 24:4; Jr 22:17
[i]**26:17** Ac 5:34
[j]**26:18** Mc 1:1,14
[k]2Kg 16:20; 18:4–21:3; Is 36:1–39:8
[l]Mc 3:12
[m]**26:19** 2Ch 32:26
[n]Ex 32:14; 2Sm 24:16
[o]**26:20** Jos 9:17; 1Sm 6:21; 7:2
[p]**26:22** Jr 36:12
[q]**26:24** 2Kg 22:12,14; Jr 39:14; 40:5–43:6
[r]**27:2** Jr 28:10-13

Jeremiah Released

16Then the officials and all the people told
the priests and prophets, "This man doesn't
deserve the death sentence, for he has spoken
to us in the name of Yahweh our God!"

17Some of the elders of the land stood up[i]
and said to all the assembled people, 18"Micah the Moreshite[j] prophesied in the days of
Hezekiah king of Judah[k] and said to all the
people of Judah, 'This is what the LORD of
·Hosts says:

·Zion will be plowed like a field,
Jerusalem will become ruins,
and the temple mount a forested hill.'[l]

19Did Hezekiah king of Judah and all the
people of Judah put him to death? Did he
not ·fear the LORD and plead for the LORD's
favor,[C,m] and did not the LORD relent concerning the disaster He had pronounced against
them?[n] We are about to bring great harm on
ourselves!"

The Prophet Uriah

20Another man was also prophesying in the
name of Yahweh—Uriah son of Shemaiah
from Kiriath-jearim.[o] He prophesied against
this city and against this land in words like
all those of Jeremiah. 21King Jehoiakim, all
his warriors, and all the officials heard his
words, and the king tried to put him to death.
When Uriah heard, he fled in fear and went
to Egypt. 22But King Jehoiakim sent men to
Egypt: Elnathan son of Achbor[p] and certain
other men with him went to Egypt. 23They
brought Uriah out of Egypt and took him to
King Jehoiakim, who executed him with the
sword and threw his corpse into the burial
place of the common people.[D]

24But Ahikam[q] son of Shaphan supported
Jeremiah, so he was not handed over to the
people to be put to death.

The Yoke of Babylon

27 At the beginning of the reign of Zedekiah[E] son of Josiah, king of Judah,
this word came to Jeremiah from the LORD:[F]
2"This is what the LORD said to me: Make
chains and yoke bars[r] for yourself and put

[A]**26:5** Lit *you, rising early and sending* [B]**26:10** Some Hb mss, Syr, Tg, Vg add *of the house* [C]**26:19** Or *and appease the LORD* [D]**26:23** Lit *the sons of the people*

[E]**27:1** Some Hb mss, Syr, Arabic; other Hb mss, DSS read *Jehoiakim* [F]**27:1** LXX omits this v.

them on your neck. 3 Send word to the king of Edom, the king of Moab, the king of the Ammonites, the king of Tyre, and the king of Sidon[a] through messengers who are coming to Zedekiah king of Judah in Jerusalem. 4 Command them to go to their masters, saying: This is what the LORD of ·Hosts, the God of Israel, says: This is what you must say to your masters: 5 By My great strength and outstretched arm,[b] I made the earth,[c] and the people, and animals on the face of the earth. I give it to anyone I please.[A,d] 6 So now I have placed all these lands under the authority of My servant[e] Nebuchadnezzar,[f] king of Babylon. I have even given him the wild animals to serve him. 7 All nations will serve him, his son, and his grandson until the time for his own land comes, and then many nations and great kings will enslave him.[g]

8 "As for the nation or kingdom that does not serve Nebuchadnezzar king of Babylon and does not place its neck under the yoke of the king of Babylon, that nation I will punish by sword, famine, and plague"—this is the LORD's declaration—"until through him I have destroyed it. 9 But as for you, do not listen to your prophets, diviners,[h] dreamers, fortune-tellers,[i] or sorcerers[j] who say to you, 'Don't serve the king of Babylon!' 10 for they prophesy a lie to you so that you will be removed from your land. I will banish you, and you will perish. 11 But as for the nation that will put its neck under the yoke of the king of Babylon and serve him, I will leave it in its own land, and that nation will cultivate[B] it and reside in it." This is the LORD's declaration.

Warning to Zedekiah

12 I spoke to Zedekiah king of Judah[k] in the same way: "Put your necks under the yoke of the king of Babylon, serve him and his people, and live! 13 Why should you and your people die[l] by the sword, famine, or plague as the LORD has threatened against any nation that does not serve the king of Babylon? 14 Do not listen to the words of the prophets who are telling you, 'You must not serve the king of Babylon,' for they are prophesying a lie to you.[m] 15 'I have not sent them'—this is the LORD's declaration—'and they are prophesying falsely in My name; therefore, I will banish you, and you will perish—you and the prophets who are prophesying to you.'"

16 Then I spoke to the priests and all these people, saying, "This is what the LORD says: 'Do not listen to the words of your prophets. They are prophesying to you, claiming, "Look, very soon now the articles of the LORD's temple will be brought back from Babylon."[n] They are prophesying a lie to you. 17 Do not listen to them. Serve the king of Babylon and live! Why should this city become a ruin?[o] 18 If they are indeed prophets and if the word of the LORD is with them, let them intercede with the LORD of Hosts not to let the articles that remain in the LORD's temple, in the palace of the king of Judah, and in Jerusalem go to Babylon.' 19 For this is what the LORD of Hosts says about the pillars, the sea, the water carts,[p] and the rest of the articles that still remain in this city, 20 those Nebuchadnezzar king of Babylon did not take when he deported Jeconiah[C] son of Jehoiakim, king of Judah, from Jerusalem to Babylon along with all the nobles of Judah[q] and Jerusalem. 21 Yes, this is what the LORD of Hosts, the God of Israel, says about the articles that remain in the temple of the LORD, in the palace of the king of Judah, and in Jerusalem: 22 'They will be brought to Babylon and will remain there until I attend to them again.'[r] This is the LORD's declaration. 'Then I will bring them up and restore them to this place.'"[s]

Hananiah's False Prophecy

28 In that same year, at the beginning of the reign of King Zedekiah of Judah,[t] in the fifth month of the fourth year, the prophet Hananiah son of Azzur from Gibeon[u] said to me in the temple of the LORD in the presence of the priests and all the people, 2 "This is what the LORD of ·Hosts, the God of Israel, says: 'I have broken the yoke of the king of Babylon.[v] 3 Within two years I will restore to this place all the articles of the LORD's temple[w] that King Nebuchadnezzar of Babylon took from here and transported to Babylon. 4 And I will restore to this place Jeconiah[C] son of Jehoiakim, king

[a] **27:3** Jr 25:21-22
[b] **27:5** Dn 4:17
[c] Is 45:12
[d] Ps 115:15-16
[e] **27:6** Jr 25:9
[f] 2Kg 24:11; 25:22; 2Ch 36:6-13
[g] **27:7** Jr 25:12
[h] **27:9** Dt 18:10,14; Jr 14:14; 29:8
[i] Lv 19:26; Dt 18:10,14; 2Ch 33:6
[j] Ex 7:11; Dt 18:10; 2Ch 33:6
[k] **27:12** Jr 28:1; 38:17
[l] **27:13** Ezk 18:31
[m] **27:14** Jr 14:14
[n] **27:16** 2Kg 24:13; 2Ch 36:7,10; Jr 28:3
[o] **27:17** Jr 7:34
[p] **27:19** 2Kg 25:13,16; Jr 52:17,20
[q] **27:20** Neh 6:17; 13:17; Jr 39:6
[r] **27:22** Jr 29:10; 32:5
[s] Ezr 1:7-11; 5:13-15; 7:19
[t] **28:1** Jr 27:12
[u] Jos 9:3
[v] **28:2** Jr 27:12
[w] **28:3** Jr 27:16

[A] **27:5** Lit *to whomever is upright in My eyes* [B] **27:11** Lit *work* [C] **27:20; 28:4** = Jehoiachin

of Judah, and all the exiles from Judah[a] who
went to Babylon' — this is the LORD's declaration — 'for I will break the yoke of the king
of Babylon.'"

Jeremiah's Response to Hananiah

5The prophet Jeremiah replied to the
prophet Hananiah in the presence of the
priests and all the people who were standing in the temple of the LORD. 6The prophet
Jeremiah said, "'Amen![b] May the LORD do
so. May the LORD make the words you have
prophesied come true and may He restore the
articles of the LORD's temple and all the exiles from Babylon to this place! 7Only listen
to this message I am speaking in your hearing and in the hearing of all the people. 8The
prophets who preceded you and me from
ancient times prophesied war, disaster,[A] and
plague against many lands and great kingdoms. 9As for the prophet who prophesies
peace — only when the word of the prophet
comes true will the prophet be recognized as
one the LORD has truly sent."[c]

Hananiah Breaks Jeremiah's Yoke

10The prophet Hananiah then took the yoke
bar from the neck of Jeremiah the prophet
and broke it.[d] 11In the presence of all the people Hananiah proclaimed, "This is what the
LORD says: 'In this way, within two years I will
break the yoke of King Nebuchadnezzar of
Babylon from the neck of all the nations.'"
Jeremiah the prophet then went on his way.

The LORD's Word against Hananiah

12The word of the LORD came to Jeremiah
after Hananiah the prophet had broken
the yoke bar from the neck of Jeremiah the
prophet: 13"Go say to Hananiah: This is what
the LORD says, 'You broke a wooden yoke bar,
but in its place you will make an iron yoke
bar.' 14For this is what the LORD of Hosts, the
God of Israel, says, 'I have put an iron yoke on
the neck of all these nations that they might
serve King Nebuchadnezzar of Babylon,[e] and
they will serve him.[f] I have also put the wild
animals under him.'"[g]

15The prophet Jeremiah said to the prophet
Hananiah, "Listen, Hananiah! The LORD did
not send you, but you have led these people
to trust in a lie.[h] 16Therefore, this is what the
LORD says: 'I am about to send you off the
face of the earth. You will die this year because you have spoken rebellion against the
LORD.'"[i] 17And the prophet Hananiah died
that year in the seventh month.

Jeremiah's Letter to the Exiles

29 This is the text of the letter[j] that Jeremiah the prophet sent from Jerusa-
lem to the rest of the elders of the exiles, the
priests, the prophets, and all the people Nebuchadnezzar[k] had deported from Jerusalem
to Babylon. 2This was after King Jeconiah,[B,l]
the queen mother, the court officials, the officials of Judah and Jerusalem, the craftsmen,
and the metalsmiths had left Jerusalem. 3The
letter was sent by Elasah son of Shaphan and
Gemariah son of Hilkiah[m] whom Zedekiah
king of Judah had sent to Babylon to Nebuchadnezzar king of Babylon. The letter
stated:

4This is what the LORD of *Hosts, the God
of Israel, says to all the exiles I deported
from Jerusalem to Babylon: 5"Build
houses and live in them.[n] Plant gardens
and eat their produce. 6Take wives and
have sons and daughters. Take wives for
your sons and give your daughters to
men in marriage so that they may bear
sons and daughters. Multiply there; do
not decrease. 7Seek the welfare of the city
I have deported you to. Pray to the LORD
on its behalf,[o] for when it has prosperity,
you will prosper."

8For this is what the LORD of Hosts, the
God of Israel, says: "Don't let your prophets who are among you[p] and your diviners deceive you,[q] and don't listen to the
dreams you elicit from them, 9for they
are prophesying falsely to you in My
name. I have not sent them."[r] This is the
LORD's declaration.

10For this is what the LORD says: "When
70 years for Babylon are complete,[s] I
will attend to you and will confirm My
promise concerning you to restore you

[a]**28:4** 2Kg 24:10-17
[b]**28:6** 1Kg 1:36
[c]**28:9** Dt 18:20-22
[d]**28:10** Jr 27:2
[e]**28:14** Dt 28:48
[f]Jr 25:11
[g]Jr 27:6
[h]**28:15** Jr 29:31; Ezk 13:22
[i]**28:16** Dt 13:5; Is 59:13; Jr 29:32
[j]**29:1** 2Sm 11:14-15; 1Kg 21:8-11
[k]2Kg 24:11; 25:22; 2Ch 36:6-13
[l]**29:2** Jr 24:1; 27:20; 28:4
[m]**29:3** 1Ch 6:13
[n]**29:5** Jr 29:28
[o]**29:7** Ezr 6:10; 1Tm 2:1-2
[p]**29:8** Jr 27:9
[q]Jr 27:15
[r]**29:9** Jr 29:31
[s]**29:10** Jr 25:12; Dn 9:2

[A]**28:8** Some Hb mss, Vg read *famine* [B]**29:2** = Jehoiachin

to this place. 11For I know the plans I
have for you"[a] — this is the LORD's declaration — "plans for your welfare, not
for disaster, to give you a future and a
hope. 12You will call to Me and come
and pray to Me, and I will listen to you.[b]
13You will seek Me[c] and find Me when
you search for Me with all your heart.
14I will be found by you" — this is the
LORD's declaration — "and I will restore

[a]29:11 Ps 33:10; Jr 26:3; 36:3 [b]29:12 Dt 30:1-10; Jr 3:12 [c]29:13 Dt 4:29; 1Ch 28:9; 2Ch 15:2

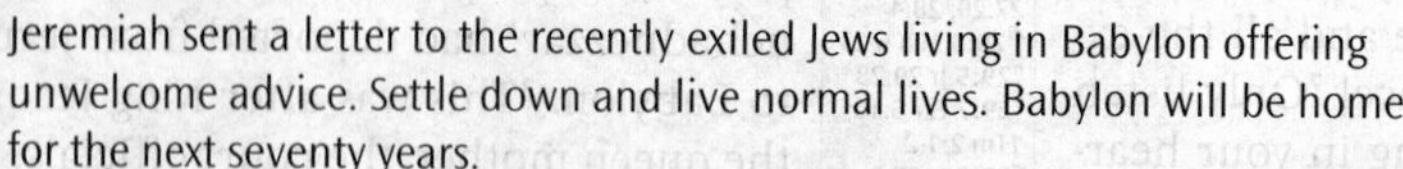

Dwelling and Working for the Good of the City

Glenn A. Barth, Jr.

Jeremiah sent a letter to the recently exiled Jews living in Babylon offering unwelcome advice. Settle down and live normal lives. Babylon will be home for the next seventy years.

Deported to a foreign city, the Jews were face-to-face with Babylon's people and its unfamiliar culture. Hoping for a speedy return to Jerusalem, Jeremiah's message was that they should unpack their boxes. They needed to change their perspective and behave like this was their home. The prophet's instructions in Jeremiah 29:5-7 outline some steps to doing this, including, "Seek the welfare of the city I have deported you to. Pray to the LORD on its behalf, for when it has prosperity, you will prosper."

It is hard for newcomers to call their new city "home." In many cities, people with family and kinship ties settle together in ethnic neighborhoods. For example, over 90,000 Hmong live in the Minneapolis/St. Paul metro area. The Hmong were U.S. allies in Laos during the Vietnam War and fled under communist persecution shortly thereafter. These refugees from a semi-tropical rural Cambodian hill country now live in a northern, urban, English speaking context. It is as though Jeremiah's advice to the Hebrews reached the Hmong as they have built homes, sold produce at farmer's markets, and formed extended families.

Over 90 percent of the world's nations are experiencing rapid urbanization. Cities are today's missional focal point. What should our response be?

First, make the city where you live "home." It may be a new place, where you may not plan to stay long, but perhaps God has other plans. When you treat the place you live like your home, you will begin to be treated like you belong there too. People will see that you care about the well-being of the city and its people. This approach will engage you in an incarnational witness in word and deed.

Second, seek the peace and prosperity of your city. Cities are centers of prosperity. We can act on those things that will make our city or community a better place to live. Prayerfully consider how your gifts and strengths can be used for the good of your city. Seek out leaders and ask them what they are trying to accomplish and how you can help. Places to start might include a local school, fire department, city hall, a nonprofit service organization, or hospital.

Third, pray for the peace of the city where you live. Pray regularly and systematically for the elected leaders, for leaders of the schools, businesses, churches, nonprofits, and for service organizations, and media members. Pray for people in your neighborhood or apartment building. Pray for the poor and oppressed. If it did not seem like home before, through prayer, God will give you a heart for your city and its people.

Fourth, keep in mind that in every city, there are newcomers. Part of our role is to welcome these newcomers into our city in the spirit of the second part of great commandment, "love your neighbor as yourself."

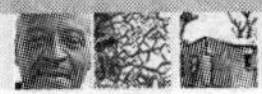

your fortunes[A,a] and gather you from all the nations and places where I banished you" — this is the LORD's declaration. "I will restore you to the place I deported you from."[b]

15 You have said, "The LORD has raised up prophets for us in Babylon!" 16 But this is what the LORD says concerning the king sitting on David's throne and concerning all the people living in this city — that is, concerning your brothers who did not go with you into exile. 17 This is what the LORD of Hosts says: "I am about to send against them sword, famine, and plague[c] and will make them like rotten figs that are inedible because they are so bad. 18 I will pursue them with sword, famine, and plague. I will make them a horror to all the kingdoms of the earth — a curse and a desolation, an object of scorn and a disgrace among all the nations where I have banished them.[d] 19 I will do this because they have not listened to My words" — this is the LORD's declaration — "that I sent to them with My servants the prophets time and time again.[B,e] And you too have not listened." This is the LORD's declaration.

20 Hear the word of the LORD, all you exiles I have sent from Jerusalem to Babylon.[f] 21 This is what the LORD of Hosts, the God of Israel, says to Ahab son of Kolaiah and to Zedekiah son of Maaseiah, the ones prophesying a lie to you in My name:[g] "I am about to hand them over to Nebuchadnezzar king of Babylon, and he will kill them before your very eyes. 22 Based on what happens to them, all the exiles of Judah who are in Babylon will create a curse[h] that says, 'May the LORD make you like Zedekiah and Ahab, whom the king of Babylon roasted in the fire!'[i] 23 because they have committed an outrage[j] in Israel by committing adultery with their neighbors' wives and have spoken a lie in My name, which I did not command them. I am He who knows, and I am a witness." This is the LORD's declaration.

[a] **29:14** Jb 42:10; Jr 32:44
[b] Dt 30:3; Jr 30:3
[c] **29:17** Jr 14:12; 21:9; 24:10
[d] **29:18** Dt 30:1; Jr 8:3; 16:15
[e] **29:19** Jr 26:5
[f] **29:20** Jr 24:5
[g] **29:21** Jr 14:14; 29:9
[h] **29:22** Is 65:15
[i] Dn 3:6
[j] **29:23** Gn 34:7; Dt 22:21; Jos 7:15
[k] **29:25** Jr 21:1; 37:3; 52:24-27
[l] **29:26** 2Ch 31:13; Jr 20:1
[m] 2Kg 9:11; Hs 9:7
[n] 2Ch 16:10; Jr 20:2
[o] **29:27** Jr 1:1
[p] **29:28** Jr 29:5
[q] **29:31** Jr 27:10,14-16; 28:15; 29:9,21,23
[r] **29:32** Jr 17:6
[s] Jr 28:16
[t] **30:2** Hab 2:2
[u] **30:3** Ezk 37:15-23

24 To Shemaiah the Nehelamite you are to say, 25 "This is what the LORD of Hosts, the God of Israel, says: You[C] in your own name have sent out letters to all the people of Jerusalem, to the priest Zephaniah[k] son of Maaseiah, and to all the priests, saying: 26 'The LORD has appointed you priest in place of Jehoiada the priest to be the chief officer[l] in the temple of the LORD, responsible for every madman[m] who acts like a prophet. You must confine him in the stocks[n] and an iron collar. 27 So now, why have you not rebuked Jeremiah of Anathoth who has been acting like a prophet among you?[o] 28 For he has sent word to us in Babylon, claiming, "The exile will be long. Build houses and settle down. Plant gardens and eat their produce." ' "[p]

29 Zephaniah the priest read this letter in the hearing of Jeremiah the prophet.

A Message about Shemaiah

30 Then the word of the LORD came to Jeremiah: 31 "Send a message to all the exiles, saying: This is what the LORD says concerning Shemaiah the Nehelamite. Because Shemaiah prophesied to you, though I did not send him, and made you trust a lie,[q] 32 this is what the LORD says: I am about to punish Shemaia h the Nehelamite and his descendants. There will not be even one of his descendants living among these people,[r] nor will any ever see the good that I will bring to My people" — this is the LORD's declaration — "for he has preached rebellion against the LORD."[s]

Restoration from Captivity

30 This is the word that came to Jeremiah from the LORD. 2 This is what the LORD, the God of Israel, says: "Write down on a scroll all the words that I have spoken to you,[t] 3 for the days are certainly coming" — this is the LORD's declaration — "when I will restore the fortunes[D] of My people Israel and Judah"[u] — the LORD's declaration. "I will restore them to the land I gave to their ancestors and they will possess it."

4 These are the words the LORD spoke to

[A] **29:14** Or *will end your captivity* [B] **29:19** Lit *prophets, rising up early and sending* [C] **29:25** Lit *Because you* [D] **30:3** Or *will end the captivity*

Israel and Judah. [5]Yes, this is what the LORD
says:

We have heard a cry of terror,
of dread — there is no peace.
6 Ask and see
whether a male can give birth.
Why then do I see every man
with his hands on his stomach
like a woman in labor
and every face turned pale?
7 How awful that day will be![a]
There will be none like it![b]
It will be a time of trouble for Jacob,
but he will be delivered out of it.

[8]"On that day" — this is the declaration of
the LORD of ·Hosts — "I will break his yoke
from your neck[c] and tear off your chains[d] so
strangers will never again enslave him.[e] [9]They
will serve the LORD their God and I will raise
up David their king for them."[f]

10 As for you, My servant Jacob,[g]
do not be afraid —
this is the LORD's declaration —
and do not be dismayed, Israel,
for without fail I will save you
from far away,
your descendants, from the land
of their captivity!
Jacob will return and have calm
and quiet
with no one to frighten him.[h]
11 For I will be with you —
this is the LORD's declaration —
to save you![i]
I will bring destruction
on all the nations
where I have scattered you;
however, I will not bring destruction
on you.
I will discipline you justly,
and I will by no means
leave you unpunished.[j]

Healing Zion's Wounds

[12]For this is what the LORD says:

Your injury is incurable;
your wound most severe.[k]
13 No one takes up the case for your sores.[l]
There is no healing for you.
14 All your lovers have forgotten you;
they no longer look for you,
for I have struck
you as an enemy would,
with the discipline[m] of someone cruel,[n]
because of your enormous ·guilt
and your innumerable sins.
15 Why do you cry out about your injury?
Your pain has no cure!
I have done these things to you
because of your enormous guilt
and your innumerable sins.
16 Nevertheless, all who devoured you
will be devoured,[o]
and all your adversaries —
all of them —
will go off into exile.
Those who plunder you
will be plundered,
and all who raid you will be raided.
17 But I will bring you health[p]
and will heal you of your wounds —
this is the LORD's declaration —
for they call you Outcast,
·Zion whom no one cares about.

Restoration of the Land

[18]This is what the LORD says:

I will certainly restore the fortunes[A]
of Jacob's tents[q]
and show compassion on his dwellings.
Every city will be rebuilt on its mound;
every citadel will stand
on its proper site.
19 Thanksgiving will come out of them,
a sound of celebration.
I will multiply them,
and they will not decrease;[r]
I will honor them, and they will not
be insignificant.
20 His children will be as in past days;
his congregation will be established
in My presence.
I will punish all his oppressors.[s]
21 Jacob's leader will be one of them;
his ruler will issue from him.
I will invite him to Me, and he will
approach Me,[t]

[a]**30:7** Jl 2:11; Zph 1:14
[b]Dn 12:1
[c]**30:8** Jr 2:20
[d]Jr 27:2
[e]Ezk 34:27
[f]**30:9** Is 55:3-5; Ezk 34:23-24; 37:24-25; Hs 3:5; Lk 1:69; Ac 13:23,34
[g]**30:10** Is 41:8; 44:2; 45:4
[h]Jr 46:27; Ezk 39:26
[i]**30:11** 2Kg 19:34; Is 37:35; Jr 15:20
[j]**30:10-11** Jr 46:27-28
[k]**30:12** Jr 10:19; 15:18; 17:9
[l]**30:13** Hs 5:13
[m]**30:14** Jr 2:30; 5:3; 7:28
[n]Is 13:9
[o]**30:16** Jr 10:25
[p]**30:17** Is 58:8; Jr 8:22; 33:6
[q]**30:18** Jr 30:3
[r]**30:19** Jr 29:6
[s]**30:20** Jdg 10:12; Is 19:20-25
[t]**30:21** Nm 16:5

[A]**30:18** Or *certainly end the captivity*

for who would otherwise risk his life
to approach Me?
This is the LORD's declaration.
22 You will be My people,
and I will be your God.[a]

The Wrath of God

23 Look, a storm from the LORD![b]
Wrath has gone out,
a churning storm.
It will whirl about the heads
of the wicked.
24 The LORD's burning anger will not
turn back
until He has completely fulfilled
the purposes of His heart.
In time to come you will
understand it.[c]

God's Relationship with His People

31 "At that time"—this is the LORD's declaration—"I will be the God of all the
families of Israel,[d] and they will be My people."
2 This is what the LORD says:

They found favor in the wilderness[e]—
the people who survived the sword.
When Israel went to find rest,
3 the LORD appeared to him[A]
from far away.
I have loved you
with an everlasting love;
therefore, I have continued to extend
faithful love to you.[f]
4 Again I will build you so that you will
be rebuilt,
Virgin Israel.
You will take up
your tambourines again[g]
and go out in joyful dancing.
5 You will plant vineyards again
on the mountains of Samaria;
the planters will plant and will enjoy
the fruit.[h]
6 For there will be a day when watchmen
will call out
in the hill country of Ephraim,
"Get up, let's go up to 'Zion,[i]
to 'Yahweh our God!"

[a] **30:22** Jr 11:4; 24:7; 31:33
[b] **30:23** Ps 83:15; Is 29:6; Zch 9:14
[c] **30:23-24** Jr 23:19-20
[d] **31:1** Jr 30:22
[e] **31:2** Ex 33:12-17
[f] **31:3** Ps 36:10; 109:12
[g] **31:4** Ex 15:20; Jdg 11:34; 1Sm 18:6
[h] **31:5** Lv 19:23,25; Dt 20:6; 28:30
[i] **31:6** Is 2:3
[j] **31:7** Ps 28:9; Hab 3:13; Zch 8:7
[k] **31:8** Jr 6:22; 25:32; 50:41
[l] Ezk 38:15
[m] **31:9** Jb 15:11
[n] Pr 4:12; Is 63:13; Ezk 36:15
[o] **31:10** Is 40:15; Jr 25:22; 47:4
[p] **31:11** Is 44:23; 48:20
[q] **31:12** Ps 34:5; Is 60:5
[r] Is 2:2; Jr 51:44; Mc 4:1
[s] Nm 18:12; Dt 7:13; Hg 1:11

God's People Brought Home

7 For this is what the LORD says:

Sing with joy for Jacob;
shout for the chief of the nations!
Proclaim, praise, and say,
"LORD, save Your people,[j]
the remnant of Israel!"
8 Watch! I am going to bring them
from the northern land.
I will gather them from remote regions
of the earth[k]—
the blind and the lame will be with them,
along with those who are pregnant
and those about to give birth.
They will return here
as a great assembly![l]
9 They will come weeping,
but I will bring them back
with consolation.[B,m]
I will lead them to 'wadis filled
with water
by a smooth way where
they will not stumble,[n]
for I am Israel's Father,
and Ephraim is My firstborn.
10 Nations, hear the word of the LORD,
and tell it among the
far off coastlands![o]
Say: The One who scattered Israel
will gather him.
He will watch over him as a shepherd
guards his flock,
11 for the LORD has ransomed Jacob
and redeemed him from the power
of one stronger than he.[p]
12 They will come and shout for joy
on the heights of Zion;
they will be radiant with joy[q]
because of[r] the LORD's goodness,
because of the grain, the new wine,
the fresh oil,[s]
and because of the young of the flocks
and herds.
Their life will be
like an irrigated garden,
and they will no longer grow weak
from hunger.
13 Then the young woman will rejoice
with dancing,

[A] **31:3** LXX; MT reads *me* [B] **31:9** LXX; MT reads *supplications*

while young and old men
rejoice together.
I will turn their mourning into joy,[a]
give them consolation,
and bring happiness out of grief.
14 I will refresh the priests
with an abundance,[A,b]
and My people will be satisfied
with My goodness.
This is the LORD's declaration.

Lament Turned to Joy

15 This is what the LORD says:

A voice was heard in Ramah,
a lament with bitter weeping—
Rachel weeping for her children,
refusing to be comforted
for her children
because they are no more.[c]

16 This is what the LORD says:

Keep your voice from weeping
and your eyes from tears,
for the reward for your work
will come—
this is the LORD's declaration—
and your children will return
from the enemy's land.
17 There is hope for your future[d]—
this is the LORD's declaration—
and your children will return
to their own territory.
18 I have heard Ephraim moaning,
"You disciplined me,
and I have been disciplined
like an untrained calf.
Restore me, and I will return,
for you, LORD, are my God.[e]
19 After I returned, I repented;
After I was instructed, I struck my thigh
in grief.[f]
I was ashamed and humiliated
because I bore the disgrace of my youth."
20 Isn't Ephraim a precious son to Me,
a delightful child?
Whenever I speak against him,
I certainly still think about him.
Therefore, My inner being yearns
for him;
I will truly have compassion on him.
This is the LORD's declaration.

[a]**31:13** Ps 105:43; Is 35:10; 51:3,11 [b]**31:14** Dt 31:20; Ps 36:8; Is 30:23 [c]**31:15** Mt 2:18 [d]**31:17** Jr 5:31; 23:20; 29:11 [e]**31:18** Ps 40:5; Jr 3:22 [f]**31:19** Ezk 21:12 [g]**31:21** 2Kg 23:17; Ezk 39:15 [h]**31:22** Jr 3:14,22; 49:4 [i]**31:23** Jb 8:6; Jr 50:7 [j]Ps 2:6; 3:4; 48:1; 99:9 [k]**31:27** Ezk 36:9,11; Hs 2:23 [l]**31:28** Jr 1:10; 18:7-10; 44:27 [m]**31:29** Ezk 18:2 [n]**31:30** Dt 24:6; Ezk 18:20 [o]**31:31** Ezk 37:26; Lk 22:20; 1Co 11:25; 2Co 3:6; Heb 9:15; 12:24

Repentance and Restoration

21 Set up road markers[g] for yourself;
establish signposts!
Keep the highway in mind,
the way you have traveled.
Return, Virgin Israel!
Return to these cities of yours.
22 How long will you turn here and there,
faithless daughter?[h]
For the LORD creates something new
in the land[B]—
a female[C] will shelter[D] a man.

23 This is what the LORD of ˚Hosts, the God
of Israel, says: "When I restore their fortunes,[E]
they will once again speak this word in the
land of Judah and in its cities, 'May the LORD
bless you, righteous settlement,[i] holy mountain.'[j] 24 Judah and all its cities will live in it together—also farmers and those who move[F]
with the flocks— 25 for I satisfy the thirsty
person and feed all those who are weak."
26 At this I awoke and looked around. My
sleep had been most pleasant to me.
27 "The days are coming"—this is the
LORD's declaration—"when I will sow the
house of Israel[k] and the house of Judah with
the seed of man and the seed of beast. 28 Just
as I watched over them to uproot and to tear
them down, to demolish and to destroy, and
to cause disaster, so will I be attentive to build
and to plant them,"[l] says the LORD. 29 "In those
days, it will never again be said:

The fathers have eaten sour grapes,
and the children's teeth are set
on edge.[m]

30 Rather, each will die for his own wrongdoing.[n] Anyone who eats sour grapes—his own
teeth will be set on edge.

The New Covenant

31 "Look, the days are coming"—this is the
LORD's declaration—"when I will make a
new covenant[o] with the house of Israel and
with the house of Judah. 32 This one will not
be like the covenant I made with their an-

[A]**31:14** Lit *fatness* [B]**31:22** Or *new on earth* [C]**31:22** Or *woman* [D]**31:22** Or *female surrounds*, or *female courts*; Hb obscure [E]**31:23** Or *I end their captivity* [F]**31:24** Tg, Vg, Aq, Sym; MT reads *and they will move*

cestors when I took them by the hand to
bring them out of the land of Egypt — a covenant they broke even though I had married
them"[a] — the LORD's declaration. 33"Instead,
this is the covenant I will make with the
house of Israel after those days" — the LORD's
declaration. "I will put My teaching within
them and write it on their hearts. I will be
their God, and they will be My people. 34No
longer will one teach his neighbor or his
brother, saying, 'Know the LORD,'[b] for they
will all know Me, from the least to the greatest of them" — this is the LORD's declaration.
"For I will forgive their wrongdoing[c] and
never again remember their sin."[d]

35This is what the LORD says:

The One who gives the sun for light
by day,
the fixed order of moon and stars
for light by night,
who stirs up the sea and makes
its waves roar[e] —
Yahweh of Hosts is His name:
36 If this fixed order departs
from My presence —
this is the LORD's declaration —
then also Israel's descendants
will cease
to be a nation before Me forever.[f]

37This is what the LORD says:

If the heavens above can be measured
and the foundations
of the earth below explored,
I will reject all of Israel's descendants
because of all they have done —
this is the LORD's declaration.

38"Look, the days are coming" — the LORD's
declaration — "when the city[A] from the
Tower of Hananel[g] to the Corner Gate[h] will
be rebuilt for the LORD. 39A measuring line
will once again stretch out straight to the hill
of Gareb[i] and then turn toward Goah. 40The
whole valley — the corpses, the ashes, and all
the fields as far as the Kidron Valley[j] to the
corner of the Horse Gate[k] to the east — will
be holy to the LORD. It will never be uprooted
or demolished again."

[a]**31:32** Is 54:4; 62:4; Mal 2:11
[b]**31:34** Jdg 2:10; 1Sm 3:7; Hs 2:20
[c]Nm 14:19; Ps 103:3; Jr 36:3
[d]**31:31-34** Heb 8:8-12; 10:16-17
[e]**31:35** Ps 46:3; Is 51:15; Jr 5:22
[f]**31:36** Jr 33:18; 35:19
[g]**31:38** Neh 3:1; 12:39
[h]2Kg 14:13; 2Ch 26:9; Zch 14:10
[i]**31:39** Zch 2:1
[j]**31:40** 2Kg 23:4
[k]Neh 3:28
[l]**32:1** 2Kg 24:17-20; 2Ch 36:10-12; Jr 27:1-11
[m]Jr 29:1
[n]**32:2** Neh 3:25; Jr 33:1; 37:21; 38:6; 39:14
[o]**32:4** Jr 34:3
[p]**32:3-5** Jr 21:3-7; 27:22; 34:2-3
[q]**32:7** 1Kg 2:26; Jr 1:1; 11:21,23
[r]Lv 25:24-52; Ru 4:1-7
[s]**32:9** Gn 23:16; Zch 11:12
[t]**32:10** Jr 32:44
[u]**32:12** Jr 36:4-32; 43:3,6; 45:1-2

Jeremiah's Land Purchase

32 This is the word that came to Jeremiah
from the LORD in the tenth year of
Zedekiah[l] king of Judah, which was the eighteenth year of Nebuchadnezzar.[m] 2At that
time, the army of the king of Babylon was besieging Jerusalem, and Jeremiah the prophet
was imprisoned in the guard's courtyard[n] in
the palace of the king of Judah. 3Zedekiah
king of Judah had imprisoned him, saying:
"Why are you prophesying, 'This is what the
LORD says: Look, I am about to hand this city
over to Babylon's king, and he will capture
it. 4Zedekiah king of Judah will not escape
from the Chaldeans; indeed, he will certainly
be handed over to Babylon's king. They will
speak face to face[B] and meet eye to eye.[o] 5He
will take Zedekiah to Babylon where he will
stay until I attend to him' — this is the LORD's
declaration. 'You will fight the Chaldeans,
but you will not succeed'?"[p]

6Jeremiah replied, "The word of the LORD
came to me: 7Watch! Hanamel, the son of
your uncle Shallum, is coming to you to say,
'Buy my field in Anathoth[q] for yourself, for
you own the right of redemption[r] to buy it.'
8"Then my cousin Hanamel came to the
guard's courtyard as the LORD had said and
urged me, 'Please buy my field in Anathoth in
the land of Benjamin, for you own the right of
inheritance and redemption. Buy it for yourself.' Then I knew that this was the word of
the LORD. 9So I bought the field in Anathoth
from my cousin Hanamel, and I weighed out
to him the money[s] — 17 ·shekels[C] of silver. 10I
recorded it on a scroll,[t] sealed it, called in
witnesses, and weighed out the silver in the
scales. 11I took the purchase agreement — the
sealed copy with its terms and conditions
and the open copy — 12and gave the purchase
agreement to Baruch[u] son of Neriah, son of
Mahseiah. I did this in the sight of my cousin[D]
Hanamel, the witnesses who were signing the
purchase agreement, and all the Judeans sitting in the guard's courtyard.

13"I instructed Baruch in their sight, 14'This
is what the LORD of ·Hosts, the God of Israel, says: Take these scrolls — this purchase
agreement with the sealed copy and this open
copy — and put them in an earthen storage

[A]**31:38** = Jerusalem [B]**32:4** Lit *His mouth will speak with his mouth* [C]**32:9** About 7 ounces [D]**32:12** Some Hb mss, LXX, Syr; other Hb mss read *uncle*

jar so they will last a long time. 15 For this is
what the LORD of Hosts, the God of Israel,
says: Houses, fields, and vineyards will again
be bought in this land.'[a]
16 "After I had given the purchase agreement to Baruch, son of Neriah, I prayed to
the LORD: 17 Oh, Lord GOD! You Yourself made
the heavens and earth[b] by Your great power[c]
and with Your outstretched arm. Nothing
is too difficult for You! 18 You show faithful
love to thousands but lay the fathers' sins on
their sons' laps after them,[d] great and mighty
God[e] whose name is •Yahweh of Hosts, 19 the
One great in counsel and mighty in deed,
whose eyes are on all the ways of the sons of
men in order to give to each person according to his ways and the result of his deeds.[f]
20 You performed signs and wonders in the
land of Egypt[g] and do so to this very day both
in Israel and among mankind. You made a
name[h] for Yourself, as is the case today. 21 You
brought Your people Israel out of Egypt with
signs and wonders, with a strong hand and
an outstretched arm, and with great terror.[i]
22 You gave them this land You swore to give
to their ancestors, a land flowing with milk
and honey.[j] 23 They entered and possessed it,
but they did not obey Your voice or live according to Your instructions.[k] They failed to
perform all You commanded them to do,[l] and
so You have brought all this disaster on them.
24 Look! Siege ramps[m] have come against the
city to capture it, and the city, as a result of
the sword, famine, and plague, has been
handed over to the Chaldeans who are fighting against it. What You have spoken has happened. Look, You can see it! 25 Yet You, Lord
GOD, have said to me: Buy the field with silver
and call in witnesses — even though the city
has been handed over to the Chaldeans!"
26 Then the word of the LORD came to Jeremiah: 27 "Look, I am Yahweh, the God of
all flesh.[n] Is anything too difficult for Me?
28 Therefore, this is what the LORD says: I
am about to hand this city over to the Chaldeans,[o] to Babylon's king Nebuchadnezzar,
and he will capture it. 29 The Chaldeans who
are going to fight against this city will come,
set this city on fire, and burn it along with
the houses where incense has been burned to
•Baal on their rooftops and where •drink offerings have been poured out to other gods
to provoke Me to anger.[p] 30 From their youth,
the Israelites and Judeans have done nothing but what is evil in My sight! They have
done nothing but provoke Me to anger by
the work of their hands"[q] — this is the LORD's
declaration — 31 "for this city has caused My
wrath and fury from the day it was built until
now. I will therefore remove it from My presence,[r] 32 because of all the evil the Israelites
and Judeans have done to provoke Me to anger — they, their kings,[s] their officials, their
priests, and their prophets, the men of Judah,
and the residents of Jerusalem. 33 They have
turned their backs to Me and not their faces.
Though I taught them time and time again,[A,t]
they do not listen and receive discipline.
34 They have placed their detestable things[u] in
the house that is called by My name and have
defiled it. 35 They have built the •high places
of Baal in the Valley of Hinnom to make their
sons and daughters pass through the fire to
•Molech[v] — something I had not commanded
them. I had never entertained the thought[B]
that they do this detestable act causing Judah
to sin!
36 "Now therefore, this is what the LORD,
the God of Israel, says to this city about
which you said, 'It has been handed over to
Babylon's king through sword, famine, and
plague': 37 I am about to gather them from
all the lands where I have banished them in
My anger, rage and great wrath, and I will return them to this place and make them live
in safety.[w] 38 They will be My people, and I will
be their God. 39 I will give them one heart[x] and
one way so that for their good and for the
good of their descendants after them, they
will •fear Me always.
40 "I will make an everlasting covenant
with them:[y] I will never turn away from doing good to them, and I will put fear of Me
in their hearts so they will never again turn
away from Me. 41 I will take delight in them
to do what is good for them, and with all My
heart and mind I will faithfully plant them in
this land.[z]
42 "For this is what the LORD says: Just as I

[a] **32:15** Jr 32:43
[b] **32:17** 2Kg 19:15; 2Ch 2:12; Is 37:16
[c] Dt 4:37; Neh 1:10; Jr 27:5
[d] **32:18** Ex 20:5-6; 34:7; Nm 14:18; Dt 5:9-10
[e] Neh 9:32
[f] **32:19** Jr 17:10
[g] **32:20** Ex 1–15; Dt 6:22; Neh 9:10
[h] Is 63:12,14; Dn 9:15
[i] **32:21** Dt 4:34; 26:8
[j] **32:22** Ex 3:8,17; Lv 20:24; Nm 13:27; Dt 26:9
[k] **32:23** Ps 78:10; Is 42:24; Jr 44:10
[l] Jr 11:8
[m] **32:24** 2Kg 25:1; Jr 6:6; Ezk 4:2
[n] **32:27** Nm 16:22
[o] **32:28** Jr 32:3
[p] **32:29** Jr 11:17; 44:3,8
[q] **32:30** Jr 25:7
[r] **32:31** 2Kg 23:27; 24:3
[s] **32:32** Jr 2:26
[t] **32:33** Jr 25:3
[u] **32:34** Jr 4:1; 7:30; Ezk 5:11
[v] **32:35** Lv 20:2-5; Dt 18:10; 2Kg 23:10; Jr 7:31
[w] **32:37** Dt 12:10; Ezk 28:26; 34:25,28
[x] **32:39** Ezk 11:19
[y] **32:40** Gn 17:7,13,19; Is 55:3; Jr 50:5
[z] **32:41** Jr 24:6

[A] **32:33** Lit *them, rising up early and teaching* [B] **32:35** Lit *them, and it did not arise on My heart*

have brought all this great disaster on these
people,[a] so am I about to bring on them all
the good I am promising them. 43 Fields will
be bought in this land about which you are
saying,[b] 'It's a desolation[c] without man or
beast; it has been handed over to the Chaldeans!' 44 Fields will be purchased with silver, the transaction written on a scroll and
sealed,[d] and witnesses will be called on in the
land of Benjamin,[e] in the areas surrounding
Jerusalem, and in Judah's cities — the cities of
the hill country, the cities of the Judean foothills, and the cities of the •Negev — because I
will restore their fortunes."[A]
This is the LORD's declaration.

Israel's Restoration

33 While he was still confined in the
guard's courtyard,[f] the word of the LORD
came to Jeremiah a second time: 2 "The LORD
who made the earth,[B] the LORD who forms it
to establish it, •Yahweh is His name,[g] says this:
3 Call to Me and I will answer you[h] and tell
you great and incomprehensible things you
do not know.[i] 4 For this is what the LORD, the
God of Israel, says concerning the houses of
this city and the palaces of Judah's kings, the
ones torn down for defense against the siege
ramps and the sword:[j] 5 The people coming to
fight the Chaldeans will fill the houses with
the corpses of their own men that I strike
down in My wrath and rage. I have hidden
My face[k] from this city because of all their
evil. 6 Yet I will certainly bring health[l] and
healing to it and will indeed heal them. I will
let them experience the abundance[C] of peace
and truth.[m] 7 I will restore the fortunes[D] of
Judah and of Israel and will rebuild them as
in former times.[n] 8 I will purify them from all
the wrongs they have committed against Me,[o]
and I will forgive all the wrongs they have
committed against Me, rebelling against Me.
9 This city will bear on My behalf a name of
joy, praise, and glory[p] before all the nations of
the earth, who will hear of all the good I will
do for them. They will tremble with awe because of all the good and all the peace[q] I will
bring about for them.
10 "This is what the LORD says: In this place,
which you say is a ruin,[r] without man or

[a]32:42 Jr 31:28
[b]32:43 Jr 32:15
[c]Jr 33:10
[d]32:44 Jr 32:10
[e]Jr 17:26
[f]33:1 Jr 32:2
[g]33:2 Ex 6:3
[h]33:3 Ps 91:15; Jr 29:12
[i]Is 48:6
[j]33:4 Jr 32:24
[k]33:5 Dt 31:17; 32:20; Is 54:8
[l]33:6 Is 58:8; Jr 8:22; 30:17
[m]2Kg 20:19; Est 9:30; Is 39:8
[n]33:7 Is 1:26
[o]33:8 Ps 51:2; Ezk 36:25; Heb 9:11-14
[p]33:9 Dt 26:19; Jr 13:11; Zph 3:19-20
[q]Jr 8:15; 14:19
[r]33:10 Jr 32:43

GOD'S HEART FOR THE WORLD

Trembling at Goodness

They will tremble with awe because of all the good and all the peace I will bring about for them. (Jeremiah 33:9)

Israel was God's chosen vehicle to declare His glory, His character, to the nations. Over and over we see God calling out to them, making Himself present to them, providing for them, and showing them how to live in the world He created. And over and over again, we see Israel going its own way and rebelling against God. Jeremiah 33:1-9 confronts us with the terrible reality that God let them go their own way. If the people will not seek His face, He will hide it from them, and they will descend into the chaos that comes from Yahweh's absence.

But what God wants the nations to see, and what they will see (v. 9), is that despite Israel's penchant to rebel, God does not turn His face away forever. He is still above all the healer, cleanser, forgiver, and rebuilder. He brings order out of chaos. He brings life out of death. In a city that has rejected His presence, He cleanses and forgives so that they can again enjoy His goodness. He restores what they have broken down. They will be called Joy, Peace, and Glory. In the end, the nations will "tremble with awe," not because of God's power to destroy, but because of His overwhelming love, "because of all the good and all the peace" He will bring.

[A]32:44 Or *will end their captivity* [B]33:2 LXX; MT reads *made it* [C]33:6 Or *fragrance*; Hb obscure [D]33:7 Or *will end the captivity*

beast — that is, in Judah's cities and Jerusalem's streets that are a desolation without man, without inhabitant, and without
beast — there will be heard again 11 a sound
of joy and gladness, the voice of the groom
and the bride,[a] and the voice of those saying,

> Praise the LORD of ·Hosts,
> for the LORD is good;
> His faithful love endures forever

as they bring thank offerings to the temple
of the LORD. For I will restore the fortunes[A]
of the land as in former times, says the LORD.
12 "This is what the LORD of Hosts says:
In this desolate place — without man or
beast — and in all its cities there will once
more be a grazing land where shepherds may
rest flocks.[b] 13 The flocks will again pass under
the hands of the one who counts them[c] in
the cities of the hill country,[d] the cities of the
Judean foothills, the cities of the ·Negev, the
land of Benjamin — the cities surrounding
Jerusalem and Judah's cities, says the LORD.

God's Covenant with David

14 "Look, the days are coming" —
this is the LORD's declaration —
"when I will fulfill the good promises
that I have spoken
concerning the house of Israel
and the house of Judah.[e]
15 In those days and at that time
I will cause a Righteous Branch[f]
to sprout up for David,
and He will administer justice
and righteousness in the land.
16 In those days Judah will be saved,
and Jerusalem will dwell securely,[g]
and this is what she will be named:
Yahweh Our Righteousness.

17 "For this is what the LORD says: David will
never fail to have a man sitting on the throne
of the house of Israel.[h] 18 The Levitical priests
will never fail to have a man always before Me
to offer ·burnt offerings, to burn ·grain offerings, and to make sacrifices."[i]
19 The word of the LORD came to Jeremiah:
20 "This is what the LORD says: If you can break
My covenant with the day and My covenant
with the night so that day and night cease to
come at their regular time,[j] 21 then also My
covenant with My servant David[k] may be broken so that he will not have a son reigning on
his throne, and the Levitical priests will not
be My ministers.[l] 22 The hosts of heaven cannot be counted; the sand of the sea cannot be
measured.[m] So, too, I will make the descendants of My servant David and the Levites
who minister to Me innumerable."
23 The word of the LORD came to Jeremiah:
24 "Have you not noticed what these people
have said? They say, 'The LORD has rejected
the two families He had chosen.'[n] My people
are treated with contempt and no longer
regarded as a nation among them. 25 This is
what the LORD says: If I do not keep My covenant with the day and with the night and
fail to establish the fixed order of heaven and
earth,[o] 26 then I might also reject the ·seed of
Jacob and of My servant David — not taking
from his descendants rulers over the descendants of Abraham, Isaac, and Jacob. Instead, I
will restore their fortunes[B] and have compassion on them."[p]

Jeremiah's Word to King Zedekiah

34 This is the word that came to Jeremiah
from the LORD when Nebuchadnez-
zar, king of Babylon,[q] all his army, all the
earthly kingdoms under his control,[r] and all
other nations were fighting against Jerusalem and all its surrounding cities: 2 "This is
what the LORD, the God of Israel, says: Go,
speak to Zedekiah, king of Judah, and tell
him: This is what the LORD says: I am about
to hand this city over to the king of Babylon,[s]
and he will burn it down. 3 As for you, you will
not escape from his hand but are certain to
be captured and handed over to him. You will
meet the king of Babylon eye to eye and speak
face to face;[C,t] you will go to Babylon.
4 "Yet hear the LORD's word, Zedekiah, king
of Judah. This is what the LORD says concerning you: You will not die by the sword; 5 you
will die peacefully. There will be a burning
ceremony for you just like the burning ceremonies for your fathers, the former kings
who preceded you.[u] 'Our king is dead!'[D] will
be the lament for you, for I have spoken this
word." This is the LORD's declaration.

[a] **33:11** Jr 7:34; 16:9; 25:10
[b] **33:12** Is 65:10; Ezk 34:12-15
[c] **33:13** Lv 27:32
[d] Jr 17:26
[e] **33:14** Jos 21:45; Jr 23:5-6
[f] **33:15** Is 4:2; Zch 3:8
[g] **33:16** Dt 33:12
[h] **33:17** 1Kg 2:4; 8:25; 9:5
[i] **33:18** Jr 31:36; 35:19
[j] **33:20** Gn 8:22; Is 54:9-10; Jr 31:35-37
[k] **33:21** 2Sm 7:11-16; 2Ch 21:7; Ps 89:3
[l] Is 61:6; Ezk 45:4-5; Jl 1:9,13
[m] **33:22** Gn 22:17
[n] **33:24** Dt 7:6; 14:2
[o] **33:25** Ps 74:16-17
[p] **33:26** Jr 33:7
[q] **34:1** 2Kg 25:1; Jr 39:1; 52:4
[r] Jr 1:15
[s] **34:2** Jr 32:3,28
[t] **34:3** Jr 32:4
[u] **34:5** 2Ch 16:14; 21:19

[A] **33:11** Or *will end the captivity* [B] **33:26** Or *Instead, I will end their captivity* [C] **34:3** Lit *and his mouth will speak to your mouth* [D] **34:5** Lit *Alas, lord*

6So Jeremiah the prophet related all these
words to Zedekiah king of Judah in Jerusalem
7while the king of Babylon's army was attacking Jerusalem and all of Judah's remaining
cities — against Lachish and Azekah,[a] for they
were the only ones left of Judah's fortified cities.

The People and Their Slaves

8This is the word that came to Jeremiah
from the LORD after King Zedekiah made a
covenant with all the people who were in Jerusalem to proclaim freedom[b] to them, 9so
each man would free his male and female
Hebrew slaves and no one would enslave his
Judean brother.[c] 10All the officials and people
who entered into covenant to free their male
and female slaves — in order not to enslave
them any longer — obeyed and freed them.
11Afterward, however, they changed their
minds and took back their male and female
slaves they had freed and forced them to become slaves again.

12Then the word of the LORD came to Jeremiah from the LORD: 13"This is what the
LORD, the God of Israel, says: I made a covenant[d] with your ancestors when I brought
them out of the land of Egypt, out of the place
of slavery, saying: 14At the end of seven years,
each of you must free his Hebrew brother
who sold himself[A] to you. He may serve you
six years, but then you must send him out
free from you.[e] But your ancestors did not
obey Me or pay any attention. 15Today you repented and did what pleased Me, each of you
proclaiming freedom for his neighbor. You
made a covenant before Me[f] at the temple
called by My name.[g] 16But you have changed
your minds[h] and profaned My name.[i] Each
has taken back his male and female slaves
who had been freed to go wherever they
wanted, and you have again subjugated them
to be your slaves.

17"Therefore, this is what the LORD says: You
have not obeyed Me by proclaiming freedom,
each man for his brother and for his neighbor.
I hereby proclaim freedom for you"[j] — this is
the LORD's declaration — "to the sword, to
plague, and to famine! I will make you a horror to all the earth's kingdoms. 18As for those
who disobeyed My covenant,[k] not keeping
the terms of the covenant they made before
Me, I will treat them like the calf they cut in
two in order to pass between its pieces.[l] 19The
officials of Judah and Jerusalem, the court officials, the priests, and all the people of the
land who passed between the pieces of the
calf 20will be handed over to their enemies,
to those who want to take their life. Their
corpses will become food for the birds of the
sky and for the wild animals of the land.[m] 21I
will hand Zedekiah king of Judah and his officials over to their enemies, to those who
want to take their lives, to the king of Babylon's army that is withdrawing. 22I am about
to give the command" — this is the LORD's
declaration — "and I will bring them back to
this city. They will fight against it, capture it,
and burn it down.[n] I will make Judah's cities a
desolation,[o] without inhabitant."

The Rechabites' Example

35 This is the word that came to Jeremiah
from the LORD in the days of Jehoia-
kim[p] son of Josiah, king of Judah: 2"Go to the
house of the Rechabites, speak to them,[q] and
bring them to one of the chambers[r] of the
temple of the LORD to offer them a drink of
wine."

3So I took Jaazaniah son of Jeremiah, son
of Habazziniah, and his brothers and all his
sons — the entire house of the Rechabites —
4and I brought them into the temple of the
LORD to a chamber occupied by the sons of
Hanan son of Igdaliah, a man of God,[s] who
had a chamber near the officials' chamber,
which was above the chamber of Maaseiah
son of Shallum the doorkeeper. 5I set jars
filled with wine and some cups before the
sons of the house of the Rechabites and said
to them, "Drink wine!"

6But they replied, "We do not drink wine,
for Jonadab,[t] son of our ancestor Rechab,
commanded: 'You and your sons must never
drink wine. 7You must not build a house or
sow seed or plant a vineyard. Those things
are not for you. Rather, you must live in
tents your whole life, so you may live a long
time on the soil where you stay as a temporary resident.'[u] 8We have obeyed the voice of

[a]**34:7** Jos 10:3-35
[b]**34:8** Lv 25:10; Is 61:1; Ezk 46:17
[c]**34:9** Lv 25:39
[d]**34:13** Jr 31:32
[e]**34:14** Ex 21:2-6; Dt 15:12-17
[f]**34:15** 2Kg 23:3
[g]Jr 7:10-11
[h]**34:16** Jr 34:11
[i]Lv 19:12
[j]**34:17** Mt 7:2
[k]**34:18** Jos 7:11; 2Kg 18:12
[l]Gn 15:10,17-18
[m]**34:20** Dt 28:26; Is 18:6; Jr 7:33
[n]**34:22** Jr 37:8
[o]Jr 4:7; 9:11
[p]**35:1** 2Kg 23:34–24:19; 2Ch 36:4-8
[q]**35:2** 1Ch 2:55
[r]1Kg 6:5,8; 1Ch 9:26,33
[s]**35:4** Dt 33:1
[t]**35:6** 2Kg 10:15,23
[u]**35:7** Ex 20:12; Eph 6:2-3

[A]**34:14** Or *who was sold*

Jonadab, son of our ancestor Rechab, in all
he commanded us. So we haven't drunk wine
our whole life—we, our wives, our sons, and
our daughters. 9 We also have not built houses
to live in and do not have vineyard, field, or
seed. 10 But we have lived in tents and have
obeyed and done as our ancestor Jonadab
commanded us. 11 However, when Nebuchadnezzar king of Babylon marched into the
land,[a] we said: Come, let's go into Jerusalem
to get away from the Chaldean and Aramean
armies. So we have been living in Jerusalem."
12 Then the word of the LORD came to Jeremiah: 13 "This is what the LORD of •Hosts,
the God of Israel, says: Go, say to the men of
Judah and the residents of Jerusalem: Will
you not accept discipline[b] by listening to My
words?"—this is the LORD's declaration.
14 "The words of Jonadab, son of Rechab, have
been carried out. He commanded his sons
not to drink wine, and they have not drunk
to this very day because they have obeyed
their ancestor's command. But I have spoken
to you time and time again,[A,c] and you have
not obeyed Me! 15 Time and time again[B] I have
sent you all My servants the prophets, proclaiming: Turn, each one from his evil way of
life,[d] and correct your actions. Stop following
other gods to serve them.[e] Live in the land
that I gave you and your ancestors. But you
would not pay attention or obey Me.[f] 16 Yes,
the sons of Jonadab son of Rechab carried
out their ancestor's command he gave them,
but these people have not obeyed Me. 17 Therefore, this is what the LORD, the God of Hosts,
the God of Israel, says: I will certainly bring to
Judah and to all the residents of Jerusalem all
the disaster I have pronounced against them
because I have spoken to them, but they have
not obeyed, and I have called to them, but
they would not answer."
18 Jeremiah said to the house of the Rechabites: "This is what the LORD of Hosts, the
God of Israel, says: 'Because you have obeyed
the command of your ancestor Jonadab and
have kept all his commands and have done
all that he commanded you, 19 this is what the
LORD of Hosts, the God of Israel, says: Jonadab son of Rechab will never fail to have a
man to always stand before Me.'"[g]

Jeremiah Dictates a Scroll

36 In the fourth year of Jehoiakim son of
Josiah,[h] king of Judah, this word came
to Jeremiah from the LORD: 2 "Take a scroll,[i]
and write on it all the words I have spoken to
you concerning Israel, Judah, and all the nations from the time I first spoke to you during Josiah's reign until today. 3 Perhaps when
the house of Judah hears about all the disaster I am planning to bring on them, each one
of them will turn from his evil way. Then I
will forgive their wrongdoing[j] and their sin."
4 So Jeremiah summoned Baruch[k] son of
Neriah. At Jeremiah's dictation,[C] Baruch
wrote on a scroll all the words the LORD had
spoken to Jeremiah. 5 Then Jeremiah commanded Baruch, "I am restricted;[l] I cannot
enter the temple of the LORD, 6 so you must go
and read from the scroll—which you wrote
at my dictation[D]—the words of the LORD in
the hearing of the people at the temple of
the LORD on a day of fasting. You must also
read them in the hearing of all the Judeans
who are coming from their cities. 7 Perhaps
their petition will come before the LORD,[m]
and each one will turn from his evil way, for
the anger and fury that the LORD has pronounced against this people are great." 8 So
Baruch son of Neriah did everything Jeremiah the prophet had commanded him. At
the LORD's temple he read the LORD's words
from the scroll.

Baruch Reads the Scroll

9 In the fifth year of Jehoiakim son of Josiah, king of Judah, in the ninth month,[n] all
the people of Jerusalem and all those coming in from Judah's cities into Jerusalem proclaimed a fast before the LORD.[o] 10 Then at
the LORD's temple, in the chamber of Gemariah son of Shaphan the scribe,[p] in the upper
courtyard at the opening of the New Gate[q] of
the LORD's temple, in the hearing of all the
people, Baruch read Jeremiah's words from
the scroll.
11 When Micaiah son of Gemariah, son of
Shaphan, heard all the words of the LORD
from the scroll, 12 he went down to the scribe's
chamber in the king's palace. All the officials
were sitting there—Elishama the scribe, De-

[a] **35:11** 2Kg 24:1-2
[b] **35:13** Jr 31:18; 32:33
[c] **35:14** Jr 25:3
[d] **35:15** Jr 18:11
[e] Jr 7:6
[f] Jr 34:14
[g] **35:19** Jr 31:36; 33:18
[h] **36:1** Jr 25:1; 45:1
[i] **36:2** Ps 40:7; Ezk 2:9
[j] **36:3** Jr 31:34; 33:8; 36:31
[k] **36:4** Jr 32:12-16; 43:3,6; 45:1-2
[l] **36:5** Jr 32:2; 33:1
[m] **36:7** 1Kg 8:28,45,49; Ps 119:170
[n] **36:9** Jr 36:22
[o] 2Ch 20:3
[p] **36:10** 2Kg 22:3-14; 2Ch 34:8-20; Jr 29:3
[q] Jr 26:10

[A] **35:14** Lit *you, rising up early and speaking* [B] **35:15** Lit *Rising up early and sending* [C] **36:4** Lit *From Jeremiah's mouth* [D] **36:6** Lit *wrote from my mouth*

laiah son of Shemaiah, Elnathan son of Achbor,[a] Gemariah son of Shaphan, Zedekiah son
of Hananiah, and all the other officials. 13 Mi-
caiah reported to them all the words he had heard when Baruch read from the scroll in
the hearing of the people. 14 Then all the offi-
cials sent word to Baruch through Jehudi son of Nethaniah, son of Shelemiah, son of Cushi, saying, "Bring the scroll that you read in the hearing of the people, and come." So Baruch son of Neriah took the scroll and went to
them. 15 They said to him, "Sit down and read it in our hearing." So Baruch read it in their hearing.
16 When they had heard all the words, they turned to each other in fear and said to Baruch, "We must surely tell the king all these
things." 17 Then they asked Baruch, "Tell us—how did you write all these words? At his dictation?"[A]
18 Baruch said to them, "At his dictation.[A] He recited all these words to me while I was writing on the scroll in ink."

Jehoiakim Burns the Scroll

19 The officials said to Baruch, "You and Jeremiah must hide yourselves and tell no one
where you are." 20 Then they came to the king at the courtyard, having deposited the scroll in the chamber of Elishama the scribe, and reported everything in the hearing of the
king. 21 The king sent Jehudi to get the scroll, and he took it from the chamber of Elishama the scribe. Jehudi then read it in the hearing of the king and all the officials who were
standing by the king. 22 Since it was the ninth month, the king was sitting in his winter quarters[b] with a fire burning in front of him.
23 As soon as Jehudi would read three or four columns, Jehoiakim would cut the scroll[B] with a scribe's knife and throw the columns into the blazing fire until the entire scroll
was consumed by the fire in the brazier. 24 As they heard all these words, the king and all of his servants did not become terrified[c] or
tear their garments. 25 Even though Elnathan, Delaiah, and Gemariah had urged the king not to burn the scroll, he would not listen
to them. 26 Then the king commanded Jerahmeel the king's son, Seraiah son of Azriel, and Shelemiah son of Abdeel to seize Baruch the scribe and Jeremiah the prophet, but the LORD had hidden them.

Jeremiah Dictates Another Scroll

27 After the king had burned the scroll with the words Baruch had written at Jeremiah's dictation,[C] the word of the LORD came to Jeremiah: 28 "Take another scroll, and once again write on it the very words that were on the original scroll that Jehoiakim king of Judah
burned. 29 You are to proclaim concerning Jehoiakim king of Judah: This is what the LORD says: You have burned the scroll, saying, 'Why have you written on it:[d] The king of Babylon will certainly come and destroy this land and
cause it to be without man or beast?' 30 There-
fore, this is what the LORD says concerning Jehoiakim king of Judah: He will have no one to sit on David's throne, and his corpse will be thrown out to be exposed to the heat of day
and the frost of night.[e] 31 I will punish him, his descendants, and his officers for their wrongdoing. I will bring on them, on the residents of Jerusalem, and on the men of Judah all the disaster, which I warned them about but they did not listen."
32 Then Jeremiah took another scroll and gave it to Baruch son of Neriah, the scribe, and he wrote on it at Jeremiah's dictation[C] all the words of the scroll that Jehoiakim,[f] Judah's king, had burned in the fire. And many other words like them were added.

Jerusalem's Last Days

37 Zedekiah son of Josiah[g] reigned as king in the land of Judah[h] in place of Jehoiachin[D,i] son of Jehoiakim, for Nebuchadnezzar king of Babylon made him king. 2 He and
his officers and the people of the land did not obey the words of the LORD[j] that He spoke through Jeremiah the prophet.
3 Nevertheless, King Zedekiah sent Jehucal[k] son of Shelemiah and Zephaniah[l] son of Maaseiah, the priest, to Jeremiah the prophet, requesting, "Please pray to the LORD our God
for us!" 4 Jeremiah was going about his daily tasks[E] among the people, for they had not yet
put him into the prison.[m] 5 Pharaoh's army had left Egypt,[n] and when the Chaldeans, who

[a] 36:12 Jr 26:22
[b] 36:22 Am 3:15
[c] 36:24 Jr 36:16
[d] 36:29 Jr 26:9
[e] 36:30 Gn 31:40
[f] 36:32 Jr 36:4,18
[g] 37:1 2Kg 24:17; 2Ch 36:10
[h] Ezk 17:12-21
[i] Jr 22:24
[j] 37:2 2Ch 36:12-16
[k] 37:3 Jr 38:1
[l] 2Kg 25:18-21; Jr 21:1; 29:24-29
[m] 37:4 Jr 32:2-3
[n] 37:5 Ezk 17:15

[A] 36:17,18 Lit *From his mouth* [B] 36:23 Lit *columns, he would tear it* [C] 36:27,32 Lit *written from Jeremiah's mouth* [D] 37:1 = Coniah [E] 37:4 Lit *was coming in and going out* were besieging Jerusalem, heard the report, they withdrew from Jerusalem.

6 The word of the LORD came to Jeremiah the prophet: 7 "This is what the LORD, the God of Israel, says: This is what you will say to Judah's king,[a] who is sending you to inquire of Me: Watch: Pharaoh's army, which has come out to help you,[b] is going to return to its own land of Egypt. 8 The Chaldeans will then return and fight against this city. They will capture it and burn it down.[c] 9 This is what the LORD says: Don't deceive yourselves by saying, 'The Chaldeans will leave us for good,' for they will not leave. 10 Indeed, if you were to strike down the entire Chaldean army that is fighting with you,[d] and there remained among them only the badly wounded[A] men, each in his tent, they would get up and burn this city down."

Jeremiah's Imprisonment

11 When the Chaldean army withdrew from Jerusalem because of Pharaoh's army, 12 Jeremiah started to leave Jerusalem to go to the land of Benjamin to claim his portion there[e] among the people. 13 But when he was at the Benjamin Gate,[f] an officer of the guard was there, whose name was Irijah son of Shelemiah, son of Hananiah, and he apprehended Jeremiah the prophet, saying, "You are deserting to the Chaldeans."

14 "That's a lie," Jeremiah replied. "I am not deserting to the Chaldeans!" Irijah would not listen to him but apprehended Jeremiah and took him to the officials. 15 The officials were angry at Jeremiah and beat him and placed him in jail in the house of Jonathan[g] the scribe, for it had been made into a prison. 16 So Jeremiah went into a cell in the dungeon[h] and stayed there many days.

Jeremiah Summoned by Zedekiah

17 King Zedekiah later sent for him and received him, and in his house privately asked him, "Is there a word from the LORD?"[i]

"There is," Jeremiah responded, and he continued, "You will be handed over to the king of Babylon."[j] 18 Then Jeremiah said to King Zedekiah, "How have I sinned against you or your servants or these people that you have put me in prison? 19 Where are your prophets who prophesied to you, claiming, 'The king of Babylon will not come against you and this land'?[k] 20 So now please listen, my lord the king. May my petition come before you.[l] Don't send me back to the house of Jonathan the scribe, or I will die there."

21 So King Zedekiah gave orders, and Jeremiah was placed in the guard's courtyard.[m] He was given a loaf of bread each day from the baker's street until all the bread was gone from the city. So Jeremiah remained in the guard's courtyard.

Jeremiah Thrown into a Cistern

38 Now Shephatiah son of Mattan, Gedaliah son of Pashhur, Jucal[B] son of Shelemiah,[n] and Pashhur son of Malchijah heard the words Jeremiah was speaking to all the people: 2 "This is what the LORD says: 'Whoever stays in this city will die by the sword, famine, and plague, but whoever surrenders to the Chaldeans will live. He will keep his life like the spoils of war and will live.'[o] 3 This is what the LORD says: 'This city will most certainly be handed over to the king of Babylon's army,[p] and he will capture it.'"

4 The officials then said to the king, "This man ought to die, because he is weakening the morale of the warriors who remain in this city and of all the people by speaking to them in this way. This man is not seeking the well-being of this people, but disaster."[q]

5 King Zedekiah said, "Here he is; he's in your hands since the king can't do anything against you." 6 So they took Jeremiah and dropped him into the cistern of Malchiah the king's son, which was in the guard's courtyard, lowering Jeremiah with ropes. There was no water in the cistern, only mud, and Jeremiah sank in the mud.[r]

7 But Ebed-melech, a ·Cushite court official employed in the king's palace, heard Jeremiah had been put into the cistern. While the king was sitting at the Benjamin Gate,[s] 8 Ebed-melech went from the king's palace and spoke to the king: 9 "My lord the king, these men have been evil in all they have done to Jeremiah the prophet. They have dropped him into the cistern where he will die from hunger, because there is no more bread in the city."[t]

[a] **37:7** Jr 21:1-2 [b] Lm 4:17 [c] **37:8** Jr 21:10; 34:2,22; 38:18 [d] **37:10** Jr 21:4-5 [e] **37:12** Jr 32:1-15 [f] **37:13** Jr 38:7; Zch 14:10 [g] **37:15** Jr 38:26 [h] **37:16** Gn 40:15; Is 24:22; Zch 9:11 [i] **37:17** Jr 38:14-16 [j] Jr 21:7 [k] **37:19** Jr 28:1-17 [l] **37:20** Jr 38:26 [m] **37:21** Jr 32:2 [n] **38:1** Jr 37:3 [o] **38:2** Jr 21:9; 39:18; 45:5 [p] **38:3** Jr 32:3-5 [q] **38:4** Jr 29:11 [r] **38:6** Gn 37:20-24 [s] **38:7** Jr 20:2; Ezk 48:32; Zch 14:10 [t] **38:9** Jr 37:21

[A] **37:10** Lit *the pierced* [B] **38:1** = Jehucal in Jr 37:3

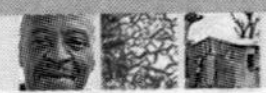

10So the king commanded Ebed-melech,
the Cushite, "Take from here 30 men under
your authority and pull Jeremiah the prophet
up from the cistern before he dies."
11So Ebed-melech took the men under his
authority and went to the king's palace to a
place below the storehouse.[A] From there he
took old rags and worn-out clothes and lowered them by ropes to Jeremiah in the cistern.
12Ebed-melech the Cushite cried out to Jeremiah, "Place these old rags and clothes between your armpits and the ropes." Jeremiah
did so, 13and they pulled him up with the
ropes and lifted him out of the cistern, but
he continued to stay in the guard's courtyard.

Zedekiah's Final Meeting with Jeremiah

14King Zedekiah sent for Jeremiah the
prophet and received him at the third entrance of the LORD's temple. The king said to
Jeremiah, "I am going to ask you something;
don't hide anything from me."
15Jeremiah replied to Zedekiah, "If I tell
you, you will kill me, won't you? Besides, if I
give you advice, you won't listen to me any-
way."
16King Zedekiah swore to Jeremiah in private,[a] "As the LORD lives, who has given us this
life,[b] I will not kill you or hand you over to
these men who want to take your life."
17Jeremiah therefore said to Zedekiah,
"This is what the LORD, the God of •Hosts, the
God of Israel, says: 'If indeed you surrender
to the officials of the king of Babylon,[c] then
you will live, this city will not be burned
down, and you and your household will survive. 18But if you do not surrender to the officials of the king of Babylon, then this city
will be handed over to the Chaldeans. They
will burn it down, and you yourself will not
escape from them.'"
19But King Zedekiah said to Jeremiah, "I
am worried about the Judeans who have deserted to the Chaldeans. They may hand me
over to the Judeans to abuse me."[d]
20"They will not hand you over," Jeremiah
replied. "Obey the voice of the LORD in what
I am telling you, so it may go well for you and
you can live. 21But if you refuse to surrender,
this is the verdict[B] that the LORD has shown
me: 22'All the women[C] who remain in the palace of Judah's king will be brought out to the
officials of the king of Babylon and will say:

> Your trusted friends[D] misled[E] you
> and overcame you.
> Your feet sank into the mire,
> and they deserted you.

23All your wives and sons will be brought
out to the Chaldeans.[e] You yourself will not
escape from them, for you will be seized by
the king of Babylon and this city will burn
down.'"
24Then Zedekiah warned Jeremiah, "Don't
let anyone know about these things or you
will die. 25If the officials hear that I have spoken with you[f] and come and demand of you,
'Tell us what you said to the king; don't hide
anything from us and we won't kill you. Also,
what did the king say to you?' 26then you will
tell them, 'I was bringing before the king my
petition that he not return me to the house
of Jonathan to die there.'"[g] 27When all the officials came to Jeremiah and questioned him,
he reported the exact words to them the king
had commanded, and they quit speaking
with him because nothing had been heard.
28Jeremiah remained in the guard's courtyard
until the day Jerusalem was captured, and he
was there when it happened.[F]

The Fall of Jerusalem to Babylon

39 In the ninth year of Zedekiah king of
Judah, in the tenth month, King Nebuchadnezzar of Babylon advanced against Jerusalem with his entire army and laid siege
to it. 2In the fourth month of Zedekiah's eleventh year, on the ninth day of the month, the
city was broken into. 3All the officials of the
king of Babylon entered and sat at the Middle Gate: Nergal-sharezer, Samgar, Nebusar-
sechim[G] the Rab-saris, Nergal-sharezer the
Rab-mag, and all the rest of the officials of
Babylon's king.
4When he saw them, Zedekiah king of Judah and all the soldiers fled. They left the city
at night by way of the king's garden through
the gate between the two walls. They left

[a]**38:16** Jr 37:17
[b]Is 57:16
[c]**38:17** 2Kg 24:12; Jr 27:12; 38:2; 39:3
[d]**38:19** Jdg 19:25; 1Sm 31:4
[e]**38:23** Jr 39:6; 41:10
[f]**38:25** Jr 38:4-6
[g]**38:26** Jr 37:20

[A]**38:11** Or *treasury* [B]**38:21** Or *promise*; lit *word* [C]**38:22** Or *wives* [D]**38:22** Lit *The men of your peace* [E]**38:22** Or *incited* [F]**38:28** Or *captured. This is what happened when Jerusalem was captured:* [G]**39:3** LXX; MT reads *Samgar-nebu, Sarsechim*

along the route to the ·Arabah.[a] 5 However, the Chaldean army pursued them and overtook Zedekiah in the plains[A] of Jericho, arrested him, and brought him to Nebuchadnezzar, Babylon's king, at Riblah in the land of Hamath. The king passed sentence on him there.

6 At Riblah the king of Babylon slaughtered Zedekiah's sons before his eyes, and he also slaughtered all Judah's nobles. 7 Then he blinded Zedekiah and put him in bronze chains to take him to Babylon.[b] 8 The Chaldeans next burned down the king's palace and the people's houses and tore down the walls of Jerusalem. 9 Nebuzaradan, the commander of the guards,[c] deported the rest of the people to Babylon — those who had remained in the city and those deserters who had defected to him along with the rest of the people who had remained. 10 However, Nebuzaradan, the commander of the guards, left in the land of Judah some of the poor people who owned nothing, and he gave them vineyards and fields at that time.[d]

Jeremiah Freed by Nebuchadnezzar

11 Speaking through Nebuzaradan, captain of the guard, King Nebuchadnezzar of Babylon gave orders concerning Jeremiah, saying: 12 "Take him, look after him, and don't let any harm come to him; do for him whatever he says." 13 Nebuzaradan, captain of the guard, Nebushazban the Rab-saris, Nergal-sharezer the Rab-mag, and all the captains of the king of Babylon 14 had Jeremiah brought from the guard's courtyard[e] and turned him over to Gedaliah[f] son of Ahikam,[g] son of Shaphan, to take him home. So he settled among his own people.

15 Now the word of the LORD had come to Jeremiah when he was confined in the guard's courtyard:[h] 16 "Go tell Ebed-melech the ·Cushite:[i] This is what the LORD of ·Hosts, the God of Israel, says: I am about to fulfill My words for harm and not for good against this city. They will take place before your eyes on that day. 17 But I will rescue you on that day" — this is the LORD's declaration — "and you will not be handed over to the men you fear. 18 Indeed, I will certainly deliver you so that you do not fall by the sword. Because you have trusted in Me, you will keep your life like the spoils of war."[j] This is the LORD's declaration.

Jeremiah Stays in Judah

40 This is the word that came to Jeremiah from the LORD after Nebuzaradan, captain of the guard, released him at Ramah.[k] When he found him, he was bound in chains with all the exiles of Jerusalem and Judah who were being exiled to Babylon. 2 The captain of the guard took Jeremiah and said to him, "The LORD your God decreed this disaster on this place,[l] 3 and the LORD has fulfilled it. He has done just what He decreed. Because you people have sinned against the LORD[m] and have not obeyed Him, this thing has happened. 4 Now pay attention: Today I am setting you free from the chains that were on your hands.[n] If it pleases you to come with me to Babylon, come, and I will take care of you. But if it seems wrong to you to come with me to Babylon, go no farther.[B] Look — the whole land is in front of you.[o] Wherever it seems good and right for you to go, go there." 5 When Jeremiah had not yet turned to go, Nebuzaradan said to him: "Return[C] to Gedaliah son of Ahikam, son of Shaphan, whom the king of Babylon has appointed over the cities of Judah, and stay with him among the people or go wherever you want to go." So the captain of the guard gave him a ration[p] and a gift[q] and released him. 6 Jeremiah therefore went to Gedaliah son of Ahikam at Mizpah,[r] and he stayed with him among the people who remained in the land.

Gedaliah Advises Peace

7 When all the commanders of the armies in the field — they and their men — heard that the king of Babylon had appointed Gedaliah son of Ahikam over the land and that he had put him in charge of the men, women, and children from the poorest of the land who had not been deported to Babylon, 8 they came to Gedaliah at Mizpah. The commanders included Ishmael[s] son of Nethaniah, Johanan and Jonathan the sons of Kareah, Seraiah son of Tanhumeth, the sons of Ephai the Netophathite, and Jezaniah son of the Maacathite — they and their men.

[a] **39:4** Dt 2:8; 2Sm 4:7
[b] **39:1-7** 2Kg 25:1-7; Jr 52:4-11
[c] **39:9** 2Kg 25:8-20; Jr 52:12-30; Dn 2:14
[d] **39:8-10** 2Kg 25:9-12; Jr 52:13-16
[e] **39:14** Jr 38:28; 40:1-6
[f] Jr 40:5
[g] 2Kg 22:12
[h] **39:15** Jr 33:1
[i] **39:16** Jr 38:1-13
[j] **39:18** Jr 21:9; 38:2; 45:5
[k] **40:1** 1Kg 15:17-22; 2Ch 16:1-6
[l] **40:2** Dt 29:24-28
[m] **40:3** Dn 9:10-12
[n] **40:4** Jr 39:12
[o] Gn 20:15
[p] **40:5** 2Kg 25:30; Jr 52:34
[q] 2Sm 11:8
[r] **40:6** Jdg 20:1-3; 1Sm 7:5-16; Jr 41:1-16
[s] **40:8** Jr 41:1,9

[A] **39:5** Lit *Arabah* [B] **40:4** Lit *Babylon, stop* [C] **40:5** LXX reads *But if not, run, return*; Hb obscure

9 Gedaliah son of Ahikam, son of Shaphan, swore an oath to them and their men, assuring them, "Don't be afraid to serve the Chaldeans. Live in the land and serve the king of Babylon, and it will go well for you.[a] 10 As for me, I am going to live in Mizpah to represent[A] you before the Chaldeans[b] who come to us. As for you, gather wine, summer fruit, and oil, place them in your storage jars, and live in the cities you have captured."

11 When all the Judeans in Moab[c] and among the Ammonites and in[d] Edom and in all the other lands[e] also heard that the king of Babylon had left a remnant in Judah and had appointed Gedaliah son of Ahikam, son of Shaphan, over them, 12 they all returned from all the places where they had been banished[f] and came to the land of Judah, to Gedaliah at Mizpah, and harvested a great amount of wine and summer fruit.

13 Meanwhile, Johanan son of Kareah and all the commanders of the armies in the field came to Gedaliah at Mizpah 14 and warned him, "Don't you realize that Baalis, king of the Ammonites, has sent Ishmael son of Nethaniah[g] to kill you?" But Gedaliah son of Ahikam would not believe them. 15 Then Johanan son of Kareah suggested to Gedaliah in private at Mizpah, "Let me go kill Ishmael son of Nethaniah. No one will know it. Why should he kill you and scatter all of Judah that has gathered to you so that the remnant of Judah would perish?"[h]

16 But Gedaliah son of Ahikam responded to Johanan son of Kareah, "Don't do that! What you're saying about Ishmael is a lie."

Gedaliah Assassinated by Ishmael

41 In the seventh month, Ishmael son of Nethaniah, son of Elishama, of the royal family and one of the king's chief officers, came with 10 men to Gedaliah son of Ahikam at Mizpah. They ate a meal together there in Mizpah, 2 but then Ishmael son of Nethaniah and the 10 men who were with him got up and struck down Gedaliah son of Ahikam, son of Shaphan, with the sword; he killed the one the king of Babylon had appointed in the land. 3 Ishmael also struck down all the Judeans who were with Gedaliah at Mizpah, as well as the Chaldean soldiers who were there.[i]

4 On the second day after he had killed Gedaliah, when no one knew yet, 5 80 men came from Shechem, Shiloh,[j] and Samaria[k] who had shaved their beards,[l] torn their garments, and gashed themselves, and who were carrying *grain and incense offerings to bring to the temple of the LORD.[m] 6 Ishmael son of Nethaniah came out of Mizpah to meet them, weeping as he came. When he encountered them, he said: "Come to Gedaliah son of Ahikam!" 7 But when they came into the city, Ishmael son of Nethaniah and the men with him slaughtered them and threw them into[B] a cistern.

8 However, there were 10 men among them who said to Ishmael, "Don't kill us, for we have hidden treasure in the field—wheat, barley, oil, and honey!" So he stopped and did not kill them along with their companions. 9 Now the cistern where Ishmael had thrown all the corpses of the men he had struck down was a large one[C] that King Asa had made in the encounter with Baasha king of Israel.[n] Ishmael son of Nethaniah filled it with the slain.

10 Then Ishmael took captive all the remnant of the people of Mizpah including the daughters of the king—all those who remained in Mizpah over whom Nebuzaradan, captain of the guard, had appointed Gedaliah son of Ahikam. Ishmael son of Nethaniah took them captive and set off to cross over to the Ammonites.[o]

The Captives Rescued by Johanan

11 When Johanan son of Kareah and all the commanders of the armies[p] with him heard of all the evil that Ishmael son of Nethaniah had done, 12 they took all their men and went to fight with Ishmael son of Nethaniah and found him by the great pool in Gibeon.[q] 13 When all the people with Ishmael saw Johanan son of Kareah and all the commanders of the army with him, they rejoiced, 14 and all the people whom Ishmael had taken captive from Mizpah turned around and rejoined Johanan son of Kareah. 15 But Ishmael son of Nethaniah escaped from Johanan with eight

[a] **40:7-9** 2Kg 25:22-24
[b] **40:10** Dt 1:38
[c] **40:11** Nm 22:1
[d] 1Sm 11:1; 12:12
[e] Gn 36:8
[f] **40:12** Jr 23:3,8; 29:14; 32:37
[g] **40:14** Jr 41:10
[h] **40:15** Jr 42:2
[i] **41:1-3** 2Kg 25:25
[j] **41:5** Jos 18:1
[k] 1Kg 16:24
[l] Dt 14:1
[m] 2Kg 25:9
[n] **41:9** 1Kg 15:16-22
[o] **41:10** Jr 40:14
[p] **41:11** Jr 40:7-8,13-16
[q] **41:12** 2Sm 2:13

[A] **40:10** Lit *to stand* [B] **41:7** Syr; MT reads *slaughtered them in* [C] **41:9** LXX; MT reads *down by the hand of Gedaliah*

men and went to the Ammonites. 16 Johanan son of Kareah and all the commanders of the armies with him then took from Mizpah all the remnant of the people whom he had recovered from Ishmael son of Nethaniah after Ishmael had killed Gedaliah son of Ahikam — men, soldiers, women, children, and court officials whom he brought back from Gibeon. 17 They left, stopping in Geruth Chimham,[a] which is near Bethlehem, in order to make their way into Egypt, 18 away from the Chaldeans. For they feared them because Ishmael son of Nethaniah had struck down Gedaliah son of Ahikam, whom the king of Babylon had appointed in the land.[b]

The People Seek Jeremiah's Counsel

42 Then all the commanders of the armies, along with Johanan son of Kareah,[c] Jezaniah son of Hoshaiah, and all the people from the least to the greatest,[d] approached 2 Jeremiah the prophet and said, "May our petition come before you;[e] pray to the LORD your God on our behalf,[f] on behalf of this entire remnant (for few of us remain out of the many,[g] as you can see with your own eyes), 3 that the LORD your God may tell us the way we should walk and the thing we should do."

4 So Jeremiah the prophet said to them, "I have heard. I will now pray to the LORD your God according to your words, and every word that the LORD answers you I will tell you; I won't withhold a word from you."[h]

5 And they said to Jeremiah, "As for every word the LORD your God sends you to tell us, if we don't act accordingly, may the LORD be a true and faithful witness against us.[i] 6 Whether it is pleasant or unpleasant, we will obey the voice of the LORD our God to whom we are sending you so that it may go well with us.[j] We will certainly obey the voice of the LORD our God!"

Jeremiah's Advice to Stay

7 Now at the end of 10 days, the word of the LORD came to Jeremiah, 8 and he summoned Johanan son of Kareah, all the commanders of the armies who were with him, and all the people from the least to the greatest.

9 He said to them, "This is what the LORD says, the God of Israel to whom you sent me to bring your petition before Him: 10 'If you will indeed stay in this land, then I will rebuild and not demolish you,[k] and I will plant and not uproot you, because I relent concerning the disaster[l] that I have brought on you. 11 Don't be afraid of the king of Babylon[m] whom you now fear; don't be afraid of him' — this is the LORD's declaration — 'because I am with you to save you[n] and deliver you from him. 12 I will grant you compassion,[o] and he[A] will have compassion on you and allow you to return to your own soil. 13 But if you say, 'We will not stay in this land,'[p] so as not to obey the voice of the LORD your God, 14 and if you say, 'No, instead we'll go to the land of Egypt[q] where we will not see war or hear the sound of the ram's horn[r] or hunger for food, and we'll live there,' 15 then hear the word of the LORD, remnant of Judah! This is what the LORD of ·Hosts, the God of Israel, says: If you are firmly resolved to go to Egypt[s] and live there for a while, 16 then the sword[t] you fear will overtake you there in the land of Egypt, and the famine you are worried about will follow on your heels[B] there to Egypt, and you will die there. 17 All who resolve to go to Egypt to live there for a while will die by the sword, famine, and plague. They will have no one escape or survive from the disaster I will bring on them.'

18 "For this is what the LORD of Hosts, the God of Israel, says: 'Just as My anger and fury were poured out on Jerusalem's residents,[u] so will My fury pour out on you if you go to Egypt. You will become an object of cursing, scorn,[v] execration, and disgrace, and you will never see this place again.' 19 The LORD has spoken concerning you, remnant of Judah: 'Don't go to Egypt.' Know for certain that I have warned you today![w] 20 You have led your own selves astray because you are the ones who sent me to the LORD your God, saying, 'Pray to the LORD our God on our behalf, and as for all that the LORD our God says, tell it to us, and we'll act accordingly.' 21 For I have told you today, but you have not obeyed the voice of the LORD your God in everything He has sent me to tell you. 22 Now therefore, know for

[a] **41:17** 2Sm 19:37-38
[b] **41:18** 2Kg 25:26; Jr 40:5
[c] **42:1** Jr 40:13; 41:11
[d] Jr 6:13
[e] **42:2** Jr 36:7
[f] 1Sm 7:8; 12:19; Is 37:4; Jr 42:20
[g] Lv 26:22
[h] **42:4** 1Sm 3:17-18
[i] **42:5** Gn 31:50; Jdg 11:10
[j] **42:6** Jr 7:23
[k] **42:10** Jr 24:6
[l] Jr 18:7-8
[m] **42:11** Jr 41:18
[n] Rm 8:31
[o] **42:12** Neh 1:11
[p] **42:13** Jr 44:16-17
[q] **42:14** Jr 41:17
[r] Jr 4:19,21
[s] **42:15** Dt 17:16; Jr 44:12-14
[t] **42:16** Ezk 11:8
[u] **42:18** Jr 7:20
[v] Jr 18:16
[w] **42:19** Ezk 2:5

[A] **42:12** LXX reads *I* [B] **42:16** Lit *will cling after you*

certain that by the sword, famine, and plague you will die in the place where you desired to go to live for a while."

Jeremiah's Counsel Rejected

43 When Jeremiah had finished speaking to all the people all the words of the LORD their God—all these words the LORD their God had sent him to give them—2then Azariah[A] son of Hoshaiah,[a] Johanan son of Kareah, and all the other arrogant men responded to Jeremiah, "You are speaking a lie! The LORD our God has not sent you to say, 'You must not go to Egypt to live there for a while!' 3Rather, Baruch son of Neriah is inciting you against us to hand us over to the Chaldeans to put us to death or to deport us to Babylon!"

4So Johanan son of Kareah and all the commanders of the armies did not obey the voice of the LORD to stay in the land of Judah. 5Instead, Johanan son of Kareah and all the commanders of the armies took the whole remnant of Judah,[b] those who had returned from all the nations where they had been banished to live in the land of Judah for a while—6the men, women, children, king's daughters, and everyone whom Nebuzaradan, captain of the guard, had allowed to remain with Gedaliah son of Ahikam son of Shaphan,[c] along with Jeremiah the prophet and Baruch son of Neriah—7and they went to the land of Egypt because they did not obey the voice of the LORD. They went as far as Tahpanhes.[d]

God's Sign to the People in Egypt

8Then the word of the LORD came to Jeremiah at Tahpanhes: 9"Pick up some large stones and set them in the mortar of the brick pavement that is at the opening of Pharaoh's palace at Tahpanhes. Do this in the sight of the Judean men 10and tell them: This is what the LORD of ˙Hosts, the God of Israel, says: I will send for My servant Nebuchadnezzar king of Babylon, and I will place his throne on these stones that I have embedded, and he will pitch his pavilion over them. 11He will come and strike down the land of Egypt[e]—those destined for death, to death; those destined for captivity, to captivity; and those destined for the sword,[f] to the sword. 12I[B] will kindle a fire in the temples of Egypt's gods,[g] and he will burn them and take them prisoner. He will ˙clean the land of Egypt as a shepherd picks lice off[C] his garment,[h] and he will leave there unscathed. 13He will smash the sacred pillars of the sun temple[D,E] in the land of Egypt and burn down the temples of the Egyptian gods."

God's Judgment against His People in Egypt

44 This is the word that came to Jeremiah for all the Jews living in the land of Egypt—at Migdol,[i] Tahpanhes,[j] Memphis,[k] and in the land of Pathros:[l] 2"This is what the LORD of ˙Hosts, the God of Israel, says: You have seen all the disaster I brought against Jerusalem and all Judah's cities; look, they are a ruin today without an inhabitant in them 3because of their evil ways that provoked Me to anger,[m] going and burning incense to serve other gods[n] that they, you, and your fathers did not know. 4So I sent you all My servants the prophets time and time again,[F] saying: Don't do this detestable thing that I hate. 5But they did not listen or pay attention; they did not turn from their evil or stop burning incense to other gods. 6So My fierce wrath poured out and burned in Judah's cities and Jerusalem's streets[o] so that they became the desolate ruin they are today.

7"So now, this is what the LORD, the God of Hosts, the God of Israel, says: Why are you doing such great harm to yourselves? You are cutting off man and woman, child and infant[p] from Judah, leaving yourselves without a remnant. 8You are provoking Me to anger by the work of your hands. You are burning incense to other gods in the land of Egypt where you have gone to live for a while. As a result, you will be cut off and become an object of cursing and insult among all the nations of earth.[q] 9Have you forgotten the evils of your fathers, the evils of Judah's kings, the evils of their wives, your own evils, and the evils of your wives that were committed in the land of Judah and in the streets of

[a]43:2 Jr 42:1 [b]43:5 Jr 40:11-12 [c]43:6 Jr 39:10; 40:7 [d]43:7-8 Jr 2:16; 44:1 [e]43:11 Jr 44:13; 46:13-26 [f]Jr 15:2 [g]43:12 Ex 12:12; Is 19:1; Jr 46:25; Ezk 30:13 [h]Ps 104:2; Is 49:18 [i]44:1 Ex 14:2 [j]Jr 43:7 [k]Jr 46:14 [l]Is 11:11 [m]44:3 Jr 7:19 [n]Jr 19:4 [o]44:6 Jr 7:34 [p]44:7 1Sm 15:3; 22:19 [q]44:8 Jr 42:18

A43:2 = Jezaniah B43:12 LXX, Syr, Vg read *He* C43:12 Or *will wrap himself in the land of Egypt as a shepherd wraps himself in* D43:13 Or *Beth-shemesh* E43:13 = of Heliopolis F44:4 Lit *prophets, rising up early and sending*

Jerusalem? 10They have not become humble
to this day, and they have not ·feared or followed My instruction or My statutes that I set
before you and your ancestors.
11"Therefore, this is what the LORD of
Hosts, the God of Israel, says: I am about to
turn against you to bring disaster,[a] to cut off
all Judah. 12And I will take away the remnant
of Judah,[b] those who have resolved to go to
the land of Egypt to live there for a while;
they will meet their end. All of them in the
land of Egypt will fall by the sword; they will
meet their end by famine. From the least to
the greatest, they will die by the sword and by
famine. Then they will become an object of
cursing, scorn,[c] execration, and disgrace. 13I
will punish those living in the land of Egypt
just as I punished Jerusalem by sword, famine, and plague. 14Then the remnant of Judah — those going to live for a while there in
the land of Egypt — will have no fugitive or
survivor to return to the land of Judah where
they are longing[A] to return to live,[d] for they
will not return except for a few fugitives."

The People's Stubborn Response

15However, all the men who knew that
their wives were burning incense to other
gods, all the women standing by — a great
assembly — and all the people who were living in the land of Egypt at Pathros answered
Jeremiah, 16"As for the word you spoke to us
in the name of ·Yahweh, we are not going to
listen to you! 17Instead, we will do everything
we said we would: burn incense to the queen
of heaven[B] and offer ·drink offerings to her
just as we, our fathers, our kings, and our officials did in Judah's cities[e] and in Jerusalem's
streets. Then we had enough food and good
things and saw no disaster, 18but from the
time we ceased to burn incense to the queen
of heaven and to offer her drink offerings, we
have lacked everything, and through sword
and famine we have met our end."
19And the women said,[C] "When we burned
incense to the queen of heaven and poured
out drink offerings to her, was it apart from
our husbands' knowledge[f] that we made sacrificial cakes in her image and poured out
drink offerings to her?"

20But Jeremiah responded to all the people — the men, women, and all the people
who were answering him: 21"As for the incense you burned in Judah's cities[g] and in
Jerusalem's streets — you, your fathers, your
kings, your officials, and the people of the
land — did the LORD not remember them?
He brought this to mind. 22The LORD can no
longer bear your evil deeds and the detestable
acts you have committed, so your land has become a waste, a desolation, and an object of
cursing, without inhabitant, as you see today.
23Because you burned incense and sinned
against the LORD and didn't obey the LORD's
voice[h] and didn't follow His instruction, His
statutes, and His testimonies, this disaster
has come to you, as you see today."
24Then Jeremiah said to all the people, including all the women, "Hear the word of the
LORD, all Judah who are in the land of Egypt.[i]
25This is what the LORD of Hosts, the God of
Israel, says: 'As for you and your wives, you
women have spoken with your mouths, and
you men fulfilled it by your deeds, saying,
"We will keep our vows that we have made to
burn incense to the queen of heaven and to
pour out drink offerings for her." Go ahead,
confirm your vows! Pay your vows!'
26"Therefore, hear the word of the LORD,
all you Judeans who live in the land of Egypt:
'I have sworn by My great name,[j] says Yahweh, that My name will never again be invoked by anyone of Judah in all the land of
Egypt,[k] saying, "As the Lord GOD lives." 27I am
watching over them for disaster and not for
good,[l] and every man of Judah who is in the
land of Egypt will meet his end by sword or
famine until they are finished off. 28Those
who escape the sword will return from the
land of Egypt to the land of Judah only few
in number,[m] and the whole remnant of Judah, the ones going to the land of Egypt to
live there for a while, will know whose word
stands, Mine or theirs! 29This will be a sign to
you' — this is the LORD's declaration — 'that I
am about to punish you in this place, so you
may know that My words of disaster concerning you will certainly come to pass.[n] 30This is
what the LORD says: I am about to hand over
Pharaoh Hophra,[o] Egypt's king, to his ene-

[a]**44:11** Jr 21:10 [b]**44:12** Jr 42:15-18 [c]Jr 18:16 [d]**44:14** Jr 22:26-27 [e]**44:17** Jr 7:18 [f]**44:19** Nm 30:6-7 [g]**44:21** Ezk 8:10-11 [h]**44:23** Jr 40:3 [i]**44:24** Jr 43:7 [j]**44:26** Jr 22:5 [k]Ezk 20:39 [l]**44:27** Jr 31:28 [m]**44:28** Is 27:12-13 [n]**44:29** Pr 19:21 [o]**44:30** Ezk 29:3; 30:21

[A]**44:14** Lit *lifting up their soul* [B]**44:17** = Ashtoreth, or Astarte [C]**44:19** LXX, Syr; MT omits *And the women said*

mies, to those who want to take his life, just
as I handed over Judah's King Zedekiah[a] to
Babylon's King Nebuchadnezzar, who was his
enemy, the one who wanted to take his life.'"

The LORD's Message to Baruch

45 This is the word that Jeremiah the
prophet spoke to Baruch son of
Neriah[b] when he wrote these words on a
scroll at Jeremiah's dictation[A,c] in the fourth
year of Jehoiakim son of Josiah, king of Judah:[d] 2"This is what the LORD, the God of
Israel, says to you, Baruch: 3'You have said,
"Woe is me, because the LORD has added misery to my pain! I am worn out with[B] groaning
and have found no rest."'[e]
4"This is what you are to say to him: 'This
is what the LORD says: What I have built I am
about to demolish, and what I have planted I
am about to uproot[f] — the whole land! 5But as
for you, do you seek great things for yourself?
Stop seeking! For I am about to bring disaster
on every living creature' — this is the LORD's
declaration — 'but I will grant you your life
like the spoils of war[g] wherever you go.'"

PROPHECIES AGAINST THE NATIONS

46 The word of the LORD that came to Jeremiah the prophet about the nations:[h]

Prophecies against Egypt

2About Egypt and the army of Pharaoh
Neco, Egypt's king,[i] which was defeated at
Carchemish[j] on the Euphrates River by Nebuchadnezzar king of Babylon in the fourth
year of Judah's King Jehoiakim son of Josiah:[k]

3 Deploy small shields[l] and large;
draw near for battle!
4 Harness the horses;
mount the steeds;[C]
take your positions with helmets on!
Polish the lances;
put on armor![m]
5 Why have I seen this?
They are terrified,
they are retreating,
their warriors are crushed,
they flee headlong,
they never look back,
terror is on every side![n]
This is the LORD's declaration.
6 The swift cannot flee,
and the warrior cannot escape!
In the north by the bank
of the Euphrates River,
they stumble and fall.[o]
7 Who is this, rising like the Nile,[p]
like rivers whose waters churn?
8 Egypt rises like the Nile,
and its waters churn like rivers.
He boasts, "I will go up, I will cover
the earth;
I will destroy cities
with their residents."
9 Rise up, you cavalry!
Race furiously, you chariots!
Let the warriors go out —
·Cush and Put,[q]
who are able to handle shields,
and the Ludim,[r]
who are able to handle and string
the bow.[s]
10 That day belongs to the Lord, the GOD
of ·Hosts,
a day of vengeance to avenge Himself
against His adversaries.
The sword will devour and be satisfied;
it will drink its fill of their blood,
because it will be a sacrifice[t]
to the Lord, the GOD of Hosts,
in the northern land
by the Euphrates River.
11 Go up to Gilead and get balm,[u]
Virgin Daughter Egypt!
You have multiplied remedies in vain;
there is no healing for you.
12 The nations have heard
of your dishonor,[v]
and your outcry fills the earth,
because warrior stumbles
against warrior
and together both of them have fallen.

13This is the word the LORD spoke to Jeremiah the prophet about the coming of Nebuchadnezzar king of Babylon to defeat the
land of Egypt:[w]

[a]**44:30** Jr 39:5-7
[b]**45:1** Jr 32:12
[c]Jr 36:4,18
[d]Jr 36:1
[e]**45:3** Ps 6:6
[f]**45:4** Jr 24:6
[g]**45:5** Jr 21:9; 38:2; 39:18
[h]**46:1** Jr 25:15-38
[i]**46:2** 2Kg 23:29
[j]2Ch 35:20
[k]Jr 45:1
[l]**46:3** Jr 51:11
[m]**46:4** Jb 41:13; Jr 51:3
[n]**46:5** Jr 6:25; 20:3-4,10; 49:29
[o]**46:6** Dn 11:19
[p]**46:7** Jr 47:2
[q]**46:9** Gn 10:6; Ezk 30:5
[r]Gn 10:13; 1Ch 1:11
[s]Is 66:19
[t]**46:10** Is 34:5-8; Ezk 39:17-20; Zph 1:7
[u]**46:11** Gn 37:25; Jr 8:22; 51:8
[v]**46:12** Jr 13:26; Hs 4:7; Nah 3:5
[w]**46:13** Jr 43:8-13

[A]**45:1** Lit *scroll from Jeremiah's mouth* [B]**45:3** Lit *I labored in my* [C]**46:4** Or *mount up, riders*

14 Announce it in Egypt, and proclaim it
in Migdol![a]
Proclaim it in Memphis
and in Tahpanhes!
Say: Take positions! Prepare yourself,
for the sword devours all around you.[b]
15 Why have your strong ones
been swept away?
Each has not stood,
for the LORD has thrust him down.
16 He continues to stumble.[c]
Indeed, each falls over the other.
They say, "Get up! Let's return
to our people
and to the land of our birth,
away from the sword that oppresses."[d]
17 There they will cry out,
"Pharaoh king of Egypt was all noise;
he let the opportune moment pass."
18 As I live —
this is the King's declaration;
•Yahweh of Hosts is His name.[e]
He will come like Tabor
among the mountains
and like Carmel by the sea.
19 Get your bags ready for exile,
inhabitant of Daughter Egypt![f]
For Memphis will become a desolation,
uninhabited ruins.
20 Egypt is a beautiful young cow,[g]
but a horsefly from the north is coming
against her.[A,h]
21 Even her mercenaries among her
are like stall-fed calves.
They too will turn back;
together they will flee;
they will not take their stand,
for the day of their calamity is coming
on them,
the time of their punishment.[i]
22 Egypt will hiss like a slithering snake,[B]
for the enemy will come with an army;
with axes they will come against her
like those who cut trees.[j]
23 They will cut down her forest —
this is the LORD's declaration —
though it is dense,
for they are more numerous
than locusts;
they cannot be counted.[k]
24 Daughter Egypt will be put to shame,
handed over to a northern people.[l]

25 The LORD of Hosts, the God of Israel, says:
"I am about to punish Amon, god of Thebes,[m]
along with Pharaoh, Egypt, her gods, and her
kings — Pharaoh and those trusting in him.
26 I will hand them over to those who want to
take their lives[n] — to Nebuchadnezzar king of
Babylon and his officers. But after this,[o] it will
be inhabited again as in ancient times."
This is the LORD's declaration.

Reassurance for Israel

27 But you, My servant Jacob,
do not be afraid,[p]
and do not be discouraged, Israel,
for without fail I will save you
from far away
and your descendants, from the land
of their captivity!
Jacob will return and have calm
and quiet
with no one to frighten him.
28 And you, My servant Jacob,
do not be afraid —
this is the LORD's declaration —
for I will be with you.[q]
I will bring destruction
on all the nations
where I have banished you,
but I will not bring destruction on you.
I will discipline you with justice,
and I will by no means
leave you unpunished.[r]

Prophecies against the Philistines

47 This is the word of the LORD that came
to Jeremiah the prophet about the Philistines[s] before Pharaoh defeated Gaza.[t] 2 This
is what the LORD says:

Look, waters are rising from the north
and becoming an overflowing •wadi.
They will overflow the land
and everything in it,[u]
the cities and their inhabitants.
The people will cry out,
and every inhabitant of the land
will wail.

[a] **46:14** Jr 44:1
[b] Jr 46:10
[c] **46:16** Lv 26:36-37
[d] Jr 50:16
[e] **46:18** Jr 48:15; 51:57
[f] **46:19** Jr 48:18
[g] **46:20** Hs 10:11
[h] Jr 1:13-14
[i] **46:21** Jr 50:27,31
[j] **46:22** Ps 74:5
[k] **46:23** Jdg 6:5; 7:12
[l] **46:24** Jr 1:15
[m] **46:25** Ezk 30:14-16
[n] **46:26** Jr 44:30; Ezk 32:11
[o] Ezk 29:8-14
[p] **46:27** Is 41:8; 44:2; 45:4
[q] **46:28** Jr 1:8,19; 30:11; 42:11
[r] **46:27-28** Jr 30:10-11
[s] **47:1** Jr 25:20
[t] Am 1:6-7; Zph 2:4
[u] **47:2** Is 8:7-8

[A] **46:20** Some Hb mss, LXX, Syr; other Hb mss read *is coming, coming* [B] **46:22** Lit *Her sound, she will go like a snake*

3 At the sound of the stomping hooves
of his stallions,[a]
the rumbling of his chariots,
and the clatter of their wheels,[b]
fathers will not turn back
for their sons,
because they will be
utterly helpless[A]
4 on account of the day that is coming
to destroy all the Philistines,
to cut off from Tyre and Sidon
every remaining ally.[c]
Indeed, the LORD is about to destroy
the Philistines,
the remnant of the islands
of Caphtor.[B,d]
5 Baldness is coming to Gaza.[e]
Ashkelon will become silent,[f]
a remnant of their valley.
How long will you gash yourself?
6 Oh, sword of the LORD![g]
How long will you be restless?
Go back to your sheath;
be still; be silent!
7 How can it[C] rest
when the LORD has given it
a command?[h]
He has assigned it[i]
against Ashkelon and the shore
of the sea.

Prophecies against Moab

48 About Moab,[j] this is what the LORD of
·Hosts, the God of Israel, says:

Woe to Nebo,[k] because it is
about to be destroyed;
Kiriathaim will be put to shame;[l]
it will be taken captive.
The fortress will be put to shame
and dismayed!
2 There is no longer praise for Moab;
they plan harm against her
in Heshbon:[m]
Come, let's cut her off
from nationhood.
Also, Madmen,[D] you will be silenced;
the sword will pursue you.
3 A voice cries out from Horonaim,[n]
"devastation and great disaster!"
4 Moab will be shattered;
her little ones will cry out.
5 For on the Ascent to Luhith
they will be weeping continually,[E]
and on the descent to Horonaim
will be heard cries of distress
over the destruction:[o]
6 Flee! Save your lives!
Be like a juniper bush[F,p]
in the wilderness.
7 Because you trust in your works[G]
and treasures,
you will be captured also.
Chemosh[q] will go into exile
with his priests and officials.
8 The destroyer will move
against every town;
not one town will escape.
The valley will perish,
and the plain will be annihilated,[r]
as the LORD has said.
9 Make Moab a salt marsh,[H,s]
for she will run away;[I]
her towns will become a desolation,
without inhabitant.
10 The one who does
the LORD's business deceitfully[J]
is cursed,[t]
and the one who withholds
his sword from bloodshed is cursed.
11 Moab has been left quiet
since his youth,
settled like wine on its dregs.[u]
He hasn't been poured
from one container to another
or gone into exile.
So his taste has remained the same,
and his aroma hasn't changed.
12 Therefore look, the days
are coming —
this is the LORD's declaration —
when I will send those to him,
who will pour him out.
They will empty his containers
and smash his jars.
13 Moab will be put to shame
because of Chemosh,

[a]47:3 Jdg 5:22; Jr 8:16; 50:11 [b]Nah 3:2-3 [c]47:4 Jr 25:22; Jl 3:4; Am 1:8-10 [d]Gn 10:14; Am 9:7 [e]47:5 Jr 48:37 [f]Jdg 1:18; Jr 25:20 [g]47:6 Ezk 21:3-5 [h]47:7 Ezk 14:17 [i]Mc 6:9 [j]48:1 Is 15:1; Ezk 25:9 [k]Nm 32:3; Jr 48:22 [l]Nm 32:37; Jr 48:23; Ezk 25:9 [m]48:2 Jr 48:34,45; 49:3 [n]48:3 Is 15:5; Jr 48:34 [o]48:5 Is 15:5 [p]48:6 Jr 17:6 [q]48:7 Jdg 11:24; 1Kg 11:7,33; Jr 48:45-47 [r]48:8 Jos 13:9,17,21 [s]48:9 Jdg 9:45 [t]48:10 1Kg 20:42 [u]48:11 Ps 75:8; Zph 1:12

A47:3 Lit *because of laziness of hands* B47:4 Probably Crete C47:7 LXX, Vg; MT reads *you* D48:2 A city in Moab E48:5 Lit *Luhith, weeping goes up with weeping* F48:6 Or *like Aroer*; Is 17:2; Jr 48:19 G48:7 LXX reads *strongholds* H48:9 LXX reads *a sign*; Vg reads *a flower*; Syr, Tg read *a crown* I48:9 Hb obscure J48:10 Or *negligently*

just as the house of Israel was
put to shame
because of Bethel[a] that they trusted in.

14 How can you say, "We are warriors —
mighty men ready for battle"?
15 The destroyer of Moab and its towns
has come up,[A]
and the best of its young men
have gone down to slaughter.
This is the King's declaration;
·Yahweh of Hosts is His name.[b]
16 Moab's calamity is near at hand;
his disaster is rushing swiftly.
17 Mourn for him,
all you surrounding nations,
everyone who knows his name.
Say: How the mighty scepter[c]
is shattered,
the glorious staff!

18 Come down from glory;
sit on parched ground,
resident of the daughter of Dibon,[d]
for the destroyer of Moab has come
against you;
he has destroyed your fortresses.
19 Stand by the highway and look,
resident of Aroer![e]
Ask him who is fleeing or her
who is escaping:[f]
What happened?
20 Moab is put to shame, indeed dismayed.
Wail and cry out!
Declare by the Arnon
that Moab is destroyed.

21 "Judgment has come to the land of the
plateau[g] — to Holon, Jahzah, Mephaath, 22 Dibon, Nebo, Beth-diblathaim, 23 Kiriathaim,
Beth-gamul, Beth-meon,[h] 24 Kerioth,[i] Bozrah,
and all the towns of the land of Moab, those
far and near. 25 Moab's ·horn is chopped off;[j]
his arm is shattered."
This is the LORD's declaration.
26 "Make him drunk, because he has exalted
himself against the LORD.[k] Moab will wallow
in his own vomit, and he will also become a
laughingstock. 27 Wasn't Israel a laughingstock to you?[l] Was he ever found among
thieves?[m] For whenever you speak of him you
shake your head."

28 Abandon the towns! Live in the cliffs,
residents of Moab!
Be like a dove
that nests inside the mouth of a cave.[n]
29 We have heard of Moab's pride,
great pride, indeed —
his insolence, arrogance, pride,
and haughty heart.
30 I know his outburst.
This is the LORD's declaration.
It is empty.
His boast is empty.
31 Therefore, I will wail over Moab.
I will cry out for Moab, all of it;
he will moan for the men of Kir-heres.
32 I will weep for you, vine of Sibmah,
with more than the weeping for Jazer.
Your tendrils have extended to the sea;
they have reached to the sea
and to Jazer.[B]
The destroyer has fallen
on your summer fruit
and grape harvest.
33 Joy and celebration are taken
from the fertile field
and from the land of Moab.
I have stopped the flow of wine
from the winepresses;
no one will tread with shouts of joy.
The shouting is not a shout of joy.[o]

34 "There is a cry from Heshbon to Elealeh;
they raise their voices as far as Jahaz[p] — from
Zoar to Horonaim and Eglath-shelishi-
yah — because even the waters of Nimrim
have become desolate. 35 In Moab, I will
stop" — this is the LORD's declaration — "the
one who offers sacrifices on the ·high place
and burns incense to his gods.[q] 36 Therefore,
My heart moans like flutes for Moab,[r] and My
heart moans like flutes for the people of Kir-
heres. And therefore, the wealth he has gained
has perished. 37 Indeed, every head is bald and
every beard clipped;[s] on every hand is a gash
and ·sackcloth around the waist. 38 On all the
rooftops of Moab and in her public squares,
everyone is mourning because I have shattered Moab like a jar no one wants."[t] This is
the LORD's declaration. 39 "How broken it is!
They wail! How Moab has turned his back!

[a] **48:13** Hs 4:15; Am 3:14; 4:4
[b] **48:15** Jr 46:18; 51:57
[c] **48:17** Ps 110:2; Ezk 19:11-12,14
[d] **48:18** Jos 13:8-9
[e] **48:19** Dt 2:36
[f] 1Sm 4:13,16
[g] **48:21** Jos 13:17-19
[h] **48:23** Jos 13:17
[i] **48:24** Jr 48:41; Am 2:2
[j] **48:25** Ps 75:10
[k] **48:26** Jr 48:42
[l] **48:27** Lm 2:15-17
[m] Jr 2:26
[n] **48:28** Is 2:19-21
[o] **48:31-33** Is 16:7-10
[p] **48:34** Is 15:4-6
[q] **48:35** Jr 11:12-13; 18:15
[r] **48:36** Is 15:5
[s] **48:37-38** Is 15:2-3
[t] **48:38** Jr 22:28

[A] **48:15** Or *Moab is destroyed; he has come up against its city* [B] **48:32** Some Hb mss read *reached as far as Jazer*

He is ashamed. Moab will become a laughingstock and a shock to all those around him."[a]
40 For this is what the LORD says:

He will swoop down like an eagle
and spread his wings against Moab.[b]
41 The towns have[A] been captured,
and the strongholds seized.
In that day the heart of Moab's warriors
will be like the heart of a woman
with contractions.[c]
42 Moab will be destroyed as a people
because he has exalted himself
against the LORD.[d]
43 Panic, pit, and trap
await you, resident of Moab.
This is the LORD's declaration.
44 He who flees from the panic will fall
in the pit,
and he who climbs from the pit
will be captured in the trap,
for I will bring against Moab
the year of their punishment.
This is the LORD's declaration.[e]

45 Those who flee will stand exhausted
in Heshbon's shadow
because fire has come out
from Heshbon
and a flame from within Sihon.
It will devour Moab's forehead
and the skull of the noisemakers.
46 Woe to you, Moab!
The people of Chemosh have perished
because your sons have been
taken captive
and your daughters have gone
into captivity.[f]
47 Yet, I will restore the fortunes[B] of Moab
in the last days.[g]
This is the LORD's declaration.
The judgment on Moab ends here.

Prophecies against Ammon

49 About the Ammonites,[h] this is what
the LORD says:

Does Israel have no sons?
Is he without an heir?
Why then has ˙Milcom[C,D]
dispossessed Gad[i]
and his people settled in their cities?
2 Therefore look, the days are coming —
this is the LORD's declaration —
when I will make the shout
of battle[j] heard
against Rabbah of the Ammonites.
It will become a desolate mound,
and its villages will be burned down.
Israel will dispossess
their dispossessors,
says the LORD.
3 Wail, Heshbon,[k] for Ai is devastated;
cry out, daughters of Rabbah!
Clothe yourselves with ˙sackcloth,[l]
and lament;
run back and forth within your walls,[E]
because Milcom will go into exile
together with his priests and officials.[m]
4 Why do you brag about your valleys,
your flowing valley,[F]
you faithless daughter?
You who trust in your treasures
and boast, "Who can attack me?"
5 Look, I am about to bring terror
on you[n] —
this is the declaration of
the Lord GOD of ˙Hosts —
from all those around you.
You will be banished,
each man headlong,
with no one to gather up the fugitives.
6 But after that, I will restore
the fortunes[B] of the Ammonites.[o]
This is the LORD's declaration.

Prophecies against Edom

7 About Edom, this is what the LORD of
Hosts says:

Is there no longer wisdom in Teman?[G]
Has counsel perished
from the prudent?
Has their wisdom rotted away?[p]
8 Run! Turn back! Lie low,
residents of Dedan,[q]
for I will bring Esau's calamity on him
at the time I punish him.[r]
9 If grape harvesters came to you,
wouldn't they leave some gleanings?[s]
Were thieves to come in the night,

[a] 48:29-39 Is 16:6-11; Zph 2:9-10
[b] 48:40 Dt 28:49; Jr 49:22
[c] 48:41 Is 13:8
[d] 48:42 Jr 48:26
[e] 48:43-44 Is 24:17-18
[f] 48:45-46 Nm 21:28-29
[g] 48:47 Jr 49:39
[h] 49:1 Ezk 21:28-32; 25:2-10; Am 1:13-15
[i] 1Kg 11:5,33
[j] 49:2 Jr 4:19
[k] 49:3 Jr 48:2
[l] Jr 48:37
[m] Jr 48:7
[n] 49:5 Jr 48:43-44
[o] 49:6 Jr 48:47; 49:39
[p] 49:7 Ob 8-9
[q] 49:8 Gn 25:1-3; Ezk 25:13
[r] Jr 6:15; 8:12; Ob 8-13
[s] 49:9 Dt 24:21

A 48:41 Or *Kerioth has* B 48:47; 49:6 Or *will end the captivity* C 49:1 LXX, Syr, Vg; MT reads *Malkam* D 49:1 = Molech E 49:3 Or *sheep pens* F 49:4 Or *about your strength, your ebbing strength* G 49:7 = a region or city in Edom

they would destroy only
what they wanted.[a]
10 But I will strip Esau bare;
I will uncover his secret places.[b]
He will try to hide himself,
but he will be unable.
His descendants will be destroyed
along with his relatives and neighbors.
He will exist no longer.
11 Abandon your fatherless;
I will preserve them;
let your widows trust in Me.[c]

12 "For this is what the LORD says: If those
who do not deserve to drink the cup must
drink it, you possibly remain unpunished? You will not remain unpunished,
for you must drink it too. 13 For by Myself
I have sworn" — this is the LORD's declaration — "Bozrah[A] will become a desolation, a
disgrace, a ruin, and a curse, and all her cities
will become ruins forever."[d]

14 I have heard a message from the LORD;
a messenger has been sent
among the nations:
Assemble yourselves to come
against her.
Rise up for war!
15 Look, I will certainly make you
insignificant among the nations,
despised among humanity.
16 As to the terror you cause,[B]
your presumptuous heart
has deceived you.
You who live in the clefts of the rock,[C]
you who occupy the mountain summit,
though you elevate your nest
like the eagle,
even from there I will bring you down.
This is the LORD's declaration.[e]

17 "Edom will become a desolation. Everyone who passes by her will be horrified and
scoff because of all her wounds.[f] 18 As when
Sodom and Gomorrah were overthrown
along with their neighbors,"[g] says the LORD,
"no one will live there; no human being will
even stay in it as a temporary resident.[h]
19 "Look, it will be like a lion coming from
the thickets[D] of the Jordan to the watered
grazing land. Indeed, I will chase Edom away
from her land in a flash. I will appoint whoever is chosen for her. For who is like Me?
Who will summon Me?[i] Who is the shepherd
who can stand against Me?"
20 Therefore, hear the plans that the LORD
has drawn up against Edom and the strate-
gies He has devised against the people of Teman:[j] The flock's little lambs will certainly be
dragged away,[k] and their grazing land will
be made desolate because of them. 21 At the
sound of their fall the earth will quake; the
sound of her cry will be heard at the ·Red
Sea.[l] 22 Look! It will be like an eagle soaring
upward, then swooping down and spreading
its wings over Bozrah. In that day the hearts
of Edom's warriors will be like the heart of a
woman with contractions.[m]

Prophecies against Damascus

23 About Damascus:[n]

Hamath and Arpad are put to shame,[o]
for they have heard a bad report
and are agitated;
in the sea there is anxiety that cannot
be calmed.
24 Damascus has become weak;
she has turned to run;
panic has gripped her.
Distress and labor pains
have seized her
like a woman in labor.
25 How can the city of praise
not be abandoned,[p]
the town that brings Me joy?
26 Therefore, her young men will fall
in her public squares;
all the warriors will perish in that day.
This is the declaration of
the LORD of Hosts.[q]
27 I will set fire to the wall of Damascus;
it will consume Ben-hadad's citadels.[r]

Prophecies against Kedar and Hazor

28 About Kedar[s] and the kingdoms of Hazor,
which Nebuchadnezzar,[t] Babylon's king, defeated, this is what the LORD says:

Rise up, go against Kedar,
and destroy the people of the east!

[a] **49:9** Ob 5
[b] **49:10** Jr 23:24; Ob 6
[c] **49:11** Dt 10:18; Ps 68:5
[d] **49:12-13** Jr 25:28-29; Am 1:12
[e] **49:14-16** Ob 1-4
[f] **49:17** Jr 19:8
[g] **49:18** Gn 19:24-25
[h] Jr 49:33; 50:40; Zph 2:9
[i] **49:19** Jb 9:19; Jr 12:5; 50:44; Zch 11:3
[j] **49:20** Jr 49:30
[k] Jr 15:3; 22:19
[l] **49:18-21** Jr 50:40,44-46
[m] **49:22** Jr 48:40-41
[n] **49:23** Is 17:1; Am 1:3
[o] 2Kg 18:34
[p] **49:25** Jr 33:9
[q] **49:26** Jr 50:30
[r] **49:27** Am 1:4
[s] **49:28** Ps 120:5; Is 21:16-17; Jr 2:10
[t] 2Kg 24:11; 25:22; 2Ch 36:6-13

[A] **49:13** = Edom's capital [B] **49:16** Lit *Your horror* [C] **49:16** = Petra [D] **49:19** Lit *pride*

29 They will take their tents
and their flocks
along with their tent curtains
and all their equipment.
They will take their camels
for themselves.
They will call out to them:
Terror is on every side![a]
30 Run! Escape quickly! Lie low,
residents of Hazor —
this is the LORD's declaration —
for Nebuchadnezzar king of Babylon
has drawn up a plan against you;
he has devised a strategy against you.

31 Rise up, go up against a nation at ease,
one living in security.
This is the LORD's declaration.
They have no doors, not even a gate bar;
they live alone.[b]
32 Their camels will become plunder,
and their massive herds of cattle will
become spoil.[c]
I will scatter them to the wind
in every direction,
those who shave their temples;
I will bring calamity on them
across all their borders.
This is the LORD's declaration.
33 Hazor will become a jackals' den,[d]
a desolation forever.
No one will live there;
no human being will even stay in it as a
temporary resident.[e]

Prophecies against Elam

34This is the word of the LORD that came
to Jeremiah the prophet about Elam[A] at the
beginning of the reign of Zedekiah king of
Judah.[f] 35This is what the LORD of Hosts says:

I am about to shatter Elam's bow,[g]
the source[B] of their might.
36 I will bring the four winds
against Elam
from the four corners of the heavens,
and I will scatter them
to all these winds.
There will not be a nation
to which Elam's banished ones
will not go.

[a]49:29 Ps 31:13; Jr 6:25; 20:3-4,10
[b]49:31 Jdg 18:7-10; Ezk 38:10-11
[c]49:32 Is 10:6; Ezk 25:7; Nah 2:9
[d]49:33 Jr 9:11; 10:22; 51:37
[e]Jr 49:18; 50:40
[f]49:34 Jr 27:12; 28:1; 29:3
[g]49:35 Is 22:6
[h]49:37 Jr 9:16
[i]49:39 Jr 48:47
[j]50:1 Is 13:1
[k]50:2 Ps 60:4; Is 5:26; 18:3
[l]Is 46:1; Jr 51:44
[m]50:3 Is 41:25; Jr 1:14-15; 6:1,22
[n]50:4 2Ch 11:16; 15:4; Hs 3:5
[o]50:5 Gn 9:16; 17:7,19; Is 55:3
[p]50:6 Is 53:6

37 I will devastate Elam
before their enemies,
before those who want to take
their lives.
I will bring disaster on them,
My burning anger.
This is the LORD's declaration.
I will send the sword after them[h]
until I finish them off.
38 I will set My throne in Elam,
and I will destroy the king and officials
from there.
This is the LORD's declaration.

39 In the last days,
I will restore the fortunes[C] of Elam.[i]
This is the LORD's declaration.

Prophecies against Babylon

50 The word the LORD spoke about
Babylon,[j] the land of the Chaldeans,
through Jeremiah the prophet:

2 Announce to the nations;
proclaim and raise up a signal flag;[k]
proclaim, and hide nothing.
Say: Babylon is captured;
Bel[l] is put to shame;
Marduk is devastated;
her idols are put to shame;
her false gods, devastated.
3 For a nation from the north will come
against her;[m]
it will make her land desolate.
No one will be living in it —
both man and beast will escape.[D]
4 In those days and at that time —
this is the LORD's declaration —
the Israelites and Judeans
will come together,
weeping as they come,
and will seek the LORD their God.[n]
5 They will ask about ·Zion,
turning their faces to this road.
They will come and join themselves[E]
to the LORD
in an everlasting covenant[o] that will
never be forgotten.
6 My people are lost sheep;[p]
their shepherds have led them astray,

[A]49:34 = modern Iran [B]49:35 Lit *first* [C]49:39 Or *will end the captivity* [D]50:3 Lit *escape; they will walk* [E]50:5 LXX; MT reads *Come and join yourselves*

guiding them the wrong way
in the mountains.[a]
They have wandered from mountain
to hill;
they have forgotten their resting place.
7 All who found them devoured them.
Their adversaries said,
"We're not ·guilty;
instead, they have sinned
against the LORD,
their righteous grazing land,[b]
the hope of their ancestors,[c] the LORD."

8 Escape from Babylon;[d]
depart from the Chaldeans' land.
Be like the rams that lead the flock.
9 For I will soon stir up and bring
against Babylon
an assembly of great nations
from the north country.
They will line up in battle formation
against her;
from there she will be captured.
Their arrows will be like those
of a skilled[A] warrior
who does not return empty-handed.
10 The Chaldeans will become plunder;
all Babylon's plunderers will be
fully satisfied.
This is the LORD's declaration.
11 Because you rejoice,
because you sing in triumph—
you who plundered My inheritance—
because you frolic like a young cow
treading grain
and neigh like stallions,[e]
12 your mother will be utterly humiliated;
she who bore you will be put to shame.
Look! She will lag behind
all[B] the nations—
a dry land, a wilderness,[f] an ·Arabah.
13 Because of the LORD's wrath,
she will not be inhabited;
she will become a desolation, every bit
of her.
Everyone who passes through Babylon
will be horrified
and scoff because of all her wounds.[g]
14 Line up in battle formation
around Babylon,
all you archers!
Shoot at her! Do not spare an arrow,
for she has sinned against the LORD.
15 Raise a war cry against her
on every side!
She has thrown up her hands
in surrender;
her defense towers have fallen;
her walls are demolished.[h]
Since this is the LORD's vengeance,[i]
take out your vengeance on her;
as she has done, do the same to her.
16 Cut off the sower from Babylon
as well as him who wields the sickle
at harvest time.
Because of the oppressor's sword,[j]
each will turn to his own people,[k]
each will flee to his own land.

The Return of God's People

17 Israel is a stray lamb, chased by lions.[l]
The first who devoured him was
the king of Assyria;
the last one who crushed his bones
was Nebuchadnezzar king of Babylon.[m]

18 Therefore, this is what the LORD of ·Hosts,
the God of Israel, says: "I am about to punish
the king of Babylon[n] and his land just as I
punished the king of Assyria.

19 I will return Israel to his grazing land,
and he will feed on Carmel and Bashan;
he will be satisfied
in the hill country of Ephraim
and of Gilead.[o]
20 In those days and at that time—
this is the LORD's declaration—
one will search for Israel's guilt,
but there will be none,
and for Judah's sins,
but they will not be found,
for I will forgive[p] those I leave
as a remnant.[q]

The Invasion of Babylon

21 "Go against the land of Merathaim,
and against those living in Pekod.
Put them to the sword;
·completely destroy them—
this is the LORD's declaration—

[a] 50:6 Ezk 34:6
[b] 50:7 Jr 31:23; 40:2-3
[c] Jr 14:8
[d] 50:8 Jr 51:6; Rv 18:4
[e] 50:11 Jdg 5:22; Jr 8:16; 47:3
[f] 50:12 Jr 51:43
[g] 50:13 Jr 19:8; 49:17
[h] 50:15 Jr 51:58
[i] Jr 46:10
[j] 50:16 Jr 46:16
[k] Is 13:14
[l] 50:17 Jr 2:15; 4:7
[m] 2Kg 24:10-12; 25:1-7
[n] 50:18 Is 10:12
[o] 50:19 Is 33:9; Mc 7:14; Nah 1:4
[p] 50:20 Nm 14:20; Jr 31:34; 36:3
[q] Jr 39:10; 52:16; Zph 3:12

[A] 50:9 Some Hb mss, LXX, Syr; other Hb mss read *bereaving* [B] 50:12 Lit *Look! The last of*

do everything I have commanded you.[a]
22 The sound of war is in the land[b] —
a great destruction.
23 How the hammer of the whole earth
is cut down and smashed!
What a horror Babylon has become
among the nations![c]
24 Babylon, I laid a trap for you, and you
were caught,[d]
but you did not even know it.
You were found and captured
because you fought against the LORD.
25 The LORD opened His armory
and brought out His weapons
of wrath,[e]
because it is a task of the Lord GOD
of Hosts
in the land of the Chaldeans.
26 Come against her
from the most distant places.[A]
Open her granaries;
pile her up like mounds of grain
and completely destroy her.
Leave her no survivors.
27 Put all her young bulls to the sword;
let them go down to the slaughter.
Woe to them, because their day
has come,
the time of their punishment.[f]

The Humiliation of Babylon

28 "There is a voice of fugitives
and those who escape
from the land of Babylon
announcing in Zion the vengeance
of the LORD our God,
the vengeance for His temple.[g]
29 Summon the archers to Babylon,
all who string the bow;
camp all around her; let none escape.
Repay her according to her deeds;[h]
just as she has done, do the same
to her,
for she has acted arrogantly
against the LORD,
against the Holy One of Israel.[i]
30 Therefore, her young men will fall
in her public squares;
all the warriors will perish in that day.
This is the LORD's declaration.[j]

[a]50:21 1Kg 9:4; 2Kg 21:8; 2Ch 7:17
[b]50:22 Jr 51:54-56
[c]50:23 Jr 51:41
[d]50:24 Jr 51:31; Dn 5:30-31
[e]50:25 Is 13:5
[f]50:27 Jr 46:21
[g]50:28 2Kg 18:16; 23:4; 24:13
[h]50:29 Jr 25:14
[i]Ps 71:22
[j]50:30 Jr 49:26
[k]50:32 Jr 21:14
[l]50:33 Is 14:17
[m]50:34 Pr 23:11; Is 47:4
[n]Mc 4:10
[o]50:37 Jr 25:20
[p]Jr 51:30
[q]50:38 Ex 15:16; 23:27; Jb 20:25

31 Look, I am against you,
you arrogant one —
this is the declaration of
the Lord GOD of Hosts —
because your day has come,
the time when I will punish you.
32 The arrogant will stumble and fall
with no one to pick him up.
I will set fire to his cities,
and it will consume everything
around him."[k]

The Desolation of Babylon

33 This is what the LORD of Hosts says:

Israelites and Judeans alike
have been oppressed.
All their captors hold them fast;[l]
they refuse to release them.
34 Their Redeemer is strong;
˙Yahweh of Hosts is His name.
He will fervently plead their case[m]
so that He might bring rest to the earth
but turmoil to those who live
in Babylon.[n]
35 A sword is over the Chaldeans —
this is the LORD's declaration —
against those who live in Babylon,
against her officials, and against
her sages.
36 A sword is against the diviners,
and they will act foolishly.
A sword is against her heroic warriors,
and they will be terrified.
37 A sword is against his horses
and chariots
and against all the foreigners
among them,[o]
and they will be like women.[p]
A sword is against her treasuries,
and they will be plundered.
38 A drought will come on her waters,
and they will be dried up.
For it is a land of carved images,
and they go mad because of
terrifying things.[B,q]
39 Therefore, desert creatures[C] will live
with hyenas,
and ostriches will also live in her.
It will never again be inhabited

[A]50:26 Lit *from the end* [B]50:38 Or *of dreaded gods* [C]50:39 Or *desert demons*

or lived in through all generations.[a]
40 Just as God demolished Sodom
and Gomorrah
and their neighboring towns[b] —
this is the LORD's declaration —
so no one will live there;
no human being will even stay in it
as a temporary resident.[c]

The Conquest of Babylon

41 Look! A people comes
from the north.
A great nation and many kings will be
stirred up
from the remote regions
of the earth.[d]
42 They grasp bow and javelin.
They are cruel and show no mercy.
Their voice roars like the sea,[e]
and they ride on horses,
lined up like men in battle formation
against you, Daughter Babylon.
43 The king of Babylon has heard reports
about them,
and his hands fall helpless.
Distress has seized him —
pain, like a woman in labor.[f]

44 "Look, it will be like a lion coming from
the thickets[A,g] of the Jordan to the watered
grazing land. Indeed, I will chase Babylon[B]
away from her land in a flash. I will appoint
whoever is chosen for her. For who is like Me?
Who will summon Me? Who is the shepherd
who can stand against Me?"
45 Therefore, hear the plans that the LORD
has drawn up against Babylon and the strat-
egies He has devised against the land of the
Chaldeans: Certainly the flock's little lambs
will be dragged away; certainly the grazing
land will be made desolate because of them.
46 At the sound of Babylon's conquest the
earth will quake; a cry will be heard among
the nations.[h]

God's Judgment on Babylon

51 This is what the LORD says:

I am about to stir up
a destructive wind[C] against Babylon[i]
and against the population
of Leb-qamai.[D,E]
2 I will send strangers to Babylon
who will scatter her and strip
her land bare,[j]
for they will come against her
from every side in the day of disaster.
3 Don't let the archer string his bow;
don't let him put on[F] his armor.[k]
Don't spare her young men;
·completely destroy her entire army!
4 Those who were slain will fall
in the land of the Chaldeans,
those who were pierced through,
in her streets.[l]
5 For Israel and Judah are not left widowed
by their God, the LORD of ·Hosts,
though their land is full of ·guilt
against the Holy One of Israel.[m]

6 Leave Babylon;[n]
save your lives, each of you![o]
Don't perish because of her guilt.
For this is the time
of the LORD's vengeance —
He will pay her what she deserves.[p]
7 Babylon was a gold cup
in the LORD's hand,[q]
making the whole earth drunk.
The nations drank her wine;[r]
therefore, the nations go mad.[s]
8 Suddenly Babylon fell
and was shattered.
Wail for her;
get balm[t] for her wound —
perhaps she can be healed.

9 We tried to heal Babylon,
but she could not be healed.
Abandon her!
Let each of us go to his own land,[u]
for her judgment extends to the sky
and reaches as far as the clouds.[v]

10 The LORD has brought about
our vindication;[w]
come, let's tell in ·Zion
what the LORD our God
has accomplished.[x]

11 Sharpen the arrows!
Fill the quivers!

[a] 50:39 Is 13:20-21; 34:13-14
[b] 50:40 Gn 19:24-25
[c] Jr 49:18,33
[d] 50:41 Jr 6:22; 25:32; 31:8
[e] 50:42 Is 5:30; 17:12
[f] 50:41-43 Jr 6:22-24
[g] 50:44 Zch 11:3
[h] 50:44-46 Jr 49:19-21
[i] 51:1 Jr 4:11-12
[j] 51:2 Jr 15:7; Mt 3:12
[k] 51:3 Jb 41:13; Jr 46:4
[l] 51:4 Jr 51:47,52
[m] 51:5 Ps 78:41; Is 37:23; Jr 50:29
[n] 51:6 Jr 50:8; Rv 18:4
[o] Jr 48:6; 51:45
[p] Ps 28:4; 137:8; Is 66:6
[q] 51:7 Rv 17:4
[r] Rv 14:8; 18:3
[s] Jr 25:16
[t] 51:8 Jr 8:22; 46:11
[u] 51:9 Is 13:14
[v] Rv 18:5
[w] 51:10 Ps 37:6
[x] Jr 50:28

[A] 50:44 Lit *pride* [B] 50:44 Lit *them* [C] 51:1 Or *stir up the spirit of a destroyer* [D] 51:1 Lit *heart of my adversaries* [E] 51:1 = Chaldeans [F] 51:3 Hb obscure

The LORD has put it into the mind
of the kings of the Medes
because His plan is aimed at Babylon
to destroy her,
for it is the LORD's vengeance,
vengeance for His temple.[a]
12 Raise up a signal flag[b]
against the walls of Babylon;
fortify the watch post;
set the watchmen in place;
prepare the ambush.
For the LORD has both planned
and accomplished
what He has threatened
against those who live in Babylon.
13 You who reside by many waters,[c]
rich in treasures,
your end has come,
your life thread is cut.

14 The LORD of Hosts has sworn by Himself:

I will fill you up with men
as with locusts,
and they will sing the victory song
over you.

15 He made the earth by His power,
established the world[d] by His wisdom,[e]
and spread out the heavens
by His understanding.[f]
16 When He thunders,[A]
the waters in the heavens are
in turmoil,[g]
and He causes the clouds
to rise from the ends of the earth.
He makes lightning for the rain
and brings the wind
from His storehouses.[h]

17 Everyone is stupid and ignorant.
Every goldsmith is put to shame
by his carved image,[i]
for his cast images are a lie;[j]
there is no breath in them.[k]
18 They are worthless,[l] a work
to be mocked.
At the time of their punishment
they will be destroyed.[m]
19 Jacob's Portion[B] is not like these
because He is the One who formed
all things.[n]
Israel is the tribe of His inheritance;[o]
Yahweh of Hosts is His name.[p]

20 You are My battle club,
My weapons of war.
With you I will smash nations;
with you I will bring kingdoms to ruin.
21 With you I will smash the horse
and its rider;
with you I will smash the chariot
and its rider.
22 With you I will smash man
and woman;[q]
with you I will smash the old man
and the youth;
with you I will smash the young man
and the young woman.
23 With you I will smash the shepherd
and his flock;
with you I will smash the farmer
and his ox-team.[C]
With you I will smash governors
and officials.

24 "I will repay Babylon and all the residents
of Chaldea for all their evil they have done in
Zion before your very eyes."[r]

This is the LORD's declaration.

25 Look, I am against you,
devastating mountain —
this is the LORD's declaration —
you devastate the whole earth.
I will stretch out My hand against you,[s]
roll you down from the cliffs,
and turn you into a charred mountain.
26 No one will be able to retrieve
a cornerstone
or a foundation stone from you,
because you will become
desolate forever.
This is the LORD's declaration.

27 Raise a signal flag[t] in the land;
blow a ram's horn among the nations;
set apart the nations against her.[u]
Summon kingdoms against her —
Ararat, Minni, and Ashkenaz.
Appoint a marshal against her;
bring up horses like a swarm[D]
of locusts.

[a] **51:11** Jr 50:28 [b] **51:12** Ps 60:4; Is 5:26; 18:3 [c] **51:13** Rv 17:1 [d] **51:15** Jb 38:4; Ps 93:1; 96:10 [e] Pr 3:19-20; 8:22-29 [f] Jb 9:8; Ps 104:2; Is 45:12 [g] **51:16** Jr 5:22; 31:35 [h] Jb 38:25-30,34-38; Ps 135:7 [i] **51:17** Is 40:18-31; 46:1-7 [j] Is 41:29 [k] Hab 2:19 [l] **51:18** Jr 10:3,8 [m] Jr 6:15; 10:15; 49:8 [n] **51:19** Gn 2:7-8,19; Ps 95:5; Is 43:1 [o] Dt 32:8-9; Ps 74:2; Is 63:17 [p] **51:15-19** Jr 10:12-16 [q] **51:22** 2Ch 36:17; Is 13:15-18 [r] **51:24** Jr 50:15,29 [s] **51:25** Jr 15:6; Ezk 6:14; 25:7 [t] **51:27** Ps 60:4; Is 5:26; 18:3 [u] Jr 6:4; 22:7; 50:9

[A] **51:16** Lit *At His giving of the voice* [B] **51:19** = the LORD [C] **51:23** Lit *yoke* [D] **51:27** Hb obscure

28 Set apart the nations for battle
against her —
the kings of Media,
her governors and all her officials,
and all the lands they rule.
29 The earth quakes[a] and trembles
because the LORD's intentions
against Babylon stand:
to make the land of Babylon
an uninhabited desolation.
30 Babylon's warriors have
stopped fighting;[b]
they sit in their strongholds.
Their might is exhausted;
they have become like women.
Babylon's homes have been set ablaze,
her gate bars are shattered.[c]
31 Messenger races to meet messenger,[d]
and herald to meet herald,
to announce to the king of Babylon
that his city has been captured
from end to end.
32 The fords have been seized,[e]
the marshes set on fire,
and the soldiers are terrified.

33 For this is what the LORD of Hosts, the
God of Israel, says:

Daughter Babylon is
like a threshing floor
at the time it is trampled.[f]
In just a little while her harvest time
will come.[g]
34 "Nebuchadnezzar of Babylon
has devoured me;
he has crushed me.
He has set me aside
like an empty dish;
he has swallowed me
like a sea monster;[h]
he filled his belly with my delicacies;
he has vomited me out,"[A]
35 says the inhabitant of Zion;
"Let the violence done to me
and my family be done to Babylon.
Let my blood be on the inhabitants
of Chaldea,"
says Jerusalem.

36 Therefore, this is what the LORD says:

I am about to plead your case[i]
and take vengeance on your behalf;
I will dry up her sea[j]
and make her fountain run dry.
37 Babylon will become a heap of rubble,
a jackals' den,
a desolation and an object of scorn,[k]
without inhabitant.
38 They will roar together like young lions;
they will growl like lion cubs.
39 While they are flushed with heat,
I will serve them a feast,
and I will make them drunk so that
they revel.[B,l]
Then they will fall asleep forever
and never wake up.
This is the LORD's declaration.
40 I will bring them down like lambs
to the slaughter,
like rams together with male goats.[m]
41 How Sheshach has been captured,
the praise[n] of the whole earth seized.
What a horror Babylon has become
among the nations![o]
42 The sea has risen over Babylon;[p]
she is covered with its turbulent waves.
43 Her cities have become a desolation,[q]
a dry and arid land,
a land where no one lives,
where no human being passes through.
44 I will punish Bel[r] in Babylon.
I will make him vomit
what he swallowed.
The nations will no longer stream
to him;
even Babylon's wall will fall.
45 Come out from among her,
My people![s]
Save your lives, each of you,
from the LORD's burning anger.
46 May you not become cowardly
and fearful
when the report is proclaimed
in the land,
for the report will come one year,
and then another the next year.
There will be violence in the land
with ruler against ruler.
47 Therefore, look, the days are coming

[a] **51:29** Ps 18:7; Is 13:13; Jr 50:46 [b] **51:30** Jr 50:37 [c] Lm 2:9; Nah 3:13 [d] **51:31** 2Ch 30:6 [e] **51:32** Jdg 12:5 [f] **51:33** Is 21:10 [g] Is 17:5; Jl 3:13; Rv 14:15 [h] **51:34** Ps 74:13; Is 27:1; Ezk 29:3 [i] **51:36** 1Sm 24:15; Pr 23:11; Jr 50:34 [j] Ex 14:16–15:21 [k] **51:37** 2Ch 29:8; Jr 18:16; 19:8 [l] **51:39** Jr 51:57 [m] **51:40** Is 34:6; Ezk 39:18 [n] **51:41** Jr 33:9; 49:25 [o] Jr 50:23 [p] **51:42** Is 8:7-8 [q] **51:43** Jr 50:12 [r] **51:44** Is 46:1; Jr 50:2 [s] **51:45** Jr 51:6

[A] **51:34** Lit *has rinsed me off* [B] **51:39** LXX reads *pass out*

when I will punish
Babylon's carved images.[a]
Her entire land will suffer shame,
and all her slain will lie fallen
within her.[b]
48 Heaven and earth and everything
in them
will shout for joy[c] over Babylon
because the destroyers from the north
will come against her.
This is the LORD's declaration.
49 Babylon must fall because of the slain
of Israel,
even as the slain of all the earth fell
because of Babylon.
50 You who have escaped the sword,[d]
go and do not stand still!
Remember the LORD from far away,
and let Jerusalem come to your mind.
51 We are ashamed
because we have heard insults.[e]
Humiliation covers our faces
because foreigners have entered
the holy places of the LORD's temple.[f]
52 Therefore, look, the days are coming—
this is the LORD's declaration—
when I will punish her carved images,
and the wounded will groan
throughout her land.
53 Even if Babylon should ascend
to the heavens[g]
and fortify her tall fortresses,
destroyers will come against her
from Me.
This is the LORD's declaration.
54 The sound of a cry from Babylon![h]
The sound of great destruction
from the land of the Chaldeans!
55 For the LORD is going
to devastate Babylon;
He will silence her mighty voice.
Their waves roar
like abundant waters;
the tumult of their voice resounds,
56 for a destroyer is coming against her,
against Babylon.
Her warriors will be captured,
their bows shattered,
for the LORD is a God of retribution;
He will certainly repay.
57 I will make her princes
and sages drunk,
along with her governors, officials,
and warriors.
Then they will fall asleep forever
and never wake up.[i]
This is the King's declaration;
Yahweh of Hosts is His name.[j]

58 This is what Yahweh of Hosts says:
Babylon's thick walls will be
totally demolished,
and her high gates consumed by fire.
The peoples will have labored
for nothing;[k]
the nations will exhaust themselves
only to feed the fire.

59 This is what Jeremiah the prophet commanded Seraiah son of Neriah son of Mahseiah,[l] the quartermaster, when he went to
Babylon with King Zedekiah of Judah in the
fourth year of Zedekiah's reign. 60 Jeremiah
wrote on one scroll about all the disaster
that would come to Babylon;[m] all these words
were written against Babylon.
61 Jeremiah told Seraiah, "When you get to
Babylon, see that you read all these words
aloud. 62 You must say, 'LORD, You have threatened to cut off[n] this place so that no one will
live in it—man or beast. Indeed, it will remain desolate forever.' 63 When you have finished reading this scroll, tie a stone to it and
throw it into the middle of the Euphrates
River.[o] 64 Then say, 'In the same way, Babylon
will sink and never rise again because of the
disaster I am bringing on her. They will grow
weary.'"

The words of Jeremiah end here.

The Fall of Jerusalem

52 Zedekiah was 21 years old when he
became king and reigned 11 years in
Jerusalem. His mother's name was Hamutal
daughter of Jeremiah; she was from Libnah.
2 Zedekiah did what was evil in the LORD's
sight just as Jehoiakim had done.[p] 3 Because
of the LORD's anger, it came to the point in
Jerusalem and Judah that He finally banished
them from His presence. Nevertheless, Zedekiah rebelled against the king of Babylon.[q]
4 In the ninth year of Zedekiah's reign, on

[a] 51:47 Jr 50:2 [b] Jr 50:12 [c] 51:48 Is 44:23; 49:13 [d] 51:50 Jr 44:28 [e] 51:51 Ps 44:15 [f] Lm 1:10 [g] 51:53 Is 14:12-14; Jr 49:16 [h] 51:54 Jr 50:22 [i] 51:57 Jr 51:39 [j] Jr 46:18; 48:15 [k] 51:58 Hab 2:13 [l] 51:59 Jr 32:12 [m] 51:60 Jr 36:2 [n] 51:62 Jr 50:3 [o] 51:63 Jr 19:10-11; Rv 18:21 [p] 52:2 2Kg 23:34–24:6; 2Ch 36:4-8 [q] 52:1-3 2Kg 24:18-20; 2Ch 36:11-13

the tenth day of the tenth month, King Nebuchadnezzar of Babylon advanced against Jerusalem with his entire army. They laid siege
to the city and built a siege wall all around it.
5 The city was under siege until King Zedekiah's eleventh year.
6 By the ninth day of the fourth month the
famine was so severe in the city that the people of the land had no food. 7 Then the city was
broken into, and all the warriors fled. They
left the city by night by way of the gate between the two walls near the king's garden,
though the Chaldeans surrounded the city.
They made their way along the route to the
'Arabah.[a] 8 The Chaldean army pursued the
king and overtook Zedekiah in the plains of
Jericho. Zedekiah's entire army was scattered
from him. 9 The Chaldeans seized the king
and brought him to the king of Babylon at
Riblah in the land of Hamath, and he passed
sentence on him.
10 At Riblah the king of Babylon slaughtered Zedekiah's sons before his eyes and also
slaughtered the Judean commanders. 11 Then
he blinded Zedekiah and bound him with
bronze chains. The king of Babylon brought
Zedekiah to Babylon, where he kept him in
custody[A] until his dying day.[b]
12 On the tenth day of the fifth month — which
was the nineteenth year of King Nebuchadnezzar, king of Babylon — Nebuzaradan, the
commander of the guards, entered Jerusalem
as the representative of[B] the king of Babylon.
13 He burned the LORD's temple, the king's palace, all the houses of Jerusalem, and all the
houses of the nobles. 14 The whole Chaldean
army with the commander of the guards tore
down all the walls surrounding Jerusalem.[c]
15 Nebuzaradan, the commander of the guards,
deported some of the poorest of the people, as
well as the rest of the people who were left in
the city, the deserters who had defected to the
king of Babylon, and the rest of the craftsmen.
16 But some of the poorest people of the land
Nebuzaradan, the commander of the guards,
left to be vinedressers and farmers.[d]
17 Now the Chaldeans broke into pieces the
bronze pillars for the LORD's temple and the
water carts and the bronze reservoir that

[a]**52:7** Dt 2:8
[b]**52:4-11** 2Kg 25:1-7; Jr 39:1-7
[c]**52:13-14** 2Ch 36:19
[d]**52:12-16** 2Kg 25:8-12; Jr 39:8-10
[e]**52:17** 1Kg 7:23,27
[f]**52:19** Ex 25:29; 37:16; Nm 4:7
[g]**52:22** 1Kg 7:16-20,41-42; 2Ch 4:12-13
[h]**52:17-27** 2Kg 25:13-21
[i]**52:28** 2Kg 24:12-16

were in the LORD's temple,[e] and carried all the
bronze to Babylon. 18 They took the pots, shovels, wick trimmers, sprinkling basins, dishes,
and all the bronze articles used in the temple
service. 19 The commander of the guards took
away the bowls, firepans, sprinkling basins,
pots, lampstands, pans, and 'drink offering
bowls[f] — whatever was gold or silver.
20 As for the two pillars, the one reservoir,
and the 12 bronze bulls under the water carts
that King Solomon had made for the LORD's
temple, the weight of the bronze of all these
articles was beyond measure. 21 One pillar was
27 feet[C] tall, had a circumference of 18 feet,[D]
was hollow — four fingers thick — 22 and had
a bronze capital on top of it.[g] One capital,
encircled by bronze latticework and pomegranates, stood 7 1/2 feet[E] high. The second pillar was the same, with pomegranates. 23 Each
capital had 96 pomegranates all around it.
All the pomegranates around the latticework
numbered 100.
24 The commander of the guards also took
away Seraiah the chief priest, Zephaniah
the priest of the second rank, and the three
doorkeepers. 25 From the city he took a
court official who had been appointed over
the warriors; seven trusted royal aides[F]
found in the city; the secretary of the commander of the army, who enlisted the people of the land for military duty; and 60
men from the common people who were
found within the city. 26 Nebuzaradan, the
commander of the guards, took them and
brought them to the king of Babylon at Riblah. 27 The king of Babylon put them to
death at Riblah in the land of Hamath. So
Judah went into exile from its land.[h]
28 These are the people Nebuchadnezzar deported:[i] in the seventh year, 3,023 Jews; 29 in
his eighteenth year,[G] 832 people from Jerusalem; 30 in Nebuchadnezzar's twenty-third
year, Nebuzaradan, the commander of the
guards, deported 745 Jews. All together 4,600
people were deported.

Jehoiachin Pardoned

31 On the twenty-fifth day of the twelfth
month of the thirty-seventh year of the ex-

[A]**52:11** Lit *in a house of guards* [B]**52:12** Lit *Jerusalem; he stood before* [C]**52:21** Lit *18 cubits* [D]**52:21** Lit *12 cubits* [E]**52:22** Lit *five cubits* [F]**52:25** Lit *seven men who look on the king's face* [G]**52:29** Some Hb mss, Syr add *he deported*

ile of Judah's King Jehoiachin, Evil-merodach king of Babylon, in the first year of his
reign, pardoned King Jehoiachin of Judah
and released him from prison. 32 He spoke
kindly to him and set his throne above the
thrones of the kings who were with him
in Babylon. 33 So Jehoiachin changed his
prison clothes, and he dined regularly in
the presence of the king of Babylon for
the rest of his life. 34 As for his allowance,
a regular allowance was given to him by
the king of Babylon, a portion for each day
until the day of his death, for the rest of
his life.[a]

[a]52:31-34 2Kg 25:27-30

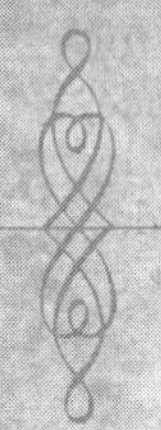

■ **AUTHOR:** Jeremiah

■■ **DATE:** After the fall of Jerusalem (around 586 B.C.)

Great moments in history are often remembered in song, poetry, speeches, or symbols. National histories celebrate military victories with holiday proclamations, but the losses and heroes' sacrifices are remembered too. "Remember the Alamo"—a military slaughter that became the battle cry for Sam Houston's army. "Never again"—the Holocaust. "Remember Pearl Harbor"—the shattering blow of the attack on Pearl Harbor. "9/11"—a numeric that touches hearts all over the world, owing to the events of September 11, 2001.

Lamentations contains five laments—poems of grief—about the fall of Jerusalem after the invasion of Babylon in sixth century B.C. But Lamentations' author—more

LAMENTATIONS

than likely the prophet Jeremiah—records the contempt of the Israelites for God's law and their indifference to God's mission. This is what led to their severe judgment. Behind Babylon's takeover is the sovereign hand of God. No power is independent of God and no turn of the journey unknown to him. Because of this assurance, Lamentations urges God's people to look through their tears to the love of God and to the promise of God: "Because of the LORD's faithful love we do not perish, for His mercies never end. They are new every morning; great is Your faithfulness!" (3:22-23).

To lament is the only proper action in the wake of utter devastation. Hope is the only proper horizon for people who know God, for "even if He causes suffering, He will show compassion according to His abundant, faithful love" (3:32). Lamentations shows emotional devastation and spiritual maturity, a mixture of grief and confidence that God's mission will rise again. When and how are questions for tomorrow.

We cannot hurry God's mission, but we can with confidence place our own losses under God's sure control. God knows us and walks with us. We can cry out in anguish and hope. "Joy has left our hearts; . . . LORD, restore us to Yourself, so we may return; renew our days as in former times," the writer pleads (5:15, 21). Such cries as this are reminders of things yet to come, memorials not of the past, but of the promise of God to save and redeem.

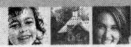

Lament over Jerusalem

א *Alef*

1 How[A] she sits alone,[a]
the city[b] once crowded with people!
She who was great among the nations
has become like a widow.[c]
The princess among the provinces
has been put to forced labor.

ב *Bet*

2 She weeps aloud during the night,[d]
with tears on her cheeks.
There is no one to offer her comfort,
not one from all her lovers.[B,e]
All her friends have betrayed her;
they have become her enemies.

ג *Gimel*

3 Judah has gone into exile
following[C] affliction and harsh slavery;
she lives among the nations
but finds no place to rest.[f]
All her pursuers have overtaken her
in narrow places.

ד *Dalet*

4 The roads to ˙Zion[g] mourn,
for no one comes
to the appointed festivals.[h]
All her gates are deserted;
her priests groan,
her young women grieve,
and she herself is bitter.

ה *He*

5 Her adversaries have become
her masters;[i]
her enemies are at ease,[j]
for the LORD has made her suffer
because of her many transgressions.
Her children have gone away
as captives before the adversary.

ו *Vav*

6 All her splendor[k] has vanished
from Daughter Zion.[l]
Her leaders are like stags
that find no pasture;
they walk away exhausted
before the hunter.[m]

ז *Zayin*

7 During the days of her affliction
and homelessness[n]
Jerusalem remembers all
her precious belongings
that were hers in days of old.
When her people fell
into the adversary's hand,
she had no one to help.
The adversaries looked at her,
laughing over her downfall.

ח *Khet*

8 Jerusalem has sinned grievously;
therefore, she has become an object
of scorn.[D]
All who honored her now despise her,
for they have seen her nakedness.
She herself groans and turns away.

ט *Tet*

9 Her uncleanness stains her skirts.[o]
She never considered her end.
Her downfall was astonishing;[p]
there was no one to comfort her.
LORD, look on my affliction,
for the enemy triumphs!

י *Yod*

10 The adversary has seized
all her precious belongings.
She has even seen the nations
enter her sanctuary—
those You had forbidden
to enter Your assembly.[q]

כ *Kaf*

11 All her people groan
while they search for bread.[r]
They have traded
their precious belongings for food
in order to stay alive.[s]
LORD, look and see
how I have become despised.

ל *Lamed*

12 Is this nothing to you, all you
who pass by?[t]
Look and see!
Is there any pain like mine,

[a]**1:1** Lm 3:28 [b]Lm 1:17 [c]Ex 22:22; Dt 10:18; 24:19-21; Is 1:17; 47:8-9 [d]**1:2** Ps 6:6 [e]Jr 3:1; 22:20-22 [f]**1:3** Dt 28:65; Ps 116:7 [g]**1:4** 2Sm 5:7; Ps 20:2; Jr 51:35 [h]Dt 16:16; 2Ch 8:13; Ps 84:5; Is 1:11-17 [i]**1:5** Dt 28:13,44 [j]Jb 3:26; 12:6; Jr 12:1 [k]**1:6** Ezk 27:10 [l]Lm 2:1,4,8; 4:22 [m]Jr 39:4-7 [n]**1:7** Is 58:7; Lm 3:19 [o]**1:9** Jr 13:22,26; Nah 3:5 [p]Dt 28:43 [q]**1:10** Dt 23:3; Neh 13:1-3; Ezk 44:9 [r]**1:11** Jr 38:9; 52:6 [s]Lm 1:19; 2:20; 4:10 [t]**1:12** Ps 89:41; Jr 22:8

A**1:1** The stanzas in Lm 1–4 form an ˙acrostic. B**1:2** = Jerusalem's political allies C**1:3** Or *because of* D**1:8** Or *become impure*

which was dealt out to me,
which the LORD made me suffer
on the day of His burning anger?[a]

מ *Mem*

13 He sent fire from heaven[b]
into my bones;
He made it descend.[A,c]
He spread a net for my feet[d]
and turned me back.
He made me desolate,
sick all day long.

נ *Nun*

14 My transgressions have been formed
into a yoke,[B,C,e]
fastened together by His hand;
they have been placed on my neck,
and the Lord has broken my strength.
He has handed me over
to those I cannot withstand.

ס *Samek*

15 The Lord has rejected[f]
all the mighty men within me.
He has summoned an army[D]
against me
to crush my young warriors.
The Lord has trampled
Virgin Daughter Judah[g]
like grapes in a winepress.[h]

ע *Ayin*

16 I weep because of these things;
my eyes flow[E] with tears.[i]
For there is no one nearby
to comfort me,[j]
no one to keep me alive.
My children are desolate
because the enemy has prevailed.

פ *Pe*

17 Zion stretches out her hands;
there is no one to comfort her.
The LORD has issued a decree
against Jacob
that his neighbors should be
his adversaries.
Jerusalem has become
something impure[k] among them.

[a]**1:12** Am 5:18 [b]**1:13** Gn 19:24; Hs 8:14; Am 1:4–2:5 [c]1Kg 18:38; 2Kg 1:10,12; Jb 30:30; Jr 20:9 [d]Ps 35:7; Is 51:20; Ezk 12:13; Hs 7:12 [e]**1:14** Gn 27:40; Lv 26:13; Dt 28:48; 2Ch 10:3-11; Is 9:4; Jr 27:2,6-11 [f]**1:15** Ps 119:118 [g]Lm 2:2,5 [h]Is 63:1-6; Jl 3:12-15; Rv 14:17-20; 19:15 [i]**1:16** Jr 9:1,18; Lm 2:11,18; 3:48-49 [j]Is 40:1 [k]**1:17** Lv 15:19-20; Ezk 7:19-20; 18:6 [l]**1:18** Neh 9:33 [m]Dt 28:41; 2Ch 29:9; Ezr 9:7; Jr 48:46 [n]**1:19** Lm 1:2 [o]Lm 1:11 [p]**1:20** Jb 30:27 [q]Dt 32:25; Ezk 7:15 [r]**1:21** Lm 1:4,8 [s]Lm 2:15-17 [t]Is 62:8–63:6; Ezk 38–39; Jl 3:1-3; Mc 7:8-13; Zch 14:1-9 [u]**1:22** Lm 4:21-22

צ *Tsade*

18 The LORD is just,
for I have rebelled
against His command.[l]
Listen, all you people;
look at my pain.
My young men and women
have gone into captivity.[m]

ק *Qof*

19 I called to my lovers,[n]
but they betrayed me.
My priests and elders
perished in the city
while searching for food
to keep themselves alive.[o]

ר *Resh*

20 LORD, see how I am in distress.
I am churning within;[p]
my heart is broken,[F]
for I have been very rebellious.
Outside, the sword takes the children;
inside, there is death.[q]

שׁ *Shin*

21 People have heard me groaning,[r]
but there is no one to comfort me.
All my enemies have heard
of my misfortune;
they are glad that You have caused it.[s]
Bring on the day You have announced,
so that they may become like me.[t]

ת *Tav*

22 Let all their wickedness come
before You,
and deal with them
as You have dealt with me
because of all my transgressions.[u]
For my groans are many,
and I am sick at heart.

Judgment on Jerusalem

א *Alef*

2 How the Lord has overshadowed
Daughter ·Zion with His anger!
He has thrown down Israel's glory
from heaven to earth.

[A]**1:13** DSS, LXX; MT reads *bones, and it prevailed against them* [B]**1:14** Some Hb mss, LXX read *He kept watch over my transgressions* [C]**1:14** Or *The yoke of my transgressions is bound*; Hb obscure [D]**1:15** Or *has announced an appointed time* [E]**1:16** Lit *my eye, my eye flows* [F]**1:20** Lit *is turned within me*

He has abandoned His footstool[A,a]
in the day of His anger.[b]

ב *Bet*

2 Without compassion[c] the Lord
has swallowed up
all the dwellings of Jacob.
In His wrath He has demolished
the fortified cities[d]
of Daughter Judah.
He brought them to the ground
and defiled the kingdom
and its leaders.[e]

ג *Gimel*

3 He has cut off every ·horn[f] of Israel
in His burning anger
and withdrawn His right hand[g]
in the presence of the enemy.
He has blazed against Jacob
like a flaming fire
that consumes everything.[h]

ד *Dalet*

4 He has bent His bow like an enemy;[i]
His right hand is positioned
like an adversary.
He has killed everyone
who was loved,[B]
pouring out His wrath like fire
on the tent of Daughter Zion.

ה *He*

5 The Lord is like an enemy;
He has swallowed up Israel.
He swallowed up all its palaces
and destroyed its fortified cities.
He has multiplied mourning
and lamentation
within Daughter Judah.[j]

ו *Vav*

6 He has done violence to His temple[C]
as if it were a garden booth,
destroying His place of meeting.[k]
The LORD has abolished
appointed festivals and Sabbaths
in Zion.
He has despised king and priest
in His fierce anger.

ז *Zayin*

7 The Lord has rejected His altar,
repudiated His sanctuary;[l]
He has handed the walls of her palaces
over to the enemy.
They have raised a shout in the house
of the LORD
as on the day of an appointed festival.

ח *Khet*

8 The LORD determined to destroy
the wall of Daughter Zion.
He stretched out a measuring line[m]
and did not restrain Himself
from destroying.
He made the ramparts and walls grieve;
together they waste away.

ט *Tet*

9 Zion's gates have fallen to the ground;[n]
He has destroyed and shattered
the bars on her gates.
Her king and her leaders live
among the nations,
instruction[D] is no more,
and even her prophets receive
no vision from the LORD.[o]

י *Yod*

10 The elders of Daughter Zion
sit on the ground in silence.
They have thrown dust on their heads[p]
and put on ·sackcloth.
The young women of Jerusalem
have bowed their heads to the ground.[q]

כ *Kaf*

11 My eyes are worn out from weeping;[r]
I am churning within.
My heart is poured out in grief[E,s]
because of the destruction
of my dear people,[t]
because children and infants faint
in the streets of the city.[u]

ל *Lamed*

12 They cry out to their mothers:
Where is the grain and wine?[v]
as they faint like the wounded

[a]**2:1** 1Ch 28:2; Ps 99:5; 132:7 [b]Jb 20:28; Ps 110:5; Zph 2:2-3 [c]**2:2** Jb 16:13; Lm 3:43; Ezk 8:18 [d]Is 2:12,15 [e]Ps 89:39; Is 43:28; 47:6 [f]**2:3** Ps 75:5,10; Jr 48:25 [g]Ex 6:6; Dt 4:34 [h]Dt 4:24; Heb 12:29 [i]**2:4** Ps 7:12; Lm 3:12 [j]**2:5** Is 29:2 [k]**2:6** Ps 74:4 [l]**2:7** Ps 89:39 [m]**2:8** 2Kg 21:13; Is 28:17; 34:11,17 [n]**2:9** Neh 1:3; Jr 14:2 [o]Ezk 7:26; Mc 3:6 [p]**2:10** Gn 37:34; Jos 7:6; Neh 9:1; Jb 2:12-13; Ezk 27:30 [q]Jb 10:15; Is 58:5 [r]**2:11** Ps 69:3; Jr 9:1; 14:17; Lm 3:48-49 [s]Ps 22:14; Jr 4:19 [t]Lm 3:48 [u]Jr 44:7 [v]**2:12** Dt 28:51; Hs 2:8-9; 7:14

[A]**2:1** Either the ark of the covenant or the temple [B]**2:4** Lit *killed all the delights of the eye*; Ezk 24:16 [C]**2:6** Lit *booth* [D]**2:9** Or *the law* [E]**2:11** Lit *My liver is poured out on the ground*

in the streets of the city,
as their lives fade away
in the arms of their mothers.

מ *Mem*

13 What can I say on your behalf?
What can I compare you to,
Daughter Jerusalem?
What can I liken you to,
so that I may console you,
Virgin Daughter Zion?
For your ruin is as vast as the sea.
Who can heal you?[a]

נ *Nun*

14 Your prophets saw visions for you
that were empty and deceptive;[b]
they did not reveal your ·guilt
and so restore your fortunes.[c]
They saw ·oracles for you
that were empty and misleading.

ס *Samek*

15 All who pass by
scornfully clap their hands[d] at you.
They mock[A,e] and shake their heads[f]
at Daughter Jerusalem:
Is this the city that was called
the perfection of beauty,[g]
the joy of the whole earth?[h]

פ *Pe*

16 All your enemies
open their mouths against you.[i]
They hiss and gnash their teeth,[j]
saying, "We have swallowed
her up.[k]
This is the day we have waited for!
We have lived to see it."

ע *Ayin*

17 The LORD has done
what He planned;
He has accomplished His decree,
which He ordained in days of old.
He has demolished
without compassion,[l]
letting the enemy gloat over you
and exalting the horn
of your adversaries.

[a]**2:13** Nah 3:19 [b]**2:14** Jr 5:12-13; 23:9-40; 28:1-4; 29:29-32; Ezk 13:8-16 [c]Dt 30:1-3; Jr 29:11-14; 30:1-3 [d]**2:15** Nm 24:10; Ezk 25:6 [e]1Kg 9:8; Jr 19:8 [f]Ps 22:7; 109:25; Mk 15:29 [g]Ps 50:2 [h]Ps 48:2 [i]**2:16** Dt 28:37; Jb 16:10; Ps 22:13; Lm 3:46 [j]Jb 16:9; Ps 35:16; 37:12 [k]Lm 2:2,5,8 [l]**2:17** Lm 2:2,21; 3:43; Ezk 7:8-9 [m]**2:18** Lm 2:8 [n]Jr 4:31; 14:17 [o]**2:19** Ps 42:4; 62:8; 77:2; 84:2; 142:2 [p]Is 51:20 [q]**2:20** Lv 26:27-29; Dt 28:53-57; 2Kg 6:24-31; Jr 19:9; Lm 4:10 [r]**2:21** Lm 2:2,17; 3:43 [s]**2:22** Ps 31:13; Jr 6:25; 20:10

צ *Tsade*

18 The hearts of the people cry out
to the Lord.
Wall of Daughter Zion,[m]
let your tears run down like a river
day and night.[n]
Give yourself no relief
and your[B] eyes no rest.

ק *Qof*

19 Arise, cry out in the night
from the first watch of the night.
Pour out your heart like water
before the Lord's presence.[o]
Lift up your hands to Him
for the lives of your children
who are fainting from hunger
on the corner of every street.[p]

ר *Resh*

20 LORD, look and consider
who You have done this to.
Should women eat their own children,[q]
the infants they have nurtured?[C]
Should priests and prophets
be killed in the Lord's sanctuary?

ש *Shin*

21 Both young and old
are lying on the ground in the streets.
My young men and women
have fallen by the sword.
You have killed them in the day
of Your anger,
slaughtering without compassion.[r]

ת *Tav*

22 You summoned my attackers[D]
on every side,[s]
as if for an appointed festival day;
on the day of the LORD's anger
no one escaped or survived.
My enemy has destroyed
those I nurtured[E] and reared.

Hope through God's Mercy

א *Alef*

3 I am the man who has seen affliction
under the rod of God's wrath.
2 He has driven me away and forced me
to walk

[A]**2:15** Lit *hiss* [B]**2:18** Lit *and the daughter of your* [C]**2:20** Or *infants in a healthy condition*; Hb obscure [D]**2:22** Or *terrors* [E]**2:22** Or *I bore healthy*; Hb obscure

in darkness instead of light.[a]
3 Yes, He repeatedly turns His hand
against me all day long.

ב *Bet*

4 He has worn away my flesh and skin;[b]
He has shattered my bones.[c]
5 He has laid siege against me,[d]
encircling me with bitterness
and hardship.[e]
6 He has made me dwell in darkness
like those who have been dead for ages.[f]

ג *Gimel*

7 He has walled me in
so I cannot escape;[g]
He has weighed me down with chains.
8 Even when I cry out and plead
for help,
He rejects my prayer.[h]
9 He has walled in my ways
with cut stones;[i]
He has made my paths crooked.[j]

ד *Dalet*

10 He is[A] a bear waiting in ambush,
a lion in hiding.[k]
11 He forced me off my way and tore me
to pieces;
He left me desolate.
12 He strung His bow[l]
and set me as the target for His arrow.

ה *He*

13 He pierced my kidneys
with His arrows.[m]
14 I am a laughingstock[n]
to all my people,[B]
mocked by their songs[o] all day long.
15 He filled me with bitterness,
satiated me with •wormwood.[p]

ו *Vav*

16 He ground my teeth on gravel[q]
and made me cower[C] in the dust.
17 My soul has been deprived[D] of peace;[r]
I have forgotten what happiness is.
18 Then I thought: My future[E] is lost,
as well as my hope from the LORD.

ז *Zayin*

19 Remember[F] my affliction
and my homelessness,[s]
the wormwood and the poison.[t]
20 I continually remember them
and have become depressed.[G,u]
21 Yet I call this to mind,
and therefore I have hope:[v]

ח *Khet*

22 Because of the LORD's faithful love[w]
we do not perish,[H]
for His mercies never end.
23 They are new every morning;
great is Your faithfulness![x]
24 I say: The LORD is my portion,[y]
therefore I will put my hope in Him.

ט *Tet*

25 The LORD is good to those who wait[z]
for Him,

[a]**3:2** Jb 12:25; Am 5:18,20 [b]**3:4** Jb 13:28; Ps 32:3; 38:3; 49:14; Mc 3:1-3 [c]Ps 51:8; Is 38:13 [d]**3:5** Jb 19:8,12 [e]Lm 3:19 [f]**3:6** Jb 10:20-22; Ps 88:6; 143:3 [g]**3:7** Jb 19:8 [h]**3:8** Jb 30:20; Ps 22:2; Is 59:2; Lm 3:44 [i]**3:9** Jb 13:27; 23:12; Is 63:17; Hs 2:6 [j]Jb 19:8; Ps 23:3; Pr 2:15; 3:6,17; 4:11 [k]**3:10** Hs 13:7-8 [l]**3:12** Ps 7:12; Lm 2:4 [m]**3:13** Jb 16:13; Pr 7:23 [n]**3:14** Jb 12:4; Jr 20:7; Lm 1:7 [o]Jb 30:9; Ps 69:12 [p]**3:15** Jr 9:15; 23:15 [q]**3:16** Ps 3:7; 58:6; Pr 20:17 [r]**3:17** Ps 88:15; Lm 3:31 [s]**3:19** Is 58:7; Lm 1:7 [t]Dt 29:18; Jr 9:15; 23:15 [u]**3:20** Ps 42:5-6,11; 43:5; 44:25 [v]**3:21** Jb 13:15; Ps 33:22; 71:14; 130:5; Mc 7:7 [w]**3:22** Ps 89:1; 103:17; Is 63:7 [x]**3:23** Ps 36:5; 89:1-8; 100:5 [y]**3:24** Nm 18:20; Ps 73:26; 142:5; Jr 10:16 [z]**3:25** Ps 25:3; Is 40:31; 49:23

Text Message

TEXT MESSAGES

The jubilation of many psalms carries different feelings than the horror of these words in Lamentations, written by Jeremiah as Israel trudged off to captivity. The gospel message necessarily brings joy but also its own level of sorrow—true words of judgment juxtaposed with promises of forgiveness and reconciliation. The messenger must tell the entire story. The Lord is good, faithful, and loving. Judgment is real, but His promises are ever and always true. He is the joyful answer. "Because of the LORD's faithful love we do not perish, for His mercies never end."

[A]**3:10** Lit *is to me* [B]**3:14** Some Hb mss, LXX, Vg; other Hb mss, Syr read *all peoples* [C]**3:16** Or *and trampled me* [D]**3:17** Syr, Vg; MT reads *You deprived my soul* [E]**3:18** Or *splendor* [F]**3:19** Or *I remember* [G]**3:20** Ancient Jewish tradition reads *and You cause me to collapse* [H]**3:22** One Hb mss, Syr, Tg read *The LORD's faithful love, indeed, does not perish*

to the person who seeks Him.
26 It is good to wait quietly[a]
for deliverance from the LORD.[b]
27 It is good for a man to bear the yoke[c]
while he is still young.

י *Yod*

28 Let him sit alone and be silent,[d]
for God has disciplined him.
29 Let him put his mouth in the dust[e] —
perhaps there is still hope.
30 Let him offer his cheek
to the one who would strike him;[f]
let him be filled with shame.

כ *Kaf*

31 For the Lord
will not reject us forever.
32 Even if He causes suffering,
He will show compassion
according to His abundant,
faithful love.[g]
33 For He does not enjoy
bringing affliction[h]
or suffering on ·mankind.

ל *Lamed*

34 Crushing all the prisoners of the land[A]
beneath one's feet,
35 denying justice to a man[i]
in the presence of the ·Most High,
36 or suppressing a person's lawsuit[j] —
the Lord does not approve
of these things.

מ *Mem*

37 Who is there who speaks
and it happens,
unless the Lord has ordained it?[k]
38 Do not both adversity and good
come from the mouth
of the Most High?[l]
39 Why should any living
person complain,
any man, because of the punishment
for his sins?

נ *Nun*

40 Let us search out and examine
our ways,
and turn back to the LORD.[m]
41 Let us lift up our hearts and our hands[n]
to God in heaven:
42 We have sinned and rebelled;
You have not forgiven.[o]

ס *Samek*

43 You have covered Yourself in anger
and pursued us;
You have killed without compassion.[p]
44 You have covered Yourself
with a cloud
so that no prayer can pass through.[q]
45 You have made us disgusting filth
among the peoples.[r]

פ *Pe*

46 All our enemies
open their mouths against us.[s]
47 We have experienced panic
and pitfall,[t]
devastation and destruction.
48 My eyes flow with streams of tears
because of the destruction
of my dear people.

ע *Ayin*

49 My eyes overflow unceasingly,
without end,[u]
50 until the LORD looks down
from heaven and sees.[v]
51 My eyes bring me grief
because of the fate of all the women
in my city.

צ *Tsade*

52 For no apparent reason, my enemies[B]
hunted me like a bird.[w]
53 They dropped me alive into[C] a pit[x]
and threw stones at me.
54 Water flooded over my head,[y]
and I thought: I'm going to die![z]

ק *Qof*

55 I called on Your name, ·Yahweh,
from the depths of the ·Pit.[aa]
56 You hear my plea:
Do not ignore my cry for relief.
57 You come near when I call on You;
You say: "Do not be afraid."

[a]**3:26** Ps 37:7; 130:5,7; 1Th 5:10; 2Tm 4:8; 2Pt 3:14 [b]Ps 37:39; 119:81; Is 46:13 [c]**3:27** Jr 27:11; Lm 1:14 [d]**3:28** Jr 15:17 [e]**3:29** Nm 22:31; Jos 7:6; 1Sm 25:23 [f]**3:30** Is 50:6; Mt 5:39; Lk 6:29 [g]**3:32** Ps 106:43-45; Ac 14:22; 2Co 4:17; Heb 12:6 [h]**3:33** Heb 12:10-11 [i]**3:35** Ex 23:6; Dt 16:19; 24:17; Mal 3:5 [j]**3:36** Ex 23:2-3 [k]**3:37** Ps 33:9-11 [l]**3:38** Gn 50:20; 1Sm 16:14; Jb 2:10; Ps 78:49; Is 45:7; Jr 1:14; 32:42; Am 3:6 [m]**3:40** Ps 119:5; 139:23-24 [n]**3:41** Ps 25:1 [o]**3:42** Dt 29:20; 2Kg 24:4; Jr 5:7 [p]**3:43** Lm 2:2,17,21; Ezk 7:8-9; 8:18 [q]**3:44** Lm 3:8 [r]**3:45** 1Co 4:13 [s]**3:46** Lm 2:16 [t]**3:47** Is 24:17; Jr 48:43 [u]**3:48-49** Jr 9:1,18; Lm 1:16; 2:11 [v]**3:50** Ps 14:2; 102:19 [w]**3:52** Ps 35:7 [x]**3:53** Gn 37:20-29; Jr 38:6-13 [y]**3:54** Ps 42:7; 69:1-2; Jnh 2:3,5 [z]Ezk 37:11 [aa]**3:55** Ps 88:6; Jnh 2:6

[A]**3:34** Or *earth* [B]**3:52** Or *Those who were my enemies for no reason* [C]**3:53** Or *They ended my life in*; Hb obscure

ר *Resh*

58 You defend my cause, Lord;[a]
You redeem my life.[b]
59 LORD, You see the wrong done to me;
judge my case.
60 You see all their malice,
all their plots against me.[c]

ש *Sin* / ש *Shin*

61 LORD, You hear their insults,[d]
all their plots against me.
62 The slander[A] and murmuring
of my opponents
attack me all day long.
63 When they sit and when
they rise, look,
I am mocked by their songs.[e]

ת *Tav*

64 You will pay them back
what they deserve, LORD,
according to the work
of their hands.[f]
65 You will give them a heart
filled with anguish.[B,g]
May Your curse be on them!
66 You will pursue them in anger
and destroy them
under Your heavens.[C,D,h]

Terrors of the Besieged City

א *Alef*

4 How the gold has become tarnished,
the fine gold become dull!
The stones of the temple[E] lie scattered
at the corner of every street.[i]

ב *Bet*

2 •Zion's precious people —
once worth their weight
in pure gold[j] —
how they are regarded as clay jars,
the work of a potter's hands!

ג *Gimel*

3 Even jackals offer their breasts
to nurse their young,
but my dear people have become cruel
like ostriches[k] in the wilderness.

ד *Dalet*

4 The nursing infant's tongue
clings to the roof of his mouth
from thirst.[l]
Little children beg for bread,
but no one gives them any.

ה *He*

5 Those who used to eat delicacies
are destitute in the streets;
those who were reared
in purple garments[m]
huddle in garbage heaps.

ו *Vav*

6 The punishment of my dear people
is greater than that of Sodom,[n]
which was overthrown in an instant
without a hand laid on it.

ז *Zayin*

7 Her dignitaries were brighter
than snow,
whiter than milk;
their bodies[F] were more ruddy
than coral,
their appearance like sapphire.[G]

ח *Khet*

8 Now they appear darker than soot;[o]
they are not recognized in the streets.
Their skin has shriveled on their bones;
it has become dry like wood.

ט *Tet*

9 Those slain by the sword are better off
than those slain by hunger,
who waste away, pierced with pain
because the fields lack produce.

י *Yod*

10 The hands of compassionate women
have cooked their own children;[p]
they became their food
during the destruction
of my dear people.[q]

כ *Kaf*

11 The LORD has exhausted His wrath,
poured out His burning anger;

[a]3:58 Ps 43:1; Pr 23:11; Jr 50:34 [b]Ps 103:4; 119:154 [c]3:60 Jr 11:19 [d]3:61 Lm 5:1 [e]3:63 Jb 30:9; Ps 69:12; Lm 3:14 [f]3:64 Ps 28:4; Rm 2:6; Rv 20:12-13 [g]3:65 Is 6:10 [h]3:66 Ps 8:3 [i]4:1 Ezk 7:19-20 [j]4:2 Is 62:3; Zch 9:16 [k]4:3 Jb 39:13-18 [l]4:4 Ps 22:15 [m]4:5 Jdg 8:26; Est 8:15 [n]4:6 Gn 18–19; Is 3:9; Jr 23:14 [o]4:8 Jb 30:30; Lm 5:10 [p]4:10 Dt 28:53; 2Kg 6:9 [q]Jr 8:11,21; Lm 2:11; 3:48

A3:62 Lit *lips* B3:65 Or *them an obstinate heart*; Hb obscure C3:66 LXX, Syr, Vg read *heavens, LORD* D3:66 Lit *under the LORD's heavens* E4:1 Or *The sacred gems* F4:7 Lit *bones* G4:7 Or *lapis lazuli*

He has ignited a fire in Zion,
and it has consumed her foundations.[a]

ל *Lamed*

12 The kings of the earth
and all the world's inhabitants
did not believe
that an enemy or adversary
could enter Jerusalem's gates.[b]

מ *Mem*

13 Yet it happened because of the sins
of her prophets
and the ·guilt of her priests,
who shed the blood of the righteous
within her.[c]

נ *Nun*

14 Blind, they stumbled in the streets,[d]
defiled by this blood,[e]
so that no one dared
to touch their garments.

ס *Samek*

15 "Stay away! ·Unclean!" people shouted
at them.
"Away, away! Don't touch us!"[f]
So they wandered aimlessly.[g]
It was said among the nations,
"They can stay here no longer."

פ *Pe*

16 The LORD Himself has scattered them;
He regards them no more.
The priests are not respected;
the elders find no favor.

ע *Ayin*

17 All the while our eyes were failing
as we looked in vain for assistance;[h]
we watched from our towers
for a nation[A] that refused to help.

צ *Tsade*

18 Our steps were closely followed
so that we could not walk in our streets.
Our end drew near;[i] our time ran out.
Our end had come!

ק *Qof*

19 Those who chased us were swifter
than eagles in the sky;[j]
they relentlessly pursued us
over the mountains
and ambushed us in the wilderness.

ר *Resh*

20 The LORD's anointed,[B] the breath
of our life,[C,k]
was captured in their traps.
We had said about him,
"We will live under his protection
among the nations."

ש *Sin*

21 So rejoice and be glad, Daughter Edom,[l]
you resident of the land of Uz![m]
Yet the cup[n] will pass to you as well;
you will get drunk and expose yourself.

ת *Tav*

22 Daughter Zion, your punishment
is complete;
He will not lengthen your exile.[D]
But He will punish your iniquity,
Daughter Edom,
and will expose your sins.[o]

Prayer for Restoration

5 ·Yahweh, remember
what has happened to us.
Look, and see our disgrace![p]
2 Our inheritance has been turned over
to strangers,
our houses to foreigners.
3 We have become orphans, fatherless;
our mothers are widows.
4 We must pay for the water we drink;
our wood comes at a price.
5 We are closely pursued;
we are tired, and no one offers us rest.
6 We made a treaty with[E] Egypt
and with Assyria, to get enough food.[q]
7 Our fathers sinned;
they no longer exist,
but we bear their punishment.
8 Slaves rule over us;[r]
no one rescues us from their hands.
9 We secure our food at the risk
of our lives
because of the sword in the wilderness.

[a] **4:11** Lm 2:3-4
[b] **4:12** 2Sm 5:6-8; Ps 48:1-5
[c] **4:13** Ps 106:38-39; Ezk 22:1-5
[d] **4:14** Dt 28:29; Is 59:10; Zph 1:17
[e] Lv 21:11
[f] **4:15** Lv 13:45-46
[g] Gn 4:12
[h] **4:17** Jr 37:7-8
[i] **4:18** Ezk 7:2-12; Am 8:2
[j] **4:19** Jr 4:13; Hab 1:8
[k] **4:20** Gn 2:7; 2Kg 25:7
[l] **4:21** Ezk 35:15; Ob 12
[m] Jr 25:20
[n] Is 51:17; Jr 25:15-16; Hab 2:16
[o] **4:22** Ps 137:7; Ezk 25:12-14; Jl 3:19
[p] **5:1** Ps 74:18,22; 89:50-51
[q] **5:6** Hs 12:1
[r] **5:8** Pr 30:21-23; Ec 10:7

[A] **4:17** Probably Egypt [B] **4:20** = King Zedekiah [C] **4:20** Lit *nostrils* [D] **4:22** Or *not deport you again* [E] **5:6** Lit *We gave the hand to*

10 Our skin is as hot[A] as an oven[a]
from the ravages of hunger.
11 Women are raped in ·Zion,
girls in the cities of Judah.
12 Princes are hung up by their hands;
elders are shown no respect.[b]
13 Young men labor at millstones;[c]
boys stumble under loads of wood.
14 The elders have left the city ·gate,
the young men, their music.[d]
15 Joy has left our hearts;[e]
our dancing has turned to mourning.
16 The crown has fallen from our head.[f]
Woe to us, for we have sinned.[g]
17 Because of this, our heart is sick;
because of these, our eyes grow dim:[h]
18 because of Mount Zion,
which lies desolate
and has jackals prowling in it.[i]
19 You, LORD, are enthroned forever;
Your throne endures from generation
to generation.[j]
20 Why have You forgotten us forever,[k]
abandoned us for our entire lives?
21 LORD, restore us to Yourself, so we
may return;[l]
renew our days as in former times,
22 unless You have completely
rejected us
and are intensely angry with us.

[a] **5:10** Lm 4:8
[b] **5:12** Lm 4:16
[c] **5:13** Ex 11:5; Jdg 16:21; Is 47:2
[d] **5:14** Is 24:8
[e] **5:15** Am 8:10
[f] **5:16** Jb 19:9; Is 28:3; Jr 13:18
[g] Jr 8:14; 14:20; Dn 9:11
[h] **5:17** Ps 69:23; Ec 12:3
[i] **5:18** Is 13:19-22; 34:11-15
[j] **5:19** Ps 9:7; 45:6; 102:12; Ezk 43:7; Heb 1:8; Rv 4:9-10; 5:13
[k] **5:20** Ps 13:1
[l] **5:21** Jr 15:19; 31:18

[A] **5:10** Or *black*; Hb obscure

■ **AUTHOR:** Ezekiel

■■ **DATE:** Ezekiel prophesied during the time of the exile (around 598–571 B.C.)

Ezekiel's life was rough, politically and emotionally. He spoke God's message to a nation who refused to heed. Leader after leader drove the nation farther from God, their source of hope. Finally, the Babylonians sacked Jerusalem. A deathly quiet rested on the ruined city. Its people—Ezekiel included—were marched into exile in 597 B.C.

If this were not difficult enough, Ezekiel was called to live a kind of prophetic drama, at great cost to him. As Jerusalem lay under siege, Ezekiel's wife became terminally ill and died an premature early death. Ezekiel lived personally what God's people were living naturally—loss of delight, hope, and home. The mission of God required it. A rebellious people would come to their senses in no other way. God was determined to be heard, known, and worshiped. Destruction and exile were His sovereign means of getting the people's attention and bringing them to repentance, and renewal.

EZEKIEL

Ezekiel's book is a literary masterpiece of form and balance. God is angry, Ezekiel shows, but God's vision is to restore and rebuild. God judges and punishes sin, but comforts and encourages all the while. God rebukes the nation for careless disregard of the commandments, then consoles the nation for the hurt and misery their lack of loyalty has caused. Parents and children will see in these portrayals the love and discipline, the total care and tempered punishment that upward growth requires. A good parent would not allow a spoiled child to ruin his or her life. Israel's good God will not be idle when His ambassadors to the world make His mission a laughing-stock.

Ezekiel sees the magnitude of the recovery needed here; he never gives up hope that God will eventually restore His people, though he does counsel a kind of quiet acceptance during the first years of exile.

The mission of God follows two tracks in Ezekiel. The geo-political track follows the loss of city, temple, home, and country. The nation will rise again, but such a prophecy is far-off. A long interim of soul-searching will bring the people a new perspective on their role in God's work.

The personal track offers a possibility of near-term renewal. Transformed personally, the people will be able to assess their history and do better with God's gifts if granted another opportunity. The images Ezekiel uses for this personal change are the textures of stones and flesh. A rock-hard heart will be changed by God's grace to a "heart of flesh" (36:26) as the Spirit of God enters their lives, moving people to cheerfully obey His will. No more legalistic drudgery (which never should have been) and no more compromise with false worship (an irrational act clutching at bad bargains offered by religious imposters).

The personal renewal Ezekiel sees will create new life and fresh capacity to know God. Eagerness will replace obligation, and success at doing God's work will overcome the setbacks and calamity of ignoring God's mission. A new team is forming. God is not finished yet.

1 In the thirtieth year, in the fourth month,
on the fifth day of the month, while I was
among the exiles by the Chebar Canal,[a] the
heavens opened[b] and I saw visions of God.[c]
2On the fifth day of the month — it was the
fifth year of King Jehoiachin's exile[d] — 3the
word of the LORD came[e] directly to Ezekiel[f]

[a]**1:1** Ezk 3:15,23; 10:15,20,22 [b]Mt 3:16; Mk 1:10; Lk 3:21; Jn 1:51; Ac 7:56; 10:11; Rv 4:1; 19:11

[c]Ex 24:10; Nm 12:6; Ezk 8:3; 11:24; 40:2 [d]**1:2** 2Kg 24:8,12,15,17; 25:27,29 [e]**1:3** Gn 15:1; 1Sm 15:10; 2Sm 7:4; 1Kg 6:11; 21:17; Is 38:4; Jr 1:2; Jnh 1:1; Hg 1:1; Zch 1:1 [f]Ezk 24:24

WORLDVIEW

The Mission of God in Africa

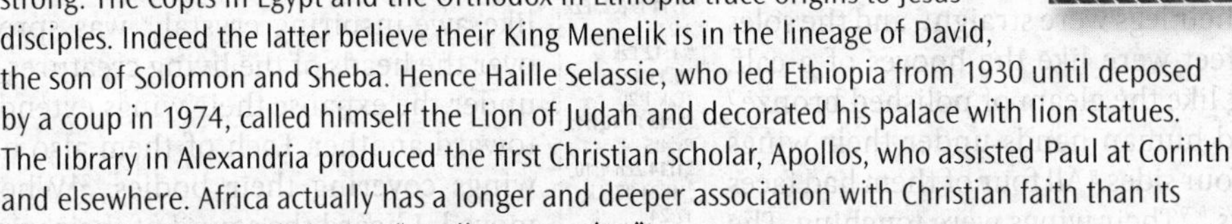

Sometimes Western Christians begin the story of Africa's explosive church growth with the arrival of missionaries during the nineteenth century. But African scholars will cordially note that the continent's first churches were early and strong. The Copts in Egypt and the Orthodox in Ethiopia trace origins to Jesus' disciples. Indeed the latter believe their King Menelik is in the lineage of David, the son of Solomon and Sheba. Hence Haille Selassie, who led Ethiopia from 1930 until deposed by a coup in 1974, called himself the Lion of Judah and decorated his palace with lion statues. The library in Alexandria produced the first Christian scholar, Apollos, who assisted Paul at Corinth and elsewhere. Africa actually has a longer and deeper association with Christian faith than its nineteenth-century missionary "sending countries."

What made the African continent fertile soil for the mission of God? The continent is too complex for generalizations across cultures or peoples. Northern Africa is now largely Muslim, while sub-Sahara nations are often known for disease, violence, and tyranny—the favorite trio of reporting media. The gospel was eagerly received in both North and South. In sub-Sahara Africa especially, churches are full of enthusiastic believers.

Ubuntu explains some of the readiness of Africa for God's message of peace and fellowship. Ubuntu is social continuity, village cohesion, hospitality, and commitment to others that typifies African tribal groups. In the West, an emphasis on individualism makes coming to faith quite a personal matter, a change of relations between individuals and God. In Africa, where identity and focus is on "we," not "I," entire villages received the gospel in faith, rapidly spreading the message, often outpacing the capacity of Christian leaders to follow-up and train new converts. This "we"-sense of African Ubuntu made the message of God's Kingdom—a new family of faith and hope—entirely sensible. People moved together toward God, then stayed together in churches to worship and learn. In Africa today, there is a palpable eagerness to know and follow God.

Ubuntu helps explain how large groups came to faith, but Africa's subsistence economy may better explain why its faith shows a "daily walk with God." The Lord's prayer, "Give us today our daily bread," is easily spoken in Europe and America, where "bread" is stored up for the month and easily accessible. In rural Africa, "daily bread" is hard won and never guaranteed. The maize and beans that sustain life depend on rain (a gift from God), sun (lots of it there, another gift), and sufficient political stability to see a planting through to harvest. From nature's provisions to social peace, Africans have long been accustomed to imploring the deities on nearby mountains for help. African Traditional Religion (ATR) is both pragmatic (what works is best practice) and deeply spiritual (the gods control everything). When God's message of love and forgiveness is set against this survival economy, people believe in order to live. When God's promise of eternal life reaches people who struggle for daily bread, hearts are open, grateful, and eager.

The mission of God has taken such root in African soil that in many cities in Europe and America, you can find pastors and missionaries from Africa, now helping diminished churches of the West recover their vitality.

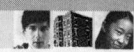

the priest, the son of Buzi, in the land of the Chaldeans[a] by the Chebar Canal. And the LORD's hand was on him there.[b]

Vision of the LORD's Glory

4 I looked and there was a whirlwind[c] coming from the north, a great cloud with fire flashing back and forth and brilliant light all around it. In the center of the fire, there was a gleam like amber.[d] 5 The form of four living creatures came from it.[e] And this was their appearance: They had human form, 6 but each of them had four faces and four wings. 7 Their legs were straight, and the soles of their feet were like the hooves of a calf, sparkling like the gleam of polished bronze.[f] 8 They had human hands under their wings on their four sides.[g] All four of them had faces and wings.[h] 9 Their wings were touching. The creatures did not turn as they moved; each one went straight ahead.[i] 10 The form of each of their faces was that of a man,[j] and each of the four had the face of a lion on the right, the face of an ox on the left, and the face of an eagle.[k] 11 That is what their faces were like. Their wings were spread upward; each had two wings touching that of another and two wings covering its body.[l] 12 Each creature went straight ahead.[m] Wherever the Spirit[A] wanted to go, they went without turning as they moved.[n]

13 The form of the living creatures was like the appearance of burning coals of fire and torches.[o] Fire was moving back and forth between the living creatures; it was bright, with lightning coming out of it. 14 The creatures were darting back and forth[p] like flashes of lightning.[q]

15 When I looked at the living creatures, there was one wheel on the ground beside each creature that had four faces. 16 The appearance of the wheels[r] and their craftsmanship was like the gleam of beryl,[s] and all four had the same form. Their appearance and craftsmanship was like a wheel within a wheel. 17 When they moved, they went in any of the four directions, without pivoting as they moved. 18 Their rims were large and frightening. Each of their four rims were full of eyes[t] all around. 19 So when the living creatures moved,[u] the wheels moved beside them, and when the creatures rose from the earth, the wheels also rose. 20 Wherever the Spirit[A] wanted to go, the creatures went in the direction the Spirit was moving. The wheels rose alongside them, for the spirit of the living creatures was in the wheels. 21 When the creatures moved, the wheels moved; when the creatures stood still, the wheels stood still; and when the creatures rose from the earth, the wheels rose alongside them, for the spirit of the living creatures was in the wheels.

22 The shape of an expanse,[v] with a gleam like awe-inspiring crystal,[w] was spread out over the heads of the living creatures.[x] 23 And under the expanse their wings extended one toward another. Each of them also had two wings covering their bodies. 24 When they moved, I heard the sound of their wings like the roar of mighty waters,[y] like the voice of the ·Almighty,[z] and a sound of commotion like the noise of an army.[aa] When they stood still, they lowered their wings.

25 A voice came from above the expanse over their heads; when they stood still, they lowered their wings. 26 The shape of a throne with the appearance of sapphire[B] stone was above the expanse.[C,ab] There was a form with the appearance of a human on the throne high above.[ac] 27 From what seemed to be His waist up, I saw a gleam like amber, with what looked like fire enclosing it all around.[ad] From what seemed to be His waist down, I also saw what looked like fire. There was a brilliant light all around Him. 28 The appearance of the brilliant light all around was like that of a rainbow in a cloud on a rainy day.[ae] This was the appearance of the form of the LORD's glory.[af] When I saw it, I fell facedown and heard a voice speaking.[ag]

Mission to Rebellious Israel

2 He said to me, "Son of man, stand up on your feet[ah] and I will speak with you." 2 As He spoke to me, the Spirit entered me and set me on my feet,[ai] and I listened to the One who was speaking to me. 3 He said to me: "Son of man, I am sending you to the Israelites, to[D] the rebellious pagans[E] who have rebelled against Me. The Israelites and their ancestors have

[a] **1:3** Gn 11:28 [b] 1Kg 18:46; 2Kg 3:15; 1Ch 28:19; Ezk 3:14-22; 37:1; 40:1; Ezr 7:6,28 [c] **1:4** 2Kg 2:1; Jb 38:1; 40:6; Ps 77:18; Is 66:15; Nah 1:3 [d] Ezk 1:27; 8:2 [e] **1:5** Ezk 10:14,21; Rv 4:6-8 [f] **1:7** Dn 10:6; Rv 1:15 [g] **1:8** Ezk 1:17; 10:11 [h] Ezk 10:8,21 [i] **1:9** Ezk 10:22 [j] **1:10** Rv 4:7 [k] Ezk 10:14-21 [l] **1:11** Is 6:2; Ezk 1:23 [m] **1:12** Ezk 10:11,22 [n] Ezk 1:20 [o] **1:13** Ps 104:4; Rv 4:5 [p] **1:14** Zch 4:10 [q] Mt 24:27; Lk 17:24 [r] **1:16** Ezk 10:9-11 [s] Dn 10:6 [t] **1:18** Ezk 10:12; Rv 4:6,8 [u] **1:19-21** Ezk 10:16-17,19 [v] **1:22** Gn 1:6-8 [w] Rv 4:6 [x] Ezk 10:1 [y] **1:24** Ezk 43:2; Rv 1:15; 19:6 [z] Ezk 10:5 [aa] Dn 10:6 [ab] **1:26** Ezk 10:1 [ac] Is 6:1; Ezk 24:10 [ad] **1:27** Ezk 1:4; 8:2 [ae] **1:28** Gn 9:13; Rv 4:3; 10:1 [af] Ex 24:16; Ezk 8:4; 11:22-23; 43:4-5 [ag] Gn 17:3; Ezk 3:23; Dn 8:17; Rv 1:17 [ah] **2:1** Dn 10:11 [ai] **2:2** Ezk 3:24; Dn 8:18

[A] **1:12,20** Or *spirit* [B] **1:26** Or *lapis lazuli* [C] **1:26** Lit *expanse that was over their head* [D] **2:3** Or *Israelites and to* [E] **2:3** LXX omits *to the rebellious pagans*

transgressed against Me to this day.[a] 4 The
children are obstinate[A] and hardhearted.[b] I
am sending you to them, and you must say
to them, 'This is what the Lord GOD says.'
5 Whether they listen or refuse to listen[c] — for
they are a rebellious house — they will know
that a prophet has been among them.[d]
6 "But you, son of man, do not be afraid
of them or their words,[e] though briers and
thorns are beside you and you live among
scorpions.[f] Don't be afraid of their words or
be discouraged by the look on their faces, for
they are a rebellious house. 7 But speak My
words to them whether they listen or refuse
to listen,[g] for they are rebellious.
8 "And you, son of man, listen to what I tell
you: Do not be rebellious like that rebellious
house. Open your mouth and eat what I am
giving you."[h] 9 So I looked and saw a hand
reaching out to me,[i] and there was a written
scroll in it.[j] 10 When He unrolled it before me,
it was written on the front and back; words of
lamentation, mourning, and woe were written on it.

3 He said to me: "Son of man, eat what you
find here. Eat this scroll,[k] then go and
speak to the house of Israel." 2 So I opened
my mouth, and He fed me the scroll. 3 "Son of
man," He said to me, "eat[B] and fill your stomach with this scroll I am giving you." So I ate
it,[l] and it was as sweet as honey in my mouth.[m]
4 Then He said to me: "Son of man, go to the
house of Israel and speak My words to them.
5 For you are not being sent to a people of unintelligible speech or difficult language but
to the house of Israel. 6 You are not being sent
to many peoples of unintelligible speech or
difficult language, whose words you cannot
understand. No doubt, if I sent you to them,
they would listen to you.[n] 7 But the house of
Israel will not want to listen to you because
they do not want to listen to Me.[o] For the
whole house of Israel is hardheaded and
hardhearted. 8 Look, I have made your face as
hard as their faces and your forehead as hard
as their foreheads.[p] 9 I have made your forehead like a diamond, harder than flint. Don't
be afraid of them or discouraged by the look
on their faces, even though they are a rebellious house."

[a]**2:3** Ezk 20:18,30
[b]**2:4** Ezk 3:7
[c]**2:5** Ezk 3:11,27
[d]Ezk 33:33
[e]**2:6** Jr 1:8,17; Ezk 3:9
[f]2Sm 23:6; Ezk 28:24; Mc 7:4
[g]**2:7** Jr 1:7,17
[h]**2:8** Jr 15:16; Ezk 3:3; Rv 10:9
[i]**2:9** Ezk 8:3
[j]Jr 36:2; Ezk 3:1
[k]**3:1** Ezk 2:8-9
[l]**3:3** Jr 15:16
[m]Ps 19:10; 119:103; Rv 10:9-10
[n]**3:6** Mt 11:21,23
[o]**3:7** Jn 15:20
[p]**3:8** Jr 1:18; 5:3
[q]**3:11** Ezk 2:5,7
[r]**3:12** Ezk 8:3; Ac 8:39
[s]**3:13** Ezk 1:24
[t]Ezk 1:15; 10:16-17
[u]**3:14** 2Kg 3:15
[v]**3:15** Jb 2:13; Ps 137:1
[w]**3:16** Jr 42:7
[x]**3:17** Is 52:8; 56:10; 62:6; Jr 6:17; Ezk 33:7-9
[y]2Ch 19:10; Is 58:1
[z]**3:18-19** Ezk 33:3,6,8-9
[aa]**3:19** Ezk 14:14,20; Ac 18:6; 1Tm 4:16
[ab]**3:20** Ezk 18:24
[ac]Jr 6:21
[ad]**3:22** Ezk 8:4
[ae]Ac 9:6
[af]**3:23** Ezk 1:28; Ac 7:55

10 Next He said to me: "Son of man, listen
carefully to all My words that I speak to you
and take them to heart. 11 Go to your people,
the exiles, and speak to them. Tell them, 'This
is what the Lord GOD says,' whether they listen or refuse to listen."[q]
12 The Spirit then lifted me up,[r] and I heard
a great rumbling sound behind me — praise
the glory of the LORD in His place! — 13 with
the[C] sound of the living creatures' wings
brushing against each other[s] and the sound
of the wheels beside them,[t] a great rumbling
sound. 14 So the Spirit lifted me up and took
me away. I left in bitterness and in an angry
spirit, and the LORD's hand was on me powerfully.[u] 15 I came to the exiles at Tel-abib, who
were living by the Chebar Canal, and I sat
there among them stunned for seven days.[v]

Ezekiel as a Watchman

16 Now at the end of seven days the word of
the LORD came to me:[w] 17 "Son of man, I have
made you a watchman over the house of Israel.[x] When you hear a word from My mouth,
give them a warning from Me.[y] 18 If I say to
the wicked person,[z] 'You will surely die,' but
you do not warn him — you don't speak out
to warn him about his wicked way in order
to save his life — that wicked person will die
for his iniquity. Yet I will hold you responsible for his blood. 19 But if you warn a wicked
person and he does not turn from his wickedness or his wicked way, he will die for his
iniquity, but you will have saved your life.[aa]
20 Now if a righteous person turns from his
righteousness and practices iniquity,[ab] and I
put a stumbling block in front of him, he will
die.[ac] If you did not warn him, he will die because of his sin and the righteous acts he did
will not be remembered. Yet I will hold you
responsible for his blood. 21 But if you warn
the righteous person that he should not sin,
and he does not sin, he will indeed live because he listened to your warning, and you
will have saved your life."
22 Then the hand of the LORD was on me
there, and He said to me, "Get up, go out to
the plain,[ad] and I will speak with you there."[ae]
23 So I got up and went out to the plain. The
LORD's glory was present there,[af] like the

[A]**2:4** Lit *hard of face* [B]**3:3** Lit *feed your belly* [C]**3:12-13** Some emend to *behind me as the glory of the LORD rose from His place:* [13]*the* glory I had seen by the Chebar Canal,[a] and I fell facedown. 24The Spirit entered me and set me on my feet.[b] He spoke with me and said: "Go, shut yourself inside your house. 25And you, son of man, they will put ropes on you[c] and bind you with them so you cannot go out among them. 26I will make your tongue stick to the roof of your mouth,[d] and you will be mute[e] and unable to rebuke them, for they are a rebellious house. 27But when I speak with you, I will open your mouth,[f] and you will say to them, 'This is what the Lord GOD says.' Let the one who listens, listen, and let the one who refuses, refuse—for they are a rebellious house.

Jerusalem's Siege Dramatized

4 "Now you, son of man, take a brick, set it in front of you, and draw the city of Jerusalem on it. 2Then lay siege against it:[g] construct a siege wall, build a ramp, pitch military camps, and place battering rams against it on all sides. 3Take an iron plate and set it up as an iron wall between yourself and the city. Turn your face toward it so that it is under siege, and besiege it. This will be a sign for the house of Israel.[h]

4"Then lie down on your left side and place the iniquity[A] of the house of Israel on it. You will bear their iniquity for the number of days you lie on your side. 5For I have assigned you the years of their iniquity according to the number of days you lie down, 390 days; so you will bear the iniquity of the house of Israel.[i] 6When you have completed these days, lie down again, but on your right side, and bear the iniquity of the house of Judah. I have assigned you 40 days, a day for each year. 7You must turn your face toward the siege of Jerusalem with your arm bared, and prophesy against it. 8Be aware that I will put cords on you so you cannot turn from side to side until you have finished the days of your siege.[j]

9"Also take wheat, barley, beans, lentils, millet, and spelt. Put them in a single container and make them into bread for yourself. You are to eat it during the number of days you lie on your side, 390 days. 10The food you eat each day will be eight ounces[B] by weight; you will eat it from time to time.[C] 11You are also to drink water by measure, a sixth of a gallon,[D] which you will drink from time to time. 12You will eat it as you would a barley cake and bake it over dried human excrement in their sight." 13The LORD said, "This is how the Israelites will eat their bread—ceremonially ·unclean—among the nations where I will banish them."[k]

14But I said, "Oh, Lord GOD, I have never been defiled. From my youth until now I have not eaten anything that died naturally or was mauled by wild beasts.[l] And impure meat has never entered my mouth."[m]

15He replied to me, "Look, I will let you use cow dung instead of human excrement, and you can make your bread over that." 16Then He said to me, "Son of man, I am going to cut off the supply of bread in Jerusalem.[n] They will anxiously eat bread rationed by weight and in dread drink water by measure.[o] 17So they will lack bread and water; everyone will be devastated and waste away because of their iniquity.[p]

Ezekiel Dramatizes Jerusalem's Fall

5 "Now you, son of man, take a sharp sword,[q] use it as you would a barber's razor, and shave your head and beard. Then take a set of scales and divide the hair. 2You are to burn up a third of it in the city when the days of the siege have ended;[r] you are to take a third and slash it with the sword all around the city; and you are to scatter a third to the wind, for I will draw a sword to chase after them. 3But you are to take a few strands from the hair and secure them in the folds of your robe.[s] 4Take some more of them, throw them into the fire, and burn them in it.[t] A fire will spread from it to the whole house of Israel.

5"This is what the Lord GOD says: I have set this Jerusalem in the center of the nations, with countries all around her. 6But she has rebelled against My ordinances with more wickedness than the nations, and against My statutes more than the countries that surround her. For her people have rejected My ordinances and have not walked in My statutes.

7"Therefore, this is what the Lord GOD says: Because you have been more insubordinate than the nations around you[u]—you have not

[a] **3:23** Ezk 1:1
[b] **3:24** Ezk 2:2
[c] **3:25** Ezk 4:8
[d] **3:26** Ps 22:15
[e] Lk 1:20,22
[f] **3:27** Ezk 24:27; 33:22
[g] **4:2** Jr 6:6; Ezk 21:22
[h] **4:3** Is 8:18; 20:3; Ezk 12:6,11; 24:24-27
[i] **4:5** Nm 14:34
[j] **4:8** Ezk 3:25
[k] **4:13** Dn 1:8; Hs 9:3
[l] **4:14** Lv 17:15; 22:8; Ezk 44:31
[m] Ac 10:14
[n] **4:16** Lv 26:26; Ezk 5:16; 14:13
[o] Ezk 12:19
[p] **4:17** Lv 26:39; Ezk 24:23; 33:10
[q] **5:1** Lv 21:5; Is 7:20; Ezk 44:20
[r] **5:2** Ezk 4:2-8
[s] **5:3** Jr 40:6; 52:16
[t] **5:4** Jr 44:14
[u] **5:7** Jr 2:10-11

[A] **4:4** Or *punishment* [B] **4:10** Lit *20 shekels* [C] **4:10** Or *it at set times* [D] **4:11** Lit *hin*

walked in My statutes or kept My ordinances; you have not even kept the ordinances of the nations around you — [8]therefore, this is what the Lord GOD says: See, I am against you, Jerusalem, and I will execute judgments within you in the sight of the nations. [9]Because of all your detestable practices, I will do to you what I have never done before and what I will never do again.[a] [10]As a result, fathers will eat their sons[b] within Jerusalem,[A] and sons will eat their fathers. I will execute judgments against you and scatter all your survivors to every direction of the wind.

[11]"Therefore, as I live" — this is the declaration of the Lord GOD — "I am going to cut you off and show you no pity, because you have defiled My sanctuary[c] with all your detestable practices and abominations.[d] Yes, I will not spare you. [12]A third of your people will die by plague and be consumed by famine within you;[e] a third will fall by the sword all around you; and I will scatter a third to every direction of the wind, and I will draw a sword to chase after them.[f] [13]When My anger is spent and I have vented My wrath on them, I will be appeased.[g] Then after I have spent My wrath on them, they will know that I, ·Yahweh, have spoken in My jealousy.[h]

[14]"I will make you a ruin and a disgrace among the nations around you, in the sight of everyone who passes by. [15]So you[B] will be a disgrace and a taunt, a warning and a horror, to the nations around you when I execute judgments against you in anger,[i] wrath, and furious rebukes. I, Yahweh, have spoken. [16]When I shoot deadly arrows of famine at them, arrows for destruction that I will send to destroy you, inhabitants of Jerusalem, I will intensify the famine against you and cut off your supply of bread. [17]I will send famine and dangerous animals against you. They will leave you childless, Jerusalem. Plague and bloodshed will sweep through you, and I will bring a sword against you. I, Yahweh, have spoken."[j]

Prophecy against Israel's Idolatry

6 The word of the LORD came to me: [2]"Son of man, turn your face toward the mountains of Israel[k] and prophesy against them. [3]You are to say: Mountains of Israel, hear the word of the Lord GOD! This is what the Lord GOD says to the mountains and the hills, to the ravines and the valleys: I am about to bring a sword against you, and I will destroy your ·high places.[l] [4]Your altars will be desolated and your incense altars smashed. I will throw down your slain in front of your idols. [5]I will lay the corpses of the Israelites in front of their idols and scatter your bones around your altars. [6]Wherever you live the cities will be in ruins and the high places will be desolate, so that your altars will lie in ruins and be desecrated,[C] your idols smashed and obliterated, your incense altars cut down, and your works wiped out. [7]The slain will fall among you, and you will know that I am ·Yahweh.

[8]"Yet I will leave a remnant when you are scattered among the nations, for throughout the countries there will be some of you who will escape the sword.[m] [9]Then your survivors will remember Me among the nations where they are taken captive,[n] how I was crushed by their promiscuous hearts that turned away from Me and by their eyes that lusted after their idols.[o] They will loathe themselves because of the evil things they did,[p] their detestable practices of every kind. [10]And they will know that I am the LORD; I did not threaten to bring this disaster on them without a reason.

Lament over the Fall of Jerusalem

[11]"This is what the Lord GOD says: Clap your hands, stamp your feet,[q] and cry out over all the evil and detestable practices of the house of Israel, who will fall by the sword, famine, and plague.[r] [12]The one who is far off will die by plague; the one who is near will fall by the sword; and the one who remains and is spared[D] will die of famine. In this way I will exhaust My wrath on them.[s] [13]You will all know that I am Yahweh when their slain lie among their idols around their altars,[t] on every high hill,[u] on all the mountaintops, and under every green tree and every leafy oak — the places where they offered pleasing aromas to all their idols. [14]I will stretch out My hand against them,[v] and wherever they live I will make the land a desolate waste,

[a]**5:9** Dn 9:12; Am 3:2
[b]**5:10** Lv 26:29; Dt 28:53-57; Jr 19:9
[c]**5:11** Jr 7:9-11; Ezk 8:5-6,16
[d]Ezk 7:20; 11:18,21
[e]**5:12** Jr 15:2; 21:9; Ezk 5:17; 6:11-12
[f]Jr 15:2; 43:10-11; 44:27
[g]**5:13** Is 1:24
[h]Ezk 36:5-6; 38:19
[i]**5:15** Ps 79:3-10; Ezk 22:4
[j]**5:17** Lv 26:6; Dt 32:23-25
[k]**6:2** Ezk 36:1
[l]**6:3-4** Lv 26:30
[m]**6:8** Jr 44:14,28; Ezk 7:16
[n]**6:9** Dt 4:29
[o]Ps 78:40
[p]Ezk 20:43; 36:31
[q]**6:11** Ezk 21:14,17; 25:6
[r]Ezk 5:12
[s]**6:12** Ezk 5:13
[t]**6:13** Ezk 6:4-7
[u]Is 57:5-7; Jr 2:20; Ezk 20:28; Hs 4:13
[v]**6:14** Is 5:25

[A]**5:10** Lit *you* [B]**5:15** DSS, LXX, Syr, Tg, Vg; MT reads *she* [C]**6:6** Hb obscure [D]**6:12** Or *besieged*

from the wilderness to Diblah.[A] Then they will know that I am Yahweh."

Announcement of the End

7 And the word of the LORD came to me:
[2]"Son of man, this is what the Lord GOD
says to the land of Israel:

An end! The end has come
on the four corners of the land.[a]
[3] The end is now upon you;
I will send My anger against you
and judge you according to your ways.
I will punish you for all
your detestable practices.
[4] I will not look on you with pity
or spare you,[b]
but I will punish you for your ways[c]
and for your detestable practices
within you.
Then you will know that I am
·Yahweh."[d]

[5]This is what the Lord GOD says:

Look, one disaster after another
is coming![e]
[6] An end has come; the end has come!
It has awakened against you.
Look, it is coming!
[7] Doom[B] has come on you,[f]
inhabitants of the land.
The time has come; the day is near.
There will be panic on the mountains
and not celebration.[g]
[8] I will pour out My wrath on you
very soon;[h]
I will exhaust My anger against you
and judge you according to your ways.
I will punish you for all your
detestable practices.
[9] I will not look on you with pity
or spare you.
I will punish you for your ways
and for your detestable practices
within you.
Then you will know
that it is I, Yahweh, who strikes.

[10] Look, the day is coming!
Doom has gone out.[i]
The rod has blossomed;[j]
arrogance has bloomed.[k]
[11] Violence has grown into a rod
of wickedness.[l]
None of them will remain:
none of their multitude,
none of their wealth,
and none of the eminent[C] among them.
[12] The time has come; the day has arrived.
Let the buyer not rejoice[m]
and the seller not mourn,
for wrath is on all her masses.[n]
[13] The seller will certainly not return
to what was sold
as long as he and the buyer
remain alive.[D]
For the vision concerning all its people
will not be revoked,
and none of them will preserve
his life because of his iniquity.
[14] They have blown the trumpet[o]
and prepared everything,
but no one goes to war,
for My wrath is on all her masses.
[15] The sword is on the outside;[p]
plague and famine are on the inside.
Whoever is in the field will die
by the sword,
and famine and plague will devour
whoever is in the city.
[16] The survivors among them will escape[q]
and live on the mountains
like doves of the valley,
all of them moaning,
each over his own iniquity.
[17] All their hands will become weak,[r]
and all their knees will turn to water.
[18] They will put on ·sackcloth,
and horror will overwhelm them.
Shame will cover all their faces,
and all their heads will be bald.[s]
[19] They will throw their silver
into the streets,
and their gold will seem like
something filthy.[t]
Their silver and gold will be unable
to save them

[a]7:2 Am 8:2,10 [b]7:4 Ezk 5:11 [c]Ezk 11:21 [d]Ezk 6:7,14 [e]7:5 2Kg 21:12-13 [f]7:7 Ezk 7:10 [g]Jl 2:1-2; Am 5:18-20; Zph 1:14-15 [h]7:8 Ezk 20:8,21 [i]7:10 Ezk 7:7 [j]Nm 17:8 [k]Is 10:5; Mt 24:32-33 [l]7:11 Ps 73:8; 125:3 [m]7:12 Pr 20:14 [n]Is 24:2 [o]7:14 Nm 10:9 [p]7:15 Jr 14:18; Ezk 6:11-12 [q]7:16 Ezk 6:8; 14:22 [r]7:17 Is 13:7; Ezk 21:7 [s]7:18 Is 15:2-3; Am 8:10 [t]7:19 Is 2:20; 30:22

[A]6:14 Some Hb mss, some LXX mss read *Riblah*; 2Kg 23:33; Jr 39:5
[B]7:7 Hb obscure [C]7:11 Some Hb mss, Syr, Vg read *and no rest*
[D]7:13 Lit *sold, while still in life is their life*

in the day of the LORD's wrath.[a]
They will not satisfy their appetites
or fill their stomachs,
for these were the stumbling blocks[b]
that brought about their iniquity.
20 He appointed His beautiful ornaments
for majesty,
but[A] they made their abhorrent images
from them,
their detestable things.[c]
Therefore, I have made these
into something filthy for them.
21 I will hand these things over
to foreigners as plunder[d]
and to the wicked of the earth as spoil,
and they will profane them.
22 I will turn My face from the wicked
as they profane My treasured place.
Violent men will enter it and profane it.

23 Forge the chain,[e]
for the land is filled with crimes
of bloodshed,
and the city is filled with violence.[f]
24 So I will bring the most evil of nations[g]
to take possession of their houses.
I will put an end to the pride
of the strong,
and their sacred places
will be profaned.[h]
25 Anguish is coming!
They will seek peace,
but there will be none.
26 Disaster after disaster will come,[i]
and there will be rumor after rumor.[j]
Then they will seek a vision
from a prophet,[k]
but instruction will perish
from the priests
and counsel from the elders.[l]
27 The king will mourn;
the prince will be clothed in grief;
and the hands of the people of the land
will tremble.
I will deal with them according to
their own conduct,
and I will judge them
by their own standards.[m]
Then they will know that I am Yahweh.

[a]**7:19** Pr 11:4; Zph 1:18 [b]Ezk 14:3 [c]**7:20** Jr 7:30; Ezk 16:17 [d]**7:21** 2Kg 24:13 [e]**7:23** Jr 27:2 [f]Ezk 8:17; 9:9 [g]**7:24** Ezk 21:31; 28:7 [h]2Ch 7:20; Ezk 24:21 [i]**7:26** Is 47:11; Jr 4:20 [j]Ezk 21:7 [k]Jr 21:2; 37:17 [l]Ps 74:9; Mc 3:6 [m]**7:27** Mt 7:2 [n]**8:1** Ezk 14:1; 20:1 [o]Ezk 1:3 [p]**8:2** Ezk 1:27 [q]Ezk 1:4,27 [r]**8:3** Ezk 11:1,24; 40:2; 2Co 12:1-4 [s]Ex 20:4; Dt 32:16 [t]**8:4** Ezk 9:3 [u]Ezk 1:28; 3:22-23 [v]**8:6** Ezk 5:11; 8:9,17; 23:4-5 [w]**8:10** Ex 20:4; Dt 4:16-18; Rm 1:23 [x]**8:11** Nm 11:16,25; Lk 10:1

Visionary Journey to Jerusalem

8 In the sixth year, in the sixth month, on
the fifth day of the month, I was sitting
in my house and the elders of Judah were sitting in front of me,[n] and there the hand of the
Lord GOD came down on me.[o] 2 I looked, and
there was a form that had the appearance of
a man.[B] From what seemed to be His waist
down was fire, and from His waist up was
something that looked bright,[p] like the gleam
of amber.[q] 3 He stretched out what appeared
to be a hand and took me by the hair of my
head. Then the Spirit lifted me up between
earth and heaven and carried me in visions of
God[r] to Jerusalem, to the entrance of the inner gate that faces north, where the offensive
statue that provokes jealousy[s] was located. 4 I
saw the glory of the God of Israel[t] there, like
the vision I had seen in the plain.[u]

Pagan Practices in the Temple

5 The LORD said to me, "Son of man, look toward the north." I looked to the north, and
there was this offensive statue north of the
altar gate, at the entrance. 6 He said to me,
"Son of man, do you see what they are doing
here, more detestable things that the house
of Israel is committing,[v] so that I must depart
from My sanctuary? You will see even more
detestable things."
7 Then He brought me to the entrance of
the court, and when I looked there was a
hole in the wall. 8 He said to me, "Son of man,
dig through the wall." So I dug through the
wall, and there was a doorway. 9 He said to
me, "Go in and see the terrible and detestable
things they are committing here." 10 I went in
and looked, and there engraved all around
the wall was every form of detestable thing,
crawling creatures and beasts, as well as all
the idols of the house of Israel.[w]
11 Seventy elders from the house of Israel
were standing before them, with Jaazaniah
son of Shaphan[x] standing among them. Each
had a firepan in his hand, and a fragrant
cloud of incense was rising up. 12 Then He
said to me, "Son of man, do you see what the
elders of the house of Israel are doing in the
darkness, each at the shrine of his idol? For
they are saying, 'The LORD does not see us.

[A]**7:20** Or *They turned their beautiful ornaments into objects of pride, and* [B]**8:2** LXX; MT, Vg read *of fire*

The LORD has abandoned the land.'"[a] 13 Again He said to me, "You will see even more detestable things, which they are committing."

14 So He brought me to the entrance of the north gate of the LORD's house, and I saw women sitting there weeping for Tammuz. 15 And He said to me, "Do you see this, son of man? You will see even more detestable things than these."

16 So He brought me to the inner court of the LORD's house, and there were about 25 men at the entrance of the LORD's temple, between the portico and the altar,[b] with their backs to the LORD's temple and their faces turned to the east.[c] They were bowing to the east in worship of the sun.[d] 17 And He said to me, "Do you see this, son of man? Is it not enough for the house of Judah to commit the detestable things they are practicing here, that they must also fill the land with violence[e] and repeatedly provoke Me to anger,[f] even putting the branch to their nose?[A,B] 18 Therefore I will respond with wrath.[g] I will not show pity or spare them.[h] Though they cry out in My ears with a loud voice,[i] I will not listen to them."

Vision of Slaughter in Jerusalem

9 Then He called to me directly with a loud voice, "Come near, executioners of the city, each of you with a destructive weapon in his hand." 2 And I saw six men coming from the direction of the Upper Gate,[j] which faces north, each with a war club in his hand. There was another man among them, clothed in linen,[k] with writing equipment at his side. They came and stood beside the bronze altar.

3 Then the glory of the God of Israel[l] rose from above the ·cherub where it had been, to the threshold of the temple. He called to the man clothed in linen with the writing equipment at his side. 4 "Pass throughout the city of Jerusalem," the LORD said to him, "and put a mark on the foreheads[m] of the men who sigh and groan[n] over all the detestable practices committed in it."

5 He spoke as I listened to the others, "Pass through the city after him and start killing; do not show pity or spare them![o] 6 Slaughter the old men, the young men and women, as well as the older women and little children,[p] but do not come near anyone who has the mark.[q] Now begin at My sanctuary."[r] So they began with the elders who were in front of the temple. 7 Then He said to them, "Defile the temple and fill the courts with the slain.[s] Go!" So they went out killing people in the city.

8 While they were killing, I was left alone. And I fell facedown and cried out, "Oh, Lord GOD![t] Are You going to destroy the entire remnant of Israel when You pour out Your wrath on Jerusalem?"

9 He answered me: "The iniquity of the house of Israel and Judah is extremely great; the land is full of bloodshed,[u] and the city full of perversity. For they say, 'The LORD has abandoned the land;[v] He does not see.'[w] 10 But as for Me, I will not show pity or spare them.[x] I will bring their actions down on their own heads."[y] 11 Then the man clothed in linen with the writing equipment at his side reported back, "I have done as You commanded me."

God's Glory Leaves the Temple

10 Then I looked, and there above the expanse over the heads[z] of the ·cherubim was something like sapphire[C] stone resembling the shape of a throne that appeared above them. 2 The LORD spoke to the man clothed in linen and said, "Go inside the wheelwork beneath the cherubim. Fill your hands with hot coals from among the cherubim and scatter them over the city."[aa] So he went in as I watched.

3 Now the cherubim were standing to the south of the temple when the man went in, and the cloud[ab] filled the inner court.[ac] 4 Then the glory of the LORD rose from above the cherub to the threshold of the temple.[ad] The temple was filled with the cloud,[ae] and the court was filled with the brightness of the LORD's glory.[af] 5 The sound of the cherubim's wings could be heard as far as the outer court; it was like the voice of ·God Almighty when He speaks.

6 After the LORD commanded the man clothed in linen, saying, "Take fire from inside the wheelwork, from among the cherubim," the man went in and stood beside a wheel. 7 Then the cherub reached out his

[a] 8:12 Ps 14:1; Is 29:15; Ezk 9:9
[b] 8:16 Jl 2:17
[c] Jr 2:27; 32:33
[d] Dt 4:19; 17:3
[e] 8:17 Ezk 7:11,23; 9:9
[f] Jr 7:18-19
[g] 8:18 Ezk 5:13
[h] Ezk 5:11
[i] Mc 3:4
[j] 9:2 2Kg 15:35; Jr 20:2
[k] Lv 16:4
[l] 9:3 Ezk 10:4,18; 11:22-23
[m] 9:4 Rv 7:2-3; 9:4; 14:1
[n] Ps 119:53,136; Jr 13:17
[o] 9:5 Ezk 5:11
[p] 9:6 2Ch 36:17
[q] Rv 9:4
[r] Jr 25:29
[s] 9:7 Ezk 7:20-22
[t] 9:8 Ezk 11:13
[u] 9:9 2Kg 21:16
[v] Ezk 8:12
[w] Is 29:15
[x] 9:10 Ezk 5:11; 7:4; 8:18
[y] Ezk 11:21
[z] 10:1 Ezk 1:22,26
[aa] 10:2 Ezk 1:13; Rv 8:5
[ab] 10:3 1Kg 8:10-11
[ac] Ezk 8:3,16
[ad] 10:4 Ezk 9:3; 10:18; 11:22-23; 43:2-5; 44:4
[ae] Ex 40:34-35; Is 6:1-4; Rv 15:8
[af] Ezk 1:28; Hg 2:7

[A] 8:17 Ancient Jewish tradition reads *My nose* [B] 8:17 Possibly a pagan ritual or a euphemism for offensive behavior [C] 10:1 Or *lapis lazuli*

hand to the fire that was among them. He
took some, and put it into the hands of the
man clothed in linen, who took it and went
out. 8 The cherubim appeared to have the
form of human hands under their wings.[a]
9 I looked, and there were four wheels beside the cherubim,[b] one wheel beside each
cherub. The luster of the wheels was like the
gleam of beryl.[c] 10 In appearance, all four had
the same form, like a wheel within a wheel.
11 When they moved, they would go in any of
the four directions,[d] without pivoting as they
moved. But wherever the head faced, they
would go in that direction,[A] without pivoting
as they went. 12 Their entire bodies,[e] including their backs, hands, wings, and the wheels
that the four of them had, were full of eyes all
around.[f] 13 As I listened the wheels were called
"the wheelwork." 14 Each one had four faces:[g]
the first face was that of a cherub, the second
that of a man, the third that of a lion, and the
fourth that of an eagle.
15 The cherubim ascended; these were the
living creatures I had seen by the Chebar
Canal.[h] 16 When the cherubim moved, the
wheels moved beside them, and when they
lifted their wings to rise from the earth, even
then the wheels did not veer away from them.
17 When the cherubim stood still,[i] the wheels
stood still, and when they ascended, the
wheels ascended with them, for the spirit of
the living creatures was in them.
18 Then the glory of the LORD moved away
from the threshold of the temple[j] and stood
above the cherubim.[k] 19 The cherubim lifted
their wings and ascended from the earth
right before my eyes;[l] the wheels were beside
them as they went. The glory of the God of
Israel was above them, and it stood at the
entrance to the eastern gate of the LORD's
house.
20 These were the living creatures I had
seen[m] beneath the God of Israel by the Chebar Canal,[n] and I recognized that they were
cherubim. 21 Each had four faces and each had
four wings,[o] with the form of human hands
under their wings. 22 Their faces looked like
the same faces I had seen[p] by the Chebar Canal. Each creature went straight ahead.

[a] 10:8 Ezk 1:8
[b] 10:9 Ezk 1:15-17
[c] Dn 10:6
[d] 10:11 Ezk 1:17
[e] 10:12 Rv 4:6,8
[f] Ezk 1:18
[g] 10:14 Ezk 1:6,10; 10:21
[h] 10:15 Ezk 1:3,5
[i] 10:17 Ezk 1:21
[j] 10:18 Ezk 10:4
[k] Ps 18:10
[l] 10:19 Ezk 11:22
[m] 10:20 Ezk 1:5,22,26; 10:15
[n] Ezk 1:1
[o] 10:21 Ezk 1:6,8; 10:14; 41:18-19
[p] 10:22 Ezk 1:10
[q] 11:1 Ezk 3:12,14; 8:3
[r] 11:2 Gn 6:5; Ps 36:4; Pr 14:2; Mc 2:1
[s] 11:3 Jr 29:28; Am 3:15; Zph 1:13
[t] Jr 1:13; Ezk 24:3,6
[u] 11:5 Jr 17:10; Ezk 2:2
[v] 11:6 Ezk 7:23; 22:2-6,9,12,27
[w] 11:7 Ezk 24:3-13; Mc 3:2-3
[x] Ezk 11:9
[y] 11:8 Pr 10:24; Is 66:4
[z] Jb 3:25; Is 24:17-18
[aa] 11:9 Ezk 5:8
[ab] 11:10 Jr 39:6; 52:9-10
[ac] 2Kg 14:25
[ad] 11:11 Ezk 11:3,7
[ae] 11:12 Ezk 8:10,14,16
[af] 11:13 Ac 5:5
[ag] Ezk 9:8

Vision of Israel's Corrupt Leaders

11 The Spirit then lifted me up[q] and
brought me to the eastern gate of the
LORD's house, which faces east, and at the
gate's entrance were 25 men. Among them I
saw Jaazaniah son of Azzur, and Pelatiah son
of Benaiah, leaders of the people. 2 The LORD
said to me, "Son of man, these are the men
who plan evil[r] and give wicked advice in this
city. 3 They are saying, 'Isn't the time near to
build houses?[B,s] The city is the pot,[t] and we are
the meat.' 4 Therefore, prophesy against them.
Prophesy, son of man!"
5 Then the Spirit of the LORD came on me,
and He told me, "You are to say: This is what
the LORD says: That is what you are thinking,
house of Israel; and I know the thoughts that
arise in your mind.[u] 6 You have multiplied
your slain in this city,[v] filling its streets with
the dead.
7 "Therefore, this is what the Lord GOD says:
The slain you have put within it are the meat,[w]
and the city is the pot, but I[C] will remove you
from it.[x] 8 You fear the sword,[y] so I will bring
the sword against you."[z] This is the declaration of the Lord GOD. 9 "I will bring you out
of the city and hand you over to foreigners;
I will execute judgments against you.[aa] 10 You
will fall by the sword,[ab] and I will judge you
at the border of Israel.[ac] Then you will know
that I am ·Yahweh. 11 The city will not be a pot
for you,[ad] and you will not be the meat within
it. I will judge you at the border of Israel, 12 so
you will know that I am Yahweh, whose statutes you have not followed and whose ordinances you have not practiced. Instead, you
have acted according to the ordinances of the
nations around you."[ae]
13 Now while I was prophesying, Pelatiah
son of Benaiah died.[af] Then I fell facedown
and cried out with a loud voice: "Oh, Lord
GOD![ag] Will You bring to an end the remnant
of Israel?"

Promise of Israel's Restoration

14 The word of the LORD came to me again:
15 "Son of man, your own relatives, those who
have the right to redeem you,[D,E] and the entire
house of Israel, all of them, are those that the

[A] 10:11 Lit *go after it* [B] 11:3 Or *The time is not near to build houses.* [C] 11:7 Some Hb mss, LXX, Syr, Tg, Vg; other Hb mss read *He* [D] 11:15 LXX, Syr read *your relatives, your fellow exiles* [E] 11:15 Or *own brothers, your relatives* residents of Jerusalem have said this to, 'Stay away from the LORD; this land has been given to us as a possession.'

16 "Therefore say: This is what the Lord GOD says: Though I sent them far away among the nations and scattered them among the countries, yet for a little while I have been a sanctuary for them[a] in the countries where they have gone.

17 "Therefore say: This is what the Lord GOD says: I will gather you from the peoples[b] and assemble you from the countries where you have been scattered, and I will give you the land of Israel.

18 "When they arrive there, they will remove all its[c] detestable things[d] and practices from it. 19 And I will give them one heart[e] and put a new spirit within them; I will remove their heart of stone[f] from their bodies[A] and give them a heart of flesh,[g] 20 so they may follow My statutes,[h] keep My ordinances, and practice them. Then they will be My people, and I will be their God.[i] 21 But as for those whose hearts pursue their desire for detestable things and practices, I will bring their actions down on their own heads."[j] This is the declaration of the Lord GOD.

God's Glory Leaves Jerusalem

22 Then the •cherubim, with the wheels beside them, lifted their wings,[k] and the glory of the God of Israel was above them. 23 The glory of the LORD[l] rose up from within the city and stood on the mountain[m] east of the city.[B,n] 24 The Spirit lifted me up[o] and brought me to Chaldea and to the exiles in a vision from the Spirit of God. After the vision I had seen left me, 25 I spoke to the exiles about all the things the LORD had shown me.

Ezekiel Dramatizes the Exile

12 The word of the LORD came to me: 2 "Son of man, you are living among a rebellious house.[p] They have eyes to see but do not see, and ears to hear but do not hear,[q] for they are a rebellious house.[r]

3 "Son of man, get your bags ready for exile and go into exile in their sight during the day. You will go into exile from your place to another place while they watch; perhaps they will understand, though they are a rebellious house. 4 During the day, bring out your bags like an exile's bags while they look on. Then in the evening go out in their sight like those going into exile. 5 As they watch, dig through the wall and take the bags out through it. 6 And while they look on, lift the bags to your shoulder and take them out in the dark; cover your face so that you cannot see the land. For I have made you a sign to the house of Israel."[s]

7 So I did just as I was commanded. In the daytime I brought out my bags like an exile's bags. In the evening I dug through the wall by hand; I took them out in the dark, carrying them on my shoulder in their sight.

8 Then the word of the LORD came to me in the morning: 9 "Son of man, hasn't the house of Israel, that rebellious house,[t] asked you, 'What are you doing?'[u] 10 Say to them: This is what the Lord GOD says: This •oracle is about the prince[C] in Jerusalem and all the house of Israel who are living there.[D] 11 You are to say, 'I am a sign for you. Just as I have done, so it will be done to them; they will go into exile,[v] into captivity.' 12 The prince who is among[w] them will lift his bags to his shoulder in the dark and go out. They[E] will dig through the wall to bring him out through it. He will cover his face so he cannot see the land with his eyes. 13 But I will spread My net over him, and he will be caught in My snare. I will bring him to Babylon, the land of the Chaldeans, yet he will not see it,[x] and he will die there. 14 I will also scatter all the attendants who surround him and all his troops to every direction of the wind,[y] and I will draw a sword to chase after them. 15 They will know that I am •Yahweh[z] when I disperse them among the nations and scatter them among the countries.[aa] 16 But I will spare a few of them from the sword,[ab] famine, and plague so they can tell about all their detestable practices among the nations where they go. Then they will know that I am Yahweh."

Ezekiel Dramatizes Israel's Anxiety

17 The word of the LORD came to me: 18 "Son of man, eat your bread with[ac] trembling and drink your water with shaking and anxiety. 19 Then say to the people of the land: This is

[a] **11:16** Is 8:14
[b] **11:17** Ezk 20:34,41-42; 28:25
[c] **11:18** Ezk 37:23
[d] Ezk 5:11
[e] **11:19** Jr 32:39
[f] Zch 7:12
[g] Ps 51:10; Jr 31:33; Ezk 36:26; 2Co 3:3
[h] **11:20** Ps 105:45; Ezk 36:27
[i] Ezk 36:28
[j] **11:21** Ezk 9:10
[k] **11:22** Ezk 10:19
[l] **11:23** Ezk 8:4
[m] Zch 14:4
[n] **11:22-23** Ezk 10:4
[o] **11:24** Ezk 8:3
[p] **12:2** Ezk 2:3,5
[q] Jr 5:21
[r] Ezk 2:5-8
[s] **12:6** Ezk 4:3; 24:24
[t] **12:9** Ezk 2:5-8
[u] Ezk 17:12; 20:49; 24:19
[v] **12:11** Jr 15:2; 52:15,28-30
[w] **12:12** 2Kg 25:1-7; Jr 39:4; 52:7
[x] **12:13** Jr 39:7; 52:11
[y] **12:14** Ezk 5:2; 17:21
[z] **12:15** Ezk 6:7,14
[aa] Ezk 22:15; 29:12; 30:23
[ab] **12:16** Ezk 6:8-9
[ac] **12:18** Ezk 4:16

[A] **11:19** Lit *flesh* [B] **11:23** = the Mount of Olives [C] **12:10** = King Zedekiah [D] **12:10** Lit *are among them* [E] **12:12** LXX, Syr read *He*

what the Lord GOD says about the residents of
Jerusalem in the land of Israel: They will eat
their bread with anxiety and drink their water in dread, for their[A,B] land will be stripped
of everything[a] in it because of the violence
of all who live there. 20 The inhabited cities
will be destroyed, and the land will become
a desolation. Then you will know that I am
Yahweh."

A Deceptive Proverb Stopped

21 Again the word of the LORD came to me:
22 "Son of man, what is this proverb you people have about the land of Israel,[b] which goes:

> The days keep passing by,[c]
> and every vision fails?

23 Therefore say to them: This is what the
Lord GOD says: I will put a stop to this proverb, and they will not use it again in Israel.[d]
But say to them: The days draw near,[e] as well
as the fulfillment of every vision. 24 For there
will no longer be any false vision or flattering
·divination[f] within the house of Israel. 25 But
I, Yahweh, will speak whatever message I will
speak, and it will be done.[g] It will no longer be
delayed.[h] For in your days, rebellious house,
I will speak a message and bring it to pass."
This is the declaration of the Lord GOD.

26 The word of the LORD came to me: 27 "Son
of man, notice that the house of Israel is saying, 'The vision that he sees concerns many
years from now;[i] he prophesies about distant
times.' 28 Therefore say to them: This is what
the Lord GOD says: None of My words will be
delayed any longer. The message I speak will
be fulfilled." This is the declaration of the
Lord GOD.

Israel's False Prophets Condemned

13 The word of the LORD came to me:
2 "Son of man, prophesy against the
prophets of Israel who[j] are prophesying. Say
to those who prophesy out of their own imagination:[k] Hear the word of the LORD! 3 This is
what the Lord GOD says: Woe to the foolish
prophets who follow their own spirit and
have seen nothing. 4 Your prophets, Israel, are
like jackals among ruins. 5 You did not go up to
the gaps[l] or restore the wall around the house
of Israel so that it might stand in battle on the
day of the LORD. 6 They see false visions and
speak lying ·divinations.[m] They claim, 'This is
the LORD's declaration,' when the LORD did
not send them,[n] yet they wait for the fulfillment of their message. 7 Didn't you see a false
vision and speak a lying divination when you
proclaimed, 'This is the LORD's declaration,'
even though I had not spoken?

8 "Therefore, this is what the Lord GOD
says: I am against you because you have spoken falsely and had lying visions." This is the
declaration of the Lord GOD. 9 "My hand will
be against the prophets who see false visions
and speak lying divinations.[o] They will not
be present in the fellowship of My people or
be recorded in the register of the house of
Israel, and they will not enter the land of Israel. Then you will know that I am the Lord
·Yahweh.

10 "Since they have led My people astray
saying, 'Peace,'[p] when there is no peace, for
when someone builds a wall they plaster it
with whitewash,[q] 11 therefore, tell those who
plaster it that it will fall. Torrential rain will
come,[r] and I will send hailstones plunging[C]
down, and a windstorm will be released.
12 Now when the wall has fallen, will you not
be asked, 'Where is the coat of whitewash
that you put on it?'

13 "So this is what the Lord GOD says: I will
release a windstorm in My wrath. Torrential
rain will come in My anger, and hailstones
will fall in destructive fury. 14 I will tear down
the wall you plastered with whitewash and
knock it to the ground so that its foundation
is exposed.[s] The city will fall, and you will
be destroyed within it. Then you will know
that I am Yahweh. 15 After I exhaust My wrath
against the wall and against those who plaster it with whitewash, I will say to you: The
wall is no more and neither are those who
plastered it — 16 those prophets of Israel who
prophesied to Jerusalem and saw a vision of
peace for her when there was no peace."[t] This
is the declaration of the Lord GOD.

17 "Now, son of man, turn[D] toward the
women of your people who prophesy[u] out
of their own imagination. Prophesy against
them[v] 18 and say: This is what the Lord GOD

[a] **12:19** Zch 7:14
[b] **12:22** Ezk 16:44; 18:2-3
[c] Jr 5:12; Ezk 11:3; 12:27; 2Pt 3:4,9
[d] **12:23** Ezk 18:3
[e] Zph 1:14
[f] **12:24** Ezk 13:6,23
[g] **12:25** Is 14:24
[h] Is 7:16
[i] **12:27** Ezk 12:22; Dn 10:14
[j] **13:2** Ezk 22:25,28
[k] Jr 23:16,26
[l] **13:5** Ps 106:23; Ezk 22:30
[m] **13:6** Ezk 22:28
[n] Jr 14:14; 23:21; 28:15
[o] **13:9** Jr 20:3-6; 28:15-17
[p] **13:10** Jr 6:14; 8:11; 14:13; Mc 3:5
[q] Ezk 22:28; Mt 23:27; Ac 23:3
[r] **13:11** Ezk 38:22; Mt 7:27
[s] **13:14** 1Co 3:10-15
[t] **13:16** Jr 6:14; 8:11
[u] **13:17** Jdg 4:4; 2Kg 22:14; Ac 21:9
[v] Ezk 13:2

[A] **12:19** Lit *its* [B] **12:19** = Jerusalem's [C] **13:11** One Hb ms, LXX, Vg; other Hb mss read *and you, hailstones, will plunge* [D] **13:17** Lit *set your face*

says: Woe to the women who sew magic bands on the wrist of every hand and who make veils for the heads of people of every height in order to ensnare lives. Will you ensnare the lives of My people but preserve your own?[a] [19]You profane Me in front of My people for handfuls of barley[b] and scraps of bread; you kill those who should not die and spare those who should not live, when you lie to My people, who listen to lies.

[20]"Therefore, this is what the Lord GOD says: I am against your magic bands that you ensnare people with like birds, and I will tear them from your arms. I will free the people you have ensnared like birds. [21]I will also tear off your veils and deliver My people from your hands,[c] so that they will no longer be prey in your hands. Then you will know that I am Yahweh. [22]Because you have disheartened the righteous person with lies, even though I have not caused him grief,[d] and because you have encouraged the wicked[e] person not to turn from his evil way to save his life, [23]therefore you will no longer see false visions or practice divination.[f] I will deliver My people from your hands. Then you will know that I am Yahweh."

Idolatrous Elders Punished

14 Some of the elders of Israel came[g] to me and sat down in front of me.[h] [2]Then the word of the LORD came to me: [3]"Son of man, these men have set up idols in their hearts and have put sinful stumbling blocks before their faces.[i] Should I be consulted by them at all?[j]

[4]"Therefore, speak to them and tell them: This is what the Lord GOD says: When anyone from the house of Israel sets up idols in his heart, puts a sinful stumbling block before his face, and then comes to the prophet, I, •Yahweh, will answer him appropriately.[A] I will answer him according to his many idols, [5]so that I may take hold of the house of Israel by their hearts. They are all estranged from Me because of their idols.

[6]"Therefore, say to the house of Israel: This is what the Lord GOD says: Repent and turn away[k] from your idols; turn your faces away from all your detestable things. [7]For when anyone from the house of Israel or from the foreigners who reside in Israel separates himself from Me, setting up idols in his heart and putting a sinful stumbling block before his face, and then comes to the prophet to inquire of Me,[B] I, Yahweh, will answer him Myself. [8]I will turn against that one and make him a sign and a proverb; I will cut him off from among My people.[l] Then you will know that I am Yahweh.

[9]"But if the prophet is deceived and speaks a message, it was I, Yahweh, who deceived that prophet.[m] I will stretch out My hand against him and destroy him from among My people Israel.[n] [10]They will bear their punishment — the punishment of the one who inquires will be the same as that of the prophet — [11]in order that the house of Israel may no longer stray from following Me and no longer defile themselves[o] with all their transgressions. Then they will be My people and I will be their God."[p] This is the declaration of the Lord GOD.

Four Devastating Judgments

[12]The word of the LORD came to me: [13]"Son of man, if a land sins against Me by acting faithlessly, and I stretch out My hand against it to cut off its supply of bread,[q] to send famine through it, and to wipe out both man and animal from it, [14]even if these three men[r] — Noah,[s] Daniel,[t] and Job[u] — were in it, they would deliver only themselves by their righteousness." This is the declaration of the Lord GOD.

[15]"If I allow dangerous animals[v] to pass through the land and depopulate it so that it becomes desolate, with no one passing through it for fear of the animals, [16]even if these three men were in it, as I live" — the declaration of the Lord GOD — "they could not deliver their sons or daughters. They alone would be delivered, but the land would be desolate.[w]

[17]"Or if I bring a sword[x] against that land and say: Let a sword pass through it, so that I wipe out both man and animal from it,[y] [18]even if these three men were in it, as I live" — the declaration of the Lord GOD — "they could not deliver their sons or daughters, but they alone would be delivered.

[a]**13:18** 2Pt 2:14 [b]**13:19** Pr 28:21; Mc 3:5 [c]**13:21** Ps 91:3; 124:7 [d]**13:22** Jr 28:15 [e]Jr 23:14 [f]**13:23** Mc 3:5-6 [g]**14:1** Ezk 8:1; 20:1 [h]Ezk 33:31-32 [i]**14:3** Ezk 7:19 [j]Ezk 20:3,31 [k]**14:6** 1Sm 7:3; Neh 1:9; Is 2:20; 30:22; 55:6-7; Ezk 18:30 [l]**14:8** Is 65:15; Jr 44:11; Ezk 5:15; 15:7 [m]**14:9** Jdg 9:23; 1Sm 16:14; 1Kg 22:23; Jr 20:7; 2Th 2:11 [n]Jr 6:14-15; 14:15 [o]**14:11** Ezk 11:18; 37:23 [p]Ezk 36:28 [q]**14:13** Lv 26:26; Is 3:1; Ezk 4:16 [r]**14:14** Jr 15:1 [s]Gn 6:8 [t]Ezk 28:3; Dn 1:6 [u]Jb 1:1,5; 42:8-9 [v]**14:15** Lv 26:22; Nm 21:6; 2Kg 17:25; Ezk 5:17 [w]**14:16** Gn 19:29; Ezk 18:20 [x]**14:17** Lv 26:25; Ezk 5:12; 21:3-4 [y]Ezk 25:13; Zph 1:3

[A]**14:4** Alt Hb tradition reads *him who comes* [B]**14:7** Lit *Me for himself*

19"Or if I send a plague into that land[a] and pour out My wrath on it with bloodshed to wipe out both man and animal from it, 20even if Noah, Daniel, and Job were in it, as I live"—the declaration of the Lord GOD—"they could not deliver their son or daughter. They would deliver only themselves by their righteousness.

21"For this is what the Lord GOD says: How much worse will it be when I send My four[b] devastating judgments against Jerusalem—sword, famine, dangerous animals, and plague—in order to wipe out both man and animal from it! 22Even so, there will be survivors left in it, sons and daughters who will be brought out. Indeed, they will come out to you, and you will observe their conduct and actions.[c] Then you will be consoled about the devastation I have brought on Jerusalem, about all I have brought on it. 23They will bring you consolation when you see their conduct and actions, and you will know that it was not without cause that I have done what I did to it."[d] This is the declaration of the Lord GOD.

Parable of the Useless Vine

15 Then the word of the LORD came to me: 2"Son of man, how does the wood of the vine,[e] that branch among the trees of the forest, compare to any other wood? 3Can wood be taken from it to make something useful? Or can anyone make a peg from it to hang things on? 4In fact, it is put into the fire as fuel.[f] The fire devours both of its ends, and the middle is charred. Can it be useful for anything? 5Even when it was whole it could not be made into a useful object. How much less can it ever be made into anything useful when the fire has devoured it and it is charred!

6"Therefore, this is what the Lord GOD says: Like the wood of the vine among the trees of the forest, which I have given to the fire as fuel, so I will give up the residents of Jerusalem. 7I will turn against them.[g] They may have escaped from the fire, but it will still consume them.[h] And you will know that I am •Yahweh when I turn against them. 8I will make the land desolate because they have acted unfaithfully." This is the declaration of the Lord GOD.

Parable of God's Adulterous Wife

16 The word of the LORD came to me again: 2"Son of man, explain Jerusalem's detestable practices to her.[i] 3You are to say: This is what the Lord GOD says to Jerusalem: Your origin and your birth were in the land of the Canaanites. Your father was an Amorite and your mother a Hittite.[j] 4As for your birth, your umbilical cord wasn't cut on the day you were born,[k] and you weren't washed •clean[A] with water. You were not rubbed with salt or wrapped in cloths.[l] 5No one cared enough about you to do even one of these things out of compassion for you. But you were thrown out into the open field because you were despised on the day you were born.

6"I passed by you and saw you lying in your blood, and I said to you as you lay in your blood: Live! Yes, I said to you as you lay in your blood: Live![B] 7I made you thrive[C] like plants of the field.[m] You grew up and matured and became very beautiful.[D] Your breasts were formed and your hair grew, but you were stark naked.

8"Then I passed by you and saw you, and you were indeed at the age for love. So I spread the edge of My garment over you and covered your nakedness.[n] I pledged Myself to you,[o] entered into a covenant with you, and you became Mine."[p] This is the declaration of the Lord GOD. 9"I washed you with water, rinsed off your blood, and anointed you with oil. 10I clothed you in embroidered cloth and provided you with leather sandals. I also wrapped you in fine linen and covered you with silk. 11I adorned you with jewelry, putting bracelets on your wrists and a chain around your neck. 12I put a ring in your nose,[q] earrings on your ears, and a beautiful tiara on your head. 13So you were adorned with gold and silver,[r] and your clothing was made of fine linen, silk, and embroidered cloth. You ate fine flour, honey, and oil. You became extremely beautiful and attained royalty. 14Your

[a]14:19 2Sm 24:15; Ezk 38:22
[b]14:21 Ezk 5:17; 33:27; Am 4:6-10; Rv 6:8
[c]14:22 Ezk 6:8; 12:16; 20:43; 36:20
[d]14:23 Jr 22:8-9
[e]15:2 Ps 80:8-16; Is 5:1-7; Hs 10:1
[f]15:4 Jn 15:6
[g]15:7 Ezk 14:8
[h]Is 24:18
[i]16:2 Is 58:1; Ezk 20:4; 22:2
[j]16:3 Dt 7:1; Jdg 3:5; 1Kg 9:20-21; Ezk 16:45
[k]16:4 Hs 2:3
[l]Lk 2:12
[m]16:7 Ex 1:7
[n]16:8 Ru 3:9; Jr 2:2
[o]Gn 22:16-18
[p]Ex 19:5; 24:7-8
[q]16:11-12 Gn 24:22,47
[r]16:13 Dt 32:13-14; Ps 45:13-14

A16:4 Hb obscure B16:6 Some Hb mss, LXX, Syr omit *Yes, I said to you as you lay in your blood: Live!* C16:7 LXX reads *Thrive; I made you* D16:7 Or matured *and developed the loveliest of ornaments* fame spread among the nations because of your beauty, for it was perfect through My splendor,[a] which I had bestowed on you." This is the declaration of the Lord GOD.

15 "But you were confident in your beauty and acted like a prostitute because of your fame.[b] You lavished your sexual favors on everyone who passed by.[c] Your beauty became his.[A] 16 You took some of your garments and made colorful ·high places for yourself, and you engaged in prostitution on them. These places should not have been built, and this should never have happened![A] 17 You also took your beautiful jewelry made from the gold and silver I had given you,[d] and you made male images so that you could engage in prostitution with them. 18 Then you took your embroidered garments to cover them, and set My oil and incense before them. 19 You also set before them as a pleasing aroma the food I gave you — the fine flour, oil, and honey that I fed you.[e] That is what happened." This is the declaration of the Lord GOD.

20 "You even took your sons and daughters you bore to Me and sacrificed them to these images as food.[f] Wasn't your prostitution enough? 21 You slaughtered My children and gave them up when you passed them through the fire[g] to the images. 22 In all your detestable practices and acts of prostitution, you did not remember the days of your youth[h] when you were stark naked and lying in your blood.

23 "Then after all your evil — Woe, woe to you!" — the declaration of the Lord GOD — 24 "you built yourself a mound and made yourself an elevated place in every square.[i] 25 You built your elevated place at the head of every street[j] and turned your beauty into a detestable thing. You spread your legs to everyone who passed by and increased your prostitution. 26 You engaged in promiscuous acts with Egyptian men, your well-endowed neighbors, and increased your prostitution[k] to provoke Me to anger.

27 "Therefore, I stretched out My hand against you and reduced your provisions. I gave you over to the desire of those who hate you, the Philistine women,[l] who were embarrassed by your indecent behavior. 28 Then you engaged in prostitution with the Assyrian men because you were not satisfied.[m] Even though you did this with them, you were still not satisfied. 29 So you extended your prostitution to Chaldea,[n] the land of merchants, but you were not even satisfied with this!

30 "How your heart was inflamed with lust" — the declaration of the Lord GOD — "when you did all these things, the acts of a brazen prostitute, 31 building your mound at the head of every street and making your elevated place in every square. But you were unlike a prostitute because you scorned payment.[o] 32 You adulterous wife, who receives strangers instead of her husband! 33 Men give gifts to all prostitutes, but you gave gifts to all your lovers. You bribed them to come to you from all around for your sexual favors. 34 So you were the opposite of other women in your acts of prostitution; no one solicited you. When you paid a fee instead of one being paid to you, you were the opposite.

35 "Therefore, you prostitute, hear the word of the LORD! 36 This is what the Lord GOD says: Because your lust was poured out and your nakedness exposed by your acts of prostitution with your lovers, and because of all your detestable idols and the blood of your children that you gave to them,[p] 37 I am therefore going to gather all the lovers you pleased[q] — all those you loved as well as all those you hated. I will gather them against you from all around and expose your nakedness[r] to them so they see you completely naked. 38 I will judge you the way adulteresses and those who shed blood are judged.[s] Then I will bring about your bloodshed in wrath and jealousy.[t] 39 I will hand you over to them, and they will level your mounds and tear down your elevated places. They will strip off your clothes,[u] take your beautiful jewelry, and leave you stark naked. 40 They will bring a mob against you[v] to stone you and cut you to pieces with their swords. 41 Then they will burn down your houses and execute judgments against you in the sight of many women. I will stop you from being a prostitute,[w] and you will never again pay fees for lovers. 42 So I will satisfy My wrath against you,[x] and My jealousy will turn away from

[a] **16:14** Lm 2:15
[b] **16:15** Is 57:8; Jr 2:20
[c] Pr 7:8-13
[d] **16:17** Ex 12:35; 32:2-4
[e] **16:19** Hs 2:8
[f] **16:20** Jr 7:31; 19:5; Ezk 23:37
[g] **16:21** Lv 18:21; Dt 18:10; 2Kg 17:17; Ezk 20:31
[h] **16:22** Jr 2:2
[i] **16:24** Jr 11:13
[j] **16:25** Pr 9:14
[k] **16:26** Ezk 23:19-20
[l] **16:27** Ezk 16:57
[m] **16:28** 2Kg 16:7,10-18; 2Ch 28:16,20-23; Jr 2:18,36
[n] **16:29** Ezk 23:14-16
[o] **16:31** Is 52:3
[p] **16:36** Jr 2:34
[q] **16:37** Jr 13:22,26; Ezk 23:9,22
[r] Is 47:3
[s] **16:38** Ezk 23:45
[t] Gn 9:6; Ezk 23:25
[u] **16:39** Ezk 23:26; Hs 2:3
[v] **16:40** Ezk 23:47
[w] **16:41** Ezk 23:48
[x] **16:42** Ezk 5:13; 21:17

[A] **16:15,16** Hb obscure

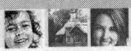

you. Then I will be silent and no longer angry. 43 Because you did not remember the
days[a] of your youth but enraged Me with all
these things, I will also bring your actions
down on your own head."[b] This is the declaration of the Lord GOD. "Haven't you committed immoral acts in addition to all your
detestable practices?
44 "Look, everyone who uses proverbs will
say this proverb about you:

Like mother, like daughter.

45 You are the daughter of your mother, who
despised her husband and children. You are
the sister of your sisters,[c] who despised their
husbands and children. Your mother was a
Hittite and your father an Amorite.[d] 46 Your
older sister was Samaria,[e] who lived with
her daughters to the north of you, and your
younger sister was Sodom, who lived with
her daughters to the south of you. 47 Didn't
you walk in their ways and do their detestable
practices? It was only a short time before you
behaved more corruptly than they did.[A,f]
48 "As I live"—the declaration of the Lord
GOD—"your sister Sodom and her daughters have not behaved as you and your daughters have.[g] 49 Now this was the iniquity of
your sister Sodom: she and her daughters
had pride, plenty of food,[h] and comfortable
security, but didn't support the poor and
needy. 50 They were haughty and did detestable things before Me, so I removed them
when I saw this.[B,i] 51 But Samaria did not commit even half your sins. You have multiplied
your detestable practices beyond theirs and
made your sisters appear righteous by all the
detestable things you have committed. 52 You
must also bear your disgrace, since you have
been an advocate for your sisters. For they
appear more righteous than you because of
your sins, which you committed more abhorrently than they did. So you also, be ashamed
and bear your disgrace, since you have made
your sisters appear righteous.
53 "I will restore their fortunes,[j] the fortunes
of Sodom and her daughters and those of Samaria and her daughters. I will also restore[C]
your fortunes among them,[k] 54 so you will
bear your disgrace and be ashamed of all you
did when you comforted them.[l] 55 As for your
sisters, Sodom and her daughters and Samaria and her daughters will return to their
former state. You and your daughters will
also return to your former state. 56 Didn't you
treat your sister Sodom as an object of scorn
when you were proud, 57 before your wickedness was exposed? It was like the time you
were scorned by the daughters of Aram[D,m]
and all those around her, and by the daughters of the Philistines—those who treated
you with contempt from every side. 58 You
yourself must bear the consequences of your
indecency and detestable practices"[n]—this is
the LORD's declaration.
59 "For this is what the Lord GOD says: I will
deal with you according to what you have
done, since you have despised the oath by
breaking the covenant.[o] 60 But I will remember the covenant I made with you in the days
of your youth, and I will establish an everlasting covenant with you.[p] 61 Then you will
remember your ways[q] and be ashamed when
you[E] receive your older and younger sisters. I
will give them to you as daughters, but not because of your covenant. 62 I will establish My
covenant with you,[r] and you will know that
I am •Yahweh, 63 so that when I make •atone-
ment for all you have done, you will remember and be ashamed,[s] and never open your
mouth again because of your disgrace."[t] This
is the declaration of the Lord GOD.

Parable of the Eagles

17 The word of the LORD came to me:
2 "Son of man, pose a riddle and speak a
parable to the house of Israel.[u] 3 You are to say:
This is what the Lord GOD says:

A great eagle with great wings,[v]
long pinions,
and full plumage of many colors
came to Lebanon and took the top
of the cedar.[w]
4 He plucked off its topmost shoot,
brought it to the land of merchants,
and set it in a city of traders.
5 Then he took some of the land's seed
and put it in a fertile field;[x]

[a] 16:43 Ps 78:42
[b] Ezk 11:21; 22:31
[c] 16:45 Ezk 23:2
[d] Ezk 16:31
[e] 16:46 Ezk 23:4,33
[f] 16:47 Ezk 5:6
[g] 16:48 Mt 10:15; 11:23-24
[h] 16:49 Gn 13:10
[i] 16:50 Gn 18:20-21
[j] 16:53 Is 1:9
[k] Jr 20:16
[l] 16:54 Ezk 14:22-23
[m] 16:57 2Kg 16:5-7
[n] 16:58 Ezk 23:49
[o] 16:59 Ezk 17:19
[p] 16:60 Is 55:3; Jr 32:38-41
[q] 16:61 Ezk 6:9
[r] 16:62 Hs 2:19-20
[s] 16:63 Ezk 36:31-32
[t] Rm 3:19
[u] 17:2 Ezk 20:49; 24:3
[v] 17:3 Jr 48:40
[w] Ezk 17:12
[x] 17:5 Dt 8:7-9

[A] 16:47 Lit *they in all your ways* [B] 16:50 Or *them as you have seen* [C] 16:53 LXX, Vg; MT reads *Samaria and her daughters and the fortunes of* [D] 16:57 Some Hb mss, Syr read *Edom* [E] 16:61 Some LXX mss, Syr read *I*

he set it like a willow,[a]
a plant[A] by abundant waters.
6 It sprouted and became
a spreading vine,
low in height with its branches turned
toward him,[b]
yet its roots stayed under it.
So it became a vine,
produced branches,
and sent out shoots.
7 But there was another great eagle
with great wings and thick plumage.
And this vine bent its roots
toward him!
It stretched out its branches to him
from its planting bed,[c]
so that he might water it.
8 It had been planted
in a good field by abundant waters
in order to produce branches,
bear fruit, and become a splendid vine.

9You are to say: This is what the Lord GOD
says:

Will it flourish?
Will he not tear out its roots[d]
and strip off its fruit
so that it shrivels?
All its fresh leaves will wither!
Great strength and many people
will not be needed to pull it
from its roots.
10 Even though it is planted,
will it flourish?
Won't it completely wither
when the east wind strikes it?[e]
It will wither on the bed
where it sprouted."

11The word of the LORD came to me: 12"Now
say to that rebellious house:[f] Don't you know
what these things mean? Tell them: The king
of Babylon came to Jerusalem, took its king
and officials,[g] and brought them back with
him to Babylon. 13He took one of the royal
family[h] and made a covenant with him, putting him under oath.[i] Then he took away
the leading men of the land, 14so the kingdom might be humble and not exalt itself[j]
but might keep his covenant in order to endure. 15However, this king revolted against
him[k] by sending his ambassadors to Egypt so
they might give him horses and a large army.[l]
Will he flourish? Will the one who does such
things escape? Can he break a covenant and
still escape?

16"As I live"—this is the declaration of the
Lord GOD—"he will die in Babylon, in the
land of the king who put him on the throne,[m]
whose oath he despised and whose covenant
he broke. 17Pharaoh will not help him with
his great army and vast horde in battle,[n] when
ramps are built and siege walls constructed to
destroy many lives. 18He despised the oath by
breaking the covenant. He did all these things
even though he gave his hand in pledge.[o] He
will not escape!"

19Therefore, this is what the Lord GOD says:
"As I live, I will bring down on his head My
oath that he despised and My covenant that
he broke. 20I will spread My net over him,[p]
and he will be caught in My snare.[q] I will
bring him to Babylon and execute judgment
on him there for the treachery he committed against Me.[r] 21All the fugitives[B] among his
troops will fall by the sword, and those who
survive will be scattered to every direction of
the wind.[s] Then you will know that I, •Yah-
weh, have spoken."

22This is what the Lord GOD says:

I will take a sprig
from the lofty top of the cedar
and plant it.[t]
I will pluck a tender sprig
from its topmost shoots,
and I will plant it
on a high towering mountain.
23 I will plant it on Israel's high mountain[u]
so that it may bear branches,
produce fruit,
and become a majestic cedar.
Birds of every kind will nest under it,[v]
taking shelter in the shade
of its branches.
24 Then all the trees of the field will know
that I am Yahweh.
I bring down the tall tree,
and make the low tree tall.[w]
I cause the green tree to wither

[a]**17:5** Is 44:4
[b]**17:6** Ezk 17:14
[c]**17:7** Ezk 31:4
[d]**17:9** 2Kg 25:7
[e]**17:10** Gn 41:6; 2Kg 19:26; Ezk 19:12; Hs 13:15; Jnh 4:8
[f]**17:12** Ezk 2:3-5; 12:9-11
[g]2Kg 24:11-15
[h]**17:13** 2Kg 24:17
[i]2Ch 36:13
[j]**17:14** Ezk 29:14
[k]**17:15** 2Kg 24:20; 2Ch 36:13
[l]Dt 17:16
[m]**17:16** Ezk 12:13
[n]**17:17** Jr 37:5,7
[o]**17:18** 1Ch 29:24
[p]**17:20** Ezk 12:13
[q]2Kg 25:5-6; Jr 39:5
[r]Ezk 20:35-36
[s]**17:21** Ezk 5:10
[t]**17:22** Ps 2:6
[u]**17:23** Ezk 20:40
[v]Dn 4:12
[w]**17:24** Is 40:4

[A]**17:5** Hb obscure [B]**17:21** Some Hb mss, LXX, Syr, Tg read *choice men*

and make the withered tree thrive.[a]
I, Yahweh, have spoken
and I will do it.[b]

Personal Responsibility for Sin

18 The word of the LORD came to me: 2 "What do you mean by using this proverb concerning the land of Israel:

The fathers eat sour grapes,[c]
and the children's teeth are set
on edge?[d]

3 As I live" — this is the declaration of the Lord GOD — "you will no longer use this proverb in Israel.[e] 4 Look, every life belongs to Me.[f] The life of the father is like the life of the son — both belong to Me. The person who sins is the one who will die.[g]

5 "Now suppose a man is righteous and does what is just and right: 6 He does not eat at the mountain shrines[h] or raise his eyes to the idols of the house of Israel. He does not defile his neighbor's wife[i] or come near a woman during her menstrual impurity.[j] 7 He doesn't oppress anyone[k] but returns his collateral to the debtor.[l] He does not commit robbery, but gives his bread to the hungry[m] and covers the naked with clothing. 8 He doesn't lend at interest or for profit[n] but keeps his hand from wrongdoing and carries out true justice between men.[o] 9 He follows My statutes and keeps My ordinances, acting faithfully. Such a person is righteous; he will certainly live."[p] This is the declaration of the Lord GOD.

10 "Now suppose the man has a violent son, who sheds blood[q] and does any of these things, 11 though the father has done none of them. Indeed, when the son eats at the mountain shrines and defiles his neighbor's wife, 12 and when he oppresses the poor and needy, commits robbery, and does not return collateral, and when he raises his eyes to the idols, commits detestable acts,[r] 13 and lends at interest or for profit, will he live? He will not live! Since he has committed all these detestable acts, he will certainly die. His blood will be on him.[s]

14 "Now suppose he has a son who sees all the sins his father has committed, and though he sees them, he does not do likewise. 15 He does not eat at the mountain shrines or raise his eyes to the idols of the house of Israel. He does not defile his neighbor's wife. 16 He doesn't oppress anyone, hold collateral, or commit robbery. He gives his bread to the hungry and covers the naked with clothing. 17 He keeps his hand from harming the poor, not taking interest or profit on a loan. He practices My ordinances and follows My statutes. Such a person will not die for his father's iniquity. He will certainly live.

18 "As for his father, he will die for his own iniquity because he practiced fraud, robbed his brother, and did what was wrong among his people.[t] 19 But you may ask, 'Why doesn't the son suffer punishment for the father's iniquity?'[u] Since the son has done what is just and right, carefully observing all My statutes, he will certainly live. 20 The person who sins is the one who will die.[v] A son won't suffer punishment for the father's iniquity, and a father won't suffer punishment for the son's iniquity.[w] The righteousness of the righteous person will be on him,[x] and the wickedness of the wicked person will be on him.[y]

21 "Now if the wicked person turns from all the sins he has committed,[z] keeps all My statutes, and does what is just and right, he will certainly live; he will not die. 22 None of the transgressions he has committed will be held against him.[aa] He will live because of the righteousness he has practiced.[ab] 23 Do I take any pleasure in the death of the wicked?"[ac] This is the declaration of the Lord GOD. "Instead, don't I take pleasure when he turns from his ways and lives? 24 But when a righteous person turns from his righteousness[ad] and practices iniquity, committing the same detestable acts that the wicked do, will he live? None of the righteous acts he did will be remembered.[ae] He will die because of the treachery he has engaged in and the sin he has committed.

25 "But you say, 'The Lord's way isn't fair.'[af] Now listen, house of Israel: Is it My way that is unfair? Instead, isn't it your ways that are unfair? 26 When a righteous person turns from his righteousness and practices iniquity, he will die for this. He will die because of the iniquity he has practiced. 27 But if a wicked person turns from the wickedness he has committed and does what is just and right, he will preserve his life. 28 He will certainly

[a] 17:24 Am 9:11
[b] Nm 14:35; Ps 33:9; Is 46:11; 55:11; Ezk 17:24; 22:14; 24:14; 36:36; 37:14
[c] 18:2 Lm 5:7
[d] Jr 31:29
[e] 18:3 Ezk 12:23
[f] 18:4 Nm 16:22; 27:16
[g] Dt 24:16; Ezk 18:20; Rm 6:23
[h] 18:6 Ezk 22:9
[i] Ex 20:17-18; Lv 20:10
[j] Lv 18:19-20
[k] 18:7 Ex 22:21
[l] Dt 24:12-13
[m] Mt 25:35-40
[n] 18:8 Ex 22:25; Lv 25:35-37
[o] Zch 8:16
[p] 18:9 Am 5:4
[q] 18:10 Nm 35:31
[r] 18:12 Ezk 8:6,17
[s] 18:13 Lv 20:9,11
[t] 18:18 Ezk 3:18
[u] 18:19 Ex 20:5
[v] 18:20 Ezk 18:4
[w] Dt 24:16; Jn 9:2
[x] Is 3:10-11
[y] Rm 2:6-9
[z] 18:21 Ezk 33:12,19
[aa] 18:22 Ezk 33:16
[ab] Ps 18:20-24
[ac] 18:23 Ezk 33:11
[ad] 18:24 Ezk 3:20; 33:18
[ae] 2Pt 2:20
[af] 18:25 Ezk 18:29; 33:17,20

live because he thought it over and turned
from all the transgressions he had committed; he will not die. 29 But the house of Israel
says, 'The Lord's way isn't fair.' Is it My ways
that are unfair, house of Israel? Instead, isn't
it your ways that are unfair?
30 "Therefore, house of Israel, I will judge
each one of you according to his ways."[a] This
is the declaration of the Lord GOD. "Repent
and turn from all your transgressions, so they
will not be a stumbling block that causes your
punishment. 31 Throw off all the transgressions you have committed, and get yourselves
a new heart and a new spirit.[b] Why should
you die, house of Israel? 32 For I take no pleasure in anyone's death." This is the declaration of the Lord GOD. "So repent and live!

A Lament for Israel's Princes

19 "Now, lament for the princes of Israel[c]
2 and say:

What was your mother? A lioness!
She lay down among the lions;
she reared her cubs
among the young lions.
3 She brought up one of her cubs,
and he became a young lion.[d]
After he learned to tear prey,
he devoured people.
4 When the nations heard about him,
he was caught in their pit.
Then they led him away with hooks
to the land of Egypt.[e]
5 When she saw that she waited in vain,
that her hope was lost,
she took another of her cubs
and made him a young lion.
6 He prowled among the lions,[f]
and he became a young lion.
After he learned to tear prey,
he devoured people.
7 He devastated their strongholds[A]
and destroyed their cities.
The land and everything
in it shuddered
at the sound of his roaring.
8 Then the nations from
the surrounding provinces
set out against him.[g]
They spread their net over him;
he was caught in their pit.
9 They put a wooden yoke on him[B]
with hooks[h]
and led him away to the king
of Babylon.
They brought him into the fortresses
so his roar could no longer be heard
on the mountains of Israel.[i]

10 Your mother was like a vine
in your vineyard,[C,j]
planted by the water;
it was fruitful and full of branches[k]
because of plentiful waters.
11 It had strong branches, fit for
the scepters of rulers;
its height towered among the clouds.[D]
So it was conspicuous for its height
as well as its many branches.
12 But it was uprooted in fury,[l]
thrown to the ground,
and the east wind dried up its fruit.
Its strong branches were torn off
and dried up;[m]
fire consumed them.
13 Now it is planted in the wilderness,[n]
in a dry and thirsty land.
14 Fire has gone out from its main branch[E]
and has devoured its fruit,
so that it no longer has a strong branch,
a scepter for ruling.[o]

This is a lament and should be used as a lament."

Israel's Rebellion

20 In the seventh year, in the fifth month,
on the tenth day of the month, some
of Israel's elders came to consult the LORD,[p]
and they sat down in front of me. 2 Then the
word of the LORD came to me: 3 "Son of man,
speak with the elders of Israel and tell them:
This is what the Lord GOD says: Are you coming to consult Me? As I live, I will not be consulted by you."[q] This is the declaration of the
Lord GOD.
4 "Will you pass judgment against them,
will you pass judgment, son of man? Explain

[a] 18:30 Ezk 7:3,8; 33:20
[b] 18:31 Jr 32:39
[c] 19:1 Ezk 26:17; 27:2
[d] 19:3 2Kg 23:31-32
[e] 19:4-5 2Kg 23:34
[f] 19:6 Jr 22:13-17
[g] 19:8 2Kg 24:2,11
[h] 19:9 2Ch 36:6
[i] Ezk 6:2
[j] 19:10 Ps 80:8-11
[k] Dt 8:7-9
[l] 19:12 Jr 31:28
[m] Hs 13:15
[n] 19:13 2Kg 24:12-16; Hs 2:3
[o] 19:14 Lm 2:5
[p] 20:1 Ezk 8:1,11-12; 14:1
[q] 20:3 Ezk 14:3

[A] 19:7 Tg, Aq; MT reads *knew their widows* [B] 19:9 Or *put him in a cage*
[C] 19:10 Some Hb mss; other Hb mss read *blood* [D] 19:11 Or *thick foliage*
[E] 19:14 Lit *from the branch of its parts*

the detestable practices of their fathers to them.[a] 5 Say to them: This is what the Lord GOD says: On the day I chose Israel, I swore an oath[A,b] to the descendants of Jacob's house and made Myself known to them in the land of Egypt. I swore to them, saying: I am •Yahweh your God.[c] 6 On that day I swore[B] to them that I would bring them out[d] of the land of Egypt into a land I had searched out for them, a land flowing with milk and honey,[e] the most beautiful of all lands.[f] 7 I also said to them: Each of you must throw away the detestable things that are before your eyes and not defile yourselves with the idols of Egypt.[g] I am Yahweh your God.[h]

8 "But they rebelled against Me and were unwilling to listen to Me. None of them threw away the detestable things that were before their eyes, and they did not forsake the idols of Egypt. So I considered pouring out My wrath on them,[i] exhausting My anger against them within the land of Egypt. 9 But I acted because of My name,[j] so that it would not be profaned in the eyes of the nations they were living among, in whose sight I had made Myself known to Israel by bringing them out of Egypt.

10 "So I brought them out of the land of Egypt and led them into the wilderness.[k] 11 Then I gave them My statutes and explained My ordinances to them—the person who does them will live by them.[l] 12 I also gave them My Sabbaths to serve as a sign between Me and them,[m] so they will know that I am Yahweh who sets them apart as holy.

13 "But the house of Israel rebelled against Me in the wilderness.[n] They did not follow My statutes and they rejected My ordinances—the person who does them will live by them.[o] They also completely profaned My Sabbaths.[p] So I considered pouring out My wrath on them in the wilderness to put an end to them.[q] 14 But I acted because of My name, so that it would not be profaned in the eyes of the nations in whose sight I had brought them out. 15 However, I swore[B] to them[r] in the wilderness that I would not bring them into the land I had given them—the most beautiful of all lands, flowing with milk and honey— 16 because they rejected My ordinances, profaned My Sabbaths, and did not follow My statutes. For their hearts went after their idols.[s] 17 But I spared them from destruction and did not bring them to an end in the wilderness.[t]

18 "Then I said to their children in the wilderness: Don't follow the statutes of your fathers, defile yourselves with their idols, or keep their ordinances.[u] 19 I am Yahweh your God. Follow My statutes, keep My ordinances, and practice them.[v] 20 Keep My Sabbaths holy,[w] and they will be a sign between Me and you, so you may know that I am Yahweh your God.

21 "But the children rebelled against Me.[x] They did not follow My statutes or carefully keep My ordinances—the person who does them will live by them. They also profaned My Sabbaths. So I considered pouring out My wrath on them and exhausting My anger against them in the wilderness. 22 But I withheld My hand and acted because of My name, so that it would not be profaned in the eyes of the nations in whose sight I brought them out. 23 However, I swore[B] to them in the wilderness that I would disperse them among the nations and scatter them among the countries.[y] 24 For they did not practice My ordinances but rejected My statutes and profaned My Sabbaths, and their eyes were fixed[z] on their fathers' idols. 25 I also gave them statutes that were not good and ordinances[aa] they could not live by. 26 When they made every firstborn pass through the fire,[ab] I defiled them through their gifts in order to devastate them so they would know that I am Yahweh.[ac]

27 "Therefore, son of man, speak to the house of Israel, and tell them: This is what the Lord GOD says: In this way also your fathers blasphemed Me by[ad] committing treachery against Me: 28 When I brought them into the land that I swore[B] to give them and they saw any high hill or leafy tree,[ae] they offered their sacrifices and presented their offensive offerings there. They also sent up their pleasing aromas and poured out their •drink offerings there. 29 So I asked them: What is this •high place you are going to? And it is called High Place to this day.

30 "Therefore say to the house of Israel: This is what the Lord GOD says: Are you defiling

[a] 20:4 Ezk 16:2; 22:2
[b] 20:5 Ex 6:6-8
[c] Ex 6:2-3
[d] 20:6 Jr 32:22
[e] Ex 3:8
[f] Ps 16:6; 48:2; 50:2; Jr 3:19
[g] 20:7 Lv 18:3
[h] Ex 20:2
[i] 20:8 Ezk 5:13; 7:8
[j] 20:9 Ezk 36:21-22
[k] 20:10 Ex 13:18,20
[l] 20:11 Lv 18:5; Rm 10:5; Gl 3:12
[m] 20:12 Ex 31:13
[n] 20:13 Nm 14:11-12,22
[o] Lv 18:5
[p] Ezk 22:8; 23:38; 44:24
[q] Ex 32:10; Dt 9:8
[r] 20:15 Nm 14:28-30
[s] 20:16 Ezk 11:21; 14:3-7
[t] 20:17 Ezk 11:13
[u] 20:18 Mt 15:1-3
[v] 20:19 Dt 5:32-33
[w] 20:20 Jr 17:22
[x] 20:21 Nm 21:5; 25:1-3
[y] 20:23 Lv 26:33
[z] 20:24 Ezk 6:9
[aa] 20:25 Ps 81:12; Rm 1:21-25,28
[ab] 20:26 Lv 18:21
[ac] Ezk 6:7
[ad] 20:27 Rm 2:24
[ae] 20:28 Ezk 6:13

A 20:5 Lit *I lifted My hand* B 20:6,15,23,28 Lit *lifted My hand* yourselves the way your fathers did,[a] and prostituting yourselves with their detestable things? 31 When you offer your gifts, making your children pass through the fire,[b] you continue to defile yourselves with all your idols to this day. So should I be consulted by you, house of Israel? As I live"—this is the declaration of the Lord GOD—"I will not be consulted by you!

Israel's Restoration

32 "When you say, 'Let us be like the nations, like the peoples of other countries, worshiping wood and stone,'[c] what you have in mind will never happen.[d] 33 As I live"—the declaration of the Lord GOD—"I will rule over you with a strong hand, an outstretched arm,[e] and outpoured wrath. 34 I will bring you from the peoples and gather you from the countries where you were scattered,[f] with a strong hand, an outstretched arm,[g] and outpoured wrath. 35 I will lead you into the wilderness of the peoples[h] and enter into judgment with you there face to face. 36 Just as I entered into judgment with your fathers in the wilderness of the land of Egypt,[i] so I will enter into judgment with you." This is the declaration of the Lord GOD. 37 "I will make you pass under the rod[j] and will bring you into the bond of the covenant. 38 And I will also purge you of those who rebel and transgress against Me.[k] I will bring them out of the land where they live as foreign residents, but they will not enter the land of Israel. Then you will know that I am Yahweh.

39 "As for you, house of Israel, this is what the Lord GOD says: Go and serve your idols, each of you. But afterward you will surely listen to Me, and you will no longer defile My holy name with your gifts and idols.[l] 40 For on My holy mountain, Israel's high mountain"—the declaration of the Lord GOD—"there the entire house of Israel, all of them,[m] will serve Me in the land. There I will accept them and will require your contributions and choicest gifts,[n] all your holy offerings. 41 When I bring you from the peoples and gather you from the countries where you have been scattered, I will accept you as a pleasing aroma. And I will demonstrate My holiness through you in the sight of the nations.[o] 42 When I lead you into the land of Israel, the land I swore[A] to give your fathers, you will know that I am Yahweh.[p] 43 There you will remember your ways and all your deeds that you have defiled yourselves with,[q] and you will loathe yourselves for all the evil things you have done.[r] 44 You will know that I am Yahweh,[s] house of Israel, when I have dealt with you because of My name[t] rather than according to your evil ways and corrupt acts." This is the declaration of the Lord GOD.

Fire in the South

45[B] The word of the LORD came to me: 46 "Son of man, face the south and preach against it. Prophesy against the forest land in the ·Negev,[u] 47 and say to the forest there: Hear the word of the LORD! This is what the Lord GOD says: I am about to ignite a fire in you, and it will devour every green tree and every dry tree in you. The blazing flame will not be extinguished, and every face from the south to the north will be scorched by it. 48 Then all people will see that I, Yahweh, have kindled it.[v] It will not be extinguished."

49 Then I said, "Oh, Lord GOD, they are saying of me, 'Isn't he just posing riddles?'"[w]

God's Sword of Judgment

21 [C] The word of the LORD came to me again: 2 "Son of man, turn your face toward[x] Jerusalem and preach against the sanctuaries. Prophesy against the land of Israel, 3 and say to it: This is what the LORD says: I am against you.[y] I will draw My sword from its sheath and cut off both the righteous and the wicked from you. 4 Since I will cut off[D] both the righteous and the wicked, My sword will therefore come out of its sheath against everyone from the south to the north.[z] 5 So all the people will know that I, ·Yahweh, have taken My sword from its sheath—it will not be sheathed again.[aa]

6 "But you, son of man, groan! Groan bitterly with a broken heart[E] right before their eyes. 7 And when they ask you, 'Why are you groaning?' then say: Because of the news that is coming.[ab] Every heart will melt, and every hand will become weak. Every spirit will be

[a] **20:30** Jdg 2:19; Jr 7:26; 16:12
[b] **20:31** Ezk 16:20
[c] **20:32** Dt 4:28; 2Kg 19:18; Rv 9:20
[d] Ezk 11:5
[e] **20:33** Jr 21:5
[f] **20:34** Jr 31:8; Ezk 36:24; 37:21
[g] Ex 6:6; Dt 4:34
[h] **20:35** Ezk 19:13
[i] **20:36** Nm 14:21-23,28
[j] **20:37** Lv 27:32; Jr 33:13
[k] **20:38** Ezk 34:17-22
[l] **20:39** Is 1:13-15; Ezk 23:38-39
[m] **20:40** Ezk 37:22,24
[n] Is 60:7; Ezk 43:27
[o] **20:41** Is 5:16; Ezk 28:25; 2Co 6:17
[p] **20:42** Ezk 36:23; 38:23
[q] **20:43** Ezk 6:9; 16:61,63
[r] Ezk 36:31
[s] **20:44** Ezk 24:24
[t] Ezk 36:22
[u] **20:46** Ezk 21:2
[v] **20:48** Jr 21:14
[w] **20:49** Ezk 17:2
[x] **21:2** Ezk 20:46
[y] **21:3** Ezk 5:8
[z] **21:4** Ezk 7:2; 20:47
[aa] **21:5** Ezk 21:30
[ab] **21:7** Ezk 7:26

[A] **20:42** Lit *lifted My hand* [B] **20:45** Ezk 21:1 in Hb [C] **21:1** Ezk 21:6 in Hb [D] **21:4** Lit *off from you* [E] **21:6** Lit *with broken loins*

discouraged, and every knee will turn to water. Yes, it is coming and it will happen." This is the declaration of the Lord GOD.

8 The word of the LORD came to me: 9 "Son of man, prophesy: This is what the Lord says! You are to proclaim:

A sword![a] A sword is sharpened
and also polished.[b]
10 It is sharpened for slaughter,
polished to flash like lightning!
Should we rejoice?
The scepter of My son,
the sword despises every tree.[A]
11 The sword is given to be polished,
to be grasped in the hand.
It is sharpened, and it is polished,
to be put in the hand of the slayer.[c]
12 Cry out and wail, son of man,
for it is against My people.
It is against all the princes of Israel!
They are given over to the sword
with My people.
Therefore strike your thigh in grief.[d]
13 Surely it will be a trial!
And what if the sword despises
even the scepter?
The scepter will not continue.[A]
This is the declaration
of the Lord GOD.

14 Therefore, son of man, prophesy
and clap your hands together.[e]
Let the sword strike two times,
even three.
It is a sword for massacre,
a sword for great massacre —
it surrounds[B] them!
15 I have appointed a sword[f] for slaughter[A]
at all their gates,
so that their hearts may melt
and many may stumble.
Yes! It is ready to flash like lightning;[g]
it is drawn[A] for slaughter.
16 Slash to the right;
turn to the left —
wherever your blade is directed.
17 I also will clap My hands together,
and I will satisfy My wrath.[h]
I, Yahweh, have spoken."

[a]21:9 Dt 32:41 [b]Jr 46:4 [c]21:11 Ezk 21:19 [d]21:12 Jr 31:19 [e]21:14 Nm 24:10 [f]21:15 Ezk 32:20 [g]Ezk 21:28 [h]21:17 Ezk 5:13 [i]21:20 Jr 49:2 [j]21:22 Ezk 4:2; 26:9 [k]21:23 Ezk 17:16,18 [l]21:25 2Kg 24:20 [m]Ezk 21:29 [n]21:26 Ezk 17:24; Lk 1:52 [o]21:27 Jr 23:5-6

18 Then the word of the LORD came to me:
19 "Now you, son of man, mark out two roads
that the sword of Babylon's king can take.
Both of them should originate from the same
land. And make a signpost at the fork in the
road to each city. 20 Mark out a road that the
sword can take to Rabbah of the Ammonites[i]
and to Judah into fortified Jerusalem. 21 For
the king of Babylon stands at the split in the
road, at the fork of the two roads, to practice
•divination: he shakes the arrows, consults the idols, and observes the liver. 22 The
answer marked[C] Jerusalem appears in his
right hand, indicating that he should set up
battering rams,[j] give the order to[D] slaughter,
raise a battle cry, set battering rams against
the gates, build a ramp, and construct a siege
wall. 23 It will seem like false divination in the
eyes of those who have sworn an oath to the
Babylonians,[E,k] but it will draw attention to
their •guilt so that they will be captured.

24 "Therefore, this is what the Lord GOD says: Because you have drawn attention to your guilt, exposing your transgressions, so that your sins are revealed in all your actions, since you have done this, you will be captured by them.

25 And you, profane and wicked prince
of Israel,[F,l]
the day has come[m]
for your punishment."[G]

26 This is what the Lord GOD says:

Remove the turban, and take off
the crown.
Things will not remain
as they are;[H]
exalt the lowly and bring down
the exalted.[n]
27 A ruin, a ruin,
I will make it a ruin!
Yet this will not happen
until He comes;[o]
I have given the judgment to Him.[I]

28 "Now prophesy, son of man, and say: This is what the Lord GOD says concerning the Ammonites and their contempt. You are to proclaim:

[A]21:10,13,15 Hb obscure [B]21:14 Or *penetrates* [C]21:22 Lit *The divination for* [D]21:22 Lit *rams, open the mouth in* [E]21:23 Lit *them* [F]21:25 = King Zedekiah [G]21:25 Lit *come in the time of the punishment of the end* [H]21:26 Lit *This not this* [I]21:27 Or *comes to whom it rightfully belongs, and I will give it to Him*

A sword! A sword
is drawn for slaughter,
polished to consume,[a] to flash
like lightning.
29 While they offer false visions[b]
and lying divinations about you,
the time has come to put you
to the necks of the profane
wicked ones;
the day has come
for your punishment.[A]
30 Return it to its sheath![c]
I will judge you[B]
in the place where you were created,
in the land of your origin.
31 I will pour out My indignation on you;
I will blow the fire of My fury on you.[d]
I will hand you over to brutal men,
skilled at destruction.
32 You will be fuel for the fire.
Your blood will be spilled in the land.
You will not be remembered,[e]
for I, Yahweh, have spoken."

Indictment of Sinful Jerusalem

22 The word of the LORD came to me:
2"As for you, son of man, will you pass
judgment? Will you pass judgment against
the city of blood? Then explain all her detestable practices to her.[f] 3You are to say: This
is what the Lord GOD says: A city that sheds
blood[g] within her walls so that her time of
judgment has come and who makes idols for
herself so that she is defiled! 4You are •guilty
of the blood you have shed,[h] and you are defiled from the idols you have made. You have
brought your judgment days near and have
come to your years of punishment. Therefore,
I have made you a disgrace to the nations and
a mockery to all the lands. 5Those who are
near and those far away from you will mock
you, you infamous one full of turmoil.
6"Look, every prince of Israel[i] within you
has used his strength to shed blood. 7Father
and mother are treated with contempt,[j] and
the foreign resident is exploited within you.
The fatherless and widow are oppressed in
you.[k] 8You despise My holy things and profane My Sabbaths.[l] 9There are men within you
who slander in order to shed blood.[m] People
who live in you eat at the mountain shrines;
they commit immoral acts within you. 10Men
within you have sexual intercourse with their
father's wife and violate women during their
menstrual impurity.[n] 11One man within you
commits a detestable act with his neighbor's
wife;[o] another wickedly defiles his daughter-
in-law; and yet another violates his sister, his
father's daughter.[p] 12People who live in you
accept bribes in order to shed blood.[q] You
take interest and profit on a loan and brutally
extort your neighbors.[r] You have forgotten
Me."[s] This is the declaration of the Lord GOD.
13"Now look, I clap My hands together
against the dishonest profit you have made[t]
and against the blood shed among you.
14Will your courage endure[u] or your hands
be strong in the days when I deal with you? I,
•Yahweh, have spoken, and I will act.[v] 15I will
disperse you among the nations and scatter
you among the countries;[w] I will purge your
uncleanness.[x] 16You[C] will be profaned in the
sight of the nations. Then you will know that
I am Yahweh."[y]

Jerusalem as God's Furnace

17The word of the LORD came to me: 18"Son
of man, the house of Israel has become dross
to Me.[z] All of them are copper, tin, iron, and
lead inside the furnace;[aa] they are the dross of
silver. 19Therefore, this is what the Lord GOD
says: Because all of you have become dross, I
am about to gather you into Jerusalem. 20Just
as one gathers silver, copper, iron, lead, and
tin into the furnace to blow fire[ab] on them
and melt them, so I will gather you in My anger and wrath, put you inside, and melt you.
21Yes, I will gather you together and blow on
you with the fire of My fury, and you will be
melted within the city. 22As silver is melted
inside a furnace, so you will be melted inside
the city. Then you will know that I, Yahweh,
have poured out My wrath on you."[ac]

Indictment of a Sinful Land

23The word of the LORD came to me: 24"Son
of man, say to her: You are a land that has not
been cleansed,[ad] that has not received rain
in the day of indignation. 25The conspiracy

[a]21:28 Is 31:8; Jr 12:12; 46:10,14
[b]21:29 Ezk 13:6-9; 22:28
[c]21:30 Jr 47:6-7
[d]21:31 Ezk 22:20-21
[e]21:32 Ezk 25:10
[f]22:2 Ezk 16:2; 20:4
[g]22:3 Ezk 22:6,27; 23:37,45
[h]22:4 2Kg 21:16
[i]22:6 Is 1:23
[j]22:7 Ex 20:12; Lv 20:9; Dt 27:16
[k]Ex 22:22
[l]22:8 Lv 19:30; Ezk 20:13
[m]22:9 Lv 19:16
[n]22:10 Lv 18:7-8,19
[o]22:11 Ex 20:17; Ezk 18:11
[p]Lv 18:9,15; 20:17
[q]22:12 Ex 23:8
[r]Lv 19:13; 25:36; Dt 23:19
[s]Ezk 23:35
[t]22:13 Ezk 21:14,17
[u]22:14 Ezk 21:7
[v]Ezk 17:24
[w]22:15 Dt 4:27; Ezk 12:15
[x]Ezk 23:27,48
[y]22:16 Ps 83:18; Ezk 6:7
[z]22:18 Ps 119:119; Is 1:22
[aa]Pr 17:3
[ab]22:20 Is 1:25
[ac]22:22 Ezk 20:8,33
[ad]22:24 Ezk 24:13

[A]21:29 Lit *come in the time of the punishment of the end* [B]21:30 = the Ammonites [C]22:16 One Hb ms, LXX, Syr, Vg read *I*

of her prophets[a] within her is[A] like a roaring
lion tearing its prey: they devour people, seize
wealth and valuables, and multiply the widows within her. 26 Her priests do violence to
My instruction and profane My holy things.[b]
They make no distinction between the holy
and the common, and they do not explain
the difference between the •clean and the
•unclean.[c] They disregard[B] My Sabbaths, and
I am profaned among them.
27 "Her officials within her are like wolves
tearing their prey, shedding blood, and destroying lives in order to make profit dishonestly. 28 Her prophets plaster with whitewash
for them by seeing false visions and lying
•divinations,[d] and they say, 'This is what the
Lord GOD says,' when the LORD has not spoken. 29 The people of the land have practiced
extortion and committed robbery.[e] They have
oppressed the poor and needy and unlawfully
exploited the foreign resident. 30 I searched
for a man among them who would repair the
wall[f] and stand in the gap before Me on behalf of the land so that I might not destroy
it,[g] but I found no one. 31 So I have poured out
My indignation on them and consumed them
with the fire of My fury. I have brought their
actions down on their own heads."[h] This is
the declaration of the Lord GOD.

The Two Immoral Sisters

23 The word of the LORD came to me
again: 2 "Son of man, there were two
women,[i] daughters of the same mother, 3 who
acted like prostitutes in Egypt,[j] behaving
promiscuously in their youth. Their breasts
were fondled there, and their virgin nipples
caressed. 4 The older one was named Oholah,[C]
and her sister was Oholibah.[D] They became
Mine and gave birth to sons and daughters.
As for their names, Oholah represents Samaria and Oholibah represents Jerusalem.
5 "Oholah acted like a prostitute even
though she was Mine. She lusted after her lovers, the Assyrians:[k] warriors 6 dressed in blue,
governors and prefects, all of them desirable
young men, horsemen riding on steeds. 7 She
offered her sexual favors to them; all of them
were the elite of Assyria. She defiled herself
with all those she lusted after and with all
their idols. 8 She didn't give up her promiscuity that began in Egypt,[l] when men slept with
her in her youth, caressed her virgin nipples,
and poured out their lust on her. 9 Therefore,
I handed her over to her lovers,[m] the Assyrians she lusted for. 10 They exposed her nakedness, seized her sons and daughters, and
killed her with the sword. Since they executed
judgment against her, she became notorious
among women.
11 "Now her sister Oholibah saw this, but
she was even more depraved in her lust than
Oholah, and made her promiscuous acts
worse than those of her sister.[n] 12 She lusted
after the Assyrians:[o] governors and prefects,
warriors splendidly dressed, horsemen riding on steeds, all of them desirable young
men. 13 And I saw that she had defiled herself;
both of them had taken the same path. 14 But
she increased her promiscuity when she
saw male figures carved on the wall,[p] images
of the Chaldeans, engraved in vermilion,[q]
15 wearing belts on their waists and flowing
turbans on their heads; all of them looked
like officers, a depiction of the Babylonians in
Chaldea, the land of their birth. 16 At the sight
of them[E] she lusted after them and sent messengers to them in Chaldea.[r] 17 Then the Babylonians came to her,[s] to the bed of love, and
defiled her with their lust. But after she was
defiled by them, she turned away from them
in disgust. 18 When she flaunted her promiscuity and exposed her nakedness, I turned
away from her in disgust just as I turned away
from her sister.[t] 19 Yet she multiplied her acts
of promiscuity, remembering the days of her
youth when she acted like a prostitute in the
land of Egypt 20 and lusted after their lovers,
whose sexual members were like those of
donkeys and whose emission was like that
of stallions. 21 So you revisited the indecency
of your youth, when the Egyptians caressed
your nipples to enjoy your youthful breasts.[u]
22 "Therefore Oholibah, this is what the
Lord GOD says: I am going to incite your lovers against you, those you turned away from
in disgust. I will bring them against you from
every side: 23 the Babylonians and all the Chaldeans; Pekod, Shoa, and Koa;[v] and all the Assyrians with them — desirable young men, all

[a] **22:25** Jr 11:9; Hs 6:9
[b] **22:26** 1Sm 2:12-17,22
[c] Lv 10:10
[d] **22:28** Ezk 13:10-15
[e] **22:29** Ezk 9:9; 22:7
[f] **22:30** Ezk 13:5
[g] Ex 32:11-14; Ps 106:23
[h] **22:31** Ezk 7:3,8-9; 9:10
[i] **23:2** Ezk 16:46
[j] **23:3** Lv 17:7; Jr 3:9
[k] **23:5** 2Kg 15:19; 16:7; 17:3; Ezk 16:28; Hs 5:13; 8:9-10
[l] **23:8** Ex 32:4; 1Kg 12:28; 2Kg 10:29; 17:16
[m] **23:9** Ezk 16:37; 23:22
[n] **23:11** Jr 3:8-11; Ezk 16:51
[o] **23:12** 2Kg 16:7-20
[p] **23:14** Ezk 8:10
[q] Ezk 16:29
[r] **23:16** Is 57:9
[s] **23:17** 2Kg 24:17
[t] **23:18** Ps 78:59; 106:40; Jr 12:8
[u] **23:21** Ezk 16:26
[v] **23:23** Jr 50:21

[A] **22:24-25** LXX reads *indignation*, [25] *whose princes within her are* [B] **22:26** Lit *close their eyes from* [C] **23:4** = Her Tent [D] **23:4** = My Tent Is in Her [E] **23:16** Lit *of her eyes*

of them governors and prefects, officers and administrators, all of them riding on horses.
[24]They will come against you with an alliance of nations and with weapons, chariots, and[A] wagons. They will set themselves against you on every side with shields, bucklers, and helmets. I will delegate judgment to them, and they will judge you by their own standards.
[25]When I vent My jealous rage on you,[a] they will deal with you in wrath. They will cut off your nose and ears, and your descendants will fall by the sword. They will seize your sons and daughters, and your descendants will be consumed by fire. [26]They will strip off your clothes and take your beautiful jewelry.[b]
[27]So I will put an end to your indecency and sexual immorality, which began in the land of Egypt, and you will not look longingly at them or remember Egypt anymore.
[28]"For this is what the Lord GOD says: I am going to hand you over to those you hate, to those you turned away from in disgust.
[29]They will treat you with hatred, take all you have worked for, and leave you stark naked,[c] so that the shame of your debauchery will be exposed, both your indecency and promiscuity. [30]These things will be done to you because you acted like a prostitute with the nations,[d] defiling yourself with their idols. [31]You have followed the path of your sister, so I will put her cup in your hand."[e]
[32]This is what the Lord GOD says:

You will drink your sister's cup,[f]
which is deep and wide.
You will be an object of[B] ridicule
and scorn,
for it holds so much.[g]
[33] You will be filled with drunkenness
and grief,
with a cup of devastation and desolation,
the cup of your sister Samaria.
[34] You will drink it and drain it;
then you will gnaw its broken pieces,
and tear your breasts.
For I have spoken.
This is the declaration
of the Lord GOD.

[35]Therefore, this is what the Lord GOD says: "Because you have forgotten Me[h] and cast Me behind your back,[i] you must bear the consequences of your indecency and promiscuity."
[36]Then the LORD said to me: "Son of man, will you pass judgment against Oholah and Oholibah?[j] Then declare their detestable practices to them.[k] [37]For they have committed adultery, and blood is on their hands; they have committed adultery with their idols. They have even made the children they bore to Me pass through the fire as food for the idols.[l] [38]They also did this to Me: they defiled My sanctuary[m] on that same day and profaned My Sabbaths.[n] [39]On the same day they slaughtered their children for their idols, they entered My sanctuary to profane it.[o] Yes, that is what they did inside My house.
[40]"In addition, they sent for men who came from far away when a messenger was dispatched to them. And look how they came! You bathed, painted your eyes,[p] and adorned yourself with jewelry for them.[q] [41]You sat on a luxurious couch with a table spread before it,[r] on which you had set My incense and oil.
[42]The sound of a carefree crowd was there. Drunkards[C] from the desert were brought in, along with common men. They put bracelets on the women's hands and beautiful crowns on their heads. [43]Then I said concerning this woman worn out by adultery: Will they now have illicit sex with her, even her? [44]Yet they had sex with her as one does with a prostitute. This is how they had sex with Oholah and Oholibah, those obscene women. [45]But righteous men will judge them the way adulteresses[s] and those who shed blood are judged, for they are adulteresses and blood is on their hands.
[46]"This is what the Lord GOD says: Summon[D] an assembly against them and consign them to terror and plunder.[t] [47]The assembly will stone them and cut them down with their swords.[u] They will kill their sons and daughters and burn their houses with fire.
[48]So I will put an end to indecency in the land, and all the women will be admonished not to imitate your indecent behavior. [49]They will repay you for your indecency,[v] and you will bear the consequences for your sins of idolatry. Then you will know that I am the Lord Yahweh."

[a]**23:25** Ex 34:14; Ezk 5:13; 8:17-18; Zph 1:18
[b]**23:26** Ezk 16:39
[c]**23:29** Ezk 16:7,22,39
[d]**23:30** Ezk 6:9
[e]**23:31** 2Kg 21:13; Jr 7:14-15
[f]**23:32** Ps 75:8; Is 51:17; Jr 25:15; Lm 4:21; Hab 2:16; Zch 12:2; Mt 20:22; 26:39; Rv 14:10
[g]Ezk 22:4-5
[h]**23:35** Is 17:10; Jr 3:21; Ezk 22:12; Hs 8:14; 13:6
[i]1Kg 14:9; Jr 2:27; 32:33
[j]**23:36** Jr 1:10; Ezk 20:4; 22:2
[k]Is 58:1; Ezk 16:2; Mc 3:8
[l]**23:37** Ezk 16:20-21; 20:26,31
[m]**23:38** 2Kg 21:4,7
[n]Ezk 20:13
[o]**23:39** Jr 7:9-11
[p]**23:40** 2Kg 9:30; Jr 4:30
[q]Is 3:18-23; Ezk 16:13-16
[r]**23:41** Is 57:7
[s]**23:45** Ezk 16:38
[t]**23:46** Jr 15:4; 24:9; 29:18
[u]**23:47** Lv 20:10; Ezk 16:40
[v]**23:49** Is 59:18; Ezk 7:4,9; 9:10

[A]**23:24** LXX reads *nations, from the north, chariots and*; Hb obscure [B]**23:32** Or *It will bring* [C]**23:42** Or *Sabeans* [D]**23:46** Or *I will summon*

Parable of the Boiling Pot

24 The word of the LORD came to me in
the ninth year, in the tenth month,
on the tenth day of the month: 2 "Son of man,
write down today's date, this very day. The
king of Babylon has laid siege to Jerusalem
this very day.[a] 3 Now speak a parable[b] to the
rebellious house. Tell them: This is what the
Lord GOD says:

Put the pot[c] on the fire —
put it on,
and then pour water into it!
4 Place the pieces of meat in it,
every good piece —
thigh and shoulder.
Fill it with choice bones.
5 Take the choicest of the flock
and also pile up the fuel[A] under it.
Bring it to a boil
and cook the bones in it."

6 Therefore, this is what the Lord GOD says:

Woe to the city of bloodshed,[d]
the pot that has rust inside it,
and whose rust will not come off!
Empty it piece by piece;
lots should not be cast for its contents.
7 For the blood she shed[B] is still within her.
She put it out on the bare rock;
she didn't pour it on the ground
to cover it with dust.[e]
8 In order to stir up wrath
and take vengeance,[f]
I have put her blood on the bare rock,
so that it would not be covered.

9 Therefore, this is what the Lord GOD says:

Woe to the city of bloodshed![g]
I Myself will make the pile
of kindling large.
10 Pile on the logs and kindle the fire!
Cook the meat well
and mix in the spices![C,D]
Let the bones be burned!
11 Set the empty pot on its coals
so that it becomes hot
and its copper glows.
Then its impurity will melt inside it;
its rust will be consumed.[h]
12 It has frustrated every effort;[E]
its thick rust will not come off.
Into the fire with its rust!
13 Because of the indecency
of your uncleanness —
since I tried to purify you,
but you would not be purified
from your uncleanness —
you will not be pure again
until I have satisfied My wrath on you.[i]
14 I, Yahweh, have spoken.
It is coming, and I will do it![j]
I will not refrain, I will not show pity,
and I will not relent.
I[F] will judge you
according to your ways and deeds.[k]
This is the declaration
of the Lord GOD.

The Death of Ezekiel's Wife: A Sign

15 Then the word of the LORD came to me:
16 "Son of man, I am about to take the delight
of your eyes[l] away from you with a fatal blow.
But you must not lament or weep or let your
tears flow.[m] 17 Groan quietly; do not observe
mourning rites for the dead.[n] Put on your
turban and strap your sandals on your feet;
do not cover your mustache or eat the bread
of mourners."[G,o]
18 I spoke to the people in the morning, and
my wife died in the evening. The next morning I did just as I was commanded. 19 Then
the people asked me, "Won't you tell us what
these things you are doing mean for us?"
20 So I answered them: "The word of the
LORD came to me: 21 'Say to the house of Israel:
This is what the Lord GOD says: I am about
to desecrate My sanctuary, the pride of your
power, the delight of your eyes, and the desire of your heart. Also, the sons and daughters you left behind will fall by the sword.[p]
22 Then you will do just as I have done: You
will not cover your mustache or eat the bread
of mourners.[G] 23 Your turbans will remain on
your heads and your sandals on your feet.
You will not lament or weep[q] but will waste
away[r] because of your sins and will groan to
one another. 24 Now Ezekiel will be a sign for
you.[s] You will do everything that he has done.

[a] **24:2** 2Kg 25:1 [b] **24:3** Ezk 17:2; 20:49 [c] Jr 1:13-14; Ezk 11:3,7,11 [d] **24:6** Ezk 22:2-3,27 [e] **24:7** Lv 17:13-14; Dt 12:16,24 [f] **24:8** Is 26:21 [g] **24:9** Hab 2:12 [h] **24:11** Ezk 22:15; 23:27 [i] **24:13** Ezk 5:13; 8:18 [j] **24:14** Ezk 17:24 [k] Ezk 18:30; 36:19 [l] **24:16** Pr 5:18; Ec 9:9; Sg 7:10 [m] Jr 16:5; 22:10 [n] **24:17** Lv 21:10-12 [o] Jr 16:7; Hs 9:4 [p] **24:21** Jr 6:11; 16:3-4; Ezk 23:25,47 [q] **24:23** Jb 27:15; Ps 78:64 [r] Lv 26:39 [s] **24:24** Ezk 4:3; Lk 11:29-30

[A] **24:5** Lit *bones* [B] **24:7** Lit *For her blood* [C] **24:10** Some Hb mss read *well; remove the broth*; LXX reads *fire so that the meat may be cooked and the broth may be reduced* [D] **24:10** Or *and stir the broth* [E] **24:12** Hb obscure [F] **24:14** Some Hb mss, LXX, Syr, Tg, Vg; other Hb mss read *They* [G] **24:17,22** Lit *men*

When this happens, you will know that I am
the Lord Yahweh.
25 “‘Son of man, know that on the day I take
their stronghold from them, their pride and
joy, the delight of their eyes and the longing of their hearts, as well as their sons and
daughters, 26 on that day a fugitive will come
to you and report the news.[a] 27 On that day
your mouth will be opened to talk with him;
you will speak and no longer be mute.[b] So you
will be a sign for them, and they will know
that I am Yahweh.’”

PROPHECIES AGAINST THE NATIONS

Judgment against Ammon

25 Then the word of the LORD came to me:
2 “Son of man, turn your face toward
the Ammonites and prophesy against them.[c]
3 Say to the Ammonites: Hear the word of the
Lord GOD: This is what the Lord GOD says:
Because you said, ‘Good!’[d] about My sanctuary when it was desecrated, about the land of
Israel when it was laid waste, and about the
house of Judah when they went into exile,
4 therefore I am about to give you to the people of the east as a possession. They will set
up their encampments and pitch their tents
among you. They will eat your fruit and drink
your milk. 5 I will make Rabbah a pasture[e] for
camels and Ammon a sheepfold. Then you
will know that I am *Yahweh.”
6 For this is what the Lord GOD says: “Because you clapped your hands,[f] stamped your
feet, and rejoiced over the land of Israel with
wholehearted contempt, 7 therefore I am
about to stretch out My hand against you[g]
and give you as plunder to the nations. I will
cut you off from the peoples and eliminate
you from the countries. I will destroy you,
and you will know that I am Yahweh.”

Judgment against Moab

8 This is what the Lord GOD says: “Because
Moab and Seir said,[h] ‘Look, the house of Judah is like all the other nations,’ 9 therefore I
am about to expose Moab’s flank beginning
with its[A] frontier cities, the pride of the land:
Beth-jeshimoth, Baal-meon,[i] and Kiriathaim.
10 I will give it along with Ammon to the people of the east as a possession, so that Ammon
will not be remembered among the nations.
11 So I will execute judgments against Moab,
and they will know that I am Yahweh.”

Judgment against Edom

12 This is what the Lord GOD says: “Because
Edom acted vengefully against the house of
Judah[j] and incurred grievous *guilt by taking revenge on them, 13 therefore this is what
the Lord GOD says: I will stretch out My hand
against Edom and cut off both man and animal from it. I will make it a wasteland; they
will fall by the sword from Teman to Dedan.
14 I will take My vengeance[k] on Edom through
My people Israel, and they will deal with
Edom according to My anger and wrath. So
they will know My vengeance.” This is the
declaration of the Lord GOD.

Judgment against Philistia

15 This is what the Lord GOD says: “Because
the Philistines acted in vengeance and took
revenge with deep contempt,[l] destroying
because of their ancient hatred, 16 therefore
this is what the Lord GOD says: I am about to
stretch out My hand against the Philistines,[m]
cutting off the Cherethites and wiping out
what remains of the coastal peoples.[B,n] 17 I
will execute great vengeance against them
with furious rebukes. They will know that I
am Yahweh[o] when I take My vengeance on
them.”

The Downfall of Tyre

26 In the eleventh year, on the first day of
the month, the word of the LORD came
to me: 2 “Son of man, because Tyre[p] said about
Jerusalem, ‘Good![q] The gateway to the peoples is shattered. She has been turned over to
me. I will be filled now that she lies in ruins,’
3 therefore this is what the Lord GOD says: See,
I am against you, Tyre![r] I will raise up many
nations against you, just as the sea raises its
waves. 4 They will destroy the walls of Tyre
and demolish her towers. I will scrape the soil
from her and turn her into a bare rock. 5 She
will become a place in the sea to spread nets,
for I have spoken.” This is the declaration of
the Lord GOD. “She will become plunder for
the nations,[s] 6 and her villages on the main-

[a] **24:26** Ezk 33:21-22
[b] **24:27** Ezk 3:26-27
[c] **25:2** Jr 49:1-6
[d] **25:3** Ezk 21:28; 26:2
[e] **25:5** Jr 49:2; Ezk 21:20
[f] **25:6** Jb 27:23; Nah 3:19
[g] **25:7** Zph 1:4
[h] **25:8** Is 15:1; Jr 48:1; Am 2:1-2
[i] **25:9** Jr 48:23
[j] **25:12** 2Ch 28:17; Ps 137:7; Jr 49:7-22
[k] **25:14** Is 11:14
[l] **25:15** Is 14:29-31
[m] **25:16** Jr 25:20; 47:1-7
[n] 1Sm 30:14; Zph 2:5
[o] **25:17** Ps 9:16
[p] **26:2** 2Sm 5:11; Jl 3:4
[q] Ezk 25:3
[r] **26:3** Is 23:3; Ezk 26:17; 28:2; Am 1:9; Zch 9:2; Mt 11:22
[s] **26:5** Ezk 25:7; 29:19

[A] **25:9** Lit *with the cities, with its* [B] **25:16** Lit *the seacoast*

land will be slaughtered by the sword.[a] Then
they will know that I am ·Yahweh."
7For this is what the Lord GOD says: "See, I
am about to bring King Nebuchadnezzar of
Babylon, king of kings,[b] against Tyre from
the north with horses, chariots, cavalry, and
a vast company of troops. 8He will slaughter
your villages on the mainland with the sword.
He will set up siege works against you,[c] and
will build a ramp[A] and raise a wall of shields
against you. 9He will direct the blows of his
battering rams against your walls and tear
down your towers with his iron tools. 10His
horses will be so numerous that their dust
will cover you. When he enters your gates as
an army entering a breached city, your walls
will shake from the noise of cavalry, wagons, and chariots. 11He will trample all your
streets with the hooves of his horses.[d] He will
slaughter your people with the sword, and
your mighty pillars will fall to the ground.
12They will take your wealth as spoil and plunder your merchandise.[e] They will also demolish your walls and tear down your beautiful
homes. Then they will throw your stones,
timber, and soil into the water. 13I will put an
end to the noise of your songs,[f] and the sound
of your lyres will no longer be heard. 14I will
turn you into a bare rock, and you will be a
place to spread nets. You will never be rebuilt,
for I, Yahweh, have spoken."[g] This is the declaration of the Lord GOD.
15This is what the Lord GOD says to Tyre:
"Won't the coasts and islands quake at the
sound of your downfall,[h] when the wounded
groan and slaughter occurs within you? 16All
the princes of the sea will descend from their
thrones,[i] remove their robes, and strip off
their embroidered garments. They will clothe
themselves with trembling; they will sit on
the ground, tremble continually, and be appalled[j] at you. 17Then they will lament[k] for you
and say of you:

How you have perished, city of renown,
you who were populated
from the seas![B]
She who was powerful on the sea,
she and all of her inhabitants
inflicted their terror.[C]
18 Now the coastlands tremble[l]
on the day of your downfall;
the islands in the sea
are alarmed by your demise."

19For this is what the Lord GOD says: "When
I make you a ruined city like other deserted
cities, when I raise up the deep against you
so that the mighty waters cover you, 20then I
will bring you down to be with those who descend to the ·Pit,[m] to the people of antiquity. I
will make you dwell in the underworld[D] like[E]
the ancient ruins, with those who descend to
the Pit, so that you will no longer be inhabited or display your splendor[F] in the land of
the living.[n] 21I will make you an object of horror, and you will no longer exist.[o] You will be
sought but will never be found again." This is
the declaration of the Lord GOD.

The Sinking of Tyre

27 The word of the LORD came to me:
2"Now, son of man, lament for Tyre.[p]
3Say to Tyre, who is located at the entrance
of the sea, merchant of the peoples[q] to many
coasts and islands: This is what the Lord GOD
says:

Tyre, you declared,
'I am perfect in beauty.'
4 Your realm was in the heart of the sea;
your builders perfected your beauty.
5 They constructed all your planking
with pine trees from Senir.[G,r]
They took a cedar from Lebanon
to make a mast for you.
6 They made your oars of oaks
from Bashan.
They made your deck of cypress wood
from the coasts of Cyprus,[s]
inlaid with ivory.
7 Your sail was made of
fine embroidered linen from Egypt,
and served as your banner.
Your awning was of blue
and purple fabric
from the coasts of Elishah.
8 The inhabitants of Sidon and Arvad[t]
were your rowers.

[a]**26:6** Ezk 16:46,53; 26:8 [b]**26:7** Jr 52:32; Dn 2:37,47 [c]**26:8** Ezk 21:22 [d]**26:11** Hab 1:8 [e]**26:12** Ezk 27:3-27 [f]**26:13** Is 23:16; 24:8-9; Am 6:5 [g]**26:14** Is 14:27 [h]**26:15** Jr 49:21 [i]**26:16** Jnh 3:6 [j]Ezk 27:35 [k]**26:17** Ezk 27:2,32; 28:12 [l]**26:18** Ezk 26:15 [m]**26:20** Jb 33:28; Ps 28:1; 30:3; Is 14:15; Ezk 28:8; 31:14; 32:18-30 [n]Jr 33:9; Zch 2:8 [o]**26:21** Ezk 27:36; 28:19 [p]**27:2** Ezk 28:12; 32:2 [q]**27:3** Is 23:2 [r]**27:5** Dt 3:9 [s]**27:6-7** Gn 10:4; 1Ch 1:7 [t]**27:8** Gn 10:18

[A]**26:8** Lit *ramp against you* [B]**26:17** Some LXX mss read *How you were destroyed from the seas, city of renown!* [C]**26:17** Lit *and all her inhabitants who put their terror on all her inhabitants*; Hb obscure [D]**26:20** Lit *the lower parts of the earth* [E]**26:20** Some Hb mss, LXX; other Hb mss, Syr read *in* [F]**26:20** LXX reads *or appear* [G]**27:5** = Mount Hermon

Your wise men were within you, Tyre;
they were your captains.
9 The elders of Gebal and its wise men[a]
were within you, repairing your leaks.

All the ships of the sea and their sailors
came to[A] you to barter for your goods.
10 Men of Persia, Lud, and Put[b]
were in your army, serving
as your warriors.
They hung shields and helmets in you;
they gave you splendor.
11 Men of Arvad and Helech
were stationed on your walls
all around,
and Gammadites were in your towers.
They hung their shields[B] all around
your walls;
they perfected your beauty.

12 "Tarshish[c] was your trading partner because of your great wealth of every kind. They
exchanged silver, iron, tin, and lead for your
merchandise. 13 Javan, Tubal, and Meshech[d]
were your merchants. They exchanged slaves[C]
and bronze utensils for your goods. 14 Those
from Beth-togarmah[e] exchanged horses, war
horses, and mules for your merchandise.
15 Men of Dedan[D,f] were also your merchants;
many coasts and islands were your regular
markets. They brought back ivory tusks[g] and
ebony as your payment. 16 Aram[E,F] was your
trading partner because of your numerous
products. They exchanged turquoise,[G] purple
and embroidered cloth, fine linen, coral,[G] and
rubies[G] for your merchandise. 17 Judah and the
land of Israel were your merchants. They exchanged wheat from Minnith,[h] meal,[H] honey,
oil, and balm, for your goods. 18 Damascus was
also your trading partner because of your numerous products and your great wealth of
every kind, trading in wine from Helbon and
white wool.[I] 19 Vedan[J] and Javan from Uzal[G,i]
dealt in your merchandise; wrought iron,
cassia,[j] and aromatic cane were exchanged
for your goods. 20 Dedan[k] was your merchant
in saddlecloths for riding. 21 Arabia and all the
princes of Kedar were your business[K] partners, trading with you in lambs, rams, and
goats. 22 The merchants of Sheba[l] and Raamah traded with you. They exchanged gold,
the best of all spices, and all kinds of precious
stones for your merchandise.[m] 23 Haran, Can-
neh, Eden,[n] the merchants of Sheba, Asshur,[o]
and Chilmad traded with you. 24 They were
your merchants in choice garments, cloaks
of blue and embroidered materials, and mul-
ticolored carpets,[G] which were bound and secured with cords in your marketplace. 25 Ships
of Tarshish[p] were the carriers for your goods.

So you became full and heavily loaded[L]
in the heart of the sea.
26 Your rowers have brought you
onto the high seas,[q]
but the east wind has shattered you
in the heart of the sea.
27 Your wealth, merchandise, and goods,
your sailors and captains,
those who repair your leaks,
those who barter for your goods,
and all the warriors within you,
with all the other people on board,[M]
sink into the heart of the sea
on the day of your downfall.
28 The countryside shakes
at the sound of your sailors' cries.[r]
29 All those who handle an oar
disembark from their ships.
The sailors and all the captains
of the sea
stand on the shore.
30 They raise their voices over you
and cry out bitterly.
They throw dust on their heads;[s]
they roll in ashes.
31 They shave their heads because of you
and wrap themselves in ˚sackcloth.
They weep over you
with deep anguish
and bitter mourning.
32 In their wailing they lament for you,[t]
mourning over you:
Who was like Tyre,
silenced[G] in the middle of the sea?
33 When your merchandise was unloaded
from the seas,
you satisfied many peoples.

[a] 27:9 1Kg 5:18 [b] 27:10 Ezk 30:5; 38:5 [c] 27:12 Gn 10:4; Ezk 38:13 [d] 27:13 Gn 10:2; Ezk 38:2; 39:1 [e] 27:14 Gn 10:3; Ezk 38:6 [f] 27:15 Ezk 38:13 [g] 1Kg 10:22 [h] 27:17 Jdg 11:33 [i] 27:19 Gn 10:27 [j] Ex 30:24 [k] 27:20 Ezk 38:13 [l] 27:22 Gn 10:7; Ezk 38:13 [m] 1Kg 10:1-2; Rv 18:12 [n] 27:23 2Kg 19:12; Is 37:12 [o] Gn 25:3 [p] 27:25 1Kg 10:22; 22:48; Is 2:16 [q] 27:26 Ezk 26:19 [r] 27:28 Ezk 26:10,15 [s] 27:30 Rv 18:17-19 [t] 27:32 Ezk 26:17

[A] 27:9 Lit *sailors were with* [B] 27:11 Or *quivers*; Hb obscure [C] 27:13 Lit *souls of men* [D] 27:15 LXX reads *Rhodes* [E] 27:16 Some Hb mss, Aq, Syr read *Edom* [F] 27:16 = Syria [G] 27:16,19,24,32 Hb obscure [H] 27:17 Or *resin*; Hb obscure [I] 27:18 Or *and wool from Zahar* [J] 27:19 Or *Dan* [K] 27:21 Lit *trading* [L] 27:25 Or *and very glorious* [M] 27:27 Lit *with all your assembly among you*

You enriched the kings of the earth
with your abundant wealth and goods.
34 Now you are shattered by the sea
in the depths of the waters;
your goods and the people within you
have gone down.
35 All the inhabitants of the coasts
and islands
are appalled[a] at you.
Their kings shudder with fear;
their faces are contorted.
36 Those who trade among the peoples
mock[A,b] you;
you have become an object of horror
and will never exist again."[c]

The Fall of Tyre's Ruler

28 The word of the LORD came to me:
2"Son of man, say to the ruler of Tyre:
This is what the Lord GOD says:

Your[B] heart is proud,
and you have said, 'I am a god;[d]
I sit in the seat of gods
in the heart of the sea.'
Yet you are a man and not a god,
though you have regarded your heart
as that of a god.
3 Yes, you are wiser than Daniel;[e]
no secret is hidden from you!
4 By your wisdom and understanding
you have acquired wealth for yourself.
You have acquired gold and silver
for your treasuries.[f]
5 By your great skill in trading
you have increased your wealth,
but your heart has become proud
because of your wealth."

6Therefore this is what the Lord GOD says:

Because you regard your heart as that
of a god,
7 I am about to bring strangers
against you,
ruthless men from the nations.
They will draw their swords
against your magnificent wisdom
and will defile your splendor.[g]
8 They will bring you down to the 'Pit,[h]
and you will die a violent death
in the heart of the sea.
9 Will you still say, 'I am a god,'
in the presence of those who kill[C] you?
Yet you will be only a man, not a god,
in the hands of those who kill you.
10 You will die the death
of the uncircumcised[i]
at the hands of strangers.[j]
For I have spoken.
This is the declaration
of the Lord GOD.

A Lament for Tyre's King

11The word of the LORD came to me: 12"Son
of man, lament[k] for the king of Tyre and say
to him: This is what the Lord GOD says:

You were the seal[D] of perfection,[E]
full of wisdom and perfect in beauty.[l]
13 You were in Eden,[m] the garden of God.
Every kind of precious stone
covered you:
carnelian, topaz, and diamond,[E]
beryl, onyx, and jasper,
sapphire,[F] turquoise[G] and emerald.[H]
Your mountings and settings
were crafted in gold;[n]
they were prepared on the day
you were created.
14 You were an anointed guardian cherub,[o]
for[I] I had appointed you.
You were on the holy mountain of God;
you walked among the fiery stones.
15 From the day you were created
you were blameless in your ways
until wickedness was found in you.
16 Through the abundance of your trade,
you were filled with violence,
and you sinned.
So I expelled you in disgrace
from the mountain of God,
and banished you, guardian cherub,[J]
from among the fiery stones.
17 Your heart became proud because of
your beauty;[p]
For the sake of your splendor
you corrupted your wisdom.
So I threw you down to the earth;

[a]27:35 Ezk 26:15-16 [b]27:36 1Kg 9:8; Jr 19:8; Zph 2:15 [c]Ezk 26:21; 28:19 [d]28:2 Is 14:14; Ac 12:22-23; 2Th 2:4 [e]28:3 Dn 1:20; 2:20-23,28; 5:11-12 [f]28:4 Ezk 27:33; Zch 9:2-3 [g]28:7 Ezk 30:11; 31:12; 32:12 [h]28:8 Ezk 26:20 [i]28:10 Ezk 31:18; 32:30 [j]Ezk 30:12 [k]28:12 Ezk 27:2 [l]Ezk 27:3 [m]28:13 Gn 2:8; Ezk 31:9,16,18; 36:35 [n]Ex 39:10-13 [o]28:14 Ex 25:18-22 [p]28:17 Ezk 28:2

A27:36 Lit *hiss* B28:2 Lit *Because your* C28:9 Some Hb mss, LXX, Syr, Vg; other Hb mss read *of the one who kills* D28:12 Or *sealer* E28:12,13 Hb obscure F28:13 Or *lapis lazuli* G28:13 Or *malachite*, or *garnet* H28:13 Or *beryl* I28:14 Or *With an anointed guardian cherub* J28:16 Or *and the guardian cherub banished you*

I made you a spectacle before kings.
18 You profaned your sanctuaries
by the magnitude of your iniquities
in your dishonest trade.
So I made fire come from within you,
and it consumed you.[a]
I reduced you to ashes on the ground
in the sight of everyone watching you.
19 All those who know you
among the nations
are appalled at you.
You have become an object of horror
and will never exist again."[b]

A Prophecy against Sidon

20The word of the LORD came to me: 21"Son
of man, turn your face toward Sidon[c] and
prophesy against it. 22You are to say: This is
what the Lord GOD says:

Look! I am against you, Sidon,[d]
and I will display My glory within you.
They will know that I am ·Yahweh
when I execute judgments
against her[e]
and demonstrate My holiness
through her.
23 I will send a plague against her[f]
and bloodshed in her streets;
the slain will fall within her,
while the sword is against her[A]
on every side.
Then they will know that I am Yahweh.

24"The house of Israel will no longer be
hurt by[B] prickly briers or painful thorns[g]
from all their neighbors who treat them with
contempt. Then they will know that I am the
Lord Yahweh.

25"This is what the Lord GOD says: When I
gather the house of Israel[h] from the peoples
where they are scattered and demonstrate
My holiness through them in the sight of the
nations, then they will live in their own land,
which I gave to My servant Jacob. 26They will
live there securely,[i] build houses, and plant
vineyards.[j] They will live securely when I execute judgments[k] against all their neighbors
who treat them with contempt. Then they
will know that I am Yahweh their God."

[a]**28:18** Ezk 19:14 [b]**28:19** Ezk 26:21; 27:36 [c]**28:21** Gn 10:19; Is 23:2; Jl 3:4 [d]**28:22** Ezk 26:3; Zch 9:2; Mt 11:22 [e]Ezk 30:19 [f]**28:23** Ezk 38:22 [g]**28:24** Nm 33:55 [h]**28:25** Ps 106:47; Ezk 20:41; 34:13 [i]**28:26** Jr 23:6; Ezk 34:25,28; 38:8 [j]Jr 32:15; Ezk 11:3 [k]Ezk 25:11 [l]**29:2** Is 19:1-17; Jr 46:2-26; Ezk 30–32 [m]**29:3** Ps 74:13; Is 27:1; Ezk 32:2 [n]**29:4** Jb 41:2; Ezk 38:4 [o]**29:5** Ezk 32:4-6 [p]Jr 8:2; 25:33 [q]Ezk 39:4 [r]**29:7** 2Kg 18:21; Is 36:6 [s]**29:8** Ezk 14:17 [t]**29:9** Ezk 30:7-8

A Prophecy of Egypt's Ruin

29 In the tenth year, in the tenth month
on the twelfth day of the month, the
word of the LORD came to me: 2"Son of man,
turn your face toward Pharaoh king of Egypt
and prophesy against him and against all of
Egypt.[l] 3Speak to him and say: This is what the
Lord GOD says:

Look, I am against you, Pharaoh
king of Egypt,
the great monster[C,m] lying in the middle
of his Nile,
who says, 'My Nile is my own;
I made it for myself.'
4 I will put hooks in your jaws[n]
and make the fish of your streams
cling to your scales.
I will haul you up
from the middle of your Nile,
and all the fish of your streams
will cling to your scales.
5 I will leave you in the desert,[o]
you and all the fish of your streams.
You will fall on the open ground
and will not be taken away
or gathered for burial.[p]
I have given you
to the beasts of the earth
and the birds of the sky as food.[q]

6 Then all the inhabitants of Egypt
will know that I am ·Yahweh,
for they[D] have been a staff made of reed
to the house of Israel.
7 When Israel grasped you by the hand,
you splintered,[r] tearing all
their shoulders;
when they leaned on you,
you shattered and made all
their hips unsteady.[E]

8"Therefore this is what the Lord GOD says:
I am going to bring a sword[s] against you and
wipe out man and animal from you. 9The land
of Egypt will be a desolate ruin.[t] Then they will
know that I am Yahweh. Because you[F] said,
'The Nile is my own; I made it,' 10therefore,
I am against you and your Nile. I will turn
the land of Egypt into ruins, a desolate waste
from Migdol to Syene, as far as the border of

[A]**28:23** Or *within her by the sword* [B]**28:24** Lit *longer have* [C]**29:3** Or *crocodile* [D]**29:6** LXX, Syr, Vg read *you* [E]**29:7** LXX, Syr, Vg; MT reads *and you caused their hips to stand* [F]**29:9** LXX, Syr, Vg; MT reads *he*

·Cush. 11 No human foot will pass through it,
and no animal foot will pass through it.[a] It
will be uninhabited for 40 years. 12 I will make
the land of Egypt a desolation among[A] desolate lands, and its cities will be a desolation
among[B] ruined cities[b] for 40 years. I will disperse the Egyptians among the nations and
scatter them across the countries.[c]
13 "For this is what the Lord GOD says: At the
end of 40 years I will gather the Egyptians
from the nations where they were dispersed.[d]
14 I will restore the fortunes of Egypt and
bring them back to the land of Pathros, the
land of their origin. There they will be a lowly
kingdom. 15 Egypt will be the lowliest of kingdoms and will never again exalt itself over the
nations. I will make them so small they cannot rule over the nations. 16 It will never again
be an object of trust[e] for the house of Israel,
drawing attention to their sin of turning to
the Egyptians. Then they will know that I am
the Lord Yahweh."

Babylon Receives Egypt as Compensation

17 In the twenty-seventh year in the first
month, on the first day of the month, the
word of the LORD came to me: 18 "Son of man,
Nebuchadnezzar king of Babylon made his
army labor strenuously against Tyre.[f] Every head was made bald and every shoulder chafed, but he and his army received no
compensation from Tyre for the labor he ex-
pended against it. 19 Therefore this is what the
Lord GOD says: I am going to give the land of
Egypt to Nebuchadnezzar king of Babylon,[g]
who will carry off its wealth, seizing its spoil
and taking its plunder. This will be his army's
compensation. 20 I have given him the land
of Egypt as the pay he labored for, since they
worked for Me." This is the declaration of the
Lord GOD. 21 "In that day I will cause a ·horn
to sprout[h] for the house of Israel, and I will
enable you to speak out[i] among them. Then
they will know that I am Yahweh."

Egypt's Doom

30 The word of the LORD came to me:
2 "Son of man, prophesy and say: This
is what the Lord GOD says:

[a] 29:11 Ezk 32:13
[b] 29:12 Ezk 30:7
[c] Ezk 12:15; 30:15,23,26
[d] 29:13 Is 19:22-23
[e] 29:16 Is 20:5; 30:1-3; Ezk 17:15
[f] 29:18 Ezk 26:7-12
[g] 29:19 Ezk 30:10,24-25; 32:11
[h] 29:21 1Sm 2:10; Ps 92:10; 132:17
[i] Ezk 3:27; 24:27; 33:22
[j] 30:2 Is 13:6; Ezk 21:12; Jl 1:11,13
[k] 30:3 Jl 2:1; Ob 15
[l] Ezk 32:7; 34:12
[m] 30:5 Jr 46:9
[n] 30:7 Ezk 29:12
[o] 30:8 Ezk 22:31
[p] 30:9 Is 18:1-2
[q] 30:11 Ezk 28:7; 31:12
[r] 30:12 Is 19:4

Wail:[j] Woe for the day!
3 For a day is near;
a day belonging to the LORD is near.[k]
It will be a day of clouds,[l]
a time of doom for the nations.
4 A sword will come against Egypt,
and there will be anguish in ·Cush
when the slain fall in Egypt,
and its wealth is taken away,
and its foundations are torn down.
5 Cush, Put, and Lud,[m]
and all the various foreign troops,[C]
plus Libya[D] and the men
of the covenant land[E]
will fall by the sword along with them.
6 This is what the LORD says:
Those who support Egypt will fall,
and its proud strength will collapse.
From Migdol to Syene
they will fall within it by the sword.
This is the declaration
of the Lord GOD.
7 They will be desolate
among[B] desolate lands,
and their cities will lie
among ruined[F] cities.[n]
8 They will know that I am ·Yahweh
when I set fire to Egypt[o]
and all its allies are shattered.

9 On that day, messengers will go out from Me
in ships[p] to terrify confident Cush. Anguish
will come over them on the day of Egypt's
doom. For indeed it is coming."
10 This is what the Lord GOD says:

I will put an end to the hordes[G] of Egypt
by the hand of Nebuchadnezzar
king of Babylon.
11 He along with his people,
ruthless men from the nations,
will be brought in to destroy the land.
They will draw their swords
against Egypt
and fill the land with the slain.[q]
12 I will make the streams dry
and sell the land into the hands
of evil men.[r]
I will bring desolation
on the land and everything in it

[A] 29:12 Or *Egypt the most desolate of* [B] 29:12; 30:7 Or *be the most desolate of* [C] 30:5 Or *all Arabia* [D] 30:5 Lit *Cub*; Hb obscure [E] 30:5 Probably Israel [F] 30:7 Or *will be the most ruined of* [G] 30:10 Or *pomp, or wealth*

by the hands of foreigners.
I, Yahweh, have spoken.

13 This is what the Lord GOD says:

I will destroy the idols and put an end
to the false gods in Memphis.[a]
There will no longer be
a prince from the land of Egypt.
So I will instill fear in that land.
14 I will make Pathros[b] desolate,
set fire to Zoan,
and execute judgments on Thebes.
15 I will pour out My wrath on Pelusium,
the stronghold of Egypt,
and will wipe out the crowds[A]
of Thebes.
16 I will set fire to Egypt;
Pelusium will writhe in anguish,
Thebes will be breached,
and Memphis will face foes
in broad daylight.[B]
17 The young men of On[C] and Pi-beseth
will fall by the sword,
and those cities[D] will go into captivity.
18 The day will be dark[E] in Tehaphnehes,
when I break the yoke of Egypt there
and its proud strength
comes to an end in the city.
A cloud[c] will cover Tehaphnehes,[F]
and its villages will go into captivity.
19 So I will execute judgments
against Egypt,
and they will know that I am Yahweh.

Pharaoh's Power Broken

20 In the eleventh year, in the first month,
on the seventh day of the month, the word of
the LORD came to me: 21 "Son of man, I have
broken the arm[d] of Pharaoh king of Egypt.
Look, it has not been bandaged—no medicine has been applied and no splint put on to bandage it so that it can grow strong enough
to handle a sword. 22 Therefore this is what
the Lord GOD says: Look! I am against Pharaoh king of Egypt. I will break his arms, both the strong one and the one already broken, and will make the sword fall from his hand.
23 I will disperse the Egyptians among the nations and scatter them among the countries.[e]
24 I will strengthen the arms of Babylon's king
and place My sword[f] in his hand. But I will break the arms of Pharaoh, and he will groan
before him as a mortally wounded man. 25 I
will strengthen the arms of Babylon's king, but Pharaoh's arms will fall. They will know that I am Yahweh when I place My sword in the hand of Babylon's king and he wields it
against the land of Egypt. 26 When I disperse
the Egyptians among the nations and scatter them among the countries, they will know that I am Yahweh."

Downfall of Egypt and Assyria

31 In the eleventh year,[g] in the third month, on the first day of the month,
the word of the LORD came to me: 2 "Son of
man, say to Pharaoh king of Egypt and to his hordes:

Who are you like in your greatness?
3 Think of Assyria, a cedar in Lebanon,[h]
with beautiful branches
and shady foliage
and of lofty height.
Its top was among the clouds.[G]
4 The waters caused it to grow;
the underground springs made it tall,
directing their rivers all around
the place where the tree was planted
and sending their channels
to all the trees of the field.
5 Therefore the cedar became greater
in height
than all the trees of the field.[i]
Its branches multiplied,
and its boughs grew long
as it spread them out
because of the plentiful water.[j]
6 All the birds of the sky
nested in its branches,[k]
and all the animals of the field
gave birth beneath its boughs;
all the great nations lived in its shade.
7 It was beautiful in its greatness,
in the length of its limbs,
for its roots extended
to abundant water.
8 The cedars in God's garden could not
rival it;[l]

[a] **30:13** Jr 43:12-13 [b] **30:14** Jr 44:1,15; Ezk 29:14 [c] **30:18** Ezk 34:12 [d] **30:21** Ps 10:15; 37:17 [e] **30:23** Ezk 29:12 [f] **30:24** Zph 2:12 [g] **31:1** Ezk 30:20 [h] **31:3** Is 10:33-34; Ezk 17:3-4,22; 31:16 [i] **31:5** Dn 4:11 [j] Ezk 17:5 [k] **31:6** Ezk 17:23; Dn 4:12,21; Mt 13:32 [l] **31:8** Gn 2:8; Is 51:3; Ezk 28:13

[A] **30:15** Or *pomp*, or *wealth* [B] **30:16** Or *foes daily* [C] **30:17** LXX, Vg; MT reads *iniquity* [D] **30:17** Or *and the women*; lit *and they* [E] **30:18** Some Hb mss, LXX, Syr, Tg, Vg; other Hb mss read *will withhold* [F] **30:18** Or *Egypt* [G] **31:3** Or *thick foliage*

the pine trees couldn't compare
with its branches,
nor could the plane trees match
its boughs.
No tree in the garden of God
could compare with it in beauty.
9 I made it beautiful with its many limbs,
and all the trees of Eden,
which were in God's garden, envied it.

10 "Therefore this is what the Lord GOD says:
Since it[A] became great in height and set its top
among the clouds,[B] and it[C] grew proud[a] on account of its height, 11 I determined to hand it
over to a ruler of nations;[b] he would surely
deal with it. I banished it because of its wickedness. 12 Foreigners, ruthless men from the
nations,[c] cut it down and left it lying. Its limbs
fell on the mountains and in every valley; its
boughs lay broken in all the earth's ravines.
All the peoples of the earth left its shade and
abandoned it. 13 All the birds of the sky nested
on its fallen trunk, and all the animals of the
field were among its boughs. 14 This happened
so that no trees planted beside water would
become great in height and set their tops
among the clouds,[B] and so that no other well-
watered trees would reach them in height.
For they have all been consigned to death, to
the underworld, among the •people who descend to the •Pit.[d]

15 "This is what the Lord GOD says: I caused
grieving on the day the cedar went down to
•Sheol.[e] I closed off the underground deep because of it:[D] I held back the rivers of the deep,
and its abundant waters were restrained. I
made Lebanon mourn on account of it, and
all the trees of the field fainted because of it.
16 I made the nations quake at the sound of its
downfall, when I threw it down to Sheol to
be with those who descend to the Pit. Then
all the trees of Eden,[f] all the well-watered
trees, the choice and best of Lebanon, were
comforted[g] in the underworld. 17 They too
descended with it to Sheol, to those slain by
the sword. As its allies[E,F] they had lived in its
shade among the nations.

18 "Who then are you like in glory and greatness among Eden's trees? You also will be
brought down to the underworld to be with
the trees of Eden. You will lie among the uncircumcised with those slain by the sword.[h]
This is Pharaoh and all his hordes" — the declaration of the Lord GOD.

A Lament for Pharaoh

32 In the twelfth year, in the twelfth
month, on the first day of the month,
the word of the LORD came to me: 2 "Son of
man, lament[i] for Pharaoh king of Egypt and
say to him:

You compare yourself to a lion
of the nations,
but[G] you are like a monster[j] in the seas.
You thrash about in your rivers,
churn up the waters with your feet,
and muddy the[H] rivers."

3 This is what the Lord GOD says:

I will spread My net over you[k]
with an assembly of many peoples,
and they[I] will haul you up in My net.
4 I will abandon you on the land
and hurl you on the open field.
I will cause all the birds of the sky
to settle on you
and let the beasts of the entire earth
eat their fill of you.[l]
5 I will put your flesh on the mountains[m]
and fill the valleys with your carcass.
6 I will drench the land
with the flow of your blood,
even to the mountains;
the ravines will be filled with your gore.
7 When I snuff you out,
I will cover the heavens
and darken their stars.
I will cover the sun with a cloud,[n]
and the moon will not give its light.
8 I will darken all the shining lights
in the heavens over you,
and will bring darkness on your land.
This is the declaration
of the Lord GOD.

9 I will trouble the hearts of many peoples,
when I bring about your destruction
among the nations,
in countries you do not know.

[a] **31:10** Ezk 28:17; Dn 5:20
[b] **31:11** Ezk 30:10-11; Dn 5:18-19
[c] **31:12** Ezk 28:7; 32:12
[d] **31:14** Ezk 26:20
[e] **31:15** Ezk 32:22-23
[f] **31:16** Ezk 26:15; 27:28; Hg 2:7
[g] Ezk 32:31
[h] **31:18** Ezk 28:10; 32:19,21
[i] **32:2** Ezk 19:1; 27:2; 28:12
[j] Is 27:1
[k] **32:3** Ezk 12:13
[l] **32:4** Ezk 29:3-5
[m] **32:5** Ezk 31:12
[n] **32:7** Jl 2:2,31; 3:15; Am 8:9; Mt 24:29; Rv 6:12; 8:12

[A] **31:10** Syr, Vg; MT, LXX read *you* [B] **31:10,14** Or *thick foliage* [C] **31:10** Lit *its heart* [D] **31:15** Or *I covered it with the underground deep* [E] **31:17** LXX, Syr read *offspring* [F] **31:17** Lit *arm* [G] **32:2** Or *Lion of the nations, you are destroyed;* [H] **32:2** Lit *their* [I] **32:3** LXX, Vg read *I*

10 I will cause many nations to be appalled
at you,
and their kings will shudder with fear
because of you[a]
when I brandish My sword
in front of them.
On the day of your downfall
each of them will tremble
every moment[b] for his life.

11 For this is what the Lord GOD says:

The sword of Babylon's king
will come against you!
12 I will make your hordes fall
by the swords of warriors,
all of them ruthless men
from the nations.[c]
They will ravage Egypt's pride,
and all its hordes will be destroyed.
13 I will slaughter all its cattle
that are beside many waters.
No human foot will churn them again,
and no cattle hooves will disturb them.[d]
14 Then I will let their waters settle
and will make their rivers flow like oil.
This is the declaration
of the Lord GOD.
15 When I make the land of Egypt
a desolation,
so that it is emptied of everything in it,
when I strike down all who live there,
then they will know that I am ˚Yahweh.[e]

16 "This is a lament that will be chanted;[f] the
women of the nations will chant it. They will
chant it over Egypt and all its hordes." This is
the declaration of the Lord GOD.

Egypt in Sheol

17 In the twelfth year,[A] on the fifteenth day
of the month, the word of the LORD came to
me: 18 "Son of man, wail over the hordes of
Egypt and bring Egypt and the daughters of
mighty nations down to the underworld,[B] to
be with those who descend to the ˚Pit:[g]

19 Who do you surpass in loveliness?
Go down and be laid to rest
with the uncircumcised!
20 They will fall among those slain
by the sword.
A sword is appointed![h]
They drag her and all her hordes away.
21 Warrior leaders will speak
from the middle of ˚Sheol
about him[C] and his allies:
They have come down;
the uncircumcised lie
slain by the sword.[i]
22 Assyria is there with all her company;
her graves are all around her.
All of them are slain, fallen
by the sword.
23 Her graves are set
in the deepest regions of the Pit,
and her company is all around
her burial place.
All of them are slain, fallen
by the sword—
those who once spread terror
in the land of the living.
24 Elam[j] is there
with all her hordes around her grave.
All of them are slain, fallen
by the sword—
those who went down
to the underworld[B] uncircumcised,
who once spread their terror
in the land of the living.
They bear their disgrace
with those who descend to the Pit.
25 Among the slain
they prepare a resting place for Elam
with all her hordes.
Her graves are all around her.
All of them are uncircumcised,
slain by the sword,
although their terror was once spread
in the land of the living.
They bear their disgrace
with those who descend to the Pit.
They are placed among the slain.
26 Meshech and Tubal[D,k] are there,
with all their hordes.
Their graves are all around them.
All of them are uncircumcised,
slain by the sword,
although their terror was once spread
in the land of the living.

[a] 32:10 Ezk 27:35
[b] Ezk 26:16
[c] 32:12 Ezk 28:7; 31:12
[d] 32:13 Ezk 29:11
[e] 32:15 Ex 7:5
[f] 32:16 2Sm 1:17; 2Ch 35:25; Jr 9:17; Ezk 26:17
[g] 32:18 Ezk 26:20
[h] 32:20 Ezk 21:15
[i] 32:21 Is 14:9-11; Ezk 31:15-18
[j] 32:24 Gn 10:22
[k] 32:26 Gn 10:2; Ezk 27:13; 38:2-3

A 32:17 LXX reads *year, in the first month,* B 32:18,24 Lit *the lower parts of the earth* C 32:21 Either Pharaoh or Egypt D 32:26 Lit *Meshech-tubal*

27 They do not lie down
with the fallen warriors
of the uncircumcised,[A]
who went down to Sheol
with their weapons of war,
whose swords were placed
under their heads.[B]
The punishment for their sins
rested on their bones,
although the terror of these warriors
was once in the land of the living.
28 But you will be shattered
and will lie down
among the uncircumcised,
with those slain by the sword.[a]
29 Edom[b] is there, her kings and all
her princes,
who, despite their strength,
have been placed
among those slain by the sword.
They lie down with the uncircumcised,
with those who descend to the Pit.
30 All the leaders of the north[c]
and all the Sidonians[d] are there.
They went down in shame with the slain,
despite the terror their strength inspired.
They lie down uncircumcised
with those slain by the sword.
They bear their disgrace
with those who descend to the Pit.
31 Pharaoh will see them
and be comforted[e] over all his hordes —
Pharaoh and all his army,
slain by the sword.
This is the declaration
of the Lord God.
32 For I will spread My[C] terror
in the land of the living,
so Pharaoh and all his hordes
will be laid to rest
among the uncircumcised,
with those slain by the sword."
This is the declaration
of the Lord God.

Ezekiel as Israel's Watchman

33 The word of the Lord came to me:
2"Son of man, speak to your people
and tell them: Suppose I bring the sword
against a land, and the people of that land
select a man from among them, appointing him as their watchman, 3and he sees the
sword coming against the land and blows his
trumpet[f] to warn the people. 4Then, if anyone
hears the sound of the trumpet but ignores
the warning,[g] and the sword comes and takes
him away, his blood will be on his own head.
5Since he heard the sound of the trumpet but
ignored the warning, his blood is on his own
hands.[D] If he had taken warning, he would
have saved his life. 6However, if the watchman sees the sword coming but doesn't
blow the trumpet, so that the people aren't
warned, and the sword comes and takes away
their lives, then they have been taken away
because of their iniquity, but I will hold the
watchman accountable for their blood.
7"As for you, son of man, I have made you
a watchman for the house of Israel.[h] When
you hear a word from My mouth, give them
a warning from Me. 8If I say to the wicked,
'Wicked one, you will surely die,'[i] but you do
not speak out to warn him about his way, that
wicked person will die for his iniquity, yet I
will hold you responsible for his blood. 9But
if you warn a wicked person to turn from his
way and he doesn't turn from it, he will die
for his iniquity, but you will have saved your
life.
10"Now as for you, son of man, say to the
house of Israel: You have said this, 'Our
transgressions and our sins are heavy on us,
and we are wasting away because of them![j]
How then can we survive?'[k] 11Tell them: As I
live" — the declaration of the Lord God — "I
take no pleasure in the death of the wicked,
but rather that the wicked person should
turn from his way and live.[l] Repent, repent
of your evil ways! Why will you die, house of
Israel?
12"Now, son of man, say to your people: The
righteousness of the righteous person will
not save him on the day of his transgression;
neither will the wickedness of the wicked
person cause him to stumble on the day he
turns from his wickedness. The righteous
person won't be able to survive by his righteousness on the day he sins. 13When I tell the
righteous person that he will surely live, but

[a]**32:28** Is 14:18 [b]**32:29** Ezk 25:12-14 [c]**32:30** Ezk 38:6,15; 39:2 [d]Ezk 28:21-23 [e]**32:31** Ezk 31:16-18 [f]**33:3** Nm 10:9 [g]**33:4** Zch 1:4 [h]**33:7** Ezk 3:17-19 [i]**33:8** Ezk 18:4 [j]**33:10** Lv 26:39; Ezk 4:17; 24:23 [k]Ezk 37:11 [l]**33:11** Ezk 18:23,30-32; Hs 11:8; 1Tm 2:4; 2Pt 3:9

[A]**32:27** LXX reads *of antiquity* [B]**32:27** Or *Do they not . . . heads?* [C]**32:32** Alt Hb tradition, LXX, Syr read *his* [D]**33:5** Lit *on him*

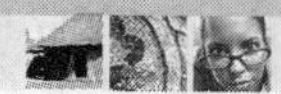

he trusts in his righteousness and commits iniquity, then none of his righteousness will be remembered, and he will die because of the iniquity he has committed.[a]

14“So when I tell the wicked person, ‘You will surely die,’ but he repents of his sin and does what is just and right — 15he returns collateral, makes restitution for what he has stolen, and walks in the statutes of life[b] without practicing iniquity — he will certainly live; he will not die. 16None of the sins he committed will be held against him. He has done what is just and right; he will certainly live.[c]

17“But your people say, ‘The Lord’s way isn’t fair,’[d] even though it is their own way that isn’t fair. 18When a righteous person turns from his righteousness and commits iniquity, he will die on account of this. 19But if a wicked person turns from his wickedness and does what is just and right, he will live because of this. 20Yet you say, ‘The Lord’s way isn’t fair.’ I will judge each of you according to his ways, house of Israel.”

The News of Jerusalem’s Fall

21In the twelfth year of our exile, in the tenth month, on the fifth day of the month, a fugitive from Jerusalem came to me and reported, “The city has been taken!” 22Now the hand of the LORD had been on me the evening before the fugitive arrived, and He opened my mouth before the man came to me in the morning. So my mouth was opened and I was no longer mute.[e]

Israel’s Continued Rebellion

23Then the word of the LORD came to me: 24“Son of man, those who live in the[A] ruins in the land of Israel are saying, ‘Abraham was only one person,[f] yet he received possession of the land.[g] But we are many; the land has been given to us as a possession.’[h] 25Therefore say to them: This is what the Lord GOD says: You eat meat with blood in it,[i] raise your eyes to your idols, and shed blood. Should you then receive possession of the land? 26You have relied on your swords, you have committed detestable acts, and each of you has defiled his neighbor’s wife. Should you then receive possession of the land?[j]

27“Tell them this: This is what the Lord GOD says: As surely as I live, those who are in the ruins will fall by the sword, those in the open field I have given to wild animals to be devoured, and those in the strongholds and caves will die by plague.[k] 28I will make the land a desolate waste,[l] and its proud strength will come to an end.[m] The mountains of Israel[n] will become desolate, with no one passing through. 29They will know that I am *Yahweh when I make the land a desolate waste because of all the detestable acts they have committed.

30“Now, son of man, your people are talking about you near the city walls and in the doorways of their houses. One person speaks to another, each saying to his brother, ‘Come and hear what the message is that comes from the LORD!’ 31So My people come to you in crowds,[B] sit in front of you, and hear your words, but they don’t obey them. Although they express love with their mouths, their hearts pursue dishonest profit. 32Yes, to them you are like a singer of love songs who has a beautiful voice and plays skillfully on an instrument. They hear your words, but they don’t obey them. 33Yet when it comes[o] — and it will definitely come — then they will know that a prophet has been among them.”

The Shepherds and God’s Flock

34 The word of the LORD came to me: 2“Son of man, prophesy against the shepherds of Israel. Prophesy, and say to them: This is what the Lord GOD says to the shepherds: Woe to the shepherds of Israel, who have been feeding themselves![p] Shouldn’t the shepherds feed their flock? 3You eat the fat, wear the wool, and butcher the fattened animals, but you do not tend the flock.[q] 4You have not strengthened the weak, healed the sick, bandaged the injured, brought back the strays, or sought the lost.[r] Instead, you have ruled them with violence and cruelty. 5They were scattered for lack of a shepherd;[s] they became food for all the wild animals[t] when they were scattered. 6My flock went astray on all the mountains and every high hill.[u] They were scattered over the whole face of the earth,

[a]**33:13** Ezk 3:20; 18:24,26
[b]**33:15** Lv 18:5; Dt 5:33; 1Kg 3:14; Ezk 20:11
[c]**33:16** Is 1:18; 43:25; Ezk 18:21-22
[d]**33:17** Ezk 18:25-30
[e]**33:22** Ezk 3:26-27; 24:26-27
[f]**33:24** Is 51:2
[g]Gn 15:7; 28:4
[h]Ezk 36:2
[i]**33:25** Lv 19:26
[j]**33:26** Ezk 18:6,10-11,15
[k]**33:27** Ezk 5:12
[l]**33:28** Ezk 35:3
[m]Ezk 7:24
[n]Ezk 6:2
[o]**33:33** Jr 28:9; Ezk 33:29
[p]**34:2** Jr 23:1
[q]**34:3** Pr 27:23
[r]**34:4** Zch 11:16; Lk 15:4
[s]**34:5** Nm 27:17; 1Kg 22:17; Jr 10:21; 23:2; 50:6; Mt 9:36
[t]Ezk 34:28
[u]**34:6** 1Pt 2:25

[A]**33:24** Lit *these* [B]**33:31** Lit *you like the coming of a people*

and there was no one searching or seeking
for them.
[7]"Therefore, you shepherds, hear the word
of the LORD. [8]As I live" — the declaration of
the Lord GOD — "because My flock has become prey and food for every wild animal
since they lack a shepherd, for My shepherds
do not search for My flock, and because the
shepherds feed themselves rather than My
flock, [9]therefore, you shepherds, hear the
word of the LORD!
[10]"This is what the Lord GOD says: Look,
I am against the shepherds.[a] I will demand
My flock from them[A] and prevent them from
shepherding the flock. The shepherds will no
longer feed themselves, for I will rescue My
flock from their mouths so that they will not
be food for them.
[11]"For this is what the Lord GOD says: See, I
Myself will search for My flock and look for
them. [12]As a shepherd looks for his sheep on
the day he is among his scattered flock, so I
will look for My flock. I will rescue them from
all the places where they have been scattered[b]
on a cloudy and dark day. [13]I will bring them
out from the peoples, gather them from the
countries, and bring them into their own
land. I will shepherd them on the mountains
of Israel, in the ravines, and in all the inhabited places of the land. [14]I will tend them with
good pasture, and their grazing place will be
on Israel's lofty mountains. There they will lie
down in a good grazing place; they will feed
in rich pasture on the mountains of Israel. [15]I
will tend My flock and let them lie down."[c]
This is the declaration of the Lord GOD. [16]"I
will seek the lost,[d] bring back the strays, bandage the injured,[e] and strengthen the weak,
but I will destroy[B] the fat and the strong. I will
shepherd them with justice.
[17]"The Lord GOD says to you, My flock: I
am going to judge between one sheep and
another, between the rams and male goats.[f]
[18]Isn't it enough for you to feed on the good
pasture? Must you also trample the rest of
the pasture with your feet? Or isn't it enough
that you drink the clear water? Must you also
muddy the rest with your feet? [19]Yet My flock
has to feed on what your feet have trampled,
and drink what your feet have muddied.

[a]34:10 Jr 21:13; Ezk 5:8; 13:8
[b]34:12 Jr 23:3
[c]34:15 Ps 23:1-2
[d]34:16 Ps 119:176; Lk 19:10
[e]Ps 147:3; Is 30:26; Hs 6:1
[f]34:17 Mt 25:31-33
[g]34:23 Ps 78:70-71; Jn 10:11,16
[h]34:24 Jr 30:9; Ezk 37:24
[i]34:25 Ezk 37:26
[j]Is 11:6-9
[k]Ezk 28:26
[l]34:26 Ps 2:6; 15:1; 133:3; Is 27:13; Jr 31:23
[m]Dt 11:13-14; 28:12
[n]34:27 Lv 26:13; Is 52:2-3; Jr 30:8
[o]34:29 Ezk 36:3,6,15
[p]34:30 Ex 6:7; Lv 26:12; Dt 29:13; Jr 30:22; 31:33; Ezk 11:20; 36:28; 37:23,27; Zch 8:8; 2Co 6:16; Heb 8:10; Rv 21:3
[q]34:31 Ps 100:3; Jr 23:1
[r]35:2 Ezk 25:12-14
[s]35:3 Ezk 6:14

[20]"Therefore, this is what the Lord GOD says
to them: See, I Myself will judge between the
fat sheep and the lean sheep. [21]Since you have
pushed with flank and shoulder and butted
all the weak ones with your horns until you
scattered them all over, [22]I will save My flock,
and they will no longer be prey for you. I will
judge between one sheep and another. [23]I will
appoint over them a single shepherd, My servant David, and he will shepherd them. He
will tend them himself and will be their shepherd.[g] [24]I, Yahweh, will be their God, and My
servant David[h] will be a prince among them.
I, Yahweh, have spoken.
[25]"I will make a covenant of peace[i] with
them and eliminate dangerous animals[j] in
the land, so that they may live securely[k] in
the wilderness and sleep in the forest. [26]I will
make them and the area around My hill[l] a
blessing: I will send down showers in their
season[m] — showers[C] of blessing. [27]The trees
of the field will give their fruit, and the land
will yield its produce; My flock will be secure
in their land. They will know that I am Yahweh when I break the bars of their yoke and
rescue them from the hands of those who
enslave them.[n] [28]They will no longer be prey
for the nations, and the wild animals of the
land will not consume them. They will live securely, and no one will frighten them. [29]I will
establish for them a place renowned for its
agriculture,[D] and they will no longer be victims of famine in the land. They will no longer endure the insults of the nations.[o] [30]Then
they will know that I, Yahweh their God, am
with them, and that they, the house of Israel,
are My people."[p] This is the declaration of the
Lord GOD. [31]"You are My flock, the human
flock of My pasture, and I am your God." This
is the declaration of the Lord GOD.[q]

A Prophecy against Edom

35 The word of the LORD came to me:
[2]"Son of man, turn your face toward
Mount Seir[r] and prophesy against it. [3]Say to
it: This is what the Lord GOD says:

Look! I am against you, Mount Seir.
I will stretch out My hand against you
and make you a desolate waste.[s]

[A]34:10 Lit *their hand* [B]34:16 Some Hb mss, LXX, Syr, Vg read *watch over* [C]34:26 Lit *season; they will be showers* [D]34:29 LXX, Syr read *a plant of peace*

4 I will turn your cities into ruins,
and you will become a desolation.
Then you will know that I am ·Yahweh.

5 "Because you maintained an ancient hatred[a] and handed over the Israelites to the
power of the sword in the time of their disaster, the time of final punishment,[b] 6 therefore,
as I live"— this is the declaration of the Lord
GOD—"I will destine you for bloodshed, and
it will pursue you. Since you did not hate
bloodshed, it will pursue you.[c] 7 I will make
Mount Seir a desolate waste and will cut off
from it those who come and go.[d] 8 I will fill
its mountains with the slain;[e] those slain by
the sword will fall on your hills, in your valleys, and in all your ravines. 9 I will make you
a perpetual desolation; your cities will not be
inhabited. Then you will know that I am Yahweh.

10 "Because you said, 'These two nations
and two lands will be mine, and we will possess them'— though the LORD was there[f]—
11 therefore, as I live"— the declaration of the
Lord GOD—"I will treat you according to
the anger and jealousy you showed in your
hatred of them. I will make Myself known
among them[A] when I judge you. 12 Then you
will know that I, Yahweh, have heard all the
blasphemies you uttered against the mountains of Israel, saying, 'They are desolate.
They have been given to us to devour!' 13 You
boasted against Me[g] with your mouth, and
spoke many words against Me. I heard it Myself!

14 "This is what the Lord GOD says: While the
whole world rejoices, I will make you a desolation. 15 Just as you rejoiced over the inheritance of the house of Israel because it became
a desolation, so I will deal with you: you will
become a desolation, Mount Seir, and so will
all Edom in its entirety. Then they will know
that I am Yahweh.

Restoration of Israel's Mountains

36 "Son of man, prophesy to the mountains of Israel and say: Mountains
of Israel, hear the word of the LORD.[h] 2 This
is what the Lord GOD says: Because the enemy has said about you, 'Good!'[i] The ancient
heights[j] have become our possession,' 3 therefore, prophesy and say: This is what the Lord
GOD says: Because they have made you desolate and have trampled you from every side,
so that you became a possession for the rest
of the nations and an object of people's gossip and slander,[k] 4 therefore, mountains of Israel, hear the word of the Lord GOD. This is
what the Lord GOD says to the mountains and
hills, to the ravines and valleys, to the desolate ruins and abandoned cities, which have
become plunder[l] and a mockery to the rest of
the nations all around.

5 "This is what the Lord GOD says: Certainly
in My burning zeal I speak against the rest
of the nations and all of Edom,[m] who took[B]
My land as their own possession with wholehearted rejoicing and utter contempt[n] so that
its pastureland became[C] plunder. 6 Therefore,
prophesy concerning the land of Israel and
say to the mountains and hills, to the ravines
and valleys: This is what the Lord GOD says:
Look, I speak in My burning zeal[o] because
you have endured the insults of the nations.
7 Therefore this is what the Lord GOD says: I
swear[D] that the nations all around you will
endure their own insults.[p]

8 "You, mountains of Israel, will produce
your branches[q] and bear your fruit for My
people Israel, since their arrival is near.
9 Look! I am on your side; I will turn toward
you,[r] and you will be tilled and sown. 10 I will
fill you with people, with the whole house of
Israel in its entirety.[s] The cities will be inhabited and the ruins rebuilt. 11 I will fill you with
people and animals,[t] and they will increase
and be fruitful. I will make you inhabited as
you once were and make you better off than
you were before. Then you will know that I
am ·Yahweh.[u] 12 I will cause people, My people
Israel, to walk on you; they will possess you,[v]
and you will be their inheritance. You will no
longer deprive them of their children.

13 "This is what the Lord GOD says: Because
people are saying to you, 'You devour men and
deprive your nation of children,'[w] 14 therefore,
you will no longer devour men and deprive
your nation of children."[E] This is the declaration of the Lord GOD. 15 "I will no longer allow

[a] **35:5** Ps 137:7; Ezk 25:15 [b] Ezk 7:2; 21:25,29 [c] **35:6** Is 63:2-6; Ezk 16:38; 32:6 [d] **35:7** Ezk 33:28 [e] **35:8** Ezk 31:12; 32:4-5 [f] **35:10** Ps 48:1-3; Ezk 48:35 [g] **35:13** Jr 48:26,42; Ob 12; Zph 2:8 [h] **36:1** Ezk 6:2 [i] **36:2** Ezk 25:3; 26:2 [j] Dt 32:13 [k] **36:3** Ezk 35:13 [l] **36:4** Ezk 34:8,28 [m] **36:5** Dt 4:24 [n] Ezk 35:10,15 [o] **36:6** Ps 74:10; 123:3-4 [p] **36:7** Ezk 20:5 [q] **36:8** Ezk 17:23 [r] **36:9** Lv 26:9 [s] **36:10** Ezk 37:21-22 [t] **36:11** Jr 33:12 [u] Is 51:3 [v] **36:12** Ob 17 [w] **36:13** Nm 13:32

[A] **35:11** LXX reads *you* [B] **36:5** Lit *gave* [C] **36:5** Or *contempt, to empty it of*; Hb obscure [D] **36:7** Lit *lift up My hand* [E] **36:14** Alt Hb tradition reads *and cause your nation to stumble*

the insults of the nations to be heard against
you, and you will not have to endure the reproach of the peoples anymore;[a] you will no
longer cause your nation to stumble."[A] This is
the declaration of the Lord GOD.

Restoration of Israel's People

16 The word of the LORD came to me: 17 "Son
of man, while the house of Israel lived in
their land, they defiled it with their conduct
and actions.[b] Their behavior before Me was
like menstrual impurity.[c] 18 So I poured out
My wrath[d] on them because of the blood they
had shed on the land, and because they had
defiled it with their idols. 19 I dispersed them
among the nations, and they were scattered
among the countries.[e] I judged them according to their conduct and actions.[f] 20 When
they came to the nations where they went,
they profaned My holy name,[g] because it was
said about them, 'These are the people of
Yahweh, yet they had to leave His land in exile.' 21 Then I had concern for My holy name,[h]
which the house of Israel profaned among
the nations where they went.

22 "Therefore, say to the house of Israel: This
is what the Lord GOD says: It is not for your
sake that I will act,[i] house of Israel, but for My
holy name,[j] which you profaned among the
nations where you went. 23 I will honor the
holiness of My great name, which has been
profaned among the nations—the name you
have profaned among them. The nations will
know that I am Yahweh"—the declaration of
the Lord GOD—"when I demonstrate My holiness through you in their sight.[k]

24 "For I will take you from the nations and
gather you from all the countries, and will
bring you into your own land.[l] 25 I will also
sprinkle clean water on you, and you will be
•clean.[m] I will cleanse you from all your impurities and all your idols.[n] 26 I will give you a
new heart and put a new spirit within you;[o] I
will remove your heart of stone[B] and give you
a heart of flesh.[p] 27 I will place My Spirit within
you[q] and cause you to follow My statutes and
carefully observe My ordinances.[r] 28 Then you
will live in the land that I gave your fathers;[s]
you will be My people, and I will be your God.[t]

29 I will save you from all your uncleanness.
I will summon the grain and make it plentiful, and will not bring famine on you.[u] 30 I will
also make the fruit of the trees and the produce of the field plentiful, so that you will no
longer experience reproach among the nations on account of famine.

31 "Then you will remember your evil ways
and your deeds that were not good,[v] and you
will loathe yourselves for your iniquities and
detestable practices.[w] 32 It is not for your sake
that I will act"[x]—the declaration of the Lord
GOD—"let this be known to you. Be ashamed
and humiliated because of your ways, house
of Israel!

33 "This is what the Lord GOD says: On the
day I cleanse you from all your iniquities, I
will cause the cities to be inhabited, and the
ruins will be rebuilt.[y] 34 The desolate land will
be cultivated instead of lying desolate in the
sight of everyone who passes by. 35 Then they
will say, 'This land that was desolate has become like the garden of Eden.[z] The cities that
were once ruined, desolate, and destroyed are
now fortified and inhabited.' 36 Then the nations that remain around you will know that
I, Yahweh, have rebuilt what was destroyed
and have replanted what was desolate. I, Yahweh, have spoken and I will do it.[aa]

37 "This is what the Lord GOD says: I will respond to the house of Israel and do this for
them:[ab] I will multiply them in number like a
flock.[C] 38 So the ruined cities will be filled with
a flock of people, just as the flock of sheep for
sacrifice[ac] is filled[D] in Jerusalem during its appointed festivals. Then they will know that I
am Yahweh."

The Valley of Dry Bones

37 The hand of the LORD was on me,[ad]
and He brought me out by His Spirit[ae]
and set me down in the middle of the valley;
it was full of bones. 2 He led me all around
them. There were a great many of them on
the surface of the valley, and they were very
dry. 3 Then He said to me, "Son of man, can
these bones live?"

I replied, "Lord GOD, only You know."[af]

4 He said to me, "Prophesy concerning these

[a] 36:15 Ezk 34:29
[b] 36:17 Jr 2:7
[c] Lv 15:19
[d] 36:18 Ezk 16:36; 22:3
[e] 36:19 Dt 28:64; Ezk 22:15
[f] Rm 2:6
[g] 36:20 Is 52:5; Rm 2:24
[h] 36:21 Is 48:9; Ezk 20:44
[i] 36:22 Dt 9:5
[j] Ps 115:1; Is 43:25; 48:11; Ezk 20:9; Dn 9:18-19
[k] 36:23 Ezk 20:41; 38:23; 39:7,25
[l] 36:24 Ezk 34:13; 37:21
[m] 36:25 Ps 51:7; Heb 9:13,19; 10:22
[n] Jr 33:8
[o] 36:26 Ezk 18:31; Jl 2:28
[p] Dt 30:6; Ezk 11:19; 2Co 3:3
[q] 36:27 Ezk 37:14
[r] Jr 24:7; 31:33; 32:40
[s] 36:28 Ezk 37:23-25
[t] Ezk 34:30
[u] 36:29-30 Ezk 34:27,29
[v] 36:31 Ezk 16:61-63
[w] Ezk 6:9; 20:43
[x] 36:32 Dt 9:5
[y] 36:33 Ezk 36:10
[z] 36:35 Is 51:3; Jl 2:3
[aa] 36:36 Ezk 17:24
[ab] 36:37 Ezk 14:3
[ac] 36:38 2Ch 35:7-9
[ad] 37:1 Ezk 1:3
[ae] Ezk 8:3; 11:24
[af] 37:3 Dt 32:39; 1Sm 2:6

[A] 36:15 Some Hb mss, Tg read *no longer bereave your nation of children*
[B] 36:26 Lit *stone from your flesh* [C] 36:37 Lit *flock of people* [D] 36:38 Lit *the flock of consecrated things, as the flock*

bones and say to them: Dry bones, hear the
word of the LORD! 5 This is what the Lord GOD
says to these bones: I will cause breath to enter you, and you will live.[a] 6 I will put tendons
on you, make flesh grow on you, and cover
you with skin. I will put breath in you so that
you come to life. Then you will know that I
am ˙Yahweh."[b]
7 So I prophesied as I had been commanded.
While I was prophesying, there was a noise, a
rattling sound, and the bones came together,
bone to bone. 8 As I looked, tendons appeared
on them, flesh grew, and skin covered them,
but there was no breath in them. 9 He said to
me, "Prophesy to the breath,[A] prophesy, son
of man. Say to it: This is what the Lord GOD
says: Breath, come from the four winds and
breathe into these slain so that they may
live!"[c] 10 So I prophesied as He commanded
me; the breath[A] entered them,[d] and they came
to life and stood on their feet, a vast army.
11 Then He said to me, "Son of man, these
bones are the whole house of Israel.[e] Look
how they say, 'Our bones are dried up,[f] and
our hope has perished;[g] we are cut off.'[h]
12 Therefore, prophesy and say to them: This
is what the Lord GOD says: I am going to open
your graves and bring you up from them,[i] My
people, and lead you into the land of Israel.
13 You will know that I am Yahweh, My people, when I open your graves and bring you
up from them.[j] 14 I will put My Spirit in you,[k]
and you will live, and I will settle you in your
own land. Then you will know that I am Yahweh. I have spoken, and I will do it."[l] This is
the declaration of the LORD.

The Reunification of Israel

15 The word of the LORD came to me: 16 "Son
of man, take a single stick and write on it:[m]
Belonging to Judah and the Israelites associated with him. Then take another stick and
write on it: Belonging to Joseph—the stick
of Ephraim—and all the house of Israel associated with him.[n] 17 Then join them together
into a single stick so that they become one
in your hand.[o] 18 When your people ask you,
'Won't you explain to us what you mean by
these things?'[p]— 19 tell them: This is what the
Lord GOD says: I am going to take the stick of
Joseph, which is in the hand of Ephraim, and
the tribes of Israel associated with him, and
put them together with the stick of Judah. I
will make them into a single stick so that they
become one in My hand.
20 "When the sticks you have written on are
in your hand and in full view of the people,[q]
21 tell them: This is what the Lord GOD says:
I am going to take the Israelites out of the
nations where they have gone.[r] I will gather
them from all around and bring them into
their own land. 22 I will make them one nation
in the land,[s] on the mountains of Israel, and
one king will rule over all of them.[t] They will
no longer be two nations and will no longer
be divided into two kingdoms. 23 They will not
defile themselves anymore with their idols,[u]
their detestable things, and all their transgressions.[v] I will save them from all their
apostasies by which[B] they sinned,[w] and I will
cleanse them. Then they will be My people,
and I will be their God.[x] 24 My servant David
will be king over them, and there will be one
shepherd for all of them.[y] They will follow My
ordinances, and keep My statutes and obey
them.[z]
25 "They will live in the land that I gave to
My servant Jacob,[aa] where your fathers lived.
They will live in it forever with their children
and grandchildren, and My servant David
will be their prince forever.[ab] 26 I will make a
covenant of peace with them;[ac] it will be an
everlasting covenant[ad] with them. I will establish and multiply them and will set My
sanctuary among them forever. 27 My dwelling place will be with them;[ae] I will be their
God, and they will be My people.[af] 28 When My
sanctuary is among them forever, the nations
will know that I, Yahweh, sanctify Israel."[ag]

The Defeat of Gog

38 The word of the LORD came to me:
2 "Son of man, turn your face toward
Gog, of the land of Magog,[ah] the chief prince
of[C] Meshech and Tubal.[ai] Prophesy against
him 3 and say: This is what the Lord GOD says:
Look, I am against you, Gog, chief prince of
Meshech and Tubal. 4 I will turn you around,
put hooks in your jaws,[aj] and bring you out
with all your army, including horses and rid-

[a] **37:5** Gn 2:7; Ps 104:29-30
[b] **37:6** Jl 2:27; 3:17
[c] **37:9** Ps 104:30
[d] **37:10** Rv 11:11
[e] **37:11** Ezk 36:10
[f] Ps 141:7
[g] Eph 2:12
[h] Is 49:14; Lm 3:54
[i] **37:12** Is 26:19; 66:14; Hs 13:14; Rm 11:15
[j] **37:13** Jn 5:28-29; 1Co 15:21-22; Rv 20:4-5
[k] **37:14** Ezk 36:27
[l] Ezk 17:24
[m] **37:16** Nm 17:2-3
[n] 2Ch 11:11-17
[o] **37:17** Is 11:13; Hs 1:11
[p] **37:18** Ezk 12:9; 24:19
[q] **37:20** Ezk 12:3
[r] **37:21** Ezk 36:24
[s] **37:22** Jr 3:18
[t] Ezk 34:23-24
[u] **37:23** Ezk 36:25
[v] Ezk 36:28-29
[w] Rm 11:26
[x] Ezk 36:38
[y] **37:24** Ezk 34:23-24; Jn 10:16
[z] Ezk 36:27
[aa] **37:25** Is 60:21
[ab] Jn 12:34
[ac] **37:26** Is 55:3; Ezk 34:25
[ad] Is 55:3; Jr 32:40; Ezk 16:60; Heb 13:20
[ae] **37:27** Jn 1:14
[af] Ezk 36:28
[ag] **37:28** Ezk 20:12
[ah] **38:2** Gn 10:2; Ezk 39:1; Rv 20:8
[ai] Ezk 27:13
[aj] **38:4** 2Kg 19:28; Ezk 29:4

[A] **37:9,10** Or *wind*, or *spirit* [B] **37:23** Some Hb mss, LXX, Sym; other Hb mss read *their settlements where* [C] **38:2** Or *the prince of Rosh,*

ers,[a] who are all splendidly dressed, a huge
company armed with shields and bucklers, all of them brandishing swords. 5 Persia,[b] ˚Cush, and Put are with them, all of them
with shields and helmets; 6 Gomer[c] with all
its troops; and Beth-togarmah[d] from the remotest parts of the north along with all its
troops — many peoples are with you.

7 "Be prepared and get yourself ready, you
and all your company who have been mobilized around you; you will be their guard.
8 After a long time you will be summoned. In
the last years you will enter a land that has
been restored from war[A] and regathered
from many peoples to the mountains of Israel, which had long been a ruin.[e] They were
brought out from the peoples, and all of them
now live securely. 9 You, all of your troops, and
many peoples with you will advance, coming
like a thunderstorm; you will be like a cloud
covering the land.

10 "This is what the Lord GOD says: On that
day, thoughts will arise in your mind, and
you will devise an evil plan. 11 You will say, 'I
will go up against a land of open villages; I
will come against a tranquil people who are
living securely,[f] all of them living without
walls and without bars or gates[g] — 12 in order
to seize spoil and carry off plunder,[h] to turn
your hand against ruins now inhabited and
against a people gathered from the nations,
who have been acquiring cattle and possessions and who live at the center of the world.'
13 Sheba[i] and Dedan[j] and the merchants of
Tarshish[k] with all its rulers[B] will ask you,
'Have you come to seize spoil? Have you assembled your hordes to carry off plunder, to
make off with silver and gold, to take cattle
and possessions, to seize great spoil?'

14 "Therefore prophesy, son of man, and say
to Gog: This is what the Lord GOD says: On
that day when My people Israel are dwelling
securely,[l] will you not know this 15 and come
from your place in the remotest parts of the
north[m] — you and many peoples with you,
who are all riding horses — a mighty horde,
a huge army? 16 You will advance against My
people Israel like a cloud covering the land.
It will happen in the last days, Gog, that I
will bring you against My land so that the nations may know Me, when I show Myself holy
through you in their sight.[n]

17 "This is what the Lord GOD says: Are
you the one I spoke about in former times
through My servants, the prophets of Israel,
who for years prophesied in those times that
I would bring you against them? 18 Now on
that day, the day when Gog comes against
the land of Israel" — this is the declaration of
the Lord GOD — "My wrath will flare up.[C] 19 I
swear in My zeal and fiery rage:[o] On that day
there will be a great earthquake in the land
of Israel. 20 The fish of the sea, the birds of the
sky, the animals of the field, every creature
that crawls on the ground, and every human
being on the face of the earth will tremble
before Me. The mountains will be thrown
down, the cliffs will collapse, and every wall
will fall to the ground. 21 I will call for a sword
against him on all My mountains" — the declaration of the Lord GOD — "and every man's
sword will be against his brother.[p] 22 I will
execute judgment on him with plague and
bloodshed. I will pour out torrential rain,
hailstones, fire, and brimstone on him, as
well as his troops and the many peoples who
are with him.[q] 23 I will display My greatness
and holiness, and will reveal Myself in the
sight of many nations.[r] Then they will know
that I am ˚Yahweh.

The Disposal of Gog

39 "As for you, son of man, prophesy
against Gog and say: This is what the
Lord GOD says: Look, I am against you, Gog,
chief prince of[D] Meshech and Tubal.[s] 2 I will
turn you around, drive you on,[t] and lead you
up from the remotest parts of the north. I
will bring you against the mountains of Israel. 3 Then I will knock your bow from your
left hand and make your arrows drop from
your right hand. 4 You, all your troops, and
the peoples who are with you will fall on the
mountains of Israel. I will give you as food to
every kind of predatory bird and to the wild
animals. 5 You will fall on the open field,[u] for
I have spoken." This is the declaration of the
Lord GOD.

6 "I will send fire against Magog[v] and those
who live securely on the coasts and islands.

[a] 38:4 Dn 11:40
[b] 38:5 Ezk 27:10
[c] 38:6 Gn 10:2
[d] Gn 10:3
[e] 38:8 Ezk 36:8-11
[f] 38:11 Jdg 18:7
[g] Jr 49:31
[h] 38:12 Is 10:6; Ezk 29:19
[i] 38:13 Ezk 27:22
[j] Ezk 27:20
[k] Ezk 27:12
[l] 38:14 Jr 23:6
[m] 38:15 Ezk 39:2
[n] 38:16 Ezk 28:22
[o] 38:19 Ezk 36:6
[p] 38:21 Ezk 14:17
[q] 38:22 Rv 16:18-21
[r] 38:23 Ezk 37:28
[s] 39:1 Ezk 38:2-3
[t] 39:2 Ezk 38:4
[u] 39:5 Ezk 32:4
[v] 39:6 Am 1:4,7,10

[A] 38:8 Lit *from the sword* [B] 38:13 Lit *young lions*, or *villages* [C] 38:18 Lit *up in My anger* [D] 39:1 Or *Gog, prince of Rosh,*

Then they will know that I am ·Yahweh. 7 So I will make My holy name known among My people Israel and will no longer allow it to be profaned. Then the nations will know that I am Yahweh, the Holy One in Israel.[a] 8 Yes, it is coming, and it will happen." This is the declaration of the Lord GOD. "This is the day I have spoken about.

9 "Then the inhabitants of Israel's cities will go out, kindle fires, and burn the weapons — the bucklers and shields, the bows and arrows, the clubs and spears. For seven years they will use them to make fires. 10 They will not gather wood from the countryside or cut it down from the forests, for they will use the weapons to make fires. They will take the loot from those who looted them and plunder those who plundered them."[b] This is the declaration of the Lord GOD.

11 "Now on that day I will give Gog a burial place there in Israel — the Valley of the Travelers[A] east of the Sea. It will block those who travel through, for Gog and all his hordes will be buried there. So it will be called the Valley of Hamon-gog.[B] 12 The house of Israel will spend seven months burying them in order to cleanse the land.[c] 13 All the people of the land will bury them and their fame will spread[d] on the day I display My glory."[e] This is the declaration of the Lord GOD.

14 "They will appoint men on a full-time basis to pass through the land and bury the invaders[C] who remain on the surface of the ground, in order to cleanse it. They will make their search at the end of the seven months. 15 When they pass through the land and one of them sees a human bone, he will set up a marker next to it until the buriers have buried it in the Valley of Hamon-gog. 16 There will even be a city named Hamonah[D] there. So they will cleanse the land.

17 "Son of man, this is what the Lord GOD says: Tell every kind of bird and all the wild animals: Assemble and come! Gather from all around to My sacrificial feast that I am slaughtering for you, a great feast on the mountains of Israel;[f] you will eat flesh and drink blood. 18 You will eat the flesh of mighty men and drink the blood of the earth's princes: rams, lambs, male goats, and all the fattened bulls of Bashan. 19 You will eat fat until you are satisfied[g] and drink blood until you are drunk, at My sacrificial feast that I have prepared for you. 20 At My table you will eat your fill of horses and riders, of mighty men and all the warriors." This is the declaration of the Lord GOD.

Israel's Restoration to God

21 "I will display My glory among the nations,[h] and all the nations will see the judgment I have executed and the hand I have laid on them. 22 From that day forward the house of Israel will know that I am Yahweh their God. 23 And the nations will know that the house of Israel went into exile on account of their iniquity, because they dealt unfaithfully with Me.[i] Therefore, I hid My face from them and handed them over to their enemies, so that they all fell by the sword. 24 I dealt with them according to their uncleanness and transgressions, and I hid My face from them.

25 "So this is what the Lord GOD says: Now I will restore the fortunes of Jacob[j] and have compassion on the whole house of Israel,[k] and I will be jealous for My holy name. 26 They will feel remorse for[E,F] their disgrace[l] and all the unfaithfulness they committed against Me, when they live securely in their land with no one to frighten them. 27 When I bring them back from the peoples and gather them from the countries of their enemies, I will demonstrate My holiness through them in the sight of many nations.[m] 28 They will know that I am Yahweh their God when I regather them to their own land after having exiled them among the nations. I will leave none of them behind.[G] 29 I will no longer hide My face from them, for I will pour out My Spirit on the house of Israel."[n] This is the declaration of the Lord GOD.

The New Temple

40 In the twenty-fifth year of our exile, at the beginning of the year, on the tenth day of the month in the fourteenth year after Jerusalem had been captured,[o] on that very day the LORD's hand was on me,[p] and He

[a] **39:7** Ezk 36:20-23
[b] **39:10** Is 14:2; 33:1
[c] **39:12** Dt 21:23
[d] **39:13** Jr 33:9; Zph 3:19-20
[e] Ezk 28:22
[f] **39:17** Rv 19:17-18
[g] **39:19** Rv 19:21
[h] **39:21** Ezk 36:23; 38:16,23
[i] **39:23** Ezk 36:18-20,23
[j] **39:25** Is 27:12-13; Jr 33:7; Ezk 34:13
[k] Ezk 36:10; 37:21-22; Hs 1:11
[l] **39:26** Ezk 16:53-54,63
[m] **39:27** Ezk 20:41; 38:23
[n] **39:29** Ezk 36:27; 37:14; Jl 2:28
[o] **40:1** 2Kg 25:1-7; Jr 39:1-9; 52:4-11; Ezk 33:21
[p] Ezk 1:3; 3:14,22; 37:1

[A] **39:11** Hb obscure [B] **39:11** = Hordes of Gog [C] **39:14** Or *basis, some to pass through the land, and with them some to bury those* [D] **39:16** In Hb, Hamonah is related to the word "horde." [E] **39:26** Some emend to *will forget* [F] **39:26** Lit *will bear* [G] **39:28** Lit *behind there any longer*

brought me there. 2 In visions of God[a] He took
me to the land of Israel and set me down on
a very high mountain.[b] On its southern slope
was a structure resembling a city. 3 He brought
me there, and I saw a man whose appearance
was like bronze,[c] with a linen cord and a measuring rod in his hand.[d] He was standing by
the gate. 4 He spoke to me: "Son of man, look
with your eyes, listen with your ears,[e] and pay
attention to everything I am going to show
you, for you have been brought here so that I
might show it to you. Report everything you
see to the house of Israel."[f]

The Wall and Outer Gates

5 Now there was a wall surrounding the
outside of the temple.[g] The measuring rod
in the man's hand was six units of 21 inches;[A]
each unit was the standard length plus three
inches.[B] He measured the thickness of the
wall structure; it was about 10 feet,[C] and its
height was the same.[C] 6 Then he came to the
gate that faced east and climbed its steps.[h]
He measured the threshold of the gate; it
was 10 feet deep—the first threshold was
10 feet deep. 7 Each recess was about 10 feet[C]
long and 10 feet[D] deep, and there was a space
of 8¾ feet[E] between the recesses. The inner
threshold of the gate on the temple side next
to the gate's portico was about 10 feet.[C] 8 Next
he measured the portico of the gate; 9 it[F] was
14 feet,[G] and its pilasters were 3½ feet.[H] The
portico of the gate was on the temple side.

10 There were three recesses on each side of
the east gate, each with the same measurements, and the pilasters on either side also
had the same measurements. 11 Then he measured the width of the gate's entrance; it was
17½ feet,[I] while the width[J] of the gateway was
22¾ feet.[K] 12 There was a barrier of 21 inches[L]
in front of the recesses on both sides, and the
recesses on each side were 10½ feet[M] square.
13 Then he measured the gateway from the
roof of one recess to the roof of the opposite
one; the distance was 43¾ feet.[N] The openings of the recesses faced each other. 14 Next,
he measured the pilasters—105 feet.[O] The
gate extended around to the pilaster of the
court.[P] 15 The distance from the front of the
gate at the entrance to the front of the gate's
portico on the inside was 87½ feet.[Q] 16 The
recesses and their pilasters had beveled windows all around the inside of the gateway.[i]
The porticoes also had windows all around
on the inside. Each pilaster was decorated
with palm trees.[j]

17 Then he brought me into the outer court,[k]
and there were chambers and a paved surface
laid out all around the court.[l] Thirty chambers faced the pavement, 18 which flanked the
gates and corresponded to the length of the
gates; this was the lower pavement. 19 Then he
measured the distance from the front of the
lower gate to the exterior front of the inner
court; it was 175 feet.[R] This was the east; next
the north is described.

20 He measured the gate of the outer court
facing north, both its length and width. 21 Its
three recesses on each side, its pilasters, and
its portico had the same measurements as
the first gate: 87½ feet[Q] long and 43¾ feet[N]
wide. 22 Its windows, portico, and palm trees
had the same measurements as those of the
gate that faced east. Seven steps led up to
the gate, and its portico was ahead of them.
23 The inner court had a gate facing the north
gate, like the one on the east. He measured
the distance from gate to gate; it was 175 feet.[R]

24 He brought me to the south side, and
there was also a gate on the south. He measured its pilasters and portico; they had the
same measurements as the others. 25 Both the
gate and its portico had windows all around,
like the other windows. It was 87½ feet[Q] long
and 43¾ feet[N] wide. 26 Its stairway had seven
steps, and its portico was ahead of them. It
had palm trees on its pilasters, one on each
side. 27 The inner court had a gate on the
south. He measured from gate to gate on the
south; it was 175 feet.[R]

The Inner Gates

28 Then he brought me to the inner court
through the south gate. When he measured
the south gate, it had the same measurements
as the others. 29 Its recesses, pilasters, and

[a] **40:2** Ezk 1:1; 8:3; Dn 7:1,7 [b] Is 2:2-3; Ezk 17:23; 20:40; 37:22; Mc 4:1; Rv 21:10 [c] **40:3** Ezk 1:7; Dn 10:6; Rv 1:15 [d] Ezk 47:3; Zch 2:1-2; Rv 11:1; 21:15 [e] **40:4** Ezk 2:1,3,6,8; 44:5 [f] Ezk 43:10 [g] **40:5** Is 26:1; Ezk 42:20 [h] **40:6** Ezk 43:1 [i] **40:16** 1Kg 6:4; Ezk 41:16,26 [j] 1Kg 6:29,32,35; 2Ch 3:5; Ezk 41:18-20,25-26 [k] **40:17** Ezk 10:5; 42:1; 46:21; Rv 11:2 [l] 2Kg 23:11; 1Ch 9:26; 23:28; 2Ch 31:11

A **40:5** = a long cubit B **40:5** Lit *six cubits by the cubit and a handbreadth* C **40:5,7** Lit *was one rod* D **40:7** Lit *and one rod* E **40:7** Lit *five cubits* F **40:8-9** Some Hb mss, Syr, Vg; other Hb mss read *gate facing the temple side; it was one rod. 9 Then he measured the portico of the gate; it* G **40:9** Lit *eight cubits* H **40:9** Lit *two cubits* I **40:11** Lit *10 cubits* J **40:11** Lit *length* K **40:11** Lit *13 cubits* L **40:12** Lit *one cubit* M **40:12** Lit *six cubits* N **40:13,21,25** Lit *25 cubits* O **40:14** Lit *60 cubits* P **40:14** Hb obscure Q **40:15,21,25** Lit *50 cubits* R **40:19,23,27** Lit *100 cubits*

portico had the same measurements as the others. Both it and its portico had windows all around. It was 87½ feet[A] long and 43¾ feet[B] wide. 30(There were porticoes all around, 43¾ feet long and 8¾ feet[C] wide.[D]) 31Its portico faced the outer court, and its pilasters were decorated with palm trees. Its stairway had eight steps.

32Then he brought me to the inner court on the east side. When he measured the gate, it had the same measurements as the others. 33Its recesses, pilasters, and portico had the same measurements as the others. Both it and its portico had windows all around. It was 87½ feet[A] long and 43¾ feet[B] wide. 34Its portico faced the outer court, and its pilasters were decorated with palm trees on each side. Its stairway had eight steps.

35Then he brought me to the north gate.[a] When he measured it, it had the same measurements as the others, 36as did its recesses, pilasters, and portico. It also had windows all around. It was 87½ feet[A] long and 43¾ feet[B] wide. 37Its portico[E] faced the outer court, and its pilasters were decorated with palm trees on each side. Its stairway had eight steps.

Rooms for Preparing Sacrifices

38There was a chamber whose door opened into the portico of the gate.[F] The •burnt offering was to be washed there.[b] 39Inside the portico of the gate there were two tables on each side, on which to slaughter the burnt offering, •sin offering,[c] and •restitution offering.[d] 40Outside, as one approaches the entrance of the north gate, there were two tables on one side and two more tables on the other side of the gate's portico. 41So there were four tables inside the gate and four outside, eight tables in all on which the slaughtering was to be done. 42There were also four tables of cut stone for the burnt offering,[e] each 31½ inches[G] long, 31½ inches wide, and 21 inches[H] high. The utensils used to slaughter the burnt offerings and other sacrifices were placed on them. 43There were three-inch[I] hooks[J] fastened all around the inside of the room, and the flesh of the offering was to be laid on the tables.

Rooms for Singers and Priests

44Outside the inner gate, within the inner court, there were chambers for the singers:[K,f] one[L] beside the north gate, facing south, and another beside the south[M] gate, facing north. 45Then the man said to me: "This chamber that faces south is for the priests who keep charge of the temple.[g] 46The chamber that faces north is for the priests who keep charge of the altar. These are the sons of Zadok,[h] the ones from the sons of Levi who may approach the LORD to serve Him."[i] 47Next he measured the court. It was square, 175 feet[N] long and 175 feet wide. The altar[j] was in front of the temple.

48Then he brought me to the portico of the temple and measured the pilasters of the portico; they were 8¾ feet[C] thick on each side. The width of the gateway was 24½ feet,[O] and the side walls of the gate were[P] 5¼ feet[Q] wide on each side. 49The portico was 35 feet[R] across and 21[S] feet[T] deep, and 10 steps led[U] up to it.[k] There were pillars by the pilasters, one on each side.[l]

Inside the Temple

41 Next he brought me into the great hall and measured the pilasters;[m] on each side the width of the pilaster was 10½ feet.[V,W] 2The width of the entrance was 17½ feet,[X] and the side walls of the entrance were 8¾ feet[C] wide on each side. He also measured the length of the great hall, 70 feet,[Y] and the width, 35 feet.[R,n] 3He went inside the next room and measured the pilasters at the entrance;[o] they were 3½ feet[Z] wide. The entrance was 10½ feet[W] wide, and the width of the entrance's side walls on each side[AA] was 12¼ feet.[AB] 4He then measured the length of the room adjacent to the great hall, 35 feet,[R] and the width, 35 feet.[p] And he said to me, "This is the most holy place."[q]

a40:35 Ezk 47:2 b40:38 2Ch 4:6 c40:39 Lv 1:3-4; 4:2-3 dLv 5:1-6 e40:42 Ex 20:25 f40:44 1Ch 6:31-32; 16:41-43; 25:1-7 g40:45 1Ch 9:23; Ps 134:1 h40:46 1Kg 2:35 iLv 6:12-13; Ezk 43:19; 44:15 j40:47 Ezk 43:13-17 k40:49 1Kg 6:3 l1Kg 7:15-22; 2Ch 3:17; Jr 52:17-23; Rv 3:12 m41:1 Ezk 40:2-3,17 n41:2 1Kg 6:2,17 o41:3 Ezk 40:16 p41:4 1Kg 6:20 q1Kg 6:16

A40:29,33,36 Lit *50 cubits* B40:29,33,36 Lit *25 cubits* C40:30,48; 41:2 Lit *five cubits* D40:30 Some Hb mss, LXX omit v. 30 E40:37 LXX; MT reads *pilasters* F40:38 Text emended; MT reads *door was by the pilasters, at the gates* G40:42 Lit *one and a half cubits* H40:42 Lit *one cubit* I40:43 Lit *one handbreadth* J40:43 Or *ledges* K40:44 LXX reads *were two chambers* L40:44 LXX; MT reads *singers, which was* M40:44 LXX; MT reads *east* N40:47 Lit *100 cubits* O40:48 Lit *14 cubits* P40:48 LXX; MT omits *24½ feet, and the side walls of the gate were* Q40:48 Lit *three cubits* R40:49; 41:2,4 Lit *20 cubits* S40:49 LXX; MT reads *19¼* T40:49 Lit *12 cubits* U40:49 MT reads *and it was on steps that they would go* V41:1 LXX; MT reads *pilasters; they were 10½ feet wide on each side — the width of the tabernacle* W41:1,3 Lit *six cubits* X41:2 Lit *10 cubits* Y41:2 Lit *40 cubits* Z41:3 Lit *two cubits* AA41:3 LXX; MT reads *width of the entrance* AB41:3 Lit *seven cubits*

Outside the Temple

5 Then he measured the wall of the temple;
it was 10 1/2 feet[A] thick. The width of the side
rooms all around the temple was seven feet.[B,a]
6 The side rooms were arranged one above
another in three stories of 30 rooms each.[C]
There were ledges on the wall of the temple
all around to serve as supports for the side
rooms, so that the supports would not be in
the temple wall itself.[b] 7 The side rooms surrounding the temple widened at each successive story, for the structure surrounding the
temple went up by stages. This was the reason
for the temple's broadness as it rose. And so,
one would go up from the lowest story to the
highest by means of the middle one.[D,c]

8 I saw that the temple had a raised platform surrounding it; this foundation for the
side rooms was 10 1/2 feet high.[E,d] 9 The thickness of the outer wall of the side rooms was
8 3/4 feet.[F] The free space between the side
rooms of the temple 10 and the outer chambers was 35 feet[G] wide all around the temple.[e]
11 The side rooms opened into the free space,
one entrance toward the north and another
to the south. The area of free space was 8 3/4
feet[F] wide all around.

12 Now the building that faced the temple
yard toward the west was 122 1/2 feet[H] wide.
The wall of the building was 8 3/4 feet[F] thick
on all sides, and the building's length was
157 1/2 feet.[I]

13 Then the man measured the temple; it
was 175 feet[J] long.[f] In addition, the temple
yard and the building, including its walls,
were 175 feet long. 14 The width of the front
of the temple along with the temple yard to
the east was 175 feet. 15 Next he measured the
length of the building facing the temple yard
to the west, with its galleries[K] on each side;[g] it
was 175 feet.

Interior Wooden Structures

The interior of the great hall and the porticoes of the court — 16 the thresholds, the beveled windows,[h] and the balconies all around
with their three levels opposite the threshold — were overlaid with wood on all sides.[i]
They were paneled from the ground to the
windows (but the windows were covered),
17 reaching to the top of the entrance, and as
far as the inner temple and on the outside.
On every wall all around, on the inside and
outside, was a pattern 18 carved with •cheru-
bim and palm trees.[j] There was a palm tree
between each pair of cherubim.[k] Each cherub
had two faces: 19 a human face turned toward
the palm tree on one side,[l] and a lion's face
turned toward it on the other. They were
carved throughout the temple on all sides.
20 Cherubim and palm trees were carved from
the ground to the top of the entrance and on
the wall of the great hall.

21 The doorposts of the great hall were
square,[m] and the front of the sanctuary had
the same appearance. 22 The altar was[L] made
of wood, 5 1/4 feet[M] high and 3 1/2 feet[N] long.[O]
It had corners, and its length[P] and sides were
of wood.[n] The man told me, "This is the table
that stands before the LORD."[o]

23 The great hall and the sanctuary each had
a double door,[p] 24 and each of the doors had
two swinging panels.[q] There were two panels
for one door and two for the other. 25 Cherubim and palm trees were carved on the doors
of the great hall like those carved on the
walls. There was a wooden canopy[D,r] outside,
in front of the portico. 26 There were beveled
windows and palm trees on both sides,[s] on
the side walls of the portico, the side rooms
of the temple, and the canopies.[D]

The Priests' Chambers

42 Then the man led me out by way of
the north gate into the outer court.[t]
He brought me to the group of chambers
opposite the temple yard and opposite the
building[u] to the north. 2 Along the length of
the chambers, which was 175 feet,[I,v] there
was an entrance on the north; the width
was 87 1/2 feet.[Q] 3 Opposite the 35 foot space[G]
belonging to the inner court and opposite
the paved surface[w] belonging to the outer
court, the structure rose gallery by gallery[x]
in three tiers. 4 In front of the chambers
was a walkway toward the inside,[y] 17 1/2 feet[R]

[a] 41:5 1Kg 6:5-10
[b] 41:6 1Kg 6:6
[c] 41:7 1Kg 6:8
[d] 41:8 Ezk 40:5
[e] 41:10 Ezk 40:17
[f] 41:13 Ezk 40:47
[g] 41:15 Ezk 42:3,5
[h] 41:16 1Kg 6:4; Ezk 40:16,25
[i] 1Kg 6:15
[j] 41:18 1Kg 6:29
[k] 2Ch 3:5; Ezk 40:16
[l] 41:19 Ezk 1:10; 10:14
[m] 41:21 1Kg 6:33; Ezk 40:9,14,16; 41:1
[n] 41:22 Ex 30:1-3; 1Kg 6:20; Rv 8:3
[o] Ex 25:23,30; Lv 24:6; Ezk 23:41; 44:16; Mal 1:7,12
[p] 41:23 1Kg 6:31-35
[q] 41:24 1Kg 6:34
[r] 41:25 1Kg 7:6
[s] 41:26 Ezk 40:16
[t] 42:1 Ezk 40:17,28,48; 41:1
[u] Ezk 41:12; 42:10,13
[v] 42:2 Ezk 41:13
[w] 42:3 Ezk 40:17
[x] Ezk 41:15-16
[y] 42:4 Ezk 46:19

A 41:5 Lit *six cubits* B 41:5 Lit *four cubits* C 41:6 Lit *another three and 30 times* D 41:7,25,26 Hb obscure E 41:8 Lit *a full rod of six cubits of a joint*; Hb obscure F 41:9,11,12 Lit *five cubits* G 41:10; 42:3 Lit *20 cubits* H 41:12 Lit *70 cubits* I 41:12 Lit *90 cubits* J 41:13; 42:2 Lit *100 cubits* K 41:15 Or *ledges*

L 41:21-22 Or *and in front of the sanctuary was something that looked like* 22 *an altar* M 41:22 Lit *three cubits* N 41:22 Lit *two cubits* O 41:22 LXX reads *long and 3 1/2 feet wide* P 41:22 LXX reads *base* Q 42:2 Lit *50 cubits* R 42:4 Lit *10 cubits* wide and 175 feet[A] long,[B] and their entrances were on the north. 5The upper chambers were narrower because the galleries took away more space from them than from the lower and middle stories of the building. 6For they were arranged in three stories and had no pillars like the pillars of the courts;[a] therefore the upper chambers were set back from the ground more than the lower and middle stories. 7A wall on the outside ran in front of the chambers, parallel to them, toward the outer court; it was 87 1/2 feet[C] long. 8For the chambers on the outer court were 87 1/2 feet long, while those facing the great hall were 175 feet[A] long.[b] 9At the base of these chambers there was an entryway on the east side as one enters them from the outer court.[c]

10In the thickness of the wall of the court toward the south,[D] there were chambers facing the temple yard[d] and the western building, 11with a passageway in front of them, just like the chambers that faced north.[e] Their length and width, as well as all their exits, measurements, and entrances, were identical. 12The entrance at the beginning of the passageway, the way in front of the corresponding[E] wall as one enters on the east side, was similar to the entrances of the chambers that were on the south side.

13Then the man said to me, "The northern and southern chambers that face the temple yard are the holy chambers where the priests who approach the LORD will eat[f] the most holy offerings.[g] There they will deposit the most holy offerings—the •grain offerings, •sin offerings, and •restitution offerings—for the place is holy.[h] 14Once the priests have entered, they must not go out from the holy area to the outer court until they have removed the clothes they minister in, for these are holy.[i] They are to put on other clothes before they approach the public area."[j]

Outside Dimensions of the Temple Complex

15When he finished measuring inside the temple complex, he led me out by way of the gate that faced east and measured all around the complex.[k]

16He measured the east side with a
measuring rod;
it was 875 feet[F] by the measuring rod.[G]
17He[H] measured the north side;
it was 875 feet[F] by the measuring rod.[G]
18He[I] measured the south side;
it was 875 feet[F] by the measuring rod.[G]
19Then he turned to the west side
and measured 875 feet[F] by the
measuring rod.[G]

20He measured the temple complex on all four sides. It had a wall all around it,[l] 875 feet long and 875 feet[m] wide, to separate the holy from the common.[n]

Return of the LORD's Glory

43 He led me to the gate,[o] the one that faces east, 2and I saw the glory of the God of Israel[p] coming from the east.[q] His voice sounded like the roar of mighty waters,[r] and the earth shone with His glory.[s] 3The vision I saw[t] was like the one I had seen when He[J] came to destroy the city,[u] and like the ones I had seen by the Chebar Canal.[v] I fell facedown.[w] 4The glory of the LORD entered the temple by way of the gate that faced east.[x] 5Then the Spirit lifted me up[y] and brought me to the inner court, and the glory of the LORD filled the temple.[z]

6While the man was standing beside me, I heard someone speaking to me from the temple.[aa] 7He said to me: "Son of man, this is the place of My throne and the place for the soles of My feet,[ab] where I will dwell among the Israelites forever.[ac] The house of Israel and their kings will no longer defile My holy name by their religious prostitution and by the corpses[K,ad] of their kings at their •high places.[L,ae] 8Whenever they placed their threshold next to My threshold and their doorposts beside My doorposts, with only a wall between Me and them, they were defiling My holy name by the detestable acts they committed.[af] So I destroyed them in My anger. 9Now let them remove their prostitution and the

[a]42:6 Ezk 41:6 [b]42:8 Ezk 41:13-14 [c]42:9 Ezk 44:5; 46:19 [d]42:10 Ezk 42:1 [e]42:11 Ezk 42:4 [f]42:13 Lv 10:3; Dt 21:5; Ezk 40:46 [g]Ex 29:31; Lv 7:6; 10:13-14,17 [h]Lv 6:25,29; 14:13; Nm 18:9-10 [i]42:14 Ex 29:4-9; Lv 8:7,13; Is 61:10; Zch 3:4-5 [j]Ezk 44:19 [k]42:15 Ezk 40:6; 43:1 [l]42:20 Is 60:18; Ezk 40:5; Zch 2:5 [m]Ezk 45:2; Rv 21:16 [n]Ezk 22:26; 44:23; 48:15 [o]43:1 Ezk 10:19; 40:6; 42:15; 44:1 [p]43:2 Is 6:3; Ezk 1:28; 3:23; 10:18-19 [q]Ezk 11:22-23 [r]Ezk 1:24; Rv 1:15 [s]Ezk 1:28; 10:4; Rv 18:1 [t]43:3 Ezk 1:4-28 [u]Jr 1:10; Ezk 9:1 [v]Ezk 1:3 [w]Ezk 1:28; 3:23 [x]43:4 Ezk 10:19 [y]43:5 Ezk 3:14; 2Co 12:2-4 [z]Ezk 10:4 [aa]43:6 Ezk 1:26 [ab]43:7 Ps 47:8 [ac]Ezk 37:26-28 [ad]Lv 26:30; Ezk 6:5,13 [ae]Ezk 6:3-5 [af]43:8 Ezk 8:3

A42:4,8 Lit *100 cubits* B42:4 LXX, Syr; MT reads *wide, a way of one cubit* C42:7 Lit *50 cubits* D42:10 LXX; MT reads *east* E42:12 Or *protective*; Hb obscure F42:16,17,18,19 Lit *500 in rods* G42:16,17,18,19 Lit *rod all around* H42:17 LXX reads *Then he turned to the north and* I42:18 LXX reads *Then he turned to the south and* J43:3 Some Hb mss, Theod, Vg; other Hb mss, LXX, Syr read *I* K43:7 Or *monuments* L43:7 Some Hb mss, Theod, Tg read *their death*

corpses[A,a] of their kings far from Me, and I will
dwell among them forever.[b]
10 "As for you, son of man, describe the temple to the house of Israel,[c] so that they may be
ashamed of their iniquities.[d] Let them measure its pattern,[e] 11 and they will be ashamed
of all that they have done. Reveal[B] the design
of the temple to them—its layout with its
exits and entrances[f]—its complete design
along with all its statutes, design specifications, and laws. Write it down in their sight[g]
so that they may observe its complete design
and all its statutes and may carry them out.[h]
12 This is the law of the temple: all its surrounding territory on top of the mountain[i]
will be especially holy. Yes, this is the law of
the temple.

The Altar

13 "These are the measurements of the altar[j]
in units of length (each unit being the standard length plus three inches[k]):[C] the gutter
is 21 inches[D] deep and 21 inches wide, with
a rim of nine inches[E] around its edge. This is
the base[F] of the altar. 14 The distance from the
gutter on the ground to the lower ledge is 3 1/2
feet,[G] and the width of the ledge is 21 inches.[D]
There are seven feet[H] from the small ledge to
the large ledge, whose width is also 21 inches.
15 The altar hearth[I] is seven feet[H] high, and
four horns[l] project upward from the hearth.
16 The hearth is square, 21 feet[J] long by 21 feet
wide.[m] 17 The ledge is 24 1/2 feet[K] long by 24 1/2
feet wide, with four equal sides.[n] The rim all
around it is 10 1/2 inches,[L] and its gutter is 21
inches[D] all around it. The altar's steps face
east."[o]
18 Then He said to me: "Son of man,[p] this is
what the Lord GOD says: These are the statutes for the altar on the day it is constructed,
so that ·burnt offerings[q] may be sacrificed on
it and blood may be sprinkled on it:[r] 19 You are
to give a bull from the herd[s] as a ·sin offering[t]
to the Levitical priests who are from the offspring of Zadok,[u] who approach Me in order
to serve Me."[v] This is the declaration of the
Lord GOD. 20 "You must take some of its blood
and apply it to the four horns[w] of the altar,

[a]43:9 Ezk 18:30 [b]Ezk 37:26-28 [c]43:10 Ezk 40:4 [d]Ezk 16:61-63 [e]Ezk 28:12 [f]43:11 Ezk 44:5 [g]Ezk 12:3 [h]Ezk 11:20 [i]43:12 Ezk 40:2 [j]43:13 Ex 27:1-8; 2Ch 4:1 [k]Ezk 40:5 [l]43:15 Ex 27:2; Lv 9:9; 1Kg 1:50; Ps 118:27 [m]43:16 Ex 27:1 [n]43:17 Ex 20:26 [o]Ezk 40:6 [p]43:18 Ezk 2:1 [q]Ex 40:29 [r]Lv 1:5,11; Heb 9:21-22 [s]43:19 Lv 4:3 [t]Ezk 45:19; Heb 7:27 [u]1Kg 2:35; Ezk 40:46 [v]Nm 16:5 [w]43:20 Lv 8:15; 9:9 [x]Lv 16:19 [y]43:21 Ex 29:14; Lv 4:12; Heb 13:11 [z]43:23 Ex 29:1,10; Ezk 45:18 [aa]Ex 29:1 [ab]43:24 Lv 2:13; Nm 18:19; Mk 9:49-50; Col 4:6 [ac]43:25 Ex 29:35-37; Lv 8:33 [ad]43:27 Lv 9:1 [ae]Ezk 20:40 [af]44:2 Ezk 43:2-4 [ag]44:3 Gn 31:54; Ex 24:9-11 [ah]Ezk 46:2,8-10 [ai]44:4 Is 6:3; Ezk 3:23; 43:5 [aj]Ezk 1:28; 43:3 [ak]44:5 Dt 32:46; Ezk 40:4 [al]Dt 12:32; Ezk 43:10-11

the four corners of the ledge, and all around
the rim. In this way you will purify the altar
and make ·atonement for it.[x] 21 Then you must
take away the bull for the sin offering, and it
must be burned outside the sanctuary in the
place appointed for the temple.[y]
22 "On the second day you are to present an
unblemished male goat as a sin offering. They
will purify the altar just as they did with the
bull. 23 When you have finished the purification, you are to present a young, unblemished bull[z] and an unblemished ram from
the flock.[aa] 24 You must present them before
the LORD; the priests will throw salt on them
and sacrifice them as a burnt offering to the
LORD.[ab] 25 You will offer a goat for a sin offering each day for seven days.[ac] A young bull and
a ram from the flock, both unblemished, must
also be offered. 26 For seven days the priests are
to make atonement for the altar and cleanse
it. In this way they will consecrate it[M] 27 and
complete the days of purification. Then on
the eighth day[ad] and afterward, the priests
will offer your burnt offerings and ·fellow-
ship offerings on the altar, and I will accept
you."[ae] This is the declaration of the Lord GOD.

The Prince's Privilege

44 The man then brought me back toward the sanctuary's outer gate that
faced east, and it was closed. 2 The LORD said
to me: "This gate will remain closed. It will
not be opened, and no one will enter through
it, because the LORD, the God of Israel, has
entered through it.[af] Therefore it will remain
closed. 3 The prince himself will sit in the
gateway to eat a meal before the LORD.[ag] He
must enter by way of the portico[ah] of the gate
and go out the same way."
4 Then the man brought me by way of the
north gate to the front of the temple. I looked,
and the glory of the LORD filled His temple.[ai]
And I fell facedown.[aj] 5 The LORD said to me:
"Son of man, pay attention;[ak] look with your
·eyes and listen with your ears to everything I
tell you about all the statutes and laws of the
LORD's temple.[al] Take careful note of the entrance of the temple along with all the exits
of the sanctuary.

[A]43:9 Or *monuments* [B]43:10-11 LXX, Vg; MT reads *pattern.* [11]*And if they are ashamed . . . done, reveal* [C]43:13 Lit *in cubits (a cubit being a cubit plus a handbreadth)* [D]43:13,14,17 Lit *one cubit* [E]43:13 Lit *one span* [F]43:13 LXX reads *height* [G]43:14 Lit *two cubits* [H]43:14,15 Lit *four cubits* [I]43:15 Hb obscure [J]43:16 Lit *12 cubits* [K]43:17 Lit *14 cubits* [L]43:17 Lit *one-half cubit* [M]43:26 Lit *will fill its hands*

The Levites' Duties and Privileges

6 “Say to the rebellious people,[a] the house of Israel: This is what the Lord GOD says: I have had enough[b] of all your detestable practices, house of Israel. 7 When you brought in foreigners,[c] uncircumcised in both heart and flesh,[d] to occupy My sanctuary, you defiled My temple while you offered My food — the fat and the blood. You[A] broke My covenant by all your detestable practices. 8 You have not kept charge of My holy things[e] but have appointed others to keep charge of My sanctuary for you.

9 “This is what the Lord GOD says: No foreigner, uncircumcised in heart and flesh, may enter My sanctuary, not even a foreigner who is among the Israelites. 10 Surely the Levites who wandered away from Me when Israel went astray, and who strayed from Me after their idols,[f] will bear the consequences of their sin.[g] 11 Yet they will occupy My sanctuary, serving as guards at the temple gates[h] and ministering at the temple. They will slaughter the ˙burnt offerings[i] and other sacrifices for the people and will stand before them to serve them.[j] 12 Because they ministered to the house of Israel before their idols and became a sinful stumbling block to them, therefore I swore an oath[B] against them”[k] — this is the declaration of the Lord GOD — “that they would bear the consequences of their sin. 13 They must not approach Me to serve Me as priests[l] or come near any of My holy things or the most holy things. They will bear their disgrace and the consequences of the detestable acts they committed. 14 Yet I will make them responsible for the duties of the temple[m] — for all its work and everything done in it.

The Priests' Duties and Privileges

15 “But the Levitical priests descended from Zadok,[n] who kept charge of My sanctuary when the Israelites went astray from Me, will approach Me to serve Me. They will stand before Me to offer Me fat and blood.” This is the declaration of the Lord GOD. 16 “They are the ones who may enter My sanctuary[o] and draw near to My table to serve Me.[p] They will keep My mandate. 17 When they enter the gates of the inner court they must wear linen garments;[q] they must not have on them anything made of wool when they minister at the gates of the inner court and within it. 18 They must wear linen turbans on their heads and linen undergarments around their waists.[r] They are not to put on anything that makes them sweat. 19 Before they go out to the outer court,[C] to the people, they must take off the clothes they have been ministering in, leave them in the holy chambers, and dress in other clothes[s] so that they do not transmit holiness to the people through their clothes.[t]

20 “They may not shave their heads[u] or let their hair grow long,[v] but must carefully trim their hair. 21 No priest may drink wine before he enters the inner court.[w] 22 He is not to marry a widow or a divorced woman, but must marry a virgin from the offspring of the house of Israel,[x] or a widow who is the widow of a priest. 23 They must teach My people the difference between the holy and the common, and explain to them the difference between the ˙clean and the ˙unclean.[y]

24 “In a dispute, they will officiate as judges and decide the case according to My ordinances.[z] They must observe My laws and statutes regarding all My appointed festivals, and keep My Sabbaths holy.[aa] 25 A priest may not come near a dead person so that he becomes defiled.[ab] However, he may defile himself for a father, a mother, a son, a daughter, a brother, or an unmarried sister. 26 After he is cleansed, he is to count off seven days for himself.[ac] 27 On the day he goes into the sanctuary, into the inner court[ad] to minister in the sanctuary, he must present his ˙sin offering.” This is the declaration of the Lord GOD.

28 “This will be their inheritance: I am their inheritance.[ae] You are to give them no possession in Israel: I am their possession. 29 They will eat the ˙grain offering, the sin offering,[af] and the ˙restitution offering. Everything in Israel that is permanently dedicated to the LORD will belong to them.[ag] 30 The best of all the ˙firstfruits of every kind and contribution of every kind from all your gifts will belong to the priests.[ah] You are to give your first batch of dough to the priest[ai] so that a blessing may rest on your homes.[aj] 31 The priests may not

[a]**44:6** Ezk 2:5-7; 3:9
[b]Ezk 45:9; 1Pt 4:3
[c]**44:7** Lv 22:25
[d]Lv 26:41; Dt 10:16; Jr 4:4; 9:26
[e]**44:8** Lv 22:2; Nm 18:7
[f]**44:10** 2Kg 23:8-9
[g]Nm 18:23
[h]**44:11** 1Ch 26:1-19
[i]2Ch 29:34; 30:17
[j]Nm 16:9
[k]**44:12** Ps 106:26
[l]**44:13** 2Kg 23:9
[m]**44:14** Nm 18:4; 1Ch 23:28-32
[n]**44:15** Ezk 40:46
[o]**44:16** Nm 18:5,7-8
[p]Ezk 41:22
[q]**44:17** Ex 28:42-43; 39:27-29
[r]**44:18** Ex 28:40
[s]**44:19** Ezk 42:14
[t]Lv 6:27
[u]**44:20** Lv 21:5
[v]Nm 6:5
[w]**44:21** Lv 10:9
[x]**44:22** Lv 21:7,13-14
[y]**44:23** Lv 10:10; Ezk 22:26
[z]**44:24** Dt 17:8-9; 2Ch 19:8
[aa]Ezk 20:20; 22:26
[ab]**44:25** Lv 21:1-4
[ac]**44:26** Nm 19:11-19
[ad]**44:27** Lv 5:3,6
[ae]**44:28** Nm 18:20; Dt 18:2; Jos 13:33
[af]**44:29** Nm 18:9,14; Jos 13:14
[ag]Lv 27:21,28
[ah]**44:30** Nm 18:8-13; Neh 10:35-37
[ai]Nm 15:20-21
[aj]Mal 3:10

[A]**44:7** LXX, Syr, Vg; MT reads *They* [B]**44:12** Lit *I lifted My hand* [C]**44:19** Some Hb mss, LXX, Syr, Vg; other Hb mss read *court, to the outer court*

eat any bird or animal that died naturally or
was mauled by wild beasts.[a]

The Sacred Portion of the Land

45 "When you divide the land by lot as
an inheritance,[b] you must set aside a
donation to the LORD, a holy portion of the
land,[c] $8\frac{1}{3}$ miles[A] long and $6\frac{2}{3}$ miles[B] wide.
This entire tract of land will be holy. 2 In this
area there will be a square section[C] for the
sanctuary, 875 by 875 feet,[D,d] with $87\frac{1}{2}$ feet[E]
of open space all around it. 3 From this holy
portion,[F] you will measure off an area $8\frac{1}{3}$
miles[A] long and $3\frac{1}{3}$ miles[G] wide, in which the
sanctuary, the most holy place,[e] will stand.[H]
4 It will be a holy area of the land to be used
by the priests who minister in the sanctuary,
who draw near to serve the LORD.[f] It will be a
place for their houses, as well as a holy area
for the sanctuary. 5 There will be another area
$8\frac{1}{3}$ miles[A] long and $3\frac{1}{3}$ miles[G] wide for the
Levites who minister in the temple;[g] it will be
their possession for towns to live in.[I]

6 "As the property of the city, you must
set aside an area $1\frac{2}{3}$ of a mile[J] wide and $8\frac{1}{3}$
miles[A] long, adjacent to the holy donation of
land.[h] It will be for the whole house of Israel.
7 And the prince will have the area on each
side of the holy donation of land and the
city's property, adjacent to the holy donation
and the city's property, stretching to the west
on the west side and to the east on the east
side.[i] Its length will correspond to one of the
tribal portions from the western boundary to
the eastern boundary. 8 This will be his land
as a possession in Israel. My princes will no
longer oppress My people[j] but give the rest of
the land to the house of Israel according to
their tribes.

9 "This is what the Lord GOD says: You have
gone too far,[K,k] princes of Israel! Put away violence and oppression and do what is just and
right.[l] Put an end to your evictions of My people." This is the declaration of the Lord GOD.
10 "You must have honest scales, an honest dry
measure,[L] and an honest liquid measure.[M,m]
11 The dry measure[N] and the liquid measure[O]
will be uniform, with the liquid measure
containing $5\frac{1}{2}$ gallons[P] and the dry measure
holding half a bushel.[P] Their measurement
will be a tenth of the standard larger capacity
measure.[Q] 12 The ·shekel will weigh 20 *gerahs*.[n]
Your mina will equal 60 shekels.

The People's Contribution to the Sacrifices

13 "This is the contribution you are to offer: Three quarts[R] from five bushels[S] of wheat
and[T] three quarts from five bushels of barley.
14 The quota of oil in liquid measures[U] will be
one percent of every[V] cor. The cor equals 10
liquid measures or one standard larger capacity measure,[W] since 10 liquid measures equal
one standard larger capacity measure. 15 And
the quota from the flock is one animal out
of every 200 from the well-watered pastures
of Israel. These are for the ·grain offerings,
·burnt offerings, and ·fellowship offerings,
to make ·atonement for the people."[o] This is
the declaration of the Lord GOD. 16 "All the
people of the land must take part in this contribution for the prince in Israel. 17 Then the
burnt offerings, grain offerings, and ·drink
offerings for the festivals, New Moons, and
Sabbaths—for all the appointed times of the
house of Israel—will be the prince's responsibility. He will provide the ·sin offerings,
grain offerings, burnt offerings, and fellowship offerings to make atonement on behalf
of the house of Israel.

18 "This is what the Lord GOD says: In the
first month, on the first day of the month,
you are to take a young, unblemished bull
and purify the sanctuary. 19 The priest must
take some of the blood from the sin offering
and apply it to the temple doorposts, the four
corners of the altar's ledge, and the doorposts
of the gate to the inner court.[p] 20 You must
do the same thing on the seventh day of the
month for everyone who sins unintentionally or through ignorance.[q] In this way you
will make atonement for the temple.

21 "In the first month, on the fourteenth day
of the month, you are to celebrate the ·Pass-
over, a festival of seven days during which

[a] 44:31 Lv 22:8 [b] 45:1 Ezk 47:21; 48:29 [c] Ezk 48:8-9 [d] 45:2 Ezk 42:20 [e] 45:3 Ezk 43:12 [f] 45:4 Ezk 48:10-11 [g] 45:5 Ezk 48:13 [h] 45:6 Ezk 48:15-18 [i] 45:7 Ezk 48:21 [j] 45:8 Ezk 19:7; 22:27 [k] 45:9 Ezk 44:6 [l] Jr 22:3 [m] 45:10 Lv 19:36; Dt 25:15 [n] 45:12 Ex 30:13; Lv 27:25 [o] 45:15 Lv 1:4; 6:30 [p] 45:19 Ezk 43:20 [q] 45:20 Lv 4:2; 5:17

[A] 45:1,3,5,6 Lit *25,000 cubits* [B] 45:1 LXX reads *20,000 cubits*; MT reads *10,000 cubits* [C] 45:2 Lit *square all around* [D] 45:2 Lit *500 by 500 cubits* [E] 45:2 Lit *50 cubits* [F] 45:3 Lit *this measured portion* [G] 45:3,5 Lit *10,000 cubits* [H] 45:3 Lit *be* [I] 45:5 LXX; MT, Syr, Tg, Vg read *possession—20 chambers* [J] 45:6 Lit *5,000 cubits* [K] 45:9 Lit *Enough of you* [L] 45:10 Lit *an honest ephah* [M] 45:10 Lit *and an honest bath* [N] 45:11 Lit *the ephah* [O] 45:11 Lit *the bath* [P] 45:11 Lit *one-tenth of a homer* [Q] 45:11 Lit *be based on the homer* [R] 45:13 Lit *One-sixth of an ephah* [S] 45:13 Lit *a homer* [T] 45:13 LXX, Vg; MT reads *and you are to give* [U] 45:14 Lit *oil, the bath, the oil* [V] 45:14 Lit *be a tenth of the bath from the* [W] 45:14 Lit *10 baths, a homer*

unleavened bread will be eaten.[a] 22 On that
day the prince will provide a bull as a sin offering on behalf of himself and all the people of the land. 23 During the seven days of
the festival, he will provide seven bulls and
seven rams without blemish as a burnt offering to the LORD on each of the seven days,
along with a male goat each day for a sin offering. 24 He will also provide a grain offering
of half a bushel[A] per bull and half a bushel per
ram, along with a gallon[B] of oil for every half
bushel. 25 At the festival that begins on the fifteenth day of the seventh month,[C,b] he will
provide the same things for seven days — the
same sin offerings, burnt offerings, grain offerings, and oil.

Sacrifices at Appointed Times

46 "This is what the Lord GOD says: The
gate of the inner court that faces east
must be closed during the six days of work,
but it will be opened on the Sabbath day[c] and
opened on the day of the New Moon. 2 The
prince should enter from the outside by way
of the gate's portico and stand at the doorpost of the gate while the priests sacrifice his
•burnt offerings and •fellowship offerings.
He will bow in worship at the threshold of
the gate and then depart, but the gate must
not be closed until evening. 3 The people of
the land will also bow in worship before the
LORD at the entrance of that gate on the Sabbaths and New Moons.
4 "The burnt offering that the prince presents to the LORD[d] on the Sabbath day is to be
six unblemished lambs[e] and an unblemished
ram. 5 The •grain offering will be half a bushel[A]
with the ram,[f] and the grain offering with the
lambs will be whatever he wants to give, as well
as a gallon[B] of oil for every half bushel. 6 On
the day of the New Moon, the burnt offering
is to be a young, unblemished bull, as well as
six lambs and a ram without blemish. 7 He will
provide a grain offering of half a bushel[A] with
the bull, half a bushel with the ram, and whatever he can afford with the lambs, together
with a gallon[B] of oil for every half bushel.
8 When the prince enters,[g] he must go in by way
of the gate's portico and go out the same way.
9 "When the people of the land come before
the LORD at the appointed times,[D,h] whoever
enters by way of the north gate to worship
must go out by way of the south gate, and
whoever enters by way of the south gate must
go out by way of the north gate. No one must
return through the gate by which he entered,
but must go out by the opposite gate. 10 When
the people enter, the prince will enter with
them, and when they leave, he will leave. 11 At
the festivals and appointed times, the grain
offering will be half a bushel[A] with the bull,
half a bushel with the ram, and whatever he
wants to give with the lambs, along with a gallon[B] of oil for every half bushel.
12 "When the prince makes a freewill offering, whether a burnt offering or a fellowship
offering as a freewill offering to the LORD,[i]
the gate that faces east must be opened for
him. He is to offer his burnt offering or fellowship offering just as he does on the Sabbath day. Then he will go out, and the gate
must be closed after he leaves.
13 "You must offer an unblemished year-
old male lamb as a daily burnt offering to
the LORD; you will offer it every morning.[j]
14 You must also prepare a grain offering every morning along with it: three quarts,[E]
with one-third of a gallon[F] of oil to moisten
the fine flour — a grain offering to the LORD.
This is a permanent statute to be observed
regularly. 15 They will offer the lamb, the grain
offering, and the oil every morning as a regular burnt offering.

Transfer of Royal Lands

16 "This is what the Lord GOD says: If the
prince gives a gift to each of his sons as their
inheritance, it will belong to his sons. It will
become their property by inheritance. 17 But
if he gives a gift from his inheritance to one
of his servants, it will belong to that servant
until the year of freedom,[k] when it will re-
vert to the prince. His inheritance belongs
only to his sons; it is theirs. 18 The prince
must not take any of the people's inheritance, evicting them from their property.[l]
He is to provide an inheritance for his sons
from his own property, so that none of My

[a] **45:21** Ex 12:18; Lv 23:4-8; Nm 28:16-17; Dt 16:1
[b] **45:25** Lv 23:33-43; Dt 16:13-15
[c] **46:1** Ex 20:9-10
[d] **46:4** Ezk 45:17
[e] Nm 28:9
[f] **46:5** Nm 28:12; Ezk 45:24
[g] **46:8** Ezk 44:3
[h] **46:9** Ex 23:14-17
[i] **46:12** Lv 23:38
[j] **46:13** Ex 29:38
[k] **46:17** Lv 25:10
[l] **46:18** Ezk 45:8-9

[A] **45:24; 46:5,7,11** Lit *an ephah* [B] **45:24; 46:5,7,11** Lit *a hin* [C] **45:25** = the Festival of Booths [D] **46:9** Or *the festivals* [E] **46:14** Lit *one-sixth of an ephah* [F] **46:14** Lit *one-third of a hin*

people will be displaced from his own property."

The Temple Kitchens

[19]Then he brought me through the entrance[a] that was at the side of the gate, into the priests' holy chambers, which faced north. I saw a place there at the far western end. [20]He said to me, "This is the place where the priests will boil the ˙restitution offering and the ˙sin offering,[b] and where they will bake the grain offering,[c] so that they do not bring them into the outer court and transmit holiness to the people." [21]Next he brought me into the outer court and led me past its four corners. There was a separate court in each of its corners. [22]In the four corners of the outer court there were enclosed[A] courts, 70 feet[B] long by 52 1/2 feet[C] wide. All four corner areas had the same dimensions. [23]There was a stone wall[D] around the inside of them, around the four of them, with ovens built at the base of the walls on all sides. [24]He said to me: "These are the kitchens where those who minister at the temple will cook the people's sacrifices."

The Life-Giving River

47 Then he brought me back to the entrance of the temple and there was water flowing from under the threshold of the temple toward the east, for the temple faced east. The water was coming down from under the south side of the threshold of the temple, south of the altar.[d] [2]Next he brought me out by way of the north gate and led me around the outside to the outer gate that faced east; there the water was trickling from the south side. [3]As the man went out east with a measuring line in his hand,[e] he measured off a third of a mile[E] and led me through the water. It came up to my ankles. [4]Then he measured off a third of a mile[E] and led me through the water. It came up to my knees. He measured off another third of a mile[E] and led me through the water. It came up to my waist. [5]Again he measured off a third of a mile[E], and it was a river that I could not cross on foot. For the water had risen; it was deep enough to swim in, a river that could not be crossed on foot.

[6]He asked me, "Do you see this, son of man?" Then he led me back to the bank of the river. [7]When I had returned, I saw a very large number of trees along both sides of the riverbank.[f] [8]He said to me, "This water flows out to the eastern region and goes down to the ˙Arabah. When it enters the sea, the sea of foul water,[F,G] the water of the sea becomes fresh.[g] [9]Every kind of living creature that swarms will live wherever the river flows,[H] and there will be a huge number of fish because this water goes there. Since the water will become fresh, there will be life everywhere the river goes. [10]Fishermen will stand beside it from En-gedi to En-eglaim.[I] These will become places where nets are spread out to dry. Their fish will consist of many different kinds, like the fish of the Mediterranean Sea.[h] [11]Yet its swamps and marshes will not be healed; they will be left for salt. [12]All kinds of trees providing food will grow along both banks of the river. Their leaves will not wither, and their fruit will not fail.[i] Each month they will bear fresh fruit because the water comes from the sanctuary. Their fruit will be used for food and their leaves for medicine."[j]

The Borders of the Land

[13]This is what the Lord GOD says: "This is[J] the border you will use to divide the land[k] as an inheritance for the 12 tribes of Israel. Joseph will receive two shares.[l] [14]You will inherit it in equal portions, since I swore[K] to give it to your ancestors.[m] So this land will fall to you as an inheritance.

[15]"This is to be the border of the land:

On the north side[n] it will extend from the Mediterranean Sea by way of Hethlon and Lebo-hamath to Zedad,[L] [16]Berothah, and Sibraim (which is between the border of Damascus and the border of Hamath), as far as Hazer-hatticon, which is on the border of Hauran. [17]So the border will run from the sea to Hazar-enon at the border[o] of Damascus, with the territory of Hamath to the north. This will be the northern side.

[a]**46:19** Ezk 42:9 [b]**46:20** 2Ch 35:13; Ezk 44:29 [c]Lv 2:4-7 [d]**47:1** Ps 46:4; Zch 14:8; Rv 22:1 [e]**47:3** Ezk 40:3 [f]**47:7** Rv 22:2 [g]**47:8** Ex 15:26; 2Kg 2:21 [h]**47:10** Nm 34:3; Ezk 48:28 [i]**47:12** Ps 1:3 [j]Rv 22:2 [k]**47:13** Nm 34:2-12 [l]Gn 48:15-16 [m]**47:14** Dt 1:8; Ezk 20:6 [n]**47:15** Nm 34:7-9; Ezk 48:1 [o]**47:17** Nm 34:9

[A]**46:22** Hb obscure [B]**46:22** Lit *40 cubits* [C]**46:22** Lit *30 cubits* [D]**46:23** Or *a row* [E]**47:3,4,5** Lit *1,000 cubits* [F]**47:8** Or *enters the sea, being brought out to the sea*; Hb obscure [G]**47:8** = the Dead Sea [H]**47:9** LXX, Vg; MT reads *the two rivers flow* [I]**47:10** Two springs near the Dead Sea [J]**47:13** Tg, Vg; Syr reads *The valley of* [K]**47:14** Lit *lifted My hand* [L]**47:15** LXX; MT reads *and Lebo to Zedad, Hamath*; Ezk 48:1

18On the east side it will run between
Hauran and Damascus, along the Jordan
between Gilead and the land of Israel;
you will measure from the northern border to the eastern sea.[A] This will be the
eastern side.

19On the south side it will run from
Tamar to the waters of Meribath-kadesh,[B]
and on to the Brook of Egypt[a] as far as
the Mediterranean Sea.[b] This will be the
southern side.

20On the west side the Mediterranean
Sea will be the border, from the southern border up to a point opposite Lebo-
hamath. This will be the western side.

21"You are to divide this land among yourselves according to the tribes of Israel.[c] 22You
will allot it as an inheritance for yourselves
and for the foreigners living among you,[d]
who have fathered children among you. You
will treat them[C] like native-born Israelites;
along with you, they will be allotted an inheritance among the tribes of Israel. 23In whatever tribe the foreigner lives, you will assign
his inheritance there." This is the declaration
of the Lord GOD.

The Tribal Allotments

48 "Now these are the names of the
tribes:

From the northern end, along the road
of Hethlon, to Lebo-hamath as far as
Hazar-enon, at the northern border
of Damascus, alongside Hamath and
extending from the eastern side to the
sea, will be Dan—one portion.
2Next to the territory of Dan, from
the east side to the west, will be
Asher—one portion.
3Next to the territory of Asher, from
the east side to the west, will be
Naphtali—one portion.
4Next to the territory of Naphtali,
from the east side to the west, will be
Manasseh—one portion.
5Next to the territory of Manasseh,
from the east side to the west, will be
Ephraim—one portion.
6Next to the territory of Ephraim,
from the east side to the west, will be
Reuben—one portion.
7Next to the territory of Reuben,
from the east side to the west, will be
Judah—one portion.

8"Next to the territory of Judah, from the
east side to the west, will be the portion you
donate to the LORD, 8 1/3 miles[D] wide, and as
long as one of the tribal portions from the
east side to the west.[e] The sanctuary will be in
the middle of it.

9"The special portion you donate to the
LORD will be 8 1/3 miles[D] long and 3 1/3 miles[E]
wide. 10This holy donation will be set apart
for the priests alone. It will be 8 1/3 miles[D] long
on the northern side, 3 1/3 miles[E] wide on the
western side, 3 1/3 miles[E] wide on the eastern
side, and 8 1/3 miles[D] long on the southern
side. The LORD's sanctuary will be in the middle of it. 11It is for the consecrated priests, the
sons of Zadok, who kept My charge[f] and did
not go astray as the Levites did when the Israelites went astray. 12It will be a special donation for them out of the holy donation of the
land, a most holy place adjacent to the territory of the Levites.

13"Next to the territory of the priests, the
Levites will have an area 8 1/3 miles[D] long and
3 1/3 miles[E] wide. The total length will be 8 1/3
miles[D] and the width 3 1/3 miles.[E,g] 14They must
not sell or exchange any of it, and they must
not transfer this choice part of the land, for it
is holy to the LORD.[h]

15"The remaining area, 1 2/3 of a mile[F] wide
and 8 1/3 miles[D] long, will be for common use
by the city,[i] for both residential and open
space. The city will be in the middle of it.
16These are the city's measurements:

1 1/2 miles[G] on the north side;
1 1/2 miles[G] on the south side;
1 1/2 miles[G] on the east side;
and 1 1/2 miles[G] on the west side.

17The city's open space will extend:

425 feet[H] to the north,
425 feet[H] to the south,
425 feet[H] to the east,
and 425 feet[H] to the west.

[a]47:19 Nm 34:5; 1Kg 8:65; Is 27:12 [b]Ezk 48:28 [c]47:21 Ezk 45:1 [d]47:22 Ac 11:18; 15:9; Eph 2:12-14; 3:6; Col 3:11 [e]48:8-9 Ezk 45:1-5 [f]48:11 Ezk 44:10,15 [g]48:13 Ezk 45:1 [h]48:14 Lv 25:34; 27:28 [i]48:15 Ezk 45:6

[A]47:18 = the Dead Sea [B]47:19 = Kadesh-barnea [C]47:22 Lit *They will be to you* [D]48:8,9,10,13,15 Lit *25,000 cubits* [E]48:9,13 Lit *10,000 cubits* [F]48:15 Lit *5,000 cubits* [G]48:16 Lit *4,500 cubits* [H]48:17 Lit *250 cubits*

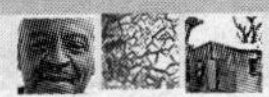

[18]"The remainder of the length alongside
the holy donation will be 3 1/3 miles[A] to the
east and 3 1/3 miles[A] to the west. It will run
alongside the holy donation. Its produce will
be food for the workers of the city. [19]The city's
workers from all the tribes of Israel will cultivate it.[a] [20]The entire donation will be 8 1/3
miles[B] by 8 1/3 miles;[B] you are to set apart the
holy donation along with the city property as
a square area.

[21]"The remaining area on both sides of the
holy donation and the city property will belong to the prince.[b] He will own the land adjacent to the tribal portions, next to the 8 1/3
miles[B] of the donation as far as the eastern
border and[C] next to the 8 1/3 miles[B] of the donation as far as the western border. The holy
donation and the sanctuary of the temple
will be in the middle of it. [22]Except for the Levitical property and the city property in the
middle of the area belonging to the prince,
the area between the territory of Judah and
that of Benjamin will belong to the prince.[c]

[23]"As for the rest of the tribes:

From the east side to the west, will be
Benjamin — one portion.
[24]Next to the territory of Benjamin,
from the east side to the west, will be
Simeon — one portion.
[25]Next to the territory of Simeon,
from the east side to the west, will be
Issachar — one portion.
[26]Next to the territory of Issachar,
from the east side to the west, will be
Zebulun — one portion.
[27]Next to the territory of Zebulun,
from the east side to the west, will be
Gad — one portion.

[28]Next to the territory of Gad toward the south
side, the border will run from Tamar to the
waters[d] of Meribath-kadesh, to the Brook of
Egypt, and out to the Mediterranean Sea. [29]This
is the land you are to allot as an inheritance
to Israel's tribes,[e] and these will be their portions." This is the declaration of the Lord God.

The New City

[30]"These are the exits of the city:

On the north side, which measures 1 1/2
miles,[D] [31]there will be three gates facing
north, the gates of the city being named
for the tribes of Israel: one, the gate
of Reuben; one, the gate of Judah; and
one, the gate of Levi.
[32]On the east side, which is 1 1/2 miles,[D]
there will be three gates: one, the gate
of Joseph; one, the gate of Benjamin;
and one, the gate of Dan.
[33]On the south side, which measures
1 1/2 miles,[D] there will be three gates:
one, the gate of Simeon; one, the gate of
Issachar; and one, the gate of Zebulun.
[34]On the west side, which is 1 1/2 miles,[D]
there will be three gates: one, the gate
of Gad; one, the gate of Asher; and one,
the gate of Naphtali.

[35]The perimeter of the city will be six miles,[E]
and the name of the city from that day on will
be: Yahweh Is There."[f]

[a] **48:19** Ezk 45:6 [b] **48:21** Ezk 34:24; 45:7 [c] **48:22** Jos 18:21-28 [d] **48:28** 2Ch 20:2 [e] **48:29** Ezk 47:13-20 [f] **48:35** Is 12:6; 14:32; 24:23; Jr 3:17; 8:19; 14:9; Ezk 35:10; Jl 3:21; Zch 2:10; Rv 21:3; 22:3

[A] **48:18** Lit *10,000 cubits* [B] **48:20,21** Lit *25,000 cubits* [C] **48:21** Lit *border, and to the west,* [D] **48:30,32,33,34** Lit *4,500 cubits* [E] **48:35** Lit *18,000 cubits*

■ **AUTHOR:** Daniel

■■ **DATE:** Daniel prophesied during the time of the exile, serving under leaders of two world empires: Babylon and Medo-Persia (around 605–530 B.C.). The book was written around 536 B.C.

The prophecy of Daniel is one of the Old Testament's most fascinating descriptions of God's mission to the world. It is divisible into two parts: the first six chapters about the adventures of Daniel and his three friends, and the second six chapters containing the majestic prophecies Daniel received from the Lord.

Both parts have a dual theme: first, the wonderful height of human service when it flows from personal godliness, faith, and commitment; second, God's great protective power and faithfulness to His people. Daniel's service, and that of his three friends in the face of great odds, shows a consistent response to the Lord's promises and provisions.

DANIEL

The friends grew up in the region of Judah. In the third year of the reign of King Jehoiakim (605 B.C.) the land was invaded by King Nebuchadnezzar. Among those carried into exile to Babylon were Daniel and his companions. Throughout the amazing events that followed, they faithfully depend on their God, who crowns their service with good success.

The book begins with the friends' request that they be exempted from the king's table, an act that openly establishes their loyalty to Israel's God.

From the outset Daniel is aware of being part of God's great mission in Babylon. Guided by God's prophetic gift he interprets Nebuchadnezzar's dream and is rewarded with a high position in the land. Serving God comes with great personal risks, however. Who does not recall the story of the three friends walking through the fiery furnace, or Daniel in the lion's den protected by God's angel?

The second half of the book of Daniel is composed of the great prophecies Daniel receives form the Lord. Daniel predicts that a succession of kingdoms will follow, ushering in chaotic times with much bloodshed, but with God promising protection for His people.

The two main themes (service and protection) are interspersed with several sub-themes. One example is the reference to Daniel's prayer patterns. Three times a day he prays with his face toward Jerusalem. The implication is clear: the Messiah, the Christ of God, will come from the people of Israel. He is the ultimate goal of the Babylonian experience. Also striking is that Daniel repeatedly humbles himself, confessing his sins and the sins of the people, and pleading for God's grace.

In chapters 10 and 12, God reveals to Daniel the larger cosmic dimensions of the kingdoms: God's angels battling the forces of darkness. God rules the nations with an eye toward the completion of the Kingdom of His Son. The great victory of the divine forces is still ours to own and to confess, as we struggle to live lives of obedience with the foretaste of the great victory to come.

When Jesus predicts the great tribulation of the end times, He makes reference to Daniel (Mt 24:15; Mk 13:14). In Hebrews 11:33–34, the experiences of Daniel and friends in the fiery furnace and the lion's den are singled out for honorable mention.

Daniel's Captivity in Babylon

1 In the third year of the reign of Jehoiakim[a] king of Judah, Nebuchadnezzar[A,b] king of Babylon came to Jerusalem and laid siege to it. 2 The Lord handed Jehoiakim king of Judah over to him, along with some of the vessels from the house of God.[c] Nebuchadnezzar carried them to the land of Babylon,[B,d] to the house of his god,[C] and put the vessels in the treasury of his god.

3 The king ordered Ashpenaz, the chief of his court officials,[D] to bring some of the Israelites from the royal family[e] and from the nobility — 4 young men without any physical defect, good-looking, suitable for instruction in all wisdom,[f] knowledgeable, perceptive, and capable of serving in the king's palace[g] — and to teach them the Chaldean language[h] and literature. 5 The king assigned them daily provisions from the royal food and from the wine that he drank.[i] They were to be trained for three years, and at the end of that time they were to serve in the king's court.[E,j] 6 Among them, from the descendants of Judah, were Daniel,[k] Hananiah, Mishael, and Azariah. 7 The chief official gave them other names: he gave the name Belteshazzar to Daniel, Shadrach to Hananiah, Meshach to Mishael, and Abednego to Azariah.[l]

Faithfulness in Babylon

8 Daniel determined that he would not defile himself with the king's food[m] or with the wine he drank. So he asked permission from the chief official not to defile himself.[n] 9 God had granted Daniel favor and compassion from the chief official,[o] 10 yet he said to Daniel, "My lord the king assigned your food and drink. I'm afraid of what would happen if he saw your faces looking thinner than those of the other young men your age. You would endanger my life[F] with the king."

11 So Daniel said to the guard whom the chief official had assigned to Daniel, Hananiah, Mishael, and Azariah, 12 "Please test your servants for 10 days. Let us be given vegetables to eat and water to drink. 13 Then examine our appearance and the appearance of the young men who are eating the king's food, and deal with your servants based on what you see." 14 He agreed with them about this and tested them for 10 days. 15 At the end of 10 days they looked better and healthier[G] than all the young men who were eating the king's food.[p] 16 So the guard continued to remove their food and the wine they were to drink and gave them vegetables.

Faithfulness Rewarded

17 God gave these four young men knowledge and understanding[q] in every kind of literature and wisdom. Daniel also understood visions and dreams[r] of every kind. 18 At the end of the time that the king had said to present them, the chief official presented them to Nebuchadnezzar. 19 The king interviewed them, and among all of them, no one was found equal to Daniel, Hananiah, Mishael, and Azariah.[s] So they began to serve in the king's court. 20 In every matter of wisdom and understanding that the king consulted them about, he found them 10 times[H,t] better than all the diviner-priests and mediums[u] in his entire kingdom. 21 Daniel remained there until the first year of King Cyrus.[v]

Nebuchadnezzar's Dream

2 In the second year of his reign, Nebuchadnezzar had dreams[w] that troubled him, and sleep deserted him.[x] 2 So the king gave orders to summon the diviner-priests, mediums, sorcerers, and Chaldeans[I,y] to tell the king his dreams. When they came and stood before the king, 3 he said to them, "I have had a dream and am anxious to understand it."

4 The Chaldeans spoke to the king (Aramaic[J,z] begins here): "May the king live forever.[aa] Tell your servants the dream, and we will give the interpretation."

5 The king replied to the Chaldeans, "My word is final: If you don't tell me the dream and its interpretation, you will be torn limb from limb,[K] and your houses will be made a garbage dump.[ab] 6 But if you make the dream and its interpretation known to me, you'll receive

[a] **1:1** 2Kg 24:1-2; 2Ch 36:5-6 [b] Jr 25:1; 52:12,28-30 [c] **1:2** 2Kg 24:13; 2Ch 36:7-10; Ezr 5:14; Jr 27:19-22; Dn 5:2 [d] Gn 10:10; 11:2; Is 11:11; Zch 5:11 [e] **1:3** 2Kg 20:18; 24:15; Is 39:7; Dn 1:9 [f] **1:4** Dn 9:22 [g] Is 39:7 [h] Jr 5:15 [i] **1:5** 2Kg 25:30; Dn 11:26 [j] Gn 41:46; 1Sm 16:22 [k] **1:6** Ezk 14:14,20; 28:3 [l] **1:7** 2Kg 23:34; 24:17; Dn 4:8,19; 5:12; 10:1 [m] **1:8** Pr 23:1-2 [n] Lv 3:17; 11:47; Ps 141:4; Ezk 4:13; Hs 9:3; Ac 10:11-15 [o] **1:9** Gn 39:21; 1Kg 8:50; Jb 5:15; Ps 106:46; Pr 16:7; Ac 7:10 [p] **1:15** Ex 23:25 [q] **1:17** Jb 32:8; Ac 7:22; Jms 1:5 [r] 1Kg 3:10-12; Dn 2:19,30; 4:18-19; 7:1 [s] **1:18-19** Gn 41:37-39 [t] **1:20** Gn 31:7; Nm 14:22; Jb 19:3 [u] Pr 3:13-18; Dn 5:11-12 [v] **1:21** Ezr 1:1-2; Is 45:1; Dn 6:28; 10:1 [w] **2:1** Gn 40:5-8; Dn 4:5; 5:9 [x] Gn 41:1,8; Est 6:1; Dn 6:18 [y] **2:2** Dt 18:10,11; 2Ch 33:6; Is 47:9,12 [z] **2:4** Ezr 4:7; Is 36:11 [aa] 1Kg 1:31; Dn 3:9; 5:10; 6:6,21 [ab] **2:5** Ezr 6:11; Dn 3:29

[A] **1:1** Or *Nebuchadrezzar* [B] **1:2** Lit *Shinar* [C] **1:2** Or *gods* [D] **1:3** Or *his eunuchs* [E] **1:5** Lit *to stand before the king* [F] **1:10** Lit *would make my head guilty* [G] **1:15** Lit *fatter of flesh* [H] **1:20** Lit *hands* [I] **2:2** In this chap. Chaldeans are influential Babylonian wise men. [J] **2:4** Dn 2:4–7:28 is written in Aram. [K] **2:5** Lit *be made into limbs* gifts, a reward, and great honor from me.[a] So make the dream and its interpretation known to me."

[7]They answered a second time, "May the king tell the dream to his servants, and we will give the interpretation."

[8]The king replied, "I know for certain you are trying to gain some time, because you see that my word is final. [9]If you don't tell me the dream, there is one decree for you.[b] You have conspired to tell me something false or fraudulent until the situation changes. So tell me the dream and I will know you can give me its interpretation."

[10]The Chaldeans answered the king, "No one on earth can make known what the king requests.[c] Consequently, no king, however great and powerful, has ever asked anything like this of any diviner-priest, medium, or Chaldean. [11]What the king is asking is so difficult that no one can make it known to him except the gods, whose dwelling is not with mortals."[d] [12]Because of this, the king became violently angry[e] and gave orders to destroy all the wise men of Babylon. [13]The decree was issued that the wise men were to be executed, and they searched for Daniel and his friends, to execute them.

[14]Then Daniel responded with tact and discretion to Arioch, the commander of the king's guard,[A,f] who had gone out to execute the wise men of Babylon. [15]He asked Arioch, the king's officer, "Why is the decree from the king so harsh?"[B,g] Then Arioch explained the situation to Daniel. [16]So Daniel went and asked the king to give him some time, so that he could give the king the interpretation.

[17]Then Daniel went to his house and told his friends Hananiah, Mishael, and Azariah about the matter, [18]urging them to ask the God of heaven[h] for mercy[i] concerning this mystery, so Daniel and his friends would not be killed with the rest of Babylon's wise men.[j] [19]The mystery was then revealed to Daniel in a vision[k] at night, and Daniel praised the God of heaven [20]and declared:

May the name of God
be praised forever and ever,[l]
for wisdom[m] and power belong to Him.
[21] He changes the times and seasons;
He removes kings
and establishes kings.[n]
He gives wisdom to the wise
and knowledge to those
who have understanding.[o]
[22] He reveals the deep
and hidden things;
He knows what is in the darkness,[p]
and light dwells with Him.[q]
[23] I offer thanks and praise to You,
God of my fathers,[r]
because You have given me
wisdom and power.
And now You have let me know
what we asked of You,
for You have let us know[s]
the king's mystery.[C]

[24]Therefore Daniel went to Arioch,[t] whom the king had assigned to destroy the wise men of Babylon. He came and said to him, "Don't kill the wise men of Babylon! Bring me before the king, and I will give him the interpretation."[u]

[25]Then Arioch quickly brought Daniel before the king and said to him, "I have found a man among the Judean exiles[v] who can let the king know the interpretation."

[26]The king said in reply to Daniel, whose name was Belteshazzar,[w] "Are you able to tell me the dream I had and its interpretation?"[x]

[27]Daniel answered the king: "No wise man, medium, diviner-priest, or astrologer[y] is able to make known to the king the mystery he asked about. [28]But there is a God in heaven who reveals mysteries, and He has let King Nebuchadnezzar know what will happen in the last days.[z] Your dream and the visions that came into your mind as you lay in bed[aa] were these: [29]Your Majesty, while you were in your bed, thoughts came to your mind about what will happen in the future.[D,ab] The revealer of mysteries[ac] has let you know what will happen. [30]As for me, this mystery has been revealed to me,[ad] not because I have more wisdom than anyone living, but in order that the interpretation might be made known to the king, and that you may understand the thoughts of your mind.[ae]

[a]2:6 Dn 5:7,16 [b]2:9 Is 41:23 [c]2:10 Dn 5:11-16 [d]2:11 Ex 29:45; Is 57:15 [e]2:12 Ps 76:10; Dn 2:24; 3:13,19 [f]2:14 Gn 37:36 [g]2:15 Dn 3:22 [h]2:18 Mt 18:19 [i]Jr 33:3 [j]Mal 3:18 [k]2:19 Nm 12:6; Jb 33:15-16; Am 3:7 [l]2:20 1Ch 29:10; Ps 72:18; Lk 1:68 [m]Jb 12:13; Is 28:29 [n]2:21 1Ch 29:11-12; Dn 4:17; Rm 13:1 [o]Jb 12:16-22 [p]2:22 Jb 12:22; Ps 139:12; Jr 23:24; Am 4:13; Heb 4:13 [q]Jn 1:4-5; 1Tm 6:16; Jms 1:17; 1Jn 1:5 [r]2:23 Gn 31:42; Ex 3:15; Dt 26:7; 1Ch 12:17; 29:18 [s]Dn 1:17-18 [t]2:24 Dn 2:14-15 [u]Ac 27:24 [v]2:25 Ezr 4:1; 6:16,19-20; 10:7,16; Dn 5:13 [w]2:26 Dn 1:7; 5:12 [x]Dn 5:16 [y]2:27 Dn 1:20; 4:7; 5:7,11 [z]2:28 Is 2:2; Dn 10:14; Hs 3:5; Mc 4:1 [aa]Dn 4:5; 7:15 [ab]2:29 Rv 1:1 [ac]Jb 12:20-22; Dn 2:45 [ad]2:30 Eph 3:3 [ae]Gn 41:16; Ec 3:18; Am 4:13; Ac 3:12

A2:14 Or *executioners* B2:15 Or *urgent* C2:23 Lit *matter* D2:29 Lit *happen after this*

The Dream's Interpretation

[31]"My king, as you were watching, a colossal
statue appeared. That statue, tall and dazzling,
was standing in front of you, and its appearance was terrifying. [32]The head of the statue
was pure gold, its chest and arms were silver,
its stomach and thighs were bronze, [33]its legs
were iron, and its feet were partly iron and
partly fired clay. [34]As you were watching, a
stone broke off without a hand touching it,[A,a]
struck the statue[b] on its feet of iron and fired
clay, and crushed them.[c] [35]Then the iron, the
fired clay, the bronze, the silver, and the gold
were shattered and became like chaff[d] from
the summer threshing floors. The wind carried them away, and not a trace of them could
be found. But the stone that struck the statue
became a great mountain and filled[e] the
whole earth.
[36]"This was the dream; now we will tell
the king its interpretation. [37]Your Majesty,
you are king of kings.[f] The God of heaven
has given you sovereignty, power,[g] strength,
and glory. [38]Wherever people live — or wild
animals, or birds of the air — He has handed
them over to you and made you ruler over
them all.[h] You are the head of gold.
[39]"After you, there will arise another kingdom, inferior to yours, and then another, a
third kingdom, of bronze, which will rule
the whole earth.[i] [40]A fourth kingdom will be
as strong as iron; for iron crushes and shatters everything, and like iron that smashes,
it will crush and smash all the others.[B,j] [41]You
saw the feet and toes, partly of a potter's
fired clay and partly of iron — it will be a divided kingdom, though some of the strength
of iron will be in it. You saw the iron mixed
with clay, [42]and that the toes of the feet were
partly iron and partly fired clay — part of the
kingdom will be strong, and part will be brittle. [43]You saw the iron mixed with clay — the
peoples will mix with one another[C] but will
not hold together, just as iron does not mix
with fired clay.
[44]"In the days of those kings, the God of
heaven will set up a kingdom that will never
be destroyed,[k] and this kingdom will not be
left to another people. It will crush all these
kingdoms[l] and bring them to an end, but will
itself endure forever. [45]You saw a stone[m] break
off from the mountain without a hand touching it,[D,n] and it crushed the iron, bronze, fired
clay, silver, and gold. The great God has told
the king what will happen in the future.[E,o] The
dream is true, and its interpretation certain."

[a]2:34 Jb 34:20; Lm 4:6; Dn 8:25; 2Co 5:1 [b]Mt 21:44; Lk 20:18 [c]Ps 2:9; Is 60:12 [d]2:35 Ps 1:4; Is 17:13; 41:15,16; Hs 13:3 [e]Is 2:2; Mc 4:1 [f]2:37 Is 47:5; Jr 27:6,7; Ezk 26:7 [g]Pr 8:15 [h]2:38 Ps 50:10; Jr 27:6; 28:14; Dn 4:21 [i]2:39 Dn 5:28,31; 7:6 [j]2:40 Dn 7:7,23 [k]2:44 Ps 145:13; Ezk 37:25; Dn 4:3; 6:26; 7:14; Lk 1:33 [l]Ps 2:9; Mt 21:44 [m]2:45 Is 28:16 [n]Dn 2:34 [o]Jr 32:18-19; Dn 2:29; Mal 1:11 [p]2:46 Mt 8:2; Ac 10:25; 14:13; Rv 19:10; 22:8 [q]2:47 Dt 10:17; Ps 136:2,3; 1Tm 6:15; Rv 17:14; 19:16 [r]Am 3:7 [s]2:48 Gn 41:41; Dn 3:1,12,30 [t]2:49 Dn 1:17; 3:12 [u]Est 2:19,21; Am 5:15 [v]3:1 1Kg 12:28; Is 46:6; Jr 16:20; Hs 2:8; 8:4; Hab 2:19 [w]Gn 11:2; Dn 2:48-49 [x]3:2 Ezr 8:36; Dn 2:48; 6:1-7 [y]3:5 Dn 2:46

Nebuchadnezzar's Response

[46]Then King Nebuchadnezzar fell down,
paid homage to Daniel, and gave orders to
present an offering and incense to him.[p]
[47]The king said to Daniel, "Your God is indeed
God of gods, Lord of kings,[q] and a revealer of
mysteries,[r] since you were able to reveal this
mystery." [48]Then the king promoted Daniel
and gave him many generous gifts. He made
him ruler over the entire province of Babylon
and chief governor over all the wise men of
Babylon.[s] [49]At Daniel's request, the king appointed Shadrach, Meshach, and Abednego[t]
to manage the province of Babylon. But Daniel remained at the king's court.[u]

Nebuchadnezzar's Gold Statue

3 King Nebuchadnezzar made a gold
statue,[v] 90 feet high and nine feet wide.[F]
He set it up on the plain of Dura in the province of Babylon.[w] [2]King Nebuchadnezzar
sent word to assemble the satraps, prefects,
governors, advisers, treasurers, judges, magistrates, and all the rulers[x] of the provinces
to attend the dedication of the statue King
Nebuchadnezzar had set up. [3]So the satraps, prefects, governors, advisers, treasurers, judges, magistrates, and all the rulers of
the provinces assembled for the dedication
of the statue the king had set up. Then they
stood before the statue Nebuchadnezzar had
set up.
[4]A herald loudly proclaimed, "People of
every nation and language, you are commanded: [5]When you hear the sound of the
horn, flute, zither,[G] lyre,[H] harp, drum,[I] and
every kind of music, you are to fall down
and worship[y] the gold statue that King
Nebuchadnezzar has set up. [6]But whoever does not fall down and worship will

[A]2:34 Lit *off not by hands* [B]2:40 Lit *all these* [C]2:43 Lit *another in the seed of men* [D]2:45 Lit *mountain, not by hands* [E]2:45 Lit *happen after this* [F]3:1 Lit *statue, its height 60 cubits, its width six cubits* [G]3:5 Or *lyre* [H]3:5 Or *sambuke* [I]3:5 Or *pipe*

immediately be thrown into a furnace of
blazing fire."[a]
7Therefore, when all the people heard the
sound of the horn, flute, zither, lyre, harp,
and every kind of music, people of every nation and language fell down and worshiped
the gold statue that King Nebuchadnezzar
had set up.

[a]3:6 Jr 29:22; Mt 13:42,50; Rv 9:2 [b]3:8 Ezr 4:12-16; Est 3:8-9; Dn 6:12,24 [c]3:10 Dn 4:6; 6:26

The Furnace of Blazing Fire

8Some Chaldeans took this occasion to
come forward and maliciously accuse[A,b] the
Jews. 9They said to King Nebuchadnezzar,
"May the king live forever. 10You as king have
issued a decree[c] that everyone who hears the
sound of the horn, flute, zither, lyre, harp,
drum, and every kind of music must fall

WORLDVIEW

The Mission of God in Prisons

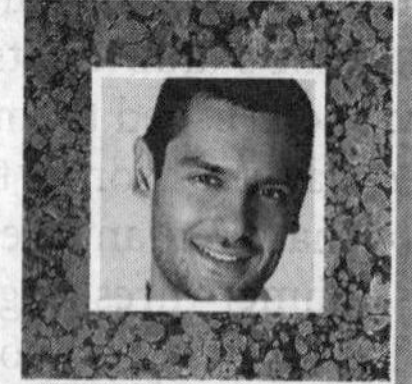

Prisons are set-apart cultures in nearly every nation, and prisoners live under a confinement that few would voluntarily choose. How does the gospel find reception among prison populations? Hear a former prisoner speak to the point:

Most prisoners give little thought to the gospel of Jesus. Many live in their own little world. They have lost wives, homes, jobs, cars. They see no light at the end of the tunnel. It can feel hopeless.

Many blame God, family, and everyone else for their situation, instead of looking at themselves and taking responsibility for their actions.

Some use religion as a crutch. If guards and the parole board come to think you are religious, there's hope of getting out sooner. You may go to all the religious meetings. It's to show, not for real.

Real Christians are sincere and dedicated. They witness to others. They study the Bible. They give a helping hand. Even in prison, they show joy.

Prisoners know they only have so many choices and it takes real commitment to surrender and follow Jesus. Prison is a world of its own, nothing like the outside world. The warden controls everything. What the warden says, goes. Some allow volunteers to come in and conduct Christian services. Some wardens allow as many as four to five men to sit at tables to do Bible study together. Some wardens frown on singing hymns out in the yard.

At times, prison routine can be a real downer. Men (ladies too, in other prisons) feel defeated even while practicing their faith. Some prisoners have been so battered by life that they lose all hope in everything, including God. And others find new life in God. Those are the ones able to carry on and encourage and uplift the others.

Prison can be a blessing, yes—a time to share, meditate, look at your life, and follow Jesus in joy and hope.

Jesus taught: "Then the King will say to those on His right, 'Come, you who are blessed by My Father, inherit the kingdom prepared for you from the foundation of the world. For . . . I was in prison and you visited Me" (Mt 25:34–35). Prisons, no place anyone wants to be, can be a place where God is found, embraced, and followed. God's mission reaches there, over the walls and despite the labels. "Convicts" find conviction there, "stewards" serve the living Lord, the "scum" or "garbage" of the world (as Paul called himself in 1Co 4:13) find God's purpose there.

[A]3:8 Lit *and eat the pieces of*

down and worship the gold statue. [11]Who-
ever does not fall down and worship will be
thrown into a furnace of blazing fire. [12]There
are some Jews you have appointed to manage
the province of Babylon: Shadrach, Meshach,
and Abednego.[a] These men have ignored
you,[b] the king; they do not serve your gods or
worship the gold statue you have set up."

[13]Then in a furious rage[c] Nebuchadnezzar
gave orders to bring in Shadrach, Meshach,
and Abednego. So these men were brought
before the king. [14]Nebuchadnezzar asked
them, "Shadrach, Meshach, and Abednego, is
it true that you don't serve my gods or worship the gold statue[d] I have set up? [15]Now if
you're ready, when you hear the sound of the
horn, flute, zither, lyre, harp, drum, and every kind of music, fall down and worship the
statue I made. But if you don't worship it, you
will immediately be thrown into a furnace of
blazing fire—and who is the god who can
rescue you from my power?"[e]

[16]Shadrach, Meshach, and Abednego replied to the king, "Nebuchadnezzar, we don't
need to give you an answer to this question.
[17]If the God we serve exists,[A] then He can rescue[f] us from the furnace of blazing fire, and
He can rescue us from the power of you, the
king. [18]But even if He does not rescue us,[B] we
want you as king to know that we will not
serve[g] your gods[h] or worship the gold statue
you set up."

[19]Then Nebuchadnezzar was filled with
rage,[i] and the expression on his face changed
toward Shadrach, Meshach, and Abednego.
He gave orders to heat the furnace seven
times more than was customary, [20]and he
commanded some of the strongest soldiers
in his army to tie up Shadrach, Meshach, and
Abednego and throw them into the furnace of
blazing fire. [21]So these men, in their trousers,
robes, head coverings,[C] and other clothes,
were tied up and thrown into the furnace of
blazing fire. [22]Since the king's command was
so urgent[D,j] and the furnace extremely hot,
the raging flames[E] killed those men who carried Shadrach, Meshach, and Abednego up.
[23]And these three men, Shadrach, Meshach,
and Abednego fell, bound, into the furnace of
blazing fire.

Delivered from the Fire

[24]Then King Nebuchadnezzar jumped up
in alarm.[k] He said to his advisers, "Didn't we
throw three men, bound, into the fire?"

"Yes, of course, Your Majesty," they replied
to the king.

[25]He exclaimed, "Look! I see four men, not
tied, walking around in the fire unharmed;[l]
and the fourth looks like a son of the gods."[F,m]

[26]Nebuchadnezzar then approached the
door of the furnace of blazing fire and called:
"Shadrach, Meshach, and Abednego, you servants of the ·Most High God—come out!"
So Shadrach, Meshach, and Abednego came
out of the fire.[n] [27]When the satraps, prefects,
governors, and the king's advisers gathered
around, they saw that the fire had no effect[o]
on[G] the bodies of these men: not a hair of
their heads was singed, their robes were unaffected, and there was no smell of fire on
them. [28]Nebuchadnezzar exclaimed, "Praise
to the God of Shadrach, Meshach, and Abednego! He sent His angel[H,p] and rescued His servants who trusted in Him.[q] They violated the
king's command and risked their lives rather
than serve or worship any god except their
own God.[r] [29]Therefore I issue a decree[s] that
anyone of any people, nation, or language
who says anything offensive against the God
of Shadrach, Meshach, and Abednego will be
torn limb from limb and his house made a
garbage dump.[t] For there is no other god who
is able to deliver like this." [30]Then the king rewarded Shadrach, Meshach, and Abednego in
the province of Babylon.[u]

Nebuchadnezzar's Proclamation

4 [1] King Nebuchadnezzar,

To those of every people, nation, and language, who live in all the earth:[v]

May your prosperity increase.[w] [2]I am
pleased to tell you about the miracles
and wonders[x] the ·Most High God has
done for me.

[a]**3:12** Dn 1:7 [b]Dn 6:13 [c]**3:13** Dn 2:12 [d]**3:14** Jr 50:2 [e]**3:15** Ex 5:20; 2Kg 18:35; Is 36:18 [f]**3:17** 1Sm 17:37; Jb 5:19; Jr 15:20,21; 2Co 1:10 [g]**3:18** Heb 11:25 [h]Jos 24:15 [i]**3:19** Est 7:7 [j]**3:22** Dn 2:15 [k]**3:24** Dn 4:19 [l]**3:25** Ps 91:3-9; Is 43:2 [m]Mt 14:33; Mk 1:1; Lk 1:35; Jn 3:18; Ac 9:20 [n]**3:26** Dn 4:2 [o]**3:27** Heb 11:34 [p]**3:28** Heb 1:14 [q]Ps 34:7; Is 37:36; Ac 5:19; 12:7 [r]Ps 22:4-5; Is 12:2; 26:3-4; Jr 17:7 [s]**3:29** Dn 4:6 [t]Ezr 6:11; Dn 2:5 [u]**3:30** Dn 2:48-49 [v]**4:1** Dn 6:25 [w]2Pt 1:2 [x]**4:2** Dn 6:27; Jn 4:48

[A]**3:17** They do not doubt God's existence as 3:18 shows. The "if" is part of an argument used to defend their refusal to serve Babylonian gods. [B]**3:18** Lit *But if not* [C]**3:21** The identity of these articles of clothing is uncertain. [D]**3:22** Or *harsh* [E]**3:22** Lit *the flame of the fire* [F]**3:25** Or *of a divine being* [G]**3:27** Lit *fire had not overcome* [H]**3:28** Or *messenger* [I]**4:1** Dn 3:31 in Hb

3 How great are His miracles,
and how mighty His wonders![a]
His kingdom is an eternal kingdom,[b]
and His dominion is from generation
to generation.

The Dream

4[A]I, Nebuchadnezzar, was at ease in my
house and flourishing in my palace.[c] 5I had
a dream, and it frightened me; while in my
bed, the images and visions in my mind
alarmed me.[d] 6So I issued a decree[e] to bring
all the wise men of Babylon to me in order
that they might make the dream's interpretation known to me.[f] 7When the diviner-priests,
mediums, Chaldeans, and astrologers came
in, I told them the dream, but they could not
make its interpretation known to me.[g]
8Finally Daniel, named Belteshazzar[h] after
the name of my god—and the spirit of the
holy gods is in him[i]—came before me. I told
him the dream: 9"Belteshazzar, head of the diviners, because I know that you have a spirit
of the holy gods[j] and that no mystery puzzles
you,[k] explain to me the visions of my dream
that I saw, and its interpretation. 10In the visions of my mind as I was lying in bed, I saw
this:

There was a tree in the middle
of the earth,
and its height was great.
11 The tree grew large and strong;
its top reached to the sky,
and it was visible to the ends
of the[B] earth.
12 Its leaves were beautiful, its fruit
was abundant,
and on it was food for all.
Wild animals found shelter under it,
the birds of the air[l] lived
in its branches,
and every creature was fed from it.[m]

13"As I was lying in my bed, I also saw in the
visions of my mind an observer, a holy one,[C,n]
coming down from heaven. 14He called out
loudly:

Cut down the tree and chop off
its branches;
strip off its leaves and scatter
its fruit.
Let the animals flee from under it,
and the birds from its branches.[o]
15 But leave the stump with its roots
in the ground,[p]
and with a band of iron and bronze
around it,
in the tender grass of the field.
Let him be drenched with dew
from the sky
and share the plants of the earth[q]
with the animals.
16 Let his mind be changed from that
of a man,
and let him be given the mind
of an animal
for seven periods of time.[D,E,r]
17 This word is by decree
of the observers;
the matter is a command
from the holy ones.
This is so the living will know
that the Most High is ruler
over the kingdom of men.
He gives it to anyone He wants
and sets the lowliest of men over it.[s]

18This is the dream that I, King Nebuchadnezzar, had. Now, Belteshazzar, tell me the interpretation, because none of the wise men of
my kingdom can make the interpretation
known to me.[t] But you can, because you have
the spirit of the holy gods."

The Dream Interpreted

19Then Daniel, whose name is Belteshazzar,
was stunned for a moment, and his thoughts
alarmed him. The king said, "Belteshazzar,
don't let the dream or its interpretation
alarm you."
Belteshazzar answered, "My lord, may the
dream apply to those who hate you, and its
interpretation to your enemies![u] 20The tree
you saw, which grew large and strong, whose
top reached to the sky and was visible to all
the earth, 21whose leaves were beautiful and
its fruit abundant—and on it was food for
all, under it the wild animals lived, and in its
branches the birds of the air lived— 22that

[a]4:3 Ps 105:27; Is 25:1 [b]Dn 2:44 [c]4:4 Ps 30:6; Is 47:7-8 [d]4:5 Dn 2:28; 7:15 [e]4:6 Dn 3:10,29 [f]Gn 41:8; Dn 2:12 [g]4:7 Dn 2:2 [h]4:8 Dn 1:7 [i]Gn 41:38; Dn 2:11 [j]4:9 Dn 5:11 [k]Ezk 28:3 [l]4:12 Ezk 17:23; Mt 13:32; Lk 13:9 [m]Ezk 31:3-6 [n]4:13 Dt 33:2; Ps 89:7; Zch 14:5; Jd 14 [o]4:14 Ezk 31:10-14 [p]4:15 Jb 14:7-9 [q]Gn 3:18 [r]4:16 Dn 7:25 [s]4:17 1Sm 2:8; Ps 9:16; Jr 27:5-7; Dn 5:21 [t]4:18 Gn 41:8; Dn 5:8 [u]4:19 2Sm 18:32

[A]4:4 Dn 4:1 in Hb [B]4:11 Lit *of all the* [C]4:13 = an angel [D]4:16 Lit *animal as seven times pass over him* [E]4:16 Perhaps 7 years

tree is you, the king. For you have become
great and strong: your greatness has grown
and even reaches the sky, and your dominion
extends to the ends of the earth.[a]
23 "The king saw an observer, a holy one,
coming down from heaven and saying, 'Cut
down the tree and destroy it, but leave the
stump with its roots in the ground and with
a band of iron and bronze around it, in the
tender grass of the field. Let him be drenched
with dew from the sky, and share food with
the wild animals for seven periods of time.'
24 This is the interpretation, Your Majesty, and
this is the sentence of the Most High that has
been passed against my lord the king:[b] 25 You
will be driven away from people to live with
the wild animals. You will feed on grass like
cattle[c] and be drenched with dew from the
sky for seven periods of time, until you acknowledge that the Most High is ruler over
the kingdom of men, and He gives it to anyone He wants.[d] 26 As for the command to leave
the tree's stump with its roots, your kingdom
will be restored[A] to you as soon as you acknowledge that Heaven[B] rules.[e] 27 Therefore,
may my advice seem good to you my king.
Separate yourself from your sins by doing
what is right,[f] and from your injustices by
showing mercy to the needy.[g] Perhaps there
will be an extension of your prosperity."[h]

The Sentence Executed

28 All this happened to King Nebuchadnezzar.[i] 29 At the end of 12 months, as he was walking on the roof of the royal palace in Babylon,
30 the king exclaimed, "Is this not Babylon the
Great that I have built by my vast power to be
a royal residence and to display my majestic
glory?"[j]
31 While the words were still in the king's
mouth, a voice came from heaven: "King
Nebuchadnezzar, to you it is declared that
the kingdom has departed from you.[k] 32 You
will be driven away from people to live with
the wild animals, and you will feed on grass
like cattle for seven periods of time, until you
acknowledge that the Most High is ruler over
the kingdom of men, and He gives it to anyone He wants."
33 At that moment the sentence against Nebuchadnezzar was executed. He was driven
away from people. He ate grass like cattle,
and his body was drenched with dew from
the sky, until his hair grew like eagles' feathers and his nails like birds' claws.[l]

Nebuchadnezzar's Praise

34 But at the end of those days, I, Nebuchadnezzar, looked up to heaven, and my sanity
returned to me. Then I praised the Most High
and honored and glorified Him who lives forever:[m]

For His dominion is
an everlasting dominion,
and His kingdom is from generation
to generation.[n]
35 All the inhabitants of the earth
are counted as nothing,
and He does what He wants[o]
with the army of heaven
and the inhabitants of the earth.
There is no one who can hold back
His hand
or say to Him, "What have You done?"[p]

36 At that time my sanity returned to me, and
my majesty and splendor returned to me for
the glory of my kingdom. My advisers and
my nobles sought me out, I was reestablished
over my kingdom, and even more greatness came to me.[q] 37 Now I, Nebuchadnezzar,
praise, exalt, and glorify the King of heaven,
because all His works are true and His ways
are just.[r] He is able to humble[s] those who walk
in pride.[t]

Belshazzar's Feast

5 King Belshazzar[u] held a great feast for
1,000 of his nobles and drank wine in
their presence. 2 Under the influence of[C] the
wine, Belshazzar gave orders to bring in the
gold and silver vessels[v] that his predecessor[D]
Nebuchadnezzar had taken from the temple
in Jerusalem, so that the king and his nobles,
wives, and concubines could drink from
them. 3 So they brought in the gold[E] vessels
that had been taken from the temple, the
house of God in Jerusalem, and the king and
his nobles, wives, and concubines drank from
them. 4 They drank the wine and praised their

[a] **4:22** Jr 27:6-8; Ezk 31:3
[b] **4:24** Jb 40:11-12; Ps 107:40
[c] **4:25** Ps 106:20; Jr 27:5
[d] Ps 83:18; Dn 5:21
[e] **4:26** Dn 2:37
[f] **4:27** Pr 28:13; Ac 8:22
[g] Ps 41:1-3; Is 58:6,7; Ezk 18:7
[h] Jr 18:8; Jn 3:10
[i] **4:28** Nm 23:19; Zch 1:6
[j] **4:30** Hab 2:4
[k] **4:31** Lk 12:20
[l] **4:32-33** Dn 5:21
[m] **4:34** Dn 6:26; 12:7; Rv 4:10
[n] Ps 145:13; Jr 10:10; Mc 4:7
[o] **4:35** Jb 9:12; 42:2; Ps 115:3; 135:6; Rm 9:20
[p] Is 40:17; 43:13; 45:9; Rm 9:20
[q] **4:36** 2Ch 33:12-13; Pr 22:4
[r] **4:37** Dt 32:4; Ps 33:4; Rv 15:3
[s] Ex 18:11; Jb 40:11-12
[t] Ps 18:27; Pr 16:18; Jms 4:6
[u] **5:1** Dn 7:1; 8:1
[v] **5:2** 1Kg 7:51; Jr 52:19

[A] **4:26** Lit *enduring* [B] **4:26** = God [C] **5:2** Or *When he tasted* [D] **5:2** Or *father*, or *grandfather* [E] **5:3** Theod, Vg add *and silver* gods made of gold and silver, bronze, iron, wood, and stone.[a]

The Handwriting on the Wall

5 At that moment the fingers of a man's hand appeared and began writing on the plaster of the king's palace wall next to the lampstand. As the king watched the hand[A] that was writing, 6 his face turned pale,[B] and his thoughts so terrified him that his hip joints shook and his knees knocked together. 7 The king called out to bring in the mediums, Chaldeans, and astrologers. He said to these wise men of Babylon, "Whoever reads this inscription and gives me its interpretation will be clothed in purple, have a gold chain around his neck,[b] and have the third highest position in the kingdom." 8 So all the king's wise men came in, but none could read the inscription or make its interpretation known to him. 9 Then King Belshazzar became even more terrified, his face turned pale,[C] and his nobles were bewildered.[c]

10 Because of the outcry of the king and his nobles, the queen[D] came to the banquet hall. "May the king live forever," she said. "Don't let your thoughts terrify you or your face be pale.[E] 11 There is a man in your kingdom who has the spirit of the holy gods in him.[d] In the days of your predecessor he was found to have insight, intelligence, and wisdom like the wisdom of the gods. Your predecessor, King Nebuchadnezzar, appointed him chief of the diviners, mediums, Chaldeans, and astrologers. Your own predecessor, the king, 12 did this because Daniel, the one the king named Belteshazzar, was found to have an extraordinary spirit, knowledge and perception, and the ability to interpret dreams, explain riddles, and solve problems.[e] Therefore, summon Daniel, and he will give the interpretation."

Daniel before the King

13 Then Daniel was brought before the king. The king said to him, "Are you Daniel, one of the Judean exiles that my predecessor the king brought from Judah?[f] 14 I've heard that you have the spirit of the gods in you, and that you have insight, intelligence, and extraordinary wisdom. 15 Now the wise men and mediums were brought before me to read this inscription and make its interpretation known to me, but they could not give its interpretation. 16 However, I have heard about you that you can give interpretations and solve problems. Therefore, if you can read this inscription and give me its interpretation, you will be clothed in purple, have a gold chain around your neck, and have the third highest position in the kingdom."[g]

17 Then Daniel answered the king, "You may keep your gifts, and give your rewards to someone else;[h] however, I will read the inscription for the king and make the interpretation known to him. 18 Your Majesty, the •Most High God gave sovereignty,[i] greatness, glory, and majesty to your predecessor Nebuchadnezzar.[j] 19 Because of the greatness He gave him, all peoples, nations, and languages[k] were terrified and fearful of him. He killed anyone he wanted and kept alive anyone he wanted; he exalted anyone he wanted and humbled anyone he wanted. 20 But when his heart was exalted and his spirit became arrogant,[l] he was deposed from his royal throne and his glory was taken from him.[m] 21 He was driven away from people,[n] his mind was like an animal's, he lived with the wild donkeys,[o] he was fed grass like cattle, and his body was drenched with dew from the sky until he acknowledged that the Most High God is ruler over the kingdom of men and sets anyone He wants over it.[p]

22 "But you his successor, Belshazzar, have not humbled your heart,[q] even though you knew all this. 23 Instead, you have exalted yourself against the Lord of heaven. The vessels from His house were brought to you, and as you and your nobles, wives, and concubines drank wine from them,[r] you praised the gods made of silver and gold, bronze, iron, wood, and stone, which do not see or hear or understand.[s] But you have not glorified the God who holds your life-breath in His hand and who controls the whole course of your life.[F] 24 Therefore, He sent the hand, and this writing was inscribed.

[a] **5:4** Is 46:6
[b] **5:7** Gn 41:42
[c] **5:9** Dn 2:1; 5:6; 7:28
[d] **5:11** Dn 4:8-9,18
[e] **5:12** Gn 41:11-15; Dn 6:3
[f] **5:13** Dn 1:3-4; 2:25
[g] **5:16** Gn 40:8; Dn 5:7,29
[h] **5:17** 2Kg 5:15-16
[i] **5:18** Dn 4:2
[j] Jr 27:5-7
[k] **5:19** Dn 2:12-13; 3:6
[l] **5:20** Ex 9:17; Jb 15:25; Dn 4:30-31
[m] Jr 13:18
[n] **5:21** Ex 9:17; Jb 15:25
[o] Jb 39:5-8
[p] Dn 4:30-31
[q] **5:22** Ex 10:3; 2Ch 33:23; 36:12
[r] **5:23** Jr 51:39,57
[s] Dn 5:3-4; Is 2:12; 37:23; Jr 50:29

[A] **5:5** Lit *part of the hand* [B] **5:5-6** Lit *writing, [6] the king's brightness changed*
[C] **5:9** Lit *his brightness changed on him* [D] **5:10** Perhaps the queen mother
[E] **5:10** Lit *your brightness change* [F] **5:23** Lit *and all your ways belong to Him*

The Inscription's Interpretation

25 "This is the writing that was inscribed:

MENE, MENE, TEKEL, PARSIN.

26 This is the interpretation of the message:

> MENE[A] means that God has numbered the days of your kingdom and brought it to an end.
>
> 27 TEKEL[B] means that you have been weighed in the balance and found deficient.
>
> 28 PERES[C,D] means that your kingdom has been divided and given to the Medes and Persians."

29 Then Belshazzar gave an order, and they clothed Daniel in purple, placed a gold chain around his neck,[a] and issued a proclamation concerning him that he should be the third ruler in the kingdom.

30 That very night Belshazzar the king of the Chaldeans was killed, 31[E] and Darius the Mede[b] received the kingdom at the age of 62.

The Plot against Daniel

6 Darius decided[F] to appoint 120 satraps over the kingdom, stationed throughout the realm, 2 and over them three administrators, including Daniel.[c] These satraps would be accountable to them so that the king would not be defrauded.[d] 3 Daniel[G] distinguished himself above the administrators and satraps because he had an extraordinary spirit,[e] so the king planned to set him over the whole realm.[f] 4 The administrators and satraps, therefore, kept trying to find a charge against Daniel[g] regarding the kingdom. But they could find no charge or corruption,[h] for he was trustworthy, and no negligence or corruption was found in him. 5 Then these men said, "We will never find any charge against this Daniel unless we find something against him concerning the law of his God."[i]

6 So the administrators and satraps went together to the king and said to him, "May King Darius live forever.[j] 7 All the administrators of the kingdom,[k] the prefects, satraps, advisers, and governors have agreed that the king should establish an ordinance and enforce an edict that for 30 days, anyone who petitions any god or man except you, the king, will be thrown into the lions' den.[l] 8 Therefore, Your Majesty, establish the edict[m] and sign the document so that, as a law of the Medes and Persians, it is irrevocable and cannot be changed."[n] 9 So King Darius signed the document.[o]

Daniel in the Lions' Den

10 When Daniel learned that the document had been signed, he went into his house. The windows in its upper room opened toward Jerusalem,[p] and three times a day he got down on his knees, prayed, and gave thanks to his God,[q] just as he had done before. 11 Then these men went as a group and found[r] Daniel petitioning and imploring his God. 12 So they approached the king[s] and asked about his edict: "Didn't you sign an edict that for 30 days any man who petitions any god or man except you, the king, will be thrown into the lions' den?"

The king answered, "As a law of the Medes and Persians, the order stands and is irrevocable."[t]

13 Then they replied to the king, "Daniel, one of the Judean exiles, has ignored you,[u] the king, and the edict you signed, for he prays three times a day." 14 As soon as the king heard this, he was very displeased; he set his mind on rescuing Daniel[v] and made every effort until sundown to deliver him.

15 Then these men went to the king and said to him, "You as king know it is a law of the Medes and Persians that no edict or ordinance the king establishes can be changed."[w]

16 So the king gave the order, and they brought Daniel and threw him into the lions' den.[x] The king said to Daniel, "May your God, whom you serve continually,[y] rescue you!" 17 A stone was brought and placed over the mouth of the den.[z] The king sealed it with his own signet ring and with the signet rings of his nobles, so that nothing in regard to Daniel could be changed. 18 Then the king went to his palace and spent the night fasting.[aa] No diversions[H] were brought to him, and he could not sleep.[ab]

[a] **5:29** Dn 5:7,16 [b] **5:31** Dn 6:1; 9:1; 11:1 [c] **6:2** Dn 2:48-49; 5:16,29 [d] Ezr 4:22; Est 7:4 [e] **6:3** Dn 5:12,14; 9:23 [f] Gn 41:40; Est 10:3 [g] **6:4** Gn 43:18; Jdg 14:4; Jr 20:10; Dn 3:8; Lk 20:20 [h] Dn 6:22; Lk 20:26; 23:14; Php 2:15; 1Pt 2:12; 3:16 [i] **6:5** Ac 24:13-16,20-21 [j] **6:6** Neh 2:3; Dn 2:4; 5:10; 6:21 [k] **6:7** Dn 3:2,27 [l] Ps 10:9; Dn 3:6; 6:16 [m] **6:8** Est 3:12; 8:10; Is 10:1 [n] Est 1:9; 8:8; Dn 6:12,15 [o] **6:9** Ps 118:9; 146:3 [p] **6:10** 1Kg 8:44-49; Ps 5:7; Jnh 2:4 [q] Ps 34:1; Dn 9:4-19; Php 4:6; 1Th 5:17-18 [r] **6:11** Ps 37:32,33; Dn 6:6 [s] **6:12** Dn 3:8-12; Ac 16:19-21 [t] Est 1:19; Dn 6:8,15 [u] **6:13** Est 3:8; Dn 3:12; Ac 5:29 [v] **6:14** Mk 6:26 [w] **6:15** Est 8:8; Ps 94:20,21; Dn 6:8,12 [x] **6:16** 2Sm 3:39; Jr 38:5; Dn 6:7 [y] Jb 5:19; Ps 37:39-40; Is 41:10; 2Co 1:10 [z] **6:17** Lm 3:53; Mt 27:66 [aa] **6:18** 2Sm 12:16,17 [ab] Est 6:1; Ps 77:4; Dn 2:1

[A] **5:26** Or *a mina* [B] **5:27** Or *a shekel* [C] **5:28** Or *half a shekel* [D] **5:28** In Aram, the word *peres* is the sg form of "parsin" in v. 25. [E] **5:31** Dn 6:1 in Hb [F] **6:1** Lit *It was pleasing before Darius* [G] **6:3** Lit *Now this Daniel* [H] **6:18** Hb obscure

Daniel Released

19 At the first light of dawn the king got up and hurried to the lions' den. 20 When he reached the den, he cried out in anguish to Daniel. "Daniel, servant of the living God," the king said,[A] "has your God whom you serve continually been able to rescue you[a] from the lions?"

21 Then Daniel spoke with the king: "May the king live forever. 22 My God sent His angel[b] and shut the lions' mouths. They haven't hurt me, for I was found innocent before Him. Also, I have not committed a crime against you my king."

23 The king was overjoyed and gave orders to take Daniel out of the den. So Daniel was taken out of the den, uninjured, for he trusted in his God.[c] 24 The king then gave the command, and those men who had maliciously accused Daniel[B,d] were brought and thrown into the lions' den—they, their children, and their wives.[e] They had not reached the bottom of the den before the lions overpowered them and crushed all their bones.

Darius Honors God

25 Then King Darius wrote to those of every people, nation, and language who live in all the earth: "May your prosperity abound.[f] 26 I issue a decree[g] that in all my royal dominion, people must tremble in fear before the God of Daniel:[h]

For He is the living God,
and He endures forever;
His kingdom will never be destroyed,[i]
and His dominion has no end.
27 He rescues and delivers;
He performs signs and wonders
in the heavens and on the earth,[j]
for He has rescued Daniel
from the power of the lions."

28 So Daniel prospered[k] during the reign of Darius and[C] the reign of Cyrus the Persian.[l]

Daniel's Vision of the Four Beasts

7 In the first year of Belshazzar king of Babylon, Daniel had a dream with visions in his mind[m] as he was lying in his bed. He wrote down the dream,[n] and here is the summary[D] of his account. 2 Daniel said, "In my vision at night I was watching, and suddenly the four winds of heaven[o] stirred up the great sea. 3 Four huge beasts[p] came up from the sea,[q] each different from the other.

4 "The first was like a lion[r] but had eagle's wings. I continued watching until its wings were torn off. It was lifted up from the ground, set on its feet like a man, and given a human mind.

5 "Suddenly, another beast appeared, a second one, that looked like a bear.[s] It was raised up on one side, with three ribs in its mouth between its teeth. It was told, 'Get up! Gorge yourself on flesh.'

6 "While I was watching, another beast appeared. It was like a leopard[t] with four wings of a bird on its back. It had four heads[u] and was given authority to rule.

7 "While I was watching in the night visions, a fourth beast[v] appeared, frightening and dreadful, and incredibly strong, with large iron teeth. It devoured and crushed, and it trampled with its feet whatever was left. It was different from all the beasts before it, and it had 10 horns.[w]

8 "While I was considering the horns, suddenly another horn,[x] a little one, came up among them, and three of the first horns were uprooted before it. There were eyes in this horn like a man's, and it had a mouth that spoke arrogantly.[y]

The Ancient of Days and the Son of Man

9 "As I kept watching,
thrones were set in place,[z]
and the Ancient of Days took His seat.
His clothing was white like snow,[aa]
and the hair of His head
like whitest wool.[ab]
His throne was flaming fire;[ac]
its wheels were blazing fire.[ad]
10 A river of fire was flowing,
coming out from His presence.
Thousands upon thousands[ae] served Him;
ten thousand times ten thousand[af]
stood before Him.
The court was convened,[ag]
and the books were opened.[ah]

[a]**6:20** Gn 18:14; Nm 11:23; Jr 32:17; Dn 3:17
[b]**6:22** Nm 20:16; Is 63:9; Dn 3:28; Ac 12:11; Heb 1:14
[c]**6:23** 1Ch 5:20; 2Ch 20:20; Ps 118:8,9; Is 26:3; Dn 3:17-18
[d]**6:24** Dn 3:8; 6:12-13
[e]Dt 24:16; 2Kg 14:6; Est 9:10
[f]**6:25** Ezr 4:17; 1Pt 1:2
[g]**6:26** Ezr 6:8-12; 7:13,21; Dn 3:29; 4:6
[h]Dn 5:19
[i]Ps 93:1,2; Dn 2:44; 7:14; Mal 3:6
[j]**6:27** Dn 4:2,3
[k]**6:28** Dn 1:21
[l]2Ch 36:22,23; Dn 10:1
[m]**7:1** Jb 33:14-16; Dn 1:17; 2:1; 4:5-9; Jl 2:28
[n]Jr 36:4,32
[o]**7:2** Ezk 37:9; Zch 2:6; Rv 7:1
[p]**7:3** Dn 7:17
[q]Rv 13:1; 17:8
[r]**7:4** Jr 4:7; 25:9; Rv 13:2
[s]**7:5** Rv 13:2
[t]**7:6** Hab 1:8; Rv 13:2
[u]Dn 8:22
[v]**7:7** Dn 7:19,23
[w]Dn 7:20,24; Rv 12:3; 13:1
[x]**7:8** Dn 7:11,20-26; 8:9
[y]Rv 13:5,6
[z]**7:9** Mt 19:28; Rv 20:4
[aa]Mk 9:3
[ab]Is 1:18; Rv 1:14
[ac]Ezk 1:13,26
[ad]Ezk 10:2,6
[ae]**7:10** Dt 33:2; 1Kg 22:19; Rv 5:11
[af]Ps 96:11-13; Rv 9:16
[ag]Dn 7:26
[ah]Dn 12:1; Rv 20:11-15

[A]**6:20** Lit *said to Daniel* [B]**6:24** Lit *had eaten his pieces* [C]**6:28** Or *Darius, even* [D]**7:1** Lit *beginning*

11"I watched, then, because of the sound of
the arrogant words the horn was speaking.
As I continued watching, the beast was killed
and its body destroyed and given over to the
burning fire.[a] 12As for the rest of the beasts,
their authority to rule was removed, but an
extension of life was granted to them for a
certain period of time.[b] 13I continued watching in the night visions,

and I saw One like a son of man[c]
coming with the clouds of heaven.[d]
He approached the Ancient of Days
and was escorted before Him.
14 He was given authority to rule,[e]
and glory, and a kingdom;
so that those of every people,
nation, and language[f]
should serve[g] Him.
His dominion is
an everlasting[h] dominion
that will not pass away,
and His kingdom is one
that will not be destroyed.

Interpretation of the Vision

15"As for me, Daniel, my spirit was deeply
distressed within me,[A] and the visions in
my mind terrified me.[i] 16I approached one
of those who were standing by and asked
him[j] the true meaning of all this. So he let
me know the interpretation of these things:[k]
17'These huge beasts, four in number, are four
kings who will rise from the earth. 18But the
holy ones of the ·Most High will receive the
kingdom and possess it forever, yes, forever
and ever.'[l]
19"Then I wanted to know the true meaning
of the fourth beast,[m] the one different from
all the others, extremely terrifying, with iron
teeth and bronze claws, devouring, crushing,
and trampling with its feet whatever was left.
20I also wanted to know about the 10 horns[n]
on its head and about the other horn that
came up, before which three fell — the horn
that had eyes, and a mouth that spoke arrogantly,[o] and that was more visible than the
others. 21As I was watching, this horn waged
war[p] against the holy ones and was prevailing over them 22until the Ancient of Days arrived and a judgment[q] was given in favor of
the holy ones of the Most High, for the time
had come, and the holy ones took possession
of the kingdom.
23"This is what he said: 'The fourth beast
will be a fourth kingdom on the earth, different from all the other kingdoms. It will devour the whole earth, trample it down, and
crush it. 24The 10 horns[r] are 10 kings who
will rise from this kingdom. Another, different from the previous ones, will rise after
them and subdue three kings. 25He will speak
words against the Most High[s] and oppress[B]
the holy ones[t] of the Most High. He will intend to change religious festivals[C] and laws,[u]
and the holy ones will be handed over to him
for a time, times, and half a time.[D,v] 26But the
court will convene,[w] and his dominion will be
taken away, to be completely destroyed forever.[x] 27The kingdom, dominion, and greatness of the kingdoms under all of heaven will
be given to the people, the holy ones of the
Most High. His kingdom will be an everlasting kingdom,[y] and all rulers will serve and
obey Him.'
28"This is the end of the interpretation.
As for me, Daniel, my thoughts terrified me
greatly,[z] and my face turned pale,[E] but I kept
the matter to myself."[aa]

The Vision of a Ram and a Goat

8 In the third year of King Belshazzar's[ab]
reign, a vision appeared to me, Daniel, after the one that had appeared to me earlier.[ac]
2I saw the vision, and as I watched, I was in
the fortress city of Susa,[ad] in the province of
Elam.[ae] I saw in the vision that I was beside
the Ulai Canal. 3I looked up,[F] and there was a
ram[af] standing beside the canal. He had two
horns. The two horns were long, but one was
longer than the other, and the longer one
came up last. 4I saw the ram charging to the
west, the north, and the south.[ag] No animal
could stand against him, and there was no
rescue from his power. He did whatever he
wanted[ah] and became great.
5As I was observing, a male goat appeared,
coming from the west across the surface of
the entire earth without touching the ground.

[a]7:11 Dn 7:26; Rv 19:20; 20:10 [b]7:12 Ps 75:6-7; Dn 2:21 [c]7:13 Mt 16:27-28; 24:30; Lk 21:27; Ac 7:56; Rv 1:7,13; 14:14 [d]Mt 26:64; Mk 13:26; 14:62 [e]7:14 Jn 3:35; 1Co 15:27; Eph 1:20-22; Php 2:9; Rv 1:6; 11:15 [f]Ps 72:11; 102:22; Rv 10:11 [g]Dn 3:14,17-18,28; 6:17,21; 7:27 [h]Heb 12:28 [i]7:15 Dn 4:19; 7:1,28 [j]7:16 Zch 1:9,19; Rv 5:5; 7:13-14 [k]Dn 7:3 [l]7:18 Ps 149:5-9; Is 60:12-14; Rv 2:26-27; 11:15; 22:5 [m]7:19 Dn 7:7-8 [n]7:20 Rv 12:3 [o]Dn 7:8; 2Th 2:9-10 [p]7:21 Rv 11:7; 13:7 [q]7:22 Dn 7:10; 1Co 6:2-3 [r]7:24 Dn 7:7; Rv 17:12 [s]7:25 Dn 11:36; Rv 13:1-6 [t]Rv 13:7; 18:24 [u]Dn 2:21 [v]Dn 12:7; Rv 11:2; 12:14 [w]7:26 Dn 7:10 [x]Rv 17:14; 19:20 [y]7:27 Ps 145:13; Is 9:7; Lk 1:33; Rv 11:15; 22:5 [z]7:28 Dn 4:19 [aa]Lk 2:19,51 [ab]8:1 Dn 5:1 [ac]Dn 7:1 [ad]8:2 Ezr 4:9; Neh 1:1; Est 1:2; 2:8 [ae]Gn 10:22; 14:1; Is 11:11; Jr 25:25; Ezk 33:24 [af]8:3 Dn 8:20 [ag]8:4 Dt 33:17; 1Kg 22:11; Ezk 34:21 [ah]Dn 11:3

[A]7:15 Lit *was distressed in the middle of its sheath* [B]7:25 Lit *wear out* [C]7:25 Lit *change times* [D]7:25 Or *for three and a half years* [E]7:28 Lit *my brightness changed on me* [F]8:3 Lit *I lifted my eyes and looked*

The goat had a conspicuous horn[A] between
his eyes.[a] 6 He came toward the two-horned
ram I had seen standing beside the canal and
rushed at him with savage fury. 7 I saw him
approaching the ram, and infuriated with
him, he struck the ram, shattering his two
horns, and the ram was not strong enough to
stand against him. The goat threw him to the
ground and trampled him, and there was no
one to rescue the ram from his power. 8 Then
the male goat became very great,[b] but when
he became powerful, the large horn was shattered.[c] Four conspicuous horns came up in
its place, pointing toward the four winds of
heaven.[d]

The Little Horn

9 From one of them a little horn[e] emerged
and grew extensively toward the south and
the east and toward the beautiful land.[B,f]
10 It grew as high as the heavenly •host, made
some of the stars and some of the host fall to
the earth,[g] and trampled them.[h] 11 It made itself great,[i] even up to the Prince of the host;[j]
it removed His daily sacrifice[k] and overthrew
the place of His sanctuary. 12 Because of rebellion, a host, together with the daily sacrifice,
will be given over. The horn will throw truth
to the ground and will be successful[l] in whatever it does.

13 Then I heard a holy one speaking,[m] and
another holy one said to the speaker, "How
long will the events of this vision last[n] — the
daily sacrifice, the rebellion that makes desolate, and the giving over of the sanctuary and
of the host to be trampled?"[o]

14 He said to me,[C] "For 2,300 evenings and
mornings; then the sanctuary will be restored."

Interpretation of the Vision

15 While I, Daniel, was watching the vision
and trying to understand it, there stood before me someone who appeared to be a man.[p]
16 I heard a human voice calling from the middle of the Ulai: "Gabriel,[q] explain the vision to
this man."

17 So he approached where I was standing;
when he came near, I was terrified and fell
facedown.[r] "Son of man," he said to me, "understand that the vision refers to the time
of the end."[s] 18 While he was speaking to me,
I fell into a deep sleep,[t] with my face to the
ground. Then he touched me, made me stand
up,[u] 19 and said, "I am here to tell you what
will happen at the conclusion of the time of
wrath, because it refers to the appointed time
of the end.[v] 20 The two-horned ram[w] that you
saw represents the kings of Media and Persia. 21 The shaggy goat represents the king of
Greece, and the large horn between his eyes
represents the first king.[D] 22 The four horns
that took the place of the shattered horn represent four kingdoms. They will rise from
that nation, but without its power.

23 Near the end of their kingdoms,
when the rebels have reached
the full measure of their sin,[E]
an insolent king, skilled in intrigue,[F]
will come to the throne.
24 His power will be great,
but it will not be his own.
He will cause terrible destruction[x]
and succeed in whatever he does.
He will destroy the powerful
along with the holy people.[y]
25 He will cause deceit to prosper
through his cunning
and by his influence,
and in his own mind he will
make himself great.
He will destroy many in a
time of peace;
he will even stand against the Prince
of princes.
Yet he will be shattered — not by
human hands.[z]
26 The vision of the evenings
and the mornings
that has been told is true.
Now you must seal up the vision[aa]
because it refers to many days
in the future."

27 I, Daniel, was overcome and lay sick for
days.[ab] Then I got up and went about the
king's business.[ac] I was greatly disturbed by
the vision and could not understand it.

[a]**8:5** Dn 8:21
[b]**8:8** 2Ch 26:16; Dn 5:20
[c]Dn 8:22
[d]Dn 7:2; Rv 7:1
[e]**8:9** Dn 7:8; 8:23
[f]Ps 48:2; Dn 11:16,41
[g]**8:10** Is 14:13; Jr 48:26; Rv 12:4
[h]Dn 7:7
[i]**8:11** 2Kg 19:22-23; 2Ch 32:15-17; Is 37:23; Dn 11:36-37
[j]Jos 5:13-15
[k]Ezk 46:14; Dn 11:31; 12:11
[l]**8:12** Is 59:14; Dn 11:36
[m]**8:13** Dn 4:13,23; 1Pt 1:12
[n]Ps 74:10; 79:5; Is 6:11; Dn 12:6,8; Rv 6:10
[o]Is 63:18; Jr 12:10; Lk 21:24; Heb 10:29; Rv 11:2
[p]**8:15** Dn 7:13; 10:16,18
[q]**8:16** Dn 9:21; Lk 1:19,26
[r]**8:17** Ezk 1:28; 44:4; Dn 2:46; Rv 1:17
[s]Dn 11:35,40
[t]**8:18** Dn 10:9; Lk 9:32
[u]Ezk 2:2; Dn 10:10,16,18
[v]**8:19** Mt 13:7
[w]**8:20** Dn 8:3
[x]**8:24** Dn 11:36; 12:7
[y]Dn 7:27
[z]**8:25** Jb 34:20; Dn 2:34,45
[aa]**8:26** Ezk 12:27; Dn 12:4,9; Rv 10:4; 22:10
[ab]**8:27** Dn 7:28; 8:17; Hab 3:16
[ac]Dn 2:48

[A]**8:5** Lit *a horn of a vision* [B]**8:9** = Israel [C]**8:14** LXX, Theod, Syr, Vg read *him* [D]**8:21** = Alexander the Great [E]**8:23** Lit *have become complete* [F]**8:23** Lit *king, and understanding riddles*

Daniel's Prayer

9 In the first year of Darius,[a] the son of
Ahasuerus, a Mede by birth, who was
ruler over the kingdom of the Chaldeans: 2In
the first year of his reign, I, Daniel, understood from the books according to the word
of the LORD to Jeremiah the prophet that the
number of years for the desolation of Jerusalem would be 70.[b] 3So I turned my attention
to the Lord God to seek Him by prayer and
petitions, with fasting, •sackcloth, and ashes.[c]
4I prayed to the LORD my God and confessed:

Ah, Lord — the great and awe-inspiring
God[d] who keeps His gracious covenant[e]
with those who love Him[f] and keep His
commands[g] — 5we have sinned,[h] done
wrong, acted wickedly, rebelled,[i] and
turned away from Your commands and
ordinances.[j] 6We have not listened to
Your servants the prophets,[k] who spoke
in Your name to our kings, leaders, fathers, and all the people of the land.

7Lord, righteousness belongs to You,[l] but
this day public shame belongs to us: the
men of Judah, the residents of Jerusalem,
and all Israel — those who are near and
those who are far, in all the countries
where You have dispersed them because
of the disloyalty they have shown toward
You. 8LORD, public shame[m] belongs to us,
our kings, our leaders, and our fathers,
because we have sinned against You.[n]
9Compassion and forgiveness belong to
the Lord our God, though we have rebelled against Him 10and have not obeyed
the voice of the LORD our God by following His instructions that He set before us
through His servants[o] the prophets.
11All Israel has broken Your law and
turned away,[p] refusing to obey You. The
promised curse[A] written in the law of Moses,[q] the servant of God, has been poured
out on us because we have sinned against
Him. 12He has carried out His words[r] that
He spoke against us and against our rulers[B,s] by bringing on us so great a disaster
that nothing like what has been done to
Jerusalem has ever been done[t] under all
of heaven. 13Just as it is written in the law
of Moses,[u] all this disaster has come on
us, yet we have not appeased[v] the LORD
our God by turning from our iniquities
and paying attention to Your truth.[w] 14So
the LORD kept the disaster in mind and
brought it on us, for the LORD our God is
righteous in all He has done. But we have
not obeyed Him.

15Now, Lord our God, who brought Your
people out of the land of Egypt with a
mighty hand[x] and made Your name renowned[y] as it is this day, we have sinned,
we have acted wickedly. 16Lord, in keeping with all Your righteous acts, may
Your anger and wrath[z] turn away from
Your city Jerusalem, Your holy mountain;[aa] for because of our sins and the
iniquities of our fathers, Jerusalem and
Your people have become an object of
ridicule to all those around us.

17Therefore, our God, hear the prayer and
the petitions of Your servant. Show Your
favor[ab] to Your desolate sanctuary[ac] for
the Lord's sake. 18Listen,[C] my God, and
hear. Open Your eyes and see our desolations and the city called by Your name.
For we are not presenting our petitions
before You based on our righteous acts,
but based on Your abundant compassion. 19Lord, hear! Lord, forgive! Lord,
listen and act! My God, for Your own
sake, do not delay,[ad] because Your city
and Your people are called by Your name.

The 70 Weeks of Years

20While I was speaking, praying, confessing my sin and the sin of my people Israel,[ae]
and presenting my petition before •Yahweh
my God concerning the holy mountain of my
God — 21while I was praying, Gabriel,[af] the
man I had seen in the first vision,[ag] came to
me in my extreme weariness, about the time
of the evening offering.[ah] 22He gave me this
explanation: "Daniel, I've come now to give
you understanding.[ai] 23At the beginning of
your petitions an answer went out, and I have
come to give it, for you are treasured by God.[aj]

[a]9:1 Dn 5:31; 6:1; 11:1
[b]9:2 2Ch 36:21; Ezr 1:1; Jr 25:11-12; 29:10; Zch 7:5
[c]9:3 Neh 1:4; Jb 2:8; Is 61:3; Lk 10:13
[d]9:4 Dt 7:21; Neh 9:32
[e]Dt 7:9
[f]1Jn 4:20
[g]Dt 7:9; Neh 1:5
[h]9:5 1Kg 8:48; Neh 9:33; Ps 106:6; Is 64:5-7; Jr 14:7
[i]Lm 1:18,20
[j]Ps 119:176; Is 53:6; Dn 9:11
[k]9:6 2Ch 36:16; Jr 44:4-5
[l]9:7 Jr 23:6; 33:16; Dn 9:18
[m]9:8 Ps 37:1-2
[n]Ps 78:56-64
[o]9:10 2Kg 17:13-15; 18:12
[p]9:11 Is 1:3-4; Jr 8:5-10
[q]Dt 28:15-68; 29:16–30:20; Lk 2:22
[r]9:12 Is 44:26; Jr 44:2-6; Lm 2:17; Zch 1:6
[s]Jb 12:17; Ps 82:2-7; 148:11
[t]Lm 1:12; 2:13; Ezk 5:9
[u]9:13 Lv 26:14-45; Dt 28:15-68; Dn 9:11
[v]Jb 36:13; Is 9:13; Jr 2:30; 5:3; Mal 1:9
[w]Jr 31:18
[x]9:15 Dt 5:15
[y]Neh 9:10; Jr 32:20
[z]9:16 Jr 32:31-32
[aa]Ps 87:1-3; Dn 9:20; Jl 3:17; Zch 8:3
[ab]9:17 Nm 6:25; Ps 31:17; 67:2
[ac]Lm 5:18
[ad]9:19 Ps 44:23; 74:10-11
[ae]9:20 Ps 145:18; Is 58:9; Dn 9:3; 10:12
[af]9:21 Dn 8:16; Lk 1:19,26
[ag]Dn 8:1,15
[ah]Ex 29:39; 1Kg 18:36; Ezr 9:4
[ai]9:22 Dn 8:16; 10:21; Zch 1:9
[aj]9:23 Dn 10:11,19

[A]9:11 Lit *The curse and the oath* [B]9:12 Lit *against rulers who ruled us* [C]9:18 Lit *Stretch out Your ear*

So consider the message and understand the
vision:[a]

24 Seventy weeks[A] are decreed[b]
about your people and your holy city—
to bring the rebellion to an end,
to put a stop to sin,
to wipe away iniquity,
to bring in everlasting righteousness,[c]
to seal up vision and prophecy,
and to anoint the most holy place.
25 Know and understand this:
From the issuing of the decree
to restore and rebuild Jerusalem[d]
until ·Messiah[e] the Prince[B]
will be seven weeks and 62 weeks.[C]
It will be rebuilt with a plaza
and a moat,
but in difficult times.
26 After those 62 weeks[D]
the Messiah will be cut off[f]
and will have nothing.
The people of the coming prince
will destroy the city[g] and the sanctuary.
The[E] end will come with a flood,[h]
and until the end there will be[F] war;
desolations are decreed.
27 He will make a firm covenant[G]
with many for one week,[H]
but in the middle of the week
he will put a stop to sacrifice
and offering.
And the abomination of desolation[i]
will be on a wing[j] of the temple[I,J]
until the decreed destruction[k]
is poured out on the desolator."

Vision of a Glorious One

10 In the third year of Cyrus king of Persia,[l] a message was revealed to Daniel,
who was named Belteshazzar.[m] The message
was true and was about a great conflict. He
understood the message and had understanding of the vision.[n]
2 In those days I, Daniel, was mourning for
three full weeks.[o] 3 I didn't eat any rich food,[p]
no meat or wine entered my mouth, and I
didn't put any oil on my body until the three
weeks were over. 4 On the twenty-fourth day
of the first month,[K] as I was standing on the
bank of the great river,[q] the Tigris, 5 I looked
up, and there was a man dressed in linen,[r]
with a belt of gold[s] from Uphaz[L,t] around his
waist. 6 His body was like topaz,[M] his face like
the brilliance of lightning, his eyes like flaming torches,[u] his arms and feet like the gleam
of polished bronze, and the sound of his
words like the sound of a multitude.[v]
7 Only I, Daniel, saw the vision.[w] The men
who were with me did not see it,[x] but a great
terror fell on them,[y] and they ran and hid. 8 I
was left alone, looking at this great vision.[z]
No strength was left in me; my face grew
deathly pale,[N,aa] and I was powerless. 9 I heard
the words he said, and when I heard them I
fell into a deep sleep,[O,ab] with my face to the
ground.

Angelic Conflict

10 Suddenly, a hand touched me and raised
me to my hands and knees. 11 He said to me,
"Daniel, you are a man treasured by God.[ac]
Understand the words that I'm saying to you.
Stand on your feet,[ad] for I have now been sent
to you."[ae] After he said this to me, I stood
trembling.
12 "Don't be afraid,[af] Daniel," he said to me,
"for from the first day that you purposed to
understand and to humble yourself before
your God,[ag] your prayers were heard. I have
come because of your prayers.[ah] 13 But the
prince of the kingdom of Persia opposed me
for 21 days. Then Michael,[ai] one of the chief
princes, came to help me after I had been left
there with the kings of Persia.[aj] 14 Now I have
come to help you understand what will happen to your people in the last days,[ak] for the
vision refers to those days."[al]
15 While he was saying these words to me, I
turned my face toward the ground and was
speechless.[am] 16 Suddenly one with human likeness[an] touched my lips.[ao] I opened my mouth
and said to the one standing in front of me,
"My lord, because of the vision, anguish overwhelms me and I am powerless.[ap] 17 How can
someone like me,[aq] your servant,[P] speak with

[a] **9:23** Mt 24:15 [b] **9:24** Lv 25:8; Nm 14:34; Ezk 4:5-6 [c] Is 51:6,8; 56:1; Jr 23:5-6; Rm 3:21-22 [d] **9:25** Ezr 4:24; 6:1-15; Neh 2:1-8; 3:1 [e] Mt 1:17; Jn 1:41; 4:25 [f] **9:26** Is 53:8; Mk 9:12; Lk 24:26 [g] Mt 24:2; Mk 13:2; Lk 19:43-44 [h] Nah 1:8 [i] **9:27** Dn 11:31; Mt 24:15; Mk 13:14; Lk 21:20 [j] Is 7:7-8; Mt 4:5 [k] Is 10:23; 28:22 [l] **10:1** Dn 1:21; 6:28 [m] Dn 1:7 [n] Dn 1:17: 2:21 [o] **10:2** Ezr 9:4-5; Neh 1:4 [p] **10:3** Dn 6:18; Am 6:6; Mt 6:17 [q] **10:4** Ezk 1:3; Dn 8:2 [r] **10:5** Ezk 9:2; Dn 12:6-7 [s] Rv 1:13; 15:6 [t] Jr 10:9 [u] **10:6** Rv 1:14; 2:18; 19:12 [v] Rv 19:6 [w] **10:7** 2Kg 6:17-20 [x] Ac 9:7 [y] Ezk 12:18 [z] **10:8** Gn 32:24 [aa] Dn 7:28; 8:27; Hab 3:16 [ab] **10:9** Gn 15:12; Jb 4:13; Dn 8:18 [ac] **10:11** Dn 9:23; 10:19 [ad] Ezk 2:2; Dn 8:18 [ae] Heb 11:14 [af] **10:12** Is 41:10,14; Dn 10:19 [ag] Dn 9:2-23; 10:2-3 [ah] Ac 10:30-31 [ai] **10:13** Dn 10:21; 12:1; Jd 9; Rv 12:7 [aj] Dn 7:17; 8:21 [ak] **10:14** Dt 31:29; Dn 2:28 [al] Dn 8:26; 12:4,9 [am] **10:15** Ezk 3:26; 24:27; Lk 1:20 [an] **10:16** Dn 8:15 [ao] Is 6:7; Jr 1:9 [ap] Dn 7:15,28; 8:17,27; 10:8-9 [aq] **10:17** Ex 24:10-11; Is 6:1-5

[A] **9:24** = 490 years [B] **9:25** Or *until an anointed one, a prince* [C] **9:25** = 49 years and 434 years [D] **9:26** = 434 years [E] **9:26** Lit *Its*, or *His* [F] **9:26** Or *end of a* [G] **9:27** Or *will enforce a covenant* [H] **9:27** = 7 years [I] **9:27** LXX; MT reads *of abominations* [J] **9:27** Or *And the desolator will be on the wing of abominations,* or *And the desolator will come on the wings of monsters* (or *of horror*); Hb obscure [K] **10:4** = Nisan (March–April) [L] **10:5** Some Hb mss read *Ophir* [M] **10:6** The identity of this stone is uncertain. [N] **10:8** Lit *my splendor was turned on me to ruin* [O] **10:9** Lit *a sleep on my face* [P] **10:17** Lit *Can I, a servant of my lord*

someone like you, my lord? Now I have no strength, and there is no breath in me."

18 Then the one with human likeness touched me again and strengthened me.[a] 19 He said, "Don't be afraid,[b] you who are[A] treasured by God.[c] Peace to you; be very strong!"[d]

As he spoke to me, I was strengthened and said, "Let my lord speak, for you have strengthened me."[e]

20 He said, "Do you know why I've come to you? I must return at once to fight against the prince of Persia, and when I leave, the prince of Greece will come.[f] 21 No one has the courage to support me against them except Michael,[g] your prince. However, I will tell you what is recorded in the book of truth.

11 1 In the first year of Darius the Mede,[h] I stood up to strengthen and protect him. 2 Now I will tell you the truth.[i]

Prophecies about Persia and Greece

"Three more kings will arise in Persia, and the fourth will be far richer than the others. By the power he gains through his riches, he will stir up everyone against the kingdom of Greece.[j] 3 Then a warrior king will arise; he will rule a vast realm and do whatever he wants.[k] 4 But as soon as he is established, his kingdom will be broken up and divided to the four winds of heaven,[l] but not to his descendants; it will not be the same kingdom that he ruled, because his kingdom will be uprooted and will go to others besides them.[m]

Kings of the South and the North

5 "The king of the South[n] will grow powerful, but one of his commanders will grow more powerful and will rule a kingdom greater than his. 6 After some years they will form an alliance, and the daughter of the king of the South will go to the king of the North[o] to seal the agreement. She will not retain power, and his strength will not endure. She will be given up, together with her entourage, her father,[B] and the one who supported her during those times. 7 In the place of the king of the South, one from her family[C] will rise up, come against the army, and enter the fortress of the king of the North. He will take action against them and triumph. 8 He will take even their gods captive to Egypt, with their metal images and their precious articles of silver and gold.[p] For some years he will stay away from the king of the North, 9 who will enter the kingdom of the king of the South and then return to his own land.

10 "His sons will mobilize for war and assemble a large number of armed forces. They will advance, sweeping through like a flood,[D,q] and will again wage war as far as his fortress. 11 Infuriated, the king of the South will march out to fight with the king of the North who will raise a large army but they will be handed over to his enemy. 12 When the army is carried off, he will become arrogant and cause tens of thousands to fall, but he will not triumph. 13 The king of the North will again raise a multitude larger than the first. After some years[E,r] he will advance with a great army and many supplies.

14 "In those times many will rise up against the king of the South. Violent ones among your own people will assert themselves to fulfill a vision, but they will fail. 15 Then the king of the North will come, build up an assault ramp,[s] and capture a well-fortified city. The forces of the South will not stand; even their select troops will not be able to resist. 16 The king of the North who comes against him will do whatever he wants,[t] and no one can oppose him. He will establish himself in the beautiful land[F,u] with total destruction in his hand. 17 He will resolve[v] to come with the force of his whole kingdom and will reach an agreement with him.[G] He will give him a daughter in marriage[H] to destroy it,[I] but she will not stand with him or support him. 18 Then he will turn his attention to the coasts and islands[J,w] and capture many. But a commander will put an end to his taunting; instead, he will turn his taunts against him.[x] 19 He will turn his attention back to the fortresses of his own land, but he will stumble, fall,[y] and be no more.[z]

20 "In his place one will arise who will send out a tax collector[aa] for the glory of the

[a] 10:18 Is 35:3-4 [b] 10:19 Jdg 6:23; Is 43:1; Dn 10:12 [c] Dn 9:23; 10:11 [d] Jos 1:6-7,9; Is 35:4 [e] Ps 138:2; 2Co 12:9 [f] 10:20 Dn 8:21; 11:2 [g] 10:21 Dn 10:13; Rv 12:7 [h] 11:1 Dn 5:31; 9:1 [i] 11:2 Dn 8:26; 10:1,21 [j] Dn 8:21; 10:20 [k] 11:3 Dn 5:19; 8:4; 11:16,36 [l] 11:4 Jr 49:36; Ezk 37:9; Dn 7:2; 8:8; Zch 2:6; 6:5; Rv 7:1 [m] Jr 12:15,17; 18:7 [n] 11:5 Dn 11:9, 11,14,25,40 [o] 11:6 Dn 11:13,15,40 [p] 11:8 Is 37:19; 46:1-2; Jr 43:12-13 [q] 11:10 Is 8:8; Jr 46:7,8; 51:42; Dn 11:26,40 [r] 11:13 Dn 4:16; 12:7 [s] 11:15 Jr 6:6; Ezk 4:2; 17:17 [t] 11:16 Dn 5:19; 11:3,36 [u] Dn 8:9; 11:41 [v] 11:17 2Kg 12:17; Ezk 4:3,7 [w] 11:18 Gn 10:5; Is 66:19; Jr 2:10; 31:10; Zph 2:11 [x] Hs 12:14 [y] 11:19 Ps 27:2; Jr 46:6 [z] Jb 20:8; Ps 37:36; Ezk 26:21 [aa] 11:20 2Kg 23:35

[A] 10:19 Lit *afraid, man* [B] 11:6 Some Hb mss, Theod read *the child*; Syr, Vg read *her children* [C] 11:7 Lit *from the shoot of her roots* [D] 11:10 Lit *advance and overflow and pass through* [E] 11:13 Lit *At the end of the times* [F] 11:16 = Israel [G] 11:17 = the king of the South [H] 11:17 Lit *him the daughter of women* [I] 11:17 Perhaps the kingdom [J] 11:18 of the Mediterranean

kingdom; but within a few days he will be
shattered, though not in anger[A] or in battle.
21“In his place a despised[a] person will arise;
royal honors will not be given to him, but he
will come during a time of peace[B,b] and seize
the kingdom by intrigue. 22A flood of forces
will be swept away before him; they will be
shattered, as well as the covenant prince. 23After an alliance is made with him, he will act
deceitfully. He will rise to power with a small
nation.[C] 24During a time of peace,[D] he will come
into the richest parts of the province[c] and do
what his fathers and predecessors never did.
He will lavish plunder, loot, and wealth on his
followers, and he will make plans against fortified cities, but only for a time.
25“With a large army he will stir up his
power and his courage against the king of the
South. The king of the South will prepare for
battle with an extremely large and powerful
army, but he will not succeed, because plots
will be made against him. 26Those who eat his
provisions[d] will destroy him; his army will be
swept away, and many will fall slain. 27The
two kings, whose hearts are bent on evil, will
speak lies[e] at the same table but to no avail,
for still the end will come at the appointed
time.[f] 28The king of the North will return to
his land with great wealth, but his heart will
be set against the holy covenant;[E] he will take
action, then return to his own land.
29“At the appointed time he will come
again to the South, but this time[F] will not be
like the first. 30Ships of Kittim[G,g] will come
against him, and being intimidated, he will
withdraw. Then he will rage against the holy
covenant and take action. On his return, he
will favor those who abandon the holy covenant. 31His forces will rise up and desecrate
the temple fortress. They will abolish the
daily sacrifice[h] and set up the abomination
of desolation.[i] 32With flattery he will corrupt
those who act wickedly toward the covenant,
but the people who know their God will be
strong and take action.[j] 33Those who are wise
among the people[k] will give understanding to many, yet they will die by sword and
flame,[l] and be captured and plundered for a
time. 34When defeated, they will be helped
by some, but many others will join them insincerely.[m] 35Some of the wise will fall so that
they may be refined,[n] purified, and cleansed[o]
until the time of the end, for it will still come
at the appointed time.
36“Then the king will do whatever he
wants.[p] He will exalt and magnify himself
above every god,[q] and he will say outrageous
things against the God of gods.[r] He will be
successful until the time of wrath is completed,[s] because what has been decreed will
be accomplished. 37He will not show regard
for the gods[H] of his fathers, the god longed
for by women, or for any other god,[t] because
he will magnify himself above all. 38Instead,
he will honor a god of fortresses — a god his
fathers did not know — with gold, silver, precious stones, and riches. 39He will deal with
the strongest fortresses with the help of a
foreign god. He will greatly honor those who
acknowledge him,[I] making them rulers over
many and distributing land as a reward.
40“At the time of the end, the king of the
South will engage him in battle, but the king
of the North will storm against him[u] with
chariots, horsemen, and many ships. He will
invade countries and sweep through them
like a flood.[v] 41He will also invade the beautiful land,[w] and many will fall. But these will
escape from his power: Edom, Moab, and the
prominent people[J] of the Ammonites.[x] 42He
will extend his power against the countries,
and not even the land of Egypt will escape.
43He will get control over the hidden treasures of gold and silver and over all the riches
of Egypt. The Libyans and *Cushites will also
be in submission.[K,y] 44But reports from the
east[z] and the north will terrify him, and he
will go out with great fury to annihilate and
*completely destroy many. 45He will pitch his
royal tents between the sea and[L] the beautiful holy mountain,[aa] but he will meet his end
with no one to help him.

12 At that time
Michael[ab] the great prince
who stands watch over your people
will rise up.

[a]**11:21** Is 53:3 [b]Dn 8:25; 11:24 [c]**11:24** Nm 13:20; Neh 9:25; Ezk 34:14 [d]**11:26** Dn 1:5,8,13,15 [e]**11:27** Ps 12:2; Jr 9:3-5; 41:1-3 [f]Dn 8:19; 11:35,40; Hab 2:3 [g]**11:30** Gn 10:4; Nm 24:24; 1Ch 1:7; Is 23:1,12; Jr 2:10 [h]**11:31** Dn 8:11-13; 12:11 [i]Dn 9:27; 12:11; Mt 24:15; Mk 13:14 [j]**11:32** Mc 5:7-9; Zch 9:13-16; 10:3-6 [k]**11:33** Mal 2:7 [l]Mt 24:9; Jn 16:2; Heb 11:36-38 [m]**11:34** Dn 11:21,32; Mt 7:15; Ac 20:29,30; Rm 16:18 [n]**11:35** Dt 8:16; Pr 17:3; Dn 12:10; Zch 13:9; Mal 3:2-3 [o]Dn 12:10 [p]**11:36** Dn 5:19; 11:3,16 [q]Is 14:13; Dn 5:20; 8:11,25; 2Th 2:4 [r]Rv 13:5-6 [s]Is 10:25; 26:20; Dn 8:19 [t]**11:37** 1Co 8:5-6 [u]**11:40** Is 5:28; Jr 4:13 [v]Dn 11:10,26; Zch 9:14 [w]**11:41** Is 11:14; Dn 8:9; 11:16 [x]Jr 48:47; 49:6 [y]**11:43** 2Ch 12:3; Ezk 30:4; Nah 3:9 [z]**11:44** Rv 16:12 [aa]**11:45** Is 11:9; 27:13; 65:25; 66:20; Dn 9:16,20 [ab]**12:1** Dn 10:13,21; Jd 9; Rv 12:7

A**11:20** Or *not openly* B**11:21** Or *come without warning* C**11:23** Or *a few people* D**11:24** Or *Without warning* E**11:28** Or *the Jewish people and religion* F**11:29** Lit *but the last* G**11:30** = the Romans H**11:37** Or *God* I**11:39** Or *those he acknowledges* J**11:41** Lit *the first* K**11:43** Lit *Cushites at his steps* L**11:45** Or *the seas at*

There will be a time of distress[a]
such as never has occurred[b]
since nations came into being
until that time.[c]
But at that time all your people
who are found written in the book[d]
will escape.[e]
2 Many of those who sleep in the dust[f]
of the earth will awake,
some to eternal life,[g]
and some to shame
and eternal contempt.[h]
3 Those who are wise will shine
like the bright expanse of the heavens,[i]
and those who lead many
to righteousness,[j]
like the stars forever and ever.

4 "But you, Daniel, keep these words secret[k]
and seal the book[l] until the time of the end.[m]
Many will roam about,[n] and knowledge will
increase."[A]
5 Then I, Daniel, looked, and two others
were standing there, one on this bank of the
river and one on the other. 6 One of them
said to the man dressed in linen,[o] who was
above the waters of the river,[p] "How long until the end[q] of these extraordinary things?"
7 Then I heard the man dressed in linen, who
was above the waters of the river. He raised
both his hands[B,r] toward heaven and swore
by Him who lives eternally[s] that it would
be for a time, times, and half a time.[t] When
the power of the holy people is shattered, all
these things will be completed.
8 I heard but did not understand. So I asked,
"My lord, what will be the outcome of these
things?"[u]
9 He said, "Go on your way, Daniel, for the
words are secret[v] and sealed until the time of
the end.[w] 10 Many will be purified,[x] cleansed,
and refined,[y] but the wicked will act wickedly;[z] none of the wicked will understand,
but the wise will understand.[aa] 11 From the
time the daily sacrifice is abolished and the
abomination of desolation[ab] is set up,[ac] there
will be 1,290 days. 12 The one who waits[ad] for
and reaches 1,335 days is blessed. 13 But as for
you, go on your way to the end;[C] you will rest,
then rise[ae] to your destiny at the end of the
days."

[a] 12:1 Mt 24:21; Mk 13:19 [b] Jr 30:7; Ezk 5:9; Dn 9:12 [c] Rv 16:18 [d] Dn 7:10; 10:21; Rv 20:12 [e] Php 4:3; Rv 20:12; 21:27 [f] 12:2 Is 26:19; Ezk 37:12-14 [g] Mt 25:46; Jn 5:28-29 [h] Is 66:24 [i] 12:3 Gn 1:6; Ps 19:1; Jn 5:35 [j] Is 53:11; Dn 11:33 [k] 12:4 Dn 8:26; 12:9; Rv 10:4 [l] Is 8:16; Jr 32:9-12; Rv 22:10 [m] Dn 8:17; 12:9,13 [n] 2Ch 16:9; Jr 5:1; Am 8:12 [o] 12:6 Ezk 9:2; Dn 10:5 [p] Dn 8:16 [q] Dn 8:13; Mt 24:3; Mk 13:4 [r] 12:7 Ezk 20:5; Rv 10:5-6 [s] Dn 4:34 [t] Dn 7:25; Rv 11:2; 12:14 [u] 12:8 1Th 5:10; 2Pt 3:10-14 [v] 12:9 Rv 10:4 [w] Dn 12:4 [x] 12:10 Zch 13:9; Ac 1:6-7; 2Th 2:7-12 [y] Dn 11:35 [z] Is 32:6-7; Rv 22:11 [aa] Dn 12:3; Hs 14:9; Jn 7:17; 8:47 [ab] 12:11 Dn 9:27 [ac] Dn 11:31; Mt 24:15; Mk 13:14 [ad] 12:12 Is 30:18 [ae] 12:13 Is 57:2; Rv 14:13

[A] 12:4 LXX reads *and the earth will be filled with unrighteousness* [B] 12:7 Lit *raised his right and his left* [C] 12:13 LXX omits *to the end*

AUTHOR: Hosea

DATE: Hosea prophesied during the reigns of the last six kings of Israel (Zechariah, Shallum, Menahem, Pekahiah, Pekah, and Hoshea—around 750–722 B.C.)

HOSEA

The book of Hosea is the first of the twelve Minor Prophets. These announcements of God's mission to the world are limited in length but not in passion and importance. It is possible that the actual prophecies as delivered are only partially recorded in Scripture. That may also explain why the various sections of the prophecy appear disjointed here and there.

Hosea was a citizen of the northern kingdom of Israel. The names Hosea and Joshua mean "salvation" just as Jesus does in the Greek. Hosea prophesied during the reign of King Uzziah who lived seven centuries before Christ. His was a long ministry of preaching, perhaps close to forty years. Reading the fourteen chapters of Hosea's writing one cannot help being impressed with the forcefulness of his messages. His style is powerful, his words colorful, and his understanding of life wide and varied. The riches of his language betokens that he is a man of considerable education. He confines his ministry mainly to Israel (which he often calls "Ephraim"), but on several occasions he addresses the nation of Judah (the two tribes of Israel's southern kingdom.)

Hosea fearlessly points out the sins of the people and urgently announces God's inevitable judgment. Both sin and judgment are described in great detail. But throughout the prophet also brings the good news: repentance will be honored with forgiveness.

All these rich facets of Hosea's message are still strikingly relevant to modern life. Here are some examples. Sin goes deep, it is part of the ponderings of the heart; sin is cruel, the princes exploiting the poor and defenseless; sin is greed, people hankering for luxury; sin is relational, people angrily pursuing conflict; sin is vice, with immorality and wantonness widespread; sin is injustice, magistrates soliciting bribes; sin defiles public administration, kings seeking support from evil allies; sin is fraud, merchants using false weights. Hosea added that sin even corrupts Israel's worship.

Hosea's prophecy is also replete with urgent warnings from God's heart. In stirring words Hosea announces judgment upon the people and their rulers if they will not repent. The swiftness of the punishment finds its climactic expression in one sentence, where God says: "So I will be like a lion to them; I will lurk like a leopard on the path" (13:7). But the nation's heartfelt repentance will open God's great heart of mercy and forgiveness. Once restored to covenant love, God's children will reap rich blessings, as foretold in the last chapter: "I will heal their apostasy; I will freely love them, for My anger will have turned from him" (14:4).

Hosea announces this redemption in the same comprehensive way: God's grace will bring healing in life's intimate relationships as well as the affairs of the nation.

1 The word of the LORD that came to Hosea son of Beeri during the reigns of Uzziah,[a] Jotham,[b] Ahaz,[c] and Hezekiah,[d] kings of Judah, and of Jeroboam[e] son of Jehoash, king of Israel.

Hosea's Marriage and Children

2 When the LORD first spoke to Hosea, He said this to him:

Go and marry a promiscuous wife[f]
and have children of promiscuity,
for the land is committing
blatant acts of promiscuity
by abandoning the LORD.

3 So he went and married Gomer daughter
of Diblaim, and she conceived and bore him
a son.[g] 4 Then the LORD said to him:

Name him Jezreel,[h] for in a little while
I will bring the bloodshed of Jezreel[i]
on the house of Jehu[j]
and put an end to the kingdom
of the house of Israel.
5 On that day I will break the bow
of Israel[k]
in the Valley of Jezreel.[A,l]

6 She conceived again and gave birth to a daughter, and the LORD said to him:

Name her No Compassion,[B]
for I will no longer have compassion
on the house of Israel.
I will certainly take them away.
7 But I will have compassion
on the house of Judah,[m]
and I will deliver them by
the LORD their God.[n]
I will not deliver them by bow, sword,
or war,
or by horses and cavalry.[o]

8 After Gomer had weaned No Compassion,
she conceived and gave birth to a son. 9 Then
the LORD said:

Name him Not My People,[C]
for you are not My people,
and I will not be your God.[D,p]
10[E] Yet the number of the Israelites
will be like the sand of the sea,[q]
which cannot be measured or counted.
And in the place where they were told:
You are not My people,
they will be called:
Sons of the living God.[r]
11 And the Judeans and the Israelites
will be gathered together.[s]
They will appoint for themselves
a single ruler[t]
and go up from[F] the land.
For the day of Jezreel[u] will be great.

2 [G] Call[H] your brothers: My People
and your sisters: Compassion.

Israel's Adultery Rebuked

2 Rebuke your mother; rebuke her.[v]
For she is not My wife and I am not
her husband.[w]
Let her remove the promiscuous look
from her face[x]
and her adultery
from between her breasts.
3 Otherwise, I will strip her naked[y]
and expose her as she was on the day
of her birth.
I will make her like a desert[z]
and like a parched land,
and I will let her die of thirst.[aa]
4 I will have no compassion
on her children[ab]
because they are the children
of promiscuity.
5 Yes, their mother is promiscuous;
she conceived them
and acted shamefully.[ac]
For she thought, "I will go
after my lovers,[ad]
the men who give me my food
and water,
my wool and flax, my oil and drink."[ae]
6 Therefore, this is what I will do:
I will block her[I] way[af] with thorns;[ag]
I will enclose her with a wall,
so that she cannot find her paths.[ah]
7 She will pursue her lovers
but not catch them;[ai]
she will seek them but not find them.
Then she will think,
"I will go back to my former husband,[aj]

[a] 1:1 2Ch 26:1-23; Is 1:1; Am 1:1
[b] 2Kg 15:5; 2Ch 27:1-9
[c] 2Kg 16:1-20; 2Ch 28:1-27; Is 1:1; 7:1-17; Mc 1:1
[d] 2Kg 18:1–20:21; 2Ch 29:1–32:33; Mc 1:1
[e] 2Kg 13:13; 14:23-29; Am 1:1
[f] 1:2 Hs 3:1
[g] 1:3 Ezk 23:4
[h] 1:4 Hs 2:22
[i] 2Kg 9:24–10:11
[j] 2Kg 9:7; 10:30; 15:10
[k] 1:5 Gn 49:24; Jb 29:20; Jr 49:35
[l] Jos 17:16; Jdg 6:33
[m] 1:7 Is 30:18
[n] Jr 25:5-6; Zch 9:9-10
[o] Ps 44:3-7
[p] 1:9 Ex 6:7; Lv 26:12; Jr 7:23; 11:4; 30:22; Ezk 36:28
[q] 1:10 Gn 22:17; Jr 33:22
[r] Rm 9:25-27
[s] 1:11 Jr 23:5-6; 50:4-5; Ezk 37:18-25; Hs 3:5
[t] Jr 30:21; Hs 3:5
[u] Ezk 36:9-11
[v] 2:2 Ezk 23:45
[w] Is 50:1
[x] Jr 3:1,9,13
[y] 2:3 Ezk 16:7,22,39
[z] Is 32:13-14; Hs 13:15
[aa] Jr 14:3; Am 8:11-13
[ab] 2:4 Jr 13:14
[ac] 2:5 Is 1:21; Hs 3:1
[ad] Jr 2:25
[ae] Jr 44:17-18
[af] 2:6 Jb 19:8
[ag] Hs 9:6; 10:8
[ah] Jr 18:15
[ai] 2:7 Hs 5:13
[aj] Jr 2:2; 3:1; Ezk 16:8; 23:4

A 1:5 = God sows B 1:6 Or *Lo-ruhamah* C 1:9 Or *Lo-ammi* D 1:9 Lit *not be yours* E 1:10 Hs 2:1 in Hb F 1:11 Or *and flourish in*; Hb obscure G 2:1 Hs 2:3 in Hb H 2:1 Lit *Say to* I 2:6 LXX, Syr; MT reads *your*

for then it was better for me
than now."[a]
8 She does not recognize[b]
that it is I who gave her the grain,[c]
the new wine, and the oil.
I lavished silver and gold on her,
which they used for ˚Baal.
9 Therefore, I will take back My grain
in its time[d]
and My new wine in its season;
I will take away My wool and linen,
which were to cover her nakedness.
10 Now I will expose her shame[e]
in the sight of her lovers,
and no one will rescue her
from My hands.
11 I will put an end to all her celebrations:[f]
her feasts,[g] New Moons,[h]
and Sabbaths —
all her festivals.
12 I will devastate her vines and fig trees.[i]
She thinks that these are her wages
that her lovers have given her.
I will turn them into a thicket,[j]
and the wild animals will eat them.[k]
13 And I will punish her for the days
of the Baals[l]
when she burned incense to them,[m]
put on her rings and jewelry,[n]
and went after her lovers,
but forgot Me.[o]
This is the LORD's declaration.

Israel's Adultery Forgiven

14 Therefore, I am going to persuade her,
lead her to the wilderness,[p]
and speak tenderly to her.[A]
15 There I will give her vineyards
back to her[q]
and make the Valley of Achor[B,r]
into a gateway of hope.
There she will respond as she did
in the days of her youth,[s]
as in the day she came out of the land
of Egypt.
16 In that day —
this is the LORD's declaration —
you will call Me, "My husband,"[t]
and no longer call Me, "My Baal."[C]

[a]**2:7** Jr 14:22; Hs 13:6 [b]**2:8** Is 1:3 [c]Ezk 16:19 [d]**2:9** Hs 8:7; 9:2 [e]**2:10** Ezk 16:37 [f]**2:11** Jr 7:34; 16:9 [g]Hs 3:4; Am 5:21; 8:10 [h]Is 1:13-14 [i]**2:12** Jr 5:17; 8:13 [j]Ps 80:12; Is 5:5; 7:23 [k]Is 32:13-15 [l]**2:13** Hs 4:13; 11:2 [m]Jr 7:9 [n]Ezk 16:12,17; 23:40 [o]Hs 4:6; 8:14; 13:6 [p]**2:14** Ezk 20:33-38 [q]**2:15** Ezk 28:25-26 [r]Jos 7:26 [s]Jr 2:1-3 [t]**2:16** Is 54:5 [u]**2:18** Jb 5:23; Is 11:6-9; Ezk 34:25 [v]Ezk 39:1-10 [w]Ezk 34:25 [x]**2:19** Is 62:4-5 [y]Is 1:27; 54:6-8 [z]**2:20** Hs 6:6; 13:4 [aa]**2:21** Is 55:10; Zch 8:12; Mal 3:10-11 [ab]**2:22** Jr 31:12; Jl 2:19 [ac]**2:23** Jr 31:37 [ad]Hs 1:6 [ae]Rm 9:25 [af]Hs 1:9 [ag]Hs 2:1 [ah]**3:1** Hs 1:2 [ai]2Sm 6:19; 1Ch 16:3; Sg 2:5 [aj]**3:2** Ru 4:10 [ak]**3:4** Hs 13:10-11 [al]Dn 9:27; 11:31; 12:11; Hs 2:11 [am]Hs 10:1-2 [an]Ex 28:4-12; 1Sm 23:9-12

17 For I will remove the names of the Baals
from her mouth;
they will no longer be remembered
by their names.
18 On that day I will make a covenant
for them
with the wild animals, the birds
of the sky,
and the creatures that crawl
on the ground.[u]
I will shatter bow, sword,
and weapons of war in the land[D,v]
and will enable the people
to rest securely.[w]
19 I will take you to be My wife forever.[x]
I will take you to be My wife
in righteousness,
justice, love, and compassion.[y]
20 I will take you to be My wife
in faithfulness,
and you will know ˚Yahweh.[z]
21 On that day I will respond[aa] —
this is the LORD's declaration.
I will respond to the sky,
and it will respond to the earth.
22 The earth will respond to the grain,[ab]
the new wine, and the oil,
and they will respond to Jezreel.
23 I will sow her[E] in the land for Myself,[ac]
and I will have compassion[ad]
on No Compassion;
I will say[ae] to Not My People:[af]
You are My people,[ag]
and he will say, "You are My God."

Waiting for Restoration

3 Then the LORD said to me, "Go again;
show love to a woman who is loved by another man and is an adulteress,[ah] just as the
LORD loves the Israelites though they turn to
other gods and love raisin cakes."[ai]
2 So I bought her for 15 ˚shekels of silver and
five bushels of barley.[F,G,aj] 3 I said to her, "You
must live with me many days. Don't be promiscuous or belong to any man, and I will act
the same way toward you."
4 For the Israelites must live many days
without king or prince,[ak] without sacrifice[al]
or sacred pillar,[am] and without ˚ephod[an] or

[A]**2:14** Lit *speak to her heart* [B]**2:15** = Trouble [C]**2:16** Or *My master* [D]**2:18** Or *war on the earth* [E]**2:23** = Israel [F]**3:2** LXX reads *barley and a measure of wine* [G]**3:2** Lit *silver, a homer of barley, and a lethek of barley*

household idols.[a] 5Afterward, the people of
Israel will return[b] and seek the LORD their
God and David their king.[c] They will come
with awe to the LORD[d] and to His goodness
in the last days.

God's Case against Israel

4 Hear the word of the LORD,[e]
people of Israel,
for the LORD has a case[f]
against the inhabitants of the land:
There is no truth,[g] no faithful love,[h]
and no knowledge of God[i]
in the land!
2 Cursing,[j] lying,[k] murder,[l] stealing,[m]
and adultery[n] are rampant;
one act of bloodshed follows another.[o]
3 For this reason the land mourns,[p]
and everyone who
lives in it languishes,
along with the wild animals[q]
and the birds of the sky;
even the fish of the sea disappear.[r]
4 But let no one dispute;[s]
let no one argue,
for My case is against you priests.[A,B,t]
5 You will stumble by day;[u]
the prophet will also stumble with you
by night.
And I will destroy your mother.[v]
6 My people are destroyed for lack
of knowledge.[w]
Because you have rejected knowledge,[x]
I will reject you[y] from serving
as My priest.
Since you have forgotten the law
of your God,[z]
I will also forget your sons.
7 The more they multiplied,[aa]
the more they sinned against Me.
I[C] will change their honor[D]
into disgrace.[ab]
8 They feed on the sin[E] of My people;[ac]
they have an appetite
for their transgressions.[ad]
9 The same judgment will happen
to both people and priests.[ae]
I will punish them for their ways[af]
and repay them for their deeds.
10 They will eat but not be satisfied;[ag]
they will be promiscuous[ah]
but not multiply.
For they have abandoned
their devotion to the LORD.[ai]
11 Promiscuity,[aj] wine, and new wine
take away one's understanding.[ak]
12 My people consult
their wooden idols,[al]
and their divining rods inform them.
For a spirit of promiscuity
leads them astray;[am]
they act promiscuously[an]
in disobedience to[F] their God.
13 They sacrifice on the mountaintops,[ao]
and they burn offerings on the hills,[ap]
and under oaks, poplars,
and terebinths,[aq]
because their shade is pleasant.
And so your daughters
act promiscuously
and your daughters-in-law
commit adultery.
14 I will not punish your daughters
when they act promiscuously
or your daughters-in-law
when they commit adultery,
for the men themselves go off
with prostitutes[ar]
and make sacrifices
with cult prostitutes.[as]
People without discernment
are doomed.[at]

Warnings for Israel and Judah

15 Israel, if you act promiscuously,
don't let Judah become *guilty!
Do not go to Gilgal[au]
or make a pilgrimage to Beth-aven,[G,av]
and do not swear an oath:
As the LORD lives![aw]
16 For Israel is as obstinate
as a stubborn cow.[ax]
Can the LORD now shepherd them
like a lamb in an open meadow?[ay]
17 Ephraim is attached to idols;[az]
leave him alone![ba]
18 When their drinking is over,
they turn to promiscuity.

[a] **3:4** Gn 31:19,34; Jdg 17:5; 18:14,17
[b] **3:5** Jr 50:4-5
[c] Is 11:1-10; Jr 23:5-6; 33:15-16; Ezk 34:24; Rm 11:23
[d] Jr 31:9
[e] **4:1** Hs 5:1
[f] Hs 12:2; Mc 6:2
[g] Is 59:4; Jr 7:28
[h] Hs 6:6
[i] Hs 5:4
[j] **4:2** Hs 10:4
[k] Hs 7:3; 10:13; 11:12
[l] Hs 6:9
[m] Hs 7:1
[n] Hs 7:4
[o] Hs 6:8; 12:14
[p] **4:3** Is 24:4; 33:9
[q] Jr 4:25
[r] Gn 1:20-25
[s] **4:4** Ezk 3:26; Am 5:10,13
[t] Dt 17:12-13
[u] **4:5** Ezk 14:3; Hs 5:5
[v] Hs 2:2,5
[w] **4:6** Is 5:13
[x] Mal 2:7-8
[y] Zch 11:8-9,15-17
[z] Hs 2:13; 8:14; 13:6
[aa] **4:7** Hs 10:1; 13:6
[ab] Hab 2:16
[ac] **4:8** Hs 10:13
[ad] Is 56:11; Mc 3:11
[ae] **4:9** Is 24:2; Jr 5:31
[af] Hs 8:13; 9:9
[ag] **4:10** Lv 26:26; Is 65:13; Mc 6:14
[ah] Hs 7:4
[ai] Hs 9:17
[aj] **4:11** Hs 5:4
[ak] Is 5:12; 28:7
[al] **4:12** Is 44:19; Jr 2:27
[am] Hs 5:4
[an] Hs 9:1
[ao] **4:13** Jr 3:6
[ap] Hs 2:13; 11:2
[aq] Jr 2:20
[ar] **4:14** Hs 4:18; 7:4
[as] Dt 23:17
[at] Hs 5:4
[au] **4:15** Hs 9:15; 12:1
[av] 1Kg 12:28-29; Hs 5:8; 10:5,8
[aw] Jr 5:2; 44:26
[ax] **4:16** Ps 78:8
[ay] Is 5:17; 7:25
[az] **4:17** Hs 13:2
[ba] Ps 81:12; Hs 4:4

A **4:4** Text emended; MT reads *argue, and your people are like those contending with a priest* B **4:4** Hb obscure C **4:7** Alt Hb tradition, Syr, Tg read *They* D **4:7** Ancient Jewish tradition reads *My honor* E **4:8** Or *sin offerings* F **4:12** Lit *promiscuously from under* G **4:15** = House of Wickedness

Israel's leaders[A] fervently love disgrace.[B]
19 A wind with its wings will
carry them off,[C,a]
and they will be ashamed
of their sacrifices.

5 Hear this, priests![b]
Pay attention, house of Israel!
Listen, royal house!
For the judgment applies to you
because you have been a snare
at Mizpah[c]
and a net spread out on Tabor.
2 Rebels[d] are deeply involved
in slaughter;[e]
I will be a punishment for all of them.[B]
3 I know Ephraim,[f]
and Israel is not hidden from Me.
For now, Ephraim,[g]
you have acted promiscuously;
Israel is defiled.
4 Their actions do not allow them
to return to their God,[h]
for a spirit of promiscuity
is among them,[i]
and they do not know the LORD.[j]
5 Israel's arrogance testifies
against them.[D,k]
Both Israel and Ephraim stumble
because of their wickedness;[l]
even Judah will stumble with them.[m]
6 They go with their flocks and herds
to seek the LORD[n]
but do not find Him;[o]
He has withdrawn from them.[p]
7 They betrayed the LORD;[q]
indeed, they gave birth
to illegitimate children.[r]
Now the New Moon[s] will devour them
along with their fields.[t]
8 Blow the horn in Gibeah,[u]
the trumpet in Ramah;[v]
raise the war cry in Beth-aven:[w]
After you, Benjamin![x]
9 Ephraim will become a desolation[y]
on the day of punishment;[z]
I announce what is certain
among the tribes of Israel.[aa]
10 The princes of Judah are like those
who move boundary markers;[ab]
I will pour out My fury[ac] on them
like water.[ad]
11 Ephraim is oppressed,
crushed in judgment,[ae]
for he is determined to follow
what is worthless.[E]
12 So I am like rot to Ephraim[af]
and like decay to the house of Judah.
13 When Ephraim saw his sickness
and Judah his wound,
Ephraim went to Assyria[ag]
and sent a delegation
to the great king.[F,ah]
But he cannot cure you or heal
your wound.[ai]
14 For I am like a lion to Ephraim[aj]
and like a young lion to the house
of Judah.
Yes, I will tear them to pieces
and depart.[ak]
I will carry them off,
and no one can rescue them.[al]
15 I will depart and return to My place
until they recognize their ·guilt
and seek My face;[am]
they will search for Me
in their distress.[an]

A Call to Repentance

6 Come, let us return to the LORD.[ao]
For He has torn us,[ap]
and He will heal us;[aq]
He has wounded us,
and He will bind up our wounds.[ar]
2 He will revive us after two days,[as]
and on the third day He will raise us up
so we can live in His presence.[at]
3 Let us strive to know the LORD.[au]
His appearance is as sure as the dawn.[av]
He will come to us like the rain,[aw]
like the spring showers that water
the land.

The LORD's First Lament

4 What am I going to do
with you, Ephraim?[ax]
What am I going to do with you, Judah?
Your loyalty is like the morning mist[ay]

[a]**4:19** Hs 12:1; 13:5
[b]**5:1** Hs 4:1
[c]Hs 9:8
[d]**5:2** Hs 9:15
[e]Hs 4:2; 6:9
[f]**5:3** Hs 6:4; 7:1; Am 3:2; 5:12
[g]Hs 6:10
[h]**5:4** Hs 4:11
[i]Hs 4:12
[j]Hs 4:6,11,14
[k]**5:5** Hs 7:10
[l]Hs 4:5
[m]Ezk 23:31-35
[n]**5:6** Hs 8:13; Mc 6:6-7
[o]Is 1:15; Jr 14:12
[p]Ezk 8:6
[q]**5:7** Is 48:8; Hs 6:7
[r]Hs 2:4
[s]Hs 2:11
[t]Is 1:14
[u]**5:8** Hs 9:9; 10:9
[v]Is 10:29; Jr 31:15
[w]Hs 4:15
[x]Jdg 5:14
[y]**5:9** Is 28:1-4; Hs 9:11-17
[z]Is 37:3
[aa]Is 46:10; Zch 1:6
[ab]**5:10** Dt 27:17
[ac]Ezk 7:8
[ad]Ps 32:6; 93:3-4
[ae]**5:11** Hs 9:16
[af]**5:12** Ps 39:11; Is 51:8
[ag]**5:13** Hs 7:11; 8:9; 12:1
[ah]Hs 10:6
[ai]Hs 14:3
[aj]**5:14** Ps 7:2; Hs 13:7; Am 3:4
[ak]Ps 50:22
[al]Mc 5:8
[am]**5:15** Is 64:7-9; Jr 3:13-14
[an]Ps 50:15, 78:34; Jr 2:27; Hs 3:5
[ao]**6:1** Jr 50:4-5
[ap]Hs 5:14
[aq]Hs 14:4
[ar]Is 30:26
[as]**6:2** Ps 30:5
[at]Dt 32:39
[au]**6:3** Is 2:3; Mc 4:2
[av]Ps 19:6; Mc 5:2
[aw]Jl 2:23
[ax]**6:4** Hs 7:1; 11:8
[ay]Ps 78:34-37

[A]**4:18** Lit *Her shields*; Ps 47:9; 89:18 [B]**4:18; 5:2** Hb obscure [C]**4:19** Lit *wind will bind it in its wings* [D]**5:5** Lit *against his face* [E]**5:11** Or *follow a command*; Hb obscure [F]**5:13** Or *to King Yareb*

and like the early dew that vanishes.
5 This is why I have used the prophets
to cut them down;[A,a]
I have killed them with the words
of My mouth.
My judgment strikes like lightning.[B]
6 For I desire loyalty and not sacrifice,
the knowledge of God[b] rather than
•burnt offerings.[c]

7 But they, like Adam,[C] have violated
the covenant;[d]
there they have betrayed Me.[e]
8 Gilead is a city of evildoers,[f]
tracked with bloody footprints.[g]
9 Like raiders who wait in ambush
for someone,[h]
a band of priests murders on the road
to Shechem.[i]
They commit atrocities.[j]
10 I have seen something horrible[k]
in the house of Israel:
Ephraim's promiscuity is there;[l]
Israel is defiled.
11 A harvest is also appointed
for you, Judah.[m]

When I[D] return My people
from captivity,[n]

7

1 when I heal Israel,[o]
the sins of Ephraim[p] and the crimes
of Samaria[q]
will be exposed.
For they practice fraud;[r]
a thief breaks in;
a raiding party pillages outside.[s]
2 But they never consider
that I remember all their evil.[t]
Now their sins are all around them;[u]
they are right in front of My face.

Israel's Corruption

3 They please the king with their evil,[v]
the princes with their lies.[w]
4 All of them commit adultery;[x]
they are like an oven heated by a baker
who stops stirring the fire
from the kneading of the dough
until it is leavened.
5 On the day of our king,
the princes are sick with the heat
of wine[y] —
there is a conspiracy with traitors.[E]
6 For they — their hearts like an oven —
draw him into their oven.
Their anger smolders all night;
in the morning it blazes
like a flaming fire.
7 All of them are as hot as an oven,[z]
and they consume their rulers.[aa]
All their kings fall;
not one of them calls on Me.[F]

8 Ephraim has allowed himself
to get mixed up with the nations.
Ephraim is unturned bread
baked on a griddle.
9 Foreigners consume his strength,[ab]
but he does not notice.[ac]
Even his hair is streaked with gray,
but he does not notice.
10 Israel's arrogance testifies
against them,[G,ad]
yet they do not return to •Yahweh
their God,[ae]
and for all this, they do not seek Him.

11 So Ephraim has become like a silly,
senseless dove;[af]
they call to Egypt,[ag] and they go
to Assyria.[ah]
12 As they are going, I will spread My net
over them;[ai]
I will bring them down like birds
of the sky.
I will discipline them in accordance
with the news that reaches[H]
their assembly.

The LORD's Second Lament

13 Woe to them,[aj] for they fled from Me;[ak]
destruction to them, for they rebelled
against Me!
Though I want to redeem them,[al]
they speak lies against Me.
14 They do not cry to Me
from their hearts;
rather, they wail on their beds.
They slash themselves[I,am] for grain
and new wine;[an]

[a]6:5 1Sm 15:32-33; Jr 1:10,18; 5:14
[b]6:6 Hs 4:1
[c]Mt 9:13; 12:7
[d]6:7 Hs 8:1
[e]Hs 5:7
[f]6:8 Hs 12:11
[g]Hs 4:2
[h]6:9 Hs 7:1
[i]Jr 7:9-10; Hs 4:2
[j]Ezk 22:9; 23:27; Hs 2:10
[k]6:10 Jr 5:30-31; 23:14
[l]Hs 5:3
[m]6:11 Jr 51:33; Jl 3:13
[n]Zph 2:7
[o]7:1 Ezk 24:13; Hs 6:4; 7:13; 11:8
[p]Hs 5:3
[q]Hs 8:5-6; 10:5,7; 13:16
[r]Hs 4:2
[s]Hs 6:9
[t]7:2 Ps 25:7; Jr 14:10; 17:1; Am 8:7
[u]Jr 2:19; 4:18; Hs 4:9
[v]7:3 Jr 28:1-4; Mc 7:3
[w]Hs 4:2; 11:12
[x]7:4 Jr 9:2; 23:10
[y]7:5 Is 28:1,7-8
[z]7:7 Ps 21:9
[aa]Hs 13:10
[ab]7:9 Is 1:7
[ac]Hs 4:6
[ad]7:10 Hs 5:5
[ae]Hs 5:4
[af]7:11 Hs 4:6,11,14; 5:4
[ag]Hs 8:13; 9:3,6
[ah]Hs 5:13; 8:9; 12:1
[ai]7:12 Ezk 12:13
[aj]7:13 Hs 9:12
[ak]Jr 14:10; Hs 9:17
[al]Jr 51:9; Hs 7:1; Mt 23:37
[am]7:14 1Kg 18:28
[an]Am 2:8

[A]6:5 Or *have cut down the prophets* [B]6:5 LXX, Syr, Tg; MT reads *Your judgments go out as light* [C]6:7 Or *they, as at Adam,* or *they, like men,* [D]6:11 Or *you. Judah, when I* [E]7:5 Lit *wine — he stretches out his hand to scorners*; Hb obscure

[F]7:3-7 These vv. may refer to a king's assassination; Hb obscure. [G]7:10 Lit *against his face* [H]7:12 Lit *news to* [I]7:14 Some Hb mss, LXX; other Hb mss read *They stay*

they turn away from Me.
15 I trained and strengthened their arms,[a]
but they plot evil against Me.[b]
16 They turn, but not to what is above;[A]
they are like a faulty bow.[c]
Their leaders will fall by the sword
because of the cursing
of their tongue.[d]
They will be ridiculed for this
in the land of Egypt.[e]

Israel's False Hopes

8 Put the horn to your mouth![f]
One like an eagle comes
against the house of the LORD,[g]
because they transgress My covenant[h]
and rebel against My law.[i]
2 Israel cries out to Me,[j]
"My God, we know You!"
3 Israel has rejected what is good;[k]
an enemy will pursue him.

4 They have installed kings,[l]
but not through Me.
They have appointed leaders,
but without My approval.
They make their silver and gold[m]
into idols for themselves
for their own destruction.[B]
5 Your calf-idol[C,n] is rejected, Samaria.[o]
My anger burns against them.
How long will they be incapable
of innocence?[p]
6 For this thing is from Israel—
a craftsman made it,[q] and it is not God.
The calf of Samaria will be smashed
to bits!

7 Indeed, they sow the wind[r]
and reap the whirlwind.[s]
There is no standing grain;
what sprouts fails to yield flour.[t]
Even if they did,
foreigners would swallow it up.
8 Israel is swallowed up![u]
Now they are among the nations
like discarded pottery.[v]
9 For they have gone up to Assyria[w]
like a wild donkey going off on its own.
Ephraim has paid for love.[x]

10 Even though they hire lovers
among the nations,
I will now round them up,
and they will begin to decrease
in number[y]
under the burden of the king
and leaders.[z]

11 When Ephraim multiplied his altars
for sin,[aa]
they became his altars for sinning.
12 Though I were to write out for him
ten thousand points of My instruction,[ab]
they would be[D] regarded
as something strange.
13 Though they offer sacrificial gifts[E,ac]
and eat the flesh,[ad]
the LORD does not accept them.
Now He will remember their ·guilt[ae]
and punish their sins;[af]
they will return to Egypt.[ag]
14 Israel has forgotten his Maker[ah]
and built palaces;[ai]
Judah has also multiplied
fortified cities.
I will send fire on their cities,[aj]
and it will consume their citadels.

The Coming Exile

9 Israel, do not rejoice jubilantly
as the nations do,[ak]
for you have acted promiscuously,[al]
leaving your God.
You have loved the wages of a prostitute
on every grain-threshing floor.[am]
2 Threshing floor and wine vat will not
sustain them,[an]
and the new wine will fail them.
3 They will not stay in the land
of the LORD.
Instead, Ephraim will return to Egypt,[ao]
and they will eat ·unclean food[ap]
in Assyria.[aq]

4 They will not pour out
their wine offerings to the LORD,[ar]
and their sacrifices will not please Him.
Their food will be like the bread
of mourners;
all who eat it become defiled.[as]

[a]7:15 Hs 11:3 [b]Nah 1:9 [c]7:16 Ps 78:57 [d]Ps 12:3-4; 17:10; Dn 7:25; Mal 3:13-14 [e]Ezk 23:32 [f]8:1 Hs 5:8 [g]Dt 28:49 [h]Hs 6:7 [i]Hs 4:6; 8:12 [j]8:2 Hs 7:14 [k]8:3 Hs 3:5 [l]8:4 Hs 13:10-11 [m]Hs 2:8; 13:1-2 [n]8:5 Hs 10:5; 13:2 [o]1Kg 12:28-29; Hs 7:1 [p]Ps 19:13; Jr 13:27 [q]8:6 Hs 13:2 [r]8:7 Hs 10:13 [s]Is 66:15; Nah 1:3 [t]Hs 2:9 [u]8:8 Jr 51:34 [v]Jr 25:34; Hs 13:15 [w]8:9 Hs 7:11 [x]Ezk 16:33 [y]8:10 Jr 42:2 [z]Is 10:8 [aa]8:11 Hs 10:1; 12:11 [ab]8:12 Hs 4:6 [ac]8:13 Hs 5:6; 9:4 [ad]Jr 6:20; 7:21 [ae]Hs 7:2; Lk 12:2; 1Co 4:5 [af]Hs 4:9; 9:7 [ag]Hs 9:3,6 [ah]8:14 Hs 2:13; 4:6; 13:6 [ai]Is 9:9-10 [aj]Jr 17:27 [ak]9:1 Is 22:12-13; Hs 10:5 [al]Hs 4:12 [am]Hs 7:14 [an]9:2 Hs 2:9 [ao]9:3 Hs 7:16; 8:13 [ap]Ezk 4:13 [aq]Hs 11:7 [ar]9:4 Nm 15:5,7,10 [as]Nm 19:11-14; Dt 26:12-14; Jr 16:5-7

[A]7:16 Some emend to *turn to what is useless* [B]8:4 Lit *themselves that it might be cut off* [C]8:5 Lit *calf* [D]8:12 Or *Though I wrote out . . . instruction, they are* [E]8:13 Hb obscure

For their bread will be
for their appetites alone;
it will not enter the house of the LORD.
5 What will you do on a festival day,[a]
on the day of the LORD's feast?[b]
6 For even if they flee from devastation,
Egypt will gather them, and Memphis
will bury them.[c]
Thistles will take possession
of their precious silver;
thorns will invade their tents.[d]

7 The days of punishment have come;[e]
the days of retribution have come.[f]
Let Israel recognize it!
The prophet is a fool,[g]
and the inspired man is insane,[h]
because of the magnitude
of your ·guilt and hostility.[i]
8 Ephraim's watchman is with my God.
The prophet encounters
a fowler's snare
on all his ways.[j]
Hostility is in the house of his God!
9 They have deeply corrupted themselves[k]
as in the days of Gibeah.[l]
He will remember their guilt;
He will punish their sins.[m]

Ephraim Bereaved of Offspring

10 I discovered Israel
like grapes in the wilderness.[n]
I saw your fathers
like the first fruit of the fig tree
in its first season.[o]
But they went to Baal-peor,[p]
consecrated themselves to Shame,[A,q]
and became detestable,[r]
like the thing they loved.
11 Ephraim's glory will fly away
like a bird:[s]
no birth, no gestation, no conception.[t]
12 Even if they raise children,
I will bereave them of each one.
Yes, woe to them when I depart
from them![u]
13 I have seen Ephraim like Tyre,[v]
planted in a meadow,
so Ephraim will bring out his children
to the executioner.

14 Give them, LORD—
What should You give?
Give them a womb that miscarries
and breasts that are dry![w]

15 All their evil appears at Gilgal,[x]
for there I came to hate them.
I will drive them from My house
because of their evil, wicked actions.[y]
I will no longer love them;
all their leaders are rebellious.[z]
16 Ephraim[aa] is struck down;
their roots are withered;
they cannot bear fruit.[ab]
Even if they bear children,
I will kill the precious offspring
of their wombs.[ac]
17 My God will reject them
because they have not listened to Him;[ad]
they will become wanderers
among the nations.[ae]

The Vine and the Calf

10 Israel is a lush[B] vine;[af]
it yields fruit for itself.
The more his fruit increased,
the more he increased the altars.[ag]
The better his land produced,
the better they made the sacred pillars.[ah]
2 Their hearts are devious;[C,ai]
now they must bear their ·guilt.[aj]
The LORD will break down their altars[ak]
and demolish their sacred pillars.
3 In fact, they are now saying,
"We have no king!
For we do not ·fear the LORD.[al]
What can a king do for us?"
4 They speak mere words,
taking false oaths
while making covenants.[am]
So lawsuits break out
like poisonous weeds in the furrows
of a field.[an]

5 The residents of Samaria[ao]
will have anxiety
over the calf[ap] of Beth-aven.[aq]
Indeed, its idolatrous priests rejoiced
over it;
the people will mourn over it,
over its glory.[ar]

[a] **9:5** Is 10:3; Jr 5:31 [b] Hs 2:11; Jl 1:13 [c] **9:6** Is 19:13; Jr 2:16; 44:1; 46:14,19; Ezk 30:13,16 [d] Is 5:6; 7:23; Hs 10:8 [e] **9:7** Is 10:3; Jr 10:15; Mc 7:4 [f] Is 34:8; Jr 16:18; 25:14 [g] Lm 2:14 [h] Is 44:25 [i] Ezk 14:9-10 [j] **9:8** Pr 29:5-6; Hs 5:1 [k] **9:9** Is 31:6 [l] Jdg 19–21; Hs 5:8; 10:9 [m] Hs 7:2; 8:13 [n] **9:10** Mc 7:1 [o] Jr 24:2 [p] Nm 25:1-9 [q] Jr 11:13; Hs 4:18 [r] Ezk 20:8 [s] **9:11** Hs 4:7; 10:4 [t] Hs 4:10 [u] **9:12** Hs 7:13 [v] **9:13** Ezk 27:3-4 [w] **9:14** Gn 49:25 [x] **9:15** Hs 4:15; 12:11 [y] Hs 4:9; 7:2; 12:2 [z] Hs 5:2 [aa] **9:16** Hs 5:11 [ab] Hs 8:7 [ac] Ezk 24:21 [ad] **9:17** Hs 4:10 [ae] Hs 7:13 [af] **10:1** Is 5:1-7; Ezk 15:1-6 [ag] Hs 8:11; 12:11 [ah] 1Kg 14:23; Hs 3:4 [ai] **10:2** 1Kg 18:21; Zph 1:5 [aj] Hs 13:16 [ak] Mc 5:13 [al] **10:3** Ps 12:4; Is 5:19 [am] **10:4** Ezk 17:13-19; Hs 4:2 [an] Dt 31:16-17; 2Kg 17:3-4 [ao] **10:5** Hs 7:1 [ap] Hs 8:5-6 [aq] Hs 4:15; 5:8 [ar] Hs 9:11

[A] **9:10** = Baal [B] **10:1** Or *ravaged* [C] **10:2** Or *divided*

It will certainly depart from them.
6 The calf itself will be taken to Assyria[a]
as an offering to the great king.[A,b]
Ephraim will experience shame;[c]
Israel will be ashamed of its counsel.[d]
7 Samaria's king will disappear[B,e]
like foam[C] on the surface of the water.
8 The ·high places[f] of Aven,
the sin of Israel,[g]
will be destroyed;
thorns and thistles will grow
over their altars.[h]
They will say to the mountains,[i]
"Cover us!"
and to the hills, "Fall on us!"[j]

Israel's Defeat because of Sin

9 Israel, you have sinned
since the days of Gibeah;[k]
they have taken their stand there.
Will not war against the unjust
overtake them in Gibeah?
10 I will discipline[l] them
at My discretion;[m]
nations will be gathered against them
to put them in bondage[D]
for their two crimes.[n]

11 Ephraim is a well-trained calf[o]
that loves to thresh,
but I will place a yoke on[E] her
fine neck.[p]
I will harness Ephraim;[q]
Judah will plow;
Jacob will do the final plowing.
12 Sow righteousness for yourselves[r]
and reap faithful love;
break up your unplowed ground.[s]
It is time to seek the LORD[t]
until He comes[u]
and sends righteousness
on you like the rain.[v]

13 You have plowed wickedness
and reaped injustice;[w]
you have eaten the fruit of lies.[x]
Because you have trusted
in your own way[F]
and in your large number of soldiers,[y]
14 the roar of battle will rise
against your people,
and all your fortifications
will be demolished[z]
in a day of war,
like Shalman's destruction
of Beth-arbel.
Mothers will be dashed to pieces
along with their children.[aa]
15 So it will be done to you, Bethel,[ab]
because of your extreme evil.
At dawn the king of Israel will be
totally destroyed.

The LORD's Love for Israel

11 When Israel was a child, I loved him,[ac]
and out of Egypt I called My son.[ad]
2 The more they[G] called them,[H,ae]
the more they[H] departed from Me.[I]
They kept sacrificing to the ·Baals[af]
and burning offerings to idols.[ag]
3 It was I who taught Ephraim to walk,[ah]
taking them[J] in My arms,[ai]
but they never knew
that I healed them.[aj]
4 I led them with human cords,
with ropes of love.[ak]
To them I was like one
who eases the yoke from their jaws;[al]
I bent down to give them food.[am]
5 Israel will not return to the land
of Egypt
and Assyria will be his king,[an]
because they refused to repent.[ao]
6 A sword will whirl through his cities;[ap]
it will destroy and devour the bars
of his gates,[K,aq]
because of their schemes.[ar]
7 My people are bent on turning
from Me.[as]
Though they call to Him on high,
He will not exalt them at all.
8 How can I give you up, Ephraim?[at]
How can I surrender you, Israel?
How can I make you like Admah?[au]
How can I treat you like Zeboiim?[av]
I have had a change of heart;
My compassion is stirred!

[a]**10:6** Hs 11:5 [b]Hs 5:13 [c]Hs 4:7 [d]Is 30:3; Jr 7:24 [e]**10:7** Hs 13:11 [f]**10:8** Dt 12:2; Hs 4:13 [g]1Kg 12:28-30; 13:34 [h]Is 32:13; Hs 9:6 [i]Lk 23:30; Rv 6:16 [j]Rv 6:16 [k]**10:9** Hs 5:8; 9:9 [l]**10:10** Hs 4:9 [m]Ezk 5:13 [n]Jdg 19–21; 1Kg 12:28-30 [o]**10:11** Jr 5:11; Hs 4:16 [p]Jr 28:14 [q]Ps 66:12 [r]**10:12** Pr 11:18 [s]Jr 4:3 [t]Hs 4:1; 12:6 [u]Hs 6:3 [v]Is 44:3; 45:8 [w]**10:13** Jb 4:8; Gl 6:7 [x]Hs 4:2; 7:3; 11:12 [y]Ps 33:16 [z]**10:14** Is 17:3 [aa]Hs 13:16 [ab]**10:15** Hs 4:15; 10:5 [ac]**11:1** Dt 4:37; 7:6-8; 10:14-15; Ps 78:68; Is 41:8; Am 3:2; Mal 1:2 [ad]Ex 4:22-23; Dt 32:5-6,18-20; Ps 103:13; Jr 3:19; Hs 1:10; Mt 2:15 [ae]**11:2** 2Kg 17:13-15 [af]Hs 2:13; 4:13 [ag]Is 65:7; Jr 18:15 [ah]**11:3** Hs 7:15 [ai]Dt 1:31; 32:10-11 [aj]Ex 15:26 [ak]**11:4** Jr 31:2-3 [al]Hs 10:11 [am]Ex 16:32 [an]**11:5** Hs 7:16; 8:13; 9:3; 10:6 [ao]Hs 7:16 [ap]**11:6** Hs 13:16 [aq]Lm 2:9 [ar]Hs 4:16-17 [as]**11:7** Jr 8:5 [at]**11:8** Hs 6:4; 7:1 [au]Gn 14:8; Dt 29:23 [av]Gn 14:2; 19:1-29; Dt 29:23

[A]**10:6** Or *to King Yareb* [B]**10:7** Or *will be cut off* [C]**10:7** Or *a stick* [D]**10:10** LXX, Syr, Vg read *against them when they are disciplined* [E]**10:11** Lit *will pass over* [F]**10:13** LXX reads *your chariots* [G]**11:2** Perhaps the prophets [H]**11:2** = Israel [I]**11:2** LXX; MT reads *them* [J]**11:3** LXX, Syr, Vg; MT reads *him* [K]**11:6** Or *devour his empty talkers*, or *devour his limbs*; Hb obscure

9 I will not vent the full fury
of My anger;[a]
I will not turn back
to destroy Ephraim.[b]
For I am God and not man,
the Holy One among you;[c]
I will not come in rage.[A]
10 They will follow the LORD;[d]
He will roar like a lion.[e]
When He roars,
His children will come trembling
from the west.[f]
11 They will be roused like birds
from Egypt
and like doves[g] from the land
of Assyria.[h]
Then I will settle them in their homes.[i]
This is the LORD's declaration.

12B Ephraim surrounds me with lies,[j]
the house of Israel, with deceit.
Judah still wanders with God
and is faithful to the holy ones.[C,D]

God's Case against Jacob's Heirs

12 Ephraim chases[E] the wind[k]
and pursues the east wind.[l]
He continually multiplies lies
and violence.
He makes a covenant with Assyria,[m]
and olive oil is carried to Egypt.[n]

2 The LORD also has a dispute
with Judah.
He is about to punish Jacob
according to his ways;[o]
He will repay him based on his actions.
3 In the womb he grasped
his brother's heel,[p]
and as an adult he wrestled with God.[q]
4 Jacob struggled with the Angel
and prevailed;
he wept and sought His favor.[r]
He found him[F] at Bethel,[s]
and there He spoke with him.[G,t]
5 ·Yahweh is the God of ·Hosts;
Yahweh is His name.[u]
6 But you must return to your God.[v]
Maintain love and justice,[w]
and always put your hope in God.[x]

[a] **11:9** Dt 13:17
[b] Jr 26:3; 30:11
[c] Is 5:24; 12:6; 41:14,16
[d] **11:10** Hs 3:5; 6:1-3
[e] Is 31:4; Jl 3:16; Am 1:2
[f] Is 66:2-5
[g] **11:11** Is 60:8; Hs 7:11
[h] Is 11:11
[i] Ezk 34:27-28
[j] **11:12** Hs 4:2; 7:3
[k] **12:1** Jr 22:22; Hs 4:19
[l] Gn 41:6; Ezk 17:10
[m] Hs 5:13; 7:11; 8:9
[n] 2Kg 17:4
[o] **12:2** Hs 4:9; 7:2
[p] **12:3** Gn 25:26; 27:36
[q] Gn 32:24-28
[r] **12:4** Gn 32:26
[s] Gn 28:13-15; 35:10-15
[t] Gn 28:10-22; 35:1-14
[u] **12:5** Ex 3:15
[v] **12:6** Hs 6:1-3; 10:12
[w] Hs 6:6
[x] Mc 7:7
[y] **12:7** Hs 7:14
[z] Pr 11:1; Am 8:5; Mc 6:11
[aa] **12:8** Ps 62:10; Hs 13:6
[ab] Hs 4:8; 14:1; Am 3:15; 6:4-6
[ac] **12:9** Hs 11:1; 13:3
[ad] Lv 23:42
[ae] **12:10** Jr 7:25
[af] Ezk 17:2; 20:49
[ag] **12:11** Hs 6:8
[ah] Hs 4:15; 9:15
[ai] Hs 8:11; 10:1-2
[aj] **12:12** Gn 28:5
[ak] Gn 29:20
[al] Gn 29:1-20
[am] **12:13** Ex 14:19-22; Is 63:11-14
[an] **12:14** 2Kg 17:7-18
[ao] Ezk 18:10-13
[ap] Dn 11:18; Mc 6:16
[aq] **13:1** Jb 29:21-22
[ar] Jdg 8:1; 12:1
[as] Hs 2:8-17; 11:2
[at] **13:2** Is 46:6; Jr 10:4; Hs 2:8
[au] Is 44:17-20
[av] Hs 8:6
[aw] Hs 8:5-6; 10:5

7 A merchant loves to extort[y]
with dishonest scales in his hands.[z]
8 But Ephraim says:
"How rich I have become;[aa]
I made it all myself.
In all my earnings,
no one can find any crime in me[ab]
that I can be punished for!"[H]

Judgment on Apostate Israel

9 I have been Yahweh your God
ever since[I] the land of Egypt.[ac]
I will make you live in tents again,[ad]
as in the festival days.
10 I spoke through the prophets[ae]
and granted many visions;
I gave parables through the prophets.[af]
11 Since Gilead is full of evil,[ag]
they will certainly come to nothing.
They sacrifice bulls in Gilgal;[ah]
even their altars will be like heaps
of rocks[ai]
on the furrows of a field.

Further Indictment of Jacob's Heirs

12 Jacob fled to the land of Aram.[aj]
Israel worked to earn a wife;[ak]
he tended flocks for a wife.[al]
13 The LORD brought Israel from Egypt
by a prophet,[am]
and Israel was tended by a prophet.
14 Ephraim has provoked bitter anger,[an]
so his Lord will leave his bloodguilt
on him[ao]
and repay him for his contempt.[ap]

13 When Ephraim spoke,[aq]
there was trembling;
he was exalted in Israel.[ar]
But he incurred ·guilt through ·Baal[as]
and died.

2 Now they continue to sin
and make themselves a cast image,[at]
idols skillfully made from their silver,[au]
all of them the work of craftsmen.[av]
People say about them,
"Let the men who sacrifice[J] kiss
the calves."[aw]

[A] **11:9** Or *come into any city*; Hb obscure [B] **11:12** Hs 12:1 in Hb [C] **11:12** Or *to the Holy One*; Hb obscure [D] **11:12** Possibly angels, or less likely, pagan gods or idols [E] **12:1** Or *feeds on*, or *tends* [F] **12:4** Or *Him* [G] **12:4** LXX, Syr; MT reads *us*

[H] **12:8** Lit *crime which is sin* [I] **12:9** LXX reads *God who brought you out of* [J] **13:2** Or *Those who make human sacrifices*

3 Therefore, they will be
like the morning mist,[a]
like the early dew that vanishes,
like chaff blown
from a threshing floor,[b]
or like smoke from a window.[c]

Death and Resurrection

4 I have been ·Yahweh your God[d]
ever since[A] the land of Egypt;
you know no God but Me,[e]
and no Savior exists besides Me.[f]
5 I knew[B] you in the wilderness,[g]
in the land of drought.
6 When they had pasture,
they became satisfied;[h]
they were satisfied,
and their hearts became proud.[i]
Therefore they forgot Me.[j]
7 So I will be like a lion[k] to them;
I will lurk like a leopard[l] on the path.
8 I will attack them
like a bear robbed of her cubs
and tear open the rib cage
over their hearts.
I will devour them there like a lioness,[m]
like a wild beast that would rip
them open.
9 I will destroy you, Israel;
you have no help but Me.[C,n]
10 Where now is your king,[D,o]
that he may save you in all your cities,
and the[E] rulers[F,p] you
demanded, saying,
"Give me a king and leaders"?
11 I give you a king in My anger[q]
and take away a king in My wrath.[r]
12 Ephraim's guilt is preserved;
his sin is stored up.[s]
13 Labor pains come on him.[t]
He is not a wise son;[u]
when the time comes,
he will not be born.[G,v]

14 I will ransom them from the power
of ·Sheol.
I will redeem[H] them from death.[w]
Death, where are your barbs?
Sheol, where is your sting?[x]
Compassion is hidden from My eyes.[y]

The Coming Judgment

15 Although he flourishes
among his brothers,[I,z]
an east wind will come,[aa]
a wind from the LORD rising up
from the desert.
His water source will fail,
and his spring will run dry.[ab]
The wind[J] will plunder the treasury[ac]
of every precious item.

16[K] Samaria[ad] will bear her guilt[ae]
because she has rebelled
against her God.[af]
They will fall by the sword;[ag]
their little ones will be dashed
to pieces,[ah]
and their pregnant women
ripped open.[ai]

A Plea to Repent

14 Israel, return to ·Yahweh your God,[aj]
for you have stumbled in your sin.[ak]
2 Take words of repentance with you[al]
and return to the LORD.
Say to Him: "Forgive all our sin
and accept what is good,
so that we may repay You
with praise[L] from our[M] lips.[am]
3 Assyria will not save us,[an]
we will not ride on horses,[ao]
and we will no longer proclaim,
'Our gods!'[ap]
to the work of our hands.[aq]
For the fatherless receives compassion
in You."[ar]

A Promise of Restoration

4 I will heal their apostasy;[as]
I will freely love them,[at]
for My anger will have turned from him.[au]
5 I will be like the dew to Israel;[av]
he will blossom like the lily[aw]
and take root like
the cedars of Lebanon.[ax]

[a]**13:3** Hs 6:4 [b]Ps 1:4; Is 17:13; Dn 2:35 [c]Ps 68:2 [d]**13:4** Hs 12:9 [e]Ex 20:3; 2Kg 18:35 [f]Is 43:11; 45:21-22 [g]**13:5** Dt 32:10 [h]**13:6** Dt 8:12,14; 32:13-15; Jr 5:7 [i]Hs 7:14 [j]Hs 2:13; 4:6; 8:14 [k]**13:7** Hs 5:14 [l]Jr 5:6 [m]**13:8** Ps 50:22 [n]**13:9** Jr 2:17,19; Hs 6:1-2; Mal 1:12-13 [o]**13:10** 2Kg 17:4; Hs 8:4 [p]Hs 7:7 [q]**13:11** 1Sm 8:7 [r]1Kg 14:7-10; Hs 10:7 [s]**13:12** Dt 32:34-35; Jb 14:17; Rm 2:5 [t]**13:13** Mc 4:9-10 [u]Dt 32:6; Hs 5:4 [v]Is 37:3; 66:9 [w]**13:14** Hs 6:1-2 [x]1Co 15:55 [y]Jr 20:16; 31:35-37 [z]**13:15** Gn 49:22; Hs 10:1 [aa]Gn 41:6; Jr 4:11-12; Ezk 17:10; 19:12 [ab]Jr 51:36 [ac]Jr 20:5 [ad]**13:16** Hs 7:1 [ae]Hs 10:2 [af]Hs 7:14 [ag]Hs 11:6 [ah]Hs 10:14 [ai]2Kg 15:16 [aj]**14:1** Hs 6:1; 10:12; 12:6 [ak]Hs 4:8; 5:5; 9:7 [al]**14:2** Mc 7:18-19 [am]Heb 13:15 [an]**14:3** Hs 5:13 [ao]Is 31:1 [ap]Hs 4:12 [aq]Hs 8:6; 13:2 [ar]Ps 68:5 [as]**14:4** Is 57:18; Hs 6:1 [at]Zph 3:17 [au]Is 12:1 [av]**14:5** Is 26:19 [aw]Sg 2:1; Mt 6:28 [ax]Is 35:2

[A]**13:4** DSS, LXX read *God who brought you out of* [B]**13:5** LXX, Syr read *fed* [C]**13:9** LXX reads *At your destruction, Israel, who will help you?* [D]**13:10** LXX, Syr, Vg; MT reads *I will be your king* [E]**13:10** Lit *your* [F]**13:10** Or *judges* [G]**13:13** Lit *he will not present himself at the opening of the womb for sons* [H]**13:14** Or *Should I ransom . . . Should I redeem . . . ?* [I]**13:15** Or *among reeds* [J]**13:15** Probably the Assyrian king [K]**13:16** Hs 14:1 in Hb [L]**14:2** LXX reads *with the fruit* [M]**14:2** Lit *repay the bulls of our*

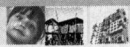

6 His new branches will spread,
and his splendor will be
like the olive tree,[a]
his fragrance, like
the forest of Lebanon.[b]
7 The people will return and live
beneath his shade.[c]
They will grow grain[d]
and blossom like the vine.
His renown will be like the wine
of Lebanon.
8 Ephraim, why should I[A] have
anything more
to do with idols?[e]
It is I who answer and watch
over him.
I am like a flourishing pine tree;[f]
your fruit comes from Me.[g]
9 Let whoever is wise[h] understand
these things,
and whoever is insightful
recognize them.
For the ways of the LORD
are right,[i]
and the righteous walk in them,[j]
but the rebellious stumble in them.[k]

[a]14:6 Jr 11:16
[b]Sg 4:11
[c]14:7 Ezk 17:23
[d]Hs 2:21-22
[e]14:8 Jb 34:32
[f]Is 41:19
[g]Ezk 17:13
[h]14:9 Ps 107:43; Jr 9:12
[i]Ps 111:7-8; Zph 3:5
[j]Is 26:7
[k]Is 1:28

GOD WHO SENDS

The Effects of Sin

Although sin and its consequences had to be dealt with because God is just, his mercy shines through, and in that mercy a promise emerges—despite the vagueness of its original expression. God has such love and concern for his disobedient children, he has such a vested interest in them, they are so much a part of him, they are so crucial and ultimate to his purpose—that the agenda of God is now shaped by this predicament. That agenda assumes many expressions in the Old Testament, but it is the New Testament which establishes this agenda in its most decisive form. The Bible does not speculate about what it would have been like had the fall not come. The Scriptures are concerned with the reality of what the fall brought and the question of what a just and loving God would do about it.

(DUBOSE, 79)

[A]14:8 LXX reads *he*

■ **AUTHOR:** Joel

■■ **DATE:** Joel prophesied during the time of the kings of Judah, perhaps sometime between 835–789 B.C.

The name Joel means "Yahweh is God." Joel's prophecy demonstrates the truth of God's name. Other than the fact that his father's name was Pethuel, little else is known about the prophet Joel. His prophecy was directed to the people of Judah and was written in elegant but powerful poetry.

In three short chapters Joel lays out basic themes found elsewhere in the books of prophecy: sin and evil inevitably lead to God's judgment while repentance reaps forgiveness; forgiveness and faithfulness will be followed by blessings. Joel prophesies events that either took place in Jewish history or are yet to come in the end times.

JOEL

Chapter one contains the fascinating description of the locust plague. Generations to come would still talk about it. The language is totally captivating in its simplicity: "What the devouring locust has left, the swarming locust has eaten; what the swarming locust has left, the young locust has eaten; and what the young locust has left, the destroying locust has eaten" (1:4).

The description of the horrors of the plague is interspersed with urgent calls to sinners to repent. Among the sinners are the priests and other dignitaries.

We must note that the plague was sent by divine appointment as a consequence of the people's sin. This we see against the background of the Old Testament dispensation. God confined His works of salvation to the nation Israel to whom He gave the Promised Land. The very ground on which they walked was part of that redemptive program. And so the land groaned with the people under God's punishment. In the New Testament dispensation God establishes His rule in Christ internationally. No longer can we identify any specific calamity as being God's punishment for any specific people group. Now, under the broader Kingdom rule, when disasters strike, the unfortunate may claim the help of the fortunate.

Again we note the immense sweep of Joel's prophecy. The nations that attack Israel will tremble before God's thunderous judgment. But all through these chapters of suffering and judgment Joel speaks of repentance followed by the Lord's promised blessings. Those, too, expand across history. The Old Testament epoch culminates in the glorious fulfillment of God's promises of redemption and the worldwide order of the New Testament church: "I will pour out My Spirit on all humanity; then your sons and your daughters will prophesy, your old men will have dreams, and your young men will see visions" (2:28).

But that event, fulfilled at Pentecost, does not stand by itself. Joel links it to the fearsome end times: "I will display wonders in the heavens and on the earth: blood, fire, and columns of smoke. The sun will be turned to darkness and the moon to blood" (2:30-31).

1 The word of the LORD that came[a] to Joel
son of Pethuel:

A Plague of Locusts

2 Hear this,[b] you elders;
listen, all you inhabitants of the land.
Has anything like this ever happened
in your days[c]
or in the days of your ancestors?
3 Tell your children about it,[d]
and let your children tell their children,
and their children the next generation.
4 What the devouring locust[e] has left,
the swarming locust has eaten;
what the swarming locust has left,
the young locust[f] has eaten;
and what the young locust has left,
the destroying locust[g] has eaten.

5 Wake up, you drunkards,[h] and weep;
wail, all you wine drinkers,
because of the sweet wine,
for it has been taken
from your mouth.
6 For a nation has invaded My land,[i]
powerful and without number;
its teeth are the teeth of a lion,
and it has the fangs of a lioness.[j]
7 It has devastated My grapevine
and splintered My fig tree.
It has stripped off its bark
and thrown it away;
its branches have turned white.
8 Grieve like a young woman dressed
in ·sackcloth,[k]
mourning for the husband
of her youth.
9 ·Grain and ·drink offerings have been
cut off[l]
from the house of the LORD;
the priests, who are ministers
of the LORD, mourn.[m]
10 The fields are destroyed;[n]
the land grieves;
indeed, the grain is destroyed;
the new wine is dried up;[o]
and the olive oil fails.[p]
11 Be ashamed, you farmers,[q]
wail, you vinedressers,[A]
over the wheat and the barley,
because the harvest of the field
has perished.[r]
12 The grapevine is dried up,[s]
and the fig tree is withered;
the pomegranate,[t] the date palm,[u]
and the apple[v] —
all the trees
of the orchard — have withered.
Indeed, human joy has dried up.[w]

13 Dress in sackcloth and lament,[x]
you priests;[y]
wail,[z] you ministers of the altar.
Come and spend the night
in sackcloth,[aa]
you ministers of my God,
because grain and drink offerings
are withheld from the house
of your God.
14 Announce a sacred fast;[ab]
proclaim an assembly!
Gather the elders[ac]
and all the residents of the land
at the house of the LORD your God,[ad]
and cry out to the LORD.[ae]

The Day of the LORD

15 Woe because of that day![af]
For the Day of the LORD is near
and will come as devastation
from the ·Almighty.[ag]
16 Hasn't the food been cut off
before our eyes,[ah]
joy and gladness[ai]
from the house of our God?
17 The seeds lie shriveled
in their casings.[B,aj]
The storehouses are in ruin,
and the granaries are broken down,
because the grain has withered away.
18 How the animals groan![ak]
The herds of cattle wander in confusion
since they have no pasture.
Even the flocks of sheep
suffer punishment.
19 I call to You, LORD,[al]
for fire has consumed
the pastures of the wilderness,[am]
and flames have devoured
all the trees of the countryside.

[a] **1:1** Hs 1:1; Mc 1:1; Zph 1:1
[b] **1:2** Hs 4:1; 5:1
[c] Dt 4:32; Jr 2:10; Mk 2:12
[d] **1:3** Ex 10:2; Jos 4:22; Ps 78:4
[e] **1:4** Ex 10:4; Jl 2:25; Am 4:9
[f] Ps 105:34; Nah 3:15-16
[g] Ps 78:46; Is 33:4
[h] **1:5** Jl 3:3
[i] **1:6** Jl 2:2,11,25
[j] Rv 9:7-8
[k] **1:8** Is 22:12; Jr 4:8; 6:26
[l] **1:9** Hs 9:4; Jl 2:14
[m] Hs 10:5; Jl 2:17
[n] **1:10** Is 24:4
[o] Hs 9:2
[p] Dt 28:51; Hs 2:8-13; Hg 1:11
[q] **1:11** Jr 14:4; 51:23; Am 5:16
[r] Is 17:11; Jr 9:12
[s] **1:12** Hab 3:17
[t] Hg 2:19
[u] Sg 7:8
[v] Sg 2:3
[w] Is 16:10; 24:11
[x] **1:13** Jr 4:8; Ezk 7:18
[y] Jl 2:17
[z] Jr 9:10
[aa] 1Kg 21:27
[ab] **1:14** Jl 2:15-16
[ac] Jl 1:2
[ad] 2Ch 20:3; Neh 9:1; Jr 36:6,9
[ae] Jnh 3:8
[af] **1:15** Jr 30:7; Am 5:16
[ag] Is 13:6,9; Ezk 30:2-3; Jl 2:1-2,11,31
[ah] **1:16** Is 3:7
[ai] Is 16:10; Jr 48:33
[aj] **1:17** Is 17:10-11
[ak] **1:18** 1Kg 18:5; Jr 12:4; 14:5-6; Hs 4:3
[al] **1:19** Ps 50:15; Mc 7:7
[am] Jr 9:10; Am 7:4

[A] **1:11** Or *The farmers are dismayed, the vinedressers wail* [B] **1:17** Or *clods*; Hb obscure

20 Even the wild animals cry out to[A] You,[a]
for the river beds are dried up,[b]
and fire has consumed
the pastures of the wilderness.

2 Blow the horn in ·Zion;[c]
sound the alarm on My holy mountain!
Let all the residents of the land tremble,
for the Day of the LORD is coming;[d]
in fact, it is near —
2 a day of darkness and gloom,[e]
a day of clouds and dense overcast,[f]
like the dawn spreading
over the mountains;
a great and strong people[g] appears,
such as never existed in ages past[h]
and never will again
in all the generations to come.[i]
3 A fire destroys[B] in front of them,[j]
and behind them a flame devours.
The land in front of them
is like the Garden of Eden,[k]
but behind them,
it is like a desert wasteland;[l]
there is no escape from them.
4 Their appearance is like that
of horses,[m]
and they gallop like war horses.
5 They bound on the tops
of the mountains.
Their sound is like the sound
of chariots,[n]
like the sound of fiery flames
consuming stubble,[o]
like a mighty army deployed for war.
6 Nations writhe in horror before them;[p]
all faces turn pale.
7 They attack as warriors attack;
they scale walls as men of war do.
Each goes on his own path,[q]
and they do not change their course.
8 They do not push each other;
each man proceeds on his own path.
They dodge the arrows, never stopping.
9 They storm the city;
they run on the wall;
they climb into the houses;[r]
they enter through the windows
like thieves.[s]

[a]**1:20** Ps 104:21; 147:9 [b]1Kg 17:7; 18:5 [c]**2:1** Jl 2:15; Jr 4:5; 51:27 [d]Jl 1:15; 2:11,31; 3:14 [e]**2:2** Jl 2:31; Zph 1:15 [f]Is 60:2; Zph 1:15 [g]Jl 1:6; 2:11,25 [h]Lm 1:12; Dn 9:12; 12:1; Jl 1:2 [i]Ex 10:14 [j]**2:3** Ps 97:3; Is 9:18-19 [k]Gn 2:8-15; Ezk 36:35 [l]Ex 10:5,15; Ps 105:34-35 [m]**2:4** Rv 9:7 [n]**2:5** Rv 9:9 [o]Is 5:24; 30:30 [p]**2:6** Is 13:8; Nah 2:10 [q]**2:7** Pr 30:27 [r]**2:9** Ex 10:6 [s]Jr 9:21 [t]**2:10** Ps 18:7; Nah 1:5 [u]Is 13:10; 34:4; Jr 4:23; Ezk 32:7-8; Mt 24:29; Rv 8:12 [v]Jl 3:15 [w]**2:11** Ps 46:6; Is 13:4 [x]Jl 2:25 [y]Jr 50:34; Rv 18:8 [z]Jl 1:15; 2:31; 3:14 [aa]Ezk 22:14 [ab]**2:12** 1Kg 8:35-40; 2Ch 7:14 [ac]Est 4:3 [ad]**2:13** Ps 51:17; Is 57:15 [ae]Jr 41:5 [af]Ex 34:6; Nm 14:18; 1Ch 21:15; Neh 9:17; Ps 86:15; 103:8; 145:8; Jr 18:8; Jnh 4:2 [ag]**2:14** Jnh 3:9 [ah]Hg 2:19 [ai]Jl 1:9,13 [aj]**2:15** Jl 2:1 [ak]2Kg 10:20 [al]**2:16** 1Sm 16:5; 2Ch 29:5 [am]**2:15-16** 2Ch 20:3; Neh 9:1; Jr 36:6,9 [an]**2:16** Ps 19:5 [ao]**2:17** Jl 1:9 [ap]Hs 10:5; Jl 1:13 [aq]Is 37:20; Am 7:2,5 [ar]Ps 44:13; 74:10 [as]Ps 42:3,10; 79:10; 115:2

10 The earth quakes before them;[t]
the sky shakes.
The sun and moon grow dark,[u]
and the stars cease their shining.[v]
11 The LORD raises His voice[w]
in the presence of His army.[x]
His camp is very large;
Those who carry out His command
are powerful.[y]
Indeed, the Day of the LORD is terrible
and dreadful[z] —
who can endure it?[aa]

God's Call for Repentance

12 Even now —
this is the LORD's declaration —
turn to Me with all your heart,[ab]
with fasting, weeping, and mourning.[ac]
13 Tear your hearts,[ad]
not just your clothes,[ae]
and return to the LORD your God.
For He is gracious and compassionate,
slow to anger, rich in faithful love,
and He relents from sending disaster.[af]
14 Who knows? He may turn and relent[ag]
and leave a blessing behind Him,[ah]
so you can offer grain and wine
to the LORD your God.[ai]
15 Blow the horn in Zion![aj]
Announce a sacred fast;[ak]
proclaim an assembly.
16 Gather the people;
sanctify the congregation;[al]
assemble the aged;[C,am]
gather the children,
even those nursing at the breast.
Let the groom leave his bedroom,[an]
and the bride her honeymoon chamber.
17 Let the priests,[ao] the LORD's ministers,
weep between the portico
and the altar.[ap]
Let them say:
"Have pity on Your people, LORD,[aq]
and do not make Your inheritance
a disgrace,[ar]
an object of scorn among the nations.
Why should it be said
among the peoples,
'Where is their God?' "[as]

[A]**1:20** Or *animals pant for*; Hb obscure [B]**2:3** Lit *consumes* [C]**2:16** Or *elders*

God's Response to His People

18 Then the LORD became jealous for His
land[a] and spared His people.[b] 19 The LORD answered His people:

Look, I am about to send you
grain, new wine, and olive oil.[c]
You will be satiated with them,
and I will no longer make you
a disgrace among the nations.[d]

20 I will drive the northerner
far from you[e]
and banish him to a dry
and desolate land,
his front ranks into the Dead Sea,[f]
and his rear guard
into the Mediterranean Sea.[g]
His stench will rise;
yes, his rotten smell will rise,[h]
for he has done catastrophic things.

21 Don't be afraid, land;[i]
rejoice and be glad,
for the LORD has done great things.[j]

22 Don't be afraid, wild animals,
for the wilderness pastures
have turned green,[k]
the trees bear their fruit,
and the fig tree and grapevine yield
their riches.

23 Children of Zion,[l] rejoice and be glad
in the LORD your God,[m]
because He gives you the autumn rain
for your vindication.[A,n]
He sends showers for you,
both autumn and spring rain[o]
as before.

24 The threshing floors will be full
of grain,[p]
and the vats will overflow
with new wine and olive oil.

25 I will repay you for the years
that the swarming locust ate,[q]
the young locust, the destroying locust,
and the devouring locust —
My great army that I sent against you.

26 You will have plenty to eat
and be satisfied.[r]
You will praise the name
of ·Yahweh your God,[s]
who has dealt wondrously with you.[t]
My people will never again be put
to shame.[u]

27 You will know that I am present
in Israel[v]
and that I am Yahweh your God,
and there is no other.[w]
My people will never again be put
to shame.[x]

God's Promise of His Spirit

28B After this[y]
I will pour out My Spirit[z]
on all humanity;[aa]
then your sons and your daughters
will prophesy,
your old men will have dreams,
and your young men will see visions.

29 I will even pour out My Spirit
on the male and female slaves
in those days.[ab]

30 I will display wonders
in the heavens and on the earth:[ac]
blood, fire, and columns of smoke.

31 The sun will be turned to darkness
and the moon to blood[ad]
before the great and awe-inspiring Day
of the LORD comes.[ae]

32 Then everyone who calls
on the name of Yahweh will be saved,[af]
for there will be an escape
for those on Mount Zion
and in Jerusalem,
as the LORD promised,[ag]
among the survivors the LORD calls.

Judgment of the Nations

3 C Yes, in those days and at that time,
when I restore the fortunes of Judah
and Jerusalem,[ah]

2 I will gather all the nations[ai]
and take them to the Valley
of Jehoshaphat.[D,aj]
I will enter into judgment
with them there[ak]
because of My people,
My inheritance Israel.
The nations have scattered
the Israelites
in foreign countries[al]

[a] 2:18 Ezk 36:5,6; Zch 1:14; 8:2
[b] Is 60:10; 63:9,15
[c] 2:19 Jr 31:12; Hs 2:21-22
[d] Ezk 34:29; 36:15
[e] 2:20 Jr 1:14-15
[f] Zch 14:8
[g] Dt 11:24
[h] Is 34:3; Am 4:10
[i] 2:21 Jl 1:10
[j] Ps 126:2-3
[k] 2:22 Ps 65:12; Jr 9:10; Jl 1:19
[l] 2:23 Ps 149:2
[m] Is 12:2-6
[n] Dt 11:13-15
[o] Hs 6:3; Zch 10:1
[p] 2:24 Lv 26:10; Am 9:13; Mal 3:10
[q] 2:25 Jl 1:4-7; 2:2-11
[r] 2:26 Dt 11:15; Is 62:9
[s] Ps 113:1; 135:1; 148:5,13
[t] Ps 126:2; Is 25:1
[u] Is 45:17
[v] 2:27 Jl 3:17,21
[w] Dt 4:35,39; 1Kg 8:60; Is 45:5-6
[x] Is 49:23
[y] 2:28-32 Ac 2:17-21
[z] 2:28 Is 32:15; 44:3; Ezk 39:29
[aa] Is 40:5; 49:26
[ab] 2:29 1Co 12:13
[ac] 2:30 Lk 21:11,25-26
[ad] 2:31 Is 13:9-10; 34:4; Mt 24:29; Mk 13:24
[ae] Zph 1:14-16; Mal 4:1,5
[af] 2:32 Rm 10:13
[ag] Ob 17
[ah] 3:1 Jr 32:44; 33:7,11; Ezk 39:25
[ai] 3:2 Is 66:18; Mc 4:12
[aj] Jl 3:12,14
[ak] Is 66:16; Jr 25:31
[al] Jr 50:17; Ezk 34:6

A 2:23 Or *righteousness* B 2:28 Jl 3:1 in Hb C 3:1 Jl 4:1 in Hb D 3:2 = The LORD Will Judge

and divided up My land.[a]
3 They cast lots for My people;[b]
they bartered a boy for a prostitute
and sold a girl for wine to drink.[c]

4And also: Tyre,[d] Sidon, and all the territories of Philistia[e]—what are you to Me? Are
you paying Me back or trying to get even
with Me? I will quickly bring retribution
on your heads.[f] 5For you took My silver and
gold and carried My finest treasures[g] to your
temples. 6You sold the people of Judah and
Jerusalem to the Greeks[h] to remove them far
from their own territory. 7Look, I am about to
rouse them up from the place where you sold
them;[i] I will bring retribution on your heads.
8I will sell your sons and daughters into the
hands of the people of Judah,[j] and they will
sell them to the Sabeans,[A,k] to a distant nation,
for the LORD has spoken.

9 Proclaim this among the nations:[l]
Prepare for holy war;[m]
rouse the warriors;[n]
let all the men of war advance
and attack!
10 Beat your plows into swords
and your pruning knives into spears.[o]
Let even the weakling say, "I am
a warrior."
11 Come quickly,[B] all
you surrounding nations;
gather yourselves.[p]
Bring down
Your warriors there, LORD.[q]
12 Let the nations be roused
and come to the Valley of Jehoshaphat,
for there I will sit down
to judge all the surrounding nations.[r]
13 Swing the sickle
because the harvest is ripe.[s]
Come and trample the grapes
because the winepress is full;[t]
the wine vats overflow
because the wickedness of the nations
is great.[u]
14 Multitudes, multitudes[v]
in the valley of decision!
For the Day of the LORD is near[w]
in the valley of decision.
15 The sun and moon will grow dark,
and the stars will cease their shining.[x]
16 The LORD will roar from ·Zion[y]
and raise His voice from Jerusalem;[z]
heaven and earth will shake.[aa]
But the LORD will be a refuge
for His people,[ab]
a stronghold for the Israelites.[ac]

Israel Blessed

17 Then you will know
that I am ·Yahweh your God,[ad]
who dwells in Zion, My holy mountain.[ae]
Jerusalem will be holy,[af]
and foreigners will never
overrun it again.[ag]
18 In that day
the mountains will drip
with sweet wine,[ah]
and the hills will flow with milk.[ai]
All the streams of Judah will flow
with water,[aj]
and a spring will issue
from the LORD's house,[ak]
watering the Valley of Acacias.[C,al]
19 Egypt will become desolate,
and Edom a desert wasteland,
because of the violence done
to the people of Judah[am]
in whose land they shed
innocent blood.
20 But Judah will be inhabited forever,[an]
and Jerusalem from generation
to generation.
21 I will pardon their bloodguilt,[D,ao]
which I have not pardoned,
for the LORD dwells in Zion.

[a]**3:2** Ezk 35:10; 36:1-5 [b]**3:3** Ob 11; Nah 3:10 [c]Am 2:6 [d]**3:4** Am 1:9; Zch 9:2-4 [e]Am 1:6-8; Zch 9:5-7 [f]Ps 28:4 [g]**3:5** 1Kg 20:6; 2Ch 36:19; Lm 1:10-11 [h]**3:6** Is 66:19; Ezk 27:13 [i]**3:7** Zch 9:13 [j]**3:8** Is 14:2; 60:14 [k]Jb 1:15; Ps 72:10; Ezk 38:13 [l]**3:9** Jr 51:27-28 [m]Jr 6:4; Mc 3:5 [n]Is 8:9-10; Jr 46:3-4; Zch 14:2-3 [o]**3:10** Is 2:4; Mc 4:3 [p]**3:11** Ezk 38:15-16 [q]Is 13:3 [r]**3:12** Ps 7:6; 98:9; Is 3:13 [s]**3:13** Jr 51:33; Hs 6:11 [t]Is 63:3; Lm 1:15 [u]Gn 18:20; Rv 19:14-16 [v]**3:14** Is 34:2-8 [w]Jl 1:15; 2:1,11 [x]**3:15** Jl 2:10,31 [y]**3:16** Hs 11:10; Am 1:2 [z]Jr 25:30; Am 1:2 [aa]Ezk 38:19; Jl 2:10; Hg 2:6 [ab]Ps 46:1; 62:8; Pr 14:26 [ac]Jr 16:19; Nah 1:7 [ad]**3:17** Ex 6:7; 29:46; Ezk 20:20 [ae]Is 11:9; 56:7; Ezk 20:40 [af]Is 4:3; Ob 17 [ag]Is 52:1; Nah 1:15 [ah]**3:18** Am 9:13 [ai]Ex 3:8 [aj]Is 30:25; 35:6 [ak]Ezk 47:1-12 [al]Nm 25:1; Ezk 47:8 [am]**3:19** Ob 10 [an]**3:20** Ezk 37:25; Am 9:15 [ao]**3:21** Is 4:4

A**3:8** Probably the south Arabian kingdom of Sheba (modern Yemen) B**3:11** LXX, Syr, Tg read *Gather yourselves and come*; Hb obscure C**3:18** Or *Shittim* D**3:21** LXX, Syr read *I will avenge their blood*

AUTHOR: Amos

DATE: During the time of the kings Uzziah of Judah and Jeroboam II of Israel—prophesying between 765–760 B.C.

God called Amos to his mission straight from his farm near the town of Tekoa in Judah. Most of his ministry, however, took place in the northern kingdom of Israel.

Amos prophesied during the reigns of Uzziah of Judah and Jeroboam of Israel (around 750 B.C.). He lived "two years before the earthquake" (1:1). The prophet Zechariah also refers to that event (Zch 14:5), but it is not known when it took place. But for God's people that designation was enough. Who could forget the date of that terrible earthquake?

Amos's style is as simple as it is eloquent. To Amos, the mission of God is clear and its aims vital. The nine chapters of Amos expose sin for what it is and issue a clarion call for repentance. Amos begins his prophecy with a stern judgment against the surrounding nations and city-states: Syria, Palestine, Tyre, Edom, and Ammon. The measure of their immorality, and their cruelty to Israel, is full.

AMOS

All that is only an introduction to the extensive prophecies against Israel and, in lesser measure, Judah. Striking in Amos' messages is the detailed description of the various sins of the people. That is probably linked to the unparalleled prosperity of the nation. The people live to the full and sin to the full. None of these specific sins are foreign to us: thanklessness, oppression of the poor, materialism, religious deformation, bribery, injustice, greed, idolatry, sham-worship, immorality, drunkenness, pride, cheating in the market place, and exploitation of the needy.

Amos announces God's judgment in equally detailed ways. Enemies will overrun the land. Great unrest will trouble the hearts of the people. The public square will be filled with anguish. Great food shortages will make prosperous times a dim memory. Droughts will cause people to stagger around in the hopes of a drink. Pestilence will stalk the cities. Plagues of locusts will follow. The royal house will know death. All of these forms of punishment will be as inevitable as prey before a roaring lion. When there appears to be no repentance, the prophet announces the severest judgment: exile.

Included in the many judgments is one directed to the sanctuary of the Golden Calf at Bethel, which King Jeroboam had erected so that the people did not have to travel to Jerusalem. Amos's stern message, delivered right at the sanctuary in Bethel, is particularly galling to chief priest Amaziah. He pointedly tells Amos to go back to Judah and do his preaching there.

But the conclusion of Amos's prophecy is a song of the triumph of God's grace. The people will turn back to the Lord. The transition from judgment to forgiveness is disarmingly sudden. Forgiveness, says Amos, will bring glorious healing and well-being in its wake. The language implies a vision of Israel's return from exile: "I will restore the fortunes of My people Israel. They will rebuild and occupy ruined cities, plant vineyards and drink their wine, make gardens and eat their produce" (Am 9:14). And for good measure Amos adds that never again will such a severe judgment come upon God's people.

1 The words of Amos, who was one of the sheep breeders[A,a] from Tekoa[b]—what he saw regarding Israel in the days of Uzziah,[c] king of Judah, and Jeroboam[d] son of Jehoash, king of Israel, two years before the earthquake.[e]

[2] He said:

The LORD roars[f] from *Zion
and raises His voice from Jerusalem;
the pastures of the shepherds mourn,[B,g]
and the summit of Carmel[h] withers.

Judgment on Israel's Neighbors

[3] The LORD says:

I will not relent
from punishing Damascus[i]
for three crimes, even four,[j]
because they threshed Gilead
with iron sledges.
[4] Therefore, I will send fire
against Hazael's palace,
and it will consume
Ben-hadad's[k] citadels.
[5] I will break down the gates[C,l]
of Damascus.
I will cut off the ruler
from the Valley of Aven,
and the one who wields the scepter
from Beth-eden.
The people of Aram will be exiled
to Kir.[m]
The LORD has spoken.

[6] The LORD says:

I will not relent from punishing Gaza[n]
for three crimes, even four,
because they exiled
a whole community,
handing them over to Edom.
[7] Therefore, I will send fire
against the walls of Gaza,
and it will consume its citadels.
[8] I will cut off the ruler from Ashdod,[o]
and the one who wields the scepter
from Ashkelon.[p]
I will also turn My hand against Ekron,
and the remainder of the Philistines[q]
will perish.
The Lord GOD has spoken.

[9] The LORD says:

I will not relent from punishing Tyre[r]
for three crimes, even four,
because they handed over
a whole community of exiles to Edom
and broke[D] a treaty of brotherhood.[s]
[10] Therefore, I will send fire[t]
against the walls of Tyre,
and it will consume its citadels.

[11] The LORD says:

I will not relent from punishing Edom[u]
for three crimes, even four,
because he pursued his brother
with the sword.[v]
He stifled his compassion,
his anger tore at them[w] continually,
and he harbored his rage incessantly.
[12] Therefore, I will send fire
against Teman,[x]
and it will consume the citadels
of Bozrah.

[13] The LORD says:

I will not relent from punishing
the Ammonites[y]
for three crimes, even four,
because they ripped open
the pregnant women of Gilead[z]
in order to enlarge their territory.[aa]
[14] Therefore, I will set fire to the walls
of Rabbah,[ab]
and it will consume its citadels.
There will be shouting on the day
of battle[ac]
and a violent wind on the day
of the storm.[ad]
[15] Their king and his princes
will go into exile together.[ae]
The LORD has spoken.

2 The LORD says:

I will not relent from punishing Moab[af]
for three crimes, even four,
because he burned the bones
of the king of Edom to lime.[ag]
[2] Therefore, I will send fire against Moab,
and it will consume the citadels
of Kerioth.[ah]

[a] **1:1** 2Kg 3:4; Am 7:14-15 [b] 2Sm 14:2; Jr 6:1 [c] 2Kg 15:1-7; 2Ch 26:1-23; Is 1:1; Hs 1:1 [d] 2Kg 14:23-29 [e] Zch 14:5 [f] **1:2** Is 42:13; Jr 25:30; Jl 3:16; Am 3:8 [g] Is 24:4-7; Jr 12:4; 23:10; Jl 1:10,18-19 [h] Am 9:3 [i] **1:3** Is 17:1-3 [j] Pr 30:15-29; Am 2:1,4,6 [k] **1:4** 2Kg 8:11-15; 13:3,22,24 [l] **1:5** Gn 22:17; Neh 1:3; Lm 2:9; Hs 11:6; Nah 3:13 [m] 2Kg 16:9; Am 9:7 [n] **1:6** Jr 47:1,4-5; Ezk 25:15-17 [o] **1:8** 2Ch 26:6; Am 3:9; Zch 9:6 [p] Jr 47:5; Zph 2:4 [q] Is 14:29-31; Ezk 25:16 [r] **1:9** Is 23; Ezk 26:1–28:19 [s] 1Kg 5:1,12; 9:11-14 [t] **1:10** Zch 9:4 [u] **1:11** Jr 49:8-22; Ezk 25:12-14 [v] Nm 20:14; Dt 2:4; 23:7; Ob 10-14 [w] Gn 37:33; Ps 7:2; Hs 5:14 [x] **1:12** Jr 49:7,20 [y] **1:13** Jr 49:1-6; Ezk 25:1-7; Zph 2:8-11 [z] 2Kg 8:12; 15:16; Hs 13:16 [aa] Is 5:8; Ezk 35:10 [ab] **1:14** 1Ch 20:1; Jr 49:2 [ac] Ezk 21:22; Am 2:2 [ad] Is 29:6; 30:30 [ae] **1:15** Jr 49:3 [af] **2:1** Is 15–16; Jr 48; Ezk 25:8-11 [ag] Lv 20:14; 21:9 [ah] **2:2** Jr 48:24,41

[A] **1:1** Or *the shepherds* [B] **1:2** Or *dry up* [C] **1:5** Lit *gate bars* [D] **1:9** Lit *and did not remember*

Moab will die with a tumult,[a]
with shouting and the sound
of the ram's horn.
3 I will cut off the judge[b] from the land
and kill all its officials[c] with him.
The LORD has spoken.

Judgment on Judah

4 The LORD says:

I will not relent from punishing Judah[d]
for three crimes, even four,
because they have rejected
the instruction of the LORD[e]
and have not kept His statutes.[f]
The lies[g] that their ancestors followed[h]
have led them astray.
5 Therefore, I will send fire[i]
against Judah,
and it will consume the citadels
of Jerusalem.

Judgment on Israel

6 The LORD says:

I will not relent from punishing Israel[j]
for three crimes, even four,
because they sell a righteous person
for silver
and a needy person for a pair
of sandals.[k]
7 They trample the heads of the poor[l]
on the dust of the ground
and block the path of the needy.[m]
A man and his father
have sexual relations
with the same girl,[n]
profaning My holy name.[o]
8 They stretch out beside every altar[p]
on garments taken as collateral,[q]
and in the house of their God,
they drink wine obtained
through fines.[r]
9 Yet I destroyed the Amorite[s]
as Israel advanced;
his height[t] was like the cedars,
and he was as sturdy as the oaks;
I destroyed his fruit[u] above
and his roots beneath.
10 And I brought you from the land
of Egypt[v]
and led you 40 years in the wilderness[w]
in order to possess the land
of the Amorite.[x]
11 I raised up some of your sons
as prophets[y]
and some of your young men
as Nazirites.[z]
Is this not the case, Israelites?
This is the LORD's declaration.
12 But you made the Nazirites drink wine
and commanded the prophets,
"Do not prophesy."[aa]
13 Look, I am about to crush[A] you
in your place[ab]
as a wagon full of sheaves crushes grain.
14 Escape will fail the swift,[ac]
the strong one will not prevail
by his strength,[ad]
and the brave will not save his life.
15 The archer will not stand his ground,[ae]
the one who is swift of foot
will not save himself,
and the one riding a horse will not save
his life.[af]
16 Even the most courageous
of the warriors
will flee naked on that day[ag] —
this is the LORD's declaration.

God's Reasons for Punishing Israel

3 Listen to this message that the LORD has
spoken against you, Israelites, against the
entire clan that I brought from the land of
Egypt:[ah]

2 I have known only you[ai]
out of all the clans of the earth;
therefore, I will punish you for all
your iniquities.[aj]
3 Can two walk together[ak]
without agreeing to meet?[B]
4 Does a lion roar[al] in the forest
when it has no prey?
Does a young lion growl from its lair
unless it has captured something?
5 Does a bird land in a trap
on the ground
if there is no bait for it?
Does a trap spring from the ground
when it has caught nothing?

[a] **2:2** Jr 48:45
[b] **2:3** Ps 2:10; 141:6
[c] Jb 12:21; Is 40:23
[d] **2:4** 2Kg 17:19; Hs 2:12; Am 3:2
[e] Jdg 2:17-20; 2Kg 22:11-17; Jr 6:19; 8:9
[f] Jr 44:10; Ezk 5:7
[g] Is 9:15-16; Jr 11:10-13; 23:14,21-22
[h] Jr 9:14; 16:11-12; Ezk 20:18,24,30
[i] **2:5** Jr 17:27; 21:10
[j] **2:6** 2Kg 18:12
[k] Dt 16:18-20; Am 5:12; 8:6
[l] **2:7** Am 5:11; 8:4; Mc 2:2,9
[m] Jb 24:4
[n] Hs 4:14
[o] Lv 18:21; Pr 30:9; Ezk 36:20-23
[p] **2:8** Am 3:14
[q] Ex 22:26
[r] Am 4:1; 6:6
[s] **2:9** Jos 10:12
[t] Nm 13:28-33
[u] Ezk 17:9; Mal 4:1
[v] **2:10** Ex 20:2; Am 3:1; 9:7
[w] Dt 2:7
[x] Nm 21:25
[y] **2:11** Dt 18:18-19; Jr 1:4-5; Am 7:14-15
[z] Nm 6:1-21; Jdg 13:2-5; 1Sm 1:11
[aa] **2:12** Jr 11:21; Am 7:13,16
[ab] **2:13** Jl 3:13
[ac] **2:14** Is 30:16-17
[ad] Jr 9:23
[ae] **2:15** Jr 51:56; Ezk 39:3
[af] Is 31:3
[ag] **2:16** Jdg 4:17
[ah] **3:1** Am 2:10
[ai] **3:2** Ex 19:5-6; Dt 4:32-37
[aj] Jr 14:10; Ezk 20:36; Dn 9:12
[ak] **3:3** Lv 26:23-24
[al] **3:4** Ps 104:21; Hs 5:14; 11:10

[A] **2:13** Or *hinder*; Hb obscure [B] **3:3** LXX reads *without meeting*

6 If a ram's horn[a] is blown in a city,
aren't people afraid?[b]
If a disaster[c] occurs in a city,
hasn't the LORD done it?[d]
7 Indeed, the Lord GOD does nothing
without revealing His counsel
to His servants the prophets.[e]
8 A lion has roared;[f]
who will not fear?
The Lord GOD has spoken;[g]
who will not prophesy?[h]
9 Proclaim on the citadels in Ashdod[i]
and on the citadels in the land of Egypt:
Assemble on the mountains of Samaria[j]
and see the great turmoil in the city
and the acts of oppression within it.[k]
10 The people are incapable
of doing right[l] —
this is the LORD's declaration —
those who store up violence
and destruction[m]
in their citadels.

11 Therefore, the Lord GOD says:

An enemy[n] will surround the land;
he will destroy[o] your strongholds
and plunder your citadels.[p]

12 The LORD says:

As the shepherd snatches two legs
or a piece of an ear
from the lion's mouth,[q]
so the Israelites who live in Samaria
will be rescued
with only the corner of a bed[r]
or the[A] cushion[B] of a couch.[C,s]
13 Listen and testify[t] against the house
of Jacob —
this is the declaration
of the Lord GOD,
the God of •Hosts.
14 I will punish the altars of Bethel[u]
on the day I punish Israel for its crimes;
the horns of the altar[v] will be cut off
and fall to the ground.[w]
15 I will demolish the winter house[x]
and the summer house;[y]
the houses inlaid with ivory[z]
will be destroyed,
and the great houses[aa] will come
to an end.
This is the LORD's declaration.

Social and Spiritual Corruption

4 Listen to this message, you cows
of Bashan[ab]
who are on the hill of Samaria,
women who oppress the poor
and crush the needy,[ac]
who say to their husbands,
"Bring us something to drink."[ad]

2 The Lord GOD has sworn[ae] by His holiness:[af]

Look, the days are coming[D]
when you will be taken away
with hooks,[ag]
every last one of you with fishhooks.[ah]
3 You will go through breaches
in the wall,[ai]
each woman straight ahead,
and you will be driven along
toward Harmon.
This is the LORD's declaration.

4 Come to Bethel and rebel;
rebel even more at Gilgal![aj]
Bring your sacrifices every morning,[ak]
your tenths every three days.
5 Offer leavened bread as
a thank offering,[al]
and loudly proclaim
your freewill offerings,[am]
for that is what you Israelites
love to do![an]
This is the LORD's declaration.

God's Discipline and Israel's Apostasy

6 I gave you absolutely nothing to eat[E,ao]
in all your cities,
a shortage of food in all
your communities,
yet you did not return to Me.[ap]
This is the LORD's declaration.

7 I also withheld the rain from you[aq]
while there were still three months
until harvest.
I sent rain on one city
but no rain on another.[ar]

[a] **3:6** Jr 4:5,19,21; 6:1; Hs 5:8; Zph 1:16 [b] Nm 10:9; Jr 4:19; Jl 2:1 [c] Is 14:24-27; 45:7 [d] Lm 3:37-39 [e] **3:7** Gn 18:17; Jr 23:18,22; Jnh 1:2 [f] **3:8** Am 1:2 [g] Jnh 1:1-3; 3:1-3 [h] Jr 6:10-11; 20:9 [i] **3:9** 1Sm 5:1; Am 1:8 [j] Am 4:1; 6:1 [k] Am 5:11; 6:8 [l] **3:10** Ps 14:4; Jr 4:22; Am 5:7; 6:12 [m] Hab 2:8-10; Zph 1:9; Zch 5:3-4 [n] **3:11** Am 6:14 [o] Am 2:14 [p] 2Kg 17:5-6; 18:9-12 [q] **3:12** 1Sm 17:34-37 [r] Ps 132:3 [s] Est 1:6; 7:8; Am 6:4 [t] **3:13** Ezk 2:7 [u] **3:14** Hs 10:5-8,14-15; Am 4:4; 5:5-6; 7:10,13 [v] Lv 8:15; 16:18-19; 1Kg 1:50-51; 2:28; Ps 118:27 [w] Hs 10:1-2 [x] **3:15** Jr 36:22 [y] Jdg 3:20 [z] 1Kg 22:39; 2Ch 9:17; Am 6:4 [aa] Am 2:5; 6:11 [ab] **4:1** Ps 22:12; Ezk 39:18 [ac] Ex 23:3,6; Lv 19:15; 25:35; Dt 15:4-11; Am 5:11; 8:6 [ad] Am 2:8; 6:6 [ae] **4:2** Am 6:8; 8:7 [af] Ps 89:35 [ag] Is 37:29; Ezk 38:4 [ah] 2Kg 19:28; 2Ch 33:10-11 [ai] **4:3** Jr 52:7 [aj] **4:4** Am 5:5 [ak] Am 5:21-22 [al] **4:5** Lv 7:12 [am] Lv 22:18-21 [an] Jr 7:9-10; Hs 9:1,10 [ao] **4:6** Is 3:1; Jr 14:18 [ap] Is 9:13; Jr 5:3; Hg 2:17 [aq] **4:7** Jr 3:1-3; 5:23-25 [ar] Ex 9:4,26; 10:22-23

[A] **3:12** Or *Israelites will be rescued, those who sit in Samaria on a corner of a bed or a* [B] **3:12** Hb obscure [C] **3:12** LXX, Aq, Sym, Theod, Syr, Tg, Vg read *or in Damascus* [D] **4:2** Lit *coming on you* [E] **4:6** Lit *you cleanness of teeth*

One field received rain
while a field with no rain withered.[a]
8 Two or three cities staggered
to another city to drink water[b]
but were not satisfied,[c]
yet you did not return[d] to Me.
This is the LORD's declaration.

9 I struck you with blight and mildew;[e]
the locust devoured[f]
your many gardens and vineyards,
your fig trees and olive trees,[g]
yet you did not return to Me.[h]
This is the LORD's declaration.

10 I sent plagues like those of Egypt;[i]
I killed your young men
with the sword,[j]
along with your captured horses.[k]
I caused the stench of your camp
to fill your nostrils,[l]
yet you did not return to Me.[m]
This is the LORD's declaration.

11 I overthrew some of you
as I[A] overthrew Sodom and Gomorrah,[n]
and you were like a burning stick
snatched from a fire,[o]
yet you did not return to Me[p]—
this is the LORD's declaration.

12 Therefore, Israel, that is what I will do
to you,
and since I will do that to you,
Israel, prepare to meet your God![q]
13 He is here:
the One who forms the mountains,[r]
creates the wind,[s]
and reveals His[B] thoughts to man,[t]
the One who makes the dawn
out of darkness
and strides on the heights of the earth.[u]
•Yahweh, the God of •Hosts,
is His name.[v]

Lamentation for Israel

5 Listen to this message that I am singing
for you, a lament,[w] house of Israel:

2 She has fallen;
Virgin Israel[x] will never rise again.[y]
She lies abandoned on her land,
with no one to raise her up.[z]

3 For the Lord GOD says:

The city that marches out
a thousand strong
will have only a hundred left,[aa]
and the one that marches out
a hundred strong
will have only ten left[ab] in the house
of Israel.

Seek God and Live

4 For the LORD says to the house of Israel:

Seek Me and live![ac]
5 Do not seek Bethel[ad]
or go to Gilgal[ae]
or journey to Beer-sheba,[af]
for Gilgal will certainly go into exile,
and Bethel will come to nothing.
6 Seek •Yahweh[ag] and live,
or He will spread like fire[ah]
throughout the house of Joseph;
it will consume everything,
with no one at Bethel to extinguish it.[ai]
7 Those who turn justice
into •wormwood[aj]
throw righteousness to the ground.
8 The One who made the Pleiades
and Orion,[ak]
who turns darkness[C] into dawn[al]
and darkens day into night,[am]
who summons the waters of the sea[an]
and pours them out over the face
of the earth[ao]—
Yahweh is His name.[ap]
9 He brings destruction[D] on the strong,[E,aq]
and it falls on the stronghold.[ar]
10 They hate the one who convicts
the •guilty[as]
at the city •gate
and despise[at] the one who speaks
with integrity.
11 Therefore, because you trample on
the poor[au]
and exact a grain tax from him,
you will never live in the houses
of cut stone[av]
you have built;
you will never drink the wine
from the lush vineyards

[a]**4:7** Lv 26:18-19; Jl 1:10-12 [b]**4:8** 1Kg 18:5; Jr 14:4 [c]Ezk 4:16; Hg 1:6 [d]Jr 3:7 [e]**4:9** Dt 28:22; Hg 2:17 [f]Jl 1:4; Am 7:1-2 [g]Dt 28:38-42; Jl 1:4-7,12 [h]Jr 3:10 [i]**4:10** Ex 11:4-5; Dt 28:27,60 [j]Jr 11:22; 18:21; 48:15 [k]2Kg 13:3,7 [l]Is 34:3 [m]Is 9:13 [n]**4:11** Gn 19:24-25 [o]Zch 3:1-2 [p]Is 9:13 [q]**4:12** Is 32:11; 64:2; Jr 5:22 [r]**4:13** Jb 38:4-7; Ps 65:6; Is 40:12 [s]Ps 135:7 [t]Ps 139:2; Dn 2:30 [u]Mc 1:3 [v]Am 5:8-9,27; 9:5-6 [w]**5:1** Jr 7:29; 9:10,17; Ezk 19:1 [x]**5:2** Jr 14:17; 31:4,21 [y]Am 8:14 [z]Is 51:18 [aa]**5:3** Is 6:13 [ab]Am 6:9 [ac]**5:4** Dt 4:29; 32:46-47 [ad]**5:5** 1Kg 12:28-29 [ae]1Sm 7:16; 11:14 [af]Gn 21:31-33 [ag]**5:6** Is 55:3,6-7 [ah]Dt 4:24; 32:22; Heb 12:29 [ai]Is 33:14; 66:24; Jr 4:4 [aj]**5:7** Am 6:12 [ak]**5:8** Jb 9:9; 38:31 [al]Gn 1:2-3; Jb 38:12 [am]Am 8:9 [an]Ps 104:6-9; Jr 10:13 [ao]Jb 36:27-30 [ap]Am 4:13; 9:5-6 [aq]**5:9** Is 29:5 [ar]Mc 5:11 [as]**5:10** Is 29:21 [at]Is 59:15 [au]**5:11** Am 3:9; 8:6; Jms 1:27 [av]Am 3:15; 6:11

[A]**4:11** Lit *God* [B]**4:13** Or *his* [C]**5:8** Or *turns the shadow of death* [D]**5:9** Hb obscure [E]**5:9** Or *stronghold*

you have planted.[a]
12 For I know your crimes are many
and your sins innumerable.
They oppress the righteous,[b]
take a bribe,
and deprive the poor of justice[c]
at the gates.
13 Therefore, the wise person
will keep silent[A,d]
at such a time,
for the days are evil.
14 Seek good and not evil
so that you may live,
and the LORD, the God of ˙Hosts,

[a]5:11 Dt 28:30; Mc 6:15; Zph 1:13 [b]5:12 Is 1:23; 5:23 [c]Am 2:6-7 [d]5:13 Ec 3:7; Hs 4:4

Justice and the Mission of God

Linda Bergquist

The most complete perspective of justice in the Bible is presented in Amos 5. A humble goat herder with no credentials as a prophet seemed an unlikely candidate to confront wealthy Israelites about their sins of social injustice, but God chose Amos for the task. This was a time of national prosperity, and many owned fine homes and productive farmlands. God had always intended that His blessings be shared among all of His people, but now, the rich were shamelessly taking advantage of the poor. They took bribes, imposed unfair taxes, and took away what rightly belonged to the weak (vv. 11,12). God was angry and offended, so He sent Amos to warn the people and remind them about what really matters to Him.

Two Hebrew words that appear many times in the Old Testament are often linked together to refer to justice. These words, *mishpat* and *tsedeq*, are used in the same sentence twice in this chapter (vv. 7,24). *Mishpat*, also used in verse 15, is translated each time as "justice." It is used around 400 times in the Bible, and is even one of God's names, *Elohay Mishpat*, or God of Justice (Is 30:18). This means that it is within the Lord's nature and purposes to choose justice. *Mishpat* is tied into the Hebraic legal code, and means that the law of justice is both extended and applied evenly to everyone. Amos knew that people who are the most at risk and unprotected needed to be defended by God's loving justice, while offenders should all be punished fairly.

Tsedeq, translated righteousness in Amos 5, is connected to *mishpat*, but it means uprightness, doing what is right, or finding a way to make it right. It is used in reference to justice over 60 times in the Bible. Verses 7 and 24 are examples of the poetic tool of connecting parallel phrases for emphasis. Amos spoke about "Those who turn justice (*mishpat*) into wormwood (a bitter plant) and throw righteousness (*tsedeq*) to the ground" (v. 7). The two words are used together again in verse 24: "But let justice (*mishpat*) flow like water, and righteousness (*tsedeq*), like an unfailing stream." Amos grieved that so many people were disobeying God and disrespecting others. He called their injustice evil and told them that only if they repented and sought goodness, would they live (v. 14).

Amos also pointed out that all the while that the Israelites were living unjustly they continued to observe their religious ceremonies. God used strong words to describe how unacceptable their hypocrisy was to Him. He said that He hates, despises, will not accept, and has no regard for their religious rituals and that it was all just noise to Him (vv. 21-23). The sacrifice He really wants from His people is the sacrifice that comes from a regular lifestyle of practicing justice. Justice is not simply an add-on, a social program, or a missions activity. It is a reflection of God's character that is indispensable to God's mission on earth.

[A]5:13 Or *the prudent will perish*

will be with you,
as you have claimed.[a]
15 Hate evil and love good;[b]
establish justice in the gate.[c]
Perhaps the LORD, the God of Hosts,
will be gracious[d]
to the remnant of Joseph.[e]

16 Therefore Yahweh, the God of Hosts, the
Lord, says:

There will be wailing in all
the public squares;[f]
they will cry out in anguish[A] in all
the streets.
The farmer will be called on
to mourn,[g]
and professional mourners[B,h]
to wail.
17 There will be wailing in all
the vineyards,[i]
for I will pass among you.[j]
The LORD has spoken.

The Day of the LORD

18 Woe to you who long for the Day
of the LORD![k]
What will the Day of the LORD
be for you?
It will be darkness and not light.[l]
19 It will be like a man who flees
from a lion[m]
only to have a bear confront him.
He goes home and rests his hand
against the wall
only to have a snake bite him.
20 Won't the Day of the LORD
be darkness rather than light,[n]
even gloom without any brightness
in it?[o]
21 I hate, I despise your feasts![p]
I can't stand the stench
of your solemn assemblies.[q]
22 Even if you offer Me
your ·burnt offerings
and ·grain offerings,[r]
I will not accept them;[s]
I will have no regard
for your ·fellowship offerings
of fattened cattle.[t]
23 Take away from Me the noise
of your songs!
I will not listen to the music
of your harps.[u]
24 But let justice flow like water,
and righteousness,
like an unfailing stream.[v]

25 "House of Israel, was it sacrifices and
grain offerings that you presented to Me during the 40 years in the wilderness?[w] 26 But you
have taken up[C] Sakkuth[D,E] your king[F] and Kai-
wan[G] your star god, images you have made for
yourselves.[x] 27 So I will send you into exile beyond Damascus."[y] Yahweh, the God of Hosts,
is His name.[z] He has spoken.

Woe to the Complacent

6 Woe to those who are at ease in ·Zion[aa]
and to those who feel secure on the hill
of Samaria —
the notable people in this first
of the nations,
those the house of Israel comes to.
2 Cross over to Calneh[ab] and see;
go from there to great Hamath;[ac]
then go down to Gath[ad] of the Philistines.
Are you better than these kingdoms?
Is their territory larger than yours?
3 You dismiss any thought of the evil day[ae]
and bring in a reign of violence.[af]
4 They lie on beds inlaid with ivory,[ag]
sprawled out on their couches,[ah]
and dine on lambs from the flock[ai]
and calves from the stall.
5 They improvise songs[H] to the sound
of the harp[aj]
and invent[I] their own
musical instruments like David.[ak]
6 They drink wine by the bowlful[al]
and anoint themselves
with the finest oils
but do not grieve over the ruin
of Joseph.[am]
7 Therefore, they will now go into exile
as the first of the captives,[an]
and the feasting[ao] of those
who sprawl out
will come to an end.

[a]**5:14** Is 48:1-2
[b]**5:15** Rm 12:9
[c]Is 1:17
[d]Jl 2:14
[e]Mc 3:5,7-8
[f]**5:16** Jr 9:10,18-20; Am 8:3
[g]Jl 1:11
[h]Jr 9:17
[i]**5:17** Is 16:10; Jr 48:33
[j]Ex 12:12
[k]**5:18** Is 5:19; Jl 1:15; 2:1,11,31
[l]Is 5:30
[m]**5:19** Jb 20:24; Is 24:17; Jr 15:2-3
[n]**5:20** Is 13:10; Zph 1:15
[o]Jl 2:2; Zph 1:15
[p]**5:21** Is 1:11-16; 66:3; Am 6:8
[q]Lv 26:31; Jr 14:12; Hs 5:6
[r]**5:22** Mc 6:6-7
[s]Jr 14:12
[t]Lv 7:11-15
[u]**5:23** Is 5:12
[v]**5:21-24** Mc 6:6-8
[w]**5:25** Dt 32:17; Jos 24:14; Neh 9:18-21; Ac 7:42-43
[x]**5:26** Is 44:12-20
[y]**5:25-27** 2Kg 17:5-6; Ac 7:42-43
[z]**5:27** Am 4:13
[aa]**6:1** Is 32:9-11; Zph 1:12
[ab]**6:2** Gn 10:10; Is 10:9
[ac]1Kg 8:65; 2Kg 18:34; Is 10:9
[ad]1Sm 5:8; 2Ch 26:6
[ae]**6:3** Am 9:10
[af]Am 3:10
[ag]**6:4** Am 3:15
[ah]Am 3:12
[ai]Ezk 34:2-3
[aj]**6:5** Am 5:23; 8:10
[ak]1Ch 15:16
[al]**6:6** Am 2:8; 4:1
[am]Jr 8:21; Lm 2:11
[an]**6:7** Am 7:11,17
[ao]1Kg 20:16-21; Dn 5:4-6,30

A**5:16** Lit *will say, "Alas! Alas!"* B**5:16** Lit *and those skilled in lamentation* C**5:26** Or *you will lift up* D**5:26** LXX, Sym, Syr, Vg read *the tent*; Ac 7:43 E**5:26** Probably a Mesopotamian war god also called Adar or Ninurta F**5:26** LXX reads *up the tent of Molech and Rephan*; Ac 7:43 G**5:26** Probably a Mesopotamian god identified with Saturn H**6:5** Hb obscure I**6:5** Or *compose on*

Israel's Pride Judged

8 The Lord God has sworn by Himself[a] — this is the declaration of ˙Yahweh, the God of ˙Hosts:

I loathe Jacob's pride[b]
and hate his citadels,[c]
so I will hand over the city[d]
and everything in it.

9 And if there are 10 men left in one house, they will die.[e] 10 A close relative[A] and burner[B,f] will remove his corpse[C] from the house. He will call to someone in the inner recesses of the house, "Any more with you?"

That person will reply, "None."

Then he will say, "Silence, because Yahweh's name must not be invoked."[g]

11 For the Lord commands:

The large house will be smashed
to pieces,
and the small house to rubble.[h]

12 Do horses gallop on the cliffs;
does anyone plow there with oxen?[D]
Yet you have turned justice
into poison[i]
and the fruit of righteousness
into ˙wormwood[j] —
13 you who rejoice over Lo-debar[k]
and say, "Didn't we capture Karnaim
for ourselves by our own strength?"[l]
14 But look, I am raising up a nation
against you, house of Israel[m] —
this is the declaration of the Lord,
the God of Hosts —
and they will oppress you
from the entrance of Hamath[E,n]
to the Brook of the ˙Arabah.[F]

First Vision: Locusts

7 The Lord God showed me this: He was forming a swarm of locusts[o] at the time the spring crop first began to sprout — after the cutting of the king's hay. 2 When the locusts finished eating the vegetation of the land,[p] I said, "Lord God, please forgive![q] How will Jacob survive since he is so small?"[r]

3 The Lord relented concerning this.[s] "It will not happen," He said.

Second Vision: Fire

4 The Lord God showed me this: The Lord God was calling for a judgment by fire.[t] It consumed the great deep and devoured the land. 5 Then I said, "Lord God, please stop![u] How will Jacob survive since he is so small?"

6 The Lord relented concerning this.[v] "This will not happen either," said the Lord God.

Third Vision: A Plumb Line

7 He showed me this: The Lord was standing there by a vertical wall with a plumb line in His hand. 8 The Lord asked me, "What do you see, Amos?"[w]

I replied, "A plumb line."

Then the Lord said, "I am setting a plumb line among My people Israel;[x] I will no longer spare them:[y]

9 Isaac's ˙high places[z] will be deserted,
and Israel's sanctuaries
will be in ruins;[aa]
I will rise up
against the house of Jeroboam
with a sword."

Amaziah's Opposition

10 Amaziah the priest[ab] of Bethel sent word to Jeroboam king of Israel, saying, "Amos has conspired against you[ac] right here in the house of Israel. The land cannot endure all his words, 11 for Amos has said this: 'Jeroboam will die by the sword, and Israel will certainly go into exile from its homeland.'"[ad]

12 Then Amaziah said to Amos, "Go away, you seer![ae] Flee to the land of Judah. Earn your living[G] and give your prophecies there, 13 but don't ever prophesy[af] at Bethel again, for it is the king's sanctuary[ag] and a royal temple."

14 So Amos answered Amaziah, "I was[H] not a prophet or the son of a prophet;[I,ah] rather, I was[H] a herdsman,[ai] and I took care of sycamore figs. 15 But the Lord took me from following the flock[aj] and said to me, 'Go, prophesy to My people Israel.'"[ak]

16 Now hear the word of the Lord. You say:

Do not prophesy[al] against Israel;
do not preach[am] against the house
of Isaac.

[a] 6:8 Gn 22:16; Jr 22:5; 51:14
[b] Lv 26:30; Dt 32:19; Ps 106:40
[c] Am 3:10-11
[d] Hs 11:6
[e] 6:9 Am 5:3
[f] 6:10 1Sm 31:12; 2Ch 16:14; Jr 34:5
[g] Is 48:1; Jr 44:26; Hs 4:15
[h] 6:11 Am 1:1; 9:9
[i] 6:12 1Kg 21:7-13; Is 59:13-14
[j] Is 5:20; Am 5:7; Rv 8:11
[k] 6:13 Jb 8:14-15; Ps 2:2-4; Lk 12:19-20
[l] Ps 75:4; Is 28:14-15
[m] 6:14 Am 3:11
[n] Nm 34:7-8; 2Kg 14:25
[o] 7:1 Ex 10:12-15; Dt 28:38,42; Jl 1:4
[p] 7:2 Ex 10:15
[q] Jr 14:7,20-21; Ezk 9:8; 11:13
[r] Is 37:4; Jr 42:2
[s] 7:3 Jr 26:19; Hs 11:8
[t] 7:4 Am 1:3–2:5
[u] 7:5 Ps 85:4; Jl 2:17
[v] 7:6 Ps 106:45; Jnh 3:10
[w] 7:8 Jr 1:11; Am 8:2
[x] Is 28:17; 34:11; Lm 2:8
[y] Am 8:2
[z] 7:9 2Kg 17:9-13; Hs 10:8
[aa] Lv 26:31; Is 63:18; Jr 51:51
[ab] 7:10 1Kg 12:31-32; 13:33
[ac] Jr 26:8-11; 38:4
[ad] 7:11 Am 5:27
[ae] 7:12 Mt 8:34
[af] 7:13 Am 2:12; Ac 4:18
[ag] 1Kg 12:29; Am 7:9
[ah] 7:14 2Kg 2:3; 4:38; 2Ch 19:2
[ai] Am 1:1
[aj] 7:15 2Sm 7:8
[ak] Jr 1:7; Ezk 2:3-4
[al] 7:16 Am 2:12
[am] Mc 2:6

A 6:10 Lit *His uncle* B 6:10 A burner of incense, a memorial fire, or a body; Hb obscure C 6:10 Lit *remove bones* D 6:12 Some emend to *plow the sea* E 6:14 Or *from Lebo-hamath* F 6:14 Probably the Valley of Zared at the southeast end of the Dead Sea G 7:12 Lit *Eat bread* H 7:14 Or *am* I 7:14 = a prophet's disciple or a member of a prophetic guild

[17]Therefore, this is what the LORD says:

Your wife will be a prostitute
in the city,[a]
your sons and daughters will fall
by the sword,[b]
and your land will be divided up
with a measuring line.
You yourself will die on pagan[A] soil,[c]
and Israel will certainly go into exile[d]
from its homeland.

Fourth Vision: A Basket of Summer Fruit

8 The Lord GOD showed me this: A basket
of summer fruit. [2]He asked me, "What do
you see, Amos?"[e]
I replied, "A basket of summer fruit."[f]
The LORD said to me, "The end has come
for My people Israel;[g] I will no longer spare
them.[h] [3]In that day the temple[B] songs[i] will
become wailing"[j]—this is the Lord GOD's
declaration. "Many dead bodies, thrown everywhere![k] Silence!"[l]

4 Hear this, you who trample
on the needy[m]
and do away with the poor of the land,[n]
5 asking, "When will the New Moon
be over
so we may sell grain,[o]
and the Sabbath,
so we may market wheat?[p]
We can reduce the measure
while increasing the price[C]
and cheat with dishonest scales.[q]
6 We can buy the poor with silver
and the needy for a pair of sandals[r]
and even sell the chaff!"

[7]The LORD has sworn[s] by the Pride of Jacob:[D,t]

I will never forget all their deeds.[u]
8 Because of this, won't the land quake[v]
and all who dwell in it mourn?[w]
All of it will rise like the Nile;[x]
it will surge and then subside
like the Nile in Egypt.[y]

9 And in that day—
this is the declaration
of the Lord GOD—
I will make the sun go down at noon;[z]
I will darken the land in the daytime.[aa]
10 I will turn your feasts into mourning[ab]
and all your songs into lamentation;[ac]
I will cause everyone[E]
to wear ·sackcloth[ad]
and every head to be shaved.[ae]
I will make that grief
like mourning for an only son[af]
and its outcome like a bitter day.

11 Hear this! The days are coming—
this is the declaration
of the Lord GOD—
when I will send a famine
through the land:
not a famine of bread or a thirst
for water,
but of hearing the words of the LORD.[ag]
12 People will stagger from sea to sea
and roam from north to east,
seeking the word of the LORD,[ah]
but they will not find it.
13 In that day
the beautiful young women,[ai]
the young men also, will faint
from thirst.[aj]
14 Those who swear by the ·guilt
of Samaria[ak]
and say, "As your god lives, Dan,"[al]
or "As the way[F,G] of Beer-sheba lives"[am]—
they will fall, never to rise again.[an]

Fifth Vision: The LORD beside the Altar

9 I saw the Lord standing beside the altar,[ao]
and He said:

Strike the capitals of the pillars[ap]
so that the thresholds shake;
knock them down on the heads of all
the people.
Then I will kill the rest of them
with the sword.[aq]
None of those who flee will get away;[ar]
none of the fugitives will escape.
2 If they dig down to ·Sheol,[as]
from there My hand will take them;
if they climb up to heaven,[at]
from there I will bring them down.
3 If they hide themselves

[a]**7:17** Hs 4:13-14 [b]Jr 14:16 [c]2Kg 17:6; Ezk 4:13; Hs 9:3 [d]Jr 36:29-31 [e]**8:2** Am 7:8 [f]Jr 24:3 [g]Ezk 7:2-3,6 [h]Am 7:8 [i]**8:3** Am 5:23; 6:4-5 [j]Am 5:16 [k]Is 34:3; Jr 33:5; Nah 3:3 [l]Am 6:10 [m]**8:4** Am 2:7; 5:11-12 [n]Is 10:2 [o]**8:5** Nm 28:11; 2Kg 4:23 [p]Ex 31:13-17 [q]Dt 25:13-15; Pr 20:23; Hs 12:7 [r]**8:6** Am 2:6 [s]**8:7** Am 4:2; 6:8 [t]Dt 33:26,29; Ps 47:4 [u]Ps 10:11; Hs 7:2; 8:13 [v]**8:8** Ps 18:7; 60:2; Is 5:25; Am 1:1 [w]Hs 4:3 [x]Jr 46:7-8 [y]Am 9:5 [z]**8:9** Is 13:10; Ezk 32:7; Jl 2:10,31 [aa]Is 59:9-10; Am 4:13; 5:8; Mt 27:45 [ab]**8:10** Jb 20:23; Am 5:21 [ac]Lm 5:15; Hs 2:11; Jms 4:9 [ad]Ezk 7:18 [ae]Is 22:12; Jr 48:37; Ezk 7:18 [af]Zch 12:10-14 [ag]**8:9-11** Mc 3:6-7 [ah]**8:12** Ezk 20:3,31 [ai]**8:13** Lm 1:18; 2:21 [aj]Is 41:17; Hs 2:3 [ak]**8:14** Hs 8:5 [al]1Kg 12:28-29 [am]Am 5:5 [an]Am 5:2; Jr 25:27 [ao]**9:1** Am 3:14 [ap]Zph 2:14 [aq]Jos 5:13-15; Am 7:9,17 [ar]Jr 11:11 [as]**9:2** Ps 139:8 [at]Jr 51:53; Ob 4

[A]**7:17** Lit *unclean* [B]**8:3** Or *palace* [C]**8:5** Lit *reduce the ephah and make the shekel great* [D]**8:7** = the LORD or the promised land [E]**8:10** Lit *every loin* [F]**8:14** LXX reads *god* [G]**8:14** Or *power*

on the top of Carmel,
from there I will track them down[a]
and seize them;
if they conceal themselves
from My sight on the sea floor,[b]
from there I will command
the sea serpent to bite them.[c]
4 And if they are driven
by their enemies into captivity,[d]
from there I will command
the sword to kill them.[e]
I will fix My eyes on them
for harm and not for good.[f]
5 The Lord, the GOD of ·Hosts —
He touches the earth;[g]
it melts, and all who dwell in it mourn;
all of it rises like the Nile
and subsides like the Nile of Egypt.[h]
6 He builds His upper chambers
in the heavens[i]
and lays the foundation of His vault
on the earth.[j]
He summons the waters of the sea
and pours them out on the face
of the earth.[k]
·Yahweh is His name.[l]

Announcement of Judgment

7 Israelites, are you not like the ·Cushites
to Me?[m]
This is the LORD's declaration.
Didn't I bring Israel from the land
of Egypt,
the Philistines from Caphtor,[A,n]
and the Arameans from Kir?[o]
8 Look, the eyes of the Lord GOD
are on the sinful kingdom,[p]
and I will destroy it
from the face of the earth.[q]
However, I will not totally destroy
the house of Jacob[r] —
this is the LORD's declaration —
9 for I am about to give the command,
and I will shake the house of Israel[s]
among all the nations,
as one shakes a sieve,
but not a pebble
will fall to the ground.
10 All the sinners among My people[t]
who say: "Disaster will never overtake[B]
or confront us,"[u]
will die by the sword.

Announcement of Restoration

11 In that day
I will restore the fallen booth[v]
of David:[w]
I will repair its gaps,
restore its ruins,[x]
and rebuild it as in the days of old,[y]
12 so that they may possess
the remnant of Edom[z]
and all the nations
that are called by My name[C,aa] —
this is the LORD's declaration —
He will do this.

13 Hear this! The days are coming —
this is the LORD's declaration —
when the plowman will overtake
the reaper[ab]
and the one who treads grapes,
the sower of seed.
The mountains will drip
with sweet wine,
and all the hills will flow with it.[ac]
14 I will restore the fortunes
of My people Israel.[D,ad]
They will rebuild and occupy
ruined cities,[ae]
plant vineyards and drink their wine,
make gardens and eat their produce.[af]
15 I will plant them on their land,
and they will never again be uprooted
from the land I have given them.[ag]
Yahweh your God has spoken.

[a]9:3 Jb 34:22; Ps 139:9-10 [b]Jnh 2:2-6 [c]Is 27:1 [d]9:4 Lv 26:33 [e]9:2-4 Jb 34:21-22; Ps 139:7-12; Jr 23:24 [f]9:4 Jr 21:10; 44:27 [g]9:5 Ps 104:32; 144:5; Is 64:1 [h]Am 8:8 [i]9:6 Ps 104:3,13 [j]Ps 102:25; Is 48:13; 51:13 [k]Ps 104:6 [l]Am 4:13; 5:8-9 [m]9:7 2Ch 14:9,12; Is 20:4; 43:3 [n]Dt 2:23; Jr 47:4 [o]2Kg 16:9; Is 22:6 [p]9:8 Am 9:4 [q]Am 3:12 [r]Jr 5:10; 30:11; 31:35-36; Jl 2:32 [s]9:9 Is 30:28; Lk 22:31 [t]9:10 Is 33:14; Zch 13:8 [u]Jr 5:12; 23:17; Am 6:3 [v]9:11 Lv 23:42-43; 2Sm 11:11; 1Kg 20:12; Is 4:6 [w]2Sm 7:11-16; Jr 23:5; Ezk 34:23-24; Zch 9:9-10; Lk 1:32; Rv 5:5 [x]Is 44:26 [y]Is 63:11; Jr 46:26 [z]9:12 Ezk 36:5; Ob 21 [aa]9:11-12 Is 43:6-7; Mal 1:11; Ac 15:15-18 [ab]9:13 Lv 26:5 [ac]Jl 2:24; 3:18 [ad]9:14 Dt 30:3; Jr 31:23; 32:42-44 [ae]Jr 30:18; 33:10-11 [af]Is 65:21; Jr 31:5 [ag]9:15 2Sm 7:10; Jr 24:6

A9:7 Probably Crete B9:10 Or *You will not let disaster come near* C9:12 LXX reads *so that the remnant of man and all the nations . . . may seek Me*; Ac 15:17 D9:14 Or *restore My people Israel from captivity*

AUTHOR: Obadiah

DATE: Obadiah wrote his book between 585 and 550 B.C.—not long after the fall of Jerusalem but before the fall of Edom

Obadiah is the shortest book in the Old Testament. Nothing is known about the author outside this book. No explicit information is given about the time of writing, but most consider Obadiah 10-14 is best explained against the background of the fall of Jerusalem to the Babylonians in 586 B.C. Since the book prophesies the desolation of Edom, which probably occurred late in the sixth century B.C., Obadiah would have been written about the middle of that century.

Most of Obadiah's prophecy addresses Edom, the nation that stemmed from Esau, the brother of Jacob. Though Edom and Judah were neighbors, their relationship was never cordial, in keeping with the struggles between Esau and Jacob.

OBADIAH

As with the other Minor Prophets, the message of Obadiah is one of judgment, and it is expressed with detail and force. Addressing the Edomites directly, the prophet chides them for the pride that kept them from recognizing their misery. They believed themselves to be a strong nation safe in their highlands. But they would soon be invaded and devastated because of the way they treated the people of Jacob. When Judah was conquered, Edom did not come to its aid, but rather joined the enemies of God's people. The Edomites proudly marched through Jerusalem's gates and grabbed their share of the spoil. When the inhabitants of Jerusalem were sold down the roads around the city, the Edomites conveniently made bids for slaves.

God remembers all. It is a fearful thing to oppose the mission of God. As the book of Obadiah shows, the punishment fits the crime. "As you have done, so it will be done to you" (v. 15). "The house of Esau will be stubble" (v. 18), swiftly consumed by fire. But while proud Edom reaps a punishment, a humbled Judah will be blessed: "But there will be a deliverance on Mount Zion, and it will be holy" (v. 17). Once again the Lord establishes that godly holiness is the only foundation for a nation's well-being.

The vision of Obadiah.

Edom's Certain Judgment

This is what the Lord GOD has said about Edom:[a]

We have heard a message
from the LORD;[b]
a messenger has been sent[c]
among the nations:
"Rise up,[d] and let us go to war
against her."[A]
2 Look, I will make you insignificant[e]
among the nations;
you will be deeply despised.
3 Your presumptuous heart
has deceived you,[f]
you who live in clefts of the rock[B,C,g]
in your home on the heights,
who say to yourself,
"Who can bring me down
to the ground?"[h]
4 Though you seem to soar[D]
like an eagle[i]
and make your nest among the stars,[j]
even from there I will bring you down.
This is the LORD's declaration.
5 If thieves came to you,[k]
if marauders by night —
how ravaged you would be! —
wouldn't they steal only
what they wanted?
If grape pickers came to you,
wouldn't they leave some grapes?[l]
6 How Esau will be pillaged,[m]
his hidden treasures searched out![n]
7 Everyone who has a treaty with you[o]
will drive you to the border;
everyone at peace with you
will deceive and conquer you.
Those who eat your bread[p]
will set[E] a trap for you.
He will be unaware of it.[q]
8 In that day —
this is the LORD's declaration —
will I not eliminate the wise ones
of Edom[r]
and those who understand
from the hill country of Esau?
9 Teman,[F,s] your warriors[t] will be terrified
so that everyone
from the hill country of Esau
will be destroyed by slaughter.[u]

Edom's Sins against Judah

10 You will be covered with shame
and destroyed forever
because of violence done
to your brother Jacob.[v]
11 On the day you stood aloof,[w]
on the day strangers captured
his wealth,[G]
while foreigners entered his •gate
and cast lots for Jerusalem,[x]
you were just like one of them.[y]
12 Do not[H] gloat over your brother[z]
in the day of his calamity;
do not rejoice over the people
of Judah[aa]
in the day of their destruction;
do not boastfully mock[I,ab]
in the day of distress.[ac]
13 Do not enter the gate of My people
in the day of their disaster.[ad]
Yes, you — do not gloat
over their misery
in the day of their disaster
and do not appropriate
their possessions[ae]
in the day of their disaster.
14 Do not stand at the crossroads[J,af]
to cut off their fugitives,
and do not hand over their survivors
in the day of distress.

Judgment of the Nations

15 For the Day of the LORD[ag] is near,
against all the nations.[ah]
As you have done,[ai] so it will be done
to you;
what you deserve will return
on your own head.[aj]
16 As you have drunk
on My holy mountain,[ak]
so all the nations will
drink continually.[al]
They will drink and gulp down
and be as though they had never been.

[a]**1** Gn 25:30; Ps 137:7; Is 21:11-12; 34:1-17; 63:1-6; Ezk 25:12-14; Am 1:11-12; Mal 1:2-5
[b]**1-4** Jr 49:14-16
[c]**1** Is 18:2; 30:4
[d]Jr 6:4-5
[e]**2** Nm 24:18; Is 23:9
[f]**3** Is 16:6
[g]2Kg 14:7; 2Ch 25:12
[h]Is 14:13-15
[i]**4** Jb 20:6-7; Hab 2:9
[j]Is 14:12-15
[k]**5** Jr 49:9
[l]Lv 19:10; 25:5,11
[m]**6** Jr 49:10
[n]Mal 1:2-3
[o]**7** Ps 55:20; Jr 30:14; Am 1:9
[p]Ps 41:9
[q]Jr 49:7
[r]**8** Jb 4:1; 5:12-14
[s]**9** Gn 36:11; 1Ch 1:45; Jb 2:11; Hab 3:3
[t]Jr 49:22
[u]Is 34:5-8; 63:1-3; Jr 49:7,20; Ezk 25:13; Am 1:12; Ob 5
[v]**10** Ezk 25:12-14; Jl 3:19; Am 1:11
[w]**11** Ps 83:5-6; 137:7; Am 1:6,9
[x]Jl 3:3; Nah 3:10
[y]2Ch 21:17; Ezk 35:10
[z]**12** Mc 4:11; 7:10
[aa]Ps 83:1-6; 137:7-9; Lm 4:21-22; Ezk 35:15; 36:5
[ab]Ps 31:18; Ezk 35:12
[ac]Gn 35:3; Ps 50:15; Jr 16:19
[ad]**13** Ezk 35:5
[ae]Ezk 35:10; 36:2-3
[af]**14** Is 16:3-4
[ag]**15** Jl 1:15; 2:1,11,31; Am 5:18,20
[ah]Is 13:6; Jl 3:14; Zph 1:7,14
[ai]Jr 50:29; 51:56
[aj]Jr 50:15; Ezk 35:11
[ak]**16** Jr 49:12
[al]Is 51:22-23

[A]**1** = Edom [B]**3** Or *in Sela*; probably = Petra [C]**3** Probably Petra [D]**4** Or *to build high* [E]**7** Some LXX mss, Sym, Tg, Vg; MT reads *They will set your bread as* [F]**9** = a region or city in Edom [G]**11** Or *forces* [H]**12-14** Or *You should not* throughout vv. 12-14 [I]**12** Lit *not make your mouth big* [J]**14** Hb obscure

17 But there will be a deliverance
on Mount ·Zion,[a]
and it will be holy;[b]
the house of Jacob will dispossess[c]
those who dispossessed them.[A,d]
18 Then the house of Jacob will be
a blazing fire,[e]
and the house of Joseph,
a burning flame,
but the house of Esau will be stubble;
Jacob[B] will set them on fire
and consume Edom.[C]
Therefore no survivor will remain[f]
of the house of Esau,
for the LORD has spoken.

Future Blessing for Israel

19 People from the ·Negev will possess[g]
the hill country of Esau;[h]
those from the Judean foothills
will possess
the land of the Philistines.[i]
They[D] will possess
the territories of Ephraim
and Samaria,[j]
while Benjamin will possess Gilead.
20 The exiles of the Israelites who are
in Halah[E]
and who are among the Canaanites
as far as Zarephath[k]
as well as the exiles of Jerusalem
who are in Sepharad
will possess the cities
of the Negev.[l]
21 Saviors[F] will ascend Mount Zion[m]
to rule over the hill country
of Esau,
but the kingdom will be the LORD's.[n]

[a]17 Is 4:2-3 [b]16-17 Is 66:20; Jl 2:32 [c]17 Is 14:1-2; Am 9:11-15 [d]Ezk 36:2-5 [e]18 Is 5:24; 9:18-19; Am 1:12; Zch 12:6 [f]Jr 11:23 [g]19 Is 11:14 [h]Am 9:11-12 [i]Is 11:14 [j]Jr 31:5; 32:44 [k]20 1Kg 17:9-10; Lk 4:26 [l]Jr 32:44; 33:13 [m]21 Neh 9:27; Is 4:5; 18:7; 24:23; Dn 2:44; Mc 4:7 [n]Ps 22:28; 47:7-9; 67:4; Zch 14:9

[A]17 DSS, LXX, Syr, Vg, Tg; MT reads *Jacob will possess its inheritance* [B]18 Lit *they* [C]18 Lit *them* [D]19 = The house of Jacob [E]20 Or *of this host of the Israelites*; Hb obscure [F]21 Or *Those who have been delivered*

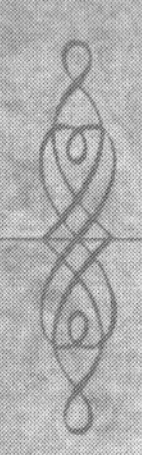

AUTHOR: Jonah

DATE: During the reign of Jeroboam II (around 793–753 B.C.); Jonah could have gone to Nineveh at any point during Jeroboam's reign or shortly after the king died

The book of Jonah constitutes a change of pace. Instead of a prophecy addressed to a specific nation or nations, the book features a dramatic episode in the prophet's life—one that many learn about in Sunday school. This little book was written as a third person account; only Jonah's prayer in the second chapter is a first person account. It is possible that he recorded his own experiences later; it is also possible, as some Bible scholars think, that another scribe recorded them.

JONAH

Jonah hailed from Gath-hepher in Galilee in the northern kingdom of Israel (see 2Kg 14:25). This prophecy was written as a historical account. Some of the main events are clearly miraculous. Some commentators believe Jonah's prophecy should be read as an allegorical lesson of God's mission in the ancient world. However, in Matthew 12:39-41, Jesus refers to Jonah's narrative as actual history. From the biblical perspective it is no surprise to see God back His mission with signs and wonders.

The book of Jonah is also a highly remarkable prophecy for its content. Here the Spirit lays out some challenging realities which are central to the mission of the church of all ages:

1. Though much of God's mission was initially limited to the nation of Israel, He is the God of all nations.

2. God is as much concerned about the salvation of the world's population as He is about the salvation of His ancient covenant people.

3. Israel has a responsibility toward its neighboring nations to share God's Word.

4. The message of grace is powerful in leading people to repentance.

5. God's children are not always His best representatives. Sent to preach a message of destruction to the people of Nineveh, Jonah chose to run in the opposite direction. But Jonah had a motive. Nineveh was the capital of the Assyrians—the enemies of Israel. The Assyrians were known for their cruelty. Jonah knew that a compassionate God would rather warn than destroy. And as a result of Jonah's curt preaching, the whole city repents!

The closing chapter is devoted to God's pastoral ministry to Jonah. Jonah's priorities need drastic revision. Personal comfort seems more important to him than the salvation of a large community of people. In the concluding verse God eloquently corrects Jonah and encourages the readers through the ages: "Should I not care about the great city of Nineveh, which has more than 120,000 people who cannot distinguish between their right and their left, as well as many animals?" (4:11).

Jonah's Flight

1 The word of the LORD came to Jonah son
of Amittai:[a] 2"Get up![b] Go to the great city[c]
of Nineveh[d] and preach against it,[e] because
their wickedness[f] has confronted[A] Me."[g]
3However, Jonah got up to flee to Tarshish[h]
from the LORD's presence.[i] He went down[j] to
Joppa[k] and found a ship going to Tarshish. He
paid the fare and went down into it to go with
them to Tarshish, from the LORD's presence.
4Then the LORD hurled[l] a violent wind on
the sea,[m] and such a violent storm arose on
the sea that the ship threatened to break
apart. 5The sailors were afraid, and each cried
out to his god.[n] They threw the ship's cargo
into the sea to lighten the load.[o] Meanwhile,
Jonah had gone down to the lowest part of
the vessel and had stretched out and fallen
into a deep sleep.[p]
6The captain approached him and said,
"What are you doing sound asleep? Get up!
Call to your god.[B,q] Maybe this god will consider us,[r] and we won't perish."
7"Come on!" the sailors said to each other.
"Let's cast lots.[s] Then we'll know who is to
blame for this trouble we're in." So they cast
lots, and the lot singled out Jonah.[t] 8Then
they said to him, "Tell us who is to blame for
this trouble we're in.[u] What is your business[v]
and where are you from? What is your country and what people are you from?"
9He answered them, "I'm a Hebrew.[w] I worship[C] ·Yahweh,[x] the God of the heavens,[y] who
made the sea[z] and the dry land."
10Then the men were even more afraid and
said to him, "What is this you've done?" The
men knew he was fleeing from the LORD's
presence,[aa] because he had told them. 11So
they said to him, "What should we do to you
to calm this sea that's against us?" For the sea
was getting worse and worse.
12He answered them, "Pick me up and
throw me into the sea[D] so it may quiet down
for you, for I know that I'm to blame[ab] for this
violent storm that is against you." 13Neverthe-
less, the men rowed hard to get back to dry
land, but they couldn't because the sea was
raging against them more and more.
14So they called out to the LORD:[ac] "Please,
Yahweh, don't let us perish because of this
man's life, and don't charge us with innocent
blood! For You, Yahweh, have done just as You
pleased."[ad] 15Then they picked up Jonah and
threw him into the sea, and the sea stopped
its raging.[ae] 16The men ·feared the LORD[af] even
more, and they offered a sacrifice to the LORD
and made vows.[ag]
17[E]Now the LORD had appointed a huge
fish[ah] to swallow Jonah, and Jonah was in[F] the
fish three days and three nights.[ai]

[a]1:1 2Kg 14:25; Jnh 3:1; Mt 12:39-41; 16:4; Lk 11:29-30,32 [b]1:2 Nm 22:20; Dt 10:11; Jos 7:10 [c]Jnh 3:2-3; 4:11 [d]Gn 10:11; 2Kg 19:36; Is 37:37; Nah 1:1; Zph 2:13 [e]Dt 15:9; 24:15; 2Kg 23:17; Is 58:1 [f]Jnh 3:8 [g]Gn 18:20; Hs 7:2 [h]1:3 Is 23:1,6,10; Jr 10:9 [i]Gn 4:16; Ps 139:7,9-10 [j]Jnh 2:6 [k]2Ch 2:16; Ezr 3:7; Ac 9:36,43 [l]1:4 1Sm 18:11; 20:33; Is 22:17; Jr 22:26-28 [m]Ps 107:25-28; 135:7 [n]1:5 1Kg 18:26 [o]Ac 27:18-19,38 [p]Gn 2:21; 15:12; Jdg 4:21; Dn 8:18; 10:9; 1Th 5:6 [q]1:6 Ps 107:28 [r]2Sm 12:22; Am 5:15; Jnh 3:9 [s]1:7 Jos 7:14-18; 1Sm 10:20-21; 14:41-42; Pr 16:33; Ac 1:23-26 [t]Nm 32:23; Pr 16:33 [u]1:8 Jos 7:19; 1Sm 14:43 [v]Gn 47:3; 1Sm 30:13 [w]1:9 Gn 14:13; 39:14; Ex 1:15; 2:13; 1Sm 4:6 [x]2Kg 17:25,28,32-33 [y]Gn 24:3,7; Ezr 1:2; Neh 1:4; Ps 136:26; Dn 2:18 [z]Neh 9:6; Ps 95:5; 146:6 [aa]1:10 Jb 27:22; Jnh 1:3 [ab]1:12 2Sm 24:17; 1Ch 21:17 [ac]1:14 Ps 107:28 [ad]Ps 51:18; 115:3; 135:6; Pr 21:1; Is 55:11; Lm 3:37-39; Dn 4:34-35; Mt 11:25 [ae]1:15 Ps 65:7; 93:3-4; 107:29 [af]1:16 Is 59:19; Mc 7:17; Zph 2:11; Mal 1:14; Lk 8:22-25 [ag]Ps 50:14; 66:13-14; 76:11; 116:17-18 [ah]1:17 Gn 9:2; Nm 11:22; 1Kg 4:33; Ps 8:8 [ai]Mt 12:40; 16:4; Lk 11:29-30; Jn 11:6,14

GOD WHO SENDS

The Sending and the Genius of the Biblical Message

The theological insight gained from the sending texts, therefore, is definitive in its nature, ultimate in its implication, and total in its impact. These passages not only relate vitally to the mainstream of the essential redemptive message of the Scriptures but they also provide significant insight into the unique biblical understanding of fundamental philosophical questions. Moreover, they contain a wealth of theological understanding relating to the broad spectrum of total biblical concern, both at the point of meaning and of function. The chief significance of the language of the sending is in the fact that this language of sending is necessary to convey explicitly the theological ideas which are inherent in the biblical message. The concept of the sending is, therefore, inherent in the very nature of the unique character of biblical revelation.

(DUBOSE, 54)

[A]1:2 Or *has come up to* [B]1:6 Or *God* [C]1:9 Or *fear* [D]1:12 Lit *sea that's against you* [E]1:17 Jnh 2:1 in Hb [F]1:17 Lit *in the belly of*

Jonah's Prayer

2 Jonah prayed to the LORD his God from
inside[A] the fish:[a]

2 I called to the LORD
in my distress,[b]
and He answered me.
I cried out for help in the belly
of ·Sheol;[c]
You heard my voice.[d]
3 You threw me into the depths,[e]
into the heart of the seas,[f]
and the current[B] overcame me.
All Your breakers and Your billows
swept over me.[g]
4 But I said: I have been banished[h]
from Your sight,[i]
yet I will look once more[C]
toward Your holy temple.[j]
5 The waters engulfed me up
to the neck;[D,k]
the watery depths overcame me;
seaweed was wrapped around my head.[l]
6 I sank to the foundations
of the mountains;[m]
the earth with its prison bars closed
behind me forever![n]
But You raised my life[o] from the ·Pit,
LORD my God![p]
7 As my life was fading away,[q]
I remembered ·Yahweh.[r]
My prayer came to You,[s]
to Your holy temple.[t]
8 Those who cling
to worthless idols[u]
forsake faithful love,[v]
9 but as for me, I will sacrifice[w]
to You
with a voice of thanksgiving.[x]
I will fulfill[y] what I have vowed.
Salvation[E] is from the LORD![z]

10 Then the LORD commanded the fish,[aa]
and it vomited Jonah onto dry land.

Jonah's Preaching

3 Then the word of the LORD came to Jonah
a second time:[ab] 2 "Get up! Go to the great
city of Nineveh[ac] and preach[ad] the message
that I tell you." 3 So Jonah got up and went to
Nineveh according to the LORD's command.
Now Nineveh was an extremely large
city,[F,ae] a three-day walk.[G] 4 Jonah set out on
the first day of his walk in the city and proclaimed,[af] "In 40 days Nineveh will be demolished!" 5 The men of Nineveh believed in
God.[H] They proclaimed a fast[ag] and dressed in
·sackcloth — from the greatest of them to the
least.

6 When word reached the king of Nineveh,
he got up from his throne, took off his royal
robe, put on sackcloth,[ah] and sat in ashes.
7 Then he issued a decree[ai] in Nineveh:

> By order of the king and his nobles: No
> man or beast, herd or flock, is to taste
> anything at all. They must not eat or
> drink water. 8 Furthermore, both man
> and beast must be covered with sack-
> cloth, and everyone must call out ear-
> nestly to God.[aj] Each must turn from
> his evil ways[ak] and from the violence[I] he
> is doing.[J] 9 Who knows?[al] God may turn
> and relent; He may turn from His burn-
> ing anger so that we will not perish.[am]

10 Then God saw their actions — that they
had turned from their evil ways[an] — so God
relented from the disaster[ao] He had threatened to do to them. And He did not do it.

Jonah's Anger

4 But Jonah was greatly displeased and became furious.[ap] 2 He prayed to the LORD:[aq]
"Please, LORD, isn't this what I said while I
was still in my own country? That's why I fled
toward Tarshish in the first place.[ar] I knew
that You are a merciful and compassionate
God,[as] slow to become angry, rich in faithful
love, and One who relents from sending disaster.[at] 3 And now, LORD, please take my life
from me,[au] for it is better for me to die than
to live."[av]

4 The LORD asked, "Is it right for you to be
angry?"

5 Jonah left the city and sat down east of it.[aw]
He made himself a shelter there and sat in its

[a] **2:1** Jb 13:15; Ps 130:1-2; Lm 3:53-56 [b] **2:2** 1Sm 30:6; Ps 18:4-6; 22:24; 120:1 [c] Ps 18:5-6; 86:13; 88:1-7; Is 28:15; 38:18 [d] Ps 34:7 [e] **2:3** Ps 69:1-2,14-15; Lm 3:54 [f] Neh 9:11 [g] Ps 42:7 [h] **2:4** Lv 21:7 [i] Ps 31:22-23; Jr 7:15 [j] 1Kg 8:38; 2Ch 6:38; Ps 5:7; 138:2 [k] **2:5** Ps 69:1-2; 105:18; Pr 23:2; Lm 3:54 [l] Ps 18:4-5 [m] **2:6** Ps 116:3 [n] Jb 38:10; Ps 9:13; Is 38:10; Mt 16:18 [o] Jb 33:28; Ps 16:10; 30:3; Is 38:17 [p] Ps 30:3; 86:13 [q] **2:7** Ps 142:3 [r] 2Sm 14:11; Ps 77:10-11; 143:5 [s] 2Ch 30:27; Ps 18:6 [t] Ps 11:4; 65:4; 88:2; Mc 1:2; Hab 2:20 [u] **2:8** 2Kg 17:15; Ps 31:6; Jr 16:18 [v] Ps 31:6 [w] **2:9** Ps 50:14,23; Jr 33:11; Hs 14:2 [x] Ps 26:7 [y] Jb 22:27; Ps 22:25; 116:14,18; Ec 5:4-5 [z] Ps 3:8; Is 12:2; 45:17; Rv 7:10 [aa] **2:10** Jnh 1:17 [ab] **3:1** Jnh 1:1 [ac] **3:2** Zph 2:13-15 [ad] Jr 1:17; Ezk 2:7 [ae] **3:3** Gn 10:11-12; Jnh 1:2; 4:11 [af] **3:4** 2Kg 18:26-28; Mt 12:41; Lk 11:32 [ag] **3:5** Dn 9:3; Jl 1:14 [ah] **3:6** 1Kg 21:27; Est 4:1-4; Jr 6:26; Ezk 27:30-31 [ai] **3:7** 2Ch 20:3; Ezr 8:21 [aj] **3:8** Ps 130:1; Jnh 1:6,14 [ak] Is 1:16-19; 55:6-7; Jr 18:11 [al] **3:9** 2Sm 12:22; Jl 2:14 [am] Jr 18:7-8 [an] **3:10** 1Kg 21:27-29; 2Kg 17:13; 2Ch 7:14; Jr 18:11; 31:18 [ao] Ex 32:14; Am 7:3,6 [ap] **4:1** Jnh 4:9; Mt 20:15; Lk 15:28 [aq] **4:2** Jr 20:7 [ar] Jnh 1:3 [as] Ex 34:6; Nm 14:18; Ps 86:5,15; Jl 2:13 [at] Neh 9:17 [au] **4:3** 1Kg 19:4; Jb 6:8-9 [av] Jb 7:15-16; Ec 7:1 [aw] **4:5** 1Kg 19:9,13

[A] **2:1** Lit *from the belly of* [B] **2:3** Lit *river* [C] **2:4** LXX reads *said: Indeed, will I look . . . ?* [D] **2:5** Or *me, threatening my life* [E] **2:9** Or *Deliverance* [F] **3:3** Or *was a great city to God* [G] **3:3** Probably the time required to cover the city on foot [H] **3:5** Or *believed God* [I] **3:8** Or *injustice* [J] **3:8** Lit *violence in their hands*

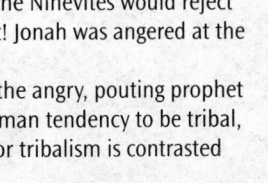

shade to see what would happen to the city.
[6]Then the LORD God appointed a plant,[A] and
it grew up to provide shade over Jonah's head
to ease his discomfort.[B] Jonah was greatly
pleased with the plant. [7]When dawn came
the next day, God appointed a worm that attacked the plant, and it withered.[a]
[8]As the sun was rising, God appointed a
scorching east wind.[b] The sun beat down so
much on Jonah's head[c] that he almost fainted,

[a]4:7 Jl 1:12 [b]4:8 Ezk 19:12; Hs 13:15 [c]Ps 121:6; Is 49:10

Jonah and the Mission of God

Trevin Wax

Although Jonah initially refused to answer God's call (chaps. 1-2), he was given another chance. In chapter 1, the prophet rose to flee; in chapter 3, the prophet rose to obey. Jonah reluctantly obeyed God's command to warn the people of Nineveh of God's impending judgment. In response to Jonah's preaching, all the Ninevites—from the king to the peasant—fell on their faces in humble repentance. Jonah became the instrument by which God orchestrated one of the greatest revivals in history.

The reader might expect the narrative to end with Jonah's triumph. Instead, this book ends with a twist: Jonah was angered by the turn of events. In 4:1, Jonah is described as "greatly displeased" and "furious." The Hebrew word *hārâ* indicates a blaze of anger.

In one of the most bewildering prayers recorded in Scripture, Jonah revealed his true intention for running from God's call. He had not run away because he was afraid the Ninevites would reject his message; he had run away because he was afraid they might accept it! Jonah was angered at the thought that God might actually forgive the wretched people of Nineveh.

Notice the contrast between the compassionate God of verse 2 and the angry, pouting prophet of verse 1. In this scene, the reader catches a glimpse of the universal human tendency to be tribal, self-centered, and focused on self-preservation. This human propensity for tribalism is contrasted with the gracious and merciful heart of God (v. 2).

In his prayer, Jonah rightly described God as a "merciful and compassionate God, slow to become angry, rich in faithful love, and One who relents from sending disaster." This description of God goes back to Yahweh's revelation of Himself to Moses on Mount Sinai. The children of Israel had sinned by worshipping a golden calf they had fashioned for themselves. Moses interceded on their behalf and begged God for mercy. He then asked to see God's glory (Ex 33:18). In response, God placed Moses in a cave and "passed in front of him," proclaiming about Himself the very words that Jonah would repeat centuries later (Ex 34:6-7).

It is interesting to note that Jonah does not pray the last part of God's revelation to Moses: "But He will not leave the guilty unpunished." This omission is telling. Jonah's prayer demonstrates that he found no offense in the thought of God justly punishing evildoers. It was the grace and mercy of God that was scandalous to him. Because the Ninevites responded to God with repentance, they had been spared the judgment they deserved. Mercy triumphed over judgment (Jms 2:13), and mercy made Jonah angry.

Jonah's temper tantrum reveals his small, unmerciful heart. The picture of God, however, stands in stark contrast to the prophet's bitterness. God breaks down walls and leads His people out into the world with good news: forgiveness is possible through repentance and faith. Tribal attitudes melt away when constantly exposed to the warm embrace of our missionary God.

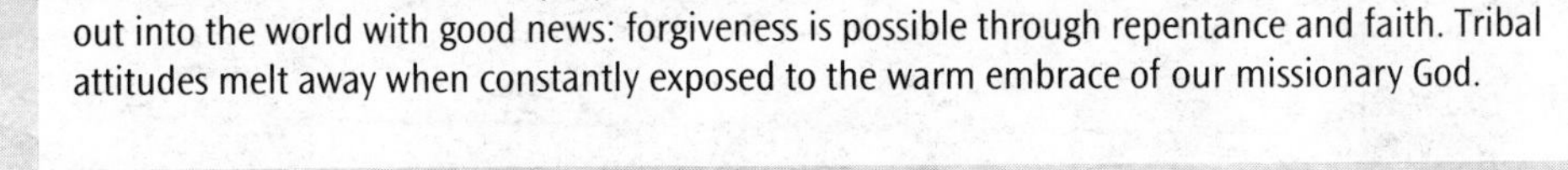

[A]4:6 A castor-oil plant or a climbing gourd [B]4:6 Lit *to deliver him from his evil*

and he wanted to die. He said, "It's better for
me to die than to live."[a]
9Then God asked Jonah, "Is it right for you
to be angry about the plant?"
"Yes," he replied. "It is right. I'm angry
enough to die!"
10So the LORD said, "You cared about the
plant, which you did not labor over and did
not grow. It appeared in a night and perished in a night.
11Should I not care about the
great city of Nineveh,[b] which has more than
120,000 people[A] who cannot distinguish between their right and their left,[c] as well as
many animals?"[d]

[a]4:8 Jnh 4:3
[b]4:11 Jnh 3:10
[c]Dt 1:39; Is 7:16
[d]Ps 36:6

A4:11 Or *men*

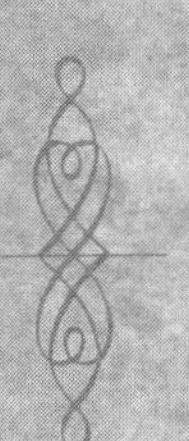

■ **AUTHOR:** Micah

■■ **DATE:** During the reigns of Jotham, Ahaz, and Hezekiah (around 750–686 B.C.)

Micah's hometown was Moresheth in Judah—the tribal area of Gath close to the Philistine border. His prophecy is directed to Jerusalem and Samaria, the main cities of Israel's divided kingdom. He was a contemporary of the prophet Isaiah, who directed his message mostly to Jerusalem. This places them around the year 700 B.C.

Micah shares the burdens of the other prophets: in view of the sins of the people he must bring tidings of judgment. In Micah's prophecy the litany of sin is spelled out in even more detail: the people follow false gods, they are greedy, they exploit the poor, they are immoral, they neglect the Word of the Lord, they oppress the defenseless, and they do not shrink back from murder. Even prophets and judges accept bribes.

MICAH

Following the patterns of his fellow prophets, Micah announces God's severe punishment. Great destruction and ruin will come upon Jerusalem and Samaria. Darkness and shame will cover the land because of the corruption of its leaders. So thorough will the judgment be that "Zion will be plowed like a field, Jerusalem will become ruins, and the hill of the temple mount will be a thicket" (3:12).

We note two characteristics of the man Micah. One is his singular courage. By identifying these sinners so specifically, he makes many enemies among the most powerful citizens in the land. The secret of Micah's courage lay in his total reliance on God. The other quality we may recognize is the great compassion he harbors toward those under judgment. It is as if he himself experiences the pain of the punishment he announces. He weeps for the people and the suffering of the land.

Perhaps because of that compassion, the Lord affords him the privilege of announcing deliverance to the people. If they will show true repentance, the Lord will shower blessings upon them. Great joy will be theirs when their enemies are vanquished and goodness returns to the land. Best of all, their iniquities will be "cast . . . into the depths of the sea" (7:19).

The mission of God often requires prophets to issue bad news, but never as the last word. Though Micah announces the great exile of his people, he also has good news: his people will return from exile and again possess the land. But the best news of all is Micah's prophecy concerning the Messiah's advent: "Bethlehem Ephrathah, you are small among the clans of Judah; One will come from you to be ruler over Israel for Me. His origin is from antiquity, from eternity" (5:2).

1 The word of the LORD that came[a] to Micah[b] the Moreshite[c]—what he saw regarding Samaria and Jerusalem in the days of Jotham,[d] Ahaz,[e] and Hezekiah,[f] kings of Judah.

Coming Judgment on Israel

2 Listen, all you peoples;[g]
pay attention, earth[A] and everyone in it![h]
The Lord GOD will be a witness
against you,[i]
the Lord, from His holy temple.[j]
3 Look, the LORD is leaving His place[k]
and coming down to trample
the heights[B] of the earth.[l]
4 The mountains will melt beneath Him,
and the valleys will split apart,
like wax near a fire,[m]
like water cascading down
a mountainside.
5 All this will happen because of
Jacob's rebellion
and the sins of the house of Israel.
What is the rebellion of Jacob?
Isn't it Samaria?[n]
And what is the •high place of Judah?[o]
Isn't it Jerusalem?
6 Therefore, I will make Samaria
a heap of ruins[p] in the countryside,
a planting area[q] for a vineyard.
I will roll her stones[r] into the valley
and expose her foundations.[s]
7 All her carved images will be smashed[t]
to pieces;
all her wages[u] will be burned in the fire,
and I will destroy all her idols.
Since she collected the wages
of a prostitute,[v]
they will be used again for a prostitute.

Micah's Lament

8 Because of this I will lament and wail;
I will walk barefoot and naked.[w]
I will howl like the jackals[x]
and mourn like ostriches.[C]
9 For her wound is incurable[y]
and has reached even Judah;[z]
it has approached the gate
of my people,[aa]
as far as Jerusalem.
10 Don't announce it in Gath,[ab]
don't weep at all.
Roll in the dust in Beth-leaphrah.
11 Depart in shameful nakedness,[ac]
you residents of Shaphir;
the residents of Zaanan[ad] will not
come out.
Beth-ezel is lamenting;
its support[D] is taken from you.
12 Though the residents of Maroth
anxiously wait for something good,[ae]
disaster has come from the LORD[af]
to the gate of Jerusalem.
13 Harness the horses to the chariot,
you residents of Lachish.[ag]
This was the beginning of sin
for Daughter •Zion,
because Israel's acts of rebellion[ah]
can be traced to you.
14 Therefore, send farewell gifts[ai]
to Moresheth-gath;
the houses of Achzib[aj] are a deception[ak]
to the kings of Israel.
15 I will again bring a conqueror
against you who live in Mareshah.[al]
The nobility[E] of Israel will come
to Adullam.[am]
16 Shave yourselves bald and cut off
your hair[an]
in sorrow for your precious children;
make yourselves as bald as an eagle,
for they have been taken from you
into exile.[ao]

Oppressors Judged

2 Woe to those who dream up wickedness
and prepare evil plans[ap] on their beds!
At morning light[aq] they accomplish it
because the power is in their hands.[ar]
2 They covet fields[as] and seize them;[at]
they also take houses.
They deprive a man of his home,[au]
a person of his inheritance.[av]
3 Therefore, the LORD says:
I am now planning[aw] a disaster
against this nation;[ax]
you cannot free your necks from it.[ay]

[a]1:1 Hs 1:1; Jl 1:1; Zph 1:1 [b]2Ch 29:5-11; 32:24-26; Jr 26:18 [c]Mc 1:14 [d]2Kg 15:5,32-38; 2Ch 27:1-9; Is 1:1; Hs 1:1 [e]2Kg 16:1-20; 2Ch 28:1-27; Is 7:1-12 [f]2Kg 18:1-20; 2Ch 29:1-31 [g]1:2 1Kg 22:28; 2Ch 18:27; Jr 6:19; 22:29 [h]Ps 24:1; Is 34:1; Jr 47:2 [i]1Sm 12:5-6; Ps 50:7; Jr 42:5; Mal 3:5 [j]Ps 11:4; Hab 2:20 [k]1:3 Is 26:21 [l]Am 4:13 [m]1:4 Ps 97:5; Is 64:1-2; Nah 1:5 [n]1:5 Is 7:9; Am 8:14 [o]2Ch 34:3-4 [p]1:6 Mc 3:12 [q]Jr 31:5; Am 5:11 [r]Lm 4:1 [s]Ezk 13:14 [t]1:7 Dt 9:21; 2Ch 34:7 [u]Dt 23:18 [v]Dt 23:18 [w]1:8 Is 20:2-4; 32:11 [x]Is 13:21-22 [y]1:9 Is 3:26; Jr 30:12,15 [z]2Kg 18:13-16; 19:31-37; Is 8:7-8 [aa]Mc 1:12 [ab]1:10 2Sm 1:20 [ac]1:11 Ezk 23:29 [ad]Jos 15:37 [ae]1:12 Is 59:9-11; Jr 14:19 [af]Jdg 2:15; 2Kg 17:7; 21:12; Is 45:7; Mc 2:3 [ag]1:13 Jos 10:3; 2Kg 14:19; Is 36:2 [ah]Mc 1:5 [ai]1:14 2Kg 16:8 [aj]Jos 15:44 [ak]Jr 15:18 [al]1:15 Jos 15:44 [am]Jos 12:15; 15:35; 1Sm 22:1; 2Sm 23:13 [an]1:16 Jb 1:20; Is 22:12; Jr 7:29 [ao]2Kg 17:6; Am 7:11,17 [ap]2:1 Ps 36:4; Is 32:7; Nah 1:11 [aq]Hs 7:6-7 [ar]Gn 31:29; Dt 28:32; Pr 3:27 [as]2:2 Jr 22:17; Am 8:4 [at]Is 5:8 [au]1Kg 21:1-15 [av]Ex 20:17; Is 5:8 [aw]2:3 Dt 28:48; Jr 18:11 [ax]Jr 8:3; Am 3:1-2 [ay]Lm 1:14; 5:5

[A]1:2 Or *land* [B]1:3 Or *high places* [C]1:8 Or *eagle owls*; lit *daughters of the desert* [D]1:11 Lit *its standing place*; Hb obscure [E]1:15 Lit *glory*

Then you will not walk so proudly[a]
because it will be an evil time.[b]
4 In that day one will take up[c] a taunt
against you,
and lament mournfully,[d] saying,
"We are totally ruined![e]
He measures out the allotted land
of my people.
How He removes it from me!
He allots our fields[f] to traitors."
5 Therefore, there will be no one
in the assembly of the LORD
to divide the land by casting lots.[A,g]

God's Word Rejected

6 "Quit your preaching,"[h] they[B] preach.
"They should not preach
these things;[i]
shame will not overtake us."[C,j]
7 House of Jacob, should it be asked,
"Is the Spirit of the LORD impatient?[k]
Are these the things He does?"
Don't My words bring good[l]
to the one who walks uprightly?[m]
8 But recently My people have risen up
like an enemy:[n]
You strip off the splendid robe[o]
from those who are
passing through confidently,[p]
like those returning from war.
9 You force[q] the women of My people
out of their comfortable homes,
and you take My blessing[D,r]
from their children forever.
10 Get up and leave,
for this is not your place of rest,[s]
because defilement[t]
brings destruction —
a grievous destruction![u]
11 If a man of wind[E] comes
and invents lies:[v]
"I will preach to you about wine
and beer,"[w]
he would be just the preacher
for this people![x]

The Remnant Regathered

12 I will indeed gather[y] all of you, Jacob;
I will collect the remnant of Israel.[z]

[a]2:3 Is 2:11-12
[b]Am 5:13
[c]2:4 Hab 2:6
[d]Jr 9:10,17-21; Mc 1:8
[e]Is 6:11; 24:3; Jr 4:13
[f]Jr 6:12; 8:10
[g]2:5 Nm 34:13,16-29; Jos 18:4,10
[h]2:6 Is 30:10; Am 2:12; 7:16
[i]Is 29:10; Mc 3:6
[j]Mc 6:16
[k]2:7 Is 50:2; 59:1
[l]Ps 119:65,68,116; Jr 15:16
[m]Ps 15:2; 84:11
[n]2:8 Jr 12:8
[o]Mc 3:2-3; 7:2-3
[p]Ps 120:6-7
[q]2:9 Jr 10:20
[r]Ezk 39:21; Hab 2:14
[s]2:10 Dt 3:19-20; 12:8-10
[t]Ps 106:38
[u]Lv 18:25-28
[v]2:11 Jr 5:13,31
[w]Is 28:7
[x]Is 30:10-11
[y]2:12 Mc 4:6-7
[z]2Kg 19:31; Mc 5:7-8; 7:18
[aa]Jr 23:3; Ezk 36:35-38
[ab]3:1 Is 1:10; Mc 3:9
[ac]Ps 82:1-5; Jr 5:5
[ad]3:2 Ps 53:4; Ezk 22:27; Mc 2:8; 7:2-3
[ae]3:3 Ps 14:4; 27:2; Zph 3:3
[af]Ezk 11:3,6-7
[ag]3:4 Ps 18:41; Pr 1:28; Is 1:15; Jr 11:11
[ah]Dt 31:17; Is 59:2
[ai]3:5 Is 3:12; 9:15-16; Jr 14:14-15
[aj]Jr 6:14
[ak]3:6 Is 8:20-22; 29:10-12
[al]Dt 18:10; Jos 13:22
[am]Is 59:10

I will bring them together like sheep
in a pen,
like a flock in the middle of its fold.
It will be noisy with people.[aa]
13 One who breaks open the way
will advance before them;
they will break out, pass
through the gate,
and leave by it.
Their King will pass through
before them,
the LORD as their leader.

Unjust Leaders Judged

3 Then I said, "Now listen,[ab]
leaders of Jacob,
you rulers of the house of Israel.
Aren't you supposed to know
what is just?[ac]
2 You hate good and love evil.
You tear off people's skin[ad]
and strip their flesh from their bones.
3 You eat the flesh[ae] of my people
after you strip their skin from them
and break their bones.
You chop them up[af]
like flesh for the cooking pot,
like meat in a cauldron."
4 Then they will cry out[ag] to the LORD,
but He will not answer them.
He will hide His face from them
at that time[ah]
because of the crimes
they have committed.

False Prophets Judged

5 This is what the LORD says
concerning the prophets
who lead my people astray,[ai]
who proclaim[aj] peace
when they have food to sink
their teeth into
but declare war against the one
who puts nothing in their mouths.
6 Therefore, it will be night[ak] for you —
without visions;
it will grow dark for you —
without *divination.[al]
The sun will set[am] on these prophets,

A2:5 Lit *LORD stretching the measuring line by lot* B2:6 = the prophets
C2:6 Text emended; MT reads *things. Shame will not depart.*
D2:9 Perhaps the land E2:11 Or *spirit*

and the daylight will turn black
over them.
7 Then the seers will be ashamed[a]
and the diviners disappointed.[b]
They will all cover their mouths[A,c]
because there will be no answer
from God.[d]

8 As for me, however, I am filled
with power[e]
by the Spirit of the LORD,
with justice and courage,
to proclaim to Jacob his rebellion
and to Israel his sin.[f]

Zion's Destruction

9 Listen to this, leaders of the house
of Jacob,[g]
you rulers of the house of Israel,
who abhor justice[h]
and pervert everything that is right,
10 who build •Zion with bloodshed[i]
and Jerusalem with injustice.
11 Her leaders issue rulings for a bribe,[j]
her priests teach for payment,[k]
and her prophets practice divination
for money.
Yet they lean on the LORD, saying,
"Isn't the LORD[l] among us?
No disaster will overtake us."
12 Therefore, because of you,
Zion will be plowed like a field,
Jerusalem will become ruins,[m]
and the hill of the temple mount[n]
will be a thicket.[o]

The LORD's Rule from Restored Zion

4 In the last days[p]
the mountain of the LORD's house[q]
will be established
at the top of the mountains
and will be raised above the hills.
Peoples will stream to it,[r]
2 and many nations will come and say,[s]
"Come, let us go up to the mountain
of the LORD,[t]
to the house of the God of Jacob.
He will teach us about His ways[u]
so we may walk in His paths."
For instruction will go out of •Zion[v]
and the word of the LORD
from Jerusalem.
3 He will settle disputes
among many peoples[w]
and provide arbitration
for strong nations
that are far away.
They will beat their swords into plows,
and their spears into pruning knives.
Nation will not take up the sword
against nation,
and they will never again train for war.
4 But each man will sit
under his grapevine[x]
and under his fig tree
with no one to frighten him.[y]
For the mouth of the LORD[z] of •Hosts
has promised this.
5 Though all the peoples each walk
in the name of their gods,[aa]
we will walk[ab] in the name
of •Yahweh our God
forever and ever.[ac]

6 On that day—
this is the LORD's declaration—
I will assemble the lame
and gather the scattered,[ad]
those I have injured.
7 I will make the lame into a remnant,[ae]
those far removed into a strong nation.
Then the LORD will rule over them[af]
in Mount Zion
from this time on and forever.
8 And you, watchtower for the flock,[ag]
fortified hill[B] of Daughter Zion,
the former rule[ah] will come to you,
sovereignty will come
to Daughter Jerusalem.

From Exile to Victory

9 Now, why are you shouting loudly?[ai]
Is there no king with you?
Has your counselor perished[aj]
so that anguish grips you like a woman
in labor?
10 Writhe and cry out,[C,ak] Daughter Zion,
like a woman in labor,
for now you will leave the city[al]
and camp in the open fields.

[a]**3:7** Zch 13:4 [b]Is 44:25; 47:12-14 [c]Lv 13:45; Lm 4:13-15; Ezk 24:17,22; Mc 7:16 [d]1Sm 28:6; Is 29:9-12; Mc 3:4 [e]**3:8** Is 61:1-2; Jr 1:18 [f]Is 58:1 [g]**3:9** Mc 3:1 [h]Ps 58:1-2; Is 1:23 [i]**3:10** Jr 22:13,17; Hab 2:12 [j]**3:11** Is 1:23; Mc 7:3 [k]Jr 6:13 [l]Is 48:2 [m]**3:12** Jr 9:11 [n]Mc 4:1 [o]Jr 26:18 [p]**4:1-3** Is 2:2-4; Dn 2:28; 10:14; Hs 3:5; Mc 5:10 [q]**4:1** Ezk 43:12; Mc 3:12; Zch 8:3 [r]Ps 22:27; 86:9; Jr 3:17 [s]**4:2** Zch 2:11; 14:16 [t]Is 56:6-7; Jr 31:6 [u]Ps 25:8-9,12; Is 54:13 [v]Is 42:1-4; Zch 14:8-9 [w]**4:3** Is 11:3-5 [x]**4:4** 1Kg 4:25; Zch 3:10 [y]Lv 26:6; Jr 30:10 [z]Is 1:20; 40:5 [aa]**4:5** 2Kg 17:29 [ab]Zch 10:12 [ac]Jos 24:15; Is 26:8,13 [ad]**4:6** Is 35:6; Jr 31:8; Mc 2:12; Zph 3:19 [ae]**4:7** Mc 5:7-8; 7:18; Mt 11:5; Lk 14:21 [af]Is 24:23 [ag]**4:8** Ps 48:3,12; 61:3 [ah]Is 1:26; Zch 9:10 [ai]**4:9** Jr 8:19 [aj]Is 3:1-3 [ak]**4:10** Mc 5:3 [al]2Kg 20:18; Hs 2:14

A**3:7** Lit *mustache* B**4:8** Or *flock, Ophel* C**4:10** Hb obscure

You will go to Babylon;
there you will be rescued;[a]
there the LORD will redeem you[b]
from the power of your enemies!
11 Many nations have now assembled
against you;[c]
they say, "Let her be defiled,
and let us feast our eyes on Zion."
12 But they do not know
the LORD's intentions[d]
or understand His plan,
that He has gathered them
like sheaves to the threshing floor.
13 Rise and thresh,[e] Daughter Zion,
for I will make your horns iron
and your hooves bronze,
so you can crush many peoples.[f]
Then you[A] will ˚set apart their plunder[g]
to the LORD for destruction,
their wealth to the Lord of all the earth.

From Defeated Ruler to Conquering King

5 [B] Now, daughter who is under attack,
you slash yourself in grief;
a siege is set against us!
They are striking the judge[h] of Israel
on the cheek with a rod.
2[C] Bethlehem Ephrathah,[i]
you are small among the clans of Judah;
One will come from you[j]
to be ruler over Israel for Me.[k]
His origin[D] is from antiquity,[l]
from eternity.[E]
3 Therefore, He will abandon them[m]
until the time
when she who is in labor[n]
has given birth;
then the rest of His brothers[o]
will return
to the people of Israel.[p]
4 He will stand and shepherd them[q]
in the strength of ˚Yahweh,
in the majestic name of Yahweh His God.
They will live securely,
for then His greatness will extend
to the ends of the earth.[r]
5 He will be their peace.[s]
When Assyria invades our land,[t]
when it marches against our fortresses,
we will raise against it seven shepherds,
even eight leaders of men.
6 They will shepherd[u] the land of Assyria
with the sword,
the land of Nimrod[v]
with a drawn blade.[F]
So He will rescue us[w] from Assyria
when it invades our land,
when it marches against our territory.

The Glorious and Purified Remnant

7 Then the remnant of Jacob[x]
will be among many peoples
like dew from the LORD,[y]
like showers on the grass,[z]
which do not wait for anyone
or linger for ˚mankind.
8 Then the remnant of Jacob
will be among the nations,
among many peoples,
like a lion among animals of the forest,[aa]
like a young lion among flocks of sheep,
which tramples[ab] and tears[ac]
as it passes through,
and there is no one to rescue them.[ad]
9 Your hand will be lifted up
against your adversaries,[ae]
and all your enemies will be destroyed.
10 In that day —
this is the LORD's declaration —
I will remove your horses from you[af]
and wreck your chariots.
11 I will remove the cities of your land[ag]
and tear down all your fortresses.[ah]
12 I will remove sorceries
from your hands,[ai]
and you will not have
any more fortune-tellers.
13 I will remove your carved images[aj]
and sacred pillars from you
so that you will not bow down again
to the work of your hands.
14 I will pull up the ˚Asherah poles[ak]
from among you[al]
and demolish your cities.[G]
15 I will take vengeance in anger
and wrath[am]
against the nations that have not
obeyed Me.

[a] **4:10** Is 43:14; 45:13; Mc 7:8-12
[b] Is 48:20; 52:9-12
[c] **4:11** Is 5:25-30; 17:12-14
[d] **4:12** Ps 147:19-20
[e] **4:13** Is 41:15
[f] Jr 51:20-23
[g] Is 60:9
[h] **5:1** 1Kg 22:24; Jb 16:10; Lm 3:30
[i] **5:2** Gn 35:19; Ru 4:11; 1Sm 17:12; Mt 2:6
[j] Is 11:1; Lk 2:4
[k] 2Ch 7:18; Is 11:1; Jr 30:21; Zch 9:9; Mt 2:6
[l] Ps 74:2; 102:25; Pr 8:22-23; Hab 1:12
[m] **5:3** Hs 11:8; Mc 4:10; 7:13
[n] Mc 4:9-10
[o] Is 10:20-22; Mc 5:7-8
[p] Mc 4:6-7
[q] **5:4** Is 40:11; 49:9; Ezk 34:13-15,23-24; Mc 7:14
[r] Is 45:22; 52:10
[s] **5:5** Is 9:6
[t] Is 8:7-8; 10:24-27
[u] **5:6** Nah 2:11-13; Zph 2:13
[v] Gn 10:8-12
[w] Is 14:25; 37:36-37
[x] **5:7** Is 10:21; Mc 2:12; 4:7; 7:18
[y] Dt 32:2; 2Sm 17:12; Ps 110:3; Hs 14:5
[z] Ps 72:6; Is 44:3
[aa] **5:8** Gn 49:9; Nm 24:9
[ab] Ps 44:5; Is 41:15-16; Mc 4:13; Zch 10:5
[ac] Hs 5:14
[ad] Ps 50:22
[ae] **5:9** Ps 10:12; 21:8; Is 26:11
[af] **5:10** Dt 17:16; Is 2:7; Hs 14:3
[ag] **5:11** Is 1:7; 6:11
[ah] Is 2:12-17; Hs 10:14; Am 5:9
[ai] **5:12** Dt 18:10-12; Is 2:6; 8:19
[aj] **5:13** Is 2:18,20; 17:8; Ezk 6:9
[ak] **5:14** Dt 16:21
[al] Ex 34:13; Is 27:9
[am] **5:15** Is 1:24; 65:12

[A] **4:13** LXX, Syr, Tg; MT reads *I* [B] **5:1** Mc 4:14 in Hb [C] **5:2** Mc 5:1 in Hb [D] **5:2** Lit *His going out* [E] **5:2** Or *from ancient times* [F] **5:6** Aq, Vg; MT, Sym read *Nimrod at its gateways* [G] **5:14** Or *shrines*

Haik Hovsepianmehr Mehr (1945–1994)

On January 6, 1945, Haik Hovsepianmehr Mehr was born in Tehran, Iran, the eldest son in a middle-class Armenian family. At the age of 15, he accepted Christ as his Savior. While a teen, he became a pastor of a church in Majidieh near Tehran. After marrying Takoosh Ginagosian in 1966, he moved to Gorgan in the northern province of Iran and pastored a church he established during his tour of duty in the military.

Mehr was ordained and later became the bishop of the *Jama'at-e Rabbani* church, which is part of the Assemblies of God denomination. The life of a follower of Christ is seldom easy, however. In 1969, while Mehr traveled with his wife and an American Christian couple, their car rear-ended a tractor trailer. While all of the adults survived, none of the four children in the car did.

Mehr worked diligently to preach Christ to the Muslims of Iran. Refusing to keep silent about the violation of the rights of Christians, Mehr refused to sign a statement in 1993 claiming that no violation of Christians' rights had occurred. Also, he refused to sign another statement disallowing Muslim converts in his church. Instead, Mehr, the Chairman of the Council of Protestant Ministers and Secretary-General of the Assembly of God Churches, urged a special representative of the United Nations to meet with Protestant leaders in Iran on this issue.

Mehr protested the treatment of Mehdi Dibaj, a friend and colleague oppressed and jailed by the government. On January 19, 1994, Bishop Mehr was reported missing while on his way to the airport. Eleven days after he was reported missing, the Tehran police asked his son to identify his body based on a photograph. His death was reported to have taken place on January 20—the apparent victim of execution.

Mehr was reported to say, "I am ready to die for the cause of the Church so that others will be able to worship their Lord peacefully and without so much fear." [1] Truer words were never spoken.

[1] Haik Hovsepianmehr Mehr quoted in "One Person's Story," OMID: A Memorial in Defense of Human Rights (http://www.iranrights.org/english/memorial-case-12863.php). Copyright © 2011, Abdorrahman Boroumand Foundation.

God's Lawsuit against Judah

6 Now listen to what the LORD is saying:
Rise, plead your case
before the mountains,
and let the hills hear your voice.
2 Listen to the LORD's lawsuit,[a]
you mountains
and enduring foundations
of the earth,[b]
because the LORD has a case
against His people,[c]
and He will argue it against Israel.
3 My people,[d] what have I done to you,[e]
or how have I wearied you?[f]
Testify against Me!
4 Indeed, I brought you up[g]
from the land of Egypt
and redeemed you[h] from that place
of slavery.[i]
I sent Moses,[j] Aaron, and Miriam[k]
ahead of you.
5 My people,
remember what Balak
king of Moab[l] proposed,
what Balaam son of Beor
answered him,[m]
and what happened from
the Acacia Grove[A,n] to Gilgal[o]
so that you may acknowledge
the LORD's righteous acts.[p]
6 What should I bring before the LORD[q]
when I come to bow before God
on high?
Should I come before Him
with ·burnt offerings,[r]
with year-old calves?
7 Would the LORD be pleased
with thousands of rams[s]
or with ten thousand streams of oil?
Should I give my firstborn
for my transgression,[t]
the child of my body for my own sin?
8 Mankind, He has told you what is good[u]
and what it is the LORD requires of you:[v]
to act justly,[w]
to love faithfulness,[x]
and to walk humbly with your God.[y]

[a]**6:2** Is 3:13; Jr 2:9
[b]2Sm 22:16; Ps 104:5
[c]Is 1:18; Hs 4:1; 12:2
[d]**6:3** Ps 50:7
[e]Jr 2:5
[f]Is 43:22-23
[g]**6:4** Ex 12:51; 20:2
[h]Dt 7:8
[i]Ex 20:2
[j]Ps 77:20
[k]Ex 15:20
[l]**6:5** Nm 22:5-6
[m]Nm 22–24
[n]Nm 25:1; Jos 2:1; 3:1
[o]Jos 4:19; 5:9-10
[p]1Sm 12:7; Ps 103:6; Is 1:27
[q]**6:6** Ps 40:6-8
[r]Ps 51:16-17
[s]**6:7** Ps 50:9; Is 40:16
[t]Lv 18:21; 20:1-5; Jr 7:31
[u]**6:8** Dt 30:15
[v]Dt 10:12
[w]Is 56:1; Jr 22:3; Mt 23:23
[x]Hs 6:6
[y]Is 57:15; 66:2
[z]**6:10** Jr 5:26-27; Am 3:10
[aa]Ezk 45:9-10; Am 8:5
[ab]**6:11** Lv 19:36; Hs 12:7
[ac]**6:12** Is 1:23; 5:7; Am 6:3-4; Mc 2:1-2
[ad]Jr 9:2-6,8; Hs 7:13; Am 2:4
[ae]Is 3:8
[af]**6:13** Mc 1:9
[ag]Is 1:7; 6:11
[ah]**6:14** Is 9:20
[ai]Is 30:6
[aj]**6:15** Dt 28:38-40; Jr 12:13
[ak]Am 5:11; Zph 1:13
[al]**6:16** 1Kg 16:25-34; 2Kg 21:3; 2Ch 21:6,13; Jr 7:24
[am]Jr 18:16
[an]Jr 19:8; 25:9,18; 29:18
[ao]Ps 44:13; Jr 51:51; Hs 12:14

Verdict of Judgment

9 The voice of ·Yahweh calls out
to the city[B]
(and it is wise to ·fear Your name):
"Pay attention to the rod
and the One who ordained it.[C]
10 Are there still[D] the treasures
of wickedness[z]
and the accursed short measure[aa]
in the house of the wicked?
11 Can I excuse wicked scales
or bags of deceptive weights?[ab]
12 For the wealthy of the city are full
of violence,[ac]
and its residents speak lies;[ad]
the tongues in their mouths
are deceitful.[ae]
13 "As a result, I have begun to strike
you severely,[E,af]
bringing desolation because of
your sins.[ag]
14 You will eat but not be satisfied,[ah]
for there will be hunger
within you.
What you acquire, you cannot save,[ai]
and what you do save,
I will give to the sword.[D]
15 You will sow but not reap;[aj]
you will press olives
but not anoint yourself with oil;
and you will tread grapes
but not drink the wine.[ak]
16 The statutes of Omri
and all the practices
of Ahab's house
have been observed;
you have followed their policies.[al]
Therefore, I will make you
a desolate place[am]
and the city's[F] residents an object
of contempt;[G,an]
you will bear the scorn
of My people."[H,ao]

Israel's Moral Decline

7 How sad for me!
For I am like one who —
when the summer fruit
has been gathered

[A]6:5 Or *Shittim* [B]6:9 = Jerusalem [C]6:9 Or *attention, you tribe. Who has ordained it?*; Hb obscure [D]6:10,14 Hb obscure [E]6:13 LXX, Aq, Theod, Syr, Vg; MT reads *I have made you sick by striking you down* [F]6:16 Lit *and its* [G]6:16 Lit *residents a hissing* [H]6:16 LXX reads *of the peoples*

after the gleaning
of the grape harvest[a] —
finds no grape cluster to eat,
no early fig, which I crave.[b]
2 Godly people have vanished
from the land;[c]
there is no one upright
among the people.[d]
All of them wait in ambush
to shed blood;[e]
they hunt each other with a net.[f]
3 Both hands are good[g]
at accomplishing evil:
the official and the judge demand
a bribe;[h]
when the powerful man communicates
his evil desire,
they plot it together.
4 The best of them is like a brier;[i]
the most upright is worse than a hedge
of thorns.[j]
The day of your watchmen,
the day of your punishment,
is coming;[k]
at this time their panic is here.[l]
5 Do not rely on a friend;[m]
don't trust in a close companion.
Seal your mouth
from the woman who lies
in your arms.
6 Surely a son considers his father a fool,[n]
a daughter opposes her mother,
and a daughter-in-law is
against her mother-in-law;
a man's enemies are the men
of his own household.
7 But I will look to the LORD;[o]
I will wait for the God of my salvation.[p]
My God will hear me.[q]

Zion's Vindication

8 Do not rejoice over me,[r] my enemy!
Though I have fallen, I will stand up;[s]
though I sit in darkness,
the LORD will be my light.[t]
9 Because I have sinned against Him,
I must endure the LORD's rage
until He argues my case[u]
and establishes justice for me.[v]
He will bring me into the light;[w]

[a]**7:1** Is 24:13
[b]Is 28:4; Hs 9:10
[c]**7:2** Is 57:1
[d]1Kg 19:10
[e]Is 59:7; Mc 3:10
[f]Jr 5:26; Hs 5:1
[g]**7:3** Pr 4:16-17
[h]Am 5:12; Mc 3:11
[i]**7:4** Ezk 2:6; 28:24
[j]Nah 1:10
[k]Is 10:3; Hs 9:7
[l]Is 22:5
[m]**7:5** Jr 9:4
[n]**7:6** Mt 10:21,35-36; Lk 12:53
[o]**7:7** Hab 2:1
[p]Ps 130:5; Is 25:9
[q]Ps 4:3
[r]**7:8** Ob 12
[s]Am 9:11
[t]Ps 27:1; Is 9:2
[u]**7:9** Jr 50:34
[v]Jb 23:3-7; Lm 3:58
[w]Ps 37:6; Is 42:7,16
[x]Is 46:13; 56:1
[y]**7:10** Ps 42:3,10; 79:10; 115:2; Jl 2:17
[z]Ps 18:42; Zch 10:5
[aa]**7:11** Is 54:11; Am 9:11
[ab]Zph 2:2
[ac]**7:12** Is 19:23-25; 60:4,9
[ad]**7:13** Jr 25:11; Mc 6:13
[ae]Is 3:10-11; Mc 3:4
[af]**7:14** Ps 95:7; Is 40:11; 49:10; Mc 5:4
[ag]Lv 27:32; Ps 23:4
[ah]Nm 23:9; Dt 33:28
[ai]Jr 50:19
[aj]Am 9:11
[ak]**7:15** Ex 3:20; 34:10; Ps 78:11-16
[al]**7:16** Mc 3:7
[am]**7:17** Ps 72:9; Is 49:23
[an]Ps 18:45
[ao]Dt 32:24
[ap]Is 25:3; 59:19
[aq]**7:18** Ex 15:11; Ps 71:19; Is 40:18
[ar]Ex 34:7,9; Is 43:25; Rm 3:25

I will see His salvation.[A,x]
10 Then my enemy will see,
and she will be covered with shame,
the one who said to me,
"Where is the LORD your God?"[y]
My eyes will look at her in triumph;
at that time she will be trampled
like mud in the streets.[z]

11 A day will come for rebuilding
your walls;[aa]
on that day your boundary
will be extended.[ab]
12 On that day people will come to you[ac]
from Assyria and the cities of Egypt,
even from Egypt to the Euphrates River
and from sea to sea
and mountain to mountain.
13 Then the earth will become
a wasteland[ad]
because of its inhabitants
and as a result of their actions.[ae]

Micah's Prayer Answered

14 Shepherd Your people[af]
with Your staff,[ag]
the flock that is Your possession.
They live alone[ah] in a woodland
surrounded by pastures.
Let them graze in Bashan and Gilead[ai]
as in ancient times.[aj]
15 I will perform miracles for them[B]
as in the days of your exodus
from the land of Egypt.[ak]
16 Nations will see and be ashamed
of[C] all their power.
They will put their hands
over their mouths;[al]
and their ears will become deaf.
17 They will lick the dust like a snake;[am]
they will come trembling out of
their hiding places[an]
like reptiles slithering on the ground.[ao]
They will tremble in the presence
of Yahweh our God;[ap]
they will stand in awe of You.
18 Who is a God like You,[aq]
removing iniquity and passing
over rebellion[ar]

[A]**7:9** Or *righteousness* [B]**7:15** = Israel [C]**7:16** Or *ashamed in spite of*

for the remnant of His inheritance?[a]
He does not hold on
to His anger forever,[b]
because He delights in faithful love.[c]
19 He will again have compassion on us;
He will vanquish our iniquities.[d]
You will cast all our[A] sins
into the depths of the sea.[e]
20 You will show loyalty to Jacob[f]
and faithful love to Abraham,
as You swore to our fathers[g]
from days long ago.

[a]**7:18** Mc 2:12; 4:7; 5:7-8 [b]Ps 103:8-9,13 [c]Jr 32:41 [d]**7:19** Jr 50:20 [e]**7:18-19** Ps 103:9-12; Is 38:17; 43:25; Jr 31:34 [f]**7:20** Gn 24:27; 32:10 [g]Dt 7:8,12

[A]**7:19** Some Hb mss, LXX, Syr, Vg; other Hb mss read *their*

AUTHOR: Nahum

DATE: Between the destruction of Thebes and the destruction of Nineveh (around 663–612 B.C.)

Nahum ("Comforter") is from the town of Elkosh in northern Galilee, though the exact location cannot be pinpointed. He prophesied during the decline of Assyria, around 650 B.C. foretelling the destruction of Nineveh by the Babylonians—which was fulfilled in 612 B.C.

Fearsome invasions by the Assyrian raiders, shortages everywhere, and suffering unimaginable form the backdrop of Nahum's life and ministry. History has recorded great excesses of human cruelty, but nothing quite equals that of the Assyrians. Their savagery is unparalleled. Their victims chose death rather than face torture by their captors. Seldom before did a nation slide so fast from repentance (as shown in response to Jonah's prophecy) to brutality.

NAHUM

Enter the prophet Nahum. He is not your typical prophet. He is a poet, God's bard. Before he begins his prophecy against Assyria he needs a lot of personal reassurance. So he writes poetry, celebrating God's greatness and power. He sings, as it were, courage into his own soul. Chapter 1 is one great hymn extolling the glory, justice, and greatness of his Sender. "The LORD is a jealous and avenging God; the LORD takes vengeance and is fierce in wrath. The LORD takes vengeance against His foes; He is furious with His enemies" (1:2).

Nahum prophesies judgment against Nineveh, the capital of the Assyrians. But that message comes in precise summaries. It begins with a reference to the disarray of Assyria's picked troops. Next, God will drain all courage from the hearts of the special units. Their commanders will stumble on their way, their hearts will melt, every face growing pale. Their wealth, of which they never had enough, will vanish, and their efforts to recruit help will come to naught.

All that is just an introduction. In the third and last chapter of Nahum's message the actual judgment is spelled out. God's forces will attack Assyria. Assyria's casualties will be so many that the soldiers will stumble over the corpses. All her allies will forsake her. There will be no healing for Nineveh this time.

All the while Nahum has good news for Judah and Israel. Upon confession of sin, the Lord will send relief and remove their affliction. Even more: the Lord will restore the splendor of olden days.

As Nahum ends his prophecy, he once more provides the main reason for Assyria's judgment: "All who hear the news about you will clap their hands because of you, for who has not experienced your constant cruelty?" (3:19).

1 The •oracle concerning Nineveh.[a] The book of the vision of Nahum the Elkoshite.

God's Vengeance

2 The LORD is a jealous and avenging God;
the LORD takes vengeance
and is fierce in[A] wrath.
The LORD takes vengeance
against His foes;
He is furious with His enemies.[b]
3 The LORD is slow to anger but great
in power;
the LORD will never leave
the •guilty unpunished.[c]
His path is in the whirlwind
and storm,
and clouds are the dust
beneath His feet.
4 He rebukes the sea so that it dries up,
and He makes all the rivers run dry.[d]
Bashan and Carmel wither;[e]
even the flower of Lebanon withers.
5 The mountains quake before Him,
and the hills melt;
the earth trembles[B,C] at His presence—
the world and all who live in it.[f]
6 Who can withstand His indignation?
Who can endure His burning anger?[g]
His wrath is poured out like fire,
even rocks are shattered before Him.

Destruction of Nineveh

7 The LORD is good,
a stronghold in a day of distress;
He cares for those who take refuge[h]
in Him.
8 But He will completely
destroy Nineveh[D]
with an overwhelming flood,[i]
and He will chase His enemies
into darkness.
9 Whatever you[E] plot against the LORD,
He will bring it
to complete destruction;[j]
oppression will not rise up
a second time.
10 For they will be consumed
like entangled thorns,[k]
like the drink of a drunkard
and like straw that is fully dry.[F]
11 One has gone out from you,[G]
who plots evil against •Yahweh,
and is a wicked counselor.

Promise of Judah's Deliverance

12 This is what the LORD says:

Though they are strong[H]
and numerous,
they will still be mowed down,
and he[I] will pass away.
Though I have afflicted you,[J,l]
I will afflict you no longer.[m]
13 For I will now break off his yoke
from you
and tear off your shackles.

The Assyrian King's Demise

14 The LORD has issued an order concerning
you:

There will be no offspring
to carry on your name.[K,n]
I will eliminate the carved idol
and cast image
from the house of your gods;[o]
I will prepare your grave,
for you are contemptible.

15[L] Look to the mountains—
the feet of one bringing good news[p]
and proclaiming peace!
Celebrate your festivals, Judah;
fulfill your vows.
For the wicked one will never again
march through you;
he will be entirely wiped out.

Attack against Nineveh

2 One who scatters is coming up
against you.
Man the fortifications!
Watch the road!
Brace[M] yourself!
Summon all your strength![q]
2 For the LORD will restore the majesty
of Jacob,
yes,[N] the majesty of Israel,

[a] **1:1** Jnh 3:3-4; 4:11; Nah 2:8; Zph 2:13
[b] **1:2** Dt 6:15; Ps 94:1; Is 63:1-6; Jr 46:10; 50:28-29; Mc 5:15; Zph 1:18
[c] **1:3** Ex 34:6-7; Nm 14:18
[d] **1:4** 2Sm 22:16; Ps 106:9; Is 50:2
[e] Is 33:9
[f] **1:5** Ps 18:7; Jr 4:24; Am 8:8
[g] **1:6** Ps 7:11; 69:24; 78:49
[h] **1:7** 2Sm 22:3; Ps 17:7; 34:8
[i] **1:8** Nah 2:6
[j] **1:9** Ps 2:1-4
[k] **1:10** Mal 4:1
[l] **1:12** Is 10:5-34
[m] Ps 30:5; 103:9; Is 54:8
[n] **1:14** Lv 20:3; 1Sm 24:21; Ps 89:4; Is 48:19; 66:22
[o] Dt 27:15; Jdg 18:14
[p] **1:15** Is 52:7; 61:1; Rm 10:15
[q] **2:1** Am 2:14

[A] **1:2** Lit *is a master of* [B] **1:5** Some emend to *earth is laid waste* [C] **1:5** Lit *lifts* [D] **1:8** Lit *her place* [E] **1:9** = Nineveh [F] **1:10** Hb obscure [G] **1:11** Possibly Nineveh [H] **1:12** Lit *intact* [I] **1:12** Either the king of Assyria or his army [J] **1:12** = Judah [K] **1:14** Lit *It will not be sown from your name any longer* [L] **1:15** Nah 2:1 in Hb [M] **2:1** Lit *Strengthen* [N] **2:2** Or *like*

though ravagers have ravaged them
and ruined their vine branches.[a]
3 The shields of his[A] warriors
are dyed red;
the valiant men are dressed in scarlet.[b]
The fittings of the chariot flash like fire
on the day of its battle preparations,
and the spears are brandished.
4 The chariots dash madly
through the streets;
they rush around in the plazas.
They look like torches;
they dart back and forth like lightning.
5 He gives orders to his officers;
they stumble as they advance.
They race to its wall;
the protective shield is set in place.
6 The river gates are opened,
and the palace erodes away.[c]
7 Beauty[B] is stripped,[C]
she is carried away;
her ladies-in-waiting moan
like the sound of doves,[d]
and beat their breasts.
8 Nineveh has been like a pool of water
from her first days,[C]
but they are fleeing.
"Stop! Stop!" they cry,
but no one turns back.
9 "Plunder the silver! Plunder the gold!"
There is no end to the treasure,
an abundance of every precious thing.[e]
10 Desolation, decimation, devastation!
Hearts melt,[f]
knees tremble,
loins shake,
every face grows pale![g]
11 Where is the lions' lair,[h]
or the feeding ground
of the young lions,
where the lion and lioness prowled,
and the lion's cub,
with nothing to frighten them away?[i]
12 The lion mauled whatever
its cubs needed
and strangled prey for its lionesses.
It filled up its dens with the kill,
and its lairs with mauled prey.[j]

[a]**2:2** Ps 80:12-15; Jr 12:10 [b]**2:3** Ezk 23:14 [c]**2:6** Nah 1:8 [d]**2:7** Is 38:14; 59:11 [e]**2:9** 2Ch 32:27; 36:10; Dn 11:8; Nah 3:3 [f]**2:10** Dt 20:8; Jos 7:5; Is 13:7; 19:1; Ezk 21:7,15 [g]Is 21:3; Jl 2:6 [h]**2:11** Is 2:15; 5:26-29; Jr 4:7; 5:6; 50:17; 51:38; Jl 1:6; Am 3:12 [i]Lv 26:6; Dt 28:26; Jr 7:33 [j]**2:12** Jb 38:39-40 [k]**2:13** Jr 21:13; 50:31; 51:25; Nah 3:5 [l]**3:1** Ezk 24:6,9 [m]Nah 2:9 [n]**3:2** Jdg 5:22; Jb 39:24; Jr 47:3 [o]**3:3** Nah 2:9 [p]**3:4** 2Kg 9:22; Pr 7:10-23; Ezk 16:15; 23:1-21; Rv 17:3-6 [q]**3:5** Nah 2:13 [r]Jr 13:22,26; Ezk 16:37 [s]**3:8** Jr 46:25; Ezk 30:14-16

13 Beware, I am against you.[k]
This is the declaration
of the LORD of ˙Hosts.
I will make your chariots go up
in smoke[D]
and the sword will devour
your young lions.
I will cut off your prey from the earth,
and the sound of your messengers
will never be heard again.

Nineveh's Downfall

3 Woe to the city of blood,[l]
totally deceitful,
full of plunder,
never without prey.[m]
2 The crack of the whip
and rumble of the wheel,
galloping horse
and jolting chariot![n]
3 Charging horseman,
flashing sword,
shining spear;
heaps of slain,
mounds of corpses,
dead bodies without end[o]—
they stumble over their dead.
4 Because of the continual prostitution
of the prostitute,
the attractive mistress of sorcery,
who betrays nations by her prostitution
and clans by her witchcraft,[p]
5 I am against you.[q]
This is the declaration
of the LORD of ˙Hosts.
I will lift your skirts over your face
and display your nakedness to nations,
your shame to kingdoms.[r]
6 I will throw filth on you
and treat you with contempt;
I will make a spectacle of you.
7 Then all who see you will recoil
from you, saying,
"Nineveh is devastated;
who will show sympathy to her?"
Where can I find anyone
to comfort you?
8 Are you better than Thebes[E,s]
that sat along the Nile

[A]**2:3** = the army commander attacking Nineveh [B]**2:7** Text emended; MT reads *Huzzab* [C]**2:7,8** Hb obscure [D]**2:13** Lit *will burn her chariots in smoke* [E]**3:8** Or *No-amon*

with water surrounding her,
whose rampart was the sea,
the river[A,B] her wall?
9 ·Cush and Egypt were
her endless source of strength;
Put and Libya were among her[C] allies.
10 Yet she became an exile;
she went into captivity.
Her children were also dashed
to pieces[a]
at the head of every street.
They cast lots for her dignitaries,[b]
and all her nobles were bound
in chains.
11 You[D] also will become drunk;
you will hide yourself.[E]
You also will seek refuge
from the enemy.

12 All your fortresses are fig trees
with figs that ripened first;
when shaken, they fall —
right into the mouth of the eater!

13 Look, your troops are like women
among you;
the gates of your land
are wide open to your enemies.
Fire will devour the bars of your gates.

14 Draw water for the siege;
strengthen your fortresses.
Step into the clay and tread the mortar;

[a]3:10 2Kg 8:12; Is 13:16; Hs 10:14
[b]Ob 11
[c]3:15 Jl 1:4
[d]3:16 Ezk 27:3,13,20,23-24
[e]3:18 1Kg 22:17
[f]3:19 Jr 10:19; 14:17; 30:12

take hold of the brick-mold!
15 The fire will devour you there;
the sword will cut you down.
It will devour you like the young locust.[c]
Multiply yourselves
like the young locust,
multiply like the swarming locust!
16 You have made your merchants[d]
more numerous than the stars
of the sky.
The young locust strips[F] the land
and flies away.
17 Your court officials are
like the swarming locust,
and your scribes like clouds of locusts,
which settle on the walls on a cold day;
when the sun rises, they take off,
and no one knows where they are.

18 King of Assyria,
your shepherds slumber;
your officers sleep.
Your people are scattered
across the mountains
with no one to gather them together.[e]
19 There is no remedy for your injury;
your wound is severe.[f]
All who hear the news about you
will clap their hands because of you,
for who has not experienced
your constant cruelty?

[A]3:8 LXX, Syr, Vg read *water* [B]3:8 Lit *sea from sea* [C]3:9 Lit *your* [D]3:11 = Nineveh [E]3:11 Or *will be overcome* [F]3:16 Or *sheds its skin*

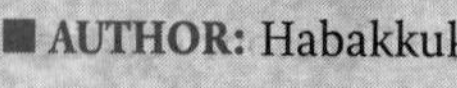

■ **AUTHOR:** Habakkuk

■■ **DATE:** After the destruction of Nineveh, but before Nebuchadnezzar's invasion of Judah (around 610 B.C.)

Habakkuk lived in Israel's southern kingdom (Judah). Not much is known about him. His message focuses on the days when Babylon has become the archenemy of Assyria, which will result in the latter's defeat at Carchemish, 605 B.C. These are critical times as nations go through great upheavals.

The name Habakkuk means "embracer" and "wrestler." Habakkuk was a deeply sensitive and peaceful man who was troubled by the chaos of his age and the moral decay of his people. He shows a sense of justice and goodwill as he describes the sin of his people and pleads for divine intervention. In that sense he is an embracer. But when God announces that He will use the cruel empire of Babylon to punish Judah, Habakkuk struggles to understand God's decision and how it relates to God's overall mission. In that sense he is a wrestler. He knows he must submit to God and that God is holy. But how could God allow such a catastrophe to befall Judah?

HABAKKUK

In the ensuing dialogue Habakkuk continues to express his loyalty to God but also his difficulty with God's disciplinary action. Gradually he finds a measure of peace. He clings to every word of assurance in God's answers. The Lord will keep the godly people of Judah in His safety. In the end that is enough for Habakkuk. God sums it up for His troubled servant: "the righteous one will live by his faith" (2:4).

As with Habakkuk, God wants His people to trust Him, even when they don't understand His plans. Habakkuk is the spokesman for many generations of believers deeply troubled by the question "Why do You tolerate those who are treacherous?" (1:13). While God may not answer that question, He does assure His children that He will never fail them. His mission in their lives will never be destroyed by the enemy.

We can make Habakkuk's final confession our own and rest in his God, even "though the fig tree does not bud and there is no fruit on the vines, though the olive crop fails and the fields produce no food, though there are no sheep in the pen and no cattle in the stalls, yet I will triumph in Yahweh; I will rejoice in the God of my salvation!" (3:17-18)

1 The •oracle that Habakkuk the prophet saw.[a]

Habakkuk's First Prayer

2 How long,[b] LORD, must I call for help[c]
and You do not listen
or cry out to You about violence
and You do not save?
3 Why do You force me to look
at injustice?[d]
Why do You tolerate[A] wrongdoing?
Oppression and violence are right
in front of me.
Strife is ongoing,
and conflict escalates.
4 This is why the law is ineffective
and justice never emerges.
For the wicked restrict[e] the righteous;
therefore, justice[f] comes out perverted.

God's First Answer

5 Look at the nations[B,g] and observe[h] —
be utterly astounded![i]
For something is taking place
in your days
that you will not believe[j]
when you hear about it.[k]
6 Look! I am raising up[l] the Chaldeans,[C]
that bitter,[m] impetuous nation
that marches across
the earth's open spaces
to seize territories not its own.
7 They are fierce[n] and terrifying;
their views of justice and sovereignty
stem from themselves.
8 Their horses are swifter[o] than leopards[p]
and more fierce[D] than wolves
of the night.
Their horsemen charge ahead;
their horsemen come
from distant lands.
They fly like an eagle,
swooping to devour.[q]
9 All of them come to do violence;
their faces[r] are set in determination.[E]
They gather[s] prisoners like sand.[t]
10 They mock[u] kings,
and rulers are a joke to them.
They laugh[v] at every fortress
and build siege ramps to capture[w] it.
11 Then they sweep[x] by like the wind
and pass through.
They are •guilty;[F] their strength
is their god.

Habakkuk's Second Prayer

12 Are You not from eternity,
•Yahweh my God?
My Holy One,[y] You[G] will not die.
LORD, You appointed them
to execute judgment;
my Rock,[z] You destined them
to punish us.
13 Your eyes[aa] are too pure[ab] to look on evil,
and You cannot tolerate wrongdoing.
So why do You tolerate those
who are treacherous?[ac]
Why are You silent
while one[H] who is wicked swallows up
one[I] who is more righteous
than himself?
14 You have made mankind
like the fish of the sea,[ad]
like marine creatures that have
no ruler.
15 The Chaldeans pull them all up
with a hook,
catch them in their dragnet,[ae]
and gather them in their fishing net;
that is why they are glad and rejoice.
16 That is why they sacrifice
to their dragnet
and burn incense to their fishing net,
for by these things
their portion is rich
and their food plentiful.[af]
17 Will they therefore empty their net[J]
and continually slaughter nations
without mercy?

Habakkuk Waits for God's Response

2 I will stand at my guard post
and station myself
on the lookout tower.[ag]
I will watch to see what He will say
to me[ah]
and what I should[K] reply
about my complaint.

[a] 1:1 Nm 24:4; Jb 19:26; Is 13:1 [b] 1:2 Ps 4:2; 6:3; 13:1 [c] Jb 19:7; Ps 5:2; Lm 3:8 [d] 1:3 Jb 4:8; Ps 5:5; Is 5:7 [e] 1:4 Jdg 20:43; Ps 22:12 [f] Ex 23:6 [g] 1:5 Ps 2:1 [h] Gn 15:5 [i] Gn 43:33; Ps 48:5; Ec 5:8 [j] Gn 15:6 [k] Ac 13:41 [l] 1:6 Ru 4:5 [m] Jdg 18:25 [n] 1:7 Sg 6:4,10 [o] 1:8 2Sm 1:23 [p] Is 11:6; Jr 5:6; 13:23; Hs 13:7 [q] Dt 28:49 [r] 1:9 Gn 48:11 [s] Dt 11:14 [t] Jos 11:4 [u] 1:10 2Kg 2:23 [v] 2Ch 30:10 [w] Nm 21:32 [x] 1:11 Is 8:8 [y] 1:12 Is 1:4 [z] Dt 32:4; Ps 18:2 [aa] 1:13 2Ch 6:20; 16:9 [ab] Ex 25:11; Ps 12:6; 19:9; 51:10; Pr 22:11; Ezk 36:25 [ac] Jdg 9:23 [ad] 1:14 Ec 9:12 [ae] 1:15 Jr 16:16; Am 4:2 [af] 1:16 Dt 8:17; Is 10:13; 37:24-25 [ag] 2:1 Is 21:6-9 [ah] Ps 85:8

[A] 1:3 Lit *observe* [B] 1:5 DSS, LXX, Syr read *Look, you treacherous people* [C] 1:6 = the Babylonians [D] 1:8 Or *and quicker* [E] 1:9 Hb obscure [F] 1:11 Or *wind, and transgress and incur guilt* [G] 1:12 Ancient Jewish tradition reads *we* [H] 1:13 = Babylon [I] 1:13 = Judah [J] 1:17 DSS read *sword* [K] 2:1 Syr reads *what He will*

God's Second Answer

2 The LORD answered me:

Write down this vision;[a]
clearly inscribe it on tablets
so one may easily read it.[A]
3 For the vision is yet
for the appointed time;
it testifies about the end
and will not lie.
Though it delays, wait for it,
since it will certainly come and not
be late.[b]
4 Look, his ego is inflated;[B]
he is without integrity.
But the righteous one will live
by his faith.[C,c]
5 Moreover, wine[D] betrays;
an arrogant man is never at rest.[E]
He enlarges his appetite like ·Sheol,
and like Death he is never satisfied.[d]
He gathers all the nations to himself;
he collects all the peoples for himself.

The Five Woe Oracles

6 Won't all of these take up a taunt
against him,
with mockery and riddles about him?
They will say:

Woe to him who amasses
what is not his —
how much longer? —
and loads himself with goods
taken in pledge.[e]
7 Won't your creditors suddenly arise,
and those who disturb you wake up?
Then you will become spoil for them.[f]
8 Since you have plundered
many nations,
all the peoples who remain
will plunder you —
because of human bloodshed
and violence against lands, cities,
and all who live in them.[g]
9 Woe to him who dishonestly makes
wealth for his house[F]
to place his nest on high,
to escape from the reach of disaster![h]
10 You have planned shame for your house
by wiping out many peoples
and sinning against your own self.
11 For the stones will cry out[i]
from the wall,
and the rafters will answer them
from the woodwork.
12 Woe to him who builds a city
with bloodshed
and founds a town with injustice![j]
13 Is it not from the LORD of ·Hosts
that the peoples labor only to fuel
the fire
and countries exhaust themselves
for nothing?[k]
14 For the earth will be filled
with the knowledge of the LORD's glory,
as the waters cover the sea.[l]
15 Woe to him who gives
his neighbors drink,
pouring out your wrath[G]
and even making them drunk,
in order to look at their nakedness!
16 You will be filled with disgrace
instead of glory.
You also — drink,
and expose your uncircumcision![H]
The cup in the LORD's right hand
will come around to you,
and utter disgrace will cover
your glory.[m]
17 For your violence against Lebanon
will overwhelm you;
the destruction of animals
will terrify you[I]
because of your human bloodshed
and violence
against lands, cities, and all who live
in them.
18 What use is a carved idol
after its craftsman carves it?
It is only a cast image, a teacher of lies.
For the one who crafts its shape
trusts in it
and makes idols that cannot speak.
19 Woe to him who says to wood:
Wake up!
or to mute stone: Come alive!
Can it teach?

[a]2:2 1Sm 3:1; Ps 89:19; Pr 29:18; Is 1:1 [b]2:3 Dn 10:1,14; 11:35; Heb 10:36-37; 2Pt 3:9; Rv 22:10 [c]2:4 Rm 1:17; Gl 3:11 [d]2:5 Pr 27:20; 30:15-16; Is 5:14 [e]2:6 Dt 24:10-13 [f]2:7 2Kg 21:14; Is 42:22,24 [g]2:8 Is 33:1; Jr 25:12,14; Rv 13:10 [h]2:9 Pr 11:28; Jr 22:13; 49:16; Ob 4; Rv 18:7 [i]2:11 Lk 19:40 [j]2:12 Ezk 22:2-3; Mc 3:10 [k]2:13 Jr 51:58 [l]2:14 Ps 72:19; Is 6:3; 11:9 [m]2:15-16 Rv 14:8-10

[A]2:2 Lit *one who reads in it may run* [B]2:4 Hb obscure [C]2:4 Or *faithfulness* [D]2:5 DSS read *wealth* [E]2:5 Or *man does not endure*; Hb obscure [F]2:9 Or *dynasty* [G]2:15 Or *venom* [H]2:16 DSS, LXX, Aq, Syr, Vg read *and stagger* [I]2:17 DSS, LXX, Aq, Syr, Tg, Vg; MT reads *them*

Look! It may be plated with gold
and silver,
yet there is no breath in it at all.

20 But the LORD is in His holy temple;
let everyone on earth
be silent in His presence.[a]

Habakkuk's Third Prayer

3 A prayer of Habakkuk the prophet. According to *Shigionoth*.[A,b]

2 LORD, I have heard the report
about You;
LORD, I stand in awe of Your deeds.
Revive Your work in these years;
make it known in these years.
In Your wrath remember mercy!

3 God comes from Teman,
the Holy One from Mount Paran.[c]
Selah

His splendor covers the heavens,
and the earth is full of His praise.[d]
4 His brilliance is like light;
rays are flashing from His hand.
This is where His power is hidden.
5 Plague goes before Him,
and pestilence follows in His steps.
6 He stands and shakes[B] the earth;
He looks and startles the nations.
The age-old mountains break apart;
the ancient hills sink down.
His pathways are ancient.
7 I see the tents of Cushan[C] in distress;
the tent curtains of the land
of Midian tremble.
8 Are You angry at the rivers, LORD?
Is Your wrath against the rivers?
Or is Your rage against the sea
when You ride on Your horses,
Your victorious chariot?
9 You took the sheath from Your bow;
the arrows are ready[D] to be used
with an oath.[E,e] *Selah*
You split the earth with rivers.
10 The mountains see You and shudder;[f]
a downpour of water sweeps by.
The deep roars with its voice[g]
and lifts its waves[F] high.
11 Sun and moon stand still
in their lofty residence,[h]
at the flash of Your flying arrows,
at the brightness
of Your shining spear.
12 You march across the earth
with indignation;
You trample down the nations
in wrath.
13 You come out to save Your people,
to save Your anointed.[G]
You crush the leader of the house
of the wicked
and strip him from foot[H] to neck. *Selah*
14 You pierce his head
with his own spears;
his warriors storm out to scatter us,
gloating as if ready to secretly devour
the weak.
15 You tread the sea with Your horses,
stirring up the great waters.[i]

Habakkuk's Confidence in God Expressed

16 I heard, and I trembled within;[j]
my lips quivered at the sound.
Rottenness entered my bones;
I trembled where I stood.
Now I must quietly wait for the day
of distress
to come against the people invading us.
17 Though the fig tree does not bud
and there is no fruit on the vines,
though the olive crop fails
and the fields produce no food,
though there are no sheep in the pen
and no cattle in the stalls,
18 yet I will triumph in Yahweh;
I will rejoice in the God
of my salvation![k]
19 Yahweh my Lord is my strength;
He makes my feet like those of a deer[l]
and enables me to walk
on mountain heights![m]

For the choir director: on[I] stringed instruments.

[a]2:20 Zph 1:7; Zch 2:13 [b]3:1 Ps 7 title [c]3:3 Dt 33:2; Jdg 5:4-5 [d]Jb 37:22; Ps 148:13; Is 42:10 [e]3:9 Dt 32:40-43 [f]3:10 Ps 77:16 [g]Ex 19:18 [h]3:11 Jos 10:12-13 [i]3:15 Ps 77:19 [j]3:16 Dn 10:4-9; Rv 1:17 [k]3:18 Ps 73:25 [l]3:19 Ps 18:33 [m]2Sm 22:34; Ps 18:33

A3:1 Perhaps a passionate song with rapid changes of rhythm, or a dirge B3:6 Or *surveys* C3:7 = Midian D3:9 Or *set* E3:9 Hb obscure F3:10 Lit *hands* G3:13 The Davidic king or the nation of Israel H3:13 Lit *foundation* I3:19 Lit *on my*

■ **AUTHOR:** Zephaniah

■■ **DATE:** During the reign of Josiah (around 625 B.C.)

Zephaniah's prophecy has a unique beginning: we read that four of his forefathers were of princely blood. We may assume that he was a man of distinction among his people. We also learn that he prophesied during the reign of King Josiah of Judah, 639–608 B.C.

We further learn that Josiah, a good and godly king, was the son of Amon, a king who followed the evil pathways of his forefathers. Josiah cleaned up after his father by inaugurating two reformations (2Ch 34). But our prophet does not refer to the good work of King Josiah. He describes the evil found in Judah and Israel and in the surrounding nations. Zephaniah's prophecies may have preceded the reformations of Josiah. It is also possible that the first reformation was not fully completed and evil continued its course,

ZEPHANIAH

thus making the second reformation necessary. In that case, Zephaniah prophesied in between the two reformations.

Zephaniah's prophecy is directed as much to the surrounding nations as to Judah and Israel. What looms large, internationally, is the decline of Assyria and the ascent of Babylon, the land of the Chaldeans. In the great ensuing clash of those two world powers, Nineveh, the capital of Assyria, will be destroyed. It is likely that Zephaniah prophesied just before that event. Nothing can stop the Chaldeans. Judah and Israel will soon quake with fear in the face of the approaching hordes from the East.

All these developments play a role in Zephaniah's prophecy. The Lord will use the Babylonians to punish His people. Before he addresses the other nations, the prophet devotes the entire first chapter to the sins of Judah. The people, led by "the king's sons" (1:8), have followed Baal and Milcom and worshiped the heavenly host.

The impending punishment will be severe. The prophet speaks of the "Day of the LORD" (1:14), an expression occurring several times in this short prophecy. The "Day of the LORD" refers to three major judgments that God will send upon His people and the world. First, the exile of the people of Judah to Babylon; second, the destruction of Jerusalem by the Romans in A.D. 70; third, we may recognize the overtones of the day of Christ's return to judge the nations.

Zephaniah stipulates that the evil neighbors of God's people will fully share in these judgments. He singles out Philistia, Moab, Ammon, Cush, and Assyria. Their ruin will be complete.

But the mission of God will not be in vain. There will be repentance. A "remnant" will be saved and restored to the Lord's favor. The end of the prophecy is a lovely prediction of the joy of God and His people communing together. "On that day it will be said to Jerusalem: 'Do not fear; Zion, do not let your hands grow weak. Yahweh your God is among you, a warrior who saves. He will rejoice over you with gladness. He will bring you quietness with His love. He will delight in you with shouts of joy" (3:16-17).

1 The word of the LORD that came to Zephaniah son of Cushi, son of Gedaliah, son of
Amariah, son of Hezekiah, in the days of Josiah[a] son of Amon, king of Judah.

The Great Day of the LORD

2 I will completely
sweep away everything
from the face of the earth[b] —
this is the LORD's declaration.
3 I will sweep away man and animal;[c]
I will sweep away the birds of the sky
and the fish of the sea,
and the ruins[A] along with the wicked.[d]
I will cut off mankind
from the face of the earth.
This is the LORD's declaration.

4 I will stretch out My hand[e]
against Judah
and against all the residents
of Jerusalem.
I will cut off every vestige of ˙Baal[f]
from this place,
the names of the pagan priests[g]
along with the priests;
5 those who bow in worship
on the rooftops[h]
to the heavenly host;
those who bow and pledge loyalty
to the LORD[i]
but also pledge loyalty to ˙Milcom;[B,j]
6 and those who turn back
from following the LORD,
who do not seek the LORD or inquire
of Him.
7 Be silent in the presence
of the Lord GOD,[k]
for the Day of the LORD is near.[l]
Indeed, the LORD has prepared
a sacrifice;[m]
He has consecrated His guests.[n]

8 On the day of the LORD's sacrifice
I will punish the officials,
the king's sons,
and all who are dressed
in foreign clothing.
9 On that day[o] I will punish
all who skip over the threshold,[C,p]
who fill their master's house
with violence and deceit.

10 On that day —
this is the LORD's declaration —
there will be an outcry
from the Fish Gate,[q]
a wailing from the Second District,[r]
and a loud crashing from the hills.
11 Wail, you residents of the Hollow,[D]
for all the merchants[E] will be silenced;
all those loaded with silver will be
cut off.

12 And at that time I will search Jerusalem
with lamps
and punish the men
who settle down comfortably,[F,s]
who say to themselves:
The LORD will not do good or evil.
13 Their wealth will become plunder
and their houses a ruin.
They will build houses but never live
in them,
plant vineyards but never drink
their wine.[t]

14 The great Day of the LORD is near,[u]
near and rapidly approaching.
Listen, the Day of the LORD —
then the warrior's cry is bitter.
15 That day is a day of wrath,
a day of trouble and distress,
a day of destruction and desolation,
a day of darkness[v] and gloom,
a day of clouds and blackness,[w]
16 a day of trumpet blast and battle cry
against the fortified cities,
and against the high corner towers.
17 I will bring distress on mankind,
and they will walk like the blind[x]
because they have sinned
against the LORD.
Their blood will be poured out like dust
and their flesh like dung.
18 Their silver and their gold
will not be able to rescue them
on the day of the LORD's wrath.[y]
The whole earth will be consumed
by the fire of His jealousy.[z]
For He will make a complete,

[a]**1:1** 2Kg 22:1–23:30; 2Ch 34:1–36:1; Jr 1:2
[b]**1:2** Gn 6:7; 7:4
[c]**1:3** 1Kg 14:10; Ezk 14:17
[d]Is 13:9-12; Mt 13:41
[e]**1:4** Ex 3:20; Ps 138:7; Ezk 14:9; 25:7,16; Zph 2:13
[f]1Kg 16:30-32
[g]2Kg 23:5
[h]**1:5** Jr 19:13; 32:29
[i]Dt 6:13; Is 48:1
[j]1Kg 11:5; 2Kg 23:13; Jr 49:1,3
[k]**1:7** Nm 13:30; Jdg 3:19; Hab 2:20; Zch 2:13
[l]Zph 1:14,18; 2:2-3
[m]Is 34:6; Jr 46:10
[n]Lv 7:11-21; 1Sm 16:5; 2Ch 35:5-13; Jr 22:17
[o]**1:9** Zph 1:10; 3:11,16
[p]1Sm 5:5
[q]**1:10** 2Ch 33:14; Neh 3:3; 12:39
[r]2Kg 22:14; 2Ch 34:22
[s]**1:12** Ex 15:8; Is 25:6; Jr 48:11
[t]**1:13** Dt 28:30; Am 5:11; Mc 6:15
[u]**1:14** Is 13:6,9; Jl 1:15; 2:1,11,31; 3:14; Am 5:18,20; Ob 15; Zch 14:1; Mal 4:5
[v]**1:15** Am 5:18-20
[w]Ps 97:2; Ezk 34:12; Jl 2:2
[x]**1:17** Lm 4:14
[y]**1:18** Ezk 7:19
[z]Ex 34:14

A**1:3** Perhaps objects connected with idolatry B**1:5** Some LXX mss, Syr, Vg; MT, other LXX mss read *their king* C**1:9** Hb obscure D**1:11** Or *the market district* E**1:11** Or *Canaanites* F**1:12** Lit *who thicken on their dregs*

yes, a horrifying end
of all the inhabitants of the earth.

A Call to Repentance

2 Gather yourselves together;
gather together, undesirable[A] nation,
2 before the decree[a] takes effect
and the day passes like chaff,
before the burning of the LORD's anger
overtakes you,
before the day of the LORD's anger
overtakes you.
3 Seek the LORD,[b] all you humble[c]
of the earth,
who carry out what He commands.
Seek righteousness, seek humility;
perhaps you will be concealed[d]
on the day of the LORD's anger.

Judgment against the Nations

4 For Gaza will be abandoned,
and Ashkelon will become a ruin.
Ashdod will be driven out at noon,
and Ekron will be uprooted.[e]
5 Woe, inhabitants of the seacoast,
nation of the Cherethites![B,f]
The word of the LORD is against you,
Canaan, land of the Philistines:
I will destroy you until there is
no one left.
6 The seacoast will become pasturelands
with caves for shepherds and folds
for sheep.
7 The coastland will belong
to the remnant of the house of Judah;
they will find pasture there.
They will lie down in the evening
among the houses of Ashkelon,
for the LORD their God will return
to them
and restore their fortunes.

8 I have heard the taunting of Moab
and the insults of the Ammonites,[g]
who have taunted My people
and threatened their territory.
9 Therefore, as I live —
this is the declaration
of the LORD of ·Hosts,
the God of Israel —
Moab will be like Sodom
and the Ammonites like Gomorrah[h] —
a place overgrown with weeds,
a salt pit, and a perpetual wasteland.
The remnant of My people
will plunder them;
the remainder of My nation
will dispossess them.
10 This is what they get for their pride,
because they have taunted
and acted arrogantly[i]
against the people of the LORD of Hosts.
11 The LORD will be terrifying to them
when He starves all the gods
of the earth.
Then all the distant coastlands
of the nations
will bow in worship to Him,
each in its own place.

12 You ·Cushites will also be slain
by My sword.[j]

13 He will also stretch out His hand
against the north
and destroy Assyria;
He will make Nineveh a desolate ruin,[k]
dry as the desert.
14 Herds will lie down in the middle of it,
every kind of wild animal.[C]
Both the desert owl[D] and the screech owl[E]
will roost in the capitals of its pillars.
Their calls will sound[F]
from the window,
but devastation[G] will be
on the threshold,
for He will expose the cedar work.[H]
15 This is the self-assured[l] city
that lives in security,
that thinks to herself:
I exist, and there is no one else.
What a desolation she has become,
a place for wild animals to lie down!
Everyone who passes by her
jeers[I] and shakes his fist.

Woe to Oppressive Jerusalem

3 Woe to the city that is rebellious[J,m]
and defiled,[n]
the oppressive city!

[a]2:2 Ps 2:7; 148:6 [b]2:3 Am 5:14 [c]Nm 12:3; Ps 25:9; 37:11; 76:9; Am 8:4 [d]Gn 4:14; Ex 3:6; Ps 17:8 [e]2:4 Jr 25:20; Am 1:6-8; Zch 9:5-7 [f]2:5 Ezk 25:16 [g]2:8 Am 1:13 [h]2:9 Gn 19:24-25 [i]2:10 Jr 48:42 [j]2:12 Is 18:1-7 [k]2:13 Nah 2:8; 3:7 [l]2:15 Is 13:3; 22:2; 23:7; 24:8; 32:13; Zph 3:11 [m]3:1 Ex 23:21; Dt 9:24; Ps 106:43 [n]Is 59:3

A2:1 Or *shameless* B2:5 = Sea Peoples C2:14 Lit *every wild animal of a nation* D2:14 Or *the pelican* E2:14 Or *the hedgehog* F2:14 Lit *sing* G2:14 LXX, Vg read *ravens* H2:14 Hb obscure I2:15 Or *hisses* J3:1 Or *filthy*

2 She has not obeyed;[a]
she has not accepted discipline.[b]
She has not trusted[c] in •Yahweh;
she has not drawn near to her God.
3 The[A] princes within her are
roaring lions;[d]
her judges are wolves of the night,[e]
which leave nothing for[B] the morning.
4 Her prophets are reckless[f] —
treacherous men.
Her priests profane the sanctuary;
they do violence to instruction.[g]
5 The righteous LORD is in her;[h]
He does no wrong.[i]
He applies His justice morning
by morning;
He does not fail at dawn,
yet the one who does wrong
knows no shame.[j]

6 I have cut off nations;
their corner towers[k] are destroyed.
I have laid waste their streets,
with no one to pass through.
Their cities lie devastated,
without a person,
without an inhabitant.[l]
7 I thought: You will certainly •fear Me
and accept correction.
Then her dwelling place[C]
would not be cut off
based on all that I had allocated to her.
However, they became more corrupt
in all their actions.
8 Therefore, wait for Me[m] —
this is the LORD's declaration —
until the day I rise up for plunder.[D]
For My decision is to gather nations,
to assemble kingdoms,
in order to pour out My indignation[n]
on them,
all My burning anger;
for the whole earth will be consumed
by the fire of My jealousy.[o]

Final Restoration Promised

9 For I will then restore
pure[p] speech to the peoples
so that all of them may call
on the name of Yahweh
and serve Him with a single purpose.[E]
10 From beyond the rivers of •Cush[q]
My supplicants, My dispersed people,
will bring an offering to Me.
11 On that day you[F] will not be put
to shame[r]
because of everything you have done
in rebelling[s] against Me.
For then I will remove
your proud,[t] arrogant people
from among you,
and you will never again be haughty
on My holy mountain.[u]
12 I will leave
a meek and humble people[v] among you,
and they will take refuge in the name
of Yahweh.
13 The remnant[w] of Israel will no longer
do wrong or tell lies;
a deceitful tongue will not be found
in their mouths.
But they will pasture and lie down,
with nothing to make them afraid.[x]

14 Sing for joy, Daughter •Zion;
shout loudly, Israel!
Be glad and rejoice with all your heart,
Daughter Jerusalem!
15 The LORD has removed
your punishment;
He has turned back your enemy.
The King of Israel, Yahweh,
is among you;
you need no longer fear harm.
16 On that day it will be said to Jerusalem:
"Do not fear;
Zion, do not let your hands grow weak.[y]
17 Yahweh your God is among you,
a warrior[z] who saves.
He will rejoice over you[aa] with gladness.
He will bring you quietness[G]
with His love.
He will delight in you with shouts
of joy."[ab]

18 I will gather those
who have been driven[ac]
from the appointed festivals;
they will be a tribute from you[H]
and a reproach on her.[I]

[a] **3:2** 1Sm 15:22 [b] Jb 5:17 [c] Pr 3:5 [d] **3:3** Ezk 22:25 [e] Hab 1:8; Mt 7:15; Ac 20:29 [f] **3:4** Jdg 9:4 [g] Ezk 22:26 [h] **3:5** Ps 129:4 [i] Ps 92:15 [j] Jr 8:12 [k] **3:6** Zph 1:16 [l] Jr 44:2; Zph 2:5 [m] **3:8** Jb 3:21; Ps 33:20; Is 8:17; 30:18; 64:4 [n] Ps 69:24; Ezk 21:31; 22:31; Nah 1:6 [o] Dt 29:20; Ps 79:5; Zch 1:14; 8:2 [p] **3:9** Dn 12:10 [q] **3:10** Is 18:1-3 [r] **3:11** Gn 2:25; 2Sm 19:5; Ps 25:3 [s] Is 1:2 [t] Jr 48:29 [u] Is 11:9 [v] **3:12** Is 66:2 [w] **3:13** Gn 45:7; 2Kg 19:31; Jr 23:3 [x] Gn 42:28; Jr 50:19; Ezk 34:14; Mc 4:4; 7:14 [y] **3:16** Jr 6:24; 50:43 [z] **3:17** Jos 1:14; Jb 16:14; Ps 78:65 [aa] Dt 28:63; 30:9 [ab] Ps 30:5 [ac] **3:18** Lm 1:4-5; 3:33

[A] **3:3** Lit *Her* [B] **3:3** Or *that had nothing to gnaw in* [C] **3:7** LXX, Syr read *her eyes* [D] **3:8** LXX, Syr read *for a witness*; Vg reads *up forever* [E] **3:9** Lit *with one shoulder* [F] **3:11** = Israel [G] **3:17** LXX, Syr read *He will renew you* [H] **3:18** = Jerusalem [I] **3:18** Hb obscure

19 Yes, at that time
I will deal with all who afflict you.
I will save the lame[a] and gather
the scattered;[b]
I will make those who were disgraced
throughout the earth
receive praise and fame.

20 At that time I will bring you[A] back,
yes, at the time I will gather you.
I will give you fame and praise
among all the peoples of the earth,
when I restore your fortunes[c]
before your eyes.
Yahweh has spoken.

[a]3:19 Ex 14:30
[b]Mc 4:6
[c]3:20 Jb 42:10; Jr 29:14; Ezk 39:25; Hs 6:11; Jl 3:1

[A]3:20 = people of Israel

■ **AUTHOR:** Haggai

■■ **DATE:** After the exile (around 520 B.C.)

The prophet Haggai assumes a unique place among the twelve Minor Prophets. He addresses the remnant of God's people soon after they returned to Jerusalem from captivity in Babylon. (See the book of Ezra for more details.) Haggai appears on the scene some eighteen years after the return of the remnant, during the second year of Darius (also called Darius Hystaspes), king of Persia. The year is about 520 B.C.

Not much is known about the prophet Haggai. His name may have been derived from a root that means "happiness." Haggai's prophecy concerns the fact that the people stopped building the temple in Jerusalem. The people thought they had a good reason to put the Lord's building program on hiatus: their own needs were urgent. They had fairly recently finished the long trek from Babylon. Having a roof over their heads was a priority. It had probably not occurred to them that fifteen years had passed by with little or no progress on the building project.

HAGGAI

Haggai quotes the naysayers. "These people say: The time has not come for the house of the LORD to be rebuilt" (1:2). As it was, they had hoped to get their "paneled houses" finished first (1:3).

The prophet then launches into some very practical teaching. He asks the people if they had noticed that so many things had gone wrong in their lives. Crops are minimal, clothes give no warmth, and food and drink fail to satisfy. There is no doubt about Haggai's message: shortchanging God reaps shortchanges in life.

Next comes the challenge: go back to the renovation! God promised to provide if they obeyed. God pricked the hearts of two good leaders: Zerubbabel, governor of Judah, and Joshua, the high priest. Once they and the other leaders accepted Haggai's message, the people followed through and started work on the temple once more.

The second half of the prophecy is one glorious reassurance from the Lord. He will fill this temple with His peace and glory. Haggai's reference to the glory of this temple was fulfilled in the coming of the Messiah.

The conclusion of this short prophecy is even more personal than the beginning. The Lord singles out Zerubbabel, His faithful servant, for a special message. He tells him that he will be "like My signet ring" (2:23)—honored. God rewards this humble leader with special powers, as His envoy among His people. Thus Zerubbabel foreshadowed Christ.

God's children have that honor today: in Christ they are God's signet ring, representing Him in the world. Good leaders, good goals, but all the people must work together. God's mission is far from done.

Command to Rebuild the Temple

1 In the second year of King Darius,[A,a] on the
first day of the sixth month, the word of
the LORD came through Haggai[b] the prophet
to Zerubbabel son of Shealtiel,[c] the governor
of Judah, and to Joshua son of Jehozadak, the
high priest:[d]

2"The LORD of ·Hosts says this: These people say: The time has not come for the house
of the LORD to be rebuilt."[e]

3The word of the LORD came through Haggai the prophet: 4"Is it a time for you yourselves to live in your paneled houses,[f] while
this house[B] lies in ruins?" 5Now, the LORD of
Hosts says this: "Think carefully[g] about[C] your
ways:

6 You have planted much
but harvested little.
You eat
but never have enough
to be satisfied.
You drink
but never have enough
to become drunk.
You put on clothes
but never have enough to get warm.
The wage earner puts his wages
into a bag with a hole in it."[h]

7The LORD of Hosts says this: "Think carefully about[C] your ways. 8Go up into the hills,
bring down lumber, and build the house.
Then I will be pleased with it and be glorified," says the LORD. 9"You expected much,
but then it amounted to little. When you
brought the harvest to your house, I ruined[D]
it. Why?" This is the declaration of the LORD
of Hosts. "Because My house still lies in ruins, while each of you is busy with his own
house.

10 So on your account,[E]
the skies have withheld the dew
and the land its crops.[i]
11 I have summoned a drought
on the fields and the hills,
on the grain, new wine, olive oil,
and whatever the ground yields,
on man and beast,
and on all that your hands produce."

[a]**1:1** Ezr 4:5; Neh 12:22; Dn 9:11; 11:1; Hg 1:15; 2:10; Zch 1:1,7; 7:1
[b]Ezr 5:1; 6:14
[c]1Ch 3:19; Ezr 3:2,8; 5:2; Neh 12:1; Hg 1:12,14; 2:2,23; Lk 3:27
[d]Hg 1:12,14; 2:2,4; Zch 3:1,8; 6:11
[e]**1:2** Ezr 1:3
[f]**1:4** 1Kg 7:7; Jr 22:14
[g]**1:5** Hg 2:15,18
[h]**1:6** Lv 26:20; Dt 28:38-40
[i]**1:10** Lv 26:20; Dt 11:17
[j]**1:12** 1Ch 13:9; Ezr 3:8; Neh 12:1; Hg 2:2; Zch 4:6
[k]Is 10:20-21; Jr 41:10; Hg 2:2
[l]Ex 14:31; Dt 4:10; 1Sm 12:18
[m]**1:13** Hg 2:4
[n]**1:14** 1Ch 5:26; Ezr 1:1,5; Is 13:17; 14:9; 41:10; 45:13; Jr 51:11
[o]**2:1** Lv 23:33-43; 2Ch 7:8-10
[p]**2:3** 1Kg 5:13-16; 6:38; 1Ch 29:1-8; Ezr 3:10-13; Zch 4:10
[q]**2:4** Jos 1:6-9; 1Ch 28:10,20
[r]Hg 1:13; Zch 8:9
[s]**2:5** Ex 33:14-17
[t]**2:6** Hg 2:21
[u]Is 64:2; Ezk 38:19-20; Heb 12:26-28
[v]**2:7** Ex 40:34-35; 1Kg 8:10-11; Is 60:1-13
[w]**2:9** Mt 12:42

The People's Response

12Then Zerubbabel[j] son of Shealtiel, the
high priest Joshua son of Jehozadak, and
the entire remnant of the people[k] obeyed the
voice of the LORD their God and the words of
the prophet Haggai, because the LORD their
God had sent him. So the people ·feared the
LORD.[l]

13Haggai, the LORD's messenger, delivered
the LORD's message to the people, "I am with
you"[m] — this is the LORD's declaration.

14The LORD stirred up the spirit[n] of Zerubbabel son of Shealtiel, governor of Judah,
the spirit of the high priest Joshua son of Jehozadak, and the spirit of all the remnant of
the people. They began work on the house of
·Yahweh of Hosts, their God, 15on the twenty-
fourth day of the sixth month, in the second
year of King Darius.

Encouragement and Promise

2 On the twenty-first day of the seventh
month,[o] the word of the LORD came
through Haggai the prophet: 2"Speak to
Zerubbabel son of Shealtiel, governor of
Judah, to the high priest Joshua son of Jehozadak, and to the remnant of the people:
3Who is left among you who saw this house
in its former glory? How does it look to you
now? Doesn't it seem like nothing to you?[F,p]
4Even so, be strong, Zerubbabel" — this is the
LORD's declaration.[q] "Be strong, Joshua son
of Jehozadak, high priest. Be strong, all you
people of the land" — this is the LORD's declaration. "Work! For I am with you"[r] — the declaration of the LORD of ·Hosts. 5"This is the
promise I made to you when you came out of
Egypt,[s] and My Spirit is present among you;
don't be afraid."

6For the LORD of Hosts says this: "Once
more, in a little while, I am going to shake
the heavens and the earth,[t] the sea and the
dry land.[u] 7I will shake all the nations so that
the treasures of all the nations will come,
and I will fill this house with glory,"[v] says the
LORD of Hosts. 8"The silver and gold belong to
Me" — this is the declaration of the LORD of
Hosts. 9"The final glory of this house[G] will be
greater than the first,"[w] says the LORD of Hosts.

[A]**1:1** King of Persia reigned 522–486 B.C. [B]**1:4** = the temple [C]**1:5,7** Lit *Place your heart on* [D]**1:9** Lit *blew on* [E]**1:10** Or *So above you* [F]**2:3** Lit *Is it not in your eyes?* [G]**2:9** Or *The glory of this latter house*

"I will provide peace in this place"[a] — this is
the declaration of the LORD of Hosts.

From Deprivation to Blessing

10On the twenty-fourth day of the ninth
month, in the second year of Darius, the word
of the LORD came to Haggai the prophet:
11"This is what the LORD of Hosts says: Ask
the priests for a ruling.[b] 12If a man is carrying
consecrated meat in the fold of his garment,
and it touches bread, stew, wine, oil, or any
other food, does it become holy?"[c]
The priests answered, "No."
13Then Haggai asked, "If someone defiled
by contact with a corpse touches any of these,
does it become defiled?"[d]
The priests answered, "It becomes defiled."
14Then Haggai replied, "So is this people, and
so is this nation before Me" — this is the LORD's
declaration. "And so is every work of their
hands; even what they offer there is defiled.
15"Now, reflect back from this day: Before one stone was placed on another in
the LORD's temple, 16what state were you
in?[A] When someone came to a grain heap
of 20 measures, it only amounted to 10;
when one came to the winepress to dip 50
measures from the vat, it only amounted
to 20. 17I struck you — all the work of your
hands — with blight, mildew,[e] and hail,[f] but
you didn't turn to Me" — this is the LORD's
declaration. 18"Consider carefully[g] from this
day forward; from the twenty-fourth day of
the ninth month, from the day the foundation of the LORD's temple was laid; consider
it carefully. 19Is there still seed left in the gra-
nary? The vine, the fig, the pomegranate, and
the olive tree have not yet produced. But from
this day on I will bless you."[h]

Promise to Zerubbabel

20The word of the LORD came to Haggai a
second time on the twenty-fourth day of the
month: 21"Speak to Zerubbabel, governor of
Judah: I am going to shake the heavens and
the earth.[i] 22I will overturn royal thrones
and destroy the power of the Gentile kingdoms.[j] I will overturn chariots and their riders. Horses and their riders will fall, each by
his brother's sword. 23On that day" — this is
the declaration of the LORD of Hosts — "I will
take you, Zerubbabel son of Shealtiel, My servant" — this is the LORD's declaration — "and
make you like My signet ring,[k] for I have chosen you."[l] This is the declaration of the LORD
of Hosts.

[a]**2:9** Is 60:18
[b]**2:11** Mal 2:7
[c]**2:12** Jr 11:15
[d]**2:13** Lv 11:39; 22:4-6; Nm 19:11-13,22
[e]**2:17** Dt 28:22; 1Kg 8:37; Am 4:9
[f]Ps 105:32-33
[g]**2:18** Hg 1:5,7
[h]**2:19** Zch 8:9-13
[i]**2:21** Hg 2:6-7; Ezk 38:19-20
[j]**2:22** Gn 19:25; Am 4:11
[k]**2:23** Est 8:8; Jr 22:23-25
[l]Mt 1:12-13

[A]**2:16** Hb obscure

AUTHOR: Zechariah

DATE: After the exile (around 520–518 B.C.)

Zechariah ("Yahweh remembers") and Haggai were contemporaries who came to Jerusalem at about the same time. As a prophet Zechariah was in a class by himself. He was of a priestly family, the only prophet-priest in this line-up of Minor Prophets. What also sets him apart is the beauty of his writings, which include rich imagery and a huge scope. At fourteen chapters the book of Zechariah is the longest of the minor prophecies.

Zechariah's prophecy can be divided into two parts: chapters 1—8 and 9—14. The first eight chapters are composed of eight visions: the four horsemen; the four horns and craftsmen; the surveyor; the high priest and branch; the golden lampstand; the flying scroll; the measuring basket; and the four chariots. The meaning is rich and varied. Though God's people have failed, He will forgive their sins and protect them as they patiently wait on Him. "'Not by strength or by might, but by My Spirit,' says the LORD of Hosts" (4:6).

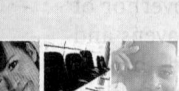

ZECHARIAH

As in the previous prophecies, the scope broadens. The people of Israel are in a sense the beginning of the world church. God's people are His ambassadors to the nations. A great reformation will result and God will send healing to the nations. The reference to Joshua, the high priest, implies a reference to Christ, God's great high priest: "This is what the LORD of Hosts says: Here is a man whose name is Branch; He will branch out from His place and build the LORD's temple" (6:12).

Chapters 9—14 differ in style and content from the previous ones. Some commentators have suggested that they were actually written by other scribes. Others, however, have observed that, though the style is different, the concerns of the second half are consistent with those of the first half. Perhaps Zechariah wrote these chapters later in life.

The prophet urges the people to continue the good reforms they had begun. Practical advice is woven into the text. Fasting is good but mercy is better. Judgment is pronounced upon the godless nations but their repentance will lead to blessings. Following the people's negligence in building the temple, their enemies make life hard for them, but God promises victory in the end. False shepherds will be judged. More references to the world church follow.

Though Jerusalem has suffered at the hands of her enemies, God "will defend the inhabitants of Jerusalem" (12:8) and "destroy all the nations that come against Jerusalem" (12:9). These glorious promises are reminiscent of Galatians 4:26: "But the Jerusalem above is free, and she is our mother."

Zechariah speaks as a true priest: God's grace leads to forgiveness and He is pleased with holy living. God's mission moves forward, despite people's hesitations and malfunctions.

A Plea for Repentance

1 In the eighth month, in the second year of
Darius,[a] the word of the LORD came to the
prophet Zechariah[b] son of Berechiah, son of
Iddo: 2"The LORD was extremely angry with
your ancestors. 3So tell the people: This is what
the LORD of ·Hosts says: Return to Me"—this
is the declaration of the LORD of Hosts—"and
I will return to you, says the LORD of Hosts.
4Do not be like your ancestors; the earlier

[a]1:1 Zch 7:1
[b]Ezr 5:1; 6:14

Return to Me: The Mission of God in the Minor Prophets

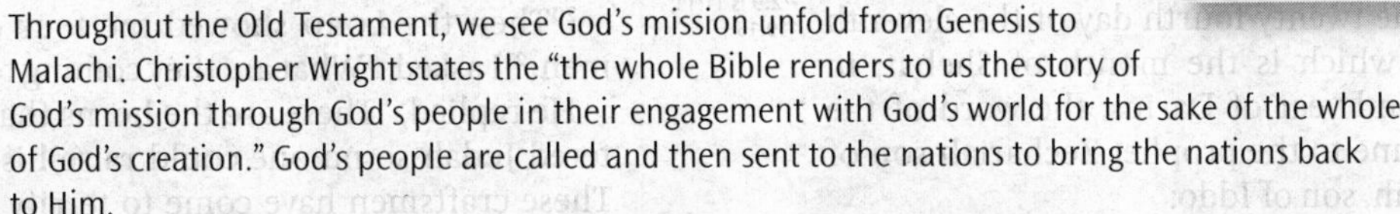

Raymond Y. Chang

Throughout the Old Testament, we see God's mission unfold from Genesis to Malachi. Christopher Wright states the "the whole Bible renders to us the story of God's mission through God's people in their engagement with God's world for the sake of the whole of God's creation." God's people are called and then sent to the nations to bring the nations back to Him.

No more is this evident than in the last twelve books of the Old Testament, formally labeled as the Minor Prophets. These twelve books are rich in theological and missiological content. While the Hebrew canon has these twelve books as one book, "The Twelve," each book is written from a unique perspective and historical context. But, there are themes that are common to all books in the light of the mission of God.

The twelve books can be separated into two periods: pre-exilic (pre-Babylonian exile) and post-exilic (post-Babylonian exile). The pre-exilic books would include Obadiah, Joel, Jonah, Amos, Hosea, Micah, Nahum, Zephaniah, and Habakkuk. The post-exilic books are Haggai, Zechariah, and Malachi.

There are three key themes uniting the Minor Prophets in the light of God's mission. First is the call to repentance from sin, especially the sin of idolatry. Second is the call to return to a full devotion of God and God's covenant. And finally, there is a call to restoration where God will ultimately be triumphant.

The pattern in both the pre-exilic and post-exilic books is the same. There is impending judgment coming because of sin often displayed in idolatry and rebellion against God's covenant. Following a description of judgment is a call for repentance. This is a key focus of the prophets. As they repent and return to God, God will bring about final restoration often in an eschatological vision for the future.

What also makes the Minor Prophets unique is that the call to repentance and return is extended to nations other than Israel. Three of the prophets speak to other nations: Obadiah to Edom, Jonah and Nahum to Nineveh. Jonah in particular is unique in that it focuses exclusively on a nation other than Israel. In Jonah, we see the self-righteousness of the prophet and sinfulness of an idolatrous nation and call for repentance under the backdrop of God's grace. Ultimately, God is given the hope of restoration of a nation that returns back to Him.

In summary, the centerpiece of God's mission in the Minor Prophets is God's desire that all nations return to Him in repentance, with the outcome that God's restoration would extend to all nations both in the present and future. Through the Minor Prophets, we see the hope of the fulfillment of Malachi 1:11. "'For My name will be great among the nations, from the rising of the sun to its setting. Incense and pure offerings will be presented in My name in every place because My name will be great among the nations,' says Yahweh of Hosts."

1 Christopher Wright, Mission of God, p. 51.

prophets proclaimed to them: This is what the
LORD of Hosts says: Turn from your evil ways
and your evil deeds.[a] But they did not listen or
pay attention to Me" — this is the LORD's declaration. 5 "Where are your ancestors now?
And do the prophets live forever? 6 But didn't
My words and My statutes that I commanded
My servants the prophets overtake your ancestors? They repented and said: As the LORD
of Hosts purposed to deal with us for our ways
and deeds, so He has dealt with us."[b]

THE NIGHT VISIONS

7 On the twenty-fourth day of the eleventh
month, which is the month of Shebat, in
the second year of Darius, the word of the
LORD came to the prophet Zechariah son of
Berechiah, son of Iddo:

First Vision: Horsemen

8 I looked out in the night and saw a man
riding on a red horse. He was standing among
the myrtle trees in the valley. Behind him
were red, sorrel, and white horses. 9 I asked,
"What are these, my lord?"

The angel who was talking to me replied, "I
will show you what they are."

10 Then the man standing among the myrtle
trees explained, "They are the ones the LORD
has sent to patrol the earth."

11 They reported to the Angel of the LORD
standing among the myrtle trees, "We have
patrolled the earth, and right now the whole
earth is calm and quiet."[c]

12 Then the Angel of the LORD responded,
"How long, LORD of Hosts, will You withhold mercy from Jerusalem and the cities of
Judah that You have been angry with these
70 years?"[d] 13 The LORD replied with kind
and comforting words to the angel who was
speaking with me.

14 So the angel who was speaking with me
said, "Proclaim: The LORD of Hosts says: I am
extremely jealous[e] for Jerusalem and ·Zion.
15 I am fiercely angry with the nations that are
at ease, for I was a little angry, but they made
it worse. 16 Therefore, this is what the LORD
says: In mercy, I have returned to Jerusalem;
My house will be rebuilt within it" — this is
the declaration of the LORD of Hosts — "and
a measuring line will be stretched out over
Jerusalem.

17 "Proclaim further: This is what the LORD
of Hosts says: My cities will again overflow
with prosperity; the LORD will once more
comfort Zion and again choose Jerusalem."[f]

Second Vision: Four Horns and Craftsmen

18 [A] Then I looked up and saw four ·horns.
19 So I asked the angel who was speaking with
me, "What are these?"

And he said to me, "These are the horns
that scattered Judah, Israel, and Jerusalem."

20 Then the LORD showed me four craftsmen. 21 I asked, "What are they coming to do?"

He replied, "These are the horns that scattered Judah so no one could raise his head.
These craftsmen have come to terrify them,
to cut off the horns of the nations that raised
their horns against the land of Judah to scatter it."

Third Vision: Surveyor

2 [B] I looked up and saw a man with a measuring line in his hand. 2 I asked, "Where
are you going?"

He answered me, "To measure Jerusalem to
determine its width and length."

3 Then the angel who was speaking with me
went out, and another angel went out to meet
him. 4 He said to him, "Run and tell this young
man: Jerusalem will be inhabited without
walls because of the number of people and
livestock in it."[g] 5 The declaration of the LORD:
"I will be a wall[h] of fire around it, and I will be
the glory within it."

6 "Get up! Leave the land of the north"[i] — this
is the LORD's declaration — "for I have scattered you like the four winds of heaven" — this
is the LORD's declaration. 7 "Go, ·Zion! Escape,
you who are living with Daughter Babylon."
8 For the LORD of ·Hosts says this: "He has sent
Me[C] for His glory against the nations who are
plundering you, for anyone who touches you
touches the pupil[D] of His[E] eye. 9 I will move
against them with My[F] power, and they will
become plunder for their own servants.[j] Then
you will know that the LORD of Hosts has sent
Me.[C]

10 "Daughter Zion, shout for joy and be glad,

[a] 1:4 2Kg 17:13; 2Ch 7:14; Ezk 33:9,11
[b] 1:6 Jr 51:12; Lm 2:17; Zch 8:14-15
[c] 1:11 Jos 11:23; Jdg 5:31; Is 14:7
[d] 1:12 Jr 25:11-12; 29:10
[e] 1:14 Ex 20:5; 34:14; Dt 5:9
[f] 1:17 2Ch 6:6; Is 40:1; Zch 2:12
[g] 2:4 Is 49:19; Jr 31:27; Ezk 36:11
[h] 2:5 Is 26:1
[i] 2:6 Jr 6:22; 10:22; 50:9
[j] 2:9 Is 11:15; 19:16

A 1:18 Zch 2:1 in Hb B 2:1 Zch 2:5 in Hb C 2:8,9 Or *me* D 2:8 Or *apple* E 2:8 Ancient Jewish tradition reads *My* F 2:9 Or *my*

for I am coming to dwell among you" — this is the LORD's declaration. 11 "Many nations will join themselves to the LORD on that day and become My[A] people.[a] I will dwell among you, and you will know that the LORD of Hosts has sent Me[B] to you. 12 The LORD will take possession of Judah as His portion in the Holy Land, and He will once again choose Jerusalem.[b] 13 Let all people be silent[c] before the LORD, for He is coming from His holy dwelling."

Fourth Vision: High Priest and Branch

3 Then he showed me Joshua[d] the high priest standing before the Angel of the LORD,[e] with Satan[C,f] standing at his right side to accuse him. 2 The LORD[D] said to Satan: "The LORD rebuke you, Satan! May the LORD who has chosen Jerusalem rebuke you! Isn't this man a burning stick snatched from the fire?"[g]

3 Now Joshua was dressed with filthy[E] clothes[h] as he stood before the Angel.[i] 4 So the Angel of the LORD[F] spoke to those[G] standing before Him, "Take off his filthy clothes!" Then He said to him, "See, I have removed your •guilt from you,[j] and I will clothe you with splendid robes."

5 Then I said, "Let them put a •clean turban[k] on his head." So a clean turban was placed on his head, and they clothed him in garments while the Angel of the LORD was standing nearby.

6 Then the Angel of the LORD charged Joshua: 7 "This is what the LORD of •Hosts says: If you walk in My ways and keep My instructions, you will both rule My house and take care of My courts; I will also grant you access among these who are standing here.

8 "Listen, Joshua the high priest, you and your colleagues sitting before you; indeed, these men are a sign that I am about to bring My servant, the Branch.[l] 9 Notice the stone[m] I have set before Joshua; on that one stone are seven eyes.[n] I will engrave an inscription on it" — this is the declaration of the LORD of Hosts — "and I will take away the guilt of this land in a single day. 10 On that day, each of you will invite his neighbor to sit under his vine and fig tree."[o] This is the declaration of the LORD of Hosts.

[a]2:10-11 Ps 47:9; Is 42:6; Mc 4:2 [b]2:12 2Ch 6:6; Zch 1:17; 3:2 [c]2:13 Hab 2:20 [d]3:1 Hg 1:1,12,14; 2:4; Zch 6:11 [e]Gn 16:7-13; 21:17; 22:11-16; 31:11-13 [f]1Ch 21:1; Jb 1:6-12; Rv 12:10 [g]3:2 Dt 4:20; Am 4:11 [h]3:3 Dt 23:13; Is 4:4 [i]Lv 22:3 [j]3:4 2Sm 24:10; Jb 7:21; Mc 7:18 [k]3:5 Ex 28:36-38 [l]3:8 Is 4:2; 11:1; Jr 23:5; 33:15; Ezk 17:22-24; Zch 6:12 [m]3:9 Ps 118:22-23; Is 8:14; 28:16; Dn 2:35,45; Zch 4:10; Rv 5:6 [n]Zch 4:10 [o]3:10 1Kg 4:25; 2Kg 18:31; Mc 4:1-8 [p]4:6 Hs 1:7; Hg 2:4-5 [q]4:7 Mt 17:20; 21:21; 1Co 13:2 [r]Is 40:4 [s]4:8 Zch 6:9 [t]4:9 Ezr 3:8-11; 5:16 [u]4:10 Hg 2:3-4 [v]2Ch 16:9; Ps 34:15; Pr 15:3; Am 9:8; 1Pt 3:12 [w]4:14 Jr 33:17-22 [x]Rv 11:3-4 [y]5:1 Ezk 2:9-10; Rv 5:1; 10:2 [z]5:2 Ex 26:15-25; 1Kg 6:3; 1Pt 4:17

Fifth Vision: Gold Lampstand

4 The angel who was speaking with me then returned and roused me as one awakened out of sleep. 2 He asked me, "What do you see?"

I replied, "I see a solid gold lampstand there with a bowl on its top. It has seven lamps on it and seven channels for each of[H] the lamps on its top. 3 There are also two olive trees beside it, one on the right of the bowl and the other on its left."

4 Then I asked the angel who was speaking with me, "What are these, my lord?"

5 "Don't you know what they are?" replied the angel who was speaking with me.

I said, "No, my lord."

6 So he answered me, "This is the word of the LORD to Zerubbabel: 'Not by strength or by might, but by My Spirit,'[p] says the LORD of •Hosts. 7 'What are you, great mountain?[q] Before Zerubbabel you will become a plain.[r] And he will bring out the capstone accompanied by shouts of: Grace, grace to it!'"

8 Then the word of the LORD came to me:[s] 9 "Zerubbabel's hands have laid the foundation of this house,[t] and his hands will complete it. Then you will know that the LORD of Hosts has sent me to you. 10 For who scorns the day of small things?[u] These seven eyes of the LORD, which scan throughout the whole earth, will rejoice when they see the plumb line[I] in Zerubbabel's hand."[v]

11 I asked him, "What are the two olive trees on the right and left of the lampstand?" 12 And I questioned him further, "What are the two olive branches beside the two gold conduits, from which golden oil pours out?"

13 Then he inquired of me, "Don't you know what these are?"

"No, my lord," I replied.

14 "These are the two anointed ones,"[J,w] he said, "who stand by the Lord of the whole earth."[x]

Sixth Vision: Flying Scroll

5 I looked up again and saw a flying scroll.[y] 2 "What do you see?" he asked me.

"I see a flying scroll," I replied, "30 feet[K] long and 15 feet[L] wide."[z]

[A]2:11 LXX, Syr read *His* [B]2:11 Or *me* [C]3:1 Or *the adversary* [D]3:2 Syr reads *The Angel of the LORD* [E]3:3 Probably stained with human excrement [F]3:4 Lit *He* [G]3:4 = the angels [H]4:2 Or *seven lips to* [I]4:10 Lit *the tin stone* [J]4:14 = Joshua and Zerubbabel [K]5:2 Lit *20 cubits* [L]5:2 Lit *10 cubits*

3 Then he said to me, "This is the curse[a]
that is going out over the whole land, for every thief will be removed according to what
is written on one side, and everyone who
swears falsely will be removed according to
what is written on the other side. 4 I will send
it out,"[b] — this is the declaration of the LORD
of ·Hosts — "and it will enter the house of the
thief and the house of the one who swears
falsely by My name. It will stay inside his
house and destroy it along with its timbers
and stones."[c]

Seventh Vision: Woman in the Basket

5 Then the angel who was speaking with me
came forward and told me, "Look up and see
what this is that is approaching."
6 So I asked, "What is it?"
He responded, "It's a measuring basket[A]
that is approaching." And he continued, "This
is their iniquity[B] in all the land." 7 Then a lead
cover was lifted, and there was a woman[d] sitting inside the basket.[e] 8 "This is Wickedness,"
he said. He shoved her down into the basket
and pushed the lead weight over its opening. 9 Then I looked up and saw two women
approaching with the wind in their wings.
Their wings were like those of a stork,[f] and
they lifted up the basket between earth and
sky.
10 So I asked the angel who was speaking
with me, "Where are they taking the basket?"
11 "To build a shrine for it in the land of ·Shi-
nar,"[g] he told me. "When that is ready, the basket will be placed there on its pedestal."

Eighth Vision: Four Chariots

6 Then I looked up again and saw four
chariots coming from between two
mountains. And the mountains were made
of bronze. 2 The first chariot had red horses,[h]
the second chariot black horses,[i] 3 the third
chariot white horses,[j] and the fourth chariot
dappled[k] horses — all strong horses. 4 So I inquired of the angel who was speaking with
me, "What are these, my lord?"
5 The angel told me, "These are the four
spirits[C,l] of heaven going out after presenting
themselves to the Lord of the whole earth.
6 The one with the black horses is going to the
land of the north, the white horses are going
after them, but the dappled horses are going to the land of the south." 7 As the strong
horses went out, they wanted to go patrol
the earth, and the LORD said, "Go, patrol the
earth." So they patrolled the earth. 8 Then He
summoned me saying, "See, those going to
the land of the north have pacified My Spirit
in the northern land."

Crowning of the Branch

9 The word of the LORD came to me:[m]
10 "Take an offering from the exiles, from Heldai, Tobijah, and Jedaiah, who have arrived
from Babylon, and go that same day to the
house of Josiah son of Zephaniah. 11 Take silver and gold, make crowns and place them
on the head of Joshua son of Jehozadak,
the high priest. 12 You are to tell him: This is
what the LORD of ·Hosts says: Here is a man
whose name is Branch;[n] He will branch out

[a] 5:3 Dt 11:26-28; 28:15-68 [b] 5:4 Ps 147:15; Is 55:11 [c] Ezr 6:11; Dn 2:5; 3:29 [d] 5:7 Hs 9:15; Rv 17:1 [e] Lv 19:36; Dt 25:14; Pr 20:10; Ezk 45:10; Am 8:5 [f] 5:9 Jr 8:7 [g] 5:11 Gn 11:9 [h] 6:2 Rv 6:4 [i] Rv 6:5-6 [j] 6:3 Rv 6:2; 19:11 [k] Gn 31:10,12 [l] 6:5 Jr 49:36; Rv 7:1-3 [m] 6:9 Zch 4:8 [n] 6:12 Zch 3:8

Text Message

TEXT MESSAGES

The picture here is straight from the prophet's exotic imagination, inspired by God. God had a message for His people, and the pictures and interpretations are vivid and unmistakable. Throughout Scripture, God used creative languages and true-to-the-culture examples to get His message across. Clearly we too can be creative as we share the gospel message. Effective evangelism is not a formula to always be repeated. God's truth must always be uncompromised, but the ways that truth can be told are many. Use your voice, pen, palate, instrument, or even skateboard to tell of God's faithfulness and love in Jesus Christ.

[A] 5:6 Lit *It's an ephah* [B] 5:6 One Hb ms, LXX, Syr; other Hb mss read *eye* [C] 6:5 Or *winds*

from His place and build the LORD's temple.
[13]Yes, He will build the LORD's temple; He will
be clothed in splendor[a] and will sit on His
throne and rule. There will also be a priest on
His throne, and there will be peaceful counsel between the two of them.[b] [14]The crown
will reside in the LORD's temple as a memorial to Heldai, Tobijah, Jedaiah, and Hen[A] son
of Zephaniah. [15]People who are far off will
come and build the LORD's temple, and you
will know that the LORD of Hosts has sent Me
to you. This will happen when you fully obey
the LORD your God."[c]

Disobedience and Fasting

7 In the fourth year of King Darius,[d] the
word of the LORD came to Zechariah on
the fourth day of the ninth month, which is
Chislev. [2]Now the people of Bethel had sent
Sharezer, Regem-melech, and their men to
plead for the LORD's favor[e] [3]by asking the
priests who were at the house of the LORD
of ·Hosts as well as the prophets, "Should we
mourn and fast in the fifth month as we have
done these many years?"

[4]Then the word of the LORD of Hosts came
to me: [5]"Ask all the people of the land and the
priests: When you fasted and lamented in the
fifth and in the seventh months for these 70
years, did you really fast for Me?[f] [6]When you
eat and drink, don't you eat and drink simply for yourselves?[g] [7]Aren't these the words
that the LORD proclaimed through the earlier prophets when Jerusalem was inhabited
and secure,[B] along with its surrounding cities, and when the southern region and the
Judean foothills were inhabited?"

[8]The word of the LORD came to Zechariah:
[9]"The LORD of Hosts says this: Make fair decisions.[h] Show faithful love and compassion[i]
to one another. [10]Do not oppress the widow
or the fatherless, the foreigner or the poor,[j]
and do not plot evil in your hearts against one
another.[k] [11]But they refused to pay attention[l]
and turned a stubborn shoulder; they closed
their ears so they could not hear.[m] [12]They
made their hearts like a rock so as not to obey
the law or the words that the LORD of Hosts
had sent by His Spirit through the earlier
prophets.[n] Therefore great anger came from
the LORD of Hosts. [13]Just as He had called, and
they would not listen, so when they called, I
would not listen," says the LORD of Hosts. [14]"I
scattered them with a windstorm over all the
nations that had not known them, and the
land was left desolate behind them, with no
one coming or going. They turned a pleasant
land into a desolation."

Obedience and Feasting

8 The word of the LORD of ·Hosts came:
[2]"The LORD of Hosts says this: I am extremely jealous[o] for ·Zion; I am jealous for
her with great wrath." [3]The LORD says this:
"I will return to Zion and live in Jerusalem.
Then Jerusalem will be called the Faithful
City,[p] the mountain of the LORD of Hosts,
and the Holy Mountain." [4]The LORD of Hosts
says this: "Old men and women will again sit
along the streets of Jerusalem, each with a
staff in hand because of advanced age. [5]The
streets of the city will be filled with boys and
girls playing in them." [6]The LORD of Hosts
says this: "Though it may seem incredible
to the remnant of this people in those days,
should it also seem incredible to Me?" — this
is the declaration of the LORD of Hosts. [7]The
LORD of Hosts says this: "I will save My people
from the land of the east and the land of the
west. [8]I will bring them back[q] to live in Jerusalem. They will be My people, and I will be
their faithful and righteous God."[r]

[9]The LORD of Hosts says this: "Let your
hands be strong, you who now hear these
words that the prophets spoke when the foundations were laid for the rebuilding of the
temple, the house of the LORD of Hosts. [10]For
prior to those days neither man nor beast had
wages. There was no safety from the enemy
for anyone who came or went, for I turned everyone against his neighbor. [11]But now, I will
not treat the remnant of this people as in the
former days" — this is the declaration of the
LORD of Hosts. [12]"For they will sow in peace:
the vine will yield its fruit, the land will yield
its produce, and the skies will yield their dew.
I will give the remnant of this people all these
things as an inheritance.[s] [13]As you have been a
curse among the nations,[t] house of Judah and
house of Israel, so I will save you, and you will

[a]**6:13** 1Ch 16:27; 29:25; Ps 96:6
[b]Ps 45:6-7; 110:1-7; Dn 7:9-14; Heb 1:3,13; Rv 5:6
[c]**6:15** Dt 28:1
[d]**7:1** Zch 1:1
[e]**7:2** Zch 8:21-22
[f]**7:5** Is 58:1-7
[g]**7:6** 1Co 10:31
[h]**7:9** Ex 18:19-23; Zch 8:16
[i]Jr 7:5-7; Hs 10:12; Mc 6:8
[j]**7:10** Dt 14:29; 16:11
[k]Mt 22:39; Jms 3:5-6
[l]**7:11** Zch 1:4
[m]Is 6:10
[n]**7:12** Jr 7:13,24
[o]**8:2** Zch 1:14
[p]**8:3** Is 1:26
[q]**8:8** Is 11:11-12; Mc 2:12-13
[r]Gn 17:7-8; Dt 26:17-18; Rv 21:3
[s]**8:12** Dt 31:7; Jos 1:6; Is 49:8
[t]**8:13** Dt 21:23; 2Kg 22:19

[A]**6:14** Probably Josiah [B]**7:7** Or *prosperous*

be a blessing.[a] Don't be afraid; let your hands
be strong." 14 For the LORD of Hosts says this:
"As I resolved to treat you badly when your
fathers provoked Me to anger, and I did not
relent," says the LORD of Hosts, 15 "so I have resolved again in these days to do what is good
to Jerusalem and the house of Judah.[b] Don't
be afraid. 16 These are the things you must do:
Speak truth to one another; make true and
sound decisions within your ·gates. 17 Do not
plot evil[c] in your hearts against your neighbor,[d] and do not love perjury,[e] for I hate all
this"—this is the LORD's declaration.
18 Then the word of the LORD of Hosts came
to me: 19 "The LORD of Hosts says this: The fast
of the fourth month,[f] the fast of the fifth, the
fast of the seventh, and the fast of the tenth[g]
will become times of joy, gladness, and cheerful festivals for the house of Judah. Therefore,
love truth and peace." 20 The LORD of Hosts
says this: "Peoples will yet come, the residents of many cities; 21 the residents of one
city will go to another, saying: Let's go at once
to plead for the LORD's favor and to seek the
LORD of Hosts. I am also going. 22 Many peoples and strong nations will come to seek the
LORD of Hosts in Jerusalem and to plead for
the LORD's favor."[h] 23 The LORD of Hosts says
this: "In those days, 10 men from nations of
every language will grab the robe of a Jewish
man tightly, urging: Let us go with you,[i] for
we have heard that God is with you."

Judgment of Zion's Enemies

9 An ·Oracle
The word of the LORD
is against the land of Hadrach,
and Damascus[j] is its resting place—
for the eyes of men
and all the tribes of Israel
are on the LORD[A]—
2 and also against Hamath,[k]
which borders it,
as well as Tyre[l] and Sidon,[m]
though they are very shrewd.
3 Tyre has built herself a fortress;
she has heaped up silver like dust
and gold like the dirt of the streets.
4 Listen! The Lord will impoverish her
and cast her wealth into the sea;
she herself will be consumed by fire.[n]
5 Ashkelon will see it and be afraid;
Gaza too, and will writhe in great pain,
as will Ekron, for her hope will fail.
There will cease to be a king in Gaza,
and Ashkelon will become uninhabited.
6 A mongrel people will live in Ashdod,
and I will destroy the pride
of the Philistines.[o]
7 I will remove the blood
from their mouths
and the detestable things[p]
from between their teeth.
Then they too will become a remnant
for our God;
they will become like a clan in Judah
and Ekron like the Jebusites.[q]
8 I will set up camp at My house
against an army,[B]
against those who march
back and forth,
and no oppressor will march
against them again,
for now I have seen with My own eyes.

The Coming of Zion's King

9 Rejoice greatly, Daughter ·Zion!
Shout in triumph, Daughter Jerusalem!
Look, your King is coming to you;
He is righteous and victorious,[C]
humble and riding on a donkey,
on a colt, the foal of a donkey.[r]
10 I will cut off the chariot from Ephraim
and the horse from Jerusalem.
The bow of war will be removed,
and He will proclaim peace
to the nations.
His dominion will extend from sea
to sea,
from the Euphrates River
to the ends of the earth.[s]
11 As for you,
because of the blood of your covenant,[t]
I will release your prisoners
from the waterless cistern.[u]
12 Return to a stronghold,
you prisoners who have hope;
today I declare that I will restore
double to you.[v]

[a] **8:13** Gn 12:2-3 [b] **8:15** Dt 8:16; Jr 32:40-41; Ezk 36:11 [c] **8:17** Mc 2:1 [d] Dt 10:12-22; Mt 22:39 [e] Lv 5:4; Nm 30:2; Jr 5:2 [f] **8:19** 2Kg 25:3-4; Jr 39:2 [g] 2Kg 25:1; Jr 39:1 [h] **8:20-22** Is 2:2-3; Jr 16:19; Mc 4:1-3; Mal 1:11-14 [i] **8:23** Is 4:1 [j] **9:1** Gn 15:2; 1Kg 11:24; Sg 7:4; Is 7:8; Am 1:3 [k] **9:2** 2Kg 14:25 [l] Jos 19:29; Is 23:1 [m] Gn 10:15 [n] **9:4** Ezk 26:4-6; 27:27 [o] **9:6** Am 1:6-8; Zph 2:4-6 [p] **9:7** Lv 11:10; Dt 29:17; Dn 11:31 [q] 2Sm 5:6-10; 24:16-25 [r] **9:9** Is 62:11; Mt 21:5; Jn 12:15 [s] **9:10** Ps 72:8; Mc 7:12 [t] **9:11** Heb 10:29; 13:20 [u] Gn 37:24; Jr 38:6 [v] **9:12** Jb 42:10; Is 61:7; Jr 16:18

[A] **9:1** Or *eyes of the LORD are on mankind—* [B] **9:8** Or *house as a guard* [C] **9:9** Or *and has salvation*

13 For I will bend Judah as My bow;
I will fill that bow with Ephraim.
I will rouse your sons, Zion,
against your sons, Greece.[A,a]
I will make you like a warrior's sword.
14 Then the LORD will appear over them,
and His arrow will fly like lightning.
The Lord GOD will sound the trumpet
and advance
with the southern storms.[b]
15 The LORD of ·Hosts will defend them.
They will consume and conquer
with slingstones;
they will drink and be rowdy as if
with wine.[c]
They will be as full as
the sprinkling basin,[d]
like those at the corners of the altar.[e]
16 The LORD their God will save them
on that day
as the flock of His people;[f]
for they are like jewels in a crown,[g]
sparkling over His land.
17 How lovely and beautiful they will be!
Grain will make
the young men flourish,
and new wine, the young women.

The LORD Restores His People

10 Ask the LORD for rain
in the season of spring rain.
The LORD makes the rain clouds,
and He will give them showers of rain
and crops in the field for everyone.[h]
2 For the idols speak falsehood,
and the diviners[i] see illusions;
they relate empty dreams
and offer empty comfort.
Therefore the people wander
like sheep;
they suffer affliction because there is
no shepherd.
3 My anger burns against the shepherds,
so I will punish the leaders.[B]
For the LORD of ·Hosts has tended
His flock,
the house of Judah;
He will make them
like His majestic steed in battle.
4 The cornerstone[j] will come from Judah.[C]
The tent peg[k] will come from them
and also the battle bow[l] and
every[D] ruler.
Together 5 they will be like warriors
in battle
trampling down the mud of the streets.
They will fight because the LORD is
with them,
and they will put horsemen to shame.
6 I will strengthen the house of Judah
and deliver the house of Joseph.[E]
I will restore[F] them
because I have compassion on them,
and they will be
as though I had never rejected them.[m]
For I am ·Yahweh their God,
and I will answer them.
7 Ephraim[n] will be like a warrior,
and their hearts will be glad as if
with wine.
Their children will see it and be glad;[o]
their hearts will rejoice in Yahweh.
8 I will whistle[p] and gather them
because I have redeemed[q] them;
they will be as numerous as
they once were.
9 Though I sow[r] them among the nations,
they will remember[s] Me
in the distant lands;
they and their children will live
and return.
10 I will bring them back from the land
of Egypt
and gather them from Assyria.
I will bring them to the land of Gilead[t]
and to Lebanon,
but it will not be enough for them.
11 Yahweh[G] will pass through the sea
of distress
and strike the waves of the sea;
all the depths of the Nile will dry up.[u]
The pride of Assyria will be
brought down,
and the scepter of Egypt will come
to an end.
12 I will strengthen[v] them in Yahweh,
and they will march[w] in His name —
this is Yahweh's declaration.

[a] **9:13** Dn 8:21; 10:20
[b] **9:14** Ps 83:15
[c] **9:15** Nm 23:24
[d] Ex 27:3
[e] Lv 1:5,11; 3:2
[f] **9:16** Ezk 36:38
[g] Lv 8:9
[h] **10:1** Dt 28:12; Is 30:23; Jr 51:16
[i] **10:2** Jr 27:9; Mc 3:7
[j] **10:4** Jdg 20:2; 1Sm 14:38; Ps 118:22; Is 28:16
[k] Jdg 4:21
[l] 2Kg 13:15-17; Rv 6:2
[m] **10:6** Ps 103:12
[n] **10:7** Is 7:8
[o] Ex 4:14; Ps 16:9
[p] **10:8** Is 5:26; 7:18
[q] Ex 13:13; 21:8; 34:20; Jb 5:20; Ps 130:8; Is 51:11; Mc 6:4
[r] **10:9** Gn 26:12; Ex 23:16; Ps 126:5
[s] Gn 40:23; Jos 1:13
[t] **10:10** Gn 31:21; Dt 34:1; Ps 60:7
[u] **10:11** Gn 8:7; Jos 2:10; 4:23; 1Kg 17:7; Jb 12:15; Ps 74:15; Pr 17:22
[v] **10:12** Zch 10:6
[w] Jos 6:3; Ps 68:7; Jr 46:9

[A] **9:13** Lit *Javan* [B] **10:3** Lit *male goats* [C] **10:4** Lit *them* [D] **10:4** Lit *also from them the . . . , from them every* [E] **10:6** = the northern kingdom [F] **10:6** Other Hb mss, LXX read *settle* [G] **10:11** Lit *He*

Israel's Shepherds: Good and Bad

11 Open your gates, Lebanon,
and fire will consume your cedars.[a]
2 Wail, cypress,[b] for the cedar has fallen;
the glorious trees are destroyed!
Wail, oaks of Bashan,[c]
for the stately forest has fallen!
3 Listen to the wail[d] of the shepherds,
for their glory is destroyed.
Listen to the roar of young lions,[e]
for the thickets of the Jordan[f]
are[A] destroyed.

4 ·Yahweh my God says this: "Shepherd the
flock intended for slaughter. 5 Those who buy
them slaughter them but are not punished.[g]
Those who sell them say: Praise the LORD because I have become rich! Even their own
shepherds have no compassion for them. 6 Indeed, I will no longer have compassion on the
inhabitants of the land" — this is the LORD's
declaration. "Instead, I will turn everyone
over to his neighbor and his king. They will
devastate the land, and I will not deliver it
from them."[h]

7 So I shepherded the flock intended for
slaughter, the afflicted of the flock.[B] I took
two staffs, calling one Favor[i] and the other
Union, and I shepherded the flock. 8 In one
month I got rid of three shepherds. I became
impatient with them, and they also detested
me. 9 Then I said, "I will no longer shepherd
you. Let what is dying die, and let what is going astray go astray; let the rest devour each
other's flesh." 10 Next I took my staff called Favor and cut it in two, annulling the covenant
I had made with all the peoples. 11 It was annulled on that day, and so the afflicted of the
flock[C] who were watching me knew that it was
the word of the LORD. 12 Then I said to them,
"If it seems right to you, give me my wages;
but if not, keep them." So they weighed my
wages, 30 pieces of silver.[j]

13 "Throw it to the potter,"[D] the LORD said
to me — this magnificent price I was valued
by them. So I took the 30 pieces of silver and
threw it into the house of the LORD, to the
potter.[E,k] 14 Then I cut in two my second staff,
Union, annulling the brotherhood between
Judah and Israel.

15 The LORD also said to me: "Take the equipment of a foolish shepherd. 16 I am about to
raise up a shepherd in the land who will not
care for those who are going astray, and he
will not seek the lost[F] or heal the broken. He
will not sustain the healthy,[G] but he will devour the flesh of the fat sheep[l] and tear off
their hooves.

17 Woe to the worthless shepherd
who deserts the flock![m]
May a sword strike[H] his arm
and his right eye!
May his arm wither away
and his right eye go completely blind!"

Judah's Security

12 An ·Oracle

The word of the LORD
concerning Israel.
A declaration of the LORD,
who stretched out the heavens,[n]
laid the foundation of the earth,[o]
and formed the spirit of man
within him.

2 "Look, I will make Jerusalem a cup that
causes staggering[p] for the peoples who surround the city. The siege against Jerusalem
will also involve Judah. 3 On that day I will
make Jerusalem a heavy stone for all the peoples; all who try to lift it will injure themselves
severely when all the nations of the earth
gather against her.[q] 4 On that day" — this is
the LORD's declaration — "I will strike every
horse with panic and its rider with madness.[r]
I will keep a watchful eye on[s] the house of Judah but strike all the horses of the nations
with blindness. 5 Then each of the leaders of
Judah will think to himself: The residents of
Jerusalem are my strength through the LORD
of ·Hosts, their God. 6 On that day I will make
the leaders of Judah like a firepot in a wood-
pile, like a flaming torch among sheaves; they
will consume all the peoples around them on
the right and the left, while Jerusalem continues to be inhabited on its site, in Jerusalem.
7 The LORD will save the tents of Judah first, so
that the glory of David's house and the glory
of Jerusalem's residents may not be greater

[a] **11:1** Jdg 9:15; 2Kg 19:23; Ps 29:5; Sg 5:15; Is 2:13
[b] **11:2** Is 14:8
[c] Is 2:13; Ezk 27:6
[d] **11:3** Is 15:8; Zph 1:10
[e] Jb 4:10; Ps 34:10; Is 5:29; Nah 2:11
[f] Jr 49:19
[g] **11:5** Ps 34:22
[h] **11:6** Jr 13:14; Lm 2:2,17,21; Ezk 7:4,9
[i] **11:7** Ps 90:17; Zch 11:10
[j] **11:12** Ex 21:32
[k] **11:13** Mt 26:15; 27:3-10
[l] **11:16** Ezk 34:3-4
[m] **11:17** Jr 23:2
[n] **12:1** Is 45:12; 51:13; Jr 10:12; 51:15
[o] Jb 38:4; Heb 1:10
[p] **12:2** Is 51:22-23; Jr 25:15-16; Rv 16:19
[q] **12:3** Jl 3:1-2
[r] **12:4** Dt 28:28
[s] Is 37:17; Jr 32:19

[A] **11:3** Lit *for the majesty of the Jordan is* [B] **11:7** LXX reads *slaughter that belonged to the sheep merchants* [C] **11:11** LXX reads *and the sheep merchants* [D] **11:13** Syr reads *treasury* [E] **11:13** One Hb ms, Syr read *treasury* [F] **11:16** Lit *young* [G] **11:16** Or *exhausted* [H] **11:17** Lit *be against*

than that of Judah. 8 On that day the LORD will
defend the inhabitants of Jerusalem, so that
on that day the one who is weakest among
them will be like David on that day, and the
house of David will be like God, like the Angel
of the LORD, before them. 9 On that day I will
set out to destroy all the nations that come
against Jerusalem.

Mourning for the Pierced One

10 "Then I will pour out a spirit[A,a] of grace
and prayer on the house of David and the residents of Jerusalem, and they will look at[B] Me
whom they pierced. They will mourn for Him
as one mourns for an only child and weep bitterly for Him as one weeps for a firstborn.[b]
11 On that day the mourning in Jerusalem
will be as great as the mourning of Hadad-
rimmon in the plain of Megiddo. 12 The land
will mourn, every family by itself: the family
of David's house by itself and their women by
themselves; the family of Nathan's[C,c] house
by itself and their women by themselves;
13 the family of Levi's house by itself and their
women by themselves; the family of Shimei[D,d]
by itself and their women by themselves; 14 all
the remaining families, every family by itself,
and their women by themselves.

God's People Cleansed

13 "On that day a fountain will be opened
for the house of David and for the
residents of Jerusalem, to wash away sin and
impurity.[e] 2 On that day"—this is the declaration of the LORD of ·Hosts—"I will erase the
names of the idols from the land, and they
will no longer be remembered. I will remove
the prophets[E] and the ·unclean spirit from
the land. 3 If a man still prophesies, his father
and his mother who bore him will say to him:
You cannot remain alive because you have
spoken falsely in the name of ·Yahweh. When
he prophesies, his father and his mother who
bore him will pierce him through.[f] 4 On that
day every prophet will be ashamed of his vision when he prophesies; they will not put
on a hairy cloak[g] in order to deceive. 5 He will
say: I am not a prophet; I work the land, for

[a] 12:10 Ezk 39:29; Jl 2:28-29; Zch 4:6
[b] Jn 19:37; Rv 1:7
[c] 12:12 2Sm 5:14; Lk 3:31
[d] 12:13 Ex 6:17; Nm 3:18; 1Ch 6:17
[e] 13:1 Zch 3:1-10
[f] 13:3 Dt 13:5; 18:20; Jr 14:14
[g] 13:4 1Kg 19:13,19; 2Kg 2:8
[h] 13:5 Am 7:14
[i] 13:6 1Kg 18:28
[j] 13:7 Mt 26:31; Mk 14:27
[k] 14:2 Jl 3:2; Zch 12:2-3
[l] 14:3 Rv 19:11-21
[m] 14:4 Ezk 11:23; Ac 1:11-12
[n] 14:5 Am 1:1
[o] Ps 89:5-7; Mt 25:31

a man purchased[F] me as a servant since my
youth.[h] 6 If someone asks him: What are these
wounds[i] on your chest?[G]—then he will answer: I received the wounds in the house of
my friends.

7 Sword, awake against My shepherd,
against the man who is
My associate—
this is the declaration of the LORD
of Hosts.
Strike the shepherd, and the sheep
will be scattered;[j]
I will also turn My hand
against the little ones.
8 In the whole land—
this is the LORD's declaration—
two-thirds[H] will be cut off and die,
but a third will be left in it.
9 I will put this third through the fire;
I will refine them as silver is refined
and test them as gold is tested.
They will call on My name,
and I will answer them.
I will say: They are My people,
and they will say: Yahweh is our God."

The LORD's Triumph and Reign

14 A day of the LORD is coming when your
plunder will be divided in your presence. 2 I will gather all the nations against Jerusalem for battle.[k] The city will be captured,
the houses looted, and the women raped.
Half the city will go into exile, but the rest of
the people will not be removed from the city.
3 Then the LORD will go out to fight against
those nations as He fights on a day of battle.[l] 4 On that day His feet will stand on the
·Mount of Olives,[m] which faces Jerusalem on
the east. The Mount of Olives will be split in
half from east to west, forming a huge valley, so that half the mountain will move to
the north and half to the south. 5 You will flee
by My mountain valley,[I] for the valley of the
mountains will extend to Azal. You will flee as
you fled[J] from the earthquake in the days of
Uzziah king of Judah.[n] Then the LORD my God
will come and all the holy ones with Him.[K,o]
6 On that day there will be no light; the

[A] 12:10 Or *out the Spirit* [B] 12:10 Or *to* [C] 12:12 = a son of David [D] 12:13 = a descendant of Levi [E] 13:2 = false prophets [F] 13:5 Or *sold* [G] 13:6 Lit *wounds between your hands* [H] 13:8 Lit *two-thirds in it* [I] 14:5 Some Hb mss, LXX, Sym, Tg read *You will be blocked—the valley of My mountains—* [J] 14:5 LXX reads *It will be blocked as it was blocked* [K] 14:5 Some Hb mss, LXX, Vg, Tg, Syr; other Hb mss read *you*

sunlight and moonlight[A] will diminish.[B,a] 7It
will be a day known only to ·Yahweh,[b] without day or night, but there will be light at evening.
8On that day living water will flow out
from Jerusalem,[c] half of it toward the eastern
sea[C] and the other half toward the western
sea,[D] in summer and winter alike. 9On that
day Yahweh will become King over all the
earth[d] — Yahweh alone, and His name alone.[e]
10All the land from Geba[f] to Rimmon[g] south
of Jerusalem will be changed into a plain. But
Jerusalem will be raised up and will remain[E]
on its site from the Benjamin Gate[h] to the
place of the First Gate,[F] to the Corner Gate,
and from the Tower of Hananel to the royal
winepresses.[i] 11People will live there, and
never again will there be a curse of ·complete
destruction. So Jerusalem will dwell in security.
12This will be the plague the LORD strikes all
the peoples with, who have warred against Jerusalem: their flesh will rot while they stand
on their feet, their eyes will rot in their sock-
ets, and their tongues will rot in their mouths.
13On that day a great panic from the LORD
will be among them, so that each will seize
the hand of another, and the hand of one will
rise against the other. 14Judah will also fight
at Jerusalem, and the wealth of all the sur-

[a]**14:6** Is 13:10; Jl 2:10; 3:15
[b]**14:7** Mt 24:36
[c]**14:8** Ezk 41:7; 47:1-12; Jl 3:18; Rv 8:8-9; 16:3
[d]**14:9** Mt 25:31
[e]Dt 4:35,39; 6:4; Is 45:5
[f]**14:10** 2Kg 23:8
[g]Neh 11:29
[h]Jr 37:13
[i]Neh 3:1; 12:39; Jr 31:38-40
[j]**14:14** Mc 4:13; Hg 2:7
[k]**14:16** Lv 23:33-36
[l]**14:20** Ex 28:36; 39:30

rounding nations will be collected: gold, silver, and clothing in great abundance.[j] 15The
same plague as the previous one will strike[G]
the horses, mules, camels, donkeys, and all
the animals that are in those camps.
16Then all the survivors from the nations
that came against Jerusalem will go up year
after year to worship the King, the LORD
of ·Hosts, and to celebrate the Festival of
Booths.[k] 17Should any of the families of the
earth not go up to Jerusalem to worship the
King, the LORD of Hosts, rain will not fall on
them. 18And if the people[H] of Egypt will not go
up and enter, then rain will not fall on them;
this will be the plague the LORD inflicts on the
nations who do not go up to celebrate the Festival of Booths. 19This will be the punishment
of Egypt and all the nations that do not go up
to celebrate the Festival of Booths.
20On that day, the words

HOLY TO THE LORD

will be on the bells of the horses.[l] The pots in
the house of the LORD will be like the sprinkling basins before the altar. 21Every pot in Jerusalem and in Judah will be holy to the LORD
of Hosts. Everyone who sacrifices will come
and take some of the pots to cook in. And on
that day there will no longer be a Canaanite[I]
in the house of the LORD of Hosts.

[A]**14:6** Lit *light; the precious things* [B]**14:6** LXX, Sym, Syr, Tg, Vg read *no light or cold or ice* [C]**14:8** = the Dead Sea [D]**14:8** = the Mediterranean Sea [E]**14:10** Or *will be inhabited* [F]**14:10** Or *the former gate* [G]**14:15** Lit *be on* [H]**14:18** Lit *family* [I]**14:21** Or *merchant*

■ **AUTHOR:** Malachi

■■ **DATE:** After the fall of Edom (around 420 B.C.)

Malachi, whose name means "messenger," was God's messenger in Judah. The building project of the temple, begun during the leadership of Zerubbabel and Josiah, has been completed. Haggai and Zechariah have concluded their ministries. A new generation has come. And, as often happened in the history of the church, their passion for the Lord's cause has grown dim. It is against this background that Malachi addresses the people of Judah.

In the first section of Malachi's message he rebukes the priests for the widespread corruption marring their ministry. Instead of selecting the best animals for sacrifices in the temple, the priests permit the people to bring blind, crippled, and diseased animals. Undoubtedly they all share in the material advantages thus gained. But Malachi uncovers the underlying cause: their heart is not in their service. His prophecy is seasoned with God's strong moral outrage. The Lord enters into a dispute with His wayward people. Would they have dared to present the governor with such sickly animals? God then offers His own answers to the questions asked.

MALACHI

In the course of his prophecy, Malachi lists more sins, most of which we can relate to in our day. The actions he censures are not isolated sins; rather, they constitute a pattern. Covenant breaking is widespread. Laborers are defrauded of their wages. Widows and orphans are oppressed and foreign citizens deprived of justice. Divorce is commonplace, immorality rampant.

This is Malachi's burden: the tragic disconnect between the people's confession and their practice. He challenges the people to make their believing and their doing seamless. As God declares: "If I am a father, where is My honor?" (1:6)

But in the end God's grace triumphs. The concluding chapters are filled with promises of victory made memorable by their Messianic beauty: "'See, I am going to send My messenger, and he will clear the way before Me. Then the Lord you seek will suddenly come to His temple, the Messenger of the covenant you desire—see, He is coming,' says the LORD of Hosts . . . He will be like a refiner and purifier of silver; He will purify the sons of Levi and refine them like gold and silver" (3:1, 3). Also: "For you who fear My name, the sun of righteousness will rise with healing in its wings" (4:2).

Malachi adds a great promise to those who desire the mission of God to be realized in their lives. God hurls the challenge at the people: "'Bring the full tenth into the storehouse so that there may be food in My house. Test Me in this way,' says the LORD of Hosts. 'See if I will not open the floodgates of heaven and pour out a blessing for you without measure'" (3:10).

The Lord's Love for Israel

1 An ·oracle:[a] The word of the LORD[b] to Israel through[c] Malachi.[A]
2 “I have loved you,”[d] says the LORD.
But you ask: “How have You loved us?”
“Wasn't Esau Jacob's brother?”[e] This is the
LORD's declaration. “Even so, I loved Jacob,
3 but I hated Esau.[f] I turned his mountains
into a wasteland, and gave his inheritance to
the desert jackals.”[g]
4 Though Edom says: “We have been devastated, but we will rebuild[B] the ruins,” the
LORD of ·Hosts says this: “They may build, but
I will demolish. They will be called a wicked
country[h] and the people the LORD has cursed[C]
forever.[i] 5 Your own eyes will see this, and you
yourselves will say, ‘The LORD is great, even
beyond[D] the borders of Israel.’[j]

Disobedience of the Priests

6 “A son honors his father, and a servant
his master. But if I am a father, where is My
honor? And if I am a master, where is your
·fear of Me?[k] says ·Yahweh of Hosts to you
priests, who despise My name.”
Yet you ask: “How have we despised Your
name?”
7 “By presenting defiled food on My altar.”
You ask: “How have we defiled You?”[l]
When you say: “The LORD's table is contemptible.”[m]
8 “When you present a blind animal for sacrifice, is it not wrong? And when you present
a lame or sick animal, is it not wrong?[n] Bring
it to your governor! Would he be pleased with
you or show you favor?” asks the LORD of
Hosts. 9 “And now ask for God's favor. Will He
be gracious to us?[o] Since this has come from
your hands, will He show any of you favor?”[p]
asks the LORD of Hosts. 10 “I wish one of you
would shut the temple doors,[q] so you would
no longer kindle a useless fire on My altar![r]
I am not pleased with you,” says the LORD of
Hosts, “and I will accept[s] no offering from
your hands.[t]
11 “For My name will be great among the nations,[u] from the rising of the sun to its setting.
Incense[E] and pure offerings will be presented
in My name in every place because My name
will be great among the nations,”[F] says Yahweh of Hosts.
12 But you are profaning it[v] when you say:
“The Lord's table is defiled, and its product,
its food, is contemptible.” 13 You also say:
“Look, what a nuisance!” “And you scorn[G]
it,”[H,w] says the LORD of Hosts. “You bring stolen,[I,x] lame, or sick animals. You bring this as
an offering! Am I to accept that from your
hands?” asks the LORD.
14 “The deceiver is cursed who has an acceptable male in his flock and makes a vow
but sacrifices a defective animal to the Lord.[y]
For I am a great King,” says Yahweh of Hosts,
“and My name[J] will be feared among the nations.

Warning to the Priests

2 “Therefore, this decree[z] is for you priests:
2 If you don't listen, and if you don't take
it to heart[aa] to honor My name,” says ·Yahweh
of ·Hosts, “I will send a curse among you, and
I will curse your blessings.[ab] In fact, I have already begun to curse them because you are
not taking it to heart.
3 “Look, I am going to rebuke your descendants,[ac] and I will spread animal waste[K] over
your faces, the waste from your festival sacrifices,[ad] and you will be taken away with
it. 4 Then you will know that I sent you this
decree so My covenant with Levi[ae] may continue,” says the LORD of Hosts. 5 “My covenant
with him was one of life and peace,[af] and I
gave these to him; it called for reverence,
and he revered Me and stood in awe of My
name.[ag] 6 True instruction was in his mouth,
and nothing wrong was found on his lips.
He walked with Me[ah] in peace and fairness
and turned many from sin.[ai] 7 For the lips of
a priest should guard knowledge, and people
should seek instruction from his mouth,
because he is the messenger of the LORD of
Hosts.[aj]
8 “You, on the other hand, have turned from
the way.[ak] You have caused many to stumble[al]

[a]**1:1** Is 13:1; Zch 9:1; 12:1 [b]Hs 1:1; Jl 1:1; Mc 1:1; Zph 1:1 [c]Jr 37:2; Hg 1:1 [d]**1:2** Dt 4:37; 7:6-8; 10:14-15; Neh 13:26; Ps 78:68 [e]Gn 25:25-26; 36:19 [f]**1:3** Gn 25:23; Rm 9:10-13 [g]Is 34:5-17; Jr 49:7-22; Ezk 35:1-15 [h]**1:4** Mal 3:12,15 [i]Is 34:5-17; Jr 49:17-18; Mal 1:14; 2:2; 3:9; 4:6 [j]**1:5** Ps 67:1-7; 72:8-11; Ezk 39:7; Zch 12:1-10; Rm 11:11-12 [k]**1:6** 1Sm 2:30; Dn 5:23; Hg 1:8 [l]**1:7** Ezk 22:26 [m]Ezk 41:22; 44:16 [n]**1:8** Lv 22:18-25; Dt 15:21; 17:1 [o]**1:9** 1Sm 13:12; Pr 19:6; Dn 9:13 [p]Nm 6:25-26 [q]**1:10** 2Ch 28:24 [r]Pr 1:17; Is 1:14 [s]Lv 22:19-21 [t]Is 1:10-17; Jr 6:20; Am 5:21-23; Mc 6:6-8 [u]**1:11** Ps 113:3; Is 45:6; 59:19; Mt 8:11 [v]**1:12** Lv 22:2; Ezk 13:19; 22:26; 36:20-23; Mal 2:10-11 [w]**1:13** 1Sm 2:29 [x]2Sm 24:24 [y]**1:14** Lv 22:18-25; 27:9-10; Nm 30:2; Dt 23:21-23; Ec 5:4-7 [z]**2:1** Nah 1:14 [aa]**2:2** Is 42:25; 57:1; Jr 12:11 [ab]Dt 28:20; Pr 3:33; 28:27; Mal 3:9 [ac]**2:3** Hs 4:6-8 [ad]Ex 29:14; Lv 16:27 [ae]**2:4** Nm 25:11-13; Dt 10:8; 33:8-11; Neh 13:29; Jr 33:17-22 [af]**2:5** 1Sm 25:6; Pr 3:2 [ag]Mal 1:6 [ah]**2:6** Gn 5:22,24; 6:9; Mc 6:8 [ai]Is 53:6; Jr 23:22; Ezk 3:19-20 [aj]**2:7** 2Ch 36:15-16; Hg 1:13 [ak]**2:8** Ex 32:8; Dt 31:29; Mal 3:7 [al]Pr 4:16; Is 8:14-15; Hs 14:1

[A]**1:1** = My Messenger [B]**1:4** Or *will return and build* [C]**1:4** Or *LORD is angry with* [D]**1:5** Or *great over* [E]**1:11** Or *Burnt offerings* [F]**1:11** Or *is great . . . are presented . . . is great* [G]**1:13** Lit *blow at* [H]**1:13** Ancient Jewish tradition reads *Me* [I]**1:13** Or *injured* [J]**1:14** Or *Because I am . . . Yahweh of Hosts, My name* [K]**2:3** Dung or entrails

by your instruction. You have violated[A] the
covenant of Levi," says the LORD of Hosts.
9"So I in turn have made you despised[a] and
humiliated before all the people because you
are not keeping My ways but are showing partiality in your instruction."[b]

Judah's Marital Unfaithfulness

10Don't all of us have one Father?[c] Didn't
one God create us?[d] Why then do we act
treacherously against one another,[e] profaning[f] the covenant of our fathers?[g] 11Judah has
acted treacherously, and a detestable[h] thing
has been done in Israel and in Jerusalem. For
Judah has profaned[i] the LORD's sanctuary,[B,j]
which He loves,[k] and has married the daughter of a foreign god.[C,l] 12To the man who
does this, may the LORD cut off[m] any descendants[D,E,n] from the tents of Jacob, even if they
present an offering to the LORD of Hosts.

13And this is another thing you do: you
cover the LORD's altar with tears, with weeping and groaning,[o] because He no longer respects your offerings or receives them gladly
from your hands.[p]

14Yet you ask, "For what reason?" Because
the LORD has been a witness[q] between you
and the wife of your youth.[r] You have acted
treacherously against her, though she was
your marriage partner[s] and your wife by covenant.[t] 15Didn't the one God make us with a
remnant of His life-breath? And what does
the One seek?[F] A godly ·offspring. So watch
yourselves carefully,[G,u] and do not act treacherously against the wife of your youth.

16"If he hates[v] and divorces his wife,[w]" says
the LORD God of Israel, "he[H] covers his garment with injustice,"[x] says the LORD of Hosts.
Therefore, watch yourselves carefully,[I] and do
not act treacherously.

Judgment at the LORD's Coming

17You have wearied the LORD[y] with your
words.

Yet you ask, "How have we wearied Him?"

When you say, "Everyone who does what
is evil is good in the LORD's sight, and He is
pleased with them,"[z] or "Where is the God of
justice?"[aa]

3 "See, I am going to send My messenger,[ab]
and he will clear the way before Me.[ac]
Then the Lord you seek[ad] will suddenly come
to His temple,[ae] the Messenger of the covenant you desire — see, He is coming," says the
LORD of ·Hosts. 2But who can endure the day
of His coming? And who will be able to stand
when He appears?[af] For He will be like a refiner's fire[ag] and like cleansing lye.[ah] 3He will
be like a refiner and purifier of silver; He will
purify the sons of Levi and refine them like
gold and silver.[ai] Then they will present offerings to the LORD in righteousness. 4And the
offerings of Judah and Jerusalem will please
the LORD as in days of old[aj] and years gone by.
5"I will come to you in judgment, and I will
be ready to witness against sorcerers and
adulterers; against those who swear falsely;
against those who oppress the widow and
the fatherless, and cheat the wage earner;
and against those who deny justice to the
foreigner.[ak] They do not ·fear Me,"[al] says the
LORD of Hosts. 6"Because I, ·Yahweh, have not
changed,[am] you descendants of Jacob have not
been destroyed.[an]

Robbing God

7"Since the days of your fathers, you have
turned from My statutes; you have not kept
them.[ao] Return to Me,[ap] and I will return to
you,"[aq] says the LORD of Hosts.

But you ask: "How can we return?"

8"Will a man rob[ar] God? Yet you are robbing Me!"

You ask: "How do we rob You?"

"By not making the payments of the tenth
and the contributions.[as] 9You are suffering under a curse, yet you — the whole nation — are still robbing Me. 10Bring the full
tenth into the storehouse[at] so that there may
be food in My house.[au] Test Me in this way,"[av]

[a]**2:9** Mal 1:6-7 [b]Lv 19:15; Dt 10:17; Ps 82:2; Mt 22:16; 1Tm 5:21; Jms 2:1,9 [c]**2:10** Ex 4:22-23; Is 63:16; Hs 11:1; Mal 1:6; Jn 8:41 [d]Dt 32:6; Is 43:1-7; 64:8 [e]Ex 21:8; Jdg 9:23; Jb 6:15; Is 21:2; Jr 3:20 [f]Nm 30:2; Ps 55:20; 89:34; Mal 1:12 [g]1Kg 8:21 [h]**2:11** Lv 18:22-30; Ezr 9:1-14; Neh 13:4-9 [i]Jr 16:18; Ezk 44:7 [j]Ex 36:1-6; Zph 3:4 [k]Ps 78:68-69 [l]Dt 7:3-4; Ezr 9:1-2,10-14; Neh 13:23-30 [m]**2:12** Ex 12:19; 31:14 [n]Ru 4:10; 1Sm 24:21 [o]**2:13** Ps 6:6-10 [p]1Kg 8:28-30; Is 56:7 [q]**2:14** Gn 31:50-53; Jdg 11:10; 1Sm 12:5 [r]Pr 2:16-17; 5:18; Is 54:6 [s]Ec 4:10 [t]Ezk 16:8,59-62; Hs 2:16-20 [u]**2:15** Ex 23:13; Jos 23:11 [v]**2:16** Gn 29:31; Dt 21:15-17; 22:13,16; Jdg 15:2; Pr 30:23 [w]Dt 24:1-4 [x]Gn 6:11,13; Ps 73:6; Jr 22:3; Hab 1:2-3 [y]**2:17** Is 43:22-24 [z]Dt 25:16; Mal 3:15 [aa]Neh 9:33; Is 40:27 [ab]**3:1** Ex 23:20; 33:2; 2Ch 36:15-16 [ac]Is 40:3; Mk 1:2; Lk 1:76 [ad]Hs 5:6 [ae]Ps 24:7-10 [af]**3:2** Rv 6:17 [ag]Dt 4:24; Is 1:25; Zch 13:9 [ah]Jr 2:22 [ai]**3:3** Ps 12:6; Pr 17:3; Ezk 22:22 [aj]**3:4** Am 9:11 [ak]**3:5** Ex 20:14,16; 22:18-24; Dt 18:10; 24:14,17; Jr 5:2,7; 7:6,9 [al]Dt 10:17-20; Mal 2:5

[am]**3:6** Nm 23:19; 1Sm 15:29; Ps 33:11; 119:89-91; Rm 11:29; Heb 6:17-18; Jms 1:17 [an]Ps 124; Hs 11:9 [ao]**3:7** Jos 1:7; 23:6; 1Kg 8:58; 2Kg 17:15; Ezr 9:7; Am 2:4; Mal 2:8 [ap]Dt 4:30; 30:2; 2Ch 30:6,9; Is 55:7; Jl 2:13; Zch 1:3 [aq]1Kg 8:33; Jr 15:19; 24:7 [ar]**3:8** Pr 22:22-23 [as]Lv 7:14,32-33; 27:30-32; Nm 18:8-24; Dt 12:5-19; 14:22-29; 26:12 [at]**3:10** Jos 6:19,24; 1Kg 7:51 [au]2Ch 31:4-10; Neh 10:34-39; Ezk 44:28-31 [av]Ex 4:1-9; Jdg 6:36-40

[A]**2:8** Lit *corrupted* [B]**2:11** Or *profaned what is holy to the LORD* [C]**2:11** = a woman who worshiped a foreign god [D]**2:12** One Hb ms, LXX, DSS read *off one witnessing or answering* [E]**2:12** Lit *off one waking or answering*; Hb obscure [F]**2:15** Or *Did the One not make them? So their flesh and spirit belong to Him,* or *No one who does this even has a remnant of the Spirit in him*; Hb obscure [G]**2:15** Lit *So guard yourselves in your spirit* [H]**2:16** Or *The LORD God of Israel says that He hates divorce and the one who* [I]**2:16** Lit *Therefore, guard yourselves in your spirit*

On the Frontlines

Larry Elliott, Jean Elliott, Karen Watson, David McDonnall (all died 2004)

On March 15, 2004, five missionaries from the United States serving with the Southern Baptist International Mission Board were scouting sites for a water purification project and delivering supplies to a refugee camp in northern Iraq. They were hoping to find a way to provide clean water to the city of Mosul. Suddenly, out of nowhere came a group of Iraqi militants who ambushed their vehicle and gunned them down with their AK-47 rifles. Only David McDonnall's wife, Carrie, survived.

The McDonnalls had arrived in Iraq in November 2003. God used them in a variety of ways—helping volunteer teams, building pharmaceutical cabinets for a medical clinic, being involved in a food distribution project giving food to both Kurdish and Arab people living in camps for internally displaced people (IDPs) who were forced out of their homes during the reign of Saddam Hussein. Carrie was involved in a mostly female volunteer group that worked with an Iraqi women's project to teach women the basics of reading, writing, and arithmetic as well as teaching them a skill, such as sewing, that would help them become self-sufficient and earn and income. David was 28; Carrie was 26 at the time.

Larry and Jean Elliott were the oldest in the group, at ages 60 and 58 respectively, and were scouting the best location in Iraq for a water purification project. They understood that their work in Iraq needed to help with basic human needs—like clean water—as well as ministering to people's souls.

Karen Watson had been a detention officer in Bakersfield, California, before joining the Southern Baptist Mission board in 2003. She went to Iraq to help the Elliotts and others study how best to allocate the mission board's humanitarian efforts. She was 38.

These Southern Baptist workers had responded to God's call to Iraq. They wanted to help the Kurds rebuild their lives, gain access to clean water, and discover God's love. Four of them gave their lives.

says the LORD of Hosts. "See if I will not open the floodgates of heaven[a] and pour out a blessing for you without measure.[b] 11 I will rebuke the devourer[A,c] for you, so that it will not ruin the produce of your land and your vine in your field will not fail to produce fruit," says the LORD of Hosts. 12 "Then all the nations will consider you fortunate, for you will be a delightful land," says the LORD of Hosts.

The Righteous and the Wicked

13 "Your words against Me are harsh,"[d] says the LORD.

Yet you ask: "What have we spoken against You?"

14 You have said: "It is useless to serve God. What have we gained by keeping His requirements[e] and walking mournfully[f] before the LORD of Hosts? 15 So now we consider the arrogant[g] to be fortunate.[h] Not only do those who commit wickedness prosper, they even test God[i] and escape."[j]

16 At that time those who feared the LORD spoke to one another. The LORD took notice and listened. So a book of remembrance[k] was written before Him for those who feared Yahweh and had high regard for His name. 17 "They will be Mine," says the LORD of Hosts,[l] "a special possession on the day I am preparing. I will have compassion on them as a man has compassion on his son who serves him.[m] 18 So you will again see the difference between the righteous and the wicked, between one who serves God and one who does not serve Him.

The Day of the LORD

4 [B] "For indeed, the day is coming, burning like a furnace, when all the arrogant and everyone who commits wickedness will become stubble. The coming day will consume them," says the LORD of ·Hosts, "not leaving them root or branches. 2 But for you who ·fear My name, the sun of righteousness will rise with healing in its wings,[n] and you will go out and playfully jump like calves from the stall.[C] 3 You will trample the wicked, for they will be ashes under the soles of your feet on the day I am preparing," says the LORD of Hosts.

A Final Warning

4 "Remember the instruction of Moses My servant, the statutes and ordinances I commanded him at Horeb[o] for all Israel. 5 Look, I am going to send you Elijah the prophet[p] before the great and awesome Day of the LORD comes.[q] 6 [D] And he will turn the hearts of fathers to their children and the hearts of children to their fathers.[r] Otherwise, I will come and strike the land[E] with a curse."

[a] **3:10** Gn 7:11; 8:2; Dt 11:16-17
[b] Dt 28:12; Is 41:18-20; Jl 2:18-32; Am 9:13-15
[c] **3:11** Jl 1:4; 2:25
[d] **3:13** Ps 119:23; Ezk 35:13
[e] **3:14** Lv 8:35; Dt 11:1
[f] Ps 35:14; 38:6
[g] **3:15** Ps 119:21,85; Is 13:11; Jr 43:2
[h] Gn 30:13; Ps 72:17; Pr 31:28
[i] Ps 78:18,41,56; 95:9
[j] Ezk 17:15
[k] **3:16** Ex 32:32; Est 6:1; Dn 12:1
[l] **3:17** Ex 19:5; Dt 7:6; 14:2; 26:18; Ps 135:4
[m] Ps 103:13; Jl 2:18; Zch 11:5-6
[n] **4:2** Ps 37:6; Is 58:8
[o] **4:4** Dt 4:10,15; 5:2
[p] **4:5** Mt 11:13-14
[q] Jl 2:31; Ac 2:20
[r] **4:6** Lk 1:17

[A] **3:11** Perhaps locusts [B] **4:1** Mal 3:19 in Hb [C] **4:2** Or *like stall-fed calves* [D] **4:6** Mal 3:24 in Hb [E] **4:6** Or *earth*

NEW TESTAMENT

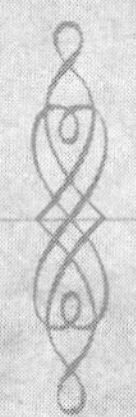

■ **AUTHOR:** Matthew, a Jewish tax collector and disciple of Jesus

■■ **DATE:** Written in A.D. 60–65, the Gospel of Matthew covers events leading up to the birth of Jesus through His crucifixion and resurrection

The mission of God now bursts onto the world scene with greater clarity and authority than ever before. Jesus Christ, born of Mary, in the line of David, speaks God's word with greater authority than kings, priests, or prophets of Old Israel. He was Immanuel—God with us. He announces God's future. He commissions missionary-disciples to spread the Word to everyone, everywhere. No matter how far afield His missionaries may travel, Jesus promises to be with them always. These astounding claims can only identify Jesus as the Messiah of God, the promised Servant of Isaiah, whose advent was predicted throughout the Old Testament. That is exactly Matthew's intention: to make the case, first to Greek-speaking Jews then to others throughout the known world, that Jesus of Nazareth is the hope to which all the Scriptures point. He is the miracle-working Teacher who is God's mission in person. Jesus is the one who tells the good news of God's Kingdom and invites all people to believe and obey.

MATTHEW

Matthew frames the story of Jesus around five great teachings or discourses. Matthew's purpose may have been to suggest to readers that Jesus' words are the new Torah (Genesis through Deuteronomy), and Jesus is the new Moses. But Jesus far surpasses Moses in His teachings on life and His power over death. Jesus is the new interpreter of God's law, superior to Moses and the prophets. With the repeated phrase, "You have heard. . . . But I tell you," Jesus speaks with authority in His Sermon on the Mount (5:21-22). This challenge to old ways caused the religious leaders who had followed the Torah (often burdening it with dogmatic, incorrect interpretations) for centuries to feel threatened.

Three years into His teaching ministry, Jesus is arraigned, tried, and executed for His claims. His death on the cross, horrible and unjust, is the heart of God's mission. On Jesus was placed the penalty for sin. His death was the substitute for ours. Jesus bore God's holy anger at sin, paid its price, and opened the gates of God's Kingdom to people who could not have entered on their own record—which is all of us.

But the death of Jesus was not the end of Him. On the first day of the week, Matthew records, Jesus rose from the grave—something Moses could not have done. The power of God was victorious over death in the resurrected life of Jesus. His resurrection was the core message Jesus sent His disciples into the world to tell.

Matthew's Gospel includes the oft-quoted Sermon on the Mount (which includes the Beatitudes) and many of Jesus' parables on the Kingdom of God. These teachings challenge the normal goals most people set for themselves: acquire wealth, become intelligent, be powerful, find love. In Jesus' teaching, the meek and powerless inherit God's Kingdom. The person who relies on God instead of worrying over money is the person who "has it all." The Kingdom arrives in the small and unexpected. It is subversive to the world's system. Jesus urged His listeners to know God and to diligently seek Him.

That's God's mission—building a family of faith and a Kingdom of praise, changing the world into all it should be through the power of God.

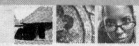

The Genealogy of Jesus Christ

1 The[a] historical record[A,b] of Jesus Christ, the Son of David,[c] the Son of Abraham:[d]

From Abraham to David

2 Abraham fathered[B] Isaac,
Isaac fathered Jacob,
Jacob fathered Judah and his brothers,[e]
3 Judah fathered Perez and Zerah
by Tamar,
Perez fathered Hezron,
Hezron fathered Aram,[f]
4 Aram fathered Amminadab,
Amminadab fathered Nahshon,
Nahshon fathered Salmon,
5 Salmon fathered Boaz by Rahab,
Boaz fathered Obed by Ruth,
Obed fathered Jesse,[g]
6 and Jesse fathered King David.

From David to the Babylonian Exile

Then[C] David fathered Solomon
by Uriah's wife,[h]
7 Solomon fathered Rehoboam,
Rehoboam fathered Abijah,
Abijah fathered Asa,[D]
8 Asa[D] fathered Jehoshaphat,
Jehoshaphat fathered Joram,[E]
Joram fathered Uzziah,[i]
9 Uzziah fathered Jotham,
Jotham fathered Ahaz,
Ahaz fathered Hezekiah,
10 Hezekiah fathered Manasseh,
Manasseh fathered Amon,[F]
Amon fathered Josiah,[j]
11 and Josiah fathered Jechoniah
and his brothers
at the time of the exile to Babylon.[k]

From the Exile to the Messiah

12 Then after the exile to Babylon
Jechoniah fathered Shealtiel,
Shealtiel fathered Zerubbabel,
13 Zerubbabel fathered Abiud,
Abiud fathered Eliakim,
Eliakim fathered Azor,[l]
14 Azor fathered Zadok,
Zadok fathered Achim,
Achim fathered Eliud,
15 Eliud fathered Eleazar,
Eleazar fathered Matthan,
Matthan fathered Jacob,
16 and Jacob fathered Joseph the husband
of Mary,
who gave birth to[G] Jesus who is called
the •Messiah.[m]

17 So all the generations from Abraham to
David were 14 generations; and from David
until the exile to Babylon, 14 generations; and
from the exile to Babylon until the Messiah,
14 generations.[n]

The Nativity of the Messiah

18 The birth of Jesus Christ came about this
way: After His mother Mary had been •en-
gaged to Joseph, it was discovered before they
came together that she was pregnant by the
Holy Spirit.[o] 19 So her husband Joseph, being a
righteous man,[p] and not wanting to disgrace
her publicly, decided to divorce her secretly.[q]
20 But after he had considered these things,
an angel of the Lord suddenly appeared to

[a]**1:1-6** Ru 4:18-22; 2Sm 7:12-16; 1Ch 2:1-15; Lk 3:32-34
[b]**1:1** Mk 12:26; Lk 3:4; Ac 1:20; Php 4:3; Rv 3:5
[c]Ps 89:3; Is 9:6; Lk 1:32,69
[d]Gn 22:18; Mt 9:7; Rm 1:3; Gl 3:16
[e]**1:2** Gn 29:35; Ps 14:7; 105:9; Mt 8:11; 22:32; Jms 2:21
[f]**1:3** Gn 38:29-30; 46:12; Lk 3:33
[g]**1:5** Ru 1:4; 2:1; Lk 3:32
[h]**1:6** 1Sm 16:1; 17:12; 2Sm 11:27; 12:24
[i]**1:7-8** 1Kg 11:43; 14:31; 15:8,24; 22:50; 2Kg 14:21
[j]**1:9-10** 2Kg 15:5,38; 16:20; 20:21; 21:18,24
[k]**1:11** 2Kg 24:6,14; Is 5:13; Jr 27:20; Ezk 1:1; Mt 1:17
[l]**1:12-13** Gn 10:10; 1Ch 3:17; Lk 3:27,30
[m]**1:16** Mt 27:17,22; Lk 2:11; Jn 1:45; 4:25
[n]**1:17** 2Kg 24:14; Jr 27:20; Dn 9:25-26; Mk 8:29; Ac 2:31,36,38
[o]**1:18** Mt 12:46; Lk 1:27,35
[p]**1:19** Mt 13:17; Mk 10:12; Lk 2:36; 1Co 14:35; 2Co 11:2; Gl 4:27
[q]Dt 22:20-24; 24:1-4; Mt 2:7; Lk 16:18; Jn 8:4-5

GOD WHO SENDS

The Incarnation

In Jesus Christ, this divine-human relationship reaches a sublime level. The people are able to see in the man Jesus—Emmanuel, God with us (Mt 1:23)—what God was like. The whole behavioral pattern of Christ's followers was based not so much upon external commandments based on Christ's moral nature but upon his relationship to them. Moreover, his sending, first the twelve, then the seventy, and finally all of his followers, brought to an exalted level the missional dimension of that relationship.

(DUBOSE, 84)

[A]**1:1** Or *The book of the genealogy* [B]**1:2** In vv. 2-16 either a son, as here, or a later descendant, as in v. 8 [C]**1:6** Other mss add *King* [D]**1:7,8** Other mss read *Asaph* [E]**1:8** = Jehoram [F]**1:10** Other mss read *Amos* [G]**1:16** Lit *Mary, from whom was born*

him in a dream, saying, "Joseph, son of David, don't be afraid to take Mary as your wife,
because what has been conceived in her is by
the Holy Spirit.[a] 21She will give birth to a son,
and you are to name Him Jesus,[A,b] because He
will save His people from their sins."[c]
22Now all this took place to fulfill what was
spoken by the Lord through the prophet:

23 **See, the virgin will become pregnant**
and give birth to a son,
and they will name Him Immanuel,[B]

which is translated "God is with us."[d]
24When Joseph got up from sleeping, he
did as the Lord's angel had commanded him.
He married her[e] 25but did not know her intimately until she gave birth to a son.[C] And he
named Him Jesus.[f]

Wise Men Seek the King

2 After Jesus was born in Bethlehem of Judea in the days of King ·Herod, ·wise men
from the east arrived unexpectedly in Jerusalem,[g] 2saying, "Where is He who has been
born King of the Jews?[h] For we saw His star
in the east[D,i] and have come to worship Him."[E]
3When King Herod heard this, he was
deeply disturbed, and all Jerusalem with him.
4So he assembled all the ·chief priests and
·scribes[j] of the people and asked them where
the ·Messiah would be born.
5"In Bethlehem of Judea," they told him,
"because this is what was written by the
prophet:

6 **And you, Bethlehem,** in the land
of Judah,
are by no means **least**
among the leaders of Judah:
because out of you will come a leader
who will shepherd My people Israel."[F,k]

7Then Herod secretly summoned the wise
men and asked them the exact time the star
appeared. 8He sent them to Bethlehem and
said, "Go and search carefully for the child.
When you find Him, report back to me so
that I too can go and worship Him."[G,l]
9After hearing the king, they went on their

[a]**1:20** 2Ch 1:1; Mt 13:49; 27:19; Jn 6:20; Rm 1:3 [b]**1:21** Lk 1:31; 2:21; Jn 10:25; 1Jn 2:12 [c]Lk 2:11; Jn 1:29; Ac 4:12; 5:31; 13:23,38-39 [d]**1:22-23** Is 7:14; Mt 21:1-4; Lk 24:44; Rm 1:2-4 [e]**1:24** Mt 1:6; 13:49; Lk 1:1; 19:32; Jd 5 [f]**1:25** Gn 4:1,17; Ex 13:2; Jdg 11:39; 1Sm 1:19; Lk 2:7,21 [g]**2:1** Gn 25:6; 1Kg 4:30; Lk 1:5; 2:4-7 [h]**2:2** Jr 23:5; 30:9; Zch 9:9; Mt 27:11; Lk 19:38; Jn 1:49 [i]Nm 24:17; Rv 22:16 [j]**2:4** Mt 16:21; 20:18; 21:15; 27:41; Lk 9:22 [k]**2:6** 2Sm 5:2; Mc 5:2; Jn 7:42; 21:16 [l]**2:7-8** Mk 5:6; Lk 1:7; Ac 13:6; Rv 1:16

GOD'S HEART FOR THE WORLD

Wise Astrologers

Where is He who has been born King of the Jews? For we saw His star in the east and have come to worship Him. (Matthew 2:2)

Most of us have gotten very used to the nativity scene. But the figures we see in those serene-looking mangers set out on mantles and in front of neighborhood churches are actually a scandalous group. The only one who would have been considered fit to be in the presence of a King is Joseph, a Jewish man, and he didn't have much choice in the matter. Mary is just a particularly obedient teenager, the shepherds are the down-and-outs of Jewish society, and then there are the "wise men."

Somehow we began to call them wise men, even kings, but they are astrologers. They are also foreigners. Even seeing a star, how did they come to know that the One who was being born was the King of the Jews? And that He was not just a human king, but one to be worshiped? Most importantly, why did they think this had anything to do with them?

The beauty of this story is that it had everything to do with them. Matthew says that these unlikely characters are the first to come and greet this King, and to worship Him. Matthew wants us to see that the gospel that Jesus brings is not just for insiders. It is for the down-and-outs, the foreigners, prostitutes, lepers, astrologers. It is for the outcasts. Even as a baby, Jesus begins His redemption, not just of Israel, but of the whole world.

A**1:21** *Jesus* is the Gk form of the Hb name "Joshua," which = "The LORD saves" or "Yahweh saves." B**1:23** Is 7:14 C**1:25** Other mss read *to her firstborn son* D**2:2** Or *star at its rising* E**2:2** Or *to pay Him homage* F**2:6** Mc 5:2 G**2:8** Or *and pay Him homage*

way. And there it was — the star they had
seen in the east![A] It led them until it came
and stopped above the place where the child
was. 10 When they saw the star, they were overjoyed beyond measure. 11 Entering the house,
they saw the child with Mary His mother, and
falling to their knees, they worshiped Him.[B]
Then they opened their treasures and presented Him with gifts: gold, frankincense,
and myrrh.[a] 12 And being warned[b] in a dream
not to go back to Herod, they returned to
their own country by another route.

The Flight into Egypt

13 After they were gone, an angel of the Lord
suddenly appeared to Joseph in a dream, saying, "Get up! Take the child and His mother,
flee to Egypt, and stay there until I tell you. For
Herod is about to search for the child to destroy Him."[c] 14 So he got up, took the child and
His mother during the night, and escaped to
Egypt. 15 He stayed there until Herod's death,
so that what was spoken by the Lord through
the prophet might be fulfilled: **Out of Egypt I**
called My Son.[C,d]

The Massacre of the Innocents

16 Then Herod, when he saw that he had
been outwitted by the wise men, flew into a
rage. He gave orders to massacre all the male
children in and around Bethlehem who were
two years[D] old and under, in keeping with
the time he had learned from the wise men.[e]
17 Then what was spoken through Jeremiah
the prophet was fulfilled:

18 **A voice was heard in Ramah,**
weeping,[E] and great mourning,
Rachel weeping for her children;
and she refused to be consoled,
because they were no more.[F,f]

The Holy Family in Nazareth

19 After Herod died, an angel of the Lord suddenly appeared in a dream to Joseph in Egypt,[g]
20 saying, "Get up! Take the child and His
mother and go to the land of Israel, because
those who sought the child's life are dead."
21 So he got up, took the child and His mother,
and entered the land of Israel. 22 But when he
heard that Archelaus[G] was ruling over Judea in
place of his father Herod, he was afraid to go
there. And being warned in a dream, he withdrew to the region of Galilee.[h] 23 Then he went
and settled in a town called Nazareth to fulfill
what was spoken through the prophets, that
He will be called a ·Nazarene.[i]

The Messiah's Herald

3 In those days John the Baptist came,[j]
preaching in the Wilderness of Judea[k]
2 and saying, "Repent, because the kingdom
of heaven has come near!"[l] 3 For he is the one
spoken of through the prophet Isaiah, who
said:

A voice of one crying out
in the wilderness:
Prepare the way for the Lord;
make His paths straight![H,m]

4 John himself had a camel-hair garment
with a leather belt around his waist, and
his food was locusts and wild honey. 5 Then
people from Jerusalem, all Judea, and all the
vicinity of the Jordan were flocking to him,
6 and they were baptized by him in the Jordan
River as they confessed their sins.[n]
7 When he saw many of the ·Pharisees and
·Sadducees[o] coming to the place of his baptism,[I] he said to them, "Brood of vipers! Who
warned you to flee from the coming wrath?[p]
8 Therefore produce fruit[q] consistent with[J] repentance. 9 And don't presume to say to yourselves, 'We have Abraham as our father.'[r] For
I tell you that God is able to raise up children
for Abraham from these stones! 10 Even now
the ax is ready to strike the root of the trees!
Therefore, every tree that doesn't produce
good fruit will be cut down and thrown into
the fire.[s]
11 "I baptize you with[K] water for repentance,[L,t] but the One who is coming after me
is more powerful than I. I am not worthy to
remove[M] His sandals. He Himself will baptize you with[K] the Holy Spirit and fire.[u] 12 His
winnowing shovel[N] is in His hand, and He

[a] **2:11** Ps 72:10; Is 60:6; Mt 1:18; 12:46; Mk 5:6
[b] **2:12** Mt 27:19; Lk 2:26; Ac 10:22; Heb 8:5; 11:7
[c] **2:13** Mt 1:20; 13:49; Mk 11:18; Jms 4:7
[d] **2:15** Ex 4:22; Nm 24:8; Hs 11:1
[e] **2:16** Is 59:7; Mk 10:34; Ac 13:6; 25:3; Rv 12:4
[f] **2:18** Gn 35:19; Jdg 4:5; Jr 31:15; Ac 8:2; 2Co 7:7
[g] **2:19** Mt 1:20; 13:49; Lk 1:11; Jd 5
[h] **2:22** Mt 17:22; Lk 1:5; Ac 27:29; Col 3:21; Heb 8:5
[i] **2:23** Mk 1:24; Lk 1:26; Jn 1:45-46
[j] **3:1-12** Mk 1:3-8; Lk 3:2-17; Jn 1:6-8,19-28
[k] **3:1** Jos 15:61; Jdg 1:16
[l] **3:2** Dn 2:44; Mt 4:17; 6:10; 10:7; Mk 1:15; Lk 10:9; 11:20; 21:31
[m] **3:3** Is 40:3; Lk 1:17,76; Jn 1:23
[n] **3:5-6** Mt 23:37; Mk 1:5; Lk 3:3; Jn 15:22; Ac 19:18
[o] **3:7** Mt 16:1; 22:23; 23:15; Ac 4:1; 5:17; 23:6
[p] Mt 12:34; 23:33; Rm 5:9; 1Th 1:10
[q] **3:8** Mt 3:10; 12:33; 13:8,26; 21:19,34,41,43; Mk 11:14
[r] **3:9** Lk 3:8; Jn 8:33,39; Ac 13:26; Rm 4:1
[s] **3:10** Mt 7:19; Lk 13:7,9; Jn 15:2,6
[t] **3:11** Mk 1:4,8; Jn 1:26; Ac 1:5
[u] Is 4:4; Jn 1:33; Ac 2:3-4; 11:16; Ti 3:5

[A] 2:9 Or *star . . . at its rising* [B] 2:11 Or *they paid Him homage* [C] 2:15 Hs 11:1 [D] 2:16 Lit *were from two years* [E] 2:18 Other mss read *Ramah, lamentation, and weeping,* [F] 2:18 Jr 31:15 [G] 2:22 A son of Herod the Great who ruled a portion of his father's kingdom 4 B.C.–A.D. 6 [H] 3:3 Is 40:3 [I] 3:7 Lit *to his baptism* [J] 3:8 Lit *fruit worthy of* [K] 3:11 Or *in* [L] 3:11 Baptism was the means by which repentance was expressed publicly. [M] 3:11 Or *to carry* [N] 3:12 A wooden farm implement used to toss threshed grain into the wind so the lighter chaff would blow away and separate from the heavier grain

will clear His threshing floor and gather His
wheat into the barn. But the chaff He will
burn up with fire that never goes out."[a]

The Baptism of Jesus

13 Then Jesus came from Galilee to John at
the Jordan, to be baptized by him.[b] 14 But John
tried to stop Him, saying, "I need to be baptized by You, and yet You come to me?"
15 Jesus answered him, "Allow it for now,
because this is the way for us to fulfill all
righteousness." Then he allowed Him to be
baptized.
16 After Jesus was baptized, He went up immediately from the water. The heavens[c] suddenly opened for Him,[A] and He saw the Spirit
of God descending like a dove and coming
down on Him.[d] 17 And there came a voice from
heaven:

This is My beloved Son.
I take delight in Him![e]

The Temptation of Jesus

4 Then[f] Jesus was led up by the Spirit into
the wilderness to be tempted by the
Devil.[g] 2 After He had fasted 40 days and 40
nights,[h] He was hungry. 3 Then the tempter
approached Him and said, "If You are the Son
of God, tell these stones to become bread."[i]
4 But He answered, "It is written:

Man must not live on bread alone
but on every word that comes
from the mouth of God."[B,j]

5 Then the Devil took Him to the holy city,[C]
had Him stand on the pinnacle of the temple,[k] 6 and said to Him, "If You are the Son of
God, throw Yourself down. For it is written:

He will give His angels[l] **orders**
concerning you,
and **they will support you**
with their hands
so that you will not strike
your foot against a stone."[D,m]

7 Jesus told him, "It is also written: **Do not**
test the Lord your God."[E,n]
8 Again, the Devil took Him to a very high
mountain and showed Him all the kingdoms
of the world and their splendor. 9 And he said
to Him, "I will give You all these things if You
will fall down and worship me."[F]
10 Then Jesus told him, "Go away,[G] Satan! For
it is written:

Worship the Lord your God,
and serve only[o] **Him.**"[H]

11 Then the Devil left Him, and immediately
angels came and began to serve Him.[p]

Ministry in Galilee

12 When He heard that John had been arrested,[q] He withdrew into Galilee.[r] 13 He left
Nazareth behind and went to live in Capernaum[s] by the sea, in the region of Zebulun
and Naphtali. 14 This was to fulfill what was
spoken through the prophet Isaiah:

15 **Land of Zebulun and land of Naphtali,**
along the sea road, beyond the Jordan,
Galilee of the Gentiles!
16 **The people who live in darkness**
have seen a great light,
and for those living in the shadowland
of death,
light has dawned.[I,J,t]

17 From then on Jesus began to preach, "Repent, because the kingdom of heaven[u] has
come near!"

The First Disciples

18 As[v] He was walking along the Sea of Galilee,[w] He saw two brothers, Simon, who was
called Peter, and his brother Andrew. They
were casting a net into the sea, since they were
fishermen. 19 "Follow Me," He told them, "and
I will make you fish for[K] people!" 20 Immediately they left their nets and followed Him.
21 Going on from there, He saw two other
brothers, James the son of Zebedee, and his
brother John. They were in a boat with Zebedee their father, mending their nets, and He
called them. 22 Immediately they left the boat
and their father and followed Him.

Teaching, Preaching, and Healing

23 Jesus was going all over Galilee,[x] teaching in their •synagogues, preaching the good

[a] **3:12** Is 30:24; Mt 13:30; Mk 9:43,48; Lk 3:17
[b] **3:13-17** Mk 1:9-11; Lk 3:21-22; Jn 1:31-34
[c] **3:16** Mt 24:35; Lk 12:33; Ac 17:24; Eph 6:9; Rv 21:10
[d] Is 11:2; Jn 1:32; Ac 7:56; 2Pt 1:17
[e] **3:17** Ps 2:7; Is 42:1; Lk 9:35; Jn 12:28
[f] **4:1-11** Mk 1:12-13; Lk 4:1-13
[g] **4:1** Jos 15:61; Jdg 1:16; Jn 1:6-7; Jms 1:14
[h] **4:2** Ex 34:28; 1Kg 19:8; Jn 9:4
[i] **4:3** Mk 3:11; 5:7; Lk 1:35; 4:41; Jn 1:34,49; Ac 9:20
[j] **4:4** Dt 8:3
[k] **4:5** Neh 11:1,18; Dn 9:24; Mt 27:53
[l] **4:6** Gn 16:7; Mt 13:49; Lk 1:11; Ac 5:19; Rv 14:6
[m] Ps 91:11-12; 1Pt 2:8
[n] **4:7** Dt 6:16; 1Sm 7:3; 1Ch 21:1
[o] **4:10** Dt 6:13; 1Ch 21:1
[p] **4:11** Mt 26:53; Lk 22:43; Heb 1:14
[q] **4:12** Mt 14:3; Mk 1:14; Lk 3:20; Jn 3:24
[r] Lk 4:14; Jn 1:43; 2:11
[s] **4:13** Mk 1:21; 2:1; Lk 4:23; Jn 2:12; 4:46
[t] **4:15-16** Is 9:1-2; 42:7; Lk 2:32
[u] **4:17** Mt 3:2; 5:3,10,19-20; 7:21; 8:11; Mk 1:14
[v] **4:18-22** Mk 1:16-20; Lk 5:2-11; Jn 1:40-42
[w] **4:18** Mt 15:29; Mk 7:31; Lk 5:1; Jn 6:1
[x] **4:23-25** Mk 1:35-39; Lk 4:42-44

[A] **3:16** Other mss omit *for Him* [B] **4:4** Dt 8:3 [C] **4:5** = Jerusalem [D] **4:6** Ps 91:11-12 [E] **4:7** Dt 6:16 [F] **4:9** Or *and pay me homage* [G] **4:10** Other mss read *Get behind Me* [H] **4:10** Dt 6:13 [I] **4:16** Lit *dawned on them* [J] **4:15-16** Is 9:1-2 [K] **4:19** Lit *you fishers of*

The Trinitarian Nature of the Mission of God

Enoch Wan

The mission of God as described in Scripture is tailor-made to the nature of our triune God. This essay will present evidences for this conclusion. We begin by offering a definition of mission that notes both the individuality and plurality involved in the task.

> "Mission" is the Christian (individual) and the church (institutional) continuing on and carrying out the *missio dei* of the triune God at both individual and institutional levels, spiritually (saving souls) and socially (ushering in shalom), for redemption, reconciliation and transformation.[1]

As this definition makes clear, each Christian (individual) is involved in a larger community (a plurality) that works to fulfill the mission of God. This resembles the way in which each member of the Trinity has individual identity and tasks while being unified in the corporate identity and purpose of the godhead.

There is strong Scriptural evidence that God is Trinity and that the mission of God is also Trinitarian. Listed below are theological descriptions of God and mission both being trinitarian, along with biblical references.

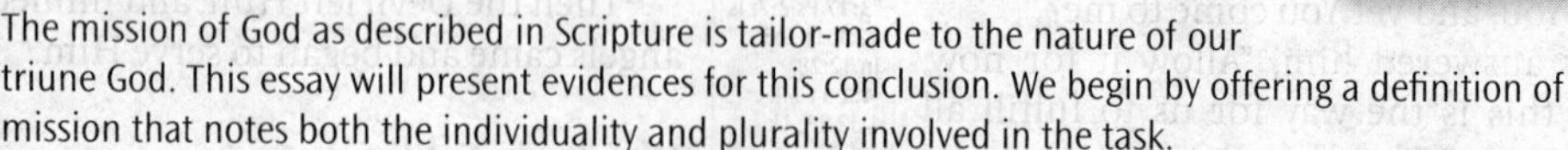

God Is Trinitarian

Jesus' baptism: Jesus' baptism in the Jordan River presents us with some of the clearest evidence for God's triune nature. In the same setting and essentially simultaneously, the voice of the Father booms from heaven, the Son stands in the water with John the Baptist, and the Spirit visibly descends upon Jesus (Mt 3:13-17; Mk 1:9-11; Lk 3:21-22; Jn 1:29-34).

Baptismal formula: The baptismal formula in the Great Commission is trinitarian (Mt 28:19-20).

Pauline literature: Paul's benediction (2Co 13:14), his doxological expressions (Eph 1:3-14; 1Tm 3:14-16) and theological articulations (Rm 8:12-30; Eph 1:3-14; 3:14-19; 4:1-7; 1Tm 3:14-16) indicate the trinitarian nature of God.

Johannine literature: Evidence of trinitarianism is found in John's expressions (1Jn 4:1-15) and his quotation of the sayings of Jesus (Jn 8:18; 14:9-21,25-26; 15:20-27; 16:1-16).

Christian greetings: The Christian manner of greeting one another offers evidence of God's triune nature (Rm 1:1-8; 1Pt 1:2).

Mission Is Trinitarian

Salvation: The election of the Father (Rm 8:29-30; Eph 1:4; 2Tm 1:8-9; 1Pt 1:2), incarnation of the Son for the provision of salvation (Php 2:6-11; Heb 2:9-18), implementation of salvation by the Spirit (Rm 8:9-14; Jn 3:5-8), and trinitarian redemption (Heb 9:11-24) are evidence for mission being triune.

Sending or being sent: The Father sends the Son (Lk 4:43; Jn 5:24; 12:49) to be the Savior (1Jn 4:14), sends the Spirit in the name of the Son (Jn 14:26), and together Father and Son send the Spirit (Jn 14:16-17,26). Further, the Father sends the Son who likewise sends the disciples (Jn 17:18).

God showing forth His nature: *Missio dei* is God pressing Himself out, thus showing forth His nature (glory). For example, the Son (Mt 9:8; 17:1-8; Lk 13:13; Jn 1:14,18; 12:28; 13:32; 17:1,4,5,10,24; 21:19) the Spirit (Jn 14:16) and being the foundation of Christian unity (Jn 17:11-12, 21-24; Eph 4:1-6) and for Christian witness (Jn 1:4-8; 3:17-21; 5:32-37; 8:12-18; 15:26; 16:1-18; 21:24).

Witnessing: Jesus said "the Father who sent Me testifies about Me" (Jn 8:18); the Holy Spirit witnesses about the Son (Jn 15:26; 1Jn 4:2-6) and helped the disciples recall the words of the Son (Jn 14:26). Further, the Father elects those who are to witness for Him (Ac 20:41).

Empowering: The Father empowered the Son by the Spirit in ministry, brought about the resurrection and exaltation of the Son (Ac 10:37; Rm 1:4; Php 3:9-10; Heb 13:20), and the Holy Spirit empowering Christians to witness (Lk 24:47-49; Ac 1:8).

Glorifying: The Father glorified the Son (Jn 12:28; Ac 3:13), the Son glorified the Father (Jn 12:28; 13:31-32; 14:31; 17:4), the Holy Spirit glorified the Son (Jn 16:14), the disciples glorified God (Ac 10:41-48; 11:15-18; 21:20), and Christians should glorify God (1Co 6:11-20; 2Co 3:3-18).

Reconciling: God in Jesus Christ reconciled the world to Himself (Rm 11:5; 2Co 18-19) and committed the message of reconciliation to Christian disciples, making us ambassadors of Christ (2Co 5:19-20) and the Holy Spirit reconciled Gentiles to God (Rm 15:16-18; 1Co 2:9-12).

Grace & gifts: The trinitarian nature of mission is seen in the gifts endowed upon believers by Christ and the Holy Spirit (1Co 12:7-11; Eph 4:7-12), and the empowering of witnesses to be fruitful to the Gospel (Jn 15:1-5; Ac 1:8; 13:2; 2Co 4:7-11; Eph 4:7-12; 1Pt 1:12). Gifts are endowed by Christ and the Spirit upon all Christians as recipients and vessels of God's grace (Rm 9:19-26; 2Co 4:5-15), and as laborers and messengers of the Gospel (Rm 10:10-15; 2Co 3:5-15). Paul described his evangelization efforts as being through the ministry of the Trinity (Rm 15:14-21).

Conclusion

Christopher Wright has said of God's mission: "There is one God at work in the universe and in human history, and . . . this God has a goal, a purpose, a mission that will ultimately be accomplished by the power of God's Word and for the glory of God's name. This is the mission of the biblical God."[2]

The mission of the one God is seen throughout the Scriptures as a work fully engaged upon by all three members of the Trinity. As members of the church, it is to our benefit to hold tightly to that work which is a priority to God the Father, God the Son, and God the Holy Spirit. As we continue to invest our lives into that which is the work of God, we will better know Him and all of the blessings of His kingdom.

[1] "'Mission' and Missio Dei: Response to Charles Van Engen's 'Mission' Defined and Described," in *Missionshift: Global Mission Issues in the Third Millennium* (Nashville: B&H Publishing Group, 2010), 45.

[2] Christopher J. H. Wright, *The Mission of God,* (2006:64).

news of the kingdom, and healing every[A] disease and sickness among the people.[a] 24 Then
the news about Him spread throughout
Syria.[b] So they brought to Him all those who
were afflicted, those suffering from various
diseases and intense pains, the demon-possessed, the epileptics, and the paralytics.[c]
And He healed them. 25 Large crowds followed
Him from Galilee, ·Decapolis, Jerusalem, Judea, and beyond the Jordan.[d]

THE SERMON ON THE MOUNT

5 When He saw the crowds, He went up on
the mountain,[e] and after He sat down,
His disciples came to Him. 2 Then[B] He began
to teach them, saying:[f]

The Beatitudes

3 "The poor in spirit are blessed,[g]
for the kingdom of heaven[h] is theirs.
4 Those who mourn are blessed,[i]
for they will be comforted.
5 The gentle are blessed,[j]
for they will inherit the earth.
6 Those who hunger and thirst
for righteousness are blessed,[k]
for they will be filled.
7 The merciful are blessed,
for they will be shown mercy.[l]
8 The pure in heart are blessed,
for they will see God.[m]
9 The peacemakers are blessed,
for they will be called sons of God.[n]
10 Those who are persecuted
for righteousness are blessed,
for the kingdom of heaven[o] is theirs.

11 "You are blessed when they insult and persecute you and falsely say every kind of evil
against you because of Me. 12 Be glad and rejoice, because your reward is great in heaven.
For that is how they persecuted[p] the prophets
who were before you.[q]

Believers Are Salt and Light

13 "You are the salt of the earth. But if the
salt should lose its taste, how can it be made

[a] 4:23 Mt 13:54; 24:14; Ac 10:38 [b] 4:24 Lk 2:2; Ac 15:23; Gl 1:21 [c] Mt 8:16; 9:32; Mk 5:15; Jn 10:21 [d] 4:25 Mk 3:7; 5:20; Lk 6:17 [e] 5:1 Mk 3:13; Lk 9:28; Jn 6:3,15 [f] 5:2 Ac 8:35; 10:34; 18:14 [g] 5:3 Is 57:15; 66:2 [h] Mt 19:14; 25:34; Mk 10:14; Lk 6:20 [i] 5:4 Is 61:2; Mt 11:29; 21:5; Jn 16:20; Rv 7:17 [j] 5:5 Ps 37:11; Rm 4:13; Rv 21:7 [k] 5:6 Is 55:1-2; Jn 4:14; 6:48; 7:37 [l] 5:7 Pr 11:17; Mt 18:33; Lk 6:36; 2Tm 1:16 [m] 5:8 Ps 24:4; Heb 12:14; 1Jn 3:2; Rv 22:4 [n] 5:9 Mt 5:45; Lk 6:35; Rm 8:14; Jms 3:18; 1Jn 3:1 [o] 5:10 Mt 19:14; 25:34; Mk 10:14; Lk 6:20; 22:29 [p] 5:12 Mt 2:23; 2Tm 3:12 [q] Mt 23:37; Ac 7:52; 1Th 2:15

Persecuted for the Sake of Righteousness

PRAYING FOR THE WORLD

It has been said that persecution of Christians today is more widespread than it has ever been in history. Many Christians all over the globe cannot freely own a Bible or worship in a church or share their faith without painful or deadly consequences.

There is a difference between simply knowing about our brothers and sisters who are suffering for their faith and feeling the pain along with them, suffering as a part of the body of Christ—when one part suffers, all parts suffer. Those of us in relative comfort and ease must never forget those who suffer for their faith, who give their lives rather than turn away from Christ. We must pray for them, encourage them, and honor them.

Pray that they stand strong and that their lives would be a courageous witness to all.

Savior of Your people, we remember those persecuted for the faith, those in dungeons, those in torture chambers, those forgotten in jails, those separated from loved ones, those disowned by communities. Many forget them, but we do not, Lord. They are a part of Your body, a part of our family, and we pray for You to protect them and give them Your surpassing peace.

Help us Lord, not to shrink back from knowing their pain and darkness. Give them the company of angels, soothe their wounds, and give them grace to forgive even their tormentors. Holy Spirit, surround Your own. Amen.

[A] 4:23 Or *every kind of* [B] 5:2 Lit *Then opening His mouth*

salty? It's no longer good for anything but to
be thrown out and trampled on by men.[a]
14"You are the light of the world. A city situated on a hill cannot be hidden.[b] 15No one
lights a lamp[c] and puts it under a basket,[A] but
rather on a lampstand, and it gives light for
all who are in the house.[d] 16In the same way,
let your light shine[B] before men, so that they
may see your good works and give glory to
your Father in heaven.[e]

Christ Fulfills the Law

17"Don't assume that I came to destroy the
Law or the Prophets. I did not come to destroy but to fulfill.[f] 18For ·I assure you: Until
heaven and earth pass away, not the smallest
letter[C] or one stroke of a letter will pass from
the law until all things are accomplished.
19Therefore, whoever breaks one of the least
of these commands and teaches people to
do so will be called least in the kingdom of
heaven. But whoever practices and teaches
these commands will be called great in the
kingdom of heaven.[g] 20For I tell you, unless
your righteousness surpasses that of the
·scribes and ·Pharisees, you will never enter
the kingdom of heaven.

Murder Begins in the Heart

21"You have heard that it was said to our ancestors,[D] **Do not murder**,[E,h] and whoever murders will be subject to judgment.[i] 22But I tell
you, everyone who is angry with his brother[F]
will be subject to judgment. And whoever
says to his brother, 'Fool!'[G] will be subject to
the ·Sanhedrin. But whoever says, 'You mo-
ron!' will be subject to ·hellfire.[H,j] 23So if you
are offering your gift on the altar, and there
you remember that your brother has something against you, 24leave your gift there in
front of the altar. First go and be reconciled
with your brother, and then come and offer
your gift. 25Reach a settlement quickly with
your adversary while you're on the way with
him, or your adversary will hand you over to
the judge, the judge to[I] the officer, and you
will be thrown into prison.[k] 26I assure you:
You will never get out of there until you have
paid the last penny![J]

Adultery in the Heart

27"You have heard that it was said, **Do not
commit adultery.**[K,l] 28But I tell you, everyone
who looks at a woman to lust for her has already committed adultery with her in his
heart.[m] 29If your right eye ·causes you to sin,[n]
gouge it out and throw it away. For it is better that you lose one of the parts of your body
than for your whole body to be thrown into
hell.[o] 30And if your right hand causes you to
sin, cut it off and throw it away. For it is better that you lose one of the parts of your body
than for your whole body to go into hell!

Divorce Practices Censured

31"It was also said, **Whoever divorces[p] his
wife must give her a written notice of divorce.**[L,q] 32But I tell you, everyone who divorces his wife, except in a case of sexual
immorality,[M] causes her to commit adultery.
And whoever marries a divorced woman
commits adultery.[r]

Tell the Truth

33"Again, you have heard that it was said
to our ancestors,[N] **You must not break your
oath, but you must keep your oaths to the
Lord.**[O,s] 34But I tell you, don't take an oath
at all: either by heaven, because it is God's
throne; 35or by the earth, because it is His
footstool; or by Jerusalem, because it is the
city of the great King.[t] 36Neither should you
swear by your head, because you cannot
make a single hair white or black. 37But let
your word 'yes' be 'yes,' and your 'no' be 'no.'[P]
Anything more than this is from the evil one.[u]

Go the Second Mile

38"You have heard that it was said, **An eye
for an eye** and **a tooth for a tooth.**[Q,v] 39But I tell
you, don't resist[R] an evildoer. On the contrary,
if anyone slaps you on your right cheek, turn

[a]**5:13** Mk 9:50; Lk 14:34
[b]**5:14** Pr 4:18; Jn 8:12; Php 2:15
[c]**5:15** Jn 5:35; Rv 21:23
[d]Mk 4:21; Lk 8:16; 11:33
[e]**5:16** Mt 9:8; Jn 15:8; 1Pt 2:12
[f]**5:17** Mt 7:12; Rm 3:31; 10:4; 13:8; Gl 3:24
[g]**5:18-19** Mt 11:11; 24:35; Lk 16:17; Jms 2:10
[h]**5:21** Ex 20:13; Dt 5:17
[i]Mt 19:18; 23:31,35; Mk 10:19; Lk 18:20; Rm 13:9; Jms 2:11
[j]**5:22** Mt 18:9; Mk 9:43; Jms 3:6; 1Jn 3:15
[k]**5:25** Pr 25:8; Lk 12:58
[l]**5:27** Ex 20:14; Dt 5:18
[m]**5:28** 2Sm 11:2; Jb 31:1; Pr 6:25
[n]**5:29** Mt 18:9; Mk 9:47
[o]Mt 10:28; 23:15,33; Lk 12:5
[p]**5:31** Jr 3:1; Mt 19:7; Mk 10:4
[q]Dt 24:1
[r]**5:32** Mt 19:9; Mk 10:11; Lk 16:18; Rm 7:3; 1Co 7:11
[s]**5:33** Lv 19:12; Nm 30:2; Dt 23:21; Mt 23:16
[t]**5:34-35** Ps 48:2; Is 66:1; Mt 23:22; Ac 7:49; Jms 5:12
[u]**5:37** Mt 6:13; 13:19,38; Jn 17:15; 2Th 3:3
[v]**5:38** Ex 21:24; Lv 24:20; Dt 19:21

[A]**5:15** A large basket used to measure grain [B]**5:16** Or *way, your light must shine* [C]**5:18** Or *not one iota*; *iota* is the smallest letter of the Gk alphabet. [D]**5:21** Lit *to the ancients* [E]**5:21** Ex 20:13; Dt 5:17 [F]**5:22** Other mss add *without a cause* [G]**5:22** Lit *Raca*, an Aram term of abuse similar to "airhead" [H]**5:22** Lit *the gehenna of fire* [I]**5:25** Other mss read *judge will hand you over to* [J]**5:26** Lit *quadrans*, the smallest and least valuable Roman coin, worth 1/64 of a daily wage [K]**5:27** Ex 20:14; Dt 5:18 [L]**5:31** Dt 24:1 [M]**5:32** Gk *porneia* = fornication, or possibly a violation of Jewish marriage laws [N]**5:33** Lit *to the ancients* [O]**5:33** Lv 19:12; Nm 30:2; Dt 23:21 [P]**5:37** Say what you mean and mean what you say [Q]**5:38** Ex 21:24; Lv 24:20; Dt 19:21 [R]**5:39** Or *don't set yourself against*, or *don't retaliate against*

the other to him also.[a] 40As for the one who
wants to sue you and take away your shirt,[A]
let him have your coat[B] as well. 41And if anyone forces[C] you to go one mile, go with him
two. 42Give to the one who asks you, and don't
turn away from the one who wants to borrow
from you.[b]

Love Your Enemies

43"You have heard that it was said, **Love**
your neighbor[D,c] and hate your enemy. 44But I
tell you, love your enemies[E] and pray for those
who[F] persecute you,[d] 45so that you may be[G]
sons of your Father in heaven. For He causes
His sun to rise on the evil and the good, and
sends rain on the righteous and the unrighteous.[e] 46For if you love those who love you,
what reward will you have? Don't even the
tax collectors do the same? 47And if you greet
only your ·brothers, what are you doing out
of the ordinary?[H,f] Don't even the Gentiles[I]
do the same? 48Be perfect,[g] therefore, as your
heavenly Father is perfect.

How to Give

6 "Be careful not to practice your righteousness[J] in front of people, to be seen
by them. Otherwise, you will have no reward
from your Father in heaven. 2So whenever
you give to the poor, don't sound a trumpet
before you, as the hypocrites do in the ·syna-
gogues and on the streets, to be applauded
by people. ·I assure you: They've got their reward![h] 3But when you give to the poor, don't
let your left hand know what your right hand
is doing, 4so that your giving may be in secret. And your Father who sees in secret will
reward you.[K,i]

How to Pray

5"Whenever you pray, you must not be
like the hypocrites, because they love to pray
standing in the synagogues and on the street
corners to be seen by people. I assure you:
They've got their reward![j] 6But when you
pray, go into your private room, shut your

[a]**5:39** Lk 6:29-30; Rm 12:17; 1Co 6:7; 1Pt 3:9
[b]**5:42** Dt 15:8; Lk 6:34
[c]**5:43** Lv 19:18; Dt 23:6; Lk 10:29
[d]**5:44** Lk 6:27; 23:34; Ac 7:60; Rm 12:20; 1Co 4:12; 1Pt 2:23
[e]**5:45** Jb 25:3; Mt 5:9; Lk 6:35; Ac 14:17
[f]**5:47** Mt 5:37; Mk 6:51; Jn 10:10; Rm 3:1; 2Co 9:1
[g]**5:48** Gn 17:1; Lv 19:2; Php 3:15; Col 4:12; Jms 1:4; 1Pt 1:15
[h]**6:1-2** Mt 23:5; Lk 6:24
[i]**6:4** Jr 17:10; Lk 14:14; Col 3:23-24; Heb 4:13
[j]**6:5** Mt 6:16; Mk 11:25; Lk 6:24; 18:11
[k]**6:6** 2Kg 4:33; Is 26:20; Mt 6:18
[l]**6:7** 1Kg 18:26; Ec 5:2
[m]**6:8** Mt 9:12; Mk 2:17; Lk 5:31; 9:11; 10:42; Ac 2:45
[n]**6:9-13** Lk 11:1-13
[o]**6:9** Lk 11:2; 1Co 7:14
[p]**6:10** Ps 103:20; Mt 3:2; 4:17; 26:42; Lk 22:42; Ac 21:14
[q]**6:11-12** Pr 30:8; Rm 4:4; Gl 5:3
[r]**6:13** Mt 26:41; 1Co 10:13; 2Pt 2:9
[s]Mt 5:37; Jn 17:15; 2Th 3:3; 2Tm 4:18
[t]**6:14** Mk 11:25; Eph 4:32; Col 3:13
[u]**6:15-16** Is 58:5; Mt 18:35; Jms 2:13
[v]**6:17** Ru 3:3; 2Sm 12:20; Dn 10:3
[w]**6:19** Pr 23:4; Heb 13:5
[x]**6:20** Mt 19:21; Lk 12:33; 18:22; 1Tm 6:19

door, and pray to your Father who is in secret. And your Father who sees in secret will
reward you.[L,k] 7When you pray, don't babble
like the idolaters,[M] since they imagine they'll
be heard for their many words.[l] 8Don't be like
them, because your Father knows the things
you need before you ask Him.[m]

The Model Prayer

9"Therefore, you should pray like this:[n]

Our Father in heaven,
Your name be honored as holy.[o]
10 Your kingdom come.
Your will be done
on earth as it is in heaven.[p]
11 Give us today our daily bread.[N]
12 And forgive us our debts,
as we also have forgiven our debtors.[q]
13 And do not bring us into[O] temptation,[r]
but deliver us from the evil one.[P,s]
[For Yours is the kingdom
and the power
and the glory forever. ·Amen.][Q]

14"For if you forgive people their wrongdoing,[R] your heavenly Father will forgive you as
well.[t] 15But if you don't forgive people,[S] your
Father will not forgive your wrongdoing.[R]

How to Fast

16"Whenever you fast, don't be sad-faced
like the hypocrites. For they make their faces
unattractive[T,u] so their fasting is obvious to
people. I assure you: They've got their reward!
17But when you fast, put oil on your head, and
wash your face,[v] 18so that you don't show your
fasting to people but to your Father who is in
secret. And your Father who sees in secret
will reward you.[L]

God and Possessions

19"Don't collect for yourselves treasures[U]
on earth, where moth and rust destroy and
where thieves break in and steal.[w] 20But collect for yourselves treasures in heaven,[x]
where neither moth nor rust destroys, and
where thieves don't break in and steal. 21For

[A]**5:40** Lit *tunic*; = inner garment [B]**5:40** Or *garment*; lit *robe*; = outer garment [C]**5:41** Roman soldiers could require people to carry loads for them. [D]**5:43** Lv 19:18 [E]**5:44** Other mss add *bless those who curse you, do good to those who hate you,* [F]**5:44** Other mss add *mistreat you and* [G]**5:45** Or *may become*, or *may show yourselves to be* [H]**5:47** Or *doing that is superior*; lit *doing more* [I]**5:47** Other mss read *tax collectors* [J]**6:1** Other mss read *charitable giving* [K]**6:4** Other mss read *will Himself reward you openly* [L]**6:6,18** Other mss add *openly* [M]**6:7** Or *Gentiles*, or *nations*, or *heathen*, or *pagans* [N]**6:11** Or *our necessary bread*, or *our bread for tomorrow* [O]**6:13** Or *do not cause us to come into* [P]**6:13** Or *from evil* [Q]**6:13** Other mss omit bracketed text [R]**6:14,15** Or *trespasses* [S]**6:15** Other mss add *their wrongdoing* [T]**6:16** Or *unrecognizable*, or *disfigured* [U]**6:19** Or *valuables*

where your treasure is, there your heart will
be also.
[22]"The eye is the lamp of the body. If your
eye is good, your whole body will be full of
light. [23]But if your eye is bad, your whole body
will be full of darkness. So if the light within
you is darkness — how deep is that darkness![a]
[24]"No one can be a *slave of two masters,
since either he will hate one and love the
other, or be devoted to one and despise the
other. You cannot be slaves of God and of
money.[b]

The Cure for Anxiety

[25]"This is why I tell you:[c] Don't worry about
your life, what you will eat or what you will
drink; or about your body, what you will
wear. Isn't life more than food and the body
more than clothing?[d] [26]Look at the birds of
the sky: They don't sow or reap or gather into
barns, yet your heavenly Father feeds them.
Aren't you worth more than they?[e] [27]Can
any of you add a single *cubit to his height[A]
by worrying? [28]And why do you worry about
clothes? Learn how the wildflowers of the
field grow: they don't labor or spin thread.
[29]Yet I tell you that not even Solomon in all
his splendor was adorned like one of these!
[30]If that's how God clothes the grass of the
field, which is here today and thrown into the
furnace tomorrow, won't He do much more
for you — you of little faith?[f] [31]So don't worry,
saying, 'What will we eat?' or 'What will we
drink?' or 'What will we wear?' [32]For the
idolaters[B] eagerly seek all these things, and
your heavenly Father knows that you need
them. [33]But seek first the kingdom of God[C,g]
and His righteousness,[h] and all these things
will be provided for you.[i] [34]Therefore don't
worry about tomorrow, because tomorrow
will worry about itself. Each day has enough
trouble[j] of its own.

Do Not Judge

7 "Do not judge, so that you won't be
judged.[k] [2]For with the judgment you
use,[D] you will be judged, and with the measure you use,[E] it will be measured to you.[l]
[3]Why do you look at the speck in your brother's eye but don't notice the log in your own
eye?[m] [4]Or how can you say to your brother,
'Let me take the speck out of your eye,' and

[a]**6:23** Mt 4:16; 8:12; 22:13; 25:30; 27:45
[b]**6:24** Lk 16:13; Gl 1:10; Jms 4:4
[c]**6:25-33** Lk 12:22-31
[d]**6:25** Lk 10:41; Php 4:6; 1Pt 5:7
[e]**6:26** Jb 38:41; Ps 147:9; Mt 10:29-31
[f]**6:29-30** 1Kg 10:4-7; Mt 8:26; 14:31; 16:8
[g]**6:33** Mk 1:15; Ac 20:25
[h]Mt 27:19; Lk 7:29; 23:41,47; Jn 5:30; 17:25; Ac 3:14
[i]1Kg 3:13; Mt 19:28; Mk 10:29; Lk 18:29; 1Tm 4:8
[j]**6:34** Mt 6:25; Lk 10:41; Php 4:6; 1Pt 5:7
[k]**7:1-5** Mk 4:24-25; Lk 6:37-42
[l]**7:2** Mk 4:24; Lk 6:38; Rm 2:1; 14:10; Jms 2:13
[m]**7:3** Lk 6:41; Jn 8:7-9

GOD'S HEART FOR THE WORLD

Your Kingdom Come

Your kingdom come. Your will be done on earth as it is in heaven. (Matthew 6:10)

It is common to pray that God would change our hearts so that we would know and do God's will, but in this prayer, Jesus asks us to expand our vision. We do not just pray for God's will to be done in "me" or in "us" or even in "the church" but "on earth." That's quite a request.

Can you imagine it being answered in full? The whole earth living in submission to God's reign? It is a beautiful picture. This prayer comes in the middle of the Sermon on the Mount; look through the different passages and imagine the world following God's will as it is laid out here. The poor are given the Kingdom. Those who mourn over loss and pain have their tears wiped away. No more hate, no more lies, no more pride. People are completely faithful to one another, and they give with a generosity that outstrips the need. It would be a miracle to find even one person who was genuinely that trustworthy, that loving, but imagine the whole earth! This incredible scene is what God longs for in the world, what Jesus asks us to pray for, and what we ask God to bring.

With Jesus' "Amen" and the end of His prayer, we can know that this world is not just in our imaginations. God is making it a reality. His Kingdom arrived when He arrived, and yet it is still coming, for we look forward to the day when His will shall be done on earth, as it is in heaven.

[A]**6:27** Or *add one moment to his life-span* [B]**6:32** Or *Gentiles*, or *nations*, or *heathen*, or *pagans* [C]**6:33** Other mss omit *of God* [D]**7:2** Lit *you judge* [E]**7:2** Lit *you measure* look, there's a log in your eye? 5Hypocrite! First take the log out of your eye, and then you will see clearly to take the speck out of your brother's eye. 6Don't give what is holy to dogs or toss your pearls before pigs,[a] or they will trample them with their feet, turn, and tear you to pieces.

Keep Asking, Searching, Knocking

7"Keep asking,[A,b] and it will be given to you.[c] Keep searching,[B] and you will find. Keep knocking,[C] and the door[D] will be opened to you. 8For everyone who asks receives, and the one who searches finds,[d] and to the one who knocks, the door[E] will be opened. 9What man among you, if his son asks him for bread, will give him a stone? 10Or if he asks for a fish, will give him a snake? 11If you then, who are evil,[e] know how to give good gifts to your children, how much more will your Father in heaven give good things to those who ask Him! 12Therefore, whatever you want others to do for you, do also the same for them—this is the Law and the Prophets.[F,f]

Entering the Kingdom

13"Enter through the narrow gate.[g] For the gate is wide and the road is broad that leads to destruction,[h] and there are many who go through it. 14How narrow is the gate and difficult the road that leads to life, and few find it.

15"Beware of false prophets[i] who come to you in sheep's[j] clothing[k] but inwardly are ravaging wolves.[l] 16You'll recognize them by their fruit.[m] Are grapes gathered from thornbushes or figs from thistles?[n] 17In the same way, every good tree produces good fruit, but a bad tree produces bad fruit. 18A good tree can't produce bad fruit; neither can a bad tree produce good fruit. 19Every tree that doesn't produce good fruit is cut down and thrown into the fire.[o] 20So you'll recognize them by their fruit.[p]

21"Not everyone who says to Me, 'Lord, Lord!' will enter the kingdom of heaven,[q] but only the one who does the will[r] of My Father in heaven.[s] 22On that day many will say to Me, 'Lord, Lord, didn't we prophesy in Your name, drive out demons[t] in Your name, and do many miracles in Your name?'[u] 23Then I will announce to them, 'I never knew you! **Depart from Me, you lawbreakers!**'[G,H,v]

The Two Foundations

24"Therefore,[w] everyone who hears these words[x] of Mine and acts on them will be like a sensible man who built his house on the rock. 25The rain fell, the rivers rose, and the winds blew and pounded that house. Yet it didn't collapse, because its foundation was on the rock. 26But everyone who hears these words of Mine and doesn't act on them will be like a foolish man who built his house on the sand. 27The rain fell, the rivers rose, the winds blew and pounded that house, and it collapsed. And its collapse was great!"

28When Jesus had finished this sermon,[I,y] the crowds were astonished at His teaching,[z] 29because He was teaching them like one who had authority, and not like their ·scribes.

A Man Cleansed

8 When He came down from the mountain, large crowds[aa] followed Him. 2Right away[ab] a man with a serious skin disease came up and knelt before Him,[ac] saying, "Lord, if You are willing, You can make me ·clean."

3Reaching out His hand He touched him, saying, "I am willing; be made clean." Immediately his disease was healed.[J] 4Then Jesus told him, "See that you don't tell anyone;[ad] but go, show yourself to the priest, and offer the gift that Moses prescribed, as a testimony to them."[ae]

A Centurion's Faith

5When He entered Capernaum,[af] a ·centurion came to Him, pleading with Him, 6"Lord, my servant is lying at home paralyzed, in terrible agony!"

7"I will come and heal him," He told him.

8"Lord," the centurion replied, "I am not worthy to have You come under my roof. But only say the word, and my servant will be

a7:6 Pr 9:7-8; 23:9; Mt 15:26 b7:7-11 Lk 11:9-13 c7:7 Mt 18:22; Mk 11:24; Jn 14:13-14; 15:7; 16:24; Jms 1:5; 1Jn 3:22; 5:14 d7:8 Pr 8:17; Is 55:6; Jr 29:12-13 e7:11 Gn 6:5; 8:21 f7:12 Mt 22:40; Lk 6:31; Rm 13:8; Gl 5:14 g7:13-14 Lk 13:23-24 h7:13 Mt 26:8; Mk 14:4; Jn 17:12; Ac 8:20; Rm 9:22; Php 1:28 i7:15 Mt 24:11,24; Mk 13:22; Lk 6:26; Ac 13:6; 2Pt 2:1 jMt 9:36; 10:6,16; 12:11-12; 15:24; 18:12-13 kMc 3:5; 2Tm 3:5 lEzk 22:27; Jn 10:12; Ac 20:29 m7:16-21 Pr 11:30; Mt 12:33; Lk 6:43-44; Jn 4:36; Jms 3:12 n7:16 Mt 13:7; Heb 6:8 o7:19 Jr 11:19; Mt 3:10; Lk 3:9; 13:7; Jn 15:2; Jd 12 p7:20 Mt 7:16; 12:33; Lk 6:44; Jms 3:12 q7:21 Mt 3:2; 18:3; Mk 9:43 rPs 143:10; Pr 16:9; Mt 12:50; Gl 1:4; Eph 1:9; 1Jn 2:17 sHs 8:2; Mt 25:11; Lk 6:46; Rm 2:13; Jms 1:22 t7:22 Mk 3:15; Rv 9:20; 18:2 uNm 24:4; Mt 10:15; Lk 13:25; Jn 11:51; 1Co 13:2 v7:23 Ps 5:5; 6:8; Mt 25:12,41; Lk 13:25-27 w7:24-27 Lk 6:47-49; Jms 1:22-25 x7:24 Mt 12:36; Mk 4:14; Lk 6:47; 8:21; Jn 1:1; 2:22 y7:28 Mt 11:1; 13:53; 19:1; 26:1 zMt 13:54; 22:23; Mk 1:22; 6:2; 11:18; Lk 4:32; Jn 7:46 aa8:1 Mt 5:1; Lk 3:7 ab8:2-4 Mk 1:40-44; Lk 5:12-14 ac8:2 Mt 9:18; 15:25; 18:26; 20:20; Jn 9:38; Ac 10:25 ad8:4 Mt 9:30; 17:9; Mk 5:43; 7:36; 8:30 aeLv 14:3-4,10; Lk 5:14; 17:14 af8:5-13 Lk 7:1-10; Jn 4:46-54

A7:7 Or *Ask* B7:7 Or *Search* C7:7 Or *Knock* D7:7 Lit *and it* E7:8 Lit *knocks, it* F7:12 When capitalized, the Law and the Prophets = the OT G7:23 Lit *you who work lawlessness* H7:23 Ps 6:8 I7:28 Lit *had ended these words* J8:3 Lit *cleansed*

cured.[a] 9 For I too am a man under authority,
having soldiers under my command.[A] I say to
this one, 'Go!' and he goes; and to another,
'Come!' and he comes; and to my •slave, 'Do
this!' and he does it."
10 Hearing this, Jesus was amazed and said
to those following Him, "•I assure you: I have
not found anyone in Israel with so great a
faith! 11 I tell you that many will come from
east and west, and recline at the table with
Abraham, Isaac, and Jacob in the kingdom of
heaven.[b] 12 But the sons of the kingdom will be
thrown into the outer darkness. In that place
there will be weeping and gnashing of teeth."[c]
13 Then Jesus told the centurion, "Go. As you
have believed,[d] let it be done for you." And his
servant was cured that very moment.[B]

Healings at Capernaum

14 When Jesus went into Peter's house,[e] He
saw his mother-in-law lying in bed with a fever. 15 So He touched her hand, and the fever
left her. Then she got up and began to serve
Him. 16 When evening came, they brought to
Him many who were demon-possessed. He
drove out the spirits[f] with a word and healed
all who were sick,[g] 17 so that what was spoken
through the prophet Isaiah might be fulfilled:

He Himself took our weaknesses
and carried our diseases.[C,h]

Following Jesus

18 When Jesus saw large crowds[D,i] around
Him, He gave the order to go to the other side of
the sea.[E] 19 A •scribe approached Him and said,[j]
"Teacher, I will follow You wherever You go!"
20 Jesus told him, "Foxes have dens and birds
of the sky have nests, but the Son of Man[k] has
no place to lay His head."
21 "Lord," another of His disciples said, "first
let me go bury my father."[F]
22 But Jesus told him, "Follow Me, and let the
dead bury their own dead."

Wind and Wave Obey the Master

23 As He got into the[G] boat,[l] His disciples[m]
followed Him. 24 Suddenly, a violent storm
arose on the sea, so that the boat was being
swamped by the waves. But He was sleeping.
25 So the disciples came and woke Him up, saying, "Lord, save us! We're going to die!"
26 But He said to them, "Why are you fearful,
you of little faith?" Then He got up and rebuked the winds and the sea.[n] And there was
a great calm.
27 The men were amazed and asked, "What
kind of man is this? — even the winds and the
sea obey[o] Him!"

Demons Driven Out by the Master

28 When He had come to the other side,[p] to
the region of the Gadarenes,[H] two demon-
possessed men met Him as they came out of
the tombs. They were so violent that no one
could pass that way. 29 Suddenly they shouted,
"What do You have to do with us,[I,J] Son of
God? Have You come here to torment us before the time?"[q]
30 Now a long way off from them, a large
herd of pigs was feeding. 31 "If You drive us
out," the demons begged Him, "send us into
the herd of pigs."
32 "Go!" He told them. So when they had
come out, they entered the pigs. And suddenly
the whole herd rushed down the steep bank
into the sea and perished in the water. 33 Then
the men who tended them fled. They went
into the city and reported everything — especially what had happened to those who were
demon-possessed. 34 At that, the whole town
went out to meet Jesus. When they saw Him,
they begged Him to leave their region.[r]

The Son of Man Forgives and Heals

9 So He got into a boat, crossed over, and
came to His own town.[s] 2 Just then[t] some
men[K] brought to Him a paralytic lying on a
mat. Seeing their faith, Jesus told the paralytic, "Have courage, son, your sins are forgiven."[u]
3 At this, some of the •scribes said among
themselves, "He's blaspheming!"[v]
4 But perceiving their thoughts,[w] Jesus said,
"Why are you thinking evil things in your
hearts?[L] 5 For which is easier: to say, 'Your
sins are forgiven,' or to say, 'Get up and walk'?

[a]**8:8** Ps 107:20; Lk 15:19,21
[b]**8:11** Is 49:12; 59:19; Mk 1:11; Lk 13:29; Eph 3:6
[c]**8:12** Mt 13:42,50; 22:13; 24:51; 25:30; Lk 13:28
[d]**8:13** Mt 9:22,29; Jn 4:53
[e]**8:14-16** Mk 1:29-34; Lk 4:38-41
[f]**8:16** Mk 3:15; 1Tm 4:1; 1Jn 4:1
[g]Mt 4:24; 8:33; Ac 19:12
[h]**8:17** Is 53:4; Mt 1:22
[i]**8:18** Mt 14:22; Mk 4:35; Lk 8:22; Jn 6:15-17
[j]**8:19-22** Lk 9:57-60
[k]**8:20** Dn 7:14; Mt 9:6; 12:8; 13:41; Mk 8:31
[l]**8:23-27** Mk 4:36-41; Lk 8:22-25; Jn 6:16-21
[m]**8:23** Mt 10:1; 26:56; Mk 3:7; 16:20; Lk 6:13; Jn 12:16
[n]**8:26** Ps 65:7; 89:9; 107:29; Mt 6:30; Lk 4:39
[o]**8:27** Mk 1:27; Lk 5:9
[p]**8:28-34** Mk 5:1-17; Lk 8:26-37
[q]**8:29** Jdg 11:12; 2Sm 16:10; Mk 1:24; Lk 4:34; Jn 2:4; Ac 8:7
[r]**8:34** 1Kg 17:18; Lk 5:8; Ac 16:39
[s]**9:1** Mt 4:13; Mk 5:21
[t]**9:2-8** Mk 2:3-12; Lk 5:18-26
[u]**9:2** Mt 4:24; 8:10,13; 9:22; Lk 7:48; Jn 16:33
[v]**9:3** Mt 26:65; Jn 10:36
[w]**9:4** Mt 12:25; Lk 6:8; 9:47; 11:17

[A]**8:9** Lit *under me* [B]**8:13** Or *that hour*; lit *very hour* [C]**8:17** Is 53:4 [D]**8:18** Other mss read *saw a crowd* [E]**8:18** = Sea of Galilee [F]**8:21** Not necessarily meaning his father was already dead [G]**8:23** Other mss read *to a* [H]**8:28** Other mss read *Gergesenes* [I]**8:29** Other mss add *Jesus* [J]**8:29** Lit *What to us and to You* [K]**9:2** Lit *then they* [L]**9:4** Or *minds*

6 But so you may know that the ·Son of Man
has authority on earth to forgive sins" — then
He told the paralytic, "Get up, pick up your
mat, and go home." 7 And he got up and went
home. 8 When the crowds saw this, they were
awestruck[A,B] and gave glory[a] to God who had
given such authority to men.

The Call of Matthew

9 As Jesus went on from there,[b] He saw a
man named Matthew sitting at the tax office,
and He said to him, "Follow Me!" So he got up
and followed Him.[c]
10 While He was reclining at the table in the
house, many tax collectors and sinners came
as guests to eat[C] with Jesus and His disciples.[d]
11 When the ·Pharisees saw this, they asked His
disciples, "Why does your Teacher eat with
tax collectors and sinners?"[e]
12 But when He heard this, He said, "Those
who are well don't need a doctor, but the sick
do.[f] 13 Go and learn what this means: **I desire
mercy and not sacrifice.**[D,g] For I didn't come
to call the righteous, but sinners."[E]

A Question about Fasting

14 Then John's disciples came to Him, saying, "Why do we and the Pharisees fast often,
but Your disciples do not fast?"[h]
15 Jesus said to them, "Can the wedding guests[F]
be sad while the groom is with them? The time[G]
will come when the groom will be taken away
from them, and then they will fast. 16 No one
patches an old garment with unshrunk cloth,
because the patch pulls away from the garment
and makes the tear worse. 17 And no one puts[H]
new wine into old wineskins. Otherwise, the
skins burst, the wine spills out, and the skins
are ruined. But they put new wine into fresh
wineskins, and both are preserved."

A Girl Restored and a Woman Healed

18 As He was telling them these things,[i]
suddenly one of the leaders[I] came and knelt

[a]9:8 Mt 5:16; 15:31; Lk 7:16; 13:13; Jn 15:8; Ac 4:21
[b]9:9-17 Mk 2:14-22; Lk 5:27-38
[c]9:9 Mt 10:3; Mk 2:14; 3:18; Lk 6:15; Ac 1:13
[d]9:10 Mt 10:42; 28:19; Lk 14:26; Jn 8:31; 13:35; 15:8; Ac 6:1
[e]9:11 Mt 11:19; Lk 5:30; 15:2; Gl 2:15
[f]9:12 Mk 2:17; Lk 5:31
[g]9:13 Hs 6:6; Mc 6:6-8; Mt 12:7
[h]9:14 Mt 11:2; 14:12; 15:2; Lk 11:1; 18:12
[i]9:18-26 Mk 5:22-43; Lk 8:41-56

PRAYING FOR THE WORLD

A Passion for Lost Souls

It was our Lord's final instruction before He returned to heaven: "Go, therefore, and make disciples of all nations" (Mt 28:19). So, we His messengers are charged with telling the lost world that they have already been found—they need only to step from the darkness and into the Light of the world.

But we get so comfortable, don't we? We spend our time worrying about our internal programs and our church façades while forgetting the lost who have yet to darken the doors of even the most beautiful church. Our passions are too often misplaced.

Let us never forget that we too were once lost until someone brought us the Good News. Our churches, no matter what our differences, all have the same mission. Indeed, "the harvest is abundant, but the workers are few. Therefore, pray to the Lord of the harvest to send out workers into His harvest" (Mt 9:37–38).

Savior of sinners, mobilize believers everywhere to share the Good News with the lost. Let our very lives be a testimony to Your love. Give us a passion for the lost, Lord, and a deep desire to share Your glorious Good News with those who haven't heard.

As Jesus told us, Lord, we pray that You will send workers into the harvest. Give us a passion. Lord, send us! Like Isaiah, help us to say, "Here I am. Send me" (Is 6:8). Amen.

A 9:8 Other mss read *amazed* B 9:8 Lit *afraid* C 9:10 Lit *came, they were reclining* (at the table); at important meals the custom was to recline on a mat at a low table and lean on the left elbow. D 9:13 Hs 6:6 E 9:13 Other mss add *to repentance* F 9:15 Lit *the sons of the bridal chamber* G 9:15 Lit *days* H 9:17 Lit *And they do not put* I 9:18 A leader of a synagogue; Mk 5:22

down before Him, saying, "My daughter is near death,[A] but come and lay Your hand on her, and she will live."[a] 19 So Jesus and His disciples got up and followed[b] him.

20 Just then, a woman who had suffered from bleeding for 12 years approached from behind and touched the •tassel on His robe,[c] 21 for she said to herself, "If I can just touch His robe, I'll be made well!"[B,d]

22 But Jesus turned and saw her. "Have courage, daughter," He said. "Your faith has made you well."[C,e] And the woman was made well from that moment.[D]

23 When Jesus came to the leader's house, He saw the flute players and a crowd lamenting loudly.[f] 24 "Leave," He said, "because the girl isn't dead, but sleeping."[g] And they started laughing at Him. 25 But when the crowd had been put outside, He went in and took her by the hand, and the girl got up.[h] 26 And this news spread throughout that whole area.[i]

Healing the Blind

27 As Jesus went on from there, two blind men followed Him, shouting, "Have mercy on us, Son of David!"[j]

28 When He entered the house, the blind men approached Him, and Jesus said to them, "Do you believe[k] that I can do this?"

"Yes, Lord," they answered Him.

29 Then He touched their eyes, saying, "Let it be done for you according to your faith!" 30 And their eyes were opened. Then Jesus warned them sternly, "Be sure that no one finds out!"[E,l] 31 But they went out and spread the news about Him throughout that whole area.

Driving Out a Demon

32 Just as they were going out, a demon-possessed man who was unable to speak was brought to Him.[m] 33 When the demon had been driven out, the man[F] spoke. And the crowds were amazed, saying, "Nothing like this has ever been seen in Israel!"

34 But the Pharisees said, "He drives out demons by the ruler of the demons!"[n]

The Lord of the Harvest

35 Then Jesus went to all the towns and villages, teaching in their •synagogues, preaching the good news of the kingdom,[o] and healing every[G] disease and every sickness.[H] 36 When He saw the crowds, He felt compassion for them, because they were weary and worn out,[p] like sheep without a shepherd.[q] 37 Then He said to His disciples,[r] "The harvest is abundant, but the workers are few. 38 Therefore, pray to the Lord of the harvest to send out workers into His harvest."

Commissioning the Twelve

10 Summoning His 12 disciples,[s] He gave them authority over •unclean spirits, to drive them out and to heal every[H] disease and sickness.[t] 2 These are the names of the 12 apostles:[u]

First, Simon, who is called Peter,
and Andrew his brother;
James the son of Zebedee,
and John his brother;
3 Philip and Bartholomew;[I]
Thomas and Matthew the tax collector;
James the son of Alphaeus,
and Thaddaeus;[J]
4 Simon the Zealot,[K] and Judas Iscariot,[L]
who also betrayed Him.[v]

5 Jesus sent out these 12 after giving them instructions: "Don't take the road leading to other nations, and don't enter any •Samaritan[w] town. 6 Instead, go to the lost sheep[x] of the house of Israel.[y] 7 As you go, announce this: 'The kingdom of heaven has come near.'[z] 8 Heal the sick, raise the dead, cleanse those with skin diseases, drive out demons.[aa] You have received free of charge; give free of charge. 9 Don't take along gold, silver, or copper for your money-belts.[ab] 10 Don't take a traveling bag for the road, or an extra shirt, sandals, or a walking stick, for the worker[ac] is worthy of his food.

11 "When you enter any town or village, find out who is worthy, and stay there until you

[a] **9:18** Mt 8:2-3; Mk 5:23 [b] **9:19** Lk 5:11; Jn 8:12 [c] **9:20** Lv 15:25; Nm 15:38; Dt 22:12; Mt 14:36; 23:5 [d] **9:21** Mt 14:36; Mk 3:10; Lk 6:19 [e] **9:22** Mt 15:28; Mk 10:52; Lk 7:50; 17:19; 18:42 [f] **9:23** 2Ch 35:25; Jr 9:17; 16:6; Ezk 24:17; Rv 18:22 [g] **9:24** Jn 11:13; Ac 20:10 [h] **9:25** Mk 9:27; Ac 3:7; 9:40-41 [i] **9:26** Mt 4:24; 9:31; 14:1; Mk 1:28; Lk 4:14 [j] **9:27** Mt 1:1; 12:23; 15:22; 20:30-31; Mk 10:47; Lk 18:38-39 [k] **9:28** Mk 11:24; Jn 3:16; Ac 10:43; Rm 10:9; 1Pt 1:8-10 [l] **9:29-30** Mt 8:4,13; 9:22; Mk 8:25; Jn 9:26 [m] **9:32-34** Mt 12:22-24; Lk 11:14-15 [n] **9:34** Mk 3:22; Jn 7:20 [o] **9:35** Mt 4:23; Mk 1:15 [p] **9:36** Mt 14:14; 15:32; Mk 6:34; 8:2 [q] Nm 27:17; 1Kg 22:17; Ezk 34:5; Zch 10:2 [r] **9:37** Mt 10:1; 26:56; Mk 3:7; 16:20; Lk 6:13; Jn 12:16 [s] **10:1-4** Mk 3:13-19; 6:13-16 [t] **10:1** Mt 9:35; Mk 6:7; Lk 9:1 [u] **10:2** Mt 4:18,21; 16:18; Jn 1:42 [v] **10:4** Mt 26:14; Lk 22:3; Jn 6:71; 13:2,26 [w] **10:5** 2Kg 17:24; Lk 9:52; 17:16; Jn 4:9; Ac 8:25 [x] **10:6** Ps 119:36; Is 53:6; Jr 50:6; Mt 9:36; 18:12 [y] Ac 2:36; 7:42; Heb 8:8,10 [z] **10:7** Mt 3:2-3; 4:17; Lk 10:9 [aa] **10:8** Mk 3:15; Rv 9:20; 18:2 [ab] **10:9-15** Mk 6:6-8; Lk 9:3-5; 10:4-12

[ac] **10:10** Lk 10:7; 1Co 9:14; 1Tm 5:18

[A] **9:18** Lit *daughter has now come to the end* [B] **9:21** Or *be delivered* [C] **9:22** Or *has saved you* [D] **9:22** Lit *hour* [E] **9:30** Lit *no one knows* [F] **9:33** Lit *the man who was unable to speak* [G] **9:35; 10:1** Or *every kind of* [H] **9:35** Other mss add *among the people* [I] **10:3** Probably the Nathanael of Jn 1:45-51 [J] **10:3** Other mss read *and Lebbaeus, whose surname was Thaddaeus* [K] **10:4** Lit *the Cananaean* [L] **10:4** *Iscariot* is probably "a man of Kerioth," a town in Judea.

leave. 12 Greet a household when you enter
it,[a] 13 and if the household is worthy, let your
peace be on it. But if it is unworthy, let your
peace return to you.[b] 14 If anyone will not welcome you or listen to your words, shake the
dust off your feet[c] when you leave that house
or town. 15 •I assure you: It will be more tolerable on the day of judgment[d] for the land of
Sodom and Gomorrah than for that town.[e]

Persecutions Predicted

16 "Look, I'm sending you out like sheep
among wolves. Therefore be as shrewd as
serpents and as harmless as doves.[f] 17 Because
people will hand you over to sanhedrins[A]
and flog you in their •synagogues,[g] beware of
them. 18 You will even be brought before governors and kings because of Me, to bear witness to them and to the nations.[h] 19 But when
they hand you over, don't worry about how or
what you should speak.[i] For you will be given
what to say at that hour, 20 because you are
not speaking, but the Spirit[j] of your Father is
speaking through you.[k]

21 "Brother will betray brother to death, and
a father his child. Children will even rise up
against their parents and have them put to
death.[l] 22 You will be hated by everyone because of My name.[m] But the one who endures
to the end will be delivered.[B,n] 23 When they
persecute you in one town, escape to another.[o]
For I assure you: You will not have covered
the towns of Israel before the •Son of Man
comes. 24 A disciple[C] is not above his teacher,
or a •slave above his master.[p] 25 It is enough
for a disciple to become like his teacher and
a slave like his master. If they called the head
of the house '•Beelzebul,' how much more the
members of his household![q]

Fear God

26 "Therefore,[r] don't be afraid of them, since
there is nothing covered that won't be uncovered and nothing hidden that won't be made
known.[s] 27 What I tell you in the dark, speak in
the light. What you hear in a whisper,[D] proclaim on the housetops.[t] 28 Don't fear those
who kill the body but are not able to kill the
soul;[u] rather, fear Him who is able to destroy
both soul and body in •hell.[v] 29 Aren't two sparrows sold for a penny?[E] Yet not one of them
falls to the ground without your Father's[w] consent.[F] 30 But even the hairs of your head have all
been counted.[x] 31 So don't be afraid therefore;
you are worth more than many sparrows.[y]

Acknowledging Christ

32 "Therefore, everyone who will acknowledge Me before men, I will also acknowledge
him before My Father in heaven.[z] 33 But whoever denies Me before men,[aa] I will also deny
him before My Father in heaven. 34 Don't assume that I came to bring peace on the earth.
I did not come to bring peace, but a sword.[ab]
35 For I came to turn

a man against his father,
a daughter against her mother,
a daughter-in-law against
her mother-in-law;
36 **and a man's enemies will be**
the members of his household.[G,ac]

37 The person who loves father or mother
more than Me is not worthy of Me;[ad] the per-

The *Modus Operandi* of God

GOD WHO SENDS

The sending, therefore, is the methodology of God, the divine *modus operandi*. The transcendent God of the Scriptures manifests his compassionate immanence through his providential sendings designed to bless, through his judgmental sendings designed to correct, and through his salvific sendings designed to redeem.

(DUBOSE, 60-61)

[a] **10:12** 1Sm 25:6; 1Ch 12:18; Ps 122:7-8 [b] **10:13** Ps 35:13; Mt 8:8; Ac 16:15 [c] **10:14** Neh 5:13; Lk 10:11; Ac 13:51 [d] **10:15** Mt 12:36; Ac 17:31; Heb 10:25; 2Pt 2:9; 1Jn 4:17 [e] Mt 11:22,24; 2Pt 2:6; Jd 6-7 [f] **10:16** Gn 3:1; Lk 10:3; Rm 16:19; Php 2:15 [g] **10:17** Mk 13:9,11; Lk 12:11-12; Ac 5:40; 26:11 [h] **10:18** Mt 28:19; Rm 1:5; Gl 1:16 [i] **10:19** Ex 4:12; Nm 23:5; Dt 18:18; Mt 6:25 [j] **10:20** Ps 51:11; Jn 1:33; Ac 2:4; Rm 8:9; Gl 5:25; Ti 3:5 [k] **10:20** Lk 12:12; Ac 4:8; 13:9; 2Co 13:3 [l] **10:21** Mc 7:6; Mt 10:35-36; Mk 13:12 [m] **10:22** Mt 24:9; Lk 21:17; Jn 15:18 [n] Mt 24:13; Mk 13:13; Jn 12:12-13 [o] **10:23** Mt 12:15; Ac 8:1; 9:25; 14:6; 17:10 [p] **10:24** Lk 6:40; Jn 13:16; 15:20 [q] **10:25** 2Kg 1:2; Mt 12:24,27; Mk 3:22; Lk 11:15,18-19 [r] **10:26-33** Lk 12:2-9 [s] **10:26** Mk 4:22; Lk 8:17; 12:2 [t] **10:27** Mt 24:17; Lk 5:19; 12:3; Ac 5:20 [u] **10:28** Is 8:12-13; 51:12-13; Jr 1:8; 1Pt 3:14 [v] Mt 5:22; Lk 12:5; Heb 10:31; Jms 4:12 [w] **10:29** Mt 5:16; 11:27; Lk 11:13; Jn 8:42 [x] **10:30** 1Sm 14:45; 2Sm 14:11; Lk 21:18; Ac 27:34 [y] **10:31** Mt 6:26; 12:12 [z] **10:32** Lk 12:8; Rm 10:9-10; Rv 3:5 [aa] **10:33** Mk 8:38; Lk 9:26; 2Tm 2:12; 2Pt 2:1 [ab] **10:34-36** Lk 12:51-53 [ac] **10:36** Ps 41:9; 55:12-13; Mc 7:6; Jn 13:18 [ad] **10:37-39** Lk 14:25-27

[A] **10:17** Local Jewish courts or local councils [B] **10:22** Or *saved* [C] **10:24** Or *student* [D] **10:27** Lit *in the ear* [E] **10:29** Gk *assarion*, a small copper coin [F] **10:29** Lit *ground apart from your Father* [G] **10:35-36** Mc 7:6

son who loves son or daughter more than Me
is not worthy of Me. 38 And whoever doesn't
take up his cross and follow[A] Me is not worthy of Me. 39 Anyone finding[B] his life will lose
it,[a] and anyone losing[C] his life because of Me
will find it.[b]

A Cup of Cold Water

40 "The one who welcomes you welcomes
Me,[c] and the one who welcomes Me welcomes Him who sent Me.[d] 41 Anyone who[D]
welcomes a prophet[e] because he is a prophet[E]
will receive a prophet's reward. And anyone
who[F] welcomes a righteous person because
he's righteous[G] will receive a righteous person's reward. 42 And whoever gives[f] just a cup
of cold water to one of these little ones because he is a disciple[H,g]—I assure you: He
will never lose his reward!"

In Praise of John the Baptist

11 When Jesus had finished giving orders
to His 12 disciples, He moved on from
there to teach and preach in their towns.[h]
2 When John heard in prison what the •Mes-
siah was doing, he sent a message by his disciples[i] 3 and asked Him, "Are You the One who is
to come, or should we expect someone else?"[j]

4 Jesus replied to them, "Go and report to
John what you hear and see: 5 the blind see,
the lame walk, those with skin diseases are
healed,[I] the deaf hear, the dead are raised,
and the poor are told the good news.[k] 6 And
if anyone is not •offended because of Me, he
is blessed."[l]

7 As these men went away, Jesus began to
speak to the crowds about John: "What did
you go out into the wilderness to see? A reed
swaying in the wind?[m] 8 What then did you
go out to see? A man dressed in soft clothes?
Look, those who wear soft clothes are in kings'
palaces. 9 But what did you go out to see? A
prophet? Yes, I tell you, and far more than a
prophet.[n] 10 This is the one it is written about:

> **Look, I am sending My messenger**
> **ahead of You;[J]**
> **he will prepare Your way before You.[K,o]**

[a] 10:39 Mt 16:25; Mk 8:35; Lk 9:24; 17:33; Jn 12:25
[b] Mt 9:9; Jn 8:12; 12:26; 21:19
[c] 10:40 Mt 18:5; Lk 10:16; Jn 13:20; Gl 4:14
[d] Mk 9:37; Lk 9:48; Jn 12:44
[e] 10:41 1Kg 17:10-15; 18:4; 2Kg 4:8; 3Jn 5-8
[f] 10:42 Mt 25:40; Mk 9:41; Heb 6:10
[g] Mt 28:19; Lk 14:26; Jn 8:31; 13:35; 15:8; Ac 6:1
[h] 11:1 Mt 7:28; 9:35; Lk 23:5
[i] 11:2-19 Lk 7:18-35
[j] 11:3 Ps 118:26; Jn 6:14; 11:27; Heb 10:37
[k] 11:5 Is 35:5; 61:1; Lk 4:18; Jms 2:5
[l] 11:6 Is 8:14-15; Mt 13:21; Jn 6:61; 16:1
[m] 11:7 Mt 3:1; Eph 4:14
[n] 11:9 Mt 14:5; 21:26; Lk 1:76
[o] 11:10 Mal 3:1; Mk 1:2
[p] 11:14 Mal 4:5; Mt 17:10-13; Mk 9:11-13; Lk 1:17; Jn 1:21
[q] 11:15 Mt 13:9; Mk 4:23; Lk 8:8; 14:35; Rv 2:7
[r] 11:18 Mt 3:4; Lk 1:15
[s] 11:19 Mt 9:10; Lk 7:36; 14:1; Jn 2:1; 12:2
[t] Mt 9:11; 18:17; Lk 15:2; 19:7
[u] 11:21-24 Lk 10:12-15
[v] 11:21 Mk 6:45; Lk 9:10; Jn 12:21
[w] Mt 15:21; Lk 6:17; Ac 12:20
[x] 11:22 Ezk 28:2-4; Am 1:9-10; Mt 10:15; 15:21; Mk 3:8
[y] 11:23 Is 14:13,15; Mt 4:13
[z] 11:25-27 Lk 10:21-22

11 "I assure you: Among those born of
women no one greater than John the Baptist
has appeared,[L] but the least in the kingdom of
heaven is greater than he. 12 From the days of
John the Baptist until now, the kingdom
of heaven has been suffering violence,[M] and
the violent have been seizing it by force. 13 For
all the prophets and the Law prophesied until
John; 14 if you're willing to accept it, he is the
Elijah who is to come.[p] 15 Anyone who has
ears[N] should listen![q]

An Unresponsive Generation

16 "To what should I compare this generation? It's like children sitting in the marketplaces who call out to each other:

> 17 We played the flute for you,
> but you didn't dance;
> we sang a lament,
> but you didn't mourn![O]

18 For John did not come eating or drinking,
and they say, 'He has a demon!'[r] 19 The •Son
of Man came eating and drinking, and they
say, 'Look, a glutton and a drunkard,[s] a friend
of tax collectors and sinners!'[t] Yet wisdom is
vindicated[P] by her deeds."[Q]

20 Then He proceeded to denounce the
towns where most of His miracles were done,
because they did not repent: 21 "Woe to you,
Chorazin![u] Woe to you, Bethsaida![v] For if the
miracles that were done in you had been done
in Tyre and Sidon,[w] they would have repented
in •sackcloth and ashes long ago! 22 But I tell
you, it will be more tolerable for Tyre and
Sidon on the day of judgment[x] than for you.
23 And you, Capernaum, will you be exalted to
heaven? You will go down to •Hades.[y] For if
the miracles that were done in you had been
done in Sodom, it would have remained until
today. 24 But I tell you, it will be more tolerable
for the land of Sodom on the day of judgment
than for you."

The Son Gives Knowledge and Rest

25 At that time Jesus said,[z] "I praise[R] You, Father, Lord of heaven and earth, because You
have hidden these things from the wise and

[A] 10:38 Lit *follow after* [B] 10:39 Or *The one who finds* [C] 10:39 Or *and the one who loses* [D] 10:41 Or *The one who* [E] 10:41 Lit *prophet in the name of a prophet* [F] 10:41 Or *And the one who* [G] 10:41 Lit *person in the name of a righteous person* [H] 10:42 Lit *little ones in the name of a disciple* [I] 11:5 Lit *cleansed* [J] 11:10 Lit *messenger before Your face* [K] 11:10 Mal 3:1 [L] 11:11 Lit *arisen* [M] 11:12 Or *has been forcefully advancing* [N] 11:15 Other mss add *to hear* [O] 11:17 Or *beat your breasts* [P] 11:19 Or *declared right* [Q] 11:19 Other mss read *children* [R] 11:25 Or *thank* learned and revealed them to infants.[a] 26Yes, Father, because this was Your good pleasure.[A] 27All things have been entrusted to Me by My Father. No one knows[B] the Son except the Father, and no one knows the Father except the Son and anyone to whom the Son desires[C] to reveal Him.[b]

28"Come to Me, all of you who are weary and burdened, and I will give you rest.[c] 29All of you, take up My yoke and learn from Me,[d] because I am gentle and humble in heart, and you will find rest for yourselves.[e] 30For My yoke is easy and My burden is light."

Lord of the Sabbath

12 At that time Jesus passed through the grainfields on the Sabbath.[f] His disciples[g] were hungry and began to pick and eat some heads of grain. 2But when the •Pharisees saw it, they said to Him, "Look, Your disciples are doing what is not lawful[h] to do on the Sabbath!"

3He said to them, "Haven't you read what David did when he and those who were with him were hungry — 4how he entered the house of God, and they ate[D] the •sacred bread, which is not lawful for him or for those with him to eat, but only for the priests?[i] 5Or haven't you read in the Law[E] that on Sabbath days the priests in the temple violate the Sabbath and are innocent?[j] 6But I tell you that something greater than the temple is here![k] 7If you had known what this means: **I desire mercy and not sacrifice**,[F,l] you would not have condemned the innocent. 8For the •Son of Man is Lord of the Sabbath."[m]

The Man with the Paralyzed Hand

9Moving on from there, He entered their •synagogue.[n] 10There He saw a man who had a paralyzed hand. And in order to accuse Him they asked Him, "Is it lawful to heal on the Sabbath?"[o]

11But He said to them, "What man among you, if he had a sheep[G] that fell into a pit on the Sabbath, wouldn't take hold of it and lift it out?[p] 12A man is worth far more than a sheep,[q] so it is lawful to do what is good on the Sabbath."

[a]**11:25** Ps 8:2; Lk 22:42; Jn 11:41; 1Co 1:26; 2Co 3:14
[b]**11:27** Mt 28:18; Jn 1:18; 7:29; 8:19; 10:15; 17:25-26
[c]**11:28** Jr 31:25; Jn 7:37
[d]**11:29** Jn 13:15; Eph 4:20; Php 2:5; 1Pt 2:21; 1Jn 2:6
[e]Jr 6:16; Zch 9:9; 2Co 10:1; Php 2:7-8
[f]**12:1-8** Mk 2:23-28; Lk 6:1-5
[g]**12:1** Mt 10:1; 26:56; Mk 3:7; 16:20; Lk 6:13; Jn 12:16
[h]**12:2** Mt 12:10; Lk 13:14; 14:3; Jn 5:10; 7:23; 9:16
[i]**12:4** Ex 25:30; Lv 24:5-9; 1Sm 21:6
[j]**12:5** Nm 28:9-10; 1Ch 9:32; Jn 7:22-23
[k]**12:6** 2Ch 6:18; Mal 3:1; Mt 12:41-42
[l]**12:7** Hs 6:6; Mc 6:8; Mt 9:13
[m]**12:8** Mt 8:20; 9:6; 12:32,40
[n]**12:9-14** Mk 3:1-6; Lk 6:6-11
[o]**12:10** Mt 12:2; Lk 13:14; 14:3; Jn 9:16
[p]**12:11** Ex 23:4-5; Dt 22:4; Lk 14:5
[q]**12:12** Mt 6:26; 10:31
[r]**12:13** 1Kg 13:4; Mt 8:3; Ac 28:8
[s]**12:14** Mt 26:4; 27:1; Mk 3:6; Lk 6:11; Jn 10:39; 11:53
[t]**12:15** Mt 4:23; 10:23; 19:2; Mk 3:7
[u]**12:16** Mt 8:4; 9:30
[v]**12:18** Mt 3:17; 17:5; Lk 4:18; Jn 3:34
[w]**12:18-21** Is 42:1-4; Jn 10:25
[x]**12:22-24** Lk 11:14-15
[y]**12:22** Mt 4:24; 9:32-34
[z]**12:23** 2Ch 1:1; Mt 1:1; Rm 1:3
[aa]**12:24** Mt 9:34; 10:25; Mk 3:22
[ab]**12:25-29** Mk 3:23-27; Lk 11:17-22
[ac]**12:26** Mt 4:1,10; 13:19; Ac 13:10
[ad]**12:27** 2Kg 2:7; Ac 19:13

13Then He told the man, "Stretch out your hand." So he stretched it out, and it was restored,[r] as good as the other. 14But the Pharisees went out and plotted against Him, how they might destroy Him.[s]

The Servant of the Lord

15When Jesus became aware of this, He withdrew from there. Huge crowds[H] followed Him, and He healed them all.[t] 16He warned them not to make Him known,[u] 17so that what was spoken through the prophet Isaiah might be fulfilled:

18 Here is My Servant
whom I have chosen,
My beloved in whom My soul delights;
I will put My Spirit on Him,
and He will proclaim justice
to the nations.[v]
19 He will not argue or shout,
and no one will hear His voice
in the streets.
20 He will not break a bruised reed,
and He will not put out
a smoldering wick,
until He has led justice to victory.[I]
21 The nations will put their hope
in His name.[J,w]

A House Divided

22Then a demon-possessed man[x] who was blind and unable to speak was brought to Him. He healed him, so that the man[K] could both speak and see.[y] 23And all the crowds were astounded and said, "Perhaps this is the Son of David!"[z]

24When the Pharisees heard this, they said, "The man drives out demons only by •Beelzebul, the ruler of the demons."[aa]

25Knowing their thoughts,[ab] He told them: "Every kingdom divided against itself is headed for destruction, and no city or house divided against itself will stand. 26If Satan[ac] drives out Satan, he is divided against himself. How then will his kingdom stand? 27And if I drive out demons by Beelzebul, who is it your sons drive them out by? For this reason they will be your judges.[ad] 28If I drive out de-

[A]**11:26** Lit *was well-pleasing in Your sight* [B]**11:27** Or *knows exactly* [C]**11:27** Or *wills*, or *chooses* [D]**12:4** Other mss read *he ate* [E]**12:5** = The Torah (the Pentateuch) [F]**12:7** Hs 6:6 [G]**12:11** Or *had one sheep* [H]**12:15** Other mss read *Many* [I]**12:20** Or *until He has successfully put forth justice* [J]**12:18-21** Is 42:1-4 [K]**12:22** Lit *mute*

mons by the Spirit of God, then the kingdom
of God has come to you.[a] 29 How can someone enter a strong man's house and steal his
possessions unless he first ties up[b] the strong
man? Then he can rob his house. 30 Anyone
who is not with Me is against Me,[c] and anyone who does not gather with Me scatters.
31 Because of this,[d] I tell you, people will be
forgiven every sin and blasphemy,[e] but the
blasphemy against[A] the Spirit will not be forgiven.[B] 32 Whoever speaks a word against the
Son of Man,[f] it will be forgiven him. But whoever speaks against the Holy Spirit, it will not
be forgiven him, either in this age or in the
one to come.[g]

A Tree and Its Fruit

33 "Either make the tree good and its fruit
good, or make the tree bad[C] and its fruit bad;
for a tree is known by its fruit.[h] 34 Brood of vipers! How can you speak good things when
you are evil? For the mouth speaks from the
overflow[i] of the heart. 35 A good man produces good things from his storeroom of
good,[D] and an evil man produces evil things
from his storeroom of evil.[j] 36 I tell you that
on the day of judgment[k] people will have to
account[l] for every careless word they speak.[E]
37 For by your words you will be acquitted, and
by your words you will be condemned."

The Sign of Jonah

38 Then some of the ˙scribes and Pharisees
said to Him, "Teacher, we want to see a sign
from You."[m]

39 But He answered them,[n] "An evil and
adulterous generation demands a sign, but
no sign will be given to it except the sign of
the prophet Jonah.[o] 40 For as Jonah was in the
belly of the huge fish three days and three
nights,[p] so the Son of Man will be in the heart
of the earth three days and three nights.
41 The men of Nineveh will stand up at the
judgment with this generation and condemn
it,[q] because they repented at Jonah's proclamation; and look—something greater than
Jonah is here![r] 42 The queen of the south[s] will
rise up at the judgment with this generation
and condemn it, because she came from the
ends of the earth to hear the wisdom of Solomon; and look—something greater than
Solomon is here!

An Unclean Spirit's Return

43 "When an ˙unclean spirit comes out of
a man, it roams through waterless places
looking for rest but doesn't find any.[t] 44 Then
it says, 'I'll go back to my house that I came
from.' And returning, it finds the house vacant, swept, and put in order. 45 Then off it
goes and brings with it seven other spirits
more evil than itself, and they enter and settle
down there. As a result, that man's last condition is worse than the first.[u] That's how it will
also be with this evil generation."

True Relationships

46 He[v] was still speaking to the crowds when
suddenly His mother and brothers were
standing outside wanting to speak to Him.[w]
47 Someone told Him, "Look, Your mother and
Your brothers are standing outside, wanting
to speak to You."[F]

48 But He replied to the one who told Him,
"Who is My mother and who are My brothers?" 49 And stretching out His hand toward
His disciples,[x] He said, "Here are My mother
and My brothers! 50 For whoever does the will
of My Father in heaven, that person is My
brother and sister and mother."[y]

The Parable of the Sower

13 On that day Jesus went out of the house
and was sitting by the sea.[z] 2 Such large
crowds gathered around Him that He got
into a boat and sat down, while the whole
crowd stood on the shore.[aa]

3 Then He told them many things in parables,[ab] saying: "Consider the sower who went
out to sow. 4 As he was sowing, some seed fell
along the path, and the birds came and ate
them up. 5 Others fell on rocky ground, where
there wasn't much soil, and they sprang up
quickly since the soil wasn't deep. 6 But when
the sun came up they were scorched, and
since they had no root, they withered. 7 Others fell among thorns, and the thorns came
up and choked them. 8 Still others fell on good

[a] **12:28** Lk 17:21; 1Jn 3:8
[b] **12:29** Is 49:24; 53:12
[c] **12:30** Mk 9:40; Lk 9:50; 11:23
[d] **12:31-32** Mk 3:28-30; Lk 12:10
[e] **12:31** Heb 6:4-6; 10:26; 1Jn 5:16
[f] **12:32** Mt 11:19; Mk 2:10; Jn 7:12; 9:24
[g] Mk 10:30; Lk 12:10; 20:34-35; Eph 1:21; Ti 2:12; Heb 6:5
[h] **12:33** Mt 7:18-19,23; Lk 6:43-44; Jn 15:4-7
[i] **12:34** 1Sm 24:13; Mt 3:7; 23:33; Lk 6:45; Eph 4:29
[j] **12:35** Mt 13:52; Col 4:6
[k] **12:36** Mt 12:41; Jn 5:29; 1Jn 4:17
[l] Lk 16:2; Ac 19:40; Rm 14:12; Heb 13:17; 1Pt 4:5
[m] **12:38** Mt 16:1; Mk 8:11-12; Lk 11:16; Jn 2:18; 6:30; 1Co 1:22
[n] **12:39** Mk 8:11-12; Lk 11:29-32
[o] Is 57:3; Mt 16:4; Mk 8:38
[p] **12:40** Jnh 1:17
[q] **12:41** Jr 3:11; Ezk 16:51; Rm 2:27
[r] Jnh 1:2; 3:5
[s] **12:42** 1Kg 10:1; 2Ch 9:1
[t] **12:43-45** Lk 11:24-26
[u] **12:45** Heb 6:4; 2Pt 2:20
[v] **12:46-50** Mk 3:31-35; Lk 8:19-21
[w] **12:46** Mt 13:55; Mk 6:3; Jn 2:12; Ac 1:14; 1Co 9:5; Gl 1:19
[x] **12:49** Mt 10:42; 28:19; Lk 14:26; Jn 8:31; 13:35; 15:8; Ac 6:1
[y] **12:50** Mt 6:1; 7:21; Jn 15:14; Heb 2:11
[z] **13:1-15** Mk 4:1-12; Lk 8:4-10
[aa] **13:2** Mk 3:9; Lk 5:3
[ab] **13:3** Mt 13:10,34-36; 15:15; 21:33,45; 22:1; 24:32; Mk 4:2

[A] **12:31** Or *of* [B] **12:31** Other mss add *people* [C] **12:33** Or *decayed;* lit *rotten*
[D] **12:35** Other mss read *from the storehouse of his heart* [E] **12:36** Lit *will speak*
[F] **12:47** Other mss omit this v.

ground and produced a crop: some 100, some 60, and some 30 times what was sown.[a] 9 Anyone who has ears[A] should listen!"[b]

Why Jesus Used Parables

10 Then the disciples[c] came up and asked Him, "Why do You speak to them in parables?"[d]

11 He answered them, "Because the •secrets of the kingdom of heaven have been given for you to know,[e] but it has not been given to them. 12 For whoever has, more will be given to him, and he will have more than enough. But whoever does not have, even what he has will be taken away from him.[f] 13 For this reason I speak to them in parables, because looking they do not see,[g] and hearing they do not listen or understand.[h] 14 Isaiah's prophecy is fulfilled in them, which says:

You will listen and listen,
yet never understand;
and you will look and look,
yet never perceive.[i]
15 **For this people's heart**
has grown callous;
their ears are hard of hearing,
and they have shut their eyes;
otherwise they might see
with their eyes
and hear with their ears,
understand with their hearts
and turn back —
and I would cure them.[B,j]

16 "But your eyes are blessed[k] because they do see, and your ears because they do hear![l] 17 For •I assure you: Many prophets and righteous people longed to see the things you see yet didn't see them; to hear the things you hear yet didn't hear them.[m]

The Parable of the Sower Explained

18 "You, then, listen to the parable of the sower:[n] 19 When anyone hears the word[C] about the kingdom and doesn't understand it, the evil one comes and snatches away what was sown in his heart. This is the one sown along the path.[o] 20 And the one sown on rocky ground — this is one who hears the word and immediately receives it with joy.[p] 21 Yet he has no root in himself, but is short-lived. When pressure or persecution[q] comes because of the word, immediately he stumbles. 22 Now the one sown among the thorns — this is one who hears the word, but the worries of this age[r] and the seduction[D] of wealth[s] choke the word, and it becomes unfruitful. 23 But the one sown on the good ground — this is one who hears and understands the word, who does bear fruit and yields: some 100, some 60, some 30 times what was sown."

The Parable of the Wheat and the Weeds

24 He presented another parable to them: "The kingdom of heaven may be compared to a man who sowed good seed in his field.[t] 25 But while people were sleeping, his enemy came, sowed weeds[E] among the wheat, and left. 26 When the plants sprouted and produced grain, then the weeds also appeared. 27 The landowner's •slaves[u] came to him and said, 'Master, didn't you sow good seed in your field? Then where did the weeds come from?'

28 "'An enemy did this!' he told them.

"'So, do you want us to go and gather them up?' the slaves asked him.

29 "'No,' he said. 'When you gather up the weeds, you might also uproot the wheat with them. 30 Let both grow together until the harvest. At harvest time I'll tell the reapers: Gather the weeds first and tie them in bundles to burn them, but store the wheat in my barn.'"

The Parables of the Mustard Seed and of the Yeast

31 He[v] presented another parable to them: "The kingdom of heaven[w] is like a mustard seed that a man took and sowed in his field. 32 It's the smallest of all the seeds, but when grown, it's taller than the vegetables and becomes a tree, so that the birds of the sky come and nest in its branches."[x]

33 He told them another parable: "The kingdom of heaven is like yeast that a woman took and mixed into 50 pounds[F] of flour until it spread through all of it."[G,y]

[a] **13:8** Gn 26:12; Mt 13:23
[b] **13:9** Mt 11:15; 13:43; Lk 8:8; 14:35; Rv 2:7,11,17,29; 3:6,13,22
[c] **13:10** Mt 9:10; Mk 10:10; Lk 6:1; Jn 6:3; Ac 6:1
[d] Mt 13:35; 15:15; 21:33,45; 22:1; 24:32
[e] **13:11** Mt 11:25; 19:11; Jn 6:65; 1Co 2:10; Col 1:27; 1Jn 2:20,27
[f] **13:12** Mt 25:29; Lk 8:18; 19:26; Jn 15:2; Jms 4:6
[g] **13:13** Dt 29:4; Is 42:19-20; Jr 5:21; Ezk 12:2
[h] Mt 15:10; 16:12; 17:13; Mk 8:21
[i] **13:14** Is 6:9; Mk 4:12; Lk 8:10; Jn 12:40; Ac 28:26-27; Rm 11:8
[j] **13:15** Is 6:10; Mt 15:8; Heb 5:11
[k] **13:16-17** Lk 10:23-24
[l] **13:16** Mt 16:17; Jn 20:29
[m] **13:17** Jn 8:56; Heb 11:13; 1Pt 1:10-12
[n] **13:18-23** Mk 4:13-20; Lk 8:11-15
[o] **13:19** Mt 4:23; 5:37; 6:13
[p] **13:20** Is 58:2; Ezk 33:31-32; Mk 6:20; Jn 5:35
[q] **13:21** Mk 4:17; 10:30; Ac 8:1; 13:50; Rm 8:35; 2Co 12:10
[r] **13:22** Rm 12:2; 2Tm 4:10; 1Jn 2:15
[s] Mt 19:23; Mk 10:23; 1Tm 6:9-10; 2Tm 4:10
[t] **13:24** Mt 18:23; 20:1; 25:1; Mk 4:26,30
[u] **13:27** Mt 10:24; Col 3:11; 4:1; Rv 1:1
[v] **13:31-32** Mk 4:30-32; Lk 13:18-19
[w] **13:31** Mt 13:24; 17:20; Lk 17:6
[x] **13:32** Ps 104:12; Ezk 17:23; 31:6; Dn 4:12
[y] **13:33** Gn 18:6; Lk 13:21; Gl 5:9

[A] **13:9** Other mss add *to hear* [B] **13:14-15** Is 6:9-10 [C] **13:19** Gk *logos* = *word*, or *message*, or *saying*, or *thing* [D] **13:22** Or *pleasure*, or *deceitfulness* [E] **13:25** Or *darnel*, a weed similar in appearance to wheat in the early stages [F] **13:33** Lit *3 sata*; about 40 quarts [G] **13:33** Or *until all of it was leavened*

Using Parables Fulfills Prophecy
[34]Jesus told the crowds all these things in
parables, and He would not speak anything
to them without a parable,[a] [35]so that what
was spoken through the prophet might be
fulfilled:

> **I will open My mouth in parables;**
> **I will declare things kept secret**
> **from the foundation of the world.**[A,b]

Jesus Interprets the Wheat and the Weeds
[36]Then He dismissed the crowds and went
into the house. His disciples approached Him
and said, "Explain the parable of the weeds in
the field to us."[c]
[37]He replied: "The One who sows the good
seed is the •Son of Man; [38]the field is the world;
and the good seed — these are the sons of the
kingdom. The weeds are the sons of the evil
one,[d] [39]and the enemy who sowed them is the
Devil. The harvest is the end of the age, and
the harvesters are angels.[e] [40]Therefore, just
as the weeds are gathered and burned in the
fire, so it will be at the end of the age.[f] [41]The
Son of Man will send out His angels, and they
will gather from His kingdom everything
that causes sin[B] and those •guilty of lawlessness.[C,g] [42]They will throw them into the blazing furnace[h] where there will be weeping and
gnashing of teeth.[i] [43]Then the righteous will
shine like the sun in their Father's kingdom.
Anyone who has ears[D] should listen![j]

The Parables of the Hidden Treasure and of the Priceless Pearl
[44]"The kingdom of heaven is like treasure,
buried in a field, that a man found and rebur-
ied. Then in his joy he goes and sells everything he has and buys that field.[k]
[45]"Again, the kingdom of heaven is like a
merchant in search of fine pearls. [46]When he
found one priceless[E] pearl, he went and sold
everything he had, and bought it.[l]

The Parable of the Net
[47]"Again, the kingdom of heaven is like a
large net thrown into the sea. It collected every kind of fish,[m] [48]and when it was full, they
dragged it ashore, sat down, and gathered the
good fish into containers, but threw out the
worthless ones. [49]So it will be at the end of
the age. The angels will go out, separate the
evil people from the righteous,[n] [50]and throw
them into the blazing furnace. In that place
there will be weeping and gnashing of teeth.[o]

The Storehouse of Truth
[51]"Have you understood all these things?"[F]
"Yes," they told Him.
[52]"Therefore," He said to them, "every student of Scripture[G] instructed in the kingdom
of heaven is like a landowner who brings out
of his storeroom what is new and what is
old."[p] [53]When Jesus had finished these parables, He left there.

Rejection at Nazareth
[54]He went to His hometown[q] and began to
teach them in their •synagogue, so that they
were astonished and said, "How did this wisdom and these miracles come to Him?[r] [55]Isn't
this the carpenter's son?[s] Isn't His mother
called Mary, and His brothers James,[t] Joseph,[H] Simon, and Judas?[u] [56]And His sisters,
aren't they all with us? So where does He get
all these things?" [57]And they were •offended
by Him.
But Jesus said to them, "A prophet is not
without honor except in his hometown and
in his household."[v] [58]And He did not do many
miracles there because of their unbelief.

John the Baptist Beheaded
14 At that time[w] •Herod the tetrarch[x]
heard the report about Jesus. [2]"This is
John the Baptist!" he told his servants. "He
has been raised from the dead, and that's why
supernatural powers are at work in him."[y]
[3]For Herod had arrested John, chained[I]
him, and put him in prison on account of
Herodias, his brother Philip's wife,[z] [4]since
John had been telling him, "It's not lawful[aa]
for you to have her!" [5]Though he wanted to
kill him, he feared the crowd, since they regarded him as a prophet.[ab]
[6]But when Herod's birthday celebration
came, Herodias's daughter danced before
them[J] and pleased Herod. [7]So he promised

[a]**13:34** Mk 4:34; Jn 10:6; 16:25
[b]**13:35** Ps 78:2; Rm 16:25-26; 1Co 2:7; Eph 3:9; Col 1:26
[c]**13:36** Mt 13:3; 15:15; 21:33,45; 22:1; 24:32
[d]**13:38** Mt 8:12; Jn 8:44; Ac 13:10; 1Jn 3:10
[e]**13:39** Jl 3:13; Heb 9:26; Rv 14:15
[f]**13:40** Mt 24:3; 28:20
[g]**13:41** Zph 1:3; Mt 8:20; 18:7; 24:31
[h]**13:42** Rv 1:15; 9:2
[i]Mt 8:12; Rv 19:20; 20:10
[j]**13:43** Dn 12:3; Mt 11:15; 1Co 15:42
[k]**13:44** Is 55:1; Php 3:7-8; Rv 3:18
[l]**13:46** Pr 2:4; Mt 7:6
[m]**13:47** Mt 3:2; 13:44; 22:10
[n]**13:49** Mt 13:39-40; 25:32
[o]**13:50** Mt 8:12; 13:42
[p]**13:52** Mt 12:35; 28:19
[q]**13:54-58** Mk 6:1-6; Lk 4:16-30
[r]**13:54** Mt 2:23; 4:23; 7:28
[s]**13:55** Mt 13:55; Mk 6:3; Lk 3:23; Jn 6:42
[t]Jms 1:1; Jd 1
[u]Mt 12:46; Jn 7:5
[v]**13:57** Jr 11:21; 12:6; Lk 4:24; Jn 4:44
[w]**14:1-12** Mk 6:14-29; Lk 9:7-9
[x]**14:1** Mk 8:15; Lk 3:19; 13:31; 23:7; Ac 4:27; 12:1; 13:1
[y]**14:2** Mt 16:14; Mk 6:14; Lk 9:7
[z]**14:3** Mt 4:12; 11:2; Jn 3:24
[aa]**14:4** Lv 18:16; 20:21
[ab]**14:5** Mt 11:9; 21:26,46

[A]**13:35** Ps 78:2 [B]**13:41** Or *stumbling* [C]**13:41** Or *those who do lawlessness* [D]**13:43** Other mss add *to hear* [E]**13:46** Or *very precious* [F]**13:51** Other mss add *Jesus asked them* [G]**13:52** Or *every scribe* [H]**13:55** Other mss read *Joses*; Mk 6:3 [I]**14:3** Or *bound* [J]**14:6** Lit *danced in the middle*

with an oath to give her whatever she might
ask. 8 And prompted by her mother, she answered, "Give me John the Baptist's head here
on a platter!" 9 Although the king regretted it,
he commanded that it be granted because of
his oaths and his guests. 10 So he sent orders
and had John beheaded in the prison. 11 His
head was brought on a platter and given to
the girl, who carried it to her mother. 12 Then
his disciples came, removed the corpse,[A] buried it, and went and reported to Jesus.

Feeding 5,000

13 When Jesus heard about it,[a] He withdrew
from there by boat to a remote place to be
alone. When the crowds heard this, they followed Him on foot from the towns. 14 As He
stepped ashore,[B] He saw a huge crowd, felt
compassion for them, and healed their sick.[b]
15 When evening came, the disciples[c] approached Him and said, "This place is a
wilderness, and it is already late.[C] Send the
crowds away so they can go into the villages
and buy food for themselves."
16 "They don't need to go away," Jesus told
them. "You give them something to eat."
17 "But we only have five loaves and two fish
here," they said to Him.
18 "Bring them here to Me," He said. 19 Then
He commanded the crowds to sit down[D] on
the grass. He took the five loaves and the two
fish, and looking up to heaven, He blessed
them. He broke the loaves and gave them to
the disciples, and the disciples gave them to
the crowds.[d] 20 Everyone ate and was filled.
Then they picked up 12 baskets full of leftover pieces![e] 21 Now those who ate were about
5,000 men, besides women and children.

Walking on the Water

22 Immediately[f] He[E] made the disciples get
into the boat and go ahead of Him to the
other side, while He dismissed the crowds.
23 After dismissing the crowds, He went up
on the mountain by Himself to pray. When
evening came, He was there alone.[g] 24 But the
boat was already over a mile[F] from land,[G] battered by the waves, because the wind was
against them. 25 Around three in the morning,[H] He came toward them walking on the
sea.[h] 26 When the disciples saw Him walking
on the sea, they were terrified. "It's a ghost!"
they said, and cried out in fear.
27 Immediately Jesus spoke to them. "Have
courage! It is I. Don't be afraid."[i]
28 "Lord, if it's You," Peter answered Him,
"command me to come to You on the water."
29 "Come!" He said.
And climbing out of the boat, Peter started
walking on the water and came toward Jesus.
30 But when he saw the strength of the wind,[I]
he was afraid. And beginning to sink he cried
out, "Lord, save me!"
31 Immediately Jesus reached out His hand,
caught hold of him, and said to him, "You of
little faith, why did you doubt?"[j] 32 When they
got into the boat, the wind ceased. 33 Then
those in the boat worshiped Him and said,
"Truly You are the Son of God!"[k]

Miraculous Healings

34 Once they crossed over,[l] they came to land
at Gennesaret.[m] 35 When the men of that place
recognized Him, they alerted[J] the whole vicinity and brought to Him all who were sick.
36 They were begging Him that they might only
touch the ˙tassel on His robe. And as many as
touched it were made perfectly well.[n]

The Tradition of the Elders

15 Then[o] ˙Pharisees and ˙scribes came
from Jerusalem to Jesus and asked,[p]
2 "Why do Your disciples[q] break the tradition
of the elders? For they don't wash their hands
when they eat!"[K,r]
3 He answered them, "And why do you break
God's commandment because of your tradition? 4 For God said:[L]

Honor your father
and your mother;[M,s] and,
The one who speaks evil of father
or mother
must be put to death.[N,t]

5 But you say, 'Whoever tells his father or
mother, "Whatever benefit you might have

[a] **14:13-21** Mk 6:32-44; Lk 9:10-17; Jn 6:1-13
[b] **14:14** Mt 4:23; 9:36
[c] **14:15** Mt 10:1, 26:56; Mk 3:7; 16:20; Lk 6:13; Jn 12:16
[d] **14:19** 1Sm 9:13; Mt 26:26; Mk 8:7; 14:22; Lk 24:30; Ac 27:35
[e] **14:20** Mt 16:9; Mk 6:43; 8:19; Lk 9:17; Jn 6:13
[f] **14:22-33** Mk 6:45-51; Jn 6:15-21
[g] **14:23** Lk 6:12; 9:48
[h] **14:25** Mt 24:23; Mk 13:35
[i] **14:27** Dt 31:6; Is 41:13; 43:1-2; Mt 17:7; Lk 2:10; Rv 1:17
[j] **14:31** Mt 6:30; 8:26; 16:8
[k] **14:33** Ps 2:7; Mt 16:16; 26:63; Mk 1:1; Lk 4:41; Jn 11:4
[l] **14:34-36** Mk 6:53-56; Jn 6:24-25
[m] **14:34** Mk 6:5; Lk 5:1
[n] **14:36** Mt 9:20; Mk 3:10; Lk 6:19; Ac 5:15
[o] **15:1-20** Mk 7:1-23
[p] **15:1** Mk 3:22; Jn 1:19
[q] **15:2** Mt 10:1; 26:56; Mk 3:7; 16:20; Lk 6:13; Jn 12:16
[r] Lk 11:38; Gl 1:14; Col 2:8; Heb 11:2
[s] **15:4** Ex 20:12; Dt 5:16; Eph 6:2
[t] Ex 21:17; Lv 20:9

[A] **14:12** Other mss read *body* [B] **14:14** Lit *Coming out* (of the boat) [C] **14:15** Lit *and the time* (for the evening meal) *has already passed* [D] **14:19** Lit *to recline* [E] **14:22** Other mss read *Jesus* [F] **14:24** Lit *already many stadia*; 1 *stadion* = 600 feet [G] **14:24** Other mss read *already in the middle of the sea* [H] **14:25** Lit *fourth watch of the night* = 3 to 6 a.m. [I] **14:30** Other mss read *saw the wind* [J] **14:35** Lit *sent into* [K] **15:2** Lit *eat bread* = eat a meal [L] **15:4** Other mss read *commanded, saying* [M] **15:4** Ex 20:12; Dt 5:16 [N] **15:4** Ex 21:17; Lv 20:9

received from me is a gift committed to the temple" — 6 he does not have to honor his father.'[A] In this way, you have revoked God's word[B] because of your tradition. 7 Hypocrites! Isaiah prophesied correctly about you when he said:

> **8 These people[C] honor Me with their lips,**
> **but their heart is far from Me.**
> **9 They worship Me in vain,**
> **teaching as doctrines the commands**
> **of men."[D,a]**

Defilement Is from Within

10 Summoning the crowd, He told them, "Listen and understand: 11 It's not what goes into the mouth that defiles[b] a man, but what comes out of the mouth, this defiles a man."[c]

12 Then the disciples came up and told Him, "Do You know that the Pharisees took offense when they heard this statement?"

13 He replied, "Every plant that My heavenly Father didn't plant will be uprooted.[d] 14 Leave them alone! They are blind guides.[E] And if the blind guide the blind, both will fall into a pit."[e]

15 Then Peter replied to Him, "Explain this parable to us."[f]

16 "Are even you still lacking in understanding?" He[F] asked. 17 "Don't you realize[G] that whatever goes into the mouth passes into the stomach and is eliminated?[H] 18 But what comes out of the mouth comes from the heart, and this defiles a man.[g] 19 For from the heart come evil thoughts, murders, adulteries, sexual immoralities, thefts, false testimonies,[h] blasphemies.[i] 20 These are the things that defile a man, but eating with unwashed hands does not defile a man."[j]

A Gentile Mother's Faith

21 When Jesus left there,[k] He withdrew to the area of Tyre and Sidon.[l] 22 Just then a Canaanite woman from that region came and kept crying out,[I] "Have mercy on me, Lord, Son of David! My daughter is cruelly tormented by a demon."[m]

23 Yet He did not say a word to her. So His disciples[n] approached Him and urged Him, "Send her away because she cries out after us."[J]

24 He replied, "I was sent only to the lost sheep of the house of Israel."[o]

25 But she came, knelt before Him, and said, "Lord, help me!"

26 He answered, "It isn't right to take the children's bread and throw it to their dogs."[p]

27 "Yes, Lord," she said, "yet even the dogs eat the crumbs that fall from their masters' table!"

28 Then Jesus replied to her, "Woman, your faith is great. Let it be done for you as you want." And from that moment[K] her daughter was cured.[q]

Healing Many People

29 Moving on from there,[r] Jesus passed along the Sea of Galilee.[s] He went up on a mountain and sat there, 30 and large crowds came to Him, having with them the lame, the blind, the deformed, those unable to speak, and many others. They put them at His feet, and He healed them. 31 So the crowd was amazed when they saw those unable to speak talking, the deformed restored, the lame walking, and the blind seeing.[t] And they gave glory to the God of Israel.

Feeding 4,000

32 Now Jesus summoned His disciples and said,[u] "I have compassion on the crowd, because they've already stayed with Me three days and have nothing to eat. I don't want to send them away hungry; otherwise they might collapse on the way."

33 The disciples said to Him, "Where could we get enough bread in this desolate place[v] to fill such a crowd?"

34 "How many loaves do you have?" Jesus asked them.

"Seven," they said, "and a few small fish."

35 After commanding the crowd to sit down on the ground, 36 He took the seven loaves and the fish, and He gave thanks, broke them, and kept on giving them to the disciples, and the disciples gave them to the crowds.[w] 37 They all ate and were filled. Then they collected

[a] **15:8-9** Is 29:13; Ezk 33:31; Col 2:22; Ti 1:14
[b] **15:11** Mt 15:18; Mk 7:15; Ac 21:28; Heb 9:13
[c] Ac 10:14-15; 1Tm 4:3
[d] **15:13** Is 60:21; 61:3; Jn 15:2; 1Co 3:9
[e] **15:14** Mal 2:8; Mt 23:16,24; Lk 6:39
[f] **15:15** Mt 13:36; Mk 7:17
[g] **15:18** Mt 12:34; Jms 3:6
[h] **15:19** Eph 4:31; Col 3:8; 1Tm 6:4
[i] Ex 20:13-16; Gl 5:19-21; Jms 2:4
[j] **15:20** Mt 11:18; Mk 7:2,5; 1Co 6:9-10
[k] **15:21-28** Mk 7:24-30
[l] **15:21** Mt 11:21; Mk 7:24
[m] **15:22** Gn 10:15,19; Jdg 1:30-33; Mt 4:24; 9:27
[n] **15:23** Mt 10:1; 26:56; Mk 3:7; 16:20; Lk 6:13; Jn 12:16
[o] **15:24** Mt 10:6,23; Jn 4:22; Rm 15:8
[p] **15:26** Ex 22:31; 2Kg 9:10; Mt 8:2; Php 3:2
[q] **15:28** Mt 9:22; 17:18; Jn 4:52-53
[r] **15:29-31** Mk 7:31-37
[s] **15:29** Mt 9:8; 18:8; Mk 9:43
[t] **15:31** Is 29:23; Lk 1:68; Ac 13:17
[u] **15:32-39** Mt 14:14-21; Mk 8:1-10
[v] **15:33** Mk 8:4; 2Co 11:26; Heb 11:38
[w] **15:36** Mt 26:27; Lk 22:17; Jn 6:11,23; Ac 27:35; Rm 14:6; 1Co 10:30

[A] 15:6 Other mss read *then he does not have to honor his father or mother* [B] 15:6 Other mss read *commandment* [C] 15:8 Other mss add *draw near to Me with their mouths, and* [D] 15:8-9 Is 29:13 LXX [E] 15:14 Other mss add *for the blind* [F] 15:16 Other mss read *Jesus* [G] 15:17 Other mss add *yet* [H] 15:17 Lit *and goes out into the toilet* [I] 15:22 Other mss read *and cried out to Him* [J] 15:23 Lit *she is yelling behind us* or *after us* [K] 15:28 Lit *hour*

the leftover pieces — seven large baskets full.
38 Now those who ate were 4,000 men, besides
women and children. 39 After dismissing the
crowds, He got into the boat and went to the
region of Magadan.[A,a]

The Yeast of the Pharisees and the Sadducees

16 The ·Pharisees and ·Sadducees approached,[b] and as a test, asked Him to
show them a sign from heaven.[c]
2 He answered them: "When evening comes
you say, 'It will be good weather because the
sky is red.' 3 And in the morning, 'Today will
be stormy because the sky is red and threatening.' You[B] know how to read the appearance of the sky, but you can't read the signs
of the times.[C] 4 An evil and adulterous generation demands a sign, but no sign will be given
to it except the sign of[D] Jonah."[d] Then He left
them and went away.
5 The disciples reached the other shore,[E]
and they had forgotten to take bread.
6 Then Jesus told them, "Watch out and beware of the yeast[F] of the Pharisees and Sadducees."[e]
7 And they discussed among themselves,
"We didn't bring any bread."
8 Aware of this, Jesus said, "You of little
faith![f] Why are you discussing among yourselves that you do not have bread? 9 Don't you
understand yet? Don't you remember the
five loaves for the 5,000 and how many baskets you collected? 10 Or the seven loaves for
the 4,000 and how many large baskets you
collected?[g] 11 Why is it you don't understand
that when I told you, 'Beware of the yeast of
the Pharisees and Sadducees,' it wasn't about
bread?"[h] 12 Then they understood that He did
not tell them to beware of the yeast in bread,
but of the teaching of the Pharisees and Sadducees.[i]

Peter's Confession of the Messiah

13 When Jesus came to the region of Caesarea Philippi,[G,j] He asked His disciples, "Who
do people say that the ·Son of Man is?"[H]
14 And they said, "Some say John the Baptist;
others, Elijah; still others, Jeremiah or one of
the prophets."[k]
15 "But you," He asked them, "who do you say
that I am?"
16 Simon Peter answered, "You are the ·Mes-
siah, the Son of the living God!"[l]
17 And Jesus responded, "Simon son of Jonah,[I,m] you are blessed because flesh and
blood did not reveal this to you, but My Father in heaven.[n] 18 And I also say to you that
you are Peter,[J] and on this rock[K] I will build
My church,[o] and the forces[L] of ·Hades will
not overpower it. 19 I will give you the keys of
the kingdom of heaven,[p] and whatever you
bind on earth is already bound[M] in heaven,
and whatever you loose on earth is already
loosed[N] in heaven."
20 And He gave the disciples orders to tell no
one that He was[O] the Messiah.[q]

His Death and Resurrection Predicted

21 From[r] then on Jesus began to point out
to His disciples that He must go to Jerusalem
and suffer many things from the elders, ·chief
priests, and ·scribes, be killed, and be raised
the third day.[s] 22 Then Peter took Him aside
and began to rebuke Him, "Oh no,[P] Lord! This
will never happen to You!"
23 But He turned and told Peter, "Get behind
Me, Satan! You are an offense to Me because
you're not thinking about God's concerns,[Q]
but man's."[t]

Take Up Your Cross

24 Then Jesus said to His disciples, "If anyone
wants to come with Me, he must deny himself, take up his cross, and follow Me.[u] 25 For
whoever wants to save his ·life will lose it, but
whoever loses his life because of Me will find
it.[v] 26 What will it benefit a man if he gains the
whole world yet loses his life? Or what will a
man give in exchange for his life?[w] 27 For the
Son of Man is going to come with His angels
in the glory of His Father,[x] and then He will
reward each according to what he has done.
28 ·I assure you: There are some standing here

[a] **15:39** Mk 3:9; 8:10
[b] **16:1-12** Mt 12:38-39; Mk 8:11-21; Lk 12:54-56
[c] **16:1** Lk 11:16; 1Co 1:22
[d] **16:4** Mt 4:13; 21:17; Lk 11:29
[e] **16:6** Mt 3:7; 8:15; Lk 12:1; 1Co 5:6-8; Gl 5:9
[f] **16:8** Mt 6:30; 8:26; 14:31; Lk 12:28
[g] **16:9-10** Mt 14:17-21; 15:34-38
[h] **16:11** Mt 3:7; 16:6; Mk 8:15; Lk 12:1
[i] **16:12** Mt 5:20; 17:13; 23:3
[j] **16:13-16** Mk 8:27-29; Lk 9:18-20
[k] **16:14** Mt 14:2; 17:10; Mk 6:15; Lk 9:8; Jn 1:21
[l] **16:16** Mt 1:16; Jn 11:27
[m] **16:17** Jn 1:42; 21:15-17
[n] 1Co 15:50; Gl 1:16; Eph 6:12; Heb 2:14
[o] **16:18** Mt 18:17; Ac 5:11; 7:38; 8:1,3; 9:31; 11:22,26
[p] **16:19** Is 22:22; Mt 18:18; Jn 20:23; Rv 1:18; 3:7
[q] **16:20** Mk 8:30; Lk 9:21
[r] **16:21-28** Mk 8:31–9:1; Lk 9:22-27
[s] **16:21** Mt 17:9; 20:18; 27:63; Lk 24:7; Jn 2:19
[t] **16:23** 2Sm 19:22; Rm 8:5,7; Php 2:5; 3:19; Col 3:2
[u] **16:24** Mt 10:38; Lk 14:27
[v] **16:25** Mt 10:39; Jn 12:25
[w] **16:26** Ps 49:7-8; Lk 12:20
[x] **16:27** Mt 26:64; Mk 8:38; Ac 1:11; 1Th 1:10; 4:16; Rv 1:7

[A] **15:39** Other mss read *Magdala* [B] **16:3** Other mss read *Hypocrites! You* [C] **16:2-3** Other mss omit *When* (v. 2) through end of v. 3 [D] **16:4** Other mss add *the prophet* [E] **16:5** Lit *disciples went to the other side* [F] **16:6** Or *leaven* [G] **16:13** A town north of Galilee at the base of Mount Hermon [H] **16:13** Other mss read *that I, the Son of Man, am* [I] **16:17** Or *son of John* [J] **16:18** *Peter* (Gk *Petros*) = a specific stone or rock [K] **16:18** *Rock* (Gk *petra*) = a rocky crag or bedrock [L] **16:18** Lit *gates* [M] **16:19** Or *earth will be bound* [N] **16:19** Or *earth will be loosed* [O] **16:20** Other mss add *Jesus* [P] **16:22** Lit *Mercy to You* = *May God have mercy on You* [Q] **16:23** Lit *about the things of God*

who will not taste death until they see the Son
of Man coming in His kingdom."[a]

The Transfiguration

17 After six days[b] Jesus took Peter, James,
and his brother John and led them up
on a high mountain by themselves.[c] 2 He was
transformed[A] in front of them, and His face
shone like the sun. Even His clothes became
as white as the light.[d] 3 Suddenly, Moses and
Elijah appeared to them, talking with Him.

4 Then Peter said to Jesus, "Lord, it's good
for us to be here! If You want, I will make[B]
three •tabernacles here: one for You, one for
Moses, and one for Elijah."[e]

5 While he was still speaking, suddenly a
bright cloud covered[C] them, and a voice from
the cloud said:

> This is My beloved Son.
> I take delight in Him.
> Listen to Him![f]

6 When the disciples[g] heard it, they fell facedown and were terrified.

7 Then Jesus came up, touched them, and
said, "Get up; don't be afraid."[h] 8 When they
looked up they saw no one except Him[D]—
Jesus alone. 9 As they were coming down from
the mountain, Jesus commanded them,[i]
"Don't tell anyone about the vision until the
•Son of Man is raised[E] from the dead."

10 So the disciples questioned Him, "Why
then do the •scribes say that Elijah must come
first?"[j]

11 "Elijah is coming[F] and will restore everything," He replied.[G,k] 12 "But I tell you: Elijah
has already come, and they didn't recognize
him. On the contrary, they did whatever they
pleased to him. In the same way the Son of
Man is going to suffer at their hands."[H,l]
13 Then the disciples understood that He
spoke to them about John the Baptist.

The Power of Faith over a Demon

14 When they reached the crowd,[m] a man
approached and knelt down before Him.
15 "Lord," he said, "have mercy on my son, because he has seizures[I] and suffers severely. He
often falls into the fire and often into the water. 16 I brought him to Your disciples, but they
couldn't heal him."[n]

17 Jesus replied, "You unbelieving and rebellious[J] generation! How long will I be with
you? How long must I put up with you? Bring
him here to Me."[o] 18 Then Jesus rebuked the
demon,[K] and it[L] came out of him,[p] and from
that moment[M] the boy was healed.

19 Then the disciples approached Jesus privately and said, "Why couldn't we drive it
out?"

20 "Because of your little faith," He[N] told
them. "For •I assure you: If you have faith
the size of[O] a mustard seed, you will tell this
mountain, 'Move from here to there,' and it
will move.[q] Nothing will be impossible for
you.[r] [21 However, this kind does not come out
except by prayer and fasting.]"[P]

The Second Prediction of His Death

22 As[s] they were meeting[Q] in Galilee, Jesus
told them, "The Son of Man is about to be betrayed into the hands of men. 23 They will kill
Him, and on the third day He will be raised
up." And they were deeply distressed.

Paying the Temple Tax

24 When they came to Capernaum, those
who collected the double-drachma tax[R] approached Peter and said, "Doesn't your
Teacher pay the double-drachma tax?"[t]

25 "Yes," he said.

When he went into the house, Jesus spoke
to him first,[S] "What do you think, Simon?
Who do earthly kings collect tariffs or taxes
from? From their sons or from strangers?"[T,u]

26 "From strangers," he said.[U]

"Then the sons are free," Jesus told him.
27 "But, so we won't •offend them, go to the sea,
cast in a fishhook, and take the first fish that
you catch. When you open its mouth you'll
find a coin.[V] Take it and give it to them for Me
and you."[v]

[a] **16:28** Mt 4:23; 10:23; Ac 20:25
[b] **17:1-8** Mk 9:2-8; Lk 9:28-36
[c] **17:1** Mt 26:37; Mk 5:37
[d] **17:2** Ps 104:2; Dn 7:9; Mt 28:3; 2Co 3:18; Rv 1:16; 10:1
[e] **17:4** Mk 9:5; Lk 9:33
[f] **17:5** Is 42:1; Mt 3:17; Mk 1:11; Lk 3:22; Ac 3:22; 2Pt 1:16-18
[g] **17:6** Mt 10:1; 26:56; Mk 3:7; 16:20; Lk 6:13; Jn 12:16
[h] **17:7** Dn 8:18; 9:21; 10:10; Mt 14:27
[i] **17:9-13** Mk 9:9-13
[j] **17:10** Mal 4:5; Mt 11:14
[k] **17:11** Mal 4:6; Lk 1:16-17
[l] **17:12** Mt 14:3,10; 16:21
[m] **17:14-21** Mk 9:14-29; Lk 9:37-43
[n] **17:16** Mt 10:1; Mk 6:7; Lk 10:17
[o] **17:17** Jn 14:9; 20:27; Php 2:15
[p] **17:18** Zch 3:2; Mt 8:26; Mk 1:25; Lk 4:35; Jd 9
[q] **17:20** Mt 21:21-22; Mk 11:23; Lk 17:6; Jn 11:40; 1Co 13:2
[r] Mk 9:23; 13:31
[s] **17:22-23** Mt 16:21; 20:17; Mk 8:31; 9:30-32; Lk 9:44-45
[t] **17:24** Ex 30:13; 38:26; Mk 9:33
[u] **17:25** Mt 22:17,19; Mk 12:14; Rm 13:7
[v] **17:27** Mt 5:29; Jn 6:61

[A] **17:2** Or *transfigured* [B] **17:4** Other mss read *wish, let's make* [C] **17:5** Or *enveloped*; Ex 40:34-35 [D] **17:8** Other mss omit *Him* [E] **17:9** Other mss read *Man has risen* [F] **17:11** Other mss add *first* [G] **17:11** Other mss read *Jesus said to them* [H] **17:12** Lit *suffer by them* [I] **17:15** Lit *he is moonstruck*; thought to be a form of epilepsy [J] **17:17** Or *corrupt*, or *perverted*, or *twisted*; Dt 32:5 [K] **17:18** Lit *rebuked him* or *it* [L] **17:18** Lit *the demon* [M] **17:18** Lit *hour* [N] **17:20** Other mss read *your unbelief," Jesus* [O] **17:20** Lit *faith like* [P] **17:21** Other mss omit bracketed text; Mk 9:29 [Q] **17:22** Other mss read *were staying* [R] **17:24** Jewish men paid this tax to support the temple; Ex 30:11-16. A double-drachma could purchase 2 sheep. [S] **17:25** Lit *Jesus anticipated him by saying* [T] **17:25** Or *foreigners* [U] **17:26** Other mss read *Peter said to Him* [V] **17:27** Gk *stater*, worth 2 double-drachmas

Who Is the Greatest?

18 At that time[A,a] the disciples[b] came to
Jesus and said, "Who is greatest in the
kingdom of heaven?"[c]
2 Then He called a child to Him and had him
stand among them. 3 "•I assure you," He said,
"unless you are converted[B] and become like
children,[d] you will never enter the kingdom
of heaven.[e] 4 Therefore, whoever humbles
himself like this child — this one is the greatest in the kingdom of heaven. 5 And whoever
welcomes[C] one child like this in My name welcomes Me.
6 "But whoever •causes the downfall of one
of these little ones who believe in Me — it
would be better for him if a heavy millstone[D]
were hung around his neck and he were
drowned in the depths of the sea![f] 7 Woe to
the world because of •offenses. For offenses
must come, but woe to that man by whom
the offense comes.[g] 8 If your hand or your foot
causes your downfall, cut it off and throw it
away. It is better for you to enter life maimed
or lame, than to have two hands or two feet
and be thrown into the eternal fire.[h] 9 And if
your eye causes your downfall, gouge it out
and throw it away. It is better for you to enter
life with one eye, rather than to have two eyes
and be thrown into •hellfire![E,i]

The Parable of the Lost Sheep

10 "See that you don't look down on one of
these little ones,[j] because I tell you that in
heaven their angels[k] continually view the
face of My Father in heaven.[l] [11 For the •Son
of Man[m] has come to save the lost.][F] 12 What do
you think?[n] If a man has 100 sheep, and one
of them goes astray, won't he leave the 99 on
the hillside and go and search for the stray?[o]
13 And if he finds it, I assure you: He rejoices
over that sheep[G] more than over the 99 that
did not go astray. 14 In the same way, it is not
the will of your Father in heaven that one of
these little ones perish.

Restoring a Brother

15 "If your brother sins against you,[H] go and
rebuke him in private.[I] If he listens to you,
you have won your brother.[p] 16 But if he won't
listen, take one or two more with you, so that
**by the testimony[J] of two or three witnesses
every fact may be established.**[K,q] 17 If he pays
no attention to them, tell the church.[L,r] But if
he doesn't pay attention even to the church,
let him be like an unbeliever[M] and a tax collector to you.[s] 18 I assure you: Whatever you
bind on earth is already bound[N] in heaven,
and whatever you loose on earth is already
loosed[O] in heaven.[t] 19 Again, I assure you: If
two of you on earth agree about any matter
that you[P] pray for, it will be done for you[Q]
by My Father in heaven. 20 For where two or
three are gathered together in My name, I am
there among them."

The Parable of the Unforgiving Slave

21 Then Peter came to Him and said, "Lord,
how many times could my brother sin
against me and I forgive him? As many as
seven times?"[u]
22 "I tell you, not as many as seven," Jesus
said to him, "but 70 times seven.[R] 23 For this
reason, the kingdom of heaven can be compared to a king who wanted to settle accounts
with his •slaves. 24 When he began to settle accounts, one who owed 10,000 talents[S] was
brought before him. 25 Since he had no way to
pay it back, his master commanded that he,
his wife, his children, and everything he had
be sold to pay the debt.[v]
26 "At this, the slave fell facedown before
him and said, 'Be patient with me, and I will
pay you everything!' 27 Then the master of
that slave had compassion, released him, and
forgave him the loan.
28 "But that slave went out and found
one of his fellow slaves who owed him 100
•denarii.[T,w] He grabbed him, started choking
him, and said, 'Pay what you owe!'
29 "At this, his fellow slave fell down[U] and
began begging him, 'Be patient with me, and
I will pay you back.' 30 But he wasn't willing.
On the contrary, he went and threw him into
prison until he could pay what was owed.
31 When the other slaves saw what had taken

[a] **18:1-5** Mk 9:33-37; Lk 9:46-48 [b] **18:1** Mt 9:10; Mk 10:10; Lk 6:1; Jn 6:3; Ac 6:1 [c] Mt 22:24; Jn 3:35; 13:20 [d] **18:3** Mt 19:14; Mk 10:15; Lk 18:17; 1Co 14:20; 1Pt 2:2 [e] Mt 5:20; 7:21; 19:23-24; Mk 9:47; Jn 3:5 [f] **18:6** Mk 9:42; Lk 17:2; 1Co 8:12 [g] **18:7** Mt 26:24; Lk 17:1; 1Co 11:19 [h] **18:8** Mt 5:30; 25:41; Mk 9:43 [i] **18:9** Mt 5:22,29; Mk 9:47 [j] **18:10** Est 1:14; Lk 1:19; Rv 8:2 [k] Ps 34:7; 91:11; Heb 1:14 [l] Mt 6:29; 25:40,45; Lk 15:7,10 [m] **18:11** Mk 2:10; Jn 2:25 [n] **18:12-14** Lk 15:1-7 [o] **18:12** Mt 17:25; 21:28 [p] **18:15** Lv 19:17; Lk 17:3; Gl 6:1; 2Th 3:15; Jms 5:19; 1Pt 3:1 [q] **18:16** Nm 35:30; Jn 8:17; 2Co 13:1; 1Tm 5:19; Heb 10:28 [r] **18:17** Mt 16:18; 1Co 14:4; Rv 1:4 [s] Rm 16:17; 1Co 5:9; 6:1-6; 2Th 3:6,14; 2Jn 10 [t] **18:18** Mt 16:19; Jn 20:23 [u] **18:21** Lk 17:3-4; Col 3:13 [v] **18:25** Ex 21:2; Lv 25:39; 2Kg 4:1; Neh 5:5,8; Lk 7:42 [w] **18:28** Mt 20:2: 22:19; Mk 6:37; 14:5; Lk 7:41; 10:35; Jn 6:7

[A] **18:1** Lit *hour* [B] **18:3** Or *are turned around* [C] **18:5** Or *receives* [D] **18:6** A millstone turned by a donkey [E] **18:9** Lit *gehenna of fire* [F] **18:11** Other mss omit bracketed text [G] **18:13** Lit *over it* [H] **18:15** Other mss omit *against you* [I] **18:15** Lit *him between you and him alone* [J] **18:16** Lit *mouth* [K] **18:16** Dt 19:15 [L] **18:17** Or *congregation* [M] **18:17** Or *like a Gentile* [N] **18:18** Or *earth will be bound* [O] **18:18** Or *earth will be loosed* [P] **18:19** Lit *they* [Q] **18:19** Lit *for them* [R] **18:22** Or *but 77 times* [S] **18:24** A huge sum of money that could never be repaid by a slave; a talent = 6,000 denarii [T] **18:28** A small sum compared to 10,000 talents [U] **18:29** Other mss add *at his feet*

place, they were deeply distressed and went and reported to their master everything that had happened.

32“Then, after he had summoned him, his master said to him, ‘You wicked slave! I forgave you all that debt because you begged me. 33Shouldn’t you also have had mercy on your fellow slave, as I had mercy on you?’[a] 34And his master got angry and handed him over to the jailers to be tortured until he could pay everything that was owed. 35So My heavenly Father will also do to you if each of you does not forgive his brother[A] from his[B] heart.”[b]

The Question of Divorce

19 When Jesus had finished this instruction,[c] He departed from Galilee and went to the region of Judea across the Jordan.[d] 2Large crowds followed Him, and He healed them there.[e] 3Some ·Pharisees approached Him to test Him. They asked, “Is it lawful for a man to divorce his wife on any grounds?”[f]

4“Haven’t you read,” He replied, “that He who created[C] them in the beginning **made them male and female**,”[D,g] 5and He also said:

> **“For this reason a man will leave**
> **his father and mother**
> **and be joined to his wife,**
> **and the two will become one flesh**?[E,h]

6So they are no longer two, but one flesh. Therefore, what God has joined together, man must not separate.”

7“Why then,” they asked Him, “did Moses command us to give divorce papers[i] and to send her away?”

8He told them, “Moses permitted you to divorce your wives because of the hardness of your hearts. But it was not like that from the beginning. 9And I tell you, whoever divorces his wife, except for sexual immorality, and marries another, commits adultery.”[F,j]

10His disciples[k] said to Him, “If the relationship of a man with his wife is like this, it’s better not to marry!”

11But He told them, “Not everyone can accept this saying, but only those it has been given[l] to. 12For there are eunuchs who were born that way from their mother’s womb, there are eunuchs who were made by men, and there are eunuchs who have made themselves that way because of the kingdom of heaven. Let anyone accept this who can.”

Blessing the Children

13Then children were brought to Him so He might put His hands on them and pray. But the disciples rebuked them.[m] 14Then Jesus said, “Leave the children alone, and don’t try to keep them from coming to Me, because the kingdom of heaven is made up of people like this.”[G,n] 15After putting His hands on them, He went on from there.

The Rich Young Ruler

16Just then someone came up and asked Him,[o] “Teacher, what good must I do to have eternal life?”[p]

17“Why do you ask Me about what is good?”[H] He said to him. “There is only One who is good.[I] If you want to enter into life, keep the commandments.”[q]

18“Which ones?” he asked Him. Jesus answered:

> **Do not murder;**
> **do not commit adultery;**
> **do not steal;**
> **do not bear false witness;**[r]
> 19 **honor your father and your mother;**
> **and love your neighbor as yourself.**[J,s]

20“I have kept all these,”[K] the young man told Him. “What do I still lack?”

21“If you want to be perfect,”[L] Jesus said to him, “go, sell your belongings and give to the poor,[t] and you will have treasure in heaven. Then come, follow Me.”

22When the young man heard that command, he went away grieving, because he had many possessions.

Possessions and the Kingdom

23Then Jesus said to His disciples, “·I assure you: It will be hard for a rich person to enter the kingdom of heaven![u] 24Again I tell you, it is easier for a camel to go through the eye of

[a]18:33 Mt 6:12; Eph 4:32; Col 3:13; 1Jn 4:11 [b]18:35 Pr 21:13; Mt 6:14; Jms 2:13 [c]19:1-9 Mk 10:1-12 [d]19:1 Mt 7:28; Lk 9:51; Jn 10:40 [e]19:2 Mt 4:23; 12:15 [f]19:3 Mt 5:31; Jn 8:6 [g]19:4 Gn 2:18; Mt 21:16 [h]19:5 Gn 2:24; Mal 2:15; 1Co 6:16; Eph 5:31 [i]19:7 Dt 24:1-4; Mt 5:31 [j]19:9 Mt 5:32; Lk 16:18 [k]19:10 Mt 10:1; 26:56; Mk 3:7; 16:20; Lk 6:13; Jn 12:16 [l]19:11 Mt 13:11; 1Co 7:7 [m]19:13-15 Mk 10:13-16; Lk 18:15-17 [n]19:14 Mt 18:3; 1Pt 2:2 [o]19:16-29 Mk 10:17-30; Lk 10:25-28; 18:18-30 [p]19:16 Mk 10:17; Jn 12:25; Ac 13:48 [q]19:17 Lv 18:5; Neh 9:29; Ezk 20:21 [r]19:18 Ex 20:13-16; Dt 5:17-20 [s]19:19 Ex 20:12; Lv 19:18; Dt 5:16; Mt 5:43; 22:39; Gl 5:14; Jms 2:8 [t]19:21 Lk 12:33; 16:9; Ac 2:45; 4:35; 1Tm 6:18 [u]19:23 Mt 13:22; Mk 10:23; 1Co 1:26; 1Tm 6:9

[A]18:35 Other mss add *his trespasses* [B]18:35 Lit *your* [C]19:4 Other mss read *made* [D]19:4 Gn 1:27; 5:2 [E]19:5 Gn 2:24 [F]19:9 Other mss add *Also whoever marries a divorced woman commits adultery*; Mt 5:32 [G]19:14 Lit *heaven is of such ones* [H]19:17 Other mss read *Why do you call Me good?* [I]19:17 Other mss read *No one is good but One — God* [J]19:18-19 Ex 20:12-16; Lv 19:18; Dt 5:16-20 [K]19:20 Other mss add *from my youth* [L]19:21 Or *complete*

a needle than for a rich person to enter the
kingdom of God."[a]
25 When the disciples heard this, they were
utterly astonished and asked, "Then who can
be saved?"
26 But Jesus looked at them and said, "With
men this is impossible, but with God all
things are possible."[b]
27 Then Peter responded to Him, "Look, we
have left everything and followed You. So
what will there be for us?"
28 Jesus said to them, "I assure you: In the
Messianic Age,[A,c] when the •Son of Man sits on
His glorious throne,[d] you who have followed
Me will also sit on 12 thrones, judging the 12
tribes of Israel. 29 And everyone who has left
houses, brothers or sisters, father or mother,[B]
children, or fields because of My name will
receive 100 times more and will inherit eternal
life.[e] 30 But many who are first will be last,
and the last first.[f]

The Parable of the Vineyard Workers

20 "For the kingdom of heaven is like a
landowner who went out early in the
morning to hire workers for his vineyard.[g]
2 After agreeing with the workers on one
•denarius for the day, he sent them into his
vineyard. 3 When he went out about nine in
the morning,[C] he saw others standing in the
marketplace doing nothing. 4 To those men
he said, 'You also go to my vineyard, and I'll
give you whatever is right.' So off they went.
5 About noon and at three,[D] he went out again
and did the same thing. 6 Then about five[E] he
went and found others standing around,[F] and
said to them, 'Why have you been standing
here all day doing nothing?'
7 "'Because no one hired us,' they said to
him.
"'You also go to my vineyard,' he told them.[G]
8 When evening came, the owner of the vineyard
told his foreman, 'Call the workers and
give them their pay,[h] starting with the last
and ending with the first.'[H]
9 "When those who were hired about five[E]
came, they each received one denarius. 10 So
when the first ones came, they assumed they
would get more, but they also received a denarius
each. 11 When they received it, they began
to complain to the landowner: 12 'These
last men put in one hour, and you made them
equal to us who bore the burden of the day
and the burning heat!'[i]
13 "He replied to one of them, 'Friend, I'm
doing you no wrong. Didn't you agree with
me on a denarius?[j] 14 Take what's yours and
go. I want to give this last man the same as I
gave you. 15 Don't I have the right to do what I
want with my business?[I] Are you jealous[J] because
I'm generous?'[K,k]
16 "So the last will be first, and the first
last."[L,l]

The Third Prediction of His Death

17 While going up to Jerusalem,[m] Jesus took
the 12 disciples aside privately and said to
them on the way: 18 "Listen! We are going up
to Jerusalem. The •Son of Man will be handed
over to the •chief priests and •scribes, and
they will condemn Him to death.[n] 19 Then
they will hand Him over to the Gentiles[o] to
be mocked, flogged,[M] and crucified, and He
will be resurrected[N] on the third day."

Suffering and Service

20 Then the mother of Zebedee's sons approached
Him with her sons.[p] She knelt
down to ask Him for something.[q] 21 "What do
you want?" He asked her.
"Promise,"[O] she said to Him, "that these two
sons of mine may sit, one on Your right and
the other on Your left, in Your kingdom."[r]
22 But Jesus answered, "You don't know
what you're asking. Are you able to drink the
cup[P] that I am about to drink?"[Q,s]
"We are able," they said to Him.
23 He told them, "You will indeed drink My
cup.[R] But to sit at My right and left is not Mine
to give; instead, it belongs to those for whom
it has been prepared by My Father."[t] 24 When
the 10 disciples heard this, they became in-

[a] **19:24** Mt 12:28; Mk 10:25; Lk 18:25
[b] **19:26** Gn 18:14; Jb 42:2; Jr 32:17; Zch 8:6; Mk 10:27; Lk 18:27
[c] **19:28** Is 65:17; 66:22; 2Pt 3:13; Rv 21:1
[d] Ps 45:6; Mt 25:31; Heb 1:8; Rv 3:21; 22:1,3
[e] **19:29** Mt 6:33; Mk 10:29; Lk 18:29
[f] **19:30** Mt 20:16; 21:31; Mk 10:31; Lk 13:30
[g] **20:1** Mt 13:24; 21:28,33
[h] **20:8** Lv 19:13; Dt 24:15
[i] **20:12** Jnh 4:8; Lk 12:55; Jms 1:11
[j] **20:13** Mt 22:12; 26:50
[k] **20:15** Dt 15:9; Pr 23:6; Mt 6:23; Mk 7:22
[l] **20:16** Mt 19:30; Mk 10:31; Lk 13:30
[m] **20:17-19** Mk 10:32-34; Lk 18:31-33
[n] **20:18** Mt 16:21; 26:66; Jn 19:7
[o] **20:19** Mt 27:2; Ac 2:23; 3:13; 4:27; 21:11
[p] **20:20-28** Mk 10:35-45; Lk 22:24-27
[q] **20:20** Mt 4:21; 8:2
[r] **20:21** Mt 16:28; 19:28; 25:31,34; Lk 23:42
[s] **20:22** Is 51:22; Jr 49:12; Mk 14:36
[t] **20:23** Ac 12:2; Rv 1:9

[A] **19:28** Lit *the regeneration* [B] **19:29** Other mss add *or wife* [C] **20:3** Lit *about the third hour* [D] **20:5** Lit *about the sixth hour and the ninth hour* [E] **20:6,9** Lit *about the eleventh hour* [F] **20:6** Other mss add *doing nothing* [G] **20:7** Other mss add *'and you'll get whatever is right.'* [H] **20:8** Lit *starting from the last until the first* [I] **20:15** Lit *with what is mine* [J] **20:15** Lit *Is your eye evil*; an idiom for jealousy or stinginess [K] **20:15** Lit *good* [L] **20:16** Other mss add *For many are called, but few are chosen."* [M] **20:19** Or *scourged* [N] **20:19** Other mss read *will rise again* [O] **20:21** Lit *Say* [P] **20:22** Figurative language referring to His coming suffering; Mt 26:39; Jn 18:11 [Q] **20:22** Other mss add *and (or) to be baptized with the baptism that I am baptized with?"* [R] **20:23** Other mss add *and be baptized with the baptism that I am baptized with.*

dignant with the two brothers. [25]But Jesus called them over and said, "You know that the rulers of the Gentiles dominate them, and the men of high position exercise power over them. [26]It must not be like that among you. On the contrary, whoever wants to become great among you must be your servant,[a] [27]and whoever wants to be first among you must be your ˙slave; [28]just as the Son of Man did not come to be served, but to serve,[b] and to give His life — a ransom for many."[c]

Two Blind Men Healed

[29]As they were leaving Jericho, a large crowd followed Him.[d] [30]There were two blind men sitting by the road. When they heard that Jesus was passing by, they cried out, "Lord, have mercy on us, Son of David!" [31]The crowd told them to keep quiet, but they cried out all the more, "Lord, have mercy on us, Son of David!"[e]

[32]Jesus stopped, called them, and said, "What do you want Me to do for you?"

[33]"Lord," they said to Him, "open our eyes!" [34]Moved with compassion, Jesus touched their eyes. Immediately they could see, and they followed Him.

The Triumphal Entry

21 When they approached Jerusalem[f] and came to Bethphage at the ˙Mount of Olives,[g] Jesus then sent two disciples, [2]telling them, "Go into the village ahead of you. At once you will find a donkey tied there, and a colt with her. Untie them and bring them to Me. [3]If anyone says anything to you, you should say that the Lord needs them, and immediately he will send them."

[4]This took place so that what was spoken through the prophet might be fulfilled:

> [5] **Tell Daughter ˙Zion,**
> **"Look, your King is coming to you,**
> **gentle, and mounted on a donkey,**
> **even on a colt,**
> **the foal of a beast of burden."**[A,h]

[6]The disciples went and did just as Jesus directed them. [7]They brought the donkey and the colt; then they laid their robes on them, and He sat on them. [8]A very large crowd spread their robes on the road; others were cutting branches from the trees and spreading them on the road. [9]Then the crowds who went ahead of Him and those who followed kept shouting:

> ˙***Hosanna*** to the Son of David!
> **He who comes in the name**
> **of the Lord is the blessed One!**[B]
> ***Hosanna*** in the highest heaven![i]

[10]When He entered Jerusalem, the whole city was shaken, saying, "Who is this?" [11]And the crowds kept saying, "This is the prophet Jesus[j] from Nazareth in Galilee!"

Cleansing the Temple Complex

[12]Jesus went into the ˙temple complex[C,k] and drove out all those buying and selling in the temple. He overturned the money changers' tables and the chairs of those selling doves.[l] [13]And He said to them, "It is written, **My house will be called a house of prayer.**[D] But you are making it **a den of thieves!**"[E,m]

Children Praise Jesus

[14]The blind and the lame came to Him in the temple complex, and He healed them. [15]When the ˙chief priests and the ˙scribes saw the wonders that He did and the children shouting in the temple complex, "*Hosanna* to the Son of David!" they were indignant [16]and said to Him, "Do You hear what these children are saying?"

"Yes," Jesus told them. "Have you never read:

> **You have prepared**[F] **praise**[n]
> **from the mouths of children**
> **and nursing infants?"**[G]

[17]Then He left them, went out of the city to Bethany,[o] and spent the night there.

The Barren Fig Tree

[18]Early in the morning,[p] as He was returning to the city, He was hungry. [19]Seeing a lone fig tree by the road, He went up to it and found nothing on it except leaves. And He said to it, "May no fruit ever come from you again!" At once the fig tree withered.

[20]When the disciples saw it, they were

[a] **20:26** Mt 23:11; Mk 9:35
[b] **20:28** Lk 22:27; Jn 13:13-15; 2Co 8:9; Php 2:7
[c] Mt 26:28; 1Tm 2:6; Ti 2:14; Heb 9:28
[d] **20:29-34** Mk 10:46-52; Lk 18:35-43
[e] **20:30-31** Mt 9:27; 21:9; 22:42
[f] **21:1-9** Mk 11:1-10; Lk 19:28-38; Jn 12:12-19
[g] **21:1** Zch 14:4; Mt 24:3; 26:30; Lk 19:29,37; 21:37; Jn 8:1; Ac 1:12
[h] **21:5** Is 62:11; Zch 9:9
[i] **21:9** Ps 118:25; Mt 9:27; 23:39; Lk 2:14
[j] **21:11** Mk 6:15; Lk 7:16; 13:33; 24:19; Jn 1:21; 4:19; 6:14
[k] **21:12-16** Mk 11:15-18; Lk 19:45-47; Jn 2:14-16
[l] **21:12** Ex 30:13; Lv 1:14; 5:7; 12:8; Dt 14:25
[m] **21:13** Jr 7:11
[n] **21:16** Ps 8:2; Mt 11:25; 12:3,5; 19:4; 22:31
[o] **21:17** Mt 26:6; Mk 11:1; Lk 19:29; 24:50; Jn 11:18
[p] **21:18-22** Mk 11:12-14,20-24

[A]**21:5** Is 62:11; Zch 9:9 [B]**21:9** Ps 118:25-26 [C]**21:12** Other mss add *of God* [D]**21:13** Is 56:7 [E]**21:13** Jr 7:11 [F]**21:16** Or *restored* [G]**21:16** Ps 8:2

amazed and said, "How did the fig tree wither so quickly?"

21 Jesus answered them, "I assure you: If you have faith and do not doubt, you will not only do what was done to the fig tree, but even if you tell this mountain, 'Be lifted up and thrown into the sea,' it will be done.[a] 22 And if you believe, you will receive[b] whatever you ask for in prayer."

Messiah's Authority Challenged

23 When He entered the temple complex,[c] the chief priests and the elders of the people came up to Him as He was teaching and said, "By what authority are You doing these things? Who gave You this authority?"[d]

24 Jesus answered them, "I will also ask you one question, and if you answer it for Me, then I will tell you by what authority I do these things. 25 Where did John's baptism come from? From heaven or from men?"

They began to argue among themselves, "If we say, 'From heaven,' He will say to us, 'Then why didn't you believe him?'[e] 26 But if we say, 'From men,' we're afraid of the crowd,[f] because everyone thought John was a prophet."[g] 27 So they answered Jesus, "We don't know."

And He said to them, "Neither will I tell you by what authority I do these things.

The Parable of the Two Sons

28 "But what do you think? A man had two sons. He went to the first and said, 'My son, go, work in the vineyard today.'[h]

29 "He answered, 'I don't want to!' Yet later he changed his mind and went. 30 Then the man went to the other and said the same thing.

"'I will, sir,' he answered. But he didn't go.

31 "Which of the two did his father's will?"

"The first," they said.

Jesus said to them, "I assure you: Tax collectors and prostitutes are entering the kingdom of God before you! 32 For John came to you in the way of righteousness,[i] and you didn't believe him. Tax collectors and prostitutes did believe him, but you, when you saw it, didn't even change your minds then and believe him.

The Parable of the Vineyard Owner

33 "Listen[j] to another parable:[k] There was a man, a landowner, who planted a vineyard, put a fence around it, dug a winepress in it, and built a watchtower.[l] He leased it to tenant farmers and went away.[m] 34 When the grape harvest[A] drew near, he sent his ·slaves to the farmers to collect his fruit. 35 But the farmers took his slaves, beat one, killed another, and stoned a third.[n] 36 Again, he sent other slaves, more than the first group, and they did the same to them. 37 Finally, he sent his son to them. 'They will respect my son,' he said.

38 "But when the tenant farmers saw the son, they said among themselves, 'This is the heir. Come, let's kill him and take his inheritance!'[o] 39 So they seized him, threw him out of the vineyard, and killed him. 40 Therefore, when the owner of the vineyard comes, what will he do to those farmers?"

41 "He will completely destroy those terrible men," they told Him, "and lease his vineyard to other farmers who will give him his produce at the harvest."[B,p]

42 Jesus said to them, "Have you never read in the Scriptures:

> **The stone that the builders rejected**
> **has become the cornerstone.**[C]
> **This came from the Lord**
> **and is wonderful in our eyes?**[D,q]

43 Therefore I tell you, the kingdom of God will be taken away from you and given to a nation producing its[E] fruit. [44 Whoever falls on this stone will be broken to pieces;[r] but on whoever it falls, it will grind him to powder!]"[F]

45 When the chief priests and the ·Pharisees heard His parables,[s] they knew He was speaking about them. 46 Although they were looking for a way to arrest Him, they feared the crowds, because they[G] regarded Him as a prophet.[t]

The Parable of the Wedding Banquet

22 Once more Jesus spoke to them in parables: 2 "The kingdom of heaven[u] may be compared to a king who gave a wedding banquet for his son.[v] 3 He sent out his ·slaves

[a]21:21 Mt 17:20; Lk 17:6; 1Co 13:2; Jms 1:6
[b]21:22 Mt 7:7-8; Jn 11:22
[c]21:23-27 Mk 11:27-33; Lk 20:1-8
[d]21:23 Ex 2:14; Mt 26:55; Ac 4:7; 7:27
[e]21:25 Mt 13:54; Lk 7:30; 15:18,21; Jn 3:27
[f]21:26 Mt 14:5; 21:46; Mk 11:32; 12:12
[g]Mt 11:9; Mk 6:20
[h]21:28 Mt 20:1
[i]21:32 Pr 8:20; Mt 3:8-12; 2Pt 2:21
[j]21:33-46 Mk 12:1-12; Lk 20:9-19
[k]21:33 Mt 13:3,34-36; 15:15; 22:1; 24:32
[l]Is 5:1-2; Lk 14:28
[m]Ps 80:8; Sg 8:11-12; Mt 25:14
[n]21:35 2Ch 24:21; Neh 9:26; Mt 5:12; 23:34,37; Ac 7:52; 1Th 2:15; Heb 11:36-37
[o]21:38 Ps 2:8; Heb 1:2
[p]21:41 Mt 8:11; Ac 13:46; 18:6; 28:28
[q]21:42 Ps 118:22-23; Ac 4:11; Rm 9:33; 1Pt 2:7
[r]21:44 Is 8:14-15; Rm 9:32-33; 1Pt 2:8
[s]21:45 Mt 13:3,35; 15:15; 21:33; 22:1; 24:32
[t]21:46 Mt 26:4; Mk 11:18; Lk 19:47-48; Jn 7:25,30,44
[u]22:2-14 Lk 14:16-24
[v]22:2 Mt 13:24; Lk 12:36; Jn 2:2; Rv 19:7

[A]21:34 Lit *the season of fruits* [B]21:41 Lit *him the fruits in their seasons* [C]21:42 Lit *the head of the corner* [D]21:42 Ps 118:22-23 [E]21:43 = the kingdom's [F]21:44 Other mss omit bracketed text [G]21:46 = the crowds

to summon those invited to the banquet,[a] but
they didn't want to come. 4 Again, he sent out
other slaves, and said, 'Tell those who are invited: Look, I've prepared my dinner; my oxen
and fattened cattle have been slaughtered,
and everything is ready. Come to the wedding
banquet.'[b]

5 "But they paid no attention and went away,
one to his own farm, another to his business.
6 And the others seized his slaves, treated
them outrageously and killed them. 7 The
king[A] was enraged, so he sent out his troops,
destroyed those murderers, and burned
down their city.

8 "Then he told his slaves, 'The banquet is
ready, but those who were invited were not
worthy.[c] 9 Therefore go to where the roads
exit the city and invite everyone you find to
the banquet.'[d] 10 So those slaves went out on
the roads and gathered everyone they found,
both evil and good. The wedding banquet was
filled with guests.[B] 11 But when the king came
in to view the guests, he saw a man there who
was not dressed for a wedding.[e] 12 So he said to
him, 'Friend,[f] how did you get in here without
wedding clothes?' The man was speechless.

13 "Then the king told the attendants, 'Tie
him up hand and foot,[C] and throw him into
the outer darkness, where there will be weeping and gnashing of teeth.'

14 "For many are invited, but few are chosen."[g]

God and Caesar

15 Then the ·Pharisees went and plotted how
to trap Him by what He said.[D,h] 16 They sent
their disciples to Him, with the ·Herodians.[i]
"Teacher," they said, "we know that You are
truthful and teach truthfully the way of God.
You defer to no one, for You don't show partiality.[E,j] 17 Tell us, therefore, what You think. Is
it lawful to pay taxes to Caesar[k] or not?"

18 But perceiving their malice, Jesus said,
"Why are you testing Me, hypocrites? 19 Show
Me the coin used for the tax." So they brought
Him a ·denarius. 20 "Whose image and in-
scription is this?" He asked them.

21 "Caesar's," they said to Him.

Then He said to them, "Therefore give back
to Caesar the things that are Caesar's, and to
God the things that are God's."[l] 22 When they
heard this, they were amazed. So they left
Him and went away.

The Sadducees and the Resurrection

23 The same day some ·Sadducees,[m] who say
there is no resurrection, came up to Him and
questioned Him:[n] 24 "Teacher, Moses said, **if
a man dies, having no children, his brother
is to marry his wife and raise up offspring
for his brother.**[F,o] 25 Now there were seven
brothers among us. The first got married
and died. Having no offspring, he left his
wife to his brother. 26 The same happened to
the second also, and the third, and so to all
seven.[G] 27 Then last of all the woman died. 28 In
the resurrection, therefore, whose wife will
she be of the seven? For they all had married
her."[H]

29 Jesus answered them, "You are deceived,
because you don't know the Scriptures or the
power of God. 30 For in the resurrection they
neither marry nor are given in marriage but
are like[I] angels in heaven.[p] 31 Now concerning
the resurrection of the dead, haven't you read
what was spoken to you by God: 32 **I am the
God of Abraham and the God of Isaac and
the God of Jacob?**[J,q] He[K] is not the God of the
dead, but of the living."

33 And when the crowds heard this, they
were astonished at His teaching.

The Primary Commands

34 When[r] the Pharisees heard that He had
silenced the Sadducees, they came together.
35 And one of them, an expert in the law, asked
a question to test Him:[s] 36 "Teacher, which
command in the law is the greatest?"[L]

37 He said to him, "**Love the Lord your God
with all your heart, with all your soul, and
with all your mind.**[M,t] 38 This is the greatest
and most important[N] command. 39 The second is like it: **Love your neighbor as yourself.**[O,u] 40 All the Law and the Prophets depend[P]
on these two commands."[v]

[a] **22:3** Est 6:14; Pr 9:3,5
[b] **22:4** Pr 9:2; Mt 21:36
[c] **22:8** Mt 10:11; Ac 13:46
[d] **22:9** Ezk 21:21; Ob 14
[e] **22:11** Rv 19:8; 22:14
[f] **22:12** Mt 20:13; 26:50
[g] **22:14** Mt 20:16; Rv 17:14
[h] **22:15-22** Mk 12:13-17; Lk 20:20-26
[i] **22:16** Mk 2:8; 3:6; 8:15
[j] Jn 3:2; Ac 10:34; 13:10; 18:26
[k] **22:17** Mk 12:14,16-17; Lk 2:1; 3:1; 20:22,24-25; Jn 19:12,15
[l] **22:21** Mt 17:25; Rm 13:7
[m] **22:23-32** Mk 12:18-27; Lk 20:27-38
[n] **22:23** Mt 3:7; Ac 4:1; 23:8
[o] **22:24** Dt 25:5
[p] **22:30** Mt 24:38; Lk 17:27
[q] **22:32** Ex 3:6; Ac 7:32
[r] **22:34-40** Mk 12:28-33; Lk 10:25-28
[s] **22:35** Lk 7:30; 10:25; 11:45; 14:3
[t] **22:37** Dt 6:5; Lk 10:27
[u] **22:39** Lv 19:18; Mt 19:19
[v] **22:40** Mt 7:12; Rm 13:8-10; Gl 5:14

[A] **22:7** Other mss read *But when the (that) king heard about it he* [B] **22:10** Lit *those reclining* (to eat) [C] **22:13** Other mss add *take him away* [D] **22:15** Lit *trap Him in a word* [E] **22:16** Lit *don't look on the face of men*; that is, on the outward appearance [F] **22:24** Dt 25:5 [G] **22:26** Lit *so until the seven* [H] **22:28** Lit *all had her* [I] **22:30** Other mss add *God's* [J] **22:32** Ex 3:6,15-16 [K] **22:32** Other mss read *God* [L] **22:36** Lit *is great* [M] **22:37** Dt 6:5 [N] **22:38** Lit *and first* [O] **22:39** Lv 19:18 [P] **22:40** Or *hang*

The Question about the Messiah

41While the Pharisees were together,
Jesus questioned them,[a] 42"What do you think
about the ·Messiah? Whose Son is He?"
"David's," they told Him.
43He asked them, "How is it then that David, inspired by the Spirit,[A] calls Him 'Lord'[b]:

> 44 **The Lord declared to my Lord,**
> **'Sit at My right hand**
> **until I put Your enemies**
> **under Your feet'?**[B,C,c]

45"If David calls Him 'Lord,' how then can
the Messiah be his Son?" 46No one was able to
answer Him at all,[D] and from that day no one
dared to question Him anymore.[d]

Religious Hypocrites Denounced

23 Then[e] Jesus spoke to the crowds and to
His disciples:[f] 2"The ·scribes and the
·Pharisees are seated in the chair of Moses.[E,g]
3Therefore do whatever they tell you, and observe it. But don't do what they do,[F] because
they don't practice what they teach.[h] 4They tie
up heavy loads that are hard to carry[G] and put
them on people's shoulders, but they themselves aren't willing to lift a finger[H] to move
them.[i] 5They do everything[I] to be observed by
others: They enlarge their phylacteries[J,j] and
lengthen their ·tassels.[K,k] 6They love the place
of honor at banquets, the front seats in the
·synagogues,[l] 7greetings in the marketplaces,
and to be called '·Rabbi' by people.
8"But as for you, do not be called 'Rabbi,' because you have one Teacher,[L] and you are all
·brothers.[m] 9Do not call anyone on earth your
father, because you have one Father, who is in
heaven.[n] 10And do not be called masters either,
because you have one Master,[M] the ·Messiah.
11The greatest among you will be your servant.[o]
12Whoever exalts himself will be humbled,
and whoever humbles himself will be exalted.[p]
13"But woe to you, scribes and Pharisees,
hypocrites! You lock up the kingdom of
heaven from people. For you don't go in, and
you don't allow those entering to go in.[q]
[14"Woe to you, scribes and Pharisees, hypocrites! You devour widows' houses and make
long prayers just for show.[N] This is why you
will receive a harsher punishment.][O]
15"Woe to you, scribes and Pharisees, hypocrites! You travel over land and sea to make
one ·proselyte,[r] and when he becomes one,
you make him twice as fit for ·hell[P] as you are!
16"Woe to you, blind guides,[s] who say, 'Whoever takes an oath by the sanctuary, it means
nothing. But whoever takes an oath[t] by the
gold of the sanctuary is bound by his oath.'[Q]
17Blind fools![R] For which is greater, the gold
or the sanctuary that sanctified the gold?
18Also, 'Whoever takes an oath by the altar,
it means nothing. But whoever takes an oath
by the gift that is on it is bound by his oath.'[Q]
19Blind people![S] For which is greater, the gift
or the altar that sanctifies the gift?[u] 20There-
fore, the one who takes an oath by the altar
takes an oath by it and by everything on it.
21The one who takes an oath by the sanctuary
takes an oath by it and by Him who dwells[v] in
it. 22And the one who takes an oath by heaven
takes an oath by God's throne[w] and by Him
who sits on it.[x]
23"Woe to you, scribes and Pharisees, hypocrites! You pay a tenth of[T] mint, dill, and
cumin,[U] yet you have neglected the more important matters of the law—justice,[y] mercy,
and faith. These things should have been done
without neglecting the others. 24Blind guides![z]
You strain out a gnat, yet gulp down a camel!
25"Woe to you, scribes and Pharisees, hypocrites! You ·clean the outside of the cup and
dish, but inside they are full of greed[V] and
self-indulgence![aa] 26Blind Pharisee! First
clean the inside of the cup,[W] so the outside of
it[X] may also become clean.
27"Woe to you, scribes and Pharisees, hypocrites! You are like whitewashed tombs,[ab]
which appear beautiful on the outside, but
inside are full of dead men's bones and every
impurity. 28In the same way, on the outside

[a]**22:41-46** Mk 12:35-37; Lk 20:41-44 [b]**22:43** 2Sm 23:2; Rv 1:10; 4:2 [c]**22:44** Ps 110:1; Ac 2:34-35; 1Co 15:25; Heb 1:13; 10:13 [d]**22:46** Mk 12:34; Lk 14:6; 20:40 [e]**23:1-7** Mk 12:38-39; Lk 20:45-46 [f]**23:1** Mt 10:42; 28:19; Lk 14:26; Jn 8:31; 13:35; 15:8; Ac 6:1 [g]**23:2** Ezr 7:6,25; Neh 8:4 [h]**23:3** Mt 5:20; 15:3-9; Rm 2:17-23 [i]**23:4** Lk 11:46; Ac 15:10; Gl 6:13 [j]**23:5** Ex 13:9; Dt 6:8; 11:18; Mt 6:1,5,16 [k]Mt 9:20; 14:36; Mk 6:56; Lk 8:44 [l]**23:6** Lk 11:43; 14:7; 20:46 [m]**23:7-8** Mk 9:5; 10:51; Jn 1:38,49; 11:8; Jms 3:1 [n]**23:9** Mal 1:6; Mt 6:9; 7:11 [o]**23:11** Mt 20:26-27; Mk 9:35; 3Jn 9 [p]**23:12** Pr 29:23; Ezk 21:26; Lk 14:11; 18:14; Jms 4:6,10; 1Pt 5:5-6 [q]**23:13** Mt 23:15,23,25; Lk 11:52 [r]**23:15** Ac 2:11; 6:5; 13:43 [s]**23:16** Mt 15:14; 23:24; Ac 1:16; Rm 2:19 [t]Lv 19:12; Nm 30:2; Dt 23:21; Mt 5:33; 14:7; 26:63,72 [u]**23:19** Ex 29:37; 30:29 [v]**23:21** 1Kg 8:13; 2Ch 6:2; Ps 26:8; 132:14 [w]**23:22** Ex 17:16; Ps 11:4; Mt 5:34; Heb 8:1 [x]Ps 47:8; Mt 19:28; Rv 4:2 [y]**23:23** 1Sm 15:22; Ps 33:5; Jr 5:1; Mc 6:8; Zch 7:9; Lk 11:42 [z]**23:24** Mt 15:14; 23:16 [aa]**23:25** Mk 7:4; Lk 11:39 [ab]**23:27** Lk 11:44; Ac 23:3

[A]**22:43** Lit *David in Spirit* [B]**22:44** Other mss read *until I make Your enemies Your footstool* [C]**22:44** Ps 110:1 [D]**22:46** Lit *answer Him a word* [E]**23:2** Perhaps a special chair for teaching in synagogues, or a metaphorical phrase for teaching with Moses' authority [F]**23:3** Lit *do according to their works* [G]**23:4** Other mss omit *that are hard to carry* [H]**23:4** Lit *lift with their finger* [I]**23:5** Lit *do all their works* [J]**23:5** Small leather boxes containing OT texts, worn by Jews on their arms and foreheads [K]**23:5** Other mss add *on their robes* [L]**23:8** Other mss add *the Messiah* [M]**23:10** Or *Teacher* [N]**23:14** Or *prayers with false motivation* [O]**23:14** Other mss omit bracketed text [P]**23:15** Lit *twice the son of gehenna* [Q]**23:16,18** Lit *is obligated* [R]**23:17** Lit *Fools and blind* [S]**23:19** Other mss read *Fools and blind* [T]**23:23** Or *You tithe* [U]**23:23** A plant whose seeds are used as a seasoning [V]**23:25** Or *full of violence* [W]**23:26** Other mss add *and dish* [X]**23:26** Other mss read *of them* you seem righteous to people, but inside you are full of hypocrisy and lawlessness.

29“Woe to you, scribes and Pharisees, hypocrites! You build the tombs of the prophets and decorate the monuments of the righteous, 30and you say, ‘If we had lived in the days of our fathers, we wouldn’t have taken part with them in shedding the prophets’ blood.’[A] 31You, therefore, testify against yourselves that you are sons of those who murdered the prophets. 32Fill up, then, the measure of your fathers’ sins![B,a]

33“Snakes! Brood of vipers! How can you escape being condemned to hell?[C,b] 34This is why I am sending you prophets,[c] sages, and scribes. Some of them you will kill and crucify, and some of them you will flog in your synagogues[d] and hound from town to town. 35So all the righteous blood shed on the earth will be charged to you,[D] from the blood of righteous Abel to the blood of Zechariah,[e] son of Berechiah, whom you murdered between the sanctuary and the altar.[f] 36·I assure you: All these things will come on this generation![g]

Jesus’ Lamentation over Jerusalem

37“Jerusalem, Jerusalem![h] She who kills the prophets and stones those who are sent to her. How often I wanted to gather your children together, as a hen gathers her chicks[E] under her wings, yet you were not willing![i] 38See, your house is left to you desolate.[j] 39For I tell you, you will never see Me again until you say, **‘He who comes in the name of the Lord is the blessed One’**!”[F,k]

Destruction of the Temple Predicted

24 As Jesus left and was going out of the ·temple complex,[l] His disciples[m] came up and called His attention to the temple buildings. 2Then He replied to them, “Don’t you see all these things? ·I assure you: Not one stone will be left here on another that will not be thrown down!”

Signs of the End of the Age

3While He was sitting on the ·Mount of Olives, the disciples approached Him privately and said, “Tell us, when will these things happen? And what is the sign of Your coming and of the end of the age?”[n]

4Then Jesus replied to them: “Watch out that no one deceives[o] you. 5For many will come in My name, saying, ‘I am the ·Messiah,’ and they will deceive many.[p] 6You are going to hear of wars and rumors of wars. See that you are not alarmed, because these things must take place, but the end is not yet. 7For nation will rise up against nation, and kingdom against kingdom. There will be famines[G,q] and earthquakes in various places.[r] 8All these events are the beginning of birth pains.[s]

Persecutions Predicted

9“Then they will hand you over for persecution,[H] and they will kill you. You will be hated by all nations because of My name.[t] 10Then many will ·take offense, betray one another and hate one another. 11Many false prophets[u] will rise up and deceive many. 12Because lawlessness[v] will multiply, the love of many will grow cold. 13But the one who endures to the end will be delivered.[I] 14This good news of the kingdom will be proclaimed in all the world[J] as a testimony to all nations.[w] And then the end will come.[x]

The Great Tribulation

15“So when you see **the abomination that causes desolation**,[K,L] spoken of by the prophet Daniel,[y] standing in the holy place”[z] (let the reader understand[M]), 16“then those in Judea must flee to the mountains! 17A man on the housetop[N] must not come down to get things out of his house.[aa] 18And a man in the field must not go back to get his clothes. 19Woe to pregnant women and nursing mothers in those days! 20Pray that your escape may not be in winter or on a Sabbath. 21For at that time there will be great tribulation,[ab] the kind that hasn’t taken place from the beginning of the world until now and never will again! 22Unless those days were limited, no one would[O] survive.[P] But those days will be limited because of the elect.[ac]

[a]23:31-32 Gn 15:16; Ac 7:51; 1Th 2:15-16
[b]23:33 Mt 3:7; 5:22; 12:34
[c]23:34 Ac 13:1; 1Co 12:28
[d]2Ch 36:15-16; Mt 10:17; Ac 22:19
[e]23:35 2Ch 24:21; Zch 1:1
[f]Gn 4:8; Heb 11:4; 1Jn 3:12; Rv 18:24
[g]23:36 Mt 10:23; 16:28; 24:34
[h]23:37-39 Lk 13:34-35
[i]23:37 Dt 32:11-12; Ru 2:12; Mt 5:12
[j]23:38 1Kg 9:7; Is 64:11; Jr 12:7; 22:5
[k]23:39 Ps 118:26; Mt 21:9
[l]24:1-51 Mk 13:1-37; Lk 21:5-36
[m]24:1 Mt 9:10; Mk 10:10; Lk 6:1; Jn 6:3; 12:16
[n]24:3 Mt 21:1; 24:27,37,39
[o]24:4 Jr 29:8; Eph 5:6; Col 2:8; 2Th 2:3
[p]24:5 Mt 1:17; Eph 5:2
[q]24:7 Ac 11:28; Rv 6:8
[r]2Ch 15:6; Is 19:2
[s]24:8-20 Lk 21:12-24
[t]24:9 Mt 10:17,22; Jn 16:2
[u]24:11 Is 44:25; Mt 7:15; 24:24; Mk 13:22; Lk 6:26; Ac 13:6; 2Pt 2:1; 1Jn 4:1
[v]24:12 Mt 13:41; 2Th 2:3
[w]24:14 Mt 4:23; Rm 10:18; Col 1:6,23; 1Th 1:8
[x]Lk 2:1; 4:5; Ac 11:28; 17:6; Rv 3:10; 16:14
[y]24:15 Dn 9:27; 11:31; 12:11; Mk 13:14; Lk 21:20
[z]Ac 6:13; 21:28
[aa]24:17 1Sm 9:25; Mt 10:27; Lk 5:19; 12:3; 17:31; Ac 10:9
[ab]24:21 Dn 12:1; Jl 2:2; Mt 24:29; Rv 7:14
[ac]24:22 Mt 22:14; 24:24,31; Mk 13:20,22,27; 1Tm 5:21; 2Tm 2:10; Rv 17:14

[A]23:30 Lit *have been partakers with them in the blood of the prophets* [B]23:32 Lit *the measure of your fathers* [C]23:33 Lit *escape from the judgment of gehenna* [D]23:35 Lit *will come on you* [E]23:37 Or *as a mother bird gathers her young* [F]23:39 Ps 118:26 [G]24:7 Other mss add *epidemics* [H]24:9 Or *tribulation*, or *distress* [I]24:13 Or *be saved* [J]24:14 Or *in all the inhabited earth* [K]24:15 Or *abomination of desolation*, or *desolating sacrilege* [L]24:15 Dn 9:27 [M]24:15 These are, most likely, Matthew’s words to his readers. [N]24:17 Or *roof* [O]24:22 Lit *short, all flesh would not* [P]24:22 Or *be saved* or *delivered*

[23]"If anyone tells you then, 'Look, here is the Messiah!'[a] or, 'Over here!' do not believe it![b] [24]False messiahs[A] and false prophets will arise and perform great signs and wonders to lead astray,[c] if possible, even the elect. [25]Take note: I have told you in advance. [26]So if they tell you, 'Look, He's in the wilderness!' don't go out; 'Look, He's in the inner rooms!' do not believe it. [27]For as the lightning comes from the east and flashes as far as the west, so will be the coming of the ˙Son of Man.[d] [28]Wherever the carcass is, there the vultures[B] will gather.[e]

The Coming of the Son of Man

[29]"Immediately after the tribulation[f] of those days:

> The sun will be darkened,
> and the moon will not shed its light;
> the stars will fall from the sky,
> and the celestial powers will be shaken.

[30]"Then the sign of the Son of Man will appear in the sky, and then all the peoples of the earth[C] will mourn;[D] and they will see the Son of Man coming on the clouds of heaven with power and great glory.[g] [31]He will send out His angels with a loud trumpet,[h] and they will gather His elect from the four winds,[i] from one end of the sky to the other.

The Parable of the Fig Tree

[32]"Now learn this parable[j] from the fig tree: As soon as its branch becomes tender and sprouts leaves, you know that summer is near. [33]In the same way, when you see all these things, recognize[E] that He[F] is near—at the door![k] [34]I assure you: This generation will certainly not pass away until all these things take place.[l] [35]Heaven and earth will pass away,[m] but My words will never pass away.[n]

No One Knows the Day or Hour

[36]"Now concerning that day and hour no one knows—neither the angels in heaven, nor the Son[G]—except the Father only.[o] [37]As the days of Noah were, so the coming of the Son of Man will be. [38]For in those days before the flood they were eating and drinking, marrying and giving in marriage, until the day Noah boarded the ark.[p] [39]They didn't know[H] until the flood came and swept them all away. So this is the way the coming of the Son of Man will be: [40]Then two men will be in the field: one will be taken and one left. [41]Two women will be grinding at the mill: one will be taken and one left.[q] [42]Therefore be alert, since you don't know what day[I] your Lord is coming.[r] [43]But know this: If the homeowner had known what time[J] the thief was coming, he would have stayed alert and not let his house be broken into.[s] [44]This is why you also must be ready, because the Son of Man is coming at an hour you do not expect.[t]

Faithful Service to the Messiah

[45]"Who then is a faithful and sensible ˙slave,[u] whom his master has put in charge of his household, to give them food at the proper time?[v] [46]That slave whose master finds him working[w] when he comes will be rewarded. [47]I assure you: He will put him in charge of all his possessions. [48]But if that wicked slave says in his heart, 'My master is delayed,' [49]and starts to beat his fellow slaves, and eats and drinks with drunkards,[x] [50]that slave's master will come on a day he does not expect and at an hour he does not know. [51]He will cut him to pieces[K] and assign him a place with the hypocrites. In that place there will be weeping and gnashing of teeth.

The Parable of the 10 Virgins

25 "Then the kingdom of heaven will be like 10 virgins[L] who took their lamps and went out to meet the groom.[y] [2]Five of them were foolish and five were sensible.[z] [3]When the foolish took their lamps, they didn't take olive oil with them. [4]But the sensible ones took oil in their flasks with their lamps. [5]Since the groom was delayed, they all became drowsy and fell asleep.

[6]"In the middle of the night there was a shout: 'Here's the groom! Come out to meet him.'

[7]"Then all those virgins got up and trimmed

[a]**24:23** Lk 17:3; 21:28 [b]Mk 11:24; Jn 6:64 [c]**24:24** Dt 13:1-3; Mt 24:11; Ac 8:9; 2Th 2:9-11; Rv 13:13-14; 16:14; 19:20 [d]**24:27** Zch 9:14; Mt 8:20; 24:3,37,39; Lk 17:24 [e]**24:28** Jb 39:30; Lk 17:37 [f]**24:29** Is 13:10; 24:23; Ezk 32:7; Jl 2:10,31; 3:15; Zph 1:15; Rv 6:12-13 [g]**24:30** Dn 7:13; Zch 12:12; Mt 24:3; Rv 1:7 [h]**24:31** Is 27:13; 1Co 15:52; 1Th 4:16; Rv 8:2; 11:15 [i]Dn 7:2; Zch 2:6; Rv 7:1 [j]**24:32** Mt 13:3,34-36; 15:15; 21:33,45; 22:1 [k]**24:33** Jms 5:9; Rv 3:20 [l]**24:34** Mt 10:23; 16:28; 23:36 [m]**24:35** Ps 102:26; Is 51:6; Mt 5:18; Heb 12:27; 2Pt 3:10 [n]Ps 119:89; Is 40:8; Mk 13:31; Lk 21:33; 1Pt 1:23,25 [o]**24:36** Zch 14:7; Mt 25:13; Mk 13:32; Ac 1:7; 1Th 5:1-2 [p]**24:37-38** Gn 6:5; 7:6-23; Mt 22:30; Lk 17:26 [q]**24:41** Ex 11:5; Is 47:2; Lk 17:35 [r]**24:42** Mt 25:13; Lk 12:40; 21:36 [s]**24:43** Lk 12:39; 1Th 5:2; Rv 3:3 [t]**24:44** Mt 25:10; 1Th 5:6 [u]**24:45-51** Lk 12:42-46 [v]**24:45** Mt 7:24; 10:16; 25:2,21 [w]**24:46** Jn 13:17; Rv 16:15 [x]**24:49** Ac 2:15; 1Co 11:21; 1Th 5:7; Rv 17:6 [y]**25:1** Mt 13:24; Ac 20:8; Rv 4:5; 19:7; 21:2,9 [z]**25:2** Mt 7:24; 10:16; 24:45

[A]**24:24** Or *False christs* [B]**24:28** Or *eagles* [C]**24:30** Or *all the tribes of the land* [D]**24:30** Lit *will beat*; that is, beat their breasts [E]**24:33** Or *things, you know* [F]**24:33** Or *it*; that is, summer [G]**24:36** Other mss omit *nor the Son* [H]**24:39** They didn't know the day and hour of the coming judgment. [I]**24:42** Other mss read *hour*; = time [J]**24:43** Lit *watch*; a division of the night in ancient times [K]**24:51** Lit *him in two* [L]**25:1** Or *bridesmaids*

their lamps. 8 But the foolish ones said to the
sensible ones, 'Give us some of your oil, because our lamps are going out.'
9 "The sensible ones answered, 'No, there
won't be enough for us and for you. Go instead to those who sell, and buy oil for yourselves.'
10 "When they had gone to buy some, the
groom arrived. Then those who were ready
went in with him to the wedding banquet,
and the door was shut.[a]
11 "Later the rest of the virgins also came
and said, 'Master, master, open up for us!'
12 "But he replied, 'I assure you: I do not
know you!'
13 "Therefore be alert, because you don't
know either the day or the hour.[A]

The Parable of the Talents

14 "For it is just like a man going on a journey.[b] He called his own ˙slaves and turned
over his possessions to them. 15 To one he gave
five talents;[B] to another, two; and to another,
one — to each according to his own ability.
Then he went on a journey.[c] Immediately
16 the man who had received five talents went,
put them to work, and earned five more. 17 In
the same way the man with two earned two
more. 18 But the man who had received one
talent went off, dug a hole in the ground, and
hid his master's money.
19 "After a long time the master of those
slaves came and settled accounts with them.
20 The man who had received five talents approached, presented five more talents, and
said, 'Master, you gave me five talents. Look,
I've earned five more talents.'
21 "His master said to him, 'Well done, good
and faithful slave! You were faithful over a
few things; I will put you in charge of many
things. Share your master's joy!'[d]
22 "Then the man with two talents also approached. He said, 'Master, you gave me two
talents. Look, I've earned two more talents.'
23 "His master said to him, 'Well done, good
and faithful slave! You were faithful over a
few things; I will put you in charge of many
things. Share your master's joy!'
24 "Then the man who had received one tal-

[a]**25:10** Mt 22:2; Lk 13:25
[b]**25:14-30** Lk 19:12-27
[c]**25:15** Mt 18:24; Lk 19:13; Rm 12:6; 1Co 12:11; Eph 4:7
[d]**25:21** Mt 24:45,47; Lk 12:44; 22:28; Heb 12:2
[e]**25:24** 1Sm 25:3; 2Co 8:12
[f]**25:26** Pr 20:4; Mt 18:32; Rm 12:11
[g]**25:29** Mt 13:12; Mk 4:25; Lk 8:18; 19:26; Jn 15:2
[h]**25:30** Mt 8:12; 22:13; Lk 13:28
[i]**25:31** Gn 16:7; Mt 5:34; 13:49; Lk 1:11; Ac 5:19; Rv 14:6
[j]Mt 16:27; 19:28; 2Th 1:7; Jd 14; Rv 1:7
[k]**25:32** Jl 3:12; Mt 24:14; 28:19; Rm 1:5; Gl 1:16
[l]Ezk 34:17,20; Mt 13:49
[m]**25:34** Mt 19:29; Lk 12:32; 1Co 15:50; Gl 5:21; Jms 2:5; 1Pt 3:9; Rv 21:7
[n]Mt 13:35; 20:23; 1Co 2:9; Heb 4:3; 9:26; 11:16; Rv 13:8; 17:8
[o]**25:35-36** Jb 31:32; Is 58:7; Ezk 18:7; 2Tm 1:16; Heb 13:2; Jms 1:27; 2:15-16

ent also approached and said, 'Master, I know
you. You're a difficult man, reaping where
you haven't sown and gathering where you
haven't scattered seed.[e] 25 So I was afraid and
went off and hid your talent in the ground.
Look, you have what is yours.'
26 "But his master replied to him, 'You evil,
lazy slave![f] If you knew that I reap where
I haven't sown and gather where I haven't
scattered, 27 then[C] you should have deposited my money with the bankers. And when
I returned I would have received my money[D]
back with interest.
28 " 'So take the talent from him and give
it to the one who has 10 talents. 29 For to everyone who has, more will be given, and he
will have more than enough. But from the
one who does not have, even what he has will
be taken away from him.[g] 30 And throw this
good-for-nothing slave into the outer darkness.[h] In that place there will be weeping and
gnashing of teeth.'

The Sheep and the Goats

31 "When the ˙Son of Man comes in His
glory, and all the angels[E,i] with Him, then He
will sit on the throne of His glory.[j] 32 All the
nations[F,k] will be gathered before Him, and
He will separate them one from another, just
as a shepherd separates the sheep from the
goats.[l] 33 He will put the sheep on His right
and the goats on the left. 34 Then the King will
say to those on His right, 'Come, you who are
blessed by My Father, inherit the kingdom[m]
prepared for you from the foundation of the
world.[n]

35 For I was hungry
and you gave Me something to eat;
I was thirsty
and you gave Me something to drink;
I was a stranger and you took Me in;
36 I was naked and you clothed Me;
I was sick and you took care of Me;
I was in prison and you visited Me.'[o]

37 "Then the righteous will answer Him,
'Lord, when did we see You hungry and feed
You, or thirsty and give You something to
drink? 38 When did we see You a stranger and

[A]**25:13** Other mss add *in which the Son of Man is coming.* [B]**25:15** Worth a very large sum of money; a talent = 6,000 ˙denarii [C]**25:26-27** Or *So you knew . . . scattered? Then* (as a question) [D]**25:27** Lit *received what is mine* [E]**25:31** Other mss read *holy angels* [F]**25:32** Or *the Gentiles* take You in, or without clothes and clothe You? 39When did we see You sick, or in prison, and visit You?'

40"And the King will answer them, 'I assure you: Whatever you did for one of the least of these ·brothers of Mine, you did for Me.'[a] 41Then He will also say to those on the left, 'Depart from Me, you who are cursed, into the eternal fire prepared for the Devil and his angels![b]

42 For I was hungry
and you gave Me nothing to eat;
I was thirsty
and you gave Me nothing to drink;
43 I was a stranger
and you didn't take Me in;
I was naked
and you didn't clothe Me,
sick and in prison
and you didn't take care of Me.'

44"Then they too will answer, 'Lord, when did we see You hungry, or thirsty, or a stranger, or without clothes, or sick, or in prison, and not help You?'

45"Then He will answer them, 'I assure you: Whatever you did not do for one of the least of these, you did not do for Me either.'[c]

46"And they will go away into eternal punishment, but the righteous into eternal life."[d]

The Plot to Kill Jesus

26 When Jesus had finished saying all this,[e] He told His disciples, 2"You know[A] that the ·Passover takes place after two days, and the ·Son of Man will be handed over to be crucified."[f]

3Then the ·chief priests[B] and the elders of the people assembled in the palace of the high priest, who was called Caiaphas,[g] 4and they conspired to arrest Jesus in a treacherous way and kill Him.[h] 5"Not during the festival," they said, "so there won't be rioting among the people."

The Anointing at Bethany

6While Jesus was in Bethany at the house of Simon,[i] a man who had a serious skin disease, 7a woman approached Him with an alabaster jar of very expensive fragrant oil. She poured it on His head as He was reclining at the table. 8When the disciples[j] saw it, they were indignant. "Why this waste?" they asked. 9"This might have been sold for a great deal and given to the poor."

10But Jesus, aware of this, said to them, "Why are you bothering this woman? She has done a noble thing for Me. 11You always have the poor with you, but you do not always have Me.[k] 12By pouring this fragrant oil on My body, she has prepared Me for burial. 13·I assure you: Wherever this gospel[l] is proclaimed in the whole world, what this woman has done will also be told in memory of her."

14Then[m] one of the Twelve—the man called Judas Iscariot—went to the chief priests[n] 15and said, "What are you willing to give me if I hand Him over to you?" So they weighed out 30 pieces of silver for him.[o] 16And from that time he started looking for a good opportunity to betray Him.

Betrayal at the Passover

17On the first day of ·Unleavened Bread[p] the disciples came to Jesus and asked, "Where do You want us to prepare the Passover so You may eat it?"

18"Go into the city to a certain man," He said, "and tell him, 'The Teacher says: My time is near; I am celebrating the Passover at your place[C] with My disciples.'"[q] 19So the disciples did as Jesus had directed them and prepared the Passover. 20When evening came, He was reclining at the table with the Twelve. 21While they were eating, He said, "I assure you: One of you will betray Me."[r]

22Deeply distressed, each one began to say to Him, "Surely not I, Lord?"

23He replied, "The one who dipped his hand with Me in the bowl—he will betray Me. 24The Son of Man will go just as it is written about Him,[s] but woe to that man by whom the Son of Man is betrayed! It would have been better for that man if he had not been born."

25Then Judas, His betrayer, replied, "Surely not I, ·Rabbi?"[t]

"You have said it," He told him.

[a]**25:40** Pr 19:17; Mt 10:42; 25:34; Heb 6:10
[b]**25:41** Mt 7:23; 13:40,42; Mk 9:48; 2Pt 2:4; Jd 6-7
[c]**25:45** Pr 14:31; 17:5; Ac 9:5
[d]**25:46** Dn 12:2; Jn 5:21; Ac 24:15; Rm 2:7
[e]**26:1-5** Mk 14:1-2; Lk 22:1-2; Jn 11:47-53
[f]**26:2** Jn 11:55; 13:1
[g]**26:3** Ps 2:2; Mt 26:57; Lk 3:2; Jn 11:47; 18:13,15; Ac 4:6
[h]**26:4** Mt 21:46; Jn 11:53
[i]**26:6-13** Mk 14:3-9; Jn 12:1-8
[j]**26:8** Mt 10:1; 26:56; Mk 3:7; 16:20; Lk 6:13; Jn 12:16
[k]**26:11** Dt 15:11; Jn 12:8
[l]**26:13** Mt 24:14; Mk 1:1; 13:10
[m]**26:14-16** Mk 14:10-11; Lk 22:3-6
[n]**26:14** Mt 10:4; Jn 6:71; 12:4; 13:30; Ac 1:16
[o]**26:15** Ex 21:32; Zch 11:12-13; Mt 27:3
[p]**26:17-19** Mk 14:12-16; Lk 22:7-13
[q]**26:18** Jn 7:6,8; 8:20; 13:1; 17:1
[r]**26:21-24** Mk 14:17-21; Lk 22:21-23; Jn 13:21-26
[s]**26:24** Dn 9:26; Mk 9:12; Lk 24:25-27; Ac 17:2-3; 26:22-23; 1Co 15:3; 1Pt 1:10
[t]**26:25** Lk 22:70; Jn 1:38

[A]**26:2** Or *Know* (as a command) [B]**26:3** Other mss add *and the scribes* [C]**26:18** Lit *Passover with you*

The First Lord's Supper

26As they were eating,[a] Jesus took bread,
blessed and broke it, gave it to the disciples,[b]
and said, "Take and eat it; this is My body."[c]
27Then He took a cup, and after giving thanks,
He gave it to them and said, "Drink from it,
all of you. 28For this is My blood that establishes the covenant;[A] it is shed for many for
the forgiveness of sins.[d] 29But I tell you, from
this moment I will not drink of this fruit of
the vine until that day when I drink it in a
new way[B] in My Father's kingdom[e] with you."
30After singing psalms,[C] they went out to the
·Mount of Olives.[f]

Peter's Denial Predicted

31Then Jesus said to them, "Tonight all of
you will run away[D] because of Me, for it is
written:

I will strike the shepherd,
and the sheep of the flock
will be scattered.[E,g]

32But after I have been resurrected, I will go
ahead of you to Galilee."[h]
33Peter told Him, "Even if everyone runs
away because of You, I will never run away!"
34"I assure you," Jesus said to him, "tonight,
before the rooster crows, you will deny Me
three times!"[i]
35"Even if I have to die with You," Peter told
Him, "I will never deny You!" And all the disciples said the same thing.

The Prayer in the Garden

36Then Jesus came with them to a place
called Gethsemane,[F,j] and He told the disciples, "Sit here while I go over there and pray."
37Taking along Peter and the two sons of Zebedee, He began to be sorrowful and deeply
distressed.[k] 38Then He said to them, "My soul
is swallowed up in sorrow[G]—to the point
of death.[H] Remain here and stay awake with
Me."[l] 39Going a little farther,[I] He fell facedown and prayed, "My Father! If it is possible,
let this cup pass from Me. Yet not as I will, but
as You will."[m]

[a]**26:26-29** Mk 14:22-25; Lk 22:17-20: 1Co 11:23-25
[b]**26:26** Mt 10:1; 26:56; Mk 3:7; 16:20; Lk 6:13; Jn 12:16
[c]Mt 14:19; 1Co 10:16
[d]**26:28** Ex 24:8; Mt 20:28; Mk 1:4; Heb 9:20
[e]**26:29** Mt 4:23; Mk 1:15; Ac 20:25
[f]**26:30** Mt 21:1; Lk 22:39; Jn 18:1
[g]**26:31** Zch 13:7; Mt 11:6; Jn 16:32
[h]**26:32** Mt 28:7,10,16; Mk 16:7
[i]**26:34** Mt 26:75; Lk 22:34; Jn 13:38
[j]**26:36-46** Mk 14:32-42; Lk 22:40-46
[k]**26:37** Mt 4:21; 17:1
[l]**26:38** Ps 42:5-6; Mt 24:42; Jn 12:27
[m]**26:39** Mt 20:22; Jn 5:30; 6:38; Php 2:8; Heb 5:7
[n]**26:42** Mt 26:39; Mk 14:36; Lk 22:42; Jn 6:38
[o]**26:45** Jn 12:27; 13:1
[p]**26:47-56** Mk 14:43-50; Lk 22:47-53; Jn 18:3-11
[q]**26:50** Mt 20:13; 22:12
[r]**26:51** Lk 22:38; Jn 18:10
[s]**26:52** Gn 9:6; Rv 13:10
[t]**26:53** 2Kg 6:17; Dn 7:10; Mt 4:11; Lk 8:30
[u]**26:54** Mt 1:22; 26:24

40Then He came to the disciples and found
them sleeping. He asked Peter, "So, couldn't
you[J] stay awake with Me one hour? 41Stay
awake and pray, so that you won't enter into
temptation. The spirit is willing, but the flesh
is weak."
42Again, a second time, He went away and
prayed, "My Father, if this[K] cannot pass[L] unless I drink it, Your will be done."[n] 43And He
came again and found them sleeping, because they could not keep their eyes open.[M]
44After leaving them, He went away again
and prayed a third time, saying the same
thing once more. 45Then He came to the disciples and said to them, "Are you still sleeping and resting?[N] Look, the time is near. The
Son of Man is being betrayed into the hands
of sinners.[o] 46Get up; let's go! See, My betrayer
is near."

The Judas Kiss

47While He was still speaking, Judas, one of
the Twelve, suddenly arrived.[p] A large mob,
with swords and clubs, was with him from
the chief priests and elders of the people.
48His betrayer had given them a sign: "The
One I kiss, He's the One; arrest Him!" 49So he
went right up to Jesus and said, "Greetings,
Rabbi!" and kissed Him.
50"Friend,"[q] Jesus asked him, "why have you
come?"[O]
Then they came up, took hold of Jesus, and
arrested Him. 51At that moment one of those
with Jesus reached out his hand and drew his
sword. He struck the high priest's ·slave and
cut off his ear.[r]
52Then Jesus told him, "Put your sword back
in its place because all who take up a sword
will perish by a sword.[s] 53Or do you think that
I cannot call on My Father, and He will provide Me at once with more than 12 legions[P] of
angels?[t] 54How, then, would the Scriptures be
fulfilled[u] that say it must happen this way?"
55At that time Jesus said to the crowds,
"Have you come out with swords and clubs,
as if I were a criminal,[Q] to capture Me? Every

[A]**26:28** Other mss read *new covenant* [B]**26:29** Or *drink new wine*; lit *drink it new* [C]**26:30** Pss 113–118 were sung during and after the Passover meal. [D]**26:31** Or ·*stumble* [E]**26:31** Zch 13:7 [F]**26:36** A garden east of Jerusalem at the base of the Mount of Olives; Gethsemane = olive oil press [G]**26:38** Or *I am deeply grieved*, or *I am overwhelmed by sorrow*; Ps 42:6,11; 43:5 [H]**26:38** Lit *unto death* [I]**26:39** Other mss read *Drawing nearer* [J]**26:40** = all 3 disciples because the verb in Gk is pl [K]**26:42** Other mss add *cup* [L]**26:42** Other mss add *from Me* [M]**26:43** Lit *because their eyes were weighed down* [N]**26:45** Or *Sleep on now and take your rest.* [O]**26:50** Or *Jesus told him, "do what you have come for."* (as a statement) [P]**26:53** A Roman legion contained up to 6,000 soldiers. [Q]**26:55** Lit *as against a criminal*

day I used to sit, teaching in the •temple complex, and you didn't arrest Me.[a] 56 But all this
has happened so that the prophetic Scriptures[A,b] would be fulfilled." Then all the disciples[c] deserted Him and ran away.

Jesus Faces the Sanhedrin

57 Those[d] who had arrested Jesus led Him
away to Caiaphas[e] the high priest, where the
•scribes and the elders had convened. 58 Meanwhile, Peter was following Him at a distance
right to the high priest's courtyard.[B] He went
in and was sitting with the temple police[C] to
see the outcome.[D,f]

59 The chief priests and the whole •Sanhe-
drin were looking for false testimony against
Jesus so they could put Him to death.[g] 60 But
they could not find any, even though many
false witnesses[h] came forward.[E] Finally, two[F]
who came forward 61 stated, "This man said, 'I
can demolish God's sanctuary[i] and rebuild it
in three days.'"

62 The high priest then stood up and said
to Him, "Don't You have an answer to what
these men are testifying against You?" 63 But[j]
Jesus kept silent.[k] Then the high priest said
to Him, "By the living God I place You under
oath:[l] tell us if You are the •Messiah, the Son
of God!"[m]

64 "You have said it,"[G] Jesus told him. "But
I tell you, in the future[H] you will see **the Son
of Man seated at the right hand** of the Power
and **coming on the clouds of heaven**."[I,n]

65 Then the high priest tore his robes and
said, "He has blasphemed![o] Why do we still
need witnesses? Look, now you've heard the
blasphemy![p] 66 What is your decision?"[J]

They answered, "He deserves death!"[q]
67 Then they spit in His face[r] and beat Him;
others slapped Him 68 and said, "Prophesy to
us, Messiah! Who hit You?"[s]

Peter Denies His Lord

69 Now Peter was sitting outside in the courtyard.[t] A servant approached him and she said,
"You were with Jesus the Galilean too."

70 But he denied it in front of everyone: "I
don't know what you're talking about!"

71 When he had gone out to the gateway, another woman saw him and told those who
were there, "This man was with Jesus the
•Nazarene!"[u]

72 And again he denied it with an oath,[v] "I
don't know the man!"

73 After a little while those standing there
approached and said to Peter, "You certainly
are one of them, since even your accent[K] gives
you away."

74 Then he started to curse[L] and to swear
with an oath, "I do not know the man!" Immediately a rooster crowed, 75 and Peter remembered the words Jesus had spoken,
"Before the rooster crows, you will deny Me
three times."[w] And he went outside and wept
bitterly.

Jesus Handed Over to Pilate

27 When daybreak came, all the •chief
priests and the elders of the people
plotted against Jesus to put Him to death.[x]
2 After tying Him up, they led Him away and
handed Him over to •Pilate,[M] the governor.[y]

Judas Hangs Himself

3 Then Judas, His betrayer, seeing that He
had been condemned, was full of remorse
and returned the 30 pieces of silver to the
chief priests and elders.[z] 4 "I have sinned by
betraying innocent blood," he said.

"What's that to us?" they said. "See to it
yourself!"

5 So he threw the silver into the sanctuary[aa]
and departed. Then he went and hanged himself.

6 The chief priests took the silver and said,
"It's not lawful[ab] to put it into the temple treasury,[N] since it is blood money."[O] 7 So they conferred together and bought the potter's field
with it as a burial place for foreigners. 8 Therefore that field has been called "Blood Field" to
this day. 9 Then what was spoken through the
prophet Jeremiah was fulfilled:

> **They took the 30 pieces of silver, the
> price of Him whose price was set by the**

[a]26:55 Mk 12:35; Lk 21:37; Jn 7:19; 8:2; 18:20 [b]26:56 Mt 26:54; Rm 1:2; 2Pt 1:20 [c]Mt 10:1; 26:56; Mk 3:7; 16:20; Lk 6:13; Jn 12:16 [d]26:57-68 Mk 14:53-65; Jn 18:12-13,19-24 [e]26:57 Mt 26:3; Jn 11:49 [f]26:58 Jn 7:32; 18:15 [g]26:59 Mt 5:22; Ac 6:11 [h]26:60 Dt 19:15; Ps 27:12; 35:11; Ac 6:13 [i]26:61 Mt 27:40; Jn 2:19; Ac 6:14 [j]26:63-66 Lk 22:67-71 [k]26:63 Is 53:7; Mt 27:12,14; Jn 19:9 [l]Lv 19:12; Nm 30:2; Dt 23:21; Mt 5:33; 14:7; 23:16 [m]Lv 5:1; 1Sm 14:24,26; Mt 16:16 [n]26:64 Ps 110:1; Dn 7:13; Mt 16:27; 24:30; Rv 1:7 [o]26:65 Mk 3:29; Jn 10:33 [p]Nm 14:6; Mk 14:63; Ac 14:14 [q]26:66 Lv 24:16; Jn 19:7 [r]26:67 Mt 27:30; Mk 10:34; Lk 22:63-65; Jn 18:22 [s]26:68 Mk 14:65; Lk 22:64 [t]26:69-75 Mk 14:66-72; Lk 22:55-62; Jn 18:16-18,25-27 [u]26:71 Mk 14:67; Ac 6:14 [v]26:72 Lv 19:12; Nm 30:2; Dt 23:21; Mt 5:33; 14:7; 23:16 [w]26:75 Mt 26:34; Jn 13:38; Ac 3:13-14 [x]27:1 Mk 15:1; Lk 22:66; Jn 18:28 [y]27:2 Mt 20:19; Lk 13:1; Ac 3:13; 1Tm 6:13 [z]27:3 Mt 21:29; 26:14-15 [aa]27:5 2Sm 17:23; Lk 1:19,21; Ac 1:18 [ab]27:6 Mk 2:24; Jn 18:31

[A]26:56 Or *the Scriptures of the prophets* [B]26:58 Or *high priest's palace* [C]26:58 Or *the officers*, or *the servants* [D]26:58 Lit *end* [E]26:60 Other mss add *they found none* [F]26:60 Other mss add *false witnesses* [G]26:64 Or *That is true*, an affirmative oath; Mt 27:11; Mk 15:2 [H]26:64 Lit *you, from now* [I]26:64 Ps 110:1; Dn 7:13 [J]26:66 Lit *What does it seem to you?* [K]26:73 Or *speech* [L]26:74 To call down curses on himself if what he said weren't true [M]27:2 Other mss read *Pontius Pilate* [N]27:6 See Mk 7:11 where the same Gk word (*Corban*) means a gift pledged to the temple. [O]27:6 Lit *the price of blood*

Israelites, 10and they gave them for the potter's field, as the Lord directed me.[A,a]

Jesus Faces the Governor

11Now Jesus stood before the governor.[b] "Are You the King of the Jews?" the governor asked Him.

Jesus answered, "You have said it."[B,c] 12And while He was being accused by the chief priests and elders, He didn't answer.[d]

13Then Pilate said to Him, "Don't You hear how much they are testifying against You?" 14But He didn't answer him on even one charge, so that the governor was greatly amazed.[e]

Jesus or Barabbas

15At the festival[f] the governor's custom was to release to the crowd a prisoner they wanted. 16At that time they had a notorious prisoner called Barabbas.[C] 17So when they had gathered together, Pilate said to them, "Who is it you want me to release for you — Barabbas,[C] or Jesus who is called ˙Messiah?"[g] 18For he knew they had handed Him over because of envy.

19While he was sitting on the judge's bench, his wife sent word to him, "Have nothing to do with that righteous man, for today I've suffered terribly in a dream because of Him!"[h]

20The chief priests and the elders, however, persuaded the crowds to ask for Barabbas and to execute Jesus. 21The governor asked them, "Which of the two do you want me to release for you?"

"Barabbas!" they answered.

22Pilate asked them, "What should I do then with Jesus, who is called Messiah?"

They all answered, "Crucify Him!"[D,i]

23Then he said, "Why? What has He done wrong?"

But they kept shouting, "Crucify Him!" all the more.[j]

24When Pilate saw that he was getting nowhere,[E] but that a riot was starting instead, he took some water, washed his hands in front of the crowd, and said, "I am innocent of this man's blood.[F] See to it yourselves!"[k]

25All the people answered, "His blood be on us[l] and on our children!" 26Then he released Barabbas to them. But after having Jesus flogged,[G] he handed Him over to be crucified.[m]

Mocked by the Military

27Then[n] the governor's soldiers took Jesus into ˙headquarters and gathered the whole ˙company around Him.[o] 28They stripped Him and dressed Him in a scarlet military robe.[p] 29They twisted together a crown of thorns, put it on His head, and placed a reed in His right hand. And they knelt down before Him and mocked Him: "Hail, King of the Jews!" 30Then they spit on Him, took the reed, and kept hitting Him on the head. 31When they had mocked Him, they stripped Him of the robe, put His clothes on Him, and led Him away to crucify Him.[q]

Crucified Between Two Criminals

32As they were going out, they found a Cyrenian man named Simon. They forced this man to carry His cross.[r] 33When they came to a place called *Golgotha*[s] (which means Skull Place), 34they gave Him wine[H] mixed with gall to drink. But when He tasted it, He would not drink it. 35After crucifying Him they divided His clothes by casting lots.[I,t] 36Then they sat down and were guarding Him there. 37Above His head they put up the charge against Him in writing:

THIS IS JESUS
THE KING OF THE JEWS.

38Then two criminals[J] were crucified with Him, one on the right and one on the left.[u] 39Those who passed by were yelling insults at[K] Him, shaking their heads[v] 40and saying, "The One who would demolish the sanctuary and rebuild it in three days, save Yourself! If You are the Son of God, come down from the cross!"[w] 41In the same way the chief priests, with the ˙scribes and elders,[L] mocked Him and said, 42"He saved others, but He cannot save Himself! He is the King of Israel![X] Let

*a*27:9-10 Jr 32:6-9; Zch 11:12-13; Mt 1:22
*b*27:11-14 Mk 15:2-5; Lk 23:2-3; Jn 18:29-38
*c*27:11 Mt 2:2; 1Tm 6:13
*d*27:12 Mt 26:63; Jn 19:9
*e*27:14 Mk 15:5; Lk 23:9
*f*27:15-26 Mk 15:6-15; Lk 23:16-25; Jn 18:39-40; 19:16
*g*27:17 Mt 1:16; 27:22
*h*27:19 Gn 20:6; Nm 12:6; Jb 33:14-16; Mt 2:12; Jn 19:13
*i*27:22 Mt 1:16; Ac 13:28
*j*27:23 Lk 23:41; Jn 8:46
*k*27:24 Dt 21:6-8; Ps 26:6; Mt 26:5; 27:4,19
*l*27:25 Jos 2:19; Ac 5:28
*m*27:26 Is 53:5; Mk 15:15; Lk 23:16; Jn 19:1
*n*27:27-31 Mk 15:16-20; Jn 19:2-3
*o*27:27 Jn 18:28,33; 19:9; Ac 10:1
*p*27:28 Lk 23:11; Jn 19:2
*q*27:30-31 Is 53:7; Mt 26:67
*r*27:32 Nm 15:35; Mk 15:21; Lk 23:26; Heb 13:12
*s*27:33-44 Mk 15:22-32; Lk 23:33-43; Jn 19:17-24
*t*27:34-35 Ps 22:17; 69:21
*u*27:38 Is 53:12; Mt 20:21; Jn 18:40
*v*27:39 Jb 16:4; Ps 22:7; 109:25; Lm 2:15; Mk 15:29
*w*27:40 Mt 4:3,6; 26:61,63; Jn 2:19
*x*27:42 Jn 1:49; 12:13

A27:9-10 Jr 32:6-9; Zch 11:12-13 B27:11 Or *That is true*, an affirmative oath; Mt 26:64; Mk 15:2 C27:16,17 Other mss read *Jesus Barabbas* D27:22 Lit *"Him — be crucified!"* E27:24 Lit *that it availed nothing* F27:24 Other mss read *this righteous man's blood* G27:26 Roman flogging was done with a whip made of leather strips embedded with pieces of bone or metal that brutally tore the flesh. H27:34 Other mss read *sour wine* I27:35 Other mss add *that what was spoken by the prophet might be fulfilled: "They divided My clothes among them, and for My clothing they cast lots."* J27:38 Or *revolutionaries* K27:39 Lit *passed by blasphemed* or *were blaspheming* L27:41 Other mss add *and Pharisees*

Resurrection

Adrian Warnock

The word "mission" is derived from the Latin word *missio,* which means "sending forth." Thus, the first question we should ask when we think about being on a mission is: who sent us? In the closing verses of Matthew 28, the risen Jesus Himself gave the Great Commission to the 12 disciples and told them to enlist others in the task. But what did Jesus send the disciples to proclaim? The sermons recorded in the book of Acts have a single key message: the resurrection of Jesus. Sermon after sermon declares that all the benefits of our salvation flow to us because Jesus rose again.

Belief in Jesus' bodily resurrection has always been a distinguishing mark of groups who claim to be Christian. Christians of all denominations agree: Jesus died, rose again, and now reigns over all creation.

The early Christians had a simple mission strategy. They would enter a town and proclaim, in essence: "Jesus has risen from the dead and demands your obedience." They would then discuss the implications of this truth with their hearers. They always got a response. Some would believe on the spot, others would want to hear more, and some hated them, wishing them dead. If we told people today that we genuinely believe that Jesus is alive, we might well receive the same varied responses. Yet, it seems easier to debate the existence of God with people.

We must not omit the message of the resurrection from our preaching and witnessing in order to make it more acceptable to today's culture. People find it difficult to believe such a miracle, but the first century world found it equally impossible to comprehend. Outside of Judaism, no one believed in resurrection. The OT reveals enough about resurrection that the Pharisees believed that there would be a bodily resurrection on the final day, but others, such as the Sadducees, could not accept this.

Only three resurrections are recorded in the entire OT. Furthermore, they are fundamentally different from what happened to Jesus since the people who were raised eventually died again, whereas Jesus rose again with a body that could never die. Very few people have ever witnessed a resurrection. No wonder then that only the supernatural power of the Holy Spirit working in our lives can enable us to believe in something that seems so astonishing.

There is an inherent power in the message we find in the first few verses of Matthew 28. Read the words slowly, meditating on how the women would have felt knowing that Jesus was dead. Imagine the depth of their sorrow and despair. Picture the extent of their love for Jesus, which compelled them to get up as early as possible to anoint His lifeless body. Consider their shock when the angel told them "He is not here, for He has risen." Realize afresh the intensity of their joy when they saw Jesus Himself, alive once more.

It is remarkable that, despite the testimonies of women being not generally accepted in Jesus' times, He chose to reveal Himself first to these women. It is a strong argument for the genuineness of the account since no one would have invented a story with women as the initial witnesses. Jesus even appointed them as the first messengers of the good news of His resurrection. This is the task of every follower of Jesus.

Some Christians today emphasize only the cross in their proclamation of the good news. The resurrection is often assumed and neglected. Many gospel presentations speak of sin, death, and punishment, but if we leave Jesus on the cross or in the grave, what hope do we have? His death is not good news without His resurrection.

If you need convincing that Jesus' resurrection stands at the very heart of the gospel, ask yourself whether the Church would exist if Jesus had remained in the tomb? Imagine the 12

disciples, most of whom were poorly educated fisherman, suddenly plucking up the courage to start the biggest and fastest-growing movement the world has ever seen. They had just run away to escape being killed with their leader. Nothing other than Him appearing alive could empower them to defy the Jewish and Roman leaders and declare, "Christ is risen!"

We would have no good news if the life of our prophet and great leader had permanently ended on a Roman cross. Paul tells is in 1 Corinthians 15:17 that we would still be in our sins if Jesus had not been raised. It is through His resurrection that we are justified (Rm 4:25).

Christians experience the new birth by the same power that raised Jesus. This is a foretaste of our future, physical resurrection. "He has given us a new birth into a living hope through the resurrection of Jesus Christ from the dead" (1Pt 1:3). We have been made spiritually alive. Paul regularly prayed that his readers would be filled with the same Holy Spirit who raised Jesus.

Because Jesus was raised, we also can have hope that one day we too will be raised. There is no valid Christian faith without the hope of a real, physical, literal reunion with both our Savior and our loved ones who have already died "in Christ." We will meet again. With our own eyes, we will see both each other and the one who loved us so much that He lived a perfect life among us and then died and rose again for us. Jesus' resurrection is also the first act of the new creation. The universe itself will one day similarly be renewed.

This is such a glorious message that we must never be apologetic or timid about it! Death has been conquered. We need not fear the one thing that every human being dreads to even think or speak of. We have the solution to the biggest problem people face today: our own impending deaths. Because of Jesus, we can live forever!

Him[A] come down now from the cross, and we
will believe in Him. 43 He has put His trust in
God; let God rescue Him now — if He wants
Him![B] For He said, 'I am God's Son.'" 44 In the
same way even the criminals who were crucified with Him kept taunting Him.[a]

The Death of Jesus

45 From noon until three in the afternoon[C]
darkness came over the whole land.[D,b] 46 About
three in the afternoon Jesus cried out with a
loud voice, ***"Elí, Elí, lemá*[E] *sabachtháni?"*** that
is, **"My God, My God, why have You forsaken**[F]
Me?"[G,c]
47 When some of those standing there heard
this, they said, "He's calling for Elijah!"
48 Immediately one of them ran and got a
sponge, filled it with sour wine, fixed it on a
reed, and offered Him a drink.[d] 49 But the rest
said, "Let's see if Elijah comes to save Him!"
50 Jesus shouted again with a loud voice and
gave up His spirit.[e] 51 Suddenly, the curtain of
the sanctuary[H,f] was split in two from top to
bottom; the earth quaked and the rocks were
split. 52 The tombs were also opened[g] and
many bodies of the ˙saints who had fallen
˙asleep were raised. 53 And they came out of
the tombs after His resurrection, entered the
holy city, and appeared to many.
54 When the ˙centurion and those with him,
who were guarding Jesus, saw the earthquake
and the things that had happened, they were terrified and said, "This man really was God's Son!"[I,h]
55 Many women who had followed Jesus
from Galilee and ministered to Him were
there, looking on from a distance.[i] 56 Among
them were ˙Mary Magdalene, Mary the
mother of James and Joseph, and the mother
of Zebedee's sons.[j]

The Burial of Jesus

57 When it was evening,[k] a rich man from
Arimathea named Joseph came, who himself had also become a disciple[l] of Jesus. 58 He

[a]27:43-44 Ps 22:8; Lk 23:39-43
[b]27:45-56 Mk 15:33-41; Lk 23:44-49; Jn 19:28-30
[c]27:46 Ps 22:1; Heb 5:7
[d]27:48 Ps 69:21; Mk 15:36; Lk 23:36; Jn 19:29
[e]27:50 Mk 15:37; Lk 23:46; Jn 10:18; 19:30
[f]27:51 Ex 26:31-33; 2Ch 3:14; Heb 9:3
[g]27:52 Ezk 37:12
[h]27:54 Jn 5:19; Heb 1:2
[i]27:55 Ps 38:11; Lk 8:2-3; Jn 19:25
[j]27:56 Mt 20:20; Mk 15:40; Jn 19:25
[k]27:57-61 Mk 15:42-47; Lk 23:50-56; Jn 19:38-42
[l]27:57 Mt 10:42; 28:19; Lk 14:26; Jn 8:31; 13:35; 15:8; Ac 6:1

[A]27:42 Other mss read *If He . . . Israel, let Him* [B]27:43 Or *if He takes pleasure in Him* [C]27:45 Lit *From the sixth hour to the ninth hour* [D]27:45 Or *whole earth* [E]27:46 Some mss read *lama*; other mss read *lima* [F]27:46 Or *abandoned* [G]27:46 Ps 22:1 [H]27:51 A heavy curtain separated the inner room of the temple from the outer. [I]27:54 Or *the Son of God*

approached Pilate and asked for Jesus' body. Then Pilate ordered that it[A] be released. [59]So Joseph took the body, wrapped it in ·clean, fine linen, [60]and placed it in his new tomb, which he had cut into the rock. He left after rolling a great stone against the entrance of the tomb.[a] [61]Mary Magdalene and the other Mary were seated there, facing the tomb.

[a]27:60 Is 53:9; Mt 27:66; 28:2; Mk 16:4

The Closely Guarded Tomb

[62]The next day, which followed the preparation day, the chief priests and the ·Phari-

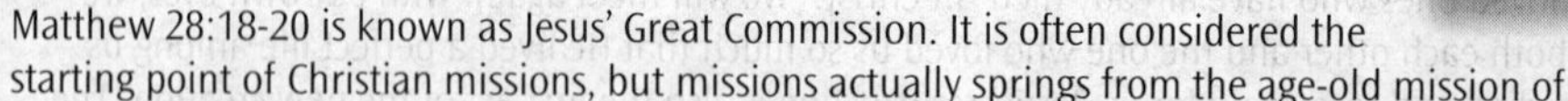

The Mission of God and Missions in the Church

Michael Pocock

Matthew 28:18-20 is known as Jesus' Great Commission. It is often considered the starting point of Christian missions, but missions actually springs from the age-old mission of God.

God has always had a missionary purpose. Missions thinkers and theologians have called this the *Missio Dei*, literally "the sending of God," or the purposeful program of God. He always had the object of making Himself known, glorifying Himself and blessing all peoples of the world, which He would do through His own people (Gn 12:1-3; Ps 19:1-4). When Jesus gave the Great Commission in Matthew 28:18-20, He actually restated what God had always wanted.

Jesus is God, a member of the Trinity. He has the same character, objectives, and authority as His Father. When Jesus gave this order to make disciples of all the peoples of the world, it must have seemed an incredible challenge. But Jesus says in verse 18: "All authority has been given to Me in heaven and on earth. Go, therefore, ..." Missions is the organized effort to do what Jesus commands here; it is not our idea or our project, it is God's. We are privileged to share in it.

The Great Commission was given to the Apostles, who in turn were to teach everyone who accepted their Gospel to do everything Jesus had told them to do (v. 20). This certainly included this last thing He commanded! Because the Apostles were the foundation of the Church (Eph 2:20), the orders given to them apply to the whole church.

What did Jesus command in Matthew 28:18-20? They were to "make disciples" (v.19). They were to do this in three ways: by going, by baptizing, and by teaching. They were to move out beyond their own people and comfort zone to reach others with the Gospel. They were to baptize everyone who believed, and do it in the name of the Father, the Son, and the Holy Spirit. The Gospel and salvation through Jesus was flowing out of the Trinity, and in line with the ages-old mission of God. God is a missionary God, so it makes sense that Jesus would send His followers in the church just as He had been sent. Baptism is a declaration or sign that new believers have fully identified with Christ.

The Apostles were to make disciples among all peoples. (That's over 9,000 language groups and a total of about 16,000 distinct peoples!) Jesus' Great Commission must have seemed close to impossible to the Apostles, but Jesus assured them in this text that He would accompany them everywhere they went until the whole task was finished. Elsewhere (Ac 1:8) Jesus told them they, and therefore the whole church, would have the ability to carry out His commission when the Holy Spirit came into them. The record in Acts and throughout history shows it can be done. People from every tribe, language, and nation will be around God's throne in the future—a picture of the completed task that Jesus gave the church to do (Rv 7:9).

[A]27:58 Other mss read *that the body*

sees gathered before Pilate[a] 63 and said, "Sir, we remember that while this deceiver was still alive He said, 'After three days I will rise again.'[b] 64 Therefore give orders that the tomb be made secure until the third day. Otherwise, His disciples[c] may come, steal Him, and tell the people, 'He has been raised from the dead.' Then the last deception will be worse than the first."

65 "You have[A] a guard of soldiers,"[B] Pilate told them. "Go and make it as secure as you know how." 66 Then they went and made the tomb secure by sealing the stone and setting the guard.[C,d]

Resurrection Morning

28 After the Sabbath,[e] as the first day of the week was dawning, ·Mary Magdalene and the other Mary went to view the tomb. 2 Suddenly there was a violent earthquake, because an angel of the Lord descended from heaven and approached the tomb. He rolled back the stone and was sitting on it.[f] 3 His appearance was like lightning, and his robe was as white as snow.[g] 4 The guards were so shaken from fear of him that they became like dead men.

5 But the angel told the women, "Don't be afraid, because I know you are looking for Jesus who was crucified.[h] 6 He is not here! For He has been resurrected, just as He said. Come and see the place where He lay.[i] 7 Then go quickly and tell His disciples,[j] 'He has been raised from the dead. In fact, He is going ahead of you to Galilee; you will see Him there.' Listen, I have told you."[k]

8 So, departing quickly from the tomb with fear and great joy, they ran to tell His disciples the news. 9 Just then[D] Jesus met them and said, "Good morning!" They came up, took hold of His feet, and worshiped Him.[l] 10 Then Jesus told them, "Do not be afraid. Go and tell

[a] **27:62** Mk 15:42; Lk 23:54; Jn 19:14,31,42
[b] **27:63** Mt 16:21; 17:22-23; 20:19; Mk 8:31; 10:34; Lk 9:22; 18:33
[c] **27:64** Mt 10:1, 26:56; Mk 3:7; 16:20; Lk 6:13; Jn 12:16
[d] **27:66** Dn 6:17; Mt 28:2,11
[e] **28:1-8** Mk 16:1-8; Lk 24:1-10; Jn 20:1-8
[f] **28:2** Lk 24:4; Jn 20:12
[g] **28:3** Dn 7:9; 10:6; Mk 9:3; Jn 20:12; Ac 1:10
[h] **28:5** Mt 14:27; 28:10; Rv 1:17
[i] **28:6** Mt 12:40; 16:21; 27:63
[j] **28:7** Mt 10:1; 26:56; Mk 3:7; 16:20; Lk 6:13; Jn 12:16
[k] Mt 26:32; Mk 16:7
[l] **28:9** Mk 16:9; Jn 20:14

GOD'S HEART FOR THE WORLD

Go Therefore

Then Jesus came near and said to them, "All authority has been given to Me in heaven and on earth. Go, therefore, and make disciples of all nations baptizing them in the name of the Father and of the Son and of the Holy Spirit, teaching them to observe everything I have commanded you. And remember, I am with you always, to the end of the age." (Matthew 28:18-20)

God is not confused about who we are. While He delights to use people to do His work in the world, He remembers our weakness. He is not surprised when we make mistakes or when we fall into sin, and He does not expect us to fulfill His mission out of our own strength. The promise that Jesus will be with us is not just a promise of comfort, but of power.

The "go" in this passage might seem to be an overwhelming, impossible command if we do not read it carefully. "Go to *all* the nations? Baptize them and teach them to observe *everything* Jesus commanded? I'm a friendly person, but I'm just not that convincing!" Thanks be to God that He is not relying on our powers of persuasion.

The task becomes much more manageable when we remember to pay attention to the "therefore" of Jesus' statement. "Go, *therefore,* and make disciples . . ." We are to go to all nations because Jesus has been given "all authority . . . in heaven and on earth." We are to go because Jesus, the King of kings and the Lord of lords, goes with us, making our work fruitful.

Out of love for us and for the whole world Jesus goes with His church until the end of the age, transforming the feeble work of our hands into something mighty and powerful.

[A] **27:65** Or *"Take* [B] **27:65** It is uncertain whether this guard consisted of temple police or Roman soldiers. [C] **27:66** Lit *stone with the guard* [D] **28:9** Other mss add *as they were on their way to tell the news to His disciples*

My brothers to leave for Galilee, and they will see Me there."[a]

The Soldiers Are Bribed to Lie

[11]As they were on their way, some of the guards came into the city and reported to the •chief priests everything that had happened. [12]After the priests[A] had assembled with the elders and agreed on a plan, they gave the soldiers a large sum of money [13]and told them, "Say this, 'His disciples came during the night and stole Him while we were sleeping.' [14]If this reaches the governor's ears,[B] we will deal with[C] him and keep you out of trouble."[b] [15]So they took the money and did as they were instructed. And this story has been spread among Jewish people to this day.[c]

The Great Commission

[16]The 11 disciples traveled to Galilee, to the mountain where Jesus had directed them.[d] [17]When they saw Him, they worshiped,[D] but some doubted. [18]Then Jesus came near and said to them, "All authority has been given to Me in heaven and on earth.[e] [19]Go, therefore, and make disciples[f] of[E] all nations,[g] baptizing[h] them in the name of the Father and of the Son and of the Holy Spirit, [20]teaching them to observe everything I have commanded you. And remember,[F] I am with you always,[G] to the end of the age."[i]

[a]28:10 Jn 20:17; Rm 8:29; Heb 2:11-12,17
[b]28:14 Mt 27:2; Ac 12:20
[c]28:15 Mt 9:31; 27:8; Mk 1:45
[d]28:16 Mt 26:32; 28:7
[e]28:18 Dn 7:13-14; Jn 17:2; Rm 14:9; Eph 1:20-22; Php 2:9-10; Col 2:10; 1Pt 3:22
[f]28:19 Mt 10:42; 28:19; Lk 14:26; Jn 8:31; 13:35; 15:8; Ac 6:1
[g]28:19 Mk 16:15; Lk 24:47
[h]28:19 Ac 2:38; 8:16
[i]28:20 Mt 13:39; 18:20; Ac 1:2; 2:42; 18:10

[A]28:12 Lit *After they* [B]28:14 Lit *this is heard by the governor* [C]28:14 Lit *will persuade* [D]28:17 Other mss add *Him* [E]28:19 Or *and disciple*; lit *and instruct* [F]28:20 Lit *look* [G]28:20 Lit *all the days*

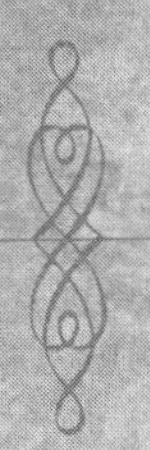

■ **AUTHOR:** John Mark

■■ **DATE:** Written around A.D. 55–65, the Gospel of Mark covers events of the ministry of John the Baptist through the ministry, crucifixion, and resurrection of Jesus

The first words of the Gospel of Mark are "The beginning of the gospel of Jesus Christ, the Son of God" (1:1). It amounts to a headline: Good news: Jesus, the Son of God, begins the mission of God.

Mark wastes no time launching into the story. The author, widely held to be John Mark (Ac 12:12,25), bypasses the genealogy and nativity reports found in Matthew. Immediately we read of the preparation for Jesus enacted by John the Baptist, Jesus' cousin. And John the Baptist is immediately linked to the Old Testament (OT) prophets.

MARK

Make no mistake, Mark insists, this Jesus is the one foretold in the OT, the One God sent to secure salvation for those who will believe. He is more than God's messenger; He is the core of the mission. He is not here to proclaim the gospel; He is the gospel. Every word of God before Him points *to* Him. Every miracle and conversion after Jesus' ascension to heaven is enabled by Him. The people who believe His message are His disciples, and become part of His body, the church.

The mission of God is apparently not conversion only, but spiritual maturation. Coming to faith should result with developing in faith. Therefore, descriptions of Jesus as a rabbi or teacher occur thirty-nine times in Mark as Jesus taught His listeners how to grow in faith.

Yet Mark frequently mentions the secret of Jesus' identity. Following a healing or a teaching point with Jesus' twelve disciples, Jesus often insisted that people keep their exposure to His power and authority to themselves. Jesus was not interested in public relations, but instead was interested in an event that would help people see God's mission even more clearly. Mark leads directly to it. The great act—or mission—of Jesus the Son of God is the ignominious place to which He was led: a Roman cross at Golgotha, the aptly named "Skull Place" (Mk 15:22). There the great teacher dies in obedience to God's will. There the reproach of God is evident to all who behold this rabbi. The miracles Jesus enacted healed people for a time; but the healer is now dying on a cross. God does not save Him. Instead, Jesus saves the world through His death. Then seeing Jesus resurrected, His disciples realized that He really was God in the flesh. His resurrected life is ours through God's gracious gift.

This Gospel ends abruptly, as if in the middle of a scene. Take that ending and jump to your story—your life of faith—and discover God's power in your life. Is that where Mark's Gospel ends? Not really. It's a story to be continued.

The Messiah's Herald

1 The beginning[a] of the gospel[b] of Jesus
Christ, the Son of God.[c] 2 As it is written in
Isaiah[d] the prophet:[A,e]

Look, I am sending My messenger[f]
ahead of You,
who will prepare Your way.[B]
3 **A voice of one crying out**
in the wilderness:[g]
Prepare the way for the Lord;[h]
make His paths straight![C,i]

4 John came baptizing[D,j] in the wilderness[k]
and preaching a baptism of repentance[E,l] for
the forgiveness[m] of sins.[n] 5 The whole Judean
countryside and all the people of Jerusalem[o]
were flocking to him, and they were baptized
by him in the Jordan[p] River as they confessed[q]
their sins.[r] 6 John wore a camel-hair garment
with a leather belt around his waist and ate
locusts[s] and wild honey.[t] 7 He was preaching:
"Someone more powerful[u] than I will come
after me.[v] I am not worthy[w] to stoop down
and untie the strap of His sandals.[x] 8 I have
baptized you with[F] water,[y] but He will baptize
you with the Holy Spirit."[z]

The Baptism of Jesus

9 In[aa] those days Jesus came from Nazareth[ab]
in Galilee[ac] and was baptized in the Jordan
by John. 10 As soon as He came up out of the
water, He saw the heavens[ad] being torn open
and the Spirit descending to Him like a dove.
11 And a voice[ae] came from heaven:[af]

You are My beloved[ag] Son;[ah]
I take delight[ai] in You![G]

The Temptation of Jesus

12 Immediately[aj] the Spirit[ak] drove[al] Him
into the wilderness.[am] 13 He was in the wilderness 40 days, being tempted[an] by Satan.[ao] He
was with the wild animals,[ap] and the angels[aq]
began to serve Him.

Ministry in Galilee

14 After[ar] John was arrested,[as] Jesus went to
Galilee,[at] preaching[au] the good news[H,I,av] of
God:[J,aw] 15 "The time[ax] is fulfilled, and the kingdom of God[ay] has come[az] near.[ba] Repent[bb] and
believe[bc] in the good news!"

The First Disciples

16 As[bd] He was passing along by the Sea of
Galilee,[be] He saw Simon[bf] and Andrew,[bg] Simon's brother. They were casting a net into
the sea,[bh] since they were fishermen.
17 "Follow Me,"[bi] Jesus told them, "and I will
make you fish for[K,bj] people!"[bk] 18 Immediately
they left their nets and followed[bl] Him.[bm]
19 Going on a little farther, He saw James[bn] the
son of Zebedee[bo] and his brother John.[bp] They
were in their boat mending their nets. 20 Immediately He called them, and they left their
father Zebedee in the boat with the hired
men and followed Him.[bq]

Driving Out an Unclean Spirit

21 Then[br] they went into Capernaum,[bs] and
right away He entered the •synagogue[bt] on the

[a] **1:1** Jn 1:1; Php 4:15 [b] **1:1-8** Mt 3:1-12; Lk 3:1-18 [c] **1:1** Jn 5:19; Heb 1:2 [d] **1:2** Mt 3:3; 4:14; 12:17 [e] Lk 16:29 [f] Mt 13:49 [g] **1:3** Jn 1:23 [h] Lk 10:1; 17:5 [i] **1:2-3** Is 40:3; Mal 3:1 [j] **1:4** Lk 7:29; Ac 22:16 [k] Rv 12:6 [l] Lk 3:3; Ac 13:24; 19:4; 26:20 [m] Mt 9:2; Lk 24:47 [n] Jn 15:22; Ac 26:18 [o] **1:5** Mt 23:37; Jn 11:36 [p] Gn 13:10; Ps 114:3; Lk 3:3 [q] Ac 19:18 [r] Jn 15:22; Rm 6:23; 1Pt 4:1 [s] **1:6** Rv 9:3,7 [t] Rv 10:9-10 [u] **1:7** Rv 18:8 [v] Jn 1:15 [w] Mt 3:11 [x] Lk 3:16; Ac 13:23-25 [y] **1:8** Jn 1:26,31,33; Ac 1:5; 8:36; 11:16 [z] Jn 1:33 [aa] **1:9-11** Mt 3:13-17; Lk 3:21-23 [ab] **1:9** Mt 2:23; 4:13; 21:11; Lk 1:26; 2:4,39,51; 4:16; Jn 1:45-46 [ac] Mt 17:22 [ad] **1:10** Mt 24:35; Lk 12:33; Ac 17:24; Eph 6:9; Rv 21:10 [ae] **1:11** Jn 5:37 [af] Rv 14:13 [ag] Lk 20:13; Eph 1:6; Phm 1 [ah] Ps 2:7 [ai] Is 42:1 [aj] **1:12-13** Mt 4:1-11; Lk 4:1-13 [ak] **1:12** Jn 1:33 [al] 3Jn 10 [am] Mt 3:1; Rv 12:6 [an] **1:13** Jms 1:13 [ao] Mt 4:1,10; Ac 13:10 [ap] Rv 6:8 [aq] Mt 13:49; Ac 5:19; Rv 14:6 [ar] **1:14-15** Mt 4:17; Jn 4:45 [as] **1:14** Mt 3:12; Lk 3:20; 9:7-9; Jn 3:24 [at] Mt 17:22 [au] Mk 13:10 [av] Mk 1:1 [aw] Rm 15:16; 1Th 2:2,8-9 [ax] **1:15** Ps 37:39; Lk 20:10; Jn 7:8 [ay] Mt 3:2; 6:33; 12:28; 19:24; 21:31,43; Mk 4:11; 9:1; 10:14; 12:34; 14:25; 15:43 [az] Mk 9:1 [ba] Rm 13:11; 1Pt 4:7 [bb] Ac 3:19; 26:20 [bc] Mk 11:24; Jn 3:16; Ac 10:43; Rm 10:9; 1Pt 1:8-10 [bd] **1:16-20** Mt 4:18-22; Lk 5:1-11 [be] **1:16** Mt 4:18; 15:29; Jn 6:1 [bf] Mt 16:17 [bg] Jn 6:8 [bh] Mk 7:31 [bi] **1:17** Mt 4:19 [bj] Mt 4:18-19; Lk 5:2 [bk] Mt 4:19 [bl] **1:18** Lk 5:11; Jn 8:12 [bm] Lk 18:28 [bn] **1:19** Ac 12:2 [bo] Jn 21:2 [bp] Jn 21:7 [bq] **1:20** Lk 18:28 [br] **1:21-26** Lk 4:31-35 [bs] **1:21** Lk 10:15 [bt] Mk 3:1; Jms 2:2

GOD WHO SENDS

The Kingdom Is Near

We have been redeemed through the transforming power of the Christ event. The eschaton has broken into history. The kingdom has invaded our world. The very life of God himself has come down to us in the Christ gift. But we still wait for the final benefits of the eschaton, the final triumph of the kingdom victory, the full release of the divine life into our lives.

(DUBOSE, 14)

[A] **1:2** Other mss read *in the prophets* [B] **1:2** Other mss add *before You* [C] **1:2-3** Is 40:3; Mal 3:1 [D] **1:4** Or *John the Baptist came*, or *John the Baptizer came* [E] **1:4** Or *a baptism based on repentance* [F] **1:8** Or *in* [G] **1:11** Or *In You I am well pleased* [H] **1:14** Other mss add *of the kingdom* [I] **1:14** Or *gospel* [J] **1:14** Either *from God* or *about God* [K] **1:17** Lit *you to become fishers of*

Sabbath[a] and began to teach.[b] 22They were astonished[c] at His teaching[d] because, unlike the
·scribes,[e] He was teaching them as one having
authority.
23Just then a man with an ·unclean[f]
spirit[g] was in their synagogue.[h] He cried
out,[A] 24"What do You have to do with us,[B]
Jesus—Nazarene?[i] Have You come to destroy[j] us? I know who You are—the Holy[k]
One of God!"[l]
25But Jesus rebuked[m] him and said, "Be
quiet,[C,n] and come out of him!" 26And the unclean spirit convulsed him,[o] shouted with a
loud voice, and came out of him.
27Then they were all amazed,[p] so they began
to argue[q] with one another, saying, "What is
this? A new teaching[r] with authority![D,s] He
commands even the unclean[t] spirits,[u] and they
obey Him." 28News about Him then spread
throughout the entire vicinity of Galilee.[v]

Healings at Capernaum

29As[w] soon as they left the synagogue,[x] they
went into Simon[y] and Andrew's[z] house[aa] with
James[ab] and John.[ac] 30Simon's mother-in-law
was lying in bed with a fever, and they told
Him about her at once. 31So He went to her,
took her by the hand, and raised her up.[ad]
The fever[ae] left her,[E] and she began to serve[af]
them.[ag]
32When[ah] evening came, after the sun had
set, they began bringing to Him all those who
were sick[ai] and those who were demon-possessed.[aj] 33The whole town was assembled at
the door, 34and He healed[ak] many who were
sick with various diseases[al] and drove out[am]
many demons.[an] But He would not permit the
demons to speak, because they knew Him.[ao]

Preaching in Galilee

35Very[ap] early in the morning, while it was
still dark, He got up, went out, and made His
way to a deserted place.[aq] And He was praying[ar] there. 36Simon[as] and his companions
went searching for Him. 37They found Him
and said, "Everyone's looking for You!"
38And He said to them, "Let's go on to the
neighboring villages so that I may preach[at]
there too. This is why I have come." 39So He
went into all of Galilee,[au] preaching in their
synagogues[av] and driving out demons.

A Man Cleansed

40Then[aw] a man with a serious skin disease[ax]
came to Him and, on his knees,[F,ay] begged
Him: "If You are willing, You can make me
·clean."[az]
41Moved with compassion,[ba] Jesus reached
out His hand and touched[bb] him. "I am willing," He told him. "Be made clean." 42Im-
mediately the disease[bc] left him, and he was
healed.[G] 43Then He sternly warned[bd] him
and sent him away[be] at once, 44telling him,
"See that you say nothing to anyone;[bf] but go
and show[bg] yourself to the priest,[bh] and offer[bi] what Moses prescribed for your cleansing,[bj] as a testimony[bk] to them." 45Yet he went
out and began to proclaim[bl] it widely and to
spread the news,[bm] with the result that Jesus
could no longer enter a town openly. But He
was out in deserted places, and they would
come to Him from everywhere.

The Son of Man Forgives and Heals

2 When[bn] He entered Capernaum[bo] again
after some days, it was reported that He
was at home. 2So many people gathered together that there was no more room, not
even in the doorway, and He was speaking
the message[bp] to them. 3Then they came to
Him bringing a paralytic,[bq] carried by four
men. 4Since they were not able to bring him
to[H] Jesus because of the crowd, they removed
the roof above where He was. And when they
had broken through, they lowered the mat on
which the paralytic was lying.
5Seeing their faith,[br] Jesus told the paralytic, "Son, your sins[bs] are forgiven."[bt]
6But some of the ·scribes[bu] were sitting
there, thinking[bv] to themselves:[I] 7"Why does
He speak like this? He's blaspheming![bw] Who
can forgive[bx] sins[by] but God alone?"[bz]

[a] **1:21** Mk 2:23; Lk 13:10 [b] Mt 28:20; Ac 4:2; 2Tm 4:11 [c] **1:22** Mk 6:2 [d] Mt 7:28; 22:33; Mk 11:18; Lk 4:32; Ac 2:42; 17:19 [e] Mt 2:4 [f] **1:23** 2Co 6:17 [g] Lk 11:24 [h] Jms 2:2 [i] **1:24** Mk 14:67 [j] Jn 6:27 [k] 1Co 7:14 [l] Lk 4:34; Jn 6:69; Eph 4:30 [m] **1:25** 2Tm 4:2 [n] Mt 22:12 [o] **1:26** Mk 9:26; Lk 9:39 [p] **1:27** Mk 10:24,32 [q] Mk 8:11 [r] Mk 11:18; Ac 2:42 [s] Jd 25 [t] 2Co 6:17 [u] Lk 11:24 [v] **1:28** Mt 17:22 [w] **1:29-31** Mt 8:14-15; Lk 4:38-39 [x] **1:29** Jms 2:2 [y] Mt 16:17 [z] Jn 6:8 [aa] Mk 9:33 [ab] Ac 12:2 [ac] Jn 21:7 [ad] **1:31** Mk 5:41 [ae] Lk 4:38 [af] Phm 13 [ag] Rm 12:13 [ah] **1:32-34** Mt 8:16-17; Lk 4:40-41 [ai] **1:32** Lk 5:31 [aj] Mt 9:32 [ak] **1:34** Ac 8:7 [al] Ac 19:12 [am] 3Jn 10 [an] Rv 9:20; 18:2 [ao] Mk 3:11-12; 5:7 [ap] **1:35-38** Mt 4:23-25; Lk 4:42-44 [aq] **1:35** Mt 14:13; Mk 6:31-32; Lk 4:42; 9:12; Rv 12:6 [ar] Mt 5:44; Ac 12:12 [as] **1:36** Mt 16:17 [at] **1:38** Mk 1:4 [au] **1:39** Mt 17:22 [av] Mk 3:1 [aw] **1:40-44** Mt 8:2-4; Lk 5:12-14 [ax] **1:40** Mt 11:5 [ay] Mt 17:14 [az] 1Jn 1:7 [ba] **1:41** Lk 15:20 [bb] Jn 20:17 [bc] **1:42** Lk 5:12 [bd] **1:43** Mt 9:30; Mk 14:5; Jn 11:33,38 [be] 3Jn 10 [bf] **1:44** Mk 5:43; 7:36; 8:26,30; 9:9; 16:8; Lk 5:14 [bg] Rv 1:1 [bh] Ac 4:1 [bi] Heb 5:1; 8:3 [bj] Lv 13–14; Heb 1:3 [bk] Mk 6:11; 1Tm 2:6 [bl] **1:45** Mk 1:4; Jn 18:32 [bm] Mk 4:14 [bn] **2:1-12** Mt 9:1-8; Lk 5:17-26 [bo] **2:1** Lk 10:15 [bp] **2:2** Mk 4:14; Jn 18:32 [bq] **2:3** Mt 4:24; 8:6; 9:2,6; Mk 2:3-10 [br] **2:5** Mt 8:10; Ac 3:16; Rm 1:8; 1Co 2:5; Gl 2:16; 1Tm 1:2; Heb 4:2 [bs] Jn 15:22 [bt] Mt 9:2,5; Lk 5:20,23; 7:48 [bu] **2:6** Mt 2:4 [bv] Mk 9:33 [bw] **2:7** Ex 22:28; Mk 3:29; Rv 13:6 [bx] Ps 25:11; Mt 9:2 [by] Jn 15:22 [bz] Ex 34:6-7; Is 43:25; 44:2

[A] **1:23** Other mss add to the beginning of v. 24: *"Leave us alone.* [B] **1:24** Lit *What to us and to You* [C] **1:25** Or *Be muzzled* [D] **1:27** Other mss read *What is this? What is this new teaching? For with authority* [E] **1:31** Other mss add *at once* [F] **1:40** Other mss omit *on his knees* [G] **1:42** Lit *made clean* [H] **2:4** Other mss read *able to get near* [I] **2:6** Or *thinking in their hearts*

The Kingdom of God

Tullian Tchividjian

According to Jesus, it's impossible for Christians to properly understand the practical nature of the Christian life without properly understanding the nature of their citizenship in God's kingdom. In fact, one of the primary biblical descriptions of Christians is that they're citizens in God's kingdom.

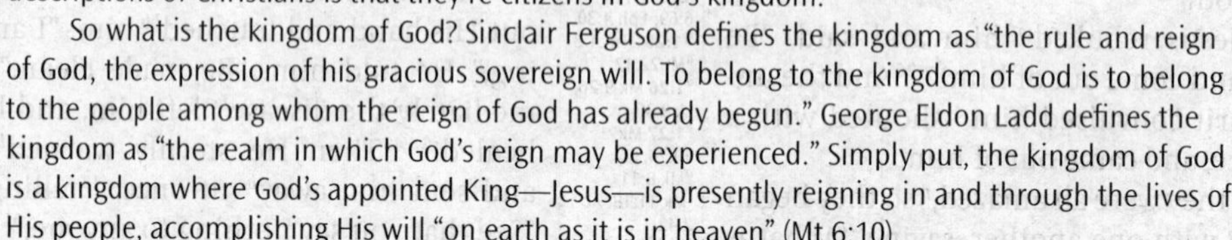

So what is the kingdom of God? Sinclair Ferguson defines the kingdom as "the rule and reign of God, the expression of his gracious sovereign will. To belong to the kingdom of God is to belong to the people among whom the reign of God has already begun." George Eldon Ladd defines the kingdom as "the realm in which God's reign may be experienced." Simply put, the kingdom of God is a kingdom where God's appointed King—Jesus—is presently reigning in and through the lives of His people, accomplishing His will "on earth as it is in heaven" (Mt 6:10).

The presence and purpose of God's kingdom undergird the teaching of the whole Bible, exhibiting God's plan—past, present, and future—for this world. The most exhaustive description of God's kingdom, though, is given to us by Jesus in the Sermon on the Mount (Mt 5–7), where He shows the kingdom of God to be central to His teaching and to the mission of God. Throughout this sermon, Jesus descriptively shows what kingdom living in a fallen world looks like, as the kingdom shapes our experience here and now.

It's helpful to think of the Kingdom of God in three stages: inauguration, continuation, and consummation.

The Kingdom's Inauguration

With the arrival of King Jesus to earth, God's kingdom was inaugurated "on earth as it is in heaven." To be sure, Jesus had always been Lord over all creation. "For everything was created by Him . . . He is before all things, and by Him all things hold together" (Col 1:16-17). Since the dawn of time, there has never been a moment when the Lord hasn't reigned over all that He has made. But God's reign and rule were demonstrated in new and dramatic ways when Jesus brought it from heaven to earth in a paradigm-shattering manner.

Previously, "He looked down from his holy heights—the LORD gazed out from heaven to earth" (Ps 102:19). Prior to the incarnation, the Lord ruled from afar (although His providential activity on earth never ceases). But then Jesus came and announced, "The time is fulfilled, and the kingdom of God has come near" (Mk 1:15). The time had come; God's kingdom was here with us. Here was God's kingdom earthed.

With Christ's first coming, God began the process of reversing the curse of sin and redeeming all things. In Christ, God was moving in a new way. All of Jesus' ministry—the words He spoke, the miracles He performed—showed there was a new order: God's order. When Jesus healed the diseased, raised the dead, and forgave the desperate, He did so to show that with the arrival of God in the flesh came the restoration of the way God intended things to be.

Tim Keller observes that Christ's miracles were not the *suspension* of the natural order but the *restoration* of the natural order. They were a reminder of what once was prior to the fall and a preview of what will eventually be a universal reality once again—a world of peace and justice, without death, disease, or conflict.

The inauguration of God's kingdom through Jesus began the "great reversal"—repealing the curse of sin and death, ensuring that God had begun the process of recreating all things.

The Kingdom's Continuation

The continuation stage of the kingdom of God is the stage we are in now—living in between Christ's first and second coming. It's a stage marked by tension between present and future. We're in the period of redemptive history often referred to as "already and not yet": the kingdom is already here in true form, but not yet full form; it's present in its beginnings, but still future in its fullness.

This guards us from an under-realized eschatology (expecting no change now) and an over-realized eschatology (expecting all change now). In this stage, we embrace the reality that while we're not yet what we will be, we're also no longer what we used to be. We're like Israel during her wilderness wanderings—we've left Egypt, but haven't yet entered the Promised Land.

The Kingdom's Consummation

The third stage, the kingdom's consummation, will take place when Jesus comes back and the process of reversing the curse of sin and recreating all things is completed (1Co 15:51-58). When our King returns there'll be no more sickness, death, tears, division, or tension. The "peace on earth" which the angels announced the night Christ was born will become a universal actuality. God's cosmic rescue mission will be complete. The fraying fabric of our fallen world will be fully and perfectly rewoven. Everything and everyone will live in perfect harmony. *Shalom* will rule. Isaiah 11:6-9 pictures it this way:

> The wolf will live with the lamb, and the leopard will lie down with the goat. The calf, the young lion, and the fatling will be together, and a child will lead them. The cow and the bear will graze, their young ones will like down together, and the lion will eat straw like the ox. An infant will play beside the cobra's pit, and a toddler will put his hand into a snake's den. None will harm or destroy another on My entire holy mountain, for the land will be as full of the knowledge of the LORD as the sea is filled with water.

For the pardoned children of God, there will be complete harmony when Jesus comes back. We'll work and worship in a perfectly renewed earth without the interference of sin. We who believe the gospel will enjoy sinless hearts and minds along with disease-free bodies. All that causes us pain and discomfort will be destroyed, and we will live forever. We'll finally be able "to enjoy what is most enjoyable with unbounded energy and passion forever." Until then, the resistance remains; the combat carries on. But we can press on faithfully knowing that for citizens in God's Kingdom, the best is yet to come.

8 Right away[a] Jesus understood in His
spirit[b] that they were thinking like this
within themselves and said to them, "Why
are you thinking these things in your
hearts?[A] 9 Which is easier:[c] to say to the paralytic,[d] 'Your sins are forgiven,' or to say, 'Get
up, pick up your mat, and walk'?[e] 10 But so
you may know that the ·Son of Man[f] has authority[g] on earth to forgive sins,"[h] He told the
paralytic, 11 "I tell you: get up,[i] pick up your
mat, and go home."

[a]**2:8** Mk 10:52 [b]Lk 5:22; 16:15; Jn 2:25 [c]**2:9** Lk 16:17; 18:25 [d]Mk 2:3 [e]Mt 11:5 [f]**2:10** Ps 8:4; Lk 5:24; Ac 7:56 [g]Mt 28:18; Mk 1:22 [h]Jn 15:22 [i]**2:11** Mk 5:41 [j]**2:12** Ac 10:45 [k]Jn 11:4; 17:1; 1Pt 2:12 [l]Lk 2:14 [m]Mt 9:33

12 Immediately he got up, picked up the mat,
and went out in front of everyone. As a result,
they were all astounded[j] and gave glory[k] to
God,[l] saying, "We have never seen anything
like this!"[m]

The Call of Matthew

13 Then[n] Jesus went out again beside the sea.
The whole crowd was coming to Him, and
He taught[o] them. 14 Then, moving on, He saw

[n]**2:13-17** Mt 9:9-13; Lk 5:27-32 [o]**2:13** Mt 28:20; Ac 4:2; 2Tm 4:11

[A]**2:8** Or *minds*

Levi[a] the son of Alphaeus sitting at the tax office,[b] and He said to him, "Follow Me!"[c] So he
got up and followed[d] Him.

Dining with Sinners

15 While He was reclining at the table in
Levi's house, many tax collectors[e] and sinners[f] were also guests[A,g] with Jesus and His
disciples, because there were many who were
following Him. 16 When the scribes[h] of the
•Pharisees[B,i] saw that He was eating[j] with sinners[k] and tax collectors,[l] they asked His disciples, "Why does He eat[C] with tax collectors
and sinners?"

17 When Jesus heard this, He told them,
"Those who are well don't need[m] a doctor,[n]
but the sick[o] do need one. I didn't come to call
the righteous,[p] but sinners."[q]

A Question about Fasting

18 Now[r] John's[s] disciples[t] and the Pharisees[D,u] were fasting.[v] People came and asked
Him, "Why do John's disciples and the Pharisees' disciples fast, but Your disciples do not
fast?"

19 Jesus said to them, "The wedding guests[E]
cannot fast while the groom[w] is with them,
can they? As long as they have the groom
with them, they cannot fast. 20 But the time[F]
will come[x] when the groom is taken away
from them,[y] and then they will fast[z] in that
day. 21 No one sews a patch of unshrunk cloth
on an old garment. Otherwise, the new patch
pulls away from the old cloth,[aa] and a worse
tear is made. 22 And no one puts new wine[ab]
into old wineskins. Otherwise, the wine will
burst[ac] the skins, and the wine is lost as well
as the skins.[G] But new wine is for fresh wineskins."

Lord of the Sabbath

23 On[ad] the Sabbath He was going through
the grainfields, and His disciples[ae] began to
make their way picking some heads of grain.
24 The Pharisees[af] said to Him, "Look, why are
they doing what is not lawful[ag] on the Sabbath?"

25 He said to them, "Have you never read
what David[ah] and those who were with him
did when he was in need[ai] and hungry[aj]—
26 how he entered the house of God in the
time of Abiathar[ak] the high priest[al] and ate the
•sacred bread[am]—which is not lawful for anyone to eat except the priests[an]—and also gave
some to his companions?" 27 Then He told
them, "The Sabbath was made for[H] man and
not man for[H] the Sabbath.[ao] 28 Therefore, the
Son of Man[ap] is Lord[aq] even of the Sabbath."[ar]

The Man with the Paralyzed Hand

3 Now[as] He entered the •synagogue[at] again,
and a man was there who had a para-
lyzed[au] hand. 2 In order to accuse[av] Him, they
were watching Him closely[aw] to see whether
He would heal[ax] him on the Sabbath.[ay] 3 He
told the man with the paralyzed hand, "Stand
before us."[I] 4 Then He said to them, "Is it lawful[az] on the Sabbath to do what is good[ba] or
to do what is evil,[bb] to save life[bc] or to kill?"[bd]
But they were silent.[be] 5 After looking around
at them with anger[bf] and sorrow at the
hardness[bg] of their hearts, He told the man,
"Stretch out your hand." So he stretched it
out, and his hand was restored.[bh] 6 Immediately the •Pharisees[bi] went out and started
plotting[bj] with the •Herodians[bk] against Him,
how they might destroy[bl] Him.

Ministering to the Multitude

7 Jesus[bm] departed with His disciples to the
sea, and a large crowd followed from Galilee,[bn] Judea,[bo] 8 Jerusalem,[bp] Idumea, beyond
the Jordan,[bq] and around Tyre[br] and Sidon.[bs]
The large crowd came to Him because they
heard about everything He was doing. 9 Then
He told His disciples to have a small boat[bt]
ready for Him, so the crowd would not crush
Him. 10 Since He had healed[bu] many, all who
had diseases were pressing toward Him to
touch[bv] Him. 11 Whenever the •unclean[bw] spirits[bx] saw Him, those possessed fell down[by] before Him and cried out, "You are the Son of
God!"[bz] 12 And He would strongly warn[ca] them
not to make Him known.[cb]

[a] **2:14** Lk 5:27,29 [b] Lk 5:27 [c] Lk 5:27 [d] Lk 5:11; Jn 8:12 [e] **2:15** Lk 3:12; 18:13 [f] Mt 9:10; 1Tm 1:15 [g] Mt 14:9; Rm 12:13 [h] **2:16** Mt 2:4 [i] Mk 7:3 [j] Mt 11:18 [k] 1Tm 1:15 [l] Lk 3:12 [m] **2:17** Mt 6:8 [n] Col 4:14 [o] Lk 5:31 [p] Mt 13:17; Rm 1:17 [q] Lk 5:32 [r] **2:18-22** Mt 9:14-17; Lk 5:33-39 [s] **2:18** Mk 1:4 [t] Jn 3:25 [u] Mk 7:3 [v] Lk 18:12; Ac 13:2 [w] **2:19** Jn 2:9 [x] **2:20** Mk 13:24 [y] Lk 17:22; Jn 16:16-20 [z] Lk 18:12 [aa] **2:21** Lk 19:36 [ab] **2:22** Lk 5:37 [ac] Jn 6:27 [ad] **2:23-28** Mt 12:1-8; Lk 6:1-5 [ae] **2:23** Mk 10:10 [af] **2:24** Mk 7:3 [ag] Lk 6:2 [ah] **2:25** Lk 1:27 [ai] Ac 2:45 [aj] Rv 7:16 [ak] **2:26** 1Sm 21:1-6 [al] Lv 16:32 [am] Ex 25:30 [an] Ac 4:1 [ao] **2:27** Col 2:16 [ap] **2:28** Mk 2:10 [aq] Rm 7:25; 1Co 8:6; Col 3:22 [ar] Lk 6:5 [as] **3:1-6** Mt 12:9-14; Lk 6:6-11 [at] **3:1** Mk 1:21,39; Jms 2:2 [au] Mk 4:6; 5:29; 9:18; 11:20-21 [av] **3:2** Rv 12:10 [aw] Lk 6:7; 14:1; 20:20 [ax] Ac 8:7 [ay] Mk 2:23; Lk 13:10; 14:3 [az] **3:4** Jn 18:31 [ba] Ps 34:14; Lk 18:18 [bb] Ps 34:12-16; 1Pt 3:17 [bc] Php 2:12; Jms 5:20 [bd] Lk 20:15 [be] Lk 1:20; 19:40 [bf] **3:5** Jms 1:19 [bg] Ex 7:13; Rm 11:25 [bh] Mk 8:25 [bi] **3:6** Mk 7:3 [bj] Mt 12:14; Mk 15:1 [bk] Mt 22:16; Mk 12:13 [bl] Mk 11:18; Jn 5:18; 6:27 [bm] **3:7-12** Mt 4:24-25; 12:15-16; Lk 6:17-19 [bn] **3:7** Mt 17:22 [bo] Lk 1:5 [bp] **3:8** Mt 23:37 [bq] Lk 3:3 [br] Ac 21:7 [bs] Gn 49:13 [bt] **3:9** Jn 21:8 [bu] **3:10** Ac 8:7 [bv] Jn 20:17 [bw] **3:11** 2Co 6:17 [bx] Lk 11:24 [by] Lk 8:47 [bz] Lk 4:34,41 [ca] **3:12** 2Tm 4:2 [cb] Mk 1:34

[A] **2:15** Lit *reclining* (at the table); at important meals the custom was to recline on a mat at a low table and lean on the left elbow. [B] **2:16** Other mss read *scribes and Pharisees* [C] **2:16** Other mss add *and drink* [D] **2:18** Other mss read *the disciples of John and of the Pharisees* [E] **2:19** Lit *The sons of the bridal chamber* [F] **2:20** Lit *the days* [G] **2:22** Other mss read *the wine spills out and the skins will be ruined* [H] **2:27** Or *because of* [I] **3:3** Lit *Rise up in the middle*

The 12 Apostles

13Then[a] He went up the mountain[b] and
summoned those He wanted, and they came
to Him. 14He also appointed 12—He also
named them apostles[A,c]—to be with Him, to
send them out to preach,[d] 15and to have authority to[B] drive out demons.

16He appointed the Twelve:[C,e]

To Simon,[f] He gave the name Peter;[g]
17 and to James[h] the son of Zebedee,[i]
and to his brother John,[j]
He gave the name "Boanerges"
(that is, "Sons of Thunder"[k]);
18 Andrew;[l]
Philip[m] and Bartholomew;
Matthew[n] and Thomas;[o]
James the son of Alphaeus,
and Thaddaeus;
Simon the Zealot,[D]
19 and Judas Iscariot,[E,p]
who also betrayed Him.

A House Divided

20Then He went home, and the crowd gathered again so that they were not even able to
eat.[F] 21When His family[q] heard this, they set
out to restrain Him, because they said, "He's
out of His mind."[r]

22The •scribes[s] who had come down from
Jerusalem said, "He has •Beelzebul[t] in Him!"
and, "He drives out[u] demons[v] by the ruler[w] of
the demons!"[x]

23So He summoned[y] them and spoke to
them in parables:[z] "How can Satan[aa] drive out
Satan?[ab] 24If a kingdom[ac] is divided against itself, that kingdom cannot stand. 25If a house
is divided against itself, that house cannot
stand. 26And if Satan rebels against himself
and is divided, he cannot stand but is finished![G]

27"On the other hand, no one can enter a
strong man's house and rob his possessions
unless he first ties up[ad] the strong man. Then
he will rob his house. 28•I assure you: People
will be forgiven for all sins[H] and whatever
blasphemies[ae] they may blaspheme. 29But
whoever blasphemes[af] against the Holy Spirit
never has forgiveness,[ag] but is •guilty[ah] of an
eternal sin"[I,ai]— 30because they were saying,
"He has an unclean spirit."[aj]

True Relationships

31Then[ak] His mother[al] and His brothers[am]
came, and standing outside, they sent word
to Him and called Him. 32A crowd was sitting around Him and told Him, "Look, Your
mother, Your brothers,[an] and Your sisters[J] are
outside asking for You."

33He replied to them, "Who are My mother
and My brothers?" 34And looking about at
those who were sitting in a circle around
Him, He said, "Here are My mother and My
brothers![ao] 35Whoever does the will of God[ap]
is My brother and sister and mother."

The Parable of the Sower

4 Again[aq] He began to teach[ar] by the sea,
and a very large crowd gathered around
Him. So He got into a boat on the sea and
sat down, while the whole crowd was on the
shore facing the sea. 2He taught them many
things in parables,[as] and in His teaching[at] He
said to them: 3"Listen! Consider the sower
who went out to sow.[au] 4As he sowed, this occurred: Some seed fell along the path,[av] and
the birds came and ate[aw] it up. 5Other seed fell
on rocky ground where it didn't have much
soil, and it sprang up right away,[ax] since it
didn't have deep soil. 6When the sun came
up, it was scorched, and since it didn't have
a root, it withered.[ay] 7Other seed fell among
thorns, and the thorns came up and choked
it, and it didn't produce a crop. 8Still others
fell on good ground and produced a crop that
increased[az] 30, 60, and 100 times what was
sown."[ba] 9Then He said, "Anyone who has ears
to hear should listen!"[bb]

Why Jesus Used Parables

10When He was alone with the Twelve,[bc]
those who were around Him asked Him
about the parables.[bd] 11He answered them,
"The •secret[be] of the kingdom of God[bf] has
been given to you, but to those outside,[bg] everything comes in parables 12so that

[a]**3:13-19** Mt 10:2-4; Lk 6:12-16 [b]**3:13** Mt 4:8 [c]**3:14** Ac 1:2; Jd 17 [d]Mk 1:4 [e]**3:16** Mk 11:11; Jn 1:35-51 [f]Mt 16:17 [g]Ac 10:32 [h]**3:17** Ac 12:2 [i]Jn 21:2 [j]Jn 21:7 [k]Rv 6:1 [l]**3:18** Jn 6:8 [m]Jn 1:43-48; 6:5,7; 12:21-22; 14:8-9 [n]Ac 1:13 [o]Jn 11:16; 14:5; 20:24,26-28; 21:2 [p]**3:19** Mk 14:10,43; Ac 1:16,25 [q]**3:21** Jn 7:3 [r]Lk 2:48; Jn 2:3-4; 7:3-5 [s]**3:22** Mt 2:4 [t]Mt 10:25; 12:24,27; Lk 11:15-19 [u]3Jn 10 [v]Rv 9:20; 18:2 [w]Lk 12:58 [x]Mt 9:34; 12:24; Lk 11:15 [y]**3:23** Lk 18:16 [z]Mk 12:1 [aa]Mk 1:13; 4:15; 8:33 [ab]**3:23-27** Mt 12:25-29; Lk 11:17-22 [ac]**3:24** Lk 4:5 [ad]**3:27** Mk 15:1 [ae]**3:28-30** Mt 12:31-32; Lk 12:10 [af]**3:29** Ac 7:51 [ag]Heb 6:4-6; 10:26-29; 1Jn 5:16 [ah]Mk 14:64 [ai]1Jn 5:16 [aj]**3:30** Lk 11:24 [ak]**3:31-35** Mt 12:46-50; Lk 8:19-21 [al]**3:31** Mt 1:16 [am]Jn 2:12 [an]**3:32** Mk 6:3 [ao]**3:34** Ac 9:30 [ap]**3:35** Rm 8:27; Gl 1:4; Eph 1:9; 1Jn 2:17 [aq]**4:1-12** Mt 13:1-15; Lk 8:4-10 [ar]**4:1** Mt 28:20; Ac 4:2; 2Tm 4:11 [as]**4:2** Mk 12:1 [at]Mk 11:18; Ac 2:42; 17:19 [au]**4:3** Gl 6:7 [av]**4:4** Mk 8:27 [aw]Gl 5:15 [ax]**4:5** Mk 10:52 [ay]**4:6** Mk 3:1 [az]**4:8** 1Pt 2:2

[ba]Jn 15:5; Col 1:6 [bb]**4:9** Is 6:9; Jr 5:21; Ezk 12:2; Mk 8:18; Lk 14:35 [bc]**4:10** Mk 11:11 [bd]Mk 12:1 [be]**4:11** 1Co 2:7 [bf]Mk 1:15 [bg]Rm 9:27

[A]**3:14** Other mss omit *He also named them apostles* [B]**3:15** Other mss add *heal diseases, and to* [C]**3:16** Other mss omit *He appointed the Twelve* [D]**3:18** Lit *the Cananaean* [E]**3:19** *Iscariot* is probably "a man of Kerioth," a town in Judea.

[F]**3:20** Or *eat a meal*; lit *eat bread* [G]**3:26** Lit *but he has an end* [H]**3:28** Lit *All things will be forgiven the sons of men* [I]**3:29** Other mss read *is subject to eternal judgment* [J]**3:32** Other mss omit *and Your sisters*

they may look and look,
yet not perceive;
they may listen and listen,
yet not understand;[a]
otherwise, they might turn back —
and be forgiven."[A,B,b]

The Parable of the Sower Explained

13 Then[c] He said to them: "Don't you understand this parable?[d] How then will you understand any of the parables? 14 The sower sows[e] the word.[f] 15 These[C] are the ones along the path[g] where the word is sown: when they hear, immediately Satan[h] comes and takes away the word[i] sown in them.[D] 16 And these are[E] the ones sown on rocky ground: when they hear the word, immediately they receive it with joy.[j] 17 But they have no root in themselves; they are short-lived. When pressure[k] or persecution comes because of the word, they immediately 'stumble.[l] 18 Others are sown among thorns; these are the ones who hear the word, 19 but the worries[m] of this age,[n] the seduction[F,o] of wealth,[p] and the desires[q] for other things enter in and choke the word, and it becomes unfruitful.[r] 20 But the ones sown on good ground are those who hear the word,[s] welcome it, and produce a crop:[t] 30, 60, and 100 times what was sown."

Using Your Light

21 He[u] also said to them, "Is a lamp brought in to be put under a basket or under a bed?[v] Isn't it to be put on a lampstand?[w] 22 For nothing is concealed except to be revealed,[x] and nothing hidden except to come to light. 23 If anyone has ears to hear, he should listen!"[y] 24 Then He said to them, "Pay attention to what you hear. By the measure[z] you use,[G,aa] it will be measured and added[ab] to you. 25 For to the one who has, it will be given, and from the one who does not have, even what he has will be taken away."[ac]

The Parable of the Growing Seed

26 "The kingdom of God[ad] is like this," He said. "A man scatters seed on the ground; 27 he sleeps[ae] and rises[af] — night[ag] and day, and the seed sprouts and grows — he doesn't know how. 28 The soil produces a crop[ah] by itself — first the blade, then the head, and then the ripe grain[ai] on the head. 29 But as soon as the crop is ready, he sends for the sickle,[aj] because the harvest[ak] has come."

The Parable of the Mustard Seed

30 And[al] He said: "How can we illustrate the kingdom of God,[am] or what parable[an] can we use to describe it? 31 It's like a mustard seed[ao] that, when sown in the soil, is smaller than all the seeds on the ground. 32 And when sown,[ap] it comes up and grows taller than all the vegetables,[aq] and produces large branches, so that the birds of the sky[ar] can nest in its shade."

Using Parables

33 He would speak the word[as] to them with many parables[at] like these, as they were able to understand.[au] 34 And He did not speak to them without a parable. Privately, however, He would explain everything to His own disciples.[av]

Wind and Wave Obey the Master

35 On[aw] that day, when evening had come, He told them, "Let's cross over to the other side of the sea." 36 So they left the crowd and took Him along since He was already in the boat. And other boats were with Him. 37 A fierce windstorm[ax] arose, and the waves[ay] were breaking over the boat, so that the boat was already being swamped. 38 But He was in the stern, sleeping[az] on the cushion. So they woke Him up[ba] and said to Him, "Teacher! Don't You care that we're going to die?"[bb]

39 He got up, rebuked[bc] the wind, and said to the sea, "Silence![bd] Be still!" The wind ceased, and there was a great calm. 40 Then He said to them, "Why are you fearful?[be] Do you still have no faith?"

41 And they were terrified[bf] and asked one another, "Who then is this? Even the wind and the sea obey[bg] Him!"[bh]

Demons Driven Out by the Master

5 Then[bi] they came to the other side of the sea, to the region of the Gerasenes.[H] 2 As soon as He got out of the boat, a man with an

[a] **4:12** Mk 7:18 [b] Is 6:9-10 [c] **4:13-20** Mt 13:18-23; Lk 8:9-15 [d] **4:13** Mk 12:1 [e] **4:14** Gl 6:7 [f] Mk 16:20 [g] **4:15** Mk 8:27 [h] Mt 4:10 [i] Lk 6:47 [j] **4:16** Jn 5:43; 15:11 [k] **4:17** 2Co 1:4 [l] Jn 16:1 [m] **4:19** 1Pt 5:7 [n] Lk 16:8; Eph 1:21 [o] Mt 13:22 [p] Mt 13:22; Lk 8:14 [q] 2Pt 1:4; 2:10 [r] Rm 1:13; Ti 3:14; Jd 12 [s] **4:20** Lk 6:47 [t] Col 1:10 [u] **4:21-25** Lk 8:16-18 [v] **4:21** Lk 5:18 [w] Rv 1:12 [x] **4:22** 2Co 4:11 [y] **4:23** Mk 4:9 [z] **4:24** 2Co 10:13 [aa] Mt 7:2; Lk 6:38 [ab] Lk 17:5 [ac] **4:25** Mt 25:29; Lk 19:26 [ad] **4:26** Mk 1:15 [ae] **4:27** Mt 9:24 [af] Mk 5:41 [ag] Jn 9:4 [ah] **4:28** Col 1:10 [ai] Lk 16:7 [aj] **4:29** Jl 3:13; Rv 14:14-19 [ak] Rv 14:15 [al] **4:30-34** Mt 13:31-35; Lk 13:18-21 [am] **4:30** Mk 1:15 [an] Mk 12:1 [ao] **4:31** Mt 17:20; Lk 17:6 [ap] **4:32** Gl 6:7 [aq] Lk 11:42 [ar] Mt 24:35; Lk 12:33; Ac 17:24; Eph 6:9; Rv 21:10 [as] **4:33** Lk 6:47; Jn 18:32 [at] Mk 12:1 [au] Jn 16:12 [av] **4:34** Mt 9:10; Mk 10:10; Lk 6:1; Jn 6:3; Ac 6:1 [aw] **4:35-41** Mt 8:23-27; Lk 8:22-25 [ax] **4:37** Ps 107:25; Jnh 1:5-6 [ay] Jd 13 [az] **4:38** Mt 9:24 [ba] Mk 5:41 [bb] Jn 6:27 [bc] **4:39** 2Tm 4:2 [bd] Mt 22:12; Mk 3:4 [be] **4:40** Mt 8:26; Rv 21:8 [bf] **4:41** Rv 11:11 [bg] Mk 1:27

[bh] Jnh 1:10,16; Mk 6:50-51 [bi] **5:1-20** Mt 8:28-34; Lk 8:26-39

[A] **4:12** Other mss read *and their sins be forgiven them* [B] **4:12** Is 6:9-10 [C] **4:15** Some people [D] **4:15** Other mss read *in their hearts* [E] **4:16** Other mss read *are like* [F] **4:19** Or *pleasure*, or *deceitfulness* [G] **4:24** Lit *you measure* [H] **5:1** Some mss read *Gadarenes*; other mss read *Gergesenes*

·unclean[a] spirit[b] came out of the tombs[c] and
met Him. 3 He lived in the tombs.[d] No one was
able to restrain him anymore—even with
chains[e]— 4 because he often had been bound
with shackles and chains, but had snapped
off the chains and smashed[f] the shackles. No
one was strong enough to subdue[g] him. 5 And
always, night[h] and day, he was crying out
among the tombs[i] and in the mountains[j] and
cutting himself with stones.

6 When he saw Jesus from a distance, he ran
and knelt down before Him. 7 And he cried
out with a loud voice, "What do You have to
do with me,[A] Jesus, Son[k] of the Most High
God?[l] I beg[B] You before God, don't torment[m]
me!" 8 For He had told him, "Come out of the
man, you unclean[n] spirit!"[o]

9 "What is your name?" He asked him.

"My name is Legion,"[C,p] he answered Him,
"because we are many." 10 And he kept begging
Him not to send them out of the region.

11 Now a large herd of pigs[q] was there, feeding[r] on the hillside. 12 The demons[D] begged
Him, "Send us to the pigs, so we may enter
them." 13 And He gave them permission. Then
the unclean[s] spirits[t] came out and entered the
pigs, and the herd of about 2,000 rushed down
the steep bank into the sea and drowned there.
14 The men who tended them[E] ran off[u] and reported it in the town and the countryside, and
people went to see what had happened. 15 They
came to Jesus and saw the man who had been
demon-possessed[v] by the legion,[w] sitting there,
dressed and in his right mind;[x] and they were
afraid.[y] 16 The eyewitnesses described to them
what had happened to the demon-possessed[z]
man and told about the pigs. 17 Then they began to beg Him to leave their region.

18 As He was getting into the boat, the man
who had been demon-possessed kept begging
Him to be with Him. 19 But He would not let
him; instead, He told him, "Go back home to
your own people, and report to them how
much the Lord[aa] has done[ab] for you and how
He has had mercy on you." 20 So he went out
and began to proclaim[ac] in the ·Decapolis[ad]
how much Jesus had done for him, and they
were all amazed.[ae]

A Girl Restored and a Woman Healed

21 When[af] Jesus had crossed over again by
boat to the other side, a large crowd[ag] gathered
around Him while He was by the sea. 22 One of
the ·synagogue leaders, named Jairus,[ah] came,
and when he saw Jesus, he fell at His feet[ai]
23 and kept begging Him, "My little daughter
is at death's door.[F] Come and lay Your hands
on[aj] her so she can get well[ak] and live."

24 So Jesus went with him, and a large crowd
was following and pressing against Him. 25 A
woman suffering from bleeding[al] for 12 years
26 had endured[am] much under many doctors.[an]
She had spent everything she had and was not
helped at all. On the contrary, she became
worse. 27 Having heard about Jesus, she came
behind Him in the crowd and touched[ao] His
robe.[ap] 28 For she said, "If I can just touch His
robes, I'll be made well!"[aq] 29 Instantly her
flow of blood ceased, and she sensed in her
body that she was cured[ar] of her affliction.

30 At once Jesus realized in Himself that
power[as] had gone out from Him. He turned
around in the crowd[at] and said, "Who
touched My robes?"[au]

31 His disciples said to Him, "You see the
crowd pressing against You, and You say,
'Who touched Me?'"

32 So He was looking around to see who had
done this. 33 Then the woman, knowing what
had happened to her, came with fear and
trembling, fell down[av] before Him, and told
Him the whole truth.[aw] 34 "Daughter," He said
to her, "your faith[ax] has made you well.[G,ay] Go
in peace and be free[H,az] from your affliction."[ba]

35 While He was still speaking, people came
from the synagogue leader's house and said,
"Your daughter is dead. Why bother the
Teacher[bb] anymore?"

36 But when Jesus overheard what was
said, He told the synagogue leader, "Don't be
afraid.[bc] Only believe." 37 He did not let anyone accompany Him except Peter,[bd] James,[be]
and John,[bf] James's brother. 38 They came to
the leader's house, and He saw a commotion—people weeping and wailing loudly.
39 He went in and said to them, "Why are you
making a commotion and weeping?[bg] The
child[bh] is not dead but asleep."[bi]

[a] **5:2** 2Co 6:17 [b] Lk 11:24 [c] Jn 5:28 [d] **5:3** Lk 23:53 [e] Mk 15:1 [f] **5:4** Rm 16:20; Rv 2:27 [g] Jms 3:7-8 [h] **5:5** Jn 9:4 [i] Lk 23:53 [j] Mt 4:8 [k] **5:7** Jn 5:19; Heb 1:2 [l] Ps 78:35 [m] Rv 20:10 [n] **5:8** 2Co 6:17 [o] Lk 11:24 [p] **5:9** Mt 26:53; Lk 8:30 [q] **5:11** Mt 7:6; 8:30-32; Lk 8:32-33; 15:15-16 [r] Jn 21:15 [s] **5:13** 2Co 6:17 [t] Lk 11:24 [u] **5:14** Jms 4:7 [v] **5:15** Mt 9:32 [w] Mk 5:9 [x] 1Pt 4:7 [y] Ps 147:11; Pr 1:7; Rv 14:7 [z] **5:16** Mt 9:32 [aa] **5:19** Col 4:1; Jd 5 [ab] Lk 1:25; 8:39; Ac 15:17; Rm 9:28 [ac] **5:20** Mk 1:4 [ad] Mt 4:25; Mk 7:31 [ae] Rv 17:6 [af] **5:21-43** Mt 9:18-26; Lk 8:40-56 [ag] **5:21** Mk 2:4 [ah] **5:22** Lk 8:41 [ai] Rv 19:10 [aj] **5:23** 1Tm 5:22 [ak] Mk 6:56 [al] **5:25** Lk 8:43 [am] **5:26** Php 1:29 [an] Col 4:14 [ao] **5:27** Jn 20:17 [ap] Lk 19:36 [aq] **5:28** Mk 6:56; Ac 16:31 [ar] **5:29** Lk 7:7 [as] **5:30** Lk 5:17; 6:19; 8:46 [at] Mk 2:13 [au] Lk 19:36 [av] **5:33** Lk 8:47 [aw] Jn 14:6 [ax] **5:34** Mt 8:10 [ay] Mt 9:22; Mk 6:56 [az] Ac 4:10 [ba] Mk 5:29 [bb] **5:35** Mk 4:38; Eph 4:11 [bc] **5:36** Jn 6:20 [bd] **5:37** Lk 6:14 [be] Ac 12:2 [bf] Jn 21:7 [bg] **5:39** Mt 9:23 [bh] Lk 1:7 [bi] Mt 9:24

[A] **5:7** Lit *What to me and to You* [B] **5:7** Or *adjure* [C] **5:9** A Roman legion contained up to 6,000 soldiers; here legion indicates a large number. [D] **5:12** Other mss read *All the demons* [E] **5:14** Other mss read *tended the pigs* [F] **5:23** Lit *My little daughter has it finally*; = to be at the end of life [G] **5:34** Or *has saved you* [H] **5:34** Lit *healthy*

40 They started laughing at Him, but He put them all outside. He took the child's father,[a] mother, and those who were with Him, and entered the place where the child was. 41 Then He took the child[b] by the hand and said to her, "*Talitha koum!*"[A] (which is translated, "Little girl, I say to you, get up!"[c]). 42 Immediately the girl got up[d] and began to walk.[e] (She was 12 years old.) At this they were utterly astounded.[f] 43 Then He gave them strict orders that no one should know about this[g] and said that she should be given something to eat.

Rejection at Nazareth

6 He[h] went away from there and came to His hometown,[i] and His disciples[j] followed Him. 2 When the Sabbath[k] came, He began to teach[l] in the •synagogue,[m] and many who heard Him were astonished. "Where did this man get these things?" they said. "What is this wisdom[n] given to Him, and how are these miracles[o] performed by His hands? 3 Isn't this the carpenter,[p] the son of Mary,[q] and the brother of James,[r] Joses, Judas,[s] and Simon? And aren't His sisters here with us?" So they were •offended[t] by Him.

4 Then Jesus said to them, "A prophet[u] is not without honor[v] except in his hometown, among his relatives, and in his household." 5 So He was not able to do any miracles[B,w] there, except that He laid His hands on[x] a few sick[y] people and healed[z] them. 6 And He was amazed[aa] at their unbelief.[ab]

Commissioning the Twelve

Now He was going around the villages in a circuit, teaching.[ac] 7 He[ad] summoned[ae] the Twelve[af] and began to send[ag] them out in pairs and gave them authority over •unclean[ah] spirits.[ai] 8 He instructed them to take nothing for the road except a walking stick: no bread, no traveling bag,[aj] no money in their belts. 9 They were to wear sandals, but not put on an extra shirt.[ak] 10 Then He said to them, "Whenever you enter a house, stay there until you leave that place. 11 If any place does not welcome[al] you and people refuse to listen to you, when you leave there, shake the dust off your feet[am] as a testimony[an] against them."[C]

12 So they went out and preached[ao] that people should repent.[ap] 13 And they were driving out many demons,[aq] anointing[ar] many sick[as] people with olive oil,[at] and healing them.[au]

John the Baptist Beheaded

14 King[av] •Herod[aw] heard of this, because Jesus' name[ax] had become well known. Some[D] said, "John the Baptist[ay] has been raised from the dead,[az] and that's why supernatural powers[ba] are at work[bb] in him." 15 But others said, "He's Elijah."[bc] Still others said, "He's a prophet[E]—like one of the prophets."[bd]

16 When Herod[be] heard of it, he said, "John,[bf] the one I beheaded, has been raised!"[bg] 17 For[bh] Herod himself had given orders to arrest John and to chain[bi] him in prison on account of Herodias,[bj] his brother Philip's wife, whom he had married.[bk] 18 John had been telling Herod, "It is not lawful[bl] for you to have your brother's wife!"[bm] 19 So Herodias held a grudge against him and wanted to kill[bn] him. But she could not, 20 because Herod was in awe[bo] of[F] John and was protecting him, knowing he was a righteous[bp] and holy[bq] man. When Herod heard him he would be very disturbed,[G,br] yet would hear him gladly.[bs]

21 Now an opportune time came on his birthday, when Herod gave a banquet[bt] for his nobles,[bu] military commanders,[bv] and the leading men of Galilee.[bw] 22 When Herodias's own daughter[H] came in and danced,[bx] she pleased Herod and his guests. The king said to the girl, "Ask me whatever you want, and I'll give it to you." 23 So he swore[by] oaths[bz] to her: "Whatever you ask me I will give you, up to half my kingdom."[ca]

24 Then she went out and said to her mother, "What should I ask for?"

"John the Baptist's[cb] head!" she said.

25 Immediately she hurried to the king and said, "I want you to give me John the Baptist's[cc] head on a platter[cd]—right now!"

26 Though the king was deeply distressed,[ce] because of his oaths[cf] and the guests[I] he did

[a] **5:40** Col 3:21 [b] **5:41** Lk 1:7 [c] Mk 1:31; 2:11; 4:27,38; 9:27; 14:41-42 [d] **5:42** Mk 9:27 [e] Mt 11:5 [f] Mk 16:8; Ac 10:45 [g] **5:43** Mk 1:44; Lk 8:56 [h] **6:1-6** Mt 13:53-58 [i] **6:1** Mk 1:9 [j] Mt 9:10; Mk 10:10; Lk 6:1; Jn 6:3; Ac 6:1 [k] **6:2** Mk 2:23; Lk 13:10 [l] Mt 28:20; Ac 4:2; 2Tm 4:11 [m] Jms 2:2 [n] Pr 3:19; Ac 7:22; 1Co 1:21 [o] Ac 19:11 [p] **6:3** Mt 13:55 [q] Mt 1:16 [r] Jms 1:1; Jd 1 [s] Mt 13:55; Jd 1 [t] Jn 16:1 [u] **6:4** Mt 2:23 [v] Mt 13:57; 1Co 4:10; 12:23 [w] **6:5** Ac 19:11 [x] 1Tm 5:22 [y] 1Co 11:30 [z] Ac 8:7 [aa] **6:6** Rv 17:6 [ab] Heb 3:12,19 [ac] Mt 28:20; Ac 4:2; 2Tm 4:11 [ad] **6:7-13** Mt 10:5-42; Lk 9:1-6 [ae] **6:7** Lk 18:16 [af] Mk 11:11 [ag] Mk 3:14 [ah] 2Co 6:17 [ai] Lk 11:24 [aj] **6:8** Lk 10:4 [ak] **6:9** Jn 19:23 [al] **6:11** Ac 17:11 [am] Mt 10:14; Lk 9:5; 10:11; Ac 13:51 [an] 1Tm 2:6 [ao] **6:12** Mk 1:4 [ap] Ac 3:19; 26:20 [aq] **6:13** Mk 3:15; Rv 9:20; 18:2 [ar] Mk 16:1 [as] 1Co 11:30 [at] Jms 5:14 [au] Ac 8:7 [av] **6:14-16** Lk 9:7-9 [aw] **6:14** Mt 14:1 [ax] Jn 10:25 [ay] Mk 1:4 [az] Mt 17:9; Jn 21:14 [ba] Mk 5:30 [bb] 1Co 12:6 [bc] **6:15** Mk 8:28 [bd] Mt 2:23; Ac 7:52 [be] **6:16** Mt 14:1 [bf] Mk 1:4 [bg] Mt 26:32 [bh] **6:17-29** Mt 14:6-12 [bi] **6:17** Mk 15:1 [bj] Mt 14:3,6; Lk 3:19 [bk] 1Tm 5:14 [bl] **6:18** Mk 2:24; Jn 18:31 [bm] Lv 18:16; 20:21 [bn] **6:19** Lk 20:15 [bo] **6:20** Ps 147:11; Pr 1:7; Rv 14:7 [bp] Mt 13:17 [bq] Ps 20:6; 1Co 7:14 [br] Lk 24:4; Jn 13:22; Ac 25:20; 2Co 4:8; Gl 4:20 [bs] 2Co 11:19 [bt] **6:21** Jn 13:2 [bu] Rv 6:15 [bv] Ac 21:31 [bw] Mt 17:22 [bx] **6:22** Mt 11:17 [by] **6:23** Heb 6:16 [bz] Mt 5:34 [ca] Lk 4:5 [cb] **6:24** Mk 1:4 [cc] **6:25** Lk 7:20 [cd] Mt 14:8 [ce] **6:26** Mt 26:38; Mk 14:34 [cf] Mt 5:33

[A] **5:41** An Aram expression [B] **6:5** Lit *miracle* [C] **6:11** Other mss add *I assure you, it will be more tolerable for Sodom or Gomorrah on judgment day than for that town.* [D] **6:14** Other mss read *He* [E] **6:15** Lit *Others said, "A prophet* [F] **6:20** Or *Herod feared* [G] **6:20** Other mss read *When he heard him, he did many things* [H] **6:22** Other mss read *When his daughter Herodias* [I] **6:26** Lit *and those reclining at the table*

Jim Elliot, Ed McCully, Roger Youderian, Pete Fleming, Nate Saint (all died 1956)

These five young missionaries died in remote Ecuador in 1956. Their story has been told in books and motion pictures, but on the day they went missing, there was no media nearby, no speeches of tribute, no memorials. Only the quietness of a radio at their home base in Shell Mera. Only wives and families waiting. And at "Palm Beach" where their small aircraft had landed to make contact with the Auca tribe, only the quiet river streaming over their bodies.

The missed radio contact was Monday, January 6. By Friday, a search team had found four of the five bodies and buried them. Five widows, eight children, and a stunned world mourned. Two years after this tragedy, Elisabeth Elliot and Rachel Saint (Nate's sister) made friendly contact with that same tribe, established a mission there, and today a church thrives. Steve Saint, young son of Nate, became an adopted son of the tribe and lived for a time with them.

Elements of the five martyrs' story took years to come to light. The missionaries had spent several months contacting the Waodani people (also known as Auca), dropping gifts from the airplane and establishing, as best they could, a friendly exchange. What they could not know were the internal issues which turned tribal leaders from curious friends into murderers. The missionaries were armed, but none used his weapon. Several of those in the killing party later reported hearing strange voices and seeing moving lights in the sky during the attack. Was this supernatural oversight of the mission of God, however violent for the men and tragic for surviving family members? Had angels gathered to welcome home these "sent ones," their mission now fulfilled? What seemed very clear to those with eyes of faith was that God had turned the deaths of five servants into victory over a culture of fear and violence that the Waodani had lived in to that point in their history. Years later, the Auca "father" of Steve Saint, retelling the story (he himself had been on the beach with a spear and club that day), was still amazed that the missionary team had not fought back.

Through the years, the sacrifice of the five young missionaries has produced a spiritual harvest of many souls. A people once driven by suspicion are transformed. Their encounter with civilization beyond the river has been mediated and successful. The mission of God to the Waodani has come full circle. Missionaries from that tribe have told others of God's love and forgiveness. More tribal violence in that equatorial river basin has by now claimed Waodani lives. They too are now martyrs for the Lord. The people survive, however. By faith, the Word of God speaks with hope to the yearning of an isolated people group, and they now have capacity for peaceful co-existence and mature leadership for their churches.

not want to refuse[a] her. 27 The king immediately sent for an executioner and commanded
him to bring John's head. So he went and beheaded him in prison, 28 brought his head on
a platter, and gave it to the girl. Then the girl
gave it to her mother. 29 When his disciples[A,b]
heard about it, they came and removed his
corpse and placed it in a tomb.[c]

Feeding 5,000

30 The[d] apostles[e] gathered around Jesus
and reported to Him all that they had done
and taught. 31 He said to them, "Come away
by yourselves to a remote place and rest for
a while." For many people were coming and
going, and they did not even have time to eat.
32 So they went away in the boat by themselves
to a remote place, 33 but many saw them leaving and recognized them. People ran there
by land from all the towns and arrived ahead
of them.[B] 34 So as He stepped ashore, He saw
a huge crowd and had compassion[f] on them,
because they were like sheep[g] without a shepherd. Then He began to teach them many
things.

35 When it was already late, His disciples[h]
approached Him and said, "This place is a
wilderness,[i] and it is already late! 36 Send them
away, so they can go into the surrounding
countryside and villages to buy themselves
something to eat."

37 "You give them something to eat," He responded.

They said to Him, "Should we go and buy
200 ˙denarii[j] worth of bread and give them
something to eat?"

38 And He asked them, "How many loaves do
you have? Go look."

When they found out they said, "Five, and
two fish."

39 Then He instructed them to have all the
people sit down[C] in groups on the green grass.
40 So they sat down in ranks of hundreds and
fifties. 41 Then He took the five loaves and
the two fish, and looking up to heaven, He
blessed and broke the loaves. He kept giving
them to His disciples to set before the people.
He also divided the two fish among them all.
42 Everyone ate and was filled.[k] 43 Then they
picked up 12 baskets full of pieces of bread
and fish. 44 Now those who ate the loaves were
5,000 men.

Walking on the Water

45 Immediately[l] He made His disciples get
into the boat and go ahead of Him to the
other side, to Bethsaida,[m] while He dismissed
the crowd. 46 After He said good-bye to them,
He went away to the mountain[n] to pray.[o]
47 When evening came, the boat was in the
middle of the sea, and He was alone on the
land. 48 He saw them being battered[p] as they
rowed,[D] because the wind was against them.
Around three in the morning[E] He came toward them walking on the sea and wanted to
pass by them. 49 When they saw Him walking
on the sea, they thought it was a ghost[q] and
cried out; 50 for they all saw Him and were terrified.[r] Immediately He spoke with them and
said, "Have courage![s] It is I.[t] Don't be afraid."[u]
51 Then He got into the boat with them, and
the wind ceased. They were completely astounded,[F] 52 because they had not understood
about the loaves. Instead, their hearts were
hardened.[v]

Miraculous Healings

53 When they had crossed over, they came
to land at Gennesaret[w] and beached the boat.
54 As they got out of the boat, people immediately recognized Him. 55 They hurried
throughout that vicinity and began to carry
the sick[x] on mats to wherever they heard He
was. 56 Wherever He would go, into villages,
towns, or the country, they laid the sick in
the marketplaces and begged Him that they
might touch just the ˙tassel[y] of His robe.[z] And
everyone who touched it was made well.

The Traditions of the Elders

7 The[aa] ˙Pharisees[ab] and some of the
˙scribes[ac] who had come from Jerusalem[ad]
gathered around Him. 2 They observed that
some of His disciples were eating their bread
with ˙unclean[ae] — that is, unwashed — hands.
3 (For the Pharisees, in fact all the Jews, will
not eat unless they wash their hands ritually,
keeping the tradition of the elders. 4 When

[a] **6:26** 1Th 4:8 [b] **6:29** Mk 10:10; Jn 3:25 [c] Jn 5:28 [d] **6:30-44** Mt 14:13-21; Lk 9:10-17; Jn 6:1-15 [e] **6:30** Ac 1:2; Jd 17 [f] **6:34** Lk 15:20 [g] Mt 7:15 [h] **6:35** Mk 10:10 [i] Jn 1:23; Rv 12:6 [j] **6:37** Mt 18:28 [k] **6:42** Mt 5:6 [l] **6:45-56** Mt 14:22-36; Jn 6:16-21 [m] **6:45** Jn 12:21 [n] **6:46** Mt 4:8 [o] Mt 5:44; Ac 12:12 [p] **6:48** Rv 20:10 [q] **6:49** Mt 14:26 [r] **6:50** Jn 5:7 [s] Jn 16:33 [t] Ex 3:14; Ps 45:8; Jn 8:24 [u] Jn 6:20 [v] **6:52** Mk 8:17; Heb 3:8 [w] **6:53** Mt 14:34; Lk 5:1 [x] **6:55** Lk 5:31 [y] **6:56** Mt 23:5 [z] Mt 9:20; 14:36; Lk 8:44; 19:36 [aa] **7:1-23** Mt 15:1-20 [ab] **7:1** Mk 7:3 [ac] Mt 2:4 [ad] Mt 23:37 [ae] **7:2** Ac 10:28

[A] **6:29** = John's disciples [B] **6:33** Other mss add *and gathered around Him* [C] **6:39** Lit *people recline* [D] **6:48** Or *them struggling as they rowed* [E] **6:48** Lit *Around the fourth watch of the night* = 3 to 6 a.m. [F] **6:51** Lit *were astounded in themselves*

they come from the marketplace,[a] they do not
eat unless they have washed.[b] And there are
many other customs they have received and
keep, like the washing of cups, jugs, copper
utensils, and dining couches.[A,c]) 5 Then the
Pharisees[d] and the scribes[e] asked Him, "Why
don't Your disciples live according to the tradition of the elders,[f] instead of eating bread
with ritually unclean[B] hands?"
6 He answered them, "Isaiah[g] prophesied[h]
correctly about you hypocrites,[i] as it is written:[j]

These people honor[k] Me with their lips,
but their heart is far from Me.
7 **They worship Me in vain,**
teaching[l] as doctrines[m] the commands[n]
of men.[C,o]

8 Disregarding the command of God, you
keep the tradition of men."[D] 9 He also said to
them, "You completely invalidate God's command in order to maintain[E] your tradition!
10 For Moses[p] said:

Honor your father
and your mother;[F,q] and
Whoever speaks evil of father
or mother
must be put to death.[G,r]

11 But you say, 'If a man tells his father or
mother: Whatever benefit[s] you might have
received from me is Corban'" (that is, a gift[t]
committed to the temple), 12 "you no longer
let him do anything for his father or mother.
13 You revoke God's word[u] by your tradition
that you have handed[v] down. And you do
many other similar things." 14 Summoning[w]
the crowd again, He told them, "Listen to Me,
all of you, and understand:[x] 15 Nothing that
goes into a person from outside can defile
him, but the things that come out of a person
are what defile him. [16 If anyone has ears to
hear, he should listen!]"[H]
17 When He went into the house away from
the crowd, the disciples asked Him about the
parable. 18 And He said to them, "Are you also
as lacking in understanding? Don't you realize that nothing going into a man from the
outside can defile him? 19 For it doesn't go
into his heart but into the stomach[y] and is
eliminated."[I] (As a result, He made all foods
·clean.[J,z]) 20 Then He said, "What comes out
of a person—that defiles him. 21 For from
within, out of people's hearts, come evil
thoughts, sexual immoralities,[aa] thefts, murders,[ab] 22 adulteries,[ac] greed,[ad] evil actions, deceit,[ae] promiscuity,[af] stinginess,[K] blasphemy,[ag]
pride,[ah] and foolishness.[ai] 23 All these evil
things come from within and defile a person."

A Gentile Mother's Faith

24 He got up and departed from[aj] there to
the region of Tyre[ak] and Sidon.[L,al] He entered
a house and did not want anyone to know it,
but He could not escape notice. 25 Instead, immediately after hearing about Him, a woman
whose little daughter had an unclean spirit[am]
came and fell at His feet.[an] 26 Now the woman
was Greek,[ao] a Syrophoenician by birth, and
she kept asking Him to drive the demon[ap] out
of her daughter. 27 He said to her, "Allow the
children to be satisfied first, because it isn't
right to take the children's bread and throw
it to the dogs."[aq]
28 But she replied to Him, "Lord,[ar] even
the dogs under the table eat the children's
crumbs."
29 Then He told her, "Because of this reply, you may go. The demon has gone out of
your daughter." 30 When she went back to her
home, she found her child lying on the bed,
and the demon was gone.

Jesus Does Everything Well

31 Again, leaving the region of Tyre,[as] He
went by way of Sidon to the Sea of Galilee,[at]
through[M] the region of the ·Decapolis.[au]
32 They brought to Him a deaf[av] man who also
had a speech difficulty,[aw] and begged Jesus to
lay His hand on[ax] him. 33 So He took him away
from the crowd privately. After putting His
fingers in the man's ears and spitting,[ay] He
touched his tongue. 34 Then, looking up to
heaven,[az] He sighed deeply and said to him,
"Ephphatha!"[N] (that is, "Be opened!"). 35 Immediately his ears were opened,[ba] his speech

[a] **7:4** Mk 6:56
[b] Heb 6:2; 9:10
[c] Lk 5:18
[d] **7:5** Mk 7:3
[e] Mt 2:4
[f] 3Jn 1
[g] **7:6** Mt 3:3; 4:14; 12:17
[h] Jn 11:51
[i] Lk 6:42
[j] Ac 15:15
[k] 1Tm 5:3
[l] **7:7** Mt 28:20; Ac 4:2; 2Tm 4:11
[m] Rm 15:4
[n] Col 2:22
[o] **7:6-7** Is 29:13
[p] **7:10** Ps 77:20; Mt 8:4; Heb 3:2
[q] Ex 20:12; Dt 5:16
[r] Ex 21:17; Lv 20:9
[s] **7:11** Mk 5:26
[t] Heb 5:1; 9:9; 11:4
[u] **7:13** Mk 4:14; Lk 8:21; Jn 18:32
[v] Jd 3
[w] **7:14** Lk 18:16
[x] Mt 13:13
[y] **7:19** Php 3:19
[z] 1Jn 1:7
[aa] **7:21** 1Th 4:3
[ab] Pr 1:16
[ac] **7:22** Nm 5:11
[ad] Eph 5:3
[ae] Ps 10:7
[af] Rm 13:13; 2Co 12:21; Gl 5:19; Eph 4:19; 1Pt 4:3; 2Pt 2:2,7,18
[ag] Jn 10:33; Rv 13:6
[ah] Ps 17:10
[ai] 2Co 11:1
[aj] **7:24-30** Mt 15:21-28
[ak] **7:24** Ac 21:7
[al] Gn 49:13
[am] **7:25** Lk 11:24
[an] Lk 8:47
[ao] **7:26** Ac 17:12
[ap] Mk 3:15; Rv 9:20; 18:2
[aq] **7:27** Ex 22:31
[ar] **7:28** Lk 10:1
[as] **7:31** Ac 21:7
[at] Mt 4:18; 15:29; Mk 1:16; Jn 6:1
[au] Mt 4:25; Mk 5:20
[av] **7:32** Lk 7:22
[aw] Ex 4:11; Is 35:6; 56:10
[ax] 1Tm 5:22
[ay] **7:33** Jn 9:6
[az] **7:34** Mt 24:35; Lk 12:33; Ac 17:24; Eph 6:9; Rv 21:10
[ba] **7:35** Phm 10

A **7:4** Other mss omit *and dining couches* B **7:5** Other mss read *with unwashed* C **7:6-7** Is 29:13 D **7:8** Other mss add *The washing of jugs, and cups, and many other similar things you practice.* E **7:9** Other mss read *to establish* F **7:10** Ex 20:12; Dt 5:16 G **7:10** Ex 21:17; Lv 20:9 H **7:16** Other mss omit bracketed text
I **7:19** Lit *goes out into the toilet* J **7:19** Other mss read *is eliminated, making all foods clean."* K **7:22** Lit *evil eye* L **7:24** Other mss omit *and Sidon* M **7:31** Or *into* N **7:34** An Aram expression

difficulty was removed,[A] and he began to
speak clearly.[a] 36 Then He ordered them to tell
no one,[b] but the more He would order them,
the more they would proclaim[c] it.
37 They were extremely astonished and
said, "He has done everything well![d] He even
makes deaf[e] people hear, and people unable
to speak,[f] talk!"

Feeding 4,000

8 In[g] those days there was again a large
crowd, and they had nothing to eat. He
summoned[h] the disciples[i] and said to them,
2 "I have compassion[j] on the crowd, because
they've already stayed with Me three days and
have nothing to eat. 3 If I send them home
hungry,[B] they will collapse on the way,[k] and
some of them have come a long distance."
4 His disciples answered Him, "Where can
anyone get enough bread here in this desolate place to fill[l] these people?"
5 "How many loaves do you have?" He asked
them.
"Seven," they said. 6 Then He commanded
the crowd to sit down on the ground. Taking
the seven loaves, He gave thanks, broke[m] the
loaves, and kept on giving them to His disciples to set before the people. So they served
the loaves to the crowd. 7 They also had a few
small fish, and when He had blessed them,
He said these were to be served as well. 8 They
ate and were filled. Then they collected seven
large baskets of leftover pieces. 9 About 4,000
men were there. He dismissed them 10 and immediately got into the boat with His disciples
and went to the district of Dalmanutha.[C]

The Yeast of the Pharisees and Herod

11 The[n] ·Pharisees[o] came out and began to
argue with Him, demanding of Him a sign[p]
from heaven[q] to test[r] Him. 12 But sighing
deeply in His spirit,[s] He said, "Why does this
generation[t] demand a sign? ·I assure you:[u] No
sign will be given to this generation!" 13 Then
He left them, got on board the boat again,
and went to the other side.
14 They had forgotten to take bread and had
only one loaf with them in the boat. 15 Then[v]
He commanded them: "Watch out! Beware
of the yeast[w] of the Pharisees and the yeast of
·Herod."[x]
16 They were discussing among themselves
that they did not have any bread. 17 Aware of
this, He said to them, "Why are you discussing that you do not have any bread? Don't you
understand or comprehend? Is your heart
hardened?[y] 18 **Do you have eyes, and not see,
and do you have ears, and not hear?**[D,z] And do
you not remember?[aa] 19 When I broke the five
loaves for the 5,000, how many baskets full of
pieces of bread did you collect?"
"Twelve," they told Him.
20 "When I broke the seven loaves for the
4,000, how many large baskets full of pieces
of bread did you collect?"
"Seven," they said.
21 And He said to them, "Don't you understand yet?"[ab]

Healing a Blind Man

22 Then they came to Bethsaida.[ac] They
brought a blind[ad] man to Him and begged
Him to touch him. 23 He took the blind man by
the hand and brought him out of the village.
Spitting[ae] on his eyes and laying His hands on[af]
him, He asked him, "Do you see anything?"
24 He looked up and said, "I see people
— they look to me like trees walking."[ag]
25 Again Jesus placed His hands on the man's
eyes, and he saw distinctly. He was cured and
could see everything clearly. 26 Then He sent[ah]
him home, saying, "Don't even go into the village."[E,ai]

Peter's Confession of the Messiah

27 Jesus[aj] went out with His disciples to the
villages of Caesarea Philippi. And on the road
He asked His disciples, "Who do people say
that I am?"
28 They answered Him, "John the Baptist;[ak]
others, Elijah; still others, one of the prophets."[al]
29 "But you," He asked them again, "who do
you say that I am?"
Peter[am] answered Him, "You are the ·Mes-
siah!"[an]
30 And He strictly warned[ao] them to tell no
one about Him.

[a] **7:35** Lk 20:21
[b] **7:36** Mk 1:44; Lk 8:56
[c] Mk 1:4
[d] **7:37** Gn 1:31
[e] Lk 7:22
[f] Mk 9:17
[g] **8:1-10** Mt 15:29-38
[h] **8:1** Lk 18:16
[i] Mt 9:10; Mk 10:10; Lk 6:1; Jn 6:3; Ac 6:1
[j] **8:2** Lk 15:20
[k] **8:3** Mk 8:27
[l] **8:4** Mt 5:6; 15:33
[m] **8:6** Mk 14:22
[n] **8:11-12** Mt 16:1-4
[o] **8:11** Mk 7:3
[p] Mk 13:22; Jn 2:11; Heb 2:4
[q] Mt 24:35; Lk 12:33; Ac 17:24; Eph 6:9; Rv 21:10
[r] Jms 1:13
[s] **8:12** Ps 51:12
[t] Lk 11:29
[u] Rv 22:21
[v] **8:15-21** Mt 16:5-12
[w] **8:15** Lk 13:21; Gl 5:9
[x] Mt 14:1
[y] **8:17** Mk 6:52; Jn 12:40; Rm 11:7; 2Co 3:14
[z] **8:18** Jr 5:21; Ezk 12:2; Mk 4:9,40
[aa] Rv 2:5
[ab] **8:21** Mk 4:40
[ac] **8:22** Jn 12:21
[ad] Mt 15:14
[ae] **8:23** Mk 7:33; 8:23; Jn 9:6
[af] 1Tm 5:22
[ag] **8:24** Mt 11:5
[ah] **8:26** Mk 3:14
[ai] Mk 1:44
[aj] **8:27-30** Mt 16:13-20; Lk 9:18-20
[ak] **8:28** Mk 1:4; Lk 7:20
[al] Mt 2:23; Ac 7:52
[am] **8:29** Lk 6:14
[an] Mt 1:17; Eph 5:2
[ao] **8:30** 2Tm 4:2

[A] **7:35** Lit *opened, the bond of his tongue was untied* [B] **8:3** Or *fasting*
[C] **8:10** Probably on the western shore of the Sea of Galilee [D] **8:18** Jr 5:21; Ezk 12:2 [E] **8:26** Other mss add *or tell anyone in the village*

His Death and Resurrection Predicted

31 Then[a] He began to teach them that the •Son of Man[b] must suffer many things and be rejected[c] by the elders,[d] the •chief priests, and the •scribes,[e] be killed, and rise[f] after three days.[g] 32 He was openly talking about this. So Peter took Him aside and began to rebuke Him.

33 But turning around and looking at His disciples, He rebuked Peter and said, "Get behind Me, Satan,[h] because you're not thinking about God's concerns,[A] but man's!"

Take Up Your Cross

34 Summoning the crowd along with His disciples, He said to them, "If anyone wants to be My follower, he must deny himself,[i] take up his cross,[j] and follow Me.[k] 35 For whoever wants to save[l] his •life will lose it,[m] but whoever loses[n] his life[o] because of Me[p] and the gospel[q] will save it.[r] 36 For what does it benefit[s] a man to gain[t] the whole world[u] yet lose[v] his life?[w] 37 What can a man give in exchange for his life?[x] 38 For whoever is ashamed[y] of Me and of My words[z] in this adulterous and sinful[aa] generation,[ab] the Son of Man will also be ashamed of him when He comes in the glory[ac] of His Father[ad] with the holy[ae] angels."[af]

9 Then He said to them, "•I assure you:[ag] There are some standing here who will not taste death[ah] until they see the kingdom of God come in power."[ai]

The Transfiguration

2 After[aj] six days[ak] Jesus took Peter, James, and John[al] and led them up on a high mountain[am] by themselves to be alone. He was transformed[B,an] in front of them, 3 and His clothes[ao] became dazzling—extremely white[ap] as no launderer on earth could whiten[aq] them. 4 Elijah[ar] appeared to them with Moses,[as] and they were talking with Jesus.

5 Then Peter said to Jesus, "•Rabbi,[at] it's good[au] for us to be here! Let us make three •tabernacles:[av] one for You, one for Moses, and one for Elijah"— 6 because he did not know what he should say,[aw] since they were terrified.[ax]

7 A cloud[ay] appeared, overshadowing[az] them, and a voice[ba] came from the cloud:[bb]

This is My beloved[bc] Son;[bd]
listen to Him![be]

8 Then suddenly, looking around, they no longer saw anyone with them except Jesus alone.

9 As[bf] they were coming down from the mountain,[bg] He ordered them to tell no one what they had seen[bh] until the •Son of Man[bi] had risen[bj] from the dead.[bk] 10 They kept this word[bl] to themselves, discussing what "rising from the dead" meant.

11 Then they began to question Him, "Why do the •scribes[bm] say that Elijah must come first?"[bn]

12 "Elijah does come first and restores[bo] everything,"[bp] He replied. "How then is it written[bq] about the Son of Man that He must suffer[br] many things and be treated with contempt?[bs] 13 But I tell you that Elijah really has come, and they did whatever they pleased to him, just as it is written[bt] about him."

The Power of Faith over a Demon

14 When[bu] they came to the disciples, they saw a large crowd around them and scribes disputing[bv] with them. 15 All of a sudden, when the whole crowd saw Him, they were amazed[C] and ran to greet Him. 16 Then He asked them, "What are you arguing with them about?"

17 Out of the crowd, one man answered Him, "Teacher,[bw] I brought my son to You. He has a spirit[bx] that makes him unable to speak.[by] 18 Wherever it seizes him, it throws him down, and he foams at the mouth, grinds his teeth, and becomes rigid. So I asked Your disciples to drive it out, but they couldn't."

19 He replied to them, "You unbelieving[bz] generation! How long will I be with you? How long must I put up with you? Bring him to Me." 20 So they brought him to Him. When the spirit saw Him, it immediately convulsed the boy. He fell to the ground and rolled around, foaming at the mouth. 21 "How long has this been happening to him?" Jesus asked his father.

[a] **8:31–9:1** Mt 16:21-28; Lk 9:21-27 [b] **8:31** Mk 2:10 [c] Mt 21:42; Mk 12:10; Lk 9:22; 17:25; 20:17; Heb 12:17; 1Pt 2:4,7 [d] 3Jn 1 [e] Mt 2:4 [f] Mt 16:21; Lk 18:33; Ac 2:24 [g] Lk 9:22 [h] **8:33** Mt 4:1,10; Ac 13:10 [i] **8:34** Mk 10:45 [j] Lk 9:23 [k] Jn 8:12; 3Jn 9 [l] **8:35** Ac 16:30; Jms 5:20; Jd 23 [m] 1Jn 3:16 [n] Mt 16:26 [o] Mt 10:39 [p] Mk 10:29; Rm 8:36 [q] Mk 1:1; Php 1:5 [r] Mt 16:25; Lk 9:24 [s] **8:36** Mk 5:26 [t] Mt 16:26 [u] Mt 13:38 [v] 1Co 3:15; Php 3:7 [w] Rm 15:1 [x] **8:37** Mt 20:28 [y] **8:38** Rm 1:16 [z] Mk 4:14; Jn 18:32 [aa] 1Tm 1:15 [ab] Mt 12:39; Lk 11:29 [ac] Lk 9:32; Jn 17:24; 2Co 3:18; 2Pt 3:18 [ad] Mt 5:16; 11:27; Jn 8:42 [ae] 1Co 7:14 [af] Mt 13:49; Ac 5:19; Jd 14; Rv 14:6 [ag] **9:1** Ps 72:19; Rv 22:21 [ah] Mk 13:28-32; 14:25; Jn 21:22-23; 2Pt 3:4 [ai] Lk 6:19 [aj] **9:2-8** Mt 17:1-8; Lk 9:28-36 [ak] **9:2** Ex 24:15-18; Hs 6:2 [al] Mt 10:2; Mk 5:37; 13:3; 14:33; Ac 1:13 [am] Mt 4:8; 2Pt 1:18 [an] Rm 12:2; 2Co 3:18 [ao] **9:3** Lk 19:36 [ap] Rv 3:4 [aq] Rv 7:14 [ar] **9:4** Mk 8:28 [as] Ps 77:20; Mt 8:4; Heb 3:2 [at] **9:5** Jn 11:8 [au] Gn 1:31 [av] Ex 25:9 [aw] **9:6** Mk 14:40 [ax] Heb 12:21 [ay] **9:7** Ex 24:15; Mt 26:64 [az] Lk 1:35 [ba] Jn 5:37 [bb] 2Pt 1:16-18 [bc] Eph 1:6; Phm 1 [bd] Lk 20:13; Jn 5:19 [be] Dt 18:15 [bf] **9:9-13** Mt 17:9-13 [bg] **9:9** Mt 4:8 [bh] Lk 8:56 [bi] Mk 2:10 [bj] Mt 16:21; Lk 18:33 [bk] Jn 20:9 [bl] **9:10** Mk 4:14 [bm] **9:11** Mt 2:4 [bn] Mal 4:5 [bo] **9:12** Mk 8:25 [bp] Lk 1:17 [bq] Ac 15:15 [br] Mk 8:31 [bs] Lk 23:11 [bt] **9:13** Mk 1:2 [bu] **9:14-29** Mt 17:14-21; Lk 9:37-42 [bv] **9:14** Mk 8:11 [bw] **9:17** Mk 4:38; Eph 4:11 [bx] Lk 11:24; 1Tm 4:1; 1Jn 4:1 [by] Mk 7:37 [bz] **9:19** Lk 12:46

[A] **8:33** Lit *about the things of God* [B] **9:2** Or *transfigured* [C] **9:15** Or *surprised*

“From childhood,” he said. 22 “And many times it has thrown him into fire or water to destroy[a] him. But if You can do anything, have compassion[b] on us and help us.”

23 Then Jesus said to him, “‘If You can’?[A,B] Everything is possible[c] to the one who believes.”[d]

24 Immediately the father of the boy cried out, “I do believe! Help my unbelief.”

25 When Jesus saw that a crowd was rapidly coming together, He rebuked[e] the ·unclean[f] spirit, saying to it, “You mute and deaf[g] spirit,[C] I command you: come out of him and never enter him again!”

26 Then it came out, shrieking and convulsing[h] him[D] violently. The boy became like a corpse, so that many said, “He’s dead.” 27 But Jesus, taking him by the hand, raised him,[i] and he stood up.

28 After He went into a house, His disciples asked Him privately, “Why couldn’t we drive it out?”

29 And He told them, “This kind can come out by nothing but prayer[j] [and fasting].”[E,k]

The Second Prediction of His Death

30 Then[l] they left that place and made their way through Galilee, but He did not want anyone to know it.[m] 31 For He was teaching[n] His disciples and telling them, “The Son of Man[o] is being betrayed[F] into the hands of men. They will kill Him, and after He is killed, He will rise[p] three days later.”[q] 32 But they did not understand this statement, and they were afraid to ask Him.[r]

Who is the Greatest?

33 Then[s] they came to Capernaum.[t] When He was in the house,[u] He asked them, “What were you arguing about on the way?”[v] 34 But they were silent,[w] because on the way they had been arguing with one another about who was the greatest.[x] 35 Sitting down, He called the Twelve[y] and said to them, “If anyone wants to be first, he must be last of all and servant of all.”[z] 36 Then He took a child,[aa] had him stand among them, and taking him in His arms, He said to them, 37 “Whoever welcomes[G] one little child such as this in My name[ab] welcomes Me. And whoever welcomes Me does not welcome Me, but Him who sent[ac] Me.”[ad]

In His Name

38 John[ae] said to Him, “Teacher,[af] we saw someone[H] driving out demons[ag] in Your name,[ah] and we tried to stop him because he wasn’t following us.”[ai]

39 “Don’t stop him,” said Jesus, “because there is no one who will perform a miracle[aj] in My name who can soon afterward speak evil of Me. 40 For whoever is not against us is for us.[ak] 41 And whoever gives you a cup of water to drink[al] because of My name,[I] since you belong to the ·Messiah[am]—I assure you:[an] He will never lose his reward.[ao]

Warnings from Jesus

42 “But whoever ·causes the downfall of one of these little ones who believe in Me[ap]—it would be better for him if a heavy millstone[J,aq] were hung around his neck and he were thrown into the sea. 43 And if your hand causes your downfall, cut it off.[ar] It is better for you to enter life maimed[as] than to have two hands and go to ·hell—the unquenchable fire,[at] [44 where

Their worm does not die,
and the fire is not quenched.][E,K,au]

45 And if your foot causes your downfall,[av] cut it off. It is better for you to enter life lame[aw] than to have two feet and be thrown into hell—[the unquenchable fire,[ax] 46 where

Their worm does not die,
and the fire is not quenched.][E,K,ay]

47 And if your eye causes your downfall, gouge it out. It is better for you to enter the kingdom of God[az] with one eye than to have two eyes and be thrown[ba] into hell,[bb] 48 where

Their worm does not die,
and the fire is not quenched.[K]

49 For everyone will be salted with fire.[L,M,bc] 50 Salt is good, but if the salt should lose its flavor,

[a]**9:22** Jn 6:27 [b]Lk 15:20 [c]**9:23** Mt 17:20; Jn 11:40 [d]Jn 3:16; Ac 10:43; Rm 10:9; 1Pt 1:8-10 [e]**9:25** 2Tm 4:2 [f]2Co 6:17 [g]Lk 7:22 [h]**9:26** Mk 1:26 [i]**9:27** Mk 1:31 [j]**9:29** Ac 12:5; 16:13; Phm 22 [k]Lk 18:12 [l]**9:30-32** Mt 17:22-23; Lk 9:43-45 [m]**9:30** Mk 1:44 [n]**9:31** Mt 28:20; Ac 4:2; 2Tm 4:11 [o]Mk 2:10 [p]Mt 16:21; Lk 18:33; Ac 2:24 [q]Mk 8:31; Lk 9:22 [r]**9:32** Mk 4:40; Lk 2:50 [s]**9:33-50** Mt 18:1-11; Lk 9:46-50 [t]**9:33** Lk 10:15 [u]Mk 1:29 [v]Mk 8:27 [w]**9:34** Mk 3:4 [x]Lk 22:24-27; Ac 8:9 [y]**9:35** Mk 11:11 [z]Mt 20:16-27; 23:11; Mk 10:43-44; Lk 22:26 [aa]**9:36** Lk 1:7 [ab]**9:37** Jn 10:25 [ac]Mt 15:24; Mk 12:6; Jn 3:16-17 [ad]Mt 10:40 [ae]**9:38** Jn 21:7 [af]Mk 4:38 [ag]Mk 3:15; Rv 9:20 [ah]Jn 10:25; 14:13 [ai]Nm 11:26-30 [aj]**9:39** Ac 19:11 [ak]**9:40** Mt 12:30; Lk 11:23 [al]**9:41** Mt 10:42; 25:35-42; Rm 12:20 [am]Mt 1:17; Eph 5:2 [an]Rv 22:21 [ao]Mt 10:42; 2Pt 2:13 [ap]**9:42** Ex 23:33; Jn 6:35 [aq]Jdg 9:53; Mt 24:41; Rv 18:22 [ar]**9:43** Mt 5:29-30 [as]Mt 15:30-31 [at]Mt 3:12; 5:22; 25:41; 2Th 1:8 [au]**9:44** Is 66:24 [av]**9:45** Jn 16:1 [aw]Jn 5:3 [ax]2Th 1:8 [ay]**9:46** Is 66:24 [az]**9:47** Mk 1:15 [ba]3Jn 10 [bb]Jms 3:6 [bc]**9:49** Lv 2:13; Ezk 43:24

[A]**9:23** Other mss add *believe* [B]**9:23** Jesus appears to quote the father’s words in v. 22 and then comment on them. [C]**9:25** A spirit that caused the boy to be deaf and unable to speak [D]**9:26** Other mss omit *him* [E]**9:29,44,46** Other mss omit bracketed text [F]**9:31** Or *handed over* [G]**9:37** Or *Whoever receives* [H]**9:38** Other mss add *who didn’t go along with us* [I]**9:41** Lit *drink in the name* [J]**9:42** A millstone turned by a donkey [K]**9:44,46,48** Is 66:24 [L]**9:49** Other mss add *and every sacrifice will be salted with salt* [M]**9:49** Lv 2:13; Ezk 43:24

how can you make it salty?[a] Have salt[b] among
yourselves and be at peace[c] with one another."

The Question of Divorce

10 He[d] set out from there and went to the
region of Judea[e] and across the Jordan.[f]
Then crowds converged on Him again and, as
He usually did, He began teaching[g] them once
more. 2 Some ·Pharisees[h] approached Him to
test[i] Him. They asked, "Is it lawful[j] for a man
to divorce[k] his wife?"[l]
3 He replied to them, "What did Moses[m]
command you?"
4 They said, "Moses permitted us to write divorce papers[n] and send her away."[o]
5 But Jesus told them, "He wrote this command for you because of the hardness of your
hearts.[p] 6 But from the beginning[q] of creation[r]
God[A] **made them male and female.**[B,s]

7 **For this reason a man will leave**[t]
his father and mother
[and be joined to his wife],[C]
8 **and the two will become one flesh.**[D,u]

So they are no longer two, but one flesh.
9 Therefore what God has joined together,
man must not separate."[v]
10 Now in the house the disciples questioned
Him again about this matter. 11 And He said to
them, "Whoever divorces his wife[w] and marries[x] another commits adultery[y] against her.
12 Also, if she divorces her husband[z] and marries another, she commits adultery."

Blessing the Children

13 Some[aa] people were bringing little children[ab] to Him so He might touch them, but
His disciples rebuked[ac] them. 14 When Jesus
saw it, He was indignant[ad] and said to them,
"Let the little children come to Me.[ae] Don't
stop[af] them, for the kingdom of God[ag] belongs
to such as these. 15 ·I assure you:[ah] Whoever
does not welcome[E,ai] the kingdom of God like
a little child[aj] will never enter it." 16 After taking them in His arms, He laid His hands on[ak]
them and blessed[al] them.

The Rich Young Ruler

17 As[am] He was setting out on a journey,[an] a
man ran up, knelt down[ao] before Him, and

[a]**9:50** Mt 5:13; Lk 14:34 [b]Ex 30:35; 2Kg 2:19-23; Col 4:6 [c]Mt 5:9; Rm 12:18; 14:13; 2Co 13:11; 1Th 5:13; Heb 12:14 [d]**10:1-12** Mt 19:1-2 [e]**10:1** Lk 1:5 [f]Mt 4:15,25; Lk 3:3; Jn 1:28; 3:26; 10:40 [g]Mt 28:20; Ac 4:2; 2Tm 4:11 [h]**10:2** Mk 7:3 [i]Jms 1:13 [j]Jn 18:31 [k]Lv 21:7 [l]1Pt 3:1 [m]**10:3** Ps 77:20; Mt 8:4; Heb 3:2 [n]**10:4** Mt 5:31 [o]Dt 24:1,3 [p]**10:5** Mk 16:14 [q]**10:6** Jn 1:1; Ac 26:4 [r]Jn 1:3; Rv 3:14 [s]Gn 1:27; 5:2 [t]**10:7** Lk 15:4 [u]**10:7-8** Gn 2:24 [v]**10:9** 1Co 7:10-15; Heb 7:26 [w]**10:11** 1Pt 3:1 [x]1Tm 5:14 [y]Mt 5:27-28 [z]**10:12** Mt 1:19 [aa]**10:13-16** Mt 19:13-15; Lk 18:15-17 [ab]**10:13** Lk 1:7 [ac]2Tm 4:2 [ad]**10:14** Lk 13:14 [ae]Lk 14:26 [af]1Co 14:39 [ag]Mk 1:15 [ah]**10:15** Ps 72:19; Rv 22:21 [ai]Ac 17:11 [aj]Lk 1:7 [ak]**10:16** 1Tm 5:22 [al]Gn 48:15 [am]**10:17-31** Mt 19:16-30; Lk 18:18-30 [an]**10:17** Mk 8:27 [ao]Mt 17:14; 27:29; Mk 1:40 [ap]Gn 1:31 [aq]Mk 4:38; Eph 4:11 [ar]Rv 21:7 [as]Lk 10:25-28; Jn 12:25; Ac 13:48 [at]**10:18** Ps 69:16 [au]**10:19** Mt 5:21 [av]Mt 5:27-28 [aw]Eph 4:28 [ax]Pr 6:19 [ay]1Co 6:7-8; 7:5; 1Tm 6:5; Jms 5:4 [az]1Tm 5:3 [ba]Ex 21:15 [bb]**10:20** Mk 4:38; Eph 4:11 [bc]**10:21** Lk 6:35;

asked Him, "Good[ap] Teacher,[aq] what must I do
to inherit[ar] eternal life?"[as]
18 "Why do you call Me good?" Jesus asked
him. "No one is good but One—God.[at] 19 You
know the commandments:

Do not murder;[au]
do not commit adultery;[av]
do not steal;[aw]
do not bear false witness;[ax]
do not defraud;[ay]
honor[az] **your father and mother.**"[F,ba]

20 He said to Him, "Teacher,[bb] I have kept all
these from my youth."
21 Then, looking at him, Jesus loved him[bc]
and said to him, "You lack one thing: Go, sell
all you have and give to the poor,[bd] and you
will have treasure[be] in heaven.[bf] Then come,[G]
follow Me."[bg] 22 But he was stunned[H] at this demand, and he went away grieving,[bh] because
he had many possessions.[bi]

Possessions and the Kingdom

23 Jesus looked around and said to His disciples, "How hard it is for those who have
wealth[bj] to enter the kingdom of God!"[bk]
24 But the disciples were astonished at His
words. Again Jesus said to them, "Children,[bl]
how hard it is[I] to enter the kingdom of God!
25 It is easier for a camel to go through the eye
of a needle than for a rich[bm] person to enter
the kingdom of God."
26 So they were even more astonished, saying
to one another, "Then who can be saved?"[bn]
27 Looking at them, Jesus said, "With men it
is impossible,[bo] but not with God, because all
things are possible with God."
28 Peter[bp] began to tell Him, "Look, we have
left everything and followed You."
29 "I assure you,"[bq] Jesus said, "there is no
one who has left house, brothers or sisters,
mother or father,[J] children, or fields because
of Me and the gospel,[br] 30 who will not receive
100 times[bs] more, now at this time[bt]—houses,
brothers and sisters, mothers and children,
and fields, with persecutions[bu]—and eternal

2Th 2:13; Heb 12:6 [bd]Mk 14:7; Rm 15:26 [be]2Co 4:7 [bf]Mt 6:20; 13:44; Lk 12:33 [bg]Jn 8:12 [bh]**10:22** 2Co 2:2 [bi]Ac 2:45; 5:1 [bj]**10:23** Ac 4:37; 8:18,20; 24:26 [bk]Mk 1:15 [bl]**10:24** Lk 1:7 [bm]**10:25** Gn 24:35; Rv 2:9 [bn]**10:26** Ac 16:30; Eph 2:8 [bo]**10:27** Heb 6:4 [bp]**10:28** Lk 6:14; Ac 10:32 [bq]**10:29** Rv 22:21 [br]Mk 1:1; Php 1:5 [bs]**10:30** Lk 21:8 [bt]Lk 20:10 [bu]Mt 13:21

[A]**10:6** Other mss omit *God* [B]**10:6** Gn 1:27; 5:2 [C]**10:7** Other mss omit bracketed text [D]**10:7-8** Gn 2:24 [E]**10:15** Or *not receive* [F]**10:19** Ex 20:12-16; Dt 5:16-20 [G]**10:21** Other mss add *taking up the cross, and* [H]**10:22** Or *he became gloomy* [I]**10:24** Other mss add *for those trusting in wealth* [J]**10:29** Other mss add *or wife*

life[a] in the age to come.[b] 31But many who are
first will be last, and the last first."[c]

The Third Prediction of His Death

32They[d] were on the road, going up to Jerusalem,[e] and Jesus was walking ahead of
them. They were astonished, but those who
followed Him were afraid.[f] Taking the Twelve
aside again, He began to tell them the things
that would happen to Him.[g]
33"Listen! We are going up to Jerusalem.
The •Son of Man[h] will be handed over to the
•chief priests and the •scribes,[i] and they will
condemn Him to death. Then they will hand
Him over to the Gentiles,[j] 34and they will
mock Him, spit on Him, flog[A] Him, and kill
Him, and He will rise[k] after three days."[l]

Suffering and Service

35Then[m] James[n] and John,[o] the sons of Zebedee,[p] approached Him and said, "Teacher,[q] we
want You to do something for us if we ask You."
36"What do you want Me to do for you?" He
asked them.
37They answered Him, "Allow us to sit at
Your right and at Your left in Your glory."[r]
38But Jesus said to them, "You don't know
what you're asking.[s] Are you able to drink the
cup[t] I drink or to be baptized with the baptism[u] I am baptized with?"[v]
39"We are able," they told Him.
Jesus said to them, "You will drink the cup I
drink, and you will be baptized with the baptism I am baptized with.[w] 40But to sit at My
right or left is not Mine to give; instead, it is
for those it has been prepared for." 41When
the other 10 disciples heard this, they began
to be indignant with James and John.[x]
42Jesus called them over and said to them,
"You know that those who are regarded as rulers of the Gentiles dominate[y] them, and their
men of high positions exercise power over
them. 43But it must not be like that among
you.[z] On the contrary, whoever wants to become great among you must be your servant,[aa]
44and whoever wants to be first among you
must be a •slave[ab] to all. 45For even the Son of
Man[ac] did not come to be served, but to serve,[ad]
and to give His life[ae] — a ransom[af] for many."[B,ag]

A Blind Man Healed

46They[ah] came to Jericho.[ai] And as He was
leaving Jericho with His disciples and a large
crowd, Bartimaeus (the son of Timaeus),
a blind[aj] beggar,[ak] was sitting by the road.[al]
47When he heard that it was Jesus the •Naza-
rene,[am] he began to cry out, "Son of David,[an]
Jesus, have mercy[ao] on me!"[ap] 48Many people
told him to keep quiet, but he was crying out
all the more, "Have mercy on me,[aq] Son of David!"
49Jesus stopped and said, "Call him."
So they called the blind man and said to
him, "Have courage![ar] Get up; He's calling for
you." 50He threw off his coat,[as] jumped up,
and came to Jesus.
51Then Jesus answered him, "What do you
want[at] Me to do for you?"
"*Rabbouni*,"[C,au] the blind man told Him, "I
want to see!"
52"Go your way," Jesus told him. "Your faith
has healed you."[av] Immediately he could see
and began to follow Him on the road.

The Triumphal Entry

11 When[aw] they approached Jerusalem,[ax]
at Bethphage and Bethany[ay] near the
•Mount of Olives, He sent two of His disciples
2and told them, "Go into the village ahead of
you. As soon as you enter it, you will find a
young donkey tied there, on which no one
has ever sat. Untie it and bring it here. 3If anyone says to you, 'Why are you doing this?' say,
'The Lord needs it and will send it back here
right away.'"
4So they went and found a young donkey
outside in the street, tied by a door. They untied it, 5and some of those standing there
said to them, "What are you doing, untying
the donkey?" 6They answered them just as
Jesus had said, so they let them go. 7Then they
brought the donkey to Jesus and threw their
robes on it, and He sat on it.
8Many people spread their robes on the
road,[az] and others spread leafy branches cut
from the fields.[D] 9Then those who went ahead
and those who followed kept shouting:

[a]**10:30** Jn 12:25; Ac 13:48 [b]Mt 12:32; Lk 20:35; Eph 1:21; 2:7 [c]**10:31** Mk 9:35 [d]**10:32-34** Mt 20:17-19; Lk 18:31-34 [e]**10:32** Ps 79:1; Mt 23:37 [f]Ps 147:11; Pr 1:7; Rv 14:7 [g]Jn 6:61 [h]**10:33** Mk 2:10 [i]Mt 2:4 [j]**10:33-34** Mk 8:31; 9:31 [k]**10:34** Mt 16:21; Ac 2:24 [l]Lk 9:22 [m]**10:35-45** Mt 20:20-28 [n]**10:35** Ac 12:2 [o]Jn 21:7 [p]Jn 21:2 [q]Mk 4:38; Eph 4:11 [r]**10:37** Mt 19:28; Lk 9:26 [s]**10:38** Jn 11:22 [t]Ps 75:8 [u]Lk 12:50; Ac 22:16 [v]Lk 12:50; Rm 6:3; 2Co 4:10-11; Gl 2:20 [w]**10:39** Ac 12:2; Rv 1:9 [x]**10:41** Jn 21:7 [y]**10:42** Ac 19:16; 1Pt 5:3 [z]**10:43** Mk 9:35; 10:45 [aa]**10:43-44** Lk 22:26 [ab]**10:44** Mt 10:24; Php 2:7; Rv 1:1 [ac]**10:45** Mk 2:10 [ad]Jn 13:13-15; Php 2:7 [ae]Jn 6:51; 10:15; Gl 2:20 [af]Lv 27:31; Ps 49:8; Mt 26:28; Eph 1:7 [ag]Is 52:13–53:12; Mt 20:28 [ah]**10:46-52** Mt 20:29-34; Lk 18:35-43 [ai]**10:46** Nm 22:1 [aj]Mt 15:14 [ak]Jn 9:8 [al]Mk 8:27 [am]**10:47** Mk 14:67 [an]2Ch 1:1; Mt 1:1; Rm 1:3 [ao]Mt 5:7; Mk 5:19; Lk 1:50 [ap]Mt 15:22; 17:15; Mk 10:48; Lk 16:24 [aq]**10:48** Mk 10:47 [ar]**10:49** Jn 16:33 [as]**10:50** Lk 19:36 [at]**10:51** Mk 1:40 [au]Jn 20:16 [av]**10:52** Mt 9:22; Mk 6:56; Lk 5:20 [aw]**11:1-11** Mt 21:1-11; Lk 19:28-44; Jn 12:12-19 [ax]**11:1** Mt 23:37; Ac 8:1 [ay]Mt 26:6; Lk 24:50; Jn 11:1,18; 12:1 [az]**11:8** Mk 8:27

[A]**10:34** Or *scourge* [B]**10:45** Or *in the place of many*; Is 53:10-12 [C]**10:51** Hb word for *my teacher* [D]**11:8** Other mss read *others were cutting leafy branches from the trees and spreading them on the road*

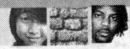

•***Hosanna!***
He who comes in the name[a]
of the Lord is the blessed One![A,b]
10 The coming kingdom[c]
of our father David[d] is blessed!
Hosanna[e] in the highest heaven!

11 And He went into Jerusalem[f] and into the
•temple complex.[g] After looking around at
everything, since it was already late, He went
out to Bethany[h] with the Twelve.

The Barren Fig Tree Is Cursed

12 The[i] next day when they came out from
Bethany, He was hungry. 13 After seeing in the
distance a fig[j] tree with leaves, He went to
find out if there was anything on it. When He
came to it, He found nothing but leaves, because it was not the season for figs. 14 He said
to it, "May no one ever eat fruit[k] from you
again!"[l] And His disciples[m] heard it.

Cleansing the Temple Complex

15 They came to Jerusalem,[n] and He went
into the temple complex[o] and began to throw out those buying and selling in the temple. He overturned the money changers'[p] tables and the chairs of those selling doves,
16 and would not permit anyone to carry goods through the temple complex.
17 Then He began to teach them: "Is it not written,[q] **My house[r] will be called a house of prayer[s] for all nations?**[B] But you have made it **a den of thieves!**"[C,t]
18 Then the •chief priests and the •scribes[u] heard it and started looking for a way to destroy Him. For they were afraid[v] of Him, because the whole crowd was astonished by His teaching.
19 And whenever evening came, they would go out of the city.

The Barren Fig Tree Is Withered

20 Early[w] in the morning, as they were passing by, they saw the fig tree withered from the roots up.
21 Then Peter[x] remembered and said to Him, "•Rabbi,[y] look! The fig tree that You cursed[z] is withered."

[a] 11:9 Jn 10:25
[b] Lk 1:42; Heb 6:14
[c] 11:10 Mk 1:15; 9:1
[d] Lk 1:27; Ac 2:29; 4:25
[e] Mk 11:9
[f] 11:11 Mt 23:37
[g] Ac 21:26
[h] Mk 11:1
[i] 11:12-19 Mt 21:12-19; Lk 19:45-48
[j] 11:13 Lk 6:44; Jn 1:48
[k] 11:14 Mt 3:8; 7:16-21
[l] Jr 8:13
[m] Mk 10:10
[n] 11:15 Mt 23:37
[o] Ac 21:26
[p] Jn 2:15
[q] 11:17 Mk 1:2; Ac 15:15
[r] Lk 11:51; Jn 2:17
[s] Ac 12:5; 16:13
[t] Jr 7:11
[u] 11:18 Mt 2:4
[v] Ps 147:11; Pr 1:7; Rv 14:7
[w] 11:20-26 Mt 21:19-22
[x] 11:21 Lk 6:14; Ac 10:32
[y] Jn 11:8
[z] Jms 3:9

GOD'S HEART FOR THE WORLD

My House

Is it not written, My house will be called a house of prayer for all nations? But you have made it a den of thieves! (Mark 11:17)

It makes sense that there would be some "buying and selling" near the temple. Jews from all over would make the pilgrimage to Jerusalem to offer sacrifices to Yahweh, and sometimes, rather than bringing a sacrifice with them, they would purchase a goat or a lamb when they got there.

But Jesus' anger also makes sense when we realize that this buying and selling was not happening *near* the temple, it was happening *in* the temple, specifically in the court of the Gentiles, a place reserved for non-Israelites to come to worship Yahweh. It was a place for the outsider. Also, the only sale item Mark mentions is doves, which were to be a free offering for those who could not afford a more expensive one. The prophets had repeatedly called Israel to care for the foreigner, the widow, the orphan, those who were poor and the outcasts of society, and Jesus is driving out those who are not heeding their words.

Exclusion and exploitation have no place in the gospel. With His death on the cross, Jesus would bring anyone who came to Him, not just into the outer courts of the temple, but into the holy of holies, the presence of God Himself. The holy of holies would no longer be reserved for one priest once a year, but would be opened to every people in every nation. How could He not be angry with those who were ignoring the provisions for which He was about to die?

[A] 11:9 Ps 118:26 [B] 11:17 Is 56:7 [C] 11:17 Jr 7:11

22 Jesus replied to them, "Have faith in
God.[a] 23 I assure you:[b] If anyone says to this
mountain, 'Be lifted up and thrown into the
sea,' and does not doubt[c] in his heart, but believes[d] that what he says will happen, it will
be done for him.[e] 24 Therefore I tell you, all
the things you pray[f] and ask for[g]—believe
that you have received[A,h] them, and you will
have them. 25 And whenever you stand[i] praying, if you have anything against anyone, forgive[j] him, so that your Father[k] in heaven[l] will
also forgive[m] you your wrongdoing. [26 But if
you don't forgive, neither will your Father in
heaven[n] forgive your wrongdoing.]"[B,C]

Messiah's Authority Challenged

27 They[o] came again to Jerusalem.[p] As He was
walking in the temple complex,[q] the chief
priests, the scribes,[r] and the elders[s] came
28 and asked Him, "By what authority[t] are You
doing these things? Who gave You this authority to do these things?"

29 Jesus said to them, "I will ask you one
question;[u] then answer Me, and I will tell you
by what authority I am doing these things.
30 Was John's baptism[v] from heaven or from
men? Answer Me."

31 They began to argue among themselves:
"If we say, 'From heaven,' He will say, 'Then
why didn't you believe[w] him?' 32 But if we say,
'From men'"—they were afraid of the crowd,
because everyone thought that John was a
genuine prophet.[x] 33 So they answered Jesus,
"We don't know."

And Jesus said to them, "Neither will I tell
you by what authority I do these things."

The Parable of the Vineyard Owner

12 Then[y] He began to speak to them in
parables: "A man planted a vineyard,[z]
put a fence around it, dug out a pit for a winepress, and built a watchtower. Then he leased
it to tenant farmers and went away. 2 At harvest time he sent[aa] a ·slave[ab] to the farmers
to collect some of the fruit[ac] of the vineyard
from the farmers. 3 But they took him, beat[ad]
him, and sent him away empty-handed.[ae]
4 Again he sent another slave to them, and
they[D] hit him on the head and treated him
shamefully.[E] 5 Then he sent another, and they
killed that one. He also sent many others;
they beat some and they killed some.

6 "He still had one to send, a beloved[af] son.
Finally[ag] he sent him to them, saying, 'They
will respect my son.'

7 "But those tenant farmers said among
themselves, 'This is the heir. Come, let's kill
him, and the inheritance will be ours!' 8 So
they seized him, killed him, and threw him
out of the vineyard.

9 "Therefore, what will the owner[F,ah] of
the vineyard do? He will come and destroy
the farmers and give the vineyard to others.
10 Haven't you read this Scripture:[ai]

The[aj] stone that
the builders rejected
has become the cornerstone.[G,ak]
11 **This came from the Lord**[al]
and is wonderful in our eyes?"[H]

12 Because they knew He had said this parable against them, they were looking for a
way to arrest Him, but they were afraid of the
crowd. So they left Him and went away.

God and Caesar

13 Then[am] they sent some of the ·Phari-
sees[an] and the ·Herodians[ao] to Him to trap
Him by what He said.[I,ap] 14 When they came,
they said to Him, "Teacher, we know You are
truthful and defer to no one, for You don't
show partiality[J,aq] but teach truthfully the
way of God. Is it lawful to pay taxes[ar] to Caesar or not? 15 Should we pay, or should we
not pay?"

But knowing their hypocrisy,[as] He said to
them, "Why are you testing[at] Me? Bring Me a
·denarius[au] to look at." 16 So they brought one.
"Whose image[av] and inscription[aw] is this?" He
asked them.

"Caesar's," they said.

17 Then Jesus told them, "Give back to Caesar the things that are Caesar's, and to God
the things that are God's."[ax] And they were
amazed[ay] at Him.

[a] 11:22 Mt 17:20 [b] 11:23 Ps 72:19; Rv 22:21 [c] Ac 10:20 [d] Jn 3:16; Ac 10:43; Rm 10:9; 1Pt 1:8-10 [e] Mk 9:23; Jn 11:22 [f] 11:24 Mt 5:44; Ac 12:12 [g] Jn 14:13; Jms 1:5 [h] Mt 7:8 [i] 11:25 Lk 18:11 [j] Mt 6:12; 9:2 [k] Mt 5:16; Lk 11:13 [l] Mt 6:1; Lk 12:33 [m] Ps 25:11; Mt 9:2 [n] 11:26 Mt 24:35; Ac 17:24; Eph 6:9; Rv 21:10 [o] 11:27-33 Mt 21:23-27; Lk 20:1-8 [p] 11:27 Mt 23:37 [q] Ac 21:26 [r] Mt 2:4 [s] 3Jn 1 [t] 11:28 Mk 1:22 [u] 11:29 Mk 4:14 [v] 11:30 Lk 7:29; Ac 18:25; 19:3 [w] 11:31 1Jn 5:10 [x] 11:32 Mt 2:23; Ac 7:52 [y] 12:1-12 Mt 21:33-46; Lk 20:9-19 [z] 12:1 Gn 9:20 [aa] 12:2 Mk 3:14 [ab] Mt 10:24 [ac] Mt 3:8; 7:16 [ad] 12:3 Lk 22:63 [ae] Col 2:8 [af] 12:6 Eph 1:6; Phm 1 [ag] Heb 1:1-2 [ah] 12:9 Col 3:22 [ai] 12:10 Mt 26:54; 2Pt 1:20 [aj] 12:10-11 Ps 118:22-23 [ak] Ac 4:11; 1Pt 2:7 [al] 12:11 Col 4:1; Jd 5 [am] 12:13-17 Mt 22:15-22; Lk 20:20-26 [an] 12:13 Mk 7:3 [ao] Mk 3:6 [ap] Lk 11:54 [aq] 12:14 Dt 1:17 [ar] Mt 17:25 [as] 12:15 Mt 23:28; Lk 12:1; Gl 2:13; 1Tm 4:2; 1Pt 2:1 [at] Jms 1:13 [au] Mt 18:28 [av] 12:16 Rv 13:14 [aw] Mk 15:26; Lk 23:38

[ax] 12:17 Rm 13:7 [ay] Rv 17:6

[A] 11:24 Some mss read *you receive*; other mss read *you will receive* [B] 11:26 Other mss omit bracketed text [C] 11:25-26 These are the only uses of this word in Mk. It means "the violation of the Law" or "stepping over a boundary" or "departing from the path" or "trespass." [D] 12:4 Other mss add *threw stones and* [E] 12:4 Other mss add *and sent him off* [F] 12:9 Or *lord* [G] 12:10 Lit *the head of the corner* [H] 12:10-11 Ps 118:22-23 [I] 12:13 Lit *trap Him in (a) word* [J] 12:14 Lit *don't look on the face of men*; that is, on the outward appearance

The Sadducees and the Resurrection

[18]Some[a] ·Sadducees,[b] who say there is no
resurrection,[c] came to Him and questioned
Him: [19]"Teacher,[d] Moses[e] wrote for us that **if
a man's brother dies**, leaves his wife behind,
and **leaves no child,[f] his brother should take
the wife[g] and produce ·offspring for his
brother.**[A,h] [20]There were seven brothers. The
first took a wife, and dying, left no offspring.
[21]The second also took her, and he died, leaving no offspring. And the third likewise. [22]So
the seven[B] left no offspring. Last of all, the
woman died too. [23]In the resurrection, when
they rise,[C] whose wife will she be, since the
seven had married her?"[D]

[24]Jesus told them, "Are you not deceived
because you don't know the Scriptures[i] or
the power[j] of God?[k] [25]For when they rise[l]
from the dead,[m] they neither marry nor are
given in marriage[n] but are like angels[o] in
heaven. [26]Now concerning the dead being
raised—haven't you read in the book of Moses, in the passage about the burning bush,
how God spoke to him: **I[p] am the God of
Abraham[q] and the God of Isaac[r] and the God
of Jacob**?[E,s] [27]He is not God of the dead but of
the living. You are badly deceived."

The Primary Commands

[28]One[t] of the ·scribes[u] approached. When
he heard them debating and saw that Jesus
answered them well, he asked Him, "Which
command is the most important of all?"[F]

[29]"This is the most important,"[G] Jesus answered:

> **Listen, Israel! The Lord[v] our God, the
> Lord[w] is One.**[H] [30]**Love[x] the Lord your
> God[y] with all your heart, with all your
> soul, with all your mind,[z] and with all
> your strength.**[I,J,aa]

[31]"The second is: **Love your neighbor[ab] as
yourself.**[K,ac] There is no other command[ad]
greater than these."

[32]Then the scribe said to Him, "You are
right, Teacher! You have correctly said that
He is One, and there is no one[ae] else except
Him.[af] [33]And to love[ag] Him with all your heart,
with all your understanding,[L] and with all
your strength, and to love your neighbor as
yourself, is far more important than all the
burnt offerings and sacrifices."[ah]

[34]When Jesus saw that he answered intelli-
gently, He said to him, "You are not far from
the kingdom of God."[ai] And no one dared[aj] to
question Him any longer.

The Question about the Messiah

[35]So[ak] Jesus asked this question as He taught
in the ·temple complex,[al] "How can the
scribes[am] say that the ·Messiah[an] is the Son of
David?[ao] [36]David[ap] himself says by the Holy
Spirit:[aq]

> **The Lord[ar] declared to my Lord,
> 'Sit at My right hand[as]
> until I put Your enemies
> under Your feet.'**[M,at]

[37]David himself calls Him 'Lord'; how then
can the Messiah be his Son?" And the large
crowd was listening to Him with delight.

Warning against the Scribes

[38]He[au] also said in His teaching, "Beware
of the scribes, who want to go around in
long robes,[av] and who want greetings in the
marketplaces,[aw] [39]the front seats[ax] in the
·synagogues,[ay] and the places of honor[az] at
banquets.[ba] [40]They devour[bb] widows'[bc] houses
and say long prayers[bd] just for show. These
will receive harsher punishment."

The Widow's Gift

[41]Sitting[be] across from the temple treasury,[bf]
He watched how the crowd dropped money
into the treasury. Many rich[bg] people were
putting in large sums. [42]And a poor[bh] widow
came and dropped in two tiny coins worth
very little.[N] [43]Summoning His disciples,[bi] He
said to them, "·I assure you:[bj] This poor widow
has put in more than all those giving to the
temple treasury.[bk] [44]For they all gave out of
their surplus,[bl] but she out of her poverty[bm]

[a]**12:18-27** Mt 22:23-33; Lk 20:27-40 [b]**12:18** Ac 23:6 [c]Ac 1:22 [d]**12:19** Mk 4:38; Eph 4:11 [e]Ps 77:20; Mt 8:4; Heb 3:2 [f]Lk 1:7 [g]Mt 1:6 [h]Gn 38:8; Dt 25:5-10 [i]**12:24** Mt 26:54; 2Pt 1:20 [j]Lk 1:35; 6:19 [k]2Co 13:4; Rv 11:17 [l]**12:25** Lk 18:33 [m]Jn 5:25; 20:9 [n]1Tm 5:14 [o]Mt 13:49; Ac 5:19; Rv 14:6 [p]**12:26** Ex 3:6,15-16 [q]Gl 3:6 [r]Jms 2:21 [s]Mt 1:2; Lk 1:33 [t]**12:28-34** Mt 22:34-40 [u]**12:28** Mt 2:4 [v]**12:29** Col 4:1; Jd 5 [w]Dt 6:4 [x]**12:30** Lk 6:35 [y]Dt 6:5; Lk 10:27 [z]1Jn 5:20 [aa]Dt 6:4-5; Jos 22:5 [ab]**12:31** Lk 10:29 [ac]Lv 19:18; 1Jn 4:21 [ad]Mk 7:8 [ae]**12:32** Rm 3:30 [af]Dt 4:35,39; 6:4; Is 37:20; 43:10; 44:6; 45:21 [ag]**12:33** Lk 6:35 [ah]1Sm 15:22; Ps 51:16; Hs 6:6; Am 5:22; Mc 6:6-8 [ai]**12:34** Mk 1:15 [aj]Lk 20:40 [ak]**12:35-37** Mt 22:41-46; Lk 20:41-44 [al]**12:35** Ac 21:26 [am]Mt 2:4 [an]Mt 1:17; Eph 5:2 [ao]2Ch 1:1; Mt 1:1; Rm 1:3 [ap]**12:36** Lk 1:27 [aq]Jn 1:33; Ac 19:21 [ar]Lk 17:5 [as]Mt 20:21 [at]Ps 110:1 [au]**12:38-40** Mt 23:1-36; Lk 20:45-47 [av]**12:38** Rv 7:14 [aw]Mk 6:56 [ax]**12:39** Lk 11:43 [ay]Jms 2:2 [az]Lk 14:7-8 [ba]Jn 13:2 [bb]**12:40** Gl 5:15 [bc]Jms 1:27 [bd]Mt 5:44; Ac 12:12 [be]**12:41-44** Lk 21:1-4 [bf]**12:41** Jn 8:20 [bg]Gn 24:35; Rv 2:9 [bh]**12:42** Mk 14:7 [bi]**12:43** Mt 9:10; Mk 10:10; Lk 6:1; Jn 6:3; Ac 6:1 [bj]Ps 72:19; Rv 22:21 [bk]Jn 8:20 [bl]**12:44** 1Co 15:58 [bm]Php 4:11

[A]**12:19** Gn 38:8; Dt 25:5 [B]**12:22** Other mss add *had taken her and* [C]**12:23** Other mss omit *when they rise* [D]**12:23** Lit *the seven had her as a wife* [E]**12:26** Ex 3:6,15-16 [F]**12:28** Lit *Which command is first of all?* [G]**12:29** Other mss add *of all the commands* [H]**12:29** Or *The Lord our God is one Lord.* [I]**12:30** Other mss add *This is the first commandment.* [J]**12:30** Dt 6:4-5; Jos 22:5 [K]**12:31** Lv 19:18 [L]**12:33** Other mss add *with all your soul* [M]**12:36** Ps 110:1 [N]**12:42** Lit *dropped in two lepta, which is a quadrans*; the *lepton* was the smallest and least valuable Gk coin in use. The *quadrans*, 1/64 of a daily wage, was the smallest Roman coin.

has put in everything she possessed[a] — all she
had to live on."[b]

Destruction of the Temple Predicted

13 As[c] He was going out of the •temple
complex,[d] one of His disciples said to
Him, "Teacher,[e] look! What massive stones!
What impressive buildings!"[f]
2 Jesus said to him, "Do you see these great
buildings?[g] Not one stone will be left here on
another that will not be thrown down!"

Signs of the End of the Age

3 While He was sitting on the •Mount of Olives[h] across from the temple complex,[i] Peter,[j]
James,[k] John,[l] and Andrew[m] asked Him privately, 4 "Tell us, when will these things happen? And what will be the sign when all these
things are about to take place?"
5 Then Jesus began by telling them: "Watch
out that no one deceives you. 6 Many will
come in My name,[n] saying, 'I am He,'[o] and they
will deceive[p] many. 7 When you hear of wars
and rumors of wars,[q] don't be alarmed;[r] these
things must take place,[s] but the end is not
yet. 8 For nation will rise up against nation,
and kingdom against kingdom.[t] There will be
earthquakes in various places, and famines.[A]
These are the beginning[u] of birth pains.[v]

Persecutions Predicted

9 "But you, be on your guard! They will
hand you over to sanhedrins,[B,w] and you
will be flogged[x] in the •synagogues.[y] You will
stand before governors and kings[z] because
of Me,[aa] as a witness[ab] to them.[ac] 10 And the
good news[C,ad] must first be proclaimed to all
nations. 11 So when they arrest you and hand
you over, don't worry beforehand what you
will say. On the contrary, whatever is given
to you in that hour — say it. For it isn't you
speaking, but the Holy Spirit. 12 Then brother
will betray[ae] brother to death,[af] and a father
his child. Children will rise up against parents and put them to death. 13 And you will
be hated by everyone because of My name.[ag]
But the one who endures to the end will be
delivered.[D,ah]

The Great Tribulation

14 "When you see the **abomination that
causes desolation**[E,ai] standing where it should
not" (let the reader understand[F]), "then those
in Judea[aj] must flee to the mountains! 15 A man
on the housetop must not come down or go
in to get anything out of his house.[ak] 16 And a
man in the field must not go back to get his
clothes.[al] 17 Woe[am] to pregnant women and
nursing mothers in those days! 18 Pray[an] it[G]
won't happen in winter. 19 For those will be
days of tribulation,[ao] the kind that hasn't been
from the beginning[ap] of the world,[H,aq] which
God created, until now and never will be
again! 20 Unless the Lord[ar] limited those days,[as]
no one would survive.[I] But He limited those
days because of the elect,[at] whom He chose.[au]
21 "Then if anyone tells you, 'Look, here is
the •Messiah![av] Look — there!' do not believe
it! 22 For false messiahs[J] and false prophets
will rise up and will perform signs and wonders[aw] to lead astray, if possible, the elect.
23 And you must watch! I have told you everything in advance.

The Coming of the Son of Man

24 "But in those days, after that tribulation:[ax]

The sun will be darkened,
and the moon will not shed its light;
25 the stars[ay] will be falling from the sky,
and the celestial powers will be shaken.[az]

26 Then they will see the •Son of Man[ba] coming[bb] in clouds[bc] with great power[bd] and
glory.[be] 27 He will send out the angels[bf] and
gather His elect[bg] from the four winds, from
the end of the earth to the end of the sky.[bh]

The Parable of the Fig Tree

28 "Learn[bi] this parable[bj] from the fig[bk]
tree: As soon as its branch becomes tender and sprouts leaves, you know that summer is near.[bl] 29 In the same way, when you
see these things happening, know[K] that He[L]
is near — at the door! 30 •I assure you:[bm] This
generation will certainly not pass away un-

[a] **12:44** Lk 15:12 [b] 1Jn 3:17 [c] **13:1-37** Mt 24:1-51; Lk 21:5-38 [d] **13:1** Ac 21:26 [e] Mk 4:38 [f] 1Co 14:3 [g] **13:2** Mk 14:58 [h] **13:3** Mt 21:1 [i] Ac 21:26 [j] Lk 6:14; Ac 10:32 [k] Ac 12:2 [l] Jn 21:7 [m] Jn 6:8 [n] **13:6** Jn 10:25; 14:13 [o] Ex 3:14; Ps 45:8; Jn 8:24 [p] 1Jn 4:6 [q] **13:7** Jr 51:46; Dn 11:44 [r] 2Th 2:2 [s] Dn 2:28-29 [t] **13:8** Is 19:2 [u] Ac 26:4 [v] Gl 4:19 [w] **13:9** Mt 10:17 [x] Lk 22:63; Ac 5:40; 16:19-23,37 [y] Jms 2:2 [z] Ac 24:10-27; 25:1-12,23-27 [aa] Rm 8:36 [ab] Mk 6:11; 1Tm 2:6 [ac] Php 1:12 [ad] **13:10** Mk 1:1; Php 1:5 [ae] **13:12** Jn 13:21 [af] Is 19:2; Mc 7:6 [ag] **13:13** Mt 10:22; Lk 6:22; Jn 15:18-21 [ah] 1Co 4:12; 2Th 1:4; 2Tm 2:12; Jms 1:12 [ai] **13:14** Dn 9:27; 11:31; 12:11 [aj] Lk 1:5 [ak] **13:15** Lk 17:22-36 [al] **13:16** Lk 19:36 [am] **13:17** Rv 9:12 [an] **13:18** Mt 5:44; Ac 12:12 [ao] **13:19** 1Co 1:4 [ap] Ac 26:4 [aq] Jn 1:3; Rv 3:14 [ar] **13:20** Col 4:1; Jd 5 [as] Is 60:21-22 [at] Mt 24:22 [au] Eph 1:4 [av] **13:21** Mt 1:17; Eph 5:2 [aw] **13:22** Ex 7:3; Dn 6:27; Jn 4:48; Ac 4:30; Rm 15:19; 2Th 2:9; Heb 2:4 [ax] **13:24** 2Co 1:4 [ay] **13:25** Rv 1:16 [az] **13:24-25** Is 13:10; 34:4; Jl 2:10,31; 3:15 [ba] **13:26** Mk 2:10 [bb] Mk 8:38; 1Th 4:16 [bc] Dn 7:13-14 [bd] Lk 6:19 [be] Mk 10:37; Lk 9:32 [bf] **13:27** Mt 13:49; Ac 5:19; Rv 14:6 [bg] Mt 22:14,22 [bh] Zch 2:6 [bi] **13:28** Jn 7:15 [bj] Mk 12:1 [bk] Jn 1:48 [bl] Rv 1:1 [bm] **13:30** Ps 72:19; Rv 22:21

[A] **13:8** Other mss add *and disturbances* [B] **13:9** Local Jewish courts or local councils [C] **13:10** Or *the gospel* [D] **13:13** Or *saved* [E] **13:14** Dn 9:27 [F] **13:14** These are, most likely, Mark's words to his readers. [G] **13:18** Other mss read *pray that your escape* [H] **13:19** Lit *creation* [I] **13:20** Lit *days, all flesh would not survive* [J] **13:22** Or *false christs* [K] **13:29** Or *you know* [L] **13:29** Or *it*; = summer

til all these things take place. 31 Heaven and earth[a] will pass away,[b] but My words will never pass away.[c]

No One Knows the Day or Hour

32 "Now concerning that day[d] or hour no one knows—neither the angels[e] in heaven nor the Son[f]—except the Father.[g] 33 Watch! Be alert![A] For you don't know when the time[h] is coming.[i] 34 It is like[j] a man on a journey, who left his house, gave authority to his •slaves,[k] gave each one his work, and commanded the doorkeeper to be alert. 35 Therefore be alert,[l] since you don't know when the master[m] of the house is coming—whether in the evening or at midnight or at the crowing of the rooster or early in the morning. 36 Otherwise, he might come suddenly and find you sleeping.[n] 37 And what I say to you, I say to everyone: Be alert!"

The Plot to Kill Jesus

14 After[o] two days it was the •Passover[p] and the Festival[q] of •Unleavened Bread.[r] The •chief priests and the •scribes[s] were looking for a treacherous[t] way to arrest and kill Him.[u] 2 "Not during the festival," they said, "or there may be rioting among the people."

The Anointing at Bethany

3 While[v] He was in Bethany[w] at the house of Simon who had a serious skin disease,[x] as He was reclining at the table,[y] a woman came with an alabaster jar of pure and expensive fragrant oil of nard. She broke the jar and poured it on His head.[z] 4 But some were expressing indignation to one another: "Why has this fragrant oil been wasted? 5 For this oil might have been sold for more than 300 •denarii[aa] and given to the poor."[ab] And they began to scold her.

6 Then Jesus said, "Leave her alone. Why are you bothering her? She has done a noble thing[ac] for Me. 7 You always have the poor[ad] with you, and you can do what is good for them whenever you want, but you do not always have Me.[ae] 8 She has done what she could; she has anointed My body[af] in advance for burial.[ag] 9 •I assure you:[ah] Wherever the gospel[ai] is proclaimed in the whole world,[aj] what this woman has done will also be told in memory of her."

10 Then[ak] Judas Iscariot,[al] one of the Twelve,[am] went to the chief priests[an] to hand Him over[ao] to them. 11 And when they heard this, they were glad and promised to give him silver.[B,ap] So he started looking for a good opportunity to betray[aq] Him.

Preparation for Passover

12 On[ar] the first day of Unleavened Bread, when they sacrifice the Passover lamb,[as] His disciples[at] asked Him, "Where do You want us to go and prepare the Passover so You may eat it?"

13 So He sent two of His disciples and told them, "Go into the city, and a man carrying a water jug will meet you. Follow him. 14 Wherever he enters, tell the owner of the house, 'The Teacher[au] says, "Where is the guest room for Me to eat the Passover with My disciples?"' 15 He will show you a large room upstairs, furnished and ready. Make the preparations for us there." 16 So the disciples[av] went out, entered the city, and found it just as He had told them, and they prepared the Passover.

Betrayal at the Passover

17 When[aw] evening came, He arrived with the Twelve.[ax] 18 While they were reclining and eating, Jesus said, "I assure you: One of you will betray Me—one who is eating with Me!"

19 They began to be distressed and to say to Him one by one, "Surely not I?"

20 He said to them, "It is one of the Twelve—the one who is dipping bread with Me in the bowl. 21 For the •Son of Man[ay] will go just as it is written[az] about Him,[ba] but woe[bb] to that man by whom the Son of Man is betrayed! It would have been better for that man if he had not been born."

The First Lord's Supper

22 As[bc] they were eating, He took bread,[bd] blessed and broke[be] it, gave it to them,[bf] and said, "Take it;[C] this is My body."[bg]

---

[a] **13:31** Lk 10:21 [b] 2Pt 3:10 [c] Ps 102:25-27; Is 40:6-8; 51:6; Mt 5:18; Lk 16:17 [d] **13:32** Mt 25:13 [e] Mt 13:49 [f] Jn 5:19; Heb 1:2 [g] Mt 5:16; 11:27; Jn 8:42 [h] **13:33** Lk 20:20 [i] Ac 1:7; 1Th 5:1-2; 1Pt 5:6 [j] **13:34** Lk 12:35-40 [k] Mt 10:24 [l] **13:35** Rv 16:15 [m] Col 3:22 [n] **13:36** Pr 6:4 [o] **14:1-2** Mt 26:1-5; Lk 22:1-2 [p] **14:1** Ex 12:11 [q] Jn 5:1 [r] Ex 23:15 [s] Mt 2:4 [t] Ps 10:7 [u] Jn 5:18 [v] **14:3-9** Mt 26:6-13; Jn 12:2-8 [w] **14:3** Mk 11:1 [x] Mt 11:5 [y] Lv 19:34 [z] Rm 12:13 [aa] **14:5** Mt 18:28 [ab] Rm 15:26 [ac] **14:6** 1Pt 2:12 [ad] **14:7** Dt 15:11 [ae] Lk 10:38-42 [af] **14:8** Lk 12:4 [ag] Jn 19:40 [ah] **14:9** Ps 72:19; Rv 22:21 [ai] Mk 1:1; Php 1:5 [aj] Mt 13:38; 1Jn 2:2 [ak] **14:10-11** Mt 26:14-16; Lk 22:3-6 [al] **14:10** Mk 3:19 [am] Mk 11:11 [an] Mt 2:4 [ao] Mk 9:31 [ap] **14:11** Lk 19:15 [aq] Jn 13:21 [ar] **14:12-16** Mt 26:17-19; Lk 22:7-13 [as] **14:12** Ex 12:21 [at] Mt 9:10; Mk 10:10; Lk 6:1; Jn 6:3; Ac 6:1 [au] **14:14** Mk 4:38; Eph 4:11 [av] **14:16** Mk 10:10 [aw] **14:17-21** Mt 26:20-25; Lk 22:21-23; Jn 13:21-30 [ax] **14:17** Mk 11:11 [ay] **14:21** Mk 2:10 [az] Mk 1:2; Ac 15:15 [ba] Dn 7:21,25; 9:26 [bb] Rv 9:12 [bc] **14:22-26** Mt 26:26-30; Lk 22:17-20; 1Co 11:23-25 [bd] **14:22** 1Co 10:16 [be] Mt 14:19; 15:36; Ac 2:46; 20:7,11; 27:35 [bf] Lk 24:30 [bg] Lk 12:4; Jn 2:21; 6:51

[A] **13:33** Other mss add *and pray* [B] **14:11** Or *money*; in Mt 26:15 it is specified as 30 pieces of silver; see Zch 11:12-13 [C] **14:22** Other mss add *eat;*

Lottie Moon (1840–1912)

From Tunchow, China in 1887, Charlotte "Lottie" Moon wrote "I would I had a thousand lives that I might give them to . . . China!"[1] And, in many ways she did give a thousand lives to China. Moon gave everything of the one she had, and her letters and story still inspire others to give their lives and their money to furthering missions in China and around the world.

Christianity had seemed irrelevant to Moon until the Spirit moved her heart at a revival meeting when she was eighteen. As one of the only women of her time in the southern states to receive a master's level education, she spent the next years teaching at a girls' school, and ministering to poor families in Georgia. When she was thirty-three, the Spirit used another sermon to move her to give her life to missions and to China.

In all, Moon spent thirty-nine years in China. For the first ten years she was a teacher, but her frustration that her gifts were not being used to their full potential led her to write letters and articles arguing for single female missionaries to be given more freedom on the mission field. Eventually, she left the school and moved to the Chinese inland to be an evangelist. Adopting Chinese customs and clothing, Moon preached the gospel, bringing hundreds to faith in Jesus Christ. Moon's love for the Chinese people grew as she faced war and famine alongside them. Near the end of her life, as she watched those around her starving to death, she shared everything she had to the point that it endangered her own life. By 1912, Moon was starving along with them. Other missionaries tried to help her by bringing her back to the United States, but Moon died along the way. Following Christ's example, she gave her life for those she loved.

Moon's influence extended beyond the borders of China. Her articles and letters prompted women in the United States to organize mission societies and fundraise in order to send more missionaries. In 1888, at her suggestion, the week before Christmas became a week of giving money to missions within the Southern Baptist Convention. This offering, named after her in 1918, now raises half of the Southern Baptist Mission budget each year, and since 1888 has raised more than 1.5 billion dollars.

As she had done with her own life, she called for others to give everything for the sake of God's mission in the world. "Why should we not . . . instead of the paltry offerings we make, do something that will prove that we are really in earnest in claiming to be followers of him who, though he was rich, for our sake became poor?"[2]

Through her work and her pleas for others to join her, one could say Moon has given more than a thousand lives to furthering missions in China and throughout the world.

[1] Lottie Moon, Zhenjiang, China, August 27, 1888, http://www.imb.org/main/give/page.asp?StoryID=5530&LanguageID=1709 (accessed May 18, 2011).

[2] Lottie Moon, Tungchow, China, Sept. 15, 1887, http://www.imb.org/main/give/page.asp?StoryID=5530&LanguageID=1709 (accessed May 18, 2011).

23 Then He took a cup, and after giving
thanks,[a] He gave it to them, and so they all
drank from it. 24 He said to them, "This is My
blood that establishes the covenant;[A,b] it is
shed[c] for many.[d] 25 I assure you:[e] I will no longer drink of the fruit of the vine[f] until that
day when I drink it in a new[g] way[B] in the kingdom of God."[h] 26 After singing psalms,[C] they
went out to the •Mount of Olives.[i]

Peter's Denial Predicted

27 Then[j] Jesus said to them, "All of you will
run away,[D,E] because it is written:[k]

I will strike the shepherd,
and the sheep[l] will be scattered.[F,m]

28 But after I have been resurrected,[n] I will go
ahead of you to Galilee."[o]
29 Peter[p] told Him, "Even if everyone runs
away, I will certainly not!"
30 "I assure you," Jesus said to him, "today,
this very night, before the rooster crows
twice, you will deny Me three times!"[q]
31 But he kept insisting, "If I have to die with
You, I will never deny You!" And they all said
the same thing.

The Prayer in the Garden

32 Then[r] they came to a place named Gethsemane, and He told His disciples,[s] "Sit here
while I pray."[t] 33 He took Peter,[u] James,[v] and
John[w] with Him, and He began to be deeply
distressed and horrified. 34 Then He said
to them, "My soul is swallowed up in sorrow[G] — to the point of death. Remain here
and stay awake."[x] 35 Then He went a little farther, fell to the ground, and began to pray
that if it were possible, the hour[y] might pass
from Him. 36 And He said, "•*Abba*,[z] Father![aa]
All things are possible[ab] for You. Take this
cup[ac] away from Me. Nevertheless, not what
I will, but what You will."
37 Then He came and found them sleeping.
"Simon,[ad] are you sleeping?" He asked Peter.[ae]
"Couldn't you stay awake one hour? 38 Stay
awake and pray[af] so that you won't enter into
temptation.[ag] The spirit[ah] is willing, but the
flesh[ai] is weak."
39 Once again He went away and prayed,
saying the same thing. 40 And He came again
and found them sleeping, because they could
not keep their eyes open.[H] They did not know
what to say to Him.[aj] 41 Then He came a third
time and said to them, "Are you still sleeping
and resting? Enough! The time has come.
Look, the Son of Man[ak] is being betrayed into
the hands of sinners.[al] 42 Get up;[am] let's go!
See — My betrayer is near."

The Judas Kiss

43 While[an] He was still speaking, Judas,[ao] one
of the Twelve,[ap] suddenly arrived. With him
was a mob, with swords and clubs, from the
chief priests, the scribes,[aq] and the elders.[ar]
44 His betrayer had given them a signal. "The
One I kiss," he said, "He's the One; arrest Him
and take Him away under guard." 45 So when
he came, he went right up to Him and said,
"•Rabbi!"[as] — and kissed Him. 46 Then they
took hold of Him and arrested Him. 47 And
one of those who stood by drew his sword,
struck the high priest's •slave, and cut off his
ear.
48 But Jesus said to them, "Have you come
out with swords and clubs, as though I were
a criminal,[I] to capture Me? 49 Every day I was
among you, teaching in the •temple complex,[at] and you didn't arrest Me. But the
Scriptures[au] must be fulfilled."[av] 50 Then they
all deserted Him and ran away.[aw]
51 Now a certain young man,[J] having a linen
cloth wrapped around his naked body, was
following Him. They caught hold of him,
52 but he left the linen cloth behind and ran
away naked.[ax]

Jesus Faces the Sanhedrin

53 They[ay] led Jesus away to the high priest,[az]
and all the chief priests, the elders, and the
scribes[ba] convened.[bb] 54 Peter[bc] followed Him
at a distance, right into the high priest's
courtyard. He was sitting with the temple police,[K,bd] warming himself by the fire.[L]
55 The chief priests and the whole •Sanhe-
drin[be] were looking for testimony against

[a]**14:23** Mk 8:6 [b]**14:24** Ex 24:8; Zch 9:11; Heb 9:18-20; 10:29; 13:20 [c]Gn 4:11; Nm 35:33; Lm 4:13; Mt 23:35 [d]Is 52:13–53:12 [e]**14:25** Rv 22:21 [f]Is 32:12; Hab 3:17; Jms 3:12 [g]Is 25:6; Lk 13:28-29; 14:15-24 [h]Mk 1:15 [i]**14:26** Mt 21:1 [j]**14:27-31** Mt 26:31-35; Lk 22:31-38; Jn 13:31-38 [k]**14:27** Ac 15:15 [l]Mt 7:15 [m]Zch 13:7 [n]**14:28** 1Co 15:4 [o]Mt 17:22 [p]**14:29** Lk 6:14; Ac 10:32 [q]**14:30** Mk 14:72 [r]**14:32-42** Mt 26:36-46; Lk 22:39-46 [s]**14:32** Mk 10:10 [t]Mt 5:44; Ac 12:12 [u]**14:33** Lk 6:14 [v]Ac 12:2 [w]Jn 21:7 [x]**14:34** Rv 16:15 [y]**14:35** Jn 2:4 [z]**14:36** Rm 8:15; Gl 4:6 [aa]Mt 5:16; 11:27; Jn 8:42 [ab]Mt 19:26; Mk 9:23 [ac]Ps 11:6; Is 51:17,22; Lm 4:21; Ezk 23:32-34; Mk 10:38-39; Jn 18:11 [ad]**14:37** Mt 16:17 [ae]Lk 6:14 [af]**14:38** Mt 5:44 [ag]Mt 6:13; Lk 4:13 [ah]Ps 51:12 [ai]Php 3:3 [aj]**14:40** Mk 4:40 [ak]**14:41** Mk 2:10 [al]Mk 8:31; 9:31; 10:33-34 [am]**14:42** Mk 5:41 [an]**14:43-52** Mt 26:47-56; Lk 22:47-53; Jn 18:1-2 [ao]**14:43** Mk 3:19 [ap]Mk 11:11 [aq]Mt 2:4 [ar]3Jn 1 [as]**14:45** Jn 11:8 [at]**14:49** Ac 21:26 [au]2Pt 1:20 [av]Mt 1:22; Mk 9:12 [aw]**14:50** Mk 4:40; Jms 4:7 [ax]**14:52** Am 2:16 [ay]**14:53-65** Mt 26:57-68; Lk 22:54,63-65; Jn 18:24 [az]**14:53** Mt 26:3 [ba]Mt 2:4 [bb]Mk 8:31; 10:33 [bc]**14:54** Lk 6:14 [bd]Jn 18:18 [be]**14:55** Mk 13:9

A**14:24** Other mss read *the new covenant* B**14:25** Or *drink new wine*; lit *drink it new* C**14:26** Pss 113–118 were sung during and after the Passover meal. D**14:27** Other mss add *because of Me this night* E**14:27** Or •*stumble* F**14:27** Zch 13:7 G**14:34** Or *I am deeply grieved* H**14:40** Lit *because their eyes were weighed down* I**14:48** Lit *as against a criminal* J**14:51** Perhaps John Mark who later wrote this Gospel K**14:54** Or *the officers*; lit *the servants* L**14:54** Lit *light*

Jesus to put Him to death,[a] but they could
find none. 56 For many were giving false testimony[b] against Him, but the testimonies did
not agree. 57 Some stood up and were giving
false testimony against Him, stating, 58 "We
heard Him say, 'I will demolish this sanctuary
made by human hands,[c] and in three days I
will build another not made by hands.'" 59 Yet
their testimony did not agree[d] even on this.

60 Then the high priest stood up before
them all and questioned Jesus, "Don't You
have an answer to what these men are testifying against You?" 61 But He kept silent and did
not answer anything.[e] Again the high priest
questioned Him, "Are You the ·Messiah,[f] the
Son[g] of the Blessed[h] One?"

62 "I am,"[i] said Jesus, "and all of you[A] will see
the Son of Man[j] seated at the right hand[k] of
the Power and **coming with the clouds[l] of
heaven**."[B,m]

63 Then the high priest[n] tore his robes[o] and
said, "Why do we still need witnesses?[p] 64 You
have heard the blasphemy![q] What is your decision?"[C]

And they all condemned Him to be deserving of death.[r] 65 Then some began to spit on
Him, to blindfold Him, and to beat Him, saying, "Prophesy!"[s] The temple police[t] also took
Him and slapped Him.

Peter Denies His Lord

66 While[u] Peter[v] was in the courtyard below, one of the high priest's servants came.
67 When she saw Peter warming himself, she
looked at him and said, "You also were with
that ·Nazarene,[w] Jesus."

68 But he denied it: "I don't know or understand what you're talking about!" Then
he went out to the entryway, and a rooster
crowed.[D]

69 When the servant saw him again she began to tell those standing nearby, "This man
is one of them!"

70 But again he denied it. After a little while
those standing there said to Peter again, "You
certainly are one of them, since you're also a
Galilean!"[E,x]

71 Then he started to curse[F] and to swear
with an oath,[y] "I don't know this man you're
talking about!"

72 Immediately a rooster crowed a second
time,[z] and Peter remembered when Jesus had
spoken the word to him, "Before the rooster
crows twice, you will deny Me three times."
When he thought about it, he began to weep.[G]

Jesus Faces Pilate

15 As[aa] soon as it was morning, the ·chief
priests had a meeting with the elders,[ab]
·scribes,[ac] and the whole ·Sanhedrin.[ad] After
tying Jesus up, they led Him away and handed
Him over to ·Pilate.[ae]

2 So Pilate asked Him, "Are You the King[af] of
the Jews?"[ag]

He answered him, "You have said it."[H]

3 And the chief priests began to accuse Him
of many things. 4 Then Pilate[ah] questioned
Him again, "Are You not answering anything?
Look how many things they are accusing You
of!" 5 But Jesus still did not answer anything,
so Pilate was amazed.

Jesus or Barabbas

6 At[ai] the festival[aj] it was Pilate's[ak] custom
to release for the people a prisoner they requested. 7 There was one named Barabbas,
who was in prison with rebels who had committed murder[al] during the rebellion.[am] 8 The
crowd came up and began to ask Pilate to do
for them as was his custom. 9 So Pilate answered them, "Do you want me to release the
King[an] of the Jews[ao] for you?" 10 For he knew
it was because of envy[ap] that the chief priests
had handed Him over. 11 But the chief priests
stirred up the crowd so that he would release
Barabbas to them instead.

12 Pilate asked them again, "Then what do
you want me to do with the One you call the
King of the Jews?"

13 Again they shouted, "Crucify Him!"

14 Then Pilate said to them, "Why? What has
He done wrong?"

But they shouted, "Crucify Him!" all the
more.

15 Then, willing to gratify the crowd, Pilate
released Barabbas to them. And after having

[a] **14:55** Mt 10:21
[b] **14:56** Pr 6:19; 1Jn 5:10
[c] **14:58** Col 2:11
[d] **14:59** Nm 35:30; Dt 17:6; 19:15; Php 2:6
[e] **14:61** Is 53:7; Mt 27:12,14; Mk 15:5; Lk 23:9; Jn 19:9
[f] Mt 1:17; Eph 5:2
[g] Jn 5:19; Heb 1:2
[h] Lk 1:68; Rm 1:25; 9:5; 2Co 1:3; 11:31; Eph 1:3; 1Pt 1:3
[i] **14:62** Ex 3:14; Ps 45:8; Jn 8:24
[j] Mk 2:10; Ac 7:56
[k] Mt 20:21
[l] Mt 26:64; Mk 13:26
[m] Ps 110:1; Dn 7:13
[n] **14:63** Mt 26:3
[o] Lv 10:6; 21:10; Nm 14:6; Jn 19:23
[p] Heb 12:1
[q] **14:64** Jn 10:33 Rv 13:6
[r] Mk 10:33
[s] **14:65** Jn 11:51
[t] Jn 18:18
[u] **14:66-72** Mt 26:69-75; Lk 22:54-62; Jn 18:15-18,25-27
[v] **14:66** Lk 6:14
[w] **14:67** Mk 1:24; 10:47; 16:6; Lk 4:34; 24:19
[x] **14:70** Jn 4:45
[y] **14:71** Mt 5:34
[z] **14:72** Mk 14:30
[aa] **15:1-5** Mt 27:2,11-14; Lk 23:25; Jn 18:28-38
[ab] **15:1** 3Jn 1
[ac] Mt 2:4
[ad] Mk 13:9
[ae] 1Tm 6:13
[af] **15:2** Lk 19:38
[ag] Jn 19:21
[ah] **15:4** 1Tm 6:13
[ai] **15:6-15** Mt 27:15-26; Lk 23:13-25; Jn 18:39–19:6
[aj] **15:6** Mk 14:1
[ak] 1Tm 6:13
[al] **15:7** Pr 1:16
[am] Ac 23:7
[an] **15:9** Lk 19:38
[ao] Jn 19:21
[ap] **15:10** Ps 37:1

[A] **14:62** Lit *and you* [B] **14:62** Ps 110:1; Dn 7:13 [C] **14:64** Lit *How does it appear to you?* [D] **14:68** Other mss omit *and a rooster crowed* [E] **14:70** Other mss add *and your speech shows it* [F] **14:71** To call down curses on himself if what he said weren't true [G] **14:72** Or *he burst into tears,* or *he broke down* [H] **15:2** Or *That is true,* an affirmative oath; Mt 26:64; 27:11

Jesus flogged,[A] he handed Him over to be crucified.

Mocked by the Military

16 Then[a] the soldiers led Him away into
the courtyard (that is, ·headquarters[b]) and
called the whole ·company together. 17 They
dressed Him in a purple[c] robe, twisted together a crown[d] of thorns, and put it on Him.
18 And they began to salute Him, "Hail,[e] King[f]
of the Jews!" 19 They kept hitting Him on the
head with a reed and spitting on Him. Getting down on their knees,[g] they were paying Him homage. 20 When they had mocked[h]
Him, they stripped Him of the purple robe,
put His clothes on Him, and led Him out to
crucify Him.

Crucified between Two Criminals

21 They[i] forced a man coming in from the
country, who was passing by, to carry Jesus'
cross.[j] He was Simon, a Cyrenian,[k] the father
of Alexander and Rufus.[l] 22 And[m] they brought
Jesus to the place called *Golgotha* (which
means Skull Place[n]). 23 They tried to give Him
wine[o] mixed with myrrh,[p] but He did not take
it. 24 Then they crucified Him and divided
His clothes, casting lots[q] for them to decide
what each would get. 25 Now it was nine in the
morning[B] when they crucified Him. 26 The inscription of the charge written against Him
was:

THE KING[r] OF THE JEWS.[s]

27 They[t] crucified two criminals[C,u] with Him,
one on His right and one on His left. [28 So
the Scripture was fulfilled that says: **And He
was counted among outlaws.**][D,E,v] 29 Those[w]
who passed by were yelling insults[x] at[F] Him,
shaking their heads,[y] and saying, "Ha! The
One who would demolish the sanctuary and
build it in three days,[z] 30 save Yourself by coming down from the cross!"[aa] 31 In the same
way, the chief priests with the scribes[ab] were
mocking Him to one another and saying, "He
saved others; He cannot save Himself! 32 Let
the ·Messiah,[ac] the King[ad] of Israel,[ae] come
down now from the cross,[af] so that we may
see and believe."[ag] Even those who were crucified with Him were taunting Him.

The Death of Jesus

33 When[ah] it was noon,[G] darkness came
over the whole land[H] until three in the afternoon.[I,ai] 34 And at three[I] Jesus cried out with
a loud voice, ***"Eloi, Eloi, lemá[J] sabachtháni?"***
which is translated, "**My God, My God, why
have You forsaken Me?**"[K,aj]
35 When some of those standing there heard
this, they said, "Look, He's calling for Elijah!"
36 Someone ran and filled a sponge with sour
wine, fixed it on a reed, offered Him a drink,[ak]
and said, "Let's see if Elijah comes to take Him
down!"
37 But Jesus let out a loud cry and breathed
His last. 38 Then the curtain[al] of the sanctuary[L]
was split in two from top to bottom. 39 When
the ·centurion, who was standing opposite
Him, saw the way He[M] breathed His last, he
said, "This man really was God's Son!"[N,am]
40 There[an] were also women looking on
from a distance. Among them were ·Mary
Magdalene,[ao] Mary the mother of James the
younger and of Joses, and Salome. 41 When He
was in Galilee,[ap] they would follow Him and
help Him. Many other women had come up
with Him to Jerusalem.[aq]

The Burial of Jesus

42 When[ar] it was already evening, because it
was preparation day (that is, the day before
the Sabbath), 43 Joseph of Arimathea, a prominent member of the Sanhedrin who was
himself looking forward[as] to the kingdom
of God,[at] came and boldly went in to Pilate[au]
and asked for Jesus' body.[av] 44 Pilate was surprised that He was already dead. Summoning
the centurion, he asked him whether He had
already died. 45 When he found out from the
centurion, he gave the corpse to Joseph. 46 After he bought some fine linen, he took Him
down and wrapped Him in the linen. Then he
placed Him in a tomb[aw] cut out of the rock,

[a] **15:16-20** Mt 27:27-31 [b] **15:16** Jn 18:28,33; 19:9; Ac 23:35; Php 1:13 [c] **15:17** Mk 15:20; Lk 16:19; Rv 18:12 [d] Jn 19:2,5; Rv 12:1 [e] **15:18** Mt 26:49; Lk 1:28; Jn 19:3 [f] Lk 19:38 [g] **15:19** Mk 5:6; Lk 22:41; Eph 3:14 [h] **15:20** Mk 10:34 [i] **15:21** Mt 27:32; Lk 23:26-31 [j] Lk 9:23 [k] Ac 6:9 [l] Rm 16:13 [m] **15:22-26** Mt 27:33-37; Lk 22:32-34; Jn 19:17-24 [n] **15:22** Jn 19:17 [o] **15:23** Gn 9:21; Dt 7:13; Ps 4:7; Pr 3:10; Lk 5:37 [p] Ps 69:21 [q] **15:24** Ps 22:18 [r] **15:26** Lk 19:38 [s] Jn 11:36 [t] **15:27-28** Mt 27:38,44; Lk 23:39-43 [u] **15:27** Mk 14:48 [v] **15:28** Is 53:12 [w] **15:29-32** Mt 27:39-43; Lk 23:35-38 [x] **15:29** Ex 22:28; Mk 3:29; Rv 13:6 [y] Ps 22:7 [z] Jn 2:19 [aa] **15:30** Lk 23:26 [ab] **15:31** Mt 2:4 [ac] **15:32** Mt 1:17; Eph 5:2 [ad] Lk 19:38 [ae] Jn 1:49 [af] Lk 23:26 [ag] Mk 8:11-12; 11:24; Jn 3:16; Ac 10:43; Rm 10:9; 1Pt 1:8-10 [ah] **15:33-39** Mt 27:45-54; Lk 23:44-48; Jn 19:28-30 [ai] **15:33** Am 8:9 [aj] **15:34** Ps 22:1 [ak] **15:36** Ps 69:21 [al] **15:38** Ex 26:31-33; 2Ch 3:14; Heb 6:19; 9:3; 10:20 [am] **15:39** Jn 5:19; Heb 1:2 [an] **15:40-41** Mt 27:55-56; Lk 23:49; Jn 19:25-27 [ao] **15:40** Mt 28:1; Mk 16:1,9; Lk 8:2; 24:10; Jn 20:1-18 [ap] **15:41** Mt 17:22 [aq] Mt 23:37 [ar] **15:42-46** Mt 27:57-60; Lk 23:50-54; Jn 19:38-42 [as] **15:43** Jd 21 [at] Mk 1:15 [au] 1Tm 6:13 [av] Lk 12:4; Jn 2:21 [aw] **15:46** Jn 5:28; 11:38; Ac 13:29

[A] **15:15** Roman flogging was done with a whip made of leather strips embedded with pieces of bone or metal that brutally tore the flesh. [B] **15:25** Lit *was the third hour* [C] **15:27** Or *revolutionaries* [D] **15:28** Other mss omit bracketed text [E] **15:28** Is 53:12 [F] **15:29** Lit *passed by blasphemed* [G] **15:33** Lit *the sixth hour* [H] **15:33** Or *whole earth* [I] **15:33,34** Lit *the ninth hour* [J] **15:34** Some mss read *lama*; other mss read *lima* [K] **15:34** Ps 22:1 [L] **15:38** A heavy curtain separated the inner room of the temple from the outer. [M] **15:39** Other mss read *saw that He cried out like this and* [N] **15:39** Or *the Son of God*; Mk 1:1

and rolled a stone[a] against the entrance to the tomb. 47 Now[b] Mary Magdalene and Mary the mother of Joses were watching where He was placed.

Resurrection Morning

16 When[c] the Sabbath was over, ˚Mary Magdalene,[d] Mary the mother of James, and Salome bought spices, so they could go and anoint Him. 2 Very early in the morning, on the first day of the week,[e] they went to the tomb[f] at sunrise. 3 They were saying to one another, "Who will roll away the stone from the entrance to the tomb for us?" 4 Looking up, they observed that the stone — which was very large — had been rolled away. 5 When[g] they entered the tomb,[h] they saw a young man[A,i] dressed[j] in a long white[k] robe sitting on the right side; they were amazed and alarmed.

6 "Don't be alarmed," he told them. "You are looking for Jesus the ˚Nazarene,[l] who was crucified. He has been resurrected![m] He is not here! See the place where they put Him. 7 But go, tell His disciples and Peter,[n] 'He is going ahead of you to Galilee;[o] you will see Him there just as He told you.'"

8 So they went out and started running from the tomb,[p] because trembling and astonishment overwhelmed them. And they said nothing to anyone,[q] since they were afraid.

Appearances of the Risen Lord

[9 Early[r] on the first day of the week,[s] after He had risen,[t] He appeared first to Mary Magdalene,[u] out of whom He had driven seven demons.[v] 10 She went and reported to those who had been with Him, as they were mourning and weeping. 11 Yet, when they heard that He was alive and had been seen by her, they did not believe it.[w] 12 Then after this, He appeared[x] in a different form to two of them walking on their way into the country.[y] 13 And they went and reported it to the rest, who did not believe them either.

The Great Commission

14 Later, He appeared to the Eleven[z] themselves as they were reclining at the table. He rebuked their unbelief and hardness of heart, because they did not believe those who saw Him after He had been resurrected.[aa] 15 Then[ab] He said to them, "Go into all the world[ac] and preach the gospel to the whole creation.[ad] 16 Whoever believes[ae] and is baptized will be saved,[af] but whoever does not believe will be condemned.[ag] 17 And these signs will accompany those who believe: In My name they will drive out demons; they will speak in new languages; 18 they will pick up snakes;[B,ah] if they should drink anything deadly, it will never harm[ai] them; they will lay hands on[aj] the sick, and they will get well."

The Ascension

19 Then after speaking to them, the Lord Jesus[ak] was taken up into heaven[al] and sat down at the right hand[am] of God. 20 And they went out and preached everywhere, the Lord working with them and confirming the word by the accompanying signs.][C]

[a] **15:46** Jn 20:1
[b] **15:47** Mt 27:61-66; Lk 23:55-56
[c] **16:1-4** Mt 28:1; Lk 24:1-2
[d] **16:1** Mk 15:40
[e] **16:2** Ac 20:7; 1Co 16:2
[f] Jn 5:28
[g] **16:5-8** Mt 28:5-8; Lk 24:3-8; Jn 20:1-2
[h] **16:5** Jn 5:28
[i] Lk 7:14
[j] Lk 12:27
[k] Rv 3:4
[l] **16:6** Mk 14:67
[m] 1Co 15:4
[n] **16:7** Lk 6:14
[o] Mt 17:22
[p] **16:8** Jn 5:28
[q] Mk 1:44; 4:40
[r] **16:9-11** Jn 20:11-18
[s] **16:9** Lk 24:1; Ac 20:7; 1Co 16:2
[t] Lk 18:33; Ac 2:24
[u] Mk 15:40
[v] Mk 3:15; Lk 8:2
[w] **16:11** Lk 24:5,11,23
[x] **16:12** Jn 21:1; 2Co 4:11
[y] Lk 24:13-35
[z] **16:14** Lk 24:9
[aa] Lk 24:38,41
[ab] **16:15-18** Mt 28:16-20
[ac] **16:15** Mt 13:38; 1Jn 2:2
[ad] Rm 8:22
[ae] **16:16** Mk 11:24; Jn 3:16; Ac 10:43; Rm 10:9; 1Pt 1:8-10
[af] Ac 2:38; 22:16
[ag] Mt 12:41; Jn 3:18,36; 5:11; 20:23
[ah] **16:18** Lk 10:19; Ac 28:3-6
[ai] Ac 28:5
[aj] Ac 9:12,17; 1Tm 5:22
[ak] **16:19** Lk 24:3
[al] Lk 24:51; Ac 1:2,11,22; 1Tm 3:16
[am] Lk 22:69; Heb 10:12

A **16:5** In Mt 28:2, the young man = an angel B **16:18** Other mss add *with their hands* C **16:9-20** Other mss omit bracketed text

■ **AUTHOR:** Luke, a Gentile physician who traveled with Paul on his missionary journeys

■■ **DATE:** Written around A.D. 60, the Gospel of Luke covers the birth of John the Baptist through the birth, ministry, crucifixion and resurrection of Jesus

This Gospel, written by Luke, is the first of a two-volume work on the mission of God as it sweeps through the world through the person of Jesus Christ. In volume two (the book of Acts), followers of Jesus take God's message to distant lands, empowered by the Holy Spirit.

Luke, the only Gentile author in the New Testament, was a physician and friend of Paul the apostle, with whom he traveled. His ordered mind and intelligence is everywhere evident in the Gospel of Luke. Three main divisions describe Jesus' ministry in Galilee, Judea and Perea, and then Jerusalem. First, however, Luke writes of Jesus' birth in words now famous—the Nativity—from which Christmas celebrations still take much of their artistry and mystique.

LUKE

Through the Gospel of Luke, God urges generations of readers to consider the life of Jesus, especially His death and resurrection, as pivotal for the world and for them personally. Nothing here is cold historical fact. Everything here is alive with the pulse of God's breakthrough and the glaring light of His Son's teaching. This is history with purpose. A new age is dawning.

Who is the Jesus Luke presents? A special child first. His birth was foretold and preceded by another special birth, that of John the Baptist, who would announce Jesus' mission. Angels sung at Jesus' birth, and Jewish leaders who knew the Scriptures recognized this child as the long-promised one.

Jesus grew to be a special teacher. Much of His teaching was through parables. His lessons would be illustrated by reference to doors, seeds, coins, sheep, wayward sons, and generous Samaritans. Those who heard Jesus' parables were often left to themselves to untangle His meaning, and if they dared, to make a personal application.

Jesus was a healer. This part of Jesus' work must have been especially fascinating to Luke. His first-century education in medicine could not come close to Jesus' ability to root out sickness and restore health. But even Jesus' healings were parables of a sort. Jesus' power and mercy were evident in these miracles, but His purpose was not in merely restoring the body but in reconciling the soul to God.

In a twist that still confounds the world's wisest people, Jesus was treated like a criminal, accused by religious authorities of violating the most sacred laws of God—the very God whose precious Son He happened to be. By state authorities He was declared a non-threat to the realm, yet given the supreme death sentence: crucifixion. God validated Jesus' mission by raising Him from the dead.

This was the mission of God all along. Everything beforehand pointed to Jesus. God's mission was achieved and launched at the same time. Angels and everyone can sing to that.

The Dedication to Theophilus

1 Many have undertaken to compile a narrative about the events that have been
fulfilled[A] among us,[a] 2 just as the original eyewitnesses[b] and servants of the word[c] handed
them down to us. 3 It also seemed good to me,
since I have carefully investigated everything
from the very first, to write to you in an orderly sequence, most honorable[d] Theophilus,[e] 4 so that you may know the certainty of
the things about which you have been instructed.[B,f]

Gabriel Predicts John's Birth

5 In the days of King ·Herod[g] of Judea, there
was a priest of Abijah's division[C,h] named
Zechariah. His wife was from the daughters
of Aaron, and her name was Elizabeth. 6 Both
were righteous in God's sight,[i] living without
blame[j] according to all the commands and
requirements of the Lord. 7 But they had no
children[D] because Elizabeth could not conceive,[E] and both of them were well along in
years.[F]
8 When his division was on duty[k] and he
was serving as priest before God, 9 it happened that he was chosen by lot, according
to the custom of the priesthood, to enter the
sanctuary of the Lord and burn incense.[l] 10 At
the hour of incense the whole assembly of the
people was praying outside. 11 An angel of the
Lord[m] appeared to him, standing to the right
of the altar of incense. 12 When Zechariah saw
him, he was startled and overcome with fear.[G]
13 But the angel said to him:

Do not be afraid,[n] Zechariah,
because your prayer has been heard.
Your wife Elizabeth will bear you a son,
and you will name him John.[o]
14 There will be joy and delight for you,
and many will rejoice at his birth.
15 For he will be great in the sight
of the Lord
and will never drink wine or beer.[p]
He will be filled with the Holy Spirit
while still in his mother's womb.[q]
16 He will turn many of the sons of Israel
to the Lord their God.
17 And he will go before Him
in the spirit and power of Elijah,
to turn the hearts of fathers
to their children,[r]
and the disobedient
to the understanding of the righteous,
to make ready for the Lord
a prepared people.[s]

18 "How can I know this?" Zechariah asked
the angel. "For I am an old man, and my wife
is well along in years."[H]
19 The angel answered him, "I am Gabriel,[t]
who stands in the presence of God,[u] and I
was sent to speak to you and tell you this
good news. 20 Now listen! You will become silent and unable to speak until the day these
things take place, because you did not believe
my words, which will be fulfilled in their
proper time."
21 Meanwhile, the people were waiting for
Zechariah, amazed that he stayed so long in
the sanctuary. 22 When he did come out, he
could not speak to them. Then they realized
that he had seen a vision in the sanctuary. He
kept making signs to them[v] and remained
speechless. 23 When the days of his ministry
were completed, he went back home.
24 After these days his wife Elizabeth conceived and kept herself in seclusion for five
months. She said, 25 "The Lord has done this
for me. He has looked with favor in these days
to take away my disgrace[w] among the people."

Gabriel Predicts Jesus' Birth

26 In the sixth month, the angel Gabriel[x] was
sent by God to a town in Galilee called Nazareth,[y] 27 to a virgin ·engaged[z] to a man named
Joseph, of the house of David.[aa] The virgin's
name was Mary. 28 And the angel came to her
and said, "Rejoice, favored woman! The Lord is
with you."[I] 29 But she was deeply troubled[ab] by
this statement, wondering what kind of greeting this could be. 30 Then the angel told her:

Do not be afraid, Mary,[ac]
for you have found favor with God.
31 Now listen:
You will conceive and give birth to
a son,

[a] **1:1** Rm 4:21; 14:5; Col 2:2; 4:12; 1Th 1:5; 2Tm 4:17; Heb 6:11; 10:22
[b] **1:2** Jn 15:27; Ac 1:21; 2Pt 1:16; 1Jn 1:1
[c] Ac 26:16; 1Co 4:1; Heb 2:3
[d] **1:3** Ac 23:26; 24:3; 26:25
[e] Ac 1:1
[f] **1:4** Ac 18:25; Rm 2:18; 1Co 14:19; Gl 6:6
[g] **1:5** Mt 2:1
[h] 1Ch 24:10
[i] **1:6** Gn 7:1; Ac 2:25; 8:21
[j] Php 2:15; 3:6; 1Th 3:13
[k] **1:8** 1Ch 24:19; 2Ch 8:14; 31:2
[l] **1:9** Ex 30:7-8
[m] **1:11** Mt 2:13-14; 28:2; Lk 2:9; Ac 5:19; 8:26; 12:7
[n] **1:13** Gn 15:1; Mt 14:27; Lk 1:30
[o] Gn 16:11; 17:19; Lk 1:60,63
[p] **1:13-15** Nm 6:3; Jdg 13:3-5; Mt 11:18; Lk 7:33
[q] **1:15** Is 44:2; Lk 1:41,44
[r] **1:16-17** Mal 4:5-6
[s] **1:17** Lk 1:76
[t] **1:19** Dn 8:16; 9:21; Lk 1:26
[u] Mt 18:10
[v] **1:22** Lk 1:62
[w] **1:25** Gn 30:23; Is 4:1; 25:8
[x] **1:26** Lk 1:19
[y] Mt 2:23
[z] **1:27** Dt 21:23; Is 7:14; Mt 1:18,23
[aa] Mt 1:20; Lk 2:4
[ab] **1:29** Lk 1:12
[ac] **1:30** Mt 14:27; Lk 1:13

[A] **1:1** Or *events that have been accomplished*, or *events most surely believed* [B] **1:4** Or *informed* [C] **1:5** One of the 24 divisions of priests appointed by David for temple service; 1Ch 24:10 [D] **1:7** Lit *child* [E] **1:7** Lit *Elizabeth was sterile* or *barren* [F] **1:7** Lit *in their days* [G] **1:12** Lit *and fear fell on him* [H] **1:18** Lit *in her days* [I] **1:28** Other mss add *blessed are you among women*

and you will call His name Jesus.[a]
32 He will be great
and will be called the Son of
the Most High,[b]
and the Lord God will give Him
the throne of His father David.[c]
33 He will reign over the house of Jacob[d]
forever,
and His kingdom will have no end.[e]

34 Mary asked the angel, "How can this be,
since I have not been intimate with a man?"[A]
35 The angel replied to her:

"The Holy Spirit will come upon you,[f]
and the power of the Most High
will overshadow you.
Therefore, the holy One to be born
will be called the Son of God.[g]

36 And consider your relative Elizabeth — even
she has conceived a son in her old age, and
this is the sixth month for her who was called
childless. 37 For nothing will be impossible
with God."[h]
38 "I am the Lord's ·slave,"[B] said Mary. "May it
be done to me according to your word." Then
the angel left her.

Mary's Visit to Elizabeth

39 In those days Mary set out and hurried to
a town in the hill country of Judah 40 where
she entered Zechariah's house and greeted
Elizabeth. 41 When Elizabeth heard Mary's
greeting, the baby leaped inside her,[C] and
Elizabeth was filled with the Holy Spirit.[i]
42 Then she exclaimed with a loud cry:

"You are the most blessed of women,
and your child will be blessed![D]

43 How could this happen to me, that the
mother of my Lord should come to me? 44 For
you see, when the sound of your greeting
reached my ears, the baby leaped for joy inside me![E] 45 She who has believed is blessed
because what was spoken to her by the Lord
will be fulfilled!"

Mary's Praise

46 And Mary said:

[a]1:31 Is 7:14; Mt 1:21,25; Lk 2:21
[b]1:32 Lk 1:76; 6:35; 8:28; Ac 7:48
[c]2Sm 7:12-13; 1Kg 2:12; Ps 132:11; Is 9:7; Jr 33:17
[d]1:33 Ex 19:3; Ps 114:1; Is 14:1; 29:22; 46:3
[e]Is 9:6 LXX; Dn 7:14
[f]1:35 Mt 1:18
[g]Mt 14:33; Lk 4:3,9,41; 22:70
[h]1:37 Gn 18:14; Lk 18:27
[i]1:41 Lk 1:67; Ac 2:4; 4:8; 9:17; 13:9
[j]1:46-53 1Sm 2:1-10
[k]1:47 Ps 35:9; Hab 3:18
[l]1Tm 1:1; 2:3; Ti 1:3; 2:10; 3:4; Jd 25
[m]1:48 Lk 11:27
[n]1:49 Ps 89:8; Zph 3:17
[o]Ps 71:19; 126:2-3
[p]Ps 99:3; 111:9; Is 57:15
[q]1:50 Ps 100:5; 103:11,17
[r]1:51 Ps 89:10; 98:1; 118:15
[s]1:53 Ps 34:10; 107:9; Lk 6:21,24-25
[t]1:58 Gn 19:19
[u]1:59 Gn 17:12; Lv 12:3; Lk 2:21; Php 3:5
[v]1:60 Lk 1:13,63
[w]1:62 Lk 1:22

My soul proclaims the greatness
of[F] the Lord,[j]
47 and my spirit has rejoiced[k] in God
my Savior,[l]
48 because He has looked with favor
on the humble condition of His slave.
Surely, from now on all generations
will call me blessed,[m]
49 because the Mighty One[n]
has done great things for me,[o]
and His name[p] is holy.
50 His mercy is from generation
to generation[q]
on those who fear Him.
51 He has done a mighty deed
with His arm;[r]
He has scattered the proud
because of the thoughts of their hearts;
52 He has toppled the mighty
from their thrones
and exalted the lowly.
53 He has satisfied the hungry
with good things[s]
and sent the rich away empty.
54 He has helped His servant Israel,
mindful of His mercy,[G]
55 just as He spoke to our ancestors,
to Abraham and his
descendants[H] forever.

56 And Mary stayed with her about three
months; then she returned to her home.

The Birth and Naming of John

57 Now the time had come for Elizabeth
to give birth, and she had a son. 58 Then her
neighbors and relatives heard that the Lord
had shown her His great mercy,[I,t] and they rejoiced with her.
59 When they came to circumcise the child
on the eighth day,[u] they were going to name
him Zechariah, after his father. 60 But his
mother responded, "No! He will be called
John."[v]
61 Then they said to her, "None of your relatives has that name." 62 So they motioned to
his father[w] to find out what he wanted him to
be called. 63 He asked for a writing tablet and
wrote:

A1:34 Lit *since I do not know a man* B1:38 Lit *Look, the Lord's slave* C1:41 Lit *leaped in her abdomen* or *womb* D1:42 Lit *and the fruit of your abdomen* (or *womb*) *is blessed* E1:44 Lit *in my abdomen* or *womb* F1:46 Or *soul magnifies* G1:54 Because He remembered His mercy; Ps 98:3 H1:55 Or *offspring*; lit *seed* I1:58 Lit *the Lord magnified His mercy with her*

HIS NAME IS JOHN.

And they were all amazed. 64 Immediately his
mouth was opened[a] and his tongue set free,
and he began to speak, praising God. 65 Fear
came on all those who lived around them,
and all these things were being talked about
throughout the hill country of Judea. 66 All
who heard about him[b] took it to heart, saying, "What then will this child become?" For,
indeed, the Lord's hand was with him.

Zechariah's Prophecy

67 Then his father Zechariah was filled with
the Holy Spirit[c] and prophesied:[d]

68 Praise the Lord, the God of Israel,[e]
because He has visited
and provided ·redemption
for His people.[f]
69 He has raised up a ·horn of salvation[A]
for us[g]
in the house of His servant David,[h]
70 just as He spoke by the mouth
of His holy prophets in ancient times;[i]
71 salvation from our enemies
and from the clutches[B] of those
who hate us.
72 He has dealt mercifully
with our fathers[j]
and remembered His holy covenant[k]—
73 the oath that He swore to our father
Abraham.[l]
He has given us the privilege,
74 since we have been rescued
from our enemies' clutches,[C]
to serve Him without fear
75 in holiness and righteousness
in His presence all our days.
76 And child, you will be called
a prophet of the Most High,[m]
for you will go before the Lord
to prepare His ways,[n]
77 to give His people knowledge
of salvation
through the forgiveness of their sins.[o]
78 Because of our God's merciful
compassion,
the Dawn from on high[p] will visit us
79 to shine on those who live in darkness
and the shadow of death,[q]
to guide our feet into the way of peace.

80 The child grew up and became spiritually
strong,[r] and he was in the wilderness until
the day of his public appearance to Israel.

The Birth of Jesus

2 In those days a decree went out from Caesar Augustus[D,s] that the whole empire[E]
should be registered. 2 This first registration
took place while[F] Quirinius was governing
Syria.[t] 3 So everyone went to be registered,
each to his own town.

4 And Joseph also went up from the town
of Nazareth in Galilee, to Judea, to the city of
David, which is called Bethlehem, because he
was of the house and family line of David,[u]
5 to be registered along with Mary, who was
·engaged to him[G] and was pregnant. 6 While
they were there, the time came for her to give
birth. 7 Then she gave birth to her firstborn
Son, and she wrapped Him snugly in cloth
and laid Him in a feeding trough—because
there was no room for them at the lodging
place.

The Shepherds and the Angels

8 In the same region, shepherds were staying out in the fields and keeping watch at
night over their flock. 9 Then an angel of the
Lord[v] stood before[H] them,[w] and the glory of
the Lord shone around them, and they were
terrified.[I] 10 But the angel said to them, "Don't
be afraid,[x] for look, I proclaim to you good
news of great joy that will be for all the people:[J] 11 Today a Savior,[y] who is ·Messiah[z] the
Lord,[aa] was born for you in the city of David.
12 This will be the sign for you:[ab] You will find
a baby wrapped snugly in cloth and lying in a
feeding trough."
13 Suddenly there was a multitude of the
heavenly host with the angel, praising God
and saying:

14 Glory to God in the highest heaven,[ac]
and peace on earth[ad] to people
He favors![K,L,ae]

[a]**1:64** Lk 1:20
[b]**1:66** Ac 11:21
[c]**1:67** Lk 1:41
[d]Jl 2:28
[e]**1:68** Ps 41:13
[f]Lk 1:71; 2:38; Heb 9:12
[g]**1:69** 1Sm 2:1,10; Ps 18:2; 89:17; 132:17; Ezk 29:21
[h]2Sm 7:26; Ps 89:3,20; Ezk 34:23-24; 37:24-25
[i]**1:70** Ac 3:21; Rm 1:2
[j]**1:72** Mc 7:20
[k]Ps 105:8-9,42; 106:45
[l]**1:73** Gn 22:16-17; Heb 6:13
[m]**1:76** Mt 11:9
[n]Mal 3:1; Lk 1:17
[o]**1:77** Jr 31:34; Mk 1:4
[p]**1:78** Is 58:8; Jr 23:5; Zch 3:8; 6:12 LXX; Mal 4:2; Lk 24:49; Eph 4:8; 2Pt 1:19
[q]**1:79** Is 9:2; 60:2-3
[r]**1:80** Lk 2:40
[s]**2:1** Mt 22:17; Lk 3:1
[t]**2:2** Mt 4:24
[u]**2:4** Lk 1:27
[v]**2:9** Lk 1:11; Ac 5:19
[w]Lk 24:4; Ac 12:7
[x]**2:10** Mt 14:27
[y]**2:11** Mt 1:21; Jn 4:42; Ac 5:31
[z]Mt 1:16; 16:16,20; Jn 11:27
[aa]Lk 1:43; Ac 2:36; 10:36
[ab]**2:12** 1Sm 2:34; 2Kg 19:29; 20:8-9; Is 7:11,14
[ac]**2:14** Mt 21:9; Lk 19:38
[ad]Lk 12:51
[ae]Lk 3:22; Eph 1:9; Php 2:13

[A]**1:69** = a strong Savior [B]**1:71** Lit *the hand* [C]**1:74** Lit *from the hand of enemies* [D]**2:1** Emperor who ruled the Roman Empire 27 B.C.–A.D. 14; also known as Octavian, he established the peaceful era known as the *Pax Romana*; Caesar was a title of Roman emperors. [E]**2:1** Or *the whole inhabited world* [F]**2:2** Or *This registration was the first while*, or *This registration was before* [G]**2:5** Other mss read *was his engaged wife* [H]**2:9** Or *Lord appeared to* [I]**2:9** Lit *they feared a great fear* [J]**2:10** Or *the whole nation* [K]**2:14** Other mss read *earth good will to people* [L]**2:14** Or *earth to men of good will*

15 When the angels had left them and returned to heaven, the shepherds said to one
another, "Let's go straight to Bethlehem and
see what has happened, which the Lord has
made known to us."
16 They hurried off and found both Mary
and Joseph, and the baby who was lying in the
feeding trough. 17 After seeing them, they reported the message they were told about this
child, 18 and all who heard it were amazed at
what the shepherds said to them. 19 But Mary
was treasuring up all these things[A] in her
heart[a] and meditating on them. 20 The shepherds returned, glorifying and praising God[b]
for all they had seen and heard, just as they
had been told.

The Circumcision and Presentation of Jesus

21 When the eight days were completed for
His circumcision,[c] He was named Jesus[d] —
the name given by the angel before He was
conceived.[B] 22 And when the days of their purification according to the law of Moses were
finished,[e] they brought Him up to Jerusalem to present Him to the Lord 23 (just as it
is written in the law of the Lord: **Every firstborn male[C] will be dedicated[D] to the Lord**[E,f])
24 and to offer a sacrifice (according to what is
stated in the law of the Lord: **a pair of turtledoves or two young pigeons**[F,g]).

Simeon's Prophetic Praise

25 There was a man in Jerusalem whose
name was Simeon. This man was righteous
and devout,[h] looking forward to Israel's consolation,[G,i] and the Holy Spirit was on him. 26 It
had been revealed to him by the Holy Spirit[j]
that he would not see death before he saw
the Lord's Messiah.[k] 27 Guided by the Spirit,
he entered[H] the ·temple complex. When the
parents brought in the child Jesus to perform
for Him what was customary under the law,
28 Simeon took Him up in his arms, praised
God, and said:

29 Now, Master,
You can dismiss Your ·slave in peace,
as You promised.
30 For my eyes have seen Your salvation.[l]
31 You have prepared it
in the presence of all peoples —
32 a light for revelation to the Gentiles[I,m]
and glory to Your people Israel.[n]

33 His father and mother[J] were amazed
at what was being said about Him. 34 Then
Simeon blessed them and told His mother
Mary: "Indeed, this child is destined to cause
the fall and rise of many in Israel[o] and to
be a sign that will be opposed[K] — 35 and a
sword will pierce your own soul — that the
thoughts[L] of many hearts may be revealed."

Anna's Testimony

36 There was also a prophetess,[p] Anna, a
daughter of Phanuel, of the tribe of Asher.[q]
She was well along in years,[M] having lived
with her husband seven years after her marriage,[N,r] 37 and was a widow for 84 years.[O] She
did not leave the temple complex, serving
God night and day with fasting and prayers.[s]
38 At that very moment,[P] she came up and began to thank God and to speak about Him to
all who were looking forward to the ·redemp-
tion of Jerusalem.[Q,t]

The Family's Return to Nazareth

39 When they had completed everything according to the law of the Lord, they returned
to Galilee, to their own town of Nazareth.[u]
40 The boy grew up and became strong, filled
with wisdom, and God's grace was on Him.[v]

In His Father's House

41 Every year His parents traveled to Jerusalem for the ·Passover Festival.[w] 42 When He
was 12 years old, they went up according to
the custom of the festival.[x] 43 After those days
were over,[y] as they were returning, the boy
Jesus stayed behind in Jerusalem, but His
parents[J] did not know it. 44 Assuming He was
in the traveling party, they went a day's journey. Then they began looking for Him among
their relatives and friends. 45 When they did
not find Him, they returned to Jerusalem to
search for Him. 46 After three days, they found

[a] **2:19** Lk 2:51 [b] **2:20** Mt 9:8 [c] **2:21** Lk 1:59 [d] Lk 1:31 [e] **2:22** Lv 12:6-8 [f] **2:23** Ex 13:2,12 [g] **2:24** Lv 5:11; 12:8 [h] **2:25** Lk 1:6 [i] Mk 15:43; Lk 2:38; 23:51 [j] **2:26** Mt 2:12 [k] Ps 89:48; Jn 8:51; Heb 11:5 [l] **2:30** Ps 119:166,174; Is 52:10; Lk 3:6 [m] **2:32** Is 42:6; 49:6,9; Ac 13:47; 26:23 [n] Is 46:13 LXX [o] **2:34** Mt 21:44; 1Co 1:23; 2Co 2:16; 1Pt 2:8 [p] **2:36** Lk 2:38; Ac 21:9 [q] Jos 19:24 [r] 1Tm 5:9 [s] **2:37** Lk 5:33; Ac 13:3; 14:23; 1Tm 5:5 [t] **2:38** Is 52:9; Lk 1:68; 2:25 [u] **2:39** Mt 2:23; Lk 1:26; 2:51; 4:16 [v] **2:40** Lk 1:80; 2:52 [w] **2:41** Ex 12:11; 23:15; Dt 16:1-6 [x] **2:42** Dt 16:16-17 [y] **2:43** Ex 12:15

[A] **2:19** Lit *these words* [B] **2:21** Or *conceived in the womb* [C] **2:23** Lit *"Every male that opens a womb* [D] **2:23** Lit *be called holy* [E] **2:23** Ex 13:2,12 [F] **2:24** Lv 5:11; 12:8 [G] **2:25** The coming of the Messiah with His salvation for the nation; Is 40:1; 61:2; Lk 2:26,30 [H] **2:27** Lit *And in the Spirit, he came into* [I] **2:32** Or *the nations* [J] **2:33,43** Other mss read *But Joseph and His mother* [K] **2:34** Or *spoken against* [L] **2:35** Or *schemes* [M] **2:36** Lit *in many days* [N] **2:36** Lit *years from her virginity* [O] **2:37** Or *she was a widow until the age of 84* [P] **2:38** Lit *very hour* [Q] **2:38** Other mss read *in Jerusalem*

Him in the temple complex sitting among the teachers, listening to them and asking them questions. [47]And all those who heard Him were astounded at His understanding and His answers. [48]When His parents saw Him, they were astonished, and His mother said to Him,[a] "Son, why have You treated us like this? Your father and I have been anxiously searching for You."[b]

[49]"Why were you searching for Me?" He asked them. "Didn't you know that I had to be in My Father's house?"[A] [50]But they did not understand what He said to them.[c]

In Favor with God and with People

[51]Then He went down with them and came to Nazareth and was obedient to them. His mother kept all these things in her heart.[d] [52]And Jesus increased in wisdom and stature, and in favor with God and with people.[e]

The Messiah's Herald

3 In the fifteenth year of the reign of Tiberius Caesar,[B] while Pontius ·Pilate was governor of Judea,[f] ·Herod was tetrarch[C] of Galilee,[g] his brother Philip tetrarch of the region of Iturea[D] and Trachonitis,[D] and Lysanias tetrarch of Abilene,[E] [2]during the high priesthood of Annas[h] and Caiaphas,[i] God's word came to John the son of Zechariah in the wilderness.[j] [3]He went into all the vicinity of the Jordan,[k] preaching a baptism of repentance[F] for the forgiveness of sins, [4]as it is written in the book of the words of the prophet Isaiah:

A voice of one crying out
in the wilderness:
Prepare the way for the Lord;
make His paths straight!
[5] **Every valley will be filled,**
and every mountain and hill will be
made low;[G]
the crooked will become straight,
the rough ways smooth,
[6] **and everyone**[H] **will see the salvation**
of God.[I,l]

[7]He then said to the crowds who came out to be baptized by him, "Brood of vipers![m] Who warned you to flee from the coming wrath? [8]Therefore produce fruit consistent with repentance. And don't start saying to yourselves, 'We have Abraham as our father,'[n] for I tell you that God is able to raise up children for Abraham from these stones! [9]Even now the ax is ready to strike[J] the root of the trees! Therefore, every tree that doesn't produce good fruit will be cut down and thrown into the fire."[o]

[10]"What then should we do?"[p] the crowds were asking him.

[11]He replied to them, "The one who has two shirts[K] must share with someone who has none, and the one who has food must do the same."[q]

[12]Tax collectors also came to be baptized, and they asked him, "Teacher, what should we do?"[r]

[13]He told them, "Don't collect any more than what you have been authorized."

[14]Some soldiers also questioned him: "What should we do?"

He said to them, "Don't take money from anyone by force or false accusation; be satisfied with your wages."

[15]Now the people were waiting expectantly, and all of them were debating in their minds[L] whether John might be the ·Messiah.[s] [16]John answered them all,[t] "I baptize you with[M] water, but One is coming who is more powerful than I. I am not worthy to untie the strap of His sandals. He will baptize you with[M] the Holy Spirit and fire. [17]His winnowing shovel[N,u] is in His hand to clear His threshing floor and gather the wheat into His barn, but the chaff He will burn up with a fire that never goes out."[v] [18]Then, along with many other exhortations, he proclaimed good news to the people. [19]But Herod the tetrarch,[w] being rebuked by him about Herodias, his brother's wife, and about all the evil things Herod had done,[x] [20]added this to everything else—he locked John up in prison.[y]

The Baptism of Jesus

[21]When all the people were baptized,[z] Jesus also was baptized. As He was praying,[aa]

[a]**2:48** Mt 12:46 [b]Lk 2:49; 3:23; 4:22 [c]**2:50** Mk 9:32; Lk 9:45; 18:34 [d]**2:51** Lk 2:19 [e]**2:52** Lk 2:40 [f]**3:1** Mt 27:2 [g]Mt 14:1 [h]**3:2** Jn 18:13,24; Ac 4:6 [i]Mt 26:3 [j]**3:2-10** Mt 3:1-10; Mk 1:3-5 [k]**3:3** Mt 3:5 [l]**3:4-6** Is 40:3-5 [m]**3:7** Mt 12:34; 23:33 [n]**3:8** Jn 8:33 [o]**3:9** Mt 7:19; Lk 13:6-9 [p]**3:10** Ac 2:37-38 [q]**3:11** Is 58:7 [r]**3:12** Mt 9:10-11; 21:31-32; Lk 5:29-30; 7:29; 15:1 [s]**3:15** Jn 1:19-20 [t]**3:16-17** Mt 3:11-12; Mk 1:7-8 [u]**3:17** Is 30:24 [v]Mk 9:43,48 [w]**3:19** Mt 14:3; Mk 6:17 [x]Mt 14:1; Lk 3:1 [y]**3:20** Jn 3:24 [z]**3:21-22** Mt 3:13-17; Mk 1:9-11 [aa]**3:21** Mt 14:23; Lk 5:16; 9:18,28-29

[A]**2:49** Or *be involved in My Father's interests* (or *things*), or *be among My Father's people* [B]**3:1** Emperor who ruled the Roman Empire A.D. 14–37 [C]**3:1** Or *ruler* [D]**3:1** A small province northeast of Galilee [E]**3:1** A small Syrian province [F]**3:3** Or *baptism based on repentance* [G]**3:5** Lit *be humbled* [H]**3:6** Lit *all flesh* [I]**3:4-6** Is 40:3-5 [J]**3:9** Lit *the ax lies at* [K]**3:11** Lit *tunics* [L]**3:15** Or *hearts* [M]**3:16** Or *in* [N]**3:17** A wooden farm implement used to toss threshed grain into the wind so the lighter chaff would blow away and separate from the heavier grain

heaven opened, 22 and the Holy Spirit descended on Him in a physical appearance like
a dove. And a voice came from heaven:

You are My beloved Son.
I take delight in You![a]

The Genealogy of Jesus Christ

23 As He began His ministry, Jesus was about
30 years old and was thought to be[A] the

son of Joseph,[b] son[B] of Heli,
24 son of Matthat, son of Levi,
son of Melchi, son of Jannai,
son of Joseph, 25 son of Mattathias,
son of Amos, son of Nahum,
son of Esli, son of Naggai,
26 son of Maath, son of Mattathias,
son of Semein, son of Josech,
son of Joda, 27 son of Joanan,
son of Rhesa, son of Zerubbabel,[c]
son of Shealtiel, son of Neri,
28 son of Melchi, son of Addi,
son of Cosam, son of Elmadam,
son of Er, 29 son of Joshua,
son of Eliezer, son of Jorim,
son of Matthat, son of Levi,
30 son of Simeon, son of Judah,
son of Joseph, son of Jonam,
son of Eliakim, 31 son of Melea,
son of Menna, son of Mattatha,
son of Nathan, son of David,
32 son of Jesse,[d] son of Obed,
son of Boaz, son of Salmon,[C]
son of Nahshon, 33 son of Amminadab,
son of Ram,[D] son of Hezron,
son of Perez, son of Judah,
34 son of Jacob, son of Isaac,
son of Abraham,[e] son of Terah,
son of Nahor, 35 son of Serug,
son of Reu, son of Peleg,
son of Eber, son of Shelah,
36 son of Cainan, son of Arphaxad,
son of Shem, son of Noah,[f]
son of Lamech, 37 son of Methuselah,
son of Enoch, son of Jared,
son of Mahalaleel, son of Cainan,
38 son of Enos, son of Seth,
son of Adam, son of God.

[a]**3:22** Ps 2:7; Is 42:1; Mt 3:17; 17:5; Mk 1:11; Lk 9:35; 2Pt 1:17
[b]**3:23** Mt 1:16
[c]**3:27** Mt 1:12
[d]**3:32-34** Mt 1:1-6
[e]**3:34-36** Gn 11:26-30; 1Ch 1:24-27
[f]**3:36-38** Gn 5:3-32; 1Ch 1:1-4
[g]**4:1-13** Mt 4:1-11; Mk 1:12-13
[h]**4:1** Lk 3:3
[i]**4:4** Dt 8:3
[j]**4:6** 1Jn 5:19
[k]**4:8** Dt 6:13
[l]**4:10** Ps 91:11
[m]**4:11** Ps 91:12
[n]**4:12** Dt 6:16
[o]**4:14** Mt 4:12
[p]Mt 9:26; Lk 4:37
[q]**4:15** Mt 4:23
[r]**4:16** Lk 2:39,51
[s]Mt 13:54; Mk 6:1-2
[t]Ac 13:14-16

The Temptation of Jesus

4 Then Jesus[g] returned from the Jordan,[h]
full of the Holy Spirit, and was led by the
Spirit in the wilderness 2 for 40 days to be
tempted by the Devil. He ate nothing during
those days, and when they were over,[E] He was
hungry. 3 The Devil said to Him, "If You are the
Son of God, tell this stone to become bread."
4 But Jesus answered him, "It is written:
Man must not live on bread alone."[F,G,i]
5 So he took Him up[H] and showed Him all
the kingdoms of the world in a moment of
time. 6 The Devil said to Him, "I will give You
their splendor and all this authority, because
it has been given over to me,[j] and I can give it
to anyone I want. 7 If You, then, will worship
me,[I] all will be Yours."
8 And Jesus answered him,[J] "It is written:

Worship the Lord your God,
and serve[k] Him only."[K]

9 So he took Him to Jerusalem, had Him
stand on the pinnacle of the temple, and said
to Him, "If You are the Son of God, throw
Yourself down from here. 10 For it is written:

He will give His angels orders
concerning you,
to protect you,[L,l] 11 and
they will support you with their hands,
so that you will not strike
your foot against a stone."[M,m]

12 And Jesus answered him, "It is said: **Do
not test the Lord your God.**"[N,n]
13 After the Devil had finished every temptation, he departed from Him for a time.

Ministry in Galilee

14 Then Jesus returned to Galilee in the
power of the Spirit,[o] and news about Him
spread throughout the entire vicinity.[p] 15 He
was teaching in their ˙synagogues,[q] being ac-
claimed[O] by everyone.

Rejection at Nazareth

16 He came to Nazareth, where He had been
brought up.[r] As usual, He entered the synagogue on the Sabbath day[s] and stood up to
read.[t] 17 The scroll of the prophet Isaiah was

[A]**3:23** People did not know about His virgin birth; Mt 1:18-25; Lk 1:26-38
[B]**3:23** The relationship in some cases may be more distant than a son.
[C]**3:32** Other mss read *Sala* [D]**3:33** Other mss read *Amminadab, son of Aram, son of Joram*; other mss read *Amminadab, son of Admin, son of Arni* [E]**4:2** Lit *were completed* [F]**4:4** Other mss add *but on every word of God* [G]**4:4** Dt 8:3
[H]**4:5** Other mss read *So the Devil took Him up on a high mountain* [I]**4:7** Lit *will fall down before me* [J]**4:8** Other mss add *"Get behind Me, Satan!* [K]**4:8** Dt 6:13
[L]**4:10** Ps 91:11 [M]**4:11** Ps 91:12 [N]**4:12** Dt 6:16 [O]**4:15** Or *glorified*

given to Him, and unrolling the scroll, He found the place where it was written:

18 **The Spirit of the Lord is on Me,**
because He has anointed Me
to preach good news to the poor.
He has sent Me[A]
to proclaim freedom[B] **to the captives**
and recovery of sight to the blind,
to set free the oppressed,
19 **to proclaim the year**
of the Lord's favor.[C,D,a]

20 He then rolled up the scroll, gave it back to the attendant, and sat down.[b] And the eyes of everyone in the synagogue were fixed on Him. 21 He began by saying to them, "Today as you listen, this Scripture has been fulfilled."

22 They were all speaking well of Him[E] and were amazed by the gracious words that came from His mouth, yet they said, "Isn't this Joseph's son?"[c]

23 Then He said to them, "No doubt you will quote this proverb[F] to Me: 'Doctor, heal yourself. So all we've heard that took place in Capernaum,[d] do here in Your hometown also.'"

24 He also said, "•I assure you: No prophet is accepted in his hometown.[e] 25 But I say to you, there were certainly many widows in Israel in Elijah's days,[f] when the sky was shut up for three years and six months while a great famine came over all the land. 26 Yet Elijah was not sent to any of them—but to a widow at Zarephath in Sidon. 27 And in the prophet Elisha's time, there were many in Israel who had serious skin diseases, yet not one of them was healed[G]—only Naaman the Syrian."[g]

28 When they heard this, everyone in the synagogue was enraged. 29 They got up, drove Him out of town,[h] and brought Him to the edge[H] of the hill that their town was built on, intending to hurl Him over the cliff. 30 But He passed right through the crowd and went on His way.[i]

Driving Out an Unclean Spirit

31 Then He went down to Capernaum,[j] a town in Galilee, and was teaching them on the Sabbath. 32 They were astonished at His teaching because His message had authority.[k]

33 In the synagogue there was a man with an •unclean demonic spirit who cried out with a loud voice,[l] 34 "Leave us alone![I] What do You have to do with us,[J] Jesus—•Nazarene? Have You come to destroy us? I know who You are—the Holy One of God!"

35 But Jesus rebuked him[m] and said, "Be quiet and come out of him!"

And throwing him down before them, the demon came out of him without hurting him at all. 36 Amazement came over them all, and they kept saying to one another, "What is this message? For He commands the unclean spirits with authority and power, and they come out!" 37 And news about Him began to go out to every place in the vicinity.

Healings at Capernaum

38 After He left the synagogue, He entered Simon's house.[n] Simon's mother-in-law was suffering from a high fever, and they asked Him about her. 39 So He stood over her and rebuked the fever, and it left her. She got up immediately and began to serve them.

40 When the sun was setting, all those who had anyone sick with various diseases brought them to Him. As He laid His hands on each one of them, He would heal them.[o] 41 Also, demons were coming out of many, shouting and saying, "You are the Son of God!"[p] But He rebuked them and would not allow them to speak, because they knew He was the •Messiah.[q]

Preaching in Galilee

42 When it was day, He went out and made His way to a deserted place.[r] But the crowds were searching for Him. They came to Him and tried to keep Him from leaving them. 43 But He said to them, "I must proclaim the good news about the kingdom of God to the other towns also, because I was sent for this purpose." 44 And He was preaching in the synagogues of Galilee.[K,s]

The First Disciples

5 As the crowd was pressing in on Jesus to hear God's word,[t] He was standing by Lake Gennesaret.[L,u] 2 He saw two boats at the

[a] **4:18-19** Is 61:1-2; Mt 11:5; 12:18; Jn 3:34
[b] **4:20** Mt 26:55
[c] **4:22** Mt 13:55; Mk 6:3; Jn 6:42
[d] **4:23** Mt 11:23; Mk 2:1-12; Jn 4:46-53
[e] **4:24** Mt 13:57; Mk 6:4; Jn 4:44
[f] **4:25** 1Kg 17:1; 18:1; Jms 5:17
[g] **4:27** 2Kg 5:1-14
[h] **4:29** Nm 15:35; Ac 7:58; Heb 13:12
[i] **4:30** Jn 10:39
[j] **4:31-37** Mk 1:21-28
[k] **4:32** Mt 7:28-29; Mk 1:22; Jn 7:46
[l] **4:33-37** Mk 1:23-28
[m] **4:35** Mt 8:26; Mk 4:39; Lk 4:39,41; 8:24
[n] **4:38-41** Mt 8:14-17; Mk 1:29-34
[o] **4:40** Mt 4:23; Mk 5:23
[p] **4:41** Mt 4:3
[q] Mt 8:16; Mk 1:34; 3:11-12
[r] **4:42-43** Mk 1:35-38
[s] **4:44** Mt 4:23; Mk 1:39
[t] **5:1-11** Mt 4:18-22; Mk 1:16-20; Jn 1:40-42
[u] **5:1** Nm 34:11; Dt 3:17; Jos 12:3; 13:27; Mt 4:18

[A] **4:18** Other mss add *to heal the brokenhearted,* [B] **4:18** Or *release,* or *forgiveness* [C] **4:19** The time of messianic grace [D] **4:18-19** Is 61:1-2 [E] **4:22** Or *They were testifying against Him* [F] **4:23** Or *parable* [G] **4:27** Lit *cleansed* [H] **4:29** Lit *brow* [I] **4:34** Or *Ha!*, or *Ah!* [J] **4:34** Lit *What to us and to You* [K] **4:44** Other mss read *Judea* [L] **5:1** = Sea of Galilee

edge of the lake;[A] the fishermen had left them
and were washing their nets. 3He got into
one of the boats,[a] which belonged to Simon,
and asked him to put out a little from the
land. Then He sat down and was teaching the
crowds from the boat.
4When He had finished speaking, He said
to Simon, "Put out into deep water and let
down[B] your nets for a catch."[b]
5"Master,"[c] Simon replied, "we've worked
hard all night long and caught nothing! But
at Your word, I'll let down the nets."[C]
6When they did this, they caught a great
number of fish, and their nets[C] began to tear.
7So they signaled to their partners in the
other boat to come and help them; they came
and filled both boats so full that they began
to sink.
8When Simon Peter saw this, he fell at
Jesus' knees and said, "Go away from me,
because I'm a sinful man, Lord!" 9For he
and all those with him were amazed[D] at the
catch of fish they took, 10and so were James
and John, Zebedee's sons, who were Simon's
partners.
"Don't be afraid,"[d] Jesus told Simon. "From
now on you will be catching people!"[e] 11Then
they brought the boats to land, left everything, and followed Him.[f]

A Man Cleansed

12While He was in one of the towns, a man
was there who had a serious skin disease all
over him.[g] He saw Jesus, fell facedown, and
begged Him: "Lord, if You are willing, You can
make me •clean."
13Reaching out His hand, He touched him,
saying, "I am willing; be made clean," and immediately the disease left him. 14Then He ordered him to tell no one: "But go and show
yourself to the priest, and offer what Moses
prescribed for your cleansing as a testimony
to them."
15But the news[E] about Him spread even
more, and large crowds would come together
to hear Him and to be healed of their sicknesses. 16Yet He often withdrew to deserted
places and prayed.[h]

The Son of Man Forgives and Heals

17On one of those days while He was teaching, •Pharisees and teachers of the law[i] were
sitting there who had come from every village of Galilee and Judea, and also from Jerusalem. And the Lord's power to heal was
in Him.[j] 18Just then some men came,[k] carrying on a mat a man who was paralyzed. They
tried to bring him in and set him down before Him. 19Since they could not find a way to
bring him in because of the crowd, they went
up on the roof and lowered him on the mat
through the roof tiles into the middle of the
crowd before Jesus.
20Seeing their faith He said, "Friend,[F] your
sins are forgiven you."
21Then the •scribes and the Pharisees[l] began to think: "Who is this man who speaks
blasphemies? Who can forgive sins but God
alone?"[m]
22But perceiving their thoughts, Jesus replied to them, "Why are you thinking this in
your hearts?[G] 23Which is easier: to say, 'Your
sins are forgiven you,' or to say, 'Get up and
walk'? 24But so you may know that the •Son
of Man has authority on earth to forgive
sins"—He told the paralyzed man, "I tell you:
Get up, pick up your mat, and go home."
25Immediately he got up before them,
picked up what he had been lying on, and
went home glorifying God. 26Then everyone
was astounded, and they were giving glory to
God. And they were filled with awe[n] and said,
"We have seen incredible things today!"

The Call of Matthew

27After this, Jesus went out and saw a tax
collector named Levi sitting at the tax office,[o]
and He said to him, "Follow Me!" 28So, leaving everything behind, he got up and began
to follow Him.

Dining with Sinners

29Then Levi hosted a grand banquet for Him
at his house. Now there was a large crowd of
tax collectors and others who were guests[H]
with them.[p] 30But the Pharisees and their
scribes[q] were complaining to His disciples,

[a]**5:3** Mt 13:2; Mk 3:9-10; 4:1 [b]**5:4-6** Jn 21:3-6 [c]**5:5** Lk 8:24; 9:33,49; 17:13 [d]**5:10** Mt 14:27 [e]2Tm 2:26 [f]**5:11** Mt 4:20,22; 19:29; Mk 1:18,20; Lk 5:28 [g]**5:12-14** Mt 8:2-4; Mk 1:40-44 [h]**5:16** Mt 14:23; Mk 1:35; Lk 6:12 [i]**5:17** Ac 5:34; 1Tm 1:7 [j]Mk 5:30; Lk 6:19; 8:46 [k]**5:18-26** Mt 9:2-8; Mk 2:3-12 [l]**5:21** Mt 23:2; Lk 11:53; Jn 8:3 [m]Is 43:25 [n]**5:26** Lk 1:65; 7:16 [o]**5:27-39** Mt 9:9-17; Mk 2:14-22 [p]**5:29** Lk 15:1 [q]**5:30** Mk 2:16; Ac 23:9

A**5:2** Lit *boats standing by the lake* B**5:4** Lit *and you* (pl in Gk) *let down* C**5:5,6** Other mss read *net* (Gk sg) D**5:9** Lit *For amazement had seized him and all those with him* E**5:15** Lit *the word* F**5:20** Lit *Man* G**5:22** Or *minds*

H**5:29** Lit *were reclining* (at the table); at important meals the custom was to recline on a mat at a low table and lean on the left elbow.

"Why do you eat and drink with tax collectors and sinners?"

31 Jesus replied to them, "The healthy don't need a doctor, but the sick do. 32 I have not come to call the righteous, but sinners to repentance."

A Question about Fasting

33 Then they said to Him, "John's disciples fast often and say prayers, and those of the Pharisees do the same, but Yours eat and drink."[A]

34 Jesus said to them, "You can't make the wedding guests[B] fast while the groom is with them, can you? 35 But the time[C] will come[a] when the groom will be taken away from them—then they will fast in those days."

36 He also told them a parable: "No one tears a patch from a new garment and puts it on an old garment. Otherwise, not only will he tear the new, but also the piece from the new garment will not match the old. 37 And no one puts new wine into old wineskins. Otherwise, the new wine will burst the skins, it will spill, and the skins will be ruined. 38 But new wine should be put into fresh wineskins.[D] 39 And no one, after drinking old wine, wants new, because he says, 'The old is better.'"[E]

Lord of the Sabbath

6 On a Sabbath,[F] He passed through the grainfields.[b] His disciples were picking heads of grain, rubbing them in their hands, and eating them. 2 But some of the ·Pharisees said, "Why are you doing what is not lawful on the Sabbath?"

3 Jesus answered them, "Haven't you read what David and those who were with him did when he was hungry—4 how he entered the house of God, and took and ate the ·sacred bread, which is not lawful for any but the priests to eat?[c] He even gave some to those who were with him."[d] 5 Then He told them, "The ·Son of Man is Lord of the Sabbath."

The Man with the Paralyzed Hand

6 On another Sabbath[e] He entered the ·synagogue and was teaching. A man was there whose right hand was paralyzed. 7 The ·scribes and Pharisees were watching Him closely,[f] to see if He would heal on the Sabbath, so that they could find a charge against Him.[g] 8 But He knew their thoughts[h] and told the man with the paralyzed hand, "Get up and stand here."[G] So he got up and stood there. 9 Then Jesus said to them, "I ask you: Is it lawful on the Sabbath to do what is good or to do what is evil, to save life or to destroy it?"[i] 10 After looking around at them all,[j] He told him, "Stretch out your hand."[k] He did so, and his hand was restored.[H] 11 They, however, were filled with rage and started discussing with one another what they might do to Jesus.

The 12 Apostles

12 During those days He went out to the mountain to pray[l] and spent all night in prayer to God. 13 When daylight came, He summoned His disciples,[m] and He chose 12 of them—He also named them apostles:[n]

14 Simon, whom He also named Peter,
and Andrew his brother;
James and John;
Philip and Bartholomew;
15 Matthew and Thomas;[o]
James the son of Alphaeus,
and Simon called the Zealot;
16 Judas the son of James,
and Judas Iscariot, who became
a traitor.

Teaching and Healing

17 After coming down with them, He stood on a level place with a large crowd of His disciples and a great number of people from all Judea and Jerusalem and from the seacoast of Tyre and Sidon.[p] 18 They came to hear Him and to be healed of their diseases; and those tormented by ·unclean spirits were made well. 19 The whole crowd was trying to touch Him,[q] because power was coming out from Him and healing them all.[r]

The Beatitudes

20 Then looking up at[I] His disciples, He said:[s]

[a] **5:35** 1Sm 2:31; Ps 37:13; Ec 2:16; 12:1; Lk 17:22
[b] **6:1-5** Mt 12:1-8; Mk 2:23-28
[c] **6:4** Ex 25:30; Lv 24:5-9
[d] 1Sm 21:6
[e] **6:6-11** Mt 12:9-14; Mk 3:1-6
[f] **6:7** Mk 3:2; Lk 14:1; 20:20
[g] Jn 8:6
[h] **6:8** Mt 9:4
[i] **6:9** Lk 14:3
[j] **6:10** Mk 3:5
[k] 1Kg 13:4
[l] **6:12** Mt 14:23; Lk 5:16; 9:18,28
[m] **6:13-16** Mt 10:2-4; Mk 3:16-19; Ac 1:13
[n] **6:13** Mk 6:30
[o] **6:15** Mt 9:9
[p] **6:17** Mt 11:21
[q] **6:19** Mt 9:21; 14:36; Mk 3:10
[r] Lk 5:17
[s] **6:20-23** Mt 5:3-12

[A] **5:33** Other mss read *"Why do John's . . . drink?"* (as a question) [B] **5:34** Or *the friends of the groom*; lit *sons of the bridal chamber* [C] **5:35** Lit *days* [D] **5:38** Other mss add *And so both are preserved.* [E] **5:39** Other mss read *is good* [F] **6:1** Other mss read *a second-first Sabbath*; perhaps a special Sabbath [G] **6:8** Lit *stand in the middle* [H] **6:10** Other mss add *as sound as the other* [I] **6:20** Lit *Then lifting up His eyes to*

You who are poor are blessed,
because the kingdom of God is yours.
21 You who are now hungry are blessed,
because you will be filled.
You who now weep are blessed,
because you will laugh.
22 You are blessed when people hate you,
when they exclude you,[a] insult you,
and slander your name as evil[b]
because of the Son of Man.[c]

23 "Rejoice in that day and leap for joy! Take note — your reward is great in heaven, for this is the way their ancestors used to treat the prophets.[d]

Woe to the Self-Satisfied

24 But woe to you who are rich,
for you have received your comfort.
25 Woe to you who are now full,
for you will be hungry.
Woe to you[A] who are now laughing,
for you will mourn and weep.
26 Woe to you[A]
when all people speak well of you,
for this is the way their ancestors
used to treat the false prophets.[e]

Love Your Enemies

27 "But I say to you who listen: Love your enemies, do what is good to those who hate you, 28 bless those who curse you, pray for those who mistreat you.[f] 29 If anyone hits you on the cheek,[g] offer the other also. And if anyone takes away your coat, don't hold back your shirt either. 30 Give to everyone who asks you, and from one who takes your things, don't ask for them back. 31 Just as you want others to do for you, do the same for them.[h] 32 If you love those who love you, what credit is that to you? Even sinners love those who love them.[i] 33 If you do what is good to those who are good to you, what credit is that to you? Even sinners do that. 34 And if you lend to those from whom you expect to receive, what credit is that to you?[j] Even sinners lend to sinners to be repaid in full. 35 But love your enemies, do what is good, and lend, expecting nothing in return. Then your reward will be great, and you will be sons of the Most High.[k] For He is gracious to the ungrateful and evil. 36 Be merciful, just as your Father also is merciful.[l]

Do Not Judge

37 "Do not judge, and you will not be judged.[m] Do not condemn, and you will not be condemned. Forgive, and you will be forgiven.[n] 38 Give, and it will be given to you; a good measure — pressed down, shaken together, and running over — will be poured into your lap.[o] For with the measure you use,[B] it will be measured back to you."[p]

39 He also told them a parable: "Can the blind guide the blind? Won't they both fall into a pit?[q] 40 A disciple is not above his teacher, but everyone who is fully trained will be like his teacher.[r]

41 "Why do you look at the speck in your brother's eye, but don't notice the log in your own eye? 42 Or how can you say to your brother, 'Brother, let me take out the speck that is in your eye,' when you yourself don't see the log in your eye? Hypocrite! First take the log out of your eye, and then you will see clearly to take out the speck in your brother's eye.

A Tree and Its Fruit

43 "A good tree doesn't produce bad fruit; on the other hand, a bad tree doesn't produce good fruit.[s] 44 For each tree is known by its own fruit. Figs aren't gathered from thornbushes, or grapes picked from a bramble bush. 45 A good man produces good out of the good storeroom of his heart. An evil man produces evil out of the evil storeroom, for his mouth speaks from the overflow of the heart.

The Two Foundations

46 "Why do you call Me 'Lord, Lord,' and don't do the things I say?[t] 47 I will show you what someone is like who comes to Me, hears My words, and acts on them:[u] 48 He is like a man building a house, who dug deep[C] and laid the foundation on the rock. When the flood came, the river crashed against that house and couldn't shake it, because it was well built. 49 But the one who hears and does not act is like a man who built a house on the ground without a foundation. The

[a] **6:22** Jn 9:22; 16:2
[b] Heb 11:26; 1Pt 4:14
[c] Jn 15:21
[d] **6:23** Neh 9:26; Ezk 2:1-7; Ac 7:52
[e] **6:26** Jr 5:12-13; 6:13-15; Mc 2:11
[f] **6:28** Mt 5:44
[g] **6:29-30** Mt 5:39-42
[h] **6:31** Mt 7:12
[i] **6:32** Mt 5:46
[j] **6:34** Pr 19:17; Mt 5:42; Lk 14:12-14
[k] **6:35** Mt 5:45; Lk 1:32
[l] **6:36** Mt 5:7,48; Jms 5:11
[m] **6:37-42** Mt 7:1-5
[n] **6:37** Mt 6:14; 18:23-35; Lk 23:16; Ac 3:13
[o] **6:38** Ps 79:12; Is 65:6-7; Jr 32:18
[p] Mk 4:24
[q] **6:39** Mt 15:14
[r] **6:40** Mt 10:24; Jn 13:16; 15:20
[s] **6:43-44** Mt 7:16,18,20; 12:33-35
[t] **6:46** Mal 1:6; Mt 7:21
[u] **6:47-49** Mt 7:24-27

[A] **6:25,26** Other mss omit *to you* [B] **6:38** Lit *you measure* [C] **6:48** Lit *dug and went deep*

river crashed against it, and immediately it
collapsed. And the destruction of that house
was great!"[a]

A Centurion's Faith

7 When He had concluded all His sayings
in the hearing of the people, He entered
Capernaum.[b] 2A ·centurion's ·slave, who was
highly valued by him, was sick and about to
die. 3When the centurion heard about Jesus,
he sent some Jewish elders to Him, requesting Him to come and save the life of his slave.
4When they reached Jesus, they pleaded with
Him earnestly, saying, "He is worthy for You
to grant this, 5because he loves our nation
and has built us a ·synagogue."[c] 6Jesus went
with them, and when He was not far from[A]
the house, the centurion sent friends to tell
Him, "Lord, don't trouble Yourself, since I am
not worthy to have You come under my roof.
7That is why I didn't even consider myself
worthy to come to You. But say the word, and
my servant will be cured.[B,d] 8For I too am a
man placed under authority, having soldiers
under my command.[C] I say to this one, 'Go!'
and he goes; and to another, 'Come!' and
he comes; and to my slave, 'Do this!' and he
does it."

9Jesus heard this and was amazed at him,
and turning to the crowd following Him, He
said, "I tell you, I have not found so great a
faith even in Israel!" 10When those who had
been sent returned to the house, they found
the slave in good health.

A Widow's Son Raised to Life

11Soon afterward He was on His way to a
town called Nain. His disciples and a large
crowd were traveling with Him. 12Just as He
neared the gate of the town, a dead man was
being carried out. He was his mother's only
son, and she was a widow.[e] A large crowd
from the city was also with her. 13When the
Lord saw her, He had compassion on her[f]
and said, "Don't cry." 14Then He came up and
touched the open coffin,[D] and the pallbear-
ers stopped. And He said, "Young man, I tell
you, get up!"[g]

15The dead man sat up and began to speak,
and Jesus gave him to his mother.[h] 16Then fear[E]
came over everyone,[i] and they glorified God,[j]
saying, "A great prophet has risen among us,"[k]
and "God has visited[F] His people."[l] 17This report about Him went throughout Judea and
all the vicinity.

In Praise of John the Baptist

18Then John's disciples told him about all
these things.[m] So John summoned two of his
disciples 19and sent them to the Lord, asking,
"Are You the One[n] who is to come, or should
we look for someone else?"

20When the men reached Him, they said,
"John the Baptist sent us to ask You, 'Are You
the One who is to come, or should we look for
someone else?'"

21At that time Jesus healed many people of
diseases,[o] plagues, and evil spirits,[p] and He
granted sight to many blind people.[q] 22He
replied to them, "Go and report to John the
things you have seen and heard: The blind
receive their sight, the lame walk, those with
skin diseases are healed,[G] the deaf hear,[r] the
dead are raised, and the poor are told the
good news.[s] 23And anyone who is not ·of-
fended because of Me is blessed." 24After
John's messengers left, He began to speak to
the crowds about John: "What did you go out
into the wilderness to see? A reed swaying
in the wind? 25What then did you go out to
see? A man dressed in soft robes? Look, those
who are splendidly dressed[H] and live in luxury are in royal palaces. 26What then did you
go out to see? A prophet?[t] Yes, I tell you, and
far more than a prophet. 27This is the one it is
written about:

> **Look, I am sending My messenger**
> **ahead of You;**[I]
> **he will prepare Your way before You.**[J,u]

28I tell you, among those born of women no
one is greater than John,[K] but the least in the
kingdom of God is greater than he."

29(And when all the people, including the
tax collectors, heard this, they acknowledged
God's way of righteousness,[L] because they
had been baptized with John's baptism.[v]

[a] 6:49 Ezk 13:10-16
[b] 7:1-10 Mt 8:5-13
[c] 7:5 Ac 10:22
[d] 7:7 Ps 107:20; Mt 8:16
[e] 7:12 Jdg 11:34; Lk 8:42; 9:38; Heb 11:17
[f] 7:13 Mt 20:34
[g] 7:14 Mt 11:5; Mk 5:41; Lk 7:22; 8:54; Jn 11:43; Ac 9:40
[h] 7:15 1Kg 17:23; 2Kg 4:36
[i] 7:16 Lk 5:26
[j] Mt 5:16; Lk 2:20; 13:13; 23:47; Ac 4:21; 11:18
[k] Dt 18:15; Mt 21:11; Lk 7:39; Jn 7:40
[l] Lk 1:68
[m] 7:18-35 Mt 11:2-19
[n] 7:19 Jn 4:25; 6:14; 11:27; Rm 5:14; Heb 10:37
[o] 7:21 Mt 4:23
[p] Mk 1:34
[q] Mt 9:30; 12:22; Mk 8:25; Lk 18:42; Jn 9:7
[r] 7:22 Is 29:18; 35:5-6
[s] Is 61:1; Lk 4:18
[t] 7:26 Mt 14:5; Lk 1:76; 20:6
[u] 7:27 Mal 3:1; Mt 11:10; Mk 1:2; Lk 1:17
[v] 7:29 Mt 21:32; Lk 3:12; Ac 18:25; 19:3

[A] 7:6 Lit *and He already was not far from* [B] 7:7 Other mss read *and let my servant be cured* [C] 7:8 Lit *under me* [D] 7:14 Or *the bier* [E] 7:16 Or *awe* [F] 7:16 Or *come to help* [G] 7:22 Lit *cleansed* [H] 7:25 Or *who have glorious robes* [I] 7:27 Lit *messenger before Your face* [J] 7:27 Mal 3:1 [K] 7:28 Other mss read *women is not a greater prophet than John the Baptist* [L] 7:29 Lit *they justified God*

30 But since the ·Pharisees and experts in the
law[a] had not been baptized by him, they rejected the plan of God for themselves.[b])

An Unresponsive Generation

31 "To what then should I compare the people of this generation, and what are they like?
32 They are like children sitting in the marketplace and calling to each other:

We played the flute for you,
but you didn't dance;
we sang a lament,
but you didn't weep!

33 For John the Baptist did not come eating
bread or drinking wine,[c] and you say, 'He has
a demon!' 34 The ·Son of Man has come eating and drinking, and you say, 'Look, a glutton and a drunkard, a friend of tax collectors
and sinners!'[d] 35 Yet wisdom is vindicated[A] by
all her children."

Much Forgiveness, Much Love

36 Then one of the Pharisees invited Him to
eat with him. He entered the Pharisee's house
and reclined at the table.[e] 37 And a woman in
the town who was a sinner found out that
Jesus was reclining at the table in the Pharisee's house.[f] She brought an alabaster jar of
fragrant oil 38 and stood behind Him at His
feet, weeping, and began to wash His feet
with her tears. She wiped His feet with the
hair of her head, kissing them and anointing
them with the fragrant oil.[g]
39 When the Pharisee who had invited
Him saw this, he said to himself, "This man,
if He were a prophet, would know who and
what kind of woman this is who is touching
Him — she's a sinner!"[h]
40 Jesus replied to him, "Simon, I have something to say to you."
"Teacher," he said, "say it."
41 "A creditor had two debtors. One owed
500 ·denarii,[i] and the other 50. 42 Since they
could not pay it back,[j] he graciously forgave
them both. So, which of them will love him
more?"
43 Simon answered, "I suppose the one he
forgave more."
"You have judged correctly," He told him.

[a] **7:30** Mt 22:35; Lk 10:25; 11:45-46,52; 14:3
[b] Mt 21:25,32; 23:13; Mk 7:9
[c] **7:33** Lk 1:15
[d] **7:34** Mt 9:10-11; Lk 15:2; 19:7
[e] **7:36** Lk 11:37; 14:1
[f] **7:37-39** Mt 26:6-13; Mk 14:3-9; Jn 12:1-8
[g] **7:38** Jn 11:2
[h] **7:39** Lk 7:16; Jn 4:19
[i] **7:41** Mt 18:28; Mk 6:37
[j] **7:42** Mt 18:25
[k] **7:44** Gn 18:4; 19:2; 43:24; Jdg 19:21; 1Tm 5:10
[l] **7:45** 2Sm 15:5; 19:39; 20:9
[m] **7:46** 2Sm 12:20; Ps 23:5; Ec 9:8; Dn 10:3
[n] **7:48** Mt 9:2; Mk 2:5; Lk 5:20; Jms 5:15; 1Jn 2:12
[o] **7:49** Lk 5:21
[p] **7:50** Mt 9:22; Mk 10:52; Lk 17:19; 18:42
[q] 1Sm 1:17; Mk 5:34; Lk 8:48
[r] **8:1** Mk 6:6
[s] Mt 4:23; Lk 4:43
[t] **8:2** Mt 27:55; Mk 15:40-41; Lk 23:49,55; Ac 1:14
[u] Mt 27:56,61; 28:1; Mk 16:9; Lk 24:10; Jn 19:25; 20:1,18
[v] **8:4-8** Mt 13:3-9; Mk 4:3-9
[w] **8:8** Gn 26:12
[x] Mt 11:15; Lk 13:34
[y] **8:9-10** Mt 13:10-11; Mk 4:10-11

44 Turning to the woman, He said to Simon,
"Do you see this woman? I entered your
house; you gave Me no water for My feet,[k] but
she, with her tears, has washed My feet and
wiped them with her hair. 45 You gave Me no
kiss,[l] but she hasn't stopped kissing My feet
since I came in. 46 You didn't anoint My head
with olive oil,[m] but she has anointed My feet
with fragrant oil. 47 Therefore I tell you, her
many sins have been forgiven; that's why[B] she
loved much. But the one who is forgiven little, loves little." 48 Then He said to her, "Your
sins are forgiven."[n]
49 Those who were at the table with Him
began to say among themselves, "Who is this
man who even forgives sins?"[o]
50 And He said to the woman, "Your faith
has saved you.[p] Go in peace."[q]

Many Women Support Christ's Work

8 Soon afterward He was traveling from
one town and village to another,[r] preaching and telling the good news of the kingdom
of God.[s] The Twelve were with Him, 2 and also
some women who had been healed of evil
spirits and sicknesses:[t] Mary, called ·Magda-
lene (seven demons had come out[u] of her);
3 Joanna the wife of Chuza, ·Herod's steward;
Susanna; and many others who were supporting them from their possessions.

The Parable of the Sower

4 As a large crowd was gathering, and people were flocking to Him from every town, He
said in a parable:[v] 5 "A sower went out to sow
his seed. As he was sowing, some fell along
the path; it was trampled on, and the birds of
the sky ate it up. 6 Other seed fell on the rock;
when it sprang up, it withered, since it lacked
moisture. 7 Other seed fell among thorns;
the thorns sprang up with it and choked it.
8 Still other seed fell on good ground; when it
sprang up, it produced a crop: 100 times what
was sown."[w] As He said this, He called out,
"Anyone who has ears to hear should listen!"[x]

Why Jesus Used Parables

9 Then His disciples asked Him, "What does
this parable mean?"[y] 10 So He said, "The ·se-
crets of the kingdom of God have been given

[A] 7:35 Or *wisdom is declared right* [B] 7:47 Her love shows that she has been forgiven

for you[a] to know, but to the rest it is in parables, so that

> **Looking they may not see,**
> **and hearing they may**
> **not understand.**[A,b]

The Parable of the Sower Explained

11 "This is the meaning of the parable:[B,c] The seed is the word of God.[d] 12 The seed along the path are those who have heard and then the Devil comes and takes away the word from their hearts, so that they may not believe and be saved. 13 And the seed on the rock are those who, when they hear, welcome the word with joy. Having no root, these believe for a while and depart in a time of testing.[e] 14 As for the seed that fell among thorns, these are the ones who, when they have heard, go on their way and are choked with worries, riches, and pleasures of life,[f] and produce no mature fruit. 15 But the seed in the good ground — these are the ones who,[C] having heard the word with an honest and good heart, hold on to it and by enduring,[g] bear fruit.

Using Your Light

16 "No one, after lighting a lamp,[h] covers it with a basket or puts it under a bed, but puts it on a lampstand so that those who come in may see its light.[i] 17 For nothing is concealed that won't be revealed, and nothing hidden that won't be made known and come to light.[j] 18 Therefore take care how you listen. For whoever has, more will be given to him;[k] and whoever does not have, even what he thinks he has will be taken away from him."

True Relationships

19 Then His mother and brothers[l] came to Him,[m] but they could not meet with Him because of the crowd. 20 He was told, "Your mother and Your brothers are standing outside, wanting to see You."

21 But He replied to them, "My mother and My brothers are those who hear and do the word of God."[n]

Wind and Wave Obey the Master

22 One day He and His disciples got into a boat,[o] and He told them, "Let's cross over to the other side of the lake."[p] So they set out, 23 and as they were sailing He fell asleep. Then a fierce windstorm came down on the lake; they were being swamped and were in danger. 24 They came and woke Him up, saying, "Master, Master, we're going to die!" Then He got up and rebuked the wind and the raging waves. So they ceased, and there was a calm.[q] 25 He said to them, "Where is your faith?"

They were fearful and amazed, asking one another, "Who can this be?[D,r] He commands even the winds and the waves, and they obey Him!"

Demons Driven Out by the Master

26 Then they sailed to the region of the Gerasenes,[E,s] which is opposite Galilee. 27 When He got out on land, a demon-possessed man from the town met Him. For a long time he had worn no clothes and did not stay in a house but in the tombs. 28 When he saw Jesus, he cried out,[t] fell down before Him, and said in a loud voice, "What do You have to do with me,[F,u] Jesus, You Son of the Most High God?[v] I beg You, don't torment me!" 29 For He had commanded the •unclean spirit to come out of the man. Many times it had seized him, and though he was guarded, bound by chains and shackles, he would snap the restraints and be driven by the demon into deserted places.

30 "What is your name?" Jesus asked him.

"Legion,"[w] he said — because many demons had entered him. 31 And they begged Him not to banish them to the •abyss.[x]

32 A large herd of pigs was there, feeding on the hillside. The demons begged Him to permit them to enter the pigs, and He gave them permission. 33 The demons came out of the man and entered the pigs, and the herd rushed down the steep bank into the lake and drowned. 34 When the men who tended them saw what had happened, they ran off and reported it in the town and in the countryside. 35 Then people went out to see what had happened. They came to Jesus and found the man the demons had departed from, sitting at Jesus' feet,[y] dressed and in his right mind. And they were afraid. 36 Meanwhile, the eyewitnesses reported to them how the demon-

[a] **8:10** Mt 19:11
[b] Is 6:9
[c] **8:11-15** Mt 13:18-23; Mk 4:13-20
[d] **8:11** Lk 8:21; 11:28; Ac 18:11; Jms 1:21; 1Pt 1:23
[e] **8:13** Ezk 33:31-32; Gl 1:6
[f] **8:14** Mt 6:25
[g] **8:15** Heb 10:36; Jms 5:7
[h] **8:16** Mt 5:15-16; Lk 11:33
[i] **8:16-18** Mk 4:21-25
[j] **8:17** Mt 10:26; Lk 12:2; 1Tm 5:25
[k] **8:18** Mt 13:12
[l] **8:19** Mt 13:55; Mk 6:3; Jn 2:12; 7:3,5,10; Ac 1:14; 1Co 9:5; Gl 1:19
[m] **8:19-21** Mt 12:46-50; Mk 3:31-35
[n] **8:21** Lk 11:28; Jms 1:22
[o] **8:22-25** Mt 8:23-27; Mk 4:36-41; Jn 6:16-21
[p] **8:22** Lk 5:1
[q] **8:24** Ps 65:7; 104:7; Mt 14:32; Mk 6:51; Lk 4:39
[r] **8:25** Mt 21:10; Lk 1:66; 5:21; 7:49; 9:9
[s] **8:26-39** Mt 8:28-34; Mk 5:1-20
[t] **8:28** Lk 4:33-34; Ac 8:7
[u] Jn 2:4
[v] Gn 14:18; Ps 57:2; Dn 3:26; Lk 1:32; Ac 16:17
[w] **8:30** Mt 26:53
[x] **8:31** Ps 140:10; Rm 10:7; Rv 9:1-2,11; 11:7; 17:8; 20:1,3
[y] **8:35** Lk 8:41; 10:39

[A] **8:10** Is 6:9 [B] **8:11** Lit *But this is the parable:* [C] **8:15** Or *these are the kind who* [D] **8:25** Lit *Who then is this?* [E] **8:26** Other mss read *the Gadarenes* [F] **8:28** Lit *What to me and to You*

possessed man was delivered.[a] 37Then all the
people of the Gerasene region[A] asked Him
to leave them,[b] because they were gripped
by great fear. So getting into the boat, He returned.

38The man from whom the demons had
departed kept begging Him to be with Him.
But He sent him away and said, 39"Go back
to your home, and tell all that God has
done for you." And off he went, proclaiming
throughout the town all that Jesus had done
for him.

A Girl Restored and a Woman Healed

40When Jesus returned, the crowd welcomed Him,[c] for they were all expecting
Him.[d] 41Just then, a man named Jairus came.
He was a leader of the •synagogue.[e] He fell
down at Jesus' feet and pleaded with Him to
come to his house, 42because he had an only
daughter[f] about 12 years old, and she was at
death's door.[B]

While He was going, the crowds were
nearly crushing Him.[g] 43A woman suffering from bleeding[h] for 12 years,[i] who had
spent all she had on doctors[C] yet could not
be healed by any, 44approached from behind
and touched the •tassel of His robe.[j] Instantly
her bleeding stopped.

45"Who touched Me?" Jesus asked.

When they all denied it, Peter[D] said, "Master,[k] the crowds are hemming You in and
pressing against You."[E]

46"Someone did touch Me," said Jesus. "I
know that power has gone out from Me."[l]
47When the woman saw that she was discovered,[F] she came trembling and fell down before Him. In the presence of all the people,
she declared the reason she had touched Him
and how she was instantly cured. 48"Daughter," He said to her, "your faith has made you
well.[G] Go in peace."[m]

49While He was still speaking,[n] someone
came from the synagogue leader's house, saying, "Your daughter is dead. Don't bother[o] the
Teacher[p] anymore."

50When Jesus heard it, He answered him,
"Don't be afraid. Only believe, and she will be

[a]**8:36** Mt 4:24
[b]**8:37** 1Kg 17:18; Lk 5:8; Ac 16:39
[c]**8:40** Lk 9:11
[d]**8:40-42** Mt 9:18-19; Mk 5:21-24
[e]**8:41** Lk 13:14; Ac 13:15; 18:8,17
[f]**8:42** Lk 7:12
[g]Mk 3:9
[h]**8:43** Lv 15:25
[i]**8:43-48** Mt 9:20-22; Mk 5:25-34
[j]**8:44** Nm 15:38-39; Dt 22:12; Mt 14:36; 23:5
[k]**8:45** Lk 5:5
[l]**8:46** Lk 5:17; 6:19; Ac 10:38
[m]**8:48** Lk 7:50
[n]**8:49-56** Mt 9:23-26; Mk 5:35-43
[o]**8:49** Lk 7:6
[p]Jn 11:28
[q]**8:51** Mk 3:17; 14:33; Lk 9:28
[r]**8:52** Lk 7:13
[s]Mt 11:17; Lk 23:27
[t]Jn 11:4,11; Ac 20:10
[u]**8:54** Mk 1:31
[v]Mt 11:5; Lk 7:14,22; Jn 11:43
[w]**8:55** Jdg 15:19; 1Sm 30:12
[x]**8:56** Mt 8:4
[y]**9:1** Lk 6:12-16
[z]Mt 10:1; Mk 3:13-15; 6:7
[aa]**9:2** Mt 10:5,7-8; Lk 4:43; 9:11,60; 10:1,9
[ab]**9:3-5** Mt 10:9-15; Mk 6:8-11; Lk 10:4-12; 22:35
[ac]**9:3** Mk 6:8
[ad]**9:5** Neh 5:13; Ac 13:51; 18:6
[ae]**9:7** Lk 3:1,19; 13:31; 23:7; Ac 13:1
[af]**9:7-9** Mt 14:1-2; Mk 6:14-16
[ag]**9:8** Mt 11:14; 16:14; 17:3-4,10-12; Lk 1:17; 4:26
[ah]Mk 6:15
[ai]**9:9** Lk 23:8
[aj]**9:10-17** Mt 14:13-21; Mk 6:32-44; Jn 6:5-13
[ak]**9:10** Mk 6:30
[al]Mt 11:21; Mk 8:22; Jn 1:44; 12:21

made well." 51After He came to the house, He
let no one enter with Him except Peter, John,
James,[q] and the child's father and mother.
52Everyone was crying[r] and mourning for
her.[s] But He said, "Stop crying, for she is not
dead but asleep."[t]

53They started laughing at Him, because
they knew she was dead. 54So He[H] took her
by the hand[u] and called out, "Child, get up!"[v]
55Her spirit returned,[w] and she got up at once.
Then He gave orders that she be given something to eat. 56Her parents were astounded,
but He instructed them to tell no one what
had happened.[x]

Commissioning the Twelve

9 Summoning the Twelve,[y] He gave them
power and authority over all the demons,
and power to heal[I] diseases.[z] 2Then He sent
them to proclaim the kingdom of God and to
heal the sick.[aa]

3"Take nothing for the road,"[ab] He told
them, "no walking stick,[ac] no traveling bag,
no bread, no money; and don't take an extra
shirt. 4Whatever house you enter, stay there
and leave from there. 5If they do not welcome
you, when you leave that town, shake off the
dust from your feet as a testimony against
them."[ad] 6So they went out and traveled from
village to village, proclaiming the good news
and healing everywhere.

Herod's Desire to See Jesus

7•Herod the tetrarch[ae] heard about everything that was going on.[af] He was perplexed,
because some said that John had been raised
from the dead, 8some that Elijah had appeared,[ag] and others that one of the ancient
prophets had risen.[ah] 9"I beheaded John,"
Herod said, "but who is this I hear such things
about?" And he wanted to see Him.[ai]

Feeding 5,000

10When the apostles returned,[aj] they reported to Jesus all that they had done.[ak] He
took them along and withdrew privately to
a[J] town called Bethsaida.[al] 11When the crowds
found out, they followed Him. He welcomed

[A]**8:37** Other mss read *the Gadarenes* [B]**8:42** Lit *she was dying* [C]**8:43** Other mss omit *who had spent all she had on doctors* [D]**8:45** Other mss add *and those with him* [E]**8:45** Other mss add *and You say, 'Who touched Me?'* [F]**8:47** Lit *she had not escaped notice* [G]**8:48** Or *has saved you* [H]**8:54** Other mss add *having put them all outside* [I]**9:1** In this passage, different Gk words are translated as heal. In Eng, "to heal" or "to cure" are synonyms with little distinction in meaning. Technically, we do not heal or cure diseases. People are healed or cured from diseases. [J]**9:10** Other mss add *deserted place near a* them,[a] spoke to them about the kingdom of God, and cured[A] those who needed healing.

12 Late in the day,[B,b] the Twelve approached and said to Him, "Send the crowd away,[c] so they can go into the surrounding villages and countryside to find food and lodging, because we are in a deserted place here."

13 "You give them something to eat," He told them.

"We have no more than five loaves[d] and two fish," they said, "unless we go and buy food for all these people." **14** (For about 5,000 men were there.)

Then He told His disciples, "Have them sit down[C] in groups of about 50 each." **15** They did so, and had them all sit down. **16** Then He took the five loaves and the two fish, and looking up to heaven,[e] He blessed and broke them.[f] He kept giving them to the disciples to set before the crowd. **17** Everyone ate and was filled. Then they picked up[D] 12 baskets of leftover pieces.

Peter's Confession of the Messiah

18 While He was praying in private[g] and His disciples were with Him, He asked them, "Who do the crowds say that I am?"

19 They answered, "John the Baptist; others, Elijah; still others, that one of the ancient prophets has come back."[E,h]

20 "But you," He asked them, "who do you say that I am?"

Peter answered, "God's ·Messiah!"[i]

His Death and Resurrection Predicted

21 But He strictly warned and instructed them to tell this to no one,[j] **22** saying,[k] "The ·Son of Man[l] must suffer many things[m] and be rejected[n] by the elders, ·chief priests, and ·scribes,[o] be killed, and be raised the third day."[p]

Take Up Your Cross

23 Then He said to them all, "If anyone wants to come with[F] Me, he must deny himself,[q] take up his cross daily,[G] and follow Me.[r] **24** For whoever wants to save his ·life will lose it, but whoever loses his life because of Me will save it.[s] **25** What is a man benefited if he gains the whole world, yet loses or forfeits himself?[t] **26** For whoever is ashamed of Me and My words,[u] the Son of Man will be ashamed of him when He comes in His glory[v] and that of the Father and the holy angels.[w] **27** I tell you the truth: There are some standing here who will not taste death[x] until they see the kingdom of God."[y]

The Transfiguration

28 About eight days after these words,[z] He took along Peter, John, and James[aa] and went up on the mountain to pray.[ab] **29** As He was praying, the appearance of His face changed,[ac] and His clothes became dazzling white.[ad] **30** Suddenly, two men were talking with Him—Moses and Elijah. **31** They appeared in glory and were speaking of His death,[H] which He was about to accomplish in Jerusalem.

32 Peter and those with him were in a deep sleep,[I,ae] and when they became fully awake, they saw His glory and the two men who were standing with Him. **33** As the two men were departing from Him, Peter said to Jesus, "Master,[af] it's good for us to be here! Let us make three ·tabernacles: one for You, one for Moses, and one for Elijah"—not knowing what he said.[ag]

34 While he was saying this, a cloud appeared and overshadowed[ah] them. They became afraid as they entered the cloud. **35** Then a voice came from the cloud,[ai] saying:

> This is My Son,[aj] the Chosen One;[J,ak]
> listen to Him![al]

36 After the voice had spoken, only Jesus was found. They kept silent, and in those days told no one what they had seen.

The Power of Faith over a Demon

37 The next day,[am] when they came down from the mountain, a large crowd met Him. **38** Just then a man from the crowd cried out, "Teacher, I beg You to look at my son, because he's my only child.[an] **39** Often a spirit seizes him; sud-

[a] **9:11** Lk 8:40 [b] **9:12** Lk 24:29 [c] Mt 15:23 [d] **9:13** Mt 16:9; Mk 8:19 [e] **9:16** Mk 7:34; Jn 11:41; 17:1 [f] Mt 26:26; Mk 8:7; 14:22; Lk 24:30 [g] **9:18-20** Mt 16:13-16; Mk 8:27-29 [h] **9:19** Lk 9:7-8 [i] **9:20** Mt 1:17; Lk 23:35; Ac 3:18; Rv 12:10 [j] **9:21** Mt 12:16; 16:20; Mk 7:36; 8:30; 9:9; Lk 5:14; 8:56 [k] **9:22-27** Mt 16:21-28; Mk 8:31–9:1 [l] **9:22** Lk 13:33; 18:31 [m] Mt 17:12,22-23; Lk 24:7 [n] Lk 17:25; 20:17; 1Pt 2:4 [o] Lk 20:1; 22:66 [p] Mt 27:63; Jn 2:19 [q] **9:23** 2Tm 2:12-13 [r] Mt 10:38-39; Lk 14:27; 1Co 15:31 [s] **9:24** Lk 17:33; Jn 12:25 [t] **9:25** Lk 12:20 [u] **9:26** Mt 10:33; Rm 1:16; 2Tm 1:8; Heb 11:16; 1Jn 2:28 [v] Dn 7:10; Zch 14:5; Mt 24:30; Jn 1:51; Ac 1:11; 1Th 1:10 [w] Lk 12:9; Rv 14:10 [x] **9:27** Jn 8:52; Heb 2:9 [y] Mt 10:23; 23:36; 24:34; Mk 13:30; Lk 21:31-32 [z] **9:28-36** Mt 17:1-8; Mk 9:2-8 [aa] **9:28** Mk 14:33; Lk 8:51 [ab] Mt 14:23; Lk 3:21; 5:16; 6:12; 9:18 [ac] **9:29** Mk 16:12 [ad] Ps 104:2; Dn 7:9; Mt 28:3 [ae] **9:32** Gn 2:21; 15:12; 1Sm 26:12; Dn 8:18; 10:9; Mt 26:43 [af] **9:33** Lk 5:5; 9:49 [ag] Mk 14:40 [ah] **9:34** Lk 1:35; Ac 5:15 [ai] **9:35** Ex 24:15-16; 2Pt 1:16-18 [aj] Ex 4:23; Ps 2:7; Hs 11:1; Ac 13:33; Heb 1:5 [ak] Ps 89:3; Is 42:1; Lk 23:35 [al] Ac 3:22 [am] **9:37-42** Mt 17:14-18; Mk 9:14-27 [an] **9:38** Lk 7:12

[A] **9:11** Or *healed*; in this passage, different Gk words are translated as heal. In Eng, "to heal" or "to cure" are synonyms with little distinction in meaning. Technically, we do not heal or cure diseases. People are healed or cured from diseases. [B] **9:12** Lit *When the day began to decline* [C] **9:14** Lit *them recline* [D] **9:17** Lit *Then were picked up by them* [E] **9:19** Lit *has risen* [F] **9:23** Lit *come after* [G] **9:23** Other mss omit *daily* [H] **9:31** Or *departure*; Gk *exodus* [I] **9:32** Lit *were weighed down with sleep* [J] **9:35** Other mss read *the Beloved*

denly he shrieks, and it throws him into convulsions until he foams at the mouth;[A] wounding[B] him, it hardly ever leaves him. [40]I begged Your disciples to drive it out, but they couldn't."[a]

[41]Jesus replied, "You unbelieving and rebellious[C] generation![b] How long will I be with you and put up with you?[c] Bring your son here."

[42]As the boy was still approaching, the demon knocked him down and threw him into severe convulsions. But Jesus rebuked the ˙unclean spirit, cured the boy,[d] and gave him back to his father.[e] [43]And they were all astonished at the greatness of God.[f]

The Second Prediction of His Death

While everyone was amazed at all the things He was doing,[g] He told His disciples, [44]"Let these words sink in:[D] The Son of Man is about to be betrayed into the hands of men."[h]

[45]But they did not understand this statement;[i] it was concealed from them so that they could not grasp it,[j] and they were afraid to ask Him about it.[E]

[a]**9:40** Lk 9:1; 10:17 [b]**9:41** Php 2:15 [c]Jn 14:9 [d]**9:42** Zch 3:2; Mt 8:26; Mk 1:25; Lk 4:35,39; Jd 9 [e]Lk 7:15 [f]**9:43** 2Pt 1:16 [g]**9:43-45** Mt 17:22-23; Mk 9:30-32 [h]**9:44** Lk 9:22 [i]**9:45** Mk 6:52; Lk 2:50; 18:34; 24:25; Jn 10:6; 12:16; 16:17-19 [j]Lk 18:34; 24:16 [k]**9:46-48** Mt 18:1-5; Mk 9:33-37; Lk 22:24 [l]**9:47** Mt 9:4 [m]**9:48** Mt 10:40,42; Lk 10:16; Jn 13:20 [n]Lk 22:26 [o]**9:49-50** Mk 9:38-40 [p]**9:49** Mt 7:22; 12:27; Mk 16:17; Lk 10:17; Ac 19:13 [q]Nm 11:28 [r]**9:50** Mt 12:30; Lk 11:23 [s]**9:51** Mk 16:19 [t]2Kg 12:17; Is 50:7; Jr 42:15 [u]Lk 13:22; 17:11; 18:31; 19:11,28

Who Is the Greatest?

[46]Then an argument started among them about who would be the greatest of them.[k] [47]But Jesus, knowing the thoughts of their hearts,[l] took a little child and had him stand next to Him. [48]He told them, "Whoever welcomes[F] this little child in My name welcomes Me. And whoever welcomes Me welcomes Him who sent Me.[m] For whoever is least among you — this one is great."[n]

In His Name

[49]John responded,[o] "Master, we saw someone driving out demons in Your name,[p] and we tried to stop him because he does not follow us."[q]

[50]"Don't stop him," Jesus told him, "because whoever is not against you is for you."[G,r]

The Journey to Jerusalem

[51]When the days were coming to a close for Him to be taken up,[H,s] He determined[I,t] to journey to Jerusalem.[u] [52]He sent messengers

GOD'S HEART FOR THE WORLD

Still Setting His People Free

Suddenly, two men were talking with Him—Moses and Elijah. They appeared in glory and were speaking of His death, which He was about to accomplish in Jerusalem. (Luke 9:30–31)

The Transfiguration is a strange scene. Jesus prays, He changes, and two ancient prophets appear. Peter, half asleep, blurts out nonsense about tents, the voice of the Father speaks from a cloud, and the whole thing is over. It is easy to identify with Peter, not understanding what we are seeing, but Luke gives us clues.

The presence of Moses and Elijah shows us that Jesus' work is the culmination of all that God has been planning to do to bring His fallen people back to Himself. The story also reminds us of Moses' work. He too climbed a mountain, and his face shone like the sun.

God's heart for the world has not changed. In Moses' time God was releasing captives, and he is still setting people free. Jesus' death, His exodus, is about releasing not just Israel, but all of creation from captivity. This time the enemy is not Pharaoh, but the powers of sin and death. Soon Jesus will climb another hill to reveal His glory from the cross, and His exodus will release the captives from bondage. His death will set us free. This is why Matthew, Mark and Luke follow the Transfiguration with the healing of a demon-possessed boy. The freeing of the boy is a picture of what Jesus' death did for the whole world.

[A]**9:39** Lit *convulsions with foam* [B]**9:39** Or *bruising*, or *mauling* [C]**9:41** Or *corrupt*, or *perverted*, or *twisted*; Dt 32:5 [D]**9:44** Lit *Put these words in your ears* [E]**9:45** Lit *about this statement* [F]**9:48** Or *receives*, throughout the verse [G]**9:50** Other mss read *against us is for us* [H]**9:51** His ascension [I]**9:51** Lit *He stiffened His face to go*; Is 50:7

ahead of Him,[a] and on the way they entered a village of the ·Samaritans[b] to make preparations for Him. 53 But they did not welcome Him, because He determined to journey to Jerusalem.[c] 54 When the disciples James and John saw this, they said, "Lord, do You want us to call down fire from heaven to consume them?"[A,d]

55 But He turned and rebuked them,[B] 56 and they went to another village.

Following Jesus

57 As they were traveling on the road someone said to Him,[e] "I will follow You wherever You go!"

58 Jesus told him, "Foxes have dens, and birds of the sky[C] have nests, but the Son of Man has no place to lay His head." 59 Then He said to another, "Follow Me."

"Lord," he said, "first let me go bury my father."[D]

60 But He told him, "Let the dead bury their own dead, but you go and spread the news of the kingdom of God."[f]

61 Another also said, "I will follow You, Lord, but first let me go and say good-bye to those at my house."[g]

62 But Jesus said to him, "No one who puts his hand to the plow and looks back is fit for the kingdom of God."

Sending Out the Seventy

10 After this, the Lord appointed 70[E] others, and He sent them ahead of Him in pairs to every town and place where He Himself was about to go. 2 He told them:[h] "The harvest[i] is abundant, but the workers[j] are few. Therefore, pray to the Lord of the harvest to send out workers into His harvest.[k] 3 Now go; I'm sending you out like lambs among wolves.[l] 4 Don't carry a money-bag,[m] traveling bag,[n] or sandals;[o] don't greet anyone along the road. 5 Whatever house you enter, first say, 'Peace[p] to this household.' 6 If a son of peace[F] is there, your peace[q] will rest on him; but if not, it will return to you. 7 Remain in the same house, eating and drinking what they offer, for the worker is worthy of his wages.[r] Don't be moving from house to house. 8 When you enter any town, and they welcome you, eat the things set before you.[s] 9 Heal the sick[t] who are there, and tell them, 'The kingdom of God[u] has come near[v] you.' 10 When you enter any town, and they don't welcome you, go out into its streets and say, 11 'We are wiping off as a witness against you[w] even the dust of your town that clings to our feet. Know this for certain: The kingdom of God has come near.' 12 I tell you, on that day[x] it will be more tolerable for Sodom[y] than for that town.[z]

Unrepentant Towns

13 "Woe[aa] to you,[ab] Chorazin![ac] Woe to you, Bethsaida![ad] For if the miracles[ae] that were done in you had been done in Tyre and Sidon,[af] they would have repented long ago, sitting in ·sackcloth and ashes![ag] 14 But it will be more tolerable for Tyre and Sidon at the judgment[ah] than for you. 15 And you, Capernaum,[ai] will you be exalted to heaven?[aj] No, you will go down to ·Hades![ak] 16 Whoever listens to you listens to Me.[al] Whoever rejects you rejects Me.[am] And whoever rejects Me rejects the One who sent Me."[an]

The Return of the Seventy

17 The Seventy[G,ao] returned with joy, saying,[ap] "Lord, even the demons[aq] submit to us in Your name."[ar]

18 He said to them, "I watched Satan[as] fall from heaven like a lightning flash.[at] 19 Look, I have given you the authority[au] to trample[av] on snakes[aw] and scorpions[ax] and over all the power of the enemy;[ay] nothing will ever harm you.[az] 20 However, don't rejoice that[H] the spirits[ba] submit to you,[bb] but rejoice that your names are written[bc] in heaven."

The Son Reveals the Father

21 In that same hour[bd] He[I] rejoiced in the Holy[J] Spirit[be] and said, "I praise[K] You, Father,[bf]

[a] **9:52** Lk 10:1 [b] Mt 10:5 [c] **9:53** Jn 4:9,20 [d] **9:54** 2Kg 1:9-16; Rv 13:13 [e] **9:57-60** Mt 8:19-22 [f] **9:60** Lk 8:1; 9:2; 16:16 [g] **9:61** 1Kg 19:20 [h] **10:2** Mt 9:37-38; Jn 4:35 [i] Rv 14:15 [j] Mt 20:1 [k] 2Th 3:1 [l] **10:3** Mt 7:15; 10:16; Jn 10:12; Ac 20:29 [m] **10:4** Lk 12:33; 22:35-36 [n] Mk 6:8; Lk 9:3; 22:35-36 [o] Mt 10:9-10 [p] **10:5** Mt 11:26; Lk 10:21; 12:51 [q] **10:6** Lk 7:50; 8:48; 24:36; Jn 20:19; Ac 15:33; 1Co 16:11; Jms 2:16 [r] **10:7** Mt 10:10; 1Tm 5:18; 2Pt 2:13 [s] **10:8** 1Co 10:27 [t] **10:9** Mt 10:8; 1Th 5:14 [u] Mt 12:28; Lk 11:20; 17:20 [v] Mt 10:7; Mk 1:15; 1Pt 4:7 [w] **10:11** Mt 10:14; Mk 6:11; Lk 9:5; Ac 13:51; 18:6 [x] **10:12** Mt 7:22; 13:1; Lk 17:31; 2Pt 3:10 [y] Rv 11:8 [z] Mt 10:15; 11:22,24; Lk 10:14 [aa] **10:13-15** Mt 11:20-24 [ab] **10:13** Ezk 16:23; Mt 23:13-16; Lk 6:24; Rv 9:12 [ac] Mt 11:21 [ad] Jn 12:21 [ae] Ex 3:20; Lk 19:37; Ac 2:22 [af] Ezr 3:7; Jr 25:22; 47:4; Jl 3:4; Lk 6:17 [ag] Est 4:1,3; Dn 9:3; Jnh 3:6 [ah] **10:14** Ps 1:5; Mt 12:41 [ai] **10:15** Mt 4:13; Lk 4:23,31; 7:1 [aj] Ac 2:33 [ak] Is 14:12-15; Ac 2:27 [al] **10:16** Mt 10:40; Jn 13:20 [am] Mt 25:45; Lk 9:48; Jn 12:48 [an] Jn 5:23; 1Th 4:8 [ao] **10:17** Ezk 8:11 [ap] **10:17-20** Mk 16:17-18; Jn 12:31 [aq] **10:17** Rv 9:20 [ar] Jn 10:25; 14:13 [as] **10:18** Mt 4:1,10; Ac 13:10; Rv 12:9 [at] Mt 28:3; Col 2:15 [au] **10:19** Mk 1:22 [av] Lk 21:24; Rv 11:2 [aw] Gn 3:16; Mt 23:33; Rv 9:19 [ax] Lk 11:12; Rv 9:3 [ay] Mt 13:39; 1Co 15:25 [az] Ps 91:13; Mk 16:18; Ac 28:5 [ba] **10:20** 1Tm 4:1; 1Jn 4:1 [bb] Mt 7:22-23 [bc] Ex 32:32; Neh 9:38; Mal 3:16 [bd] **10:21-24** Mt 11:25-27; 13:16-17 [be] **10:21** Lk 2:27; 4:1; 19:21; Ac 2:4 [bf] Mt 7:21; Lk 23:34,46; Jn 8:42; 11:41; 12:27-28; 17:1-25

[A] **9:54** Other mss add *as Elijah also did* [B] **9:55-56** Other mss add *and said, "You don't know what kind of spirit you belong to. 56 For the Son of Man did not come to destroy people's lives but to save them,"* [C] **9:58** Wild birds, as opposed to domestic birds [D] **9:59** Not necessarily meaning his father was already dead [E] **10:1** Other mss read *72* [F] **10:6** A peaceful person; one open to the message of the kingdom [G] **10:17** Other mss read *The Seventy-two* [H] **10:20** Lit *don't rejoice in this, that* [I] **10:21** Other mss read *Jesus* [J] **10:21** Other mss omit *Holy* [K] **10:21** Or *thank*, or *confess*

Lord of heaven and earth,[a] because You have
hidden these things from the wise and the
learned[b] and have revealed them to infants.[c]
Yes, Father, because this was Your good pleasure.[A,d] 22 All things have[B] been entrusted to
Me by My Father. No one knows who the Son
is except the Father, and who the Father is
except the Son, and anyone to whom the Son
desires[C] to reveal Him."[e]
23 Then turning to His disciples He said privately, "The eyes that see the things you see
are blessed! 24 For I tell you that many prophets and kings wanted to see the things you see
yet didn't see them; to hear the things you
hear yet didn't hear them."[f]

The Parable of the Good Samaritan

25 Just[g] then an expert in the law[h] stood up
to test[i] Him, saying, "Teacher,[j] what must I do
to inherit eternal life?"[k]
26 "What is written in the law?" He asked
him. "How do you read it?"
27 He answered:

Love the Lord your God[l] with all your heart, with all your soul, with all your strength, and with all your mind;[m] and your neighbor as yourself.[D,n]

28 "You've answered correctly," He told him.
"Do this and you will live."[o]
29 But wanting to justify himself,[p] he asked
Jesus, "And who is my neighbor?"[q]
30 Jesus took up the question and said: "A
man was going down from Jerusalem to
Jericho and fell into the hands of robbers.
They stripped him, beat him up, and fled,
leaving him half dead. 31 A priest happened
to be going down that road. When he saw
him, he passed by on the other side. 32 In the
same way, a Levite, when he arrived at the
place and saw him, passed by on the other
side. 33 But a •Samaritan[r] on his journey
came up to him, and when he saw the man,
he had compassion.[s] 34 He went over to him
and bandaged his wounds, pouring on olive
oil[t] and wine. Then he put him on his own
animal, brought him to an inn, and took
care of him. 35 The next day[E] he took out two
•denarii, gave them to the innkeeper, and
said, 'Take care of him. When I come back
I'll reimburse you for whatever extra you
spend.'
36 "Which of these three do you think
proved to be a neighbor to the man who fell
into the hands of the robbers?"
37 "The one who showed mercy[u] to him," he
said.
Then Jesus told him, "Go and do the same."

Martha and Mary

38 While they were traveling, He entered a
village, and a woman named Martha[v] welcomed Him into her home.[F] 39 She had a sister named Mary, who also sat at the Lord's[G]
feet[w] and was listening to what He said.[H] 40 But
Martha was distracted by her many tasks, and
she came up and asked, "Lord, don't You care[x]
that my sister has left me to serve alone? So
tell her to give me a hand."[I,y]
41 The Lord[J] answered her, "Martha, Martha, you are worried and upset about many
things,[z] 42 but one thing is necessary.[aa] Mary
has made the right choice,[K] and it will not be
taken away from her."

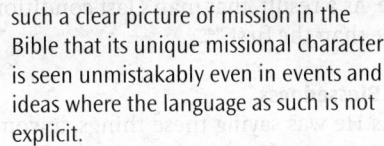

Missional and "Go"

GOD WHO SENDS

The explicit language of the sending, therefore, establishes such a clear picture of mission in the Bible that its unique missional character is seen unmistakably even in events and ideas where the language as such is not explicit.

The extensive vocabulary of "go," in both Old and New Testaments, is the imperative mood of the missional idea. It expresses through mandate form what the sending expresses in description and idea through the indicative mood.

(DuBose, 55)

[a] **10:21** Gn 14:19; Ac 17:24 [b] Is 44:25; Jr 8:9; Ac 13:7; 1Co 1:19-27; 3:19-20 [c] Ps 8:2; Mt 21:16 [d] Lk 2:14 [e] **10:22** Jn 1:18; 6:46; 7:29; 8:19; 10:15; 17:25-26 [f] **10:24** Jn 8:56; Heb 11:13; 1Pt 1:10-12 [g] **10:25-28** Mt 22:34-40; Mk 12:28-34 [h] **10:25** Lk 7:30 [i] Mt 16:1; 19:3 [j] Mt 8:19; Lk 3:12; Jn 1:38 [k] Mt 19:29; Lk 18:18; Jn 12:25; Rv 21:7 [l] **10:27** Lk 4:8 [m] Dt 6:5 [n] Lv 19:18 [o] **10:28** Lv 18:5; Neh 9:29; Ezk 20:11; Rm 10:5; Gl 3:12 [p] **10:29** Lk 16:15 [q] Ex 20:16-17; Lv 6:2; 19:13-18; Pr 3:28-29; Mt 5:43; 19:19; Rm 13:9-10 [r] **10:33** Mt 10:5; Lk 9:52; Ac 1:8 [s] Lk 7:13; 15:20 [t] **10:34** Is 1:6; Jms 5:14 [u] **10:37** Mt 23:23; Lk 1:72; Jms 2:13 [v] **10:38** Jn 11:1,19-20; 12:2-3 [w] **10:39** Lk 8:35; Ac 22:3 [x] **10:40** Mk 4:38; 1Pt 5:7 [y] Rm 8:26 [z] **10:41** Lk 12:22; 1Co 7:32; Php 4:6 [aa] **10:42** Ps 16:5; 27:4; Jn 6:27

[A] **10:21** Lit *was well-pleasing in Your sight* [B] **10:22** Other mss read *And turning to the disciples, He said, "Everything has* [C] **10:22** Or *wills*, or *chooses* [D] **10:27** Lv 19:18; Dt 6:5 [E] **10:35** Other mss add *as he was leaving* [F] **10:38** Other mss omit *into her home* [G] **10:39** Other mss read *at Jesus'* [H] **10:39** Lit *to His word* or *message* [I] **10:40** Or *tell her to help me* [J] **10:41** Other mss read *Jesus* [K] **10:42** Lit *has chosen the good part*

The Model Prayer

11 He was praying[a] in a certain place, and
when He finished, one of His disciples
said to Him, "Lord, teach us to pray, just as
John also taught his disciples."[b]
2 He said to them, "Whenever you pray, say:[c]

Father,[A,d]
Your name[e] be honored as holy.[f]
Your kingdom come.[B,g]
3 Give us each day our daily bread.[C,h]
4 And forgive us our sins,[i]
for we ourselves also forgive everyone
in debt to us.[D,j]
And do not bring us into temptation."[E,k]

Keep Asking, Searching, Knocking

5 He also said to them: "Suppose one of you[F]
has a friend and goes to him at midnight and
says to him, 'Friend, lend me three loaves of
bread, 6 because a friend of mine on a journey
has come to me, and I don't have anything to
offer him.'[G] 7 Then he will answer from inside
and say, 'Don't bother me! The door is already
locked, and my children and I have gone to
bed. I can't get up to give you anything.' 8 I tell
you, even though he won't get up and give
him anything because he is his friend, yet because of his friend's persistence,[H] he will get
up and give him as much as he needs.[l]
9 "So[m] I say to you, keep asking,[I,n] and it will
be given to you. Keep searching,[J,o] and you
will find. Keep knocking,[K,p] and the door will
be opened to you. 10 For everyone who asks receives, and the one who searches finds, and to
the one who knocks, the door will be opened.
11 What father among you, if his son[L] asks for
a fish, will give him a snake instead of a fish?
12 Or if he asks for an egg, will give him a scorpion? 13 If you then, who are evil,[q] know how
to give good gifts to your children, how much
more will the heavenly Father[r] give[M] the Holy
Spirit[s] to those who ask Him?"

A House Divided

14 Now[t] He was driving out a demon[u] that
was mute.[N,v] When the demon came out, the
man who had been mute, spoke, and the
crowds were amazed. 15 But some of them
said, "He drives out demons by ·Beelzebul,[w]
the ruler[x] of the demons!"[y] 16 And others, as
a test,[z] were demanding of Him a sign[aa] from
heaven.
17 Knowing their thoughts,[ab] He told them:
"Every kingdom divided[ac] against itself is
headed for destruction, and a house divided against itself falls. 18 If Satan[ad] also is
divided against himself, how will his kingdom[ae] stand? For you say I drive out demons
by Beelzebul. 19 And if I drive out demons by
Beelzebul, who is it your sons[O,af] drive them
out by? For this reason they will be your
judges. 20 If I drive out demons by the finger
of God,[ag] then the kingdom of God[ah] has come
to you. 21 When a strong man, fully armed,
guards his estate, his possessions are secure.[P]
22 But when one stronger than he attacks and
overpowers[ai] him, he takes from him all his
weapons[Q,aj] he trusted[ak] in, and divides up
his plunder.[al] 23 Anyone who is not with Me
is against Me,[am] and anyone who does not
gather with Me scatters.

An Unclean Spirit's Return

24 "When[an] an ·unclean spirit[ao] comes out
of a man, it roams through waterless places
looking for rest,[ap] and not finding rest, it
then[R] says, 'I'll go back to my house where
I came from.' 25 And returning, it finds the
house swept and put in order. 26 Then it goes
and brings seven other spirits[aq] more evil
than itself, and they enter and settle down
there. As a result, that man's last condition is
worse than the first."[ar]

True Blessedness

27 As He was saying these things, a woman
from the crowd[as] raised her voice and said to
Him, "The womb that bore You and the one
who nursed You[at] are blessed!"
28 He said, "Even more, those who hear the
word of God[au] and keep it[av] are blessed!"

[a] **11:1** Lk 3:21 [b] Lk 5:33 [c] **11:2-13** Mt 6:9-13 [d] **11:2** Jn 20:17; 1Pt 1:17 [e] Ps 9:10; Jn 10:25; 17:6 [f] Is 29:23; Lk 1:49; 1Pt 3:15 [g] Mk 9:1 [h] **11:3** Pr 30:8 [i] **11:4** Lk 6:12; 7:48; 24:47 [j] Mt 18:23-35 [k] Mt 26:41; Lk 4:13; 22:40,46; 1Co 10:1 [l] **11:8** Lk 18:1-6 [m] **11:9-13** Mt 7:7-11; Jn 14:13-14; 15:7; 16:24 [n] **11:9** Mt 18:19; 21:22; Mk 11:24; Jms 1:5-6,17; 1Jn 3:22; 5:14-15 [o] Dt 4:29; 1Ch 28:9; 2Ch 15:2; Pr 8:17; Is 55:6; Jr 29:13 [p] Lk 11:10; 12:36; 13:25; Ac 12:13,16; Rv 3:20 [q] **11:13** Rm 12:17; 1Th 5:22; 2Tm 3:13 [r] Mt 5:48 [s] Ps 51:11; Jn 1:33; Ac 2:4,38; Rm 8:9 [t] **11:14-23** Mt 9:32-34; 12:22-30; Mk 3:22-27; Jn 7:20; 8:48,52; 10:20 [u] **11:14** Mk 7:26 [v] Mk 7:37; 9:15-25; Lk 7:22 [w] **11:15** 2Kg 1:2; Mt 10:25 [x] Lk 12:58 [y] Jn 12:31; 14:30; 16:11; Eph 2:2 [z] **11:16** Lk 10:25 [aa] Jn 2:11; 8:6 [ab] **11:17** Lk 5:22; Php 2:6 [ac] Dn 5:28; 11:4; Lk 12:52-53 [ad] **11:18** Mt 4:1,10; Ac 13:10 [ae] Lk 4:5 [af] **11:19** Gl 3:7; 1Pt 5:13 [ag] **11:20** Ex 8:19; 31:18; Dt 9:10; Ps 8:3 [ah] Mt 19:24; 21:31,43; Lk 17:21 [ai] **11:22** Jn 16:33; 1Jn 2:13 [aj] Eph 6:11,13 [ak] Ac 26:28 [al] Is 49:24-26

[am] **11:23** Mk 9:40; Lk 9:50 [an] **11:24-26** Mt 12:43-45 [ao] **11:24** Mk 1:23-27; Lk 8:29; 9:42; Rv 18:2 [ap] Mt 11:29; Rv 4:8; 14:11 [aq] **11:26** Lv 26:18-28; Dt 7:1; Pr 6:31; 26:25; Lk 8:2 [ar] Jn 5:14; 2Pt 2:20-22 [as] **11:27** Lk 12:3 [at] Lk 1:48; 23:29 [au] **11:28** Lk 5:1; 8:21; Ac 13:7 [av] Lv 22:31; Jn 13:17; Jms 1:22; Rv 1:3; 22:7

[A] **11:2** Other mss read *Our Father in heaven* [B] **11:2** Other mss add *Your will be done on earth as it is in heaven* [C] **11:3** Or *our bread for tomorrow* [D] **11:4** Or *everyone who wrongs us* [E] **11:4** Other mss add *But deliver us from the evil one* [F] **11:5** Lit *Who of you* [G] **11:6** Lit *I have nothing to set before him* [H] **11:8** Or *annoying persistence*, or *shamelessness* [I] **11:9** Or *you, ask* [J] **11:9** Or *Search* [K] **11:9** Or *Knock* [L] **11:11** Other mss read *son asks for bread, would give him a stone? Or if he* [M] **11:13** Lit *the Father from heaven will give* [N] **11:14** A demon that caused the man to be mute [O] **11:19** Your exorcists [P] **11:21** Lit *his possessions are in peace* [Q] **11:22** Gk *panoplia*, the armor and weapons of a foot soldier; Eph 6:11,13 [R] **11:24** Other mss omit *then*

The Sign of Jonah

[29]As the crowds were increasing, He began saying: "This generation[a] is an evil generation.[b] It demands a sign,[c] but no sign will be given to it except the sign of Jonah.[A,d] [30]For just as Jonah became a sign to the people of Nineveh, so also the ˙Son of Man[e] will be to this generation. [31]The queen of the south[f] will rise up at the judgment[g] with the men of this generation and condemn[h] them, because she came from the ends of the earth to hear the wisdom of Solomon,[i] and look — something greater than Solomon is here! [32]The men of Nineveh will rise up at the judgment with this generation and condemn it, because they repented at Jonah's proclamation, and look — something greater than Jonah is here!

The Lamp of the Body

[33]"No[j] one lights a lamp[k] and puts it in the cellar or under a basket,[B] but on a lampstand, so that those who come in may see its light. [34]Your eye is the lamp of the body.[l] When your eye is good, your whole body is also full of light. But when it is bad,[m] your body is also full of darkness. [35]Take care then, that the light in you is not darkness. [36]If, therefore, your whole body is full of light, with no part of it in darkness, it will be entirely illuminated, as when a lamp shines its light on you."[C]

Religious Hypocrisy Denounced

[37]As He was speaking, a ˙Pharisee[n] asked Him to dine with him. So He went in and reclined at the table. [38]When the Pharisee saw this, he was amazed that He did not first perform the ritual washing[D,o] before dinner.[p] [39]But the Lord said to him: "Now you Pharisees ˙clean the outside of the cup and dish, but inside you are full of greed[q] and evil.[r] [40]Fools![s] Didn't He who made the outside make the inside too? [41]But give from what is within to the poor,[E,t] and then everything is clean[u] for you.

[42]"But woe[v] to you Pharisees! You give a tenth[F,w] of mint, rue, and every kind of herb, and you bypass[G] justice[x] and love for God.[H,y] These things you should have done without neglecting the others.

[43]"Woe to you Pharisees! You love the front seat[z] in the ˙synagogues[aa] and greetings in the marketplaces.

[44]"Woe to you![I] You are like unmarked graves;[ab] the people who walk over them don't know it."

[45]One of the experts in the law[ac] answered Him, "Teacher, when You say these things You insult us too."

[46]Then He said: "Woe also to you experts in the law! You load people with burdens[ad] that are hard to carry, yet you yourselves don't touch these burdens with one of your fingers.[ae]

[47]"Woe to you! You build monuments[J] to the prophets,[af] and your fathers killed[ag] them. [48]Therefore, you are witnesses[ah] that you approve[K,ai] the deeds of your fathers, for they killed them, and you build their monuments.[L] [49]Because of this, the wisdom of God[aj] said, 'I will send them prophets and apostles,[ak] and some of them they will kill and persecute,'[al] [50]so that this generation[am] may be held responsible for the blood of all the prophets shed since the foundation of the world[M,an] — [51]from the blood of Abel[ao] to the blood of Zechariah,[ap] who perished between the altar and the sanctuary.

"Yes, I tell you, this generation will be held responsible.[N]

[52]"Woe to you experts in the law! You have taken away the key of knowledge![aq] You didn't go in yourselves, and you hindered[ar] those who were going in."

[53]When He left there,[O] the ˙scribes and the Pharisees began to oppose[as] Him fiercely and to cross-examine Him about many things; [54]they were lying in wait[at] for Him to trap Him in something He said.[P,au]

[a]**11:29** Lk 7:31; 17:25; 21:32 [b]**11:29-32** Mt 12:39-42; Mk 8:12 [c]**11:29** Lk 11:16 [d]Jnh 1:1–4:9; Mt 16:4 [e]**11:30** Mk 2:10; Lk 5:24 [f]**11:31** 1Kg 10:1; 2Ch 9:1 [g]Lk 10:14 [h]Heb 11:7 [i]1Kg 4:34; Pr 1:1 [j]**11:33** Mt 5:15; Mk 4:21 [k]Lk 8:16 [l]**11:34-36** Mt 6:22-23 [m]**11:34** Jr 24:8; Mt 7:17 [n]**11:37** Lk 7:36 [o]**11:38** Heb 6:2 [p]Mt 15:2; Mk 7:2-5 [q]**11:39** Mt 23:25; Lk 12:20; 16:14; Heb 10:34 [r]Mk 7:22 [s]**11:40** Mt 23:17; Lk 12:20 [t]**11:41** Lk 12:33; Ac 24:17 [u]Ps 24:4; Ti 1:15 [v]**11:42** Lk 10:13 [w]Dt 14:22; Lk 18:12 [x]Mc 6:8; Zch 7:9; Mt 12:18,20; Jn 7:24; Ac 8:33 [y]Dt 6:5; Lk 10:27; Jn 5:42; 2Th 3:5 [z]**11:43** Mt 23:6; Mk 12:39; Lk 20:46 [aa]Jms 2:2 [ab]**11:44** Mt 23:27 [ac]**11:45** Lk 7:30 [ad]**11:46** Mt 23:4; Ac 27:10; Gl 6:5 [ae]Mt 11:28-30; Ac 15:10 [af]**11:47** Mt 2:23; Ac 7:52 [ag]Lk 20:15 [ah]**11:48** Mt 23:31 [ai]Ac 22:20; Rm 1:32 [aj]**11:49** Pr 1:20-33; 8:1-36; Mt 23:34 [ak]Lk 11:27; 13:1; 15:32; 21:9-10; Jn 13:16; Ac 1:2 [al]1Th 2:15; 2Tm 3:12 [am]**11:50** Lk 11:29 [an]Heb 9:26; Rv 18:24

[ao]**11:51** Gn 4:9-10; Heb 12:24; 1Jn 3:12 [ap]2Ch 24:20-22 [aq]**11:52** 1Co 14:6 [ar]1Co 14:39 [as]**11:53** Mk 6:19; Gl 5:1 [at]**11:54** Ac 23:21 [au]Is 29:21; Mt 22:15; Mk 3:2; 12:13; Lk 20:20; Jn 8:6

[A]**11:29** Other mss add *the prophet* [B]**11:33** Other mss omit *or under a basket* [C]**11:36** Or *shines on you with its rays* [D]**11:38** Lit *He did not first wash* [E]**11:41** Or *But donate from the heart as charity* [F]**11:42** Or *a tithe* [G]**11:42** Or *neglect* [H]**11:42** Lit *the justice and the love of God* [I]**11:44** Other mss read *you scribes and Pharisees, hypocrites!* [J]**11:47** Or *graves* [K]**11:48** Lit *witnesses and approve* [L]**11:48** Other mss omit *their monuments* [M]**11:50** Lit *so that the blood of all . . . world may be required of this generation,* [N]**11:51** Lit *you, it will be required of this generation* [O]**11:53** Other mss read *And as He was saying these things to them* [P]**11:54** Other mss add *so that they might bring charges against Him*

Beware of Religious Hypocrisy

12 In these circumstances,[A] a crowd of many thousands came together, so that they were trampling[a] on one another. He began to say to His disciples first:[b] "Be on your guard[c] against the yeast[B,d] of the ·Pharisees, which is hypocrisy.[e] 2 There is nothing covered that won't be uncovered,[f] nothing hidden that won't be made known.[g] 3 Therefore, whatever you have said in the dark will be heard in the light, and what you have whispered in an ear in private rooms[h] will be proclaimed on the housetops.[i]

Fear God

4 "And I say to you, My friends,[j] don't fear[k] those who kill the body, and after that can do nothing more. 5 But I will show you the One to fear: Fear[l] Him who has authority to throw people into ·hell[m] after death. Yes, I say to you, this is the One to fear! 6 Aren't five sparrows sold for two pennies?[C] Yet not one of them is forgotten in God's sight.[n] 7 Indeed, the hairs of your head are all counted. Don't be afraid; you are worth more than many sparrows!

Acknowledging Christ

8 "And I say to you, anyone who acknowledges[o] Me before men, the ·Son of Man[p] will also acknowledge him before the angels of God,[q] 9 but whoever denies Me before men will be denied before the angels of God.[r] 10 Anyone who speaks a word against the Son of Man will be forgiven,[s] but the one who blasphemes against the Holy Spirit[t] will not be forgiven. 11 Whenever[u] they bring you before ·synagogues and rulers and authorities,[v] don't worry[w] about how you should defend[x] yourselves or what you should say. 12 For the Holy Spirit will teach you at that very hour what must be said."[y]

The Parable of the Rich Fool

13 Someone from the crowd said to Him, "Teacher,[z] tell my brother to divide the inheritance with me."

[a] **12:1** Lk 8:5 [b] Mt 16:5-6; Mk 8:14-15 [c] Jr 9:4; Lk 17:3; Ac 20:28 [d] Lk 13:21; Gl 5:9 [e] Mt 23:28; Mk 12:15; Gl 2:13; 1Pt 2:1 [f] **12:2-9** Mt 10:26-33; Mk 4:22; Lk 8:17 [g] **12:2** Lk 6:44 [h] **12:3** Mt 6:6; 24:26; Lk 12:24 [i] Ac 10:9 [j] **12:4** Ac 27:3 [k] Is 8:13; 51:12; Jr 1:8; Jn 6:20 [l] **12:5** Ps 147:11; Pr 1:7; Ac 10:2; Rv 14:7 [m] Mk 9:43; Jms 3:6 [n] **12:6** Ps 50:11 [o] **12:8** Mt 7:23; Jn 9:22 [p] Lk 5:24; 11:30 [q] Lk 15:10; Jn 1:51; Ac 10:3; Rm 10:9; Rv 3:5 [r] **12:9** Lk 9:26 [s] **12:10** Mt 12:31-32; Mk 3:28-30 [t] Lk 1:15,35; 2:25-26; 3:22 [u] **12:11-12** Mt 10:19-20; Mk 13:11; Lk 21:14-15 [v] **12:11** Lk 20:20; Eph 3:10; Col 2:15 [w] Php 4:6 [x] Ac 26:24 [y] **12:12** Pr 1:23; Jn 14:26 [z] **12:13** Lk 11:45

PRAYING FOR THE WORLD

Helping Those in Need

Most of us do not understand the extent of suffering around the world—or even in our own neighborhoods. We do not know the full pain of famines. We live easily past the aching hurt of the poverty line. We are unaware of the cruelty perpetrated on women. We don't know the financial difficulties faced by our neighbors and others near us who may be in need.

We must learn from Jesus.

Jesus said, "Much will be required of everyone who has been given much" (Luke 12:48). Privilege has been given for service; many people loved by God need help. Are we ready to lend a hand? How might we show Jesus' kind of compassion to those who need our help?

Merciful Savior, we have been greatly blessed, but we do not to forget our brothers and sisters who are less fortunate. We realize that many needy people live less than a street away. Countless more populate regions elsewhere on the globe. Have mercy on them, dear Lord. Hear their cries. Come to the rescue of mothers who have nothing to give their children. Guide the homeless to havens of relief. Stir our hearts to be ready to come to their aid. Show us how to help.

We pray that the rich and powerful in the earth make caring for the poor a priority. Curb all forms of exploitation and corruption. Reach into the communities of the weak and helpless. May your justice prevail. Amen.

[A] **12:1** Or *Meanwhile*, or *At this time*, or *During this period* [B] **12:1** Or *leaven* [C] **12:6** Lit *two assaria*; the *assarion* (sg) was a small copper coin

14 "Friend,"[A] He said to him, "who appointed Me a judge or arbitrator over you?" 15 He then told them, "Watch out and be on guard[a] against all greed[b] because one's life is not in the abundance of his possessions."[c]

16 Then He told them a parable:[d] "A rich[e] man's land was very productive. 17 He thought to himself, 'What should I do, since I don't have anywhere to store my crops? 18 I will do this,' he said. 'I'll tear down my barns and build bigger ones and store all my grain and my goods there. 19 Then I'll say to myself, "You[B] have many goods stored up for many years. Take it easy;[f] eat, drink, and enjoy yourself."'[g]

20 "But God said to him, 'You fool![h] This very night your ˙life is demanded of you. And the things you have prepared — whose will they be?'[i]

21 "That's how it is with the one who stores up treasure[j] for himself and is not rich toward God."[k]

The Cure for Anxiety

22 Then He said to His disciples: "Therefore I tell you,[l] don't worry about your life, what you will eat; or about the body, what you will wear.[m] 23 For life is more than food and the body more than clothing. 24 Consider the ravens:[n] They don't sow or reap; they don't have a storeroom or a barn; yet God feeds them.[o] Aren't you worth much more than the birds? 25 Can any of you add a ˙cubit to his height[C] by worrying?[p] 26 If then you're not able to do even a little thing, why worry about the rest?

27 "Consider how the wildflowers grow: They don't labor or spin thread. Yet I tell you, not even Solomon[q] in all his splendor was adorned like one of these! 28 If that's how God clothes the grass, which is in the field today and is thrown into the furnace tomorrow, how much more will He do for you — you of little faith?[r] 29 Don't keep striving for what you should eat and what you should drink, and don't be anxious. 30 For the Gentile world eagerly seeks[s] all these things, and your Father[t] knows that you need them.

31 "But seek His kingdom,[u] and these things will be provided for you.[v] 32 Don't be afraid,[w] little flock,[x] because your Father delights[y] to give you the kingdom.[z] 33 Sell[aa] your possessions and give to the poor.[ab] Make money-bags[ac] for yourselves that won't grow old, an inexhaustible treasure[ad] in heaven, where no thief comes near and no moth destroys. 34 For where your treasure is, there your heart will be also.[ae]

Ready for the Master's Return

35 "Be ready for service[D] and have your lamps lit.[af] 36 You must be like people waiting for their master[ag] to return[E] from the wedding banquet[ah] so that when he comes and knocks, they can open the door for him at once.[ai] 37 Those ˙slaves the master will find alert[aj] when he comes will be blessed. ˙I assure you: He will get ready,[F] have them recline at the table, then come and serve them.[ak] 38 If he comes in the middle of the night, or even near dawn,[G] and finds them alert, those slaves are blessed. 39 But know this: If the homeowner had known at what hour the thief was coming,[al] he would not have let his house be broken into. 40 You also be ready,[am] because the Son of Man[an] is coming at an hour that you do not expect."[ao]

Rewards and Punishment

41 "Lord," Peter asked, "are You telling this parable to us or to everyone?"

42 The Lord said: "Who then is the faithful and sensible manager[ap] his master will put in charge of his household servants to give them their allotted food[aq] at the proper time? 43 That slave whose master finds him working when he comes will be rewarded. 44 I tell you the truth: He will put him in charge of all his possessions. 45 But if that slave says in his heart, 'My master is delaying his coming,'[ar] and starts to beat the male and female slaves, and to eat and drink and get drunk, 46 that slave's master will come on a day he does not expect him and at an hour he does not know. He will cut him to pieces[H] and assign him a place with the unbelievers.[I] 47 And that slave who knew his master's will and didn't prepare himself or do it[J] will be severely beaten.[as] 48 But the

[a] **12:15** 1Tm 6:20; 2Tm 1:14; 4:15; 2Pt 3:17; 1Jn 5:21 [b] Eph 5:3 [c] Gn 12:5; Jb 20:20; 31:24; Ps 62:10 [d] **12:16** Lk 5:36; 8:11 [e] Lk 6:24; 16:19; 18:23; 19:2; 21:1 [f] **12:19** Mt 11:28; Mk 6:31; Rv 6:11; 14:13 [g] Ec 2:24 [h] **12:20** Jr 17:11; Lk 11:40 [i] Ps 39:6; 49:10; Jr 17:11; Mt 16:26 [j] **12:21** 2Pt 3:7 [k] Mt 6:19-20 [l] **12:22-32** Mt 6:25-34 [m] **12:22** Pr 31:25 [n] **12:24** 1Kg 17:4,6; Jb 38:41; Ps 147:9; Pr 30:17 [o] Rv 12:6 [p] **12:25** Php 4:6 [q] **12:27** 1Kg 10:4-7 [r] **12:28** Mt 8:26; 14:31; 16:8 [s] **12:30** Heb 11:14; 13:14 [t] Mt 5:16; 6:1; 11:27; Jn 8:42 [u] **12:31** Mt 5:6,20; Lk 11:2 [v] 1Kg 3:11-14; Mt 19:29; Mk 10:29-30 [w] **12:32** Lk 12:4,7 [x] Is 40:11; Ac 20:28; 1Pt 5:2-3 [y] Mt 11:26; Lk 10:21; Eph 1:5,9; Php 2:13 [z] Mt 13:19; 25:34; Lk 22:29 [aa] **12:33-34** Mt 6:19-21 [ab] **12:33** Ac 24:17 [ac] Lk 10:4 [ad] Mk 10:21; 2Co 4:7 [ae] **12:34** 1Pt 1:4 [af] **12:35-48** Mt 24:42-51; 25:1-13; Mk 13:33-37; Jn 13:4-5 [ag] **12:36** 2Pt 3:12 [ah] Jn 2:1 [ai] Rv 3:20 [aj] **12:37** Rm 13:11 [ak] Lk 17:8; 22:27 [al] **12:39** 1Th 5:2 [am] **12:40** Lk 21:36 [an] Mk 2:10 [ao] 1Th 5:2; 2Pt 3:10; Rv 3:3; 16:15 [ap] **12:42** Lk 16:1 [aq] 1Tm 6:8 [ar] **12:45** 1Jn 2:28 [as] **12:47** Dt 25:2; Jms 4:17

[A] **12:14** Lit *Man* [B] **12:19** Lit *say to my soul, "Soul, you* [C] **12:25** Or *add one moment to his life-span* [D] **12:35** Lit *Let your loins be girded*; an idiom for tying up loose outer clothing in preparation for action; Ex 12:11 [E] **12:36** Lit *master, when he should return* [F] **12:37** Lit *will gird himself* [G] **12:38** Lit *even in the second or third watch* [H] **12:46** Lit *him in two* [I] **12:46** Or *unfaithful*, or *untrustworthy* [J] **12:47** Lit *or do toward his will* one who did not know and did things deserving[a] of blows will be beaten lightly. Much will be required of everyone who has been given much. And even more will be expected of the one who has been entrusted with more.[A,b]

Not Peace but Division

49 "I came[c] to bring fire on the earth, and how I wish it were already set ablaze! 50 But I have a baptism to be baptized with,[d] and how it consumes[e] Me until it is finished![f] 51 Do you think that I came here to give peace to the earth?[g] No, I tell you, but rather division! 52 From now on, five in one household will be divided: three against two, and two against three.

53 **They will be divided, father against son,**
son against father,
mother against daughter,
daughter against mother,
mother-in-law against
her daughter-in-law,
and daughter-in-law
against mother-in-law."[B,h]

Interpreting the Time

54 He also said to the crowds:[i] "When you see a cloud rising in the west, right away you say, 'A storm is coming,' and so it does.[j] 55 And when the south wind is blowing, you say, 'It's going to be a scorcher!' and it is. 56 Hypocrites![k] You know how to interpret the appearance of the earth and the sky, but why don't you know how to interpret this time?[l]

Settling Accounts

57 "Why don't you judge for yourselves what is right?[m] 58 As you are going with your adversary[n] to the ruler, make an effort to settle with him on the way. Then he won't drag you before the judge,[o] the judge hand you over to the bailiff, and the bailiff throw you into prison.[p] 59 I tell you, you will never get out of there until you have paid the last cent."[C,q]

Repent or Perish

13 At that time,[r] some people came and reported to Him about the Galileans[s] whose blood ·Pilate[t] had mixed with their sacrifices. 2 And He[D] responded to them, "Do you think that these Galileans were more sinful than all Galileans because they suffered these things?[u] 3 No, I tell you; but unless you repent, you will all perish as well! 4 Or those 18 that the tower in Siloam[v] fell on and killed — do you think they were more sinful than all the people who live in Jerusalem? 5 No, I tell you; but unless you repent, you will all perish as well!"

The Parable of the Barren Fig Tree

6 And He told this parable:[w] "A man had a fig tree that was planted in his vineyard. He came looking for fruit on it and found none.[x] 7 He told the vineyard worker, 'Listen, for three years I have come looking for fruit on this fig tree and haven't found any. Cut it down![y] Why should it even waste the soil?'[z]

8 "But he replied to him, 'Sir,[E] leave it this year also, until I dig around it and fertilize it.[aa] 9 Perhaps it will bear fruit next year, but if not, you can cut it down.'"

Healing a Daughter of Abraham

10 As He was teaching in one of the ·synagogues on the Sabbath,[ab] 11 a woman was there who had been disabled by a spirit[F,ac] for over 18 years. She was bent over and could not straighten up at all.[G] 12 When Jesus saw her, He called out to her,[H] "·Woman, you are free of your disability." 13 Then He laid His hands on her,[ad] and instantly she was restored[ae] and began to glorify God.[af]

14 But the leader of the synagogue, indignant[ag] because Jesus had healed on the Sabbath, responded by telling the crowd, "There are six days when work should be done;[ah] therefore come on those days and be healed and not on the Sabbath day."

15 But the Lord answered him and said, "Hypocrites![ai] Doesn't each one of you untie his ox[aj] or donkey from the feeding trough[ak] on the Sabbath and lead it to water?[al] 16 Satan[am] has bound[an] this woman, a daughter of Abraham,[ao] for 18 years — shouldn't she be untied from this bondage on the Sabbath day?"

17 When He had said these things, all His adversaries[ap] were humiliated,[aq] but the whole

[a] **12:48** Lv 5:17; Nm 15:29
[b] Lv 5:17; Mt 13:12; Rm 1:20; 2:14; 1Tm 1:13
[c] **12:49-53** Mt 10:34-36; Mk 10:38
[d] **12:50** Ac 22:16; Rm 6:3; Eph 4:5
[e] 2Co 5:14
[f] Jn 19:28; 19:30
[g] **12:51** Lk 2:14
[h] **12:53** Mc 7:6
[i] **12:54-56** Mt 16:2-3
[j] **12:54** 1Kg 18:43-44
[k] **12:56** Lk 6:42
[l] Lk 20:10; 21:8,30
[m] **12:57-59** Mt 5:25-26
[n] **12:58** 1Pt 5:8
[o] 2Tm 4:8
[p] Pr 25:8
[q] **12:59** Lk 21:2
[r] **13:1** Mt 21:18-19; Mk 11:12-14
[s] Jn 4:45
[t] Mt 27:2
[u] **13:2** Jn 9:2
[v] **13:4** Jn 9:7
[w] **13:6** Lk 5:35; 12:16
[x] Mt 21:18-19; Mk 11:13
[y] **13:7** Mt 7:19; Lk 3:9; Jn 15:2; Rm 11:22
[z] Is 5:2
[aa] **13:8** Lk 16:3
[ab] **13:10** Lk 4:31; 6:6
[ac] **13:11** Mt 8:17; Lk 4:33; 6:18; 7:21; 8:2,29; 9:39
[ad] **13:13** Mt 19:15; Mk 5:23; 6:2,5; 8:23; Lk 4:40
[ae] Ac 15:16; Heb 12:12
[af] Jn 11:4
[ag] **13:14** Mt 20:24; 21:15; 26:8; Mk 10:14,41; 14:4
[ah] Ex 20:9; Ezk 46:1
[ai] **13:15** Lk 6:42
[aj] Lk 14:5,19; 1Co 9:9
[ak] Lk 2:7,12,16
[al] Mt 12:11; Lk 14:5
[am] **13:16** Mt 4:1,10; Ac 13:10
[an] Mk 5:3; 15:1; 2Tm 2:9
[ao] Gn 16:15; Jn 8:37; Heb 2:16
[ap] **13:17** Lk 21:5; 1Co 16:9; Php 1:28; 1Tm 5:14
[aq] Ps 132:18; Is 45:16 LXX; 1Pt 3:16

[A] **12:48** Or *much* [B] **12:53** Mc 7:6 [C] **12:59** Gk *lepton*, the smallest and least valuable copper coin in use [D] **13:2** Other mss read *Jesus* [E] **13:8** Or *Lord* [F] **13:11** Lit *had a spirit of disability* [G] **13:11** Or *straighten up completely* [H] **13:12** Or *He summoned her*

crowd was rejoicing over all the glorious things He was doing.[a]

The Parables of the Mustard Seed and of the Yeast

18 He said, therefore, "What is the kingdom of God like,[b] and what can I compare it to? 19 It's like a mustard seed that a man took and sowed in his garden. It grew and became a tree, and the birds of the sky nested in its branches."

20 Again He said, "What can I compare the kingdom of God[c] to? 21 It's like yeast[d] that a woman took and mixed into 50 pounds[A] of flour until it spread through the entire mixture."[B]

The Narrow Way

22 He went through one town and village after another, teaching and making His way to Jerusalem.[e] 23 "Lord," someone asked Him, "are there few being saved?"[C,f]

He said to them, 24 "Make every effort to enter through the narrow door,[g] because I tell you, many will try to enter and won't be able 25 once the homeowner gets up and shuts the door.[h] Then you will stand[D] outside and knock on the door, saying, 'Lord, open up for us!' He will answer you, 'I don't know you or where you're from.' 26 Then you will say,[E] 'We ate and drank in Your presence, and You taught in our streets!' 27 But He will say, 'I tell you, I don't know you or where you're from. Get away from Me,[i] all you workers of unrighteousness!' 28 There will be weeping and gnashing of teeth[j] in that place,[k] when you see Abraham, Isaac, Jacob, and all the prophets in the kingdom of God,[l] but yourselves thrown out. 29 They will come from east and west, from north and south, and recline at the table[m] in the kingdom of God. 30 Note this: Some are last who will be first, and some are first who will be last."[n]

Jesus and Herod Antipas

31 At that time some ·Pharisees came and told Him, "Go, get out of here! ·Herod[o] wants to kill You!"[p]

32 He said to them, "Go tell that fox, 'Look! I'm driving out demons and performing healings today and tomorrow, and on the third day[F] I will complete My work.'[G,q] 33 Yet I must[r] travel today, tomorrow, and the next day, because it is not possible for a prophet[s] to perish[t] outside of Jerusalem!

Jesus' Lamentation over Jerusalem

34 "Jerusalem, Jerusalem![u] She who kills the prophets and stones[v] those who are sent to her.[w] How often I wanted to gather your children[x] together, as a hen gathers her chicks under her wings,[y] but you were not willing![z] 35 See, your house[H] is abandoned to you.[aa] And I tell you, you will not see Me until the time comes when you say, '**He who comes in the name of the Lord is the blessed One**'!"[I,ab]

A Sabbath Controversy

14 One Sabbath, when He went to eat[J] at the house of one of the leading ·Pharisees,[ac] they were watching Him closely.[ad] 2 There in front of Him was a man whose body was swollen with fluid.[K] 3 In response, Jesus asked the law experts[ae] and the Pharisees, "Is it lawful to heal on the Sabbath or not?"[af] 4 But they kept silent. He took the man, healed him, and sent him away. 5 And to them, He said, "Which of you whose son or ox falls into a well, will not immediately pull him out on the Sabbath day?"[ag] 6 To this they could find no answer.

Teachings on Humility

7 He told a parable[ah] to those who were invited, when He noticed how they would choose the best places[ai] for themselves: 8 "When you are invited by someone to a wedding banquet, don't recline at the best place, because a more distinguished person[aj] than you may have been invited by your host.[L] 9 The one who invited both of you may come and say to you, 'Give your place to this man,' and then in humiliation, you will proceed to take the lowest place.

10 "But when you are invited, go and recline in the lowest place, so that when the one who

[a] **13:17** Is 12:5
[b] **13:18-19** Mt 13:31-32; Mk 4:30-32
[c] **13:20-21** Mt 13:33
[d] **13:21** Mt 16:6,11-12; Mk 8:15; Lk 12:1; 1Co 5:6-8; Gl 5:9
[e] **13:22** Lk 9:51
[f] **13:23** Mt 22:14; Lk 18:26; Ac 2:21; Rm 9:27; Eph 2:8; 1Pt 3:20; Rv 3:4
[g] **13:24** Mt 7:13-14
[h] **13:25** Mt 7:22-23; 10:33; 25:12
[i] **13:27** Ps 6:8; 2Tm 2:19; Heb 3:12
[j] **13:28** Mt 13:42,50; 22:13; 24:51; 25:30
[k] **13:28-29** Mt 8:11-12
[l] **13:28** Mk 1:15; Lk 4:43
[m] **13:29** Lk 12:37
[n] **13:30** Mt 19:30; 20:16; Mk 10:31
[o] **13:31** Mt 14:1
[p] Mt 14:5; Mk 6:19; Jn 7:19-25; Ac 5:33
[q] **13:32** Heb 2:10; 5:9; 7:28
[r] **13:33** Ac 3:21; 17:3
[s] Mt 2:23; 21:11
[t] Mk 8:31
[u] **13:34-35** Mt 23:37-39; Lk 19:41-44
[v] **13:34** Heb 11:37
[w] 2Ch 24:20-22; Mt 21:35; Lk 20:15
[x] Ps 147:2; Is 62:1,4
[y] Dt 32:11; Ps 17:8; 36:7
[z] Jn 5:40
[aa] **13:35** Is 64:11; Jr 12:7; 22:1-8
[ab] Ps 118:26; Mt 21:9; Lk 19:38; Jn 12:13
[ac] **14:1** Lk 7:36; 11:37
[ad] Mk 3:2; Lk 6:7; 20:20
[ae] **14:3** Lk 7:30; 14:30
[af] Mt 12:2; Mk 3:4; Lk 6:2,9; 13:14; Jn 5:10
[ag] **14:5** Ex 21:33; Dt 22:4; Mt 12:11; Lk 13:15
[ah] **14:7** Lk 5:36; 13:6
[ai] Lk 11:43
[aj] **14:8** Lk 7:2; Php 2:29; 1Pt 2:4

[A] **13:21** Lit *3 sata*; about 40 quarts [B] **13:21** Or *until all of it was leavened* [C] **13:23** Or *are the saved few?* (in number); lit *are those being saved few?* [D] **13:25** Lit *you will begin to stand* [E] **13:26** Lit *you will begin to say* [F] **13:32** Very shortly [G] **13:32** Lit *I will be finished* [H] **13:35** Probably the temple; Jr 12:7; 22:5 [I] **13:35** Ps 118:26 [J] **14:1** Lit *eat bread*; = eat a meal [K] **14:2** Afflicted with dropsy or edema [L] **14:8** Lit *by him*

invited you comes, he will say to you, 'Friend,
move up higher.' You will then be honored[a]
in the presence of all the other guests.[b] 11For
everyone who exalts himself will be humbled,
and the one who humbles himself will be exalted."[c]
12He also said to the one who had invited
Him, "When you give a lunch or a dinner,
don't invite your friends, your •brothers,
your relatives, or your rich neighbors, because they might invite you back, and you
would be repaid. 13On the contrary, when
you host a banquet,[d] invite those who are
poor, maimed, lame, or blind.[e] 14And you will
be blessed, because they cannot repay you;
for you will be repaid[f] at the resurrection of
the righteous."[g]

The Parable of the Large Banquet

15When[h] one of those who reclined at the
table with Him heard these things, he said to
Him, "The one who will eat bread in the kingdom of God[i] is blessed!"
16Then He told him: "A man was giving a
large banquet and invited many. 17At the time
of the banquet, he sent his •slave to tell those
who were invited, 'Come, because everything
is now ready.'
18"But without exception[A] they all began
to make excuses. The first one said to him, 'I
have bought a field, and I must go out and see
it. I ask you to excuse me.'
19"Another said, 'I have bought five yoke of
oxen, and I'm going to try them out. I ask you
to excuse me.'
20"And another said, 'I just got married,[B,j]
and therefore I'm unable to come.'
21"So the slave came back and reported
these things to his master. Then in anger, the
master of the house told his slave, 'Go out
quickly into the streets and alleys of the city,
and bring in here the poor, maimed, blind,
and lame!'[k]
22"'Master,' the slave said, 'what you ordered has been done, and there's still room.'
23"Then the master told the slave, 'Go out
into the highways and lanes and make them
come in, so that my house may be filled. 24For
I tell you, not one of those men who were invited will enjoy my banquet!'"

[a]**14:10** Jn 5:44; 7:18; Rm 2:7
[b]Pr 25:6-7; 29:23
[c]**14:11** Ezk 21:26; Mt 18:4; 23:12; Lk 1:51; 3:5; 18:14; Jms 4:10; 1Pt 5:5-6
[d]**14:13** Lk 5:29
[e]Lv 22:22; Lk 14:21
[f]**14:14** Rm 11:35; 12:19; 1Th 3:9; 2Th 1:6; Heb 10:30
[g]Ac 24:15
[h]**14:15-24** Mt 22:1-14
[i]**14:15** Lk 13:29; 22:16,30; Rv 19:9
[j]**14:20** Dt 24:5
[k]**14:21** Lk 14:13
[l]**14:25-33** Mt 10:37-38
[m]**14:26** Mt 11:28; Mk 10:14; Lk 6:47; Jn 5:40
[n]Dt 21:15; 22:13; 24:3; Lk 16:13
[o]**14:27** Jn 19:17
[p]**14:28** Pr 24:27
[q]**14:33** Mt 19:21; Php 3:7; Heb 11:26
[r]**14:34-35** Mt 5:13; Mk 9:49-50
[s]**14:34** Jdg 9:45; Mk 9:50
[t]**14:35** Mt 11:15; 13:9; Mk 4:9
[u]**15:1-7** Mt 18:12-14
[v]**15:1** Mt 11:19; Lk 5:29
[w]**15:2** Lk 5:30; 7:39; Ac 11:3; Gl 2:12
[x]**15:3** Mk 12:1
[y]**15:4** Ps 119:176; Jr 50:6; Zc 11:16; Mt 10:6; 15:24
[z]**15:7** Jr 51:48; Rv 18:20

The Cost of Following Jesus

25Now[l] great crowds were traveling with
Him. So He turned and said to them: 26"If
anyone comes to Me[m] and does not hate[n] his
own father and mother, wife and children,
brothers and sisters—yes, and even his own
life—he cannot be My disciple. 27Whoever
does not bear his own cross[o] and come after
Me cannot be My disciple.
28"For which of you, wanting to build a
tower, doesn't first sit down and calculate
the cost[p] to see if he has enough to complete
it? 29Otherwise, after he has laid the foundation and cannot finish it, all the onlookers
will begin to make fun of him, 30saying, 'This
man started to build and wasn't able to finish.'
31"Or what king, going to war against another king, will not first sit down and decide
if he is able with 10,000 to oppose the one
who comes against him with 20,000? 32If
not, while the other is still far off, he sends
a delegation and asks for terms of peace. 33In
the same way, therefore, every one of you who
does not say good-bye to[C] all his possessions[q]
cannot be My disciple.
34"Now,[r] salt[s] is good, but if salt should lose
its taste, how will it be made salty? 35It isn't fit
for the soil or for the manure pile; they throw
it out. Anyone who has ears to hear should listen!"[t]

The Parable of the Lost Sheep

15 All[u] the tax collectors[v] and sinners
were approaching to listen to Him.
2And the •Pharisees and •scribes were complaining, "This man welcomes sinners[w] and
eats with them!"
3So He told them this parable:[x] 4"What man
among you, who has 100 sheep and loses one
of them,[y] does not leave the 99 in the open
field[D] and go after the lost one until he finds
it? 5When he has found it, he joyfully puts it
on his shoulders, 6and coming home, he calls
his friends and neighbors together, saying to
them, 'Rejoice with me, because I have found
my lost sheep!' 7I tell you, in the same way,
there will be more joy in heaven[z] over one
sinner who repents than over 99 righteous
people who don't need repentance.

[A]**14:18** Lit *And from one* (voice) [B]**14:20** Lit *I have married a woman* [C]**14:33** Or *does not renounce* or *leave* [D]**15:4** Or *the wilderness*

The Parable of the Lost Coin

[8]"Or what woman who has 10 silver coins,[A]
if she loses one coin, does not light a lamp,
sweep the house, and search carefully until
she finds it? [9]When she finds it, she calls her
women friends and neighbors together, saying, 'Rejoice with me, because I have found
the silver coin I lost!' [10]I tell you, in the same
way, there is joy in the presence of God's angels[a] over one sinner who repents."

[a]15:10 Lk 2:10 [b]15:13 Lk 16:1 [c]Rm 6:2; 8:12; Gl 2:14; Col 3:7

The Parable of the Lost Son

[11]He also said: "A man had two sons. [12]The
younger of them said to his father, 'Father,
give me the share of the estate I have coming
to me.' So he distributed the assets[B] to them.
[13]Not many days later, the younger son gathered together all he had and traveled to a distant country, where he squandered[b] his estate
in foolish living.[c] [14]After he had spent everything, a severe famine struck that country,

The Parable of the Lost Sheep

Afshin Ziafat

The parable of the lost sheep is the first of three consecutive parables Jesus shares with his disciples to show us the heart of God and the mission of Christ. God's mission in Christ is to seek and to save the lost (Lk 19:10). This story challenges us to look at our own hearts, to see God's heart, and to move with compassion to reach the lost with the hope of Christ.

This parable comes on the heels of the Pharisees and scribes grumbling over the fact that Jesus receives sinners. It ends with Jesus speaking of the 99 righteous persons who need no repentance. Scripture is clear that there are none who are righteous apart from Christ (Rm 3:10), therefore this last statement is intended to refer to people who think they are righteous and do not need to repent. The Gospel teaches that we are not righteous in our own works and we are indebted to the grace and mercy of Christ for our righteousness (Lk 18:9-14). We are all sinners and were lost before Christ saved us!

Jesus contrasts the grumbling of the "religious elite" with the rejoicing in heaven over one sinner who repents. Through this parable, we see the intense focus of our God in heaven for those who are still lost. It is a humbling reminder that God is not just interested in us but also in those who do not know Him. After Jesus reveals Himself to be the Good Shepherd who lays His life down for the sheep, He goes on to say, "I have other sheep that are not of this fold; I must bring them also, and they will listen to My voice. Then there will be one flock, one shepherd" (Jn 10:16). The work of salvation God started in us was not intended to end with us but to go out to other "sheep." God told Abraham that He would make him a great nation and that "all the peoples on earth will be blessed through you" (Gn 12:3). It is imperative for us to know that we serve a God who is constantly on mission to save the one lost sheep.

The astonishing thought of the mission of God is that He has chosen to use us as His ambassadors to accomplish this mission. Those who are reconciled to God through Christ are given the ministry of reconciliation and as ambassadors for Christ they are given the message of reconciliation (2Co 5:18-20). In this parable, the shepherd leaves the 99 in the open field to go after the one lost sheep. Jesus couches this idea in a question in verse four that is meant to draw the hearer to action. Will we leave the 99 and go after the one lost sheep? Jesus emptied Himself, took the form of a servant, and became obedient to the point of death to save us. In order to participate in this mission of God, we too must leave behind some things and go after those who have not yet been reconciled to Him. We must leave our comfort zones and selfish desires behind to join God in His mission for the lost sheep!

[A]15:8 Gk *10 drachmas*; a *drachma* was a silver coin = a °denarius [B]15:12 Or *living*; lit *livelihood*

and he had nothing.[A] 15 Then he went to work for[B] one of the citizens of that country, who sent him into his fields to feed pigs.[a] 16 He longed to eat his fill from[C] the carob pods[D] the pigs were eating, but no one would give him any. 17 When he came to his senses,[E] he said, 'How many of my father's hired hands have more than enough food, and here I am dying of hunger![F] 18 I'll get up, go to my father, and say to him, Father, I have sinned[b] against heaven[c] and in your sight. 19 I'm no longer worthy[d] to be called your son. Make me like one of your hired hands.' 20 So he got up and went to his father. But while the son was still a long way off, his father saw him and was filled with compassion.[e] He ran, threw his arms around his neck,[G] and kissed[f] him. 21 The son said to him, 'Father, I have sinned against heaven and in your sight. I'm no longer worthy to be called your son.'

22 "But the father told his ˚slaves, 'Quick! Bring out the best robe[g] and put it on him; put a ring[h] on his finger[H] and sandals[i] on his feet. 23 Then bring the fattened calf[j] and slaughter it, and let's celebrate with a feast, 24 because this son of mine was dead and is alive again;[k] he was lost and is found!' So they began to celebrate.

25 "Now his older son was in the field; as he came near the house, he heard music and dancing. 26 So he summoned one of the servants and asked what these things meant. 27 'Your brother is here,' he told him, 'and your father has slaughtered the fattened calf because he has him back safe and sound.'[I]

28 "Then he became angry and didn't want to go in. So his father came out and pleaded with him. 29 But he replied to his father, 'Look, I have been slaving many years for you, and I have never disobeyed your orders, yet you never gave me a young goat so I could celebrate with my friends. 30 But when this son of yours came, who has devoured your assets[J] with prostitutes,[l] you slaughtered the fattened calf for him.'

31 "'Son,'[K] he said to him, 'you are always with me,[m] and everything I have is yours. 32 But we had to celebrate and rejoice, because this brother of yours was dead and is alive again; he was lost and is found.'"

[a] **15:15** Lv 11:7; Dt 14:8
[b] **15:18** Ex 10:16
[c] Mt 21:25; Jn 3:27
[d] **15:19** Lk 7:6-7
[e] **15:20** Mt 9:36; Mk 1:41; Lk 7:13; 10:33
[f] Gn 29:13; 33:4; 45:15; 2Sm 14:33
[g] **15:22** Zch 3:3-5
[h] Gn 41:42; Est 3:10; 8:2
[i] Ezk 16:10
[j] **15:23** 1Sm 28:24
[k] **15:24** Lk 15:32; Rm 11:15; 2Co 4:10; Col 2:13
[l] **15:30** Pr 29:3
[m] **15:31** Jn 8:35
[n] **16:1** Lk 16:19
[o] Lk 12:42
[p] Lk 15:13
[q] **16:2** 1Tm 1:4
[r] **16:8** Lk 18:6
[s] Mt 12:32; Lk 20:34
[t] Jn 12:46; Eph 5:8; 1Th 5:5
[u] **16:9** Lk 11:41
[v] Mt 6:24; 1Tm 6:10
[w] **16:10** Mt 25:21-23
[x] Lk 19:17
[y] **16:13** Mt 6:24
[z] Lk 14:26

The Parable of the Dishonest Manager

16 He also said to the disciples: "There was a rich[n] man who received an accusation that his manager[o] was squandering[p] his possessions. 2 So he called the manager in and asked, 'What is this I hear about you? Give an account of your management,[q] because you can no longer be my manager.'

3 "Then the manager said to himself, 'What should I do, since my master is taking the management away from me? I'm not strong enough to dig; I'm ashamed to beg. 4 I know what I'll do so that when I'm removed from management, people will welcome me into their homes.'

5 "So he summoned each one of his master's debtors. 'How much do you owe my master?' he asked the first one.

6 "'A hundred measures of olive oil,' he said.

"'Take your invoice,' he told him, 'sit down quickly, and write 50.'

7 "Next he asked another, 'How much do you owe?'

"'A hundred measures of wheat,' he said.

"'Take your invoice,' he told him, 'and write 80.'

8 "The master praised the unrighteous manager[r] because he had acted astutely. For the sons of this age[s] are more astute than the sons of light[t] in dealing with their own people.[L] 9 And I tell you, make friends[u] for yourselves by means of the unrighteous money[v] so that when it fails,[M] they may welcome you into eternal dwellings. 10 Whoever is faithful[w] in very little[x] is also faithful in much, and whoever is unrighteous in very little is also unrighteous in much. 11 So if you have not been faithful with the unrighteous money, who will trust you with what is genuine? 12 And if you have not been faithful with what belongs to someone else, who will give you what is your own? 13 No[y] household slave can be the ˚slave of two masters, since either he will hate[z] one and love the other, or he will be devoted to one and despise the

[A] 15:14 Lit *and he began to be in need* [B] 15:15 Lit *went and joined with* [C] 15:16 Other mss read *to fill his stomach with* [D] 15:16 Seed casings of a tree used as food for cattle, pigs, and sometimes the poor [E] 15:17 Lit *to himself* [F] 15:17 Or *dying in the famine*; v. 14 [G] 15:20 Lit *He ran, fell on his neck* [H] 15:22 Lit *hand* [I] 15:27 Lit *him back healthy* [J] 15:30 Lit *livelihood*, or *living* [K] 15:31 Or *Child* [L] 16:8 Lit *own generation* [M] 16:9 Other mss read *when you fail* or *pass away*

other. You can't be slaves to both God and
money."

Kingdom Values

[14]The •Pharisees, who were lovers of money,[a] were listening to all these things and
scoffing[b] at Him. [15]And He told them: "You
are the ones who justify[c] yourselves in the
sight of others, but God knows your hearts.[d]
For what is highly admired by people is revolting[e] in God's sight.

[16]"The[f] Law and the Prophets[g] were[A] until
John; since then, the good news of the kingdom of God[h] has been proclaimed, and everyone is strongly urged to enter it.[B] [17]But it
is easier[i] for heaven and earth to pass away
than for one stroke of a letter in the law to
drop out.

[18]"Everyone[j] who divorces[k] his wife and
marries another woman commits adultery,[l]
and everyone who marries a woman divorced
from her husband commits adultery.

The Rich Man and Lazarus

[19]"There was a rich man who would dress
in purple and fine linen,[m] feasting lavishly
every day. [20]But a poor man named Lazarus, covered with sores, was left at his gate.[n]
[21]He longed to be filled[o] with what fell from
the rich man's table,[p] but instead the dogs[q]
would come and lick his sores. [22]One day the
poor man died and was carried away by the
angels to Abraham's side.[C,r] The rich man also
died and was buried. [23]And being in torment[s]
in •Hades,[t] he looked up and saw Abraham a
long way off, with Lazarus at his side. [24]'Father Abraham!'[u] he called out, 'Have mercy
on me and send Lazarus to dip the tip of his
finger in water and cool my tongue, because
I am in agony[v] in this flame!'

[25]"'Son,'[D] Abraham said, 'remember that during your life you received your good things,[w]
just as Lazarus received bad things, but now
he is comforted here,[x] while you are in agony.
[26]Besides all this, a great chasm has been fixed
between us and you, so that those who want to
pass over from here to you cannot; neither can
those from there cross over to us.'

[27]"'Father,' he said, 'then I beg you to send
him to my father's house — [28]because I have
five brothers — to warn[y] them, so they won't
also come to this place of torment.'

[29]"But Abraham said, 'They have Moses and
the prophets;[z] they should listen to them.'

[30]"'No, father Abraham,' he said. 'But if
someone from the dead goes to them, they
will repent.'

[31]"But he told him, 'If they don't listen to
Moses and the prophets, they will not be persuaded if someone rises from the dead.'"[aa]

Warnings from Jesus

17 He[ab] said to His disciples, "Offenses[E] will
certainly come,[F] but woe[ac] to the one
they come[ad] through! [2]It would be better for
him if a millstone[G] were hung around his neck
and he were thrown into the sea than for him
to cause one of these little ones to •stumble.[ae]
[3]Be[af] on your guard. If your brother sins,[H] rebuke[ag] him, and if he repents, forgive[ah] him.
[4]And if he sins against you seven times in a
day, and comes back to you seven times, saying, 'I repent,' you must forgive him."

Faith and Duty

[5]The[ai] apostles[aj] said to the Lord, "Increase
our faith."[ak]

[6]"If you have faith the size of[I] a mustard
seed,"[al] the Lord said, "you can say to this
mulberry tree, 'Be uprooted and planted in
the sea,' and it will obey you.

[7]"Which one of you having a •slave tending sheep or plowing will say to him when he
comes in from the field, 'Come at once and sit
down to eat'? [8]Instead, will he not tell him, 'Prepare something for me to eat, get ready,[J] and
serve me while I eat and drink; later you can eat
and drink'?[am] [9]Does he thank that slave because
he did what was commanded?[K] [10]In the same
way, when you have done all that you were
commanded, you should say, 'We are good-for-
nothing[an] slaves; we've only done our duty.'"

Ten Men Healed

[11]While traveling to Jerusalem,[ao] He passed
between[L] Samaria and Galilee.[ap] [12]As He

[a]**16:14** 2Tm 3:2 [b]Lk 23:35 [c]**16:15** Lk 10:29; 18:9 [d]1Sm 16:7; Ps 17:3; Pr 21:2; Rm 8:27 [e]Dt 24:4 [f]**16:16-17** Mt 5:18; 11:12-13; 24:35; Mk 13:31 [g]**16:16** Mt 7:12; 22:40; Ac 13:15; Rm 3:21 [h]Mt 4:23 [i]**16:17** Mt 5:18 [j]**16:18** Mt 5:32; 19:9; Mk 10:11-12 [k]Mt 1:19; 19:9 [l]Ex 20:14; Lv 20:10; Pr 6:32; 2Pt 2:14 [m]**16:19** Ex 28:6; 35:35; Est 8:15; Pr 31:22; Ezk 27:16; Rv 18:16 [n]**16:20** Ac 3:2 [o]**16:21** Lv 15:16 [p]Mt 15:27 [q]1Kg 21:19 [r]**16:22** Jn 13:23 [s]**16:23** Is 50:11 [t]Mt 11:23 [u]**16:24** Lk 3:8; 16:30; 19:9; Jn 8:33,39,53 [v]Is 66:24; Mt 25:41 [w]**16:25** Lk 6:24 [x]Mt 11:28 [y]**16:28** Ac 2:40; 8:25 [z]**16:29** Lk 24:27,44; Jn 1:45; Ac 26:22; 28:23 [aa]**16:31** Mt 28:11-15; Jn 12:10-11 [ab]**17:1-3** Mt 18:6-7; Mk 9:42; 1Co 11:19 [ac]**17:1** Lk 22:22 [ad]Mt 13:41 [ae]**17:2** 1Co 8:9 [af]**17:3-4** Mt 18:15,21-22 [ag]**17:3** Lv 19:17 [ah]Mt 6:14 [ai]**17:5-6** Mt 17:19-21; Mk 9:28-29 [aj]**17:5** Lk 6:13 [ak]Mk 9:24 [al]**17:6** Mt 13:31; Mk 4:31; Lk 13:19 [am]**17:8** Lk 12:35-37 [an]**17:10** Jb 22:2-3; 35:7; Mt 25:30; Rm 11:35 [ao]**17:11** Lk 9:51 [ap]Jn 4:3-4

[A]16:16 Perhaps *were proclaimed*, or *were in effect* [B]16:16 Or *everyone is forcing his way into it* [C]16:22 Or *to Abraham's bosom*; lit *to the fold of Abraham's robe*; Jn 13:23 [D]16:25 Lit *Child* [E]17:1 Or *Traps*, or *Bait-sticks*, or *Causes of stumbling*, or *Causes of sin* [F]17:1 Lit *It is impossible for offenses not to come* [G]17:2 Large stone used for grinding grains into flour [H]17:3 Other mss add *against you* [I]17:6 Lit *faith like* [J]17:8 Or *eat, gird yourself*; lit *eat, tuck in your robe* [K]17:9 Other mss add *I don't think so* [L]17:11 Or *through the middle of*

entered a village, 10 men with serious skin
diseases[a] met Him. They stood at a distance
13 and raised their voices, saying, "Jesus, Master,[b] have mercy on us!"
14 When He saw them, He told them, "Go
and show yourselves to the priests."[c] And
while they were going, they were healed.[A]
15 But one of them, seeing that he was
healed, returned and, with a loud voice, gave
glory to God.[d] 16 He fell facedown[e] at His feet,
thanking Him. And he was a ·Samaritan.[f]
17 Then Jesus said, "Were not 10 cleansed?
Where are the nine? 18 Didn't any return[B]
to give glory to God except this foreigner?"
19 And He told him, "Get up and go on your
way. Your faith has made you well."[C,g]

The Coming of the Kingdom

20 Being[h] asked by the ·Pharisees when the
kingdom of God will come,[i] He answered
them, "The kingdom of God is not coming
with something observable; 21 no one will
say,[D] 'Look here!' or 'There!' For you see, the
kingdom of God is among you."
22 Then He told the disciples: "The days are
coming[j] when you will long to see one of the
days of the ·Son of Man, but you won't see it.[k]
23 They will say to you,[l] 'Look there!' or 'Look
here!' Don't follow or run after them.[m] 24 For
as the lightning flashes from horizon to horizon and lights up the sky, so the Son of Man
will be in His day.[n] 25 But first He must suffer
many things and be rejected by this generation.[o]
26 "Just as it was in the days of Noah,[p] so it
will be in the days of the Son of Man: 27 People
went on eating, drinking, marrying and giving in marriage[q] until the day Noah boarded
the ark,[r] and the flood came and destroyed
them all. 28 It will be the same as it was in the
days of Lot:[s] People went on eating, drinking,
buying, selling, planting, building. 29 But on
the day Lot left Sodom, fire and sulfur rained
from heaven and destroyed[t] them all. 30 It[u]
will be like that on the day the Son of Man is
revealed.[v] 31 On that day, a man on the housetop, whose belongings are in the house, must
not come down to get them. Likewise the
man who is in the field must not turn back.
32 Remember Lot's wife![w] 33 Whoever tries to
make his ·life secure[E,F] will lose it, and whoever loses his life will preserve it.[x] 34 I tell you,
on that night[y] two will be in one bed: One
will be taken and the other will be left. 35 Two
women will be grinding grain together: One
will be taken and the other left. [36 Two will
be in a field: One will be taken, and the other
will be left.][G]
37 "Where, Lord?"[z] they asked Him.
He said to them, "Where the corpse is, there
also the vultures[aa] will be gathered."

The Parable of the Persistent Widow

18 He then told them a parable on the
need for them to pray[ab] always and not
become discouraged:[ac] 2 "There was a judge
in a certain town who didn't fear God[ad] or
respect man. 3 And a widow[ae] in that town
kept coming to him, saying, 'Give me justice
against my adversary.'
4 "For a while he was unwilling, but later
he said to himself, 'Even though I don't fear
God or respect man, 5 yet because this widow
keeps[af] pestering me,[H] I will give her justice,
so she doesn't wear me out[I] by her persistent
coming.'"
6 Then the Lord said, "Listen to what the unjust judge says. 7 Will not God grant justice[ag]
to His elect[ah] who cry out to Him day and
night?[ai] Will He delay[aj] to help them?[J] 8 I tell
you that He will swiftly grant them justice.
Nevertheless, when the ·Son of Man comes,[ak]
will He find that faith[K] on earth?"

The Parable of the Pharisee and the Tax Collector

9 He[al] also told this parable to some who
trusted in themselves[am] that they were righteous[an] and looked down[ao] on everyone else:
10 "Two men went up to the ·temple complex
to pray,[ap] one a ·Pharisee and the other a tax
collector. 11 The Pharisee took his stand[L,aq] and
was praying like this: 'God, I thank You that

[a] **17:12** Lv 13:45-46 [b] **17:13** Lk 5:5 [c] **17:14** Lv 13:2–14:32; Mt 8:4; Lk 5:14 [d] **17:15** Mt 9:8; Mk 2:12; Lk 2:14; 5:26; Jn 9:24; Ac 4:21; 12:23; Rm 4:20 [e] **17:16** 1Sm 20:41; 2Sm 14:22; Mt 17:6; 1Co 14:25 [f] Mt 10:5; Jn 4:9 [g] **17:19** Mt 9:22; Mk 10:52; Lk 5:20; 18:42 [h] **17:20-21** Mt 24:23; Mk 13:21 [i] **17:20** Lk 19:11; Ac 1:6 [j] **17:22** Dt 32:35; Is 2:12; Jr 7:32; Am 4:2; Lk 5:35; 19:43; 21:6; 23:29 [k] Am 5:18 [l] **17:23-24** Mt 24:23,27; Mk 13:21 [m] **17:23** Lk 21:8 [n] **17:24** 1Co 1:8 [o] **17:25** Mt 16:21; Lk 9:22 [p] **17:26-27** Mt 24:37-38 [q] **17:27** Lk 20:34-35 [r] Gn 6:14 [s] **17:28** Gn 19:1-26 [t] **17:29** Gn 19:24-25 [u] **17:30-35** Mt 24:17,39-41; Mk 13:15 [v] **17:30** Mt 16:27; 24:44; 1Co 1:7; 2Th 1:7; 1Pt 1:7; 4:13 [w] **17:32** Gn 19:26 [x] **17:33** Mt 10:39; Jn 12:25 [y] **17:34** Lk 1:78-79 [z] **17:37** Lk 17:20 [aa] Ezk 29:5; 32:4; 39:17-20 [ab] **18:1** Lk 11:5-13; 21:36; 1Th 5:17 [ac] 2Co 4:1 [ad] **18:2** Ps 147:11; Pr 1:7; Ac 10:2; Rv 14:7 [ae] **18:3** Lk 2:37; 4:26; 7:12; 21:2 [af] **18:5** Lk 11:8 [ag] **18:7** Is 63:4; Rv 6:10 [ah] Mt 24:22; Rm 8:33; 2Tm 2:10; Ti 1:1 [ai] Ps 88:1 [aj] 2Pt 3:9 [ak] **18:8** Dn 7:13; Lk 9:26; 12:40 [al] **18:9-14** Mt 18:4; 23:12; Lk 14:11 [am] **18:9** Mt 5:20; 2Co 1:9 [an] Lk 16:15 [ao] Lk 23:11; Ac 4:11; Rm 14:3,10 [ap] **18:10** 1Kg 10:5; 2Kg 20:5,8; Ac 3:1 [aq] **18:11** Mt 6:5; Mk 11:25

[A] **17:14** Lit *cleansed* [B] **17:18** Lit *Were they not found returning* [C] **17:19** Or *faith has saved you* [D] **17:21** Lit *they will not say* [E] **17:33** Other mss read *to save his life* [F] **17:33** Or *tries to retain his life* [G] **17:36** Other mss omit bracketed text [H] **18:5** Lit *widow causes me trouble* [I] **18:5** Or *doesn't give me a black eye*, or *doesn't ruin my reputation* [J] **18:7** Or *Will He put up with them?* [K] **18:8** Or *faith*, or *that kind of faith*, or *any faith*, or *the faith*, or *faithfulness*; the faith that persists in prayer for God's vindication [L] **18:11** Or *Pharisee stood by himself*

I'm not like other people[A]—greedy,[a] unrighteous,[b] adulterers,[c] or even like this tax collector. 12 I fast[d] twice a week; I give a tenth[B,e] of
everything I get.'
13 "But the tax collector, standing far off,[f]
would not even raise his eyes to heaven[g] but
kept striking his chest[C,h] and saying, 'God,
turn Your wrath from me[D,i]—a sinner!'[j] 14 I
tell you, this one went down to his house
•justified[k] rather than the other; because everyone who exalts himself will be humbled,
but the one who humbles himself will be exalted."[l]

Blessing the Children

15 Some[m] people were even bringing infants to Him so He might touch them, but
when the disciples saw it, they rebuked them.
16 Jesus, however, invited them: "Let the little
children come to Me,[n] and don't stop them,
because the kingdom of God belongs to such
as these. 17 •I assure you:[o] Whoever does not
welcome[p] the kingdom of God like a little
child[q] will never enter it."

The Rich Young Ruler

18 A[r] ruler[s] asked Him, "Good Teacher, what
must I do to inherit eternal life?"[t]
19 "Why do you call Me good?" Jesus asked
him. "No one is good but One—God. 20 You
know the commandments:

Do not commit adultery;
do not murder;
do not steal;
do not bear false witness;
honor your father and mother."[E,u]

21 "I have kept all these from my youth," he
said.
22 When Jesus heard this, He told him, "You
still lack one thing: Sell all that you have and
distribute it to the poor,[v] and you will have
treasure in heaven.[w] Then come, follow Me."[x]
23 After he heard this, he became extremely
sad,[y] because he was very rich.

Possessions and the Kingdom

24 Seeing that he became sad,[F] Jesus said,
"How hard it is for those who have wealth to
enter the kingdom of God! 25 For it is easier
for a camel to go through the eye of a needle
than for a rich person to enter the kingdom
of God."
26 Those who heard this asked, "Then who
can be saved?"[z]
27 He replied, "What is impossible with men
is possible with God."[aa]
28 Then Peter said, "Look, we have left what
we had and followed[ab] You."
29 So He said to them, "I assure you: There is
no one who has left a house, wife or •broth-
ers, parents or children because of the kingdom of God, 30 who will not receive many
times more at this time,[ac] and eternal life in
the age to come."

The Third Prediction of His Death

31 Then[ad] He took the Twelve aside and told
them, "Listen! We are going up to Jerusalem.[ae] Everything that is written[af] through the
prophets about the Son of Man will be accomplished.[ag] 32 For He will be handed over to the
Gentiles,[ah] and He will be mocked,[ai] insulted,
spit[aj] on; 33 and after they flog Him, they will
kill Him, and He will rise on the third day."[ak]
34 They understood none of these things.[al]
This saying[G,am] was hidden[an] from them, and
they did not grasp what was said.

A Blind Man Receives His Sight

35 As[ao] He drew near Jericho, a blind man
was sitting by the road begging. 36 Hearing
a crowd passing by, he inquired what this
meant. 37 "Jesus the •Nazarene[ap] is passing by,"
they told him.
38 So he called out,[aq] "Jesus, Son of David,[ar]
have mercy[as] on me!" 39 Then those in front
told him to keep quiet,[H] but he kept crying
out all the more, "Son of David, have mercy
on me!"
40 Jesus stopped and commanded that he
be brought to Him. When he drew near, He
asked him, 41 "What do you want Me to do for
you?"
"Lord," he said, "I want to see!"

[a] **18:11** Mt 7:15; 1Co 5:10-11; 6:10 [b] Lk 16:10 [c] Ex 20:14; 1Co 6:9; Heb 13:4 [d] **18:12** Lk 5:33-35; Ac 13:2-3 [e] Lk 11:42 [f] **18:13** Lk 17:12 [g] Ezr 9:6 [h] Lk 23:48 [i] Heb 2:17 [j] 1Tm 1:15 [k] **18:14** Lk 16:15; Php 3:8 [l] Is 2:11; Lk 1:52; 3:5; 14:11 [m] **18:15-17** Mt 18:3; 19:13-15; Mk 10:13-16 [n] **18:16** Lk 14:26 [o] **18:17** Ps 72:19; Rv 22:21 [p] Lk 8:13 [q] 1Co 14:20; 1Pt 2:2 [r] **18:18-30** Mt 19:16-30; Mk 10:17-31; Lk 22:28-30 [s] **18:18** Lk 8:41; 12:58 [t] Lk 10:25; Jn 3:15 [u] **18:20** Ex 20:12-16; Dt 5:16-20 [v] **18:22** Lk 12:33; 19:8; Ac 2:45; 4:34 [w] Mt 6:19-20; Lk 5:11; 12:33 [x] Lk 5:27 [y] **18:23** Mt 26:38; Mk 6:26; 14:34 [z] **18:26** Lk 18:42; Eph 2:8 [aa] **18:27** Gn 18:14; Jb 42:2; Jr 32:17; Zch 8:6; Lk 1:37; Rm 4:21; 11:22 [ab] **18:28** Lk 5:11; Jn 8:12 [ac] **18:30** Jb 42:10; Mt 6:33; Lk 21:8 [ad] **18:31-34** Mt 20:17-19; Mk 10:32-34 [ae] **18:31** Lk 9:51 [af] Ps 22; Is 52:13–53:12; Mt 1:22; 26:24 [ag] Lk 22:37; Jn 19:28 [ah] **18:32** Mt 27:2; Jn 18:30-31; Ac 3:13 [ai] Mt 27:26-31 [aj] Mt 26:67; Mk 14:65; 15:19 [ak] **18:33** Mt 16:21; Lk 9:22 [al] **18:34** Mk 9:32; Lk 2:50; 9:45 [am] Lk 1:29 [an] Lk 24:16

[ao] **18:35-43** Mt 20:29-34; Mk 10:46-52 [ap] **18:37** Mt 2:23; Jn 18:5; 19:19; Ac 2:22 [aq] **18:38** Lk 18:7 [ar] Mt 1:1; 9:27; Lk 1:32; Rm 1:3 [as] Lk 16:24

[A] **18:11** Or *like the rest of men* [B] **18:12** Or *give tithes* [C] **18:13** = mourning [D] **18:13** Lit *God, be propitious to me*; = May Your wrath be turned aside by the sacrifice [E] **18:20** Ex 20:12-16; Dt 5:16-20 [F] **18:24** Other mss omit *he became sad* [G] **18:34** The meaning of the saying [H] **18:39** Or *those in front rebuked him*

42“Receive your sight!”[a] Jesus told him.
“Your faith has healed you.”[A,b] 43Instantly he
could see, and he began to follow Him, glorifying God.[c] All the people,[d] when they saw it,
gave praise to God.

Jesus Visits Zacchaeus

19 He entered Jericho and was passing
through. 2There was a man named
Zacchaeus who was a chief tax collector,
and he was rich. 3He was trying to see who
Jesus was, but he was not able because of the
crowd, since he was a short man. 4So running
ahead, he climbed up a sycamore tree to see
Jesus, since He was about to pass that way.
5When Jesus came to the place, He looked
up and said to him, “Zacchaeus, hurry and
come down because today I must stay at your
house.”

6So he quickly came down and welcomed
Him joyfully. 7All who saw it began to complain,[e] “He’s gone to lodge with a sinful
man!”

8But Zacchaeus stood there and said to the
Lord, “Look, I’ll give[B] half of my possessions
to the poor,[f] Lord! And if I have extorted[g] anything from anyone, I’ll pay[C] back four times
as much!”[h]

9“Today salvation[i] has come to this house,”
Jesus told him, “because he too is a son of
Abraham.[j] 10For the ˙Son of Man has come to
seek and to save the lost.”[D,k]

The Parable of the 10 Minas

11As[l] they were listening to this, He went on
to tell a parable because He was near Jerusalem,[m] and they thought the kingdom of God
was going to appear right away.[n]

12Therefore He said: “A nobleman traveled
to a far country to receive for himself authority to be king[E] and then return. 13He called
10 of his ˙slaves, gave them 10 minas,[F] and
told them, ‘Engage in business until I come
back.’

14“But his subjects hated him and sent a delegation after him, saying, ‘We don’t want this
man to rule over us!’

15“At his return, having received the authority to be king,[E] he summoned those slaves he
had given the money to, so he could find out
how much they had made in business. 16The
first came forward and said, ‘Master, your
mina has earned 10 more minas.’

17“ ‘Well done, good[G] slave!’ he told him. ‘Because you have been faithful[o] in a very small
matter, have authority over 10 towns.’

18“The second came and said, ‘Master, your
mina has made five minas.’

19“So he said to him, ‘You will be over five
towns.’

20“And another came and said, ‘Master, here
is your mina. I have kept it hidden away in a
cloth 21because I was afraid of you, for you’re
a tough man: you collect what you didn’t deposit and reap what you didn’t sow.’[p]

22“He told him, ‘I will judge you by what
you have said,[H] you evil slave! If you knew I
was a tough man, collecting what I didn’t deposit and reaping what I didn’t sow, 23why
didn’t you put my money in the bank? And
when I returned, I would have collected it
with interest!’ 24So he said to those standing
there, ‘Take the mina away from him and give
it to the one who has 10 minas.’

25“But they said to him, ‘Master, he has 10
minas.’

26“ ‘I tell you, that to everyone who has,
more will be given; and from the one who
does not have, even what he does have will be
taken away.[q] 27But bring here these enemies
of mine,[r] who did not want me to rule over
them, and slaughter[I] them in my presence.’ ”

The Triumphal Entry

28When[s] He had said these things, He went
on ahead, going up to Jerusalem.[t] 29As He
approached Bethphage and Bethany, at the
place called the ˙Mount of Olives,[u] He sent
two of the disciples 30and said, “Go into the
village ahead of you. As you enter it, you will
find a young donkey tied there, on which no
one has ever sat. Untie it and bring it here. 31If
anyone asks you, ‘Why are you untying it?’
say this: ‘The Lord needs it.’ ”

32So those who were sent left and found it
just as He had told them.[v] 33As they were untying the young donkey, its owners said to
them, “Why are you untying the donkey?”

[a]18:42 Lk 7:22; Jn 9:11; Ac 9:12
[b]Mt 9:22; Lk 5:20; 7:50; 8:48; 17:19; 18:26
[c]18:43 Lk 7:16; 13:13
[d]Lk 2:10
[e]19:7 Lk 15:2
[f]19:8 Lk 18:22
[g]Lk 3:14
[h]Ex 22:1; 2Sm 12:6
[i]19:9 Lk 1:77
[j]Lk 3:8; 13:16; Gl 3:7,29
[k]19:10 Ezk 34:16; Mt 9:13; 10:6; 15:24; 18:12; Lk 15:4
[l]19:11-27 Mt 25:14-30; Mk 13:34
[m]19:11 Lk 9:51
[n]Lk 17:20; Ac 1:6
[o]19:17 Lk 16:10; 1Co 4:2
[p]19:21 2Co 8:12
[q]19:26 Mt 13:12; Mk 4:25; Lk 8:18
[r]19:27 Lk 19:14
[s]19:28-44 Mt 21:1-11; Mk 11:1-11
[t]19:28 Lk 9:51
[u]19:29 2Sm 15:30; Zch 14:4; Lk 21:37; 22:39
[v]19:32 Lk 22:13

[A]18:42 Or *has saved you* [B]19:8 Or *I give* [C]19:8 Or *I pay* [D]19:10 Or *save what was lost* [E]19:12,15 Lit *to receive for himself a kingdom* or *sovereignty* [F]19:13 = Gk coin worth 100 drachmas or about 100 days’ wages [G]19:17 Or *capable* [H]19:22 Lit *you out of your mouth* [I]19:27 Or *execute*

34 "The Lord needs it," they said. 35 Then[a]
they brought it to Jesus, and after throwing
their robes on the donkey, they helped Jesus
get on it.[b] 36 As He was going along, they were
spreading their robes on the road.[c] 37 Now He
came near the path down the Mount of Olives, and the whole crowd of the disciples began to praise God joyfully with a loud voice
for all the miracles they had seen:

38 **The King[d] who comes**
in the name of the Lord[A,B,e]
is the blessed One.
Peace in heaven
and glory[f] in the highest heaven![g]

39 Some of the ·Pharisees from the crowd
told Him, "Teacher, rebuke Your disciples."
40 He answered, "I tell you, if they were to
keep silent, the stones would cry out!"[h]

Jesus' Love for Jerusalem

41 As He approached and saw the city, He
wept[i] over it, 42 saying, "If you knew[j] this day
what would bring peace — but now it is hidden[k] from your eyes. 43 For the days will come
on you[l] when your enemies will build an em-
bankment against you, surround you, and
hem you in on every side.[m] 44 They will crush
you and your children within you to the
ground,[n] and they will not leave one stone on
another[o] in you, because you did not recognize the time of your visitation."[p]

Cleansing the Temple Complex

45 He[q] went into the ·temple complex and
began to throw out those who were selling,[C]
46 and He said, "It is written, **My house will be**
a house of prayer,[r] but you have made it **a den**
of thieves!"[D,s]
47 Every day He was teaching[t] in the temple
complex. The ·chief priests, the ·scribes, and
the leaders of the people were looking for
a way to destroy[u] Him, 48 but they could not
find a way to do it, because all the people[v]
were captivated by what they heard.[E]

The Authority of Jesus Challenged

20 One[w] day[F] as He was teaching[x] the
people in the ·temple complex and
proclaiming the good news,[y] the ·chief priests
and the ·scribes, with the elders,[z] came up
2 and said to Him: "Tell us, by what authority are You doing these things? Who is it who
gave You this authority?"
3 He answered them, "I will also ask you a
question. Tell Me, 4 was the baptism of John
from heaven or from men?"
5 They discussed it among themselves: "If
we say, 'From heaven,' He will say, 'Why didn't
you believe him?' 6 But if we say, 'From men,'
all the people[aa] will stone us, because they are
convinced that John was a prophet."[ab]
7 So they answered that they did not know
its origin.[G]
8 And Jesus said to them, "Neither will I tell
you by what authority I do these things."

The Parable of the Vineyard Owner

9 Then[ac] He began to tell the people this
parable: "A man planted a vineyard,[ad] leased
it to tenant farmers, and went away for a long
time. 10 At harvest time he sent a ·slave to the
farmers so that they might give him some
fruit from the vineyard. But the farmers beat
him and sent him away empty-handed. 11 He
sent yet another slave, but they beat that
one too, treated him shamefully, and sent
him away empty-handed. 12 And he sent yet
a third, but they wounded this one too and
threw him out.
13 "Then the owner of the vineyard said,
'What should I do? I will send my beloved[ae]
son. Perhaps[H] they will respect him.'
14 "But when the tenant farmers saw him,
they discussed it among themselves and said,
'This is the heir. Let's kill him, so the inheritance will be ours!'[af] 15 So they threw him out
of the vineyard and killed him.
"Therefore, what will the owner of the
vineyard do to them? 16 He will come and destroy[ag] those farmers and give the vineyard to
others."
But when they heard this they said, "No —
never!"[ah]
17 But He looked at them and said, "Then
what is the meaning of this Scripture:[I,ai]

The stone that the builders rejected —
this has become the cornerstone?[J,K,aj]

[a] **19:35-38** Jn 12:12-15
[b] **19:35** Zch 9:9
[c] **19:36** 2Kg 9:13
[d] **19:38** Mt 2:2; 25:34
[e] Ps 118:26; Lk 13:35
[f] Lk 2:14
[g] Jb 16:19; Ps 148:1; Mt 21:9; Mk 11:10; Lk 2:14
[h] **19:40** Hab 2:11
[i] **19:41** Lk 13:34-35; Jn 11:35; Heb 5:7
[j] **19:42** Lk 23:34
[k] Lk 8:9-10; 10:21
[l] **19:43** Lk 17:22
[m] Is 29:3; Jr 6:6; Ezk 4:2; Lk 21:20
[n] **19:44** Mt 24:2; Mk 13:2
[o] Lk 21:6
[p] Ex 3:16; Lk 1:68; 7:16; 1Pt 2:12
[q] **19:45-48** Mt 21:12-19; Mk 11:12-19; Jn 2:13-17; 8:1-2; 11:45-53
[r] **19:46** Is 56:7
[s] Jr 7:11
[t] **19:47** Mt 26:55; Lk 20:1
[u] Lk 6:11; 11:53-54; 20:19
[v] **19:48** Lk 18:43; 20:6
[w] **20:1-8** Mt 21:23-27; Mk 11:27-33
[x] **20:1** Lk 19:47
[y] Lk 4:18; 8:1
[z] Lk 9:22; 22:66
[aa] **20:6** Lk 19:48
[ab] Mt 11:9; Lk 7:29-30
[ac] **20:9-19** Mt 21:33-46; Mk 12:1-12
[ad] **20:9** Is 5:1-7
[ae] **20:13** Mt 17:5; Lk 3:22
[af] **20:14** Lk 16:16
[ag] **20:16** Lk 19:27
[ah] Rm 3:4; 1Co 6:15; Gl 2:17
[ai] **20:17** Lk 4:17; 18:31; 21:22,37; 24:44
[aj] Ps 118:22; Ac 4:11; Eph 2:20; 1Pt 2:4-7

[A] **19:38** Luke substitutes "the King" for "He" in Ps 118:26. [B] **19:38** Ps 118:26 [C] **19:45** Other mss add *and buying in it* [D] **19:46** Is 56:7; Jr 7:11 [E] **19:48** Lit *people hung on what they heard* [F] **20:1** Lit *It happened on one of the days* [G] **20:7** Or *know where it was from* [H] **20:13** Other mss add *when they see him* [I] **20:17** Lit *What then is this that is written* [J] **20:17** Lit *the head of the corner* [K] **20:17** Ps 118:22

18 Everyone who falls on that stone will be broken to pieces, and if it falls on anyone, it will
grind him to powder!"[a]
19 Then the scribes and the chief priests[b]
looked for a way to get their hands on Him[c]
that very hour, because they knew He had
told this parable against them, but they
feared the people.[d]

God and Caesar

20 They[A,e] watched closely[f] and sent spies[g]
who pretended to be righteous,[B] so they could
catch Him in what He said,[C,h] to hand Him[i]
over to the governor's[j] rule and authority.
21 They questioned Him, "Teacher, we know
that You speak and teach correctly,[k] and You
don't show partiality,[D,l] but teach truthfully
the way of God.[m] 22 Is it lawful[n] for us to pay
taxes[o] to Caesar[p] or not?"
23 But detecting their craftiness, He said to
them,[E] 24 "Show Me a ·denarius. Whose image
and inscription does it have?"
"Caesar's," they said.
25 "Well then," He told them, "give back to
Caesar[q] the things that are Caesar's and to
God the things that are God's."
26 They were not able to catch Him in what
He said[C] in public,[F] and being amazed at His
answer, they became silent.[r]

The Sadducees and the Resurrection

27 Some[s] of the ·Sadducees, who say there
is no resurrection,[t] came up and questioned
Him: 28 "Teacher, Moses wrote for us that **if a
man's brother** has a wife, and **dies childless,
his brother should take the wife and produce
·offspring for his brother.**[G,u] 29 Now there
were seven brothers. The first took a wife and
died without children. 30 Also the second[H]
31 and the third took her. In the same way, all
seven died and left no children. 32 Finally, the
woman died too. 33 In the resurrection, therefore, whose wife will the woman be? For all
seven had married her."[I]
34 Jesus told them, "The sons of this age[v]
marry and are given in marriage.[w] 35 But those
who are counted worthy[x] to take part in that
age[y] and in the resurrection from the dead
neither marry nor are given in marriage.
36 For they cannot die anymore,[z] because they
are like angels and are sons of God,[aa] since
they are sons of the resurrection. 37 Moses
even indicated in the passage about the burning bush that the dead are raised, where he
calls the Lord **the God of Abraham and the
God of Isaac and the God of Jacob.**[J,ab] 38 He is
not God of the dead but of the living, because
all are living to[K] Him."[ac]
39 Some of the scribes answered, "Teacher,
You have spoken well." 40 And they no longer
dared to ask Him anything.

The Question about the Messiah

41 Then[ad] He said to them, "How can they say
that the ·Messiah is the Son of David?[ae] 42 For
David himself says in the Book of Psalms:[af]

> **The Lord declared to my Lord,**
> **'Sit at My right hand**
> 43 **until I make Your enemies**
> **Your footstool.'**[L,ag]

44 David calls Him 'Lord'; how then can the
Messiah be his Son?"[ah]

Warning against the Scribes

45 While[ai] all the people were listening,
He said to His disciples, 46 "Beware[aj] of the
scribes, who want to go around in long robes
and who love greetings in the marketplaces,
the front seats in the ·synagogues, and the
places of honor at banquets.[ak] 47 They devour
widows' houses and say long prayers just
for show. These will receive greater punishment."[M]

The Widow's Gift

21 He[al] looked up and saw the rich dropping their offerings into the temple
treasury.[am] 2 He also saw a poor widow dropping in two tiny coins.[N,an] 3 "I tell you the truth,"
He said. "This poor widow has put in more
than all of them.[ao] 4 For all these people have
put in gifts out of their surplus, but she out of
her poverty has put in all she had to live on."

[a] **20:18** Is 8:14-15; Dn 2:34-35,44-45; Rm 9:32-33; 1Pt 2:8 [b] **20:19** Mt 2:4; 20:18; 21:15; Lk 22:2; 23:10 [c] Lk 19:47; 21:12 [d] Lk 22:2 [e] **20:20-26** Mt 20:15-22; Mk 12:13-17 [f] **20:20** Lk 6:7; 14:1 [g] Mt 22:15-16 [h] Lk 11:54 [i] Lk 24:20; Ac 3:13; Rm 8:32 [j] Mt 27:2; Lk 21:12 [k] **20:21** Jn 3:2 [l] Dt 1:17; 10:17; Mal 2:9; Mt 22:16 [m] Ac 13:10; 18:25-26 [n] **20:22** Lk 6:9; 14:3 [o] Mt 17:25; Lk 23:2; Rm 13:6-7 [p] Lk 2:1; 3:1; 20:24-25; 23:2 [q] **20:25** Mt 22:21 [r] **20:26** Lk 9:36; 14:4 [s] **20:27-40** Mt 22:23-33,46; Mk 12:18-27,34 [t] **20:27** Ac 23:6 [u] **20:28** Dt 25:5 [v] **20:34** Lk 16:8 [w] Lk 17:27 [x] **20:35** Ac 5:41; 2Th 1:5 [y] Mk 10:30 [z] **20:36** 1Co 15:54-55; Rv 21:4 [aa] Ps 82:6; Mt 5:45; Rm 8:14,19; Gl 3:26 [ab] **20:37** Ex 3:6,15-16; 4:5; Mt 1:2; Ac 3:13; 7:30-32 [ac] **20:38** Rm 6:10-11; 14:7-8; 2Co 5:14-15; Gl 2:19-20; 1Th 4:14; 5:10 [ad] **20:41-44** Mt 22:41-46; Mk 12:34-37 [ae] **20:41** Mt 1:1,17; Lk 1:27; Rm 1:3; Eph 5:2 [af] **20:42** Lk 24:44; Ac 1:20 [ag] **20:42-43** Ps 110:1; Ac 2:34-35; 1Co 15:25; Heb 1:13; 10:13 [ah] **20:44** Rm 1:3-4 [ai] **20:45-47** Mt 23:1-36; Mk 12:37-40 [aj] **20:46** Mt 16:6

[ak] Lk 11:43 [al] **21:1-4** Mk 12:41-44 [am] **21:1** 2Kg 12:9; Mt 27:6; Jn 8:20 [an] **21:2** Lk 12:59 [ao] **21:3** 2Co 8:2,12

[A] **20:20** The scribes and chief priests of v. 19 [B] **20:20** Or *upright*; that is, loyal to God's law [C] **20:20,26** Lit *catch Him in a word* [D] **20:21** Lit *You don't receive a face* [E] **20:23** Other mss add *"Why are you testing Me?* [F] **20:26** Lit *in front of the people* [G] **20:28** Dt 25:5 [H] **20:30** Other mss add *took her as wife, and he died without children* [I] **20:33** Lit *had her as wife* [J] **20:37** Ex 3:6,15 [K] **20:38** Or *with* [L] **20:42-43** Ps 110:1 [M] **20:47** Or *judgment* [N] **21:2** Lit *two lepta*; the *lepton* was the smallest and least valuable Gk coin in use.

Destruction of the Temple Predicted

5As[a] some were talking about the ·temple complex, how it was adorned with beautiful stones and gifts dedicated to God,[A] He said, 6"These things that you see — the days will come[b] when not one stone will be left on another that will not be thrown down!"[c]

Signs of the End of the Age

7"Teacher," they asked Him, "so when will these things be? And what will be the sign when these things are about to take place?"[d]

8Then He said, "Watch out that you are not deceived.[e] For many will come in My name,[f] saying, 'I am He,'[g] and, 'The time is near.' Don't follow them.[h] 9When you hear of wars and rebellions,[B] don't be alarmed. Indeed, these things must take place first, but the end won't come right away."

10Then He told them: "Nation will be raised up against nation, and kingdom against kingdom.[i] 11There will be violent earthquakes,[j] and famines and plagues[k] in various places, and there will be terrifying sights and great signs from heaven.[l] 12But before all these things, they will lay their hands on you[m] and persecute[n] you. They will hand you over to the ·synagogues[o] and prisons,[p] and you will be brought before kings and governors[q] because of My name. 13It will lead to an opportunity for you to witness.[C,r] 14Therefore make up your minds[D] not to prepare your defense ahead of time,[s] 15for I will give you such words[E,t] and a wisdom[u] that none of your adversaries will be able to resist or contradict.[v] 16You will even be betrayed by parents, brothers, relatives, and friends.[w] They will kill some of you. 17You will be hated by everyone because of My name,[x] 18but not a hair of your head will be lost.[y] 19By your endurance gain[F] your ·lives.[z]

The Destruction of Jerusalem

20"When you see Jerusalem surrounded by armies,[aa] then recognize that its desolation[ab] has come near. 21Then those in Judea must flee[ac] to the mountains![ad] Those inside the city[G] must leave it, and those who are in the country must not enter it, 22because these are days of vengeance[ae] to fulfill all the things that are written. 23Woe to pregnant women and nursing mothers in those days,[af] for there will be great distress in the land[H] and wrath against this people. 24They will fall by the edge of the sword[ag] and be led captive into all the nations, and Jerusalem will be trampled by the Gentiles[I,ah] until the times of the Gentiles[ai] are fulfilled.

The Coming of the Son of Man

25"Then there will be signs in the sun, moon, and stars;[aj] and there will be anguish on the earth among nations bewildered by the roaring sea and waves.[ak] 26People will faint from fear and expectation of the things that are coming on the world, because the celestial powers will be shaken.[al] 27Then they will see the ·Son of Man coming in a cloud[am] with power and great glory.[an] 28But when these things begin to take place, stand up and lift up your heads, because your ·redemption is near!"[ao]

The Parable of the Fig Tree

29Then He told them a parable: "Look at the fig tree, and all the trees. 30As soon as they put out leaves you can see for yourselves and recognize that summer is already near. 31In the same way, when you see these things happening, recognize[J] that the kingdom of God is near. 32·I assure you: This generation will certainly not pass away until all things take place.[ap] 33Heaven and earth will pass away,[aq] but My words will never pass away.[ar]

The Need for Watchfulness

34"Be on your guard,[as] so that your minds are not dulled[K] from carousing,[L] drunkenness,[at] and worries of life,[au] or that day will come on you unexpectedly[av] 35like a trap. For it will come on all who live on the face of the whole earth. 36But be alert at all times,[aw] praying that you may have strength[M] to

[a]**21:5-38** Mt 24:1-51; Mk 13:1-37 [b]**21:6** Lk 17:22 [c]Lk 19:44 [d]**21:7** Ac 1:6-7 [e]**21:8** Jr 29:8; Eph 5:6; 2Th 2:3 [f]Jr 14:14; 1Jn 2:18 [g]Jn 8:24 [h]Lk 17:23 [i]**21:10** 2Ch 15:6; Is 19:2 [j]**21:11** Is 29:6; Zch 14:5; Rv 6:12 [k]Rv 6:8 [l]Lk 11:16; 12:33 [m]**21:12-17** Mt 10:19-22; Mk 13:11-13 [n]**21:12** Ps 119:84 [o]Ac 22:19; 26:11 [p]Ac 4:3; 5:18; 8:3; 12:4; 16:23 [q]Ac 17:6; 18:12; 24:1,27; 25:6; 27:24; 2Co 11:23 [r]**21:13** Php 1:12-19 [s]**21:14** Lk 12:11 [t]**21:15** Ex 4:12 [u]Ac 6:10 [v]Ac 4:14 [w]**21:16** Mt 10:35; Lk 12:53 [x]**21:17** Lk 6:22; Jn 15:18-19 [y]**21:18** 1Sm 14:45; Mt 10:30; Lk 12:7; Jn 10:28 [z]**21:19** Mt 10:22; 24:13; Rm 2:7; 5:3; Heb 10:36; Jms 1:3 [aa]**21:20** Lk 19:43 [ab]Dn 9:27 [ac]**21:21** Lk 17:31 [ad]Mt 4:8 [ae]**21:22** Is 34:8; 63:4; Dn 9:24-27; Hs 9:7; Lk 18:7-8 [af]**21:23** Lk 23:29 [ag]**21:24** Heb 11:34 [ah]Ps 79:1; Is 63:18; Dn 8:13; Rv 11:2 [ai]Dn 12:7; Rm 11:25 [aj]**21:25** Is 13:10; 24:23; Ezk 32:7; Jl 2:10; 3:15; Ac 2:20; Rv 6:12-13 [ak]Ps 46:2-3; 65:7; Is 17:12; Jl 2:30-31 [al]**21:26** Is 34:4; Hg 2:6

[am]**21:27** Dn 7:13; Rv 1:7 [an]Mt 16:27; 26:64; Mk 9:1 [ao]**21:28** Lk 2:38; 24:21; Rm 8:23; 13:11 [ap]**21:32** Lk 9:27 [aq]**21:33** Ps 102:26; Is 51:6; 2Pt 3:10 [ar]Ps 119:89; Is 40:8; Mt 5:18; Lk 16:17; 1Pt 1:23,25 [as]**21:34** Lk 17:3 [at]Rm 13:13 [au]Mt 13:22; Mk 4:19; 1Th 5:6-7; 1Pt 4:7 [av]Lk 12:40; 1Th 5:3 [aw]**21:36** Mt 25:13; 26:41; Mk 14:34-38; Lk 12:37; Ac 20:31; 1Co 16:13; Eph 6:18; 1Th 5:6; 1Pt 5:8 [a]**21:36** Rm 2:3; 1Th 5:3; Heb 2:3

[A]**21:5** Gifts given to the temple in fulfillment of vows to God [B]**21:9** Or *insurrections*, or *revolutions* [C]**21:13** Lit *lead to a testimony for you* [D]**21:14** Lit *Therefore place* (determine) *in your hearts* [E]**21:15** Lit *you a mouth* [F]**21:19** Other mss read *endurance you will gain* [G]**21:21** Lit *inside her* [H]**21:23** Or *the earth* [I]**21:24** Or *nations* [J]**21:31** Or *you know* [K]**21:34** Lit *your hearts are not weighed down* [L]**21:34** Or *hangovers* [M]**21:36** Other mss read *you may be counted worthy*

escape[a] all these things that are going to take
place and to stand before the Son of Man."
37 During[b] the day, He was teaching in the
temple complex,[c] but in the evening He
would go out and spend the night on what
is called the ·Mount of Olives.[d] 38 Then all the
people would come early in the morning to
hear Him in the temple complex.[e]

The Plot to Kill Jesus

22 The[f] Festival of ·Unleavened Bread,[g]
which is called ·Passover,[h] was drawing near. 2 The ·chief priests and the ·scribes
were looking for a way to put Him to death,[i]
because they were afraid of the people.[j]
3 Then[k] Satan entered Judas,[l] called Iscariot,[m] who was numbered among the Twelve.
4 He went away and discussed with the chief
priests and temple police[n] how he could
hand Him over[o] to them. 5 They were glad and
agreed to give him silver.[A] 6 So he accepted the
offer and started looking for a good opportunity to betray Him to them when the crowd
was not present.

Preparation for Passover

7 Then[p] the Day of Unleavened Bread came
when the Passover lamb had to be sacrificed.[q]
8 Jesus sent Peter and John,[r] saying, "Go and
prepare the Passover meal for us, so we can
eat it."
9 "Where do You want us to prepare it?"
they asked Him.
10 "Listen," He said to them, "when you've entered the city, a man carrying a water jug will
meet you. Follow him into the house he enters.
11 Tell the owner of the house, 'The Teacher asks
you, "Where is the guest room where I can eat
the Passover with My disciples?"' 12 Then he
will show you a large, furnished room upstairs.[s] Make the preparations there."
13 So they went and found it just as He had
told them,[t] and they prepared the Passover.

The First Lord's Supper

14 When[u] the hour came, He reclined at the
table, and the apostles with Him. 15 Then He
said to them, "I have fervently desired to eat
this Passover with you before I suffer. 16 For I
tell you, I will not eat it again[B] until it is fulfilled in the kingdom of God."[v] 17 Then He
took a cup,[w] and after giving thanks,[x] He said,
"Take this and share it among yourselves.
18 For I tell you, from now on I will not drink
of the fruit of the vine until the kingdom of
God comes."
19 And He took bread, gave thanks, broke it,
gave it to them, and said, "This is My body,[y]
which is given for you. Do this in remembrance[z] of Me."
20 In the same way He also took the cup after supper and said, "This cup is the new covenant[aa] established by My blood;[ab] it is shed
for you.[C] 21 But[ac] look, the hand of the one betraying Me is at the table with Me![ad] 22 For the
·Son of Man will go away as it has been determined,[ae] but woe to that man by whom He is
betrayed!"
23 So they began to argue[af] among themselves which of them it could be who was going to do this thing.

The Dispute over Greatness

24 Then a dispute also arose among them
about who should be considered the greatest.[ag] 25 But He said to them,[ah] "The kings of
the Gentiles dominate them, and those who
have authority over them are called[D] 'Bene-
factors.'[E] 26 But it must not be like that among
you. On the contrary, whoever is greatest
among you must become like the youngest,[ai]
and whoever leads, like the one serving. 27 For
who is greater, the one at the table or the one
serving? Isn't it the one at the table? But I am
among you as the One who serves.[aj] 28 You are
the ones who stood by Me in My trials.[ak] 29 I
bestow on you a kingdom,[al] just as My Father
bestowed one on Me, 30 so that you may eat
and drink at My table in My kingdom.[am] And
you will sit on thrones judging the 12 tribes
of Israel.[an]

Peter's Denial Predicted

31 "Simon, Simon,[F] look out! Satan[ao] has
asked to sift you[G] like wheat.[ap] 32 But I have

[b]21:37-38 Jn 8:1-2 [c]21:37 Mt 26:55 [d]Mt 21:1; Lk 22:39; Jn 8:1; 18:2 [e]21:38 Jn 8:2 [f]22:1-2 Mt 26:1-5; Mk 14:1-2 [g]22:1 Ex 23:15 [h]Ex 12:11; Jn 6:4; 11:55; 13:1 [i]22:2 Mt 12:14; 21:46 [j]Lk 19:47-48; 20:19 [k]22:3-6 Mt 26:14-16; Mk 14:10-11 [l]22:3 Jn 13:2,27; Ac 5:3 [m]Lk 6:16 [n]22:4 Lk 22:52; Ac 4:1; 5:24,26; 16:20,22,35-36,38 [o]Mk 9:31 [p]22:7-13 Mt 26:17-19; Mk 14:12-16 [q]22:7 Ex 12:21; 1Co 5:7 [r]22:8 Ac 3:1; 8:14 [s]22:12 Ac 1:13 [t]22:13 Lk 19:32 [u]22:14 Mt 26:20; Mk 14:17 [v]22:16 Lk 14:15; Rv 19:9 [w]22:17-20 Mt 26:26-29; Mk 14:22-25; 1Co 11:23-25 [x]22:17 Mt 14:19; 15:36 [y]22:19 Jn 6:51-53 [z]Heb 10:3 [aa]22:20 Ex 24:8; Jr 31:31; Zch 9:11; 1Co 11:25; 2Co 3:6; Heb 7:22; 8:8,13; 9:15; 12:24; 13:20 [ab]1Co 10:16 [ac]22:21-23 Mt 26:21-24; Mk 14:18-21; Jn 13:18-26 [ad]22:21 Ps 41:9 [ae]22:22 Ac 2:23; 10:42; 17:26,31 [af]22:23 Mt 21:25; Mk 9:10; Lk 24:15 [ag]22:24 Mk 9:34; Lk 1:32 [ah]22:25-27 Mt 20:25-28; Mk 10:42-45 [ai]22:26 Lk 9:48; 1Pt 5:3 [aj]22:27 Mt 20:28; Jn 13:1-17 [ak]22:28 Heb 2:18; 4:15

[al]22:29 Mt 25:34; 2Tm 2:12 [am]22:30 Lk 22:16 [an]Mt 19:28 [ao]22:31 Mt 4:10 [ap]Am 9:9

[A]22:5 Or *money*; Mt 26:15 specifies 30 pieces of silver; Zch 11:12-13 [B]22:16 Other mss omit *again* [C]22:19-20 Other mss omit *which is given for you* (v. 19) through the end of v. 20 [D]22:25 Or *them call themselves* [E]22:25 Title of honor given to those who benefited the public good [F]22:31 Other mss read *Then the Lord said, "Simon, Simon* [G]22:31 In Gk, the word *you* is pl prayed[a] for you[A] that your faith may not fail. And you, when you have turned back, strengthen[b] your brothers."

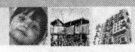

33"Lord,"[c] he told Him, "I'm ready to go with You both to prison and to death!"

34"I tell you, Peter," He said, "the rooster will not crow today until[B] you deny three times that you know Me!"

Be Ready for Trouble

35He also said to them, "When I sent you out[d] without money-bag, traveling bag, or sandals, did you lack anything?"

"Not a thing," they said.

36Then He said to them, "But now, whoever has a money-bag should take it, and also a traveling bag. And whoever doesn't have a sword should sell his robe and buy one. 37For I tell you, what is written must be fulfilled in Me: **And He was counted among the outlaws.**[C,e] Yes, what is written about Me is coming to its fulfillment."[f]

38"Lord," they said, "look, here are two swords."

"Enough of that!"[D] He told them.

The Prayer in the Garden

39He went out and made His way[g] as usual[h] to the ·Mount of Olives,[i] and the disciples followed Him. 40When He reached the place,[j] He told them, "Pray that you may not enter into temptation."[k] 41Then He withdrew from them about a stone's throw, knelt down, and began to pray,[l] 42"Father, if You are willing, take this cup[m] away from Me—nevertheless, not My will, but Yours, be done."

[43Then an angel from heaven[n] appeared to Him, strengthening Him. 44Being in anguish,[o] He prayed more fervently, and His sweat became like drops of blood falling to the ground.][E] 45When He got up from prayer and came to the disciples, He found them sleeping, exhausted from their grief.[F] 46"Why are you sleeping?" He asked them. "Get up and pray, so that you won't enter into temptation."

The Judas Kiss

47While[p] He was still speaking, suddenly a mob was there, and one of the Twelve named Judas was leading them. He came near Jesus to kiss Him, 48but Jesus said to him, "Judas, are you betraying the Son of Man with a kiss?"

49When those around Him saw what was going to happen, they asked, "Lord, should we strike with the sword?" 50Then one of them struck the high priest's ·slave and cut off his right ear.

51But Jesus responded, "No more of this!"[G] And touching his ear, He healed him. 52Then Jesus said to the chief priests, temple police, and the elders who had come for Him, "Have you come out with swords and clubs as if I were a criminal?[H] 53Every day while I was with you in the ·temple complex,[q] you never laid a hand on Me. But this is your hour[r]—and the dominion of darkness."[s]

Peter Denies His Lord

54They seized Him, led Him away, and brought Him into the high priest's house. Meanwhile Peter[t] was following at a distance. 55They[u] lit a fire in the middle of the

Text Message

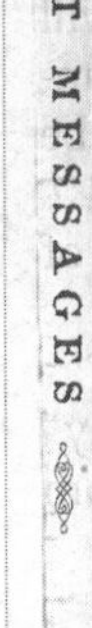

This scene is one of the great failures the Bible shares with us, for two reasons: (1) to avoid repeating it, and (2) to learn that such mistakes do not cancel us out from God's work. Why does failure happen? Peter allowed distance between himself and Jesus. Distance breeds bewilderment, doubt, and perhaps even resignation from one's commitment to follow. Peter recovered from this bleak episode to be a forceful evangelist of the risen Christ. Jesus welcomed him back, even singled him out for special reconciliation. Mistakes or retreats need not mean distance forever.

[a]**22:32** Jn 17:9-15; Rm 8:34 [b]Jn 21:15-17; 1Co 1:9; Php 1:6; 1Th 5:24; 2Tm 2:13 [c]**22:33-34** Mt 26:33-35; Mk 14:29-31; Jn 13:37-38 [d]**22:35** Mt 10:9-10; Mk 6:8; Lk 9:3; 10:4 [e]**22:37** Is 53:12 [f]Jn 17:4; 19:30 [g]**22:39** Mt 26:30; Mk 14:26; Lk 4:30; Jn 18:1 [h]Lk 21:37 [i]Mt 21:1 [j]**22:40-46** Mt 26:36-46; Mk 14:32-42 [k]**22:40** Mt 6:13; Lk 4:13; 11:4 [l]**22:41** Lk 18:11 [m]**22:42** Jn 18:11 [n]**22:43** Mt 4:11; Heb 1:14 [o]**22:44** Heb 5:7 [p]**22:47-53** Mt 26:47-56; Mk 14:43-50; Jn 18:3-12 [q]**22:53** Lk 2:46; Jn 18:20 [r]Jn 12:27; 16:4 [s]Ac 26:18; Eph 6:12; Col 1:13 [t]**22:54** Mt 26:58; Mk 14:54; Jn 18:15 [u]**22:55-62** Mt 26:69-75; Mk 14:66-72; Jn 18:16-18,25-27

A**22:32** In Gk, the word you is sg B**22:34** Other mss read *before* C**22:37** Is 53:12 D**22:38** Or *It is enough!* E**22:43-44** Other mss omit bracketed text F**22:45** Lit *sleeping from grief* G**22:51** Lit *Permit as far as this* H**22:52** Lit *as against a criminal*

courtyard[a] and sat down together, and Peter
sat among them. 56 When a servant saw him
sitting in the firelight, and looked closely at
him, she said, "This man was with Him too."
57 But he denied it: "Woman, I don't know
Him!"
58 After a little while, someone else saw him
and said, "You're one of them too!"
"Man, I am not!" Peter said.
59 About an hour later, another kept insisting, "This man was certainly with Him, since
he's also a Galilean."
60 But Peter said, "Man, I don't know what
you're talking about!" Immediately, while he
was still speaking, a rooster crowed. 61 Then
the Lord turned and looked at Peter.[b] So Peter remembered the word of the Lord, how
He had said to him, "Before the rooster crows
today, you will deny Me three times."[c] 62 And
he went outside and wept bitterly.

Jesus Mocked and Beaten

63 The men who were holding Jesus started
mocking and beating Him.[d] 64 After blindfold-
ing Him, they kept[A] asking, "Prophesy! Who
hit You?" 65 And they were saying many other
blasphemous[e] things against Him.

Jesus Faces the Sanhedrin

66 When daylight came,[f] the elders[B] of the
people, both the chief priests and the scribes,[g]
convened and brought Him before their ·San-
hedrin.[h] 67 They said,[i] "If You are the ·Messiah,
tell us."
But He said to them, "If I do tell you, you will
not believe. 68 And if I ask you, you will not answer. 69 But from now on, the Son of Man will be
seated at the right hand of the Power of God."[j]
70 They all asked, "Are You, then, the Son of
God?"[k]
And He said to them, "You say that I am."[l]
71 "Why do we need any more testimony,"
they said, "since we've heard it ourselves from
His mouth?"

Jesus Faces Pilate

23 Then[m] their whole assembly rose up
and brought Him before ·Pilate. 2 They
began to accuse Him, saying, "We found this

[a] **22:55** Mt 26:3
[b] **22:61** Mk 10:21
[c] Lk 22:31-34; Ac 3:13-14
[d] **22:63-65** Mt 26:67-68; Mk 14:65; Jn 18:22-23
[e] **22:65** Mk 3:29
[f] **22:66** Mt 27:1; Mk 15:1; Jn 18:28
[g] Lk 9:22; 20:1
[h] Mk 13:9
[i] **22:67-71** Mt 26:63-66; Mk 14:61-64; Jn 18:19-21
[j] **22:69** Ps 110:1; Mk 16:19; Ac 7:56; Heb 1:3
[k] **22:70** Mt 4:3; Lk 1:32,35
[l] Mt 26:64; 27:11; Lk 23:3
[m] **23:1-5** Mt 27:1,11-14; Mk 15:1-5; Jn 18:28-38
[n] **23:2** Lk 20:22-25
[o] **23:3** Mt 27:11; Mk 15:2
[p] Mt 2:2; Lk 23:37-38; Jn 18:39; 19:3
[q] **23:4** Mt 27:24; Lk 23:14,22; Jn 19:4,6; 1Pt 2:22
[r] **23:5** Ac 17:5-8,13
[s] Mt 4:12,23; Lk 4:14; Jn 1:43; 2:11
[t] **23:6** 1Tm 6:13
[u] **23:7** Lk 3:1; 9:7-9; 13:31
[v] **23:9** Is 53:7; Mt 27:12,14; Mk 15:4-5; Jn 19:9
[w] **23:11** Is 53:3; Mk 9:12; Lk 18:32; Ac 4:11
[x] Mt 27:28; Mk 15:17
[y] **23:12** Ps 2:2; Ac 4:27
[z] **23:13** Lk 23:35; 24:20; Jn 7:26,48; 12:42
[aa] **23:14** Lk 23:2
[ab] Lk 23:4
[ac] **23:16** Jn 19:1; Ac 5:40
[ad] **23:17** Mt 27:15; Mk 15:6; Jn 18:39
[ae] **23:18-23** Mt 27:15-23; Mk 15:6-14; Jn 18:40
[af] **23:18** Ac 21:36; 22:22

man subverting our nation, opposing payment of taxes[n] to Caesar, and saying that He
Himself is the ·Messiah, a King."
3 So Pilate asked Him,[o] "Are You the King of
the Jews?"[p]
He answered him, "You have said it."[C]
4 Pilate then told the ·chief priests and the
crowds, "I find no grounds[q] for charging this
man."
5 But they kept insisting, "He stirs up the
people,[r] teaching throughout all Judea, from
Galilee[s] where He started even to here."

Jesus Faces Herod Antipas

6 When Pilate[t] heard this,[D] he asked if the
man was a Galilean. 7 Finding that He was
under ·Herod's jurisdiction, he sent Him to
Herod,[u] who was also in Jerusalem during
those days. 8 Herod was very glad to see Jesus;
for a long time he had wanted to see Him because he had heard about Him and was hoping to see some miracle[E] performed by Him.
9 So he kept asking Him questions, but Jesus
did not answer him.[v] 10 The chief priests and
the ·scribes stood by, vehemently accusing Him. 11 Then Herod, with his soldiers,
treated Him with contempt, mocked[w] Him,
dressed Him in a brilliant robe,[x] and sent
Him back to Pilate. 12 That very day Herod
and Pilate became friends.[F,y] Previously, they
had been hostile toward each other.

Jesus or Barabbas

13 Pilate called together the chief priests,
the leaders, and the people,[z] 14 and said to
them, "You have brought me this man as one
who subverts the people.[aa] But in fact, after examining Him in your presence, I have
found no grounds[ab] to charge this man with
those things you accuse Him of. 15 Neither
has Herod, because he sent Him back to us.
Clearly, He has done nothing to deserve death.
16 Therefore, I will have Him whipped[G,ac] and
then release Him." [17 For according to the festival he had to release someone to them.][H,ad]
18 Then[ae] they all cried out together, "Take
this man away![af] Release Barabbas to us!"
19 (He had been thrown into prison for a re-

[A] **22:64** Other mss add *striking Him on the face and* [B] **22:66** Or *council of elders* [C] **23:3** Or *That is true*; an affirmative oath [D] **23:6** Other mss read *heard "Galilee"* [E] **23:8** Or *sign* [F] **23:12** Lit *friends with one another* [G] **23:16** Gk *paideuo*; to discipline or "teach a lesson"; 1Kg 12:11,14 LXX; 2Ch 10:11,14; perhaps a way of referring to the Roman scourging; Lat *flagellatio* [H] **23:17** Other mss omit bracketed text

bellion that had taken place in the city, and
for murder.)
20 Pilate, wanting to release Jesus,[a] addressed them again, 21 but they kept shouting,
"Crucify! Crucify Him!"
22 A third time he said to them, "Why? What
has this man done wrong?[b] I have found in
Him no grounds[c] for the death penalty.
Therefore, I will have Him whipped and then
release Him."
23 But they kept up the pressure, demanding with loud voices that He be crucified. And
their voices[A] won out. 24 So[d] Pilate decided to
grant their demand[e] 25 and released the one
they were asking for, who had been thrown
into prison for rebellion and murder. But he
handed Jesus over to their will.[f]

The Way to the Cross

26 As[g] they led Him away, they seized Simon,
a Cyrenian,[h] who was coming in from the
country, and laid the cross[i] on him to carry
behind Jesus. 27 A large crowd of people followed Him, including women who were
mourning and lamenting Him.[j] 28 But turning
to them, Jesus said, "Daughters of Jerusalem,[k]
do not weep for Me, but weep for yourselves
and your children. 29 Look, the days are coming[l] when they will say, 'The women without
children, the wombs that never bore and the
breasts that never nursed, are fortunate!'[m]
30 Then they will begin **to say to the mountains, 'Fall on us!' and to the hills, 'Cover
us!'**[B,n] 31 For if they do these things when the
wood is green, what will happen when it is
dry?"[o]

Crucified between Two Criminals

32 Two others—criminals[p]—were also led
away to be executed with Him. 33 When[q] they
arrived at the place called The Skull, they crucified Him there, along with the criminals,
one on the right and one on the left. [34 Then
Jesus said, "Father,[r] forgive[s] them, because
they do not know what they are doing."[t]][C]
And they divided His clothes and cast lots.[u]
35 The[v] people stood watching, and even
the leaders kept scoffing:[w] "He saved others;
let Him save Himself if this is God's Messiah,
the Chosen One!"[x] 36 The soldiers also mocked
Him. They came offering Him sour wine[y]
37 and said, "If You are the King of the Jews,[z]
save Yourself!"
38 An inscription was above Him:[D]

THIS IS THE KING OF THE JEWS.

39 Then[aa] one of the criminals hanging there
began to yell insults at[E] Him: "Aren't You the
Messiah? Save Yourself and us!"
40 But the other answered, rebuking him:
"Don't you even fear God,[ab] since you are undergoing the same punishment? 41 We are
punished justly, because we're getting back

[a] **23:20** Ac 3:13-14
[b] **23:22** Jn 8:46
[c] Lk 23:4
[d] **23:24-25** Mt 27:24-26; Mk 15:15; Jn 19:16
[e] **23:24** Php 4:6
[f] **23:25** Lk 24:20; Ac 4:24-28
[g] **23:26-32** Mt 27:31-32; Mk 15:20-21; Jn 19:17
[h] **23:26** Rm 16:3
[i] Lk 9:23; 14:27
[j] **23:27** Lk 8:52; Ac 8:2; Rv 1:7; 18:9
[k] **23:28** Sg 1:5; 2:7
[l] **23:29** Lk 17:22
[m] Mt 24:19; Mk 13:17; Lk 11:27; 21:23
[n] **23:30** Hs 10:8
[o] **23:31** Ezk 20:47; Lk 19:41
[p] **23:32** Is 53:12; Mt 27:38; Mk 15:27; Lk 22:37; Jn 19:18
[q] **23:33-34** Mt 27:33-38; Mk 15:22-27; Jn 19:17-24
[r] **23:34** Mt 5:16; 6:1; 11:27; Jn 8:42
[s] Mt 11:25; Lk 6:29,35; 22:42
[t] Ac 3:17; 1Co 2:6-8
[u] Ps 22:18
[v] **23:35-38** Mt 27:43,48; Mk 15:26,29-32; Jn 19:19,29
[w] **23:35** Ps 22:7,17; Lk 16:14; 23:13
[x] Is 42:1; Mt 1:17; 12:18; Lk 9:20,35; 1Pt 2:4
[y] **23:36** Ps 69:21
[z] **23:37** Lk 23:3
[aa] **23:39-43** Mt 27:44; Mk 15:32
[ab] **23:40** Ps 147:11; Pr 1:7; Ac 10:2; Rv 14:7

The Beauty of the Cross

GOD WHO SENDS

We may easily see the resurrection as a thing of beauty in the sense of the value and inspiration it brought to the discouraged followers of Christ. But how do we see the cross, the first principle and reality of the gospel, as a thing of beauty, that is, in its original historical reality as a cruel method of execution? The answer, of course, is in the fact that this ugly act of suffering became beautiful because it was vicarious (on behalf of others) and salvific (for a redemptive purpose). The ornamental beauty of a jeweled cross in a comfortable Christendom is not the biblical meaning of the beauty of the cross. The New Testament meaning of beauty is the beauty of missional purpose—the vicarious and redemptive suffering of Jesus which was the climactic act of the mission of God through his Son.

(DUBOSE, 95)

[A] **23:23** Other mss add *and those of the chief priests* [B] **23:30** Hs 10:8
[C] **23:34** Other mss omit bracketed text [D] **23:38** Other mss add *written in Greek, Latin, and Hebrew letters* [E] **23:39** Or *began to blaspheme*

what we deserve for the things we did, but this man has done nothing wrong."[a] 42 Then he said, "Jesus, remember me[A,b] when You come into Your kingdom!"[c]

43 And He said to him, "•I assure you: Today you will be with Me in paradise."[d]

The Death of Jesus

44 It[e] was now about noon,[B] and darkness came over the whole land[C] until three,[D] 45 because the sun's light failed.[E] The curtain[f] of the sanctuary was split down the middle. 46 And Jesus called out with a loud voice, "Father, **into Your hands I entrust My spirit.**"[F,g] Saying this, He breathed His last.

47 When the •centurion saw what happened, he began to glorify[h] God, saying, "This man really was righteous!" 48 All the crowds that had gathered for this spectacle, when they saw what had taken place, went home, striking their chests.[G,i] 49 But[j] all who knew Him, including the women who had followed Him from Galilee, stood at a distance,[k] watching these things.

The Burial of Jesus

50 There[l] was a good and righteous man named Joseph, a member of the •Sanhedrin, 51 who had not agreed with their plan[m] and action. He was from Arimathea, a Judean town, and was looking forward to the kingdom of God.[n] 52 He approached Pilate and asked for Jesus' body. 53 Taking it down, he wrapped it in fine linen and placed it in a tomb cut into the rock, where no one had ever been placed.[H,o] 54 It was preparation day, and the Sabbath was about to begin.[I] 55 The women[p] who had come with Him from Galilee followed along and observed the tomb and how His body was placed. 56 Then they returned and prepared spices and perfumes.[q] And they rested on the Sabbath according to the commandment.[r]

Resurrection Morning

24 On[s] the first day of the week,[t] very early in the morning, they[J] came to the tomb, bringing the spices they had prepared. 2 They found the stone rolled away from the tomb. 3 They went in but did not find the body[u] of the Lord Jesus.[v] 4 While they were perplexed about this, suddenly two men stood by them in dazzling[w] clothes. 5 So the women were terrified and bowed down to the ground.[K]

"Why are you looking for the living among the dead?" asked the men. 6 "He is not here, but He has been resurrected![x] Remember how He spoke to you when He was still in Galilee,[y] 7 saying, 'The •Son of Man must be betrayed[z] into the hands of sinful men, be crucified, and rise[aa] on the third day'?" 8 And they remembered His words.

9 Returning from the tomb, they reported all these things to the Eleven[ab] and to all the rest. 10 •Mary Magdalene, Joanna, Mary the mother of James,[ac] and the other women with them were telling the apostles[ad] these things. 11 But these words seemed like nonsense to them, and they did not believe[ae] the women. 12 Peter,[af] however, got up and ran to the tomb. When he stooped to look in, he saw only the linen cloths.[L,ag] So he went home, amazed[ah] at what had happened.

The Emmaus Disciples

13 Now[ai] that same day two of them were on their way to a village called[M] Emmaus, which was about seven miles[N,aj] from Jerusalem.[ak] 14 Together they were discussing everything that had taken place. 15 And while they were discussing and arguing, Jesus Himself came near and began to walk along with them. 16 But they[O] were prevented from recognizing Him.[al] 17 Then He asked them, "What is this dispute that you're having[P] with each other as you are walking?" And they stopped walking and looked discouraged.

18 The one named Cleopas answered Him, "Are You the only visitor in Jerusalem who doesn't know the things that happened there in these days?"[am]

19 "What things?" He asked them.

So they said to Him, "The things concerning

[a]23:41 Lk 23:4 [b]23:42 Jdg 16:28; 1Sm 25:31; Neh 5:19; Jb 14:13; Ps 106:4 [c]Mk 8:38; Ac 20:25 [d]23:43 2Co 12:4; Rv 2:7 [e]23:44-49 Mt 27:45-56; Mk 15:33-41 [f]23:45 Ex 26:31-33; Heb 6:19 [g]23:46 Ps 31:5; Is 53:12; Jn 19:30; 1Co 15:55; 1Pt 4:19 [h]23:47 Lk 13:13 [i]23:48 Lk 18:13 [j]23:49 Mt 27:55-56; Mk 15:40-41; Jn 19:25 [k]Ps 38:11; 88:8 [l]23:50-56 Mt 27:57-61; Mk 15:42-47; Jn 19:38-42 [m]23:51 Ac 2:23 [n]Lk 2:25,38 [o]23:53 Is 53:9; Mk 11:2 [p]23:55 Lk 1:42 [q]23:56 Mk 16:1; Lk 24:1 [r]Ex 20:10; Dt 5:14 [s]24:1-12 Mt 28:1-10; Mk 16:1-11; Jn 20:1-18 [t]24:1 Ac 20:7; 1Co 16:2 [u]24:3 Lk 12:4 [v]Lk 7:13; Ac 1:21 [w]24:4 Lk 2:9; 17:24; Ac 12:7 [x]24:6 Mt 26:32; Mk 5:41; 9:27; Jn 2:19; 1Co 15:4 [y]Mt 17:22-23; Mk 9:30-31; Lk 9:22,44 [z]24:7 Lk 9:22,31,44; 18:32-33; 23:21 [aa]Mt 17:9,23; Mk 8:31; 9:31; 10:34; Lk 18:33; 24:46 [ab]24:9 Ac 1:15-26; 2:14 [ac]24:10 Mk 15:40; 16:1; Lk 8:2-3 [ad]Lk 6:13 [ae]24:11 Mt 28:17; Lk 24:41; Jn 20:25,27 [af]24:12 Lk 6:14; Ac 10:32 [ag]Lk 23:53 [ah]Lk 1:21,63; 2:18,33; 4:22; Ac 2:7; 3:12 [ai]24:13 Mk 16:12-13 [aj]Rv 21:16 [ak]Mt 23:37; Ac 8:1 [al]24:16 Lk 9:45; 18:34; Jn 20:14-15; 21:4 [am]24:18 Ac 26:26

A23:42 Other mss add *Lord* B23:44 Lit *about the sixth hour* C23:44 Or *whole earth* D23:44 Lit *the ninth hour* E23:45 Other mss read *three, and the sun was darkened* F23:46 Ps 31:5 G23:48 = mourning H23:53 Or *interred,* or *laid* I23:54 Lit *was dawning*; not in the morning but at sundown Friday J24:1 Other mss add *and other women with them* K24:5 Lit *and inclined their faces to the ground* L24:12 Other mss add *lying there* M24:13 Lit *village, which name is* N24:13 Lit *about 60 stadia*; 1 *stadion* = 600 feet O24:16 Lit *their eyes* P24:17 Lit *What are these words that you are exchanging*

Jesus the ·Nazarene,[a] who was a Prophet[b] powerful in action and speech[c] before God and all
the people,[d] 20 and how our ·chief priests and
leaders[e] handed Him over to be sentenced to
death,[f] and they crucified Him.[g] 21 But we were
hoping that He was the One who was about to
·redeem[h] Israel. Besides all this, it's the third
day[i] since these things happened. 22 Moreover,
some women from our group astounded us.
They arrived early at the tomb, 23 and when
they didn't find His body, they came and reported that they had seen a vision of angels
who said He was alive. 24 Some of those who
were with us went to the tomb and found it
just as the women had said, but they didn't see
Him."[j]

25 He said to them, "How unwise and slow
you are to believe in your hearts all that the
prophets have spoken![k] 26 Didn't the ·Messiah
have to suffer[l] these things and enter into His
glory?"[m] 27 Then beginning with Moses[n] and
all the Prophets,[o] He interpreted for them the
things concerning Himself in all the Scriptures.[p]

28 They came near the village where they
were going, and He gave the impression that
He was going farther.[q] 29 But they urged Him:
"Stay with us, because it's almost evening, and
now the day is almost over." So He went in to
stay with them.

30 It was as He reclined at the table with
them that He took the bread, blessed and
broke[r] it, and gave it to them. 31 Then their eyes
were opened,[s] and they recognized Him, but
He disappeared from their sight.[t] 32 So they
said to each other, "Weren't our hearts ablaze
within us while He was talking with us on the
road and explaining the Scriptures[u] to us?"
33 That very hour they got up and returned to
Jerusalem. They found the Eleven[v] and those
with them gathered together, 34 who said,[A]
"The Lord has certainly been raised, and has
appeared to Simon!"[w] 35 Then they began to
describe what had happened on the road
and how He was made known to them in the
breaking of the bread.[x]

The Reality of the Risen Jesus

36 And[y] as they were saying these things,
He Himself stood among them. He said to
them, "Peace[z] to you!" 37 But they were startled
and terrified[aa] and thought they were seeing a ghost.[ab] 38 "Why are you troubled?"[ac] He
asked them. "And why do doubts arise in your
hearts? 39 Look at My hands and My feet, that
it is I Myself![ad] Touch Me and see,[ae] because a
ghost does not have flesh and bones as you can
see I have." 40 Having said this, He showed them
His hands and feet. 41 But while they still were
amazed and unbelieving because of their joy,
He asked them, "Do you have anything here to
eat?" 42 So they gave Him a piece of a broiled
fish,[B] 43 and He took it and ate in their presence.

44 Then He told them, "These are My words[af]
that I spoke to you while I was still with
you—that everything written about Me in

Sent to Be a Witness

GOD WHO SENDS

Drawing upon the long tradition of this concept in the Hebrew Scriptures, the New Testament develops a major principle of witness, especially from a salvific and evangelistic perspective. Witness has the force both of "being" and of "bearing" in the New Testament Scriptures. John 1:6–7 uses both the noun and verb to describe the missional witness of John the Baptist: "There was a man sent from God, whose name was John. He came for testimony, to bear witness to the light."

Jesus strongly affirmed the witness of his mission from the Father (John 5:35–37; etc.); and after the resurrection, he affirmed his followers as witness to his crucifixion and resurrection (Luke 24:46–49). The record of John 20:21 affirms the sending, and the record of Acts 1:8 affirms the place of the witness in the missional vocation.

(DuBose, 113-114)

[a] **24:19** Lk 4:34; 18:37; Ac 2:22
[b] Dt 18:15; Lk 4:24
[c] Lk 4:14; Ac 1:1; 2:22
[d] Lk 18:43
[e] **24:20** Lk 23:13
[f] Lk 9:44; 18:32; Ac 3:13; 13:27-28
[g] Lk 23:21,25; Ac 5:30
[h] **24:21** Lk 22:20; Ac 1:6
[i] Lk 9:22; 13:32; 18:33
[j] **24:24** Lk 24:12; Jn 20:2-10
[k] **24:25** Lk 16:31; 18:31; Ac 26:27; 2Pt 1:21
[l] **24:26** Lk 24:44-48; 1Co 15:3-5
[m] Lk 9:26,32; 21:27; 22:69; Ac 2:33; 7:55; 22:11
[n] **24:27** Gn 3:15; 12:3; 22:18; Nm 21:9; 24:17
[o] 2Sm 7:12-16; Is 7:14; 9:6; 52:13–53:12; Jr 23:5-6; Dn 7:13-14; Mc 5:2; Zch 9:9; 12:10
[p] Lk 16:16
[q] **24:28** Mk 6:48
[r] **24:30** Lk 9:16; 22:19
[s] **24:31** 2Kg 6:17; Lk 24:16
[t] Jn 20:19,26
[u] **24:32** Ac 17:3; 1Co 15:3-8
[v] **24:33** Lk 24:9
[w] **24:34** Lk 22:32; 1Co 15:4-5
[x] **24:35** Ac 2:42
[y] **24:36-44** Jn 20:19-20
[z] **24:36** Lk 2:14; 7:50; 8:48; 10:5; 19:38; Ac 10:36
[aa] **24:37** Lk 24:5; Ac 10:4; 24:25
[ab] Mt 14:26
[ac] **24:38** Jn 14:1,27
[ad] **24:39** Jn 20:25,27
[ae] Mt 28:9; Ac 2:31; 17:18,31-32; 23:6-10; 24:15,21
[af] **24:44** Lk 9:22,44; 17:25; 18:31-33; 22:37

[A] **24:34** Gk is specific that this refers to the Eleven and those with them. [B] **24:42** Other mss add *and some honeycomb* the Law of Moses, the Prophets,[a] and the Psalms[b] must be fulfilled." 45 Then He opened their minds[c] to understand[d] the Scriptures. 46 He also said to them, "This is what is written:[A] The Messiah would suffer and rise from the dead the third day,[e] 47 and repentance for[B] forgiveness of sins[f] would be proclaimed in His name to all the nations,[g] beginning at Jerusalem.[h] 48 You are witnesses[i] of these things. 49 And look, I am sending you[C] what My Father promised.[j] As for you, stay in the city[D] until you are empowered[E,k] from on high."

[a]**24:44** Ac 13:15; 28:23 [b]Ps 2:6-9; 16:10; 22:1-18; 34:20; 41:9; 69:1-9,20-21,26; 110:1-7; 118:22-26 [c]**24:45** Lk 24:27,31 [d]Lk 9:45; 18:34 [e]**24:46** Ps 16:10; Lk 9:22,44; 17:25; 18:32; Ac 8:26-40; 1Co 15:3-4 [f]**24:47** Hs 14:2; Lk 3:3; Ac 2:38; 5:31; 8:22 [g]Gn 12:3;

The Ascension of Jesus

50 Then He led them out as far as Bethany,[l] and lifting up His hands[m] He blessed them. 51 And while He was blessing them, He left them and was carried up into heaven.[n] 52 After worshiping Him,[o] they returned to Jerusalem with great joy.[p] 53 And they were continually in the •temple complex praising God.[F,q]

Ps 22:27; Is 2:2; 49:6; Hs 2:23; Mal 1:11; Mt 28:19-20; Mk 16:15 [h]**24:47-49** Ac 1:4-8 [i]**24:48** Ac 4:20,33 [j]**24:49** Is 32:15; Jl 2:28-32; Jn 14:26; Ac 2:16-21; Eph 1:13 [k]Ac 4:33; Rm 15:13 [l]**24:50** Lk 19:29; Ac 1:12 [m]Lv 9:22; 1Tm 2:8 [n]**24:51** Mk 16:19; Jn 20:17; Ac 1:9-11 [o]**24:52** Mt 28:17 [p]Lk 2:10 [q]**24:53** Ac 2:46; 3:1; 5:42

[A]**24:46** Other mss add *and thus it was necessary that* [B]**24:47** Other mss read *repentance and* [C]**24:49** Lit *upon you* [D]**24:49** Other mss add *of Jerusalem* [E]**24:49** Lit *clothed with power* [F]**24:53** Other mss read *praising and blessing God. Amen.*

Evangelism

Ed Stetzer

Evangelism is the act of witnessing to the good news that the mission of God has been accomplished in the person and work of Jesus Christ. All of God's promises in Scripture are fulfilled in the perfect life, sacrificial death, and victorious resurrection of Jesus (cf. 2Co 1:20). The Greek noun for evangelism (*euangelion*) is typically translated in the New Testament as "gospel," referring to the content of the message, but it may also be translated as a noun that implies action, like "evangelism."

Evangelism then is the act of *gospelizing*—proclaiming the message of the life and work of Jesus to the world. God has a content-shaped mission for us. The content is to share that God's mission has been accomplished in Jesus.

God's mission began at creation, and the plan for humanity was to move out from Eden to inhabit the world in order to reflect God's goodness and glory over the whole earth (Gn 1:28). This mission was challenged by sin, but not defeated.

God saves His people from the condemnation of sin and its corruption by the sacrificial death of Jesus and His victorious resurrection. Jesus then sends His followers out to reclaim all nations for God's glory (Mt 28:18).

Luke tells of Jesus walking to Emmaus with two disciples; this story captures six biblical aspects of the evangelistic mission of Jesus' disciples.

Jesus sends those who know Him as Savior (Lk 24:46,52). Jesus calls and sends those who have had a life-transforming encounter with Him. He opens the minds of the disciples, so that they would know Him. They are convinced that He is the Son of God and that He fulfills the Scriptures.

Jesus sends His disciples with a story about how He fulfills Scripture. Jesus connects the dots of the biblical story from Moses, the Prophets to the Psalms, showing that He had fulfilled Scripture (v. 46).

Jesus sends with a message that happened in history, but changes the present and future (v. 46). Days after His trial and crucifixion, Jesus appears in flesh, showing His hands and feet (vv. 39). What the cross accomplished in the past is applied in the present. Their minds are opened because they understand the meaning of the cross and resurrection. The disciples return to Jerusalem worshipping Jesus, filled with joy, and ready to be sent.

Jesus sends His disciples out with a message to be proclaimed (v. 47). The message is that repentance and forgiveness are offered in Jesus' name.

Jesus sends them on a mission for the nations—beginning in Jerusalem and going to the nations (v. 47).

Jesus sends with the power required for the mission. He says, "I am sending you what My Father promised." He describes the arrival of this promise as being "empowered from on high" (v. 49). The power is indispensible. Those sent on the mission have no control over what happens when they share gospel. Without the power of the Spirit, the ministry of evangelism is not sufficient to provoke faith in the hearer.

Evangelism is God's mission. He sends us to proclaim His message about what He has done. Evangelism is the story of God's work of salvation in action—being told by those whom God sends.

AUTHOR: John, the disciple

DATE: Written around A.D. 90, the Gospel of John covers the ministry of John the Baptist through the birth, ministry, crucifixion, and resurrection of Jesus

Jesus is the mission of God, and in this Gospel, He is the message (Word) of God. We see Him as the creator-redeemer who shows God's power at weddings and at funerals, who eats merrily with many companions, and who weeps over the death of a treasured friend. The Gospel of John portrays God's mission as uniquely embodied in Jesus Christ, who was sent so that "by believing you may have life in His name" (20:31).

While the first three Gospels are called the Synoptic Gospels in that they share key phrases and sequences of events, John's Gospel is different. John makes the mission of God clear at this important point: everyone should believe in and obey Jesus Christ, God

JOHN

incarnate. Jesus' teaching, His prayers, His miracles are for all people to behold, ponder, and then, recognizing He is the Messiah of God, to believe. Believing in Jesus is not just acknowledgment; it is also action. To believe is to follow Him and do God's will as Jesus reveals it. That is the mission of God. All the Old Testament promises and every appeal from God to "act justly, to love faithfulness, and to walk humbly with your God" (Mc 6:8) are fulfilled by becoming a disciple of Jesus Christ. He is the one God has sent, "the way, the truth, and the life" (Jn 14:6). Believe on Him, and have eternal life.

Not everyone in John believes. Oddly, some encounter Jesus and refuse, or go away (6:66). The great religious leader Nicodemus asks reasonable questions, but his position at the end of the intitial interview is indecision. The Samaritan woman at the well, however, is led to belief step by step. Like the man born blind in chapter 9, her initial skepticism becomes public faith as Jesus reveals her own life to her. People today who ask good questions should never be hustled away from church as if their inquiries are rude or inappropriate. Jesus persisted in love and conversation, and people responded in faith. That miracle of conversion still happens every day, many times worldwide, through the witness of Christians in nearly every language of the globe.

In John's Gospel, Jesus is the "light of the world" (8:12) and the "bread of life" (6:35)—powerful metaphors for the abundance to be found in a faithful relationship with Him. After Jesus' resurrection, He settles Thomas's doubt. Then He reinstates Peter, the one who denied Him, assuring Peter of his call. Jesus shuns questions about the future while urging that the way forward (in life and faith) is to follow Him.

This Word of God, Jesus, who prays so dearly (chapter 17) and transforms people so dramatically is the One who embodies God's mission, teaches God's mission, and accomplishes God's mission.

What does God want? For us to follow Jesus. And then, for all those who follow to join in the mission. The word "sent" is used consistently throughout this Gospel and finds one of its great uses in 20:21 where Jesus commissions His followers: "As the Father has sent Me, I also send you." Consider yourself commissioned.

Prologue

1 In the beginning[a] was the Word,[A,b]
and the Word was with God,
and the Word was God.[c]
2 He was with God in the beginning.[d]
3 All things were created[e] through Him,[f]
and apart from Him not one thing
was created
that has been created.
4 Life was in Him,[B,g]
and that life was the light[h] of men.
5 That light shines[i] in the darkness,
yet the darkness did not overcome[C] it.[j]

6 There was a man named John[k]
who was sent from God.
7 He came as a witness
to testify about the light,
so that all might believe through him.[D]
8 He was not the light,
but he came to testify[l] about the light.
9 The true light,[m] who gives light
to everyone,
was coming into the world.[E,n]

10 He was in the world,
and the world was created[o] through Him,
yet the ˚world did not recognize Him.
11 He came to His own,[F]
and His own people[F] did not receive Him.
12 But to all who did receive[p] Him,[q]
He gave them the right[r] to be[G]
children[s] of God,[t]
to those who believe[u] in His name,[v]

[a]**1:1** Gn 1:1; Col 1:18 [b]Jn 1:14; 1Jn 1:1; Rv 19:13 [c]Jn 20:28; Php 2:6 [d]**1:2** Jn 8:38; 17:5; Ac 26:4 [e]**1:3** Col 1:16; Heb 1:2 [f]Rm 11:36 [g]**1:4** 1Jn 2:5 [h]Ps 36:9; Jn 12:46 [i]**1:5** 1Jn 2:8 [j]Php 3:12 [k]**1:6** Mk 1:4 [l]**1:8** Jn 15:26 [m]**1:9** Jn 12:46 [n]Jn 18:37; 1Jn 2:8 [o]**1:10** Jn 1:3 [p]**1:12** 2Jn 10 [q]Jn 5:43 [r]Mk 1:22; Ac 9:14 [s]Lk 1:7 [t]Mt 5:9; Jn 11:52; Rm 8:16; 1Jn 3:1 [u]Jn 3:16 [v]Jn 10:25; 1Jn 3:23

God With Us

GOD'S HEART FOR THE WORLD

The Word became flesh and took up residence among us. We observed His glory, the glory as the One and Only Son from the Father, full of grace and truth. (John 1:14)

It can be difficult to get a clear picture of what God is like, especially with all the abstract terms we use to describe Him: infinite, invisible, impassible, omniscient, omnipresent, omnipotent, to name a few. But in Jesus, all that abstraction disappears. Suddenly God is here, walking around in the dust with sandals on His feet, eating meals and going to weddings. He wept, slept, and even got into arguments. He really is "God *with* us." When John says, "We observed His glory" he does not mean, "we squinted and scratched our heads and were able to finally get an idea of it." He means, "We walked down the street with God's glory. We talked with it. We were changed by it. We didn't just imagine it, we *saw* it."

But what did they see? What did God's glory look like? It looked like a baby, born in a manger. It looked like a man, with nothing particularly attractive about Him, wandering around Israel with a ragtag group of followers. It looked like poverty, rejection, humiliation, and finally death. It was not exactly what everyone expected.

It might not be what we expect either. But God has never been limited by what people "expect." His heart for the world is bigger than we can imagine—so big that He acted to deal with the sin problem we had created for ourselves. He acted because He loved. He acted by doing the unexpected, unimaginable, uncompromising act of sending His Son to die for us.

He continues to send His people to do the unexpected, the unimaginable, the uncompromising. He asks of His followers nothing more than He Himself did for us.

[A]**1:1** The *Word* (Gk *Logos*) is a title for Jesus as the communication and the revealer of God the Father; Jn 1:14,18; Rv 19:13. [B]**1:3-4** Other punctuation is possible:... *not one thing was created. What was created in Him was life* [C]**1:5** Or *grasp*, or *comprehend*, or *overtake*; Jn 12:35 [D]**1:7** Or *through it* (the light) [E]**1:9** Or *The true light who comes into the world gives light to everyone,* or *The true light enlightens everyone coming into the world.* [F]**1:11** The same Gk adjective is used twice in this verse: the first refers to all that Jesus owned as Creator (*to His own*); the second refers to the Jews (*His own people*). [G]**1:12** Or *become*

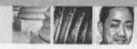

13 who were born,[a]
not of blood,[A]
or of the will[b] of the flesh,[c]
or of the will of man,[B]
but of God.[d]

[a]1:13 1Pt 1:3 [b]1Co 7:37; 16:12; Eph 2:3; 2Tm 2:26; 2Pt 1:21 [c]Php 3:3 [d]1Pt 1:3; 1Jn 2:29

14 The Word[e] became flesh[C,f]
and took up residence[D] among us.
We observed His glory,[g]

[e]1:14 Jn 1:1 [f]Php 2:7; 1Jn 4:2; 5:20 [g]Mk 10:37; Jn 17:24

Jesus in the Flesh

Hugh Halter

Imagine you live in a world where everyone holds some spiritual belief but no one knows exactly what God is like. Some would live a self-oriented existence believing the impersonal cosmos granted them justification to live any way they wanted. They would indulge every pleasure, use people for their own purposes, and freedom would be the highest value . . . even if it hurt people around them. On the other side of the fence would be people who thought they knew everything about truth and would turn their personal beliefs into religion and use it to control people, judge any and all imperfections, creating abusive social, spiritual, and religious tensions. In both cases, people are unable to find the real God.

Now, imagine you're God and your great desire is that the people you created can understand who you really are and what true life is. How would you help the disoriented find you? Could you just write a Bible and straighten everyone out? Could you create a website called "Absolute Truth For Everyone"? Could you mandate and create laws that made everyone behave the same? Would that do it?

God's approach was to leave heaven and come to earth as the first missionary. God knew He had to become perfect Grace and perfect Truth all in one person and rent an apartment in our neighborhood, become like us, live in our world. Then, maybe then, we could finally see His glory!

The incarnation means that God took on flesh. Then the concepts, opinions, and beliefs about divinity could be easily answered simply by seeing Him, talking to Him, feeling His hand upon our shoulders and hearing the inflection in His voice.

It's one thing to GO on mission, it's another thing to know "how to go, who to go to, and what we should do as we go." That's the power of Jesus taking on flesh. He showed us the how, the who, and the what.

How can we know the balance of living amongst the spiritually disoriented, the sinners, the confused? All we have to do is watch Jesus. He lived His first 30 years without starting His public ministry. This teaches us patience and how missionaries must put in their time. Listening to Him challenge the religious while also advocating, eating dinner with, and loving sinners teaches us who we should spend our time with. Observing His gentle posture and kind words models for us how a missionary wins the heart of a person; healing the real needs of people, calling us past our "church-oriented" consumer Christianity. Watching Him die shows us how to give our lives away without expecting success in return.

Our world needs to find the real God, both His Grace and His Truth. God's hope for the world now rests in the hands of a few would-be missionaries. Those who are willing to "Go" on mission in a way patterned after the incarnational way He came to us. For He said, "As the Father has sent Me, I also send you."

[A]1:13 Lit *bloods*; the pl form of *blood* occurs only here in the NT. It may refer either to lineal descent (that is, blood from one's father and mother) or to the OT sacrificial system (that is, the various blood sacrifices). Neither is the basis for birth into the family of God. [B]1:13 Or *not of human lineage, or of human capacity, or of human volition* [C]1:14 The eternally existent Word (vv. 1-2) took on full humanity but without sin; Heb 4:15. [D]1:14 Or *and dwelt in a tent*; lit *and tabernacled*; this word occurs only here in John. A related word, referring to the Festival of Tabernacles, occurs only in 7:2; Ex 40:34-38.

the glory as the •One and Only[a] Son[A]
from the Father,
full of grace and truth.
15 (John testified concerning Him
and exclaimed,
"This was the One of whom I said,
'The One coming after me[b]
has surpassed me,[c]
because He existed before me.'")[d]
16 Indeed, we have all received grace[e]
after grace
from His fullness,
17 for the law was given through Moses,[f]
grace and truth[g] came
through Jesus Christ.
18 No one has ever seen God.[B]
The One and Only[h] Son[C] —
the One who is at the Father's[i] side[D] —
He has revealed Him.[j]

John the Baptist's Testimony

19 This is John's testimony when the •Jews
from Jerusalem[k] sent priests[l] and Levites[m] to
ask him, "Who are you?"
20 He did not refuse to answer, but he declared: "I am not the •Messiah."[n]
21 "What then?" they asked him. "Are you
Elijah?"[o]
"I am not," he said.
"Are you the Prophet?"[E,p]
"No," he answered.
22 "Who are you, then?" they asked. "We
need to give an answer to those who sent us.
What can you tell us about yourself?"
23 He said, "I am a **voice of one crying out
in the wilderness: Make straight the way of
the Lord**[F,q] — just as Isaiah[r] the prophet said."
24 Now they had been sent from the •Phari-
sees.[s] 25 So they asked him, "Why then do you
baptize if you aren't the Messiah, or Elijah, or
the Prophet?"
26 "I baptize with[G] water,"[t] John answered
them. "Someone stands among you, but you
don't know Him. 27 He is the One coming after me,[H,u] whose sandal strap I'm not worthy
to untie."
28 All this happened in Bethany[I] across the
Jordan,[J,v] where John was baptizing.

The Lamb of God

29 The next day John saw Jesus coming toward him and said, "Here is the Lamb of
God,[w] who takes away the sin[x] of the world!
30 This is the One I told you about: 'After me
comes a man who has surpassed me, because
He existed before me.' 31 I didn't know Him,[y]
but I came baptizing with[G] water so He might
be revealed[z] to Israel."
32 And John testified, "I watched the Spirit[aa]
descending from heaven like a dove, and He
rested on Him.[ab] 33 I didn't know Him, but
He[K] who sent me to baptize with[G] water told
me, 'The One you see the Spirit descending
and resting on — He is the One who baptizes
with[G] the Holy Spirit.'[ac] 34 I have seen and testified that He is the Son of God!"[L,ad]
35 Again the next day, John was standing
with two of his disciples. 36 When he saw Jesus
passing by, he said, "Look! The Lamb of God!"
37 The two disciples heard him say this and
followed Jesus. 38 When Jesus turned and noticed them following Him, He asked them,
"What are you looking for?"
They said to Him, "•Rabbi"[ae] (which means
"Teacher"), "where are You staying?"
39 "Come and you'll see," He replied. So they
went and saw where He was staying, and they
stayed with Him that day. It was about 10 in
the morning.[M]
40 Andrew,[af] Simon Peter's brother, was one
of the two who heard John and followed Him.
41 He first found his own brother Simon and
told him, "We have found the Messiah!"[N,ag]
(which means "Anointed[ah] One"), 42 and he
brought Simon to Jesus.
When Jesus saw him, He said, "You are
Simon, son of John.[O] You will be called •Ce-
phas"[ai] (which means "Rock").

[a] **1:14** Heb 11:17; 1Jn 4:9
[b] **1:15** Mt 3:11; Mk 1:7; Jn 1:27,30
[c] Col 1:19
[d] Jn 3:13; 8:58; 10:30; 14:7-9,23; Php 2:6
[e] **1:16** Ac 15:11; 2Pt 3:18
[f] **1:17** Ps 77:20; Mt 8:4; Heb 3:2
[g] Ps 119:142; Jn 14:6; 2Th 2:10
[h] **1:18** 1Jn 4:9
[i] Mt 5:16; 11:27; Jn 8:42
[j] Mt 11:27; Lk 10:22; 1Jn 2:24
[k] **1:19** Mt 23:37
[l] Ac 4:1
[m] Ex 6:19; Lk 10:32
[n] **1:20** Mt 1:17; Eph 5:2
[o] **1:21** Mal 4:5; Mt 11:14; 17:10-13; Mk 8:28; Lk 1:17
[p] Dt 18:15; Mt 2:23
[q] **1:23** Is 40:3
[r] Mt 3:3; 4:14; 12:17
[s] **1:24** Mk 7:3
[t] **1:26** Mk 1:8
[u] **1:27** Jn 1:15
[v] **1:28** Mk 10:1; Lk 3:3
[w] **1:29** Is 53:7; Ac 8:32; 1Pt 1:19; Rv 5:6
[x] Jn 15:22; 1Jn 3:5
[y] **1:31** Jn 7:28
[z] 2Co 4:11; 1Jn 1:2
[aa] **1:32** Ps 51:11; Jn 1:33; Ac 2:4; Rm 8:9; Gl 5:25; Ti 3:5; 1Jn 5:8; Rv 3:22
[ab] Jms 4:5
[ac] **1:33** Mt 3:11; Mk 1:8; Lk 3:16; Ac 11:16
[ad] **1:34** Mt 3:17; 4:3; Jn 1:49; 5:19; Heb 1:2
[ae] **1:38** Jn 11:8
[af] **1:40-42** Mt 4:18-22; Mk 1:16-20; Lk 5:2-11
[ag] **1:41** Mt 1:17
[ah] Ex 29:29
[ai] **1:42** 1Co 1:12; 3:22; 9:5; 15:5; Gl 1:18; 2:9,11,14

A 1:14 *Son* is implied from the reference to the Father and from Gk usage. B 1:18 Since God is an infinite being, no one can see Him in His absolute essential nature; Ex 33:18-23. C 1:18 Other mss read *God* D 1:18 Lit *is in the bosom of the Father* E 1:21 Probably the Prophet in Dt 18:15 F 1:23 Is 40:3 G 1:26,31,33 Or *in* H 1:27 Other mss add *who came before me* I 1:28 Other mss read *in Bethabara* J 1:28 Another Bethany, near Jerusalem, was the home of Lazarus, Martha, and Mary; Jn 11:1. K 1:33 *He* refers to God the Father, who gave John a sign to help him identify the Messiah. Vv. 32-34 indicate that John did not know that Jesus was the Messiah until the Spirit descended upon Him at His baptism. L 1:34 Other mss read *is the Chosen One of God* M 1:39 Lit *about the tenth hour.* Various methods of reckoning time were used in the ancient world. John probably used a different method from the other 3 Gospels. If John used the same method of time reckoning as the other 3 Gospels, the translation would be: *It was about four in the afternoon.* N 1:41 In the NT, the word Messiah translates the Gk word *Christos* ("Anointed One"), except here and in Jn 4:25 where it translates *Messias.* O 1:42 Other mss read *Simon, son of Jonah*

Philip and Nathanael

43The next day He[A] decided to leave for Galilee. Jesus found Philip[a] and told him, "Follow
Me!"

44Now Philip was from Bethsaida,[b] the
hometown of Andrew and Peter. 45Philip
found Nathanael[B,c] and told him, "We have
found the One Moses wrote about in the Law
(and so did the prophets[d]): Jesus the son of Joseph,[e] from Nazareth!"[f]

46"Can anything good[g] come out of Nazareth?" Nathanael asked him.

"Come and see," Philip answered.

47Then Jesus saw Nathanael coming toward
Him and said about him, "Here is a true Israelite;[h] no deceit is in him."

48"How do you know me?" Nathanael
asked.

"Before Philip called you, when you were
under the fig tree, I saw you," Jesus answered.

49"Rabbi,"[i] Nathanael replied, "You are the
Son[j] of God! You are the King of Israel!"[k]

50Jesus responded to him, "Do you believe
only because I told you I saw you under the
fig tree? You[C] will see greater things than
this." 51Then He said, "I assure you: You[D] will
see heaven opened and the angels of God[l]
ascending and descending[m] on the ·Son of
Man."[n]

The First Sign: Turning Water into Wine

2 On the third day a wedding took place
in Cana[o] of Galilee.[p] Jesus' mother[q] was
there, and 2Jesus and His disciples were invited to the wedding as well. 3When the wine
ran out, Jesus' mother told Him, "They don't
have any wine."

4"What has this concern of yours to do with
Me,[E,r] ·woman?"[s] Jesus asked. "My hour[F] has
not yet come."

5"Do whatever He tells you," His mother
told the servants.

6Now six stone water jars had been set there
for Jewish purification.[t] Each contained 20
or 30 gallons.[G]

7"Fill the jars with water," Jesus told them.
So they filled them to the brim. 8Then He said
to them, "Now draw some out and take it to
the chief servant."[H] And they did.

9When the chief servant tasted the water
(after it had become wine), he did not know
where it came from—though the servants
who had drawn the water knew. He called the
groom 10and told him, "Everyone sets out the
fine wine first, then, after people have drunk
freely, the inferior. But you have kept the fine
wine until now."

11Jesus performed this first sign[I] in Cana[u]
of Galilee.[v] He displayed[w] His glory,[x] and His
disciples believed in Him.

12After this, He went down to Capernaum,[y]
together with His mother, His brothers,[z] and
His disciples, and they stayed there only a few
days.

Cleansing the Temple Complex

13The Jewish ·Passover[aa] was near, so Jesus
went up to Jerusalem.[ab] 14In the ·temple complex[ac] He found people selling oxen, sheep,
and doves, and He also found the money
changers sitting there. 15After making a whip
out of cords,[ad] He drove everyone out of
the temple complex with their sheep[ae] and
oxen. He also poured out the money changers' coins and overturned the tables. 16He
told those who were selling doves, "Get these
things out of here! Stop turning My Father's[af]
house[ag] into a marketplace!"[J,ah]

17And His disciples remembered that it is
written: **Zeal[ai] for Your house will consume[aj]
Me.**[K,ak]

18So the ·Jews replied to Him, "What sign
of authority will You show us for doing these
things?"

19Jesus answered, "Destroy this sanctuary,[al]
and I will raise it up in three days."[am]

20Therefore the Jews said, "This sanctuary
took 46 years to build, and will You raise it up
in three days?"[an]

21But He was speaking about the sanctuary
of His body.[ao] 22So when He was raised from
the dead,[ap] His disciples remembered that He
had said this.[aq] And they believed the Scripture[ar] and the statement Jesus had made.

[a]**1:43** Mk 3:18 [b]**1:44** Jn 12:21 [c]**1:45** Jn 1:46-49; 21:2 [d]Mt 2:23; Ac 7:52; Rm 3:21 [e]Mt 1:16; Lk 1:27; 2:4,16,33; 3:23; Jn 6:42 [f]Mk 1:9 [g]**1:46** Gn 1:31 [h]**1:47** 2Co 11:22 [i]**1:49** Jn 11:8 [j]Jn 5:19 [k]Mt 27:42; Mk 15:32; Jn 12:13 [l]**1:51** Lk 12:8-9; 15:10; Ac 10:3 [m]Gn 28:12 [n]Mk 2:10 [o]**2:1** Jn 2:11; 4:46; 21:2 [p]Mt 17:22 [q]Mt 1:16 [r]**2:4** 2Sm 16:10; 19:22 [s]Jn 19:26 [t]**2:6** Lv 13–14; Heb 1:3 [u]**2:11** Jn 2:1; 21:2 [v]Mt 17:22 [w]2Co 4:11; 1Jn 1:2 [x]Mk 10:37; Jn 17:24 [y]**2:12** Lk 10:15 [z]Mt 12:46-50; Mk 3:31-35; 6:3; Lk 8:19-21; Ac 1:14 [aa]**2:13** Ex 12:11 [ab]Mt 23:37 [ac]**2:14-17** Mt 21:12-13; Mk 11:15-17; Lk 19:45-46 [ad]**2:15** Ac 27:32 [ae]Mt 7:15 [af]**2:16** Mt 5:16; 11:27; Jn 8:42 [ag]Lk 11:51; Jn 2:17 [ah]Jr 7:11; Zch 14:21; Mal 3:1-3 [ai]**2:17** Nm 25:13 [aj]Gl 5:15 [ak]Ps 69:9 [al]**2:19** Lk 1:21 [am]Lk 9:22 [an]**2:20** Mk 15:29 [ao]**2:21** Mt 26:26; 27:52,58; Mk 14:22; 15:43; Lk 12:4; 22:19; 23:52,55; Jn 19:31,38,40; 20:12; 1Co 10:16; 11:23-26; Heb 10:5,10; 1Pt 2:24 [ap]**2:22** Mt 17:9; Rv 20:12 [aq]Jn 14:26 [ar]Mt 26:54; 2Pt 1:20

A**1:43** Or *he*, referring either to Simon Peter (vv. 41-42) or Andrew (vv. 40-41) B**1:45** Probably the Bartholomew of the other Gospels and Acts C**1:50** In Gk, the word you is sg and refers to Nathanael. D**1:51** In Gk, the word you is pl and refers to Nathanael and the other disciples. E**2:4** Or *You and I see things differently*; lit *What to Me and to you*; Mt 8:29; Mk 1:24; 5:7; Lk 8:28 F**2:4** The time of His sacrificial death and exaltation; Jn 7:30; 8:20; 12:23,27; 13:1; 17:1 G**2:6** Lit *2 or 3 measures* H**2:8** Lit *ruler of the table*; perhaps *master of the feast*, or *headwaiter* I**2:11** Lit *this beginning of the signs*; Jn 4:54; 20:30. Seven miraculous signs occur in John's Gospel and are so noted in the headings. J**2:16** Lit *a house of business* K**2:17** Ps 69:9

23 While He was in Jerusalem[a] at the Passover Festival,[b] many trusted in His name[c]
when they saw the signs He was doing.
24 Jesus, however, would not entrust Himself
to them, since He knew them all 25 and because He did not need anyone to testify about
man; for He Himself knew what was in man.[d]

Jesus and Nicodemus

3 There was a man from the ·Pharisees[e]
named Nicodemus,[f] a ruler[g] of the ·Jews.
2 This man came to Him at night and said,
"·Rabbi,[h] we know that You have come from
God[i] as a teacher,[j] for no one could perform
these signs You do unless God were with
him."[k]
3 Jesus replied, "·I assure you: Unless someone is born again,[A,l] he cannot see the kingdom of God."[m]
4 "But how can anyone be born when he
is old?" Nicodemus asked Him. "Can he enter his mother's womb a second time and be
born?"
5 Jesus answered, "I assure you: Unless someone is born[n] of water and the Spirit,[B,o] he cannot enter the kingdom of God. 6 Whatever is
born of the flesh[p] is flesh, and whatever is
born of the Spirit[q] is spirit. 7 Do not be amazed
that I told you that you[C] must be born[r] again.
8 The wind[D] blows where it pleases, and you
hear its sound, but you don't know where it
comes from or where it is going.[s] So it is with
everyone born of the Spirit."[t]
9 "How can these things be?" asked Nicodemus.
10 "Are you a teacher[E] of Israel and don't
know these things?" Jesus replied. 11 "I assure
you:[u] We speak what We know and We testify
to what We have seen, but you[F] do not accept
Our testimony.[G] 12 If I have told you about
things that happen on earth and you don't
believe, how will you believe if I tell you about
things of heaven? 13 No one has ascended[v]
into heaven[w] except the One who descended
from heaven[x]—the ·Son of Man.[H,y] 14 Just as

[a] **2:23** Mt 23:37 [b] Jn 5:1 [c] Jn 10:25; 1Jn 3:23 [d] **2:25** Jr 17:10 [e] **3:1** Mk 7:3 [f] Jn 3:4,9; 7:50; 19:39 [g] Lk 8:41; 12:58 [h] **3:2** Jn 11:8 [i] Mk 1:45 [j] Mk 4:38; Eph 4:11 [k] Ex 3:12; Jn 15:24; Ac 10:38; Rv 21:3 [l] **3:3** 1Pt 1:3; 1Jn 2:29 [m] Mk 1:15; 9:1 [n] **3:5** Mk 9:43 [o] Ezk 36:25-27; Ac 22:16; Ti 3:5 [p] **3:6** Php 3:3 [q] Jn 1:33 [r] **3:7** 1Pt 1:3 [s] **3:8** Jn 8:14 [t] 1Co 2:13-16 [u] **3:11** Jn 1:51; Rv 22:21 [v] **3:13** Jn 20:17 [w] Dt 30:12; Jn 6:62; Ac 2:34; Rm 10:6; 1Co 15:47; Eph 4:8-10; Rv 11:12 [x] Jn 6:38; 8:23 [y] Mk 2:10 [z] **3:14** Ps 77:20; Mt 8:4; Heb 3:2 [aa] Nm 21:4-9 [ab] **3:15** Mk 10:17; Jn 12:25; Ac 13:48 [ac] **3:16** Jn 12:43; 1Co 13:1; Gl 2:20; Col 1:13; 3:12; 1Th 1:4; 2Th 2:13,16; 1Jn 4:7-12; Jd 1 [ad] 1Jn 4:9 [ae] Jn 5:19; Heb 1:2 [af] Jn 12:25; Rm 5:8; 1Jn 3:16; 4:9-10 [ag] **3:17** Jn 8:11 [ah] **3:18** Mt 12:41; Mk 16:16 [ai] Jn 10:25; 1Jn 3:23 [aj] Jn 5:19 [ak] **3:19** Ps 36:9; Jn 12:46 [al] Jn 18:37; 1Jn 2:8 [am] **3:20** Lk 6:27; 19:14 [an] Mk 14:6; Gl 3:10; Jms 2:14-26 [ao] **3:21** Jn 5:36 [ap] **3:23** Mk 1:4 [aq] **3:24** Mk 1:14 [ar] **3:25** Mt 9:14; 11:2; 14:12; Mk 2:18; 6:29; Lk 5:33; 7:18-19;

Moses[z] lifted up the snake in the wilderness,[aa]
so the Son of Man must be lifted up, 15 so that
everyone who believes in Him will[I] have eternal life.[ab]
16 "For God loved[ac] the world in this way:[J] He
gave His ·One and Only[ad] Son,[ae] so that everyone who believes in Him will not perish but
have eternal life.[af] 17 For God did not send His
Son into the world that He might condemn[ag]
the world, but that the world might be saved
through Him. 18 Anyone who believes in Him
is not condemned, but anyone who does not
believe is already condemned,[ah] because he
has not believed in the name[ai] of the One and
Only Son[aj] of God.
19 "This, then, is the judgment: The light[ak]
has come into the world,[al] and people loved
darkness rather than the light because their
deeds were evil. 20 For everyone who practices
wicked things hates[am] the light and avoids it,[K]
so that his deeds[an] may not be exposed. 21 But
anyone who lives by[L] the truth comes to the
light, so that his works[ao] may be shown to be
accomplished by God."[M]

Jesus and John the Baptist

22 After this, Jesus and His disciples went
to the Judean countryside, where He spent
time with them and baptized. 23 John[ap] also
was baptizing in Aenon near Salim, because
there was plenty of water there. People were
coming and being baptized, 24 since John had
not yet been thrown into prison.[aq]
25 Then a dispute arose between John's disciples[ar] and a Jew[N] about purification.[as] 26 So
they came to John and told him, "Rabbi,[at] the
One you testified about, and who was with
you across the Jordan,[au] is baptizing—and
everyone is flocking to Him."[av]
27 John responded, "No one can receive a single thing unless it's given to him from heaven.
28 You yourselves can testify that I said, 'I am
not the ·Messiah,[aw] but I've been sent ahead of

11:1; Jn 1:35,37; 6:3 [as] Lv 13–14; Heb 1:3 [at] **3:26** Jn 11:8 [au] Mk 10:1; Lk 3:3 [av] Mk 1:45 [aw] **3:28** Mt 1:17; Eph 5:2

[A] **3:3** The same Gk word can mean again or from above (also in v. 7). [B] **3:5** Or *spirit*, or *wind*; the Gk word *pneuma* can mean *wind*, *spirit*, or *Spirit*, each of which occurs in this context. [C] **3:7** The pronoun is pl in Gk. [D] **3:8** The Gk word *pneuma* can mean wind, spirit, or Spirit, each of which occurs in this context. [E] **3:10** Or *the teacher* [F] **3:11** In Gk, the word you is pl here and throughout v. 12. [G] **3:11** The pronouns we and our refer to Jesus and His authority to speak for the Father. [H] **3:13** Other mss add *who is in heaven* [I] **3:15** Other mss add *not perish, but* [J] **3:16** The Gk word *houtos*, commonly translated in Jn 3:16 as "so" or "so much" occurs over 200 times in the NT. Almost without exception it is an adverb of manner, not degree (for example, see Mt 1:18). It only means "so much" when modifying an adjective (see Gl 3:3; Rv 16:18). Manner seems primarily in view in Jn 3:16, which explains the HCSB's rendering. [K] **3:20** Lit *and does not come to the light* [L] **3:21** Lit *who does* [M] **3:21** It is possible that Jesus' words end at v. 15. Ancient Gk did not have quotation marks. [N] **3:25** Other mss read *and the Jews*

Him.'[a] [29]He who has the bride[b] is the groom.
But the groom's friend, who stands by and
listens for him, rejoices greatly[A] at the groom's
voice. So this joy[c] of mine is complete. [30]He
must increase, but I must decrease."

The One from Heaven

[31]The One who comes from above[d] is above
all. The one who is from the earth is earthly
and speaks in earthly terms.[B] The One who
comes from heaven is above all.[e] [32]He testifies[f] to what He has seen and heard, yet no
one accepts His testimony. [33]The one who
has accepted His testimony has affirmed
that God is true.[g] [34]For God sent Him, and He
speaks God's words, since He[C] gives the Spirit[h]
without measure. [35]The Father loves the Son[i]
and has given all things into His hands.[j] [36]The
one who believes in the Son has eternal life,
but the one who refuses to believe in the Son
will not see life; instead, the wrath of God remains on him.[k]

Jesus and the Samaritan Woman

4 When Jesus[D] knew that the ·Pharisees[l]
heard He was making[m] and baptizing
more disciples than John[n] [2](though Jesus
Himself was not baptizing, but His disciples
were), [3]He left Judea[o] and went again to Galilee.[p] [4]He had to travel through Samaria,[q] [5]so
He came to a town of Samaria called Sychar
near the property[E] that Jacob[r] had given his
son Joseph.[s] [6]Jacob's well[t] was there, and
Jesus, worn out from His journey, sat down at
the well. It was about six in the evening.[F]

[7]A woman of Samaria came to draw water.[u]

"Give Me a drink," Jesus said to her, [8]for His
disciples had gone into town to buy food.

[9]"How is it that You, a Jew,[v] ask for a drink
from me, a ·Samaritan[w] woman?" she asked
Him. For Jews do not associate with[G] Samaritans.[H]

[10]Jesus answered, "If you knew the gift of
God,[x] and who is saying to you, 'Give Me a
drink,' you would ask Him, and He would give
you living water."[y]

[11]"Sir,"[z] said the woman, "You don't even
have a bucket, and the well is deep. So where
do You get this 'living water'? [12]You aren't
greater than our father Jacob,[aa] are You? He
gave us the well and drank from it himself, as
did his sons and livestock."

[13]Jesus said, "Everyone who drinks from
this water will get thirsty again. [14]But whoever
drinks from the water that I will give him will
never get thirsty again—ever![ab] In fact, the water I will give him will become a well[I],[ac] of water
springing up within him for eternal life."[ad]

[15]"Sir," the woman said to Him, "give me
this water so I won't get thirsty and come
here to draw water."

[16]"Go call your husband," He told her, "and
come back here."

[17]"I don't have a husband," she answered.

"You have correctly said, 'I don't have a husband,'" Jesus said. [18]"For you've had five husbands, and the man you now have is not your
husband. What you have said is true."

[19]"Sir," the woman replied, "I see that You
are a prophet. [20]Our fathers worshiped on
this mountain,[J],[ae] yet you Jews say that the
place to worship is in Jerusalem."[af]

[21]Jesus told her, "Believe Me, ·woman, an
hour is coming when you will worship the
Father neither on this mountain nor in Jerusalem. [22]You Samaritans[K] worship what you
do not know. We worship what we do know,
because salvation is from the Jews.[ag] [23]But an
hour is coming, and is now here,[ah] when the
true worshipers will worship the Father in
spirit and truth. Yes, the Father wants such
people to worship Him. [24]God is spirit,[ai] and
those who worship Him must worship in
spirit and truth."[aj]

[25]The woman said to Him, "I know that
·Messiah[L],[ak] is coming" (who is called Christ[al]).
"When He comes, He will explain everything
to us."

[26]"I am He,"[am] Jesus told her, "the One
speaking to you."

The Ripened Harvest

[27]Just then His disciples arrived, and
they were amazed that He was talking with

[a]**3:28** Lk 1:17 [b]**3:29** Rv 21:2 [c]Jn 15:11 [d]**3:31** Jms 1:17 [e]Jn 8:23; 1Jn 4:5-6 [f]**3:32** Jn 15:26; Ac 26:5 [g]**3:33** 1Jn 5:20 [h]**3:34** Jn 1:33 [i]**3:35** Jn 5:20; 10:17; 1Co 13:1 [j]Jn 5:19 [k]**3:36** Mk 16:16 [l]**4:1** Mk 7:3 [m]Mt 28:19-20 [n]Mk 1:4 [o]**4:3** Lk 1:5 [p]Mt 17:22 [q]**4:4** Ac 1:8 [r]**4:5** Ps 22:23; Mt 1:2; Lk 1:33 [s]Gn 30:24; 33:19; 48:22; 49:22 [t]**4:6** Jms 3:11 [u]**4:7** Gn 24:11-17; 29:2-12 [v]**4:9** Jn 11:36; Ac 14:1; Rv 2:9 [w]Lk 9:52; Ac 1:8 [x]**4:10** Ac 8:20 [y]Gn 26:19; Ps 36:7-9; Is 49:10; 55:1; Jr 2:13; Zch 14:8; Jn 7:38; Rv 7:17; 21:6; 22:1,17 [z]**4:11** Lk 10:1 [aa]**4:12** Mt 1:2; Lk 1:33 [ab]**4:14** Jn 6:35; 7:37; 1Co 4:11; Rv 7:16; 21:6; 22:17 [ac]Jms 3:11 [ad]Jn 12:25; Ac 13:48; Rm 8:2; 1Jn 2:25 [ae]**4:20** Dt 11:29–12:14; 27:3; Jos 24:1 [af]Mt 23:37 [ag]**4:22** Gn 12:1-7; Is 2:3; Mal 1:11; Mt 15:24; Jn 11:36; Rm 3:1-2; 9:4-5; 15:8-9 [ah]**4:23** Jn 5:25-29; 16:32 [ai]**4:24** Jn 1:33; 2Th 2:10; Jd 20 [aj]2Th 2:10 [ak]**4:25** Mt 1:17; Eph 5:2 [al]Ex 29:29; Jn 1:41 [am]**4:26** Ex 3:14; Ps 45:8; Jn 8:24

[A]**3:29** Lit *with joy rejoices* [B]**3:31** Or *of earthly things* [C]**3:34** Other mss read *since God* [D]**4:1** Other mss read *the Lord* [E]**4:5** Lit *piece of land* [F]**4:6** Lit *the sixth hour*; see note at Jn 1:39; an alt time reckoning would be *noon* [G]**4:9** Or *do not share vessels with* [H]**4:9** Other mss omit *For Jews do not associate with Samaritans.* [I]**4:14** Or *spring* [J]**4:20** Mount Gerizim, where there had been a Samaritan temple that rivaled Jerusalem's [K]**4:22** *Samaritans* is implied since the Gk verb and pronoun are pl. [L]**4:25** In the NT, the word Messiah translates the Gk word *Christos* ("Anointed One"), except here and in Jn 1:41 where it translates *Messias*.

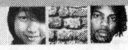

a woman. Yet no one said, "What do You
want?" or "Why are You talking with her?"
28 Then the woman left her water jar, went
into town, and told the men, 29 "Come, see
a man who told me everything I ever did!
Could this be the Messiah?"[a] 30 They left the
town and made their way to Him.[b]
31 In the meantime the disciples kept urging
Him, "•Rabbi,[c] eat something."
32 But He said, "I have food to eat that you
don't know about."
33 The disciples said to one another, "Could
someone have brought Him something to
eat?"
34 "My food is to do the will of Him[d] who
sent Me[e] and to finish His work,"[f] Jesus told
them. 35 "Don't you say, 'There are still four
more months, then comes the harvest'? Listen to what I'm telling you: Open[A] your eyes
and look at the fields, for they are ready[B] for
harvest. 36 The reaper is already receiving pay
and gathering fruit for eternal life,[g] so the
sower and reaper can rejoice together. 37 For
in this case the saying is true: 'One sows and
another reaps.'[h] 38 I sent you to reap what you
didn't labor for; others have labored, and you
have benefited from[C] their labor."

The Savior of the World

39 Now many Samaritans[i] from that town
believed in Him because of what the woman
said[D] when she testified,[j] "He told me everything I ever did." 40 Therefore, when the Samaritans came to Him,[k] they asked Him to
stay with them, and He stayed there two days.
41 Many more believed because of what He
said.[E] 42 And they told the woman, "We no longer believe because of what you said, for we
have heard for ourselves and know that this
really is the Savior[l] of the world."[F]

A Galilean Welcome

43 After two days He left there for Galilee.[m]
44 Jesus Himself testified[n] that a prophet has
no honor in his own country.[o] 45 When[p] they
entered Galilee, the Galileans[q] welcomed
Him because they had seen everything He
did in Jerusalem[r] during the festival.[s] For they
also had gone to the festival.

The Second Sign: Healing an Official's Son

46 Then He went again to Cana[t] of Galilee,
where He had turned the water into wine. There
was a certain royal official whose son was ill at
Capernaum.[u] 47 When this man heard that
Jesus had come from Judea[v] into Galilee, he
went to Him and pleaded with Him to come
down and heal his son, for he was about to die.
48 Jesus told him, "Unless you people see
signs and wonders,[w] you will not believe."[x]

[a] **4:29** Mt 1:17
[b] **4:30** Mk 1:45
[c] **4:31** Jn 11:8
[d] **4:34** Eph 1:9; 1Jn 2:17
[e] Jn 5:30
[f] Jn 5:36
[g] **4:36** Mk 10:17; Jn 12:25; Ac 13:48
[h] **4:37** Lv 26:16; Dt 20:6; Jb 31:8; Mc 6:15; Mt 25:24; Lk 19:21
[i] **4:39** Lk 9:52; Ac 1:8
[j] Jn 15:26; Ac 26:5
[k] **4:40** Mk 1:45
[l] **4:42** 2Pt 3:18
[m] **4:43** Is 9:1-2; Mt 17:22
[n] **4:44** Jn 15:26; Ac 26:5
[o] Mt 13:57; Mk 6:4; Lk 4:24
[p] **4:45** Mt 4:17; Mk 1:14-15
[q] Mt 26:69; Mk 14:70; Lk 13:1-2; 22:59; 23:6; Ac 1:11; 2:7; 5:37
[r] Mt 23:37
[s] Jn 2:23; 5:1
[t] **4:46** Jn 2:1,11; 21:2
[u] Lk 10:15
[v] **4:47** Lk 1:5
[w] **4:48** Ex 7:3-4; Mk 13:22; Jn 2:23-25; 6:26
[x] Jn 3:16; 6:64; 20:25

GOD WHO SENDS

John's Theme of Christ Sent

Almost every page of the Fourth Gospel breathes with a passage in which Jesus expressed who he is in terms of his sense of being sent, his sense of mission. He came not to do his own will but the will of the Father who sent him (4:34; 5:30; 6:38–40). He came not to speak his words but the words of the Father who sent him (7:16–18; 8:26–29; 12:49; 14:24; 17:8). He came not to do his own work but the work of the Father who sent him (4:34; 5:36; 9:4). Jesus acknowledged that his very life rested with the Father who had sent him (4:34; 6:57). The sending in John speaks to the very heart of the gospel. "For God sent the Son into the world, not to condemn the world, but that the world might be saved through him" (3:17). Of special significance in John is the fact that Jesus linked his own mission with the mission of his followers (17:18; 20:21). Finally in John are the significant references concerning the sending of the Holy Spirit. Jesus spoke of the Father sending the Holy Spirit in his name (14:26) and of his sending the Spirit from the Father (15:26).

(DuBose, 49-50)

[A] **4:35** Lit *Raise* [B] **4:35** Lit *white* [C] **4:38** Lit *you have entered into* [D] **4:39** Lit *because of the woman's word* [E] **4:41** Lit *because of His word* [F] **4:42** Other mss add *the Messiah*

49"Sir,"[a] the official said to Him, "come
down before my boy dies!"
50"Go," Jesus told him, "your son will live."
The man believed what[A] Jesus said to him and
departed.
51While he was still going down, his ·slaves
met him saying that his boy was alive. 52He
asked them at what time he got better. "Yesterday at seven in the morning[B] the fever left
him," they answered. 53The father[b] realized
this was the very hour at which Jesus had told
him, "Your son will live." Then he himself believed, along with his whole household.
54This, therefore, was the second sign[c]
Jesus performed after He came from Judea to
Galilee.[d]

The Third Sign: Healing the Sick

5 After this, a Jewish festival took place,
and Jesus went up to Jerusalem.[e] 2By
the Sheep Gate[f] in Jerusalem there is a pool,
called Bethesda[C] in ·Hebrew, which has five
colonnades.[D] 3Within these lay a large number of the sick—blind, lame, and paralyzed
[—waiting for the moving of the water, 4be-
cause an angel would go down into the pool
from time to time and stir up the water. Then
the first one who got in after the water was
stirred up recovered from whatever ailment
he had].[E]
5One man was there who had been sick for
38 years. 6When Jesus saw him lying there
and knew he had already been there a long
time,[g] He said to him, "Do you want to get
well?"
7"Sir,"[h] the sick man answered, "I don't have
a man to put me into the pool when the water
is stirred up, but while I'm coming, someone
goes down ahead of me."
8"Get up," Jesus told him, "pick up your
mat and walk!" 9Instantly the man got well,
picked up his mat, and started to walk.
Now that day was the Sabbath,[i] 10so the
·Jews[j] said to the man who had been healed,
"This is the Sabbath![k] It's illegal for you to
pick up your mat."
11He replied, "The man who made me well[l]
told me, 'Pick up your mat and walk.'"

[a]4:49 Lk 10:1
[b]4:53 Lk 11:11; Col 3:21
[c]4:54 Jn 2:11
[d]Mt 17:22
[e]5:1 Mt 23:37
[f]5:2 Neh 3:1,32; 12:39
[g]5:6 Is 46:10; Zch 14:7; Jn 5:6; 6:6; 8:14; 9:3; 11:11-15; 13:1-3,11
[h]5:7 Lk 10:1
[i]5:9 Mk 2:23
[j]5:10 Jn 11:36
[k]Lk 14:3
[l]5:11 Ti 2:8
[m]5:13 Jn 7:28
[n]5:14 Ac 21:26
[o]5:15 Ti 2:8
[p]5:16 Lk 6:28; 2Tm 3:12

12"Who is this man who told you, 'Pick up
your mat and walk'?" they asked. 13But the
man who was cured did not know who it
was,[m] because Jesus had slipped away into the
crowd that was there.[F]
14After this, Jesus found him in the ·temple
complex[n] and said to him, "See, you are well.
Do not sin anymore, so that something worse
doesn't happen to you." 15The man went and
reported to the Jews that it was Jesus who had
made him well.[o]

Honoring the Father and the Son

16Therefore, the Jews began persecuting[p]
Jesus[G] because He was doing these things on

GOD WHO SENDS

Sent to Bear a Witness

Being a witness is complemented by the bearing of a witness. We are sent both to be a witness and to bear a witness. The Gospel of John reveals a strong relationship between the idea of the sending and the idea of witness in the teachings of Jesus. The relationship is especially linked to the self-understanding and realization of Jesus. Jesus did not seek his own will but the will of the Father who sent him. If he bore witness to himself his testimony was not true (5:31–32). The works which the Father granted him to accomplish bore him witness that the Father had sent him. And the Father who sent him also had borne witness to him (5:36–37). Later, in a slightly different vein, Jesus affirmed that he did indeed bear witness to himself and that the Father also bears witness to him (8:18).

(DUBOSE, 114)

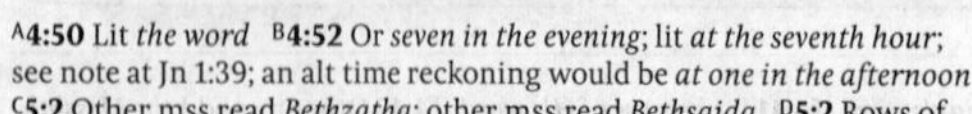
[A]4:50 Lit *the word* [B]4:52 Or *seven in the evening*; lit *at the seventh hour*; see note at Jn 1:39; an alt time reckoning would be *at one in the afternoon* [C]5:2 Other mss read *Bethzatha*; other mss read *Bethsaida* [D]5:2 Rows of columns supporting a roof [E]5:3-4 Other mss omit bracketed text [F]5:13 Lit *slipped away, there being a crowd in that place* [G]5:16 Other mss add *and trying to kill Him*

the Sabbath.[a] 17But Jesus responded to them, "My Father[b] is still working, and I am working also." 18This is why the Jews began trying all the more to kill Him:[c] Not only was He breaking the Sabbath, but He was even calling God His own Father, making Himself equal with God.

19Then Jesus replied, "·I assure you: The Son is not able to do anything on His own, but only what He sees the Father doing. For whatever the Father[A] does, the Son also does these things in the same way.[d] 20For the Father loves the Son and shows Him everything He is doing, and He will show Him greater works[e] than these so that you will be amazed. 21And just as the Father raises[f] the dead and gives them life, so the Son also gives life to anyone He wants to.[g] 22The Father,[h] in fact, judges no one but has given all judgment to the Son, 23so that all people will honor the Son just as they honor the Father.[i] Anyone who does not honor the Son does not honor the Father who sent Him.[j]

Life and Judgment

24"I assure you: Anyone who hears My word and believes Him who sent Me has eternal life[k] and will not come under judgment but has passed from death to life.

25"I assure you: An hour is coming, and is now here,[l] when the dead will hear the voice of the Son of God, and those who hear will live.[m] 26For just as the Father has life in Himself, so also He has granted to the Son[n] to have life in Himself. 27And He has granted Him the right to pass judgment,[o] because He is the ·Son of Man.[p] 28Do not be amazed at this, because a time is coming when all who are in the graves will hear His voice 29and come out—those who have done good things, to the resurrection of life, but those who have done wicked things, to the resurrection of judgment.

30"I can do nothing on My own. I judge only as I hear, and My judgment[q] is righteous,[r] because I do not seek My own will, but the will of Him who sent Me.[s]

Four Witnesses to Jesus

31"If I testify about Myself, My testimony is not valid.[B] 32There is Another who testifies about Me, and I know that the testimony He gives about Me is valid.[C,t] 33You have sent messengers to John, and he has testified to the truth.[u] 34I don't receive man's testimony, but I say these things so that you may be saved. 35John[D,v] was a burning and shining lamp,[w] and for a time you were willing to enjoy his light.[x]

36"But I have a greater testimony than John's because of the works that the Father has given Me to accomplish.[y] These very works I am doing testify about Me that the Father has sent[z] Me. 37The Father who sent Me has Himself testified[aa] about Me. You have not heard His voice at any time, and you haven't seen His form.[ab] 38You don't have His word living in you, because you don't believe the One He sent. 39You pore over[E] the Scriptures[ac] because you think you have eternal life in them, yet they testify about Me.[ad] 40And you are not willing[ae] to come to Me[af] so that you may have life.

41"I do not accept glory[ag] from men, 42but I know you—that you have no love for God[ah] within you. 43I have come in My Father's name,[ai] yet you don't accept Me.[aj] If someone else comes in his own name, you will accept him. 44How can you believe? While accepting glory from one another, you don't seek the glory that comes from the only[ak] God.[al] 45Do not think that I will accuse you to the Father. Your accuser is Moses,[am] on whom you have set your hope. 46For if you believed Moses, you would believe Me, because he wrote about Me. 47But if you don't believe his writings,[an] how will you believe My words?"[ao]

The Fourth Sign: Feeding 5,000

6 After[ap] this, Jesus crossed the Sea of Galilee[aq] (or Tiberias[ar]). 2And a huge crowd was following Him because they saw the signs that He was performing by healing the sick. 3So Jesus went up a mountain and sat down there with His disciples.

4Now the ·Passover, a Jewish festival, was near. 5Therefore, when Jesus looked up and noticed a huge crowd coming toward Him,[as] He asked Philip,[at] "Where will we buy bread

[a]**5:16** Lk 13:10 [b]**5:17** Mt 5:16; 11:27; Jn 8:42 [c]**5:18** Mt 12:14; 26:4; 27:1; Mk 3:6; 14:1; Lk 6:11; Jn 7:1,19; 10:33; 11:53 [d]**5:19** Jn 3:35; 6:38; 7:16,28; 8:26-42; 10:18,30,36-38; 12:49-50; 14:9,24,31; 15:9-10; 16:15; 17:9-10 [e]**5:20** Heb 3:9; Rv 15:3 [f]**5:21** Mk 9:27; Jn 2:19 [g]Jn 11:25-26 [h]**5:22** Mt 11:27 [i]**5:23** Jn 15:23 [j]Lk 10:16 [k]**5:24** Jn 6:53; 12:25; Ac 13:48; 1Jn 2:25 [l]**5:25** Jn 4:23 [m]Php 1:21 [n]**5:26** Jn 5:19; Col 1:19 [o]**5:27** 2Th 1:5 [p]Mk 2:10; Heb 2:6; Rv 1:13; 14:14 [q]**5:30** Mt 12:41; 2Th 1:5 [r]Mt 6:33; Jn 8:16 [s]Mt 26:39; Jn 4:34; 6:38; 7:16-18; 8:28; 14:10; Rm 8:27; Eph 1:9 [t]**5:32** 1Jn 5:20 [u]**5:33** Ps 119:142; Jn 14:6 [v]**5:35** Mk 1:4 [w]2Sm 21:17; Mt 5:14-15; Lk 12:35; 2Pt 1:19; Rv 21:23 [x]Ps 36:9; Jn 12:46 [y]**5:36** Jn 15:24 [z]Mk 9:37; Jn 1:6,33 [aa]**5:37** 1Jn 5:9 [ab]Ex 33:11; Dt 4:12; Is 6:1; Lk 3:22; Jn 1:18; 6:46-47; 14:9; 1Tm 1:17 [ac]**5:39** Mt 26:54; 2Pt 1:20 [ad]Lk 24:27,44; Ac 13:27 [ae]**5:40** Lk 13:34 [af]Lk 14:26 [ag]**5:41** Jn 17:24; Php 3:19; 1Pt 5:4 [ah]**5:42** Lk 10:27; 11:42; 1Jn 4:20 [ai]**5:43** Jn 10:25; 14:13; Ac 15:14; Rv 14:1 [aj]Mk 4:16; Jn 1:12; 12:48; 13:20; 17:8 [ak]**5:44** Dt 6:4; Jn 17:3; Rm 3:30; 16:27; 1Tm 1:17; 6:15-16; Jd 25; Rv 15:4 [al]1Th 2:4 [am]**5:45** Ps 77:20; Mt 8:4; Heb 3:2 [an]**5:47** Mt 26:54; Rm 1:2 [ao]Lk 16:29-31 [ap]**6:1-15** Mt 14:13-21; Mk 6:30-44; Lk 9:10-17 [aq]**6:1** Mk 1:16 [ar]Jn 6:23; 21:1 [as]**6:5** Mk 1:45 [at]Mk 3:18

[A]**5:19** Lit *whatever that One* [B]**5:31** Or *not true* [C]**5:32** Or *true* [D]**5:35** Lit *That man* [E]**5:39** In Gk this could be a command: *Pore over . . .*

so these people can eat?" 6He asked this to
test him,[a] for He Himself knew what He was
going to do.

7Philip answered, "Two hundred ˈdenarii[b]
worth of bread wouldn't be enough for each
of them to have a little."

8One of His disciples, Andrew,[c] Simon[d]
Peter's[e] brother, said to Him, 9"There's a
boy here who has five barley loaves and two
fish — but what are they for so many?"

10Then Jesus said, "Have the people sit
down."

There was plenty of grass in that place, so
they sat down. The men numbered about
5,000.[f] 11Then Jesus took the loaves, and after
giving thanks He distributed them to those
who were seated — so also with the fish, as
much as they wanted.[g]

12When they were full, He told His disciples, "Collect the leftovers so that nothing is
wasted."[h] 13So they collected them and filled
12 baskets with the pieces from the five barley
loaves that were left over by those who had
eaten.

14When the people saw the sign[A] He had
done, they said, "This really is the Prophet[i]
who was to come[j] into the world!"[k] 15There-
fore, when Jesus knew that they were about
to come and take Him by force to make Him
king,[l] He withdrew again[B] to the mountain by
Himself.

The Fifth Sign: Walking on Water

16When[m] evening came, His disciples went
down to the sea, 17got into a boat, and started
across the sea to Capernaum.[n] Darkness had
already set in, but Jesus had not yet come to
them. 18Then a high wind arose, and the sea
began to churn. 19After they had rowed about
three or four miles,[C] they saw Jesus walking
on the sea. He was coming near the boat, and
they were afraid.

20But He said to them, "It is I.[D,o] Don't be
afraid!" 21Then they were willing to take Him
on board, and at once the boat was at the
shore where they were heading.

The Bread of Life

22The next day, the crowd that had stayed
on the other side of the sea knew there had
been only one boat.[E,p] They also knew that
Jesus had not boarded the boat with His disciples, but that His disciples had gone off
alone. 23Some boats from Tiberias[q] came near
the place where they ate the bread after the
Lord gave thanks. 24When the crowd saw that
neither Jesus nor His disciples were there,
they got into the boats and went to Capernaum looking for Jesus.

25When they found Him on the other side
of the sea, they said to Him, "ˈRabbi,[r] when
did You get here?"

26Jesus answered, "ˈI assure you: You are
looking for Me, not because you saw[F] the
signs, but because you ate the loaves and were
filled. 27Don't work for the food that perishes[s]
but for the food that lasts for eternal life,[t]
which the ˈSon of Man[u] will give you, because
God the Father[v] has set His seal of approval
on Him."

28"What can we do to perform the works of
God?" they asked.

29Jesus replied, "This is the work[w] of
God — that you believe in the One He has
sent."[x]

30"What sign then are You going to do so we
may see and believe You?" they asked. "What
are You going to perform? 31Our fathers ate
the manna[y] in the wilderness,[z] just as it is
written: **He gave them bread from heaven to
eat.**"[G,H,aa]

32Jesus said to them, "I assure you: Moses[ab] didn't give you the bread from heaven,
but My Father gives you the real bread from
heaven. 33For the bread of God is the One who
comes down from heaven and gives life to the
world."

34Then they said, "Sir, give us this bread always!"

35"I am[ac] the bread of life," Jesus told them.
"No one who comes to Me[ad] will ever be hungry,[ae] and no one who believes in Me[af] will ever
be thirsty[ag] again. 36But as I told you, you've
seen Me,[I] and yet you do not believe. 37Every-
one the Father gives Me will come to Me, and
the one who comes to Me I will never cast
out.[ah] 38For I have come down from heaven,[ai]

[a]**6:6** Ex 15:25
[b]**6:7** Mt 18:28
[c]**6:8** Mt 4:18; 10:2; Mk 1:16,29; 3:18; 13:3; Lk 6:14; Jn 1:40,44; 12:22; Ac 1:13
[d]Mt 16:17
[e]Lk 6:14; Ac 10:32
[f]**6:10** Mt 14:21
[g]**6:11** 2Kg 4:42-44
[h]**6:12** Lk 15:4
[i]**6:14** Dt 18:15
[j]Mt 11:3; Lk 7:19-20; Rm 5:14; Heb 10:37
[k]Jn 18:37
[l]**6:15** Jn 19:21
[m]**6:16-21** Mt 14:22-36; Mk 6:45-56
[n]**6:17** Lk 10:15
[o]**6:20** Ex 3:14; Ps 45:8; Jn 8:24
[p]**6:22** Jn 21:8
[q]**6:23** Jn 6:1; 21:1
[r]**6:25** Jn 11:8
[s]**6:27** Is 55:2
[t]Jn 12:25; Ac 13:48; 1Jn 2:25
[u]Dn 7:13; Mk 2:10; Jn 6:53,62
[v]1Co 8:6; 15:24; Eph 5:20
[w]**6:29** Jn 5:36
[x]Mk 9:37; Jn 1:6
[y]**6:31** Ex 16:31
[z]Rv 12:6
[aa]Ex 16:4,15; Ps 78:24
[ab]**6:32** Ps 77:20; Mt 8:4; Heb 3:2
[ac]**6:35** Jn 8:24
[ad]Lk 14:26
[ae]Jn 4:14; Rv 7:16
[af]Mt 18:6; Mk 9:42; Jn 6:35; 7:38; 11:25-26; 12:44,46; 14:12; 16:9
[ag]Jn 7:37
[ah]**6:37** Mt 24:22
[ai]**6:38** Ex 3:8; Pr 30:4; Dn 4:13,23; Mt 28:2; Jn 1:51; 3:13; Eph 4:10; Rv 10:1; 18:1; 20:1

[A]**6:14** Other mss read *signs* [B]**6:15** A previous withdrawal is mentioned in Mk 6:31-32, an event that occurred just before the feeding of the 5,000. [C]**6:19** Lit *25 or 30 stadia*; 1 *stadion* = 600 feet [D]**6:20** Lit *I am* [E]**6:22** Other mss add *into which His disciples had entered* [F]**6:26** Or *perceived* [G]**6:31** Bread miraculously provided by God for the Israelites [H]**6:31** Ex 16:4; Ps 78:24 [I]**6:36** Other mss omit *Me*

not to do My will, but the will of Him[a] who
sent Me. 39This is the will of Him who sent
Me: that I should lose none of those He has
given Me but should raise[b] them up on the
last day. 40For this is the will of My Father:[c]
that everyone who sees the Son[d] and believes
in Him may have eternal life, and I will raise[e]
him up on the last day."

41Therefore the ·Jews started complaining
about Him because He said, "I am the bread
that came down from heaven." 42They were
saying, "Isn't this Jesus the son of Joseph,[f]
whose father and mother we know? How
can He now say, 'I have come down from
heaven'?"

43Jesus answered them, "Stop complaining
among yourselves. 44No one can come to Me
unless the Father who sent Me draws[A] him,
and I will raise him up on the last day. 45It is
written in the Prophets:[g] **And they will all be
taught by God.**[B,h] Everyone who has listened
to and learned from the Father[i] comes to
Me— 46not that anyone has seen the Father[j]
except the One who is from God.[k] He has seen
the Father.[l]

47"I assure you: Anyone who believes[C] has
eternal life. 48I am the bread of life. 49Your
fathers ate the manna[m] in the wilderness,[n]
and they died. 50This is the bread that comes
down from heaven so that anyone may eat of
it and not die.[o] 51I am the living bread that
came down from heaven. If anyone eats of
this bread he will live[p] forever.[q] The bread
that I will give for the life[r] of the world is My
flesh."[s]

52At that, the Jews argued[t] among themselves,[u] "How can this man give us His flesh
to eat?"

53So Jesus said to them, "I assure you: Unless
you eat the flesh of the Son of Man[v] and drink
His blood,[w] you do not have life in yourselves.
54Anyone who eats My flesh and drinks My
blood[x] has eternal life, and I will raise[y] him
up on the last day, 55because My flesh is real
food and My blood is real drink. 56The one
who eats My flesh and drinks My blood lives
in Me, and I in him.[z] 57Just as the living[aa] Father sent Me and I live because of the Father,
so the one who feeds on Me will live[ab] because
of Me. 58This is the bread that came down
from heaven; it is not like the manna[D] your
fathers ate—and they died. The one who eats
this bread will live forever."[ac]

59He said these things while teaching in the
·synagogue[ad] in Capernaum.[ae]

Many Disciples Desert Jesus

60Therefore, when many of His disciples
heard this, they said, "This teaching is hard!
Who can accept[E] it?"

61Jesus, knowing in Himself[af] that His disciples were complaining about this, asked
them, "Does this ·offend you? 62Then what if
you were to observe the Son of Man[ag] ascending[ah] to where He was before? 63The Spirit[ai] is
the One who gives life. The flesh doesn't help
at all. The words that I have spoken to you
are spirit and are life. 64But there are some
among you who don't believe." (For Jesus
knew from the beginning[aj] those who would
not[F] believe and the one who would betray[ak]
Him.) 65He said, "This is why I told you that
no one can come to Me[al] unless it is granted
to him by the Father."

66From that moment many of His disciples
turned back and no longer accompanied
Him. 67Therefore Jesus said to the Twelve,[am]
"You don't want to go away too, do you?"

68Simon Peter[an] answered, "Lord, who will
we go to? You have the words of eternal life.
69We have come to believe and know that You
are the Holy One of God!"[G,ao]

70Jesus replied to them, "Didn't I choose
you, the Twelve?[ap] Yet one of you is the
Devil!"[aq] 71He was referring to Judas,[ar] Simon
Iscariot's son,[H,I] one of the Twelve, because he
was going to betray[as] Him.

The Unbelief of Jesus' Brothers

7 After this, Jesus traveled in Galilee,[at] since
He did not want to travel in Judea[au] because the ·Jews[av] were trying to kill Him.[aw]
2The Jewish Festival of Tabernacles[J,K,ax] was
near, 3so His brothers[ay] said to Him, "Leave
here and go to Judea so Your disciples can
see Your works[az] that You are doing. 4For no

[a]**6:38** Eph 1:9; 1Jn 2:17 [b]**6:39** Lk 18:33 [c]**6:40** Mt 11:27 [d]Jn 5:19 [e]Mt 16:21 [f]**6:42** Jn 1:45 [g]**6:45** Mt 2:23; Ac 7:52 [h]Is 54:13 [i]1Co 2:13; 1Th 4:9; 1Jn 2:20 [j]**6:46** Ex 33:20; Jn 5:47 [k]Jn 16:27 [l]Lk 10:22; Jn 8:38; 14:9 [m]**6:49** Ex 16:12-36 [n]Rv 12:6 [o]**6:50** Jn 11:26 [p]**6:51** Php 1:21 [q]Rv 4:9 [r]Jn 5:26; 6:53 [s]Php 3:3; Heb 10:10 [t]**6:52** 2Tm 2:24 [u]Jn 9:16; 10:19 [v]**6:53** Mk 2:10 [w]Heb 9:12 [x]**6:54** Mt 26:26-29; Mk 14:22-25; Lk 22:15-20; 1Co 11:23-25 [y]Mt 16:21 [z]**6:56** Jn 15:4-5; 1Jn 3:24; 4:13-16 [aa]**6:57** Mt 25:31-46; Heb 10:31 [ab]Php 1:21; 1Pt 1:18 [ac]**6:58** Rv 4:9 [ad]**6:59** Jms 2:2 [ae]Lk 10:15 [af]**6:61** Mk 10:32; Jn 1:47-48; 2:24-25; 4:17-18; 9:3; 11:4,11; 13:10-11,38 [ag]**6:62** Mk 2:10 [ah]Jn 3:13; 20:17; Ac 1:9 [ai]**6:63** Ps 51:11; Jn 1:33; Ac 2:4; Rm 8:9; Gl 5:25; Ti 3:5; Rv 3:22 [aj]**6:64** Jn 16:30; Ac 26:4 [ak]Mt 10:4; Jn 13:21 [al]**6:65** Lk 14:26 [am]**6:67** Mk 11:11 [an]**6:68** Lk 6:14 [ao]**6:69** Mk 1:24 [ap]**6:70** Jn 13:18 [aq]Mt 4:1,10; Jn 13:2,27; Ac 13:10 [ar]**6:71** Mk 3:19 [as]Mt 10:4; Jn 13:21 [at]**7:1** Mt 17:22 [au]Lk 1:5 [av]Jn 11:36 [aw]Jn 5:18 [ax]**7:2** Ex 23:16 [ay]**7:3** Mk 3:21,31-35; 6:3; Lk 8:19 [az]Mk 6:28; Jn 5:36; Heb 3:9; Rv 15:3

[A]**6:44** Or *brings*, or *leads*; see the use of this Gk verb in Jn 12:32; 21:6; Ac 16:19; Jms 2:6. [B]**6:45** Is 54:13 [C]**6:47** Other mss add *in Me* [D]**6:58** Other mss omit *the manna* [E]**6:60** Lit *hear* [F]**6:64** Other mss omit *not* [G]**6:69** Other mss read *You are the Messiah, the Son of the Living God* [H]**6:71** Other mss read *Judas Iscariot, Simon's son* [I]**6:71** Lit *Judas, of Simon Iscariot* [J]**7:2** Or *Booths* [K]**7:2** One of 3 great Jewish religious festivals, along with Passover and Pentecost; Ex 23:14; Dt 16:16

one does anything in secret while he's seeking public recognition. If You do these things, show Yourself to the world." 5(For not even His brothers believed in Him.)

6Jesus told them, "My time[a] has not yet arrived, but your time is always at hand. 7The world cannot hate[b] you, but it does hate Me because I testify about it — that its deeds are evil. 8Go up to the festival yourselves. I'm not going up to the festival yet,[A] because My time has not yet fully come." 9After He had said these things, He stayed in Galilee.

Jesus at the Festival of Tabernacles

10After His brothers had gone up to the festival, then He also went up, not openly but secretly. 11The Jews were looking for Him at the festival and saying, "Where is He?" 12And there was a lot of discussion about Him among the crowds. Some were saying, "He's a good[c] man." Others were saying, "No, on the contrary, He's deceiving[d] the people." 13Still, nobody was talking publicly about Him because they feared the Jews.

14When the festival was already half over, Jesus went up into the ·temple complex[e] and began to teach. 15Then the Jews were amazed and said, "How does He know the Scriptures,[f] since He hasn't been trained?"

16Jesus answered them, "My teaching isn't Mine but is from the One who sent Me.[g] 17If anyone wants to do His will,[h] he will understand whether the teaching is from God or if I am speaking on My own. 18The one who speaks for himself seeks his own glory.[i] But He who seeks the glory[j] of the One who sent Him is true,[k] and there is no unrighteousness in Him.[l] 19Didn't Moses[m] give you the law? Yet none of you keeps the law![n] Why do you want to kill Me?"

20"You have a demon!" the crowd responded. "Who wants to kill You?"

21"I did one work,[o] and you are all amazed," Jesus answered. 22"Consider this: Moses has given you circumcision[p] — not that it comes from Moses but from the fathers[q] — and you circumcise a man on the Sabbath.[r] 23If a man receives circumcision on the Sabbath[s] so that the law of Moses[t] won't be broken, are you angry at Me because I made a man entirely well on the Sabbath? 24Stop judging[u] according to outward appearances; rather judge according to righteous judgment."

The Identity of the Messiah

25Some of the people of Jerusalem[v] were saying, "Isn't this the man they want to kill? 26Yet, look! He's speaking publicly and they're saying nothing to Him. Can it be true that the authorities[w] know He is the ·Messiah?[x] 27But we know where this man is from.[y] When the Messiah comes, nobody will know where He is from."

28As He was teaching in the temple complex,[z] Jesus cried out, "You know Me and you know where I am from. Yet I have not come on My own, but the One who sent Me[aa] is true. You don't know Him;[ab] 29I know Him because I am from Him, and He sent Me."[ac]

30Then they tried to seize Him. Yet no one laid a hand on Him because His hour[B] had not yet come. 31However, many from the crowd believed in Him and said, "When the Messiah comes, He won't perform more signs than this man has done,[ad] will He?"

32The ·Pharisees[ae] heard the crowd muttering these things about Him, so the ·chief priests[af] and the Pharisees sent temple police to arrest Him.

33Then Jesus said, "I am only with you for a short time.[ag] Then I'm going to the One who sent Me.[ah] 34You will look for Me, but you will not find Me; and where I am, you cannot come."[ai]

35Then the Jews[aj] said to one another, "Where does He intend to go so we won't find Him? He doesn't intend to go to the Dispersion[C,ak] among the Greeks[al] and teach the Greeks, does He? 36What is this remark He made: 'You will look for Me, and you will not find Me; and where I am, you cannot come'[am]?"

The Promise of the Spirit

37On the last and most important day of the festival,[an] Jesus stood up and cried out, "If anyone is thirsty, he should come to Me[D,ao] and drink![ap] 38The one who believes in Me,[aq] as the

[a]**7:6** Ps 37:39; Lk 20:10; Jn 7:8
[b]**7:7** Lk 6:27; 19:14
[c]**7:12** Gn 1:31
[d]Rv 20:10
[e]**7:14** Ac 21:26
[f]**7:15** Mt 26:54
[g]**7:16** Jn 5:19,30
[h]**7:17** Rm 8:27; Eph 1:9
[i]**7:18** Php 3:19
[j]Lk 9:32; Jn 17:24; 2Co 3:18; 1Pt 5:4; 2Pt 3:18
[k]Jn 8:14; 1Jn 5:20
[l]1Jn 3:5
[m]**7:19** Ps 77:20; Mt 8:4; Heb 3:2
[n]Rm 2:12-29; 3:9-10,20-23,27-28
[o]**7:21** Jn 5:36; Heb 3:9; Rv 15:3
[p]**7:22** Ac 15:1; Gl 6:15
[q]Gn 17:9-14; Lv 12:3
[r]Mk 2:23
[s]**7:23** Lk 13:10
[t]Lk 2:22
[u]**7:24** Lk 6:37; Heb 9:27
[v]**7:25** Mt 23:37
[w]**7:26** Lk 8:41; 12:58
[x]Mt 1:17; Eph 5:2
[y]**7:27** Mt 13:55; 21:11; Lk 4:22; Jn 6:42
[z]**7:28** Ac 21:26
[aa]Jn 5:19
[ab]Jn 1:26-33; 5:13; 8:14,19,55; 9:29-30; 12:35; 13:7; 14:5; 15:15,21; 20:14; Gl 4:8; 1Th 4:5; 2Th 1:8; Ti 1:16
[ac]**7:29** Mk 9:37; Lk 10:22; Jn 1:6; 9:16
[ad]**7:31** Jn 15:24
[ae]**7:32** Mk 7:3
[af]Mt 2:4
[ag]**7:33** Jn 12:35; 14:19; 16:5,16
[ah]Jn 14:12; 16:5,10,17,28
[ai]**7:34** Jn 8:21; 13:33
[aj]**7:35** Jn 11:36
[ak]Jms 1:1; 1Pt 1:1
[al]Gl 2:3
[am]**7:36** Jn 8:21
[an]**7:37** Lv 23:34-36; Nm 29:35; Dt 16:13-14; Neh 8:18; Jn 5:1
[ao]Lk 14:26
[ap]Is 55:1; Rv 22:17
[aq]**7:38** Jn 6:35

[A]**7:8** Other mss omit *yet* [B]**7:30** The time of His sacrificial death and exaltation; Jn 2:4; 8:20; 12:23,27; 13:1; 17:1 [C]**7:35** Jewish people scattered throughout Gentile lands who spoke Gk and were influenced by Gk culture [D]**7:37** Other mss omit *to Me*

Scripture[a] has said,[A] will have streams of living water[b] flow[c] from deep within him." 39He said this about the Spirit.[d] Those who believed in Jesus were going to receive the Spirit,[e] for the Spirit[B] had not yet been received[C,D] because Jesus had not yet been glorified.

The People Are Divided over Jesus

40When some from the crowd heard these words, they said, "This really is the Prophet!"[E,f] 41Others said, "This is the Messiah!" But some said, "Surely the Messiah doesn't come from Galilee, does He? 42Doesn't the Scripture[g] say that the Messiah comes from David's[h] offspring[F] and from the town of Bethlehem,[i] where David once lived?" 43So a division[j] occurred among the crowd because of Him. 44Some of them wanted to seize Him,[k] but no one laid hands on Him.

Debate over Jesus' Claims

45Then the temple police[l] came to the chief priests[m] and Pharisees, who asked them, "Why haven't you brought Him?"

46The police answered, "No man ever spoke like this!"[G,n]

47Then the Pharisees responded to them: "Are you fooled[o] too? 48Have any of the rulers[p] or Pharisees believed in Him? 49But this crowd, which doesn't know the law, is accursed!"

50Nicodemus[q] — the one who came to Him previously, being one of them — said to them, 51"Our law doesn't judge a man before it hears from him and knows what he's doing, does it?"[r]

52"You aren't from Galilee[s] too, are you?" they replied. "Investigate and you will see that no prophet arises from Galilee."[H,t]

8 [53So each one went to his house. 1But Jesus went to the ·Mount of Olives.[u]

An Adulteress Forgiven

2At dawn He went to the ·temple complex[v] again, and all the people were coming to Him.[w] He sat down[x] and began to teach them. 3Then the ·scribes and the ·Pharisees[y] brought a woman caught in adultery,[z] making her stand in the center. 4"Teacher," they said to Him, "this woman was caught in the act of committing adultery.[aa] 5In the law Moses[ab] commanded us to stone such women.[ac] So what do You say?" 6They asked this to trap Him,[ad] in order that they might have evidence to accuse Him.

Jesus stooped down and started writing on the ground with His finger. 7When they persisted in questioning Him, He stood up and said to them, "The one without sin[ae] among you[af] should be the first to throw a stone at her."[ag]

8Then He stooped down again and continued writing on the ground. 9When they heard this, they left one by one, starting with the older men. Only He was left, with the woman in the center. 10When Jesus stood up, He said to her, "·Woman, where are they? Has no one condemned you?"

11"No one, Lord,"[I] she answered.

"Neither do I condemn you,"[ah] said Jesus. "Go, and from now on do not sin anymore."][J]

The Light of the World

12Then Jesus spoke to them again: "I am[ai] the light[aj] of the world. Anyone who follows Me will never walk in the darkness but will have the light of life."[ak]

13So the Pharisees said to Him, "You are testifying about Yourself. Your testimony is not valid."[K]

14"Even if I testify about Myself," Jesus replied, "My testimony is valid,[L] because I know where I came from and where I'm going. But you don't know where I come from or where I'm going.[al] 15You judge[am] by human standards.[M,an] I judge no one.[ao] 16And if I do judge, My judgment is true, because I am not alone, but I and the Father who sent Me judge[ap] together.[aq] 17Even in your law it is written that the witness of two men is valid.[ar] 18I am the One who testifies[as] about Myself, and the Father who sent Me testifies about Me."

19Then they asked Him, "Where is Your Father?"

[a]**7:38** Mt 26:54 [b]Jn 4:10-14 [c]Ex 17:1-6; Ps 78:15-16; 105:40-41; Pr 18:4; Is 12:3; Ezk 47:1-11; Zch 14:8; Rv 22:1-2 [d]**7:39** Ps 51:11; Jn 1:33; Ac 2:4; 8:15; Rm 8:9; Gl 5:25; Ti 3:5; Rv 3:22 [e]Ac 2:33 [f]**7:40** Jn 6:14 [g]**7:42** 2Pt 1:20 [h]Lk 1:27 [i]Gn 35:19 [j]**7:43** Jn 9:16; 1Co 1:10 [k]**7:44** Jn 10:39 [l]**7:45** Jn 18:18 [m]Mt 2:4 [n]**7:46** Mt 7:28-29 [o]**7:47** Rv 20:10 [p]**7:48** Lk 8:41 [q]**7:50** Jn 3:1; 19:39 [r]**7:51** Dt 1:16; 17:6; 19:15 [s]**7:52** Mt 17:22 [t]2Kg 14:25 [u]**8:1** Mt 21:1 [v]**8:2** Ac 21:26 [w]Mk 1:45 [x]Mk 9:35 [y]**8:3** Mk 7:3 [z]Nm 5:11 [aa]**8:4** Mt 5:27-28 [ab]**8:5** Ps 77:20; Mt 8:4; Heb 3:2 [ac]Lv 20:10; Dt 22:22-24; Ezk 16:38-41 [ad]**8:6** Lk 11:54 [ae]**8:7** Rm 3:23; 6:23 [af]Rm 2:1,22 [ag]Dt 17:7 [ah]**8:11** Jn 3:17 [ai]**8:12** Ex 3:14; Jn 8:24,58 [aj]Ps 36:9; Jn 12:46; 1Jn 2:8 [ak]Ex 13:21-22; 14:19-25; Is 42:6; 49:6; 60:19-22; Zch 14:5-8; Jn 9:5; 12:46 [al]**8:14** Jn 3:8; 7:28; 9:29; 12:35; 13:3,36; 14:5; 16:5,28; 1Jn 2:11 [am]**8:15** Lk 6:37; Rv 19:11 [an]Php 3:3 [ao]Jn 3:17; 12:47 [ap]**8:16** Mt 12:41; 2Th 1:5 [aq]Jn 16:32 [ar]**8:17** Nm 35:30; Jn 8:14 [as]**8:18** 1Jn 5:7,9

[A]**7:38** Jesus may have had several OT passages in mind; Is 58:11; Ezk 47:1-12; Zch 14:8 [B]**7:39** Other mss read *Holy Spirit* [C]**7:39** Other mss read *had not yet been given* [D]**7:39** Lit *the Spirit was not yet*; the word *received* is implied from the previous clause. [E]**7:40** Probably the Prophet in Dt 18:15 [F]**7:42** Lit *seed* [G]**7:46** Other mss read *like this man* [H]**7:52** Jonah and probably other prophets did come from Galilee; 2Kg 14:25 [I]**8:11** Or *Sir*; Jn 4:15,49; 5:7; 6:34; 9:36 [J]**8:11** Other mss omit bracketed text [K]**8:13** The law of Moses required at least 2 witnesses to make a claim legally valid (v. 17). [L]**8:14** Or *true* [M]**8:15** Lit *You judge according to the flesh*

"You know neither Me nor My Father,"[a] Jesus answered. "If you knew Me, you would also know My Father."[b] 20 He spoke these words by the treasury,[A,c] while teaching in the temple complex. But no one seized Him, because His hour[B] had not come.

Jesus Predicts His Departure

21 Then He said to them again, "I'm going away;[d] you will look for Me, and you will die in your sin.[e] Where I'm going, you cannot come."[f]

22 So the •Jews said again, "He won't kill Himself, will He, since He says, 'Where I'm going, you cannot come'[g]?"

23 "You are from below," He told them, "I am from above.[h] You are of this world;[i] I am not of this •world.[j] 24 Therefore I told you that you will die in your sins. For if you do not believe that I am He,[C] you will die in your sins."

25 "Who are You?" they questioned.

"Precisely what I've been telling you from the very beginning," Jesus told them. 26 "I have many things to say and to judge about you, but the One who sent Me[k] is true, and what I have heard from Him—these things I tell the world."[l]

27 They did not know He was speaking to them about the Father. 28 So Jesus said to them, "When you lift up the •Son of Man,[m] then you will know that I am[n] He, and that I do nothing on My own.[o] But just as the Father taught Me, I say these things. 29 The One who sent Me is with Me. He has not left Me alone,[p] because I always do what pleases Him."

Truth and Freedom

30 As He was saying these things, many believed in Him. 31 So Jesus said to the Jews who had believed Him, "If you continue in My word,[D,q] you really are My disciples. 32 You will know the truth,[r] and the truth will set you free."

33 "We are descendants[E] of Abraham,"[s] they answered Him, "and we have never been enslaved to anyone. How can You say, 'You will become free'?"

34 Jesus responded, "•I assure you: Everyone who commits sin is a •slave of sin.[t] 35 A slave does not remain in the household forever,[u] but a son does remain forever.[v] 36 Therefore, if the Son sets you free, you really will be free. 37 I know you are descendants[E] of Abraham,[w] but you are trying to kill Me because My word[D] is not welcome among you. 38 I speak what I have seen[x] in the presence of the Father;[F,y] therefore, you do what you have heard from your father."

39 "Our father is Abraham!" they replied.

"If you were Abraham's children," Jesus told them, "you would do what Abraham did.[z] 40 But now you are trying to kill Me, a man who has told you the truth[aa] that I heard from God. Abraham did not do this! 41 You're doing what your father does."[ab]

"We weren't born[ac] of sexual immorality,"[ad] they said. "We have one Father—God."[ae]

42 Jesus said to them, "If God were your Father, you would love Me,[af] because I came from God[ag] and I am here. For I didn't come on My own, but He sent Me. 43 Why don't you understand what I say? Because you cannot listen to[G] My word.[ah] 44 You are of your father the Devil,[ai] and you want to carry out your father's desires. He was a murderer[aj] from the beginning[ak] and has not stood in the truth,[al] because there is no truth in him. When he tells a lie, he speaks from his own nature,[H] because he is a liar and the father of liars.[I] 45 Yet because I tell the truth, you do not believe Me. 46 Who among you can convict Me of sin?[am] If I tell the truth, why don't you believe Me? 47 The one who is from God listens to God's words. This is why you don't listen, because you are not from God."

Jesus and Abraham

48 The Jews responded to Him, "Aren't we right in saying that You're a •Samaritan[an] and have a demon?"[ao]

49 "I do not have a demon," Jesus answered. "On the contrary, I honor My Father and you dishonor Me. 50 I do not seek My glory;[ap] the One who seeks it also judges. 51 I assure you:

[a] 8:19 Jn 7:28; 1Jn 2:23
[b] Lk 10:22; Jn 17:3; 1Jn 4:8
[c] 8:20 Mk 12:41,43; Lk 21:1
[d] 8:21 Jn 14:2; 16:5
[e] Dt 24:16; Ezk 3:18; 33:8; Jn 15:22; Rm 3:23; 6:23
[f] Jn 7:34,36; 8:22; 13:33
[g] 8:22 Jn 8:21
[h] 8:23 Jn 3:13,31; 18:36; Col 3:1-2
[i] 1Jn 4:5
[j] Jn 15:19; 17:14-16; 18:36
[k] 8:26 Jn 5:19
[l] Jn 3:32; 15:15
[m] 8:28 Mk 2:10
[n] Jn 8:24
[o] Mk 6:5; Jn 9:33; 15:5
[p] 8:29 Jn 16:32; Ac 10:38
[q] 8:31 Jn 2:22; 18:32
[r] 8:32 Ps 119:142; Jn 14:6; 2Th 2:10
[s] 8:33 Gn 16:15; Jn 8:37; Heb 2:16
[t] 8:34 Rm 6:17-20; 2Pt 2:19
[u] 8:35 1Jn 2:17
[v] Gn 21:10; Lk 15:31; Gl 4:30
[w] 8:37 Lk 19:9; Jn 8:31-47; Ac 13:26; Rm 4:11,16; Gl 3:7
[x] 8:38 Jn 3:32; 5:19; 6:46
[y] Mt 5:16; 11:27; Lk 11:13; Jn 8:42
[z] 8:39 Gl 3:7,9
[aa] 8:40 Ps 119:142; Jn 14:6
[ab] 8:41 2Jn 9
[ac] 1Jn 2:29
[ad] Hs 2:4; 1Th 4:3
[ae] Dt 32:6
[af] 8:42 Dt 6:5; Lk 10:27; 1Jn 5:1
[ag] Jn 13:3; 16:27; 1Jn 5:20
[ah] 8:43 Lk 6:47; Jn 18:32
[ai] 8:44 Mt 4:1; Jn 13:2,27; Eph 2:1-3
[aj] 1Jn 3:15
[ak] Gn 3:1-4; 4:8-9; Ac 26:4; 2Co 11:3; 1Jn 3:8-15; Rv 12:9
[al] Jn 14:6; Rm 3:7
[am] 8:46 Jn 15:22; 1Jn 3:5
[an] 8:48 Lk 9:52; Ac 1:8
[ao] Jn 7:20; 10:20; Rv 9:20; 18:2
[ap] 8:50 Jn 17:24; Php 3:19; 1Pt 5:4

[A] 8:20 A place for offerings to be given, perhaps in the court of women [B] 8:20 The time of His sacrificial death and exaltation; Jn 2:4; 7:30; 12:23,27; 13:1; 17:1 [C] 8:24 Jesus claimed to be deity, but the Pharisees didn't understand His meaning. [D] 8:31,37 Or *My teaching*, or *My message* [E] 8:33,37 Or *offspring*; lit *seed*; Jn 7:42 [F] 8:38 Other mss read *of My Father* [G] 8:43 Or *cannot hear* [H] 8:44 Lit *from his own things* [I] 8:44 Lit *of it*

If anyone keeps My word,[a] he will never see
death — ever!"
52Then the Jews said, "Now we know You
have a demon. Abraham died and so did the
prophets. You say, 'If anyone keeps My word,
he will never taste death — ever!' 53Are You
greater than our father Abraham who died?
Even the prophets died. Who do You pretend
to be?"[A]
54"If I glorify Myself," Jesus answered, "My
glory is nothing. My Father — you say about
Him, 'He is our God' — He is the One who
glorifies Me. 55You've never known Him, but I
know Him. If I were to say I don't know Him,[b]
I would be a liar like you. But I do know Him,[c]
and I keep His word. 56Your father Abraham
was overjoyed that he would see My day; he
saw it[d] and rejoiced."
57The Jews replied, "You aren't 50 years old
yet, and You've seen Abraham?"[B]
58Jesus said to them, "I assure you: Before
Abraham was, I am."[C,e]
59At that, they picked up stones[f] to throw at
Him.[g] But Jesus was hidden[D,h] and went out of
the temple complex.[E,i]

The Sixth Sign: Healing a Man Born Blind

9 As He was passing by, He saw a man blind
from birth. 2His disciples questioned
Him: "•Rabbi,[j] who sinned, this man[k] or his
parents,[l] that he was born blind?"
3"Neither this man nor his parents sinned,"
Jesus answered. "This came about so that
God's works[m] might be displayed in him.
4We[F] must do the works[n] of Him who sent
Me[G] while it is day.[o] Night is coming when no
one can work. 5As long as I am in the world, I
am the light of the world."[p]
6After He said these things He spit on the
ground, made some mud[q] from the saliva,
and spread the mud on his eyes. 7"Go," He told
him, "wash in the pool of Siloam"[r] (which
means "Sent"). So he left, washed, and came
back seeing.[s]
8His neighbors and those who formerly
had seen him as a beggar said, "Isn't this the
man who sat begging?" 9Some said, "He's the
one." "No," others were saying, "but he looks
like him."

[a]8:51 Jn 8:52,55; 14:23-24; 15:20; 17:6; 18:32; 1Jn 2:5; Rv 1:3; 3:8,10; 22:7,9
[b]8:55 Jn 7:28
[c]Mt 11:27
[d]8:56 Lk 10:24; Heb 11:13-19
[e]8:58 Ex 3:14; Ps 45:8; Jn 1:15; 8:24; 17:5; Col 1:17
[f]8:59 Jn 10:33
[g]Ex 17:4; Lv 24:16; 1Sm 30:6; 1Kg 21:10-13; Jn 10:31; 11:8
[h]Lk 4:30; Jn 12:36
[i]Ac 21:26
[j]9:2 Jn 11:8
[k]Ezk 18:20
[l]Ex 20:5; Jb 21:19
[m]9:3 Jn 5:36; 6:28-29; Rm 14:20; Heb 3:9; Rv 15:3
[n]9:4 Jn 5:17; 2Jn 8
[o]Jn 11:9; 12:35; Rm 13:12
[p]9:5 Mt 5:14; Jn 8:12; 12:46
[q]9:6 Gn 2:7
[r]9:7 Lk 13:4; Jn 9:11
[s]Is 35:5
[t]9:11 Jn 9:7
[u]Ac 9:12
[v]9:13 Mk 7:3
[w]9:14 Mk 2:23
[x]9:16 Jn 7:29
[y]Mt 26:45; Lk 24:7; Jn 9:24; Rm 5:19
[z]Jn 7:43; 10:19; 1Co 1:10

He kept saying, "I'm the one!"
10Therefore they asked him, "Then how
were your eyes opened?"
11He answered, "The man called Jesus made
mud, spread it on my eyes, and told me, 'Go
to Siloam[t] and wash.' So when I went and
washed I received my sight."[u]
12"Where is He?" they asked.
"I don't know," he said.

The Healed Man's Testimony

13They brought the man who used to be
blind to the •Pharisees.[v] 14The day that Jesus
made the mud and opened his eyes was a Sabbath.[w] 15So again the Pharisees asked him how
he received his sight.
"He put mud on my eyes," he told them. "I
washed and I can see."
16Therefore some of the Pharisees said,
"This man is not from God,[x] for He doesn't
keep the Sabbath!" But others were saying,
"How can a sinful man[y] perform such signs?"
And there was a division[z] among them.

Text Message

TEXT MESSAGES

The blind beggar needed a little respect after the passing disciples essentially accused someone in his family, or himself, of gross sin. Jesus told him, "Go . . . wash." The blind beggar is challenged to trust and obey. Jesus' word to him was the right word for him: he could go and wash, and after that, obedience. Let the gospel you share be right and actionable for your audience. Let them understand that salvation is offered freely and need only be accepted. From that moment, they begin a wonderful journey with God where they no longer stumble blindly, but they see.

[A]8:53 Lit *Who do You make Yourself?* [B]8:57 Other mss read *and Abraham has seen You?* [C]8:58 *I AM* is the name God gave Himself at the burning bush; Ex 3:13-14; see note at Jn 8:24. [D]8:59 Or *Jesus hid Himself* [E]8:59 Other mss add *and having gone through their midst, He passed by* [F]9:4 Other mss read *I* [G]9:4 Other mss read *sent us*

17 Again they asked the blind man,[A] "What do you say about Him, since He opened your eyes?"

"He's a prophet,"[a] he said.

18 The ˚Jews did not believe this about him—that he was blind and received sight—until they summoned the parents of the one who had received his sight.

19 They asked them, "Is this your son, the one you say was born blind? How then does he now see?"

20 "We know this is our son and that he was born blind," his parents answered. 21 "But we don't know how he now sees, and we don't know who opened his eyes. Ask him; he's of age. He will speak for himself." 22 His parents said these things because they were afraid of the Jews, since the Jews had already agreed that if anyone confessed Him as ˚Messiah,[b] he would be banned from the ˚synagogue. 23 This is why his parents said, "He's of age; ask him."

24 So a second time they summoned the man who had been blind and told him, "Give glory[c] to God.[B,d] We know that this man is a sinner!"

25 He answered, "Whether or not He's a sinner, I don't know. One thing I do know: I was blind, and now I can see!"

26 Then they asked him, "What did He do to you? How did He open your eyes?"

27 "I already told you," he said, "and you didn't listen. Why do you want to hear it again? You don't want to become His disciples too, do you?"

28 They ridiculed him: "You're that man's disciple, but we're Moses'[e] disciples. 29 We know that God has spoken to Moses. But this man—we don't know where He's from!"[f]

30 "This is an amazing thing," the man told them. "You don't know where He is from, yet He opened my eyes! 31 We know that God doesn't listen to sinners,[g] but if anyone is God-fearing and does His will,[h] He listens to him.[i] 32 Throughout history[C] no one has ever heard of someone opening the eyes of a person born blind.[j] 33 If this man were not from God, He wouldn't be able to do anything."[k]

34 "You were born entirely in sin,"[l] they replied, "and are you trying to teach us?" Then they threw him out.[D,m]

The Blind Man's Sight and the Pharisees' Blindness

35 When Jesus heard that they had thrown the man out, He found him and asked, "Do you believe in the ˚Son of Man?"[E,n]

36 "Who is He, Sir,[o] that I may believe in Him?" he asked.

37 Jesus answered, "You have seen Him; in fact, He is the One speaking with you."

38 "I believe, Lord!" he said, and he worshiped Him.

39 Jesus said, "I came into this world[p] for judgment,[q] in order that those who do not see will see and those who do see will become blind."[r]

40 Some of the Pharisees who were with Him heard these things and asked Him, "We aren't blind too, are we?"

41 "If you were blind," Jesus told them, "you wouldn't have sin.[F,s] But now that you say, 'We see'—your sin remains.

The Ideal Shepherd

10 "˚I assure you: Anyone who doesn't enter the sheep pen by the door but climbs in some other way, is a thief and a robber.[t] 2 The one who enters by the door is the shepherd[u] of the sheep.[v] 3 The doorkeeper opens it for him, and the sheep hear his voice. He calls his own sheep by name and leads them out. 4 When he has brought all his own outside, he goes ahead of them. The sheep follow him because they recognize his voice. 5 They will never follow a stranger; instead they will run away from him, because they don't recognize the voice of strangers."

6 Jesus gave them this illustration, but they did not understand[w] what He was telling them.

The Good Shepherd

7 So Jesus said again, "I assure you: I am[x] the door of the sheep.[y] 8 All who came before Me[G] are thieves and robbers, but the sheep didn't listen to them. 9 I am the door. If anyone en-

[a] 9:17 Jn 6:14
[b] 9:22 Mt 1:17; Eph 5:2
[c] 9:24 Jn 17:24
[d] Jos 7:19; 1Sm 6:5; Is 42:12; Jr 13:16; Lk 2:14; Rm 4:20
[e] 9:28 Ps 77:20; Mt 8:4; Heb 3:2
[f] 9:29 Jn 7:27-28; 8:14
[g] 9:31 Jb 27:9; Ps 66:18; Pr 28:9; Is 1:15; 1Jn 3:21
[h] Eph 1:9
[i] Ps 34:15,16; 145:19; Pr 15:20; Jms 5:16-18; 1Jn 5:14-15
[j] 9:32 Jn 15:24
[k] 9:33 Jn 8:28
[l] 9:34 Ps 51:5
[m] Is 66:5
[n] 9:35 Mk 2:10
[o] 9:36 Lk 10:1
[p] 9:39 Jn 18:37
[q] Mk 12:40; Jn 5:22-30
[r] Lk 4:18; Jn 3:19; 12:47-50
[s] 9:41 Jn 15:22,24; 1Jn 1:8; 3:5
[t] 10:1 Jr 7:11; Hs 6:9; 1Th 5:2,4; 2Pt 3:10; Rv 3:3; 16:15
[u] 10:2 Gn 4:2; Ps 23:1
[v] Mt 7:15
[w] 10:6 Mk 9:32; Lk 2:50; 9:45; 18:34; Jn 2:24; 12:16
[x] 10:7 Ex 3:14; Ps 45:8; Jn 8:24
[y] Mt 7:15

[A] 9:17 = the man who had been blind [B] 9:24 *Give glory to God* was a solemn charge to tell the truth; Jos 7:19. [C] 9:32 Lit *From the age* [D] 9:34 = they banned him from the synagogue; v. 22 [E] 9:35 Other mss read *the Son of God* [F] 9:41 To *have sin* is an idiom that refers to guilt caused by sin. [G] 10:8 Other mss omit *before Me*

ters by Me, he will be saved and will come in
and go out and find pasture. 10 A thief comes
only to steal[a] and to kill and to destroy.[b] I have
come so that they may have life and have it in
abundance.
11 "I am the good shepherd.[c] The good shepherd lays down his life for the sheep.[d] 12 The
hired man, since he is not the shepherd and
doesn't own the sheep, leaves them[A] and runs
away when he sees a wolf[e] coming. The wolf
then snatches and scatters them. 13 This happens because he is a hired man and doesn't
care about the sheep.
14 "I am the good shepherd. I know My own
sheep, and they know Me, 15 as the Father
knows Me, and I know the Father.[f] I lay down
My life[g] for the sheep. 16 But I have other sheep[h]
that are not of this fold; I must bring them
also, and they will listen to My voice. Then
there will be one flock, one shepherd.[i] 17 This is
why the Father loves Me,[j] because I am laying
down My life[k] so I may take it up again. 18 No
one takes it from Me, but I lay it down on My
own. I have the right to lay it down, and I have
the right to take it up again. I have received
this command from My Father."[l]
19 Again a division[m] took place among the
•Jews because of these words. 20 Many of
them were saying, "He has a demon[n] and He's
crazy! Why do you listen to Him?" 21 Others
were saying, "These aren't the words of someone demon-possessed. Can a demon open the
eyes of the blind?"[o]

Jesus at the Festival of Dedication

22 Then the Festival of Dedication[B] took
place in Jerusalem, and it was winter.
23 Jesus was walking in the •temple complex in
Solomon's Colonnade.[C,p] 24 Then the Jews surrounded Him and asked, "How long are You
going to keep us in suspense?[D] If You are the
•Messiah,[q] tell us plainly."[E,r]
25 "I did tell you and you don't believe,"
Jesus answered them. "The works[s] that I do in
My Father's name testify about Me. 26 But you
don't believe because you are not My sheep.[F,t]
27 My sheep hear My voice, I know them, and
they follow Me. 28 I give them eternal life,[u] and
they will never perish[v]—ever! No one will
snatch[w] them out of My hand. 29 My Father,[x]
who has given them to Me, is greater than all.
No one is able to snatch them out of the Father's hand. 30 The Father and I are one."[G,y]

[a] **10:10** Eph 4:28 [b] Jn 6:27 [c] **10:11** Ps 23; Is 40:11; Ezk 34:12,23; 37:24; Zch 13:7; Jn 21:15-17; Heb 13:20; 1Pt 2:25; 5:4; Rv 7:17 [d] Mt 20:28; Mk 10:45; 2Co 5:21; Gl 3:13; 1Jn 3:16 [e] **10:12** Lk 10:3 [f] **10:15** Mt 11:27; Lk 10:22 [g] Mt 20:28 [h] **10:16** Is 56:8; Ezk 34:11-13; Mt 8:11,12; Jn 12:32; Ac 10:34-35; 1Pt 2:25 [i] Ezk 34:23; 37:24; Jn 11:52; 17:11,20-22; Eph 2:11-19 [j] **10:17** Jn 3:35; 5:20 [k] 1Jn 3:16 [l] **10:18** Jn 5:19 [m] **10:19** Jn 7:43; 9:16 [n] **10:20** Jn 7:20; 8:48; Rv 9:20; 18:2 [o] **10:21** Ex 4:11; Ps 146:8; Jn 9:32-33 [p] **10:23** Ac 3:11; 5:12 [q] **10:24** Mt 1:17; Eph 5:2 [r] Mt 26:63; Lk 22:67; 2Co 3:12 [s] **10:25** Jn 5:36; 6:28-29; Rm 14:20; Heb 3:9; 2Jn 8; Rv 15:3 [t] **10:26** Jn 6:37; 8:47 [u] **10:28** Jn 12:25; Ac 13:48; 1Jn 2:25 [v] Mt 10:42; Mk 9:41; Lk 21:18; Jn 3:16; 6:27,39; 17:12; 18:9; 2Co 4:9; 2Jn 8 [w] 1Th 4:17 [x] **10:29** Mt 11:27 [y] **10:30** Jn 1:15; 14:10; 17:11; 1Jn 2:24

GOD WHO SENDS

The Pilgrimage of New Life

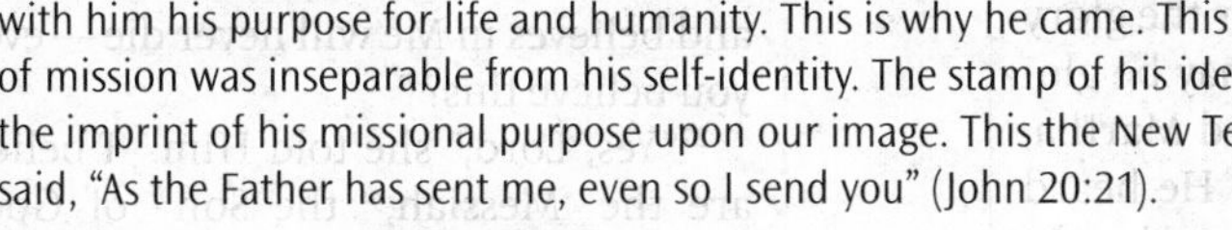

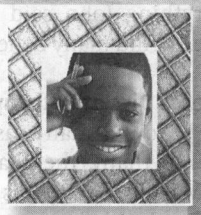

The Christian life is a spiritual pilgrimage. It is not a journey to a shrine which has limitations of space and time. It is a journey into life, a life so rich no limitation of space and time is able to contain it. Jesus came on a pilgrimage to earth to give us life. He said, "I came that they may have life, and have it abundantly" (John 10:10). This life, which he brings to us and which has its source in the Heavenly Father, is inexhaustible in its meaning. And this life he has invited us to share. This invitation into life, moreover, is an invitation to share the good news of that life with others. We join him in his pilgrimage, a journey into the glories of his kingdom, into the beauties of his family, into the limitless love of his outreached arms. He calls us into partnership, to explore with him his purpose for life and humanity. This is why he came. This is why he was sent. His sense of mission was inseparable from his self-identity. The stamp of his identity upon us leaves indelibly the imprint of his missional purpose upon our image. This the New Testament makes clear. Jesus said, "As the Father has sent me, even so I send you" (John 20:21).

(DuBose, 13)

[A] **10:12** Lit *leaves the sheep* [B] **10:22** Or *Hanukkah*, also called *the Feast of Lights*; this festival commemorated the rededication of the temple in 164 B.C. [C] **10:23** Rows of columns supporting a roof [D] **10:24** Lit *How long are you taking away our life?* [E] **10:24** Or *openly*, or *publicly* [F] **10:26** Other mss add *just as I told you* [G] **10:30** Lit *I and the Father—We are one.*

Renewed Efforts to Stone Jesus

31 Again the Jews picked up rocks to stone
Him.[a]
32 Jesus replied, "I have shown you many
good works[b] from the Father. Which of these
works are you stoning Me for?"
33 "We aren't stoning[c] You for a good work,"
the Jews answered, "but for blasphemy, because
You—being a man—make Yourself God."
34 Jesus answered them, "Isn't it written in
your scripture,[A] **I said, you are gods**?[B,d] 35 If He
called those whom the word[e] of God came to
'gods'—and the Scripture[f] cannot be broken— 36 do you say, 'You are blaspheming' to
the One the Father set apart and sent into the
world, because I said: I am the Son of God?[g]
37 If I am not doing My Father's works,[h] don't
believe Me. 38 But if I am doing them and you
don't believe Me, believe the works. This way
you will know and understand[C] that the Father is in Me and I in the Father."[i] 39 Then they
were trying again to seize Him,[j] yet He eluded
their grasp.[k]

Many beyond the Jordan Believe in Jesus

40 So He departed again across the Jordan[l]
to the place where John[m] had been baptizing
earlier, and He remained there. 41 Many came
to Him[n] and said, "John never did a sign, but
everything John said about this man was
true." 42 And many believed in Him there.

Lazarus Dies at Bethany

11 Now a man was sick, Lazarus, from
Bethany,[o] the village of Mary and her sister Martha.[p] 2 Mary was the one who anointed
the Lord with fragrant oil and wiped His feet
with her hair,[q] and it was her brother Lazarus
who was sick. 3 So the sisters sent a message to
Him: "Lord, the one You love is sick."
4 When Jesus heard it, He said, "This sickness will not end in death but is for the glory
of God,[r] so that the Son of God[s] may be glorified through it." 5 Now Jesus loved Martha,
her sister, and Lazarus. 6 So when He heard
that he was sick, He stayed two more days in
the place where He was. 7 Then after that, He
said to the disciples, "Let's go to Judea[t] again."
8 "•Rabbi,"[u] the disciples told Him, "just now
the •Jews tried to stone You,[v] and You're going
there again?"
9 "Aren't there 12 hours in a day?" Jesus answered. "If anyone walks during the day, he
doesn't stumble, because he sees the light
of this world.[w] 10 If anyone walks during the
night,[x] he does stumble, because the light is
not in him." 11 He said this, and then He told
them, "Our friend Lazarus has fallen •asleep,[y]
but I'm on My way to wake him up."
12 Then the disciples said to Him, "Lord, if
he has fallen asleep, he will get well."
13 Jesus, however, was speaking about his
death, but they thought He was speaking
about natural sleep. 14 So Jesus then told them
plainly, "Lazarus has died. 15 I'm glad for you
that I wasn't there so that you may believe.
But let's go to him."
16 Then Thomas[z] (called "Twin") said to his
fellow disciples, "Let's go so that we may die
with Him."

The Resurrection and the Life

17 When Jesus arrived, He found that Lazarus had already been in the tomb[aa] four days.
18 Bethany was near Jerusalem[ab] (about two
miles[D] away). 19 Many of the Jews had come
to Martha and Mary to comfort them about
their brother. 20 As soon as Martha heard that
Jesus was coming, she went to meet Him. But
Mary remained seated in the house.
21 Then Martha said to Jesus, "Lord, if You
had been here, my brother wouldn't have
died. 22 Yet even now I know that whatever
You ask from God, God will give You."
23 "Your brother will rise[ac] again," Jesus told
her.
24 Martha said, "I know that he will rise
again in the resurrection at the last day."[ad]
25 Jesus said to her, "I am[ae] the resurrection
and the life. The one who believes in Me,[af]
even if he dies, will live.[ag] 26 Everyone who lives
and believes in Me will never die—ever.[ah] Do
you believe this?"
27 "Yes, Lord," she told Him, "I believe You
are the •Messiah,[ai] the Son[aj] of God, who
comes into the world."[ak]

Jesus Shares the Sorrow of Death

28 Having said this, she went back and

[a] **10:31** Jn 11:8
[b] **10:32** Jn 5:36; 15:24
[c] **10:33** Lv 24:16; Mt 9:3; 26:62-66; Jn 5:18; 8:59
[d] **10:34** Ps 82:6
[e] **10:35** Lk 8:21; Jn 2:22; 18:32
[f] Mt 26:54
[g] **10:36** Jn 5:19; Heb 1:2
[h] **10:37** Jn 5:36; 15:24; Heb 3:9; Rv 15:3
[i] **10:38** Jn 14:10; 1Jn 5:20
[j] **10:39** Jn 7:44
[k] Lk 4:30
[l] **10:40** Mk 10:1; Lk 3:3
[m] Mk 1:4
[n] **10:41** Mk 1:45
[o] **11:1** Mk 11:1
[p] Lk 10:38-39,40-42
[q] **11:2** Lk 7:38; Jn 12:3
[r] **11:4** Lk 9:32; Jn 9:3; 10:38; 11:40; 17:24; 2Co 3:18; 2Pt 3:18
[s] Jn 5:19; Heb 1:2
[t] **11:7** Lk 1:5
[u] **11:8** Mt 23:7-8; 26:25,49; Mk 9:5; 11:21; 14:45; Jn 1:38,49; 3:2,26; 4:31; 6:25; 9:2
[v] Jn 10:31
[w] **11:9** Mt 5:14; Jn 8:12
[x] **11:10** Jn 9:4
[y] **11:11** Ac 13:36; 1Co 11:30
[z] **11:16** Mk 3:18
[aa] **11:17** Jn 5:28
[ab] **11:18** Mt 23:37
[ac] **11:23** Mk 9:27
[ad] **11:24** Jn 2:4; 6:39; 1Pt 1:5; 3:3; 2Pt 3:3; Jd 18
[ae] **11:25** Ex 3:14; Jn 8:24,58
[af] Jn 6:35
[ag] Php 1:21
[ah] **11:26** Jn 6:50; 8:51
[ai] **11:27** Mt 1:17; Eph 5:2
[aj] Jn 5:19
[ak] Jn 18:37

[A] **10:34** Other mss read *in the scripture* [B] **10:34** Ps 82:6 [C] **10:38** Other mss read *know and believe* [D] **11:18** Lit *15 stadia; 1 stadion* = 600 feet

called her sister Mary, saying in private, "The
Teacher is here and is calling for you."
29 As soon as she heard this, she got up
quickly and went to Him.[a] 30 Jesus had not yet
come into the village but was still in the place
where Martha had met Him. 31 The Jews who
were with her in the house consoling her saw
that Mary got up quickly and went out. So
they followed her, supposing that she was going to the tomb[b] to cry there.
32 When Mary came to where Jesus was and
saw Him, she fell at His feet[c] and told Him,
"Lord, if You had been here, my brother
would not have died!"
33 When Jesus saw her crying, and the Jews
who had come with her crying, He was angry[A]
in His spirit[d] and deeply moved. 34 "Where
have you put him?" He asked.
"Lord," they told Him, "come and see."
35 Jesus wept.[e]
36 So the Jews said, "See how He loved[f] him!"
37 But some of them said, "Couldn't He who
opened the blind man's eyes[g] also have kept
this man from dying?"

The Seventh Sign: Raising Lazarus from the Dead

38 Then Jesus, angry[B] in Himself again, came
to the tomb. It was a cave, and a stone was lying against it.[h] 39 "Remove the stone," Jesus
said.
Martha, the dead man's sister, told Him,
"Lord, he's already decaying.[C] It's been four
days."
40 Jesus said to her, "Didn't I tell you that
if you believed you would see the glory[i] of
God?"[j]
41 So they removed the stone. Then Jesus
raised His eyes and said, "Father, I thank[k] You
that You heard Me.[l] 42 I know that You always
hear Me, but because of the crowd standing
here I said this, so they may believe You sent[m]
Me." 43 After He said this, He shouted with a
loud voice, "Lazarus, come out!" 44 The dead
man came out bound hand and foot with
linen strips and with his face wrapped in a
cloth. Jesus said to them, "Loose him and let
him go."

The Plot to Kill Jesus

45 Therefore, many of the Jews who came to
Mary and saw what He did believed in Him.[n]
46 But some of them went to the ·Pharisees[o]
and told them what Jesus had done.
47 So the ·chief priests and the Pharisees
convened the ·Sanhedrin[p] and said, "What
are we going to do since this man does many
signs? 48 If we let Him continue in this way,
everyone will believe in Him! Then the Romans[q] will come and remove both our place[D]
and our nation."
49 One of them, Caiaphas,[r] who was high
priest[s] that year, said to them, "You know
nothing at all! 50 You're not considering that it
is to your[E] advantage that one man should die
for the people rather than the whole nation
perish."[t] 51 He did not say this on his own, but
being high priest that year he prophesied that
Jesus was going to die[u] for the nation, 52 and
not for the nation only, but also to unite the
scattered children[v] of God. 53 So from that day
on they plotted to kill Him.[w] 54 Therefore Jesus
no longer walked openly[x] among the Jews but
departed from there to the countryside near
the wilderness,[y] to a town called Ephraim.
And He stayed there with the disciples.
55 The Jewish ·Passover[z] was near, and many
went up to Jerusalem[aa] from the country
to purify[F] themselves before the Passover.
56 They were looking for Jesus and asking one
another as they stood in the ·temple complex:[ab] "What do you think? He won't come
to the festival,[ac] will He?" 57 The chief priests[ad]
and the Pharisees had given orders that if
anyone knew where He was, he should report
it so they could arrest Him.

The Anointing at Bethany

12 Six days before the ·Passover, Jesus
came to Bethany[ae] where Lazarus[G]
was, the one Jesus had raised from the dead.[af]
2 So[ag] they gave a dinner for Him there; Martha[ah] was serving them, and Lazarus was
one of those reclining at the table with
Him. 3 Then Mary took a pound of fragrant
oil — pure and expensive nard — anointed
Jesus' feet, and wiped His feet with her hair.[ai]

[a] **11:29** Mk 1:45
[b] **11:31** Jn 5:28
[c] **11:32** Rv 19:10
[d] **11:33** Ps 51:12
[e] **11:35** Lk 19:41
[f] **11:36** Mk 14:44; Jn 5:20
[g] **11:37** Jn 9:6-7
[h] **11:38** Mt 27:60; Mk 15:46; Lk 24:2; Jn 20:1
[i] **11:40** Jn 17:24
[j] Mk 9:23; 1Jn 3:2
[k] **11:41** Mk 8:6; Rm 1:8
[l] Jn 9:31
[m] **11:42** Mk 9:37; Jn 1:6
[n] **11:45** Jn 2:23; 12:11
[o] **11:46** Mk 7:3
[p] **11:47** Mk 13:9
[q] **11:48** Ac 16:21
[r] **11:49** Mt 26:3,57; Lk 3:2; Jn 18:13-14,24,28; Ac 4:6
[s] Lv 16:32
[t] **11:50** Is 53:8; Jn 18:14
[u] **11:51** 2Co 4:10
[v] **11:52** Lk 1:7
[w] **11:53** Jn 5:18
[x] **11:54** Jn 7:1
[y] Mt 3:1; Rv 12:6
[z] **11:55** Ex 12:11
[aa] Mt 23:37
[ab] **11:56** Ac 21:26
[ac] Jn 2:23
[ad] **11:57** Mt 2:4
[ae] **12:1** Mk 11:1
[af] Jn 11:43-44
[ag] **12:2-8** Mt 26:6-13; Mk 14:3-9
[ah] **12:2** Jn 11:1
[ai] **12:3** Mk 14:3; Jn 11:2

[A] **11:33** The Gk word is very strong and probably indicates Jesus' anger against sin's tyranny and death. [B] **11:38** See note at 11:33. [C] **11:39** Lit *he already stinks* [D] **11:48** The temple or possibly all of Jerusalem [E] **11:50** Other mss read *to our* [F] **11:55** The law of Moses required God's people to purify or cleanse themselves so they could celebrate the Passover. Jews often came to Jerusalem a week early to do this; Nm 9:4-11. [G] **12:1** Other mss read *Lazarus who died*

So the house was filled with the fragrance of the oil.

4 Then one of His disciples, Judas Iscariot[a] (who was about to betray Him), said, 5 "Why wasn't this fragrant oil sold for 300 ·denarii[A,b] and given to the poor?" 6 He didn't say this because he cared about the poor but because he was a thief.[c] He was in charge of the money-bag and would steal part of what was put in it.

7 Jesus answered, "Leave her alone; she has kept it for the day of My burial.[d] 8 For you always have the poor with you,[e] but you do not always have Me."

The Decision to Kill Lazarus

9 Then a large crowd of the Jews learned He was there. They came not only because of Jesus, but also to see Lazarus the one He had raised from the dead.[f] 10 Therefore the ·chief priests decided to kill Lazarus also 11 because he was the reason many of the Jews were deserting them[B] and believing in Jesus.

The Triumphal Entry

12 The[g] next day, when the large crowd that had come to the festival heard that Jesus was coming to Jerusalem, 13 they took palm branches[h] and went out to meet Him. They kept shouting: "·***Hosanna!***[i] **He who comes in the name of the Lord is the blessed One**[C,j] — the King of Israel!"[k]

14 Jesus found a young donkey[l] and sat on it, just as it is written: 15 **Fear no more,**[m] **Daughter ·Zion. Look, your King is coming, sitting on a donkey's colt.**[D,n]

16 His disciples did not understand these things at first. However, when Jesus was glorified, then they remembered that these things had been written about Him[o] and that they had done these things to Him. 17 Meanwhile, the crowd, which had been with Him when He called Lazarus out of the tomb[p] and raised him from the dead, continued to testify.[E] 18 This is also why the crowd met Him, because they heard He had done this sign.

19 Then the ·Pharisees said to one another, "You see? You've accomplished nothing. Look — the world has gone after Him!"[q]

Jesus Predicts His Crucifixion

20 Now some Greeks were among those who went up to worship at the festival. 21 So they came to Philip,[r] who was from Bethsaida[s] in Galilee,[t] and requested of him, "Sir,[u] we want to see Jesus."

22 Philip went and told Andrew;[v] then Andrew and Philip went and told Jesus. 23 Jesus replied to them, "The hour has come for the ·Son of Man[w] to be glorified.

24 "·I assure you: Unless a grain of wheat[x] falls to the ground and dies, it remains by itself. But if it dies, it produces a large crop.[F,y] 25 The one who loves his life will lose it,[z] and the one who hates[aa] his life[ab] in this world will keep it for eternal life. 26 If anyone serves Me, he must follow Me. Where I am, there My servant[ac] also will be.[ad] If anyone serves Me, the Father will honor[ae] him.

27 "Now My soul is troubled. What should I say — Father, save Me[af] from this hour? But that is why I came to this hour. 28 Father, glorify Your name!"[G,ag]

Then a voice[ah] came from heaven:[ai] "I have glorified it, and I will glorify it again!"[aj]

29 The crowd standing there heard it and said it was thunder. Others said that an angel had spoken to Him.

30 Jesus responded, "This voice came, not for Me, but for you.[ak] 31 Now is the judgment of this world.[al] Now the ruler of this ·world[am] will be cast out.[an] 32 As for Me, if I am lifted up[H] from the earth I will draw all people to Myself."[ao] 33 He said this to signify what kind of death He was about to die.[ap]

34 Then the crowd replied to Him, "We have heard from the scripture that the ·Messiah will remain forever.[aq] So how can You say, 'The Son of Man[ar] must be lifted up'?[H] Who is this Son of Man?"

35 Jesus answered, "The light will be with you only a little longer.[as] Walk while you have the light[at] so that darkness doesn't overtake you.[au] The one who walks in darkness doesn't know where he's going.[av] 36 While you have the light,[aw] believe in the light so that you may become sons of light." Jesus said this, then went away and hid from them.[ax]

[a] **12:4** Mt 26:14; Mk 3:19
[b] **12:5** Mt 18:28
[c] **12:6** Jn 10:1
[d] **12:7** Jn 19:40
[e] **12:8** Dt 15:11
[f] **12:9** Jn 21:14
[g] **12:12-19** Mt 21:1-11; Mk 11:1-11; Lk 19:28-44
[h] **12:13** Lv 23:40; Rv 7:9
[i] Lk 1:42
[j] Ps 118:25-26
[k] Jn 1:49
[l] **12:14** Lk 13:15
[m] **12:15** Jn 6:20
[n] Zch 9:9
[o] **12:16** Jn 2:22; 14:26
[p] **12:17** Jn 5:28
[q] **12:19** Mk 15:6-15; Lk 19:39-44; Jn 11:47-48; 12:36-43; 19:15
[r] **12:21** Mk 3:18
[s] Mt 11:21; Mk 6:45; 8:22; Lk 9:10; 10:13; Jn 1:44
[t] Mt 17:22
[u] Col 3:22
[v] **12:22** Jn 6:8
[w] **12:23** Mk 2:10
[x] **12:24** Lk 16:7
[y] 1Co 15:36
[z] **12:25** Jn 10:28
[aa] Lk 6:27; 19:14
[ab] Mt 10:39
[ac] **12:26** 1Co 3:5
[ad] Jn 14:3; 17:24; 2Co 5:8; Php 1:23; 1Th 4:17
[ae] 1Tm 5:3
[af] **12:27** Ps 3:7
[ag] **12:28** Jn 10:25; Ac 15:14; Rv 14:1
[ah] Jn 5:37
[ai] Rv 14:13
[aj] Jn 11:4; 17:1; 1Pt 2:12
[ak] **12:30** Jn 11:42
[al] **12:31** Lk 4:6
[am] Jn 3:16; 14:30; 16:11
[an] Col 2:15; 1Jn 3:8
[ao] **12:32** Jn 11:51
[ap] **12:33** Jn 18:32
[aq] **12:34** Ps 89:36; Jn 15:4; 1Jn 2:17
[ar] Mk 2:10
[as] **12:35** Ps 118:27; Jn 7:33; 9:4
[at] Ps 36:9; Jn 12:46; 1Jn 2:8
[au] Php 3:12
[av] Jn 7:28; 8:14; 1Jn 2:11
[aw] **12:36** Jn 7:33; 1Th 5:5
[ax] Lk 4:30

[A] **12:5** This amount was about a year's wages for a common worker. [B] **12:11** Lit *going away* [C] **12:13** Ps 118:25-26 [D] **12:15** Zch 9:9 [E] **12:17** Other mss read *Meanwhile the crowd, which had been with Him, continued to testify that He had called Lazarus out of the tomb and raised him from the dead.* [F] **12:24** Lit *produces much fruit* [G] **12:28** Other mss read *Your Son* [H] **12:32,34** Or *exalted*

Isaiah's Prophecies Fulfilled

37 Even though He had performed so many signs in their presence, they did not believe in Him. 38 But this was to fulfill[a] the word of Isaiah[b] the prophet, who said:[A]

> **Lord, who has believed**
> **our message?**
> **And who has the arm[c] of the Lord**
> **been revealed to?**[B,d]

39 This is why they were unable to believe, because Isaiah also said:

> 40 **He has blinded[e] their eyes**
> **and hardened their hearts,[f]**
> **so that they would not see**
> **with their eyes**
> **or understand**
> **with their hearts,**
> **and be converted,[g]**
> **and I would heal them.**[C,h]

41 Isaiah said these things because[D] he saw His glory[i] and spoke about Him.

42 Nevertheless, many did believe in Him even among the rulers,[j] but because of the Pharisees they did not confess Him, so they would not be banned from the ·synagogue. 43 For they loved praise from men[k] more than praise from God.[E,l]

A Summary of Jesus' Mission

44 Then Jesus cried out, "The one who believes in Me[m] believes not in Me, but in Him who sent Me. 45 And the one who sees Me sees Him[n] who sent Me. 46 I have come as a light into the world, so that everyone who believes in Me would not remain in darkness. 47 If anyone hears My words and doesn't keep[o] them, I do not judge him; for I did not come to judge the world[p] but to save the world.[q] 48 The one who rejects Me[r] and doesn't accept My sayings has this as his judge:[F] The word I have spoken will judge him on the last day.[s] 49 For I have not spoken on My own, but the Father[t] Himself who sent Me has given Me a command as to what I should say and what I should speak. 50 I know that His command is eternal life.[u] So the things that I speak, I speak just as the Father has told Me."[v]

[a] **12:38** Mt 1:22 [b] Mt 3:3; 4:14; 12:17 [c] Ex 15:16 [d] Is 53:1 [e] **12:40** Jn 8:59 [f] Heb 3:8 [g] Is 56:3,6; Mt 18:3; 23:15; Ac 15:3; 28:27; Rm 16:5; 1Tm 3:6 [h] Is 6:10; 1Pt 2:24 [i] **12:41** Mk 10:37; Jn 17:24 [j] **12:42** Lk 8:41 [k] **12:43** Php 3:19 [l] Lk 9:32; 2Co 3:18; 1Th 2:4; 2Pt 3:18 [m] **12:44** Jn 6:35 [n] **12:45** Jn 14:9 [o] **12:47** Lk 11:28; 2Tm 1:14; 2Pt 3:17 [p] Lk 6:37; Jn 3:18; 8:15; Rv 6:10 [q] Jn 3:17; Ac 16:30; Eph 2:8 [r] **12:48** Lk 10:16 [s] Jn 2:4; 6:39; 1Pt 1:5; 3:3; 2Pt 3:3; Jd 18 [t] **12:49** Mt 11:27 [u] **12:50** Jn 5:26; 12:25; Ac 13:48; 1Jn 2:25 [v] Jn 5:19; 14:24 [w] **13:1** Jn 10:18; 12:23; 16:28 [x] Jn 1:11; 6:37 [y] **13:2** Mt 4:1,10; Jn 8:44; Ac 13:10 [z] Mk 3:19 [aa] Mt 10:4; Jn 12:4; 13:21 [ab] **13:3** Mt 11:27; 28:18; Jn 17:2 [ac] Jn 8:42; 16:27; 17:8 [ad] Jn 8:14; 14:12; 16:28; 17:11 [ae] **13:4** Lk 19:36 [af] Lk 12:37 [ag] **13:6** Mt 16:17 [ah] **13:7** Jn 3:11; 7:28; 12:16 [ai] **13:14** 1Tm 5:10; 1Pt 5:5 [aj] **13:15** 1Pt 2:21 [ak] **13:16** Jn 15:20

Jesus Washes His Disciples' Feet

13 Before the ·Passover Festival, Jesus knew that His hour had come to depart from this world to the Father.[w] Having loved His own who were in the world,[x] He loved them to the end.[G]

2 Now by the time of supper, the Devil[y] had already put it into the heart of Judas,[z] Simon Iscariot's son, to betray[aa] Him. 3 Jesus knew that the Father had given everything into His hands,[ab] that He had come from God,[ac] and that He was going back to God.[ad] 4 So He got up from supper, laid aside His robe,[ae] took a towel, and tied it around Himself.[af] 5 Next, He poured water into a basin and began to wash His disciples' feet and to dry them with the towel tied around Him.

6 He came to Simon Peter,[ag] who asked Him, "Lord, are You going to wash my feet?"

7 Jesus answered him, "What I'm doing you don't understand now, but afterward you will know."[ah]

8 "You will never wash my feet — ever!" Peter said.

Jesus replied, "If I don't wash you, you have no part with Me."

9 Simon Peter said to Him, "Lord, not only my feet, but also my hands and my head."

10 "One who has bathed," Jesus told him, "doesn't need to wash anything except his feet, but he is completely ·clean. You are clean, but not all of you." 11 For He knew who would betray Him. This is why He said, "You are not all clean."

The Meaning of Footwashing

12 When Jesus had washed their feet and put on His robe, He reclined[H] again and said to them, "Do you know what I have done for you? 13 You call Me Teacher and Lord. This is well said, for I am. 14 So if I, your Lord and Teacher, have washed your feet, you also ought to wash one another's feet.[ai] 15 For I have given you an example[aj] that you also should do just as I have done for you.

16 "·I assure you: A ·slave is not greater than his master,[I,ak] and a messenger is not greater than the one who sent him. 17 If you know

[A] **12:38** Lit *which he said* [B] **12:38** Is 53:1 [C] **12:40** Is 6:10 [D] **12:41** Other mss read *when* [E] **12:43** Lit *loved glory of men more than glory of God*; v. 41; Jn 5:41 [F] **12:48** Lit *has the one judging him* [G] **13:1** = completely or always [H] **13:12** At important meals the custom was to recline on a mat at a low table and lean on the left elbow. [I] **13:16** Or *lord*

these things, you are blessed if you do them.[a]
18 I'm not speaking about all of you; I know
those I have chosen.[b] But the Scripture[c] must
be fulfilled:[d] **The one who eats My bread[A] has
raised his heel against Me.**[B,e]
19 "I am telling you now before it happens,[f]
so that when it does happen you will believe[g]
that I am He.[h] 20 I assure you: Whoever receives anyone I send receives Me, and the one
who receives[i] Me receives Him who sent Me."

Judas's Betrayal Predicted

21 When[j] Jesus had said this, He was troubled in His spirit[k] and testified,[l] "I assure you:
One of you will betray Me!"
22 The disciples started looking at one another — uncertain which one He was speaking about. 23 One of His disciples, the one
Jesus loved,[m] was reclining close beside
Jesus.[C] 24 Simon Peter motioned to him to find
out who it was He was talking about. 25 So he
leaned back against Jesus and asked Him,
"Lord, who is it?"
26 Jesus replied, "He's the one I give the piece
of bread to after I have dipped it."[n] When He
had dipped the bread,[o] He gave it to Judas, Simon Iscariot's son.[D] 27 After Judas ate the piece
of bread, Satan[p] entered him. Therefore Jesus
told him, "What you're doing, do quickly."
28 None of those reclining at the table knew
why He told him this. 29 Since Judas[q] kept the
money-bag, some thought that Jesus was telling him, "Buy what we need for the festival,"[r]
or that he should give something to the poor.
30 After receiving the piece of bread, he went
out immediately. And it was night.[s]

The New Command

31 When[t] he had gone out, Jesus said, "Now
the ·Son of Man[u] is glorified, and God is glorified[v] in Him.[w] 32 If God is glorified in Him,[E]
God will also glorify Him in Himself and will
glorify Him at once.
33 "Children, I am with you a little while longer.[x] You will look for Me, and just as I told the
·Jews, 'Where I am going you cannot come,'[y]
so now I tell you.
34 "I give you a new command: Love one
another. Just as I have loved you, you must
also love one another. 35 By this all people will
know that you are My disciples, if you have
love[z] for one another."

Peter's Denials Predicted

36 "Lord," Simon Peter said to Him, "where
are You going?"
Jesus answered, "Where I am going[aa] you
cannot follow Me now, but you will follow
later."
37 "Lord," Peter asked, "why can't I follow
You now? I will lay down my life[ab] for You!"[ac]
38 Jesus replied, "Will you lay down your life
for Me? I assure you: A rooster will not crow
until you have denied Me three times.

The Way to the Father

14 "Your heart must not be troubled.[ad] Believe[F] in God;[ae] believe also in Me. 2 In
My Father's house are many dwelling places;[G]
if not, I would have told you. I am going away[af]
to prepare a place for you. 3 If I go away and
prepare a place for you, I will come back[ag] and
receive you to Myself, so that where I am you
may be also.[ah] 4 You know the way to where I
am going."[H,ai]
5 "Lord," Thomas[aj] said, "we don't know
where You're going. How can we know the
way?"
6 Jesus told him, "I am[ak] the way,[al] the truth,
and the life. No one comes to the Father except through Me.

Jesus Reveals the Father

7 "If you know Me, you will also know[I] My
Father.[am] From now on you do know Him[an]
and have seen Him."
8 "Lord," said Philip,[ao] "show us the Father,
and that's enough for us."
9 Jesus said to him, "Have I been among
you all this time without your knowing Me,
Philip? The one who has seen Me has seen
the Father.[ap] How can you say, 'Show us the
Father'? 10 Don't you believe that I am in the
Father and the Father is in Me?[aq] The words I
speak to you I do not speak on My own.[ar] The

[a] **13:17** Mt 7:24-25; Lk 6:47; 11:28; Jms 1:22-25 [b] **13:18** Jn 6:70; Eph 1:4 [c] Mt 26:54 [d] Mt 1:22 [e] Ps 41:9 [f] **13:19** Jn 13:19 [g] Mk 11:24; Jn 3:16; Ac 10:43; Rm 10:9; 1Pt 1:8-10 [h] Ex 3:14; Jn 8:24,58 [i] **13:20** Jn 5:43; 2Jn 10 [j] **13:21-30** Mt 26:20-25; Mk 14:17-21; Lk 22:21-23 [k] **13:21** Ps 51:12 [l] Jn 15:26; Ac 26:5 [m] **13:23** Jn 19:26; 20:2; 21:7,20 [n] **13:26** Ps 41:9 [o] Mk 14:20 [p] **13:27** Mt 4:1,10; Jn 8:44; Ac 13:10 [q] **13:29** Mk 3:19 [r] Jn 2:23 [s] **13:30** Jn 9:4 [t] **13:31-38** Mt 26:31-35; Mk 14:27-31; Lk 22:31-38 [u] **13:31** Mk 2:10 [v] Jn 11:4; 17:1; 1Pt 2:12 [w] 2Th 1:12; 1Jn 2:5 [x] **13:33** Jn 7:33 [y] Jn 8:21-22; 14:2; 16:5 [z] **13:35** 1Co 13:1 [aa] **13:36** Jn 14:2; 16:5 [ab] **13:37** 1Jn 3:16 [ac] Mk 14:31 [ad] **14:1** Jn 14:27 [ae] Ac 16:34; 27:25; Rm 4:3,17,24; Gl 3:6; Ti 3:8; Jms 2:23; 1Jn 5:10 [af] **14:2** Jn 8:21-22; 13:33,36; 16:7 [ag] **14:3** Mk 8:38 [ah] Jn 12:26 [ai] **14:4** Jn 7:28; 8:14; 16:5; 1Jn 2:11 [aj] **14:5** Mk 3:18 [ak] **14:6** Ex 3:14; Jn 8:24,58 [al] Heb 10:20 [am] **14:7** Mt 11:27; 1Jn 2:23 [an] Jn 17:3; 1Jn 4:8 [ao] **14:8** Mk 3:18 [ap] **14:9** Jn 5:19,37; 12:45 [aq] **14:10** Jn 10:30; 14:11,20; 1Jn 2:24; 4:17 [ar] Jn 5:30

[A] **13:18** Other mss read *eats bread with Me* [B] **13:18** Ps 41:9 [C] **13:23** Lit *reclining at Jesus' breast*; that is, on His right; Jn 1:18 [D] **13:26** Other mss read *Judas Iscariot, Simon's son* [E] **13:32** Other mss omit *If God is glorified in Him* [F] **14:1** Or *You believe* [G] **14:2** The Vg used the Lat term *mansio*, a traveler's resting place. The Gk word is related to the verb *meno*, meaning *remain* or *stay*, which occurs 40 times in John. [H] **14:4** Other mss read this verse: *And you know where I am going, and you know the way* [I] **14:7** Other mss read *If you had known Me, you would have known*

Father who lives in Me does His works.[a] 11 Believe Me that I am in the Father and the Father is in Me. Otherwise, believe[A] because of the works themselves.[b]

Praying in Jesus' Name

12 "I assure you: The one who believes in Me[c] will also do the works that I do. And he will do even greater works than these,[d] because I am going to the Father.[e] 13 Whatever you ask in My name, I will do it so that the Father may be glorified[f] in the Son.[g] 14 If you ask Me[B] anything in My name,[h] I will do it.[C,i]

Another Counselor Promised

15 "If you love Me, you will keep[D] My commands.[j] 16 And I will ask the Father, and He will give you another ·Counselor[k] to be with you forever. 17 He is the Spirit[l] of truth.[m] The ·world is unable to receive Him because it doesn't see Him or know Him. But you do know Him, because He remains with you and will be[E] in you.[n] 18 I will not leave you as orphans; I am coming to you.

The Father, the Son, and the Holy Spirit

19 "In a little while the world will see Me no longer,[o] but you will see Me.[p] Because I live, you will live[q] too. 20 In that day you will know that I am in My Father,[r] you are in Me, and I am in you. 21 The one who has My commands and keeps them is the one who loves Me.[s] And the one who loves Me will be loved by My Father.[t] I also will love him and will reveal Myself to him."

22 Judas[u] (not Iscariot) said to Him, "Lord, how is it You're going to reveal Yourself to us and not to the world?"[v]

23 Jesus answered, "If anyone loves Me, he will keep My word. My Father will love him, and We will come to him and make Our home with him.[w] 24 The one who doesn't love Me will not keep My words. The word that you hear is not Mine but is from the Father who sent Me.[x]

25 "I have spoken these things to you while I remain with you. 26 But the Counselor, the Holy Spirit[y]—the Father will send[z] Him in My name—will teach you all things[aa] and remind you of everything I have told you.[ab]

Jesus' Gift of Peace

27 "Peace I leave with you. My peace I give to you. I do not give to you as the world gives. Your heart must not be troubled or fearful.[ac] 28 You have heard Me tell you, 'I am going away[ad] and I am coming to you.' If you loved Me, you would have rejoiced that I am going to the Father,[ae] because the Father is greater than I.[af] 29 I have told you now before it happens[ag] so that when it does happen you may believe. 30 I will not talk with you much longer, because the ruler of the world[ah] is coming. He has no power over Me.[F,ai] 31 On the contrary, I am going away[G] so that the world may know that I love the Father. Just as the Father commanded Me, so I do.

"Get up; let's leave this place.

The Vine and the Branches

15 "I am[aj] the true vine, and My Father is the vineyard keeper. 2 Every branch in Me that does not produce fruit He removes,[ak] and He prunes every branch that produces fruit so that it will produce more fruit. 3 You are already ·clean[al] because of the word I have spoken to you. 4 Remain in Me, and I in you. Just as a branch is unable to produce fruit by itself unless it remains on the vine, so neither can you unless you remain in Me.[am]

5 "I am the vine;[an] you are the branches. The one who remains in Me and I in him produces much fruit,[ao] because you can do nothing without Me. 6 If anyone does not remain in Me, he is thrown aside[ap] like a branch and he withers. They gather them, throw them into the fire,[aq] and they are burned.[ar] 7 If you remain in Me and My words remain in you, ask whatever you want and it will be done for you.[as] 8 My Father is glorified[at] by this: that you produce much fruit and prove to be[H] My disciples.

Christlike Love

9 "As the Father has loved Me, I have also loved you. Remain in My love.[au] 10 If you keep My commands you will remain in My love, just as I have kept My Father's commands and remain in His love.[av]

[a] **14:10** Jn 5:36; 6:28; Heb 3:9; Rv 15:3 [b] **14:11** Jn 10:38 [c] **14:12** Jn 6:35 [d] Jn 5:20 [e] Jn 7:33; 13:1,3; 16:5,10,17,28; 17:11,13; 20:17 [f] **14:13** Jn 11:4; 17:1; 1Pt 2:12 [g] Jn 5:19 [h] **14:14** Jn 10:25 [i] Jn 11:22; 15:6; 16:23-24 [j] **14:15** 1Jn 5:3 [k] **14:16** Lk 24:49; Jn 14:26; 15:26; 16:7; 1Jn 2:1; Ac 2:33 [l] **14:17** Jn 1:33 [m] Ps 119:142; 2Th 2:10; 1Jn 4:6 [n] 1Jn 4:4 [o] **14:19** Jn 7:33 [p] Jn 16:16 [q] Php 1:21 [r] **14:20** Jn 14:10 [s] **14:21** Jn 8:31; 1Jn 2:5 [t] Dt 7:12-13; Jn 16:27 [u] **14:22** Lk 6:16; Ac 1:13 [v] Ac 10:40-41 [w] **14:23** Jn 14:2; 1Jn 2:24 [x] **14:24** Jn 5:19; 7:16; 8:28; 12:49-50 [y] **14:26** Ps 51:11; Jn 1:33; Ac 2:4; Rm 8:9; Gl 5:25; Ti 3:5; Rv 3:22 [z] Lk 24:49; Jn 14:16; 15:26; 16:7; Ac 2:33 [aa] Jn 16:13; 1Co 2:10; 1Jn 2:27 [ab] Jn 2:22; 2Pt 1:21 [ac] **14:27** 2Tm 1:7 [ad] **14:28** Jn 16:5 [ae] Jn 16:10 [af] Jn 10:29; 1Jn 3:20; 4:4 [ag] **14:29** Jn 13:19; 16:4 [ah] **14:30** Mt 4:1; Jn 12:31 [ai] Lk 4:6 [aj] **15:1** Ex 3:14; Jn 8:24,58 [ak] **15:2** Mt 3:10; 7:19; 15:13; Lk 3:9; 13:6-9; Jn 15:6; Rm 11:17,22 [al] **15:3** Ps 24:4; Ti 1:15 [am] **15:4** Jn 6:56; 8:28; 1Jn 2:5 [an] **15:5** Jms 3:12 [ao] Mk 4:8 [ap] **15:6** Jn 15:2 [aq] 2Th 1:8 [ar] 1Th 1:8; 2Pt 3:7 [as] **15:7** Jn 14:14 [at] **15:8** Jn 11:4; 17:1; 1Pt 2:12 [au] **15:9** Col 1:13; 1Jn 5:20; Jd 21 [av] **15:10** Jn 5:19

[A] **14:11** Other mss read *believe Me* [B] **14:14** Other mss omit *Me* [C] **14:14** Other mss omit all of v. 14 [D] **14:15** Other mss read *If you love Me, keep* (as a command) [E] **14:17** Other mss read *and is* [F] **14:30** Lit *He has nothing in Me* [G] **14:31** Probably refers to the cross [H] **15:8** Or *and become*

11“I have spoken these things to you so that
My joy may be in you and your joy may be
complete.[a] 12This is My command: Love one
another as I have loved[b] you. 13No one has
greater love than this, that someone would
lay down his life[c] for his friends. 14You are
My friends if you do what I command you.
15I do not call you ˚slaves anymore, because
a slave doesn’t know what his master[A,d] is doing. I have called you friends, because I have
made known to you everything I have heard
from My Father. 16You did not choose Me, but
I chose you.[e] I appointed you that you should
go out and produce fruit and that your fruit
should remain, so that whatever you ask[f] the
Father in My name,[g] He will give you.[h] 17This is
what I command you: Love one another.

Persecutions Predicted

18“If the ˚world hates[i] you, understand
that it hated Me before it hated you. 19If you
were of the world, the world would love you
as its own. However, because you are not of
the world, but I have chosen[j] you out of it,
the world hates you. 20Remember the word I
spoke to you: ‘A slave is not greater than his
master.’[k] If they persecuted Me, they will also
persecute you. If they kept My word,[l] they
will also keep yours. 21But they will do all
these things to you on account of My name,[m]
because they don’t know[n] the One who sent
Me. 22If I had not come and spoken to them,
they would not have sin.[B,o] Now they have
no excuse for their sin. 23The one who hates
Me also hates My Father.[p] 24If I had not done
the works[q] among them that no one else has
done,[r] they would not have sin.[s] Now they
have seen and hated both Me and My Father.
25But this happened so that the statement
written in their scripture might be fulfilled:[t]
They hated Me for no reason.[C,u]

Coming Testimony and Rejection

26“When the ˚Counselor[v] comes, the One I
will send to you from the Father[w]—the Spirit
of truth[x] who proceeds from the Father—He
will testify about Me. 27You also will testify,[y]
because you have been with Me from the beginning.

16 “I have told you these things to keep
you from ˚stumbling. 2They will ban
you from the ˚synagogues.[z] In fact, a time is
coming when anyone who kills you will think
he is offering service[aa] to God. 3They will do
these things because they haven’t known[ab]
the Father or Me. 4But I have told you these
things so that when their time[D] comes you
may remember[ac] I told them to you. I didn’t
tell you these things from the beginning, because I was with you.

The Counselor’s Ministry

5“But now I am going away[ad] to Him who
sent Me, and not one of you asks Me, ‘Where
are You going?’[ae] 6Yet, because I have spoken
these things to you, sorrow has filled your
heart. 7Nevertheless, I am telling you the
truth.[af] It is for your benefit that I go away,
because if I don’t go away the ˚Counselor will
not come to you. If I go, I will send Him to
you.[ag] 8When He comes, He will convict the
world about sin, righteousness, and judg-

[a]**15:11** 1Jn 1:4; 2Jn 12
[b]**15:12** Jn 3:16
[c]**15:13** Rm 5:8; 1Jn 3:16
[d]**15:15** Col 3:22
[e]**15:16** Mt 24:22
[f]Jn 10:25
[g]Jn 14:13
[h]Jn 11:22; 16:23
[i]**15:18** Lk 6:27; 19:14
[j]**15:19** Eph 1:4
[k]**15:20** Jn 13:16
[l]Jn 8:51
[m]**15:21** Mk 13:13; Jn 10:25
[n]Jn 3:11; 7:28; 20:9
[o]**15:22** Ezk 2:5; 3:7; Jn 9:41; Rm 1:20; 2:1; 6:23
[p]**15:23** Jn 5:23
[q]**15:24** Jn 5:36; Heb 3:9; Rv 15:3
[r]Jn 3:2; 7:31; 9:32; 10:32,37
[s]Jn 9:41
[t]**15:25** Jn 12:38; 13:18; 17:12; 18:9,32; 19:24,36
[u]Ps 69:4
[v]**15:26** Jn 14:16
[w]Jn 14:26
[x]Ps 119:142; Jn 1:33; 14:17; 16:13; Rm 3:7; 1Jn 4:6
[y]**15:27** Ac 4:20
[z]**16:2** Jn 9:22; 12:42
[aa]Ex 12:25
[ab]**16:3** Jn 7:28
[ac]**16:4** Jn 14:29; Rv 2:5
[ad]**16:5** Jn 7:33; 8:14,21-22; 13:3,33,36; 14:4-5,28; 16:10,17
[ae]Jn 8:14
[af]**16:7** Ps 119:142
[ag]Jn 14:26

GOD WHO SENDS

Our Life of Ministry

Every Christian is called (1) “out of,” (2) “into,” (3) “in order that.” The calling is possible because of the salvific work of God. This was possible because of the sending of God. Jesus said, “I know whom I have chosen; . . . he who receives any one whom I send receives me; and he who receives me receives him who sent me” (John 13:18,20). To be called into Christ is to be called into his mission (John 17:18). Because the gospel was created out of the sending of God, to receive that gospel is to be called to share it. The call to conversion, the call to discipleship, the call to declare his wonderful deeds is the call to mission.
(DUBOSE, 103)

[A]**15:15** Or *lord* [B]**15:22** To *have sin* is an idiom that refers to guilt caused by sin. [C]**15:25** Ps 69:4 [D]**16:4** Other mss read *when the time*

ment: 9 About sin, because they do not believe
in Me; 10 about righteousness, because I am
going to the Father[a] and you will no longer
see Me; 11 and about judgment,[b] because the
ruler of this •world[c] has been judged.[d]

12 "I still have many things to tell you, but
you can't bear them now.[e] 13 When the Spirit
of truth[f] comes, He will guide you into all
the truth.[g] For He will not speak on His own,
but He will speak whatever He hears. He will
also declare to you what is to come. 14 He will
glorify Me, because He will take from what is
Mine and declare it to you. 15 Everything the
Father[h] has is Mine.[i] This is why I told you
that He takes from what is Mine and will declare it to you.[j]

Sorrow Turned to Joy

16 "A little while[k] and you will no longer see
Me;[l] again a little while and you will see Me."[A]
17 Therefore some of His disciples said to
one another, "What is this He tells us: 'A little
while and you will not see Me; again a little
while and you will see Me'; and, 'because I am
going to the Father'[m]?" 18 They said, "What is
this He is saying,[B] 'A little while'? We don't
know what He's talking about!"

19 Jesus knew they wanted to question Him,
so He said to them, "Are you asking one another about what I said, 'A little while and you
will not see Me; again a little while and you
will see Me'?

20 "I assure you: You will weep and wail,[n]
but the world will rejoice. You will become
sorrowful,[o] but your sorrow will turn to joy.
21 When a woman is in labor she has pain[p] because her time has come. But when she has
given birth to a child,[q] she no longer remembers the suffering because of the joy that a
person has been born into the world. 22 So
you also have sorrow[C] now. But I will see you
again. Your hearts will rejoice,[r] and no one
will rob you of your joy.[s] 23 In that day you will
not ask Me anything.

"I assure you: Anything you ask the Father
in My name, He will give you.[t] 24 Until now
you have asked for nothing in My name.[u] Ask
and you will receive,[v] so that your joy may be
complete.[w]

[a] **16:10** Jn 14:12,28; 16:17
[b] **16:11** Mt 12:41; Jn 5:22; 2Th 1:5; Rv 19:11
[c] Mt 4:1; Jn 12:31
[d] Col 2:15; Heb 2:14
[e] **16:12** Mk 4:33
[f] **16:13** Rm 3:7; 1Jn 4:6
[g] Jn 1:17; 14:6; 2Th 2:10
[h] **16:15** Mt 11:27
[i] Jn 17:10
[j] Jn 5:19
[k] **16:16** Jn 7:33
[l] Mk 2:20; 14:19
[m] **16:17** Jn 14:12; 16:10
[n] **16:20** Mt 11:17; Lk 7:32; 23:27
[o] Jn 16:6; 2Co 2:2
[p] **16:21** Gl 4:19
[q] Lk 1:7
[r] **16:22** Jn 20:20
[s] Jn 15:11
[t] **16:23** Jn 11:22; 14:13-14; 15:16
[u] **16:24** Jn 10:25
[v] Mt 7:8
[w] 1Jn 1:4; 2Jn 12
[x] **16:26** Jn 14:16
[y] Jn 10:25
[z] **16:27** Jn 14:21
[aa] Jn 6:46; 8:42; 13:3; 16:30
[ab] **16:28** Jn 14:12
[ac] **16:30** Mk 2:8; Jn 1:48; 2:24-25; 6:64; 21:17
[ad] Jn 16:27
[ae] **16:32** Jn 4:23
[af] Jn 8:16,29
[ag] **17:1** Jn 5:19; Heb 1:2
[ah] Jn 12:28
[ai] **17:2** Php 3:3
[aj] Jn 12:25; Ac 13:48; 1Jn 2:25
[ak] Mt 24:22
[al] **17:3** Jn 5:44; Rm 16:27
[am] Jn 4:23; 1Jn 5:20
[an] Mk 9:37; Jn 1:6
[ao] Jn 5:38; 6:29

Jesus the Victor

25 "I have spoken these things to you in figures of speech. A time is coming when I will
no longer speak to you in figures, but I will
tell you plainly about the Father. 26 In that
day you will ask[x] in My name.[y] I am not telling you that I will make requests to the Father on your behalf. 27 For the Father Himself
loves you, because you have loved[z] Me and
have believed that I came from God.[D,aa] 28 I
came from the Father and have come into the
world. Again, I am leaving the world and going to the Father."[ab]

29 "Ah!" His disciples said. "Now You're
speaking plainly and not using any figurative
language. 30 Now we know that You know everything[ac] and don't need anyone to question
You. By this we believe that You came from
God."[ad]

31 Jesus responded to them, "Do you now
believe? 32 Look: An hour is coming, and has
come,[ae] when each of you will be scattered to
his own home, and you will leave Me alone.
Yet I am not alone, because the Father is with
Me.[af] 33 I have told you these things so that in
Me you may have peace. You will have suffering in this world. Be courageous! I have conquered the world."

Jesus Prays for Himself

17 Jesus spoke these things, looked up to
heaven, and said:

Father,
the hour has come.
Glorify Your Son
so that the Son[ag]
may glorify You,[ah]
2 for You gave Him authority
over all flesh;[E,ai]
so He may give eternal life[aj]
to all You have given Him.[ak]
3 This is eternal life:
that they may know You,
the only[al] true[am] God,
and the One You have sent[an] —
Jesus Christ.[ao]
4 I have glorified You on the earth
by completing the work You gave Me
to do.

[A] **16:16** Other mss add *because I am going to the Father* [B] **16:18** Other mss omit *He is saying* [C] **16:22** Other mss read *will have sorrow* [D] **16:27** Other mss read *from the Father* [E] **17:2** Or *people*

5 Now, Father,[a] glorify Me
in Your presence
with that glory[b] I had with You
before the world existed.[c]

Jesus Prays for His Disciples

6 I have revealed Your name[d]
to the men You gave Me[e]
from the world.[f]
They were Yours, You gave them to Me,[g]
and they have kept Your word.[h]
7 Now they know that all things
You have given to Me are from You,
8 because the words that You gave Me,[i]
I have given them.
They have received them
and have known for certain
that I came from You.[j]
They have believed that You sent Me.
9 I pray[A] for them.
I am not praying for the ˚world
but for those You have given Me,[k]
because they are Yours.
10 Everything I have is Yours,
and everything You have is Mine,[l]
and I have been glorified in them.
11 I am no longer in the world,
but they are in the world,
and I am coming to You.[m]
Holy[n] Father,
protect[B] them by Your name[o]
that You have given Me,
so that they may be one[p] as We are[q] one.
12 While I was with them,
I was protecting them by Your name
that You have given Me.
I guarded[r] them and not one of them
is lost,
except the son of destruction,[C]
so that the Scripture[s] may be fulfilled.[t]
13 Now I am coming to You,
and I speak these things in the world
so that they may have My joy completed
in them.
14 I have given them Your word.
The world hated[u] them
because they are not of the world,[v]
as I am not of the world.[w]
15 I am not praying
that You take them out of the world
but that You protect them
from the evil one.[x]
16 They are not of the world,
as I am not of the world.[y]
17 ˚Sanctify[D,z] them by the truth;[aa]
Your word is truth.
18 As You sent Me into the world,[ab]
I also have sent them into the world.
19 I sanctify Myself for them,
so they also may be sanctified
by the truth.

Jesus Prays for All Believers

20 I pray not only for these,

GOD WHO SENDS

Love: The Mood and Method of Mission

Love and the sending so come together in the thought of Jesus reflected in John's Gospel as to make mood and method one. The why and the what are united. Ideology and action are wed. One cannot do mission without reflecting the spirit of mission. In his prayer Jesus linked love and the sending: "and these know that thou has sent me. I made known to them thy name, and I will make it known, that the love with which thou has love me may be in them, and I in them" (John 17:25–26).

To be loved of God and to be sent by God to share that love is for the Christian and the church the summum bonum, the highest and ultimate good. The inspiring words of Jesus linger still: "So have I loved you" (John 15:9); "So I send you" (John 20:21).

(DuBose, 135)

[a]**17:5** Mt 11:27 [b]Mk 10:37; Jn 17:24; 1Pt 5:1 [c]Pr 8:23; Jn 1:1-2; 8:58 [d]**17:6** Jn 10:25; Ac 15:14; Rv 14:1 [e]Mt 24:22; Jn 6:37 [f]Jn 8:23; 13:1; 15:19; 17:14-16; 18:36; 1Co 5:10; 1Jn 2:16; 4:5 [g]Jn 18:9 [h]Jn 8:51 [i]**17:8** Jn 14:24 [j]Jn 5:43; 13:3 [k]**17:9** Rm 9:11 [l]**17:10** Jn 16:15 [m]**17:11** Jn 13:3; 14:12 [n]Ps 20:6; 1Co 7:14 [o]Pr 18:10 [p]Jn 11:52 [q]Jn 10:16,30; 17:22; Gl 3:28 [r]**17:12** 2Tm 1:14 [s]Mt 26:54 [t]Ps 41:9; Jn 13:18; 15:25; 19:24,36 [u]**17:14** Lk 6:22,27; 19:14 [v]Jn 15:19 [w]Jn 8:23; 18:36 [x]**17:15** 2Th 3:3 [y]**17:16** Jn 18:36; 1Jn 4:17 [z]**17:17** Lk 11:2 [aa]Ps 119:142; 2Th 2:10; 1Jn 5:20 [ab]**17:18** 1Jn 4:17

[A]**17:9** Lit *ask* (throughout this passage) [B]**17:11** Lit *keep* (throughout this passage) [C]**17:12** The one destined for destruction, loss, or perdition [D]**17:17** Set apart for special use

but also for those who believe in Me
through their message.
21 May they all be one,[a]
as You, Father, are in Me and I am
in You.[b]
May they also be one[A] in Us,
so the world may believe You sent Me.
22 I have given them the glory[c]
You have given Me.
May they be one as We are one.
23 I am in them and You are in Me.[d]
May they be made completely one,
so the world may know You have
sent Me
and have loved[e] them as
You have loved Me.[f]
24 Father,
I desire those You have given Me
to be with Me where I am.[g]
Then they will see My glory,
which You have given Me
because You loved Me
before the world's foundation.
25 Righteous Father!
The world has not known You.
However, I have known You,[h]
and these have known that You sent Me.
26 I made Your name[i] known to them
and will make it known,
so the love You have loved Me with
may be in them and I may be in them.[j]

[a]**17:21** Jn 11:52; 17:11
[b]1Jn 2:24; 5:20
[c]**17:22** Mk 10:37; Jn 17:24; 1Pt 5:1,4
[d]**17:23** 1Jn 4:4
[e]Jn 3:16; 12:43; 1Co 13:1; 2Th 2:13
[f]Jn 15:9
[g]**17:24** Jn 12:26
[h]**17:25** Mt 11:27; Lk 10:22
[i]**17:26** Jn 10:25
[j]1Jn 4:4
[k]**18:1-12** Mt 26:47-56; Mk 14:43-52; Lk 22:47-53
[l]**18:2** Mk 3:19
[m]Mt 10:4; Mk 9:31; Jn 13:21
[n]**18:3** Mk 7:3
[o]**18:4** Jn 16:30
[p]**18:5** Ex 3:14; Jn 8:24,58

Jesus Betrayed

18 After[k] Jesus had said these things, He
went out with His disciples across the
Kidron Valley, where there was a garden, and
He and His disciples went into it. 2 Judas,[l] who
betrayed[m] Him, also knew the place, because
Jesus often met there with His disciples. 3 So
Judas took a ·company of soldiers and some
temple police from the ·chief priests and the
·Pharisees[n] and came there with lanterns,
torches, and weapons.
4 Then Jesus, knowing everything that was
about to happen to Him,[o] went out and said
to them, "Who is it you're looking for?"
5 "Jesus the ·Nazarene," they answered.
"I am He,"[B,p] Jesus told them.

GOD'S HEART FOR THE WORLD

Invited In

May they all be one, as You, Father, are in Me and I am in You. May they also be one in Us, so the world may believe You sent Me. (John 17:21)

In the Gospel of John, the cross is part of Jesus' ascension. He is lifted up on the cross as part of His being lifted up to the Father. When Jesus prays, "Father, the hour has come. Glorify Your Son . . . ," He speaks of both the glory that will come to Him on the cross, and as He ascends to His Father. The disciples are finally ready to see the glory of the cross, God's glory in its truest form, but still, Jesus prays for their protection, as if they might not fully understand.

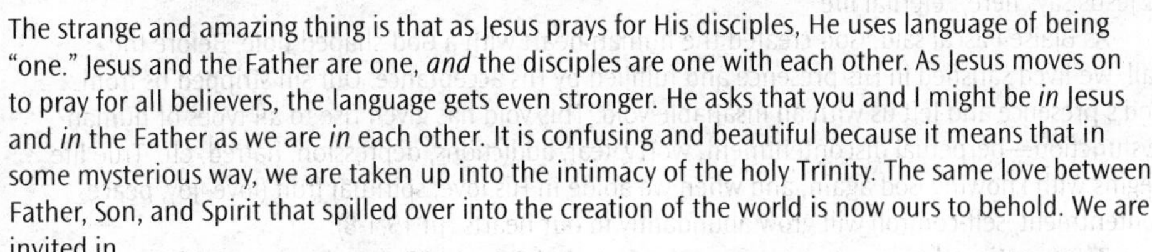

The strange and amazing thing is that as Jesus prays for His disciples, He uses language of being "one." Jesus and the Father are one, *and* the disciples are one with each other. As Jesus moves on to pray for all believers, the language gets even stronger. He asks that you and I might be *in* Jesus and *in* the Father as we are *in* each other. It is confusing and beautiful because it means that in some mysterious way, we are taken up into the intimacy of the holy Trinity. The same love between Father, Son, and Spirit that spilled over into the creation of the world is now ours to behold. We are invited in.

The glory of the cross, so foreign to a worldly glory, allows us to be one, as they are one, and that oneness is eternal life. That oneness displays God's glory to the whole world and carries us into life everlasting.

[A]**17:21** Other mss omit *one* [B]**18:5** Lit *I am*; see note at Jn 8:58.

What Is the Gospel?

J.D. Greear

In Jesus' prayer, He gives us a clear definition of salvation.

Salvation is essentially the knowledge of God. True knowledge of God is eternal life. Salvation is not simply forgiveness of sin, but more importantly restores the relationship between humans and God. Have you ever seen that bumper sticker, "Christians are not perfect; they're just forgiven"? Christians aren't perfect yet, that is true; but they are not "just forgiven." Christians have been restored to God. God has resumed again His rightful place as our master, our joy, our security. Jesus came not just to free people from hell, but to bring them back to true knowledge of God. This genuine knowledge of God is one of the things that separate the message of Jesus from that of other religions. The Gospel's prize is not just eternal safety in paradise, it is God Himself.

Salvation comes through knowing Jesus Christ. Jesus, who was both fully God and fully man (Jn 1:1-14; 2:19-22; 8:58), was uniquely able to accomplish our salvation. As man, He could be our substitute, living the life we should have lived and dying the death we had been condemned to die. As God, He had the right to forgive sin, the power to overcome death, and the ability to restore us to fellowship with the Father.

Jesus Christ suffered the full fury of God's wrath for our sins in our place. On the cross, every ounce of punishment due unto us was unleashed upon Him. For those who have repented of their sins and trusted Jesus as Savior, no more punishment remains. God cannot hold us accountable for our sin, because it would be unjust for God to demand two payments for the same sin! Jesus paid the full price for our sin once and for all on the cross.

God accomplishes salvation all by Himself (Jn 1:12-13). This also distinguishes the Gospel from other religions. We can classify all religions in two categories. In one type of religion, humans work for their salvation. This is the approach of every religion in the world—whether Islam's five pillars; Buddhism's eight-fold path; or Hinduism's scheme of karma and reincarnation. The Gospel flips these approaches on their head. The Gospel teaches that our acceptance is a gift. God has done the work; ours is only to repent and believe. Our obedience to God is not to earn favors from Him, but rather done in grateful response to what He has done for us. Religion is spelled "D-O;" the Gospel is spelled "D-O-N-E" by Jesus Christ.

Eternal life is our present possession. In the Gospel of John, "eternal life" functions as both unbounded duration and a quality of living. Not only did Jesus' work guarantee us heaven in the future, it gives us God in the present. God's presence in our lives is the abundant life (Jn 10:10)—or, as Jesus says here, "eternal life."

As Blaise Pascal said, God created the human heart with a God-shaped hole. Before the Fall, we lived satisfied in His presence and fulfilled by His acceptance. Our sin stripped us from God's presence and left us with an insatiable void. This void has given rise to all types of human dysfunction—perpetual discontentment, worry, fear, addictions, depression, hatred, etc. True life begins with knowing God again, and when we abide in His love, spiritual fruit (love, joy, peace, contentment, self-control) will grow abundantly in our hearts (Jn 15:1-8).

The question that screams out from the Gospel of John is, "Do you know Jesus?" Not, "Have you prayed a prayer?" or "Do you go to church?" or "Are you perfectly obedient to the 10 commandments?" but "Do you know the love of Jesus and have you received His free offer of salvation?"

Jesus said that many people who called Him "Lord" would be turned away from Him on the last day because He never knew them (Mt 7:21-23). I used to interpret this as a warning that only the upper 10% of "Christians" would make it into heaven and many would be cut. So, each time I read that passage, I determined that I was going to be in that upper 10%. I'd redouble my efforts to give more sacrificially, be more regular in my quiet time, and be more pure. "Then," I thought, "there's no way God could cut me from the team. I'm going to be on the Dean's List of Christians."

The people who will be turned away on the last day are people who served God. Jesus said they were plenty busy—going to church, preaching sermons, making offerings, doing miracles, and even casting out demons. Their problem is that they never knew a Jesus so gracious that He receives sinners freely. And they didn't value that Jesus enough to forsake all the treasures of this world for Him. As a result, they never rested their souls in His grace or feasted their souls on His pleasures.

Even then, on the last day, they think their religious activity will earn their right to heaven. They say, "Look, Lord... look at what we *did*!" It proves they never really knew who He was. Jesus is not known by doing enough or giving enough. Jesus is known only by believing in His compassion toward you and resting in His promise of eternal life.

The good news is that knowing Him is easy. Jesus did everything necessary to reconcile you fully to God. You simply repent and believe that what the Gospel says about Him is true. He is a God who stands ready to accept you, completely, because of what Jesus has done for you. He is a God whose mercy and love for you knows no bounds. It stretches out toward you right at this very moment. Following Jesus as Lord means that your life will change radically, as He must now rule your life, but you'll find that obedience and even sacrifice are sweet because of His presence in and with you.

Have you felt that love in your heart? Have you believed and embraced it, *personally*? Have you heard His voice in your soul saying, "*You*. You are my child. I died for *you*. I have accepted you." If not, open your heart to Him today.

Judas, who betrayed Him, was also standing with them. 6When He told them, "I am
He," they stepped back and fell to the ground.
7Then He asked them again, "Who is it
you're looking for?"
"Jesus the Nazarene," they said.
8"I told you I am He," Jesus replied. "So if
you're looking for Me, let these men go." 9This
was to fulfill[a] the words He had said: "I have
not lost one of those You have given Me."[b]
10Then Simon[c] Peter,[d] who had a sword,[e]
drew it, struck the high priest's[f] ·slave, and
cut off his right ear. (The slave's name was
Malchus.)
11At that, Jesus said to Peter, "Sheathe your
sword! Am I not to drink the cup[g] the Father
has given Me?"

Jesus Arrested and Taken to Annas

12Then the company of soldiers, the commander, and the Jewish temple police arrested Jesus and tied Him up. 13First they led
Him to Annas,[h] for he was the father-in-law
of Caiaphas,[i] who was high priest that year.
14Caiaphas was the one who had advised the
·Jews that it was advantageous that one man
should die for the people.[j]

Peter Denies Jesus

15Meanwhile, Simon Peter[k] was following
Jesus, as was another disciple. That disciple
was an acquaintance of the high priest; so he
went with Jesus into the high priest's courtyard. 16But Peter remained standing outside by the door. So the other disciple, the
one known to the high priest, went out and
spoke to the girl who was the doorkeeper and
brought Peter in.
17Then the slave girl who was the doorkeeper said to Peter, "You aren't one of this
man's disciples too, are you?"
"I am not!" he said. 18Now the slaves and

[a]**18:9** Mt 1:22
[b]Jn 17:6,12
[c]**18:10** Mt 16:17
[d]Lk 6:14; Ac 10:32
[e]Mk 14:47; Heb 4:12
[f]Lv 16:32
[g]**18:11** Is 51:22; Jr 49:12; Mt 20:22; 26:39,42; Mk 14:36; Lk 22:42
[h]**18:13** Lk 3:2; Jn 18:24; Ac 4:6
[i]Mt 26:3; Jn 11:49
[j]**18:14** Jn 11:50
[k]**18:15** Lk 6:14

the temple police had made a charcoal fire, because it was cold. They were standing there warming themselves, and Peter was standing with them, warming himself.

Jesus before Annas

19 The high priest[a] questioned Jesus about His disciples and about His teaching.

20 "I have spoken openly to the world," Jesus answered him. "I have always taught in the ·synagogue[b] and in the ·temple complex,[c] where all the Jews congregate, and I haven't spoken anything in secret. 21 Why do you question Me? Question those who heard what I told them. Look, they know what I said."

22 When He had said these things, one of the temple police standing by slapped Jesus, saying, "Is this the way you answer the high priest?"

23 "If I have spoken wrongly," Jesus answered him, "give evidence[A] about the wrong; but if rightly,[d] why do you hit Me?"

24 Then[e] Annas[f] sent Him bound to Caiaphas the high priest.

Peter Denies Jesus Twice More

25 Now Simon Peter was standing and warming himself. They said to him, "You aren't one of His disciples too, are you?"

He denied it and said, "I am not!"

26 One of the high priest's slaves, a relative of the man whose ear Peter had cut off, said, "Didn't I see you with Him in the garden?"

27 Peter then denied it again. Immediately a rooster crowed.[g]

Jesus before Pilate

28 Then[h] they took Jesus from Caiaphas to the governor's ·headquarters.[i] It was early morning. They did not enter the headquarters themselves; otherwise they would be defiled and unable to eat the ·Passover.

29 Then ·Pilate[j] came out to them and said, "What charge[k] do you bring against this man?"

30 They answered him, "If this man weren't a criminal,[B] we wouldn't have handed Him over to you."

31 So Pilate told them, "Take Him yourselves and judge Him according to your law."

"It's not legal[C] for us to put anyone to death," the Jews declared. 32 They said this so that Jesus' words might be fulfilled signifying what kind of death He was going to die.[l]

33 Then Pilate went back into the headquarters, summoned Jesus, and said to Him, "Are You the King of the Jews?"[m]

34 Jesus answered, "Are you asking this on your own, or have others told you about Me?"

35 "I'm not a Jew, am I?" Pilate replied. "Your own nation and the chief priests handed You over to me. What have You done?"

36 "My kingdom[n] is not of this ·world," said Jesus. "If My kingdom were of this world,[o] My servants[D,p] would fight, so that I wouldn't be handed over to the Jews. As it is, My kingdom does not have its origin here."[E,q]

37 "You are a king then?" Pilate asked.

"You say that I'm a king," Jesus replied. "I was born for this, and I have come into the world[r] for this: to testify[s] to the truth.[t] Everyone who is of the truth listens to My voice."

38 "What is truth?" said Pilate.

Jesus or Barabbas

After he had said this, he went out to the Jews again and told them, "I find no grounds[u] for charging Him. 39 You[v] have a custom that I release one prisoner to you at the Passover. So, do you want me to release to you the King of the Jews?"

40 They shouted back, "Not this man, but Barabbas!"[w] Now Barabbas was a revolutionary.[F,x]

Jesus Flogged and Mocked

19 Then ·Pilate took Jesus and had Him flogged. 2 The soldiers also twisted together a crown[y] of thorns, put it on His head, and threw a purple robe around Him. 3 And they repeatedly came up to Him[z] and said, "Hail, King of the Jews!" and were slapping His face.

4 Pilate went outside again and said to them, "Look, I'm bringing Him outside to you to let you know I find no grounds[aa] for charging Him."

[a] **18:19** Mt 26:3
[b] **18:20** Jms 2:2
[c] Ac 21:26
[d] **18:23** Gn 1:31
[e] **18:24-27** Mt 26:57-75; Mk 14:53-72; Lk 22:54,62-65
[f] **18:24** Jn 18:13
[g] **18:27** Jn 13:38
[h] **18:28-38** Mt 27:2,11-14; Mk 15:1-5; Lk 23:25
[i] **18:28** Mk 15:16
[j] **18:29** 1Tm 6:13
[k] 1Tm 5:19; Ti 1:6
[l] **18:32** Jn 12:32-33
[m] **18:33** Jn 19:21
[n] **18:36** Mk 1:15; Ac 20:25
[o] Jn 17:6
[p] Lk 1:2; Jn 18:18; Ac 26:16; 1Co 4:1
[q] Jn 8:23; 17:14,16
[r] **18:37** Jn 1:9; 3:19; 6:14; 9:39; 11:27; 12:46; 16:28; 1Tm 1:15
[s] Jn 15:26; Ac 26:5
[t] Ps 119:142; 2Th 2:10
[u] **18:38** Mt 27:37; Mk 15:26; Jn 19:4,6; Ac 13:28; 23:28; 25:18; 28:18
[v] **18:39–19:6** Mt 27:15-26; Mk 15:6-15; Lk 23:13-25
[w] **18:40** Mk 15:7
[x] Mk 14:48
[y] **19:2** Mk 15:17
[z] **19:3** Mk 1:45
[aa] **19:4** Jn 18:38

[A] **18:23** Or *him, testify* [B] **18:30** Lit *an evil doer* [C] **18:31** According to Roman law
[D] **18:36** Or *attendants*, or *helpers* [E] **18:36** Lit *My kingdom is not from here*
[F] **18:40** Or *robber*; see Jn 10:1,8 for the same Gk word used here

Pilate Sentences Jesus to Death

5 Then Jesus came out wearing the crown
of thorns and the purple robe.[a] Pilate said to
them, "Here is the man!"[b]
6 When the ·chief priests and the temple
police saw Him, they shouted, "Crucify! Crucify!"
Pilate responded, "Take Him and crucify
Him yourselves, for I find no grounds for
charging Him."
7 "We have a law," the ·Jews replied to him,
"and according to that law He must die,[c] because He made Himself[A] the Son of God."[d]
8 When Pilate heard this statement, he was
more afraid than ever. 9 He went back into
the ·headquarters[e] and asked Jesus, "Where
are You from?" But Jesus did not give him an
answer.[f] 10 So Pilate said to Him, "You're not
talking to me? Don't You know that I have the
authority to release You and the authority to
crucify You?"
11 "You would have no authority over Me
at all," Jesus answered him, "if it hadn't been
given you from above. This is why the one
who handed Me over to you has the greater
sin."[B,g]
12 From that moment Pilate made every effort[C] to release Him. But the Jews shouted,
"If you release this man, you are not Caesar's
friend. Anyone who makes himself a king opposes Caesar!"
13 When Pilate heard these words, he
brought Jesus outside. He sat down on the
judge's bench in a place called the Stone Pavement (but in ·Hebrew *Gabbatha*). 14 It was the
preparation day for the ·Passover, and it was
about six in the morning.[D] Then he told the
Jews, "Here is your king!"
15 But they shouted, "Take Him away! Take
Him away! Crucify Him!"
Pilate said to them, "Should I crucify your
king?"
"We have no king but Caesar!" the chief
priests answered.
16 So then, because of them, he handed Him
over to be crucified.

The Crucifixion

Therefore they took Jesus away.[E] 17 Carrying[h] His own cross,[i] He went out to what is
called Skull Place, which in Hebrew is called
Golgotha. 18 There they crucified Him and two
others with Him, one on either side, with Jesus
in the middle. 19 Pilate also had a sign lettered
and put on the cross. The inscription was:

JESUS THE NAZARENE
THE KING OF THE JEWS.

20 Many of the Jews read this sign, because
the place where Jesus was crucified was near
the city,[j] and it was written in Hebrew,[F] Latin,
and Greek. 21 So the chief priests of the Jews
said to Pilate, "Don't write, 'The King of the
Jews,'[k] but that He said, 'I am the King of the
Jews.'"
22 Pilate replied, "What I have written, I
have written."
23 When the soldiers crucified Jesus, they
took His clothes and divided them into four
parts, a part for each soldier. They also took
the tunic, which was seamless, woven in one
piece from the top. 24 So they said to one another, "Let's not tear it, but cast lots for it, to
see who gets it." They did this to fulfill[l] the
Scripture[m] that says: **They divided My clothes
among themselves, and they cast lots for My
clothing.**[G,n] And this is what the soldiers did.

Jesus' Provision for His Mother

25 Standing[o] by the cross[p] of Jesus were His
mother,[q] His mother's sister, Mary the wife
of Clopas, and ·Mary Magdalene.[r] 26 When
Jesus saw His mother and the disciple He
loved[s] standing there, He said to His mother,
"·Woman, here is your son." 27 Then He said to
the disciple, "Here is your mother." And from
that hour the disciple took her into his home.

The Finished Work of Jesus

28 After[t] this, when Jesus knew that everything was now accomplished[u] that the Scripture might be fulfilled, He said, "I'm thirsty!"[v]
29 A jar full of sour wine was sitting there; so
they fixed a sponge full of sour wine on hyssop[H,w] and held it up to His mouth.
30 When Jesus had received the sour wine,
He said, "It is finished!"[x] Then bowing His
head, He gave up His spirit.[y]

[a] **19:5** Lk 19:36 [b] Zch 6:12 [c] **19:7** Lv 24:16; Jn 10:33,36 [d] Jn 5:18; 19:12; Heb 1:2 [e] **19:9** Mk 15:16 [f] Mk 14:61 [g] **19:11** Jn 15:22; 18:13-14,19-24,28 [h] **19:17-24** Mt 27:33-37; Mk 15:22-26; Lk 23:32-34 [i] **19:17** Lk 9:23; 23:26 [j] **19:20** Heb 13:12 [k] **19:21** Mt 2:2; 27:11,29,37; Mk 15:2,9,12,18,26; Lk 23:3,37-38; Jn 18:33,39; 19:3,19 [l] **19:24** Mt 1:22 [m] Mt 26:54 [n] Ps 22:18 [o] **19:25-27** Mt 27:55-56; Mk 15:40-41; Lk 23:49 [p] **19:25** Lk 23:26 [q] Mt 1:16 [r] Mk 15:40 [s] **19:26** Jn 13:23; 21:7 [t] **19:28-30** Mt 27:45-54; Mk 15:33-39; Lk 23:44-48 [u] **19:28** Lk 12:50; 18:31; 22:37; Jn 19:30; Ac 13:29; Heb 10:14; 11:40 [v] Ps 22:15; 69:21 [w] **19:29** Ex 12:22 [x] **19:30** Lk 12:50; Jn 4:34; 17:4; 19:28 [y] 1Jn 5:8

[A] **19:7** He claimed to be [B] **19:11** To *have sin* is an idiom that refers to guilt caused by sin. [C] **19:12** Lit *Pilate was trying* [D] **19:14** Lit *the sixth hour*; see note at Jn 1:39; an alt time reckoning would be *about noon* [E] **19:16** Other mss add *and led Him out* [F] **19:20** Or *Aramaic* [G] **19:24** Ps 22:18 [H] **19:29** Or *with hyssop*

Jesus' Side Pierced

31 Since it was the preparation day,[a] the Jews did not want the bodies[b] to remain on the cross[c] on the Sabbath[d] (for that Sabbath was a special[A] day). They requested that Pilate have the men's legs broken and that their bodies be taken away.[e] 32 So the soldiers came and broke the legs of the first man and of the other one who had been crucified with Him. 33 When they came to Jesus, they did not break His legs since they saw that He was already dead.[f] 34 But one of the soldiers pierced[g] His side[h] with a spear, and at once blood and water[i] came out. 35 He who saw this has testified[j] so that you also may believe. His testimony is true, and he knows he is telling the truth.[k] 36 For these things happened so that the Scripture would be fulfilled:[l] **Not one of His bones will be broken.**[B,m] 37 Also, another Scripture says: **They will look at the One they pierced.**[C,n]

Jesus' Burial

38 After[o] this, Joseph of Arimathea, who was a disciple of Jesus—but secretly because of his fear of the Jews—asked Pilate that he might remove Jesus' body.[p] Pilate gave him permission, so he came and took His body away. 39 Nicodemus[q] (who had previously come to Him at night) also came, bringing a mixture of about 75 pounds[D] of myrrh and aloes. 40 Then they took Jesus' body[r] and wrapped it in linen cloths[s] with the aromatic spices, according to the burial[t] custom of the Jews. 41 There was a garden in the place where He was crucified. A new tomb was in the garden; no one had yet been placed in it. 42 They placed Jesus there because of the Jewish preparation and since the tomb was nearby.

The Empty Tomb

20 On[u] the first day of the week[v] ·Mary Magdalene[w] came to the tomb[x] early, while it was still dark. She saw that the stone[y] had been removed[E] from the tomb. 2 So she ran to Simon Peter[z] and to the other disciple, the one Jesus loved, and said to them, "They have taken the Lord out of the tomb,[aa] and we don't know where they have put Him!"

3 At that, Peter and the other disciple went out, heading for the tomb. 4 The two were running together, but the other disciple outran Peter and got to the tomb first. 5 Stooping down, he saw the linen cloths[ab] lying there, yet he did not go in. 6 Then, following him, Simon Peter came also. He entered the tomb and saw the linen cloths lying there. 7 The wrapping[ac] that had been on His head was not lying with the linen cloths[ad] but was folded up in a separate place by itself. 8 The other disciple, who had reached the tomb first, then entered the tomb, saw, and believed. 9 For they still did not understand the Scripture[ae] that He must rise[af] from the dead.[ag] 10 Then the disciples went home again.

Mary Magdalene Sees the Risen Lord

11 But[ah] Mary stood outside facing the tomb,[ai] crying. As she was crying, she stooped to look into the tomb. 12 She saw two angels[aj] in white sitting there, one at the head and one at the feet, where Jesus' body[ak] had been lying. 13 They said to her, "·Woman, why are you crying?"

"Because they've taken away my Lord,"[al] she told them, "and I don't know where they've put Him." 14 Having said this, she turned around and saw Jesus standing there, though she did not know it was Jesus.[am]

15 "Woman," Jesus said to her, "why are you crying? Who is it you are looking for?"

Supposing He was the gardener, she replied, "Sir, if you've removed Him, tell me where you've put Him, and I will take Him away."

16 Jesus said, "Mary."

Turning around, she said to Him in ·Hebrew, *"Rabbouni!"*[F]—which means "Teacher."[an]

17 "Don't cling to Me," Jesus told her, "for I have not yet ascended[ao] to the Father.[ap] But go to My brothers[aq] and tell them that I am ascending to My Father[ar] and your Father—to My God[as] and your God."

18 Mary Magdalene went and announced to the disciples, "I have seen the Lord!"[at] And she told them what[G] He had said to her.

[a] **19:31** Jn 19:14 [b] Lk 12:4 [c] Lk 23:26 [d] Mk 2:23 [e] Dt 21:22-23; Jos 8:29; 10:26-27 [f] **19:33** Ex 12:46; Nm 9:12; Ps 34:20 [g] **19:34** Zch 12:10; Rv 1:7 [h] Jn 20:20 [i] 1Jn 5:6-9 [j] **19:35** Jn 1:14-15,34 [k] Jn 21:24 [l] **19:36** Jn 13:18; 17:12; 19:24 [m] Ex 12:46; Nm 9:12; Ps 34:20 [n] **19:37** Zch 12:10 [o] **19:38-42** Mt 27:57-60; Mk 15:42-46; Lk 23:50-54 [p] **19:38** Lk 12:4; Jn 2:21 [q] **19:39** Jn 3:1-9; 7:50 [r] **19:40** Jn 2:21; 19:40 [s] Jn 20:5 [t] Mk 14:8 [u] **20:1-2** Mt 28:5-8; Mk 16:5-8; Lk 24:3-8 [v] **20:1** Lk 24:1; Ac 20:7; 1Co 16:2 [w] Mk 15:40 [x] Jn 5:28 [y] Mt 27:60,66; Mk 15:46 [z] **20:2** Lk 6:14; Jn 21:7; Ac 10:32 [aa] Jn 5:28 [ab] **20:5** Lk 24:12; Jn 19:40; 20:5-7 [ac] **20:7** Lk 19:20; Jn 11:44; Ac 19:12 [ad] Jn 20:5 [ae] **20:9** Mt 26:54 [af] Lk 18:33; Ac 2:24 [ag] Mk 9:9-10; 12:25; Lk 16:31; 24:46; Ac 10:41; 13:34; 17:3,31 [ah] **20:11-18** Mk 16:9-11 [ai] **20:11** Jn 5:28 [aj] **20:12** Gn 16:7; Mt 13:49; Ac 5:19; Rv 14:6 [ak] Lk 12:4; Jn 2:21 [al] **20:13** Lk 10:1; 1Co 8:6 [am] **20:14** Jn 21:4 [an] **20:16** Mk 4:38; Eph 4:11 [ao] **20:17** Lk 24:51; Jn 3:13; 6:62; Ac 1:9-11; 2:33-34; Rm 10:6; Eph 1:20-21; 4:8; 1Pt 3:22 [ap] Mt 5:16; 11:27; Jn 8:42 [aq] Ac 9:30 [ar] Jn 14:12 [as] Mt 27:46 [at] **20:18** Mk 16:10

[A] **19:31** Lit *great* [B] **19:36** Ex 12:46; Nm 9:12; Ps 34:20 [C] **19:37** Zch 12:10 [D] **19:39** Lit *100 litrai*; a Roman *litrai* = 12 ounces [E] **20:1** Lit *She saw the stone removed* [F] **20:16** *Rabbouni* is also used in Mk 10:51 [G] **20:18** Lit *these things*

The Metanarrative of God's Mission

Christopher Wright

Too often, the church has separated *theology* (as a discipline about God—what God is like, what God has said, and what God has done), from *missions* (being about us and what we do). However, our mission is derived from God's own mission—the *missio Dei*—which in turn is a reflection of what God is like, what God has said, and what God has done (and is doing and has yet to do). This unity between theology and missions is one key way of looking at the grand story of Scripture. Our theology of God must include the mission of God as a unifying metanarrative for the whole Bible.

Some people use the term *missio Dei* as referring only to the sending action of God. The reason they do this is that the "root" of the Latin verb *mitto* means "to send." However, if we reduce our focus only to the sending acts of God, we may ignore a number of important missional themes and teachings in the Bible, which are crucial for our understanding of the fullness of God's mission and our own practice of missions.

Missio Dei can have a broader sense drawn from the way the Bible paints a picture of the purposefulness of God. *The mission of God is the commitment of God to make Himself known to His creation ultimately for the purpose of redeeming and restoring all creation to its right relationship with God.* The story of God making Himself known is the grand narrative of the Bible. God's mighty acts make Him known to the peoples of the world and are predicted, proclaimed, explained, and celebrated throughout the biblical storyline.

In His election of Abraham, God makes Himself known, and launches His great agenda of bringing blessing to all nations on earth (Gn 12:1-3), repeating this promise five times in Genesis. Paul defined this great missional purpose of God as 'the good news ahead of time' (Gl 3:6-8), and understood his own mission, and the church's mission, in light of it.

Through the experience of God's grace, God makes Himself known. God declares His desire to be known through salvation (Ex 5:22-6:8, Is 46:9-10). He declares Himself to be the king over the whole earth through His redemptive acts (Ex 2:23-24, 15:18, Ezk 36:21-23). Based on His redemptive deeds, the Bible proclaims that there is "no other" god than the God of Israel (Dt 4:32-39, Is 41:22-23). Unlike the fictional gods of the other peoples, who were thought of as having limited power that allowed them to rule only over specific locations, the God of the Bible has unlimited power and extends His reign over all of creation (Jr 10:10-12; Ts 45:11-13). He is the only and only God, and the whole universe is His to rule as He pleases.

Even through the experience of judgment, God makes Himself known. Through the plagues and Red Sea, Pharaoh learns why he should obey the God of Israel (Ex 5:2). Israel and the nations learned of God's uniqueness and sovereignty over the whole earth through the exile of Israel (2Kg 18:32-35, Jr 27:4-6). Even kings who do not know the one true God are used by Him to accomplish His purposes, much as an axe is used to chop wood (Is 10:5-19). And yet God remains faithful and committed to His people even in the midst of sovereign judgment upon them (Jr 27:1-14). Their punishment is to have a redeeming and purifying purpose.

In the New Testament, Jesus fulfills God's mission to be known—identifying Himself with the God of Israel, fulfilling the promise made to Abraham by opening up the way to blessing for Jews and Gentiles alike. The biblical story reveals that God wills to be known through Jesus, His Son (Jn 1:18, 17:1-3, 2Co 4:4-6).

Making Himself known is God's purpose in creation and His purpose in redemption. "The heavens declare the glory of God, and the sky proclaims the work of His hands. Day after day they pour out speech; night after night they communicate knowledge" (Ps 19:1-2). God's "invisible attributes, that is, His eternal power and divine nature, have been clearly seen since the creation of the world, being understood through what He has made" (Rm 1:20). The whole Bible presents a God of missional activity, from His purposeful, goal-oriented act of Creation to the completion of His mission through the redemption of all Creation in the new heavens and new earth, and the creation of a new humanity in Christ, redeemed from every nation on earth though the blood of the cross.

We also find in the Bible that *humanity has a mission* (to rule and care for the earth); *Old Testament Israel had a mission* (to be the agent of God's blessing to all nations); *Jesus had a mission* (to embody and fulfill the mission of Israel, bringing blessing to the nations through bearing our sin on the Cross and anticipating the new Creation in His Resurrection); *and the church has a mission* (to participate with God in the ingathering of the nations in fulfillment of Old Testament Scriptures).

The mission of God, then, governs the story of the Bible from the brokenness of the nations in Genesis 11 to the healing of the nations in Revelation 21-22. If the grand story of the Bible and our world is God making Himself known, then this is the motivation and purpose of the church's mission. The church's missional activities, to which they are called and sent on, flows directly from God's mission. The church's missional activities are acts of humble participation in God's great work for His grand purpose.

God is on mission, and we, in that wonderful phrase of Paul's, are "coworkers with God."

The Disciples Commissioned

[19]In the evening of that first day of the
week,[a] the disciples were gathered together
with the doors locked because of their fear
of the ·Jews. Then Jesus came, stood among
them, and said to them, "Peace to you!"[b]
[20]Having said this, He showed them His
hands and His side.[c] So the disciples rejoiced
when they saw the Lord.
[21]Jesus said to them again, "Peace to you!
As the Father has sent Me,[d] I also send you."[e]
[22]After saying this, He breathed on them[f] and
said,[A] "Receive the Holy Spirit.[g] [23]If you forgive the sins of any, they are forgiven them; if
you retain the sins of any, they are retained."[h]

Thomas Sees and Believes

[24]But one of the Twelve, Thomas[i] (called
"Twin"), was not with them when Jesus came.
[25]So the other disciples kept telling him, "We
have seen the Lord!"
But he said to them, "If I don't see the mark
of the nails in His hands, put my finger into
the mark of the nails,[j] and put my hand into
His side,[k] I will never believe!"[l]
[26]After eight days His disciples were in-
doors again, and Thomas was with them.
Even though the doors were locked, Jesus
came and stood among them. He said, "Peace
to you!"
[27]Then He said to Thomas, "Put your finger
here and observe My hands. Reach out your
hand and put it into My side. Don't be an unbeliever, but a believer."[m]
[28]Thomas responded to Him, "My Lord and
my God!"
[29]Jesus said, "Because you have seen Me,
you have believed.[B] Those who believe without seeing[n] are blessed."

The Purpose of This Gospel

[30]Jesus performed many other signs[o] in the
presence of His disciples that are not written[p]
in this book.[q] [31]But these are written so that
you may believe Jesus is the ·Messiah,[r] the
Son[s] of God,[C,t] and by believing you may have
life in His name.[u]

Jesus' Third Appearance to the Disciples

21 After this, Jesus revealed[v] Himself
again to His disciples by the Sea of Tiberias.[D,w] He revealed Himself in this way:

[a]**20:19** Lk 24:1; Ac 20:7; 1Co 16:2 [b]Jn 14:27; 16:33 [c]**20:20** Lk 24:39-40; Jn 19:34; 20:25-29 [d]**20:21** Jn 3:17; 17:18; Heb 3:1 [e]Jn 13:20; Ac 1:2 [f]**20:22** Gn 2:7; Ezk 37:9 [g]Ps 51:11; Jn 1:33; 14:17; 16:7; Ac 2:4; 8:15; Rm 8:9; Gl 5:25; Ti 3:5; Rv 3:22 [h]**20:23** Mt 16:19; 18:18; Jn 9:41 [i]**20:24** Mk 3:18; Jn 11:16 [j]**20:25** Ps 22:16 [k]Jn 20:20 [l]Dt 9:23; Mk 16:11; Lk 22:67; Jn 4:48; 6:64; Ac 13:41 [m]**20:27** Nm 12:7 [n]**20:29** 2Co 5:7; 1Pt 1:8 [o]**20:30** Jn 2:11; 21:25 [p]1Jn 1:4 [q]2Tm 4:13 [r]**20:31** Mt 1:17; Ac 18:5; 1Jn 2:22; 5:1 [s]Jn 5:19 [t]Heb 1:2 [u]Jn 10:27; 1Jn 3:23

[v]**21:1** Mk 16:12; Jn 21:14; 2Co 4:11; 5:10; 1Tm 3:16; Heb 9:26; 1Pt 1:10; 1Jn 1:2; 3:5,8 [w]Jn 6:1,23

[A]**20:22** Lit *He breathed and said to them* [B]**20:29** Or *have you believed?* (as a question) [C]**20:31** Or *that the Messiah, the Son of God, is Jesus* [D]**21:1** The Sea of Galilee; *Sea of Tiberias* is used only in John; Jn 6:1,23

2 Simon Peter,[a] Thomas[b] (called "Twin"),
Nathanael[c] from Cana of Galilee,[d] Zebedee's[e]
sons, and two others of His disciples were together.
3 "I'm going fishing," Simon Peter said to
them.
"We're coming with you," they told him.
They went out and got into the boat, but that
night they caught nothing.[f]
4 When daybreak came, Jesus stood on the
shore. However, the disciples did not know it
was Jesus.[g]
5 "Men,"[A] Jesus called to them, "you don't
have any fish, do you?"
"No," they answered.
6 "Cast the net on the right side of the boat,"
He told them, "and you'll find some." So they
did,[B] and they were unable to haul it in because of the large number of fish. 7 Therefore
the disciple, the one Jesus loved, said to Peter,
"It is the Lord!"[h]
When Simon Peter heard that it was the
Lord, he tied his outer garment around him[C]
(for he was stripped) and plunged into the sea.
8 But since they were not far from land (about
100 yards[D,i] away), the other disciples came in
the boat,[j] dragging the net full of fish. 9 When
they got out on land, they saw a charcoal fire
there, with fish lying on it, and bread.
10 "Bring some of the fish you've just caught,"
Jesus told them. 11 So Simon Peter got up and
hauled the net ashore, full of large fish — 153
of them. Even though there were so many, the
net was not torn.[k]
12 "Come and have breakfast," Jesus told
them. None of the disciples dared ask Him,
"Who are You?" because they knew it was the
Lord. 13 Jesus came, took the bread, and gave it
to them. He did the same with the fish.
14 This was now the third time[E,l] Jesus appeared[F,m] to the disciples after He was raised
from the dead.

Jesus' Threefold Restoration of Peter

15 When they had eaten breakfast, Jesus
asked Simon Peter, "Simon, son of John,[G] do
you love[H] Me more than these?"
"Yes, Lord," he said to Him, "You know that
I love You."
"Feed[n] My lambs,"[o] He told him.
16 A second time He asked him, "Simon, son
of John, do you love[p] Me?"[q]
"Yes, Lord," he said to Him, "You know that
I love You."
"Shepherd[r] My sheep,"[s] He told him.
17 He asked him the third time, "Simon, son
of John, do you love[t] Me?"
Peter was grieved[u] that He asked him the
third time, "Do you love Me?" He said, "Lord,
You know everything![v] You know that I love
You."
"Feed[w] My sheep," Jesus said. 18 "•I assure
you:[x] When you were young, you would tie
your belt and walk wherever you wanted.
But when you grow old, you will stretch out
your hands and someone else will tie you and
carry you where you don't want to go." 19 He
said this to signify by what kind of death[y] he
would glorify God.[I,z] After saying this, He told
him, "Follow Me!"[aa]

Correcting a False Report

20 So Peter turned around and saw the disciple Jesus loved[ab] following them. That disciple was the one who had leaned back against
Jesus at the supper and asked, "Lord, who is
the one that's going to betray You?"[ac] 21 When
Peter saw him, he said to Jesus, "Lord — what
about him?"
22 "If I want him to remain until I come,"[ad]
Jesus answered, "what is that to you? As for
you, follow Me."
23 So this report[J] spread to the •brothers[K,ae] that
this disciple would not die.[af] Yet Jesus did not tell
him that he would not die, but, "If I want him to
remain until I come, what is that to you?"

Epilogue

24 This is the disciple who testifies to these
things and who wrote them down. We know
that his testimony is true.
25 And there are also many other things that
Jesus did, which, if they were written one by
one, I suppose not even the world itself could
contain the books[L] that would be written.[ag]

[a]**21:2** Lk 6:14; Ac 10:32
[b]Mk 3:18
[c]Jn 1:45-49
[d]Mt 17:22
[e]Mt 4:21; 10:2; 20:20; 26:37; 27:56; Mk 1:19-20; 3:17; 10:35; Lk 5:10; Jn 21:7; Ac 12:2
[f]**21:3** Lk 5:5
[g]**21:4** Jn 20:14,19,26
[h]**21:7** Lk 10:1; 1Co 8:6
[i]**21:8** Lk 12:25
[j]Mk 3:9; Jn 6:22-24
[k]**21:11** Lk 5:4-10
[l]**21:14** Jn 20:19,26
[m]Jn 21:1; 2Co 4:11; 1Jn 1:2
[n]**21:15** Mt 8:30,33; Mk 5:11,14; Lk 8:32,34; 15:15; Jn 21:17
[o]Rv 5:6
[p]**21:16** Lk 6:35; Rv 12:11
[q]Lk 10:27
[r]1Pt 5:2
[s]Mt 7:15; Jn 10:11
[t]**21:17** Mk 14:44; Jn 5:20
[u]2Co 2:2
[v]Jn 16:30
[w]Jn 21:15
[x]**21:18** Jn 1:51; Rv 22:21
[y]**21:19** 2Pt 1:14
[z]Jn 11:4; 17:1; 1Pt 2:12
[aa]Jn 1:43; 8:12; 10:27
[ab]**21:20** Jn 21:7
[ac]Jn 13:21,23-25
[ad]**21:22** Mk 8:38
[ae]**21:23** Ac 9:30
[af]Mk 9:1
[ag]**21:25** Jn 20:30

[A]**21:5** Lit *Children* [B]**21:6** Lit *they cast* [C]**21:7** Lit *he girded his garment* [D]**21:8** Lit *about 200 cubits* [E]**21:14** The other two are in Jn 20:19-29. [F]**21:14** Lit *was revealed* (v. 1) [G]**21:15-17** Other mss read *Simon, son of Jonah*; Mt 16:17; Jn 1:42 [H]**21:15-17** Two synonyms are translated *love* in this conversation: *agapao*, the first 2 times by Jesus (vv. 15-16); and *phileo*, the last time by Jesus (v. 17) and all 3 times by Peter (vv. 15-17). Peter's threefold confession of love for Jesus corresponds to his earlier threefold denial of Jesus; Jn 18:15-18,25-27. [I]**21:19** Jesus predicts that Peter would be martyred. Church tradition says that Peter was crucified upside down. [J]**21:23** Lit *this word* [K]**21:23** The word brothers refers to the late first century Christian community. [L]**21:25** Lit *scroll*

■ **AUTHOR:** Luke

■■ **DATE:** Written in A.D. 60–63, the book of Acts covers events of the early church from the ascension of Jesus through Paul's travels until he reaches Rome

This book of church history shows the mission of God empowered by the Holy Spirit as promised by Jesus at His ascension. The once fearful disciples move out from Jerusalem to all points of the compass. The risen Christ goes with them in a power heretofore unseen in creation. To describe it theoretically is impossible. It must be lived and experienced, worked with, struggled over, relied on, trusted. It is life the way God intended: reconciled to Him and living in community with His people.

Luke, a Gentile, was a physician and a missionary who traveled with the apostle Paul. Luke wrote this specialized history because the members of the newly formed church needed to know their story. If the *parousia* (Jesus' return at the end of history) were delayed for a second or third generation, then this book would instruct future believers where they came from. Many generations after Luke, we can see the value of his careful reporting.

ACTS

From the human side, the first-century church was fragile; problems were solved by prayer, trial, and error; leaders rose and fell. Paul emerges as no less an apostle than the disciples, and the one who does most to promote a world movement. Yet persecution causes Paul to spend much of his time in prison.

As Luke records, Christians did not easily scare. They did not cease praying or witnessing. Those who came alive by faith knew that God empowered them. Those watching from outside were amused, confused, or enraged. No matter. The Christian movement expanded so that even Rome itself appeared to be invaded by its power. The mission of God—saving people from sin and alienation, reconciling people to God and to each other—was already a quiet, unstoppable revolution. It falls to the church to be the rebellion against the world's rebellion.

Acts describes transitions, negotiations, sermons, imprisonments, and escape, but mostly it demonstrates that God changes people from the inside out. Life's purpose is defined through God's fame alive in a redeemed sinner. Eternity is always in view and death loses its sting. Daily habits are changing as families come to see God's blessings in new ways. Leaders recognize their role as stewards in God's world, not opportunists who ought to grab all they can.

The church is birthed and takes shape. In these pages, we witness the people of "the Way" caring deeply for one another and embarking on God's mission given by Christ at the mount of Ascension. Churches are planted, leaders are called out, and lives are eternally changed.

Boldly is an adverb that describes much of this momentum. These Christians have something new to say, and the world is beginning to take notice.

Prologue

1 I wrote the first narrative, Theophilus,
about all that Jesus began to do and teach[a]
2until the day He was taken up, after He had
given orders through the Holy Spirit to the
apostles He had chosen.[b] 3After He had suffered, He also presented Himself alive to
them by many convincing proofs, appearing
to them during 40 days and speaking about
the kingdom of God.[c]

[a]1:1 Lk 1:3; 24:19
[b]1:2 Mt 28:19-20; Lk 24:47; Jn 20:21
[c]1:3 Mt 28:17; Mk 16:14; Lk 24:34,36; Jn 20:19; 1Co 15:5-7
[d]1:4 Lk 24:49; Jn 14:1; Ac 2:33

The Holy Spirit Promised

4While He was together[A] with them, He
commanded them not to leave Jerusalem, but
to wait for the Father's promise.[d] "This," He
said, "is what you heard from Me; 5for John

Cross-Cultural Mission of God

Craig Ott

The mission of God seeks to enfold people of every nation, tribe, and language into God's kingdom. Though God has chosen to work through a particular people of His calling—Israel in the OT and the church in the NT—this calling was always with the intent that His people would become agents of His mission to all peoples. We find this beginning with the call of Abraham and the patriarchs (Gn 12:3; see also 18:18; 22:18; 26:4; 28:14). The election of God's people was never intended as an end in itself, but rather that they might become a blessing to the nations (Ps 67). Many OT passages point to the day when God would gather peoples from the nations to be included in His purposes and become agents of His kingdom (e.g. Is 56:3,6-8; 66:18-21; Zch 8:20-23).

Jesus taught that the gospel of the kingdom would be preached among all nations before His return (Mt 24:14; Mk 13:10). After His resurrection Jesus commanded His followers to preach in the power of the Spirit repentance and forgiveness through Christ, and to make disciples of all nations (Mt 28:19; Mk 16:15; Lk 24:46-47). In short, they are sent on mission into the world as Jesus Himself was sent by the Father (Jn 20:21).

After the death and resurrection of Christ and with the sending of the Holy Spirit at Pentecost, God's mission to the nations bursts forth in a new way through His new people, the church. In Acts 1:8 Jesus indicates that the Spirit would empower His people to become His witnesses "in Jerusalem, in all Judea and Samaria, and to the ends of the earth." The spread of the disciples' witness involves crossing *geographic barriers* moving outward from Jerusalem to increasingly remote regions. This sending also entails crossing *ethnic barriers* as the gospel moves from the people of Israel to the Samaritans, a people of mixed Israelite and non-Israelite lineage, and on to diverse ethnic groups culturally very different from Israel. Furthermore, *religious barriers* are crossed as the gospel moves from the people of promise, the Israelites, to the Samaritans, who had a form of OT faith, and on to Gentiles who adhered to a variety of religious beliefs.

The phrase "ends of the earth" underlines the comprehensiveness of the mission and alludes to Isaiah 49:6, which describes the Servant of the Lord: "I will also make you a light for the nations, to be my salvation to the ends of the earth." These words anticipate not only the work of Christ (Lk 2:32) but also the future witness of His disciples (Ac 13:47).

God's mission to include in His kingdom people from every nation, tribe, and language will be wonderfully fulfilled (Rv 5:9-10; 7:9). Thus the church today as God's missionary people can confidently bear witness to Christ and advance His kingdom, near and far, crossing every cultural barrier. We cannot rest until the gospel has been preached in word and deed, and the church is planted among every people, in every locality and from every religious background.

[A]1:4 Or *He was eating*, or *He was lodging*

baptized with water, but you will be baptized
with the Holy Spirit not many days from
now."[a]
6 So when they had come together, they
asked Him, "Lord, are You restoring the kingdom to Israel at this time?"
7 He said to them, "It is not for you to know
times or periods that the Father has set by His
own authority.[b] 8 But you will receive power
when the Holy Spirit has come on you, and
you will be My witnesses in Jerusalem, in all
Judea and Samaria, and to the ends[A] of the
earth."[c]

The Ascension

9 After He had said this, He was taken up as
they were watching, and a cloud took Him
out of their sight. 10 While He was going, they
were gazing into heaven, and suddenly two
men in white clothes stood by them.[d] 11 They
said, "Men of Galilee, why do you stand looking up into heaven? This Jesus, who has been
taken from you into heaven, will come in the
same way that you have seen Him going into
heaven."[e]

United in Prayer

12 Then they returned to Jerusalem from
the mount called the Mount of Olives, which
is near Jerusalem — a Sabbath day's journey
away. 13 When they arrived, they went to the
room[f] upstairs where they were staying:

Peter, John,
James, Andrew,
Philip, Thomas,
Bartholomew, Matthew,
James the son of Alphaeus,
Simon the Zealot,
and Judas the son of James.[g]

14 All these were continually united[h] in
prayer,[B] along with the women, including
Mary[C] the mother of Jesus, and His brothers.[i]

Matthias Chosen

15 During these days Peter stood up among
the •brothers[D] — the number of people who
were together was about 120 — and said:
16 "Brothers, the Scripture had to be fulfilled

[a] **1:5** Jl 3:18; Mt 3:11; Ac 11:16
[b] **1:7** Mt 24:36; Mk 13:32; 1Th 5:1
[c] **1:8** Lk 24:48; Ac 2:1,4; 4:33; 8:1,14; 13:47
[d] **1:10** Mt 28:13; Mk 16:5; Lk 24:4; Jn 20:12
[e] **1:11** Mt 16:27; Ac 2:7; 1Th 1:10; 2Th 1:10
[f] **1:13** Ac 9:37,39; 20:8
[g] Mt 10:2-4; Mk 3:16-19; Lk 6:14-16
[h] **1:14** Ac 2:46; 4:24; 5:12; 15:25; Rm 15:6
[i] Mt 12:46; Lk 23:49,55; Rm 12:12; Col 4:2
[j] **1:16** Lk 22:37,47; 24:44; Jn 13:18; 18:3
[k] **1:17** Jn 6:71; Ac 20:24; 21:19
[l] **1:18** Mt 26:14-15; 27:5,7-8
[m] **1:20** Ps 69:25; 109:8
[n] **1:22** Mk 1:4; Ac 2:31; 4:2; 17:18; 23:6; 24:15; 26:23
[o] **1:23** Ac 15:22; 18:7
[p] **1:24** Ac 6:6; 13:3
[q] 1Sm 16:7; Jr 17:10; Ac 15:8; Rv 2:23
[r] **1:25** Rm 1:5; 1Co 9:2; Gl 2:8
[s] **1:26** Mt 27:35; Mk 15:24; Lk 23:34; Jn 19:24; Ac 8:21; 26:18; Col 1:12; 1Pt 5:3
[t] **2:1** Lv 23:15; Ac 1:14; 20:16
[u] **2:2** 1Kg 19:11; Jb 38:1; Ezk 1:4
[v] Ac 4:31; 16:26
[w] **2:4** Ac 4:31; 13:52
[x] Mk 16:17; 1Co 12:10
[y] **2:5** Mt 28:19; Rm 1:5; Gl 1:16

that the Holy Spirit through the mouth of
David spoke in advance about Judas, who
became a guide to those who arrested Jesus.[j]
17 For he was one of our number and was allotted a share in this ministry."[k] 18 Now this
man acquired a field with his unrighteous
wages. He fell headfirst and burst open in the
middle, and all his insides spilled out.[l] 19 This
became known to all the residents of Jerusalem, so that in their own language that field
is called *Hakeldama* (that is, Field of Blood).
20 "For it is written in the Book of Psalms:

Let his dwelling become desolate;
let no one live in it;[E] and
Let someone else take his position.[F,m]

21 "Therefore, from among the men who
have accompanied us during the whole time
the Lord Jesus went in and out among us —
22 beginning from the baptism of John until the day He was taken up from us — from
among these, it is necessary that one become
a witness with us of His resurrection."[n]
23 So they proposed two: Joseph, called Barsabbas, who was also known as Justus, and
Matthias.[o] 24 Then they prayed,[p] "You, Lord,
know the hearts of all; show which of these
two You have chosen[q] 25 to take the place[G] in
this apostolic service[r] that Judas left to go
to his own place." 26 Then they cast lots[s] for
them, and the lot fell to Matthias. So he was
numbered with the 11 apostles.

Pentecost

2 When the day of Pentecost had arrived,
they were all together in one place.[t] 2 Suddenly a sound like that of a violent rushing
wind[u] came from heaven, and it filled the
whole house where they were staying.[v] 3 And
tongues, like flames of fire that were divided,
appeared to them and rested on each one of
them. 4 Then they were all filled[w] with the
Holy Spirit and began to speak in different
•languages, as the Spirit gave them ability for
speech.[x]
5 There were Jews living in Jerusalem, devout
men from every nation[y] under heaven. 6 When
this sound occurred, a crowd came together
and was confused because each one heard

[A] **1:8** Lit *the end* [B] **1:14** Other mss add *and petition* [C] **1:14** Or *prayer, with their wives and Mary* [D] **1:15** Other mss read *disciples* [E] **1:20** Ps 69:25 [F] **1:20** Ps 109:8

[G] **1:25** Other mss read *to share*

them speaking in his own language. 7 And they
were astounded and amazed, saying,[A] "Look,
aren't all these who are speaking Galileans?[a]
8 How is it that each of us can hear in our own
native language? 9 Parthians, Medes, Elamites;
those who live in Mesopotamia, in Judea and
Cappadocia, Pontus and •Asia,[b] 10 Phrygia and
Pamphylia, Egypt and the parts of Libya near
Cyrene; visitors from Rome, both Jews and
•proselytes,[c] 11 Cretans and Arabs — we hear
them speaking the magnificent acts of God in
our own languages." 12 They were all astounded
and perplexed, saying to one another, "What
could this be?" 13 But some sneered and said,
"They're full of new wine!"[d]

Peter's Sermon

14 But Peter stood up with the Eleven, raised
his voice, and proclaimed to them: "Men of
Judah and all you residents of Jerusalem, let
me explain this[B] to you and pay attention to
my words. 15 For these people are not drunk,
as you suppose, since it's only nine in the
morning.[C] 16 On the contrary, this is what was
spoken through the prophet Joel:

17 **And it will be** in the last days, says God,
that **I will pour out My Spirit**
on all humanity;
then your sons and your daughters
will prophesy,
your young men will see visions,
and your old men will dream dreams.[e]
18 **I will even pour out My Spirit**
on My male and female •slaves
in those days,
and they will prophesy.[f]
19 **I will display wonders**
in the heaven above
and signs on the earth below:
blood and fire and a cloud of smoke.
20 **The sun will be turned to darkness**
and the moon to blood[g]
before the great and remarkable Day of
the Lord[h] **comes.**
21 **Then everyone who calls**
on the name of the Lord will be saved.[D,i]

22 "Men of Israel, listen to these words: This
Jesus the •Nazarene was a man pointed out to
you by God with miracles, wonders, and signs
that God did among you through Him, just as
you yourselves know.[j] 23 Though He was delivered up according to God's determined plan
and foreknowledge, you used[E] lawless people[F]
to nail Him to a cross and kill Him.[k] 24 God
raised Him up, ending the pains of death,[l] because it was not possible for Him to be held
by it. 25 For David says of Him:

I saw the Lord ever before me;
because He is at my right hand,
I will not be shaken.
26 **Therefore my heart was glad,**
and my tongue rejoiced.
Moreover, my flesh will rest in hope,
27 **because You will not leave me in •Hades**
or allow Your Holy One to see decay.[m]
28 **You have revealed the paths of life**
to me;
You will fill me with gladness
in Your presence.[G,n]

29 "•Brothers, I can confidently speak to you
about the patriarch David: He is both dead
and buried, and his tomb is with us to this
day.[o] 30 Since he was a prophet, he knew that
God had sworn an oath to him to seat one
of his descendants[H,I] on his throne.[p] 31 Seeing
this in advance, he spoke concerning the resurrection of the •Messiah:

He[J] **was not left in Hades,**
and His flesh **did not**
experience decay.[K,q]

32 "God has resurrected[r] this Jesus. We are
all witnesses of this. 33 Therefore, since He
has been exalted to the right hand of God[s]
and has received from the Father the promised Holy Spirit,[t] He has poured out[u] what
you both see and hear. 34 For it was not David
who ascended into the heavens, but he himself says:

The Lord declared to my Lord,
'Sit at My right hand
35 **until I make Your enemies**
Your footstool.'[L,v]

36 "Therefore let all the house of Israel know
with certainty that God has made this Jesus,

[a] **2:7** Ac 1:11; 2:12
[b] **2:9** Gn 14:9; 2Kg 17:6
[c] **2:10** Mt 23:15; Ac 13:13; 15:38; 16:6,21; 18:23
[d] **2:13** Ac 17:32; 1Co 14:23
[e] **2:17** Is 44:3; Jn 7:38; Ac 10:45; 21:9
[f] **2:18** Ac 21:10; 1Co 12:10
[g] **2:20** Mt 24:29; 1Th 5:2
[h] Is 58:13; Ezk 13:5; Am 5:18; Ob 15; Zph 1:14; Zch 14:1; Mal 4:5
[i] **2:17-21** Jl 2:28-32; Ac 16:31; Rm 10:13
[j] **2:22** Jn 3:2; 4:48; Ac 10:38; Heb 2:4
[k] **2:23** Mt 26:24; Lk 22:22; 24:20; Ac 3:18; 4:28; 5:30
[l] **2:24** Rm 8:11; 1Co 6:14; 2Co 4:14; Eph 1:20; Col 2:12; 1Th 1:10; Heb 13:20
[m] **2:27** Mt 11:23; Lk 2:26; Ac 13:35; Heb 7:26
[n] **2:25-28** Ps 16:8-11
[o] **2:29** 1Kg 2:10; Neh 3:16; Ac 7:8-9; 13:36
[p] **2:30** 2Sm 23:2; Ps 132:11; Mt 22:43; Lk 1:32; Ac 1:8; Heb 11:32
[q] **2:31** Ps 16:10; Ac 2:27
[r] **2:32** Lk 18:33; Ac 2:24
[s] **2:33** Php 2:9; Heb 10:12
[t] Jn 7:39; 14:26; 16:7,13
[u] Ac 2:17; 10:45
[v] **2:34-35** Ps 110:1; Mt 5:35; 22:44; Mk 12:36; Lk 20:42-43; Jn 3:13; 1Co 15:25; Heb 1:13

[A] **2:7** Other mss add *to one another* [B] **2:14** Lit *let this be known* [C] **2:15** Lit *it's the third hour of the day* [D] **2:17-21** Jl 2:28-32 [E] **2:23** Other mss read *you have taken* [F] **2:23** Or *used the hand of lawless ones* [G] **2:25-28** Ps 16:8-11 [H] **2:30** Other mss add *according to the flesh to raise up the Messiah* [I] **2:30** Lit *one from the fruit of his loin* [J] **2:31** Other mss read *His soul* [K] **2:31** Ps 16:10 [L] **2:34-35** Ps 110:1

whom you crucified, both Lord and Messiah!"[a]

Forgiveness through the Messiah

37When they heard this, they came under deep conviction[A] and said to Peter and the rest of the apostles: "Brothers, what must we do?"[b]

38"Repent,"[c] Peter said to them, "and be baptized,[d] each of you, in the name[e] of Jesus Christ for the forgiveness of your sins, and you will receive the gift of the Holy Spirit.

[a]2:36 Mt 28:18; Lk 2:11; Rm 14:9; 2Co 4:5
[b]2:37 Lk 3:10; Ac 16:30
[c]2:38 Lk 24:47; Ac 3:19; 26:20
[d]Ac 8:12; 22:16
[e]Ac 3:16; 15:14

Making Disciples

Alton Garrison

There are many definitions of discipleship and many approaches to the process of "disciple making." However, the church that was birthed in Acts 2 modeled one of the last directives Jesus gave. "Go, therefore, and make disciples" (Mt 28:19). The question we must ask is: What were the characteristics of a first-century disciple, and how are they attained?

The Bible is clear regarding God's will for those who have become Christians and want to follow Christ as a disciple. First Peter 1:15-16 states, "But as the One who called you is holy, you also are to be holy in all your conduct; for it is written, Be holy, because I am holy." Holiness is an attribute possessed by God, essential to His nature, and an expected discipline of all the disciples of Christ.

It is not just an experience, status, or recognition but a distinct discipline that results in a God-reflecting quality. A fully developed disciple of Christ will have engaged in a process that may be better understood as a progressive manifestation of the Holy Spirit's indwelling, empowering a person to reflect the character of Christ. The Apostle Paul described the work of the Holy Spirit in 2 Corinthians 3:18: "We all, with unveiled faces, are looking as in a mirror at the glory of the Lord and are being transformed into the same image from glory to glory; this is from the Lord who is the Spirit." Discipleship begins with forgiveness and grace but is completed through maturity.

While we definitely have our responsibility in the process of becoming a disciple, there is obviously a necessary divine component. The first step on the discipleship journey in Acts 2 was *Holy Spirit* ***empowerment***.

After a ten-day prayer vigil in the Upper Room, the 120 faithful followers of Christ were "filled with the Holy Spirit" (Ac 2:4). This empowerment was for a special purpose: power to be witnesses for Christ and to be the church "so that God's multi-faceted wisdom may now be made known through the church (Eph 3:10). Those observing did not understand what they were seeing and hearing and said, "What could this be?" (Ac 2:12).

Following *empowerment*, Peter answered this question by ***educating*** the crowd concerning Christ and by preaching a powerful sermon (vv.14-39), and three thousand souls were saved. These people were not casual converts. They became "devoted" followers of Jesus Christ, and they engaged in a new lifestyle (vv. 42-47). What did that new lifestyle involve, and how was the first century church so effective that it impacted the world for Christ?

Luke described how they ***evolved*** into a powerful spiritual force by synergizing worship, evangelism, discipleship, fellowship, and service. These spiritual components are still essential for a church to fulfill God's directives, but the church corporately is only a reflection of the individuals in it. The goal of all believers should be to connect to God and to each other, personally grow through an intentional spiritual process, serve, commit to sharing their faith, and exalt God through daily devotion and worship.

[A]2:37 Lit *they were pierced to the heart*

39 For the promise is for you and for your children, and for all who are far off,[A,a] as many as
the Lord our God will call." 40 And with many
other words he testified and strongly urged
them, saying, "Be saved from this corrupt[B]
generation!"[b]

A Generous and Growing Church

41 So those who accepted his message were
baptized, and that day about 3,000 people
were added to them. 42 And they devoted
themselves to the apostles' teaching,[c] to the
fellowship, to the breaking of bread, and to
the prayers.[d]
43 Then fear came over everyone, and many
wonders and signs were being performed
through the apostles.[e] 44 Now all the believers were together and held all things in
common.[f] 45 They sold their possessions and
property and distributed the proceeds to
all, as anyone had a need.[C] 46 Every day they
devoted themselves to meeting together in
the ·temple complex, and broke bread from
house to house. They ate their food with a joyful and humble attitude,[g] 47 praising God and
having favor with all the people. And every
day the Lord added to them[D] those who were
being saved.[h]

Healing of a Lame Man

3 Now Peter and John were going up together to the ·temple complex at the hour
of prayer[i] at three in the afternoon.[E] 2 And a
man who was lame from birth was carried
there and placed every day at the temple gate
called Beautiful, so he could beg from those
entering the temple complex.[j] 3 When he saw
Peter and John about to enter the temple
complex, he asked for help. 4 Peter, along with
John, looked at him intently and said, "Look
at us." 5 So he turned to them,[F] expecting to
get something from them. 6 But Peter said,
"I don't have silver or gold, but what I have,
I give you: In the name of Jesus Christ the
·Nazarene, get up and walk!"[k] 7 Then, taking
him by the right hand he raised him up, and
at once his feet and ankles became strong.
8 So he jumped up, stood, and started to walk,
and he entered the temple complex with
them—walking, leaping, and praising God.[l]
9 All the people saw him walking and praising God, 10 and they recognized that he was
the one who used to sit and beg at the Beautiful Gate of the temple complex. So they were
filled with awe and astonishment at what had
happened to him.[m]

Preaching in Solomon's Colonnade

11 While he[G] was holding on to Peter and
John, all the people, greatly amazed, ran toward them in what is called Solomon's Colonnade.[n] 12 When Peter saw this, he addressed the
people: "Men of Israel, why are you amazed
at this? Or why do you stare at us, as though
we had made him walk by our own power or
godliness? 13 The God of Abraham, Isaac, and
Jacob, the God of our fathers,[o] has glorified
His Servant Jesus, whom you handed over
and denied in the presence of ·Pilate,[p] when
he had decided to release Him. 14 But you denied the Holy and Righteous One[q] and asked
to have a murderer given to you.[r] 15 You killed
the source[H] of life, whom God raised from
the dead; we are witnesses of this.[s] 16 By faith
in His name, His name has made this man
strong, whom you see and know. So the faith
that comes through Him has given him this
perfect health in front of all of you.
17 "And now, ·brothers, I know that you did
it in ignorance, just as your leaders also did.[t]
18 But what God predicted through the mouth
of all the prophets—that His ·Messiah would
suffer—He has fulfilled[u] in this way. 19 Therefore repent[v] and turn back, so that your sins
may be wiped out,[w] that seasons of refreshing may come from the presence of the Lord,[I]
20 and that He may send Jesus, who has been
appointed[x] for you as the Messiah. 21 Heaven
must welcome[J] Him until the times of the restoration of all things, which God spoke about
by the mouth of His holy prophets from the
beginning.[y] 22 Moses said:[K]

**The Lord your God will raise up for you a
Prophet like me from among your brothers. You must listen to Him in everything He will say to you. 23 And everyone**

[a] **2:39** Is 44:3; Ac 3:25; Eph 2:13
[b] **2:40** Dt 32:5; Mt 17:17; Php 2:15
[c] **2:42** Ac 5:28; 13:12; 17:19; 1Co 14:6
[d] Ac 1:14; Heb 10:25
[e] **2:43** Mk 16:17,20; Ac 5:12
[f] **2:44** Mt 19:21; Ac 4:32
[g] **2:46** Lk 24:53; Ac 5:42; 20:7
[h] **2:47** Ac 5:14; 11:24; 16:5; Rm 14:18
[i] **3:1** Ps 55:17; Mt 27:46; Ac 10:3,30
[j] **3:2** Lk 16:20; Jn 9:8; Ac 14:8
[k] **3:6** Ac 4:10; 2Co 6:10
[l] **3:8** Is 35:4-6; Ac14:10
[m] **3:10** Jn 9:8; Ac 3:2
[n] **3:11** Lk 22:8; Jn 10:23; Ac 5:12
[o] **3:13** Ac 5:30; 7:32; 22:14
[p] Mt 27:2; Lk 23:4; Jn 19:15; Ac 13:28
[q] **3:14** Mk 1:24; Ac 4:27; 7:52
[r] Mk 15:11; Lk 23:18,25
[s] **3:15** Ac 2:24; 5:31
[t] **3:17** Lk 23:34; Ac 13:27
[u] **3:18** Lk 24:27; Ac 2:23; 17:3; 26:23
[v] **3:19** Ac 2:38; 8:22; 17:30; 26:20
[w] Ps 51:1,9; Is 43:25; 44:22; Col 2:14
[x] **3:20** Ac 22:14; 26:16
[y] **3:21** Mt 17:10; Lk 1:70; Ac 1:11

[A] **2:39** For distant generations or perhaps Gentiles [B] **2:40** Or *crooked*, or *twisted* [C] **2:45** Or *to all, according to one's needs* [D] **2:47** Other mss read *to the church* [E] **3:1** Lit *at the ninth hour* [F] **3:5** Or *he paid attention to them* [G] **3:11** Other mss read *the lame man who was healed* [H] **3:15** Or *the Prince*, or *the Ruler* [I] **3:19** Some editors or translators put *that seasons . . . the Lord* in v. 20 [J] **3:21** Or *receive*, or *retain* [K] **3:22** Other mss add *to the fathers*

who will not listen to that Prophet will
be completely cut off from the people.[A,a]

24 "In addition, all the prophets who have
spoken, from Samuel and those after him,
have also announced these days. 25 You are
the sons of the prophets and of the covenant
that God made with your ancestors, saying
to Abraham, **And all the families of the earth**
will be blessed through your offspring.[B,b]
26 God raised up His Servant[C] and sent Him
first to you to bless you by turning each of
you from your evil ways."[c]

Peter and John Arrested

4 Now as they were speaking to the people,
the priests, the commander of the temple
police, and the ·Sadducees confronted them,[d]
2 because they were provoked that they were
teaching the people and proclaiming the
resurrection from the dead, using Jesus as
the example.[D,e] 3 So they seized them and put
them in custody until the next day, since it
was already evening. 4 But many of those who
heard the message believed, and the number
of the men came to about 5,000.

Peter and John Face the Jewish Leadership

5 The next day, their rulers, elders, and
·scribes assembled in Jerusalem 6 with Annas
the high priest, Caiaphas, John and Alexander, and all the members of the high-priestly
family.[E,f] 7 After they had Peter and John stand
before them, they asked the question: "By
what power or in what name have you done
this?"

8 Then Peter was filled with the Holy Spirit
and said to them, "Rulers of the people
and elders:[F,g] 9 If we are being examined today about a good deed done to a disabled
man — by what means he was healed — 10 let
it be known to all of you and to all the people
of Israel, that by the name of Jesus Christ the
·Nazarene — whom you crucified and whom
God raised from the dead — by Him this man
is standing here before you healthy.[h] 11 This
Jesus is

> **the stone rejected by you builders,**
> **which has become the cornerstone.**[G,H,i]

12 There is salvation in no one else, for there is
no other name under heaven given to people,
and we must be saved by it."[j]

The Name Forbidden

13 When they observed the boldness of Peter
and John and realized that they were unedu-
cated and untrained men, they were amazed
and recognized that they had been with
Jesus.[k] 14 And since they saw the man who
had been healed standing with them, they
had nothing to say in response. 15 After they had
ordered them to leave the ·Sanhedrin, they
conferred among themselves, 16 saying, "What
should we do with these men? For an obvious
sign, evident to all who live in Jerusalem, has
been done through them, and we cannot
deny it![l] 17 However, so this does not spread
any further among the people, let's threaten
them against speaking to anyone in this name
again." 18 So they called for them and ordered
them not to preach or teach at all in the name
of Jesus.

19 But Peter and John answered them,
"Whether it's right in the sight of God for us
to listen to you rather than to God, you decide;[m] 20 for we are unable to stop speaking
about what we have seen and heard."[n]

21 After threatening them further, they released them. They found no way to punish
them, because the people were all giving
glory to God over what had been done;[o] 22 for
this sign of healing had been performed on a
man over 40 years old.

Prayer for Boldness

23 After they were released, they went to
their own people and reported everything
the ·chief priests and the elders had said to
them. 24 When they heard this, they all raised
their voices to God and said, "Master, You are
the One who made the heaven, the earth, and
the sea, and everything in them.[p] 25 You said
through the Holy Spirit, by the mouth of our
father David Your servant:[I]

> **Why did the Gentiles rage**
> **and the peoples plot futile things?**
> 26 **The kings of the earth took their stand**

[a] **3:22-23** Dt 18:15-19; Ac 7:37
[b] **3:25** Gn 22:18; Ac 2:39; Rm 9:4
[c] **3:26** Ac 2:24; 13:46; Rm 1:16
[d] **4:1** Mt 3:7; Lk 22:4; Ac 5:24
[e] **4:2** Ac 3:15; 17:18
[f] **4:6** Mt 26:3; Lk 3:2; Jn 18:13
[g] **4:8** Lk 23:13; Ac 4:5
[h] **4:10** Ac 2:24; 3:6
[i] **4:11** 1Pt 2:7
[j] **4:12** Mt 1:21; Ac 10:43; 1Tm 2:5
[k] **4:13** Mt 11:25; Lk 22:8; Jn 7:15
[l] **4:16** Jn 11:47; Ac 3:9-10
[m] **4:19** Ac 4:13; 5:28
[n] **4:20** Ac 22:15; 1Co 9:16; 1Jn 1:1,3
[o] **4:21** Mt 9:8; 21:26; Lk 20:6,19; 22:2; Ac 5:26
[p] **4:24** Ex 20:11; 2Ch 2:12; Neh 9:6; Ps 102:25; 124:8; 134:3; 146:6; Is 37:16

[A] **3:22-23** Dt 18:15-19 [B] **3:25** Gn 12:3; 18:18; 22:18; 26:4 [C] **3:26** Other mss add *Jesus* [D] **4:2** Lit *proclaiming in Jesus the resurrection from the dead* [E] **4:6** Or *high-priestly class*, or *high-priestly clan* [F] **4:8** Other mss add *of Israel* [G] **4:11** Lit *the head of the corner* [H] **4:11** Ps 118:22 [I] **4:25** Other mss read *through the mouth of David Your servant*

and the rulers assembled together
against the Lord and
against His ·Messiah.[A,a]

27 "For, in fact, in this city both ·Herod and Pontius ·Pilate, with the Gentiles and the people[B] of Israel, assembled together against Your holy Servant Jesus, whom You anointed,[b] 28 to do whatever Your hand and Your plan had predestined to take place. 29 And now, Lord, consider their threats, and grant that Your ·slaves may speak Your message with complete boldness,[c] 30 while You stretch out Your hand for healing, signs, and wonders[d] to be performed through the name of Your holy Servant Jesus." 31 When they had prayed, the place where they were assembled was shaken, and they were all filled with the Holy Spirit and began to speak God's message with boldness.[e]

Believers Sharing

32 Now the large group of those who believed were of one heart and mind, and no one said that any of his possessions was his own, but instead they held everything in common.[f] 33 And the apostles were giving testimony with great power to the resurrection of the Lord Jesus, and great grace was on all of them.[g] 34 For there was not a needy person among them, because all those who owned lands or houses sold them, brought the proceeds of the things that were sold,[h] 35 and laid them at the apostles' feet. This was then distributed for each person's basic needs.[C,i]

36 Joseph, a Levite and a Cypriot by birth, the one the apostles called Barnabas, which is translated Son of Encouragement,[j] 37 sold a field he owned, brought the money, and laid it at the apostles' feet.[k]

Lying to the Holy Spirit

5 But a man named Ananias, with his wife Sapphira, sold a piece of property. 2 However, he kept back part of the proceeds with his wife's knowledge, and brought a portion of it and laid it at the apostles' feet.[l]

3 Then Peter said, "Ananias, why has Satan filled your heart[m] to lie to the Holy Spirit and keep back part of the proceeds from the field? 4 Wasn't it yours while you possessed it? And after it was sold, wasn't it at your disposal? Why is it that you planned this thing in your heart? You have not lied to men but to God!" 5 When he heard these words, Ananias dropped dead, and a great fear came on all who heard.[n] 6 The young men got up, wrapped his body, carried him out, and buried him.[o]

7 There was an interval of about three hours; then his wife came in, not knowing what had happened. 8 "Tell me," Peter asked her, "did you sell the field for this price?"

"Yes," she said, "for that price."

9 Then Peter said to her, "Why did you agree to test the Spirit of the Lord? Look! The feet of those who have buried your husband are at the door, and they will carry you out!"[p]

10 Instantly she dropped dead at his feet. When the young men came in, they found her dead, carried her out, and buried her beside her husband. 11 Then great fear came on the whole church and on all who heard these things.

Apostolic Signs and Wonders

12 Many signs and wonders were being done among the people through the hands of the apostles.[q] By common consent they would all meet in Solomon's Colonnade.[r] 13 None of the rest dared to join them, but the people praised them highly.[s] 14 Believers were added to the Lord in increasing numbers—crowds of both men and women. 15 As a result, they would carry the sick out into the streets and lay them on cots and mats so that when Peter came by, at least his shadow[t] might fall on some of them. 16 In addition, a large group came together from the towns surrounding Jerusalem, bringing sick people and those who were tormented by ·unclean spirits, and they were all healed.

In and Out of Prison

17 Then the high priest took action. He and all his colleagues, those who belonged to the party of the ·Sadducees, were filled with jealousy.[u] 18 So they arrested[D] the apostles and put them in the city jail.[v] 19 But an angel of the Lord opened the doors of the jail during the night, brought them out, and said,[w] 20 "Go

[a] **4:25-26** Ps 2:1-2; Dn 9:24-25; Lk 4:18; Ac 1:16; 10:38; Heb 1:9
[b] **4:27** Mt 14:1; 27:2; Lk 23:1,12
[c] **4:29** Ac 9:27; 13:46; 14:3; 19:8; Php 1:14
[d] **4:30** Jn 4:48; Ac 3:6
[e] **4:31** Ac 2:2,4; 16:26; Php 1:14
[f] **4:32** Ac 2:44; Php 1:27
[g] **4:33** Lk 24:48; Ac 1:8,22
[h] **4:34** Mt 19:21; Ac 2:45
[i] **4:35** Ac 2:45; 4:37; 5:2; 6:1
[j] **4:36** Ac 9:27; 1Co 9:6
[k] **4:37** Ac 4:35; 5:2
[l] **5:2** Ac 4:37; 5:3
[m] **5:3** Mt 4:10; Lk 22:3; Jn 13:2,27
[n] **5:5** Ezk 11:13; Ac 5:10-11
[o] **5:6** Ezk 29:5; Jn 19:40; Ac 8:2
[p] **5:9** Ac 5:3-4; 15:10; 1Co 10:9
[q] **5:12** Ac 2:43; 14:3; 19:11; Rm 15:19; 2Co 12:12; Heb 2:4
[r] Jn 10:23; Ac 4:21,32
[s] **5:13** Ac 2:47; 3:11
[t] **5:15** Mt 14:36; Ac 19:12
[u] **5:17** Ac 4:1; 15:5
[v] **5:18** Lk 21:12; Ac 4:3
[w] **5:19** Mt 1:20; Lk 1:11; Ac 8:26; 12:7; 16:26; 27:23

[A] **4:25-26** Ps 2:1-2 [B] **4:27** Lit *peoples* [C] **4:35** Lit *person as anyone had need* [D] **5:18** Lit *laid hands on*

and stand in the ·temple complex, and tell the
people all about this life."[a] 21 In obedience to
this, they entered the temple complex at daybreak and began to teach.

The Apostles on Trial Again

When the high priest and those who were
with him arrived, they convened the ·San-
hedrin—the full Senate of the sons of Israel—and sent orders to the jail to have them
brought.[b] 22 But when the temple police got
there, they did not find them in the jail, so
they returned and reported, 23 "We found the
jail securely locked, with the guards standing
in front of the doors, but when we opened
them, we found no one inside!" 24 As[A] the commander of the temple police and the ·chief
priests heard these things, they were baffled
about them, as to what could come of this.

25 Someone came and reported to them,
"Look! The men you put in jail are standing
in the temple complex and teaching the people." 26 Then the commander went with the
temple police and brought them in without
force, because they were afraid the people
might stone them.[c] 27 After they brought them
in, they had them stand before the Sanhedrin, and the high priest asked, 28 "Didn't we
strictly order you not to teach in this name?[d]
And look, you have filled Jerusalem with your
teaching and are determined to bring this
man's blood on us!"[e]

29 But Peter and the apostles replied, "We
must obey God rather than men. 30 The God
of our fathers raised up Jesus,[f] whom you had
murdered by hanging Him on a tree.[g] 31 God
exalted this man to His right hand as ruler
and Savior, to grant repentance to Israel, and
forgiveness of sins.[h] 32 We are witnesses of
these things, and so is the Holy Spirit[i] whom
God has given to those who obey Him."

Gamaliel's Advice

33 When they heard this, they were enraged and wanted to kill them.[j] 34 A ·Pharisee
named Gamaliel, a teacher of the law who
was respected by all the people, stood up in
the Sanhedrin and ordered the men[B] to be
taken outside for a little while.[k] 35 He said to
them, "Men of Israel, be careful about what
you're going to do to these men. 36 Not long
ago Theudas rose up, claiming to be somebody, and a group of about 400 men rallied
to him. He was killed, and all his partisans
were dispersed and came to nothing.[l] 37 After
this man, Judas the Galilean rose up in the
days of the census and attracted a following.[C]
That man also perished, and all his partisans
were scattered. 38 And now, I tell you, stay
away from these men and leave them alone.
For if this plan or this work is of men, it will
be overthrown;[m] 39 but if it is of God, you will
not be able to overthrow them. You may even
be found fighting against God." So they were
persuaded by him.[n] 40 After they called in the
apostles and had them flogged, they ordered
them not to speak in the name of Jesus and
released them.[o] 41 Then they went out from
the presence of the Sanhedrin, rejoicing that
they were counted worthy to be dishonored
on behalf of the Name.[D,p] 42 Every day in the
temple complex, and in various homes, they
continued teaching and proclaiming the
good news that Jesus is the ·Messiah.

Seven Chosen to Serve

6 In those days, as the number of the disciples[q] was multiplying, there arose a
complaint by the Hellenistic Jews[E] against
the Hebraic Jews[F] that their widows were
being overlooked in the daily distribution.[r]
2 Then the Twelve summoned the whole company of the disciples and said, "It would not
be right for us to give up preaching about
God to handle financial matters.[G] 3 Therefore,
·brothers, select from among you seven men
of good reputation,[s] full of the Spirit[t] and wisdom, whom we can appoint to this duty. 4 But
we will devote ourselves to prayer and to the
preaching ministry." 5 The proposal pleased
the whole company. So they chose Stephen,[u]
a man full of faith and the Holy Spirit, and
Philip, Prochorus, Nicanor, Timon, Parme-
nas, and Nicolaus, a ·proselyte from Antioch.[v]
6 They had them stand before the apostles,
who prayed[w] and laid their hands on[x] them.[H]

[a] 5:20 Jn 6:63,68; Php 2:16
[b] 5:21 Mt 5:22; Ac 4:6; 5:27,34,41
[c] 5:26 Ac 4:21; 5:13
[d] 5:28 Jn 14:13; Ac 3:16; 1Jn 3:23
[e] Mt 27:25; Ac 2:23,36; 3:15; 4:10; 7:52
[f] 5:30 Ac 2:24; 3:13
[g] Ac 10:39; 13:29; Gl 3:13; 1Pt 2:24
[h] 5:31 Ac 2:33; 3:15
[i] 5:32 Lk 24:48; Jn 15:26; Ac 15:28; Heb 2:4
[j] 5:33 Ac 2:37; 7:54
[k] 5:34 Lk 2:46; 5:17; Ac 22:3
[l] 5:36 Ac 8:9; Gl 2:6; 6:3
[m] 5:38 Mt 15:17; Mk 11:30
[n] 5:39 Pr 21:30; Ac 7:51; 11:17
[o] 5:40 Mt 10:17; Mk 13:9; Ac 4:18
[p] 5:41 Mt 5:12; Jn 15:21; 1Pt 4:13
[q] 6:1 Mt 9:10; Mk 10:10; Lk 6:1; Jn 6:3; Ac 9:1,10,19,25-26; 21:4,16
[r] Ac 2:41; 4:4,35; 5:14; 9:29,39; 11:20
[s] 6:3 Dt 1:13; 1Tm 3:7
[t] Lk 4:1; Ac 7:55; 11:19,24
[u] 6:5 Ac 6:8-9; 11:19; 22:20
[v] Mt 23:15; Ac 8:5,26; 21:8
[w] 6:6 Ac 1:24; 8:17; 13:3; 2Tm 1:6
[x] Nm 8:10; Ac 9:17; 1Tm 4:14

[A] 5:24 Other mss add *the high priest and* [B] 5:34 Other mss read *apostles*
[C] 5:37 Lit *and drew people after him* [D] 5:41 Other mss add *of Jesus*, or *of Christ*
[E] 6:1 Jews of Gk language and culture [F] 6:1 Jews of Aram or Hb language and culture [G] 6:2 Or *to serve tables* [H] 6:6 The laying on of hands signified the prayer of blessing for the beginning of a new ministry.

7 So the preaching about God flourished,
the number of the disciples in Jerusalem multiplied[a] greatly, and a large group of priests
became obedient to the faith.

Stephen Accused of Blasphemy

8 Stephen, full of grace and power, was performing great wonders and signs among
the people. 9 Then some from what is called
the Freedmen's ·Synagogue, composed of
both Cyrenians and Alexandrians, and some
from Cilicia and ·Asia, came forward and disputed with Stephen. 10 But they were unable
to stand up against his wisdom and the Spirit
by whom he was speaking.
11 Then they persuaded some men to say,
"We heard him speaking blasphemous words
against Moses and God!"[b] 12 They stirred up
the people, the elders, and the ·scribes; so
they came, dragged him off, and took him to
the ·Sanhedrin. 13 They also presented false
witnesses who said, "This man does not stop
speaking blasphemous words against this
holy place and the law.[c] 14 For we heard him
say that Jesus, this ·Nazarene, will destroy
this place and change the customs that Moses
handed down to us."[d] 15 And all who were sitting in the Sanhedrin looked intently at him
and saw that his face was like the face of an
angel.

Stephen's Sermon

7 "Is this true?"[A] the high priest asked.
2 "Brothers and fathers," he said, "listen: The God of glory appeared to our father
Abraham when he was in Mesopotamia, before he settled in Haran,[e] 3 and said to him:

> **Get out of your country**
> **and away from your relatives,**
> **and come to the land**
> **that I will show you.**[B,f]

4 "Then he came out of the land of the Chaldeans and settled in Haran. From there, after
his father died, God had him move to this
land you now live in.[g] 5 He didn't give him an
inheritance in it, not even a foot of ground,
but He promised to give it to him as a possession, and to his descendants after him,[h] even
though he was childless. 6 God spoke in this
way:

> **His descendants would be strangers**
> **in a foreign country,**
> **and they would enslave**
> **and oppress them 400 years.**
> 7 **I will judge the nation**
> **that they will serve as ·slaves,** God said.
> **After this, they will come out**
> **and worship Me in this place.**[C,i]

8 Then He gave him the covenant of circumcision. After this, he fathered Isaac and circumcised[j] him on the eighth day; Isaac did
the same with Jacob, and Jacob with the 12
patriarchs.[k]

The Patriarchs in Egypt

9 "The patriarchs became jealous of Joseph
and sold him into Egypt, but God was with
him[l] 10 and rescued him out of all his troubles.
He gave him favor and wisdom in the sight of
Pharaoh, king of Egypt, who appointed him
ruler over Egypt and over his whole household.[m] 11 Then a famine and great suffering
came over all of Egypt and Canaan,[n] and our
ancestors could find no food. 12 When Jacob
heard there was grain in Egypt, he sent our
ancestors the first time. 13 The second time,
Joseph was revealed to his brothers, and Joseph's family became known to Pharaoh. 14 Joseph then invited his father Jacob and all his
relatives, 75 people in all,[o] 15 and Jacob went
down to Egypt. He and our ancestors died
there,[p] 16 were carried back to Shechem, and
were placed in the tomb that Abraham had
bought for a sum of silver from the sons of
Hamor in Shechem.[q]

Moses, a Rejected Savior

17 "As the time was drawing near to fulfill the
promise that God had made to Abraham, the
people flourished and multiplied in Egypt[r]
18 until a different king who did not know Joseph ruled over Egypt.[D] 19 He dealt deceitfully
with our race and oppressed our ancestors by
making them leave their infants outside, so
they wouldn't survive.[E,s] 20 At this time Moses
was born, and he was beautiful in God's sight.

[a]**6:7** Ac 12:24; 19:20; Col 1:6
[b]**6:11** 1Kg 21:10,13; Mt 26:59-60
[c]**6:13** Mt 24:15; Ac 7:58; 21:28; 25:8
[d]**6:14** Dn 9:26; Ac 15:1; 21:21; 26:3; 28:17
[e]**7:2** Gn 11:31; 15:7; Ps 29:3; Ac 22:1; 1Co 2:8
[f]**7:3** Gn 12:1
[g]**7:4** Gn 11:31; 12:4-5
[h]**7:5** Gn 12:7; 13:15; 15:18; 17:8; Gl 3:16; Heb 8:8-9
[i]**7:6-7** Gn 15:13-14; Ex 3:12; 12:40
[j]**7:8** Gn 17:9-11; 21:2-4
[k]Gn 25:26; 29:31; 30:5; 35:23
[l]**7:9** Gn 37:11,28; 39:2,21; 45:4; Ps 105:17
[m]**7:10** Gn 41:37-43; 42:6; Ps 105:21
[n]**7:11** Gn 41:54; 42:5
[o]**7:13-14** Gn 45:1-4,9-10,16,27; 46:26-27; Ex 1:5; Dt 10:22
[p]**7:15** Gn 46:5; 49:33; Ex 1:6
[q]**7:16** Gn 23:16; 33:19; 50:13; Ex 13:19; Jos 24:32
[r]**7:17** Gn 15:13; Ex 1:7; Ps 105:24
[s]**7:18-19** Ex 1:8-10,22; Ps 105:25

[A]**7:1** Lit *"Are these things so?"* [B]**7:3** Gn 12:1 [C]**7:6-7** Gn 15:13-14 [D]**7:18** Other mss omit *over Egypt* [E]**7:19** A common pagan practice of population control by leaving infants outside to die

He was cared for in his father's home three
months, 21and when he was left outside, Pharaoh's daughter adopted and raised him as
her own son.[a] 22So Moses was educated in all
the wisdom of the Egyptians and was powerful in his speech and actions.[b]
23"As he was approaching the age of 40, he
decided[A] to visit his brothers, the Israelites.
24When he saw one of them being mistreated,
he came to his rescue and avenged the oppressed man by striking down the Egyptian.
25He assumed his brothers would understand that God would give them deliverance
through him, but they did not understand.
26The next day he showed up while they were
fighting and tried to reconcile them peacefully, saying, 'Men, you are brothers. Why are
you mistreating each other?'[c]
27"But the one who was mistreating his
neighbor pushed him[B] away, saying:

Who appointed you a ruler and a judge
over us? 28Do you want to kill me, the
same way you killed the Egyptian yester-
day?[C,d]

29"At this disclosure, Moses fled and became an exile in the land of Midian, where
he fathered two sons.[e] 30After 40 years had
passed, an angel[D] appeared to him in the
wilderness of Mount Sinai, in the flame of a
burning bush. 31When Moses saw it, he was
amazed at the sight. As he was approaching
to look at it, the voice of the Lord came: **32I am**
the God of your fathers — the God of Abra-
ham, of Isaac, and of Jacob.[E,f] So Moses began
to tremble and did not dare to look.
33"Then the Lord said to him:

Remove the sandals from your feet, for
the place where you are standing is holy
ground. 34I have observed the oppres-
sion of My people in Egypt; I have heard
their groaning and have come down to
rescue them. And now, come, I will send
you to Egypt.[F,g]

35"This Moses, whom they rejected when
they said, **Who appointed you a ruler and a**
judge?[C] — this one God sent as a ruler and
a redeemer by means of the angel who appeared to him in the bush.[h] 36This man led
them out and performed wonders and signs
in the land of Egypt,[i] at the Red Sea, and in the
wilderness 40 years.[j]

Israel's Rebellion against God

37"This is the Moses who said to the Israelites, **God[G] will raise up for you a Prophet like**
me from among your brothers.[H,k] 38He is the
one who was in the congregation in the wilderness together with the angel who spoke to
him on Mount Sinai, and with our ancestors.[l]
He received living oracles to give to us.[m] 39Our
ancestors were unwilling to obey him, but
pushed him away, and in their hearts turned
back to Egypt.[n] 40They told Aaron:

Make us gods who will go before us. As
for this Moses who brought us out of the
land of Egypt, we don't know what's hap-
pened to him.[I,o]

41They even made a calf in those days, offered sacrifice to the idol, and were celebrating what their hands had made.[p] 42Then God
turned away[q] and gave them up to worship[r]
the host of heaven, as it is written in the book
of the prophets:

House of Israel, did you bring Me
offerings and sacrifices
40 years in the wilderness?
43 **No, you took up the tent of Moloch**[J]
and the star of your god Rephan,[K]
the images that you made to worship.
So I will deport you beyond Babylon![L,s]

God's Real Tabernacle

44"Our ancestors had the tabernacle of the
testimony in the wilderness, just as He who
spoke to Moses commanded him to make it
according to the pattern he had seen.[t] 45Our
ancestors in turn received it and with Joshua
brought it in when they dispossessed the nations that God drove out before our fathers,[u]
until the days of David. 46He found favor in
God's sight and asked that he might provide
a dwelling place for the God[M] of Jacob.[v] 47But
it was Solomon who built Him a house.[w]
48However, the Most High does not dwell in

[a]**7:20-21** Ex 2:2-10; Heb 11:23
[b]**7:22** 1Kg 4:30; Is 19:11; Lk 24:19
[c]**7:23-26** Ex 2:11-14; Heb 11:24-26
[d]**7:27-28** Ex 2:14; Lk 12:14; Ac 7:35
[e]**7:29** Ex 2:15,22; 18:3-4
[f]**7:32** Ex 3:6; Mt 22:32; Mk 12:26; Lk 20:37
[g]**7:33-34** Ex 3:5,7-8,10
[h]**7:35** Ex 14:19; Nm 20:16
[i]**7:36** Ex 12:41; 33:1; Heb 8:9
[j]Ex 14:21; 16:35; Nm 14:33; Ps 95:10; Ac 13:18
[k]**7:37** Dt 18:15; Ac 3:22
[l]**7:38** Ex 19:17; Is 63:9; Ac 7:53
[m]Dt 5:27; 32:47; Jn 1:17; Rm 3:2; Heb 4:12; 5:12; 1Pt 4:11
[n]**7:39** Ex 16:3; Nm 11:4; 14:3-4; Ezk 20:8,24
[o]**7:40** Ex 32:1,23
[p]**7:41** Dt 9:16; Ps 106:19-20; Rv 9:20
[q]**7:42** Jos 24:20; Is 63:10
[r]Dt 4:19; 2Kg 21:3; Jr 19:13; Zph 1:5
[s]**7:42-43** 1Kg 11:7; Am 5:25-27; Ac 7:36
[t]**7:44** Ex 25:8-9,40; 38:21; Heb 8:5
[u]**7:45** Jos 3:14; 18:1; 23:9; 24:18; Ps 44:2
[v]**7:46** 2Sm 7:1,8; 1Ch 22:7; Ps 89:19; 132:5
[w]**7:47** 1Kg 6:1-2; 8:17-20; 2Ch 3:1

[A]**7:23** Lit *40, it came into his heart* [B]**7:27** Moses [C]**7:27-28,35** Ex 2:14
[D]**7:30** Other mss add *of the Lord* [E]**7:32** Ex 3:6,15 [F]**7:33-34** Ex 3:5,7-8,10
[G]**7:37** Other mss read *'The Lord your God* [H]**7:37** Dt 18:15 [I]**7:40** Ex 32:1,23
[J]**7:43** Canaanite or Phoenician sky or sun god [K]**7:43** Perhaps an Assyrian star god—the planet Saturn [L]**7:42-43** Am 5:25-27 [M]**7:46** Other mss read *house*

sanctuaries made with hands, as the prophet
says:[a]

49 Heaven is My throne,
and earth My footstool.
What sort of house will you build
for Me?
says the Lord,
or what is My resting place?
50 Did not My hand make all
these things?[A,b]

Resisting the Holy Spirit

51 "You stiff-necked[c] people with uncircumcised hearts and ears![d] You are always resisting the Holy Spirit; as your ancestors did, so
do you. 52 Which of the prophets did your fathers not persecute?[e] They even killed those
who announced beforehand the coming of
the Righteous One, whose betrayers and murderers[f] you have now become. 53 You received
the law under the direction of angels[g] and yet
have not kept it."

The First Christian Martyr

54 When they heard these things, they were
enraged in their hearts[B] and gnashed their
teeth at him. 55 But Stephen, filled by the Holy
Spirit, gazed into heaven. He saw God's glory,
with[C] Jesus standing at the right hand of
God,[h] and he said, 56 "Look! I see the heavens
opened and the ·Son of Man standing at the
right hand of God!"[i]
57 Then they screamed at the top of their
voices, covered their ears, and together
rushed against him. 58 They threw him out of
the city and began to stone[j] him. And the witnesses laid their robes at the feet of a young
man named Saul.[k] 59 They were stoning Stephen as he called out: "Lord Jesus, receive my
spirit!"[l] 60 Then he knelt down and cried out
with a loud voice,[m] "Lord, do not charge them
with this sin!" And saying this, he fell ·asleep.[n]

Saul the Persecutor

8 Saul agreed with putting him to death.
On that day a severe persecution broke
out against the church in Jerusalem, and all
except the apostles were scattered throughout the land of Judea and Samaria.[o] 2 Devout
men buried Stephen and mourned deeply
over him. 3 Saul,[p] however, was ravaging the
church. He would enter house after house,
drag off men and women, and put them in
prison.[q]

Philip in Samaria

4 So those who were scattered went on
their way preaching the message of good
news. 5 Philip went down to a[D] city in Samaria
and proclaimed the ·Messiah to them.[r] 6 The
crowds paid attention with one mind to what
Philip said, as they heard and saw the signs he
was performing. 7 For ·unclean spirits, crying
out with a loud voice, came out of many who
were possessed, and many who were paralyzed and lame were healed.[s] 8 So there was
great joy in that city.

The Response of Simon

9 A man named Simon had previously practiced sorcery in that city and astounded the
·Samaritan people, while claiming to be
somebody great.[t] 10 They all paid attention to
him, from the least of them to the greatest,
and they said, "This man is called the Great
Power of God!"[E,u] 11 They were attentive to
him because he had astounded them with his
sorceries for a long time. 12 But when they believed Philip, as he preached the good news
about the kingdom of God and the name of
Jesus Christ, both men and women were baptized.[v] 13 Then even Simon himself believed.
And after he was baptized, he went around
constantly with[F] Philip and was astounded
as he observed the signs and great miracles[w]
that were being performed.

Simon's Sin

14 When the apostles who were at Jerusalem heard that Samaria had welcomed God's
message, they sent Peter and John to them.[x]
15 After they went down there, they prayed for
them, so the Samaritans might receive the
Holy Spirit. 16 For He had not yet come down
on[G] any of them; they had only been baptized
in the name of the Lord Jesus.[y] 17 Then Peter
and John laid their hands on them, and they
received the Holy Spirit.

[a] **7:48** 1Kg 8:27; 2Ch 2:6
[b] **7:49-50** Is 66:1-2; Mt 5:34-35
[c] **7:51** Ex 32:9; Dt 10:16; Heb 3:13
[d] Lv 26:41; Jr 4:4; 6:10; 9:26
[e] **7:52** 2Ch 36:16; Mt 5:12; 21:35; 23:31,37; 1Th 2:15
[f] Ac 3:14; 5:28
[g] **7:53** Ac 7:38; Gl 3:19; Heb 2:2
[h] **7:55** Jn 12:41; Ac 6:5
[i] **7:56** Mt 3:16; Jn 1:51
[j] **7:58** Lv 24:14-16; Dt 13:9; Heb 13:12
[k] Ac 8:1; 22:20
[l] **7:59** Ps 31:5; Lk 23:46; Ac 9:14
[m] **7:60** Mt 5:44; Lk 22:41; 23:34; Ac 9:40
[n] Jn 11:11; 1Co 11:30; 1Th 4:13-15
[o] **8:1** Ac 9:31; 11:19
[p] **8:3** Ac 7:58; 22:20
[q] Ac 22:4,19; 26:10; 1Co 15:9; Gl 1:13; Php 3:6; 1Tm 1:13
[r] **8:4-5** Ac 6:5; 15:35
[s] **8:7** Mt 4:24; Mk 16:17
[t] **8:9** Ac 5:36; 13:6
[u] **8:10** Ac 14:11; 28:6
[v] **8:12** Ac 1:3; 2:38
[w] **8:13** Ac 8:6; 19:11
[x] **8:14** Lk 22:8; Ac 8:1
[y] **8:16** Mt 28:19; Ac 2:38; 10:48; 19:2

A 7:49-50 Is 66:1-2 B 7:54 Or *were cut to the quick* C 7:55 Lit *and* D 8:5 Other mss read *the* E 8:10 Or *This is the power of God called Great* F 8:13 Or *he kept close company with* G 8:16 Or *yet fallen on*

18 When Simon saw that the Holy[A] Spirit was
given through the laying on of the apostles'
hands, he offered them money, 19 saying, "Give
me this power too, so that anyone I lay hands
on may receive the Holy Spirit."
20 But Peter told him, "May your silver be
destroyed with you, because you thought the
gift of God could be obtained with money![a]
21 You have no part or share in this matter,
because your heart is not right before God.[b]
22 Therefore repent of this wickedness of
yours, and pray to the Lord that the intent
of your heart may be forgiven you. 23 For I see
you are poisoned by bitterness and bound by
iniquity."[c]
24 "Please pray[B] to the Lord for me," Simon
replied, "so that nothing you have said may
happen to me."[d]
25 Then, after they had testified and spoken
the message of the Lord, they traveled back to
Jerusalem, evangelizing many villages of the
Samaritans.

The Conversion of the Ethiopian Official

26 An angel of the Lord spoke to Philip: "Get
up and go south to the road that goes down
from Jerusalem to Gaza." (This is the desert
road.)[C,e] 27 So he got up and went. There was an
Ethiopian man, a eunuch[f] and high official of
Candace, queen of the Ethiopians,[D] who was
in charge of her entire treasury. He had come
to worship in Jerusalem[g] 28 and was sitting
in his chariot on his way home, reading the
prophet Isaiah aloud.
29 The Spirit told Philip, "Go and join that
chariot."[h]
30 When Philip ran up to it, he heard him
reading the prophet Isaiah, and said, "Do you
understand what you're reading?"
31 "How can I," he said, "unless someone
guides me?" So he invited Philip to come up
and sit with him. 32 Now the Scripture passage
he was reading was this:

He was led like a sheep to the slaughter,
and as a lamb is silent
before its shearer,
so He does not open His mouth.
33 **In His humiliation justice**
was denied Him.
Who will describe His generation?
For His life is taken from the earth.[E,i]

34 The eunuch replied to Philip, "I ask you,
who is the prophet saying this about—himself or another person?" 35 So Philip proceeded[F] to tell him the good news about Jesus,
beginning from that Scripture.[j]
36 As they were traveling down the road,
they came to some water. The eunuch said,
"Look, there's water! What would keep me
from being baptized?" [37 And Philip said, "If
you believe with all your heart you may." And
he replied, "I believe that Jesus Christ is the
Son of God."][G] 38 Then he ordered the chariot to stop, and both Philip and the eunuch
went down into the water, and he baptized
him. 39 When they came up out of the water,
the Spirit of the Lord[k] carried Philip away,
and the eunuch did not see him any longer.
But he went on his way rejoicing. 40 Philip appeared in[H] Azotus,[I] and he was traveling and
evangelizing all the towns until he came to
Caesarea.[l]

The Damascus Road

9 Meanwhile, Saul was still breathing
threats and murder against the disciples[m] of the Lord. He went to the high priest[n]
2 and requested letters[o] from him to the ˙syna-
gogues in Damascus, so that if he found any
men or women who belonged to the Way,[p] he
might bring them as prisoners to Jerusalem.
3 As[q] he traveled and was nearing Damascus,
a light from heaven suddenly flashed around
him. 4 Falling to the ground, he heard a voice
saying to him, "Saul, Saul, why are you persecuting Me?"
5 "Who are You, Lord?" he said.
"I am Jesus, the One you are persecuting,"
He replied. 6 "But get up and go into the city,
and you will be told what you must do."
7 The men who were traveling with him
stood speechless, hearing the sound but
seeing no one.[r] 8 Then Saul got up from the
ground, and though his eyes were open, he
could see nothing. So they took him by the
hand and led him into Damascus. 9 He was
unable to see for three days and did not eat
or drink.

[a] **8:20** 2Kg 5:16; Is 55:1; Dn 5:17; Mt 10:8; Ac 2:38
[b] **8:21** 2Kg 10:15; Ps 78:37
[c] **8:22-23** Is 55:6-7; Dn 4:27; 2Tm 2:25; Heb 12:15
[d] **8:24** Gn 20:7; Ex 8:8; Nm 21:7; Jms 5:16
[e] **8:26** Ac 5:19; 8:29
[f] **8:27** Ps 68:31; 87:4; Is 56:3; Zph 3:10
[g] 1Kg 8:41; Jn 12:20
[h] **8:29** Ac 10:19; 11:12; 13:2; 20:23; 21:11
[i] **8:32-33** Is 53:7-8; Php 2:8
[j] **8:35** Lk 24:27; Ac 17:2; 18:28
[k] **8:39** 1Kg 18:12; 2Kg 2:16; Ezk 3:12,14; 8:3; 11:1,24; 43:5
[l] **8:40** Ac 10:1,24; 12:19; 21:8,16; 23:23,33; 25:1,4,6,13
[m] **9:1** Mt 9:10; Mk 10:10; Lk 6:1; Jn 6:3; Ac 6:1
[n] Ac 8:3; 9:13,21
[o] **9:2** Ac 15:30; 22:5; 23:25,33
[p] Ac 19:9,23; 22:4; 24:14,22
[q] **9:3-8** Ac 22:6-11; 26:12-18; 1Co 15:8
[r] **9:7** Dn 10:7; Jn 12:29; Ac 22:9

[A] **8:18** Other mss omit *Holy* [B] **8:24** Gk words *you* and *pray* are pl [C] **8:26** Or *is a desert place* [D] **8:27** = Nubia [E] **8:32-33** Is 53:7-8 [F] **8:35** Lit *Philip opened his mouth* [G] **8:37** Other mss omit bracketed text [H] **8:40** Or *Philip was found at*, or *Philip found himself in* [I] **8:40** Or *Ashdod*

Saul's Baptism

10 There was a disciple in Damascus named Ananias. And the Lord said to him in a vision, "Ananias!"

"Here I am, Lord!" he said.[a]

11 "Get up and go to the street called Straight," the Lord said to him, "to the house of Judas, and ask for a man from Tarsus[b] named Saul, since he is praying there. 12 In a vision[A] he has seen a man named Ananias coming in and placing his hands on him so he can regain his sight."[c]

13 "Lord," Ananias answered, "I have heard from many people about this man, how much harm he has done to Your ·saints in Jerusalem.[d] 14 And he has authority here from the ·chief priests to arrest all who call on Your name."[e]

15 But the Lord said to him, "Go! For this man is My chosen instrument[f] to take My name to Gentiles,[g] kings, and the Israelites.[h] 16 I will show him how much he must suffer for My name!"[i]

17 So Ananias left and entered the house. Then he placed his hands on him and said, "Brother Saul, the Lord Jesus, who appeared to you on the road you were traveling, has sent me so that you can regain your sight and be filled with the Holy Spirit."[j]

18 At once something like scales fell from his eyes, and he regained his sight. Then he got up and was baptized. 19 And after taking some food, he regained his strength.[k]

Saul Proclaiming the Messiah

Saul was with the disciples in Damascus for some days. 20 Immediately he began proclaiming Jesus in the synagogues: "He is the Son of God."[l]

21 But all who heard him were astounded and said, "Isn't this the man who, in Jerusalem, was destroying those who called on this name and then came here for the purpose of taking them as prisoners to the chief priests?"[m]

22 But Saul grew more capable and kept confounding the Jews who lived in Damascus by proving that this One is the ·Messiah.

23 After many days had passed, the Jews conspired to kill him, 24 but their plot became known to Saul. So they were watching the gates day and night intending to kill him,[n] 25 but his disciples took him by night and lowered him in a large basket through an opening in the wall.[o]

Saul in Jerusalem

26 When he arrived in Jerusalem,[p] he tried to associate with the disciples, but they were all afraid of him, since they did not believe he was a disciple. 27 Barnabas, however, took him and brought him to the apostles and explained to them how Saul had seen the Lord on the road and that He had talked to him, and how in Damascus he had spoken boldly[q] in the name of Jesus.[r] 28 Saul was coming and going with them in Jerusalem, speaking boldly in the name of the Lord. 29 He conversed and debated with the Hellenistic Jews,[B] but they attempted to kill him.[s] 30 When the ·brothers found out, they took him down to Caesarea and sent him off to Tarsus.[t]

31 So the church[u] throughout all Judea, Galilee, and Samaria had peace, being built up and walking in the ·fear of the Lord and in the encouragement of the Holy Spirit, and it increased in numbers.

The Healing of Aeneas

32 As Peter was traveling from place to place,[C] he also came down to the saints[v] who lived in Lydda.[w] 33 There he found a man named Aeneas, who was paralyzed and had been bedridden for eight years. 34 Peter said to him, "Aeneas, Jesus Christ heals you. Get up and make your bed,"[D] and immediately he got up.[x] 35 So all who lived in Lydda and Sharon[y] saw him and turned to the Lord.

Dorcas Restored to Life

36 In Joppa[z] there was a disciple named Tabitha, which is translated Dorcas.[E] She was always doing good works[aa] and acts of charity. 37 In those days she became sick and died. After washing her, they placed her in a room upstairs. 38 Since Lydda was near Joppa, the disciples heard that Peter was there and sent two men to him who begged him, "Don't delay in coming with us." 39 So Peter got up and went with them. When he arrived, they led

[a] **9:10** Ac 10:3,17,19; 22:12
[b] **9:11** Ac 9:30; 11:25; 21:39; 22:3
[c] **9:12** Mk 5:23; Ac 9:17
[d] **9:13** Ac 8:3; 9:32; Rm 1:7; 15:25-26,31; 16:2,15
[e] **9:14** Ac 7:59; 1Co 1:2; 2Tm 2:22
[f] **9:15** Ac 13:2; Rm 1:1; Gl 1:15
[g] Mt 28:19; Rm 1:5; Gl 1:16
[h] Ac 25:22; 26:1
[i] **9:16** Ac 20:23; 21:4,11; 2Co 6:4-5; 11:23-27; 1Th 3:3
[j] **9:17** Ac 6:6; 22:13
[k] **9:19** Ac 11:26; 26:20
[l] **9:20** Mt 4:3; Ac 13:5,14
[m] **9:21** Ac 8:3; 9:13-14; Gl 1:13,23
[n] **9:24** Ac 20:3,19; 23:12,30; 25:3; 2Co 11:26
[o] **9:25** Jos 2:15; 1Sm 19:12; 2Co 11:33
[p] **9:26** Ac 22:17; 26:20; Gl 1:17
[q] **9:27** Ac 13:46; 14:3; 18:26; 19:8; 26:26; Eph 6:20; 1Th 2:2
[r] Ac 4:36; 9:3-6,20,22
[s] **9:29** Ac 6:1; 2Co 11:26
[t] **9:30** Ac 8:40; Gl 1:21
[u] **9:31** Mt 16:18; 1Co 14:4; Rv 1:4
[v] **9:32** Rm 1:7; Eph 5:3; 6:18
[w] 1Ch 8:12; Ezr 2:23; Neh 7:37; 11:35
[x] **9:34** Ac 3:6,16; 4:10
[y] **9:35** 1Ch 5:16; 27:29; Sg 2:1; Is 33:9; 35:2; 65:10
[z] **9:36** Jos 19:46; 2Ch 2:16; Ezr 3:7; Jnh 1:3; Ac 10:5
[aa] 1Tm 2:10; Ti 3:8

[A] **9:12** Other mss omit *In a vision* [B] **9:29** Lit *Hellenists*; that is, Gk-speaking Jews [C] **9:32** Lit *Peter was passing through all* [D] **9:34** Or *and get ready to eat* [E] **9:36** = Gazelle him to the room upstairs. And all the widows approached him, weeping and showing him the robes and clothes that Dorcas had made while she was with them. 40 Then Peter sent them all out of the room. He knelt down, prayed, and turning toward the body said, "Tabitha, get up!" She opened her eyes, saw Peter, and sat up.[a] 41 He gave her his hand and helped her stand up. Then he called the saints and widows and presented her alive. 42 This became known throughout Joppa, and many believed in the Lord. 43 And Peter stayed on many days in Joppa with Simon,[b] a leather tanner.[A]

Cornelius's Vision

10 There was a man in Caesarea named Cornelius, a ˚centurion of what was called the Italian ˚Regiment.[c] 2 He was a devout man and feared God along with his whole household. He did many charitable deeds for the Jewish people and always prayed to God.[d] 3 About three in the afternoon[B] he distinctly saw in a vision an angel of God who came in and said to him, "Cornelius!"[e]

4 Looking intently at him, he became afraid and said, "What is it, lord?"

The angel told him, "Your prayers and your acts of charity have come up as a memorial offering before God.[f] 5 Now send men to Joppa and call for Simon, who is also named Peter. 6 He is lodging with Simon, a tanner, whose house is by the sea."[g]

7 When the angel who spoke to him had gone, he called two of his household slaves and a devout soldier, who was one of those who attended him. 8 After explaining everything to them, he sent them to Joppa.

Peter's Vision

9 The[h] next day, as they were traveling and nearing the city, Peter went up to pray on the housetop[i] about noon.[C] 10 Then he became hungry and wanted to eat, but while they were preparing something, he went into a visionary state. 11 He saw heaven opened[j] and an object that resembled a large sheet coming down, being lowered by its four corners to the earth. 12 In it were all the four-footed animals and reptiles of the earth, and the birds of the sky. 13 Then a voice said to him, "Get up, Peter; kill and eat!"

14 "No, Lord!" Peter said. "For I have never eaten anything common[D] and ritually ˚unclean!"[k]

15 Again, a second time, a voice said to him, "What God has made ˚clean, you must not call common."[l] 16 This happened three times, and then the object was taken up into heaven.

Peter Visits Cornelius

17 While Peter was deeply perplexed about what the vision he had seen might mean, the men who had been sent by Cornelius, having asked directions to Simon's house, stood at the gate. 18 They called out, asking if Simon, who was also named Peter, was lodging there.

19 While Peter was thinking about the vision, the Spirit told him, "Three men are here looking for you.[m] 20 Get up, go downstairs, and accompany them with no doubts at all, because I have sent them."[n]

21 Then Peter went down to the men and said, "Here I am, the one you're looking for. What is the reason you're here?"

22 They said, "Cornelius, a centurion, an upright and God-fearing man, who has a good reputation with the whole Jewish nation, was divinely directed by a holy angel to call you to his house and to hear a message from you."[o] 23 Peter then invited them in and gave them lodging.

The next day he got up and set out with them, and some of the brothers from Joppa went with him.[p] 24 The following day he entered Caesarea. Now Cornelius was expecting them and had called together his relatives and close friends. 25 When Peter entered, Cornelius met him, fell at his feet, and worshiped him.

26 But Peter helped him up and said, "Stand up! I myself am also a man."[q] 27 While talking with him, he went on in and found that many had come together there. 28 Peter said to them, "You know it's forbidden for a Jewish man to associate with or visit a foreigner.[r] But God has shown me that I must not call any

[a] **9:40** Mt 9:25; Mk 5:41; Lk 22:41; Jn 11:43; Ac 7:60
[b] **9:43** Ac 10:6,17,32
[c] **10:1** Mt 27:27; Mk 15:16; Jn 18:3,12; Ac 8:40
[d] **10:2** Ac 10:22,35; 13:16,26
[e] **10:3** Ac 3:1; 5:19; 9:10; 10:17,19
[f] **10:4** Ac 9:43; 11:14
[g] **10:6** Lk 16:13; Rm 14:4; 1Pt 2:18
[h] **10:9-32** Ac 11:5-14
[i] **10:9** Ps 55:17; Jr 19:13; 32:29; Zph 1:5; Mt 24:17
[j] **10:10-11** Jn 1:51; Ac 22:17
[k] **10:14** Lv 11:4; 20:25; Dt 4:4-20; Ezk 4:14; Dn 1:8; Ac 9:5
[l] **10:15** Mt 15:11; Mk 7:19; Rm 14:14; 1Co 10:25; 1Tm 4:4; Ti 1:15
[m] **10:19** Ac 8:29; 10:3
[n] **10:20** Ac 15:7-9
[o] **10:22** Mk 8:38; Ac 10:2; 11:14
[p] **10:23** Ac 10:45; 11:12
[q] **10:26** Ac 14:15; Rv 19:10; 22:8
[r] **10:28** Jn 4:9; 18:28; Ac 11:3

[A] **9:43** Tanners were considered ritually ˚unclean because of their occupation. [B] **10:3** Lit *About the ninth hour* [C] **10:9** Lit *about the sixth hour* [D] **10:14** Perhaps *profane*, or *non-sacred*; Jews ate distinctive food according to OT law and their traditions, similar to modern kosher or non-kosher foods.

person common or unclean.[a] 29 That's why I
came without any objection when I was sent
for. So I ask: Why did you send for me?"
30 Cornelius replied, "Four days ago at this
hour, at three in the afternoon,[A] I was[B] praying in my house. Just then a man in a dazzling
robe stood before me[b] 31 and said, 'Cornelius,
your prayer has been heard, and your acts of
charity have been remembered in God's sight.
32 Therefore send someone to Joppa and invite Simon here, who is also named Peter. He
is lodging in Simon the tanner's house by the
sea.'[C] 33 Therefore I immediately sent for you,
and you did the right thing in coming. So we
are all present before God, to hear everything
you have been commanded by the Lord."

[a] 10:28 Ac 10:14-15,35; 15:8-9
[b] 10:30 Ac 1:10; 3:1

Welcome, Everyone!

Mark DeYmaz

Following Philip's evangelism among the Samaritans and the subsequent conversion of an Ethiopian (Ac 8), why did Luke feel compelled to mention the ethnicity of those being redeemed? The answer is clear: he is demonstrating to disciples both then and now that the Gospel, like the church itself, is not just for the Jews (Eph 3:3,6).

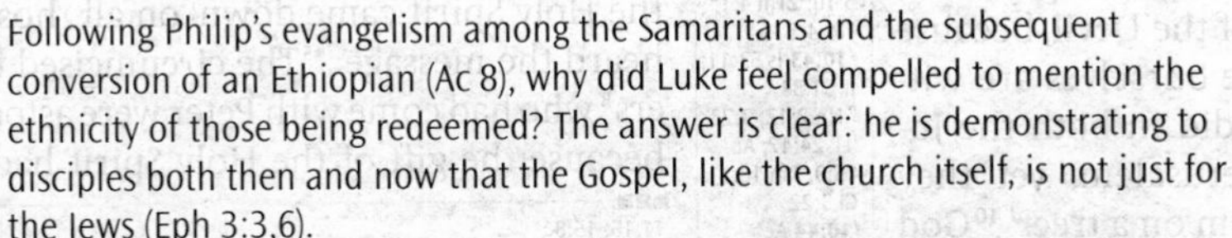

In Acts 10, Luke recounts the conversion of a Roman centurion named Cornelius. In response to Cornelius's prayers, an angel of the Lord appears and instructs him to send for a man named Simon (Peter). Meanwhile, Peter is praying and has a vision of the heavens opening up with a sheet coming down out of the sky filled with various animals deemed profane by the Jews. A voice instructs him, "Get up, Peter; kill and eat" (vv. 9-13). But Peter refuses to eat what is unholy and unclean (v. 14).

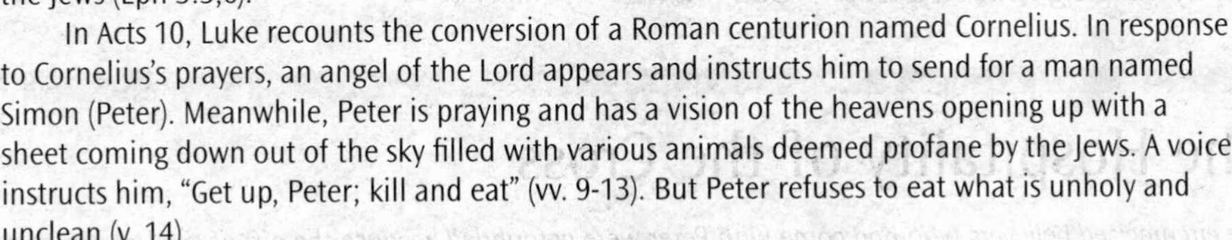

Later, in coming to the house of Cornelius, Peter sets the context for his arrival. He tells Cornelius, "You know it's forbidden for a Jewish man to associate with or visit a foreigner. But God has shown me that I must not call any person common or unclean" (v. 28).

Historically it was an unlawful breach of religious protocol for Jews to associate with Gentiles. However, at this time, the Holy Spirit is writing a new law upon Peter's heart, and he stands corrected: "Now I really understand that God doesn't show favoritism, but in every nation the person who fears Him and does righteousness is acceptable to Him" (v. 35).

As Peter then shares the Gospel with Cornelius, the Holy Spirit falls upon this Gentile and his entire household (vv. 24-48). The significance of the moment does not go unnoticed by the Jews. As Luke records, "The circumcised believers who had come with Peter were astounded because the gift of the Holy Spirit had been poured out on the Gentiles also" (v. 47).

In considering these early stories of conversion—featuring the Samaritans, an Ethiopian, and a Roman (Gentile) solider—it should cause us to ask, *If the kingdom of God is not segregated, why on earth is the local church?* Surely it breaks the heart of God that many churches in the United States are divided by race and class, and that little has changed in the more than one hundred years since it was first observed that eleven o'clock on Sunday morning is the most segregated hour of the week. Brothers and sisters, it should not be so.

In Isaiah 49:1-6, the prophet links glorifying God and the restoration of a single nation to the Jews becoming a light to the Gentiles (all other people groups). Could it be that in our own day God is calling us to walk, work, and worship Him together as one beyond the distinctions of this world? Could it be that in so doing we will bring Him greater glory and be restored as a people of credible witness in an increasingly cynical society, for the sake of the Gospel?

[A] 10:30 Lit *at the ninth hour* [B] 10:30 Other mss add *fasting and* [C] 10:32 Other mss add *When he arrives, he will speak to you.*

Good News for Gentiles

34 Then Peter began to speak: "Now I really
understand that God doesn't show favoritism,[a] 35 but in every nation the person who
fears Him and does righteousness is acceptable to Him. 36 He sent the message to the
Israelites, proclaiming the good news of
peace through Jesus Christ—He is Lord of
all.[b] 37 You know the events[A] that took place
throughout Judea, beginning from Galilee after the baptism that John preached:
38 how God anointed Jesus of Nazareth with
the Holy Spirit and with power, and how He
went about doing good and healing all who
were under the tyranny of the Devil, because
God was with Him.[c] 39 We ourselves are witnesses of everything He did in both the Judean country and in Jerusalem, yet they
killed Him by hanging Him on a tree.[d] 40 God
raised up this man on the third day and permitted Him to be seen, 41 not by all the people,
but by us, witnesses appointed beforehand by
God, who ate and drank with Him after He
rose from the dead.[e] 42 He commanded us to
preach to the people and to solemnly testify
that He is the One appointed by God to be
the Judge of the living and the dead.[f] 43 All the
prophets testify[g] about Him that through His
name[h] everyone who believes in Him will receive forgiveness of sins."[i]

Gentile Conversion and Baptism

44 While Peter was still speaking these words,
the Holy Spirit came down[j] on all those who
heard the message. 45 The circumcised believers[B] who had come with Peter were astounded
because the gift of the Holy Spirit had been

[a] **10:34** Dt 10:17; 2Ch 19:7; Rm 2:11; Gl 2:6; Eph 6:9; Col 3:25; 1Pt 1:17
[b] **10:36** Mt 28:18; Ac 2:36; 13:32; Rm 10:12; Eph 2:17; Rv 17:14
[c] **10:38** Mt 4:23; Lk 4:18; Jn 3:2; Ac 4:26
[d] **10:39** Lk 24:48; Ac 2:32; 5:30
[e] **10:41** Lk 24:43; Jn 14:17,22
[f] **10:42** Jn 5:22; Ac 17:31; Rm 14:9; 2Co 5:10; 2Tm 4:1; 1Pt 4:5
[g] **10:43** Is 53:11; Jr 31:34
[h] 1Jn 2:12; 3:23
[i] Lk 24:47; Ac 15:9; Rm 10:11; Gl 3:22
[j] **10:44** Ac 11:15; 15:8

GOD'S HEART FOR THE WORLD

The Hospitality of the Cross

The circumcised believers who had come with Peter were astounded because the gift of the Holy Spirit had been poured out on the Gentiles also. (Acts 10:45)

The disciples had not expected a Messiah like Jesus, who came in poverty and gentleness and died the death of a criminal. Repeatedly they misunderstand Him and what He came to do. Acts 10 shows us that they continued to be surprised by the work of God even after Jesus ascended and gave them the Holy Spirit.

As Jewish people, Peter and the other disciples had clear boundaries between them and "unclean" Gentiles. Israel had been given a particular way of life in order that they might show the world what it looks like when people dwell with the presence of Yahweh. But many of them had misunderstood this distinctiveness, thinking that the Messiah would come to save Israel from their human oppressors. Instead, the Messiah came to save the whole world from the oppression of the evil one.

Humans tend to over-identify with any group that we are a part of, whether it is our friends, our company, or our country. We are fortunate that God redirects His people when they go astray, just like He did for Peter. Peter was given miracles and divine appointments to show him that he "must not call any person common or unclean" (v. 28), and that the Holy Spirit is a gift that is offered to all people, regardless of who they are and where they were born. Christ's arms were spread wide on the cross to welcome all who come. Along with Peter we understand "that God doesn't show favoritism, but in every nation the person who fears Him and does righteousness is acceptable to Him. He sent the message to the sons of Israel, proclaiming the good news of peace through Jesus Christ—He is Lord of all" (vv. 34-36).

[A] **10:37** Or *word*; lit *thing* [B] **10:45** Jewish Christians who stressed circumcision; Ac 11:2; 15:5; Gl 2:12; Col 4:11; Ti 1:10

poured out on the Gentiles also.[a] 46 For they
heard them speaking in other ·languages and
declaring the greatness of[A] God.
Then Peter responded, 47 "Can anyone withhold water and prevent these people from
being baptized, who have received the Holy
Spirit just as we have?"[b] 48 And he commanded
them to be baptized in the name of Jesus
Christ.[c] Then they asked him to stay for a few
days.

Gentile Salvation Defended

11 The apostles and the ·brothers who
were throughout Judea heard that the
Gentiles had welcomed God's message also.
2 When Peter went up to Jerusalem, those who
stressed circumcision[B] argued with him,[d]
3 saying, "You visited uncircumcised men and
ate with them!"[e]
4 Peter began to explain to them in an orderly sequence, saying: 5 "I[f] was in the town
of Joppa praying, and I saw, in a visionary
state, an object that resembled a large sheet
coming down, being lowered by its four corners from heaven, and it came to me. 6 When
I looked closely and considered it, I saw the
four-footed animals of the earth, the wild
beasts, the reptiles, and the birds of the sky.
7 Then I also heard a voice telling me, 'Get up,
Peter; kill and eat!'
8 "'No, Lord!' I said. 'For nothing common
or ritually ·unclean has ever entered my
mouth!' 9 But a voice answered from heaven a
second time, 'What God has made ·clean, you
must not call common.'
10 "Now this happened three times, and then
everything was drawn up again into heaven.
11 At that very moment, three men who had
been sent to me from Caesarea arrived at the
house where we were. 12 Then the Spirit told
me to accompany them with no doubts at all.
These six brothers accompanied me, and we
went into the man's house.[g] 13 He reported to
us how he had seen the angel standing in his
house and saying, 'Send[C] to Joppa, and call
for Simon, who is also named Peter. 14 He will
speak a message[D] to you that you and all your
household[h] will be saved by.'
15 "As I began to speak, the Holy Spirit came
down on them, just as on us at the beginning.[i]
16 Then I remembered the word of the Lord,
how He said, 'John baptized with water, but
you will be baptized with the Holy Spirit.'[j]
17 Therefore, if God gave them the same gift
that He also gave to us when we believed on
the Lord Jesus Christ, how could I possibly
hinder God?"[k]
18 When they heard this they became silent.
Then they glorified God, saying, "So God has
granted repentance resulting in life[E] even to
the Gentiles!"[l]

The Church in Antioch

19 Those who had been scattered as a result
of the persecution that started because of Stephen made their way as far as Phoenicia, Cyprus, and Antioch,[m] speaking the message to
no one except Jews. 20 But there were some of
them, Cypriot and Cyrenian men, who came
to Antioch and began speaking to the Hellenists,[F,G] proclaiming the good news about the
Lord Jesus.[n] 21 The Lord's hand was with them,
and a large number who believed turned to
the Lord.[o] 22 Then the report about them was
heard by the church that was at Jerusalem,
and they sent out Barnabas to travel[H] as far as
Antioch. 23 When he arrived and saw the grace
of God, he was glad and encouraged all of
them to remain true to the Lord with a firm
resolve of the heart,[p] 24 for he was a good man,
full of the Holy Spirit[q] and of faith. And large
numbers of people were added[r] to the Lord.
25 Then he[I] went to Tarsus to search for Saul,
26 and when he found him he brought him to
Antioch. For a whole year they met with the
church and taught large numbers. The disciples[s] were first called Christians at Antioch.[t]

Famine Relief

27 In those days some prophets came down
from Jerusalem to Antioch.[u] 28 Then one of
them, named Agabus, stood up and predicted
by the Spirit that there would be a severe famine throughout the Roman world.[J] This took
place during the time of Claudius.[K,v] 29 So
each of the disciples, according to his ability,

[a] **10:45** Ac 2:33,38; 10:23; 11:18
[b] **10:47** Ac 2:4; 8:36; 11:17; 15:8
[c] **10:48** Ac 2:38; 8:16; 1Co 1:14-17
[d] **11:2** Ac 10:45; Col 4:11; 1Tm 1:10
[e] **11:3** Ac 10:28; Gl 2:12
[f] **11:5-14** Ac 10:9-32
[g] **11:12** Ac 8:29; 10:23; 15:9
[h] **11:14** Jn 4:53; Ac 10:2; 16:15,31-34; 18:8; 1Co 1:16
[i] **11:15** Ac 2:4; 10:44
[j] **11:16** Mt 3:11; Mk 1:8; Lk 3:16; Jn 1:33; Ac 1:5
[k] **11:17** Ac 5:39; 10:45,47
[l] **11:18** Rm 10:12-13; 2Co 7:10
[m] **11:19** Ac 6:5; 13:1; 14:26; 15:22-23,30,35; 18:22; Gl 2:11
[n] **11:20** Mt 27:32; Ac 4:36
[o] **11:21** Lk 1:66; Ac 2:47; 9:35
[p] **11:23** Ac 13:43; 14:26; 15:40; 20:24,32
[q] **11:24** Lk 4:1; Ac 6:5; 7:55
[r] Ac 2:41,47; 5:14
[s] **11:26** Ac 6:1; 9:1; 13:52; 14:20; 15:10; 16:1; 19:1
[t] Ac 26:28; 1Pt 4:16
[u] **11:27** Ac 13:1; 15:32; 1Co 12:28; Eph 4:11
[v] **11:28** Mt 24:14; Ac 18:2; 21:10; Gl 2:2

[A] **10:46** Or *and magnifying* [B] **11:2** Lit *those of the circumcision* [C] **11:13** Other mss add *men* [D] **11:14** Lit *speak words* [E] **11:18** Or *repentance to life* [F] **11:20** Other mss read *Greeks* [G] **11:20** In this context, a non-Jewish person who spoke Gk [H] **11:22** Other mss omit *to travel* [I] **11:25** Other mss read *Barnabas* [J] **11:28** Or *the whole world* [K] **11:28** Emperor A.D. 41–54; there was a famine A.D. 47–48.

determined to send relief to the brothers
who lived in Judea.[a] 30 They did this, sending it
to the elders[b] by means of Barnabas and Saul.

James Martyred and Peter Jailed

12 About that time King ·Herod cruelly
attacked some who belonged to the
church, 2 and he killed James,[c] John's brother,
with the sword. 3 When he saw that it pleased
the Jews, he proceeded to arrest Peter too,
during the days of ·Unleavened Bread.[d] 4 After
the arrest, he put him in prison and assigned
four squads of four soldiers each to guard
him, intending to bring him out to the people after the ·Passover. 5 So Peter was kept in
prison, but prayer was being made earnestly
to God for him by the church.

Peter Rescued

6 On the night before Herod was to bring
him out for execution, Peter, bound with two
chains, was sleeping between two soldiers,
while the sentries in front of the door guarded
the prison. 7 Suddenly an angel of the Lord[e] appeared, and a light shone in the cell. Striking
Peter on the side, he woke him up and said,
"Quick, get up!" Then the chains fell off his
wrists.[f] 8 "Get dressed," the angel told him, "and
put on your sandals." And he did so. "Wrap
your cloak around you," he told him, "and follow me." 9 So he went out and followed, and he
did not know that what took place through the
angel was real, but thought he was seeing a vision.[g] 10 After they passed the first and second
guard posts, they came to the iron gate that
leads into the city, which opened to them by
itself. They went outside and passed one street,
and immediately the angel left him.[h]
11 Then Peter came to himself and said,
"Now I know for certain that the Lord has
sent His angel and rescued me from Herod's
grasp and from all that the Jewish people expected."[i] 12 When he realized this, he went to
the house of Mary, the mother of John Mark,[A,j]
where many had assembled and were praying. 13 He knocked at the door in the gateway,
and a servant named Rhoda came to answer.
14 She recognized Peter's voice, and because
of her joy, she did not open the gate but ran
in and announced that Peter was standing at
the gateway.
15 "You're crazy!" they told her. But she kept
insisting that it was true. Then they said, "It's
his angel!"[k] 16 Peter, however, kept on knocking, and when they opened the door and saw
him, they were astounded.
17 Motioning to them with his hand[l] to be
silent, he explained to them how the Lord
had brought him out of the prison. "Report
these things to James[B,m] and the ·brothers," he
said. Then he departed and went to a different place.
18 At daylight, there was a great commotion[C]
among the soldiers as to what could have become of Peter. 19 After Herod had searched
and did not find him, he interrogated the
guards and ordered their execution. Then
Herod went down from Judea to Caesarea
and stayed there.[n]

Herod's Death

20 He had been very angry with the Tyrians and Sidonians.[D] Together they presented
themselves before him. They won over Blas-
tus, who was in charge of the king's bedroom,
and through him they asked for peace, because their country was supplied with food
from the king's country.[o] 21 So on an appointed
day, dressed in royal robes and seated on the
throne, Herod delivered a public address to
them. 22 The assembled people began to shout,
"It's the voice of a god and not of a man!" 23 At
once an angel of the Lord[p] struck him because he did not give the glory to God, and
he became infected with worms and died.[q]
24 Then God's message flourished and multiplied.[r] 25 After they had completed their relief
mission, Barnabas and Saul returned to[E] Jerusalem, taking along John who is called Mark.[s]

Preparing for the Mission Field

13 In the church that was at Antioch there
were prophets and teachers: Barnabas,
Simeon who was called Niger, Lucius the
Cyrenian, Manaen, a close friend of ·Herod
the tetrarch,[t] and Saul.
2 As they were ministering to[F] the Lord and
fasting, the Holy Spirit said, "Set apart for Me

[a] 11:29 Rm 15:26; 2Co 9:1-2; Gl 2:10
[b] 11:30 Ac 14:23; 15:2; 16:4; 20:17; 21:18; 1Tm 5:17,19; Jms 5:14; 2Jn 1
[c] 12:2 Mt 4:21; 20:23
[d] 12:3 Ex 12:15; 23:15; Ac 12:5; 20:6; 24:27; 25:9; 2Co 1:11; Eph 6:18
[e] 12:7 Lk 1:11; Col 4:1; Jd 5
[f] Lk 2:9; 5:19; 16:26; 24:4
[g] 12:9 Ps 126:1; Ac 9:10
[h] 12:10 Ac 5:19; 16:26
[i] 12:11 Ps 33:18-19; 34:7; Dn 3:28; 6:22; Lk 15:17; 2Co 1:10
[j] 12:12 Ac 12:25; 15:37,39; Col 4:10; 2Tm 4:11; Phm 24; 1Pt 5:13
[k] 12:13-15 Mt 18:10; Lk 24:21
[l] 12:17 Ac 13:16; 19:33; 21:40
[m] Ac 15:13; 21:18; Gl 1:19; 2:9,12
[n] 12:19 Ac 8:40; 16:27; 27:42
[o] 12:20 1Kg 5:11; Ezr 3:7; Ezk 27:17; Mt 11:21
[p] 12:23 Lk 1:11; Col 4:1; Jd 5
[q] 1Sm 25:38; 2Sm 24:16-17; Ps 115:1
[r] 12:24 Ac 6:7; 19:20
[s] 12:25 Ac 4:36; 11:30; 12:12
[t] 13:1 Mt 14:1; Ac 4:36; 11:19,22,27; 1Co 12:28

[A] 12:12 Lit *John who was called Mark* [B] 12:17 This was James, the Lord's brother; Mk 6:3. This was not James the apostle; Ac 12:2. [C] 12:18 Or *was no small disturbance* [D] 12:20 The people of the area of modern Lebanon [E] 12:25 Other mss read *from* [F] 13:2 Or *were worshiping*

Barnabas and Saul for the work I have called
them to."[a] 3 Then after they had fasted, prayed,
and laid hands on them, they sent them off.[b]

The Mission to Cyprus

4 Being sent out by the Holy Spirit, they
came down to Seleucia, and from there they
sailed to Cyprus. 5 Arriving in Salamis, they
proclaimed God's message in the Jewish
•synagogues. They also had John as their assistant.[c] 6 When they had gone through the
whole island as far as Paphos, they came

[a] 13:2 Ac 8:29; 9:15; Rm 1:1; Gl 1:15
[b] 13:3 Ac 6:6; 14:26
[c] 13:5 Ac 9:20; 12:12

Itinerant Ministry

Andrew Jones

Maybe it's not right, but I feel a slight pang of grief when I read of Saul and Barnabas. Despite having a secure future as church leaders, they are assigned the downwardly mobile status of itinerant ministry by the church in Antioch. Doomed to wander through places always foreign and rarely familiar, they will limp forward as borrowers and beggars, strangers and sojourners, but never settlers.

An "itinerant" travels from place to place without a home. Stereotypes are demeaning: drifters, hobos, vagrants, bums, squatters, tramps, and carnies. Some are neutral but few are positive. And yet there are some who voluntarily embrace itinerancy for the sake of the gospel, including circuit riders, pilgrims, and wandering monks. The worst examples of the latter were frowned on. Benedict called them "gyrovagues" ("Those that wander in a circle"); Augustine called them "circumcelliones" ("Those that prowl around barns").

Despite the stigma of being homeless ragamuffins, it was often the wandering missionaries who enabled the church to accelerate its mission into new spheres: extraordinary itinerants including preaching orders in the Middle Ages, Methodist circuit-riders, tent-revivalists, and the Celtic "peregrine," who one writer described as "intrepid Irish adventurers."

As an itinerant for most of my twenty-five years in mission service, I share both in the shame of this lowly disposition and the joy of freedom to travel wherever God is shining His light. I also have some perspective on why the Holy Spirit might have set such a precedent in Antioch.

Itinerancy is more effective in both cost and time, having no house to maintain or return to. Our apostolic efforts are not tempted by the idolatry of building our own empire because next week we will be somewhere else, serving another ministry project. But it's more than that. As itinerants, our dependence on others for their participation with us becomes a filter that leads us to the right people at the right time, as Jesus outlined in Luke 10. We depend on God. We depend on God's family. We even depend on the people we are sent to.

Like Abraham, we are told to go but not given a destination. We find ourselves in intimate company with the people of faith, who viewed the heavenly city as their real home. We have no house but we enjoy a hundred houses in this life and the benefits of a large and diverse spiritual family. We drink deeply of the sufferings of Christ who, having no place to lay His head, walked the same path we tread.

Recent years have seen a more positive spin on the mobile lifestyle. Partly in response to globalization and the necessity of competence in foreign cultures, many are eager to embrace new itinerant identities such as "global nomads," "existential migrants," and even "families on the road." Likewise, interest in itinerant ministry has intensified as a new generation discovers a "spirituality of the road" and new forms of missional pilgrimage.

As in Antioch, there are still Christians of export quality being sent out on itinerant journeys that are initiated by God, modeled by Christ, led by the Spirit, and given an enthusiastic thumbs-up by the church.

across a sorcerer, a Jewish false prophet
named Bar-Jesus.[a] 7He was with the ˚procon-
sul, Sergius Paulus, an intelligent man. This
man summoned Barnabas and Saul and desired to hear God's message.[b] 8But Elymas the
sorcerer (this is the meaning of his name) opposed[c] them and tried to turn the proconsul
away from the faith.[d]
9Then Saul — also called Paul — filled with
the Holy Spirit, stared straight at the sorcerer
10and said, "You son of the Devil,[e] full of all
deceit and all fraud, enemy of all righteous-

[a]**13:6** Mt 7:15; Ac 8:9
[b]**13:7** Ac 18:12; 19:38
[c]**13:8** Ex 7:11; 2Tm 3:8
[d]Ac 6:7; 8:9
[e]**13:10** Mt 13:38; Jn 8:44

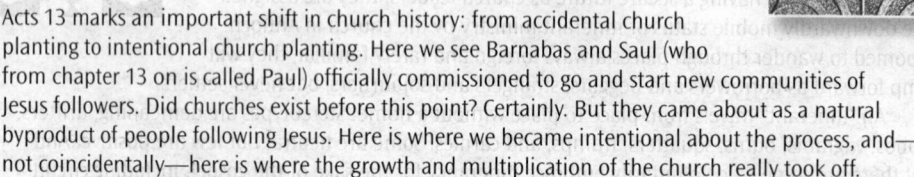

The Birth of Intentional Church Planting

Bob Logan

Acts 13 marks an important shift in church history: from accidental church planting to intentional church planting. Here we see Barnabas and Saul (who from chapter 13 on is called Paul) officially commissioned to go and start new communities of Jesus followers. Did churches exist before this point? Certainly. But they came about as a natural byproduct of people following Jesus. Here is where we became intentional about the process, and—not coincidentally—here is where the growth and multiplication of the church really took off.

Jesus is the One who builds His church (Mt 16:18). He gave us the responsibility to make disciples—more followers of Jesus (28:19-20). As we make disciples, churches are planted. The first church was planted in Jerusalem after Pentecost (Ac 2:42-47). These followers of Jesus lived incarnationally, and as they focused on making disciples, new churches were formed. The word "church" in Greek, *ecclesia*, simply means "gathered." Disciples gathered in homes, temples, and various other places.

After the killing of Stephen and the persecution that followed (7:54-8:1), believers spread out to Samaria, continuing to preach the gospel and make disciples. Wherever they went, they gathered—resulting in new churches. Some of these people went to Antioch and a church was formed there (11:19-26).

In Antioch, in Acts 13:1-3, an important but often overlooked shift takes place: the planting of new churches becomes intentional, the product of focused activity by people set aside for this particular mission. The church at Antioch became a base from which Paul and Barnabas were officially commissioned for the work of establishing churches.

From this point on we can trace the ministry of Paul as he and his companions plant new churches and multiply them, raising up new leaders as they go. They preached the gospel in Derbe, Lystra, Iconium, and Philippi, and raised up leaders such as Timothy and Lydia, then moved on to Thessalonica, Berea, Corinth, and Ephesus (chaps. 16-18). Almost every place Paul and his companions went, they planted new churches.

Eventually Paul worked out of a home base in Ephesus at the school of Tyrannus (19:8-10), training leaders who then went out to reach the whole region of Asia Minor: "And this went on for two years, so that all the inhabitants of Asia, both Jews and Greeks, heard the message about the Lord" (v. 10). Most of the letters Paul wrote in the NT provide guidance to these fledgling churches he has planted and left in the hands of others, and some to churches he has never seen in person, planted by those he trained in Ephesus.

Starting and multiplying churches is directly connected to the mission of God. As we make disciples among all people groups, we contribute to the result described in Revelation 7:9: "After this I looked, and there was a vast multitude from every nation, tribe, people, and language, which no one could number, standing before the throne and before the Lamb."

ness! Won't you ever stop perverting the
straight paths[a] of the Lord? 11Now, look! The
Lord's hand is against you.[b] You are going to
be blind, and will not see the sun for a time."
Suddenly a mist and darkness fell on him,
and he went around seeking someone to lead
him by the hand.
12Then the proconsul, seeing what happened, believed and was astonished at the
teaching about the Lord.[c]

Paul's Sermon in Antioch of Pisidia

13Paul and his companions set sail from Paphos and came to Perga in Pamphylia. John,
however, left them and went back to Jerusalem.[d] 14They continued their journey from
Perga and reached Antioch in Pisidia. On the
Sabbath day they went into the synagogue
and sat down.[e] 15After the reading of the Law
and the Prophets, the leaders of the synagogue sent word to them, saying, "Brothers,
if you have any message of encouragement
for the people, you can speak."[f]
16Then Paul stood up and motioned with
his hand and said: "Men of Israel, and you
who fear God, listen![g] 17The God of this people Israel chose our ancestors, exalted the
people during their stay in the land of Egypt,
and led them out of it with a mighty[A] arm.[h]
18And for about 40 years He put up with
them[B] in the wilderness;[i] 19then after destroying seven nations in the land of Canaan,[j] He
gave their land to them as an inheritance.
20This all took about 450 years. After this, He
gave them judges until Samuel the prophet.[k]
21Then they asked for a king, so God gave
them Saul the son of Kish, a man of the tribe
of Benjamin, for 40 years.[l] 22After removing
him,[m] He raised up David as their king and
testified about him: '**I have found David** the
son of Jesse, **a man loyal to Me,**[C,n] who will
carry out all My will.'
23"From this man's descendants, according to the promise, God brought the Savior,
Jesus,[D] to Israel.[o] 24Before He came to public
attention,[E] John had previously proclaimed a
baptism of repentance to all the people of Israel.[p] 25Then as John was completing his life's
work, he said, 'Who do you think I am? I am
not the One. But look! Someone is coming after me, and I am not worthy to untie the sandals on His feet.'[q]
26"Brothers, sons of Abraham's race, and
those among you who fear God, the message
of this salvation has been sent to us.[r] 27For the
residents of Jerusalem and their rulers, since
they did not recognize Him or the voices of
the prophets that are read every Sabbath,
have fulfilled their words[F] by condemning
Him.[s] 28Though they found no grounds for
the death penalty, they asked *Pilate to have
Him killed.[t] 29When they had fulfilled all that
had been written about Him, they took Him
down from the tree and put Him in a tomb.[u]
30But God raised Him from the dead,[v] 31and
He appeared for many days to those who
came with Him from Galilee to Jerusalem,
who are now His witnesses to the people.[w]
32And we ourselves proclaim to you the good
news of the promise that was made to our ancestors.[x] 33God has fulfilled this for us, their
children, by raising up Jesus, as it is written
in the second Psalm:

> **You are My Son;**
> **today I have become Your Father.**[G,H,y]

34Since He raised Him from the dead, never
to return to decay, He has spoken in this way,
**I will grant you the faithful covenant bless-
ings**[I] **made to David.**[J,z] 35Therefore He also
says in another passage, **You will not allow
Your Holy One to see decay.**[K,aa] 36For David,
after serving his own generation in God's
plan, fell *asleep,[ab] was buried with his fathers, and decayed.[ac] 37But the One God raised
up did not decay. 38Therefore, let it be known
to you, brothers, that through this man forgiveness of sins is being proclaimed to you,[ad]
39and everyone who believes in Him is *justified from everything that you could not be
justified from through the law of Moses.[ae]
40So beware that what is said in the prophets
does not happen to you:

> 41 **Look, you scoffers,**
> **marvel and vanish away,**
> **because I am doing a work**
> **in your days,**

[a]**13:10** Hs 14:9; 2Pt 2:15
[b]**13:11** Ex 9:3; 1Sm 5:6-7; Ps 32:4; Heb 10:31
[c]**13:12** Ac 13:49; 15:35-36
[d]**13:13** Ac 12:12; 13:6; 15:38
[e]**13:14** Ac 9:20; 14:19,21; 16:3; 17:2; 18:4
[f]**13:15** Mk 5:22; Ac 15:21
[g]**13:16** Ac 10:2; 12:17
[h]**13:17** Ex 1:6; 6:6; Dt 7:6-8; Ac 7:17
[i]**13:18** Dt 1:31; Ac 7:36
[j]**13:19** Dt 7:1; Jos 14:1; 19:51; Ps 78:55; Ac 7:45
[k]**13:20** Jdg 2:16; 1Sm 3:20; Ac 3:24
[l]**13:21** 1Sm 8:5; 9:1; 10:1
[m]**13:22** 1Sm 15:23,26; 16:13
[n]1Sm 13:14; Ps 89:20
[o]**13:23** Ps 132:1; Mt 1:1; Lk 2:11; Ac 13:32
[p]**13:24** Mt 3:1; Mk 1:4; Lk 3:3; Ac 1:22; 19:4
[q]**13:25** Mt 3:11; Mk 1:7; Lk 3:16; Jn 1:20,27; Ac 20:24
[r]**13:26** Ac 4:12; 5:20
[s]**13:27** Lk 24:27; Ac 3:17
[t]**13:28** Mt 27:22-23; Ac 3:14
[u]**13:29** Mt 27:59; Lk 23:53; Ac 5:30
[v]**13:30** Mt 28:6; Ac 2:24
[w]**13:31** Mt 28:16; Lk 24:48; Ac 1:3
[x]**13:32** Ac 5:42; 26:6; Rm 4:13; 9:4
[y]**13:33** Ps 2:7; Heb 1:5; 5:5
[z]**13:34** Is 55:3; Ac 13:30,37
[aa]**13:35** Ps 16:10; Ac 2:27
[ab]**13:36** Ac 7:60; 1Co 11:30; 15:6,18,20,51; 1Th 4:13-15
[ac]1Kg 2:10; Ac 2:29; 13:22; 20:27
[ad]**13:38** Lk 24:47; Ac 2:38
[ae]**13:39** Rm 3:28; 10:4

[A]13:17 Lit *with an uplifted* [B]13:18 Other mss read *He cared for them* [C]13:22 1Sm 13:14; Ps 89:20 [D]13:23 Other mss read *brought salvation* [E]13:24 Lit *Before the face of His entrance* [F]13:27 Lit *fulfilled them* [G]13:33 Or *I have begotten You* [H]13:33 Ps 2:7 [I]13:34 Lit *faithful holy things* [J]13:34 Is 55:3 [K]13:35 Ps 16:10

> **a work that you will never believe,**
> **even if someone were to explain it**
> **to you."[A,a]**

Paul and Barnabas in Antioch

42 As they[B] were leaving, the people[C] begged that these matters be presented to them the following Sabbath. 43 After the synagogue had been dismissed, many of the Jews and devout ˙proselytes followed Paul and Barnabas, who were speaking with them and persuading them to continue in the grace of God.[b]

44 The following Sabbath almost the whole town assembled to hear the message of the Lord.[D] 45 But when the Jews saw the crowds, they were filled with jealousy and began to oppose what Paul was saying by insulting him.[c]

46 Then Paul and Barnabas boldly said: "It was necessary that God's message be spoken to you first. But since you reject it and consider yourselves unworthy of eternal life, we now turn to the Gentiles![d] 47 For this is what the Lord has commanded us:

> **I have made you**
> **a light for the Gentiles**
> **to bring salvation**
> **to the ends[E] of the earth."[F,e]**

The Salvific Ending

GOD WHO SENDS

The language of the New Testament is equally explicit in describing the ultimate salvation through the sending of Jesus. The God of the Bible is more than "the One who is" and "the One who speaks," he is "the One who acts"; the way he acts is through the sending. The God of the Bible is "the One who sends." And his ultimate sending is his salvific sending.

(DUBOSE, 63-64)

[a] 13:41 Is 29:14; Hab 1:5
[b] 13:43 Ac 11:23; 14:22
[c] 13:45 Ac 18:6; 1Th 2:16; 1Pt 4:4; Jd 10
[d] 13:46 Mt 21:43; Ac 3:26; 18:6; 22:21; 28:28
[e] 13:47 Is 42:6; 49:6; Lk 2:32
[f] 13:50 Ac 14:2,19; 2Tm 3:11
[g] 13:51 Mt 10:14; Mk 6:11; Lk 9:5; Ac 18:6
[h] Ac 14:1,19,21; 16:2; 2Tm 3:11
[i] 13:52 Mt 5:12; Jn 16:22; Ac 2:4
[j] 14:1 Ac 13:5,51; 14:19
[k] 14:2 Jn 3:36; Ac 13:50
[l] 14:3 Mk 16:20; Jn 4:48; Ac 4:29; 20:32; Heb 2:4
[m] 14:4 Ac 17:4-5; 19:9; 28:24
[n] 14:6 Mt 10:23; 2Tm 3:11
[o] 14:7 Ac 14:15,21; 16:10
[p] 14:8-10 Mk 6:56; Php 2:12
[q] 14:11 Ac 8:10; 28:6

48 When the Gentiles heard this, they rejoiced and glorified the message of the Lord, and all who had been appointed to eternal life believed. 49 So the message of the Lord spread through the whole region. 50 But the Jews incited the prominent women, who worshiped God, and the leading men of the city. They stirred up persecution against Paul and Barnabas and expelled them from their district.[f] 51 But they shook the dust off their feet[g] against them[h] and went to Iconium. 52 And the disciples were filled with joy and the Holy Spirit.[i]

Growth and Persecution in Iconium

14 The same thing happened in Iconium; they entered the Jewish ˙synagogue and spoke in such a way that a great number of both Jews and Greeks believed.[j] 2 But the Jews who refused to believe stirred up and poisoned the minds of the Gentiles against the brothers.[k] 3 So they stayed there for some time and spoke boldly in reliance on the Lord, who testified to the message of His grace by granting that signs and wonders be performed through them.[l] 4 But the people of the city were divided, some siding with the Jews and some with the apostles.[m] 5 When an attempt was made by both the Gentiles and Jews, with their rulers, to assault and stone them, 6 they found out about it and fled to the Lycaonian towns called Lystra and Derbe, and to the surrounding countryside.[n] 7 And there they kept evangelizing.[o]

Mistaken for Gods in Lystra

8 In Lystra a man without strength in his feet, lame from birth,[G] and who had never walked, sat 9 and heard Paul speaking. After observing him closely and seeing that he had faith to be healed, 10 Paul said in a loud voice, "Stand upright on your feet!" And he jumped up and started to walk around.[p]

11 When the crowds saw what Paul had done, they raised their voices, saying in the Lycaonian language, "The gods have come down to us in the form of men!"[q] 12 And they started to call Barnabas, Zeus, and Paul, Hermes, because he was the main speaker. 13 Then the

[A] 13:41 Hab 1:5 [B] 13:42 Paul and Barnabas [C] 13:42 Other mss read *they were leaving the synagogue of the Jews, the Gentiles* [D] 13:44 Other mss read *of God* [E] 13:47 Lit *the end* [F] 13:47 Is 49:6 [G] 14:8 Lit *from his mother's womb*

priest of Zeus, whose temple was just outside
the town, brought oxen and garlands to the
gates. He, with the crowds, intended to offer
sacrifice.
14 The apostles Barnabas and Paul tore their
robes when they heard this and rushed into
the crowd, shouting:[a] 15 "Men! Why are you
doing these things? We are men also, with the
same nature as you, and we are proclaiming
good news to you, that you should turn from
these worthless things[b] to the living God,
**who made the heaven, the earth, the sea,
and everything in them.**[A,c] 16 In past generations He allowed all the nations[d] to go their
own way, 17 although He did not leave Himself
without a witness,[e] since He did what is good
by giving you rain from heaven and fruitful
seasons[f] and satisfying your[B] hearts with food
and happiness." 18 Even though they said these
things, they barely stopped the crowds from
sacrificing to them.
19 Then some Jews came from Antioch and
Iconium, and when they had won over the
crowds and stoned Paul, they dragged him
out of the city, thinking he was dead.[g] 20 After
the disciples surrounded him, he got up and
went into the town. The next day he left with
Barnabas for Derbe.[h]

Church Planting

21 After they had evangelized that town and
made many disciples, they returned to Lystra,
to Iconium, and to Antioch,[i] 22 strengthening
the[C] disciples by encouraging them to continue in the faith[j] and by telling them, "It is
necessary to pass through many troubles[k] on
our way into the kingdom of God."
23 When they had appointed elders[l] in every
church and prayed with fasting, they committed them to the Lord in whom they had
believed. 24 Then they passed through Pisidia
and came to Pamphylia. 25 After they spoke
the message in Perga, they went down to Attalia. 26 From there they sailed back to Antioch
where they had been entrusted to the grace of
God for the work they had now completed.[m]
27 After they arrived and gathered the church
together, they reported everything God had
done with them[n] and that He had opened
the door[o] of faith to the Gentiles. 28 And they
spent a considerable time[D] with the disciples.

Dispute in Antioch

15 Some men[p] came down from Judea and
began to teach the brothers: "Unless
you are circumcised[q] according to the custom
prescribed by Moses,[r] you cannot be saved!"
2 But after Paul and Barnabas had engaged
them in serious argument and debate, the
church arranged for Paul and Barnabas and
some others of them to go up to the apostles
and elders in Jerusalem concerning this con-
troversy.[s] 3 When they had been sent on their
way by the church,[t] they passed through both
Phoenicia and Samaria, explaining in detail
the conversion of the Gentiles, and they created great joy among all the brothers.
4 When they arrived at Jerusalem, they were
welcomed by the church, the apostles, and
the elders, and they reported all that God had
done with them.[u] 5 But some of the believers
from the party of the ·Pharisees stood up and
said, "It is necessary to circumcise them and
to command them to keep the law of Moses!"

The Jerusalem Council

6 Then the apostles and the elders assembled
to consider this matter. 7 After there had been
much debate, Peter stood up and said to them:
"Brothers, you are aware that in the early days
God made a choice among you,[E] that by my
mouth the Gentiles would hear the gospel
message and believe. 8 And God, who knows
the heart, testified to them by giving[F] the Holy
Spirit, just as He also did to us.[v] 9 He made no
distinction between us and them,[w] cleansing
their hearts by faith.[x] 10 Now then, why are you
testing God by putting a yoke on the disciples'
necks[y] that neither our ancestors nor we have
been able to bear? 11 On the contrary, we believe we are saved through the grace[z] of the
Lord Jesus in the same way they are."
12 Then the whole assembly fell silent and
listened to Barnabas and Paul describing all
the signs and wonders God had done through
them among the Gentiles.[aa] 13 After they
stopped speaking, James responded: "Brothers, listen to me! 14 Simeon[G] has reported how

[a]**14:14** Mt 26:65; Mk 14:63
[b]**14:15** 1Sm 12:21; 1Co 8:4; 1Th 1:9
[c]Gn 1:1; Ex 20:11; Ps 146:6; Jr 14:22; Rv 14:7
[d]**14:16** Ps 81:2; Mc 4:5; Ac 17:30; 1Pt 4:3
[e]**14:17** Ac 17:26-27; Rm 1:19-20
[f]Lv 26:4; Dt 11:14; 28:12; Jb 5:10; Ps 65:10; 147:8; Ezk 34:26; Jl 2:23
[g]**14:19** Ac 13:45,51; 2Co 11:25; 2Tm 3:11
[h]**14:20** Ac 11:26; 14:22,28
[i]**14:21** Mt 28:19; Ac 13:51
[j]**14:22** Ac 11:23; 13:43
[k]Lk 22:48; Jn 15:20; 16:33; Ac 9:16; Rm 8:17; 1Th 3:3; 2Tm 3:12
[l]**14:23** Ac 11:30; 13:3; 20:32; Ti 1:5
[m]**14:26** Ac 11:19; 13:3
[n]**14:27** Ac 15:12; 21:19
[o]1Co 16:9; 2Co 2:12; Col 4:3; Rv 3:8
[p]**15:1** Ac 15:24; Gl 2:12
[q]Ac 15:5; 16:3; 21:21; 1Co 7:18; Gl 5:2
[r]Lv 12:3; Ac 6:14
[s]**15:2** Ac 11:30; 16:4; Gl 2:1-2
[t]**15:3** Ac 11:18; 21:5; Rm 15:24; 1Co 16:6,11; 2Co 1:16; Ti 3:13; 3Jn 6
[u]**15:4** Ac 14:27; 15:12
[v]**15:8** Ac 1:24; 10:44,47
[w]**15:9** Ac 10:28,34; 11:12
[x]Ac 10:43; 1Pt 1:22
[y]**15:10** Mt 23:4; Gl 5:1
[z]**15:11** Rm 3:24; Eph 2:5-8; Ti 2:11
[aa]**15:12** Jn 4:48; Ac 14:27; 15:4

[A]**14:15** Ex 20:11; Ps 146:6 [B]**14:17** Other mss read *our* [C]**14:22** Lit *the souls of the* [D]**14:28** Or *spent no little time* [E]**15:7** Other mss read *us* [F]**15:8** Other mss add *them* [G]**15:14** Simon (Peter)

God first intervened to take from the Gentiles
a people for His name.[a] 15And the words of
the prophets agree with this, as it is written:

16 **After these things I will return**
and rebuild David's fallen tent.
I will rebuild its ruins
and set it up again,
17 **so the rest of humanity**
may seek the Lord —
even all the Gentiles
who are called by My name,
declares the Lord who does
these things,
18 **known from long ago.**[A,B,b]

19Therefore, in my judgment, we should not
cause difficulties for those among the Gentiles who turn to God, 20but instead we should
write to them to abstain from things polluted
by idols, from sexual immorality,[c] from eating anything that has been strangled, and
from blood. 21For since ancient times, Moses
has had those who proclaim him in every city,
and every Sabbath day he is read aloud in the
*synagogues."[d]

The Letter to the Gentile Believers

22Then the apostles and the elders, with
the whole church, decided to select men who
were among them and to send them to Antioch with Paul and Barnabas: Judas, called
Barsabbas, and Silas,[e] both leading men
among the brothers. 23They wrote this letter
to be delivered by them:[C]

From the apostles and the elders, your
brothers,
To the brothers among the Gentiles in
Antioch, Syria, and Cilicia:[f]
Greetings.
24Because we have heard that some without our authorization went out from us[g]
and troubled you with their words and
unsettled your hearts,[D,h] 25we have unanimously[i] decided to select men and send
them to you along with our dearly loved
Barnabas and Paul, 26who have risked
their lives[j] for the name of our Lord
Jesus Christ. 27Therefore we have sent Judas and Silas, who will personally report
the same things by word of mouth.[E] 28For
it was the Holy Spirit's decision — and
ours — to put no greater burden on you
than these necessary things:[k] 29that you
abstain from food offered to idols, from
blood, from eating anything that has
been strangled, and from sexual immorality.[l] You will do well if you keep yourselves from these things.
Farewell.

The Outcome of the Jerusalem Letter

30Then, being sent off, they went down to
Antioch, and after gathering the assembly,

GOD WHO SENDS

Nature of the Church: Sending and Receiving

Mission as sending affirms that in the deepest theological sense every church is both a "receiving" and a "sending" church. To dichotomize the church by defining it one way in one part of the world and another way in another part of the world has been to fail to understand the fundamental New Testament meaning both of the church and of the sending and, therefore, of mission. The church was created out of mission and for mission. Therefore, every church in the clearest New Testament meaning is a sending church. Moreover, now that a maturing world Christian community is rising above the paternalism and other stifling influences of the past, we need a renewed sense of being sent as the common vocation of every Christian and every church.

(DuBose, 140)

[a]15:13-14 Ac 12:17; 15:7 [b]15:16-18 Is 45:21; Jr 14:9; Dn 9:19; Am 9:11-12 [c]15:20 1Co 8:7,13; 10:7-8,14-28; Rv 2:14,20 [d]15:21 Ac 13:15; 2Co 3:14 [e]15:22 Ac 1:23; 15:2; 1Pt 5:12 [f]15:23 Ac 15:1; 23:26; Jms 1:1 [g]15:24 Gl 2:4; 5:12; Ti 1:10 [h]Gl 1:7; 5:10 [i]15:25 Ac 1:14; 2:46; 4:24; 5:12; 7:57; 8:6; 12:20; 18:12; 19:29 [j]15:26 Ac 9:23-25; 14:19 [k]15:28 Ac 5:32; 15:8 [l]15:29 Ac 15:20; 21:25; Rv 2:14,20

A15:17-18 Other mss read *says the Lord who does all these things. Known to God from long ago are all His works.* B15:16-18 Am 9:11-12; Is 45:21 C15:23 Lit *Writing by their hand:* D15:24 Other mss add *by saying, "Be circumcised and keep the law,"* E15:27 Lit *things through word*

they delivered the letter. 31 When they read it,
they rejoiced because of its encouragement.
32 Both Judas and Silas, who were also prophets themselves, encouraged the brothers and
strengthened them with a long message.[a]
33 After spending some time there, they were
sent back in peace[b] by the •brothers to those
who had sent them.[A,B] 35 But Paul and Barnabas, along with many others, remained in
Antioch teaching and proclaiming the message of the Lord.[c]

Paul and Barnabas Part Company

36 After some time had passed, Paul said to
Barnabas, "Let's go back and visit the brothers in every town[d] where we have preached
the message of the Lord and see how they're
doing." 37 Barnabas wanted to take along John
Mark.[C] 38 But Paul did not think it appropriate to take along this man who had deserted
them in Pamphylia and had not gone on with
them to the work. 39 There was such a sharp
disagreement that they parted company, and
Barnabas took Mark[e] with him and sailed off
to Cyprus. 40 Then Paul chose Silas and departed, after being commended to the grace
of the Lord by the brothers.[f] 41 He traveled
through Syria[g] and Cilicia, strengthening the
churches.

Paul Selects Timothy

16 Then he went on to Derbe and Lystra,
where there was a disciple named Timothy,[h] the son of a believing Jewish woman,[i]
but his father was a Greek. 2 The •brothers
at Lystra and Iconium spoke highly of him.[j]
3 Paul wanted Timothy[D] to go with him, so he
took him and circumcised[k] him because of
the Jews who were in those places, since they
all knew that his father was a Greek. 4 As they
traveled through the towns, they delivered
the decisions reached by the apostles and elders at Jerusalem for them to observe.[l] 5 So the
churches were strengthened in the faith and
increased in number daily.[m]

Evangelization of Europe

6 They went through the region of Phrygia
and Galatia and were prevented by the Holy

[a]**15:32** Ac 14:22; 15:1
[b]**15:33** Mk 5:34; Ac 16:36; 1Co 16:11; Heb 11:31
[c]**15:35** Ac 8:4; 13:1
[d]**15:36** Ac 13:4,13-14,51; 14:6,24
[e]**15:37-39** Ac 12:12; 13:13; Col 4:10
[f]**15:40** Ac 11:23; 14:26; 15:22
[g]**15:41** Ac 6:9; 15:23; 16:5
[h]**16:1** Ac 17:14-15; 18:5; 19:22; 20:4; Rm 16:21; 1Co 4:17; Php 2:19; 1Th 3:2,6
[i]2Tm 1:5; 3:15
[j]**16:2** Ac 13:51; 16:40
[k]**16:3** Gl 2:3
[l]**16:4** Ac 11:30; 15:2,28
[m]**16:5** Ac 2:47; 9:31; 15:41
[n]**16:6** Ac 2:9; 18:23; Gl 1:2; 3:1
[o]**16:7** Ac 8:29; Rm 8:9; Gl 4:6; Php 1:19; 1Pt 1:11
[p]**16:8** Ac 16:11; 20:5-6; 2Co 2:12; 2Tm 4:13
[q]**16:9** Ac 9:10; 20:1,3
[r]**16:10-17** Ac 20:5-15; 21:1-18; 27:1–28:16
[s]**16:12** Ac 20:6; Php 1:1; 1Th 2:2
[t]**16:14** Lk 24:45; Ac 18:7; Rv 1:11
[u]**16:15** Gn 19:3; Lk 24:29; Ac 11:14
[v]**16:16** Lv 19:31; Dt 18:11; 1Sm 28:3,7
[w]**16:17-18** Mk 5:7; 16:17
[x]**16:19** Mt 10:18; Ac 8:3; 15:22; 17:6-8; 19:25-26; 21:30; Jms 2:6

Spirit from speaking the message in •Asia.[n]
7 When they came to Mysia, they tried to go
into Bithynia, but the Spirit of Jesus[o] did not
allow them. 8 So, bypassing Mysia, they came
down to Troas.[p] 9 During the night a vision
appeared to Paul: A Macedonian man was
standing and pleading with him, "Cross over
to Macedonia and help us!"[q] 10 After[r] he had
seen the vision, we[E] immediately made efforts
to set out for Macedonia, concluding that
God had called us to evangelize them.

Lydia's Conversion

11 Then, setting sail from Troas, we ran a
straight course to Samothrace, the next day
to Neapolis, 12 and from there to Philippi,[s]
a Roman colony, which is a leading city of
that district of Macedonia. We stayed in
that city for a number of days. 13 On the Sabbath day we went outside the city gate by the
river, where we thought there was a place of
prayer. We sat down and spoke to the women
gathered there. 14 A woman named Lydia, a
dealer in purple cloth from the city of Thyatira, who worshiped God, was listening. The
Lord opened her heart to pay attention to
what was spoken by Paul.[t] 15 After she and her
household were baptized, she urged us, "If
you consider me a believer in the Lord, come
and stay at my house."[u] And she persuaded us.

Paul and Silas in Prison

16 Once, as we were on our way to prayer, a
•slave girl met us who had a spirit of prediction.[F,v] She made a large profit for her owners
by fortune-telling. 17 As she followed Paul and
us she cried out, "These men, who are proclaiming to you[G] the way of salvation, are the
slaves of the Most High God." 18 And she did
this for many days.

But Paul was greatly aggravated and turning to the spirit, said, "I command you in the
name of Jesus Christ to come out of her!" And
it came out right away.[H,w]

19 When her owners saw that their hope of
profit was gone, they seized Paul and Silas[x]
and dragged them into the marketplace to
the authorities. 20 Bringing them before the
chief magistrates, they said, "These men are

[A]**15:33** Other mss read *the brothers to the apostles* [B]**15:33** Other mss add v. 34: *But Silas decided to stay there.* [C]**15:37** Lit *John who was called Mark* [D]**16:3** Lit *wanted this one* [E]**16:10** The use of we in this passage probably indicates that the author Luke is joining Paul's missionary team here. [F]**16:16** Or *a spirit by which she predicted the future* [G]**16:17** Other mss read *us* [H]**16:18** Lit *out this hour*

seriously disturbing our city. They are Jews
21 and are promoting customs that are not legal for us as Romans to adopt or practice."[a]
22 Then the mob joined in the attack against
them, and the chief magistrates stripped off
their clothes and ordered them to be beaten
with rods.[b] 23 After they had inflicted many
blows on them, they threw them in jail, ordering the jailer to keep them securely guarded.
24 Receiving such an order, he put them into
the inner prison and secured their feet in the
stocks.[c]

A Midnight Deliverance

25 About midnight Paul and Silas were praying and singing hymns to God, and the prisoners were listening to them. 26 Suddenly
there was such a violent earthquake that the
foundations of the jail were shaken, and immediately all the doors were opened, and everyone's chains came loose.[d] 27 When the jailer
woke up and saw the doors of the prison
open, he drew his sword and was going to kill
himself, since he thought the prisoners had
escaped.
28 But Paul called out in a loud voice, "Don't
harm yourself, because all of us are here!"
29 Then the jailer called for lights, rushed
in, and fell down trembling before Paul and
Silas. 30 Then he escorted them out and said,
"Sirs, what must I do to be saved?"[e]
31 So they said, "Believe on the Lord Jesus,
and you will be saved—you and your household."[f] 32 Then they spoke the message of the
Lord to him along with everyone in his house.
33 He took them the same hour of the night
and washed their wounds. Right away he and
all his family were baptized. 34 He brought
them into his house, set a meal before them,
and rejoiced because he had believed God
with his entire household.[g]

An Official Apology

35 When daylight came, the chief magistrates sent the police to say, "Release those
men!"
36 The jailer reported these words to Paul:
"The magistrates have sent orders for you to be
released. So come out now and go in peace."[h]
37 But Paul said to them, "They beat us in
public without a trial, although we are Roman citizens, and threw us in jail. And now
are they going to smuggle us out secretly?
Certainly not! On the contrary, let them
come themselves and escort us out!"[i]
38 Then the police reported these words to
the magistrates. They were afraid when they
heard that Paul and Silas were Roman citizens. 39 So they came and apologized to them,
and escorting them out, they urged them to
leave town. 40 After leaving the jail, they came
to Lydia's house where they saw and encouraged the brothers, and departed.[j]

A Short Ministry in Thessalonica

17 Then they traveled through Amphipolis and Apollonia and came to Thessalonica,[k] where there was a Jewish •synagogue.
2 As usual, Paul went to the synagogue, and on
three Sabbath days reasoned with them from
the Scriptures,[l] 3 explaining and showing that
the •Messiah had to suffer and rise from the
dead: "This Jesus I am proclaiming to you is
the Messiah."[m] 4 Then some of them were persuaded and joined Paul and Silas, including a
great number of God-fearing Greeks, as well
as a number[A] of the leading women.[n]

Riot in the City

5 But the Jews became jealous, and they
brought together some scoundrels from the
marketplace, formed a mob, and started a
riot in the city. Attacking Jason's house, they
searched for them to bring them out to the
public assembly.[o] 6 When they did not find
them, they dragged Jason and some of the
•brothers before the city officials, shouting,
"These men who have turned the world upside down have come here too, 7 and Jason
has received them as guests! They are all acting contrary to Caesar's decrees,[p] saying that
there is another king—Jesus!"[q] 8 The Jews
stirred up the crowd and the city officials
who heard these things. 9 So taking a security bond from Jason and the others, they released them.

The Bereans Search the Scriptures

10 As soon as it was night, the brothers sent
Paul and Silas off to Berea.[r] On arrival, they

[a] **16:21** Est 3:8; Ac 16:12
[b] **16:22** 2Co 6:5; 11:25; 1Th 2:2
[c] **16:24** Jb 13:27; 33:11; Jr 20:2-3; 29:26
[d] **16:26** Ac 4:31; 5:19; 12:7,10
[e] **16:30** Ac 2:37; 22:10
[f] **16:31** Mk 16:16; Ac 11:14
[g] **16:34** Ac 11:14; 16:15
[h] **16:36** Ac 15:33; 16:27
[i] **16:37** Ac 22:25-29
[j] **16:39-40** Mt 8:34; Ac 16:14
[k] **17:1** Ac 20:4; Php 4:16; 1Th 1:1; 2Tm 4:10
[l] **17:2** Ac 8:35; 9:20; 13:13-14
[m] **17:3** Lk 24:26; Jn 20:9; Ac 3:18; 9:22; 18:28
[n] **17:4** Jn 7:35; Ac 14:4; 15:22
[o] **17:5** Ac 17:13; Rm 16:21; 1Th 2:14-16
[p] **17:7** Lk 2:1; Rm 1:32; Eph 2:15
[q] Lk 23:2; Jn 19:12
[r] **17:10** Ac 17:13-14; 20:4

[A] **17:4** Lit *as well as not a few*

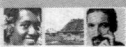

went into the synagogue of the Jews. [11]The
people here were more open-minded than
those in Thessalonica, since they welcomed
the message with eagerness and examined
the Scriptures[a] daily to see if these things
were so. [12]Consequently, many of them be-

[a]17:11 Is 34:16; Lk 16:29; Jn 5:39

lieved, including a number of the prominent
Greek women as well as men. [13]But when
the Jews from Thessalonica found out that
God's message had been proclaimed by Paul
at Berea, they came there too, agitating and
disturbing[A] the crowds. [14]Then the brothers

Cultural Engagement

Joe Thorn

As the church is faithful to the mission given to her by Jesus Christ she will, out of necessity, "engage culture." Of course, engaging culture is not our mission, but "making disciples of all nations" is what our Lord has called us to do. Yet, this sacred work cannot be done in a vacuum outside of the cultural milieu in which people live.

Paul's experience in Athens (Ac 17:16-34) is helpful as it demonstrates how he approached people and ministry in a particular culture. The Apostle found himself in Athens, not through the careful planning and execution of a detailed ministry strategy, but in the providence of God as he encountered opposition to his ministry. And, while he was there, Paul was not idle. He was led by God to push forward with the gospel into a unique time and place. Here we see three things that characterized Paul's ministry as he engaged culture.

Paul was provoked by the lostness and idolatry of the people. He was struck by the deep and pervasive idolatry of the people in Athens. These were men and women who were created to know and reflect the glory of God, but they had rejected the Creator and instead chose to worship created and imaginary gods. Paul engaged the culture not because he loved culture, but because he loved God and loved people made in God's image, and because it is a necessary aspect of carrying out the mission of the church.

Paul focused on the grand narrative of God that culminates in the work of Jesus. His response to people and culture in Athens was to do what he always did in every city—proclaim Jesus Christ as Lord. He first went to the Synagogue where the Scripture was available to be read and expounded upon. He didn't develop a totally new approach to engage the people God had surprisingly sent him to. Rather, he continued to fulfill his calling to preach Christ crucified. As the Athenians heard this message they became curious or incredulous.

Paul showed the Athenians how their culture and lives were both connected to and yet disconnected from the truth of God. He could do this because he understood their religion and worldview enough to point out the need for redemption from within their own belief system, as he brought the good news to them from outside of it.

Cultural engagement is not the thoughtless consumption or uncritical reception of things in culture, but a pressing into the lives of people who live in a particular cultural context with an understanding of their world and how the gospel ultimately answers their brokenness and alienation from God. Cultural engagement is not the goal of ministry, but a necessary component of faithful gospel proclamation. It means we work to know the beliefs, values, and idols of the people, determining where, what, and how they worship. It means we work to clearly articulate the supremacy of Jesus over these things. It means we remain focused on the mission Christ gave the church.

[A]17:13 Other mss omit *and disturbing*

immediately sent Paul away to go to the
sea, but Silas and Timothy[a] stayed on there.
15 Those who escorted Paul brought him as far
as Athens, and after receiving instructions for
Silas and Timothy to come to him as quickly
as possible, they departed.[b]

Paul in Athens

16 While Paul was waiting for them in Athens, his spirit was troubled within him when
he saw that the city was full of idols. 17 So he
reasoned in the synagogue with the Jews and
with those who worshiped God and in the
marketplace every day with those who happened to be there.[c] 18 Then also, some of the
Epicurean and Stoic philosophers argued
with him. Some said, "What is this pseudo-
intellectual[A] trying to say?"
Others replied, "He seems to be a preacher
of foreign deities" — because he was telling
the good news about Jesus and the Resurrection.[B,d]
19 They took him and brought him to the Areopagus,[C] and said, "May we learn about this
new teaching you're speaking of?[e] 20 For what
you say sounds strange to us, and we want to
know what these ideas mean." 21 Now all the
Athenians and the foreigners residing there
spent their time on nothing else but telling
or hearing something new.

The Areopagus Address

22 Then Paul stood in the middle of the Areopagus and said: "Men of Athens! I see that
you are extremely religious in every respect.
23 For as I was passing through and observing
the objects of your worship, I even found an
altar on which was inscribed:

TO AN UNKNOWN GOD.

Therefore, what you worship in ignorance,
this I proclaim to you. 24 The God who made
the world and everything in it[f] — He is Lord
of heaven and earth[g] and does not live in
shrines made by hands.[h] 25 Neither is He
served by human hands, as though He needed
anything,[i] since He Himself gives everyone
life and breath and all things.[j] 26 From one
man[D] He has made every nationality to live
over the whole earth and has determined
their appointed times and the boundaries of
where they live.[k] 27 He did this so they might
seek God, and perhaps they might reach out
and find Him, though He is not far from each
one of us.[l] 28 For in Him we live and move and
exist, as even some of your own poets have
said, 'For we are also His offspring.'[E,m] 29 Being
God's offspring then, we shouldn't think that
the divine nature is like gold or silver or
stone, an image fashioned by human art and
imagination.[n]
30 "Therefore, having overlooked[o] the times
of ignorance, God now commands all people
everywhere to repent, 31 because He has set a
day when He is going to judge the world in
righteousness by the Man He has appointed.
He has provided proof of this to everyone by
raising Him from the dead."[p]
32 When they heard about resurrection of
the dead, some began to ridicule him. But
others said, "We'd like to hear from you again
about this." 33 Then Paul left their presence.
34 However, some men joined him and believed, including Dionysius the Areopagite,
a woman named Damaris, and others with
them.

Founding the Corinthian Church

18 After this, he[F] left Athens and went to
Corinth,[q] 2 where he found a Jewish
man named Aquila,[r] a native of Pontus, who
had recently come from Italy with his wife
Priscilla because Claudius[G] had ordered all
the Jews to leave Rome. Paul came to them,
3 and being of the same occupation, stayed
with them and worked, for they were tentmakers[H] by trade.[s] 4 He reasoned in the ˙syna-
gogue every Sabbath and tried to persuade
both Jews and Greeks.[t]
5 When Silas and Timothy came down from
Macedonia, Paul was occupied with preaching the message[I] and solemnly testified to the
Jews that Jesus is the ˙Messiah.[u] 6 But when
they resisted and blasphemed,[v] he shook his
robe[J,w] and told them, "Your blood is on your
own heads![x] I am innocent.[K] From now on I

[a] **17:14** Mt 10:23; Ac 15:22; 16:1
[b] **17:15** Ac 18:1,5; 1Th 3:1
[c] **17:16-17** Ac 9:20; 2Pt 2:8
[d] **17:18** Ac 4:2; 17:31-32
[e] **17:19** Mk 1:27; Ac 17:22
[f] **17:24** Is 42:5; Ac 14:15
[g] Dt 10:14; Ps 115:16; Mt 11:25
[h] Ac 7:48
[i] **17:25** Jb 22:2; Ps 50:10-12
[j] Gn 2:7; Jb 27:3; 33:4; Zch 12:1
[k] **17:26** Dt 32:8; Jb 12:23; Mal 2:10
[l] **17:27** Dt 4:7; Jr 23:23-24; Ac 14:17
[m] **17:28** Jb 12:10; Dn 5:23; Ti 1:12
[n] **17:29** Is 40:18-19; Rm 1:23
[o] **17:30** Lk 24:47; Ac 14:16; Rm 3:25; Ti 2:11-12; 1Pt 1:14; 4:3
[p] **17:31** Ps 9:8; 98:9; Mt 10:15; Ac 2:24; Rm 2:16
[q] **18:1** Ac 17:15; 19:1; 1Co 1:2; 2Co 1:1,23; 2Tm 4:20
[r] **18:2** Ac 18:18,26; Rm 16:3-5; 1Co 16:19; 2Tm 4:19
[s] **18:3** Ac 20:34; 1Co 4:12; 9:15; 2Co 11:7; 12:13; 1Th 2:9; 2Th 3:8
[t] **18:4** Ac 9:20; 13:14; 14:1; 18:19
[u] **18:5** Jb 32:18; Ac 15:22; 16:1,9; 17:3,14-15; 18:28; 1Th 3:6
[v] **18:6** Ac 13:45; Rm 3:8; 1Co 4:13; Ti 3:2
[w] Neh 5:13; Mt 10:14; Ac 13:51
[x] 2Sm 1:16; Ezk 18:13; 33:4; Mt 27:25

[A] **17:18** Lit *this seed picker*; = one who picks up scraps [B] **17:18** = Gk *Anastasis* [C] **17:19** Or *Mars Hill*, the oldest and most famous court in Athens with jurisdiction in moral, religious, and civil matters [D] **17:26** Other mss read *one blood* [E] **17:28** This citation is from Aratus, a third-century B.C. Gk poet.

[F] **18:1** Other mss read *Paul* [G] **18:2** Roman emperor A.D. 41–54; he expelled all Jews from Rome in A.D. 49. [H] **18:3** Or *leatherworkers*, or less likely *manufacturers of theatrical properties* [I] **18:5** Other mss read *was urged by the Spirit* [J] **18:6** A symbolic display of protest; Mt 10:14; Ac 13:51 [K] **18:6** Lit ˙*clean*

Marketplace Mission

Larry E. McCrary

In many parts of the world, some of the most effective missionaries are not officially labeled as missionaries at all. Instead, they form part of the marketplace and share the gospel in the context of their work and community, living their lives with intentionality.

This is the case with Aquila and Priscilla, who are introduced in Acts 18 as transnational marketplace workers. A few quick facts about this couple:

- Aquila was from Pontus, which is located in modern-day northern Turkey
- He and Priscilla were expelled from Rome
- They met Paul in Corinth; they shared the same profession and even accompanied him to Ephesus
- Wherever they were placed by God, they seemed to make the most of their opportunities

Aquila and Priscilla were tentmakers by trade. Neither Luke nor Paul ever mentioned in their writings that Aquila and Priscilla were in full-time ministry, leading us to conclude they were involved in marketplace ministry. They evidently had the skills and ability to move from place to place and practice their trade.

As marketplace workers, their intentionality was crucial. No matter where they lived, they were engaged in the work of the gospel.

- They were coworkers with Paul in Christ Jesus (Rm 16:3)
- They risked their lives for Paul (Rm 16:4)
- The church was grateful for them (Rm 16:3)
- They assisted Paul in Ephesus (Ac 18:18-28)
- They hosted a church in their own home (Rm 16:3-5; 1Co 16:19)
- They instructed Apollos privately to help him learn more about Jesus (Ac 18:26)

"Here is a perfect example before us—by Christians like Aquila and Priscilla traveling the routes of trade and commerce and carrying their faith wherever they went," writes New Testament scholar John Polhill (*The New American Commentary*, Acts, p. 383).

In her book, *Tentmakers*, author Ruth Siemens writes this about life on the mission field: "The secular job is not an inconvenience, but the God-given context in which tentmakers live out the gospel in a winsome, wholesome, nonjudgmental way, demonstrating personal integrity, doing quality work and developing caring relationships."

The intentionality shown by Aquila and Priscilla went beyond their workplace. It also extended into their community, as they showed hospitality, especially in their home. In Scripture we see the following examples of their hospitality:

- A church met in their home (Rm 16:5; 1Co 16:19)
- Paul stayed with them as they shared the same trade (Ac 18:3)
- Apollos was invited to their house so they could explain more about Jesus to him (Ac 18:26)

Marketplace professionals do many things on the mission field, and each of us can learn from their examples as to how we can live as missionaries in our own marketplaces. They lead or help with the planting of new churches, minister to those in need, involve their sending churches in partnering overseas, and start Bible studies. They make intentional choices in their daily lives and come alongside one another to pray, encourage, mentor, and learn as they serve in the marketplace, carrying on the legacy left by Aquila and Priscilla.

will go to the Gentiles."[a] 7So he left there and
went to the house of a man named Titius Justus, a worshiper of God, whose house was
next door to the synagogue. 8Crispus, the
leader of the synagogue, believed the Lord,
along with his whole household.[b] Many of the
Corinthians, when they heard, believed and
were baptized.
9Then the Lord said to Paul in a night vision, "Don't be afraid, but keep on speaking
and don't be silent. 10For I am with you, and
no one will lay a hand on you to hurt you, because I have many people in this city."[c] 11And
he stayed there a year and six months, teaching the word of God among them.
12While Gallio was ·proconsul of Achaia,
the Jews made a united attack against Paul
and brought him to the judge's bench.[d]
13"This man," they said, "persuades people to
worship God contrary to the law!"
14As Paul was about to open his mouth, Gallio said to the Jews, "If it were a matter of a
crime or of moral evil, it would be reasonable
for me to put up with you Jews. 15But if these
are questions about words, names, and your
own law, see to it yourselves. I don't want to
be a judge of such things."[e] 16So he drove them
from the judge's bench. 17Then they all[A] seized
Sosthenes,[f] the leader of the synagogue, and
beat him in front of the judge's bench. But
none of these things concerned Gallio.

The Return Trip to Antioch

18So Paul, having stayed on for many days,
said good-bye to the ·brothers and sailed
away to Syria. Priscilla and Aquila were
with him. He shaved his head at Cenchreae
because he had taken a vow.[g] 19When they
reached Ephesus[h] he left them there, but he
himself entered the synagogue and engaged
in discussion with[B] the Jews. 20And though
they asked him to stay for a longer time, he
declined, 21but he said good-bye and stated,[C]
"I'll come back to you again, if God wills."[i]
Then he set sail from Ephesus.
22On landing at Caesarea, he went up and
greeted the church[D] and went down to Antioch.[j] 23And after spending some time there,
he set out, traveling through one place after
another in the Galatian territory and Phrygia,
strengthening all the disciples.[k]

The Eloquent Apollos

24A Jew named Apollos,[l] a native Alexandrian, an eloquent man who was powerful
in the use of the Scriptures, arrived in Ephesus. 25This man had been instructed in the
way of the Lord; and being fervent in spirit,[E]
he spoke and taught the things about Jesus
accurately, although he knew only John's
baptism.[m] 26He began to speak boldly in the
synagogue. After Priscilla and Aquila heard
him, they took him home[F] and explained the
way of God to him more accurately.[n] 27When
he wanted to cross over to Achaia, the brothers wrote to the disciples urging them to welcome him. After he arrived, he greatly helped
those who had believed through grace.[o] 28For
he vigorously refuted the Jews in public, demonstrating through the Scriptures that Jesus
is the Messiah.[p]

Twelve Disciples of John the Baptist

19 While Apollos was in Corinth, Paul
traveled through the interior regions
and came to Ephesus. He found some disciples[q] 2and asked them, "Did you receive the
Holy Spirit when you believed?"
"No," they told him, "we haven't even heard
that there is a Holy Spirit."[r]
3"Then what baptism were you baptized
with?" he asked them.
"With John's baptism," they replied.
4Paul said, "John baptized with a baptism
of repentance, telling the people that they
should believe in the One who would come
after him, that is, in Jesus."[s]
5When they heard this, they were baptized
in the name of the Lord Jesus. 6And when
Paul had laid his hands on[t] them, the Holy
Spirit came on them, and they began to speak
in other ·languages and to prophesy.[u] 7Now
there were about 12 men in all.

In the Lecture Hall of Tyrannus

8Then he entered the ·synagogue and
spoke boldly over a period of three months,
engaging in discussion and trying to per-

[a] **18:6** Ezk 3:18; Ac 13:46
[b] **18:8** Mk 5:22; Ac 11:14; 1Co 1:14
[c] **18:9-10** Mt 28:20; Ac 23:11
[d] **18:12** Ac 13:7; 18:27
[e] **18:15** Ac 23:29; 25:11,19
[f] **18:17** 1Co 1:1
[g] **18:18** Nm 6:2,5,9,18; Ac 21:24; Rm 16:1
[h] **18:19** Ac 19:1; 20:16; 1Co 15:32; 1Tm 1:3; 2Tm 1:18
[i] **18:21** Rm 1:10; 1Co 4:19; 16:7; Heb 6:3; Jms 4:15; 1Pt 3:17
[j] **18:22** Ac 8:40; 11:19
[k] **18:23** Ac 14:22; 16:6
[l] **18:24** Ac 19:1; 1Co 1:12; 3:5; 4:6; 16:12; Ti 3:13
[m] **18:25** Lk 7:29; Ac 9:2; 19:3; Rm 12:11
[n] **18:26** Mt 2:8; Lk 1:3; Ac 18:25; 23:15,20; 24:22; Eph 5:15; 1Th 5:2
[o] **18:27** Ac 18:12,18; 1Co 3:6
[p] **18:28** Ac 9:22; 17:2-3; 18:5
[q] **19:1** Ac 18:1,24; 1Co 1:12; 3:5-6
[r] **19:2** Jn 7:39; Ac 8:16; 11:16
[s] **19:4** Mt 3:11; Jn 1:7,27; Ac 13:24-25
[t] **19:6** Ac 6:6; 8:17
[u] Mk 16:17; Ac 2:4; 10:46

[A] **18:17** Other mss read *Then all the Greeks* [B] **18:19** Or *and addressed*
[C] **18:21** Other mss add *"By all means it is necessary to keep the coming festival in Jerusalem. But* [D] **18:22** The church in Jerusalem [E] **18:25** Or *in the Spirit*
[F] **18:26** Lit *they received him*

suade them about the things of the kingdom
of God.[a] 9 But when some became hardened
and would not believe, slandering the Way in
front of the crowd, he withdrew from them
and met separately with the disciples, conducting discussions every day in the lecture
hall of Tyrannus.[b] 10 And this went on for two
years, so that all the inhabitants of •Asia, both
Jews and Greeks, heard the message about the
Lord.[c]

Demonism Defeated at Ephesus

11 God was performing extraordinary miracles by Paul's hands, 12 so that even facecloths
or work aprons[A] that had touched his skin
were brought to the sick, and the diseases left
them, and the evil spirits came out of them.[d]
13 Then some of the itinerant Jewish exorcists attempted to pronounce the name of
the Lord Jesus over those who had evil spirits,
saying, "I command you by the Jesus that Paul
preaches!"[e] 14 Seven sons of Sceva, a Jewish
•chief priest, were doing this. 15 The evil spirit
answered them, "I know Jesus, and I recognize Paul — but who are you?" 16 Then the
man who had the evil spirit leaped on them,
overpowered them all, and prevailed against
them, so that they ran out of that house naked and wounded. 17 This became known to
everyone who lived in Ephesus, both Jews and
Greeks. Then fear fell on all of them, and the
name of the Lord Jesus was magnified.[f] 18 And
many who had become believers came confessing and disclosing their practices, 19 while
many of those who had practiced magic collected their books and burned them in front
of everyone. So they calculated their value
and found it to be 50,000 pieces of silver.
20 In this way the Lord's message flourished
and prevailed.[g]

The Riot in Ephesus

21 When these events were over, Paul resolved in the Spirit to pass through Macedonia and Achaia and go to Jerusalem. "After
I've been there," he said, "I must see Rome as
well!"[h] 22 So after sending two of those who
assisted him, Timothy and Erastus, to Macedonia, he himself stayed in Asia for a while.[i]

23 During that time there was a major[B]
disturbance about the Way.[j] 24 For a person
named Demetrius, a silversmith who made
silver shrines of Artemis,[C] provided a great
deal of[D] business for the craftsmen. 25 When
he had assembled them, as well as the workers engaged in this type of business, he said:
"Men, you know that our prosperity is derived from this business. 26 You both see and
hear that not only in Ephesus, but in almost
all of Asia, this man Paul has persuaded and
misled a considerable number of people by
saying that gods made by hand are not gods![k]
27 So not only do we run a risk that our business may be discredited, but also that the
temple of the great goddess Artemis may be
despised and her magnificence come to the
verge of ruin — the very one all of Asia and
the world adore."
28 When they had heard this, they were
filled with rage and began to cry out, "Great
is Artemis of the Ephesians!" 29 So the city was
filled with confusion, and they rushed all together into the amphitheater, dragging along
Gaius[l] and Aristarchus,[m] Macedonians who
were Paul's traveling companions. 30 Though
Paul wanted to go in before the people, the
disciples did not let him. 31 Even some of the
provincial officials of Asia, who were his
friends, sent word to him, pleading with him
not to take a chance by going[E] into the amphitheater. 32 Meanwhile, some were shouting one thing and some another, because
the assembly was in confusion, and most of
them did not know why they had come together. 33 Then some of the crowd gave Alexander advice when the Jews pushed him to
the front. So motioning with his hand, Alexander wanted to make his defense to the people.[n] 34 But when they recognized that he was
a Jew, a united cry went up from all of them
for about two hours: "Great is Artemis of the
Ephesians!"
35 However, when the city clerk had calmed
the crowd down, he said, "Men of Ephesus!
What man is there who doesn't know that
the city of the Ephesians is the temple guardian of the great[F] Artemis, and of the image
that fell from heaven? 36 Therefore, since

[a] **19:8** Ac 1:3; 9:20; 28:23
[b] **19:9** Ac 9:2; 11:26; 14:4; 19:23,30
[c] **19:10** Ac 19:8,22,26-27; 20:31
[d] **19:11-12** Ac 5:15; 8:13
[e] **19:13** Mt 12:27; Mk 9:38; Lk 11:19
[f] **19:17** Ac 5:5,11; 18:19
[g] **19:20** Ac 6:6-7; 12:24
[h] **19:21** Ac 16:9; 18:12; 20:16,22; Rm 15:24-25,28
[i] **19:22** Ac 13:5; 16:1,23; 19:10; 2Tm 4:20
[j] **19:23** Ac 9:2; 2Co 1:8
[k] **19:26** Dt 4:28; Ps 115:4; Is 44:10-20; Jr 10:3; Ac 17:29; 1Co 8:4; Rv 9:20
[l] **19:29** Rm 16:23; 1Co 1:14
[m] Ac 20:4; 27:2; Col 4:10; Phm 24
[n] **19:32-33** Ac 12:17; 21:34

[A] **19:12** Or *that also sweatbands and sweatcloths* or *handkerchiefs* [B] **19:23** Lit *was not a little* [C] **19:24** Artemis was the ancient Gk mother goddess believed to control all fertility. [D] **19:24** Lit *provided not a little* [E] **19:31** Lit *not to give himself* [F] **19:35** Other mss add *goddess*

these things are undeniable, you must keep
calm and not do anything rash. 37 For you have
brought these men here who are not temple
robbers or blasphemers of our[A] goddess. 38 So
if Demetrius and the craftsmen who are with
him have a case against anyone, the courts
are in session, and there are ·proconsuls. Let
them bring charges against one another.[a]
39 But if you want something else, it must
be decided in a legal assembly. 40 In fact, we
run a risk of being charged with rioting for
what happened today, since there is no ·justi-
fication that we can give as a reason for this
disorderly gathering." 41 After saying this, he
dismissed the assembly.

Paul in Macedonia

20 After the uproar was over, Paul sent
for the disciples, encouraged them,
and after saying good-bye, departed to go
to Macedonia.[b] 2 And when he had passed
through those areas and exhorted them at
length, he came to Greece 3 and stayed three
months. When he was about to set sail for
Syria, a plot was devised against him by
the Jews, so a decision was made to go back
through Macedonia.[c] 4 He was accompanied[B]
by Sopater son of Pyrrhus[C] from Berea, Aristarchus and Secundus from Thessalonica,
Gaius from Derbe, Timothy,[d] and Tychicus[e]
and Trophimus[f] from ·Asia. 5 These men went
on ahead and waited for us in Troas,[g] 6 but we
sailed away from Philippi after the days of
·Unleavened Bread.[h] In five days we reached
them at Troas, where we spent seven days.

Eutychus Revived at Troas

7 On the first day of the week, we[D] assembled to break bread.[i] Paul spoke to them, and
since he was about to depart the next day, he
extended his message until midnight. 8 There
were many lamps in the room upstairs where
we were assembled, 9 and a young man named
Eutychus was sitting on a window sill and
sank into a deep sleep as Paul kept on speaking. When he was overcome by sleep, he fell
down from the third story and was picked
up dead. 10 But Paul went down, fell on him,
embraced him, and said, "Don't be alarmed,
for his ·life is in him!"[j] 11 After going upstairs,
breaking the bread, and eating, Paul conversed a considerable time until dawn. Then
he left. 12 They brought the boy home alive
and were greatly comforted.

From Troas to Miletus

13 Then we went on ahead to the ship and
sailed for Assos, intending to take Paul on
board there. For these were his instructions,
since he himself was going by land. 14 When
he met us at Assos, we took him on board
and came to Mitylene. 15 Sailing from there,
the next day we arrived off Chios. The following day we crossed over to Samos, and[E] the
day after, we came to Miletus.[k] 16 For Paul had
decided to sail past Ephesus so he would not
have to spend time in Asia, because he was
hurrying to be in Jerusalem, if possible, for
the day of Pentecost.[l]

Farewell Address to the Ephesian Elders

17 Now from Miletus, he sent to Ephesus
and called for the elders of the church. 18 And
when they came to him, he said to them: "You
know, from the first day I set foot in Asia,
how I was with you the whole time[m] — 19 serving the Lord with all humility, with tears,
and with the trials that came to me through
the plots of the Jews[n] — 20 and that I did not
shrink back from proclaiming to you anything that was profitable or from teaching
it to you in public and from house to house.
21 I testified to both Jews and Greeks about repentance toward God[o] and faith in our Lord
Jesus.[p]

22 "And now I am on my way to Jerusalem,
bound in my spirit,[F] not knowing what I will
encounter there,[q] 23 except that in town after town the Holy Spirit testifies to me that
chains and afflictions are waiting for me.[r]
24 But I count my life of no value to myself, so
that I may finish my course[G] and the ministry[s] I received from the Lord Jesus,[t] to testify
to the gospel of God's grace.

25 "And now I know that none of you will
ever see my face again — everyone I went
about preaching the kingdom to. 26 Therefore
I testify to you this day that I am innocent[H]

[a] **19:37-38** Ac 13:7; Rm 2:22
[b] **20:1** Ac 11:26; 16:9; 19:21; 2Co 2:12-13
[c] **20:3** Ac 9:23; 20:19; 23:12; 25:3; 2Co 11:26
[d] **20:4** Ac 14:6; 16:1; 17:1; 19:29
[e] Eph 6:21; Col 4:7; 2Tm 4:12; Ti 3:12
[f] Ac 21:29; 2Tm 4:20
[g] **20:5** Ac 16:8,10; 20:6-8,13-15
[h] **20:6** Ex 12:14-15; 23:15
[i] **20:7** Ac 2:42; 1Co 10:16
[j] **20:10** 1Kg 17:21; 2Kg 4:34; Mt 9:23-24; Mk 5:39
[k] **20:15** Ac 20:17; 2Tm 4:20
[l] **20:16** Ac 2:1; 18:19; 19:21; 1Co 16:8
[m] **20:18** Ac 18:19; 19:1,10
[n] **20:19-20** Ac 20:3,27
[o] **20:21** Mk 1:15; Ac 2:38; 18:5
[p] Ac 24:24; 26:18; Eph 1:15; Col 2:5; Phm 5
[q] **20:22** Ac 17:16; 20:16
[r] **20:23** Ac 9:16; 21:4,11; 1Th 3:3
[s] **20:24** Ac 1:17; 21:13; 2Co 4:1; 2Tm 4:7
[t] Gl 1:1; Ti 1:3

[A] **19:37** Other mss read *your* [B] **20:4** Other mss add *to Asia* [C] **20:4** Other mss omit *son of Pyrrhus* [D] **20:7** Other mss read *the disciples* [E] **20:15** Other mss add *after staying at Trogyllium* [F] **20:22** Or *in the Spirit* [G] **20:24** Other mss add *with joy* [H] **20:26** Lit ·*clean*

of everyone's blood,[a] 27For I did not shrink
back from declaring to you the whole plan of
God.[b] 28Be on guard for yourselves and for all
the flock[c] that the Holy Spirit has appointed
you to as ·overseers,[d] to shepherd the church
of God,[A] which He purchased with His own
blood.[e] 29I know that after my departure savage wolves will come in among you, not sparing the flock. 30And men will rise up from
your own number with deviant doctrines
to lure the disciples into following them.[f]
31Therefore be on the alert, remembering
that night and day for three years I did not
stop warning each one of you with tears.[g]

32"And now[B] I commit you to God and to the
message of His grace,[h] which is able to build
you up and to give you an inheritance[i] among
all who are ·sanctified. 33I have not coveted
anyone's silver or gold or clothing.[j] 34You
yourselves know that these hands have provided for my needs and for those who were
with me.[k] 35In every way I've shown you that
by laboring like this, it is necessary to help
the weak and to keep in mind the words of
the Lord Jesus, for He said, 'It is more blessed
to give than to receive.'"

36After he said this, he knelt down and
prayed with all of them.[l] 37There was a great
deal of weeping by everyone. They embraced
Paul and kissed him, 38grieving most of all
over his statement that they would never see
his face again. Then they escorted him to the
ship.[m]

Warnings on the Journey to Jerusalem

21 After[n] we tore ourselves away from
them and set sail, we came by a direct
route to Cos, the next day to Rhodes, and from
there to Patara. 2Finding a ship crossing over
to Phoenicia, we boarded and set sail. 3After
we sighted Cyprus, leaving it on the left, we
sailed on to Syria and arrived at Tyre, because
the ship was to unload its cargo there. 4So we
found some disciples and stayed there seven
days. Through the Spirit they told Paul not to
go to Jerusalem.[o] 5When our days there were
over, we left to continue our journey, while
all of them, with their wives and children, escorted us out of the city. After kneeling down
on the beach to pray, 6we said good-bye to one
another. Then we boarded the ship, and they
returned home.

7When we completed our voyage from Tyre,
we reached Ptolemais, where we greeted the
·brothers and stayed with them one day.[p]
8The next day we left and came to Caesarea,
where we entered the house of Philip[q] the
evangelist,[r] who was one of the Seven, and
stayed with him. 9This man had four virgin
daughters who prophesied.[s]

10While we were staying there many days, a
prophet named Agabus came down from Judea. 11He came to us, took Paul's belt, tied his
own feet and hands, and said, "This is what
the Holy Spirit says: 'In this way the Jews in Jerusalem will bind the man who owns this belt
and deliver him into Gentile hands.'"[t] 12When
we heard this, both we and the local people
begged him not to go up to Jerusalem.

13Then Paul replied, "What are you doing,
weeping and breaking my heart? For I am
ready not only to be bound but also to die in
Jerusalem for the name of the Lord Jesus."[u]

14Since he would not be persuaded, we
stopped talking and simply said, "The Lord's
will be done!"[v]

Conflict over the Gentile Mission

15After these days we got ready and went
up to Jerusalem. 16Some of the disciples from
Caesarea also went with us and brought us to
Mnason, a Cypriot and an early disciple, with
whom we were to stay.[w]

17When we reached Jerusalem, the brothers
welcomed us gladly.[x] 18The following day Paul
went in with us to James, and all the elders
were present.[y] 19After greeting them, he related in detail what God did among the Gentiles through his ministry.[z]

20When they heard it, they glorified God
and said, "You see, brother, how many thousands of Jews there are who have believed, and
they are all zealous[aa] for the law. 21But they
have been told about you that you teach all
the Jews who are among the Gentiles to abandon Moses, by telling them not to circumcise
their children or to walk in our customs.[ab] 22So
what is to be done?[C] They will certainly hear

[a]**20:25-26** Ac 18:6; 20:38; 28:31
[b]**20:27** Lk 7:30; Ac 20:20; Eph 1:11
[c]**20:28** Lk 12:32; Jn 10:16; 1Co 9:7; 1Pt 5:2-3
[d]Php 1:1; 1Tm 3:2; Ti 1:7; 1Pt 2:25
[e]Eph 1:7,14; Heb 9:12; 1Pt 1:19; Rv 5:9
[f]**20:30** Ac 11:26; 1Tm 1:20; 1Jn 2:19
[g]**20:31** Ac 19:10; 20:19
[h]**20:32** Ac 14:23; Heb 13:9
[i]Ac 26:18; Eph 1:14; Col 1:12; 3:24; Heb 9:15; 1Pt 1:4
[j]**20:33** 1Sm 12:3; 1Co 9:12; 2Co 7:2; 11:9; 12:17
[k]**20:34** Ac 18:3; 19:22
[l]**20:36** Lk 22:41; Ac 7:60; 21:5
[m]**20:37-38** Ac 15:3; 20:25
[n]**21:1** Ac 16:10-11
[o]**21:4** Ac 11:26; 20:23; 21:11
[p]**21:7** Jn 21:23; Ac 12:20
[q]**21:8** Ac 6:5; 8:5
[r]Eph 4:11; 2Tm 4:5
[s]**21:9** Lk 2:36; Ac 2:7; 13:1; 1Co 11:5
[t]**21:11** 1Kg 22:11; Jr 13:1-11; Mt 20:19; Ac 20:23; 21:33
[u]**21:13** Ac 5:41; 9:16; 20:24
[v]**21:14** Mt 6:10; Lk 22:42
[w]**21:16** Ac 8:40; 21:3-4
[x]**21:17** Ac 15:4; 21:7
[y]**21:18** Ac 11:30; 12:17; 15:13
[z]**21:19** Ac 1:17; 14:27; Rm 15:18-19
[aa]**21:20** Ac 22:3; Rm 10:12; Gl 1:14
[ab]**21:21** Ac 6:14; 15:19-20; 21:28; 1Co 7:18

[A]**20:28** Other mss read *church of the Lord*; other mss read *church of the Lord and God* [B]**20:32** Other mss add *brothers,* [C]**21:22** Other mss add *A multitude has to come together, since*

that you've come. 23Therefore do what we tell
you: We have four men who have obligated
themselves with a vow. 24Take these men, purify yourself along with them, and pay for
them to get their heads shaved. Then everyone
will know that what they were told about you
amounts to nothing, but that you yourself are
also careful about observing the law.[a] 25With
regard to the Gentiles who have believed, we
have written a letter containing our decision
that[A] they should keep themselves from food
sacrificed to idols, from blood, from what is
strangled, and from sexual immorality."

The Riot in the Temple Complex

26Then the next day, Paul took the men,
having purified himself along with them, and
entered the temple, announcing the completion of the purification days when the offering for each of them would be made.[b] 27As the
seven days were about to end, the Jews from
•Asia saw him in the •temple complex, stirred
up the whole crowd, and seized him,[c] 28shout-
ing, "Men of Israel, help! This is the man who
teaches everyone everywhere against our
people, our law, and this place. What's more,
he also brought Greeks into the temple and
has profaned this holy place."[d] 29For they had
previously seen Trophimus the Ephesian in
the city with him, and they supposed that
Paul had brought him into the temple complex.[B,e]
30The whole city was stirred up, and the
people rushed together. They seized Paul,
dragged him out of the temple complex,
and at once the gates were shut.[f] 31As they
were trying to kill him, word went up to the
commander of the •regiment that all Jerusalem was in chaos. 32Taking along soldiers
and •centurions, he immediately ran down
to them. Seeing the commander and the soldiers, they stopped beating Paul. 33Then the
commander came up, took him into custody, and ordered him to be bound with two
chains.[g] He asked who he was and what he
had done. 34Some in the mob were shouting
one thing and some another. Since he was not
able to get reliable information because of
the uproar, he ordered him to be taken into
the barracks.[h] 35When Paul got to the steps, he
had to be carried by the soldiers because of
the mob's violence, 36for the mass of people
followed, yelling, "Take him away!"[i]

Paul's Defense before the Jerusalem Mob

37As he was about to be brought into the
barracks, Paul said to the commander, "Am I
allowed to say something to you?"
He replied, "Do you know Greek? 38Aren't
you the Egyptian who raised a rebellion some
time ago and led 4,000 Assassins[C,D] into the
wilderness?"[j]
39Paul said, "I am a Jewish man from Tarsus of Cilicia,[k] a citizen of an important city.[E]
Now I ask you, let me speak to the people."
40After he had given permission, Paul stood
on the steps and motioned with his hand to
the people. When there was a great hush, he
22 addressed them in the •Hebrew language:[l] 1"Brothers and fathers, listen
now to my defense before you." 2When they
heard that he was addressing them in the Hebrew language, they became even quieter.[m]
3He[n] continued, "I am a Jewish man, born in
Tarsus of Cilicia but brought up in this city[F]
at the feet of Gamaliel[o] and educated according to the strict view of our patriarchal law.
Being zealous for God, just as all of you are
today,[p] 4I persecuted this Way[q] to the death,
binding and putting both men and women
in jail,[r] 5as both the high priest and the whole
council of elders can testify about me. After
I received letters from them to the brothers,
I traveled to Damascus to bring those who
were prisoners there to be punished in Jerusalem.[s]

Paul's Testimony

6"As[t] I was traveling and near Damascus,
about noon an intense light from heaven suddenly flashed around me. 7I fell to the ground
and heard a voice saying to me, 'Saul, Saul,
why are you persecuting Me?'
8"I answered, 'Who are You, Lord?'
"He said to me, 'I am Jesus the •Nazarene,
the One you are persecuting!' 9Now those

[a]**21:24** Jn 11:55; Ac 18:18; 21:26; 24:18
[b]**21:26** Nm 6:13; Ac 24:18
[c]**21:27** Ac 24:18; 26:21
[d]**21:28** Mt 24:15; Ac 24:6
[e]**21:29** Ac 18:19; 20:4
[f]**21:30** 2Kg 11:15; Ac 16:19; 26:21
[g]**21:33** Ac 12:6; 20:23; 21:11; Eph 6:20; 2Tm 1:16; 2:9
[h]**21:34** Ac 19:32; 23:10
[i]**21:36** Lk 23:18; Jn 19:15; Ac 22:22
[j]**21:38** Mt 24:26; Ac 5:36
[k]**21:39** Ac 9:11; 22:3
[l]**21:40** Jn 5:2; Ac 12:17
[m]**22:1-2** Ac 7:2; 21:40
[n]**22:3-16** Ac 9:1-22; 26:9-18
[o]**22:3** Dt 33:3; Ac 5:34; 9:11; 21:39; 2Co 11:22; Php 3:5
[p]Ac 26:5; Rm 10:2; Php 3:6
[q]**22:4** Ac 9:2; 24:14,22
[r]Ac 8:3; 22:19-20; 26:10
[s]**22:5** Lk 22:66; Ac 13:26; 1Tm 4:14
[t]**22:6-11** Ac 9:3-8; 26:12-18

[A]**21:25** Other mss add *they should observe no such thing, except that* [B]**21:29** The inner temple court for Jewish men [C]**21:38** Lit *4,000 men of the Assassins* [D]**21:38** In Lat, the word *Sicarii* is similar to the Eng word "cut-throats." [E]**21:39** Lit *of no insignificant city* [F]**22:3** Probably Jerusalem, but others think Tarsus

who were with me saw the light,[A] but they did
not hear the voice of the One who was speaking to me.[a]
10"Then I said, 'What should I do, Lord?'
"And the Lord told me, 'Get up and go into
Damascus, and there you will be told about
everything that is assigned for you to do.'
11"Since I couldn't see because of the brightness of that light, I was led by the hand by
those who were with me, and came into Damascus.[b] 12Someone named Ananias, a devout man according to the law, having a good
reputation with all the Jews residing there,[c]
13came and stood by me and said, 'Brother
Saul, regain your sight.' And in that very hour
I looked up and saw him. 14Then he said, 'The
God of our fathers has appointed[d] you to
know His will, to see[e] the Righteous One,[f] and
to hear the sound of His voice.[B] 15For you will
be a witness for Him to all people of what you
have seen and heard.[g] 16And now, why delay?
Get up and be baptized, and wash away your
sins[h] by calling on His name.'[i]
17"After I came back to Jerusalem and was
praying in the ·temple complex, I went into
a visionary state[j] 18and saw Him telling me,
'Hurry and get out of Jerusalem quickly, because they will not accept your testimony
about Me!'
19"But I said, 'Lord, they know that in ·syna-
gogue after synagogue I had those who believed in You imprisoned and beaten.[k] 20And
when the blood of Your witness Stephen was
being shed, I was standing by and approving,[C]
and I guarded the clothes of those who killed
him.'[l]
21"Then He said to me, 'Go, because I will
send you far away to the Gentiles.'"[m]

Paul's Roman Protection

22They listened to him up to this word. Then
they raised their voices, shouting, "Wipe this
person off the earth — it's a disgrace for him
to live!"[n]
23As they were yelling and flinging aside
their robes and throwing dust into the air,[o]
24the commander ordered him to be brought
into the barracks, directing that he be examined with the scourge, so he could discover
the reason they were shouting against him
like this. 25As they stretched him out for the
lash, Paul said to the ·centurion standing by,
"Is it legal for you to scourge a man who is a
Roman citizen and is uncondemned?"[p]
26When the centurion heard this, he went
and reported to the commander, saying,
"What are you going to do? For this man is a
Roman citizen."
27The commander came and said to him,
"Tell me — are you a Roman citizen?"
"Yes," he said.
28The commander replied, "I bought this
citizenship for a large amount of money."
"But I was born a citizen," Paul said.
29Therefore, those who were about to examine him withdrew from him at once. The
commander too was alarmed when he realized Paul was a Roman citizen and he had
bound him.[q]

Paul before the Sanhedrin

30The next day, since he wanted to find out
exactly why Paul was being accused by the
Jews, he released him[D] and instructed the
·chief priests and all the ·Sanhedrin to convene.[r] Then he brought Paul down and placed
23 him before them. 1Paul looked intently at the ·Sanhedrin and said,
"Brothers, I have lived my life before God in
all good conscience[s] until this day." 2But the
high priest Ananias ordered those who were
standing next to him to strike him on the
mouth.[t] 3Then Paul said to him, "God is going
to strike you, you whitewashed wall! You are
sitting there judging me according to the law,
and in violation of the law are you ordering
me to be struck?"[u]
4And those standing nearby said, "Do you
dare revile God's high priest?"
5"I did not know, brothers, that he was the
high priest," replied Paul. "For it is written,
**You must not speak evil of a ruler of your
people.**"[E,v] 6When Paul realized that one
part of them were ·Sadducees and the other
part were ·Pharisees, he cried out in the Sanhedrin, "Brothers, I am a Pharisee, a son of
Pharisees![w] I am being judged because of
the hope of the resurrection of the dead!"[x]
7When he said this, a dispute broke out between the Pharisees and the Sadducees, and

[a]**22:9** Dn 10:7; Ac 9:7; 26:13
[b]**22:10-11** Ac 9:8; 16:30
[c]**22:12** Ac 9:10,17; 10:22
[d]**22:14** Ac 3:13; 9:15; 26:16
[e]1Co 9:1; 15:8
[f]Ac 3:14; 7:52
[g]**22:15** Ac 23:11; 26:16
[h]**22:16** Ac 2:38; 1Co 6:11; Heb 10:22
[i]Ac 9:14; Rm 10:13
[j]**22:17** Ac 9:26; 10:10
[k]**22:19** Mt 10:17; Ac 8:3; 22:4
[l]**22:20** Ac 7:58; 8:1; Rm 1:32
[m]**22:21** Ac 9:15; 13:46
[n]**22:22** Ac 21:36; 25:24
[o]**22:23** 2Sm 16:13; Ac 7:58
[p]**22:24-25** Ac 16:37; 21:34; 22:29
[q]**22:29** Ac 16:38; 21:33
[r]**22:30** Mt 5:22; Ac 23:3-8
[s]**23:1** Ac 24:16; 1Co 4:4; 1Tm 3:9; 2Tm 1:5; Heb 13:18; 1Pt 3:16
[t]**23:2** 1Kg 22:24; Jn 18:22; Ac 24:1
[u]**23:3** Lv 19:15; Dt 25:1-2; Mt 23:27; Jn 7:51
[v]**23:5** Ex 22:28; Ac 24:17
[w]**23:6** Ac 26:5; Php 3:5
[x]Ac 24:15,21; 26:6-8; 28:20

[A]**22:9** Other mss add *and were afraid* [B]**22:14** Lit *to hear a voice from His mouth* [C]**22:20** Other mss add *of his murder* [D]**22:30** Other mss add *from his chains* [E]**23:5** Ex 22:28

the assembly was divided. 8 For the Sadducees
say there is no resurrection,[a] and no angel or
spirit, but the Pharisees affirm them all.
9 The shouting grew loud, and some of the
·scribes of the Pharisees'[b] party got up and
argued vehemently: "We find nothing evil in
this man.[c] What if a spirit or an angel has spoken to him?"[A,d] 10 When the dispute became
violent, the commander feared that Paul
might be torn apart by them and ordered the
troops to go down, rescue him from them,
and bring him into the barracks.[e]

The Plot against Paul

11 The following night, the Lord stood by
him and said, "Have courage! For as you have
testified about Me in Jerusalem, so you must
also testify in Rome."[f]
12 When it was day, the Jews formed a conspiracy and bound themselves under a curse:
neither to eat nor to drink until they had
killed Paul.[g] 13 There were more than 40 who
had formed this plot. 14 These men went to the
·chief priests and elders and said, "We have
bound ourselves under a solemn curse that we
won't eat anything until we have killed Paul.
15 So now you, along with the Sanhedrin, make
a request to the commander that he bring him
down to you[B] as if you were going to investigate his case more thoroughly. However, before he gets near, we are ready to kill him."[h]
16 But the son of Paul's sister, hearing about
their ambush, came and entered the barracks
and reported it to Paul. 17 Then Paul called one
of the ·centurions and said, "Take this young
man to the commander, because he has something to report to him."
18 So he took him, brought him to the commander, and said, "The prisoner Paul called
me and asked me to bring this young man to
you, because he has something to tell you."
19 Then the commander took him by the
hand, led him aside, and inquired privately,
"What is it you have to report to me?"
20 "The Jews," he said, "have agreed to ask
you to bring Paul down to the Sanhedrin tomorrow, as though they are going to hold a
somewhat more careful inquiry about him.
21 Don't let them persuade you, because there
are more than 40 of them arranging to ambush him, men who have bound themselves
under a curse not to eat or drink until they
kill him. Now they are ready, waiting for a
commitment from you."[i]
22 So the commander dismissed the young
man and instructed him, "Don't tell anyone
that you have informed me about this."

To Caesarea by Night

23 He summoned two of his centurions and
said, "Get 200 soldiers ready with 70 cavalry
and 200 spearmen to go to Caesarea at nine
tonight.[C,j] 24 Also provide mounts so they can
put Paul on them and bring him safely to Felix the governor."
25 He wrote a letter of this kind:
26 Claudius Lysias,
To the most excellent governor Felix:
Greetings.[k]
27 When this man had been seized by the
Jews and was about to be killed by them, I
arrived with my troops and rescued him
because I learned that he is a Roman citizen.[l] 28 Wanting to know the charge they
were accusing him of, I brought him
down before their Sanhedrin. 29 I found
out that the accusations were about disputed matters in their law,[m] and that
there was no charge that merited death
or chains.[n] 30 When I was informed that
there was a plot against the man,[D,o] I sent
him to you right away. I also ordered his
accusers[p] to state their case against him
in your presence.[E]

31 Therefore, the soldiers took Paul during
the night and brought him to Antipatris as
they were ordered. 32 The next day, they returned to the barracks, allowing the cavalry
to go on with him. 33 When these men entered Caesarea and delivered the letter to the
governor, they also presented Paul to him.[q]
34 After he[F] read it, he asked what province he
was from. So when he learned he was from
Cilicia,[r] 35 he said, "I will give you a hearing
whenever your accusers get here too." And
he ordered that he be kept under guard in
·Herod's ·palace.[s]

[a] **23:8** Mt 22:23; Mk 12:18; Lk 20:27
[b] **23:9** Mk 2:16; Lk 5:30
[c] Ac 23:29; 25:25; 26:31
[d] Jn 12:29; Ac 22:7,17-18
[e] **23:10** Ac 21:34; 23:16,32
[f] **23:11** Ac 18:9; 19:21; 27:23
[g] **23:12** Ac 23:14,21,30; 25:3
[h] **23:15** Ac 22:30; 23:1
[i] **23:21** Lk 11:54; Ac 23:12,14
[j] **23:23** Ac 8:40; 23:33
[k] **23:26** Lk 1:3; Ac 15:23; 24:3; 26:25
[l] **23:27** Ac 21:32-33; 22:25-29
[m] **23:29** Ac 18:15; 25:19
[n] Ac 25:25; 26:31
[o] **23:30** Ac 9:24; 23:12,20
[p] Ac 24:19; 25:16
[q] **23:33** Ac 8:40; 23:23-24,26
[r] **23:34** Ac 6:9; 21:39; 25:1
[s] **23:35** Mt 27:27; Ac 24:27; 25:16

[A] **23:9** Other mss add *Let us not fight God.* [B] **23:15** Other mss add *tomorrow*
[C] **23:23** Lit *at the third hour tonight* [D] **23:30** Other mss add *by the Jews*
[E] **23:30** Other mss add *Farewell* [F] **23:34** Other mss read *the governor*

The Accusation against Paul

24 After five days Ananias the high priest came down with some elders and a lawyer[A] named Tertullus. These men presented their case against Paul to the governor.[a] 2 When he was called in, Tertullus began to accuse him and said: "Since we enjoy great peace because of you, and reforms are taking place for the benefit of this nation by your foresight, 3 we acknowledge this in every way and everywhere, most excellent[b] Felix, with utmost gratitude. 4 However, so that I will not burden you any further, I beg you in your graciousness to give us a brief hearing. 5 For we have found this man to be a plague,[c] an agitator[d] among all the Jews throughout the Roman world, and a ringleader of the sect of the ·Nazarenes! 6 He even tried to desecrate the temple, so we apprehended him [and wanted to judge him according to our law. 7 But Lysias the commander came and took him from our hands with great force, 8 commanding his accusers to come to you.][B] By examining him yourself you will be able to discern all these things we are accusing him of." 9 The Jews also joined in the attack, alleging that these things were so.

Paul's Defense before Felix

10 When the governor motioned to him to speak, Paul replied: "Because I know you have been a judge of this nation for many years, I am glad to offer my defense in what concerns me.[e] 11 You are able to determine that it is no more than 12 days since I went up to worship in Jerusalem.[f] 12 They didn't find me disputing with anyone or causing a disturbance among the crowd, either in the ·temple complex or in the ·synagogues or anywhere in the city.[g] 13 Neither can they provide evidence to you of what they now bring against me. 14 But I confess this to you: I worship my fathers' God according to the Way,[h] which they call a sect, believing all the things that are written in the Law and in the Prophets.[i] 15 And I have a hope in God, which these men themselves also accept, that there is going to be a resurrection,[C,j] both of the righteous and the unrighteous.[k] 16 I always do my best to have a clear conscience[l] toward God and men. 17 After many years, I came to bring charitable gifts and offerings to my nation,[m] 18 and while I was doing this, some Jews from ·Asia found me ritually purified in the temple, without a crowd and without any uproar.[n] 19 It is they who ought to be here before you to bring charges, if they have anything against me. 20 Either let these men here state what wrongdoing they found in me when I stood before the ·Sanhedrin, 21 or about this one statement I cried out while standing among them, 'Today I am being judged before you concerning the resurrection of the dead.'"

The Verdict Postponed

22 Since Felix was accurately informed about the Way,[o] he adjourned the hearing, saying, "When Lysias the commander comes down, I will decide your case." 23 He ordered that the ·centurion keep Paul[D] under guard, though he could have some freedom, and that he should not prevent any of his friends from serving[E] him.[p]

24 After some days, when Felix came with his wife Drusilla, who was Jewish, he sent for Paul and listened to him on the subject of faith in Christ Jesus. 25 Now as he spoke about righteousness, self-control, and the judgment to come,[q] Felix became afraid and replied, "Leave for now, but when I find time I'll call for you." 26 At the same time he was also hoping that money would be given to him by Paul.[F] For this reason he sent for him quite often and conversed with him.

27 After two years had passed, Felix received a successor, Porcius Festus,[r] and because he wished to do a favor for the Jews,[s] Felix left Paul in prison.[t]

Appeal to Caesar

25 Three days after Festus arrived in the province, he went up to Jerusalem from Caesarea.[u] 2 Then the ·chief priests and the leaders of the Jews presented their case against Paul to him; and they appealed,[v] 3 asking him to do them a favor against Paul,[G] that

[a] **24:1** Ac 21:27; 23:2,24,30
[b] **24:3** Lk 1:3; Ac 23:26; 26:25
[c] **24:5** Ac 16:20; 17:6
[d] Ac 21:28; 26:5; 28:22
[e] **24:9-10** Ac 23:24; 1Th 2:16
[f] **24:11** Ac 21:27; 24:1
[g] **24:12** Ac 25:8; 28:17
[h] **24:14** Ac 9:2; 22:4; 24:22
[i] Ac 3:13; 26:22; 28:23
[j] **24:15** Ac 23:6; 28:20
[k] Dn 12:2; Jn 5:28-29
[l] **24:16** Ac 23:1; 1Co 4:4; 1Tm 3:9; 2Tm 1:5; Heb 13:18; 1Pt 3:16
[m] **24:17** Ac 11:29; Rm 15:25-28; 1Co 16:1-3; 2Co 8:1-4; Gl 2:10
[n] **24:18** Ac 21:26-27; 26:21
[o] **24:22** Ac 9:2; 22:4; 24:14
[p] **24:23** Ac 23:35; 27:3; 28:16
[q] **24:25** Gl 5:23; Ti 2:12; 2Pt 1:6
[r] **24:27** Ac 25:1,4,9; 26:24
[s] Ac 12:3; 25:9
[t] Ac 23:35; 25:14
[u] **25:1** Ac 8:40; 23:34
[v] **25:2** Ac 24:1; 25:15

A **24:1** In Gk, the word *rhetor* is similar to the Eng "rhetoric." In this situation, a rhetorician who was skilled in public speaking in the Gk language was needed.
B **24:6-8** Other mss omit bracketed text
C **24:15** Other mss add *of the dead*
D **24:23** Lit *him*
E **24:23** Other mss add *or visiting*
F **24:26** Other mss add *so that he might release him*
G **25:3** Lit *asking a favor against him*

he might summon him to Jerusalem. They
were preparing an ambush along the road
to kill him. 4However, Festus answered that
Paul should be kept at Caesarea, and that
he himself was about to go there shortly.[a]
5"Therefore," he said, "let the men of authority among you go down with me and accuse
him, if there is any wrong in this man."
6When he had spent not more than eight
or 10 days among them, he went down to
Caesarea. The next day, seated at the judge's
bench, he commanded Paul to be brought
in.[b] 7When he arrived, the Jews who had come
down from Jerusalem stood around him and
brought many serious charges that they were
not able to prove,[c] 8while Paul made the defense that, "Neither against the Jewish law,[d]
nor against the temple, nor against Caesar
have I sinned at all."
9Then Festus, wanting to do a favor for the
Jews,[e] replied to Paul, "Are you willing to go
up to Jerusalem, there to be tried before me
on these charges?"
10But Paul said: "I am standing at Caesar's
tribunal, where I ought to be tried. I have
done no wrong to the Jews, as even you can
see very well. 11If then I am doing wrong, or
have done anything deserving of death, I do
not refuse to die, but if there is nothing to
what these men accuse me of, no one can give
me up to them. I appeal to Caesar!"[f]
12After Festus conferred with his council,
he replied, "You have appealed to Caesar; to
Caesar you will go!"

King Agrippa and Bernice Visit Festus

13After some days had passed, King Agrippa[A]
and Bernice arrived in Caesarea and paid a
courtesy call on Festus. 14Since they stayed
there many days, Festus presented Paul's case
to the king, saying, "There's a man who was
left as a prisoner by Felix. 15When I was in Jerusalem, the chief priests and the elders of
the Jews presented their case and asked for
a judgment against him.[g] 16I answered them
that it's not the Romans' custom to give any
man up[B] before the accused confronts the
accusers face to face and has an opportunity
to give a defense concerning the charges.[h]
17Therefore, when they had assembled here, I
did not delay. The next day I sat at the judge's
bench and ordered the man to be brought in.
18Concerning him, the accusers stood up and
brought no charge of the sort I was expecting. 19Instead they had some disagreements[i]
with him about their own religion and about
a certain Jesus, a dead man Paul claimed to
be alive. 20Since I was at a loss in a dispute
over such things, I asked him if he wished to
go to Jerusalem and be tried there concerning these matters. 21But when Paul appealed
to be held for trial by the Emperor, I ordered
him to be kept in custody until I could send
him to Caesar."
22Then Agrippa said to Festus, "I would like
to hear the man myself."
"Tomorrow you will hear him," he replied.[j]

Paul before Agrippa

23So the next day, Agrippa and Bernice[k]
came with great pomp and entered the au-
ditorium with the commanders and prominent men of the city. When Festus gave the
command, Paul was brought in. 24Then Festus said: "King Agrippa and all men present
with us, you see this man about whom the
whole Jewish community has appealed to
me, both in Jerusalem and here, shouting
that he should not live any longer.[l] 25Now I realized that he had not done anything deserving of death, but when he himself appealed
to the Emperor, I decided to send him.[m] 26I
have nothing definite to write to my lord
about him. Therefore, I have brought him
before all of you, and especially before you,
King Agrippa, so that after this examination
is over, I may have something to write. 27For it
seems unreasonable to me to send a prisoner
and not to indicate the charges against him."

Paul's Defense before Agrippa

26 Agrippa said to Paul, "It is permitted
for you to speak for yourself."
Then Paul stretched out his hand and began his defense: 2"I consider myself fortunate, King Agrippa, that today I am going to
make a defense before you about everything
I am accused of by the Jews, 3especially since
you are an expert in all the Jewish customs

[a]**25:3-4** Ac 9:24; 24:23 [b]**25:6** Mt 27:19; Ac 25:10,17 [c]**25:7** Mk 15:3; Lk 23:2,10; Ac 24:5,13 [d]**25:8** Ac 6:13; 24:12; 28:17 [e]**25:9** Ac 24:27; 25:20 [f]**25:11** Ac 25:21,25; 26:32; 28:19 [g]**25:14-15** Ac 24:27; 25:2 [h]**25:16** Ac 23:30; 24:4-5 [i]**25:19** Ac 18:15; 23:29 [j]**25:20-22** Ac 9:15; 25:9,11 [k]**25:23** Ac 25:13; 26:30 [l]**25:24** Ac 22:22; 25:2,7 [m]**25:25** Ac 23:29; 25:11-12

[A]**25:13** Herod Agrippa II ruled Palestine A.D. 52–ca 95. [B]**25:16** Other mss add *to destruction*

and controversies. Therefore I beg you to listen to me patiently.

4 "All the Jews know my way of life from my youth, which was spent from the beginning among my own nation and in Jerusalem.[a] 5 They had previously known me for quite some time, if they were willing to testify, that according to the strictest party of our religion I lived as a ·Pharisee.[b] 6 And now I stand on trial for the hope[c] of the promise[d] made by God to our fathers, 7 the promise our 12 tribes hope to attain as they earnestly serve Him night and day. King Agrippa, I am being accused by the Jews because of this hope.[e] 8 Why is it considered incredible by any of you that God raises the dead? 9 In fact, I myself supposed it was necessary to do many things in opposition to the name of Jesus the ·Nazarene.[f] 10 I actually did this in Jerusalem, and I locked up many of the ·saints in prison, since I had received authority for that from the ·chief priests. When they were put to death, I cast my vote against them.[g] 11 In all the ·synagogues I often tried to make them blaspheme by punishing them.[h] I even pursued them to foreign cities since I was greatly enraged at them.

Paul's Account of His Conversion and Commission

12 "I was traveling to Damascus under[i] these circumstances with authority and a commission from the chief priests. 13 King Agrippa, while on the road at midday, I saw a light from heaven brighter than the sun, shining around me and those traveling with me. 14 We all fell to the ground, and I heard a voice speaking to me in the ·Hebrew language, 'Saul, Saul, why are you persecuting Me? It is hard for you to kick against the goads.'[A,j]

15 "Then I said, 'Who are You, Lord?'

"And the Lord replied: 'I am Jesus, the One you are persecuting. 16 But get up and stand on your feet. For I have appeared to you for this purpose, to appoint you as a servant and a witness of what you have seen[B] and of what I will reveal to you.[k] 17 I will rescue you from the people and from the Gentiles. I now send you to them[l] 18 to open their eyes[m] so they may turn from darkness to light and from the power of Satan to God, that by faith in Me they may receive forgiveness of sins and a share among those who are ·sanctified.'[n]

19 "Therefore, King Agrippa, I was not disobedient to the heavenly vision. 20 Instead, I preached to those in Damascus first, and to those in Jerusalem and in all the region of Judea, and to the Gentiles, that they should repent and turn to God, and do works worthy of repentance.[o] 21 For this reason the Jews seized me in the ·temple complex and were trying to kill me. 22 To this very day, I have obtained help that comes from God, and I stand and testify to both small and great, saying nothing else than what the prophets and Moses said would take place[p] — 23 that the ·Messiah must suffer, and that as the first to rise from the dead, He would proclaim light to our people and to the Gentiles."[q]

Not Quite Persuaded

24 As he was making his defense this way, Festus exclaimed in a loud voice, "You're out of your mind,[r] Paul! Too much study is driving you mad!"

25 But Paul replied, "I'm not out of my mind, most excellent Festus. On the contrary, I'm speaking words of truth and good judgment.[s] 26 For the king knows about these matters. It is to him I am actually speaking boldly. For I am convinced that none of these things escapes his notice, since this was not done in a corner. 27 King Agrippa, do you believe the prophets? I know you believe."

28 Then Agrippa said to Paul, "Are you going to persuade me to become a Christian so easily?"

29 "I wish before God," replied Paul, "that whether easily or with difficulty, not only you but all who listen to me today might become as I am — except for these chains."[t]

30 So the king, the governor, Bernice, and those sitting with them got up, 31 and when they had left they talked with each other and said, "This man is doing nothing that deserves death or chains."[u]

32 Then Agrippa said to Festus, "This man could have been released if he had not appealed to Caesar."[v]

[a] **26:3-4** Ac 6:14; 25:19; Gl 1:13
[b] **26:5** Ac 22:3; 23:6; Php 3:5
[c] **26:6** Ac 24:15; 28:20
[d] Ac 13:32; Rm 15:8
[e] **26:7** Php 3:11; 1Th 3:10; 1Tm 5:5; Jms 1:1
[f] **26:9** Jn 16:2; 1Tm 1:13
[g] **26:10** Ac 8:3; 9:13-14,21; 22:5,20
[h] **26:11** Ac 25:21,25; 26:32; 28:19
[i] **26:12-18** Ac 9:3-8; 22:6-11
[j] **26:14** Ac 9:7; 21:40
[k] **26:16** Ezk 2:1; Dn 10:11; Ac 22:14-15
[l] **26:17** 1Ch 16:35; Jr 1:8,19; Ac 9:15
[m] **26:18** Is 35:5; 42:7
[n] Ac 20:32; Eph 5:8; Col 1:13; 1Pt 2:9
[o] **26:20** Mt 3:8; Lk 3:8; Ac 9:19-20,22,26-29; 13:46; 22:17-20
[p] **26:22** Lk 24:27; Ac 10:43; 24:14
[q] **26:23** Lk 24:26; 1Co 15:20,23; Col 1:18; Rv 1:5
[r] **26:24** 2Kg 9:11; Jn 10:20; 1Co 1:23; 2:14; 4:10
[s] **26:25** Ac 23:26; 24:3
[t] **26:28-29** Ac 11:26; 21:33; 1Co 7:7
[u] **26:30-31** Ac 23:9,29; 25:23
[v] **26:32** Ac 25:11; 28:18

[A] **26:14** Sharp sticks used to prod animals, such as oxen in plowing [B] **26:16** Other mss read *things in which you have seen Me*

Sailing for Rome

27 When it was decided that we were to sail to Italy, they handed over Paul and some other prisoners to a ·centurion named Julius, of the Imperial ·Regiment.[a] 2 So when we had boarded a ship of Adramyttium, we put to sea, intending to sail to ports along the coast of ·Asia. Aristarchus, a Macedonian of Thessalonica, was with us.[b] 3 The next day we put in at Sidon, and Julius treated Paul kindly and allowed him to go to his friends to receive their care.[c] 4 When we had put out to sea from there, we sailed along the northern coast[A] of Cyprus because the winds were against us. 5 After sailing through the open sea off Cilicia and Pamphylia, we reached Myra in Lycia.[d] 6 There the centurion found an Alexandrian ship sailing for Italy and put us on board. 7 Sailing slowly for many days, we came with difficulty as far as Cnidus. Since the wind did not allow us to approach it, we sailed along the south side[A] of Crete off Salmone. 8 With yet more difficulty we sailed along the coast and came to a place called Fair Havens near the city of Lasea.

Paul's Advice Ignored

9 By now much time had passed, and the voyage was already dangerous. Since the Fast[B,e] was already over, Paul gave his advice 10 and told them, "Men, I can see that this voyage is headed toward damage and heavy loss, not only of the cargo and the ship but also of our lives." 11 But the centurion paid attention to the captain and the owner of the ship rather than to what Paul said.[f] 12 Since the harbor was unsuitable to winter in, the majority decided to set sail from there, hoping somehow to reach Phoenix, a harbor on Crete[g] open to the southwest and northwest, and to winter there.

Storm-Tossed Ship

13 When a gentle south wind sprang up, they thought they had achieved their purpose. They weighed anchor and sailed along the shore of Crete. 14 But not long afterward, a fierce wind called the "northeaster"[C] rushed down from the island. 15 Since the ship was caught and was unable to head into the wind, we gave way to it and were driven along. 16 After running under the shelter of a little island called Cauda,[D] we were barely able to get control of the skiff. 17 After hoisting it up, they used ropes and tackle and girded the ship. Then, fearing they would run aground on the Syrtis,[E] they lowered the drift-anchor, and in this way they were driven along. 18 Because we were being severely battered by the storm, they began to jettison the cargo the next day.[h] 19 On the third day, they threw the ship's gear overboard with their own hands.

20 For many days neither sun nor stars appeared, and the severe storm kept raging. Finally all hope that we would be saved was disappearing. 21 Since many were going without food, Paul stood up among them and said, "You men should have followed my advice not to sail from Crete and sustain this damage and loss. 22 Now I urge you to take courage, because there will be no loss of any of your lives, but only of the ship. 23 For this night an angel of the God I belong to and serve stood by me,[i] 24 and said, 'Don't be afraid, Paul. You must stand before Caesar. And, look! God has graciously given you all those who are sailing with you.' 25 Therefore, take courage, men, because I believe God that it will be just the way it was told to me.[j] 26 However, we must run aground on a certain island."[k]

27 When the fourteenth night came, we were drifting in the Adriatic Sea,[F] and in the middle of the night the sailors thought they were approaching land.[G] 28 They took a sounding and found it to be 120 feet[H] deep; when they had sailed a little farther and sounded again, they found it to be 90 feet[I] deep. 29 Then, fearing we might run aground in some rocky place, they dropped four anchors from the stern and prayed for daylight to come.

30 Some sailors tried to escape from the ship; they had let down the skiff into the sea, pretending that they were going to put out anchors from the bow. 31 Paul said to the centurion and the soldiers, "Unless these men stay in the ship, you cannot be saved." 32 Then the soldiers cut the ropes holding the skiff and let it drop away.

[a] 27:1 Ac 10:1; 16:10; 25:12,25
[b] 27:2 Ac 17:1; 19:29
[c] 27:3 Ac 24:23; 27:43; 28:16
[d] 27:5 Ac 6:9; 13:13
[e] 27:9 Lv 16:29-31; 23:27-29; Nm 29:7
[f] 27:10-11 Ac 27:21; Rv 18:17
[g] 27:12 Ac 2:11; Ti 1:5
[h] 27:18 Jnh 1:5; Ac 27:38
[i] 27:23 Dn 6:16; Ac 18:9; 23:11; Rm 1:9; 2Tm 4:17
[j] 27:25 Ac 27:22,36; Rm 4:20-21
[k] 27:26 Ac 27:17,29; 28:1

[A] 27:4,7 Lit *sailed under the lee* [B] 27:9 The Day of Atonement [C] 27:14 Lit *Euraquilo*, a violent northeast wind [D] 27:16 Or *Clauda* [E] 27:17 = sandbanks or sandbars near North Africa [F] 27:27 Part of the northern Mediterranean Sea; not the modern Adriatic Sea east of Italy [G] 27:27 Lit *thought there was land approaching them* [H] 27:28 Lit *20 fathoms* [I] 27:28 Lit *15 fathoms*

33 When it was about daylight, Paul urged
them all to take food, saying, "Today is the
fourteenth day that you have been waiting
and going without food, having eaten nothing. 34 Therefore I urge you to take some food.
For this has to do with your survival, since
none of you will lose a hair from your head."[a]
35 After he said these things and had taken
some bread, he gave thanks to God in the
presence of all of them, and when he broke
it, he began to eat.[b] 36 They all became encouraged and took food themselves. 37 In all there
were 276 of us on the ship.[c] 38 When they had
eaten enough, they began to lighten the ship
by throwing the grain overboard into the sea.

Shipwreck

39 When daylight came, they did not recognize the land but sighted a bay with a beach.
They planned to run the ship ashore if they
could.[d] 40 After casting off the anchors, they
left them in the sea, at the same time loosen-
ing the ropes that held the rudders. Then they
hoisted the foresail to the wind and headed
for the beach. 41 But they struck a sandbar and
ran the ship aground. The bow jammed fast
and remained immovable, while the stern began to break up by the pounding of the waves.
42 The soldiers' plan was to kill the prisoners
so that no one could swim away and escape.
43 But the centurion kept them from carrying out their plan because he wanted to save
Paul, so he ordered those who could swim to
jump overboard first and get to land. 44 The
rest were to follow, some on planks and some
on debris from the ship. In this way, everyone
safely reached the shore.[e]

Malta's Hospitality

28 Once ashore, we[f] then learned that
the island was called Malta.[g] 2 The local people[h] showed us extraordinary kindness, for they lit a fire and took us all in,
since it was raining and cold. 3 As Paul gathered a bundle of brushwood and put it on
the fire, a viper came out because of the heat
and fastened itself to his hand. 4 When the
local people saw the creature hanging from
his hand, they said to one another, "This
man is probably a murderer, and though he
has escaped the sea, Justice[A] does not allow
him to live!"[i] 5 However, he shook the creature off into the fire and suffered no harm.[j]
6 They expected that he would swell up or
suddenly drop dead. But after they waited a
long time and saw nothing unusual happen
to him, they changed their minds and said
he was a god.[k]

Ministry in Malta

7 Now in the area around that place was
an estate belonging to the leading man of
the island, named Publius, who welcomed
us and entertained us hospitably for three
days. 8 Publius's father was in bed suffering
from fever and dysentery. Paul went to him,
and praying and laying his hands on him, he
healed him.[l] 9 After this, the rest of those on
the island who had diseases also came and
were cured. 10 So they heaped many honors
on us, and when we sailed, they gave us what
we needed.

Rome at Last

11 After three months we set sail in an Alexandrian ship that had wintered at the island,
with the Twin Brothers[B] as its figurehead.
12 Putting in at Syracuse, we stayed three days.
13 From there, after making a circuit along the
coast,[C] we reached Rhegium. After one day a
south wind sprang up, and the second day we
came to Puteoli. 14 There we found believers[D,m]
and were invited to stay with them for seven
days.

And so we came to Rome. 15 Now the believers[D] from there had heard the news about us
and had come to meet us as far as the Forum
of Appius and the Three Taverns. When Paul
saw them, he thanked God and took courage.
16 When we entered Rome,[E] Paul was permitted to stay by himself with the soldier who
guarded him.[n]

Paul's First Interview with Roman Jews

17 After three days he called together the
leaders of the Jews. When they had gathered he said to them: "Brothers, although I
have done nothing against our people or the

[a] **27:34** 1Kg 1:52; Mt 10:30; Lk 21:18
[b] **27:35** Mt 14:19; 15:36
[c] **27:37** Ac 2:41; 7:14; Rm 13:1; 1Pt 3:20
[d] **27:38-39** Ac 27:18; 28:1
[e] **27:41-44** Ac 12:19; 27:3,22; 2Co 11:25
[f] **28:1** Ac 16:10; 27:1
[g] Ac 27:26,39
[h] **28:2** Rm 1:14; 1Co 14:11; Col 3:11
[i] **28:4** Lk 13:2,4; Jn 9:2
[j] **28:5** Mk 16:18; Lk 10:19
[k] **28:6** Ac 8:10; 14:11
[l] **28:8** Ac 9:40; Jms 5:14-15
[m] **28:14** Jn 21:23; Ac 1:16
[n] **28:16** Ac 24:23; 27:3

[A] **28:4** Gk *Dike*, a goddess of justice [B] **28:11** Gk *Dioscuri*, twin sons of Zeus [C] **28:13** Other mss read *From there, casting off,* [D] **28:14,15** Lit *brothers* [E] **28:16** Other mss add *the centurion turned the prisoners over to the military commander; but*

customs of our ancestors, I was delivered as
a prisoner from Jerusalem into the hands of
the Romans.[a] 18After they examined me, they
wanted to release me, since I had not committed a capital offense.[b] 19Because the Jews
objected, I was compelled to appeal to Caesar;[c] it was not as though I had any accusation against my nation. 20For this reason I've
asked to see you and speak to you. In fact, it
is for the hope of Israel that I'm wearing this
chain."[d]

21Then they said to him, "We haven't received any letters about you from Judea.
None of the brothers has come and reported
or spoken anything evil about you. 22But we
would like to hear from you what you think.
For concerning this sect, we are aware that it
is spoken against everywhere."[e]

The Response to Paul's Message

23After arranging a day with him, many
came to him at his lodging. From dawn to
dusk he expounded and witnessed about
the kingdom of God. He tried to persuade
them concerning Jesus from both the Law of
Moses and the Prophets.[f] 24Some were persuaded by what he said, but others did not
believe.[g]

25Disagreeing among themselves, they began to leave after Paul made one statement:
"The Holy Spirit correctly spoke through the
prophet Isaiah to your[A] ancestors 26when He
said,

Go to these people and say:
You will listen and listen,
yet never understand;
and you will look and look,
yet never perceive.
27 **For the hearts of these people**
have grown callous,
their ears are hard of hearing,
and they have shut their eyes;
otherwise they might see
with their eyes
and hear with their ears,
understand with their heart,
and be converted,
and I would heal them.[B,h]

28Therefore, let it be known to you that this
saving work of God has been sent to the Gentiles; they will listen!"[i] [29After he said these
things, the Jews departed, while engaging in a
prolonged debate among themselves.][C]

Paul's Ministry Unhindered

30Then he stayed two whole years in his
own rented house. And he welcomed all who
visited him, 31proclaiming the kingdom of
God[j] and teaching the things concerning
the Lord Jesus Christ with full boldness[k] and
without hindrance.

[a]**28:17** Ac 6:14; 25:8
[b]**28:18** Ac 22:24; 23:29; 26:31
[c]**28:19** Ac 25:11; 26:32
[d]**28:20** Ac 21:33; 26:6-7,29; Eph 6:20; 2Tm 1:16
[e]**28:22** Lk 2:34; Ac 24:5; 1Pt 2:12; 4:14
[f]**28:23** Ac 8:35; 17:3; 19:8; 26:22; Phm 22
[g]**28:24** Ac 14:4; 19:9
[h]**28:26-27** Ps 119:70; Is 6:9-10; Mt 13:14-15; Mk 4:12; Lk 8:10; Jn 12:40; Rm 11:8
[i]**28:28** Lk 2:30; Ac 13:26,46; Rm 11:11
[j]**28:31** Mt 4:23; Ac 20:25; 28:23
[k]Ac 4:29,31; 2Tm 2:9

[A]**28:25** Other mss read *our* [B]**28:26-27** Is 6:9-10 [C]**28:29** Other mss omit bracketed text

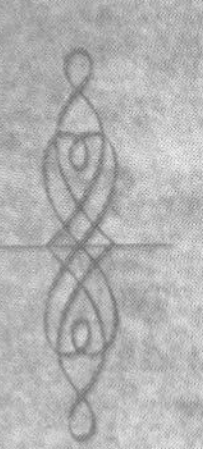

AUTHOR: Paul (Saul of Tarsus)

DATE: Written in A.D. 57 from Corinth during Paul's third missionary journey

Jesus' life, death, and resurrection shocked God's covenant people—faithful Jews—and proved such a confounding paradox to the Gentiles that someone needed to provide an explanation. God chose a Pharisee named Saul to do it. First, Saul (later Paul) must become a follower of Jesus (see Ac 9). Then he must apply his considerable intelligence and immense heart to the questions roiling on both sides of his world, among the religious elites—he was one himself—and among the self-infatuated secularists—another world he could partially identify with through his Roman citizenship. The Epistle to the Romans is the result. God's mission to the world becomes clearer and more compelling in Paul's account of the significance of sin, grace, and the law.

ROMANS

The Epistle to the Romans has three parts. Section 1 (Rm 1–8) explains the horrific consequences of human disregard for God. Paul does not exclude himself from this mess, as if he alone was enlightened. In one of Paul's most passionate paragraphs, he refers to his own situation as wretched, totally bottom of the barrel (chap. 7). This section concludes with stirring promises embraced by generations of Christians: nothing can separate us from the love of God in Christ the Lord (chap. 8). If this single chapter of the Bible was all that was known of God's work in the world, it would be more than enough to fuel lives with hope, purpose, and devotion to God.

The second part of Romans (9:11) spotlights God's mission among the chosen people Israel. Clearly the mission of God is to all nations. In the days of Moses, descendants of Jacob knew they had been singled out for a special purpose. Since then, a robust set of laws, teachings, and rituals had kept the worship of Yahweh alive, even if at low ebb from time to time. What of all that now? Paul insists that God still loves the children of Jacob and wants their love and worship, now as always. But for Paul, nothing is academic. He so wants his Israelite brothers to believe the good news of Christ that He offers to take God's judgment on Himself.

The third section of Romans (12:16) is about service. In the light of grace, sin's power is broken forever, and the living Christ enables our steadfast service to God. Here as before, Paul's heart and pen are stirred as he contemplates the change this Gospel brings. "Be transformed," he proclaims in Romans 12:2. God's mercy brings such freedom, such a future, that our best response is to eagerly accept this grace and live by the power of His Spirit in the pleasure of His holiness. Days of self-absorption are over; sincere love for others is reasonable. More than reasonable, it's delightful, because it is fueled by joy, patience, zeal, and steadfastness. This is God's new way of life.

Here is your part in God's mission: live as one transformed. God is with you. You are "more than victorious" (8:37). Go now, Paul urges. You are the missionaries of God. Tell and show everyone, for God's glory.

God's Good News for Rome

1 Paul, a ·slave of Christ Jesus, called as an apostle[A,a] and singled out[b] for God's good news[c] — 2 which He promised long ago[d] through His prophets[e] in the Holy Scriptures — 3 concerning His Son, Jesus Christ our Lord, who was a descendant of David[B,f] according to the flesh[g] 4 and who has been declared to be the powerful[h] Son of God[i] by the resurrection from the dead according to the Spirit of holiness.[C] 5 We have received grace and apostleship[j] through Him to bring about[D] the obedience[k] of faith[E] among all the nations,[F,l] on behalf of His name, 6 including yourselves who also belong to Jesus Christ by calling:[m]

7 To all who are in Rome, loved by God,[n] called[o] as ·saints.[p]

Grace to you and peace from God our Father and the Lord Jesus Christ.

Paul's Desire to Visit Rome

8 First, I thank my God through Jesus Christ for all of you because the news of your faith[G] is being reported in all the world.[q] 9 For God, whom I serve with my spirit[r] in telling the good news about His Son, is my witness[s] that I constantly mention you,[t] 10 always asking in my prayers that if it is somehow in God's will, I may now at last succeed in coming to you.[u] 11 For I want very much to see you,[v] so I may impart to you some spiritual gift to strengthen you, 12 that is, to be mutually encouraged by each other's faith, both yours and mine.

13 Now I want you to know,[H,w] ·brothers, that I often planned to come to you (but was prevented until now[x]) in order that I might have a fruitful ministry[I] among you,[y] just as among the rest of the Gentiles. 14 I am obligated both to Greeks and barbarians,[J,z] both to the wise and the foolish. 15 So I am eager to preach the good news[aa] to you also who are in Rome.

The Righteous Will Live by Faith

16 For I am not ashamed of the gospel,[K,ab] because it is God's power for salvation[ac] to everyone who believes, first to the Jew,[ad] and also to the Greek.[ae] 17 For in it God's righteousness is revealed from faith to faith,[L,af] just as it is written: **The righteous will live by faith.**[M,N,ag]

The Guilt of the Gentile World

18 For God's wrath[ah] is revealed from heaven against all godlessness and unrighteousness of people who by their unrighteousness suppress the truth,[ai] 19 since what can be known[O] about God is evident among them,[aj] because God has shown it to them. 20 For His invisible attributes, that is, His eternal power and divine nature, have been clearly seen since the creation of the world,[ak] being understood through what He has made.[al] As a result, people are without excuse. 21 For though they knew God, they did not glorify Him as God or show gratitude. Instead, their thinking became nonsense, and their senseless minds were darkened.[am] 22 Claiming to be wise, they became fools[an] 23 and exchanged the glory of the immortal God for images resembling

[a]**1:1** 1Co 1:1; 9:1; 2Co 1:1 [b]Ac 9:15; 13:2; Gl 1:15 [c]Mk 1:14 [d]**1:2** Ti 1:2 [e]Lk 1:70; Rm 3:21; 16:26 [f]**1:3** Mt 1:1 [g]Jn 1:14; Rm 4:1; 9:3,5; 1Co 10:18 [h]**1:4** Ac 10:38; 13:33; 17:31; 26:23 [i]Mt 4:3 [j]**1:5** Ac 1:25; Gl 1:16 [k]Ac 6:7; Rm 16:26 [l]Ac 9:15 [m]**1:6** Jd 1; Rv 17:14 [n]**1:7** Rm 5:5; 8:39; 1Th 1:4 [o]Rm 8:28; 1Co 1:24 [p]1Co 1:2-4 [q]**1:8** Rm 16:19 [r]**1:9** 2Tm 1:3 [s]Rm 9:1; 2Co 1:23; 11:31; Php 1:8; 1Th 2:5,10 [t]Eph 1:16; Php 1:3-5; 1Th 1:2; 2Tm 1:3; Phm 4 [u]**1:10** Ac 18:21; Rm 15:32 [v]**1:11** Ac 19:21; Rm 15:23 [w]**1:13** 1Co 10:1; 11:3 [x]Ac 19:21 [y]Jn 4:36; Rm 15:16; Php 1:22; Col 1:6 [z]**1:14** Ac 28:2 [aa]**1:15** Rm 15:20; 1Co 9:16 [ab]**1:16** 2Tm 1:8,12,16 [ac]1Co 1:18,24 [ad]Ac 3:26; Rm 2:9 [ae]Jn 7:35 [af]**1:17** Rm 3:21; 9:30; Php 3:9 [ag]Hab 2:4; Gl 3:11; Heb 10:38 [ah]**1:18** Rm 5:9; Eph 5:6; Col 3:6 [ai]2Th 2:6-10 [aj]**1:19** Ac 14:17; 17:24-27 [ak]**1:20** Mk 10:6 [al]Jb 12:7-9; Ps 19:1-6; Jr 5:21-22 [am]**1:21** 2Kg 17:15; Jr 2:5; Eph 4:17-20 [an]**1:22** Jr 10:14; 1Co 1:20

GOD WHO SENDS

Redemption and Society

Christians are compelled to see all of life not simply from a theological but from a missiological perspective. That is, they must bring to society a value system based upon principles of justice which the moral nature of God demands. Moreover, Christians must have a sense of purpose in these societal relationships—a sense of being sent to the kingdom for the opportunity to be redemptive for such times as the providence of God may allow.

(DuBose, 85)

[A]**1:1** Or *Jesus, a called apostle* [B]**1:3** Lit *was of the seed of David* [C]**1:4** Or *the spirit of holiness*, or *the Holy Spirit* [D]**1:5** Or *Him for*; lit *Him into* [E]**1:5** Or *the obedience that is faith*, or *the faithful obedience*, or *the obedience that comes from faith*; Rm 16:26 [F]**1:5** Or *Gentiles* [G]**1:8** Or *because your faith* [H]**1:13** Lit *I don't want you to be unaware* [I]**1:13** Lit *have some fruit* [J]**1:14** Or *non-Greeks* [K]**1:16** Other mss add *of Christ* [L]**1:17** Or *revealed out of faith into faith* [M]**1:17** Or *The one who is righteous by faith will live* [N]**1:17** Hab 2:4 [O]**1:19** Or *what is known* mortal man, birds, four-footed animals, and reptiles.[a]

24 Therefore God delivered them over in the cravings of their hearts[b] to sexual impurity, so that their bodies were degraded among themselves. 25 They exchanged the truth of God for a lie,[c] and worshiped and served something created instead of the Creator, who is praised forever.[d] •Amen.

From Idolatry to Depravity

26 This is why God delivered them over to degrading passions.[e] For even their females exchanged natural sexual relations[A] for unnatural ones. 27 The males in the same way also left natural relations[A] with females and were inflamed in their lust for one another. Males committed shameless acts with males[f] and received in their own persons[B] the appropriate penalty of their error.

28 And because they did not think it worthwhile to acknowledge God, God delivered them over to a worthless mind to do what is morally wrong. 29 They are filled with all unrighteousness,[C] evil, greed, and wickedness. They are full of envy, murder, quarrels, deceit, and malice. They are gossips,[g] 30 slanderers, God-haters, arrogant, proud, boastful,[h] inventors of evil, disobedient to parents,[i] 31 undiscerning, untrustworthy, unloving,[D,j] and unmerciful. 32 Although they know full well God's just sentence—that those who practice such things deserve to die[E,k]—they not only do them, but even applaud[F,l] others who practice them.

God's Righteous Judgment

2 Therefore, any one of you[G,m] who judges is without excuse.[n] For when you judge another,[o] you condemn yourself, since you, the judge, do the same things. 2 We know that God's judgment on those who do such things is based on the truth. 3 Do you really think—anyone of you who judges those who do such things yet do the same—that you will escape God's judgment? 4 Or do you despise the riches of His kindness,[p] restraint,[q] and patience,[r] not recognizing[H] that God's kindness[s] is intended to lead you to repentance? 5 But because of your hardness and unrepentant heart you are storing up wrath[t] for yourself in the day of wrath,[u] when God's righteous judgment is revealed. 6 **He will repay each one according to his works:**[I,v] 7 eternal life[w] to those who by persistence in doing good[x] seek glory, honor,[y] and immortality;[z] 8 but wrath and indignation to those who are self-seeking[aa] and disobey the truth[ab] but are obeying unrighteousness; 9 affliction and distress[ac] for every human being who does evil, first to the Jew, and also to the Greek;[ad] 10 but glory, honor, and peace for everyone who does what is good, first to the Jew, and also to the Greek. 11 There is no favoritism with God.[ae]

12 All those who sinned without the law[af] will also perish without the law, and all those who sinned under the law will be judged by the law. 13 For the hearers of the law[ag] are not righteous before God, but the doers of the law will be declared righteous.[J] 14 So, when Gentiles, who do not have the law, instinctively[ah] do what the law demands, they are a law to themselves even though they do not have the law. 15 They show that the work of the law[K] is written on their hearts.[ai] Their consciences confirm this. Their competing thoughts will either accuse or excuse them[L] 16 on the day when God judges[aj] what people have kept secret, according to my gospel through Christ Jesus.[ak]

Jewish Violation of the Law

17 Now if[M] you call yourself a Jew, and rest in the law,[al] boast in God, 18 know His will, and approve the things that are superior,[am] being instructed from the law, 19 and if you are convinced that you are a guide for the blind, a light to those in darkness, 20 an instructor of the ignorant, a teacher of the immature, having the full expression[N] of knowledge and truth[an] in the law— 21 you then, who teach another,[ao] don't you teach yourself? You who preach, "You must not steal"—do you steal? 22 You who say, "You must not commit adultery"—do you commit adultery? You who detest idols, do you rob their temples?[ap] 23 You

[a] **1:23** Ps 106:20; Jr 2:11; Ac 17:29
[b] **1:24** Eph 2:3; 4:19
[c] **1:25** Is 44:20; Jr 10:14; 13:25; 16:19
[d] Rm 9:5; 2Co 11:31
[e] **1:26** 1Th 4:5
[f] **1:27** Lv 18:22; 20:13; 1Co 6:9
[g] **1:29** 2Co 12:20
[h] **1:30** Ps 5:5
[i] 2Tm 3:2
[j] **1:31** 2Tm 3:3
[k] **1:32** Rm 6:21
[l] Lk 11:48; Ac 8:1; 22:20
[m] **2:1** Lk 12:14; Rm 9:20
[n] Rm 1:20
[o] 2Sm 12:5-7; Mt 7:1; Rm 14:22
[p] **2:4** Rm 11:22
[q] Rm 3:25
[r] Ex 34:6; Rm 9:22; 1Tm 1:16; 1Pt 3:20; 2Pt 3:15
[s] 2Pt 3:9
[t] **2:5** Dt 32:34; Pr 1:18
[u] Ps 110:5; 2Co 5:10; 2Th 1:5; Jd 6
[v] **2:6** Ps 62:12; Pr 24:12, Mt 16:27
[w] **2:7** 1Co 15:42,50,53
[x] Lk 8:15; Heb 10:36
[y] Heb 2:7; 1Pt 1:7
[z] Mt 25:46
[aa] **2:8** 2Co 12:20; Gl 5:20; Php 2:3; Jms 3:14,16
[ab] 2Th 2:12
[ac] **2:9** Rm 8:35
[ad] Ac 3:26; Rm 1:16; 1Pt 4:17
[ae] **2:11** Dt 10:17; Ac 10:34
[af] **2:12** 1Co 9:21
[ag] **2:13** Mt 7:21,24; Jn 13:17; Jms 1:22
[ah] **2:14** Ac 10:35; Rm 1:19
[ai] **2:15** Rm 2:27
[aj] **2:16** Ac 10:42; 17:31; Rm 3:6; 14:10
[ak] Rm 16:25; 1Co 15:1; Gl 1:11; 1Tm 1:11; 2Tm 2:8
[al] **2:17** Mc 3:11; Jn 5:45; Rm 9:4
[am] **2:18** Php 1:10
[an] **2:20** Is 2:1-4; 42:6-7; 49:6
[ao] **2:21** Mt 23:3-7
[ap] **2:22** Ac 19:37

[A] **1:26,27** Lit *natural use* [B] **1:27** Or *in themselves* [C] **1:29** Other mss add *sexual immorality* [D] **1:31** Other mss add *unforgiving* [E] **1:32** Lit *things are worthy of death* [F] **1:32** Lit *even take pleasure in* [G] **2:1** Lit *Therefore, O man, every one* [H] **2:4** Or *patience, because you do not recognize* [I] **2:6** Ps 62:12; Pr 24:12 [J] **2:13** Or *will be justified* or *acquitted* [K] **2:15** The code of conduct required by the law [L] **2:15** Internal debate, either in a person or among the pagan moralists [M] **2:17** Other mss read *Look—* [N] **2:20** Or *the embodiment*

who boast in the law,[a] do you dishonor God
by breaking the law? 24 For, as it is written:
**The name of God is blasphemed among the
Gentiles because of you.**[A,b]

Circumcision of the Heart

25 For circumcision benefits you if you observe the law, but if you are a lawbreaker,
your circumcision has become uncircumcision.[c] 26 Therefore if an uncircumcised[d] man
keeps the law's requirements,[e] will his uncircumcision not be counted as circumcision?
27 A man who is physically uncircumcised,
but who fulfills the law, will judge you[f] who
are a lawbreaker in spite of having the letter
of the law and circumcision. 28 For a person
is not a Jew who is one outwardly,[g] and true
circumcision is not something visible in the
flesh. 29 On the contrary, a person is a Jew
who is one inwardly,[h] and circumcision is
of the heart — by the Spirit, not the letter.[B,i]
That man's praise[C] is not from men but from
God.[j]

Paul Answers an Objection

3 So what advantage does the Jew have?
Or what is the benefit of circumcision?
2 Considerable in every way. First, they were
entrusted[k] with the spoken words of God.[l]
3 What then? If some did not believe,[m] will
their unbelief cancel God's faithfulness? 4 Absolutely not![n] God must be true, even if everyone is a liar,[o] as it is written:

That You may be justified
in Your words
and triumph when You judge.[D,p]

5 But if our unrighteousness highlights[E] God's
righteousness,[q] what are we to say?[r] I use a
human argument:[F,s] Is God unrighteous to
inflict wrath? 6 Absolutely not! Otherwise,
how will God judge the world?[t] 7 But if by
my lie God's truth is amplified to His glory,
why am I also still judged as a sinner?[u] 8 And
why not say, just as some people slanderously
claim we say, "Let us do what is evil so that
good may come"?[v] Their condemnation is deserved!

The Whole World Guilty before God

9 What then? Are we any better?[G] Not at
all! For we have previously charged that both
Jews[w] and Gentiles[H,x] are all under sin,[I,y] 10 as
it is written:[J]

There is no one righteous,
not even one.
11 **There is no one who understands;**
there is no one who seeks God.
12 **All have turned away;**
all alike have become useless.
There is no one who does what is good,
not even one.[K,z]
13 **Their throat is an open grave;**
they deceive with their tongues.[L,aa]
Vipers' venom is under their lips.[M,ab]
14 **Their mouth is full of cursing**
and bitterness.[N,ac]
15 **Their feet are swift to shed blood;**
16 **ruin and wretchedness are**
in their paths,
17 **and the path of peace**
they have not known.[O,ad]
18 **There is no fear of God**
before their eyes.[P,ae]

19 Now we know that whatever the law
says[af] speaks to those who are subject to the
law,[Q,ag] so that every mouth may be shut and
the whole world may become subject to God's
judgment.[R,ah] 20 For no one will be ·justified[S]
in His sight by the works of the law,[ai] because
the knowledge of sin comes through the law.[aj]

God's Righteousness through Faith

21 But now, apart from the law, God's righteousness has been revealed[ak] — attested
by the Law and the Prophets[T,al] 22 — that is,
God's righteousness through faith[am] in Jesus
Christ,[U,an] to all who believe,[ao] since there is no
distinction.[ap] 23 For all have sinned[aq] and fall
short of the[V] glory of God. 24 They are justified
freely by His grace[ar] through the ·redemp-
tion that is in Christ Jesus.[as] 25 God presented

[a] **2:23** Mc 3:11; Jn 5:45; Rm 9:4
[b] **2:24** Is 52:5; Ezk 36:20-23; 2Pt 2:2
[c] **2:25** Jr 4:4; 9:25
[d] **2:26** Rm 3:30; 1Co 7:19; Eph 2:11
[e] Rm 8:4
[f] **2:27** Mt 12:41
[g] **2:28** Jn 8:39; Rm 9:6; Gl 6:15
[h] **2:29** Php 3:3; Col 2:11
[i] Rm 7:6; 2Co 3:6
[j] Jn 5:44; 12:43; 1Co 4:5; 2Co 10:18
[k] **3:2** Dt 4:8; Ps 147:19; Rm 9:4
[l] Ac 7:38
[m] **3:3** Rm 10:16; Heb 4:2
[n] **3:4** Lk 20:16; Rm 3:31
[o] Ps 116:11
[p] Ps 51:4
[q] **3:5** Rm 5:8; 2Co 6:4; Gl 2:18
[r] Rm 4:1; 7:7; 8:31; 9:14,30
[s] Rm 6:19; 1Co 9:8; 15:32; Gl 3:15
[t] **3:6** Rm 2:16
[u] **3:7** Rm 9:19
[v] **3:8** Rm 6:1
[w] **3:9** Rm 2:1-29
[x] Rm 1:18-32
[y] Rm 3:19,23; 11:32; Gl 3:22
[z] **3:10-12** Ps 14:1-3; 53:1-3; Ec 7:20
[aa] **3:13** Ps 5:9
[ab] Ps 140:3
[ac] **3:14** Ps 10:7
[ad] **3:15-17** Is 59:7-8
[ae] **3:18** Ps 36:1
[af] **3:19** Jn 10:34
[ag] Rm 2:12
[ah] Rm 2:9
[ai] **3:20** Ps 143:2; Ac 13:39; Gl 2:16
[aj] Rm 4:15; 5:13,20; 7:7
[ak] **3:21** Rm 1:17; 9:30
[al] Ac 10:43; Rm 1:2
[am] **3:22** Rm 4:5
[an] Ac 3:16; Gl 2:16,20; 3:22; Eph 3:12
[ao] Rm 4:11,16; 10:4
[ap] Rm 10:12; Gl 3:28; Col 3:11
[aq] **3:23** Rm 3:9
[ar] **3:24** Rm 4:4,16; Eph 2:8
[as] 1Co 1:30; Eph 1:7; Col 1:14; Heb 9:15

[A] **2:24** Is 52:5 [B] **2:29** Or *heart — spiritually, not literally* [C] **2:29** In Hb, the words Jew, Judah, and praise are related. [D] **3:4** Ps 51:4 [E] **3:5** Or *shows*, or *demonstrates* [F] **3:5** Lit *I speak as a man* [G] **3:9** Are we Jews any better than the Gentiles? [H] **3:9** Lit *Greeks* [I] **3:9** Under sin's power or dominion [J] **3:10** Paul constructs this charge from a chain of OT quotations, mainly from the Psalms. [K] **3:10-12** Ps 14:1-3; 53:1-3; Ec 7:20 [L] **3:13** Ps 5:9 [M] **3:13** Ps 140:3 [N] **3:14** Ps 10:7 [O] **3:15-17** Is 59:7-8 [P] **3:18** Ps 36:1 [Q] **3:19** Lit *those in the law* [R] **3:19** Or *become guilty before God*, or *may be accountable to God* [S] **3:20** Or *will be declared righteous*, or *will be acquitted* [T] **3:21** When capitalized, *the Law and the Prophets* = OT [U] **3:22** Or *through the faithfulness of Jesus Christ* [V] **3:23** Or *and lack the*

Him as a ˚propitiation[A,a] through faith in His
blood,[b] to demonstrate His righteousness,
because in His restraint God[c] passed over the
sins previously committed.[d] 26 God presented
Him to demonstrate His righteousness at the
present time, so that He would be righteous
and declare righteous[B] the one who has faith
in Jesus.

Boasting Excluded

27 Where then is boasting?[e] It is excluded.
By what kind of law?[C,f] By one of works? No,
on the contrary, by a law[D] of faith. 28 For we
conclude that a man is justified by faith apart
from the works of the law.[g] 29 Or is God for
Jews only?[h] Is He not also for Gentiles? Yes,
for Gentiles too, 30 since there is one God[i] who
will justify the circumcised by faith[j] and the
uncircumcised through faith. 31 Do we then
cancel the law through faith? Absolutely
not![k] On the contrary, we uphold the law.[l]

Abraham Justified by Faith

4 What then can we say that Abraham, our
physical ancestor,[E,m] has found? 2 If Abraham was ˚justified[F] by works,[n] he has something to brag about—but not before God.[G]
3 For what does the Scripture say?

> **Abraham believed God,**
> **and it was credited to him**
> **for righteousness.**[H,o]

4 Now to the one who works,[p] pay is not considered as a gift, but as something owed. 5 But
to the one who does not work, but believes
on Him who declares the ungodly to be righteous,[I,q] his faith is credited for righteousness.

David Celebrating the Same Truth

6 Likewise, David also speaks of the blessing of the man God credits righteousness to
apart from works:

> 7 **How joyful are those whose lawless**
> **acts are forgiven**
> **and whose sins are covered!**
> 8 **How joyful is the man**
> **the Lord will never charge with sin!**[J,r]

[a]**3:25** 1Jn 2:2; 4:10 [b]1Co 5:7; Heb 9:14,28; 1Pt 1:19; Rv 1:5 [c]Rm 2:4 [d]Ac 17:30; 14:16 [e]**3:27** Rm 2:17,23; 4:2; 1Co 1:29-31 [f]Rm 9:31 [g]**3:28** Ac 13:39; Rm 9:31; Eph 2:9; Jms 2:20,24,26 [h]**3:29** Ac 10:34; Rm 9:24; 10:12; 15:9; Gl 3:28 [i]**3:30** Rm 10:12 [j]Rm 4:11,16; Gl 3:8 [k]**3:31** Lk 20:16; Rm 3:4 [l]Mt 5:17; Rm 4:3; 8:4 [m]**4:1** Rm 1:3 [n]**4:2** 1Co 1:31 [o]**4:3** Gn 15:6; Gl 3:6; Jms 2:23 [p]**4:4** Rm 11:6 [q]**4:5** Jn 3:33; Rm 3:22 [r]**4:7-8** Ps 32:1-2; 2Co 5:19 [s]**4:9** Rm 3:30 [t]Gn 15:6 [u]**4:11** Gn 17:10-11 [v]Jn 3:33 [w]Lk 19:9 [x]Rm 3:22 [y]**4:13** Rm 9:8; Gl 3:16; Heb 6:15,17; 7:6; 11:9,17 [z]Gn 17:4-6; 21:17-18 [aa]**4:14** Gl 3:18 [ab]**4:15** Rm 7:7,10-25; 1Co 15:56; Gl 3:10 [ac]Rm 3:20 [ad]**4:16** Rm 3:24 [ae]Rm 9:8; 15:8 [af]**4:17** Gn 17:5 [ag]Jn 5:21 [ah]Is 48:13; 51:2 [ai]1Co 1:28 [aj]**4:18** Gn 17:5 [ak]Gn 15:5 [al]**4:19** Heb 11:12 [am]Gn 17:17 [an]Gn 18:11 [ao]**4:20** Mt 9:8 [ap]**4:21** Rm 14:5

Abraham Justified before Circumcision

9 Is this blessing only for the circumcised,[s]
then? Or is it also for the uncircumcised?
For we say, **Faith was credited to Abraham**
for righteousness.[H,t] 10 In what way then was
it credited—while he was circumcised, or
uncircumcised? Not while he was circumcised, but uncircumcised. 11 And he received
the sign of circumcision[u] as a seal of the righteousness that he had by faith[K,v] while still
uncircumcised. This was to make him the father[w] of all who believe[x] but are not circumcised, so that righteousness may be credited
to them also. 12 And he became the father of
the circumcised, who are not only circumcised but who also follow in the footsteps of
the faith our father Abraham had while he
was still uncircumcised.

The Promise Granted through Faith

13 For the promise to Abraham[y] or to his descendants that he would inherit the world[z]
was not through the law, but through the
righteousness that comes by faith.[K] 14 If those
who are of the law are heirs,[aa] faith is made
empty and the promise is canceled. 15 For the
law produces wrath.[ab] And where there is no
law,[ac] there is no transgression.

16 This is why the promise is by faith, so
that it may be according to grace,[ad] to guarantee it to all the descendants[ae]—not only
to those who are of the law[L] but also to those
who are of Abraham's faith. He is the father
of us all 17 in God's sight. As it is written: **I have**
made you the father of many nations.[M,af] He
believed in God, who gives life to the dead[ag]
and calls[ah] things into existence that do not
exist.[ai] 18 He believed, hoping against hope, so
that he became **the father of many nations**[M,aj]
according to what had been spoken: **So will**
your descendants be.[N,ak] 19 He considered[O]
his own body to be already dead[al] (since he
was about 100 years old)[am] and also considered the deadness of Sarah's womb,[an] without
weakening in the faith. 20 He did not waver in
unbelief at God's promise but was strengthened in his faith and gave glory to God,[ao] 21 because he was fully convinced[ap] that what He

[A]**3:25** Or *as a propitiatory sacrifice*, or *as an offering of atonement*, or *as a mercy seat*; 2Co 5:21; Heb 9:5 [B]**3:26** Or *and justify*, or *and acquit* [C]**3:27** Or *what principle?* [D]**3:27** Or *a principle* [E]**4:1** Lit *our ancestor according to the flesh* [F]**4:2** Or *was declared righteous*, or *was acquitted* [G]**4:2** He has no reason for boasting in God's presence. [H]**4:3,9** Gn 15:6 [I]**4:5** Or *who acquits*, or *who justifies* [J]**4:7-8** Ps 32:1-2 [K]**4:11,13** Lit *righteousness of faith* [L]**4:16** Or *not to those who are of the law only* [M]**4:17,18** Gn 17:5 [N]**4:18** Gn 15:5 [O]**4:19** Other mss read *He did not consider* had promised He was also able to perform.[a] 22 Therefore, **it was credited to him for righteousness.**[A,b] 23 Now **it was credited to him** was not written for Abraham alone,[c] 24 but also for us. It will be credited to us who believe in Him[d] who raised Jesus our Lord from the dead.[e] 25 He was delivered up for[B] our trespasses[f] and raised for[B] our justification.[C,g]

Faith Triumphs

5 Therefore, since we have been declared righteous by faith,[h] we have peace[D] with God through our Lord Jesus Christ.[i] 2 We have also obtained access through Him[j] by faith[E] into this grace in which we stand,[k] and we rejoice in the hope of the glory of God. 3 And not only that,[l] but we also rejoice in our afflictions,[m] because we know that affliction produces endurance,[n] 4 endurance produces proven character,[o] and proven character produces hope. 5 This hope will not disappoint us,[p] because God's love has been poured out in our hearts[q] through the Holy Spirit who was given to us.

GOD WHO SENDS

The Metanarrative

The God of the Bible is ever present in his world because of humanity, the crown of his creation. Man—male and female—was made in the image of God. But that image has been marred by sin. Yet God's loving reach to his creatures is never ending—to restore that full image through redemption. The story of the Bible is the story of God's loving reach for men and women, to restore them to fellowship with himself. And his method in accomplishing this restoration and redemption is the sending.

(DUBOSE, 67)

[a] **4:21** Gn 18:14; Heb 11:19
[b] **4:22** Gn 15:6; Rm 4:3
[c] **4:23** Rm 15:4; 1Co 9:9; 10:11; 2Tm 3:16
[d] **4:24** Rm 10:9; 1Pt 1:21
[e] Ac 2:24
[f] **4:25** Rm 5:6,8; 8:32; Gl 2:20; Eph 5:2
[g] Rm 5:18; 1Co 15:17; 2Co 5:15
[h] **5:1** Rm 3:28
[i] Rm 5:11
[j] **5:2** Eph 2:18; 3:12; Heb 10:19-20; 1Pt 3:18
[k] 1Co 15:1
[l] **5:3** Rm 5:11; 8:23; 9:10; 2Co 8:19
[m] Mt 5:12; Jms 1:2-3
[n] Lk 21:19
[o] **5:4** Php 2:22; Jms 1:12
[p] **5:5** Ps 119:116; Rm 9:33; Heb 6:18-20
[q] Ac 2:33; 10:45; Gl 4:6; Ti 3:6
[r] **5:6** Gl 4:4
[s] **5:8** Rm 3:5
[t] Jn 3:16; 15:13; Rm 8:39
[u] **5:9** Rm 3:25
[v] Rm 1:18; 1Th 1:10
[w] **5:10** Rm 11:28; 2Co 5:18-20; Eph 2:3; Col 1:21
[x] Rm 8:34; Heb 7:25
[y] **5:11** Rm 11:15; 2Co 5:18-20
[z] **5:12** Gn 2:17; 3:6,19; 1Co 15:21
[aa] Rm 6:23; 1Co 15:56; Jms 1:15
[ab] Rm 5:19,21; 1Co 15:22
[ac] **5:13** Rm 4:15
[ad] **5:14** Hs 6:7
[ae] 1Co 15:45
[af] **5:15** Ac 15:11
[ag] **5:16** 1Co 11:32
[ah] **5:17** 2Tm 2:12; Rv 22:5
[ai] **5:18** Rm 4:25

Those Declared Righteous Are Reconciled

6 For while we were still helpless, at the appointed moment,[r] Christ died for the ungodly. 7 For rarely will someone die for a just person—though for a good person perhaps someone might even dare to die. 8 But God proves[s] His own love for us[t] in that while we were still sinners, Christ died for us! 9 Much more then, since we have now been declared righteous by His blood,[u] we will be saved through Him from wrath.[v] 10 For if, while we were enemies,[w] we were reconciled to God through the death of His Son, then how much more, having been reconciled, will we be saved by His life![x] 11 And not only that, but we also rejoice in God through our Lord Jesus Christ. We have now received this reconciliation through Him.[y]

Death through Adam and Life through Christ

12 Therefore, just as sin entered the world through one man,[z] and death through sin,[aa] in this way death spread to all men,[ab] because all sinned.[F] 13 In fact, sin was in the world before the law, but sin is not charged to a person's account when there is no law.[ac] 14 Nevertheless, death reigned from Adam to Moses, even over those who did not sin in the likeness of Adam's transgression.[ad] He is a prototype[G] of the Coming One.[ae]

15 But the gift is not like the trespass. For if by the one man's trespass the many died, how much more have the grace of God and the gift overflowed to the many by the grace of the one man,[af] Jesus Christ. 16 And the gift is not like the one man's sin, because from one sin came the judgment,[ag] resulting in condemnation, but from many trespasses came the gift, resulting in •justification.[C] 17 Since by the one man's trespass, death reigned through that one man, how much more will those who receive the overflow of grace and the gift of righteousness reign in life[ah] through the one man, Jesus Christ.

18 So then, as through one trespass there is condemnation for everyone, so also through one righteous act there is life-giving justification[H,ai] for everyone. 19 For just as through one

[A] **4:22** Gn 15:6 [B] **4:25** Or *because of* [C] **4:25; 5:16** Or *acquittal* [D] **5:1** Other mss read *faith, let us have peace,* which can also be translated *faith, let us grasp the fact that we have peace* [E] **5:2** Other mss omit *by faith* [F] **5:12** Or *have sinned* [G] **5:14** Or *figure,* or *pattern*; = an OT person or thing that prefigures a NT person or thing [H] **5:18** Lit *is justification of life*

man's disobedience the many were made sinners,[a] so also through the one man's obedience[b] the many will be made righteous. 20 The
law came along to multiply the trespass.[c] But
where sin multiplied, grace multiplied even
more[d] 21 so that, just as sin reigned in death,[e]
so also grace will reign[f] through righteousness, resulting in eternal life through Jesus
Christ our Lord.

The New Life in Christ

6 What should we say then?[g] Should we
continue in sin so that grace may multiply?[h] 2 Absolutely not![i] How can we who died
to sin[j] still live in it? 3 Or are you unaware that
all of us who were baptized[k] into Christ Jesus
were baptized into His death?[l] 4 Therefore
we were buried with Him by baptism into
death,[m] in order that, just as Christ was raised
from the dead[n] by the glory of the Father,[o] so
we too may ·walk in a new way[A] of life.[p] 5 For if
we have been joined with Him in the likeness
of His death,[q] we will certainly also be[B] in the
likeness of His resurrection. 6 For we know
that our old self[C,r] was crucified with Him[s] in
order that sin's dominion over the body[D] may
be abolished,[t] so that we may no longer be enslaved to sin, 7 since a person who has died[u]
is freed[E] from sin's claims.[F] 8 Now if we died
with Christ,[v] we believe that we will also live
with Him, 9 because we know that Christ, having been raised from the dead,[w] will not die
again. Death no longer rules over Him.[x] 10 For
in light of the fact that He died, He died to
sin once for all; but in light of the fact that He
lives, He lives to God. 11 So, you too consider
yourselves dead to sin[y] but alive to God in
Christ Jesus.[G]

12 Therefore do not let sin reign in your
mortal body, so that you obey[H] its desires.
13 And do not offer any parts[I] of it to sin[z] as
weapons for unrighteousness. But as those

[a]5:19 Rm 11:32 [b]Php 2:8 [c]5:20 Rm 3:20; 7:7; Gl 3:19 [d]Rm 6:1; 1Tm 1:14 [e]5:21 Rm 5:12,14 [f]Jn 1:17; Rm 6:23 [g]6:1 Rm 3:5 [h]Rm 3:8; 6:15 [i]6:2 Lk 20:16 [j]Rm 7:4,6; Gl 2:19; Col 2:20; 3:3; 1Pt 2:24 [k]6:3 Mt 28:19; 1Co 1:13-17; 12:13; Gl 3:27 [l]Ac 2:38; 8:16; 19:5 [m]6:4 Col 2:12 [n]Ac 2:24 [o]Jn 11:40; 2Co 13:4 [p]Rm 7:6; 2Co 5:17; Gl 6:15; Eph 4:23-24; Col 3:10 [q]6:5 2Co 4:10; Php 3:10; Col 2:12; 3:1 [r]6:6 Eph 4:22; Col 3:9 [s]Gl 2:20; 5:24; 6:14 [t]Rm 7:24

[u]6:7 1Pt 4:1 [v]6:8 2Co 4:10; 2Tm 2:11 [w]6:9 Ac 2:24 [x]Rv 1:18 [y]6:11 Rm 7:4,6; Gl 2:19; Col 2:20; 3:3; 1Pt 2:24 [z]6:13 Rm 7:5; Col 3:5

GOD'S HEART FOR THE WORLD

A Hope We Can Count On

But God proves His own love for us in that while we were still sinners, Christ died for us! (Romans 5:8)

Hope is a dangerous feeling. When we hope we long for and anticipate something good: a marriage, a job, a child or grandchild, a gift. But hope opens us up to the potential for hurt. What if these good things do not come? What if we "get our hopes up" and get let down? Often people will protect themselves from hurt by trying to keep from hoping at all.

But Paul, knowing this fear, encourages us that "this hope," the hope of entering into the glorious presence of God, "does not disappoint" (v. 5). We can trust it; it will not let us down. We can be sure of the hope we place in God because the proof is in Christ's death. Paul says that God didn't just show His love for those who were doing everything right, but for those who were doing everything wrong. Jesus died for the world of sinners even though we did not honor or trust Him. Colossians 1 even says that we were God's enemies, and yet He gave Himself to us. His promise was not flippant or half-hearted; it cost Him His life.

Jesus' death for the ungodly gives us such confidence in God's salvation that we can not only have hope, but can boast about that hope. We can boast even as we suffer through terrible circumstances because God's love for the world can be trusted.

The proof is in the cross.

[A]6:4 Or *in newness* [B]6:5 Be joined with Him [C]6:6 Lit *man*; = the person before conversion [D]6:6 Lit *that the body of sin* [E]6:7 Or *justified*; lit *acquitted* [F]6:7 Lit *from sin* [G]6:11 Other mss add *our Lord* [H]6:12 Other mss add *sin* (lit *it*) *in* [I]6:13 Or *members*

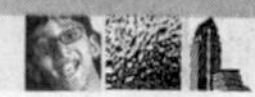

who are alive from the dead, offer yourselves
to God,[a] and all the parts[A] of yourselves to
God as weapons for righteousness. 14For sin
will not rule over you, because you are not
under law[b] but under grace.[c]

From Slaves of Sin to Slaves of God

15What then? Should we sin because we are
not under law but under grace?[d] Absolutely
not![e] 16Don't you know that if you offer yourselves to someone[B] as obedient ·slaves,[f] you
are slaves of that one you obey[g]—either of sin
leading to death[h] or of obedience leading to
righteousness? 17But thank God that, although
you used to be slaves of sin,[i] you obeyed from
the heart that pattern of teaching you were
transferred[C] to,[j] 18and having been liberated
from sin,[k] you became enslaved to righteousness. 19I am using a human analogy[D,l] because
of the weakness of your flesh.[E] For just as you
offered the parts[A] of yourselves as slaves to
moral impurity, and to greater and greater
lawlessness, so now offer them as slaves to
righteousness, which results in ·sanctification.
20For when you were slaves of sin, you were
free from allegiance to righteousness.[F,m] 21So
what fruit was produced[G] then from the things
you are now ashamed of?[n] For the end of those
things is death.[o] 22But now, since you have been
liberated from sin and have become enslaved
to God,[p] you have your fruit, which results in
sanctification[H,q]—and the end is eternal life![r]
23For the wages of sin is death, but the gift of
God is eternal life in Christ Jesus our Lord.[s]

An Illustration from Marriage

7 Since I am speaking to those who understand law, ·brothers,[t] are you unaware
that the law has authority over someone as
long as he lives? 2For example, a married
woman is legally bound to her husband while
he lives.[u] But if her husband dies, she is released from the law regarding the husband.
3So then, if she gives herself to another man
while her husband is living, she will be called
an adulteress. But if her husband dies, she is
free from that law. Then, if she gives herself to
another man, she is not an adulteress.

4Therefore, my brothers, you also were
put to death[v] in relation to the law[w] through
the crucified body of the ·Messiah,[x] so that
you may belong to another—to Him who
was raised from the dead—that we may
bear fruit for God. 5For when we were in the
flesh,[I,y] the sinful passions operated through
the law in every part of us[J,z] and bore fruit for
death. 6But now we have been released from
the law, since we have died to what held us,
so that we may serve in the new way[K] of the
Spirit[aa] and not in the old letter of the law.

Sin's Use of the Law

7What should we say then?[ab] Is the law sin?
Absolutely not![ac] On the contrary, I would not
have known sin if it were not for the law.[ad] For
example, I would not have known what it is to
covet if the law had not said, **Do not covet.**[L,ae]
8And sin, seizing an opportunity through the
commandment,[af] produced in me coveting of
every kind. For apart from the law sin is dead.[ag]
9Once I was alive apart from the law, but
when the commandment came, sin sprang
to life 10and I died. The commandment that
was meant for life[ah] resulted in death for me.
11For sin, seizing an opportunity through the
commandment, deceived me,[ai] and through it
killed me. 12So then, the law is holy,[aj] and the
commandment is holy and just and good.

The Problem of Sin in Us

13Therefore, did what is good cause my
death?[M] Absolutely not![ak] On the contrary, sin,
in order to be recognized as sin, was producing death in me through what is good, so that
through the commandment, sin might become sinful beyond measure. 14For we know
that the law is spiritual,[al] but I am made out of
flesh,[N] sold[am] into sin's power.[an] 15For I do not
understand what I am doing,[ao] because I do
not practice what I want to do,[ap] but I do what
I hate. 16And if I do what I do not want to do, I
agree with the law that it is good. 17So now I am
no longer the one doing it, but it is sin living in
me. 18For I know that nothing good lives in me,
that is, in my flesh.[aq] For the desire to do what
is good is with me, but there is no ability to do

[a]**6:13** Rm 12:1; 2Co 5:14; 1Pt 2:24
[b]**6:14** Rm 5:18; 7:4,6; Gl 4:21
[c]Rm 5:17,21
[d]**6:15** Rm 6:1
[e]Lk 20:16
[f]**6:16** Rm 11:2; 1Co 3:16; 5:6; 6:2-3,9,15-16,19; 9:13,24
[g]Jn 8:34; 2Pt 2:19
[h]Rm 6:23
[i]**6:17** Rm 1:8; 2Co 2:14
[j]2Tm 1:3
[k]**6:18** Jn 8:32; Rm 8:2
[l]**6:19** Rm 3:5
[m]**6:20** Mt 6:24
[n]**6:21** Jr 12:13; Ezk 16:63; Rm 7:5
[o]Rm 1:32; 5:12; 8:6,13; Gl 6:8
[p]**6:22** 1Co 7:22; 1Pt 2:16
[q]Rm 7:4
[r]1Pt 1:9
[s]**6:23** Mt 25:46; Rm 5:21; 8:39
[t]**7:1** Rm 1:13
[u]**7:2** 1Co 7:39
[v]**7:4** Rm 6:2
[w]Rm 8:2; Gl 2:19; 5:18
[x]Col 1:22
[y]**7:5** Rm 8:8-10; 2Co 10:3
[z]Rm 6:13,21,23
[aa]**7:6** Rm 2:29
[ab]**7:7** Rm 3:5
[ac]Lk 20:16
[ad]Rm 4:15; 5:20
[ae]Ex 20:17
[af]**7:8** Rm 3:20
[ag]1Co 15:56
[ah]**7:10** Lv 18:5; Lk 10:28; Rm 10:5; Gl 3:12
[ai]**7:11** Gn 3:13
[aj]**7:12** 1Tm 1:8
[ak]**7:13** Lk 20:16
[al]**7:14** 1Co 3:1
[am]1Kg 21:20,25; 2Kg 17:17; Rm 6:6; Gl 4:3
[an]Rm 3:9
[ao]**7:15** Jn 15:15
[ap]Gl 5:17
[aq]**7:18** Jn 3:6; Rm 8:3

[A]**6:13,19** Or *members* [B]**6:16** Lit *that to whom you offer yourselves* [C]**6:17** Or *entrusted* [D]**6:19** Lit *I speak humanly*; Paul is personifying sin and righteousness as slave masters. [E]**6:19** Or *your human nature* [F]**6:20** Lit *free to righteousness* [G]**6:21** Lit *what fruit do you have* [H]**6:22** Or *holiness*

[I]**7:5** = a person's life before accepting Christ [J]**7:5** Lit *of our members* [K]**7:6** Lit *in newness* [L]**7:7** Ex 20:17 [M]**7:13** Lit *good become death to me?* [N]**7:14** Other mss read *I am carnal*

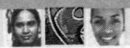

it. 19 For I do not do the good that I want to do,
but I practice the evil that I do not want to do.
20 Now if I do what I do not want, I am no longer the one doing it, but it is the sin that lives
in me. 21 So I discover this principle:[A,a] When I
want to do what is good, evil is with me. 22 For
in my inner self[B] I joyfully agree with God's
law.[b] 23 But I see a different law in the parts of
my body,[C,c] waging war against the law of my
mind and taking me prisoner to the law of sin
in the parts of my body.[C] 24 What a wretched
man I am! Who will rescue me from this dying body?[d] 25 I thank God through Jesus Christ
our Lord![D,e] So then, with my mind I myself am
a slave to the law of God, but with my flesh, to
the law of sin.

The Life-Giving Spirit

8 Therefore, no condemnation[f] now exists
for those in[g] Christ Jesus,[E,h] 2 because the
Spirit's law of life[i] in Christ Jesus has set you[F]
free from the law of sin and of death.[j] 3 What
the law could not do[k] since it was limited[G] by
the flesh,[l] God did. He condemned sin in the
flesh by sending His own Son in flesh like ours[m]
under sin's domain,[H] and as a sin offering,[n] 4 in
order that the law's requirement would be accomplished[o] in us who do not •walk according
to the flesh[p] but according to the Spirit. 5 For
those who live[I] according to the flesh think
about the things of the flesh,[q] but those who
live[I] according to the Spirit, about the things
of the Spirit. 6 For the mind-set of the flesh[r] is
death,[s] but the mind-set of the Spirit is life and
peace. 7 For the mind-set of the flesh is hostile[t] to God because it does not submit itself
to God's law, for it is unable to do so. 8 Those
who are in the flesh[u] cannot please God. 9 You,
however, are not in the flesh, but in the Spirit,
since[J] the Spirit of God lives in you.[v] But if anyone does not have the Spirit of Christ,[w] he does
not belong to Him. 10 Now if Christ is in you,[x]
the body is dead[K] because of sin, but the Spirit[L]
is life because of righteousness. 11 And if the
Spirit of Him who raised Jesus from the dead[y]
lives in you, then He who raised Christ from
the dead will also bring your mortal bodies to
life through[M] His Spirit who lives in you.

[a]7:21 Rm 8:2 [b]7:22 2Co 4:16; Eph 3:16; 1Pt 3:4 [c]7:23 Rm 6:19; Gl 5:17; Jms 4:1; 1Pt 2:11 [d]7:24 Rm 6:6; 8:2; Col 2:11 [e]7:25 1Co 15:57 [f]8:1 Rm 5:16; 8:34 [g]Rm 8:9-10 [h]Rm 8:11,39; 16:3 [i]8:2 1Co 15:45 [j]Jn 8:32,36; Rm 6:14,18; 7:4 [k]8:3 Ac 13:39; Heb 10:1-2 [l]Rm 7:18; Heb 7:18 [m]Php 2:7; Heb 2:14,17; 4:15 [n]Lv 5:6-7,11; 14:31; Is 53:10 [o]8:4 Lk 1:6; Rm 2:26 [p]Gl 5:16 [q]8:5 Gl 5:19-25 [r]8:6 Gl 6:8 [s]Rm 6:21 [t]8:7 Jms 4:4 [u]8:8 Rm 7:5 [v]8:9 Jn 14:23; 1Co 3:16; 6:19; 2Co 6:16; 2Tm 1:14 [w]Jn 14:17; Gl 4:6; Php 1:19; 1Jn 4:13 [x]8:10 Jn 17:23; Gl 2:20; Eph 3:17; Col 1:27 [y]8:11 Ac 2:24; Rm 6:4 [z]8:13 Col 3:5 [aa]8:14 Gl 5:18 [ab]Hs 1:10; Mt 5:9; Jn 1:12; Rm 9:8,26; 2Co 6:18; Gl 3:26; 1Jn 3:1; Rv 21:7 [ac]8:15 2Tm 1:7; Heb 2:15 [ad]Gl 4:5 [ae]Mk 14:36; Gl 4:6

The Holy Spirit's Ministries

12 So then, •brothers, we are not obligated
to the flesh to live according to the flesh, 13 for
if you live according to the flesh, you are going to die. But if by the Spirit you put to death
the deeds of the body,[z] you will live. 14 All those
led by God's Spirit[aa] are God's sons.[ab] 15 For you
did not receive a spirit of slavery to fall back
into fear,[ac] but you received the Spirit of adoption,[ad] by whom we cry out, "•*Abba*, Father!"[ae]

GOD WHO SENDS

Imago Dei and *Missio Dei*

In Romans 8 Paul began his classic theological statement by emphasizing that it was through the sending of God that his redemption came to sinful humanity (v. 3). As he moved toward the conclusion of this powerful statement on the salvific work of God, he emphasized that God's purpose was that the redeemed might be "conformed to the image of his Son" (v. 29). Consequently, just as God's first mission ("the incipient sending") was to deal with the problem of the broken image of God in the first family, so God's final mission in Scripture (the ultimate sending in Jesus Christ) was to restore that image of God in the new family of the redeemed. Moreover, it all comes about because of the activity of God and humanity's experience with God's redemptive reality. And significantly, the method behind the recovery of the *imago Dei* is the *missio Dei*—the incipient sending of Genesis and the ultimate sending of the New Covenant.

(DUBOSE, 79-80)

[A]7:21 Or *law* [B]7:22 Lit *inner man* [C]7:23 Lit *my members* [D]7:25 Or *Thanks be to God—(it is done) through Jesus Christ our Lord!* [E]8:1 Other mss add *who do not walk according to the flesh but according to the Spirit* [F]8:2 Other mss read *me* [G]8:3 Or *weak* [H]8:3 Lit *in the likeness of sinful flesh* [I]8:5 Or *those who are* [J]8:9 Or *provided that* [K]8:10 Or *the body will die* [L]8:10 Or *spirit* [M]8:11 Other mss read *because of*

16 The Spirit Himself testifies together with our
spirit[a] that we are God's children, 17 and if children, also heirs[b] — heirs of God and coheirs
with Christ — seeing that[A] we suffer with Him[c]
so that we may also be glorified with Him.

From Groans to Glory

18 For I consider that the sufferings of this
present time are not worth comparing[d] with
the glory[e] that is going to be revealed to us.
19 For the creation eagerly waits with anticipation[f] for God's sons[g] to be revealed. 20 For
the creation was subjected[h] to futility[i] — not
willingly, but because of Him who subjected
it[j] — in the hope 21 that the creation itself[k]
will also be set free from the bondage of corruption into the glorious freedom of God's
children. 22 For we know that the whole creation has been groaning together with labor
pains[l] until now. 23 And not only that,[m] but
we ourselves who have the Spirit as the ·first-
fruits[n] — we also groan within ourselves,[o] eagerly waiting for adoption,[p] the ·redemption
of our bodies.[q] 24 Now in this hope[r] we were
saved, yet hope[s] that is seen is not hope, because who hopes for what he sees? 25 But if we
hope for what we do not see,[t] we eagerly wait
for it with patience.

26 In the same way the Spirit also joins to
help in our weakness, because we do not
know what to pray for as we should,[u] but the
Spirit Himself intercedes for us[B,v] with unspoken groanings. 27 And He who searches the
hearts[w] knows the Spirit's mind-set, because
He intercedes for the ·saints according to the
will of God.

28 We know that all things work together[C] for
the good[D] of those who love God: those who
are called according to His purpose.[x] 29 For
those He foreknew He also predestined[y] to be
conformed to the image of His Son,[z] so that He
would be the firstborn among many brothers.[aa] 30 And those He predestined, He also
called; and those He called, He also ·justified;[ab]
and those He justified, He also glorified.[ac]

The Believer's Triumph

31 What then are we to say
about these things?[ad]
If God is for us, who is against us?[ae]
32 He did not even spare His own Son[af]
but offered Him up for us all;[ag]
how will He not also with Him grant
us everything?
33 Who can bring an accusation
against God's elect?[ah]
God is the One who justifies.[ai]
34 Who is the one who condemns?[aj]
Christ Jesus is the One who died,[ak]
but even more, has been raised;[al]
He also is at the right hand of God[am]
and intercedes for us.[an]
35 Who can separate us from the love
of Christ?
Can affliction[ao] or anguish
or persecution[ap]
or famine or nakedness or danger
or sword?
36 As it is written:
Because of You
we are being put to death all day long;[aq]
we are counted as sheep
to be slaughtered.[E,ar]
37 No, in all these things we are
more than victorious[as]
through Him who loved us.[at]
38 For I am persuaded that not even
death or life,[au]
angels or rulers,[av]
things present or things to come,[aw]
hostile powers,
39 height or depth, or any other
created thing
will have the power to separate us
from the love of God[ax] that is
in Christ Jesus our Lord![ay]

Israel's Rejection of Christ

9 I speak the truth in Christ[az] — I am not
lying; my conscience is testifying to me
with the Holy Spirit[F] — 2 that I have intense
sorrow and continual anguish in my heart.
3 For I could almost wish[ba] to be cursed[bb] and
cut off[G] from the ·Messiah for the benefit of
my ·brothers, my own flesh and blood. 4 They

[a] **8:16** Ac 5:32 [b] **8:17** Ac 20:32; Gl 3:29; 4:7; Eph 3:6; Ti 3:7; Heb 1:14; Rv 21:7 [c] 2Co 1:5,7; Php 3:10; Col 1:24; 2Tm 2:12 [d] **8:18** 2Co 4:17; 1Pt 4:13 [e] Rm 1:5; Col 3:4; Ti 2:13; 1Pt 5:1 [f] **8:19** Php 1:20 [g] 1Co 1:7; Col 3:4; 1Pt 1:7,13; 1Jn 3:2 [h] **8:20** Gn 3:17-19 [i] Ps 39:5; Ec 1:2 [j] Gn 3:17; 5:29 [k] **8:21** Ac 3:21; 2Pt 3:13; Rv 21:1 [l] **8:22** Jr 12:4,11 [m] **8:23** Rm 5:3 [n] Nm 15:17-21; 1Co 16:15; 2Co 1:22 [o] 2Co 5:2,4 [p] Gl 5:5 [q] Rm 7:24 [r] **8:24** 1Th 5:8; Ti 3:7 [s] Rm 4:18; 2Co 5:7; Heb 11:1 [t] **8:25** 1Th 1:3 [u] **8:26** Mt 20:22; 2Co 12:8 [v] Jn 14:16; Rm 8:15-16; Eph 6:18 [w] **8:27** Ps 139:1-5; Lk 16:15; Ac 1:24; Rv 2:23 [x] **8:28** Rm 9:24; 11:29; 1Co 1:9; Gl 1:6,15; 5:8; Eph 1:11; 3:11; 2Th 2:14; Heb 9:15; 1Pt 2:9; 3:9 [y] **8:29** Rm 9:23; 1Co 2:7; Eph 1:5,11 [z] 1Co 15:49; Php 3:21; Col 3:10; 1Jn 3:2 [aa] Col 1:18; Heb 1:6 [ab] **8:30** 1Co 6:11 [ac] Jn 17:22; Rm 9:23; 1Co 2:7 [ad] **8:31** Rm 3:5; 4:1 [ae] Ps 118:6; Mt 1:23 [af] **8:32** Jn 3:16; Rm 5:8 [ag] Rm 4:25 [ah] **8:33** Lk 18:7 [ai] Is 50:8-9 [aj] **8:34** Rm 8:1 [ak] Rm 5:6-8 [al] Ac 2:24 [am] Mk 16:19 [an] Heb 7:25; 9:24; 1Jn 2:1 [ao] **8:35** Rm 2:9; 2Co 4:8 [ap] 1Co 4:11; 2Co 11:26-27 [aq] **8:36** Ac 20:24; 1Co 4:9; 15:30-31; 2Co 1:9; 6:9; 11:23 [ar] Is 53:7; Zch 11:4,7 [as] **8:37** Jn 16:33; 1Co 15:57 [at] Gl 2:20; Eph 5:2; Rv 1:5 [au] **8:38** 1Co 3:22 [av] 1Co 15:24; Eph 1:21; 1Pt 3:22 [aw] 1Co 3:22 [ax] **8:39** Rm 5:8 [ay] Rm 8:1 [az] **9:1** Rm 1:9; 2Co 11:10; Gl 1:20; 1Tm 2:7 [ba] **9:3** Ex 32:32 [bb] 1Co 12:3; 16:22; Gl 1:8,9

[A] **8:17** Or *provided that* [B] **8:26** Some mss omit *for us* [C] **8:28** Other mss read *that God works together in all things* [D] **8:28** The ultimate good [E] **8:36** Ps 44:22 [F] **9:1** Or *testifying with me by the Holy Spirit* [G] **9:3** Lit *were anathema*

are Israelites,[a] and to them belong the adoption,[b] the glory,[c] the covenants,[d] the giving of
the law,[e] the temple service,[f] and the promises.[g] 5 The ancestors are theirs,[h] and from
them, by physical descent,[A] came the Messiah,[i] who is God[j] over all,[k] praised forever.[B,l]
·Amen.

God's Gracious Election of Israel

6 But it is not as though the word of God has
failed.[m] For not all who are descended from Israel are Israel.[n] 7 Neither are they all children
because they are Abraham's descendants.[C,o]
On the contrary, **your ·offspring will be
traced[D] through Isaac.**[E,p] 8 That is, it is not the
children by physical descent[F] who are God's
children,[q] but the children of the promise[r]
are considered to be the offspring. 9 For this
is the statement of the promise: **At this time I
will come, and Sarah will have a son.**[G,s] 10 And
not only that,[t] but also Rebekah received a
promise when she became pregnant[H,u] by
one man, our ancestor Isaac. 11 For though her
sons had not been born yet or done anything
good or bad, so that God's purpose according
to election might stand —[v] 12 not from works
but from the One who calls — she was told:
The older will serve the younger.[I,w] 13 As it is
written: **I have loved Jacob, but I have hated
Esau.**[J,x]

God's Selection Is Just

14 What should we say then?[y] Is there injustice with God?[z] Absolutely not![aa] 15 For He tells
Moses:

> **I will show mercy**
> **to whom I will show mercy,**
> **and I will have compassion**
> **on whom I will have compassion.**[K,ab]

16 So then it does not depend on human will
or effort[L,ac] but on God who shows mercy.[ad]
17 For the Scripture tells Pharaoh:

> **I raised you up for this reason**
> **so that I may display My power in you**
> **and that My name may be proclaimed**
> **in all the earth.**[M,ae]

18 So then, He shows mercy to those He wants
to, and He hardens those He wants to harden.[af]
19 You will say to me,[ag] therefore, "Why then
does He still find fault?[ah] For who can resist
His will?"[ai] 20 But who are you, a mere man, to
talk back to God?[aj] Will what is formed say to
the one who formed it, "Why did you make me
like this?"[ak] 21 Or has the potter no right over
the clay,[al] to make from the same lump one
piece of pottery for honor and another for dishonor? 22 And what if God, desiring to display
His wrath and to make His power known, endured with much patience[am] objects of wrath
ready for destruction?[an] 23 And what if He did
this to make known the riches of His glory[ao]
on objects of mercy[ap] that He prepared beforehand for glory[aq] — 24 on us, the ones He also
called,[ar] not only from the Jews but also from
the Gentiles?[as] 25 As He also says in Hosea:

> **I will call Not My People, My People,**
> **and she who is Unloved, Beloved.**[N,at]
> 26 **And it will be in the place where**
> **they were told,**
> **you are not My people,**
> **there they will be called sons**
> **of the living God.**[O,au]

27 But Isaiah cries out concerning Israel:

> **Though the number of Israel's sons**
> **is like the sand of the sea,**[av]
> **only the remnant will be saved;**[aw]
> 28 **for the Lord will execute**
> **His sentence**
> **completely and decisively**
> **on the earth.**[P,Q,ax]

29 And just as Isaiah predicted:

> **If the Lord of ·Hosts[R] had not left**
> **us offspring,**[ay]
> **we would have become like Sodom,**
> **and we would have been made**
> **like Gomorrah.**[S,az]

Israel's Present State

30 What should we say then?[ba] Gentiles,
who did not pursue righteousness, have

[a]**9:4** Rm 8:6 [b]Ex 4:22; Rm 8:15 [c]Ex 40:34; 1Kg 8:11; Ezk 1:28; Heb 9:5 [d]Gn 17:2; Dt 29:14; Lk 1:72; Ac 3:25; Eph 2:12 [e]Dt 4:13-14; Ps 147:19 [f]Dt 7:6; 14:1; Heb 9:1,6 [g]Ac 2:39; 13:32; Eph 2:12 [h]**9:5** Ac 3:13; Rm 11:28 [i]Mt 1:1-16; Rm 1:3 [j]Jn 1:1; Col 2:9 [k]Col 1:16-19 [l]Rm 1:25 [m]**9:6** Nm 23:19 [n]Jn 1:47; Rm 2:28-29; Gl 6:16 [o]**9:7** Jn 8:33,39; Gl 4:23 [p]Gn 21:12; Heb 11:18 [q]**9:8** Rm 8:14 [r]Rm 4:13,16; Gl 3:29; 4:28; Heb 11:11 [s]**9:9** Gn 18:10,14 [t]**9:10** Rm 5:3 [u]Gn 25:21 [v]**9:11** Rm 4:17; 8:28 [w]**9:12** Gn 25:23 [x]**9:13** Mal 1:2-3 [y]**9:14** Rm 3:5 [z]2Ch 19:7; Rm 2:11 [aa]Lk 20:16 [ab]**9:15** Ex 33:19 [ac]**9:16** Gl 2:2 [ad]Eph 2:8 [ae]**9:17** Ex 9:16 [af]**9:18** Ex 4:21; 7:3; 9:12; 10:20,27; 11:10; 14:4,7; Dt 2:30; Jos 11:20; Jn 12:40; Rm 11:7,25 [ag]**9:19** Rm 11:19; 1Co 15:25; Jms 2:18 [ah]Rm 3:7 [ai]2Ch 20:6; Jb 9:12; Dn 4:35 [aj]**9:20** Jb 33:13 [ak]Is 29:16; 45:9; 64:8; Jr 18:6; 2Tm 2:20 [al]**9:21** Is 64:8; Jr 18:6 [am]**9:22** Rm 2:4 [an]Pr 16:4; 1Pt 2:8 [ao]**9:23** Rm 2:4; Eph 3:16 [ap]Ac 9:15 [aq]Rm 8:29 [ar]**9:24** Rm 8:28 [as]Rm 3:29 [at]**9:25** Hs 2:23; 1Pt 2:10 [au]**9:26** Hs 1:10; Mt 16:16

[av]**9:27** Gn 22:17 [aw]Rm 11:5 [ax]**9:27-28** Is 10:22-23; 28:22 [ay]**9:29** Jms 5:4 [az]Dt 29:23; Is 1:9; 13:19; Jr 49:18; 50:40; Am 4:11 [ba]**9:30** Rm 9:14

A**9:5** Lit *them, according to the flesh* B**9:5** Or *the Messiah, the One who is over all, the God who is blessed forever*, or *Messiah. God, who is over all, be blessed forever* C**9:7** Lit *seed* D**9:7** Lit *called* E**9:7** Gn 21:12 F**9:8** Lit *children of the flesh* G**9:9** Gn 18:10,14 H**9:10** Or *Rebekah conceived by the one act of sexual intercourse* I**9:12** Gn 25:23 J**9:13** Mal 1:2-3 K**9:15** Ex 33:19 L**9:16** Or *on the one running*; lit *on the one willing* M**9:17** Ex 9:16 N**9:25** Hs 2:23 O**9:26** Hs 1:10 P**9:28** Or *land* Q**9:27-28** Is 10:22-23; 28:22; Hs 1:10 R**9:29** Gk *Sabaoth*; this word is a transliteration of the Hb word for *Hosts*, or *Armies*. S**9:29** Is 1:9

obtained righteousness — namely the righteousness that comes from faith.[a] 31But Israel, pursuing the law for righteousness,[b]
has not achieved the righteousness of the
law.[A,c] 32Why is that? Because they did not
pursue it by faith, but as if it were by works.[B]
They stumbled over the stumbling stone.[d]
33As it is written:

[a]9:30 Rm 1:17; 3:21; 10:6; Gl 2:16; 3:24; Php 3:9; Heb 11:7 [b]9:31 Is 51:1; Rm 10:2,20; 11:7 [c]Gl 5:4 [d]9:32 1Pt 2:6,8

Consumerism and the Mission of God

Skye Jethani

Critiques of consumerism usually focus on the dangers of idolatry—the temptation to make material goods the center of life rather than God. But this misses the real threat consumerism poses. As contingent beings we must consume resources to survive. The problem is not consuming to live, but rather living to consume.

We find ourselves in a culture that defines our relationships and actions primarily through a matrix of consumption. As the philosopher Baudrillard explains, "Consumption is a system of meaning." We assign value to ourselves and others based on the goods we purchase and how useful they are to us. One's identity is now constructed by the clothes you wear, the vehicle you drive, and the music on your iPod. In short, you are what you consume.

When this understanding of the world and self is brought into Christian faith, two very damaging things occur. First, consumerism reduces God from a deity to a commodity. His value, like everything else, is determined by His usefulness to the user (i.e. the Christian). In consumerism, personal desires and their fulfillment are paramount, therefore everything and everyone—including God—exists to satisfy these cravings. This is precisely the opposite of what Scripture teaches. We are called to live in submission to God and walk humbly with Him. Consumerism, however, reduces God so that He becomes a means to an end. He is presented as a useful tool that supplies us with our desires and expectations. As one sociologist noted, in our consumer culture we have come to view God as part cosmic therapist and part divine butler.

Secondly, consumerism reduces Jesus Christ from Lord to a label. When the early Christians declared "Christ is Lord" they were subverting the popular belief of the day that "Caesar is Lord." It was a proclamation of Jesus' authority and power over all things, and it was a declaration of allegiance to our heavenly King.

But in consumerism the customer is king, not Jesus. As a result Christianity becomes just one more brand we integrate and display along with Gap, Apple, and Starbucks to express our identity. So Christians no longer carry an expectation of obedience and allegiance to Christ, but rather the perpetual consumption of Christian merchandise and experiences—music, books, t-shirts, conferences, and jewelry. And rather than living out the values and ethics of the Kingdom of God, we share the values of our consumer culture while our identity as Christians remains a veneer.

Ultimately the powerful influence of consumerism in our contemporary culture forces us to ask hard questions about our faith. Are we truly seeking a life with God? Or are we simply trying to use Him? And is our allegiance to Christ and His Kingdom? Or is "Christian" simply a label we identify with but with no real impact on our lives or behaviors? And as we pursue the mission of the Gospel, are we presenting Jesus Christ as the goal and treasure of life? Or is He being packaged and sold as a commodity to help consumers achieve lesser desires?

A9:31 Other mss read *the law for righteousness* B9:32 Other mss add *of the law*

Look! I am putting a stone in ˙Zion
to stumble over
and a rock to trip over,
yet the one who believes on Him[a]
will not be put to shame.[A,b]

Righteousness by Faith Alone

10 ˙Brothers, my heart's desire and prayer
to God concerning them[B] is for their
salvation! 2 I can testify about them that they
have zeal for God,[c] but not according to
knowledge. 3 Because they disregarded the
righteousness from God[d] and attempted to
establish their own righteousness, they have
not submitted themselves to God's righteousness. 4 For Christ is the end[C] of the law for
righteousness[e] to everyone who believes.[f]
5 For Moses writes about the righteousness
that is from the law: **The one who does these
things will live by them.**[D,g] 6 But the righteousness that comes from faith[h] speaks like this:
**Do not say in your heart, "Who will go up to
heaven?"**[E,i] that is, to bring Christ down 7 or,
"Who will go down into the ˙abyss?"[F,j] that is,
to bring Christ up from the dead.[k] 8 On the
contrary, what does it say? **The message is
near you, in your mouth and in your heart.**[G,l]
This is the message of faith that we proclaim:
9 If you confess with your mouth, "Jesus is
Lord,"[m] and believe in your heart[n] that God
raised Him from the dead,[o] you will be saved.
10 One believes with the heart, resulting in
righteousness, and one confesses with the
mouth, resulting in salvation. 11 Now the
Scripture says, **Everyone who believes on
Him will not be put to shame,**[H,p] 12 for there is
no distinction between Jew and Greek,[q] since
the same Lord[r] of all[s] is rich to all who call on
Him. 13 For **everyone who calls on the name of
the Lord will be saved.**[I,t]

Israel's Rejection of the Message

14 But how can they call on Him they have
not believed in? And how can they believe
without hearing about Him?[u] And how can
they hear without a preacher?[v] 15 And how
can they preach unless they are sent? As it is
written: **How beautiful[J] are the feet of those[K]
who announce the gospel of good things!**[L,w]
16 But all did not obey the gospel.[x] For Isaiah
says, **Lord, who has believed our message?**[M,y]
17 So faith comes from what is heard,[z] and
what is heard comes through the message
about Christ.[N,aa] 18 But I ask, "Did they not
hear?" Yes, they did:

Their voice has gone out to all
the earth,
and their words to the ends
of the inhabited world.[O,ab]

19 But I ask, "Did Israel not understand?"
First, Moses said:

I will make you jealous
of those who are not a nation;[ac]
I will make you angry by a nation
that lacks understanding.[P,ad]

20 And Isaiah says boldly:

I was found
by those who were not looking for Me;
I revealed Myself
to those who were not asking for Me.[Q,ae]

21 But to Israel he says: **All day long I have
spread out My hands to a disobedient and
defiant people.**[R,af]

[a] 9:33 Rm 10:11
[b] Is 8:14; 28:16; Rm 5:5
[c] 10:2 Ac 21:20
[d] 10:3 Rm 1:17
[e] 10:4 Rm 7:1-4; Gl 3:24; 4:5
[f] Rm 3:22
[g] 10:5 Lv 18:5; Neh 9:29; Ezk 20:11,13,21; Rm 7:10
[h] 10:6 Rm 9:30
[i] Dt 9:4; 30:12
[j] 10:7 Dt 30:13; Lk 8:31
[k] Heb 13:20
[l] 10:8 Dt 30:14
[m] 10:9 Mt 10:32; Lk 12:8; Rm 14:9; 1Co 12:3; Php 2:11
[n] Ac 16:31; Rm 4:24
[o] Ac 2:24
[p] 10:11 Is 28:16
[q] 10:12 Rm 3:22,29
[r] Ac 10:36
[s] Rm 3:29
[t] 10:13 Jl 2:32; Ac 2:21; 7:59
[u] 10:14 Eph 2:17; 4:21
[v] Ac 8:31; Ti 1:3
[w] 10:15 Is 52:7; Nah 1:15; Rm 1:15; 15:20
[x] 10:16 Rm 3:3
[y] Is 53:1; Jn 12:38
[z] 10:17 Gl 3:2,5
[aa] Col 3:16
[ab] 10:18 Ps 19:4; Rm 1:8; Col 1:16,23; 1Th 1:8
[ac] 10:19 Rm 11:11,14
[ad] Dt 32:21
[ae] 10:20 Is 65:1; Rm 9:30
[af] 10:21 Is 65:2

GOD WHO SENDS

Evangelism

In Romans 10:15 Paul wrote: "And how can men preach [*kerusso*] unless they are sent? [*apostello*] As it is written, 'How beautiful are the feet of those who preach good news (*euaggelizo*)!'" In this passage it is clear that the preacher is sent to proclaim the good news. Proclamation, therefore is clearly the content of the mission, and this means that evangelism is one of the basic purposes of the sending.

(DUBOSE, 119)

[A] 9:33 Is 8:14; 28:16 [B] 10:1 Other mss read *God for Israel* [C] 10:4 Or *goal* [D] 10:5 Lv 18:5 [E] 10:6 Dt 9:4; 30:12 [F] 10:7 Dt 30:13 [G] 10:8 Dt 30:14 [H] 10:11 Is 28:16 [I] 10:13 Jl 2:32 [J] 10:15 Or *welcome*, or *timely* [K] 10:15 Other mss read *feet of those who announce the gospel of peace, of those* [L] 10:15 Is 52:7; Nah 1:15 [M] 10:16 Is 53:1 [N] 10:17 Other mss read *God* [O] 10:18 Ps 19:4 [P] 10:19 Dt 32:21 [Q] 10:20 Is 65:1 [R] 10:21 Is 65:2

Israel's Rejection Not Total

11 I ask, then, has God rejected His people?[a] Absolutely not![b] For I too am an
Israelite, a descendant of Abraham,[c] from
the tribe of Benjamin. 2God has not rejected
His people whom He foreknew.[d] Or don't
you know[e] what the Scripture says in the passage about Elijah — how he pleads with God
against Israel?

3 **Lord, they have killed Your prophets**
and torn down Your altars.
I am the only one left,
and they are trying to take my life![A,f]

4But what was God's reply to him? **I have left**
7,000 men for Myself who have not bowed
down to ˙Baal.[B,g] 5In the same way, then, there
is also at the present time a remnant chosen
by grace.[h] 6Now if by grace,[i] then it is not by
works; otherwise grace ceases to be grace.[C]
7What then? Israel did not find what it was
looking for,[j] but the elect did find it. The rest
were hardened,[k] 8as it is written:

God gave them a spirit of insensitivity,[D]
eyes that cannot see
and ears that cannot hear,
to this day.[E,l]

9And David says:

Let their feasting[F] **become a snare**
and a trap,
a pitfall and a retribution to them.
10 **Let their eyes be darkened**
so they cannot see,
and their backs be bent continually.[G,m]

Israel's Rejection Not Final

11I ask, then, have they stumbled in order
to fall? Absolutely not! On the contrary, by
their stumbling,[H] salvation has come to the
Gentiles[n] to make Israel jealous. 12Now if
their stumbling[H] brings riches for the world,
and their failure riches for the Gentiles, how
much more will their full number bring![o]
13Now I am speaking to you Gentiles. In
view of the fact that I am an apostle to the
Gentiles,[p] I magnify my ministry, 14if I can
somehow make my own people[I,q] jealous
and save some of them.[r] 15For if their rejection brings reconciliation[s] to the world, what
will their acceptance mean but life from the
dead?[t] 16Now if the ˙firstfruits offered up are
holy,[u] so is the whole batch. And if the root is
holy, so are the branches.
17Now if some of the branches were broken off,[v] and you, though a wild olive branch,
were grafted in among them[w] and have come
to share in the rich root[J] of the cultivated olive tree, 18do not brag that you are better than
those branches. But if you do brag — you do
not sustain the root, but the root sustains
you.[x] 19Then you will say,[y] "Branches were broken off so that I might be grafted in." 20True
enough; they were broken off by unbelief,
but you stand by faith.[z] Do not be arrogant,
but be afraid.[aa] 21For if God did not spare
the natural branches, He will not spare you
either. 22Therefore, consider God's kindness
and severity: severity toward those who have
fallen but God's kindness[ab] toward you — if
you remain in His kindness.[ac] Otherwise you
too will be cut off.[ad] 23And even they, if they
do not remain in unbelief,[ae] will be grafted
in, because God has the power to graft them
in again. 24For if you were cut off from your
native wild olive and against nature were
grafted into a cultivated olive tree, how much
more will these — the natural branches — be
grafted into their own olive tree?
25So that you will not be conceited,[af] ˙broth-
ers, I do not want you to be unaware[ag] of this
˙mystery:[ah] A partial hardening has come to
Israel[ai] until the full number of the Gentiles
has come in.[aj] 26And in this way all[K] Israel will
be saved, as it is written:

The Liberator will come from ˙Zion;
He will turn away godlessness
from Jacob.
27 **And this will be My covenant**
with them[L,ak]
when I take away their sins.[M,al]

28Regarding the gospel, they are enemies for
your advantage,[am] but regarding election,
they are loved because of the patriarchs,[an]
29since God's gracious gifts and calling[ao] are

[a] 11:1 1Sm 12:22; Jr 33:24-26
[b] Lk 20:16
[c] 2Co 11:22; Php 3:5
[d] 11:2 1Sm 12:22; Ps 94:14; Rm 8:29; 1Pt 1:2
[e] Rm 6:16
[f] 11:3 1Kg 19:10,14; 1Th 2:14
[g] 11:4 1Kg 19:18
[h] 11:5 2Kg 19:4; Rm 9:27
[i] 11:6 Rm 4:4
[j] 11:7 Rm 9:31
[k] Mk 6:52; Rm 9:18; 11:25; 2Co 2:14
[l] 11:8 Dt 29:4; Is 29:10; Mt 13:13-14
[m] 11:9-10 Ps 69:22-23
[n] 11:11 Ac 28:28
[o] 11:12 Rm 11:25
[p] 11:13 Ac 9:15
[q] 11:14 Gn 29:14; 2Sm 19:12-13; Rm 9:3
[r] 1Co 1:21; 7:16; 9:22; 1Tm 1:15; 2:4; 2Tm 1:9; Ti 3:5
[s] 11:15 Rm 5:11
[t] Lk 15:24,32
[u] 11:16 Nm 15:17-21; Neh 10:37; Ezk 44:30
[v] 11:17 Jr 11:16; Jn 15:2
[w] Eph 2:12-13
[x] 11:18 Jn 4:22
[y] 11:19 Rm 9:19
[z] 11:20 Rm 5:2; 1Co 10:12; 2Co 1:24
[aa] Rm 12:16; 1Tm 6:17; 1Pt 1:17
[ab] 11:22 Rm 2:4
[ac] 1Co 15:2; Heb 3:6,14
[ad] Jn 15:2
[ae] 11:23 2Co 3:16
[af] 11:25 Rm 12:16
[ag] Rm 1:13
[ah] Mt 13:11; Rm 16:25; 1Co 2:7-10; Eph 3:3-5,9
[ai] Rm 11:7
[aj] Lk 21:24; Jn 10:16
[ak] 11:26-27 Is 59:20-21
[al] 11:27 Jr 31:31-34; Heb 8:10,12
[am] 11:28 Rm 5:10
[an] Dt 7:8; 10:15; Rm 9:5
[ao] 11:29 Rm 8:28; 1Co 1:26; Eph 1:18; 4:1,4; Php 3:14; 2Th 1:11; 2Tm 1:9; Heb 3:1; 2Pt 1:10

[A] 11:3 1Kg 19:10,14 [B] 11:4 1Kg 19:18 [C] 11:6 Other mss add *But if of works it is no longer grace; otherwise work is no longer work.* [D] 11:8 Lit *stupification* [E] 11:8 Dt 29:4; Is 29:10 [F] 11:9 Lit *table* [G] 11:9-10 Ps 69:22-23 [H] 11:11,12 Or *transgression* [I] 11:14 Lit *flesh* [J] 11:17 Other mss read *the root and the richness* [K] 11:26 Or *And then all* [L] 11:26-27 Is 59:20-21 [M] 11:27 Jr 31:31-34

irrevocable.[A,a] 30 As you once disobeyed God,
but now have received mercy through their
disobedience, 31 so they too have now disobeyed, resulting in mercy to you, so that
they also now[B] may receive mercy. 32 For God
has imprisoned all in disobedience,[b] so that
He may have mercy on all.

A Hymn of Praise

33 Oh, the depth of the riches[c]
both of the wisdom and the knowledge
of God![d]
How unsearchable His judgments[e]
and untraceable His ways!
34 **For who has known the mind**
of the Lord?[f]
Or who has been His counselor?
35 **Or who has ever first given to Him,**
and has to be repaid?[C,g]
36 For from Him and through Him
and to Him are all things.[h]
To Him be the glory forever. ·Amen.

A Living Sacrifice

12 Therefore, ·brothers, by the mercies of
God, I urge you[i] to present your bodies
as a living sacrifice,[j] holy and pleasing to God;
this is your spiritual worship.[D] 2 Do not be
conformed[k] to this age,[l] but be transformed
by the renewing of your mind,[m] so that you
may discern what is the good, pleasing, and
perfect will[n] of God.

Many Gifts but One Body

3 For by the grace[o] given to me, I tell everyone among you not to think of himself more
highly than he should think.[p] Instead, think
sensibly, as God has distributed a measure
of faith[q] to each one. 4 Now as we have many
parts in one body,[r] and all the parts do not
have the same function, 5 in the same way we
who are many[s] are one body in Christ[t] and individually members of one another. 6 According to the grace given to us, we have different
gifts:[u]

If prophecy,[v]
use it according to the standard
of one's[E] faith;
7 if service,[w] in service;
if teaching,[x] in teaching;
8 if exhorting,[y] in exhortation;
giving, with generosity;[z]
leading,[aa] with diligence;
showing mercy, with cheerfulness.[ab]

Christian Ethics

9 Love must be without hypocrisy.[ac] Detest
evil;[ad] cling to what is good. 10 Show family affection to one another with brotherly love.[ae]
Outdo one another in showing honor.[af] 11 Do
not lack diligence; be fervent in spirit;[ag] serve
the Lord.[ah] 12 Rejoice in hope;[ai] be patient in
affliction;[aj] be persistent in prayer.[ak] 13 Share
with the ·saints in their needs;[al] pursue hospitality.[am] 14 Bless those who persecute you;[an]
bless and do not curse. 15 Rejoice with those
who rejoice;[ao] weep with those who weep.
16 Be in agreement with one another.[ap] Do not
be proud;[aq] instead, associate with the humble. Do not be wise in your own estimation.[ar]
17 Do not repay anyone evil for evil.[as] Try to
do what is honorable[at] in everyone's eyes. 18 If
possible, on your part, live at peace with everyone.[au] 19 Friends, do not avenge yourselves;
instead, leave room for His[F] wrath. For it is
written: **Vengeance belongs to Me; I will re-**
pay,[G,av] says the Lord. 20 But

If your enemy is hungry, feed him.[aw]
If he is thirsty, give him something
to drink.
For in so doing
you will be heaping fiery coals
on his head.[H,ax]

21 Do not be conquered by evil, but conquer
evil with good.

A Christian's Duties to the State

13 Everyone must submit to the governing
authorities,[ay] for there is no authority
except from God,[az] and those that exist are instituted by God. 2 So then, the one who resists
the authority is opposing God's command,
and those who oppose it will bring judgment

[a] **11:29** Heb 7:21 [b] **11:32** Rm 3:9; Gl 3:22-23 [c] **11:33** Rm 2:4; Eph 3:8 [d] Col 2:3; Eph 3:10 [e] Jb 5:9; 11:7; 15:8 [f] **11:34** Is 40:13-14; 1Co 2:16 [g] **11:34-35** Jb 35:7; 41:11; Is 40:13; Jr 23:18 [h] **11:36** 1Co 8:6; 11:12; Col 1:16; Heb 2:10 [i] **12:1** 1Co 1:10; 2Co 10:2; Eph 4:1; 1Pt 2:11 [j] Rm 6:13,16,19; 1Co 6:20; Heb 13:15; 1Pt 2:5 [k] **12:2** 1Pt 1:14 [l] Mt 13:22; Gl 1:4; 1Jn 2:15 [m] Eph 4:23; Ti 3:5 [n] Eph 5:10,17; Col 1:9 [o] **12:3** Rm 1:5; 15:15; 1Co 3:10; 15:10; Gl 2:9; Eph 3:7-8 [p] Rm 11:20 [q] 1Co 7:17; 2Co 10:13; Eph 4:7; 1Pt 4:11 [r] **12:4** 1Co 12:12-14; Eph 4:4,16 [s] **12:5** 1Co 10:17,23 [t] 1Co 12:20,27; Eph 4:12,25 [u] **12:6** 1Co 7:7; 12:4; 1Pt 4:10-11 [v] Ac 13:1; 1Co 12:10 [w] **12:7** Ac 6:1; 1Co 12:28 [x] Ac 13:1; 1Co 14:26 [y] **12:8** Ac 4:36; 11:23; 13:15 [z] 2Co 8:2; 9:11,13 [aa] 1Co 12:28; 1Tm 5:17 [ab] 2Co 9:7 [ac] **12:9** 2Co 6:6; 1Tm 1:5 [ad] 1Th 5:21-22 [ae] **12:10** Jn 13:34; 1Th 4:9; Heb 13:1; 2Pt 1:7 [af] Rm 13:7; Php 2:3; 1Pt 2:17 [ag] **12:11** Ac 18:25 [ah] Ac 20:19 [ai] **12:12** Rm 5:2 [aj] Heb 10:32,36 [ak] Ac 1:14 [al] **12:13** Rm 15:25; 1Co 16:15; 2Co 9:1; Heb 6:10 [am] Mt 25:35; 1Tm 3:2 [an] **12:14** Mt 5:44; Lk 6:22; 1Co 4:12 [ao] **12:15** Job 30:25; Heb 13:3 [ap] **12:16** Rm 15:5; 2Co 13:11; Php 2:2; 4:2; 1Pt 3:8 [aq] Rm 11:20 [ar] Rm 11:25; Pr 3:7 [as] **12:17** Pr 20:22; 24:29 [at] 2Co 8:21 [au] **12:18** Mk 9:50; Rm 14:19 [av] **12:19** Dt 32:35; Ps 94:1; 1Th 4:6; Heb 10:30 [aw] **12:20** Mt 5:44; Lk 6:27 [ax] 2Kg 6:22; Pr 25:21-22 [ay] **13:1** Ti 3:1; 1Pt 2:13 [az] Dn 2:21; 4:17; Jn 19:1

A **11:29** Or *are not taken back* B **11:31** Other mss omit *now* C **11:34-35** Jb 41:11; Is 40:13; Jr 23:18 D **12:1** Or *your reasonable service* E **12:6** Or *the* F **12:19** Lit *the* G **12:19** Dt 32:35 H **12:20** Pr 25:21-22

on themselves. 3 For rulers are not a terror[a] to
good conduct, but to bad. Do you want to be
unafraid of the authority? Do what is good,
and you will have its approval. 4 For government is God's servant for your good. But if
you do wrong, be afraid, because it does not
carry the sword for no reason. For government is God's servant, an avenger[b] that brings
wrath on the one who does wrong. 5 Therefore, you must submit, not only because of
wrath, but also because of your conscience.[c]
6 And for this reason you pay taxes, since the
authorities are God's public servants, continually attending to these tasks.[A] 7 Pay your obligations[d] to everyone: taxes to those you owe
taxes,[e] tolls to those you owe tolls, respect to
those you owe respect,[f] and honor to those
you owe honor.

Love, Our Primary Duty

8 Do not owe anyone anything,[B] except to
love one another, for the one who loves another has fulfilled the law.[g] 9 The commandments:

Do not commit adultery;
do not murder;
do not steal;[C]
do not covet;[D,h]

and whatever other commandment—all are
summed up by this: **Love your neighbor as
yourself.**[E,i]
10 Love does no wrong to a neighbor. Love,
therefore, is the fulfillment of the law.

Put On Christ

11 Besides this, knowing the time, it is already the hour[j] for you[F] to wake up from
sleep,[k] for now our salvation is nearer than
when we first believed.[l] 12 The night is nearly
over, and the daylight is near,[m] so let us discard the deeds of darkness[n] and put on
the armor of light.[o] 13 Let us •walk with decency,[p] as in the daylight: not in carousing
and drunkenness;[q] not in sexual impurity
and promiscuity; not in quarreling and jealousy. 14 But put on the Lord Jesus Christ,[r] and
make no plans to satisfy the fleshly desires.[s]

[a]**13:3** 1Pt 2:14 [b]**13:4** 1Th 4:6 [c]**13:5** 1Pt 2:13,19 [d]**13:7** Mt 22:21 [e]Lk 20:22; 23:2 [f]Mt 17:25 [g]**13:8** Mt 7:12; 22:39; Jn 13:34; Rm 12:10; Gl 5:14; Jms 2:8 [h]**13:9** Ex 20:13-17; Dt 5:17-21 [i]Lv 19:18; Mt 19:19 [j]**13:11** 1Co 7:29; 10:11; Jms 5:8; 1Pt 4:7; 2Pt 3:9,11; 1Jn 2:18; Rv 1:3; 22:10 [k]Mk 13:37; 1Co 15:34; Eph 5:14; 1Th 5:6 [l]Ac 19:2; 1Co 3:5; 15:2 [m]**13:12** Heb 10:25; 1Jn 2:8; Rv 1:3; 22:10 [n]Eph 5:11 [o]2Co 6:7; 10:4; Eph 6:11,13; 1Th 5:8 [p]**13:13** 1Th 4:12 [q]Lk 21:34; Gl 5:21; Eph 5:18; 1Pt 4:3 [r]**13:14** Jb 29:14; Gl 3:27; Eph 4:24; Col 3:10,12 [s]Gl 5:16; 1Pt 2:11 [t]**14:1** Ac 28:2; Rm 11:15; 12:3; 15:7 [u]Rm 15:1; 1Co 8:9-11; 9:22 [v]**14:2** Rm 14:14 [w]**14:3** Lk 18:9 [x]Col 2:16 [y]Ac 28:2; Rm 11:15; 15:7 [z]**14:4** Rm 9:20; Jms 4:12 [aa]**14:5** Gl 4:10 [ab]Lk 1:1; Rm 4:21 [ac]**14:6** Mt 14:19; 1Co 10:30; 1Tm 4:3-4 [ad]**14:7** Rm 8:38; 2Co 5:15; Gl 2:20; Php 1:20 [ae]**14:8** Lk 20:38; Php 1:20; 1Th 5:10; Rv 14:13 [af]**14:9** Rv 1:18; 2:8 [ag]Mt 28:18; Jn 12:24; Php 2:11; 1Th 5:10 [ah]**14:10** Rm 2:16; 2Co 5:10 [ai]**14:11** Php 2:10-11 [aj]Is 45:23; 49:18 [ak]**14:12** Mt 12:36; 16:27; 1Pt 4:5

The Law of Liberty

14 Accept[t] anyone who is weak in faith,[G,u]
but don't argue about doubtful issues.
2 One person believes he may eat anything,[v]
but one who is weak eats only vegetables.
3 One who eats must not look down on one
who does not eat,[w] and one who does not eat
must not criticize one who does,[x] because
God has accepted him.[y] 4 Who are you to criticize[z] another's household slave? Before his
own Lord he stands or falls. And he will stand.
For the Lord is able[H] to make him stand.
5 One person considers one day to be above
another day.[aa] Someone else considers every
day to be the same. Each one must be fully
convinced in his own mind.[ab] 6 Whoever observes the day, observes it for the honor of the
Lord.[I] Whoever eats, eats for the Lord, since
he gives thanks to God;[ac] and whoever does
not eat, it is for the Lord that he does not eat
it, yet he thanks God. 7 For none of us lives to
himself, and no one dies to himself.[ad] 8 If we
live, we live for the Lord; and if we die, we die
for the Lord. Therefore, whether we live or
die, we belong to the Lord.[ae] 9 Christ died and
came to life[af] for this: that He might rule over
both the dead and the living.[ag] 10 But you, why
do you criticize your brother? Or you, why do
you look down on your brother? For we will
all stand before the tribunal of God.[J,ah] 11 For
it is written:

As I live, says the Lord,
every knee will bow to Me,[ai]
and every tongue will give praise
to God.[K,aj]

12 So then, each of us will give an account of
himself to God.[ak]

The Law of Love

13 Therefore, let us no longer criticize one
another.[al] Instead decide never to put a stumbling block or pitfall in your brother's way.[am]
14 (I know and am persuaded by the Lord
Jesus that nothing is •unclean in itself.[an] Still,
to someone who considers a thing to be unclean, to that one it is unclean.[ao]) 15 For if your

[al]**14:13** Mt 7:1; Rm 14:3 [am]1Co 8:13 [an]**14:14** Ac 10:15; Rm 14:2,20 [ao]1Co 8:7

[A]13:6 Lit *to this very thing* [B]13:8 Or *Leave no debt outstanding to anyone* [C]13:9 Other mss add *you shall not bear false witness* [D]13:9 Ex 20:13-17; Dt 5:17-21 [E]13:9 Lv 19:18 [F]13:11 Other mss read *for us* [G]14:1 Or *weak in the Faith* [H]14:4 Other mss read *For God has the power* [I]14:6 Other mss add *but whoever does not observe the day, it is to the Lord that he does not observe it* [J]14:10 Other mss read *of Christ* [K]14:11 Is 45:23; 49:18

brother is hurt by what you eat, you are no longer ·walking according to love.[a] Do not destroy that one Christ died for by what you eat.[b] 16 Therefore, do not let your good be slandered,[c] 17 for the kingdom of God is not eating and drinking,[d] but righteousness, peace, and joy[e] in the Holy Spirit. 18 Whoever serves Christ[f] in this way is acceptable to God and approved by men.[g]

19 So then, we must pursue what promotes peace[h] and what builds up one another.[i] 20 Do not tear down God's work because of food. Everything is ·clean, but it is wrong for a man to cause stumbling by what he eats.[j] 21 It is a noble thing not to eat meat, or drink wine, or do anything that makes your brother stumble.[A] 22 Do you have a conviction?[B] Keep it to yourself before God. The man who does not condemn himself by what he approves is blessed.[k] 23 But whoever doubts stands condemned if he eats,[l] because his eating is not from a conviction,[C] and everything that is not from a conviction[C] is sin.

Pleasing Others, Not Ourselves

15 Now we who are strong have an obligation to bear the weaknesses of those without strength,[m] and not to please ourselves. 2 Each one of us must please his neighbor for his good, to build him up.[n] 3 For even the ·Messiah did not please Himself.[o] On the contrary, as it is written, **The insults of those who insult You have fallen on Me.**[D,p] 4 For whatever was written in the past was written for our instruction,[q] so that we may have hope through endurance and through the encouragement from the Scriptures. 5 Now may the God who gives[E] endurance and encouragement[r] allow you to live in harmony with one another,[s] according to the command of Christ Jesus, 6 so that you may glorify the God and Father of our Lord Jesus Christ[t] with a united mind and voice.

Glorifying God Together

7 Therefore accept one another,[u] just as the Messiah also accepted you, to the glory of God. 8 For I say that the Messiah became a servant of the circumcised[F] on behalf of God's truth,[v] to confirm the promises to the fathers,[w] 9 and so that Gentiles[x] may glorify God for His mercy.[y] As it is written:

Therefore I will praise You
among the Gentiles,
and I will sing psalms to Your name.[G,z]

10 Again it says: **Rejoice, you Gentiles, with His people!**[H,aa] 11 And again:

Praise the Lord, all you Gentiles;
all the peoples should praise Him![I,ab]

12 And again, Isaiah says:

The root of Jesse[ac] **will appear,**
the One who rises to rule
the Gentiles;
the Gentiles will hope in Him.[J,ad]

13 Now may the God of hope fill you with all joy and peace as you believe in Him[ae] so that you may overflow with hope by the power of the Holy Spirit.[af]

From Jerusalem to Illyricum

14 My ·brothers, I myself am convinced about you that you also are full of goodness,[ag] filled with all knowledge,[ah] and able to instruct one another. 15 Nevertheless, I have written to remind you more boldly on some points[K] because of the grace given me by God[ai] 16 to be a minister of Christ Jesus to the Gentiles,[aj] serving as a priest of God's good news.[ak] My purpose is that the offering of the Gentiles may be acceptable,[al] ·sanctified by the Holy Spirit. 17 Therefore I have reason to boast in Christ Jesus[am] regarding what pertains to God.[an] 18 For I would not dare say anything except what Christ has accomplished through me[ao] to make the Gentiles obedient by word and deed, 19 by the power of miraculous signs and wonders,[ap] and by the power of God's Spirit. As a result, I have fully proclaimed the good news about the Messiah from Jerusalem[aq] all the way around to Illyricum.[L,ar] 20 My aim is to evangelize where Christ has not been named,[as] so that I will not build on someone else's foundation,[at] 21 but, as it is written:

a 14:15 Eph 5:2
b 1Co 8:11
c 14:16 1Co 10:30; Ti 2:5
d 14:17 1Co 8:8
e Rm 15:13; Gl 5:22
f 14:18 Rm 16:18
g 2Co 8:21; Php 4:8; 1Pt 2:12
h 14:19 Ps 34:14; Rm 12:18; 1Co 7:15; 2Tm 2:22; Heb 12:14
i Rm 15:2; 1Co 10:23; 14:3,26; 2Co 12:19; Eph 4:12,29
j 14:20 1Co 8:9-13
k 14:22 1Jn 3:21
l 14:23 Rm 14:5
m 15:1 Rm 14:1; Gl 6:2; 1Th 5:14
n 15:2 1Co 9:22; 10:24,33; 2Co 13:9
o 15:3 2Co 8:9
p Ps 69:9
q 15:4 Rm 4:23; 2Tm 3:16
r 15:5 2Co 1:3
s Rm 12:16
t 15:6 Rv 1:6
u 15:7 Rm 14:1
v 15:8 Mt 15:24; Ac 3:26
w Rm 4:16; 2Co 1:20
x 15:9 Rm 3:29; 11:30
y Mt 9:8
z 2Sm 22:50; Ps 18:49
aa 15:10 Dt 32:43
ab 15:11 Ps 117:1
ac 15:12 Rv 5:5; 22:16
ad Is 11:10; Mt 12:21
ae 15:13 Rm 14:17
af 1Co 2:4; 1Th 1:5
ag 15:14 Eph 5:9; 2Th 1:11
ah 1Co 1:5; 8:1,7,10; 12:8; 13:2
ai 15:15 Rm 12:3
aj 15:16 Ac 9:15; Rm 11:13
ak Rm 1:1
al Rm 12:1; Eph 5:2; Php 2:17
am 15:17 Php 3:3
an Heb 2:17; 5:1
ao 15:18 Ac 15:12; 21:19; Rm 1:5; 2Co 3:5
ap 15:19 Jn 4:48
aq Ac 22:17-21
ar Ac 20:1
as 15:20 Rm 1:15; 10:15
at 1Co 3:10; 2Co 10:15-16

A 14:21 Other mss add *or offended or weakened* B 14:22 Lit *have faith* C 14:23 Or *faith* D 15:3 Ps 69:9 E 15:5 Lit *God of* F 15:8 The Jews G 15:9 2Sm 22:50; Ps 18:49 H 15:10 Dt 32:43 I 15:11 Ps 117:1 J 15:12 Is 11:10 K 15:15 Other mss add *brothers* L 15:19 A Roman province northwest of Greece on the eastern shore of the Adriatic Sea

Those who were not told about Him
will see,
and those who have not heard
will understand.[A,a]

Paul's Travel Plans

22 That is why I have been prevented many
times from coming to you.[b] 23 But now I no
longer have any work to do in these provinces,[B] and I have strongly desired for many
years to come to you[c] 24 whenever I travel
to Spain.[C] For I hope to see you when I pass
through, and to be assisted by you for my
journey there,[d] once I have first enjoyed your
company[e] for a while. 25 Right now I am traveling to Jerusalem[f] to serve the •saints,[g] 26 for
Macedonia[h] and Achaia[D,i] were pleased to
make a contribution for the poor among the
saints in Jerusalem. 27 Yes, they were pleased,
and indeed are indebted to them. For if the
Gentiles have shared in their spiritual benefits,[j] then they are obligated to minister to
Jews in material needs. 28 So when I have finished this and safely delivered the funds[E] to
them,[k] I will visit you on the way to Spain. 29 I
know that when I come to you, I will come in
the fullness of the blessing[F] of Christ.
30 Now I appeal to you, brothers, through
our Lord Jesus Christ and through the love of
the Spirit,[l] to join with me in fervent prayers
to God on my behalf.[m] 31 Pray that I may be
rescued from the unbelievers in Judea,[n] that
the gift I am bringing to[G] Jerusalem[o] may be
acceptable to the saints,[p] 32 and that, by God's
will,[q] I may come to you with joy[r] and be refreshed together with you.
33 The God of peace be with all of you.[s]
•Amen.

Urgency for Contextualized Ministry

GOD WHO SENDS

The contextualized style of proclamation today and tomorrow no doubt will vary (perhaps radically) from many traditional patterns of evangelistic communication. However, the primacy of evangelism in the emerging world agenda grows out of the primacy of the evangel. Good news is for telling. The concern for reaching the unreached, for evangelism, and for church growth are not only authentic concerns but are also mandatory implications of our mission. They will always be relevant, as long as they are balanced with concern for the prophetic witness to justice and other vital concerns of Christian faith and practice.

(DUBOSE, 156)

Paul's Commendation of Phoebe

16 I commend to you[t] our sister Phoebe,
who is a servant[H] of the church in Cenchreae.[u] 2 So you should welcome her in the
Lord[v] in a manner worthy of the •saints and
assist her in whatever matter she may require
your help. For indeed she has been a benefac-
tor of many — and of me also.

Greeting to Roman Christians

3 Give my greetings to Prisca[I] and
Aquila,[w] my coworkers in[x] Christ Jesus,[y]
4 who risked their own necks for my life.
Not only do I thank them, but so do all
the Gentile churches.
5 Greet also the church that meets in
their home.[z]
Greet my dear friend Epaenetus, who
is the first convert[J,aa] to Christ from
•Asia.[K,ab]
6 Greet Mary,[L] who has worked very
hard for you.[M]
7 Greet Andronicus and Junia,[N] my
fellow countrymen[ac] and fellow
prisoners.[ad] They are noteworthy in the

[a] 15:21 Is 52:15 [b] 15:22 Rm 1:13; 1Th 2:18 [c] 15:23 Ac 19:21; Rm 1:10 [d] 15:24 Ac 15:3 [e] Rm 1:12 [f] 15:25 Ac 19:21 [g] Ac 24:17 [h] 15:26 Ac 16:9; 1Co 16:5; 2Co 1:16; 2:13; 7:5; 8:1; 9:2,4; 11:9; Php 4:15; 1Th 1:7; 4:10; 1Tm 1:3 [i] Ac 18:12; 19:21 [j] 15:27 1Co 9:11 [k] 15:28 Jn 3:33 [l] 15:30 Gl 5:22; Col 1:8 [m] 2Co 1:11; Col 4:12 [n] 15:31 2Co 1:10; 2Th 3:2; 2Tm 3:11; 4:17 [o] 2Co 8:4; 9:1 [p] Ac 9:13; Rm 15:15 [q] 15:32 Ac 18:21; Rm 1:10 [r] Rm 15:23 [s] 15:33 Rm 16:20; 2Co 13:11; Php 4:9; 1Th 5:23; 2Th 3:16; Heb 13:20 [t] 16:1 2Co 3:1 [u] Ac 18:18 [v] 16:2 Php 2:29 [w] 16:3 Ac 18:2 [x] Rm 8:11; 2Co 5:17; 12:2; Gl 1:22 [y] Rm 8:1 [z] 16:5 1Co 16:19; Col 4:15; Phm 2 [aa] 1Co 16:15 [ab] Ac 16:6 [ac] 16:7 Rm 9:3; 16:21 [ad] Col 4:10; Phm 23

[A] 15:21 Is 52:15 [B] 15:23 Lit *now, having no longer a place in these parts* [C] 15:24 Other mss add *I will come to you.* [D] 15:26 The churches of these provinces [E] 15:28 Lit *delivered this fruit* [F] 15:29 Other mss add *of the gospel* [G] 15:31 Lit *that my service for* [H] 16:1 Others interpret this term in a technical sense: *deacon*, or *deaconess*, or *minister*, or *courier* [I] 16:3 Traditionally, *Priscilla*, as in Ac 18:2,18,26 [J] 16:5 Lit *the firstfruits* [K] 16:5 Other mss read *Achaia* [L] 16:6 Or *Maria* [M] 16:6 Other mss read *us* [N] 16:7 Either a feminine name or "Junias," a masculine name

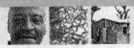

eyes of the apostles,[A,B] and they were
also in Christ before me.
[8]Greet Ampliatus, my dear friend in the
Lord.
[9]Greet Urbanus, our coworker in
Christ, and my dear friend Stachys.
[10]Greet Apelles, who is approved in
Christ.
Greet those who belong to the
household of Aristobulus.[a]
[11]Greet Herodion, my fellow
countryman.
Greet those who belong to the household
of Narcissus who are in the Lord.
[12]Greet Tryphaena and Tryphosa, who
have worked hard in the Lord.
Greet my dear friend Persis, who has
worked very hard in the Lord.
[13]Greet Rufus,[b] chosen in the Lord; also
his mother — and mine.
[14]Greet Asyncritus, Phlegon, Hermes,
Patrobas, Hermas, and the •brothers
who are with them.
[15]Greet Philologus and Julia, Nereus
and his sister, and Olympas, and all the
saints who are with them.[c]
[16]Greet one another with a holy kiss.[d]
All the churches of Christ send you
greetings.

Warning against Divisive People

[17]Now I urge you, brothers, to watch out for
those who cause dissensions and obstacles
contrary to the doctrine you have learned.[e]
Avoid them,[f] [18]for such people do not serve
our Lord Christ[g] but their own appetites.[C,h]
They deceive the hearts of the unsuspecting
with smooth talk and flattering words.[i]

Paul's Gracious Conclusion

[19]The report of your obedience has reached
everyone.[j] Therefore I rejoice over you. But I
want you to be wise about what is good, yet
innocent about what is evil.[k] [20]The God of
peace[l] will soon crush Satan[m] under your feet.
The grace of our Lord Jesus be with you.[n]
[21]Timothy,[o] my coworker, and Lucius,[p] Jason,[q] and Sosipater,[r] my fellow countrymen,
greet you.

[a]**16:10** 1Co 1:11
[b]**16:13** Mk 15:21
[c]**16:15** Rm 16:2
[d]**16:16** 1Co 16:20; 2Co 13:12; 1Th 5:26; 1Pt 5:14
[e]**16:17** 1Tm 1:3; 6:3
[f]Mt 7:15; Gl 1:8-9; 2Th 3:6,14; Ti 3:10; 2Jn 10
[g]**16:18** Rm 14:18
[h]Php 3:19
[i]Col 2:4; 2Pt 2:3
[j]**16:19** Rm 1:8
[k]Jr 4:22; Mt 10:16; 1Co 14:20
[l]**16:20** Rm 15:33
[m]Mt 4:10
[n]1Co 16:23; 2Co 13:13; Gl 6:18; Php 4:23; 1Th 5:28; 2Th 3:18; Rv 22:21
[o]**16:21** Ac 16:1
[p]Ac 13:1
[q]Ac 17:5
[r]Ac 20:4
[s]**16:22** 1Co 16:21; Gl 6:11; Col 4:18; 2Th 3:17; Phm 19
[t]**16:23** Ac 20:4; 1Co 1:14
[u]Ac 19:22
[v]**16:25** Eph 3:20; Jd 24
[w]Rm 2:16
[x]Mt 13:35; Rm 11:25; 1Co 2:1,7; 4:1; Eph 1:9; 3:3,9; 6:19; Col 1:26; 2:2; 4:3; 1Tm 3:16
[y]2Tm 1:9; Ti 1:2
[z]**16:26** Rm 1:2
[aa]Rm 1:5
[ab]**16:27** Rm 11:36

[22]I Tertius, who wrote this letter,[s] greet you
in the Lord.[D]
[23]Gaius,[t] who is host to me and to the whole
church, greets you. Erastus,[u] the city treasurer, and our brother Quartus greet you.
[[24]The grace of our Lord Jesus Christ be
with you all.][E]

Glory to God

[25]Now to Him who has power to strengthen
you[v] according to my gospel and the proclamation about Jesus Christ,[w] according to the
revelation of the •mystery kept silent[x] for long
ages[y] [26]but now revealed and made known
through the prophetic Scriptures,[z] according to the command of the eternal God to
advance the obedience of faith[F,aa] among all
nations — [27]to the only wise God, through
Jesus Christ — to Him be the glory forever![G,ab]
•Amen.

Developing a Missional Theology

GOD WHO SENDS

The growing prominence of mission in modern theology has not prevented the development of missiology as a parallel discipline. In recent years there has been much reflection on the theology of mission. However, the growing feeling is that we need to return to the more primal relation of mission and theology in the sense of their meaning in Scripture and in the early church. What is needed is not so much a theology of mission but a missional theology. In other words, mission does not so much need to be justified theologically as theology needs to be understood missiologically.

(DUBOSE, 148-149)

[A]**16:7** Or *are outstanding among* [B]**16:7** "The apostles" is not always a technical term referring to the 12; cp. 2Co 8:23; Php 2:25 where this word is translated as "messenger." [C]**16:18** Lit *belly* [D]**16:22** Or *letter in the Lord, greet you* [E]**16:24** Other mss omit bracketed text; cp. v. 20 [F]**16:26** Or *the obedience that is faith*, or *the faithful obedience*, or *the obedience that comes from faith*; Rm 1:5 [G]**16:25-27** Other mss have these vv. at the end of chap 14 or 15.

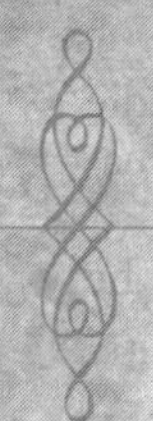

AUTHOR: Paul (Saul of Tarsus)

DATE: Written around A.D. 54 in Ephesus

If churches were filled with nothing but fully transformed people—loving, caring, other-centered servants of Christ—who would not want this new life in the power of God and joy in the praise of God?

But churches are far from paradise. They are populated by less-than-perfect people like you and me. Paul's first letter to the church in Corinth shows this all too plainly. Early in the experience of the community of God, ugliness shows up. Greed, gluttony, sexual immorality, an overemphasis on hyper-spirituality, litigation between people who worship together—the list goes on. This church appears wrecked. Far from giving up, Paul sees such splendid promise in them that he writes some of the most treasured

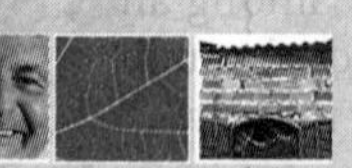

1 CORINTHIANS

chapters of the Bible: on the gifts of the Spirit (chap. 12), on love (chap. 13), on Christ's resurrection (chap. 15). God's mission to these people is not going away. It's going deeper and growing stronger.

Paul writes this book to set the church's affairs in order and to discipline those refusing to repent. He reminds them that the body is a "sanctuary of the Holy Spirit" (6:19)—the earthly home of God. Paul also writes with a hint of solace for a struggling religious minority. The great Greek thinkers dismiss the gospel as nonsense: God crucified? Preposterous! Paul stirs the flagging confidence of the Corinthian Christians. "God's foolishness is wiser than human wisdom," he writes (1:25). In other words, faith does not rest on Greek wisdom and logic, but on God's power. Trust God and walk by the Spirit. The gospel delivered through you may be derided today but ultimately cannot be denied in eternity.

God's message to the world is Christ, who died, was risen, and is coming again. This mission is to tell all people about Him. Paul's key chapters on love and life in the body of Christ finally resolve into practical concerns for needy people, for friends, and for people he has not met but considers his kin in faith. We are taught that every believer has a place in the care for those around us. Empowered by God's Spirit—by His presence and gifting—we are privileged to serve in His mission to all people.

The closing chapter (chap. 16) is filled with warmth and care. Paul never diminishes people into a great collective. He treasures the community of faith that together praises the Lord and serves God's mission—building up faith in every way, loving the world as God does.

Greeting

1 Paul,[a] called as an apostle[b] of Christ Jesus
by God's will,[c] and Sosthenes our brother:[d]
2To God's church at Corinth,[e] to those who
are ·sanctified[f] in Christ Jesus and called[g] as
·saints, with all those in every place who call
on the name[h] of Jesus Christ our Lord—both
their Lord and ours.
3Grace to you and peace from God our Father[i] and the Lord Jesus Christ.

Thanksgiving

4I always thank[j] my God for you because
of God's grace given to you in Christ Jesus,
5that by Him you were enriched[k] in everything—in all speech and all knowledge.[l]
6In this way, the testimony about Christ was
confirmed among you,[m] 7so that you do not
lack any spiritual gift as you eagerly wait[n] for
the revelation[o] of our Lord Jesus Christ. 8He
will also strengthen you to the end,[p] so that
you will be blameless in the day of our Lord
Jesus Christ.[q] 9God is faithful;[r] you were
called by Him[s] into fellowship with His Son,[t]
Jesus Christ our Lord.

Divisions at Corinth

10Now I urge you, ·brothers, in the name
of our Lord Jesus Christ, that all of you agree
in what you say, that there be no divisions
among you, and that you be united with the
same understanding and the same conviction. 11For it has been reported to me about
you, my brothers, by members of Chloe's
household, that there is rivalry[u] among you.
12What I am saying is this: Each of you says,
"I'm with Paul," or "I'm with Apollos,"[v] or
"I'm with ·Cephas,"[w] or "I'm with Christ."[x] 13Is
Christ divided?[y] Was it Paul who was crucified for you? Or were you baptized in Paul's
name? 14I thank God[A,B] that I baptized none
of you except Crispus[z] and Gaius,[aa] 15so that
no one can say you were baptized in my
name. 16I did, in fact, baptize the household[ab]
of Stephanas;[ac] beyond that, I don't know if
I baptized anyone else. 17For Christ did not
send me to baptize, but to evangelize—not
with clever words, so that the cross[ad] of Christ
will not be emptied of its effect.

Christ the Power and Wisdom of God

18For the message of the cross is foolishness
to those who are perishing, but it is God's
power to us who are being saved.[ae] 19For it is
written:

> **I will destroy the wisdom of the wise,**
> **and I will set aside the understanding**
> **of the experts.**[C,af]

20Where is the philosopher?[D] Where is the
scholar? Where is the debater of this age?[ag]
Hasn't God made the world's wisdom foolish? 21For since, in God's wisdom, the ·world
did not know God through wisdom, God was
pleased to save those who believe through the
foolishness of the message preached. 22For
the Jews ask for signs[ah] and the Greeks seek
wisdom, 23but we preach Christ crucified,[ai] a
stumbling block to the Jews and foolishness
to the Gentiles.[E] 24Yet to those who are called,[aj]
both Jews and Greeks, Christ is God's power
and God's wisdom, 25because God's foolishness is wiser than human wisdom, and God's
weakness is stronger than human strength.

Boasting Only in the Lord

26Brothers, consider your calling: Not many
are wise from a human perspective,[F] not
many powerful,[ak] not many of noble birth.
27Instead, God has chosen[al] what is foolish
in the world to shame the wise, and God has
chosen what is weak in the world to shame
the strong. 28God has chosen what is insignificant and despised in the world[am]—what
is viewed as nothing—to bring to nothing
what is viewed as something, 29so that no
one[G] can boast in His presence.[an] 30But it is
from Him that you are in Christ Jesus, who
became God-given wisdom for us—our righteousness,[ao] sanctification,[ap] and ·redemp-
tion,[aq] 31in order that, as it is written:[ar] **The**
one who boasts must boast in the Lord.[H,as]

Paul's Proclamation

2 When I came to you, ·brothers, announcing the testimony[I] of God to you, I did not
come with brilliance[at] of speech[au] or wisdom.
2For I didn't think it was a good idea to know

[a]1:1 Ac 13:9 [b]Rm 1:1 [c]2Co 1:1; Eph 1:1; Col 1:1; 2Tm 1:1 [d]Ac 18:17 [e]1:2 Ac 18:1; 19:1; 2Co 1:1,23; 2Tm 4:20 [f]Ac 20:32; 26:18; 1Co 6:11; Heb 10:10 [g]Rm 1:6-7 [h]Gn 4:26; Ps 79:6; Jn 10:25; Ac 9:14; 15:14; Rv 14:1 [i]1:3 Rm 1:7; 2Co 1:2; Gl 1:3; Eph 1:2; Php 1:2; 2Th 1:2; Ti 1:4 [j]1:4 Rm 1:8; Php 1:3; Col 1:3; 1Th 1:2; 2Th 1:3; 2Tm 1:3; Phm 4 [k]1:5 2Co 8:9; 9:11 [l]Rm 15:14; 1Co 12:8; 2Co 8:7; 1Jn 2:20 [m]1:6 2Th 1:10; 1Tm 2:6; 2Tm 1:8; Rv 1:2 [n]1:7 Lk 17:30; Rm 8:19; Php 3:20; Heb 9:28; 2Pt 3:12 [o]1Pt 4:13 [p]1:8 Php 1:6; 1Th 3:13 [q]Lk 17:24; 1Co 5:5; 2Co 1:14; Php 2:16; Col 1:22 [r]1:9 Dt 7:9; Is 49:7; 1Co 10:13; 2Co 1:18 [s]Rm 8:28 [t]Jn 5:19; Heb 1:2; 1Jn 1:3 [u]1:11 Ti 3:9 [v]1:12 Ti 3:13 [w]Jn 1:42 [x]Mt 23:9-10 [y]1:13 1Co 12:5; 2Co 11:4; Eph 4:5 [z]1:14 Ac 18:8 [aa]Rm 16:23 [ab]1:16 Rm 16:5 [ac]1Co 16:15,17 [ad]1:17 Lk 23:26; Php 3:18 [ae]1:18 Ac 19:11; Rm 1:16; 2Co 13:4 [af]1:19 Is 29:14 [ag]1:20 Lk 16:8 [ah]1:22 Mt 12:38 [ai]1:23 Lk 23:26; 1Co 2:2; Gl 3:1; 5:11 [aj]1:24 Rm 1:6 [ak]1:26 Ac 25:5 [al]1:27 Mt 24:22; Eph 1:4 [am]1:28 Lk 18:9 [an]1:29 Ac 7:46 [ao]1:30 Mt 6:33; Rm 1:17; 2Pt 1:1 [ap]1Th 4:3 [aq]Eph 1:7 [ar]1:31 Mk 1:2 [as]Jr 9:23-24 [at]2:1 1Tm 2:2 [au]Col 4:6

A1:14 Other mss omit *God* B1:14 Or *I am thankful* C1:19 Is 29:14 D1:20 Or *wise* E1:23 Other mss read *Greeks* F1:26 Lit *wise according to the flesh* G1:29 Lit *that not all flesh* H1:31 Jr 9:24 I2:1 Other mss read *mystery*

anything among you except Jesus Christ and
Him crucified.[a] 3 I came to you in weakness,[b]
in fear,[c] and in much trembling.[d] 4 My speech[e]
and my proclamation were not with persuasive[f] words of wisdom[A] but with a powerful
demonstration by the Spirit, 5 so that your
faith might not be based on men's wisdom
but on God's power.[g]

Spiritual Wisdom

6 However, we do speak a wisdom among
the mature,[h] but not a wisdom of this age, or
of the rulers[i] of this age, who are coming to
nothing.[j] 7 On the contrary, we speak God's
hidden wisdom in a ·mystery, a wisdom God
predestined[k] before the ages for our glory.[l]
8 None of the rulers of this age knew this wisdom, for if they had known it, they would not
have crucified the Lord of glory.[m] 9 But as it is
written:

What eye did not see and ear
did not hear,
and what never entered
the human mind —
God prepared this for those
who love Him.[B,n]

10 Now God has revealed these things to us
by the Spirit, for the Spirit searches everything,[o] even the depths of God.[p] 11 For who
among men knows the thoughts[C] of a man
except the spirit[q] of the man that is in him?
In the same way, no one knows[r] the thoughts[C]
of God except the Spirit of God. 12 Now we
have not received the spirit of the ·world, but
the Spirit who comes from God, so that we
may understand what has been freely given
to us by God. 13 We also speak these things,
not in words[s] taught by human wisdom,
but in those taught by the Spirit, explaining
spiritual things to spiritual people.[D] 14 But the
unbeliever[E] does not welcome what comes
from God's Spirit, because it is foolishness to
him; he is not able to understand it since it
is evaluated[F] spiritually. 15 The spiritual person, however, can evaluate[G] everything, yet
he himself cannot be evaluated[F] by anyone.
16 For

who has known the Lord's mind,
that he may instruct Him?[H,t]

But we have the mind of Christ.[u]

The Problem of Immaturity

3 ·Brothers, I was not able to speak to you
as spiritual people but as people of the
flesh, as babies in Christ.[v] 2 I gave you milk
to drink, not solid food, because you were
not yet ready for it. In fact, you are still not
ready, 3 because you are still fleshly. For since
there is envy[w] and strife[I,x] among you, are you
not fleshly and living like unbelievers?[J] 4 For
whenever someone says, "I'm with Paul," and
another, "I'm with Apollos,"[y] are you not unspiritual people?[K,L]

The Role of God's Servants

5 What then is Apollos? And what is Paul?
They are servants through whom you believed, and each has the role the Lord has
given. 6 I planted,[z] Apollos watered, but God
gave the growth. 7 So then neither the one who
plants nor the one who waters is anything,
but only God who gives the growth. 8 Now the
one planting and the one watering are one in
purpose, and each will receive his own reward
according to his own labor. 9 For we are God's
coworkers.[M] You are God's field, God's building.[aa] 10 According to God's grace that was given
to me, I have laid a foundation as a skilled master builder, and another builds on it. But each
one must be careful how he builds on it. 11 For
no one can lay any other foundation[ab] than
what has been laid down. That foundation is
Jesus Christ. 12 If anyone builds on that foundation with gold, silver,[ac] costly stones,[ad] wood,
hay, or straw, 13 each one's work will become
obvious, for the day[N] will disclose it, because
it will be revealed by fire;[ae] the fire will test the
quality of each one's work.[af] 14 If anyone's work
that he has built survives, he will receive a reward. 15 If anyone's work is burned up, it will
be lost, but he will be saved;[ag] yet it will be like
an escape through fire.[O,ah]
16 Don't you yourselves know that you are
God's sanctuary[ai] and that the Spirit of God

[a] **2:2** 1Co 1:23-24; Gl 6:14
[b] **2:3** 2Co 11:30
[c] Rv 11:11
[d] Php 2:12
[e] **2:4** Mt 12:37
[f] Php 1:25
[g] **2:5** Mk 5:30; Lk 1:35; 6:19; Ac 19:11; 2Co 13:4; 2Tm 1:7; Rv 11:17
[h] **2:6** Mt 5:48
[i] Lk 12:58
[j] Heb 2:14
[k] **2:7** Eph 1:5
[l] Lk 24:26; 1Pt 5:1,4
[m] **2:8** Ps 24:7
[n] **2:9** Is 52:15; 64:4; Lk 10:27; 1Jn 4:20
[o] **2:10** Ps 17:3; Jn 14:26
[p] Rm 8:39; 11:33; Eph 3:18
[q] **2:11** Rm 1:9
[r] 1Jn 4:8
[s] **2:13** Mt 12:37
[t] **2:16** Is 40:13
[u] Col 2:2
[v] **3:1** 1Co 14:20; Heb 5:13; 1Pt 2:2
[w] **3:3** Jms 3:14,16
[x] Ti 3:9
[y] **3:4** Ti 3:13
[z] **3:6** Ac 18:4-11; 1Co 4:15; 9:1; 15:1
[aa] **3:9** 1Pt 2:5
[ab] **3:11** Is 28:16; Rm 15:20; 2Co 10:16; 11:4; Gl 1:6-9
[ac] **3:12** Jms 5:3
[ad] Rv 17:4
[ae] **3:13** 2Th 1:8; 1Pt 1:7
[af] Ps 62:12; Pr 24:12; Mt 16:27; 2Co 5:10; 1Pt 1:17
[ag] **3:15** Mt 9:22; Ac 16:30; Eph 2:8
[ah] Jd 23
[ai] **3:16** Lk 1:21

[A] **2:4** Other mss read *human wisdom* [B] **2:9** Is 52:15; 64:4 [C] **2:11** Or *things* [D] **2:13** Or *things with spiritual words* [E] **2:14** Or *unspiritual*; lit *natural* [F] **2:14,15** Or *judged, or discerned* [G] **2:15** Or *judge, or discern* [H] **2:16** Is 40:13 [I] **3:3** Other mss add *and divisions* [J] **3:3** Lit *and walking according to man* [K] **3:4** Other mss read *are you not carnal* [L] **3:4** Lit *not just human* [M] **3:9** Or *are coworkers belonging to God* [N] **3:13** The day of Christ's judgment of believers [O] **3:15** Lit *yet so as through fire*

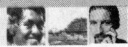

lives in you?[a] 17 If anyone destroys God's sanctuary, God will destroy him;[b] for God's sanctuary is holy,[c] and that is what you are.

The Folly of Human Wisdom

18 No one should deceive[d] himself. If anyone among you thinks he is wise in this age,[e]
he must become foolish[f] so that he can become wise.[g] 19 For the wisdom of this ˈworld is
foolishness[h] with God, since it is written:[i] **He
catches the wise in their craftiness;**[A,j] 20 and
again, **The Lord knows that the reasonings**[k]
of the wise are meaningless.[B,l] 21 So no one
should boast in human leaders, for everything is yours[m]— 22 whether Paul or Apollos
or ˈCephas[n] or the world or life[o] or death[p] or
things present or things to come[q]—everything is yours, 23 and you belong to Christ,[r]
and Christ belongs to God.

The Faithful Manager

4 A person should consider us in this way:
as servants[s] of Christ and managers[t] of
God's ˈmysteries.[u] 2 In this regard, it is expected of managers that each one of them be
found faithful.[v] 3 It is of little[w] importance to
me that I should be evaluated[x] by you or by
any human court.[C] In fact, I don't even evaluate myself. 4 For I am not conscious of anything against myself, but I am not justified[y]
by this. The One who evaluates me is the Lord.
5 Therefore don't judge[z] anything prematurely, before the Lord comes,[aa] who will both
bring to light what is hidden in darkness and
reveal the intentions of the hearts. And then
praise will come to each one from God.[ab]

The Apostles' Example of Humility

6 Now, ˈbrothers,[ac] I have applied these
things to myself and Apollos[ad] for your benefit, so that you may learn from us the saying:
"Nothing beyond what is written."[D] The purpose is that none of you will be inflated with
pride in favor of one person over another.
7 For who makes you so superior? What do
you have that you didn't receive? If, in fact,
you did receive it, why do you boast as if you
hadn't received it? 8 You are already full! You
are already rich! You have begun to reign as
kings without us—and I wish you did reign,

[a] **3:16** Lv 26:11; Jms 4:5
[b] **3:17** Heb 6:8
[c] Ps 20:6; 1Co 7:14
[d] **3:18** 2Co 11:3
[e] Lk 16:8
[f] Mt 5:22
[g] Is 5:21; Jr 8:8-9; Gl 6:3
[h] **3:19** 1Co 1:18
[i] Ac 15:15; Gl 4:22
[j] Jb 5:13; Lk 20:23
[k] **3:20** Mt 15:19; 1Tm 2:8
[l] Ps 94:11
[m] **3:21** Rm 8:32
[n] **3:22** Jn 1:42
[o] 1Jn 5:12
[p] Mt 10:21; Jn 8:51; Php 3:10
[q] Rm 8:38
[r] **3:23** Nm 3:12
[s] **4:1** Jn 18:36
[t] Lk 16:1
[u] 1Co 2:7
[v] **4:2** Nm 12:7
[w] **4:3** Mt 5:19
[x] 1Co 2:14
[y] **4:4** Ac 13:39
[z] **4:5** Lk 6:37
[aa] Mk 8:38; 1Pt 5:6
[ab] 2Co 10:18
[ac] **4:6** Ac 9:30
[ad] Ti 3:13
[ae] **4:10** 1Pt 5:14
[af] **4:12** 2Jn 8
[ag] Ac 18:3
[ah] **4:13** Is 64:6; Lm 3:45
[ai] **4:14** 1Th 2:11; Phm 1
[aj] **4:15** Gl 4:19; Phm 10

so that we could also reign with you! 9 For I
think God has displayed us, the apostles, in
last place, like men condemned to die: We
have become a spectacle to the world and to
angels and to men. 10 We are fools for Christ,
but you are wise in Christ![ae] We are weak, but
you are strong! You are distinguished, but we
are dishonored! 11 Up to the present hour we
are both hungry and thirsty; we are poorly
clothed, roughly treated, homeless; 12 we labor, working[af] with our own hands.[ag] When
we are reviled, we bless; when we are persecuted, we endure it; 13 when we are slandered,
we respond graciously. Even now, we are like
the world's garbage, like the dirt everyone
scrapes off their sandals.[ah]

Paul's Fatherly Care

14 I'm not writing this to shame you, but to
warn you as my dear children.[ai] 15 For you can
have 10,000 instructors in Christ, but you
can't have many fathers. For I became your
father[aj] in Christ Jesus through the gospel.
16 Therefore I urge you to imitate me. 17 This

TEXT MESSAGES

Text Message

Can you hear Paul's anger at the people of this church? His biting sarcasm seems out of character for a seasoned missionary. Is tough talk sometimes appropriate in God's mission to the world? Yes. Paul models it here. But just as quickly, Paul changes his tone to resemble a loving dad speaking to children. Point duly noted. When tough talk is necessary, follow it with reminders of God's great love.

The invitation to repent and believe is always a homecoming, a reconciliation, initiated by the Father to wandering children.

[A] **3:19** Jb 5:13 [B] **3:20** Ps 94:11 [C] **4:3** Lit *a human day* [D] **4:6** The words in quotation marks could = the OT, a Jewish maxim, or a popular proverb.

is why I have sent[a] Timothy to you. He is my
dearly loved and faithful[b] son in the Lord.
He will remind you about my ways in Christ
Jesus, just as I teach everywhere in every
church. 18 Now some are inflated with pride,
as though I were not coming to you. 19 But I
will come to you soon,[c] if the Lord wills, and
I will know not the talk but the power of
those who are inflated with pride. 20 For the
kingdom of God is not a matter of talk but of
power. 21 What do you want? Should I come
to you with a rod,[d] or in love and a spirit of
gentleness?[e]

Immoral Church Members

5 It is widely reported that there is sexual
immorality[f] among you, and the kind
of sexual immorality that is not even tolerated[A] among the Gentiles[g] — a man is living
with his father's wife.[h] 2 And you are inflated
with pride, instead of filled with grief[i] so that
he who has committed this act might be removed from your congregation. 3 For though
I am absent in body but present in spirit,[j] I
have already decided about the one who has
done this thing as though I were present.
4 When you are assembled in the name of
our Lord Jesus with my spirit and with the
power of our Lord Jesus, 5 turn that one over
to Satan for the destruction of the flesh,[k] so
that his spirit may be saved in the Day of the
Lord.[l]
6 Your boasting is not good. Don't you know
that a little yeast[m] permeates the whole batch
of dough?[n] 7 ·Clean out the old yeast so that
you may be a new batch. You are indeed unleavened, for Christ our ·Passover[o] has been
sacrificed.[B] 8 Therefore, let us observe the
feast, not with old yeast or with the yeast
of malice and evil[p] but with the unleavened
bread of sincerity and truth.

Church Discipline

9 I wrote to you in a letter not to associate[q]
with sexually immoral people.[r] 10 I did not
mean the immoral people of this ·world or
the greedy[s] and swindlers[t] or idolaters; otherwise you would have to leave the world.[u]

[a] **4:17** 2Co 9:3; Eph 6:21-22; Col 4:7-8; Phm 12
[b] Nm 12:7
[c] **4:19** Ac 19:21; 1Co 16:5; 2Co 1:15-16
[d] **4:21** 2Co 1:23; 2:1,3; 12:20-21; 13:2,10
[e] Jms 3:13
[f] **5:1** 1Th 4:3
[g] Gl 1:16
[h] Lv 18:8; Dt 22:30; 27:20
[i] **5:2** Lk 6:25
[j] **5:3** Col 2:5; 1Th 2:17
[k] **5:5** 1Jn 5:16
[l] Mt 25:13; Ac 2:20; Php 1:6
[m] **5:6** Lk 13:21; Gl 5:9
[n] **5:6-8** Lk 13:21
[o] **5:7** Ex 12
[p] **5:8** Mk 7:22; Rm 1:29
[q] **5:9** 2Th 3:14
[r] 1Co 6:9; Eph 5:5; 1Tm 1:10; Heb 12:16; 13:4; Rv 21:8; 22:15
[s] **5:10** Eph 5:5
[t] Lk 18:11
[u] Jn 17:6
[v] **5:11** 2Th 3:6
[w] 1Co 6:10
[x] **5:12** Lk 6:37
[y] **5:13** Dt 17:7
[z] **6:1** Mt 18:15-17
[aa] **6:4** Lk 18:9
[ab] **6:5** 1Co 4:14
[ac] Ac 9:30
[ad] **6:6** Lk 12:46
[ae] **6:7** Rm 11:12
[af] Rv 2:11
[ag] Mk 10:19
[ah] **6:9** Lk 16:10
[ai] Mk 1:15; Ac 20:25
[aj] Eph 5:5
[ak] Lk 18:11
[al] Gn 19:5
[am] **6:10** Jn 10:1
[an] Eph 5:5
[ao] 1Co 5:11
[ap] Lk 18:11
[aq] **6:11** Eph 2:2-3; 4:22; 5:8; Ti 3:3
[ar] Lk 11:2
[as] **6:12** Jn 18:31

11 But now I am writing[C] you not to associate
with anyone who claims to be a believer[D,v]
who is sexually immoral or greedy, an idolater or verbally abusive, a drunkard[w] or a swindler. Do not even eat with such a person. 12 For
what business is it of mine to judge[x] outsiders? Don't you judge those who are inside?
13 But God judges outsiders. **Put away the evil
person from among yourselves.**[E,y]

Lawsuits among Believers

6 If any of you has a legal dispute against
another, do you dare go to court[z] before
the unrighteous,[F] and not before the ·saints?
2 Or don't you know that the saints will judge
the ·world? And if the world is judged by
you, are you unworthy to judge the smallest
cases? 3 Don't you know that we will judge angels — not to mention ordinary matters? 4 So
if you have cases pertaining to this life, do you
select those[G] who have no standing[aa] in the
church to judge? 5 I say this to your shame![ab]
Can it be that there is not one wise person
among you who is able to arbitrate between
his ·brothers?[ac] 6 Instead, believer[H] goes to
court against believer, and that before unbelievers![ad]
7 Therefore, to have legal disputes against
one another is already a moral failure for
you.[ae] Why not rather put up with injustice?[af]
Why not rather be cheated?[ag] 8 Instead, you
act unjustly and cheat — and you do this to
believers! 9 Don't you know that the unrighteous[ah] will not inherit God's kingdom?[ai] Do
not be deceived: No sexually immoral people,
idolaters,[aj] adulterers,[ak] or anyone practicing homosexuality,[I,al] 10 no thieves,[am] greedy[an]
people, drunkards, verbally abusive people,[ao]
or swindlers[ap] will inherit God's kingdom.
11 And some of you used to be like this.[aq] But
you were washed, you were ·sanctified,[ar] you
were ·justified in the name of the Lord Jesus
Christ and by the Spirit of our God.

Glorifying God in Body and Spirit

12 "Everything is permissible[as] for me,"[J] but
not everything is helpful. "Everything is permissible for me," but I will not be brought un-

[A] **5:1** Other mss read *named* [B] **5:7** Other mss add *for us* [C] **5:11** Or *now I wrote* [D] **5:11** Lit *anyone named a brother* [E] **5:13** Dt 17:7 [F] **6:1** Unbelievers; v. 6 [G] **6:4** Or *life, appoint those* (as a command) [H] **6:6-8** Lit *brothers* [I] **6:9** Lit *adulterers, passive homosexual partners, active homosexual partners* [J] **6:12-13** The words in quotation marks are most likely slogans used by some Corinthian Christians and corrected by Paul.

der the control of anything. 13 "Food[a] for the
stomach and the stomach for food," but God
will do away with both of them.[A] The body is
not for sexual immorality[b] but for the Lord,
and the Lord for the body. 14 God raised up the
Lord and will also raise us up by His power.[c]
15 Don't you know that your bodies are a part
of Christ's body?[d] So should I take a part of
Christ's body and make it part of a prostitute? Absolutely not! 16 Don't you know that
anyone joined to a prostitute is one body with
her? For Scripture says, **The two will become
one flesh.**[B,e] 17 But anyone joined[f] to the Lord is
one spirit[g] with Him.
18 Run[h] from sexual immorality! "Every sin
a person can commit is outside the body."[C]
On the contrary, the person who is sexually
immoral[i] sins against his own body. 19 Don't
you know that your body is a sanctuary[j] of
the Holy Spirit[k] who is in you,[l] whom you
have from God? You are not your own, 20 for
you were bought[m] at a price. Therefore glorify
God in your body.[D]

Principles of Marriage

7 Now in response to the matters you
wrote[E] about: "It is good for a man not
to have relations with[F] a woman."[G] 2 But because sexual immorality is so common,[H,n]
each man should have his own wife,[o] and
each woman should have her own husband.
3 A husband should fulfill his marital responsibility[p] to his wife, and likewise a wife to her
husband. 4 A wife does not have the right over
her own body, but her husband does. In the
same way, a husband does not have the right
over his own body, but his wife does. 5 Do
not deprive[q] one another sexually—except
when you agree for a time, to devote yourselves to[I] prayer. Then come together again;
otherwise, Satan may tempt you because of
your lack of self-control. 6 I say the following[J]
as a concession, not as a command. 7 I wish
that all people were just like me. But each has
his own gift[r] from God, one person in this
way and another in that way.

A Word to the Unmarried

8 I say to the unmarried and to widows:[s] It
is good for them if they remain as I am. 9 But
if they do not have self-control,[t] they should
marry, for it is better to marry[u] than to burn
with desire.

About Married People

10 I command the married[v]—not I, but the
Lord—a wife is not to leave[K] her husband.
11 But if she does leave, she must remain unmarried or be reconciled to her husband—and a
husband is not to leave his wife.[w] 12 But I (not
the Lord)[L] say to the rest: If any brother[x] has
an unbelieving wife and she is willing to live
with him, he must not leave her. 13 Also, if any
woman has an unbelieving husband and he is
willing to live with her, she must not leave her
husband. 14 For the unbelieving husband is set
apart for God[y] by the wife, and the unbelieving wife is set apart for God by the husband.[M]
Otherwise your children would be corrupt,
but now they are set apart for God. 15 But if
the unbeliever leaves, let him leave. A brother
or a sister is not bound in such cases. God has
called you[N] to live in peace. 16 For you, wife,
how do you know whether you will save your
husband? Or you, husband, how do you know
whether you will save your wife?

Various Situations of Life

17 However, each one must live his life in
the situation the Lord assigned when God
called[z] him.[O] This is what I command in all
the churches. 18 Was anyone already circumcised when he was called? He should not
undo his circumcision. Was anyone called
while uncircumcised? He should not get
circumcised. 19 Circumcision does not matter and uncircumcision does not matter, but
keeping God's commands does. 20 Each person should remain in the life situation[P] in
which he was called. 21 Were you called while
a ˙slave? It should not be a concern to you.
But if you can become free, by all means take
the opportunity.[Q] 22 For he who is called by the

[a] **6:13** 1Tm 6:8 [b] 1Th 4:3 [c] **6:14** Mk 5:30; Lk 1:35; 6:19; Ac 19:11; 2Co 13:4; Rv 11:17 [d] **6:15** Rm 12:5; 1Co 12:27; Eph 5:30 [e] **6:16** Gn 2:24 [f] **6:17** Jn 11:52 [g] Ps 51:12 [h] **6:18** Jms 4:7 [i] 1Co 10:8 [j] **6:19** Lk 1:21 [k] Rm 8:9,23; 1Co 7:40; 2Co 4:13; Jd 19 [l] Jms 4:5; 1Jn 4:4 [m] **6:20** 2Pt 2:1 [n] **7:2** 1Th 4:3 [o] Mt 1:6; 1Pt 3:1 [p] **7:3** Rm 13:7 [q] **7:5** Mk 10:19 [r] **7:7** 2Co 1:11 [s] **7:8** Jms 1:27 [t] **7:9** 1Co 9:25 [u] 1Tm 5:14 [v] **7:10** 1Tm 5:14 [w] **7:11** Dt 22:19 [x] **7:12** Ac 9:30 [y] **7:14** Lk 11:2 [z] **7:17** Col 3:15

[A] **6:13** Lit *both it and them* [B] **6:16** Gn 2:24 [C] **6:18** See note at 1Co 6:12-13. [D] **6:20** Other mss add *and in your spirit, which belong to God.* [E] **7:1** Other mss add *to me* [F] **7:1** Lit *not to touch* [G] **7:1** The words in quotation marks are a principle that the Corinthians wrote to Paul about to ask for his view. [H] **7:2** Lit *because of immoralities* [I] **7:5** Other mss add *fasting and to* [J] **7:6** Lit *say this*; some interpret the word as referring to v. 2, vv. 2-5, v. 5 (wholly or in part), or v. 6 [K] **7:10** Or *separate from*, or *divorce* [L] **7:12** Jesus did not address the situation of a marriage in the Gentile world where only one person is a believer. [M] **7:14** Lit *the brother* [N] **7:15** Other mss read *us* [O] **7:17** Lit *called each* [P] **7:20** Lit *in the calling* [Q] **7:21** Or *But even though you can become free, make the most of your position as a slave.*

Lord as a slave[a] is the Lord's freedman.[A] Likewise he who is called as a free man[B] is Christ's
slave. 23 You were bought[b] at a price; do not become slaves of men. 24 Brothers, each person
should remain with God in whatever situation he was called.

About the Unmarried and Widows

25 About virgins: I have no command from
the Lord, but I do give an opinion as one who
by the Lord's mercy[c] is trustworthy.[d] 26 Therefore I consider this to be good because of the
present distress: It is fine for a man to remain as he is. 27 Are you bound to a wife? Do
not seek to be loosed. Are you loosed from a
wife? Do not seek a wife. 28 However, if you
do get married,[e] you have not sinned, and if
a virgin marries, she has not sinned. But such
people will have trouble in this life,[C] and I am
trying to spare you. 29 And I say this, brothers:
The time is limited,[f] so from now on those
who have wives should be as though they had
none, 30 those who weep as though they did
not weep, those who rejoice[g] as though they
did not rejoice, those who buy as though
they did not possess, 31 and those who use the
world as though they did not make full use of
it. For this world in its current form is passing away.[h]

32 I want you to be without concerns. An unmarried man is concerned about the things
of the Lord—how he may please[i] the Lord.
33 But a married man is concerned about the
things of the world—how he may please his
wife— 34 and his interests are divided. An
unmarried woman or a virgin is concerned
about the things of the Lord,[j] so that she may
be holy both in body and in spirit. But a married woman is concerned about the things
of the world—how she may please her husband. 35 Now I am saying this for your own
benefit, not to put a restraint on you, but because of what is proper and so that you may
be devoted to the Lord without distraction.

36 But if any man thinks he is acting improperly toward his virgin,[D] if she is past
marriageable age,[E] and so it must be, he can
do what he wants. He is not sinning; they can
get married. 37 But he who stands firm in his
heart (who is under no compulsion, but has
control over his own will[k]) and has decided
in his heart to keep his own virgin, will do
well. 38 So then he who marries[F] his virgin
does well, but he who does not marry[G] will
do better.

39 A wife is bound[H] as long as her husband
is living. But if her husband dies, she is free
to be married to anyone she wants—only in
the Lord.[I] 40 But she is happier if she remains
as she is, in my opinion. And I think that I also
have the Spirit of God.

Food Offered to Idols

8 About food offered to idols:[l] We know
that "we all have knowledge."[J] Knowledge
inflates with pride,[m] but love[n] builds up. 2 If
anyone thinks he knows anything, he does
not yet know it as he ought to know it.[o] 3 But
if anyone loves God,[p] he is known[q] by Him.

4 About eating food offered to idols, then,
we know that "an idol is nothing in the
world," and that "there is no God but one."[r]
5 For even if there are so-called gods,[s] whether
in heaven or on earth—as there are many
"gods" and many "lords"—

6 yet for us there is one God, the Father.[t]
All things are from Him,[u]
and we exist for Him.
And there is one Lord, Jesus Christ.
All things are through Him,
and we exist through Him.[v]

7 However, not everyone has this knowledge.
In fact, some have been so used to idolatry up
until now that when they eat food offered to
an idol, their conscience, being weak, is defiled. 8 Food will not make us acceptable to
God. We are not inferior if we don't eat, and
we are not better if we do eat.[w] 9 But be careful
that this right of yours in no way becomes a
stumbling block[x] to the weak. 10 For if someone sees you, the one who has this knowledge,
dining in an idol's temple, won't his weak
conscience be encouraged to eat food offered
to idols? 11 Then the weak person, the brother
for whom Christ died,[y] is ruined[K,z] by your
knowledge.[aa] 12 Now when you sin like this

[a] **7:22** Rm 1:1; 2Tm 2:24 [b] **7:23** 2Pt 2:1 [c] **7:25** Mt 5:7; Mk 5:19; Lk 1:50 [d] Nm 12:7 [e] **7:28** 1Tm 5:14 [f] **7:29** Rm 13:11 [g] **7:30** Php 1:18 [h] **7:31** Mk 13:7; 1Jn 2:8 [i] **7:32** 1Th 4:1 [j] **7:34** 1Tm 5:5 [k] **7:37** Jn 1:13 [l] **8:1** Ac 15:29; 21:25; 1Co 10:19; Rv 2:14,20 [m] 1Co 4:6 [n] 1Co 13:1-13 [o] **8:2** 1Co 3:18; 13:8-12; 1Tm 6:4 [p] **8:3** Dt 6:5; Lk 10:27 [q] Pr 2:6 [r] **8:4** Dt 6:4 [s] **8:5** 2Th 2:4 [t] **8:6** Mt 5:16; 11:27; Lk 11:13; Jn 8:42; Eph 5:20 [u] Ps 104:24; Col 1:16; Rv 3:14 [v] Jn 1:3 [w] **8:8** Rm 14:17 [x] **8:9** Ex 23:33; Rm 14:20 [y] **8:11** Jn 11:51; Rm 5:6,8; 8:34; 14:9,15; 1Co 15:3; Gl 2:21; Eph 5:2; 1Th 5:10 [z] Heb 6:8 [aa] Mt 25:45

[A] **7:22** A former slave [B] **7:22** A man who was never a slave [C] **7:28** Lit *in the flesh* [D] **7:36** = a man's fiancée, or his daughter, or his Levirate wife, or a celibate companion [E] **7:36** Or *virgin, if his passions are strong,* [F] **7:38** Or *marries off* [G] **7:38** Or *marry her off* [H] **7:39** Other mss add *by law* [I] **7:39** Only a believer [J] **8:1** See note at 1Co 6:12-13. [K] **8:11** Or *destroyed*

against the ·brothers and wound their weak
conscience, you are sinning against Christ.
13Therefore, if food causes my brother to fall,
I will never again eat meat,[a] so that I won't
cause my brother to fall.

Paul's Example as an Apostle

9 Am I not free? Am I not an apostle? Have
I not seen Jesus our Lord? Are you not my
work in the Lord? 2If I am not an apostle to
others, at least I am to you, for you are the
seal[b] of my apostleship in the Lord. 3My defense to those who examine me is this: 4Don't
we have the right to eat and drink?[c] 5Don't we
have the right to be accompanied by a Christian wife[A] like the other apostles,[d] the Lord's
brothers, and ·Cephas?[e] 6Or do Barnabas[f]
and I alone have no right to refrain from
working? 7Who ever goes to war at his own
expense?[g] Who plants a vineyard and does
not eat its fruit? Or who shepherds a flock
and does not drink the milk from the flock?
8Am I saying this from a human perspective?
Doesn't the law also say the same thing? 9For
it is written in the law of Moses, **Do not muz-**
zle an ox[h] while it treads out grain.[B,i] Is God
really concerned with oxen? 10Or isn't He
really saying it for us? Yes, this is written for
us,[j] because he who plows ought to plow in
hope,[k] and he who threshes should do so in
hope of sharing the crop.[l] 11If we have sown
spiritual things for you, is it too much if we
reap material benefits from you? 12If others
have this right to receive benefits from you,
don't we even more?

However, we have not made use of this
right; instead we endure everything[m] so
that we will not hinder the gospel of Christ.
13Don't you know that those who perform the
temple services eat the food from the temple,
and those who serve at the altar[n] share in the
offerings of the altar? 14In the same way, the
Lord has commanded that those who preach
the gospel should earn their living by the gospel.[o]

15But I have used none of these rights, and
I have not written this to make it happen
that way for me. For it would be better for
me to die than for anyone to deprive me of
my boast! 16For if I preach the gospel, I have
no reason to boast, because an obligation
is placed on me. And woe to me if I do not
preach the gospel! 17For if I do this willingly,
I have a reward, but if unwillingly, I am entrusted[p] with a stewardship. 18What then is
my reward? To preach the gospel and offer
it free of charge and not make full use of my
authority in the gospel.[q]

19Although I am a free man and not anyone's ·slave, I have made myself a slave to everyone, in order to win[r] more people. 20To
the Jews I became like a Jew, to win Jews;
to those under the law, like one under the
law—though I myself am not under the
law[C]—to win those under the law.[s] 21To those
who are without that law,[t] like one without
the law—not being without God's law but
within Christ's law—to win those without

[a] 8:13 Dt 12:15
[b] 9:2 Rv 5:1
[c] 9:4 2Th 3:8-9
[d] 9:5 Jd 17
[e] Jn 1:42
[f] 9:6 Ac 4:36
[g] 9:7 Lk 3:14
[h] 9:9 Lk 13:15
[i] Dt 25:4
[j] 9:10 Rm 4:24
[k] Ac 23:6; 1Th 1:3
[l] 2Tm 2:6
[m] 9:12 Ac 20:33-35; 2Co 6:3-10; 11:7-12
[n] 9:13 Lv 6:16,26; 7:6,31-32; Nm 5:9-10; 18:8-20,31; Dt 18:1
[o] 9:14 Mt 10:8-10; Lk 10:7
[p] 9:17 Lk 16:11
[q] 9:18 2Co 11:7; 12:13
[r] 9:19 1Pt 3:1
[s] 9:20 Ac 16:3; 21:23-26
[t] 9:21 Rm 2:12,14; Gl 2:3; 3:2

GOD WHO SENDS

Motivation for Mission

The deepest inward impulse relates to our sense of being and identity in Christ and the sense of missional purpose which emanates inevitably from that sense of who we are (John 17:18). As our deepest sense of identity as Christians is involved in our sense of mission, so our most satisfying pursuits in life are involved in being on mission. Out of a solid sense of self-identity comes an integrated wholeness which makes for strong motivation. To have a sense of mission built into the very fabric of our being as Christians is to have the stuff of which Christian motivation is made. The Christian's pursuit of purpose is linked inseparably with the divine impulse—that interlocking relation of which mission is an inextricable part.

(DuBose, 100-101)

[A] 9:5 Lit *a sister as a wife* [B] 9:9 Dt 25:4 [C] 9:20 Other mss omit *though I myself am not under law*

Contextualization and the Mission of God

Keith Whitfield

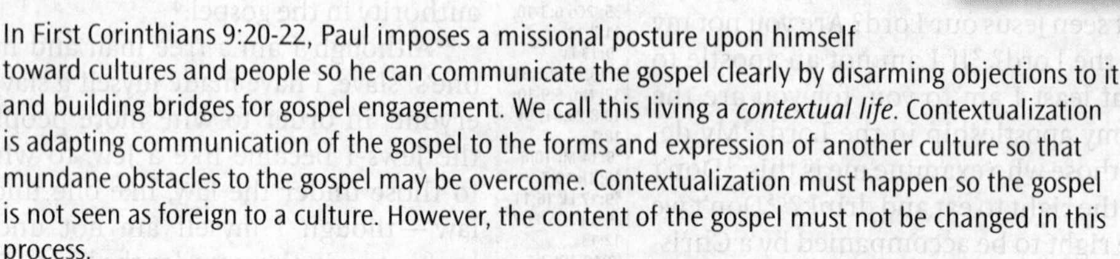

In First Corinthians 9:20-22, Paul imposes a missional posture upon himself toward cultures and people so he can communicate the gospel clearly by disarming objections to it and building bridges for gospel engagement. We call this living a *contextual life*. Contextualization is adapting communication of the gospel to the forms and expression of another culture so that mundane obstacles to the gospel may be overcome. Contextualization must happen so the gospel is not seen as foreign to a culture. However, the content of the gospel must not be changed in this process.

Contextualization has largely been the work of cross-cultural missions. But as societies change throughout the world, contextualizing the gospel has become a necessity even for those sharing the gospel in their own cultural context. Because the gospel is about God's redemptive story confronting humanity's story of rebellion, everyone seeking to share the gospel faces barriers to communicating the message—whether linguistic, cultural, or both.

A culture is a group of people with shared social and linguistic identity. This identity is shaped by beliefs about what it means to be human, assessment of what is wrong in their world, possible solutions, and views on how to appropriate the solutions. A culture's prevailing worldview affects logic, prejudices what evidence one considers, and dictates what types of solutions are viable options. The task of contextualization is to use what is good, just, and beautiful in a culture to establish a clear communication of the gospel, in order to overcome obstacles to understanding and to confront idols that oppose the truth. By contextualizing our communication, the hope is to see people and cultures redeemed and restored with the gospel, that they may "turn to God from idols to serve the living and true God" (1Th 1:9).

We find in Acts numerous examples of Paul contextualizing the gospel. He communicates the gospel in a synagogue to God-fearing Jews with the Scriptures and the words of John the Baptist (Ac 13:23-25). He engages working class pagans with the gospel by appealing to general revelation (14:16-17). In Acts 17, he enters another context where he provokes pagan philosophers to consider their own claims against the story of the gospel. In these texts, Paul communicates the gospel contextually and faithfully by accessing the native culture and emphasizing different biblical doctrines surrounding the gospel. In all of it, he communicates a universal, monotheistic God who is not served by human hands (17:24-29), but in fact reveals Himself (14:16-17).

Paul proclaims the sovereign goodness of God (Ac 13:16-22; 14:17), points to the work of God for salvation over against the works of men (13:37-38; 14:15; 17:18, 30), and confronts human efforts to save themselves through moralism (13:39) and idolatry (14:15; 17:23). All are called to repentance (13:39-41; 14:14-18; 17:30).

Contextualization is consistent with the call of Christians to be a light in the world. The church is called to love those who are living differing stories. The church is also called to persuade those who are living differing stories of the truthfulness of the gospel. To pursue this calling, our message must be understandable.

the law. 22 To the weak I became weak, in order to win the weak. I have become all things
to all people, so that I may by every possible
means save some.[a] 23 Now I do all this because
of the gospel, so I may become a partner in
its benefits.[A]

24 Don't you know that the runners in a
stadium all race,[b] but only one receives the
prize? Run in such a way to win the prize.[c]
25 Now everyone who competes exercises self-
control[d] in everything. However, they do it to
receive a crown[e] that will fade away,[f] but we a
crown that will never fade away. 26 Therefore I
do not run like one who runs aimlessly or box
like one beating the air. 27 Instead, I discipline
my body and bring it under strict control, so
that after preaching to others, I myself will
not be disqualified.[g]

Warnings from Israel's Past

10 Now I want you to know, ·brothers,
that our fathers[h] were all under the
cloud,[i] all passed through the sea,[j] 2 and all
were baptized[k] into Moses[l] in the cloud and in
the sea. 3 They all ate the same spiritual food,[m]
4 and all drank the same spiritual drink. For
they drank from a spiritual rock[n] that followed them, and that rock was Christ.[o] 5 But
God was not pleased with most of them, for
they were struck down in the wilderness.[p]

6 Now these things became examples for
us, so that we will not desire[q] evil things as
they did.[B,r] 7 Don't become idolaters[s] as some
of them were; as it is written, **The people sat
down to eat and drink, and got up to play.**[C,D,t]
8 Let us not commit sexual immorality[u] as
some of them did,[E] and in a single day 23,000
people fell dead.[v] 9 Let us not test Christ as
some of them did[F] and were destroyed by
snakes.[w] 10 Nor should we complain[x] as some
of them did,[G,y] and were killed by the destroyer.[H,z] 11 Now these things happened to
them as examples, and they were written
as a warning to us,[aa] on whom the ends of
the ages[ab] have come.[ac] 12 So, whoever thinks
he stands must be careful not to fall.[ad] 13 No
temptation has overtaken you except what is
common to humanity. God is faithful,[ae] and
He will not allow you to be tempted beyond
what you are able, but with the temptation
He will also provide a way of escape[af] so that
you are able to bear it.

Warning against Idolatry

14 Therefore, my dear friends, flee from idolatry. 15 I am speaking as to wise people. Judge for
yourselves what I say. 16 The cup[ag] of blessing[ah]
that we give thanks for, is it not a sharing in the
blood of Christ? The bread[ai] that we break, is it
not a sharing in the body of Christ? 17 Because
there is one bread, we who are many are one[aj]
body, for all of us share that one bread. 18 Look
at the people of Israel.[I] Do not those who eat
the sacrifices participate in what is offered on
the altar?[ak] 19 What am I saying then? That food
offered to idols is anything, or that an idol is
anything? 20 No, but I do say that what they[J]
sacrifice, they sacrifice to demons and not to
God. I do not want you to participate with demons! 21 You cannot drink the cup of the Lord
and the cup of demons. You cannot share in
the Lord's table and the table of demons. 22 Or
are we provoking the Lord to jealousy? Are we
stronger than He?[al]

Christian Liberty

23 "Everything is permissible,"[K,L] but not
everything is helpful. "Everything is permissible,"[K] but not everything builds up. 24 No one
should seek his own good, but the good of the
other person.[am]

25 Eat everything that is sold in the meat
market, asking no questions for conscience'
sake, 26 for **the earth is the Lord's,**[an] **and all
that is in it.**[M,ao] 27 If one of the unbelievers invites you over and you want to go, eat everything that is set before you, without raising
questions of conscience. 28 But if someone
says to you, "This is food offered to an idol,"
do not eat it,[ap] out of consideration for the
one who told you, and for conscience' sake.[N]
29 I do not mean your own conscience, but
the other person's. For why is my freedom
judged[aq] by another person's conscience? 30 If
I partake with thanks,[ar] why am I slandered
because of something I give thanks for?

[a] **9:22** Rm 11:14; 1Co 7:16
[b] **9:24** Jd 3
[c] Col 2:18
[d] **9:25** Gl 5:23
[e] 1Pt 5:4
[f] 1Pt 1:18
[g] **9:27** Heb 6:8
[h] **10:1** Ps 44:1; Ac 7:11
[i] Ex 13:21
[j] Ex 14:29
[k] **10:2** Ac 22:16
[l] Ps 77:20; Mt 8:4; Heb 3:2
[m] **10:3** Ex 16:31
[n] **10:4** Ex 17:6; Nm 20:7-13
[o] Jn 4:14; 6:30-35
[p] **10:5** Jd 5
[q] **10:6** Mt 27:23; Jms 4:2
[r] Nm 11:4,33-34; Ps 78:18; 106:14
[s] **10:7** Eph 5:5
[t] Ex 32:6
[u] **10:8** 1Co 6:18; Rv 2:14,20; 17:2; 18:3,9
[v] Nm 25:1-18; Ps 106:29
[w] **10:9** Nm 21:6
[x] **10:10** Jn 6:41; Jd 16
[y] Nm 16:41-50
[z] Ex 12:23; 2Sm 24:16; 1Ch 21:15; Ps 78:49
[aa] **10:11** Ps 102:18
[ab] Mk 13:7
[ac] Mk 10:30
[ad] **10:12** Pr 24:16; Heb 6:8
[ae] **10:13** Nm 12:7
[af] 2Pt 2:9
[ag] **10:16** Mt 26:27; Mk 14:23; Lk 22:17,20; 1Co 11:25-26
[ah] Mk 6:41; Gl 3:14
[ai] Mt 26:26; Mk 14:22; Lk 22:19; Ac 2:42,46; 20:7
[aj] **10:17** Jn 11:52; Eph 4:4
[ak] **10:18** Gn 8:20; Lv 1:5; Nm 3:26; Dt 12:27; 1Sm 2:28; 1Ch 6:49; Ps 26:6; Ezk 8:15; Heb 7:13
[al] **10:22** Ec 6:10
[am] **10:24** Mk 10:45; Php 2:4
[an] **10:26** Mk 13:19
[ao] Ps 24:1
[ap] **10:28** Lk 10:8
[aq] **10:29** Lk 6:37
[ar] **10:30** Mk 8:6; Rm 1:8

[A] **9:23** Lit *partner of it* [B] **10:6** Lit *they desired* [C] **10:7** Or *to dance* [D] **10:7** Ex 32:6 [E] **10:8** Lit *them committed sexual immorality* [F] **10:9** Lit *them tested* [G] **10:10** Lit *them complained* [H] **10:10** Or *the destroying angel* [I] **10:18** Lit *Look at Israel according to the flesh* [J] **10:20** Other mss read *Gentiles* [K] **10:23** Other mss add *for me* [L] **10:23** See note at 1Co 6:12-13. [M] **10:26** Ps 24:1 [N] **10:28** Other mss add *"For the earth is the Lord's and all that is in it."*

31 Therefore, whether you eat or drink, or whatever you do, do everything for God's glory.[a] 32 Give no offense[b] to the Jews or the Greeks or the church of God, 33 just as I also try to please all people in all things, not seeking my own profit, but the profit of many,[c] so that they may be saved. 11 1 Imitate me, as I also imitate Christ.[d]

Instructions about Head Coverings

2 Now I praise you[A] because you always remember me and keep the traditions[e] just as I delivered[f] them to you. 3 But I want you to know that Christ is the head[g] of every man, and the man is the head of the woman,[B,h] and God is the head of Christ.[i] 4 Every man who prays or prophesies with something on his head dishonors[j] his head. 5 But every woman who prays or prophesies with her head uncovered dishonors her head, since that is one and the same as having her head shaved.[k] 6 So if a woman's head[C] is not covered, her hair should be cut off. But if it is disgraceful for a woman to have her hair cut off or her head shaved, she should be covered.

7 A man, in fact, should not cover his head, because he is God's image[l] and glory,[m] but woman is man's glory. 8 For man did not come from woman, but woman came from man.[n] 9 And man was not created for woman, but woman for man. 10 This is why a woman should have a symbol of authority on her head, because of the angels. 11 In the Lord, however, woman is not independent of man, and man is not independent of woman. 12 For just as woman came from man, so man comes through woman, and all things come from God.[o]

13 Judge[p] for yourselves: Is it proper for a woman to pray to God with her head uncovered? 14 Does not even nature itself teach[q] you that if a man has long hair it is a disgrace[r] to him, 15 but that if a woman has long hair, it is her glory?[s] For her hair is given to her[D] as a covering. 16 But if anyone wants to argue about this, we have no other[E] custom, nor do the churches of God.

The Lord's Supper

17 Now in giving the following instruction I do not praise you, since you come together not for the better but for the worse. 18 For to begin with, I hear that when you come together as a church there are divisions among you, and in part I believe it. 19 There must, indeed, be factions[t] among you, so that those who are approved may be recognized among you. 20 Therefore, when you come together, it is not really to eat the Lord's Supper.[u] 21 For at the meal, each one eats his own supper ahead of others. So one person is hungry while another gets drunk! 22 Don't you have houses to eat and drink in? Or do you look down on the church of God and embarrass those who have nothing? What should I say to you? Should I praise you? I do not praise you for this!

23 For I received from the Lord what I also passed on to you:[v] On the night when He was betrayed, the Lord Jesus took bread, 24 gave thanks, broke it, and said,[F] "This is My body, which is[G] for you. Do this in remembrance of Me."[w]

25 In the same way, after supper He also took the cup and said, "This cup is the new covenant[x] established by My blood.[y] Do this, as often as you drink it, in remembrance of Me." 26 For as often as you eat this bread and drink the cup, you proclaim the Lord's death[z] until He comes.[aa]

Self-Examination

27 Therefore, whoever eats the bread or drinks the cup of the Lord in an unworthy way will be •guilty of sin against the body[H] and blood of the Lord. 28 So a man should examine himself; in this way he should eat the bread and drink from the cup. 29 For whoever eats and drinks without recognizing the body,[I] eats and drinks judgment[ab] on himself. 30 This is why many are sick and ill among you, and many have fallen •asleep.[ac] 31 If we were properly evaluating ourselves, we would not be judged, 32 but when we are judged,[ad] we are disciplined by the Lord, so that we may not be condemned[ae] with the •world.

33 Therefore, my •brothers, when you come together to eat, wait for one another. 34 If anyone is hungry, he should eat at home, so that when you gather together you will not come

[a] 10:31 Mk 10:37; Lk 9:32; Jn 17:24; 2Co 3:18; 2Pt 3:18
[b] 10:32 Ac 24:16; Php 1:10
[c] 10:33 Mk 10:45
[d] 11:1 Php 2:5; 1Pt 2:21
[e] 11:2 2Th 2:15; 3:6
[f] Jd 3
[g] 11:3 Eph 1:22; 4:15; Col 1:18; 2:10,19
[h] Gn 3:16; Eph 5:23
[i] 1Co 3:23
[j] 11:4 1Pt 3:16
[k] 11:5 Dt 21:11-12
[l] 11:7 Gn 1:27
[m] Mk 10:37; Lk 9:32; Jn 17:24; 2Co 3:18; 2Pt 3:18
[n] 11:8 Gn 2:21-23; 1Tm 2:13
[o] 11:12 Ps 104:24; Rv 3:14
[p] 11:13 Jn 5:22-30
[q] 11:14 Mt 28:20; Ac 4:2; 2Tm 4:11
[r] 2Co 6:8
[s] 11:15 Php 3:19
[t] 11:19 2Pt 2:1
[u] 11:20 Mt 26:26-29; Mk 14:22-25; Lk 22:14-20; 1Co 10:14-22
[v] 11:23 Jd 3
[w] 11:24 Lk 22:19
[x] 11:25 Lk 22:20
[y] Jn 6:54
[z] 11:26 Php 2:8; 3:10
[aa] Mk 8:38
[ab] 11:29 Mk 12:40; 1Jn 5:16
[ac] 11:30 Jn 11:11; Ac 7:60; 1Th 4:13-15
[ad] 11:32 Jn 5:22-30
[ae] Mt 12:41; Jn 5:22

[A] 11:2 Other mss add *brothers,* [B] 11:3 Or *the husband is the head of the wife* [C] 11:6 Lit *a woman* [D] 11:15 Other mss omit *to her* [E] 11:16 Or *no such* [F] 11:24 Other mss add *"Take, eat.* [G] 11:24 Other mss add *broken* [H] 11:27 Lit *be guilty of the body* [I] 11:29 Other mss read *drinks unworthily, not discerning the Lord's body*

under judgment. And I will give instructions
about the other matters whenever I come.[a]

Diversity of Spiritual Gifts

12 Now concerning what comes from the
Spirit:[A] ·brothers, I do not want you to
be unaware. 2 You know that when you were
pagans, you used to be led off to the idols[b] that
could not speak.[c] 3 Therefore I am informing
you that no one speaking by the Spirit of God
says, "Jesus is cursed," and no one can say,
"Jesus is Lord," except by the Holy Spirit.
4 Now there are different gifts,[d] but the
same Spirit. 5 There are different ministries,
but the same Lord. 6 And there are different
activities, but the same God activates each
gift in each person.[B] 7 A demonstration of
the Spirit is given to each person[e] to produce
what is beneficial:

8 to one[f] is given a message of wisdom[g]
through the Spirit,
to another, a message of knowledge
by the same Spirit,
9 to another, faith by the same Spirit,
to another, gifts of healing[h]
by the one Spirit,
10 to another, the performing of miracles,[i]
to another, prophecy,[j]
to another, distinguishing
between spirits,[k]
to another, different kinds
of ·languages,
to another, interpretation of languages.

11 But one and the same Spirit is active in all
these, distributing to each person as He wills.

Unity Yet Diversity in the Body

12 For as the body is one[l] and has many
parts, and all the parts of that body, though
many, are one body—so also is Christ.[m] 13 For
we were all baptized by[C] one Spirit into one
body—whether Jews or Greeks, whether
·slaves or free—and we were all made to
drink of one Spirit.[n] 14 So the body is not one
part but many. 15 If the foot should say, "Because I'm not a hand, I don't belong to the
body," in spite of this it still belongs to the
body. 16 And if the ear should say, "Because
I'm not an eye, I don't belong to the body,"
in spite of this it still belongs to the body. 17 If
the whole body were an eye, where would the
hearing be? If the whole body were an ear,
where would the sense of smell be? 18 But now
God has placed each one of the parts in one
body just as He wanted.[o] 19 And if they were
all the same part, where would the body be?
20 Now there are many parts, yet one body.
21 So the eye cannot say to the hand, "I
don't need you!" Or again, the head can't
say to the feet, "I don't need you!" 22 But even
more, those parts of the body that seem to be
weaker are necessary. 23 And those parts of the
body that we think to be less honorable,[p] we
clothe these with greater honor, and our un-
presentable parts have a better presentation.
24 But our presentable parts have no need of
clothing. Instead, God has put the body together, giving greater honor to the less honorable, 25 so that there would be no division[q]
in the body, but that the members would
have the same concern for each other. 26 So
if one member suffers, all the members suffer with it; if one member is honored, all the
members rejoice with it.
27 Now you are the body of Christ,[r] and individual members of it. 28 And God has placed
these in the church:[s]

first apostles, second prophets,
third teachers,[t] next miracles,[u]
then gifts of healing,[v] helping,
managing, various kinds of languages.
29 Are all apostles? Are all prophets?
Are all teachers? Do all do miracles?
30 Do all have gifts of healing?
Do all speak in other languages?
Do all interpret?[w]

31 But desire[x] the greater gifts. And I will show
you an even better way.

Love: The Superior Way

13 If I speak human or angelic
·languages
but do not have love,[y]
I am a sounding gong[z]
or a clanging cymbal.
2 If I have the gift of prophecy[aa]
and understand all ·mysteries
and all knowledge,

[a] **11:34** 1Co 4:19
[b] **12:2** 1Co 8:4
[c] Ac 8:32; 1Co 14:10; 2Pt 2:16
[d] **12:4** Rm 12:6; 1Co 14:1; Eph 4:8; Heb 2:4; 1Pt 4:10
[e] **12:7** Jms 4:5
[f] **12:8-10** Rm 12:7-8; Eph 4:11; 1Pt 4:11
[g] **12:8** 1Co 2:6-7
[h] **12:9** Lk 13:32; Ac 4:22,30; 10:38
[i] **12:10** Ac 19:11
[j] 1Co 13:2
[k] 1Jn 4:1-3
[l] **12:12** Jn 11:52
[m] Eph 4:4
[n] **12:13** Gl 3:28; Eph 2:13-18; Col 3:11
[o] **12:18** Ps 143:10; Pr 16:9; Jn 5:30; Gl 1:4; Eph 1:9; 1Jn 2:17
[p] **12:23** Mk 6:4; 1Pt 2:7
[q] **12:25** 1Co 1:10
[r] **12:27** Eph 1:23; Col 1:18
[s] **12:28** Mt 16:18; 1Co 14:4; Rv 1:4
[t] Eph 4:11; Jms 3:1
[u] Mk 13:22
[v] 1Co 12:9
[w] **12:30** Lk 24:27
[x] **12:31** Nm 25:13; Jms 4:2
[y] **13:1** Jn 13:35; 1Jn 4:7-12
[z] Mt 10:9
[aa] **13:2** 1Co 14:1,3-6,22-39; Eph 4:11; 1Th 5:20

[A] **12:1** Or *concerning spiritual things*, or *spiritual gifts* [B] **12:6** Lit *God acts all things in all* [C] **12:13** Or *with*, or *in*

The Gifts of the Spirit

Ed Stetzer

Jesus promised His disciples that He would send them the Spirit, and with the Spirit, He promised His followers that they would be able to do more for the kingdom than He had (Jn 14:12). With this promise, Jesus was indicating that by being empowered by His Spirit, His disciples will minister to more people and will see the kingdom expand further. When the kingdom arrived, a kingdom-people emerged. A tangible, local gathering of redeemed people called the church. This body of people was called to represent and extend the reign of God on the earth.

The nature, identity, and mission of the church is seen in its relationship to Jesus as His body, and also in its relationship to the Spirit as the temple of the Spirit. The church is a missional instrument of God's Spirit and a sign of God's reign on the earth, as the Spirit empowers it and transforms it. The Spirit and His gifts are dispensed to equip the church, empowering its members to continue in the ministry of Jesus and to advance His kingdom (Rm 12:3; 1Co 12:7,12-31; 14:12; 1Pt 4:10). The presence of spiritual gifts is evidence of the Spirit's presence among the body (1Co 12:7,13). The Spirit's works are visible through the public ministries of the church—corporate worship, the preaching of the Word, the practice of the ordinances, the laying on of hands, and church discipline (1Co 14). In these ministries, people encounter the gospel and can be transformed by its power. As the church ministers through the empowerment of the Spirit, the unredeemed are introduced to their need for salvation and believers are edified in their life with Christ. The church is built up as a body and continues in its obedience to God's mission through actively engaging in the gifts given by the Spirit.

The search for one's spiritual gifts for personal spiritual fulfillment overlooks, therefore, what is fundamental about the function of these gifts—the edification and equipping of the body. These gifts are given to individuals, and for the common good of the entire body. But, if spiritual gifts are given to build up the entire body, individuals will personally benefit from them. The communal and personal blessings of spiritual gifts result from individuals using their gifts and from individuals being served by others as they use their gifts.

The Spirit, according to His sovereign will, disperses gifts to individual members of the church for the common good of the church. There are different kinds of gifts, acts of service, and actions (1Co 12:4). In 1 Corinthians 12:8-10, thirteen different gifts are listed. Seven gifts are given in Romans 12:6-8. Though many interpret the gifts noted in Ephesians 4:11 as referring to gifted people in particular ministry positions rather than gifts distributed by the Spirit, it is worth noting that Paul states these gifts serve the same purpose as those listed in Romans 12 and 1 Corinthians 12. Since the lists overlap and are not identical, it appears the Bible is not giving us a definitive list of the gifts; the focus is on the Giver of these gifts.

It is important to see in the different gifts listed in the NT is that they come from the same source, and the recipients of the gifts share the same identity and purpose. Paul claims that each person of the Trinity is involved in the dispersing of the gifts (1Co 12:4-11). The gifts are given by the wise and good plan of God, and applied to individuals through the empowering of the Spirit. Paul also states that all the gifts are valuable to the church, because each person shares in the same identity—members of one body (1Co 12:12-31). One gift is not more significant than another one, because the purpose for all of them is the common good of the church.

The purpose for the spiritual gifts is accomplished, because the presence and application

of the gifts announce—to those who can discern it—that Jesus Christ is Lord over all people and things (1Co 12:3). This proclamation stirs up and strengthens faith.

To those who are spiritually unable to discern the presence of the Spirit and His gifts in the church, the use of the gifts is a means of witnessing to the world that the kingdom is here in the people of God (1Co 14:23-25). These gifts also serve to build up the church for its mission—as it is sent to extend the presence and power of the Spirit throughout the earth (Heb 10:19-39). Ultimately, the gifts are given to assist the church in its mission to see God glorified in all things (1Pt 4:10-11).

and if I have all faith
so that I can move mountains[a]
but do not have love, I am nothing.
3 And if I donate all my goods to feed
the poor,
and if I give my body in order to boast[A]
but do not have love, I gain nothing.
4 Love is patient,[b] love is kind.
Love does not envy,[c]
is not boastful, is not conceited,[d]
5 does not act improperly,
is not selfish,[e] is not provoked,[f]
and does not keep a record of wrongs.
6 Love finds no joy in unrighteousness
but rejoices in the truth.[g]
7 It bears all things, believes all things,
hopes all things, endures[h] all things.

8 Love never ends.[i]
But as for prophecies,
they will come to an end;
as for languages, they will cease;
as for knowledge, it will come
to an end.
9 For we know in part,
and we prophesy in part.
10 But when the perfect comes,
the partial will come to an end.
11 When I was a child,
I spoke like a child,
I thought like a child,
I reasoned like a child.
When I became a man,
I put aside childish things.
12 For now we see indistinctly,[B] as
in a mirror,[C]
but then face to face.[j]
Now I know in part,
but then I will know fully,[k]
as I am fully known.[l]
13 Now these three remain:
faith, hope,[m] and love.
But the greatest of these is love.

Prophecy: A Superior Gift

14 Pursue love and desire spiritual gifts,
and above all that you may prophesy.
2 For the person who speaks in another ˙lan-
guage[n] is not speaking to men but to God,
since no one understands him; however, he
speaks ˙mysteries in the Spirit.[D] 3 But the person who prophesies speaks to people for edification, encouragement, and consolation.
4 The person who speaks in another language
builds himself up, but he who prophesies
builds up the church. 5 I wish all of you spoke
in other languages, but even more that you
prophesied. The person who prophesies
is greater than the person who speaks in
languages, unless he interprets so that the
church may be built up.
6 But now, ˙brothers, if I come to you
speaking in other languages, how will I
benefit you unless I speak to you with a revelation[o] or knowledge or prophecy or teaching? 7 Even inanimate things that produce
sounds—whether flute or harp[p]—if they
don't make a distinction in the notes, how
will what is played on the flute or harp be
recognized? 8 In fact, if the trumpet makes an
unclear sound, who will prepare for battle?[q]
9 In the same way, unless you use your tongue
for intelligible speech, how will what is spoken be known? For you will be speaking into
the air. 10 There are doubtless many different

[a]13:2 Mt 17:20 [b]13:4 1Th 5:14 [c]Nm 25:13; Gl 4:17 [d]1Co 4:6 [e]13:5 Mk 10:45; Php 2:4 [f]Ac 17:16 [g]13:6 Ps 119:142; Jn 8:14; 14:6 [h]13:7 Jms 1:12 [i]13:8 Mt 7:25,27; Lk 6:49; 11:17; 13:4; 16:17; Ac 15:16; Heb 11:30; Rv 11:13; 16:19 [j]13:12 1Jn 3:2 [k]Pr 2:6; Jn 17:3; 1Jn 4:8 [l]1Co 8:3; Gl 4:9 [m]13:13 1Th 1:3 [n]14:2 1Co 12:10 [o]14:6 1Pt 4:13 [p]14:7 Rv 5:8; 14:2; 15:2 [q]14:8 Nm 10:9; Is 58:1; Jr 4:19; Ezk 33:3-6; Jl 2:1

A13:3 Other mss read *body to be burned* B13:12 Or *indirectly* C13:12 Ancient mirrors were normally made out of polished metals and were not as clear as modern ones. D14:2 Or *in spirit*, or *in his spirit*

kinds of languages in the world, and all have meaning.[A] 11 Therefore, if I do not know the meaning of the language, I will be a foreigner[B] to the speaker, and the speaker will be a foreigner to me. 12 So also you — since you are zealous[a] for spiritual gifts,[C,b] seek to excel in building up the church.

13 Therefore the person who speaks in another language should pray that he can interpret. 14 For if I pray in another language, my spirit[c] prays, but my understanding is unfruitful.[d] 15 What then? I will pray with the spirit, and I will also pray with my understanding. I will sing with the spirit, and I will also sing with my understanding. 16 Otherwise, if you praise with the spirit,[D] how will the uninformed person[E] say "Amen"[e] at your giving of thanks, since he does not know what you are saying? 17 For you may very well be giving thanks, but the other person is not being built up. 18 I thank[f] God that I speak in other languages more than all of you; 19 yet in the church I would rather speak five words[g] with my understanding, in order to teach others also, than 10,000 words in another language.

20 Brothers, don't be childish in your thinking, but be infants in regard to evil and adult in your thinking.[h] 21 It is written in the law:

> **I will speak to these people**
> **by people of other languages**
> **and by the lips of foreigners,**
> **and even then, they will not listen**
> **to Me,**[F,i]

says the Lord. 22 It follows that speaking in other languages is intended as a sign,[G] not for believers but for unbelievers. But prophecy is not for unbelievers but for believers. 23 Therefore, if the whole church assembles together and all are speaking in other languages and people who are uninformed or unbelievers come in, will they not say that you are out of your minds? 24 But if all are prophesying and some unbeliever or uninformed person comes in, he is convicted by all and is judged by all. 25 The secrets of his heart will be revealed, and as a result he will fall facedown and worship God, proclaiming, "God is really among you."[j]

Order in Church Meetings

26 What then is the conclusion, brothers? Whenever you come together, each one[H] has a psalm, a teaching, a revelation, another language, or an interpretation.[k] All things must be done for edification. 27 If any person speaks in another language, there should be only two, or at the most three, each in turn, and someone must interpret. 28 But if there is no interpreter, that person should keep silent in the church and speak to himself and to God. 29 Two or three prophets should speak, and the others should evaluate.[l] 30 But if something has been revealed to another person sitting there, the first prophet should be silent. 31 For you can all prophesy one by one, so that everyone may learn and everyone may be encouraged.[m] 32 And the prophets' spirits are under the control of the prophets, 33 since God is not a God of disorder but of peace.

As in all the churches of the ·saints,[n] 34 the women[I] should be silent in the churches,[o] for they are not permitted to speak, but should be submissive, as the law also says. 35 And if they want to learn something, they should ask their own husbands[p] at home, for it is disgraceful for a woman to speak in the church meeting. 36 Did the word of God originate from you, or did it come to you only?

37 If anyone thinks he is a prophet or spiritual, he should recognize that what I write to you is the Lord's command. 38 But if anyone ignores this, he will be ignored.[J] 39 Therefore, my brothers, be eager[q] to prophesy, and do not forbid speaking in other languages. 40 But everything must be done decently[r] and in order.

Resurrection Essential to the Gospel

15 Now ·brothers, I want to clarify[K] for you the gospel I proclaimed to you; you received it and have taken your stand[s] on it. 2 You are also saved by it, if you hold to the message I proclaimed to you — unless you be-

[a] **14:12** Nm 25:13; Gl 1:14 [b] Ps 51:11; Lk 11:34; Jn 1:33; Ac 2:4; Rm 8:9; Gl 5:25; Ti 3:5; 1Jn 4:1; Rv 3:22 [c] **14:14** Ps 51:12 [d] Gl 5:22; Ti 3:14 [e] **14:16** Ps 72:19; Rv 22:21 [f] **14:18** Rm 1:8 [g] **14:19** Mt 12:37 [h] **14:20** Ps 131:2; Is 28:9; Mt 18:3; Rm 16:19; Eph 4:14; Heb 5:12-13 [i] **14:21** Is 28:11-12 [j] **14:25** Is 45:14; Zch 8:23 [k] **14:26** 1Co 12:10 [l] **14:29** 1Jn 4:1 [m] **14:31** Lk 16:25 [n] **14:33** Eph 6:18 [o] **14:34** 1Tm 2:11-12; 1Pt 3:1 [p] **14:35** Mt 1:19; 1Pt 3:1 [q] **14:39** Nm 25:13; Gl 4:17 [r] **14:40** Rm 13:13 [s] **15:1** Pr 24:16

[A] **14:10** Lit *and none is without a sound* [B] **14:11** Gk *barbaros* = in Eng a "barbarian." To a Gk, a *barbaros* was anyone who did not speak Gk. [C] **14:12** Lit *zealous of spirits*; *spirits* = human spirits, spiritual powers, or the Holy Spirit [D] **14:16** Or *praise by the Spirit* [E] **14:16** Lit *the one filling the place of the uninformed* [F] **14:21** Is 28:11-12 [G] **14:22** Lit *that languages are for a sign* [H] **14:26** Other mss add *of you* [I] **14:34** Other mss read *your women* [J] **14:38** Other mss read *he should be ignored* [K] **15:1** Or *I make known*

lieved for no purpose.[A,a] 3 For I passed on to
you[b] as most important what I also received:

that Christ died[c] for our sins
according to the Scriptures,[d]
4 that He was buried,[e]
that He was raised on the third day[f]
according to the Scriptures,[g]
5 and that He appeared to ·Cephas,[h]
then to the Twelve.[i]
6 Then He appeared to over 500 brothers
at one time;[j]
most of them are still alive,
but some have fallen ·asleep.
7 Then He appeared to James,[k]
then to all the apostles.[l]
8 Last of all, as to one
abnormally born,[B,m]
He also appeared to me.[n]

9 For I am the least of the apostles,[o] unworthy to be called an apostle, because I persecuted[p] the church of God. 10 But by God's
grace I am what I am, and His grace toward
me was not ineffective. However, I worked
more than any of them, yet not I, but God's
grace that was with me.[q] 11 Therefore, whether
it is I or they, so we proclaim and so you have
believed.

Resurrection Essential to the Faith

12 Now if Christ is proclaimed as raised
from the dead,[r] how can some of you say,
"There is no resurrection of the dead"?[s] 13 But
if there is no resurrection of the dead, then
Christ has not been raised; 14 and if Christ
has not been raised, then our proclamation
is without foundation, and so is your faith.[C]
15 In addition, we are found to be false witnesses[t] about God, because we have testified[u]
about God that He raised up Christ — whom
He did not raise up if in fact the dead are not
raised. 16 For if the dead are not raised, Christ
has not been raised. 17 And if Christ has not
been raised, your faith is worthless; you are
still in your sins. 18 Therefore, those who have
fallen asleep in Christ[v] have also perished. 19 If
we have put our hope in Christ for this life
only, we should be pitied more than anyone.

[a] **15:2** Gl 4:11; Heb 6:8
[b] **15:3** Jd 3
[c] 1Co 8:11
[d] Mt 26:54; 1Pt 1:20
[e] **15:4** Mt 27:59-60; Mk 15:46; Lk 23:53; Jn 19:41-42
[f] 1Th 4:14
[g] Ps 16:10; Is 53:10; Hs 6:2; Mt 12:40; Jn 2:22; Ac 2:25-32; 13:33-35; 26:22-23
[h] **15:5** Lk 24:34
[i] Mk 16:14; Lk 24:36; Jn 20:19,26; Ac 10:41
[j] **15:6** Mt 28:10-20
[k] **15:7** Jms 1:1
[l] Ac 1:3-11
[m] **15:8** 1Tm 1:13-16
[n] Ac 9:1-8
[o] **15:9** Eph 3:8; 1Tm 1:16-17
[p] Php 3:6
[q] **15:10** 2Co 3:5; Php 2:13; Col 1:29
[r] **15:12** Mt 17:9
[s] Mt 22:23; Mk 12:18; Lk 20:27; Ac 23:8; 2Tm 2:18
[t] **15:15** Mt 26:60
[u] Jn 15:26
[v] **15:18** 1Th 4:16; 1Pt 5:14
[w] **15:20** Ex 23:19; Lv 2:12; Rm 8:23; Col 1:18
[x] **15:21** Mt 10:21; Jn 8:51; Php 3:10
[y] Gn 3:1-7; Rm 5:12-14
[z] Mt 28:5-6; Mk 16:6; Lk 24:5-8,34; Jn 11:25; 20:9,15-18
[aa] **15:22** Rm 14:9
[ab] **15:23** 1Th 4:17
[ac] **15:24** Mt 24:6; Mk 13:7
[ad] Mt 5:16; 11:27; Lk 11:13; Jn 8:42; Eph 5:20
[ae] Ac 8:10; Eph 1:21; 1Pt 3:22
[af] **15:25** Lk 1:33; Rv 11:15
[ag] Ps 110:1; Mt 22:44; Eph 1:22
[ah] **15:26** 2Co 5:4
[ai] **15:27** Ps 8:6
[aj] **15:28** Jn 5:19; Heb 1:2
[ak] Ps 104:24; Eph 1:23
[al] **15:31** Rm 8:36
[am] **15:32** Eph 1:1
[an] 1Th 2:19
[ao] Is 22:13
[ap] **15:34** Ti 2:12
[aq] 1Co 4:14
[ar] **15:36** Jn 12:24

Christ's Resurrection Guarantees Ours

20 But now Christ has been raised from the
dead, the ·firstfruits[w] of those who have fallen
asleep. 21 For since death[x] came through a
man,[y] the resurrection of the dead also comes
through a man.[z] 22 For as in Adam all die, so
also in Christ all will be made alive.[aa] 23 But
each in his own order:[ab] Christ, the firstfruits;
afterward, at His coming, those who belong
to Christ. 24 Then comes the end,[ac] when He
hands over the kingdom to God the Father,[ad]
when He abolishes all rule and all authority
and power.[ae] 25 For He must reign[af] until He
puts all His enemies under His feet.[ag] 26 The
last enemy to be abolished is death.[ah] 27 For
God has put everything under His feet.[D,ai] But
when it says "everything" is put under Him, it
is obvious that He who puts everything under
Him is the exception. 28 And when everything
is subject to Christ, then the Son[aj] Himself
will also be subject to the One who subjected
everything to Him, so that God may be all in
all.[ak]

Resurrection Supported by Christian Experience

29 Otherwise what will they do who are being baptized for the dead? If the dead are not
raised at all, then why are people baptized for
them?[E] 30 Why are we in danger every hour?
31 I affirm by the pride in you that I have in
Christ Jesus our Lord: I die every day![al] 32 If I
fought wild animals in Ephesus[am] with only
human hope,[F] what good did that do me?[G,an]
If the dead are not raised, **Let us eat and
drink, for tomorrow we die.**[H,ao] 33 Do not be
deceived: "Bad company corrupts good morals."[I] 34 Come to your senses[J,ap] and stop sinning, for some people are ignorant about
God. I say this to your shame.[aq]

The Nature of the Resurrection Body

35 But someone will say, "How are the dead
raised? What kind of body will they have
when they come?" 36 Foolish one! What you
sow does not come to life[ar] unless it dies.
37 And as for what you sow — you are not sowing the future body, but only a seed,[K] perhaps

[A] **15:2** Or *believed without careful thought*, or *believed in vain* [B] **15:8** Or *one whose birth was unusual, He* [C] **15:14** Or *proclamation is useless, and your faith also is useless*, or *proclamation is empty, and your faith also is empty* [D] **15:27** Ps 8:6 [E] **15:29** Other mss read *for the dead* [F] **15:32** Lit *Ephesus according to man* [G] **15:32** Lit *what to me the profit?* [H] **15:32** Is 22:13 [I] **15:33** A quotation from the poet Menander, *Thais*, 218 [J] **15:34** Lit *Sober up righteously* [K] **15:37** Lit *but a naked seed*

of wheat or another grain. 38 But God gives it
a body as He wants,[a] and to each of the seeds
its own body. 39 Not all flesh[b] is the same flesh;
there is one flesh for humans, another for
animals, another for birds, and another for
fish. 40 There are heavenly bodies and earthly
bodies, but the splendor[c] of the heavenly bodies is different from that of the earthly ones.
41 There is a splendor of the sun, another of
the moon, and another of the stars; for one
star differs from another star in splendor.
42 So it is with the resurrection of the dead:

Sown in corruption, raised
in incorruption;[d]
43 sown in dishonor,[e] raised in glory;[f]
sown in weakness, raised in power;[g]
44 sown a natural body, raised
a spiritual body.

If there is a natural body, there is also a spiritual body. 45 So it is written: **The first man**
Adam became a living being;[A,h] the last Adam[i]
became a life-giving Spirit. 46 However, the
spiritual is not first, but the natural, then the
spiritual.

47 The first man was from the earth
and made of dust;[j]
the second man is[B] from heaven.
48 Like the man made of dust,
so are those who are made of dust;
like the heavenly man,
so are those who are heavenly.[k]
49 And just as we have borne
the image[l] of the man made of dust,
we will also bear
the image of the heavenly man.[m]

Victorious Resurrection

50 Brothers, I tell you this: Flesh[n] and blood[o]
cannot inherit the kingdom of God, and corruption cannot inherit incorruption. 51 Listen! I am telling you a ·mystery:

We will not all fall asleep,
but we will all be changed,
52 in a moment, in the blink of an eye,
at the last trumpet.[p]
For the trumpet will sound,
and the dead will be
raised incorruptible,

[a] **15:38** Ps 143:10; Pr 16:9; Jn 5:30; Gl 1:4; Eph 1:9; 1Jn 2:17
[b] **15:39** Php 3:3
[c] **15:40** Lk 9:31-32; Ac 22:11
[d] **15:42** Rm 2:7; Eph 6:24; 2Tm 1:10
[e] **15:43** 2Co 6:8
[f] 1Pt 5:4
[g] Mk 5:30; Lk 1:35; 6:19; Ac 19:11; 2Co 13:4; Rv 11:17
[h] **15:45** Gn 2:7
[i] Rm 8:2
[j] **15:47** Gn 2:7; 3:19; Ps 90:3
[k] **15:48** Php 3:20-21
[l] **15:49** Gn 1:27
[m] 1Jn 3:2
[n] **15:50** Php 3:3
[o] Mt 16:17
[p] **15:52** Mt 24:31; 1Pt 1:5
[q] **15:53** Pr 31:25
[r] 1Pt 1:18
[s] **15:54** Mt 23:24
[t] Is 25:8
[u] **15:55** Hs 13:14
[v] **15:56** Rm 4:15
[w] Gl 5:4
[x] **15:57** 1Jn 5:5
[y] **15:58** Mk 14:6; Gl 3:10; Jms 2:14-26
[z] **16:1** Ac 11:30; 2Co 8:4
[aa] Gl 1:2
[ab] **16:2** Mt 28:1; Mk 16:9; Lk 24:1; Jn 20:1,19; Ac 20:7
[ac] 2Co 9:1-5
[ad] **16:3** 2Co 8:16-22
[ae] Mt 23:37; Ac 8:1
[af] **16:5** Ac 16:9
[ag] **16:7** Ps 143:10; Pr 16:9; Jn 5:30; Gl 1:4; Eph 1:9; 1Jn 2:17
[ah] **16:8** Eph 1:1
[ai] Ex 34:22
[aj] **16:9** Col 4:3

and we will be changed.
53 For this corruptible must be clothed[q]
with incorruptibility,[r]
and this mortal must be clothed
with immortality.
54 When this corruptible is clothed
with incorruptibility,
and this mortal is clothed
with immortality,
then the saying that is written
will take place:
Death has been swallowed up[s]
in victory.[C,t]
55 **Death, where is your victory?**
Death, where is your sting?[D,u]
56 Now the sting of death is sin,
and the power of sin[v] is the law.[w]
57 But thanks be to God, who gives us
the victory[x]
through our Lord Jesus Christ!

58 Therefore, my dear brothers, be steadfast,
immovable, always excelling in the Lord's
work,[y] knowing that your labor in the Lord
is not in vain.

Collection for the Jerusalem Church

16 Now about the collection[z] for the
·saints: You should do the same as I instructed the Galatian[aa] churches. 2 On the first
day of the week,[E,ab] each of you is to set something aside and save in keeping with how he
prospers, so that no collections will need to
be made when I come.[ac] 3 When I arrive, I will
send with letters[ad] those you recommend to
carry your gracious gift to Jerusalem.[ae] 4 If it
is suitable for me to go as well, they can travel
with me.

Paul's Travel Plans

5 I will come to you after I pass through
Macedonia[af] — for I will be traveling through
Macedonia — 6 and perhaps I will remain
with you or even spend the winter, so that
you may send me on my way wherever I go.
7 I don't want to see you now just in passing,
for I hope to spend some time with you, if
the Lord allows.[ag] 8 But I will stay in Ephesus[ah]
until Pentecost,[ai] 9 because a wide door[aj] for
effective ministry has opened for me[F] — yet

[A] **15:45** Gn 2:7 [B] **15:47** Other mss add *the Lord* [C] **15:54** Is 25:8 [D] **15:55** Hs 13:14 [E] **16:2** Or *Each Sunday* [F] **16:9** Lit *for a door has opened to me, great and effective*

many oppose me. 10 If Timothy comes, see that
he has nothing to fear from you, because he is
doing the Lord's work,[a] just as I am. 11 Therefore, no one should look down[b] on him. Send
him on his way in peace so he can come to me,
for I am expecting him with the brothers.[A]
12 About our brother Apollos:[c] I strongly
urged him to come to you with the brothers, but he was not at all willing to come now.
However, he will come when he has an opportunity.

Final Exhortation

13 Be alert, stand firm in the faith,[d] act like a
man, be strong. 14 Your every action must be
done with love.[e]
15 •Brothers, you know the household of
Stephanas: They are the •firstfruits[f] of Achaia[g]
and have devoted themselves to serving the
saints. I urge you 16 also to submit to such people, and to everyone who works and labors
with them. 17 I am pleased to have Stephanas,
Fortunatus, and Achaicus present, because
these men have made up for your absence.
18 For they have refreshed my spirit[h] and
yours. Therefore recognize[i] such people.

Conclusion

19 The churches of •Asia[j] greet you.[k] Aquila
and Priscilla[l] greet you warmly in the Lord,
along with the church that meets in their
home.[m] 20 All the brothers greet you. Greet
one another with a holy kiss.[n]
21 This greeting is in my own hand[B,o] — Paul.
22 If anyone does not love the Lord, a curse
be on him. *Marana tha* that is, Lord, come![C]
23 The grace of the Lord Jesus be with you.[p]
24 My love be with all of you in Christ Jesus.

[a] **16:10** Jn 5:17; 2Jn 8
[b] **16:11** Lk 18:9
[c] **16:12** Ti 3:13
[d] **16:13** Jd 3
[e] **16:14** 1Co 13:1
[f] **16:15** Lv 2:12
[g] Ac 18:12
[h] **16:18** Ps 51:12
[i] 1Th 5:12
[j] **16:19** Ac 6:9
[k] **16:19-20** Rm 16:3-23; 2Co 13:12; Php 4:21-22; Col 4:10-15; 1Th 5:26; Phm 23-24
[l] **16:19** Ac 18:2
[m] Rm 16:5
[n] **16:20** 2Co 13:12
[o] **16:21** 2Th 3:17
[p] **16:23-24** 2Co 13:13; Gl 6:18; Eph 6:23-24; Php 4:23; Col 4:18; 1Th 5:28; 2Th 3:18

[A] **16:11** *With the brothers* may connect with Paul or Timothy. [B] **16:21** Paul normally dictated his letters to a secretary, but signed the end of each letter himself; Rm 16:22; Gl 6:11; Col 4:18; 2Th 3:17. [C] **16:22** Or *Maran atha* (an Aram expression transliterated into Gk) = *Our Lord has come!*

AUTHOR: Paul (Saul of Tarsus)

DATE: Written around A.D. 55 from Macedonia

While the first letter to the Corinthians dealt with problems in the church, this letter deals with challenges to the apostle Paul's ministry. False teachers question his integrity in order to boost their own status. Some of the issue springs from a collection being taken for hard-pressed Christians in Jerusalem. The false teachers claim that Paul, the treasurer and fundraiser, is getting richer by the day.

What's an apostle to do? From Macedonia, Paul responded to these rumors and lies. His letter was to be read throughout Achaia, the Roman province covering southern Greece. He wanted to head off the false teachers before they disrupted other churches. In a volatile setting such as this, the mission of God goes forward.

2 CORINTHIANS

That should be considerable encouragement to many churches today. Books are written and seminars offered on recovery from church politics or church-based abuse. The sad truth is that many believers once loyal to a local church have withdrawn, tired of the biases and disgusted at the conduct, all done under the patina of pious faith. In the worst cases, disillusioned believers grow to doubt even the reality of God, and slip away from any relationship with Him. Habits of indifference lead to decades of forgetfulness. A once growing Christian has shriveled for lack of spiritual nourishment, all begun when the claims of the church did not match the life within it.

Even then, God has a mind to make these situations right again. In such cases the mission of God, obscured by false teachers, needs the polish of the Word, the primer of worship, and the protective coat of repentance and forgiveness. Paul urged Corinthian Christians to first examine his integrity, then recognize the fragile, faltering nature of spiritual growth, battered by opposition of many kinds. Stay close to Christ, Paul urges. Listen to mentors who have taught Christian truth and have long walked with God and show steady faith. Don't give up this friendship, don't abandon this effort. At stake is not only the welfare of distant Christians, but the trajectory of your own discovery of God. We do not learn faith by standing still, much less by jumping overboard, even when churches are sinking.

Most people are not perfect specimens of God's completed mission. Our habits of sin and sloth are too obvious to claim "arrival" at spiritual expertise. A healthy church has means and methods of addressing wrongs, and setting them right by prayer and discipline. The mission of God cannot be found in great museums or concert halls, in celebrity chasing or wealth acquisition. God's mission is focused in the preaching, teaching, and ordinances of the church.

Greeting

1 Paul, an apostle of Christ Jesus by God's
will,[a] and Timothy[b] our[A] brother:
To God's church at Corinth,[c] with all the
•saints who are throughout Achaia.[d]
2Grace to you and peace[e] from God our Father[f] and the Lord Jesus Christ.

The God of Comfort

3Praise[g] the God and Father of our Lord
Jesus Christ, the Father of mercies[h] and the
God of all comfort.[i] 4He comforts us in all
our affliction,[B] so that we may be able to comfort those who are in any kind of affliction,
through the comfort we ourselves receive
from God. 5For as the sufferings[j] of Christ[k]
overflow to us, so through Christ our comfort also overflows.[l] 6If we are afflicted,[m] it
is for your comfort and salvation. If we are
comforted, it is for your comfort, which is
experienced in your endurance of the same
sufferings that we suffer.[n] 7And our hope[o]
for you is firm, because we know that as you
share[p] in the sufferings, so you will share in
the comfort.
8For we don't want you to be unaware,
•brothers, of our affliction that took place in
•Asia:[q] we were completely overwhelmed
— beyond our strength[r] — so that we even despaired[s] of life. 9Indeed, we personally had a
death sentence within ourselves, so that we
would not trust in ourselves but in God[t] who
raises[u] the dead. 10He has delivered[v] us from
such a terrible death,[w] and He will deliver us.
We have put our hope in Him that He will deliver us again 11while you join in helping us by
your prayers. Then many will give thanks on
our[C] behalf for the gift that came to us
through the prayers of many.

A Clear Conscience

12For this is our confidence: The testimony[x]
of our conscience[y] is that we have conducted
ourselves in the world, and especially toward
you, with God-given sincerity and purity,
not by fleshly[D] wisdom[z] but by God's grace.[aa]
13Now we are writing nothing to you other
than what you can read and also understand.
I hope you will understand completely — 14as
you have partially understood us — that we
are your reason for pride,[ab] as you are ours,[ac]
in the day of our[E] Lord Jesus.[ad]

A Visit Postponed

15I planned with this confidence to come
to you first,[ae] so you could have a double benefit,[F] 16and to go on to Macedonia[af] with your
help, then come to you again from Macedonia and be given a start by you[ag] on my journey[ah] to Judea.[ai] 17So when I planned this, was
I irresponsible? Or what I plan, do I plan in
a purely human[G,aj] way so that I say "Yes, yes"
and "No, no" simultaneously? 18As God is
faithful,[ak] our message to you is not "Yes and
no." 19For the Son of God,[al] Jesus Christ, who
was preached among you by us — by me and
Silvanus[H,am] and Timothy — did not become
"Yes and no"; on the contrary, a final "Yes" has
come in Him.[an] 20For every one of God's promises[ao] is "Yes" in Him. Therefore, the "•Amen"[ap]
is also spoken through Him by us for God's
glory.[aq] 21Now it is God who strengthens us,
with you, in Christ and has anointed[ar] us.
22He has also sealed us and given us the Spirit
as a down payment[as] in our hearts.[at]
23I call on God as a witness,[au] on my life,
that it was to spare you that I did not come to
Corinth.[av] 24I do not mean that we have control
of[I] your faith, but we are workers with you for
your joy, because you stand[aw] by faith.

2 1In fact, I made up my mind about this:[J] I would
not come to you on another painful visit.[K] 2For
if I cause you pain, then who will cheer me
other than the one being hurt by me?[L] 3I wrote
this very thing so that when I came I wouldn't
have pain from those who ought to give me joy,
because I am confident[ax] about all of you that
my joy will also be yours. 4For I wrote to you
with many tears out of an extremely troubled
and anguished heart — not that you should be
hurt, but that you should know the abundant
love I have for you.

A Sinner Forgiven

5If anyone has caused pain, he has caused

[a]1:1 1Co 1:1; Eph 1:1; Col 1:1; 2Tm 1:1 [b]1Th 3:2; 1Tm 1:2 [c]1Co 1:2 [d]Ac 18:12; Php 1:1 [e]1:2 Lk 12:51; Rm 1:7; 2Tm 1:2; 3Jn 14 [f]Mt 5:16; 11:27; Lk 11:13; Jn 8:42; Eph 5:20 [g]1:3 Mk 14:61 [h]Heb 10:28 [i]Lk 2:25 [j]1:5 Gl 5:24; Php 3:10 [k]Rm 8:17; 2Co 4:10; Gl 6:17; Php 3:10; Col 1:24 [l]Php 1:29 [m]1:6 Heb 11:37 [n]Php 1:29 [o]1:7 1Th 1:3 [p]Phm 17 [q]1:8 Ac 6:9 [r]Ac 8:10; 1Co 15:24; Eph 1:21; 1Pt 3:22 [s]2Co 4:8 [t]1:9 Ps 25:2; 26:1; Jr 17:5-7; Lk 18:9 [u]Mk 9:27; Jn 2:19 [v]1:10 Mt 27:43 [w]Mt 10:21; Jn 8:51; Php 3:10 [x]1:12 1Tm 2:6 [y]Heb 13:18 [z]Pr 3:19; 1Co 1:21 [aa]Ac 23:1; 2Co 4:2; 5:12; 1Th 2:10 [ab]1:14 Rm 2:17; Gl 6:4 [ac]2Co 9:3; Php 2:16; 4:1; 1Th 2:19-20 [ad]Php 1:6 [ae]1:15 Ac 18:1-18; 1Co 4:19 [af]1:16 Ac 16:9 [ag]Ac 20:38 [ah]Ac 19:21; 1Co 16:5-7 [ai]Lk 1:5 [aj]1:17 Php 3:3; Col 3:22 [ak]1:18 Nm 23:19 [al]1:19 Jn 5:19; Heb 1:2 [am]1Th 1:1 [an]Heb 13:8 [ao]1:20 Gn 12:7 [ap]Ps 72:19; Rv 22:21 [aq]Mk 10:37; Lk 9:32; Jn 17:24; 2Co 3:18; 2Pt 3:18 [ar]1:21 Lk 4:18; 1Jn 2:20 [as]1:22 Eph 1:14 [at]Jms 4:5 [au]1:23 Rm 1:9; Php 1:8; Heb 12:1

[av]1Co 4:21; 2Co 13:2,10 [aw]1:24 Pr 24:16 [ax]2:3 Php 1:25

[A]1:1 Lit *the* [B]1:4 Or *trouble*, or *tribulation*, or *trials*, or *oppression*; the Gk word has a lit meaning of being under pressure. [C]1:11 Other mss read *your* [D]1:12 The word *fleshly* (characterized by flesh) indicates that the wisdom is natural rather than spiritual. [E]1:14 Other mss omit *our* [F]1:15 Other mss read *a second joy* [G]1:17 Or *a worldly*, or *a fleshly*, or *a selfish* [H]1:19 Or *Silas*; Ac 15:22-32; 16:19-40; 17:1-16 [I]1:24 Or *we lord it over*, or *we rule over* [J]2:1 Lit *I decided this for myself* [K]2:1 Lit *not again in sorrow to come to you* [L]2:2 Lit *the one pained*

pain not so much to me but to some degree — not to exaggerate[a] — to all of you.
6The punishment inflicted by the majority
is sufficient for that person. 7As a result, you
should instead forgive[b] and comfort him.
Otherwise, this one may be overwhelmed by
excessive grief. 8Therefore I urge you to reaffirm your love to him. 9I wrote for this purpose: to test your character[c] to see if you are
obedient[d] in everything. 10If you forgive anyone, I do too. For what I have forgiven — if I
have forgiven anything — it is for you in the
presence of Christ. 11I have done this so that
we may not be taken advantage[e] of by Satan.
For we are not ignorant of his schemes.

A Trip to Macedonia

12When I came to Troas[f] to preach the gospel of Christ, the Lord opened a door[g] for me.
13I had no rest[h] in my spirit because I did not
find my brother Titus,[i] but I said good-bye to
them and left for Macedonia.[j]

A Ministry of Life or Death

14But thanks be to God,[k] who always puts us
on display[A] in Christ[B] and through us spreads
the aroma of the knowledge of Him in every
place.[l] 15For to God we are the fragrance[m] of
Christ among those who are being saved[n] and
among those who are perishing.[o] 16To some
we are an aroma of death[p] leading to death,
but to others, an aroma of life[q] leading to life.
And who is competent for this? 17For we are
not like the many[C] who market God's message[r] for profit. On the contrary, we speak
with sincerity in Christ, as from God and before God.

Living Letters

3 Are we beginning to commend ourselves
again? Or do we need, like some, letters
of recommendation to you or from you?
2You yourselves are our letter, written on our
hearts, recognized and read by everyone.[s] 3It
is clear that you are Christ's letter,[t] produced[D]
by us, not written with ink but with the Spirit
of the living God[u] — not on stone tablets[v] but
on tablets that are hearts of flesh.[w]

Paul's Competence

4We have this kind of confidence toward
God through Christ. 5It is not that we are
competent in[E] ourselves to consider anything
as coming from ourselves, but our competence is from God.[x] 6He has made us competent to be ministers of a new covenant,[y] not of
the letter,[z] but of the Spirit. For the letter kills,
but the Spirit produces life.

New Covenant Ministry

7Now if the ministry of death, chiseled in
letters on stones, came with glory,[aa] so that
the Israelites were not able to look directly
at Moses' face because of the glory from his
face — a fading glory — 8how will the ministry of the Spirit not be more glorious? 9For
if the ministry of condemnation had glory,
the ministry of righteousness overflows with
even more glory. 10In fact, what had been
glorious is not glorious now by comparison
because of the glory that surpasses it. 11For
if what was fading away[ab] was glorious, what
endures will be even more glorious.
12Therefore, having such a hope,[ac] we use
great boldness. 13We are not like Moses, who
used to put a veil over his face[ad] so that the
Israelites could not stare at the the end of
what was fading away, 14but their minds
were closed.[F,ae] For to this day, at the reading
of the old covenant,[af] the same veil remains;
it is not lifted, because it is set aside only in
Christ.[ag] 15Even to this day, whenever Moses is
read, a veil lies over their hearts, 16but whenever a person turns[ah] to the Lord, the veil is
removed.[ai] 17Now the Lord is the Spirit, and
where the Spirit of the Lord is, there is freedom. 18We all, with unveiled faces, are looking as in a mirror at[G,aj] the glory of the Lord[ak]
and are being transformed[al] into the same
image[am] from glory to glory;[H] this is from the
Lord who is the Spirit.[I]

The Light of the Gospel

4 Therefore, since we have this ministry
because we were shown mercy,[an] we do
not give up.[ao] 2Instead, we have renounced
shameful secret things, not walking[ap] in

[a]**2:5** 2Th 3:8
[b]**2:7** Mt 6:12
[c]**2:9** Rm 5:4
[d]Php 2:8
[e]**2:11** 2Co 12:17
[f]**2:12** Ac 16:8
[g]Col 4:3
[h]**2:13** 2Th 1:7
[i]Ti 1:4
[j]Ac 16:9
[k]**2:14** 1Co 15:57
[l]Jn 17:3; 1Jn 4:8
[m]**2:15** Eph 5:2; Php 4:18
[n]Mt 9:22; Ac 16:30; Eph 2:8
[o]Jn 6:27
[p]**2:16** Mt 10:21; Jn 8:51; Php 3:10
[q]1Jn 5:12
[r]**2:17** Mt 12:36; Mk 4:14; Lk 6:47; 8:21; Jn 1:1; 2:22; 18:32; Ac 17:11; 2Tm 2:15; Heb 4:12
[s]**3:2** 1Co 9:2
[t]**3:3** Phm 13
[u]Dt 5:26
[v]Ex 24:12
[w]Pr 3:3; 7:3; Jr 17:1; 31:33; Ezk 11:19; 36:26; Heb 8:10
[x]**3:5** 1Co 15:10
[y]**3:6** Lk 22:20; Heb 7:22
[z]Rm 7:6
[aa]**3:7** Ex 34:29-35; Mk 10:37; Lk 9:32; Jn 17:24; 2Co 3:18; 2Pt 3:18
[ab]**3:11** Heb 2:14
[ac]**3:12** 1Th 1:3
[ad]**3:13** Ex 34:33
[ae]**3:14** Mk 8:17; Heb 3:13
[af]Ac 13:15; 15:21; Heb 7:22
[ag]Rm 16:7; 1Pt 5:14
[ah]**3:16** 1Pt 2:25
[ai]Ex 34:34
[aj]**3:18** 1Co 13:12
[ak]Jn 17:24; 2Co 1:20; 4:4-6; 1Tm 1:11,17
[al]Mk 9:2
[am]Gn 1:27; 1Jn 3:2
[an]**4:1** Mt 5:7; Mk 5:19; Lk 1:50
[ao]2Th 3:13
[ap]**4:2** 2Jn 6

[A]**2:14** Or *always leads us in a triumphal procession*, or *always causes us to triumph* [B]**2:14** Lit *in the Christ*, or *in the Messiah*; 1Co 15:22; Eph 1:10,12,20; 3:11 [C]**2:17** Other mss read *the rest* [D]**3:3** Lit *ministered to* [E]**3:5** Lit *from* [F]**3:14** Lit *their thoughts were hardened* [G]**3:18** Or *are reflecting* [H]**3:18** Progressive glorification or sanctification [I]**3:18** Or *from the Spirit of the Lord*, or *from the Lord, the Spirit*

deceit or distorting God's message,[a] but
commending ourselves to every person's
conscience in God's sight by an open display
of the truth.[b] 3But if our gospel is veiled, it is
veiled to those who are perishing. 4In their
case, the god of this age[c] has blinded the
minds of the unbelievers so they cannot see
the light of the gospel of the glory of Christ,[A,d]
who is the image of God.[e] 5For we are not proclaiming ourselves but Jesus Christ as Lord,[f]
and ourselves as your •slaves because of
Jesus. 6For God who said, "Let light shine out
of darkness,"[g] has shone in our hearts to give
the light of the knowledge[h] of God's glory[i] in
the face of Jesus Christ.

Treasure in Clay Jars

7Now we have this treasure in clay jars, so
that this extraordinary power[j] may be from
God and not from us. 8We are pressured in
every way but not crushed; we are perplexed
but not in despair; 9we are persecuted but
not abandoned; we are struck down but not
destroyed. 10We always carry the death of
Jesus[k] in our body, so that the life of Jesus may
also be revealed in our body. 11For we who
live are always given over to death[l] because of
Jesus, so that Jesus' life may also be revealed
in our mortal flesh. 12So death works in us,
but life in you. 13And since we have the same
spirit of faith in keeping with what is written, **I believed, therefore I spoke,**[B,m] we also
believe, and therefore speak. 14We know that
the One who raised the Lord Jesus will raise
us also with Jesus[n] and present us with you.
15Indeed, everything is for your benefit, so
that grace, extended through more and more
people, may cause thanksgiving[o] to increase
to God's glory.
16Therefore we do not give up.[p] Even
though our outer person is being destroyed,
our inner person[q] is being renewed day by
day. 17For our momentary light affliction[C,r] is
producing for us an absolutely incomparable
eternal weight of glory.[s] 18So we do not focus
on what is seen,[t] but on what is unseen. For
what is seen is temporary, but what is unseen
is eternal.

[a]4:2 2Co 2:17; 2Tm 2:15; Heb 4:12
[b]2Co 5:11-12; 6:7; 7:14
[c]4:4 Lk 16:8
[d]Mk 10:37
[e]Gn 1:27
[f]4:5 Php 2:11
[g]4:6 Gn 1:3; Mt 6:23
[h]Php 3:8; 1Jn 4:8
[i]Mk 10:37; Lk 9:32; Jn 17:24; 2Co 3:18; 2Pt 3:18
[j]4:7 Mk 5:30; Lk 1:35; 6:19; Ac 19:11; 2Co 13:4; Rv 11:17
[k]4:10 Lk 9:23; Rm 5:6-8; 6:5-8; 8:34-36; Gl 6:17
[l]4:11 Mt 10:21; Jn 8:51; Php 3:10
[m]4:13 Ps 116:10 LXX
[n]4:14 1Th 4:14
[o]4:15 2Co 9:11
[p]4:16 2Th 3:13
[q]Rm 7:22
[r]4:17 Gl 6:2
[s]Lk 24:26; 1Pt 5:1,4
[t]4:18 Rm 8:24

GOD'S HEART FOR THE WORLD

From Glory to Glory

We all, with unveiled faces, are reflecting the glory of the Lord and are being transformed into the same image from glory to glory; this is from the Lord who is the Spirit. (2 Corinthians 3:18)

It is often said that a couple that has been married for years begins to look like one another in the way they dress and present themselves. They don't try to make these changes, but they are transformed by the presence of the other. That is not unlike what is happening to believers who live in God's presence. Paul describes us as "reflecting the glory of the Lord" and "being transformed into the same image from glory to glory."

When Moses stood in the presence of God, he was transformed. His face would start to shine like the sun, but when he went down from Mount Sinai, he would cover the brightness with a veil. Paul tells us here that Moses hid his face because that glory was not lasting. It would fade away. But that is not the case for believers. We who have been given the Spirit of God and can see "the light of the gospel of the glory of Christ" (4:4) can always be in the presence of God in worship and prayer, and always have Christ within us. When we turn to the Lord, we reflect His glory, not in a transitory way like Moses, but eternally, like Christ Himself. And we are transformed by it.

Like the old couple who has begun too look like one another, as we spend time in the presence of God we are slowly transformed. We begin to look more and more like Christ, moving from one stage of glory to the next. We do not change by our own efforts, but simply by turning our eyes to Jesus.

A4:4 Or *the gospel of the glorious Christ*, or *the glorious gospel of Christ* B4:13 Ps 116:10 LXX C4:17 See note at 2Co 1:4.

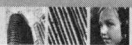

Our Future after Death

5 For we know that if our temporary,
earthly dwelling[A,a] is destroyed, we have
a building from God, an eternal dwelling[B]
in the heavens,[b] not made with hands.[c] 2In-
deed, we groan in this body, desiring[d] to put
on our dwelling from heaven, 3since, when
we are clothed,[C] we will not be found naked.[e]
4Indeed, we groan while we are in this tent,
burdened as we are, because we do not want
to be unclothed but clothed, so that mortal-
ity[f] may be swallowed up by life. 5And the One
who prepared us for this very purpose is God,
who gave us the Spirit as a down payment.
6So, we are always confident and know that
while we are at home in the body we are away
from the Lord. 7For we ·walk by faith,[g] not by
sight,[h] 8and we are confident and satisfied
to be out of the body and at home with the
Lord.[i] 9Therefore, whether we are at home or
away, we make it our aim to be pleasing[j] to
Him. 10For we must all appear before the tribunal[k] of Christ,[l] so that each may be repaid[m]
for what he has done in the body, whether
good or worthless.
11Therefore, because we know the ·fear of
the Lord,[n] we seek to persuade people. We are
completely open before God, and I hope we
are completely open to your consciences as
well. 12We are not commending ourselves to
you again, but giving you an opportunity to
be proud of us, so that you may have a reply
for those who take pride in the outward appearance[D] rather than in the heart. 13For if we
are out of our mind,[o] it is for God; if we have
a sound mind,[p] it is for you. 14For Christ's
love compels[E] us, since we have reached this
conclusion: If One died for all,[q] then all died.
15And He died for all[r] so that those who live
should no longer live for themselves,[s] but for
the One[t] who died for them and was raised.

The Ministry of Reconciliation

16From now on, then, we do not know[F] anyone in a purely human way.[G] Even if we have
known[H] Christ in a purely human way,[I] yet
now we no longer know[F] Him in this way.
17Therefore, if anyone is in Christ, he is a new
creation;[u] old things have passed away, and
look,[v] new things[J] have come.[w] 18Everything
is from God, who reconciled us to Himself
through Christ and gave us the ministry of

---

[a]**5:1** 2Pt 1:13
[b]Eph 6:9; Php 2:10
[c]Col 2:11
[d]**5:2** 1Pt 2:2
[e]**5:3** Mt 25:36; Lk 10:30
[f]**5:4** Rm 7:24; 8:23; 1Co 15:26
[g]**5:7** Mt 8:10; Ac 3:16; Rm 1:8; 1Co 2:5; Gl 2:16; 1Tm 1:2; Heb 4:2
[h]Lk 3:22
[i]**5:8** Php 1:23
[j]**5:9** Heb 13:21
[k]**5:10** Jn 5:22-30
[l]Mt 25:31-46; Php 1:6; Heb 10:31
[m]Mt 16:27
[n]**5:11** Ps 147:11; Pr 1:7; 1Pt 1:17; Rv 14:7
[o]**5:13** Ac 10:45
[p]1Pt 4:7
[q]**5:14** Jn 11:51; 2Co 4:10
[r]**5:15** Lk 20:38; Heb 2:9
[s]Rm 14:7
[t]Lk 20:38
[u]**5:17** Jn 1:3; Rv 3:14
[v]Rm 8:24
[w]Is 43:19; 65:17; Rm 6:4; Eph 4:24; Rv 21:5

GOD WHO SENDS

Human Instrumentality in the Mission

Although God always reserves the right in his sovereign pleasure to act otherwise, his basic method is to work through human instrumentality. He even sends providential blessings and judgment through people. In this regard, the final nature of the biblical theology of the sending is illustrated. One may arbitrarily select a disinterested person to accomplish any given number of missions. However, God's unique salvific mission necessitates that only those who have been the recipients of his redemptive sending qualify to become the instruments of that redemptive sending.

Moreover, not only are the redeemed the ones who are qualified to share redemption but there is also an inherent mandate to so share. Those who are the recipients of God's salvific sending become the instruments of that sending. This is more than a missional mandate however; it is a missional compulsion which emanates from the very impulse of Christian existence itself. Moreover, it relates ultimately to the divine impulse which sent the Son from the bosom of the Father.

(DUBOSE, 68)

[A]**5:1** = our present physical body [B]**5:1** = our future body [C]**5:3** Other mss read *stripped* [D]**5:12** Lit *in face* [E]**5:14** Or *For the love of Christ impels*, or *For the love of Christ controls* [F]**5:16** Or *regard* [G]**5:16** Lit *anyone according to the flesh* [H]**5:16** Or *have regarded* [I]**5:16** Lit *Christ according to the flesh* [J]**5:17** Other mss read *look, all new things*

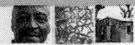

reconciliation:[a] **19**That is, in Christ, God was
reconciling the world[b] to Himself,[c] not counting their trespasses against them, and He has
committed the message of reconciliation
to us. **20**Therefore, we are ambassadors[d] for
Christ, certain that God is appealing through
us. We plead on Christ's behalf,[e] "Be reconciled to God." **21**He made the One who did not
know sin[f] to be sin[A] for us,[g] so that we might
become the righteousness of God in Him.

6 Working together[B] with Him, we also appeal to you, "Don't receive God's grace in
vain." **2**For He says:

> **I heard you in an acceptable time,**
> **and I helped you in the day**
> **of salvation.**[C,h]

Look, now is the acceptable time; now is the
day of salvation.[i]

The Character of Paul's Ministry

3We give no opportunity for stumbling
to anyone, so that the ministry will not be
blamed. **4**But as God's ministers, we commend ourselves in everything:

> by great endurance, by afflictions,
> by hardship, by difficulties,
> **5** by beatings, by imprisonments,[j]
> by riots, by labors,
> by sleepless nights, by times of hunger,
> **6** by purity,[k] by knowledge,[l]
> by patience,[m] by kindness,[n]
> by the Holy Spirit, by sincere love,[o]
> **7** by the message of truth,[p]
> by the power of God;[q]
> through weapons of righteousness
> on the right hand and the left,
> **8** through glory[r] and dishonor,
> through slander and good report;
> as deceivers yet true;
> **9** as unknown yet recognized;
> as dying and look — we live;
> as being disciplined yet not killed;
> **10** as grieving yet always rejoicing;[s]
> as poor yet enriching many;
> as having nothing yet
> possessing everything.

11We have spoken openly[D] to you, Corinthians; our heart has been opened wide. **12**You
are not limited by us, but you are limited by
your own affections. **13**I speak as to my children. As a proper response, you should also
be open to us.

Separation to God

14Do not be mismatched with unbelievers.
For what partnership is there between righteousness and lawlessness?[t] Or what fellowship does light[u] have with darkness?[v] **15**What
agreement does Christ have with Belial?[E] Or
what does a believer have in common with
an unbeliever? **16**And what agreement does
God's sanctuary have with idols?[w] For we[F] are
the sanctuary of the living God, as God said:

> **I will dwell among them**[x]
> **and walk among them,**

[a]**5:18** Rm 5:11 [b]**5:19** 2Pt 2:20 [c]Ti 2:11 [d]**5:20** Eph 6:20 [e]2Co 12:10; Php 1:29 [f]**5:21** 1Jn 3:5 [g]Rm 8:3; Gl 3:13; 1Pt 2:24 [h]**6:2** Is 49:8 [i]Is 49:8; 55:6; Lk 4:19; Heb 3:13 [j]**6:5** Jdg 16:21 [k]**6:6** 2Co 11:3 [l]Php 3:8; 1Jn 4:8 [m]Ex 34:6; 2Tm 3:10 [n]Rm 2:4; 3:12; 11:22; Gl 5:22; Eph 2:7; Col 3:12; Ti 3:4 [o]1Co 13:1 [p]**6:7** 2Th 2:10 [q]Mk 5:30; Lk 1:35; 6:19; Ac 19:11; 2Co 13:4; Rv 11:17 [r]**6:8** 1Pt 5:4 [s]**6:10** Mt 5:4; Jn 16:22; 2Co 7:4; Php 1:4,25; 2:17-18; 3:1; 4:1,4; Col 1:24; 1Th 1:6; 1Pt 1:6-8 [t]**6:14** Mt 13:41 [u]Jn 12:46 [v]Mt 6:23 [w]**6:16** Gn 31:19; 1Co 8:4 [x]Jms 4:5

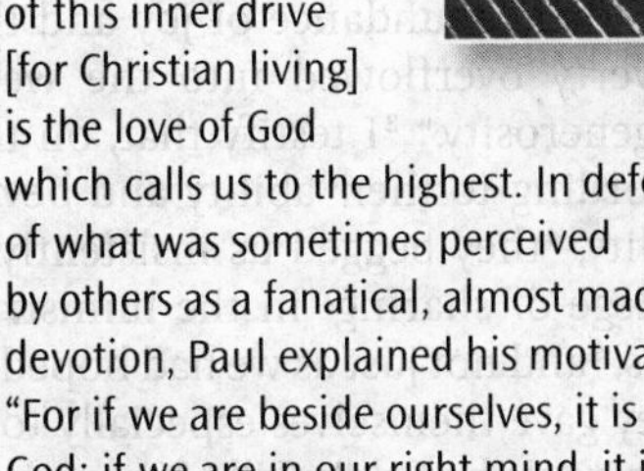

Compelled by Love

GOD WHO SENDS

The deepest element of this inner drive [for Christian living] is the love of God which calls us to the highest. In defense of what was sometimes perceived by others as a fanatical, almost mad devotion, Paul explained his motivation: "For if we are beside ourselves, it is for God; if we are in our right mind, it is for you. For the love of Christ controls us" (2Co 5:13-14). Paul was not saying that his love for Christ produced this intense life-and-death motivation, but Christ's love for him. In other words, he was so moved by the knowledge and experience of Christ's love for him that he was controlled and compelled by it. Out of that came the concept of ambassadorship (mission) which he develops in his next line of thought in 2 Corinthians 5:20.

(*DuBose*, 134)

[A]**5:21** Or *be a sin offering* [B]**6:1** Or *As we work together* [C]**6:2** Is 49:8 [D]**6:11** Lit *Our mouths have been open* [E]**6:15** Or *Beliar*, a name for the Devil or antichrist in extra-biblical Jewish writings [F]**6:16** Other mss read *you*

and I will be their God,[a]
and they will be My people.[A,b]
17 **Therefore, come out from among them**
and be separate, says the Lord;
do not touch any unclean thing,
and I will welcome you.[B,c]
18 **I will be a Father[d] to you,**
and you will be sons[e] and daughters
to Me,
says the Lord Almighty.[C,f]

7 Therefore, dear friends, since we have
such promises,[g] let us ·cleanse ourselves
from every impurity of the flesh and spirit,[h]
completing our ·sanctification[D] in the ·fear
of God.[i]

Joy and Repentance

2 Accept us.[E] We have wronged no one, corrupted[j] no one, defrauded no one. 3 I don't say
this to condemn you, for I have already said
that you are in our hearts, to live together
and to die together. 4 I have great confidence
in you; I have great pride in you. I am filled
with encouragement; I am overcome with joy
in all our afflictions.
5 In fact, when we came into Macedonia,[k]
we[F] had no rest. Instead, we were troubled
in every way: conflicts[l] on the outside, fears[m]
inside. 6 But God, who comforts the humble,[n]
comforted us by the arrival of Titus, 7 and not
only by his arrival, but also by the comfort
he received from you. He told us about your
deep longing, your sorrow,[G] and your zeal[o]
for me, so that I rejoiced even more. 8 For even
if I grieved you with my letter,[p] I do not regret
it — even though I did regret it since I saw
that the letter grieved you, yet only for a little
while. 9 Now I rejoice, not because you were
grieved, but because your grief led to repentance. For you were grieved as God willed, so
that you didn't experience any loss from us.
10 For godly grief produces a repentance not
to be regretted and leading to salvation, but
worldly grief produces death.[q] 11 For consider
how much diligence this very thing — this
grieving as God wills — has produced in you:
what a desire to clear yourselves, what indignation, what fear, what deep longing, what
zeal, what justice! In every way you showed
yourselves to be pure[r] in this matter. 12 So even
though I wrote to you, it was not because of
the one who did wrong, or because of the
one who was wronged, but in order that your
diligence for us might be made plain to you
in the sight of God. 13 For this reason we have
been comforted.
In addition to our comfort, we rejoiced
even more over the joy Titus[s] had,[H] because
his spirit was refreshed by all of you. 14 For if I
have made any boast to him about you, I have
not been embarrassed; but as I have spoken
everything to you in truth,[t] so our boasting
to Titus has also turned out to be the truth.
15 And his affection toward you is even greater
as he remembers the obedience of all of you,
and how you received him with fear and
trembling. 16 I rejoice that I have complete
confidence in you.

Appeal to Complete the Collection

8 We want you to know, ·brothers, about
the grace of God granted to the churches[u]
of Macedonia:[v] 2 During a severe testing by
affliction, their abundance of joy and their
deep poverty overflowed into the wealth
of their generosity.[w] 3 I testify that, on their
own, according to their ability and beyond
their ability, 4 they begged us insistently for
the privilege of sharing[x] in the ministry to
the ·saints, 5 and not just as we had hoped. Instead, they gave themselves especially to the
Lord, then to us by God's will.[y] 6 So we urged
Titus that just as he had begun, so he should
also complete this grace to you. 7 Now as you
excel in everything — faith, speech, knowledge,[z] and in all diligence, and in your love
for us[I] — excel also in this grace.
8 I am not saying this as a command. Rather,
by means of the diligence of others, I am testing the genuineness of your love. 9 For you
know the grace of our Lord Jesus Christ:
Though He was rich,[aa] for your sake He became poor,[ab] so that by His poverty you might
become rich. 10 Now I am giving an opinion
on this because it is profitable for you, who a
year ago began not only to do something but
also to desire it.[J,ac] 11 But now finish the task[K]

[a] **6:16** Heb 3:6 [b] Lv 26:12 [c] **6:17** Is 52:11 [d] **6:18** Mt 5:16; 11:27; Lk 11:13; Jn 8:42; Eph 5:20 [e] Mt 5:9 [f] 2Sm 7:14; Rv 1:8 [g] **7:1** Gn 12:7 [h] Ps 51:12 [i] Ps 147:11; Pr 1:7; Rv 14:7 [j] **7:2** 1Co 3:17; 15:33; 2Co 11:3; Eph 4:22; 2Pt 2:12; Jd 10; Rv 19:2 [k] **7:5** Ac 16:9 [l] Jms 4:1; Ti 3:9 [m] Jn 7:13; Ac 27:29 [n] **7:6** Mt 11:29 [o] **7:7** Nm 25:13 [p] **7:8** 2Co 2:2,4 [q] **7:10** Mt 10:21; Jn 8:51; Php 3:10 [r] **7:11** Php 4:8 [s] **7:13** Ti 1:4 [t] **7:14** Ps 119:142; Jn 8:14; 14:6; 2Co 11:10; 1Jn 5:20; 3Jn 3 [u] **8:1** Mt 16:18; 1Co 14:4; Rv 1:4 [v] Ac 16:9 [w] **8:2** Php 4:10 [x] **8:4** Ac 24:17; Rm 15:26,31; 2Co 8:19-20; 9:1,12-13 [y] **8:5** Ps 143:10; Pr 16:9; Jn 5:30; Gl 1:4; Eph 1:9; 1Jn 2:17 [z] **8:7** Php 3:8; 1Jn 4:8 [aa] **8:9** Mt 20:28; 2Co 6:10; Php 2:6-7 [ab] Php 2:7 [ac] **8:10** 1Co 16:1-4; 2Co 9:1-2

[A] **6:16** Lv 26:12; Jr 31:33; 32:38; Ezk 37:26 [B] **6:17** Is 52:11 [C] **6:18** 2Sm 7:14; Is 43:6; 49:22; 60:4; Hs 1:10 [D] **7:1** Or *spirit, perfecting holiness* [E] **7:2** Lit *Make room for us* [F] **7:5** Lit *our flesh* [G] 7:7 Or *lamentation*, or *mourning* [H] **7:13** Lit *the joy of Titus* [I] **8:7** Other mss read *in our love for you* [J] **8:10** Lit *to will* [K] **8:11** Lit *finish the doing* as well, that just as there was eagerness to desire it, so there may also be a completion from what you have. 12For if the eagerness is there, it is acceptable according to what one has, not according to what he does not have.[a] 13It is not that there may be relief for others and hardship for you, but it is a question of equality[A]— 14at the present time your surplus is available for their need, so their abundance may also become available for our need, so there may be equality. 15As it has been written:

The person who gathered much
did not have too much,
and the person who gathered little
did not have too little.[B,b]

Administration of the Collection

16Thanks be to God who put the same concern for you into the heart of Titus. 17For he accepted our urging and, being very diligent, went out to you by his own choice. 18We have sent with him the brother[c] who is praised throughout the churches for his gospel ministry.[C] 19And not only that, but he was also appointed by the churches to accompany us with this gift[D] that is being administered by us for the glory of the Lord Himself and to show our eagerness to help. 20We are taking this precaution so no one can criticize us about this large sum administered by us. 21For we are making provision[d] for what is right,[e] not only before the Lord but also before men. 22We have also sent with them our brother. We have often tested him in many circumstances and found him to be diligent—and now even more diligent because of his great confidence in you. 23As for Titus, he is my partner[f] and coworker[g] serving you; as for our brothers, they are the messengers[h] of the churches, the glory of Christ.[i] 24Therefore, show them proof before the churches of your love and of our boasting[j] about you.

[a]8:12 Lk 21:3
[b]8:15 Ex 16:18
[c]8:18 2Co 12:18
[d]8:21 1Tm 5:8
[e]1Pt 2:12
[f]8:23 Phm 17
[g]1Co 3:9
[h]Jn 13:16
[i]Mk 10:37
[j]8:24 2Co 12:5; Jms 4:16

Motivations for Giving

9 Now concerning the ministry to the saints, it is unnecessary for me to write to you. 2For I know your eagerness, and I brag

PRAYING FOR THE WORLD

Give Generously

Our financial gifts support missions. That makes us missionaries, and it is a great honor to join in being able to help those called to go to be able to have the funds to both go and be supported as they minister.

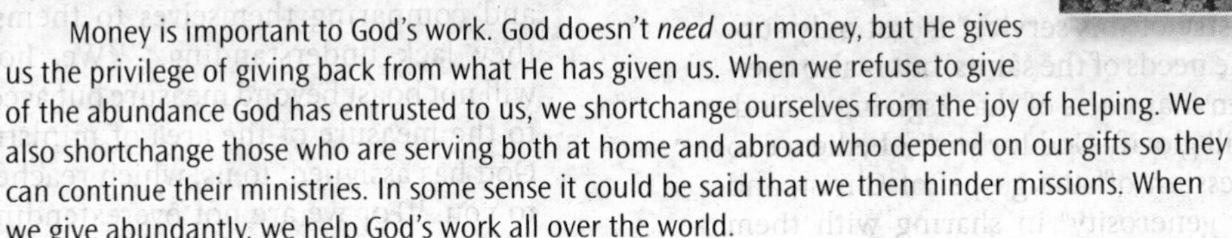

Money is important to God's work. God doesn't *need* our money, but He gives us the privilege of giving back from what He has given us. When we refuse to give of the abundance God has entrusted to us, we shortchange ourselves from the joy of helping. We also shortchange those who are serving both at home and abroad who depend on our gifts so they can continue their ministries. In some sense it could be said that we then hinder missions. When we give abundantly, we help God's work all over the world.

In addition, mission programs must expand to remain viable. The key word in missions is *growth*. The Lord will bless us for being His coworkers in the spread of the gospel when we give cheerfully so that others can hear the Good News!

Dear Lord, from Your bounty we give, for all that we have comes from Your gracious hand. In gratitude we give with joy. Remove any barriers deep inside us that obstruct giving. Help us to know of Your provision for our own needs so that we can help provide for those who are on the front lines sharing the Good News. May our generosity spring from love, vision, and joy.

Direct our gifts to the right destinations. May many believe and dedicate their lives to You. Amen.

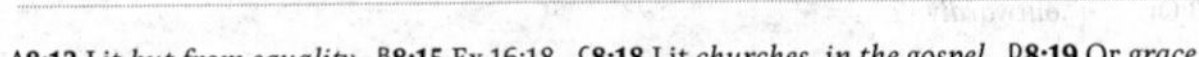

[A]8:13 Lit *but from equality* [B]8:15 Ex 16:18 [C]8:18 Lit *churches, in the gospel* [D]8:19 Or *grace*

about you to the Macedonians:[A,a] "Achaia[B,b] has been prepared since last year," and your zeal[c] has stirred up most of them.[d] 3 But I sent the brothers so our boasting about you in the matter would not prove empty, and so you would be prepared just as I said. 4 For if any Macedonians come with me and find you unprepared, we, not to mention you, would be embarrassed in that situation.[C] 5 Therefore I considered it necessary to urge the brothers to go on ahead to you and arrange in advance the generous gift[e] you promised, so that it will be ready as a gift and not as an extortion.[f]

6 Remember this:[D] The person who sows sparingly will also reap sparingly, and the person who sows generously will also reap generously. 7 Each person should do as he has decided in his heart—not reluctantly or out of necessity, for God loves[g] a cheerful giver. 8 And God is able[h] to make every grace overflow to you, so that in every way, always having everything you need, you may excel in every good work. 9 As it is written:

> **He scattered;**[i]
> **He gave to the poor;**
> **His righteousness endures forever.**[E,j]

10 Now the One who provides seed for the sower and bread for food will provide and multiply your seed and increase the harvest of your righteousness.[k] 11 You will be enriched[l] in every way for all generosity, which produces thanksgiving to God through us. 12 For the ministry of this service[m] is not only supplying the needs of the saints, but is also overflowing in many acts of thanksgiving to God. 13 They will glorify God for your obedience to the confession of[F] the gospel of Christ, and for your generosity[n] in sharing with them and with others through the proof provided by this service. 14 And they will have deep affection for[G] you in their prayers on your behalf because of the surpassing grace of God in you. 15 Thanks be to God for His indescribable gift.

Paul's Apostolic Authority

10 Now I, Paul, make a personal appeal to you by the gentleness and graciousness of Christ—I who am humble among you in person but bold toward you when absent. 2 I beg you that when I am present I will not need to be bold with the confidence by which I plan to challenge certain people who think we are behaving in an unspiritual way.[H,o] 3 For though we live in the body,[I] we do not wage war in an unspiritual way,[J] 4 since the weapons of our warfare[p] are not worldly,[K] but are powerful[q] through God for the demolition of strongholds. We demolish arguments 5 and every high-minded thing that is raised up against the knowledge[r] of God, taking every thought captive to obey Christ. 6 And we are ready to punish any disobedience, once your obedience has been confirmed.

7 Look at what is obvious.[L] If anyone is confident that he belongs to Christ,[s] he should remind himself of this: Just as he belongs to Christ, so do we. 8 For if I boast some more about our authority, which the Lord gave for building you up[t] and not for tearing you down, I am not ashamed. 9 I don't want to seem as though I am trying to terrify you with my letters. 10 For it is said, "His letters are weighty and powerful, but his physical presence is weak, and his public speaking is despicable." 11 Such a person should consider this: What we are in the words of our letters when absent, we will be in actions when present.

12 For we don't dare classify or compare ourselves with some who commend[u] themselves. But in measuring themselves by themselves and comparing themselves to themselves,[v] they lack understanding.[w] 13 We, however, will not boast beyond measure but according to the measure of the area of ministry that God has assigned[x] to us, which reaches even to you. 14 For we are not overextending ourselves, as if we had not reached you, since we have come to you with the gospel of Christ. 15 We are not bragging beyond measure about other people's labors. But we have the hope[y] that as your faith increases, our area of ministry will be greatly enlarged, 16 so that we may proclaim the good news to the regions beyond you,[z] not boasting about what has already been done in someone else's area of ministry.[aa] 17 So **the one who boasts must**

[a] **9:2** Ac 16:9 [b] Ac 18:12 [c] Nm 25:13 [d] 2Co 8:18; 12:18 [e] **9:5** Ac 11:30 [f] Eph 5:3 [g] **9:7** Lk 6:35; Jn 3:16; 12:43; 2Th 2:13; Rv 12:11 [h] **9:8** Eph 3:20 [i] **9:9** Jn 16:32 [j] Ps 112:9; 1Jn 2:17 [k] **9:10** Is 55:10-11; Hs 10:12 [l] **9:11** 1Co 1:5; 2Co 6:10 [m] **9:12** Heb 8:6 [n] **9:13** Php 4:10 [o] **10:2** Php 3:3 [p] **10:4** 1Tm 1:18 [q] Ac 25:5 [r] **10:5** Jn 17:3; 1Jn 4:8 [s] **10:7** 1Co 3:23; Gl 5:24 [t] **10:8** 1Co 14:3 [u] **10:12** Gl 2:18 [v] Pr 26:12; 27:2 [w] Mt 13:13 [x] **10:13** Rm 12:3; 1Co 7:17; Heb 7:2 [y] **10:15** 1Th 1:3 [z] **10:16** Ac 19:21 [aa] Rm 15:20

[A] **9:2** Macedonia was a Roman province in the northern area of modern Greece. [B] **9:2** Achaia was the Roman province, south of Macedonia, where Corinth was located. [C] **9:4** Or *in this confidence* [D] **9:6** Lit *And this* [E] **9:9** Ps 112:9 [F] **9:13** Or *your obedient confession to* [G] **9:14** Or *will long for* [H] **10:2** Or *are living as a non-Christian*; lit *are walking according to flesh* [I] **10:3** Lit *flesh* [J] **10:3** Lit *war according to flesh* [K] **10:4** Lit *fleshly* [L] **10:7** Or *You are looking at things outwardly*

boast in the Lord.[A,a] 18 For it is not the one
commending himself who is approved, but
the one the Lord commends.[b]

Paul and the False Apostles

11 1 I wish you would put up with a little
foolishness[c] from me. Yes, do put up
with me.[B] 2 For I am jealous[d] over you with a
godly jealousy,[e] because I have promised you
in marriage to one husband — to present a
pure[f] virgin to Christ. 3 But I fear that, as the
serpent[g] deceived[h] Eve[i] by his cunning, your
minds may be seduced from a complete and
pure[C] devotion to Christ.[j] 4 For if a person
comes and preaches another Jesus,[k] whom
we did not preach, or you receive a different
spirit,[l] which you had not received, or a different gospel,[m] which you had not accepted,
you put up with it splendidly!
5 Now I consider myself in no way inferior
to the "super-apostles."[n] 6 Though untrained
in public speaking,[o] I am certainly not untrained in knowledge.[p] Indeed, we have always made that clear to you in everything.
7 Or did I commit a sin by humbling[q] myself so that you might be exalted,[r] because
I preached the gospel of God to you free of
charge?[s] 8 I robbed other churches by taking
pay from them to minister to you. 9 When I
was present with you and in need, I did not
burden anyone, for the brothers who came
from Macedonia[t] supplied my needs.[u] I have
kept myself, and will keep myself, from burdening you in any way. 10 As the truth of Christ
is in me, this boasting of mine will not be
stopped[D] in the regions of Achaia.[v] 11 Why?
Because I don't love you? God knows I do!
12 But I will continue to do what I am doing,
in order to deny[E] the opportunity of those
who want an opportunity to be regarded
just as our equals in what they boast about.
13 For such people are false apostles,[w] deceitful
workers, disguising themselves as apostles of
Christ. 14 And no wonder! For Satan disguises
himself as an angel of light. 15 So it is no great
thing if his servants also disguise themselves
as servants of righteousness. Their destiny[F]
will be according to their works.[x]

Paul's Sufferings for Christ

16 I repeat: No one should consider me a
fool. But if you do, at least accept me as a fool,
so I too may boast a little. 17 What I say in this
matter[G] of boasting, I don't speak as the Lord
would, but foolishly. 18 Since many boast in an
unspiritual way,[H] I will also boast. 19 For you,
being so wise, gladly put up with fools![y] 20 In
fact, you put up with it if someone enslaves
you, if someone devours[z] you, if someone
captures you, if someone dominates you, or
if someone hits[aa] you in the face. 21 I say this
to our shame: We have been weak.
But in whatever anyone dares to boast — I
am talking foolishly — I also dare:

[a] **10:17** Jr 9:24
[b] **10:18** 1Th 2:4
[c] **11:1** Mk 7:22; 2Co 11:17,21
[d] **11:2** Jms 3:16
[e] Nm 25:13; Gl 4:17
[f] Php 4:8
[g] **11:3** Gn 3:1; Lk 10:19
[h] Rm 7:11; 16:18; 1Co 3:18; 2Th 2:3; 1Tm 2:14
[i] Gn 3:20
[j] 1Th 3:5
[k] **11:4** 1Co 3:11
[l] 1Jn 4:1
[m] Gl 1:6
[n] **11:5** Jd 17
[o] **11:6** 1Co 1:17
[p] Php 3:8; 1Jn 4:8
[q] **11:7** Lk 14:11
[r] Lk 1:52
[s] Ac 18:3
[t] **11:9** Ac 16:9
[u] Php 4:10
[v] **11:10** Ac 18:12
[w] **11:13** Rv 2:2
[x] **11:15** Gl 3:10
[y] **11:19** Pr 3:7
[z] **11:20** Gl 5:15
[aa] Mt 5:39

The Role of the Vocational Missionary

GOD WHO SENDS

Just as the vocational missionary has had a significant role in the past, so he and she will have a significant role in the future. Rightly directed, there is as significant a role for missionaries today as ever before. Vocational missionaries and those who send them must adopt the "fraternal" pattern rather than the "paternal." Today vocational missionaries serve more as consultants, enablers, and liaison persons than in the more dominant administrative role of the past. Whatever they do, they are fellow workers—common pilgrims with those in whose countries they are guests. The vocational missionary role has been and is changing, and it will continue to change. But it is not obsolete. In fact new and exciting prospects are before it as Christians the world over share in many ways.

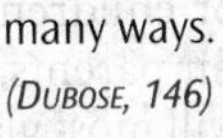

(DUBOSE, 146)

A **10:17** Jr 9:24 B **11:1** Or *Yes, you are putting up with me* C **11:3** Other mss omit *and pure* D **11:10** Or *silenced* E **11:12** Lit *cut off* F **11:15** Lit *end* G **11:17** Or *business,* or *confidence* H **11:18** Lit *boast according to the flesh*

22 Are they Hebrews?[a] So am I.
Are they Israelites? So am I.
Are they the ·seed of Abraham?[b]
So am I.
23 Are they servants of Christ?
I'm talking like a madman —
I'm a better one:
with far more labors,
many more imprisonments,
far worse beatings, near death[A]
many times.
24 Five times I received 39 lashes from Jews.[c]
25 Three times I was beaten with rods
by the Romans.[d]
Once I was stoned by my enemies.[B,e]
Three times I was shipwrecked.[f]
I have spent a night and a day
in the open sea.
26 On frequent journeys, I faced
dangers from rivers,
dangers from robbers,[g]
dangers from my own people,[h]
dangers from the Gentiles,
dangers in the city,
dangers in the open country,
dangers on the sea,
and dangers among false ·brothers;
27 labor and hardship,
many sleepless nights,
hunger and thirst,
often without food, cold,
and lacking clothing.[i]

28 Not to mention[C] other things, there is the
daily pressure on me: my care for all the
churches. 29 Who is weak, and am not weak?
Who is made to ·stumble,[j] and I do not burn
with indignation? 30 If boasting is necessary,
I will boast about my weaknesses. 31 The God
and Father[k] of the Lord Jesus, who is praised
forever, knows I am not lying. 32 In Damascus,[l]
the governor under King Aretas[D] guarded the
city of the Damascenes in order to arrest me,
33 so I was let down in a basket through a window in the wall and escaped his hands.[m]

Sufficient Grace

12 Boasting is necessary. It is not profitable, but I will move on to visions[n]
and revelations[o] of the Lord. 2 I know a man
in Christ who was caught up[p] into the third
heaven 14 years ago. Whether he was in the
body or out of the body, I don't know, God
knows. 3 I know that this man — whether in
the body or out of the body I don't know, God
knows — 4 was caught up into paradise.[q] He
heard inexpressible words, which a man is
not allowed to speak. 5 I will boast about this
person, but not about myself, except of my
weaknesses. 6 For if I want to boast, I will not
be a fool, because I will be telling the truth.[r]
But I will spare you, so that no one can credit
me with something beyond what he sees in
me or hears from me, 7 especially because
of the extraordinary revelations. Therefore,
so that I would not exalt myself, a thorn in
the flesh[s] was given to me, a messenger[E] of
Satan[t] to torment me so I would not exalt
myself. 8 Concerning this, I pleaded with the
Lord three times to take it away from me.
9 But He said to me, "My grace is sufficient for
you, for power[F,u] is perfected in weakness."[v]
Therefore, I will most gladly boast all the
more about my weaknesses, so that Christ's
power may reside in me. 10 So I take pleasure
in weaknesses, insults, catastrophes, persecutions, and in pressures, because of Christ.[w]
For when I am weak, then I am strong.[x]

Signs of an Apostle

11 I have become a fool; you forced it on me.
I should have been endorsed by you, since I
am not in any way inferior to the "super-apostles," even though I am nothing.[y] 12 The signs[z]
of an apostle[aa] were performed with great
endurance among you — not only signs but
also wonders[ab] and miracles.[ac] 13 So in what
way were you treated worse than the other
churches, except that I personally did not
burden you? Forgive me this wrong!

Paul's Concern for the Corinthians

14 Now I am ready to come to you this third
time.[ad] I will not burden you, for I am not seeking what is yours, but you. For children are
not obligated to save up for their parents, but
parents for their children. 15 I will most gladly
spend and be spent for you.[G,ae] If I love you
more, am I to be loved less? 16 Now granted, I

[a] **11:22** Php 3:5 [b] Gn 16:15; Gl 3:39 [c] **11:24** Dt 25:3 [d] **11:25** Ac 16:22 [e] Ac 14:19 [f] Ac 27:1-44; 1Tm 1:19 [g] **11:26** Mk 14:48 [h] Ac 9:23; 13:50; 14:5; 17:5; 18:12; 20:3,19; 21:27; 23:10-12; 25:3 [i] **11:27** Rm 8:35 [j] **11:29** Jn 16:1 [k] **11:31** Mt 5:16; 11:27; Lk 11:13; Jn 8:42; Eph 5:20 [l] **11:32** 2Sm 8:5 [m] **11:33** Ac 9:19-25 [n] **12:1** Lk 1:22 [o] 1Pt 4:13 [p] **12:2** 1Th 4:17 [q] **12:4** Lk 23:43 [r] **12:6** Ps 119:142; Jn 8:14; 14:6; 2Co 11:10; 1Jn 5:20; 3Jn 3 [s] **12:7** Nm 33:55; Ezk 28:24; Php 3:3 [t] Mt 4:1,10; Ac 13:10 [u] **12:9** Mk 5:30; Lk 1:35; 6:19; Ac 19:11; 2Co 13:4; Rv 11:17 [v] Is 40:29-31; 1Co 2:5; Php 4:13 [w] **12:10** Mt 5:11-12; Rm 5:3; 2Co 13:4 [x] Eph 6:10 [y] **12:11** Gl 6:3 [z] **12:12** Heb 2:4 [aa] Ac 1:2; Jd 17 [ab] Mk 13:22 [ac] Ac 19:11 [ad] **12:14** Ac 18; 2Co 2:1; 13:1 [ae] **12:15** 2Co 1:6; Php 2:17; Col 1:24; 1Th 2:8; 2Tm 2:10

[A] **11:23** Lit *and in deaths* [B] **11:25** A common Jewish method of capital punishment; Ac 14:5 [C] **11:28** Lit *Apart from* [D] **11:32** Aretus IV (9 B.C.–A.D. 40), a Nabatean Arab king [E] **12:7** Or *me, an angel* [F] **12:9** Other mss read *My power* [G] **12:15** Lit *for your souls*, or *for your lives*

have not burdened[a] you; yet sly as I am, I took
you in by deceit![b] 17 Did I take advantage of you
by anyone I sent you? 18 I urged Titus[c] to come,
and I sent the brother with him. Did Titus
take advantage of you? Didn't we ·walk in the
same spirit[d] and in the same footsteps?

19 You have thought all along that we were
defending ourselves to you.[A] No, in the sight
of God we are speaking in Christ, and everything, dear friends, is for building you up.[e]
20 For I fear that perhaps when I come I will
not find you to be what I want, and I may
not be found by you to be what you want;[B]
there may be quarreling,[f] jealousy,[g] outbursts
of anger, selfish ambitions,[h] slander,[i] gossip,
arrogance, and disorder.[j] 21 I fear that when
I come my God will again[C] humiliate me in
your presence, and I will grieve for many who
sinned before and have not repented[k] of the
moral impurity, sexual immorality,[l] and promiscuity[m] they practiced.

Final Warnings and Exhortations

13 This is the third time I am coming to
you.[n] **Every fact must be established by
the testimony[D] of two or three witnesses.**[E,o] 2 I
gave a warning when I was present the second
time, and now I give a warning[p] while I am
absent to those who sinned before and to all
the rest: If I come again, I will not be lenient,
3 since you seek proof of Christ speaking in
me.[q] He is not weak toward you, but powerful among you. 4 In fact, He was crucified[r] in
weakness, but He lives[s] by God's power. For
we also are weak in Him,[t] yet toward you we
will live[u] with Him by God's power.

5 Test[v] yourselves to see if you are in the
faith. Examine yourselves. Or do you yourselves not recognize that Jesus Christ is in
you? — unless you fail the test.[F] 6 And I hope
you will recognize that we do not fail the
test. 7 Now we pray to God that you do nothing wrong — not that we may appear to pass
the test, but that you may do what is right,[w]
even though we may appear to fail. 8 For
we are not able to do anything against the
truth,[x] but only for the truth. 9 In fact, we rejoice when we are weak and you are strong.[y]
We also pray that you become fully mature.[G]
10 This is why I am writing these things while
absent, that when I am there I will not use severity, in keeping with the authority the Lord
gave me for building up[z] and not for tearing
down.[aa]

11 Finally, ·brothers, rejoice. Become mature, be encouraged, be of the same mind,[ab]
be at peace,[ac] and the God of love[ad] and peace
will be with you. 12 Greet one another with a
holy kiss.[ae] All the ·saints greet you.

13 The grace of the Lord Jesus Christ, and the
love[af] of God, and the fellowship of the Holy
Spirit be with all of you.[H,ag]

[a] **12:16** 1Th 2:7
[b] Ps 10:7
[c] **12:18** Ti 1:4
[d] Ps 51:12
[e] **12:19** 1Co 14:3-4
[f] **12:20** Ti 3:9
[g] Jms 3:14
[h] Rm 2:8
[i] 1Pt 2:1
[j] 1Co 14:33,40
[k] **12:21** Ac 3:19
[l] 1Th 4:3
[m] Mk 7:21-22
[n] **13:1** 2Co 12:14
[o] Dt 17:6; 19:15
[p] **13:2** Gl 5:21; 1Th 3:4
[q] **13:3** Mt 10:20; 1Co 5:4
[r] **13:4** Mt 27:22; Php 2:7-8
[s] Rm 14:9; Php 1:21; 1Pt 3:18
[t] 2Co 12:10
[u] Rm 6:4,8
[v] **13:5** Jms 1:13
[w] **13:7** 1Pt 2:12
[x] **13:8** 2Th 2:10
[y] **13:9** Ac 25:5
[z] **13:10** 1Co 14:3
[aa] 2Co 10:4,8
[ab] **13:11** Rm 12:16; Php 1:7
[ac] Mk 9:50; Rm 16:20; 2Tm 1:2
[ad] 1Jn 4:16
[ae] **13:12** Rm 16:16; 1Co 16:20; 1Th 5:26; 1Pt 5:14
[af] **13:13** 1Co 13:1; 1Jn 4:16
[ag] 2Th 3:16

[A] **12:19** Or *Have you thought . . . to you?* [B] **12:20** Lit *be as you want* [C] **12:21** Or *come again my God will* [D] **13:1** Lit *mouth* [E] **13:1** Dt 17:6; 19:15 [F] **13:5** Or *you are disqualified*, or *you are counterfeit* [G] **13:9** Or *become complete*, or *be restored*

[H] **13:12-13** Some translations divide these 2 vv. into 3 vv. so that v. 13 begins with *All the saints . . .* and v. 14 begins with *The grace of . . .*

■ **AUTHOR:** Paul (Saul of Tarsus)

■■ **DATE:** Possibly written in A.D. 49 before the Jerusalem Council

This truth rings throughout the good news of Jesus Christ: no one works his or her way into God's favor. All the benefits of God are given, not earned. Forgiveness of sin and incorporation into the family of God is the work of Christ, done once for all. People everywhere are invited to turn from sin, receive Christ as Lord and Savior, and experience the transformation promised by Jesus by the power of the Holy Spirit. The mission of God is the clear communication of this core message, and its fulfillment in every life.

Paul gets vigorous about it in this letter to Christians in the Roman province of Galatia. (Some scholars believe the letter's destination was north-central Asia Minor.)

GALATIANS

So agitated is Paul that he calls for eternal condemnation on anyone who teaches a "different gospel" (1:6), including himself should he ever succumb to such error.

Paul insists the gospel is not fiction. He himself did not invent it. Jesus and the disciples did not set its outlines and adapt its contours. This gospel—God's good news of redemption by faith in Christ—was always God's mission. For anyone to tamper with it or redirect it, that person is anathema. Paul himself received the gospel directly from God.

His dramatic account of his new life in Christ (2:19-20) is as clear a transition from law to grace, old life to new, opposition to glad service, self to Christ, as any ever told. Martin Luther's effort to reform the church was based on the teachings in this letter. All reforms are started on the recognition that God is the source of life and healing. We don't earn it; ours is to live it. Social boundaries separating "good people" from pagans are gone. The gospel is for all. God's family is wide and deep.

All well and good, you say. But people left to their own devices—people without rules to follow—are a people risking moral collapse. Paul is much more optimistic. Don't give up your freedom for rules. To do so is to depend on your record of obedience and not on Christ. Don't depend on ancient traditions. Live by the Spirit. Here is radical trust in God's mission. Transformed by Christ, you will be fulfilled. The virtues of spiritual maturity will grow in you: love, joy, peace, and more (5:22-23).

For the defense of God's mission Paul lays it all on the line. Do not allow spiritual deception to start a cancer in your soul. Do not give up on the calling of God. God's intentions are directed toward the gift freely offered, paid in full by Jesus, and appropriated by faith. God's mission is peace and mercy to you—a sobering and deeply comforting revelation of the divine heart. God wants the wayward back, without delay. He sent His Son to find them.

Greeting

1 Paul,[a] an apostle—not from men or by
man, but by Jesus Christ and God the Father[b] who raised Him from the dead[c]— 2and
all the ·brothers who are with me:
To the churches of Galatia.[A,d]
3Grace to you and peace from God the Father and our Lord[B] Jesus Christ, 4who gave
Himself for our sins[e] to rescue us from this
present evil age,[f] according to the will of our
God and Father.[g] 5To whom be the glory forever and ever. ·Amen.

No Other Gospel

6I am amazed that you are so quickly turning away from Him who called[h] you by the
grace of Christ and are turning to a different
gospel— 7not that there is another gospel,[i]
but there are some[j] who are troubling you
and want to change the good news[C] about the
·Messiah. 8But even if we or an angel[k] from
heaven should preach to you a gospel other
than what we have preached to you,[l] a curse
be on him![D] 9As we have said before, I now
say again: If anyone preaches to you a gospel
contrary to what you received,[m] a curse be on
him!
10For am I now trying to win the favor of
people, or God?[n] Or am I striving to please
people? If I were still trying to please people,
I would not be a ·slave of Christ.

Paul Defends His Apostleship

11Now I want you to know, brothers, that
the gospel preached by me is not based on human thought.[E] 12For I did not receive it from
a human source and I was not taught it, but it
came by a revelation[o] from Jesus Christ.[p]
13For you have heard about my former
way of life[q] in Judaism:[r] I persecuted[s] God's
church to an extreme degree and tried to
destroy it. 14I advanced in Judaism beyond
many contemporaries among my people, because I was extremely zealous for the traditions of my ancestors.[t] 15But when God, who
from my birth set me apart and called[u] me by
His grace, was pleased 16to reveal His Son[v] in
me, so that I could preach Him among the
Gentiles, I did not immediately consult with
anyone.[F] 17I did not go up to Jerusalem[w] to
those who had become apostles[x] before me;
instead I went to Arabia[y] and came back to
Damascus.[z]
18Then after three years I did go up to Jerusalem[aa] to get to know ·Cephas,[G,ab] and
I stayed with him 15 days. 19But I didn't see
any of the other apostles except James,[ac] the
Lord's brother. 20Now I am not lying in what
I write to you. God is my witness.[H]
21Afterward, I went to the regions of Syria[ad]
and Cilicia.[ae] 22I remained personally unknown to the Judean churches in Christ;
23they simply kept hearing: "He who formerly
persecuted[af] us now preaches the faith[ag] he
once tried to destroy." 24And they glorified
God because of me.

Paul Defends His Gospel at Jerusalem

2 Then after 14 years I went up again[ah] to
Jerusalem with Barnabas,[ai] taking Titus[aj]
along also. 2I went up according to a revelation[ak] and presented to them the gospel I
preach among the Gentiles—but privately to
those recognized as leaders—so that I might
not be running, or have run the race, in vain.
3But not even Titus who was with me, though
he was a Greek, was compelled to be circumcised. 4This issue arose because of false brothers[al] smuggled in, who came in secretly to spy
on the freedom that we have in Christ Jesus,
in order to enslave us. 5But we did not give up
and submit to these people for even an hour,
so that the truth[am] of the gospel would be preserved for you.
6Now from those recognized as important
(what they really were makes no difference to
me; God does not show favoritism[I,an])—they
added nothing to me. 7On the contrary, they
saw that I had been entrusted with the gospel
for the uncircumcised,[ao] just as Peter[ap] was for
the circumcised, 8since the One at work in Peter
for an apostleship to the circumcised was also
at work in me for the Gentiles. 9When James,[aq]
·Cephas,[ar] and John,[as] recognized as pillars,[at]
acknowledged the grace that had been given
to me, they gave the right hand of fellowship

[a]**1:1** Ac 13:9 [b]Mt 5:16; 6:1; 11:27; Jn 8:42 [c]Ac 9:6; 20:24; 22:10-21; 26:16 [d]**1:2** Ac 16:6; 18:23; 1Co 16:1; 2Tm 4:10; 1Pt 1:1 [e]**1:4** Rm 6:23; Ti 2:14 [f]Mt 20:28; Rm 4:25; 1Co 15:3; Gl 2:20 [g]Php 4:20; 1Th 1:3; 3:11,13; Heb 10:7; 1Pt 3:17; Rv 10:7 [h]**1:6** Col 3:15; 1Pt 1:15 [i]**1:7** Ac 4:12; 1Co 3:11 [j]Jd 4 [k]**1:8** Gn 16:7; Mt 13:49; Lk 1:11; Ac 5:19; Rv 14:6 [l]Rm 15:20 [m]**1:9** Jd 3 [n]**1:10** 1Th 2:4 [o]**1:12** 1Pt 4:13 [p]1Co 11:23; 15:3 [q]**1:13** 2Pt 3:11 [r]Ac 8:1–9:2; 26:4; Php 3:5-6 [s]Php 3:6; 2Tm 3:12 [t]**1:14** Mk 7:3 [u]**1:15** Mt 24:22; Col 3:15 [v]**1:16** Jn 5:19; Heb 1:2 [w]**1:17** Mt 23:37; Ac 8:1 [x]Jd 17 [y]Is 21:13; Jr 25:24; Ezk 27:21; Gl 4:25 [z]2Sm 8:5 [aa]**1:18** Ac 9:26 [ab]Jn 1:42 [ac]**1:19** Jd 1 [ad]**1:21** Nm 23:7; Lk 2:2 [ae]Ac 9:30; 11:25-26 [af]**1:23** Ac 8:1-3 [ag]Jd 3 [ah]**2:1** Ac 15:2-30 [ai]Ac 4:36 [aj]Ti 1:4 [ak]**2:2** 1Pt 4:13 [al]**2:4** 2Pt 2:1 [am]**2:5** 2Th 2:10 [an]**2:6** Dt 16:19 [ao]**2:7** Col 3:11 [ap]Lk 6:14; Ac 10:32 [aq]**2:9** Jd 1 [ar]Jn 1:42 [as]Jn 21:7 [at]1Tm 3:15; Rv 3:12; 10:1

[A]**1:2** A Roman province in what is now Turkey [B]**1:3** Other mss read *God our Father and the Lord* [C]**1:7** Or *gospel* [D]**1:8** Or *you, let him be condemned*, or *you, let him be condemned to hell*; Gk *anathema* [E]**1:11** Lit *not according to man* [F]**1:16** Lit *flesh and blood* [G]**1:18** Other mss read *Peter* [H]**1:20** Lit *Behold, before God* [I]**2:6** Or *God is not a respecter of persons*; lit *God does not receive the face of man*

David Brainerd (1718—1747)

David Brainerd's short life has been an inspiration to many. Once he came to know what God wanted, he did it—despite tuberculosis, depression, loneliness, and hunger. Brainerd's mission was to take the gospel to Native Americans, people who knew of God's power but not His love that was demonstrated in the suffering of His Son.

Brainerd was orphaned as a teenager. Inherited farmland was his means of making a living. But living, for Brainerd, was not baling hay. It was preaching and evangelizing. At age twenty-one, he was converted. He enrolled at Yale College to study theology but became critical of his instructors and was expelled for rudeness, an act he later regretted. His sense of mission survived this setback, however, and he was given an opportunity to do missionary work among New England Indian tribes by the Society in Scotland for Propagating Christian Knowledge. First near Nassau, New York, and then among the Delaware Indians in Pennsylvania, Brainerd lived and taught, partially translating the Psalms, but with a worsening cough and weakened stamina.

Come back to a church and relieve these symptoms, he was told. But no, Brainerd knew where he belonged despite chronic coughing. For three and a half years he lived among Native Americans, learning their language, founding schools, and establishing churches. In 1746, he could go on no longer. Brainerd eventually resided with the family of Jonathan Edwards in Northhampton, Massachusetts. There he was nursed by Edwards' young daughter Jerusha, who contracted tuberculosis herself and died soon after Brainerd.

At the age of 29, Brainerd died. He was not a theologian, and his mission among Native Americans was only a little longer than short term in today's missionary movement. But he left a journal—a record of his prayers and his battles with sickness.

Two years later, in 1749, Edwards used Brainerd's journal to publish *An Account of the Life of the Late Reverend Mr. David Brainerd*. The book has become a legacy in itself, profoundly influential in the spiritual growth of many Christians. After several editions, it has never been out of print. Many have said that Brainerd's *Life* and the *Bible* are the two books that gave them strength during trials and the courage to keep the mission when circumstances would have sent their lives into detour.

Today Brainerd Hall at Yale is the only building there named after a student who has been expelled. From God's mission, only deteriorating health and eventually death could expel Brainerd. Yet nothing could expel Brainerd from his walk with God.

to me and Barnabas, agreeing that we should
go to the Gentiles and they to the circumcised.
10 They asked only that we would remember the
poor,[a] which I made every effort to do.

Freedom from the Law

11 But when Cephas[A] came to Antioch, I
opposed him to his face because he stood
condemned.[B] 12 For he regularly ate with
the Gentiles before certain men came from
James. However, when they came, he withdrew and separated himself, because he
feared those from the circumcision party.
13 Then the rest of the Jews[b] joined his hypocrisy,[c] so that even Barnabas was carried away
by their hypocrisy. 14 But when I saw that they
were deviating from the truth of the gospel,
I told Cephas[A] in front of everyone, "If you,
who are a Jew, live like a Gentile[d] and not like
a Jew,[e] how can you compel Gentiles to live[f]
like Jews?"[C]
15 We who are Jews by birth and not "Gentile sinners" 16 know that no one is •justi-
fied by the works of the law[g] but by faith in
Jesus Christ.[D] And we have believed in Christ
Jesus so that we might be justified by faith in
Christ[E] and not by the works of the law, because by the works of the law no human being will[F] be justified. 17 But if we ourselves are
also found to be "sinners" while seeking to
be justified by Christ,[h] is Christ then a pro-
moter[G,i] of sin? Absolutely not![j] 18 If I rebuild[k]
the system[H] I tore down, I show myself to be
a lawbreaker.[l] 19 For through the law I have
died to the law,[m] so that I might live for God.[n]
I have been crucified with Christ[I] 20 and I no
longer live, but Christ lives in me.[o] The life I
now live in the body,[J] I live by faith in the Son
of God,[p] who loved[q] me[r] and gave Himself[s] for
me.[t] 21 I do not set aside the grace of God, for if
righteousness comes through the law,[u] then
Christ died[v] for nothing.

Justification through Faith

3 You foolish[w] Galatians! Who has hypno-
tized you,[K] before whose eyes Jesus Christ
was vividly portrayed[L] as crucified?[x] 2 I only
want to learn this from you: Did you receive
the Spirit by the works of the law or by hearing with faith?[M] 3 Are you so foolish? After
beginning with the Spirit, are you now going
to be made complete by the flesh?[N] 4 Did you
suffer[y] so much for nothing—if in fact it was
for nothing? 5 So then, does God supply you
with the Spirit and work miracles[z] among
you by the works of the law or by hearing
with faith?[M]
6 Just as Abraham **believed God,**[aa] **and it was
credited to him for righteousness,**[O,ab] 7 then
understand that those who have faith are
Abraham's sons.[ac] 8 Now the Scripture saw in
advance that God would •justify the Gentiles
by faith and told the good news ahead of time
to Abraham,[ad] saying, **All the nations will be
blessed through you.**[P,ae] 9 So those who have
faith are blessed with Abraham,[af] who had
faith.[Q]

Law and Promise

10 For all who rely on the works of the law
are under a curse,[ag] because it is written:[ah]
**Everyone who does not continue doing ev-
erything written in the book of the law is
cursed.**[R,ai] 11 Now it is clear that no one is justified before God by the law, because **the righteous will live**[aj] **by faith.**[S,ak] 12 But the law is
not based on faith; instead, **the one who does
these things will live by them.**[T,al] 13 Christ has
•redeemed us from the curse of the law by becoming a curse for us,[am] because it is written:
Everyone who is hung on a tree is cursed.[U,an]
14 The purpose was that the blessing of Abraham would come to the Gentiles by Christ
Jesus, so that we could receive the promised
Spirit through faith.[ao]
15 •Brothers, I'm using a human illustration.[V] No one sets aside or makes additions
to even a human covenant[W] that has been
ratified. 16 Now the promises were spoken to
Abraham and to his •seed. He does not say
"and to seeds," as though referring to many,
but referring to one, **and to your seed,**[X,ap] who
is Christ. 17 And I say this: The law, which came

[a] **2:10** Mk 14:7; Rm 15:26
[b] **2:13** Rm 2:28-29
[c] Mk 12:15
[d] **2:14** Rm 1:13
[e] Rm 14:2
[f] Rm 6:2
[g] **2:16** Rm 3:20; Gl 3:2,5,10
[h] **2:17** Rm 6:23; 1Tm 1:15
[i] 1Co 3:5
[j] Lk 20:16
[k] **2:18** Ac 20:32
[l] Rm 2:25,27; Jms 2:9,11
[m] **2:19** Rm 7:4; 1Pt 2:24
[n] Php 1:21
[o] **2:20** Mk 10:38; 2Co 13:5
[p] Jn 5:19; Heb 1:2
[q] Jn 3:16
[r] 2Th 2:13
[s] Ti 2:14
[t] Lk 20:38; Rm 14:8
[u] **2:21** Rm 7:5; 9:31; Gl 5:4; Php 3:6
[v] 1Co 8:11; Php 3:10
[w] **3:1** Rm 1:14
[x] Mt 27:22
[y] **3:4** Php 1:29
[z] **3:5** Mk 13:22
[aa] **3:6** Jn 14:1
[ab] Gn 15:6
[ac] **3:7** Jn 8:37,39
[ad] **3:8** Gn 16:15; Jn 8:37; Heb 2:16
[ae] Gn 12:3; 18:18
[af] **3:9** Jn 8:39
[ag] **3:10** Jms 3:10
[ah] Ac 15:15
[ai] Dt 27:26; Rm 4:15
[aj] **3:11** Php 1:21
[ak] Hab 2:4
[al] **3:12** Lv 18:5
[am] **3:13** 1Pt 2:24
[an] Dt 21:23; Ac 5:30
[ao] **3:14** Rm 4:16
[ap] **3:16** Gn 12:7; 13:15; 17:8; 24:7

[A] **2:11,14** Other mss read *Peter* [B] **2:11** Or *he was in the wrong* [C] **2:14** Some translations continue the quotation through v. 16 or v. 21. [D] **2:16** Or *by the faithfulness of Jesus Christ* [E] **2:16** Or *by the faithfulness of Christ* [F] **2:16** Lit *law all flesh will not* [G] **2:17** Or *servant* [H] **2:18** Lit *rebuild those things that* [I] **2:19** Other textual traditions place *I have been crucified with Christ* in v. 20. [J] **2:20** Or *flesh* [K] **3:1** Other mss add *not to obey the truth* [L] **3:1** Other mss add *among you* [M] **3:2,5** Lit *by law works or faith hearing* or *hearing the message* [N] **3:3** By human effort [O] **3:6** Gn 15:6 [P] **3:8** Gn 12:3; 18:18 [Q] **3:9** Or *with believing Abraham* [R] **3:10** Dt 27:26 [S] **3:11** Hab 2:4 [T] **3:12** Lv 18:5 [U] **3:13** Dt 21:23 [V] **3:15** Lit *I speak according to man* [W] **3:15** Or *will, or testament* [X] **3:16** Gn 12:7; 13:15; 17:8; 24:7

430 years later,[a] does not revoke a covenant
that was previously ratified by God[A] and cancel the promise. 18For if the inheritance is
from the law, it is no longer from the promise; but God granted it to Abraham through
the promise.

The Purpose of the Law

19Why then was the law given?[b] It was
added because of transgressions until the
Seed to whom the promise was made would
come. The law was put into effect through
angels[c] by means of a mediator.[d] 20Now a mediator is not for just one person, but God is
one.[e] 21Is the law therefore contrary to God's
promises? Absolutely not! For if a law had
been given that was able to give life, then
righteousness would certainly be by the law.
22But the Scripture has imprisoned everything under sin's power,[B,f] so that the promise by faith in Jesus Christ[g] might be given to
those who believe.[h] 23Before this faith[i] came,
we were confined under the law, imprisoned
until the coming faith was revealed.[j] 24The
law, then, was our guardian[C] until Christ,[k] so
that we could be justified by faith. 25But since
that faith[l] has come, we are no longer under a guardian, 26for you are all sons of God
through faith in Christ Jesus.

Sons and Heirs

27For as many of you as have been baptized
into Christ have put on Christ like a garment.[m] 28There is no Jew or Greek, •slave or
free,[n] male or female;[o] for you are all one[p] in
Christ Jesus. 29And if you belong to Christ,
then you are Abraham's seed, heirs[q] according
4 to the promise.[r] 1Now I say that as long
as the heir[s] is a child, he differs in no way
from a •slave, though he is the owner[t] of everything. 2Instead, he is under guardians and
stewards until the time set by his father. 3In
the same way we also, when we were children,
were in slavery under the elemental forces[D] of
the world.[u] 4When the time came to completion, God sent His Son,[v] born of a woman,[w]
born under the law, 5to •redeem those under
the law, so that we might receive adoption
as sons.[x] 6And because you are sons, God has
sent the Spirit of His Son[y] into our[E] hearts,
crying, "•*Abba*,[z] Father!"[aa] 7So you are no longer a slave[ab] but a son,[ac] and if a son, then an
heir[ad] through God.

Paul's Concern for the Galatians

8But in the past, when you didn't know
God,[ae] you were enslaved to things[F] that by
nature are not gods. 9But now, since you know
God,[af] or rather have become known by God,
how can you turn back again to the weak and
bankrupt[ag] elemental forces?[ah] Do you want
to be enslaved to them all over again? 10You
observe special days, months, seasons, and
years.[ai] 11I am fearful for you, that perhaps my
labor for you has been wasted.

12I beg you, •brothers: Become like me, for
I also became like you. You have not wronged
me; 13you know that previously I preached
the gospel to you because of a physical illness.
14You did not despise or reject me though my
physical condition was a trial for you.[G] On the
contrary, you received me as an angel of God,
as Christ Jesus Himself.

15What happened to this sense of being
blessed you had? For I testify to you that,
if possible, you would have torn out your
eyes and given them to me. 16Have I now become your enemy by telling you the truth?[aj]
17They[H] are enthusiastic about you, but not
for any good. Instead, they want to isolate
you so you will be enthusiastic about them.
18Now it is always good to be enthusiastic
about good—and not just when I am with
you. 19My children,[ak] I am again suffering labor pains[al] for you until Christ is formed in
you. 20I would like to be with you right now
and change my tone of voice, because I don't
know what to do about you.

Sarah and Hagar: Two Covenants

21Tell me, those of you who want to be under the law, don't you hear the law? 22For it
is written that Abraham[am] had two sons, one
by a slave[an] and the other by a free woman.
23But the one by the slave was born according to the impulse of the flesh, while the one

[a] **3:17** Gn 15:13; Ex 12:40; Ac 7:6
[b] **3:19** Rm 4:15; 5:20
[c] Gn 16:7; Mt 13:49; Lk 1:11; Ac 5:19; Rv 14:6
[d] Heb 8:6
[e] **3:20** Dt 6:4
[f] **3:22** Rm 6:23
[g] Rm 3:22
[h] Mk 11:24; Jn 3:16; Ac 10:43; Rm 10:9; 1Pt 1:8-10
[i] **3:23** Jd 3
[j] Lk 10:21
[k] **3:24** Mt 5:17; Col 2:17; Heb 9:10
[l] **3:25** Jd 3
[m] **3:27** Pr 31:25
[n] **3:28** Jn 8:33
[o] Rm 10:12; 1Co 12:13; Gl 5:6
[p] Jn 17:11
[q] **3:29** Rm 4:14; 8:17
[r] Rm 4:13
[s] **4:1** Nm 26:52-62
[t] Col 3:22
[u] **4:3** Rm 7:6; 2Pt 2:20
[v] **4:4** Jn 5:19; Heb 1:2
[w] Gn 3:15; Lk 2:7; Php 2:7
[x] **4:5** Dt 14:1; Mt 5:9
[y] **4:6** Ac 16:7; Rm 5:5,20; 8:9,16; 2Co 3:17
[z] Mk 14:36; Rm 8:15
[aa] Mt 5:16; 6:1; 11:27; Jn 8:42
[ab] **4:7** Mt 10:24; Rv 1:1
[ac] Dt 14:1; Mt 5:9
[ad] Nm 26:52-62; Rm 4:14; 8:17
[ae] **4:8** Jn 7:28; Php 3:8
[af] **4:9** Pr 2:6; Php 3:8
[ag] Mk 14:17; Rm 15:26
[ah] Col 2:8
[ai] **4:10** Rm 14:5; Col 2:16
[aj] **4:16** Eph 4:15
[ak] **4:19** 1Th 2:11
[al] 1Co 4:15; Jms 1:18
[am] **4:22** Gn 16:15; Jn 8:37; Heb 2:16
[an] Rm 8:15,21; Heb 2:15

[A] **3:17** Other mss add *in Christ* [B] **3:22** Lit *under sin* [C] **3:24** The word translated *guardian* in vv. 24-25 is different from the word in Gl 4:2. In our culture, we do not have a slave who takes a child to and from school, protecting the child from harm or corruption. In Gk the word *paidogogos* described such a slave. This slave was not a teacher. [D] **4:3** Or *spirits*, or *principles* [E] **4:6** Other mss read *your* [F] **4:8** Or *beings* [G] **4:14** Other mss read *me* [H] **4:17** The false teachers

by the free woman was born as the result of a promise. 24 These things are illustrations,[A] for the women represent the two covenants. One is from Mount Sinai[a] and bears children into slavery — this is Hagar.[b] 25 Now Hagar is Mount Sinai in Arabia[c] and corresponds to the present Jerusalem,[d] for she is in slavery with her children. 26 But the Jerusalem above[e] is free, and she is our mother. 27 For it is written:[f]

> **Rejoice, childless woman,**[g]
> **who does not give birth.**
> **Burst into song and shout,**
> **you who are not in labor,**
> **for the children of the desolate**
> **are many,**
> **more numerous than those**
> **of the woman who has**
> **a husband.**[B,h]

28 Now you, brothers, like Isaac,[i] are children of promise.[j] 29 But just as then the child born according to the flesh persecuted the one born according to the Spirit,[k] so also now.[l] 30 But what does the Scripture say?

> **Drive out the slave and her son, for the son of the slave will never be a coheir with the son of the free woman.**[C,m]

31 Therefore, brothers, we are not children of the slave but of the free woman.[n]

Freedom of the Christian

5 Christ has liberated us to be free. Stand firm[o] then and don't submit again to a yoke of slavery.[p] 2 Take note! I, Paul, tell you that if you get yourselves circumcised, Christ will not benefit you at all. 3 Again I testify to every man who gets himself circumcised that he is obligated to keep the entire law. 4 You who are trying to be ˙justified by the law are alienated from Christ; you have fallen from grace.[q] 5 For through the Spirit, by faith, we eagerly wait[r] for the hope[s] of righteousness. 6 For in Christ Jesus neither circumcision nor uncircumcision accomplishes anything; what matters is faith[t] working through love.[u]

7 You were running well. Who prevented you from obeying the truth?[v] 8 This persuasion did not come from the One who called you.[w] 9 A little yeast leavens the whole lump of dough. 10 I have confidence in the Lord you will not accept any other view. But whoever it is that is confusing you will pay the penalty.[x] 11 Now ˙brothers, if I still preach circumcision, why am I still persecuted? In that case the offense of the cross[y] has been abolished. 12 I wish those who are disturbing you might also get themselves castrated!

13 For you were called[z] to be free, brothers; only don't use this freedom as an opportunity for the flesh, but serve one another through love. 14 For the entire law is fulfilled[aa] in one statement: **Love your neighbor as yourself.**[D,ab] 15 But if you bite and devour[ac] one another, watch out, or you will be consumed by one another.

The Spirit versus the Flesh

16 I say then, ˙walk by the Spirit[ad] and you will not carry out the desire of the flesh. 17 For the flesh desires[ae] what is against the Spirit, and the Spirit desires what is against the flesh; these are opposed to each other, so that you don't do what you want.[af] 18 But if you are led by the Spirit, you are not under the law.

19 Now the works of the flesh are obvious:[E,F] sexual immorality,[ag] moral impurity,[ah] promiscuity,[ai] 20 idolatry,[aj] sorcery,[ak] hatreds,[al] strife,[am] jealousy,[an] outbursts of anger,[ao] selfish ambitions,[ap] dissensions,[aq] factions,[ar] 21 envy,[G,as] drunkenness, carousing,[at] and anything similar. I tell you about these things in advance — as I told you before — that those who practice such things will not inherit the kingdom of God.[au]

22 But the fruit of the Spirit[av] is love,[aw] joy,[ax] peace, patience,[ay] kindness,[az] goodness, faith,[H] 23 gentleness,[ba] self-control.[bb] Against such things there is no law. 24 Now those who belong to Christ Jesus[bc] have crucified the flesh[bd] with its passions and desires.[be] 25 Since we live[bf] by the Spirit, we must also follow the Spirit. 26 We must not become conceited, provoking one another, envying one another.[bg]

[a] 4:24 Ex 16:1 [b] Gn 16:1 [c] 4:25 Is 21:13; Jr 25:24; Ezk 27:21; Gl 1:17 [d] Mt 23:37; Ac 8:1 [e] 4:26 Heb 12:22; Rv 3:12; 21:2,10 [f] 4:27 Ac 15:15 [g] Gn 11:30; Lk 1:7 [h] Is 54:1 [i] 4:28 Ps 105:9; Jms 2:21 [j] Gn 12:7; Rm 9:8; Gl 3:29 [k] 4:29 Ps 51:11; Jn 1:33; Ac 2:4; Rm 8:9; Gl 5:25; Ti 3:5; Rv 3:22 [l] Gn 21:9 [m] 4:30 Gn 21:10 [n] 4:31 1Pt 3:6 [o] 5:1 Rm 14:4; Php 1:27 [p] 4:21–5:1 Gl 4:22 [q] 5:4 2Pt 3:18 [r] 5:5 Jd 21 [s] Rm 8:23-25; 1Th 1:3 [t] 5:6 1Th 1:3 [u] 1Co 13:1; Jms 2:18-22 [v] 5:7 Jn 8:14; 1Jn 5:20 [w] 5:8 Col 3:15; 1Pt 1:15 [x] 5:10 Mk 12:40 [y] 5:11 Lk 9:23 [z] 5:13 Col 3:15 [aa] 5:14 Mt 1:22 [ab] Lv 19:18; Mt 7:12; 19:19; 22:37-40; Jn 13:34 [ac] 5:15 Gl 5:20; Php 3:2,20 [ad] 5:16 Rm 8:4; 1Tm 3:16; 2Pt 1:4; 2:10 [ae] 5:17 1Pt 2:11 [af] Rm 7:15,23; Php 2:13 [ag] 5:19 Mk 7:21; 1Th 4:3 [ah] 1Th 4:7 [ai] Mk 7:22 [aj] 5:20 Col 3:5; 1Pt 4:3 [ak] Rv 18:23 [al] Rm 8:7 [am] Ti 3:9 [an] Jms 3:4 [ao] Rv 14:19 [ap] Rm 2:8 [aq] Rm 16:17 [ar] 2Pt 2:1 [as] 5:21 Rm 1:29 [at] Rm 13:13; 1Pt 4:3 [au] 1Co 6:10; 15:50 [av] 5:22 Mt 7:16-20; Rm 6:21; 7:4; 8:5; Eph 5:9 [aw] 1Co 13:1; Phm 5 [ax] Jn 15:11; 2Co 6:10 [ay] Ex 34:6; 2Tm 3:10 [az] Ps 25:6; 2Co 6:6 [ba] 5:23 Jms 3:13 [bb] 2Pt 1:6 [bc] 5:24 Nm 3:12 [bd] Rm 8:12 [be] 2Pt 1:4; 2:10 [bf] 5:25 Php 1:21; 3:16 [bg] 5:26 Php 2:3

A 4:24 Typology or allegory B 4:27 Is 54:1 C 4:30 Gn 21:10 D 5:14 Lv 19:18 E 5:19 Other mss add *adultery* F 5:19 Lit *obvious, which are:* G 5:21 Other mss add *murders* H 5:22 Or *faithfulness*

Carry One Another's Burdens

6 1Brothers, if someone is caught in any
wrongdoing, you who are spiritual
should restore such a person with a gentle[a]
spirit,[b] watching out for yourselves so you
also won't be tempted.[c] 2Carry one another's
burdens; in this way you will fulfill the law
of Christ.[d] 3For if anyone considers himself
to be something when he is nothing,[e] he deceives himself.
4But each person should examine his own work,[f] and then he will have a
reason for boasting in himself alone, and not
in respect to someone else. 5For each person
will have to carry his own load.

[a]6:1 Jms 3:13 [b]Ps 51:12 [c]Jms 1:13 [d]6:2 1Co 9:21 [e]6:3 1Co 3:18; 2Co 12:11; Gl 2:6 [f]6:4 Mk 14:6; Gl 3:10; Jms 2:14-26

WORLDVIEW

The Mission of God in Latin America

Contemporary Latin America projects a paradox of cultural energies. Considering the history of the region, it is no surprise that festive joy and bitter violence, distinctive music and hard-scrabble economies, all live side by side.

Religiously, Latin America is Catholic and Pentecostal, with many smaller pockets of believers of all types. Catholic leaders are known for their courageous stands on matters of land reform and justice to peasants. Pentecostal churches have flourished as people seek the help of an active God, alive and alert, ready to save.

The gospel is widely known and loudly celebrated. Latin America's celebrity drug lords contradict its teaching, yet claim their own version of allegiance, in similar manner to Sicily's famed mob dons. Parts of the continent are dangerous to Christian believers who must resist the cycle of violence associated with Latin America's most successful exports. The Christ statue overlooking Brazil's Rio speaks to the public presence of the church, but does the Spirit of Christ find welcoming hearts and willing hands there?

The gospel is the Word spoken and gladly received, the Good News of Christ crucified and risen, now alive in the church through the Holy Spirit. Latin Americans love to celebrate the joy of life, and among world citizens they seem the most buoyant and hopeful. No doubt this "open door" to the heart explains the surge of church growth among Christians emphasizing the power and presence of God. A faith with daily access to the God who made us, cares for us, and satisfies the soul's needs for comfort in sorrow and sustenance in joy—this is a faith that speaks the heart-language of Latin America. At the same time, exuberant faith must face squarely the inequities of centuries of land mismanagement, imperialism, radical political movements, and the ever-present interests of Latin America's powerful northern neighbor. The Monroe Doctrine, articulated by America's fifth president, warns any nation away from alliances which subvert or challenge the interests of the United States in this hemisphere. Latin America has long lived in the shadow of the world's greatest super-power. Yet her faith reflects a robust regional flavor, one that northern churches may profit from imbibing. And indeed they have. Mission excursions by the thousands have developed bonds of brotherhood between local congregations, and many of Latin America's outstanding pastor-theologians have helped world churches understand the mission of God with greater clarity.

The Christian call to social justice has had no greater champions than those leaders who have fought to end slavery, to establish literacy, and to campaign for uniform enforcement of justice in a region rife with corruption and political oppression. While the gospel reshapes the heart of Jesus' followers, it also calls for mercy and equity in the administration of God's world. These struggles have tested the resolve of Latin American leaders and given the world many models for the cost of doing the work of God.

6 The one who is taught the message must
share[a] all his good things with the teacher.
7 Don't be deceived: God is not mocked. For
whatever a man sows he will also reap, 8 because the one who sows to his flesh will reap
corruption from the flesh, but the one who
sows to the Spirit[b] will reap eternal life[c] from
the Spirit. 9 So we must not get tired[d] of doing
good,[e] for we will reap at the proper time if
we don't give up. 10 Therefore, as we have opportunity, we must work[f] for the good[g] of all,
especially for those who belong to the household[h] of faith.[i]

Concluding Exhortation

11 Look at what large letters I use as I write
to you in my own handwriting. 12 Those who
want to make a good impression in the flesh[j]
are the ones who would compel you to be circumcised[k]—but only to avoid being persecuted[l] for the cross[m] of Christ. 13 For even the
circumcised don't keep[n] the law themselves;
however, they want you to be circumcised in
order to boast about your flesh. 14 But as for
me, I will never boast about anything except
the cross of our Lord Jesus Christ. The •world
has been crucified to me through the cross,
and I to the world. 15 For[A] both circumcision
and uncircumcision[o] mean nothing; what
matters instead is a new creation.[p] 16 May
peace come to all those who follow this standard, and mercy to the Israel[q] of God!

17 From now on, let no one cause me trouble, because I bear on my body scars for the
cause of Jesus.[r] 18 Brothers, the grace of our
Lord Jesus Christ be with your spirit.[s] •Amen.

[a] **6:6** Rm 15:27; 1Pt 5:2
[b] **6:8** Ps 51:11; Jn 1:33; Ac 2:4; Rm 8:9; Gl 5:25; Ti 3:5; Rv 3:22
[c] Jn 12:25; Ac 13:48
[d] **6:9** 2Th 3:13
[e] Lk 18:18; Jms 4:17
[f] **6:10** 2Jn 8
[g] Gn 1:31; 3Jn 11
[h] 1Tm 5:8
[i] Jd 3
[j] **6:12** Php 3:3
[k] Ac 15:1
[l] 2Tm 3:12
[m] Php 3:18
[n] **6:13** Lk 11:28
[o] **6:15** Col 3:11
[p] Jn 1:3; Rv 3:14
[q] **6:16** Lk 3:8
[r] **6:17** Php 3:10
[s] **6:18** Ps 51:12

A **6:15** Other mss add *in Christ Jesus*

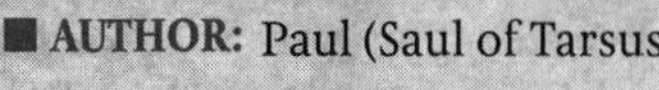

EPHESIANS

■ **AUTHOR:** Paul (Saul of Tarsus)

■■ **DATE:** Written around A.D. 60 in Rome while imprisoned

The mission of God to the world, Paul writes, is a mystery which God has shown Paul and which he passes along in this letter meant for the church in Ephesus and the surrounding region. Not a "mystery" as in a tangle of clues finally solved but a mystery in that its plan and purpose, hidden in the heart of God, is now revealed. People who know the Scriptures will see hints pointing toward it, even prototypes illustrating it.

The mystery is this: Jesus Christ explains the character of God and fulfills the plan of God as no one before or after can. The world was created because God loved the Son. The world was saved because God the Father and God the Son love the world. The triune God will bring everything in history and creation to a climax centered on Christ. In the time remaining, a body of believers will be formed and developed which reflects the unity and love of the three-in-one God. It is a dazzling scenario.

Paul answers the big question in Ephesians. Why did God make all this? "He made known to us the mystery of His will, according to His good pleasure that He planned in Him" (1:9). Why did God forgive the sins of all who trust Christ? It was "according to His favor and will" (1:5). Why did the Christian movement begin in Jerusalem and from there spread around the world? It was to bring "praise to His glory" (1:12). And why did this all happen when it did? Because the times had reached their fulfillment (1:10). God did it all, in His time and way, because the triune God wanted to build a "beloved" community (1:6) to enjoy His eternal Kingdom of joy and peace. Paul is trying to fashion in language what will only come together when it is experienced. The picture is overwhelming.

Many other questions find resolution here. Could God be frustrated or His plans sidetracked? Many times, the Bible records, God's good plans were hijacked by petulant people who lost sight of the truth. Always, however, God's sovereign oversight would bring recovery to the train wreck, and the mission would be reenergized. God's mission was "predestined according to the purpose of the One who works out everything in agreement with the decision of His will, so that we who had already put our hope in the Messiah might bring praise to His glory" (1:11-12). Temporary setbacks could never become permanent stalls.

Another big question: How is conversion managed, as so many people appear quite resistant, indifferent, or ignorant of God's plan? It is managed by a transition from death to life, Paul teaches, brought about by God's own will and grace (2:8). Are people not free to believe or walk away? Many do walk away, but those who believe are "sealed" by the Holy Spirit (1:13) who protects God's people from the Evil One. The result is safe access to God (2:18). God's people pray assured that their prayers are heard.

The mission of God is Christ magnified. It is God's pleasure done God's way in good time. Paul himself seems overwhelmed as he tells this mystery to the church and points to the object of His great love, Jesus the Son. That same love is never remote from you, never hidden, never beyond access. God can change your life—His mission all along.

Greeting

1 Paul,[a] an apostle of Christ Jesus by God's will:[b]

To the faithful ·saints[c] in Christ Jesus at Ephesus.[A,d]

2 Grace to you and peace from God our Father and the Lord Jesus Christ.

God's Rich Blessings

3 Praise the God and Father of our Lord Jesus Christ, who has blessed us in Christ with every spiritual blessing in the heavens.[e] 4 For He chose us in Him, before the foundation of the world, to be holy and blameless in His sight.[B,f] In love[C] 5 He predestined us to be adopted through Jesus Christ for Himself, according to His favor and will, 6 to the praise of His glorious grace[g] that He favored us with in the Beloved.[h]

7 We have ·redemption in Him[i] through His blood, the forgiveness[j] of our trespasses, according to the riches of His grace 8 that He lavished on us with all wisdom and understanding. 9 He made known to us the ·mystery of His will,[k] according to His good pleasure that He planned in Him[l] 10 for the administration[D] of the days of fulfillment[E]—to bring everything together in the ·Messiah,[m] both things in heaven and things on earth[n] in Him.[o]

11 We have also received an inheritance[F] in Him, predestined[p] according to the purpose of the One who works out everything in agreement with the decision of His will, 12 so that we who had already put our hope[q] in the Messiah might bring praise to His glory.[r]

13 When you heard the message of truth,[s] the gospel of your salvation, and when you believed in Him, you were also sealed with the promised Holy Spirit.[t] 14 He is the down payment[u] of our inheritance, for the redemption of the possession,[G] to the praise of His glory.

Prayer for Spiritual Insight

15 This is why, since I heard about your faith in the Lord Jesus and your love for all the saints, 16 I never stop giving thanks for you as I remember you in my prayers. 17 I pray that the God of our Lord Jesus Christ, the glorious Father,[H] would give you a spirit[I,v] of wisdom and revelation[w] in the knowledge of Him. 18 I pray that the perception of your mind[J] may be enlightened so you may know what is the hope[x] of His calling,[y] what are the glorious riches of His inheritance among the saints, 19 and what is the immeasurable greatness of His power[z] to us who believe, according to the working of His vast strength.

God's Power in Christ

20 He demonstrated this power in the Messiah by raising Him from the dead and seating Him at His right hand[aa] in the heavens[ab]—21 far above every ruler and authority, power and dominion, and every title given,[K,ac] not only in this age but also in the one to come.[ad] 22 And **He put everything under His feet**[L,ae] and appointed Him as head[af] over everything for the church, 23 which is His body,[ag] the fullness[ah] of the One who fills all things[ai] in every way.

From Death to Life

2 And you were dead[aj] in your trespasses and sins 2 in which you previously ·walked according to the ways of this world,[ak] according to the ruler who exercises authority over the lower heavens,[M,al] the spirit[am] now working in the disobedient.[N] 3 We too all previously lived among them in our fleshly[an] desires, carrying out the inclinations[ao] of our flesh and thoughts, and we were by nature children under wrath[ap] as the others were also. 4 But God, who is rich in mercy,[aq] because of His great love[ar] that He had for us,[O] 5 made us alive[as] with the ·Messiah even though we were dead[at] in trespasses. You are saved by grace! 6 Together with Christ Jesus He also raised us up and seated us in the heavens,[au] 7 so that in the coming ages[av] He might display the immeasurable riches[aw] of His grace through His kindness[ax] to us in Christ Jesus. 8 For you are saved by grace[ay] through faith, and this is not from yourselves; it is God's gift— 9 not from

[a] **1:1** Ac 13:9
[b] Eph 1:9
[c] Eph 5:2
[d] Ac 18:19-21; 19:9-10; 20:3,17; 1Co 15:32; Rv 2:1
[e] **1:3** Eph 1:20; 2:6; 3:10; 6:12
[f] **1:4** Jd 24
[g] **1:6** Jn 1:14; Rm 5:2; 2Co 4:15
[h] Mt 3:17; Jn 3:35; 10:17; Col 1:13
[i] **1:7** Heb 9:12
[j] Ps 25:11; Mt 9:2; Mk 2:5; Lk 24:47
[k] **1:9** Rm 11:25; 16:25; Eph 3:3; Col 1:27
[l] Rm 9:11
[m] **1:10** Mt 1:17; Eph 5:2
[n] Php 2:10
[o] Col 1:16
[p] **1:11** Pr 19:21
[q] **1:12** 1Th 1:3
[r] Mk 10:37
[s] **1:13** Col 1:5; 2Th 2:10
[t] Ps 51:11; Jn 1:33; Ac 2:4; Rm 8:9; Gl 5:25; Ti 3:5; Rv 3:22
[u] **1:14** Gn 38:17-18,20; 2Co 1:22; 5:5
[v] **1:17** Ps 51:12
[w] 1Pt 4:13
[x] **1:18** 1Th 1:3
[y] Col 3:15
[z] **1:19** Ac 4:33
[aa] **1:20** Php 2:9
[ab] Jn 20:17; Eph 1:3; 2:6; 3:10; 6:12; Php 2:10; 1Pt 3:22
[ac] **1:21** 2Tm 2:19
[ad] Mk 10:30
[ae] **1:22** Ps 8:6; Rm 13:1; 1Co 15:27; 1Pt 3:22
[af] Col 2:10
[ag] **1:23** Eph 4:4
[ah] Jn 1:16
[ai] Col 3:11
[aj] **2:1** Jn 5:25
[ak] **2:2** 2Pt 2:20
[al] 2Pt 2:10; Jd 8
[am] 1Co 2:12; 1Tm 4:1
[an] **2:3** Php 3:3
[ao] Mt 21:31; Lk 12:47; 23:25; Jn 1:13; 1Co 7:37; 2Pt 1:21
[ap] Rm 2:5; Rv 6:16
[aq] **2:4** Lk 1:50
[ar] 1Co 13:1; 1Jn 4:16
[as] **2:5** Col 2:13; 1Tm 5:6
[at] Jn 5:25
[au] **2:6** Eph 1:3,20; 3:10; 6:12; Php 2:10; 1Pt 3:22
[av] **2:7** Mk 10:30
[aw] Lk 8:14; 2Co 8:9
[ax] Ps 25:6
[ay] **2:8** Rm 3:24; 6:14; 11:6; Gl 2:21; 2Tm 1:9

[A] **1:1** Other mss omit *at Ephesus* [B] **1:4** Vv. 3-14 are 1 sentence in Gk. [C] **1:4** Or *In His sight in love* [D] **1:10** Or *dispensation*; lit *house law* (Gk *oikonomia*) [E] **1:10** Lit *the fulfillment of times* [F] **1:11** Or *we also were chosen as an inheritance*, or *we were also made an inheritance* [G] **1:14** *The possession* could be either man's or God's [H] **1:17** Or *the Father of glory* [I] **1:17** Or *you the Spirit* [J] **1:18** Lit *the eyes of your heart* [K] **1:21** Lit *every name named* [L] **1:22** Ps 8:6 [M] **2:2** Lit *ruler of the domain of the air* [N] **2:2** Lit *sons of disobedience* [O] **2:4** Lit *love with which He loved us*

works, so that no one can boast. 10 For we are
His creation, created[a] in Christ Jesus for good
works, which God prepared ahead of time[b] so
that we should walk in them.

Unity in Christ

11 So then, remember that at one time you
were Gentiles in the flesh — called "the uncircumcised" by those called "the circumcised,"[c]
which is done in the flesh by human hands.[d]
12 At that time you were without the Messiah,
excluded from the citizenship of Israel, and
foreigners to the covenants of the promise,[e]
without hope[f] and without God in the world.
13 But now in Christ Jesus, you who were far
away have been brought near by the blood[g]
of the Messiah. 14 For He is our peace, who
made both groups one[h] and tore down the
dividing wall of hostility. In His flesh, 15 He
made of no effect the law consisting of commands and expressed in regulations, so that
He might create[i] in Himself one[j] new man
from the two, resulting in peace. 16 He did
this so that He might reconcile both to God
in one body[k] through the cross and put the
hostility to death by it.[A] 17 When the Messiah
came, He proclaimed the good news[l] of peace
to you who were far away and peace to those
who were near.[m] 18 For through Him we both
have access[n] by one Spirit to the Father.[o] 19 So
then you are no longer foreigners and strangers, but fellow citizens with the ·saints, and
members of God's household, 20 built on the
foundation of the apostles and prophets,[p]
with Christ Jesus Himself as the cornerstone.
21 The whole building, being put together[q]
by Him, grows into a holy sanctuary in the
Lord.[r] 22 You also are being built together[s] for
God's dwelling[t] in the Spirit.

Paul's Ministry to the Gentiles

3 For this reason, I, Paul, the prisoner[u] of
Christ Jesus on behalf of you Gentiles —
2 you have heard, haven't you, about the administration of God's grace that He gave to
me for you? 3 The ·mystery was made known
to me by revelation,[v] as I have briefly written above. 4 By reading this you are able to
understand my insight about the mystery of
the ·Messiah.[w] 5 This was not made known to
people[B] in other generations as it is now revealed to His holy apostles and prophets[x] by
the Spirit: 6 The Gentiles are coheirs, members of the same body, and partners of the
promise[y] in Christ Jesus through the gospel.
7 I was made a servant of this gospel by the
gift of God's grace that was given to me by the
working of His power.[z]
8 This grace was given to me — the least of
all the ·saints — to proclaim to the Gentiles
the incalculable riches[aa] of the Messiah, 9 and
to shed light for all about the administration of the mystery hidden for ages in God
who created[ab] all things. 10 This is so God's
multi-faceted wisdom[ac] may now be made
known through the church to the rulers and
authorities in the heavens.[ad] 11 This is according to His eternal purpose[ae] accomplished in
the Messiah, Jesus our Lord. 12 In Him we have
boldness and confident access[af] through faith
in Him.[C] 13 So then I ask you not to be discouraged[ag] over my afflictions on your behalf, for
they are your glory.[ah]

[a]**2:10** Jn 1:3; Rv 3:14
[b]Rm 9:23
[c]**2:11** Gl 6:15
[d]Php 3:3
[e]**2:12** Gn 12:7
[f]1Th 1:3; 4:13
[g]**2:13** Heb 9:12
[h]**2:14** Rm 10:12; Gl 3:28
[i]**2:15** Rv 3:14
[j]Jn 11:52
[k]**2:16** Eph 4:4
[l]**2:17** Lk 4:18; 1Pt 1:12
[m]Is 57:19
[n]**2:18** Jn 10:7-9; Rm 5:2; Eph 3:12
[o]Jn 4:23; 1Co 12:13; Eph 4:4; Col 1:12
[p]**2:20** 1Co 12:28; Eph 3:5
[q]**2:21** Eph 4:16
[r]1Pt 2:5
[s]**2:22** Rm 11:18
[t]1Pt 2:5
[u]**3:1** 2Tm 1:8
[v]**3:3** 1Pt 4:13
[w]**3:4** Col 4:3
[x]**3:5** 1Co 12:28-29; Eph 2:20
[y]**3:6** Gn 12:7
[z]**3:7** Mk 5:30; Lk 1:35; 6:19; Ac 19:11; 2Co 13:4; Rv 11:17
[aa]**3:8** Rm 1:15; 10:12; 11:12; 1Pt 1:12
[ab]**3:9** Mk 13:19
[ac]**3:10** Pr 3:19; Rm 11:33; 1Co 1:21,24; Rv 7:12
[ad]Eph 1:3,20; 2:6; 6:12; Php 2:10
[ae]**3:11** Pr 19:21
[af]**3:12** Rm 5:2
[ag]**3:13** 2Th 3:13
[ah]Jn 5:44; 7:18; Rm 2:7; 1Pt 5:4

GOD WHO SENDS

The New Humanity

Humanization has always been implied in biblical salvation and, therefore, must always be a vital concern of mission. The New Testament speaks of the church as the new humanity and the Christian as the new human person (Eph 2:15-16; 4:24; Col 3:9-10; 1Pt 2:9; 2Co 5:17). The church as community embodies this new humanity. The Christian ashrams, the basic ecclesial communities, the house churches, and numerous other renewed forms of the contextualized church around the world today are glowing witness to the church as community and the embodiment of the new humanity.

(DUBOSE, 154-155)

[A]**2:16** Or *death in Himself* [B]**3:5** Lit *to the sons of men* [C]**3:12** Or *through His faithfulness*

Prayer for Spiritual Power

14 For this reason I kneel[a] before the Father[A]
15 from whom every family in heaven and on
earth is named. 16 I pray that He may grant you,
according to the riches[b] of His glory,[c] to be
strengthened with power[d] in the inner man[e]
through His Spirit, 17 and that the Messiah
may dwell in your hearts through faith. I pray
that you, being rooted and firmly established
in love, 18 may be able to comprehend with all
the saints what is the length and width, height
and depth of God's love,[f] 19 and to know the
Messiah's love that surpasses knowledge, so
you may be filled with all the fullness of God.

[a] **3:14** Php 2:10
[b] **3:16** Lk 8:14; 2Co 8:9
[c] Lk 9:32; Jn 17:24; 2Co 3:18; 2Pt 3:18
[d] 2Tm 1:7
[e] Rm 7:22; Php 4:13
[f] **3:18** Jb 11:7-9; Ps 103:11-14

The Church as God's Missionary Agent

Ed Stetzer

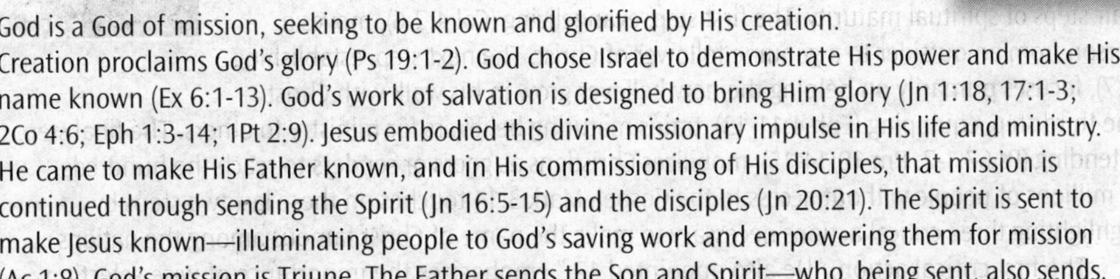

God is a God of mission, seeking to be known and glorified by His creation. Creation proclaims God's glory (Ps 19:1-2). God chose Israel to demonstrate His power and make His name known (Ex 6:1-13). God's work of salvation is designed to bring Him glory (Jn 1:18, 17:1-3; 2Co 4:6; Eph 1:3-14; 1Pt 2:9). Jesus embodied this divine missionary impulse in His life and ministry. He came to make His Father known, and in His commissioning of His disciples, that mission is continued through sending the Spirit (Jn 16:5-15) and the disciples (Jn 20:21). The Spirit is sent to make Jesus known—illuminating people to God's saving work and empowering them for mission (Ac 1:8). God's mission is Triune. The Father sends the Son and Spirit—who, being sent, also sends.

If we see God as a missionary God, viewing the church as a missionary people is intuitive. God—the source of the mission—gives the church its missionary call and impulse. God, to see His mission fulfilled, empowers us by His Spirit to join Him on mission (Eph 1:20-22, 3:10). The redeemed people of God do not follow Christ as individuals. The Spirit gathers them together into local covenant communities, where they are found "standing firm in one spirit, with one mind, working side by side for the faith that comes from the gospel " (Php 1:27). Through the ministry of the church, the mission of Jesus is extended, for it is His body—called to make disciples of all nations.

In Ephesians 3:1-10, Paul positions his whole ministry in light of the churches' role in God's mission. The reason for his calling to share the gospel with the Gentiles, he states, is to serve God's purpose for the church. Paul envisions that churches will be planted as a result of his mission, and he claims that by these local gatherings, God will accomplish His mission, for God's purpose for the church is to make known His "multifaceted wisdom" in the mystery of the gospel (v. 10).

Peter echoes this when he writes to the scattered church throughout Pontus, Galatia, Cappadocia, Asia, and Bithynia. Peter calls them exiles in this world, but a chosen, royal, holy people—who belong to God. They have received mercy for a divine purpose—that they may proclaim God's praises (1Pt 2:9) and that by their lives others may glorify God (1Pt 2:12).

In His mission, God is redeeming people and restoring the world for His glory. In commissioning His disciples, Jesus points out that there are no limitations to the scope of His mission (Mt 28:18). This is reinforced when Jesus instructed the disciples to wait for the Spirit to come, and then, His mission would extend beyond Israel (Ac 1:8). Jesus not only gives the scope of His mission for the church, He assures them of its success. He promises that the gates of Hades cannot prevent the advance of the church (Mt 16:18), so God's will will be accomplished in the world for His glory through the church.

[A] **3:14** Other mss add *of our Lord Jesus Christ*

20 Now to Him who is able[a] to do above and
beyond all that we ask or think[b] according to
the power[c] that works in us— 21 to Him be
glory in the church and in Christ Jesus to all
generations, forever and ever. ·Amen.[d]

Unity and Diversity in the Body of Christ

4 Therefore I, the prisoner for the Lord,[e]
urge you to ·walk worthy of the calling you have received, 2 with all humility[f]
and gentleness, with patience,[g] accepting[A,h]
one another in love,[i] 3 diligently keeping the
unity[j] of the Spirit[k] with the peace[l] that binds
us. 4 There is one body and one Spirit[m]—just
as you were called to one hope[B,n] at your call-

[a] **3:20** Rm 16:25; 2Co 9:8; Jd 24 [b] Mk 14:36 [c] Rm 15:13; 16:25; 2Tm 1:7; Jd 24 [d] **3:21** Php 4:20 [e] **4:1** 2Tm 1:8 [f] **4:2** Col 3:12 [g] Ex 34:6; 2Tm 3:10 [h] Heb 13:22 [i] 1Co 13:1

[j] **4:3** Eph 4:13 [k] Ps 51:11; Jn 1:33; Ac 2:4; Rm 8:9; Gl 5:25; Ti 3:5; Rv 3:22 [l] Lk 12:51; Rm 1:7; 2Tm 1:2; 3Jn 14 [m] **4:4** Rm 12:4-5; 1Co 10:17; 12:9,12-13; Eph 2:16,18; Col 3:15 [n] Ac 26:6-7; 28:20; Rm 5:2; 8:23-25; Eph 1:18; Col 1:5; 1Th 1:3

Developing Missional Leaders

Bill Jones

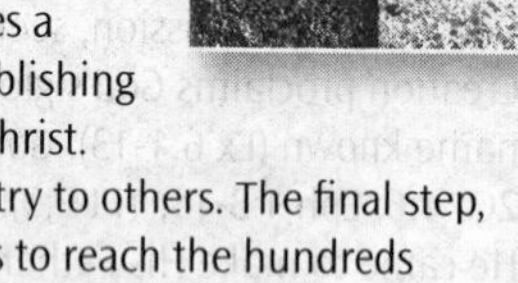

Scripture provides clear direction for Christ's followers to help others move up the stair steps of spiritual maturity. The first step, evangelizing (Col 4:2-6), moves a person from an outsider to a genuine follower of Christ. The next step, establishing (2:7), focuses primarily on helping the new believer grow in his walk with Christ. The third step, equipping (Eph 4:11-13), trains maturing believers for ministry to others. The final step, extending (Ps 67:1-2; Rm 10:14-15), mobilizes Christians as goers or senders to reach the hundreds of millions of people without access to the Gospel. Mark 3:14 touches on these last two steps by highlighting three critical actions necessary to make the name of Christ famous among the nations.

The first critical action, "He also appointed 12," emphasizes the importance of wise selection. Luke 6:12-13 notes that before Jesus selected His team, He spent the entire previous night in prayer. Further, when He chose His team, Jesus did not choose strangers. He had met five of them through John the Baptist about a year earlier (Jn 1:35-51). He even went on a ministry trip with four of them (Mk 1:13-14) before selecting them. Note, too, that from His many disciples (2:15), He only selected twelve. Having a small number allowed for personalized training. Similarly, as the Church equips future missional leaders, we must follow Christ's example by covering the selection in prayer, choosing only those whom we know well, and limiting the training to a small number in order to maximize the impact.

The second necessary action, "to be with Him," focuses on Jesus' preferred method of preparation. They experienced on-the-job training. They watched the Lord as He ministered in public and listened as He debriefed them in private (4:10). Later, as His team developed, Jesus sent them out to practice ministry two by two (6:7,12). Likewise, we must realize that no better training method exists than involving future world-changers in ministry with us: no contact, no impact.

The final action, "to send them out to preach," stresses Jesus' ultimate goal, the mobilization of effective workers who could reach the nations with the message of the Gospel. Throughout His ministry, Christ demonstrated God's love not only for the Jews, but also for the Samaritans (Jn 4) as well as the Gentiles (Mk 7:24-30). Later, as this vision of God's heart for all peoples grew into a sense of urgency, the Twelve traveled to the ends of the earth proclaiming God's love and forgiveness. For the missional leaders we train, we also must continually emphasize God's love for every tongue, tribe, and nation by involving them in cross-cultural ministry.

Declaring God's glory among all peoples will require the mobilization of large numbers of believers firmly established in their walk with Christ and effectively equipped for their work as His co-laborers. By wisely selecting, properly training, and strategically launching missional laborers, the Church can fulfill the task of taking the gospel to all the nations of the world.

[A] **4:2** Or *tolerating* [B] **4:4** Lit *called in one hope*

ing — 5 one Lord,[a] one faith,[b] one baptism,
6 one God[c] and Father[d] of all, who is above all
and through all and in all.[e]
7 Now grace was given to each one of us[f] according to the measure of the ·Messiah's gift.
8 For it says:

When He ascended[g] on high,
He took prisoners into captivity;[A]
He gave gifts to people.[B,h]

9 But what does "He ascended" mean except
that He[C] descended to the lower parts of the
earth?[D,i] 10 The One who descended is also the
One who ascended far above all the heav-
ens,[j] that He might fill[E] all things.[k] 11 And He
personally gave some to be apostles, some
prophets, some evangelists, some pastors and
teachers, 12 for the training of the ·saints in
the work of ministry, to build up the body of
Christ,[l] 13 until we all reach unity in the faith
and in the knowledge of God's Son,[m] growing
into a mature man with a stature[n] measured
by Christ's fullness. 14 Then we will no longer
be little children, tossed by the waves and
blown around by every wind of teaching,[o] by
human cunning with cleverness in the tech-
niques of deceit. 15 But speaking the truth in
love, let us grow in every way into Him who
is the head[p] — Christ. 16 From Him the whole
body, fitted and knit together[q] by every supporting ligament, promotes the growth[r] of
the body for building up itself in love by the
proper working of each individual part.

Living the New Life

17 Therefore, I say this and testify in the
Lord: You should no longer walk as the Gentiles walk, in the futility of their thoughts.
18 They are darkened in their understanding,
excluded from the life of God, because of the
ignorance that is in them and because of the
hardness of their hearts. 19 They became callous and gave themselves over to promiscuity for the practice of every kind of impurity[s]
with a desire for more and more.[F]
20 But that is not how you learned about the
Messiah, 21 assuming you heard about Him
and were taught by Him, because the truth[t]
is in Jesus. 22 You took off[G,u] your former way
of life,[v] the old self[H,w] that is corrupted by deceitful desires; 23 you are being renewed[I] in
the spirit[x] of your minds; 24 you put on[J,y] the
new self, the one created[z] according to God's
likeness[aa] in righteousness and purity of the
truth.
25 Since you put away[ab] lying, **Speak the
truth, each one to his neighbor,**[K,ac] because
we are members of one another. 26 **Be angry
and do not sin.**[L,ad] Don't let the sun go down
on your anger, 27 and don't give the Devil an
opportunity. 28 The thief must no longer steal.
Instead, he must do honest work with his own
hands, so that he has something to share[ae]
with anyone in need. 29 No foul language is to
come from your mouth, but only what is good
for building up someone in need,[M] so that it
gives grace to those who hear. 30 And don't
grieve God's Holy Spirit.[af] You were sealed by
Him[N] for the day of ·redemption.[ag] 31 All bitterness, anger and wrath, shouting and slander must be removed from you, along with all
malice. 32 And be kind[ah] and compassionate[ai]
to one another, forgiving[aj] one another, just
as God also forgave you[O] in Christ.

5 Therefore, be imitators of God, as dearly
loved children. 2 And ·walk in love, as the
·Messiah also loved us and gave Himself for
us,[ak] a sacrificial and fragrant offering to
God. 3 But sexual immorality[al] and any impurity[am] or greed[an] should not even be heard of[P]
among you, as is proper for ·saints. 4 Coarse
and foolish talking or crude joking are not
suitable, but rather giving thanks. 5 For know
and recognize this: Every sexually immoral[ao]
or impure[ap] or greedy[aq] person, who is an
idolater, does not have an inheritance in the
kingdom[ar] of the Messiah and of God.

Light versus Darkness

6 Let no one deceive you with empty arguments, for God's wrath[as] is coming on the
disobedient[Q] because of these things. 7 Therefore, do not become their partners. 8 For you
were once darkness, but now you are light[at]
in the Lord. Walk as children of light[au] — 9 for

[a] **4:5** 1Co 1:13; 8:6 [b] Jd 3 [c] **4:6** Dt 6:4 [d] Mt 5:16; 11:27; Lk 11:13; Jn 8:42 [e] Ps 104:24 [f] **4:7** 1Co 12:7-11 [g] **4:8** Jn 20:17 [h] Ps 68:18 [i] **4:9** Jn 3:13; 6:62; Rm 10:6-7; Php 2:6-11 [j] **4:10** Jn 3:13; 6:38 [k] Eph 1:23; Heb 4:14; 7:26; 9:24 [l] **4:12** Rm 7:4; 1Co 10:16; 12:27; Col 2:17 [m] **4:13** Jn 5:19; Heb 1:2 [n] Lk 2:52 [o] **4:14** Rm 15:4; Heb 13:9 [p] **4:15** Col 2:10 [q] **4:16** Col 2:2 [r] Col 2:19 [s] **4:19** 1Th 4:17 [t] **4:21** 2Th 2:10 [u] **4:22** Rm 13:12 [v] 2Pt 3:11 [w] Rm 6:6; 7:6; 1Co 5:7-8; 2Co 3:14; Col 3:9 [x] **4:23** Ps 51:12 [y] **4:24** Rm 13:12 [z] Mk 13:19; Jn 1:3; Rv 3:14 [aa] Col 3:10; 2Pt 1:4 [ab] **4:25** Pr 31:25 [ac] Zch 8:16 [ad] **4:26** Ps 4:4; 37:8; Mt 18:21; Jms 1:19-20 [ae] **4:28** 1Th 2:8; 1Tm 6:18 [af] **4:30** Ps 51:11; Jn 1:33; Ac 2:4; Rm 8:9; Gl 5:25; Ti 3:5; Rv 3:22 [ag] Php 1:6 [ah] **4:32** Mt 11:30; Lk 5:39; 6:35; Rm 2:4; 1Co 15:33; 1Pt 2:3 [ai] 1Pt 3:8 [aj] Ps 25:11; Mt 9:2; Mk 2:5; Lk 24:47; Col 3:12-13 [ak] **5:2** 2Th 2:13; Ti 2:14 [al] **5:3** 1Th 4:3 [am] 1Th 4:7 [an] Lk 12:15; Rm 1:29; Eph 4:19; Col 3:5; 1Th 2:5; 2Pt 2:3,14 [ao] **5:5** 1Co 5:9 [ap] 2Co 6:17 [aq] 1Co 5:10-11; 6:10 [ar] Mk 1:15 [as] **5:6** Rm 2:5; Rv 6:16 [at] **5:8** Ps 36:9; Jn 12:46 [au] Is 2:5; Lk 16:8; Jn 12:35-36

[A] **4:8** Or *He led the captives* [B] **4:8** Ps 68:18 [C] **4:9** Other mss add *first* [D] **4:9** Or *the lower parts, namely, the earth* [E] **4:10** Or *fulfill*; Eph 1:23 [F] **4:19** Lit *with greediness* [G] **4:21-22** Or *Jesus. This means: take off* (as a command) [H] **4:22** Lit *man*; = a person before conversion [I] **4:22-23** Or *desires; renew* (as a command) [J] **4:23-24** Or *minds; and put on* (as a command) [K] **4:25** Zch 8:16 [L] **4:26** Ps 4:4 [M] **4:29** Lit *for the building up of the need* [N] **4:30** Or *Spirit, by whom you were sealed* [O] **4:32** Other mss read *us* [P] **5:3** Or *be named* [Q] **5:6** Lit *sons of disobedience*

the fruit of the light[A] results in all goodness,
righteousness, and truth[a]— [10]discerning[b]
what is pleasing[c] to the Lord. [11]Don't participate in the fruitless[d] works of darkness, but
instead expose them. [12]For it is shameful even
to mention what is done by them in secret.
[13]Everything exposed by the light is made
clear,[e] [14]for what makes everything clear is
light. Therefore it is said:

> Get up, sleeper,[f] and rise up
> from the dead,[g]
> and the Messiah will shine on you.[B,h]

Consistency in the Christian Life

[15]Pay careful attention, then, to how you
walk—not as unwise people but as wise—
[16]making the most of the time,[C,i] because the
days are evil. [17]So don't be foolish, but understand[j] what the Lord's will[k] is. [18]And don't get
drunk[l] with wine,[m] which leads to reckless actions, but be filled by the Spirit:[n]

> [19] speaking to one another
> in psalms, hymns, and spiritual songs,
> singing and making music
> from your heart to the Lord,
> [20] giving thanks always for everything
> to God the Father
> in the name of our Lord Jesus Christ,
> [21] submitting to one another
> in the fear of Christ.[o]

Wives and Husbands

[22]Wives,[p] submit[D,q] to your own husbands[r]
as to the Lord, [23]for the husband is the head
of the wife[s] as Christ is the head[t] of the
church. He is the Savior of the body.[u] [24]Now
as the church submits to Christ, so wives are
to submit to their husbands in everything.
[25]Husbands, love your wives,[v] just as Christ
loved[w] the church and gave Himself[x] for her
[26]to make her holy, cleansing[E] her with the
washing of water by the word. [27]He did this
to present the church to Himself in splendor, without spot or wrinkle or anything like
that, but holy and blameless.[y] [28]In the same
way, husbands are to love their wives as their
own bodies. He who loves his wife loves himself. [29]For no one ever hates his own flesh but
provides and cares for it, just as Christ does
for the church, [30]since we are members of His
body.[F]

> [31] **For this reason a man will leave**
> **his father and mother**
> **and be joined to his wife,**[z]
> **and the two will become**
> **one flesh.**[G,aa]

[32]This ·mystery[ab] is profound, but I am talking about Christ and the church. [33]To sum up,
each one of you is to love his wife as himself,
and the wife is to respect her husband.

Children and Parents

6 Children, obey[ac] your parents as you
would the Lord,[H] because this is right.
[2]**Honor your father and mother**, which is
the first commandment[I] with a promise, [3]**so
that it may go well with you and that you may
have a long life in the land.**[J,K,ad] [4]Fathers, don't
stir up anger[ae] in your children, but bring
them up in the training[af] and instruction of
the Lord.

Sent Into the World

GOD WHO SENDS

On the stage of the world, the drama of the divine sendings transpires. It is not in some heavenly realm nor in some isolated "holy" place that God acts. He is present in the real world of people. He sent Moses into the midst of the thriving activities and teeming multitudes of Egypt. He sent his Son into the midst of Palestinian life—into the streets, the public places, the homes and hearts of the people. God sent his Son into the world. He sends us into the world as the medium of his message.
(DuBose, 69)

---

[a]**5:9** Eph 5:17 [b]**5:10** Rm 12:2 [c]Lk 18:18 [d]**5:11** Gl 5:22; Ti 3:14 [e]**5:13** 1Jn 1:2 [f]**5:14** Pr 6:4 [g]Jn 5:25 [h]Is 26:19; 51:17; 52:1; 60:1; Mal 4:2; Lk 1:78-79; Rm 13:11 [i]**5:16** Col 4:5 [j]**5:17** Jr 31:31-34; Ezk 36:26-27; Rm 12:2; Php 1:9-10; 1Th 5:21 [k]Ps 143:10; Pr 16:9; Gl 1:4; Eph 1:9 [l]**5:18** Lk 12:45; Jn 2:10; 1Th 5:7; Rv 17:2 [m]Gn 9:21; Dt 7:13; Ps 4:7; Pr 3:10; Lk 5:37 [n]Lk 1:15; Ac 13:52 [o]**5:18-21** Col 3:16-17; 1Pt 1:17 [p]**5:22** 1Pt 3:1 [q]Gn 3:16; 1Co 11:3,7-9,11-12; Col 3:18; Ti 2:4-5; 1Pt 3:1-6 [r]1Pt 3:1 [s]**5:23** 1Co 11:3 [t]Col 2:10 [u]Col 3:18–4:1 [v]**5:25** Col 3:19; 1Pt 3:7 [w]Jn 3:16; 1Co 13:1; 2Th 2:13 [x]Ti 2:14 [y]**5:27** Jd 24 [z]**5:31** 1Pt 3:1 [aa]Gn 2:24 [ab]**5:32** 1Co 2:7 [ac]**6:1** Pr 1:8; 6:20; 23:22; Col 3:20 [ad]**6:2-3** Ex 20:12 [ae]**6:4** Rm 10:19 [af]Heb 12:5

[A]5:9 Other mss read *fruit of the Spirit* [B]5:14 This poem may have been an early Christian hymn based on several passages in Isaiah; Is 9:2; 26:19; 40:1; 51:17; 52:1; 60:1. [C]5:16 Lit *buying back the time* [D]5:22 Other mss omit *submit* [E]5:26 Or *having cleansed* [F]5:30 Other mss add *and of His flesh and of His bones* [G]5:31 Gn 2:24 [H]6:1 Lit *parents in the Lord* [I]6:2 Or *is a preeminent commandment* [J]6:3 Or *life on the earth* [K]6:2-3 Ex 20:12

Prayer and the Mission of God

Philip Nation

Prayer is used by God to bring His people into alignment with His mission. It is critical that we remember that prayer is not a power by which we force God to act according to our will. Rather, by communicating with God, His passions can become our passions. Believers have the opportunity to both listen to and speak to the God of the universe in prayer to receive guidance by His Spirit. It is not just an activity of our faith but is a portion of the relationship we have with Christ.

Prayer is an activity often thought of as driving only the personal side of the believer's life. If we view prayer merely as an internal discipline, we can lose sight of how God might use prayer as a means of engaging us in His mission in ways that extend beyond our own spiritual development. As our maturity in Christ develops through the relational activity of prayer, it should consequently cause us to see the world and humanity as Christ does.

The mission assigned to the church has its originations in the mind of God and must therefore be directed by Him. It is in prayer oftentimes that Christians will come to a place of complete abandonment to God's Spirit. In Ephesians 6:18, believers are directed to "pray at all times in the Spirit." By praying according the passions and in the power of the Holy Spirit, we surrender our will to His plan and purposes.

We should also remember that, through prayer, God connects us to His heart for the church as well. In 6:18, Paul also wrote that we are to intercede "for all the saints." A significant portion of God's mission is the building of His church. In the larger context of Ephesians 6:10-20, the teaching presented is about spiritual warfare against believers and the church. In Paul's teaching to the Ephesians, prayer plays a prominent role in the defense of our fellow believers.

In regards to activity in the mission, Paul requests prayer so that he will engage in speaking about the gospel well and with boldness (verses 19-20). Doubtlessly, the church must learn to understand its culture and minister with kindness to the people around us. But the proverbial point of the spear for us is to speak about the greatness of Christ's work on our behalf. We are ambassadors who speak on behalf of our King and with His authority. To do so well, just as Paul requested, we must have the benefit of intercessory prayer by the church. Believers should both pray for one another and request prayer from one another to effectively engage in God's mission.

The act and results of prayer are a mysterious occurrence. God has chosen this medium by which He will subsequently embolden believers for His mission and mature them in the faith. Are you being emboldened through prayer?

Slaves and Masters

5 •Slaves, obey your human[A] masters[a] with
fear and trembling,[b] in the sincerity[c] of your
heart, as to Christ. 6 Don't work only while
being watched, in order to please men, but
as slaves of Christ, do God's will[d] from your
heart.[B] 7 Serve with a good attitude, as to the
Lord and not to men,[e] 8 knowing that whatever good each one does, slave or free, he will
receive this back from the Lord. 9 And masters, treat your slaves the same way, without
threatening[f] them, because you know that
both their Master and yours is in heaven, and
there is no favoritism[g] with Him.[h]

Christian Warfare

10 Finally, be strengthened by the Lord and
by His vast strength.[i] 11 Put on[j] the full armor[k]
of God so that you can stand against the tactics[C] of the Devil. 12 For our battle is not
against flesh[l] and blood, but against the rulers, against the authorities,[m] against the
world powers of this darkness, against the
spiritual forces of evil[n] in the heavens.[o] 13 This
is why you must take up the full armor[p] of
God, so that you may be able to resist[q] in the
evil day, and having prepared everything, to
take your stand. 14 Stand,[r] therefore,

with truth[s] like a belt
  around your waist,
righteousness[t] like armor
  on your chest,[u]
15 and your feet sandaled with readiness
  for the gospel of peace.[D]
16 In every situation take the shield[v]
  of faith,[w]
and with it you will be able
  to extinguish
all the flaming arrows
  of the evil one.[x]
17 Take the helmet[y] of salvation,
and the sword[z] of the Spirit,[aa]
which is God's word.

18 Pray[ab] at all times in the Spirit[ac] with every
prayer and request, and stay alert[ad] in this
with all perseverance and intercession for all
the •saints. 19 Pray also for me, that the message may be given to me when I open my
mouth to make known with boldness[ae] the
•mystery of the gospel. 20 For this I am an ambassador[af] in chains. Pray that I might be bold
enough in Him to speak as I should.

Paul's Farewell

21 Tychicus,[ag] our dearly loved brother and
faithful servant[E] in the Lord, will tell you all
the news about me so that you may be informed. 22 I am sending him to you for this
very reason, to let you know how we are and
to encourage[ah] your hearts.[ai]
23 Peace to the •brothers, and love with
faith, from God the Father[aj] and the Lord
Jesus Christ. 24 Grace be with all who have undying love for our Lord Jesus Christ.[F,G]

[a] 6:5 Col 3:22; 1Pt 2:18 [b] Php 2:12 [c] 2Co 9:11 [d] 6:6 Ps 143:10; Pr 16:9; Gl 1:4; Eph 1:9 [e] 6:7 Col 3:23 [f] 6:9 Ac 4:29; 9:1 [g] Col 3:25 [h] Col 4:1 [i] 6:10 Ac 4:33 [j] 6:11 Pr 31:25 [k] Eph 6:11-17 [l] 6:12 Php 3:3 [m] 1Pt 3:22 [n] Mt 6:13; Jn 17:15 [o] Eph 1:3,20; 2:6; 3:10; Php 2:10 [p] 6:13 1Th 5:8 [q] 2Tm 4:15; 1Pt 5:9 [r] 6:14 Pr 24:16; Php 1:27 [s] Jn 14:6; 1Jn 5:20 [t] Mt 6:33; Rm 1:17; 2Pt 1:1 [u] 1Th 5:8 [v] 6:16 Gn 15:1 [w] Mt 8:10; Ac 3:16; Rm 1:8; 1Co 2:5; Gl 2:16; 1Tm 1:2; Heb 4:2 [x] 2Th 3:3 [y] 6:17 1Th 5:8 [z] Mk 14:47 [aa] Ps 51:11; Jn 1:33; Ac 2:4; Rm 8:9; Gl 5:25; Ti 3:5; Rv 3:22 [ab] 6:18 Mt 5:44; Ac 12:12 [ac] Jd 20 [ad] Pr 6:4 [ae] 6:19 2Co 3:12 [af] 6:20 2Co 5:20 [ag] 6:21 Ti 3:12 [ah] 6:22 Lk 16:25 [ai] Col 4:8 [aj] 6:23 Mt 5:16; 11:27; Lk 11:13; Jn 8:42

[A] 6:5 Lit *according to the flesh* [B] 6:6 Lit *from soul* [C] 6:11 Or *schemes*, or *tricks* [D] 6:15 Ready to go tell others about the gospel [E] 6:21 Or *deacon* [F] 6:24 Other mss add *Amen.* [G] 6:24 Lit *all who love our Lord Jesus Christ in incorruption*

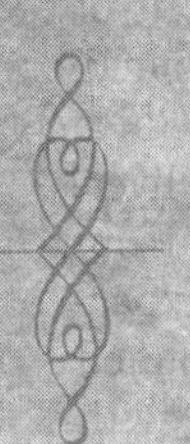

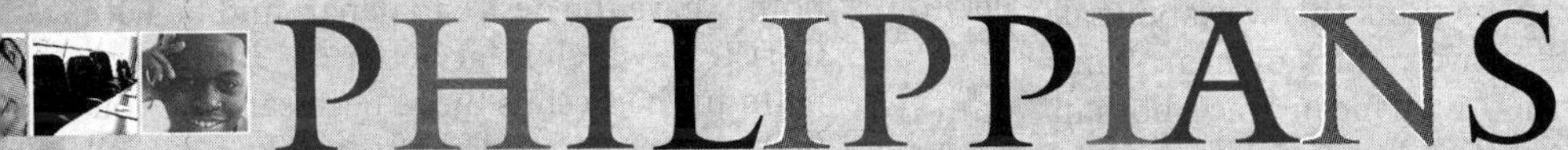

PHILIPPIANS

■ **AUTHOR:** Paul (Saul of Tarsus)

■■ **DATE:** Written around A.D. 60 in Rome while imprisoned

God's premier missionary sits in a Roman jail awaiting trial in front of a Roman judge whose first loyalty is to Caesar. A cause for dejection? Paul instead celebrates the Lord Christ, urging the church in Philippi (a Roman city where army veterans were given retirement villas) to be joyful despite all appearances. Real power is not in Rome, but in heaven.

Paul's mission may or may not be complete. He believes he will be freed but concedes that his trial's outcome may result in his being "with Christ—which is far better" (1:23). God's mission, Paul knows, is not complete. More territories need to hear the gospel. More people need to learn of God's redemption, won by the death and secured by the resurrection of Jesus Christ. That's the main reason for the rejoicing Paul urges the church to do. The Day of Christ is coming. All the losses and struggles will be covered by the great joy of God's victory over evil at the return of Christ. Until then, God's mission requires unity—no more disputes and divisions in the church. As Paul wrote, "Fulfill my joy by thinking the same way" (2:2). This doesn't mean having identical opinions on all matters, but being together on the mission, witnessing to God's glory, and teaching new believers to live as citizens in God's world.

In the middle of this letter stands a remarkable seven verses (2:5-11) describing the posture of Jesus with respect to His own mission. The verses are called the Christ Hymn because they were likely part of early Christian praise, used here by Paul to make this point: God comes to us humbly, not wielding universal power, but showing instead universal love through sacrificial obedience and death. God does this through Christ, Paul explains, not because death is grand, but rather to show us that God Himself lives through our worst experience and greatest fear. Death came into human experience because of sin; God knows that and shows His victory over death by dying and rising. Victory over death is now ours by faith. What could a Roman judge possibly say to intimidate someone who understands that God has died and was raised, and we will be raised too? Believe in God, trust in God's total goodness, and don't worry about anything, Paul says. God's mission is sure to succeed. Be a part of it.

Troubles threaten to wreck the church in Philippi. Paul speaks sternly to people who twist God's mission into their own misconceived religious imaginations. No, Paul says, do not follow these inflated egos and their ideas of self-promotion. Then Paul displays his own curriculum vita as one which, by human standards, would qualify him as well educated and impressive (3:4-6). Paul regards all that as waste and points people back to Christ as God's only way to relieve sin's trouble. Christ is our gateway to kinship with God.

Paul knows that one's past is no judge of success in life. Where are you heading? Forget past mistakes, lost years, bad times. Keep moving forward. Press on for the prize: God's call on your life, partnership in God's mission, and deep joy along the way.

Greeting

1 Paul[a] and Timothy,[b] slaves of Christ Jesus:
To all the ·saints in Christ Jesus who are
in Philippi,[c] including the ·overseers[d] and
deacons.[e]
2 Grace to you and peace from God our Father and the Lord Jesus Christ.

Thanksgiving and Prayer

3 I give thanks to my God for every remembrance of you,[A] 4 always praying with joy for
all of you in my every prayer, 5 because of your
partnership in the gospel from the first day[f]
until now.[g] 6 I am sure of this, that He who
started a good work[h] in you[B] will carry it on
to completion[i] until the day of Christ Jesus.
7 It is right[j] for me to think this way about all
of you, because I have you in my heart,[C] and
you are all partners with me in grace, both in
my imprisonment[k] and in the defense[l] and
establishment of the gospel. 8 For God is my
witness,[m] how deeply I miss all of you[n] with
the affection of Christ Jesus. 9 And I pray
this: that your love[o] will keep on growing[p] in
knowledge and every kind of discernment,[q]
10 so that you can approve the things that are
superior[r] and can be pure[s] and blameless[t]
in[D] the day of Christ,[u] 11 filled with the fruit[v]
of righteousness[w] that comes through Jesus
Christ to the glory[x] and praise of God.

Advance of the Gospel

12 Now I want you to know, ·brothers, that
what has happened to me has actually resulted in the advance of the gospel,[y] 13 so that
it has become known throughout the whole
imperial guard,[E] and to everyone else, that
my imprisonment is in the cause of Christ.
14 Most of the brothers in the Lord have gained
confidence from my imprisonment and dare
even more to speak the message[F,z] fearlessly.
15 To be sure, some preach Christ out of envy
and strife,[aa] but others out of good will.[G]
16 These do so out of love,[ab] knowing that I
am appointed for the defense of the gospel;
17 the others proclaim Christ out of rivalry,[ac]
not sincerely, seeking to cause me anxiety
in my imprisonment.[H] 18 What does it matter? Just that in every way, whether out of
false motives[ad] or true, Christ is proclaimed.
And in this I rejoice. Yes, and I will rejoice
19 because I know this will lead to my deliverance[I,ae] through your prayers and help from
the Spirit[af] of Jesus Christ.[ag] 20 My eager expectation and hope[ah] is that I will not be ashamed
about anything, but that now as always, with
all boldness, Christ will be highly honored in
my body, whether by life[ai] or by death.[aj]

Living Is Christ

21 For me, living is Christ[ak] and dying is gain.[al]
22 Now if I live on in the flesh, this means fruitful[am] work[an] for me; and I don't know which
one I should choose. 23 I am pressured by
both. I have the desire to depart and be with
Christ[ao] — which is far better[ap] — 24 but to remain in the flesh is more necessary for you.
25 Since I am persuaded of this, I know that I

[a] **1:1** Ac 13:9 [b] Ac 16:1; 1Tm 1:2 [c] Ac 16:12-40; 20:3-6; 1Th 2:2 [d] Ac 20:28; Ti 1:7 [e] 1Co 3:5 [f] **1:5** Ac 16:12-40 [g] 1Co 9:15-18; 2Co 11:7-9; Php 4:10,16,18 [h] **1:6** 2Co 9:8; Gl 3:10 [i] 2Co 7:1 [j] **1:7** Rm 1:17 [k] Php 1:13-14,17-20,25,30; 2:17,24; 4:22 [l] Ac 22:1 [m] **1:8** Rm 1:9 [n] 1Th 3:6 [o] **1:9** 1Co 13:1 [p] 1Co 15:58 [q] Eph 5:17 [r] **1:9-10** Rm 12:2 [s] **1:10** 2Pt 3:1 [t] Ac 24:16; 1Co 10:32 [u] Php 1:6,15 [v] **1:11** Mt 3:8; Gl 5:22 [w] Rm 1:17 [x] Lk 9:32; Jn 17:24; 2Co 3:18; 2Pt 3:18 [y] **1:12** Mk 13:9; Ac 21–26 [z] **1:14** Lk 8:21; Jn 18:32; Ac 17:11; Heb 4:12 [aa] **1:15** Rm 1:29; Ti 3:9 [ab] **1:16** 1Co 13:1 [ac] **1:17** Rm 2:8 [ad] **1:18** 1Th 2:5 [ae] **1:19** Jb 13:16-18 [af] Gl 5:25 [ag] Ac 16:7; Rm 8:9; 1Pt 1:11 [ah] **1:20** Ac 23:6; 1Th 1:3 [ai] 1Jn 5:12 [aj] Jn 8:51 [ak] **1:21** Rm 14:7-9; Gl 2:19-20; Php 1:11,15; Col 2:6–3:11 [al] Rm 8:38-39; Php 3:7 [am] **1:22** Mt 3:8; Rm 1:13; Gl 5:22 [an] Mk 14:6; Gl 3:10; Jms 2:14-26 [ao] **1:23** Rm 6:8; 2Co 4:14; 13:4-5; 1Th 4:14; 5:9-10 [ap] Jn 12:26

TEXT MESSAGES

Text message

Did Paul say that gospel messengers whose motives are twisted are okay, so long as the message gets out? Paul seems unusually tolerant, when we might expect him to admonish and correct. The gospel message is so important that some tolerance is in order, even when the messenger is less than perfect. Paul does not insist that every messenger do as he does. As long as the core message is broadcast, good can come. What bothers you about God's messengers?

Be tolerant of peripheral differences in style when the essential message is clear and true: Christ crucified and risen for our salvation.

[A] **1:3** Or *for your every remembrance of me* [B] **1:6** Or *work among you* [C] **1:7** Or *because you have me in your heart* [D] **1:10** Or *until* [E] **1:13** Lit *praetorium*, a Lat word that can also refer to a military headquarters, to the governor's palace, or to Herod's palace. [F] **1:14** Other mss add *of God* [G] **1:15** The good will of men, or God's good will or favor [H] **1:17** Lit *sincerely, intending to raise tribulation to my bonds* [I] **1:19** Or *vindication*

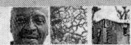

will remain and continue with all of you for
your progress and joy in the faith,[a] 26 so that,
because of me, your confidence may grow[b] in
Christ Jesus[c] when I come to you again.
27 Just one thing: Live your life[d] in a manner
worthy of the gospel of Christ. Then, whether
I come and see you or am absent, I will hear
about you that you are standing firm[e] in one[f]
spirit, with one mind,[A] working side by side
for the faith[g] that comes from the gospel,
28 not being frightened in any way by your
opponents.[h] This is a sign of destruction for

[a]1:25 Mt 8:10; Ac 3:16; Rm 1:8; 1Co 2:5; Gl 2:16; 1Tm 1:2; Heb 4:2; Jd 3 [b]1:26 1Co 15:58 [c]Rm 16:7; Eph 2:6; 1Pt 5:14 [d]1:27 Ac 23:1 [e]1Co 16:13; Gl 5:1; Eph 6:13-17; Php 4:1; 2Th 2:15 [f]Jn 11:52 [g]1Tm 3:9; 4:1,6; 5:8; 6:10,21 [h]1:28 1Co 16:9

Mission as a Linguistic Thread in Scripture

Ed Stetzer

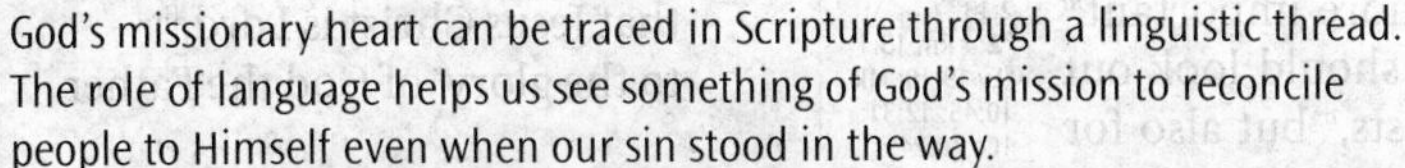

God's missionary heart can be traced in Scripture through a linguistic thread. The role of language helps us see something of God's mission to reconcile people to Himself even when our sin stood in the way.

The Lord commanded Noah, "Be fruitful and multiply and fill the earth" (Gn 9:1). However, humanity rebelled and attempted to live in one location. They decided to settle down and make a name for themselves. "Otherwise, we will be scattered over the face of the whole earth" (Gn 11:4).

At our rebellion, God pressed His mission forward by confusing the language, causing people to scatter. It was God's intent to keep us from our self-glorifying activity so that He could once again lead us to Himself. God divided the language and scattered the people in order to fill the earth.

Throughout the OT, Israel was to bring the nations "up to" Jerusalem to worship the one true God. Israel was not faithful to that mission. Moving forward several thousand years, we arrive at Pentecost in Acts 2. As was the custom of all Jews, the apostles and early believers gathered in Jerusalem, the center point of religious practice and the place where Jesus completed His ministry.

At Pentecost God gathered the nations to hear about His redemptive work through Peter's sermon. God delivered His gospel declaration to the masses and His Spirit upon those who believed in Christ. When the Spirit came, people spoke in other tongues, but they heard everything in one voice. Babel had been the place where God divided language and Jerusalem was now the place where the nations heard God's redemption in one voice.

From the linguistic miracle in Jerusalem, they are sent "out from" Jerusalem. In the OT, they were to bring the nations to Jerusalem. As the Spirit came in power, He accomplished what Israel could not—the tongues of the nations praised God's name in Jerusalem. Then they understood what Jesus had said just a chapter earlier. Jesus reversed the direction—"up to Jerusalem" in the OT became "out from Jerusalem" in the NT. Jesus said His work would move from Jerusalem, to Judea, to Samaria, and to the uttermost part of the earth.

As the church of today, we are under the commission to carry the gospel to all the people groups of the world. Though we hold no illusions that by our wit and abilities this task can be done, we can look with hope to the end of the Scriptures about what will occur. In Revelation 7:9, John wrote that he saw a "vast multitude from every nation, tribe, people, and language, which no one could number, standing before the throne and before the Lamb" for the purpose of worshiping the God of salvation. We wait for the day when we see what John saw. One day every tongue, tribe, and nation will be united around the throne of God singing one message: "Salvation belongs to our God, who is seated on the throne, and to the Lamb" (Rv 7:10).

[A]1:27 Lit *soul*

them,[a] but of your deliverance[b]—and this is
from God. 29 For it has been given to you on
Christ's behalf not only to believe[c] in Him,
but also to suffer for Him, 30 having the same
struggle that you saw I had and now hear that
I have.

Christian Humility

2 If then there is any encouragement in
Christ, if any consolation of love,[d] if any
fellowship with the Spirit,[e] if any affection
and mercy,[f] 2 fulfill my joy by thinking the
same way,[g] having the same love,[h] sharing
the same feelings, focusing on one[i] goal. 3 Do
nothing out of rivalry[j] or conceit,[k] but in humility[l] consider others as more important[m]
than yourselves. 4 Everyone should look out
not only for his own interests,[n] but also for
the interests of others.[o]

Christ's Humility and Exaltation

5 Make your own attitude that of Christ
Jesus,

6 who, existing in the form of God,
did not consider equality with God[p]
as something to be used
for His own advantage.[A]
7 Instead He emptied Himself[q]
by assuming the form of a ·slave,[r]
taking on the likeness of men.[s]
And when He had come as a man
in His external form,
8 He humbled Himself
by becoming obedient
to the point of death—
even to death on a cross.[t]
9 For this reason God
highly exalted Him[u]
and gave Him the name
that is above every name,
10 so that at the name of Jesus
every knee will bow[v]—
of those who are in heaven[w]
and on earth
and under the earth[x]—
11 and every tongue[y] should confess
that Jesus Christ is Lord,[B]
to the glory[z] of God the Father.

Lights in the World

12 So then, my dear friends,[aa] just as you have
always obeyed,[ab] not only in my presence, but
now even more in my absence, work out your
own salvation with fear and trembling. 13 For
it is God who is working in you, enabling you
both to desire and to work out His good purpose. 14 Do everything without grumbling[ac]
and arguing,[ad] 15 so that you may be blameless[ae]
and pure,[af] children of God who are faultless[ag] in a crooked[ah] and perverted[ai] generation,[aj] among whom you shine like stars in the
world. 16 Hold firmly to[C] the message[ak] of life.
Then I can boast[al] in the day of Christ[am] that I
didn't run or labor for nothing. 17 But even if I
am poured out[an] as a ·drink offering[ao] on the
sacrifice and service of your faith, I am glad
and rejoice with all of you. 18 In the same way
you should also be glad and rejoice with me.

Timothy and Epaphroditus

19 Now I hope in the Lord Jesus[ap] to send
Timothy[aq] to you soon so that I also may be
encouraged when I hear news about you.
20 For I have no one else like-minded who
will genuinely care about your interests; 21 all
seek their own interests,[ar] not those of Jesus
Christ.[as] 22 But you know his proven character,
because he has served with me in the gospel

GOD WHO SENDS

The Beauty of Mission

To be on mission as God's messenger to bring his good news is a thing of beauty because it is participation in his redemptive purpose. It is being God's instrument to bring the good news his salvation provides. It is the beauty not just of purpose, but of the sending purpose.

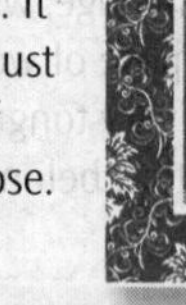

(DUBOSE, 95)

[a] **1:28** Mt 7:13; Rm 9:22 [b] Ac 4:12; 2Co 7:10; Heb 5:9 [c] **1:29** Mk 11:24; Jn 3:16; Ac 10:43; Rm 10:9; 1Pt 1:8-10 [d] **2:1** Rm 5:8; 15:30; 2Th 2:16; 1Jn 3:16; 4:9-10,16 [e] 1Co 12:13; 2Co 13:13; Eph 4:3 [f] Col 3:12 [g] **2:2** Rm 12:16; 15:5; 2Co 13:11; Php 4:2 [h] 2Th 1:3; 1Jn 3:16 [i] Jn 11:52 [j] **2:3** Rm 2:8 [k] Gl 5:26 [l] Col 3:12 [m] Rm 13:1; Php 3:8; 4:7; 1Pt 2:13 [n] **2:4** Rm 15:1 [o] Lv 19:18; Mk 10:45; 12:31; 1Co 10:24; 13:5; Php 2:21 [p] **2:6** Is 9:6; Jn 1:1,14; 20:28; Rm 9:5; Col 1:15-16; Ti 2:13; Heb 1:2-13; 2Pt 1:1; 1Jn 4:14-15 [q] **2:7** Mk 9:12; 2Co 8:9; 13:4 [r] Is 42:1; 53:12; Mt 20:28; Mk 10:45 [s] Jn 1:14; Rm 8:3; Gl 4:4; 1Tm 2:5; Heb 2:17 [t] **2:8** Lk 23:26; Php 3:10 [u] **2:9** Is 52:13; 53:12; Dn 7:14; Ac 2:32,33; 5:30,31; Eph 1:20-21; Heb 2:9 [v] **2:10** Is 45:23 [w] 2Co 5:1; Eph 1:20; 2:6; 3:10; 6:12; Heb 3:1; 12:22 [x] Mt 28:18; Eph 1:10; Rv 5:13 [y] **2:11** Is 45:23; Rm 10:9; 14:11; 1Co 12:3 [z] Lk 9:32; Jn 17:24; 2Co 3:18; 2Pt 3:18 [aa] **2:12** Phm 1 [ab] Mk 1:27; Ac 16:14,32,33; Rm 6:12 [ac] **2:14** Jn 7:12; Ac 6:1; 1Pt 4:9 [ad] 1Tm 2:8 [ae] **2:15** Lk 1:6 [af] Mt 10:16; Rm 16:19 [ag] Jd 24 [ah] Lk 3:5; Ac 2:40; 1Pt 2:18 [ai] Mt 17:17 [aj] Dt 32:5 [ak] **2:16** Lk 8:21; Jn 18:32; Ac 17:11; Heb 4:12 [al] Rm 2:17; Gl 6:4; Php 1:26 [am] Php 1:6,15 [an] **2:17** Php 1:7 [ao] Ex 25:29; Nm 28:7 [ap] **2:19** Lk 24:3 [aq] Ac 16:1; 1Tm 1:2 [ar] **2:21** Rm 15:1; 2Tm 3:2 [as] 1Co 10:24; Php 1:15

[A] **2:6** Or *to be grasped*, or *to be held on to* [B] **2:11** Gk *kurios* = Yahweh; Is 42:8 LXX [C] **2:16** Or *Offer*, or *Hold out*

ministry like a son with a father. 23 Therefore, I hope to send him as soon as I see how things go with me. 24 I am convinced in the Lord that I myself will also come quickly.[a]

25 But I considered it necessary to send you Epaphroditus[b] — my brother, coworker, and fellow soldier, as well as your messenger and minister to my need[c] — 26 since he has been longing for all of you and was distressed because you heard that he was sick. 27 Indeed, he was so sick that he nearly died. However, God had mercy on him, and not only on him but also on me, so that I would not have one grief on top of another. 28 For this reason, I am very eager to send him so that you may rejoice when you see him again and I may be less anxious. 29 Therefore, welcome him in the Lord with all joy and hold men like him in honor, 30 because he came close to death for the work[d] of Christ, risking his life to make up what was lacking in your ministry to me.

Knowing Christ

3 Finally, my ·brothers, rejoice[e] in the Lord. To write to you again about this is no trouble for me and is a protection for you.

2 Watch out for "dogs,"[A] watch out for evil[f] workers, watch out for those who mutilate the flesh. 3 For we are the circumcision,[g] the ones who serve by the Spirit[h] of God, boast in Christ Jesus,[i] and do not put confidence in the flesh — 4 although I once also had confidence in the flesh. If anyone else thinks he has grounds for confidence in the flesh, I have more: 5 circumcised the eighth day;[j] of the nation of Israel,[k] of the tribe of Benjamin,[l] a Hebrew born of Hebrews; regarding the law,[m] a ·Pharisee; 6 regarding zeal,[n] persecuting[o] the church; regarding the righteousness that is in the law,[p] blameless.[q]

7 But everything that was a gain to me, I have considered to be a loss because of Christ. 8 More than that, I also consider everything to be a loss in view of the surpassing value[r] of knowing Christ[s] Jesus my Lord. Because of Him I have suffered the loss of all things and consider them filth, so that I may gain Christ[t] 9 and be found in Him, not having a righteousness of my own from the law,[u] but one that is through faith in Christ[B] — the righteousness from God based on faith.[v] 10 My goal is to know Him and the power of His resurrection and the fellowship of His sufferings,[w] being conformed to His death,[x] 11 assuming that I will somehow reach the resurrection from among the dead.

Reaching Forward to God's Goal

12 Not that I have already reached the goal or am already fully mature, but I make every effort to take hold[y] of it because I also have been taken hold of by Christ Jesus. 13 Brothers, I do not[C] consider myself to have taken hold of it. But one thing I do: Forgetting what is behind[z] and reaching forward to what is ahead, 14 I pursue as my goal the prize promised by God's heavenly[D] call in Christ Jesus.[aa] 15 Therefore, all who are mature should think this way. And if you think differently about anything, God will reveal[ab] this also to you. 16 In any case, we should live up to whatever truth we have attained. 17 Join in imitating me, brothers, and observe those who live according to the example you have in us. 18 For I have often told you, and now say again with tears, that many live as enemies of the cross[ac] of Christ. 19 Their end is destruction; their god is their stomach; their glory[ad] is in their shame. They are focused on earthly things, 20 but our citizenship is in heaven, from which we also eagerly wait for a Savior, the Lord Jesus Christ. 21 He will transform the body of our humble condition into the likeness of His glorious[ae] body,[af] by the power that enables Him to subject everything to Himself.

Practical Counsel

4 So then, my ·brothers, you are dearly loved and longed for — my joy and crown.[ag] In this manner stand firm[ah] in the Lord, dear friends. 2 I urge Euodia and I urge Syntyche to agree in the Lord. 3 Yes, I also ask you, true partner,[E] to help these women who have contended for the gospel at my side, along with Clement and the rest of my coworkers whose names are in the book of life. 4 Rejoice in the Lord always. I will say it again: Rejoice! 5 Let

[a] **2:24** Php 1:7
[b] **2:25** Php 4:18
[c] Mt 6:8
[d] **2:30** Mk 14:6; 2Co 9:8; Gl 3:10; Jms 2:14-26
[e] **3:1** Rm 12:12; 2Co 6:10; Php 1:18
[f] **3:2** 2Co 13:7
[g] **3:3** Gl 6:15
[h] Rm 8:4; Gl 5:25; 1Tm 3:16
[i] Rm 16:7; Eph 2:6; Php 1:1,15; 1Pt 5:14
[j] **3:5** Gn 17:12,25; 21:4; Lv 12:3; Lk 1:59; 2:21
[k] Rm 9:6
[l] Ps 68:27
[m] Ac 5:34; 22:3; Gl 1:14; 5:4
[n] **3:6** Rm 10:2
[o] Ac 22:2-5; 26:9-11; 1Co 15:9; Gl 1:13; 1Tm 1:13; 2Tm 3:12
[p] Rm 3:21; 9:31; 10:4-5; Gl 2:21; 3:21
[q] Lk 1:6; Rm 7:9-10
[r] **3:8** Php 2:3
[s] Jn 17:3; 2Co 4:6; Gl 4:8-9; Php 1:15; Col 2:2; 1Jn 4:8
[t] 1Pt 3:1
[u] **3:9** Rm 10:5
[v] Rm 3:22; 10:4; Gl 2:21; Heb 11:7
[w] **3:10** Rm 8:17; 2Co 1:5-7; Col 1:24; 1Pt 4:13; 5:1,9
[x] Rm 6:5; 8:36; 2Co 4:7-12; 12:9-10; Gl 6:17
[y] **3:12** Jn 1:5; 12:35; Rm 9:30; 1Co 9:24; Eph 3:18
[z] **3:13** Lk 9:62; 17:31
[aa] **3:14** Rm 16:7; Eph 2:6; Php 1:1,15; 1Pt 5:14
[ab] **3:15** Lk 10:21
[ac] **3:18** Lk 23:26; 1Co 1:17; Gl 6:12
[ad] **3:19** Lk 14:10; Jn 5:41,44; 8:50,54; 12:43; Rm 9:4; 1Co 11:15; 2Co 6:8; 1Th 2:6
[ae] **3:21** 1Pt 5:4
[af] 1Co 6:13; 1Jn 3:2
[ag] **4:1** Rv 12:1
[ah] Rm 14:4; 1Co 16:13; Php 1:27; 2:2

A **3:2** An expression of contempt for the unclean, those outside the people of God B **3:9** Or *through the faithfulness of Christ* C **3:13** Other mss read *not yet* D **3:14** Or *upward* E **4:3** Or *true Syzygus*, possibly a person's name your graciousness be known to everyone. The Lord is near.[a] 6 Don't worry about anything, but in everything, through prayer and petition with thanksgiving, let your requests be made known to God. 7 And the peace of God, which surpasses[b] every thought, will guard your hearts and minds in Christ Jesus.[c]

8 Finally brothers, whatever is true,[d] whatever is honorable,[e] whatever is just,[f] whatever is pure,[g] whatever is lovely, whatever is commendable — if there is any moral excellence[h] and if there is any praise — dwell on these things. 9 Do what you have learned and received[i] and heard and seen in me, and the God of peace will be with you.

Appreciation of Support

10 I rejoiced in the Lord greatly that once again[j] you renewed your care for me.[k] You were, in fact, concerned about me but lacked the opportunity to show it. 11 I don't say this out of need, for I have learned to be content in whatever circumstances I am. 12 I know both how to have a little, and I know how to have a lot.[l] In any and all circumstances I have learned the secret of being content — whether well fed or hungry, whether in abundance or in need. 13 I am able to do all things through Him[A] who strengthens me.[m] 14 Still, you did well by sharing with me in my hardship.

15 And you Philippians[n] know that in the early days of the gospel,[o] when I left Macedonia,[p] no church shared with me in the matter of giving and receiving except you alone. 16 For even in Thessalonica[q] you sent gifts for my need[r] several times. 17 Not that I seek the gift, but I seek the profit[B,s] that is increasing to your account. 18 But I have received everything in full,[t] and I have an abundance. I am fully supplied, having received from Epaphroditus[u] what you provided — a fragrant offering, an acceptable sacrifice, pleasing[v] to God. 19 And my God[w] will supply all your needs according to His riches in glory in Christ Jesus. 20 Now to our God and Father[x] be glory forever and ever.[y] •Amen.[z]

Final Greetings

21 Greet every •saint in Christ Jesus. Those brothers who are with me greet you. 22 All the saints greet you, but especially those from Caesar's[aa] household.[ab] 23 The grace of the Lord Jesus Christ be with your spirit.[C,ac]

[a] **4:5** 1Co 16:22; Php 1:6; Heb 10:24-25; Jms 5:8; Rv 1:7; 3:11; 22:20 [b] **4:7** Php 2:3 [c] Rm 16:7; Eph 2:6; Php 1:1,15; 1Pt 5:14 [d] **4:8** Jn 8:14 [e] 1Tm 3:8,11; Ti 2:2 [f] Rm 1:17 [g] 2Co 7:11; 11:2; 1Tm 5:22; Ti 2:5; Jms 3:17; 1Pt 3:2; 1Jn 3:3 [h] 1Pt 2:9; 2Pt 1:3,5 [i] **4:9** Jd 3 [j] **4:10** Php 1:5 [k] 2Co 8:1-2; 11:9 [l] **4:12** 1Co 15:58 [m] **4:13** 2Co 12:9; Eph 3:16; Col 1:11; 1Tm 1:12; 2Tm 4:17 [n] **4:15** Php 1:1 [o] Ac 16:6-40; Php 1:5 [p] Ac 16:9 [q] **4:16** Ac 17:1 [r] Mt 6:8 [s] **4:17** Mt 3:8; Rm 1:13; Gl 5:22 [t] **4:18** Php 1:5 [u] Php 2:25 [v] Heb 13:21 [w] **4:19** Mt 27:46; Rm 1:8; Php 1:8 [x] **4:20** Gl 1:4; 1Th 1:3; 3:11,13 [y] Gl 1:5; 1Tm 1:17; 2Tm 4:18; Heb 13:21 [z] Rm 11:36; Rv 22:21 [aa] **4:22** Mt 22:17; Lk 20:22 [ab] Php 1:7 [ac] **4:23** Rm 1:9

[A] **4:13** Other mss read *Christ* [B] **4:17** Lit *fruit* [C] **4:23** Other mss add *Amen.*

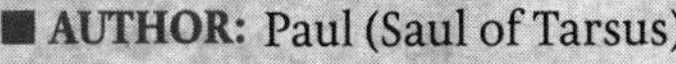

■ **AUTHOR:** Paul (Saul of Tarsus)

■■ **DATE:** Written around A.D. 60 in Rome while Paul was imprisoned

The mission of God is that Christ be praised as Savior and Lord. So when the worship of Christ begins to fade, the mission of God is in jeopardy. Church buildings erected without a confession of Christ as Lord are wasted space. Courts may dispense justice and markets may set fair prices with no acknowledgment of Christ as head of creation—nice, but likely to fail.

Paul writes this letter to a church which has begun to cease its worship of Christ. He warns them about their spiritual myopia and urges them to see again what God has done—what His sovereign plan has provided—in the person of Jesus, the Son of Man and Son of God. Christ has effected the great rescue (1:13). Stay strongly attached

COLOSSIANS

to Him, the One crucified and raised to life by God's power. The kingdom of God is the place of "all power" (1:11).

Who is this Christ to whom we must give our trust and praise? Paul answers in ways that will stir the soul and challenge the mind (chap. 1). God's mission is to build a kingdom not threatened by sin or fatigue, and to do it all for love. God desires that Christ, His Son, be known as Lord and King. God desires that all He has made eagerly and freely recognize and believe in Christ, delight in Christ, and find pleasure in following Christ.

As in Ephesians, Paul reminds readers that sin made them dead to God. They could not appropriate life; they were unwilling to confess Christ as King. But only God could made them alive—religious duties and periods of penance could never bring about life. Once alive, their roots sink deep into the soil of the Scriptures; their life is rebuilt by God's power, and they are thankful. It is a huge turnabout. As Paul reminds them: believe Him and give your life to Him. The rest will be found along the path that God will unfold. All you do, do it for God (3:17, 23). In that way the mission of God will become your life, and you will know God as friend and sovereign Lord.

Paul closes his letter with practical advice and personal appeals. His eloquent descriptions of God's mission turns to quite simple matters of putting feet to the task, living in the light of God's promises and power. Family members are to support and respect each another. Obedience to those in authority is another way of putting feet to the task. All of us have a Master in heaven (4:1).

Paul has seen the mission of God clearly. He wrestled to put his vision of it into words; yet Paul had needs too. His own path involved writing from a prison cell in Rome. Yet the mission of God had a hold on his heart that four dim walls could not imprison.

Greeting

1 Paul, an apostle of Christ Jesus by God's
will,[a] and Timothy[b] our[A] brother:
2 To the •saints in Christ at Colossae, who
are faithful •brothers.
Grace to you and peace from God our Father.[B]

Thanksgiving

3 We always thank God, the Father of our
Lord Jesus Christ, when we pray for you, 4 for
we have heard of your faith in Christ Jesus
and of the love you have for all the saints 5 because of the hope reserved for you in heaven.
You have already heard about this hope in the
message of truth,[c] the gospel 6 that has come
to you. It is bearing fruit[d] and growing all
over the world,[e] just as it has among you since
the day you heard it and recognized God's
grace[f] in the truth.[C,g] 7 You learned this from
Epaphras,[h] our dearly loved fellow •slave. He
is a faithful servant of the •Messiah[i] on your[D]
behalf, 8 and he has told us about your love in
the Spirit.[j]

Prayer for Spiritual Growth

9 For this reason also, since the day we
heard this, we haven't stopped praying for
you. We are asking[k] that you may be filled
with the knowledge[l] of His will[m] in all wisdom and spiritual understanding,[E] 10 so that
you may •walk worthy of the Lord, fully pleasing to Him, bearing fruit in every good work[n]
and growing in the knowledge of God.[o] 11 May
you be strengthened[p] with all power,[q] according to His glorious[r] might, for all endurance
and patience, with joy 12 giving thanks to the
Father, who has enabled you[F] to share in the
saints'[G] inheritance in the light.[s] 13 He has rescued[t] us from the domain of darkness and
transferred us into the kingdom[u] of the Son[v]
He loves.[w] 14 We have •redemption,[H] the forgiveness of sins, in Him.

The Centrality of Christ

15 He is the image of the invisible God,[x]
the firstborn over all creation.[I,y]
16 For everything was created by Him,[z]
in heaven and on earth,
the visible and the invisible,
whether thrones or dominions
or rulers or authorities—
all things have been created
through Him and for Him.[aa]
17 He is before all things,[ab]
and by Him all things[ac] hold together.
18 He is also the head of the body,
the church;
He is the beginning,[ad]
the firstborn from the dead,[ae]
so that He might come to have
first place in everything.
19 For God was pleased to have
all His fullness[af] dwell in Him,[ag]
20 and through Him to reconcile
everything to Himself
by making peace[ah]
through the blood[ai] of His cross[J,aj]—
whether things on earth or things
in heaven.

21 Once you were alienated and hostile in
your minds because of your evil actions.
22 But now He has reconciled you by His physical body[K] through His death,[ak] to present
you holy, faultless,[al] and blameless before
Him[am]— 23 if indeed you remain grounded
and steadfast in the faith[an] and are not shifted
away from the hope[ao] of the gospel that you
heard. This gospel has been proclaimed in all
creation[ap] under heaven,[aq] and I, Paul,[ar] have
become a servant of it.

Paul's Ministry

24 Now I rejoice in my sufferings[as] for you,
and I am completing in my flesh what is lacking in Christ's afflictions for His body,[at] that
is, the church. 25 I have become its servant,
according to God's administration that was
given to me for you, to make God's message
fully known, 26 the •mystery hidden for ages
and generations but now revealed to His
saints. 27 God wanted to make known among
the Gentiles the glorious wealth of this mystery, which is Christ[au] in you, the hope[av]

[a] **1:1** 1Co 1:1; 2Co 1:1; Eph 1:1; 2Tm 1:1 [b] Ac 16:1; 1Tm 1:2 [c] **1:5** Ps 119:142; Jn 14:6; 2Co 11:10; Eph 1:13; 2Tm 2:15; 3Jn 3 [d] **1:6** Mk 4:8 [e] Mt 13:38; 24:14; Rm 3:6; 2Pt 2:20 [f] 2Pt 3:18 [g] 2Th 2:10 [h] **1:7** Col 4:12; Phm 23 [i] Mt 1:17; Eph 5:2 [j] **1:8** Ps 51:11; Jn 1:33; Ac 2:4; Rm 8:9; Ti 3:5; Rv 1:10; 3:22 [k] **1:9** Jn 14:13; Jms 1:5 [l] Pr 2:6; Col 3:10 [m] Eph 1:9 [n] **1:10** 2Co 9:8; Gl 3:10 [o] Pr 2:6; Jn 17:3; 2Pt 1:2; 1Jn 4:8 [p] **1:11** Php 4:13 [q] Ac 4:33; 2Co 13:4 [r] Lk 9:32; Jn 17:24; 2Co 3:18; 2Pt 3:18 [s] **1:12** Ps 36:9; Jn 12:46 [t] **1:13** Mt 27:43 [u] Mt 3:2; Mk 1:15; Ac 20:25 [v] Jn 5:19; Heb 1:2 [w] Mt 3:17; Jn 3:16; 15:10; 17:26; 1Jn 4:16 [x] **1:15** Php 2:6 [y] Jn 1:3; Rv 3:14 [z] **1:16** Gn 1:1; Mk 13:19 [aa] Jn 1:3; Rm 11:36; 1Co 8:6; Eph 1:10,21 [ab] **1:17** Jn 1:1-2; 8:58; Heb 1:2-3 [ac] Ps 104:24 [ad] **1:18** Gn 1:1; Mk 1:1; Jn 1:1; Ac 26:4 [ae] Ac 26:23; 1Co 15:20,23; Rv 1:5 [af] **1:19** Ps 72:19; Is 6:3; Jr 23:24; Ezk 43:5; 44:4; Jn 1:14,16; Eph 3:19; Php 2:6; Col 2:9 [ag] Dt 12:5 [ah] **1:20** Ac 7:26; Eph 2:14 [ai] Heb 9:12 [aj] Lk 9:23; 23:26 [ak] **1:22** Php 2:8 [al] Jd 24 [am] 2Co 4:14 [an] **1:23** Gl 2:16; Jd 3 [ao] 1Th 1:3

[ap] Rv 3:14 [aq] Rm 10:18; Eph 6:9 [ar] Ac 13:9 [as] **1:24** 2Co 1:4; Php 1:29; 3:10 [at] Eph 4:4 [au] **1:27** Col 2:2 [av] 1Th 1:3

[A] **1:1** Lit *the* [B] **1:2** Other mss add *and the Lord Jesus Christ* [C] **1:6** Or *and truly recognized God's grace* [D] **1:7** Other mss read *our* [E] **1:9** Or *all spiritual wisdom and understanding* [F] **1:12** Other mss read *us* [G] **1:12** Or *holy ones'* [H] **1:14** Other mss add *through His blood* [I] **1:15** The One who is preeminent over all creation [J] **1:20** Other mss add *through Him* [K] **1:22** His body of flesh on the cross

The Centrality of Christ in Mission

Philip Nation

The person and work of Jesus is essential to our exploration of the mission of God. In fact, without Jesus, the exploration would be fruitless as He is the central figure of the redemptive work of God. When we discuss the gospel and God's mission, it is tempting to focus solely on theological statements and activities done by the church. However, at the core of the gospel is not an idea but a person—Christ. At the core of God's mission is not an action by humans but the work accomplished by God the Son through His incarnation. Christ is the center of God's mission and we are the beneficiaries of who He is and what He has done.

The Incarnation of Jesus

In Colossians 1:15-20, we are brought face-to-face with the fact that Jesus is God in the flesh. The man born in Bethlehem and reared in Nazareth is "the image of the invisible God" (v.15) and had the fullness of God dwelling in Him (v.19). The incarnation is a nearly impossible idea to comprehend. The fact that the eternal God chose to live in a human body is amazing and mind-boggling. Yet, for God's mission to be accomplished, this was the necessary action.

The incarnation is both merciful and necessary. It is merciful in that through God's arrival on Earth in human form, He will take up the sacrificial work that is impossible for everyone else. For thousands of years, blood had been spilt upon the altars of the Temple in Jerusalem and the tabernacles of worship used by the Hebrew people. They had placed their faith in the Lord that He would accept them and deliver a Messiah to set all things right between God and man.

In the incarnation, God Himself takes up the work. It is a task that no mere mortal can accomplish. Thus, God humbles Himself and condescends to our level of existence. He was born as we are, lived as we do, experienced life in the same manner as us all yet without sin. He was born as a man but He never—not once—succumbs to temptation. He is a man but has the very nature of God.

Uniquely Capable of Reconciliation

It is only through the work of Christ that people and creation can be reconciled to God. There are a number of reasons for His solitary ability to accomplish this task. As 1:16 states, He is the One who created all things and holds all things together. As the only One with authority over the created order, God is the only One capable of redeeming us since we have fallen into sin. Though we might be puzzled by all of this power residing in this one Man, it is vital to remember that Jesus is not whom we often make Him out to be. Though He taught, He is more than a great teacher. Though He performed miracles, He was not just a magical figure. Though He lived perfectly, He was not just an ethics professor. Jesus the Messiah was the Creator God in flesh and was the only One capable of reconciling creation to Himself.

Also, Christ is stated to be the "firstborn over all creation" (1:15). The phrase means that Jesus, as Messiah, ranks as preeminent over all other people. By virtue of His divine nature, He is the greatest of all who have been born among humanity. Being in very nature God, Christ has the unique character to reconcile us to God. "Firstborn" is also associated with His resurrection in verse 18, describing Him as "the firstborn from the dead." He is supreme not only in His place among the living but also in His place among those who have died. Jesus is solitary in His ability to defeat death and thus bring peace to those who trust him.

Making Peace Through the Cross

The life of Jesus is without doubt the most important period of time in history. As He is central to the mission of God, His life is central to our existence. However, we can hone in even further to say that it is the death and resurrection of Christ that are the key events within the existence of our created order. Paul wrote in 1:20 that Jesus makes peace between Himself and people "through the blood of His cross."

The crucifixion and resurrection event in the life of Jesus is central to the mission of God because it is through this unique work that God reconciles us to Himself. He is the only person born before, during, or after His time on earth that can accomplish the work done through the cross. Throughout the passage, it is important to note how the personal pronouns are used in reference to Jesus. From the act of creation to the work of making peace between God and man, it is only possible through Jesus because He is the Messiah, fully God and fully man.

Head of the Church

The passage points to one other central role held by Christ: "head of the body, the church" (v.18). As we begin to act upon the mission that has been entrusted to us, we do so with the understanding that it is an inherited mission. We are given the work of proclaiming reconciliation that was accomplished by someone else, namely Jesus. He has completed the work and we now bear witness to that work under His direction.

As members of the church, we should be encouraged that He has not left us to our own devices. Rather, Jesus remains engaged with the reconciling work still to take place between God and individuals who hear the gospel. He fits believers together as members of the church, indwelt by His Spirit, to proclaim His salvation and serve so that others might see a portrait of His grace in our lives. The mission is accomplished because Jesus is uniquely the Savior who has died in our place and empowers His church.

of glory. 28 We proclaim Him, warning and
teaching everyone with all wisdom, so that
we may present everyone mature in Christ.
29 I labor for this, striving[a] with His strength
that works powerfully in me.[b]

2 For I want you to know how great a struggle[c] I have for you, for those in Laodicea,[d]
and for all who have not seen me in person.
2 I want their hearts to be encouraged[e] and
joined together in love, so that they may
have all the riches of assured understanding and have the knowledge of God's ·mys-
tery[f] — Christ.[A,g] 3 All the treasures of wisdom[h]
and knowledge[i] are hidden in Him.

Christ versus the Colossian Heresy

4 I am saying this so that no one will deceive
you with persuasive arguments. 5 For I may be
absent in body, but I am with you in spirit,[j]
rejoicing to see how well ordered you are and
the strength of your faith in Christ.

6 Therefore, as you have received[k] Christ
Jesus the Lord,[l] ·walk in Him, 7 rooted and
built up in Him[m] and established in the faith,
just as you were taught,[n] overflowing with
gratitude.

8 Be careful that no one takes you captive
through philosophy and empty deceit based
on human tradition,[o] based on the elemental
forces of the world, and not based on Christ.[p]
9 For the entire fullness[q] of God's nature[B]
dwells bodily[C] in Christ, 10 and you have been
filled by Him, who is the head[r] over every
ruler and authority. 11 You were also circumcised in Him with a circumcision not done
with hands, by putting off the body of flesh,[s]
in the circumcision of the ·Messiah.[D,t] 12 Having been buried with Him[u] in baptism, you

[a] **1:29** Jd 3 [b] 1Co 15:10 [c] **2:1** 2Tm 4:7 [d] Col 4:13-16; Rv 1:11; 3:14 [e] **2:2** Lk 16:25; Col 4:8 [f] Php 3:8 [g] Col 1:27 [h] **2:3** Pr 3:19; Is 11:2; 45:3; Jr 23:5; Ac 7:22; 1Co 1:21 [i] 1Co 14:6 [j] **2:5** Ps 51:12; 1Th 2:17 [k] **2:6** Jd 3 [l] Eph 3:11 [m] **2:7** Eph 2:20 [n] Eph 4:21; Heb 13:9 [o] **2:8** Mk 7:3 [p] 1Tm 6:20 [q] **2:9** Php 2:6; Col 1:19 [r] **2:10** 1Co 11:3; Eph 1:22; 4:15; 5:23 [s] **2:11** Col 1:22; 3:9 [t] Mt 1:17; Eph 5:2 [u] **2:12** Rm 6:4

[A] **2:2** Other mss read *mystery of God, both of the Father and of Christ*; other ms variations exist on this v. [B] **2:9** Or *of the deity* [C] **2:9** Or *nature lives in a human body* [D] **2:11** = His death

were also raised with Him[a] through faith in the working of God, who raised Him from the dead.[b] 13 And when you were dead in trespasses and in the uncircumcision of your flesh, He made you alive with Him and forgave us all our trespasses. 14 He erased the certificate of debt, with its obligations, that was against us and opposed to us, and has taken it out of the way by nailing it to the cross.[c] 15 He disarmed the rulers and authorities and disgraced them publicly; He triumphed over them by Him.[A,d]

16 Therefore, don't let anyone judge[e] you in regard to food and drink[f] or in the matter of a festival or a new moon[g] or a Sabbath day.[B] 17 These are a shadow[h] of what was to come;[i] the substance is[C] the Messiah.[j] 18 Let no one disqualify you,[D,k] insisting on ascetic practices[l] and the worship of angels, claiming access to a visionary realm and inflated[m] without cause by his unspiritual[E] mind. 19 He doesn't hold on to the head, from whom the whole body,[n] nourished and held together by its ligaments and tendons, develops with growth from God.

20 If you died with the Messiah[o] to the elemental forces of this world, why do you live as if you still belonged to the world? Why do you submit to regulations: 21 "Don't handle, don't taste, don't touch"? 22 All these regulations refer to what is destroyed by being used up; they are commands and doctrines of men. 23 Although these have a reputation of wisdom[p] by promoting ascetic practices, humility, and severe treatment of the body, they are not of any value in curbing self-indulgence.[F,q]

The Life of the New Man

3 So if you have been raised with the •Messiah, seek what is above, where the Messiah is, seated at the right hand of God.[r] 2 Set your minds on what is above, not on what is on the earth.[s] 3 For you have died,[t] and your life is hidden with the Messiah in God. 4 When the Messiah, who is your[G] life, is revealed,[u] then you also will be revealed with Him in glory.[v]

[a]2:12 Eph 2:6; Col 3:1 [b]Mt 17:9; Jn 5:25; 20:9; 21:14; Ac 2:24 [c]2:14 Lk 9:23; 23:26 [d]2:15 Lk 10:18; Jn 12:31; 16:11; Eph 6:12; Heb 2:14 [e]2:16 Lk 6:37 [f]Jn 6:55; Rm 14:3,17; 1Co 8:4; Heb 9:10 [g]Ps 81:3 [h]2:17 Heb 8:5; 10:1 [i]Rm 8:38 [j]Gl 3:24; 5:2 [k]2:18 1Co 9:24; Php 3:14 [l]Col 3:12 [m]1Co 4:6 [n]2:19 1Co 6:13; Eph 4:4 [o]2:20 Rm 6:8; 1Pt 2:24 [p]2:23 Ac 7:22 [q]1Tm 4:8 [r]3:1 Heb 10:12 [s]3:2 Php 3:19 [t]3:3 Rm 6:8 [u]3:4 2Co 4:11; 1Jn 1:2; 2:28 [v]Lk 9:32; Jn 17:24; 2Co 3:18; 2Pt 3:18 [w]3:5 1Th 4:3,7 [x]Rm 1:26; 1Th 4:5 [y]Eph 5:3 [z]1Co 10:14; Gl 5:20; 1Pt 4:3 [aa]3:6 Jms 1:19; Rv 6:16 [ab]3:7 Lk 15:13; Rm 6:2 [ac]3:8 Rm 13:12 [ad]Jms 1:19 [ae]Rv 14:19 [af]1Co 14:20 [ag]Jn 10:33; Rv 13:6 [ah]Eph 4:22-31 [ai]3:9 Lv 19:11; 1Tm 2:7 [aj]Col 2:15 [ak]Eph 4:22 [al]3:10 Pr 31:25 [am]Mk 13:19; Jn 1:3; Rv 3:14 [an]3:11 Eph 1:23 [ao]3:12 Jn 3:16; 2Th 2:13; Rv 12:11 [ap]2Co 6:6 [aq]Ac 20:19; Eph 4:2; Php 2:3; Col 2:18,23; 1Pt 5:5 [ar]Jms 3:13 [as]2Tm 3:10 [at]3:13 2Co 2:7,10; 12:13; Eph 4:32 [au]3:15 Jn 14:27; 1Co 7:15; Php 4:7 [av]3:17 Jn 14:13; Php 2:10 [aw]3:18–4:1 Eph

5 Therefore, put to death what belongs to your worldly nature:[H] sexual immorality, impurity,[w] lust,[x] evil desire, and greed,[y] which is idolatry.[z] 6 Because of these, God's wrath[aa] comes on the disobedient,[I] 7 and you once •walked in these things when you were living[ab] in them. 8 But now you must also put away[ac] all the following: anger,[ad] wrath,[ae] malice,[af] slander,[ag] and filthy language from your mouth.[ah] 9 Do not lie[ai] to one another, since you have put off[aj] the old self[J,ak] with its practices 10 and have put on[al] the new self. You are being renewed in knowledge according to the image of your[K] Creator.[am] 11 In Christ[L] there is not Greek and Jew, circumcision and uncircumcision, barbarian, Scythian,[M] •slave and free; but Christ is all and in all.[an]

The Christian Life

12 Therefore, God's chosen ones, holy and loved,[ao] put on heartfelt compassion, kindness,[ap] humility,[aq] gentleness,[ar] and patience,[as] 13 accepting one another and forgiving one another if anyone has a complaint against another. Just as the Lord has forgiven you, so you must also forgive.[at] 14 Above all, put on love — the perfect bond of unity. 15 And let the peace of the Messiah, to which you were also called[au] in one body, control your hearts. Be thankful. 16 Let the message about the Messiah dwell richly among you, teaching and admonishing one another in all wisdom, and singing psalms, hymns, and spiritual songs, with gratitude in your hearts to God. 17 And whatever you do, in word or in deed, do everything in the name[av] of the Lord Jesus, giving thanks to God the Father through Him.

Christ in Your Home

18 Wives, be submissive to your
husbands, as is fitting in the Lord.[aw]
19 Husbands,[ax] love your wives[ay] and
don't be bitter[az] toward them.
20 Children,[ba] obey your parents in
everything, for this pleases the Lord.
21 Fathers,[bb] do not exasperate[bc] your

5:22–6:9 [ax]3:19 1Pt 3:1 [ay]Eph 5:25; 1Pt 3:1 [az]Rv 8:11; 10:9-10 [ba]3:20 Gn 3:16; Lv 10:14; Dt 31:12; Ps 37:25; Pr 20:7; Lk 1:7; Ac 2:39; Heb 2:13 [bb]3:21 Ps 103:13; Eph 6:4; Heb 11:23 [bc]2Co 9:2

A2:15 Or *them through it*; = through the cross B2:16 Or *or sabbaths* C2:17 Or *substance belongs to* D2:18 Or *no one cheat us out of your prize* E2:18 Lit *fleshly* F2:23 Lit *value against indulgence of the flesh* G3:4 Other mss read *our* H3:5 Lit *death the members on the earth* I3:6 Other mss omit *on the disobedient* J3:9 Lit *man*; = a person before conversion K3:10 Lit *his* L3:11 Lit *Where* M3:11 A term for a savage

Perpetua and Felicity (died 203)

Three women, arrested during the seasonal Roman persecutions of Christians, were each charged with treason for worshiping something other than the Roman emperor. Emperor Septimius Severus (A.D. 193–211) forbade his subjects to become Christians or Jews. Perpetua came from a home of wealth and status. Her pagan father begged her to renounce her Christian faith and save herself for the sake of the family. (Fathers had near absolute family control in Roman culture.) But Perpetua refused. Her personal account, written in the first person, describes the events leading up to her martyrdom. An eyewitness then appended the account of her death, along with the deaths of others who had been imprisoned along with her.

Perpetua had a young child who was not yet weaned when she was put in prison. Her mother was allowed to bring the child to her, and the father tried to use the child to get Perpetua to deny her faith. She steadfastly refused, as did the others. All of them were condemned to be torn to pieces by wild beasts.

Felicity was eight months pregnant. Two days before the scheduled games, she gave birth to a child who was adopted by a Christian woman.

All of them were then taken into the arena where wild beasts were released. The mission of God had so changed these women that neither public humiliation nor the fury of wild beasts would dissuade them. Christ was their Savior and companion even in the amphitheater in Carthage.

Stories of that day tell of Perpetua holding a wounded Felicity in her arms, bravely anticipating their death together. But the bull whose horns had begun to tear their flesh now seemed indifferent to the slaughter. Thousands of onlookers urged the beast to charge. The animal stood still. To finish the grim work, gladiators rushed forward. Felicity perished quickly. Then, stunned like the bull, the gladiator facing Perpetua hesitated. She herself, it is said, helped guide his sword, a picture of poise amid the shouting and chaos. So loyal were these women to Jesus Christ that several spectators, including the governor of Rome, reportedly converted.

Early martyrs showed a jaundiced world that the mission of God would not be turned back, no matter the threat. The presence of the living Christ would see them through to heaven's side when this rough world could hold them no longer.

children, so they won't become
discouraged.
22 Slaves, obey your human[a] masters
in everything. Don't work only while
being watched, in order to please
men, but work wholeheartedly,
fearing the Lord.[b]
23 Whatever you do, do it
enthusiastically,[A] as something
done for the Lord and not for men,[c]
24 knowing that you will receive the
reward of an inheritance from the
Lord. You serve the Lord Christ.
25 For the wrongdoer[d] will be paid
back for whatever wrong he has
done, and there is no favoritism.

4 Masters,[e] supply your ·slaves with what
is right and fair, since you know that
you too have a Master in heaven.

Speaking to God and Others

2 Devote yourselves[f] to prayer; stay alert in
it with thanksgiving. 3 At the same time, pray
also for us that God may open a door[g] to us
for the message, to speak the ·mystery of the
·Messiah,[h] for which I am in prison,[i] 4 so that
I may reveal it as I am required to speak. 5 Act
wisely toward outsiders, making the most of
the time.[j] 6 Your speech should always be gracious, seasoned with salt,[k] so that you may
know how you should answer each person.[l]

Christian Greetings

7 Tychicus,[m] our dearly loved brother, faithful[n] servant, and fellow slave in the Lord, will
tell you all the news about me. 8 I have sent
him to you for this very purpose, so that you
may know how we are[B] and so that he may encourage[o] your hearts.[p] 9 He is with Onesimus,[q]
a faithful and dearly loved brother, who is
one of you. They will tell you about everything here.
10 Aristarchus, my fellow prisoner, greets
you, as does Mark,[r] Barnabas's[s] cousin (concerning whom you have received instructions: if he comes to you, welcome him),
11 and so does Jesus who is called Justus. These
alone of the circumcision are my coworkers
for the kingdom of God, and they have been
a comfort to me. 12 Epaphras,[t] who is one of
you, a slave of Christ Jesus, greets you. He is
always contending[u] for you in his prayers,
so that you can stand mature and fully assured[C] in everything God wills.[v] 13 For I testify
about him that he works hard[D,w] for you, for
those in Laodicea,[x] and for those in Hierapolis. 14 Luke, the dearly loved physician, and
Demas[y] greet you. 15 Give my greetings to the
·brothers in Laodicea, and to Nympha and
the church in her home.[z] 16 When this letter
has been read among you, have it read also
in the church of the Laodiceans; and see that
you also read the letter from Laodicea. 17 And
tell Archippus,[aa] "Pay attention to the ministry you have received in the Lord, so that you
can accomplish it."[ab]
18 This greeting is in my own hand — Paul.
Remember my imprisonment.[ac] Grace be
with you.[E,ad]

[a] **3:22** Rm 1:3; 4:1; 8:4-5,12-13; 9:3,5; 1Co 1:26; 10:18; 2Co 1:17; 5:16; 10:2-3; 11:18; Gl 4:23,29; Eph 6:5
[b] Pr 1:7; Rv 14:7
[c] **3:23** Eph 6:7
[d] **3:25** Rv 2:11
[e] **4:1** Col 3:22
[f] **4:2** Rm 12:12
[g] **4:3** Ac 14:27; 1Co 16:9; 2Co 2:12
[h] 1Co 2:7; Eph 3:4; 5:2
[i] Ac 27:2; 28:16,30; Eph 6:18-20
[j] **4:5** Eph 5:15-17
[k] **4:6** Mk 9:50; Lk 14:34
[l] 1Pt 3:15
[m] **4:7** Ac 20:4; Ti 3:12
[n] Nm 23:19
[o] **4:8** Lk 16:25
[p] Eph 6:21-22; Col 2:2
[q] **4:9** Phm 10,16
[r] **4:10** Phm 24
[s] Ac 4:36
[t] **4:12** Col 1:7; Phm 23
[u] Jd 3
[v] Gl 1:4; Eph 1:9
[w] **4:13** Jd 3
[x] Col 2:1
[y] **4:14** 2Tm 4:10
[z] **4:15** Ac 12:12; Rm 16:5
[aa] **4:17** Phm 2
[ab] 2Tm 4:5
[ac] **4:18** Php 1:7
[ad] 1Tm 6:21; 2Tm 4:22; Ti 3:15

A **3:23** Lit *do it from the soul* B **4:8** Other mss read *that he may know how you are* C **4:12** Other mss read *and complete* D **4:13** Other mss read *he has a great zeal* E **4:18** Other mss add *Amen.*

■ **AUTHOR:** Paul (Saul of Tarsus)

■■ **DATE:** Both letters were written around A.D. 51 from Corinth

The two letters of Paul to new converts in Thessalonica, the major city in Macedonia, are among his earliest writings. According to Acts 17, Paul and Silas left their ministry in Thessalonica quickly, perhaps too fast for the new Christians then without leadership. The intent of Paul's letters is to encourage his small church, teach them, urge certain behavioral adjustments, and leave them with a more certain hope.

These letters are God's mission in action. Paul and his companions are telling the good news to Jews and Gentiles in a bustling city, likely at the synagogue first, then wherever willing people gather. The message is a radical change of vision. The true

1 THESSALONIANS

God loves them. In Jesus Christ God has saved them. Their faithful response to God is assurance that they have been forgiven, adopted into God's family, and given a mission of their own. They must learn to praise Jesus in all they do, and trust Jesus in all that they face.

Paul's approach in these letters carries an important lesson concerning the mission of God. Imagine Paul's predicament. He left new believers with less teaching than a longer visit would have afforded. Some of them knew the Old Testament well, but knew little about the power of God now operating through the Holy Spirit. Now without Paul, their questions must be many, and the pressure to abandon this new way must be continuous and heavy. Paul picks up his pen, and does just the opposite of what we might expect. Instead of getting into lessons vital to understanding faith, he writes about personal matters and his strong feelings for the believers. Paul is well over half way done with 1 Thessalonians before he offers any teaching at all!

Relationships have priority over lessons. Paul's bonds of affection with these new Christians come first, then the lessons unfold. There is a lesson in that, too.

In both letters, the big lesson concerns Jesus' return. Today there is hardly a more controversial topic than this. So many ideas on how and when and what follows—it's a wonder Paul even approached the subject.

Leadership consultants know that the big issue for most people is the future. Will we survive? Will our children prosper? Can we know what tomorrow brings? And the biggest of all—what's after death? Paul teaches the all-important truths of how God's mission reaches its end-point. Here is good news for every person. Jesus will return. Before that, the death of God's people is a time of transition leading to joy. Encourage one another, he says, for God's mission turns fear into freedom.

Greeting

1 Paul, Silvanus,[A,a] and Timothy:[b]
To the church of the Thessalonians[c] in
God the Father and the Lord Jesus Christ.
Grace to you and peace.[B]

Thanksgiving

2We always thank God for all of you, remembering you constantly in our prayers.
3We recall, in the presence of our God and
Father,[d] your work of faith,[e] labor of love, and
endurance of hope in our Lord Jesus Christ,[f]
4knowing your election,[g] *brothers loved[h] by
God.[i] 5For our gospel did not come to you
in word only, but also in power, in the Holy
Spirit,[j] and with much assurance. You know
what kind of men we were among you[k] for
your benefit, 6and you became imitators of
us and of the Lord when, in spite of severe
persecution, you welcomed the message[l]
with joy from the Holy Spirit. 7As a result,
you became an example to all the believers in
Macedonia[m] and Achaia.[n] 8For the Lord's message rang out from you, not only in Macedonia and Achaia, but in every place that your
faith[C,o] in God has gone out. Therefore, we
don't need to say anything, 9for they themselves report[D] what kind of reception[p] we
had from you: how you turned[q] to God from
idols[r] to serve the living[s] and true[t] God 10and
to wait[u] for His Son[v] from heaven, whom He
raised from the dead[w] — Jesus, who rescues
us[x] from the coming wrath.[y]

Paul's Conduct

2 For you yourselves know, *brothers, that
our visit[z] with you was not without result.
2On the contrary, after we had previously suffered,[aa] and we were treated outrageously in
Philippi,[ab] as you know, we were emboldened
by our God to speak the gospel of God to you
in spite of great opposition. 3For our exhortation didn't come from error or impurity[ac]
or an intent to deceive.[ad] 4Instead, just as we
have been approved by God to be entrusted[ae]
with the gospel,[af] so we speak, not to please
men, but rather God,[ag] who examines our
hearts.[ah] 5For we never used flattering speech,
as you know, or had greedy[ai] motives[aj] — God
is our witness[ak] — 6and we didn't seek glory[al]
from people, either from you or from others. 7Although we could have been a burden
as Christ's apostles,[am] instead we were gentle[E]
among you, as a nursing mother nurtures
her own children. 8We cared so much for you
that we were pleased to share with you not
only the gospel of God but also our own lives,
because you had become dear to us. 9For you
remember our labor and hardship, brothers.
Working[an] night and day so that we would not
burden any of you, we preached God's gospel
to you. 10You are witnesses,[ao] and so is God,
of how devoutly, righteously,[ap] and blame-
lessly[aq] we conducted ourselves with you believers. 11As you know, like a father with his
own children,[ar] 12we encouraged, comforted,
and implored each one of you to *walk worthy of God,[as] who calls you into His own kingdom[at] and glory.[au]

Reception and Opposition to the Message

13This is why we constantly thank God, because when you received the message about
God that you heard from us, you welcomed
it not as a human message, but as it truly is,[av]
the message of God,[aw] which also works effectively in you believers. 14For you, brothers, became imitators of God's churches in
Christ Jesus that are in Judea,[ax] since you have
also suffered[ay] the same things from people
of your own country,[az] just as they did from
the Jews 15who killed both the Lord Jesus[ba]
and the prophets and persecuted us;[bb] they
displease God and are hostile to everyone,
16hindering us from speaking to the Gentiles
so that they may be saved. As a result, they are
always completing the number of their sins,[bc]
and wrath has overtaken them at last.[F]

Paul's Desire to See Them

17But as for us, brothers, after we were
forced to leave you for a short time (in person, not in heart[bd]), we greatly desired and
made every effort to return[be] and see you face
to face. 18So we wanted to come to you — even
I, Paul, time and again — but Satan[bf] hindered

[a]**1:1** Ac 15:22; 2Co 1:19; 2Th 1:1; 1Pt 5:12 [b]Ac 16:1; 1Tm 1:2 [c]Ac 17:1 [d]**1:3** Php 4:20 [e]Rm 3:28; 9:32; Gl 2:16; 5:6; 2Th 1:11; Heb 6:1; Jms 2:14-26; Rv 2:19 [f]Ac 15:26 [g]**1:4** Mt 24:22; Eph 1:4 [h]Jn 3:16; Rv 12:11 [i]Dt 33:12; 2Th 2:13 [j]**1:5** Jn 1:33; Ac 2:4; Rm 8:9; 1Co 2:4; Gl 5:25; Ti 3:5; Rv 3:22 [k]Ac 20:18; 1Th 2:10 [l]**1:6** Heb 4:12 [m]**1:7** Ac 16:9 [n]Ac 18:12 [o]**1:8** Gl 2:16 [p]**1:9** Ac 17:1-9 [q]1Pt 2:25 [r]Gn 31:19; 1Co 8:4 [s]Dt 5:26 [t]Jn 4:23; 1Jn 5:20 [u]**1:10** Jd 21 [v]Heb 1:2 [w]Mt 17:9; Jn 5:25 [x]Mt 27:43 [y]Rm 2:5; 1Th 5:9; Rv 6:16 [z]**2:1** Ac 17:1-9 [aa]**2:2** Ac 16:19-24 [ab]Php 1:1 [ac]**2:3** 1Th 4:7 [ad]Ps 10:7 [ae]**2:4** Lk 16:11 [af]Ac 15:7; Gl 2:7; 1Tm 1:11 [ag]Jn 5:44; 12:43; 1Co 4:5; 2Co 10:18; Gl 1:10; Php 3:19; 1Th 2:15; 1Pt 3:4 [ah]Ps 17:3; Pr 21:2; Rm 8:27 [ai]**2:5** Eph 5:3 [aj]Mk 12:40; Lk 20:47; Jn 15:22; Ac 27:30; Php 1:18 [ak]Rm 1:9 [al]**2:6** Php 3:19 [am]**2:7** Ac 1:2; Jd 17 [an]**2:9** 2Jn 8 [ao]**2:10** Rm 1:9 [ap]Ti 2:12 [aq]1Th 5:23 [ar]**2:11** 1Co 4:14; Gl 4:19; 1Tm 1:2; Phm 10 [as]**2:12** 3Jn 6 [at]Mk 1:15; Ac 20:25 [au]Lk 9:32; 24:26; Jn 17:24; 2Co 3:18; 1Pt 5:1; 2Pt 3:18 [av]**2:13** 2Th 3:1 [aw]Lk 8:21 [ax]**2:14** Lk 1:5 [ay]Php 1:29 [az]Ac 17:5 [ba]**2:15** Lk 24:20 [bb]Rm 11:3 [bc]**2:16** Mt 23:30-32 [bd]**2:17** Col 2:5 [be]1Th 3:10 [bf]**2:18** Mt 4:1,10; Ac 13:10

[A]**1:1** Or *Silas*; Ac 15:22-32; 16:19-40; 17:1-16 [B]**1:1** Other mss add *from God our Father and the Lord Jesus Christ* [C]**1:8** Or *in every place news of your faith* [D]**1:9** Lit *report about us* [E]**2:7** Other mss read *infants* [F]**2:16** Or *to the end*

WORLDVIEW

The Mission of God in Post-Modern Europe

"Post-modern" refers to the idea that the "modern" era has passed, and something has replaced it. That modern era was the reckoning of certain bright European minds who found exquisite order in the universe. About the starry skies, calculations and mathematical laws could reveal patterns of order. About the human body and mind, rational systems explained universal human nature. In modern Europe, a gospel mediated by sacred orderliness fit quite well. A rational God created an ordered universe and properly designed an orderly way for people to worship.

Now much has changed. In art, literature, philosophy, and even politics, Europe has led the charge toward post-modernity, questioning both the self-congratulatory West (Europe has the best and brightest) and the fundamentals of physics and human nature. A post-modern climate insists that final answers are impossible, absolutes are only temporary, and moral options are entirely based on social-cultural needs, some of them quite subconscious. The best humanity can do is hobble forward, groping for an improved future through trial and error. Neither the ordered heavens nor human reason (and certainly not the claims of religion) are reliable guides, as once thought. We are orphans in a vast cosmos. Make your adjustment.

The mission of God in this post-modern climate, at first glance, faces considerable obstacles. Yet doors have opened as people have reckoned with their moorings and grown dissatisfied with the paucity of moral and spiritual assurance offered by post-modern advocates. Moreover, the church has made adjustments and shown a much more contemporary face. Old is not sacred merely for its arches and organs. New approaches carry the hope that old media never explored:

- Two devastating world wars have taught Europe the dangers of demagoguery. Europeans cautiously avoid messages framed as absolutes aimed at heightening public fear.
- A long history of religious wars, including Eastern Europe's recent slaughter in Kosovo, has created a visceral retrenchment from religious messages targeting minority peoples.
- Strong centrally controlled economies have bureaucratized life in most European countries. People find their groove, and government covers most exigencies. "Daily bread" is a state obligation.
- Faith groups do not make easy neighbors. Will Muslim dress be permitted in Europe? France says no; others must decide.

Europe has produced the most influential teachers of Christendom, both Catholic and Protestant, yet post-modern Europe seems superficially content to keep religion at a distance. Tradition requires some observance, but many are wary of religious enthusiasm.

The mission of God brings to post-modern Europe the vibrancy of a genuinely caring community (the church) together with the "impossible" claim of resurrection power. The Spirit of God is not bounded by rationalism or statism. Creative freedom abounds as God reaches a new generation indifferent to church but alive to spiritual reality. The poor and meek of Jesus' Beatitudes contrast sharply with towering cathedrals and vested dignitaries. But in the contrast, a hunger for spiritual experience is born anew.

us. 19 For who is our hope or joy[a] or crown[b] of
boasting[c] in the presence of our Lord[d] Jesus at
His coming?[e] Is it not you?[f] 20 For you are our
glory[g] and joy!

Anxiety in Athens

3 Therefore, when we could no longer
stand it, we thought it was better to be left
alone in Athens.[h] 2 And we sent Timothy,[i] our
brother and God's coworker[A] in the gospel
of Christ,[j] to strengthen and encourage you
concerning your faith, 3 so that no one will be
shaken by these persecutions. For you yourselves know that we are appointed to[B] this.
4 In fact, when we were with you, we told you
previously that we were going to suffer persecution, and as you know, it happened. 5 For
this reason, when I could no longer stand it,
I also sent him to find out about your faith,
fearing that the tempter had tempted you
and that our labor might be for nothing.

Encouraged by Timothy

6 But now Timothy has come to us[k] from you
and brought us good news about your faith
and love and reported that you always have
good memories of us, wanting to see us, as we
also want to see you.[l] 7 Therefore, ˙brothers, in
all our distress and persecution, we were encouraged about you through your faith. 8 For
now we live, if you stand firm[m] in the Lord.
9 How can we thank God for you in return for
all the joy[n] we experience before our God because of you, 10 as we pray very earnestly night
and day to see you face to face[o] and to complete what is lacking in your faith?[p]

Prayer for the Church

11 Now may our God and Father[q] Himself,
and our Lord Jesus,[r] direct our way to you.
12 And may the Lord cause you to increase
and overflow with love[s] for one another[t]
and for everyone, just as we also do for
you. 13 May He make your hearts blameless[u]
in holiness[v] before our God and Father at
the coming[w] of our Lord[x] Jesus with all His
˙saints. ˙Amen.[C]

[a] **2:19** Jn 15:11; 2Co 6:10 [b] Rv 12:1 [c] 2Co 12:5; Jms 4:16 [d] Rv 11:8 [e] 1Th 1:10; 1Jn 2:28 [f] 1Co 15:31; 2Co 1:14; Php 4:1; 2Th 1:4 [g] **2:20** Jn 12:43; Php 3:19 [h] **3:1** Ac 17:15 [i] **3:2** Ac 16:1; 1Tm 1:2 [j] Php 1:27 [k] **3:6** Ac 18:5 [l] 1Co 11:2; Php 1:8 [m] **3:8** Rm 14:4; 1Co 16:13; Php 1:27 [n] **3:9** Jn 15:11; 2Co 6:10; Php 1:18 [o] **3:10** 1Th 2:17 [p] Col 1:24 [q] **3:11** Jn 8:42; Php 4:20 [r] Ac 20:21 [s] **3:12** Lk 7:42 [t] Rm 13:8 [u] **3:13** Lk 1:6 [v] Rm 1:4; 1Co 7:14; 2Co 7:1 [w] 1Th 1:10; 1Jn 2:28 [x] Rv 11:8 [y] **4:3** 1Th 5:18 [z] Rm 6:19,22; 1Co 1:30; 2Th 2:13; 1Tm 2:15; Heb 12:14; 1Pt 1:2 [aa] 1Tm 4:3 [ab] **4:5** 2Pt 1:4; 2:10 [ac] **4:6** 2Co 12:17 [ad] **4:7** Mt 23:27; 2Co 12:21; Gl 5:19; Eph 4:19; 5:3; Col 3:5; 1Th 2:3 [ae] **4:8** Ps 51:11; Jn 1:33; Ac 2:4; Rm 8:9; Gl 5:25; Ti 3:5; 1Jn 5:8; Rv 3:22 [af] **4:9** Jn 6:45 [ag] 1Jn 3:11 [ah] **4:10** Ac 16:9 [ai] **4:11** Lk 14:4; 23:56; Ac 11:18; 21:14 [aj] 2Th 3:12; 2Jn 8 [ak] **4:12** Rm 13:13; 1Co 14:40 [al] Eph 4:28 [am] **4:13** Jr 14:19; Eph 2:12; 1Th 1:3 [an] **4:14** Lk 18:33 [ao] Rm 14:9,15; 1Co 8:11; 15:3-4; 2Co 5:15 [ap] Jn 14:19; Rm 8:11; 1Co 6:14; 15:18-20; 2Co 4:14; Php 1:23 [aq] **4:15** 2Pt 1:21; Rv 11:8

The Call to Sanctification

4 Finally then, ˙brothers, we ask and encourage you in the Lord Jesus, that as you
have received from us how you must ˙walk
and please God — as you are doing[D] — do so
even more. 2 For you know what commands
we gave you through the Lord Jesus.
3 For this is God's will,[y] your ˙sanctification:[z]
that you abstain[aa] from sexual immorality,
4 so that each of you knows how to control his
own body[E] in sanctification and honor, 5 not
with lustful desires,[ab] like the Gentiles who
don't know God. 6 This means one must not
transgress against and defraud[ac] his brother
in this matter, because the Lord is an avenger
of all these offenses,[F] as we also previously
told and warned you. 7 For God has not called
us to impurity[ad] but to sanctification. 8 Therefore, the person who rejects this does not
reject man, but God, who also gives you His
Holy Spirit.[ae]

Loving and Working

9 About brotherly love: You don't need
me to write you because you yourselves are
taught by God[af] to love one another.[ag] 10 In
fact, you are doing this toward all the brothers in the entire region of Macedonia.[ah] But
we encourage you, brothers, to do so even
more, 11 to seek to lead a quiet life,[ai] to mind
your own business,[G] and to work[aj] with your
own hands, as we commanded you, 12 so that
you may walk properly[H,ak] in the presence of
outsiders[I] and not be dependent on anyone.[J,al]

The Comfort of Christ's Coming

13 We do not want you to be uninformed,
brothers, concerning those who are ˙asleep,
so that you will not grieve like the rest, who
have no hope.[am] 14 Since we believe that Jesus
died and rose[an] again,[ao] in the same way God
will bring with Him those who have fallen
asleep through[K] Jesus.[ap] 15 For we say this to you
by a revelation from the Lord:[L,aq] We who are
still alive at the Lord's coming[ar] will certainly
have no advantage over[M] those who have
fallen asleep.[as] 16 For the Lord Himself will

[ar] 1Jn 2:28 [as] 1Co 15:51

[A] **3:2** Other mss read *servant* [B] **3:3** Or *are destined for* [C] **3:13** Other mss omit *Amen.* [D] **4:1** Lit *walking* [E] **4:4** Or *to acquire his own wife*; lit *to possess his own vessel* [F] **4:6** Lit *things* [G] **4:11** Lit *to practice one's own things* [H] **4:12** Or *may live respectably* [I] **4:12** Non-Christians [J] **4:12** Or *not need anything*, or *not be in need* [K] **4:14** Or *in* [L] **4:15** Or *a word of the Lord* [M] **4:15** Or *certainly not precede*

descend from heaven with a shout,[A,a] with
the archangel's[b] voice, and with the trumpet
of God, and the dead in Christ[c] will rise first.
17 Then[d] we who are still alive will be caught
up together with them in the clouds[e] to meet
the Lord in the air and so we will always be
with the Lord. 18 Therefore encourage[B] one
another with these words.

The Day of the Lord

5 About the times and the seasons:[f] ·Broth-
ers, you do not need anything to be written to you. 2 For you yourselves know very well
that the Day of the Lord[g] will come just like a
thief[h] in the night. 3 When they say, "Peace and
security," then sudden destruction[i] comes on
them, like labor pains come on a pregnant
woman, and they will not escape. 4 But you,
brothers, are not in the dark, for this day to
overtake you like a thief.[j] 5 For you are all sons
of light and sons of the day. We do not belong
to the night or the darkness.[k] 6 So then, we
must not sleep, like the rest, but we must stay
awake and be serious. 7 For those who sleep,
sleep at night, and those who get drunk are
drunk at night. 8 But since we belong to the
day, we must be serious[l] and put the armor[m]
of faith and love on our chests, and put on a
helmet[n] of the hope of salvation. 9 For God did
not appoint us to wrath, but to obtain salvation through our Lord[o] Jesus Christ,[p] 10 who
died for us,[q] so that whether we are awake
or ·asleep,[r] we will live together with Him.[s]
11 Therefore encourage one another and build
each other up as you are already doing.

[a]**4:16** Jn 5:25 [b]Jd 9 [c]Rm 16:7; 1Co 15:18; 1Pt 5:14; Rv 14:13; 20:5 [d]**4:17** 1Co 15:23,51-52 [e]Mt 26:64 [f]**5:1** Dn 2:21; Ac 1:7 [g]**5:2** Jl 2:1; Mt 25:13; Ac 2:20; Php 1:6 [h]Jn 10:1 [i]**5:3** 2Th 1:9 [j]**5:4** Jb 24:13-17 [k]**5:5** Col 1:13 [l]**5:8** 1Pt 5:8 [m]Eph 6:14; Rv 9:9,17 [n]1Sm 17:5,38; Ps 60:7; 108:8; Is 59:17; Eph 6:17 [o]**5:9** Rv 11:8 [p]Ac 15:26 [q]**5:10** Jn 11:51; Rm 14:9; 1Co 8:11; Gl 1:4 [r]1Th 5:6 [s]Lk 20:38; Php 1:23 [t]**5:12** 1Co 16:18; Php 2:29 [u]**5:13** Mk 9:50 [v]**5:14** 2Th 3:15 [w]Mt 18:26,29; Lk 18:7; 1Co 13:4; Heb 6:15; Jms 5:7-8; 2Pt 3:9 [x]**5:15** Mt 5:44; Rm 12:17; 1Pt 3:9 [y]Lk 7:47 [z]Rm 12:9; Gl 6:10; 1Th 5:21 [aa]**5:16** 2Co 6:10; Php 1:18 [ab]**5:18** Eph 6:6; 1Th 4:3; 1Pt 2:15; 4:2; 1Jn 2:17 [ac]**5:21** Eph 5:17 [ad]**5:22** 1Tm 4:3 [ae]**5:23** Rm 15:33 [af]Ps 51:12 [ag]1Th 1:10

Exhortations and Blessings

12 Now we ask you, brothers, to give recognition[t] to those who labor among you and
lead you in the Lord and admonish you, 13 and
to regard them very highly in love because of
their work. Be at peace[u] among yourselves.
14 And we exhort you, brothers:[v] warn those
who are irresponsible,[C] comfort the discouraged, help the weak, be patient[w] with everyone. 15 See to it that no one repays evil for evil[x]
to anyone,[y] but always pursue what is good
for one another and for all.[z]

16 Rejoice[aa] always!
17 Pray constantly.
18 Give thanks in everything,
for this is God's will[ab] for you
in Christ Jesus.
19 Don't stifle the Spirit.
20 Don't despise prophecies,
21 but test all things.[ac]
Hold on to what is good.
22 Stay away[ad] from every kind of evil.

23 Now may the God of peace[ae] Himself
·sanctify you completely. And may your
spirit,[af] soul, and body be kept sound and
blameless for the coming[ag] of our Lord[ah]
Jesus Christ.[ai] 24 He who calls[aj] you[ak] is faithful, who also will do it. 25 Brothers, pray for us
also. 26 Greet all the brothers with a holy kiss.
27 I charge you by the Lord that this letter be
read to all the brothers.[al] 28 The grace of our
Lord Jesus Christ be with you.

[ah]Rv 11:8 [ai]1Jn 2:28 [aj]**5:24** Col 3:15 [ak]1Pt 1:15 [al]**5:27** Col 4:16

A**4:16** Or *command* B**4:18** Or *comfort* C**5:14** Or *who are disorderly, or who are undisciplined*

2 THESSALONIANS

For the introduction to the book of 2 Thessalonians, see the introduction to the book of 1 Thessalonians, page 1256.

Greeting

1 Paul, Silvanus,[A,a] and Timothy:[b] To the church of the Thessalonians[c] in God our Father and the Lord Jesus Christ.

2 Grace to you and peace from God our Father and the Lord Jesus Christ.

God's Judgment and Glory

3 We must always thank God for you, •brothers. This is right, since your faith is flourishing and the love[d] each one of you has for one another[e] is increasing.[f] 4 Therefore, we ourselves boast[g] about you among God's churches — about your endurance and faith in all the persecutions and afflictions you endure. 5 It is a clear evidence of God's righteous[h] judgment[i] that you will be counted worthy of God's kingdom, for which you also are suffering,[j] 6 since it is righteous for God to repay with affliction those who afflict you 7 and to reward with rest you who are afflicted, along with us. This will take place at the revelation of the Lord Jesus from heaven with His powerful angels, 8 taking vengeance with flaming fire[k] on those who don't know God[l] and on those who don't obey the gospel of our Lord Jesus.[m] 9 These will pay the penalty of eternal destruction[n] from the Lord's presence[o] and from His glorious strength[p] 10 in that day when He comes[q] to be glorified[r] by His •saints[s] and to be admired by all those who have believed, because our testimony among you was believed. 11 And in view of this, we always pray for you that our God will consider you worthy of His calling,[t] and will, by His power, fulfill every desire for goodness and the work of faith,[u] 12 so that the name[v] of our Lord Jesus will be glorified[w] by you, and you by Him,[x] according to the grace of our God and the Lord Jesus Christ.

The Man of Lawlessness

2 Now concerning the coming[y] of our Lord[z] Jesus Christ and our being gathered to Him: We ask you, •brothers, 2 not to be easily upset in mind or troubled, either by a spirit[aa] or by a message or by a letter as if from us, alleging that the Day of the Lord[B,ab] has come.[ac] 3 Don't let anyone deceive you in any way. For that day will not come unless the apostasy[C] comes first and the man of lawlessness[D] is revealed, the son of destruction. 4 He opposes and exalts himself above every so-called god[ad] or object of worship,[ae] so that he sits[E] in God's sanctuary,[F] publicizing that he himself is God.

5 Don't you remember that when I was still with you I told you about this? 6 And you know what currently restrains him, so that he will be revealed in his time.[af] 7 For the •mystery of lawlessness[ag] is already at work, but the one now restraining will do so until he is out of the way, 8 and then the lawless one will be revealed. The Lord Jesus will destroy him with the breath of His mouth[ah] and will bring him to nothing with the brightness of His coming. 9 The coming of the lawless one is based on Satan's working, with all kinds of false miracles, signs, and wonders,[ai] 10 and with every unrighteous deception among those who are perishing. They perish because they did not accept the love of the truth in order to be saved.[aj] 11 For this reason God sends them a strong delusion so that they will believe what is false, 12 so that all will be condemned[ak] — those who did not believe[al] the truth but enjoyed unrighteousness.

Stand Firm

13 But we must always thank God for you, brothers loved by the Lord, because from the beginning[G] God has chosen[am] you for salvation

[a] 1:1 Ac 15:22; 2Co 1:19; 1Th 1:1; 1Pt 5:12 [b] Ac 16:1; 1Tm 1:2 [c] Ac 17:1 [d] 1:3 1Co 13:1; 1Jn 4:16 [e] Php 2:2 [f] 1Th 4:10 [g] 1:4 2Co 12:5 [h] 1:5 1Jn 1:9 [i] Mt 12:41; Jn 5:22,27,30; 8:16; 16:11; Heb 9:27; Jms 2:13; 2Pt 3:7; Rv 14:7; 16:7; 19:2 [j] Php 1:29 [k] 1:8 1Co 3:13; Heb 10:27; 12:29; 2Pt 3:7; Rv 14:10 [l] Ps 79:6; Is 66:15; Jr 10:25 [m] 1Pt 4:17 [n] 1:9 1Tm 6:9 [o] Gn 4:14 [p] Is 2:10,19,21 [q] 1:10 Mk 8:38 [r] Jn 17:10; Rm 8:17 [s] Eph 5:3; 6:18 [t] 1:11 Eph 4:1; Col 3:15 [u] Gl 2:16; 1Th 1:3 [v] 1:12 Jn 14:13; Ac 3:16; 15:14; Php 2:10 [w] Is 24:15; 49:3; 66:5; Mal 1:11; 2Co 8:23 [x] Jn 13:31 [y] 2:1 1Th 1:10; 1Jn 2:28 [z] Rv 11:8 [aa] 2:2 1Jn 4:1 [ab] Mt 25:13; Ac 2:20; Php 1:6 [ac] 2Tm 2:18; 1Jn 2:28 [ad] 2:4 1Co 8:5 [ae] Is 14:12-15; Ezk 28:2; Ac 17:23 [af] 2:6 Lk 21:8 [ag] 2:7 Mt 13:41 [ah] 2:8 Is 11:4; 30:28 [ai] 2:9 Mt 24:24; Mk 13:22; Rv 13:13 [aj] 2:10 Ac 16:30; Eph 2:8 [ak] 2:12 Jn 5:22-30 [al] Jn 6:64 [am] 2:13 Rm 9:11; 11:5; Eph 1:4; 1Th 1:4

[A] **1:1** Or *Silas*; Ac 15:22-32; 16:19-40; 17:1-16 [B] **2:2** Other mss read *Christ* [C] **2:3** Or *rebellion* [D] **2:3** Other mss read *man of sin* [E] **2:4** Other mss add *as God* [F] **2:4** Or *temple* [G] **2:13** Other mss read *because as a firstfruit*

through •sanctification[a] by the Spirit and
through belief in the truth. 14 He called you
to this through our gospel, so that you might
obtain the glory[b] of our Lord Jesus Christ.
15 Therefore, brothers, stand firm[c] and hold
to the traditions you were taught,[d] either by
our message or by our letter.
16 May our Lord Jesus Christ Himself and

[a]2:13 Rm 6:19; 1Co 1:30; 1Th 4:3; 1Tm 2:15; Heb 12:14; 1Pt 1:2 [b]2:14 Lk 9:32; Jn 17:24; 2Co 3:18; 1Pt 5:1,4; 2Pt 3:18 [c]2:15 Rm 14:4; 1Co 16:13; Php 1:27 [d]Mk 7:3; 1Tm 4:11; Jd 3

WORLDVIEW

The Mission of God in India

Home to Buddhism, Hinduism, and other religions, India presents a landscape of gods, deities, lords, and castes, all of which lead the seeker toward the yoga principle of serenity through "emptying" the mind of its cares and dwelling instead on the eternal void. "Emptying" is a significant feature of Paul's description of Jesus, creating at once a contrast to Indian spirituality and filling the void with divine care and purpose.

In Buddhist practice, meditation seeks to relinquish all that causes suffering, all one's disappointments and unattainables, all desperate and futile dreams. Buddhists strive to avoid suffering by denying the reality of all that causes it. Seeking a simplicity that contrasts sharply to modern consumerist culture, millions of Buddhists follow a non-violent, anti-greed ethic that promises eventual arrival in nirvana.

Hinduism presents such a vast array of beliefs—from many gods to none—that summarizing its core is nearly impossible. The easier task is to observe its outcomes, most famously captured in a caste system that perpetuates social differences between Brahmins and Shudras. An array of teachers and dogma have created a complex system of worship and practice, often bewildering to outsiders, yet beautiful in many respects, particularly in its statuary and architecture.

To those seeking tranquility, the gospel offers grace and peace as dominant themes. Jesus, motivated entirely by the love of God (indeed, the highest expression of God's love), effects for believers a dramatic change: once enemies of God by virtue of sin, Jesus' followers are brought into a relationship of peace with God, a total reconciliation based on divine initiative and validated by the Christian believer's transformed life. Unlike Buddhism, peace with God through Christ is never an offer of tranquility during life on earth. Indeed, quite the opposite is Jesus' promise. John 16:33 says: "I have told you these things so that in Me you may have peace. You will have suffering in this world. Be courageous! I have conquered the world." This realistic prospect of peace amid struggle offers substantial help to people who, no matter their meditative practices, face the common human end (death) and the all too common setbacks that precede it.

In place of the Hindu deities and the life-determining caste system, the gospel offers transformation—the last shall be first (Mt 20:16)—and a critical focus on God's word revealed in the unique Son, Jesus Christ (Jn 14:6). God's favor is not to be won by impossible devotion, nor is God's favor parceled out as a birthright. All are invited to believe, indeed, that is God's very intention (3:16). No factors of birth hinder a person from experiencing abundant life in fellowship with God. Likewise, no factors of birth guarantee it. In the gospel, Jesus is the pioneer of eternal salvation, open to all. This liberating freedom is also humankind's most important responsibility—to live in trust and gratitude.

All hope is offered by Jesus Christ. Throughout this huge sub-continent, laden with gods and encrusted by traditions, the Indian church celebrates this hope and invites its neighbors to "come and see" the Christ, the Word of God.

God our Father, who has loved[a] us and
given us eternal encouragement and good
hope by grace, 17 encourage your hearts and
strengthen you in every good work and word.

Pray for Us

3 Finally, ·brothers, pray for us that the
Lord's message may spread rapidly and be
honored, just as it was with you,[b] 2 and that we
may be delivered[c] from wicked and evil men,
for not all have faith.[A] 3 But the Lord is faithful; He will strengthen and guard you from
the evil one.[d] 4 We have confidence in the Lord
about you, that you are doing and will do
what we command. 5 May the Lord direct
your hearts to God's love and Christ's endurance.[e]

Warning against Irresponsible Behavior

6 Now we command you, brothers, in the
name[f] of our Lord Jesus Christ, to keep away
from every brother[g] who ·walks irresponsibly
and not according to the tradition[h] received[i]
from us. 7 For you yourselves know how you
must imitate[j] us: We were not irresponsible
among you; 8 we did not eat[k] anyone's food[B]
free of charge;[l] instead, we labored[m] and
struggled,[n] working[o] night and day, so that
we would not be a burden[p] to any of you. 9 It is
not that we don't have the right[q] to support,
but we did it to make ourselves an example
to you so that you would imitate[r] us. 10 In fact,
when we were with you, this is what we commanded you: "If anyone isn't willing to work,
he should not eat."[s] 11 For we hear that there
are some among you who walk irresponsibly,
not working at all, but interfering with the
work of others.[t] 12 Now we command and exhort such people by the Lord Jesus Christ that
quietly working, they may eat their own food.[B]
13 Brothers, do not grow weary[u] in doing good.
14 And if anyone does not obey our instruction in this letter, take note of that person;
don't associate with him, so that he may be
ashamed. 15 Yet don't treat him as an enemy,
but warn him as a brother.

Final Greetings

16 May the Lord of peace[v] Himself give
you peace always in every way.[w] The Lord be
with all of you.[x] 17 This greeting is in my own
hand[y] — Paul. This is a sign in every letter;
this is how I write. 18 The grace of our Lord
Jesus Christ be with all of you.

[a] **2:16** Jn 3:16; Rv 12:11
[b] **3:1** 1Th 2:13
[c] **3:2** Mt 27:43; Rm 15:31
[d] **3:3** Mt 5:37; 6:13; 13:19,38; Jn 17:15; Eph 6:16; 1Jn 2:13-14; 3:12; 5:18-19
[e] **3:5** Rm 15:5; Rv 13:10
[f] **3:6** Jn 14:13; Ac 3:16; 15:14; Php 2:10
[g] Mt 18:17; 1Co 5:11; 2Tm 3:5; 2Jn 10
[h] Mk 7:3
[i] Jd 3
[j] **3:7** 3Jn 11
[k] **3:8** 1Co 10:25
[l] 1Th 2:7
[m] Rv 14:13
[n] 2Co 11:27; 1Th 2:9
[o] Ac 18:3; Eph 4:28; 2Jn 8
[p] 2Co 2:5; 1Th 2:9
[q] **3:9** Mk 1:22; Ac 9:14; Rm 13:1; 1Co 9:4-14
[r] Heb 8:5
[s] **3:10** 1Th 4:11
[t] **3:11** 1Tm 5:13
[u] **3:13** Lk 18:1; 2Co 4:1,16; Gl 6:9; Eph 3:13
[v] **3:16** 1Th 5:23
[w] Nm 6:26; Eph 6:23
[x] Rm 15:33; 1Co 16:24; 2Co 13:13; Ti 3:15; Heb 13:25
[y] **3:17** 1Co 16:21

[A] **3:2** Or *for the faith is not in everyone* [B] **3:8,12** Or *bread*

■ **AUTHOR:** Paul (Saul of Tarsus)

■■ **DATE:** Written around A.D. 60–64 from either Rome or Macedonia

These three letters of Paul—1 and 2 Timothy and Titus—are called the pastoral epistles. They contain instructions for Timothy in Ephesus and for Titus on Crete on how to lead a church. As we read, it's clear that church problems common today are not new. The lessons Paul offers concerning church officers, age group needs, handling money, guarding the gospel, are applicable today. God's mission in the world between the resurrection of Christ and His return in glory makes the church this era's most significant institution.

Readers will note that not all of Paul's advice is observed in today's churches. For example, women are usually allowed to attend church with braided hair or wearing gold or pearls (2:9). How then are Christians today to receive these instructions? Three pointers are as follows.

1 TIMOTHY

Focus on the core message. Paul expresses the core in what he identifies as "trustworthy" sayings. In 1 Timothy 1:15, for instance, the "saying" establishes the mission of God for all times and places. Every church should faithfully teach this good news. Next to Jesus Christ saving sinners, all else is second tier. Hold steady there, Paul writes, or your church will sink like a rock (1Tm 1:19). Other "trustworthy" sayings can be found in 1 Timothy 3:1 and 4:9; 2 Timothy 2:11; and Titus 3:8. Once the core message is clear, there may be contextual applications of it, culture to culture.

Face pressing problems with clear, caring answers that maintain church unity and keep the core mission strong. Missionaries and pastors in every era have had to faithfully follow and apply these principles in nurturing the church. Where mechanical applications occur without cultural sensitivity, the church usually shows fissures and eventually, irreconcilable conflicts. Not every problem has only one solution. Wisdom is required; God's Spirit must do the leading.

Test every church strategy through a process of submission to wise Christian authority, and comply as much as possible with established civil authority. God's mission is not advanced by wild tirades conducted by fringe movements working in the name of Christ but shamefully discrediting Christ by their petulance and immaturity. Whatever a church's governing structure and whatever a church's niche mission, all must be accountable to the plan of God to redeem people and restore the world through Jesus Christ.

In the world's churches there are many faces. The one head is Christ, and the tasks are preaching, teaching, and living the good news. American and European churches are just now discovering that southern hemisphere Christians have much to teach them about core mission. This is as it should be—Christians constantly learning what God wants. Paul describes it as fighting a battle (1Tm 1:18), and indeed faithful service to Christ can be a fight against powerful adversaries. But it is also a pleasure and privilege. Live it so that you, like Paul, can say: "I have fought the good fight, I have finished the race, I have kept the faith" (2Tm 4:7).

Greeting

1 Paul,[a] an apostle of Christ Jesus by the
command[b] of God our Savior[c] and of
Christ Jesus our hope:[d]
2 To Timothy,[e] my true son in the faith.
Grace, mercy, and peace from God the[A] Father and Christ Jesus our Lord.

False Doctrine and Misuse of the Law

3 As I urged you when I went to Macedonia,[f] remain in Ephesus[g] so that you may instruct certain people[h] not to teach different
doctrine 4 or to pay attention to myths[i] and
endless genealogies. These promote empty
speculations rather than God's plan,[j] which
operates by faith. 5 Now the goal of our instruction is love[k] that comes from a pure
heart,[l] a good conscience,[m] and a sincere
faith.[n] 6 Some have deviated from these and
turned aside to fruitless discussion. 7 They
want to be teachers of the law, although they
don't understand what they are saying or
what they are insisting on. 8 But we know that
the law is good,[o] provided one uses it legiti-
mately. 9 We know that the law is not meant
for a righteous person, but for the lawless
and rebellious,[p] for the ungodly and sinful,
for the unholy and irreverent, for those who
kill their fathers and mothers, for murderers,
10 for the sexually immoral[q] and homosexu-
als,[r] for kidnappers,[B] liars,[s] perjurers, and for
whatever else is contrary to the sound teaching[t] 11 based on the glorious gospel[u] of the
blessed God,[v] which was entrusted to me.[w]

Paul's Testimony

12 I give thanks to Christ Jesus our Lord who
has strengthened[x] me, because He considered me faithful, appointing me to the ministry— 13 one who was formerly a blasphemer,[y]
a persecutor,[z] and an arrogant man.[aa] But I
received mercy because I acted out of ignorance in unbelief. 14 And the grace of our Lord
overflowed, along with the faith and love
that are in Christ Jesus. 15 This saying is trustworthy[ab] and deserving of full acceptance:
"Christ Jesus came into the world[ac] to save sinners"[ad]—and I am the worst of them.[ae] 16 But I
received mercy[af] for this reason, so that in me,
the worst of them, Christ Jesus might demonstrate His extraordinary patience[ag] as an example to those who would believe in Him for
eternal life.[ah] 17 Now to the King[ai] eternal,[aj] immortal,[ak] invisible, the only[C] God,[al] be honor[am]
and glory[an] forever and ever. Amen.[ao]

Engage in Battle

18 Timothy, my son, I am giving you this instruction in keeping with the prophecies[ap] previously made about you, so that by them you
may strongly engage in battle, 19 having faith[aq]
and a good conscience.[ar] Some[as] have rejected
these and have suffered the shipwreck of their
faith. 20 Hymenaeus[at] and Alexander[au] are among
them, and I have delivered them to Satan,[av] so
that they may be taught not to blaspheme.

Instructions on Prayer

2 First of all, then, I urge that petitions,
prayers, intercessions, and thanksgivings
be made for everyone, 2 for kings and all those
who are in authority,[aw] so that we may lead a
tranquil and quiet life in all godliness[ax] and
dignity.[ay] 3 This is good, and it pleases God our
Savior,[az] 4 who wants everyone[ba] to be saved[bb]
and to come to the knowledge of the truth.[bc]

5 For there is one God[bd]
and one mediator[be] between God
and humanity,
Christ Jesus, Himself human,[bf]
6 who gave Himself—a ransom for all,[bg]
a testimony at the proper time.

7 For this I was appointed a herald, an apostle[bh] (I am telling the truth;[D] I am not lying),
and a teacher of the Gentiles[bi] in faith and
truth.

Instructions to Men and Women

8 Therefore, I want the men in every place
to pray, lifting up holy hands without anger
or argument.[bj] 9 Also, the women are to dress
themselves in modest clothing,[bk] with decency
and good sense, not with elaborate hairstyles,
gold,[bl] pearls, or expensive apparel, 10 but with
good works,[bm] as is proper for women who

[a] 1:1 Ac 13:9 [b] Rm 16:26; Ti 1:3 [c] 1Tm 2:3; Ti 1:3; 2:10; 3:4; Jd 25 [d] 1Co 15:19; Col 1:27; 1Th 1:3; 1Pt 1:3,13 [e] 1:2 Ac 16:1; 20:4; 1Co 4:17; 16:10 [f] 1:3 Ac 16:9 [g] Eph 1:1 [h] Jd 4 [i] 1:4 1Tm 4:7; 2Tm 4:4; Ti 1:14; 2Pt 1:16 [j] Eph 1:10; 3:2,9; Col 1:25 [k] 1:5 Rm 13:10 [l] Ps 24:4; 2Tm 2:22; 1Pt 1:22 [m] Ac 23:1; 24:16; Rm 9:1; 2Co 1:12; 1Tm 1:19; 3:9; Heb 10:22; 1Pt 3:21 [n] 2Tm 1:5 [o] 1:8 Rm 7:12,16 [p] 1:9 Ti 1:6,10; Heb 2:8 [q] 1:10 1Co 5:9 [r] Gn 19:5; Rm 1:27; 1Co 6:9 [s] Jn 8:44 [t] 1Tm 6:3; 2Tm 1:13; Ti 1:9; 2:1 [u] 1:11 2Co 4:4 [v] 1Tm 6:15 [w] Lv 6:4; Lk 12:48; 1Co 9:17; Gl 2:7; 1Th 2:4; 1Tm 1:11; 6:20; 2Tm 1:12,14; Ti 1:3 [x] 1:12 Ac 9:22; Php 4:13 [y] 1:13 Ac 6:11; 2Tm 3:2; 2Pt 2:11 [z] Php 3:6 [aa] 1Co 15:8 [ab] 1:15 1Tm 3:1; 4:9; 2Tm 2:11; Ti 3:8 [ac] Jn 3:17; 12:46; 18:37; 1Jn 4:9 [ad] Mk 2:17; Lk 19:10; Rm 11:4 [ae] 1Co 15:9 [af] 1:16 Lk 1:50 [ag] Ex 34:6; Rm 2:4 [ah] Jn 12:25; Ac 13:48 [ai] 1:17 Ps 47:7 [aj] Ps 90:2 [ak] 1Co 9:25 [al] Jn 5:44; 1Co 8:6; Eph 4:6; 1Tm 2:5; 6:15; Jd 25 [am] 2Pt 1:17; Rv 5:12 [an] Mk 10:37 [ao] Php 4:20; 1Tm 6:16; Rv 22:21 [ap] 1:18 1Co 13:2; 1Tm 4:14; 2Tm 1:6 [aq] 1:19 Eph 3:12; 6:16; Col 1:23; 2:5; 1Th 5:8; 1Tm 3:13; 6:12; 2Tm 4:7; 1Jn 5:4

[ar] Heb 10:22 [as] 2Tm 2:18; Jd 4 [at] 1:20 2Tm 2:17 [au] 2Tm 4:14 [av] 1Co 5:5 [aw] 2:2 Ezr 6:10; Rm 13:1; 1Co 2:1 [ax] 2Pt 1:3 [ay] 1Tm 3:4; Ti 2:7 [az] 2:3 1Tm 1:1 [ba] 2:4 Ti 2:11 [bb] Ezk 18:23,32; Jn 3:17; 1Tm 4:10; Ti 2:11; 2Pt 3:9 [bc] Jn 14:6,17 [bd] 2:5 Dt 6:4; Gl 3:20 [be] Heb 8:6 [bf] Jn 1:14; Php 2:7; 3:3; 1Jn 4:2; 5:20 [bg] 2:6 Mt 20:28; Gl 1:4 [bh] 2:7 Eph 3:7-8; 1Tm 1:11; 2Tm 1:11 [bi] Ac 9:15 [bj] 2:8 Mk 7:21; Lk 9:46-47; 24:38; Rm 14:1; Php 2:14 [bk] 2:9 1Pt 3:3 [bl] Rv 3:18 [bm] 2:10 2Co 9:8; Gl 3:10

[A] 1:2 Other mss read *our* [B] 1:10 Or *slave traders* [C] 1:17 Other mss add *wise* [D] 2:7 Other mss add *in Christ*

Chester "Chet" Bitterman III (1952–1981)

Chet and his wife Brenda asked God to make clear to them their part in His worldwide mission. Their mission would be the delivery of the Word of God in mother tongues, native languages that could reach the heart with the message of salvation in Christ. Speakers of unwritten languages waited for translators to create alphabets and then teach them literacy skills. Here was a significant work and a mission far from complete. The impact of Bible translation work worldwide was plain: Where the Bible is read in the mother tongue, people testify to the nearness of God. Love expressed in a native language is undeniably persuasive. Chet and Brenda applied to serve with Wycliffe Bible Translators. Assignment: Colombia, South America.

Their tribal group was to be the Carijonas. To prepare, Chet and Brenda studied language and offered to help with logistics at Wycliffe's Loma Linda base. That meant days of shopping and searching markets for the supplies needed for frontier missions work. At the Bogota office on January 18, 1981, they put their two baby daughters to bed and prayed for God's help in the work before them. It would be their last night together.

Early the next morning, M-19 guerillas entered the compound and kidnapped Chet, holding him hostage for two demands: first, their message must be published in world newspapers; second, all Wycliffe translators must leave Colombia within thirty days. That or Chet's life.

World attention that week was not on Colombia. Ronald Reagan became president on January 20, and the high-profile American hostages in Tehran, Iran, were released the same day. They were the last group of the original sixty-six Americans who had been held by Islamic fundamentalists for over a year. All eyes were on the Middle East. Yet the eye and ear of God knew of events in Colombia, for many prayers were sent heavenward on behalf of Wycliffe's young hostage. Brenda prayed that Chet would be encouraged by the many Scriptures they had committed to memory, and if God willed, they would put those Scriptures into the Carijona language. A letter from Chet released by M-19 reassured his family and colleagues: "The Lord brought 2 Corinthians 2:14 to mind. 'But thanks be to God, who always leads us in triumph through the Lord Jesus Christ.'" Even in captivity, Chet's passion was to see God's mission done. Colombian media printed the full text of Chet's letter. The worldwide Christian mission was headline news as the drama unfolded. Then, suddenly, forty-eight days after abduction, demands from M-19 ceased. Chet was shot dead, his body left on a bus. Chet's role in God's mission was done.

Chet's love for the Colombian people, and Wycliffe's commitment to bring them God's Word, was never in doubt throughout the ordeal, nor is it today. The Bitterman family paid a high price, but the price paid for them was higher still, the Son of God's life on a cross—the mission of God to save.

affirm that they worship God. 11 A woman
should learn in silence with full submission.[a]
12 I do not allow a woman to teach or to have
authority over a man; instead, she is to be silent.
13 For Adam was created first, then Eve.[b]
14 And Adam was not deceived, but the woman
was deceived and transgressed.[c] 15 But she will
be saved through childbearing, if she continues[A] in faith, love, and holiness,[d] with good
judgment.

Qualifications of Church Leaders

3 This saying is trustworthy:[B,e] "If anyone
aspires to be an ·overseer,[f] he desires a
noble work." 2 An overseer,[g] therefore, must

[a]2:11 1Co 14:34; Ti 2:5 [b]2:13 Gn 2:7,22; 3:16; 1Co 11:8-12 [c]2:14 Gn 3:6,13; 2Co 11:3 [d]2:15 1Th 3:12–4:10 [e]3:1 1Tm 1:15; 4:9 [f]Ac 20:28; Php 1:1; Ti 1:7 [g]3:2-4 Ti 1:6-8

The Reproduction of Leaders

Dave Ferguson

We have the privilege of reading some of the Apostle Paul's strategic thinking for accomplishing the mission of God—reproducing apprentices of Jesus. Paul, who literally gave his life for the mission of Jesus, was motivated by Jesus' call to *"Go, therefore, and make disciples of all nations"* (Mt 28:19) and to see them reproduced from *"Jerusalem, in all Judea and Samaria, and to the ends of the earth"* (Ac 1:8). Though not present when the Great Commission was given, Paul received his own commission (Ac 9) and it inspired him to bring alongside himself a young apprentice in the faith, Timothy. Paul apprenticed Timothy as a follower of Jesus and laid out a strategy of reproducing apprentices of Jesus that could catalyze a movement.

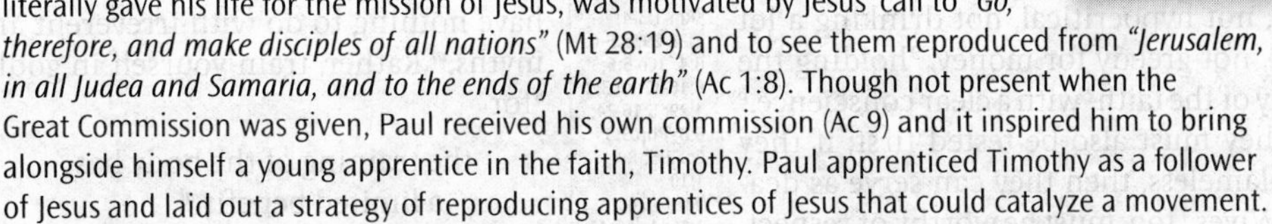

Reproducing was not a new idea to Paul. The Bible shows reproduction as God's creative intention that everything living would reproduce. In Genesis God instructed all creatures to be fruitful and multiply (Gn 1:28). Jesus gave that same message of reproducing to His followers (Mt 28:19) and the challenge to reproduce disciples to the ends of the earth (Ac 1:8). Responding to Jesus' commission the church grew to at least 3,000 on Pentecost (2:41), more than 5,000 a short time later (4:4), and was clearly a movement as *"believers were added to the Lord in increasing numbers"* (5:14). This first century movement of reproducing apprentices of Jesus moved beyond Jerusalem and started multiplying churches in Samaria (8:5,12-13); took the gospel to Africa (8:26-28); to the Gentile world (chap. 10) and beyond.

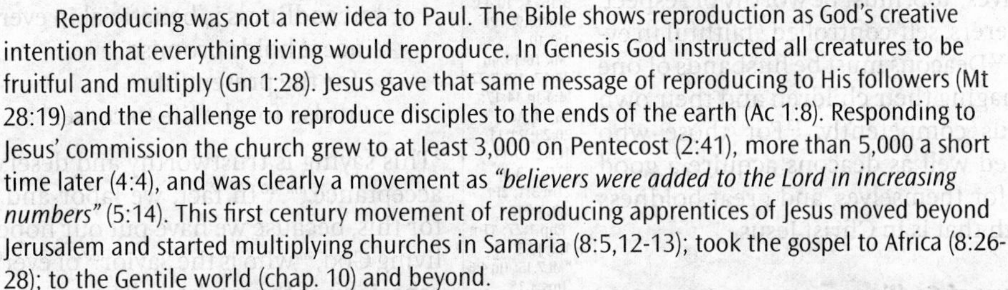

Reproducing apprentices of Jesus requires intentional relationship building. Right after Jesus calls His first followers, John 3:22 tell us, *"After this, Jesus and His disciples went to the Judean countryside, where He spent some time with them and baptized."* The word for "spend time" is the Greek word *diatribo* which is a composite of two words: *dia* which means "through," and *tribo* which means "to rub." So *diatribo* may imply that they spent time rubbing through to each other, meaning they influenced one another. *Diatribo* occurs in an apprenticeship. Paul was apprenticing Timothy the same way that Jesus did His followers: through intentional relationship building.

Reproducing apprentices of Jesus means passing on the profound and simple truth of the gospel. Paul passed on to Timothy gospel truths that were so profound that he would never forget them. They gripped Timothy's heart and mind forever. But at the same time, these truths were so simple that Timothy could in turn pass them on to others who could then pass them on to others.

Reproducing apprentices of Jesus results in generations of changed lives. Paul was clear with Timothy that if he were successful at apprenticing other followers of Jesus it would not end with him or the next generation or even the following. Paul challenges Timothy with a vision of four generations of reproduction: from Paul to Timothy; from Timothy to reliable men; and then from reliable men to others. Through reproducing apprentices of Jesus, generations of lives would be changed, accomplishing the mission of God.

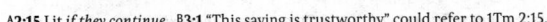

A2:15 Lit *if they continue* B3:1 "This saying is trustworthy" could refer to 1Tm 2:15.

be above reproach, the husband of one wife, self-controlled, sensible,[a] respectable, hospitable,[b] an able teacher,[A] 3 not addicted to wine, not a bully but gentle, not quarrelsome, not greedy[c] — 4 one who manages his own household competently, having his children under control with all dignity. 5 (If anyone does not know how to manage his own household, how will he take care of God's church?) 6 He must not be a new convert, or he might become conceited and fall into the condemnation of the Devil.[d] 7 Furthermore, he must have a good reputation among outsiders, so that he does not fall into disgrace and the Devil's[e] trap.

8 Deacons,[f] likewise, should be worthy of respect, not hypocritical, not drinking a lot of wine, not greedy for money, 9 holding the *mystery of the faith[g] with a clear conscience.[h] 10 And they must also be tested first; if they prove blameless, then they can serve as deacons. 11 Wives,[i] too, must be worthy of respect, not slanderers, self-controlled,[j] faithful in everything. 12 Deacons must be husbands of one wife, managing their children and their own households competently. 13 For those who have served well as deacons acquire a good standing for themselves, and great boldness in the faith that is in Christ Jesus.

The Mystery of Godliness

14 I write these things to you, hoping to come[k] to you soon. 15 But if I should be delayed, I have written so that you will know how people ought to act in God's household,[l] which is the church of the living God,[m] the pillar and foundation of the truth.[n] 16 And most certainly, the mystery of godliness[o] is great:

He[B] was manifested in the flesh,[p]
vindicated in the Spirit,[q]
seen by angels,
preached among the nations,
believed[r] on in the world,
taken up in glory.[s]

Demonic Influence

4 Now the Spirit[t] explicitly says that in later times[u] some will depart from the faith,[v] paying attention to deceitful spirits[w] and the teachings of demons,[x] 2 through the hypocrisy[y] of liars whose consciences[z] are seared. 3 They forbid marriage[aa] and demand abstinence[ab] from foods that God created[ac] to be received with gratitude by those who believe and know the truth. 4 For everything created by God is good,[ad] and nothing should be rejected if it is received with thanksgiving,[ae] 5 since it is sanctified by the word of God[af] and by prayer.

A Good Servant of Jesus Christ

6 If you point these things out to the *brothers, you will be a good servant of Christ Jesus, nourished by the words of the faith[ag] and the good teaching that you have followed.[ah] 7 But have nothing to do with irreverent and silly myths.[ai] Rather, train yourself in godliness,[aj] 8 for

the training of the body has
a limited benefit,[ak]
but godliness is beneficial in every way,
since it holds promise
for the present life
and also for the life to come.[al]

9 This saying is trustworthy and deserves full acceptance.[am] 10 In fact, we labor and strive[C] for this, because we have put our hope in the living God,[an] who is the Savior[ao] of everyone,[ap] especially of those who believe.

Instructions for Ministry

11 Command and teach these things. 12 Let no one despise your youth; instead, you should be an example to the believers in speech,[aq] in conduct,[ar] in love,[D,as] in faith, in purity.[at] 13 Until I come,[au] give your attention to public reading, exhortation, and teaching. 14 Do not neglect the gift that is in you; it was given to you through prophecy,[av] with the laying on of hands[aw] by the council of elders. 15 Practice these things; be committed to them, so that your progress may be evident to all. 16 Pay close attention to your life and your teaching; persevere in these things, for by doing this you will save[ax] both yourself and your hearers.[ay]

[a] **3:2** Ti 2:2,5 [b] Lv 19:34; 1Pt 4:9; 2Jn 10 [c] **3:3** 1Tm 6:10 [d] **3:6** 1Tm 5:12; 2Pt 2:3; Rv 20:1-15 [e] **3:7** Ac 13:10 [f] **3:8** Php 1:1 [g] **3:9** Php 1:27; 1Tm 1:2,19; Jd 3 [h] Heb 13:18 [i] **3:11** 1Pt 3:1-6 [j] Ti 2:2 [k] **3:14** 1Tm 4:13 [l] **3:15** 1Co 3:16; 2Co 6:16; Eph 2:21-22; 1Pt 2:5; 4:17 [m] Mt 16:16; 1Tm 4:10 [n] Ps 119:142; 2Co 11:10; 2Th 2:10 [o] **3:16** 2Pt 1:3 [p] Jn 1:14; Php 2:7; 1Jn 4:2; 5:20 [q] Rm 1:3-4; 2:28-29; 7:5-6; 8:4; 1Co 5:5; 6:16-17; Gl 3:3; 4:29; 5:16-24; 6:8; Php 3:3; Col 2:5; Rv 1:10 [r] Mt 11:24; Jn 3:16; Ac 10:43; Rm 10:9; 1Pt 1:8-10 [s] Mk 16:19; Jn 20:17; 1Pt 3:22 [t] **4:1** Jn 14:17; 16:13; Ac 20:23; 21:11; 1Co 2:10-11 [u] 2Th 2:3-9; 2Tm 3:1; 2Pt 3:3; Jd 18 [v] Php 1:27; 1Tm 1:2; Jd 3 [w] Mt 7:15; 1Jn 4:6 [x] Jms 3:15 [y] **4:2** Mk 12:15 [z] Heb 13:18 [aa] **4:3** 1Tm 5:14; Heb 13:4 [ab] Rm 14:6; Col 2:16,23; 1Th 4:3; 5:22; 1Pt 2:11 [ac] Gn 1:29; 9:3 [ad] **4:4** Gn 1:31 [ae] Ac 10:15 [af] **4:5** Lk 8:21; 1Tm 2:1; Heb 4:12 [ag] **4:6** Php 1:27; 1Tm 1:2; Jd 3 [ah] 2Tm 3:10-15 [ai] **4:7** 1Tm 1:4; 2Tm 4:4; Ti 1:14; 2Pt 1:16 [aj] 2Pt 1:3 [ak] **4:8** Col 2:23 [al] Ps 37:9,11; Pr 19:23; 22:4; Mt 6:33; Mk 10:30; Jn 12:25; Ac 13:48; 1Pt 3:9 [am] **4:9** 1Tm 1:15; 3:1; 2Tm 2:11 [an] **4:10** Dt 5:26; Jos 3:10; 1Sm 17:26; Ps 42:2; Jr 10:10; Dn 6:20; Ac 14:15; 1Tm 3:15 [ao] 1Tm 1:1 [ap] 1Tm 2:4; Ti 2:11 [aq] **4:12** Pr 12:6 [ar] 2Pt 3:11 [as] 1Co 13:1 [at] 1Tm 5:2 [au] **4:13** 1Tm 3:14 [av] **4:14** 1Co 13:2; 1Tm 1:18; 2Tm 1:6 [aw] 1Tm 5:22 [ax] **4:16** Eph 2:8; Jd 23 [ay] Ezk 33:9; Ac 20:28; Rm 11:14

[A] **3:2** Or *hospitable, skillful in teaching* [B] **3:16** Other mss read *God* [C] **4:10** Other mss read *and suffer reproach* [D] **4:12** Other mss add *in spirit*

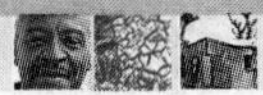

5 Do not rebuke an older man, but exhort him as a father, younger men as brothers, 2 older women as mothers, and with all propriety, the younger women as sisters.

The Support of Widows

3 Support[A] widows[a] who are genuinely widows. 4 But if any widow has children or grandchildren, they must learn to practice godliness toward their own family first and to repay their parents, for this pleases God. 5 The real widow, left all alone, has put her hope in God[b] and continues night and day in her petitions and prayers; 6 however, she who is self-indulgent is dead even while she lives.[c] 7 Command this also, so they won't be blamed. 8 But if anyone does not provide[d] for his own, that is his own household, he has denied the faith[e] and is worse than an unbeliever.

9 No widow should be placed on the official support list[B] unless she is at least 60 years old, has been the wife of one husband, 10 and is well known for good works[f]—that is, if she has brought up children, shown hospitality,[g] washed the •saints' feet,[h] helped the afflicted,[i] and devoted herself to every good work.[j] 11 But refuse to enroll younger widows, for when they are drawn away from Christ by desire, they want to marry[k] 12 and will therefore receive condemnation[l] because they have renounced their original pledge. 13 At the same time, they also learn to be idle, going from house to house; they are not only idle, but are also gossips[m] and busybodies, saying things they shouldn't say. 14 Therefore, I want younger women to marry,[n] have children, manage their households, and give the adversary no opportunity to accuse us.[o] 15 For some have already turned away[p] to follow Satan. 16 If any[C] believing woman has widows in her family, she should help them, and the church should not be burdened, so that it can help those who are genuinely widows.

Honoring the Elders

17 The elders who are good leaders should be considered worthy of an ample honorarium,[D] especially those who work hard[q] at preaching and teaching. 18 For the Scripture says:

> **Do not muzzle an ox**
> **while it is treading out the grain,**[E,r] and,
> the worker is worthy of his wages.[s]

19 Don't accept an accusation against an elder unless it is supported by two or three witnesses.[t] 20 Publicly rebuke those who sin, so that the rest will also be afraid. 21 I solemnly charge you before God and Christ Jesus and the elect angels to observe[u] these things without prejudice, doing nothing out of favoritism. 22 Don't be too quick to appoint[F,v] anyone as an elder, and don't share in the sins of others. Keep yourself pure.[w] 23 Don't continue drinking only water, but use a little wine because of your stomach and your frequent illnesses. 24 Some people's sins are obvious, going before them to judgment,[x] but the sins of others surface[G] later. 25 Likewise, good works are obvious, and those that are not obvious cannot remain hidden.

Honoring Masters

6 All who are under the yoke as •slaves must regard their own masters[H] to be worthy of all respect, so that God's name[y] and His teaching will not be blasphemed. 2 Those who have believing masters should not be disrespectful to them because they are •brothers, but should serve them better, since those who benefit from their service are believers and dearly loved.[z]

False Doctrine and Human Greed

Teach and encourage these things. 3 If anyone teaches other doctrine and does not agree with the sound teaching of our Lord[aa] Jesus Christ and with the teaching that promotes godliness,[ab] 4 he is conceited, understanding nothing, but has a sick interest in disputes and arguments over words.[ac] From these come envy,[ad] quarreling,[ae] slander,[af] evil suspicions, 5 and constant disagreement among people whose minds are depraved and deprived of the truth, who imagine that godliness[I] is a way to material gain.[J,ag] 6 But godliness with contentment is a great gain.[ah]

> 7 For we brought nothing into the world,
> and[K] we can take nothing out.[ai]

[a] 5:3 Ex 22:22; Jms 1:27
[b] 5:5 1Co 7:34
[c] 5:6 Lk 15:24; Eph 2:1,5; 5:14; Rv 3:1
[d] 5:8 Rm 12:17; 2Co 8:21
[e] Mt 10:33; Php 1:27; 1Tm 1:2; 2Pt 2:1; Jd 4; Rv 2:13
[f] 5:10 Mk 14:6; 2Co 9:8; Gl 3:10; Jms 2:14-26
[g] 2Jn 10
[h] Lk 7:44; Jn 13:5-14
[i] Heb 11:37
[j] 2Co 9:8
[k] 5:11 1Tm 5:14
[l] 5:12 Mk 12:40
[m] 5:13 Pr 17:9; 3Jn 10
[n] 5:14 Gn 2:18-25; 1Co 7:9-10; 1Tm 4:3; 5:11
[o] Ti 2:4-5
[p] 5:15 Heb 12:13
[q] 5:17 1Th 5:12
[r] 5:18 Dt 25:4; 1Co 9:9
[s] Lv 19:13; Dt 24:14-15; Mt 10:10; Lk 10:7; 1Co 9:4-14; 2Pt 2:13
[t] 5:19 Dt 19:15
[u] 5:21 Lk 11:28
[v] 5:22 Ex 29:10; Lv 4:15; Lk 4:40; Ac 6:6; 28:8; 1Tm 4:14; Heb 6:2
[w] Php 4:8
[x] 5:24 Mt 12:41; Jn 5:22-30; Heb 9:27
[y] 6:1 Jn 10:25; Ac 15:14; Rv 14:1
[z] 6:2 2Th 2:12; 1Jn 4:16
[aa] 6:3 Rv 11:8
[ab] 2Pt 1:3
[ac] 6:4 2Tm 2:14,23; Ti 3:9
[ad] Ps 37:1
[ae] Ti 3:9
[af] Rv 13:6
[ag] 6:5 Eph 4:22; 2Tm 3:8; Ti 1:11,15
[ah] 6:6 Ps 37:16; Pr 15:16; 16:8; Php 4:11; Heb 13:5
[ai] 6:7 Jb 1:21; Ps 49:17; Ec 5:15

[A] **5:3** Lit *Honor* [B] **5:9** Lit *be enrolled* [C] **5:16** Other mss add *believing man or* [D] **5:17** Or *of respect and remuneration*; lit *of double honor* [E] **5:18** Dt 25:4 [F] **5:22** Lit *to lay hands on* = to ordain [G] **5:24** Lit *follow* [H] **6:1** Or *owners*

[I] **6:5** Referring to religion as a means of financial gain [J] **6:5** Other mss add *From such people withdraw yourself.* [K] **6:7** Other mss add *it is clear that*

8 But if we have food and clothing,[A]
we will be content with these.

9 But those who want to be rich fall into
temptation, a trap, and many foolish and
harmful desires, which plunge people into
ruin and destruction. 10 For the love of money
is a root[B] of all kinds of evil, and by craving
it, some have wandered away from the faith[a]
and pierced themselves with many pains.

[a]6:10 Php 1:27; 1Tm 1:2; Jd 3 [b]6:11 1Co 13:1 [c]Rv 13:10 [d]6:12 2Tm 4:7; Jd 3 [e]1Jn 5:12

Fight the Good Fight

11 But you, man of God, run
from these things,
and pursue righteousness,
godliness, faith,
love,[b] endurance,[c] and gentleness.
12 Fight the good fight[d]
for the faith;
take hold of eternal life[e]

The Mission of God in the Pacific Rim

WORLDVIEW

In the varied cultures that make up the Pacific Rim, diversity is the most obvious marker. The Rim includes island nations such as Fiji and Japan, Samoa and the Philippines, but also countries along the western side of the Americas, Mexico, and Chile among them.

It was in the Rim nation of Papua New Guinea that missionaries Don and Carol Richardson discovered one of modern missions' most important theses: God's mission is woven into cultures in one or more central values, which help illustrate God's love and prepare that culture for the gospel. Richardson called these cultural bridges "redemptive analogies" in his book *Peace Child*, originally published in 1975. The Richardsons were missionaries among the cannibalistic Sawi people on (then) Dutch New Guinea when tribal warfare seemed unsolvable. Despite their best peace-making efforts, the day came when the Richardsons felt they could no longer stay. Tribal war was ruining their work. They confronted the chiefs and later, to their astonishment, witnessed the peace-child ceremony—the surrender of a child from one tribe to another as a guarantee of friendly relations. The chiefs could make peace no other way.

This ceremony has led to much creative anthropology as missiologists began to uncover similar analogies elsewhere. What should and perhaps should not qualify as a redemptive analogy is as wide a question today as any. But the effort to locate these bridges has proved important to the worldwide mission of God, as understood by churches and sending agencies.

The stories of God's mission around the Pacific basin, with its isolated cultures in seemingly endless varieties, are hardly possible to summarize. The Rim has every major religion in it, hundreds of languages, and a history of conflict as its landmass has passed through waves of aggressive exploitation. James Michener's novel *Hawaii* was made into an epic motion picture in 1966. Central to the plot was a narrow-hearted missionary (played by Max Von Sydow) and his winsome wife (played by Julie Andrews) who managed to disrupt and corrupt the culture beyond recognition, all in the name of the gospel. But the story of the growth of the church in the Pacific was not as Michener told it. There was sacrifice, setback, and steady development such that today the Rim, in its wide variety, trains its own pastors, has its own national Christian movements, and sends missionaries to all other parts of the world.

As the region is diverse, so is the church in it. Differences have presented temporary but never permanent setbacks. Today the Pacific Rim is the site of energetic Christian churches, theological training, and missionary work.

[A]6:8 Or *food and shelter* [B]6:10 Or *is the root*

that you were called to
and have made a good
confession about
in the presence of many witnesses.

13 In the presence of God, who gives life to all,[a]
and of Christ Jesus, who gave a good confession before Pontius ·Pilate,[b] I charge you 14 to
keep the command without fault or failure
until the appearing[c] of our Lord[d] Jesus Christ.
15 God will bring this about in His own time.[e]
He is

the blessed and only[f] Sovereign,
the King of kings,[g]
and the Lord of lords,[h]
16 the only One who has immortality,
dwelling in unapproachable light;[i]
no one has seen or can see Him,[j]
to Him be honor and eternal might.[k]
·Amen.[l]

Instructions to the Rich

17 Instruct those who are rich in the present
age not to be arrogant[m] or to set their hope
on the uncertainty of wealth, but on God,[A]
who richly provides us with all things[n] to enjoy. 18 Instruct them to do what is good, to be
rich in good works,[o] to be generous, willing
to share,[p] 19 storing up for themselves a good
reserve[B] for the age to come,[q] so that they may
take hold of life that is real.

Guard the Heritage

20 Timothy, guard what has been entrusted
to you,[r] avoiding[s] irreverent, empty speech
and contradictions from the "knowledge"
that falsely bears that name.[t] 21 By professing
it, some[u] people have deviated from the faith.[v]
Grace be with all of you.

[a] **6:13** Mk 13:19; Rm 1:25 [b] Mt 27:11-14 [c] **6:14** Ti 2:13; 1Jn 2:28 [d] Rv 11:8 [e] **6:15** Lk 21:8 [f] Rm 16:27 [g] Rv 17:14 [h] Dt 10:17; Ps 136:2-3; Rv 17:14; 19:16 [i] **6:16** Ps 36:9; 104:2; Jn 12:46 [j] Ex 33:20; Jn 1:18 [k] Jd 25 [l] 1Tm 1:17; Rv 22:21 [m] **6:17** 1Sm 2:3; Ec 7:8; Rm 11:20; 12:16 [n] Ac 17:25 [o] **6:18** Mk 14:6; Gl 3:10; Jms 2:14-26; 1Pt 2:12 [p] Rm 12:8,13; Eph 4:28 [q] **6:19** Mt 6:20 [r] **6:20** 1Tm 1:11; 2Tm 1:12,14; Ti 1:3 [s] Heb 12:13

[t] Col 2:8; 2Tm 2:16; 4:4; Ti 1:14 [u] **6:21** 2Tm 2:18 [v] Php 1:27; 1Tm 1:2

[A] **6:17** Other mss read *on the living God* [B] **6:19** Or *foundation*

2 TIMOTHY

For the introduction to the book of 2 Timothy, see the introduction to the book of 1 Timothy, page 1264.

Greeting

1 Paul,[a] an apostle of Christ Jesus by God's
will,[b] for the promise of life[c] in Christ
Jesus:
2To Timothy, my dearly loved son.
Grace, mercy, and peace[d] from God the Father and Christ Jesus our Lord.

Thanksgiving

3I thank God, whom I serve with a clear
conscience[e] as my ancestors did, when I constantly remember you in my prayers night
and day.[f] 4Remembering your tears, I long
to see you so that I may be filled with joy,
5clearly recalling your sincere faith[g] that first
lived in your grandmother Lois, then in your
mother Eunice,[h] and that I am convinced is
in you also.
6Therefore, I remind you to keep ablaze[A]
the gift of God that is in you through the laying on of my hands.[i] 7For God has not given
us a spirit[B] of fearfulness,[j] but one of power,[k]
love,[l] and sound judgment.

Not Ashamed of the Gospel

8So don't be ashamed[m] of the testimony
about our Lord,[n] or of me His prisoner.[o] Instead, share in suffering for the gospel, relying on the power[p] of God.

9 He has saved us and called us
with a holy calling,[q]
not according to our works,[r]
but according to His own purpose[s]
and grace,
which was given to us in Christ Jesus
before time began.
10 This has now been made evident
through the appearing[t] of our Savior
Christ Jesus,
who has abolished death[u]
and has brought life[v] and immortality
to light
through the gospel.

11For this gospel I was appointed[w] a herald,
apostle, and teacher,[C] 12and that is why I suffer[x] these things. But I am not ashamed, because I know the One I have believed in and
am persuaded that He is able to guard what
has been entrusted to me[D,y] until that day.[z]

Be Loyal to the Faith

13Hold on to the pattern of sound teaching[aa]
that you have heard from me,[ab] in the faith and
love that are in Christ Jesus. 14Guard, through
the Holy Spirit who lives in us, that good thing
entrusted to you. 15This you know: All those in
·Asia[ac] have turned away from me,[ad] including
Phygelus and Hermogenes. 16May the Lord
grant mercy[ae] to the household of Onesiphorus,[af] because he often refreshed me[ag] and was
not ashamed of my chains.[ah] 17On the contrary,
when he was in Rome,[ai] he diligently searched
for me and found me. 18May the Lord grant
that he obtain mercy[aj] from Him on that day.
And you know very well how much he ministered at Ephesus.[ak]

Be Strong in Grace

2 You, therefore, my son, be strong in the
grace[al] that is in Christ Jesus. 2And what
you have heard from me[am] in the presence
of many witnesses, commit to faithful[an] men
who will be able to teach others also.
3Share in suffering as a good soldier of
Christ Jesus.[ao] 4No one serving as a soldier
gets entangled in the concerns of civilian life;
he seeks to please the recruiter. 5Also, if anyone competes as an athlete, he is not crowned

[a]1:1 Ac 13:9 [b]1Co 1:1; Eph 1:1; Col 1:1 [c]1Jn 2:25; 5:12 [d]1:2 1Tm 1:2; 2Jn 3 [e]1:3 Ac 23:1; 24:16; Rm 9:1; 2Co 1:12; 1Tm 1:19; 3:9; Heb 10:22; 1Pt 3:21 [f]Eph 1:6 [g]1:5 1Tm 1:5 [h]Ac 16:1 [i]1:6 1Tm 4:14; 5:22 [j]1:7 Jn 7:13; 14:27; Rm 8:15 [k]Lk 1:35; 4:14; 24:49; Ac 1:8; 4:33; Rm 15:13,19; 1Co 2:4; Eph 3:16,20; 1Th 1:5 [l]1Co 13:1 [m]1:8 Mk 8:38; Rm 1:16; 2Tm 1:12,16 [n]Ac 4:33; 1Co 1:6; Rv 1:2,9; 12:17; 19:10; 20:4 [o]Eph 3:1; 4:1; Phm 1,9 [p]Lk 1:35; 2Co 13:4 [q]1:9 Rm 8:28; 11:14,29; Heb 3:1 [r]Eph 2:9 [s]Pr 19:21; Is 42:6; 46:10; Ac 2:23; 4:28; 26:16; Rm 8:28; 9:11; Eph 1:11; Php 2:13 [t]1:10 Lk 21:8; 2Tm 4:1; 1Jn 2:28 [u]Jn 8:51; Php 3:10 [v]1Jn 5:12 [w]1:11 1Tm 2:7 [x]1:12 Php 1:29; 2Tm 2:9 [y]1Tm 1:11; 6:20; Ti 1:3 [z]Php 1:6; 2Tm 4:8 [aa]1:13 1Tm 1:10; 6:3; Ti 1:9; 2:1 [ab]2Tm 2:2; 3:14 [ac]1:15 Ac 6:9; 16:6 [ad]2Tm 4:10-16 [ae]1:16 Lk 1:50 [af]2Tm 4:19 [ag]Phm 7,20 [ah]Ac 16:26; 20:23; 21:33; 23:29; 26:29; Eph 6:20; Phm 10 [ai]1:17 Rm 1:7 [aj]1:18 Lk 1:50 [ak]Eph 1:1 [al]2:1 Gl 1:6; 2Pt 3:18 [am]2:2 2Tm 1:13 [an]Nm 12:7 [ao]2:3 1Tm 1:18

[A]1:6 Or *to rekindle* [B]1:7 Or *us the Spirit* [C]1:11 Other mss add *of the Gentiles* [D]1:12 Or *guard what I have entrusted to Him*, or *guard my deposit*

unless he competes according to the rules.
6 The hardworking farmer ought to be the
first to get a share of the crops.[a] 7 Consider
what I say, for the Lord will give you understanding in everything.
8 Keep your attention on Jesus Christ as
risen from the dead[b] and descended from David. This is according to my gospel. 9 I suffer
for it to the point of being bound like a criminal, but God's message is not bound. 10 This is
why I endure[c] all things for the elect:[d] so that
they also may obtain salvation, which is in
Christ Jesus, with eternal glory.[e] 11 This saying
is trustworthy:[f]

For if we have died with Him,[g]
we will also live with Him;
12 if we endure, we will also reign[h] with Him;

[a] **2:6** 1Co 9:10
[b] **2:8** Mt 17:9; Jn 21:14
[c] **2:10** Jms 1:12
[d] Mt 24:22
[e] Lk 9:32; 24:26; Jn 17:24; 2Co 3:18; 1Pt 5:1,4; 2Pt 3:18
[f] **2:11** 1Tm 1:15; 3:1; 4:9; Ti 3:8
[g] Jn 8:51
[h] **2:12** Rv 20:4

Passing on the Mission

Earl Creps

God entrusts an eternal mission to temporary human beings. Every generation of believers faces the challenge of transmitting these redemptive purposes to the next. In 2 Timothy 2:2, the Apostle Paul instructs his protégé to make their relationship a pattern for passing on the mission of God. Paul's writings depict four kinds or relationship between current and future leaders that are essential to this transition.

Paternal relationship: "my dearly loved son" (2 Tm 1:2)—The nature of the bond between the two men is evident in the five times the Apostle refers to Timothy as his son. Paul loves this younger man, who may have grown up without a father, as if he were his own child. Timothy responds with missionary sacrifices, as exemplified in being circumcised to avoid offending their Jewish audiences (Ac 16:3). Passing on the mission begins with older leaders becoming spiritual parents to their successors.

Fraternal relationship: "our brother" (Col 1:1)—The Apostle speaks of Timothy three times as "our brother," part of the household of faith, and of equal value with all of the other members—including Paul himself. In fact, the Apostle refers to himself and Timothy together simply as "slaves of Christ Jesus" (Php 1:1). No one can feel superior when all of us humble ourselves before the same God. Treating the next generation with the respect due to members of the same family helps form the bonds through which the mission can be transmitted.

Ministerial relationship: "my coworker" (Rm 16:21)—Paul developed Timothy into a fully functioning minister of the gospel, traveling with him, serving as an emissary, leading the Ephesian church Paul founded, and enduring hardship for the faith. To the Thessalonians, Paul described him as "our brother and God's coworker in the gospel of Christ" (1Th 3:2). Timothy learned the ministry by sharing Paul's life and teaching as they traveled the roads and oceans of the Roman Empire. Mission legacies are formed as future leaders share in real apostolic responsibilities right now.

Supernatural relationship: "man of God" (1Tm 6:11)—The Apostle recognized that God will work in a unique way in this younger minister, reminding him of the prophetic basis of his ministry (1Tm 1:18) and encouraging him to "keep ablaze" the gift within him (2Tm 1:6). As a "man of God," Timothy will have to find God's plan for his own times, as Paul did for his. We cannot foresee the conditions our successors will encounter any more than Paul and Timothy could have anticipated the Internet. The Lord we trust in our generation will have to be the Lord disciples trust for the next generation as men and women of the everlasting God.

Timothy grew into a seasoned leader who extended the mission of God long after the Apostle's passing. When future leaders begin as sons, become brothers, develop into coworkers, and are recognized as real men and women of God, they don't just own the mission, the mission owns them.

if we deny Him, He will also deny us;
13 if we are faithless, He remains faithful,
for He cannot deny Himself.

An Approved Worker

[14]Remind them of these things, charging
them before God[A] not to fight about words;[a]
this is in no way profitable and leads to the
ruin of the hearers. [15]Be diligent to present
yourself approved to God, a worker who
doesn't need to be ashamed, correctly teaching the word of truth.[b] [16]But avoid irreverent,
empty speech, for this will produce an even
greater measure of godlessness.[c] [17]And their
word will spread like gangrene; Hymenaeus[d]
and Philetus are among them. [18]They have
deviated from the truth, saying that the resurrection has already taken place,[e] and are
overturning the faith of some.[f] [19]Neverthe-
less, God's solid foundation stands firm, having this inscription:[g]

The Lord knows those
who are His,[B,h] and

Everyone who names the name[i]
of the Lord
must turn away from unrighteousness.[j]

[20]Now in a large house there are not only
gold and silver bowls,[k] but also those of wood
and clay, some for honorable[C] use, some for
dishonorable.[D,l] [21]So if anyone purifies himself from anything dishonorable,[E] he will be
a special[F] instrument, set apart, useful to the
Master, prepared for every good work.[m]

[22]Flee[n] from youthful passions, and pursue righteousness, faith, love, and peace,[o]
along with those who call on the Lord[p] from
a pure heart. [23]But reject foolish and ignorant
disputes, knowing that they breed quarrels.
[24]The Lord's[q] •slave must not quarrel,[r] but
must be gentle to everyone, able to teach,[G]
and patient, [25]instructing his opponents with
gentleness.[s] Perhaps God will grant them repentance[t] leading them to the knowledge
of the truth. [26]Then they may come to their

[a]**2:14** 1Tm 6:4 [b]**2:15** Eph 1:13; Col 1:5; Jms 1:18 [c]**2:16** Jd 18 [d]**2:17** 1Tm 1:20 [e]**2:18** Ac 17:32; 1Co 15:12-17; 2Th 2:1-2 [f]1Tm 1:19; 6:21 [g]**2:19** Jos 23:7; Est 9:4; Is 26:13; Rm 15:20; Eph 1:21 [h]Nm 16:5; Pr 2:6; Jn 10:14,27; 1Co 8:3 [i]Ac 15:14 [j]Lv 24:11,16; Nm 16:26-27; Jos 23:7; Ps 6:9; 33:15; Pr 3:7; Is 26:13; 52:11; Jr 20:9 [k]**2:20** Rm 9:21 [l]Rm 9:21 [m]**2:21** 2Co 9:8; Gl 3:10; 1Tm 5:10 [n]**2:22** 1Tm 4:12; 6:11; Jms 4:7 [o]Lk 12:51; 2Tm 1:2; Heb 12:14; 3Jn 14 [p]Gn 13:4 [q]**2:24** Rv 11:8 [r]Jn 6:52; Ac 7:26; Jms 4:2 [s]**2:25** Jms 3:13 [t]Ac 26:20; Rm 2:4; 2Co 7:9-10

PRAYING FOR THE WORLD

The Good Goal of Maturity

Some people read Scripture and say they believe it, but their hearts remain cold and unchanged. Jesus referred to such folks in the parable of the sower: They are like seed that sprouts quickly but dies back because it has no depth of soil (Mt 13:5).

The world urgently needs mature believers who are "doers of the word and not hearers only" (Jms 1:22), mature believers who are "correctly teaching the word of truth" (2Tm 2:15). Mature believers understand God's Word and thus can discern truth from false teaching. They speak what God speaks and not their own interpretations. They know that they don't know everything, but they allow Scripture to interpret Scripture and they have a grasp of the big picture of God's Word.

Such spiritual maturity is vital for all believers—for we are all witnesses of our faith in every place and to every person with whom we have contact. To be God's representatives, we must know and do His Word.

Holy Spirit, teach us the value of deep and constant study. Bring Your Word to mind as we move through each day. Help us to recognize its power. When we feel weary and listless, bring us back to the Bible passages we once cherished so dearly. When we feel depressed, remind us of Your promises. When we're afraid, remind us of those who did mighty deeds in Your name with Your strength. Help us to be not just hearers of Your Word, but doers as well. Help us to correctly handle Your Word so that we teach the truth alone. Amen.

[A]**2:14** Other mss read *before the Lord* [B]**2:19** Nm 16:5 [C]**2:20** Or *special* [D]**2:20** Or *ordinary* [E]**2:21** Lit *from these* [F]**2:21** Or *an honorable* [G]**2:24** Or *everyone, skillful in teaching*

senses and escape the Devil's trap,[a] having
been captured by him to do his will.[b]

Difficult Times Ahead

3 But know this: Difficult times will come
in the last days.[c] 2 For people will be lovers of self,[d] lovers of money,[e] boastful, proud,[f]
blasphemers, disobedient to parents, ungrateful, unholy,[g] 3 unloving, irreconcilable,
slanderers,[h] without self-control, brutal,
without love for what is good,[i] 4 traitors,[j] reckless,[k] conceited,[l] lovers of pleasure[m] rather
than lovers of God, 5 holding to the form of
godliness but denying its power.[n] Avoid these
people![o]

6 For among them are those who worm
their way into households and capture idle
women burdened down with sins, led along
by a variety of passions,[p] 7 always learning
and never able to come to a knowledge of the
truth.[q] 8 Just as Jannes and Jambres[r] resisted
Moses,[s] so these also resist the truth, men
who are corrupt in mind,[t] worthless[u] in regard to the faith. 9 But they will not make further progress, for their lack of understanding
will be clear to all, as theirs[A] was also.

Struggles in the Christian Life

10 But you have followed my teaching, conduct, purpose,[v] faith, patience, love,[w] and endurance, 11 along with the persecutions and
sufferings[x] that came to me in Antioch,[y] Iconium,[z] and Lystra.[aa] What persecutions I endured! Yet the Lord rescued me from them
all. 12 In fact, all those who want to live a godly
life in Christ Jesus will be persecuted.[ab] 13 Evil
people and impostors will become worse, deceiving[ac] and being deceived. 14 But as for you,
continue in what you have learned and firmly
believed. You know those who taught you,[ad]
15 and you know that from childhood you
have known the sacred Scriptures,[ae] which
are able to give you wisdom for salvation[af]
through faith in Christ Jesus. 16 All Scripture
is inspired by God[B,ag] and is profitable for
teaching, for rebuking, for correcting, for
training in righteousness, 17 so that the man
of God may be complete, equipped for every
good work.[ah]

[a]**2:26** 1Tm 3:7 [b]Jn 1:13 [c]**3:1** Jn 6:39; Php 1:6; 1Pt 1:5; 2Pt 3:3; Jd 18 [d]**3:2** Php 2:21; 1Tm 6:4 [e]Lk 16:14; 1Tm 3:3; 6:10 [f]Pr 16:18; Lk 1:51; Rm 1:30 [g]1Tm 1:9 [h]**3:3** Jn 14:6 [i]Ti 1:8 [j]**3:4** Lk 6:16; Ac 7:52 [k]Ac 19:36 [l]1Tm 3:6; 6:4 [m]Php 3:19 [n]**3:5** 1Co 4:20; 2Co 13:4; Ti 1:16 [o]Mt 7:15; 2Th 3:6 [p]**3:6** 2Pt 1:4; 2:10 [q]**3:7** 2Co 11:10; 1Tm 2:4; 2Tm 2:25; Ti 1:1 [r]**3:8** Ex 7:11-12; 8:18; 9:11 [s]Ps 77:20; Mt 8:4; Heb 3:2 [t]1Co 14:14; Php 4:7 [u]2Co 13:5-7 [v]**3:10** Pr 19:21; Ac 11:23 [w]1Co 13:1; 1Jn 4:16 [x]**3:11** Gl 5:24; Php 3:10 [y]Ac 13:14; 14:19,21 [z]Ac 13:51; 16:2 [aa]Ac 14:6,8; 27:5 [ab]**3:12** Jn 15:20; Ac 14:22; 2Co 4:9-10 [ac]**3:13** Rv 20:10 [ad]**3:14** 2Tm 1:13 [ae]**3:15** Mt 26:54; 2Pt 1:20-21 [af]Ac 4:12; 2Co 7:10; Heb 5:9 [ag]**3:16** 2Pt 1:20-21 [ah]**3:17** 2Co 9:8; Gl 3:10; 1Tm 5:10; 2Tm 2:21 [ai]**4:1** Jn 5:22-30; Rm 5:18; 1Pt 4:5 [aj]Jn 5:25; Rm 14:9; 1Pt 4:5; Rv 18:8; 19:11 [ak]Mk 1:15; Ac 20:25 [al]**4:3** Rm 15:4 [am]**4:4** 1Tm 1:4; 4:7; Ti 1:14; 2Pt 1:16 [an]**4:5** Ac 21:8; Eph 4:11 [ao]**4:6** Gn 35:14; Php 2:17 [ap]**4:8** Jn 15:17; Rv 12:1 [aq]Lk 18:2,6; Jn 5:22-30; Ac 10:42; Heb 12:23

Fulfill Your Ministry

4 I solemnly charge you before God and
Christ Jesus, who is going to judge[ai] the
living and the dead,[aj] and because of His appearing and His kingdom:[ak] 2 Proclaim the
message; persist in it whether convenient
or not; rebuke, correct, and encourage with
great patience and teaching. 3 For the time
will come when they will not tolerate sound
doctrine,[al] but according to their own desires, will multiply teachers for themselves
because they have an itch to hear something
new.[C] 4 They will turn away from hearing the
truth and will turn aside to myths.[am] 5 But as
for you, be serious about everything, endure
hardship, do the work of an evangelist,[an] fulfill your ministry.

6 For I am already being poured out as a
•drink offering,[ao] and the time for my departure is close. 7 I have fought the good fight, I
have finished the race, I have kept the faith.
8 There is reserved for me in the future the
crown[ap] of righteousness, which the Lord,
the righteous Judge,[aq] will give me on that
day, and not only to me, but to all those who
have loved His appearing.[ar]

Final Instructions

9 Make every effort to come to me soon,[as]
10 for Demas[at] has deserted me,[au] because he
loved this present world, and has gone to
Thessalonica.[av] Crescens has gone to Galatia,[aw] Titus[ax] to Dalmatia. 11 Only Luke[ay] is with
me. Bring Mark[az] with you, for he is useful to
me in the ministry. 12 I have sent Tychicus[ba] to
Ephesus. 13 When you come, bring the cloak
I left in Troas[bb] with Carpus, as well as the
scrolls, especially the parchments. 14 Alexander[bc] the coppersmith did great harm to
me. The Lord will repay him according to his
works. 15 Watch out[bd] for him yourself because
he strongly opposed our words.

16 At my first defense, no one stood by me,
but everyone deserted me.[be] May it not be
counted against them. 17 But the Lord stood
with me and strengthened me, so that the
proclamation might be fully made through

[ar]Ti 2:13; 1Jn 2:28 [as]**4:9** Ti 3:12 [at]**4:10** Col 4:14; Phm 24 [au]2Tm 1:15 [av]Ac 17:1 [aw]Gl 1:2 [ax]Ti 1:4 [ay]**4:11** Col 4:14; Phm 24 [az]Ac 15:37-39 [ba]**4:12** Ac 20:4; Ti 3:12 [bb]**4:13** Ac 16:8 [bc]**4:14** 1Tm 1:20 [bd]**4:15** 2Tm 1:14; 2Pt 3:17 [be]**4:16** 2Tm 1:15

[A]3:9 = Jannes and Jambres [B]3:16 Lit *breathed out by God*; the Scripture is the product of God's Spirit working through men; 2Pt 1:20-21. [C]4:3 Or *to hear what they want to hear*; lit *themselves, itching in the hearing*

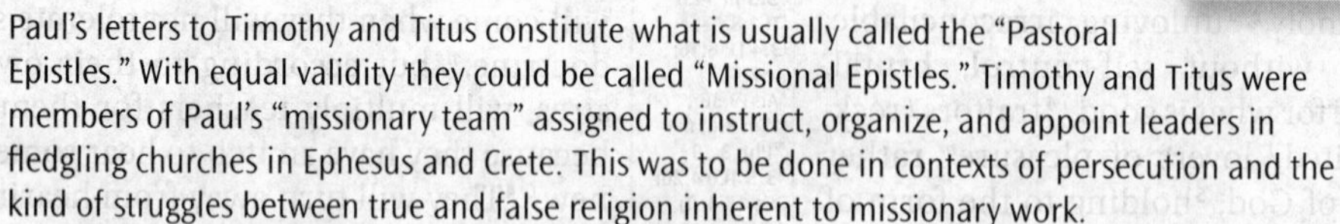

The Authority of Scripture and the Christian Mission

David Hesselgrave

Paul's letters to Timothy and Titus constitute what is usually called the "Pastoral Epistles." With equal validity they could be called "Missional Epistles." Timothy and Titus were members of Paul's "missionary team" assigned to instruct, organize, and appoint leaders in fledgling churches in Ephesus and Crete. This was to be done in contexts of persecution and the kind of struggles between true and false religion inherent to missionary work.

Timothy had a Jewish mother and a Greek father. Of the latter we know little but we are told that his grandmother Lois and his mother Eunice had instructed him in the Sacred Scriptures. These writings are crucial to missionary ministry. In the text before us the Apostle Paul explains why.

The Message of Scripture. The world of the first century was well supplied with a wide variety of so-called holy books. The Scriptures to which Paul refers were writings of an entirely different genre—namely, the Torah, Psalms, and Prophets of the OT. He refers to them as "holy writings," a rabbinic expression associated with Hellenistic Judaism and for that reason especially appropriate in that missionary context. Even though they antedated the birth of Christ, the OT writings were able to instruct Timothy concerning salvation that comes through faith in Christ because they prophesied Christ's coming and redemptive work. The message of Christ is one of inestimable value to people of all times and places because Christ is the only way to salvation (Jn 14:6; Ac 4:12).

The Inspiration of Scripture. The books of the NT, including Paul's letters to Timothy and Titus, were received as Scripture. All biblical books taken together constitute the "Canon" or "measure" by which all truth claims are to be tested. Rival books such as the Hindu Vedas, Buddhist Sutras, Kojiki of Shintoism, the Qur'an of Islam, and the Book of Mormon are of human origin. Ongoing investigation of Bible manuscripts and biblical history reveals that the Bible is completely trustworthy and true. The Apostle Peter writes, "No prophecy of Scripture comes from one's own interpretation, because no prophecy ever came by the will of man; instead, men spoke from God as they were moved by the Holy Spirit" (2 Pt 1:20). The Apostle Paul says, "All Scripture is inspired by God" (2Tm 3:16). The Greek word *theopneustos* literally means "breathed out" by God. Because that is so, God intends Scripture to be carefully expounded, faithfully obeyed, and fervently defended.

The Dynamic of Scripture. The Bible is not only true; it is also powerful. When God breathed into Adam's nostrils Adam became a "living being" (Gn 2:7). Similarly, as the product of the creative breath of God, Scripture has the ability to effect the salvation of sinners. Now Paul adds another dynamic. He adds that Scripture is beneficial in spiritual ministries designed to produce healthy believers and healthy churches. These ministries include: (1) *teaching:* teaching is the primary means of discipling believers in accordance with the Great Commission in Matthew 28:19-20; (2) *rebuking:* the Holy Spirit uses Scripture to rebuke or convict us concerning sin, righteousness, and judgment according to John 16:8; (3) *correcting:* the Greek word contains the root *ortho* indicating that God's people are to "measure up" biblically and be "straight," or orthodox, in doctrine and practice; and, (4) *training in righteousness:* in the context of Scripture, righteousness has to do not only with a right relationship with fellow human beings but also and especially with God Himself as Paul says in 2 Corinthians 5:21. Finally, Paul adds still another dimension to the dynamic of Scripture: the Bible is profitable for the man of God because when God's messenger employs Scripture in the foregoing ways he himself is made "complete" or "competent" and "equipped for every good work" (2Tm 3:17).

Application and Conclusion. Leaders of the ancient church grappled with the doctrine of *Incarnation*—that, as the Son of God, Jesus Christ was fully man and fully God. However, both Scripture and Christ Himself taught the doctrine and it has been confirmed repeatedly in Christian creeds and church councils, including the Council of Chalcedon in 451. In recent times leaders of the modern church have grappled with the doctrine of *Inspiration*—that the original texts of Scripture could be the words of human authors as well as the words of God. However, both Christ and Scripture teach the doctrine and it has been confirmed repeatedly in Christian creeds and by various Christian councils, including the International Council on Biblical Inerrancy in 1978.

The Incarnation of Christ and the Inspiration of Scripture are interwoven and interdependent doctrines. Both are quintessential to missions and God's plan for world evangelization. It was in obedience to God the Father that Jesus came to accomplish redemption. It is in obedience to God the Son that disciples herald the Christian gospel by reducing oral languages to writing; translating the Bible into new languages; revising archaic translations; preaching, teaching, and modeling biblical doctrine and righteous living; and planting, organizing, and enabling leadership in newly planted churches. This is a daunting task made all the more difficult by virtue of the fact that, until Christ returns, our world continues to be a world of heart-rending needs of all kinds—economic, educational, medical, social, and political as well as spiritual. Responding to these needs with ameliorative deeds is inherent to missionary work because Christ commanded His followers, "Let your light shine before men, so that they may see your good works and give glory to your Father in heaven" (Mt 5:16). Indeed, Paul's exhortation is, "As we have opportunity, we must work for the good of all, especially for those who belong to the household of faith" (Gl 6:10).

But first things first! The essence of the task to be carried out by God's "messenger-missionaries" is to employ Scripture to the salvation of sinners, the formation of the church, the defense of truth, and the unmasking of error. That is what makes missionaries (and pastors, and all of "God's messengers" for that matter) competent and that is what equips them and those who hear them to do "every good work" as well as to share every good "word" (2Th 2:17).

me and all the Gentiles might hear. So I was
rescued from the lion's mouth. 18The Lord
will rescue me from every evil work and will
bring me safely into His heavenly kingdom.[a]
To Him be the glory forever and ever! ·Amen.

Benediction

19Greet Prisca and Aquila,[b] and the household of Onesiphorus.[c] 20Erastus[d] has remained at Corinth; I left Trophimus[e] sick at
Miletus.[f] 21Make every effort to come before
winter. Eubulus greets you, as do Pudens,
Linus, Claudia, and all the ·brothers.

22The Lord be with your spirit. Grace be
with you.

[a]4:18 Mk 1:15; Ac 20:25 [b]4:19 Ac 18:2 [c]2Tm 1:16 [d]4:20 Ac 19:22; Rm 16:23 [e]Ac 20:4; 21:29 [f]Ac 20:15,17

Preaching and the Mission of God

Matt Chandler

God's way of reminding His people of what He means to accomplish has always been through the calling of men and women to serve as vessels or conduits through which His voice and power would flow. Whether we look at Moses, the prophets, John the Baptist, Peter at Pentecost, or the church planting genius of the Apostle Paul, God's way of letting people know of His grace made available in Christ is the preaching of His Word. In 2 Timothy 4:1-5 Paul, close to his death, writes to his prize student that this methodology isn't changing. Paul makes it explicitly clear that Timothy is to preach and

proclaim God's word and that to do so is a very serious thing. He charges him "before God and Christ Jesus, who is going to judge the living and the dead" and by "His Kingdom." Is there anything more serious than these things? If all of existence is about and for God's Kingdom and if we will all be judged by Him, how important is the proclamation of God's Word? Important enough that Paul charges Timothy (and by extension, us) with a weighty charge.

On top of the weight of the charge, Paul tells us to proclaim the gospel whether our listeners like it or not. He tells Timothy that people aren't going to like it and will instead look for teachers who will tell them what they want to hear. According to the text there are five stated goals when it comes to preaching and the mission of God:

- **Reprove**—To reprove is to point out error. When we preach we let the Scriptures show us where we have believed lies and where we are living in rebellion. The Scriptures show us where we are outside of God's design for how life and relationships were meant to work.
- **Rebuke**—To rebuke is to correct. How cruel would it be if the Scriptures taught us what was wrong but not what was right? We aren't left wondering what to do but rather are led to what is right, led into how God designed life and relationships to work. When we preach, we aren't commanded to point out only the wrong but to push towards the right as well.
- **Exhort**—To exhort is to encourage. When we preach we encourage disciples to move away from error and toward how God designed for us to live. We don't beat people up but rather build people up.
- **With Patience**—Sanctification is a slower process than most of us want to admit. When we preach the Word we are to do so in such a way that shows patience with those who listen and an understanding that maturation is a process.
- **Teaching**—Simply put, this is the application of the Word. "How" should be a question answered at some level when we preach the word. We can't just answer the "why", "where" and "when" and leave people guessing when it comes to the application of those truths.

TITUS

For the introduction to the book of Titus, see the introduction to the book of 1 Timothy, page 1264.

Greeting

1 Paul,[a] a •slave of God[b] and an apostle of Jesus Christ, to build up[A] the faith of God's elect[c] and their knowledge of the truth[d] that leads[B] to godliness,[e] 2 in the hope of eternal life[f] that God, who cannot lie,[g] promised before time began.[h] 3 In His own time He has revealed[i] His message[j] in the proclamation that I was entrusted[k] with by the command[l] of God our Savior:[m]

4 To Titus,[n] my true son[o] in our common faith.

Grace and peace from God the Father and Christ Jesus our Savior.[p]

Titus's Ministry in Crete

5 The reason I left you in Crete[q] was to set right what was left undone and, as I directed you, to appoint elders[r] in every town: 6 one[s] who is blameless,[t] the husband of one wife, having faithful[C] children not accused of wildness or rebellion. 7 For an •overseer,[u] as God's administrator, must be blameless, not arrogant, not hot-tempered, not addicted to wine, not a bully, not greedy for money, 8 but hospitable, loving what is good, sensible, righteous, holy, self-controlled, 9 holding to the faithful message as taught,[v] so that he will be able both to encourage with sound teaching[w] and to refute those who contradict it.

10 For there are also many rebellious people, full of empty talk and deception, especially those from Judaism.[D] 11 It is necessary to silence them; they overthrow whole households by teaching what they shouldn't in order to get money dishonestly. 12 One of their very own prophets said,

> Cretans are always liars, evil beasts,
> lazy gluttons.[E]

13 This testimony is true.[x] So, rebuke them sharply,[y] that they may be sound in the faith 14 and may not pay attention to Jewish myths[z] and the commands of men who reject the truth.[aa]

15 To the pure, everything is pure, but to those who are defiled and unbelieving nothing is pure; in fact, both their mind and conscience[ab] are defiled. 16 They profess to know God,[ac] but they deny Him by their works.[ad] They are detestable, disobedient, and disqualified for any good work.[ae]

Sound Teaching and Christian Living

2 But you must say the things that are consistent with sound teaching.[af] 2 Older men[ag] are to be level headed, worthy of respect, sensible, and sound in faith, love,[ah] and endurance. 3 In the same way, older women[ai] are to be reverent in behavior, not slanderers, not addicted to much wine. They are to teach what is good, 4 so they may encourage the young women to love their husbands and to love their children, 5 to be self-controlled, pure, homemakers, kind, and submissive[aj] to their husbands, so that God's message[ak] will not be slandered.

6 In the same way, encourage the young men[al] to be self-controlled 7 in everything. Make yourself an example of good works with integrity and dignity[F] in your teaching. 8 Your message is to be sound beyond reproach,[am] so that the opponent will be ashamed, having nothing bad to say about us.

9 •Slaves are to be submissive to their masters[an] in everything, and to be well-pleasing,[ao] not talking back 10 or stealing, but demonstrating utter faithfulness, so that they may

[a] **1:1** Ac 13:9 [b] Ac 16:17; Rm 1:1; Eph 6:6; Jms 1:1; 1Pt 2:16; Rv 1:1 [c] Mt 22:14; 24:22; Lk 18:7; Rm 8:33; Col 3:12; 1Co 1:27-28; 1Th 1:4; Jms 2:5 [d] 1Tm 2:4; 2Tm 3:7 [e] 1Tm 6:3 [f] **1:2** 1Co 15:19; Ti 3:7; Heb 9:15 [g] Nm 23:19; Heb 6:18 [h] Rm 1:2; 2Tm 1:9 [i] **1:3** Jn 21:1; 2Co 4:11; 1Pt 5:4; 1Jn 1:2 [j] Jn 1:1; 2:22; 2Tm 2:15; Heb 4:12 [k] 1Tm 1:11; 6:20; 2Tm 1:12,14 [l] 1Tm 1:1 [m] 1Tm 1:1; 2:3; Ti 2:10; 3:4; Jd 25 [n] **1:4** 2Co 2:13; 7:6,13-14; 8:6,16,23; 12:18; Gl 2:1,3; 2Tm 4:10 [o] 1Tm 1:2 [p] Rm 1:7; 1Co 1:3 [q] **1:5** Ac 27:7,12-13 [r] 1Tm 3:1-7; 5:17 [s] **1:6-8** 1Tm 3:2-4 [t] **1:6** Col 1:22 [u] **1:7** Ac 20:28; Php 1:1; 1Pt 2:25 [v] **1:9** Ac 2:42 [w] 1Tm 1:10; 6:3; 2Tm 1:13; Ti 2:1 [x] **1:13** Jn 8:14 [y] 2Co 13:10 [z] **1:14** 1Tm 1:4; 4:7; 2Tm 4:4; 2Pt 1:16 [aa] 2Tm 4:4 [ab] **1:15** Heb 13:18 [ac] **1:16** Jn 7:28 [ad] Mk 14:6; 2Co 9:8; Gl 3:10; Jms 2:14-26 [ae] 2Co 9:8 [af] **2:1** Ti 1:9 [ag] **2:2** 1Tm 5:1

[ah] 1Co 13:1; 1Jn 4:16 [ai] **2:3** 1Tm 5:2 [aj] **2:5** Lk 10:17; Eph 5:22 [ak] Lk 8:21; 2Tm 2:15; Heb 4:12 [al] **2:6** 1Tm 5:1; 1Pt 5:5; 1Jn 2:13-14 [am] **2:8** 1Tm 2:2 [an] **2:9** Eph 6:5-9; Col 3:22; 1Tm 6:1; 1Pt 2:18; Jd 4 [ao] Heb 13:21

A **1:1** Or *according to* B **1:1** Or *corresponds* C **1:6** Or *believing* D **1:10** Lit *the circumcision* E **1:12** This saying is from the Cretan poet Epimenides (6th century B.C.). F **2:7** Other mss add *incorruptibility*

William Tyndale (1494–1536)

Born around 1494 near the Welsh border, English scholar William Tyndale had a heart and mind like a sponge, eager for learning, especially when learning led to truth. Truth he wanted more than anything, and not merely for his own intellectual pleasure but for all people. He believed his quest for truth would be satisfied in the study of the Bible, but in that day study of the Bible was carefully guarded by church-run universities, and the church controlled access to the Scriptures themselves. Ninety years before his birth, the English Bible had been banned in England by the church.

By the time he was thirty years of age, Tyndale's life mission was set: to work from the best available Greek and Hebrew Bible texts, translating them into vernacular English so readable that any English speaker could be confident that God was speaking and that the Bible was God's Word. In England, Tyndale could find neither help nor a protective bishop for translation work, so he set sail for Germany in 1525 where he completed a New Testament. Pursued there by English bounty hunters, he moved to Antwerp and completed the first five Old Testament books: Genesis through Deuteronomy. There he mixed easily with a group of English merchants, relaxing his guard. It proved to be a fatal mistake. A "friend" eager for the bounty betrayed Tyndale to English agents in May 1535.

Tyndale spent eighteen months in confinement, charged with the "crime" of believing that faith alone justifies and was enough for salvation. With no legal remedy and no defense (since the charges were true), he worked hard to complete the English Bible, helped by a sympathetic warden.

In August 1536, Tyndale was defrocked and condemned. In October, he was tied to a stake and burned as a heretic and an outcast. Mercifully, the executioner strangled him before flames consumed his body. His last words: "Lord, open the King's eyes."

That king, the infamous Henry VIII, would eventually support the distribution of the English Bible as part of his own rebellion against Rome. The scholars who created what would become the King James Version of the Bible depended heavily on Tyndale's work. The translator's last wish—and his life's calling—was thereby fulfilled. Since that day, an English Bible has been available in multiple translations throughout the world.

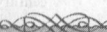

adorn the teaching of God our Savior[a] in everything.
11 For the grace of God has appeared with
salvation[A] for all people,[b] 12 instructing us to
deny godlessness[c] and worldly lusts[d] and to
live in a sensible, righteous,[e] and godly[f] way
in the present age, 13 while we wait for the
blessed hope[g] and appearing of the glory[h] of
our great God and Savior, Jesus Christ. 14 He
gave Himself for us[i] to •redeem us from all
lawlessness and to cleanse for Himself a people for His own possession,[j] eager to do good
works.
15 Say these things, and encourage and rebuke with all authority. Let no one disregard[B]
you.

Christian Living among Outsiders

3 Remind them to be submissive[k] to rulers and authorities, to obey, to be ready
for every good work, 2 to slander no one, to
avoid fighting, and to be kind, always showing gentleness[l] to all people. 3 For we too were
once foolish, disobedient, deceived, enslaved
by various passions[m] and pleasures,[n] living in
malice and envy, hateful, detesting one another.

4 But when the
kindness of God our Savior
and His love
for mankind appeared,[o]
5 He saved us[p] —
not by works of righteousness
that we had done,[q]
but according to His mercy[r] —
through the washing of regeneration[s]
and renewal by the Holy Spirit.[t]
6 He poured out this Spirit
on us abundantly[u]
through Jesus Christ our Savior
7 so that, having been •justified
by His grace,[v]
we may become heirs with the hope
of eternal life.[w]

8 This saying is trustworthy.[x] I want you to insist on these things, so that those who have
believed God might be careful to devote
themselves to good works. These are good
and profitable for everyone. 9 But avoid foolish debates,[y] genealogies,[z] quarrels,[aa] and disputes about the law, for they are unprofitable
and worthless. 10 Reject a divisive[ab] person after a first and second warning,[ac] 11 knowing
that such a person is perverted and sins, being self-condemned.

Final Instructions and Closing

12 When I send Artemas or Tychicus to you,[ad]
make every effort to come to me[ae] in Nicopolis, for I have decided to spend the winter
there. 13 Diligently help Zenas the lawyer and
Apollos[af] on their journey, so that they will
lack[ag] nothing.
14 And our people must also learn to devote
themselves to good works for cases of urgent
need, so that they will not be unfruitful.[ah]
15 All those who are with me greet you. Greet
those who love us in the faith. Grace be with
all of you.[ai]

[a] 2:10 1Tm 1:1; 2:3; Ti 1:3; 3:4; Jd 25
[b] 2:11 Ac 1:8; Rm 10:14; 2Co 5:18-21; 1Tm 2:4; 4:10; 2Pt 3:9
[c] 2:12 Jd 18
[d] 2Tm 4:10; 2Pt 1:4; 2:10
[e] Lk 23:41; 1Co 15:34; 1Th 2:10; 1Pt 2:24
[f] 2Tm 3:12
[g] 2:13 Ac 23:6; 1Th 1:3
[h] Lk 9:32; Jn 17:1,24; 2Co 3:18; 2Pt 3:18
[i] 2:14 Mt 20:28; Mk 10:45; Rm 8:32; Gl 1:4; 2:20; Eph 5:2,25; 1Tm 2:6
[j] Ex 19:5; Lk 1:68
[k] 3:1 Rm 13:1-7; 1Pt 2:13-14
[l] 3:2 Jms 3:13
[m] 3:3 2Pt 1:4; 2:10
[n] Jms 4:1
[o] 3:4 1Tm 1:1; 2:3; Ti 1:3; 2:10; Jd 25
[p] 3:5 Rm 11:14; 2Tm 1:9
[q] Eph 2:9
[r] Eph 2:4; 1Pt 1:3
[s] Jn 3:5; Eph 5:26; 1Pt 3:21
[t] Rm 12:2
[u] 3:6 Jl 2:28; Ac 2:33; 10:45; Rm 5:5
[v] 3:7 Ac 13:43; 15:11; 1Co 8:1; Gl 1:6; 1Pt 4:10
[w] Ti 1:2
[x] 3:8 1Tm 1:15; 3:1; 4:9; 2Tm 2:11
[y] 3:9 1Tm 6:4
[z] 1Tm 1:4
[aa] Rm 1:29; 13:13; 1Co 1:11; 3:3; 2Co 12:20; Gl 5:20; Php 1:15; 1Tm 6:4

[ab] 3:10 1Tm 1:9 [ac] Mt 18:15; 2Th 3:15 [ad] 3:12 Ac 20:4; Eph 6:21; Col 4:7; 2Tm 4:12 [ae] Lk 14:26; 2Tm 4:9 [af] 3:13 Ac 18:24; 19:1; 1Co 1:12; 3:4-6,22; 4:6; 16:12 [ag] Jms 2:15 [ah] 3:14 Mt 13:22; Mk 4:19; 1Co 14:14; Gl 5:22; Eph 5:11; 2Pt 1:8; Jd 12 [ai] 3:15 Col 4:18; 2Th 3:16

[A] 2:11 Or *appeared, bringing salvation*; or *appeared with saving power* [B] 2:15 Or *despise*

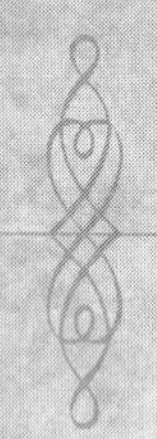

■ **AUTHOR:** Paul (Saul of Tarsus)

■■ **DATE:** Written around A.D. 60 while Paul was imprisoned in Rome

Paul's short, personal letter to a believer named Philemon demonstrates that God's mission to the world changes everything. Relationships carefully defined by civilized culture (and encrusted through time, diminished by greed, enforced by power) are totally reconstructed. The gospel of Jesus Christ works a quiet, persistent revolution in how people think of themselves and others. As Paul explains to Philemon, neither he (with strong social advantages) nor Philemon's runaway slave Onesimus (without any advantages) can approach each other as they did before, now that each is a brother of Jesus Christ, and thus a brother to the other.

PHILEMON

These changes will not be easy or automatic. Each party will have to confront a new identity in Jesus Christ. The slave can no longer be "owned," since he belongs to Christ. The master can no longer pull his socially sanctioned power plays, or even grasp for his full legal rights, since his master is Jesus Christ. Each party will have to work at this change and discover in the transitions new possibilities for mutual flourishing.

Take that difficult lesson into contemporary cultures. Ask how the mission of God refashions community today. Is the disabled person really not able, or able in different ways? How are these abilities incorporated and nurtured by churches? New converts on parole from prison, refugees with language barriers, the depressed and other challenged Christians who want to worship Christ and serve the church: are opportunities found or created? Paul challenges Philemon to adapt to new relationships with a heartfelt celebration that echoes the joy in heaven over a once distant son or daughter of God at last come home. Every church can apply that challenge to its own circumstances, and every person to his or her identity and calling. Jesus Christ revamps the charts of where we stand and how we present ourselves. Let the slave be as a freeman. Let the master be as a partner. Let the rich be wholly dependent on God's grace and the poor be well supplied.

God's mission to the world takes the social boundaries that separate us from one another and challenges believers to find mutual strength and creativity by refreshing these relationships. The refreshment comes from love, grace, joy, and peace—all gifts from God.

Greeting

Paul,[a] a prisoner[b] of Christ Jesus,[c] and Timothy[d] our brother:

To Philemon our dear friend and coworker, 2 to Apphia our sister,[A] to Archippus[e] our fellow soldier,[f] and to the church that meets in your home.[g]

3 Grace to you and peace from God our Father and the Lord Jesus Christ.

Philemon's Love and Faith

4 I always thank my God when I mention you in my prayers, 5 because I hear of your love[h] and faith toward[B] the Lord Jesus and for all the •saints. 6 I pray that your participation in the faith may become effective[i] through knowing every good thing[j] that is in us[C] for the glory of Christ. 7 For I have great joy and encouragement from your love, because the hearts of the saints have been refreshed[k] through you, brother.

An Appeal for Onesimus

8 For this reason, although I have great boldness in Christ to command you to do what is right, 9 I appeal to you, instead, on the basis of love. I, Paul, as an elderly man[D] and now also as a prisoner[l] of Christ Jesus, 10 appeal to you for my son,[m] Onesimus.[E,n] I fathered[F,o] him while I was in chains. 11 Once he was useless to you, but now he is useful both to you and to me. 12 I am sending him back to you as a part of myself.[G,H] 13 I wanted to keep him with me, so that in my imprisonment for the gospel he might serve me in your place. 14 But I didn't want to do anything without your consent, so that your good deed might not be out of obligation, but of your own free will. 15 For perhaps this is why he was separated from you for a brief time, so that you might get him back permanently, 16 no longer as a •slave, but more than a slave—as a dearly loved brother. He is especially so to me, but even more to you, both in the flesh[p] and in the Lord.[I,q]

17 So if you consider me a partner, accept[r] him as you would me. 18 And if he has wronged you in any way, or owes you anything, charge that to my account.[s] 19 I, Paul, write this with my own hand:[t] I will repay it—not to mention to you that you owe me even your own self. 20 Yes, brother, may I have joy from you in the Lord; refresh my heart in Christ. 21 Since I am confident of your obedience, I am writing to you, knowing that you will do even more than I say. 22 But meanwhile, also prepare a guest room for me, for I hope that through your prayers I will be restored to you.

Final Greetings

23 Epaphras,[u] my fellow prisoner in Christ Jesus, greets you, and so do 24 Mark,[v] Aristarchus,[w] Demas, and Luke,[x] my coworkers.

25 The grace of the Lord[J,y] Jesus Christ be with your spirit.[z]

[a] 1 Ac 13:9 [b] 2Tm 1:8; Heb 13:3 [c] Rm 1:1 [d] Ac 16:1; 1Tm 1:2 [e] 2 Col 4:17 [f] Php 2:25 [g] Ac 12:12; Rm 16:5 [h] 5 Dt 6:5; Mt 22:37; Gl 5:6,22; Eph 6:23; 1Th 1:3; 3:6; 5:8; 1Tm 1:14; 1Jn 4:20 [i] 6 Gl 5:6 [j] Gn 1:31; 18:18; 3Jn 11 [k] 7 Lk 12:19; 2Tm 1:16 [l] 9 2Tm 1:8; Heb 13:3 [m] 10 1Th 2:11 [n] Col 4:9 [o] 1Co 4:15 [p] 16 Php 3:3 [q] 1Co 16:19; Rv 11:8 [r] 17 Rm 14:1 [s] 18 Rm 5:13 [t] 19 1Co 16:21 [u] 23 Col 1:7; 4:12 [v] 24 Ac 12:12,25; 15:37,39; Col 4:10; 2Tm 4:11; 1Pt 5:13 [w] Ac 19:29 [x] Col 4:14; 2Tm 4:10-11 [y] 25 2Th 3:18; Rv 11:8 [z] Ps 51:12

A2 Other mss read *our beloved* B5 Lit *faith that you have toward* C6 Other mss read *in you* D9 Or *an ambassador* E10 In Gk, Onesimus means useful. F10 Referring to the fact that Paul led him to Christ; 1Co 4:15 G12 Other mss read *him back. Receive him as a part of myself.* H12 Lit *you—that is, my inward parts* I16 Both physically and spiritually J25 Other mss read *our Lord*

■ AUTHOR: Unknown (some possible authors: Paul, Luke, Apollos, Priscilla, Clement of Rome, Barnabas)

■■ DATE: Written sometime between A.D. 60 and 96

God's mission is the total supremacy and sufficiency of Jesus Christ, expressed eloquently in this letter by an unknown author. (Speculation of who wrote Hebrews still continues.) Christ is supreme above angels, priests, and the great Old Testament heroes. Moses and Melchizedek are mentioned, along with a faith "hall of fame" in chapter 11. Jesus Christ is the One through whom God has spoken.

If God's mission has been consistently described as the building of God's family, the salvation of all who believe, then Jesus is the means to that end. At one time, animal sacrifice—which foreshadowed a future work of God—was the way God forgave sin and built His kingdom. Now the revealed means to this end is Jesus. Hebrews deepens the means-ends issue and reminds us of God's great joy at Jesus' obedience. In fact, the elevation of Jesus to God's "right hand" (1:3, 13; 8:1; 10:12) seems every bit as much the goal of God's mission as the salvation of humankind. Jesus Christ is the purpose of God's work in human history, as much as His once-for-all sacrifice by which the power of sin is beaten and eternal life given.

HEBREWS

This sermon (as Hebrews is widely regarded) drives home its points by referencing Jewish worship and Old Testament Scriptures. Much of the book's argument appears nowhere else in the Bible: Jesus compared to angels, then to the mysterious priest Melchizedek whom Abraham honored (Gn 14:17-24). A modern reader who is literate in Old Testament practice will follow the sermon's logic. But everyone will notice the sermon's warnings. As good and benevolent as God is, there will come a day when His patience gives way to a holy anger. Do not oppose God on that day, Hebrews warns. Do not "harden your hearts" (Heb 3:15) to God's word nor ignore the salvation God presents as the way to life. This sermon pulls no punches.

Hebrews portrays life as a journey. People are searching as Abraham did for a "better city" where God is closer, sorrow farther, where stress and doubt are completely settled in God's kindness. Hebrews calls it a search for Sabbath rest, where God's peace reigns. Modern readers may find "Sabbath rest" a bit antiquated. Even for the devout, the modern Sabbath (day of worship) is crowded with sports, parties, and work. Not much of it feels like rest, or even a change of pace. Hebrews' point is that God's mission is to bring about His Sabbath rest—peace, friendship, plenty, health, joy, and love. It's God's plan to make eternity a "new heaven" of sumptuous delights and re-made relationships, pleasures hard to imagine. It's our longing for such life that drives us to "a better place" (11:16) and the only sure guide is the One already there: Jesus, set on high, anointed by God.

It is the work of believers to show others the appeal of this journey with Christ. Having been enamored by the sacrifice made on our behalf, now we turn toward the world that is satisfied with the stuff of earth and help them enter the Kingdom that is here and yet to come.

The Nature of the Son

1 Long ago God spoke[a] to the fathers by the
prophets[b] at different times and in different ways.[c] 2 In these last days,[d] He has spoken
to us by His Son. God has appointed Him heir
of all things and made the universe[A,e] through
Him. 3 The Son is the radiance[B] of God's glory
and the exact expression[C] of His nature, sus-
taining all things by His powerful word. After
making purification for sins,[D] He sat down at
the right hand of the Majesty on high.[E,f] 4 So
He became higher in rank than the angels,
just as the name He inherited is superior to
theirs.[g]

The Son Superior to Angels

5 For to which of the angels did He ever say,
You are My Son; today I have become Your
Father,[F,G] or again, **I will be His Father, and**
He will be My Son?[H,h] 6 When He again[I] brings
His firstborn into the world,[i] He says, **And**
all God's angels must worship Him.[J,j] 7 And
about the angels He says:

He makes His angels winds,[K]
and His servants[L] **a fiery flame,**[M,k]

8 but to[N] the Son:

Your throne, God,
is forever and ever,
and the scepter of Your kingdom
is a scepter of justice.[l]
9 **You have loved righteousness**
and hated lawlessness;
this is why God, Your God,
has anointed You
with the oil of joy[m]
rather than Your companions.[O,P]

10 And:

In the beginning, Lord,
You established the earth,
and the heavens are the works
of Your hands;[n]
11 **they will perish, but You remain.**
They will all wear out like clothing;[o]
12 **You will roll them up like a cloak,**[Q]
and they will be changed like a robe.
But You are the same,
and Your years will never end.[R,p]

13 Now to which of the angels has He ever said:

Sit at My right hand
until I make Your enemies
Your footstool?[S,T,q]

14 Are they not all ministering spirits sent out
to serve those who are going to inherit salvation?[r]

Warning against Neglect

2 We must, therefore, pay even more attention to what we have heard, so that we
will not drift away. 2 For if the message spoken
through angels was legally binding[U,s] and every transgression and disobedience received
a just punishment,[t] 3 how will we escape if we
neglect such a great salvation? It was first
spoken by the Lord and was confirmed to us
by those who heard Him.[u] 4 At the same time,
God also testified by signs and wonders, various miracles, and distributions of gifts from
the Holy Spirit according to His will.[v]

Jesus and Humanity

5 For He has not subjected to angels the
world to come that we are talking about. 6 But
one has somewhere testified:

What is man that You remember him,
or the son of man that You care
for him?
7 **You made him lower than the angels**
for a short time;
You crowned him with glory
and honor[V]
8 **and subjected everything**
under his feet.[W]

For in **subjecting everything** to him, He left
nothing that is not subject to him. As it is, we
do not yet see **everything subjected** to him.[w]
9 But we do see Jesus — **made lower than the**
angels for a short time so that by God's grace
He might taste death for everyone — crowned
with glory and honor[x] because of His suffering in death.[y]

[a]**1:1** Jn 9:29; Heb 2:2-3 [b]Ac 2:30; 3:21 [c]Nm 12:6,8; Jl 2:28 [d]**1:2** 2Pt 3:3; Jd 18 [e]Ps 2:8; Jn 1:3 [f]**1:3** Mk 16:19; Col 1:17 [g]**1:4** Eph 1:21; Php 2:9 [h]**1:5** 2Sm 7:14; Ps 2:7; Ac 13:33 [i]**1:6** Rm 8:29; Heb 10:5 [j]Dt 32:43; Ps 97:7 [k]**1:7** Ps 104:4 [l]**1:8** Ps 45:6-7 [m]**1:9** Is 61:1,3; Php 2:9 [n]**1:10** Ps 102:25 [o]**1:11** Is 50:9; 51:6 [p]**1:12** Ps 102:26-27; Heb 13:8 [q]**1:13** Jos 10:24; Ps 110:1; Mt 22:44; Mk 12:36; Ac 2:34-35; Heb 10:13 [r]**1:14** Ps 103:20; Mt 18:10; Heb 5:9 [s]**2:2** Dt 33:2; Ac 7:53; Heb 1:1 [t]Nm 15:30; Heb 10:28 [u]**2:3** Lk 1:2; Heb 1:2; 10:29 [v]**2:4** Jn 4:48; Ac 2:22; 1Co 12:4; Eph 1:5 [w]**2:6-8** Jb 7:17; Ps 8:4-6; 1Co 15:25 [x]**2:9** Ac 2:33; 3:13 [y]Jn 3:16; 2Co 5:15; Php 2:9

[A]**1:2** Lit *ages* [B]**1:3** Or *reflection* [C]**1:3** Or *representation*, or *copy*, or *reproduction* [D]**1:3** Other mss read *for our sins by Himself* [E]**1:3** Or *He sat down on high at the right hand of the Majesty* [F]**1:5** Or *have begotten You* [G]**1:5** Ps 2:7 [H]**1:5** 2Sm 7:14; 1Ch 17:13 [I]**1:6** Or *And again, when He* [J]**1:6** Dt 32:43 LXX; Ps 97:7 [K]**1:7** Or *spirits* [L]**1:7** Or *ministers* [M]**1:7** Ps 104:4 [N]**1:8** Or *about* [O]**1:9** Or *associates* [P]**1:8-9** Ps 45:6-7 [Q]**1:12** Other mss omit *like a cloak* [R]**1:10-12** Ps 102:25-27 [S]**1:13** Or *enemies a footstool for Your feet* [T]**1:13** Ps 110:1 [U]**2:2** Or *valid*, or *reliable* [V]**2:7** Other mss add *and set him over the works of your hands* [W]**2:6-8** Ps 8:5-7 LXX

10 For in bringing many sons to glory, it was
entirely appropriate that God — all things exist for Him and through Him — should make
the source[A] of their salvation perfect through
sufferings.[a] 11 For the One who ·sanctifies and
those who are sanctified all have one Father.[B]
That is why Jesus is not ashamed to call them
·brothers,[b] 12 saying:

I will proclaim Your name
to My brothers;
I will sing hymns to You
in the congregation.[C,c]

13 Again, **I will trust in Him.**[D] And again, **Here**
I am with the children God gave Me.[E,d]
14 Now since the children have flesh and
blood in common, Jesus also shared in these,
so that through His death He might destroy
the one holding the power of death — that is,
the Devil[e] — 15 and free those who were held
in slavery all their lives by the fear of death.[f]
16 For it is clear that He does not reach out to
help angels, but to help Abraham's offspring.
17 Therefore, He had to be like His brothers in
every way, so that He could become a merciful and faithful high priest in service[F] to God,
to make ·propitiation[g] for the sins of the people.[h] 18 For since He Himself was tested and
has suffered, He is able to help those who are
tested.

Our Apostle and High Priest

3 Therefore, holy ·brothers and companions in a heavenly calling, consider Jesus,
the apostle and high priest of our confession;[i]
2 He was faithful to the One who appointed
Him, just as Moses was in all God's household. 3 For Jesus is considered worthy of more
glory than Moses, just as the builder has more
honor than the house. 4 Now every house is
built by someone, but the One who built everything is God.[j] 5 Moses was faithful as a servant[k] in all God's household, as a testimony to
what would be said in the future. 6 But Christ
was faithful as a Son over His household. And
we are that household if we hold on to the
courage and the confidence of our hope.[G,l]

[a]**2:10** Lk 13:32; 24:26; Rm 11:36; Heb 7:28
[b]**2:11** Mt 28:10; Jn 20:17; Ac 17:28; Heb 10:10
[c]**2:12** Ps 22:22; Heb 12:23
[d]**2:13** Ps 18:2; Is 8:17-18; 12:2; Jn 10:29
[e]**2:14** Jn 1:14; 1Co 15:54-56; Col 2:15; 2Tm 1:10; 1Jn 3:8
[f]**2:15** Rm 8:15; 2Tm 1:7
[g]**2:17** 2Co 5:21
[h]Php 2:7; Heb 4:15; 5:1-2; 7:26-28
[i]**3:1** Rm 15:8; Php 3:14; Heb 2:11,17; 4:14-15
[j]**3:4** Eph 2:10; 3:9
[k]**3:5** Ex 14:31; Nm 12:7; Dt 18:19
[l]**3:6** Mt 10:22; Rm 5:2; 11:22; 1Co 3:16; Heb 1:2
[m]**3:7-11** Ps 95:7-11; Ac 7:36; Heb 4:3,5
[n]**3:13** Eph 4:22; Heb 10:24
[o]**3:14** 1Co 15:2; Heb 3:6; 10:23; 11:1
[p]**3:15** Ps 95:7-8
[q]**3:16** Nm 14:2; Dt 1:35-38
[r]**3:17** Nm 14:29; Ps 106:26
[s]**4:1-2** 1Th 2:13; Heb 12:15

Warning against Unbelief

7 Therefore, as the Holy Spirit says:

Today, if you hear His voice,
8 **do not harden your hearts**
as in the rebellion,
on the day of testing in the wilderness,
9 **where your fathers tested Me,**
tried Me,
and saw My works 10 **for 40 years.**
Therefore I was provoked
with that generation
and said, "They always go astray
in their hearts,
and they have not known My ways."
11 **So I swore in My anger,**
"They will not enter My rest."[H,m]

12 Watch out, brothers, so that there won't be
in any of you an evil, unbelieving heart that
departs from the living God. 13 But encourage
each other daily, while it is still called **today**,
so that none of you is hardened by sin's deception.[n] 14 For we have become companions
of the ·Messiah if we hold firmly until the end
the reality[I] that we had at the start.[o] 15 As it is
said:

Today, if you hear His voice,
do not harden your hearts
as in the rebellion.[J,p]

16 For who heard and rebelled? Wasn't it
really all who came out of Egypt under Moses?[q] 17 And who was He provoked with for
40 years? Was it not with those who sinned,
whose bodies fell in the wilderness?[r] 18 And
who did He swear to that they would not enter His rest, if not those who disobeyed? 19 So
we see that they were unable to enter because
of unbelief.

The Promised Rest

4 Therefore, while the promise to enter His
rest remains, let us fear that none of you
should miss it.[K] 2 For we also have received the
good news just as they did; but the message
they heard did not benefit them, since they
were not united with those who heard it in
faith[L,s] 3 (for we who have believed enter the
rest), in keeping with what[M] He has said:

[A]**2:10** Or *pioneer*, or *leader* [B]**2:11** Or *father*, or *origin*, or *all are of one* [C]**2:12** Ps 22:22 [D]**2:13** 2Sm 22:3 LXX; Is 8:17 LXX; 12:2 LXX [E]**2:13** Is 8:18 LXX [F]**2:17** Lit *things* [G]**3:6** Other mss add *firm to the end* [H]**3:7-11** Ps 95:7-11 [I]**3:14** Or *confidence* [J]**3:15** Ps 95:7-8 [K]**4:1** Or *that any of you might seem to have missed it* [L]**4:2** Other mss read *since it was not united by faith in those who heard* [M]**4:3** Or *rest), just as*

So I swore in My anger,
they will not enter My rest.[A,a]

And yet His works have been finished since
the foundation of the world, [4]for somewhere
He has spoken about the seventh day in this
way:

And on the seventh day
God rested from all His works.[B,b]

[5]Again, in that passage He says, **They will
never enter My rest.**[A] [6]Since it remains for
some to enter it, and those who formerly received the good news did not enter because
of disobedience,[c] [7]again, He specifies a certain day — **today** — speaking through David
after such a long time, as previously stated:

Today, if you hear His voice,
do not harden your hearts.[C,d]

[8]For if Joshua[e] had given them rest, God
would not have spoken later about another
day. [9]Therefore, a Sabbath rest remains for
God's people. [10]For the person who has entered His rest has rested from his own works,
just as God did from His.[f] [11]Let us then make
every effort to enter that rest, so that no one
will fall into the same pattern of disobedience.

[12]For the word of God is living and effective[g] and sharper than any double-edged
sword,[h] penetrating as far as the separation
of soul and spirit, joints and marrow. It is
able to judge the ideas and thoughts of the
heart.[i] [13]No creature is hidden from Him, but
all things are naked and exposed to the eyes
of Him to whom[j] we must give an account.

Our Great High Priest

[14]Therefore, since we have a great high
priest who has passed through the heavens — Jesus the Son of God — let us hold fast
to the confession.[k] [15]For we do not have a high
priest who is unable to sympathize with our
weaknesses, but One who has been tested in
every way as we are,[l] yet without sin.[m] [16]There-
fore let us approach the throne of grace with
boldness, so that we may receive mercy and
find grace to help us at the proper time.

The Messiah, a High Priest

5 For every high priest taken from men
is appointed in service[D] to God for the
people, to offer both gifts and sacrifices for
sins. [2]He is able to deal gently with those who
are ignorant and are going astray, since he is
also subject to weakness.[n] [3]Because of this, he
must make a sin offering for himself as well
as for the people.[o] [4]No one takes this honor
on himself; instead, a person is called by God,
just as Aaron was.[p] [5]In the same way, the •Mes-
siah did not exalt Himself to become a high
priest, but the One who said to Him, **You are
My Son; today I have become Your Father,**[E,q]
[6]also said in another passage, **You are a priest
forever in the order of Melchizedek.**[F,r]

[7]During His earthly life,[G] He offered prayers
and appeals[s] with loud cries and tears[t] to the
One who was able to save Him from death,
and He was heard because of His reverence.
[8]Though He was God's Son, He learned obedience through what He suffered.[u] [9]After He
was perfected, He became the source of eternal salvation for all who obey Him, [10]and He

[a]**4:3** Ps 95:11; Heb 3:11
[b]**4:4** Gn 2:2; Ex 20:11
[c]**4:5-6** Ps 95:11; Heb 3:19
[d]**4:7** Ps 95:7-8; Heb 3:7
[e]**4:8** Jos 22:4
[f]**4:10** Heb 4:4; Rv 14:13
[g]**4:12** Jr 23:29; 1Pt 1:23
[h]Is 49:2; Eph 6:17; Rv 1:16; 2:12
[i]1Co 14:24-25
[j]**4:13** 2Ch 16:9; Jb 26:6; 34:21; Ps 33:13-15
[k]**4:14** Heb 3:1; 6:20; 10:23
[l]**4:15** Is 53:3; Heb 2:18
[m]2Co 5:21; 1Pt 2:22
[n]**5:2** Heb 2:18; 4:15; 7:28
[o]**5:3** Lv 4:3; 9:7; Heb 9:7
[p]**5:4** Ex 28:1; 1Ch 23:18
[q]**5:5** Ps 2:7; Jn 8:54; Heb 1:1
[r]**5:6** Ps 110:4; Heb 7:17
[s]**5:7** Mt 26:39; Mk 14:36
[t]Ps 22:1; Mt 27:46,50; Mk 15:34,37; Lk 23:46
[u]**5:8** Php 2:7-8; Heb 1:2

TEXT MESSAGES

Text Message

God is at work through His Word. Many are the styles, images, pictures, and metaphors that messengers may use to tell the core message that God sent His Son to save us. The variety of approaches adds creativity and color, and helps relate the gospel to earth's many cultures, but it is this core message that God brings alive to each person individually. We messengers must do our best to share the message with whatever giftedness we have been given. If we fumble, we trust that God's power overshadows our stuttering. His Word can change the world.

[A]**4:3,5** Ps 95:11 [B]**4:4** Gn 2:2 [C]**4:7** Ps 95:7-8 [D]**5:1** Lit *things* [E]**5:5** Ps 2:7 [F]**5:6** Gn 14:18-20; Ps 110:4 [G]**5:7** Lit *In the days of His flesh*

was declared by God a high priest in the order of Melchizedek.

The Problem of Immaturity

11 We have a great deal to say about this, and
it's difficult to explain, since you have become too lazy to understand. 12 Although by
this time you ought to be teachers, you need
someone to teach you the basic principles
of God's revelation again. You need milk,
not solid food.[a] 13 Now everyone who lives
on milk is inexperienced with the message
about righteousness, because he is an infant.
14 But solid food is for the mature—for those
whose senses have been trained to distinguish between good and evil.[b]

Warning against Regression

6 Therefore, leaving the elementary message about the ·Messiah, let us go on to
maturity, not laying again the foundation of
repentance from dead works, faith in God,[c]
2 teaching about ritual washings,[A] laying on
of hands, the resurrection of the dead, and
eternal judgment.[d] 3 And we will do this if God
permits.

4 For it is impossible to renew to repentance
those who were once enlightened, who tasted
the heavenly gift, became companions with
the Holy Spirit,[e] 5 tasted God's good word
and the powers of the coming age, 6 and who
have fallen away, because,[B] to their own harm,
they are recrucifying the Son of God and
holding Him up to contempt.[f] 7 For ground
that has drunk the rain that has often fallen
on it and that produces vegetation useful to
those it is cultivated for receives a blessing
from God. 8 But if it produces thorns and thistles, it is worthless and about to be cursed,
and will be burned at the end.[g]

9 Even though we are speaking this way,
dear friends, in your case we are confident of
the better things connected with salvation.
10 For God is not unjust; He will not forget
your work and the love[C] you showed for His
name when you served the ·saints—and you
continue to serve them.[h] 11 Now we want each
of you to demonstrate the same diligence for
the final realization of your hope, 12 so that
you won't become lazy but will be imitators
of those who inherit the promises through
faith and perseverance.[i]

Inheriting the Promise

13 For when God made a promise to Abraham, since He had no one greater to swear by,
He swore by Himself:

> 14 **I will indeed bless you,**
> **and I will greatly multiply you.**[D,j]

15 And so, after waiting patiently, Abraham[E]
obtained the promise. 16 For men swear by
something greater than themselves, and for
them a confirming oath ends every dispute.
17 Because God wanted to show His unchangeable purpose even more clearly to the heirs of
the promise, He guaranteed it with an oath,[k]
18 so that through two unchangeable things,
in which it is impossible for God to lie, we
who have fled for refuge might have strong
encouragement to seize the hope set before
us.[l] 19 We have this hope as an anchor for
our lives, safe and secure. It enters the inner
sanctuary behind the curtain.[m] 20 Jesus has
entered there on our behalf as a forerunner,[n]
because He has become a high priest forever
in the order of Melchizedek.[o]

The Greatness of Melchizedek

7 For this Melchizedek—

> King of Salem, priest of the Most High
> God,
> who met Abraham and blessed him
> as he returned from defeating the kings,
> 2 and Abraham gave him a tenth
> of everything;
> first, his name means
> king of righteousness,
> then also, king of Salem,
> meaning king of peace;
> 3 without father, mother, or genealogy,
> having neither beginning of days
> nor end of life,
> but resembling the Son of God[p]—

remains a priest forever.

4 Now consider how great this man
was—even Abraham the patriarch[q] gave a
tenth of the plunder to him! 5 The sons of Levi
who receive the priestly office have a com-

[a] **5:12** 1Co 3:2; Heb 6:1; 1Pt 2:21
[b] **5:14** Is 7:15; 1Co 2:6
[c] **6:1** Php 3:13; Heb 5:12; 9:14
[d] **6:2** Jn 3:25; Ac 6:6; 17:31-32; 19:4-6
[e] **6:4** Gl 3:3; Eph 2:8; Heb 10:32
[f] **6:6** Heb 10:29; 2Pt 2:21; 1Jn 5:16
[g] **6:7-8** Gn 3:17-18; Ps 65:10; Is 5:6
[h] **6:10** Pr 19:17; Mt 10:42; 25:40; 2Co 8:4; 1Th 1:3; 2Tm 1:18
[i] **6:12** Heb 10:36; 13:7
[j] **6:13-15** Gn 21:5; 22:16-17; Lk 1:73
[k] **6:16-17** Ex 22:11; Heb 11:9
[l] **6:18** Ti 1:2; Heb 12:1
[m] **6:19** Lv 16:2,15; Heb 9:7
[n] **6:20** Heb 4:14; 8:1; 9:24
[o] Heb 5:6,10; 7:17
[p] **7:1-3** Gn 14:18-20; Mt 4:3; Mk 5:7; Heb 7:6
[q] **7:4** Gn 14:20; Ac 2:29; 7:8-9

[A] **6:2** Or *about baptisms* [B] **6:6** Or *while* [C] **6:10** Other mss read *labor of love* [D] **6:14** Gn 22:17 [E] **6:15** Lit *he*

mand according to the law to collect a tenth
from the people[a] — that is, from their ·broth-
ers — though they have also descended from
Abraham.[A] 6 But one without this[B] lineage
collected tenths from Abraham and blessed
the one who had the promises.[b] 7 Without a
doubt,[C] the inferior is blessed by the superior.
8 In the one case, men who will die receive
tenths, but in the other case, Scripture testifies that he lives.[c] 9 And in a sense Levi himself,
who receives tenths, has paid tenths through
Abraham, 10 for he was still within his ancestor[D] when Melchizedek met him.

A Superior Priesthood

11 If then, perfection came through the Levitical priesthood (for under it the people received the law[d]), what further need was there
for another priest to appear, said to be in the
order of Melchizedek and not in the order of
Aaron?[e] 12 For when there is a change of the
priesthood, there must be a change of law as
well. 13 For the One these things are spoken
about belonged to a different tribe. No one
from it has served at the altar. 14 Now it is evident that our Lord came from Judah,[f] and
Moses said nothing about that tribe concerning priests.

15 And this becomes clearer if another priest
like Melchizedek appears, 16 who did not become a priest based on a legal command concerning physical[E] descent but based on the
power of an indestructible life. 17 For it has
been testified:

> **You are a priest forever**
> **in the order of Melchizedek.**[F,g]

18 So the previous command is annulled because it was weak and unprofitable[h] 19 (for
the law perfected[i] nothing), but a better hope
is introduced, through which we draw near
to God.[j]

20 None of this happened without an oath.
For others became priests without an oath,
21 but He became a priest with an oath made
by the One who said to Him:

> **The Lord has sworn,**
> **and He will not change His mind,**
> **You are a priest forever.**[F,k]

22 So Jesus has also become the guarantee of a
better covenant.[l]

23 Now many have become Levitical priests,
since they are prevented by death from remaining in office. 24 But because He remains
forever, He holds His priesthood permanently. 25 Therefore, He is always able to save[G]
those who come to God through Him, since
He always lives to intercede[m] for them.

26 For this is the kind of high priest we need:
holy, innocent, undefiled, separated from
sinners, and exalted above the heavens.[n] 27 He
doesn't need to offer sacrifices every day, as
high priests do — first for their own sins,
then for those of the people. He did this once
for all when He offered Himself.[o] 28 For the
law appoints as high priests men who are
weak, but the promise of the oath, which
came after the law, appoints a Son,[p] who has
been perfected[q] forever.

A Heavenly Priesthood

8 Now the main point of what is being said
is this: We have this kind of high priest,
who sat down at the right hand of the throne
of the Majesty in the heavens,[r] 2 a minister of
the sanctuary and the true tabernacle that
was set up by the Lord and not man.[s] 3 For every high priest is appointed to offer gifts[t] and
sacrifices; therefore it was necessary for this
priest also to have something to offer. 4 Now
if He were on earth, He wouldn't be a priest,
since there are those[H] offering the gifts prescribed by the law. 5 These serve as a copy and
shadow[u] of the heavenly things, as Moses was
warned when he was about to complete the
tabernacle. For God said, **Be careful that you
make everything according to the pattern
that was shown to you on the mountain.**[I,v]
6 But Jesus has now obtained a superior ministry, and to that degree He is the mediator[w]
of a better covenant,[x] which has been legally
enacted on better promises.[y]

A Superior Covenant

7 For if that first covenant had been faultless, there would have been no occasion for a
second one. 8 But finding fault with His people,[J] He says:[K]

[a] **7:5** Nm 18:21,26; 2Ch 31:4-5
[b] **7:6** Gn 14:19; Rm 4:13
[c] **7:8** Heb 5:6; 6:20
[d] **7:11** Gl 2:21; Heb 7:18-19; 8:7
[e] Heb 7:17; 10:1
[f] **7:14** Is 11:1; Mc 5:2; Mt 1:3; Lk 3:33; Rv 5:5
[g] **7:17** Ps 110:4; Heb 5:6; 6:20; 7:21
[h] **7:18** Rm 8:3; Gl 4:9
[i] **7:19** Ac 13:39; Rm 3:20; Heb 9:9
[j] Heb 4:16; 6:18
[k] **7:21** 1Sm 15:29; Ps 110:4
[l] **7:22** Heb 8:6-10; 9:15; 12:24; 13:20
[m] **7:25** Rm 8:34; Heb 9:24
[n] **7:26** 2Co 5:21; Heb 4:15
[o] **7:27** Eph 5:2; Heb 5:1,3; 9:12,28
[p] **7:28** Heb 1:2; 2:10; 5:2,9
[q] Php 3:12; Heb 10:14; 11:40
[r] **8:1** Col 3:1; Heb 2:17
[s] **8:2** Ex 33:7; Heb 9:11,24
[t] **8:3** Eph 5:2; Heb 5:1; 9:14
[u] **8:5** Col 2:17; Heb 9:23; 10:1
[v] Ex 25:40; Heb 11:7; 12:25
[w] **8:6** Jb 33:23; Is 29:1; Gl 3:19-20; 1Tm 2:5; Heb 9:15; 12:24
[x] Heb 7:22; 9:15; 12:24; 13:20
[y] Lk 22:20; 2Co 3:6,8

[A] **7:5** Lit *have come out of Abraham's loins* [B] **7:6** Lit *their* [C] **7:7** Or *Beyond any dispute* [D] **7:10** Lit *still in his father's loins* [E] **7:16** Or *fleshly* [F] **7:17,21** Ps 110:4 [G] **7:25** Or *He is able to save completely* [H] **8:4** Other mss read *priests* [I] **8:5** Ex 25:40 [J] **8:8** Lit *with them* [K] **8:8** Other mss read *finding fault, He says to them*

Look, the days are coming,
says the Lord,
when I will make a new covenant
with the house of Israel
and with the house of Judah —
9 not like the covenant
that I made with their ancestors
on the day I took them by their hands
to lead them out of the land of Egypt.
I disregarded them, says the Lord,
because they did not continue
in My covenant.
10 But this is the covenant
that I will make with the house
of Israel
after those days, says the Lord:
I will put My laws into their minds
and write them on their hearts.
I will be their God,
and they will be My people.[a]
11 And each person will not teach
his fellow citizen,[A]
and each his brother, saying,
"Know the Lord,"
because they will all know Me,
from the least to the greatest of them.[b]
12 For I will be merciful
to their wrongdoing,
and I will never again remember
their sins.[B,C,c]

13 By saying, **a new covenant**, He has declared
that the first is old. And what is old and aging
is about to disappear.[d]

Old Covenant Ministry

9 Now the first covenant also had regulations for ministry and an earthly sanctuary. 2 For a tabernacle was set up, and in the
first room, which is called the holy place,
were the lampstand, the table, and the presentation loaves.[e] 3 Behind the second curtain, the tabernacle was called the most holy
place.[f] 4 It contained the gold altar of incense
and the ark of the covenant, covered with
gold on all sides, in which there was a gold jar
containing the manna, Aaron's staff that budded, and the tablets of the covenant.[g] 5 The
•cherubim of glory were above it overshadowing the •mercy seat. It is not possible to
speak about these things in detail right now.[h]
6 With these things set up this way, the
priests enter the first room repeatedly, performing their ministry.[i] 7 But the high priest
alone enters the second room, and he does
that only once a year, and never without
blood, which he offers for himself and for the
sins of the people committed in ignorance.[j]
8 The Holy Spirit was making it clear that the
way into the most holy place had not yet been
disclosed while the first tabernacle was still
standing.[k] 9 This is a symbol for the present
time, during which gifts and sacrifices are
offered that cannot perfect the worshiper's
conscience.[l] 10 They are physical regulations
and only deal with food, drink, and various
washings imposed until the time of restoration.[m]

New Covenant Ministry

11 But the •Messiah has appeared, high
priest of the good things that have come.[D]
In the greater and more perfect tabernacle
not made with hands (that is, not of this creation[n]), 12 He entered the most holy place once
for all, not by the blood of goats and calves,
but by His own blood, having obtained eternal •redemption.[o] 13 For if the blood of goats
and bulls and the ashes of a young cow, sprinkling those who are defiled, sanctify for the
purification of the flesh,[p] 14 how much more
will the blood of the Messiah, who through
the eternal Spirit[q] offered Himself without
blemish to God, cleanse our[E] consciences
from dead works to serve the living God?[r]
15 Therefore, He is the mediator[s] of a new
covenant,[F,t] so that those who are called
might receive the promise[u] of the eternal inheritance, because a death has taken
place for redemption from the transgressions committed under the first covenant.[v]
16 Where a will exists, the death of the one
who made it must be established. 17 For a will
is valid only when people die, since it is never
in force while the one who made it is living.
18 That is why even the first covenant was inaugurated with blood. 19 For when every command had been proclaimed by Moses to all

[a] **8:10** Zch 8:8; 2Co 3:3; Heb 10:16
[b] **8:11** Is 54:13; Jn 6:45; 1Jn 2:27
[c] **8:12** Jr 31:31-34; Rm 11:27; Heb 10:17
[d] **8:13** 2Co 5:17
[e] **9:2** Ex 25:8-9,23-39; 26:1; Lv 24:5-8
[f] **9:3** Ex 26:31-33; 40:3
[g] **9:4** Ex 16:33; 25:10,16; 30:1-5; Nm 17:10; Dt 10:2
[h] **9:5** Ex 25:18-19; Lv 16:2
[i] **9:6** Nm 28:3
[j] **9:7** Ex 30:10; Lv 16:15,34; Heb 5:3
[k] **9:8** Jn 14:6; Heb 10:19-20
[l] **9:9** Heb 5:1; 7:19
[m] **9:10** Lv 11:2-3; Col 2:16
[n] **9:11** Heb 2:17; 8:2; 10:1
[o] **9:12** Dn 9:24; Heb 7:27; 10:4
[p] **9:13** Lv 16:14-15; Nm 19:2,9,17-18
[q] **9:14** 1Pt 3:18; 1Jn 1:7
[r] Ti 2:14; Heb 6:1; 10:2,22
[s] **9:15** 1Tm 2:5; Heb 8:6; 12:24
[t] Jr 31:31-34; 1Co 11:25; 2Co 3:6; Heb 7:22; 8:8; 13:20
[u] Gn 12:7; Rm 8:28; Gl 3:19; Heb 4:1
[v] Rm 3:25; 5:6

[A] **8:11** Other mss read *neighbor* [B] **8:12** Other mss add *and their lawless deeds* [C] **8:8-12** Jr 31:31-34 [D] **9:11** Other mss read *that are to come* [E] **9:14** Other mss read *your* [F] **9:15** The Gk word used here and in vv. 15-18 can be translated covenant, will, or testament.

the people according to the law, he took the blood of calves and goats, along with water, scarlet wool, and hyssop, and sprinkled the scroll itself and all the people,[a] 20 saying, **This is the blood of the covenant that God has commanded for you.**[A,b] 21 In the same way, he sprinkled the tabernacle and all the articles of worship with blood.[c] 22 According to the law almost everything is purified with blood, and without the shedding of blood there is no forgiveness.[d]

23 Therefore it was necessary for the copies of the things in the heavens to be purified with these sacrifices, but the heavenly things themselves to be purified with better sacrifices than these.[e] 24 For the Messiah did not enter a sanctuary made with hands (only a model[B] of the true one) but into heaven itself, so that He might now appear in the presence of God for us.[f] 25 He did not do this to offer Himself many times, as the high priest enters the sanctuary yearly with the blood of another.[g] 26 Otherwise, He would have had to suffer many times since the foundation of the world. But now He has appeared one time, at the end of the ages,[h] for the removal of sin by the sacrifice of Himself.[i] 27 And just as it is appointed for people to die once—and after this, judgment[j]— 28 so also the Messiah, having been offered once to bear the sins of many,[k] will appear a second time,[l] not to bear sin, but[C] to bring salvation to those who are waiting for Him.[m]

The Perfect Sacrifice

10 Since the law has only a shadow of the good things[n] to come, and not the actual form of those realities, it can never perfect the worshipers by the same sacrifices they continually offer year after year. 2 Otherwise, wouldn't they have stopped being offered, since the worshipers, once purified, would no longer have any consciousness of sins? 3 But in the sacrifices there is a reminder of sins every year. 4 For it is impossible for the blood of bulls and goats to take away sins.

5 Therefore, as He was coming into the world, He said:

> **You did not want sacrifice and offering,**
> **but You prepared a body for Me.**
> 6 **You did not delight**
> **in whole burnt offerings**
> **and sin offerings.**
> 7 **Then I said, "See—**
> **it is written about Me**
> **in the volume of the scroll—**
> **I have come to do Your will, God!"**[D,o]

8 After He says above, **You did not want or delight in sacrifices and offerings, whole burnt offerings and sin offerings** (which are offered according to the law[p]), 9 He then says, **See, I have come to do Your will.**[E] He takes away the first to establish the second. 10 By this will of God, we have been ·sanctified through the offering of the body of Jesus Christ once and for all.[q]

11 Every priest stands day after day ministering and offering the same sacrifices time after time, which can never take away sins.[r] 12 But this man, after offering one sacrifice for sins forever, sat down at the right hand of God.[s] 13 He is now waiting until His enemies are made His footstool.[t] 14 For by one offering He has perfected forever those who are sanctified. 15 The Holy Spirit also testifies to us about this. For after He says:

> 16 **This is the covenant I will make**
> **with them**
> **after those days, says the Lord:**
> **I will put My laws on their hearts**
> **and write them on their minds,**

17 He adds:

> **I will never again remember**
> **their sins and their lawless acts.**[F,u]

18 Now where there is forgiveness of these, there is no longer an offering for sin.

Exhortations to Godliness

19 Therefore, ·brothers, since we have boldness to enter the sanctuary through the blood of Jesus,[v] 20 by a new and living way He has opened for us through the curtain (that is, His flesh[w]), 21 and since we have a great high priest over the house of God,[x] 22 let us draw near with a true heart in full assurance of faith, our hearts sprinkled ·clean from an evil conscience and our bodies washed in pure water.[y] 23 Let us hold on to the

[a] 9:19 Ex 24:6-8; Lv 14:4-6
[b] 9:20 Ex 24:8; Mt 26:28
[c] 9:21 Ex 29:12; Lv 8:15
[d] 9:22 Lv 17:11
[e] 9:23 Heb 8:5
[f] 9:24 Rm 8:34; Heb 7:25; 8:2
[g] 9:25 Heb 9:7; 10:19
[h] 9:26 Mt 24:3; 28:20; 1Co 10:11
[i] Heb 4:3; 7:27
[j] 9:27 Gn 3:19; 2Co 5:10
[k] 9:28 Is 53:12; 1Pt 2:24
[l] Mk 8:38; 1Th 4:16
[m] Mt 26:28; 1Co 1:7; Ti 2:13
[n] 10:1 Col 2:17; Heb 8:5; 9:11
[o] 10:5-7 Ps 40:6-8; Jr 36:2; Heb 1:6
[p] 10:8 Mk 12:33; Heb 10:5-6
[q] 10:10 Jn 17:19; Heb 7:27; 9:12
[r] 10:11 Nm 28:3; Heb 5:1
[s] 10:12 Rm 8:34; Eph 1:20; Col 3:1; Heb 1:3; 8:1; 12:2; 1Pt 3:22
[t] 10:13 Ps 110:1; Mt 22:44; Mk 12:36; Lk 20:43; Ac 2:34-35; 1Co 15:25; Heb 1:13
[u] 10:16-17 Jr 31:33-34: Heb 8:10,12
[v] 10:19 Eph 2:18; Heb 9:25
[w] 10:20 Jn 10:9; Heb 9:3,8
[x] 10:21 Heb 2:17; 4:14
[y] 10:22 Ezk 36:25; Heb 9:14

[A] **9:20** Ex 24:8 [B] **9:24** Or *antitype*, or *figure* [C] **9:28** Lit *time, apart from sin,* [D] **10:5-7** Ps 40:6-8 [E] **10:9** Other mss add *God* [F] **10:16-17** Jr 31:33-34

confession of our hope without wavering,
for He who promised is faithful.[a] 24 And let us
be concerned about one another in order to
promote love and good works, 25 not staying
away from our worship meetings, as some
habitually do, but encouraging each other,[b]
and all the more as you see the day drawing
near.

[a] 10:23 1Co 1:9; Heb 3:6 [b] 10:25 Ac 2:42; Rm 13:11; Heb 3:13 [c] 10:26 Nm 15:30; Dt 17:12; Heb 6:4; 2Pt 2:20-21; 1Jn 5:16 [d] 10:27 Is 26:11; Zph 1:18; 2Th 1:8

Warning against Deliberate Sin

26 For if we deliberately sin after receiving
the knowledge of the truth, there no longer
remains a sacrifice for sins,[c] 27 but a terrifying expectation of judgment and the fury of
a fire about to consume the adversaries.[d] 28 If
anyone disregards Moses' law, he dies without mercy, based on the testimony of two or

Biblical Community on Mission

Steve Gladen

Why is it important that people gather in community and join God on His mission? It is important because all throughout Scripture, community is integral for the carrying out of God's mission. God chooses to work through people to redeem His world. People reaching people. We undertake the mission of God together because by God's design there is power in "together."

Community existed even before the beginning of time and is rooted in the eternal Trinity. In Genesis 1:26 God says: "Let Us make man in Our image." Our communal nature reflects the communal aspect of God. So fundamental is community that even in the most perfect environment mankind ever experienced, the Garden of Eden, "alone" was deemed "not good" (Gn 2:18). Ecclesiastes describes the importance of not being alone: "Two are better than one," and "A cord of three strands is not quickly broken" (Ecc 4:9,12). That's why in prison the highest form of punishment is solitary confinement!

Jesus' entire journey was undertaken through community. He modeled togetherness by starting community with twelve disciples who would carry out His mission. Jesus created a reproducible and strategic model for the mission to continue. The early church took community seriously and saw great fulfillments of the Great Commission (Mt 28:19-20) and the Great Commandment (22:36-40). In Acts 2:42-47 we see what community looked like and what it did. It fellowshipped, discipled believers, served, evangelized, and worshipped. The result: God's mission spread. The events of Acts 2 occurred within months of the Great Commission. The Lord added to their number daily because these early believers were modeling what Jesus had done among them.

How exactly did God add to their number daily? He did it through their involvement in "the temple complex" and "in various homes" (Ac 5:42). These represent gatherings of people, both publicly and privately. The phrase "one another" is used 58 times in Scripture. Jesus sent the disciples out in pairs (Mk 6:7). There is repeated emphasis on close relationships and community. Mission is fulfilled through togetherness and partnership among believers.

In Luke 5, four men broke through the roof of a synagogue to lower their paralyzed friend to Jesus. Sometimes it takes something as radical as that to fulfill God's mission and lead someone to Jesus! As we are taught in Romans 12, we are a part of one body and we need one another.

How can your community help you see God's mission fulfilled? Your community helps you (1) care about people who don't know Jesus, (2) believe God can reach the impossible person, (3) make a plan for God's mission to happen, (4) overcome difficulties that try to stop God's mission, (5) have courage to do something different to accomplish God's mission, (6) work together to get God's mission done, and (7) be willing to pay the cost to do God's mission.

Are you involved in a relational community of believers? If not, you'll miss God's design for His mission to be fulfilled.

three witnesses.[a] 29 How much worse punishment do you think one will deserve who
has trampled on the Son of God, regarded as
profane[A] the blood of the covenant by which
he was sanctified, and insulted the Spirit of
grace?[b] 30 For we know the One who has said,
Vengeance belongs to Me, I will repay,[B,C] and
again, **The Lord will judge His people.**[D,c] 31 It
is a terrifying thing to fall into the hands of
the living God![d]

32 Remember the earlier days when, after
you had been enlightened, you endured a
hard struggle with sufferings.[e] 33 Sometimes
you were publicly exposed to taunts and afflictions, and at other times you were companions of those who were treated that way.[f]
34 For you sympathized with the prisoners[E]
and accepted with joy the confiscation of your
possessions, knowing that you yourselves
have a better and enduring possession.[F,g] 35 So
don't throw away your confidence, which has
a great reward.[h] 36 For you need endurance, so
that after you have done God's will, you may
receive what was promised.[i]

37 For yet in **a very little while,**
the Coming One will come
and not delay.
38 **But My righteous one**[G] **will live by faith;**
and if he draws back,
I have no pleasure in him.[H,j]

39 But we are not those who draw back and
are destroyed, but those who have faith and
obtain life.

Heroes of Faith

11 Now faith is the reality[I] of what is
hoped for, the proof[J] of what is not
seen.[k] 2 For our ancestors won God's approval
by it.

3 By faith we understand that the universe
was[K] created by God's command,[L,l] so that
what is seen has been made from things that
are not visible.

4 By faith Abel offered to God a better sacrifice than Cain did. By faith he was approved
as a righteous man, because God approved

[a]**10:28** Dt 17:6; Heb 2:2
[b]**10:29** Mt 12:31-32; Eph 4:30; Heb 6:6
[c]**10:30** Dt 32:35-36; Ps 135:14; Rm 12:19
[d]**10:31** Mt 16:16; Lk 12:5
[e]**10:32** Php 1:29-30; Heb 6:4
[f]**10:33** 1Co 4:9; Php 4:14; 1Th 2:14
[g]**10:34** Mt 5:12; 1Pt 1:4-5
[h]**10:35** Heb 2:2; 11:26
[i]**10:36** Lk 21:19; Heb 12:1
[j]**10:37-38** Hab 2:3-4; Lk 18:8; Rm 1:17; Gl 3:11; Rv 22:20
[k]**11:1** Rm 8:24; 2Co 4:18
[l]**11:3** Gn 1:1; Jn 1:3; 2Pt 3:5
[m]**11:4** Gn 4:4; 1Jn 3:12
[n]**11:5** Gn 5:21-24; 2Kg 2:11
[o]**11:7** Gn 6:13-22; 1Pt 3:20
[p]**11:8** Gn 12:1-4,7; Ac 7:2-4
[q]**11:9** Gn 12:8; 18:1; Ac 7:5; Heb 6:17
[r]**11:10** Heb 12:22; 13:14; Rv 21:2,10,14
[s]**11:11** Gn 17:19; 18:11-14; 21:2
[t]**11:12** Gn 22:17; Rm 4:19
[u]**11:13** Mt 13:17; Jn 8:56; Heb 11:39
[v]Gn 23:4; 1Ch 29:15; Ps 39:12; 1Pt 1:17
[w]**11:16** Ex 3:6,15; Mk 8:38; 2Tm 4:18; Heb 13:14
[x]**11:17** Gn 22:1-10; Jms 2:21

his gifts, and even though he is dead, he still
speaks through his faith.[m]

5 By faith Enoch was taken away so he did
not experience death, and **he was not to be**
found because God took him away.[M] For
prior to his removal he was approved, since
he had pleased God.[n] 6 Now without faith it
is impossible to please God, for the one who
draws near to Him must believe that He exists
and rewards those who seek Him.

7 By faith Noah, after he was warned about
what was not yet seen and motivated by godly
fear, built an ark to deliver his family. By faith
he condemned the world and became an heir
of the righteousness that comes by faith.[o]

8 By faith Abraham, when he was called,
obeyed and went out to a place he was going
to receive as an inheritance. He went out, not
knowing where he was going.[p] 9 By faith he
stayed as a foreigner in the land of promise,
living in tents with Isaac and Jacob, coheirs of
the same promise.[q] 10 For he was looking forward to the city that has foundations, whose
architect and builder is God.[r]

11 By faith even Sarah herself, when she was
unable to have children, received power to
conceive offspring, even though she was past
the age, since she[N] considered that the One
who had promised was faithful.[s] 12 Therefore
from one man — in fact, from one as good as
dead — came offspring as numerous as the
stars of heaven and as innumerable as the
grains of sand by the seashore.[t]

13 These all died in faith without having received the promises, but they saw them from
a distance,[u] greeted them, and confessed
that they were foreigners and temporary
residents on the earth.[v] 14 Now those who say
such things make it clear that they are seeking a homeland. 15 If they were thinking about
where they came from, they would have had
an opportunity to return. 16 But they now desire a better place — a heavenly one. Therefore God is not ashamed to be called their
God, for He has prepared a city for them.[w]

17 By faith Abraham, when he was tested,
offered up Isaac.[x] He received the promises
and he was offering his unique son, 18 the

[A]**10:29** Or *ordinary* [B]**10:30** Other mss add *says the Lord* [C]**10:30** Dt 32:35
[D]**10:30** Dt 32:36 [E]**10:34** Other mss read *sympathized with my imprisonment*
[F]**10:34** Other mss add *in heaven* [G]**10:38** Other mss read *the righteous one*
[H]**10:37-38** Is 26:20 LXX; Hab 2:3-4 [I]**11:1** Or *assurance* [J]**11:1** Or *conviction*
[K]**11:3** Or *the worlds were*, or *the ages were* [L]**11:3** Or *word* [M]**11:5** Gn 5:21-24
[N]**11:11** Or *By faith Abraham, even though he was past age — and Sarah herself was barren — received the ability to procreate since he*

one it had been said about, **Your ˙seed will**
be traced[A] **through Isaac.**[B,a] 19 He considered
God to be able even to raise someone from
the dead,[b] and as an illustration,[C] he received
him back.
20 By faith Isaac blessed Jacob and Esau[c]
concerning things to come. 21 By faith Jacob,
when he was dying, blessed each of the sons
of Joseph, and **he worshiped, leaning on the**
top of his staff.[D,d] 22 By faith Joseph, as he was
nearing the end of his life, mentioned the
exodus of the Israelites and gave instructions
concerning his bones.[e]
23 By faith, after Moses was born, he was
hidden by his parents for three months, because they saw that the child was beautiful,
and they didn't fear the king's edict.[f] 24 By
faith Moses, when he had grown up, refused
to be called the son of Pharaoh's daughter
25 and chose to suffer with the people of God
rather than to enjoy the short-lived pleasure
of sin.[g] 26 For he considered the reproach because of the ˙Messiah to be greater wealth
than the treasures of Egypt, since his attention was on the reward.[h]
27 By faith he left Egypt behind, not being
afraid of the king's anger, for Moses persevered as one who sees Him who is invisible.[i]
28 By faith he instituted the ˙Passover and
the sprinkling of the blood, so that the destroyer of the firstborn might not touch the
Israelites. 29 By faith they crossed the Red Sea
as though they were on dry land. When the
Egyptians attempted to do this, they were
drowned.[j]
30 By faith the walls of Jericho fell down after being encircled by the Israelites for seven
days. 31 By faith Rahab the prostitute received
the spies in peace and didn't perish with
those who disobeyed.[k]
32 And what more can I say? Time is too
short for me to tell about Gideon, Barak, Samson, Jephthah,[l] David, Samuel, and the prophets,[m] 33 who by faith conquered kingdoms,[n]
administered justice, obtained promises, shut
the mouths of lions,[o] 34 quenched the raging
of fire, escaped the edge of the sword, gained
strength after being weak, became mighty
in battle, and put foreign armies to flight.[p]
35 Women received their dead—they were
raised to life again. Some men were tortured,
not accepting release, so that they might gain a
better resurrection, 36 and others experienced
mockings and scourgings, as well as bonds
and imprisonment.[q] 37 They were stoned,[E,r]
they were sawed in two, they died by the
sword, they wandered about in sheepskins, in
goatskins,[s] destitute, afflicted, and mistreated.
38 The ˙world was not worthy of them. They
wandered in deserts and on mountains, hiding in caves and holes in the ground.
39 All these were approved through their
faith, but they did not receive what was
promised, 40 since God had provided something better for us, so that they would not be
made perfect without us.[t]

The Call to Endurance

12 Therefore, since we also have such a
large cloud of witnesses[u] surrounding
us, let us lay aside every weight and the sin
that so easily ensnares us. Let us run with endurance[v] the race that lies before us, 2 keeping
our eyes on Jesus,[F] the source and perfecter[G]
of our faith, who for the joy that lay before
Him[H] endured a cross and despised the
shame[w] and has sat down at the right hand
of God's throne.

Fatherly Discipline

3 For consider Him who endured such hostility from sinners against Himself, so that
you won't grow weary and lose heart.[x] 4 In
struggling against sin, you have not yet resisted to the point of shedding your blood.
5 And you have forgotten the exhortation that
addresses you as sons:

> **My son, do not take the Lord's**
> **discipline lightly**
> **or faint when you are reproved by Him,**
> 6 **for the Lord disciplines the one He loves**
> **and punishes every son He receives.**[I,y]

7 Endure suffering as discipline: God is dealing with you as sons. For what son is there
that a father does not discipline? 8 But if
you are without discipline—which all[J] re-

[a]**11:18** Gn 21:12; Rm 9:7 [b]**11:19** Rm 4:17 [c]**11:20** Gn 25:25; 27:26-40 [d]**11:21** Gn 47:31; 48:1,5,16,20 [e]**11:22** Gn 50:24-25; Ex 13:19 [f]**11:23** Ex 1:16,22; 2:2 [g]**11:24-25** Ex 2:10-11; Ps 84:10 [h]**11:26** Heb 10:35; 13:13 [i]**11:27** Rm 1:20; Col 1:15-16; 1Tm 1:17 [j]**11:29** Ex 14:22-30 [k]**11:31** Jos 2:1; 6:23 [l]**11:32** Jdg 4:6; 11:1; 13:24 [m]1Sm 1:20; 16:1,13 [n]**11:33** 2Sm 7:11; 8:1-3 [o]Jdg 14:5-6; 1Sm 17:34-37; Dn 6:22 [p]**11:34** Jdg 15:8; 2Kg 20:7; Dn 3:25 [q]**11:36** Gn 39:20; Jr 20:2 [r]**11:37** 1Kg 21:13; 2Ch 24:20-21 [s]1Kg 19:10; 2Kg 1:8 [t]**11:40** Heb 11:16; Rv 6:11 [u]**12:1** Heb 11:2,4-5,39 [v]1Co 9:24; Heb 10:36 [w]**12:2** Lk 24:26; Php 2:8-9; Heb 13:13 [x]**12:3** Mt 10:24; Gl 6:9 [y]**12:5-6** Jb 5:17; Ps 94:12; Pr 3:11-12; Rv 3:16

[A]**11:18** Lit *called* [B]**11:18** Gn 21:12 [C]**11:19** Or *a foreshadowing*, or *a parable*, or *a type* [D]**11:21** Gn 47:31 [E]**11:37** Other mss add *they were tempted* [F]**12:2** Or *us, looking to Jesus* [G]**12:2** Or *the founder and completer* [H]**12:2** Or *who instead of the joy lying before Him*; that is, the joy of heaven [I]**12:6** Pr 3:11-12 [J]**12:8** = Christians

ceive[A]—then you are illegitimate children and not sons.[a] 9 Furthermore, we had natural fathers discipline us, and we respected them. Shouldn't we submit even more to the Father of spirits and live?[b] 10 For they disciplined us for a short time based on what seemed good to them, but He does it for our benefit, so that we can share His holiness.[c] 11 No discipline seems enjoyable at the time, but painful. Later on, however, it yields the fruit of peace[d] and righteousness to those who have been trained by it.[e]

12 Therefore strengthen your tired hands and weakened knees,[f] 13 and make straight paths for your feet, so that what is lame may not be dislocated[B] but healed instead.[g]

Warning against Rejecting God's Grace

14 Pursue peace with everyone, and holiness[h]—without it no one will see the Lord.[i] 15 Make sure that no one falls short of the grace of God and that no root of bitterness springs up, causing trouble and by it, defiling many.[j] 16 And make sure that there isn't any immoral or irreverent[k] person like Esau, who sold his birthright in exchange for one meal.[l] 17 For you know that later, when he wanted to inherit the blessing, he was rejected because he didn't find any opportunity for repentance, though he sought it with tears.[m]

18 For you have not come to what could be touched, to a blazing fire, to darkness, gloom, and storm, 19 to the blast of a trumpet, and the sound of words. (Those who heard it begged that not another word be spoken to them, 20 for they could not bear what was commanded: **And if even an animal touches the mountain, it must be stoned!**[C,n] 21 The appearance was so terrifying that Moses said, **I am terrified and trembling.**[D,o]) 22 Instead, you have come to Mount ˙Zion, to the city of the living God (the heavenly Jerusalem), to myriads of angels in festive gathering,[p] 23 to the assembly of the firstborn whose names have been written[E] in heaven, to God who is the Judge of all, to the spirits of righteous people made perfect,[q] 24 to Jesus (mediator[r] of a new covenant[s]), and to the sprinkled blood, which says better things than the blood of Abel.[t]

25 Make sure that you do not reject the One who speaks. For if they did not escape when they rejected Him who warned them on earth, even less will we if we turn away from Him who warns us from heaven.[u] 26 His voice shook the earth at that time, but now He has promised, **Yet once more I will shake not only the earth but also heaven.**[F,v] 27 This expression, "Yet once more," indicates the removal of what can be shaken[w]—that is, created things—so that what is not shaken might remain. 28 Therefore, since we are receiving a kingdom that cannot be shaken, let us hold on to grace.[G] By it, we may serve God acceptably, with reverence and awe,[x] 29 for our God is a consuming fire.[y]

Final Exhortations

13 Let brotherly love[z] continue. 2 Don't neglect to show hospitality, for by doing this some have welcomed angels as guests without knowing it.[aa] 3 Remember the prisoners, as though you were in prison with them, and the mistreated, as though you yourselves were suffering bodily.[H] 4 Marriage must be respected by all, and the marriage bed kept undefiled, because God will judge immoral people and adulterers.[ab] 5 Your life should be free from the love of money. Be satisfied with what you have, for He Himself has said, **I will never leave you or forsake you.**[I,ac] 6 Therefore, we may boldly say:

The Lord is my helper;
I will not be afraid.
What can man do to me?[J,ad]

7 Remember your leaders who have spoken God's word to you. As you carefully observe the outcome of their lives, imitate their faith.[ae] 8 Jesus Christ is the same yesterday, today, and forever.[af] 9 Don't be led astray by various kinds of strange teachings; for it is good for the heart to be established by grace and not by foods, since those involved in them have not benefited.[ag] 10 We have an altar from which those who serve the tabernacle do not have a right to eat.[ah] 11 For the bodies of those animals whose blood is brought into the most holy place by the high priest[ai] as a sin

[a] **12:7-8** Dt 8:5; 1Pt 5:9 [b] **12:9** Nm 16:22; Is 38:16 [c] **12:10** Lv 11:44; 2Pt 1:4 [d] **12:11** Is 32:17; Jms 3:17-18 [e] 1Pt 1:6 [f] **12:12** Jb 4:3-4; Is 35:3 [g] **12:13** Pr 4:26; Gl 6:1 [h] **12:14** Rm 6:22; 14:19 [i] Mt 5:8; 2Co 7:1 [j] **12:15** 2Co 6:1; Gl 5:4; Heb 3:12; 10:39 [k] **12:16** 1Tm 1:9; 4:7; 6:20; 2Tm 2:16 [l] Gn 25:33 [m] **12:17** Gn 27:34-38 [n] **12:18-20** Ex 19:12-13,18; 20:18-21; Dt 4:11; 5:5,25 [o] **12:21** Dt 9:19 [p] **12:22** Gl 4:26; Heb 11:10 [q] **12:23** Ps 94:2; Lk 10:20; Php 3:12 [r] **12:24** 1Tm 2:5; Heb 7:22; 8:6; 9:15 [s] 1Co 11:25; 2Co 3:6; Heb 13:20 [t] Gn 4:10; Heb 11:4 [u] **12:25** Heb 2:2-4; 8:5; 11:7 [v] **12:26** Ex 19:18; Hg 2:6 [w] **12:27** 1Co 7:31; 2Pt 3:10 [x] **12:28** Dn 2:44; Heb 13:15 [y] **12:29** Dt 4:24; 2Th 1:8 [z] **13:1** Rm 12:10; 1Pt 1:22 [aa] **13:2** Gn 18:3; Mt 25:35 [ab] **13:3-4** Mt 25:36; 1Co 6:9 [ac] **13:5** Dt 31:6,8; Jos 1:5; Php 4:11 [ad] **13:6** Ps 27:1; 56:4,11; 118:6 [ae] **13:7** Heb 6:12; 13:17,24 [af] **13:8** Jn 8:58; Heb 1:12 [ag] **13:9** Eph 4:14; Col 2:16 [ah] **13:10** 1Co 9:13; 10:18 [ai] **13:11** 1Co 9:13; 10:18

[A] **12:8** Lit *discipline, of which all have become participants* [B] **12:13** Or *so that the lame will not be turned aside* [C] **12:20** Ex 19:12 [D] **12:21** Dt 9:19 [E] **12:23** Or *registered* [F] **12:26** Hg 2:6 [G] **12:28** Or *let us give thanks*, or *let us have grace* [H] **13:3** Or *mistreated, since you are also in a body* [I] **13:5** Dt 31:6 [J] **13:6** Ps 118:6

offering are burned outside the camp.[a]
12 Therefore Jesus also suffered outside the
gate,[b] so that He might •sanctify[A] the people
by His own blood. 13 Let us then go to Him
outside the camp, bearing His disgrace.[c]
14 For we do not have an enduring city here;
instead, we seek the one to come.[d] 15 Therefore, through Him let us continually offer up
to God a sacrifice of praise, that is, the fruit
of our lips that confess His name.[e] 16 Don't
neglect to do what is good and to share, for
God is pleased with such sacrifices.[f] 17 Obey
your leaders[B] and submit to them, for they
keep watch[g] over your souls as those who
will give an account, so that they can do this
with joy and not with grief, for that would
be unprofitable for you. 18 Pray for us; for
we are convinced that we have a clear conscience, wanting to conduct ourselves honorably in everything.[h] 19 And I especially urge
you to pray[C] that I may be restored to you
very soon.

Benediction and Farewell

20 Now may the God of peace, who brought
up from the dead our Lord Jesus — the great
Shepherd of the sheep[i] — with the blood of
the everlasting covenant,[j] 21 equip[D] you with
all that is good to do His will, working in us
what is pleasing in His sight, through Jesus
Christ. Glory belongs to Him forever and
ever.[E,k] •Amen.
22 •Brothers, I urge you to receive this message of exhortation, for I have written to you
briefly. 23 Be aware that our brother Timothy
has been released. If he comes soon enough,
he will be with me when I see you. 24 Greet all
your leaders and all the •saints. Those who
are from Italy greet you. 25 Grace be with all
of you.[l]

[a] **13:11** Ex 29:14; Lv 16:27 [b] **13:12** Jn 19:17; Ac 7:58 [c] **13:13** Heb 11:26; 1Pt 4:14 [d] **13:14** Mc 3:10; Heb 12:22 [e] **13:15** Lv 7:12; Hs 14:2; Eph 5:20 [f] **13:16** Rm 12:13; Php 4:18 [g] **13:17** Is 62:6; Ezk 3:17; Ac 20:28 [h] **13:18** Ac 23:1; 1Th 5:25 [i] **13:20** Jn 10:11; Ac 2:24; Rm 15:33 [j] Zch 9:11; Heb 7:22; 8:6-10; 9:15; 12:24 [k] **13:21** Rm 11:36; Php 2:13; 1Pt 5:10 [l] **13:22-25** Ac 16:1; Col 4:18; 1Th 3:2; Heb 13:7,17; 1Pt 5:12

PRAYING FOR THE WORLD

Rise Up, O Men of God!

Great leaders are required in all segments of society. For good reason. And how much more so in the church! Christ is the head of the church, His body, and He calls gifted members to lead. Great leaders take the mission of God to another level. That is why God made special requirements for leadership in the church—calling upon people who have both qualifications and qualities that will allow them to handle the responsibilities of church leadership.

Leadership is never easy. Church leaders necessarily find themselves to be Satan's targets, for they are on the front lines leading the charge. Thus, we should continually pray for those in leadership, and beyond that, ask for God to give His unmistakable call and courage to many others who can step up and lead churches of every size in every place around the world.

Today, Lord, we pray for our church leaders. We know the special call You have given them, and the heavy responsibility they carry. Help them lead with wisdom, discernment, humility, grace, and love for the people You have placed in their care.

And we pray Lord that You will give Your call and courage to many who can step in and fill the shoes of those in established churches who are getting older. May they be mentored and prepared to continue the work already begun. We pray for others who will strike out and lead new churches in needy places—around the corner and around the world. Amen.

[A] 13:12 Or *set apart*, or *consecrate* [B] 13:17 Or *rulers* [C] 13:19 Lit *to do this* [D] 13:21 Or *perfect* [E] 13:21 Other mss omit *and ever*

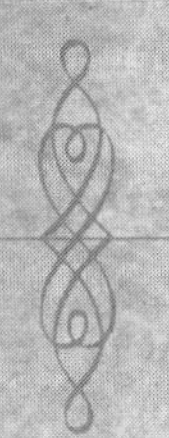

■ **AUTHOR:** James, the half-brother of Jesus, and the leader of the church in Jerusalem

■■ **DATE:** Written before the Jewish council on circumcision in Jerusalem (A.D. 49)

Never imagine that following Jesus is to punt away the active life you seek. James describes the faithful life as action and passion—even to the point of posing what might seem like a glaring counterpoint to other New Testament teachings. Can faith save you, James asks? No, faith alone cannot save you. You must show it, live it, and walk in it before faith saves you, because only then is faith real. Tough talk from the brother of Jesus.

For James, faith is always expressed. Be faithful with your speech, he insists. Be faithful with fair treatment of everybody. Don't favor the rich as if they are special. Pray for each other. Solve your quarrels quickly, before friends drift apart. Be generous, as God is. In these ways show your faith. Then it will be so much more than pious self-indulgence.

JAMES

Faith that wants to shine a light on itself is not faith. Let service to others be your first word, your show of faith. Faith that works for God is authentic. It rings true.

God's mission to the world is faith that makes a difference. Active people sorting out the Lordship of Jesus Christ in daily living are God's agents in the world and missionaries in the best sense. Active faith points to God's way as *the* way. On that journey, Jesus is the forerunner; all who follow are torch bearers showing the way.

James works through some very practical life issues. Knowing that words are weapons, he urges his readers to aim for God's work, not self-promotion, in all speech. He also urges well-to-do readers to stop misusing God's gifts and instead to look to the service wealth could provide. Prayer is another concern. Many prayers seem to bounce off the walls, unheard by God. Many worthy requests (for healing, a job, a break, a favorable outcome) seem ineffective. How should we pray, then? James offers wisdom on finding God's mission at the center of your conversations with God.

None of these "do-it" points are faith substitutes. God wants our worship and trust. But belief without action is a false claim, James insists. Live in faith, practice the life of faith, know God by trust and action, and discover the vitality and security of friendship with God.

If God is at work in you, then believe and don't doubt. Instead, align yourself with the part of God's mission you are specially designed to help.

Greeting

1 James,[a] a ·slave of God[b] and of the Lord
Jesus Christ:
To the 12 tribes[c] in the Dispersion.[A,d]
Greetings.[e]

Trials and Maturity

2 Consider it a great joy, my ·brothers,
whenever you experience various trials,[f]
3 knowing that the testing of your faith produces endurance. 4 But endurance must do its
complete work, so that you may be mature
and complete, lacking nothing.
5 Now if any of you lacks wisdom, he should
ask God, who gives to all generously and without criticizing, and it will be given to him.[g]
6 But let him ask in faith without doubting.
For the doubter is like the surging sea, driven
and tossed by the wind. 7 That person should
not expect to receive anything from the Lord.
8 An indecisive[B] man is unstable in all his
ways.[h]
9 The brother of humble circumstances
should boast in his exaltation, 10 but the one
who is rich should boast in his humiliation
because he will pass away like a flower of the
field.[i] 11 For the sun rises with its scorching
heat and dries up the grass; its flower falls off,
and its beautiful appearance is destroyed. In
the same way, the rich man will wither away
while pursuing his activities.[j]
12 A man who endures trials[C] is blessed, because when he passes the test he will receive
the crown[k] of life that God[D] has promised to
those who love Him.[l]
13 No one undergoing a trial should say, "I
am being tempted by God." For God is not
tempted by evil,[E] and He Himself doesn't
tempt anyone. 14 But each person is tempted
when he is drawn away and enticed by his
own evil desires.[m] 15 Then after desire has conceived, it gives birth to sin, and when sin is
fully grown, it gives birth to death.[n]
16 Don't be deceived, my dearly loved brothers.[o] 17 Every generous act and every perfect
gift is from above, coming down from the
Father of lights; with Him there is no variation or shadow cast by turning.[p] 18 By His own
choice, He gave us a new birth by the message
of truth[F] so that we would be the ·firstfruits
of His creatures.[q]

Hearing and Doing the Word

19 My dearly loved brothers, understand
this: Everyone must be quick to hear, slow to
speak, and slow to anger,[r] 20 for man's anger
does not accomplish God's righteousness.
21 Therefore, ridding yourselves of all moral
filth and evil,[G] humbly receive the implanted
word, which is able to save you.[H,s]
22 But[t] be doers of the word and not hearers
only, deceiving yourselves. 23 Because if any-

[a]1:1 Mt 13:55; Mk 6:3; Ac 12:17; 15:13; 21:18; Gl 1:19; 2:9,12; Jd 1
[b]Ac 16:17; Rm 1:1; Eph 6:6; Jms 1:1; 1Pt 2:16; Rv 1:1
[c]Gn 49:28; Ex 24:4; Ezk 47:13; Mt 19:28; Ac 26:7; Rv 21:12
[d]Jn 7:35; 1Pt 1:1
[e]Ti 1:1
[f]1:2 Mt 5:12; 1Pt 1:6
[g]1:5 1Kg 3:9; Pr 2:3-6; Mt 7:7
[h]1:8 Jms 4:8; 2Pt 2:14
[i]1:10 1Co 7:31; 1Pt 1:24
[j]1:11 Ps 102:4,11; Is 40:7
[k]1:12 1Co 9:25; 2Tm 4:8; 1Pt 5:4; Rv 2:10; 3:11
[l]Mt 10:22; Jms 2:5
[m]1:14 Pr 7:6-23
[n]1:15 Jb 15:35; Ps 7:14; Is 59:4; Rm 6:23
[o]1:16 1Co 6:9; Jms 1:19
[p]1:17 Nm 23:19; Mal 3:6; Jn 3:27; 1Jn 1:5
[q]1:18 Jn 1:13; Eph 1:12
[r]1:19 Pr 10:19; 17:27; Ec 5:1-2
[s]1:21 Eph 1:13; 4:22; Col 3:8
[t]1:22-25 Mt 7:24-27; Rm 2:13; Jms 2:14-20

GOD WHO SENDS

Mature in Faith and Mission

To separate nurture and mission is a dangerous theological fallacy. The idea that we first teach and train people then send them meaningfully on mission is not the New Testament pattern. Mission must be experienced as well as taught. The identity of both experience and understanding emanate from the very nature of Christian existence. Out of this comes the expression in life of both experience and understanding borne on the wings of purpose. This, as we have observed, is the missional impulse. As impulse compels expression, the missional purpose comes to fruition. As our very being is constituted of the divine mission, so the full flowering of who and what we are can only come in the living out of the divine missional purpose. Only "in" and "on" mission are we able fully to mature.

(DUBOSE, 129)

A1:1 Jewish people scattered throughout Gentile lands who spoke Gk and were influenced by Gk culture B1:8 Or *A doubting*, or *A double-minded* C1:12 Lit *trial*, used as a collective D1:12 Other mss read *that the Lord* E1:13 Or *evil persons*, or *evil things* F1:18 = the gospel G1:21 Lit *evil excess* H1:21 Lit *save your souls*

one is a hearer of the word and not a doer,
he is like a man looking at his own face[A] in a
mirror. 24 For he looks at himself, goes away,
and immediately forgets what kind of man
he was. 25 But the one who looks intently into
the perfect law of freedom and perseveres
in it, and is not a forgetful hearer but one
who does good works — this person will be
blessed in what he does.[a]

26 If anyone[B] thinks he is religious without
controlling his tongue,[b] then his religion is
useless and he deceives himself. 27 Pure and
undefiled religion before our[C] God and Father is this: to look after orphans and widows[c] in their distress and to keep oneself
unstained by the ·world.[d]

The Sin of Favoritism

2 My ·brothers, do not show favoritism
as you hold on to the faith in our glorious Lord Jesus Christ.[e] 2 For example, a man
comes into your meeting wearing a gold
ring and dressed in fine clothes, and a poor
man dressed in dirty clothes also comes in.
3 If you look with favor on the man wearing
the fine clothes and say, "Sit here in a good
place," and yet you say to the poor man,
"Stand over there," or, "Sit here on the floor
by my footstool," 4 haven't you discriminated
among yourselves and become judges with
evil thoughts?

5 Listen, my dear brothers: Didn't God
choose the poor in this world[f] to be rich in
faith[g] and heirs[h] of the kingdom that He has
promised to those who love Him? 6 Yet you
dishonored that poor man.[i] Don't the rich
oppress you and drag[j] you into the courts?
7 Don't they blaspheme the noble name that
was pronounced over you at your baptism?[k]

8 Indeed, if you keep the royal law prescribed in the Scripture, **Love your neighbor
as yourself**,[D,l] you are doing well. 9 But if you
show favoritism,[m] you commit sin and are
convicted by the law as transgressors. 10 For
whoever keeps the entire law, yet fails in one
point, is ·guilty of breaking it all.[n] 11 For He
who said, **Do not commit adultery**,[E] also said,
Do not murder.[F,o] So if you do not commit
adultery, but you do murder, you are a lawbreaker.

12 Speak and act as those who will be judged
by the law of freedom.[p] 13 For judgment is
without mercy to the one who hasn't shown
mercy.[q] Mercy triumphs over judgment.

Faith and Works

14 What good is it, my brothers, if someone
says he has faith but does not have works?
Can his faith[G] save him?

15 If a brother or sister is without clothes
and lacks daily food 16 and one of you says to
them, "Go in peace, keep warm, and eat well,"
but you don't give them what the body needs,
what good is it?[r] 17 In the same way faith, if it
doesn't have works, is dead by itself.

18 But someone will say, "You have faith, and
I have works."[H] Show me your faith without
works, and I will show you faith from my
works.[I,s] 19 You believe that God is one; you
do well. The demons also believe — and they
shudder.[t]

20 Foolish man! Are you willing to learn that
faith without works is useless? 21 Wasn't Abraham our father justified by works when he offered Isaac his son on the altar? 22 You see that
faith was active together with his works, and
by works, faith was perfected.[u] 23 So the Scripture was fulfilled that says, **Abraham believed
God, and it was credited to him for righteousness**,[J,v] and he was called God's friend.[w]
24 You see that a man is ·justified by works
and not by faith alone. 25 And in the same way,
wasn't Rahab the prostitute also justified by
works when she received the messengers and
sent them out by a different route?[x] 26 For just
as the body without the spirit is dead, so also
faith without works is dead.

Controlling the Tongue

3 Not many should become teachers, my
·brothers, knowing that we will receive
a stricter judgment,[y] 2 for we all stumble in
many ways.[z] If anyone does not stumble in
what he says,[K] he is a mature man who is also
able to control his whole body.[L,aa]
3 Now when we put bits into the mouths

[a] **1:25** Jn 13:17; Jms 2:12
[b] **1:26** Ps 34:13; 39:1; 141:3; Jms 3:2-3; 1Pt 3:10
[c] **1:27** Jb 31:17; Is 1:17,23; Mt 25:36
[d] Rm 12:2; 1Jn 5:18
[e] **2:1** Lv 19:15; Dt 1:17; Ac 10:34; Rm 2:11; Eph 6:9; Col 3:25
[f] **2:5** Jb 34:19; 1Co 1:27
[g] Lk 12:21; Rv 2:9
[h] Rm 4:13-14; 8:17; Gl 3:29; 4:7; Ti 3:7; Heb 1:2; 11:7
[i] **2:6** 1Co 11:22
[j] Ac 8:3; 17:6; 18:12
[k] **2:7** Is 63:19; 65:1; Am 9:12; Ac 15:17
[l] **2:8** Lv 19:18; Mt 22:39
[m] **2:9** Lv 19:15; Dt 1:17; Ac 10:34; Rm 2:11; Eph 6:9; Col 3:25
[n] **2:10** Mt 5:10; Gl 3:10
[o] **2:11** Ex 20:13-14; Dt 5:17-18
[p] **2:12** Mt 7:12,24-29; 19:17-21; 22:36-40; 28:20
[q] **2:13** Jb 22:6; Pr 21:13; Mt 5:7; 18:32-35
[r] **2:14-16** Mt 25:35-36; Lk 3:11; 1Jn 3:16-18
[s] **2:18** Rm 3:28; Heb 11:33; Jms 3:13
[t] **2:19** Dt 6:4; Mt 8:29; Lk 4:34
[u] **2:21-22** Gn 22:9; 1Th 1:3; Heb 11:17
[v] **2:23** Gn 15:6; Rm 4:3; Gl 3:6
[w] 2Ch 20:7; Is 41:8
[x] **2:25** Jos 2:4,6,15; Heb 11:31
[y] **3:1** Mt 23:8; Rm 2:20-21; 1Tm 1:7
[z] **3:2** 1Kg 8:46; Pr 20:9; Jms 2:10
[aa] Mt 12:37; Jms 1:26; 1Pt 3:10

[A] **1:23** Lit *at the face of his birth* [B] **1:26** Other mss add *among you* [C] **1:27** Or *before the* [D] **2:8** Lv 19:18 [E] **2:11** Ex 20:14; Dt 5:18 [F] **2:11** Ex 20:13; Dt 5:17 [G] **2:14** Or *Can faith*, or *Can that faith*, or *Can such faith* [H] **2:18** The quotation may end here or after v. 18b or v. 19. [I] **2:18** Other mss read *Show me your faith from your works, and from my works I will show you my faith.* [J] **2:23** Gn 15:6 [K] **3:2** Lit *in word* [L] **3:2** Lit *to bridle the whole body*

William Carey (1761–1834)

William Carey's work in England and India lives up to his motto: "Expect great things from God. Attempt great things for God."[1] He began as a shoemaker, ended as a scholar, linguist, and missionary, and is now known as the father of modern missions.

God's training is evident throughout Carey's life. Before traveling to India he worked as a cobbler, a schoolteacher, and a pastor, each position furthering his call to missions. Carey had an affinity for languages and used his time at his cobbler's bench to teach himself Latin, Greek, Hebrew, French, Italian, and Dutch. He was rarely without a book. Surprisingly, it was in the pages of the adventures of Captain James Cook that Carey began to sense the importance of bringing the message of Christ to those who had not yet heard His name. As a teacher Carey learned about the populations of the world and their religions. As a pastor, Carey was able to put all of this together in his *Enquiry into the Obligation of Christians to Use Means for the Conversion of the Heathens*, which outlined theological and practical reasons for Christians to engage in missions and eventually led to the creation of the Baptist Missionary Society (BMS).

In 1793, supported by the BMS, Carey boarded a ship to India along with his wife, three small children, and a medical missionary. He had no plans to return. Their first Hindu convert to Christianity did not come until 1800, seven years after they arrived. This did not sway Carey, who saw his primary strength in his ability to "plod" regardless of the circumstances. This perseverance allowed him to press on even when he faced his wife's nervous breakdown, her subsequent mental instability, her eventual death, the deaths of two children, and then the death of his second wife as well as the disease that kept him bedridden for seven months.

Despite this adversity and discouragement, Carey achieved great things for God. In the Western world, he changed the face of missions. During Carey's time, Christians tended to be indifferent or outright resistant to missions, but his example influenced the creation of several missionary societies and led many to the mission field. He also opened the doors to India within the East India Company, which had previously refused missionaries access to Calcutta until 1831 when they revised their policy.

Carey succeeded in his desire to found the Church in India. He created a lifestyle of communal living and self-support for the missionaries and trained indigenous leaders for the pastorate. He used his language proficiency to translate the Bible, in whole or in part, into over thirty-five Indian languages and dialects, allowing Christians across India to read Scripture in their own language.

Carey also influenced social change in India. Through his work, the practices of child sacrifice and Suttee (the voluntary or forced burning of widows on the funeral pyre of their deceased husband) were outlawed. The caste system, which ensured that the poor remained both poor and marginalized in society, was challenged through participation in communion, inter-caste marriages, and schools that were made available to people regardless of their place in society. Carey also participated in the installation of the first degree-granting college in Asia.

We might be tempted to regard Carey as an amazing man, but Carey would direct our gaze elsewhere. On his deathbed he chastised another missionary, "You have been speaking about Dr. Carey; when I am gone say nothing about Dr. Carey—speak about Dr. Carey's God."[2]

[1] William Carey quoted in Florence Huntington Jensen, *Hearts Aflame* (Waukesha, WI: Metropolitan Church Association, 1932).

[2] Ibid.

of horses to make them obey us,[a] we also guide the whole animal.[A] **4**And consider ships: Though very large and driven by fierce winds, they are guided by a very small rudder wherever the will of the pilot directs. **5**So too, though the tongue is a small part of the body, it boasts great things.[b] Consider how large a forest a small fire ignites. **6**And the tongue is a fire. The tongue, a world of unrighteousness, is placed among the parts of our bodies. It pollutes the whole body,[c] sets the course of life on fire, and is set on fire by •hell.

7Every sea creature, reptile, bird, or animal is tamed and has been tamed by man, **8**but no man can tame the tongue. It is a restless evil, full of deadly poison.[d] **9**We praise our[B] Lord and Father with it, and we curse men who are made in God's likeness with it.[e] **10**Praising and cursing come out of the same mouth. My brothers, these things should not be this way. **11**Does a spring pour out sweet and bitter water from the same opening? **12**Can a fig tree produce olives, my brothers, or a grapevine produce figs? Neither can a saltwater spring yield fresh water.

The Wisdom from Above

13Who is wise and has understanding among you? He should show his works by good conduct with wisdom's gentleness.[f] **14**But if you have bitter envy and selfish ambition in your heart, don't brag and deny the truth.[g] **15**Such wisdom does not come from above but is earthly, unspiritual, demonic.[h] **16**For where envy and selfish ambition exist, there is disorder and every kind of evil. **17**But the wisdom from above is first pure, then peace-loving, gentle, compliant, full of mercy and good fruits, without favoritism and hypocrisy.[i] **18**And the fruit of righteousness[j] is sown in peace by those who cultivate peace.

Proud or Humble

4 What is the source of wars and fights among you? Don't they come from the cravings[k] that are at war within you?[C] **2**You desire and do not have. You murder and covet and cannot obtain. You fight and war. You do not have because you do not ask. **3**You ask and don't receive because you ask with wrong motives, so that you may spend it on your evil desires.[l]

4Adulteresses![D,E] Don't you know that friendship with the •world is hostility toward God? So whoever wants to be the world's friend becomes God's enemy.[m] **5**Or do you think it's without reason the Scripture says that the Spirit who lives in us yearns jealously?[F,n]

6But He gives greater grace. Therefore He says:

> **God resists the proud,**
> **but gives grace to the humble.**[G,o]

7Therefore, submit to God. But resist the Devil, and he will flee from you.[p] **8**Draw near to God, and He will draw near to you. Cleanse your hands, sinners, and purify your hearts, double-minded people![q] **9**Be miserable and mourn and weep. Your laughter must change to mourning and your joy to sorrow.[r] **10**Humble yourselves before the Lord, and He will exalt you.

11Don't criticize one another, •brothers. He who criticizes a brother or judges his brother criticizes the law and judges the law. But if you judge the law, you are not a doer of the law but a judge.[s] **12**There is one lawgiver and judge[H] who is able to save and to destroy. But who are you to judge your neighbor?[t]

Our Will and His Will

13Come now, you who say, "Today or tomorrow we will travel to such and such a city and spend a year there and do business and make a profit."[u] **14**You don't even know what tomorrow will bring—what your life will be! For you are like smoke that appears for a little while, then vanishes.[v]

15Instead, you should say, "If the Lord wills, we will live and do this or that." **16**But as it is, you boast in your arrogance. All such boasting is evil.[w] **17**So it is a sin for the person who knows to do what is good and doesn't do it.[x]

Warning to the Rich

5 Come now, you rich[y] people! Weep and wail over the miseries that are coming on you. **2**Your wealth is ruined and your clothes

[a]**3:3** Ps 32:9; 39:1
[b]**3:5** Ps 12:3-4; 73:8-9
[c]**3:6** Ps 120:2-3; Pr 16:27; Mt 15:11,18
[d]**3:8** Ps 140:3; Ec 10:11; Rm 3:13
[e]**3:9** Gn 1:26; 1Co 11:7
[f]**3:13** Jms 1:21; 2:18
[g]**3:14** Rm 2:8; 13:13; 2Co 12:20
[h]**3:15** 2Th 2:9; 1Tm 4:1; Jms 1:17; Rv 2:24
[i]**3:17** Lk 6:36; Rm 12:9; 1Co 2:6; Heb 12:11; Jms 2:4
[j]**3:18** Pr 11:18; Is 32:17; Hs 10:12; Am 6:12; Gl 6:8; Php 1:11
[k]**4:1** Rm 7:23; Ti 3:9
[l]**4:3** Ps 18:41; 1Jn 3:22; 5:14
[m]**4:4** Jn 15:19; Jms 1:27; 1Jn 2:15
[n]**4:5** 1Co 6:19; 2Co 6:16
[o]**4:6** Ps 138:6; Pr 3:34; Mt 23:12
[p]**4:7** Eph 4:27; 6:11; 1Pt 5:8-9
[q]**4:8** 2Ch 15:2; Is 1:16; Jms 1:8
[r]**4:9** Mt 5:4; Lk 6:25
[s]**4:11** Mt 7:1; Jms 1:22; 1Pt 2:1
[t]**4:12** Mt 10:28; Rm 14:4
[u]**4:13** Pr 27:1; Lk 12:18-20
[v]**4:14** Jb 7:7; Ps 102:3
[w]**4:15-16** Ac 18:21; 1Co 5:6
[x]**4:17** Lk 12:47-48; Jn 9:41; 2Pt 2:21
[y]**5:1** Pr 11:28; Lk 6:24

[A]**3:3** Lit *whole body* [B]**3:9** Or *praise the* [C]**4:1** Lit *war in your members* [D]**4:4** Other mss read *Adulterers and adulteresses* [E]**4:4** Or *Unfaithful people!* [F]**4:5** Or *He who caused the Spirit to live in us yearns jealously*, or *the spirit He caused to live in us yearns jealously*, or *He jealously yearns for the Spirit He made to live in us* [G]**4:6** Pr 3:34 [H]**4:12** Other mss omit *and judge* are moth-eaten.[a] 3 Your silver and gold are corroded, and their corrosion will be a witness against you and will eat your flesh like fire. You stored up treasure in the last days![b] 4 Look! The pay that you withheld from the workers[c] who reaped your fields cries out, and the outcry of the harvesters has reached the ears of the Lord of •Hosts.[A,d] 5 You have lived luxuriously on the land and have indulged yourselves. You have fattened your hearts[e] for[B] the day of slaughter.[f] 6 You have condemned — you have murdered — the righteous man; he does not resist you.[g]

Waiting for the Lord

7 Therefore, •brothers, be patient until the Lord's coming. See how the farmer waits for the precious fruit of the earth and is patient with it until it receives the early and the late rains.[h] 8 You also must be patient. Strengthen your hearts, because the Lord's coming is near.[i]

9 Brothers, do not complain about one another, so that you will not be judged. Look, the judge stands at the door![j]

10 Brothers, take the prophets who spoke in the Lord's name as an example of suffering and patience. 11 See, we count as blessed those who have endured.[C] You have heard of Job's endurance[k] and have seen the outcome from the Lord. The Lord is very compassionate and merciful.[l]

Truthful Speech

12 Now above all, my brothers, do not swear, either by heaven or by earth or with any other oath.[m] Your "yes" must be "yes," and your "no" must be "no," so that you won't fall under judgment.[D]

Effective Prayer

13 Is anyone among you suffering? He should pray. Is anyone cheerful? He should sing praises.[n] 14 Is anyone among you sick? He should call for the elders of the church, and they should pray over him after anointing him with olive oil in the name of the Lord.[o] 15 The prayer of faith will save the sick person, and the Lord will restore him to health; if he has committed sins, he will be forgiven.[p] 16 Therefore, confess your sins to one another and pray for one another, so that you may be healed. The urgent request of a righteous person is very powerful in its effect.[q] 17 Elijah was a man with a nature like ours; yet he prayed earnestly that it would not rain, and for three years and six months it did not rain on the land.[r] 18 Then he prayed again, and the sky gave rain and the land produced its fruit.[s]

19 My brothers, if any among you strays from the truth,[t] and someone turns him back,[u] 20 let him know that whoever turns a sinner from the error of his way will save his •life from death and cover a multitude of sins.[v]

[a] **5:2** Jb 13:28; Is 50:9; Mt 6:19-20
[b] **5:3** Rm 2:5; Jms 5:8
[c] **5:4** Lv 19:13; Jb 24:10-11; Jr 22:13; Mal 3:5
[d] Dt 24:15; Rm 9:29
[e] **5:5** Jb 21:13; Am 6:1
[f] Jr 12:3; 25:34
[g] **5:6** Heb 10:38; Jms 4:2
[h] **5:7** Dt 11:14; Jr 5:24; Hos 6:3
[i] **5:8** Rm 13:11; Php 4:5; 1Pt 4:7
[j] **5:9** Mt 24:33; 1Co 4:5; Jms 4:12; 1Pt 4:5
[k] **5:11** Jb 1:21-22; 2:10; 42:10-12
[l] Ex 34:6; Nm 14:18; Mt 5:10
[m] **5:12** Mt 5:33-37; 23:16-22; Mk 7:9-13
[n] **5:13** Ps 50:15; Col 3:16
[o] **5:14** Mk 6:13; 16:18
[p] **5:15** Is 33:24; Mt 9:2; Mk 2:5; Lk 24:47
[q] **5:16** Nm 11:2; Mt 3:6; Jn 9:31; 1Pt 2:24
[r] **5:17** 1Kg 17:1; 18:1; Lk 4:25; Ac 14:15
[s] **5:18** 1Kg 18:41-45; Jms 3:17-18
[t] **5:19** Mt 18:15; Gl 6:1; Jms 3:14
[u] Ps 51:13; Dn 12:3; Mal 2:6; Lk 1:16
[v] **5:20** Pr 10:12; Rm 11:14; 1Pt 4:8

A 5:4 Gk *Sabaoth*; this word is a transliteration of the Hb word for *Hosts*, or *Armies*. B 5:5 Or *hearts in* C 5:11 Or *have persevered* D 5:12 Other mss read *fall into hypocrisy*

■ **AUTHOR:** Simon Peter, the disciple

■■ **DATE:** First Peter was written between A.D. 62 and 64 in Rome with 2 Peter coming three years after 1 Peter.

The marvel of God's mission to the world is that gifts and talents—personal competencies—which often seem so limited can be so useful. Who would have guessed that Jesus' twelve disciples could start a worldwide movement, or that one disciple named Peter who acquired the Greek language later in life could write so beautifully about faith in these two letters.

The sheer beauty of these two letters has caused many to doubt that Jesus' impetuous disciple had anything to do with composing them. Peter likely used Silvanus (also called Silas) to help with the manuscript (1Pt 5:12), a common practice in his day. From the old fisherman's mind, heart, and pen comes magnificent teaching about the quality of life God intends for everyone, the new relationships God wants people to enjoy, the resiliency God gives us so we can weather storms and troubles. Set your hope on the day of Christ's return, when all hardship will be vindicated and God's victory over evil complete.

1 PETER

Who besides Christians have a time-line like that—a day when all is made right and God's triumph is made plain? Who can describe such things, so deeply spiritual and visionary, yet still so sure? A fisherman can, by God's Spirit enabled.

These letters were written after A.D. 60 and before 68 when Nero ordered Peter killed. Peter describes living well in the first letter, and persevering well in the second. Living well means knowing your identity and mission. Persevering (Peter likely approached his death as he wrote) means discerning false hope from true, and false teaching from the genuine gospel. God's mission rides on God's good news, not versions of it perverted by slanderous amendments (2Pt 2:11). As if to speak to contemporary critics, Peter insists that he follows no "cleverly contrived myths" (1:16) but the very power of God revealed in Jesus Christ. He was an eyewitness, and he knows what he saw and heard.

Peter's vision is forward-looking, in the trajectory of God's mission. He knows that trouble bites at the heels of Jesus' followers like a hungry dog. He has seen his share of "brute beast" imposters aiming to dissuade people from Christ. But a day is coming, when "the heavens will pass away with a loud noise, the elements will burn and be dissolved, and the earth and the works on it will be disclosed" (3:10). Until that day, Christians are to grow in grace.

Peter's great image of the mission of God should be familiar to all believers: a light shining in a dark place (1Pt 2:9). The "light" imagines that God's revelation in Jesus Christ—God's Word of salvation to all people—is like a beacon showing the way. Fog, mist, and starless night depict a world where relationships are bent and broken, violence rules, and greed spoils even the best plans of good people. In that place, light shines on a path to new life, God's life. For a time, the darkness will persist around the lighted path. God's people, light bearers, are to live and tell God's truth as stars foretell dawn. That beautiful image should plant God's mission firmly in your vision, with the same joy and peace of the generation who knew Jesus personally.

Read here the transformation that Peter experienced, turning his many dawns on the lake fishing toward the great dawn of Jesus' victory—God's mission accomplished.

Greeting

1 Peter,[a] an apostle of Jesus Christ:

To the temporary residents[b] dispersed[A,c] in Pontus, Galatia, Cappadocia, ·Asia, and Bithynia,[d] chosen[e] 2according to the foreknowledge[f] of God the Father and set apart by the Spirit[g] for obedience[h] and for sprinkling with the blood[i] of Jesus Christ.

May grace and peace be multiplied to you.

A Living Hope

3Praise the God and Father of our Lord Jesus Christ.[j] According to His great mercy,[k] He has given us a new birth[l] into a living hope[m] through the resurrection of Jesus Christ from the dead[n] 4and into an inheritance that is imperishable,[o] uncorrupted, and unfading, kept in heaven[p] for you. 5You are being protected by God's power[q] through faith for a salvation that is ready to be revealed in the last time.[r] 6You rejoice in this,[B] though now for a short time you have had to struggle in various trials[s] 7so that the genuineness of your faith[t] — more valuable than gold, which perishes though refined by fire[u] — may result[v] in[C] praise, glory, and honor[w] at the revelation of Jesus Christ.[x] 8You love Him,[y] though you have not seen[z] Him. And though not seeing Him now, you believe in Him and rejoice[aa] with inexpressible and glorious joy, 9because you are receiving the goal of your[D] faith, the salvation of your souls.[E]

10Concerning this salvation, the prophets[ab] who prophesied about the grace that would come to you searched and carefully investigated. 11They inquired into what time or what circumstances[F] the Spirit of Christ[ac] within them was indicating when He testified in advance[ad] to the messianic sufferings[G,ae] and the glories[af] that would follow.[H] 12It was revealed to them that they were not serving themselves but you. These things have now been announced to you through those who preached the gospel to you[ag] by the Holy Spirit sent from heaven.[ah] Angels desire to look into these things.

A Call to Holy Living

13Therefore, with your minds ready for action,[I,ai] be serious[aj] and set your hope[ak] completely on the grace to be brought to you at the revelation[al] of Jesus Christ. 14As obedient children,[am] do not be conformed to the desires of your former ignorance. 15But as the One who called you[an] is holy,[ao] you also are to be holy in all your conduct; 16for it is written, **Be holy, because I am holy.**[J,ap]

17And if you address as Father the One who judges impartially[aq] based on each one's work,[ar] you are to conduct yourselves in fear[as] during the time of your temporary residence. 18For you know that you were ·redeemed from your empty way of life[at] inherited from the fathers, not with perishable things like silver or gold,[au] 19but with the precious blood of Christ,[av] like that of a lamb[aw] without defect or blemish. 20He was chosen[K,ax] before the foundation of the world but was revealed at the end of the times[ay] for you 21who through Him are believers in God,[az] who raised Him from the dead[ba] and gave Him glory,[bb] so that your faith and hope are in God.

22By obedience to the truth,[L] having purified yourselves[M] for sincere love of the ·brothers, love one another[bc] earnestly[N] from a pure[O] heart,[bd] 23since you have been born again[be] — not of perishable seed[bf] but of imperishable — through the living and enduring word of God.[bg] 24For

All flesh is like grass,
and all its glory[bh] like a flower of the grass.
The grass withers, and the flower falls,
25 **but the word of the Lord**
endures forever.[P,bi]

And this is the word that was preached as the gospel to you.

The Living Stone and a Holy People

2 So rid yourselves of[bj] all malice, all deceit, hypocrisy, envy, and all slander.[bk] 2Like newborn infants, desire the pure spir-

[a]**1:1** Lk 6:14; Ac 10:32 [b]Gn 23:4; Ps 39:12; Heb 11:9,13; 1Pt 2:11 [c]Jn 7:35; Jms 1:1 [d]Ac 2:9; 6:9; 16:6-7; Gl 1:2 [e]Mt 22:14; 24:22; Ti 1:1 [f]**1:2** Rm 8:29; 1Pt 1:20 [g]2Th 2:13 [h]1Pt 1:14,22 [i]Heb 9:12; 10:22; 12:24 [j]**1:3** 2Co 1:3; Eph 1:3 [k]Gl 6:16; Ti 3:5 [l]Jn 1:13; 3:3,7; Jms 1:18; 1Pt 1:23 [m]Ac 23:6; 1Th 1:3 [n]1Co 15:20; 1Pt 3:21 [o]**1:4** Ac 20:32; Rm 8:17; Col 3:24 [p]2Tm 4:8 [q]**1:5** Jn 10:28; Php 4:7 [r]Rm 8:18; 2Co 4:17; Heb 12:11; 1Pt 4:13; 5:1,10; Rv 15:1; 21:9 [s]**1:6** Jms 1:2; 1Pt 4:12 [t]**1:7** Jms 1:3 [u]Is 48:10; Zch 13:9; Mal 3:3; 1Co 3:13 [v]2Co 5:3; Php 3:9; Rv 14:5 [w]Rm 2:7,10,29; 1Co 4:5 [x]Lk 17:30 [y]**1:8** 1Jn 4:20 [z]Ex 33:20; Rm 8:24 [aa]Jn 15:11; 2Co 6:10 [ab]**1:10** Lk 1:70; 10:24; 16:16,29; 18:31; 24:25,27,44 [ac]**1:11** Rm 8:9 [ad]Mt 26:24 [ae]Mk 8:31; Lk 24:26; Php 3:10 [af]Lk 24:26 [ag]**1:12** Mk 16:15; 1Co 9:14; 2Co 10:16 [ah]Jn 14:26; 15:26; Ac 1:8; 2:2-4; 13:4 [ai]**1:13** Ex 12:11 [aj]1Pt 5:8 [ak]Mt 12:21; Rm 8:24; 1Th 1:3 [al]1Pt 4:13; 5:4 [am]**1:14** Heb 2:13 [an]**1:15** Gl 1:6; 5:8; 1Th 2:12; 5:24; 1Pt 5:10

[ao]Lk 1:49; 1Co 7:14 [ap]**1:16** Lv 11:44-45; 19:2; 20:7 [aq]**1:17** Ac 10:34; Rm 2:11; Gl 2:6; Eph 6:9 [ar]1Co 3:12 [as]Ac 9:31; Rm 3:18; 2Co 5:11; 7:1; Eph 5:21; Php 2:12 [at]**1:18** 2Pt 3:11 [au]Is 52:3; 1Co 6:20; Ti 2:14; Heb 9:12 [av]**1:19** Jn 6:53; Ac 20:28; 1Co 10:16; Eph 2:13; Heb 10:19 [aw]Ex 12:5; Lv 4:32; Is 53:7; Jn 1:29 [ax]**1:20** Ac 2:23; Eph 1:4; 1Pt 1:2; Rv 13:8 [ay]2Pt 3:3; Jd 18 [az]**1:21** Ac 10:45; Rm 4:24; 10:9; Eph 1:1; 1Tm 4:12; 6:2 [ba]Ac 2:24; Rm 10:9 [bb]Jn 17:5,24; 1Tm 3:16; Heb 2:9 [bc]**1:22** Zch 7:9; Jn 13:34; Rm 12:10; 1Th 4:9; 1Jn 4:7 [bd]1Tm 1:5 [be]**1:23** 1Pt 1:3 [bf]1Jn 3:9 [bg]Lk 8:21; Heb 4:12 [bh]**1:24** 1Pt 5:4 [bi]**1:24-25** Is 40:6-8; Lk 21:33; Jms 1:10-11; 1Jn 2:17 [bj]**2:1** Rm 13:12 [bk]2Co 12:20

[A]**1:1** Jewish people scattered throughout Gentile lands who spoke Gk and were influenced by Gk culture [B]**1:6** Or *In this fact rejoice* [C]**1:7** Lit *may be found for* [D]**1:9** Other mss read *our*, or they omit the possessive pronoun [E]**1:9** Or *your lives* [F]**1:11** Or *inquired about the person or time* [G]**1:11** Or *the sufferings of Christ* [H]**1:11** Lit *the glories after that* [I]**1:13** Lit *Therefore, when you have the loins of your mind girded* [J]**1:16** Lv 11:44-45; 19:2; 20:7 [K]**1:20** Or *foreknown* [L]**1:22** Other mss add *through the Spirit* [M]**1:22** Or *purified your souls* [N]**1:22** Or *intensely* [O]**1:22** Other mss omit *pure* [P]**1:24-25** Is 40:6-8

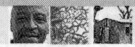

itual milk,[a] so that you may grow by it for
your salvation,[A] 3 since **you have tasted**[b] **that
the Lord is good.**[B,c] 4 Coming to Him, a living stone — rejected by men but chosen and
valuable to God — 5 you yourselves, as living
stones, are being built into a spiritual house
for a holy priesthood to offer spiritual sacrifices acceptable to God[d] through Jesus Christ.
6 For it is contained in Scripture:

> **Look! I lay a stone in ˈZion,**[e]
> **a chosen and honored**[C] **cornerstone,**[D,f]
> **and the one who believes in Him**
> **will never be put to shame!**[E,F,g]

7 So honor will come to you who believe, but
for the unbelieving,

> **The stone that the builders rejected —**
> **this One has become the cornerstone,**[G,h]

[a] **2:2** 1Co 3:2; 9:7; Heb 5:12-13
[b] **2:3** Heb 6:4-5
[c] Ps 34:8; Ti 3:4
[d] **2:5** Rm 12:1; Heb 13:15
[e] **2:6** Ps 9:11; Heb 12:22
[f] Eph 2:20
[g] Is 28:16; Rm 9:33; 10:11
[h] **2:7** Ps 118:22; Mt 21:42; Lk 20:17; Ac 4:11

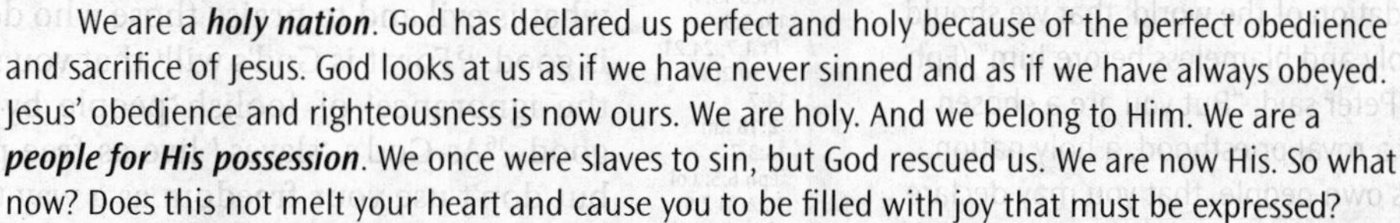

Identity in Christ

Eric Geiger

Peter appeals to our identity in Christ as a motivating factor to join God on His mission of bringing people to Himself (1Pt 2:9-12). First, Peter reminds us that God chose us. We are a ***chosen race***. God pulled us to Himself when we pursued everything else. We are also His ***royal priesthood***. We are able to enjoy the presence of God, to speak with Him directly; something the original readers of Peter's letter knew was deeply sacred. They were accustomed to the "priest" being the individual who on one day a year could enter the "Most Holy Place" in the temple and quickly exit out of sheer terror. Now because Christ tore the temple veil, we may continually enjoy the presence of God.

We are a ***holy nation***. God has declared us perfect and holy because of the perfect obedience and sacrifice of Jesus. God looks at us as if we have never sinned and as if we have always obeyed. Jesus' obedience and righteousness is now ours. We are holy. And we belong to Him. We are a ***people for His possession***. We once were slaves to sin, but God rescued us. We are now His. So what now? Does this not melt your heart and cause you to be filled with joy that must be expressed?

Notice the phrase "so that" in verse nine. God gave you a brand new identity in Him when you came to faith ***"so that you may proclaim the praises of the One who called you out of darkness into His marvelous light."*** Ultimately God has given you your great identity so that you will proclaim His praises. Your life is to be a living advertisement, a walking billboard of the grace of God. Because of what He has done in you and for you, your life should be a constant statement of the transforming power of the gospel. By living the reality of your identity, you will proclaim His greatness. Live as His chosen child by trusting Him in all things. Live as a priest by spending time in His presence. Live as His holy bride because you are deeply grateful that He has made you pure. As you live your new identity people will encounter the grace of God in your life.

And where do you live? Look at verses 11-12 for another statement of your identity. You are ***strangers and temporary residents*** here. You do not belong to the kingdom of this world because you are now a member of God's Kingdom. However, God has you here—on mission among people. God wants you to live your new identity, conducting yourself honorably "among the Gentiles." These verses challenge us to abstain from sin, not from sinful people. In His providence, God has placed you in your career, home, neighborhood, and city to live your new identity among people who do not know Him. To live only among believers is to forsake God's mission and your identity as a stranger in this world. Live the reality of your identity among people whom God is seeking to rescue.

[A] **2:2** Other mss omit *in your salvation* [B] **2:3** Ps 34:8 [C] **2:6** Or *valuable* [D] **2:6** Lit *head of the corner* [E] **2:6** Or *be disappointed* [F] **2:6** Is 28:16 LXX [G] **2:7** Ps 118:22

[8]and

A stone to stumble over,[A]
and a rock to trip over.[B,C,a]

They stumble because they disobey the message; they were destined[b] for this.

9 But you are **a chosen race,**[D,E,c]
a royal priesthood,[F,d]
a holy nation,[G,e] **a people**
for His possession,[H,f]
so that you may proclaim the praises[I,J,g]
of the One who called you
out of darkness
into His marvelous light.[h]
10 Once you were not a people,
but now you are God's people;
you had not received mercy,[i]
but now you have received mercy.

A Call to Good Works

[11]Dear friends, I urge you as strangers and
temporary residents[j] to abstain[k] from fleshly[l]
desires that war against you.[K,m] [12]Conduct[n]
yourselves honorably among the Gentiles,[L]
so that in a case where they speak against you
as those who do what is evil, they will, by observing your good works, glorify God on the
day of visitation.[M,o]

[13]Submit[p] to every human authority[N] because of the Lord, whether to the Emperor[O]
as the supreme authority[q] [14]or to governors as
those sent out by him to punish those who do
what is evil and to praise those who do what
is good. [15]For it is God's will[r] that you silence
the ignorance[s] of foolish people by doing
good. [16]As God's ˙slaves,[t] live as free people,
but don't use your freedom as a way to conceal evil.[u] [17]Honor everyone. Love[v] the brotherhood.[w] Fear God.[x] Honor the Emperor.[O]

Submission of Slaves to Masters

[18]Household slaves, submit with all fear[y]
to your masters,[z] not only to the good and
gentle but also to the cruel.[P,aa] [19]For it brings
favor[Q] if, mindful of God's will,[R,S] someone
endures grief from suffering unjustly. [20]For
what credit is there if you sin and are punished, and you endure it? But when you do
what is good and suffer,[ab] if you endure it, this
brings favor with God.

21 For you were called to this,
because Christ also suffered[ac] for you,
leaving you an example,[ad]
so that you should follow[ae] in His steps.
22 He **did not commit sin,**[af]

---

[a]**2:8** Is 8:14; Rm 9:33; 14:20
[b]Ac 2:23; 4:27-28; Rm 9:22; 11:7; Jd 4
[c]**2:9** Dt 7:6; 10:15; Is 43:20
[d]Is 61:6; Rv 1:6; 5:10; 20:6
[e]Ex 19:6
[f]Ex 34:9; Dt 7:6; Ps 33:12; Is 43:21; Ti 2:14
[g]Is 42:12; 43:21
[h]Is 9:2; Ac 26:18; Eph 5:8; Col 1:12-13
[i]**2:10** Mt 5:7; Mk 5:19; Lk 1:50
[j]**2:11** 1Pt 1:1
[k]1Tm 4:3
[l]Rm 7:23; Php 3:3
[m]Gl 5:17; Jms 4:1
[n]**2:12** 2Pt 3:11
[o]Is 10:3; Jr 6:15; 8:12; 10:15; Lk 1:68; 7:16; 19:44
[p]**2:13-14** Rm 13:1-7; Ti 3:1
[q]**2:13** Rm 13:1
[r]**2:15** Gl 1:4; Eph 1:9
[s]1Pt 3:16
[t]**2:16** Rm 1:1; Ti 1:1; Rv 2:20
[u]1Co 14:20
[v]**2:17** Rv 12:11
[w]Heb 13:1; 1Pt 5:9
[x]Pr 1:7; 24:21; Ac 10:2; Rv 14:7
[y]**2:18** Rm 13:3,7
[z]Eph 6:5; Col 3:22; Ti 2:9; Jd 4
[aa]Php 2:15
[ab]**2:20** 1Pt 4:14
[ac]**2:21** Mk 8:31; 1Pt 3:18; 1Jn 3:16
[ad]Jn 13:15
[ae]Jn 8:12
[af]**2:22** 1Pt 4:1; 1Jn 3:5

The Call to Mission and Ministry

GOD WHO SENDS

The missional call common to all Christians has its roots in the purposeful intent of the Christian call. All Christians are called, and inherent in that call is the ingredient of purpose. Jesus said, "I chose you and appointed you that you should go and bear fruit" (Jn 15:16). Paul said, "He chose us in him before the foundation of the world, that we should be holy and blameless before him" (Eph 1:4). Peter said, "But you are a chosen race, a royal priesthood, a holy nation, God's own people, that you may declare the wonderful deeds of him who called you out of darkness into his marvelous light" (1Pt 2:9). John emphasized the fruitful intent of the Christian calling. Paul accented the moral intent of the Christian calling. Peter affirmed the full missional purpose of the calling. We are called not simply to bear fruit and to be holy. We are called "out of" darkness, "into" light, "that" ("in order that") we may declare his wonderful deeds.

(DUBOSE, 103)

[A]**2:8** Or *a stone causing stumbling* [B]**2:8** Or *a rock to trip over* [C]**2:8** Is 8:14 [D]**2:9** Or *generation*, or *nation* [E]**2:9** Dt 7:6; 10:15; Is 43:20 LXX [F]**2:9** Ex 19:6; 23:22 LXX; Is 61:6 [G]**2:9** Ex 19:6; 23:22 LXX [H]**2:9** Ex 19:5; 23:22 LXX; Dt 4:20; 7:6; Is 43:21 LXX [I]**2:9** Or *the mighty deeds* [J]**2:9** Is 42:12; 43:21 [K]**2:11** Or *against the soul* [L]**2:12** Or *among the nations*, or *among the pagans* [M]**2:12** The day when God intervenes in human history, either in grace or in judgment [N]**2:13** Or *creature* [O]**2:13,17** Lit *king* [P]**2:18** Or *unscrupulous*; lit *crooked* [Q]**2:19** Other mss add *with God* [R]**2:19** Other mss read *if, because of a good conscience* [S]**2:19** Lit *if, because of conscience toward God*

and no deceit[a] **was found**
in His mouth;[A,b]
23 when He was reviled,
He did not revile in return;
when He was suffering,
He did not threaten
but entrusted Himself to the One
who judges[c] justly.
24 He Himself bore our sins[d]
in His body[e] on the tree,[f]
so that, having died to sins,[g]
we might live for righteousness;[h]
you have been healed
by **His wounds.**[B,i]
25 For you **were like sheep**
going astray,[C,j]
but you have now returned
to the Shepherd[k] and Guardian[D]
of your souls.

Wives and Husbands

3 In the same way, wives,[l] submit yourselves to your own husbands so that, even
if some disobey the Christian message,[m] they
may be won over[E,n] without a message by the
way their wives live[o] 2 when they observe your
pure, reverent lives.[p] 3 Your beauty should not
consist of outward things like elaborate hairstyles and the wearing of gold ornaments[F]
or fine clothes.[q] 4 Instead, it should consist
of what is inside[G] the heart[r] with the imperishable quality of a gentle[s] and quiet[t] spirit,
which is very valuable in God's eyes. 5 For
in the past, the holy[u] women who put their
hope[v] in God also beautified themselves in
this way, submitting to their own husbands,
6 just as Sarah[w] obeyed Abraham, calling him
lord. You have become her children when
you do what is good and are not frightened
by anything alarming.[x]
7 Husbands,[y] in the same way, live with your
wives with an understanding of their weaker
nature[H,z] yet showing them honor as coheirs
of the grace of life, so that your prayers will
not be hindered.

Do No Evil

8 Now finally, all of you should be like-
minded and sympathetic, should love believers,[I,aa] and be compassionate[ab] and humble,[J]
9 not paying back evil for evil[ac] or insult for insult but, on the contrary, giving a blessing,[ad]
since you were called for this, so that you can
inherit a blessing.

10 For the[ae] **one who wants to love life**
and to see good days
must keep his tongue from evil[af]
and his lips from speaking deceit,[ag]
11 **and he must turn away**[ah] **from evil**
and do what is good.
He must seek peace[ai]
and pursue it,
12 **because the eyes of the Lord are**
on the righteous
and His ears are open
to their request.
But the face of the Lord is against
those who do what is evil.[K]

[a]**2:22** 2Pt 2:1 [b]Is 53:9 [c]**2:23** Rv 18:8; 19:11 [d]**2:24** Heb 7:27-28; 9:27-28 [e]Is 53:4-5,12; Jn 2:21 [f]Ac 5:30; 10:39; 13:29; Gl 3:13 [g]Rm 6:2,8-11; 7:6; Gl 2:19; Col 2:20; 3:3 [h]Rm 6:2,11; Ti 2:12 [i]Is 53:5; Mt 13:15; Jn 12:40; Ac 28:27 [j]**2:25** Ps 119:176; Is 53:6 [k]Gn 48:15; 49:24; Ps 23:1; Jr 31:10 [l]**3:1** Eph 5:22-33; Col 3:18-19; 1Tm 3:11 [m]1Co 7:16 [n]1Co 9:19-22; Php 3:8 [o]2Pt 3:11 [p]**3:2** Ti 2:5 [q]**3:3** Is 3:18-24; 1Tm 2:9 [r]**3:4** Rm 2:29; 7:22 [s]Mt 5:5 [t]1Tm 2:2 [u]**3:5** Ps 20:6; 1Co 7:14 [v]1Tm 5:5; 1Pt 1:3 [w]**3:6** Gn 17:15-21; 18:6-15; Heb 11:11 [x]Pr 3:25 [y]**3:7** Mt 1:19; 1Co 14:35; Eph 5:22-28; Col 3:18-19; Ti 2:4-5 [z]1Th 4:4 [aa]**3:8** Heb 13:1 [ab]Eph 4:32 [ac]**3:9** Rm 12:17 [ad]Lk 6:28; Rm 12:14; 1Co 4:12 [ae]**3:10-12** Ps 34:12-16 [af]**3:10** Jms 1:26 [ag]Rm 3:13; Jms 3:5-8 [ah]**3:11** Ps 37:27 [ai]Lk 12:51; 2Tm 1:2; Heb 12:14; 3Jn 14

GOD WHO SENDS

The Cost of Witness and Service

The mission of God has always required radical commitment. Witness the vulnerable Moses. Witness the vulnerable Jesus—the ultimate vulnerability of the cross!

A comfortable Western Christianity finds little identification with the radical commitment reflected in Jesus' identification with the Servant of the Lord and his mission to release the captives and liberate the oppressed. The missional mandate emerging from the very nature of the Christian faith calling for the witness of redemptive deeds reflective of the nature of God himself is beginning to find expression around the world.

(DuBose, 123)

[A]**2:22** Is 53:9 [B]**2:24** Is 53:5 [C]**2:25** Is 53:6 [D]**2:25** Or *Overseer* [E]**3:1** Lit *may be gained* [F]**3:3** Lit *and of putting around of gold items* [G]**3:4** Lit *Instead, the hidden man of* [H]**3:7** Lit *understanding as the weaker vessel* [I]**3:8** Lit *sympathetic, loving the brothers* [J]**3:8** Other mss read *courteous* [K]**3:10-12** Ps 34:12-16

Undeserved Suffering

13 And who will harm[A] you if you are deeply
committed to what is good?[B] 14 But even if
you should suffer for righteousness,[a] you are
blessed. **Do not fear what they fear[b] or be disturbed,**[C,c] 15 but honor[D] the ˚Messiah[E] as Lord
in your hearts. Always be ready to give a defense to anyone who asks you for a reason[F]
for the hope that is in you.[d] 16 However, do this
with gentleness and respect, keeping your
conscience clear,[G,H,e] so that when you are accused,[I] those who denounce your Christian
life[J] will be put to shame. 17 For it is better to
suffer[f] for doing good, if that should be God's
will,[K] than for doing evil.

18 For Christ also suffered[g] for sins
once for all,[L,h]
the righteous for the unrighteous,[M]
that He might bring you[N] to God,[i]
after being put to death
in the fleshly realm[O,j]
but made alive in the spiritual realm.[P]

19 In that state[Q] He also went and made a
proclamation to the spirits[k] in prison[R] 20 who
in the past were disobedient, when God patiently waited in the days of Noah[l] while an
ark was being prepared. In it a few—that is,
eight people[S,m]—were saved through water.
21 Baptism, which corresponds to this, now
saves you (not the removal of the filth of the
flesh,[n] but the pledge[T] of a good conscience
toward God) through the resurrection of
Jesus Christ.[o] 22 Now that He has gone into
heaven,[p] He is at God's right hand[q] with angels, authorities, and powers subject to Him.[r]

[a]**3:14** Mt 6:33; Rm 1:17; 2Pt 1:1 [b]Jn 6:20; 7:13 [c]**3:14-15** Is 8:12-13 [d]**3:15** 1Jn 4:4 [e]**3:16** Ac 23:1; 24:16; Rm 9:1; 2Co 1:12; 1Tm 1:5,19; 3:9; Heb 10:22; 1Pt 3:21 [f]**3:17** Php 1:29; 1Pt 2:19 [g]**3:18** Mk 8:31; Rm 5:8 [h]Rm 6:10; Heb 9:28; 10:10; 1Pt 2:21; 4:1 [i]Rm 5:2 [j]Eph 2:14 [k]**3:19** 1Jn 4:1 [l]**3:20** Gn 5:29 [m]Gn 5:32; 6:18; 7:7,13; 8:16,18 [n]**3:21** Heb 9:14; 10:22 [o]1Pt 1:3 [p]**3:22** Ac 1:10,12; 1Tm 3:16; Heb 4:14; 6:20 [q]Ps 110:1; Mk 16:19; Ac 2:33-34; Rm 8:34; Heb 10:12 [r]Eph 1:20-22

PRAYING FOR THE WORLD

Always Be Ready

When we have some good news to share, we often can hardly wait to share it. However, many of us have the Best News of all, and we are too often reticent to tell others. We have our excuses. We don't want to offend. We don't really know what to say. The timing doesn't feel right. We fear that we can't answer the follow-up questions. We don't want to lose friends. We don't want to look weird or sound pushy.

Perhaps it will help if we consider sharing the Good News as we would any good news—simply because it's so good and we want those we care about to hear it!

Bottom line: Our job is to speak, the Holy Spirit will convict and convince. We would do well to heed Peter's advice: "Always be ready to give a defense to anyone who asks you for a reason for the hope that is in you" (1Pt 3:15).

Savior, we do not feel ready to be Your witnesses. Dissolve our fear and timidity. Open our hearts to Your power. Around us are so many who have not heard the message of salvation. Help us to recognize them and to know what to say and when to say it. Cleanse our hearts from prejudice. By Your grace may we be welcoming, winsome, and inviting in all our ways. Give us an excitement to share You with others!

Bear up those who have worked hard in the gospel ministry but have seen little results. Steel their resolve. Help us to partner with them in this privilege of sharing Your story of salvation. Amen.

[A]**3:13** Or *mistreat, or do evil to* [B]**3:13** Or *you are partisans for the good*; lit *you are zealots* [C]**3:14** Is 8:12 [D]**3:15** Or *sanctify*; lit *set apart* [E]**3:15** Other mss read *set God* [F]**3:15** Or *who demands of you an accounting* [G]**3:16** Lit *good* [H]**3:16** Or *keeping a clear conscience* [I]**3:16** Other mss read *when they speak against you as evildoers* [J]**3:16** Lit *your good behavior in Christ* [K]**3:17** Lit *if the will of God should will* [L]**3:18** Other mss read *died for sins on our behalf*; other mss read *died for our sins*; other mss read *died for sins on your behalf* [M]**3:18** Or *the Righteous One in the place of the unrighteous many* [N]**3:18** Other mss read *us* [O]**3:18** Or *in the flesh* [P]**3:18** Or *in the spirit*, or *in the Spirit* [Q]**3:19** Or *In whom*, or *At that time*, or *In which* [R]**3:19** Perhaps fallen supernatural beings or angels; 2Pt 2:4; Jd 6 [S]**3:20** Lit *souls* [T]**3:21** Or *the appeal*

Following Christ

4 Therefore, since Christ suffered[A] in the
flesh,[B] equip[C] yourselves also with the
same resolve[D]—because the one who suffered in the flesh has finished[a] with sin[E]—
2 in order to live the remaining time in the
flesh, no longer for human desires,[F] but
for God's will.[b] 3 For there has already been
enough time spent in doing what the pagans
choose to do:[G] carrying on in unrestrained
behavior, evil desires,[c] drunkenness, orgies,[d]
carousing, and lawless idolatry. 4 So they are
surprised that you don't plunge with them
into the same flood[H] of wild living—and they
slander you. 5 They will give an account to the
One who stands ready to judge the living and
the dead.[e] 6 For this reason the gospel was also
preached to those who are now dead,[f] so that,
although they might be judged by men in the
fleshly[g] realm,[I] they might live[h] by God in the
spiritual realm.[J]

End-Time Ethics

7 Now the end of all things is near;[i] therefore, be serious and disciplined[j] for prayer.
8 Above all, maintain an intense love[k] for each
other, since **love covers a multitude of sins.**[K,l]
9 Be hospitable[m] to one another without complaining. 10 Based on the gift each one has
received, use it to serve others,[n] as good managers of the varied grace of God. 11 If anyone
speaks, it should be as one who speaks God's
words; if anyone serves, it should be from the
strength God provides,[o] so that God may be
glorified through Jesus Christ in everything.
To Him belong the glory and the power forever and ever. ·Amen.

Christian Suffering

12 Dear friends, don't be surprised when
the fiery ordeal[L] comes among you to test you
as if something unusual were happening to
you.[p] 13 Instead, rejoice as you share in the sufferings of the ·Messiah,[q] so that you may also
rejoice with great joy at the revelation[r] of His
glory. 14 If you are ridiculed for the name of
Christ,[s] you are blessed, because the Spirit[t]
of glory and of God rests on you.[M] 15 None of
you, however, should suffer as a murderer, a
thief, an evildoer, or a meddler.[N] 16 But if anyone suffers as a "Christian," he should not be
ashamed but should glorify God in having
that name. 17 For the time has come for judgment[u] to begin with God's household,[v] and if
it begins with us, what will the outcome be
for those who disobey the gospel of God?

18 And **if a righteous person is saved**
with difficulty,
what will become of the ungodly
and the sinner?[O,w]

19 So those who suffer according to God's will
should, while doing what is good, entrust
themselves[x] to a faithful Creator.

About the Elders

5 Therefore, as a fellow elder and witness[y] to the sufferings of the ·Messiah
and also a participant in the glory about to
be revealed,[z] I exhort the elders among you:
2 Shepherd God's flock among you,[aa] not
overseeing[P] out of compulsion but freely, according to God's will;[Q] not for the money but
eagerly; 3 not lording it over those entrusted
to you, but being examples to the flock. 4 And
when the chief Shepherd[ab] appears, you will
receive the unfading crown[ac] of glory.
5 In the same way, you younger men, be subject to the elders. And all of you clothe yourselves with[R] humility toward one another,
because

God resists the proud
but gives grace to the humble.[S,ad]

6 Humble[ae] yourselves, therefore, under the
mighty hand[af] of God, so that He may exalt
you at the proper time,[T] 7 casting all your care
on Him, because He cares about you.[ag]

Conclusion

8 Be serious![ah] Be alert![ai] Your adversary the
Devil[aj] is prowling around like a roaring lion,
looking for anyone he can devour. 9 Resist
him[ak] and be firm in the faith, knowing that

[a]**4:1** Rm 6:10; Heb 4:15; 7:26; 9:28 [b]**4:2** Mk 3:35; Rm 6:11; 12:2 [c]**4:3** Mk 7:22 [d]Rm 13:13; Gl 5:21 [e]**4:5** Ac 10:42; Rm 14:9; 2Tm 4:1 [f]**4:6** Jn 5:25 [g]1Pt 3:18 [h]Php 1:21 [i]**4:7** Rm 13:11-12; Heb 9:26; Jms 5:8; 1Jn 2:18; Rv 1:3 [j]1Pt 5:8 [k]**4:8** 1Pt 1:22 [l]Pr 10:12; Jms 5:20 [m]**4:9** 1Tm 3:2; Ti 1:8 [n]**4:10** 1Co 12:7 [o]**4:11** Rm 12:6-8; 1Co 15:58 [p]**4:12** 1Pt 1:6-7 [q]**4:13** Gl 5:24; Php 3:10 [r]1Co 1:7; Eph 1:17; 2Th 1:7; 1Pt 1:7,13 [s]**4:14** Ps 89:50-51; Ac 5:41; 1Pt 2:20 [t]Ac 4:33; Rv 3:22 [u]**4:17** Mk 12:40; Jn 5:22; Heb 10:27; 13:4 [v]Gl 6:10; Eph 2:19; 1Tm 3:15; Heb 3:2 [w]**4:18** Pr 11:31 [x]**4:19** Ps 10:14; 2Co 1:9 [y]**5:1** Ac 4:20 [z]Rm 8:18; Col 3:4 [aa]**5:2** Jr 3:15; 23:1; Jn 21:16; Ac 20:28 [ab]**5:4** Jn 10:11,14; 21:15-17; Heb 13:20; 1Pt 2:25 [ac]1Co 9:25; Rv 12:1 [ad]**5:5** Pr 3:34; Jms 4:6 [ae]**5:6** Lk 14:11 [af]1Kg 8:42; 2Ch 6:32; Dn 9:15 [ag]**5:7** Ps 55:22 [ah]**5:8** 1Th 5:6,8; 2Tm 4:5; 1Pt 1:13; 4:7 [ai]Rv 16:15 [aj]Mt 4:1,10; Ac 13:10 [ak]**5:9** Eph 6:13-14; Jms 4:7

[A]**4:1** Other mss read *suffered for us* [B]**4:1** The phrase "in the flesh" probably means in human experience. [C]**4:1** Or *arm* [D]**4:1** Or *perspective*, or *attitude* [E]**4:1** Or *the one who has suffered in the flesh has ceased from sin* [F]**4:2** Lit *for desires of human beings* [G]**4:3** Or *Gentiles* [H]**4:4** Lit *you don't run with them into the same pouring out* [I]**4:6** Or *in the flesh* [J]**4:6** Or *in the spirit* [K]**4:8** Pr 10:12 [L]**4:12** Lit *the burning* [M]**4:14** Other mss add *He is blasphemed because of them, but He is glorified because of you.* [N]**4:15** Or *as one who defrauds others* [O]**4:18** Pr 11:31 LXX [P]**5:2** Other mss omit *overseeing* [Q]**5:2** Other mss omit *according to God's will* [R]**5:5** Lit *you tie around yourselves* [S]**5:5** Pr 3:34 LXX [T]**5:6** Lit *in time*

the same sufferings are being experienced by
your fellow believers throughout the world.
10 Now the God of all grace, who called you
to His eternal glory[a] in Christ Jesus, will personally[A] restore, establish, strengthen, and
support you after you have suffered a little.[B]
11 The dominion[C] belongs to Him forever.[D]
•Amen.

12 I have written you this brief letter
through Silvanus[E,b] (I know him to be a faithful brother) to encourage you and to testify
that this is the true grace of God. Take your
stand in it! 13 The church in Babylon,[F,c] also
chosen, sends you greetings, as does Mark,
my son. 14 Greet one another with a kiss of
love.[d] Peace[e] to all of you who are in Christ.[G]

[a] **5:10** 1Pt 5:1,4; 2Pt 3:18
[b] **5:12** Ac 15:22; 1Th 1:1; 2Th 1:1
[c] **5:13** Rv 14:8; 16:19; 17:5,18; 18:2,10,21
[d] **5:14** Rm 16:16; 1Co 16:20; 2Co 13:12; 1Th 5:26
[e] Eph 6:23

[A] **5:10** Lit *Himself* [B] **5:10** Or *a little while*, or *to a small extent* [C] **5:11** Other mss read *dominion and glory*; other mss read *glory and dominion* [D] **5:11** Other mss read *forever and ever* [E] **5:12** Or *Silas*; Ac 15:22-32; 16:19-40; 17:1-16 [F] **5:13** Probably refers to Rome [G] **5:14** Other mss read *Christ Jesus. Amen.*

2 PETER

For the introduction to the book of 2 Peter, see the introduction to the book of 1 Peter, page 1303.

Greeting

1 Simeon[A] Peter,[a] a ·slave and an apostle[b] of Jesus Christist:

To those who have obtained a faith of equal privilege with ours[B] through the righteousness[c] of our God and Savior[d] Jesus Christ.

[2]May grace and peace be multiplied to you through the knowledge of God[e] and of Jesus our Lord.

Growth in the Faith

[3]His[C] divine power[f] has given us everything required for life and godliness through the knowledge[g] of Him who called[h] us by[D] His own glory and goodness. [4]By these He has given us very great and precious promises,[i] so that through them you may share in the divine nature,[j] escaping the corruption that is in the world because of evil desires. [5]For this very reason, make every effort to supplement your faith with goodness, goodness with knowledge, [6]knowledge with self-control,[k] self-control with endurance, endurance with godliness, [7]godliness with brotherly affection,[l] and brotherly affection with love. [8]For if these qualities are yours and are increasing, they will keep you from being useless[m] or unfruitful[n] in the knowledge of our Lord Jesus Christ. [9]The person who lacks these things is blind and shortsighted and has forgotten the cleansing from his past sins. [10]Therefore, ·brothers, make every effort to confirm your calling and election,[o] because if you do these things you will never stumble. [11]For in this way, entry into the eternal kingdom[p] of our Lord and Savior Jesus Christ will be richly supplied to you.

[12]Therefore I will always remind you about these things, even though you know them and are established in the truth[q] you have. [13]I consider it right, as long as I am in this bodily tent,[E,r] to wake you up with a reminder, [14]knowing that I will soon lay aside my tent, as our Lord Jesus Christ has also shown me.[s] [15]And I will also make every effort that you may be able to recall these things at any time after my departure.[F]

The Trustworthy Prophetic Word

[16]For we did not follow cleverly contrived myths when we made known to you the power and coming of our Lord Jesus Christ;[t] instead, we were eyewitnesses of His majesty.[u] [17]For when He received honor and glory from God the Father, a voice came to Him from the Majestic Glory:

> This is My beloved Son.[G]
> I take delight in Him![H,v]

[18]And we heard this voice when it came from heaven while we were with Him on the holy mountain.[w] [19]So we have the prophetic word strongly confirmed. You will do well to pay attention to it, as to a lamp shining in a dismal place,[x] until the day dawns[y] and the morning star[z] rises in your hearts. [20]First of all, you should know this: No prophecy of Scripture comes from one's own interpretation, [21]because no prophecy ever came by the will of man;[aa] instead, men spoke from God as they were moved by the Holy Spirit.[ab]

The Judgment of False Teachers

2 But there were also false prophets[ac] among the people, just as there will be false teachers[ad] among you. They will secretly bring in destructive heresies, even denying the Master who bought[ae] them, and will bring swift destruction on themselves. [2]Many

[a]**1:1** Mt 16:17; Lk 6:14; Ac 10:32; 15:14 [b]Rm 1:1; Ti 1:1 [c]Rm 5:17,21; Php 1:11 [d]Ti 2:13 [e]**1:2** Jn 17:3; Php 3:8; 2Pt 1:3,8; 2:20; 3:18 [f]**1:3** 1Pt 1:5 [g]Jn 17:3; Php 3:8; 2Pt 1:2,8; 2:20; 3:18 [h]1Th 2:12; 2Th 2:14; 1Pt 5:10 [i]**1:4** Jos 21:45; 1Kg 8:56; Is 38:16; Jr 33:14; Rm 9:4; 15:8; 2Co 7:1 [j]Eph 4:24; Heb 12:10; 1Jn 3:2 [k]**1:6** Ac 24:25; Gl 5:23 [l]**1:7** Rm 12:10; Heb 13:1; 1Pt 1:22 [m]**1:8** Jms 2:20 [n]Mt 7:16-21; Gl 5:22; Ti 3:14 [o]**1:10** Mt 22:14; Rm 11:29; 2Pt 1:3 [p]**1:11** Col 1:13; 2Tm 4:18 [q]**1:12** 2Co 11:10; Col 1:5-6; 2Jn 2; 3Jn 3-4 [r]**1:13** 2Co 5:1-4 [s]**1:14** Jn 21:18-23 [t]**1:16** Mk 13:26; 14:62; 1Th 2:19 [u]Mt 17:1-6 [v]**1:17** Is 42:1; Mt 3:17; 17:5; Mk 1:11; 9:7; Lk 3:22 [w]**1:18** Ps 2:6; Mt 17:1; Mk 9:2; Lk 9:28 [x]**1:19** Ps 119:105 [y]Mal 4:2; Rm 13:12; 2Pt 3:18 [z]Nm 24:17; Rv 22:16 [aa]**1:21** Jr 23:26; 2Tm 3:16 [ab]2Sm 23:2; Lk 1:70; Ac 1:16; 3:18; 1Pt 1:11 [ac]**2:1** Dt 13:1-5; Mt 7:15 [ad]Ac 20:29; 2Co 11:13-15; Gl 2:4; 1Tm 4:1; 2Tm 4:3 [ae]1Co 6:20; 7:23

[A]**1:1** Other mss read *Simon* [B]**1:1** Or *obtained a faith of the same kind as ours* [C]**1:3** Lit *As His* [D]**1:3** Or *to* [E]**1:13** = Peter's body [F]**1:15** Or *my death* [G]**1:17** Other mss read *My Son, My Beloved* [H]**1:17** = Christ's transfiguration; Mt 17:5

will follow their unrestrained ways, and the
way of truth will be blasphemed because of
them.[a] 3 They will exploit[b] you in their greed[c]
with deceptive words. Their condemnation,[d]
pronounced long ago, is not idle, and their
destruction does not sleep.
4 For if God didn't spare[e] the angels who
sinned but threw them down into Tartarus[A,f]
and delivered them to be kept in chains[B] of
darkness until judgment;[g] 5 and if He didn't
spare the ancient world, but protected Noah,[h]
a preacher of righteousness, and seven others,[C,i] when He brought a flood on the world
of the ungodly; 6 and if He reduced the cities
of Sodom and Gomorrah[j] to ashes and condemned them to ruin,[D] making them an example to those who were going to be ungodly;[E,k]
7 and if He rescued righteous Lot,[l] distressed
by the unrestrained behavior of the immoral
8 (for as he lived among them, that righteous
man tormented himself day by day with the
lawless deeds he saw and heard[m]) — 9 then the
Lord knows how to rescue[n] the godly from
trials and to keep the unrighteous under punishment until the day of judgment,[o] 10 especially those who follow the polluting desires
of the flesh and despise authority.[p]

Bold, arrogant people! They do not tremble when they blaspheme the glorious ones;
11 however, angels, who are greater in might
and power, do not bring a slanderous charge
against them before the Lord.[F] 12 But these
people, like irrational animals — creatures of instinct born to be caught and destroyed — speak blasphemies about things
they don't understand, and in their destruction they too will be destroyed, 13 suffering
harm as the payment for unrighteousness.
They consider it a pleasure to carouse in
the daytime. They are spots and blemishes,
delighting in their deceptions[G] as they feast
with you. 14 They have eyes full of adultery[q]
and are always looking for sin. They seduce
unstable people and have hearts trained in
greed. Children under a curse![r] 15 They have
gone astray by abandoning the straight path[s]
and have followed the path of Balaam,[t] the
son of Bosor,[H] who loved the wages of unrighteousness[u] 16 but received a rebuke for his
transgression: A donkey that could not talk
spoke with a human voice and restrained the
prophet's irrationality.[v]
17 These people are springs without water,
mists driven by a whirlwind. The gloom of
darkness has been reserved for them.[w] 18 For by
uttering boastful, empty words,[x] they seduce,
with fleshly desires and debauchery, people
who have barely escaped[I] from those who
live in error. 19 They promise them freedom,
but they themselves are ˚slaves of corruption,
since people are enslaved to whatever defeats
them.[y] 20 For if, having escaped the world's
impurity through the knowledge of our Lord
and Savior Jesus Christ,[z] they are again entangled in these things and defeated, the last
state is worse for them than the first.[aa] 21 For
it would have been better for them not to
have known the way of righteousness[ab] than,
after knowing it, to turn back from the holy
command[ac] delivered[ad] to them.[ae] 22 It has happened to them according to the true proverb:
A dog returns to its own vomit,[J,af] and, "a sow,
after washing itself, wallows in the mud."

The Day of the Lord

3 Dear friends, this is now the second letter[ag] I have written to you; in both letters,
I want to develop a genuine[ah] understanding
with a reminder, 2 so that you can remember the words previously spoken by the holy
prophets and the command of our Lord and
Savior given through your apostles. 3 First, be
aware of this: Scoffers will come in the last
days[ai] to scoff, living according to their own
desires, 4 saying, "Where is the promise of His
coming?[aj] Ever since the fathers fell ˚asleep,[ak]
all things continue as they have been since
the beginning of creation." 5 They willfully ignore this: Long ago the heavens and the earth
were brought about from water and through
water[al] by the word of God.[am] 6 Through these
waters the world of that time perished when
it was flooded.[an] 7 But by the same word,[ao] the
present heavens and earth are stored up for
fire, being kept until the day of judgment[ap]
and destruction of ungodly men.

[a] **2:2** Rm 2:24 [b] **2:3** Jms 4:13 [c] Eph 5:3 [d] Mt 12:41; 23:33; Rm 3:8 [e] **2:4** Rm 8:32; Jd 6 [f] Rv 20:2-3,10 [g] Mt 25:41 [h] **2:5** Gn 5:29 [i] 1Pt 3:20 [j] **2:6** Gn 19:24; Jd 7 [k] Is 1:9; Jd 15 [l] **2:7** Gn 19:16 [m] **2:8** Ps 119:136,158; Ezk 9:4 [n] **2:9** 1Co 10:13 [o] Mt 10:15; Jd 6 [p] **2:10-13** Jd 8-12 [q] **2:14** Mt 5:27-28 [r] Jr 23:14; Hs 4:2; Eph 2:3; Heb 2:13 [s] **2:15** Ac 13:10 [t] Nm 22:5-7; Dt 23:4; Neh 13:2; Jd 11; Rv 2:14 [u] Hs 9:1; Mc 1:7; Ac 1:18 [v] **2:16** Nm 22:22-35 [w] **2:17** Jd 13 [x] **2:18** Jd 16 [y] **2:19** Jn 8:34; Rm 6:16; 7:5 [z] **2:20** 2Pt 1:2 [aa] Mt 12:45; Lk 11:26 [ab] **2:21** Pr 8:20; 12:28; 16:31; 21:21; Mt 21:32 [ac] Rm 7:12; 1Tm 6:14 [ad] Jd 3 [ae] Ezk 18:1-32; Heb 6:4-6; 10:26-27 [af] **2:22** Pr 26:11 [ag] **3:1** 1Pt 1:1 [ah] Php 1:10 [ai] **3:3** 2Tm 3:1; Heb 1:2; Jms 5:3; 1Pt 1:20 [aj] **3:4** 1Th 2:19; 2Pt 3:12 [ak] Ac 7:60 [al] **3:5** Ps 24:1-2; 33:6-7; 136:5-6; Pr 8:24-29 [am] Gn 1:3-30; Ps 148:5; Jn 1:1-3; Heb 4:12; 11:3 [an] **3:6** 2Pt 2:5 [ao] **3:7** Is 66:15-16; Ezk 38:22; Am 7:4; Zph 1:18; Mal 4:1 [ap] Php 1:6; 2Th 1:5; 1Jn 4:17

[A] **2:4** = Gk name for a place of divine punishment in the underworld. [B] **2:4** Other mss read *in pits* [C] **2:5** Lit *righteousness, as the eighth* [D] **2:6** Other mss omit *to ruin* [E] **2:6** Other mss read *an example of what is going to happen to the ungodly* [F] **2:11** Other mss read *them from the Lord* [G] **2:13** Other mss read *delighting in the love feasts* [H] **2:15** Other mss read *Beor* [I] **2:18** Or *people who are barely escaping* [J] **2:22** Pr 26:11

[8]Dear friends, don't let this one thing escape you: With the Lord one day is like a
thousand years, and a thousand years like
one day.[a] [9]The Lord does not delay His promise,[b] as some understand delay, but is patient
with you, not wanting any[c] to perish[d] but all
to come to repentance.[e]
[10]But the Day of the Lord[f] will come like
a thief;[A,g] on that day the heavens will pass
away[h] with a loud noise, the elements will
burn and be dissolved,[i] and the earth and
the works on it will be disclosed.[B] [11]Since all
these things are to be destroyed in this way, it
is clear what sort of people you should be in
holy conduct and godliness [12]as you wait for
and earnestly desire the coming[C] of the day
of God.[j] The heavens will be on fire and be
dissolved because of it, and the elements will
melt with the heat. [13]But based on His promise, we wait for the new heavens and a new
earth,[k] where righteousness will dwell.[l]

Conclusion

[14]Therefore, dear friends, while you wait
for these things, make every effort to be
found at peace with Him without spot or
blemish.[m] [15]Also, regard the patience of our
Lord as an opportunity for salvation, just as
our dear brother Paul has written to you according to the wisdom given to him.[n] [16]He
speaks about these things in all his letters in
which there are some matters that are hard to
understand. The untaught and unstable twist
them to their own destruction,[o] as they also
do with the rest of the Scriptures.
[17]Therefore, dear friends, since you know
this in advance, be on your guard,[p] so that
you are not led away by the error of lawless
people and fall from your own stability. [18]But
grow in the grace and knowledge[q] of our Lord
and Savior Jesus Christ. To Him be the glory
both now and to the day of eternity.[D,r] Amen.[E]

TEXT MESSAGES

Text message

We wonder what is taking so long—when will Christ return and straighten out this mess? He is delaying to give folks a bit more time to come to Him, and by extension, giving us a bit more time to share His Good News. What amazing compassion from God who is "not wanting any to perish, but all to come to repentance" (2Pt 3:9). We must go, for "how can they call on Him in whom they have not believed? And how can they believe without hearing about Him? And how can they hear without a preacher?" (Rm 10:14).

[a]**3:8** Ps 90:4 [b]**3:9** Hab 2:3 [c]Ti 2:11 [d]Ezk 18:23,32; 33:11; 1Tm 2:4 [e]Jl 2:12-13; Jnh 3:10; 4:2; Ac 17:31; Rm 2:4 [f]**3:10** Php 1:6 [g]Mt 24:43; Lk 12:39; 1Th 5:2 [h]Mt 5:18; 24:35; Rv 21:1 [i]Is 24:19; Mc 1:4 [j]**3:12** Lk 12:36; 1Co 1:7; 1Th 1:10; Ti 2:13; Jd 21 [k]**3:13** Is 65:17; 66:22; Mt 19:28; Rm 8:21; Rv 21:1 [l]Is 32:16; Rm 14:17 [m]**3:14** Php 2:15; 1Th 5:23; 1Tm 6:14; Jms 1:27 [n]**3:15** Ac 9:17; 15:25; 2Pt 3:2 [o]**3:16** Heb 5:11; 2Pt 2:14 [p]**3:17** Lk 12:15; 2Tm 1:14; 4:15 [q]**3:18** 2Pt 1:2 [r]Rm 11:36; 2Tm 4:18; Rv 1:6

[A]**3:10** Other mss add *in the night* [B]**3:10** Other mss read *will be burned up* [C]**3:12** Or *and speed the coming* [D]**3:18** Or *now and forever* [E]**3:18** Other mss omit *Amen.*

■ **AUTHOR:** John, the disciple

■■ **DATE:** First John was written between A.D. 85 and 90 in Ephesus; 2 and 3 John were written around A.D. 90 in Ephesus

These endearing letters from the old disciple John to younger believers carry a powerful lesson to every reader: Watch your step, follow the truth, don't fall victim to false religion. Despite frequent references to God's love and the love of friends (including the author's love), these letters challenge heresies associated with incipient Gnosticism, one of the most prevalent "bad road" theories threatening the beliefs of first-century Christians. John had harsh words for those who gave an ear to these silver-tongued imposters. The mission of God is Jesus Christ as Savior and Lord, not the Gnostic perversion.

1 JOHN

Why did the Gnostics pose such a threat? *Gnosis* is Greek for "knowledge," hence the name of these dangerous false teachers who claimed that special knowledge would free soul from body and lead to enlightenment. The danger of this idea was the split it created in the mission of God. After creating the material world, God called it good, Genesis affirms. The Gnostics called it bad and impermanent. When Jesus came as a child of Mary, God the Son took flesh and blood, a human body. Gnostics taught that the body was flawed; spirit alone was good. To follow the Gnostic way, you had to believe that Jesus was not really human, that the world was inherently bad, and that salvation was to be achieved by adopting this ethereal philosophy. Gnosticism had some appeal—secret special knowledge has always been alluring.

In 1 John, John advises that teachers of this program are antichrists—enemies of the gospel. Their teaching must be rejected, and any inroad into the church must be resisted. God's Spirit would enable Christians to stay loyal to Jesus, who really died and rose from the dead. Jesus, the whole person, would come again soon. ("It is the last hour"—2:18). Life is found only through faith in Jesus. John's frequent use of "dear friends" (3:21; 4:1,7) and "little children" (2:1,18,28) should not mask his firm opposition to Gnostic error.

In 2 John, the same author urges discernment concerning the ancient value of hospitality. Should false teachers show up, do not open your home or help their cause. To do so would be giving aid and support to people undermining the truth. God's mission requires drawing lines, observing boundaries. John never advises hatefulness or violence, just no aid to Gnostics. Focus your generosity on people and causes that proclaim Jesus.

In 3 John, a church member named Diotrephes, who was headstrong and full of himself, needs the discipline of the church. On the other hand, Gaius lived the truth, to the joy of John. God's mission rests with people like Gaius. Guard your character. Grow in grace and peace.

Prologue: Our Declaration

1 What was from the beginning,[a]
what we have heard,
what we have seen with our eyes,
what we have observed
and have touched with our hands,
concerning the Word[b] of life—
[2] that life was revealed,[c]
and we have seen it
and we testify and declare to you
the eternal life that was with the Father
and was revealed to us[d]—
[3] what we have seen and heard
we also declare to you,
so that you may have fellowship[e]
along with us;
and indeed our fellowship is
with the Father[f]
and with His Son Jesus Christ.
[4] We are writing these things[A]
so that our[B] joy[g] may be complete.

Fellowship with God

[5]Now this is the message we have heard
from Him and declare to you: God is light,[h]
and there is absolutely no darkness in Him.[i]
[6]If we say, "We have fellowship[j] with Him," yet
we •walk in darkness,[k] we are lying and are not
practicing[C] the truth.[l] [7]But if we walk in the
light[m] as He Himself is in the light, we have
fellowship with one another, and the blood of
Jesus[n] His Son cleanses us from all sin. [8]If we
say, "We have no sin,"[o] we are deceiving ourselves, and the truth is not in us. [9]If we confess our sins, He is faithful and righteous to
forgive[p] us our sins and to cleanse us from all
unrighteousness. [10]If we say, "We don't have
any sin," we make Him a liar, and His word[q]
is not in us.[r]

2 My little children, I am writing you these
things so that you may not sin. But if anyone does sin, we have an •advocate[s] with the
Father—Jesus Christ the Righteous One. [2]He
Himself is the •propitiation[t] for our sins, and
not only for ours, but also for those of the
whole world.[u]

God's Commands

[3]This is how we are sure[v] that we have come
to know Him: by keeping His commands.[w]
[4]The one who says, "I have come to know
Him," yet doesn't keep His commands, is a
liar, and the truth is not in him. [5]But whoever
keeps His word,[x] truly in him the love of God
is perfected.[D] This is how we know we are in
Him:[y] [6]The one who says he remains in Him[z]
should •walk just as He walked.

[7]Dear friends, I am not writing you a new
command[aa] but an old command that you have
had from the beginning. The old command is
the message[ab] you have heard. [8]Yet I am writing
you a new command, which is true in Him and
in you, because the darkness is passing away[ac]
and the true light[ad] is already shining.[ae]
[9]The one who says he is in the light but hates
his brother[af] is in the darkness until now.
[10]The one who loves his brother[ag] remains in
the light, and there is no cause for stumbling
in him.[E] [11]But the one who hates his brother[ah]
is in the darkness, walks in the darkness,[ai] and
doesn't know where he's going,[aj] because the
darkness has blinded his eyes.

Reasons for Writing

[12] I am writing to you, little children,
because your sins have been forgiven
because of Jesus' name.[ak]
[13] I am writing to you, fathers,
because you have come to know
the One who is from the beginning.[al]
I am writing to you, young men,
because you have had victory
over the evil one.[am]
[14] I have written to you, children,
because you have come to know
the Father.
I have written to you, fathers,
because you have come to know
the One who is from the beginning.
I have written to you, young men,
because you are strong,
God's word[an] remains in you,
and you have had victory
over the evil one.

A Warning about the World

[15]Do not love the •world[ao] or the things
that belong to[F] the world. If anyone loves the

[a]**1:1** Jn 1:1; 1Jn 2:13-14 [b]Ps 119:25; Jn 1:1,4; 5:24; Php 2:16 [c]**1:2** Jn 1:31; 21:1,14; Col 3:4; 1Pt 5:4; 1Jn 2:28; 3:5,8 [d]1Jn 5:20 [e]**1:3** Php 3:10 [f]Mt 11:27 [g]**1:4** 2Co 2:3; Php 1:4,25; 2:18 [h]**1:5** Ps 27:1; 36:9; Jn 12:46; 1Tm 6:16 [i]1Jn 2:5 [j]**1:6** 2Co 8:4 [k]Pr 2:13; Is 9:2; 50:10; Jn 8:12; 12:35; 1Jn 2:11 [l]Jn 14:6; 2Co 11:10; 3Jn 3 [m]**1:7** Eph 5:8-14; Col 1:12-14; Php 2:15; 1Th 5:5 [n]Heb 10:19; 12:24; 1Pt 1:2,19; Rv 1:5 [o]**1:8** Pr 20:9; Jr 2:35; Rm 3:9-23; Jms 3:2 [p]**1:9** Ps 103:3; Jr 31:34; Mt 9:6; 26:28; Col 1:14; Jms 5:15 [q]**1:10** Lk 8:21; Heb 4:12 [r]Jn 8:37 [s]**2:1** Jn 14:26 [t]**2:2** Rm 3:25; 2Co 5:21; Heb 2:17; 1Jn 4:10 [u]Mt 26:13; 28:19-20; Mk 14:9; Rm 1:8 [v]**2:3** Jn 13:35; 1Jn 2:5; 3:19,24; 4:2,6,13; 5:2 [w]Jn 14:15; 15:10 [x]**2:5** Jn 14:23 [y]Jn 6:56; 14:20; 15:1-7; Rm 8:1; 2Co 5:17; Eph 2:10; Php 1:1 [z]**2:6** Jn 15:4-7; 1Jn 2:24,27-28; 3:6,24; 4:13,15-16 [aa]**2:7** Mk 7:8; Jn 13:34; 2Jn 5 [ab]Lk 6:47; Jn 1:1 [ac]**2:8** Rm 13:12; 1Co 7:31; 1Jn 2:17 [ad]Jn 1:9; 3:19-21; 8:12; 12:46 [ae]Jn 1:5; 12:35-36; Rv 22:5 [af]**2:9** 1Jn 2:11; 3:15; 4:20 [ag]**2:10** Rm 12:10; 1Th 4:9; Heb 13:1; 1Pt 1:22; 1Jn 3:10,14-17; 4:20-21 [ah]**2:11** Lv 19:17; 1Jn 3:15; 4:20 [ai]1Jn 1:6 [aj]Jn 14:6 [ak]**2:12** Ps 25:11; Lk 24:47; Ac 2:38; 10:43 [al]**2:13** 1Jn 1:1 [am]Jn 16:33; 17:15; Eph 6:10; 1Jn 2:14; 4:4; 5:4-5; Rv 2:7 [an]**2:14** 1Jn 1:10 [ao]**2:15** Jn 15:19; 17:16; Rm 12:2; Jms 1:27; 4:4

[A]**1:4** Other mss add *to you* [B]**1:4** Other mss read *your* [C]**1:6** Or *not living according to* [D]**2:5** Or *truly completed* [E]**2:10** Or *in it* [F]**2:15** Lit *things in* world, love for the Father is not in him. 16 For everything that belongs to[A] the world — the lust of the flesh,[a] the lust of the eyes,[b] and the pride[c] in one's lifestyle — is not from the Father, but is from the world. 17 And the world with its lust is passing away,[d] but the one who does God's will[e] remains forever.[f]

The Last Hour

18 Children, it is the last hour.[g] And as you have heard, "Antichrist[h] is coming," even now many antichrists have come. We know from this that it is the last hour. 19 They went out from us, but they did not belong to us; for if they had belonged to us, they would have remained with us. However, they went out so that it might be made clear that none of them belongs to us.

20 But you have an anointing[i] from the Holy One,[j] and all of you have knowledge.[B] 21 I have not written to you because you don't know the truth, but because you do know it, and because no lie comes from the truth. 22 Who is the liar, if not the one who denies that Jesus is the •Messiah?[k] This one is the antichrist: the one who denies the Father and the Son. 23 No one who denies the Son can have the Father;[l] he who confesses the Son has the Father as well.[m]

Remaining with God

24 What you have heard from the beginning must remain in you. If what you have heard from the beginning remains in you, then you will remain in the Son[n] and in the Father.[o] 25 And this is the promise that He Himself made to us: eternal life.[p] 26 I have written these things to you about those who are trying to deceive you.

27 The anointing you received from Him remains in you, and you don't need anyone to teach you. Instead, His anointing teaches you about all things[q] and is true and is not a lie; just as He has taught you, remain in Him.[r]

God's Children

28 So now, little children, remain in Him, so that when He appears[s] we may have boldness and not be ashamed before Him at His coming.[t] 29 If you know that He is righteous, you know this as well: Everyone who does what is right[u] has been born of Him.[v]

3 1 Look at how great a love[C] the Father has given us that we should be called God's children. And we are! The reason the •world does not know us is that it didn't know Him. 2 Dear friends, we are God's children now, and what we will be has not yet been revealed.[w] We know that when He appears, we will be like Him[x] because we will see Him as He is.[y] 3 And everyone who has this hope[z] in Him purifies himself just as He is pure.[aa]

4 Everyone who commits sin also breaks the law;[D] sin is the breaking of law. 5 You know that He was revealed so that He might take away sins,[E,ab] and there is no sin in Him.[ac] 6 Everyone who remains in Him[ad] does not sin;[F,ae] everyone who[G] sins has not seen Him or known Him.

7 Little children, let no one deceive you! The one who does what is right is righteous, just as He is righteous. 8 The one who commits[H] sin is of the Devil, for the Devil has sinned from the beginning. The Son of God[af] was revealed[ag] for this purpose: to destroy the Devil's works. 9 Everyone who has been born of God[ah] does not sin,[I] because His[J] seed[ai] remains in him; he is not able to sin,[K] because he has been born of God. 10 This is how God's children — and the Devil's children — are made evident.

The Command to Love

Whoever does not do what is right is not of God, especially the one who does not love his brother.[aj] 11 For this is the message you have heard from the beginning: We should love one another, 12 unlike Cain,[ak] who was of the evil one[al] and murdered[L] his brother. And why did he murder him? Because his works were evil, and his brother's were righteous. 13 Do not be surprised, •brothers, if the world hates[am] you. 14 We know that we have passed from death to life because we love our brothers.

[a] **2:16** Rm 13:14; Eph 2:3; 1Pt 4:2; 2Pt 2:18 [b] Gn 3:6; Pr 27:20 [c] Jms 4:16 [d] **2:17** 1Jn 2:8 [e] Mk 3:35; Eph 6:6; 1Th 4:3; 1Pt 2:15 [f] Jn 8:35; 12:34; 2Co 9:9; 1Pt 1:25 [g] **2:18** Jn 2:4; 1Pt 4:7 [h] Mt 24:5,24; 1Jn 2:22; 4:3; 2Jn 7 [i] **2:20** 2Co 1:21 [j] Ps 89:18; Mk 1:24; Ac 10:38 [k] **2:22** Jn 20:31; Ac 18:5; Eph 5:2; 1Jn 5:1 [l] **2:23** Jn 5:23 [m] Jn 8:19; 16:3; 17:3; 1Jn 4:15; 5:1; 2Jn 9 [n] **2:24** Jn 15:4-7; 1Jn 2:6,27-28; 3:6,24; 4:13,15-16 [o] Jn 10:38; Col 3:3; 1Th 1:1; 1Jn 4:15-16 [p] **2:25** Jn 4:14; 1Tm 4:8; 2Tm 1:1; Ti 1:2 [q] **2:27** Jn 14:26 [r] Jn 15:4-7; 1Jn 2:6; 3:6,24; 4:13,15-16 [s] **2:28** Lk 17:30; Col 3:4; 1Jn 3:2 [t] 1Th 2:19 [u] **2:29** Gn 18:19; Dt 6:18; 1Jn 3:7,10 [v] Jn 1:12-13; 3:3-7; 8:41; 1Jn 3:9; 4:7; 5:1,4,18 [w] **3:2** 2Co 4:11; 1Pt 5:4; 1Jn 2:28 [x] Rm 8:29; 1Co 15:49; 2Co 3:18; Php 3:21; 2Pt 1:4 [y] 1Co 13:12; Heb 12:14; Rv 22:4 [z] **3:3** Ac 23:6; 1Th 1:3 [aa] Php 4:8 [ab] **3:5** Jn 1:29; 1Co 15:3; Heb 10:4; 1Pt 2:24 [ac] 2Co 5:21; Heb 4:15; 7:26; 1Pt 2:21-22; 3:18; 1Jn 2:29 [ad] **3:6** Jn 15:4-7; 1Jn 2:6,24,27-28; 3:24; 4:13,15-16 [ae] Rm 6:11-12; 1Jn 2:29; 5:18 [af] **3:8** Mk 1:11 [ag] Jn 21:1; 2Co 4:11; 1Pt 5:4; 1Jn 5:20 [ah] **3:9** 1Jn 2:29

[ai] 1Pt 1:23 [aj] **3:10** 1Jn 2:10; 3:14-17; 4:20-21 [ak] **3:12** Gn 4:1; Jd 11 [al] 2Th 3:3 [am] **3:13** Jn 17:14

[A] 2:16 Lit *that is in* [B] 2:20 Other mss read *and you know all things* [C] 3:1 Or *at what sort of love* [D] 3:4 Or *also commits iniquity* [E] 3:5 Other mss read *our sins* [F] 3:6 Or *not keep on sinning* [G] 3:6 Or *who keeps on sinning* [H] 3:8 Or *practices* [I] 3:9 Or *not practice sin* [J] 3:9 God's [K] 3:9 Or *to keep on sinning* [L] 3:12 Or *slaughtered*

Bill Wallace (1908—1951)

Jesus commissioned His disciples to "go, therefore, and make disciples of all nations, baptizing them in the name of the Father and of the Son and of the Holy Spirit" (Mt 28:19). He also said, "I have told you these things so that in Me you may have peace. You will have suffering in this world. Be courageous! I have conquered the world" (Jn 16:33). When Bill Wallace, a doctor's son, decided to obey the Great Commission at the age of 17 on July 5, 1925, little did he know that he would discover the suffering of which Jesus spoke. Ten years later, after finishing medical school, Wallace went to Wuchow, China, in 1935 to serve as a medical missionary. He went as a representative of the Foreign Mission Board of the Southern Baptist Convention and served at the Stout Memorial Hospital in Wuchow. The prayers of many Christians in China for a medical missionary were answered.

In 1935, the world teetered on the brink of war. In the ensuing years, China remained a hotbed of change due to the Boxer Rebellion, the invasion of the Japanese during World War II, and the growth of Communism. But through all of the chaos, Wallace continued to perform surgeries and witness for Christ.

Even when asked to leave China for his own safety, Wallace refused. Instead, he moved the hospital when necessary.

In the early morning of December 19, 1950, the Communists raided his home and took Wallace to prison. A gun had been found under his pillow, Wallace was told, a claim that led to a charge of espionage. After interrogation and beatings, Wallace was forced to sign a false confession.

Although his imprisonment took a toll on his spirits, Wallace continued to bear witness to his Lord. Two months after his imprisonment, however, his body was found hanging in his cell. While his Communist jailers claimed suicide, his badly beaten body told another story.

Chinese Christians buried him in a grave marked by the words of the apostle Paul: "For Me to Live Is Christ." [1]

In 1963, Jesse C. Fletcher wrote a biography on him entitled *Bill Wallace of China*. In 1967, the motion picture, *Bill Wallace of China* was released.

[1] Source: Wallace Memorial Baptist Church (http://www.wmbc.net/templates/cuswallace/details.asp?id=31704&PID=322415).

The one who does not love remains in death.[a]
15 Everyone who hates his brother[b] is a murderer,[c] and you know that no murderer has
eternal life residing in him.

Love in Action

16 This is how we have come to know love: He
laid down His life[d] for us.[e] We should also lay
down our lives for our brothers.[f] 17 If anyone
has this world's goods[g] and sees his brother in
need[h] but closes his eyes[i] to his need—how
can God's love reside in him?[j]
18 Little children, we must not love with
word or speech, but with truth and action.[k]
19 This is how we will know we belong to the
truth[l] and will convince our conscience in
His presence, 20 even if our conscience condemns us, that God is greater than our conscience, and He knows all things.[m]
21 Dear friends, if our conscience doesn't
condemn us, we have confidence before God
22 and can receive whatever we ask from Him
because we keep His commands[n] and do what
is pleasing in His sight. 23 Now this is His command: that we believe in the name[o] of His Son
Jesus Christ, and love one another as He commanded us. 24 The one who keeps His commands remains in Him,[p] and He in him. And
the way we know that He remains in us[q] is
from the Spirit[r] He has given us.

The Spirit of Truth and the Spirit of Error

4 Dear friends, do not believe every spirit,
but test the spirits[s] to determine if they
are from God, because many false prophets
have gone out into the world.
2 This is how you know the Spirit of God:
Every spirit who confesses that Jesus Christ
has[A] come in the flesh[t] is from God.[u] 3 But every spirit who does not confess Jesus[B] is not
from God. This is the spirit of the antichrist;[v]
you have heard that he is coming, and he is
already in the world now.
4 You are from God, little children, and
you have conquered them, because the One
who is in you[w] is greater than the one who
is in the world.[x] 5 They are from the •world.[y]
Therefore what they say is from the world,
and the world listens to them. 6 We are from
God. Anyone who knows God listens to us;[z]
anyone who is not from God does not listen
to us. From this we know the Spirit of truth
and the spirit of deception.[aa]

Knowing God through Love

7 Dear friends, let us love one another, because love is from God, and everyone who
loves has been born of God[ab] and knows God.
8 The one who does not love does not know
God, because God is love. 9 God's love was revealed among us in this way:[C] God sent[ac] His
•One and Only Son[ad] into the world so that we
might live[ae] through Him. 10 Love consists in
this: not that we loved God, but that He loved
us[af] and sent His Son to be the[D] •propitiation[ag]
for our sins. 11 Dear friends, if God loved us
in this way, we also must love one another.[ah]
12 No one has ever seen God.[E,ai] If we love one
another, God remains in[F] us and His love is
perfected in us.
13 This is how we know that we remain in
Him[aj] and He in us: He has given assurance to
us from His Spirit.[ak] 14 And we have seen and
we testify that the Father has sent His Son[al]
as the world's Savior. 15 Whoever confesses[G,am]
that Jesus is the Son of God—God remains
in him and he in God. 16 And we have come to
know and to believe the love that God has for
us. God is love, and the one who remains in
love remains in God, and God remains in him.
17 In this, love is perfected with us so that we
may have confidence in the day of judgment,[an]
for we are as He is in this world.[ao] 18 There is
no fear in love; instead, perfect love drives out
fear,[ap] because fear involves punishment.[H] So
the one who fears has not reached perfection
in love.[aq] 19 We love[I] because He first loved us.[ar]

Keeping God's Commands

20 If anyone says, "I love God," yet hates his
brother,[as] he is a liar.[at] For the person who
does not love his brother[au] he has seen cannot love the God he has not seen.[J] 21 And we
have this command from Him: The one who
loves God must also love his brother.

[a] **3:14** Jn 8:51 [b] **3:15** 1Jn 2:9,11; 4:20 [c] Mt 5:21-22; Jn 8:44 [d] **3:16** Jn 10:11,14,17-18; 13:37-38; 15:13 [e] Is 53:10; Mk 10:45 [f] Mk 8:34-35; 1Co 11:1; Php 2:5-8 [g] **3:17** Mk 12:44; Lk 15:12; 1Jn 2:16 [h] Ac 2:45 [i] 2Co 7:15 [j] Jms 2:15-16; 1Jn 2:5 [k] **3:18** Mt 7:21; Jn 13:34-35; 15:12-17; Jms 1:22-25; 2:14-17 [l] **3:19** Jn 14:6; 2Co 11:10; 3Jn 3 [m] **3:20** Ps 139:6; Pr 2:6; Jn 14:28 [n] **3:22** Mk 7:8; Jn 14:15; 1Jn 2:3; 5:2 [o] **3:23** Ps 33:21; Is 50:10; Jn 1:12; 3:18; 1Jn 5:13 [p] **3:24** Lk 11:13; Jn 15:4-7; Ac 5:32; 15:8 [q] Jn 6:56 [r] Rm 8:9-16 [s] **4:1** 1Th 5:21 [t] **4:2** Jn 1:14; Php 2:7; 3:3 [u] 1Co 12:3 [v] **4:3** 1Jn 2:18,22; 2Jn 7 [w] **4:4** Rm 8:31; Col 1:27; 1Jn 3:20 [x] Jn 12:31 [y] **4:5** Jn 17:6; 2Pt 2:20 [z] **4:6** Jn 8:47 [aa] Mk 13:5-6; 1Co 2:12; 1Tm 4:1 [ab] **4:7** 1Jn 2:29 [ac] **4:9** Mk 9:37 [ad] Jn 1:14,18; 3:16,18 [ae] Jn 10:28 [af] **4:10** Jn 3:16 [ag] 2Co 5:21; 1Jn 2:2 [ah] **4:11** Jn 13:14; 15:12; Rm 13:8; 1Th 4:9; 1Pt 1:22 [ai] **4:12** Ex 33:20 [aj] **4:13** Jn 15:4-7; 1Jn 2:6,24,27-28; 3:6,24; 4:15-16 [ak] Rv 3:22 [al] **4:14** Rm 1:3 [am] **4:15** Jn 9:22; Php 2:6 [an] **4:17** Mt 10:15; 11:22,24; 12:36; 2Pt 2:9; 3:7; Jd 6 [ao] Jn 14:10-11; 15:9-10; 17:11,15,18 [ap] **4:18** Rm 8:15 [aq] Eph 4:11-16 [ar] **4:19** 2Th 2:13 [as] **4:20** 1Jn 2:9,11; 3:15 [at] 1Jn 1:10 [au] 1Jn 2:10; 3:10,14-17

[A] **4:2** Or *confesses Jesus to be the Christ* [B] **4:3** Other mss read *confess that Jesus has come in the flesh* [C] **4:9** Or *revealed in us* [D] **4:10** Or *a* [E] **4:12** Since God is an infinite being, no one can see Him in His absolute essential nature; Ex 33:18-23. [F] **4:12** Or *remains among* [G] **4:15** Or *acknowledges* [H] **4:18** Or *fear has its own punishment* or *torment* [I] **4:19** Other mss add *Him* [J] **4:20** Other mss read *has seen, how is he able to love . . . seen?* (as a question)

5 Everyone who believes that Jesus is the
•Messiah has been born of God,[a] and everyone who loves the Father also loves the
one born of Him. 2This is how we know that
we love God's children when we love God
and obey[A] His commands. 3For this is what
love for God is: to keep His commands. Now
His commands are not a burden,[b] 4because
whatever has been born of God conquers the
•world. This is the victory that has conquered
the world: our faith. 5And who is the one who
conquers the world[c] but the one who believes
that Jesus is the Son of God?[d]

The Certainty of God's Testimony

6Jesus Christ — He is the One who came by
water and blood, not by water only, but by
water[e] and by blood.[f] And the Spirit is the One
who testifies,[g] because the Spirit is the truth.
7For there are three that testify:[B,h] 8the Spirit,[i]
the water, and the blood[j] — and these three
are in agreement. 9If we accept the testimony
of men, God's testimony[k] is greater, because
it is God's testimony that He has given about
His Son. 10(The one who believes in the Son of
God has this testimony within him. The one
who does not believe God has made Him a
liar,[l] because he has not believed in the testimony God has given about His Son.) 11And
this is the testimony: God has given us eternal
life, and this life is in His Son.
12The one who has the Son has life.[m] The
one who doesn't have the Son of God does not
have life. 13I have written these things to you
who believe in the name[n] of the Son of God, so
that you may know that you have eternal life.

Effective Prayer

14Now this is the confidence we have before
Him: Whenever we ask[o] anything according
to His will, He hears us.[p] 15And if we know
that He hears whatever we ask,[q] we know that
we have what we have asked Him for.[r]
16If anyone sees his brother committing a
sin that does not bring death, he should ask,
and God[C] will give life to him — to those who
commit sin that doesn't bring death. There
is sin[D] that brings death. I am not saying he
should pray about that. 17All unrighteousness
is sin, and there is sin that does not bring
death.

Conclusion

18We know that everyone who has been
born of God does not sin, but the One[E] who
is born of God keeps him,[F,G,s] and the evil one
does not touch him.
19We know that we are of God, and the
whole world is under the sway of the evil one.
20And we know that the Son of God has
come[t] and has given us understanding so that
we may know the true One.[H] We are in the
true One — that is, in His Son Jesus Christ.[u]
He is the true God and eternal life.
21Little children, guard yourselves from
idols.

[a] **5:1** 1Jn 2:29
[b] **5:3** Dt 30:11; Mt 11:30; 23:4,23
[c] **5:5** 1Co 15:57; 2Pt 2:20
[d] Jn 5:19; 14:1; Heb 1:2
[e] **5:6** Mk 1:11; Jn 1:34
[f] Jn 17:1; 1Jn 1:7; 4:10
[g] Jn 15:26; Ac 26:5
[h] **5:7** Dt 19:15; Mt 18:16; Jn 8:17-18
[i] **5:8** Jn 1:32; 19:30; 20:22
[j] Jn 19:34
[k] **5:9** Jn 5:36-37; 8:18
[l] **5:10** Gn 3:4
[m] **5:12** Jn 3:15,36; 5:24; 6:40,47
[n] **5:13** 1Jn 3:23
[o] **5:14** Mt 7:7; Jn 14:13; 1Jn 3:22
[p] Mt 7:8; Jn 9:31; 11:22
[q] **5:15** Jms 1:5
[r] Jn 11:22; 16:24
[s] **5:18** Jn 17:12; 1Pt 1:5; Jd 24; Rv 3:10
[t] **5:20** Jn 1:14; 8:42; 1Jn 1:2; 3:5,8
[u] Jn 10:38; 15:9; 17:21; 1Th 1:1; 1Jn 2:23-24

A **5:2** Other mss read *keep* B **5:7-8** Other mss (Vg and a few late Gk mss) read *testify in heaven: the Father, the Word, and the Holy Spirit, and these three are One. 8And there are three who bear witness on earth:* C **5:16** Lit *He* D **5:16** Or *is a sin* E **5:18** Jesus Christ F **5:18** Other mss read *himself* G **5:18** Or *the one who is born of God keeps himself* H **5:20** Other mss read *the true God*

2 JOHN

For the introduction to the book of 2 John, see the introduction to the book of
1 John, page 1314.

Greeting

The Elder:[A]
To the elect[a] lady[B] and her children:
I love all of you in the truth — and not only
I, but also all who have come to know the
truth[b] — 2 because of the truth that remains
in us[c] and will be with us forever.
3 Grace, mercy, and peace[d] will be with us
from God the Father and from Jesus Christ,
the Son[e] of the Father, in truth and love.[f]

Truth and Deception

4 I was very glad to find some of your children 'walking in the truth,[g] in keeping with
a command we have received from the Father. 5 So now I urge you, dear lady — not as
if I were writing you a new command, but
one we have had from the beginning — that
we love one another.[h] 6 And this is love:[i] that
we walk according to His commands.[j] This is
the command as you have heard it from the
beginning: you must walk in love.[C]

7 Many deceivers have gone out into the
world; they do not confess the coming of
Jesus Christ in the flesh.[D,k] This is the deceiver
and the antichrist.[l] 8 Watch yourselves so you
don't lose what we[E] have worked for, but that
you may receive a full reward.[m] 9 Anyone who
does not remain in Christ's teaching[n] but goes
beyond it, does not have God.[o] The one who
remains[p] in that teaching, this one has both
the Father[q] and the Son.[r] 10 If anyone comes
to you and does not bring this teaching, do
not receive[s] him into your home, and don't
say, "Welcome," to him; 11 for the one who says,
"Welcome," to him shares[t] in his evil works.[u]

Farewell

12 Though I have many things to write to
you,[v] I don't want to do so with paper and ink.
Instead, I hope to be with you and talk face to
face[F] so that our joy[w] may be complete.
13 The children of your elect sister send you
greetings.

[a]**1** Rm 16:13; 1Pt 5:13; 2Jn 13
[b]Jn 8:32; 14:6; 1Tm 2:4
[c]**2** 1Jn 1:8
[d]**3** 1Tm 1:2; 2Tm 1:2
[e]Heb 1:2
[f]1Jn 4:12
[g]**4** 3Jn 3-4
[h]**5** 1Jn 3:11
[i]**6** 1Jn 2:5; 5:3
[j]Ps 103:18; Mk 7:8; Jn 14:15,21,23; 15:10
[k]**7** Php 3:3
[l]1Jn 2:18,22; 4:3
[m]**8** 2Pt 2:13
[n]**9** Jn 8:31-32; 1Jn 2:21-23,27
[o]Jn 5:12; 8:41; 1Jn 2:23
[p]Jn 15:4-16
[q]Mt 11:27
[r]Heb 1:2; 1Jn 2:23
[s]**10** Jn 1:12; 6:21; 13:20
[t]**11** 1Tm 5:22
[u]Eph 5:11; 1Tm 5:22; Jd 23
[v]**12** 3Jn 13
[w]Jn 15:11

[A]**1** Or *Presbyter* [B]**1** Or *Kyria*, a proper name; probably a literary figure for a local church known to John; the children would be its members. [C]**6** Lit *in it* [D]**7** Or *confess Jesus Christ as coming in the flesh* [E]**8** Other mss read *you* [F]**12** Lit *mouth to mouth*

3 JOHN

For the introduction to the book of 3 John, see the introduction to the book of
1 John, page 1314.

Greeting

The Elder:[a]
To my dear friend[A] Gaius: I love you in
the truth.[b]
2 Dear friend,[B] I pray that you may prosper
in every way and be in good health physically[c]
just as you are spiritually.[C] 3 For I was very glad
when some •brothers came and testified[d] to
your faithfulness to the truth — how you are
•walking in the truth.[e] 4 I have no greater joy[f]
than this: to hear that my children[g] are walking in the truth.

Gaius Commended

5 Dear friend,[B] you are showing faithfulness[D] by whatever you do for the brothers, especially when they are strangers. 6 They have
testified to your love in front of the church.[h]
You will do well to send them on their journey[i] in a manner worthy of God,[j] 7 since they
set out for the sake of the Name,[k] accepting
nothing from pagans.[l] 8 Therefore, we ought
to support such men so that we can be coworkers with[E] the truth.

Diotrephes and Demetrius

9 I wrote something to the church, but Diotrephes, who loves to have first place among
them,[m] does not receive us.[n] 10 This is why, if
I come, I will remind him of the works he is
doing, slandering[o] us with malicious words.
And he is not satisfied with that! He not only
refuses to welcome the brothers himself, but
he even stops those who want to do so and ex-
pels them from the church.
11 Dear friend,[B] do not imitate what is evil,[p]
but what is good. The one who does good is
of God;[q] the one who does evil has not seen
God.[r] 12 Demetrius has a good testimony from
everyone, and from the truth itself. And we
also testify for him, and you know[s] that our
testimony is true.[t]

Farewell

13 I have many things to write you, but I don't
want to write to you with pen and ink. 14 I hope
to see you soon, and we will talk face to face.[F]
Peace be with you. The friends send you
greetings. Greet the friends by name.

[a] 1 2Jn 1
[b] Jn 14:6; 1Jn 5:20
[c] 2 1Tm 1:10
[d] 3 Jn 15:26; Ac 26:5
[e] 2Jn 4
[f] 4 Jn 15:11
[g] 1Co 4:14; Gl 4:19; Php 2:22
[h] 6 Mt 16:18; 1Co 14:4; Rv 1:4
[i] Ac 15:3; 20:38; 21:5; Rm 15:24; 1Co 16:6; 2Co 1:16; Ti 3:13
[j] 1Co 10:31; 1Th 2:12
[k] 7 Jn 10:25; Ac 15:14; Rv 14:1
[l] 1Co 9:15-18
[m] 9 Mt 20:25-28; 23:5-12; Col 1:18; 1Pt 5:2-3; 2Jn 9
[n] Ac 18:27; Rm 16:1-2; 2Co 3:1
[o] 10 1Tm 5:13
[p] 11 1Pt 3:17
[q] 1Jn 4:4
[r] Ex 33:20
[s] 12 1Jn 2:20-21
[t] Jn 21:24

[A] 1 Or *my beloved* [B] 2,5,11 Or *Beloved* [C] 2 Lit *as your soul prospers* [D] 5 Lit *are doing a faithful thing* [E] 8 Or *coworkers for* [F] 14 Lit *mouth to mouth*

■ **AUTHOR:** Jude, the half-brother of Jesus

■■ **DATE:** Jude was probably written before 2 Peter, which was written between A.D. 62 and 64.

The brother of Jesus writes a short letter that warns loyal Christians against teachers who lead people away from Christ. Jude's language is filled with Old Testament references. Some passages closely resemble parts of 2 Peter. Who borrowed from whom is a question about which scholars still debate.

The mission of God, as this short epistle describes, is the building up of Christians in "the faith" (v. 3). By faith, Jude means the objective teaching of the gospel, not the subjective response of believers (important as that is). Jude's purpose in writing is to conserve the faith that was preached and taught, while a threatening opposition snatches the vocabulary of faith, changing it to fit the inventive falsehoods of heretical teachers.

JUDE

Who in his or her right mind challenges the mission of God, careless of the power they try to manipulate? In Jude's letter, all we know are the adjectives he uses to describe them: "ungodly" (v. 4); "dreamers" (v. 8), blasphemers and defilers (v. 8), "dangerous reefs" (v. 12); "waterless clouds" (v. 12) and more. By that roster of attributes, few people would be attracted to them. But Jude knows what all of Christian history has since shown: willful people bent on evil often adopt the appearance of "faith" as a means to gaining power. One need only recall Hitler's frequent use of Christian symbols and institutions to see how dangerous this strategy can be.

Resist them, Jude warns. Resist the lies by looking continually toward Jesus. Be fully dependent on the Holy Spirit. Pray and encourage others. Remember God's love and mercy. Give no ground to the grumblers. Their corruption is all the evidence Christians need that the mission of God has been perverted in their teaching. They follow the god of self-indulgent curiosity. Their pitch may be attractive initially, but "woe to them!" Jude writes (v. 11).

Woe? Not a very strong word these days. No one hitting his thumb with a hammer cries "woe!" For Jude, however, "woe" is the fork in the road. Follow the faith to God and eternal life. Follow "woe" to darkness, a symbolic term for the loneliness, desperation, and hopelessness of life without God. Jude sees the choice these liars have made. Every step takes them farther from the truth.

Jude ends his letter with a doxology, a formal closing that teaches, blesses, and praises (vv. 24-25). Perhaps you have heard it. Frequent worshipers will know it by heart. Now it is yours to invoke on your loved ones or friends. God's mission is expressed through doxologies like this, blessings that create wind at your back along the faith road, praises that center your day on the majesty of God and the salvation won by Jesus Christ.

In your prayers for the sick, the wandering, even for those who lean toward error—use this doxology. It will focus your prayers on the power and mission of the God who loves forevermore.

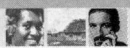

Greeting

Jude,[a] a •slave of Jesus Christ and a brother
of James:
To those who are the called,[b] loved[A,c] by God
the Father and kept by Jesus Christ.[d]
2 May mercy, peace, and love be multiplied
to you.[e]

Jude's Purpose in Writing

3 Dear friends, although I was eager to write
you about the salvation we share,[f] I found it
necessary to write and exhort you to contend
for the faith[g] that was delivered[h] to the •saints
once for all. 4 For some men, who were designated for this judgment long ago,[i] have come
in by stealth;[j] they are ungodly,[k] turning the
grace of our God into promiscuity and denying[l] Jesus Christ, our only Master and Lord.

Apostates: Past and Present

5 Now I want to remind you, though you
know all these things: The Lord[B] first[C] saved
a people out of Egypt and later destroyed
those who did not believe;[m] 6 and He has kept,
with eternal chains in darkness for the judgment of the great day, the angels[n] who did not
keep their own position but deserted their
proper dwelling. 7 In the same way, Sodom
and Gomorrah[o] and the cities around them
committed sexual immorality and practiced
perversions,[D] just as angels did, and serve as
an example by undergoing the punishment
of eternal fire.[p]
8 Nevertheless, these dreamers likewise defile their flesh, reject authority, and blaspheme
glorious ones.[q] 9 Yet Michael[r] the archangel,[s]
when he was disputing with the Devil[t] in a debate about Moses'[u] body, did not dare bring an
abusive condemnation against him but said,
"The Lord rebuke you!" 10 But these people
blaspheme anything they don't understand.
What they know by instinct like unreasoning
animals — they destroy themselves with these
things. 11 Woe to them! For they have traveled
in the way of Cain,[v] have abandoned themselves to the error of Balaam[w] for profit, and
have perished in Korah's rebellion.[x]

The Apostates' Doom

12 These are the ones who are like dangerous reefs[E] at your love feasts.[y] They feast with
you, nurturing only themselves without fear.
They are waterless clouds carried along by
winds;[z] trees in late autumn — fruitless, twice
dead, pulled out by the roots; 13 wild waves of
the sea, foaming up their shameful deeds;
wandering stars[aa] for whom the blackness of
darkness[ab] is reserved forever![ac]
14 And Enoch,[ad] in the seventh generation
from Adam, prophesied about them:

Look! The Lord comes[F]
with thousands of His holy ones[ae]
15 to execute judgment on all
and to convict them[G]
of all their ungodly[af] acts
that they have done in an ungodly way,
and of all the harsh things
ungodly sinners
have said against Him.

16 These people are discontented grumblers,
•walking according to their desires;[ag] their
mouths utter arrogant words, flattering[ah]
people for their own advantage.
17 But you, dear friends, remember what

[a] 1 Mt 13:55; Mk 6:3 [b] Rm 1:7; 1Co 1:24 [c] 1Th 1:4; 2Th 2:13 [d] Jn 17:11,15; 1Th 5:23; 1Pt 1:5 [e] 2 1Pt 1:2; 2Pt 1:2 [f] 3 Ti 1:4 [g] 1Tm 6:12; 2Tm 4:7 [h] 2Pt 2:21 [i] 4 1Pt 2:8 [j] Gl 2:4; 2Tm 3:6 [k] Mk 7:22; Rm 5:6 [l] Ti 1:16; 2Pt 2:1; 1Jn 2:22 [m] 5 1Co 10:1-11 [n] 6 Gn 6:1-4; 2Pt 2:4 [o] 7 2Pt 2:6 [p] 2Th 1:8 [q] 8 2Pt 2:10 [r] 9 Dn 10:13,21; 12:1; Rv 12:7 [s] Lk 1:19; 1Th 4:16 [t] Mt 4:1,10; Ac 13:10 [u] Ps 77:20; Mt 8:4; Heb 3:2 [v] 11 Gn 4:1-17,24-25; Heb 11:4; 1Jn 3:12 [w] Nm 22:5; 2Pt 2:15 [x] Nm 16:1 [y] 12 1Co 11:17-22; 2Pt 2:13 [z] Pr 25:14 [aa] 13 Is 14:12-15; Rv 1:16; 8:10; 9:1 [ab] Mt 6:23; Jd 6 [ac] 2Pt 2:17 [ad] 14 Gn 5:18 [ae] Dt 33:2; Dn 7:10; Mk 8:38; 1Th 3:13; 2Th 1:7; Heb 12:22 [af] 15 2Pt 2:5-6 [ag] 16 2Pt 2:10 [ah] Lv 19:15; Dt 10:17; 2Ch 19:7; Pr 28:21

TEXT MESSAGES

Text message

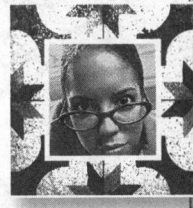

False teachers run rampant around our world, but they are not a new problem. All of the New Testament writers warned against them. Jude warned his readers to "contend for the faith that was delivered to the saints once for all" (v. 3). The message has never changed, the way of salvation is still only through Jesus Christ alone. We must test all teaching against the words of Scripture and pray for discernment. Our words must never veer from the faith that was delivered so many centuries ago "once for all."

A1 Other mss read *sanctified* B5 Other mss read *Jesus/Joshua, God,* or *God Christ* C5 Other mss place *first* after *remind you* D7 Lit *and went after other flesh* E12 Or *like spots* F14 Or *came* G15 Lit *convict all*

was predicted by the apostles of our Lord
Jesus Christ; 18 they told you, "In the end time[a]
there will be scoffers[b] walking according to
their own ungodly desires." 19 These people
create divisions and are unbelievers,[A,c] not
having the Spirit.

Exhortation and Benediction

20 But you, dear friends, as you build yourselves up in your most holy faith and pray in
the Holy Spirit,[d] 21 keep yourselves in the love
of God,[e] expecting the mercy of our Lord
Jesus Christ for eternal life. 22 Have mercy on
those who doubt; 23 save others by snatching
them from the fire;[f] have mercy on others but
with fear,[g] hating[h] even the garment[i] defiled
by the flesh.

24 Now to Him[j] who is able to protect you
from stumbling[k] and to make you stand in
the presence of His glory, blameless[l] and
with great joy, 25 to the only[m] God our Savior,
through Jesus Christ our Lord,[B] be glory, majesty, power, and authority before all time,[C]
now and forever. ·Amen.

[a] 18 1Tm 4:1; 2Tm 3:1; 1Pt 1:5,20
[b] 2Pt 3:3
[c] 19 Rm 8:9; Php 3:3
[d] 20 Rm 8:15-16,26-27; Eph 6:18
[e] 21 Jn 15:9-10; 1Jn 4:16
[f] 23 1Co 3:15; 2Th 1:8
[g] Rv 11:11
[h] Pr 6:16-19
[i] Zch 3:3-4
[j] 24 Rm 16:25; Eph 3:20
[k] Jn 17:12
[l] Eph 1:4; 5:27; Php 2:15; Col 1:22
[m] 25 Jn 5:44; Rm 16:27

A 19 Or *natural* B 25 Other mss omit *through Jesus Christ our Lord* C 25 Other mss omit *before all time*

■ **AUTHOR:** John, the disciple

■■ **DATE:** Written in A.D. 95 while exiled on Patmos

The mission of God plays out on a cosmic screen in breathtaking episodes. The struggle between God and Satan reaches its climax. Promises so long in coming, come. Jesus judges evil and protects the faithful. Complex layers of symbols teach that God's mission will succeed. There is an end-point. But the end-point is really a door to a wonderful future, for God and for all who are sons and daughters of God.

Scholars have used four interpretive frameworks to unravel Revelation's symbols. Each is a helpful, faithful effort to understand these complex layers of story and teaching. The *pretorist* framework interprets Revelation's symbols as first-century references; while *futurists* believe the symbols point to the end of history. *Idealists*

REVELATION

see the symbols as the long fight of good overcoming evil, and *historicists* believe they describe the long providence of God from creation to consummation. Each framework helps coordinate the episodes of John's vision, just as "the mission of God"—the interpretive framework of this study Bible—helps readers see the purpose of the sixty-six books that constitute the Holy Bible. How does Jacob relate to Jonah, to James, to Jehovah? How does Jerusalem relate to the Flood, to Canaan, to Bethlehem, Rome, and the heavenly city? How does the Holy Spirit relate to God the Father and God the Son? How does water relate to Spirit, and bread to wine? How do mortal men and women relate to the Infinite and Immortal? This Bible has used the "the mission of God" to weave a long, interpretive thread throughout the Bible's fascinating and challenging fabric.

The mission of God, motivated by love, has come to us through many media and communication styles. Bushes have suddenly burst into flame. Psalm-songs have been composed and sung. Prophets have preached. Fire has descended. Parchments have been buried and rediscovered. Ephods and offerings have turned eyes God-ward. Soft voices in the night have awakened faith. Jesus Christ has been the person to which all parts of the mission have pointed. And here in Revelation, it is Jesus Christ—the real person, not a symbol—who offers the final, gracious word. "He who testifies about these things says, "Yes, I am coming quickly." To which the apostle John responds: "Amen! Come, Lord Jesus! The grace of the Lord Jesus be with all the saints. Amen" (22:20-21).

Prologue

1 The revelation of[A] Jesus Christ that God gave Him to show His ·slaves[a] what must quickly[B] take place.[b] He sent it and signified it[C] through His angel[c] to His slave John,[d] 2 who testified to God's word and to the testimony[D] about Jesus Christ,[e] in all he saw.[E] 3 The one who reads this is blessed,[f] and those who hear the words of this prophecy and keep[F] what is written in it are blessed, because the time is near!

4 John:

To the seven churches in ·Asia.

Grace and peace[g] to you from[G] the One who is, who was, and who is coming;[h] from the seven spirits[H,i] before His throne; 5 and from Jesus Christ, the faithful witness, the firstborn from the dead and the ruler of the kings of the earth.

To Him who loves us and has set us free[I] from our sins by His blood, 6 and made us a kingdom,[J] priests[K,j] to His God and Father— the glory and dominion are His forever and ever. ·Amen.

7 **Look! He is coming with the clouds,**[k]
and **every eye will see Him,**
including those who pierced[L] **Him.**
And all the families of the earth[M,N,l]
will mourn over Him.[O,P,m]
This is certain. Amen.

8 "I am the ·Alpha and the Omega,"[n] says the Lord God, "the One who is, who was, and who is coming, the Almighty."

John's Vision of the Risen Lord

9 I, John, your brother and partner in the tribulation, kingdom, and endurance that are in Jesus, was on the island called Patmos because of God's word and the testimony about Jesus.[Q,o] 10 I was in the Spirit[R,S,p] on the Lord's day,[T] and I heard a loud voice behind me like a trumpet 11 saying, "Write on a scroll[U] what you see and send it to the seven churches: Ephesus, Smyrna, Pergamum, Thyatira, Sardis, Philadelphia, and Laodicea."

12 I turned to see whose voice[q] it was that spoke to me. When I turned I saw seven gold lampstands, 13 and among the lampstands was One like the ·Son of Man,[V,r] dressed in a long robe and with a gold sash wrapped around His chest. 14 His head and hair were white like wool—white as snow—and His eyes like a fiery flame. 15 His feet were like fine bronze as it is fired in a furnace, and His voice like the sound of cascading[W] waters.[s] 16 He had seven stars in His right hand; a sharp double-edged sword came from His mouth,[t] and His face was shining like the sun at midday.[X]

17 When I saw Him, I fell at His feet like a dead man. He laid His right hand on me and said, "Don't be afraid! I am the First and the Last,[u] 18 and the Living One. I was dead, but look—I am alive forever and ever, and I hold the keys of death and ·Hades. 19 Therefore write what you have seen, what is, and what will take place after this. 20 The ·secret of the seven stars you saw in My right hand and of the seven gold lampstands is this: The seven stars are the angels[Y] of the seven churches, and the seven lampstands[Z] are the seven churches.

THE LETTERS TO THE SEVEN CHURCHES

The Letter to Ephesus

2 "Write to the angel[AA] of the church in Ephesus:

"The One who holds the seven stars in His right hand and who walks among the seven gold lampstands says: 2 I know your works, your labor, and your endurance, and that you cannot tolerate evil. You have tested those who call themselves apostles and are not, and you have found them to be liars. 3 You also possess endurance and have tolerated many things because of My name and have not grown weary. 4 But I have this against you: You have abandoned the love you had at first. 5 Remember then how far you have fallen; repent, and do the works you did at first. Otherwise, I will come to you[AB] and remove your lampstand from its place—unless you repent. 6 Yet you do have this: You hate the practices of the Nicolaitans, which I also hate.

[a] **1:1** Ac 2:18; Rm 6:19; 1Pt 2:16; Rv 22:6 [b] Dn 2:28-29,45; Rv 22:6 [c] Gn 24:7; Mt 1:24; Ac 12:11 [d] Jn 21:7; Rv 22:8 [e] **1:2** 1Co 1:6; Rv 12:17; 19:10; 20:4 [f] **1:3** Rv 14:13; 16:15; 19:9; 20:6; 22:7,14 [g] **1:4** Ti 1:4 [h] Rv 1:8,17; 4:8; 16:5 [i] Rv 3:1; 4:5; 5:6 [j] **1:6** Ex 19:6 [k] **1:7** Is 19:1; Zch 12:10; Jn 19:34-37 [l] Gn 12:3; 28:14; Zch 14:17 [m] Dn 7:13; Zch 12:10 [n] **1:8** Is 44:6; Rv 21:6; 22:13 [o] **1:9** Rv 1:2; 6:9; 12:17; 19:10; 20:4 [p] **1:10** Rv 4:2; 17:3; 21:10 [q] **1:12** Ex 20:18 [r] **1:13** Dn 7:13 [s] **1:15** Ezk 1:24; 43:2; Rv 14:2; 19:6 [t] **1:16** Is 49:2; Heb 4:12; Rv 2:12,16; 19:15 [u] **1:17** Is 41:4; 44:6; 48:12; Rv 2:8; 22:13

[A] **1:1** Or *Revelation of*, or *A revelation of* [B] **1:1** Or *soon* [C] **1:1** Made it known through symbols [D] **1:2** Or *witness* [E] **1:2** Lit *as many as he saw* [F] **1:3** Or *follow*, or *obey* [G] **1:4** Other mss add *God* [H] **1:4** Or *the sevenfold Spirit* [I] **1:5** Other mss read *has washed us* [J] **1:6** Other mss read *kings and* [K] **1:6** Or *made us into* (or *to be*) *a kingdom of priests*; Ex 19:6 [L] **1:7** Or *impaled* [M] **1:7** Or *all the tribes of the land* [N] **1:7** Gn 12:3; 28:14; Zch 14:17 [O] **1:7** Or *will wail because of Him* [P] **1:7** Dn 7:13; Zch 12:10 [Q] **1:9** Lit *the witness of Jesus* [R] **1:10** Or *in spirit*; lit *I became in the Spirit* [S] **1:10** John was brought by God's Spirit into a realm of spiritual vision. [T] **1:10** Sunday [U] **1:11** Or *book* [V] **1:13** Or *like a son of man* [W] **1:15** Lit *many* [X] **1:16** Lit *like the sun shines in its power* [Y] **1:20** Or *messengers* [Z] **1:20** Other mss add *that you saw* [AA] **2:1** Or *messenger* here and elsewhere [AB] **2:5** Other mss add *quickly*

7"Anyone who has an ear should listen to
what the Spirit says to the churches. I will
give the victor[a] the right to eat from the tree
of life, which is in[A] God's paradise.[b]

[a]2:7 1Jn 5:4-5 [b]Gn 2:8-9; Lk 23:43; 2Co 12:4; Rv 22:2,14,19

The Letter to Smyrna

8"Write to the angel of the church in
Smyrna:
"The First and the Last, the One who was

Jesus' Mission: Refocusing and Renewing His Church

Mike Dodson

When Jesus' words were recorded by John under the Spirit's direction, the seven churches hadn't been in existence very long; yet, they each needed some degree of refocus or renewal. In fact, throughout its history the Church has followed that pattern: growing, decaying, and being restored. We who follow Jesus know from experience that the body of Christ will sometimes drift—drift from her first love, from Jesus and His teachings, and from His mission.

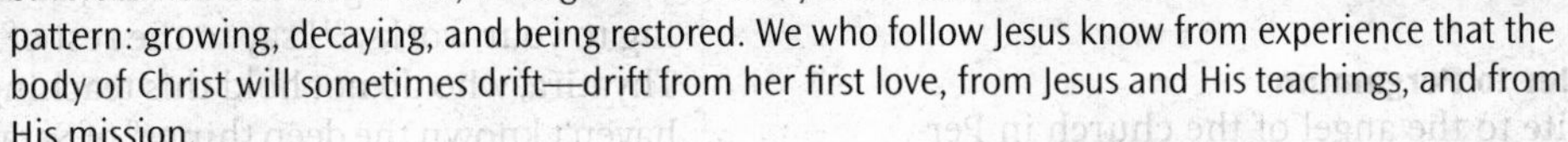

Because of this tendency, remembering who Jesus is and being renewed in His mission for the Church is vital. In Revelation 1, Jesus is revealed as the Eternal Son, Risen Lord, Sacrificial Savior, and Glorious King. The Jesus revealed in Revelation is definitely not a wimp. He calls His people to live confidently in Him. Jesus isn't passive or removed from this situation. He walks in the midst of His churches to observe, evaluate, correct, and renew because He paid the ultimate price to build an army of priests who would fulfill His mission, build His kingdom, and bring Him glory (1:5-6).

The Jesus of Revelation confronts

- the self-motivated actions of the church in Ephesus (2:1-7), calling them to repent and to be motivated by Christ's love for them (2Co 5:14-15).
- the self-reliance and self-sufficiency of Christ's people in Laodicea (3:14-22), calling them to zealous repentance and reliance upon His provisions.
- the complacency and compromise of the body of Christ in Pergamum, Thyatira, and Sardis (2:12-17,18-29; 3:1-6), calling them to repent, reject false teaching, stop being immoral, and wake up to their mission.
- any sense of self-pity that might creep into the poverty and weakness of the churches in Smyrna and Philadelphia (2:8-11; 3:7-13), affirming them and calling them to continue to be courageous, faithful, and on mission.

Not only does Jesus call it like He sees it, but He also messes with the status quo. Five of the seven churches need some radical change, and four of the seven specifically need to repent—change their mind, heart, will, and actions about some specific things. Many churches that need to change—have the need to refocus and revitalize—actually want the communities in which they live to change while they remain the same. But being the real church requires following the real Jesus revealed in these chapters of Revelation.

T. S. Eliot summed up well the church's ongoing need to be refocused and renewed: "The Church must be forever building, for it is ever decaying within and attacked from without; for this is the law of life." [1]

John summed up well the way the body of Christ can be renewed in its belief of who Jesus Christ really is and refocused on the mission Jesus has given His Church to fulfill—"To Him who loves us and has set us free from our sins by His blood, and made us a kingdom, priests to His God and Father—the glory and dominion are His forever and ever. Amen" (Rv 1:6).

[1]T. S. Eliot, *Collected Poems 1909-1962* (New York: Harcourt Brace & Company, 1991), 153-54.

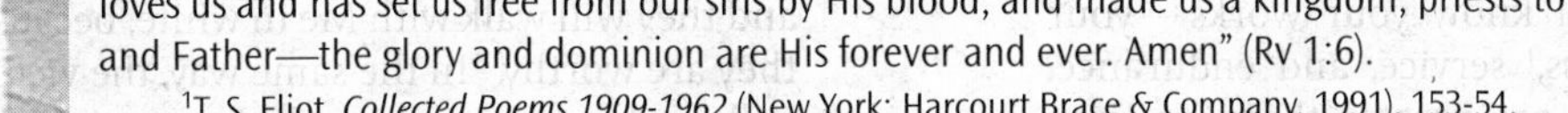

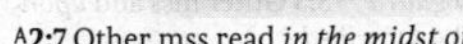

[A]2:7 Other mss read *in the midst of*

dead and came to life, says: 9 I know your[A] affliction and poverty, yet you are rich. I know
the slander of those who say they are Jews
and are not, but are a ·synagogue of Satan.
10 Don't be afraid of what you are about to suffer. Look, the Devil is about to throw some of
you into prison to test you, and you will have
affliction for 10 days. Be faithful until death,
and I will give you the crown[B] of life.
11 "Anyone who has an ear should listen
to what the Spirit says to the churches. The
victor will never be harmed by the second
death.[a]

The Letter to Pergamum

12 "Write to the angel of the church in Pergamum:
"The One who has the sharp, double-edged
sword[b] says: 13 I know[C] where you live — where
Satan's throne is! And you are holding on to
My name and did not deny your faith in Me,[D]
even in the days of Antipas, My faithful witness who was killed among you, where Satan
lives. 14 But I have a few things against you. You
have some there who hold to the teaching of
Balaam, who taught Balak to place a stumbling block[E] in front of the Israelites: to eat
meat sacrificed to idols and to commit sexual
immorality.[F] 15 In the same way, you also have
those who hold to the teaching of the Nicolaitans.[G] 16 Therefore repent! Otherwise, I will
come to you quickly and fight against them
with the sword of My mouth.
17 "Anyone who has an ear should listen to
what the Spirit says to the churches. I will give
the victor some of the hidden manna.[H,c] I will
also give him a white stone, and on the stone
a new name[d] is inscribed that no one knows
except the one who receives it.

The Letter to Thyatira

18 "Write to the angel of the church in Thyatira:
"The Son of God, the One whose eyes are
like a fiery flame and whose feet are like fine
bronze,[I] says: 19 I know your works — your
love, faithfulness,[J] service, and endurance.
Your last works are greater than the first.
20 But I have this against you: You tolerate the
woman Jezebel, who calls herself a prophetess and teaches and deceives My ·slaves to
commit sexual immorality[F] and to eat meat
sacrificed to idols. 21 I gave her time to repent,
but she does not want to repent of her sexual
immorality.[K] 22 Look! I will throw her into a
sickbed and those who commit adultery with
her into great tribulation, unless they repent
of her[L] practices. 23 I will kill her children with
the plague.[M,e] Then all the churches will know
that I am the One who examines minds[N] and
hearts, and I will give to each of you according to your works. 24 I say to the rest of you in
Thyatira, who do not hold this teaching, who
haven't known the deep things[O] of Satan — as
they say — I do not put any other burden on
you. 25 But hold on to what you have until I
come.[f] 26 The one who is victorious and keeps
My works to the end: I will give him authority
over the nations —

27 **and he will shepherd[P,g] them**
with an iron scepter;
he will shatter them like pottery[Q,h] —

just as I have received this from My Father. 28 I
will also give him the morning star.[i]
29 "Anyone who has an ear should listen to
what the Spirit says to the churches.

The Letter to Sardis

3 "Write to the angel of the church in Sardis:
"The One who has the seven spirits of God[j]
and the seven stars says: I know your works;
you have a reputation[R] for being alive, but
you are dead. 2 Be alert and strengthen[S] what
remains, which is about to die, for I have
not found your works complete before My
God. 3 Remember, therefore, what you have
received and heard; keep it, and repent. But
if you are not alert, I will come[T] like a thief,
and you have no idea at what hour I will come
against you.[U] 4 But you have a few people[V] in
Sardis who have not defiled[W] their clothes,
and they will walk with Me in white, because
they are worthy. 5 In the same way, the victor
will be dressed in white clothes, and I will

[a] 2:11 Rv 20:6,14; 21:8 [b] 2:12 Is 49:2; Heb 4:12; Rv 1:16; 2:16; 19:15 [c] 2:17 Ex 16:32-34 [d] Is 55:13; 56:5; 62:2 [e] 2:23 Ezk 33:27 [f] 2:25 Rv 3:11 [g] 2:27 Rv 19:15 [h] Ps 2:9 [i] 2:28 Is 14:12; 2Pt 1:19; Rv 22:1 [j] 3:1 Rv 1:4; 4:5; 5:6

A 2:9 Other mss add *works and* B 2:10 Or *wreath* C 2:13 Other mss add *your works and* D 2:13 Or *deny My faith* E 2:14 Or *to place a trap* F 2:14,20 Or *commit fornication* G 2:15 Other mss add *which I hate* H 2:17 Other mss add *to eat* I 2:18 Probably gleaming white hot; Rv 1:15 J 2:19 Or *faith* K 2:21 Or *her fornication* L 2:22 Other mss read *their* M 2:23 Or *I will surely kill her children* N 2:23 Lit *kidneys* O 2:24 Or *the secret things* P 2:27 Or *rule*; see 19:15 Q 2:27 Ps 2:9 R 3:1 Lit *have a name* S 3:2 Other mss read *guard* T 3:3 Other mss add *upon you* U 3:3 Or *upon you* V 3:4 Lit *few names* W 3:4 Or *soiled* never erase his name from the book of life[a] but will acknowledge his name before My Father and before His angels.

6 "Anyone who has an ear should listen to what the Spirit says to the churches.

The Letter to Philadelphia

7 "Write to the angel of the church in Philadelphia:

"The Holy One, the True One, the One who has the key of David, who opens and no one will close, and closes and no one opens[b] says: 8 I know your works. Because you have limited strength, have kept My word, and have not denied My name, look, I have placed before you an open door that no one is able to close. 9 Take note! I will make those from the ·synagogue of Satan, who claim to be Jews and are not, but are lying — note this — I will make them come and bow down at your feet, and they will know that I have loved you.[c] 10 Because you have kept My command to endure,[A] I will also keep you from the hour of testing that is going to come over the whole world to test those who live on the earth. 11 I am coming quickly. Hold on to what you have,[d] so that no one takes your crown. 12 The victor: I will make him a pillar in the sanctuary of My God, and he will never go out again. I will write on him the name of My God and the name of the city of My God — the new Jerusalem, which comes down out of heaven from My God — and My new name.[e]

13 "Anyone who has an ear should listen to what the Spirit says to the churches.

The Letter to Laodicea

14 "Write to the angel of the church in Laodicea:

"The ·Amen, the faithful and true Witness, the Originator[B,f] of God's creation says: 15 I know your works, that you are neither cold nor hot. I wish that you were cold or hot. 16 So, because you are lukewarm, and neither hot nor cold, I am going to vomit[C] you out of My mouth. 17 Because you say, 'I'm rich; I have become wealthy and need nothing,' and you don't know that you are wretched, pitiful, poor, blind, and naked, 18 I advise you to buy from Me gold refined in the fire so that you may be rich, white clothes so that you may be dressed and your shameful nakedness not be exposed, and ointment to spread on your eyes so that you may see. 19 As many as I love,

[a] 3:5 Rv 13:8; 17:8; 20:12,15; 21:27
[b] 3:7 Is 22:22
[c] 3:9 Is 45:14; 60:14
[d] 3:11 Rv 2:25
[e] 3:12 Rv 2:17
[f] 3:14 Col 1:18; Jn 1:1-5

PRAYING FOR THE WORLD

Revive Us Again

We ought to be people who change the world—turn it upside-down as it were! The distressful reality, however, is that too many people have lost the wonder and amazement of their own salvation and have become lukewarm—no longer passionate for their faith, no longer mindful of the gifts the Spirit gave for them to change their corner of the world.

We want our drinks piping hot or ice cold—not lukewarm. When Jesus speaks to the church of Laodicea, He spits them out because they are "lukewarm" (Rv 3:16). Lukewarm faith doesn't change the world. Lukewarm attitudes don't draw people to our Savior. Let's pray that the church can regain the passion for the Good News and for lost souls.

Lord, we pray that we are not among the ranks of the lukewarm, but if we are, we ask that You set us and all those with us ablaze with the passion of Your Spirit. Dispel doubt from our hearts. Lead us to unceasing prayer. Fill us with concern for the lonely and the poor. May we rejoice with those who rejoice and weep with those who weep. Remind us of all You have done for us and renew our passion for You. Give us joy and gratitude for tasks well done. Amaze us again with Your precious promises. Spirit of Christ, open our eyes to see the miracles of your grace and power. Amen.

[A] 3:10 Lit *My word of endurance* [B] 3:14 Or *Ruler*, or *Source*, or *Beginning* [C] 3:16 Or *spit*

I rebuke and discipline. So be committed[A]
and repent. 20 Listen! I stand at the door and
knock. If anyone hears My voice and opens
the door, I will come in to him and have dinner with him, and he with Me. 21 The victor: I
will give him the right to sit with Me on My
throne, just as I also won the victory and sat
down with My Father on His throne.

22 "Anyone who has an ear should listen to
what the Spirit says to the churches."

The Throne Room of Heaven

4 After this I looked, and there in heaven
was an open door. The first voice that
I had heard speaking to me like a trumpet
said, "Come up here, and I will show you what
must take place after this."

2 Immediately I was in the Spirit,[B,a] and a
throne was set there in heaven.[b] One was
seated on the throne, 3 and the One seated[C]
looked like jasper[D] and carnelian[E] stone. A
rainbow that looked like an emerald surrounded the throne. 4 Around that throne
were 24 thrones, and on the thrones sat 24
elders dressed in white clothes, with gold
crowns on their heads. 5 Flashes of lightning
and rumblings of thunder came from the
throne. Seven fiery torches were burning before the throne, which are the seven spirits of
God.[c] 6 Something like a sea of glass, similar to
crystal, was also before the throne. Four living creatures[d] covered with eyes in front and
in back were in the middle[F] and around the
throne. 7 The first living creature was like a
lion; the second living creature was like a calf;
the third living creature had a face like a man;
and the fourth living creature was like a flying eagle. 8 Each of the four living creatures
had six wings;[e] they were covered with eyes
around and inside. Day and night they never
stop,[G] saying:

> Holy, holy, holy,[H]
> Lord God, the Almighty,
> who was, who is, and who is coming.

9 Whenever the living creatures give glory,
honor, and thanks to the One seated on the
throne, the One who lives forever and ever,
10 the 24 elders fall down before the One
seated on the throne, worship the One who
lives forever and ever, cast their crowns before the throne, and say:

> 11 Our Lord and God,[I]
> You are worthy to receive
> glory and honor and power,
> because You have created all things,
> and because of Your will
> they exist and were created.

The Lamb Takes the Scroll

5 Then I saw in the right hand of the One
seated on the throne a scroll with writing
on the inside and on the back,[f] sealed with
seven seals. 2 I also saw a mighty angel proclaiming in a loud voice, "Who is worthy to
open the scroll and break its seals?" 3 But no
one in heaven or on earth or under the earth
was able to open the scroll or even to look in
it. 4 And I cried and cried because no one was
found worthy to open[J] the scroll or even to
look in it.

5 Then one of the elders said to me, "Stop
crying. Look! The Lion from the tribe of Judah,[g] the Root of David,[h] has been victorious[i]
so that He may open the scroll and[K] its seven
seals." 6 Then I saw One like a slaughtered
lamb standing between[L] the throne and the
four living creatures and among the elders.
He had seven horns and seven eyes, which are
the seven spirits of God[j] sent into all the earth.
7 He came and took the scroll[M] out of the right
hand of the One seated on the throne.

The Lamb Is Worthy

8 When He took the scroll, the four living
creatures and the 24 elders fell down before
the Lamb. Each one had a harp and gold bowls
filled with incense, which are the prayers of
the *saints. 9 And they sang a new song:[k]

> You are worthy to take the scroll
> and to open its seals,
> because You were slaughtered,
> and You *redeemed[N] people[O]
> for God by Your blood
> from every tribe and language

[a] **4:2** Rv 1:10; 17:3; 21:10 [b] Dn 7:9 [c] **4:5** Rv 1:4; 3:1; 5:6 [d] **4:6** Is 6:2-3; Ezk 1:5-28; 10:20 [e] **4:8** Is 6:2 [f] **5:1** Ezk 2:9-10 [g] **5:5** Gn 49:9 [h] Is 11:1,10; Rv 22:16 [i] Jn 16:33 [j] **5:6** Rv 1:4 [k] **5:9** Ps 40:3; 96:1; 98:1; 149:1; Is 42:10; Rv 14:3

[A] **3:19** Or *be zealous* [B] **4:2** Or *in spirit*; lit *I became in the Spirit* [C] **4:3** Other mss omit *and the One seated* [D] **4:3** A precious stone [E] **4:3** A translucent red gem [F] **4:6** Lit *In the middle of the throne* [G] **4:8** Or *they never rest* [H] **4:8** Other mss read *holy* 9 times [I] **4:11** Other mss add *the Holy One*; other mss read *Lord* [J] **5:4** Other mss add *and read* [K] **5:5** Other mss add *loose* [L] **5:6** Or *standing in the middle of* [M] **5:7** Other mss include *the scroll* [N] **5:9** Or *purchased* [O] **5:9** Other mss read *us*

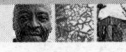

and people and nation.[a]
10 You made them a kingdom[A]
and priests to our God,[b]
and they will reign on the earth.

11Then I looked and heard the voice of
many angels around the throne, and also of
the living creatures and of the elders. Their
number was countless thousands, plus thousands of thousands. 12They said with a loud
voice:

The Lamb who was slaughtered
is worthy
to receive power and riches
and wisdom and strength
and honor and glory
and blessing!

13I heard every creature in heaven, on earth,
under the earth, on the sea, and everything
in them say:

Blessing and honor and glory
and dominion
to the One seated on the throne,
and to the Lamb, forever and ever!

14The four living creatures said, "Amen," and
the elders fell down and worshiped.

[a]5:9 Ex 19:5 [b]5:10 Ex 19:6; Rv 1:5-6 [c]6:2 Zch 6:1-3 [d]6:4 Mt 10:34

The First Seal on the Scroll

6 Then I saw[B] the Lamb open one of the
seven[C] seals, and I heard one of the four
living creatures say with a voice like thunder, "Come!"[D,E] 2I looked, and there was a
white horse.[c] The horseman on it had a bow;
a crown was given to him, and he went out as
a victor to conquer.[F]

The Second Seal

3When He opened the second seal, I heard
the second living creature say, "Come!"[D,E]
4Then another horse went out, a fiery red
one, and its horseman was empowered[G] to
take peace from the earth, so that people
would slaughter one another. And a large
sword was given to him.[d]

PRAYING FOR THE WORLD

The World Needs the Word

The great majority of the world's citizens now have a Bible in their own language. That did not just happen. Many translations actually had to begin with translators first undertaking the task of writing alphabets and grammars for oral languages. Tribes all over the world that never had written down their language now have both a written language and portions if not all of the Bible. Such translation work takes years—even decades—of immersion in a culture and a language. Wycliffe Bible Translators took the lead in this noble enterprise. They have prepared all or part of the Bible in some 700 languages. Presently their teams are working in ninety countries to complete a translation.

We rejoice with the many people groups that now have access to God's wonderful revelation of grace and salvation in their own languages.

Lord of all understanding, bless the many women and men who toil at creating a written language and then translating Your Word so that people everywhere can read Your message of salvation. Remind us, Lord, every time when we open our Bibles, that we handle a precious gift from Your hand. Raise up gifted young men and women to study linguistics to strengthen the ranks of translators around the globe. Bless the people who hold the newly-arrived copies of the Bible in their hands—may they read with understanding and discernment. We also understand, Lord, the massive tasks of having Scriptures produced and distributed. We also think of countries where governments do not allow Bibles to be distributed. Bless the spread of Your written Word. Amen.

A5:10 Other mss read *them kings* B6:1 Lit *saw when* C6:1 Other mss omit *seven* D6:1,3 Other mss add *and see* E6:1,3 Or *Go!* F6:2 Lit *went out conquering and in order to conquer* G6:4 Or *was granted*; lit *was given*

The Third Seal

5 When He opened the third seal, I heard the third living creature say, "Come!"[A,B] And I looked, and there was a black horse. The horseman on it had a set of scales in his hand. 6 Then I heard something like a voice among the four living creatures say, "A quart of wheat for a ·denarius, and three quarts of barley for a denarius — but do not harm the olive oil and the wine."

The Fourth Seal

7 When He opened the fourth seal, I heard the voice of the fourth living creature say, "Come!"[A,B] 8 And I looked, and there was a pale green[C] horse. The horseman on it was named Death, and ·Hades was following after him. Authority was given to them[D,a] over a fourth of the earth, to kill by the sword, by famine, by plague, and by the wild animals of the earth.

The Fifth Seal

9 When He opened the fifth seal, I saw under the altar the people[E] slaughtered because of God's word and the testimony they had.[F,b] 10 They cried out with a loud voice: "Lord,[G] the One who is holy and true, how long until You judge and avenge our blood from those who live on the earth?" 11 So a white robe was given to each of them, and they were told to rest a little while longer until the number would be completed of their fellow slaves and their ·brothers, who were going to be killed just as they had been.

The Sixth Seal

12 Then I saw Him open[H] the sixth seal. A violent earthquake occurred; the sun turned black like ·sackcloth[c] made of goat hair; the entire moon[I] became like blood; 13 the stars[J] of heaven fell to the earth as a fig tree drops its unripe figs when shaken by a high wind; 14 the sky separated like a scroll being rolled up; and every mountain and island was moved from its place.

15 Then the kings of the earth, the nobles, the military commanders, the rich, the powerful, and every ·slave and free person hid in the caves and among the rocks of the mountains.[d] 16 And they said to the mountains and to the rocks, "Fall on us and hide us[e] from the face of the One seated on the throne and from the wrath of the Lamb, 17 because the great day of Their[K] wrath has come! And who is able to stand?"[f]

[a]6:8 Mt 10:1; 28:18; Rv 9:3 [b]6:9 Rv 1:2,9; 12:17; 19:10; 20:4 [c]6:12 Is 50:3 [d]6:15 Is 2:10 [e]6:16 Hs 10:8 [f]6:17 Mal 3:2 [g]7:1 Is 11:12; Ezk 7:2; Rv 20:7-8

The Sealed of Israel

7 After this I saw four angels standing at the four corners of the earth,[g] restraining the four winds of the earth so that no wind could blow on the earth or on the sea or on any tree. 2 Then I saw another angel, who had the seal of the living God rise up from the east. He cried out in a loud voice to the four angels who were empowered[L] to harm the earth and the sea: 3 "Don't harm the earth or the sea or the trees until we seal the ·slaves of our God on their foreheads." 4 And I heard the number of those who were sealed:

144,000 sealed from every tree
of the Israelites:
5 12,000 sealed from the tribe of Judah,
12,000[M] from the tribe of Reuben,
12,000 from the tribe of Gad,
6 12,000 from the tribe of Asher,
12,000 from the tribe of Naphtali,
12,000 from the tribe of Manasseh,
7 12,000 from the tribe of Simeon,
12,000 from the tribe of Levi,
12,000 from the tribe of Issachar,
8 12,000 from the tribe of Zebulun,
12,000 from the tribe of Joseph,
12,000 sealed from the tribe
of Benjamin.

A Multitude from the Great Tribulation

9 After this I looked, and there was a vast multitude from every nation, tribe, people, and language, which no one could number, standing before the throne and before the Lamb. They were robed in white with palm branches in their hands. 10 And they cried out in a loud voice:

Salvation belongs to our God,
who is seated on the throne,
and to the Lamb!

[A]6:5,7 Other mss add *and see* [B]6:5,7 Or *Go!* [C]6:8 Or *a greenish gray* [D]6:8 Other mss read *him* [E]6:9 Lit *souls* [F]6:9 Other mss add *about the Lamb* [G]6:10 Or *Master* [H]6:12 Lit *I saw when He opened* [I]6:12 Or *the full moon* [J]6:13 Perhaps meteors [K]6:17 Other mss read *His* [L]7:2 Lit *angels to whom it was given* [M]7:5-8 Other mss add *sealed* after each number

[11]All the angels stood around the throne,
the elders, and the four living creatures, and
they fell facedown before the throne and
worshiped God, [12]saying:

˙Amen! Blessing and glory and wisdom
and thanksgiving and honor
and power and strength
be to our God forever and ever. Amen.

[13]Then one of the elders asked me, "Who
are these people robed in white, and where
did they come from?"
[14]I said to him, "Sir,[A] you know."
Then he told me:

These are the ones coming out
of the great tribulation.
They washed their robes
and made them white[a]
in the blood of the Lamb.
15 For this reason they are
before the throne of God,
and they serve Him day and night
in His sanctuary.
The One seated on the throne
will shelter[B] them:
16 They will no longer hunger;
they will no longer thirst;
the sun will no longer strike them,
nor will any heat.[b]
17 For the Lamb who is at the center
of the throne
will shepherd them;[c]
He will guide them to springs
of living waters,[d]
and God will wipe away every tear
from their eyes.[e]

The Seventh Seal

8 When He opened the seventh seal, there
was silence in heaven for about half an
hour. [2]Then I saw the seven angels who stand
in the presence of God; seven trumpets were
given to them. [3]Another angel, with a gold incense burner, came and stood at the altar. He
was given a large amount of incense to offer
with the prayers of all the ˙saints on the gold
altar in front of the throne. [4]The smoke of the
incense, with the prayers of the saints, went
up in the presence of God from the angel's
hand. [5]The angel took the incense burner,
filled it with fire from the altar, and hurled it
to the earth; there were rumblings of thunder, flashes of lightning, and an earthquake.
[6]And the seven angels who had the seven
trumpets prepared to blow them.

The First Trumpet

[7]The first angel[C] blew his trumpet, and hail
and fire, mixed with blood, were hurled to
the earth. So a third of the earth was burned
up, a third of the trees were burned up, and
all the green grass was burned up.

The Second Trumpet

[8]The second angel blew his trumpet, and
something like a great mountain ablaze with
fire was hurled into the sea.[f] So a third of the
sea became blood, [9]a third of the living creatures in the sea died, and a third of the ships
were destroyed.

The Third Trumpet

[10]The third angel blew his trumpet, and
a great star, blazing like a torch, fell from
heaven.[g] It fell on a third of the rivers and
springs of water. [11]The name of the star is
Wormwood, and a third of the waters became ˙wormwood. So, many of the people
died from the waters, because they had been
made bitter.

The Fourth Trumpet

[12]The fourth angel blew his trumpet, and
a third of the sun was struck, a third of the
moon, and a third of the stars, so that a third
of them were darkened. A third of the day was
without light, and the night as well.[h]
[13]I looked again and heard an eagle[D] flying high overhead, crying out in a loud
voice, "Woe![i] Woe! Woe to those who live on
the earth, because of the remaining trumpet blasts that the three angels are about to
sound!"

The Fifth Trumpet

9 The fifth angel blew his trumpet, and I
saw a star that had fallen from heaven
to earth.[j] The key to the shaft of the ˙abyss[k]
was given to him. [2]He opened the shaft of the
abyss, and smoke came up out of the shaft

[a]**7:14** Ps 51:7; Is 1:18; 43:25; 44:22
[b]**7:16** Is 49:10
[c]**7:17** Ps 23:1; Ezk 34:23
[d]Ps 23:2; Is 49:10; Jr 2:13
[e]Is 25:8; Rv 21:4
[f]**8:8** Jr 51:25
[g]**8:10** Is 14:12; Rv 9:1
[h]**8:12** Am 8:9
[i]**8:13** Rv 9:12; 11:14; 12:12
[j]**9:1** Rv 8:10
[k]Lk 8:31; Rm 10:7; Rv 9:11; 11:7; 17:8; 20:1-3

[A]**7:14** Lit *My lord* [B]**7:15** Or *will spread His tent over* [C]**8:7** Other mss include *angel* [D]**8:13** Other mss read *angel* like smoke from a great[A] furnace so that the sun and the air were darkened by the smoke from the shaft. 3 Then locusts came out of the smoke on to the earth, and power[B] was given to them[a] like the power that scorpions have on the earth. 4 They were told not to harm the grass of the earth, or any green plant, or any tree, but only people who do not have God's seal on their foreheads. 5 They were not permitted to kill them but were to torment them for five months; their torment is like the torment caused by a scorpion when it strikes a man. 6 In those days people will seek death and will not find it; they will long to die, but death will flee from them.

7 The appearance of the locusts was like horses equipped for battle.[b] Something like gold crowns was on their heads; their faces were like men's faces; 8 they had hair like women's hair; their teeth were like lions' teeth;[c] 9 they had chests like iron breastplates; the sound of their wings was like the sound of chariots with many horses rushing into battle; 10 and they had tails with stingers like scorpions, so that with their tails they had the power[B] to harm people for five months. 11 They had as their king[C] the angel of the abyss; his name in Hebrew is •Abaddon,[D] and in Greek he has the name Apollyon.[E] 12 The first woe has passed. There are still two more woes to come after this.

The Sixth Trumpet

13 The sixth angel blew his trumpet. From the four[F] horns of the gold altar[d] that is before God, I heard a voice 14 say to the sixth angel who had the trumpet, "Release the four angels bound at the great river Euphrates." 15 So the four angels who were prepared for the hour, day, month, and year were released to kill a third of the human race. 16 The number of mounted troops was 200 million;[G] I heard their number. 17 This is how I saw the horses in my vision: The horsemen had breastplates that were fiery red, hyacinth blue, and sulfur yellow. The heads of the horses were like lions' heads, and from their mouths came fire, smoke, and sulfur. 18 A third of the human race was killed by these three plagues — by the fire, the smoke, and the sulfur that came from their mouths. 19 For the power of the horses is in their mouths and in their tails, for their tails, which resemble snakes, have heads, and they inflict injury with them.

20 The rest of the people, who were not killed by these plagues, did not repent of the works of their hands to stop worshiping demons[e] and idols of gold, silver, bronze, stone, and wood, which are not able to see, hear, or walk.[f] 21 And they did not repent of their murders, their sorceries,[H] their sexual immorality, or their thefts.

The Mighty Angel and the Small Scroll

10 Then I saw another mighty angel[g] coming down from heaven, surrounded by a cloud, with a rainbow[h] over his head.[I] His face was like the sun, his legs[J] were like fiery pillars,[i] 2 and he had a little scroll opened in his hand. He put his right foot on the sea, his left on the land, 3 and he cried out with a loud voice like a roaring lion. When he cried out, the seven thunders spoke with their voices. 4 And when the seven thunders spoke, I was about to write. Then I heard a voice from heaven, saying, "Seal up what the seven thunders said,[j] and do not write it down!"

5 Then the angel that I had seen standing on the sea and on the land raised his right hand to heaven. 6 He swore an oath by the One who lives forever and ever,[k] who created heaven and what is in it, the earth and what is in it, and the sea and what is in it: "There will no longer be an interval of time,[K] 7 but in the days of the sound of the seventh angel,[l] when he will blow his trumpet, then God's •hidden plan[m] will be completed, as He announced to His servants[L] the prophets."[n]

8 Now the voice that I heard from heaven spoke to me again and said, "Go, take the scroll that lies open in the hand of the angel who is standing on the sea and on the land."

9 So I went to the angel and asked him to give me the little scroll. He said to me, "Take and

[a] **9:3** Mt 10:1; 28:18; Rv 6:8
[b] **9:7** Jl 2:4
[c] **9:8** Jl 1:6
[d] **9:13** Ex 39:38; 40:5
[e] **9:20** 1Co 10:20
[f] Ps 115:4-7; 135:15-17; Dn 5:23
[g] **10:1** Rv 5:2; 18:21
[h] Rv 4:3
[i] Rv 3:12
[j] **10:4** Dn 8:26; 12:4,9
[k] **10:6** Dn 12:7
[l] **10:7** Rv 11:15; 16:17
[m] Rv 1:20; 17:5,7
[n] 2Kg 9:7; 17:23; Ezk 38:17; Am 3:7; Zch 1:6; 1Pt 2:10-12

[A] **9:2** Other mss omit *great* [B] **9:3,10** Or *authority* [C] **9:11** Or *as king over them* [D] **9:11** Or *destruction* [E] **9:11** Or *destroyer* [F] **9:13** Other mss omit *four* [G] **9:16** Other mss read *100 million* [H] **9:21** Or *magic potions*, or *drugs*; Gk *pharmakon* [I] **10:1** Or *a halo on his head* [J] **10:1** Or *feet* [K] **10:6** Or *be a delay* [L] **10:7** Or *slaves*

eat it; it will be bitter in your stomach, but it
will be as sweet as honey in your mouth."[a]
10 Then I took the little scroll from the angel's hand and ate it. It was as sweet as honey
in my mouth, but when I ate it, my stomach
became bitter.[b] 11 And I was told,[A] "You must
prophesy again about[B] many peoples, nations, languages, and kings."[c]

The Two Witnesses

11 Then I was given a measuring reed[d] like
a rod,[C] with these words: "Go[D] and measure God's sanctuary and the altar, and count
those who worship there. 2 But exclude the
courtyard outside the sanctuary. Don't measure it, because it is given to the nations,[E] and
they will trample the holy city for 42 months.
3 I will empower[F] my two witnesses, and they
will prophesy for 1,260 days,[G,e] dressed in
•sackcloth."[H] 4 These are the two olive trees
and the two lampstands that stand before the
Lord[I] of the earth.[f] 5 If anyone wants to harm
them, fire comes from their mouths and
consumes their enemies;[g] if anyone wants
to harm them, he must be killed in this way.
6 These men have the power to close up the
sky so that it does not rain during the days
of their prophecy.[h] They also have power over
the waters to turn them into blood[i] and to
strike the earth with every plague whenever
they want.

The Witnesses Martyred

7 When they finish their testimony, the
beast[J,j] that comes up out of the •abyss will
make war with them, conquer them, and kill
them. 8 Their dead bodies[K,k] will lie in the public square[L] of the great city, which prophetically[M] is called Sodom and Egypt, where also
their Lord was crucified. 9 And representatives from[N] the peoples, tribes, languages,
and nations[l] will view their bodies for three
and a half days and not permit their bodies
to be put into a tomb. 10 Those who live on the
earth will gloat over them and celebrate and
send gifts to one another because these two
prophets brought judgment to those who live
on the earth.

[a]10:9 Ps 119:103; Jr 15:16; Ezk 2:8–3:3
[b]10:10 Nm 5:24; Ezk 3:1-3
[c]10:11 Dn 3:4,7; 4:1; 5:19; 7:14; Rv 5:9; 7:9; 11:9
[d]11:1 Ezk 40:3,5; 42:15-19; Rv 21:15
[e]11:3 Dn 12:11; Rv 12:6,14; 13:5
[f]11:4 Zch 4:3,11-14
[g]11:5 Jr 5:14
[h]11:6 1Kg 17:1
[i]Ex 7:17-21
[j]11:7 Rv 13:1,11; 17:8
[k]11:8 Is 66:24
[l]11:9 Rv 5:9; 7:9; 10:11
[m]11:11 Gn 2:7; 6:17; 7:15,22; Ezk 37:5
[n]11:12 2Kg 2:1; Mk 16:19; Lk 24:51; Ac 1:9-10
[o]11:13 Is 29:6; Ezk 38:19
[p]11:14 Rv 8:13; 9:12
[q]11:15 Is 27:13
[r]2Sm 7:16; Is 37:16; Dn 7:14,18; Lk 1:32-33
[s]11:17 Rv 1:4,8; 4:8; 16:5
[t]Lk 1:33; 1Co 15:25; Rv 19:6
[u]11:18 Ps 2:1
[v]Rv 10:7
[w]2Kg 23:2; Ps 115:13; Rv 19:5
[x]11:19 Rv 4:5; 8:5

The Witnesses Resurrected

11 But after 3½ days, the breath[O] of life[m]
from God entered them, and they stood on
their feet. So great fear fell on those who saw
them. 12 Then they heard[P] a loud voice from
heaven saying to them, "Come up here." They
went up to heaven in a cloud, while their enemies watched them.[n] 13 At that moment a violent earthquake took place,[o] a tenth of the
city fell, and 7,000 people were killed in the
earthquake. The survivors were terrified and
gave glory to the God of heaven. 14 The second
woe[p] has passed. Take note: The third woe is
coming quickly!

The Seventh Trumpet

15 The seventh angel blew his trumpet,[q] and
there were loud voices in heaven saying:

The kingdom of the •world has become
the kingdom
of our Lord and of His •Messiah,
and He will reign forever and ever![r]

16 The 24 elders, who were seated before God
on their thrones, fell facedown and worshiped God, 17 saying:

We thank You, Lord God, the Almighty,
who is and who was,[Q,s]
because You have taken
Your great power
and have begun to reign.[t]
18 The nations were angry,[u]
but Your wrath has come.
The time has come
for the dead to be judged
and to give the reward
to Your servants the prophets,[v]
to the •saints, and to those who fear
Your name,
both small and great,[w]
and the time has come to destroy
those who destroy the earth.

19 God's sanctuary in heaven was opened, and
the ark of His covenant[R] appeared in His
sanctuary. There were flashes of lightning,
rumblings of thunder,[x] an earthquake,[S] and
severe hail.

[A]10:11 Lit *And they said to me* [B]10:11 Or *prophesy again against* [C]11:1 Other mss add *and the angel stood up* [D]11:1 Lit *Arise* [E]11:2 Or *Gentiles* [F]11:3 Lit *I will give to* [G]11:3 = 3½ years of 30-day months [H]11:3 Mourning garment of coarse, often black, material [I]11:4 Other mss read *God* [J]11:7 Or *wild animal* [K]11:8 Lit *Their corpse* [L]11:8 Or *lie on the broad street* [M]11:8 Or *spiritually*, or *symbolically* [N]11:9 Lit *And from* [O]11:11 Or *spirit* [P]11:12 Other mss read *Then I heard* [Q]11:17 Other mss add *and who is to come* [R]11:19 Other mss read *ark of the covenant of the Lord* [S]11:19 Other mss omit *an earthquake*

Hudson Taylor (1832–1905)

Seeing what Hudson Taylor accomplished as a missionary in China, no one would guess that as a child he had been deemed too frail even to attend school. Yet this is often the way with our God: He does great things through the most unlikely people in order to show us His awesome power. Hudson Taylor's story is one of courage and triumph because he believed in the power of God and His promise to answer prayer.

Taylor had good reason to hold on to this hope. Having strayed from his parent's faith as a young man, he was brought back to Christ at seventeen by his mother's fervent prayer. Looking for something to read, Taylor had picked up a Bible tract while at the same moment his mother, away on a trip, was led by the Holy Spirit to intercede for him. He was converted to Christ. This beginning led Taylor to a life lived by prayer.

Shortly after his conversion, Taylor received a call to China as clearly as if he had heard an audible voice, and he dedicated himself to preparing for this mission. He studied medicine and began to learn Mandarin, but more significantly he began to train himself for the trials he would face. He moved into a poor neighborhood called Drainside for its filthy ditch, which filled with garbage until rain carried it away. He devoted himself to the poor there. Over and over again he found himself called to give up his last cent to help someone in need, trusting that "kindness to the poor is a loan to the Lord" (Pr 19:17). Over and over again he found that God truly is the provider. More than anything else, this repeated experience of God's loving provision prepared Taylor for his life in China where he would resolve to "move the hearts of men," not by his charisma or power of persuasion, but "through God, by prayer alone."[1]

In all, Hudson Taylor made eleven trips to China, spending a total of fifty-one years working there. He founded China Inland Mission (CIM), and during his time away he urgently recruited others to serve alongside him. Taylor is known for being particularly sensitive to the Chinese culture, taking on the traditional clothing and hairstyle even though that was uncommon for missionaries of his time. He learned to speak several different Chinese languages and dialects. For Taylor, there was nothing that would get in the way of spreading the Good News to the Chinese people he loved so dearly and prayed for constantly. He faced near shipwrecks, famines, riots, and sickness, but these only served to deepen his dependence on God. By the time Hudson Taylor died in 1905, CIM had 205 mission stations, 125 schools, 849 missionaries, and over 500 local workers. All of this was responsible for the more than eighteen thousand Chinese people who gave their lives to Jesus Christ.

Hudson Taylor gave his life fully and completely to God and depended upon Him in every circumstance. Every bit of his work was accomplished by the mighty arm of his Lord.

[1] Hudson Taylor, quoted in E. Myers Harrison, *Heroes of Faith on Pioneer Trails* (Chicago: Moody Press, 1945).

The Woman, the Child, and the Dragon

12 A great sign[A] appeared in heaven: a woman clothed with the sun, with the moon under her feet and a crown of 12 stars on her head.[a] 2 She was pregnant and cried out in labor and agony as she was about to give birth. 3 Then another sign[B] appeared in heaven: There was a great fiery red dragon having seven heads and 10 horns,[b] and on his heads were seven diadems.[C] 4 His tail swept away a third of the stars in heaven and hurled them to the earth.[c] And the dragon stood in front of the woman who was about to give birth, so that when she did give birth he might devour her child. 5 But she gave birth to a Son—a male who is going to shepherd[D] all nations with an iron scepter[d]—and her child was caught up to God and to His throne. 6 The woman fled into the wilderness, where she had a place prepared by God,[e] to be fed there[E] for 1,260 days.[f]

The Dragon Thrown Out of Heaven

7 Then war broke out in heaven: Michael[g] and his angels fought against the dragon. The dragon and his angels also fought, 8 but he could not prevail, and there was no place for them in heaven any longer. 9 So the great dragon was thrown out—the ancient serpent,[h] who is called the Devil[F] and Satan,[G,i] the one who deceives the whole world.[j] He was thrown to earth, and his angels with him.

10 Then I heard a loud voice in heaven say:

The salvation and the power
and the kingdom of our God
and the authority of His ·Messiah
have now come,
because the accuser[k] of our ·brothers
has been thrown out:
the one who accuses them
before our God day and night.
11 They conquered him
by the blood of the Lamb
and by the word of their testimony,
for they did not love their lives
in the face of death.[l]
12 Therefore rejoice, you heavens,
and you who dwell in them!
Woe to the earth and the sea,
for the Devil has come down to you
with great fury,
because he knows he has a short time.

The Woman Persecuted

13 When the dragon saw that he had been thrown to earth, he persecuted the woman who gave birth to the male child. 14 The woman was given two wings of a great eagle, so that she could fly from the serpent's presence to her place in the wilderness, where she was fed for a time, times, and half a time.[H,m] 15 From his mouth the serpent spewed water like a river flowing after the woman, to sweep her away in a torrent. 16 But the earth helped the woman. The earth opened its mouth and swallowed up the river that the dragon had spewed from his mouth. 17 So the dragon was furious with the woman and left to wage war[n] against the rest of her offspring[I]—those who keep God's commands and have the testimony about Jesus.[o] 18 He[J] stood on the sand of the sea.[K]

The Beast from the Sea

13 And I saw a beast coming up out of the sea.[p] He[L] had 10 horns and seven heads. On his horns were 10 diadems,[q] and on his heads were blasphemous names.[M,r] 2 The beast I saw was like a leopard, his feet were like a bear's, and his mouth was like a lion's mouth.[s] The dragon gave him his power, his throne, and great authority. 3 One of his heads appeared to be fatally wounded,[N] but his fatal wound was healed. The whole earth was amazed and followed the beast.[O,t] 4 They worshiped the dragon[u] because he gave authority to the beast. And they worshiped the beast, saying, "Who is like the beast?[v] Who is able to wage war against him?"

5 A mouth was given to him to speak boasts and blasphemies.[w] He was also given authority to act[P,Q] for 42 months.[x] 6 He began to speak[R]

[a] **12:1** Gn 37:9-10 [b] **12:3** Dn 7:7 [c] **12:4** Dn 8:10 [d] **12:5** Ps 2:7-9; Rv 19:15 [e] **12:6** 1Kg 19:3-8 [f] Dn 12:11; Rv 11:3; 12:14; 13:5 [g] **12:7** Dn 10:13,21; 12:1 [h] **12:9** Gn 3:1 [i] Lk 10:18; Rm 16:20; Rv 2:9; 3:9; 20:2,7 [j] 1Tm 5:15 [k] **12:10** Jb 1:9-11; Zch 3:1 [l] **12:11** Jn 12:25 [m] **12:14** Dn 7:25; 12:7; Rv 11:2; 13:5 [n] **12:17** Rv 11:7; 13:7 [o] Rv 1:2,9; 19:10; 20:4 [p] **13:1** Dn 7:3 [q] Rv 12:3 [r] Rv 17:3 [s] **13:2** Dn 7:4-6 [t] **13:3** Rv 17:8 [u] **13:4** Rv 12:3 [v] Ex 15:11; Is 46:5 [w] **13:5** Dn 7:8,11,20 [x] Rv 11:2

[A] **12:1** Or *great symbolic display*; see Rv 12:3 [B] **12:3** Or *another symbolic display* [C] **12:3** Or *crowns* [D] **12:5** Or *rule* [E] **12:6** Lit *God, that they might feed her there* [F] **12:9** In Gk, *diabolos* means slanderer. [G] **12:9** In Hb, Satan means adversary. [H] **12:14** This expression, occurring in Dn 7:25; 12:7, = 3½ years or 42 months (Rv 11:2; 13:5) or 1,260 days (Rv 11:3). [I] **12:17** Or *seed* [J] **12:18** Other mss read *I.* "He" is apparently a reference to the dragon. [K] **12:18** Some translations put Rv 12:18 either in Rv 12:17 or Rv 13:1. [L] **13:1** The beasts in Rv 13:1,11 are customarily referred to as "he" or "him" rather than "it." The Gk word for a beast (*therion*) is grammatically neuter. [M] **13:1** Other mss read *heads was a blasphemous name* [N] **13:3** Lit *be slain to death* [O] **13:3** Lit *amazed after the beast* [P] **13:5** Other mss read *wage war* [Q] **13:5** Or *to rule* [R] **13:6** Lit *He opened his mouth in*

blasphemies against God: to blaspheme His
name and His dwelling — those who dwell
in heaven. 7 And he was permitted to wage
war against the ·saints and to conquer them.
He was also given authority over every tribe,
people, language, and nation.[a] 8 All those who
live on the earth will worship him, everyone
whose name was not written from the foundation of the world in the book[A] of life[b] of the
Lamb who was slaughtered.[B,c]
9 If anyone has an ear, he should listen:[d]

10 If anyone is destined for captivity,
into captivity he goes.
If anyone is to be killed[C]
with a sword,
with a sword he will be killed.[e]

This demands the perseverance[D] and faith of
the saints.[f]

The Beast from the Earth

11 Then I saw another beast coming up out
of the earth; he had two horns like a lamb,[E,g]
but he sounded like a dragon. 12 He exercises
all the authority of the first beast on his behalf and compels the earth and those who
live on it to worship the first beast, whose
fatal wound was healed. 13 He also performs
great signs, even causing fire to come down
from heaven to earth in front of people. 14 He
deceives those who live on the earth[h] because
of the signs that he is permitted to perform
on behalf of the beast,[i] telling those who live
on the earth to make an image[F] of the beast
who had the sword wound and yet lived. 15 He
was permitted to give a spirit[G] to the image
of the beast, so that the image of the beast
could both speak and cause whoever would
not worship the image of the beast to be
killed. 16 And he requires everyone — small
and great, rich and poor, free and ·slave — to
be given a mark[H] on his right hand or on his
forehead,[j] 17 so that no one can buy or sell unless he has the mark: the beast's name or the
number of his name.
18 Here is wisdom:[I,k] The one who has understanding must calculate[J] the number of the
beast, because it is the number of a man.[K] His
number is 666.[L]

The Lamb and the 144,000

14 Then I looked, and there on Mount
·Zion stood the Lamb, and with Him
were 144,000 who had His name and His Father's name written on their foreheads.[l] 2 I
heard a sound[M] from heaven like the sound
of cascading waters[m] and like the rumbling of
loud thunder. The sound I heard was also like
harpists playing on their harps.[n] 3 They sang[N]
a new song[o] before the throne and before the
four living creatures and the elders,[p] but no
one could learn the song except the 144,000
who had been ·redeemed[O] from the earth.
4 These are the ones not defiled with women,
for they have kept their virginity.[q] These are the
ones who follow the Lamb wherever He goes.
They were redeemed[O,P] from the human race as
the ·firstfruits[r] for God and the Lamb. 5 No lie
was found in their mouths; they are blameless.[s]

The Proclamation of Three Angels

6 Then I saw another angel flying high overhead,[t] having the eternal gospel to announce
to the inhabitants of the earth — to every nation, tribe, language, and people.[u] 7 He spoke
with a loud voice: "Fear God and give Him
glory, because the hour of His judgment has
come. Worship the Maker of heaven and
earth, the sea and springs of water."
8 A second angel[Q] followed, saying: "It has
fallen, Babylon the Great has fallen,[R] who
made all nations drink the wine of her sexual
immorality,[S] which brings wrath."[v]
9 And a third angel[T] followed them and
spoke with a loud voice: "If anyone worships
the beast and his image and receives a mark
on his forehead or on his hand, 10 he will
also drink the wine of God's wrath, which is
mixed full strength in the cup of His anger.[w]
He will be tormented with fire and sulfur[x] in
the sight of the holy angels and in the sight of
the Lamb, 11 and the smoke of their torment
will go up forever and ever.[y] There is no rest[U]

[a] **13:7** Rv 5:9; 7:9; 11:9; 14:6 [b] **13:8** Ex 32:32-33; Ps 69:28; Php 4:3; Rv 3:5; 17:8; 20:12,15; 21:27 [c] 1Pt 1:19-20 [d] **13:9** Rv 2:7 [e] **13:10** Jr 15:2 [f] Rv 14:12 [g] **13:11** Dn 8:3 [h] **13:14** Rv 12:9 [i] 2Th 2:9-12 [j] **13:16** Rv 14:1 [k] **13:18** Rv 17:9 [l] **14:1** Rv 3:12; 7:3; 13:16 [m] **14:2** Ezk 1:24; 43:2; Rv 1:15; 19:6 [n] Rv 5:8 [o] **14:3** Rv 5:9 [p] Rv 4:4,6 [q] **14:4** 1Sm 21:4-5 [r] Ex 23:19 [s] **14:5** Zph 3:13 [t] **14:6** Rv 8:13 [u] Rv 5:9; 7:9; 11:9; 13:7 [v] **14:8** Is 21:9; Jr 51:7-8,49; Rv 18:2 [w] **14:10** Ps 75:8; Is 51:17; Jr 25:15-17 [x] Lk 17:29; Rv 20:10; 21:8 [y] **14:11** Is 1:31; 34:10; 66:24; Rv 19:3

[A] **13:8** Or *scroll* [B] **13:8** Or *written in the book of life of the Lamb who was slaughtered from the foundation of the world* [C] **13:10** Other mss read *anyone kills* [D] **13:10** Lit *Here is the perseverance* [E] **13:11** Or *ram* [F] **13:14** Or *statue*, or *likeness* [G] **13:15** Or *give breath*, or *give life* [H] **13:16** Or *stamp*, or *brand* [I] **13:18** Or *This calls for wisdom* [J] **13:18** Or *count*, or *figure out* [K] **13:18** Or *is a man's number*, or *is the number of a person* [L] **13:18** Other Gk mss read *616* [M] **14:2** Or *voice* [N] **14:3** Other mss add *as it were* [O] **14:3,4** Or *purchased* [P] **14:4** Other mss add *by Jesus* [Q] **14:8** Lit *Another angel, a second* [R] **14:8** Other mss omit the second *has fallen* [S] **14:8** Or *wine of her passionate immorality* [T] **14:9** Lit *Another angel, a third* [U] **14:11** Lit *They have no rest*

day or night for those who worship the beast
and his image, or anyone who receives the
mark of his name. 12This demands the perseverance[A] of the ·saints,[a] who keep God's commands and their faith in Jesus."[B]

13Then I heard a voice from heaven saying,
"Write: The dead who die in the Lord from
now on are blessed."[b]

"Yes," says the Spirit, "let them rest from
their labors, for their works follow them!"

Reaping the Earth's Harvest

14Then I looked, and there was a white
cloud, and One like the Son of Man[C,c] was
seated on the cloud, with a gold crown on
His head and a sharp sickle in His hand. 15An-
other angel came out of the sanctuary, crying
out in a loud voice to the One who was seated
on the cloud, "Use your sickle and reap, for
the time to reap has come, since the harvest
of the earth is ripe."[d] 16So the One seated on
the cloud swung His sickle over the earth, and
the earth was harvested.

17Then another angel who also had a sharp
sickle came out of the sanctuary in heaven.
18Yet another angel, who had authority over
fire, came from the altar, and he called with
a loud voice to the one who had the sharp
sickle, "Use your sharp sickle and gather the
clusters of grapes from earth's vineyard, because its grapes have ripened." 19So the angel
swung his sickle toward earth and gathered
the grapes from earth's vineyard, and he
threw them into the great winepress of God's
wrath.[e] 20Then the press was trampled outside the city, and blood flowed out of the
press up to the horses' bridles for about 180
miles.[D,f]

Preparation for the Bowl Judgments

15 Then I saw another great and awe-inspiring sign[E] in heaven:[g] seven angels
with the seven last plagues, for with them,
God's wrath will be completed.[h] 2I also saw
something like a sea of glass[i] mixed with
fire, and those who had won the victory over
the beast, his image,[F] and the number of
his name, were standing on the sea of glass
with harps from God.[G,j] 3They sang the song
of God's servant Moses[k] and the song of the
Lamb:

Great and awe-inspiring are
Your works,
Lord God, the Almighty;
righteous and true are Your ways,
King of the Nations.[H]
4 Lord, who will not fear
and glorify Your name?
Because You alone are holy,
for all the nations will come
and worship before You
because Your righteous acts
have been revealed.

5After this I looked, and the heavenly sanctuary—the tabernacle of testimony[l]—was
opened.[m] 6Out of the sanctuary came the
seven angels with the seven plagues, dressed
in ·clean, bright linen, with gold sashes
wrapped around their chests. 7One of the
four living creatures gave the seven angels
seven gold bowls filled with the wrath of God
who lives forever and ever. 8Then the sanctuary was filled with smoke from God's glory
and from His power,[n] and no one could enter
the sanctuary until the seven plagues of the
seven angels were completed.

The First Bowl

16 Then I heard a loud voice from the
sanctuary saying to the seven angels,
"Go and pour out the seven[I] bowls of God's
wrath on the earth." 2The first went and
poured out his bowl on the earth, and severely painful sores[J,o] broke out on the people
who had the mark of the beast and who worshiped his image.

The Second Bowl

3The second[K] poured out his bowl into the
sea. It turned to blood like a dead man's, and
all life[L] in the sea died.[p]

The Third Bowl

4The third[K] poured out his bowl into the
rivers and the springs of water, and they

[a]**14:12** Rv 13:10
[b]**14:13** Rv 1:3; 16:15; 19:9; 20:6; 22:7,14
[c]**14:14** Dn 7:13; Lk 21:27; Rv 1:13
[d]**14:15** Jl 3:13
[e]**14:19** Rv 16:19; 19:15
[f]**14:20** Is 63:1-6
[g]**15:1** Rv 12:3
[h]Rv 16:17
[i]**15:2** Rv 4:6
[j]Rv 5:8; 14:2
[k]**15:3** Ex 15:1; Dt 31:22
[l]**15:5** Ex 38:21; Nm 17:7; 18:2
[m]Rv 11:19
[n]**15:8** Is 6:4
[o]**16:2** Ex 9:9-11
[p]**16:3** Rv 8:8-9

[A]**14:12** Lit *Here is the perseverance* [B]**14:12** Or *and faith in Jesus*, or *and faithfulness to Jesus* [C]**14:14** Or *like a son of man* [D]**14:20** Lit *1,600 stadia* [E]**15:1** Or *and awesome symbolic display* [F]**15:2** Other mss add *his mark* [G]**15:2** Or *harps of God*; = harps belonging to the service of God [H]**15:3** Other mss read *ages* [I]**16:1** Other mss omit *seven* [J]**16:2** Lit *and a severely painful sore* [K]**16:3,4** Other mss add *angel* [L]**16:3** Lit *and every soul of life* became blood.[a] 5 I heard the angel of the waters say:

> You are righteous,
> who is and who was,[b] the Holy One,
> for You have decided these things.
> 6 Because they poured out
> the blood of the ·saints
> and the prophets,
> You also gave them blood to drink;
> they deserve it![c]

7 Then I heard someone from the altar say:

> Yes, Lord God, the Almighty,
> true and righteous are
> Your judgments.[d]

The Fourth Bowl

8 The fourth[A] poured out his bowl on the sun. He[B] was given the power[C] to burn people with fire, 9 and people were burned by the intense heat. So they blasphemed the name of God,[e] who had the power[C] over these plagues, and they did not repent and give Him glory.

The Fifth Bowl

10 The fifth[A] poured out his bowl on the throne of the beast,[f] and his kingdom was plunged into darkness.[g] People[D] gnawed their tongues because of their pain 11 and blasphemed the God of heaven[h] because of their pains and their sores, yet they did not repent of their actions.

The Sixth Bowl

12 The sixth[A] poured out his bowl on the great river Euphrates,[i] and its water was dried up to prepare the way for the kings from the east. 13 Then I saw three unclean spirits like frogs[j] coming from the dragon's mouth,[k] from the beast's mouth,[l] and from the mouth of the false prophet.[m] 14 For they are spirits of demons performing signs,[n] who travel to the kings of the whole world to assemble them for the battle of the great day of God, the Almighty.[o]

15 "Look, I am coming like a thief. The one who is alert and remains clothed[E,p] so that he may not go around naked and people see his shame[q] is blessed."[r]

16 So they assembled them at the place called in Hebrew, Armagedon.[F,G,s]

The Seventh Bowl

17 Then the seventh[A] poured out his bowl into the air,[H] and a loud voice came out of the sanctuary[I,t] from the throne, saying, "It is done!" 18 There were flashes of lightning and rumblings of thunder. And a severe earthquake occurred like no other since man has been on the earth—so great was the quake.[u] 19 The great city[v] split into three parts, and the cities of the nations[J] fell. Babylon the Great was remembered in God's presence; He gave her the cup filled with the wine of His fierce anger.[w] 20 Every island fled, and the mountains disappeared.[K,x] 21 Enormous hailstones, each weighing about 100 pounds,[L] fell from the sky on people, and they blasphemed God[y] for the plague of hail because that plague was extremely severe.[z]

The Woman and the Scarlet Beast

17 Then one of the seven angels who had the seven bowls[aa] came and spoke with me: "Come, I will show you the judgment of the notorious prostitute[M] who sits on many[N] waters.[ab] 2 The kings of the earth committed sexual immorality with her, and those who live on the earth became drunk on the wine of her sexual immorality."[ac] 3 So he carried me away in the Spirit[O,ad] to a desert. I saw a woman sitting on a scarlet beast that was covered[P] with blasphemous names and had seven heads and 10 horns.[ae] 4 The woman was dressed in purple and scarlet, adorned with gold, precious stones, and pearls. She had a gold cup in her hand filled with everything vile[af] and with the impurities of her[Q] prostitution. 5 On her forehead a cryptic name[ag] was written:

BABYLON THE GREAT
THE MOTHER OF PROSTITUTES
AND OF THE VILE THINGS OF THE EARTH.

[a] 16:4 Ex 7:19-21
[b] 16:5 Rv 11:17
[c] 16:6 Is 49:26
[d] 16:7 Ps 19:9; Rv 19:2
[e] 16:9 Rv 13:6
[f] 16:10 Rv 2:13; 13:2
[g] Ex 10:21
[h] 16:11 Rv 13:6
[i] 16:12 Rv 9:14
[j] 16:13 Ex 8:2-14; Lv 11:9-12,41-47
[k] Rv 12:9
[l] Rv 13:1
[m] Rv 13:11-17
[n] 16:14 2Th 2:9-10
[o] Jl 2:11; 3:2; Rv 19:11-21
[p] 16:15 Lk 12:35-40; 1Th 5:2,6-8
[q] Rv 3:18
[r] Rv 1:3; 14:13; 19:9; 20:6; 22:7,14
[s] 16:16 Jdg 5:19; 2Kg 9:27; Ezk 38:8
[t] 16:17 Is 66:6
[u] 16:18 Ex 19:16-19; Rv 4:5; 8:5; 11:19
[v] 16:19 Rv 18:10,16,18,19,21
[w] Rv 14:19; 19:15
[x] 16:20 Ezk 38:20; Rv 6:14
[y] 16:21 Rv 16:9,11
[z] Jos 10:11; Ezk 38:22
[aa] 17:1 Rv 21:9
[ab] Jr 51:13
[ac] 17:2 Is 23:16-17; Nah 3:4; Rv 14:8; 18:3
[ad] 17:3 Rv 1:10; 4:2; 21:10
[ae] Rv 13:1
[af] 17:4 Mt 24:15; Mk 13:14; Lk 16:15; Rv 21:27
[ag] 17:5 Rv 14:1

[A] 16:8,10,12,17 Other mss add *angel* [B] 16:8 Or *It* [C] 16:8,9 Or *authority* [D] 16:10 Lit *They* [E] 16:15 Or *and guards his clothes* [F] 16:16 Other mss read *Armageddon*; other mss read *Harmegedon*; other mss read *Mageddon*; other mss read *Magedon* [G] 16:16 Traditionally *the hill of Megiddo*, a great city that guarded the pass between the coast and the valley of Jezreel or Esdraelon; Jdg 5:19; 2Kg 9:27 [H] 16:17 Or *on the air* [I] 16:17 Other mss add *of heaven* [J] 16:19 Or *the Gentile cities* [K] 16:20 Lit *mountains were not found* [L] 16:21 Lit *about a talent*; talents varied in weight upwards from 75 pounds [M] 17:1 Traditionally translated *the great whore* [N] 17:1 Or *by many* [O] 17:3 Or *in spirit* [P] 17:3 Lit *was filled* [Q] 17:4 Other mss read *of earth's*

6Then I saw that the woman was drunk on
the blood of the ·saints and on the blood of
the witnesses to Jesus. When I saw her, I was
greatly astonished.

The Meaning of the Woman and of the Beast

7Then the angel said to me, "Why are you
astonished? I will tell you the ·secret meaning of the woman and of the beast, with the
seven heads and the 10 horns, that carries
her. 8The beast that you saw was, and is not,
and is about to come up from the ·abyss[a] and
go to destruction.[b] Those who live on the
earth whose names have not been written in
the book of life from the foundation of the
world[c] will be astonished when they see the
beast that was, and is not, and will be present again.[d]
9"Here is the mind with wisdom:[A,e] The
seven heads are seven mountains on which
the woman is seated. 10They are also seven
kings:[B] Five have fallen, one is, the other has
not yet come, and when he comes, he must
remain for a little while. 11The beast that was
and is not, is himself an eighth king, yet he
belongs to the seven and is going to destruction. 12The 10 horns you saw are 10 kings who
have not yet received a kingdom, but they will
receive authority as kings with the beast for
one hour. 13These have one purpose, and they
give their power and authority to the beast.
14These will make war against the Lamb, but
the Lamb will conquer them because He is
Lord of lords and King of kings.[f] Those with
Him are called, chosen, and faithful."
15He also said to me, "The waters you saw,
where the prostitute was seated, are peoples,
multitudes, nations, and languages.[g] 16The
10 horns you saw, and the beast, will hate
the prostitute.[h] They will make her desolate
and naked, devour her flesh, and burn her
up with fire.[i] 17For God has put it into their
hearts to carry out His plan by having one
purpose[j] and to give their kingdom[C] to the
beast until God's words are accomplished.
18And the woman you saw is the great city
that has an empire[D] over the kings of the
earth."

[a]**17:8** Rv 11:7 [b]Rv 1:18; 2:8 [c]Ps 69:28; Is 4:3; Rv 3:5; 13:8; 20:12,15; 21:27 [d]Rv 13:3,12,14 [e]**17:9** Rv 13:18 [f]**17:14** Dt 10:17; Ps 136:2-3; Dn 2:47 [g]**17:15** Rv 5:9; 7:9; 10:11; 11:9; 13:7; 14:6 [h]**17:16** 2Sm 13:15-20; Ezk 23:22-35 [i]Lv 20:14; 21:9 [j]**17:17** Gn 50:20 [k]**18:2** Is 21:9; Rv 14:8 [l]Is 13:20-22 [m]**18:3** Rv 14:8; 17:2 [n]**18:4** Is 52:11; Jr 50:8; 51:6,9,45; 2Co 6:17 [o]**18:5** Jr 51:9 [p]**18:6** Jr 50:29 [q]Is 40:2; Jr 16:18; 17:18 [r]Rv 14:8 [s]**18:7** Is 47:7-8

The Fall of Babylon the Great

18 After this I saw another angel with
great authority coming down from
heaven, and the earth was illuminated by his
splendor. 2He cried in a mighty voice:

It has fallen,[E]
Babylon the Great has fallen![k]
She has become a dwelling for demons,
a haunt for every ·unclean spirit,
a haunt for every unclean bird,
and a haunt[F] for every unclean
and despicable beast.[G,l]
3 For all the nations have drunk[H]
the wine of her sexual immorality,
which brings wrath.[m]
The kings of the earth
have committed sexual immorality
with her,
and the merchants of the earth
have grown wealthy
from her excessive luxury.

4Then I heard another voice from heaven:

Come out of her, My people,
so that you will not share
in her sins[n]
or receive any of her plagues.
5 For her sins are piled up[I] to heaven,[o]
and God has remembered
her crimes.
6 Pay her back the way she also paid,[p]
and double it according to her works.[q]
In the cup in which she mixed,[r]
mix a double portion for her.
7 As much as she glorified herself
and lived luxuriously,
give her that much torment and grief,
for she says in her heart,
"I sit as a queen;
I am not a widow,
and I will never see grief."[s]
8 For this reason her plagues will come
in one day[J]—
death and grief and famine.
She will be burned up with fire,
because the Lord God who judges her
is mighty.

[A]**17:9** Or *This calls for the mind with wisdom* [B]**17:10** Some editors or translators put *They are also seven kings:* in v. 9. [C]**17:17** Or *sovereignty* [D]**17:18** Or *has sovereignty* or *rulership* [E]**18:2** Other mss omit *It has fallen* [F]**18:2** Or *prison* [G]**18:2** Other mss omit the words *and a haunt for every unclean beast.* The words *and despicable* then refer to the *bird* of the previous line. [H]**18:3** Some mss read *have collapsed*; other mss read *have fallen* [I]**18:5** Or *sins have reached up* [J]**18:8** Suddenly

The World Mourns Babylon's Fall

9The kings of the earth who have committed sexual immorality and lived luxuriously
with her will weep and mourn over her when
they see the smoke of her burning. 10They will
stand far off in fear of her torment, saying:

Woe, woe, the great city,
Babylon, the mighty city!
For in a single hour[A]
your judgment has come.

11The merchants of the earth will also weep
and mourn over her, because no one buys
their merchandise any longer — 12merchan-
dise of gold, silver, precious stones, and
pearls; fine fabrics of linen, purple, silk, and
scarlet; all kinds of fragrant wood products;
objects of ivory; objects of expensive wood,
brass,[B] iron, and marble; 13cinnamon, spice,[C,D]
incense, myrrh,[E] and frankincense; wine, olive oil, fine wheat flour, and grain; cattle and
sheep; horses and carriages; and slaves[F] and
human lives.[G,a]

14 The fruit you craved has left you.
All your splendid and glamorous things
are gone;
they will never find them again.

15The merchants of these things, who became
rich from her, will stand far off in fear of her
torment, weeping and mourning, 16saying:

Woe, woe, the great city,
dressed in fine linen, purple,
and scarlet,
adorned with gold, precious stones,
and pearls,
17 for in a single hour[A]
such fabulous wealth was destroyed!

And every shipmaster, seafarer, the sailors,
and all who do business by sea, stood far off
18as they watched the smoke from her burning and kept crying out: "Who is like the great
city?"[b] 19They threw dust on their heads and
kept crying out, weeping, and mourning:[c]

Woe, woe, the great city,[d]
where all those who have ships
on the sea
became rich from her wealth,
for in a single hour[A] she was destroyed.
20 Rejoice over her, heaven,
and you ·saints, apostles, and prophets,[e]
because God has executed
your judgment on her![H]

The Finality of Babylon's Fall

21Then a mighty angel[f] picked up a stone
like a large millstone and threw it into the
sea, saying:

In this way, Babylon the great city
will be thrown down violently[g]
and never be found again.[h]
22 The sound of harpists, musicians,
flutists, and trumpeters
will never be heard in you again;[i]
no craftsman of any trade
will ever be found in you again;
the sound of a mill
will never be heard in you again;
23 the light of a lamp
will never shine in you again;
and the voice of a groom and bride
will never be heard in you again.[j]
All this will happen
because your merchants
were the nobility of the earth,
because all the nations were deceived
by your sorcery,[I]
24 and the blood of prophets and saints,
and of all those slaughtered on earth,
was found in you.[J,k]

Celebration in Heaven

19 After this I heard something like the
loud voice of a vast multitude in heav-
en, saying:

·Hallelujah![l]
Salvation, glory, and power belong
to our God,
2 because His judgments are true[K]
and righteous,[m]
because He has judged
the notorious prostitute
who corrupted the earth
with her sexual immorality;

[a]**18:13** Gn 36:6; Nm 31:32-35; 1Ch 5:21; Ezk 27:13 [b]**18:18** Ezk 27:32 [c]**18:19** Ezk 27:30 [d]Rv 18:10,16 [e]**18:20** Rv 12:12 [f]**18:21** Rv 5:2; 10:1 [g]Jr 51:59-64 [h]Rv 16:20; 18:11,14,22-23 [i]**18:22** Is 24:8 [j]**18:23** Jr 25:10 [k]**18:24** Rv 6:10; 16:6 [l]**19:1** Ps 104:35; 105:45 [m]**19:2** Jn 8:16; 19:35; Rv 16:7; 15:3

[A]**18:10,17,19** Suddenly [B]**18:12** Or *bronze*, or *copper* [C]**18:13** Other mss omit *spice* [D]**18:13** Or *amomum*, an aromatic plant [E]**18:13** Or *perfume* [F]**18:13** Or *bodies* [G]**18:13** Slaves; "bodies" was the Gk way of referring to slaves; "souls of men" was the Hb way. [H]**18:20** Or *God pronounced on her the judgment she passed on you*; see Rv 18:6 [I]**18:23** Ancient sorcery or witchcraft often used spells and drugs. Here the term may be non-literal, that is, Babylon drugged the nations with her beauty and power. [J]**18:24** Lit *in her* [K]**19:2** Valid; Jn 8:16; 19:35

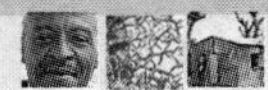

and He has avenged the blood
of His •slaves
that was on her hands.[a]
3A second time they said:

Hallelujah!
Her smoke ascends forever and ever![b]

4Then the 24 elders and the four living
creatures fell down and worshiped God,[c] who
is seated on the throne, saying:

•Amen! Hallelujah![d]

5A voice came from the throne, saying:

Praise our God,
all His slaves, who fear Him,
both small and great![e]

Marriage of the Lamb Announced

6Then I heard something like the voice of
a vast multitude, like the sound of cascading
waters,[f] and like the rumbling of loud thunder, saying:

Hallelujah, because our Lord God,
the Almighty,
has begun to reign!
7 Let us be glad, rejoice,
and give Him glory,[g]
because the marriage of the Lamb
has come,
and His wife has prepared herself.
8 She was given fine linen to wear, bright
and pure.[h]

For the fine linen represents the righteous
acts of the •saints.[i]
9Then he[A] said to me,[j] "Write: Those invited
to the marriage feast[k] of the Lamb are fortunate!" He also said to me, "These words of
God are true." 10Then I fell at his feet to worship him, but he said to me, "Don't do that! I
am a fellow slave with you and your •brothers
who have the testimony about[B] Jesus.[l] Worship God, because the testimony about Jesus
is the spirit of prophecy."[C]

The Rider on a White Horse

11Then I saw heaven opened,[m] and there was
a white horse. Its rider is called Faithful and
True,[n] and He judges and makes war in righteousness.[o] 12His eyes were like a fiery flame,
and many crowns[D] were on His head. He had a
name written that no one knows except Himself.[p] 13He wore a robe stained with blood,[E,q]
and His name is the Word of God.[r] 14The
armies that were in heaven followed Him on
white horses, wearing pure white linen. 15A
sharp[F] sword[s] came from His mouth, so that
He might strike the nations with it.[t] He will
shepherd[G] them with an iron scepter.[u] He will
also trample the winepress of the fierce anger
of God,[v] the Almighty. 16And He has a name
written on His robe and on His thigh:

**KING OF KINGS
AND LORD OF LORDS.**[w]

The Beast and His Armies Defeated

17Then I saw an angel standing on[H] the sun,
and he cried out in a loud voice, saying to all
the birds flying high overhead, "Come, gather
together for the great supper of God, 18so that
you may eat the flesh of kings, the flesh of
commanders, the flesh of mighty men, the
flesh of horses and of their riders, and the
flesh of everyone, both free and slave, small
and great."[x]
19Then I saw the beast, the kings of the
earth, and their armies[y] gathered together
to wage war against the rider on the horse
and against His army. 20But the beast was
taken prisoner, and along with him the false
prophet, who had performed the signs in his
presence. He deceived those who accepted
the mark of the beast and those who worshiped his image with these signs.[z] Both of
them were thrown alive into the lake of fire
that burns with sulfur.[aa] 21The rest were killed
with the sword that came from the mouth of
the rider on the horse, and all the birds were
filled with their flesh.

Satan Bound

20 Then I saw an angel coming down
from heaven with the key to the
•abyss[ab] and a great chain in his hand. 2He
seized the dragon, that ancient serpent who
is the Devil and Satan,[I,ac] and bound[ad] him for
1,000 years. 3He threw him into the abyss,
closed it, and put a seal on it[ae] so that he

[a]19:2 Dt 32:43; 2Kg 9:7; Rv 6:10; 16:6; 17:6; 18:24
[b]19:3 Is 34:8-10; Rv 14:11
[c]19:4 Rv 5:8
[d]Ps 106:48
[e]19:5 Ps 115:13
[f]19:6 Ezk 1:24; 43:2; Rv 1:15; 14:2
[g]19:7 Mt 5:12
[h]19:8 Rv 15:6; 19:14
[i]Eph 2:10
[j]19:9 Rv 17:1; 22:8-9
[k]Is 25:6-8; Lk 13:29
[l]19:10 Rv 1:2,9; 12:17; 20:4
[m]19:11 Rv 4:1; 11:19; 15:5
[n]Rv 3:14
[o]Ps 9:8; 96:13; Rv 16:7; 19:2
[p]19:12 Rv 2:17; 3:12
[q]19:13 Is 63:1-6
[r]Jn 1:1-5; Heb 4:12
[s]19:15 Is 49:2; Heb 4:12; Rv 1:16; 2:12,16
[t]Is 11:4; 2Th 2:8; Rv 1:16; 2:12
[u]Ps 2:9; Rv 12:5
[v]Rv 16:19; 14:19-20
[w]19:16 Dt 10:17; Dn 2:47; 1Tm 6:15; Rv 17:14
[x]19:18 Ezk 39:17-20
[y]19:19 Rv 16:13-14
[z]19:20 Rv 13:13-17
[aa]Mt 5:22; Mk 9:43; Rv 20:10,14; 21:8
[ab]20:1 Lk 8:31; Rv 9:1
[ac]20:2 Rv 12:9
[ad]Is 24:22
[ae]20:3 Dn 6:17; Mt 27:66

[A]19:9 Probably an angel; Rv 17:1; 22:8-9 [B]19:10 Or *to* [C]19:10 Or *the Spirit* [D]19:12 Or *diadems* [E]19:13 Or *a robe dipped in* [F]19:15 Other mss add *double-edged* [G]19:15 Or *rule* [H]19:17 Or *in* [I]20:2 Other mss add *who deceives the whole world*

would no longer deceive the nations[a] until
the 1,000 years were completed. After that,
he must be released for a short time.

The Saints Reign with the Messiah

4Then I saw thrones, and people seated on
them who were given authority to judge.[b]
I also saw the people[A,c] who had been beheaded[B] because of their testimony about
Jesus[d] and because of God's word, who had
not worshiped the beast or his image, and who
had not accepted the mark on their foreheads
or their hands.[e] They came to life[f] and reigned
with the ·Messiah for 1,000 years. **5**The rest of
the dead did not come to life until the 1,000
years were completed. This is the first resurrection. **6**Blessed[g] and holy is the one who
shares in the first resurrection! The second
death[h] has no power[C] over them, but they will
be priests of God and of the Messiah, and they
will reign with Him for 1,000 years.[i]

Satanic Rebellion Crushed

7When the 1,000 years are completed, Satan will be released from his prison **8**and
will go out to deceive the nations at the four
corners of the earth,[j] Gog and Magog, to
gather them for battle.[k] Their number is like
the sand of the sea. **9**They came up over the
surface of the earth and surrounded the encampment of the ·saints, the beloved city.
Then fire came down from heaven[D] and consumed them.[l] **10**The Devil who deceived them
was thrown into the lake of fire and sulfur
where the beast and the false prophet are,[m]
and they will be tormented day and night forever and ever.[n]

The Great White Throne Judgment

11Then I saw a great white throne and One
seated on it. Earth and heaven fled from His
presence, and no place was found for them.[o]
12I also saw the dead, the great and the small,
standing before the throne, and books were
opened.[p] Another book was opened, which is
the book of life,[q] and the dead were judged
according to their works[r] by what was written in the books.

[a]**20:3** Rv 12:9
[b]**20:4** Dn 7:22; Mt 19:28; 1Co 6:2-3; Rv 3:21; 6:9
[c]Rv 6:9
[d]Rv 1:2,9; 12:17; 19:10
[e]Rv 13:12-16
[f]Is 25:6-8; Mt 9:18; 26:29; Lk 13:29; Rv 2:8; 13:14
[g]**20:6** Rv 1:3; 14:13; 16:15; 19:9; 22:7,14
[h]Rv 20:14; 21:8
[i]Rv 1:6; 5:10
[j]**20:8** Is 11:12; Ezk 7:2; Rv 7:1
[k]Ezk 38–39
[l]**20:9** 2Kg 1:10,12; Ezk 38:22; 39:6; Lk 9:54
[m]**20:10** Rv 19:20
[n]Mt 25:41
[o]**20:11** Is 51:6; Mt 24:35; 2Pt 3:10; Rv 18:21
[p]**20:12** Dn 7:10
[q]Is 4:3; 34:16; Dn 12:1; Rv 3:5; 13:8; 17:8; 20:15; 21:27
[r]Ps 62:12; Jr 17:10; Rm 2:6; 1Pt 1:17
[s]**20:13** Rv 1:18; 6:8
[t]**20:14** Is 25:7-8; 1Co 15:26
[u]**21:1** Is 65:17; 66:22; 2Pt 3:13
[v]Rv 13:1
[w]**21:2** Gl 4:26; Heb 11:10; Rv 3:12
[x]Is 61:10; Rv 19:7
[y]**21:3** Lv 26:11-12; Jr 31:33; Ezk 37:27; Zch 8:8
[z]**21:4** Is 25:8; 30:19; 51:11; Rv 7:17
[aa]Hs 13:14; 1Co 15:54
[ab]Is 35:10; 60:20; 65:19
[ac]Is 42:9
[ad]**21:5** Rv 22:6
[ae]**21:6** Rv 16:17
[af]Rv 1:8; 22:13
[ag]Is 44:6; 48:12
[ah]Ps 42:1-2; Is 41:17; 44:3; 55:1; Jn 4:14; 7:37
[ai]Ps 36:9; Jr 2:13; Jn 4:14
[aj]**21:7** Rv 2:7
[ak]2Sm 7:14
[al]**21:8** Rv 19:20
[am]**21:9** Rv 16:1

13Then the sea gave up its dead, and Death
and ·Hades[s] gave up their dead; all[E] were
judged according to their works. **14**Death and
Hades were thrown into the lake of fire.[t] This
is the second death, the lake of fire.[F] **15**And
anyone not found written in the book of life
was thrown into the lake of fire.

The New Creation

21 Then I saw a new heaven and a new
earth,[u] for the first heaven and the
first earth had passed away, and the sea no
longer existed.[v] **2**I also saw the Holy City, new
Jerusalem, coming down out of heaven from
God,[w] prepared like a bride adorned for her
husband.[x]

3Then I heard a loud voice from the throne:[G]

> Look! God's dwelling[H] is with humanity,
> and He will live with them.
> They will be His people,[y]
> and God Himself will be with them
> and be their God.[I]
> **4** He will wipe away every tear
> from their eyes.[z]
> Death will no longer exist;[aa]
> grief, crying, and pain will exist
> no longer,[ab]
> because the previous things[J]
> have passed away.[ac]

5Then the One seated on the throne said,
"Look! I am making everything new." He
also said, "Write, because these words[K] are
faithful and true."[ad] **6**And He said to me, "It is
done![ae] I am the ·Alpha and the Omega,[af] the
Beginning and the End.[ag] I will give water as
a gift to the thirsty[ah] from the spring of life.[ai]
7The victor[aj] will inherit these things, and I
will be his God, and he will be My son.[ak] **8**But
the cowards, unbelievers,[L] vile, murderers,
sexually immoral, sorcerers, idolaters, and
all liars — their share will be in the lake that
burns with fire and sulfur,[al] which is the second death."

The New Jerusalem

9Then one of the seven angels, who had
held the seven bowls filled with the seven last
plagues,[am] came and spoke with me: "Come, I

[A]**20:4** Lit *souls* [B]**20:4** All who had given their lives for their faith in Christ [C]**20:6** Or *authority* [D]**20:9** Other mss add *from God* [E]**20:13** Lit *each* [F]**20:14** Other mss omit *the lake of fire* [G]**21:3** Other mss read *from heaven* [H]**21:3** Or *tent, or tabernacle* [I]**21:3** Other mss omit *and be their God* [J]**21:4** Or *the first things* [K]**21:5** Other mss add *of God* [L]**21:8** Other mss add *the sinful*

will show you the bride, the wife of the Lamb."
10 He then carried me away in the Spirit[A,a] to
a great and high mountain[b] and showed me
the holy city, Jerusalem, coming down out of
heaven from God, 11 arrayed with God's glory.[c]
Her radiance was like a very precious stone, like
a jasper stone, bright as crystal. 12 The city had a
massive high wall, with 12 gates. Twelve angels
were at the gates; the names of the 12 tribes
of Israel's sons were inscribed on the gates.
13 There were three gates on the east, three gates
on the north, three gates on the south, and
three gates on the west.[d] 14 The city wall had 12
foundations, and the 12 names of the Lamb's 12
apostles were on the foundations.

The End of All Things

The concept of the sending helps us to see that behind all we mean by mission is a life-transforming dynamic: an impulse and an identity, a passion and a purpose. Mission is more than doctrine. It is event as well as idea, process as well as content, medium as well as message, mood as well as method, mystery as well as meaning.

We began with a quest. We end with a quest. We began with the search for the implication of an idea. In the process, we have been enveloped in the dynamic of a living truth. We conclude with the realization that mission itself is a quest. Through the biblical concept of the sending, we have come to see the Christian life as a missional pilgrimage, a journey in mission—more, a journey into mission—an odyssey which will end only in the eschaton.

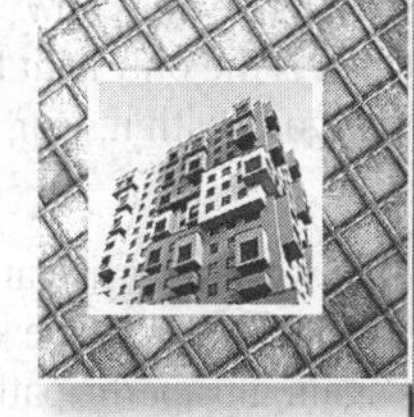

(DUBOSE, 160)

GOD WHO SENDS

15 The one who spoke with me had a gold
measuring rod[e] to measure the city, its gates,
and its wall.[f] 16 The city is laid out in a square;
its length and width are the same. He measured the city with the rod at 12,000 *stadia*.[B]
Its length, width, and height are equal. 17 Then
he measured its wall, 144 ·cubits according to
human measurement, which the angel used.
18 The building material of its wall was jasper,
and the city was pure gold like clear glass.
19 The foundations of the city wall were
adorned with every kind of precious stone:[g]

the first foundation jasper,
the second sapphire,
the third chalcedony,
the fourth emerald,
20 the fifth sardonyx,
the sixth carnelian,
the seventh chrysolite,
the eighth beryl,
the ninth topaz,
the tenth chrysoprase,
the eleventh jacinth,
the twelfth amethyst.

21 The 12 gates are 12 pearls; each individual
gate was made of a single pearl. The broad
street[C] of the city was pure gold, like transparent glass.
22 I did not see a sanctuary in it, because the
Lord God the Almighty and the Lamb are its
sanctuary. 23 The city does not need the sun or
the moon to shine on it, because God's glory
illuminates it, and its lamp is the Lamb.[h]
24 The nations[D] will walk in its light,[i] and the
kings of the earth will bring their glory into
it.[E,j] 25 Each day its gates will never close because it will never be night there. 26 They will
bring the glory and honor of the nations into
it.[F,k] 27 Nothing profane will ever enter it:[l] no
one who does what is vile or false, but only
those written in the Lamb's book of life.[m]

The Source of Life

22 Then he showed me the river[G] of living water, sparkling like crystal, flowing from the throne of God and of the Lamb[n]
2 down the middle of the broad street of the
city. The tree of life[H] was on both sides of the

[a] 21:10 Rv 1:10; 4:2; 17:3
[b] Ezk 40:2
[c] 21:11 Is 60:1-2
[d] 21:13 Ezk 48:30-34
[e] 21:15 Rv 11:1
[f] Ezk 40:3
[g] 21:19 Ex 28:15-21; Is 54:11
[h] 21:23 Is 24:23; 30:26; 60:19-20; Zch 14:6-7; Rv 22:5
[i] 21:24 Is 42:6; 49:6; 60:3,5
[j] Is 49:7,23; 60:10
[k] 21:26 Is 60:11
[l] 21:27 Is 35:8; 52:1
[m] Rv 3:5; 13:8; 17:8; 20:12,15
[n] 22:1 Ezk 47:1-2; Jl 3:18

[A] 21:10 Or *in spirit* [B] 21:16 A *stadion* (sg) = about 600 feet; 12,000 *stadia* = 1,400 miles. [C] 21:21 Or *The public square* [D] 21:24 Other mss add *of those who are saved* [E] 21:24 Other mss read *will bring to Him the nations' glory and honor* [F] 21:26 Other mss add *in order that they might go in* [G] 22:1 Other mss read *pure river* [H] 22:2 Or *was a tree of life*, or *was a tree that gives life*

river, bearing 12 kinds of fruit, producing its
fruit every month.[a] The leaves of the tree are
for healing the nations, 3and there will no
longer be any curse.[b] The throne of God and
of the Lamb will be in the city,[A] and His ·slaves
will serve Him. 4They will see His face,[c] and
His name will be on their foreheads.[d] 5Night
will no longer exist,[e] and people will not need
lamplight or sunlight, because the Lord God
will give them light. And they will reign forever and ever.

The Time Is Near

6Then he said to me, "These words are
faithful and true.[f] And the Lord, the God of
the spirits of the prophets,[B] has sent His angel to show His slaves what must quickly take
place."[C,g]
7"Look, I am coming quickly![h] The one who
keeps the prophetic words of this book is
blessed."[i]
8I, John, am the one who heard and saw
these things. When I heard and saw them, I
fell down to worship at the feet of the angel
who had shown them to me. 9But he said to
me, "Don't do that! I am a fellow slave with
you, your ·brothers the prophets, and those
who keep the words of this book. Worship
God."[j] 10He also said to me, "Don't seal the
prophetic words of this book, because the
time is near.[k] 11Let the unrighteous go on in
unrighteousness; let the filthy go on being
made filthy; let the righteous go on in righteousness; and let the holy go on being made
holy."[l]
12"Look! I am coming quickly, and My
reward is with Me[m] to repay each person
according to what he has done.[n] 13I am the ·Al-
pha and the Omega,[o] the First and the Last,[p]
the Beginning and the End.[q]
14"Blessed[r] are those who wash their robes,[D]
so that they may have the right to the tree of
life and may enter the city by the gates. 15Out-
side are the dogs, the sorcerers, the sexually
immoral, the murderers, the idolaters, and
everyone who loves and practices lying.[s]
16"I, Jesus, have sent My angel to attest these
things to you[E] for the churches. I am the Root[t]

[a]**22:2** Gn 2:9; 3:22
[b]**22:3** Gn 3:14-19; Zch 14:11
[c]**22:4** Ex 33:20; Ps 17:15; Mt 5:8
[d]Rv 7:3; 9:4; 13:16; 14:1,9; 17:5; 20:4
[e]**22:5** Zch 14:7; Rv 21:25
[f]**22:6** Rv 3:14; 19:11; 21:5
[g]Dn 2:28-29,45; Rv 1:1
[h]**22:7** Rv 3:11
[i]Rv 1:3; 14:13; 19:9; 20:6; 22:14
[j]**22:9** Rv 19:10
[k]**22:10** Dn 12:4; Rv 1:3; 10:4
[l]**22:11** Ezk 3:27; Dn 12:10
[m]**22:12** Is 40:10; 62:11
[n]Is 59:18; Jr 17:10; 25:14
[o]**22:13** Rv 1:8
[p]Rv 1:17
[q]Rv 21:6
[r]**22:14** Rv 1:3; 14:13; 16:15; 19:9; 20:6; 22:7
[s]**22:15** Rv 21:8
[t]**22:16** Rv 5:5

GOD'S HEART FOR THE WORLD

A Holy City

The city does not need the sun or the moon to shine on it, because God's glory illuminates it, and its lamp is the Lamb. (Revelation 21:23)

In the end, God's mission does not find its fulfillment with clouds, harps, and white robes, but in a city. Heaven is not an escape from the here and now. It is instead the here and now remade—brought to perfection, to completion. God is not a God who gives up on what He loves. He redeems it and makes it new again. He fixes what we have broken. The perfection that He brings takes this world into itself, and God's mission is fulfilled in a holy city, the New Jerusalem.

That city reminds us of life now, but it is also thankfully very different. God's presence is no longer limited to a temple, or even to dwelling in believers by the Spirit as He does now. Those in the city live in total intimacy with the Lamb. The light of the glory of God is the only light the city needs. Darkness has fled and everything that hides in the darkness has gone with it: fear, hatred, murder, strife. Everything has been made new.

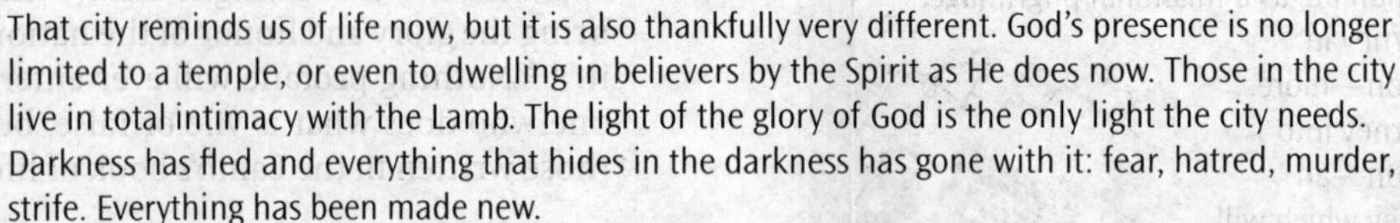

Christians hold to a beautiful hope, and part of its beauty is that we can participate in God's bringing it about. When we praise God and seek to live in His will, we are like the kings who bring their glory into the New Jerusalem. When Christ comes again, this participation will not be a struggle against sin and death, it will be life and freedom. It will not be an ending, but a new beginning.

[A]**22:3** Lit *in it* [B]**22:6** Other mss read *God of the holy prophets* [C]**22:6** Or *soon* [D]**22:14** Other mss read *who keep His commands* [E]**22:16** In Gk, *you* is pl

and the Offspring of David,[a] the Bright Morning Star."[b]
[17]Both the Spirit and the bride say, "Come!"
Anyone who hears should say, "Come!" And
the one who is thirsty should come. Whoever
desires should take the living water as a gift.[c]
[18]I testify to everyone who hears the prophetic words of this book: If anyone adds to
them, God will add to him the plagues that
are written in this book. [19]And if anyone takes
away from the words of this prophetic book,
God will take away his share of the tree of life
and the holy city, written in this book.[d]
[20]He who testifies about these things[e] says,
"Yes, I am coming quickly."
•Amen! Come, Lord Jesus![f]
[21]The grace of the Lord Jesus[A] be with all the
•saints.[B] Amen.[C]

[a]**22:16** Is 11:1,10; Rm 1:3
[b]Nm 24:17; Rv 2:28
[c]**22:17** Rv 21:6
[d]**22:19** Dt 4:2; 12:32
[e]**22:20** Rv 1:2
[f]1Co 16:22

[A]**22:21** Other mss add *Christ* [B]**22:21** Other mss omit *the saints* [C]**22:21** Other mss omit *Amen.*

HCSB Bullet Notes

The *HCSB Bullet Notes* are one of the unique features of the *Holman Christian Standard Bible*®. These notes explain frequently used biblical words or terms. These "bullet" words (for example: •abyss) are marked with a bullet only on their first occurrence in a chapter of the biblical text. Other frequently used words, like •gate, are marked with bullets only where the use of the word fits the definitions given below. A few words in footnotes, like •acrostic, also have a bullet.

Abaddon — A Hebrew word for either the grave or the realm of the dead

Abba — The Aramaic word for father

abyss — The bottomless pit or the depths (of the sea); it is the prison for Satan and the demons.

acrostic — A device in Hebrew poetry in which each verse begins with a successive letter of the Hebrew alphabet

advocate — The Greek word *parakletos* means one called alongside to help, counsel, or protect; it is used of the Holy Spirit in Jn and in 1Jn.

Almighty — The Hebrew word is *El Shaddai*; *El* means God, but the meaning of *Shaddai* is disputed; traditionally it is translated "Almighty."

Alpha and Omega — The first and last letters of the Greek alphabet; it is used to refer to God the Father in Rv 1:8 and 21:6 and to Jesus, God the Son, in Rv 22:13.

Amen — The transliteration of a Hebrew word signifying that something is certain, valid, truthful, or faithful; it is often used at the end of biblical songs, hymns, and prayers.

annihilate(d) — During periods of war in Canaan and its neighboring countries, this was the destruction of a city, its inhabitants, and their possessions, including livestock.

Arabah — The section of the Great Rift in Palestine, extending from the Jordan Valley and the Dead Sea to the Gulf of Aqabah; the Hebrew word can also be translated as "plain," referring to any plain or to any part of the Arabah.

Asaph — A musician appointed by David to oversee the music used in worship at the Temple; 12 psalms are attributed to Asaph.

Asherah(s)/ Asherah pole(s) — A Canaanite fertility goddess who was the mother of the god Baal; also the wooden poles associated with the worship of her

Ashtoreth(s) — A Canaanite goddess of fertility, love, and war, who was the daughter of Asherah and consort of Baal; the plural form of her name in Hebrew is *Ashtaroth*.

Asia — A Roman province that is now part of modern Turkey; it did not refer to the modern continent of Asia.

asleep — A term used in reference to believers who have died

atone/ atonement — A theological term for God's provision to deal with human sin; in the OT, it primarily means purification. In some contexts forgiveness, pardon, expiation, propitiation, or reconciliation is included. The basis of atonement is substitutionary sacrifice offered in faith. The OT sacrifices were types and shadows of the great and final sacrifice of Jesus on the cross.

Baal — A fertility god who was the main god of the Canaanite religion and the god of rain and thunderstorms; it is also the Hebrew word meaning "lord," "master," "owner," or "husband."

Beelzebul — A term of slander, which was variously interpreted "lord of flies," "lord of dung," or "ruler of demons"

Bread of the Presence	Bread that was offered in Yahweh's presence, that is, inside His house, not out on the altar (Lv 24:5-9)
brother(s)	The Greek word *adelphoi* can be used as a reference to males only or to groups that include males and females. It is the context of each usage that determines the proper meaning.
burnt offering(s)	Or *holocaust*; an offering completely burned to ashes; it was used in connection with worship, seeking God's favor, expiating sin, or averting judgment.
cause(s) the downfall of/ cause(s) to sin	The Greek word *skandalizo* has a root meaning of snare or trap but has no real English counterpart.
centurion	A Roman officer who commanded about 100 soldiers
Cephas	The Aramaic word for rock; it is parallel to the Greek word *petros* from which the English name Peter is derived.
cherub(im)	A class of winged angels associated with the throne of God who function as guardians and who prevented Adam and Eve from returning to the garden of Eden
chief priest(s)	A group of Jewish temple officers that included the high priest, captain of the temple, temple overseers, and treasurers
clean	When something is clean, it is holy or acceptable to God. When it is unclean, it is unholy (such as an unclean spirit). The term can be used in a ritual sense to apply to moral standards for living.
company	Or *cohort*; a Roman military unit that numbered as many as 600 men
completely destroy	During periods of war in Canaan and its neighboring countries, this was the destruction of a city, its inhabitants, and their possessions, including livestock.
Counselor	The Greek word *parakletos* means one called alongside to help, counsel, or protect; it is used of the Holy Spirit in Jn and 1Jn.
cubit(s)	An OT measurement of distance that equaled about 18 inches
Cush/Cushite	The lands of the Nile in southern Egypt, including Nubia and Northern Sudan; also the people who lived in that region
Decapolis	Originally, it referred to a federation of 10 Gentile towns east of the Jordan River.
denarius/ denarii	A small silver Roman coin, which was equal to a day's wage for a common laborer
divination	An attempt to foresee future events or discover hidden knowledge by means of physical objects such as water, arrows, flying birds, or animal livers
drink offering(s)	An offering of a specified amount of wine or beer given along with animal sacrifices; it was poured over the sacrifice before it was burned.
engaged	Jewish engagement was a binding agreement that could only be broken by divorce.
ephod	A vest-like garment extending below the waist and worn under the breastpiece; it was used by both the priests and the high priest.
everyone	Literally *sons of man* or *sons of Adam*
family redeemer	A family member who had certain obligations of marriage, redeeming an estate, and punishment of a wrongdoer
fear(s) God or the LORD/ the fear of the LORD/fear Yahweh	No single English word conveys every aspect of the word fear of includes worshipful submission, reverential awe, and obedient respect to the covenant-keeping God of Israel.

fellowship sacrifice(s) or offering(s)	An animal offering was given to maintain and strengthen a person's relationship with God. It was not required as a remedy for impurity or sin but was an expression of thanksgiving for various blessings. An important function of this sacrifice was to provide meat for the priests and the participants in the sacrifice; also called the peace offering or the sacrifice of well-being.
firstfruits	The agricultural products harvested first and given to God as an offering with more products to come in later harvests; it is also used as a metaphor for the first people to come to faith or for Jesus, the first person to rise from the dead, or for the Spirit who is given to believers as the first portion (or down payment) of our salvation with more to come in eternity.
gate(s)	The center for community discussions, political meetings, and trying of court cases
Gittith	Perhaps an instrument, musical term, tune from Gath, or song for the grape harvest
God Almighty	The Hebrew word is *El Shaddai*; *El* means God, but the meaning of *Shaddai* is disputed; traditionally it is translated "Almighty."
grain offering(s)	An offering given along with animal sacrifices or given by itself; a portion was burnt and the priests and participant ate the remainder.
guilt/guilty	The liability to be punished for a fault, a sin, an act, or an omission unless there is forgiveness or atonement; the term normally concerns an objective fact, not a subjective feeling.
Hades	The Greek word for the place of the dead; it corresponds to the Hebrew word *Sheol*.
Hallelujah!	Or *Praise the* LORD*!*; it literally means *Praise Yah!* (a shortened form of *Yahweh*).
headquarters	The Latin word *Praetorium* was used by Greek writers for the residence of the Roman governor; it may also refer to military headquarters, the imperial court, or the emperor's guard.
Hebrew	Or *Aramaic*; the translation of this word is debated since some claim Aramaic was commonly spoken in Palestine during NT times. More recently others claim that Hebrew was the spoken language.
hell/hellfire	The Greek word is *gehenna*; it is the Aramaic term for the Valley of Hinnom on the south side of Jerusalem; formerly, it was a place of human sacrifice, and in NT times, a place for the burning of garbage; it is the place of final judgment for those rejecting Christ.
Herod	Name of the Idumean family ruling Palestine from ca 37 B.C. to A.D. 95; the main rulers from this family mentioned in the NT are:
Herod I	(37 B.C.–4 B.C.) He was also known as Herod the Great; he built the great temple in Jerusalem and massacred the male babies in Bethlehem.
Herod Antipas	(4 B.C.–A.D. 39) The son of Herod the Great; he ruled one-fourth of his father's kingdom (Galilee and Perea); he killed John the Baptist and mocked Jesus.
Herod Agrippa I	(A.D. 37–44) The grandson of Herod the Great; he beheaded James the apostle and imprisoned Peter.
Herod Agrippa II	(A.D. 52–ca 95) The great-grandson of Herod the Great; he heard Paul's defense.
Herodians	They were the political supporters of Herod the Great and his family.
hidden plan	Translation of the Greek word *musterion*; it is a secret hidden in the past but now revealed.
Higgaion	Term used for a musical notation, for a device denoting a pause in an instrumental interlude, or for a murmuring harp tone
high place(s)	An ancient place of worship most often associated with pagan religions; it was usually built on an elevated location.

horn	A symbol of power based on the strength of animal horns
Hosanna	A term of praise derived from the Hebrew word for save
Host(s)	Military forces consisting of God's angels, sometimes including the sun, moon, and stars, and occasionally Israel
human race	Literally *sons of man* or *sons of Adam*
I assure you	This is a phrase used only by Jesus to testify to the certainty and importance of His words; in Mt, Mk, and Lk it is literally *Amen, I say to you*; in Jn it is literally *Amen, amen, I say to you*.
Jews	In Jn, the term Jews usually indicates those in Israel who were opposed to Jesus, particularly the Jewish authorities in Jerusalem who led the nation.
justification/ justify/ justified	The act of God as judge that declares sinners (who were in the wrong) to be right or righteous in His sight. God is just in doing this because Jesus died on the cross to take away their sins and to give them His own righteousness (2Co 5:21). The sinner receives this justification by faith and by grace when he trusts Christ's work.
language(s)	The Greek word *glossa* can refer to the tongue as the organ of speech (see Mk 7:33) or to the language the tongue produces. In certain NT passages, scholars differ on whether the term refers to human languages or to ecstatic speech capable only of divine interpretation ("speaking in tongues").
Leviathan	Or *twisting one*; a mythological sea serpent or dragon associated with the chaos at creation; sometimes it is applied to an animal such as a crocodile.
life/lives	The same Greek word *(psyche)* can be translated life or soul.
mankind	Literally *sons of man* or *sons of Adam*
Mary Magdalene	Or *Mary of Magdala*; Magdala was probably a town on the western shore of the Sea of Galilee, north of Tiberias.
Maskil	It is from a Hebrew word meaning *to be prudent* or *to have insight*; it could also mean a contemplative, instructive, or wisdom psalm.
men	Literally *sons of man* or *sons of Adam*
mercy seat	Or *place of atonement*; it was the gold lid on the ark of the covenant that was first in the tabernacle and later in the temple.
Messiah	Or *the Christ*; the Greek word is *Christos* and means *the anointed one*. Where the NT emphasizes *Christos* as a name of our Lord or has a Gentile context, "Christ" is used. Where the NT *Christos* has a Jewish context, the title "Messiah" is used.
Miktam	A musical term of uncertain meaning; it possibly denotes a plaintive style.
Milcom	An Ammonite god who was the equivalent of Baal, the Canaanite storm god
Molech	A Canaanite god associated with death and the underworld; the worship ritual of passing someone through the fire is connected with him. This ritual could have been either fire-walking or child sacrifice.
Most High	The Hebrew word is *Elyon*; it is often used with other names of God, such as Hebrew *El (God)* or *Yahweh (LORD)*; it is used to refer to God as the supreme being.
Mount of Olives	A mountain east of Jerusalem across the Kidron Valley
mystery	Translation of the Greek word *musterion*; it is a secret hidden in the past but now revealed.
Nazarene	A person from Nazareth; growing up in Nazareth was an aspect of the Messiah's humble beginnings.
Negev	An arid region in the southern part of Israel; the Hebrew word means south.
offend(ed)	The Greek word *skandalizo* has a root meaning of snare or trap but has no real English counterpart.

offspring	This term is used literally or metaphorically to refer to plants or grain, sowing or harvest, male reproductive seed, human children or physical descendants, and also to spiritual children or to Christ (see *seed*).
One and Only	Or *one of a kind*, or *incomparable*, or *only begotten*; the Greek word can refer to someone's only child as in Lk 7:12; 8:42; 9:38. It can also refer to someone's special child as in Heb 11:17.
oracle	A prophetic speech of a threatening or menacing character; it was often spoken against the nations.
overseer(s)	Or *elder(s)*, or *bishop(s)*
palace	The Latin word *Praetorium* was used by Greek writers for the residence of the Roman governor; it may also refer to military headquarters, the imperial court, or the emperor's guard.
Passover	The Israelite festival celebrated on the fourteenth day of the first month, in the early spring; it was a celebration of the deliverance of the Israelites from Egypt, commemorating the final plague on Egypt when the firstborn were killed.
people	Literally *sons of man*, or *sons of Adam*
perverted men	Literally *sons of Belial*; in Hebrew, the basic meaning of Belial is worthless.
Pharisee(s)	A religious sect of Judaism that followed the whole written and oral law
Pilate	Pontius Pilate was governor of the province of Judea A.D. 26–36.
Pit	A term for either the grave or the realm of the dead
proconsul	The chief Roman government official in a senatorial province who presided over Roman court hearings
propitiation	The removal of divine wrath; Jesus' death is the means that turns God's wrath from the sinner.
proselyte(s)	A person from another race or religion who went through a prescribed ritual to become a Jew
Rabbi	The Hebrew word means *my great one*; it is used for a recognized teacher of the Scriptures.
Rabshakeh	The title of a high-ranking Assyrian official who was the chief cupbearer to the king
Rahab	Or *boisterous one*; it is the name of a mythological sea serpent or dragon defeated at the time of creation. Scripture sometimes uses the name metaphorically to describe Egypt.
redemption/ redeemed	The deliverance from bondage by a payment or ransom (Mk 10:45; 1Pt 1:18-19)
Red Sea	Literally *Sea of Reeds*
regiment	Or *cohort*; a Roman military unit that numbered as many as 600 men
restitution offering(s)	An offering that was a penalty for unintentional sins, primarily committed in relation to the tabernacle or temple; it is traditionally translated *trespass* or *guilt offering*.
sackcloth	A garment made of poor quality material and worn as a sign of grief and mourning
sacred bread	Literally *bread of presentation*; these were 12 loaves of bread, representing the 12 tribes of Israel and put on the table in the holy place in the tabernacle and later in the temple. The priests ate the previous week's loaves.
Sadducee(s)	A religious sect of Judaism that mainly followed the first 5 books of the OT (the Torah or Pentateuch)
saint(s)/ sanctification/ sanctify/ sanctified	The work of the Holy Spirit that separates believers in Jesus from the world; at the time of saving faith in Jesus, the believer is made a saint; therefore, all believers are saints. The believer participates with the Spirit in a process of transformation that continues until glorification. The goal of sanctification is progressive conformity to the image of Jesus Christ.

Samaritan(s) A people of mixed, Gentile/Jewish ancestry who lived between Galilee and Judea and were hated by the Jews

Sanhedrin The supreme council of Judaism; it had 70 members and was patterned after Moses' 70 elders.

scribe(s) A professional group in Judaism that copied the law of Moses and interpreted it, especially in legal cases

secret Translation of the Greek word *musterion*; it is a secret hidden in the past but now revealed.

seed This term is used literally or metaphorically to refer to plants or grain, sowing or harvest, male reproductive seed, human children or physical descendants, and also to spiritual children or to Christ (Gl 3:16).

Selah A Hebrew word whose meaning is uncertain; various interpretations include: (1) a musical notation, (2) a pause for silence, (3) a signal for worshipers to fall prostrate on the ground, (4) a term for the worshipers to call out, and (5) a word meaning forever.

set apart for destruction During periods of war in Canaan and its neighboring countries, this was the destruction of a city, its inhabitants, and their possessions, including livestock.

shekel(s) In the OT the *shekel* is a measurement of weight that came to be used as money, either gold or silver.

Sheminith A musical term meaning *instruments* or *on the instrument of eight strings*

Sheol A Hebrew word for either the grave or the realm of the dead

Shinar A land in Mesopotamia, including ancient Sumer and Babylon; it is modern Iraq.

sin offering(s) Or *purification offering*; it was the most important OT sacrifice for cleansing from impurities. It provided purification from sin and certain forms of ceremonial uncleanness.

slave(s) The strong Greek word *doulos* cannot be accurately translated in English as servant or bond servant; the HCSB translates this word as slave, not out of insensitivity to the legitimate concerns of modern English speakers, but out of a commitment to accurately convey the brutal reality of the Roman Empire's inhumane institution as well as the ownership called for by Christ.

Son of Man Most frequent title Jesus used for Himself (Mt 8:20; see also Dn 7:13)

song of ascents A term that probably refers to the songs pilgrims sang as they traveled the roads going up to worship in Jerusalem (Pss 120–134)

soul The same Greek word (*psyche*) can be translated life or soul.

stumble The Greek word *skandalizo* has a root meaning of snare or trap but has no real English counterpart.

synagogue This is a place where the Jewish people met for prayer, worship, and teaching of the Scriptures.

tabernacle(s) Or *tent*, or *shelter*; a term used for temporary housing.

take offense The Greek word *skandalizo* has a root meaning of snare or trap but has no real English counterpart.

tassel Fringe put on the clothing of devout Jews to remind them to keep the law

temple complex In the Jerusalem temple, the complex included the sanctuary (the holy place and the holy of holies), at least 4 courtyards (for priests, Jews, women, and Gentiles), numerous gates, and several covered walkways.

testimony A reference to either the Mosaic law in general or to a specific section of the law, the Ten Commandments, which were written on stone tablets and placed in the ark of the covenant (also called the ark of the testimony)

Topheth A place of human sacrifice that was located outside Jerusalem in the Hinnom Valley (Jr 7:31-32)

unclean	When something is clean, it is holy or acceptable to God. When it is unclean, it is unholy (such as an unclean spirit). The term can be used in a ritual sense to apply to moral standards for living.
Unleavened Bread	A seven-day festival celebrated in conjunction with the Passover (Ex 12:1-20)
Urim & Thummim	Two objects used by Israelite priests to determine God's will
wadi	A valley, ravine, or stream that is dry except in the rainy season
walk(ed)/ walking	A term often used in a figurative way to mean "way of life" or "behavior"
wicked men	Literally *sons of Belial*; in Hebrew, the basic meaning of Belial is worthless.
wise men	The Greek word is *magoi*; the English word "magi" is based on a Persian word. They were eastern sages who observed the heavens for signs and omens.
woman	When used in direct address, "Woman" was not a term of disrespect but of honor.
world	The organized Satanic system that is opposed to God and hostile to Jesus and His followers; it also refers to the non-Christian culture including governments, educational systems, and businesses.
wormwood	A small shrub that was used as a medicinal herb and noted for its bitter taste
Yah/Yahweh	Or *The Lord;* it is the personal name of God in Hebrew; "Yah" is the shortened form. Yahweh is used in places where the personal name of God is discussed (Ps 68:4) or in places of His self-identification (Is 42:8).
Zion	Originally a term for the fortified section of Jerusalem and then, by extension, used for the temple and the city of Jerusalem both in the present time and in the future

Letter to the Church

Calvin Miller

To every Christian who reads this book: you are a missionary.

Missions is the joyous work of informing the world that it is loved. Missions is unrelenting in its desire, it pushes in flaming light against the dark walls of human ignorance. It is honest about all things eternal: we can be free only when we know the truth (Jn 8:32).

Missions is clear, cold water—a cup of grace, a draft of life in the desert. It is as free as air, yet as precious as a pearl buried deep in the brokenness of the human spirit (Mt 13:46). Missions is a message, as simple as two words Jesus Saves—one noun, one verb—and yet this simplicity is God's broad banner posted just above the gates of eternity (Lk 19:10).

Missions is ravenous in its hunger to please God. It knows no other purpose for its existence. It lives for the single pleasure of hearing God say, "Well done, good and faithful slave (Mt 25:21). You have told the truth in a false world, you have turned the iron key of liberty in the steel door of hell, and the captives are freed (Lk 4:18)! For this liberation you have been called "missionary."

Missions is a divine madness that hears the voice of God's only begotten, crying from a mountaintop, into all the world (Mt 28:18-20). It takes this cry to bed and pillow every night. It wakes at every dawn, as Christ whispers in the heart, "I was dead, but look—I am alive forever and ever, and I hold the keys of death and Hades" (Rv 1:18). You must arise for I have come to seek and to save that which was lost. There is no time to waste, the world is loved and doesn't know it. Hold out your hand and I fill it with gold, and you must go out to give the gold away, making rich all those who are poor in spirit (Mt 5:3). Tell all those who starve about the Marriage Supper of the Lamb (Rv 19:9).

To every Christian who reads this book: you are a missionary.

No matter your credentials. All who name the name of Christ have been ordained by the urgency of God's agenda in a fallen world. Missionaries are not just those special few who have accepted some certificate of some profession. They are not servants of a special calling. Missionaries are all those who have said "yes, Lord!" To say "I believe" is to understand that you have accepted the commission to go into all the world, starting right inside your home, your village, your nation, your world. You have been empowered. Christ has breathed upon you (Jn 20:22). When Christ moves in, you move out. Out where? Out there! Outside your narrow life. Anywhere is the place to start. So start. Seek! Knock! Any door will do (Mt 7:7). You need no grand beginning point.

There, it is done! You have spoken to someone the entreaty, "Come with us to Christ!" Congratulations! You are a missionary and missionaries are the merchants of hope. How beautiful upon the mountains are the feet of those who bring good news, who proclaim peace, who bring Good Tidings, who proclaim salvation, who say to Zion, Your God Reigns (Isaiah 52:7).

But be not proud! In redeeming the world all arrogance is precluded. There are no good, arrogant missionaries (2Co 12:5). Christ's ambassadors (2Co 5:20) are men and women made humble by the immense size of the message given to them by Earth's Lover. They feed on the bread they give away. They remember who they were when they met Christ, and just that little act of memory causes them to weep that that they once stumbled into grace, before they were ever called to dispense it. Now they are driven by the joy of God's call, they are the cleansed unclean, the forgiven forgivers, the wounded healers. Nothing is more important than their preachment. They live for it, they die for it (1Co 9:16). They will not change their minds and they cannot change the subject. They are intentional about one truth, "Come, see a man who told me everything I ever did" (Jn 4:29). I can baptize you only with water, but He will baptize you with fire and the Holy Spirit (Lk 3:16). Thus holding forth the world in their left hand they reach for heaven with their right hand, and the gulf between time and eternity is pulled shut (Lk 16:22). The world at hand is made one with the world that is on the way.

All we who know Him are the heralds of God, missionaries blind to our own greatness because we have served a magnificent obsession, a glorious compulsion, "Jesus lives, Jesus saves." There is no other significant, eternal truth (Ac 4:12).

The day we became missionaries we were no longer good at the sedentary life. The word "go" forbids us to settle into the plush present, for we know that the future is where we were meant to live, for only the future holds the possibility of us making our next disciple (1Co 9:19). Of course we love our last convert, but that believer has only fueled our fever to meet the next one.

Here in this volume you hold the grand marriage of the Word of God and the Commission of God. This is the book that holds the definition of forty holy men, the Bible writers, who have defined the heart of God. Missions plus the Word equals everything. You cannot serve just one of these, for to serve the Book is to serve the mission (Php 2:16). To fail to serve either of them is to choose to serve neither. Read herein what God has for you, then do all that you have read. Only then will you enter into life a whole person waiting on God, and knowing who you are. And knowing who you are you will find pleasure in your identity (Php 3:8,10).

Your life belongs to the world.
Your zip code is the globe.
You are a missionary.

Letter to the Church

Billy Graham

If Jesus Christ came into the world to save us from our sins and give us the gift of eternal life, then why doesn't God take us to Heaven the moment we trust Christ as our Lord and Savior?

Many answers might be given to this question, of course—but they all come down to this: God leaves us here because He has a mission for us to fulfill. We aren't here by accident; neither are we here simply to enjoy the good things life has to offer. We are here because God put us here, and He has a sovereign purpose in keeping us here. It's true for us as individuals, and it's true for His body, the Church, in all of its fullness. As Jesus prayed just before His arrest and trial, "I am not praying that You take them out of the world . . . As You sent Me into the world, I also have sent them into the world" (Jn 17:15,18).

But what is the mission we're sent to accomplish? What does God want His people to do?

We will never understand His mission unless we understand His revealed Word, the Bible. Apart from it we will flounder around, never understanding His mission for us and therefore never fulfilling it. Yet from one end of the Bible to the other we see God's plan at work, and our first task must be to understand it.

Apart from the Bible we will never comprehend the depth of human sin, and the horror of what it has done to the entire human race. Because of our rebellion against God, we have been cut off from the very One who created us, and have become subject instead to death and judgment and Hell. Beyond that, our lives have been twisted and marred by sin's terrible tyranny over us and over all human society. The Scripture's words are true: "There is no one righteous, not even one. There is no one who understands; there is no one who seeks God. All have turned away; all alike have become useless" (Rm 3:10-12a).

But apart from the Bible we'll also never understand the depth of God's love! We can say "God loves you." We may even think we feel His love from time to time in our hearts—but what is the proof? The proof is in the Bible's message of the Cross. In the Cross we see God's love demonstrated in all of its fullness and depth, for at the Cross God Himself, in the person of His only Son, our Lord Jesus Christ, took upon Himself the judgment that we deserve. As the Bible says, "God's love was revealed among us in this way: God sent His One and Only Son into the world so that we might live through Him" (1Jn 4:9). By His resurrection Jesus demonstrated beyond all doubt that He was indeed the Savior, sent into the world to save us from our sins and give us the gift of eternal life. And some day He will come again to conquer all evil and establish His eternal rule over all creation.

This is the message God has given us—a life-changing message that our sick and confused world desperately needs. We need to understand it . . . we need to submit our lives to it . . . and we need to share it in every way we possibly can. God did not intend for His Church—His people—to be just another social club, or a community that is concerned only with its own survival or power or internal welfare. We are called to be His instruments—His feet, His hands, His voice, His welcoming arms—in penetrating our world with the Good News of God's redeeming love in Jesus Christ.

Jesus' final command to His followers has never been rescinded, nor will it ever become outdated or unimportant or irrelevant: "All authority has been given to Me in heaven and on earth. Go, therefore, and make disciples of all nations, baptizing them in the name of the Father and of the Son and of the Holy Spirit, teaching them to observe everything I have commanded you. And remember, I am with you always, to the end of the age" (Mt 28:18-20).

This is why evangelism must be our continual priority, and this is why discipleship must be our goal. We are under divine orders, and our only logical response must be obedience. But more than that, we are under a divine compulsion—a compulsion born of love. How can we remain indifferent to those around us who are living every day of their lives "without hope and without God in the world" (Eph 2:12)? How can we remain indifferent to a world that is torn by war and injustice and racism and famine and poverty and disease?

Paul's words must become ours: "For Christ's love compels us, since we have reached this conclusion: If One died for all, then all died. And He died for all so that those who live should no longer live for themselves, but for the One who died for them and was raised. . . . Therefore, we are ambassadors for Christ, certain that God is appealing through us. We plead on Christ's behalf, 'Be reconciled to God'" (2Co 5:14-15,20).

Let God's Word, the Bible, saturate your soul every day. Let its message of hope and freedom from sin change you into the person God wants you to be—a person who reflects Christ in all you think and do and say. And then let that message send you to your knees in prayer for a dying world, and let it send you in the power of the Holy Spirit to tell others that there can be hope . . . there can be new life . . . there can be forgiveness . . . and there can be Heaven before us because of Jesus Christ, the only Savior of the world.

And in that day when we stand before Him, may we not be ashamed, but may we hear Him say, "Well done, good and faithful slave!" (Mt 25:23).

Letter to the Church

Erwin W. Lutzer

"Be alert and strengthen what remains, which is about to die, for I have not found your works complete before My God" (Rv 3:2). In these words from the lips of Jesus, we have the marching orders for the church of the 21st century; here we have commands addressed to us in our culture and in the midst of our successes and failures. Tragedy awaits us if we don't listen to what Jesus has to say.

Jesus begins this letter to this first century congregation in Sardis with this diagnosis, "you have a reputation for being alive, but you are dead" (3:1). Here was a church that was thought highly of in the community, but when Jesus applies His stethoscope to the congregation He cannot discover a heartbeat. The good works of the church members were like grave clothes that masked the marks of death. They had form without power, a reputation without life.

Today we evaluate churches on the basis of their numbers, their budgets, or by the many different opportunities they offer for worship and service. But, alas, too often our impact on the moral and spiritual decline of our culture is scarcely noticed. Tragically, in many instances churches are being closed either because of divisions, lack of funds, or declining interest. This is not a credit to Christ and His reputation is tarnished in our communities. This deserves our tears.

However, all is not lost. Although the church in Sardis was dead, Jesus did point to some signs of life, "But you have a few people in Sardis who have not defiled their clothes" (3:4). If He cannot work through the entire congregation to restore life to this church, Jesus will work through a small group of people who refused to compromise with their culture. He will work with those whose hearts are right with Him and who are faithful to their calling. Jesus now prescribes a remedy for this congregation.

First, He invites the people to wake up! In other words, they are to admit to the depressing reality of their lifelessness; they should begin by assessing their own weakness and decline of influence. They should not live with the false assurance that they are healthy when in point of fact, spiritually they are near death. Honesty is the first step.

Second, Jesus commands, "Strengthen what remains and is about to die" (v. 2). Those who had remained faithful could help restore those who had succumbed to spiritual lethargy. There were some people and programs in the church that were worth preserving, if only they were infused with new life. Today in our churches there is much that can encourage us; there are still signs of life, but too often there is also the stench of death.

Third, Jesus asks them to remember what they had received. Tragically, many in our own churches have forgotten the Gospel; they have imbibed substitutes for the one message that can breathe life into a dying corpse. If only we would remember that it is at the foot of the cross that the church lives and breathes; it is only through a clear gospel both spoken and lived out by members of the congregation that a church is saved from becoming irrelevant.

child coming before God. "In the Spirit" is a venue to be found only by those consumed with a hunger and thirst for righteousness, those with no self-concern distracting or reducing the totality of their quest for Heaven's entry into a given setting, people, or circumstance.

Thus it is that John's Lord's Day intercession unfolds in a multiple "revelation" of practical truth, (quite beside bringing forth the book by that name). John describes a voice "like a trumpet"—a phrase that must be understood as more than a reference to volume. John's Jewish upbringing gave divine authority to trumpet calls—alerting to instructive directions and awareness of an enemy's assault (see Nm 10:1-10). It was Jesus' voice, but what occurs as John is alerted and turns "to see whose voice it was that spoke to me" issues in a dual outcome: an overwhelming confrontation by Jesus Himself; following which, John receives a clear and penetrating pastoral "word" to send to the troubled congregations under his oversight. The two outcomes answer John's two primary needs: (1) his own need to be renewed in Jesus' own presence; and (2) his need for resolving issues in the troubled churches he could not reach on his own.

John's prayer-encounter brought a new discovery of the fullness of Christ Himself. John did not write verses 12-16 to report a vision but to relate an encounter, to testify to his being shaken to the root of his being. He unabashedly confesses, "I fell at His feet like a dead man!" (1:17). The reason is clear; not simply because of the profound description he so graphically gives (vv. 12-16); but rather, because of the depth of perception that suddenly burst over an apostle whose last physical encounter with Jesus was on the Mount of Olives when He ascended. Here is the Reigning Christ! And in that moment John is exclaiming, "I saw Jesus like I have never seen Him before!!"

Even in these later years of my own role as a leader, I walk in the light of John's experience, declaring, "Lord, I refuse to bank on anything of my past learning, victories, or understanding." The secret wisdom of lasting leadership is in resisting anything that takes Jesus HIMSELF out of the heart's gaze, the mind's rulership, or removes my self-measure from under His calculation, correction, and instruction. It is a call to all as leaders to resist the passivity of presuming we ever grasp even a full beginning of the magnitude and majesty of our Master; or to be regularly overwhelmed in His presence; a call to maintain that posture of soul that prostrates pride and rinses away any residue or habit that pleads for self-importance; that will never allow the potential deceit hidden within the suave, style-conscious, one-knee genuflection before the Almighty.

May God's Spirit keep me—keep us all—"face down" as we keep looking forward to His appearance, with our eyes simultaneously on the fields white for harvest.

Letter to the Church

R. T. Kendall

The Bible in a nutshell, said Martin Luther, is contained in John 3:16: "For God loved the world in this way: He gave His One and Only Son, so that everone who believes in Him will not perish but have eternal life." These words unveil the Gospel of Jesus Christ: (1) why He came—namely, to die; (2) what motivated God to send Him—His love for the world; (3) who Jesus is—God's one and only Son, the God-man; (4) how we receive His benefit—by faith alone; (5) exactly what that benefit is—eternal life; and (6) the consequence of not receiving Him—eternal punishment.

Why is our mandate to spread the Gospel of Jesus Christ so important? The answer is, because it mirrors the very heartbeat of God. It means more to God than anything else. What Jesus did by dying on a cross for our sins is the most important thing that God ever conceived or did. Whereas all things in God's creation are important to Him—its beauty, its being sustained by the word of His power (Heb 1:3), His goodness to all humankind—called 'common grace' by theologians, nothing parallels the role of His Son. In a word: God sent His Son into the world to die on a cross so that we might go to Heaven and not to Hell when we die.

Therefore if you and I want to understand the God of the Bible we need to get in touch with His heart. His beloved Son and what He did by shedding His blood means more to God Almighty than anything else. God is determined that Jesus Christ should see the agony of His death and be satisfied (Is 53:11). This satisfaction comes about essentially in two ways: (1) when the blood of Jesus pacified the wrath and justice of God, and (2) when the message of the Cross is carried to the entire world.

Had He chosen to, God could have saved the world by the death of Jesus alone—His perfect faith without our faith. This would have meant universalism, the idea that all are saved whether or not they hear and believe the

Gospel. But God designed our salvation to be carried out "from faith to faith" (Rm 1:17), that Jesus' substitutionary work on the cross be ratified by our own personal faith (Rm 3:22; Gal 2:16). Our faith—the ability to believe—comes only by hearing the message (Rm 10:17) applied by the Holy Spirit (2Th 2:13). In His infinite wisdom it pleased God by the foolishness of what is preached to save people (1Co 1:21).

This means that you and I have been given a mission. It is the most glorious calling, privilege, and responsibility in the whole world. It is carrying on what Jesus started. 'As the Father has sent Me, I also send you' (Jn 20:21). You and I have been dignified with the task of telling everybody we meet that God sent His Son into the world to die on a cross in order that we might go to Heaven and not to Hell when we die.

Have you ever wondered about the possibility that God might use you—and nobody else—to see a certain person converted? And have you ever thought about the possibility that you may be the only person who shares this Good News with that person? This is therefore a task for every one of us. We should not leave this task to the great preachers and evangelists of this world. God may use them, yes. But it is our mandate to speak to every man and woman as if no one else will do so, and then present the Gospel to them as if their destiny were in our hands.

Have you ever personally led a soul to Jesus Christ?

This matter was so important to the great Apostle Paul that he said, "To the weak I became weak, in order to win the weak. I have become all things to all people, so that I may by every possible means save some. Now I do all this because of the gospel, so I may become a partner in its benefits" (1Co 9:22-23).

This mission, then, is the chief calling of the Church. We must never forget this. It would be easy to be diverted by other things that concern us, and then forget our primary calling. We must feed the poor, be salt and light to the world, pray for our leaders, get involved in issues that reflect the righteousness that exalts a nation (Pr 4:34), yes. But at the end of the day the final direction from our Lord Jesus just before He ascended to heaven was to preach the Gospel to every person and make disciples out of them (Mt 28:19). We can learn from church history that those nations into which the Gospel penetrated were blessed in countless other ways, such as raising their standard of living.

But the main thing is to keep the main thing the main thing. That is our mission.

Letter to the Church

R. C. Sproul

The mission of the church is eternal. Its origin is in eternity and its destination is eternity. God's plan of redemption for this fallen world was not an afterthought or an expression of a plan B. Rather, before the world was even created, in all eternity God the Father, God the Son, and God the Holy Spirit had a covenant among themselves that we call the Covenant of Redemption.

It was God's eternal design to manifest His plan of redemption and the creation of His church. The Father from eternity agreed to send the second person of the Trinity, the Son, into the world to accomplish this plan of redemption. Together, the Father and the Son agreed to send the Holy Spirit to apply the accomplished work of redemption to God's people.

So the mission of the church begins with the mission of the second person of the Trinity. A mission involves a sending. The Father sends the Son into the world in order to effect God's eternal plan of redemption. That mission is accomplished by the Son. As His mission was accomplished He commanded His people, those who believed in His name, to go into all the world, to proclaim the gospel to all people, that the Kingdom of God may be made known throughout the earth and throughout the ages. The mission of the church began with a mandate given to the church, by the One whose mission was to fulfill all things that the Father sent Him to do. So He said, "As the Father sent Me so send I you." Looking backward we see that the mission of the church began in eternity with the agreement in the Godhead among the Father, the Son, and the Holy Spirit, and the end of that mission is made manifest in the eternal redemption that God's people experience.

The Kingship of Christ is one that lasts forever. He is the King of Kings, the Lord of Lords, and He shall reign forever and ever. In that eternal reign His church, which is made up of His people, will join in His triumph and participate in His glory as the kingdom of Christ lasts forever. We see then that there is no end to the mission of the church other than its eternal destiny of salvation and glory. We need to understand that the mission of the church is not a temporary matter. It's not a concern that merely began in Old Testament days and reached its conclusion at the end of the old creation. It is a mission from the ages and unto the ages and for the ages. The church must understand that her mission is one that matters eternally. It is a mission that can never be regarded as being of secondary importance.

The seeking of the kingdom of God is the central business of the church. Our Lord commanded that we should seek first the kingdom of God and His righteousness and all other things will be added unto us. So there is no higher priority for the church than the making manifest and bearing witness to the Kingdom of our Savior. This is an eternal destiny with eternal consequences and is of eternal importance. Everything that the church does today and tomorrow matters and counts forever.

The Church Unleashed

The Church Unleashed in Central Asian Villages

Submitted by a worker in Central Asia

Coming down out of the high mountains of Central Asia flows the ancient Oxus River. It runs through desolate lands where the summertime temperatures can exceed 120 degrees Fahrenheit. Just above the river valley is a desert area with a handful of very poor villages. Our humanitarian aid agency did a series of water projects for both drinking and irrigation. We mobilized the community to dig wells and canals that would vastly improve their quality of life. What they needed more than anything else however, was a relationship with the One who could give them streams of living water. Our team was made up of me and four national workers who are followers of Jesus. As we shared the Truth with the villagers, we discovered that although they were all strict Muslims none of them had even heard of Jesus.

One day our team shared with a man about how Jesus lived two thousand years ago, died on a cross, and was raised to life again. The man responded by asking what the price of meat was up in the capital city! He was not changing the subject; he just had no context to understand anything we were telling him. What could we do? We began to pray. Every day we got up, prayed, sang, and studied the Word together. All that we did was worship to our Lord in front of the villagers. At the end of seven months we had seen some amazing things, miracles and answered prayer, but no one wanted to become a follower of Jesus. We were discouraged. We moved on to other villages.

A year later we returned and found that while we had been gone the Holy Spirit continued to work. People had been reading the Bibles we had given them. Two couples had become followers of Christ and wanted to be baptized. We prayed with them, baptized them in the local canal, taught them the Lord's Supper and went on to work in other places. I was concerned that we would not be able to disciple them and train them to withstand the persecution that would come. But we had discipled them. To this day these two families meet every day, pray, sing, study the Word, and worship together. Every day they go out and proclaim the Gospel. They do exactly what they saw us doing for seven months. Every day they are persecuted for their faith. They have been criticized, ostracized, threatened, and beaten, but their love for Jesus keeps them going. I don't understand how they could stand strong for Jesus in such a dark and hostile environment with so little encouragement or support. One day we went down and one of the new believers gave a short devotion. His wife read aloud the last two chapters of Revelation, and then he said, "We are not working for these pathetic houses, or this hard barren land. We are not working for an earthly home. We are laboring for an eternal home that will be glorious forever."

The Church Unleashed in a Central Asian City

Submitted by a worker in Central Asia

In the busy streets of a city of more than 10 million people, with the hustle and bustle of business and busyness, impromptu grocery carts, street sweepers, and shop owners, God is at work. Down a tight, narrow street that serves to separate the four to six story buildings, is a side apartment where a group of migrant workers meets to worship. Economics is what brings these workers from their homeland to this city where better jobs mean vastly greater earning potential.

But this new host city, however, affords something else they lack at home: the precious privilege for them to hear the gospel and worship without fear of persecution.

Religious worship is very restricted in the countries from which these workers have come. Homes cannot contain more than a single Bible and believers have been arrested for holding worship gatherings in their homes. Pressures from family and friends to avoid conversion are intense, while government surveillance constantly seeks to stop such meetings, even restricting those who would leave the country in order to worship.

Thankfully, God uses this oppressive background of their lives to draw them to Himself. They come to our country having been poorly treated, resulting in a deep humility and openness to the gospel. We have seen "God resists the proud, but gives grace to the humble" (James 4:6) played out in real time as people have come to faith in Christ.

Our migrant workers work long hours each day, but we are often able to approach them at work if it is in a public setting like a shoe store, bakery, or hotel. They are different in appearance from the locals, so they are easy to spot in the marketplace. Our easy door opener is, "We've been to your country; we have friends in your country." Because of this touchstone, we are able to give them materials featuring THE story. They are receptive to DVDs and THE book because we can provide them in their native language.

Worship meetings of these migrant workers in our country are not large—between 15 and 30 at the primary one, and from two to five at a new gathering five miles away. What they may seem to lack in numbers, though, is more than overcome by their enthusiasm for worshiping God. People from six people groups are gathered in an apartment on a regular basis. Usually at least three languages need to be spoken for everyone to get the full message, but translation is not done in a traditional way. The speaker's words are translated by whisper from friend to friend until everyone has heard. Prayer time is similar with languages jumping several times as the gathered family prays aloud.

When we are together, the singing is in two or three different languages at the same time, yet there is no confusion. I like to think it's like heaven. Though small amid a city of so many, the church is being unleashed.

The Church Unleashed in Ecuador

J. Guy Muse

One of my favorite stories of the beginnings of evangelical work in Ecuador took place in 1892. Francisco Penzotti was a Uruguayan carpenter-turned-preacher who attempted to push several boxes of Bibles past customs inspectors in Guayaquil. The official defiantly declared: "As long as Mount Chimborazo stands, these books will never enter Ecuador!" Today, 120 years later, all around the slopes of the majestic Chimborazo, is one of the largest concentrations of Bible-believing Christians in Ecuador, with an estimated 40 percent professing faith in Jesus Christ. God, not man, has the final word, and that Word continues to spread to every corner of this nation of 14 million.

I was six years old when my parents, James and Pat Muse, arrived in Ecuador by steamboat at the very port of entry where Penzotti first attempted to bring God's Word to this country. My mom and dad came to Ecuador as part of a great wave of American missionaries arriving in response to God's call after the shocking 1956 murders of Nate Saint, Jim Elliot, Roger Youderian, Pete Fleming, and Ed McCully—the five missionaries speared by the Aucas on the Curaray River. I grew up with several of the children of the men who had given their lives in the belief that indeed, "He is no fool who gives what he cannot keep to gain what he cannot lose."

Over the span of the past 50 years my family has been blessed to witness all four stages of the Gospel planting process in Ecuador: plowing, planting, watering, and harvest. In the late 50s and 60s, they were plowing the ground in preparation for the Gospel seed. Radio HCJB, the Voice of the Andes in Quito, was a primary instrument in preparing hearts to be receptive for the Gospel seed sowing that followed throughout the 70s and continues to the present. In the 80s and 90s we "watered" the seed through the establishment of Christian schools, hospitals, seminaries, bookstores, literature ministries, encampments, radio/TV ministries, church planting, and the establishment of national church conventions and Gospel associations.

Now, my wife and I are blessed to be part of the fourth stage of bringing in God's harvest. Few nations on the earth today are as responsive to the Gospel as Ecuador. Because of the rich, fertile ground, there is a saying that if you toss a seed anywhere in Ecuador, it will sprout and bear fruit. The same holds true for spiritual seeds. Today, it is all we can do to keep up with what God is doing in this spiritually fertile land. While nobody but the Lord really knows the extent of the harvest, it is estimated that close to 15 percent of Ecuadorians are followers of Jesus Christ.

We are very close to the "tipping point" of seeing a massive spiritual awakening in this land. It is my belief that, if the Lord tarries, in our lifetime we will see Ecuador discipling other nations. Like that first great wave of arriving American missionaries, I foresee a second wave of departing Ecuadorian missionaries going to the nations from the same port city that once tried to keep Penzotti's Bibles out!

The Church Unleashed in Europe

Mark Edworthy

In 2010, I visited a colleague who serves in Wales and when we arrived at his apartment, I was surprised to see that he lives in a converted chapel that now contains several flats (apartments). Sadly, thousands of church buildings in Europe have been closed, sold, or converted into businesses over the last few decades. Yet new congregations are also being started in homes, coffee houses, and public venues. To paraphrase Mark Twain, "The reports of the death of the church in Europe are greatly exaggerated."

When the world changed on November 9, 1989 with the opening of the Berlin Wall, Europe slowly reintegrated. The churches in Eastern Europe emerged from the shadows and believers wanted to make up for lost time. Many churches closed by the communist governments were reopened and new churches started. Western Europe continued down the path of secularism but even there new expressions of church began to emerge.

The 1990s saw a pronounced rise in new groups and churches in Central and Eastern Europe. A zeal for the Lord was evident, especially in Ukraine, Romania, and Moldova. Yet new churches were also started in some of the so-called "sowing" fields of Poland, Lithuania, former Yugoslavia, and even, Albania.

In Western Europe, new forms of church are emerging in places like London and Seville. In London, Christian workers have reached out among disenfranchised young people in the district of World's End. Many youth have left their drug culture to confess the Lord and start a new community of faith. In Seville where about two tenths of a percent consider themselves evangelicals, a new church has emerged with over fifty in attendance. It has little in common with the predominant church institution of the country but is a vibrant place for new believers to grow in their faith.

Possibly the most exciting trend in European missions is the transition of several countries from mission-receiving status to mission-sending bases. Hundreds of church planters have been trained in Moldova, Romania, Ukraine, and Germany and now serve throughout Europe and the world.

I currently live in Prague, Czech Republic. Considered one of the most secular nations in the world, many church planting attempts have not been fruitful here over the past several decades. Today not only are new Czech congregations forming but other Europeans have started two "ethnic" churches for minority groups in the city. Led by Ukrainians, a Russian-speaking church has been meeting for several years and has a heart to start other Russian-speaking churches in the country. Though averaging only about 40 on Sundays, the church has already started four other churches in the Czech Republic. More recently, two Polish Roma families moved to Prague for the year to help start a new church for their people group. The first worship service was held in January 2011 and the group has over forty each week for worship. Many Roma have come to faith in the initial weeks of the church and many have a heart to reach others.

Though the center of the Christian Church may have transitioned to Africa or Asia, the "older brother" Europe is seeing signs of a turnaround that we pray will blossom into a revival.

The Church Unleashed in France

Terry and Sheila Wilbanks

So are western Europeans still interested in the message of the gospel? In France the majority of people claim to be culturally Catholic, and on university campuses the students see no reason to even believe there is such a thing as God. And yet this is where I find myself, working with French university students.

I know that the message of the gospel doesn't change, but the way that you convey that message does. It is true in whatever culture or country you live. The challenge in France is getting into natural conversations with non-Christians where one can share the truth about Christ. One way we see this working is through the idea of 3rd places and intentionality. The concept goes like this: 1st place is your home, 2nd place is your work or university, and the 3rd place is where people from different backgrounds get together on a regular basis. If you can't find a 3rd place, then you create one. It is what we did with Café Anglais.

It is a place where university students come to practice English. There is no bait and switch. We talk about

English with a lesson plan from a secular website, ending with a friendly debate relating to life issues. During the lesson, the students do not hear a gospel presentation, but they are seeing it in my life as we share life. But my witness can't stop there. I have to be intentional, to verbally share. Most French students have not seen a true follower of Christ living out their belief, so I want to be that.

After Café Anglais, I go for a coffee or bite to eat with the students, praying as I go, looking for the Lord to open up an opportunity. Before long we are talking about their spiritual beliefs and how that is working for them. One student asks if I think all religions are the same. I smile and share what I believe. Being intentional is seen in asking one of the students to play pool. We play 3 games in 15 minutes and then only 2 in the next hour because I start asking him about his spiritual beliefs. He quickly identifies that he was raised as an atheist and has no one he can turn to for questions about God. I smile and continue the conversation, playing pool, but more interested in the conversation.

Being intentional means going on campus with a picture survey in order to hear what students are thinking on spiritual things, all the time looking and believing that God is already working on the campus. I run into a girl who happens to be searching for something greater than herself. In the conversation I ask her if she knows who Jesus is. She replies that she doesn't really know much about Jesus. Then she asks if I could tell her. I smile, knowing western Europeans are still interested in the message of the Gospel.

The Church Unleashed in Istanbul

Nicholas Drake

Before arriving on the mission field, our team had the passion and conviction to facilitate reproducing house churches. Just over one year ago we established an English-speaking house church that has since become 100 percent Turkish-speaking. God, in His graciousness and mercy, has blessed us in countless ways through this fellowship.

Language and religion are two words that sum up the most significant challenges we face as a church. Because Turkish is a very difficult language for English speakers, we have struggled as a young team in learning the language to a level that is adequate for making disciples. Still, God has used us even in our inadequacy, allowing us the privilege of ministering to neighbors, friends, about 30 Muslim visitors to our fellowship, and a couple of local believers. As a Muslim nation with very few evangelical Christians, Turkey is one of the most unreached countries in the world. The resulting challenges are obvious, as there is a great deal of opposition to the gospel and much suspicion regarding what we do as a local church.

Despite these overwhelming challenges, God has blessed our church with countless opportunities. Most of our Muslim visitors have joined us for our time of worship on Sunday mornings multiple times. In fact, some of them come regularly. Only the work of the Holy Spirit can cause Muslims to repeatedly attend a Christian worship service where the Word of God is preached and is done so by us, people with broken Turkish.

The greatest blessing we enjoy as a church is the discipleship of and partnership with two local believers. One of these men, Sinan, trusted in Christ while living in another city in Eastern Turkey and joined our fellowship after moving to Istanbul. Sinan is growing in his faith and has a passion for God's Word. A couple months ago we had the privilege of baptizing the other local man, Necdet, who is now a part of our church. Through a men's Bible study and the witness of many believers, Necdet recognized his need for Christ and was saved a few months ago. Seeing how he has changed since then has been nothing short of miraculous.

As a young church serving in a hard and unreached land, our defeats have certainly outweighed our victories. Being lied to repeatedly by locals, seeing very little response to the gospel, receiving insults and ridicule from nonbelievers, and having high expectations which are regularly unmet are ways the enemy has attempted to permanently defeat and destroy our church. God's grace and the victories He brings, however, give us the strength and desire to endure. What an amazing honor it is to preach the gospel to Muslims, to see people respond (few as they may be), to baptize a new believer, to disciple Muslim-background believers and to be the church in a dark land! May the Spirit of Christ continue to change people and bring about a church planting movement amongst the Turks and Kurds of Turkey!

The Church Unleashed in Japan

Gary Fujino

JAPAN AND CHRISTIANITY: Jesuit Roman Catholic priest Francis Xavier was the first missionary to enter Japan in 1549. Initially, the faith was welcomed, but in the next century the newly transplanted religion was stamped out under fierce persecution. The great Sakoku or "closing of Japan" to many foreign nations followed for almost two and a half centuries. Later, an underground church of "hidden Christians" resurfaced in the late 1800s. But it was no longer orthodox, syncretizing into an indigenous, Christo-pagan cult.

Protestantism arrived during the Meiji Restoration when Japan's borders were reopened to the West at the end of the nineteenth century. While foreign religions were officially banned until 1873, Protestant missions began in Yokohama in 1859 after U.S. Commodore Matthew Perry's "black ships" reopened Japan's ports in 1853. Still today, however, the official count of Japanese Christians, including all types of Catholic, Protestant, Orthodox, and Christian-like cults, number less than 2 percent of all Japanese. Evangelical Christians are fewer still, comprising only 0.4 percent of a nation numbering 127 million souls.

WHAT JAPANESE BELIEVE: Japanese are good at taking influences from outside Japan and making them "Japanese." Religion is no exception. Animism, Shamanism, Shintoism, Taoism, Buddhism, Confucianism, ancestor worship, and even different forms of Christianity have all impacted Japanese religious thinking, as well as Western science, technologies, and philosophies, Chinese culture and thought, secular humanism, material wealth and prosperity, plus, a deep love for nature. Japanese believe in many different things at the same time, with no sense of contradiction. They follow horoscopes, fortune-telling, comparing blood types, using amulets, palm reading, and engage in temple or shrine rituals. Spiritually speaking, whatever directly affects daily life, and has immediate, visible results, is valued and practiced. Japanese are more "spiritual" than "religious." In short, spiritual attitudes are based on a pluralistic, "religion-ized," polytheistic and materialistic worldview. Christianity impacts this belief system but as one among many rather than as an exclusive faith.

THE CHURCH IN JAPAN TODAY: Japan has an interesting mix of mainline, evangelical, and charismatic denominations. In the summer of 2009, many churchs united to celebrate 150 years of Protestant missions in Japan. That event gave hope against disharmony, which has crippled the church for decades. The impact of its historic triple disaster—of a 9.0 earthquake, devastating tsunami waves, and a nuclear power plant emergency that affected more than 600 kilometers of the nation's eastern coastline on March 11, 2011—has likely changed Japan profoundly. Great physical and spiritual needs and opportunities have been identified because of this global tragedy. How the church in Japan responds through relief efforts and gospel witness could positively influence Japan's future.

Two facts remain clear: (1) Japan remains more than 99 percent non-Christian. The gospel is still desperately needed; (2) God's Holy Spirit is blowing through the church in Japan, birthing new leaders as well as forms of church. The Lord is preparing Japan for a great work in this generation. Pray that winds of revival and reconstruction will continue to blow throughout Japan for its return to the Lord of the harvest before He comes again.

The Church Unleashed in New Zealand

Howard McConnell

New Zealand is a small, scenic, two-island country (slightly larger than California) located southwest of Australia. It was originally populated by the Maori. When missionaries first came to evangelize the Maori, a high percentage (80–90 percent) accepted Christ, especially after their king had done so. The coming of the Europeans (now over 70 percent of the population) has eroded, and continues to erode, the presence of Christianity to the point that evangelicals now compose only 18 percent of the population. New Zealand's earlier Christian influence, along with its isloation, may account for its reputation as one of the least corrupt nations in the world.

A stable economy seems to attract immigrants from Asian countries, the South Pacific Islands, Europe, and South Africa. Past membership in the British Commonwealth explains the predominance of the European culture. Having gained its independence from Britain, New Zealand retains the British Monarch as the official head of state, but unlike Britain, there is no state church in New Zealand.

The Kiwi enjoy religious freedom; the government itself, however, has separated itself from any form of religious activity, refrains from using religious terminology, and does not publically acknowledge any specific religion. Bible classes are openly taught in public schools with members of the community encouraged to conduct these classes. Higher education is funded by the State—including Bible and missionary training institutes—thus, providing for extensive and inexpensive religious training for those who desire it.

In recent years the Maori have been demanding and obtaining certain rights they claim to be theirs as the original occupants of this mountainous nation. The European Kiwi tend to tolerate, or even encourage, the Maori Kiwi in their religious activities—some of which tend to be pagan in nature.

Though believers are dedicated to their churches, worship services have low attendance during holiday times. Summer homes near the beach lure families during school holidays—specifically planned to coordinate with Christmas and Easter. The size of the country lends itself to easy travel in any direction, including flying across the "ditch" to Australia—thus, creating a very mobile nation.

Nearly 5,000 congregations attract both young and old; old churches attract the older generation, and new churches attract the younger. The more established churches tend to remain small—maxing out at about 200 attendees, but the majority having around 50—while some new churches attract very large numbers. It is not unusual for several small congregations of differing cultures to share facilities. Evangelicals tend to be devoted to their church, have a tendency to be mission-minded, and faithfully support their missionaries—sending extra funds when needs arise.

A few years ago New Zealand was ranked fourth in the world as a missionary sending nation on a per capita basis. Church leaders want to raise the ratio to 1 in every 1,000 believers—more than doubling the current number of missionaries. A bold vision for the church unleashed in New Zealand.

The Church Unleashed among Refugees in Central Asia

M. M. Kumar

The church takes on different forms in the refugee wasteland. Spacious, gleaming sanctuaries and stained glass give way to cramped, dilapidated apartments with windows wet with humidity. There are no giant crosses or chiming bells; instead there are low profiles and secrecy. Still, the refugee church is powerful and spiritual. The refugee church values Christmas as much as any church anywhere. I have seen Christmas pageants that rival big budget Hollywood shows. Sitting in stadium chairs with thousands of others, I have witnessed the telling of the Christmas story complete with a choir, symphony, and livestock. Despite the extravagance of those Christmas services, they do not even come close to the Christmas service of 2010.

It began with a phone call from Ali (names are altered in this essay) asking me and my friend John to visit him, his brother, sister-in-law, and another refugee couple who were interested in Jesus. Despite his deep personal problems, Ali continued to share his reason for hope and his desperate confidence in Jesus. The witness had attracted Reza and Melihat. Ali specifically asked us to share about Christmas and its significance.

The drive to Ali's city was spent discussing who would share and the task fell to me. Unlike the Christmas services I experienced in America, the seven of us were crowded onto lumpy couches in a small living room. Sharing the story of Mary and Joseph, I asked the question, "If they were in Joseph's hometown, why didn't they stay with his family?" The answer seemed to be that their obedience to God's messengers cost them the love and acceptance of their family. Refugees understand being turned away by their families and communities better than I ever will. The manger was a filthy, reeking place and unfit for any child, let alone a king. Yet it was fitting because the manger reflected the condition of the world and that is where Jesus would accomplish His work of redemption. There was no choir or pageantry in Ali's living room that evening; there was only a body of believers trying to comprehend the loving act of God. After the Bible study, Reza said something to Ali, who turned to John and me and said, "My friend would like to become a follower of Jesus now."

I blinked in disbelief that John and I would receive this honor after Ali had done all the heavy lifting. John, Ali and I began discussing the book of Romans with Reza and he acknowledged his need of salvation. Ali led Reza in a prayer of confessing his faith in Christ. In the sweet silence of the room, Reza sat on the edge of the couch and cried silently. With tears running down his face he acknowledged the significance of his act, "Today is my birthday."

I looked at everyone in the room and saw the church for what it is at the very core—flawed, yet composed of redeemed men and women obeying God. I felt grateful and unworthy to be in that holy church that evening.

The Church Unleashed in the Buddhist Word

Submitted by a worker among the Buddhists

One day So Law walked out of his house and noted the many Buddhist families living around him. Being one of the few Christians in that village, his heart was moved by the lostness he saw. He asked himself a question, "Who will tell them about Jesus?" The answer was swift in coming, "Why not you!"

So Law was a layman, a former worker in a local gem mine. He had no theological training or experience in evangelism or church planting. He did not even know where to begin, but he knew his Savior. With a prayer on his lips he determined he would try. He went to a home near him and began to share the gospel. To his amazement the household responded in faith. He went to another home and another and people began to respond to his message. They had never heard the name Jesus or His love for them. Upon hearing it, many responded in faith. God was at work!

As time passed So Law enlisted other unpaid laymen to join him in sharing the gospel house to house. Significant prayer walking often preceded their visitation in new neighborhoods and villages. As they prayed God began to open many hearts to the gospel message. The work experienced major growth over the next few weeks and months. So Law and his team were now baptizing new believers every other month.

Thein joined the team as it began to grow. He had been trained at a theological seminary and brought teaching and organizational skills that were much needed. He organized the evangelists and developed a strategy for church planting in the area. Under his direction the work grew so rapidly that the team could no longer control it. They sought help from local believers of other ethnic groups who had a heart to win the Buddhists. This partnership proved strategic and the work surged.

The church planting team began to disciple the new believers and taught them to share their faith immediately. They gathered together into house church networks with worship services and prayer meetings. New believers continued to win family, friends, and neighbors to Christ. Referrals were given to evangelists to follow up and the work continued to grow. Soon there were more than 2,000 baptized Buddhist converts meeting in more than fourteen house church networks and fifteen to twenty house visitation meetings.

So Law, an untrained layman with an obedient heart, has been used mightily of the Lord to win Buddhists (one of the most resistant people groups to the gospel) for Christ. Today there are more than 3,500 baptized believers meeting in twenty-six house church networks throughout the area. This is perhaps the largest movement of Buddhists to Christ in several decades. It all began with one man who believed God not only could, but that He would! The world is still seeing, "What God can do with one man whose heart is fully yielded to Him."

The Church Unleashed in South Asia

Submitted by a worker in South Asia

A few months after my family arrived in India to serve as church planting missionaries, we were thrilled to have the opportunity to go out to a village with a national friend to share the gospel and see the church in action. With our two preschoolers in tow, we took a three-hour train ride followed by an hour on the back of motorcycles until we finally made it to our destination. That night our four-year-old sang "Jesus Loves Me" and my wife shared a Bible story with dozens of spiritually hungry village women crowded around a single lantern.

The next morning we arrived at a simple structure where we removed our shoes before joining almost a hundred people sitting on the floor—men on one side and women on the other. For the next three hours we sang praises to Jesus and studied His Word in an amazing celebration of God and His faithfulness.

Not long after that trip we read a horrifying account of another father who had taken his two sons into the village in a neighboring state to share the good news of Jesus. During the night, while they were sleeping in their vehicle, religious fundamentalists surrounded their car and set it on fire. As the man and his children tried to escape, the villagers forced them to remain in the car until they were burned alive. To misquote Dickens, in South Asia these are the best of times and the worst of times.

The Worst of Times: Across South Asia we are seeing incredible persecution. Recently a government leader was assassinated simply for saying that unjust laws should not be used to persecute Christians. Many areas are passing "anti-conversion laws" making it illegal to tell people about Jesus. At the same time religious intolerance is growing, so is religious indifference as youth are being seduced by materialism and moral relativism.

Many traditional churches are unable to respond to these challenges because they have been corrupted by liberalism and an unhealthy dependence on western culture and money. Some churches have demonstrated more faith in the American dollar than in the God of the Bible. Others credit false religions with more power than God.

The Best of Times: In spite of these challenges, however, this is perhaps the most exciting time in the history of the church in South Asia. Every day new churches are being started and people groups that never before had access to the gospel are being reached at an unprecedented rate. Men and women are being trained to take the gospel into their own communities and entire households are coming to faith.

We have had the privilege of seeing Hindus, Buddhists, Muslims, and Sikhs respond with joy as they hear for the first time of the Savior who loves them and laid down His life for them. Watching these same people gain an understanding of the Great Commission and bring the gospel to neighboring peoples is an incredible joy! Please continue to pray for God's blessings on the peoples of South Asia.

The Church Unleashed among the Nosu in South China

Submitted by a worker in South China

After praying every day for twenty years to the unknown Most High God to send someone to explain who He was, Solomon (names changed in this essay) finally received his answer. When the visiting missionary concluded the story of Christ, Solomon immediately believed and began telling others that same day. Three months later, after seeing seven others believe, Solomon was confronted by the local shaman who told him to stop sharing the gospel. Solomon refused and was cursed by the shaman—who said Solomon would die in three days. On the fourth day, he was still alive. This prompted his entire village to gather outside his home and ask, "What do you know that we don't know?" Solomon shared the gospel again, and 80 of the 160 villagers believed in Christ that day. As the news of Solomon traveled throughout the surrounding villages, more and more believed—more than 20 in one village and more than 60 in another.

Over the next nine months, as Solomon received further discipleship and in turn passed that on to the new believers in his village, one of the first churches was born among the Shengzha Nosu (an ethnic minority in China). The church began to tackle difficult issues such as whether they as Christians could continue to celebrate traditional festivals and holidays which had pagan origins, how to deal with drunkenness in their culture, and how an opium farmer who claimed to believe should be integrated into the church body. At the same time, the discipleship process did not cease with the first church. Members of this church went to the other villages in order to train the new believers. Six months later, another church was started. Several months passed and two more were started. Two young men from Solomon's village, Doug and Micah, felt God's call on their lives to travel from village to village sharing the gospel. They shared their call with the church, who supported them in prayer, and they left the next day. On their first trip, they saw two come to faith and saw new believers in twelve different villages over the next year.

Through the power of the Holy Spirit, the church has not only changed individual lives in Solomon's village, but the Nosu culture as well. As 190 of the 195 villagers are now believers, this village does not look like any other Nosu village in all of China. In most villages the men are drunk all the time and gamble away what little money they make on card games while their wives and children work the fields. In this village, the men work alongside the women. They have stopped drinking and beating their families. They gather together as a church body in some form every day of the week—for prayer, teaching the Word, fellowship, accountability, evangelism and worship. In less than five years, the church has been unleashed on this village, with results only attributable to the Most High God, who is no longer unknown among the Nosu.

The Church Unleashed in Rural Southwest China

Taylor Nicholson

Darkness arrives and with it the familiar smell of garlic and chilies frying in an old wok. Pigs squeal for their usual round of grasses and barefoot children run past cooking fires chasing friends with sticks and assorted home-made toys. It is the end of another work day in the village, Pai. More than 5,000 similar villages dot the mountainsides in this area that is home to over 22 different people groups. Their days trudge along one after another where there is no such thing as weekends—just survival.

From one of the many simple homes comes a low sound of voices singing and an occasional drumbeat. It is in this home that worship is held. It's not necessarily Sunday evening and certainly not Sunday morning. Villagers begin their day with the dawn as they tend to the land and the few livestock they have. It is only in the evenings, after dinner is cooked and cleared, that Christians gather in the home of one designated "leader." Sometimes they gather weekly, sometimes more often. They don't follow a strict schedule. Few have trained pastors. Some are blessed to have visiting a pastor travel through.

The Gospel came to this area over 60 years ago. It was brought on foot and horseback by missionaries from Europe and America. Then in 1949 the missionaries were kicked out. Believers were left to themselves to grow and share whatever knowledge they had. Many did not have Bibles, and if they did, they could scarcely read.

Now, 60 years later, there remain pockets of Christians in these remote villages who survived time and toil. Faith has been passed to their children and grandchildren but there's been little input from outside. False doctrine has gone uncorrected. The same passages may be taught hundreds of times and the same songs sung till there is little joy in their actual singing, just mindless repetition of a tune. It is only in the last 10 years that the church in China and outside missionaries are returning to these villages to strengthen what remains and share with most who have never heard. The task is slow and difficult for many reasons.

Villages are hard to reach. Just simply visiting some of these remote areas requires a trip by bus or motorcycle and then an arduous hike. Villagers are often distrustful of outsiders and when God is mentioned, they wonder which god you are talking about because the cults have had a strong presence here telling people not to eat meat or go to doctors. Additionally, the Christians in a village may be mocked by their neighbors who say, "You are still poor, how is believing in your God going to make my life better."

Yet, the church is growing, one village at a time. Groups are small and comprised mainly of elderly and their grandchildren, for many of the parents have left the area to work in factories. But now, there are new songs, correct teaching, and life is breathed into what was stagnant. It is through the raising up of farmer evangelists that the Christian landscape is changing. These young men are now being trained and equipped as they go out amongst their own people and transform the peoples for God and His purposes.

The Church Unleashed in Tibet

Submitted by a worker in Tibet

The Northern Kham Tibetans of Western China have no church among them as of yet, and only a handful of believers have turned from their Tibetan Buddhist beliefs to follow Christ as their Lord and Savior. In recent years political turmoil, ethnic tensions, and natural disaster have awakened a fresh urgency among the Chinese house churches to reach the Northern Kham Tibetans with the Gospel. Decades long ignorance and apathy among Chinese Christians has begun to melt away and is being replaced with a genuine and passionate desire to reach these remote mountain people hurt by political marginalization, bigotry, and deadly disaster.

Our God is sovereign over the nations, and over His mission to receive praise from every tongue, tribe, and people. He wills and acts through a host of divinely ordained circumstances. It is when His church recognizes this and joins Him in these circumstances that we experience the joyous victories of seeing hearts changed, ancient belief systems abandoned, and lives transformed by His loving grace.

In recent years the Chinese house church has been instrumental in seeing God's Kingdom come to the Northern Kham Tibetans. By His grace they have begun to recognize the multitude of ways that the Lord moves and are reaching out to minister through difficult circumstances such as deadly earthquakes and ethnic tension. By combining simple acts of love and compassion to the bold proclamation of the Gospel, these Chinese believers are modeling true reconciliation. Not only ethnic reconciliation but what it means to be reconciled to God Himself. Because of their powerful testimony these bold servants are seeing fruit for the first time ever among these remote and unreached people.

However, the task remains unfinished until a thriving New Testament Church is raised up among the Northern Kham Tibetans. Close attention to the Gospel message by both Chinese Christians as well as western Great Commission workers is a must. The challenge for both the Chinese and foreign cross-cultural worker alike is to remain faithful to the Gospel of justification by faith in the atoning work of Christ as the only means of salvation for the unreached. We pray that threats to biblical orthodoxy such as inclusivism will not place obstacles in the path of biblical proclamation of the gospel and the planting of healthy churches.

A humble, rigorous, and deep understanding of biblical truth as it applies to the whole of life is a challenge that needs to be maintained for the sake of the future Northern Kham Tibetan church. Lives centered on the Gospel are a must. Future challenges and obstacles are no doubt great, but greater hope can be found in the knowledge that Christ Himself tells us that He will build His church, and that not even the gates of hell will prevail against it.

Concordance

AARON
Levite, brother of Moses (Ex 4:14; 6:16-20). Spokesman for Moses (4:14-16; 7:1-2). Consecrated (Ex 29) and ordained (Lv 8) as priest (Ex 28:1; 1Ch 6:49; Heb 5:1-4; 7). Made golden calf (Ex 32). Died outside the promised land (Nm 20:1-12,22-29; 33:38-39).

ABADDON
Your faithfulness in **A**? ... Ps 88:11
Sheol and **A** lie open before
the LORD ... Pr 15:11
his name in Hebrew is **A**, ... Rv 9:11

ABANDON
I will **a** them and hide My face ... Dt 31:17
certainly not **a** the LORD ... Jos 24:16
LORD will not **a** His people, ... 1Sm 12:22
but if you **a** Him, He will **a** you. ... 2Ch 15:2
For You will not **a** me to Sheol; ... Ps 16:10
Don't **a** wisdom, ... Pr 4:6
a-ed the love you had at first. ... Rv 2:4

ABBA
He said, "***A***, Father! ... Mk 14:36
we cry out, "***A***, Father!" ... Rm 8:15
crying, "***A***, Father!" ... Gl 4:6

ABEL
Shepherd, second son of Adam; brought acceptable sacrifice; was murdered (Gn 4:2-8; Mt 23:35; Heb 11:4).

ABIGAIL
Intelligent wife of the fool Nabal; pled for his life; married David after Nabal died (1Sm 25).

ABIJAH
1. Tragic son of King Jeroboam of Israel (1Kg 14:1,13).
2. Son of Rehoboam, King of Judah (2Ch 13). Also known as Abijam (1Kg 15:1-8).

ABILITY
each according to his own **a**. ... Mt 25:15
according to their **a** ... 2Co 8:3

ABIMELECH
1. King of Gerar at the time of Abraham (Gn 20:1-18; 21:22-32).
2. King of Gerar at the time of Isaac (Gn 26:1-31).
3. Son of Gideon, tried to become king of Shechem (Jdg 9).

ABLE
count the stars, if you are **a** ... Gn 15:5
Moses chose **a** men ... Ex 18:25
God is **a** to raise up children ... Mt 3:9
Are you **a** to drink the cup ... Mt 20:22
the Lord is **a** to make him stand. ... Rm 14:4
tempted beyond what you are **a**, ... 1Co 10:13
Now to Him who is **a** to do ... Eph 3:20
to Him who is **a** to protect you ... Jd 24
a to open the scroll ... Rv 5:3

ABNER
Saul's cousin and commander of his army (1Sm 14:50). At first supported Saul's son Ish-bosheth (2Sm 2:8-9) but defected to David (3:6-21). Killed by Joab and mourned by David (3:22-39).

ABOMINATION
Milcom, the **a** of the Ammonites. ... 2Kg 23:13
and set up the **a** of desolation. ... Dn 11:31
see the **a** that causes desolation, ... Mt 24:15

ABOVE
the LORD is God in heaven **a** ... Dt 4:39
the name that is **a** every name, ... Php 2:9
Set your minds on what is **a**, ... Col 3:2

ABRAHAM
Born Abram son of Terah in Ur, Mesopotamia; married Sarai, then lived in Haran (Gn 11:31; Ac 7:2-4). Called to Canaan and given a promise of progeny and prosperity (Gn 12:1-3). Lied to Pharaoh in Egypt about Sarai (12:10-20). Separated from his nephew Lot (Gn 13). Rescued Lot (14:1-16) and was blessed by Melchizedek (14:17-20; Heb 7:1-10). God declared him righteous because of his faith (Gn 15:6; Rm 4:3,20-22; Gl 3:6; Jms 2:23).

Fathered Ishmael by Hagar (Gn 16). Name changed (17:5); circumcised (17:9-27; Rm 4:9-12). Visited by angels (Gn 18); promised a son with Sarah (18:9-14; cp. 17:15-19). Lied to Abimelech in Gerar about Sarah (Gn 20). Fathered Isaac (21:1-7). Sent Hagar away at Sarah's request (21:8-14). Tested by God concerning Isaac (Gn 22; Heb 11:17-19; Jms 2:21-24). Buried Sarah at Machpelah (Gn 23). Sent servant to find wife for Isaac (24:1-9). Died and was buried with Sarah (25:7-11).

God promised a covenant with Abraham, then made it and confirmed it (Gn 12:1-3; 13:14-17; 15; 17; 22:15-18). It was the basis of future blessings for many people (Ex 2:24; Lv 26:42; 2Kg 13:23; Ps 105:6-11; Ac 3:25).

ABSALOM
Son of David by Maacah (2Sm 3:3). Known for his looks and hair (14:25-26). Killed Amnon for raping Tamar and was banished by David (2Sm 13). Reinstated by David at Joab's insistence (2Sm 14). Rebelled, ousted David (2Sm 15–17). Killed by Joab (18:9-15) despite David's warning (18:5). Greatly mourned by David (18:33–19:4).

ABSENT
a in body but present in spirit, ... 1Co 5:3
I may be **a** in body, but ... Col 2:5

ABSTAIN
he is to **a** from wine and beer. ... Nm 6:3
a from food offered to idols, ... Ac 15:29
a from fleshly desires ... 1Pt 2:11

ABUNDANCE
Seven years of great **a** ... Gn 41:29
bearing spices, gold in great **a**, ... 1Kg 10:2
have life and have it in **a**. ... Jn 10:10

ABUNDANTLY
He poured out this [Spirit] on us **a** ... Ti 3:6

ABUSED
a her all night ... Jdg 19:25

ABYSS
not to banish them to the **a**. ... Lk 8:31
Who will go down into the **a**? ... Rm 10:7

ACCEPT
Should we **a** only good from God ... Jb 2:10
the LORD **a-ed** Job's prayer. ... Jb 42:9
My son, if you **a** my words ... Pr 2:1
A my instruction ... Pr 8:10
Not everyone can **a** this saying, ... Mt 19:11
a one another, ... Rm 15:7
a-ing one another ... Eph 4:2; Col 3:13

ACCEPTABLE
the meditation of my heart be **a** ... Ps 19:14
Look, now is the **a** time; ... 2Co 6:2
spiritual sacrifices **a** to God ... 1Pt 2:5

ACCEPTANCE
and deserving of full **a**: ... 1Tm 1:15

ACCESS
a through Him by faith into ... grace ... Rm 5:2
we both have **a** by one Spirit ... Eph 2:18

ACCOMPANY
signs will **a** those who believe: ... Mk 16:17

ACCOMPLISH
it will **a** what I please ... Is 55:11
I watch over My word to **a** it." ... Jr 1:12

ACCORDING
be done to me **a** to your word. ... Lk 1:38
who do not walk **a** to the flesh ... Rm 8:4
ask anything **a** to His will, ... 1Jn 5:14
were judged **a** to their works ... Rv 20:12

ACCOUNT
a for every careless word ... Mt 12:36

ACCUSATION
Who can bring an **a** ... Rm 8:33
an **a** against an elder ... 1Tm 5:19

ACCUSE
He will not always **a** us ... Ps 103:9
standing at his right side to **a** ... Zch 3:1
in order to **a** Him ... Mt 12:10; Mk 3:2
They began to **a** Him, ... Lk 23:2
Your **a-r** is Moses, ... Jn 5:45

ACHAN
Sinned at Jericho; stoned (Jos 7; 1Ch 2:7).

ACHISH
King of Gath before whom David feigned madness (1Sm 21:10-15). Later, he favored David (1Sm 27–29).

ACKNOWLEDGE
Then I **a-d** my sin to You ... Ps 32:5
I will also **a** him before My
Father in heaven ... Mt 10:32

ACQUIT
I know You will not **a** me. ... Jb 9:28

ACT (n)
an outstretched arm and great **a-s** ... Ex 6:6
deeds and mighty **a-s** like Yours? ... Dt 3:24
this woman was caught in the **a** ... Jn 8:4

ACT (v)
trust in Him, and He will **a**, ... Ps 37:5
these words of Mine and **a-s** ... Mt 7:24
a-ed out of ignorance in unbelief. ... 1Tm 1:13

ACTION
a-s are weighed by Him. ... 1Sm 2:3
with your minds ready for **a**, ... 1Pt 1:13

ADAM
First man. Created by God (Gn 1:26-27; 2:7). Named animals (2:18-20). Given Eve (2:21-25). Failed to obey and was evicted (1:15-17; 3:6-24; Rm 5:14; 1Co 15:22). Died at 930 years (Gn 5:3-5).

ADD
no **a-ing** to it or taking from it. ... Ec 3:14
Can any of you **a** a single cubit ... Mt 6:27
about 3,000 people were **a-ed** ... Ac 2:41

ADDICTED
not **a** to wine, ... 1Tm 3:3; Ti 1:7

ADMINISTRATION
the **a** of the mystery ... Eph 3:9

ADMONISHING
teaching and **a** one another ... Col 3:16

ADONIJAH
Son of David (2Sm 3:4). Conspired for the throne and was executed by Solomon (1Kg 1–2).

ADOPTION
but you received the Spirit of **a**, ... Rm 8:15
that we might receive **a** as sons. ... Gl 4:5

ADORN
A yourself with majesty ... Jb 40:10
as a bride **a-s** herself ... Is 61:10
it was **a-ed** with beautiful stones ... Lk 21:5
a the teaching of God our Savior ... Ti 2:10
a-ed with gold, precious stones, ... Rv 17:4
a bride **a-ed** for her husband. ... Rv 21:2

ADORNMENT
life for you and **a** for your neck. ... Pr 3:22

ADULTERER
both the **a** and the adulteress ... Lv 20:10
a-'s eye watches for twilight, ... Jb 24:15
you associate with **a-s**. ... Ps 50:18
the land is full of **a-s**; ... Jr 23:10
idolaters, **a-s**, male prostitutes, ... 1Co 6:9
judge immoral people and **a-s**, ... Heb 13:4

ADULTERESS
both the adulterer and the **a** ... Lv 20:10
an **a** goes after a precious life. ... Pr 6:26
This is the way of an **a**: she eats ... Pr 30:20
they are **a-es** ... Ezk 23:45
A-es! Don't you know ... Jms 4:4

ADULTEROUS
You **a** wife, ... Ezk 16:32
An evil and **a** generation ... Mt 12:39; 16:4
this **a** and sinful generation, ... Mk 8:38

ADULTERY
Do not commit **a**. ... Ex 20:14; Dt 5:18
already committed **a** with her ... Mt 5:28
marries another, commits **a**. ... Mt 19:9
do not commit **a**; do not steal; ... Mt 19:18
brought a woman caught in **a**, ... Jn 8:3
who said, Do not commit **a**, also ... Jms 2:11

ADVANTAGE
the **a** of wisdom ... Ec 10:10
So what **a** does the Jew have? ... Rm 3:1

ADVERSARY
You exalt me above my **a-ies**; ... Ps 18:48
give the **a** no opportunity ... 1Tm 5:14
Your **a** the Devil is prowling ... 1Pt 5:8

ADVERSITY
life and prosperity, death and **a**. ... Dt 30:15

ADVICE
rejected the elders' **a** ... 2Ch 10:13
not follow the **a** of the wicked, ... Ps 1:1

ADVISERS
with many **a** they succeed. ... Pr 15:22

ADVOCATE
we have an **a** with the Father ... 1Jn 2:1

AFFECTION
limited by your own **a-s**. ... 2Co 6:12
with the **a** of Christ Jesus. ... Php 1:8

AFFLICT
Egyptians mistreated and **a-ed** us, ... Dt 26:6
Evildoers will not **a** them ... 2Sm 7:10
He was oppressed and **a-ed**, ... Is 53:7
Though I have **a-ed** you, I will
a you no longer. ... Nah 1:12
you who are **a-ed**, along with us. ... 2Th 1:7
destitute, **a-ed**, and mistreated. ... Heb 11:37

AFFLICTED (n)
He heard the outcry of the **a** ... Jb 34:28

AFFLICTION
fruitful in the land of my **a**. ... Gn 41:52
LORD saw that the **a** of Israel ... 2Kg 14:26
Consider my **a** and trouble, ... Ps 25:18
He does not enjoy bringing **a** ... Lm 3:33
a-s are waiting for me ... Ac 20:23
a produces endurance, ... Rm 5:3
momentary light **a** is producing ... 2Co 4:17

AFRAID
I was **a** because I was naked, ... Gn 3:10
not be **a**, Abram. I am your shield ... Gn 15:1
he was **a** to look at God. ... Ex 3:6
Do not be **a**, alarmed, or terrified ... Dt 20:3
Do not be **a** or discouraged, ... Jos 1:9
of whom should I be **a**? ... Ps 27:1
When I am **a**, I will trust in You. ... Ps 56:3

She is not **a** for her household ... Pr 31:21
I will trust Him and not be **a**. ... Is 12:2
don't be **a** to take Mary ... Mt 1:20
Jesus told them, "Do not be **a**. ... Mt 28:10
Do not be **a**, Mary, ... Lk 1:30
angel said to them, "Don't be **a**, ... Lk 2:10
they were **a** of the people. ... Lk 22:2
It is I. Don't be **a**! ... Jn 6:20
they were **a** of the Jews, ... Jn 9:22

AGABUS
Early church prophet (Ac 11:28; 21:10).

AGAG
Amalekite king spared by Saul, executed by Samuel (1Sm 15).

AGAINST
who is not with Me is **a** Me, ... Mt 12:30
whoever is not **a** us is for us. ... Mk 9:40
If God is for us, who is **a** us? ... Rm 8:31

AGONY
a like a woman in labor. ... Jr 22:23
I am in **a** in this flame! ... Lk 16:24

AGREE
If two of you on earth **a** ... Mt 18:19
but the testimonies did not **a**. ... Mk 14:56
Why did you **a** to test the Spirit ... Ac 5:9
I **a** with the law that it is good ... Rm 7:16

AGREEMENT
making a binding **a** in writing ... Neh 9:38
we have made an **a** with Sheol; ... Is 28:15
a does Christ have with Belial? ... 2Co 6:15
these three are in **a**. ... 1Jn 5:8

AGRIPPA
Herodian king who heard Paul's testimony (Ac 25–26).

AHAB
Son of Omri, king of Israel (1Kg 16:28–22:40). Married Jezebel and promoted baalism (16:31-33). Killed Naboth (21:1-14). Condemned by Elijah (18:18; 21:17-24) and other prophets (20:35-43; 22:19-28). Died in disguise in battle (22:29-40).

AHASUERUS
King of Persia, son of Darius and grandson of Cyrus. Greek name is Xerxes. Dismissed Vashti and married Esther (Est 1–2). Signed Haman's decree (Est 3) then was convinced by Esther to reverse it and hang Haman (Est 4–7) and allow the Jews to defend themselves (Est 8–9).

AHAZ
Idolatrous king of Judah (2Kg 16:2-4). Son of Jotham. Attacked by Aram and Israel (16:5-6; 2Ch 28:5-7). Refused Isaiah's advice and turned to Assyria for help (Is 7). Not buried among the kings (2Ch 28:27).

AHAZIAH
1. Son of Ahab; king of Israel (1Kg 22:40). Injured in a fall; condemned by Elijah for seeking Baal (2Kg 1:2-17).
2. Son of Jehoram; king of Judah (2Kg 8:25-27). Mortally wounded by Jehu while visiting King Joram of Israel (9:27).

AHEAD
sending My messenger **a** of You; ... Mt 11:10
reaching forward to what is **a**, ... Php 3:13

AHIJAH
1. Priest at the time of Saul (1Sm 14:3-4,18).
2. Prophet from Shiloh to Jeroboam (1Kg 11:29-39).

AI
Bethel on the west and **A** on the ... Gn 12:8
they fled from the men of **A**. ... Jos 7:4

AIJALON
moon, over the valley of **A**. ... Jos 10:12
A with its pasturelands, ... Jos 21:24

AIR
box like one who beats the **a**. ... 1Co 9:26
meet the Lord in the **a**; ... 1Th 4:17
poured out his bowl into the **a**, ... Rv 16:17

ALABASTER
an **a** jar ... Mt 26:7; Mk 14:3

ALARM
sound the **a** on My holy mountain! ... Jl 2:1

ALARMED
and rumors of wars, don't be **a**; ... Mk 13:7

ALERT
be **a**, since you don't know ... Mt 24:42
Be **a**, stand firm in the faith, ... 1Co 16:13
stay **a** in this, with all perseverance ... Eph 6:18
Be sober! Be on the **a**! ... 1Pt 5:8

ALIEN
I am a resident **a** among you. ... Gn 23:4
the land where you live as an **a**, ... Gn 28:4
if you no longer oppress the **a**, ... Jr 7:6
His descendants would be **a-s** ... Ac 7:6
I urge you as **a-s** ... 1Pt 2:11

ALIENATED
are **a** from Christ; ... Gl 5:4
you were once **a** and hostile ... Col 1:21

ALIVE
to keep them **a** with you. ... Gn 6:19
when they heard that He was **a** ... Mk 16:11
He also presented Himself **a** ... Ac 1:3
dead to sin, but **a** to God ... Rm 6:11
in Christ all will be made **a**. ... 1Co 15:22
made us **a** with the Messiah ... Eph 2:5
He made you **a** with Him ... Col 2:13
Then we who are still **a** ... 1Th 4:17
made **a** in the spiritual realm. ... 1Pt 3:18
but look—I am **a** forever ... Rv 1:18

ALL
with **a** your heart, with **a** your soul, and with **a** your strength. ... Dt 6:5
search for Me with **a** your heart. ... Jr 29:13
love the Lord ... with **a** your heart, ... Lk 10:27
A have turned away, ... Rm 3:12
a have sinned and fall short ... Rm 3:23
He died to sin once for **a**; ... Rm 6:10
I am able to do **a** things ... Php 4:13
A Scripture is inspired by God ... 2Tm 3:16
but **a** to come to repentance. ... 2Pt 3:9

ALLIANCE
Solomon made an **a** with Pharaoh ... 1Kg 3:1
they will form an **a**, ... Dn 11:6

ALLOTMENT
Israel according to their **a-s**: ... Jos 12:7

ALLOW
will not **a** Your Faithful One to ... Ps 16:10
A it for now, ... Mt 3:15
a Your Holy One to see decay. ... Ac 2:27
will not **a** you to be tempted ... 1Co 10:13

ALMIGHTY
I am God **A**. ... Gn 17:1
Isaac, and Jacob as God **A**, ... Ex 6:3
dwells in the shadow of the **A**. ... Ps 91:1
holy, holy, holy, Lord God, the **A**, ... Rv 4:8
God, the **A**, has begun to reign! ... Rv 19:6

ALONE
not good for the man to be **a**. ... Gn 2:18
man does not live on bread **a** ... Dt 8:3
I **a** am left, ... 1Kg 19:10
Against You—you **a**— ... Ps 51:4
the LORD **a** will be exalted ... Is 2:11
Man must not live on bread **a** ... Mt 4:4
Who can forgive sins but God **a**? ... Mk 2:7
by works and not by faith **a**. ... Jms 2:24

ALPHA
the **A** and the Omega, ... Rv 1:8; 21:6; 22:13

ALREADY
has **a** committed adultery ... Mt 5:28
A you are full! **A** you are rich! ... 1Co 4:8
he is **a** in the world now. ... 1Jn 4:3

ALTAR
Noah built an **a** to the LORD. ... Gn 8:20
Isaac and placed him on the **a**, ... Gn 22:9
construct the **a** of acacia wood. ... Ex 27:1
tear down their **a-s**, ... Ex 34:13
take hold of the horns of the **a**. ... 1Kg 1:50
leave your gift ... in front of the **a**. ... Mt 5:24
takes an oath by the **a**, ... Mt 23:18
when he offered Isaac ... on the **a**? ... Jms 2:21
I saw under the **a** the souls ... Rv 6:9

ALWAYS
my sin is **a** before me. ... Ps 51:3
You **a** have the poor with you, ... Mt 26:11
I am with you **a**, ... Mt 28:20
Rejoice in the Lord **a**. ... Php 4:4
a be ready to give a defense ... 1Pt 3:15

AM *see* I AM

AMASA
David's nephew; commander of Absalom's army (2Sm 17:25). Reinstated by David (19:13). Killed by Joab (20:10).

AMAZED
a and asked, "What kind of man ... Mt 8:27
He was **a** at their unbelief. ... Mk 6:6
they were astounded and **a**, ... Ac 2:7

AMAZIAH
Son of Joash; king of Judah. Defeated Edom but adopted their gods (2Ch 25:11-14). Rejected God's rebuke, challenged King Jehoash of Israel, and was defeated (26:15-24). Killed by a conspiracy (26:27).

AMBASSADOR
we are **a-s** for Christ; ... 2Co 5:20
For this I am an **a** in chains. ... Eph 6:20

AMBUSH
Set an **a** behind the city. ... Jos 8:2
set up an **a** around Gibeah. ... Jdg 20:29

AMEN
all the people will reply, '**A**!' ... Dt 27:15
LORD be praised forever. **A** and **a**. ... Ps 89:52
The **A**, the faithful and true ... Rv 3:14
A! Come, Lord Jesus! ... Rv 22:20

AMNON
Oldest son of David (2Sm 3:2). Raped his sister Tamar; killed by Absalom (2Sm 13).

AMON
Son of Manasseh; king of Judah; killed by his servants (2Kg 21:18-26).

AMOS
Prophet against moral decay in Israel under Jeroboam II (Am 5:24).

ANANIAS
1. Lied about gift to the church at Jerusalem and died (Ac 5:1-6).
2. Disciple in Damascus who visited Paul (Ac 9:10-19).
3. High priest at Paul's arrest (Ac 23:1-5; 24:1).

ANCESTORS
from the day their **a** came out ... 2Kg 21:15
returned to the sins of their **a** ... Jr 11:10

ANCHOR
sure and firm **a** of the soul ... Heb 6:19

ANCIENT
Will you continue on the **a** path ... Jb 22:15
Rise up, **a** doors! ... Ps 24:7,9
Ask about the **a** paths: ... Jr 6:16
the **A** of Days took His seat. ... Dn 7:9
since **a** times, Moses ... Ac 15:21
if He didn't spare the **a** world, ... 2Pt 2:5
seized the dragon, that **a** serpent ... Rv 20:2

ANDREW
Apostle; fisherman; Peter's brother (Mt 4:18; 10:2; Mk 1:16,29; 3:18; 13:3; Lk 6:14; Jn 1:35-44; 6:8-9; 12:12; Ac 1:13).

ANGEL
two **a-s** entered Sodom ... Gn 19:1
A of the LORD called to him ... Gn 22:11
He will send His **a** before you, ... Gn 24:7
a-s were going up and down ... Gn 28:12
God sent an **a** to Jerusalem ... 1Ch 21:15
a of the LORD encamps around ... Ps 34:7
He will give His **a-s** orders ... Ps 91:11
Praise the LORD, all His **a-s** ... Ps 103:20
My God sent His **a** and shut ... Dn 6:22
Jacob struggled with the **A** ... Hs 12:4
a of the Lord suddenly appeared ... Mt 2:13
He will give His **a-s** orders ... Mt 4:6
their **a-s** continually view ... Mt 18:10
a said to them, "Don't be afraid ... Lk 2:10
the **a-s** of God ascending ... Jn 1:51
we will judge **a-s** ... 1Co 6:3
disguised as an **a** of light. ... 2Co 11:14
even if we or an **a** from heaven ... Gl 1:8
the worship of **a-s**, ... Col 2:18
some have welcomed **a-s** as guests ... Heb 13:2
A-s desire to look into ... 1Pt 1:12
if God didn't spare the **a-s** ... 2Pt 2:4
To the **a** of the church in ... Rv 2–3

ANGER
gracious God, slow to **a** ... Ex 34:6
LORD's **a** burned against Israel ... Jdg 2:14
His **a** may ignite at any moment. ... Ps 2:12
For His **a** lasts only a moment, ... Ps 30:5
A gentle answer turns away **a**, ... Pr 15:1
sun go down on your **a**, ... Eph 4:26
So I swore in My **a**, ... Heb 3:11
slow to speak, and slow to **a**, ... Jms 1:19
winepress of the fierce **a** of God, ... Rv 19:15

ANGRY
the Son, or He will be **a**, ... Ps 2:12
Be **a** and do not sin; ... Ps 4:4
who is **a** with his brother ... Mt 5:22
Be **a** and do not sin. ... Eph 4:26

ANGUISH
He will see it out of His **a**, ... Is 53:11

ANIMAL
LORD God formed ... each wild **a** ... Gn 2:19
every **a** of the forest is Mine, ... Ps 50:10
cares about his **a-'s** health, ... Pr 12:10
four-footed **a-s** and reptiles ... Ac 10:12

ANNIHILATE
a all the Jewish people ... Est 3:13

ANNOUNCE
I **a** them to you before they occur ... Is 42:9
feet of those who **a** the gospel ... Rm 10:15

ANOINT
A Aaron and his sons ... Ex 30:30
The LORD **a-ed** you king ... 1Sm 15:17
You **a** my head with oil; ... Ps 23:5
a-ed My body in advance ... Mk 14:8
a-ed Me to preach good news ... Lk 4:18
You didn't **a** My head with oil, ... Lk 7:46
a-ed Jesus' feet, ... Jn 12:3
against ... Jesus, whom You **a-ed**, ... Ac 4:27
pray over him after **a-ing** him ... Jms 5:14

ANOINTED (adj)
If the **a** priest sins, ... Lv 4:3
he will walk before My **a** one ... 1Sm 2:35
Do not touch My **a** ones ... 1Ch 16:22
against the LORD and His **A** One: ... Ps 2:2
Do not touch My **a** ones, ... Ps 105:15
an **a** guardian cherub, ... Ezk 28:14
These are the two **a** ones, ... Zch 4:14

ANOINTED (n)
lift my hand against ... LORD's **a**. ... 1Sm 24:6

ANOINTING (n)
an **a** from the Holy One, 1Jn 2:20
His **a** teaches you 1Jn 2:27
ANOTHER
Let **a** praise you, and not your Pr 27:2
I will not give My glory to **a**. Is 48:11
He will give you **a** Counselor Jn 14:16
not that there is **a** gospel, Gl 1:7
ANSWER (n)
A gentle **a** turns away anger, Pr 15:1
a of the tongue is from the LORD Pr 16:1
who gives an **a** before he listens Pr 18:13
were astounded at ... His **a-s**. Lk 2:47
ANSWER (v)
He **a-ed** him with fire 1Ch 21:26
Don't **a** a fool according to Pr 26:4
ANT
Go to the **a**, you slacker! Pr 6:6
ANTICHRIST
heard, "**A** is coming," even now
many **a-s** have come. 1Jn 2:18
He is the **a**, the one who denies 1Jn 2:22
spirit of the **a**; you have heard 1Jn 4:3
This is the deceiver and the **a**. 2Jn 7
ANTIOCH
first called Christians in **A**. Ac 11:26
reached **A** in Pisidia. Ac 13:14
ANXIOUS
don't be **a**. Lk 12:29
ANYTHING
Is **a** impossible for the LORD? Gn 18:14
Is **a** too difficult for Me? Jr 32:27
A you ask the Father Jn 16:23
APART
Set **a** for Me Barnabas and Saul Ac 13:2
a from the law ... righteousness has Rm 3:21
from my mother's womb set me **a** Gl 1:15
set **a** the Messiah as Lord 1Pt 3:15
APOLLOS
Alexandrian Jew, became a Christian apologist after being instructed in doctrine by Priscilla and Aquila in Ephesus (Ac 18:24-28). Was popular like Paul and Peter (1Co 1:12) but not a rival (3:5-6,22; 4:6; 16:12; Ti 3:13).
APOSTASY
a-ies will reprimand you. Jr 2:19
save them from all their **a-ies** Ezk 37:23
I will heal their **a**; Hs 14:4
unless the **a** comes first 2Th 2:3
APOSTLE
the names of the 12 **a-s**: Mt 10:2
I am an **a** to the Gentiles, Rm 11:13
first **a-s**, second prophets, 1Co 12:28
unworthy to be called an **a**, 1Co 15:9
some to be **a-s**, some prophets, Eph 4:11
Jesus, the **a** and high priest Heb 3:1
APOSTLESHIP
We have received grace and **a** Rm 1:5
you are the seal of my **a** 1Co 9:2
Peter in the **a** to the circumcised Gl 2:8
APPEAL (v)
I **a** to Caesar! Ac 25:11
God is **a-ing** through us, 2Co 5:20
I **a**, instead, on the basis of love. Phm 9
APPEAR
the LORD **a-ed** to Abram Gn 12:7
sign of the Son of Man will **a** Mt 24:30
all **a** before the judgment seat 2Co 5:10
until the **a-ing** of our Lord 1Tm 6:14
hope and the **a-ing** of the glory Ti 2:13
will **a** a second time, Heb 9:28
APPEARANCE
Do not look at his **a** 1Sm 16:7
no **a** that we should desire Him. Is 53:2
judging according to outward **a-s**; Jn 7:24
APPETITE
A worker's **a** works for him Pr 16:26
yet the **a** is never satisfied. Ec 6:7
Lord Christ but their own **a-s**, Rm 16:18
APPLE
Guard me as the **a** of Your eye; Ps 17:8
like golden **a-s** on a silver tray. Pr 25:11
APPOINT
These are the LORD's **a-ed** times, Lv 23:4
A a king for them. 1Sm 8:22
I will **a** peace as your guard Is 60:17
A harvest is also **a-ed** for you, Hs 6:11
the LORD **a-ed** a great fish Jnh 1:17
He also **a-ed** 12 Mk 3:14
God did not **a** us to wrath, 1Th 5:9
He has **a-ed** heir of all things Heb 1:2
it is **a-ed** for people to die once Heb 9:27
APPROACH
let us **a** the throne of grace Heb 4:16
APPROVED
and **a** by men. Rm 14:18
just as we have been **a** by God 1Th 2:4
to present yourself **a** to God, 2Tm 2:15
by it our ancestors were **a**. Heb 11:2
AQUILA
Husband of Priscilla; tentmaker; Jewish Christian; teacher; co-worker with Paul (Ac 18:2,18,26; Rm 16:3; 1Co 16:19; 2Tm 4:19).
ARABAH
in the **A** opposite Suph, Dt 1:1
the Sea of the **A** (the Dead Sea) Jos 3:16
along the route to the **A**, 2Kg 25:4
a dry land, a wilderness, an **A**. Jr 50:12
and goes down to the **A**. Ezk 47:8
ARARAT
on the mountains of **A**. Gn 8:4
ARAUNAH
Man whose threshing floor David bought (2Sm 24:15-25); also called Ornan (1Ch 21:15-28); threshing floor became site of the temple (1Ch 22:1; 2Ch 3:1).
ARCHANGEL
a shout, with the **a-'s** voice, 1Th 4:16
Michael the **a**, Jd 9
ARCHER
the **a-s** caught up with him 1Sm 31:3
The **a-s** shot King Josiah, 2Ch 35:23
like an **a** who wounds everyone Pr 26:10
ARCHITECT
whose **a** and builder is God. Heb 11:10
ARGUE
Pharisees ... to **a** with Him, Mk 8:11
don't **a** about doubtful issues. Rm 14:1
without grumbling and **a-ing**, Php 2:14
ARGUMENT
Hear now my **a**, Jb 13:6
Then an **a** started among them Lk 9:46
We demolish **a-s** 2Co 10:4
deceive you with empty **a-s**, Eph 5:6
deceive you with persuasive **a-s**. Col 2:4
holy hands without anger or **a**. 1Tm 2:8
ARISE
God **a-s**. His enemies scatter, Ps 68:1
A, my darling. Come away, Sg 2:10
A, shine, for your light has come Is 60:1
false prophets will **a** Mt 24:24
ARK
Make ... an **a** of gofer wood. Gn 6:14
make an **a** of acacia wood, Ex 25:10
Put the tablets ... into the **a**. Ex 25:16
The **a** of God was captured, 1Sm 4:11
Nothing was in the **a** except 1Kg 8:9
the day Noah boarded the **a**. Mt 24:38
ARM (n)
a strong hand and an outstretched **a**, Dt 4:34
underneath are the everlasting **a-s**. Dt 33:27
Do you have an **a** like God's? Jb 40:9
a-s can bend a bow of bronze. Ps 18:34
taking them in His **a-s**, Mk 10:16
who has the **a** of the Lord
been revealed to? Jn 12:38
ARMAGEDON
place called in Hebrew **A**. Rv 16:16
ARMOR
through the joints of his **a**. 1Kg 22:34
Put on the full **a** of God Eph 6:11
ARMY
chariots and his **a** into the sea; Ex 15:4
commander of the LORD's **a**. Jos 5:14
defied the **a-ies** of the living God. 1Sm 17:36
a great **a**, like an **a** of God. 1Ch 12:22
Though an **a** deploy against me, Ps 27:3
king is not saved by a large **a**; Ps 33:16
Jerusalem surrounded by **a-ies**, Lk 21:20
The **a-ies** that were in heaven Rv 19:14
on the horse and against His **a**. Rv 19:19
ARREST
Herod had **a-ed** John, Mt 14:3
looking for a way to **a** Him, Mt 21:46
hold of Jesus, and **a-ed** Him. Mt 26:50
he proceeded to **a** Peter too, Ac 12:3
ARROGANCE
your **a** have reached My ears, 2Kg 19:28
A leads to nothing but strife, Pr 13:10
you boast in your **a**. Jms 4:16
ARROGANT
a people have attacked me; Ps 86:14
an **a** spirit before a fall. Pr 16:18
Do not be **a**, but be afraid. Rm 11:20
ARROW
I will shoot three **a-s** beside it 1Sm 20:20
a-s of the Almighty have pierced Jb 6:4
the **a** that flies by day, Ps 91:5
a-s in the hand of a warrior Ps 127:4
He made me like a sharpened **a**; Is 49:2
Their tongues are deadly **a-s** Jr 9:8
extinguish the flaming **a-s** Eph 6:16
ARTAXERXES
King of Persia who allowed Ezra to rebuild the temple (Ezr 6:14; 7:1-26) and Nehemiah to rebuild the wall of Jerusalem (Neh 2:1-6).
ARTEMIS
Greek goddess (Ac 19:24-35).
ASA
Son of Abijam; king of Judah (1Kg 15:8). Instituted reforms (15:13). Rebuked for relying on Aram for military help and on doctors for healing rather than on the Lord (2Ch 16:1-12).
ASCEND
Who may **a** the mountain Ps 24:3
No one has **a-ed** into heaven Jn 3:13
observe the Son of Man **a-ing** Jn 6:62
not yet **a-ed** to the Father. Jn 20:17
same as the One who **a-ed** Eph 4:10
ASCRIBE
a to the LORD glory
and strength. 1Ch 16:28; Ps 96:7
A power to God. Ps 68:34
ASENATH
Wife of Joseph (Gn 41:45,50; 46:20).
ASHAMED
Jacob will no longer be **a** Is 29:22
is **a** of Me and of My words Mk 8:38
I am not **a** of the gospel, Rm 1:16
don't be **a** of the testimony 2Tm 1:8
who doesn't need to be **a**, 2Tm 2:15
not **a** to call them brothers, Heb 2:11
is not **a** to be called their God, Heb 11:16
ASHER
Jacob's eighth son, born of Zilpah (Gn 30:13; 35:26). The tribe's territory was in the northwest on the Phoenician coast (Jos 19:24-31). Also, a town (17:7).
ASHERAH
cut down the **A** pole beside it. Jdg 6:25
and the 400 prophets of **A** 1Kg 18:19
an obscene image of **A**. 2Ch 15:16
ASHES
even though I am dust and **a** Gn 18:27
Tamar put **a** on her head 2Sm 13:19
the **a** spilled off the altar, 1Kg 13:5
put on sackcloth and **a**, Est 4:1
repent in dust and **a**. Jb 42:6
a crown of beauty instead of **a**, Is 61:3
put on sackcloth, and sat in **a**. Jnh 3:6
in sackcloth and **a** long ago! Mt 11:21
ASIA
prevented from speaking ... in ... **A**. Ac 16:6
churches in the province of **A**. Rv 1:4
ASIDE
Do not turn **a** to the right or Dt 28:14
Everyone has turned **a**; Ps 53:3
let us lay **a** every weight Heb 12:1
ASK
When your children **a** you, Ex 12:26
When your son **a-s** you Dt 6:20
A of Me, and I will make Ps 2:8
Two things I **a** of You; Pr 30:7
sought by those who did not **a**; Is 65:1
Give to the one who **a-s** you, Mt 5:42
you need before you **a** Him. Mt 6:8
Keep **a-ing**, and it will be given Mt 7:7
Holy Spirit to those who **a** Lk 11:13
A and you will receive, Jn 16:24
the Jews **a** for signs 1Co 1:22
You **a** and don't receive because
you **a** wrongly, Jms 4:3
ASLEEP
The child is not dead but **a**. Mk 5:39
as they were sailing He fell **a**. Lk 8:23
Lazarus has fallen **a**, Jn 11:11
We will not all fall **a**, 1Co 15:51
concerning those who are **a**, 1Th 4:13
ASSEMBLE
a the whole community Lv 8:3
A on the mountains of Samaria Am 3:9
to gather nations, to **a** kingdoms, Zph 3:8
to **a** them for the battle Rv 16:14
ASSEMBLY
sacred **a** on the first day and another
sacred **a** on the seventh. Ex 12:16
the **a** in front of the rock, Nm 20:10
His praise in the **a** of the godly. Ps 149:1
the **a** was divided. Ac 23:7
the **a** of the firstborn Heb 12:23
ASSOCIATE
you **a** with adulterers. Ps 50:18
Don't **a** with those who drink Pr 23:20
don't **a** with rebels, Pr 24:21
a with the humble. Rm 12:16
not to **a** with anyone who bears
the name of brother 1Co 5:11
don't **a** with him, 2Th 3:14
ASSURANCE
Holy Spirit, and with much **a**. 1Th 1:5
true heart in full **a** of faith, Heb 10:22

ASSURED
stand mature and fully **a** ..... Col 4:12
ASSYRIA
From that land he went to **A** ..... Gn 10:11
The king of **A** deported the
Israelites to **A** 2Kg 18:11
ASTONISHED
were **a** and said, "How did this ..... Mt 13:54
they were **a** at His teaching. ..... Mt 22:33
were **a**. "Where did this man get ..... Mk 6:2
disciples were **a** at His words. ..... Mk 10:24
all **a** at the greatness of God. ..... Lk 9:43
ASTRAY
who rejects correction goes **a**. ..... Pr 10:17
We all went **a** like sheep; ..... Is 53:6
their shepherds have led them **a**, ... Jr 50:6
and one of them goes **a**, ... Mt 18:12
you were like sheep going **a**, ... 1Pt 2:25
ATHALIAH
Wife of Jehoram and mother of Ahaziah, kings of Judah; descendant of Omri (2Kg 8:26). Encouraged Baal worship (8:27). Killed heirs and ruled after her son's death (11:1-3). Jehoiada the priest executed her and crowned Josiah, the only surviving heir (11:4-20).
ATHENS
City in Greece (Ac 17; 1Th 3:1).
ATHLETE
if anyone competes as an **a**, ... 2Tm 2:5
ATONEMENT
priest will make **a** on their behalf, ... Lv 4:20
make **a** before the LORD ..... Lv 14:31
is the Day of **A**. ..... Lv 23:27
ATTACK (v)
he may come and **a** me, ... Gn 32:11
I will **a** him while he is weak 2Sm 17:2
a worm that **a-ed** the plant, ... Jnh 4:7
ATTEMPTED
When the Egyptians **a** to do this, ... Heb 11:29
ATTENTION
to pay **a** is better than the fat 1Sm 15:22
Pay **a** to the sound of my cry, ... Ps 5:2
My son, pay **a** to my words; ..... Pr 4:20
pay **a** to the words of the wise, ... Pr 22:17
pay **a** to myths and endless 1Tm 1:4
give your **a** to public reading, ... 1Tm 4:13
not pay **a** to Jewish myths ..... Ti 1:14
more **a** to what we have heard ..... Heb 2:1
ATTITUDE
Make your own **a** that of Christ ..... Php 2:5
AUTHORITY
like one who had **a**, ... Mt 7:29
Son of Man has **a** on earth ..... Mt 9:6
All **a** has been given to Me ..... Mt 28:18
submit to the governing **a-ies**, ... Rm 13:1
there is no **a** except from God, ... Rm 13:1
rulers, against the **a-ies**, ... Eph 6:12
teach or to have **a** over a man; 1Tm 2:12
be submissive to rulers and **a-ies**, ... Ti 3:1
glory, majesty, power, and **a** ..... Jd 25
AVENGE
do not **a** yourselves; ..... Rm 12:19
how long until You judge and **a** ..... Rv 6:10
AVENGER
cities as a refuge from the **a**, ... Nm 35:12
AVOID
a irreverent, empty speech 2Tm 2:16
But **a** foolish debates, genealogies, ... Ti 3:9
AWAKE
when I **a**, I will be satisfied ..... Ps 17:15
or **a-n** love until ..... Sg 2:7; 3:5; 8:4
I **a-ned** you under the apricot tree. ..... Sg 8:5
He **a-ns** Me each morning;
He **a-ns** My ear to listen ..... Is 50:4
in the dust of the earth will **a**, ... Dn 12:2
Couldn't you stay **a** one hour? ..... Mk 14:37
we must stay **a** and be sober. 1Th 5:6
AWE
of the world stand in **a** of Him. ..... Ps 33:8
I tremble in **a** of You; ..... Ps 119:120
stand in **a** of the God of Israel, ... Is 29:23
AWE-INSPIRING
looked like the **a** Angel of God. ..... Jdg 13:6
the great and **a** God who keeps ..... Neh 1:5
the LORD Most High is **a**, ... Ps 47:2
His acts toward mankind are **a**. ..... Ps 66:5
You are **a** in Your sanctuaries. ..... Ps 68:35
LORD—the great and **a** God ..... Dn 9:4
great and **a** Day of the LORD ..... Jl 2:31
AWESOME
What an **a** place this is! ..... Gn 28:17
the great, mighty, and **a** God, ... Dt 10:17
glorious and **a** name—Yahweh, ... Dt 28:58
great and **a** Day of the LORD ..... Mal 4:5
AX
iron **a** head fell into the water, ... 2Kg 6:5
the **a** is ready to strike ..... Mt 3:10; Lk 3:9

AZARIAH
1. Prophet (2Ch 15:1-8).
2. King of Judah, also called Uzziah (2Kg 15:1-7).
BAAL
Israel aligned itself with **B** of Peor, ... Nm 25:3
the 450 prophets of **B** 1Kg 18:19
no longer call Me: My **B**. ..... Hs 2:16
who have not bowed down to **B**. ..... Rm 11:4
BAASHA
King of Israel (1Kg 15:16–16:7). Exterminated Jeroboam's family (15:29).
BABY
the **b** leaped inside her, ... Lk 1:41
you will find a **b** wrapped ..... Lk 2:12
b who was lying in the manger. ..... Lk 2:16
BABYLON
Mesopotamian city; place of captivity (2Kg 24; Dn 1:1-6); symbol of wickedness (Rv 17:5).
Therefore its name is called **B**, ... Gn 11:9
from a distant country, from **B**. 2Kg 20:14
went up from **B** to Jerusalem. ..... Ezr 1:11
By the rivers of **B** ..... Ps 137:1
B has fallen, has fallen. ..... Is 21:9
She who is in **B**, also chosen, ... 1Pt 5:13
It has fallen, **B** the Great ..... Rv 14:8
BACK (adv)
looked **b** and became a pillar ..... Gn 19:26
ahead 10 steps or go **b** 10 steps? 2Kg 20:9
plow and looks **b** is fit for ..... Lk 9:62
BAD
but a **b** tree produces **b** fruit. ..... Mt 7:17
B company corrupts good 1Co 15:33
BAG
in each man's sack was his **b** of ..... Gn 42:35
two different weights in your **b**, ... Dt 25:13
David put his hand in the **b**, ... 1Sm 17:49
weeping, carrying the **b** of seed, ... Ps 126:6
or **b-s** of deceptive weights? ..... Mc 6:11
wages into a **b** with a hole in it. ..... Hg 1:6
BAKED
b unleavened bread for them, ... Gn 19:3
b the dough they had brought ..... Ex 12:39
a grain offering **b** in an oven, ... Lv 2:4
BAKER
Egypt's cupbearer and his **b** ..... Gn 40:1
BALAAM
Prophet hired by King Balak of Moab to curse Israel (Nm 22). His donkey talked (22:21-30; 2Pt 2:16). He blessed Israel (Nm 23–24; Jos 24:10; Neh 13:2). Executed for practicing divination (Nm 31:8; Jos 13:22; 2Pt 2:15; Jd 11; Rv 2:14).
BALAK
King of Moab who hired Balaam to curse Israel (Nm 22–24).
BALDY
chanting, "Go up, **b**! 2Kg 2:23
BALM
Is there no **b** in Gilead? ..... Jr 8:22
BANDAGE
cleansed, **b-d**, or soothed with oil. ..... Is 1:6
LORD **b-s** His people's injuries ..... Is 30:26
Look, it has not been **b-d** ..... Ezk 30:21
healed the sick, **b-d** the injured ..... Ezk 34:4
and **b-d** his wounds, ... Lk 10:34
BANISH
plans so that the one **b-ed** from
Him does not remain **b-ed**. 2Sm 14:14
nations where I will **b** them. ..... Ezk 4:13
BANQUET
the king held a week-long **b** ..... Est 1:5
He brought me to the **b** hall, ... Sg 2:4
love the place of honor at **b-s**, ... Mt 23:6
a **b**, invite those who are poor, ... Lk 14:13
BAPTISM
Sadducees coming to ... his **b**, ... Mt 3:7
Where did John's **b** come from? ..... Mt 21:25
preaching a **b** of repentance ..... Mk 1:4
with the **b** I am baptized with? ..... Mk 10:38
baptized with John's **b**. ..... Lk 7:29
he knew only John's **b**. ..... Ac 18:25
we were buried with Him by **b** ..... Rm 6:4
one Lord, one faith, one **b**, ... Eph 4:5
buried with Him in **b**, ... Col 2:12
B ... now saves you 1Pt 3:21
BAPTIST
In those days John the **B** came, ... Mt 3:1
no one greater than John the **B** ..... Mt 11:11
Give me John the **B-'s** head ..... Mt 14:8
Some say John the **B**; ..... Mt 16:14
BAPTIZE
I **b** you with water for ..... Mt 3:11
I need to be **b-d** by You, ... Mt 3:14
b-ing them in the name of ..... Mt 28:19
to be **b-d** with the baptism I ..... Mk 10:38
and is **b-d** will be saved, ... Mk 16:16
Jesus also was **b-d**. ..... Lk 3:21

b-ing more disciples than John ..... Jn 4:1
will be **b-d** with the Holy Spirit ..... Ac 1:5
repent ... and be **b-d**, ... Ac 2:38
who were **b-d** into Christ Jesus
were **b-d** into His death? ..... Rm 6:3
Christ did not send me to **b**, but 1Co 1:17
all were **b-d** into Moses 1Co 10:2
we were all **b-d** by one Spirit 1Co 12:13
are being **b-d** for the dead? 1Co 15:29
BARABBAS
Insurrectionist released by Pilate instead of Jesus (Mt 27:16-26; Mk 15:7-15; Lk 23:18; Jn 18:40).
BARAK
Reluctantly joined Deborah to fight Canaanites (Jdg 4–5; 1Sm 12:11; Heb 11:32).
BARN
sow or reap or gather into **b-s**, ... Mt 6:26
I'll tear down my **b-s** and build ..... Lk 12:18
BARNABAS
Levite from Cyprus, named Joseph (Ac 4:36). Introduced Paul to Jerusalem church (9:26-27). Worked with Paul, initially as leader in Antioch (11:19-30), then on a journey (Ac 13–14), then in Jerusalem (15:1-21). Separated from Paul over whether to bring John Mark with them again (15:36-41).
BARREN
Sarai was **b**; she had no child. ..... Gn 11:30
No woman will miscarry or be **b** ..... Ex 23:26
b woman gives birth to seven, ... 1Sm 2:5
Rejoice, **b** one, ... Is 54:1
Blessed are the **b**, ... Lk 23:29
Rejoice, O **b** woman ..... Gl 4:27
BARTHOLOMEW
Apostle (Mt 10:3; Mk 3:18; Lk 6:14; Ac 1:13), possibly also called Nathanael (Jn 1:43-51).
BARUCH
Jeremiah's scribe (Jr 36).
BASHAN
strong ones of **B** encircle me. ..... Ps 22:12
BASIN
Make a bronze **b** for washing ..... Ex 30:18
he made 10 bronze **b-s** 1Kg 7:38
poured water into a **b** and began to ..... Jn 13:5
BASKET
Three **b-s** ... were on my head ..... Gn 40:16
she got a papyrus **b** for him ..... Ex 2:3
LORD showed me two **b-s** of figs ..... Jr 24:1
A **b** of summer fruit. ..... Am 8:1
a lamp and puts it under a **b**, ... Mt 5:15
they picked up 12 **b-s** full ..... Mt 14:20
pieces—seven large **b-s** full. ..... Mt 15:37
how many **b-s** you collected? ..... Mt 16:9
BATHING
he saw a woman **b** 2Sm 11:2
BATHSHEBA
Wife of Uriah the Hittite. David committed adultery with her, then married her (2Sm 11). Solomon's mother (2Sm 12; 1Kg 1–2).
BATTLE
the **b** is the LORD's. 1Sm 17:47
the **b** is not yours, but God's. 2Ch 20:15
clothed me with strength for **b**; ..... Ps 18:39
horse is prepared for ... **b**, ... Pr 21:31
or the **b** to the strong, ... Ec 9:11
b is not against flesh and blood ..... Eph 6:12
like horses equipped for **b**. ..... Rv 9:7
Magog, to gather them for **b**. ..... Rv 20:8
BEAR (n)
Whenever a lion or a **b** came 1Sm 17:34
two female **b-s** came out 2Kg 2:24
to meet a **b** robbed of her cubs ..... Pr 17:12
The cow and the **b** will graze, ... Is 11:7
He is a **b** waiting in ambush, ... Lm 3:10
second one, that looked like a **b**. ..... Dn 7:5
BEAR (v)
you will **b** children in anguish. ..... Gn 3:16
punishment is too great to **b**! ..... Gn 4:13
wife Sarah will **b** you a son, ... Gn 17:19
that **b-s** its fruit in season ..... Ps 1:3
He Himself **bore** our sicknesses, ... Is 53:4
yet He **bore** the sin of many ..... Is 53:12
but you can't **b** them now. ..... Jn 16:12
b-s all things, believes all 1Co 13:7
offered once to **b** the sins of ..... Heb 9:28
He Himself **bore** our sins 1Pt 2:24
tree of life **b-ing** 12 kinds of fruit ..... Rv 22:2
BEAST
Four huge **b-s** came up ..... Dn 7:3
b that comes up out of the abyss ..... Rv 11:7
a **b** coming up out of the sea. ..... Rv 13:1
calculate the number of the **b**, ... Rv 13:18
who had the mark of the **b** ..... Rv 16:2
who accepted the mark of the **b** ..... Rv 19:20
BEAT
saw an Egyptian **b-ing** a Hebrew, ... Ex 2:11
gave My back to those who **b** Me, ... Is 50:6

will **b** their swords into plows, Mc 4:3
they spit in His face and **b** Him; Mt 26:67
to **b** Him, saying, "Prophesy!" Mk 14:65
they stopped **b-ing** Paul. Ac 21:32
or box like one who **b-s** the air. 1Co 9:26
Three times I was **b-en** 2Co 11:25
when you sin and are **b-en**? 1Pt 2:20

BEAUTIFUL
but Rachel was shapely and **b**. Gn 29:17
Let a search be made for **b** young Est 2:2
How **b** you are, my darling. Sg 1:15; 4:1
How **b** on the mountains are Is 52:7

BEAUTY
gazing on the **b** of the LORD Ps 27:4
is deceptive and **b** is fleeting, Pr 31:30
b should not consist of outward 1Pt 3:3

BED
if I make my **b** in Sheol, Ps 139:8
under a basket or under a **b**? Mk 4:21
the marriage **b** kept undefiled, Heb 13:4

BEDROLL
pick up your **b** and walk! Jn 5:8

BEELZEBUL
if I drive out demons by **B**, Mt 12:27

BEER
he is to abstain from wine and **b**. Nm 6:3
Wine is a mocker, **b** is a brawler, Pr 20:1
Give **b** to one who is dying, Pr 31:6
they stagger, but not with **b**. Is 29:9

BEER-SHEBA
place was called **B** because Gn 21:31
Abraham settled in **B**. Gn 22:19
All the Israelites from Dan to **B** Jdg 20:1

BEFORE
B a word is on my tongue, Ps 139:4
No god was formed **b** Me, Is 43:10
Even **b** they call, I will answer; Is 65:24
B the rooster crows twice, Mk 14:72
B Abraham was, I am. Jn 8:58
who for the joy that lay **b** Him Heb 12:2

BEGGING
or his children **b** bread. Ps 37:25

BEGINNING
In the **b** God created the heavens Gn 1:1
of the LORD is the **b** of wisdom, Pr 9:10
of a matter is better than its **b**; Ec 7:8
I declare the end from the **b**, Is 46:10
In the **b** was the Word, Jn 1:1
Omega, the **B** and the End. Rv 21:6

BEHEADED
had John **b** in the prison. Mt 14:10
souls of those who had been **b** Rv 20:4

BEHIND
told Peter, "Get **b** Me, Satan! Mt 16:23
forgetting what is **b** Php 3:13

BELIEVE
Abram **b-d** the LORD, Gn 15:6
they did not **b** God or rely on Ps 78:22
The inexperienced **b** anything, Pr 14:15
Who has **b-d** what we have heard? Is 53:1
Do you **b** that I can do this? Mt 9:28
of these little ones who **b** in Me Mt 18:6
if you **b**, you will receive. Mt 21:22
or, 'Over here!' do not **b** it! Mt 24:23
Repent and **b** in the good news! Mk 1:15
is possible to the one who **b-s**. Mk 9:23
I do **b**! Help my unbelief. Mk 9:24
not doubt in his heart, but **b-s** Mk 11:23
b that you have received them, Mk 11:24
Don't be afraid. Only **b**, Lk 8:50
slow you are to **b** in your hearts Lk 24:25
so that everyone who **b-s** in Him Jn 3:16
you **b** in the One He has sent. Jn 6:29
Anyone who **b-s** has eternal life. Jn 6:47
you don't **b** Me, **b** the works. Jn 10:38
b-s in Me will never die Jn 11:26
Lord, who has **b-d** our message? Jn 12:38
B in God; **b** also in Me. Jn 14:1
world may **b** You sent Me. Jn 17:21
entered the tomb, saw, and **b-d**. Jn 20:8
seen Me, you have **b-d**. Those who
  b without seeing are blessed. Jn 20:29
written so that you may **b** Jn 20:31
B on the Lord Jesus, Ac 16:31
in Jesus Christ, to all who **b**, Rm 3:22
Abraham **b-d** God, and it was Rm 4:3
b in your heart that God raised Rm 10:9
b-s all things, hopes all things, 1Co 13:7
Just as Abraham **b-d** God, and it Gl 3:6
Since we **b** that Jesus died and 1Th 4:14
b-d on in the world, taken up 1Tm 3:16
I know whom I have **b-d** 2Tm 1:12
must **b** that He exists Heb 11:6
You **b** that God is one; ... The
  demons also **b** Jms 2:19
Abraham **b-d** God, and it was Jms 2:23
not seeing Him now, you **b** 1Pt 1:8
do not **b** every spirit, but test 1Jn 4:1
Everyone who **b-s** that Jesus is the
  Messiah has been born of God, 1Jn 5:1

BELIEVER
intended as a sign, not to **b-s** 1Co 14:22
what does a **b** have in common 2Co 6:15

BELLY
move on your **b** and eat dust Gn 3:14
For as Jonah was in the **b** of Mt 12:40

BELONG
that **b-s** to your neighbor. Ex 20:17
hidden things **b** to the LORD our
  God, but the revealed things **b** Dt 29:29
kingship **b-s** to the LORD; Ps 22:28
the leaders of the earth **b** to God; Ps 47:9
you may **b** to another—to Him Rm 7:4
we live or die, we **b** to the Lord. Rm 14:8
you **b** to Christ, and Christ to 1Co 3:23
Salvation **b-s** to our God, Rv 7:10

BELOVED
The LORD's **b** rests securely Dt 33:12
This is My **b** Son. I take delight Mt 3:17
My **b** in whom My soul delights; Mt 12:18

BELT
with a leather **b** around his waist, Mt 3:4
with truth like a **b** around your Eph 6:14

BENAIAH
Heroic warrior in charge of David's bodyguard (2Sm 8:18; 20:23; 23:20-23). Loyal to Solomon (1Kg 1; 4:4); executed Adonijah, Joab, and Shimei (2:25-46).

BENEFIT
and do not forget all His **b-s**. Ps 103:2
What will it **b** a man if he gains Mt 16:26
you have **b-ed** from their labor. Jn 4:38
It is for your **b** that I go away, Jn 16:7
what is the **b** of circumcision? Rm 3:1
Christ will not **b** you at all. Gl 5:2

BEN-HADAD
1. King of Aram in Asa's time (1Kg 15:18-20; 2Ch 16:2-4).
2. King of Aram from Ahab's time (1Kg 20; 2Kg 6:24; 8:7-13).
3. King of Aram in Jehoash's time (2Kg 13:24-25).

BENJAMIN
Second son of Rachel, twelfth son of Jacob (Gn 35:17-18,24). Tribe with the smallest territory; Jerusalem may have originally been in it (Jos 18:16; Jdg 1:21). Nearly wiped out (Jdg 20–21). Saul and Paul were Benjaminites (1Sm 9:1; Rm 11:1; Php 3:5).

BERNICE
Wife of King Agrippa (Ac 25:13,23; 26:30).

BEREA
sent Paul and Silas off to **B**. Ac 17:10

BETHANY
to **B**, and spent the night there. Mt 21:17
He led them out as far as **B**, Lk 24:50
in **B** ... where John was baptizing. Jn 1:28
Lazarus, from **B**, Jn 11:1

BETHEL
east of **B** and pitched his tent, Gn 12:8
and named the place **B**, Gn 28:19
He set up one in **B**, 1Kg 12:29

BETHLEHEM
B Ephrathah, you are small Mc 5:2
After Jesus was born in **B** Mt 2:1

BETRAY
When you have finished **b-ing**,
  they will **b** you. Is 33:1
Brother will **b** brother to death, Mt 10:21
a good opportunity to **b** Him. Mt 26:16
One of you will **b** Me. Mt 26:21
that man by whom He is **b-ed**! Lk 22:22
b-ing the Son of Man with a kiss Lk 22:48
He knew who would **b** Him. Jn 13:11
the night when He was **b-ed**, 1Co 11:23

BETTER
to obey is **b** than sacrifice, 1Sm 15:22
Your faithful love is **b** than life. Ps 63:3
B a little with the fear of Pr 15:16
B a meal of vegetables where Pr 15:17
B a dry crust with peace Pr 17:1
B to live on the corner of a roof Pr 21:9
b a neighbor nearby Pr 27:10
nothing **b** for man than to eat, Ec 2:24
B one handful with rest, Ec 4:6
B that you do not vow Ec 5:5
Your love is much **b** than wine, Sg 4:10
it is **b** that you lose one of your Mt 5:29
b for him if a heavy millstone Mt 18:6
it is **b** to marry than to burn 1Co 7:9
I will show you an even **b** way. 1Co 12:31
be with Christ—which is far **b** Php 1:23
the guarantee of a **b** covenant. Heb 7:22
it is **b** to suffer for doing good, 1Pt 3:17

BETWEEN
hostility **b** you and the woman,
  and **b** your seed and her seed. Gn 3:15
torch ... **b** the divided animals. Gn 15:17
the LORD judge **b** me and you. Gn 16:5
and to discern **b** good and evil. 1Kg 3:9
passed **b** the pieces of the calf Jr 34:19
lifted me up **b** earth and heaven Ezk 8:3
you murdered **b** the sanctuary Mt 23:35
distinction **b** Jew and Greek, Rm 10:12

BEYOND
not too difficult or **b** your reach. Dt 30:11
able to do above and **b** all Eph 3:20
about Christ, but goes **b** it, 2Jn 9

BIND
He **bound** his son Isaac Gn 22:9
b them as a sign on your hands, Dt 11:18
and **b-s** up their wounds. Ps 147:3
Always **b** them to your heart; Pr 6:21
B up the testimony. Is 8:16
whatever you **b** on earth is already
  bound in heaven, Mt 16:19; 18:18
and **bound** him for 1,000 years. Rv 20:2

BIRD
You may eat every clean **b**, Dt 14:11
Look at the **b-s** of the sky: Mt 6:26
b-s of the sky have nests, but Mt 8:20
worth much more than the **b-s**? Lk 12:24

BIRTH
a time to give **b** and a time to die; Ec 3:2
b of Jesus Christ came about Mt 1:18

BIRTHRIGHT
First sell me your **b**. Gn 25:31
b in exchange for one meal. Heb 12:16

BITE
anyone who is **bitten** looks at it, Nm 21:8
if you **b** and devour one another, Gl 5:15

BITTER
and made their lives **b** Ex 1:14
unleavened bread and **b** herbs. Ex 12:8
water at Marah because it was **b** Ex 15:23
Almighty has made me very **b**. Ru 1:20
pour out sweet and **b** water Jms 3:11

BITTERNESS
The heart knows its own **b**, Pr 14:10
All **b**, anger and wrath, Eph 4:31
that no root of **b** springs up, Heb 12:15

BLACK
I looked, and there was a **b** horse. Rv 6:5
the sun turned **b** like sackcloth Rv 6:12

BLAMELESS
b man You prove Yourself **b**; 2Sm 22:26
happy are those whose way is **b**, Ps 119:1
b in the day of our Lord Jesus 1Co 1:8
to be holy and **b** in His sight. Eph 1:4
so that you may be **b** and pure, Php 2:15

BLASPHEME
My name is continually **b-d** Is 52:5
He has **b-d**! Mt 26:65
He's **b-ing**! Who can forgive sins Mk 2:7
b-s against the Holy Spirit Mk 3:29
God is **b-d** among the Gentiles Rm 2:24
they may be taught not to **b**. 1Tm 1:20

BLASPHEMOUS
We heard him speaking **b** words Ac 6:11
and on his heads were **b** names. Rv 13:1

BLASPHEMY
b against the Spirit will not Mt 12:31
you've heard the **b**! Mt 26:65
to speak boasts and **b-ies**. Rv 13:5

BLAZE
fire from the LORD **b-d** among Nm 11:1
mountain was **b-ing** with fire. Dt 5:23
in the morning it **b-s** like Hs 7:6

BLAZING (adj)
into the furnace of **b** fire. Dn 3:20

BLEMISH
he must present one without **b** Lv 3:1
offered Himself without **b** to God Heb 9:14
a lamb without defect or **b**. 1Pt 1:19

BLESS
God **b-ed** the seventh day Gn 2:3
I will **b** you, Gn 12:2
B me—me too, my father! Gn 27:34
let You go unless You **b** me. Gn 32:26
the LORD **b-ed** the Sabbath day Ex 20:11
LORD **b** you and protect you; Nm 6:24
since He has **b-ed**, I cannot Nm 23:20
they curse, You will **b**. Ps 109:28
A generous person will be **b-ed**, Pr 22:9
b-es his neighbor with a loud Pr 27:14
the nations will be **b-ed** by Him Jr 4:2
from this day on I will **b** you. Hg 2:19
took bread, **b-ed** and broke it, Mt 26:26
b those who curse you, Lk 6:28
families of the earth will be **b-ed**. Ac 3:25

B those who persecute you; **b** ... Rm 12:14
When we are reviled, we **b**; ... 1Co 4:12
With it we **b** our Lord ... Jms 3:9

BLESSED (adj)
May you be **b** by the LORD, ... Ps 115:15
B is he who comes in the name of the LORD. ... Ps 118:26
Let your fountain be **b**, ... Pr 5:18
sons rise up and call her **b**. ... Pr 31:28
B are the poor in spirit, ... Mt 5:3
B is He who comes in the name ... Mt 21:9
You are the most **b** of women, ... Lk 1:42
who believe without seeing are **b**. ... Jn 20:29
more **b** to give than to receive. ... Ac 20:35
while we wait for the **b** hope ... Ti 2:13
B is a man who endures trials, ... Jms 1:12
B be the God and Father ... 1Pt 1:3
B is the one who reads and **b** ... Rv 1:3
B is the one who keeps ... Rv 22:7

BLESSING (n)
you will be a **b**. ... Gn 12:2
deceitfully and took your **b**. ... Gn 27:35
set before you a **b** and a curse: ... Dt 11:26
these **b-s** will come and overtake ... Dt 28:2
God turned the curse into a **b**. ... Neh 13:2
send down ... showers of **b**. ... Ezk 34:26
and honor and glory and **b**! ... Rv 5:12

BLIND (adj)
a **b** beggar, was sitting ... Mk 10:46
I was **b**, and now I can see! ... Jn 9:25
are wretched, pitiful, poor, **b**, ... Rv 3:17

BLIND (n)
I was eyes to the **b** ... Jb 29:15
LORD opens the eyes of the **b**. ... Ps 146:8
the eyes of the **b** will be opened, ... Is 35:5
the **b** see, the lame walk, ... Mt 11:5
Can the **b** guide the **b**? ... Lk 6:39
you are a guide for the **b**, ... Rm 2:19

BLIND (v)
deafen their ears and **b** their eyes; ... Is 6:10
the god of this age has **b-ed** ... 2Co 4:4
the darkness has **b-ed** his eyes. ... 1Jn 2:11

BLOCK (n)
I will bow down to a **b** of wood. ... Is 44:19
Christ crucified, a stumbling **b** ... 1Co 1:23

BLOOD
Whoever sheds man's **b**, his **b** will be shed by man, ... Gn 9:6
see the **b**, I will pass over you. ... Ex 12:13
This is the **b** of the covenant ... Ex 24:8
life of a creature is in the **b**, ... Lv 17:11
flesh and **b** did not reveal this ... Mt 16:17
this is My **b** ... the covenant; ... Mt 26:28
field has been called "**B** Field" ... Mt 27:8
sweat became like drops of **b** ... Lk 22:44
the moon to **b**, before the great ... Ac 2:20
declared righteous by His **b**, ... Rm 5:9
the new covenant in My **b**. ... 1Co 11:25
redemption through His **b**, ... Eph 1:7
battle is not against flesh and **b**, ... Eph 6:12
not by the **b** of goats and calves, but by His own **b**, ... Heb 9:12
without ... **b** there is no forgiveness ... Heb 9:22
One who came by water and **b**; ... 1Jn 5:6
set us free from our sins by His **b**, ... Rv 1:5
conquered ... by the **b** of the Lamb ... Rv 12:11

BLOODSHED
no one is guilty of **b**. ... Ex 22:2
b defiles the land, ... Nm 35:33
absolved of responsibility for **b**. ... Dt 21:8
Save me from the guilt of **b**, ... Ps 51:14

BLOSSOM (n)
cups shaped like almond **b-s**, ... Ex 25:33
has budded, if the **b** has opened, ... Sg 7:12
their **b-s** will blow away like dust, ... Is 5:24

BLOSSOM (v)
sprouted, formed buds, **b-ed**, ... Nm 17:8
the almond tree **b-s**, ... Ec 12:5
Jacob will take root. Israel will **b** ... Is 27:6

BLOT (v)
I will destroy them and **b** out ... Dt 9:14
b out all my guilt. ... Ps 51:9

BLOW (v)
B the horn in Zion; sound the ... Jl 2:1
The wind **b-s** where it pleases, ... Jn 3:8
b-n around by every wind ... Eph 4:14
seven trumpets prepared to **b** them. ... Rv 8:6

BOAST
who puts on his armor **b** like ... 1Kg 20:11
I will **b** in the LORD; ... Ps 34:2
The man who **b-s** about a gift ... Pr 25:14
Don't **b** about tomorrow, ... Pr 27:1
the one who **b-s** should **b** in this, ... Jr 9:24
one who **b-s** must **b** in the Lord. ... 1Co 1:31
so that no one can **b**. ... Eph 2:9
it **b-s** great things. ... Jms 3:5

BOASTFUL
b cannot stand in Your presence; ... Ps 5:5
Love does not envy; is not **b**; ... 1Co 13:4

BOAT
they left the **b** and their father ... Mt 4:22
the **b** was being swamped ... Mt 8:24
climbing out of the **b**, Peter ... Mt 14:29

BOAZ
Husband of Ruth (Ru 4:13), kinsman redeemer (2:20; 3:1; 4:3-10,16-17). Ancestor of David (4:21-22; 1Ch 2:11-12) and Jesus (Mt 1:5; Lk 3:32).

BODY
The eye is the lamp of the **b**. ... Mt 6:22
Take and eat it; this is My **b**. ... Mt 26:26
rescue me from this **b** of death? ... Rm 7:24
present your **b-ies** as a living ... Rm 12:1
b-ies are the members of Christ? ... 1Co 6:15
know that your **b** is a sanctuary ... 1Co 6:19
This is My **b**, which is for you ... 1Co 11:24
b is one and has many parts, ... 1Co 12:12
sown a natural **b**, raised a spiritual **b**. ... 1Co 15:44
out of the **b** and at home with ... 2Co 5:8
There is one **b** and one Spirit, ... Eph 4:4

BODILY
fullness of God's nature dwells **b**, ... Col 2:9

BOLD
but **b** toward you when absent. ... 2Co 10:1
Pray that I might be **b** enough ... Eph 6:20

BOLDNESS
speak God's message with **b**. ... Ac 4:31
in whom we have **b**, access, ... Eph 3:12
approach the throne ... with **b**, ... Heb 4:16

BONE
This one, at last, is **b** of my **b**, ... Gn 2:23
not break any of its **b-s**. ... Ex 12:46
b-s; not one of them is broken. ... Ps 34:20
a gentle tongue can break a **b**. ... Pr 25:15
valley; it was full of **b-s**. ... Ezk 37:1
are full of dead men's **b-s** ... Mt 23:27
Not one of His **b-s** will be ... Jn 19:36

BOOK
erase me from the **b** You have ... Ex 32:32
b of instruction must not depart ... Jos 1:8
I have found the **b** of the law ... 2Kg 22:8
be erased from the **b** of life ... Ps 69:28
no end to the making of many **b-s**, ... Ec 12:12
whose names are in the **b** of life. ... Php 4:3
written in the Lamb's **b** of life. ... Rv 21:27

BOOTH
The Festival of **B-s** to the LORD ... Lv 23:34
dwell in **b-s** during the festival ... Neh 8:14

BORN
a child will be **b** for us, ... Is 9:6
LORD called me before I was **b**. ... Is 49:1
I set you apart before you were **b**. ... Jr 1:5
who has been **b** King of the Jews ... Mt 2:2
you must be **b** again. ... Jn 3:7
as to one abnormally **b**, ... 1Co 15:8
since you have been **b** again ... 1Pt 1:23
who loves has been **b** of God ... 1Jn 4:7

BORROW
wicked **b-s** and does not repay, ... Ps 37:21
the **b-er** is a slave to the lender. ... Pr 22:7
one who wants to **b** from you. ... Mt 5:42

BOUNDARY
set all the **b-ies** of the earth; ... Ps 74:17
set the sand as the **b** of the sea, ... Jr 5:22

BOW (n)
placed My **b** in the clouds, ... Gn 9:13
bent their tongues like their **b-s**; ... Jr 9:3

BOW (v)
May ... nations **b** down to you. ... Gn 27:29
and **b-ed** down to my sheaf. ... Gn 37:7
Come, let us worship and **b** down; ... Ps 95:6
Every knee will **b** to Me, ... Is 45:23
coastlands of the nations will **b** ... Zph 2:11
every knee will **b** to Me, ... Rm 14:11

BOWL
one who dipped his hand with Me in the **b** ... Mt 26:23
the seven **b-s** of God's wrath ... Rv 16:1

BOZRAH
Edomite city (Gn 36:33; 1Ch 1:44; Is 34:6; 63:1; Jr 49:13,22; Am 1:12).

BRANCH
b of the LORD will be beautiful ... Is 4:2
a **b** from his roots will bear fruit. ... Is 11:1
raise up a righteous **B** of David. ... Jr 23:5
about to bring My servant, the **B**. ... Zch 3:8
I am the vine; you are the **b-es**. ... Jn 15:5
a wild olive **b**, were grafted in ... Rm 11:17

BREAD
eat **b** by the sweat of your brow ... Gn 3:19
Festival of Unleavened **B** ... Ex 12:17
man does not live on **b** alone ... Dt 8:3
You provided **b** from heaven ... Neh 9:15
b on the surface of the waters, ... Ec 11:1
Man must not live on **b** alone ... Mt 4:4
Give us today our daily **b**. ... Mt 6:11
took **b**, blessed and broke it, ... Mt 26:26
one who is dipping **b** with Me ... Mk 14:20
I am the **b** of life, ... Jn 6:35
breaking of **b**, and to prayers. ... Ac 2:42
the Lord Jesus took **b**, ... 1Co 11:23

BREAK *see also* BROKEN (adj)
I will **b** down your strong pride. ... Lv 26:19
I will never **b** My covenant ... Jdg 2:1
will **b** them with a rod of iron; ... Ps 2:9
three strands is not easily **broken**. ... Ec 4:12
He will not **b** a bruised reed, ... Is 42:3
long ago I **broke** your yoke; ... Jr 2:20
where thieves **b** in and steal. ... Mt 6:19
He will not **b** a bruised reed, ... Mt 12:20
bread, blessed and **broke** it, ... Mt 26:26
She **broke** the jar and poured it ... Mk 14:3
the Scripture cannot be **broken** ... Jn 10:35
they did not **b** His legs ... Jn 19:33
of His bones will be **broken**. ... Jn 19:36
Branches were **broken** off so that ... Rm 11:19
gave thanks, **broke** it, ... 1Co 11:24
to open the scroll and **b** its seals? ... Rv 5:2
war **broke** out in heaven: ... Rv 12:7

BREATH
breathed the **b** of life into ... Gn 2:7
Remember that my life is but a **b**. ... Jb 7:7

BREATHE
b-d the breath of life into ... Gn 2:7
Let everything that **b-s** praise ... Ps 150:6
b into these slain so that they ... Ezk 37:9
a loud cry and **b-d** His last. ... Mk 15:37
He **b-d** on them and said, ... Jn 20:22

BRIBE
not take a **b**, for a **b** blinds ... Ex 23:8
the one who hates **b-s** will live. ... Pr 15:27
love graft and chase after **b-s**. ... Is 1:23

BRICK
They had **b** for stone ... Gn 11:3
require the same quota of **b-s** ... Ex 5:8

BRIDE
rejoices over his **b**, so your God ... Is 62:5
the **b**, the wife of the Lamb. ... Rv 21:9

BRIGHT
suddenly a **b** cloud covered ... Mt 17:5
dressed in clean, **b** linen, ... Rv 15:6
the **B** Morning Star. ... Rv 22:16

BRIGHTER
shining **b** and **b**. ... Pr 4:18

BRING
brought each to the man to see ... Gn 2:19
b into the ark two of every ... Gn 6:19
LORD who **brought** you from Ur ... Gn 15:7
B My sons from far away, ... Is 43:6
anointed Me to **b** good news ... Is 61:1
B the full 10 percent into ... Mal 3:10
brought nothing into the world, ... 1Tm 6:7

BROKEN (adj) *see also* BREAK
sacrifice pleasing to God is a **b** spirit. God, You will not despise a **b** and humbled heart. ... Ps 51:17

BROKENHEARTED
He heals the **b** and binds up ... Ps 147:3
He has sent Me to heal the **b**, ... Is 61:1

BRONZE
So Moses made a **b** snake ... Nm 21:9
my arms can bend a bow of **b**. ... 2Sm 22:35

BROOD
B of vipers! Who warned you ... Mt 3:7

BROTHER
Am I my **b-'s** guardian? ... Gn 4:9
His **b-s** were jealous of him, ... Gn 37:11
pleasant it is when **b-s** can live ... Ps 133:1
a **b** is born for a difficult time. ... Pr 17:17
friend who stays closer than a **b**. ... Pr 18:24
B will betray **b** to death, ... Mt 10:21
no one who has left house, **b-s** ... Mk 10:29
b goes to law against **b**, ... 1Co 6:6
if food causes my **b** to fall, ... 1Co 8:13
not ashamed to call them **b-s**, ... Heb 2:11

BRUISED (adj)
will not break a **b** reed, ... Is 42:3; Mt 12:20

BUILD
let us **b** ourselves a city ... Gn 11:4
So he **built** it in seven years. ... 1Kg 6:38
Unless the LORD **b-s** a house, ... Ps 127:1
Wisdom has **built** her house; ... Pr 9:1
who **built** his house on the rock. ... Mt 7:24
on this rock I will **b** My church, ... Mt 16:18
be careful how he **b-s** on it, ... 1Co 3:10
but not everything **b-s** up. ... 1Co 10:23
built on the foundation of the apostles and prophets, ... Eph 2:20

BUILDING (n)
Do you see these great **b-s**? Mk 13:2
You are God's field, God's **b**. 1Co 3:9
we have a **b** from God, 2Co 5:1
b is being fitted together in Him Eph 2:21

BUILDER
The stone that the **b-s** rejected Ps 118:22
The stone that the **b-s** rejected Mt 21:42
whose architect and **b** is God. Heb 11:10

BULL
their hands on the **b-'s** head. Ex 29:10
unblemished **b** as a sin offering Lv 4:3
Many **b-s** surround me; Ps 22:12
I will not accept a **b** from Ps 50:9
Do I eat the flesh of **b-s** Ps 50:13
no desire for the blood of **b-s**, Is 1:11
impossible for the blood of **b-s** Heb 10:4

BURDEN (n)
bear the **b** of the people, Nm 11:17
Cast your **b** on the LORD, Ps 55:22
Day after day He bears our **b-s**; Ps 68:19
yoke is easy and My **b** is light. Mt 11:30
You load people with **b-s** Lk 11:46
Carry one another's **b-s**; Gl 6:2

BURDEN (v)
have **b-ed** Me with your sins; Is 43:24
you who are weary and **b-ed**, Mt 11:28
I will not **b** you, 2Co 12:14
the church should not be **b-ed**, 1Tm 5:16

BURIAL
Give me a **b** site among you Gn 23:4
she has prepared Me for **b**. Mt 26:12

BURN
Why isn't the bush **b-ing** up? Ex 3:3
b for **b**, bruise for bruise, Ex 21:25
b-ing on the altar continually; Lv 6:13
Israel did not **b** any of the cities Jos 11:13
to **b** their sons and daughters Jr 7:31
king not to **b** the scroll, Jr 36:25
the chaff He will **b** up with fire Mt 3:12
into the fire, and they are **b-ed**. Jn 15:6
if I give my body to be **b-ed**, 1Co 13:3
a third of the earth was **b-ed** up, Rv 8:7
lake of fire that **b-s** with sulfur. Rv 19:20

BURNING (adj)
turned from His **b** anger. Jos 7:26
my loins are full of **b** pain, Ps 38:7

BURNT
If his gift is a **b** offering Lv 1:3

BURST
the watery depths **b** open, Gn 7:11
the new wine will **b** the skins, Lk 5:37
falling headfirst, he **b** open Ac 1:18

BURY
so that I can **b** my dead. Gn 23:4
Joseph's bones ... were **b-ied** Jos 24:32
let the dead **b** their own dead. Mt 8:22
were **b-ied** with Him by baptism Rm 6:4
was **b-ied**, that He was raised 1Co 15:4
b-ied with Him in baptism, Col 2:12

BUSH
the **b** was on fire but was not Ex 3:2

BUSINESS
to mind your own **b**, 1Th 4:11
and do **b** and make a profit. Jms 4:13

BUSYBODIES
are also gossips and **b**, 1Tm 5:13

BUY
B—and do not sell—truth, Pr 23:23
b wine and milk without money Is 55:1
drove out all those **b-ing** and Mt 21:12
for you were **bought** at a price; 1Co 6:20
denying the Master who **bought** 2Pt 2:1
b from Me gold refined Rv 3:18
no one can **b** or sell unless Rv 13:17

BUYER
it's worthless!" the **b** says, Pr 20:14

CAESAREA
came to the region of **C** Philippi, Mt 16:13
a man in **C** named Cornelius, Ac 10:1
Paul should be kept at **C**, Ac 25:4

CAIAPHAS
High priest, along with his father-in-law Annas, who sentenced Jesus (Mt 23:6; Lk 3:2; Jn 18:13). Spoke prophetically (Jn 11:49-52). Threatened Peter and John (Ac 4:6).

CAIN
Firstborn of Adam and Eve; crop farmer; murdered his brother; God marked and banished him (Gn 4:1-25; Heb 11:4; 1Jn 3:12; Jd 11).

CALEB
Judahite who scouted Canaan and, along with Joshua, recommended invasion (Nm 13:30–14:38). Entered the promised land (Dt 1:36); received Hebron (Jos 14:13).

CALF
made it into an image of a **c**. Ex 32:4
bring the fattened **c** and slaughter Lk 15:23
not by the blood of goats and **c-ves** Heb 9:12

CALL
the LORD **c-ed** Samuel, 1Sm 3:4
I **c-ed** to the LORD in my distress; 2Sm 22:7
c on the name of your god, and I
  will **c** on the name of Yahweh. 1Kg 18:24
people who are **c-ed** by My name 2Ch 7:14
is near all who **c** out to Him, Ps 145:18
Woe to those who **c** evil good Is 5:20
c to Him while He is near. Is 55:6
I didn't come to **c** the righteous, Mt 9:13
Why do you **c** Me 'Lord, Lord,' Lk 6:46
He **c-s** his own sheep by name Jn 10:3
I do not **c** you slaves anymore, Jn 15:15
those He **c-ed**, He also justified; Rm 8:30
everyone who **c-s** on the name of Rm 10:13
God has not **c-ed** us to impurity, 1Th 4:7

CALLING (n)
God's ... and **c** are irrevocable. Rm 11:29
Brothers, consider your **c**: 1Co 1:26
walk worthy of the **c** you have Eph 4:1
confirm your **c** and election, 2Pt 1:10

CALM (n)
And there was a great **c**. Mt 8:26

CALM (v)
I have **c-ed** and quieted myself Ps 131:2

CAMEL
easier for a **c** to go through the eye Mt 19:24
gnat, yet gulp down a **c**! Mt 23:24

CAMP (n)
Jacob said, "This is God's **c**." Gn 32:2
outside the **c** and slaughtered Nm 19:3
go to Him outside the **c**, Heb 13:13

CAMP (v)
c around the tent of meeting Nm 2:2

CANA
a wedding took place in **C** of Galilee. Jn 2:1

CANAAN
Son of Ham, his descendants, and the land they populated (Gn 9:18-27; 10:15-19). God promised the land to Abraham (12:4-7; 17:8; Ex 6:4; 1Ch 16:15-18).

CANAANITE
commanded Jacob not to marry a **C** Gn 28:6
drive out the **C-s**, Amorites, Hittites, Ex 33:2

CAPERNAUM
went to live in **C** by the sea, Mt 4:13
teaching in the synagogue in **C**. Jn 6:59

CAPTIVE
the king of Babylon took him **c** 2Kg 24:12
took many **c-s** to Damascus. 2Ch 28:5
to the heights, taking away **c-s**; Ps 68:18
to proclaim liberty to the **c-s**, Is 61:1
to proclaim freedom to the **c-s** Lk 4:18
taking every thought **c** 2Co 10:5

CARE (n)
the sheep under His **c**. Ps 95:7
I was sick and you took **c** of Me; Mt 25:36
to an inn, and took **c** of him. Lk 10:34
casting all your **c** upon Him, 1Pt 5:7

CARE (v)
what is man, that You **c** for him, Ps 144:3
son of man, that You **c** for him? Heb 2:6

CAREFUL
be **c** not to forget the LORD Dt 6:12
Be **c** to obey all these things Dt 12:28
c attention, then, to how you walk Eph 5:15

CARELESS
to account for every **c** word Mt 12:36

CARMEL
gathered the prophets at Mount **C**. 1Kg 18:20

CARMI
Son of Reuben (Gn 46:9; Nm 26:6).

CARPENTER
Isn't this the **c-'s** son? Mt 13:55
Isn't this the **c**, the son of Mary, Mk 6:3

CARRY
I **c-ied** you on eagles' wings Ex 19:4
God **c-ied** you as a man **c-ies** his son Dt 1:31
No one but the Levites may **c** 1Ch 15:2
shepherd them, and **c** them forever. Ps 28:9
lambs in His arms and **c-ies** them Is 40:11
and He **c-ied** our pains; Is 53:4
He Himself ... **c-ied** our diseases. Mt 8:17
will not **c** out the desire of the flesh. Gl 5:16

CASE
let us argue our **c** together. Is 43:26

CAST (adj)
Do not make **c** images of gods Ex 34:17
his **c** images are a lie; Jr 10:14; 51:17

CAST (v)
c spells, consult a medium or Dt 18:11
He **c** the Pur (that is, the lot) Est 9:24
they **c** lots for my clothing. Ps 22:18
C your burden on the LORD, Ps 55:22
they **c** lots for My clothing. Jn 19:24
c-ing all your care upon Him, 1Pt 5:7

CATCH
your sin will **c** up with you. Nm 32:23
C the foxes for us—the little foxes Sg 2:15
now on you will be **c-ing** people! Lk 5:10
brought a woman **caught** in adultery, Jn 8:3
be **caught** up together with them 1Th 4:17
her child was **caught** up to God Rv 12:5

CATTLE
is Mine, the **c** on a thousand hills. Ps 50:10

CAUSE (n)
For You have upheld my just **c**; Ps 9:4
upholds the just **c** of the poor, Ps 140:12

CAUSE (v)
and **c-s** grass to grow on the hills. Ps 147:8
c one of these little ones to stumble Lk 17:2

CAVE
give me the **c** of Machpelah Gn 23:9
Then Saul left the **c** and went on 1Sm 24:7
hid in the **c-s** and among the rocks Rv 6:15

CEASE
not sin ... by **c-ing** to pray for you 1Sm 12:23
He makes wars **c** Ps 46:9
as for languages, they will **c**; 1Co 13:8

CELEBRATE
King David dancing and **c-ing**, 1Ch 15:29
C His deeds among the peoples. Is 12:4

CENTURION
a **c** came to Him, pleading with Him Mt 8:5
When the **c** saw what happened, Lk 23:47
in Caesarea named Cornelius, a **c** Ac 10:1

CERTIFICATE
he may write her a divorce **c**, Dt 24:1
He erased the **c** of debt, Col 2:14

CHAFF
But the **c** He will burn up with fire Mt 3:12

CHAIN
For this I am an ambassador in **c-s**. Eph 6:20
to be kept in **c-s** of darkness 2Pt 2:4

CHALDEA
Another name for the Babylonian empire (Jr 51:24; Ezk 12:13; 23:15).

CHALDEAN
Inhabitants of Chaldea (Gn 11:28). Known as sages or magicians (Dn 2:2; 4:7). Took Judah into exile (2Kg 25; 2Ch 36:17-19; Ezr 5:12; Jr 32).

CHAMPION
a **c** named Goliath, from Gath, 1Sm 17:4

CHANGE (v)
does not lie or **c** His mind, 1Sm 15:29
Can the Cushite **c** his skin, Jr 13:23
Because I, Yahweh, have not **c-d**, Mal 3:6
but we will all be **c-d**, 1Co 15:51
and they will be **c-d** like a robe. Heb 1:12
and He will not **c** His mind, Heb 7:21

CHANGERS
He overturned the money **c'** tables Mt 21:12

CHARACTER
c, and proven **c** produces hope. Rm 5:4

CHARGE (n)
Joseph was in **c** of the country; Gn 42:6
Above His head they put up the **c** Mt 27:37
the gospel and offer it free of **c**, 1Co 9:18

CHARGE (v)
Do not **c** your brother interest Dt 23:19
c that to my account. Phm 18

CHARIOT
came back and covered the **c-s** Ex 14:28
even though they have iron **c-s** Jos 17:18
because those people had iron **c-s**. Jdg 1:19
because Jabin had 900 iron **c-s**, Jdg 4:3
a **c** of fire with horses of fire 2Kg 2:11
covered with horses and **c-s** of fire 2Kg 6:17
Some take pride in a **c**, Ps 20:7
saw four **c-s** coming Zch 6:1
I will cut off the **c** from Ephraim Zch 9:10

CHARM
C is deceptive and beauty is Pr 31:30

CHEEK
My **c-s** to those who tore out My Is 50:6
if anyone slaps you on your right **c**, Mt 5:39

CHEERFUL
God loves a **c** giver. 2Co 9:7

CHEMOSH
Moab's god (Jdg 11:24; 1Kg 11:7,33).

CHERUB
He rode on a **c** and flew, 2Sm 22:11
The first **c-'s** height was 15 feet 1Kg 6:26

CHERUBIM
He stationed **c** with a flaming, Gn 3:24
there were four wheels beside the **c**, Ezk 10:9

CHIEF
the **c-s** of David's warriors 1Ch 11:10
rejected by the elders, the **c** priests, Mk 8:31

military census (2Sm 24; 1Ch 21); Adonijah and Solomon (1Kg 1–2).
Named Solomon as successor (1Kg 1:29-30). Died (2Sm 23:1-7; 1Kg 2:10-12). Ancestor of Jesus (Mt 1:1,6); Jesus is heir to his throne forever (Mt 12:23; 21:9; Mk 11:10; Lk 1:32; Rv 22:16).

DAY
God called the light "**d**," ... Gn 1:5
pursue me all the **d-s** of my life, ... Ps 23:6
This is the **d** the LORD has made ... Ps 118:24
Give us each **d** our daily bread. ... Lk 11:3
well that the **D** of the Lord will ... 1Th 5:2
one **d** is like 1,000 years, ... 2Pt 3:8

DEACONS
D, likewise, should be ... 1Tm 3:8

DEAD
and let the **d** bury their own **d**. ... Mt 8:22
He is not the God of the **d**, ... Mt 22:32
consider yourselves **d** to sin, ... Rm 6:11
you were **d** in your trespasses ... Eph 2:1
and the **d** in Christ will rise ... 1Th 4:16
also faith without works is **d**. ... Jms 2:26

DEAD SEA
The end of the Jordan River, forming the southeastern border of Canaan (Nm 34:3; Jos 15:5); also called the Sea of the Arabah (Dt 3:17; Jos 3:16; 12:3; 2Kg 14:25) and the eastern sea (Ezk 47:18; Zch 14:8).

DEAF
On that day the **d** will hear the ... Is 29:18
the **d** hear, the dead are raised, ... Mt 11:5

DEATH
but has passed from **d** to life. ... Jn 5:24
For the wages of sin is **d**, ... Rm 6:23
I hold the keys of **d** and Hades. ... Rv 1:18

DEBORAH
Prophet and judge (Jdg 4–5).

DEBTS
forgive us our **d**, as we also ... Mt 6:12

DECEIT
disputes, **d**, and malice. ... Rm 1:29
and no **d** was found in His mouth; ... 1Pt 2:22

DECEIVE
Let no one **d** you with empty ... Eph 5:6

DECREE
In those days a **d** went out from ... Lk 2:1

DEER
As a **d** longs for streams of ... Ps 42:1
makes my feet like those of a **d** ... Hab 3:19

DEFENSE
ready to give a **d** to anyone who ... 1Pt 3:15

DEFILES
out of the mouth, this **d** a man. ... Mt 15:11

DELIGHT (n)
his **d** is in the LORD's ... Ps 1:2
beloved Son. I take **d** in Him! ... Mt 3:17

DELIGHT (v)
rescued me because He **d-ed** in me. ... Ps 18:19
I **d** to do Your will, my God; ... Ps 40:8
just as a father, the son he **d-s** in. ... Pr 3:12
My beloved in whom My soul **d-s**; ... Mt 12:18

DELIVER
but **d** us from the evil one. ... Mt 6:13
He was **d-ed** up for our trespasses ... Rm 4:25

DELIVERER
my fortress, and my **d**, ... 2Sm 22:2; Ps 18:2

DELUGE
I am bringing a **d** ... Gn 6:17

DEMOLITION
for the **d** of strongholds. ... 2Co 10:4

DEMON
The **d-s** also believe—and they ... Jms 2:19

DEN
are making it a **d** of thieves! ... Mt 21:13

DENY
he must **d** himself, take up ... Mt 16:24
you will **d** Me three times! ... Mt 26:34
of religion but **d-ing** its power. ... 2Tm 3:5

DEPART
scepter will not **d** from Judah, ... Gn 49:10
is old he will not **d** from it. ... Pr 22:6
on the left, '**D** from Me, you who ... Mt 25:41

DEPTH
the **d** of the riches both of the ... Rm 11:33

DESCEND
the Spirit **d-ing** from heaven like ... Jn 1:32
The One who **d-ed** is the same as ... Eph 4:10
Himself will **d** from heaven with ... 1Th 4:16

DESERVE
has not dealt with us as our sins **d** ... Ps 103:10

DESIRE (n)
Your **d** will be for your husband ... Gn 3:16
carry out the **d** of the flesh. ... Gl 5:16
I have the **d** to depart and be ... Php 1:23

DESIRE (v)
For I **d** loyalty and not ... Hs 6:6
I **d** mercy and not sacrifice ... Mt 9:13; 12:7

But **d** the greater gifts. ... 1Co 12:31

DESOLATE
your house is left to you **d**. ... Mt 23:38

DESOLATION
set up the abomination of **d**. ... Dn 11:31
the abomination that causes **d**, ... Mt 24:15

DESPAIR (n)
we are perplexed but not in **d**; ... 2Co 4:8

DESPAIRED
so that we even **d** of life. ... 2Co 1:8

DESPISE
So Esau **d-d** his birthright. ... Gn 25:34
fools **d** wisdom and instruction. ... Pr 1:7
He was **d-d** and rejected by men, ... Is 53:3
devoted to one and **d** the other. ... Mt 6:24
God has chosen ... **d-d** things ... 1Co 1:28
a cross and **d-d** the shame, ... Heb 12:2

DESTINED
this child is **d** to cause the ... Lk 2:34

DESTROY
who is able to **d** both soul and ... Mt 10:28
if our earthly house, a tent, is **d-ed**, ... 2Co 5:1
who is able to save and to **d**. ... Jms 4:12

DESTRUCTION
Pride comes before **d**, ... Pr 16:18
road is broad that leads to **d**, ... Mt 7:13

DETERMINES
but the LORD **d** his steps. ... Pr 16:9

DEVIL
to be tempted by the **D**. ... Mt 4:1
who is called the **D** and Satan, ... Rv 12:9

DEVOUR
You **d** widows' houses ... Mt 23:14

DIE
from it, you will certainly **d**. ... Gn 2:17
Where you **d**, I will **d**, and there I ... Ru 1:17
but fools **d** for lack of sense. ... Pr 10:21
a time to give birth and a time to **d**; ... Ec 3:2
Even if I have to **d** with You, ... Mt 26:35
believes in Me will never **d** ... Jn 11:26
moment, Christ **d-d** for the ungodly ... Rm 5:6
living is Christ and **dying** is gain. ... Php 1:21
for people to **d** once ... Heb 9:27

DINAH
Daughter of Jacob and Leah (Gn 30:21). Raped by Shechem; avenged by Simeon and Levi (Gn 34).

DINNER
in to him and have **d** with him, ... Rv 3:20

DISCIPLE
A **d** is not above his teacher, ... Mt 10:24
and make **d-s** of all nations, ... Mt 28:19
come after Me cannot be My **d**. ... Lk 14:27
My word, you really are My **d-s**. ... Jn 8:31
and the **d-s** were first called ... Ac 11:26

DISCOURAGED
Do not be afraid or **d**, ... Jos 1:9

DISCUSS
"Come, let us **d** this," says the ... Is 1:18

DISEASE
He heals all your **d-s**. ... Ps 103:3
and healing every **d** and sickness ... Mt 4:23

DISGUISED
Satan himself is **d** as an angel ... 2Co 11:14

DISHONOR (n)
sown in **d**, raised in glory; ... 1Co 15:43

DISOBEDIENCE
through one man's **d** the many were ... Rm 5:19

DISOBEDIENT
spirit now working in the **d**. ... Eph 2:2

DISORDER
is not a God of **d** but of peace. ... 1Co 14:33

DISTINCTION
believe, since there is no **d**. ... Rm 3:22

DISTINGUISHING
to another, **d** between spirits ... 1Co 12:10

DIVIDED
They **d** my garments among ... Ps 22:18
Every kingdom **d** against itself ... Mt 12:25
Him they **d** His clothes ... Mt 27:35
Is Christ **d**? Was it Paul who was ... 1Co 1:13

DIVINATION
not to practice **d** or sorcery. ... Lv 19:26

DIVINE
For His **d** power has given us ... 2Pt 1:3

DIVISIONS
that there be no **d** among you, ... 1Co 1:10

DIVORCE
If he hates and **d-s** his wife, ... Mal 2:16
permitted you to **d** your wives ... Mt 19:8

DOCTRINE
teaching as **d-s** the commands of ... Mt 15:9
they will not tolerate sound **d**, ... 2Tm 4:3

DOERS
But be **d** of the word and not ... Jms 1:22

DOG
The **d-s** will eat Jezebel in the ... 1Kg 21:23
since a live **d** is better than a ... Ec 9:4
bread and throw it to the **d-s**. ... Mk 7:27

DONKEY
riding on a **d**, on a colt, the foal of ... Zch 9:9
mounted on a **d**, even on a colt ... Mt 21:5

DOOR
and the **d** will be opened to you ... Mt 7:7
I am the **d**. If anyone enters by ... Jn 10:9
I stand at the **d** and knock. ... Rv 3:20

DOORPOSTS
blood and put it on the two **d** ... Ex 12:7
Write them on the **d** of your house ... Dt 6:9

DOUBT (v)
of little faith, why did you **d**? ... Mt 14:31
If you have faith and do not **d**, ... Mt 21:21

DOVE
he sent out a **d** to see whether ... Gn 8:8
Spirit of God descending like a **d** ... Mt 3:16
serpents and as harmless as **d-s**. ... Mt 10:16

DRAW
D near to God, and He will **d** near ... Jms 4:8

DREAMS
your old men will have **d**, and ... Jl 2:28
and your old men will dream **d**. ... Ac 2:17

DRINK (v)
and so they all **drank** from it. ... Mk 14:23
all made to **d** of one Spirit. ... 1Co 12:13

DRIVE
did not **d** them out completely. ... Jos 17:13
He **drove** everyone out of the temple ... Jn 2:15

DRUNK (adj)
And don't get **d** with wine, ... Eph 5:18

DRUNKARD
a reviler, a **d** or a swindler. ... 1Co 5:11

DRUNKENNESS
envy, **d**, carousing, and anything ... Gl 5:21

DRY (adj)
and let the **d** land appear. ... Gn 1:9
D bones, hear the word of ... Ezk 37:4

DULL
D the minds of these people; ... Is 6:10

DUST
man out of the **d** from the ground ... Gn 2:7
remembering that we are **d**. ... Ps 103:14
all come from **d**, and all return to **d**. ... Ec 3:20
shake the **d** off your feet when ... Mt 10:14

DWELL
and I will **d** in the house of the ... Ps 23:6
the Messiah may **d** in your hearts ... Eph 3:17

DWELLING
house are many **d** places; ... Jn 14:2

EAGLE
I carried you on **e-s'** wings and ... Ex 19:4
they will soar on wings like **e-s**; ... Is 40:31
the left, and the face of an **e**. ... Ezk 1:10

EAR
otherwise they ... hear with their **e-s**, ... Is 6:10
has seen and no **e** has heard, ... 1Co 2:9
who has an **e** should listen to ... Rv 2:7

EARTH
God created the heavens and the **e**. ... Gn 1:1
The **e** and everything in it, ... Ps 24:1
His glory fills the whole **e**. ... Is 6:3
they will inherit the **e**. ... Mt 5:5

EARTHLY
They are focused on **e** things, ... Php 3:19

EARTHQUAKE
but the LORD was not in the **e**. ... 1Kg 19:11
A violent **e** occurred; ... Rv 6:12

EAST
As far as the **e** is from the west ... Ps 103:12

EASY
For My yoke is **e** and My burden ... Mt 11:30

EAT
You are free to **e** from any tree ... Gn 2:16
she took some of its fruit and **ate** it; ... Gn 3:6
words were found, and I **ate** them ... Jr 15:16
E this scroll, then go and speak ... Ezk 3:1
Everyone **ate** and was filled. ... Mt 14:20
They all **ate** and were filled. ... Mt 15:37
and said, "Take and **e** it; ... Mt 26:26
Get up, Peter; kill and **e**! ... Ac 10:13

EDEN
LORD God planted a garden in **E**, ... Gn 2:8

EGYPT
sold Joseph in **E** to Potiphar, ... Gn 37:36
Out of **E** I called My Son. ... Mt 2:15

EHUD
Benjaminite judge (Jdg 3:12-30).

ELAH
Son of Baasha; king of Israel (1Kg 16:6-14).

ELDERS
The **e** who are good leaders ... 1Tm 5:17

ELEAZAR
Son of Aaron; high priest (Ex 6:23; Nm 20:25-28). Helped Joshua distribute land (Jos 14:1).

ELECTION
to confirm your calling and **e**, ... 2Pt 1:10
ELI
High priest at Samuel's birth (1Sm 1–4). Blessed Hannah (1:17; 2:20). Failed to discipline his sons (2:12-17,22-36). Died when the ark was captured (4:11-18).
ELIAKIM
1. Son of Hilkiah; Hezekiah's administrator (2Kg 18:18; Is 22:20; 36:3).
2. Son of Josiah; king of Judah. Called Jehoiakim (2Kg 23:34; 2Ch 36:4).
ELIEZER
1. Abraham's servant (Gn 15:2).
2. Son of Moses (Ex 18:4; 1Ch 23:15).
3. Ancestor of Jesus (Lk 3:29).
ELIJAH
Prophet against Ahab and Ahaziah. Predicted famine (1Kg 17:1; Jms 5:17). Fed by ravens (1Kg 17:2-7); fed by widow (17:8-16; Lk 4:26); raised widow's son (1Kg 17:17-24). Defeated prophets of Baal (18:19-40). Fled Jezebel (19:1-3). Chose Elisha to succeed him (19:16,19-21); taken up into heaven (2Kg 2:1-12).
Forerunner to the Messiah, embodied in John the Baptist (Mal 4:5; Mt 11:14; 17:10-13; Lk 1:17). Appeared with Jesus (Mt 17:3-4).
ELISHA
Prophet; successor to Elijah (1Kg 19:16-21; 2Kg 2:1-18). Made bad water good (2:19-22); called bear to punish boys (2:23-24); provided water for army (3:13-22). Provided miraculous supply of oil for widow (4:1-7); granted son to barren woman and restored him to life (4:8-37). Healed Naaman and punished Gehazi (5:1-27). Made axe head float (6:5-7). Blinded Syrian army (6:8–7:20). A man was revived by touching his dead bones (13:20-21).
Made Hazael king of Syria (8:7-15) and Jehu king of Israel (9:1-13).
ELIZABETH
Mother of John the Baptist; Mary's relative (Lk 1).
EMPTIED
He **e** Himself by assuming .... Php 2:7
EMPTY (adj)
deceive you with **e** arguments, ... Eph 5:6
END (n)
but its **e** is the way to death. .... Pr 14:12
endures to the **e** will be delivered. .... Mt 24:13
He loved them to the **e**. .... Jn 13:1
Christ is the **e** of the law for .... Rm 10:4
END (v)
Love never **e-s**. But as for 1Co 13:8
ENDURES
the one who **e** to the end will .... Mt 10:22
hopes all things, **e** all things. 1Co 13:7
ENEMY
me in the presence of my **e-ies**; .... Ps 23:5
love your **e-ies** and pray for those .... Mt 5:44
The last **e** He abolishes is death 1Co 15:26
world's friend becomes God's **e**. .... Jms 4:4
ENLIGHTENED
eyes of your heart may be **e** .... Eph 1:18
ENOCH
Father of Methuselah (Gn 5:18-21); prophet (Jd 14); walked with God, and God took him (Gn 5:22-24; Heb 11:5).
ENSLAVED
want to be **e** to them all over again? .... Gl 4:9
ENSNARES
the sin that so easily **e** us, ... Heb 12:1
ENTANGLED
soldier gets **e** in the concerns 2Tm 2:4
ENTER
you will never **e** the kingdom of .... Mt 5:20
E through the narrow gate. .... Mt 7:13
he cannot **e** the kingdom of God. .... Jn 3:5
just as sin **e-ed** the world through .... Rm 5:12
ENTHRONED
e on the praises of Israel. .... Ps 22:3
ENTRUSTED
what has been **e** to me until that 2Tm 1:12
EPHRAIM
Son of Joseph (Gn 41:52); tribe with territory north and west of Bethel (Gn 48; Jos 14:4; 16:4-5); designation for Israel (Is 11:13; Jr 7:15; Ezk 37:16; Hs 5:13).
EQUAL
making Himself **e** with God. .... Jn 5:18
EQUALITY
did not consider **e** with God as .... Php 2:6
ERROR
from the **e** of his way will .... Jms 5:20
ESAU
Son of Isaac; elder twin of Jacob (Gn 25:24-26); rejected by God (Mal 1:2-3; Rm 9:13); sold birthright (Gn 25:30-34; Heb 12:16); tricked out of blessing (Gn 27:1-30; Heb 11:20); reconciled with Jacob (Gn 33:4-16). Progenitor of Edomites in Seir (Dt 2:4-29).
ESCAPE (n)
will also provide a way of **e**, ... 1Co 10:13
ESTABLISH
But I will **e** My covenant with .... Gn 6:18
ESTHER
Persian name of Hadassah, Mordecai's cousin (Est 2:7). Chosen queen of Persia (2:16-18); interceded at great risk to foil a plot to exterminate the Jews (Est 3–9).
ETERNAL
must I do to have **e** life? .... Mt 19:16
not perish but have **e** life. .... Jn 3:16
gift of God is **e** life in Christ .... Rm 6:23
incomparable **e** weight of glory. 2Co 4:17
may know that you have **e** life. 1Jn 5:13
ETERNITY
from **e** to **e**, You are God. .... Ps 90:2
has also put **e** in their hearts .... Ec 3:11
EVALUATES
The One who **e** me is the Lord. 1Co 4:4
EVANGELIST
prophets, some **e-s**, some pastors .... Eph 4:11
the work of an **e**, fulfill your 2Tm 4:5
EVE
First woman; wife of Adam (Gn 3:20; 4:1-2,25). Gave in to temptation (3:1; 2Co 11:3; 1Tm 2:13-14).
EVIL
of the knowledge of good and **e**. .... Gn 2:9
To fear the LORD is to hate **e** .... Pr 8:13
who call **e** good and good **e**, ... Is 5:20
but deliver us from the **e** one. .... Mt 6:13
protect them from the **e** one. .... Jn 17:15
is a root of all kinds of **e**, ... 1Tm 6:10
EXALT
let us **e** His name together. .... Ps 34:3
You are **e-ed** above all the gods. .... Ps 97:9
Righteousness **e-s** a nation, but .... Pr 14:34
humbles himself will be **e-ed**. .... Mt 23:12
the Lord, and He will **e** you. .... Jms 4:10
EXAMINE
So a man should **e** himself; 1Co 11:28
EXAMPLE
given you an **e** that you also .... Jn 13:15
these things became **e-s** for us, ... 1Co 10:6
EXCUSE (n)
they have no **e** for their sin. .... Jn 15:22
As a result, people are without **e**. .... Rm 1:20
EXIST
and through whom all things **e**, ... Heb 2:10
believe that He **e-s** and rewards .... Heb 11:6
EXPECT
coming at an hour you do not **e**. .... Mt 24:44
EXPOSE
so that his deeds may not be **e-d**. .... Jn 3:20
darkness, but instead, **e** them. .... Eph 5:11
EXTINGUISH
will be able to **e** the flaming .... Eph 6:16
EYE
e for **e**, tooth for tooth, ... Ex 21:24; Lv 24:20
For the **e-s** of the LORD range 2Ch 16:9
If your right **e** causes you to .... Mt 5:29
the speck in your brother's **e** but .... Mt 7:3
I pray that the **e-s** of your heart .... Eph 1:18
EYEWITNESSES
original **e** ... handed them down to us .... Lk 1:2
we were **e** of His majesty. 2Pt 1:16
EZEKIEL
Hebrew prophet at the time of the exile, writing from Babylon (Ezk 1:1; 2Kg 24:14-16). Wrote about the fall of Jerusalem (Ezk 33:21) and the ultimate restoration of the city and temple (Ezk 40–48).
EZRA
Priest and teacher of the law; leader of the returning exiles, sent by King Artaxerxes of Persia to reestablish worship in the temple (Ezr 7–8). Nehemiah's colleague (Neh 8:2,6; 12:31-37). Made priests stop intermarriage with foreigners (Ezr 9–10).
FACE
I have seen God **f** to **f**, ... Gn 32:30
the LORD spoke with Moses **f** to **f**, ... Ex 33:11
LORD make His **f** shine on you, ... Nm 6:25
a mirror, but then **f** to **f**. 1Co 13:12
and His **f** was shining like the sun .... Rv 1:16
FAILED
as though the word of God has **f**. .... Rm 9:6
FAINT (v)
they will walk and not **f**. .... Is 40:31
FAITH
righteous one will live by his **f**. .... Hab 2:4
If you have **f** the size of a mustard .... Mt 17:20
three remain: **f**, hope, and love. 1Co 13:13
for we walk by **f**, not by sight 2Co 5:7
grace you are saved through **f**, ... Eph 2:8
finished the race, I have kept the **f**. 2Tm 4:7
Now **f** is the reality of what is .... Heb 11:1
Now without **f** it is impossible .... Heb 11:6
source and perfecter of our **f**, ... Heb 12:2
FAITHFUL
goodness and **f** love will pursue .... Ps 23:6
Well done, good and **f** slave! .... Mt 25:21
God is **f** and He will not allow 1Co 10:13
He who calls you is **f**, who also 1Th 5:24
for He who promised is **f**. .... Heb 10:23
He is **f** and righteous to forgive 1Jn 1:9
FAITHFULNESS
to heaven, Your **f** to the skies. .... Ps 36:5
great is Your **f**! .... Lm 3:23
FAITHLESS
if we are **f**, He remains faithful, ... 2Tm 2:13
FALL
have sinned and **f** short of the .... Rm 3:23
FALSE
Do not give **f** testimony against .... Ex 20:16
Beware of **f** prophets who come .... Mt 7:15
F messiahs and **f** prophets will .... Mt 24:24
FAMILY
from whom every **f** in heaven and .... Eph 3:15
FAMINE
There was a **f** in the land, ... Gn 12:10
seven years of **f** will take place .... Gn 41:30
FAST (v)
After He had **f-ed** 40 days and 40 .... Mt 4:2
Whenever you **f**, don't be .... Mt 6:16
FASTING
come out except by prayer and **f**. .... Mt 17:21
FATHER
a man leaves his **f** and mother .... Gn 2:24
Honor your **f** and your mother so .... Ex 20:12
Eternal **F**, Prince of Peace. .... Is 9:6
Our **F** in heaven, Your name be .... Mt 6:9
that I had to be in My **F-'s** house? .... Lk 2:49
Stop turning my **F's** house into .... Jn 2:16
The **F** and I are one. .... Jn 10:30
In My **F-'s** house are many dwelling .... Jn 14:2
comes to the **F** except through .... Jn 14:6
FATHERLESS
A father of the **f** and a champion .... Ps 68:5
FAULT
Why then does He still find **f**? .... Rm 9:19
FAULTLESS
who are **f** in a crooked .... Php 2:15
FAVOR (n)
Noah ... found **f** in the eyes of .... Gn 6:8
for you have found **f** with God. .... Lk 1:30
FEAR (n)
salvation with **f** and trembling. .... Php 2:12
There is no **f** in love; instead,
perfect love drives out **f**, ... 1Jn 4:18
FEAR (v)
F the LORD your God, worship Him .... Dt 6:13
darkest valley, I **f** no danger, for .... Ps 23:4
but a woman who **f-s** the LORD will .... Pr 31:30
So the one who **f-s** has not reached 1Jn 4:18
FEASTS
I hate, I despise your **f**! .... Am 5:21
FEED
"**F** My lambs," He told him. .... Jn 21:15
FEEDING
and laid Him in a **f** trough .... Lk 2:7
FEET
You put everything under his **f**: .... Ps 8:6
is a lamp for my **f** and a light .... Ps 119:105
began to wash His disciples' **f** .... Jn 13:5
FELLOWSHIP
this is the law of the **f** sacrifice .... Lv 7:11
Or what **f** does light have with 2Co 6:14
FEMALE
He created them male and **f**. .... Gn 1:27
slave or free, male or **f**; .... Gl 3:28
FEW
are invited, but **f** are chosen. .... Mt 22:14
FIELD
how the wildflowers of the **f** grow: .... Mt 6:28
out in the **f-s** and keeping watch .... Lk 2:8
your eyes and look at the **f-s**, ... Jn 4:35
You are God's **f**, God's building 1Co 3:9
FIG
so they sewed **f** leaves together .... Gn 3:7
FIGHT (n)
Fight the good **f** for the faith; 1Tm 6:12
I have fought the good **f**, I have 2Tm 4:7
FIGHT (v)
The LORD will **f** for you; .... Ex 14:14
F the good fight for the faith; 1Tm 6:12
I have **fought** the good fight, I have 2Tm 4:7
FILL (v)
Be fruitful, multiply, **f** the earth, ... Gn 1:28
the God of hope **f** you with all .... Rm 15:13
but be **f-ed** with the Spirit .... Eph 5:18
FILTH
all things and consider them **f**, ... Php 3:8
FIND
who **f-s** a wife **f-s** a good thing .... Pr 18:22

Take the **h** of salvation, ... Eph 6:17
HELP (v)
I do believe! **H** my unbelief. ...... Mk 9:24
HELPER
I will make a **h** who is like him. ...... Gn 2:18
Lord is my **h**; I will not be afraid. ...... Heb 13:6
HELPLESS
For while we were still **h**, ... Rm 5:6
HEROD
1. The Great; King in Judea at the time of Jesus' birth; executed male babies (Mt 2).
2. Archelaus; son of 1. (Mt 2:22).
3. Philip; son of 1. (Mk 6:17).
4. Antipas; son of 1.; tetrarch of Galilee; arrested and executed John the Baptist (Mt 14:1-12).
5. Agrippa I; grandson of 1.; persecuted the church; died when he didn't give glory to God (Ac 12).
6. Agrippa II; son of 5. (Ac 25:13). Heard Paul's defense (25:22–26:32).
HERODIAS
Wife of Herod Antipas, formerly of Herod Philip; requested head of John the Baptist (Mt 14:3-11; Mk 6:17-28; Lk 3:19).
HEZEKIAH
Son of Ahaz; king of Judah (2Kg 18–20; 2Ch 29-32; Is 36–39). Reformer (2Kg 18:4; 2Ch 29–31). Healed of fatal illness (2Kg 20:1-11); showed treasuries to Babylonians (20:12-19).
HIDE (v)
they **hid** themselves from the LORD ...... Gn 3:8
h me in the shadow of Your wings ...... Ps 17:8
HILL
the cattle on a thousand **h-s**. ...... Ps 50:10
situated on a **h** cannot be hidden ...... Mt 5:14
HIRAM
1. King of Tyre; helped David build his palace and Solomon build the temple (2Sm 5:11; 2Kg 5). Manned Solomon's fleet (1Kg 9:27).
2. Craftsman; helped build the temple and its furnishings (1Kg 7:13-14); also called Huram (2Ch 4:11) or Huram-abi (2:13; 4:16).
HOLINESS
Who is like You, glorious in **h**, ... Ex 15:11
HOLY *see also* **HOLY SPIRIT**
you are standing is **h** ground. ...... Ex 3:5
H, **h**, **h** is the LORD of Hosts; ...... Is 6:3
HOLY SPIRIT
Third person of the Trinity, through whom God acts, reveals His will, empowers individuals, and discloses His personal presence.
or take Your **H** from me. ...... Ps 51:11
Father and of the Son and of the **H**, ... Mt 28:19
they were all filled with the **H** ...... Ac 2:4
were sealed with the promised **H**. ...... Eph 1:13
HONEY
land flowing with milk and **h** ...... Ex 3:8
HONOR (v)
H your father and your mother ...... Ex 20:12
HOPE (n)
This **h** does not disappoint, ... Rm 5:5
three remain: faith, **h**, and love. 1Co 13:13
Christ in you, the **h** of glory. ...... Col 1:27
HOPES (v)
all things, **h** all things 1Co 13:7
HOSANNA
H in the highest heaven! ...... Mt 21:9
HOSEA
Prophet in Israel near the end of the kingdom; his marriage modeled God's love and Israel's unfaithfulness (Hs 1–3).
HOSHEA
Son of Elah; last king of Israel (2Kg 15:30; 17:1-6).
HOUSE
who built his **h** on the rock. ...... Mt 7:24
HUMBLE (adj)
Moses was a very **h** man, ... Nm 12:3
HUMBLED (v)
He **h** Himself by becoming ...... Php 2:8
HUMILITY
clothe yourselves with **h** toward one 1Pt 5:5
HUNGER (v)
Blessed are those who **h** and thirst ...... Mt 5:6
HUNGRY
For I was **h** and you gave Me ...... Mt 25:35
HURAM *see* **HIRAM**
HURAM-ABI *see* **HIRAM**
HUSBAND
"Go call your **h**," He told her, ... Jn 4:16
for the **h** is head of the wife as ...... Eph 5:23
HYMNS
in psalms, **h**, and spiritual ...... Eph 5:19
HYPOCRISY
are full of **h** and lawlessness. ...... Mt 23:28
HYPOCRITE
you must not be like the **h-s**, ... Mt 6:5
H! First take the log out of ...... Mt 7:5
scribes and Pharisees, **h-s**! ...... Mt 23:13
I AM
I WHO **I**. ...... Ex 3:14
"**I**," said Jesus, ... Mk 14:62
Before Abraham was, **I**. ...... Jn 8:58
IDOL
Do not make an **i** for yourself, ... Ex 20:4
About food offered to **i-s**: 1Co 8:1
IMAGE
Let Us make man in Our **i**, ... Gn 1:26
He is the **i** of the invisible God ...... Col 1:15
IMITATORS
I urge you, be **i** of me. 1Co 4:16
IMMANUEL
have a son, and name him **I**. ...... Is 7:14
they will name Him **I**, which is ...... Mt 1:23
IMMORAL
associate with sexually **i** people 1Co 5:9
IMMORALITY
except for sexual **i**, and marries ...... Mt 19:9
Flee from sexual **i**! 1Co 6:18
Let us not commit sexual **i** as some 1Co 10:8
that you abstain from sexual **i**, ... 1Th 4:3
IMMORTAL
the King eternal, **i**, invisible 1Tm 1:17
IMMORTALITY
mortal must be clothed with **i**. 1Co 15:53
IMPERISHABLE
crown, but we an **i** one. 1Co 9:25
INCREASE
said to the Lord, "**I** our faith." ...... Lk 17:5
INHERIT
gentle, because they will **i** the earth. ...... Mt 5:5
INIQUITY
punished Him for the **i** of us all. ...... Is 53:6
INSPIRED
All Scripture is **i** by God and is 2Tm 3:16
INSULT (v)
you when they **i** you and ...... Mt 5:11
INTERCEDE
the Spirit Himself **i-s** for us with ...... Rm 8:26
He always lives to **i** for them. ...... Heb 7:25
INTERMARRY
Do not **i** with them. ...... Dt 7:3
INTERPRETATION
Don't **i-s** belong to God? ...... Gn 40:8
to another, **i** of languages. 1Co 12:10
comes from one's own **i**, ... 2Pt 1:20
INTERPRETER
But if there is no **i**, that person 1Co 14:28
INVISIBLE
His **i** attributes, that is, His ...... Rm 1:20
He is the image of the **i** God, ... Col 1:15
immortal, **i**, the only God, ... 1Tm 1:17
INVITE
a banquet, **i** those who are poor, ... Lk 14:13
INWARD
was You who created my **i** parts; ...... Ps 139:13
IRON
I sharpens **i**, and one man ...... Pr 27:17
ISAAC
Son of Abraham and Sarah; fulfillment of a promise (Gn 17:17; 21:5). God tested Abraham by asking him to sacrifice Isaac (Gn 22; Heb 11:17-19). Married Rebekah (Gn 24). Heir to Abraham's promise (Gn 25:5,11; Ps 105:9; Rm 9:7). Father of Esau and Jacob (Gn 25:21-26); blessed Jacob (Gn 27). Lied to Abimelech in Gerar about Rebekah (26:7-11). Died in Hebron (35:27-29).
ISAIAH
Son of Amoz; prophet to four kings of Judah (Is 1:1). Called (Is 6). Sons' names were symbolic (7:3; 8:3).
ISHMAEL
Son of Abraham and Hagar (Gn 16:11-15). Received a blessing but not the promise (17:18-21). Descendants are perpetual opponents of Israel (25:18).
ISRAEL
Name God gave Jacob (Gn 32:28; 35:10). Also his descendants—God's chosen people—and their land (Ex 3:16; 1Sm 13:19; 15:35; 1Kg 4:1; Mt 2:6,20; Php 3:5). In the divided kingdom, the northern (1Kg 12:20).
ISSACHAR
Son of Jacob and Leah (Gn 30:18). Tribe with territory from Jezreel to Tabor (Jos 19:17-23); its troops who rallied to David understood the times (1Ch 12:32).
ITCH
they have an **i** to hear something 2Tm 4:3
ITHAMAR
Fourth son of Aaron (Ex 6:23; 28:1; Nm 26:20; 1Ch 6:3; 24:1); took over priesthood when their brothers died (Lv 10:6,12,16; Nm 3:4; 1Ch 24:2); in charge of the Levites (Ex 38:21; Nm 4:28,33; 7:8).
JABEZ
Israelite who asked for and received a blessing (1Ch 4:9-10).
JABIN
A king of Canaan, whose commander Sisera was defeated by Israel (Jdg 4–5).
JACOB
Son of Isaac and Rebekah; younger twin brother of Esau (Gn 25:21-26). Took birthright (25:33); fled Esau (27:41–28:5). Received the promise (28:10-22). Worked for his wives (29:1-30). Wrestled with God (32:22-32); God changed his name to Israel (32:28; 49:2). Reconciled with Esau (33:4-16). Fathered the twelve tribes (29:21–30:24; 35:16-18). Went to Egypt (46:1-7). Died there, buried in Hebron (49:29–50:14). Ancestor of Jesus (Mt 1:2).
JAIRUS
Synagogue leader whose daughter Jesus restored (Mk 5:22-43; Lk 8:41-56).
JAMES
1. Apostle; son of Zebedee; brother of John (Mt 4:21; 10:2). At transfiguration (17:1); in Gethsemane (26:36-37). Martyred (Ac 12:2).
2. Apostle; son of Alphaeus (Mt 10:3).
3. Brother of Jesus (Mt 13:55; Gl 1:19). Believed after the resurrection (Jn 7:3; Ac 1:14; 1Co 15:7). Leader of church in Jerusalem (Ac 15; 21:18; Gl 2:9). Author (Jms 1:1).
JAR
with an alabaster **j** of pure and ...... Mk 14:3
JAWBONE
He found a fresh **j** of a donkey, ... Jdg 15:15
JEALOUS
is a consuming fire, a **j** God. ...... Dt 4:24
JEHOAHAZ
1. Son of Jehu; king of Israel (2Kg 13:1-9).
2. Son of Josiah; king of Judah (2Kg 23:30-34). Called Shallum (Jr 22:11).
JEHOASH
1. Alternate name of Joash son of Ahaziah, king of Judah (2Kg 12).
2. Son of Jehoahaz; king of Israel (2Kg 13:10–14:13).
JEHOIACHIN
Son of Jehoiakim; king of Judah (2Kg 24:6). Also called Jeconiah or Coniah (Jr 22:24; 24:1). Exiled (2Kg 24:10-17) but later favored (25:27-30).
JEHOIAKIM
Son of Josiah; king of Judah. Succeeded his brother Jehoahaz; name changed from Eliakim by Neco (2Kg 23:34). Burned Jeremiah's scroll (Jr 36). Became vassal of Babylon; later rebelled and was defeated (2Kg 24:1-6; Dn 1:2).
JEHORAM
1. Alternate form of Joram, son of Ahab; king of Israel (2Kg 3:1).
2. Son of Jehoshaphat; king of Judah (2Kg 8:16-24; 2Ch 21). Ahab's son-in-law (2Kg 8:18). Edom gained independence during his reign (8:20).
JEHOSHAPHAT
1. Son of Asa; king of Judah (1Kg 15:24). Initially faithful, strong, blessed (2Ch 17). Then married Ahab's daughter Athaliah and formed alliances with Ahab and Joram, kings of Israel (1Kg 22; 2Kg 3; 8:26; 2Ch 18; 20).
2. Valley of judgment (Jl 3:2,12).
JEHU
1. Son of Hanani; prophet against Baasha king of Israel (1Kg 16:1-12).
2. Son of Jehoshaphat; king of Israel. Anointed by Elisha's servant; executed Ahaziah king of Judah, Joram, Jezebel and the house of Ahab in Israel, and the worshipers of Baal (2Kg 9–10; cp. 1Kg 19:16-17).
JEPHTHAH
Gileadite judge who made rash vow affecting his daughter (Jdg 11–12; 1Sm 12:11; Heb 11:32).
JEREMIAH
Prophet to Judah in the time leading up to the exile (Jr 1:1-3). Put in stocks (20:1-3), threatened (Jr 26), opposed (Jr 28), imprisoned (32:2; 37), censured (Jr 36), and thrown into a cistern (Jr 38). Taken to Egypt against his will (Jr 43).
JEROBOAM
1. Son of Nebat; Solomon's servant; rebelled; first king of Israel (1Kg 11:26–12:20). Judged for notorious idolatry (12:25–14:20).
2. Son of Joash, king of Israel (2Kg 14:23-29).
JERUSALEM
Formerly called Salem (Gn 14:18; Ps 76:2) or Jebus (Jos 18:28; 1Ch 11:4). David conquered it and made it his capital (2Sm 5:5-9); Solomon built temple, palace, and fortifications (1Kg 3:1). Conquered by Babylon (2Kg 24:10-12). Rebuilt and resettled after the exile (Ezr 1; Neh 12:27). Jesus visited (Mt 21:1; Jn 2:13); mourned (Mt 23:37). Important city in early church (Ac 15:4). New Jerusalem promised (Rv 3:12; 21:2,10).
JESSE
David's father (Ru 4:17-22; 1Sm 16; 1Ch 2:12-16; Mt 1:5-6; Lk 3:32).
JESUS
Messiah and Lord (Ac 2:36; Eph 3:11; 1Pt 3:15). Born in Bethlehem (Mt 1:18-25; Lk 2:1-7) to a virgin, Mary

(Mt 1:20; Lk 1:26-38). Genealogy (Mt 1:1-17; Lk 3:23-38). Raised in Nazareth (Mt 2:19-23; Lk 2:39-40). Visited the temple at age 12 (Lk 2:41-50).

Baptized by John (Mt 3:13-17; Lk 3:21). Tempted in the wilderness (Mt 4:1-11; Lk 4:1-13). Chose apostles (Lk 5:1-11,27-28; 6:12-16; Jn 1:35-51).

Transformation (Mt 17:1-9; Mk 9:2-10). Triumphal entry into Jerusalem (Mt 21:1-11; Lk 19:28-40). Betrayal and arrest (Mt 26:17-25,47-56; Mk 14:17-21,43-50; Lk 22:1-6,47-54), trial (Mt 26:57-66; 27:11-31; Mk 14:53-65; 15:1-20; Lk 22:66–23:25), crucifixion (Mt 27:32-56; Mk 15:21-39; Lk 23:32-49), and resurrection (Mt 28; Mk 16; Lk 24; Jn 20–21).

JETHRO
Priest of Midian; Moses' father-in-law and adviser (Ex 3:1; 4:18; 18). Also called Reuel (2:18).

JEW
first to the **J**, and also to the .... Rm 1:16

JEZEBEL
Wife of King Ahab of Israel, daughter of the king of Sidon; brought Baal worship to Israel (1Kg 16:31-33). Killed prophets and threatened Elijah (18:4,13; 19:1-2). Killed by Jehu (2Kg 9:30-37) in fulfillment of prophecy (1Kg 21). Name used as a label (Rv 2:20).

JOAB
Son of Zeruiah; David's nephew and commander of his troops (1Ch 2:16; 11:6). Killed Abner (2Sm 3:22-39), Absalom (2Sm 18), Amasa, and Sheba (2Sm 20). Sided with Adonijah (1Kg 1:7,19); David told Solomon to execute him (2:5-6,28-35).

JOASH
1. Son of Ahaziah; king of Judah (2Kg 12). Protected by Jehoiada (2Kg 11). Repaired temple (2Ch 24:4-14).
2. Alternate name of Jehoash son of Jehoahaz, king of Israel (2Kg 13:10).

JOB
Wealthy patriarch. His book tells of his testing (Jb 1–2), perseverance (Jb 3–37), rebuke (Jb 38–41), and vindication (Jb 42; Jms 5:11).

JOEL
Son of Pethuel; prophet who urged priests to call Judah to repentance; depicted calamities (Jl 1:1–2:11); predicted the Messiah (2:21-32; Ac 2:16).

JOHN
1. The baptizer; son of Zechariah; prophet. Annunciation and birth (Lk 1:5-25,57-66). Preached repentance, announced the coming Messiah (Mt 3:1-12; Mk 1:1-8; Lk 3:1-18; 7:27-28), and baptized Jesus (Mt 3:13-15; Mk 1:9; Lk 3:21-22). Fulfilled the role of Elijah (Mt 11:13-14; 17:12-13; Mk 9:12-13; Mt 3:4; cp. 2Kg 1:8). Asked Jesus to verify His identity (Mt 11:2-6; Lk 7:18-23). Beheaded by Herod Antipas (Mt 14:1-12; Mk 6:14-29; Lk 3:19-20; 9:7-9).
2. Apostle; son of Zebedee; brother of James. Call (Mt 4:21-22; Mk 1:19-20). Among the inner three at special occasions (Mk 9:2; 14:32-33). With James, called "Sons of Thunder" (Mk 3:17); asked for places of honor (Mk 10:35-41). Often with Peter (Ac 1:13; 3:1-11; 4:13-20; 8:14); a leader in Jerusalem (Gl 2:9). In his gospel, called the disciple Jesus loved (Jn 13:23; 19:26; 20:2; 21:7,20); also wrote three letters and Revelation.
3. John Mark *see* MARK

JOINED
what God has **j** together, ... Mt 19:6

JONAH
Son of Amittai; prophet at the time of Jeroboam II (2Kg 14:23-27). Rejected God's call to preach in Nineveh; swallowed by a great fish (Jnh 1). Prayed (Jnh 2); preached repentance in Nineveh (Jnh 3); scolded by God for his anger (Jnh 4). Used as an example (Mt 12:39-41; 16:4; Lk 11:29-32).

JONATHAN
Son of Saul; friend of David (1Sm 18:1-4; 19:1-7; 20; 23:16-18). Killed in battle (31:1-13); mourned by David (2Sm 1:17-27).

JORAM
1. Son of Ahab; king of Israel (2Kg 3). Succeeded his brother Ahaziah (1:17). Attacked Moab with the help of Judah, Edom, and Elisha (3:4-27). Wounded by Arameans (8:28); killed by Jehu (9:14-26).
2. Alternate form of Jehoram, son of Jehoshaphat; king of Judah (2Kg 8:16-24; 2Ch 21).

JORDAN
dry ground in the middle of the **J**, ... Jos 3:17
Jesus came ... to John at the **J**, ... Mt 3:13

JOSEPH
1. Son of Jacob and Rachel. Sold into slavery in Egypt (Gn 37); imprisoned on false accusations (Gn 39); became Pharaoh's second in command (41:39-45); sold grain to brothers (Gn 42–45); enabled his father and brothers to move to Egypt (Gn 46–47). Sons Ephraim and Manasseh each became tribes (Gn 48). Died in Egypt, buried in Canaan (50:22-26; Ex 13:19; Jos 24:32; Ac 7:16).
2. Husband of Mary; foster father of Jesus (Mt 1:16,20; Lk 2:4; 3:23; 4:22; Jn 1:45; 6:42). Carpenter (Mt 13:55). Told in a dream not to divorce Mary (Mt 1:18-25); told in a dream to flee to Egypt (2:13-23).
3. Of Arimathea; a righteous member of the Sanhedrin who sought the kingdom of God; put Jesus' body in his tomb (Mt 27:57-60; Mk 15:43-46; Lk 23:50-53; Jn 19:38-42).

JOSHUA
Son of Nun; successor to Moses as leader of Israelites. Leader of Moses' army (Ex 17:8-13); Moses' servant on Mt. Sinai (32:17). Scouted Canaan and, along with Caleb, recommended invasion (Nm 13:30–14:38). Chosen, commissioned, and encouraged by God (Nm 27:15-23; Dt 31:14-15,23; Jos 1:1-9).

Conquered Canaan (Jos 2–11) and distributed the land (Jos 12–21). Renewed the covenant and charged the people (Jos 23–24).

JOSIAH
Son of Amon; king of Israel. Became king at age 8 (2Kg 21:19–22:2). Found the book of the law and instituted reforms (2Kg 22–23; 2Ch 34–35). Died resisting Pharaoh Neco (2Kg 23:29-30; 2Ch 35:20-25).

JOTHAM
1. Son of Gideon (Jdg 9).
2. Son of Uzziah/Azariah; co-regent (2Kg 15:5), then king of Judah (15:32-38).

JOY
Restore the **j** of Your salvation .... Ps 51:12
news of great **j** that will be for .... Lk 2:10
who for the **j** that lay before Him .... Heb 12:2

JUDAH
Son of Jacob and Leah (Gn 29:35); tribe with large territory west and south of Jerusalem (Jos 15:20-63). Tricked by daughter-in-law (Gn 38). Ancestor of David and Jesus (Gn 49:10; 1Sm 17:12; Mt 1:3,6,16; Rv 5:5). Name of the southern part of the divided kingdom (2Kg 12:20; 14:21; 23:27; Ezk 37:15-23) and the Persian province in the restoration (Neh 5:14; Hg 1:1).

JUDAS
1. Iscariot; apostle (Mt 10:4); treasurer, miser, thief (Jn 12:4-6). Betrayed Jesus (Mt 26:21-25,44-50; Lk 22:3-6; Jn 13:21-30); committed suicide (Mt 27:3-10; Ac 1:16-20).
2. Son of James; apostle; called Thaddaeus (Mt 10:3; Mk 3:18; Lk 6:16; Jn 14:22).
3. Brother of Jesus (Mt 13:55; Mk 6:3); also called Jude.

JUDE
Brother of Jesus; also called Judas; author (Mt 13:55; Jd 1).

JUDEA
Another name for the territory of Judah.
Jesus was born in Bethlehem of **J** .... Mt 2:1
in Jerusalem, in all **J** and Samaria, ... Ac 1:8

JUDGE (n)
Won't the **J** of all the earth do .... Gn 18:25
Lord raised up **j-s**, who saved them .... Jdg 2:16

JUDGE (v)
Do not **j**, so that you won't be **j-d**. .... Mt 7:1

JUDGMENT
the wicked will not survive the **j**, ... Ps 1:5
die once—and after this, **j**— .... Heb 9:27

JUSTIFICATION
and raised for our **j**. .... Rm 4:25

JUSTIFY
But wanting to **j** himself, he .... Lk 10:29
They are **j-ied** freely by His grace .... Rm 3:24
God is the One who **j-ies**. .... Rm 8:33
no one is **j-ied** by the works of the .... Gl 2:16

KADESH
Oasis, also called Kadesh-barnea. Where Abraham fought the Amalekites (Gn 14:7). Where the Israelites camped, they sent out spies, and Moses struck the rock (Nm 13:26; 20:1,11; 27:14; 32:8; Dt 1:46; 9:23; Jdg 11:16-17). Southern limit of Judah (Nm 34:4; Jos 10:41; 15:3).

KEEP
K asking, and it will be given .... Mt 7:7
the race, I have **kept** the faith. 2Tm 4:7

KEYS
give you the **k** of the kingdom .... Mt 16:19

KILL
a time to **k** and a time to heal; .... Ec 3:3
for the letter **k-s**, but the Spirit 2Co 3:6

KIND (adj)
Love is patient; love is **k**. 1Co 13:4

KINDNESS
that God's **k** is intended to lead .... Rm 2:4

KING
days there was no **k** in Israel; .... Jdg 17:6
who has been born **K** of the Jews? .... Mt 2:2
K OF **K-S** AND LORD OF .... Rv 19:16

KINGDOM *see also* KINGDOM OF GOD; KINGDOM OF HEAVEN
Your **k** come. Your will be done .... Mt 6:10

KINGDOM OF GOD (GOD'S KINGDOM)
But seek first the **k** and His .... Mt 6:33

KINGDOM OF HEAVEN
Repent, because the **k** has come near! .... Mt 3:2
I will give you the keys of the **k**, ... Mt 16:19

KISS (n)
betraying the Son of Man with a **k**? .... Lk 22:48

KISS (v)
The One I **k**, He's the One; .... Mt 26:48

KNEE
of Jesus every **k** should bow .... Php 2:10

KNIT
You **k** me together in my mother's .... Ps 139:13

KNOCK
Keep **k-ing**, and the door will be .... Mt 7:7
I stand at the door and **k**. .... Rv 3:20

KNOW
be like God, **k-ing** good and evil. .... Gn 3:5
But I **k** my living Redeemer, ... Jb 19:25
and **k** that I am God, ... Ps 46:10
You have searched me and **k-n** me. .... Ps 139:1
Search me, God, and **k** my heart; .... Ps 139:23
your Father **k-s** the things you need .... Mt 6:8
I never **knew** you! Depart from Me, ... Mt 7:23
I **k** My own sheep, and they **k** Me, ... Jn 10:14
to **k** Him and the power of His .... Php 3:10

KNOWLEDGE
the tree of the **k** of good and evil. .... Gn 2:9
to know ... love that surpasses **k**, ... Eph 3:19

KORAH
1. Led rebellion against Moses (Nm 16; Jd 11).
2. Kohathite Levite (Ex 6:21; 1Ch 6:22); ancestor of temple singers (2Ch 20:19; Pss 42; 44–49; 84–85; 87–88).

LABAN
Rebekah's brother (Gn 24:29); father of Leah and Rachel (Gn 29:15-30).

LABOR (v)
You are to **l** six days and do all .... Ex 20:9

LABORER
The **l** is worthy of his wages. 1Tm 5:18

LACK
shepherd; there is nothing I **l**. .... Ps 23:1

LAMB
God Himself will provide the **l** .... Gn 22:8
Like a **l** led to the slaughter .... Is 53:7
L of God, who takes away the sin .... Jn 1:29
"Feed My **l-s**," He told him. .... Jn 21:15

LAMP
Your word is a **l** for my feet and .... Ps 119:105

LAND
forgive their sin, and heal their **l**. 2Ch 7:14

LANGUAGE
began to speak in different **l-s**, ... Ac 2:4
If I speak the **l-s** of men and of 1Co 13:1

LAST (adj)
are first will be **l**, and the **l** first. .... Mt 19:30
The **l** enemy He abolishes is 1Co 15:26

LAST (n)
I am the First and the **L**, ... Rv 1:17

LATER
Lord your God in **l** days and obey .... Dt 4:30

LAUGH
Why did Sarah **l**, ... Gn 18:13
The One enthroned in heaven **l-s**; .... Ps 2:4

LAW
assume that I came to destroy the **L** .... Mt 5:17
All the **L** and the Prophets depend .... Mt 22:40
are not under **l** but under grace .... Rm 6:14

LAY
I **l** down My life for the sheep. .... Jn 10:15

LAZARUS
1. Poor man in Jesus' parable (Lk 16:19-31).
2. Brother of Mary and Martha; friend of Jesus (Jn 11:1-5). Died; revived by Jesus (11:3-44). Endangered because of fame (12:9-11,17).

LEAD (v)
of cloud to **l** them on their way .... Ex 13:21
He **l-s** me beside quiet waters. .... Ps 23:2
Like a lamb **led** to the slaughter .... Is 53:7
All those **led** by God's Spirit are .... Rm 8:14

LEAH
Wife of Jacob; mother of Reuben, Simeon, Levi, Judah, Issachar, Zebulun, and Dinah (Gn 29:16-35; 30:14-21).

LEARN
take up My yoke and **l** from Me, ... Mt 11:29
for I have **l-ed** to be content in .... Php 4:11

LEAVE
This is why a man **l-s** his father .... Gn 2:24
I will never **l** you or forsake .... Heb 13:5

LEFT (adj)
don't let your **l** hand know what .... Mt 6:3
right and the goats on the **l**. .... Mt 25:33

LEGION
"My name is **L**," he answered Him .... Mk 5:9

LEND
and **l**, expecting nothing in return. .... Lk 6:35

LENDER
borrower is a slave to the **l**. .... Pr 22:7

LEVEL (v)
mountain and hill will be **l-ed**; .... Is 40:4
LEVI
1. Son of Jacob and Leah (Gn 29:34). Ancestor of priestly tribe (Ex 32:25-29; Nm 3:11-13; Dt 10:6-9); received no allotment of land, only scattered towns and cities of refuge (Nm 18:20; 35:1-8; Jos 13:14,33); supported by tithes (Nm 18:21; Heb 7:5). Assisted descendants of Aaron in worship (Nm 3:5-9; 1Ch 6:16,31-32,49; 23:24-32; 2Ch 29:12-21); taught the word of God (2Ch 17:7-9; Neh 8:9-12).
2. Apostle, called Matthew (Mk 2:14; Lk 5:27-29; cp. Mt 9:9).
LIAR
he is a **l** and the father of **l-s**. .... Jn 8:44
LIBERTY
to proclaim **l** to the captives, ... Is 61:1
LIE (v) (prevaricate)
God is not a man who **l-s**, or a .... Nm 23:19
Do not **l** to one another, since .... Col 3:9
LIE (v) (recline)
when you **l** down and when .... Dt 6:7; 11:19
He lets me **l** down in green .... Ps 23:2
cloth and **l-ing** in a feeding trough. .... Lk 2:12
LIFE
the breath of **l** into his .... Gn 2:7
then you must give **l** for **l**, ... Ex 21:23
the **l** of a creature is in the blood, ... Lv 17:11
Don't worry about your **l**, ... Mt 6:25
I am the resurrection and the **l**. .... Jn 11:25
LIFTED
so the Son of Man must be **l** up, ... Jn 3:14
LIGHT (n)
"Let there be **l**," and there was **l**. .... Gn 1:3
The LORD is my **l** and my salvation .... Ps 27:1
in darkness have seen a great **l**; .... Is 9:2
You are the **l** of the world. .... Mt 5:14
I am the **l** of the world. .... Jn 8:12
LIGHTNING
For as the **l** comes from the east .... Mt 24:27
LIKENESS
Our image, according to Our **l**. .... Gn 1:26
slave, taking on the **l** of men. .... Php 2:7
LINE
l after **l**, **l** after **l**, a little here .... Is 28:10
LION
prowling around like a roaring **l**, ... 1Pt 5:8
LIPS
His praise will always be on my **l**. .... Ps 34:1
I am a man of unclean **l** .... Is 6:5
people honor Me with their **l**, ... Mt 15:8
LISTEN
Keep **l-ing**, but do not understand; .... Is 6:9
I take delight in Him. **L** to Him! .... Mt 17:5
LIVE (v)
man does not **l** on bread alone .... Dt 8:3
on those **l-ing** in the land of darkness, ... Is 9:2
the righteous one will **l** by his faith. .... Hab 2:4
Man must not **l** on bread alone .... Mt 4:4
LIVING (adj)
and the man became a **l** being. .... Gn 2:7
But I know my **l** Redeemer, and He .... Jb 19:25
and He would give you **l** water. .... Jn 4:10
word of God is **l** and effective .... Heb 4:12
LIVING (n)
l is Christ and dying is gain. .... Php 1:21
LOAF
only have five **loaves** and two fish .... Mt 14:17
LOCUST
I will bring **l-s** into your territory. .... Ex 10:4
his food was **l-s** and wild honey. .... Mt 3:4
LOG
notice the **l** in your own eye .... Mt 7:3
LONG (adj)
How **l** will You hide Your face .... Ps 13:1
if a man has **l** hair it is a disgrace 1Co 11:14
LONGS (v)
As a deer **l** for streams of water, so .... Ps 42:1
LOOKS
everyone who **l** at a woman to .... Mt 5:28
the plow and **l** back is fit for .... Lk 9:62
LOOSE
whatever you **l** on earth is already .... Mt 16:19
LORD Ld = LORD/Yahweh *see also* YAHWEH
declaration of the **Ld** to my **L**: .... Ps 110:1
who says to Me, '**L**, **L**!, will enter .... Mt 7:21
The **L** declared to my **L**, ... Mt 22:44
with your mouth, "Jesus is **L**," .... Rm 10:9
one can say, "Jesus is **L**," except 1Co 12:3
confess that Jesus Christ is **L**, ... Php 2:11
LOSES
but whoever **l** his life because .... Mt 16:25
LOSS
everything to be a **l** in view of .... Php 3:8
LOST (adj)
go to the **l** sheep of the house .... Mt 10:6
LOST (n)
I will seek the **l**, bring back .... Ezk 34:16
come to seek and to save the **l**. .... Lk 19:10
LOT
Abraham's nephew (Gn 11:27). Separated from Abraham; settled in Sodom (13:1-13). Rescued from kings (14:1-16); from Sodom (18:16–19:29; Lk 17:28-29; 2Pt 2:7-9). Fathered Moabites and Ammonites by his daughters (Gn 19:30-38).
LOT
Pur (that is, the **l**) was cast .... Est 3:7
and they cast **l-s** for my clothing .... Ps 22:18
The **l** is cast into the lap, ... Pr 16:33
His clothes by casting **l-s**. .... Mt 27:35
LOVE (n)
His **l** is eternal. .... Ps 136:1-26
No one has greater **l** than this, ... Jn 15:13
L is patient; **l** is kind. **L** does not 1Co 13:4
LOVE (v)
but **l** your neighbor as yourself; .... Lv 19:18
L the LORD your God with all .... Dt 6:5
l your enemies and pray for .... Mt 5:44
For God **l-d** the world in this way .... Jn 3:16
new commandment: **l** one another. .... Jn 13:34
Husbands, **l** your wives, just as .... Eph 5:25
LOVELY
How **l** is Your dwelling place, ... Ps 84:1
whatever is pure, whatever is **l**, ... Php 4:8
LOYAL
LORD has found a man **l** to Him, ... 1Sm 13:14
LUKE
Companion of Paul (2Tm 4:11; Phm 24); physician (Col 4:14); author of Luke and Acts (note "we" in Ac 16:10; 28:16).
LUKEWARM
because you are **l**, and neither .... Rv 3:16
LUST (v)
looks at a woman to **l** for her has .... Mt 5:28
MAACAH
1. David's wife; mother of Absalom (2Sm 3:3; 1Ch 3:2).
2. Mother of Judah's King Abijam (1Kg 15:2); promoted Asherah worship (15:13).
MAGDALENE *see* MARY 2.
MAJESTY
He is robed in **m**; .... Ps 93:1
right hand of the **M** on high. .... Heb 1:3
MAKER
kneel before the LORD our **M**. .... Ps 95:6
MALACHI
Postexilic prophet (Mal 1:1).
MALE
He created them **m** and female. .... Gn 1:27
slave or free, **m** or female; .... Gl 3:28
MAN *see also* MAN OF GOD
God formed the **m** out of the dust .... Gn 2:7
what is **m** that You remember him, ... Ps 8:4
MAN OF GOD
so that the **m** may be complete, ... 2Tm 3:17
MANASSEH
1. Son of Joseph and Asenath (Gn 41:50-51). Adopted by Jacob as a tribe (Gn 48); allotted half of its territory east of the Jordan from Gerasa to Mt. Hermon in the far north and half west of the Jordan to the Mediterranean from the Yarkon River to Mt. Carmel (Nm 32:33-42; Jos 13:29-31; 17).
2. Son of Hezekiah; king of Judah (2Kg 21:1-18). Wickedness brought on God's judgment (21:10-15; Jr 15:4).
MANIFESTED
He was **m** in the flesh, justified 1Tm 3:16
MANNA
Israel named the substance **m**. .... Ex 16:31
fathers ate the **m** in the desert, ... Jn 6:31,49
MANTLE
him and threw his **m** over him. 1Kg 19:19
MARK, JOHN
Missionary (Ac 12:12,25); Barnabas's cousin (Col 4:10); cause of split between Paul and Barnabas (Ac 15:36-40); later apparently reconciled to Paul (Col 4:10; 2Tm 4:11; Phm 24). Also close to Peter (1Pt 5:13). Wrote the Gospel of Mark.
MARK
He placed a **m** on Cain so that .... Gn 4:15
and receives a **m** on his forehead .... Rv 14:9
MARRIAGE
nor are given in **m** but are like .... Mt 22:30
M must be respected by all, ... Heb 13:4
the **m** of the Lamb has come, ... Rv 19:7
MARRIED (adj)
a **m** man is concerned about 1Co 7:33
MARRY
the dead neither **m** nor are given .... Lk 20:35
it is better to **m** than to burn 1Co 7:9
MARTHA
Sister of Mary and Lazarus (Lk 10:38-42; Jn 11:1–12:2).
MARY
1. Mother of Jesus (Mt 1:16; Lk 1:26-56; 2:1-20,34-35). Present at the cross (Jn 19:25-27); among the believers (Ac 1:14).
2. Magdalene; delivered from demons (Lk 8:2); follower and supporter of Jesus (Mk 15:40-41). Witness to the crucifixion and resurrection (Mt 27:54–28:10; Mk 16:1-10; Lk 24:10; Jn 19:25–20:18).
3. Mother of James and Joseph/Joses; follower and supporter of Jesus (Mk 15:40-41). Witness to the crucifixion and resurrection (Mt 27:54–28:10; Mk 16:1-8; Lk 24:10).
4. Sister of Martha and Lazarus (Jn 11); anointed Jesus' feet (12:1-3).
MASTERS (n)
No one can be a slave of two **m** .... Mt 6:24
MATTHEW
Apostle; former tax collector (Mt 9:9; 10:3). Also called Levi son of Alphaeus (Mk 2:14; cp. Lk 5:27-32). Wrote a gospel.
MEASURE (n)
and with the **m** you use, it will be .... Mt 7:2
a good **m**—pressed down, shaken .... Lk 6:38
MEAT
It is a noble thing not to eat **m**, ... Rm 14:21
MEDIA
Country of the Medes, north of Elam and west of Assyria (Ezr 6:2); ally of Persia (Est 1:3; Dn 5:28; 8:20); cursed by Jeremiah (Jr 25:25).
MEDIATOR
one God and one **m** between God 1Tm 2:5
MEDICINE
A joyful heart is good **m**, ... Pr 17:22
MEDITATES
he **m** on it day and night. .... Ps 1:2
MEDITATION
mouth and the **m** of my heart .... Ps 19:14
MEDITERRANEAN SEA
Western border of Israel (Ex 23:31; Nm 34:6; Dt 11:24; 34:2; Jos 1:4; 23:4; Ezk 47:15-20), including several of the tribal territories (Jos 15:4,11,12,47; 16:3,8; 17:9).
MEDIUM
A man or woman who is a **m** .... Lv 20:27
MEET
I will **m** with you there above .... Ex 25:22
Israel, prepare to **m** your God! .... Am 4:12
in the clouds to **m** the Lord in 1Th 4:17
MELCHIZEDEK
King of Salem and priest (Gn 14:18); represents undying priesthood (Ps 110:4; Heb 5:6,10; 6:20; 7).
MELT
elements will **m** with the heat. 2Pt 3:12
MEMBER
if one **m** suffers, all the **m-s** suffer 1Co 12:26
MENAHEM
King of Israel; obtained throne by force (2Kg 15:10-16). Paid tribute to the king of Assyria (15:19-20).
MEPHIBOSHETH
Son of Jonathan; granted privilege in David's court (2Sm 4:4; 9; 16; 19).
MERCIFUL
Blessed are the **m**, because they .... Mt 5:7
MERCY
for His **m-ies** never end. .... Lm 3:22
I desire **m** and not sacrifice. .... Mt 9:13
I will show **m** to whom I show **m**, ... Rm 9:15
But God, who is abundant in **m**, ... Eph 2:4
MESSAGE
Lord, who has believed our **m**? .... Jn 12:38
MESSENGER
am sending My **m** ahead of You .... Mt 11:10
MESSIAH *see also* CHRIST
until **M** the Prince will be seven .... Dn 9:25
told him, "We have found the **M**!" .... Jn 1:41
that you may believe Jesus is the **M** .... Jn 20:31
set apart the **M** as Lord in your 1Pt 3:15
who denies that Jesus is the **M**? 1Jn 2:22
kingdom of our Lord and of His **M** .... Rv 11:15
METHUSELAH
Son of Enoch; grandfather of Noah (Gn 5:21-29; Lk 3:36-37).
MICAH
1. Ephraimite idolater (Jdg 17–18).
2. Prophet to Israel and Judah in the days of kings Jotham, Ahaz, and Hezekiah of Judah (Jr 26:18; Mc 1:1).
MICAIAH
Son of Imlah; prophet against Ahab (1Kg 22:5-28; 2Ch 18:4-27).
MICHAEL
Archangel; guardian of Israel (Dn 10:13,21; 12:1). Disputed with the Devil (Jd 9); will fight the dragon (Rv 12:7).
MICHAL
Daughter of Saul (1Sm 14:49); offered to David to endanger him (18:20-29); warned David of a plot (19:11-

17). Given to Palti (25:44); taken back (2Sm 3:12-16). Despised David dancing before the Lord (6:14-23; 1Ch 15:29).
MIGHT
Not by strength or by **m**, but by My .... Zch 4:6
MIGHTY
How the **m** have fallen! 2Sm 1:19
strong and **m**, the LORD, **m** in battle. .... Ps 24:8
Counselor, **M** God, Eternal Father .... Is 9:6
MILE
if anyone forces you to go one **m**, ... Mt 5:41
MILK
a land flowing with **m** and honey .... Ex 3:8
You need **m**, not solid food. .... Heb 5:12
MILLSTONE
better for him if a heavy **m** were .... Mt 18:6
MIND
is not man who changes his **m**. 1Sm 15:29
all your soul, and with all your **m**. .... Mt 22:37
by the renewing of your **m**, ... Rm 12:2
But we have the **m** of Christ. 1Co 2:16
MINISTRY
gave us the **m** of reconciliation: 2Co 5:18
MIRACLES
For if the **m** that were done in .... Mt 11:21
was not able to do any **m** there, ... Mk 6:5
testified by signs ... various **m**, ... Heb 2:4
MIRIAM
Sister of Moses and Aaron; daughter of Jochabed and Amram (Nm 26:59; 1Ch 6:3). Watched over baby Moses (Ex 2:4-8). Prophetess; led dancing at Red Sea (15:20-21). Struck with skin disease for criticizing Moses (Nm 12; Dt 24:9); died in Kadesh (Nm 20:1).
MIRROR
as in a **m**, but then face to face. 1Co 13:12
looking at his own face in a **m**; .... Jms 1:23
MISMATCHED
Do not be **m** with unbelievers. 2Co 6:14
MISUSE
Do not **m** the name of the LORD .... Ex 20:7
MOCKED
down before Him and **m** Him: .... Mt 27:29
God is not **m**. For whatever a man .... Gl 6:7
MOCKER
Wine is a **m**, beer is a brawler .... Pr 20:1
MOMENT
For His anger lasts only a **m**, ... Ps 30:5
in a **m**, in the twinkling of an eye, ... 1Co 15:52
MOMENTARY
For our **m** light affliction is 2Co 4:17
MONEY
cannot be slaves of God and of **m**. .... Mt 6:24
For the love of **m** is a root of 1Tm 6:10
MOON
the **m** and the stars, which You set .... Ps 8:3
you by day, or the **m** by night. .... Ps 121:6
the **m** to blood before the great .... Jl 2:31
MORALS
Bad company corrupts good **m**. 1Co 15:33
MORDECAI
Cousin and legal guardian of Esther (Est 2:7). Uncovered assassination plot (2:21-23). Offended Haman (3:1-7); Haman sought genocide (3:7-15); Mordecai led Esther to thwart the attempt (Est 4–5). Honored by the king (Est 6); wrote revenge edict (Est 8).
MORNING
but there is joy in the **m**. .... Ps 30:5
They are new every **m**; .... Lm 3:23
and the **m** star arises in your hearts. 2Pt 1:19
of David, the Bright **M** Star. .... Rv 22:16
MORTAL
and this **m** must be clothed with 1Co 15:53
MOSES
Leader of Israel; Levite; brother of Aaron and Miriam (1Ch 6:3). Born under Egyptian oppression (Ex 1); set adrift on Nile; rescued and raised by Pharaoh's daughter (2:1-10). Killed Egyptian; fled to Midian and married Zipporah (2:11-22). Called by God from burning bush (Ex 3–4). Announced ten plagues (Ex 7–11).
Divided the Red Sea (Ex 14). Brought water from a rock (17:1-7); held up God's staff and defeated Amalek (17:8-13). Delegated judging (18:13-26).
God spoke to him at Sinai: law (Ex 19–23); tabernacle, equipment, and garments (Ex 25–28; 30); consecration of priests (Ex 29). Discovered golden calf and broke tablets (Ex 32). Saw God's glory (33:12–34:28). Ordained Aaron and his sons (Lv 8–9).
Opposed by Aaron and Miram (Nm 12); opposed by Korah (Nm 16). Excluded from promised land for striking rock (20:1-13; 27:12-14; Dt 32:51). Made a bronze snake for healing (Nm 21:4-9; Jn 3:14). Wrote the book of the law (Jos 23:6; 2Ch 34:14). Saw promised land from a distance (Dt 3:23-27; 34:1-4); commissioned Joshua as successor (Nm 27:12-23); buried by God (Dt 34:5-8).
MOST HIGH
he was a priest to God **M**. .... Gn 14:18
under the protection of the **M** .... Ps 91:1
called the Son of the **M**, ... Lk 1:32
the **M** does not dwell in sanctuaries .... Ac 7:48
of Salem, priest of the **M** God, ... Heb 7:1
MOTH
where **m** and rust destroy and .... Mt 6:19
MOTHER
a man leaves his father and **m** .... Gn 2:24
Honor your father and your **m** so .... Ex 20:12
to the disciple, "Here is your **m**." .... Jn 19:27
MOUNT (n) *see also* CARMEL, MOUNT OF OLIVES, ZION
The LORD came down on **M** Sinai, ... Ex 19:20
M Zion on the slopes of the north is .... Ps 48:2
they went out to the **M** of Olives. .... Mt 26:30
Now Hagar is **M** Sinai in Arabia .... Gl 4:25
MOUNT OF OLIVES
The **M** will be split in half .... Zch 14:4
psalms, they went out to the **M**. .... Mt 26:30
made His way as usual to the **M**, ... Lk 22:39
MOUNTAIN
will be provided on the LORD's **m**. .... Gn 22:14
I raise my eyes toward the **m-s**. .... Ps 121:1
beautiful on the **m-s** are the feet .... Is 52:7
will tell this **m**, 'Move from .... Mt 17:20
all faith, so that I can move **m-s**, ... 1Co 13:2
MOURN
a time to **m** and a time to dance; .... Ec 3:4
Blessed are those who **m**, because .... Mt 5:4
MOUTH
Who made the human **m**? .... Ex 4:11
from the **m-s** of children .... Ps 8:2
May the words of my **m** and .... Ps 19:14
yet He did not open His **m**. .... Is 53:7
if you confess with your **m** .... Rm 10:9
MULTIPLY
Be fruitful, **m**, fill the earth, ... Gn 1:28
where sin **m-ied**, grace **m-ied** .... Rm 5:20
MULTITUDE
M-s, **m-s** in the valley of decision! .... Jl 3:14
and cover a **m** of sins. .... Jms 5:20
since love covers a **m** of sins. 1Pt 4:8
MURDER
Do not **m**. .... Ex 20:13
Do not **m**, and whoever **m-s** will .... Mt 5:21
MURDERER
the **m** must be put to death. .... Nm 35:16
He was a **m** from the beginning .... Jn 8:44
who hates his brother is a **m** 1Jn 3:15
MUSIC
singing and making **m** to the Lord .... Eph 5:19
MUSTARD
is like a **m** seed that a man .... Mt 13:31
faith the size of a **m** seed, ... Mt 17:20
MUZZLE
Do not **m** an ox while it treads .... Dt 25:4
You must not **m** an ox that is 1Tm 5:18
MYRRH
gold, frankincense, and **m**. .... Mt 2:11
MYSTERY
I am telling you a **m**: 1Co 15:51
the **m** of godliness is great: 1Tm 3:16
MYTHS
pay attention to **m** and endless 1Tm 1:4
contrived **m** when we made known 2Pt 1:16
NAGGING (adj)
share a house with a **n** wife .... Pr 21:9
NAHUM
Prophet against Nineveh (Nah 1:1).
NAILING (v)
the way by **n** it to the cross .... Col 2:14
NAILS (n)
finger into the mark of the **n** .... Jn 20:25
NAKED
the man and his wife were **n** .... Gn 2:25
N I came from my mother's womb, ... Jb 1:21
I was **n** and you clothed Me; .... Mt 25:36
NAME (n)
The man gave **n-s** to all the .... Gn 2:20
This is My **n** forever; .... Ex 3:15
not misuse the **n** of the LORD .... Ex 20:7
I am Yahweh, that is My **n**; .... Is 42:8
Your **n** be honored as holy. .... Mt 6:9
there is no other **n** under heaven .... Ac 4:12
the **n** that is above every **n**, ... Php 2:9
NAPHTALI
Son of Jacob and Bilhah (Gn 30:1-8). Tribe with territory north and west of the Sea of Galilee (Jos 19:32-39); praised by Deborah (Jdg 5:18); produced Hiram the craftsman (1Kg 7:13-14).
NARROW
Enter through the **n** gate. .... Mt 7:13
NATHAN
Prophet to David; told David he would never fail to have a descendant on the throne (2Sm 7:4-17); confronted David about Bathsheba (2Sm 12:1-15). Anointed Solomon (1Kg 1).
NATHANAEL
Apostle "in whom is no deceit"; invited by Philip; asked if anything good comes out of Nazareth (Jn 1:45-49; 21:2); possibly also called Bartholomew (Mt 10:3).
NATION
I will make you into a great **n** .... Gn 12:2
Happy is the **n** whose God is the .... Ps 33:12
Righteousness exalts a **n**, but sin .... Pr 14:34
For **n** will rise up against **n** .... Mt 24:7
and make disciples of all **n-s** .... Mt 28:19
NATURAL
the **n** man does not welcome 1Co 2:14
sown a **n** body, raised a 1Co 15:44
NAZARENE
that He will be called a **N**. .... Mt 2:23
NAZARETH
Hometown of Jesus (Mt 2:23; Lk 2:51; 4:16; Jn 1:45-46).
NAZIRITE
a special vow, a **N** vow, ... Nm 6:2
NEBUCHADNEZZAR
King of Babylon; defeated and exiled Judah (2Kg 24–25; 1Ch 6:15; 2Ch 36; Jr 39). Dreams interpreted by Daniel (Dn 2; 4); threw Shadrach, Meshach, and Abednego into the furnace (Dn 3); temporarily insane (Dn 4); praised God (2:47; 3:28; 4:34-37).
NEED (n)
to all, as anyone had a **n**. .... Ac 2:45
supply all your **n-s** according .... Php 4:19
NEED (v)
Father knows the things you **n** .... Mt 6:8
say to the hand, "I don't **n** you!" 1Co 12:21
NEEDLE
the eye of a **n** than for a rich .... Mt 19:24
NEGLECT
Do not **n** the gift that is in you 1Tm 4:14
we escape if we **n** such a great .... Heb 2:3
NEHEMIAH
Cupbearer to King Artaxerxes of Babylon (Neh 1:11); obtained permission for, planned, and supervised rebuilding Jerusalem's walls despite opposition (Neh 2–6). Was appointed governor of Judah (5:14). Dedicated wall (12:27-43). Promoted reforms (Neh 8–10; 13). Prayed frequently (1:4-11; 2:4; 4:4-5,9; 5:19; 6:9,14; 13:14,22,29,31).
NEIGHBOR
Do not covet your **n-'s** wife, ... Ex 20:17
but love your **n** as yourself; .... Lv 19:18
and love your **n** as yourself. .... Mt 19:19
NEW
He put a **n** song in my mouth, ... Ps 40:3
there is nothing **n** under the sun. .... Ec 1:9
you a **n** heart and put a **n** spirit .... Ezk 36:26
And no one puts **n** wine into old .... Mt 9:17
This cup is the **n** covenant .... Lk 22:20
I give you a **n** commandment: .... Jn 13:34
I am making everything **n**. .... Rv 21:5
NEWS
who brings **n** of good things, ... Is 52:7
the poor are told the good **n**. .... Mt 11:5
NICODEMUS
Pharisee and member of the Sanhedrin. Visited Jesus at night (Jn 3:1-21); defended Jesus to the Sanhedrin (7:45-52); helped prepare Jesus' body for burial (19:39).
NIGHT
and He called the darkness "**n**." .... Gn 1:5
come just like a thief in the **n**. 1Th 5:2
NINE
He was **n** feet, **n** inches tall 1Sm 17:4
NOAH
Son of Lamech; descendant of Seth; a righteous man (Gn 5:28-29; 6:9; Ezk 14:14; Heb 11:7; 2Pt 2:5). Built an ark, entered it with animals and his family, and survived the flood (Gn 6:14–8:19; 1Pt 3:20). Received God's promise (Gn 8:20–9:17). Got drunk and cursed Canaan (9:20-27). Flood a symbol of sudden judgment (Mt 24:37-38; Lk 17:26-27).
NUMBER (n)
it is the **n** of a man. His **n** is 666. .... Rv 13:18
OAKS
beside the **o** of Mamre .... Gn 13:18
and he was as sturdy as the **o**; .... Am 2:9
OATH
The LORD swore an **o** to David, ... Ps 132:11
I tell you, don't take an **o** at all: .... Mt 5:34
OBADIAH
Prophet against Edom (Ob 1).
OBEDIENCE
through the one man's **o** the many .... Rm 5:19
He learned **o** through what He .... Heb 5:8
OBEDIENT
becoming **o** to the point of death .... Php 2:8
OBEY
to **o** is better than sacrifice, ... 1Sm 15:22
the winds and the sea **o** Him! .... Mt 8:27
We must **o** God rather than men. .... Ac 5:29

OBSERVE
You must **o** My Sabbaths, Ex 31:13
When I **o** Your heavens, the work Ps 8:3
teaching them to **o** everything I Mt 28:20
You **o** special days, months, Gl 4:10
OBVIOUS
the works of the flesh are **o**: Gl 5:19
good works are **o**, and those that 1Tm 5:25
OFFEND
anyone is not **o-ed** because of Me Mt 11:6
OFFENSE
but love covers all **o-s**. Pr 10:12
that case the **o** of the cross has Gl 5:11
OFFENSIVE
if there is any **o** way in me; Ps 139:24
OFFER
and **o** him there as a burnt Gn 22:2
if you are **o-ing** your gift on Mt 5:23
once for all when He **o-ed** Himself. Heb 7:27
OFFERING (n) *see also* BURNT, FELLOWSHIP
take pleasure in burnt **o-s** ... as much as in obeying the LORD? 1Sm 15:22
You make Him a restitution **o** Is 53:10
You did not want sacrifice and **o**, Heb 10:5
OFFSPRING
I will give this land to your **o**. Gn 12:7
said, 'For we are also His **o**.' Ac 17:28
I am the Root and the **O** of David, Rv 22:16
OIL
You anoint my head with **o**; Ps 23:5
sensible ones took **o** in their flasks Mt 25:4
OLD
I have been young and now I am **o**, Ps 37:25
even when he is **o** he will not Pr 22:6
your **o** men will have dreams, Jl 2:28
puts new wine into **o** wineskins. Mt 9:17
o things have passed away, 2Co 5:17
OLDER
The **o** will serve the younger. Rm 9:12
OLIVE *see also* MOUNT OF OLIVES
was a plucked **o** leaf in her beak Gn 8:11
OMRI
Army commander; king of Israel; founded the city of Samaria (1Kg 16:15-28).
ONCE
He died to sin **o** for all; Rm 6:10
appointed for people to die **o** Heb 9:27
ONE *see* ONE AND ONLY SON
The LORD our God, the LORD is **o**. Dt 6:4
Are You the Coming **O**, Mt 11:3
The Father and I are **o**. Jn 10:30
they may be **o** as We are **o**. Jn 17:11
o Lord, **o** faith, **o** baptism, Eph 4:5
For there is **o** God and **o** mediator 1Tm 2:5
ONE AND ONLY SON
glory as the **O** from the Father, Jn 1:14
No one has ever seen God. The **O** Jn 1:18
He gave His **O**, so that everyone Jn 3:16
not believed in the name of the **O** Jn 3:18
God sent His **O** into the world so 1Jn 1:8
OPEN (v)
eyes will be **o-ed** and you will be Gn 3:5
yet He did not **o** His mouth. Is 53:7
and the door will be **o-ed** to you Mt 7:7
Who is worthy to **o** the scroll Rv 5:2
OPPORTUNITY
looking for a good **o** to betray Him. Mt 26:16
and don't give the Devil an **o**. Eph 4:27
OPPRESSED
He was **o** and afflicted, Is 53:7
to the blind, to set free the **o**, Lk 4:18
ORACLE
The **o** of Balaam son of Beor, Nm 24:3
received living **o-s** to give to us. Ac 7:38
ORDAIN
the way you will **o** Aaron and his Ex 29:9
ORDER (n)
Put your affairs in **o**, 2Kg 20:1
give His angels **o-s** concerning Mt 4:6
sin in **o** that grace may multiply? Rm 6:1
must be done decently and in **o**. 1Co 14:40
ORDINANCES
the **o** of the LORD are reliable Ps 19:9
ORNAN *see* ARAUNAH
ORPHANS
I will not leave you as **o**; Jn 14:18
OTHER
I am the LORD, and there is no **o**; Is 45:5
as you want **o-s** to do for you, Lk 6:31
OTHNIEL
Judge; defeated Arameans (Jdg 3:7-11); Caleb's nephew (Jos 15:17; Jdg 1:13).
OUTDO
O one another in showing honor. Rm 12:10
OUTRAN
other disciple **o** Peter and got Jn 20:4
OUTSIDE
You clean the **o** of the cup and Mt 23:25
Jesus also suffered **o** the gate, Heb 13:12
OUTSIDERS
properly in the presence of **o** 1Th 4:12
OUTSTRETCHED
you with an **o** arm and great acts Ex 6:6
OUTWARD
Stop judging according to **o** Jn 7:24
should not consist of **o** things 1Pt 3:3
OUTWARDLY
person is not a Jew who is one **o**, Rm 2:28
OVERCOME
yet the darkness did not **o** it. Jn 1:5
OVERFLOWS
my cup **o**. Ps 23:5
OVERPOWER
forces of Hades will not **o** it. Mt 16:18
OVERSEER
If anyone aspires to be an **o** 1Tm 3:1
OVERSHADOW
of the Most High will **o** you. Lk 1:35
OVERTAKE
my sins have **o-n** me; Ps 40:12
temptation has **o-n** you except 1Co 10:13
this day would **o** you like a thief. 1Th 5:4
OVERTURNED
o the money changers' tables Mt 21:12
OWE
one who **o-d** 10,000 talents Mt 18:24
Do not **o** anyone anything, except Rm 13:8
you **o** me even your own self. Phm 19
OWN (adj)
rely on your **o** understanding; Pr 3:5
OWN (n)
He came to His **o**, Jn 1:11
You are not your **o**, 1Co 6:19
OX
Do not muzzle an **o** while it treads Dt 25:4
not muzzle an **o** while it treads 1Co 9:9
PAIN
I will intensify your labor **p-s**; Gn 3:16
and He carried our **p-s**; Is 53:4
and **p** will exist no longer, Rv 21:4
PALM
you on the **p-s** of My hands; Is 49:16
they took **p** branches and went Jn 12:13
PARABLE
He told them many things in **p-s** Mt 13:3
Why do You speak to them in **p-s**? Mt 13:10
speak anything to them without a **p** Mt 13:34
but to the rest it is in **p-s**, so that Lk 8:10
PARADISE
you will be with Me in **p** Lk 23:43
was caught up into **p**. 2Co 12:4
PARALYTIC
brought to Him a **p** lying on a Mt 9:2
PARENTS
evil, disobedient to **p**, Rm 1:30
Children, obey your **p** in the Lord, Eph 6:1
disobedient to **p**, ungrateful, 2Tm 3:2
PART (n)
wash you, you have no **p** with Me. Jn 13:8
the body is one and has many **p-s** 1Co 12:12
know in **p**, and we prophesy in **p**. 1Co 13:9
PARTIAL
a **p** hardening has come to Israel Rm 11:25
PARTIALITY
Do not show **p** when rendering Dt 1:17
not good to show **p** Pr 18:5; 24:23; 28:21
You don't show **p** but teach Mk 12:14
PARTNERSHIP
For what **p** is there between 2Co 6:14
PASS
see the blood, I will **p** over you. Ex 12:13
when you **p** through the waters, Is 43:2
Heaven and earth will **p** away, but My words will never **p** away. Mt 24:35
let this cup **p** from Me. Mt 26:39
he **p-ed** by on the other side. Lk 10:31
but has **p-ed** from death to life. Jn 5:24
old things have **p-ed** away, 2Co 5:17
PASSIONS
Flee from youthful **p**, and pursue 2Tm 2:22
PASSOVER
it is the LORD's **P**. Ex 12:11
the **P** lamb had to be sacrificed. Lk 22:7
Christ our **P** has been sacrificed. 1Co 5:7
PASTORS
some **p** and teachers, Eph 4:11
PASTURE (n)
lets me lie down in green **p-s** Ps 23:2
His people, the sheep of His **p**. Ps 100:3
come in and go out and find **p**. Jn 10:9
PATCH
No one sews a **p** of unshrunk Mk 2:21
PATH
or take the **p** of sinners, Ps 1:1
the right **p-s** for His name's Ps 23:3
for my feet and a light on my **p**. Ps 119:105
make His **p-s** straight! Mt 3:3
some seeds fell along the **p**, Mt 13:4
PATIENCE
love, joy, peace, **p**, kindness, Gl 5:22
PATIENT
Love is **p**; love is kind. 1Co 13:4
PATIENTLY
I waited **p** for the LORD, Ps 40:1
PAUL
Early church missionary, theologian, and writer. Also called Saul (Ac 13:9). Citizen of Tarsus, a Benjaminite, raised in Jerusalem as a rabbinical student and Pharisee (21:39; 22:3,28; 26:5; Gl 1:14; Php 3:5). Persecuted Christians, including Stephen (Ac 8:1; 26:9-11); converted on the way to Damascus (9:1-19); began preaching Christ in Arabia and Damascus and was threatened (9:20-22; 2Co 11:32-33; Gl 1:17;).

Introduced to the church at Jerusalem by Barnabas (Ac 9:26-30); carried money with Barnabas from Antioch to Judea (11:27-30). Set apart with Barnabas to go through Cyprus and Galatia as missionaries (Ac 13–14); stoned (14:19-20). Focused on Gentile evangelism (9:15; Gl 2:7; Eph 3:8). Attended Jerusalem council (Ac 15). Split with Barnabas over John Mark (15:36-39).

Traveled with Silas and Timothy through Asia Minor and Greece (15:39–16:3). Hindered by the Spirit from entering Bithynia; called to Macedonia in a vision (16:7-10). Beaten, imprisoned, and released in Philippi (16:16-40). Spoke at Areopagus in Athens (17:19-34). Preached at Corinth and Ephesus (Ac 18–19). Said farewell in Ephesus (20:17-38).

Arrested at riot in Jerusalem (21:26-36); testified before the Sanhedrin (23:1-10), Governors Felix and Festus (24:10-21; 25:1-12), and King Agrippa (Ac 26); appealed to Caesar (25:11). Shipwrecked on the way to Rome (Ac 27); ministered in Malta, then Rome (Ac 28).
PAY
Is it lawful to **p** taxes to Caesar Mt 22:17
P your obligations to everyone: Rm 13:7
not **p-ing** back evil for evil or 1Pt 3:9
PAYMENT
gave us the Spirit as a down **p**. 2Co 5:5
He is the down **p** of our Eph 1:14
PEACE
favor on you and give you **p**. Nm 6:26
Pray for the **p** of Jerusalem: Ps 122:6
time for war and a time for **p**. Ec 3:8
Eternal Father, Prince of **P**. Is 9:6
and **p** on earth to people He favors! Lk 2:14
P I leave with you. My **p** I give Jn 14:27
we have **p** with God through our Rm 5:1
fruit of the Spirit is love, joy, **p**, Gl 5:22
For He is our **p**, who made both Eph 2:14
And the **p** of God, which surpasses Php 4:7
PEACEMAKERS
Blessed are the **p**, because they Mt 5:9
PEARL
or toss your **p-s** before pigs, Mt 7:6
When he found one priceless **p** Mt 13:46
PENTECOST
When the day of **P** had arrived, Ac 2:1
PEOPLE
your **p** will be my **p**, Ru 1:16
His **p**, the sheep of His pasture. Ps 100:3
a holy nation, a **p** for His possession, 1Pt 2:9
and language and **p** and nation. Rv 5:9
PERCEIVE
keep looking, but do not **p**. Is 6:9
look and look, yet never **p**. Mt 13:14
PERFECT (adj)
The instruction of the LORD is **p**, Ps 19:7
Be **p**, therefore, as your heavenly Mt 5:48
and every **p** gift is from above, Jms 1:17
instead, **p** love drives out fear, 1Jn 4:18
PERFECTED (v)
for power is **p** in weakness. 2Co 12:9
and His love is **p** in us. 1Jn 4:12
PERFECTER
the source and **p** of our faith Heb 12:2
PERISH
If I **p**, I **p**. Est 4:16
one of these little ones **p**. Mt 18:14
in Him will not **p** but have Jn 3:16
is veiled to those who are **p-ing**. 2Co 4:3
not wanting any to **p**, but all to 2Pt 3:9
PERISHABLE
do it to receive a **p** crown, 1Co 9:25
not of **p** seed but of 1Pt 1:23
PERMISSIBLE
Everything is **p** for me, 1Co 6:12
"Everything is **p**," but not 1Co 10:23

PRICE
the **p** of Him whose **p** was set by ... Mt 27:9
for you were bought at a **p**; ... 1Co 6:20
PRICELESS
When he found one **p** pearl, ... Mt 13:46
PRIDE
P comes before destruction, ... Pr 16:18
PRIEST
he was a **p** to God Most High. ... Gn 14:18
be My kingdom of **p-s** and My holy ... Ex 19:6
You are a **p** like Melchizedek. ... Ps 110:4
a great high **p** who has passed ... Heb 4:14
You are a **p** forever in the order ... Heb 5:6
PRIESTHOOD
race, a royal **p**, a holy nation ... 1Pt 2:9
PRINCE
P-s have persecuted me without ... Ps 119:161
Eternal Father, **P** of Peace. ... Is 9:6
PRISON
I was in **p** and you visited Me. ... Mt 25:36
Peter was kept in **p**, but prayer ... Ac 12:5
saw the doors of the **p** open, ... Ac 16:27
to the spirits in **p** ... 1Pt 3:19
PRISONER
The LORD frees **p-s**. ... Ps 146:7
p of Christ Jesus on behalf ... Eph 3:1
PRIZE
but only one receives the **p**? ... 1Co 9:24
as my goal the **p** promised by ... Php 3:14
PROCLAIM
and I will **p** the name Yahweh ... Ex 33:19
and the sky **p-s** the work of His ... Ps 19:1
to **p** liberty to the captives, ... Is 61:1
you **p** the Lord's death until He ... 1Co 11:26
p the message; persist in it ... 2Tm 4:2
PRODUCE (v)
A good tree can't **p** bad fruit; ... Mt 7:18
of your faith **p-s** endurance. ... Jms 1:3
PROFANE
Do not **p** the name of your God; ... Lv 18:21
PROFIT (n)
not seeking my own **p**, but the **p** ... 1Co 10:33
and do business and make a **p**. ... Jms 4:13
PROFITABLE
God and is **p** for teaching ... 2Tm 3:16
PROGRESS
so that your **p** may be evident to ... 1Tm 4:15
PROMINENT
number of the **p** Greek women ... Ac 17:12
PROMISCUITY
moral impurity, **p**, ... Gl 5:19
PROMISCUOUS
Go and marry a **p** wife ... Hs 1:2
PROMISE (n)
For the **p** is for you and for ... Ac 2:39
of God's **p-s** is "Yes" in Him. ... 2Co 1:20
since it holds **p** for the present ... 1Tm 4:8
The Lord does not delay His **p** ... 2Pt 3:9
PROMISED (adj)
from the Father the **p** Holy Spirit, ... Ac 2:33
PROMISED (v)
This is the land I **p** Abraham, ... Dt 34:4
for He who **p** is faithful. ... Heb 10:23
PRONOUNCE
he could not **p** it correctly, ... Jdg 12:6
PROOF
to them by many convincing **p-s** ... Ac 1:3
the **p** of what is not seen. ... Heb 11:1
PROPER
among you, as is **p** for saints. ... Eph 5:3
PROPERTY
his wife, sold a piece of **p**. ... Ac 5:1
PROPHECY
miracles, to another, **p**, ... 1Co 12:10
But as for **p-ies**, they will come to ... 1Co 13:8
no **p** of Scripture comes from ... 2Pt 1:20
PROPHESY
sons and your daughters will **p**, ... Jl 2:28
Lord, didn't we **p** in Your name, ... Mt 7:22
and above all that you may **p**. ... 1Co 14:1
PROPHET
God will raise up for you a **p** like ... Dt 18:15
No **p** is accepted in his hometown. ... Lk 4:24
"Are you the **P**?" "No," ... Jn 1:21
first apostles, second **p-s**, ... 1Co 12:28
PROPHETESS
There was also a **p**, Anna, ... Lk 2:36
PROPHETIC
known through the **p** Scriptures, ... Rm 16:26
we have the **p** word strongly ... 2Pt 1:19
PROPITIATION
Him as a **p** through faith ... Rm 3:25
to make **p** for the sins of the ... Heb 2:17
Himself is the **p** for our sins, ... 1Jn 2:2
Son to be the **p** for our sins. ... 1Jn 4:10

PROSELYTE
land and sea to make one **p** ... Mt 23:15
PROSPER
Whatever he does **p-s**. ... Ps 1:3
will **p** in what I send it to do. ... Is 55:11
PROSPERITY
set before you life and **p**, ... Dt 30:15
I saw the **p** of the wicked. ... Ps 73:3
PROSTITUTE (n)
a **p** named Rahab, and stayed there. ... Jos 2:1
p-s are entering the kingdom ... Mt 21:31
and make it part of a **p**? ... 1Co 6:15
PROTECT
He **p-s** His flock like a shepherd ... Is 40:11
who is able to **p** you from ... Jd 24
PROTECTION
lives under the **p** of the Most High ... Ps 91:1
PROUD
LORD, my heart is not **p**; ... Ps 131:1
God resists the **p**, but gives ... Jms 4:6
PROVEN
endurance produces **p** character, ... Rm 5:4
PROVERB
Solomon composed 3,000 **p-s**, ... 1Kg 4:32
The **p-s** of Solomon son of David, ... Pr 1:1
you will quote this **p** to Me: ... Lk 4:23
PROVIDE
God Himself will **p** the lamb ... Gn 22:8
all these things will be **p-d** for you. ... Mt 6:33
He will also **p** a way of escape, ... 1Co 10:13
if anyone does not **p** for his own ... 1Tm 5:8
richly **p-s** us with all things ... 1Tm 6:17
PROVOKED
tested God and **p** the Holy One ... Ps 78:41
is not selfish; is not **p**; ... 1Co 13:5
PROWLING
the Devil is **p** around like a ... 1Pt 5:8
PRUNES
and He **p** every branch that ... Jn 15:2
PSALMS
and the **P** must be fulfilled. ... Lk 24:44
speaking to one another in **p**, ... Eph 5:19
PUBLIC
your attention to **p** reading, ... 1Tm 4:13
PUBLICLY
not wanting to disgrace her **p** ... Mt 1:19
P rebuke those who sin, so that ... 1Tm 5:20
PUNISHED
the LORD has **p** Him for the ... Is 53:6
PUNISHMENT
My **p** is too great to bear! ... Gn 4:13
p for our peace was on Him, ... Is 53:5
son won't suffer **p** for the father's ... Ezk 18:20
they will go away into eternal **p**, ... Mt 25:46
because fear involves **p** ... 1Jn 4:18
PUPIL
guarded him as the **p** of His eye. ... Dt 32:10
PURCHASED
which He **p** with His own blood. ... Ac 20:28
PURE
can a young man keep his way **p**? ... Ps 119:9
eyes are too **p** to look on evil, ... Hab 1:13
Blessed are the **p** in heart, ... Mt 5:8
whatever is just, whatever is **p**, ... Php 4:8
PURIFICATION
After making **p** for sins, He sat ... Heb 1:3
PURIFY
P me with hyssop, and I will be ... Ps 51:7
He will **p** the sons of Levi and ... Mal 3:3
PURIM
reason these days are called **P**, ... Est 9:26
PURITY
by **p**, by knowledge, by patience, ... 2Co 6:6
PURPLE
crown of thorns and the **p** robe. ... Jn 19:5
PURPOSE
because I was sent for this **p**. ... Lk 4:43
are called according to His **p**. ... Rm 8:28
PURSUE
seek peace and **p** it. ... Ps 34:14
P peace with everyone, and ... Heb 12:14
PURSUIT
futile, a **p** of the wind. ... Ec 1:14
PUT
But **p** on the Lord Jesus Christ, ... Rm 13:14
P on the full armor of God so ... Eph 6:11
QUAIL
So at evening **q** came ... Ex 16:13
QUALITY
will test the **q** of each one's ... 1Co 3:13
QUARRELS (n)
that there are **q** among you. ... 1Co 1:11
QUARRELSOME
but gentle, not **q**, not greedy ... 1Tm 3:3
QUEEN
The **q** of Sheba heard about ... 1Kg 10:1

The **q** of the south will rise up ... Mt 12:42
QUENCHED
not die, and the fire is not **q**. ... Mk 9:44
QUICK
everyone must be **q** to hear, ... Jms 1:19
QUICKLY
What you're doing, do **q**. ... Jn 13:27
Yes, I am coming **q**. ... Rv 22:20
QUIET
He leads me beside **q** waters. ... Ps 23:2
a tranquil and **q** life in all ... 1Tm 2:2
of a gentle and **q** spirit, ... 1Pt 3:4
QUIVER
who has filled his **q** with them. ... Ps 127:5
QUOTA
require the same **q** of bricks ... Ex 5:8
RABBI
do not be called '**R**' because you ... Mt 23:8
RABBOUNI
she said to Him in Hebrew, "***R***!" ... Jn 20:16
RAB-SARIS
Title of Assyrian and Babylonian officials (2Kg 18:17; Jr 39:3,13).
RACE (n)
the **r** is not to the swift, ... Ec 9:11
I have finished the **r**, I have kept ... 2Tm 4:7
endurance the **r** that lies before ... Heb 12:1
you are a chosen **r**, a royal ... 1Pt 2:9
RACE (v)
the runners in a stadium all **r**, ... 1Co 9:24
RACHEL
Daughter of Laban; wife and cousin of Jacob (Gn 29:10,18-30); mother of Joseph and Benjamin (30:24; 35:16-20); stole her father's household idols (31:19).
R weeping for her children ... Jr 31:15; Mt 2:18
RADIANCE
He is the **r** of His glory, ... Heb 1:3
RAGE (n)
A king's **r** is like a lion's roar ... Pr 19:12
RAGE (v)
the Gentiles **r**, and the peoples ... Ac 4:25
RAHAB
Prostitute in Jericho who hid the Israelite spies (Jos 2; Heb 11:31); spared by Joshua (Jos 6:17,22-25). Mother of Boaz (Mt 1:5).
RAIN (n)
and the **r** fell on the earth 40 ... Gn 7:12
and sends **r** on the righteous and ... Mt 5:45
RAISE
I will **r** up for them a prophet ... Dt 18:18
killed, and be **r-d** the third day. ... Mt 16:21
and I will **r** it up in three days. ... Jn 2:19
that He was **r-d** on the third ... 1Co 15:4
who **r-d** the Lord Jesus will **r** us ... 2Co 4:14
RAM
up and saw a **r** caught by its ... Gn 22:13
RANSOM (n)
Yet these cannot ... pay his **r** to God ... Ps 49:7
to give His life—a **r** for many. ... Mt 20:28
RANSOM (v)
for the LORD has **r-ed** Jacob and ... Jr 31:11
RASHLY
something **r** and later to reconsider ... Pr 20:25
RAVEN
he sent out a **r**. ... Gn 8:7
Consider the **r-s**: they don't sow ... Lk 12:24
READ
Sabbath day and stood up to **r**. ... Lk 4:16
Blessed is the one who **r-s** ... Rv 1:3
READY
and always be **r** to give a ... 1Pt 3:15
REAL
My flesh is **r** food and My blood ... Jn 6:55
REALLY
Did God **r** say, 'You can't eat from ... Gn 3:1
REAP
sow in tears will **r** with shouts ... Ps 126:5
they don't sow or **r** or gather ... Mt 6:26
a man sows he will also **r**, ... Gl 6:7
REASON (n)
asks you for a **r** for the hope ... 1Pt 3:15
REASONED (v)
a child, I **r** like a child. ... 1Co 13:11
REBEKAH
Sister of Laban; wife of Isaac (Gn 24); mother of Jacob and Esau (25:21-26). Passed off as Isaac's sister (26:6-11). Encouraged Jacob to secure Isaac's blessing (27:1-17).
REBEL (v)
Only don't **r** against the LORD, ... Nm 14:9
Why do the nations **r** and the peoples ... Ps 2:1
but they have **r-led** against Me. ... Is 1:2
REBELLION
For **r** is like the sin of divination, ... 1Sm 15:23
REBUILD
to go up and **r** the LORD's house ... Ezr 1:5
Come, let's **r** Jerusalem's wall ... Neh 2:17

and the ruins will be **rebuilt**. Ezk 36:33
sanctuary and **r** it in three days. Mt 26:61

REBUKE (v)
do not **r** me in Your anger; Ps 6:1
The LORD **r** you, Satan! Zch 3:2
He got up and **r-d** the winds Mt 8:26
go and **r** him in private. Mt 18:15
Publicly **r** those who sin, 1Tm 5:20
r, correct, and encourage with 2Tm 4:2
him, but said, "The Lord **r** you!" Jd 9

RECEIVE
But to all who did **r** Him, He gave Jn 1:12
Ask and you will **r**, Jn 16:24
is more blessed to give than to **r**. Ac 20:35
What do you have that you didn't **r**? 1Co 4:7

RECOGNIZE
yet the world did not **r** Him. Jn 1:10

RECONCILE
First go and be **r-d** with your Mt 5:24
Christ's behalf, "Be **r-d** to God." 2Co 5:20
through Him to **r** everything to Col 1:20

RECONCILIATION
whom we have now received **r**. Rm 5:11
and gave us the ministry of **r**: 2Co 5:18

RECORD (n)
does not keep a **r** of wrongs; 1Co 13:5

RECRUCIFYING
they are **r** the Son of God Heb 6:6

RED
they are as **r** as crimson, Is 1:18
good weather because the sky is **r**. Mt 16:2

RED SEA
Crossed by Israel (Ex 13:18; 14:15-31; Nm 21:4; Dt 11:4; Jos 2:10; 4:23; 24:6; Neh 9:9; Ps 106:7,9-11,22; 136:13-15; Ac 7:36; Heb 11:29); southern extent of the promised land (Ex 23:31); location of Solomon's fleet (1Kg 9:26).

REDEEM
the price of **r-ing** him is too costly, Ps 49:8
He **r-s** your life from the Pit; Ps 103:4
Christ has **r-ed** us from the curse Gl 3:13
to **r** those under the law, Gl 4:5

REDEEMER
I know my living **R**, and He will Jb 19:25
LORD, my rock and my **R**. Ps 19:14
Your **R** is the Holy One of Israel. Is 41:14

REDEMPTION
because your **r** is near! Lk 21:28
adoption, the **r** of our bodies. Rm 8:23
In Him we have **r** through His Eph 1:7
having obtained eternal **r**. Heb 9:12

REED
He will not break a bruised **r**, Is 42:3
A **r** swaying in the wind? Mt 11:7

REFLECT
are **r-ing** the glory of the Lord 2Co 3:18

REFRESHING (n)
that seasons of **r** may come Ac 3:19

REFUGE
will include six cities of **r**, Nm 35:6
whose wings you have come for **r**. Ru 2:12
God is our **r** and strength, Ps 46:1
we who have fled for **r** might Heb 6:18

REFUTE
For he vigorously **r-d** the Jews in Ac 18:28

REGARD (n)
The LORD had **r** for Abel and his Gn 4:4

REGARD (v)
but we in turn **r-ed** Him stricken, Is 53:4

REGENERATION
through the washing of **r** and Ti 3:5

REGION
In the same **r**, shepherds were Lk 2:8

REGISTER
that the whole empire should be **r-ed**. Lk 2:1

REGRET
LORD **r-ted** that He had made man Gn 6:6

REGULATIONS
Why do you submit to **r**: Col 2:20

REHOBOAM
Son of Solomon; king of Judah (1Kg 11:43). Answered people harshly; the kingdom was divided (12:1-19; 2Ch 10:1-19).

REIGN
The LORD will **r** forever and ever! Ex 15:18
The LORD **r-s**! He is robed in Ps 93:1
who says to Zion, "Your God **r-s**!" Is 52:7
He will **r** over the house of Lk 1:33
do not let sin **r** in your mortal Rm 6:12
For He must **r** until He puts all 1Co 15:25
will **r** with Him for 1,000 years. Rv 20:6

REJECT
The stone the builders **r-ed** has Ps 118:22
He was despised and **r-ed** by men, Is 53:3
the builders **r-ed** has become Mt 21:42
Whoever **r-s** you **r-s** Me. Lk 10:16
of men who **r** the truth. Ti 1:14
r-ed by men but chosen and 1Pt 2:4

REJOICE
let us **r** and be glad in it. Ps 118:24
R in the Lord always. I will say it again: **R**! Php 4:4

RELATIVE
in his hometown, among his **r-s**, Mk 6:4

RELEASE (v)
do you want me to **r** for you? Mt 27:21

RELENT
but the LORD **r-ed** concerning 2Sm 24:16
may turn and **r** and leave a blessing Jl 2:14

RELIGION
holding to the form of **r** but denying 2Tm 3:5
and undefiled **r** before our God Jms 1:27

RELIGIOUS
are extremely **r** in every respect. Ac 17:22

RELY
He **r-ies** on the LORD; let Him Ps 22:8
do not **r** on your own understanding; Pr 3:5

REMAIN
the word of our God **r-s** forever. Is 40:8
R in Me, and I in you. Jn 15:4
three **r**: faith, hope, and love. 1Co 13:13

REMARKABLE
and look at this **r** sight. Ex 3:3

REMARKABLY
been **r** and wonderfully made. Ps 139:14

REMEMBER
God **r-ed** Noah, Gn 8:1
R to dedicate the Sabbath day Ex 20:8
what is man that You **r** him, Ps 8:4
made of, **r-ing** that we are dust. Ps 103:14
So **r** your Creator in the days Ec 12:1
and never again **r** their sin. Jr 31:34
R Lot's wife! Lk 17:32
asked only that we would **r** the poor, Gl 2:10
R my imprisonment. Col 4:18
will never again **r** their sins Heb 8:12; 10:17

REMEMBRANCE
there is no **r** of You in death; Ps 6:5
Do this in **r** of Me. Lk 22:19; 1Co 11:24

REMINDER
there is a **r** of sins every year. Heb 10:3

REMNANT
For a **r** will go out from 2Kg 19:31
The **r** will return, the **r** of Jacob, Is 10:21
only the **r** will be saved; Rm 9:27

REMOTE
by boat to a **r** place to be alone. Mt 14:13

REMOVAL
not the **r** of the filth of the flesh, 1Pt 3:21

REMOVE
I will **r** your heart of stone and Ezk 36:26

RENEW
and **r** a steadfast spirit within me. Ps 51:10
youth is **r-ed** like the eagle. Ps 103:5
the LORD will **r** their strength; Is 40:31
by the **r-ing** of your mind, Rm 12:2
person is being **r-ed** day by day. 2Co 4:16

REPAY
Vengeance belongs to Me; I will **r**. Dt 32:35
deserve or **repaid** us according to Ps 103:10
I will **r**, says the Lord. Rm 12:19

REPEAT
R them to your children. Dt 6:7

REPENT
and **r** in dust and ashes. Jb 42:6
R, because the kingdom of heaven Mt 3:2
R ... and be baptized, Ac 2:38

REPENTANCE
a baptism of **r** for the forgiveness Mk 1:4
r for forgiveness of sins will be Lk 24:47
godly grief produces a **r** 2Co 7:10
to perish, but all to come to **r**. 2Pt 3:9

REPRIMAND (n)
Better an open **r** than concealed Pr 27:5

REPROACH
must be above **r**, the husband of 1Tm 3:2

REQUESTS (n)
your **r** be made known to God. Php 4:6

REQUIRES
what it is the LORD **r** of you: Mc 6:8

REQUIREMENT
in order that the law's **r** would Rm 8:4

RESCUE
R those being taken off to death, Pr 24:11
His trust in God; let God **r** Him Mt 27:43
has **r-d** us from the domain of Col 1:13
r-s us from the coming wrath. 1Th 1:10
Lord knows how to **r** the godly 2Pt 2:9

RESIDE
Christ's power may **r** in me. 2Co 12:9
has eternal life **r-ing** in him. 1Jn 3:15

RESIDENCE
I will place My **r** among you, Lv 26:11
a place for Your **r** forever. 2Ch 6:2
flesh and took up **r** among us. Jn 1:14

RESIST
tell you, don't **r** an evildoer. Mt 5:39
are always **r-ing** the Holy Spirit; Ac 7:51
For who can **r** His will? Rm 9:19
may be able to **r** in the evil day Eph 6:13
have not yet **r-ed** to the point Heb 12:4
But **r** the Devil, and he will flee Jms 4:7

RESOUND
sea and all that fills it **r**. Ps 96:11
Praise Him with **r-ing** cymbals; Ps 150:5

RESPECT (n)
r to those you owe **r**, Rm 13:7
do this with gentleness and **r**, 1Pt 3:16

RESPECT (v)
Each of you is to **r** his mother Lv 19:3
'They will **r** my son,' he said. Mt 21:37

REST (n)
They will not enter My **r**. Ps 95:11
and I will give you **r**. Mt 11:28
A Sabbath **r** remains, therefore Heb 4:9

RESTED (v)
He **r** on the seventh day Gn 2:2

RESTORE
R the joy of Your salvation to me, Ps 51:12
is coming and will **r** everything, Mt 17:11
are You **r-ing** the kingdom to Israel? Ac 1:6
spiritual should **r** such a person Gl 6:1

RESTRAINS
know what currently **r** him, 2Th 2:6

RESTRAINT
because in His **r** God passed over Rm 3:25

RESURRECTED
and He will be **r** on the third Mt 20:19
For He has been **r**, just as He said. Mt 28:6
He has been **r**! He is not here! Mk 16:6

RESURRECTION
the **r** of life ... the **r** of judgment. Jn 5:29
I am the **r** and the life. Jn 11:25
if there is no **r** of the dead, 1Co 15:13
know Him and the power of His **r** Php 3:10

RETURN (v)
you are dust, and you will **r** to dust. Gn 3:19
the spirit **r-s** to God who gave Ec 12:7
mouth will not **r** to Me empty, Is 55:11
Come, let us **r** to the LORD. Hs 6:1

REUBEN
Son of Jacob and Leah; eldest (Gn 29:32). Lost birthright for sleeping with father's concubine (35:22; 49:4; 1Ch 5:1). Tried to rescue Joseph (Gn 37:21-29); offered to protect Benjamin (42:37). Tribe with territory east of the Dead Sea, north of the Arnon River (Nm 32; Jos 13:15-23).

REVEAL
blood did not **r** this to you, Mt 16:17
of his heart will be **r-ed**, 1Co 14:25

REVELATION
light for **r** to the Gentiles Lk 2:32
eagerly wait for the **r** of our Lord 1Co 1:7
has a psalm, a teaching, a **r**, 1Co 14:26
was made known to me by **r**, Eph 3:3
The **r** of Jesus Christ that God gave Rv 1:1

REVERE
descendants of Israel, **r** Him! Ps 22:23

REVERENCE
serve God acceptably, with **r** Heb 12:28

REVERENT
observe your pure, **r** lives. 1Pt 3:2

REVILE
When we are **r-d**, we bless; 1Co 4:12
when **r-d**, He did not **r** in return; 1Pt 2:23

REVIVE
Will You not **r** us again so that Ps 85:6

REVOKE
You **r** God's word by your tradition Mk 7:13

REWARD (n)
there is a **r** for the righteous! Ps 58:11
His **r** is with Him, and His gifts Is 40:10
your **r** is great in heaven. Mt 5:12
They've got their **r**! Mt 6:2,5,16
his attention was on the **r**. Heb 11:26

RIB
God made the **r** ... into a woman Gn 2:22

RICH (adj)
Don't wear yourself out to get **r**; Pr 23:4
hard for a **r** person to enter Mt 19:23
who want to be **r** fall into 1Tm 6:9
r should boast in his humiliation, Jms 1:10

RICHES
in her left, **r** and honor. Pr 3:16
the rich must not boast in his **r**. Jr 9:23
make known the **r** of His glory Rm 9:23
Oh, the depth of the **r** Rm 11:33

Jesus, because He will **s** His people Mt 1:21
whoever wants to **s** his life will Mt 16:25
and is baptized will be **s-d**, Mk 16:16
come to seek and to **s** the lost. Lk 19:10
world might be **s-d** through Him. Jn 3:17
name of the Lord will be **s-d**. Ac 2:21
the name of the Lord will be **s-d**. Rm 10:13
grace you are **s-d** through faith, Eph 2:8
came into the world to **s** sinners 1Tm 1:15

SAVIOR
They forgot God their **S**, Ps 106:21
and there is no other **S** but Me. Is 43:11
a **S**, who is Messiah the Lord. Lk 2:11
God, who is the **S** of everyone, 1Tm 4:10

SAY
who do you **s** that I am? Mt 16:15

SCALE
Dishonest **s-s** are detestable Pr 11:1
had a balance **s** in his hand. Rv 6:5

SCARLET
Though your sins are like **s**, Is 1:18
Him and dressed Him in a **s** robe. Mt 27:28

SCATTERED
sheep of the flock will be **s**. Mt 26:31

SCEPTER
s will not depart from Judah, Gn 49:10

SCOFFERS
s will come in the last days to 2Pt 3:3

SCORPION
asks for an egg, will give him a **s**? Lk 11:12

SCRIBES
authority, and not like their **s**. Mt 7:29
woe to you, **s** and Pharisees, Mt 23:13

SCRIPTURE
Today ... this **S** has been fulfilled. Lk 4:21
concerning Himself in all the **S-s**. Lk 24:27
You pore over the **S-s** because you Jn 5:39
and the **S** cannot be broken Jn 10:35
All **S** is inspired by God and is 2Tm 3:16

SEA
through the **s** on dry ground, Ex 14:22
the winds and the **s** obey Him! Mt 8:27
was something like a **s** of glass, Rv 4:6

SEAL (n)
Set me as a **s** on your heart, Sg 8:6
the scroll and break its **s-s**?" Rv 5:2

SEAL (v)
s the slaves ... on their foreheads. Rv 7:3

SEARCH
You have **s-ed** me and known me. Ps 139:1
S me, God, and know my heart; Ps 139:23
Keep **s-ing**, and you will find. Mt 7:7
And He who **s-es** the hearts knows Rm 8:27
for the Spirit **s-es** everything, 1Co 2:10

SEASON
that bears its fruit in **s** Ps 1:3
days, months, **s-s**, and years. Gl 4:10

SEAT (n)
Make a mercy **s** of pure gold, Ex 25:17
love the front **s** in the Lk 11:43
before the judgment **s** of Christ, 2Co 5:10

SEATED (v)
I saw the Lord **s** on a high and Is 6:1

SECRET
He knows the **s-s** of the heart? Ps 44:21
Father who sees in **s** will reward you. Mt 6:4
things kept **s** from the Mt 13:35
judges what people have kept **s**, Rm 2:16

SECRETLY
decided to divorce her **s**. Mt 1:19
but **s** because of his fear of the Jn 19:38

SEE
no one can **s** Me and live. Ex 33:20
in heart, because they will **s** God. Mt 5:8
No one has ever **s-n** God. Jn 1:18
who has **s-n** Me has **s-n** the Father. Jn 14:9
what we have **s-n** with our eyes, 1Jn 1:1
because we will **s** Him as He is. 1Jn 3:2

SEED
like a mustard **s** that a man took Mt 13:31
faith the size of a mustard **s**, Mt 17:20
not of perishable **s** but of 1Pt 1:23

SEEK
when you **s** Him with all your Dt 4:29
pray and **s** My face, and turn 2Ch 7:14
s peace and pursue it. Ps 34:14
S the LORD while He may be found; Is 55:6
But **s** first the kingdom of God Mt 6:33
come to **s** and to save the lost. Lk 19:10

SEEMS
a way that **s** right to a man, Pr 14:12; 16:25

SEIZE
Then they tried to **s** Him. Jn 7:30

SELF-CONTROL
you because of your lack of **s**. 1Co 7:5
knowledge with **s**, **s** with endurance, 2Pt 1:6

SELF-CONTROLLED
sensible, righteous, holy, **s**, Ti 1:8

SELFISH
is not **s**; is not provoked; 1Co 13:5
envy and **s** ambition Jms 3:14,16

SELL
You were **sold** for nothing, and you Is 52:3
joy he goes and **s-s** everything Mt 13:44
s all you have and give to the poor, Mk 10:21
one can buy or **s** unless he has Rv 13:17

SEND
I AM has **sent** me to you. Ex 3:14
Who should I **s**? ... Here I am. **S** me. Is 6:8
of the harvest to **s** out workers Mt 9:38
Me welcomes Him who **sent** Me. Mt 10:40
has **sent** Me to proclaim freedom Lk 4:18
the will of Him who **sent** Me. Jn 5:30; 6:38
If I go, I will **s** Him to you. Jn 16:7
Father has **sent** Me, I also **s** you. Jn 20:21
they preach unless they are **sent**? Rm 10:15
He loved us and **sent** His Son to be 1Jn 4:10

SENSE
who commits adultery lacks **s**; Pr 6:32

SENSIBLE
who heeds correction is **s**. Pr 15:5
were foolish and five were **s**. Mt 25:2

SEPARATE (v)
and a gossip **s-s** friends. Pr 16:28
joined together, man must not **s**. Mt 19:6
Who can **s** us from the love of Rm 8:35

SERPENT
Now the **s** was the most cunning Gn 3:1
as shrewd as **s-s** and as harmless Mt 10:16
the ancient **s**, who is called Rv 12:9

SERVANT
Speak, for Your **s** is listening. 1Sm 3:10
Give praise, you **s-s** of the LORD Ps 135:1
This is My **S**; I strengthen Him, Is 42:1
See, My **s** will act wisely; Is 52:13
Here is My **S** whom I have chosen, Mt 12:18
great among you must be your **s**, Mt 20:26
Where I am, there My **s** also will be Jn 12:26

SERVE
did not come to be **s-d**, but to **s**, Mt 20:28
but **s** one another through love. Gl 5:13

SERVICE
Render **s** with a good attitude, Eph 6:7

SET
S apart for Me Barnabas and Saul Ac 13:2

SEVEN
will be **s** weeks and 62 weeks. Dn 9:25
forgive him? As many as **s** times? Mt 18:21
To the **s** churches in the province Rv 1:4
s angels with the **s** last plagues, Rv 15:1

SEVENTH
By the **s** day, God completed His Gn 2:2
the **s** day is a Sabbath to the Ex 20:10

SEVENTY *see also* 70
S weeks are decreed about your Dn 9:24
The **S** returned with joy, saying, Lk 10:17

SEW
so they **s-ed** fig leaves together Gn 3:7
No one **s-s** a patch of unshrunk Mk 2:21

SHADE
to provide **s** over Jonah's Jnh 4:6
birds of the sky can nest in its **s**. Mk 4:32

SHADOW
Our days on earth are like a **s**, 1Ch 29:15
hide me in the **s** of Your wings Ps 17:8
dwells in the **s** of the Almighty. Ps 91:1
least his **s** might fall on some Ac 5:15
as a copy and **s** of the heavenly Heb 8:5

SHAKE
established; it cannot be **s-n**. 1Ch 16:30
of the LORD **s-s** the wilderness; Ps 29:8
s the dust off your feet when you Mt 10:14
pressed down, **s-n** together, Lk 6:38
where they were assembled was **s-n**, Ac 4:31
once more I will **s** not only the Heb 12:26

SHALLUM
1. King of Israel; assassinated Zechariah; was assassinated by Menahem (2Kg 15:10-15).
2. Alternate name for Jehoahaz (2Kg 23:30-34; Jr 22:11). *see* JEHOAHAZ 2.

SHAME
hope in Me will not be put to **s**. Is 49:23
some to **s** and eternal contempt. Dn 12:2
on Him will not be put to **s**. Rm 9:33
a cross and despised the **s**, Heb 12:2
in Him will never be put to **s**! 1Pt 2:6

SHAMEFUL
For it is **s** even to mention what Eph 5:12

SHAMELESS
Males committed **s** acts with males Rm 1:27

SHAPHAN
Josiah's court secretary or scribe (2Kg 22:3-14); his sons were friends of Jeremiah (Jr 26:24; 36:10; 39:14).

SHARE (v)
S your master's joy! Mt 25:21
two shirts must **s** with someone Lk 3:11

SHARP
There was such a **s** disagreement Ac 15:39

SHARPENS
s iron, and one man **s** another. Pr 27:17

SHARPER
and **s** than any two-edged sword, Heb 4:12

SHAVED
If I am **s**, my strength will leave Jdg 16:17
for them to get their heads **s**. Ac 21:24

SHEARER
a lamb is silent before its **s**, Ac 8:32

SHEAVES
shouts of joy, carrying his **s**. Ps 126:6

SHECHEM
1. City in the hill country of Ephraim. Simeon and Levi destroyed the city in revenge for the rape of Dinah (Gn 34); Joshua renewed the covenant there (Jos 24:1-28); served as first capital of the northern kingdom (1Kg 12:25).
2. Son of Hamor; raped Dinah (Gn 34).

SHED
Whoever **s-s** man's blood, his blood Gn 9:6
My blood; it is **s** for you. Lk 22:20
without the **s-ding** of blood there Heb 9:22

SHEEP
people, the **s** of His pasture. Ps 100:3
We all went astray like **s**; Is 53:6
like **s** without a shepherd. Mt 9:36
If a man has 100 **s**, and one Mt 18:12
separates the **s** from the goats. Mt 25:32
He calls his own **s** by name Jn 10:3
I lay down My life for the **s**. Jn 10:15
"Feed My **s**," Jesus said. Jn 21:17

SHEET
a large **s** being lowered to Ac 10:11

SHELTER
under the **s** of Your wings. Ps 61:4

SHEOL
You will not abandon me to **S**; Ps 16:10
make my bed in **S**, You are there. Ps 139:8
S and Abaddon lie open before Pr 15:11
have made an agreement with **S**; Is 28:15
S, where is your sting? Hs 13:14

SHEPHERD (n)
The LORD is my **s**; there is Ps 23:1
He protects His flock like a **s**; Is 40:11
prophesy against the **s-s** of Israel. Ezk 34:2
like sheep without a **s**. Mt 9:36
s-s were staying out in the fields Lk 2:8
I am the good **s**. The good **s** lays Jn 10:11
And when the chief **S** appears, 1Pt 5:4

SHEPHERD (v)
You will **s** My people Israel 2Sm 5:2
s God's flock among you, not 1Pt 5:2

SHIELD
He is a **s** to all who take refuge 2Sm 22:31
LORD is my strength and my **s**; Ps 28:7
situation take the **s** of faith, Eph 6:16

SHINE
the LORD make His face **s** on you, Nm 6:25
Arise, **s**, for your light has Is 60:1
let your light **s** before men, Mt 5:16
and His face **shone** like the sun. Mt 17:2
glory of the Lord **shone** around them, Lk 2:9

SHIPWRECK
Three times I was **s-ed**. 2Co 11:25
suffered the **s** of their faith. 1Tm 1:19

SHOOT (n)
a **s** will grow from the stump Is 11:1

SHORT
Is My hand too **s** to redeem? Is 50:2
the crowd, since he was a **s** man. Lk 19:3
sinned and fall **s** of the glory Rm 3:23

SHOULDERS
government will be on His **s**. Is 9:6

SHOUT (n)
descend from heaven with a **s**, 1Th 4:16

SHOUT (v)
until the time I say, '**S**!' Then you Jos 6:10
S triumphantly to the LORD, Ps 100:1
they kept **s-ing**, "Crucify Him!" Mt 27:23

SHOW
because they will be **s-n** mercy. Mt 5:7
make long prayers just for **s**. Mt 23:14
He **s-ed** them His hands and feet. Lk 24:40
s us the Father, and that's enough Jn 14:8
And I will **s** you an even better 1Co 12:31
S me your faith without works, Jms 2:18

SHOWERS
s in ... season—**s** of blessing. Ezk 34:26

SHREWD
Therefore be as **s** as serpents Mt 10:16

SHUT
and they have **s** their eyes; ... Mt 13:15
SICK
need a doctor, but the **s** do. ... Mt 9:12
I was **s** and you took care of Me; ... Mt 25:36
Is anyone among you **s**? ... Jms 5:14
SICKLE
Swing the **s** because the harvest ... Jl 3:13
and a sharp **s** in His hand. ... Rv 14:14
SICKNESS
He Himself bore our **s-es**, ... Is 53:4
SIDE
Though a thousand fall at your **s** ... Ps 91:7
pierced His **s** with a spear, ... Jn 19:34
SIFT
has asked to **s** you like wheat. ... Lk 22:31
SIGHT
The blind receive their **s**, ... Lk 7:22
for we walk by faith, not by **s** ... 2Co 5:7
SIGN
will give you a **s**: The virgin ... Is 7:14
demands a **s**, but no **s** will be given
to it except the **s** of ... Jonah. ... Mt 12:39
s of Your coming and of the end ... Mt 24:3
This will be the **s** for you: ... Lk 2:12
Jesus performed many other **s-s** ... Jn 20:30
Jews ask for **s-s** and the Greeks ... 1Co 1:22
SILAS
Early church leader and prophet; also called Silvanus. Brought news from Jerusalem to Antioch (Ac 15:22,32); worked with Paul and Peter in missions and writing letters (15:40-41; 16:19-40; 17:10-15; 18:5; 2Co 1:19; 1Th 1:1; 2Th 1:1; 1Pt 5:12).
SILENCE (n)
should learn in **s** with full ... 1Tm 2:11
there was **s** in heaven for about ... Rv 8:1
SILENCE (v)
that He had **s-d** the Sadducees, ... Mt 22:34
said to the sea, "**S**! Be still!" ... Mk 4:39
SILENT
When I kept **s**, my bones became ... Ps 32:3
considered wise when he keeps **s**, ... Pr 17:28
and like a sheep **s** before her ... Is 53:7
But Jesus kept **s**. ... Mt 26:63
and as a lamb is **s** before its ... Ac 8:32
women should be **s** in the ... 1Co 14:34
SILVER
like golden apples on a **s** tray. ... Pr 25:11
30 pieces of **s** for him. ... Mt 26:15
SIMEON
1. Son of Jacob and Leah (Gn 29:33); with Levi, avenged Dinah's rape by Shechem (34:25-31; 49:5); held as hostage by Joseph (42:24). Tribe with territory within Judah (Jos 19:1-9; Jdg 1:3,17).
2. Devout Jew who blessed the baby Jesus (Lk 2:25-35).
3. Jewish variation of Simon (Ac 15:14; 2Pt 1:1). *see* PETER
SIMON
1. Apostle Peter's original name (Mt 4:18). *see* PETER
2. Apostle; called the Zealot (Mt 10:4; Mk 3:18; Lk 6:15; Ac 1:13).
3. Sorcerer who wanted to buy the power of the Spirit (Ac 8:9-24).
SIN (n)
be sure your **s** will catch up with ... Nm 32:23
but **s** is a disgrace to any people. ... Pr 14:34
yet He bore the **s** of many ... Is 53:12
forgive us our **s-s**, for we ... Lk 11:4
takes away the **s** of the world! ... Jn 1:29
For the wages of **s** is death, ... Rm 6:23
Christ died for our **s-s** according to ... 1Co 15:3
who did not know **s** to be **s** for us, ... 2Co 5:21
way as we are, yet without **s**. ... Heb 4:15
confess our **s-s**, He is faithful ... 1Jn 1:9
s is the breaking of law. ... 1Jn 3:4
SIN (v)
You—You alone—I have **s-ned** ... Ps 51:4
so that I may not **s** against You. ... Ps 119:11
your right eye causes you to **s**, ... Mt 5:29
If your brother **s-s**, rebuke him, ... Lk 17:3
from now on do not **s** any more. ... Jn 8:11
Rabbi, who **s-ned**, this man or ... Jn 9:2
For all have **s-ned** and fall short ... Rm 3:23
SINCERE
for **s** love of the brothers, ... 1Pt 1:22
SINFUL
I was **s** when my mother conceived ... Ps 51:5
into the hands of **s** men, ... Lk 24:7
SING
I will **s** to the LORD, for He is ... Ex 15:1
S praise to God, **s** praise; ... Ps 47:6
S a new song to the LORD ... Ps 96:1; 98:1
After **s-ing** psalms, they went out ... Mt 26:30
s-ing and making music to the ... Eph 5:19
s-ing psalms, hymns, and spiritual ... Col 3:16

they **sang** a new song: You are ... Rv 5:9
SINGED
not a hair of their heads was **s**, ... Dn 3:27
SINGERS
S lead the way, with musicians ... Ps 68:25
SINK
I have **sunk** in deep mud, ... Ps 69:2
And beginning to **s** he cried out, ... Mt 14:30
SINNER
or take the path of **s-s**, ... Ps 1:1
My son, if **s-s** entice you, don't ... Pr 1:10
friend of tax collectors and **s-s**! ... Mt 11:19
in heaven over one **s** who repents ... Lk 15:7
while we were still **s-s** Christ died ... Rm 5:8
came into the world to save **s-s** ... 1Tm 1:15
SISTER
say you're my **s** ... Gn 12:13
is My brother and **s** and mother. ... Mt 12:50
SIT
the LORD **s-s** enthroned forever; ... Ps 9:7
S at My right hand until I make ... Ps 110:1
But to **s** at My right and left is ... Mt 20:23
SIX
are to labor **s** days and do all ... Ex 20:9
SKIN
clothing out of **s-s** for Adam and ... Gn 3:21
unclean; he has a **s** disease. ... Lv 13:8
"**S** for **s**!" Satan answered ... Jb 2:4
Even after my **s** has been destroyed, ... Jb 19:26
a man with a serious **s** disease came ... Mt 8:2
Otherwise, the **s-s** burst, ... Mt 9:17
SKULL
Golgotha (which means **S** Place), ... Mt 27:33
SKY
Your faithfulness to the **s-ies**. ... Ps 36:5
good weather because the **s** is red. ... Mt 16:2
the **s** separated like a scroll ... Rv 6:14
SLACKER
Go to the ant, you **s**! ... Pr 6:6
by the field of a **s** and by the ... Pr 24:30
SLANDER (n)
and whoever spreads **s** is a fool. ... Pr 10:18
hypocrisy, envy, and all **s**. ... 1Pt 2:1
SLANDER (v)
who does not **s** with his tongue, ... Ps 15:3
when we are **s-ed**, we entreat. ... 1Co 4:13
SLANDERER
behavior, not **s-s**, not addicted ... Ti 2:3
SLAP
if anyone **s-s** you on your right ... Mt 5:39
SLAUGHTER
are counted as sheep to be **s-ed**. ... Ps 44:22
Like a lamb led to the **s** ... Is 53:7
was led like a sheep to the **s**, ... Ac 8:32
The Lamb who was **s-ed** is worthy ... Rv 5:12
SLAVE
Remember that you were a **s** in ... Dt 5:15
borrower is a **s** to the lender. ... Pr 22:7
No one can be a **s** of two masters ... Mt 6:24
to my **s**, 'Do this!' and he does it. ... Mt 8:9
first among you must be your **s**; ... Mt 20:27
Well done, good and faithful **s**! ... Mt 25:21
who commits sin is a **s** of sin. ... Jn 8:34
I do not call you **s-s** anymore,
because a **s** doesn't know what ... Jn 15:15
no Jew or Greek, **s** or free, male ... Gl 3:28
by assuming the form of a **s**, ... Php 2:7
SLAVERY
out of Egypt, out of the place of **s**, ... Ex 13:3
you did not receive a spirit of **s** ... Rm 8:15
SLEEP (n)
God caused a deep **s** to come over ... Gn 2:21
A little **s**, a little slumber, ... Pr 6:10; 24:33
SLEEP (v)
of Israel does not slumber or **s**. ... Ps 121:4
the girl isn't dead, but **s-ing**. ... Mt 9:24
disciples and found them **s-ing**. ... Mt 26:40
SLING
Philistine with a **s** and a stone. ... 1Sm 17:50
SLOW
s to anger and rich in faithful ... Ex 34:6
to hear, **s** to speak, and **s** to anger, ... Jms 1:19
SLUMBER
your Protector will not **s**. ... Ps 121:3
SMALL
faithful in a very **s** matter, ... Lk 19:17
SMALLEST
It's the **s** of all the seeds, ... Mt 13:32
SMOKE
Sinai was ... enveloped in **s** ... Ex 19:18
the temple was filled with **s**. ... Is 6:4
SMOLDERING (adj)
will not put out a **s** wick ... Is 42:3; Mt 12:20
SMOOTH
S lips with an evil heart are ... Pr 26:23
straight, the rough ways **s**, ... Lk 3:5

SNAKE
the ground, and it became a **s**. ... Ex 4:3
made a bronze **s** and mounted it ... Nm 21:9
In the end it bites like a **s** ... Pr 23:32
for a fish, will give him a **s**? ... Mt 7:10
they will pick up **s-s**; ... Mk 16:18
as Moses lifted up the **s** in the ... Jn 3:14
SNARE
their gods, it will be a **s** for you. ... Ex 23:33
the **s-s** of death confronted me. ... 2Sm 22:6
will keep your foot from a **s**. ... Pr 3:26
SNATCH
No one will **s** them out of My ... Jn 10:28
SNOUT
like a gold ring in a pig's **s**. ... Pr 11:22
SNOW
and I will be whiter than **s**. ... Ps 51:7
they will be as white as **s**; ... Is 1:18
and his robe was as white as **s**. ... Mt 28:3
SNUGLY
she wrapped Him **s** in cloth and ... Lk 2:7
SOAR
will **s** on wings like eagles; ... Is 40:31
SOBER
but we must stay awake and be **s**. ... 1Th 5:6
Be **s**! Be on the alert! ... 1Pt 5:8
SODOM
City on the plain, where Lot settled (Gn 10:19; 13:10; 14:11-12); destroyed along with Gomorrah by God (Gn 18:20; 19:24).
SOIL
quickly since the **s** wasn't deep. ... Mt 13:5
SOLDIERS
The **s** also mocked Him. ... Lk 23:36
SOLID
I fed you milk, not **s** food, ... 1Co 3:2
But **s** food is for the mature ... Heb 5:14
SOLOMON
Son of David and Bathsheba; third king of Israel (2Sm 12:24; 1Kg 1:30-40). Asked for wisdom (3:5-15); knew many proverbs and songs (4:32; Pss 72; 127; Pr 1:1; 10:1; 25:1; Sg 1:1); wisdom demonstrated in child dispute (1Kg 3:16-28) and the visit of the Queen of Sheba (10:1-13). Built and dedicated the temple (1Kg 5–8). Accumulated vast wealth (9:26-28; 10:26-29); had many wives and concubines, who influenced him toward idolatry (11:1-8).
SON *see also* SON OF DAVID, SON OF GOD, SON OF MAN, SONS OF GOD
"Take your **s**," He said, "your only ... Gn 22:2
and he will be a **s** to Me. ... 2Sm 7:14
He said to Me, "You are My **S**; ... Ps 2:7
S-s are indeed a heritage from ... Ps 127:3
The virgin will conceive, have a **s**, ... Is 7:14
Out of Egypt I called My **S**. ... Mt 2:15
beloved **S**. I take delight in Him! ... Mt 3:17
This man really was God's **S**! ... Mt 27:54
called the **S** of the Most High, ... Lk 1:32
you will be **s-s** of the Most High. ... Lk 6:35
He gave His One and Only **S**, ... Jn 3:16
conformed to the image of His **S**, ... Rm 8:29
will be called **s-s** of the living ... Rm 9:26
you will be **s-s** and daughters ... 2Co 6:18
slave, but a **s**; and if a **s**, then an heir ... Gl 4:7
He has spoken to us by His **S**, ... Heb 1:2
that addresses you as **s-s**: ... Heb 12:5
loved us and sent His **S** to be ... 1Jn 4:10
The one who has the **S** has life. ... 1Jn 5:12
SON OF DAVID
Perhaps this is the **S**! ... Mt 12:23
Hosanna to the **S**! ... Mt 21:9
SON OF GOD
will be called the **S**. ... Lk 1:35
that He is the **S**! ... Jn 1:34
confesses that Jesus is the **S** ... 1Jn 4:15
SON OF MAN
s that You look after Him? ... Ps 8:4
He said to me, "**S**, ... Ezk 2:1
I saw One like a **s** coming ... Dn 7:13
S coming in His kingdom. ... Mt 16:28
When the **S** comes in His glory, ... Mt 25:31
S seated at the right hand ... Mk 14:62
so the **S** must be lifted up, ... Jn 3:14
S standing at the right hand of God! ... Ac 7:56
One like the **S** was seated on ... Rv 14:14
SONG
He put a new **s** in my mouth, ... Ps 40:3
psalms, hymns, and spiritual **s-s**, ... Eph 5:19
the **s** of the Lamb: ... Rv 15:3
SONS OF GOD
the **s** saw that the daughters of man ... Gn 6:2
peacemakers ... will be called **s**. ... Mt 5:9
you are all **s** through faith in Christ ... Gl 3:26
SORCERER
But Elymas, the **s**, which is how ... Ac 13:8

SORCERY
- interpret omens, practice **s**, — Dt 18:10
- idolatry, **s**, hatreds, strife, — Gl 5:20

SORROW
- For with much wisdom is much **s**; — Ec 1:18
- My soul is swallowed up in **s** — Mt 26:38
- but your **s** will turn to joy. — Jn 16:20

SOUL
- all your **s**, and with all your strength. — Dt 6:5
- LORD is perfect, reviving the **s**; — Ps 19:7
- to destroy both **s** and body in hell. — Mt 10:28
- Now My **s** is troubled. — Jn 12:27
- as far as to divide **s**, spirit, joints, — Heb 4:12
- shepherd and guardian of your **s-s**. — 1Pt 2:25

SOUND (n)
- voice like the **s** of cascading waters. — Rv 1:15

SOUND (v)
- **s** the alarm on My holy mountain! — Jl 2:1
- the trumpet will **s**, and the dead — 1Co 15:52

SOUR
- The fathers have eaten **s** grapes, — Jr 31:29

SOURCE
- And you killed the **s** of life, — Ac 3:15
- **s** and perfecter of our faith, — Heb 12:2

SOVEREIGN
- He is the blessed and only **S**, — 1Tm 6:15

SOW (v)
- those who **s** trouble reap the same. — Jb 4:8
- Those who **s** in tears will reap — Ps 126:5
- they don't **s** or reap or gather — Mt 6:26
- a man who **s-ed** good seed — Mt 13:24
- One **s-s** and another reaps. — Jn 4:37
- **Sown** in corruption, raised in — 1Co 15:42
- person who **s-s** sparingly will — 2Co 9:6
- whatever a man **s-s** he will also — Gl 6:7

SOWER
- Consider the **s** who went out to — Mt 13:3

SPARE
- He did not even **s** His own Son, — Rm 8:32
- if God didn't **s** the angels who — 2Pt 2:4

SPARINGLY
- person who sows **s** will also reap **s**, — 2Co 9:6

SPARROWS
- are worth more than many **s**. — Mt 10:31

SPEAK
- to be silent and a time to **s**; — Ec 3:7
- began to **s** in different languages, — Ac 2:4
- If I **s** the languages of men and — 1Co 13:1
- was a child, I **spoke** like a child, — 1Co 13:11
- Holy Spirit, men **spoke** from God. — 2Pt 1:21

SPEAR
- their **s-s** into pruning knives. — Is 2:4; Mc 4:3
- pierced His side with a **s**, — Jn 19:34

SPECIAL
- has chosen you to be His **s** people — Dt 14:2
- cleanse for Himself a **s** people, — Ti 2:14

SPECK
- the **s** in your brother's eye, — Mt 7:3

SPECTACLE
- we have become a **s** to the world — 1Co 4:9

SPEECH
- I am slow and hesitant in **s**. — Ex 4:10
- Day after day they pour out **s**; — Ps 19:2

SPICES
- cloths with the aromatic **s**, — Jn 19:40

SPIN
- they don't labor or **s** — Mt 6:28; Lk 12:27

SPIRIT *see also* **HOLY SPIRIT, SPIRIT OF GOD, SPIRIT OF THE LORD**
- an evil **s** from the LORD began — 1Sm 16:14
- Into Your hand I entrust my **s**; — Ps 31:5
- renew a steadfast **s** within me. — Ps 51:10
- the **s** returns to God who gave — Ec 12:7
- and put a new **s** within you; — Ezk 36:26
- pour out My **S** on all humanity — Jl 2:28
- Blessed are the poor in **s**, — Mt 5:3
- I will put My **S** on Him, and He — Mt 12:18
- The **s** is willing, but the flesh — Mt 26:41
- into Your hands I entrust My **s**. — Lk 23:46
- God is **s**, and those who worship Him must worship in **s** and truth. — Jn 4:24
- met us who had a **s** of prediction — Ac 16:16
- are not in the flesh, but in the **S**, — Rm 8:9
- have the **S** as the firstfruits — Rm 8:23
- different gifts, but the same **S**. — 1Co 12:4
- walk by the **S** and you will not — Gl 5:16
- There is one body and one **S**, — Eph 4:4
- but be filled with the **S**: — Eph 5:18
- Don't stifle the **S**. — 1Th 5:19
- to divide soul, **s**, joints, and — Heb 4:12
- proclamation to the **s-s** in prison — 1Pt 3:19
- not believe every **s**, but test the **s-s** — 1Jn 4:1

SPIRIT OF GOD
- **S** was hovering over the surface — Gn 1:2
- He saw the **S** descending like a dove — Mt 3:16

SPIRIT OF THE LORD
- **S** took control of David from that — 1Sm 16:13
- **S** is on Me ... He has appointed Me — Lk 4:18

SPIRITISTS
- not turn to mediums or consult **s**, — Lv 19:31

SPIRITUAL
- this is your **s** worship. — Rm 12:1
- a natural body, raised a **s** body. — 1Co 15:44
- blessed us with every **s** blessing — Eph 1:3

SPIT
- Then they **s** in His face and beat — Mt 26:67
- He **s** on the ground, made some mud — Jn 9:6

SPLENDOR
- Worship the LORD in the **s** of — Ps 29:2

SPLIT
- He **s** the rock, and water gushed — Is 48:21

SPOKESMAN
- He will be your **s**, — Ex 4:16

SPONGE
- a **s** full of sour wine on hyssop — Jn 19:29

SPOT
- without **s** or wrinkle or any such — Eph 5:27
- in peace without **s** or blemish — 2Pt 3:14

SPRAWL
- ivory, **s-ed** out on their couches, — Am 6:4
- of those who **s** out will come to — Am 6:7

SPREAD
- **s-ing** out the sky like a canopy, — Ps 104:2

SPRING (n)
- from the **s** of living water as a gift. — Rv 21:6

SPRING (v)
- **S** up, well—sing to it! — Nm 21:17
- they **sprang** up quickly since — Mt 13:5
- well of water **s-ing** up within him — Jn 4:14

SPRINKLE
- will also **s** clean water on you, — Ezk 36:25
- **s-ing** with the blood of Jesus Christ. — 1Pt 1:2

SPY (v)
- in secretly to **s** on our freedom — Gl 2:4

SQUANDERED
- he **s** his estate in foolish living. — Lk 15:13

STAFF
- threw down his **s** before Pharaoh — Ex 7:10
- rod and Your **s**—they comfort me. — Ps 23:4

STAND
- where you are **s-ing** is holy ground. — Ex 3:5
- against itself, that house cannot **s**. — Mk 3:25
- into this grace in which we **s**, — Rm 5:2
- thinks he **s-s** must be careful — 1Co 10:12
- so that you can **s** against the — Eph 6:11
- I **s** at the door and knock. — Rv 3:20

STAR
- God made ... as well as the **s-s**. — Gn 1:16
- the morning **s-s** sang together — Jb 38:7
- we saw His **s** in the east — Mt 2:2
- of David, the Bright Morning **S**. — Rv 22:16

STATURE
- look at his appearance or his **s**, — 1Sm 16:7
- Jesus increased in wisdom and **s**, — Lk 2:52

STAY
- and **s** awake with Me. — Mt 26:38

STEADFAST
- me and renew a **s** spirit within — Ps 51:10

STEAL
- Do not **s**. — Ex 20:15
- where thieves break in and **s**. — Mt 6:19
- comes only to **s** and to kill and — Jn 10:10
- The thief must no longer **s**. — Eph 4:28

STEPHEN

Foremost of the first seven deacons (Ac 6:1-7). First Christian martyr (6:8–7:60); Saul approved of his death (8:1; 22:20); start of persecution and dispersion (11:19).

STEPS
- but the LORD determines his **s**. — Pr 16:9
- you should follow in His **s**. — 1Pt 2:21

STEWARDSHIP
- I am entrusted with a **s**. — 1Co 9:17

STIFLE
- Don't **s** the Spirit. — 1Th 5:19

STILL (adj)
- reflect in your heart and be **s**. — Ps 4:4
- Silence! Be **s**!" The wind ceased — Mk 4:39

STING
- O Death, where is your **s**? — 1Co 15:55

STIR
- but a harsh word **s-s** up wrath. — Pr 15:1
- from time to time and **s** up the water. — Jn 5:4

STOMACH
- passes into the **s** and is eliminated? — Mt 15:17
- Food for the **s** and the **s** for foods, — 1Co 6:13

STONE (n)
- **s** tablets inscribed by ... God. — Ex 31:18
- five smooth **s-s** from the wadi — 1Sm 17:40
- strike your foot against a **s**. — Ps 91:12
- The **s** that the builders rejected — Ps 118:22
- have laid a **s** in Zion, a tested **s**, — Is 28:16
- strike your foot against a **s**. — Mt 4:6
- for bread, will give him a **s**? — Mt 7:9
- silent, the **s-s** would cry out! — Lk 19:40
- be the first to throw a **s** at her. — Jn 8:7
- not on **s** tablets but on tablets — 2Co 3:3
- to Him, a living **s**—rejected by — 1Pt 2:4

STOREHOUSE
- full 10 percent into the **s** — Mal 3:10

STOREROOM
- brings out of his **s** what is new and — Mt 13:52

STORM
- a violent **s** arose on the sea, — Mt 8:24

STRAIGHT
- make a **s** highway for our God in — Is 40:3
- Make **s** the way of the Lord — Jn 1:23

STRAIN
- You **s** out a gnat, yet gulp down — Mt 23:24

STRANGER
- I was a **s** and you took Me in; — Mt 25:35
- no longer foreigners and **s-s**, — Eph 2:19

STRAP
- whose sandal **s** I'm not worthy to — Jn 1:27

STRAW
- costly stones, wood, hay, or **s**, — 1Co 3:12

STREAMS (n)
- planted beside **s** of water — Ps 1:3
- its **s** delight the city of God, — Ps 46:4
- **s** of living water flow from — Jn 7:38

STREET
- Wisdom calls out in the **s**; — Pr 1:20
- on the **s** corners to be seen by people. — Mt 6:5
- **s** of the city was pure gold, — Rv 21:21

STRENGTH
- The LORD is my **s** and my song; — Ex 15:2
- does not prevail by his own **s**. — 1Sm 2:9
- I love You, LORD, my **s**. — Ps 18:1
- The LORD is my **s** and my shield; — Ps 28:7
- God is our refuge and **s**, a helper — Ps 46:1
- in the LORD will renew their **s**; — Is 40:31
- Not by **s** or by might, but by My — Zch 4:6
- your mind, and with all your **s**. — Mk 12:30

STRENGTHEN
- have turned back, **s** your brothers. — Lk 22:32
- be **s-ed** by the Lord and by His — Eph 6:10
- things through Him who **s-s** me. — Php 4:13
- Therefore **s** your tired hands — Heb 12:12

STRETCHER
- lowered the **s** on which the paralytic — Mk 2:4

STRICKEN
- but we in turn regarded Him **s**, — Is 53:4

STRIFE
- a house full of feasting with **s**. — Pr 17:1
- sorcery, hatreds, **s**, jealousy, — Gl 5:20

STRIKE
- **s** your head, and you will **s** his heel. — Gn 3:15
- you will not **s** your foot against — Ps 91:12
- The sun will not **s** you by day, — Ps 121:6
- **S** the shepherd, and the sheep will — Zch 13:7
- you will not **s** your foot against — Mt 4:6
- I will **s** the shepherd, and the — Mt 26:31

STRIPPED
- They **s** him, beat him up, — Lk 10:30

STRIVING
- Don't keep **s** for what you — Lk 12:29

STROKE
- or one **s** of a letter will pass from — Mt 5:18
- than for one **s** of a letter ... to drop — Lk 16:17

STRONG
- Be **s** and courageous; — Dt 31:6
- LORD, **s** and mighty, the LORD, — Ps 24:8
- The name of the LORD is a **s** tower; — Pr 18:10
- The boy grew up and became **s**, — Lk 2:40
- Now we who are **s** have an — Rm 15:1
- For when I am weak, then I am **s**. — 2Co 12:10

STRONGER
- God's weakness is **s** than human — 1Co 1:25

STRONGHOLD
- the God of Jacob is our **s**. — Ps 46:7,11
- way of the LORD is a **s** for the — Pr 10:29
- for the demolition of **s-s**. — 2Co 10:4

STUBBORN
- a **s** and rebellious generation, — Ps 78:8

STUDY
- and much **s** wearies the body. — Ec 12:12
- Too much **s** is driving you mad! — Ac 26:24

STUMBLE
- nothing makes them **s**. — Ps 119:165
- be a stone to **s** over and a rock — Is 8:14
- They **s-d** over the **s-ing** stone. — Rm 9:32
- We give no opportunity for **s-ing** — 2Co 6:3
- for we all **s** in many ways. — Jms 3:2
- who is able to protect you from **s-ing** — Jd 24

STUMBLING BLOCK
- but instead decide not to put a **s** — Rm 14:13
- Christ crucified, a **s** to the Jews — 1Co 1:23
- this right ... in no way becomes a **s** — 1Co 8:9

STUMP
shoot will grow from the **s** of Jesse, ... Is 11:1
STUPID
one who hates correction is **s**. ... Pr 12:1
SUBDUE
fill the earth, and **s** it. ... Gn 1:28
SUBJECT
the creation was **s-ed** to futility ... Rm 8:20
And when everything is **s** to Him, ... 1Co 15:28
SUBMISSION
learn in silence with full **s**. ... 1Tm 2:11
SUBMISSIVE
Wives, be **s** to your husbands, as ... Col 3:18
Remind them to be **s** to rulers ... Ti 3:1
SUBMIT
He **s-ted** Himself to death, ... Is 53:12
s to the governing authorities, ... Rm 13:1
Wives, **s** to your own husbands ... Eph 5:22
Therefore, **s** to God. But resist ... Jms 4:7
S to every human institution ... 1Pt 2:13
SUCCESS
He stores up **s** for the upright; ... Pr 2:7
SUE
one who wants to **s** you and take ... Mt 5:40
SUEZ
LORD will divide the Gulf of **S**. ... Is 11:15
SUFFER
Son of Man must **s** many things, ... Mk 8:31
Messiah would **s** and rise from ... Lk 24:46
we **s** with Him so that we also may ... Rm 8:17
one member **s-s**, all ... **s** with it; ... 1Co 12:26
Christ also **s-ed** for you, ... 1Pt 2:21
it is better to **s** for doing good, ... 1Pt 3:17
Christ also **s-ed** for sins once ... 1Pt 3:18
SUFFERING (n)
man of **s** who knew what sickness ... Is 53:3
the **s-s** of this present time are not ... Rm 8:18
the fellowship of His **s-s**, ... Php 3:10
SUFFICIENT
My grace is **s** for you, ... 2Co 12:9
SUMMER
it prepares its provisions in **s**; ... Pr 6:8
leaves, you know that **s** is near. ... Mt 24:32
SUN
And the **s** stood still ... Jos 10:13
the LORD God is a **s** and shield. ... Ps 84:11
there is nothing new under the **s**. ... Ec 1:9
the **s** of righteousness will rise ... Mal 4:2
For He causes His **s** to rise on ... Mt 5:45
The **s** will be darkened, ... Mt 24:29
Don't let the **s** go down on your ... Eph 4:26
His face was shining like the **s** ... Rv 1:16
not need the **s** or the moon to ... Rv 21:23
SUNLIGHT
will not need lamplight or **s**, ... Rv 22:5
SUNRISE
they went to the tomb at **s**. ... Mk 16:2
SUPERIOR
He inherited is **s** to theirs. ... Heb 1:4
inferior is blessed by the **s**. ... Heb 7:7
SUPPER
took the cup after **s** and said, ... Lk 22:20
cup, after **s**, and said, "This ... 1Co 11:25
SUPPLY (v)
And my God will **s** all your needs ... Php 4:19
SUPPORT
but the LORD was my **s**. ... 2Sm 22:19
SUPPRESS
unrighteousness **s** the truth, ... Rm 1:18
SURE
be **s** your sin will catch up with ... Nm 32:23
cornerstone, a **s** foundation; ... Is 28:16
SURELY
to say to Him, "**S** not I, Lord?" ... Mt 26:22
SURPASS
capable, but you **s** them all! ... Pr 31:29
unless your righteousness **s-es** ... Mt 5:20
love that **s-es** knowledge, ... Eph 3:19
view of the **s-ing** value of knowing ... Php 3:8
peace of God, which **s-es** every ... Php 4:7
SURROUND
Many bulls **s** me; ... Ps 22:12
large cloud of witnesses **s-ing** us, ... Heb 12:1
SURVIVE
were limited, no one would **s**. ... Mt 24:22
built **s-s**, he will receive a reward. ... 1Co 3:14
SURVIVORS
of Hosts had not left us a few **s**, ... Is 1:9
SUSTAIN
wake again because the LORD **s-s** me. ... Ps 3:5
not **s** the root, but the root **s-s** you. ... Rm 11:18
and He **s-s** all things by His ... Heb 1:3
SWALLOWED (v)
has been **s** up in victory. ... 1Co 15:54
SWEAR
By Myself I have **sworn**, says ... Gn 22:16
LORD **swore** an oath to David, ... Ps 132:11
Neither should you **s** by your head, ... Mt 5:36
swore in My anger, "They will not ... Heb 3:11
Lord has **sworn**, and He will not ... Heb 7:21
brothers, do not **s**, either by ... Jms 5:12
SWEAT
eat bread by the **s** of your brow ... Gn 3:19
His **s** became like drops of blood ... Lk 22:44
SWEEP
vacant, **swept**, and put in order. ... Mt 12:44
not light a lamp, **s** the house, ... Lk 15:8
SWEET
How **s** Your word is to my taste ... Ps 119:103
Stolen water is **s**, ... Pr 9:17
it was as **s** as honey in my mouth. ... Ezk 3:3
Does a spring pour out **s** and bitter ... Jms 3:11
SWIFT
that the race is not to the **s**, ... Ec 9:11
Their feet are **s** to shed blood; ... Rm 3:15
SWORD
flaming, whirling **s** to guard the ... Gn 3:24
Nations will not take up the **s** against ... Is 2:4
come to bring peace, but a **s**. ... Mt 10:34
who take up a **s** will perish by a **s**. ... Mt 26:52
a **s** will pierce your own soul ... Lk 2:35
and the **s** of the Spirit, ... Eph 6:17
sharper than any two-edged **s**, ... Heb 4:12
mouth came a sharp two-edged **s**; ... Rv 1:16
SYCAMORE
he climbed up a **s** tree to see ... Lk 19:4
SYMBOL
should have [a **s** of] authority ... 1Co 11:10
SYMPATHIZE
a high priest who is unable to **s** ... Heb 4:15
SYNAGOGUE
teaching in their **s-s**, preaching ... Mt 4:23
He entered the **s** on the Sabbath ... Lk 4:16
They will ban you from the **s-s**. ... Jn 16:2
reasoned in the **s** every Sabbath ... Ac 18:4
but are a **s** of Satan. ... Rv 2:9
TABERNACLE
the design of the **t** ... Ex 25:9
glory of the LORD filled the **t**. ... Ex 40:34
I will make three **t-s** here: ... Mt 17:4
Jewish Festival of **T-s** was near, ... Jn 7:2
more perfect **t** not made with ... Heb 9:11
TABLE
construct a **t** of acacia wood, ... Ex 25:23
You prepare a **t** before me in the ... Ps 23:5
overturned the money changers' **t-s** ... Mt 21:12
TABLETS
that I may give you the stone **t** ... Ex 24:12
not on stone **t** but on **t** ... 2Co 3:3
TAKE
t up My yoke and learn from Me, ... Mt 11:29
deny himself, **t** up his cross, ... Mt 16:24
T and eat it; this is My body. ... Mt 26:26
who **t-s** away the sin of the world! ... Jn 1:29
they've **taken** away my Lord, ... Jn 20:13
t up the full armor of God, ... Eph 6:13
TALENTS
To one he gave five **t**; ... Mt 25:15
TALK (v)
T about them when you sit in ... Dt 6:7
TALL
He was nine feet, nine inches **t** ... 1Sm 17:4
TAMAR
1. Judah's daughter-in-law; widow of Er and Onan; mother of Judah's sons (Gn 38).
2. Daughter of David; raped by Amnon; avenged by Absalom (2Sm 13).
TAMBOURINE
Praise Him with **t** and dance; ... Ps 150:4
TARSHISH
Distant Mediterranean port city known for sea trade (1Kg 10:22; 22:48; Ps 48:7; 72:10; Is 2:16; 23:1,6,10,14; 66:19; Jr 10:9; Ezk 27:12,25; 38:13); Jonah fled toward it (Jnh 1:3).
TASTE (v)
T and see that the LORD is good. ... Ps 34:8
who will not **t** death until they ... Mt 16:28
handle, don't **t**, don't touch"? ... Col 2:21
grace He might **t** death for ... Heb 2:9
who **t-d** the heavenly gift, ... Heb 6:4
since you have **t-d** that the Lord ... 1Pt 2:3
TAUNTING (v)
crucified with Him kept **t** Him. ... Mt 27:44
TAX COLLECTOR
Don't even the **t-s** do the same? ... Mt 5:46
a friend of **t-s** and sinners! ... Mt 11:19
T-s and prostitutes are entering ... Mt 21:31
one a Pharisee and the other a **t**. ... Lk 18:10
TAXES (n) *see also* TAX COLLECTOR
lawful to pay **t** to Caesar or not? ... Mt 22:17
t to those you owe **t**, ... Rm 13:7
TEACH
T them to your children ... Dt 4:9; 11:19
t me Your paths. ... Ps 25:4
T a youth about the way he ... Pr 22:6
t-ing them to observe everything ... Mt 28:20
t-ing them as one having authority. ... Mk 1:22
He **taught** them many things in ... Mk 4:2
t us to pray, just as John also **taught** ... Lk 11:1
Holy Spirit ... will **t** you all things ... Jn 14:26
allow a woman to **t** or to have ... 1Tm 2:12
will be able to **t** others also. ... 2Tm 2:2
correctly **t-ing** the word of truth. ... 2Tm 2:15
you don't need anyone to **t** you. ... 1Jn 2:27
TEACHER
A disciple is not above his **t**, ... Mt 10:24
if I, your Lord and **T**, have washed ... Jn 13:14
some pastors and **t-s**, ... Eph 4:11
TEACHING (n)
were astonished at His **t**, ... Mt 7:28; 22:33
and is profitable for **t**, ... 2Tm 3:16
TEAR (n)
My **t-s** have been my food day and ... Ps 42:3
Put my **t-s** in Your bottle. ... Ps 56:8
Those who sow in **t-s** will reap ... Ps 126:5
to wash His feet with her **t-s**. ... Lk 7:38
away every **t** from their eyes ... Rv 7:17; 21:4
TEAR (v)
T your hearts, not just your ... Jl 2:13
high priest **tore** his robes and ... Mt 26:65
TELL
t about all His wonderful works! ... Ps 105:2
TEMPERED
not quick **t**, not addicted to wine, ... Ti 1:7
TEMPLE
The LORD is in His holy **t**; ... Ps 11:4
But the LORD is in His holy **t**; ... Hab 2:20
something greater than the **t** is here! ... Mt 12:6
they found Him in the **t** complex ... Lk 2:46
TEMPORARY
what is seen is **t**, but what is ... 2Co 4:18
TEMPT
wilderness to be **t-ed** by the Devil. ... Mt 4:1
allow you to be **t-ed** beyond what ... 1Co 10:13
and He Himself doesn't **t** anyone. ... Jms 1:13
TEMPTATION
And do not bring us into **t**, ... Mt 6:13
No **t** has overtaken you except ... 1Co 10:13
TEMPTER
Then the **t** approached Him and ... Mt 4:3
TEN *see also* 10
covenant—the **T** Commandments. ... Ex 34:28
TENDERLY
Speak **t** to Jerusalem, and ... Is 40:2
TENT
live in Your **t** forever and ... Ps 61:4
our earthly house, a **t**, is destroyed, ... 2Co 5:1
TENTH
give to You a **t** of all that You give ... Gn 28:22
You pay a **t** of mint, dill, and ... Mt 23:23
I give a **t** of everything I get. ... Lk 18:12
TERRIFY
around them, and they were **t-ied**. ... Lk 2:9
It is a **t-ing** thing to fall into ... Heb 10:31
TERROR
not fear the **t** of the night, ... Ps 91:5
are not a **t** to good conduct ... Rm 13:3
TEST
God **t-ed** Abraham ... Gn 22:1
Do not **t** the LORD your God ... Dt 6:16
t me and know my concerns. ... Ps 139:23
stone in Zion, a **t-ed** stone, ... Is 28:16
T Me in this way," says the LORD ... Mal 3:10
Do not **t** the Lord your God. ... Mt 4:7
He asked this to **t** him, for He knew ... Jn 6:6
did you agree to **t** the Spirit ... Ac 5:9
t all things. Hold on to what ... 1Th 5:21
who has been **t-ed** in every way ... Heb 4:15
but **t** the spirits to determine ... 1Jn 4:1
TESTER
but the LORD is a **t** of hearts. ... Pr 17:3
TESTIFY
is Another who **t-ies** about Me, ... Jn 5:32
the Spirit ... He will **t** about Me. ... Jn 15:26
TESTIMONY
Do not give false **t** against your ... Ex 20:16
based on the **t** of one witness. ... Nm 35:30
the **t** of the LORD is trustworthy, ... Ps 19:7
looking for false **t** against Jesus ... Mt 26:59
We know that his **t** is true. ... Jn 21:24
THANKS
Give **t** to the LORD; ... 1Ch 16:8,34
Give **t** to the LORD, for He is good. ... Ps 136:1
and after giving **t**, He gave it ... Mt 26:27
Give **t** in everything, for this ... 1Th 5:18
THANKSGIVING
Let us enter His presence with **t**; ... Ps 95:2

Enter His gates with **t** and ... Ps 100:4
through prayer and petition with **t**, ... Php 4:6

THIEF
and where **t-ves** break in and steal. ... Mt 6:19
you are making it a den of **t-ves**! ... Mt 21:13
what time the **t** was coming, ... Mt 24:43
come just like a **t** in the night. ... 1Th 5:2
Look, I am coming like a **t**. ... Rv 16:15

THING
with God all **t-s** are possible. ... Mt 19:26
kept all these **t-s** in her heart. ... Lk 2:51
But one **t** I do: forgetting ... Php 3:13
any praise—dwell on these **t-s**. ... Php 4:8

THINK *see also* THOUGHT (n)
son of man, that You **t** of him? ... Ps 144:3
not to **t** of himself more highly than ... Rm 12:3
a child, I **thought** like a child, ... 1Co 13:11

THIRD
killed, and be raised the **t** day. ... Mt 16:21

THIRST (v)
I **t** for God, the living God. ... Ps 42:2
who hunger and **t** for righteousness, ... Mt 5:6
no longer will they **t**; ... Rv 7:16

THIRSTY
everyone who is **t**, come to the ... Is 55:1
was **t** and you gave Me something ... Mt 25:35
this water will get **t** again. ... Jn 4:13
in Me will ever be **t** again. ... Jn 6:35
If anyone is **t**, he should come ... Jn 7:37

THISTLES
produce thorns and **t** for you, ... Gn 3:18

THOMAS
Apostle; sought evidence of resurrection; made confession of faith (Jn 20:24-29).

THORN
It will produce **t-s** and thistles ... Gn 3:18
fell among **t-s**, and the **t-s** came up ... Mt 13:7
twisted together a crown of **t-s**, ... Mt 27:29
t in the flesh was given to me, ... 2Co 12:7

THOUGHT (n)
The LORD knows man's **t-s**; ... Ps 94:11
My **t-s** are not your **t-s**, ... Is 55:8
But perceiving their **t-s**, Jesus said, ... Mt 9:4
taking every **t** captive to the ... 2Co 10:5

THOUSAND *see also* 1,000
his **t-s**, but David his tens of **t-s**. ... 1Sm 18:7
the cattle on a **t** hills. ... Ps 50:10
in Your sight a **t** years are like ... Ps 90:4

THREATEN
when suffering, He did not **t**, ... 1Pt 2:23

THREE
cord of **t** strands is not easily ... Ec 4:12
For where two or **t** are gathered ... Mt 18:20
you will deny Me **t** times! ... Mt 26:34
killed, and rise after **t** days. ... Mk 8:31
Now these **t** remain: faith, hope, ... 1Co 13:13
For there are **t** that testify: ... 1Jn 5:7

THRESHING
muzzle an ox that is **t** grain, ... 1Tm 5:18

THRESHING FLOOR
David bought the **t** ... 2Sm 24:24

THROAT
their **t** is an open grave; ... Ps 5:9
Their **t** is an open grave; ... Rm 3:13

THRONE
will establish the **t** of his kingdom ... 2Sm 7:13
Your **t**, God, is forever and ever; ... Ps 45:6
seated on a high and lofty **t**, ... Is 6:1
will also sit on 12 **t-s**, judging ... Mt 19:28
let us approach the **t** of grace with ... Heb 4:16
cast their crowns before the **t**, ... Rv 4:10
great white **t** and One seated on it. ... Rv 20:11

THROW
He has **t-n** the horse and its rider ... Ex 15:1
should be the first to **t** a stone at her. ... Jn 8:7

THUNDERCLOUD
I answered you from the **t**. ... Ps 81:7

TIME
for such a **t** as this. ... Est 4:14
a **t** for every activity under heaven: ... Ec 3:1
for a **t**, **t-s**, and half a **t**. ... Dn 7:25; 12:7
Teacher says: My **t** is near; ... Mt 26:18
you will deny Me three **t-s**! ... Mt 26:34
My **t** has not yet arrived, ... Jn 7:6
making the most of the **t**. ... Col 4:5
she was fed for a **t**, **t-s**, and half a **t**. ... Rv 12:14

TIMOTHY
Companion of Paul (Ac 16–20; Rm 16:21; 2Co 1:1; 1Th 1:1; 2Th 1:1; Php 1:1; Phm 1). Sent by Paul to Corinth (1Co 4:17); to Philippi (Php 2:19); to Thessalonica (1Th 3:2). Pastored Ephesian church (1Tm 1:3). Received two letters from Paul (1Tm 1:2; 2Tm 1:2) and a plea to come (4:9).

TITUS
Gentile coworker with Paul (2Co 8:23; Gl 2:1-3). Sent to Corinth (2Co 7:13-15; 8:16-17); in charge of church in Crete (Ti 1:5); went to Dalmatia (2Tm 4:10).

TODAY
T, if you hear His voice: ... Ps 95:7
Give us **t** our daily bread. ... Mt 6:11
T you will be with Me in paradise. ... Lk 23:43
while it is still called **t**, ... Heb 3:13
T, if you hear His voice, do not ... Heb 3:15
same yesterday, **t**, and forever. ... Heb 13:8

TOLERABLE
It will be more **t** on the day of ... Mt 10:15

TOLERATE
they will not **t** sound doctrine, ... 2Tm 4:3
and that you cannot **t** evil. ... Rv 2:2

TOMB
You are like whitewashed **t-s**, ... Mt 23:27
stone rolled away from the **t**. ... Lk 24:2
already been in the **t** four days. ... Jn 11:17

TOMORROW
Don't boast about **t**, for you don't ... Pr 27:1
Let us eat and drink, for **t** we die! ... Is 22:13
Therefore don't worry about **t**, ... Mt 6:34

TONGUE
Before a word is on my **t**, You ... Ps 139:4
death are in the power of the **t**, ... Pr 18:21
every **t** will swear allegiance. ... Is 45:23
And **t-s**, like flames of fire that ... Ac 2:3
and every **t** should confess that ... Php 2:11
but no man can tame the **t**. ... Jms 3:8

TOOTH
for eye, **t** for **t**, ... Ex 21:24; Lv 24:20; Dt 19:21
for an eye and a **t** for a **t**. ... Mt 5:38
weeping and gnashing of **teeth**. ... Mt 8:12

TOP
split in two from **t** to bottom; ... Mt 27:51

TORMENTED (v)
those **t** by unclean spirits ... Lk 6:18
they will be **t** day and night ... Rv 20:10

TORRENT
the **t** would have swept over us; ... Ps 124:4

TOSS
tear it, but **t** for it, to see ... Jn 19:24
driven and **t-ed** by the wind. ... Jms 1:6

TOUCH
You must not eat it or **t** it, ... Gn 3:3
t-ed my mouth with it and said: ... Is 6:7
If I can just **t** His robe, ... Mt 9:21
to Him so He might **t** them, ... Mk 10:13
T Me and see, because a ghost ... Lk 24:39
and have **t-ed** with our hands, ... 1Jn 1:1

TOWEL
took a **t**, and tied it around Himself. ... Jn 13:4

TOWER
a **t** with its top in the sky. ... Gn 11:4
name of the LORD is a strong **t**; ... Pr 18:10

TOWN
and from the **t** of Bethlehem, ... Jn 7:42

TRADERS
When Midianite **t** passed by, ... Gn 37:28

TRADITION
You revoke God's word by your **t** ... Mk 7:13
empty deceit based on human **t**, ... Col 2:8

TRAGEDY
a sickening **t** ... Ec 5:13,16; 6:1

TRAIN
who **t-s** my hands for battle and ... Ps 144:1
will never again **t** for war. ... Is 2:4; Mc 4:3

TRAINING
them up in the **t** and instruction ... Eph 6:4
correcting, for **t** in righteousness, ... 2Tm 3:16

TRAITOR
Judas Iscariot, who became a **t**. ... Lk 6:16

TRAMPLE
pearls before pigs, or they will **t** them ... Mt 7:6
Jerusalem will be **t-d** by the ... Lk 21:24
who has **t-d** on the Son of God, ... Heb 10:29

TRAMPLING (n)
you—this **t** of My courts? ... Is 1:12

TRANSFORM
He was **t-ed** in front of them, ... Mt 17:2
be **t-ed** by the renewing of your ... Rm 12:2
are being **t-ed** into the same image ... 2Co 3:18
He will **t** the body of our humble ... Php 3:21

TRANSGRESSION
is the one whose **t** is forgiven, ... Ps 32:1
has He removed our **t-s** from us. ... Ps 103:12
was pierced because of our **t-s**, ... Is 53:5
where there is no law, there is no **t**. ... Rm 4:15

TRANSLATE
law ... **t-ing** and giving the meaning ... Neh 8:8
Immanuel ... **t-d** "God is with us." ... Mt 1:23

TRAP
their gods will be a **t** to you. ... Jdg 2:3
to **t** Him by what He said. ... Mt 22:15
into disgrace and the Devil's **t**. ... 1Tm 3:7

TREACHEROUS
looking for a **t** way to arrest and kill ... Mk 14:1

TREADS
your foot **t** will be yours. ... Dt 11:24
an ox while it **t** out grain. ... Dt 25:4
an ox while it **t** out the grain. ... 1Co 9:9

TREASURE (n)
For where your **t** is, there your ... Mt 6:21
and you will have **t** in heaven. ... Mt 19:21
Now we have this **t** in clay jars, ... 2Co 4:7
Him all the **t-s** of wisdom and ... Col 2:3

TREASURE (v)
I have **t-d** Your word in my heart ... Ps 119:11
But Mary was **t-ing** up all these ... Lk 2:19

TREATY
Make no **t** with them ... Dt 7:2

TREE *see also* TREE OF LIFE
the **t** of the knowledge of good and ... Gn 2:9
hung [on a **t**] is under God's curse. ... Dt 21:23
He is like a **t** planted beside ... Ps 1:3
all the **t-s** of the field will clap ... Is 55:12
every **t** that doesn't produce good ... Mt 3:10
At once the fig **t** withered. ... Mt 21:19
Cursed is everyone ... hung on a **t**. ... Gl 3:13
our sins in His body on the **t**, ... 1Pt 2:24

TREE OF LIFE
the **t** in the midst of the garden, ... Gn 2:9
She is a **t** to those who embrace her, ... Pr 3:18
victor the right to eat from the **t**, ... Rv 2:7
will take away his share of the **t** ... Rv 22:19

TREMBLE
t before Him, all the earth. ... 1Ch 16:30

TREMBLING (n)
your own salvation with fear and **t**. ... Php 2:12

TRESPASS
by the one man's **t** the many died, ... Rm 5:15
not counting their **t-es** against ... 2Co 5:19
you were dead in your **t-es** and sins ... Eph 2:1

TRIALS
you experience various **t**, ... Jms 1:2

TRIBE
These are the **t-s** of Israel, 12 ... Gn 49:28
He chose instead the **t** of Judah, ... Ps 78:68
judging the 12 **t-s** of Israel. ... Mt 19:28
from every **t** and language and people ... Rv 5:9

TRIBULATION
that time there will be great **t**, ... Mt 24:21
ones coming out of the great **t**. ... Rv 7:14

TRIP
over and a rock to **t** over, ... Is 8:14
a rock to **t** over, yet the one who ... Rm 9:33
and a rock that **t-s** them up. ... 1Pt 2:8

TRIUMPH
When the righteous **t**, there is great ... Pr 28:12
He **t-ed** over them by Him. ... Col 2:15
Mercy **t-s** over judgment. ... Jms 2:13

TRIVIAL
sin of Jeroboam ... were a **t** matter ... 1Kg 16:31

TROPHIMUS
and Tychicus and **T** from Asia. ... Ac 20:4
previously seen **T** the Ephesian ... Ac 21:29
T I left sick at Miletus. ... 2Tm 4:20

TROUBLE (n)
mankind is born for **t** as surely as ... Jb 5:7
is always found in times of **t**. ... Ps 46:1
Each day has enough **t** of its own. ... Mt 6:34

TROUBLE (v)
Your heart must not be **t-d**. ... Jn 14:1

TROUGH
and laid Him in a feeding **t** ... Lk 2:7

TRUE
The **t** light, who gives light to ... Jn 1:9
You, the only **t** God, and the One ... Jn 17:3
His testimony is **t** ... Jn 19:35; 21:24
God must be **t**, but everyone is a ... Rm 3:4
whatever is **t**, whatever is ... Php 4:8
these words are faithful and **t**. ... Rv 21:5; 22:6

TRULY
T You are the Son of God! ... Mt 14:33

TRUMPET
priests carry seven ram's-horn **t-s** ... Jos 6:4
Praise Him with **t** blast; ... Ps 150:3
give ... don't sound a **t** before you, ... Mt 6:2
at the last **t**. For the **t** will sound, ... 1Co 15:52
seven **t-s** were given to them. ... Rv 8:2

TRUST (n)
put His **t** in God; let God rescue ... Mt 27:43

TRUST (v)
When I am afraid, I will **t** in You. ... Ps 56:3
T in the LORD with all your ... Pr 3:5
those who **t** in the LORD will renew ... Is 40:31
Again, I will **t** in Him. ... Heb 2:13

TRUSTWORTHY
The wounds of a friend are **t**, ... Pr 27:6
This saying is **t** ... 1Tm 1:15; 3:1; 4:9

TRUTH
The entirety of Your word is **t**, ... Ps 119:160
grace and **t** came through Jesus ... Jn 1:17

more than **w-men** for the morning ... Ps 130:6
I have made you a **w** ... Ezk 3:17; 33:7

WATER (n)
w covered the earth. ... Gn 7:6
He leads me beside quiet **w-s**. ... Ps 23:2
bread on the surface of the **w-s**, ... Ec 11:1
who is thirsty, come to the **w-s**; ... Is 55:1
abandoned ... fountain of living **w**, ... Jr 2:13
that day living **w** will flow out ... Zch 14:8
a cup of cold **w** to one of these ... Mt 10:42
Peter started walking on the **w** ... Mt 14:29
is born of **w** and the Spirit, ... Jn 3:5
and He would give you living **w**. ... Jn 4:10
the One who came by **w** and blood; ... 1Jn 5:6
spring of living **w** as a gift. ... Rv 21:6

WATERED (v)
I planted, Apollos **w**, but God ... 1Co 3:6

WATERFALLS
calls to deep in the roar of Your **w**; ... Ps 42:7

WAVER
He did not **w** in unbelief at God's ... Rm 4:20
of our hope without **w-ing**, ... Heb 10:23

WAVES
was being swamped by the **w**. ... Mt 8:24
even the winds and the **w**, ... Lk 8:25

WAX
my heart is like **w**, melting within ... Ps 22:14

WAY
watches over the **w** of the righteous ... Ps 1:6
Commit your **w** to the LORD; ... Ps 37:5
can a young man keep his **w** pure? ... Ps 119:9
There is a **w** that seems right ... Pr 14:12
youth about the **w** he should go; ... Pr 22:6
Prepare the **w** of the LORD in the ... Is 40:3
we all have turned to our own **w**; ... Is 53:6
and your **w-s** are not My **w-s**. ... Is 55:8
Prepare the **w** for the Lord; ... Mt 3:3
God loved the world in this **w**: ... Jn 3:16
I am the **w**, the truth, and the life. ... Jn 14:6
will also provide a **w** of escape, ... 1Co 10:13

WEAK
spirit is willing, but the flesh is **w**. ... Mt 26:41
Accept anyone who is **w** in faith, ... Rm 14:1
God has chosen the ... **w** things ... 1Co 1:27
For when I am **w**, then I am ... 2Co 12:10

WEAKER
understanding of their **w** nature ... 1Pt 3:7

WEAKNESS
took our **w-es** and carried our ... Mt 8:17
also joins to help in our **w**, ... Rm 8:26
sown in **w**, raised in power; ... 1Co 15:43
unable to sympathize with our **w-es** ... Heb 4:15

WEALTH
They trust in their **w** ... Ps 49:6
W is not profitable on a day of ... Pr 11:4
Give me neither poverty nor **w**; ... Pr 30:8
seduction of **w** choke the word, ... Mt 13:22

WEAPONS
the **w** of our warfare are not ... 2Co 10:4

WEAR
about your body, what you will **w**. ... Mt 6:25

WEARISOME
All things are **w**; man is unable ... Ec 1:8

WEARY (adj)
they will run and not grow **w**; ... Is 40:31
Come to Me, all of you who are **w** ... Mt 11:28
do not grow **w** in doing good. ... 2Th 3:13

WEDDING
get in here without **w** clothes?' ... Mt 22:12
a **w** took place in Cana of Galilee. ... Jn 2:1

WEEDS
w among the wheat, ... Mt 13:25

WEEK
Observe the Festival of **W-s** ... Ex 34:22
Seventy **w-s** are decreed ... Dn 9:24
first day of the **w** was dawning, ... Mt 28:1

WEEP
W-ing may spend the night, but ... Ps 30:5
wept when we remembered Zion. ... Ps 137:1
a time to **w** and a time to laugh; ... Ec 3:4
Rachel **w-ing** for her children; ... Mt 2:18
there will be **w-ing** and gnashing ... Mt 8:12
Jesus **wept**. ... Jn 11:35
who rejoice; **w** with those who **w**. ... Rm 12:15

WEIGHS
but the LORD **w** the motives. ... Pr 16:2

WEIGHT
honest balances, honest **w-s**, ... Lv 19:36
incomparable eternal **w** of glory. ... 2Co 4:17
lay aside every **w** and the sin that ... Heb 12:1

WELCOMES
whoever **w** one child like this ... Mt 18:5

WELFARE
plans for your **w**, not for disaster, ... Jr 29:11

WELL (adv)
master said to him, '**W** done, ... Mt 25:21

WEST
far as the east is from the **w**, ... Ps 103:12

WHEAT
sowed weeds among the **w**, ... Mt 13:25
Unless a grain of **w** falls into ... Jn 12:24

WHEEL
was like a **w** within a **w**. ... Ezk 1:16

WHIRLWIND
Elijah up to heaven in a **w**. ... 2Kg 2:1
sow the wind and reap the **w**. ... Hs 8:7

WHISPER
there was a voice, a soft **w**. ... 1Kg 19:12
What you hear in a **w**, proclaim ... Mt 10:27

WHITE
scarlet, they will be as **w** as snow; ... Is 1:18
make a single hair **w** or black. ... Mt 5:36
head and hair were **w** like wool ... Rv 1:14
I saw a great **w** throne and One ... Rv 20:11

WHITER
and I will be **w** than snow. ... Ps 51:7

WHITEWASHED
You are like **w** tombs, ... Mt 23:27

WHO
w do you say that I am? ... Mt 16:15

WICK
will not put out a smoldering **w**, ... Mt 12:20

WICKED
does not follow the advice of the **w**, ... Ps 1:1
They made His grave with the **w**, ... Is 53:9

WICKEDNESS
saw that man's **w** was widespread ... Gn 6:5

WIDE
the gate is **w** and the road is broad ... Mt 7:13

WIDOWS
devour **w'** houses and make long ... Mt 23:14
Support **w** who are genuinely **w**. ... 1Tm 5:3

WIFE
and mother and bonds with his **w**, ... Gn 2:24
Do not covet your neighbor's **w**, ... Ex 20:17
700 **w-ves** who ... turned his heart ... 1Kg 11:3
A man who finds a **w** finds a good ... Pr 18:22
Who can find a capable **w**? ... Pr 31:10
each man should have his own **w**, ... 1Co 7:2
W-ves, submit to your ... Eph 5:22
husband of one **w**, ... 1Tm 3:2
the bride, the **w** of the Lamb. ... Rv 21:9

WILD
Without revelation people run **w**, ... Pr 29:18
food was locusts and **w** honey. ... Mt 3:4
you, though a **w** olive branch, ... Rm 11:17

WILDERNESS
Prepare the way of the LORD in the **w** ... Is 40:3
voice of one crying out in the **w**: ... Mt 3:3
into the **w** to be tempted ... Mt 4:1
fathers ate the manna in the **w**, ... Jn 6:31,49

WILDFLOWERS
Consider how the **w** grow: ... Lk 12:27

WILL (n)
I delight to do Your **w**, my God; ... Ps 40:8
Your **w** be done on earth as it is ... Mt 6:10
Yet not as I **w**, but as You **w**. ... Mt 26:39
the good, pleasing, and perfect **w** ... Rm 12:2
See, I have come to do Your **w**. ... Heb 10:9
ask anything according to His **w**, ... 1Jn 5:14

WILL (v)
say, "If the Lord **w-s**, we **w** ... Jms 4:15

WILLING (adj)
The spirit is **w**, but the flesh ... Mt 26:41

WIND
but the LORD was not in the **w**. ... 1Kg 19:11
the **w-s** and the sea obey Him! ... Mt 8:27
The **w** blows where it pleases, ... Jn 3:8

WINDSTORM
A fierce **w** arose, and the waves ... Mk 4:37

WINE
W is a mocker, beer is a brawler, ... Pr 20:1
no one puts new **w** into old ... Mt 9:17
water (after it had become **w**), ... Jn 2:9
And don't get drunk with **w**, ... Eph 5:18

WINESKINS
no one puts new wine into old **w**. ... Mt 9:17

WINGS
I carried you on eagles' **w** ... Ex 19:4
soaring on the **w** of the wind. ... 2Sm 22:11
hide me in the shadow of Your **w** ... Ps 17:8
will soar on **w** like eagles; ... Is 40:31
rise with healing in its **w**, ... Mal 4:2
gathers her chicks under her **w**, ... Mt 23:37

WINTER
Pray it won't happen in **w**. ... Mk 13:18

WIPE
She **w-d** His feet with the hair ... Lk 7:38
will **w** away every tear ... Rv 7:17; 21:4

WISDOM
God gave Solomon **w**, ... 1Kg 4:29
of the LORD is the beginning of **w**, ... Pr 9:10
Yet **w** is vindicated by all her ... Lk 7:35
Now if any of you lacks **w**, ... Jms 1:5

WISE
making the inexperienced **w**. ... Ps 19:7
w men from the east arrived ... Mt 2:1
hidden these things from the **w** ... Mt 11:25
foolish things to shame the **w**, ... 1Co 1:27

WITHER
and whose leaf does not **w**. ... Ps 1:3
The grass **w-s**, the flowers fade ... Is 40:7
At once the fig tree **w-ed**. ... Mt 21:19
grass **w-s**, and the flower drops ... 1Pt 1:24

WITNESS
the testimony of two or three **w-es**. ... Dt 19:15
many false **w-es** came forward. ... Mt 26:60
will be My **w-es** in Jerusalem, ... Ac 1:8
large cloud of **w-es** surrounding ... Heb 12:1
from Jesus Christ, the faithful **w**, ... Rv 1:5

WOE
w to you, scribes and Pharisees, ... Mt 23:13
And **w** to me if I do not preach ... 1Co 9:16

WOLVES
you out like sheep among **w**. ... Mt 10:16
savage **w** will come in ... Ac 20:29

WOMAN
this one will be called **w**, ... Gn 2:23
w who fears the LORD ... be praised. ... Pr 31:30
who looks at a **w** to lust for her ... Mt 5:28
are the most blessed of **w-en**, ... Lk 1:42
brought a **w** caught in adultery ... Jn 8:3
the man is the head of the **w**, ... 1Co 11:3
w-en should be silent in the ... 1Co 14:34
God sent His Son, born of a **w**, ... Gl 4:4
I do not allow a **w** to teach ... 1Tm 2:12

WOMB
Naked I came from my mother's **w**, ... Jb 1:21
me together in my mother's **w**. ... Ps 139:13
before I formed you in the **w**; ... Jr 1:5
his mother's **w** a second time ... Jn 3:4

WONDERFUL
My name ... since it is **w**. ... Jdg 13:18
tell about all His **w** works! ... Ps 105:2
that I may see **w** things in Your ... Ps 119:18
He will be named **W** Counselor, ... Is 9:6

WONDERFULLY
been remarkably and **w** made. ... Ps 139:14

WONDERS
I will display **w** in the heaven ... Ac 2:19

WOOD
I will bow down to a block of **w**. ... Is 44:19
costly stones, **w**, hay, or straw, ... 1Co 3:12

WOOL
as crimson, they will be like **w**. ... Is 1:18

WORD
bread alone but on every **w** that ... Dt 8:3
May the **w-s** of my mouth and the ... Ps 19:14
treasured Your **w** in my heart so ... Ps 119:11
Your **w** is a lamp for my feet ... Ps 119:105
Every **w** of God is pure; ... Pr 30:5
My **w** ... not return to Me empty, ... Is 55:11
bread alone but on every **w** that ... Mt 4:4
hears these **w-s** of Mine and acts ... Mt 7:24
but My **w-s** will never pass away. ... Mt 24:35
beginning was the **W**, and the **W** was
with God, and the **W** was God. ... Jn 1:1
The **W** became flesh and took up ... Jn 1:14
You have the **w-s** of eternal life. ... Jn 6:68
correctly teaching the **w** of truth. ... 2Tm 2:15
For the **w** of God is living and ... Heb 4:12
His name is called the **W** of God. ... Rv 19:13

WORK (n)
seventh day, God completed His **w** ... Gn 2:2
six days and do all your **w**, ... Ex 20:9
by faith apart from **w-s** of law. ... Rm 3:28
test the quality of each one's **w**. ... 1Co 3:13
because by the **w-s** of the law no ... Gl 2:16
not from **w-s**, so that no one can ... Eph 2:9
in Christ Jesus for good **w-s**, ... Eph 2:10
started a good **w** in you will ... Php 1:6
has faith, but does not have **w-s**? ... Jms 2:14

WORK (v)
Don't **w** for the food that ... Jn 6:27
that all things **w** together for ... Rm 8:28
w out your own salvation with ... Php 2:12
isn't willing to **w**, he should not eat ... 2Th 3:10

WORKER
abundant, but the **w-s** are few. ... Mt 9:37
the **w** is worthy of his wages. ... Lk 10:7
a **w** who doesn't need to be ... 2Tm 2:15

WORLD
He judges the **w** with righteousness; ... Ps 9:8
You are the light of the **w**. ... Mt 5:14
gains the whole **w** yet loses his ... Mt 16:26
Go into all the **w** and preach the ... Mk 16:15
For God loved the **w** in this way: ... Jn 3:16
I am the light of the **w**. ... Jn 8:12; 9:5

Bible Reading Plans

The *HCSB Mission of God Study Bible* offers two plans for reading through the Bible. The first plan developed by Heather Collins Grattan is structured to take a person through the Bible in three years. This plan may appeal to busy persons who have a limited amount of time each day to read the Scriptures. Reading a smaller portion each day may enable the person to spend more time reading, studying, and meditating on the passage for the day.

The second plan was developed by the late Robert Murray M'Cheyne. This plan takes the reader to four portions of Scripture each day from various parts of the Bible. Following this plan, a person will read through the Old Testament once and the New Testament twice within a year.

Approaching the Bible

In reading and studying the Bible, we draw on the same knowledge, skills, and competencies we use in reading other documents. However, with the Bible there is an added dimension. The Bible was written by human beings but the ultimate Author who worked through a variety of human authors is God Himself. In what may have been his last written words to Timothy, Paul reminded his protégé that all Scripture is inspired by God. For this reason, John Wesley said that Scripture can only be understood with the help of the Spirit who inspired these 66 books. Therefore, as believers come to read and study Scripture, they need to remember the Author of Scripture and ask for the Spirit's help in understanding what they read.

- Come to the Bible expecting to grow. It is like both milk (1Pt 2:2) and solid food (Heb 5:14) providing nourishment for both the young and those more mature.
- Come to the Bible for understanding and direction. It is like a counselor (Ps 119:24) and provides light for your journey (Ps 119:105,130).
- Come to the Bible for correction and purification. It is like:
  - a mirror in which the believer sees himself and the changes that God requires,
  - fire and a hammer (Jr 23:29),
  - a scalpel by which God performs spiritual surgery on the heart (Hb 4:12),
  - water that washes and purifies (Eph 5:26).
- Come to the Bible for pleasure. God's Word is like honey (Ps 19:9; 119:103).

Come daily to the Bible with these attitudes and expectations, and you will be changed. This is God's multifaceted instrument for conforming you to the image of His Son.

Three-Year Bible Reading Plan

Edited by Heather Collins Grattan

YEAR ONE

JANUARY

Genesis 1:1-26	1st
Genesis 1:27–2:25	2nd
Genesis 3:1-24	3rd
Genesis 4:1-26	4th
Genesis 5:1-32	5th
Genesis 6:1–7:10	6th
Genesis 7:11–8:22	7th
Genesis 9:1-29	8th
Genesis 10:1-32	9th
Genesis 11:1–12:9	10th
Genesis 12:10–13:18	11th
Genesis 14:1-24	12th
Genesis 15:1–16:16	13th
Genesis 17:1-27	14th
Genesis 18:1-15	15th
Genesis 18:16-33	16th
Genesis 19:1-29	17th
Genesis 19:30–20:18	18th
Genesis 21:1-34	19th
Genesis 22:1-24	20th
Genesis 23:1–24:14	21st
Genesis 24:15-44	22nd
Genesis 24:45-67	23rd
Genesis 25:1-18	24th
Genesis 25:19-34	25th
Genesis 26:1-25	26th
Genesis 26:26–27:20	27th
Genesis 27:21-46	28th
Genesis 28:1–29:12	29th
Genesis 29:13–30:11	30th
Genesis 30:12-43	31st

FEBRUARY

Genesis 31:1-35	1st
Genesis 31:36-55	2nd
Genesis 32:1-32	3rd
Genesis 33:1-20	4th
Genesis 34:1-31	5th
Genesis 35:1–36:8	6th
Genesis 36:9-43	7th
Genesis 37:1-36	8th
Genesis 38:1-30	9th
Genesis 39:1-23	10th
Genesis 40:1–41:14	11th
Genesis 41:15-49	12th
Genesis 41:50–42:26	13th
Genesis 42:27–43:14	14th
Genesis 43:15-34	15th
Genesis 44:1-34	16th
Genesis 45:1-28	17th
Genesis 46:1-34	18th
Genesis 47:1-31	19th
Genesis 48:1-22	20th
Genesis 49:1-28	21st
Genesis 49:29–50:26	22nd
Exodus 1:1-22	23rd
Exodus 2:1-25	24th
Exodus 3:1-22	25th
Exodus 4:1-31	26th
Exodus 5:1–6:13	27th
Exodus 6:14–7:13	28th

MARCH

Exodus 7:14–8:19	1st
Exodus 8:20–9:12	2nd
Exodus 9:13-35	3rd
Exodus 10:1-20	4th
Exodus 10:21–11:10	5th
Exodus 12:1-28	6th
Exodus 12:29–13:16	7th
Exodus 13:17–14:31	8th
Exodus 15:1-27	9th
Exodus 16:1-36	10th
Exodus 17:1-16	11th
Exodus 18:1-27	12th
Exodus 19:1-25	13th
Exodus 20:1-26	14th
Exodus 21:1-36	15th
Exodus 22:1-31	16th
Exodus 23:1-33	17th
Exodus 24:1–25:9	18th
Exodus 25:10-40	19th
Exodus 26:1-37	20th
Exodus 27:1–28:14	21st
Exodus 28:15-43	22nd
Exodus 29:1-34	23rd
Exodus 29:35–30:21	24th
Exodus 30:22–31:18	25th
Exodus 32:1-35	26th
Exodus 33:1–34:9	27th
Exodus 34:10-35	28th
Exodus 35:1–36:1	29th
Exodus 36:2-38	30th
Exodus 37:1-24	31st

APRIL

Exodus 37:25–38:20	1st
Exodus 38:21–39:7	2nd
Exodus 39:8-43	3rd
Exodus 40:1-38	4th
Leviticus 1:1–2:16	5th
Leviticus 3:1–4:12	6th
Leviticus 4:13-35	7th
Leviticus 5:1–6:7	8th
Leviticus 6:8–7:10	9th
Leviticus 7:11-38	10th
Leviticus 8:1-36	11th
Leviticus 9:1-24	12th
Leviticus 10:1–11:8	13th
Leviticus 11:9-40	14th
Leviticus 11:41–13:8	15th
Leviticus 13:9-39	16th
Leviticus 13:40-59	17th
Leviticus 14:1-32	18th
Leviticus 14:33-57	19th
Leviticus 15:1-33	20th
Leviticus 16:1-34	21st
Leviticus 17:1-16	22nd
Leviticus 18:1-30	23rd
Leviticus 19:1-37	24th
Leviticus 20:1-27	25th
Leviticus 21:1–22:16	26th
Leviticus 22:17–23:8	27th
Leviticus 23:9-32	28th
Leviticus 23:33–24:23	29th
Leviticus 25:1-17	30th

MAY

Leviticus 25:18-46	1st
Leviticus 25:47–26:13	2nd
Leviticus 26:14-46	3rd
Leviticus 27:1-34	4th
Numbers 1:1-31	5th
Numbers 1:32-54	6th
Numbers 2:1-34	7th
Numbers 3:1-39	8th
Numbers 3:40–4:20	9th
Numbers 4:21-49	10th
Numbers 5:1-31	11th
Numbers 6:1-27	12th
Numbers 7:1-35	13th
Numbers 7:36-65	14th
Numbers 7:66–8:4	15th
Numbers 8:5-26	16th
Numbers 9:1-23	17th
Numbers 10:1-36	18th
Numbers 11:1-30	19th
Numbers 11:31–13:16	20th
Numbers 13:17–14:10	21st
Numbers 14:11-38	22nd
Numbers 14:39–15:21	23rd
Numbers 15:22-41	24th
Numbers 16:1-24	25th
Numbers 16:25-50	26th
Numbers 17:1–18:7	27th
Numbers 18:8-32	28th
Numbers 19:1-22	29th
Numbers 20:1-29	30th
Numbers 21:1-20	31st

JUNE

Numbers 21:21-35 1st
Numbers 22:1-21 2nd
Numbers 22:22–23:12 3rd
Numbers 23:13–24:14 4th
Numbers 24:15–25:18 5th
Numbers 26:1-37 6th
Numbers 26:38-65 7th
Numbers 27:1–28:8 8th
Numbers 28:9–29:6 9th
Numbers 29:7-40 10th
Numbers 30:1–31:24 11th
Numbers 31:25-54 12th
Numbers 32:1-42 13th
Numbers 33:1-49 14th
Numbers 33:50–34:29 15th
Numbers 35:1-34 16th
Numbers 36:1-13 17th
Deuteronomy 1:1-25 18th
Deuteronomy 1:26-46 19th
Deuteronomy 2:1-23 20th
Deuteronomy 2:24–3:20 21st
Deuteronomy 3:21–4:14 22nd
Deuteronomy 4:15-49 23rd
Deuteronomy 5:1-33 24th
Deuteronomy 6:1-25 25th
Deuteronomy 7:1-26 26th
Deuteronomy 8:1–9:6 27th
Deuteronomy 9:7–10:11 28th
Deuteronomy 10:12–11:7 29th
Deuteronomy 11:8-32 30th

JULY

Deuteronomy 12:1-32 1st
Deuteronomy 13:1–14:21 2nd
Deuteronomy 14:22–15:23 3rd
Deuteronomy 16:1–17:7 4th
Deuteronomy 17:8–18:22 5th
Deuteronomy 19:1-21 6th
Deuteronomy 20:1–21:14 7th
Deuteronomy 21:15–22:21 8th
Deuteronomy 22:22–23:25 9th
Deuteronomy 24:1–25:4 10th
Deuteronomy 25:5–26:15 11th
Deuteronomy 26:16–27:26 12th
Deuteronomy 28:1-35 13th
Deuteronomy 28:36-68 14th
Deuteronomy 29:1-29 15th
Deuteronomy 30:1–31:8 16th
Deuteronomy 31:9-29 17th
Deuteronomy 31:30–32:25 18th
Deuteronomy 32:26-52 19th
Deuteronomy 33:1-19 20th
Deuteronomy 33:20–34:12 21st
Joshua 1:1-18 22nd
Joshua 2:1-24 23rd
Joshua 3:1-17 24th
Joshua 4:1–5:9 25th
Joshua 5:10–6:21 26th
Joshua 6:22–7:15 27th
Joshua 7:16–8:23 28th
Joshua 8:24–9:15 29th
Joshua 9:16–10:15 30th
Joshua 10:16-43 31st

AUGUST

Joshua 11:1-23 1st
Joshua 12:1–13:7 2nd
Joshua 13:8–14:5 3rd
Joshua 14:6–15:19 4th
Joshua 15:20–16:4 5th
Joshua 16:5–17:18 6th
Joshua 18:1-28 7th
Joshua 19:1-39 8th
Joshua 19:40–21:8 9th
Joshua 21:9-42 10th
Joshua 21:43–22:20 11th
Joshua 22:21–23:16 12th
Joshua 24:1-33 13th
Judges 1:1-36 14th
Judges 2:1-23 15th
Judges 3:1-31 16th
Judges 4:1–5:5 17th
Judges 5:6-31 18th
Judges 6:1-24 19th
Judges 6:25-40 20th
Judges 7:1-25 21st
Judges 8:1-35 22nd
Judges 9:1-21 23rd
Judges 9:22-57 24th
Judges 10:1–11:11 25th
Judges 11:12-40 26th
Judges 12:1-15 27th
Judges 13:1-25 28th
Judges 14:1-20 29th
Judges 15:1-20 30th
Judges 16:1-22 31st

SEPTEMBER

Judges 16:23–17:13 1st
Judges 18:1-31 2nd
Judges 19:1-30 3rd
Judges 20:1-18 4th
Judges 20:19-48 5th
Judges 21:1-25 6th
Ruth 1:1-22 7th
Ruth 2:1-23 8th
Ruth 3:1-18 9th
Ruth 4:1-22 10th
1 Samuel 1:1-28 11th
1 Samuel 2:1-26 12th
1 Samuel 2:27–3:18 13th
1 Samuel 3:19–5:5 14th
1 Samuel 5:6–6:18 15th
1 Samuel 6:19–8:9 16th
1 Samuel 8:10–9:17 17th
1 Samuel 9:18–10:16 18th
1 Samuel 10:17–11:15 19th
1 Samuel 12:1-25 20th
1 Samuel 13:1-22 21st
1 Samuel 13:23–14:30 22nd
1 Samuel 14:31-52 23rd
1 Samuel 15:1-35 24th
1 Samuel 16:1-23 25th
1 Samuel 17:1-37 26th
1 Samuel 17:38-58 27th
1 Samuel 18:1-30 28th
1 Samuel 19:1-24 29th
1 Samuel 20:1-34 30th

OCTOBER

1 Samuel 20:35–22:5 1st
1 Samuel 22:6–23:6 2nd
1 Samuel 23:7-29 3rd
1 Samuel 24:1–25:13 4th
1 Samuel 25:14-44 5th
1 Samuel 26:1–27:4 6th
1 Samuel 27:5–28:25 7th
1 Samuel 29:1–30:20 8th
1 Samuel 30:21–31:13 9th
2 Samuel 1:1-27 10th
2 Samuel 2:1–3:5 11th
2 Samuel 3:6-39 12th
2 Samuel 4:1–5:16 13th
2 Samuel 5:17–6:23 14th
2 Samuel 7:1-29 15th
2 Samuel 8:1–9:13 16th
2 Samuel 10:1-19 17th
2 Samuel 11:1-27 18th
2 Samuel 12:1-31 19th
2 Samuel 13:1-27 20th
2 Samuel 13:28–14:17 21st
2 Samuel 14:18–15:12 22nd
2 Samuel 15:13–16:4 23rd
2 Samuel 16:5-22 24th
2 Samuel 16:23–17:29 25th
2 Samuel 18:1-27 26th
2 Samuel 18:28–19:23 27th
2 Samuel 19:24–20:10 28th
2 Samuel 20:11–21:14 29th
2 Samuel 21:15–22:24 30th
2 Samuel 22:25–23:7 31st

NOVEMBER

2 Samuel 23:8-39 1st
2 Samuel 24:1-25 2nd
1 Kings 1:1-31 3rd
1 Kings 1:32–2:12 4th
1 Kings 2:13-38 5th
1 Kings 2:39–3:28 6th
1 Kings 4:1-34 7th
1 Kings 5:1-18 8th
1 Kings 6:1-38 9th
1 Kings 7:1-26 10th
1 Kings 7:27-51 11th
1 Kings 8:1-26 12th
1 Kings 8:27-43 13th

1 Kings 8:44-66 14th
1 Kings 9:1-28 15th
1 Kings 10:1-29 16th
1 Kings 11:1-25 17th
1 Kings 11:26–12:11 18th
1 Kings 12:12-33 19th
1 Kings 13:1-34 20th
1 Kings 14:1-31 21st
1 Kings 15:1-32 22nd
1 Kings 15:33–16:28 23rd
1 Kings 16:29–17:24 24th
1 Kings 18:1-35 25th
1 Kings 18:36–19:18 26th
1 Kings 19:19–20:28 27th
1 Kings 20:29–21:10 28th
1 Kings 21:11-29 29th
1 Kings 22:1-28 30th

DECEMBER

1 Kings 22:29-53 1st
2 Kings 1:1-18 2nd
2 Kings 2:1-25 3rd
2 Kings 3:1–4:7 4th
2 Kings 4:8-44 5th
2 Kings 5:1-27 6th
2 Kings 6:1-33 7th
2 Kings 7:1-20 8th
2 Kings 8:1-29 9th
2 Kings 9:1-29 10th
2 Kings 9:30–10:17 11th
2 Kings 10:18-36 12th
2 Kings 11:1-20 13th
2 Kings 11:21–12:21 14th
2 Kings 13:1-25 15th
2 Kings 14:1-29 16th

2 Kings 15:1-31 17th
2 Kings 15:32–17:6 18th
2 Kings 17:7-33 19th
2 Kings 17:34–18:18 20th
2 Kings 18:19-37 21st
2 Kings 19:1-28 22nd
2 Kings 19:29–20:21 23rd
2 Kings 21:1-26 24th
2 Kings 22:1–23:3 25th
2 Kings 23:4-27 26th
2 Kings 23:28–24:20 27th
2 Kings 25:1-30 28th
1 Chronicles 1:1-31 29th
1 Chronicles 1:32–2:9 30th
1 Chronicles 2:10-41 31st

YEAR TWO

JANUARY

1 Chronicles 2:42–3:16 1st
1 Chronicles 3:17–4:23 2nd
1 Chronicles 4:24–5:10 3rd
1 Chronicles 5:11–6:15 4th
1 Chronicles 6:16-53 5th
1 Chronicles 6:54-81 6th
1 Chronicles 7:1-29 7th
1 Chronicles 7:30–8:40 8th
1 Chronicles 9:1-34 9th
1 Chronicles 9:35–11:9 10th
1 Chronicles 11:10-47 11th
1 Chronicles 12:1-37 12th
1 Chronicles 12:38–14:17 13th
1 Chronicles 15:1–16:6 14th
1 Chronicles 16:7-43 15th
1 Chronicles 17:1-27 16th
1 Chronicles 18:1-17 17th
1 Chronicles 19:1–20:8 18th
1 Chronicles 21:1–22:1 19th
1 Chronicles 22:2–23:14 20th
1 Chronicles 23:15–24:19 21st
1 Chronicles 24:20–25:31 22nd
1 Chronicles 26:1-32 23rd
1 Chronicles 27:1-34 24th
1 Chronicles 28:1-21 25th
1 Chronicles 29:1-30 26th
2 Chronicles 1:1–2:10 27th
2 Chronicles 2:11–3:17 28th
2 Chronicles 4:1–5:1 29th
2 Chronicles 5:2–6:11 30th
2 Chronicles 6:12-31 31st

FEBRUARY

2 Chronicles 6:32–7:11 1st
2 Chronicles 7:12–8:18 2nd
2 Chronicles 9:1-31 3rd
2 Chronicles 10:1–11:4 4th
2 Chronicles 11:5–12:16 5th
2 Chronicles 13:1–14:1 6th
2 Chronicles 14:2–15:19 7th
2 Chronicles 16:1–17:19 8th
2 Chronicles 18:1-27 9th
2 Chronicles 18:28–19:11 10th
2 Chronicles 20:1-30 11th
2 Chronicles 20:31–21:20 12th
2 Chronicles 22:1–23:15 13th
2 Chronicles 23:16–24:22 14th
2 Chronicles 24:23–25:16 15th
2 Chronicles 25:17–26:10 16th
2 Chronicles 26:11–28:8 17th
2 Chronicles 28:9–29:11 18th
2 Chronicles 29:12-36 19th
2 Chronicles 30:1–31:1 20th
2 Chronicles 31:2-21 21st
2 Chronicles 32:1-31 22nd
2 Chronicles 32:32–33:25 23rd
2 Chronicles 34:1-28 24th
2 Chronicles 34:29–35:19 25th
2 Chronicles 35:20–36:8 26th
2 Chronicles 36:9-23 27th
Ezra 1:1-2:42 28th

MARCH

Ezra 2:43–3:7 1st
Ezra 3:8–4:16 2nd
Ezra 4:17–5:17 3rd
Ezra 6:1-22 4th
Ezra 7:1-28 5th
Ezra 8:1-30 6th
Ezra 8:31–9:15 7th
Ezra 10:1-17 8th
Ezra 10:18-44 9th
Nehemiah 1:1–2:10 10th
Nehemiah 2:11–3:19 11th
Nehemiah 3:20–4:14 12th
Nehemiah 4:15–5:19 13th
Nehemiah 6:1–7:3 14th
Nehemiah 7:4-60 15th
Nehemiah 7:61–8:12 16th
Nehemiah 8:13–9:18 17th
Nehemiah 9:19-37 18th
Nehemiah 9:38–10:39 19th
Nehemiah 11:1-36 20th
Nehemiah 12:1-26 21st
Nehemiah 12:27–13:5 22nd
Nehemiah 13:6-31 23rd
Esther 1:1-22 24th
Esther 2:1-23 25th
Esther 3:1–4:17 26th
Esther 5:1–6:14 27th
Esther 7:1–8:17 28th
Esther 9:1-17 29th
Esther 9:18–10:3 30th
Job 1:1–2:10 31st

APRIL

Job 2:11–4:11 1st
Job 4:12–5:27 2nd
Job 6:1-30 3rd
Job 7:1-21 4th
Job 8:1-22 5th
Job 9:1-35 6th
Job 10:1-22 7th
Job 11:1-20 8th
Job 12:1–13:19 9th
Job 13:20–14:22 10th
Job 15:1-35 11th
Job 16:1–17:16 12th
Job 18:1–19:20 13th
Job 19:21–20:29 14th

Job 21:1-34 15th
Job 22:1-30 16th
Job 23:1-17 17th
Job 24:1–25:6 18th
Job 26:1–27:23 19th
Job 28:1-28 20th
Job 29:1-25 21st
Job 30:1-31 22nd
Job 31:1-40 23rd
Job 32:1-22 24th
Job 33:1-33 25th
Job 34:1-37 26th
Job 35:1-16 27th
Job 36:1-33 28th
Job 37:1-24 29th
Job 38:1-41 30th

MAY

Job 39:1-30 1st
Job 40:1-24 2nd
Job 41:1-34 3rd
Job 42:1-17 4th
Psalms 1:1–3:8 5th
Psalms 4:1–6:10 6th
Psalms 7:1–8:9 7th
Psalm 9:1-20 8th
Psalm 10:1-18 9th
Psalms 11:1–13:6 10th
Psalms 14:1–16:11 11th
Psalms 17:1–18:15 12th
Psalm 18:16-50 13th
Psalms 19:1–21:7 14th
Psalms 21:8–22:26 15th
Psalms 22:27–24:10 16th
Psalm 25:1-22 17th
Psalms 26:1–27:14 18th
Psalms 28:1–30:12 19th
Psalm 31:1-24 20th
Psalms 32:1–33:22 21st
Psalm 34:1-22 22nd
Psalm 35:1-28 23rd
Psalms 36:1–37:20 24th
Psalms 37:21–38:12 25th
Psalms 38:13–40:10 26th
Psalms 40:11–42:4 27th
Psalms 42:5–44:16 28th
Psalms 44:17–46:3 29th
Psalms 46:4–48:14 30th
Psalm 49:1-20 31st

JUNE

Psalm 50:1-23 1st
Psalm 51:1-19 2nd
Psalms 52:1–54:7 3rd
Psalms 55:1–56:13 4th
Psalms 57:1–58:11 5th
Psalms 59:1–60:12 6th
Psalms 61:1–63:11 7th
Psalms 64:1–65:13 8th
Psalms 66:1–67:7 9th
Psalm 68:1-27 10th
Psalms 68:28–69:21 11th
Psalms 69:22–71:16 12th
Psalms 71:17–72:20 13th
Psalm 73:1-28 14th
Psalms 74:1–75:10 15th
Psalms 76:1–77:20 16th
Psalm 78:1-39 17th
Psalm 78:40-72 18th
Psalms 79:1–80:19 19th
Psalms 81:1–82:8 20th
Psalms 83:1–84:12 21st
Psalms 85:1–86:17 22nd
Psalms 87:1–88:18 23rd
Psalm 89:1-18 24th
Psalm 89:19-52 25th
Psalms 90:1–91:16 26th
Psalms 92:1–94:23 27th
Psalms 95:1–97:12 28th
Psalms 98:1–99:9 29th
Psalms 100:1–102:17 30th

JULY

Psalms 102:18–103:22 1st
Psalm 104:1-35 2nd
Psalm 105:1-45 3rd
Psalm 106:1-39 4th
Psalms 106:40–107:22 5th
Psalms 107:23–108:13 6th
Psalm 109:1-31 7th
Psalms 110:1–112:10 8th
Psalms 113:1–115:18 9th
Psalms 116:1–117:2 10th
Psalm 118:1-29 11th
Psalm 119:1-48 12th
Psalm 119:49-88 13th
Psalm 119:89-136 14th
Psalms 119:137–120:7 15th
Psalms 121:1–124:8 16th
Psalms 125:1–129:8 17th
Psalms 130:1–134:3 18th
Psalms 135:1–136:26 19th
Psalms 137:1–138:8 20th
Psalm 139:1-24 21st
Psalms 140:1–141:10 22nd
Psalms 142:1–143:12 23rd
Psalm 144:1-15 24th
Psalm 145:1-21 25th
Psalms 146:1–147:20 26th
Psalms 148:1–150:6 27th
Proverbs 1:1-33 28th
Proverbs 2:1-22 29th
Proverbs 3:1-35 30th
Proverbs 4:1-27 31st

AUGUST

Proverbs 5:1–6:19 1st
Proverbs 6:20–7:27 2nd
Proverbs 8:1-36 3rd
Proverbs 9:1-18 4th
Proverbs 10:1-32 5th
Proverbs 11:1-31 6th
Proverbs 12:1-28 7th
Proverbs 13:1-25 8th
Proverbs 14:1-35 9th
Proverbs 15:1-33 10th
Proverbs 16:1-33 11th
Proverbs 17:1-28 12th
Proverbs 18:1-24 13th
Proverbs 19:1-29 14th
Proverbs 20:1-30 15th
Proverbs 21:1-31 16th
Proverbs 22:1-29 17th
Proverbs 23:1-35 18th
Proverbs 24:1-34 19th
Proverbs 25:1-28 20th
Proverbs 26:1-28 21st
Proverbs 27:1-27 22nd
Proverbs 28:1-28 23rd
Proverbs 29:1-27 24th
Proverbs 30:1-33 25th
Proverbs 31:1-31 26th
Ecclesiastes 1:1-18 27th
Ecclesiastes 2:1-26 28th
Ecclesiastes 3:1-22 29th
Ecclesiastes 4:1-16 30th
Ecclesiastes 5:1–6:12 31st

SEPTEMBER

Ecclesiastes 7:1-29 1st
Ecclesiastes 8:1–9:10 2nd
Ecclesiastes 9:11–10:20 3rd
Ecclesiastes 11:1–12:14 4th
Song of Songs 1:1–2:7 5th
Song of Songs 2:8–3:11 6th
Song of Songs 4:1–5:2 7th
Song of Songs 5:3–6:13 8th
Song of Songs 7:1–8:14 9th
Isaiah 1:1-20 10th
Isaiah 1:21–2:11 11th
Isaiah 2:12–3:15 12th
Isaiah 3:16–5:7 13th
Isaiah 5:8-30 14th
Isaiah 6:1–7:9 15th
Isaiah 7:10–8:10 16th
Isaiah 8:11–9:7 17th
Isaiah 9:8–10:4 18th
Isaiah 10:5-26 19th
Isaiah 10:27–11:16 20th
Isaiah 12:1–13:22 21st
Isaiah 14:1-27 22nd
Isaiah 14:28–15:9 23rd
Isaiah 16:1-14 24th

Isaiah 17:1–18:7 25th
Isaiah 19:1–20:6 26th
Isaiah 21:1-17 27th
Isaiah 22:1-25 28th
Isaiah 23:1-18 29th
Isaiah 24:1-23 30th

OCTOBER

Isaiah 25:1-12 1st
Isaiah 26:1-21 2nd
Isaiah 27:1-13 3rd
Isaiah 28:1-22 4th
Isaiah 28:23–29:12 5th
Isaiah 29:13-30:7 6th
Isaiah 30:8-33 7th
Isaiah 31:1–32:20 8th
Isaiah 33:1-24 9th
Isaiah 34:1–35:3 10th
Isaiah 35:4–36:22 11th
Isaiah 37:1-20 12th
Isaiah 37:21-38 13th
Isaiah 38:1–39:8 14th
Isaiah 40:1-26 15th
Isaiah 40:27–41:16 16th
Isaiah 41:17–42:9 17th
Isaiah 42:10–43:7 18th
Isaiah 43:8–44:5 19th
Isaiah 44:6-23 20th
Isaiah 44:24–45:17 21st
Isaiah 45:18–46:13 22nd
Isaiah 47:1-15 23rd
Isaiah 48:1-22 24th
Isaiah 49:1-21 25th
Isaiah 49:22–51:3 26th
Isaiah 51:4-23 27th
Isaiah 52:1-15 28th
Isaiah 53:1-12 29th
Isaiah 54:1–55:5 30th
Isaiah 55:6–56:12 31st

NOVEMBER

Isaiah 57:1-21 1st
Isaiah 58:1-14 2nd
Isaiah 59:1-21 3rd
Isaiah 60:1-22 4th
Isaiah 61:1–62:12 5th
Isaiah 63:1-19 6th
Isaiah 64:1–65:7 7th
Isaiah 65:8–66:4 8th
Isaiah 66:5-24 9th
Jeremiah 1:1–2:3 10th
Jeremiah 2:4-25 11th
Jeremiah 2:26–3:13 12th
Jeremiah 3:14–4:4 13th
Jeremiah 4:5-31 14th
Jeremiah 5:1-19 15th
Jeremiah 5:20–6:12 16th
Jeremiah 6:13-30 17th
Jeremiah 7:1-34 18th
Jeremiah 8:1-22 19th
Jeremiah 9:1-22 20th
Jeremiah 9:23–10:18 21st
Jeremiah 10:19–11:23 22nd
Jeremiah 12:1-17 23rd
Jeremiah 13:1-27 24th
Jeremiah 14:1-22 25th
Jeremiah 15:1-21 26th
Jeremiah 16:1-21 27th
Jeremiah 17:1-27 28th
Jeremiah 18:1-23 29th
Jeremiah 19:1–20:6 30th

DECEMBER

Jeremiah 20:7–21:14 1st
Jeremiah 22:1-23 2nd
Jeremiah 22:24–23:17 3rd
Jeremiah 23:18–24:10 4th
Jeremiah 25:1-31 5th
Jeremiah 25:32–26:24 6th
Jeremiah 27:1-22 7th
Jeremiah 28:1-17 8th
Jeremiah 29:1-32 9th
Jeremiah 30:1-24 10th
Jeremiah 31:1-22 11th
Jeremiah 31:23-40 12th
Jeremiah 32:1-25 13th
Jeremiah 32:26–33:9 14th
Jeremiah 33:10–34:7 15th
Jeremiah 34:8–35:19 16th
Jeremiah 36:1-32 17th
Jeremiah 37:1–38:13 18th
Jeremiah 38:14–39:18 19th
Jeremiah 40:1–41:10 20th
Jeremiah 41:11–42:22 21st
Jeremiah 43:1–44:6 22nd
Jeremiah 44:7-30 23rd
Jeremiah 45:1–46:19 24th
Jeremiah 46:20–47:7 25th
Jeremiah 48:1-25 26th
Jeremiah 48:26-47 27th
Jeremiah 49:1-22 28th
Jeremiah 49:23-39 29th
Jeremiah 50:1-16 30th
Jeremiah 50:17-32 31st

YEAR THREE

JANUARY

Jeremiah 50:33–51:10 1st
Jeremiah 51:11-32 2nd
Jeremiah 51:33-48 3rd
Jeremiah 51:49-64 4th
Jeremiah 52:1-34 5th
Lamentations 1:1-15 6th
Lamentations 1:16–2:9 7th
Lamentations 2:10–3:9 8th
Lamentations 3:10-57 9th
Lamentations 3:58–4:15 10th
Lamentations 4:16–5:22 11th
Ezekiel 1:1-28 12th
Ezekiel 2:1–3:27 13th
Ezekiel 4:1–5:17 14th
Ezekiel 6:1–7:9 15th
Ezekiel 7:10-27 16th
Ezekiel 8:1–9:11 17th
Ezekiel 10:1–11:15 18th
Ezekiel 11:16–12:28 19th
Ezekiel 13:1–14:11 20th
Ezekiel 14:12–16:14 21st
Ezekiel 16:15-43 22nd
Ezekiel 16:44-63 23rd
Ezekiel 17:1-24 24th
Ezekiel 18:1-32 25th
Ezekiel 19:1-14 26th
Ezekiel 20:1-31 27th
Ezekiel 20:32–21:13 28th
Ezekiel 21:14-32 29th
Ezekiel 22:1-31 30th
Ezekiel 23:1-34 31st

FEBRUARY

Ezekiel 23:35–24:14 1st
Ezekiel 24:15–25:17 2nd
Ezekiel 26:1-21 3rd
Ezekiel 27:1-27 4th
Ezekiel 27:28–28:10 5th
Ezekiel 28:11-26 6th
Ezekiel 29:1-21 7th
Ezekiel 30:1-26 8th
Ezekiel 31:1–32:6 9th
Ezekiel 32:7-28 10th
Ezekiel 32:29–33:20 11th
Ezekiel 33:21–34:19 12th
Ezekiel 34:20–35:15 13th
Ezekiel 36:1-32 14th
Ezekiel 36:33–37:28 15th
Ezekiel 38:1-23 16th
Ezekiel 39:1–40:4 17th
Ezekiel 40:5-37 18th
Ezekiel 40:38–41:12 19th
Ezekiel 41:13–42:20 20th
Ezekiel 43:1-27 21st
Ezekiel 44:1-31 22nd
Ezekiel 45:1-25 23rd
Ezekiel 46:1-24 24th
Ezekiel 47:1-23 25th
Ezekiel 48:1-35 26th

Daniel 1:1–2:16 27th
Daniel 2:17-49 28th

MARCH

Daniel 3:1-30 1st
Daniel 4:1-27 2nd
Daniel 4:28–5:16 3rd
Daniel 5:17–6:18 4th
Daniel 6:19–7:14 5th
Daniel 7:15–8:22 6th
Daniel 8:23–9:19 7th
Daniel 9:20–11:4 8th
Daniel 11:5-35 9th
Daniel 11:36–12:13 10th
Hosea 1:1–2:13 11th
Hosea 2:14–4:11 12th
Hosea 4:12–5:15 13th
Hosea 6:1–7:16 14th
Hosea 8:1–9:9 15th
Hosea 9:10–10:15 16th
Hosea 11:1–12:14 17th
Hosea 13:1–14:9 18th
Joel 1:1-20 19th
Joel 2:1-17 20th
Joel 2:18-32 21st
Joel 3:1-21 22nd
Amos 1:1–2:5 23rd
Amos 2:6–3:15 24th
Amos 4:1-13 25th
Amos 5:1-27 26th
Amos 6:1-7:9 27th
Amos 7:10–8:14 28th
Amos 9:1-15 29th
Obadiah 30th
Jonah 1:1–2:10 31st

APRIL

Jonah 3:1–4:11 1st
Micah 1:1–2:5 2nd
Micah 2:6–4:2 3rd
Micah 4:3–5:9 4th
Micah 5:10–6:16 5th
Micah 7:1-20 6th
Nahum 1:1–2:10 7th
Micah 2:11–3:19 8th
Habakkuk 1:1-17 9th
Habakkuk 2:1-20 10th
Habakkuk 3:1-19 11th
Zephaniah 1:1-18 12th
Zephaniah 2:1-15 13th
Zephaniah 3:1-20 14th
Haggai 1:1-15 15th
Haggai 2:1-23 16th
Zechariah 1:1–2:13 17th
Zechariah 3:1–5:11 18th
Zechariah 6:1–7:14 19th
Zechariah 8:1–9:8 20th
Zechariah 9:9–10:12 21st
Zechariah 11:1–12:14 22nd
Zechariah 13:1–14:21 23rd
Malachi 1:1-14 24th
Malachi 2:1–3:6 25th
Malachi 3:7–4:6 26th
Matthew 1:1–2:6 27th
Matthew 2:7–3:17 28th
Matthew 4:1–5:12 29th
Matthew 5:13–6:4 30th

MAY

Matthew 6:5–7:12 1st
Matthew 7:13–8:27 2nd
Matthew 8:28–9:34 3rd
Matthew 9:35–10:31 4th
Matthew 10:32–11:30 5th
Matthew 12:1-37 6th
Matthew 12:38–13:23 7th
Matthew 13:24-58 8th
Matthew 14:1-36 9th
Matthew 15:1-39 10th
Matthew 16:1–17:13 11th
Matthew 17:14–18:20 12th
Matthew 18:21–19:15 13th
Matthew 19:16–20:19 14th
Matthew 20:20–21:22 15th
Matthew 21:23-46 16th
Matthew 22:1-46 17th
Matthew 23:1-39 18th
Matthew 24:1-35 19th
Matthew 24:36–25:30 20th
Matthew 25:31–26:25 21st
Matthew 26:26-68 22nd
Matthew 26:69–27:26 23rd
Matthew 27:27-56 24th
Matthew 27:57–28:20 25th
Mark 1:1-39 26th
Mark 1:40–2:22 27th
Mark 2:23–3:35 28th
Mark 4:1-41 29th
Mark 5:1-43 30th
Mark 6:1-29 31st

JUNE

Mark 6:30-56 1st
Mark 7:1-37 2nd
Mark 8:1–9:1 3rd
Mark 9:2-37 4th
Mark 9:38–10:22 5th
Mark 10:23–11:11 6th
Mark 11:12–12:17 7th
Mark 12:18-44 8th
Mark 13:1-37 9th
Mark 14:1-31 10th
Mark 14:32-72 11th
Mark 15:1-41 12th
Mark 15:42–16:20 13th
Luke 1:1-38 14th
Luke 1:39-80 15th
Luke 2:1-40 16th
Luke 2:41–3:20 17th
Luke 3:21–4:13 18th
Luke 4:14-44 19th
Luke 5:1-39 20th
Luke 6:1-36 21st
Luke 6:37–7:17 22nd
Luke 7:18-50 23rd
Luke 8:1-25 24th
Luke 8:26-56 25th
Luke 9:1-36 26th
Luke 9:37-62 27th
Luke 10:1-37 28th
Luke 10:38–11:28 29th
Luke 11:29-54 30th

JULY

Luke 12:1-34 1st
Luke 12:35-59 2nd
Luke 13:1-30 3rd
Luke 13:31–14:24 4th
Luke 14:25–15:32 5th
Luke 16:1-31 6th
Luke 17:1-37 7th
Luke 18:1-34 8th
Luke 18:35–19:27 9th
Luke 19:28-48 10th
Luke 20:1-26 11th
Luke 20:27–21:4 12th
Luke 21:5-38 13th
Luke 22:1-38 14th
Luke 22:39-65 15th
Luke 22:66–23:25 16th
Luke 23:26–24:12 17th
Luke 24:13-53 18th
John 1:1-34 19th
John 1:35–2:12 20th
John 2:13–3:21 21st
John 3:22–4:26 22nd
John 4:27-54 23rd
John 5:1-30 24th
John 5:31–6:24 25th
John 6:25-71 26th
John 7:1-44 27th
John 7:45–8:29 28th
John 8:30-59 29th
John 9:1-41 30th
John 10:1-42 31st

AUGUST

John 11:1-44 1st
John 11:45–12:19 2nd
John 12:20-50 3rd
John 13:1-38 4th
John 14:1-31 5th
John 15:1–16:4 6th
John 16:5-33 7th

John 17:1-26 8th
John 18:1-24 9th
John 18:25-40 10th
John 19:1-27 11th
John 19:28–20:18 12th
John 20:19–21:14 13th
John 21:15-25 14th
Acts 1:1–2:13 15th
Acts 2:14-40 16th
Acts 2:41–3:26 17th
Acts 4:1-31 18th
Acts 4:32–5:16 19th
Acts 5:17–6:7 20th
Acts 6:8–7:22 21st
Acts 7:23-53 22nd
Acts 7:54–8:25 23rd
Acts 8:26–9:9 24th
Acts 9:10-43 25th
Acts 10:1-43 26th
Acts 10:44–11:30 27th
Acts 12:1–13:3 28th
Acts 13:4-41 29th
Acts 13:42–14:7 30th
Acts 14:8-28 31st

SEPTEMBER

Acts 15:1-35 1st
Acts 15:36–16:15 2nd
Acts 16:16-40 3rd
Acts 17:1-34 4th
Acts 18:1–19:7 5th
Acts 19:8-41 6th
Acts 20:1-38 7th
Acts 21:1-36 8th
Acts 21:37–22:21 9th
Acts 22:22–23:10 10th
Acts 23:11-35 11th
Acts 24:1-27 12th
Acts 25:1-27 13th
Acts 26:1-32 14th
Acts 27:1-26 15th
Acts 27:27–28:10 16th
Acts 28:11-31 17th
Romans 1:1-32 18th
Romans 2:1-29 19th
Romans 3:1-31 20th
Romans 4:1-25 21st
Romans 5:1–6:14 22nd
Romans 6:15–7:25 23rd
Romans 8:1-39 24th
Romans 9:1-33 25th
Romans 10:1–11:10 26th
Romans 11:11-36 27th
Romans 12:1–13:14 28th
Romans 14:1–15:13 29th
Romans 15:14-33 30th

OCTOBER

Romans 16:1-27 1st
1 Corinthians 1:1–2:5 2nd
1 Corinthians 2:6–3:23 3rd
1 Corinthians 4:1–5:13 4th
1 Corinthians 6:1-20 5th
1 Corinthians 7:1-40 6th
1 Corinthians 8:1–9:27 7th
1 Corinthians 10:1–11:1 8th
1 Corinthians 11:2-34 9th
1 Corinthians 12:1–13:13 10th
1 Corinthians 14:1-40 11th
1 Corinthians 15:1-34 12th
1 Corinthians 15:35-58 13th
1 Corinthians 16:1-24 14th
2 Corinthians 1:1–2:4 15th
2 Corinthians 2:5–3:18 16th
2 Corinthians 4:1–5:15 17th
2 Corinthians 5:16–7:1 18th
2 Corinthians 7:2–8:15 19th
2 Corinthians 8:16–9:15 20th
2 Corinthians 10:1–11:15 21st
2 Corinthians 11:16–12:10 22nd
2 Corinthians 12:11–13:13 23rd
Galatians 1:1–2:10 24th
Galatians 2:11–3:26 25th
Galatians 3:27–4:31 26th
Galatians 5:1–6:18 27th
Ephesians 1:1–2:10 28th
Ephesians 2:11–3:21 29th
Ephesians 4:1–5:14 30th
Ephesians 5:15–6:24 31st

NOVEMBER

Philippians 1:1–2:11 1st
Philippians 2:12–3:11 2nd
Philippians 3:12–4:23 3rd
Colossians 1:1–2:3 4th
Colossians 2:4–3:17 5th
Colossians 3:18–4:18 6th
1 Thessalonians 1:1–2:16 7th
1 Thessalonians 2:17–4:12 8th
1 Thessalonians 4:13–5:28 9th
2 Thessalonians 1:1–2:12 10th
2 Thessalonians 2:13–3:18 11th
1 Timothy 1:1–2:15 12th
1 Timothy 3:1–5:2 13th
1 Timothy 5:3-25 14th
1 Timothy 6:1-21 15th
2 Timothy 1:1–2:13 16th
2 Timothy 2:14–3:9 17th
2 Timothy 3:10–4:22 18th
Titus 1:1–2:15 19th
Titus 3:1-15 20th
Philemon 21st
Hebrews 1:1–2:4 22nd
Hebrews 2:5–3:19 23rd
Hebrews 4:1–5:10 24th
Hebrews 5:11–7:10 25th
Hebrews 7:11–8:13 26th
Hebrews 9:1-28 27th
Hebrews 10:1-39 28th
Hebrews 11:1-40 29th
Hebrews 12:1-29 30th

DECEMBER

Hebrews 13:1-25 1st
James 1:1–2:13 2nd
James 2:14–3:18 3rd
James 4:1–5:20 4th
1 Peter 1:1-25 5th
1 Peter 2:1–3:7 6th
1 Peter 3:8–4:11 7th
1 Peter 4:12–5:14 8th
2 Peter 1:1-21 9th
2 Peter 2:1-22 10th
2 Peter 3:1-18 11th
1 John 1:1–2:17 12th
1 John 2:18–3:24 13th
1 John 4:1–5:21 14th
2 John–3 John 15th
Jude 16th
Revelation 1:1–2:7 17th
Revelation 2:8–3:6 18th
Revelation 3:7–4:11 19th
Revelation 5:1–6:11 20th
Revelation 6:12–8:6 21st
Revelation 8:7–9:21 22nd
Revelation 10:1–11:19 23rd
Revelation 12:1–13:10 24th
Revelation 13:11–14:20 25th
Revelation 15:1–16:16 26th
Revelation 16:17–17:18 27th
Revelation 18:1-24 28th
Revelation 19:1–20:6 29th
Revelation 20:7–21:27 30th
Revelation 22:1-21 31st

Daily Bread
The Word of God in a Year

Compiled by the late Rev. Robert Murray M'Cheyne, M.A.

JANUARY

This is My beloved Son. I take delight in Him. Listen to Him (Mt 17:5)!

Genesis 1	Matthew 1	1st	Ezra 1	Acts 1
Genesis 2	Matthew 2	2nd	Ezra 2	Acts 2
Genesis 3	Matthew 3	3rd	Ezra 3	Acts 3
Genesis 4	Matthew 4	4th	Ezra 4	Acts 4
Genesis 5	Matthew 5	5th	Ezra 5	Acts 5
Genesis 6	Matthew 6	6th	Ezra 6	Acts 6
Genesis 7	Matthew 7	7th	Ezra 7	Acts 7
Genesis 8	Matthew 8	8th	Ezra 8	Acts 8
Genesis 9–10	Matthew 9	9th	Ezra 9	Acts 9
Genesis 11	Matthew 10	10th	Ezra 10	Acts 10
Genesis 12	Matthew 11	11th	Nehemiah 1	Acts 11
Genesis 13	Matthew 12	12th	Nehemiah 2	Acts 12
Genesis 14	Matthew 13	13th	Nehemiah 3	Acts 13
Genesis 15	Matthew 14	14th	Nehemiah 4	Acts 14
Genesis 16	Matthew 15	15th	Nehemiah 5	Acts 15
Genesis 17	Matthew 16	16th	Nehemiah 6	Acts 16
Genesis 18	Matthew 17	17th	Nehemiah 7	Acts 17
Genesis 19	Matthew 18	18th	Nehemiah 8	Acts 18
Genesis 20	Matthew 19	19th	Nehemiah 9	Acts 19
Genesis 21	Matthew 20	20th	Nehemiah 10	Acts 20
Genesis 22	Matthew 21	21st	Nehemiah 11	Acts 21
Genesis 23	Matthew 22	22nd	Nehemiah 12	Acts 22
Genesis 24	Matthew 23	23rd	Nehemiah 13	Acts 23
Genesis 25	Matthew 24	24th	Esther 1	Acts 24
Genesis 26	Matthew 25	25th	Esther 2	Acts 25
Genesis 27	Matthew 26	26th	Esther 3	Acts 26
Genesis 28	Matthew 27	27th	Esther 4	Acts 27
Genesis 29	Matthew 28	28th	Esther 5	Acts 28
Genesis 30	Mark 1	29th	Esther 6	Romans 1
Genesis 31	Mark 2	30th	Esther 7	Romans 2
Genesis 32	Mark 3	31st	Esther 8	Romans 3

FEBRUARY

I have treasured the words of His mouth more than my daily food (Jb 23:12).

Genesis 33	Mark 4	1st	Esther 9–10	Romans 4
Genesis 34	Mark 5	2nd	Job 1	Romans 5
Genesis 35–36	Mark 6	3rd	Job 2	Romans 6
Genesis 37	Mark 7	4th	Job 3	Romans 7
Genesis 38	Mark 8	5th	Job 4	Romans 8
Genesis 39	Mark 9	6th	Job 5	Romans 9
Genesis 40	Mark 10	7th	Job 6	Romans 10
Genesis 41	Mark 11	8th	Job 7	Romans 11
Genesis 42	Mark 12	9th	Job 8	Romans 12
Genesis 43	Mark 13	10th	Job 9	Romans 13
Genesis 44	Mark 14	11th	Job 10	Romans 14
Genesis 45	Mark 15	12th	Job 11	Romans 15
Genesis 46	Mark 16	13th	Job 12	Romans 16

Genesis 47	Luke 1:1-38	14th	Job 13	1 Corinthians 1
Genesis 48	Luke 1:39-80	15th	Job 14	1 Corinthians 2
Genesis 49	Luke 2	16th	Job 15	1 Corinthians 3
Genesis 50	Luke 3	17th	Job 16–17	1 Corinthians 4
Exodus 1	Luke 4	18th	Job 18	1 Corinthians 5
Exodus 2	Luke 5	19th	Job 19	1 Corinthians 6
Exodus 3	Luke 6	20th	Job 20	1 Corinthians 7
Exodus 4	Luke 7	21st	Job 21	1 Corinthians 8
Exodus 5	Luke 8	22nd	Job 22	1 Corinthians 9
Exodus 6	Luke 9	23rd	Job 23	1 Corinthians 10
Exodus 7	Luke 10	24th	Job 24	1 Corinthians 11
Exodus 8	Luke 11	25th	Job 25–26	1 Corinthians 12
Exodus 9	Luke 12	26th	Job 27	1 Corinthians 13
Exodus 10	Luke 13	27th	Job 28	1 Corinthians 14
Exodus 11–12:21	Luke 14	28th	Job 29	1 Corinthians 15

MARCH

Mary was treasuring up all these things in her heart and meditating on them (Lk 2:19).

Exodus 12:22ff	Luke 15	1st	Job 30	1 Corinthians 16
Exodus 13	Luke 16	2nd	Job 31	2 Corinthians 1
Exodus 14	Luke 17	3rd	Job 32	2 Corinthians 2
Exodus 15	Luke 18	4th	Job 33	2 Corinthians 3
Exodus 16	Luke 19	5th	Job 34	2 Corinthians 4
Exodus 17	Luke 20	6th	Job 35	2 Corinthians 5
Exodus 18	Luke 21	7th	Job 36	2 Corinthians 6
Exodus 19	Luke 22	8th	Job 37	2 Corinthians 7
Exodus 20	Luke 23	9th	Job 38	2 Corinthians 8
Exodus 21	Luke 24	10th	Job 39	2 Corinthians 9
Exodus 22	John 1	11th	Job 40	2 Corinthians 10
Exodus 23	John 2	12th	Job 41	2 Corinthians 11
Exodus 24	John 3	13th	Job 42	2 Corinthians 12
Exodus 25	John 4	14th	Proverbs 1	2 Corinthians 13
Exodus 26	John 5	15th	Proverbs 2	Galatians 1
Exodus 27	John 6	16th	Proverbs 3	Galatians 2
Exodus 28	John 7	17th	Proverbs 4	Galatians 3
Exodus 29	John 8	18th	Proverbs 5	Galatians 4
Exodus 30	John 9	19th	Proverbs 6	Galatians 5
Exodus 31	John 10	20th	Proverbs 7	Galatians 6
Exodus 32	John 11	21st	Proverbs 8	Ephesians 1
Exodus 33	John 12	22nd	Proverbs 9	Ephesians 2
Exodus 34	John 13	23rd	Proverbs 10	Ephesians 3
Exodus 35	John 14	24th	Proverbs 11	Ephesians 4
Exodus 36	John 15	25th	Proverbs 12	Ephesians 5
Exodus 37	John 16	26th	Proverbs 13	Ephesians 6
Exodus 38	John 17	27th	Proverbs 14	Philippians 1
Exodus 39	John 18	28th	Proverbs 15	Philippians 2
Exodus 40	John 19	29th	Proverbs 16	Philippians 3
Leviticus 1	John 20	30th	Proverbs 17	Philippians 4
Leviticus 2–3	John 21	31st	Proverbs 18	Colossians 1

APRIL

Send Your light and Your truth; let them lead me (Ps 43:3).

Leviticus 4	Psalms 1–2	1st	Proverbs 19	Colossians 2
Leviticus 5	Psalms 3–4	2nd	Proverbs 20	Colossians 3
Leviticus 6	Psalms 5–6	3rd	Proverbs 21	Colossians 4
Leviticus 7	Psalms 7–8	4th	Proverbs 22	1 Thessalonians 1

Leviticus 8	Psalm 9	5th	Proverbs 23	1 Thessalonians 2
Leviticus 9	Psalm 10	6th	Proverbs 24	1 Thessalonians 3
Leviticus 10	Psalms 11–12	7th	Proverbs 25	1 Thessalonians 4
Leviticus 11–12	Psalms 13–14	8th	Proverbs 26	1 Thessalonians 5
Leviticus 13	Psalms 15–16	9th	Proverbs 27	2 Thessalonians 1
Leviticus 14	Psalm 17	10th	Proverbs 28	2 Thessalonians 2
Leviticus 15	Psalm 18	11th	Proverbs 29	2 Thessalonians 3
Leviticus 16	Psalm 19	12th	Proverbs 30	1 Timothy 1
Leviticus 17	Psalms 20–21	13th	Proverbs 31	1 Timothy 2
Leviticus 18	Psalm 22	14th	Ecclesiastes 1	1 Timothy 3
Leviticus 19	Psalms 23–24	15th	Ecclesiastes 2	1 Timothy 4
Leviticus 20	Psalm 25	16th	Ecclesiastes 3	1 Timothy 5
Leviticus 21	Psalms 26–27	17th	Ecclesiastes 4	1 Timothy 6
Leviticus 22	Psalms 28–29	18th	Ecclesiastes 5	2 Timothy 1
Leviticus 23	Psalm 30	19th	Ecclesiastes 6	2 Timothy 2
Leviticus 24	Psalm 31	20th	Ecclesiastes 7	2 Timothy 3
Leviticus 25	Psalm 32	21st	Ecclesiastes 8	2 Timothy 4
Leviticus 26	Psalm 33	22nd	Ecclesiastes 9	Titus 1
Leviticus 27	Psalm 4	23rd	Ecclesiastes 10	Titus 2
Numbers 1	Psalm 35	24th	Ecclesiastes 11	Titus 3
Numbers 2	Psalm 36	25th	Ecclesiastes 12	Philemon
Numbers 3	Psalm 37	26th	Song of Songs 1	Hebrews 1
Numbers 4	Psalm 38	27th	Song of Songs 2	Hebrews 2
Numbers 5	Psalm 39	28th	Song of Songs 3	Hebrews 3
Numbers 6	Psalms 40–41	29th	Song of Songs 4	Hebrews 4
Numbers 7	Psalms 42–43	30th	Song of Songs 5	Hebrews 5

MAY

From childhood you have known the sacred Scriptures (2Tm 3:15).

Numbers 8	Psalm 44	1st	Song of Songs 6	Hebrews 6
Numbers 9	Psalm 45	2nd	Song of Songs 7	Hebrews 7
Numbers 10	Psalms 46–47	3rd	Song of Songs 8	Hebrews 8
Numbers 11	Psalm 48	4th	Isaiah 1	Hebrews 9
Numbers 12-13	Psalm 49	5th	Isaiah 2	Hebrews 10
Numbers 14	Psalm 50	6th	Isaiah 3–4	Hebrews 11
Numbers 15	Psalm 51	7th	Isaiah 5	Hebrews 12
Numbers 16	Psalms 52–54	8th	Isaiah 6	Hebrews 13
Numbers 17–18	Psalm 55	9th	Isaiah 7	James 1
Numbers 19	Psalms 56–57	10th	Isaiah 8–9:7	James 2
Numbers 20	Psalms 58–59	11th	Isaiah 9:8–10:4	James 3
Numbers 21	Psalms 60–61	12th	Isaiah 10:5ff	James 4
Numbers 22	Psalms 62–63	13th	Isaiah 11–12	James 5
Numbers 23	Psalms 64–65	14th	Isaiah 13	1 Peter 1
Numbers 24	Psalms 66–67	15th	Isaiah 14	1 Peter 2
Numbers 25	Psalm 68	16th	Isaiah 15	1 Peter 3
Numbers 26	Psalm 69	17th	Isaiah 16	1 Peter 4
Numbers 27	Psalms 70–71	18th	Isaiah 17–18	1 Peter 5
Numbers 28	Psalm 72	19th	Isaiah 19–20	2 Peter 1
Numbers 29	Psalm 73	20th	Isaiah 21	2 Peter 2
Numbers 30	Psalm 74	21st	Isaiah 22	2 Peter 3
Numbers 31	Psalms 75–76	22nd	Isaiah 23	1 John 1
Numbers 32	Psalm 77	23rd	Isaiah 24	1 John 2
Numbers 33	Psalm 78:1-37	24th	Isaiah 25	1 John 3
Numbers 34	Psalm 78:38ff	25th	Isaiah 26	1 John 4
Numbers 35	Psalm 79	26th	Isaiah 27	1 John 5
Numbers 36	Psalm 80	27th	Isaiah 28	2 John

Deuteronomy 1	Psalms 81–82	28th	Isaiah 29	3 John
Deuteronomy 2	Psalms 83–84	29th	Isaiah 30	Jude
Deuteronomy 3	Psalm 85	30th	Isaiah 31	Revelation 1
Deuteronomy 4	Psalms 86–87	31st	Isaiah 32	Revelation 2

JUNE

The one who reads this is blessed, and those who hear the words of this prophecy and keep what is written in it are blessed (Rv 1:3).

Deuteronomy 5	Psalm 88	1st	Isaiah 33	Revelation 3
Deuteronomy 6	Psalm 89	2nd	Isaiah 34	Revelation 4
Deuteronomy 7	Psalm 90	3rd	Isaiah 35	Revelation 5
Deuteronomy 8	Psalm 91	4th	Isaiah 36	Revelation 6
Deuteronomy 9	Psalms 92–93	5th	Isaiah 37	Revelation 7
Deuteronomy 10	Psalm 94	6th	Isaiah 38	Revelation 8
Deuteronomy 11	Psalms 95–96	7th	Isaiah 39	Revelation 9
Deuteronomy 12	Psalms 97–98	8th	Isaiah 40	Revelation 10
Deuteronomy 13–14	Psalms 99–101	9th	Isaiah 41	Revelation 11
Deuteronomy 15	Psalm 102	10th	Isaiah 42	Revelation 12
Deuteronomy 16	Psalm 103	11th	Isaiah 43	Revelation 13
Deuteronomy 17	Psalm 104	12th	Isaiah 44	Revelation 14
Deuteronomy 18	Psalm 105	13th	Isaiah 45	Revelation 15
Deuteronomy 19	Psalm 106	14th	Isaiah 46	Revelation 16
Deuteronomy 20	Psalm 107	15th	Isaiah 47	Revelation 17
Deuteronomy 21	Psalms 108–109	16th	Isaiah 48	Revelation 18
Deuteronomy 22	Psalms 110–111	17th	Isaiah 49	Revelation 19
Deuteronomy 23	Psalms 112–113	18th	Isaiah 50	Revelation 20
Deuteronomy 24	Psalms 114–115	19th	Isaiah 51	Revelation 21
Deuteronomy 25	Psalm 116	20th	Isaiah 52	Revelation 22
Deuteronomy 26	Psalms 117–118	21st	Isaiah 53	Matthew 1
Deuteronomy 27–28:19	Psalm 119:1-24	22nd	Isaiah 54	Matthew 2
Deuteronomy 28:20ff	Psalm 119:25-48	23rd	Isaiah 55	Matthew 3
Deuteronomy 29	Psalm 119:49-72	24th	Isaiah 56	Matthew 4
Deuteronomy 30	Psalm 119:73-96	25th	Isaiah 57	Matthew 5
Deuteronomy 31	Psalm 119:97-120	26th	Isaiah 58	Matthew 6
Deuteronomy 32	Psalm 119:121-144	27th	Isaiah 59	Matthew 7
Deuteronomy 33–34	Psalm 119:145-176	28th	Isaiah 60	Matthew 8
Joshua 1	Psalms 120–122	29th	Isaiah 61	Matthew 9
Joshua 2	Psalms 123–125	30th	Isaiah 62	Matthew 10

JULY

They welcomed the message with eagerness and examined the Scriptures daily to see if these things were so (Ac 17:11).

Joshua 3	Psalms 126–128	1st	Isaiah 63	Matthew 11
Joshua 4	Psalms 129–131	2nd	Isaiah 64	Matthew 12
Joshua 5–6:5	Psalms 132–134	3rd	Isaiah 65	Matthew 13
Joshua 6:6ff	Psalms 135–136	4th	Isaiah 66	Matthew 14
Joshua 7	Psalms 137–138	5th	Jeremiah 1	Matthew 15
Joshua 8	Psalm 139	6th	Jeremiah 2	Matthew 16
Joshua 9	Psalms 140–141	7th	Jeremiah 3	Matthew 17
Joshua 10	Psalms 142–143	8th	Jeremiah 4	Matthew 18
Joshua 11	Psalm 144	9th	Jeremiah 5	Matthew 19
Joshua 12–13	Psalm 145	10th	Jeremiah 6	Matthew 20
Joshua 14–15	Psalms 146–147	11th	Jeremiah 7	Matthew 21
Joshua 16–17	Psalm 148	12th	Jeremiah 8	Matthew 22
Joshua 18–19	Psalms 149–150	13th	Jeremiah 9	Matthew 23
Joshua 20–21	Acts 1	14th	Jeremiah 10	Matthew 24

Joshua 22	Acts 2	15th	Jeremiah 11	Matthew 25
Joshua 23	Acts 3	16th	Jeremiah 12	Matthew 26
Joshua 24	Acts 4	17th	Jeremiah 13	Matthew 27
Judges 1	Acts 5	18th	Jeremiah 14	Matthew 28
Judges 2	Acts 6	19th	Jeremiah 15	Mark 1
Judges 3	Acts 7	20th	Jeremiah 16	Mark 2
Judges 4	Acts 8	21st	Jeremiah 17	Mark 3
Judges 5	Acts 9	22nd	Jeremiah 18	Mark 4
Judges 6	Acts 10	23rd	Jeremiah 19	Mark 5
Judges 7	Acts 11	24th	Jeremiah 20	Mark 6
Judges 8	Acts 12	25th	Jeremiah 21	Mark 7
Judges 9	Acts 13	26th	Jeremiah 22	Mark 8
Judges 10–11:11	Acts 14	27th	Jeremiah 23	Mark 9
Judges 11:12ff	Acts 15	28th	Jeremiah 24	Mark 10
Judges 12	Acts 16	29th	Jeremiah 25	Mark 11
Judges 13	Acts 17	30th	Jeremiah 26	Mark 12
Judges 14	Acts 18	31st	Jeremiah 27	Mark 13

AUGUST

"Speak, for Your servant is listening" (1Sm 3:10).

Judges 15	Acts 19	1st	Jeremiah 28	Mark 14
Judges 16	Acts 20	2nd	Jeremiah 29	Mark 15
Judges 17	Acts 21	3rd	Jeremiah 30–31	Mark 16
Judges 18	Acts 22	4th	Jeremiah 32	Psalms 1–2
Judges 19	Acts 23	5th	Jeremiah 33	Psalms 3–4
Judges 20	Acts 24	6th	Jeremiah 34	Psalms 5–6
Judges 21	Acts 25	7th	Jeremiah 35	Psalms 7–8
Ruth 1	Acts 26	8th	Jeremiah 36	Psalm 9
Ruth 2	Acts 27	9th	Jeremiah 37	Psalm 10
Ruth 3–4	Acts 28	10th	Jeremiah 38	Psalms 11–12
1 Samuel 1	Romans 1	11th	Jeremiah 39	Psalms 13–14
1 Samuel 2	Romans 2	12th	Jeremiah 40	Psalms 15–16
1 Samuel 3	Romans 3	13th	Jeremiah 41	Psalm 17
1 Samuel 4	Romans 4	14th	Jeremiah 42	Psalm 18
1 Samuel 5–6	Romans 5	15th	Jeremiah 43	Psalm 19
1 Samuel 7–8	Romans 6	16th	Jeremiah 44	Psalms 20–21
1 Samuel 9	Romans 7	17th	Jeremiah 46	Psalm 22
1 Samuel 10	Romans 8	18th	Jeremiah 47	Psalms 23–24
1 Samuel 11	Romans 9	19th	Jeremiah 48	Psalm 25
1 Samuel 12	Romans 10	20th	Jeremiah 49	Psalms 26–27
1 Samuel 13	Romans 11	21st	Jeremiah 50	Psalms 28–29
1 Samuel 14	Romans 12	22nd	Jeremiah 51	Psalm 30
1 Samuel 15	Romans 13	23rd	Jeremiah 52	Psalm 31
1 Samuel 16	Romans 14	24th	Lamentations 1	Psalm 32
1 Samuel 17	Romans 15	25th	Lamentations 2	Psalm 33
1 Samuel 18	Romans 16	26th	Lamentations 3	Psalm 34
1 Samuel 19	1 Corinthians 1	27th	Lamentations 4	Psalm 35
1 Samuel 20	1 Corinthians 2	28th	Lamentations 5	Psalm 36
1 Samuel 21–22	1 Corinthians 3	29th	Ezekiel 1	Psalm 37
1 Samuel 23	1 Corinthians 4	30th	Ezekiel 2	Psalm 38
1 Samuel 24	1 Corinthians 5	31st	Ezekiel 3	Psalm 39

SEPTEMBER

The instruction of the LORD is perfect, renewing one's life (Ps 19:7).

1 Samuel 25	1 Corinthians 6	1st	Ezekiel 4	Psalms 40–41
1 Samuel 26	1 Corinthians 7	2nd	Ezekiel 5	Psalms 42–43

1 Samuel 27	1 Corinthians 8	3rd	Ezekiel 6	Psalm 44
1 Samuel 28	1 Corinthians 9	4th	Ezekiel 7	Psalm 45
1 Samuel 29–30	1 Corinthians 10	5th	Ezekiel 8	Psalms 46–47
1 Samuel 31	1 Corinthians 11	6th	Ezekiel 9	Psalm 48
2 Samuel 1	1 Corinthians 12	7th	Ezekiel 10	Psalm 49
2 Samuel 2	1 Corinthians 13	8th	Ezekiel 11	Psalm 50
2 Samuel 3	1 Corinthians 14	9th	Ezekiel 12	Psalm 51
2 Samuel 4–5	1 Corinthians 15	10th	Ezekiel 13	Psalms 52–54
2 Samuel 6	1 Corinthians 16	11th	Ezekiel 14	Psalm 55
2 Samuel 7	2 Corinthians 1	12th	Ezekiel 15	Psalms 56–57
2 Samuel 8–9	2 Corinthians 2	13th	Ezekiel 16	Psalms 58–59
2 Samuel 10	2 Corinthians 3	14th	Ezekiel 17	Psalms 60–61
2 Samuel 11	2 Corinthians 4	15th	Ezekiel 18	Psalms 62–63
2 Samuel 12	2 Corinthians 5	16th	Ezekiel 19	Psalms 64–65
2 Samuel 13	2 Corinthians 6	17th	Ezekiel 20	Psalms 66–67
2 Samuel 14	2 Corinthians 7	18th	Ezekiel 21	Psalm 68
2 Samuel 15	2 Corinthians 8	19th	Ezekiel 22	Psalm 69
2 Samuel 16	2 Corinthians 9	20th	Ezekiel 23	Psalms 70–71
2 Samuel 17	2 Corinthians 10	21st	Ezekiel 24	Psalm 72
2 Samuel 18	2 Corinthians 11	22nd	Ezekiel 25	Psalm 73
2 Samuel 19	2 Corinthians 12	23rd	Ezekiel 26	Psalm 74
2 Samuel 20	2 Corinthians 13	24th	Ezekiel 27	Psalms 75–76
2 Samuel 21	Galatians 1	25th	Ezekiel 28	Psalm 77
2 Samuel 22	Galatians 2	26th	Ezekiel 29	Psalm 78:1-37
2 Samuel 23	Galatians 3	27th	Ezekiel 30	Psalm 78:38ff
2 Samuel 24	Galatians 4	28th	Ezekiel 31	Psalm 79
1 Kings 1	Galatians 5	29th	Ezekiel 32	Psalm 80
1 Kings 2	Galatians 6	30th	Ezekiel 33	Psalms 81–82

OCTOBER

How I love Your instruction! It is my meditation all day long (Ps 119:97).

1 Kings 3	Ephesians 1	1st	Ezekiel 34	Psalms 83–84
1 Kings 4–5	Ephesians 2	2nd	Ezekiel 35	Psalm 85
1 Kings 6	Ephesians 3	3rd	Ezekiel 36	Psalm 86
1 Kings 7	Ephesians 4	4th	Ezekiel 37	Psalms 87–88
1 Kings 8	Ephesians 5	5th	Ezekiel 38	Psalm 89
1 Kings 9	Ephesians 6	6th	Ezekiel 39	Psalm 90
1 Kings 10	Philippians 1	7th	Ezekiel 40	Psalm 91
1 Kings 11	Philippians 2	8th	Ezekiel 41	Psalms 92–93
1 Kings 12	Philippians 3	9th	Ezekiel 42	Psalm 94
1 Kings 13	Philippians 4	10th	Ezekiel 43	Psalms 95–96
1 Kings 14	Colossians 1	11th	Ezekiel 44	Psalms 97–98
1 Kings 15	Colossians 2	12th	Ezekiel 45	Psalms 99–101
1 Kings 16	Colossians 3	13th	Ezekiel 46	Psalm 102
1 Kings 17	Colossians 4	14th	Ezekiel 47	Psalm 103
1 Kings 18	1 Thessalonians 1	15th	Ezekiel 48	Psalm 104
1 Kings 19	1 Thessalonians 2	16th	Daniel 1	Psalm 105
1 Kings 20	1 Thessalonians 3	17th	Daniel 2	Psalm 106
1 Kings 21	1 Thessalonians 4	18th	Daniel 3	Psalm 107
1 Kings 22	1 Thessalonians 5	19th	Daniel 4	Psalms 108–109
2 Kings 1	2 Thessalonians 1	20th	Daniel 5	Psalms 110–111
2 Kings 2	2 Thessalonians 2	21st	Daniel 6	Psalms 112–113
2 Kings 3	2 Thessalonians 3	22nd	Daniel 7	Psalms 114–115
2 Kings 4	1 Timothy 1	23rd	Daniel 8	Psalm 116
2 Kings 5	1 Timothy 2	24th	Daniel 9	Psalms 117–118
2 Kings 6	1 Timothy 3	25th	Daniel 10	Psalm 119:1-24

2 Kings 7	1 Timothy 4	26th	Daniel 11	Psalm 119:25-48
2 Kings 8	1 Timothy 5	27th	Daniel 12	Psalm 119:49-72
2 Kings 9	1 Timothy 6	28th	Hosea 1	Psalm 119:73-96
2 Kings 10	2 Timothy 1	29th	Hosea 2	Psalm 119:97-120
2 Kings 11–12	2 Timothy 2	30th	Hosea 3–4	Psalm 119:121-144
2 Kings 13	2 Timothy 3	31st	Hosea 5–6	Psalm 119:145-176

NOVEMBER

Like newborn infants, desire the pure spiritual milk, so that you may grow by it for your salvation (1Pt 2:2).

2 Kings 14	2 Timothy 4	1st	Hosea 7	Psalms 120–122
2 Kings 15	Titus 1	2nd	Hosea 8	Psalms 123–125
2 Kings 16	Titus 2	3rd	Hosea 9	Psalms 126–128
2 Kings 17	Titus 3	4th	Hosea 10	Psalms 129–131
2 Kings 18	Philemon	5th	Hosea 11	Psalms 132–134
2 Kings 19	Hebrews 1	6th	Hosea 12	Psalms 135–136
2 Kings 20	Hebrews 2	7th	Hosea 13	Psalms 137–138
2 Kings 21	Hebrews 3	8th	Hosea 14	Psalm 139
2 Kings 22	Hebrews 4	9th	Joel 1	Psalms 140–141
2 Kings 23	Hebrews 5	10th	Joel 2	Psalm 142
2 Kings 24	Hebrews 6	11th	Joel 3	Psalm 143
2 Kings 25	Hebrews 7	12th	Amos 1	Psalm 144
1 Chronicles 1–2	Hebrews 8	13th	Amos 2	Psalm 145
1 Chronicles 3–4	Hebrews 9	14th	Amos 3	Psalms 146–147
1 Chronicles 5–6	Hebrews 10	15th	Amos 4	Psalms 148–150
1 Chronicles 7–8	Hebrews 11	16th	Amos 5	Luke 1:1-38
1 Chronicles 9–10	Hebrews 12	17th	Amos 6	Luke 1:39ff
1 Chronicles 11–12	Hebrews 13	18th	Amos 7	Luke 2
1 Chronicles 13–14	James 1	19th	Amos 8	Luke 3
1 Chronicles 15	James 2	20th	Amos 9	Luke 4
1 Chronicles 16	James 3	21st	Obadiah	Luke 5
1 Chronicles 17	James 4	22nd	Jonah 1	Luke 6
1 Chronicles 18	James 5	23rd	Jonah 2	Luke 7
1 Chronicles 19–20	1 Peter 1	24th	Jonah 3	Luke 8
1 Chronicles 21	1 Peter 2	25th	Jonah 4	Luke 9
1 Chronicles 22	1 Peter 3	26th	Micah 1	Luke 10
1 Chronicles 23	1 Peter 4	27th	Micah 2	Luke 11
1 Chronicles 24–25	1 Peter 5	28th	Micah 3	Luke 12
1 Chronicles 26–27	2 Peter 1	29th	Micah 4	Luke 13
1 Chronicles 28	2 Peter 2	30th	Micah 5	Luke 14

DECEMBER

The instruction of his God is in his heart; his steps do not falter (Ps 37:31).

1 Chronicles 29	2 Peter 3	1st	Micah 6	Luke 15
2 Chronicles 1	1 John 1	2nd	Micah 7	Luke 16
2 Chronicles 2	1 John 2	3rd	Nahum 1	Luke 17
2 Chronicles 3–4	1 John 3	4th	Nahum 2	Luke 18
2 Chronicles 5–6:11	1 John 4	5th	Nahum 3	Luke 19
2 Chronicles 6:12ff	1 John 5	6th	Habakkuk 1	Luke 20
2 Chronicles 7	2 John	7th	Habakkuk 2	Luke 21
2 Chronicles 8	3 John	8th	Habakkuk 3	Luke 22
2 Chronicles 9	Jude	9th	Zephaniah 1	Luke 23
2 Chronicles 10	Revelation 1	10th	Zephaniah 2	Luke 24
2 Chronicles 11–12	Revelation 2	11th	Zephaniah 3	John 1
2 Chronicles 13	Revelation 3	12th	Haggai 1	John 2
2 Chronicles 14–15	Revelation 4	13th	Haggai 2	John 3
2 Chronicles 16	Revelation 5	14th	Zechariah 1	John 4

2 Chronicles 17	Revelation 6	15th	Zechariah 2	John 5
2 Chronicles 18	Revelation 7	16th	Zechariah 3	John 6
2 Chronicles 19–20	Revelation 8	17th	Zechariah 4	John 7
2 Chronicles 21	Revelation 9	18th	Zechariah 5	John 8
2 Chronicles 22–23	Revelation 10	19th	Zechariah 6	John 9
2 Chronicles 24	Revelation 11	20th	Zechariah 7	John 10
2 Chronicles 25	Revelation 12	21st	Zechariah 8	John 11
2 Chronicles 26	Revelation 13	22nd	Zechariah 9	John 12
2 Chronicles 27–28	Revelation 14	23rd	Zechariah 10	John 13
2 Chronicles 29	Revelation 15	24th	Zechariah 11	John 14
2 Chronicles 30	Revelation 16	25th	Zechariah 12–13:1	John 15
2 Chronicles 31	Revelation 17	26th	Zechariah 13:2ff	John 16
2 Chronicles 32	Revelation 18	27th	Zechariah 14	John 17
2 Chronicles 33	Revelation 19	28th	Malachi 1	John 18
2 Chronicles 34	Revelation 20	29th	Malachi 2	John 19
2 Chronicles 35	Revelation 21	30th	Malachi 3	John 20
2 Chronicles 36	Revelation 22	31st	Malachi 4	John 21

Notes

Notes

Notes

Notes

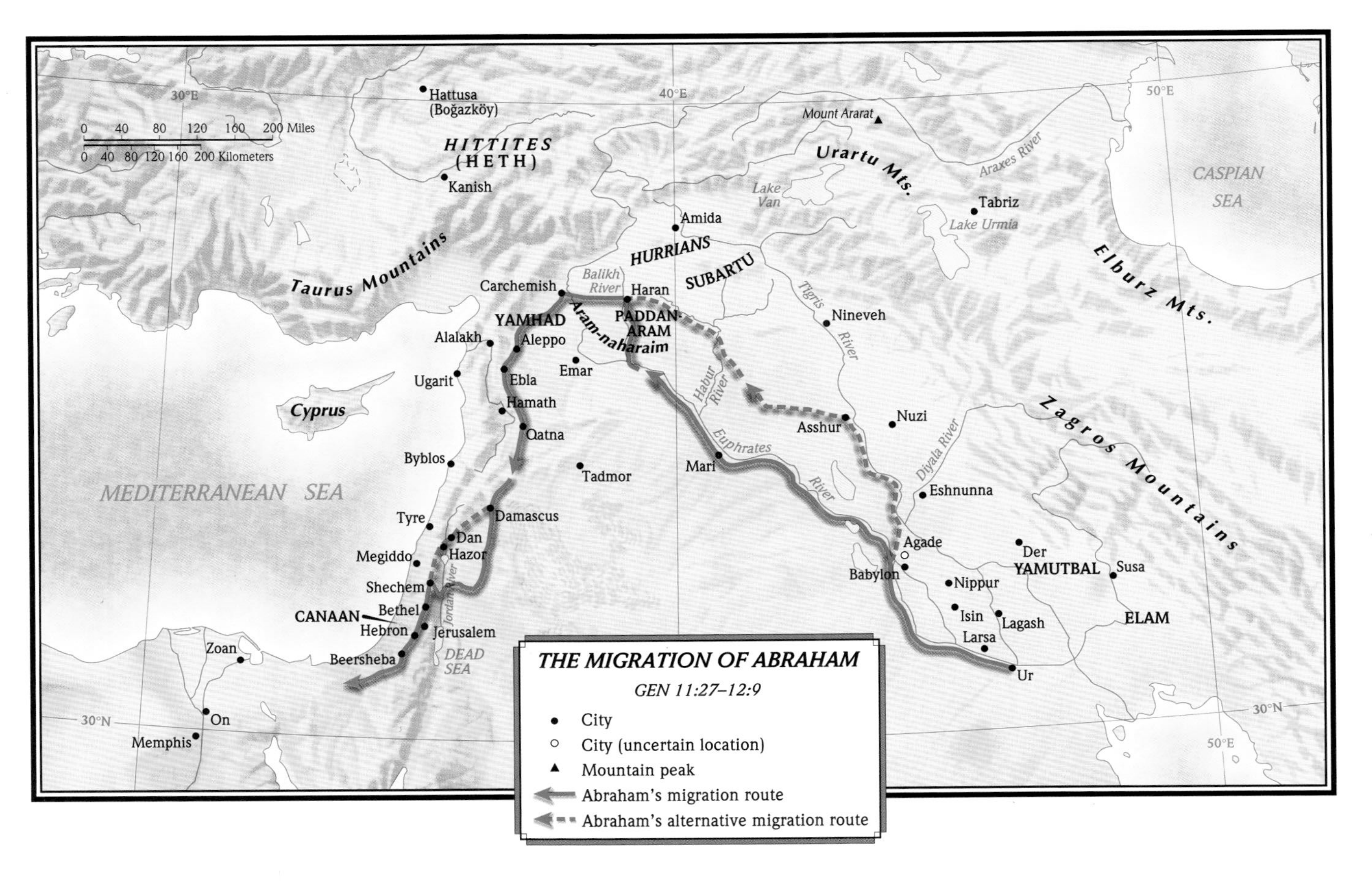
THE MIGRATION OF ABRAHAM
GEN 11:27–12:9
City
City (uncertain location)
Mountain peak
Abraham's migration route
Abraham's alternative migration route
0 40 80 120 160 200 Miles
0 40 80 120 160 200 Kilometers
30°E
40°E
50°E
30°N
Hattusa (Boğazköy)
HITTITES (HETH)
Kanish
Taurus Mountains
Mount Ararat
Urartu Mts.
Araxes River
Lake Van
Tabriz
Lake Urmia
CASPIAN SEA
Elburz Mts.
Amida
HURRIANS
SUBARTU
Balikh River
Carchemish
Haran
PADDAN-ARAM
Aram-naharaim
YAMHAD
Aleppo
Alalakh
Emar
Ugarit
Ebla
Hamath
Cyprus
Qatna
Byblos
Tadmor
Tigris River
Nineveh
Habur River
Asshur
Nuzi
Euphrates River
Mari
Diyala River
Zagros Mountains
Eshnunna
MEDITERRANEAN SEA
Tyre
Damascus
Dan
Hazor
Megiddo
Shechem
Jordan River
Bethel
CANAAN
Hebron
Jerusalem
Beersheba
DEAD SEA
Zoan
On
Memphis
Agade
Babylon
Der
YAMUTBAL
Susa
Nippur
Isin
Lagash
ELAM
Larsa
Ur

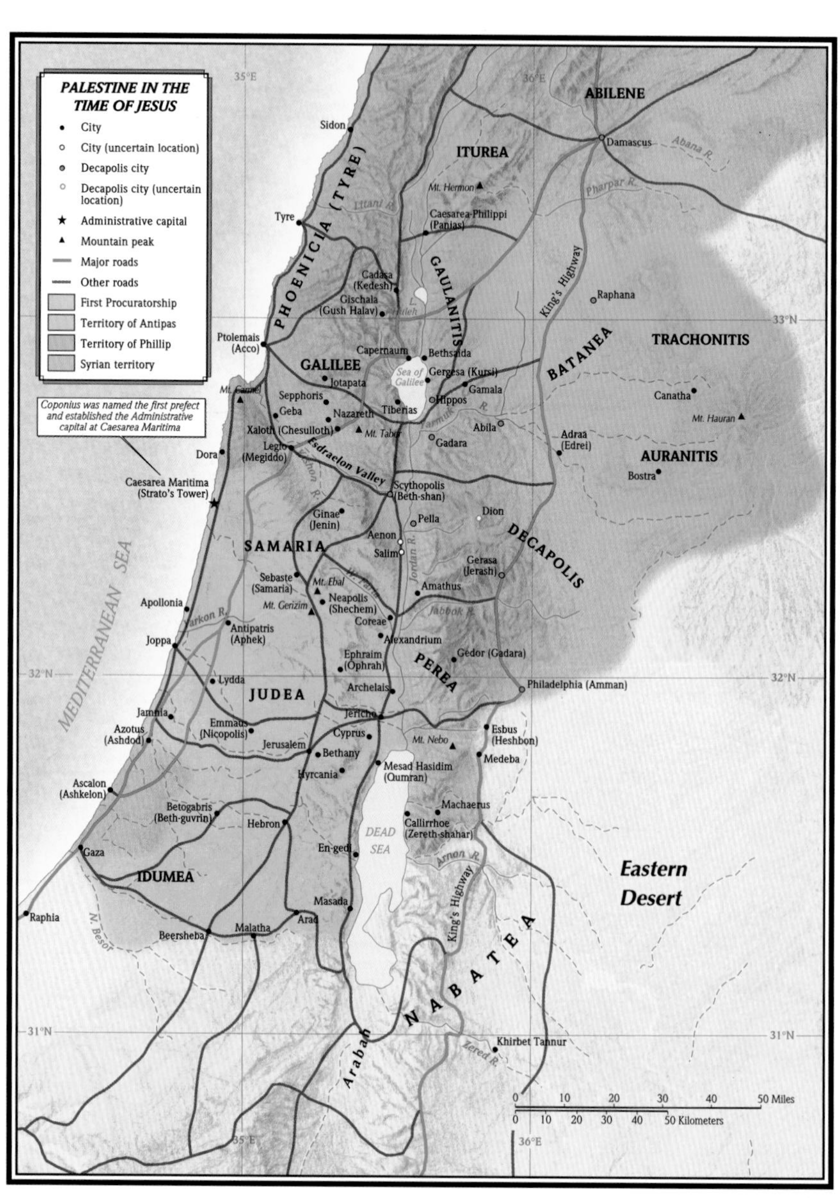

PALESTINE IN THE TIME OF JESUS
City
City (uncertain location)
Decapolis city
Decapolis city (uncertain location)
Administrative capital
Mountain peak
Major roads
Other roads
First Procuratorship
Territory of Antipas
Territory of Phillip
Syrian territory
Coponius was named the first prefect and established the Administrative capital at Caesarea Maritima
35°E
36°E
33°N
32°N
31°N
ABILENE
Damascus
Abana R.
Pharpar R.
ITUREA
Mt. Hermon
Sidon
PHOENICIA (TYRE)
Litani R.
Tyre
Caesarea-Philippi (Panias)
GAULANITIS
King's Highway
Cadasa (Kedesh)
Gischala (Gush Halav)
Raphana
Ptolemais (Acco)
Capernaum
Bethsaida
BATANEA
TRACHONITIS
GALILEE
Sea of Galilee
Gergesa (Kursi)
Gamala
Mt. Carmel
Jotapata
Sepphoris
Hippos
Canatha
Geba
Nazareth
Tiberias
Yarmuk R.
Mt. Hauran
Xaloth (Chesulloth)
Mt. Tabor
Abila
Adraa (Edrei)
Gadara
Dora
Legio (Megiddo)
Esdraelon Valley
AURANITIS
Bostra
Caesarea Maritima (Strato's Tower)
Scythopolis (Beth-shan)
Ginae (Jenin)
Pella
Dion
DECAPOLIS
MEDITERRANEAN SEA
SAMARIA
Aenon
Salim
Jordan R.
Gerasa (Jerash)
Sebaste (Samaria)
Mt. Ebal
Amathus
Mt. Gerizim
Neapolis (Shechem)
Apollonia
Yarkon R.
Coreae
Jabbok R.
Antipatris (Aphek)
Alexandrium
Joppa
Gedor (Gadara)
Ephraim (Ophrah)
PEREA
Lydda
Archelais
Philadelphia (Amman)
JUDEA
Jamnia
Jericho
Emmaus (Nicopolis)
Cyprus
Esbus (Heshbon)
Azotus (Ashdod)
Jerusalem
Mt. Nebo
Bethany
Medeba
Hyrcania
Mesad Hasidim (Qumran)
Ascalon (Ashkelon)
Betogabris (Beth-guvrin)
Machaerus
Hebron
DEAD SEA
Callirrhoe (Zereth-shahar)
Gaza
En-gedi
Arnon R.
Eastern Desert
IDUMEA
Masada
Raphia
N. Besor
Arad
Beersheba
Malatha
NABATEA
Arabah
Khirbet Tannur
Zered R.
0 10 20 30 40 50 Miles
0 10 20 30 40 50 Kilometers

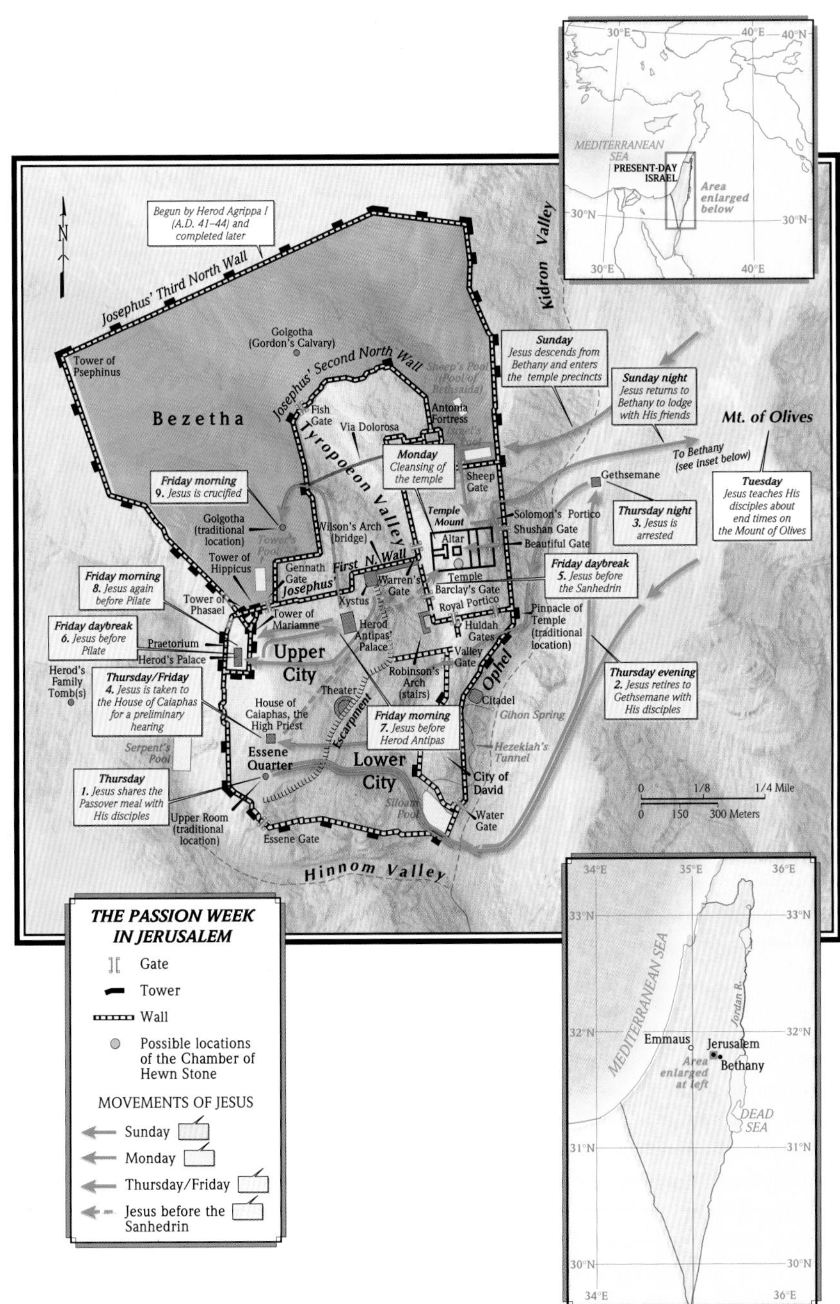

THE PASSION WEEK IN JERUSALEM
Gate
Tower
Wall
Possible locations of the Chamber of Hewn Stone
MOVEMENTS OF JESUS
Sunday
Monday
Thursday/Friday
Jesus before the Sanhedrin
N
Begun by Herod Agrippa I (A.D. 41–44) and completed later
Josephus' Third North Wall
Josephus' Second North Wall
Josephus' First N. Wall
Kidron Valley
Golgotha (Gordon's Calvary)
Tower of Psephinus
Bezetha
Sheep's Pool (Pool of Bethsaida)
Antonia Fortress
Israel's Pool
Fish Gate
Via Dolorosa
Tyropoeon Valley
Sunday Jesus descends from Bethany and enters the temple precincts
Sunday night Jesus returns to Bethany to lodge with His friends
Mt. of Olives
To Bethany (see inset below)
Monday Cleansing of the temple
Sheep Gate
Gethsemane
Friday morning 9. Jesus is crucified
Golgotha (traditional location)
Tower's Pool
Wilson's Arch (bridge)
Temple Mount
Altar
Solomon's Portico
Shushan Gate
Beautiful Gate
Thursday night 3. Jesus is arrested
Tuesday Jesus teaches His disciples about end times on the Mount of Olives
Tower of Hippicus
Gennath Gate
Warren's Gate
Temple
Barclay's Gate
Royal Portico
Friday daybreak 5. Jesus before the Sanhedrin
Friday morning 8. Jesus again before Pilate
Tower of Phasael
Tower of Mariamne
Xystus
Pinnacle of Temple (traditional location)
Friday daybreak 6. Jesus before Pilate
Praetorium
Herod's Palace
Upper City
Herod Antipas' Palace
Huldah Gates
Valley Gate
Ophel
Herod's Family Tomb(s)
Thursday/Friday 4. Jesus is taken to the House of Caiaphas for a preliminary hearing
Robinson's Arch (stairs)
Theater
Citadel
Gihon Spring
Thursday evening 2. Jesus retires to Gethsemane with His disciples
House of Caiaphas, the High Priest
Escarpment
Friday morning 7. Jesus before Herod Antipas
Serpent's Pool
Hezekiah's Tunnel
Essene Quarter
Lower City
Thursday 1. Jesus shares the Passover meal with His disciples
City of David
Siloam Pool
Upper Room (traditional location)
Essene Gate
Water Gate
Hinnom Valley
0 1/8 1/4 Mile
0 150 300 Meters
30°E
40°E
40°N
30°N
MEDITERRANEAN SEA
PRESENT-DAY ISRAEL
Area enlarged below
34°E
35°E
36°E
33°N
32°N
31°N
MEDITERRANEAN SEA
Jordan R.
Emmaus
Jerusalem
Bethany
Area enlarged at left
DEAD SEA

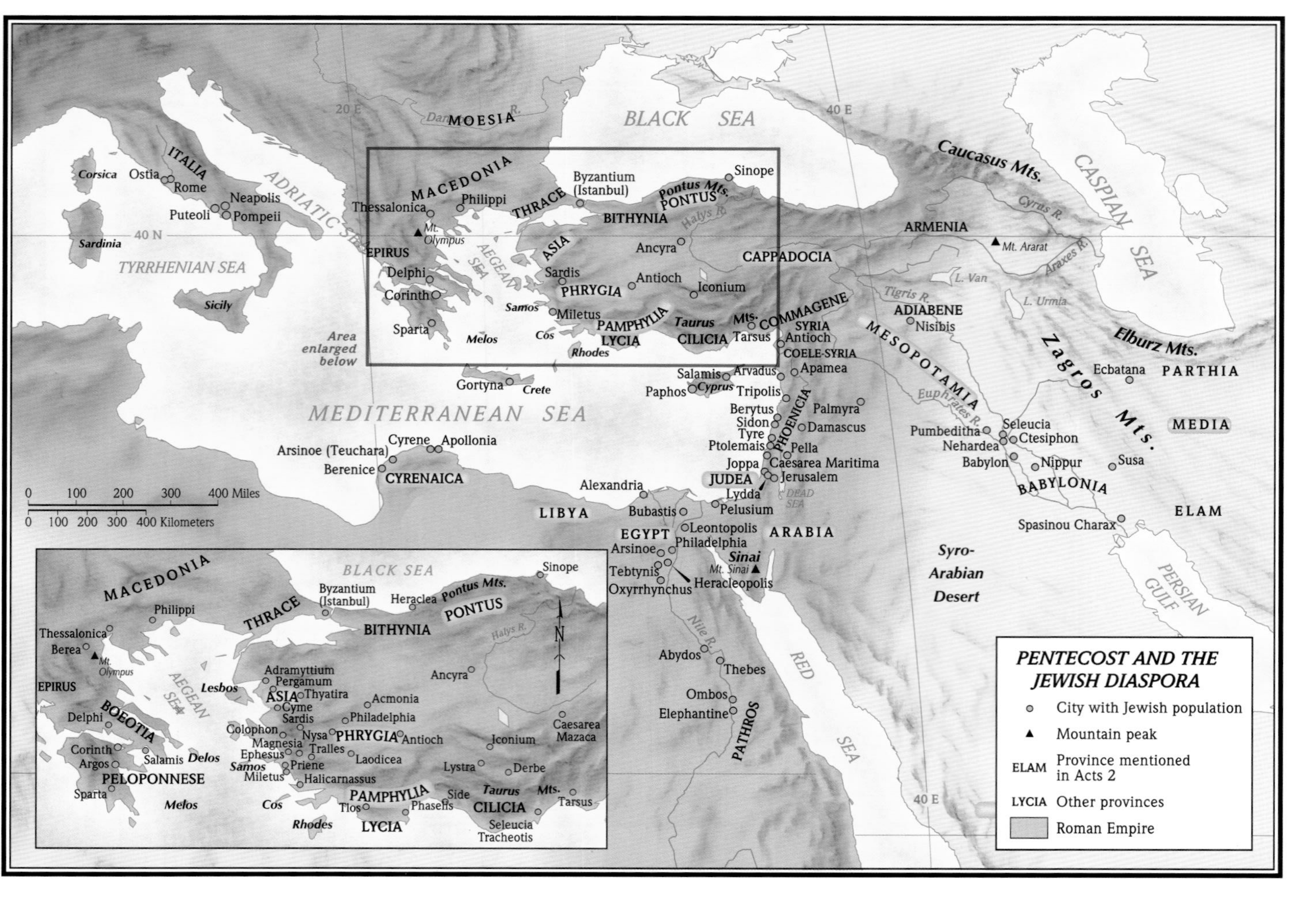

PENTECOST AND THE JEWISH DIASPORA
City with Jewish population
Mountain peak
ELAM Province mentioned in Acts 2
LYCIA Other provinces
Roman Empire
BLACK SEA
CASPIAN SEA
MEDITERRANEAN SEA
ADRIATIC SEA
TYRRHENIAN SEA
AEGEAN SEA
RED SEA
PERSIAN GULF
DEAD SEA
Caucasus Mts.
Elburz Mts.
Zagros Mts.
Pontus Mts.
Taurus Mts.
Mt. Ararat
Mt. Olympus
Mt. Sinai
Danube R.
Halys R.
Cyrus R.
Araxes R.
Tigris R.
Euphrates R.
Nile R.
L. Van
L. Urmia
MOESIA
ITALIA
MACEDONIA
THRACE
EPIRUS
ASIA
BITHYNIA
PONTUS
CAPPADOCIA
PHRYGIA
PAMPHYLIA
LYCIA
CILICIA
COMMAGENE
SYRIA
COELE-SYRIA
PHOENICIA
JUDEA
ARMENIA
ADIABENE
MESOPOTAMIA
BABYLONIA
PARTHIA
MEDIA
ELAM
ARABIA
EGYPT
LIBYA
CYRENAICA
PATHROS
Sinai
Syro-Arabian Desert
Corsica
Sardinia
Sicily
Crete
Cyprus
Rhodes
Samos
Cos
Melos
Ostia
Rome
Neapolis
Puteoli
Pompeii
Thessalonica
Philippi
Delphi
Corinth
Sparta
Byzantium (Istanbul)
Sinope
Ancyra
Sardis
Antioch
Iconium
Miletus
Tarsus
Gortyna
Salamis
Paphos
Arvadus
Tripolis
Apamea
Palmyra
Berytus
Sidon
Tyre
Ptolemais
Damascus
Pella
Joppa
Caesarea Maritima
Jerusalem
Lydda
Pelusium
Alexandria
Bubastis
Leontopolis
Philadelphia
Arsinoe
Tebtynis
Oxyrrhynchus
Heracleopolis
Abydos
Thebes
Ombos
Elephantine
Cyrene
Apollonia
Arsinoe (Teuchara)
Berenice
Nisibis
Pumbeditha
Nehardea
Babylon
Seleucia
Ctesiphon
Nippur
Susa
Ecbatana
Spasinou Charax
Area enlarged below
20 E
40 E
40 N
0 100 200 300 400 Miles
0 100 200 300 400 Kilometers
BLACK SEA
AEGEAN SEA
MACEDONIA
THRACE
BITHYNIA
PONTUS
Pontus Mts.
EPIRUS
BOEOTIA
PELOPONNESE
ASIA
PHRYGIA
PAMPHYLIA
LYCIA
CILICIA
Taurus Mts.
Halys R.
N
Thessalonica
Berea
Mt. Olympus
Philippi
Byzantium (Istanbul)
Heraclea
Sinope
Ancyra
Delphi
Corinth
Argos
Salamis
Sparta
Lesbos
Delos
Samos
Melos
Cos
Rhodes
Adramyttium
Pergamum
Thyatira
Cyme
Sardis
Acmonia
Philadelphia
Colophon
Magnesia
Ephesus
Miletus
Nysa
Tralles
Priene
Halicarnassus
Laodicea
Antioch
Iconium
Caesarea Mazaca
Lystra
Derbe
Tlos
Phaselis
Side
Seleucia Tracheotis
Tarsus

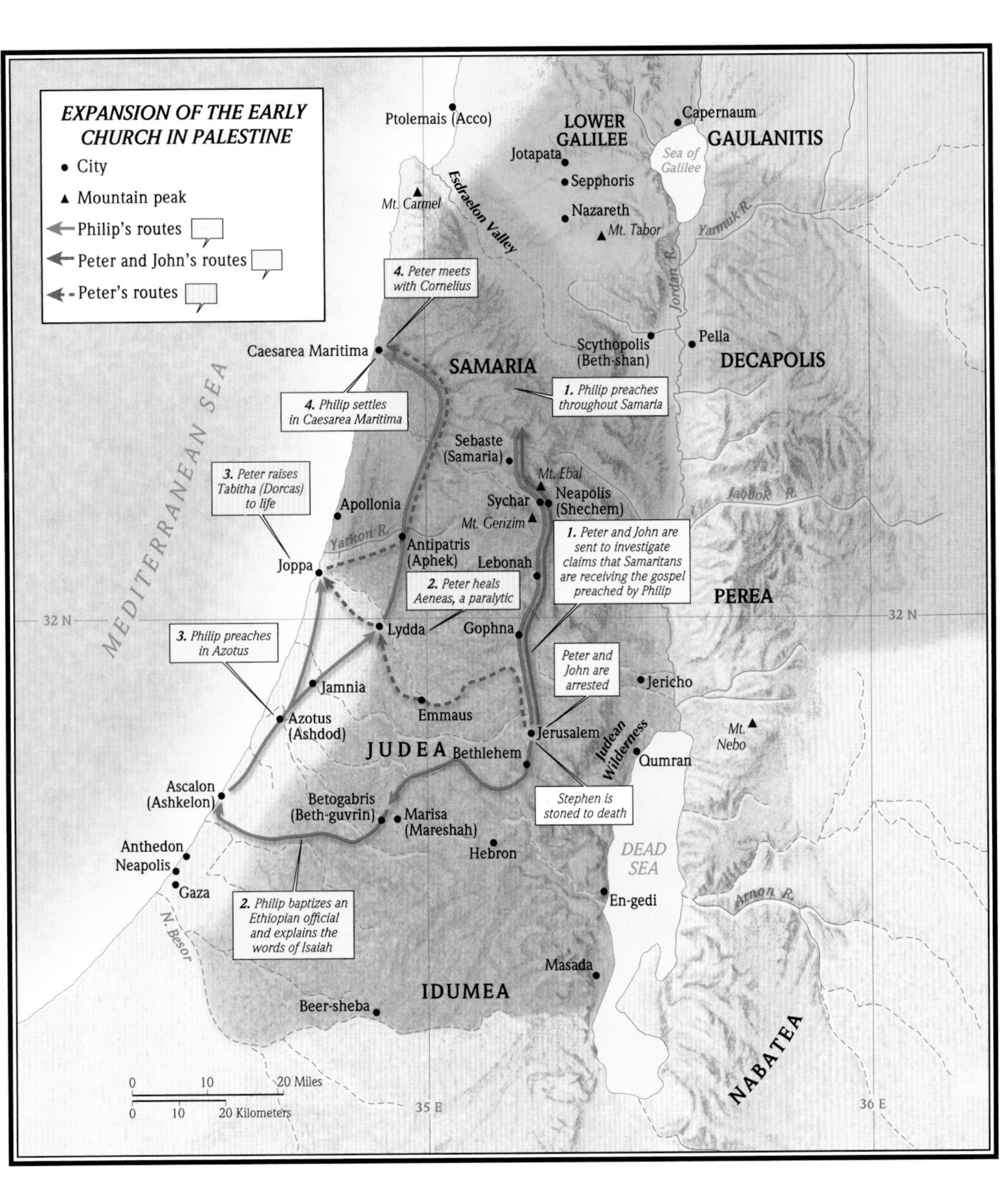
EXPANSION OF THE EARLY CHURCH IN PALESTINE
City
Mountain peak
Philip's routes
Peter and John's routes
Peter's routes
Ptolemais (Acco)
LOWER GALILEE
Capernaum
GAULANITIS
Jotapata
Sea of Galilee
Sepphoris
Mt. Carmel
Esdraelon Valley
Nazareth
Mt. Tabor
Yarmuk R.
Jordan R.
4. Peter meets with Cornelius
Scythopolis (Beth-shan)
Pella
DECAPOLIS
Caesarea Maritima
SAMARIA
MEDITERRANEAN SEA
1. Philip preaches throughout Samaria
4. Philip settles in Caesarea Maritima
Sebaste (Samaria)
3. Peter raises Tabitha (Dorcas) to life
Mt. Ebal
Sychar
Neapolis (Shechem)
Jabbok R.
Apollonia
Mt. Gerizim
Yarkon R.
Antipatris (Aphek)
1. Peter and John are sent to investigate claims that Samaritans are receiving the gospel preached by Philip
Joppa
Lebonah
2. Peter heals Aeneas, a paralytic
PEREA
32 N
Lydda
Gophna
3. Philip preaches in Azotus
Peter and John are arrested
Jamnia
Jericho
Emmaus
Azotus (Ashdod)
Jerusalem
Mt. Nebo
JUDEA
Bethlehem
Judean Wilderness
Qumran
Ascalon (Ashkelon)
Betogabris (Beth-guvrin)
Marisa (Mareshah)
Stephen is stoned to death
Anthedon
Neapolis
Hebron
DEAD SEA
Gaza
En-gedi
Arnon R.
N. Besor
2. Philip baptizes an Ethiopian official and explains the words of Isaiah
Masada
IDUMEA
Beer-sheba
NABATEA
0 10 20 Miles
0 10 20 Kilometers
35 E
36 E

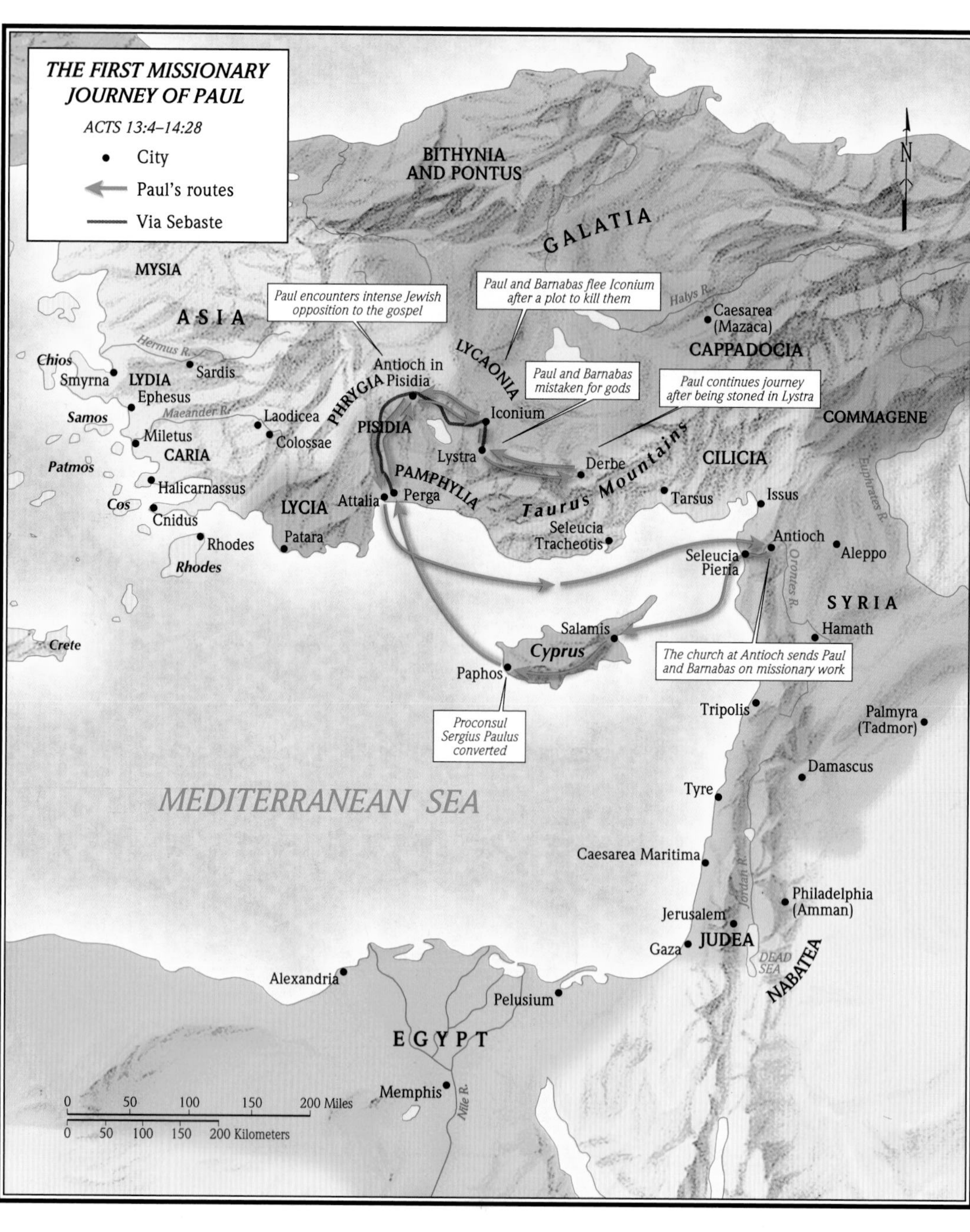
THE FIRST MISSIONARY JOURNEY OF PAUL
ACTS 13:4–14:28
City
Paul's routes
Via Sebaste
N
BITHYNIA AND PONTUS
GALATIA
MYSIA
ASIA
Paul encounters intense Jewish opposition to the gospel
Paul and Barnabas flee Iconium after a plot to kill them
Halys R.
Caesarea (Mazaca)
CAPPADOCIA
LYCAONIA
Hermus R.
Chios
Smyrna
LYDIA
Sardis
Antioch in Pisidia
PHRYGIA
Paul and Barnabas mistaken for gods
Paul continues journey after being stoned in Lystra
Ephesus
Samos
Maeander R.
Laodicea
Iconium
COMMAGENE
Miletus
Colossae
PISIDIA
CARIA
Lystra
Derbe
CILICIA
Patmos
Halicarnassus
PAMPHYLIA
Taurus Mountains
Euphrates R.
Cos
Cnidus
LYCIA
Attalia
Perga
Tarsus
Issus
Rhodes
Patara
Seleucia Tracheotis
Antioch
Aleppo
Rhodes
Seleucia Pieria
Orontes R.
SYRIA
Salamis
Hamath
Crete
Cyprus
The church at Antioch sends Paul and Barnabas on missionary work
Paphos
Tripolis
Proconsul Sergius Paulus converted
Palmyra (Tadmor)
Damascus
MEDITERRANEAN SEA
Tyre
Caesarea Maritima
Jordan R.
Philadelphia (Amman)
Jerusalem
Gaza
JUDEA
DEAD SEA
NABATEA
Alexandria
Pelusium
EGYPT
Memphis
Nile R.
0 50 100 150 200 Miles
0 50 100 150 200 Kilometers

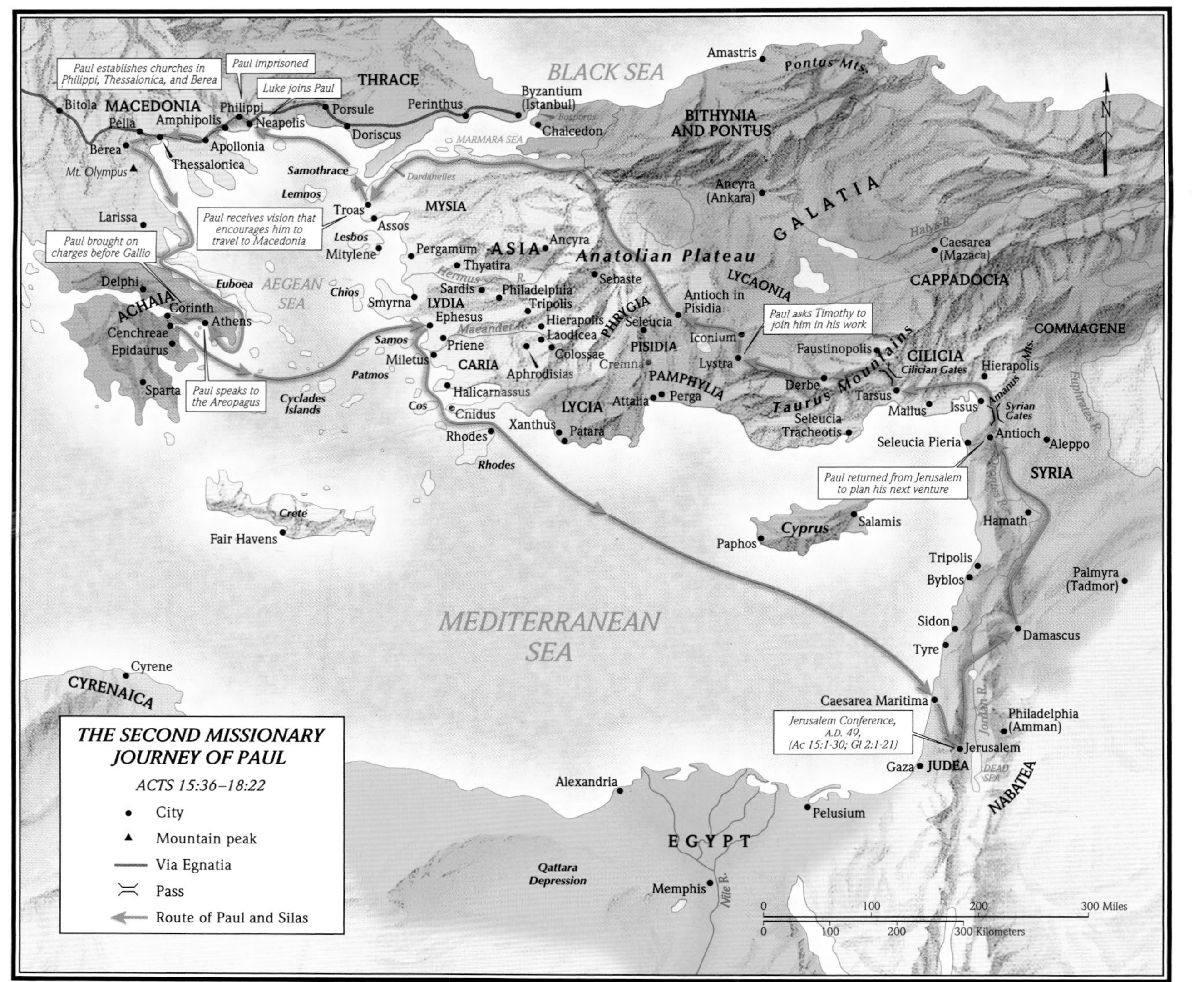
THE SECOND MISSIONARY JOURNEY OF PAUL
ACTS 15:36–18:22
City
Mountain peak
Via Egnatia
Pass
Route of Paul and Silas
Paul establishes churches in Philippi, Thessalonica, and Berea
Paul imprisoned
Luke joins Paul
Paul receives vision that encourages him to travel to Macedonia
Paul brought on charges before Gallio
Paul speaks to the Areopagus
Paul asks Timothy to join him in his work
Paul returned from Jerusalem to plan his next venture
Jerusalem Conference, A.D. 49, (Ac 15:1-30; Gl 2:1-21)
BLACK SEA
AEGEAN SEA
MEDITERRANEAN SEA
MARMARA SEA
THRACE
MACEDONIA
ACHAIA
MYSIA
ASIA
LYDIA
CARIA
LYCIA
PHRYGIA
PISIDIA
PAMPHYLIA
LYCAONIA
GALATIA
BITHYNIA AND PONTUS
CAPPADOCIA
CILICIA
COMMAGENE
SYRIA
JUDEA
NABATEA
EGYPT
CYRENAICA
Anatolian Plateau
Taurus Mountains
Pontus Mts.
Amanus Mts.
Cilician Gates
Syrian Gates
Bitola
Pella
Amphipolis
Philippi
Neapolis
Porsule
Doriscus
Perinthus
Byzantium (Istanbul)
Bosporus
Chalcedon
Amastris
Berea
Thessalonica
Apollonia
Mt. Olympus
Samothrace
Lemnos
Dardanelles
Troas
Assos
Lesbos
Mitylene
Larissa
Delphi
Euboea
Corinth
Cenchreae
Athens
Epidaurus
Sparta
Chios
Smyrna
Samos
Patmos
Cyclades Islands
Cos
Pergamum
Thyatira
Hermus R.
Sardis
Philadelphia
Ancyra
Tripolis
Ephesus
Maeander R.
Priene
Miletus
Halicarnassus
Cnidus
Rhodes
Hierapolis
Laodicea
Colossae
Aphrodisias
Xanthus
Patara
Sebaste
Antioch in Pisidia
Seleucia
Cremna
Attalia
Perga
Iconium
Lystra
Derbe
Faustinopolis
Tarsus
Mallus
Issus
Seleucia Tracheotis
Ancyra (Ankara)
Halys R.
Caesarea (Mazaca)
Hierapolis
Euphrates R.
Antioch
Aleppo
Seleucia Pieria
Orontes R.
Crete
Fair Havens
Cyprus
Salamis
Paphos
Hamath
Tripolis
Byblos
Sidon
Tyre
Damascus
Palmyra (Tadmor)
Caesarea Maritima
Jordan R.
Philadelphia (Amman)
Jerusalem
Gaza
DEAD SEA
Cyrene
Alexandria
Pelusium
Qattara Depression
Memphis
Nile R.
0 100 200 300 Miles
0 100 200 300 Kilometers
N

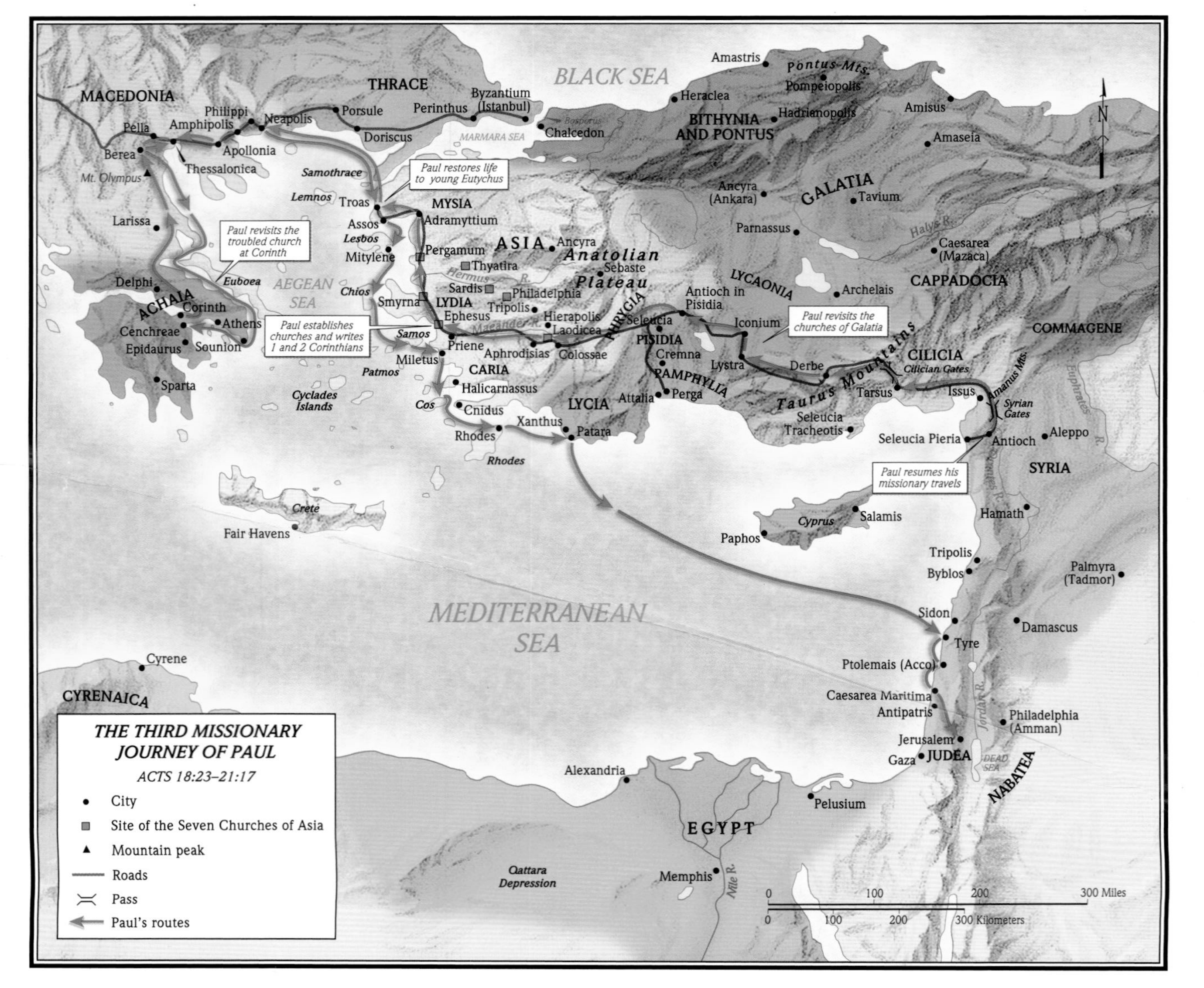
THE THIRD MISSIONARY JOURNEY OF PAUL
ACTS 18:23–21:17
City
Site of the Seven Churches of Asia
Mountain peak
Roads
Pass
Paul's routes
Paul restores life to young Eutychus
Paul revisits the troubled church at Corinth
Paul establishes churches and writes 1 and 2 Corinthians
Paul revisits the churches of Galatia
Paul resumes his missionary travels
MACEDONIA
THRACE
BLACK SEA
MARMARA SEA
Bosporus
BITHYNIA AND PONTUS
Pontus Mts.
GALATIA
CAPPADOCIA
COMMAGENE
MYSIA
ASIA
Anatolian Plateau
LYDIA
CARIA
LYCIA
PHRYGIA
PISIDIA
PAMPHYLIA
LYCAONIA
CILICIA
Taurus Mountains
Cilician Gates
Amanus Mts.
Syrian Gates
SYRIA
JUDEA
NABATEA
EGYPT
CYRENAICA
ACHAIA
AEGEAN SEA
MEDITERRANEAN SEA
Qattara Depression
Pella
Berea
Mt. Olympus
Amphipolis
Philippi
Neapolis
Apollonia
Thessalonica
Porsule
Doriscus
Perinthus
Byzantium (Istanbul)
Chalcedon
Heraclea
Amastris
Pompeiopolis
Hadrianopolis
Amisus
Amaseia
Ancyra (Ankara)
Tavium
Parnassus
Halys R.
Caesarea (Mazaca)
Archelais
Samothrace
Lemnos
Troas
Assos
Lesbos
Mitylene
Adramyttium
Pergamum
Thyatira
Ancyra
Sebaste
Hermus R.
Sardis
Philadelphia
Tripolis
Hierapolis
Laodicea
Colossae
Maeander R.
Aphrodisias
Chios
Smyrna
Ephesus
Samos
Priene
Miletus
Patmos
Halicarnassus
Cos
Cnidus
Rhodes
Xanthus
Patara
Attalia
Perga
Cremna
Seleucia
Antioch in Pisidia
Iconium
Lystra
Derbe
Tarsus
Issus
Seleucia Tracheotis
Seleucia Pieria
Antioch
Aleppo
Euphrates R.
Orontes R.
Larissa
Delphi
Euboea
Corinth
Athens
Cenchreae
Epidaurus
Sounion
Sparta
Cyclades Islands
Crete
Fair Havens
Cyprus
Salamis
Paphos
Hamath
Tripolis
Byblos
Palmyra (Tadmor)
Sidon
Tyre
Damascus
Ptolemais (Acco)
Caesarea Maritima
Antipatris
Jordan R.
Philadelphia (Amman)
Jerusalem
Gaza
DEAD SEA
Cyrene
Alexandria
Pelusium
Memphis
Nile R.
0 100 200 300 Miles
0 100 200 300 Kilometers
N

Finally, they are to repent, that is turn from sin and toward Christ. They were to ask God for a renewed love for Him and confess that their idols were an offense to the God they claimed to love. This would be painful but necessary, and in the long run their church would be revived.

Jesus taught that the church was to be in the world but not of the world. In other words, the church is to be in the world like a ship is in the ocean. But when the ocean gets into the ship, we know that there is trouble ahead. Today we must admit with sorrow that the church is taking on water. We cannot rescue men and women from the churning water if we ourselves are going under. We must repent of our acceptance of the world's values of money, self-fulfillment, and entertainment.

What is God saying to the church today? We, like many of the saints at Sardis, have soiled our garments by moral compromise. This weakens us and nullifies our witness. How can congregations awash with the guilt of moral impurity witness with credibility to the watching world? And what about the doctrinal compromises we make when we concentrate only on the more positive aspects of Christian teaching and ignore the more difficult issues of judgment and hell? We have sold out to the culture, and now are blind to our own compromises and sins.

What should we do? We must begin by embracing the words of Jesus for ourselves. Congregations must humbly assess their true spiritual state before God. We must let Jesus apply His stethoscope to our hearts and give us a true reading of our spiritual health.

This must be followed by repentance not just individually but as a corporate body. As a church we have the responsibility to identify and "strengthen what remains." This is not a one-time event but an ongoing pattern of faithfulness, continually revisiting our spiritual condition.

And if we don't do this? Jesus' warning is ominous, "But if you are not alert, I will come like a thief and you have no idea at what hour I will come against you" (3:3). This is not a reference to the return of Christ at the end of the age but rather a warning to the church that He will return to judge them. He will come to rebuke and discipline us. Today there is no church where Sardis once was; this is a reminder that we cannot take our own future for granted.

Read the promise Jesus makes to those who are faithful, "they will walk with Me in white, because they are worthy" (3:4). These people will never have their names blotted out from the book of life; further, Jesus will acknowledge their names "before My Father and before His angels" (v. 5).

Jesus ends His letter to Sardis by saying: "Anyone who has an ear should listen to what the Spirit says to the churches" (3:6).

Are we listening?

Letter to the Church

Jack Hayford

Written as an elder servant, to Christ and His Church—especially to the shepherds of the Flock of God and to all pursuing His Great Commission.

In this my 77th year, I am still privileged to speak to thousands of pastors annually. Their most asked question: "What is the secret to an abiding fruitfulness in ministry." To answer, I acknowledge the essential touchpoints: (a) fidelity to God's Eternal Word; (b) faithful devotion to one's wife and family; (c) personal purity and self-discipline in all things; and (d) to love Christ's people, humbly and respectfully acknowledging the worth of all who honor Christ, though they differ from my theology. However, I spend most of the time on the real "secret": (e) to keep a life of personal worship and intimate prayer fellowship with Jesus (1Jn 1:5-10).

I know of no better example of such a walk than the Apostle John. His long and faithful life, his spiritual impact, and his extended, faithful labors as a pastor and apostle inspire me. Often I have turned to his description of an encounter he had with Jesus late in life (Rv 1:9-20).

Revelation 1:9-21 illustrates John's applying ministry principles born of a life shaped deeply by a "Christ in you" dimension of Jesus' leader-style being incarnate in one of His servants. I see these as the essence of the "secret" to lasting leadership.

I use the word "secret" in the sense the NT word *musterion* was used of spiritual truth generally unperceived until God reveals it to human understanding and individual experience; this is a sharp contrast to the common listings of "leadership tips" today. The nature of spirit-begotten molding and shaping of Christ-as-a-Leader in us does not flow from a corporate management textbook. But John, as did other NT leaders, learned and lived in the dynamic infused by the Holy Spirit's presence flowing from Jesus' lessons and lifestyle into the fabric of their lives. Textbook leadership-methodologies cannot substitute for Spirit-begotten love, sacrifice, and self-discipline.

JOHN—A Brother…A Companion

John begins with a gentle, personal, and tenderly sensitive tone, opening with a demeanor that greets his readers as equals.

"I, John, your brother and partner . . . "

John has every reason to begin by affirming his apostolic authority but chooses to approach his delivery of so grand a disclosure of last things not as a distinguished leader but as "your brother and partner"—as one living life on the same plane as his readers. The utter absence of pretense or posturing is notable. His model leaves no room for posturing, manipulation, parading prominence, or treating "position" as though it elevated one over others rather than simply defined duty to be served as a steward without personal prestige.

". . . in the tribulation, kingdom, and endurance that are in Jesus."

John not only makes a ready reference to his own struggles, but does so in a manner that underscores his practical life as a believer. He, just as others, faced common trials and afflictions, and John affirms that the godly must face these things with "endurance." His words assert the certainty of faith's ultimate victory—enunciating the presence of Christ's kingdom at hand irrespective of whatever present trial we are facing. His leadership models a living out and engendering in others a practical, realistic walk of faith.

John demonstrates a leader "fit for the Master's use;" not only by faithful labor, but by a constancy of humility, marked by a steadfast pursuit of childlike spirituality; he was open, yielded, and teachable for a lifetime. It's precisely that spirit that Jesus cited as a qualification for receiving the Kingdom; (that is, not only saving grace but an abiding availability to lead others to maturity within that grace—see Mark 10:13-16).

It is on the foundation of this and the above baseline traits of John's character that the capstone of true leadership is unveiled. Childlikeness of spirit is essential to living within this secret place of ongoing renewal and fruitfulness because it confronts the common mistake of presuming "leadership" is essentially the fruit of an effective mix of intellectual acumen, social skills, giftedness, and public or platform presence. But whatever benefit any of these afford, truly transforming spiritual impact only flows from a leader who lives and serves with a total dependence upon and vulnerability to the Holy Spirit. His ongoing "glory to glory" metamorphosis (2Co 3:18) gives rise to our most needed leadership qualities, today and always: e.g., transparency of spirit before God; brokenness of self will; a contrite heart; an unabashed passion to know His heart and His presence; an absence of any self-sufficiency; a refusal of vain posturing or presumption of status before man. The evidence of these things having been worked in John's being is evident in the rest of the passage, beginning with the words:

"I was in the Spirit on the Lord's Day . . ."

Remember, John is an imprisoned bishop. His circumstance was one under hostile surveillance; he is subject to some labor as part of the Roman penal colony; any visitor to Patmos has learned of the dry, desert nature of the rocky isle. In this context, John—the spiritual leader—in a dry and helpless situation evidences the path to the fountain of strength for beleaguered leaders. Helpless in ourselves, there is an ever-present point of retreat. And thus is was, on a lonely Lord's Day in a penal colony on a desert island, that John found a place of prayer and entered into worship and prayer he describes as "in the Spirit."

Prayer "in the Spirit" may one moment be worship and the next be warfare. It is born of the recognition that the weapons of our warfare do not issue from human resources or skill. It is not the prayer of a reserved saint—nor the formal exercise of a person concerned about their appearance, their style, or the opinion of those preoccupied with arguing the form or acceptability of varied expressions of "Spirit-filled prayer."

It is that place that is found before God when a leader or any thirsty soul comes as a child of the Father, resting in the Son, and opens fully to the Holy Spirit's enablement in worship. As a result they step into the Throne Room of heaven. It is prayer that becomes effective, fervent intercession (see Jms 5:16b-18; Rm 8:26-27). "Prayer in the Spirit" describes neither a theologized style nor an emotional state. But it does define the chosen stance of a redeemed